
LESKO'S INFO-POWER

Second Edition

by

MATTHEW LESKO

Editor: Andrew Naprawa

Associate Editor: Mary Ann Martello

Contributing Editor: Toni Murray

Researchers:

Claire Capretta
Patricia Dickey
Laura Hovenier
Kim Walker-Klarman
Judy Marcus
Shirley Massman
Roger Munter
Daniel O'Connor
Julie Paul
Debbie Samson
Carol Sargent
Pam Schultz

Production Director: Beth Meserve

LESKO'S INFO-POWER. Copyright 1994 by Matthew Lesko. All rights reserved. Printed in the United States of America. Published by Information USA, Inc., P.O. Box E, Kensington, MD 20895

SIXTH EDITION

Cover Design: Sally Whitehead

Photo: George Tames

Library of Congress Cataloging-in-Publication Data

Lesko, Matthew.

Lesko's Info-Power sourcebook.

ISBN #1-878346-17-2 (paperback)

Other books written by Matthew Lesko:

Getting Yours: The Complete Guide to Government Money

How to Get Free Tax Help

Information USA

The Computer Data and Database Source Book

The Maternity Sourcebook

Lesko's New Tech Sourcebook

The Investor's Information Sourcebook

The Federal Data Base Finder

The State Database Finder

Government Giveaways for Entrepreneurs

The Great American Gripe Book

What To Do When You Can't Afford Health Care

TO

all the federal and state bureaucrats who

eagerly share information that empowers us

to pursue our goals and dreams

Introduction

Thank you for buying, borrowing, or stealing my book. I have spent over 20 years using and compiling government information. Even though I've written over 40 books on the subject, it is my hope that with every book, I get better at it. I believe that this is my best ever and I hope you can get good use out of *Info-Power*.

WARNING: THIS BOOK IS OUT OF DATE

You have to realize that the moment any book is printed, it is out of date. Especially this one with its 45,000 sources. A book of this size is sure to have some telephone numbers that have changed. But don't be discouraged. You can live with these small inconveniences. If you are calling a government office listed in the book and the telephone number gets you a local diner, or some other wrong number, here's what you can do.

* Call the operator for the area and ask for the number of the office you're after. The directory assistance operator can be located by dialing the area code followed by 555-1212. To inquire about a toll-free number, call directory assistance at (800) 555-1212.

* Or, call us at (301) 942-6303. We will try and help you in any way we can.

You can keep up to date with the information in this book by ordering our new editions when they become available. Each edition verifies all the sources identified in the book and includes updated information, new and expanded chapters and much more. We hope to be publishing updates every other year.

You can also keep current by accessing this information online, via computer, through CompuServe. We will be constantly updating this information on this computer service. For subscription information to CompuServe call (800) 524-3388 and ask for Representative 168. Thanks again for your interest in this book. I hope you will feel free to call with your comments and questions.

Happy Hunting,

Matthew Lesko

TABLE OF CONTENTS

INTRODUCTION

I.	**INFORMATION IS POWER**	**1**
	Information is Power	1
	How to Find Mr. Potato	4
	Coping with Misinformation	6
	Case Study: Jelly Beans	8
II.	**MY FAVORITE BUREAUCRAT**	**11**
III.	**INFO-POWER GREATEST HITS**	**26**
IV.	**INFORMATION STARTING PLACES**	**34**
	Free Help in Finding Free Experts	34
	State Information Starting Places	36
	Federal Public Information Offices	40
	Hotlines	76
	Recorded Messages	93
V.	**CONSUMER POWER**	**94**
	General Sources	94
	State Consumer Protection Offices	102
	Money, Banking, and Credit	105
	Product Safety	109
	Post Office and Mailing	113
VI.	**HOUSING AND REAL ESTATE**	**119**
	General Sources	119
	Federal Money for Housing and Real Estate	125
	State Money for Housing and Real Estate	130
	Gardening	140
VII.	**EDUCATION**	**143**
	School: Grades K-12	143
	College and Continuing Education	155
	Science Teachers and Students	161
	Innovation and Trends	166
	Money for Teachers and Schools	170
	Federal Money for Students	182
	The World's Largest Educational Database	191
	State Money for Students	195
	State Money for College Students	198
	State Education Information	230
VIII.	**CAREERS AND WORKPLACE**	**234**
	General Sources	234
	Career and Job Training Opportunities	243
	Employee Benefits and Rights	251
	Labor-Management Cooperation	256
	Occupational Health and Safety	261
	Federal Employment	268
	Federal Job Banks	277
	Research Grants in Every Field	282

IX. ARTS AND HUMANITIES **290**
Artists, Designers, Performers 290
Film, Photography, and Media Arts 294
Money for the Arts 298
Money for the Humanities 300
Historians, Scholars and Writers 303
Museums and Cultural Resources 313
State Arts Programs 322
State Money for the Arts and Artists 326

X. YOUR COMMUNITY **344**
Urban and Rural Resources 344
Neighborhood Improvements 348
Traffic and Transportation 352
Fires, Floods, and Disaster Relief 354
Money for Communities and Non-Profits 359
Volunteerism 383

XI. GOVERNMENT FINANCIAL HELP TO INDIVIDUALS **385**
Poor, Elderly, Disabled, and Unemployed 385
Veterans and Dependents 390

XII. VACATIONS AND BUSINESS TRAVEL **396**
Tourist Adventures 396
Parks and Camping 403
Boating and Fishing 410
International Travel 415
Domestic Tourism and Trends 420
State Travel Hotlines 422

XIII. INVESTMENTS AND FINANCIAL SERVICES **424**
General Sources 424
Banking 426
Money 431
Credit Unions 433
Stocks and Bonds 435
Government Bonds, Bills and Notes 445
State Banking Information 447
Commodities 451

XIV. TAXES **453**
Federal Tax Help 453
Tax Hotlines 464
Recorded Messages 466
IRS Tax Forms 470
Free Tax Publications 491
State Tax Assistance 498

XV. HEALTH AND MEDICINE **501**
Clearinghouses and Starting Points 501
Healthy Lifestyle and Physical Fitness 516
Food Facts, Nutrition, and Diets 520
Contraception and Pregnancy 526
Stress, Mental Illness, and Family Violence 532
AIDS, Cancer, and Other Diseases 537
Cigarettes and Chewing Tobacco 553
Aging and America's Elderly 556
Handicapped/Disabled Resources 563
Medical Devices, RX and Surgery 566
Chemicals, Toxins, and Other Health Hazards 571
Medical Research: Clues and Answers 573
Health Care Costs and Services 575

XVI. DRUGS AND CHEMICAL DEPENDENCE **577**
General Sources 577
Education and Prevention 588
Treatment and Rehabilitation 595
Law Enforcement and Prosecution 599

XVII. LAW AND SOCIAL JUSTICE **609**
General Sources 609
Courts and Legal Help 619
Immigration and Naturalization 623
Discrimination and Civil Rights 626

XVIII. INFORMATION ON PEOPLE, COMPANIES, AND MAILING LISTS **630**
Who Owes Money To Whom 630
Professional People and Local Businesses 635
Driver's Licenses and Motor Vehicles 641
Other Info Sources on People 646
Information On Any Company 649
Companies In Your State 657
State Company Directories 664
State Securities and Stockbrokers 668
Food and Drug Companies 671
Utility Companies 677
Weights and Measures 682
Insurance Companies and Salesmen 685
Federal Mailing Lists 689

XIX. GOVERNMENT AUCTIONS AND SURPLUS PROPERTY **695**
Government Auctions and Surplus Property 695
Donations to Non-Profit Organizations 702
Resolution Trust Company 704
State Government Auctions 705
Unclaimed Money 711

XX. SMALL BUSINESS AND ENTREPRENEURING **717**
Federal Starting Places 717
State Starting Places for Money 727
Federal Money for Business 754
Franchising: How to Select the Best Opportunity 770

XXI. BUSINESS AND INDUSTRY **774**
General Sources 774
Airlines 781
Communications 789
Shipping and Fishing 797
Mining 810
General Transportation 818
Highways, Waterways and Railways 824

XXII. SELLING TO THE GOVERNMENT **833**
Government Contracts 833
Free Local Help: The Best Place to Start to Sell
to the Government 836
Government Buys Bright Ideas From Inventors:
Small Business Innovative Research Programs (SBIR) 840
State Procurement Offices 841

XXIII. SELLING OVERSEAS: INTERNATIONAL TRADE **843**

XXIV. ECONOMICS, DEMOGRAPHICS AND STATISTICS **861**
General Sources 861
State Crime Statistics 879
State Labor Offices 883

XXIV. ECONOMICS, DEMOGRAPHICS AND STATISTICS (continued)

State Health Statistics **889**

Highway Accident Statistics **895**

State Data Centers **898**

State Statistical Abstracts **905**

State Forecasting Centers **907**

XXV. INTERNATIONAL RELATIONS AND DEFENSE 912

Foreign Policy **912**

Arms Control and World Peace **935**

Military and National Security **939**

XXVI. SCIENCE AND TECHNOLOGY 962

General Sources **962**

Aerospace Technology/Space Research **981**

Geology and Earth Science **991**

National Institute of Standards and Technology **997**

XXVII. PATENTS, TRADEMARKS AND COPYRIGHTS 1017

XXVIII. AGRICULTURE AND FARMING 1021

Management and Productivity **1021**

Food Quality and Distribution **1033**

Trade and Marketing **1037**

State Agriculture Information **1042**

XXIX. ENERGY 1049

General Sources **1049**

Fossil Fuels: Oil, Coal and Natural Gas **1067**

Nuclear Energy and Waste **1072**

XXX. WEATHER AND MAPS 1083

Climate and Forecasts **1083**

Maps and Geography **1088**

XXXI. ENVIRONMENT AND NATURE 1095

General Sources **1095**

Water and Air Quality **1108**

Forests and Land Conservation **1123**

Fish and Wildlife **1132**

Hazardous and Solid Waste **1142**

XXXII. FREEDOM OF INFORMATION ACT (FOIA) 1153

Government Records and Privacy **1153**

Federal FOIA Offices **1167**

State FOIA Offices **1174**

XXXIII. INFORMATION FROM LAWMAKERS 1177

Tracking Federal Legislation **1177**

U.S. Congress Committees **1180**

Legislative Branch Sources **1188**

Tracking State Legislation **1194**

XXXIV. BOOKS AND LIBRARIES 1199

Library of Congress **1199**

Federal Libraries **1205**

Government Printing Office **1212**

XXXV. GOVERNMENT DATABASES AND BULLETIN BOARDS 1215

Federal Government Databases **1215**

Electronic Bulletin Boards **1233**

XXXVI. MORE INFO-POWER HITS **1239**

XXXVII. THE GOVERNMENT WORKS FOR KIDS, TOO **1243**

XXXVII. CURRENT EVENTS AND HOMEWORK **1299**

XXXVIII. EXPERTS **1454**

XXXIX. INDEX **1525**

Information Is Power

Information is the key to opportunities. It's essential for all the important aspects of life:

* making the right investment,
* choosing the right career,
* seeking the latest medical cure, or
* buying at the best price.

But why, if we are living in an information society, do most of us base our decisions on hearsay, headlines, outdated or incomplete information? I think there are two reasons which explain this paradox:

* information overload, and
* poor information training.

Information overload is the more obvious of the two. We see it everywhere: the proliferation of magazines, newspapers, databases, and even television channels. I'll talk more about this later. What is an even more distressing problem is our inadequate information training.

Your Library Is Out Of Date

Today, most adults and even our children have been trained to believe that if you need information, you go to the library. That's fine for certain subjects, like literature and history, but inadequate for most of the important concerns that affect our lives everyday. Libraries are full of the traditional information resources but you will encounter major problems if you rely on these sources because:

* most books are out of date, and
* libraries represent only a fraction of the information available to us.

Books can tell you only about yesterdays, but the information needed to make critical decisions must reflect what is happening today and tomorrow, not the past. More than ever our world is changing at an ever increasing speed. What once took months, even years to change, now occurs in hours, even minutes.

Those who rely on yesterday's information are the ones who get hurt in our society. Take, for example, the steel workers who thought that they would make $25 per hour forever. What about those who believed all the hype a few years ago about how Individual Retirement Accounts (IRAs) would make their financial lives secure forever. Now the rules have changed and the tax advantage isn't what it used to be. Books published in the traditional way are out of date before they hit the bookstores. How can you depend on a book offering investment advice when the manuscript was completed 18 to 24 months ago? It takes most New York publishers 9 to 12 months just to

do the editing, proofing, and printing. With external events changing our landscape every day, like the stock market crash of 1987, or the fall of the Berlin Wall in 1989, we can no longer rely on such books.

Government Is World's Largest Source of Information

Traditional books represent only a fraction of the really powerful information that is available. Did you know that all of the major commercial publishers in our country generate approximately 50,000 books each year, but one little government publisher, the National Technical Information Service (NTIS), alone sells about 90,000 titles annually. And it's estimated that NTIS titles represent only a tiny portion of the research that is actually published by federal agencies. And computers are not much of a help either. Most databases you access are bibliographies which fail to capture the latest information.

The government is the largest source of information in the world, and very little of it is available in any library. And, more importantly, the information you get from the government is going to be superior to most anything you can ever get commercially. If you purchase a book in the bookstore, you're likely to get the result of one to two years of some author's efforts. On the other hand, if you get a government study, often you are getting the results of hundreds of man years worth of work, along with the telephone number of the actual office that conducted the research. That's just how the government works and chances are the government study will be free.

Information Opportunities

By relying on traditional information sources, you are missing out on information opportunities. Such an opportunity occurs when you have intelligence that is current, comprehensive, reliable, and even cheaper than someone else's information. There is no unique opportunity for you when your stockbroker calls about a chance to invest in some biotechnology company, because the broker probably is sharing that tip with 5,000 other "special" clients. The real opportunity occurs when you have the information before the stockbroker. And you can get it, but not from conventional sources. How can you take advantage of a new cure for your medical ailment if your doctor is not aware of the latest therapies because the *New England Journal of Medicine* hasn't published a recent article on this disease. Or perhaps some scientific journal plans to run an article revealing a potential cure, but it is still in the editing process and won't be published for another three months. You need that information today, and you can get it, but not from traditional sources.

Medicine is typical of the information overload when your doctor--the information provider--cannot possibly keep up on

Be patient. If any phone number is incorrect, call (area code) 555-1212 and request the new listing.

Information Is Power

all the latest developments. That physician has got a practice to run, and the information changes too fast and constantly. But the best health information in the world *IS* available and *YOU* can get it.

Archives vs. Information

Libraries are great storehouses for literature and archival material. They handle traditional published materials very well, but do a relatively poor job in solving more current information problems. This is a pity since we are living in an information society, and information is the most important ingredient in our lives. Doesn't it make sense that libraries should be the most important building in the community? Yet they're not, mainly because information retrieval requires a different set of skills than the archival business. Archiving is more suited for passive, non-people oriented skills, the cloistered scholars. The communication skills needed in today's information society are action-oriented and people-oriented.

The Information Winners

The winners in this information age are those who learn how to tap into non-traditional sources, and use experts. Finding non-traditional sources of information, however, is no easy task. The government is the world's largest supplier of these non-traditional sources, but it does not advertise. The government spends billions collecting information and expertise but spends barely a nickel advertising its availability. Another problem is that much of the information is not collected for the reason for which you want to use it. Even people in the government who have the information often fail to realize that it can be used to solve your particular problem. Take, for example, the Census data. Every decade we spend over $1 billion dollars collecting information on all the noses and toilets in this country--the census of population and housing. The law which requires us to collect this information is, of course, the Constitution, which mandates that we count all Americans in order to figure out the number of Members of Congress. But the unintentional fallout of this law is a billion dollar market study which no one except the government can do. Not even a Fortune 500 company can afford to collect this amount of data. But when the results come out:

* companies can use the data to identify new markets;
* banks can decide where to locate branch offices;
* families can learn which are the best neighborhoods;
* inventors can determine the demand and need for their products.

Using Experts To Solve Information Overload

Knowing how to find and use experts is not only the solution to identifying the best in non-traditional information, but it is also the key in dealing with information overload. And what's ideal about this approach is that most all the best experts cost you nothing. The government, because it is the richest source for non-traditional information in the world, is also the richest source of experts. It is full of specialists who spend entire careers studying almost any topic from futures commodities to extraterrestrials. And they are available to anyone just for the price of a telephone call.

Find Out What Will Be In Books Tomorrow

If you access a computerized database and put in a term or key word, you can get overwhelmed. Immediately it will be apparent that today anybody with a copier machine is a publisher, and once it is published, somebody with a database is indexing it. So a printout from your computer search might total 500 citations. If you want answers now, you are in worse shape than when you started. Why? Because the computer cannot distinguish the relevant articles from the bad ones. Probably you need to retrieve all the articles cited. Also, as I mentioned earlier, much of what databases contain is from outdated published material.

My theory is that in an average of seven telephone calls you can find an expert who has read all of those articles. This specialist can tell you which ones to read, or will know the answer on the spot so there will be no need to track down the articles. These experts also can tell you what will be in the database tomorrow because they are in the process of writing it or reviewing another expert's article. They are tracking developments minute by minute in their field of expertise.

And what's great about our society is that these experts are dying to talk to you. They devote their lives to studying a particular subject in a massive bureaucracy and most feel no one cares about what they do and know. I estimate that there are over 700,000 such experts in the federal government alone, and this does not count state governments, non-profit groups, and international organizations.

The real trick is in how you treat these experts. You must remember that these experts get the same paycheck whether they help you for free for two weeks, or whether they hang up on you right after you say hello. You can't think of getting information in the terms we are taught in school. The best information is no longer in some impersonal book locked up in a dusty library. It's locked up in the heads of experts and other resource people, but now you have to learn a whole new set of skills to get at it. Once you do, you will have the power of information at your fingertips. Here are a few examples of what I am talking about.

* You want to know the best industries of the 1990s to invest in? The government has over 100 industry analysts at the U.S. Department of Commerce studying all the major industries in this country and forecasting what they will be doing in the next 5 years.

* Your teenager has run up a few hundred dollars on pornographic 900 numbers? The dial-a-porn expert at the Federal Communications Commission can tell you about your legal position for not paying the bill.

* You want to know the market for polypropelene resin in 15 developing countries? There is a woman at the U.S. Department of Commerce who collects all the official export and import statistics from every country in the world, and can provide you with latest available data.

Be patient. If any phone number is incorrect, call (area code) 555-1212 and request the new listing.

Information Is Power

The Care and Feeding of Bureaucrats

There is no magic in how you treat experts. Simply remember to treat them the way you want to be treated. But, this is easy to forget when the bureaucratic runaround triggers instant frustration. While making your seven phone calls to find your expert--beware. These are common reactions.

* You get put on hold for what seems like hours.
* Everyone you talk with cannot understand your question and thinks you're off your rocker.
* After getting transferred and trying other numbers, you wind up talking with the same person twice.

What's important is not to lose your composure. Keep in mind that it will take an average of seven phone calls to find the person who can help. Otherwise, by the time you reach the expert you'll be angry and frustrated and that attitude will usually cause this information provider to end the conversation immediately. Remember that the expert wants to help you--if you give them a chance.

How High Priced Consultants Stop The World From Getting Ahead

I believe that most of us fail to pursue our dreams because we think that the information and resources needed are not available or that we are going to have to pay a lot to get it from some high-priced consultant. If more people learn the new information skills required, more of us will do what we feel is important to do. You don't have to hire a high-priced consultant to get the pertinent information you need to get started. Even if you do, these consultants usually have archaic information gathering skills and usually sell recycled information.

Let's say you have a crazy idea--selling bridal gowns through the mail and you wonder if there is a market for it. A consultant will charge you a minimum of $10,000 to do a market study. However, about $20 can translate into any State Government Data Center providing you with all the zip codes which have high concentrations of unmarried, eligible women, correlated with low concentrations of bridal gown salons, or department stores with bridal salons.

Do you want to start your own non-profit organization to change the world? If you call a local attorney, they will charge you a few thousand dollars to fill out the IRS paperwork. Or, you can call the Non-Profit Office at the IRS in Washington, DC that provides free help to anyone who runs into difficulty completing the tax-exempt forms.

Recently I even got trapped in this negative thinking when I had the idea of sponsoring "My Favorite Bureaucrat Award." I was worried about the rules and regulations for offering a cash prize. What does "Void Where Prohibited" really mean? I thought about hiring a lawyer to figure all this out until I realized that there must be someone in the government to call. And there was. I found a contest expert, an attorney at the Federal Trade Commission, who told me such a contest had the seal of approval as long as I didn't give away over $5,000. He informed me that two states require you to post a bond and complete tons of paperwork if the prize exceeds $5,000. Until I resolved all these questions I was reluctant to pursue my idea. (Incidentally, there is a lot more about the results of this contest in the My Favorite Bureaucrat Chapter.)

In my 20 years of experience, most experts will outshine private consultants both in terms of the quality of information and the cost of providing it!

How To Find Mr. Potato

The techniques for locating an expert can best be illustrated by a classic story from the days when I was struggling to start my first information brokerage company in 1975.

At the time the business amounted only to a desk and telephone crowded in the bedroom of my apartment. As so often happens in a fledgling enterprise, my first client was a friend. His problem was this: "I must have the latest information on the basic supply and demand of Maine potatoes within 24 hours."

My client represented a syndicate of commodity investors which invests millions of dollars in Maine potatoes. When he called, these potatoes were selling at double their normal price and he wanted to know why. I knew absolutely nothing about potatoes, but figured I knew where to find out. The agreement with my client was that I would be paid only if I succeeded in getting the information (no doubt you have guessed I no longer work this way).

Luck With The First Telephone Call

The first call I made was to the general information office of the U.S. Department of Agriculture (USDA). I asked to speak to an expert on potatoes. The USDA operator referred me to Mr. Charlie Porter. At that point I wondered if this Mr. Porter was a department functionary with responsibility for handling crank calls, but the operator assured me that he was an agriculture economist specializing in potatoes. I telephoned Mr. Porter and explained how I was a struggling entrepreneur who knew nothing about potatoes and needed his help to answer a client's request. Charlie graciously gave me much of the information I needed, adding that he would be happy to talk at greater length either over the phone or in person at his office. I decided to go see him.

Only Problem Was Getting Out Of Charlie's Office

For two and one half hours the next morning, the federal government's potato expert explained in intimate detail the supply and demand of Maine potatoes. Charlie Porter showed me computer printouts that reflected how the price had doubled in recent weeks. For any subject that arose during our conversation, Charlie had immediate access to a reference source. Rows of books in his office covered every conceivable aspect of the potato market. A strip of ticker tape that tracked the daily price of potatoes from all over the country lay across his desk.

Here in Charlie's office was everything anyone might ever want to know about potatoes. The problem, it turned out, was not in getting enough information, but how to leave his office gracefully. Once Charlie started talking, it was hard to stop him.

It seemed that Charlie Porter had devoted his life's work studying the supply and demand of potatoes and finally someone with a genuine need sought his expertise.

One Potato...Two Potato...

When I was finally able to let Charlie know I had to leave, he pointed across the hall in the direction of a potato statistician whose primary responsibility was to produce a monthly report on potato production and consumption in the United States. From this statistician I learned about all the categories of potatoes that are tallied. It turns out the USDA counts all the potato chips sold every month, even how many Pringle potato chips are consumed. The statistician offered to place me on the mailing list to receive all this free monthly data.

The Art Of Getting An Expert To Talk

The information explosion requires greater reliance on experts in order to sift through the expanse of data. Cultivating an expert, however, demands an entirely different set of skills than old-fashioned library or archival research. You must know how to treat people so that they are ready, willing, and able to give you the information needed. It is human nature for most anyone to want to share their knowledge, but your approach will determine whether you ultimately get the expert to open up. It is your job to create an environment that makes an individual want to share his or her expertise. Remember when dealing with both public and private sector experts, they will get the same paycheck whether they give you two weeks worth of free help or if they cut short the conversation.

Expectations: The Seven-Phone Call Rule

There is no magic to finding an expert. It is simply a numbers game which takes an average of seven telephone calls. Dial up enough people and keep asking each for a lead. Patience and persistence are essential. This is why it is essential to remember "the seven-phone call rule".

If you make several calls and get upset because you have been transferred from one person to another, you will be setting yourself up to fail once you locate the right expert. What is likely to happen is that when your "Charlie Porter" answers the telephone he is going to hear you complaining about how sick and tired you are of getting the runaround from his organization. Well, to Charlie, you don't sound like you are going to be the highlight of his day. He is going to figure out how to get rid of you.

This explains why some people are able to get information and others fail. Experienced researchers know it is going to take a

Be patient. If any phone number is incorrect, call (area code) 555-1212 and request the new listing.

How To Find Mr. Potato

number of telephone calls and they condition themselves to be patient. After all, the runaround is an unavoidable part of the information gathering process. Consequently, the first words that come out of your mouth are extremely important because they set the stage for engaging the expert on your behalf.

Ten Basic Telephone Tips

Here are a few pointers to keep in mind when you are casting about for an expert. These guidelines amount to basic common sense, but are often forgotten by the time you get to that sixth or seventh phone call.

1) Introduce Yourself Cheerfully
The way you start the conversation will set the tone for the entire interview. Your greeting and initial comment should be cordial and cheerful. Your opening should give the feeling that this is not going to be just another telephone call, but a pleasant interlude in his or her day.

2) Be Open And Candid
You should be as candid as possible with your source since you are asking the same of him. If you are evasive or deceitful in explaining your needs or motives, your source will be reluctant to provide you with information. If there are certain facts you cannot reveal such as client confidentiality, explain just that. Most people will understand.

3) Be Optimistic
Throughout the entire conversation you should exude a sense of confidence. If you call and say "You probably aren't the right person" or "You don't have any information, do you?" it's easy for the person to respond, "You're right, I cannot help you." A positive attitude will encourage your source to stretch his mind to see how he might be able to help you.

4) Be Humble And Courteous
You can be optimistic and still be humble. Remember the adage that you can catch more flies with honey than you can with vinegar. People in general, and experts in particular, love to tell others what they know, as long as their position of authority is not questioned or threatened.

5) Be Concise
State your problem simply. Be direct. A long-winded explanation may bore your contact and reduce your chances for getting a thorough response.

6) Don't Be A "Gimme"
A "gimme" is someone who expects instant answers and displays a "give me that" attitude. It is important to be considerate and sensitive to the expert's time, feelings, and even his or her eccentricities.

7) Be Complimentary
This goes hand in hand with being humble. A well-placed compliment about your source's expertise or insight will serve you well. In searching for information in large organizations, you are apt to talk to many colleagues of your source, so it wouldn't hurt to convey the respect that your "Charlie Porter" commands. For example, "Everyone I spoke to said you are the person I must talk with." It is reassuring to know you have the respect of your peers.

8) Be Conversational
Avoid spending the entire time talking about the information you need. Briefly mention a few irrelevant topics such as the weather, the Washington Redskins, or the latest political campaign. The more social you are without being too chatty, the more likely that your source will open up.

9) Return The Favor
You might share with your source information or even gossip you have picked up elsewhere. However, be certain not to betray the trust of either your client or another source. If you do not have any relevant information to share at the moment, it would still be a good idea to call back when you are further along in your research.

10) Send Thank You Notes
A short note, typed or handwritten, will help ensure that your source will be just as cooperative in the future.

Coping With Misinformation

One of the major problems encountered by researchers is determining the accuracy of the information collected. If you are doing traditional market research and using primary sources, accuracy is not that complicated. Traditional market researchers are well aware of survey methods, sampling techniques, and computing errors using statistical standard deviation analysis. However, if you are a desk researcher, like Information USA, Inc. which relies on secondary sources and expert opinion, how do you compute the standard deviation for error? The answer is that you cannot use hard statistical techniques, but you can employ other soft forms of error checking.

Major Causes for Error and Prevention Tactics

Problem #1: Lost In The Jargon

It is not uncommon for researchers to be dealing frequently in areas of expertise where they do not have complete command of the industry jargon. In such situations it is easy to believe that you have found the exact information needed only to find out later that you missed the mark considerably. This is a common trap to fall into when fishing in unfamiliar waters. And if you have to do the job quickly, it is easy to believe that you know more than you really do. Or, you avoid getting the complete explanation of specific jargon because you do not want to waste the time of the expert who is giving you the information. Here is an experience of a U.S. Department of Agriculture expert which illustrates this point.

This government expert received a call one day from an assistant at the White House. This hot shot, who acted pretty impressed with himself, said he was in a meeting with both the President and the head of the Meat Packers Association and needed to know right then the official number of cows in the United States. The livestock expert asked the presidential aide if that was exactly what he meant and then when he impatiently responded "Yes," the bureaucrat told him the figure. Within minutes the White House staffer called back and said the president of the Meat Packers Association laughed at him and claimed that there were twice as many cows. The assistant then realized he needed the number of all cows--all "male cows"--as well as all female ones.

The White House aide had a problem with semantics, probably a city slicker who never knew the difference between cows and cattle. This can happen to anyone, not only a self-assured Presidential aide. For example, if you want to know the market for computers, are you talking about free standing units or central processing units?

Solution #1: Act A Little Dumb

In order to prevent this type of embarrassment, you have to

find an expert with whom you are comfortable. When I say comfortable, I mean someone you can go to and ask dumb questions. You will get the most help if you are very humble in your approach. If you request information with the arrogance of the over confident White House staffer, you may be given only the facts you ask for and nothing more. However, if you call up an expert and say something like, "Oh God, can you please help me? I don't really know much about this, but my boss needs to know how many cows there are in the country." With more than a hint of indecision in your voice and honestly admitting you don't know much about the field, the expert is more likely to ask you some key questions that will ensure that you get the right figures.

Problem #2: Believing The Written Word Or A Computer

This is a more serious problem than the difficulties and confusion surrounding industry jargon. Mastering the terminology just requires a little homework. However, overcoming a deep seated belief that information either from a computer, in published sources, or from the government, is always accurate can be like changing your religion. It took me years, as well as dozens of professional embarrassments, to overcome this problem.

Just because a figure is in print does not make it gospel. Remember the saying, "Figures don't lie, but liars can figure." Keep this in mind before betting the farm on anything you read in print, even if it comes out of a computer. A good illustration which follows pertains to Census Bureau information.

A few years ago we were doing a market study on stereo speakers and discovered that the figures the U.S. Bureau of the Census had for this market were off by over 50 percent. No one in the industry complained to the government because the industry was small and couldn't be bothered. But most of the companies involved knew that the figure was misleading and had no use for it. Another case is a Fortune 500 company which told us that for over five years it filled out the U.S. Census form under the wrong SIC code. An important caveat--this firm ranks as the number two manufacturer in the industry.

You have to remember that number crunchers at the Census Bureau and other such organizations are not always interested in the meaning behind the numbers. Much of their work is simply taking a number from block A, adding it to the number in block B, and placing the result in block C. Verifying where the numbers come from is not their job.

Published sources are an even a bigger problem than government data. Many believe that what you read in a magazine or a newspaper or hear on television or radio must be true. Nonsense. Anyone and their brother can be interviewed

Be patient. If any phone number is incorrect, call (area code) 555-1212 and request the new listing.

Coping With Misinformation

by a magazine or newspaper, and usually what they say will get printed in a magazine or quoted on the air as long as it is not too outrageous. And, sometimes you are more likely to get it into print if it **is** outrageous. After all, most news stories are just accounts of what someone said as interpreted by a journalist.

The more general the media, the less accurate it may be about an industry. In other words, an article in the ice cream industry trade magazine is more likely to be accurate than a similar story in the *New York Times*. The trade journal will have reporters who cover that particular industry and they will more than likely be able to flush out bad data. The newspaper, on the other hand, will do only one ice cream story a year, and will print almost anything it hears. So just because someone is quoted in an article does not mean that the information is correct.

I have seen much of this firsthand when on nationwide book promotion tours. In newspaper interviews or on radio and television talk shows, I can say almost anything and they will print or broadcast it, as is. I will give countless facts and figures based on my own biased research (remember that I am trying to sell books), and hardly ever will I be questioned or seriously challenged before, during or after the fact, about their authenticity. I don't know if it is laziness, apathy, or just plain lack of time that allows so much unchallenged information to be presented in the media. I have even blatantly lied to a reporter who thought of himself as a clone of CBS' Mike Wallace of "60 Minutes." Before I started doing media interviews, I assumed that any good reporter worth his or her salt could find holes in what I presented and would expose me as some kind of fraud. I did not know how they would do it, but I guess my own insecurity prompted me to prepare for the worst. The reality is that most reporters spend little or no time studying the topic before they interview you, and if you become annoyed or angry, especially with this Mike Wallace type described above, you can blow them away with a exaggerated fact or half-truth that he will never be able to verify.

Solution #2: Find Another Industry Expert

Whether a figure comes from the Census Bureau, a trade magazine or off the tube, your best bet for determining whether the number is accurate, and also the one you need, is to track down an industry expert, other than the one quoted, and ask him to comment on the figure. What you are seeking is their biased opinion about the accuracy of the stated figure. If the expert believes the figure is correct but doesn't know why, find another expert.

Problem #3: Trusting An Expert

This may seem to contradict what I just said in the solution to problem #2, but stick with me and you will see the difference. There are many times when you cannot start with published or printed data and all you can do is pick the brains of experts within the industry. This means that you will be getting facts and figures based on the best available guess from experts. Many times this is the only way to get the information you need.

Getting this type of soft data can be full of danger. After having worked for hours trying to find a friendly soul to share with you his innermost thoughts about the facts and figures of an industry or company, you do not want to turn him off with an antagonistic remark about the accuracy of his data.

Solution #3: Ask Why?

The best way to judge whether a source is knowledgeable about the fact or figure he gave you is to ask him how he arrived at the number. Such a question will likely initiate one of the following responses:

"I don't know. It's the best I can think of."

- A response like this will be a clue that the expert may not know what he is talking about and you should continue your search for a knowledgeable and willing expert.

"This is the figure I read from an industry association study."

- This should lead you to verify that such a study was conducted and to attempt to interview people involved with the report.

"The industry figure is XX because our sales are half that and we are number two in the industry."

- This is probably one of the best types of answers you can get. Any time an industry expert gives you a figure based on something he is positive about, you can almost take it to the bank. The best you can do after this is to find other industry analysts and ask them to comment on the figure you were given.

Misinformation can lead to a decision making disaster. Following the simple techniques described above can take you a long way down the road to making near excellent decisions based on near perfect information.

Case Study: Jelly Beans

In our information society, which produces thousands of databases and other resources every day, it seems that most decision makers rely primarily on traditional information sources. More often than not, executives will spend lots of time and money trying to determine the size of a market or information about a competitor, and if the answer cannot be found through conventional sources, the corporate decision is made without the information. This does not have to be the case.

We believe that you can find solid information for almost any problem, no matter how sensitive the issue may be, if you use some unorthodox research techniques. To illustrate this point, here is a step-by-step account of how one of our researchers succeeded in gathering figures on the U.S. market for jelly beans when a Fortune 500 firm came up empty-handed after exhausting all traditional sources. The prevailing view both inside and outside the industry was that this piece of the information puzzle could not be obtained.

It should be said at the outset that the estimates Information USA, Inc. finally obtained must not be regarded as 100% accurate, but they do represent the best available figures and, most likely, come within 10% to 15% of the actual number.

Opening Round

Faced with the problem of finding the U.S. market for jelly beans, we already knew that our client had contacted the major market research firms, did some literature searches, and came up with practically no useful information. As is evident from this case study, this information hunt occurred when Ronald Reagan was President.

1) The first call was to the U.S. Department of Commerce to locate the government's jelly bean expert. We were referred to Cornelius Kenny, the confectionery industry expert. Mr. Kenny was out that day and would call us back when he returned to the office.

2) A search of Gale's *Encyclopedia of Associations* identified four relevant trade associations. However, upon contacting them we were told that they provide information only to their members.

3) The White House seemed like a good bet because of Ronald Reagan's fondness for jelly beans and all the resulting publicity. The Public Affairs office at 1600 Pennsylvania Avenue said that it never obtained statistical information on the industry but could tell us tales about a life-size water buffalo and portraits of the President constructed out of jelly beans. However, they suggested that we contact several lobbying organizations. Calls to these groups proved fruitless.

4) A call to the U.S. Bureau of the Census uncovered John Streeter, an analyst who monitors the panned candy industry. He told us:

* jelly beans have never been counted and there would be no way to get the answer;

* non-Chocolate Panned Candy category within the Bureau's Annual Confectionery Survey contains jelly beans;

* the seasonal category of the Non-Chocolate Panned Candies, according to his estimates, contains 90% jelly beans because most jelly beans are sold during Easter and they are about the only non-chocolate panned manufactured candy sold on a seasonal basis;

* $37,804,000 worth of non-chocolate panned candy was shipped by U.S. manufacturers in 1984, which represents about 48,354,000 pounds; the figures for total non-chocolate panned candy for 1984 totaled $251,525,000 and 237,308,000 pounds; and

* government regulations prohibited him from revealing the names of jelly bean manufacturers, but he did refer us to two trade associations he thought might help.

So this analyst at the Census Bureau, who tried to discourage us with warnings that no such figure for the jelly bean market existed, actually gave us quite concrete information as well as some valuable leads.

Armed and Dangerous With A Little Information

At this point we had a market estimate from one government expert based on a figure generated by the U.S. Bureau of the Census. It may have sounded like the answer we were after, but taking that figure to our client at this juncture would have been premature and possibly irresponsible. The main drawback was the estimate reflected only one person's opinion, and although he was an expert, he was not a true industry observer as one would be if they were actually in the business of selling jelly beans. At this stage in our search, our strategy was to find people in the industry who could give us their interpretation of these figures.

The Census expert referred us to one of the trade associations we already had contacted. However, when we called back saying that Mr. Streeter at the Census Bureau suggested we call them, the association promptly responded with a list of the 25 major jelly bean manufacturers. This is an example of how using the name of a government expert can get you in the door. When we phoned several manufacturers, they laughed when we told them of our effort to ascertain the market for jelly beans. Jelly beans had never been counted, they told us, and their advice was to give up.

Be patient. If any phone number is incorrect, call (area code) 555-1212 and request the new listing.

Case Study: Jelly Beans

At this point Mr. Kenny, the confectionery expert at the U.S. Department of Commerce called us back and he, too, said that the market had never been measured. However, he did hazard a guess that the jelly bean market could be roughly 50% of the total Census figure for Non-Chocolate Panned Candy.

A separate call to a private research group which does trend analysis by surveying grocery stores shared its estimate that 90% of all jelly beans are sold at Easter.

Easier To Be A Critic Than A Source

Our lack of success in dealing with a few manufacturers caused us to change tactics. Instead of asking them to estimate the size of the jelly bean market, we began asking them what they thought of the figures we received from the industry analysts at the Commerce Department as well as the Census Bureau. We decided to try to find someone who actually filled out the Census survey and get a reaction to the Census figures. We spoke with the owner of Herbert Candies, a small candy company. He gave us his 1984 jelly bean production and cost statistics, told us he filled out the Census report, and readily explained what he thought the Census statistics meant in terms of jelly bean production and cost. Furthermore, using his calculator, he helped us arrive at national figures for 1984. He also told us which companies manufacture 80% of the jelly beans produced in the country.

Now, armed with actual figures for 1984 jelly bean production, average cost per pound, average number of jelly beans in a pound, and the percentage of jelly beans produced during Easter, we resumed calling manufacturers---this time to get their opinion of our figures. This was the real turning point in dealing with the manufacturers. Because everyone in the industry knew that there were no exact numbers on the size of the jelly bean market, as professionals, they were afraid to give a figure because anyone could say it was wrong. However, because they were experts in the business, they were not afraid to criticize someone else's information. Reactions from insiders were just what we needed to help hone a good working number. The manufacturers were able to tell us why our figures were good or not and they gave us sound reasons why the numbers should be adjusted, such as "Based on our sales figures your numbers sound a little low," or "Not all manufacturers report to the Bureau of the Census so that figure may be low."

To show how this tactic prompted many manufacturers to be candid about both the industry and their sales in particular, here are highlights of our conversations with nine companies. What is presented below may seem to be too detailed, but after reviewing them we hope that it proves our point about how open business executives can be about their company.

1) Owner, Herbert Candies (small manufacturer and retailer)

* 90% of jelly beans are sold at Easter
* 60% of Census seasonal category are jelly beans
* average cost of jelly beans is $1 per pound
* when President Reagan first got into office the jelly bean market shot up 150% but now it is back to normal
* 4 companies have 80% of the market with E.J. Brach the largest at 40%, Brock the second largest, followed by Herman Goelitz and Maillard
* his company sold 30,000 pounds this past year and 90% at Easter; 10,000 were gourmet beans at $3.20 per pound and 20,000 were regular jelly beans at $2.80 per pound

2) Marketing Department, Nabisco Confectionery

* suggested we call SAMI, a private market research firm
* estimated 90% of jelly beans are sold at Easter
* confirmed that E.J. Brach has 40% of the market

3) Vice President of Marketing and Sales, Herman Goelitz (producer of "Bellies," Ronald Reagan's favorite)

* between 35% and 50% of his jelly beans are sold at Easter
* $1 per pound could be the average retail price
* a retailer can purchase jelly beans at $.60 per pound
* the retail price ranges between $1.25 and $5 per pound

4) General Manager, Burnell's Fine Candy (manufacturer of hanging bag jelly beans)

* 75% of jelly beans are sold at Easter
* $.60 to $.75 per pound is average manufacturer's price
* $1.59 is the average retail price
* 75% of Census seasonal category is probably jelly beans

5) Senior VP of Marketing and Sales, E.J. Brach (largest manufacturer)

* produces 24 million jelly beans annually at an average price of $.86 per pound
* there are approximately 100 beans per pound
* Brach's selling price is about industry average
* they have about 50% of the market
* 90% of the jelly beans sold at Easter sounds too high

6) Product Manager of Marketing Department, Brock Candy (second largest manufacturer)

* 85% to 95% of all jelly beans are sold at Easter
* average price paid by retailers is $.59 to $.99 per pound
* there are 130 to 140 jelly beans in a pound
* E.J. Brach has 40% to 50% of the jelly bean business - 32 to 45 million jelly beans sold in a year sounds correct given Brock's production figures; but probably it is closer to the high side
* Brock Candy is number 2 in the industry
* there are not many jelly bean manufacturers and basing total production on E.J. Brach's sales figures is a good way to arrive at an industry estimate

7) Traffic Manager, Powell Confectionery (medium size producer)

* 75% of jelly beans are sold at Easter judging from Powell's sales

Be patient. If any phone number is incorrect, call (area code) 555-1212 and request the new listing.

Information Is Power

* average retail price $.75 to $.80 per pound and the average manufacturer's price is $.65 to $.70 per pound
* 35 to 45 million jelly beans per year sounds reasonable
* it seems fair to double E.J. Brach production figures to get the total market because it has about 50% share of the market

8) President, Ferrara Panned Candy (largest panned candy producer)

* familiar with Census data and believes that jelly beans represent about 75% to 80% of the seasonal sales
* 80% to 90% of all jelly beans are sold at Easter
* 32 to 45 million pounds per year seems a bit low
* E.J. Brach has 50% of the packaged jelly bean market but has less than half of the bulk jelly bean market

9) New Product Development Manager, Farley Candy

* familiar with Census data and believes that the numbers are understated because not all companies report their figures
* an industry estimate of 32 to 50 million pounds per year seems low

So much for all those who discouraged us from even tackling this issue of the market for jelly beans. All the data poured forth during these telephone conversations provided more information than our Fortune 500 client ever expected.

Deciding On An Estimate

As you can see from the interviews outlined above, traffic managers all the way up to company presidents were willing to give us their best estimate of the size of the market and even divulge their own company's sales figures.

After government experts, the figure seemed to cluster around the 45 to 50 million pound range. It may not be that obvious from just reading the highlights of our interviews, but that consensus became apparent after talking with about a dozen people.

Information Exchange Is A People Business

It is just surprising what company executives and government experts are willing to tell you if they are approached in the right way. You can find the answer to any question (or at least a good estimate) as long as you expect to make many phone calls and you treat each person on the other end of the telephone in a friendly, appreciative way.

The biggest difference between those who succeed in their information quest and those who fail boils down to whether or not they believe the information exists. If you persist in thinking the information can be found, nine times out of ten you will get what you need.

My Favorite Bureaucrat Award

In 1989, Information USA awarded $5,000 to the best story submitted describing how a bureaucrat was of help to you. Two runner-up awards were also given at $500 each. We received close to 1,000 entries and each one proved once again how important and powerful government resources can be. Listed below are a selection of the stories we received. The entry number at the end of the story reflects the number assigned to the entry at the time of submission. If you would like to know about the winner, contact our office.

* Children's Book Writer Finds Success With Free Marketing, Legal and Tax Help

A man in Seattle, Washington wrote a book called "Bill the Dog and Mr. TV Head," but didn't know what to do with his great idea until he contacted his local Small Business Development Center. He read about the center in Information USA's "Government Giveaways for Entrepreneurs." He made an appointment to meet with a counselor, Bill Jacobs, the very next day. As the writer tells it, Bill Jacobs was great. He went over all the facts and asked twenty more questions that the author, himself, hadn't ever thought about. Since the product was an educational book for children, Mr. Jacobs gathered a bundle of marketing information from the U.S. Department of Education. He helped the author settle on objectives and determined how to best meet them. He also secured a government mailing list of those interested in the book, and arranged to get him lower mailing rates at the post office as well as help in filing his taxes. All these services were free of charge. (Entry #3)

* Public Works Worker Passes Buck Quickly To Save Credit Manager's Job

A credit manager for the Sherwin-Williams company had trouble collecting on an old debt of $2,220 worth of paint sold to the Public Works Department of the City of Oakland, California. His boss said that if he didn't collect the check by the end of the month, he would have to suffer the consequences, both financially and emotionally. He kept calling Public Works and didn't receive any attention until a Ms. Perle Goins heard about his predicament. Perle processed the check immediately and called him to see if he would like to come down in person to pick it up. Although the San Francisco earthquake had recently occurred making travel difficult, he went down immediately to pick up the check. The credit manager says that Perle saved his job and possibly his career because "she cares and is willing to do what it takes to get the job done." (Entry #8)

* HUD Auditor Helps Co-Op Owners In Arizona

An auditor for HUD was sent to the Concord Village Co-Op in Tempe, Arizona to investigate a report of irregularities sent into HUD's Inspector General's Office. Since his initial visit he continues to return to investigate when aggravated co-op owners call on him. The owners feel that this auditor is their only recourse in dealing with management. (Entry #16)

* State Official Returns Kidnapped Son To Mom

In August, 1979, a separated woman living in Wisconsin came home one day to find her son had been kidnapped by his father. She contacted Christopher Foley, Wisconsin's Attorney General, and found that she had very little recourse because the father and boy had left the state. A year later Mr. Foley called the mother to tell her that the laws had changed so they now had the right to go after the father and return the boy. By searching telephone records Mr. Foley was able to locate the father in Houston, Texas and had him arrested. Mom flew down to pick up her son. The mother feels she would never have had her child back if it were not for Mr. Foley's efforts to act above and beyond the call of duty by making that extra phone call one year later. (Entry #18)

* Inmate Says Welding Instructor Is Saving The World

An inmate at the Oregon State Penitentiary has a welding instructor named Joe Karvandi who is dedicated to helping inmates learn a trade or skill. Joe believes that inmates who respond to training are likely to be become productive members of society, because they've been given an example of a normal, responsible life style. The inmate feels that without this man's determination and concern for society, the percentage of repeat criminals would be much higher. He believes that Joe is reaching at least one in ten inmates and that his contribution is making our society a better and safer place to live. (Entry #30)

* County Official's House Call Is Highlight Of Plumber's Life

A woman named Sheri moved to rural Mississippi with her husband, three year old daughter, and seventy-eight year old father. Within months of moving, her father was diagnosed with throat cancer. Her father's income came from a New York plumber's union pension which needed notarized documents in order to continue sending him checks to pay his medical bills. Sheri's father was bedridden so she couldn't leave the house to see a notary. Mr. Bobby Parker, a county beat supervisor, heard about the problem. He not only took the time to drive way out to their house to see her father and handle the paperwork, but he also visited with her father and made him feel like the most important appointment on his schedule--something much needed by a lonely, terminally ill, elderly man. Her father died a few months later taking with him the memory of his last and gratefully finest outside contact. (Entry #32)

* County Commissioner Is Last Hope For Dying Cancer Victim

A woman living on the East Coast traveled 1,100 miles to Oklahoma to care for her mother who was dying of stomach cancer. When she got there she found her mother in a messy situation. Her mother was living on $400 per month and the doctors and health care providers wanted to charge as much as $92 per visit. Everywhere she turned she was told that her mother was not eligible for any special medical programs. In desperation she called a friend who in turn called County Commissioner Elton Lamb. Within an hour Elton was at her house, took one look at her mother, and within minutes returned with the county nurse. The nurse proceeded to give her morphine, along with instructions on how to administer more when needed. Mr. Lamb took the woman's daughter aside and said "No widow-lady should have to suffer like this, just because she can't afford help. I am very sorry that happened and it is all taken care of now." That night her mother died in her arms. She will never - as long as she lives - forget the compassion of County Commissioner Elton Lamb. (Entry #41)

* State Librarian Saves Government Contractor Hundreds In Documents Costs

A contracts administrator in Utah works for a business that relies on government contracts. He relies on Ferne Kelso, Procurement Consultant at Utah's Military Specification Library, to deliver military specifications quickly and inexpensively when he needs them. In recent months he has sent three different people over to her office to get documents. None had any prior knowledge about how to find the documents they needed, but by the end of their first library visit, they could easily find all of them. When they came across documents the library didn't have, Ferne directed them to the necessary sources and always recommended alternative sources with specific names and telephone numbers. Through her friendliness and wonderful, helpful attitude, she has saved his company hundreds of dollars in labor and documents costs. (Entry #44)

* Delinquent Taxpayer Finds A Helpful Hand At The IRS

A woman in Virginia Beach owed the IRS a lot of back taxes as well as penalties. Revenue Agent L.R. Phelps was assigned to find Mary and collect.

Be patient. If any phone number is incorrect, call (area code) 555-1212 and request the new listing.

My Favorite Bureaucrat

When Ms. Phelps located Mary, she was very helpful in solving her problem and worked out a payment schedule. Ms. Phelps performed her job in a manner that was friendly but professional, understanding but firm, and patient but aggressive. Mary says she is embarrassed to admit she found a helpful bureaucrat and she's glad Ms. Phelps is in the position. (Entry #53)

* Iowa Governor Keeps Trucks Rolling For Small Businessman

A dispatcher who works for Morgan Drive Away in Iowa, was trying to make sure one of the trucks loaded with gym equipment would make it in time to meet a ship in California. The ship would deliver the equipment to U.S. servicemen overseas. Along the way ,the truck driver was stopped in a southern state and told by authorities that he couldn't travel that day because it was Columbus Day. If the driver didn't travel that day, he would miss the boat. The driver called the dispatcher. The dispatcher told management and somehow Governor Terry Brandstad called Sandy to tell him that he personally talked to the Governor of the southern state involved and everything was now on its way. (Entry #54)

* Local Agency Worker Gets Money In Hours to Save Family from Losing Home

A mortgage company in South Carolina had a client who was about to lose his house if he didn't make his payment the next day. The mortgage company took the client in to see Johnny Ruth Jenkins at the local Human Resource Center. She immediately sized up the situation and realized it was an emergency. She stopped what she was doing, skipped lunch, and within a few hours was able to get the funds from another government agency to pay the bill. Since the incident, the family has been back on their feet, but would have been homeless if it weren't for Ms. Jenkins. (Entry #70)

* Motor Vehicles Clerk Shows Driver How To Beat The System

A woman in Massachusetts and her husband moved and had to change their motor vehicle registrations. The woman took the necessary paperwork for her and her husband's car to the Registry of Motor Vehicles to make the necessary changes. Changing the registration for her car was a snap. But when it came to her husband's car the clerk said, "We can't process this without your husband's signature." Her heart sank. She told the clerk it was going to take another day or two to get the signature because her husband worked a long way off. The clerk said, "Go outside, get your husband's signature and bring it back to me." The clerk kept repeating this phrase to her and she kept telling the clerk it was going to take two days. They kept going back and forth. She thought the clerk had no brains, and that there was a total breakdown in communication, so she left. On the way out the door she realized what the clerk was telling her to do. She went behind a tree and forged her husband's signature. When she came back into the office the clerk said, "You didn't have to go all the way outside." (Entry #72)

* State Tax Auditor Shows Small Business How To Reduce Tax

A woman was running a small business in New Jersey when the state tax auditor walked into her office one day and asked to see all of her records. After reviewing the documentation for several days, it was clear that she was due a heavy fine for not having the necessary paperwork to identify which customers were tax exempt, and a problem in her payroll records. However the agent was terrific. He was friendly and personable and told her exactly what to say in a letter to his supervisor to try and get the fine reduced. In a few weeks she received word that she would only have to pay a token fine. (Entry #77)

* Bureau of Mines Asbestos Researcher Saves the Day For Litigator

A legal researcher working on a class action asbestos case identified an important study at the National Archives that was 50 years old. The study concluded that asbestos is one of the most hazardous substances known to man. The study was signed, but the credentials of the author could not be found until the legal researcher contacted Bob Virta, staff asbestos researcher at the Bureau of Mines. Bob spent that afternoon in the Bureau's library and immediately faxed the researcher chapter and verse about the author in question. Bob sent articles with his comments on the side, information on his academic awards, the accession number of his correspondence file when he worked at the Bureau and even the location of the cemetery where he's buried. He also included a list of people who attended the funeral back in 1972. (Entry #78)

* Ex-Corporate Executive Saves Over $5,000 in Tax Accounting Charges by Using IRS Hotline

An ex-corporate executive in Delaware was used to having his taxes prepared by high priced tax consultants. When he retired he decided to try it himself, but ran into problem because he didn't know how to handle something called "passive activity losses". He called the IRS "800" number and found Mrs. Pat Phillips who researched his question and called him back within a day. She also followed up by sending him some sample work sheets explaining the solution in detail. The next tax season he called the IRS hotline again and continued to get excellent responses. He estimates that this free service has saved him at least $5,000 in tax consulting services. (Entry #83)

* Postal Service Consumer Affairs Gets Results for Lousy Delivery

A computer company in New Jersey moved their offices to a new location on the second floor of a building. The new postal carrier disliked having to climb up the flight of stairs and started harassing the company and obstructing mail delivery. The company called the carrier's supervisor, with no results. They contacted the regional office and also got no results. Then they called the U.S. Postal Service's Office of Consumer Affairs in Washington, DC. They wrote a letter as advised, and promptly got a visit from an official at the regional office, followed by an apology from the postal carrier. (Entry #84)

* New Jersey Chemical Company Succeeds In Business Thanks To Many Helpful Bureaucrats

A manager at Moeller Chemicals recalls Thomas Jefferson who said, "My God, how little do my countrymen know what precious blessing they are in possession of and which no other people on earth enjoy." He believes helpful bureaucrats are one of these precious blessings Jefferson referred to in his writings. He has used Nina McGlone, a clerk at the U.S. Department of Treasury, to help him through a tax problem which dates back to 1985. Special DEA Agent Leslie D. Hoppy at the U.S. Department of Justice was a great help to him in showing their company how to fight against the illicit use of chemicals for the manufacture of narcotics. And, John Markus, Chief of Manufacturing and Quality Control for FDA's Center for Veterinary Medicine, has spent many valuable hours helping him through tedious animal drug applications both over the telephone and through the mail. (Entry #84)

* Young Woman Buys Condo With Help Of Little-Known Money Program

A woman living in the District of Columbia thought that at the age of 27 she would never be able to afford her own home--but she was wrong. A little-known local program allowed her to put down 5% on a one bedroom condo, gave her a loan at 3% for $16,000, and gave her a loan at 0% interest to cover the $4,000 closing costs. The rest was financed conventionally. (Entry #93)

* Customer Service Manager For Machinery Corporation Learns Real Customer Service From Government Trade Specialist

The customer service manager for a U.S. subsidiary of a Japanese company was making calls all over the government trying to obtain the necessary forms for exporting and then re-importing repaired circuit boards from Japan. Someone eventually directed him to Mary at the U.S. Department of Commerce. She listened to the problem and said she would find the answer. She got the answer, called him back immediately and volunteered to send him the necessary forms. She also volunteered to make the calls necessary to find out where he should send the forms. She was uncommonly courteous, polite and eager to help. She also called him back in a few days after he received the forms to see if everything had gone smoothly. This customer service manager said he "learned some principles about customer service" from her. (Entry #94)

* Congressional Assistant Helps Citizens Committee Turn NIKE Site Into Community Golf Course

Ed Murnane, while working as an assistant to Congressman Philip M. Crane, worked with the Citizens Committee of Arlington Heights, IL to convince the

Be patient. If any phone number is incorrect, call (area code) 555-1212 and request the new listing.

My Favorite Bureaucrat

government to give up their plans to build a grandiose Army reserve center in the middle of their town and to instead deed the property over to the city to be used as a park. He went to bat for the community by helping to motivate, inspire and formulate a plan of action that was eventually effective. The city now has a 90 acre golf course that gets over 60,000 rounds of play a year. (Entry #97)

* Smiling Immigration and Naturalization Service Official Takes Pride In Helping Adopted Babies

A few years ago a couple in New Jersey started the long, arduous and frustrating process of filing for a foreign adoption. It involved standing in lines for hours to pick up a single form and took them to city, state and federal offices. After one year of paperwork, they got a call from their adoption agency saying there was a baby girl waiting for them in Chile. They immediately went to work on the final paperwork because they were told it would take six weeks to process. After many telephone calls to the Newark INS Office, the woman finally reached a HUMAN who asked how she could help. When she heard about the baby she said, "How wonderful - you must be so excited. Come over to my office right away." When the woman arrived she was greeted by a smiling woman, Mrs. Pollard, who had an entire wall covered with pictures of "her babies" that she had helped get adopted in the U.S.. What was supposed to take 6 weeks, this smiling bureaucrat did in only 30 minutes. On the way out the door, Mrs. Pollard wished her luck in her new role as a mother and said she expected a picture for her wall. (Entry #103)

* State Legislative Researcher Finds Money For Struggling Artists

Any time a researcher from the South Carolina Chamber of Commerce needs some information for one of her members, she calls Len Marini, researcher at the Joint Committee on Cultural Affairs. Although he has an amazing scope of professional and volunteer commitments, he always responds immediately to any of her needs. More astounding is his dedication to the cultural community at a grass roots level. He devotes much of his time to help struggling artists, actors, photographers, et. al. He is creative in seeking ways to fund their projects, as well as providing moral support and guidance. He also participates in the arts. He serves on the boards of the local theater and library, works the theater concessions, and has had leading roles in productions such as A Streetcar Named Desire. (Entry #105)

* Call To County Consumer Office Gets Two Free T-Bones

A man in Nassau County, New York was walking into a local food market when he saw a sign on the window that read "Sirloin Steak $1.19 per pound" (this was a few years ago). When he walked over to the meat counter he saw only one badly cut steak in the case. He rang the bell and asked for another cut but was told there was nothing more to cut from. He asked to speak to the meat manager and got no results. He asked to see the store manager and got no results. He went home and called James Picken, Jr., Commissioner of Consumer Affairs. Later that night after he finished dinner, the doorbell rang and standing there was the store manager with two free 2-inch sirloins as a peace offering, thanks to the commissioner's phone call to the store. (Entry #111)

* Michigan Banker Gets The Law Changed In An Afternoon On The Hill

A Michigan banker visiting Capitol Hill with other bankers overheard talk about a piece of legislation which would affect his bank and a handful of other banks in the county. After talking to his Congressman's aide, who called other congressional aides, they were able to get the legislation changed within hours. (Entry #114)

* Government Helps Firearms Entrepreneur On Consulting Fees

An Air Force employee was very active in target shooting and decided to get into the business. He realized that he needed the proper licenses from the U.S. Office of Alcohol, Tobacco and Firearms, when he saw advertisements in gun magazines for consultants who would charge big money to get this information. When he called the office directly he found that the government would send him the information for free, let him attend free seminars on the topic, and provide him with an 800 number to answer any special questions. (Entry #117)

* Bureaucrat Barred Thalidomide

During the early 1960's, thousands of pregnant women in Europe took a new sedative called thalidomide that resulted in the birth of babies without arms or legs or with other deformities. A low level GS-14 bureaucrat, Dr. Frances Lesey at the Food and Drug Administration, held off the pressures from the drug companies and even from within the FDA to approve the drug before she had finished testing it. (Entry 119)

* Coordinator of Vital Records Saves Families And Funeral Directors Valuable Time

Until recently it took 120 to 150 days to have either a major or minor correction made to a death certificate in New York City. When Mrs. Francine Benjamin went to work for the city Department of Health, she cut this time down to 10 days even though it had been done the other way for 20 years. (Entry #121)

* U.S. Attorney's Public Service Includes Towing Stranded Automobiles

Two women driving through Montana on the way to a wedding found themselves stranded in the middle of a Crow Indian Reservation. Along came a very kind man who stopped, drove them to the nearest town, got a tow chain, drove them back to their car, and towed them to a town 40 miles away where they could get help. He was the U.S. Attorney for Billings. He wouldn't take money and said he hoped they would do the same if they found someone stranded.

* Social Security Administration Tracks Down Missing Father Of 20 Years

The parents of Mr. James divorced in 1943, while he was serving in the U.S. Army Air Corps. Although he kept up with his mother, he could not find his father no matter how much searching he did through government organizations and public records. Twenty years later his congressman's office told him to write his father a letter explaining that he wanted to contact him, and they would have the Social Security Administration forward it to his last known address. In this way, confidentiality would be maintained. Within a week his father contacted him and arranged for an immediate two week visit. (Entry #124)

* Genealogy Researcher Gets A Surprise Bonanza From County Clerk

When a man in Illinois wrote to the County Clerk's office in Salem, Indiana, he was in for a pleasant surprise. His letter was a request for marriage records from the 1850's for some of his wife's ancestors. The clerk at the office not only sent him copies of the old marriage records, but gave him her home address and said that he could write her personally if he needed more information. He did write her and received so much family history information that it extended his wife's family line back to the pre-Revolutionary War era. Over the years he wrote to her a few more times and each time she responded quickly and efficiently. (Entry #135)

* State Geological Office Saves Residents From Collapsing Mines.

An area in Ohio was plagued by abandoned mines that were collapsing and seriously damaging houses. Property owners were descending on the local library to obtain precise information on the location of the mines. The library didn't have such information, but the head of reference services contacted the state Geological Survey Division and was put in touch with Mr. Rea. Mr. Rea saved the day. He patiently explained the terminology to the librarian in detail so that she could order the proper documents. There were different scale maps available and he advised her to first look at a small-scale map covering the whole county (which he sent free of charge), and then decided for which areas more detailed maps were needed. After the first phone call he even called back to explain that the maps were on light sensitive paper and should be kept away from light. Within days, and with his help, all the necessary maps were available for library patrons. (Entry #137)

* Local HUD Official Saves Mother Of Two From Living In The Streets

A young woman in Ohio living in HUD subsidized housing was about to be evicted because she was behind in rent. The woman had two children and also received aid for dependent children. Her sister called the local HUD office and

Be patient. If any phone number is incorrect, call (area code) 555-1212 and request the new listing.

My Favorite Bureaucrat

asked to make arrangements for the woman and her children to remain in their home if the rent was caught up and advance payments were made. The answer was a resounding no. The only immediate solution would have been to have her and her two children move into her mother's two bedroom apartment. Her mother had recently undergone a serious back operation and had no income, therefore the solution was not practical. Her sister called HUD again and had an opportunity to speak with Ms. Prince. Ms Prince superseded the system, allowed the woman to pay back rent, and gave her an extension on her lease pending an inspection. The woman was very grateful because she knew that once evicted from federal housing, she wouldn't be eligible to apply for subsidized rent again. If this had occurred, she would have been forced to live in a crowded situation or on the street. (Entry #138)

* Attorney General Retrieves $1,000 For Couple From Phantom Furniture Store

When a woman in Seattle got married she and her husband fell victim to a furniture scam. They paid $1,000 up front on $1,500 worth of furniture and waited for delivery. The furniture was never delivered. When they returned to the store a few days later the store was completely empty. They called the office of the state Attorney General and were told that there were many people ahead of them who had similar complaints against the company. They also told them that the owners had opened another store 20 miles away. They were given a choice of either waiting in line for legal action, or going to the new store and asking for a refund. They went to the new store, and were given a refund thanks to the information supplied by the Attorney General. (Entry #148)

* IRS Agent Shows Taxpayer How To Beat The System

A young man from Kansas who had recently married reworked his tax return dozens of times because he could not believe that he was going to owe the IRS $750. This was $750 he didn't have. He decided to go to the local IRS office and have them check it. The agent confirmed his worst fears, that he had computed his taxes correctly. But the agent also told him what to do if he couldn't pay the bill. "Do not send in your return until April 15th. Save every cent you can. Then on the 15th, go down to the post office just before midnight and mail your return. Enclose a check for as much as you have saved and a note stating that you cannot pay your tax liability in full at the present time, but you intend to as soon as possible. If you wait until the last minute to send in your return they won't get to it until July, and then it will go into a group of problem returns. They probably won't get to it until October. By then you should have saved enough to pay it off in full, plus interest on the late portion. It's all legal and you ought to come out fine." The man followed the agent's instructions, and just as the agent had predicted, it all worked out. (Entry #153)

* It Only Takes Hours For Newlyweds To Make Their First Move

A man from Detroit, Michigan married a Canadian in Winnipeg, Manitoba. He had heard many horror stories about how long they would have to be separated until they could get the proper documentation allowing his wife to reside with him in the United States. When they went to the U.S. Consulate in Winnipeg, they were met with long lines and were expecting the worst. Instead they met a consulate official named Jeffrey Baron. In less than an hour, he processed all the required paperwork to allow them to both enter the United States. He also explained everything they needed to cross the border into the United States. Instead of waiting weeks, they were able to go into the U.S. that same day. (Entry #168)

* State Senator Saves Beerman's Business

The state of Arizona passed a law which prevented a small beer business from ever doing business again. The owner thought he had lost everything until he contacted State Senator Pat Wright. She took the time to explain his rights to him and all the procedures required to change his situation. With her help and support he ended up in front of the State Senate Hearing Committee and had the law changed. (Entry #174)

* Local Official Pulls All The Stops To Help Woman Get Stop Light

A woman in Michigan wanted to get a traffic light at a dangerous corner near her home. She began collecting signatures, attending city council meetings, and writing city and state officials, but didn't get anywhere. She even collected accident data and understood the ins and out of the "Michigan Manual for

Uniform Traffic Control Devices." Then state representative Alvin J. Hoekman got involved and gave her all the assistance he could. The light was installed shortly thereafter. (Entry #178)

* Consumer Utility Official Saves Customers Money, Returns Part Of Its Budget To The Treasury And Even Offers Free Meals

A report from the Attorney General of Colorado shows that in its first three years of operation, Colorado's Office of Consumer Counsel was solely responsible for $4.7 million in savings to utility customers, and was primarily responsible for $50 million in annual savings and $73 million more in one-time savings. During this same period of time their expenditures were $1.7 million and each year they returned part of their budget to the state treasury. After long meetings far away from home, the head of the office, Ron Binz, often invited committee members to stay at his home for dinner and a night's sleep. (Entry #180)

* IRS Agents Shows How Ignorance Does Not Have To Be Taxing

A taxpayer in New Jersey had a windfall in 1988, and in April of 1989 filed and paid a tax based primarily on his windfall. Then in August he received a notice of a penalty of $1,200 for not filing an Estimated Tax Payment. He knew nothing about such a filing and called the IRS 800 number for help. Mr. LeFleur answered the telephone and spent a good deal of time explaining the rules concerning Estimated Taxes. He also read and explained the categories under which he could claim an exception and not pay the penalty. It was obvious that his situation did not fit any of the exceptions. Mr. LeFleur suggested that he write a detailed letter asking to have the penalty removed. He felt that someone reading the letter might accept "Ignorance of the Law" as an excuse. The man wrote the letter and shortly thereafter was notified that his penalty had been lifted based on his explanation. (Entry #181)

* AID Official Helps U.S. Company Get Turkish Contract

A U.S. Company was bidding on a contract in Turkey to build a national radio transmission monitoring system. However, a Canadian company was about to get the contract because the Canadian government was going to throw in a $100,000 feasibility study to sweeten the deal. The U.S. Agency for International Development (AID) decided to match the Canadian deal and, as a result the U.S. company got the contract. (Entry #182)

* Generous Census Worker Helps Woman With Marketing Plan

A woman in Omaha needed to know the concentration of people between the ages of 40 and 60 in order to develop a marketing plan. She didn't know where to start so she called the clerk of her community for help. This call led to four additional calls. All of the kind and generous people she spoke to were willing to explain what data was available and the best place for her to obtain it. Within four hours, including lunch, she was back in her office with all the latest data she needed to solve her problem. (Entry #183)

* Third Grader Gets Help For Science Project From Senator's Office

A third grader in Louisiana had to do a project for science class on a famous astronaut. He and his mom went to the library and couldn't find anything very interesting to report on. When they got home they decided to call Senator John Glenn's Office in Washington, DC for help. Within one week the boy had a wonderful autographed picture of the ex-astronaut along with a bunch of background articles to make him the envy of his class. (Entry #185)

* Transportation Secretary Gets Parachutist Out Of Jail

In October, 1986, Michael Sergio showed his enthusiasm for the Mets baseball team by parachuting into the middle of Shea Stadium during the 6th game of the World Series, without permission. The criminal court of Queens treated it as a harmless venture and sentenced Sergio to 100 hours of community service and a $500 fine. However, the FAA held Sergio in contempt of court for not revealing the name of the pilot who flew his plane and sentenced him to six months in jail and a $100 a day fine for each day he continued his silence. As soon as Michael went to jail his parents wrote a letter of appeal to the Secretary

Be patient. If any phone number is incorrect, call (area code) 555-1212 and request the new listing.

My Favorite Bureaucrat

of Transportation, Elizabeth Dole. Not only were his parents upset about the cruel and unusual punishment he was receiving, they were also very concerned because Michael's youngest brother was dying of cancer and his brother did not want Michael to be in jail when the end of his life came. Ms. Dole responded quickly and Michael was home with his brother within three weeks. (Entry #188)

* State Counselor Helps Vet When Congressman Fails

When a man from upstate New York received his military discharge, he had a service connected disability but was turned away by the Veterans Administration to receive financial compensation. He contacted his Congressman and even he couldn't help. Years later when a co-worker asked about his limping, he told him his military disability story. The co-worker suggested that he see his brother-in-law who was a veteran's counselor for the state of New York. After a thorough medical exam, a review of the paperwork, and a hearing in front of the appeal board, the Veterans Administration approved him for compensation. (Entry #202)

* Postal Supervisor Bucks The System To Get A Company Its Money Sooner

When a small company moved their offices from Hillsdale to Lakewood, New Jersey, they encountered a big problem. The business depended on the mail for its survival. All their orders and money came in by mail. But because of their move, for some reason their mail was taking up to six weeks to catch up to them. When they called their old post office to investigate the trouble, the supervisor who answered the telephone took it upon himself to change the system and have their mail handled as first class mail each day and not as forwarded mail. This meant that they received the mail within one or two days instead of six weeks. (Entry #206)

* Senator Helps Flight Trainer Business Take Off

An entrepreneur in Milwaukee had been trying for nine months to get federal, state and city agencies to look at his proposal for flight training, but no one would help him. As a last resort he sent a letter to Senator Proxmire detailing his proposal. Within a short period of time he received calls and letters of response from those agencies the Senator had contacted and his business was off and flying. (Entry #208)

* Commerce Official Bends The Rules To Refund $1,000 To Exporter

A management consultant in Chicago put down a $1,000 deposit to participate in an upcoming trade show in India sponsored by the U.S. Department of Commerce. He hoped to represent a number of U.S. companies at the show, but despite his best efforts he could not get a single company interested. When he called the Department of Commerce to cancel, he was told the registration dates had been extended and he still had time to solicit companies. The allotted time passed and he still didn't have a customer. He ask for a refund on his deposit but was informed that the 90 day stipulation had passed and that he was not entitled to the refund. He argued, however, that since they had extended the registration time he should be entitled to the refund. A letter to the supervisor of the person he had been dealing with got him his refund. (Entry #209)

* City Planner Shows Citizens How To Beat The System

A number of citizens in St. Petersburg were worried that a city ordinance might be overturned that required neighbor notification of the installation of satellite dishes. When they contacted Bernice Darling, a planner at the City Planning Department, she gave them great advice. She provided them with copies of the ordinance and the application for change. She also informed them of an upcoming city council meeting concerning the matter. With her help they were able to attend the meeting and stop the ordinance from being changed. (Entry #211)

* Federal Reserve Worker Finds Missing $10,000 For Lady From The Bronx

When a woman in the Bronx had a $20,000 Treasury Note ready to mature, she wrote to the Federal Reserve Board asking that the note be rolled over into two $10,000 notes maturing in two and four years, respectively. She also instructed them to transfer all the interest into her account at Chase Manhattan Bank. When she got her statement from Chase she noticed that she only received interest on one note for $10,000. She called the New York Federal Reserve Bank thinking that all would be lost, but instead found Carol Hayes. Carol really understood the problem completely. She asked a few questions and took her number to call her back. Carol was able to follow the money through the Federal Reserve and into the computers of Chase. During the long process Carol continued to call and give progress reports. She assured the distraught woman that she hadn't forgotten her, and that the $10,000 would be found. When she did find the funds, the lady from the Bronx thanked her to no end. Carol simply said, "Just doing my job." (Entry #212)

* IRS Lets Delinquent Taxpayer Work Out A Deal

A fellow in Oklahoma City was making payments of $1,000 per month to the IRS to satisfy back taxes. However, before he had completed his payments he had back surgery and was laid up for two months unable to earn any money. When payments stopped, the IRS issued a "Notice to Levy" and had his checking and other accounts seized. Although he was truly in the wrong, he called the IRS and spoke to a Mrs. Petrie in the Dallas office. After she listened to his problem she rescinded the "Notice to Levy" and reinstated the repayment plan at half his original monthly payments. He says "this truly was an act of compassion by a caring woman, to whom I am grateful." (Entry #216)

* Woman With Special Title Problem Gets Special Help

A woman purchased a car in Vermont and took it to New York for registration. Due to special circumstances they said it would require eight to ten weeks to process the registration. The woman needed the car for local transportation to work as well as for medical reasons for her son, so she contacted her local assemblyman for assistance. His office said they could not help because they were Republican and the Commissioner of Motor Vehicles was a Democrat. She wrote to the local Department of State and they replied saying they could do nothing. At this time she called the main office of the Division of Motor Vehicles, and after five or six transfers finally contacted Louise in the Titles Department. After explaining her situation, Louise contacted the Director of Titles and worked out a plan to personally walk her title through the bureaucracy. (Entry #217)

* Elderly Mugging Victim Gets Losses Back From State Program

While an elderly man was going through the turnstiles of the New York subway system a young punk snatched his wallet and ran away. The man pursued the culprit but he was too fast to catch. He found two transit police and the three of them spent about a half an hour looking around, but with no luck. The transit police reported the crime to the local police station. A few days later the man read in the newspaper about a state program that compensates elderly residents who are victims of violent crimes. He applied thinking that nothing would happen. Lo and behold, in a few weeks, he received a check in the mail for all the money he lost. (Entry #218)

* Labor Statistics Economist Contributes To Writer's Third Shift

A writer in Baltimore was struggling with a chapter on "How to Survive the Third Shift" for her new book about jobs. She wrote to a regional office of the Bureau of Labor Statistics and received a wonderful response from their office in Dallas. The person in charge of the office sent the writer two articles which served as the basis for the entire chapter in her book. The articles were titled "Late-Shift Employment in Manufacturing Industries" and "Workers on Late Shifts in a Changing Economy." (Entry #219)

* Balloonist Flying High With Help From FAA

When a fellow purchased a foreign registered hot air balloon he dreaded the inspection process required by the FAA. However, he was pleasantly surprised when he ran into Phil and Ernie who are specialists at the FAA. Although getting the balloon ready for inspection was a tedious process with many phone calls over a period of several months, he was very impressed by the two officials. They both had a "we want to help you get this done" attitude, and they always showed an interest in any questions or problems he had. Any forms he requested were sent out the same day and all of his phone calls were promptly returned. On the day of inspection, the balloonist was very late for his appointment, but Ernie stayed even though it put him behind schedule. Ernie also followed up the inspection to see if he was encountering any problems clearing up a few discrepancies. When he sent in his application for air worthiness, Ernie mailed back the necessary forms the following afternoon. (Entry #220)

Be patient. If any phone number is incorrect, call (area code) 555-1212 and request the new listing.

My Favorite Bureaucrat

* Management Consultant Gets The Business From Small Business Office

When a management consultant decided to try to get business from the federal government, he called over 50 small business offices in federal agencies. All but one simply sent him literature on how to do business with their agency. The one standout was Ila Burnell, Small Business Specialist at the Customs Service. She immediately made a personal appointment to meet with him, and gave him other names to contact at Customs. In addition, she referred him to procurement people at NASA where she had formerly worked for many years. Using her name, he contacted these people and was able to set up appointments immediately. Although it's too early to tell if business will come of this yet, he certainly has a running start thanks to Ila. (Entry #221)

* A Bureaucratic Belly Laugh Drops Homeowner's Taxes By $16,000

When a man in Mississippi found out that his property taxes had increased because his house was reassessed at a higher value, he called around asking how he could get his taxes reduced. The general consensus of opinion (and accompanying horselaughs) was that he talk to the county tax assessor. Not to be intimidated he called the county tax assessor, who answered his own telephone, and talked to him. When he explained that he might have been treated unfairly, the assessor asked if he was home during the day. He replied, "Hell no, I'm working two jobs to pay for my home." The tax man had an out and out belly laugh over the comment and said he would send someone out the next morning to reassess his house. The house was reassessed and the man's taxes were reduced by $16,000. (Entry #223)

* State Acts As Super Travel Agent

When a couple in Michigan wanted to travel to Niagara Falls and New York City last summer they called the 800 number for the New York State Department of Tourism. They could request packets of information by pressing numbers on their touch tone phone, and if they needed to talk to someone they were able to talk to an operator. The person answering the phone was friendly, courteous and to the point. They discussed special subjects the couple wanted information on, and the tourism official suggested other subjects they might find interesting. In a few weeks the couple had brochures showing the places of interest, maps of everything, dining and lodging information bracketed by prices, as well as helpful tips on using mass transit. Based on all this information, they made their plans and had an excellent vacation. (Entry #233)

* State Employee Gives Immediate Answers To Employer's Questions

A business owner in the state of Washington called the state capital several times for help interpreting a new state law affecting him, but didn't get anywhere. Everyone was in a meeting and he was told that someone from a local office would call him back shortly. He thought to himself, "Oh Sure." The very next day, Candy Hansen, the Employment Standards Supervisor for the local agency called him. She listened to the question, but her initial perusal of the law did not identify the section pertaining to his question. She apologized for not being able to cite chapter and verse immediately, and said that she didn't want to tie up his valuable time - could she call him back? Within a half an hour she called him back with the answer and the next day he received a copy of the bill in the mail. (Entry #236)

* Labor Official Explains New Pension Law To Taxpayer

A man from Ohio called the U.S. Department of Labor in Washington to get some information on a new pension law. The person he was directed to not only explained the law to him, but also sent him literature about the law and then called him back and quizzed him on the particulars to ensure that he really understood it. (Entry #240)

* FAA Official Keeps Aircraft Company Flying High

A few years ago a small aircraft company in Kentucky purchased the assets of another aircraft company that was going out of business. The one thing they were unable to purchase was the Type Certificate which is issued by the FAA and authorizes the company to manufacture new aircraft. They petitioned the FAA to revoke the original certificate on the grounds that it had been dormant for 25 years and to re-award it to their company. The official from the FAA assigned to the case could have easily recommended a denial of the petition on the grounds that the procedure was unprecedented, and could have saved himself a tremendous amount of work. Instead, he researched the case fully, visited the facility to see if they could support the responsibilities of a certificate, investigated the legal aspects of the case, contacted the State Corporate Commission to determine the bankruptcy status of the old company, and forwarded a detailed file to FAA headquarters with a recommendation that the petition be honored. An official from the Kentucky company told the FAA official that in 30 years of doing business he had never encountered a bureaucrat who went so far out of his way to help. The bureaucrat's response was, "The taxpayers pay me to do a service - I am just doing that." (Entry #242)

* Banking Commission Official Lowers Mortgage Rate Of Divorced Mother And Saves Her $20,000

A woman in Massachusetts had a "locked-in" deal with a bank to finance her new home at 8.75% interest. However, on the day before closing, a bank official called to tell her that because of current banking conditions they could not be held to the 8.75% rate and recalculated the rate to 11 percent. She had already paid the bank a non-refundable fee of $2,000. As a divorced mother of two, with no family in the area, and ready for settlement the following day, she felt helpless. A call to the State Banking Commission changed this. After she called, an official at the Commission made numerous calls to the bank as well as to the attorney handling the closing. The next day the woman went to the closing as advised by the Commission official, signed the mortgage, and immediately told the lawyers she wanted to cancel the mortgage she had just signed. The Commission official spent the next few days reprimanding the president of the bank. The bank president promptly sent the woman an apology along with a new mortgage at the 8.75% rate. The difference would have cost her $20,000 in extra interest.

* U.S. Border Patrol Favors Canadian Student Who Doesn't Lie

A young Canadian couple was attending a college in Michigan on student visas. They were aware of the many difficulties others had encountered with proper papers and officials at the border. Once when returning from Canada, the wife discovered she had lost her official documents she needed to cross the border that day. They knew they could lie to the border officials so that she could enter on her husband's student visa. But they decided to be honest and explain the situation to the officials. They could have been sent back to Canada, but they weren't. The officials told them that many people lie to them and that they appreciated their honesty. The officials immediately found a way they both could enter the country and get back to school. (Entry # 248)

* IRS Official Helps Woman In Illinois Turn $1,550 Loss Into $669 Gain

A woman in Illinois knew she would owe the IRS some money for the Self Employment Tax, but didn't expect to owe the $1,550 stated on a form she received from the IRS. After being unsuccessful trying to get someone at the IRS to explain why she owed that much money, she finally ran into Jean Doughty at the Kansas City IRS Office. Jean listened carefully and then offered to search out and actually look at the original document. She called back and they were going through the return together when Jean suddenly noticed that the woman had listed her income twice. She then offered to rework the whole return - all eight pages, and check it out. About two weeks later the woman in Illinois got a corrected return and a refund check for $669. (Entry # 258)

* State Insulation Expert Offers Expert Advice To New Homeowner

A lady in Scottsdale is very grateful to Dennis Craston who works for the Arizona Risk Assessment Office. Thanks to his advice, she is living in a new home, secure in the knowledge that her children will be growing up surrounded by safe housing insulation. He made himself readily available by telephone to answer all of her environmental quality questions about Urea-Formaldehyde Form insulation and different ways to test for any dangerous toxins it released into the atmosphere. He was willing to listen and not pass the buck. "He offered realistic and helpful advice on testing, how to, where to, etc. He was like finding a lighthouse in a sea of indifference." (Entry #261)

* Sam At The County Government Makes A Heroine Out Of Real Estate Consultant

A woman in Northern Virginia thanks Sam Demme at the County Department of Environmental Management for making her a success at her job. While working for a real estate management consulting firm, Sam turned her into an

Be patient. If any phone number is incorrect, call (area code) 555-1212 and request the new listing.

My Favorite Bureaucrat

expert on the general procedure, forms, and processes involved in bonding and releasing commercial real estate projects. Over the four and 1/2 years she dealt with Sam, each visit was met with a smile and each question, an answer.

* Government Librarian Overwhelms Student Seeking Fellowship

When a student from Milwaukee decided she wanted to apply for a Fulbright grant to do research in Uruguay, she was overwhelmed by the paperwork and turned to Mr. Dorn, the Hispanic Culture Specialist at the Library of Congress, for help. This specialist was able to supply what she needed to complete the application including: 1) someone in Uruguay who would collaborate with her on the project, 2) the name, address, and telephone number for the National Library in Uruguay which she contacted directly for further information; and 3) a lengthy computer search, to verify that no publication existed which might have the same results as her intended research. (Entry #272)

* State Representative Shows That One Letter Can Make A Difference In Changing the Law

A man in North Carolina who usually felt insulated against politically related problems, was upset when he read in the paper that the North Carolina Legislature was about to change the requirements for children entering elementary school. They were planning to move the cut-off date for 5-year-olds from October 15th to July 1st so that the average age of children would be 3 and 1/2 months older and they would be likely to score better than states who kept the later cut-off date. He became angry and decided to call his State representative at home. The representative came in from cutting the grass to answer the phone and told the concerned man that he just happened to be chairman of the education committee and would be discussing that proposal the coming week. He suggested that he write a letter stating his opposition. The man was relieved to hear that shortly after writing his letter, the proposal to change was dropped.

* Single Mom Realizes Dream Home Through Little-Known Government Program

A young, single parent living in Pennsylvania thought she would never be able to afford her own home. She checked out the traditional, conventional, and FHA mortgages, and quickly realized that she would not be able to do it without some kind of miracle. Then she learned about a little known program aimed at low income people which made her dream come true. This program, at the Farmers Home Administration, subsidizes her mortgage payments, and the subsidy decreases as her mortgage increases until she is able to assume the full mortgage payment. Any interest the government paid on her behalf over the years is recaptured (based on a formula) when she sells the house. (Entry #282)

* Clerk Helps Couple Outfox Foxy Lawyer In Small Claims Court

A young couple, recently out of college, was moving to another town to start a new job. All was going along smoothly until the landlord decided not to refund their deposit of $100. The couple filed in small claims court and won, but were sent back when the landlord's attorney filed an evasive legal maneuver which stopped them from receiving their money. The couple had no attorney but with the help of Eileen, a clerk at the courthouse, they blocked the attorney's smart maneuver. She spent a lot of her time at the courthouse and on the telephone ensuring that the couple had correctly filled out the proper forms, enabling them to circumvent the landlord's action and collect the judgement. (Entry #282)

* Ohio Man Sends In $100 For Info - Gets A Bunch Back Along With His Check

A man in Ohio recently sent in a request for information concerning measuring instruments to the National Institutes of Standards and Technology along with a $100 check as payment for the information. He was quite surprised to discover his refunded check enclosed inside a massive packet of information relevant to his project, along with the assurance that more information was forthcoming.

* City Clerk Shows Young Ice Cream Entrepreneur How To Fight City Hall

A young man in Colorado was trying to set up a business selling ice cream from bicycles fitted with freezers. When he inquired about getting the proper licenses from the city he was told that he would need to pay $50 for a license for each

vendor he employed. Since the turnover among adolescent drivers is rapid, the cost would have been prohibitive. A woman in the city office explained the step-by-step process to try to change the law. He followed her advice and after he presented his case to the city council, the ordinance was revised to allow his business to be licensed on a per vehicle basis. (Entry #297)

* Banker Finds A Friendly Banking Official When Starting A New Bank

When a banker in South Carolina submitted a charter for a new bank he was surprised when Mr. Fasbender, the government official assigned to handle the case, demonstrated a personal interest in the banker's efforts and took the time to explain the detailed procedures involved. He was not your "typical" government official. He maintained the high degree of professionalism required, and yet demonstrated that he truly was interested in the bank's success and that he cared. The banker says all this preceded his charter's approval. (Entry #300)

* City Clerk Helps Contest Winner Get $10,000 Prize

A man in Brooklyn was notified that he won $10,000 in a sweepstakes Money Magazine sponsored. But much to his surprise, a follow up letter a few months later informed him he was disqualified after an independent investigation into his application. The man didn't understand the disqualification and believed he was still a winner. He found help from a clerk at the New York City Office of Business Licensing who helped him compose a letter in response along with proper documentation to tell Money Magazine where they were mistaken. It worked, and he received the $10,000 prize. (Entry #305)

* Motor Vehicle Examiner's Advice Is Better Than The Doctor's

When a 70-year-old woman in California went to have her driver's license renewed she knew she would have trouble passing the exam because she had just undergone cataract surgery in one eye. She passed the written exam but was unable to read the eye chart, even with her glasses on, and was told to go see a doctor and then return. After the doctor performed some minor corrective surgery she was sent back to motor vehicles with a note from the doctor recommending that she be given a license for two years. When she went back she again failed the eye test and was tested by a cold, impersonal driving examiner who scared the heck out of her. She tried to play on the examiner's sympathies but got nowhere. He was unbelievably nasty. After her driving test he said that he would test her vision again. When she started the eye test, the examiner told her to read from the upper or distance part of the bifocals (previous examiners never told her that). Then the nasty instructor said, "I don't care what your doctor says, I'm approving your license for another four years. You can see perfectly." (Entry #307)

* Customs Official Shows Trust To Free Man's $15,000 Dust Collector

A man in Utah unwittingly purchased a BMW that was improperly cleared through U.S. Customs. As a result it sat in his garage because motor vehicles would not register it without the proper Customs form. Over the weeks he was shuffled unendingly through the Customs Offices at Terminal Island until someone finally told him what to send to obtain the form. He sent the required materials, then waited. Weeks passed and nothing happened. In a second series of calls he learned that he had been given poor advice and he was to send further materials. He sent them, and waited. Weeks passed and again, nothing happened. Finally he contacted Barbara Smith. The visits were formal at first, but soon they became chummy little talks. Then she did an amazing thing -- she decided to waive the most troubling of the paperwork, trusted in him, and sent the customs release form. Now his $15,000 dust collector is his daily transportation. (Entry #310)

* Helpful IRS Agent Shows Couple How To Appeal A Penalty

A couple in Michigan got a notice from the IRS to pay $2,583 in back taxes. After going through their paperwork, they determined that they did indeed owe the taxes, but did not think they had to pay the interest and penalty. They walked into their local IRS office and talked to Tim Whaley about the problem. He understood and explained how to write an appeal letter to get the interest and penalty removed. He worked with them over the weeks to ensure that all steps were taken properly by both the taxpayers and the IRS. The couple is now waiting for their answer. (Entry #311)

Be patient. If any phone number is incorrect, call (area code) 555-1212 and request the new listing.

My Favorite Bureaucrat

* Forest Service Ranger Helps Mountain Guide Find His Way Through The Paper Trail

When a mountain guide applied for a license in the Olympic National Forest in Washington, he knew he was in for trouble. The forest is made up of many autonomous ranger districts, creating inconsistencies in the application procedure and a monumental paper chase. Many of the districts seem most concerned with logging, and consider alternative uses of the forest an annoyance. Many districts don't even consider mountain guide applications in the same year they are submitted, and in some cases the permit fee costs more than a mountain guide can afford. This mountain guide was fortunate to have the help of Carol Both at the Quilcene Ranger Station. She discovered an obscure regulation that allowed her to create a master permit that would work in all districts of the forest. It not only saved the guide time and money, but streamlined the permit process as well. (Entry #317)

* Firehouse Gets Loan For Expansion After Being Denied

The Lawrence Township Fire Company waited years to be able to purchase a tract of land next to its firehouse. When opportunity finally knocked, they applied to the PA Emergency Management Volunteer Loan Assistance Program for a low-interest loan. The person who processed the application, for some unknown reason, by-passed normal procedure and stamped it "denied." After many calls, the fire company reached Ms. Sandra Lowan in the office of the loan program, who did some investigating. She discovered that the person who had denied the application had never even looked at it. Ms. Lowan took it upon herself to review the application again, found that it was in order, and set the necessary money aside in a special account awaiting the completion of further paperwork. (Entry #320)

* State Treasurer Sends Milwaukee Man $176 Surprise

In 1989 a man living in Wauwatosa received a letter from the State Treasurer of Wisconsin stating that if he could prove that he once lived on 78th Street in Milwaukee they would send him $176. He did so, and they sent him the money. It seems that in 1959 he owned some stock in a company called Curtis Wright. They couldn't find him to send a dividend, so the state had been sitting on his money all that time. (Entry #322)

* Social Worker Goes Out Of Her Way To Keep Brothers In Foster Home Together

Two boys had to be placed in foster homes because their mother was entering drug rehabilitation. The two boys, eight and five years old, were not able to be placed in the same house and their homes were 35 miles apart. The social worker who placed the boys tried to get them together, but when she couldn't she did the next best thing. She would personally take them together to visit their mom. She would also pick them up and take them to their grandparents for visits which would mean five or six hours on the road. The grandmother, who cares deeply for the boys, says they have responded wonderfully. (Entry # 327)

* Temporary Postmaster Didn't Give Up To Save Small Business Thousands On Postage

A small company in Wyoming was sending out their magazine to their customers at $1.05 a piece, and the postage was killing their business. They talked to their local postmaster about getting a lower rate, such as second class postage, but the local postmaster said there was no way they could ever qualify. Then one day a temporary postmaster took over and the businessman thought it couldn't hurt to ask a new person. When he asked, the temporary postmaster was excited about finding a way to get the small business to qualify for the second class postage rate. Although it took him nine months, he finally found a way, and it saved the business thousands of dollars. (Entry #333)

* Damage To Beehive From Bear Is Reimbursed From Wild Bear Attack Grant Program

A man in Denver, Colorado had his beehives broken into by a wild bear. He estimated the damage to be $8,000 and was surprised when he learned that he qualified for a grant from the Colorado Division of Wildlife which would reimburse him for the damage. In addition to immediately agreeing to repay him for his losses, they also placed traps, snares, and electric fences to prevent such an attack from happening again. (Entry # 341)

* State Attorney General Gets Retired School Teacher A Windfall After She's Stuck With Two Timeshares

A retired school teacher in Texas was talked into a time share deal, even though she already owned one time share. The salesman told her if she purchased their property, they would take over responsibility for her old property. She purchased the new property, but, of course, the smooth talking salesman was wrong, and she was still responsible for the old property. She called the state Attorney General's office and they were terrific. They worked out a deal in which the company took back their property, and paid the woman's damages--including all the payments she'd ever made on the first property plus an additional year's maintenance fee and interest. When she continued to receive literature in the mail describing how she could win a new car or $5,000 if she purchased a timeshare from this same company she'd just won a judgement from, she sent the literature to the Attorney General. A few months later she received a check for $50 from the U.S. Department of Justice. The literature she and others had received from the company, was sent on to the Department of Justice to be used to win a case against them for false advertising. The judgement was distributed among all those who had complained, just as she had. (Entry #348)

* Newspaper Man Claims State Safety Official Saved 107 Traffic Deaths Last Year

A newspaper man who covers the Montana state capital watched the Highway Traffic Safety Administrator cut the highway traffic death rate in the state from 300 to 193 last year. His research and steady advocacy were instrumental in winning stiffer anti-drunken driving laws and mandatory seat belt legislation in a climate where heavy drinking, heavier driving, and damn the torpedoes is practically a state motto. He reasoned that nothing educates better than a stern patrolman at the driver-side window, and aimed funding at boosting DWI arrests. He literally turned the DWI picture around in many communities. Many in the state's powerful tavern industry protested, but they couldn't argue with the result of his efforts--a major decrease in DWI crashes. (Entry #350)

* Government Researchers Help Student Get An A+ And Reach The Finals Of A Fulbright Scholarship

A 39-year-old woman in Florida working on a paper in Irish Studies, contacted an Irish Studies expert at the Congressional Research Service on Capitol Hill. When she contacted him about a paper she was doing he spent close to an hour providing her with information which would have taken her months to locate, if she'd been able to locate it at all. He also gave her a number of other sources which proved to be invaluable. She got an A on her paper. Shortly thereafter, she contacted him again for some information she needed in order to apply for a Fulbright Scholarship. He didn't have the esoteric information she needed, but he gave her the names of two contacts at the Irish Embassy who were able to provide her with the needed information. She didn't believe that she stood much of a chance of getting a Fulbright, but with this bureaucrat's help she is a finalist. (Entry #354)

* Alaska Natural Resources Officer Saves Mining Entrepreneur from a $25,000 Mistake

A man in Alaska was about to purchase the rights to certain mines in Alaska for $25,000. He went to the State Office of Natural Resources where a Ms. Rosenau helped him do research to see if the person selling the mines actually owned them. In her thorough investigation of the documents, she found that the apparent owner did not own clear title and could not sell the mining claims. This could have easily been a $25,000 mistake.

* Single Parent Finishes College With Financial Assistance From State Pregnant Women's Program

A single woman in Michigan in her senior year of college, found out she was pregnant. Her baby was due shortly after the end of the semester in which she would receive her degree. As her due date approached, she felt great emotional, physical, academic, and financial pressures. At that point she heard about the Pregnant Woman's Program at the State Department of Social Services. This program provided financial assistance to pregnant women in need. She definitely felt she needed help. Her case worker was wonderful. She guided her step-by-step through the application process and made sure she got the financial help she needed to finish college and have her baby with as little stress as possible. (Entry #384)

Be patient. If any phone number is incorrect, call (area code) 555-1212 and request the new listing.

My Favorite Bureaucrat

* **Office of Civil Rights Official Is The Only Person To Take Grandmother's Charge Of Sexual Harassment Seriously**

Officials at the school where a grandmother was taking courses would not take her charges against a teacher for sexual harassment seriously. Everyone she turned to in the administration thought her charge was laughable. The college ignored their harassment policies. When she took her complaint to the Community College Board of Directors they stonewalled her. She finally contacted Bera Lee at the San Francisco Office of Civil Rights who took her complaint seriously. They investigated the case but could not officially find evidence for the grandmother since the case came down to her word against his. However, she found them to be very understanding and fair. (Entry #391)

* **State Labor Official Is One Of The Best At Finding Jobs For Disabled Vets**

He works 50 to 60 hours a week and spends his own money and time to get the job done. As a result he is one of the best in the country at getting jobs for disabled veterans. Each time Dan Bloodsworth negotiates with an employer to hire a disabled veteran, another man or woman is placed on the road to a new life and not one of them is accepting something for nothing from the government. (Entry #395)

* **Apartment Manager Stuck Out His Can And Got Help From The Garbage Man**

A man in California had trouble managing an apartment building. The donut shop next door continually littered the back of his property and used his dumpster. He called the police and the city sanitation departments, but didn't get any response. He finally got in touch with Gunter Moors, an Environmental Inspector with the city, who changed the situation around. In 15 minutes he was at the donut shop, established new rules for the shop to follow, and arranged for the dumpsters to be emptied twice a week. (Entry #397)

* **When Local Government Gets Him $368 For Stolen Radio, Man Believes Paying Some Taxes May Be Worth It**

Last year a man in Brooklyn had his radio and equalizer stolen while his car was parked in a commercial parking garage. He called the police to report the accident. He spent the next month trying to get his money back from the garage company. They wouldn't pay and he didn't have time to go to small claims court. He had filed a complaint with the Department of Consumer Affairs, but had never followed up on it. A few months later he got a call from a Consumer Affairs office asking if his problem had been settled. It seemed that the garage owner was standing in the office right at that moment seeking a renewal of his owner's license. The official was calling to see if his claim had been settled. Within a few days of the call the man received a check for $368. This makes it a little easier for him to pay taxes. (Entry #399)

* **Soil Conservation Official A Friend To Farmers, Sportsmen And Environmentalists**

Mr. Lloyd Wright, a land-use planner for the U.S. Soil Conservation Service, designed an agricultural Land Evaluation and Site Assessment (LESA) system which requires federal agencies to assess the negative reaction of any federal projects on farmers. He is also responsible for the wetlands program which helps wildlife, as well as fishermen, hunters, and environmentalists, through efforts to ensure that federal farm programs do not negatively impact wetlands. (Entry #400)

* **City Tax Commissioner Gives Back More Taxes**

The City Tax Commission of the City of Norfolk has expanded their program to ensure that more people are aware of the possible ways to reduce their real estate taxes. A certain commissioner helps his staff get the limelight for the work he has done. He is very active in the community. For instance, he throws birthday parties at senior citizen homes for those patients who turn 100 years old. (Entry #413)

* **State Health Official Makes Life Easier For Parents Of Deaf Child**

A couple in Pennsylvania finally decided they were ready for children after five years of marriage. When their first child was born, they were crushed to learn that the child was deaf. The woman quit her job to take care of the child's special needs. Shortly after this, the husband lost his job because of a plant closing. The woman turned to the state government for assistance and was happy to find Mr. Tornbloom who gave them a considerable amount of time, a wealth of information about programs and possibilities, and approved payment by the state for the child's hearing aid. The couple remarked, "He genuinely seemed to value his job." (Entry #416)

* **Vital Records Supervisor Opens Express Lane For Woman In Need**

A woman living near Chicago was concerned about her sister in Indianapolis whose 14-year-old son had just died of cardiac arrest. Her sister's other son was in a hospital in Germany suffering from a collapsed lung. On the day after the funeral, the bereaved mother decided to go immediately to Germany to see her other son, but needed a passport. She called her sister and asked if she would be able to go to Chicago and pick up a copy of her birth certificate which she needed in order to get an emergency passport. The woman had to have the birth certificate in six hours so she could make her flight to Germany. The driving time alone took a good five hours, and when the woman's sister arrived at Vital Records in Chicago, she was told the process of getting a copy of the certificate would take one hour, no matter what the circumstances. She then asked for the supervisor and explained her situation. The supervisor immediately took her hand, expressed his condolences, disappeared for a few minutes and returned with the certificate saying "you better get going." (Entry #418)

* **Student In Wheel Chair Thanks Fast Moving Rehabilitation Counselor**

A student at the University of Missouri was used to bureaucratic paperwork. With a post-polio handicap, she often dealt with a state rehabilitation counsellor who drove her crazy by constantly insisting that rules be followed in minute detail. It seemed that he required every scrap of paper pertaining to her existence dating back to the time of her birth. The student got around campus in an electric wheel-chair she received from the state. One day when the batteries failed, she had to ask campus transportation to drive her around to her classes. To her surprise, when she called her counsellor about the problem, he processed the paperwork immediately and in twenty hours she had her new batteries and was able to get herself to class. (Entry #420)

* **IRS Auditor Finds Extra Bonus For Accountant**

An accountant in a Texas company was worried when she heard that she would be the one responsible for working with an IRS auditor to audit the company's profit sharing plan. However, the experience changed her mind about IRS auditors. She found the auditor to be warm, friendly and extremely professional. More importantly, during the audit, a mistake in the vesting schedule was uncovered. When the company changed its year end a few years ago, the head of the company did not count the short year as a full year for vesting as required by law. This counting of the short year made the accountant completely vested in the plan, instead of 60% vested as she was told by her employer. An unexpected windfall thanks to the IRS. (Entry #421)

* **IRS Problem Resolution Center Saves Home Over $65**

The IRS wrote letters to a lady in Baltimore telling her they were going to seize her house if she didn't pay them $65. A few years before, she and her husband had a cleaning woman once a week and erroneously filed the incorrect form when sending in her employment taxes. The poor lady tried for six months to straighten out the IRS computer with no success. Then came Mrs. Stapleton from the IRS Problem Resolution Center to the rescue. She straightened it all out for the grateful couple and they were able to save their house. (Entry #422)

* **Lead Poisoning Expert Provides Worried Mother With Expert Advice**

A woman in Maryland was frightened and confused when she learned that her daughter tested positive for lead poisoning. She called a number of different agencies attempting to discover the causes, treatments, and effects of lead poisoning. Although she found a number of offices which she thought might be able to help her, no one could give her any clear answers until she spoke with Dr. Susan Binder at the Centers For Disease Control in Atlanta. The doctor listened to her story in detail and outlined the possible causes of the poisoning. Together they arrived at the conclusion that recent house renovations were the likely culprit. She then discussed the potential long-term effects, some of the basic steps she could take to help her daughter, current research and

Be patient. If any phone number is incorrect, call (area code) 555-1212 and request the new listing.

My Favorite Bureaucrat

controversies on the subject, and sent current literature. But most importantly, Dr. Binder referred her to local experts and resources in her area where she could turn for further assistance. (Entry #423)

* State Worker Helps Couple Identify Little-Known Program To Pay For Baby's Skull Surgery

A couple in Illinois felt the financial pinch when they learned that their insurance coverage did not cover the C-section birth of their new daughter. They were also devastated to learn that their insurance would not cover the expenses associated with skull surgery which was needed immediately for their new baby. A case worker for the state Office of Crippled Children solved their problem by helping them through the maze of forms and questions needed to qualify for a program which would pay for their baby's operation. (Entry #525)

* Head Of State Surplus Property Helps With Computer Bargain

When a college professor went to Utah's Federal Surplus Division to investigate buying a used computer, the clerk was unable to provide him with enough technical information to make an educated purchase. He later called Bill Arseneau, head of the state's surplus division, who personally saw to it that the professor got all the information he needed to make his purchasing decision. (Entry #426)

* Supercrat Writes Comic Strip For State Department As Well As Saving Cambodian Refugees From The Khmer Rouge

Chip Beck, a diplomat at the State Department, is an accomplished cartoonist who writes a Doonesbury type strip for a State Department magazine which makes fun of diplomats. During the Indochina War he also found himself responsible for 40,000 people fleeing communism in central Cambodia. They were encircled by two Khmer Rouge regiments and cut off from normal supply routes. He drove Ambassador John Gunther Dean around in an open air jeep during a torrential downpour to witness the plight of the unsheltered families in the midst of a war zone. He jokingly said to the Ambassador, "Sir, I wanted you to see what these people have to endure for the next six months if we don't provide shelter in a hurry." (Entry #431)

* Social Services Official Provides Hotline For Inner-City Pastor

A Michigan pastor works closely with John Rosendall at the Michigan Department of Social Services. Over 60% of the pastor's people are on some form of public assistance. John gave the pastor a special number so that he can call him almost any time of day to handle the problems of his parishioners. He will also check on many of the people who come to the church for help to see if they really need it. Once a family came to the church's food bank for free food and the pastor, questioning their story, contacted John about their background. John found out that the family was earning more money than many of the working families in the parish and most of their money was tax free. (Entry #434)

* Export Expert Provides Fast Info To Business

Bernadine at the Chicago office of the Department of Commerce goes well beyond the requirements of her job according to a researcher who regularly uses her services. Many times she has answered a critical request from an unknown caller to get export or import numbers on some esoteric data. Her expertise is a positive reflection on all U.S. government workers and a godsend to researchers. (Entry #441)

* State Small Business Specialist Helps 20 Year Old Entrepreneur

A 20-year-old entrepreneur in New Jersey didn't have money to hire consultants to get answers to all the questions he had about starting his own business. When he called the State Business Assistance Office all his questions were taken care of for free. The woman counselor informed him of the procedures for incorporation, how to protect the name of his business, as well as what forms and fees would be required. She also counselled him on the advantages of forming a partnership, and when he was unsure of taxes she helped him fill out the necessary forms. (Entry #442)

* Poultry Industry Expert Captures Consultant To Tell Him More Than He Ever Wanted To Know About Eggs

A consultant from Silver Spring, Maryland was trying to get some information about the outlook and trends for chicken and eggs for a client who was in the business. After six telephone calls he made contact with Mr. Weimer, whom he was told from previous calls was the government's authority on the poultry industry. He made an appointment to meet with him and when he arrived, Mr. Weimer began a most in depth discussion with hand-outs, sheets and graphs that spelled everything out in a clear and concise manner. (Entry #444)

* Morton Downey Participant Gets Postal Official To Understand The Rules

While a postal worker from Brooklyn was sitting in the audience of the Morton Downey Jr. Show, he met an aging hippie from Colorado. The man in the audience said that he had difficulty cashing a $3,000 postal money order at the Lenox Hill, New York Post Office. The manager of the post office told him he needed two forms of identification when he only showed him one. The Brooklyn postal worker went home and researched the regulations and found that only one form of identification was required. He called the manager of the Lenox Hill office, and was assured that the station will now comply with regulations. (Entry #447)

* Dental Clinic Clerk Helps Homeless With Bad Teeth

A young man in Chicago who grew up in an upper middle class family found himself homeless for six years. When he finally began to get his life back together and had a full time job as a doorman he began to have problems with his teeth. His hard life had taken its toll. His teeth hurt so badly he couldn't sleep at night and he couldn't afford a dentist. He visited the dental clinic at Northwestern University whose prices were very reasonable but he still couldn't afford it. A young woman in the records office, who understood his situation, took it upon herself to call his brother and arrange payment. (Entry #451)

* FHA Official Helps Those With Late Payment Mortgages

A woman in Indiana is grateful to the woman who runs the local office of the Farmers Home Administration. Without the FHA she would not have been able to buy a home of her own. Soon after she moved in she was involved in an accident and was unable to work or pay her mortgage payments. The FHA Office was very understanding and arranged a repayment program for her once she started working again. (Entry 453)

* Postal Employee Fishes Out No Postage Birthday Cards From Mailbox - On A Sunday

A man in New Jersey waited until the very last minute to buy birthday cards for his wife. One was to be from himself, the other from his one-year-old son. His wife's birthday was on Monday and it was now Sunday. The man knew his wife only liked cards that arrived in the mail, so he drove to the next town which had a Sunday pick-up hoping they would be delivered the next day. When he reached the mailbox and started writing out the cards, an impatient motorist pulled up behind him and started blowing his horn. Hurriedly he posted the cards. When he got home he realized that he didn't place stamps on his cards. It was Sunday, but he decided to call the post office. The man who answered the phone agreed to help. When he returned to the post office the man unlocked the door and came outside to the mailbox to retrieve the cards. He also advised him that if he wanted to have his wife receive her cards by the next day, he would have a better chance if he used another Sunday pickup box near by. He did, and his wife received both of the cards the next day on her birthday, thanks to the Sunday postal official. (Entry #455)

* State Attorney General Gets Alimony Check For Retired Woman

A woman from New York was shocked when her ex-husband told her that he was no longer going to pay her alimony after he retired. He was due to retire soon and she knew she could not make it on her Social Security check alone. She contacted two lawyers to get copies of the laws regarding her situation but they never sent the right ones. When she ran out of money for lawyers, she contacted the Assistant Attorney General of New York and he sent her copies of the laws which showed that her husband had to continue his alimony. She quickly sent him what she received from the state, and he agreed to live up to his responsibility. (Entry #457)

Be patient. If any phone number is incorrect, call (area code) 555-1212 and request the new listing.

My Favorite Bureaucrat

★ Industry Expert Saves The Day For Consultant

A consultant in California received the book "Information USA" as a gift for his birthday last year only to leave it collecting dust on a shelf. The man never bothered opening up the first chapter since he believed the phrase, "I am from the government and I'm here to help you" to be one of the world's biggest lies. He changed his mind when a client walked in and wanted to buy something called Vanadium Slags. He couldn't find anyone who knew anything about them. But by chance he picked up "Information USA" and after three calls found Gordon Schmidt at the Department of Commerce. Gordon not only told him over the phone what it is, he also faxed him important information on the product within 15 minutes. The unexpected eagerness made him wonder if he was on Mars. He now believes that conscientious bureaucrats can make a big difference. (Entry #460)

★ Opera Company Gets State Grant To Perform In Nursing Homes

A new opera company that wished to perform in nursing homes went to the state arts council for help. They weren't expecting much assistance, but to their surprise, they received moral support, encouragement, and $1,100 to get their opera going. (Entry #465)

★ Official Makes State Day Center Happen With Her Own Time And Money

The Governor of Pennsylvania wanted to establish a model State Day Care Center program quickly. Jane Snyder, who was given the project, first worried about how parents, already overburdened with jobs and child care, were going to form the Parents Association required by complex regulations. Diving right in, she helped start the association herself. She paid the application fees from her own pocket and never requested reimbursement. She didn't get overtime pay, but she felt the Day Care project was worth the many extra hours she worked. She got the center running on time and under budget. When the center opened, they needed to write a newsletter but no one could do find the time to do it. That is, no one except Jane, who squeezed in the extra hours on Sunday afternoons. Gifts for the center's Christmas in July arrived compliments of Ms. Snyder as well as other incidentals which the budget didn't cover. At the grand opening, the Governor got all the attention and Jane was off camera consoling a crying youngster and helping a little boy fix his shoe laces. (Entry #476)

★ State Program Provides Van For Wheelchair Dependent Man To Pursue His Dreams

A young man in Arizona had spinal surgery at the age of twelve and was confined to a wheelchair for the rest of his life. He dreamt of getting up and putting one foot in front of another and going wherever he wanted. His life improved dramatically in his teens when he got an electric wheelchair. With his new freedom and confidence, he started to do things like play drums in the school's marching band. He began to realize that perhaps his options weren't so limited as he once believed. Later on in college he dreamt of being a sportscaster, but realized at graduation that he needed a way of transporting himself around. What he needed was his own van, so that he could start knocking on doors, meeting with people, and volunteering for internships--all requirements for getting a job in broadcasting. Believing himself unable to arrange for such a vehicle, he put his dreams of sportscasting on hold. In the meantime he took a job in telemarketing because it provided wheelchair transportation. All this changed when he met Bill Butler at the state rehabilitation department. Bill arranged for him to buy a $17,000 wheelchair equipped van so that he could pursue his choice of career. To his delight, he soon received his big break at a large local radio station. (Entry #470)

★ Bureaucrat Gives Human Response To Environmental Impact Statement

A federal official was working with a large Arizona utility company to prepare an environmental impact statement for their new coal-fired power plant. The statement had to pass muster from the state regulatory agencies. A letter of response from the state agency commented on the artist's rendering of the proposed power plant. The picture showed the main buildings, tall stacks, some landscaping, and a nondescript background with a few clouds drawn in. The letter asked if the sky would actually look like the drawing in the picture. They guessed the state was trying to imply that the sky would fill up with black smoke even though the impact statement showed millions of dollars of state of the art air pollution control equipment. The federal official wrote back to the state saying the sky would look like the picture "Only on partly cloudy days."

★ Older Arizonian Writes Governor About Setting Up A Program To Help People Like Her, and Gets A Call To Set Up The Program

An unemployed, elderly American in Arizona had trouble finding work. In desperation, she wrote directly to the Governor about her problem. In her letter she also described, in some detail, a California program called Network Employment Unlimited that was successful in solving her kind of problem and suggested there should be something like this in Arizona. She also mentioned that she would be willing to help establish such a program. To her surprise, she got an immediate call from another state office wishing to meet with her and discuss setting up the program she had described in her letter. She met with the official and is currently involved in establishing the state program she suggested. (Entry #483)

★ Writer Gets New and Old Help From IRS

When a freelance writer was working on an article about the first 1040 used 75 years ago, she got more help than she expected from Josie Downing at the IRS in Washington, DC. Josie tracked down several internal publications unavailable outside the agency, and provided her with access to the IRS's vaults and files. She provided her with desk space when she came to town and complimentary photocopies. Josie also directed her to the right official at the National Archives for a copy of the first 1040. (Entry #486)

★ A Call To The Interstate Commerce Commission Gets Goods Delivered

National Van Lines was holding the personal goods of a woman from Chicago while they disputed an apparent overcharge on the bill. The woman called the Interstate Commerce Commission in Washington, DC, which in turn contacted the moving company and showed them where they were mistaken. They quickly delivered her goods. (Entry 487)

★ Church Board Gets Census Demographics To Select New Pastor

A woman on a committee to select a new pastor for her church, took on the responsibility to find demographic information about the neighborhoods surrounding the church. She wrote to a regional office of the Bureau of the Census requesting the information. To her surprise, she received all the information she needed and more within five days. (Entry #489)

★ Controller of Currency Clears Up Credit Rating for Credit Card Holder

A man living in Arizona didn't realize that he had a bad credit rating until he applied for credit at a local shopping center. He once had a credit card with the Bank of Boston and had tried to cancel the card but never got a response from the bank. The bank continued sending him a bill for the annual fee. When he didn't pay they also charged him interest on the fee and placed it in his credit report showing that he didn't pay his bills. The man wrote to Senator Kennedy of Massachusetts who contacted the Controller of Currency in Washington, DC. The Controller wrote to the bank, which cleared up the matter immediately. The bank sent a letter of apology to the man in Arizona. (Entry #490)

★ City Code Official Helps Homeowner with Broken Bathroom

A man in Illinois accepted a $400 bid from a freelance repairman to have his bathroom re-tiled. It was considerably less than the $1,000 estimate he had received from a local store. When the freelancer started the job he kept asking for more money and he ended up charging $2,500. The homeowner later found out the man was not a licensed plumber and was wanted in another county for writing bad checks. It cost the homeowner another $2,000 to have a reputable firm repair the job. A code enforcement officer for the city encouraged the homeowner to take the freelancer to court, and helped him through the legal paperwork. He also offered consumer tips on what he did wrong and how to avoid such an incident in the future. Now, the man contacts the code enforcement officer to have him check the credentials and reputation of a tradesman before hiring. (Entry # 492)

★ Election Commission Official Helps Biographer Over Five Year Period

Kent Cooper is a public servant in the disclosure unit of the Federal Election

Be patient. If any phone number is incorrect, call (area code) 555-1212 and request the new listing.

My Favorite Bureaucrat

Commission. He believes that people who live in a democracy should be told clearly how their system of government can be used. When a young writer was living in Washington, DC, Kent was always available to help him piece together campaign finance puzzles. Even after the writer moved thousands of miles away, Kent continued to help. For five years while the writer was working on a biography of Armand Hammer, Kent, almost always on his own initiative, informed the writer about Hammer's campaign contributions on the public record. He also sent printouts of PAC reports that Hammer had directed. (Entry #496)

* Forest Ranger Fulfills Dream In Life

A 47-year-old woman with no job experience had always dreamed of working outdoors. When she applied to work as a Forest Technician at the Sierra National Forest, it was a local forest ranger who renewed her faith in truth, justice and the American way by promoting equal opportunity and hiring her. She now spends her days planting aspens in beautiful green meadows, and building fences, bridges and gully plugs in an effort to save the environment. (Entry #507)

* State Licensing Official Cut Application Process From Twelve Months To Five Weeks

A woman from Michigan moved to Illinois to work as a nurse. It wasn't until after she got her job that she realized she needed an Illinois nursing certificate to work. The process to obtain a certificate took six to twelve months and she had to start work in six weeks. A call to Ms. Paoni at the Illinois Department of Professional Regulations made it all happen in just five weeks. Ms. Paoni personally walked every piece of paperwork through the system. (Entry #508)

* Conservation Officer Gets Rid Of Raccoon Family For Sleepless Homeowner

A female raccoon decided to deliver her babies in a crawl space under a woman's bedroom in Indiana. The woman tried everything to get rid of the mother raccoon and her noisy children including traps, mothball fumes, recordings of barking dogs, and professional exterminators, but nothing worked. After six weeks of insomnia she called Phil, a friendly state conservation officer, who suggested she try rags dipped in ammonia. She did as he had recommended, and the noisy, pesky coons finally left. (Entry #509)

* Librarian Helps Visually Handicapped Want To Live

A woman in Alabama discovered that due to her failing vision she would soon be unable to read, watch television, or drive a car. She went to the local library and the woman in charge of services for the blind literally changed her life. She encouraged her to get a seeing eye dog, and told her about the many free services available through the library, such as talking books. Although her life is different than before, it is still full. (Entry #514)

* State Insurance Commissioner Shows How A Cancerous Mole Is More Serious Than Breast Enlargements

A woman in North Carolina got a notice from her insurance company that they were not going to pay for her claim to have a cancerous mole removed from her back. She knew of a fellow worker who had just been paid by the same insurance company to have her breasts enlarged and thought she was being treated unfairly. She contacted the state insurance commissioner and within the month received payment for her medical care. (Entry #527)

* FHA Official Shows Realtor How To Get Money For His Clients

A realtor in Montana gave up trying to take advantage of government programs to help his clients purchase homes. But he changed his mind fourteen months ago when John Walkup took over the FHA office. John holds monthly meetings to explain the programs that are available. He explains the need for each document, goes through the processes, and makes people feel better. He also holds educational meetings for realtors and streamlines their jobs. In just over a year he has managed to turn a clumsy, bumbling department into a thriving hub of loan activity.

* State Health Care Official Gets Money And Private Bill To Help Terminally Ill Boy

A Wisconsin couple's insurance company would not cover the medical expenses for their terminally ill son. They turned to a state counselor for help. An attorney who works for the service was able to get an insurance company to pay the $17,000 disputed bill. The attorney also got the Governor to pass a law so that their son was included in a new program. This program provided special funds that allowed him to come home from the hospital for visits three times a week when he was stable. (Entry #540)

* State Assemblyman Corrals Wild Steer With 4-Wheel Drive Bronco

A young girl watched as her prize steer, Boggie, bolted out of a California county fair gate. Several men attempted unsuccessfully to grab his rope. Boggie darted past the midway and out a gate onto Highway 86. He was on his way to becoming hamburger meat. As he ran down the highway, California highway patrolmen halted traffic and the chase continued. The steer sought refuge in an adjoining airport. Assemblyman Steve Peace was eating at a restaurant near the airport and saw the steer pursuit. He dashed from the restaurant and jumped into his Bronco to join the chase. Boggie loped down the runway with Steve in hot pursuit. The persuasive, gentle nudging of the Bronco against Boggie's hind quarters, soon coaxed him into submission against a fence. A livestock trailer was secured and Boggie returned safely to the fairgrounds. Despite the stressful event, Boggie did receive a gold ribbon. The assemblyman deserved one, too. (Entry #542)

* State Director of Children Saves Money and Children's Welfare

The former Permanency Planning Director in the state of Michigan works on behalf of children who are developmentally disabled. She has a philosophy that all children have a right to a permanent home. As a result of her work, the federal government provided a small grant to establish a state-wide program in 1983 to support families as they care for their children with special needs at home. The program is now six years old, and has benefited hundreds of children and their families. The program has also enabled the state of Michigan to recover millions of dollars by averting the cost of placing children in institutions. (Entry #545)

* USDA Instructor Teaches Woman How To Give Out Federal Money and Not Succumb to Special Interest Groups

A woman in Washington, DC was placed in charge of giving out state grants for historic preservation. She took a grant managers course at the local U.S. Department of Agriculture Extension Service. Her instructor instilled in her an attitude of fair play and honesty under pressure. On the job she quickly realized that when large amounts of public monies are at stake, there is great pressure to accommodate special interest groups. Those who do the accommodating rise rapidly on the pay scale until they are not needed anymore. She learned the valuable lesson that maintaining integrity is difficult to do, but possible. (Entry #568)

* Mayor Helps Couple Eliminate Flood Insurance

A young couple who could barely afford their Veterans Administration mortgage payments on their new house, learned that the VA required them to carry flood insurance in an area that had next to no chance of flooding. They wrote to the mayor of the town and in two weeks he sent engineers to designate the area as one that did not require flood insurance. (Entry #573)

* Free Trees Available From City Official

The head of the Tree Shade Commission of Paramus, New Jersey promotes the planting, nurturing, and appreciation of trees in the borough. He has a tree nursery where baby trees, when they are big enough, are given to homeowners free of charge. He makes house-calls free of charge to check on the trees and to see if they are sick and whether or not they can be cured. If a tree dies, he'll replace it with a new one. On Community Health Day he runs a booth demonstrating how to maintain the good health of trees and plants. His staff organizes marathons through the park, allowing the runners to pass by and enjoy the trees. He provides wonderful Paramus Mulch free of charge for gardens or lawns. His accomplishments are well known in surrounding towns, and he is often asked to speak to groups in the surrounding areas. (Entry #583)

Be patient. If any phone number is incorrect, call (area code) 555-1212 and request the new listing.

My Favorite Bureaucrat

* Chief Probation Official Saves Secretary's Life

In 1988 a woman in Michigan became painfully ill after finishing dinner in her apartment. The next morning she called her boss, the county's Chief Probation Official. He came over immediately and took her to the emergency room. After surgery it was learned that she had Chrohn's Disease and would have died if the state official hadn't gone out of his way to get her to the hospital. (Entry #584)

* Hang Up Causes Attorney To Get Satisfaction

A woman in Illinois who made a purchase by phone was dissatisfied with the product. She called the company and requested a refund, but the company hung up on her. The Illinois state Attorney General's Office got her the refund in 90 days. (Entry #585)

* Canadian Bureaucrat Helps New York

A businessman in New York praises a Canadian government official. Although the official was due to retire, he did not lose the desire to see the project he was responsible for through to the end. He was working with the state of New York to develop a new energy saving dry wall product. The dry wall absorbs heat when the room is too hot and discharges heat when the room is too cold. The project could have easily been lost in the cracks if he hadn't made it his duty to see it through to completion. (Entry #588)

* County Conservation Official Helps Homeowner Manage Runoff

When the county highway administration widened a road that ran through a woman's property in upper state New York, she was troubled because they stripped thousands of feet of vegetation away and diverted run-off water into her pond. She called the county soil and water department and spoke with Fred Sinclair who arrived within days offering his knowledge and assistance. He gave her literature on water management and lent her his personal reference materials. He even gave her his home telephone number. When she occasionally called him he was extremely helpful, even after a long day at work. He gave her free government materials to help her re-seed the land and offered his know-how to help with the planting. He has revisited the site many times and intends to do so until the problem is solved. (Entry #592)

* State Helps Single Mother Recover $55,000 In Child Support

A man left his wife and two-year-old daughter in 1977. Over time he accumulated a debt of $55,000 in child support payments. The state office of the Attorney General located him in another state through Department of Labor information files. They were also able to obtain his current salary, social security number, address, and the name of his employer. With this information they were able to serve him with a court summons and collect the money he owed for the child. (Entry #608)

* HUD Official Helps Couple Get House

The performance of Jim LaZott, a HUD official in Des Moines, Iowa was like a beacon of hope in a sea of chaos. When a young couple began working with the local HUD office to purchase a home, they found it nearly impossible to get even the basic information on HUD programs. That all changed when they met Jim. Everything was smooth sailing from there. (Entry #612)

* U.S. Agriculture Official Gives Moscow Bears A Taste Of Freedom

When the Moscow Circus was visiting the United States, an official from the Michigan Humane Society contacted the U.S. Department of Agriculture concerning the circus' violation of the federal Animal Welfare Act. Together they tried to get the circus to voluntarily comply with the laws governing the cage sizes for wild animals in captivity. The circus' performing bears were transported and housed in cages that were so small they couldn't even turn around freely, let alone stand up and stretch. The animals were exhibiting stereotypical behavior characteristic of intensive confinement. But because federal laws do not specify exact cage dimensions, circus officials attempted to play a "catch 22" game to get around the law. Although the agriculture official realized that at any moment he or his superiors could receive a call from the U.S. State Department instructing them to leave the circus alone for political reasons, he pursued his mission. After many months of negotiations he was able to work out a compromise in which the circus built a large exercise cage to the Department of Agriculture's specifications and all the bears had four hours of daily access to this cage. (Entry #619)

* States Labor Official Cuts Insurance Rates For Small Business By 30 Percent

The owners of a small foundry in Michigan cite an official from the Michigan Department of Labor as the reason their workman's compensation insurance rates are 30% lower than their competitors'. This official showed up as soon as they opened their doors for business. He pointed out many areas that had to be addressed to eliminate potential hazards and also set up a program where he made monthly visits to teach employees about safety. As a result, the company has never had an OSSA, EPA or Michigan Department of Public Health violation, and received an award for going three years in a row without a lost time accident. This exemplary safety record caused their insurance rates to be 30% lower than their nearest competitor. (Entry #621)

* A Call To Washington, DC Results In Hand Delivered Tax Forms In Arizona

A tax lawyer in Arizona had trouble getting a form from a local IRS office. He decided to contact the IRS Ombudsman's office in Washington, DC to complain about the problem. When he heard about the complaint, the Ombudsman called a local office and had an IRS agent hand deliver the form to the attorney. (Entry #626)

* Forest Service Helps Survival School Survive

A survival school located in Arizona has nothing but praise for the local forest service. They are a small business and whenever they can't meet the payments to obtain their necessary permits, the forest service allows them whatever time they need to make the payments, without penalizing them. Whenever they need to extend the range of their permit, the forest service will always accommodate them. Even when they failed to meet a deadline to sign some papers, a forest service official brought the papers to them, so they didn't have to pay a penalty. (Entry #627)

* State Nurse Helps Mothers Cope With Premature Babies

A woman in Delaware was devastated to learn that her baby would be born fourteen weeks early. She began working with a nurse from the state Early Intervention Program. After the birth of her son, the nurse visited him frequently throughout his four month hospital stay, and after the baby had returned to his home, she visited him many times to thoroughly evaluate his developmental progress. She was the first to spot his hearing loss and helped the couple obtain a state-funded hearing aid for him. She diagnosed his need for speech, physical, and occupational therapy, and helped enroll him in an excellent school. At this time the nurse was experiencing difficulties of her own at home. Her husband was dying of cancer. Despite this, she continued to be an extremely dedicated and compassionate person. (Entry #636)

* FDA Official Helps Inventor Get Clearance

The inventor of a medical device had to get clearance from the Food and Drug Administration before he could start selling his product to manufacturers. His initial call to the FDA resulted in pounds of booklets and forms. When he called back a second time, he not only got exact answers to his questions, but he also received the know-how to achieve his dream. An FDA staffer sent him samples of successful applications to copy from, and told him exactly what was required of him to be accepted by the FDA. With this help, the inventor got his approval in record time. Most companies he spoke with were surprised at how quickly he had managed to cut through the bureaucratic red tape. (Entry #646)

* Student Gets Government Doctor To Help With Term Paper

In 1983, a student studying organizational psychology used the book "Information USA" to identify a physician at the National Institutes of Health to help him obtain information for a term paper. This doctor spoke to the student for over an hour helping him gain a basic understanding of the subject matter. The doctor's assistant sent the student an index of federally funded grants on the subject, a list of publications available from their office, and a thick annotated bibliography enabling him to do further research on the subject. All of this was free of charge. He also obtained the names of other researchers to contact and references to explore. (Entry #652)

Be patient. If any phone number is incorrect, call (area code) 555-1212 and request the new listing.

My Favorite Bureaucrat

* Counselor Takes 61-Year-Old From Potential Suicide To Great Potential

A draftsman in Ohio was laid off at the age of 61. He couldn't find another job and became so depressed, he even considered suicide. By chance, he met a state vocational counselor and she changed his life. She helped him enroll in a computer aided drafting school to update his skills and found him a new job. (Entry #659)

* State Consultant Doubles Income For Small Business Owner For Free

A free consultant from Tennessee's Small Business Development Center helped a small metal products company on the verge of not making it. He helped double the company's income and gave the owner confidence in the future. The consultant suggested the business would benefit if it were to sell to the government. He showed them how to get on the state government's bidders list. Once they had been accepted, he helped them figure out the cost of materials so that they could make a proper bid. The consultant also called the state to get answers to their many unanswered questions, and helped them locate materials and get credit extensions from suppliers. He taught the owner's wife how to do the payroll and other accounting functions. When the company was filling its biggest order, the owner hurt his leg and the doctors told him to stay off of it. Hearing this, the state consultant came by after he got off work, put on a pair of cover-alls and painted grills. One day the company was having trouble with their hydropic press. The owner was so frustrated he was about to scream, when the state official stopped by on his way home from work and fixed it himself, to the owner's amazement. The consultant has been checking up on the business for six months and has gotten them on three more bidders lists. (Entry #666)

* Unemployed Couple Learns About Program Where Employer Can Get Money If They Are Hired

In 1983 a couple moved to Tonawanda, New York to try to get jobs in their respective fields. However, when they couldn't find good jobs they were forced to live on their earnings from part-time jobs and buy food stamps. Then they encountered an official with the local Jobs Training Partnership Act. He showed them how to make themselves more marketable by informing potential employers that they would be entitled to cash benefits if they hired them. This made the difference. The husband was hired and within the year he more than doubled his salary. The man realizes the Jobs Training Partnership Act was the main reason he was able to find employment. (Entry #679)

* Commerce Expert Helps Market Researcher

When a market researcher called the Material Handling Specialist at the Department of Commerce for some marketing data, he was told that the data he needed had not been collected by the government for the last three years. But the specialist, undaunted, said she would try to find some additional information and call him back. A couple of days later she called back and gave him a number of additional sources likely to provide the information he needed. She also went out of her way to apologize for not being able to help him directly and wished him luck. She encouraged him to call back if she could be of any further assistance.

* City Manager Pays For White Shirts Ruined In Washing Machine

A man in Elmhurst, Illinois got his first white collar job and purchased eight new white shirts. When his wife laundered his new shirts, to her surprise they all turned to a rust color. The called the city water department to see if there was anything wrong with the water and got a negative response. They then called the city manager trying to get a refund for his ruined shirts. After a couple of phone calls back and forth and a letter from the city attorney, his request was denied. He then showed up at the city manager's office and asked to see the water department's work sheets for the day in question. The city manager said it would take too much time to accommodate his request. After a few minutes of silence the man asked him if he would take a check for half the cost of the shirts now and the other half in about a week. (Entry #700)

* Judge Straightens Out Life Of Gambler

In 1987 a man from South Carolina found himself broke, out of a job, and in jail for writing bad checks to support his gambling habit. He was easily looking at spending the next five years in jail for his crimes. While in jail he wrote to a local judge for help. The judge called him to his office along with all the people to whom he had written bad checks. Together they worked out a payment plan

and got him a job with the water department. Within a year he was made supervisor, paid off all his debts, got married again and is raising a family.

* Fifty-Six Year Old Woman Thought She Was Unemployable

A 56 year old woman in Seattle suddenly found herself out of work and she thought she was unemployable. The Women's Bureau at the U.S. Department of Labor made an appointment for her with the Mayor's Office for Senior Employment. There a counselor showed her the worth of her skills and got her a job as an editor. (Entry #712)

* Wife Who Works With County Crippled Children Teaches Husband Meaning Of Life

A man from Grand Rapids nominates his wife, who works for the Crippled Children Division of the Kent County Health Department, for the favorite bureaucrat award. She spends a considerable amount of time working out problems, expressing love, and offering understanding to parents who learn that their children will never be like other children. Many of the children die at a very young age. Her understanding of human needs has taught him compassion and tenderness which he would never have learned without her example.

* Congressman Teaches Constituent How To Expect Good Things From People

A congressman from Michigan manages a summer vegetable stand in front of his house. He manages the stand by the honor system with a note asking patrons to place the money for the produce they purchase in an empty coffee can. A constituent recently learned while talking to the congressman, that he empties the can each night and in several years of operation he has never been cheated. The congressman said he believes that people respond to the expectations of others. If we assume others will betray us, people have nothing to lose by doing so; however, if we sincerely respect their potential for good, most people do not want to show themselves to be unworthy. (Entry #716)

* U.S. Postal Service Employees Have Special Programs To Help The Needy At Christmas

During the Christmas season a committee at a local post office goes through hundreds of letters to Santa. The requests from children who ask for food, clothing, or blankets instead of toys, are granted from a special fund set up by postal workers. Fun letters from children asking for toys are also answered personally by postal workers. Mail carriers also submit names of families on their routes that are struggling. These families are adopted by groups of postal workers who donate money to purchase groceries, clothing, and toys for them.

* Job Service Helps Homeless Ex-Marine And His Family

Last year a Vietnam Veteran and his family were homeless and broke. They were living in the back of their station wagon in West Virginia. They decided to go to Mesa, Arizona where they met a veterans affairs representative at the job service office who worked closely with the family to get them food, shelter, and work. By the end of the year, they had a Christmas tree in their own living room with presents under it. (Entry #722)

* EPA Makes Sure Woman Business Owner Gets Contract

A woman in Mississippi was running her husband's subcontracting business for some time while he was ill. When he died, a number of prime government contractors took away her business believing that she could not do the job alone. She contacted the EPA's Minority and Women's Business Representative who took up her case and made sure that the subcontracts were returned to her. She says that this official reaffirmed her belief that the compassion of an individual along with the power of a bureaucracy can protect small business in America.

* Transportation Expert Puts Inventor Into Big Business

An inventor in New Jersey had a great idea for an automobile anti-theft device. The product would enable the customer to permanently etch a federal number on car windows. This would cut down on thefts because a thief would have to replace the windows in the vehicle if he wanted to resell it. This would make car theft too expensive and time consuming. The inventor had trouble identifying

Be patient. If any phone number is incorrect, call (area code) 555-1212 and request the new listing.

insurance companies that offered premium discounts for such devices. Without this information the product would not have credibility or perceived value. He checked through Information USA newsletters for sources of assistance and came across the U.S. Department of Transportation's Office of Motor Vehicle Theft Rulemaking Group. When he contacted the group, the woman he spoke with on the phone listed the insurance companies she thought might offer the discounts he was looking for. While on the line, she located a 52-page report that had been presented to Congress concerning motor vehicle theft, which added more states to the list that required insurance companies to provide a discount for this type of anti-theft device. She also gave him contacts to obtain further information and sent him a copy of the 52-page report, which arrived two days later. One of the contacts provided a free report from the state police agencies which demonstrated how such an anti-theft device substantially increased the recovery rate of stolen vehicles from 20% to over 70%. This information was critical to the future growth and well being of this small business. (Entry #730)

* Government Expert On Paper Preservation Helps Comic Book Collector

A comic book collector in California was worried about the best way to preserve his rare, valuable comic book collection. Certain plastics used for comic storage

are intensely destructive to paper, and he had no way of knowing which plastics were this type. Advertisements in trade magazines were deceptive and confusing. Using the copy of "Information USA" he'd received for Christmas, he contacted Carole Zimmermann, head of the Preservation Office at the Library of Congress. This cheerful public servant not only identified the plastic in question to be highly destructive, but also clarified confusing advertisements, explained the latest laboratory research, and suffered his ignorant questions with grace and an easy laugh. She shared her expansive knowledge in a relaxed, personable, and enjoyable conversation and saved him hundreds of dollars in potential damages. (Entry #736)

* Rehabilitation Counselor Helps Woman in Illinois To See Again

As a result of a spinal tap, a woman in Illinois contracted Multiple Sclerosis. The effects of her disease caused her to lose her eyesight, her job, and have a car accident. In addition to the financial strains she already faced, the roof on her house also had to be replaced. She went to the state's Office of Rehabilitation to see if they could help her find employment since she was blind. The counselor questioned the diagnosis of her eye condition and paid for another eye test. As a result of the test, she had eye surgery and regained her eyesight. (Entry #756)

Be patient. If any phone number is incorrect, call (area code) 555-1212 and request the new listing.

Info-Power Greatest Hits

We've put together this quick reference guide of the hundred or so topics that people most often ask us about, whether it's money to start a business, government auctions, a vacation in the Virgin Islands, free medical care, summer jobs, or birthday cards from the President.

The list is arranged alphabetically, with key words first. You'll find a brief description of the program, a telephone number to get you started, and then a reference to the chapter in *Info-Power* where you can find more information on the topic and lots of other related sources you might also be interested in.

If you don't find what you're looking for in this section, be sure to check the index at the back of *Info-Power.* If you still can't find what you're looking for, call us at (301) 942-6303, and we'll get you headed in the right direction.

* Adopt-A-Horse
Public Affairs
Bureau of Land Management
Suite 5600, 1849 C Street, NW
Washington, DC 20240 (202) 208-5717
If you've got the proper place to put it, the Bureau of Land Management will let you adopt a burro or horse for about $125. *(See the chapter on Environment and Nature.)*

* Aerial Photos Of Your Neighborhood
EROS Data Center
Sioux Falls, SD 57198 (605) 594-6151
The government has taken aerial photos of almost every square foot of the U.S., including your neighborhood. *(See the chapter on Weather and Maps.)*

* Aerospace Workshops For Teachers
Education Division
NASA
300 E Street, SW, Code FE
Washington, DC 20546 (202) 358-1519
NASA holds free workshops all over the U.S. for teachers on astronomy, life in space, rocketry, remote sensing, and more. *(See the chapter on Science and Technology.)*

* Age Discrimination
Publications Center
Equal Employment Opportunity Commission
P.O. Box 12549
Cincinnati, Oh 45212 (800) 669-3362 (publications)
Population's getting older, but companies still want younger employees. Unfortunately, that's illegal. *(See the chapters on Careers and Workplace, and Law and Social Justice.)*

* AIDS Hotline
National AIDS Information Clearinghouse
P.O. Box 6003
Rockville, MD 20850 (800) 342-2437
Know the difference between fact and fiction when it comes to AIDS. Free publications, videos, posters, and research results. *(See the chapter on Health and Medicine.)*

* Airline Passenger Complaint Center
Consumer Affairs
U.S. Department of Transportation
Washington, DC 20590 (202) 366-2220
Was your flight attendant rude? Were you bumped off a flight even though you had a prepaid ticket? Get some action fast. *(See the chapter on Consumer Power.)*

* Air Traffic Controller Job Bank
Federal Aviation Administration
800 Independence Ave., SW
Washington, DC 20591 (800) 960-0600
Lost your airline job during the recession? Maybe you can get another through the Airline Rehire Program. *(See the chapter on Careers and Workplace.)*

* Ansel Adams Prints
National Archives
Still Picture Branch
7th and Pennsylvania Avenue, NW
Washington, DC 20408 (202) 501-5455
Want copies of selected still photos in the National Archives holdings? *(See the chapter on Books and Libraries.)*

* Artists and Creative Writers: Free Money
National Endowment for the Arts
1100 Pennsylvania Avenue, NW
Washington, DC 20506 (202) 682-5400
Starving writer or artist? The National Endowment of the Arts gives out millions in grants each year. *(See the chapter on Arts and Humanities.)*

* Art Slide Shows on Free Loan
National Gallery of Art
Slide Library
Constitution and 6th Streets, NW
Washington, DC 20565 (202) 842-6273
The National Gallery of Art loans all kinds of slides and videos on their collection. *(See the chapter on Arts and Humanities.)*

* Astronomy Hotline
See Star Gazer Hotline

* Auctions at the Postal Service
Claims and Inquiries
U.S. Postal Service
2970 Market Street
Room 531A
Philadelphia, PA 19104 (215) 895-8140
What happens to all those packages that go unclaimed through the mail? They're auctioned off. *(See the chapter on Government Auctions and Surplus Property.)*

* Auto Safety Hotline
National Highway Traffic Safety Administration
Auto Safety Hotline
NEF-11.2HL

Be patient. If any phone number is incorrect, call (area code) 555-1212 and request the new listing.

Info-Power Greatest Hits

400 7th Street, SW
Washington, DC 20590 (800) 424-9393
Safety problems with your new car and the dealer is no help? The government is a good persuader. *(See the chapter on Consumer Power.)*

* Banking Complaint Action

Federal Deposit Insurance Corporation (FDIC)
Consumer Affairs
1776 F St., NW
F 130
Washington, DC 20429 (202) 898-3542
If you've got a problem with any FDIC-insured bank, call this hotline and have it investigated. *(See the chapter on Consumer Power.)*

* Bird Watchers Paradise

See Wildlife Refuges

* Birthday Greetings from the President

White House Greetings Office
Room 39
Washington, DC 20500
The President will send anyone who's 80 or over a birthday card. To request one, write the above office. *(See the chapter on More Info-Power Hits.)*

* Boating Lessons

Commandant, (G-NAB-5)
U.S. Coast Guard Headquarters (800) 368-5647
Washington, DC 20593-0001 (202) 267-0780 in DC
The Coast Guard offers all kinds of free boating and safety courses. *(See the chapter on Vacations and Business Travel.)*

* Boating Safety Hotline

Commandant, (G-NAB-5)
U.S. Coast Guard Headquarters
Washington, DC 20593-0001 (800) 368-5647
Information on safety courses, product recalls, publications, coloring books for kids, and general complaints. *(See the chapter on Vacations and Business Travel.)*

* Burros

See Adopt-A-Horse

* Business Start-Up Money

Answer Desk
U.S. Small Business Administration (SBA)
409 Third Street, SW
Washington, DC 20416 (800) 827-5722
The SBA guarantees small business loans for those who can't qualify through their regular bank. Also contact your state's Department of Economic Development, or your local Small Business Development Center, for information on money sources closer to home. *(See the chapter on Small Business and Entrepreneuring.)*

* Business Loans for Teens

Farmer Programs Loan Making Division
Farmers Home Administration
U.S. Department of Agriculture
South Agriculture Building
Room 5420
Washington, DC 20250
Kids can get thousands to finance their own farm-related businesses from the local Farmers Home Administration, Production Loan Division. *(See the chapter on Small Business and Entrepreneuring.)*

* Cancer Answers

National Cancer Institute
Building 31, Room 10A18

9000 Rockville Pike
Bethesda, MD 20892 (800) 4-CANCER
Everything you needed to know about cancer, plus physician referrals, latest research and publications. *(See the chapter on Health and Medicine.)*

* Capitol Hill Guided Tours

U.S. Capitol
Washington, DC 20510
Before you go to Washington, DC, ask your member of congress for a VIP tour pass to get free red carpet treatment. *(See the chapter on Vacations and Business Travel.)*

* Cars

See Auctions

* Cholesterol Info-Line

National Heart, Lung, and Blood Information Center
P.O. Box 30105
Bethesda, MD 20824 (301) 251-1222
Get the newest facts and research results on cholesterol and your diet. *(See the chapter on Health and Medicine.)*

* Christmas Trees and Firewood

For a nominal permit fee, you can cut your own Christmas tree or collect firewood on public lands. Contact your nearest National Forest or local Bureau of Land Management, U.S. Department of Interior, for details. *(See the chapter on Environment and Nature.)*

* Condom Testing Results

Center for Population Research
6100 Executive Boulevard
Room 8B07
Bethesda, MD 20892 (301) 496-4924
How reliable is that brand of condom you're using? The government has expert testers. *(See the chapter on Health and Medicine.)*

* Congressional Salaries and Expenses

House Documents Room
2nd and D Street, SW
Room B18
Washington, DC 20515 (202) 225-3456
How much did your congressional representative spend on meals and entertainment last year? *(See the chapter on Information from Lawmakers.)*

* Consultants Can Make Millions

Each year government agencies spend millions on freelancers to advise them on everything from engineering and accounting problems to environmental studies and pesticides. Contact the Office of Small and Disadvantaged Business Utilization for whichever agency you're interested in for more details. *(See the chapter on Selling to the Government.)*

* Consumer Products and Toy Recall Hotline

Office of Information and Public Affairs
U.S. Consumer Product Safety Commission
Washington, DC 20207 (800) 638-2772
Want to find out if a toy you bought for your kid is being recalled because it's dangerous? *(See the chapter on Consumer Power.)*

* Country Home Loans

Fannie Mae
Public Information Office
3900 Wisconsin Avenue, NW
Washington, DC 20016-2899 (800) 732-6643
FmHA provides low-interest loans to qualified buyers to purchase homes in rural areas. *(See the chapter on Housing and Real Estate.)*

Be patient. If any phone number is incorrect, call (area code) 555-1212 and request the new listing.

Info-Power Greatest Hits

* **Country Inn Start-Up Money: $100,000**

Office of Rural Affairs and Economic Development
U.S. Small Business Administration
409 Third Street, SW
Washington, DC 20416 (202) 205-6485

A catalog called, *Working Together: A Guide to Federal and State Resources for Rural Economic Development*, describes money and ways to help start businesses in small towns. *(See the chapter on Small Business and Entrepreneuring.)*

* **Credit Counseling for Home Buyers**

If you own a HUD-insured home, and you're having trouble meeting your bills, you can receive free financial counseling. Contact your bank that handles the loan for more information. *(See the chapter on Housing and Real Estate.)*

* **Credit Repair Help for Free**

Don't pay to have your credit improved. Your local County Cooperative Extension Service will show you how to do it for free. *(See the chapter on Consumer Power.)*

* **Crime Insurance at Bargain Prices**

Federal Crime Insurance Program
P.O. Box 6301
Rockville, MD 20849-6301 (800) 638-8780

Residents in 12 states qualify for federally-subsidized crime insurance for their homes. *(See the chapter on Law and Social Justice.)*

* **Crime Victims Assistance**

A mugger stole your rent money, and you missed two weeks of work while in the hospital. Get money by contacting your state's Crime Victims Assistance office. *(See the chapter on Law and Social Justice.)*

* **Dead Beat Dads: Tracking Him Down**

He says it wasn't him. He won't pay child support he owes you. Contact your state Child Support Enforcement Office. *(See the chapter on Your Community.)*

* **Dental Care: Free and Low-Cost**

Contact your state's Dental Society or the Dental School at the university near you for information on how to get dental care at a fraction of the cost that a private dentist would charge. *(See the chapter on Health and Medicine.)*

* **Dental Implants for Free**

National Institutes of Health
Clinical Center
Bethesda, MD 20892 (301) 496-2563

Lost a tooth along the way? If government dental researchers are studying new dental implants and looking for volunteer patients, you could get one for free. *(See the chapter on Health and Medicine.)*

* **Drug Dealers' Boats and Cars**

United States Custom Service, Public Affairs
1301 Constitution Avenue, NW
Washington, DC 20229 (703) 351-7887

U.S. Customs and Marshals Services confiscate and auction cars, boats, jewelry, and real estate of drug dealers. Call the above number, and look in the Wednesday edition of *USA Today*. *(See the chapter on Government Auctions and Surplus Property.)*

* **Drugs, Free**

See Prescription Drugs

* **Earthquake Safety Checklist**

Publications
Federal Emergency Management Agency (FEMA)
500 C Street, SW

Washington, DC 20472 (202) 646-3484

Obviously you think living in California is worth it. But the FEMA still thinks you should be prepared. *(See the chapter on Your Community.)*

* **Environmental Question Line**

Environmental Protection Agency
Public Information Center
401 M Street, SW, PM-211B
Washington, DC 20460 (202) 260-7751

How should you dispose of motor oil? Indoor air quality problems? Removing asbestos? *(See the chapter on Environment and Nature.)*

* **Export Advice Hotline**

Trade Information Center
International Trade Administration
U.S. Department of Commerce
Room HCHB 7424
14th and Constitution Avenue, NW
Washington, DC 20230 (800) USA-TRADE

Want to sell your gizmo or doodad in the Soviet Union but don't know how? Experts are waiting to help. *(See the chapter on International Trade.)*

* **Family Budget Help**

See Home Economics

* **Films and Lectures on Art**

National Gallery of Art
Constitution and 6th Street, NW
Washington, DC 20565 (202) 842-6353

National Gallery holds all kinds of free lectures and films on the arts. Call the above number for a schedule. *(See the chapter on Arts and Humanities.)*

* **Firewood**

See Christmas Trees

* **Flags over the U.S. Capitol**

U.S. Capitol
Washington, DC 20515 (202) 224-3121

Want to buy a flag that's flown over the U.S. Capitol in Washington, DC? Contact your local Senator or Congressman for details, or call the above number. *(See the chapter on More Info-Power Hits.)*

* **FmHA Money Waiting for You**

Support Service Center
U.S. Department of Housing and Urban Development
P.O. Box 44372
Washington, DC 20026 (703) 235-8117

Ever taken out a FmHA-insured home loan? You may have a chunk of money waiting for you. One call will tell. *(See the chapter on Housing and Real Estate.)*

* **Foster Grandparents Volunteers**

ACTION
1100 Vermont Avenue, NW
Washington, DC 20525 (202) 606-4849

Over 60 and looking for something new? Help out under-privileged children. Call ACTION for details. *(See the chapter on Your Community.)*

* **Franchise Buying Assistance: Laws and Guidelines**

Franchise Rule Information
Federal Trade Commission
Sixth Street and Pennsylvania Avenue, NW
Washington, DC 20580 (202) 326-3220

Call the Federal Trade Commission Franchise Rule Information Hotline. *(See the chapter on Small Business and Entrepreneuring.)*

Be patient. If any phone number is incorrect, call (area code) 555-1212 and request the new listing.

Info-Power Greatest Hits

* Freelancer Artists, Writers, Consultants

The government spends millions each year on these freelance services. Contact the Office of Small and Disadvantaged Business Utilization for whichever agency you're interested in for more details. *(See the chapter on Selling to the Government.)*

* Genealogical Workshops

Attention NXI
National Archives
Washington, DC 20408 (202) 501-5525

Want to find out who your great-grandfather was? The National Archives runs three-hour workshops to show you the ropes of genealogical research for $10. The Archive's calendar of events includes registration details. *(See the chapter on Arts and Humanities, and Books and Libraries.)*

* Geographic Names Information Database

Geographic Names Branch
U.S. Geological Survey
12201 Sunrise Valley Drive
Reston, VA 22092 (703) 648-4547

Thinking of starting a new town in Alaska? Make sure there already isn't another town with the same name. *(See the chapter on Government Databases and Bulletin Boards.)*

* Health Care: Best in the World for Free

National Institutes of Health
Clinical Center
Building 10, Room 1C255
Bethesda, MD 20892 (301) 496-2563

Each year hundreds of thousands of people across the country receive free medical care for everything from breast cancer and toothache to diabetes and writer's cramp, from the best researchers in the country. *(See the chapter on Health and Medicine.)*

* Health Information Hotline

National Health Information Center
P.O. Box 1133
Washington, DC 20013 (800) 336-4797

Want to know about health care issues such as Lyme Disease, cancer, AIDS, Medicare and Medicaid? The National Health Information Center has both answers and free publications. *(See the chapter on Health and Medicine.)*

* Health Profession Scholarships From U.S. Department of Veterans Affairs

Health Professional Educational Assistance Programs
U.S. Department of Veterans Affairs
Office of Academic Affairs
810 Vermont Avenue, NW
Washington, DC 20420 (202) 535-7528

If you're willing to work for the VA for at least a year after you graduate, you might be in line for a scholarship. *(See the chapter on Health and Medicine.)*

* Historic Home Renovation Loans

History Division
National Park Service
800 N. Capitol Street, NE
Washington, DC 20002 (202) 343-8167

Think your home has local historic significance? If it makes it on the National Register, you may qualify for low-interest loans to pay for upkeep and renovation. Contact your state Historic Registration or call the number above. *(See the chapter on Your Community, and Housing and Real Estate.)*

* Historic Preservation Ideas

Superintendent of Documents
Government Printing Office
Washington, DC 20402 (202) 783-3238

Is there a special way to rehang wooden windows or put a new roof on an historic home? Get a free Government Printing Office bibliography of publications on historic preservation. *(See the chapter on Your Community and Housing and Real Estate.)*

* Home-based Business Tips

Answer Desk
U.S. Small Business Administration
409 Third Street, SW
Washington, DC 20416 (800) 827-5722

Want to run a business out of your home? Get a free start-up guide from the Small Business Administration (SBA). Contact your local SBA or call the above number. *(See the chapter on Small Business and Entrepreneuring.)*

* Home Economics Workshops

Your local County Cooperative Extension Service will help you select, prepare, and budget a healthy menu for your family. *(See the chapter on Health and Medicine.)*

* Horses To Adopt

See Adopt-A-Horse

* Housing Discrimination Hotline

Housing Discrimination Hotline
U.S. Department of Housing and Urban Development
451 Seventh Street, SW
Washington, DC 20410 (800) 669-9777

Can't get a housing loan because the house is in the "wrong" kind of neighborhood? Landlord won't rent to you after seeing you in person? *(See the chapter on Consumer Power.)*

* Houses for $1?

You probably won't get a house for a dollar, but you just may be able to get one for pennies on the dollar at HUD auctions. Consult the Real Estate section in your paper for upcoming auctions and available properties. For information on low-interest, government-insured housing loans, call your local HUD office. *(See the chapter on Housing and Real Estate.)*

* Ice Breaker Expeditions

Ice Operations
U.S. Coast Guard
2100 2nd Street, SW
Washington, DC 20593 (202) 267-1450

Need to go to the South Pole to write your next book? *(See the chapter on Vacations and Business Travel.)*

* Information on Demand

Reference
Library of Congress
1st Street and Independence Avenue, SE
Washington, DC 20540 (202) 707-5534

Got a quick question that a staff member at Library of Congress could answer? *(See the chapter on Books and Libraries.)*

* Inmate Locator Line

Federal Bureau of Prisons
Inmate Locator
320 First Street, NW
Washington, DC 20534 (202) 307-3126

You've just got to get letters to Jim Bakker and Charles Manson. *(See the chapters on Law and Social Justice, and Information on People, Companies and Mailing Lists.)*

* Insurance Complaints and Questions

Insurance company won't honor your claim? Canceled without a reason? Your state's insurance commissioner will get what's coming to you. *(See the chapter on Information on People, Companies and Mailing Lists.)*

Be patient. If any phone number is incorrect, call (area code) 555-1212 and request the new listing.

Info-Power Greatest Hits

* Interstate Land Sales Fraud-Line

Interstate Land Sales Registration Division
U.S. Department of Housing and Urban Development
451 7th Street, SW
Washington, DC 20410 (202) 708-0502

Bought some swamp land in Florida that was supposed to be luxury condos? *(See the chapter on Consumer Power.)*

* Inventors Become Millionaires

Office of Energy Related Inventions
National Institute of Standards and Technology
Building 411, Room A115
Gaithersburg, MD 20899 (301) 975-5500

The Energy Related Invention Assistance Program will evaluate your invention and help you get a grant to turn your idea into a business. *(See the chapter on Science and Technology.)*

* Job Retraining for Free

Get free technical and vocational training under a federal job training program through your local employment office. *(See the chapter on Careers and Workplace.)*

* Job Safety Inspections On-Site

Consumer Affairs
Occupational Safety and Health Administration (OSHA)
200 Constitution Avenue, NW
Room N3637
Washington, DC 20210 (800) 321-OSHA

Asbestos falling from your ceiling at work? Repetitive movements causing pain in your joints? OSHA will inspect for free. Contact your local OSHA office for information. For emergencies, contact the 800 number listed above. *(See the chapter on Careers and Workplace.)*

* Jobs With the Federal Government

Most federal agencies have job line recordings for immediate openings that need filling. Consult the U.S. Government listings in your phone book for the appropriate agency and number, or see the chapter on Federal Government Databases for the listings in Washington, DC headquarters.

* Job Trends: What's Hot, What's Not

Office of Employment Projectors
U.S. Department of Labor
2 Massachusetts Avenue, NE, Room 2135
Washington, DC 20212 (202) 606-5709

Find out what jobs will be hot and what will not before you spend money on college. *(See the chapter on Careers and Workplace.)*

* Lie Detector Reliability

National Criminal Justice Reference Service
Box 6000
Department F
Rockville, MD 20850 (301) 251-5500

How reliable are lie detector tests? The Justice Department will send you the findings of their study. *(See the chapters on Careers and Workplace, Law and Social Justice.)*

* Lost Loved Ones

See Missing People

* Medical Care: Free and Low-Cost

Office of Health Facilities
Health Resources and Services Administration
U.S. Department of Health and Human Services
5600 Fishers Lane, Room 11-03 (800) 638-0742
Rockville, MD 20857 (800) 492-0359 in MD

Under the Hill-Burton law, many low-income individuals qualify for free health care at over 2,500 health facilities. *(See the chapter on Health and Medicine.)*

* Medications, Free

See Prescription Drugs

* Missing People: Be Your Own Private Eye

Find your lost friend or loved one on your own and save big money. Use state motor vehicles records, voter registration records, armed services locator program, professional licensing offices, and much more. *(See the chapter on Information on People, Companies and Mailing Lists.)*

* Money Programs: Billions for Everyone

The federal government loans and gives away billions every year for everything from houses and businesses, to writers and painters. Look through the *Catalog of Federal Domestic Assistance* at your library. *(See the chapters on Small Business and Entrepreneuring, and Housing and Real Estate.)*

* Money to Start a Business

See Business Start-Up Money

* Moon Rocks for Teachers

Johnson Space Center
Education Coordinator
National Aeronautics and Space Administration (NASA)
Houston, TX 77058

NASA will loan science teachers lunar rock samples for classroom use after an orientation seminar. *(See the chapter on Education.)*

* Motor Vehicle Records: Locate Anyone Who Drives

Don't hire a private eye--do what they do: use your state's motor vehicle and license records to track anyone down. *(See the chapter on Information on People, Companies and Mailing Lists.)*

* NASA Space Videos

Lorain County Joint Vocational School
NASA Core
15181 Route 58 South
Oberlin, OH 44074 (216) 774-1051, ext. 293

Want some great NASA videos on moon walks, the Space Shuttle, the Apollo Missions? Get them at a fraction of retail cost directly from NASA. *(See the chapter on Education.)*

* Native American Ancestry Census

U.S. Department of the Interior
Bureau of Indian Affairs
Tribal Enrollment
Mail Stop 2611-MIV
Washington, DC 20245 (202) 208-3702

Think you might be part Cherokee or Apache? The Bureau of Indian Affairs can help you in your search. Call the Branch of Tribal Enrollment. *(See the chapter on Arts and Humanities.)*

* Neighborhood Watch Programs

National Sheriff's Association
1450 Duke Street
Alexandria, VA 22314 (703) 836-7827

Want to make your neighborhood a safer place for your kids? Get help setting up a Watch program. *(See the chapter on Law and Social Justice.)*

* Nuclear Fallout Shelter Plans

Publications
Federal Emergency Management Agency
500 C Street, SW
Washington, DC 20472 (202) 646-3484

Want to build a snack bar that also serves as a nuclear fallout shelter? Call the number above for plans. *(See the chapter on Your Community.)*

Be patient. If any phone number is incorrect, call (area code) 555-1212 and request the new listing.

Info-Power Greatest Hits

* Nuclear War Survival Guide

NETC Home Study Program
Federal Emergency Management Agency (FEMA)
16825 S. Seton Ave.
Emmsburg, MD 21727 (301) 447-1076

Still worried about the Russian A-bombs? FEMA will send a home-study course on surviving a nuclear war. *(See the chapter on Your Community.)*

* Overseas Travel Advisory Hotline

Citizens Emergency Center
Overseas Citizens Services
U.S. Department of State
2201 C Street, NW
Room 4800
Washington, DC 20520 (202) 647-5225

Before you book three weeks in Beirut or Yugoslavia, you might want to get some advice from the State Department. *(See the chapter on Vacations and Business Travel.)*

* Painters and Sculptors: Money for Your Work

(202) 501-1256

New federal buildings have to set aside a portion of construction and renovation budgets for art work. *(See the chapter on Small Business and Entrepreneuring.)*

* Paternity Testing

See Dead Beat Dads

* Peace Corps Volunteering

Peace Corps
1555 Nilson Boulevard
Room 701
Arlington, VA 22209 (703) 235-9191

Want to see Prague and Budapest but can't afford it? The Peace Corps has sent hundreds to Eastern Europe. *(See the chapter on Your Community.)*

* Pension Protection Guides for Employees

Public Affairs
Pension Benefits Guaranty Corporation
2020 K Street, NW
Washington, DC 20006 (202) 778-8840

Know your rights about pensions, including the federal program that insures certain plans. *(See the chapter on Careers and Workplace.)*

* Pesticides Hotline

National Pesticide Telecommunications Network
Texas Tech University
Thompson Hall, Room 5129
Lubbock, TX 79430 (800) 858-7378

Need to know how to safely handle and use certain pesticides in your garden? Call the Environmental Protection Agency at the above number. *(See the chapter on Environment and Nature.)*

* Plant Care Answer Line

Horto-Line (202) 576-7597

Why is your bonsai dying? Do dandelions have any medicinal use? How do you grow your own herbs? *(See the chapter on Housing and Real Estate.)*

* Plant and Lawn Workshops

You've decided you don't want a yellow lawn again this year. Call your local County Cooperative Extension Service for free expertise. *(See the chapter on Housing and Real Estate.)*

* Polar Expeditions for Civilians

Ice Operations
U.S. Coast Guard
2100 2nd Street, SW

Washington, DC 20593 (202) 267-1450

Need to go to the South Pole to write your next book? *(See the chapter on Vacations and Business Travel.)*

* Police Radar Guns

See Radar Buster Reports

* Polygraph Testing Rights

(202) 523-7640

Before you agree to taking a lie detector test at your job, you should know the law that prohibits its use. *(See the chapter on Careers and Workplace.)*

* Prescription Drugs for Free

Pharmaceutical Manufacturer's Association
1100 15th Street, NW
Washington, DC 20005 (800) 726-7504

If you have to choose between eating and taking a much-needed medication, then you might be able to get your drug prescription filled free of charge directly from the drug company. Call the Pharmaceutical Manufacturer's Association for a directory of drug companies that participate. *(See the chapter on Health and Medicine.)*

* Presidential Birthday cards

See Birthday Cards

* Prospecting for Gold

The Bureau of Mines publishes a free guide on prospecting for gold. Contact your local library and ask for Information Circular (IC) 8517. This publication can also be found in Federal Depositories, on many university campuses. *(See the chapter on Business and Industry.)*

* Puerto Rico on Uncle Sam

VISTA
1100 Vermont Avenue, NW
Washington, DC 20525 (202) 606-4824

Always wanted to spend time in Puerto Rico but couldn't afford it? Volunteer to fight poverty there and Uncle Sam will pay you to go for a year and even forgive a portion of your student loans. *(See the chapter on Your Community.)*

* Radar Buster Reports: Beating a Speeding Ticket

Office of Law Enforcement Standards
National Institute of Standards and Technology
Building 225, Room A-323
Gaithersburg, MD 20899 (301) 975-2757

Busted for speeding? A report on the reliability of police radar might be what you're looking for. *(See the chapter on Science and Technology.)*

* Radon Gas Leaks

Radon Division
ANR464
Environmental Protection Agency
401 M Street, SW
Washington, DC 20460 (800) SOS-RADON

For information on how to get your home tested for radon and locating a contractor to make any necessary repairs, call the above number. *(See the chapter on Environment and Nature.)*

* Rental Rates Across the U.S.

Valuation Branch
Multi-Family Housing
U.S. Department of Housing and Urban Development
451 7th Street, SW
Washington, DC 20410 (202) 708-0624

Negotiating a rental agreement and think the landlord is asking too much? Show him or her what the government thinks the place should go for. *(See the chapter on Housing and Real Estate.)*

Be patient. If any phone number is incorrect, call (area code) 555-1212 and request the new listing.

Info-Power Greatest Hits

* Scholarships and Internships
U.S. Capitol
Washington, DC 20510 (202) 224-3121
Millions of dollars are available to students each year in the form of fellowships and scholarships. Write your member of congress and ask for a copy of Info-Pack *Internships and Fellowships* (#IP0631) or call the above number. *(See the chapter on Education.)*

* Second Surgical Opinion Line
Health Care Financing Administration
330 Independence Avenue, SW
Washington, DC 20201 (800) 638-6833
Just maybe you don't need a hysterectomy or your gall bladder removed. If you're on Medicare or Medicaid, you can get help with a second opinion. *(See the chapter on Health and Medicine.)*

* Small Business Loans
Answer Desk
U.S. Small Business Administration (SBA)
409 Third Street, SW
Washington, DC 20416 (800) 827-5722
Everything you needed to know and more about starting and running your own small business. *(See the chapter on Small Business and Entrepreneuring.)*

* Small Business Mentors
Answer Desk
U.S. Small Business Administration (SBA)
409 Third Street, SW
Washington, DC 20416 (800) 827-5722
Need some free marketing advice or accounting help? A retired business executive will help. *(See the chapter on Small Business and Entrepreneuring.)*

* Smoking: Free Help to Quit
Building 31, Room 10A18
9000 Rockville Pike
Bethesda, MD 20892 (800) 4-CANCER
Everything you need to know about smoking and how to quit, new research, local programs, and more. *(See the chapter on Health and Medicine.)*

* Space Camp for Kids and Adults
U.S. Space Camp
P.O. Box 070015
Huntsville, AL 35807-7015 (800) 637-7223
Astronaut training, rocketry classes, simulated space missions, and everything. *(See the chapter on Education.)*

* Space Photos
EROS Data Center
Sioux Falls, SD 57198 (605) 594-6511
What does Montana look like from space? How about Sheboygan? You can buy it and hang it on your wall. *(See the chapter on Weather and Maps.)*

* Star Gazer Hotline
(202) 357-2000
When is Jupiter next visible? The next eclipse? Find out the latest astronomical news. *(See the chapter on Science and Technology.)*

* Stock Broker Complaint Line
Consumer Affairs
Securities and Exchange Commission (SEC)
Mail Stop 2-6
450 5th Street, NW
Washington, DC 20546 (202) 272-7440
Your broker drained your account and blew it in Las Vegas? The SEC can help. *(See the chapter on Investments and Finance Services.)*

* Student Loans Forgiven
VISTA
1100 Vermont Avenue, NW
Washington, DC 20525 (202) 606-4824
If you join Volunteers in Service to America (VISTA) and work to help the poor for a year, you can have a portion of your student loans forgiven; up to 50%, if you stay in for three years. *(See the chapter on Your Community.)*

* Student Loan Hotline
Federal Student Aid Information Center
P.O. Box 84
Washington, DC 20044 (800) 333-4636
Interested in finding out what federal financial aid is available for college? *(See the chapter on Education.)*

* Summer Jobs in Conservation
Forest Service
U.S. Department of Agriculture
Personnel
1621 N. Kent
Rosslyn, VA 22209 (703) 235-8102

or

Office of Human Resources
U.S. Fish and Wildlife Resources
1550 Wilson Boulevard
Arlington, VA 22209 (703) 353-2505
The Forest Service and Fish and Wildlife Service hire teens during the summer for conservation work on public lands. *(See the chapter on Careers and Workplace.)*

* Summer Jobs: Thousands for Teens and Older
Job Information Center
P.O. Box 14179
Office of Personnel Management
WEC, Room 1425
Washington, DC 20044 (202) 606-2575
Each summer the federal government hires thousands of kids across the U.S. Apply before April 15. *(See the chapter on Careers and Workplace.)*

* Tax Preparation Courses Free to All
Internal Revenue Service
1111 Constitution Avenue, NW
Public Affairs
Washington, DC 20224 (800) 829-1040
The Internal Revenue Service will train you to prepare returns in return for helping others who need tax help. *(See the chapter on Taxes.)*

* Teenage Business Loans
See Business Loans for Teens

* Term Papers: 10,000 Free for the Asking
U.S. Capitol
Washington, DC 20515
By writing your member of Congress, you can get a research paper written on practically any subject on current events. *(See the chapter on Current Events and Homework.)*

* Travel Emergency Center
Citizen Emergency Center
Overseas Citizens Services
U.S. Department of State
2201 C Street, NW
Room 4800
Washington, DC 20520 (202) 647-5225
Did your father go to Spain and not return? Need to get money to your son who's homeless in Paris? *(See the chapter on Vacations and Business Travel.)*

Be patient. If any phone number is incorrect, call (area code) 555-1212 and request the new listing.

Info-Power Greatest Hits

* Treasury Securities Info-Line

Public Affairs
U.S. Savings Bond Division
U.S. Department of Treasury
800 K Street, NW
Washington, DC 20226 (202) 874-4000

What's a T-Bill? Is it different from a Savings Bond? Can I buy one and avoid paying a broker a commission? *(See the chapter on Investments and Financial Services.)*

* Turkey Cooking Hotline

Meat and Poultry Hotline (202) 720-3333

Just how long should you cook a thirteen pound turkey to make sure it's safe to eat? The U.S. Department of Agriculture knows. *(See the chapter on Health and Medicine.)*

* Unconventional Cancer Treatments

Office of Technology Assessment (OTA)
Health Program
U.S. Congress
Washington, DC 20515-8025 (202) 228-6590

OTA is studying the safety, effectiveness, and availability of new, unconventional cancer treatments. *(See the chapter on Health and Medicine.)*

* Urban Homesteading Program

Willing to live in a run-down city neighborhood if you can get a house for $250 and agree to fix it up? Call your regional U.S. Department of Housing and Urban Development office or County Housing Community Development Office for details. *(See the chapter on Housing and Real Estate.)*

* Videos and Films: 8,000 From Uncle Sam

National Audiovisual Center
Multi-Media Publications
8700 Edgeworth Drive
Capitol Heights, MD 20743 (301) 763-1896

Looking for a video on prospecting, worker safety, or even concentration camps? Try the National Audiovisual Center. *(See the chapter on Arts and Humanities.)*

* Virgin Islands Vacation

VISTA
1100 Vermont Avenue, NW
Washington, DC 20525 (202) 606-4824

Camp out at the National Park on the Virgin Islands for a fraction of what a hotel there costs. If you want to spend a whole year there on Uncle Sam, join VISTA and request to be sent there to work on eliminating poverty. *(See the chapter on Vacations and Business Travel.)*

* Watergate Tapes and Trial Transcripts

Nixon Materials Project Staff
National Archives
Washington, DC 20408 (703) 756-6498

Want to hear Nixon, Haldeman, and Ehrlichman cooking up a conspiracy? Transcripts of tapes available, too. *(See the chapter on Arts and Humanities.)*

* Wildlife Refuges: National Guide

Superintendent of Documents
Government Printing Office (GPO)
Washington, DC 20402 (202) 783-3238

The ultimate animal watcher's vacation idea: tour some National Wildlife Refuges. Ask for *National Wildlife Refuges: A Visitor's Guide*. *(See the chapter on Vacations and Business Travel.)*

* Writers: Free Grants to Create

National Endowment for the Arts
1100 Pennsylvania Avenue, NW
Washington, DC 20506 (202) 682-5400

Starving writer? The National Endowment for the Arts gives out millions in grants each year. *(See the chapter on Arts and Humanities.)*

* Woodsy Owl Cleanup For Kids

Doris Nance, Forest Service
Forest Program Youth Project
Woodsy Owl
U.S. Department of Agriculture
P.O. Box 96090
Washington, DC 20090-6090 (202) 205-1785

Give a hoot, show kids how to not pollute with stickers, coloring sheets, patches, and song sheets. *(See the chapter on Environment and Nature.)*

Be patient. If any phone number is incorrect, call (area code) 555-1212 and request the new listing.

Information Starting Places

Free Help in Finding A Free Expert

* *See also Experts Chapter*

Not only is the world full of experts who are willing to help resolve your information problems for free, there are organizations whose sole mission is to put you in touch with these specialists. Here is a list of some of these clearinghouses arranged by subject area. Don't forget to use the Experts Chapter, which includes the names and phone numbers of experts who specialize in everything from aquaculture to zinc. Remember that these experts spend their lives studying specific areas and are waiting to help you for free. Just keep in mind that a polite, courteous phone attitude can do wonders.

* Agriculture and Commodities

Office of Public Affairs
U.S. Department of Agriculture, Room 413A
Washington, DC 20250 (202) 720-4623

A staff of research specialists are available to provide specific answers or direct you to an expert in any agricultural-related topic.

National Agricultural Library
10301 Baltimore Boulevard
Beltsville, MD 20705-2351 (301) 504-5755

This library serves as an information clearinghouse.

National Agricultural Statistics Service
U.S. Department of Agriculture, NAS
14th and Independence Avenue SW
Room 4117 S. Bldg.
Washington, DC 20250 (202) 720-3896

ASS provides contacts for agricultural production, stocks, prices and other data.

* Arts and Entertainment

Performing Arts Library
John F. Kennedy Center
Washington, DC 20566 (202) 707-6245

This center which works jointly with the Library of Congress offers reference services on any aspect of the performing arts.

* Best and Worst Industries and Companies

U.S. Department of Commerce
Washington, DC 20230 (202) 482-2000

Over 100 analysts monitor all the major industries in the U.S. and the companies within these industries ranging from athletic products to truck trailers.

Office of Industries
U.S. International Trade Commission
500 E Street SW, Room 504
Washington, DC 20436 (202) 205-3296

Experts analyze impact of world trade on U.S. industries ranging from audio components to x-ray apparatus.

* Business Advice

Roadmap Program
U.S. Department of Commerce
14th and Constitution Avenue, NW
Washington, DC 20230 (202) 482-3176

Roadmap Program provides reference services on all aspects of commerce and business.

Library
U.S. Department of Commerce
14th and Constitution Avenue, NW
Washington, DC 20230 (202) 482-5511

This library also provides reference services on all aspects of business.

* Country Experts

Country Officers
U.S. Department of State

2201 C Street NW
Washington, DC 20520 (202) 647-4000

Hundreds of experts are available to provide current political, economic, and other background information on the country they study. Call to ask for the number of a specific country officer.

U.S. Department of Commerce
International Trade Administration
Washington, DC 20230 (202) 482-2000

Teams of experts from these regions can provide information on marketing and business practices for every country in the world.

Agricultural and Trade Analysis Division
Economics Research Service
U.S. Department of Agriculture
14th and Independence Ave.
Washington, DC 20005-4788 (202) 720-8732

This office provides information on agricultural-related aspects of foreign countries.

Foreign Agricultural Services (FAS)
Information Division
U.S. Department of Agriculture
14th and Independence Avenue, SW
Washington, DC 20250 (202) 720-9461

FAS provides data on world crops, agricultural policies, and markets.

Division of International Minerals
Bureau of Mines
U.S. Department of Interior
810 7th Street, NW, MS 5205
Washington, DC 20241 (202) 501-9666

Foreign country experts monitor all aspects of foreign mineral industries.

* Crime

National Criminal Justice Reference Service
National Institute of Justice
Box 6000
Rockville, MD 20850 (301) 251-5500

Database and reference service provide bibliographies and expertise free or sometimes for a nominal fee.

Uniform Crime Reporting Section
FBI
U.S. Department of Justice
409 7th St., NW
Washington, DC 20535 (202) 324-3000

Statistics are available on eight major crimes against person and property.

* Demographics, Economic and Industry Statistics

Data Users Service Division
Bureau of the Census
Customer Service
Washington, DC 20233 (301) 763-4100

Staff will guide you to the billions of dollars worth of taxpayer supported data.

* Economics: National, Regional and International

Bureau of Economic Analysis
U.S. Department of Commerce

Be patient. If any phone number is incorrect, call (area code) 555-1212 and request the new listing.

Free Help in Finding A Free Expert

Washington, DC 20230 (202) 523-0777

This is the first place to call for economic data.

* Education

Office of Educational Research and Improvement U.S. Department of Education 555 New Jersey Ave., NW Washington, DC 20208-1235 (202) 708-5366

A network of 16 information clearinghouses that identify literature, experts, audiovisuals, funding, etc.

Educational Information Branch U.S. Department of Education/OERI 555 New Jersey Avenue, NW Washington, DC 20208 (800) 424-1616

Hotline provides referrals to other information sources on any aspect of education.

* Energy

National Energy Information Center U.S. Department of Energy 1F048 Forrestal Building 1000 Independence Ave., SW Washington, DC 20585 (202) 586-8800

This office provides general reference services on U.S. Department of Energy data.

Conservation and Renewable Energy Inquiry and Referral Service PO Box 8900 Silver Spring, MD 20907 (800) 523-2929

Free help on how to save energy as well as information on solar, wind, or any other aspect of renewable energy.

U.S. Department of Energy Office of Scientific and Technical Information PO Box 62 Oak Ridge, TN 37831 (615) 576-1301

This office provides research and other information services on all energy related topics.

* Health

ONHIC National Health Information Center PO Box 1133 (800) 336-4797 Washington, DC 20013-1133 (301) 565-4167 in MD

For leads to both public and private sector health organizations, research centers and universities.

National Center for Health Statistics U.S. Department of Health and Human Services 6525 Belcrest Rd., Room 1064 Presidential Building Hyattsville, MD 20782 (301) 436-8500

This clearinghouse can provide data on any aspect of health.

* Housing

Library and Information Services Center U.S. Department of Housing and Urban Development 451 7th Street SW Washington, DC 20410 (202) 708-2370

This library provides information on all aspects of housing and staff will direct you to a program which meets your needs.

* Import and Export Statistics

Foreign Trade Reference Room U.S. Department of Commerce

14th and Constitution Ave., NW Washington, DC 20230 (202) 482-2185

This library can provide data on many aspects of U.S. trade.

* Metals and Minerals

Division of Mineral Commodities (Domestic) Bureau of Mines U.S. Department of the Interior 810 7th Street, NW Washington, DC 20241 (202) 501-9450

Dozens of commodity specialists collect, analyze, and disseminate information on the adequacy and availability of the mineral base for the national economy.

* Prices, Employment, Productivity And Living Conditions Statistics

U.S. Department of Labor Bureau of Labor Statistics Washington, DC 20212 (202) 606-7828

There are subject specialists in such areas as plant closings, labor force projections, producer price indexes, work stoppages.

* World Import and Export Statistics

World Trade Statistics U.S. Department of Commerce Room 2233, Herbert Hoover Building 14th and Constitution Ave. Washington, DC 20230 (202) 482-5242

This is place for numbers concerning trade for most countries.

General Sources

These three offices are the places to get help in locating experts in government as well as the private sector and trade associations.

* Associations

Information Central American Society of Association Executives 1575 Eye Street NW Washington, DC 20005 (202) 626-2723

If you cannot find a relevant association after referring to *Gale's Encyclopedia of Associations* (which is available in most libraries) this organization will help find the right one.

* Government Experts

Federal Information Center P.O. Box 600 Cumberland, MD 21501-0600 (301) 722-9000

Centers are located throughout the country and the staff will find you an expert in the government on most any topic.

* Technical Research

Science and Technology Division Reference Section, Library of Congress 1st and Independence, SE Washington, DC 20540 (202) 707-5639

This reference section offers both free and fee-based reference and bibliographic services.

Be patient. If any phone number is incorrect, call (area code) 555-1212 and request the new listing.

Information Starting Places

State Starting Places For Finding Experts

If you have trouble locating the exact office you need from the listings elsewhere in the book, this is the section for you. The first place you should start is with State Information Offices listed below. The operators at these offices are normally trained to handle information requests from people who don't know where to go within the state bureaucracy. If you are not successful, try either or both of the other offices listed.

Governor's Office

Because the responsibilities of various state offices often overlap, it may be helpful to begin your data search by contacting the state governor's office. While every state has a central switchboard to field inquiries regarding state business, the number is usually helpful only if you already know which agency is responsible for gathering and interpreting the information you are after. If you are hazy in this regard, the state governor's office will certainly know the appropriate agency department and, if you are lucky, even the name of the special contact person to call.

State Library

A vast amount of research information is available from the state library. After all, it is the official repository of state agency documents and the first place to start if you want to do all of the footwork yourself. In addition, most state libraries also shelve copies of federal government documents and publications.

State libraries are paid for with tax dollars and are open to the public. Collections usually include state legal codes, state historical documents, archival records, genealogy type information, business and economic records, statistical abstracts and annual reports.

In each library these is generally a government information person who can provide telephone and personal assistance to researchers. In addition, there is often a staff specialist to help with statistical questions.

The following is a list of state operators, librarians, and governor's offices.

State Information and Governor's Offices

Alabama
State Information: (205) 242-8000

Governor's Office: Office of the Governor, Statehouse, 11 South Union St., Montgomery, AL 36130; (205) 242-7100.

State Library: Alabama Public Library Service, 6030 Monticello Drive, Montgomery, AL 36130; (205) 277-7330.

Alaska
State Information: (907) 465-2111

Governor's Office: Office of the Governor, P.O. Box 110001, Juneau, AK 99811; (907) 465-3500.

State Library: Libraries and Museums, P.O. Box 110571, Juneau, AK 99811-0571; (907) 465-2920.

Arizona
State Information: (602) 542-4900

Governor's Office: Office of the Governor, 1700 West Washington St., Phoenix, AZ 85007; (602) 542-4331.

State Library: Department of Library Archives and Public Records, State Capitol, Room 442, 1700 W. Washington St., Phoenix, AZ 85007; (602) 542-4159.

Arkansas
State Information: (501) 682-3000

Governor's Office: Office of the Governor, State Capitol Building, Room 250, Little Rock, AR 72201; (501) 682-2345.

State Library: Arkansas State Library, 1 Capitol Mall, Little Rock, AR 72201; (501) 682-1527.

California
State Information: (916) 322-9900

Governor's Office: Office of the Governor, State Capitol, Sacramento, CA 95814; (916) 445-2841.

State Library: California State Library, Library and Courts Building, Sacramento, CA 95814; (916) 654-0261.

Colorado
State Information: (303) 866-5000

Governor's Office: Office of the Governor, 136 State Capitol Building, Denver, CO 80203-1792; (303) 866-2471.

State Library: Colorado State Library, 201 East Colfax Ave., Denver, CO 80203; (303) 866-4799.

Connecticut
State Information: (203) 240-0222

Governor's Office: Office of the Governor, Executive Chambers, Room 202, Hartford, CT 06106; (203) 566-4840.

State Library: Connecticut State Library, 231 Capitol Ave., Hartford, CT 06115; (203) 566-3056.

Delaware
State Information: (302) 739-4000

Governor's Office: Office of the Governor, Tatnall Bldg., William Penn Street, Dover, DE 19901; (302) 739-4101.

Be patient. If any phone number is incorrect, call (area code) 555-1212 and request the new listing.

State Starting Places For Finding Experts

State Library: Delaware State Library, 43 South DuPont Highway, Dover, DE 19901; (302) 739-4748.

District of Columbia

Information: (202) 727-1000

Mayor's Office: Executive Office of the Mayor, 441 4th NW, Room 1100, 1 Judiciary Square, Washington, DC 20001; (202) 727-2980.

Central Library: Martin Luther King, Jr. Memorial Library, 901 G St. NW, Washington, DC 20001; (202) 727-1101.

Florida

State Information: (904) 488-1234

Governor's Office: Office of the Governor, The Capitol, Tallahassee, FL 32399-0001; (904) 488-4441.

State Library: Florida State Library, R.A. Gray Building, 500 Bruno St., Tallahassee, FL 32399; (904) 487-2651.

Georgia

State Information: (404) 656-2000

Governor's Office: Office of the Governor, 203 State Capitol, Atlanta, GA 30334; (404) 656-1776.

State Library: Georgia State Library, 156 Trinity Ave, Atlanta, GA 30303; (404) 656-2462.

Hawaii

State Information: (808) 548-6222

Governor's Office: Office of the Governor, State Capitol, Honolulu, HI 96813; (808) 548-5420.

State Library: Hawaii State Library, 478 South King St., Honolulu, HI 96813; (808) 548-4775.

Idaho

State Information: (208) 334-2411

Governor's Office: Office of the Governor, State House, Boise, ID 83720; (208) 334-2100.

State Library: Idaho State Library, 325 West State St., Boise, ID 83720; (208) 334-5124.

Illinois

State Information: (217) 782-2000

Governor's Office: Office of the Governor, State Capitol, Springfield, IL 62706; (217) 782-6830.

State Library: Illinois State Library, 300 S. 2nd Street, Springfield, IL 62701; (217) 782-7848.

Indiana

State Information: (317) 232-1000

Governor's Office: Office of the Governor, State House, 100 N. Capitol Ave. Indianapolis, IN 46204; (317) 232-4567.

State Library: Indiana State Library, 140 North Senate, Indianapolis, IN 46204; (317) 232-3675.

Iowa

State Information: (515) 281-5011

Governor's Office: Office of the Governor, State Capitol, Des Moines, IA 50319; (515) 281-5211.

State Library: Iowa State Library, East 12th and Grand Streets, Des Moines, IA 50319; (515) 281-4118.

Kansas

State Information: (913) 296-0111

Governor's Office: Office of the Governor, State House, Topeka, KS 66612; (913) 296-3232.

State Library: Kansas State Library, State House, Topeka, KS 66612; (913) 296-3296.

Kentucky

State Information: (502) 564-3130

Governor's Office: Office of the Governor, State Capitol Building, Frankfort, KY 40601; (502) 564-2611.

State Library: Kentucky State Library, 700 Capitol Ave., #200, Frankfort, KY 40601-3489; (502) 564-4848.

Louisiana

State Information: (504) 342-6600

Governor's Office: Office of the Governor, P.O. Box 94004, Baton Rouge, LA 70804; (504) 342-7015.

State Library: Louisiana State Library, P.O. Box 131, Baton Rouge, LA 70821; (504) 342-4923.

Maine

State Information: (207) 582-9500

Governor's Office: Office of the Governor, State House Station 1, Augusta, ME 04333; (207) 287-3531.

State Library: Maine State Library, State House, Station 83, Augusta, ME 04333; (207) 287-5600.

Maryland

State Information: (410) 974-2000

Governor's Office: Office of the Governor, State House, Annapolis, MD 21404; (410) 974-3901.

State Library: Maryland State Archives, Hall of Records, 350 Rowe Boulevard, Annapolis, MD 21404; (410) 974-3914.

Massachusetts

State Information: (617) 722-2000

Governor's Office: Office of the Governor, State House, Boston, MA 02133; (617) 727-3600.

State Library: 341 State Street, Boston, MA 02133; (617) 727-2590.

Michigan

State Information: (517) 373-1837

Governor's Office: Office of the Governor, State Capitol Building, Lansing, MI 48913; (517) 373-3400.

Be patient. If any phone number is incorrect, call (area code) 555-1212 and request the new listing.

Information Starting Places

State Library: Michigan State Library, 717 W. Allegan, Lansing, MI 48909; (517) 373-5400.

Minnesota

State Information: (612) 296-6013

Governor's Office: Office of the Governor, 130 State Capitol, St. Paul, MN 55155; (612) 296-3391.

State Library: Legislative Reference Library, State Office Building, St. Paul, MN 55155; (612) 296-3398.

Mississippi

State Information: (601) 359-1000

Governor's Office: Office of the Governor, P.O. Box 139, Jackson, MS 39205; (601) 359-3150.

State Library: Department of Archives and History Library, P.O. Box 571, Jackson, MS 39205; (601) 359-6850.

Missouri

State Information: (314) 751-2000

Governor's Office: Office of the Governor, State Capitol, P.O. Box 720, Jefferson City, MO 65102-0720; (314) 751-3222.

State Library: Missouri State Library, P.O. Box 387, Jefferson City, MO 65102-0387; (314) 751-3615.

Montana

State Information: (406) 444-2511

Governor's Office: Office of the Governor, State Capitol, Helena, MT 59620; (406) 444-3111.

State Library: Montana State Library, 1515 East 6th Ave., Helena, MT 59620; (406) 444-3115.

Nebraska

State Information: (402) 471-2311

Governor's Office: Office of the Governor, State Capitol, P.O. Box 94848, Lincoln, NE 68509-4848; (402) 471-2244.

State Library: Nebraska State Library, P.O. Box 98910, Lincoln, NE 68509-8910; (402) 471-3189.

Nevada

State Information: (702) 687-5000

Governor's Office: Office of the Governor, State Capitol Bldg., Carson City, NV 89710; (702) 687-5670.

State Library: Nevada State Library, 100 Sewart St., Carson City, NV 89710; (702) 687-5160.

New Hampshire

State Information: (603) 271-1110

Governor's Office: Office of the Governor, State House, Concord, NH 03301; (603) 271-2121.

State Library: New Hampshire State Library, 20 Park St., Concord, NH 03301; (603) 271-2394.

New Jersey

State Information: (609) 292-2121

Governor's Office: Office of the Governor, 125 West State St., State House, Trenton, NJ 08625; (609) 292-6000.

State Library: New Jersey State Library, State House Annex, CN 520, Trenton, NJ; (609) 292-6220.

New Mexico

State Information: (505) 827-4011

Governor's Office: Office of the Governor, State Capitol Building, Santa Fe, NM 87503; (505) 827-3000.

Governor's Office: State Library: New Mexico State Library, 325 Don Gaspar, Santa Fe, NM 87503; (505) 827-3800.

New York

State Information: (518) 474-2121

Governor's Office: Office of the Governor, State Capitol, Albany, NY 12224; (518) 474-5355.

State Library: New York State Library, Empire State Plaza, Madison Avenue, Albany, NY 12230; (518) 474-5355.

North Carolina

State Information: (919) 733-1110

Governor's Office: Office of the Governor, State Capitol, Raleigh, NC 27603; (919) 733-5811.

State Library: North Carolina State Library, 109 East Jones St., Raleigh, NC 27611; (919) 733-2570.

North Dakota

State Information: (701) 224-2000

Governor's Office: Office of the Governor, State Capitol, Bismarck, ND 58505; (701) 224-2200.

State Library: North Dakota State Library, State Capitol, Bismarck, ND 58505; (701) 224-2490.

Ohio

State Information: (614) 466-2000

Governor's Office: Office of the Governor, State House, Columbus, OH 43215; (614) 466-3555.

State Library: Ohio State Library, 65 South Front St., Columbus, OH 43266; (614) 644-7061.

Oklahoma

State Information: (405) 521-1601

Governor's Office: Office of the Governor, 212 State Capitol, Oklahoma City, OK 73105; (405) 521-2342.

State Library: Oklahoma State Library, 200 N.E. 18th St., Oklahoma City, OK 73105; (405) 521-2502.

Oregon

State Information: (503) 378-3131

Governor's Office: Office of the Governor, 254 State Capitol, Salem, OR 97310; (503) 378-3100.

Be patient. If any phone number is incorrect, call (area code) 555-1212 and request the new listing.

State Starting Places For Finding Experts

State Library: Oregon State Library, State Library Building, Salem, OR 97310; (503) 378-4274.

Pennsylvania

State Information: (717) 787-2121

Governor's Office: Office of the Governor, 225 Main Capitol Bldg., Harrisburg, PA 17120; (717) 787-5962.

State Library: Pennsylvania State Library, P.O. Box 1601, Harrisburg, PA 17105; (717) 787-5718.

Rhode Island

State Information: (401) 277-2000

Governor's Office: Office of the Governor, 222 State House, Providence, RI 02903; (401) 277-2080.

State Library: Rhode Island State Library, Room 208, State House, Providence, RI 02903; (401) 277-2473.

South Carolina

State Information: (803) 734-1000

Governor's Office: Office of the Governor, P.O. Box 11369, Columbia, SC 29211; (803) 734-9818.

State Library: South Carolina State Library, P.O. Box 11469, Columbia, SC 29225; (803) 734-8666.

South Dakota

State Information: (605) 773-3011

Governor's Office: Office of the Governor, State Capitol, Pierre, SD 57501; (605) 773-3212.

State Library: South Dakota State Library, 500 E. Capitol, Pierre, SD 57501; (605) 773-3131.

Tennessee

State Information: (615) 741-3011

Governor's Office: Office of the Governor, State Capitol, Nashville, TN 37219; (615) 741-2001.

State Library: Tennessee State Library, 403 7th Ave. North, Nashville, TN 37243; (615) 741-2764.

Texas

State Information: (512) 463-4630

Governor's Office: Office of the Governor, P.O. Box 12428, Austin, TX 78711; (512) 463-2000.

State Library: Texas State Library, P.O. Box 12927, Austin, TX 78711; (512) 463-5455.

Utah

State Information: (801) 538-3000

Governor's Office: Office of the Governor, Room 210, State Capitol, Salt Lake City, UT 84114; (801) 538-1000.

State Library: Utah State Library, 2150 South 300 West, Suite 16, Salt Lake City, UT 84115; (801) 466-5888.

Vermont

State Information: (802) 828-1110

Governor's Office: Office of the Governor, 109 State Street, Montpelier, VT 05609-0101; (802) 828-3333.

State Library: Vermont State Library, 109 State Street, Montpelier, VT 05609-0601; (802) 828-3261.

Virginia

State Information: (804) 786-0000

Governor's Office: Office of the Governor, P.O. Box 1475, Richmond, VA 23212; (804) 786-2211.

State Library: Virginia State Library, 11th St and Capitol Square, Richmond, VA 23219; (804) 786-8929.

Washington

State Information: (206) 753-5000

Governor's Office: Office of the Governor, Legislative Building, Olympia, WA 98504; (206) 753-6780.

State Library: Washington State Library, Capitol Campus, Mail Stop AJ-11, Olympia, WA 98504; (206) 753-5590.

West Virginia

State Information: (304) 558-3456

Governor's Office: Office of the Governor, Main Capitol Complex, Charleston, WV 25305; (304) 558-2000.

State Library: West Virginia State Library, Cultural Center, Charleston, WV 25305; (304) 558-2041.

Wisconsin

State Information: (608) 266-2211

Governor's Office: Office of the Governor, 115 E. Capitol, Madison, WI 53702; (608) 266-1212.

State Library: State Historical Society, 816 State St., Madison, WI 53706; (608) 264-6534.

Wyoming

State Information: (307) 777-7011

Governor's Office: Office of the Governor, State Capitol, Cheyenne, WY 82002; (307) 777-7434.

State Library: Wyoming State Library, Supreme Court Building, 23rd and Capitol, Cheyenne, WY 82002; (307) 777-7283.

Be patient. If any phone number is incorrect, call (area code) 555-1212 and request the new listing.

Information Starting Places

Federal Public Information Offices

Almost every federal department, agency, and commission has a special staff to respond to inquiries from the public and the press. These public information offices are particularly helpful in providing details about new programs, proposed legislation, data, statistics, reports and other materials. Keep in mind that the public information office may not be aware or may not be in a position to share with you information that has not been officially released by the government agency. The policy of each office differs; some public information offices like many at the National Institutes of Health tend to offer to send photocopies of medical article abstracts and also provide the names and phone numbers of experts and NIH researchers. If others are reluctant to suggest whom you should talk with, refer to the relevant chapter in *Info-Power* and place calls to other offices within the agency or department.

BRANCHES

Legislative Branch

The U.S. Senate
Washington, DC 20511
(202) 224-3121

The U.S. House of Representatives
Washington, DC 20515
(202) 224-3121

Architect of the Capitol
U.S. Capitol Building, Room SB15
Washington, DC 20515
(202) 225-1200

U.S. Botanic Garden
245 First Street, SW
Washington, DC 20024
(202) 225-8333

General Accounting Office
441 G Street, NW
Washington, DC 20548
(202) 512-3000

Government Printing Office
710 N. Capitol Street, NW
Washington, DC 20401
(202) 512-0000

Library of Congress
101 Independence Ave., SE
Washington, DC 20540
(202) 707-5000

Office of Technology Assessment
U.S. Congress
Washington, DC 20510-8025
(202) 224-8996

Congressional Budget Office
2nd and D Sts., SW
Washington, DC 20515
(202) 226-2621

Copyright Royalty Tribunal
1825 Connecticut Ave., NW, Suite 918
Washington, DC 20009
(202) 606-4400

Judicial Branch

Supreme Court of the U.S.
1 1st St., NE
Washington, DC 20543
(202) 479-3000

U.S. Court of International Trade
1 Federal Plaza
New York, NY 10007
(212) 264-2814

Judicial Panel on Multidistrict Litigation
1 Columbus Circle, NE, Room G255
Washington, DC 20002
(202) 273-2800

U.S. Claims Court
717 Madison Place, NW
Washington, DC 20005
(202) 219-9657

U.S. Court of Military Appeals
450 E. St., NW
Washington, DC 20442
(202) 272-1448

Office of Policy Development
10th and Constitution Ave., NW, Room 4258
Washington, DC 20530
(202) 514-2000

U.S. Tax Court
400 2nd St., NW
Washington, DC 20217
(202) 606-8751

Temporary Emergency Court of Appeals
801 Pennsylvania Ave., NW, Suite 625
Washington, DC 20004
(202) 535-3390

Administrative Office of the United States Court of Appeals
717 Madison Place, NW
Washington, DC 20439
(202) 633-6550

Federal Judicial Center
1 Columbus Circle, NE
Washington, DC 20002
(202) 273-4000

Executive Branch

The White House Office
1600 Pennsylvania Ave.
Washington, DC 20500
(202) 456-1414

Be patient. If any phone number is incorrect, call (area code) 555-1212 and request the new listing.

Federal Public Information Offices

Office of Management and Budget
Room 249, Old Executive Office Bldg.
17th and Pennsylvania Ave., NW
Washington, DC 20503
(202) 395-3080

Council of Economic Advisers
Room 314
Old Executive Office Bldg.
17th and Pennsylvania Ave., NW
Washington, DC 20500
(202) 395-5084

National Security Council
Old Executive Office Bldg.
17th and Pennsylvania Ave., NW
Washington, DC 20506
(202) 395-4974

Office of the U.S. Trade Representative
600 17th St., NW
Washington, DC 20506
(202) 395-3230

Council on Environmental Quality
722 Jackson Place, NW
Washington, DC 20503
(202) 395-5750

Office of Science and Technology Policy
Old Executive Office Bldg.
Room 431
Washington, DC 20500
(202) 395-7347

Office of National Drug Control Policy
Executive Office of the President
Washington, DC 20500
(202) 467-9800

National Critical Materials Council
810 7th St., NW
Mailstop 1100
Washington, DC 20241
(202) 501-3737

Office of Administration
725 17th St., NW
Washington, DC 20503
(202) 395-6963

Office of the Vice President of the United States
Old Executive Office Bldg.
Washington, DC 20501
(202) 456-2326

DEPARTMENTS

Department of Agriculture

14th and Independence Ave., SW
Washington, DC 20250
(202) 720-8732

Small Community and Rural Development
Farmers Home Administration
14th and Independence Ave., SW
Room 5037-S
Washington, DC 20250
(202) 720-4323

Rural Development Administration
USDA RDA
Attn. LAPIS
Room 5423
14th and Independence Ave., SW

Washington, DC 20250
(202) 690-2394

Rural Electrification Administration
Room 4042-S
14th and Independence, Ave., SW
Washington, DC 20250
(202) 720-1255

Federal Crop Insurance Corporation
1400 Independence Ave., SW
Washington, DC 20250
(202) 254-8460

Marketing and Inspection Services
Agricultural Cooperative Service
P.O. Box 96576
Washington, DC 20090-6576
(202) 720-2556

Agricultural Marketing Service
USDA
P.O. Box 96456
Room 3510, South
Washington, DC 20090-6456
(202) 720-8999

Animal and Plant Health Inspection Service
P.O. Box 96464
Washington, DC 20090-6464
(202) 720-3861

Food Safety and Inspection Service
14th and Independence Ave., SW
Washington, DC 20250
(202) 720-7943

Packers and Stockyards Administration
14th and Independence Ave., SW, Room 3039
Washington, DC 20250-2800
(202) 720-7051

Food and Consumer Services
Food and Nutrition Service
3101 Park Center Drive
Alexandria, VA 22302
(703) 305-2276

Human Nutrition Information Service
6505 Belcrest Road
Hyattsville, MD 20782
(301) 436-7725

Office of the Consumer Advisor
14th and Independence Ave., SW
Room 240-E
Washington, DC 20250
(202) 720-3975

Agricultural Stabilization and Conservation Service
3702 South Bldg.
P.O. Box 2415
Washington, DC 20013
(202) 720-5237

Commodity Credit Corporation
14th and Independence Ave., SW
Room 4521-S
Washington, DC 20250-1000
(202) 720-3448

Foreign Agricultural Service
14th and Independence Ave., SW
Room 213-A
Washington, DC 20250
(202) 720-3448

Be patient. If any phone number is incorrect, call (area code) 555-1212 and request the new listing.

Information Starting Places

Office of International Corporation and Development
14th and Independence Ave., SW
Room 3002
Washington, DC 20250-4300
(202) 690-1800

Science and Education
Agricultural Research Service
14th and Independence Ave., SW
302A Administration Bldg.
Washington, DC 20520-2201
(202) 720-3656

Cooperative State Research Service
14th and Independence Ave., SW
305A Administration Bldg.
Washington, DC 20250-2201
(202) 720-4423

USDA Extension Service
Room 3328 South
14th and Independence Ave., SW
Washington, DC 20250-0900
(202) 720-3029

National Agricultural Library
10301 Baltimore Blvd.
Beltsville, MD 20705-2351
(301) 504-5248

Natural Resources and Environment
Forest Service
201 14th St., SW
Washington, DC 20250
(202) 205-1760

Soil Conservation Service
P.O. Box 2890
Washington, DC 20013
(202) 205-0027

Economic Research Service
1301 New York Ave., NW
Washington, DC 20005
(202) 219-0515

National Agricultural Statistics Service
14th and Independence Ave., SW
Room 5829
Washington, DC 20250
(202) 720-4020

Office of Energy
USDA/OE
14th and Independence Ave., SW
Room 438A Administration Bldg.
Washington, DC 20250
(202) 720-2634

World Agricultural Outlook Board
Room 5143 South
14th and Independence Ave., SW
Washington, DC 20250-3800
(202) 720-6030

Economics Management Staff
1301 New York Ave., NW
Room 228
Washington, DC 20005-4789
(202) 219-0504

Graduate School, U.S. Department of Agriculture
14th and Independence Ave., SW
Room 1103
Washington, DC 20250
(202) 690-4280

Sources of Information for the Department of Agriculture
Contracts and Small Business Activities
14th and Independence Ave., SW
Room 1550, South Building
Washington, DC 20250

Films
Office of Public Affairs
Room 1614 South
14th and Independence Ave., SW
Washington, DC 20250-1300
(202) 720-6072

Waste and Fraud Hotline
14th and Independence Ave., SW
Washington, DC 20250
(800) 424-9121

Speakers
Office of Public Liaison
14th and Independence Ave., SW
Room 112A, Administration Bldg.
Washington, DC 20250-1320
(202) 720-2798

USDA Locator
14th and Independence Ave., SW
Washington, DC 20250
(202) 720-8732

Public Affairs
14th and Independence Ave., SW
Room 112A, Administration Bldg.
Washington, DC 20250-1320
(202) 720-2798

Freedom of Information Office
14th and Independence Ave., SW
Room 536-A
Washington, DC 20250-1300
(202) 720-8164

Rural Information Center
National Agricultural Library
Room 304
10301 Baltimore Blvd.
Beltsville, MD 20705
(800) 633-7701

Department of Commerce

Herbert C. Hoover Bldg.
14th and Constitution Ave., NW
Washington, DC 20230
(202) 482-2000

Office of the Secretary
14th and Constitution Ave., NW, Room 5422
Washington, DC 20230
(202) 482-2112

Competitive Assessment and Business Policy
Office of Business Analysis
HCHB Room 4885
Washington, DC 20230
(202) 482-1986

Minority Business Development Agency
14th and Constitution Ave., NW
Room 6707
Washington, DC 20230
(202) 482-1936

Bureau of the Census
Washington, DC 20233
(301) 763-7662

Be patient. If any phone number is incorrect, call (area code) 555-1212 and request the new listing.

Federal Public Information Offices

Office of Census Publications
Washington, DC 20233
(301) 763-4100

Bureau of Economic Analysis
1401 K St., NW
Washington, DC 20230
(202) 523-0777

Bureau of Export Administration
Room HCHB 3895
14th and Constitution Ave., NW
Washington, DC 20230
(202) 377-2721

Economic Development Administration
14th and Constitution Ave., NW
Room 7810
Washington, DC 20230
(202) 377-5113

International Trade Administration
14th and Constitution Ave., NW
Room 3414
Washington, DC 20230
(202) 482-3808

National Oceanic and Atmospheric Administration (NOAA)
Room 5230, 14th and Constitution Ave., NW
Washington, DC 20230
(202) 482-2985

NOAA Publications
NOAA Central Library
6009 Executive Blvd.
Rockville, MD 20852
(301) 443-8330

Patent and Trademark Office
Commission of Patents and Trademarks
Washington, DC 20231
(703) 305-8341

Technology Administration
Room 4824
14th and Constitution Ave., NW
Washington, DC 20230
(202) 482-3037

National Institute of Standards and Technology (NIST)
Gaithersburg, MD 20899-0001
(301) 975-2758

NIST Publications
Gaithersburg, MD 20899
(301) 975-3058

National Technical Information Service
5285 Port Royal Road
Springfield, VA 22161
(703) 487-4650

United States Travel and Tourism Administration
14th and Constitution Ave., NW
Room 1863
Washington, DC 20230
(202) 482-3811

Sources of Information for the Department of Commerce

Age and Citizenship Information
Bureau of the Census
P.O. Box 1545
Jeffersonville, IN 47131
(812) 285-5314

Public Affairs
Room 5058

14th and Constitution Ave., NW
Washington, DC 20230
(202) 482-4901

Locator
14th and Constitution Ave., NW
Washington, DC 20230
(202) 377-2000

Publications
Office of Secretary
Publications Division
Room 2830B
14th and Constitution Ave.
Washington, DC 20230
(202) 482-2108

Freedom of Information Office
Room 6020
14th and Constitution Ave., NW
Washington, DC 20230
(202) 482-4115

Fraud and Waste Hotline
Office of Inspector General
P.O. Box 612
Ben Franklin Station
Washington, DC 20044
(800) 424-5197

Department of Defense

Army Public Affairs Office
Defense Intelligence Agency
Attention: Executive Services Office
Pentagon
Washington, DC 20340-1038
(703) 614-7039

Naval Public Affairs Office
Defense Intelligence Agency
Pentagon, 2E340
Washington, DC 20350
(703) 697-6724

Publications Office
Office of the Assistant Secretary of Defense
(Public Affairs)
Directorate for Public Communications
Room 2 Echo 777
Pentagon
Washington, DC 20301-1400
(703) 697-5737

Freedom of Information Office
Office of the Assistant Secretary for Defense
Chief, Freedom of Information and Privacy Acts Division
Crystal Square II, Suite 201
1725 Jefferson Davis Highway
Arlington, VA 22202
(703) 697-1182

Locator
Pentagon
Washington, DC 20350
(703) 545-6700

Defense Hotline
Pentagon
Washington, DC 20301-1900
(800) 424-9098

American Forces Information Service
601 N. Fairfax St.
Suite 311
Alexandria, VA 22314
(703) 274-4839

Be patient. If any phone number is incorrect, call (area code) 555-1212 and request the new listing.

Information Starting Places

DOD Dependent Schools
2461 Eisenhower Ave.
Alexandria, VA 22331-1100
(703) 325-0885

Office of Civilian Health and Medical
Program of the Uniformed Services
Aurora, CO 80045-6900
(303) 361-8606

Office of Civilian Health and Medical
Program of the Uniformed Services
Defense Medical Systems Support Center
5109 Leesburg Pike
Skyline 6
Falls Church, VA 22041
(703) 756-2530

Office of Economic Adjustment
400 Army Navy Drive, Room 200
Arlington, VA 22202-2884
(703) 697-9155

Washington Headquarters Service
Office of Secretary of Defense
Room 3D972, Pentagon
Washington, DC 20301-1155
(703) 695-4436

Department of the Air Force
Secretary of the Air Force
Freedom of Information Office
SAF/AAIS (FOIA)
Room 4A1088C
Pentagon
Washington, DC 20330
(703) 697-8120

Department of the Army
Office of Chief of Public Affairs
Attn: SAPA-PCD
Pentagon
Washington, DC 20310
(703) 614-0739

Office of the Secretary of the Army
Room 3E718
Pentagon
Washington, DC 20310-0101
(703) 695-3211

United States Army Forces Command
Office of Public Affairs
Attn: FCPA
Ft. McPherson, GA 30330-6000
(404) 669-5607

United States Army Material Command
5001 Eisenhower Ave.
Alexandria, VA 22333-0001
(703) 274-9625

United States Army Information Systems Command
Headquarters
USAISC
Ft. Huachuca, AZ 85613-5000
(602) 538-6161

United States Army Intelligence and Security Command
Headquarters
Ft. Belvoir, VA 22060
(703) 706-1232

United States Army Health Service Command
Headquarters
Ft. Sam Houston, TX 78234
(512) 221-6313

United States Army Criminal Investigation Command
Dept of Army
5611 Columbia Pike
CIOP-PPMN
Falls Church, VA 22041-5015
(703) 756-1232

Military Traffic Management Command
5611 Columbia Pike
Falls Church, VA 22041-5050
(703) 756-1724

United States Army Military District of Washington
Building 32
Ft. McNair
Washington, DC 20319
(202) 475-0565

United States Army Corps of Engineers
Chief of Engineers
U.S. Army Corps of Engineers
Attn CECS
Washington, DC 20314-1000
(202) 272-0001

Department of the Navy
Public Affairs Office
Secretary of the Navy
Washington, DC 20350-1000
(703) 697-7491

Space and Naval Warfare Systems Command
2451 Crystal Park 5
Washington, DC 20363-5200
703-602-8768

Supply Systems
Room 1C247
Pentagon
Arlington, VA 20330-6345
(703) 697-0812

Strategic Systems
Air Force Programs
HQ USAF/SCMS
1250 Pentagon
Washington, DC 20330-1250
(703) 614-6407

Naval Computer and Tele-communications Command
4401 Massachusetts Ave., NW
Washington, DC 20394-5460
(202) 282-0356

Office of the Assistant Secretary for Defense
Freedom of Information Office
Room 2C757
Pentagon
Washington, DC 20301-1400
(703) 697-3078

Naval Inspector General
Washington Navy Yard
Building 200
Washington, DC 20374-5006
(202) 433-2000

Judge Advocate General
200 Stovall St.
Alexandria, VA 22332-2400
(703) 614-7420

Comptroller
Room 4E768
Pentagon
Washington, DC 20350-1000
(703) 697-2325

Be patient. If any phone number is incorrect, call (area code) 555-1212 and request the new listing.

Federal Public Information Offices

Auditor General
5611 Columbia Pike
Room 506B Nassas Bldg.
Falls Church, VA 22041-5080
(703) 756-2117

Office of Information
Chief of Information
Pentagon
Room 2E340
Washington DC 20350-1200
(703) 697-6724

Chief of Naval Research
800 North Quincy St.
Suite 907
Arlington, VA 22217-5660
(703) 696-4258

Personnel Boards
801 N. Randolph St.
Suite 907
Arlington, VA 22203
(703) 696-4356

Naval Records
Bureau of Naval Personnel
Office of the Files
PERS 313C1 REC
2 Navy Annex
Washington DC 20370-3130
(703) 614-1315

Naval Air Systems Command
Commander of Naval Air Systems
Washington, DC 20361-0001
(703) 692-2260

Naval Sea Systems Command
Office of the Commander
2531 Jefferson Davis Highway
Arlington, VA22242-5160
(703) 602-3328

Naval Personnel
Navy Annex
Federal Bldg., #2
S/HHRO
Washington, DC 20370-5000
(703) 614-1271

Naval Medicine
23 and E Sts., NW
Washington, DC 20372-5120
(202) 653-1327

Oceanographer of the Navy
Chief of Naval Operations (N096)
U.S. Naval Observatory
3450 Massachusetts Ave., NW
Washington, DC 20392-5421
(202) 653-1295

Naval Space Command
Building 180
Bahlgren, VA 22448-5170
(703) 663-7841

Legal Services
Judge Advocates Office
200 Stovall St.
Alexandria, VA 22332-2400
(703) 325-9820

Naval Security Group Command
Office of the Commander
3801 Nebraska Ave., NW

Washington, DC 20393-5442
(202) 282-0272

Intelligence Command
Office of Inspector General
Code OCA
4301 Suitland Road
Washington, DC 20395
(301) 763-3557

Naval Investigative Service
901 M St., SE
Building 111
Washington, DC 20388
(202) 433-9323

Chief of Naval Education and Training
250 Dallas St.
Pensacola, FL 32508-5220
(904) 452-4858

United States Marine Corps
Office of Public Affairs (PA)
Washington, DC 20380-0001
(703) 614-2344

United States Naval Academy
117 DeCater Road
Annapolis, MD 20412-5018
(800) 638-9156

Defense Agencies

Defense Advanced Research Projects Agency
3701 N. Fairfax Dr.
Arlington, VA 22203-1714
(703) 696-2444

Defense Commissary Agency
Bldg. 11200
Ft. Lee, VA 23801-6300
(804) 734-2227

Defense Contract Audit Agency
Cameron Station
Alexandria, VA 22304-6178
(703) 274-6785

Defense Finance and Accounting Service
1931 Jefferson Davis Highway
Arlington, VA 22240-5291
(703) 607-2616

Defense Information Systems Agency
701 S. Courthouse Road
Arlington, VA 22204-2199
(703) 692-9012

Defense Intelligence Agency
Public Liaison Office
Washington, DC 20340
(703) 695-0071

Defense Investigative Service
1340 Braddock Place
Alexandria, VA 22314-1651
(202) 475-0966

Defense Legal Services Agency
1600 Defense, Pentagon
Washington, DC 20301-1600
(703) 695-3341

Defense Logistics Agency
Cameron Station
Alexandria, VA 22304-6100
(703) 274-6521

Be patient. If any phone number is incorrect, call (area code) 555-1212 and request the new listing.

Information Starting Places

Defense Mapping Agency
8613 Lee Highway
Fairfax, VA 22031
(703) 285-9368

Defense Security Assistance Agency
Office of the Director
Pentagon
Room 4E841
Washington, DC 20301-2800
(703) 695-3291

National Security Agency
9800 Savage Road
Ft. George G. Mead
Washington, DC 20755-6000
(301) 688-6524

On-Site Inspection Agency
Dulles International Airport
Washington, DC 20041-0498
(703) 742-4326

Strategic Defense Initiative Organization
Room 1E1081
Pentagon
Washington, DC 20301-7100
(703) 697-4040

Joint Service Schools
Defense Intelligence College
Washington, DC 20340-5485
(202) 373-4545

Defense Systems Management College
Ft. Belvoir, VA 22060-5426
(703) 805-3360

National Defense University
National War College
Washington, DC 20319-6000
(202) 475-1776

National Defense University
Industrial College of the Armed Forces
Ft. L.J. McNair
Washington, DC 20319
(202) 475-1832

Armed Forces Staff College
7800 Hampton Blvd.
Norfolk, VA 23511-1702
(804) 444-5302

National Defense University
Information Resource Management College
Ft. Mcnair
Washington, DC 20319-6000
(202) 287-9322

Department of Education

400 Maryland Ave., SW
Washington, DC 20202
(202) 401-1576

Federally Sided Corporations
American Printing House for the Blind
P.O. Box 6085
Louisville, KY 40206
(502) 895-2405

Gallaudet University
800 Florida Ave., NE
Washington, DC 20002
(202) 651-5000

Howard University
2400 6th St., NW
Washington, DC 20059
(202) 806-6100

National Technical Institute for the Deaf
P.O. Box 9887
Rochester, NY 14623-0887
(716) 475-6400

Department of Energy

1000 Independence Ave., SW
Washington, DC 20585
(202) 586-5000

Public Affairs
1000 Independence Ave., SW
Room 7A145
Washington, DC 20585
(202) 586-4940

Office of Nuclear Safety
NS-1
1000 Independence Ave., SW
Washington, DC 20585
(202) 586-2407

Office of Energy Research
ER-60
GTN
Washington, DC 20545
(301) 903-4944

Office of Environmental Restoration and Waste Management
1000 Independence Ave., SW
Washington, DC 20585
(202) 586-2661

Assistant Secretary for Fossil Energy
FE10
Washington 20585
(301) 903-2617

Defense Programs
1000 Independence Ave., SW
Washington, DC 20585
(202) 586-2295

Nuclear Energy
Office of Public Affairs
1000 Independence Ave., SW
Washington DC 20585
(202) 586-1941

Civilian Radioactive Waste Management
1000 Independence Ave., SW
RW13
Washington, DC 20585
(202) 586-9116

New Production Reactors
1000 Independence Ave., SW
Washington, DC 20585
(202) 586-6456

National Energy Information Center
1000 Independence Ave., SW
Washington, DC 20585
(202) 586-1181

Economic Regulatory Administration
1000 Independence Ave., SW
Room 5B148
Washington, DC 20585
(202) 586-4241

Be patient. If any phone number is incorrect, call (area code) 555-1212 and request the new listing.

Federal Public Information Offices

Federal Energy Regulatory Commission
825 N. Capitol
Washington, DC 20426
(202) 208-0300

Power Administrations
Bonneville Power Administration
P.O. Box 3621
Portland, OR 97208
(503) 230-5101

Southeastern Power Administration
Samuel Elbert Bldg.
Elberton, GA 30635
(706) 283-9917

Alaska Power Administration
2770 Sherwood Lane
Suite 2B
Juno, AK 99801-8545
(907) 586-7405

Southwestern Power Administration
P.O. Box 1619
Tulsa, OK 74101
(918) 581-7474

Western Area Power Administration
P.O. Box 3402
Golden, CO 80401
(303) 231-1513

Department of Health and Human Services

200 Independence Ave., SW
Washington, DC 20201
(202) 619-0257

Administration on Aging
330 Independence Ave., SW
Suite 4661
Washington, DC 20201
(202) 619-0556

Administration for Children and Families
370 L'Enfant Promenade, SW
Suite 600
Washington, DC 20447
(202) 401-9200

Developmental Disabilities
370 L'Enfant Promenade, SW
Washington, DC 20447
(202) 690-6590

Native Americans
370 L'Enfant Promenade, SW
Washington, DC 20447
(202) 690-7776

Child Support Enforcement
370 L'Enfant Promenade, SW
Washington, DC 20447
(202) 401-9373

Community Services
5th Floor, West
370 L'Enfant Promenade, SW
Washington, DC 20447
(202) 401-9333

Program Support
370 L'Enfant Promenade, SW
Washington, DC 20447
(202) 401-9238

Office of Information Systems Management
200 Independence Ave., SW
Washington, DC 20201
(202) 401-9257

Financial Management
370 L'Enfant Plaza, SW
Washington, DC 20447
(202) 401-9238

Public Affairs
901 D St., SW
Washington, DC 20447
(202) 401-9215

Refugee Resettlement
370 L'Enfant Promenade, SW
Washington, DC 20447
(202) 401-9246

Office of Family Assistance
370 L'Enfant Promenade
Washington, DC 20447
(202) 401-9275

Public Health Service
1660 L St., NW
Suite 1200
Washington, DC 20036
(202) 673-7700

Employment
5600 Fishers Lane
Room 17A07
Rockville, MD 20857
(301) 443-6900

Films, Publications, and Other Information
Office of Communications
200 Independence Ave., SW
Room 721H
Washington, DC 20201
(202) 690-6867

Agency for Health Care Policy and Research
2101 E. Jefferson St.
Rockville, MD 20852-4908
(301) 227-8364

Grants Management
Executive Office
Suite 601
2101 E. Jefferson St.
Rockville, MD 20852
(301) 227-8447

Contracts
Executive Office Center
Suite 601
2101 E. Jefferson St.
Rockville, MD 20852
(301) 227-8443

Employment
2101 E. Jefferson St.
Suite 601
Rockville, MD 20852
(301) 227-8443

Publications
P.O. Box 8547
Silver Spring, MD 20907
(800) 358-9295

Alcohol, Drug Abuse, and Mental Health Administration
Parklawn Bldg.
5600 Fishers Lane

Be patient. If any phone number is incorrect, call (area code) 555-1212 and request the new listing.

Information Starting Places

Room 12-105
Rockville, MD 20857
(301) 443-3875

National Institute on Alcohol Abuse and Alcoholism
5600 Fishers Lane
Rockville, MD 20857
(301) 443-4373

National Institute on Drug Abuse
Room 1005
5600 Fishers Lane
Rockville, MD 20857
(301) 443-6487

National Institute of Mental Health
Extramural Programs
Parklawn Bldg.
Room 17-C08
Rockville, MD 20857
(301) 443-3877

Office for Substance Abuse Prevention
5515 Security Lane
Rockwall II Bldg.
Rockville, MD 20852
(301) 443-5266

Center For Substance Abuse Treatment
Rockwall II Bldg.
10th Floor
5600 Fishers Lane
Rockville, MD 20857
(301) 443-6501

Grants and Contracts
5600 Fishers Lane
Rockville, MD 20857
(301) 443-4147

Employment
Room 15C-12
5600 Fishers Lane
Rockville, MD 20857
(301) 443-5407

Centers for Disease Control and Prevention
Public Affairs Office
1600 Clifton Rd., NE
Atlanta, GA 30333
(404) 639-3286

Employment
1600 Clifton Rd., NE
Atlanta, GA 30333
(404) 639-3615

Films
1600 Clifton Rd., NE
Atlanta, GA 30333
(404) 639-2412

Publications
1600 Clifton Rd., NE
Atlanta, GA 30333
(404) 639-3534

Agency for Toxic Substances and Disease Registry
1600 Clifton Rd., NE
Mailstop E28
Atlanta, GA 30333
(404) 639-0727

Food and Drug Administration
5600 Fishers Lane
Rockville, MD 20857
(301) 443-1544

Office of Consumer Affairs
5600 Fishers Lane
Rockville, MD 20857
(301) 443-3170

Center for Drug Evaluation and Research
5600 Fishers Lane
(MPN 1, Room 151)
Rockville, MD 20857
(301) 295-8012

Center for Biologics Evaluations Evaluation and Research
1401 Rockville Pike
Rockville, MD 20852
(301) 496-3556

Division of Consumer Affairs and Center for Devices and Radiological Health
1901 Chapman Ave.
Rockville, MD 20857
(301) 443-4190

Center for Veterinary Medicine
Metro Park North 2
HFV1
7500 Standish Place
Rockville, MD 20855
(301) 443-3450

Regional Operations
Office of Regulatory Affairs
5600 Fishers Lane
Room 1490
Rockville, MD 20857
(301) 443-1594

Consumer Activities
Room 1685
5600 Fishers Lane
Rockville, MD 20857
(301) 443-5006

Employment
5600 Fishers Lane
Room 759
Rockville, MD 20857
(301) 443-2234

Publications
5600 Fishers Lane
Rockville, MD 20857
(301) 443-3220

Freedom of Information Office
5600 Fishers Lane
Room 12A16
Rockville, MD 20857
(301) 443-1813

Health Resources and Services Administration
Office of Communications
5600 Fishers Lane
Rockville, MD 20857
(301) 443-2086

Bureau of Health Care Delivery and Assistance
Room 7-05
Parklawn Building
5600 Fishers Lane
Rockville, MD 20857
(301) 443-2320

Bureau of Health Professions
5600 Fishers Lane
Parklawn Building
Rockville, MD 20857
(301) 443-2060

Be patient. If any phone number is incorrect, call (area code) 555-1212 and request the new listing.

Federal Public Information Offices

Bureau of Health Resources Development
5600 Fishers Lane
Room 1103
Parklawn Building
Rockville, MD 20857
(301) 443-1993

Maternal and Child Health Bureau
Room 18-05
Parklawn Building
5600 Fishers Lane
Rockville, MD 20857
(301) 443-2170

Employment
Room 14A-46
Parklawn Building
5600 Fishers Lane
Rockville, MD 20857
(301) 443-5460

Films
Room 1445
Parklawn Building
5600 Fishers Lane
Rockville, MD 20857
(301) 443-2086

Office of Communications
Room 1445
Parklawn Building
5600 Fishers Lane
Rockville, MD 20857
(301) 443-2086

Publications
Room 1445
Parklawn Building
5600 Fishers Lane
Rockville, MD 20857
(301) 443-2086

Indian Health Service
Room 6-05
Parklawn Building
5600 Fishers Lane
Rockville, MD 20857
(301) 443-1087

Employment
Room 4B-44
Parklawn Building
5600 Fishers Lane
Rockville, MD 20857
(301) 443-6520

Publications
12720 Twinbrook Parkway
Rockville, MD 20857
(301) 443-5860

Office of Communications
5600 Fishers Lane
Room 6-35
Rockville, MD 20857
(301) 443-1397

National Institutes of Health
9000 Rockville Pike
Bethesda, MD 20892
(301) 496-4000

National Cancer Institute
Building 31, Room 10A29
9000 Rockville Pike
Bethesda, MD 20892
(301) 496-6631

National Heart, Lung, and Blood Institute
Office of Communications and Public Information
Building 31, Room 4A21
9000 Rockville Pike
Bethesda, MD 20892
(301) 496-4236

National Library of Medicine
Office of Inquiries
Building 38, Room 2S10
8600 Rockville Pike
Bethesda, MD 20894

National Institute of Diabetes and Digestive and Kidney Diseases
Office of the Director
Building 31, Room 9A52
9000 Rockville Pike
Bethesda, MD 20892
(301) 496-5741

National Institute of Allergy and Infectious Diseases
Office of Communications
Building 31, Room 7A32
9000 Rockville Pike
Bethesda, MD 20892
(301) 496-5717

National Institute of Child Health and Human Development
Office of the Director
Building 31, Room 2A20
9000 Rockville Pike
Bethesda, MD 20892
(301) 496-2500

National Institute on Deafness and Other Communicative Disorders
Office of the Director
Building 31, Room 3C02
9000 Rockville Pike
Bethesda, MD 20892
(301) 402-0495

National Institute of Dental Research
Office of the Director
Building 31, Room 2C27
9000 Rockville Pike
Bethesda, MD 20892
(301) 496-6621

National Institute of Environmental Health Sciences
Office of Communications
Building 101, Room A202
Research Triangle Park, NC 27709
(919) 541-4580

National Institute of General Medical Sciences
Office of Administrative Management
Building 928
9000 Rockville Pike
Bethesda, MD 20892
(301) 496-7714

National Institute of Neurological Disorders and Stroke
Public Inquiries Section
Building 31, Room 8A06
9000 Rockville Pike
Bethesda, MD 20892
(301) 496-5751

National Eye Institute
Office of the Director
Building 31, Room 6A07
9000 Rockville Pike
Bethesda, MD 20892
(301) 496-7425

National Institute on Aging
Office of Administrative Management

Be patient. If any phone number is incorrect, call (area code) 555-1212 and request the new listing.

Information Starting Places

Building 31, Room 5C32
9000 Rockville Pike
Bethesda, MD 20892
(301) 496-5345

National Institute of Arthritis and Musculoskeletal and Skin Diseases
Office of the Director
Building 31, Room 4C32
9000 Rockville Pike
Bethesda, MD 20892
(301) 496-4353

Clinical Center
Office of the Director
Building 10, Room 2C146
9000 Rockville Pike
Bethesda, MD 20892
(301) 496-3227

Fogarty International Center
Building 31, Room B2C29
9000 Rockville Pike
Bethesda, MD 20892
(301) 496-4625

National Center for Human Genome Research
Building 38A, Room 605
9000 Rockville Pike
Bethesda, MD 20892
(301) 496-0844

National Center for Nursing Research
Westwood Building
Room 754
9000 Rockville Pike
Bethesda, MD 20892
(301) 594-9618

Division of Computer Research and Technology
Executive Office
Building 12A, Room 3025
9000 Rockville Pike
Bethesda, MD 20892
(301) 496-5206

National Center for Research Resources
Executive Office
Building 12A, Room 4003
9000 Rockville Pike
Bethesda, MD 20892
(301) 496-5605

Division of Research Grants
Executive Office
5333 Westbard Ave.
Westwood Building
Bethesda, MD 20892
(301) 594-7333

Contracts
Building 31, 1B03
9000 Rockville Pike
Bethesda, MD 20892
(301) 496-6431

Employment
Office of Personnel Management
Building 1, Room B1-60
9000 Rockville Pike
Bethesda, MD 20892
(301) 496-4197

Commissioned Officer Program
Building 31, Room B3C24
9000 Rockville Pike
Bethesda, MD 20892
(301) 496-4212

Films
National Library of Medicine
8600 Rockville Pike
Bethesda, MD 20894
(301) 496-6308

Publications
Editorial Operations Branch
Building 31, Room 2B03
9000 Rockville Pike
Bethesda, MD 20892
(301) 496-4143

Office of Communications
Building 31, Room 2B03
9000 Rockville Pike
Bethesda, MD 20892
(301) 496-4143

Health Care Financing Administration
6325 Security Blvd.
364 East Highrise Building
Baltimore, MD 21207
(410) 966-3000

Contracts and Small Business Activities
Office of Grants
364 East Highrise Bldg.
6325 Security Blvd.
Baltimore, MD 21207
(410) 966-5157

Employment
634 Highrise Building
6325 Security Blvd.
Baltimore, MD 21207
(301) 966-5489

Publications
555 E. Highrise Building
6325 Security Blvd.
Baltimore, MD 21207
(410) 966-3215

Social Security Administration
Office of Public Affairs
4th Floor, Annex Bldg.
6401 Security Blvd.
Baltimore, MD 21235
(410) 965-7700

Contracts and Small Business Activities
322 Altmeyer Building
Systems Planning and Integration
Room 322
Baltimore, MD 21235
(410) 965-5912

Reading Rooms
Room G-44
Altmeyer Building
Baltimore, MD 21235
(800)-2345-SSA

Employment
Personnel Office
6401 Security Blvd.
Baltimore, MD 21235
(410) 965-4506

Publications
4th Floor
Annex Bldg.
6401 Security Blvd.
Baltimore, MD 21235
(410) 965-7700

Be patient. If any phone number is incorrect, call (area code) 555-1212 and request the new listing.

Federal Public Information Offices

Speakers and Films
4th Floor, Annex Bldg.
6401 Security Blvd.
Baltimore, MD 21235
(410) 965-7700

Sources of Information for Health and Human Services

Civil Rights Office
330 Independence Ave., SW
Washington, DC 20201
(202) 619-0403
(202) 863-0100 (Hotline)

Consumer Activities
1620 L St., NW
Suite 700
Washington, DC 20036
(202) 634-4310

Locator
330 Independence Ave., SW
Washington, DC 20201
(202) 619-0257

Publications
Room 5259
330 Independence Ave., SW
Washington, DC 20201
(202) 619-1142

Department of Housing and Urban Development

451 Seventh St., SW
Washington, DC 20410
(202) 708-1422

HUD Hotline
Office of the Inspector General
451 Seventh St., SW
Washington, DC 20410
(800) 347-3735 or
(202) 708-4200

Program Areas

Assistant Secretary for Housing-Federal Housing Commissioner
Room 9100
451 Seventh St., SW
Washington, DC 20410-8000
(202) 708-3600

Assistant Secretary for Community Planning and Development
Room 7100
451 Seventh St., SW
Washington, DC 20410
(202) 708-2690

Assistant Secretary for Policy Development and Research
Room 8100
451 Seventh St., SW
Washington, DC 20410
(202) 708-1600

Lead-Based Paint Abatement and Poisoning Prevention
451 Seventh St., SW
Washington, DC 20410
(202) 755-1785

Assistant Secretary for Fair Housing and Equal Opportunity
Room 5100
451 Seventh St., SW
Washington, DC 20410
(202) 708-4252

Assistant Secretary for Public and Indian Housing
Room 4100
451 Seventh St., SW
Washington, DC 20410
(202) 708-0950

Government National Mortgage Association
Room 6100
451 Seventh St., SW
Washington, DC 20410
(202) 708-0926

Locator
451 Seventh St., SW
Washington, DC 20410
(202) 708-1112

Contracts
Room 5272
451 Seventh St., SW
Washington, DC 20410
(202) 708-1290

Property Disposition Division
Room 9172
451 Seventh St., SW
Washington, DC 20410
(202) 708-0740

Employment
Room 2255
451 Seventh St., SW
Washington, DC 20410
(202) 708-0408

Program Information Center
451 Seventh St., SW
Washington, DC 20410
(202) 708-1420

Freedom of Information Act Requests
Room 10139
451 Seventh St., SW
Washington, DC 20410
(202) 708-3054

Office of Public Affairs
451 Seventh St., SW
Washington, DC 20410
(202) 708-0980

Department of the Interior

1849 C St., NW
Washington, DC 20240
(202) 208-3171

Office of Inspector General
Mailstop 5341
1849 C St., NW
Washington, DC 20240
(202) 208-4356

Office of Hearings and Appeals
4015 Wilson Blvd.
Arlington, VA 22203
(703) 235-3810

Bureaus

United States Fish and Wildlife Service
1849 C St., NW
Washington, DC 20240
(202) 208-5634

Contracts
4401 N. Fairfax Dr.

Be patient. If any phone number is incorrect, call (area code) 555-1212 and request the new listing.

Information Starting Places

Room 212
Arlington, 22203
(703) 358-1728

Office of Current Information
1849 C St., NW
Washington, DC 20240
(202) 208-5634

Publications
4401 N. Fairfax Dr.
Mailstop 130, Webb Building
Arlington, VA 22203
(703) 358-1711

National Park Service
1849 C St., NW
Washington 20013-7127
(202) 208-6843

Contracts
Room 460
800 N. Capitol St.
Washington, DC 20013
(202) 523-0059

Employment
1849 C St., NW
Room 3323
Washington, DC 20013
(202) 208-5093

Publications
Harpers Ferry Historical Association
P.O. Box 197
Harpers Ferry, WV 25425
(304) 535-6881

Grants-in-Aid
800 N. Capitol St., NW
Suite 400
Washington, DC 20002
(202) 343-3700

United States Bureau of Mines
810 Seventh St., NW
Washington, DC 20241
(202) 501-9649

Contracts
Procurement Office
Mailstop 2140
810 Seventh St., NW
Washington, DC 20241
(202) 501-9256

Public Affairs
Mailstop 1040
810 Seventh St., NW
Washington, DC 20241
(202) 501-9649

Employment
Mailstop 2130
810 Seventh St., NW
Washington, DC 20241
(202) 501-9630

Publications
Publication Distributions
P.O. Box 18070
Cochrans Mill Road
Pittsburgh, PA 15236
(412) 892-4338

United States Geological Survey
National Center

12201 Sunrise Valley Drive
Reston, VA 22092
(703) 648-4460

Contracts, Grants, and Cooperative Agreements
Office of Procurement and Contracts
205 National Center
12201 Sunrise Valley Drive
Reston, VA 22092
(703) 648-7373

Employment
215 National Center
12201 Sunrise Valley Drive
Reston, VA 22092
(703) 648-6131

Exhibits
Branch of Visual Service
790 National Center
12201 Sunrise Valley Drive
Reston, VA 22092
(703) 648-4357

Films
Branch of Visual Service
790 National Center
12201 Sunrise Valley Drive
Reston, VA 22092
(703) 648-4357

Maps
Distribution Branch
Box 25286, Denver Federal Center
Denver, CO 80225
(303) 236-7477

New Media
119 National Center
12201 Sunrise Valley Drive
Reston, VA 22092
(703) 648-4460

Publications
Distribution Branch
Box 25286
Denver Federal Center
Denver, CO 80225
(303) 236-7477

Water Data
National Water Data Exchange
421 National Center
12201 Sunrise Valley Drive
Reston, VA 22092
(703) 648-5663

Office of Surface Mining Reclamation and Enforcement
1951 Constitution Ave., NW
Washington, DC 20240
(202) 208-2719

Contracts
Procurement Branch
Office of Surface Mining
1951 Constitution Ave., NW
Washington, DC 20240
(202) 343-4865

Employment
Chief
Division of Personnel
Office of Surface Mining
1951 Constitution Ave., NW
Washington, DC 20240
(202) 208-2965

Be patient. If any phone number is incorrect, call (area code) 555-1212 and request the new listing.

Federal Public Information Offices

Bureau of Indian Affairs
Department of the Interior
Washington, DC 20240
(202) 208-7315

Contracts
Chief
Contracting and Grants Administration
Department of the Interior
1951 Constitution Ave., NW
Washington, DC 20240
(202) 208-2825

Employment
Personnel Office
1951 Constitution Ave., NW
Washington, DC 20240
(202) 208-2547

Reading Room
National Resources Library
Main Interior Building
Department of the Interior
1951 Constitution Ave., NW
Washington, DC 20240
(202) 208-5815

Speakers and Films
Office of Public Affairs
1951 Constitution Ave., NW
Washington, DC 20240
(202) 208-7315

Public Affairs
Office of Public Affairs
1951 Constitution Ave., NW
Washington, DC 20240
(202) 208-7315

Minerals Management Service
1849 C St., NW
Washington, DC 20240
(202) 208-3983

Public Affairs
Room 4213
1849 C St., NW
Washington, Dc 20240
(202) 208-3983

Bureau of Land Management
Department of the Interior
1849 C St., NW
Washington, DC 20240
(202) 208-3435

Contracts
Office of Procurement
1849 C St., NW
Washington, DC 20240
(202) 208-4843

Public Affairs
1849 C St., NW
Room 5600
Washington, DC 20240
(202) 208-3435

Small Business Activities
(for Western States except Oregon)
Office of Procurement
Building 50
Denver Federal Center
P.O. Box 25047
Denver, CO 80225-0047
(303) 969-6502

Bureau of Reclamation
Office of Public Affairs
Room 7640
1849 C St., NW
Washington, DC 20240
(202) 208-4662

Contracts
Office of Procurement
Building 67
Denver Federal Center
Denver, CO 80225
(303) 236-6914

Employment
Personnel Office
Denver Federal Center
Denver, CO 80225
(303) 236-3820

Publications
Office of Publications
Denver Federal Center
Denver, CO 80225
(303) 236-6741

Speakers and Films
Office of Public Affairs
Room 7640
1849 C St., NW
Washington, DC 20240
(202) 208-4662

Office of Public Affairs
Room 7640
1849 C St., NW
Washington, DC 20240
(202) 208-4662

Sources of Information for the Department of the Interior
Contracts
Office of Acquisition and Property Management
1849 C St., NW
Mailstop 5512-MIB
Washington, DC 20240
(202) 208-6431

Departmental Museum
1849 C St., NW
Mailstop 5412-MIB
Washington, DC 20240
(202) 208-4743

Employment
Office of Personnel
1849 C St., NW
Washington, DC 20240
(202) 208-6761

Publications
Office of Printing and Publications
Mailstop 1307-MIB
1849 C St., NW
Washington, DC 20240
(202) 208-4841

Office of Public Affairs
Mailstop 7013
1849 C St., NW
Washington, DC 20240
(202) 208-3171

Freedom of Information Office
1849 C St., NW
Washington, DC 20240
(202) 208-5342

Be patient. If any phone number is incorrect, call (area code) 555-1212 and request the new listing.

Information Starting Places

Reading Room
Library Reading Room
Mailstop 1151
1849 C St., NW
Washington, DC 20240
(202) 208-5815

Locator
1849 C St., NW
Washington, DC 20240
(202) 208-7220

Department of Justice

Constitution Ave. and Tenth St., NW
Washington, DC 20530
(202) 514-2000

Community Relations Service
Suite 330, 5530 Friendship Blvd.
Chevy Chase, MD 20815
(301) 492-5929

Office for U.S. Trustees
Suite 700
901 E St., NW
Washington, DC 20530
(202) 307-1391

Divisions

Antitrust Division
FOIA Unit
10th St. and Pennsylvania Ave., NW
Washington, DC 20530
(202) 514-2692

Civil Division
Office of the Asst. Attorney General
10th St. and Pennsylvania Ave., NW
Washington, DC 20530
(202) 514-3301

Civil Rights Division
Executive Officer
10th St. and Pennsylvania Ave., NW
Washington, DC 20530
(202) 514-4224

Criminal Division
Office of the Asst. Attorney General
10th St. and Pennsylvania Ave., NW
Washington, DC 20530
(202) 514-2601

Environment and Natural Resources Division
Office of the Attorney General
10th St. and Pennsylvania Ave., NW
Washington, DC 20530
(202) 514-2701

Tax Division
Office of the Asst. Attorney General
10th St. and Pennsylvania Ave., NW
Washington, DC 20530
(202) 514- 2901

Office of Special Counsel for Immigration Related Unfair
Employment Practices
P.O. Box 65490
Washington, DC 20035-5490
(800) 255-5490

Bureaus

Drug Enforcement Administration
Department of Justice
Washington, DC 20537
(202) 307-7977

Federal Bureau of Investigation
9th St. and Pennsylvania Ave., NW
Washington, DC 20235
(202) 324-3000

Bureau of Prisons
320 First St., NW
Washington, DC 20534
(202) 307-3198

United States Marshal Service
600 Army Navy Drive
Arlington, VA 22202-4210
(202) 307-9000

United States National Central Bureau-International Criminal Police Organization
Washington, DC 20530
(202) 272-8383

Immigration and Naturalization
425 I St., NW
Washington, DC 20536
(202) 514-4316

Office of Justice Programs
633 Indiana Ave., NW
Washington, DC 20531
(202) 307-0781

Boards

Executive Office for Immigration Review
5107 Leesburg Pike
Suite 2400
Falls Church, VA 22041
(703) 305-0169

United States Parole Commission
5550 Friendship Blvd.
Chevy Chase, MD 20815
(301) 305-1171

Foreign Claims Settlement Commission of the United States
Office of the Chairman
Room 10000
601 D St., NW
Washington, DC 20579
(202) 208-7730

Sources of Information for the Department of Justice

Controlled Substances Act Registration
P.O. Box 28083
Central Station
Washington, DC 20038
(202) 307-7255

Employment
Personnel Management
Room 4311
10th St. and Constitution Ave., NW
Washington, DC 20530
(202) 653-6155

Reading Rooms

Bureau of Prisons
320 First St., NW
Washington, DC 20534
(202) 307-3029

Immigration and Naturalization
425 I St., NW
Washington, DC 20536
(202) 633-2761

Foreign Claims Settlement Commission
5550 Friendship Blvd.

Be patient. If any phone number is incorrect, call (area code) 555-1212 and request the new listing.

Federal Public Information Offices

Chevy Chase, MD 20815
(202) 492-5959

Board of Immigration Appeals
Suite 1609
5203 Leesburg Pike
Falls Church, VA 22015
(202) 756-6183

National Institute of Justice
9th Floor
633 Indiana Ave., NW
Washington, DC 20531
(202) 307-5883

Publications and Films
Room 1218
10th and Constitution Ave., NW
Washington, DC 20530
(202) 514-2007

Office of Public Affairs
Room 1218
10th and Constitution Ave., NW
Washington, DC 20530
(202) 514-2007

Freedom of Information Officer
Office of Information and Privacy
10th and Constitution Ave., NW
Room 7238
Washington, DC 20530
(202) 514-3642

Reference Service
Criminal Justice Reference Service
Box 6000
Rockville, MD 20850
(800) 851-3420

Small Business Activities
Office of Small and Disadvantaged Business Utilization
10th St. and Pennsylvania Ave., NW
Washington, DC 20530
(202) 724-6271

Locator
10th St. and Pennsylvania Ave., NW
Washington, DC 20530
(202) 514-2000

Fraud Hotline
Inspector General's Hotline
P.O. Box 28188
Central Station
Washington, DC 20038
(202) 514-0642

Aliens Inquiries Information
Office of Information
Immigration and Naturalization
425 I St., NW
Washington, DC 20536
(202) 514-4316

Department of Labor

200 Constitution Ave., NW
Washington, DC 20210
(202) 219-6666

Inspector General
200 Constitution Ave., NW
Washington, DC 20210
(800) 347-3756 or
(202) 357-0227

Public Affairs
200 Constitution Ave., NW
Room S1032
Washington, DC 20210
(202) 219-7316

Women's Bureau
200 Constitution Ave., NW
Room S3002
Washington, DC 20210
(202) 219-6611

Deputy Secretary of Labor
200 Constitution Ave., NW
Room S2018
Washington, DC 20210
(202) 219-6151

Administrative Appeals
Room S4309
200 Constitution Ave., NW
Washington, DC 20210
(202) 219-4728

Office of Small and Disadvantaged Business Utilization
Room C2318
200 Constitution Ave., NW
Washington, DC 20210
(202) 219-9148

Office of Administrative Law Judges
Suite 400
800 K St., NW
Washington, DC 20001-8001
(202) 633-0330

Benefits Review Board
Suite 500
800 K St., NW
Washington, DC 20001-8001
(202) 633-7501

Wage Appeals Board
200 Constitution Ave.
Room N1651
Washington, DC 20210
(202) 219-9039

Department of Labor Academy
Room N2305
200 Constitution Ave., NW
Washington, DC 20210
(202) 219-7401

Solicitor of Labor
Room N2414
200 Constitution Ave., NW
Washington, DC 20210
(202) 219-6863

Employment Training Administration
Room S2322
200 Constitution Ave., NW
Washington, DC 20210
(202) 219-6871

Federal Unemployment Insurance Service
Room S4231
200 Constitution Ave., NW
Washington, DC 20210
(202) 219-8600

United States Employment Service
Room N4470
200 Constitution Ave., NW
Washington, DC 20210
(202) 219-5257

Be patient. If any phone number is incorrect, call (area code) 555-1212 and request the new listing.

Information Starting Places

Office of Apprenticeship and Training
Room N4649
200 Constitution Ave., NW
Washington, DC 20210
(202) 219-6540

Office of Trade Adjustment Assistance
200 Constitution Ave., NW
Washington, DC 20210
(202) 219-5555

Job Training Partnership Act
Room N4459
200 Constitution Ave., NW
Washington, DC 20210
(202) 219-6236

Senior Community Service Employment Program
Room N4641
200 Constitution Ave., NW
Washington, DC 20210
(202) 219-5904

Planning and Policy Development
200 Constitution Ave., NW
Washington, Dc 20210
(202) 219-7664

Financial and Administrative Management Service
Room S5526
200 Constitution Ave., NW
Washington, DC 20210
(202) 219-7801

Regional Management Program
Office of Public Affairs
Room S2322, 200 Constitution Ave., NW
Washington, DC 20210
(202) 219-6871

Labor-Management Standards
Room N5402
200 Constitution Ave., NW
Washington, DC 20210
(202) 219-6098

Pension and Welfare Benefits Administration
200 Constitution Ave., NW
Washington, DC 20210
(202) 219-8784

Labor-Management Relations
Room S2203
200 Constitution Ave., NW
Washington, DC 20210
(202) 219-6045

Employment Standards Administration
Room C4325
200 Constitution Ave., NW
Washington, DC 20210
(202) 219-8743

Federal Contract Compliance Programs
200 Constitution Ave., NW
Washington, DC 20210
(202) 219-9371

Office of Workers' Compensation Program
800 N. Capitol St., NW
Washington, DC 20211
(202) 724-0713

Occupational Safety and Health Administration
200 Constitution Ave., NW
Washington, DC 20210
(202) 219-8148

Bureau of Labor Statistics
200 Constitution Ave., NW
Washington, DC 20210
(202) 606-7828

Veterans' Employment and Training Service
200 Constitution Ave., NW
Washington, DC 20210
(202) 219-9110

Sources of Information for the Department of Labor

Contracts
Room S1522
200 Constitution Ave., NW
Washington, DC 20210
(202) 219-8904

Employment
200 Constitution Ave., NW
Washington, DC 20210
(202) 219-6666

Publications
200 Constitution Ave., NW
Washington, DC 20210
(202) 219-6871

Reading Rooms
200 Constitution Ave., NW
Washington, DC 20210
(202) 219-6992

Locator
200 Constitution Ave., NW
Washington, DC 20210
(202) 219-6666

Freedom of Information Officer
Room N2428
200 Constitution Ave., NW
Washington, DC 20210
(202) 219-8188

Fraud and Waste Hotline
Office of Inspector General
Attn: CAO, Room S5514
200 Constitution Ave., NW
Washington, DC 20210
(800) 347-3756

Labor Statistics
200 Constitution Ave., NW
Washington, DC 20210
(202) 606-7000

Department of State

2201 C St., NW
Washington, DC 20520
(202) 647-4000

Functional Areas

Diplomatic Security
200 C St., NW
Washington, Dc 20520
(202) 663-0549

Economic and Business Affairs
2201 C St., NW
Washington, DC 20520
(202) 647-7971

Intelligence and Research
Room 6641
2201 C St., NW
Washington, DC 20520
(202) 647-1080

Be patient. If any phone number is incorrect, call (area code) 555-1212 and request the new listing.

Federal Public Information Offices

International Communications and Information Policy
Room 6313
220 C St., NW
Washington, DC 20520
(202) 647-5832

International Narcotics Matters
200 C St., NW
Washington, DC 20520
(202) 647-4664

International Organization Affairs
Room 6323
200 C St., NW
Washington, DC 20520
(202) 647-9600

Legislative Affairs
200 C St., NW
Washington, DC 20520
(202) 647-2163

Medical Services
Room 2906
200 C St., NW
Washington, DC 20520
(202) 647-3617

Public Affairs
Room 5831
200 C St., NW
Washington, DC 20520
(202) 647-6575

Consular Affairs
Room 5807
200 C St., NW
Washington, DC 20520
(202) 647-1488

Politico-Military Affairs
200 C St., NW
Washington, DC 20520
(202) 647-6968

Oceans and International Environmental and Scientific Affairs
200 C St., NW
Washington, DC 20520
(202) 647-3622

Protocol
Room 1046
200 C St., NW
Washington, DC 20520
(202) 647-2663

Human Rights and Humanitarian Affairs
Room 7802
200 C St., NW
Washington, DC 20520
(202) 647-2126

Refugee Programs
Room 1244
200 C St., NW
Washington, DC 20520
(202) 663-1520

Sources of Information for the Department of State

Audiovisual Materials
Video Transfer, Inc.
5710 Arundel Avenue
Rockville, MD 20552
(301) 881-0270

Conferences, Seminars, Speaking Engagements, Briefings
Office of Public Liaison

Bureau of Public Affairs
Department of State, Room 5831
Washington, DC 20520
(202) 647-1433

Contracts
Office of Acquisitions (A/OPR/ACQ)
Department of State
Washington, DC 20520
(703) 875-6000

Diplomatic and Official Passports
Passport Services
Diplomatic and Congressional Travel Branch
1425 K St., NW, Room 358
Washington, DC 20521
(202) 326-6234

Employment
Foreign Service Employment
PER/REE/REC
P.O. Box 9317
Rosslyn Station
Arlington, VA 22210
(703) 875-7108

Civil Service Positions
PER/CSP/SSD
P.O. Box 18657
Washington, DC 200236-8657
(202) 647-6132

Civil Service Job Information Line
(202) 647-7284

Freedom of Information Officer
Director, Office of Freedom of Information Privacy and Classification
2201 C St., NW
Washington, DC 20520-1512
(202) 647-8484

Missing Persons, Emergencies, Deaths of Americans Abroad
Citizens Emergency Center
200 C St., NW
Washington, DC 20520
(202) 647-5225

Citizenship, International Parental Child Abduction, Judicial Assistance, Overseas Voting
Bureau of Consular Affairs
Citizens Consular Service, Room 4817
Washington, DC 20520
(202) 647-3666

Passports
Passport Service
Bureau of Consular Affairs
1425 K St., NW
Washington, DC 20524
(202) 647-0518

Publications
Public Information
Bureau of Public Affairs
Room 5831
Washington, DC 20520
(202) 647-6575

Reading Room
2201 C St., NW
Washington, DC 20520
(202) 647-8484

Visas
2201 C St., NW
Washington, DC 20520
(202) 663-1225

Be patient. If any phone number is incorrect, call (area code) 555-1212 and request the new listing.

Information Starting Places

Locator
2201 C St., NW
Washington, DC 20520
(202) 647-4000

Fraud and Waste Hotline
Office of the Inspector General
P.O. Box 19392
Washington, DC 20036-9392
(202) 647-3320

Department of Transportation

400 Seventh St., SW
Washington, DC 20590
(202) 366-4000

United States Coast Guard
2100 Second St., SW
Washington, DC 20593-0001
(202) 267-2229

Search and Rescue
Commandant (G-NRS)
2100 Second St., SW
Washington, DC 20593
(202) 267-1948

Maritime Law Enforcement
Commandant (G-OLE)
2100 Second St., SW
Washington, DC 20593
(202) 267-1890

Marine Inspection
Merchant Vessel Inspection and Documentation Division
2100 Second St., SW
Washington, DC 20593
(202) 267-1464

Marine Licensing
2100 Second St., SW
Washington, DC 20593
(202) 267-0218

Merchant Vessel Personnel (G-MVP)
Room 1210
2100 Second St., SW
Washington, DC 20593-0001
(202) 267-0214

Marine Environmental Response
2100 Second St., SW
Washington, DC 20593
(202) 267-0518

Port Safety and Security
Room 1104
2100 Second St., SW
Washington, DC 20593
(202) 267-0489

Waterways Management
2100 Second St., SW
Washington, DC 20593
(202) 267-2267

Aids to Navigation
Room 1116
2100 Second St., SW
Washington, DC 20593
(202) 267-1965

Bridge Division
Room 1408, 2100 Second St., SW
Washington, DC 20593
(202) 267-0368

Ice Operations
Room 1202
2100 Second St., SW
Washington, DC 20593
(202) 267-1450

Deepwater Ports
2100 Second St., SW
Washington, DC 20593
(202) 267-0495

Boating Safety
2100 Second St., SW
Washington, DC 20593
(202) 267-1077

Coast Guard Auxiliary
Room 1504
2100 Second St., SW
Washington, DC 20593
(202) 267-1001

Military Readiness
Room 3300
2100 Second St., SW
Washington, DC 20593
(202) 267-2039

Reserve Training
Room 5412
2100 Second St., SW
Washington, DC 20593
(202) 267-1240

Marine Safety Regulations
Room 3406
2100 Second St., SW
Washington, DC 20593
(202) 267-1477

Information Office
Headquarters Information
2100 Second St., SW
Washington, DC 20593
(202) 267-2229

Federal Aviation Administration
Office of Public Affairs
8 Federal Aviation Administration
800 Independence Ave., SW
Washington, DC 20591
(202) 267-3484

Federal Highway Administration
400 Seventh St., SW
Washington, DC 20590
(202) 366-0660

Office of Management Systems
400 Seventh St., SW
Washington, DC 20590
(202) 366-0630

Federal Railroad Administration
400 Seventh St., SW
Washington, DC 20590
(202) 366-4000

Transportation Test Center
Pueblo, CO 81001
(303) 545-5660

Public Affairs Office
Room 8125
400 Seventh St., SW
Washington, DC 20590
(202) 366-0881

Be patient. If any phone number is incorrect, call (area code) 555-1212 and request the new listing.

Federal Public Information Offices

National Highway Traffic Safety Administration
Office of Public and Consumer Affairs
400 Seventh St., SW
Washington, DC 20590
(202) 366-9550

Federal Transit Administration
Office of Public and Consumer Affairs
400 Seventh St., SW
Washington, DC 20590
(202) 366-4043

Maritime Administration
Office of External Affairs
Room 7219, 400 Seventh St., SW
Washington, DC 20590
(202) 366-5807

Saint Lawrence Seaway Development Corporation
Director of Communications
400 Seventh St., SW
Washington, DC 20590
(202) 764-3200

Research and Special Programs Administration
400 Seventh St., SW
Washington, DC 20590
(202) 366-4433

Office of Hazardous Materials Safety
Room 8420
400 Seventh St., SW
Washington, DC 20590
(202) 366-0656

Office of Pipeline Safety
Room 8417
400 Seventh St., SW
Washington, DC 20590
(202) 366-4595

Office of Research, Technology, and Analysis
Room 8406
400 Seventh St., SW
Washington, DC 20590
(202) 366-4434

Office of Emergency Transportation
Room 8404
400 Seventh St., SW
Washington, DC 20590
(202) 366-5270

Office of Airline Statistics
Room 4125
400 Seventh St., SW
Washington, DC 20590
(202) 366-9059

Office of University Research and Education
Room 10309
400 Seventh St., SW
Washington, DC 20590
(202) 366-5442

Office of Automated Tariffs
Room 6424
400 Seventh St., SW
Washington, DC 20590
(202) 366-2414

Office of Research Policy and Technology Transfer
Room 9402
400 Seventh St., SW
Washington, DC 20590
(202) 366-4208

Volpe National Transportation Systems Center
55 Broadway, Kendall Square
Cambridge, MA 02142
(617) 494-2224

Office of Management and Administration
400 Seventh St., SW
Washington, DC 20590
(202) 366-4347

Policy and International Affairs
Room 10228
400 Seventh St., SW
Washington, DC 20590
(202) 366-4544

Budget and Programs
Room 10101
400 Seventh St., SW
Washington, DC 20590
(202) 366-9191

Office of Civil Rights
Room 10215
400 Seventh St., SW
Washington, DC 20590
(202) 366-4648

Public Affairs
Room 10413
400 Seventh St., SW
Washington, DC 20590
(202) 366-5580

Small and Disadvantaged Business Utilization
400 Seventh St., SW
Washington, DC 20590
(800) 532-1169

Contract Appeals
Room 5101
400 Seventh St., SW
Washington, DC 20590
(202) 366-4305

Commercial Space Transportation
Room 5415
400 Seventh St., SW
Washington, DC 20590
(202) 366-5770

Inspector General- Fraud and Waste
400 Seventh St., SW
Washington, DC 20590
(800) 424-9071

Sources of Information for the Department of Transportation

Coast Guard Career
U.S. Coast Guard Academy
2100 Second St. SW
Washington, DC 20590
(202) 267-2229 or
(203) 444-8444

Consumer Activities
Room 10405
2100 Second St., SW
Washington, DC 20590
(202) 366-2220

Contracts
Office of Acquisition and Grant Management
Room 9401
2100 Second St., SW
Washington, DC 20590
(202) 366-4285

Be patient. If any phone number is incorrect, call (area code) 555-1212 and request the new listing.

Information Starting Places

Employment
Room 9113, 2100 Second St., SW
Washington, DC 20590
(202) 366-9392

Environmental Affairs
Regulatory Affairs
Environmental Division
2100 Second St., SW
Washington, DC 20590
(202) 366-4366

Reading Rooms/Dockets
Room 4107
2100 Second St., SW
Washington, DC 20590
(202) 366-9322

Locator
2100 Second St., SW
Washington, DC 20590
(202) 366-4000

Publications
Office of Public Affairs
Room 8125
2100 Second St., SW
Washington, DC 20590
(202) 366-0039

Freedom of Information Officer
Room 5432
2100 Second St., SW
Washington, DC 20590
(202) 366-4542

Department of Treasury

1500 Pennsylvania Ave., NW
Washington, DC 20220
(202) 566-2000

Bureau of Alcohol, Tobacco and Firearms
Room 8290
650 Massachusetts Ave., NW
Washington, DC 20226
(202) 927-8500

Office of Public Affairs
650 Massachusetts Ave., NW
Washington, DC 20226
(202) 927-7777

Office of the Comptroller of the Currency
250 E St., SW
Washington, DC 20219
(202) 874-5000

Contracts
250 E St., SW
Washington, DC 20219
(202) 874-5000

Employment
250 E St., SW
Washington, DC 20219
(202) 874-5000

United States Customs Service
1301 Constitution Ave., NW
Washington, DC 20229
(202) 927-2095

Public Affairs
1301 Constitution Ave., NW
Washington, DC 20229
(202) 927-1770

Publications
Office of Public Affairs
1301 Constitution Ave., NW
Washington, DC 20229
(202) 927-1770

Reading Rooms
Customs Library
1301 Constitution Ave., NW
Washington, DC 20229
(202) 927-1617

Speakers
Office of Public Relations
1301 Constitution Ave., NW
Washington, DC 20229
(202) 927-1770

Contracts
Office of Contracts and Procurements
1301 Constitution Ave., NW
Washington, DC 20229
(202) 927-0990

Freedom of Information Officer
1301 Constitution Ave., NW
Washington, DC 20229
(202) 927-0860

Bureau of Engraving and Printing
14th and C Streets, SW
Washington, DC 20228
(202) 874-3019

Contracts and Small Business Activities
Office of Procurement
Room 705A, 14th and C Streets, SW
Washington, DC 20228
(202) 874-2534

Employment
Office of Personnel
14th and C Streets, SW
Washington, DC 20228
(202) 874-3747

Freedom of Information Act Requests
Room 321-A
14th and C Streets, SW
Washington, DC 20228
(202) 874-2687

Public Affairs
Room 533M
14th and C Streets, SW
Washington, DC 20228
(202) 874-3019

Product Sales
Room 533M
14th and C Streets, SW
Washington, DC 20228
(202) 874-3019

Federal Law Enforcement Training Center
Glynco, GA 31524
(912) 267-2447 or
(202) 927-8940 (Washington, DC number)

Public Affairs
Bldg. 94
Glynco, GA 31524
(912) 267-2447

Financial Management Service
Room 548
401 14th St., SW

Be patient. If any phone number is incorrect, call (area code) 555-1212 and request the new listing.

Federal Public Information Offices

Washington, DC 20227
(202) 874-6740

Office of Public Affairs
401 14th St., SW
Washington, DC 20227
(202) 874-6740

Contracts
Acquisitions
Room 109
401 14th St., SW
Washington, DC 20227
(202) 874-6910

Employment
Room 120
401 14th St., SW
Washington, DC 20227
(202) 874-7090

Internal Revenue Service
1111 Constitution Ave., NW
Washington, DC 20224
(800) 829-1040
(202) 622-5000

Contracts
Office of Procurement
Room 3425
1111 Constitution Ave., NW
Washington, DC 20224
(202) 622-8480

Educational Programs
1111 Constitution Ave., NW
Washington, DC 20224
(800) 829-1040

Employment
Office of Personnel
1111 Constitution Ave., NW
Washington, DC 20224
(202) 622-1460

Publications
P.O. Box 25866
Richmond, VA 23289
(800) 829-3676

Reading Rooms
1111 Constitution Ave., NW
Washington, DC 20224
(202) 622-5164

Taxpayer Service
1111 Constitution Ave., NW
Washington, DC 20224
(800) 829-1040

United States Mint
633 Third St., NW
Washington, DC 20220
(202) 874-6000

Office of Public Affairs
Room 74
633 Third St., NW
Washington, DC 20220
(202) 874-6450

Numismatic Services
Customer Service Department
10001 Arrowspace Drive
Lanham, MD 20706
(301) 436-7400

Bureau of the Public Debt
999 E St., NW
Washington, DC 20239-0001
(202) 219-3300

Office of Public Affairs
Room 553
E St. Bldg.
Washington, DC 20239-0001
(202) 219-3302

Employment
Office of Personnel
Room 446-4
300 13th St., SW
Washington, DC 20239
(202) 874-4010

Savings Bonds
Office of Bond Consultants
Parkersburg, WV 26106-1328
(304) 420-6112

Treasury Securities
Customer Service
300 13th St., SW
Washington, DC 20239
(202) 874-1260

United States Savings Bonds Division
800 K St., NW
Washington, DC 20226
(202) 377-7700

Office of Public Affairs
800 K St., NW
Washington, DC 20226
(202) 377-7715

Current Rate Information
800 K St., NW
Washington, DC 20226
(800) 4US-BOND

United States Secret Service
1800 G St., NW
Washington, DC 20223
(202) 435-5708

Public Affairs
1800 G St., NW
Suite 805
Washington, DC 20223
(202) 435-5708

Employment
Office of Personnel
1800 G St., NW
Washington, DC 20223
(202) 435-5708

Publications
Office of Public Affairs
1800 G St., NW
Suite 805
Washington, DC 20223
(202) 435-5708

Office of Thrift Supervision
1700 G St., NW
Washington, DC 20552
(202) 906-6000

Communications Division
1700 G St., NW
Washington, DC 20552
(202) 906-6913

Be patient. If any phone number is incorrect, call (area code) 555-1212 and request the new listing.

Information Starting Places

Sources of Information for the Department of Treasury

Contracts
Office of Procurement
1500 Pennsylvania Ave., NW
Room 6100 Annex
Washington, DC 20220
(202) 622-0510

Public Affairs
1500 Pennsylvania Ave., NW
Room 2315
Washington, DC 20220
(202) 622-2960

Reading Room
Library
1500 Pennsylvania Ave., NW
Washington, DC 20220
(202) 622-2777

Small and Disadvantaged Business Activities
1500 Pennsylvania Ave., NW
Room 6100 Annex
Washington, DC 20220
(202) 622-0195

Tax Legislative Council
Room 3064
1500 Pennsylvania Ave., NW
Washington, DC 20220
(202) 622-0140

Inspector General- Fraud and Waste Hotline
1500 Pennsylvania Ave., NW
Washington, DC 20220
(800) 359-3898

Freedom of Information Office
Room 1054
1500 Pennsylvania Ave., NW
Washington, DC 20220
(202) 622-0930

Locator
1500 Pennsylvania Ave., NW
Washington, DC 20220
(202) 622-2000

Department of Veterans Affairs

810 Vermont Ave., NW
Washington, Dc 20420
(202) 233-2300

National Cemetery System
Office of Public Affairs
MS 402-E
810 Vermont Ave., NW
Washington, DC 20420
(202) 535-7855

Veterans Benefits Administration
810 Vermont Ave., NW
Washington, DC 20420
(202) 535-7920

Veterans Health Administration
810 Vermont Ave., NW
Washington, DC 20420
(202) 535-7208

Sources of Information for the Department of Veterans Affairs

Office of Public Affairs
810 Vermont Ave., NW
Washington, DC 20420
(202) 535-8300

Audiovisual Services (037)
810 Vermont Ave., NW
Room C-76
Washington, DC 20420
(202) 233-2715

Contracts and Small Business Activities
Office of Acquisition and Review (95)
810 Vermont Ave.
Washington, DC 20420
(202) 233-3296

Employment
Office of Personnel (055)
810 Vermont Ave., NW
Washington, DC 20420
(202) 233-2694

Freedom of Information Act Requests
810 Vermont Ave., NW
Washington, DC 20420
(202) 233-3616

Medical Center Design, Construction, and Related Services
Office of Facilities
Room 407, 810 Vermont Ave., NW
Washington, DC 20420
(202) 233-3181

Reading Room
Library
810 Vermont Ave., NW
Washington, DC 20420
(202) 233-2356

Publications
Room 944
810 Vermont Ave., NW
Washington, DC 20420
(202) 233-3056

Inspector General- Fraud and Waste Hotline
810 Vermont Ave., NW
Washington, DC 20420
(800) 488-8244

Locator
810 Vermont Ave., NW
Washington, DC 20420
(202) 233-4000

INDEPENDENT AGENCIES

ACTION
1100 Vermont Ave., NW
Washington, DC 20525
(202) 606-5108

Foster Grandparents
1100 Vermont Ave., NW
Room 6100
Washington, DC 20525
(202) 606-4855

Retired Senior Volunteers
1100 Vermont Ave., NW
Room 6100
Washington, DC 20525
(202) 606-4855

Senior Companions
1100 Vermont Ave., NW
Room 6100
Washington, DC 20525
(202) 606-4855

Be patient. If any phone number is incorrect, call (area code) 555-1212 and request the new listing.

Federal Public Information Offices

Volunteers in Service to America
VISTA
Room 8100
1100 Vermont Ave., NW
Washington, DC 20525
(202) 606-4845

Student Community Service Projects
Room 8100
1100 Vermont Ave., NW
Washington, DC 20525
(202) 606-4824

Program Demonstration and Development Division
Room 8100
1100 Vermont Ave., NW
Washington, DC 20525
(202) 606-4857

Publications
1100 Vermont Ave., NW
Suite 11100
Washington, DC 20525
(202) 606-5108

Public Affairs
1100 Vermont Ave., NW
Suite 11100
Washington, DC 20525
(202) 606-5108

Administrative Conference of the United States

Suite 500
2120 L St., NW
Washington, DC 20037-1568
(202) 254-7020

African Development Foundation

7400 Eye St., NW
Washington, DC 20005
(202) 673-3916

Central Intelligence Agency

Washington, DC 20505
(703) 482-1100

Commission on Civil Rights

1121 Vermont Ave., NW
Washington, DC 20425
(202) 376-8177

Public Affairs
1121 Vermont Ave., NW
Washington, DC 20425
(202) 376-8312

Commodity Futures Trading Commission

2033 K St., NW
Washington, DC 20581
(202) 254-6970

Office of Communication and Education Services
2033 K St., NW
Washington, DC 20581
(202) 254-8630

Consumer Product Safety Commission

5401 Westbard Avenue
Bethesda, MD 20207
(301) 492-6580

Defense Nuclear Facilities Safety Board

Suite 700
625 Indiana Ave., NW
Washington, DC 20004
(202) 208-6400

Environmental Protection Agency

401 M St., SW
Washington, DC 20460
(202) 260-2090

Activities
Air and Radiation
Room 937 West Tower
401 M St., SW
Washington, DC 20460
(202) 260-7400

Office of Water
Room 1035 East Tower
401 M St., SW
Washington, DC 20460
(202) 260-5700

Solid Waste and Emergency Response
Room 363
401 M St., SW
Washington, DC 20460
(202) 260-4610

Prevention, Pesticides and Toxic Response
635 East Tower Bldg.
401 M St., SW
Washington, DC 20460
(202) 260-2902

Research and Development
913 West Tower Bldg.
401 M St., SW
Washington, DC 20460
(202) 260-7676

Sources of Information
Contracts
Procurement and Contracts Management
401 M St., SW
Washington, DC 20460
(202) 260-5020

Employment
Office of Human Resources
401 M St., SW
Washington, DC 20460
(202) 260-3144

Freedom of Information Act Requests
Freedom of Information Officer
401 M St., SW
Washington, DC 20460
(202) 260-4048

Reading Room
Information Management and Services Division
401 M St., SW
Washington, DC 20460
(202) 260-5921

Public Affairs
Office of Communications, Education and Public Affairs
401 M St., SW
Washington, DC 20460
(202) 260-7963

Public Information Center
401 M St., SW

Be patient. If any phone number is incorrect, call (area code) 555-1212 and request the new listing.

Information Starting Places

Washington, DC 20460
(202) 260-7751

Equal Employment Opportunity Commission

1801 L St., NW
Washington, DC 20507
(202) 663-4900; (800) USA-EEOC

Sources of Information

Employment
Personnel Office
1801 L St., NW
Washington, DC 20507
(202) 663-4306

General Inquiries
1801 L St., NW
Washington, DC 20507
(800) 669-EEOC

Publications
1801 L St., NW
Washington, DC 20507
(800) 669-EEOC

Reading Room
EEOC Library
1801 L St., NW
Washington, DC 20507
(202) 663-4630

Speakers
1801 L St., NW
Washington, DC 20507
(202) 663-4900

Export-Import Bank of the United States

811 Vermont Ave., NW
Washington, DC 20571
(202) 566-8990

Farm Credit Administration

1501 Farm Credit Drive
McLean, VA 22102-5090
(703) 883-4000

Public Affairs
1501 Farm Credit Drive
McLean, VA 22102-5090
(703) 883-4056

Federal Communications Commission

1919 M St., NW
Washington, DC 20544
(202) 632-7000
TDD: (202) 632-6999

Activities

Mass Media
1919 M St., NW
Washington, DC 20554
(202) 632-6460

Common Carrier Communications
1919 M St., NW
Washington, DC 20554
(202) 632-6910

Private Radio Communications
1919 M St., NW
Washington, DC 20554
(202) 632-6940

Engineering and Technology
1919 M St., NW
Washington, DC 20554
(202) 653-8103

Field Operations Bureau
1919 M St., NW
Washington, DC 20554
(202) 632-6980

Sources of Information

Advisory Committee Management
1919 M St., NW
Washington, DC 20554
(202) 632-0923

Consumer Assistance and Small Business Division
1919 M St., NW
Washington, DC 20554
(202) 632-7000

Contracts
Office of Procurement
1919 M St., NW
Washington, DC 20554
(202) 634-1528

Employment
Office of Personnel
1919 M St., NW
Washington, DC 20554
(202) 632-7104

Equal Employment Practices by Industry
1919 M St., NW
Washington, DC 20554
(202) 632-7000

Ex-Parte Presentations
Room 222, 1919 M St., NW
Washington, DC 20554
(202) 632-6390

Fee Information
Public Service Office
Room 254
1919 M St., NW
Washington, DC 20554
(202) 632-FEES

Information Available for Public Inspection
Office of the Managing Director
Room 852
1919 M St., NW
Washington, DC 20554
(202) 632-6390

Public Affairs
1919 M St., NW
Washington, DC 20554
(202) 632-7000

Federal Deposit Insurance Corporation

550 17th St., NW
Washington, DC 20429
(202) 393-8400

Sources of Information

Bank Depositors and Customers
Director
Office of Consumer Affairs
550 17th St., SW
Washington, DC 20429

Employment
Personnel Office

Be patient. If any phone number is incorrect, call (area code) 555-1212 and request the new listing.

Federal Public Information Offices

550 17th St., NW
Washington, DC 20429
(202) 898-8890

FDIC Rules and Related Acts
550 17th St., NW
Room F400
Washington, DC 20429
(202) 898-3811

Corporate Communications Office
550 17th St., NW
Washington, DC 20429
(202) 898-6996

Federal Election Commission

999 E St., NW
Washington, DC 20463
(202) 219-3420
(800) 424-9530

Sources of Information
Clearinghouse on Election Administration
999 E St., NW
Washington, DC 20463
(800) 424-9530

Public Affairs
Press Office
999 E St., NW
Washington, DC 20463
(202) 219-4155 or
(800) 424-9530

Employment
Director
Personnel and Labor Management Relations
999 E St., NW
Washington, DC 20463
(292) 219-4290

Reading Room
FEC Library
999 E St., NW
Washington, DC 20463
(800) 424-9530

Federal Emergency Management Agency

500 C St., SW
Washington, DC 20472
(202) 646-4600

Contracts
500 C St., SW
Washington, DC 20472
(202) 646-3744

Employment
500 C St., SW
Washington, DC 20472
(202) 646-3964

Freedom of Information Officer
Office of General Counsel
500 C St., SW
Washington, DC 20472
(202) 646-3840

Public Affairs
500 C St., SW
Washington, DC 20472
(202) 6464-4600

Federal Housing Finance Board

1777 F St., NW
Washington, DC 20006
(202) 408-2500

Public Affairs
1777 F St., NW
Washington, DC 20006
(202) 408-2837

Federal Labor Relations Authority

500 C St., SW
Washington, DC 20424
(202) 382-0711

Director of Information Resources and Research Services
500 C St., SW
Washington, DC 20424
(202) 382-0715

Federal Maritime Commission

1100 L St., NW
Washington, DC 20573-0001
(202) 619-5707

Employee Locator
1100 L St., NW
Washington, DC 20573-0001
(202) 619-5773

Information Complaints
1100 L St., NW
Washington, DC 20573-0001
(202) 619-5807

Office of the Secretary
1100 L St., NW
Washington, DC 20573-0001
(202) 619-5725

Federal Mediation and Conciliation Service

2100 K St., NW
Washington, DC 20427
(202) 653-5290

Office of Public and International Affairs
2100 K St., NW
Washington, DC 20427
(202) 653-5290

Mediation Services
2100 K St., SW
Washington, DC 20427
(202) 653-5240

Federal Mine Safety and Health Review Commission

1730 K St., NW
Washington, DC 20006
(202) 653-5633

Federal Reserve System

Board of Governors of the Federal Reserve System
20th St. and Constitution Ave., NW
Washington, DC 20551
(202) 452-3000

Publications Services (MS-138)
20th St. and Constitution Ave., NW
Washington, DC 20551
(202) 452-3244

Be patient. If any phone number is incorrect, call (area code) 555-1212 and request the new listing.

Information Starting Places

Reading Room
Library
20th St. and Constitution Ave., NW
Washington, DC 20551
(202) 452-3684

Office of Public Affairs
20th St. and Constitution Ave., NW
Washington, DC 20551
(202) 452-3205

Federal Retirement Thrift Investment Board

1250 8th St., NW
Washington, DC 20005
(202) 942-1600

Director of External Affairs
1250 8th St., NW
Washington, DC 20005
(202) 942-1640

Federal Trade Commission

Pennsylvania Ave. at 6th St., NW
Washington, DC 20580
(202) 326-2222

Contracts
Office of Procurement
Pennsylvania Ave. at 6th St., NW
Washington, DC 20580
(202) 326-2275

Employment
Office of Personnel
Room H-149
Pennsylvania Ave. at 6th St., NW
Washington, DC 20580
(202) 326-2022

Publications
Public Reference Branch
Pennsylvania Ave. at 6th St., NW
Washington, DC 20580
(202) 326-2222

Office of Public Affairs
Room 421
Pennsylvania Ave. at 6th St., NW
Washington, DC 20580
(202) 326-2180

General Services Administration

General Services Building
18th and F St., NW
Washington, DC 20405
(202) 708-5082

Information Resources Management Service
18th and F St., NW
Washington, DC 20405
(202) 501-1000

Federal Supply Service
General Services Administration
Washington, DC 20406
(703) 305-6667

Public Buildings Service
Room 6344
18th and F St., NW
Washington, DC 20405
(202) 501-1100

Federal Property Resources Service
18th and F St., NW
Washington, DC 20405
(202) 501-0210

Acquisition Policy
Room 4040
18th and F St., NW
Washington, DC 20405
(202) 501-1043

Small and Disadvantaged Business Utilization
Room 6029
18th and F St., NW
Washington, DC 20405
(202) 501-1021

Child Care and Development Programs
Room 6119
18th and F St., NW
Washington, DC 20405
(202) 501-3965

Governmentwide Policy Division
Room 6215
18th and F St., NW
Washington, DC 20405
(202) 501-0507

Contract Appeals
Room 7022
18th and F St., NW
Washington, DC 20405
(202) 501-0720

Information Security Oversight
Room 530
18th and F St., NW
Washington, DC 20405
(202) 634-6150

Office of the Inspector General
18th and F St., NW
Washington, DC 20405
(202) 501-0466

Fraud and Waste Hotline
18th and F St., NW
Washington, DC 20405
(800) 424-5210

Office of Administration
Room 6125
18th and F St., NW
Washington, DC 20405
(202) 501-0945

Chief Financial Officer
Room 2140
18th and F St., NW
Washington, DC 20405
(202) 501-1721

Ethics and Civil Rights
Room 5129
18th and F St., NW
Washington, DC 20405
(202) 501-0765

Federal Telecommunications System 2000
18th and F St., NW
Room 6223
Washington, DC 20405
(202) 208-7493

Office of Technical Assistance
5203 Leesburg Pike

Be patient. If any phone number is incorrect, call (area code) 555-1212 and request the new listing.

Federal Public Information Offices

Suite 400
Falls Church, VA 22041
(703) 756-4100

Office of Information Resources
Procurement
Room G44
18th and F St., NW
Washington, DC 20405
(202) 501-1072

Telecommunications Service
Suite G242
18th and F St., NW
Washington, DC 20405
(202) 501-0308

GSA Information Systems
18th and F St., NW
Washington, DC 20405
(202) 501-1800

Federal Information Center
P.O. Box 600
Cumberland, MD 21502-0600
(301) 722-9098

Domestic Assistance Catalogue
300 7th St., SW
Reporters Building
Room 101
Washington, DC 20407
(202) 708-5126

Federal Supply Service
Office of the Public Liaison
1941 Jefferson Davis Highway
Arlington, VA 22202
(703) 305-6646

Office of Real Property Development
Room 2341
18th and F St., NW
Washington, DC 20405
(202) 501-1025

Office of Real Property Management and Safety
Room 4340
18th and F St., NW
Washington, DC 20405
(202) 501-0971

Office of Physical Security and Law Enforcement
18th and F St., NW
Washington, DC 20405
(202) 501-0887

Office of Planning
Room 6331
18th and F St., NW
Washington, DC 20405
(202) 501-0638

Office of Procurement
18th and F St., NW
Washington, DC 20405
(202) 501-0907

Sources of Information for General Services Administration

Consumer Information Center
Pueblo, CO 81009
(719) 943-4000

Employment
Personnel Operations Division (CPS)
Office of Personnel

Washington, DC 20405
(202) 501-0370

Freedom of Information Act Request
Attn: Privacy Act Officer
Room 7102
Washington, DC 20405
(202) 501-2691

Publications
Director of Publications
Office of Communications (XS)
Washington, DC 20405
(202) 501-1235

Speakers
Office of Public Affairs (X)
General Services Administration
Washington, DC 20405
(202) 501-0705

Public Affairs
Office of Public Affairs (X)
General Services Administration
Washington, DC 20405
(202) 501-0705

Inter-American Foundation

901 North Stuart St.
Arlington, VA 22203
(703) 841-3800

Office of the President
10th Floor
901 North Stuart St.
Arlington, VA 22203
(703) 841-3810

Interstate Commerce Commission

12th and Constitution Ave., NW
Washington, DC 20423
(202) 927-7119

Sources of Information

Consumer Affairs
Office of Compliance and Consumer Assistance
12th and Constitution Ave., NW
Washington, DC 20423
(202) 927-5500

Contracts
Procurement and Contracting Branch
12th and Constitution Ave., NW
Washington, DC 20423
(202) 927-5370

Employment
Director of Personnel
12th and Constitution Ave., NW
Washington, DC 20423
(202) 927-7288

Public Affairs
Office of External Affairs
Room 4136
12th and Constitution Ave., NW
Washington, DC 20423
(202) 927-5350

Publications
Public Affairs
Office of External Affairs
Room 4136
12th and Constitution Ave., NW

Be patient. If any phone number is incorrect, call (area code) 555-1212 and request the new listing.

Information Starting Places

Washington, DC 20423
(202) 927-5350

Reading Rooms
Office of the Secretary
Room 2215, ICC Building
12th and Constitution Ave., NW
Washington, DC 20423
(202) 927-7428

Small Business Activities
Office of Public Assistance
Room 3119, 12th and Constitution Ave., NW
Washington, DC 20423
(202) 927-7597

Speakers
Public Affairs
Office of External Affairs
Room 4136
12th and Constitution Ave., NW
Washington, DC 20423
(202) 927-5350

Merit Systems Protection Board

8th Floor, 1120 Vermont Ave., NW
Washington, DC 20419
(202) 653-7124

National Aeronautics and Space Administration

300 E St.
Washington, DC 20546-0001
(202) 358-1000

Office of Aeronautics
NASA Headquarters
Code R
Washington, DC 20546
(202) 358-2693

Space Systems Development
NASA Headquarters
Code D
Washington, DC 20546
(202) 358-4561

Space Science and Applications
NASA Headquarters
Code S
Washington, DC 20546
(202) 358-0370

Space Flight
NASA Headquarters
Code M
Washington, DC 20546
(202) 358-2542

Space Communications
Code 9
Washington, DC 20546
(202) 358-2020

Office of Exploration
Code X
Washington, DC 20546
(202) 358-1902

Sources of Information
Contracts
Office of Procurement
Code HW
Washington, DC 20546
(202) 358-2088

Employment
Code FPH
Washington, DC 20546
(202) 358-8478

Reading Room
300 E St.
Washington, DC 20546-0001
(202) 358-1000

Headquarters Information Center
300 E St.
Washington, DC 20546-0001
(202) 358-1000

National Archives and Records Administration

National Archives Bldg.
7th St. and Pennsylvania Ave., NW
Washington, DC 20408
(202) 501-5400

References Services Branch (NNRS)
7th St. and Pennsylvania Ave., NW
National Archives Bldg.
Washington, DC 20408
(202) 501-5400

Presidential Libraries
Room 104
National Archives Bldg.
7th St. and Pennsylvania Ave., NW
Washington, DC 20408
(202) 501-5700

Federal Records Centers
7th St. and Pennsylvania Ave., NW
Washington, DC 20408
(202) 653-8450

Records Administration
601 D St., NW
9214 Patrick Henry Bldg.
Washington, DC 20408
(202) 501-6000

Office of the Federal Register
800 N. Capitol St., NW
Suite 700
Washington, DC 20408
(202) 523-5240

Public Programs
Room G12
7th St. and Pennsylvania Ave., NW
Washington, DC 20408
(202) 501-5200

National Archives Trust Fund Board
Room G5
7th St. and Pennsylvania Ave., NW
Washington, DC 20408
(202) 501-5155

National Historical Publications and Records Commission
7th St. and Pennsylvania Ave., NW
Washington, DC 20408
(202) 501-5600

Sources of Information
Calendar of Events
National Archives Building
Office of Public Affairs
7th St. and Pennsylvania Ave., NW
Washington, DC 20408
(202) 501-5525

Be patient. If any phone number is incorrect, call (area code) 555-1212 and request the new listing.

Federal Public Information Offices

Recorded Messages
7th St. and Pennsylvania Ave., NW
Washington, DC 20408
(202) 501-5000

Speakers
Office of Public Affairs
7th St. and Pennsylvania Ave., NW
Washington, DC 20408
(202) 501-5225

Workshops
Office of Education
7th St. and Pennsylvania Ave., NW
Washington, DC 20408
(202) 724-0456

Publications
Publication Services
7th and Pennsylvania Ave., NW
Washington, DC 20408
(202) 501-5240

Teaching Aids
Office of Education
7th and Pennsylvania Ave., NW
Washington, DC 20408
(202) 724-0456

Guided Tours
Room G8
7th and Pennsylvania Ave., NW
Washington, DC 20408
(202) 501-5205

Audiovisual Sales and Rentals
National Audiovisual Center
8700 Edgeworth Drive
Capitol Heights, MD 20743-3701
(800) 788-6282

Educational Opportunities
Office of Public Programs
7th and Pennsylvania Ave., NW
Washington, DC 20408
(202) 501-5212

Volunteers
National Archives Bldg.
7th and Pennsylvania Ave., NW
Washington, DC 20408
(202) 501-5205

Congressional and External Affairs
Office of Public Affairs
7th St. and Pennsylvania Ave., NW
Washington, DC 20408
(202) 501-5525

Reading Rooms
National Archives Bldg.
7th St. and Pennsylvania Ave., NW
Washington, DC 20408
(202) 756-6700

Freedom of Information Act
Policy and Program Analysis Division
7th and Pennsylvania Ave., NW
Washington, DC 20408
(202) 501-5110

Contracts
Acquisitions Management Branch
7th and Pennsylvania Ave., NW
Washington, DC 20408
(202) 501-5920

Employment
Personnel Operations Branch
Room 2002
9700 Page Blvd.
St. Louis, MO 63132
(800) 634-4898

Records Administration Information Center
7th and Pennsylvania Ave, NW
Washington, DC 20408
(202) 501-6025

National Capital Planning Commission

Suite 301
801 Pennsylvania Ave., NW
Washington, DC 20576
(202) 724-0174

National Credit Union Administration

1776 G St., NW
Washington, DC 20456
(202) 682-9600

Office of Examination and Insurance
6th Floor
1776 G St., NW
Washington, DC 20456
(202) 682-9640

Sources of Information
Employment
Personnel Information
National Credit Union Administration
Washington, DC 20456
(202) 682-9720

Federally Insured Credit Unions
Freedom of Information Officer
National Credit Union Administration
Washington, DC 20456
(202) 682-9700

Office of Public and Congressional Affairs
National Credit Union Administration
1776 G St., NW
Washington, DC 20456
(202) 682-9650

National Foundation on the Arts and the Humanities

National Endowment for the Arts
1100 Pennsylvania Ave., NW
Washington, DC 20506
(202) 682-5400

National Endowment for the Humanities
1100 Pennsylvania Ave., NW
Washington, DC 20506
(202) 606-8438

Education Grants
Division of Education Programs
1100 Pennsylvania Ave., NW
Washington, DC 20506
(202) 682-5426

Research
Division of Research Programs
1100 Pennsylvania Ave., NW
Washington, DC 20506
(202) 682-5432

State Grants
Division of State Programs

Be patient. If any phone number is incorrect, call (area code) 555-1212 and request the new listing.

Information Starting Places

1100 Pennsylvania Ave., NW
Washington, DC 20506
(202) 682-5429

Challenge Grants
Office of Challenge Grants
1100 Pennsylvania Ave., NW
Washington, DC 20506
(202) 682-5436

Public Affairs
1100 Pennsylvania Ave., NW
Washington, DC 20506
(202) 682-5400

Institute of Museum Services
Program Director
Room 609
1100 Pennsylvania Ave., NW
Washington, DC 20506
(202) 786-0536

National Labor Relations Board

1717 Pennsylvania Ave., NW
Washington, DC 20570
(202) 254-8064

Information Division
Room 710
1717 Pennsylvania Ave., NW
Washington, DC 20570
(202) 632-4950

National Mediation Board

1425 K St., NW
Washington, DC 20572
(202) 619-5920

National Railroad Passenger Corporation (AMTRAK)

60 Massachusetts Ave., NE
Washington, DC 20002
(202) 906-3000

Public Affairs
Public Affairs Department
60 Massachusetts Ave., NE
Washington, DC 20002
(202) 906-3860

National Science Foundation

1800 G St., NW
Washington, DC 20550
(202) 357-5000

Sources of Information

Board and Committee Minutes
National Science Board Office
1800 G St., NW
Washington, DC 20550
(202) 357-9582

Contracts
1800 G St., NW
Washington, DC 20550
(202) 357-7880

Employment
Division of Human Resource Management
Room 208
1800 G St., NW
Washington, DC 20550
(202) 357-9859

Fellowships
Directorate for Education and Human Resources
1800 G St., NW
Washington, DC 20550
(202) 357-7856

Freedom of Information Act
FOIA REQUEST
Office of Legislative and Public Affairs
Room 527
1800 G St., NW
Washington, DC 20550
(202) 357-9498

Inspector General
Office of Inspector General
Room 1241
1800 G St., NW
Washington, DC 20550
(202) 357-9457

Privacy Act Requests
Privacy Act Officer
1800 G St., NW
Room 208
Washington, DC 20550
(202) 357-7335

Publications
National Science Foundation
Forms and Publications
Room 232
1800 G St., NW
Washington, DC 20550
(202) 357-7861

Reading Room
National Science Foundation Library
Room 248
1800 G St., NW
Washington, DC 20550
(202) 357-7811

Small Business Activities
Office of Small Business and Disadvantaged Business Utilization
1800 G St., NW
Washington, DC 20550
(202) 653-5202

Legislative and Public Affairs
1800 G St., NW
Washington, DC 20550
(202) 357-9498

National Transportation Safety Board

490 L'Enfant Plaza, SW
Washington, DC 20594
(202) 382-6600

Sources of Information

Contracts
Contracting Officer
Financial Management Division
490 L'Enfant Plaza
Washington, DC 20594
(202) 382-6725

Employment
Human Resources Division
490 L'Enfant Plaza, SW
Washington, DC 20594
(202) 382-6717

Publications
Public Inquiries Section
490 L'Enfant Plaza, SW

Be patient. If any phone number is incorrect, call (area code) 555-1212 and request the new listing.

Federal Public Information Offices

Washington, DC 20594
(202) 382-6735

Reading Room
Public Inquiries Section
490 L'Enfant Plaza, SW
Washington, DC 20594
(202) 382-6735

Public Affairs
490 L'Enfant Plaza, SW
Washington, DC 20594
(202) 382-0660

Nuclear Regulatory Commission

Washington, DC 20555
(301) 492-7000

Source of Information

Contracts
Small and Disadvantaged Business Utilization and Civil Rights
MNBB 7217
Nuclear Regulatory Commission
Washington, DC 20555
(301) 492-4665

Employment
Office of Personnel
Nuclear Regulatory Commission
Washington, DC 20555
(301) 492-4661

Freedom of Information Act Requests
Director
Division of Freedom of Information and Publication Services
Nuclear Regulatory Commission
Washington, DC 205555
(301) 492-7211

Reading Rooms
Public Document Room
2120 L St., NW
Washington, DC 20555
(202) 634-3273

Records
Director
Division of Freedom of Information and Publication Services
Nuclear Regulatory Commission
Washington, DC 20555
(301) 492-7211

Office of Governmental and Public Affairs
Nuclear Regulatory Commission
Washington, DC 20555
(301) 504-2240

Occupational Safety and Health Review Commission

1825 K St., NW
Washington, DC 20006
(202) 634-7943

Office of Government Ethics

Suite 500
1201 New York Ave., NW
Washington, DC 20005-3917
(202) 619-5757

Office of Personnel Management

1900 E St., NW
Washington, DC 20415-0001
(202) 606-1800

Inspector General
1900 E St., NW
Room 6400
Washington, DC 20415
(202) 606-1200

Sources of Information

Contracts
Chief, Procurement Division
Administration Group
1900 E St., NW
Washington, DC 20415
(202) 606-2240

Employment
Office of Personnel
Room 1447
1900 E St., NW
Washington, DC 20415
(202) 606-2400

Publications
Chief, Issuance System Office
1900 E St., NW
Washington, DC 20415
(202) 606-1973

Office of Communications
1900 E St., NW
Washington, DC 20415-0001
(202) 606-1800

Office of Special Counsel

Suite 300
730 M St., NW
Washington, DC 20036
(202) 653-7188
(800) 872-9855

Panama Canal Commission

Room 550
2000 L St., NW
Washington, DC 20036-4996
(202) 634-6441

Peace Corps

1990 K St., NW
Washington, DC 20526
(202) 606-3886
(800) 424-8580

Sources of Information

Recruiting
Public Response Unit
1990 K St., NW
Washington, DC 20526
(800) 424-8500

Employment
Office of Personnel Management
1990 K St., NW
Washington, DC 20526
(202) 606-3336

Office of External Affairs
1990 K St., NW
Washington, DC 20526
(202) 606-3010

Pennsylvania Avenue Development Corporation

Suite 1220 North
1331 Pennsylvania Ave., NW

Be patient. If any phone number is incorrect, call (area code) 555-1212 and request the new listing.

Information Starting Places

Washington, DC 20004-1703
(202) 724-9091

Director of Corporate Affairs
Suite 1220 North
1331 Pennsylvania Ave., NW
Washington, DC 20004-1703
(202) 724-9073

Pension Benefit Guaranty Corporation

2020 K St., NW
Washington, DC 20006
(202) 778-8800

Postal Rate Commission

1333 H St., NW
Washington, DC 20268-0001
(202) 789-6800

Secretary
1333 H St., NW
Washington, DC 20268-0001
(202) 789-6840

Railroad Retirement Board

844 North Rush St.
Chicago, IL 60611-2092
(312) 751-4776

Office of Public Affairs
844 North Rush St.
Chicago, IL 60611-2092
(312) 751-4776

Washington Legislative/Liaison Office
Suite 558
2000 L St., NW
Washington, DC 20036-4998

Resolution Trust Corporation

801 17th St., NW
Washington, DC 20434
(202) 416-6900

Office of Public Affairs
801 17th St., NW
Washington, DC 20434
(202) 416-7557

Securities and Exchange Commission

450 5th St., SW
Washington, DC 20549
(202) 272-3100

Office of Public Affairs
450 5th St., SW
Washington, DC 20549
(202) 272-2650

Publications: - a monthly summary of security transactions is available through:
Superintendent of Documents
Government Printing Office
Washington, DC 20402
(202) 272-7440

Contracts
Office of Administrative Services
450 5th St., SW
Washington, DC 20549
(202) 272-7000

Employment
Office of Human Resources Management
450 5th St., SW
Washington, DC 20549
(202) 272-2519

Reading Rooms
Library
450 5th St., SW
Washington, DC 20549
(202) 272-7450

Small Business Activities
450 5th St., SW
Washington, DC 20549
(202) 272-2644

Selective Service System

National Headquarters
1023 31st St., SW
Washington, DC 20435
(202) 724-0820

Office of Public Affairs
National Headquarters
1023 31st St., SW
Washington, DC 20435
(202) 724-0790

Employment
Director, Selective Service System
Attn: RMH
Washington, DC 20435
(202) 724-0435

Procurement
Director
Selective Service System
Attn: RMC
Washington, DC 20435
(202) 724-0731

Small Business Administration

409 Third St., SW
Washington, DC 20416
(202) 205-7151

Locator
409 Third St., SW
Washington, DC 20416
(202) 205-6600

Answer Desk
409 Third St., SW
Washington, DC 20416
(800) U-ASK-SBA

Office of Financial Assistance
8th Floor
409 Third St., SW
Washington, DC 20416
(202) 205-6490

Disaster Assistance
409 Third St., SW
Washington, DC 20416
(202) 205-6734

Investment
Divesture Insurance
Suite 8100
409 Third St., SW
Washington, DC 20416
(202) 205-6734

Be patient. If any phone number is incorrect, call (area code) 555-1212 and request the new listing.

Federal Public Information Offices

Surety Guarantee
Suite 8600
409 Third St., SW
Washington, DC 20416
(202) 205-6540

Procurement Assistance
409 Third St., SW
Washington, DC 20416
(202) 205-6460

Business Initiatives, Education and Training
409 Third St., SW
Washington, DC 20416
(202) 205-6665

Minority Small Business Development
409 Third St., SW
Washington, DC 20416
(202) 205-6410

Advocacy
Suite 7800
409 Third St., SW
Washington, DC 20416
(202) 205-6533

Women's Business Ownership
409 Third St., SW
Washington, DC 20416
(202) 205-6673

Veterans Affairs
409 Third St., SW
Washington, DC 20416
(202) 205-6773

Innovation, Research and Technology
409 Third St., SW
Washington, DC 20416
(202) 205-6450

International Trade
409 Third St., SW
Washington, DC 20416
(202) 205-6720

Small Business Development Centers
409 Third St., SW
Washington, DC 20416
(202) 205-6766

Public Affairs
409 Third St., SW
Washington, DC 20416
(202) 205-6533

Tennessee Valley Authority

Room 300
412 First St., SE
Washington, DC 20444-2003
(202) 479-4412
or
400 West Summit Hill Dr.
Knoxville, TN 37902
615-632-2101

Citizen Participation
Regional Communications
ET PB 25H
400 West Summit Hill Dr.
Knoxville, TN 37902-1499
(615) 632-8000

Contracts
Division of Purchasing

CST Street
Chattanooga, TN 37401-2127
(615) 751-2624

Electric Power Supply and Rates
Power Group
LP 25 18OG
1101 Market St.
Chattanooga, TN 37402-2801
(615) 751-8678

Employment
Human Resources Services
ET 5D 93U
400 West Summit Hill Drive
Knoxville, TN 37902-1499
(615) 632-3341

Environmental and Energy Education
TVA Energy Education/Information
Forestry Bldg.
Ridgeway Road
Norris, TN 37828
(615) 632-1599

Environmental Quality
Resource Development
SPB 2S 201P
309 Walnut St.
Knoxville, TN 37902-1499
(615) 632-6578

Fertilizer and Agriculture
National Fertilizer and Environmental Research Center
Muscle Shoals, AL 35660-1010
(205) 386-2593

Employment
Office of Human Resources
400 Summit Hill Drive
Knoxville, TN 37902-1499
(615) 632-4400

Minority Economic Development
OCH E 3B 7B
601 Summit Hill Drive
Knoxville, TN 37901-1499
(615) 632-4405

Maps
Maps and Surveys Department
HB 2N 200A
311 Broad St.
Chattanooga, TN 37402-2801
(615) 751-2133

Medical Program
Medical Services
EB 6W 4A
20 East 11th St.
Chattanooga, TN 37402-2801
(615) 751-2091

Publications
Regional Communications
ET PB 25H
400 W. Summit Hill Drive
Knoxville, TN 37902-1499
(615) 632-8000

Recreation
Land Resources
Forestry Bldg.
Ridgeway Road
Norris, TN 37828
(615) 632-1802

Be patient. If any phone number is incorrect, call (area code) 555-1212 and request the new listing.

Information Starting Places

Technical Library
Technical Library Services
WT 2D 15B
400 W. Summit Hill Drive
Knoxville, TN 47902-1499
(615) 632-3033

Public Affairs
Regional Communications
Tennessee Valley Authority
400 West Summit Hill Dr.
Knoxville, TN 37902-1499
(615) 632-8000
or
Washington Office
412 1st St., SE
Washington, DC 20444-2003
(202) 479-4412

Thrift Depositor Protection Oversight Board
Suite 600
1777 F St., NW
Washington, DC 20232
(202) 786-9661

Public Affairs
Suite 800
1777 F St., NW
Washington, DC 20232
(202) 786-9672

United States Arms Control and Disarmament Agency
320 21st St, NW
Washington, DC 20451
(202) 647-8677

Contracts
Contracting Office
320 21st St., NW
Washington, DC 20451
(703) 235-3288

Public Affairs
Room 5843
320 21st St., NW
Washington, DC 20451
(202) 647-8677

Speakers
320 21st St., NW
Washington, DC 20451
(202) 647-4800

United States Information Agency
301 4th St., SW
Washington, DC 20547
(202) 619-4700

Public Affairs
Office of the Public Liaison
301 4th St., SW
Washington, DC 20547
(202) 619-4355

Administrative Regulations
Management Plans and Analysis Staff
301 4th St., SW
Washington, DC 20547
(202) 619-4700

Contracts
Office of Contracts
301 4th St., SW

Washington, DC 20547
(202) 485-6398

Employment
Special Recruitment Staff
Office of Personnel
301 4th St., SW
Washington, DC 20547
(202) 619-5618

International Audiovisual Programs
Chief Attestation Officer
301 4th St., SW
Washington, DC 20547
(202) 501-7775

United States International Development Cooperation Agency
320 21st St., NW
Washington, DC 20523-0001
(202) 647-9620

Agency for International Development
320 21st St., NW
Washington, DC 20523-0001
(202) 647-9620

Public Affairs
Office of the Public Liaison
320 21st St., NW
Washington, DC 20523-0001
(202) 647-1850

Congressional Affairs
Bureau for Legislative Affairs
Agency for International Development
320 21st St., NW
Washington, DC 20523-0001
(202) 647-8264

Employment
Recruiting Division
Office of Human Resources Development
320 21st St., NW
Washington, DC 20523-0001
(202) 663-2368

Contracts
Office of Small and Disadvantaged Business Utilization
320 21st St., NW
Washington, DC 20523-1414
(703) 875-1551

Trade and Development Program
Director
Room 309, State Annex 16
Washington, DC 20523
(703) 875-4357

Overseas Private Investment Corporation
Information Office
1100 New York Ave., NW
Washington, DC 20527
(202) 336-8400

Small Business Activities
1100 New York Ave., NW
Washington, DC 20527
(800) 424-OPIC

United States International Trade Commission
500 E St., SW
Washington, DC 20436
(202) 205-2000

Be patient. If any phone number is incorrect, call (area code) 555-1212 and request the new listing.

Federal Public Information Offices

United States Postal Service
475 L'Enfant Plaza, SW
Washington, DC 20260
(202) 268-2000

Consumer Advocate
475 L'Enfant Plaza, SW
Washington, DC 20260
(202) 268-2284

Marketing Department
475 L'Enfant Plaza, SW
Washington, DC 20260
(202) 268-3916

Postal Inspection
475 L'Enfant Plaza, SW
Washington, DC 20260
(202) 268-4293

Contracts
Procurement and Supply Department
475 L'Enfant Plaza, SW
Washington, DC 20260
(202) 268-4140

Employment
475 L'Enfant Plaza, SW
Washington, DC 20260
(202) 268-4267

Films
Communications Department
475 L'Enfant Plaza, SW
Washington, DC 20260
(202) 268-2189

Philatelic Information
Stamp Management
475 L'Enfant Plaza, SW
Washington, DC 20260-2420
(202) 268-2312

Philatelic Sales
Philatelic Sales Branch
U.S. Postal Service
Kansas City, MO 64144-9988
(816) 455-0970

Reading Rooms
11th Floor North
Library Division
475 L'Enfant Plaza, SW
Washington, DC 20260
(202) 268-2900

Speakers
Communications Department
475 L'Enfant Plaza, SW
Washington, DC 20260
(202) 268-3653

Be patient. If any phone number is incorrect, call (area code) 555-1212 and request the new listing.

Information Starting Places

Hotlines

- *A database on foreign owned agricultural land in the U.S.;*
- *Audiovisual materials on foreign language instruction;*
- *Recalls on automobiles purchased in the past 10 years;*
- *Just about any kind of map ranging from road maps to highly specialized maps;*
- *Finance records of political candidates;*
- *Inventory of houses acquired from failed savings and loan companies;*
- *Assistance to small businesses in complying with environmental regulations;*
- *Status of bills pending in State legislatures;*
- *Free eye care for the elderly;*
- *A hearing test by telephone; and*
- *Recorded messages of job vacancies in federal government agencies.*

Do you know that this kind of information can be obtained by one toll-free telephone call? These "hotline" numbers may be set up by state or federal agencies or nonprofit organizations, who are more than willing to answer your inquiries or provide you with publications, most of which will be sent to you free-of-charge.

Hotline numbers often are thought of as emergency numbers or numbers to be called in a crisis situation. Although many hotline numbers are emergency response numbers such as the Chemical Manufacturers Association chemical spills or explosions emergency assistance hotline or U.S. Department of Health and Human Services food and drug emergency advice line, the majority of hotlines are informational. They are staffed by experts who can answer your questions or are clearinghouses with personnel eager to send you their publications.

Many hotlines are simply recorded messages of information, providing the answers to the organization's most asked questions. The U.S. Department of Commerce/Bureau of Economic Analysis has four such recorded messages, including information on leading economic indicators, quarterly estimates of the gross national product, statistical information on personal income, and U.S. international transactions. The U.S. Department of Health and Human Services/Centers for Disease Control has three recorded messages on AIDS giving you statistical information such as the number of cases and deaths among age groups, the ten states with the highest number of cases, and projections of deaths by 1992.

Hotline numbers are usually, but not necessarily, toll free 800 numbers. Due to budget cuts, many numbers of the Federal government, which were previously toll-free, are now commercial numbers, although their function remains the same.

Some of the 800 numbers of hotlines listed below cannot be reached from all calling areas. An 800 number sometimes cannot be used when dialing within the same metropolitan area, state, or area code where the organization is located. In these instances, the commercial number is given in addition to the toll free number. Generally, the toll-free numbers for state government agencies are valid only within the state. There are a few exceptions to this, such as 800 numbers for State Offices of Tourism and some State tax information hotlines.

Hotlines provide many types of assistance, ranging from informational to direct financial or other types of direct intervention assistance. Here are some examples of the types of assistance individuals have received from hotline organizations:

National Health Organizations Help Disabled Child Win Medicaid and SSI Benefits

A child with congenital brain damage, mental retardation, eye problems and paralysis on the right side, was denied Supplemental Security Income (SSI) and Medicaid by the Social Security Administration based on insufficient disability. The decision was appealed and brought before the U.S. Supreme Court. The American Academy of Pediatrics, the National Organization for Rare Disorders and the Spina Bifida Association among others filed an Amicus brief on behalf of the child. Making reference to the Amicus brief, the Supreme Court ruled that Social Security benefits are improperly being denied because child claimants are held to a higher standard than adults. As a result of this decision, the child, as well as many others previously denied benefits, will now receive them.

New York State Receives Assistance with Drug Prevention Program

The State of New York's Section V (an 11-county area) decided to implement a long-range chemical health program for student athletes. The steering committee of Operation Offense, the name adopted for their program, asked State High School Associations' TARGET professionals to come to New York to train athletic directors or coaches to become workshop leaders. In the next eight months, over 5,000 coaches, parents and athletes were reached by the Operation Offense program.

Counseling and Morale Support from MADD

Parents who lost a child as a result of drunk driving phone Mothers Against Drunk Driving and talk to a counselor who lost a daughter to a drunk driver. The counselor talks to them, subsequently helps them through the criminal justice system, and even goes to court with them to provide them with morale support.

Be patient. If any phone number is incorrect, call (area code) 555-1212 and request the new listing.

Hotlines

Women's Sports Foundation Gives Financial Assistance to Athletes

Bonnie Blair, a speed skater, who received the WSF Up and Coming Athlete Award in 1986, went on to win a gold medal at the 1988 Olympics. Sheila Conover, a luger, received a grant from WSF and became a double gold medalist in the 1987 Pan American Games.

A list of hotlines follows, in alphabetical order by agency or organization under main subject headings:

Agriculture and Botany

Michigan Department of Agriculture
Michigan agricultural assistance
(800) 346-FARM (in Michigan only)

Montana Department of Agriculture
Montana financial assistance to ranchers and farmers
(800) 722-FARM

Nebraska Department of Agriculture
Nebraska agricultural promotion and publications
(800) 831-0550 (in Nebraska only)

New York Department of Agriculture and Markets
New York state fruits and vegetables marketing sources and opportunities
(800) NY-CROPS

U.S. Department of Agriculture (USDA)
Recorded message of agricultural news
(202) 488-8358

U.S. Department of Agriculture
Meat and Poultry Hotline
(800) 535-4555

U.S. Department of Agriculture
USDA Information Line
(202) 720-2791

U.S. Department of Agriculture
Office of Inspector General
(800) 424-9192

U.S. Department of Agriculture
To order publications, databases and subscriptions on agricultural trade and economics
(800) 999-6779

USDA/Agricultural Research Service
Information on activities of ARS
(202) 344-4296

USDA/Economic Research Service
To order database on Foreign Owned Agricultural Land (No. 87015)
(800) 999-6779

USDA/Foreign Agricultural Service
To access foreign agricultural news releases by FAX machine
(202) 720-3930; FAX: (202) 720-3229

USDA/National Agricultural Library (ALF)
An electronic bulletin board for the exchange of agricultural information
(301) 504-6510, 5111, 5496, 5497

U.S. Botanic Gardens
Recorded message of upcoming events
(202) 225-7099

U.S. Botanic Gardens
Talk to a botanist about plant care
(202) 225-8333; (202) 226-4082

Banks and Investments

Commodity Futures Trading Commission
To file complaints about commodity brokers
(202) 254-3067

Federal Deposit Insurance Corporation (FDIC)
For information and to file complaints about FDIC insured banks
(800) 424-5488
(800) 934-3342

Federal Reserve System
Consumer Affairs Line
(202) 452-3946

Federal Reserve Banks throughout the USA with recorded messages announcing future auctions of Treasury securities (Bills, Bonds, and Notes) and interest rates and other auction results:

Atlanta, Georgia: . . . . (404) 521-8500
Birmingham, Alabama: . . . . (205) 731-8500 x702
Boston, Massachusetts: . . . . (617) 973-3000
Buffalo, New York: . . . . (716) 849-5000
Chicago, Illinois: . . . . (312) 322-5322
Denver, Colorado: . . . . (303) 572-2300
Detroit, Michigan: . . . . (313) 961-6880
Kansas City, Missouri: . . . . (816) 881-2000
Louisville, Kentucky: . . . . (502) 568-9200
Miami, Florida: . . . . (305) 591-2065 general information
(305) 471-6257 interest rates
New Orleans, Louisiana: . . . . (504) 593-3200
N.Y., New York: . . . . (212) 720-5000
Oklahoma City, Oklahoma: . . . . (405) 270-8400
Omaha, Nebraska: . . . . (402) 221-5500
Philadelphia, Pennsylvania: . . . . (215) 574-6000
Pittsburgh, Pennsylvania: . . . . (412) 261-7800
Portland, Oregon: . . . . (503) 221-5900 (future auction schedules)
(503) 221-5921 (results of recent auctions)
Salt Lake City, Utah: . . . . (801) 322-7900
San Antonio, Texas: . . . . (512) 978-1200 x330
San Francisco, California: . . . . (415) 974-2000
Seattle, Washington: . . . . (206) 343-3600
St. Louis, Missouri: . . . . (314) 444-8444

Federal Reserve Board
Recorded message on statistical releases,
board meetings, testimony, etc.
(202) 452-3206

Federal Reserve Board
Recorded message regarding bank holding companies' applications and orders
(202) 452-3207

Securities and Exchange Commission
Recorded message of information on publications, investor inquiries/complaints, broker/dealer registration, etc.
(202) 272-3100

U.S. Department of the Treasury/Bureau of Public Debt
Recorded message on Treasury Bill, Note, and Bond offerings, auction results, U.S. Savings Bond information, etc.
(202) 874-4000

Recorded message of information on U.S. Savings Bonds, etc.
(800) US-BONDS

Books, Audiovisual Materials, Libraries, and Records

Government Printing Office (GPO)
To place an order or obtain information on new government books
(202) 783-3238 X3

Government Printing Office (GPO)
To order special publications such as regulations
(202) 512-2457

Information Starting Places

Government Printing Office (GPO)
To check on a subscription
(202) 512-2303

Library of Congress
Information about the Library of Congress and its holdings
(202) 707-5522

Library of Congress
Recorded message regarding major exhibitions on display
(202) 707-8000

Library of Congress
Recorded message on using the Library of Congress
(202) 707-6400

National Archives and Records Administration
Recorded message on events at the National Archives
(202) 501-5000

National Audiovisual Center
Audiovisual materials on foreign languages, fire safety, wildlife, etc.
(800) 222-0109

Smithsonian Institution
To order Smithsonian records and books, including *A Smithsonian Book of Comic-Book Comics*
(800) 927-7377

U.S. Department of Defense (DOD)/Public Communications
To inquire about or order DOD publications
(703) 697-5737

Business and the Economy

Nebraska Department of Economic Development
Nebraska marketing, demographic and economic information
(800) 426-6505

Senior Corps of Retired Executives (SCORE)
Information about SCORE and referrals
(202) 653-6279

Small Business Administration
Small Business facts, financing and development programs, including SCORE information
(800) 827-5722; (202) 205-6533

U.S. Department of Commerce
Information/assistance to small businesses
(202) 482-1472

U.S. Department of Labor
Recorded message of departmental news
(202) 219-6666

Civil Rights

Commission on Civil Rights
To file civil rights complaints
(202) 376-8116

Equal Employment Opportunity Commission
How to file EEO complaints
(800) 669-3362

U.S. Department of Justice
Redress information for Japanese Americans interred during World War II
(202) 219-6900

U.S. Department of Justice/Community Relations Service
Assist people with discrimination cases and hate groups in neighborhoods
(800) 347-HATE

Commerce, Interstate (For Foreign Commerce see Trade)

Interstate Commerce Commission
Recorded message giving diesel fuel price for the day
(202) 927-7600

Communications

Federal Communications Commission (FCC)
Recorded message of actions taken by FCC and public notices
(202) 632-7000

Consumer Power

Consumer Product Safety Commission
Consumer product safety information, recalls, complaints, and publications
(800) 638-2772; (800) 638-8270 TDD
(800) 492-8104 TDD in Maryland

Consumer Product Safety Commission
Recorded message announcing meetings
(301) 504-0100

Interstate Commerce Commission
Complaints about household movers
(202) 927-5500

Postal Rate Commission
Recorded message regarding hearings on postal rates and mail classifications
(202) 789-6874

State consumer protection offices for information on filing complaints and access to records, by state (all numbers are in-state only):

Alabama . . . . . (800) 392-5658; (800) 392-8050 Utility Company Complaints
Arizona . . . . . . (800) 352-8431; (800) 222-7000 Utility Company Complaints
Arkansas . . . . . (800) 482-8982; (800) 482-1164 Utility Company Complaints
California . . . . (800) 952-5225; (800) 952-5548 TDD
(800) 952-5210 Auto Repair Complaints
(800) 233-9045 Insurance Information and Complaints
Connecticut . . . . (800) 842-2649
(800) 538-2277 Lemon Law complaints for new automobile purchases
(800) 382-4586 Utility Company Complaints
Delaware . . . . (800) 443-2179 Sussex County
(800) 282-8574 Utility Company Complaints
Florida . . . . (800) 321-5366 Toll Free Lemon Law
(800) 342-2175, 2176; (800) 327-3382
(800) 342-3552 Utility Company Complaints
Georgia . . . . (800) 869-1123
(800) 282-5813 Utility Company Complaints
Illinois . . . . (800) 572-7711 900 no. complaints and information only
Idaho . . . . (800) 432-3545
Indiana . . . . (800) 382-5516; (800) 662-0027
Kansas . . . . (800) 432-2310; (800) 662-0027 Utility Company Complaints
Kentucky . . . . (800) 432-9257
Louisiana . . . . (800) 256-2413 Utility Company Complaints
Maine . . . . (800) 332-8529
Maryland . . . . . (800) 969-5766; (800) 492-0474 Utility Company Complaints
Michigan . . . . (800) 292-4204
(800) 292-9555 Utility Company Complaints; also (800) 443-8926 TDD
Minnesota . . . . (800) 652-9747 Utility Company Complaints
Mississippi . . . . . (800) 356-6428 (Utility Company Complaints North District
(800) 356-6430 Utility Company Complaints Central Districts
(800) 356-6429 Utility Company Complaints South District
Missouri . . . . (800) 392-8222
(800) 392-4211 Utility Company Complaints
Montana . . . . (800) 332-2272
Nebraska . . . . (800) 526-0017 Utility Company Complaints
Nevada . . . . (800) 992-0900
New Hampshire . . . . (800) 852-3793 Utility Company Complaints
New Jersey . . . . (800) 792-8600
(800) 242-5846 Tapes on various subjects,
including Lemon Law, Truth-in-Lending
(800) 624-0241 Utility Company Complaints
New Mexico . . . . (800) 432-2070

Be patient. If any phone number is incorrect, call (area code) 555-1212 and request the new listing.

Hotlines

New York . . . . (800) 342-3377 Utility Company Complaints
(800) 342-3355 Utility Company Complaints--unwarranted shut-off of a utility (emergencies)

North Dakota . . . . (800) 472-2600
(800) 932-2400 Utility Company Complaints

Ohio . . . . (800) 899-5253
(800) 282-0515 Business and Product Complaints
(800) 686-7826 Utility Company Complaints

Oklahoma . . . . (800) 522-8154 Utility Company Complaints

Oregon . . . . (800) 522-2404 Utility Company Complaints

Pennsylvania . . . . (800) 782-1110
(800) 441-2555

Rhode Island . . . . (800) 852-7776
(800) 341-1000

South Carolina . . . . (800) 922-1594
(800) 922-5131 Utility Company Complaints

Tennessee . . . . (800) 342-8385
(800) 422-CLUB Health Club Hotline
(800) 342-8359 Utility Company Complaints

Vermont . . . . (800) 622-4496 Utility Company Complaints

Virginia . . . . (800) 451-1525
(800) 552-7945 Utility Company Complaints

Washington . . . . (800) 551-4636
(800) 562-6150 Utility Company Complaints

West Virginia . . . . (800) 368-8808
(800) 344-5113 Utility Company Complaints
(800) 247-8789 Motor Carrier Complaints

Wisconsin . . . . (800) 422-7128
(800) 362-8189

U.S. Department of Agriculture
Food safety information and to report illness from meat, poultry or eggs
(800) 535-4555; (202) 447-3333 in Washington, DC

U.S. Department of Labor/Bureau of Labor Statistics
Recorded message regarding indicators, including consumer and producer price indexes, employment cost index, etc.
(202) 606-7828

Copyright Information

Library of Congress
Copyright information
(202) 707-3000

Courses

Boating correspondence course entitled "The Skipper's Course"
(719) 544-3142

National Credit Union
Examiner training programs
(202) 682-9640

National Federation of State High School Associations
Under TARGET Program, training seminars for teachers and other professionals on chemical use and prevention
(816) 464-5400

National Resource Center on Child Sexual Abuse
Training for professionals
(800) KIDS-006

U.S. Department of State
One day seminar on foreign policy and business opportunities abroad for Vice Presidents of companies doing business
(202) 647-1433

U.S. Department of the Treasury/Internal Revenue Service
Under VITA program, free courses in return for tax preparation and small business tax education course
(202) 566-4904

Crimes, Criminals and Criminal Law

Anonymous Witness Reporting System

To report major crimes
(800) 782-7463; (800) 78-CRIME in California

U.S. Department of Justice/Bureau of Justice Statistics
Publications providing statistical information on prisoners
(800) 732-3277

Justice/Bureau of Justice Statistics
Information on juvenile justice publications and database searches
(800) 638-8736

Justice/National Institute of Justice
Publications and database searches for criminal justice-related information, statistics and publications
(800) 851-3420

U.S. Secret Service
Information about criminal activities and protective responsibilities
(202) 395-2020

Defense and the Military

U.S. Department of Defense (Defense)
Provides assistance with employer/employee problems for members of the Guard and Reserve
(800) 274-3561

Defense/Air Force
Health Profession Scholarships in return for military service
(800) 531-5980

Defense/Army
Recorded message of information for problems with army retirees paychecks
(800) 428-2290

Defense/Civilian Health and Medical Program of the Uniformed Services
Information regarding benefits
(303) 361-3907 or 3707

Defense/Defense Mapping Agency
Guidance on obtaining maps and charts of the Defense Mapping Agency
(800) 826-0342

Defense/Defense Nuclear Agency
Radiation exposure by veterans in Hiroshima/Nagasaki or participating in nuclear tests
(800) 462-3683

Defense/Navy
Naval recruitment and opportunities
(800) 327-NAVY

U.S. Naval Reserves
Recorded message to leave name/number for someone to call back
(800) USA-USNR

U.S. Naval Academy
Recorded message (M-F 5pm-8pm, weekends and holidays) regarding admissions information, nominations and appointments, application materials, etc.
(800) 638-9156

Selective Service
Selective Service registration and status
(708) 688-6888

Veterans Administration
Prisoners of War (POW) assistance with receiving checks, hospital problems, etc.
(800) 831-6515

Veterans Administration
Information on CHAMPVA, medical benefits for dependents of disabled veterans or veterans whose death was service-related
(800) 733-8387

Be patient. If any phone number is incorrect, call (area code) 555-1212 and request the new listing.

Information Starting Places

Disaster Relief

Federal Emergency Management Agency (FEMA)
Information on National Flood Insurance Program regulations, claims, conferences and maps
(800) 638-6620; (301) 731-5300 in DC

FEMA - National Emergency Center Library
Publications and bibliographies on emergency management information
(800) 638-1821

FEMA
To order maps showing flood-prone areas
(800) 358-9616

Drugs and Chemical Dependency

Al-Anon
Referral service to support group meetings
(800) 344-2666

Alcohol and Chemical Dependency Rehabilitation for the Elderly
Treatment center at Hopedale Hall, Hopedale, Illinois
(800) 354-7089
(800) 344-0824 in Illinois

Alcohol and Drug Help Referral Hotline
Information, referrals and 24 hour a day counseling
(800) 252-6465

Just Say No! Clubs
Publications, consultations, grant information
(800) 258-2766
(415) 939-6666 in California

Mothers Against Drunk Driving (MADD)
Information, victims assistance and referrals
(800) 438-6233

Health Connection
Publications, videos, display posters on drug, alcohol, and smoking prevention and education
(800) 548-8700

National Clearinghouse for Alcohol and Drug Information
Publications and grant information
(301) 468-2600

National Cocaine Hotline
Information and referrals
(800) COC-AINE

National Council on Alcoholism
Information and publications on alcoholism and drug addiction
(800) NCA-CALL

National Drug Abuse Information and Treatment Hotline
Information and referrals in Spanish
(800) 66-AYUDA

National Federation of Parents for Drug-Free Youth
Parent information line and training
(314) 968-1322

Drug Free Workplace Helpline/U.S. Department of Health and Human Services
Assistance on implementing drug-free workplace programs
(800) 843-4971

National Institute on Drug Abuse Hotline/HHS
Information and referrals
(800) 662-HELP

Pride Institute - Chemical Dependency Treatment Center
Inpatient facility in Eden Prairie, Minnesota, treating alcohol- and/or drug-dependent lesbians and gay men
(800) 54-PRIDE

State High School Associations Target Programs
Information, publications and drug and alcohol education for K-12
(800) 366-6667

U.S. Department of Education
To order *What Works--Schools Without Drugs* and *A Parent's Guide to Prevention*
(800) 624-0100

U.S. Department of Education Regional Centers:
Assistance to state and local educational agencies with alcohol and drug abuse education and prevention programs
Southwest: . . . . (800) 234-7972; (405) 325-1454 in Oklahoma
Western: . . . . (800) 547-6339; (503) 275-9479 in Oregon

U.S. Department of Health and Human Services/Alcohol, Drug Abuse and Mental Health Administration
Information about drugs in the workplace program
(800) 843-4971

U.S. Department of the Interior/No Drugs in the Workplace
Recorded message of information regarding AIDS, alcohol, illegal drugs, drug testing procedures, personal counseling, etc.
(800) 628-DRUG

Education

Bilingual and minority language training and technical assistance:
Evaluation Assistance Center--Georgetown University
(800) 925-EACE
RMC Research Corp.
(800) 258-0802

ERIC Clearinghouse on Adult Career and Vocational Education
Adult vocational and continuing education programs
(800) 848-4815

ERIC Document Reproduction Service
To order copies of ERIC documents announced in *Resources in Education*
(800) 227-3742

National Clearinghouse for Bilingual Information
Bilingual education information for educators
(800) 321-6223

State Clearinghouses for Adult Education for these states:
Information to improve basic skills
Virginia . . . . (800) 237-0178; (804) 367-6521

U.S. Department of Education
Educational research and improvement statistics
(800) 424-1616

Education/Federal Student Aid Information Center
General and technical information regarding application process and Federal policy
(708) 559-0949

Education/Office of Educational Research and Improvement
OERI Electronic Bulletin Board for accessing education information
(800) 424-1616

Education/Office of Intergovernmental Affairs
Information regarding the application process for the President's Academic Fitness Line
(800) 438-7232

Education/Office of Postsecondary Education
Information on Pell Grant Program
(708) 559-0949

EDIC Clearinghouse for Rural Education and Small Schools
(800) 624-9120
(800) 344-6646 (in West Virginia)

ORYX Press
Publishes *Current Index to Journals in Education*, the *Thesaurus of ERIC*

Be patient. If any phone number is incorrect, call (area code) 555-1212 and request the new listing.

Hotlines

Descriptors and other ERIC publications
(800) 279-ORYX

Access ERIC
Provides referral services for the Educational Resources Information Center
(800) LET-ERIC

Employment and Job Training

ACTION/VISTA
Volunteers in Service to America information on applying or services
(800) 424-8867

Administrative Office of the U.S. Courts
Job vacancy number
(202) 786-6297

National Archives and Records Administration
Job information and vacancies
(800) 827-4898

National Science Foundation
Job information and vacancies
(800) 628-1487

Office of Personnel Management
Recorded message of information about jobs with the U.S. Government
(202) 606-2700

Peace Corps
Recorded message of information about activities, application procedures and job vacancies
(800) 424-8580 x214

U.S. Department of Labor (Labor)
Recorded message about job information and vacancies
(800) 366-2753

Labor/Employment and Training Administration
Recorded message of information on Job Corps for Youths
(800) 733-JOBS
(800) 628-2888

Labor/Women's Bureau
Technical information and papers regarding workforce quality
(800) 827-5335

U.S. Navy
Naval recruitment and opportunities
(800) 327-NAVY

Energy

Nuclear Regulatory Commission (NRC)
Recorded message announcing Nuclear Reactor Regulations meetings
(301) 492-7424

U.S. Department of Energy (Energy)
Department of Energy Local Public Document Rooms
(800) 638-8081

Energy
Conservation and renewable energy information, publications and referrals
(800) 523-2929

Energy
Energy; appropriate technology assistance service and conservation information
(800) 428-2525; (800) 428-1718 (Montana)

Energy/Bonneville Power Administration
Activated when there is a news breaking item (i.e., power failures, rate changes, etc.)
(800) 223-7883; (800) 272-3373 Oregon only

Energy/Federal Energy Regulatory Commission (FERC)
FERC Hotline Enforcement Task Force: Complaints or questions concerning gas and electric power companies or to report violations of FERC regulations
(202) 208-1390

Energy/Federal Energy Regulatory Commission (FERC)
FERC Daily Issuance Hotline: Recorded message of FERC documents and orders issued daily
(202) 208-0555

Energy/National Energy Information Center
Information, research and orders for publications
(202) 586-8800

Environment

Center for Hazardous Material Research
Waste reduction and minimization information
(800) 826-5320 (Pennsylvania); (800) 334-2467 Pennsylvania

Chemical Manufacturers Association
Chemical spills, explosions, etc., emergency response assistance
(800) 424-9300

Chemical Manufacturers Trade Association
Referrals for health and safety information on industrial chemicals
(800) CMA-8200; (202) 887-1315 in DC

Environmental Protection Agency (EPA)/Small Business Ombudsman Hotline
Asbestos handling and abatement in schools, home and workplace information and assistance to small businesses in complying with regulations
(800) 368-5888; (703) 557-1938 in Washington, DC

Environmental Protection Agency (EPA)
Chemical spills; community planning and procedural information
(800) 535-0202; (202) 479-2449 in Washington, DC

Environmental Protection Agency (EPA)
Dioxin information for contaminated areas in Missouri
(800) 892-5009

Environmental Protection Agency (EPA) Headquarters, Washington, DC
EPA/Hazardous Waste Ombudsman assistance on hazardous waste issues
(202) 415-9361

Environmental Protection Agency (EPA)
Resource Conservation and Recovery Act and the Comprehensive Environmental Response, Compensation and Liability Act information and requests for documents (Superfund)
(800) 424-9346; (202) 382-3000 in Washington, DC

Environmental Protection Agency (EPA)
Safe drinking water information
(800) 426-4791; (202) 260-7908 in Washington, DC

Environmental Protection Agency (EPA)
Toxic Substances Control Act regulations and asbestos program information
(202) 554-1404

Environmental Protection Agency program information by region:
Region I (CT, MA, VT, NH, RI)
Hazardous Waste Ombudsman . . . . (617) 565-3420
Small Business Ombudsman . . . . (617) 860-4300
Unleaded Fuel Hotline . . . . (800) 631-2700 in MA
(800) 821-1237 in other Region I states

Region II (NY, NJ, Puerto Rico and Virgin Islands)
Hazardous Waste Ombudsman . . . . (212) 264-2980
RCRA Hotline . . . . (800) 732-1223
Small Business Ombudsman . . . . (212) 264-4711
Superfund Hotline . . . . (800) 346-5009

Region III (Washington, DC; DE, MD, PA, VA, WV)
Hazardous Waste Ombudsman . . . . (215) 597-0982

Be patient. If any phone number is incorrect, call (area code) 555-1212 and request the new listing.

Information Starting Places

Small Business Ombudsman . . . . (215) 597-9817
Waste Minimization Hotline . . . . (800) 334-2467 in PA
(800) 826-5320 in other Region 3 states

Region IV (AL, FL, GA, KN, MS, NC, SC, TN)
General Number . . . . (800) 282-0239 in GA
(800) 241-1754 in other Region 4 states
Hazardous Waste Ombudsman . . . . (404) 347-7109
Small Business Ombudsman . . . . (404) 347-7109

Region V (IN, MI, IL, MN, OH, WI)
General Number . . . . (800) 572-2515 in IL
(800) 621-8431 in other Region 5 states

Region VI (AK, LA, NM, OK, TX)
Environmental Emergency Hotline--24 hours . . . . (214) 655-2222
Hazardous Waste Ombudsman . . . . (214) 655-6765
Small Business Ombudsman . . . . (214) 655-6570

Region VII (NE, IA, KS, MO)
Action Line for IA, MO, and NE residents: . . . . (800) 223-0425
Action Line for KS residents only: . . . . (800) 221-7749

Region VIII (CO, MT, ND, SD, UT, WY)
General Number . . . . (800) 759-4372
Hazardous Waste Ombudsman . . . . (303) 294-1111
Small Business Ombudsman . . . . (303) 294-1111

Region IX (AZ, CA, HI, NV, Guam, Samoa, Northern Mariana Islands, Palau, Micronesia, and Marshall Islands)
Hazardous Waste Ombudsman . . . . (415) 744-1730
RCRA Hotline . . . . (415) 744-2074
Small Business Ombudsman . . . . (415) 744-1635
Superfund Hotline . . . . (415) 744-2356

Region X (WA, OR, ID, AS)
(800) 424-EPA-4

EPA/Center for Environmental Research Information
To order EPA research reports
(513) 569-7562

EPA Institute
Clearinghouse for all EPA training activities
(202) 260-6678

EPA/Radon Office
Information on radon issues
(202) 260-9617

National Pesticide Telecommunications Network (EPA and Texas Tech University)
Pesticide information on safe use and effects
(800) 858-7378; OR (806) 743-3091 in Texas

National Small Flows Clearinghouse
Information on wastewater treatment technologies for small communities
(800) 624-8301

Nuclear Regulatory Commission
Recorded message announcing DOE/NRC meetings on waste management
(301) 492-7424

U.S. Department of Agriculture
Rural Information Center Hotline
(800) 633-7701

U.S. Department of Agriculture/Soil Conservation Service
Information on conserving soil and water resources and on volunteering
(800) THE SOIL

U.S. Department of the Interior/Mineral Management Service-Pacific Regional Office
For information about Outer Continental Shelf oil and gas exploration off California
(805) 389-7502

Interior/Office of Surface Mining Reclamation and Enforcement
Eastern Support Center
Emergency response number regarding abandoned land mines
(412) 937-2146

U.S. Department of Transportation/Coast Guard
To report adverse environmental acts (oil spills, etc.) by boats
(800) 424-8802; (202) 426-2675 in Washington DC

Wetlands Protection Hotline
Provides you with information on wetlands and their protection
(800) 832-7828

Firearms and Explosives

U.S. Department of the Treasury/Alcohol, Tobacco and Firearms Administration
Firearms, explosives, and licensing information
(800) 366-5423

Treasury/Alcohol, Tobacco and Firearms Administration
To report stolen or missing explosives
(800) 800-3855; (202) 927-7777 in DC

Fraud Hotlines

(see Whistleblower Hotlines)

Government

Bureau of National Affairs
Online access to Daily Tax Report and Daily Congressional and Presidential Calendar
(800) 862-4636

Executive Office of the President
Recorded message of information on White House tours
(202) 456-7041

Executive Office of the President
Recorded message of information on tours of the Old Executive Office Building
(202) 395-5895

Federal Election Commission
Political candidates and committees finance records
(800) 424-9530

Federal Information Centers
For information about Federal services, programs, and regulations:
Eastern time zone: . . . . (800) 347-1997
Central time zone: . . . . (800) 366-2998
Mountain time zone: . . . . (800) 359-3997
Pacific time zone: . . . . (800) 726-4995
Alaska: . . . . (800) 729-8003
Hawaii: . . . . (800) 733-5996

National Archives and Records Administration/Office of the Federal Register
Information on documents (regulations, etc.) published in the *Federal Register*
(202) 523-6641; (202) 523-5229 (TTY)

Office of Press Secretary
Recorded message of President's daily schedule
(202) 456-2343

Recorded message of First Lady's daily schedule
(202) 456-6269

Office of the Special Counsel
To report prohibited personnel practices, political activities and other violations by federal and certain state/local employees
(800) 872-9855

President's Voice on Current Issues/White House News
White House Press office actualities line (recorded message)
(800) 424-9090

Be patient. If any phone number is incorrect, call (area code) 555-1212 and request the new listing.

Hotlines

State legislatures, status, copies, etc., of bills:

Delaware . . . . (800) 282-8545
Florida . . . . (800) 342-1827
Georgia . . . . (800) 282-5803
Illinois . . . . (800) 252-6300
Maryland . . . . (800) 492-7122
Montana . . . . (800) 333-3408
Nebraska . . . . (800) 742-7456
New Jersey . . . . (800) 792-8630
New York . . . . (800) 342-9860
Ohio . . . . (800) 282-0253
South Carolina . . . . (800) 922-1539
Washington . . . . (800) 563-6000
West Virginia . . . . (800) 362-9696
Wisconsin . . . . (800) 362-9696

U.S. Congress
Recorded messages of floor votes on legislation:

U.S. House of Representatives
Democratic Cloakroom
(202) 225-7400
Republican Cloakroom
(202) 225-7430

U.S. Senate
Democratic Cloakroom
(202) 224-8541
Republican Cloakroom
(202) 224-8601

U.S. Department of the Treasury/Financial Management Services
To report lost or stolen Federal Government checks
(202) 874-8400

The White House Office
To comment on any subject
(202) 456-1111

The White House Office
Information on obtaining greeting cards from the President
(202) 456-2724

White House Switchboard
To transfer to another White House telephone line
(202) 456-1414

National Archives and Records Administration
Recorded message on visitors information
(202) 501-5000

Handicapped Services and Information

American Council of the Blind
Legislation affecting and resource materials for the blind
(800) 424-8666; (703) 467-5081 in Virginia

American Foundation for the Blind
Referral service
(800) 232-5463

Blind Children's Center
Nursery School, infant to age 5, in Los Angeles, California
(800) 222-3566; (800) 222-3567 in California

Clearinghouse on the Handicapped
Handicapped in Washington, DC; publications and referrals
(202) 732-1245

Coordinating Council for the Handicapped
Information and referrals
(312) 939-3513

Deafness Research Foundation
Information and referrals
(800) 535-3323

Devereux Foundation
Residential treatment in 11 states for emotionally disturbed, retarded or

autistic individuals
(800) 345-1292

Federation of the Handicapped
Referrals and training program for the handicapped
(212) 206-4250

Foundation for the Blind
Referral services
(800) 232-5463; (212) 620-2147 in New York

Gallaudet Library
Information about library holdings
(202) 651-5216 TTY only; (202) 651-5217 voice and TTY

Guide Dog Foundation for the Blind
Free guide dogs for the blind
(800) 548-4337

Heath Resource Center
Post-secondary education for people with disabilities
(800) 544-3284; (202) 939-9320 in Washington, DC

Information Center for Individuals with Disabilities
Information and referrals for the disabled
(617) 727-5540

Information, Protection and Advocacy Center for Handicapped Individuals
Assistance, special education and training programs for handicapped and mentally ill
(202) 547-8081

Institute of Logopedics
Residential school in Wichita, Kansas, for multiple-handicapped children
(800) 835-1043

Job Accommodation
Information/consulting referral service for accommodating people with disabilities in the workplace
(800) 526-7234; (800) 526-4698 in West Virginia; (800) 526-2262 in Canada

Library of Congress/National Library for the Blind
Provides books and tapes to individuals with sight disabilities
(800) 424-8567; (202) 707-5100

Massachusetts Commission for the Blind
Job counseling and job referral services
(800) 392-6450 (voice); (800) 392-6556 (TDD), Boston office
(800) 332-2772 (voice and TDD), Springfield office

National Association for Hearing and Speech Action Line
Consumer hearing and speech hotline
(800) 638-8255; (301) 897-0039 in HI, AR, MD

National Center for Youth with Disabilities
Information including database searches for adolescents
(800) 333-NCYD

National Down Syndrome Congress
Information and publications
(800) 232-6372

National Down Syndrome Society Hotline
Publications, information about educational, respite and research grants programs
(800) 221-4602; (212) 460-9330 in New York

National Hearing Aid Society Hearing Aid Helpline
Assistance in locating qualified hearing instrument specialists, consumer information kit, referrals for financial assistance
(800) 521-5247; (313) 478-2610 in Michigan

National Information Center for Children and Youth with Handicaps
Locating services for the handicapped and information on learning disabilities
(800) 999-5599

Information Starting Places

National Information Clearinghouse for Infants with Disabilities and Life-Threatening Conditions
Referral service for ill or seriously disabled infants
(800) 922-9234

National Information System for Health Related Services
Information regarding children born with disabilities
(800) 922-9234

National Institute on Disability and Rehabilitation Research
Research grants to individuals or institutions providing equipment to individuals with disabilities
(202) 732-1134

National Organization on Disability
Information and publications
(800) 248-ABLE

National Rehabilitation Information Center (NARIC)
Information and referral on disability and rehabilitation
(800) 346-2742

Tripod/Grapevine
Information and referral service regarding deafness in children
(800) 352-8888 voice and TDD; (800) 2-TRIPOD voice and TDD;
(800) 346-8888 in California

U.S. Department of Education/American Printing House for the Blind
Information on publications regarding the blind
(800) 223-1839

Education/Clearinghouse for the Disabled
Information, publications and referrals
(202) 732-1241

Health

Aerobics and Fitness Foundation
Information on diet and exercise
(800) BE FIT 86

AIDS Clinical Trials Information Service
Information on federally and privately sponsored clinical trials
(800) TRIALS-A

Al-Anon Family Group Headquarters
Information and counseling for family and children of alcoholics
(800) 356-9996

Alcoholism and Drug Addiction Treatment Center
(McDonald Center, La Jolla, California)
(800) 382-4357

Alcohol and Drug Information, National Clearinghouse
Publications, posters and referrals
(800) 729-6686

Allergy and Asthma Information Line
Publications and referrals
(800) 822-ASMA

Alzheimer's Disease Education Center
Information packets and referrals
(800) 438-4380

AMC Cancer Information and Counseling Line of the National Cancer Institute
Information, publications, nursing and counseling services
(800) 525-3777

American Academy of Pediatrics
Although primarily an association for pediatricians, also is an advocacy center for children
(800) 433-9016

American Association of Poison Control Centers
For information on accidental ingestion of chemicals, poisons or drugs
(unless otherwise noted, toll-free numbers are valid only within each state):

Alabama:
Children's Hospital of Alabama - Regional Poison Control Center, Birmingham
(800) 292-6678

Arizona:
Arizona Poison and Drug Information Center, Tucson
(800) 362-0101
Samaritan Regional Poison Center, Phoenix
(602) 253-3334

California:
Fresno Regional Poison Control Center
(800) 346-5922
Los Angeles County Medical Association Regional Poison Control Center
(800) 77-POISN
San Diego Regional Poison Center
(800) 876-4766
San Francisco Bay Area Regional Poison Control Center
(800) 523-2222
UCDMC Regional Poison Control Center, Sacramento
(800) 342-9293

Colorado:
Rocky Mountain Poison and Drug Center, Denver
(800) 332-3073

District of Columbia:
National Poison Control Center Hotline (Georgetown University Hospital, Washington, DC)
(202) 625-3333; (202) 784-4660 (TTY)

Florida:
Florida Poison Information Center, Tampa
(800) 282-3171

Georgia:
Georgia Poison Control Center, Atlanta
(800) 282-5846 (also valid outside Georgia); (404) 525-3323 (TTY)

Indiana:
Indiana Poison Center, Indianapolis
(800) 382-9097

Kentucky:
Kentucky Regional Poison Center of Kosair, Louisville
(800) 722-5725

Maryland:
Maryland Poison Center, Baltimore
(800) 492-2414

Massachusetts:
Massachusetts Poison Control System, Boston
(800) 682-9211

Michigan:
Poison Control Center, Children's Hospital of Michigan, Detroit
(800) 462-6642; (800) 356-3232 (TTY)

Minnesota:
Hennepin Regional Poison Center
(612) 347-3141; (612) 337-7474 (TTY)
Minnesota Regional Poison Center
(800) 222-1222

Missouri:
Cardinal Glennon Children's Hospital Regional Poison Center, St. Louis
(800) 392-9111; (800) 366-8888; (314) 577-5336 (TTY)

Montana:
Rocky Mountain Poison and Drug Center, Denver, Colorado
(800) 525-5042

Nebraska:
Mid-Plains Poison Control Center, Omaha
(800) 642-9999 (NE only); (800) 228-9515 (surrounding states)

Be patient. If any phone number is incorrect, call (area code) 555-1212 and request the new listing.

Hotlines

New Jersey:
New Jersey Poison Information and Education System, Newark
(800) 962-1253

New Mexico:
New Mexico Poison and Drug Information Center, Albuquerque
(800) 432-6866

New York:
Long Island Regional Poison Control Center, East Meadow
(516) 542-2323
New York City Poison Control Center, New York, NY
(212) 340-4494; (212) POISONS

Nevada:
Rocky Mountain Poison and Drug Center, Denver, Colorado
(800) 446-6179 for Las Vegas

Ohio:
Central Ohio Poison Center, Columbus
(800) 682-7625; (614) 228-2272 (TTY)
Regional Poison Control System, Cincinnati Drug and Poison Information Center
(800) 872-5111

Oregon:
Oregon Poison Center, Portland
(800) 452-7165

Pennsylvania:
Delaware Valley Regional Poison Control Center, Philadelphia
(215) 386-2100
Pittsburgh Poison Center
(412) 681-6669

Rhode Island:
Rhode Island Poison Center - Rhode Island Hospital, Providence
(401) 277-5727

Texas:
North Texas Poison Center, Dallas
(800) 441-0040
Texas State Poison Center, Galveston
(409) 765-1420; [(800) 392-8548--medical professionals only]

Utah:
Intermountain Regional Poison Control Center, Salt Lake City
(800) 456-7707

West Virginia:
West Virginia Poison Center, Charleston
(800) 642-3625

Wyoming:
Rocky Mountain Poison and Drug Center, Denver, Colorado
(800) 442-2702

American Cancer Society
Information, publications and referrals
(800) ACS-2345 (within each state with a divisional office)

American Cleft Palate Association
Publications and referrals
(800) 24-CLEFT

American Diabetes Association
Information and publications
(800) ADA-DISC; (703) 549-1500 in Virginia and Washington, DC

American Kidney Fund
Publications, information and financial assistance
(800) 638-8299

American Liver Foundation
Information and referrals
(800) 223-0179; (201) 256-2556

American Mental Health Fund
Call to receive brochure
(800) 433-5959; (800) 826-2336 in IL

American Paralysis Foundation
Spinal Cord Injury Hotline
Information, counseling and referral service
(800) 526-3456

American Parkinson Disease Association
Information and referrals to doctors and hospitals
(800) 223-2732

American Schizophrenia Association
To receive information packet
(800) 847-3802

American Sudden Infant Death (SIDS) Institute
Clinical research, educational seminars and treatment facilities
(800) 232-SIDS; (800) 847-7437 in Georgia

American Society of Plastic and Reconstructive Surgeons
Referral service
(800) 635-0635

American Trauma Society
Publications and information
(800) 556-7890; (301) 925-8811 in Maryland

Amyotrophic Lateral Sclerosis Association
Information, publications and referrals
(800) 782-4747

Arthritis Foundation
Information and referrals
(800) 283-7800

ASPO/Lamaze (American Society for Psychoprophylaxis in Obstetrics)
Information regarding certification of educators and class referrals
(800) 368-4404

Better Hearing Institute
Information and educational publications
(800) EAR-WELL; (703) 642-0580 in Virginia

Birth Control Care Center
Information, referrals and treatment
(800) 255-7889

Brookdale Center on Aging
Technical assistance program for instituting a respite program for individuals with Alzheimers
(800) 648-COPE

Bulimia Anorexia Crisis Intervention Hotline
Counseling, 24 hours a day
(800) 762-3334

Bulimia Anorexia Self-Help Line
Information and counseling
(800) 227-4785

Children's Hospice International
Referral network
(800) 242-4453

Clearinghouse on Child Abuse and Neglect Information
Publications and information on child abuse
(800) FYI-3366

Cooley's Anemia Foundation
Publications and referrals
(800) 221-3571; (212) 598-0911 in New York

Cornelia de Lange Syndrome Foundation
Supportive education and referrals for families with children with Cornelia de Lange syndrome

Be patient. If any phone number is incorrect, call (area code) 555-1212 and request the new listing.

Information Starting Places

(800) 223-8355; (203) 693-0159 in Connecticut
(800) 753-2357 in Canada

Cystic Fibrosis Foundation
Publications and referrals
(800) 344-4823; (301) 951-4422 in Maryland

Deafness and Other Communication Disorders, National Institute on Deafness
Publications and referrals
(800) 241-1044

Drug Free Workplace Helpline
Publications and referrals to corporations, businesses and organizations
(800) 843-4971

Drug Abuse, Information on
NIDA
(800) 662-HELP

Eldercare Hotline
Referrals to local resources nationwide
(800) 677-1116

Endometriosis Foundation
Leave name/address on recorded message to get information
(800) 992-ENDO; (414) 355-2200 in Wisconsin

Epilepsy Foundation of America
Information
(800) EFA-1000; (301) 459-3700 in Maryland

Facial Plastic Surgery Information Service
To receive information packet
(800) 332-FACE (USA); (800) 523-FACE (Canada)

Foundation Center
Information on foundations and types of grants they provide
(800) 424-9836

Hill-Burton Hospital Free Care
Information on hospitals and other health facilities with provide free care
(800) 638-0742; (800) 492-0539 (in Maryland)

Homeless and Mental Illness, National Resource Center on
Information about services for homeless and mentally ill population
(800) 444-7415

Hospice Education Institute Hospicelink
Referral network
(800) 331-1620; (203) 767-1620 in Connecticut

Human Growth Foundation
Information regarding physical growth disorders in children
(800) 451-6434

Huntington's Disease Society of America
Information Line
(800) 345-4372; (212) 242-1968 in New York

Joseph and Rose Kennedy Institute of Ethics National Reference Center for Bioethics Literature
Free online searches of database on bioethic research
(800) MED-ETHX

Juvenile Diabetes Foundation
Information, publications and volunteer programs
(800) JDF-CURE; (212) 889-7575 in New Jersey

Liberty Godparents Home
Pregnancy counseling services, maternity home, continuing education for teenagers and referrals
(800) 368-3336

The Living Bank
Organ donor registry and referral service
(800) 528-2971

Lung Line National Asthma Center
Information and publications on immune system and respiratory disorders
(800) 222-5864; (303) 355-LUNG in Denver

Lupus Foundation of America
For free information packet
(800) 558-0121

March of Dimes Birth Defects Foundation
Health services grants to individuals or institutions
(914) 428-7100

Mercer Center for Eating Disorders
Information and counseling
(800) 33-ABTEC; (301) 332-9800 in Maryland

Minority Health Resource Center, Office of
Publications, referrals and assistance
(800) 444-6472

Myasthenia Gravis Foundation
Patient and professional literature and grants for research
(800) 541-5454

Names Project
Orders for "Common Threat," a documentary on the AIDS quilt
(800) USA-NAME

National AIDS Hotline (funded by Centers for Disease Control)
AIDS information
(800) 342-AIDS; (800) 344-SIDA (Spanish);
(800) AIDS-TTY (Hearing Impaired)

National AIDS Information Clearinghouse
AIDS publications, posters, databases, videos
(800) 458-5231

National Association for Sickle Cell Disease
Publications and referrals
(800) 421-8453; (213) 936-7205 in California

National Child Safety Council
Safety materials for children
(800) 222-1464

National Eye Care Project Helpline
Assistance/care for the elderly
(800) 222-EYES

National Foundation for Depressive Illness
Information on recorded message
(800) 248-4344

National Foundation for Ileitis and Colitis
Free brochures, counseling, doctor referrals and support groups
(800) 343-3637

National Headache Foundation
Information and publications
(800) 843-2256; (800) 523-8858 in Illinois

National Health Information Clearinghouse
To obtain publications on health, such as those contained in *Healthfinder series* and referrals to laser surgery experts
(800) 336-4797

National Hepatitis Hotline of the American Liver Foundation
Information regarding tests, availability of vaccines, etc.; physicians referral service
(800) 223-0179

National Hospice Organization
Referral and information helpline on hospices
(800) 658-8898

National Information Center for Orphan Drugs and Rare Diseases
Referrals to rare disease organizations and information and application

Be patient. If any phone number is incorrect, call (area code) 555-1212 and request the new listing.

Hotlines

status regarding orphan drugs
(800) 456-3505

National Institute for Occupational Safety and Health Information
Publications/database searches on occupational safety and health, including hazards associated with fetal development and pregnancy and list of cancer-causing products
(800) 35-NIOSH

National Kidney Foundation
Information regarding organ and tissue donation
(800) ACT-GIVE

National Library of Medicine
Information and reference database searches on publications from 1913 and audiovisuals from 1970
(800) 272-4787

National Lymphedema Network
Information and referrals
(800) 541-3259

National Multiple Sclerosis Society
(800) 227-3166 for information; (800) 624-8236 for free information packet

National Native American AIDS Prevention Center/Indian AIDS Hotline
Information on AIDS and AIDS prevention
(800) 283-AIDS

National Neurofibromatosis Foundation
To receive information packet
(800) 323-7938; (212) 460-8980 in New York

National Parkinson Foundation
Information and neurologists referrals
(800) 327-4545; (800) 433-7022 in Florida; (305) 547-6666 in Maine

National Rehabilitation Information Center (NARIC)
Information and referral on disability and rehabilitation
(800) 34-2742

National Retinitis Pigmentosa Foundation
To receive information packet
(800) 638-2300

National Reyes' Syndrome Foundation
Information and referrals
(800) 233-7393; (800) 231-7393 in Ohio

National Safety Council
Recorded message of information and to leave name/address to receive publications
(800) 621-7619

National Sexually Transmitted Diseases Resource Center
Information, publications and referrals
(800) 227-8922

National Spinal Cord Injury Association
Information and referrals
(800) 962-9629

National Sudden Infant Death Syndrome (SIDS) Foundation
Publications, information and referrals
(800) 221-SIDS

National Tuberous Sclerosis Association
Research, information and referrals
(800) 225-6872; (301) 459-9888 in Maryland

Neurological Disorders and Stroke, National Institute of
Information and referrals
(800) 352-9424

Occupational Hearing Service
Hearing/screening test by telephone
(800) 222-EARS; (800) 345-EARS in Pennsylvania

Organ Donor Hotline
Information
(800) 24-DONOR

Orton Dyslexia Society
Information and referrals
(800) ABCD-123; (301) 296-0232 in Maryland

Parkinson's Education Program
(714) 250-2975 for information and referrals; (800) 344-7872 for free information packet

PMS Access
Information packet, referrals, and pharmacy
(800) 222-4767

AIDS, ARC and HIV Infection
Information packet and newsletter on experimental drugs for AIDS, ARC and HIV infection
(800) 822-7422; (800) 334-7422 (in California)

Recovery of Male Potency
Information and publications
(800) 835-7667; (313) 357-1216 in Detroit, Michigan

Sarcoidosis Family Aid and Research Foundation
Information, publications, research
(800) 223-6429

Shriner's Hospital Referral Line
(800) 237-5055; (800) 282-9161 in Florida

Simon Foundation
Information regarding loss of bladder control
(800) 23-SIMON

Spina Bifida Information and Referral
Publications, information and referrals
(800) 621-3141; (301) 770-7222 in Maryland

Sturge-Weber Foundation
Literature, Support Services and education on Sturge-Weber syndrome
(800) 627-5482

Suicide and Rape 24-Hour Emergency Services of the Humanistic Mental Health Foundation
Crisis hotline, residential treatment programs, financial assistance
(800) 333-4444

Terri Gotthelf Lupus Research Institute
Information, publications, referrals, research grants
(800) 82-LUPUS

Tourette Syndrome Association
To receive information packet
(800) 237-0717

United Scleroderma Foundation
Information and publications
(800) 722-HOPE; (408) 728-2202 in California

U.S. Department of Agriculture
Food safety information and to report illness from meat, poultry or eggs
(800) 535-4555; (202) 447-3333 in Washington, DC

U.S. Department of Health and Human Services (HHS)
Health information referral service
(800) 336-4797

HHS/Centers for Disease Control
AIDS: Recorded message on number of cases, deaths, and distribution among age groups
(404) 332-4555

HHS/Centers for Disease Control
AIDS: Recorded message on distribution of total cases among

Be patient. If any phone number is incorrect, call (area code) 555-1212 and request the new listing.

Information Starting Places

transmissions categories and among male and female adults, adolescents and children
(404) 332-4555

HHS/Centers for Disease Control
AIDS: Recorded message on ten states with highest number of cases, current public health service estimates of HIV infections and projections of cases and deaths by 1992
(404) 332-4555

HHS/Food and Drug Administration
Reporting of problems with drugs and medical devices by health professionals
(800) 638-6725; (301) 881-0256 in Maryland (call collect)

HHS/Food and Drug Administration
Food and drugs; complaints and advice on emergencies
(202) 443-1240; (202) 857-8400 weekends and holidays

HHS/Health Care Financing Administration
Referral service for second surgical opinions
(800) 638-6833; (800) 492-6603 in Maryland

HHS/National Institutes of Health/National Cancer Institute
Cancer information and publications
(800) 4-CANCER; (808) 524-1234 in Hawaii

HHS/Office of Minority Health Resource Center
Information, publications and database searches
(800) 444-6472

HHS/Social Security Administration
Information on retirement, survivor, disability, medicare and SSI benefits
(800) 234-5772

U.S. Department of Labor/Mine Safety and Health Administration
For reporting health and safety hazards
(703) 557-2020

Women's Spots Foundation
Information packet, educational travel and training grants for individual athletes
(800) 227-3988; (212) 972-9170 in New York

Y-Me Breast Cancer Support and Information
Counseling services and publications
(800) 221-2141; (708) 799-8228 in Illinois

Housing, Real Estate and Home Improvement

Cooperative Extension Service Headquarters throughout the USA, which provide home and garden assistance, information, and education:

Amherst, Massachusetts . . . . (413) 545-4800
Athens, Georgia . . . . (706) 542-3824
Auburn, Alabama . . . . (205) 844-4444
Baton Rouge, Louisiana . . . . (504) 388-6083
Blacksburg, Virginia . . . . (703) 231-6705
Bozeman, Montana . . . . (406) 994-4371
Brookings, South Dakota . . . . (605) 688-4792
Burlington, Vermont . . . . (802) 656-2980
Clemson, South Carolina . . . . (803) 656-3382
College Park, Maryland . . . . (301) 853-4746
College Station, Texas . . . . (409) 845-7967
Columbia, Missouri . . . . (314) 882-7754
Columbus, Ohio . . . . (614) 292-4067
Corvalis, Oregon . . . . (503) 737-2713
District of Columbia . . . . (202) 576-6993
Durham, New Hampshire . . . . (603) 862-1520
Fargo, North Dakota . . . . (701) 237-8944
Fairbanks, Alaska . . . . (907) 474-7246
Fort Collins, Colorado . . . . (303) 491-6281
Gainesville, Florida . . . . (904) 392-1761
Honolulu, Hawaii . . . . (808) 956-8234
Ithaca, New York . . . . (607) 255-2237
Kingston, Rhode Island . . . . (401) 792-2474
Knoxville, Tennessee . . . . (615) 974-7114
Kolonia, Pohnpei, Micronesia . . . . (691) 320-2728
Lansing, Michigan . . . . (517) 355-2308
Laramie, Wyoming . . . . (307) 766-5124
Las Cruces, New Mexico . . . . (505) 646-3016
Lincoln, Nebraska . . . . (402) 472-2966
Little Rock, Arkansas . . . . (501) 373-2575
Lexington, Kentucky . . . . (606) 257-4772
Logan, Utah . . . . (801) 750-2200
Madison, Wisconsin . . . . (608) 262-3786
Mangilao, Guam . . . . (617) 734-9162
Manhattan, Kansas . . . . (913) 532-7137
Mayaguez, Puerto Rico . . . . (809) 834-4040
Mississippi State, Mississippi . . . . (601) 325-3036
Morgantown, West Virginia . . . . (304) 293-5691
Moscow, Idaho . . . . (208) 885-6639
Newark, Delaware . . . . (302) 831-2504
New Brunswick, New Jersey . . . . (201) 932-9306
Oakland, California . . . . (510) 686-2565
Orono, Maine . . . . (207) 581-3186
Pullman, Washington . . . . (509) 335-2933
Raleigh, North Carolina . . . . (919) 515-2811
Reno, Nevada . . . . (702) 784-6611
St. Croix, Virgin Islands . . . . (809) 778-0246
Saint Paul, Minnesota . . . . (612) 624-2703
Saipan, Marianas . . . . (670) 234-9022
Stillwater, Oklahoma . . . . (405) 744-5398
Storrs, Connecticut . . . . (203) 486-2917
Tucson, Arizona . . . . (602) 621-7209
University Park, Pennsylvania . . . . (814) 865-2541
Urbana, Illinois . . . . (217) 333-2660

Federal National Mortgage Association (Fannie Mae)
Information on accessing Fannie Mae's mortgage network
(800) 752-6440

Resolution Trust Corporation
Real estate information and inventory of houses acquired from failed savings and loan companies
(800) 431-0600

State housing assistance program information for the following states:
Maine . . . . (800) 452-4668
Minnesota . . . . (800) 652-9747
Vermont . . . . (800) 287-VHFA

U.S. Department of Agriculture/Economic Research Service
To order database on Foreign Owned Agricultural Land (No. 87015)
(800) 999-6779

U.S. Department of Housing and Urban Development (HUD)
Fair housing information or complaints regarding housing discrimination
(800) 669-9777

U.S. Department of Housing and Urban Development (HUD)
Home Equity Conversion Reverse Mortgage Programs, drug information, searchable database, publications, etc.
(800) 245-2691; (301) 251-5154 in Maryland

U.S. Department of the Treasury/Office of Thrift Supervision
Recorded message of indexes used to compute mortgage rates
(202) 906-6494

Immigration

U.S. Department of Justice/Immigration and Naturalization Service
Recorded message of information on visas, passports, family fairness policy, permanent residency status, etc.
(202) 514-4316

Immigration-Related Unfair Employment Practices Hotline
To report employment problems
(800) 255-7688

Amnesty Program/Legislation General Information
To find out information regarding the process to request amnesty or become a legal immigrant
(800) 777-7700

Hotlines

Insurance

Federal Crime Insurance
Insurance coverage for robbery and burglary
(800) 638-8780; (301) 251-1660 in Washington, DC

Hill-Burton
Information on free or low cost health care, complaints about facilities or denial of treatment due to medicare/medicaid coverage
(800) 638-0742; (800) 492-0359 in Maryland

Office of Personnel Management/Office of Retirement and Insurance Policy
Recorded message of information on federal employees special benefits
(202) 606-0777

U.S. Department of Defense/Civilian Health and Medical Program of the Uniformed Services
Information regarding benefits
(303) 361-3907 or 3707

Veterans Administration
Information on CHAMPVA, medical benefits for dependents of disabled veterans or veterans whose death was service-related
(800) 733-8387

Veterans Administration
GI life insurance information
(800) 669-8477

Veterans Administration
To contact your VA regional offices
(800) 827-1000

International Organizations

Peace Corps
Recorded message of information about activities, application procedures and job vacancies
(800) 424-8580 x214

Judicial System

Administrative Office of the U.S. Courts
Recorded message regarding pending legislation affecting the courts
(202) 786-6297

U.S. Supreme Court
Information on dockets and activities
(202) 479-3011

U.S. Department of Justice
To report hate crimes
(800) 347-HATE

Maps

Federal Emergency Management Agency
To order maps showing flood-prone areas
(800) 358-9616

U.S. Department of Defense/Defense Mapping Agency
Guidance on obtaining maps and charts of the Defense Mapping Agency
(800) 826-0342

U.S. Geological Survey
To order maps: Antarctic, moon and planets, land use, photoimage, etc.
(800) USA-MAPS

U.S. Department of the Interior/National Park Service
Civil War troop movement maps
(303) 969-2130

Maritime

St. Lawrence Seaway Ship Arrival
Recorded message of shipping schedule
(315) 769-2422

U.S. Department of Transportation (DOT)/Coast Guard
Boating safety information, complaints or violations and referrals to local CG offices for subscriptions to *Local Notice to Mariners*
(800) 368-5647

U.S. Department of Transportation (DOT)/Coast Guard
Coast Guard Auxiliary public education courses
(800) 336-BOAT; or (800) 245-BOAT in Virginia

U.S. Department of Transportation (DOT)/Coast Guard
To report adverse environmental acts (oil spills, etc.) by boats
(800) 424-8802; (202) 426-2675 in Washington, DC

U.S. Department of Transportation (DOT)/Coast Guard
To report hazardous conditions, drug smuggling or improper boarding
(800) 323-7233

Money and Coins

American Eagle
To receive a free regional edition buyer's guide to U.S. mint and eagle coins
(800) USA-GOLD

Professional Ordering Service for Various Products
For information on obtaining Presidential Bicentennial Gold Coins
(800) 822-6500

U.S. Department of the Treasury/Bureau of Engraving and Printing
Recorded message of information on tours
(202) 874-3188

Patent and Trademark

U.S. Department of Commerce/Patent and Trademark Helpline
(703) 305-8747; (800) 888-8062 (Trademark Registration)

Pension Plans

Pension Benefits Guarantee Corporation
Recorded message of current interest rates on pension plans
(202) 778-8899

Tennessee Valley Authority (TVA)
Information regarding TVA retirement system
(800) 284-1309

Recreation

U.S. Department of Agriculture (USDA)/Forest Service
Reservations at National Forests
(800) 283-CAMP

U.S. Department of Agriculture (USDA)/Forest Service
Information and publications on wildlife, rangers, etc.
(202) 205-0947

U.S. Department of the Interior/National Park Service
Documents, prints of drawings, brochures, aerial photos, etc., on National Parks
(303) 969-2130

Senior Citizens Services

American Association of Retired Persons and state and Washington, DC governments
Free legal counsel for the elderly
(800) 622-2520; (800) 652-5997
(800) 252-5997; (202) 234-0970

National Eye Care Project Helpline
Assistance/care for the elderly
(800) 222-EYES

National Health Information Center
To order *Exercise for Older Americans* in *Healthfinder* series and *Healthy*

Be patient. If any phone number is incorrect, call (area code) 555-1212 and request the new listing.

Information Starting Places

Older People publications and program information
(800) 336-4797

National Technical Information Service
To order 30-page study entitled *Aging and Health Promotion: Market Research for Public Health*
(800) 553-NTIS

State agencies on aging for information on services, assistance and benefits:
Illinois . . . . (800) 252-8966
Maryland . . . . (800) 243-3425
Massachusetts . . . . (800) 882-2003; (800) 872-0166 TDD
Missouri . . . . (800) 392-0210 elderly abuse
(800) 235-5503 aging information and referrals
New Hampshire . . . . (800) 322-9191
Oregon . . . . (800) 232-3020 program monitoring
(800) 282-8096 administration of senior services (voice/TDD)
Texas . . . . (800) 252-9240

Social Services

Covenant House
Crisis counseling for adolescents, especially runaways and referrals
(800) 999-9999

Domestic Violence Hotline
Referral service for counseling, shelter, legal information, etc.
(800) 333-SAFE

Edna Gladney Center
Maternity home and adoption center
(800) 433-2922; (800) 772-2740 in Texas

Kevin Collins Foundation for Missing Children
Advice and immediate response to families of stranger-abducted children
(800) 272-0012

National Child Abuse Hotline
Information, counseling and referral service
(800) 422-4453

National Council on Child Abuse and Family Violence
Referral assistance, information and publications
(800) 222-2000

National Hotline for Missing Children
Reports from parents and law enforcement officers and sightings of missing children
(800) 843-5678

National Resource Center on Child Sexual Abuse
Child sexual abuse information, publications and training
(800) KIDS-006

Parents Anonymous Hotline
Referral service for treatment of child abuse
(800) 421-0353; (800) 352-0386 in California

Runaway hotline
With information, resources and message delivery for runaways and their parents
(800) 621-4000

Suicide and Rape 24-Hour Emergency Services of the Humanistic Mental Health Foundation
Crisis hotline, residential treatment programs, financial assistance
(800) 333-4444

Tough Love
Referral service for parents with problem children
(800) 333-1069

U.S. Department of Labor/Women's Bureau
Publications on childcare and work and family life
(800) 827-5335

Space

Smithsonian Institution
Recorded *Sky Watcher's Report* on stars and constellations
(202) 357-2000

Space and Rocket Center
Space Camp programs for children, adults, and educators
(800) 63-SPACE

Taxes

Internal Revenue Service/U.S. Department of the Treasury
To speak to a tax specialist for account-related information, to set up payment plans, etc.
(800) 829-1040

Internal Revenue Service
To order IRS forms
(800) 829-3676

Internal Revenue Service
IRS telephone assistance services for deaf taxpayers with TV/Telephone-TTY equipment
(800) 829-4059

Internal Revenue Service
Status of tax return and recorded topics
(800) 829-4477

State tax assistance numbers, which are toll-free only for the following states:
Connecticut . . . . (800) 321-7829
Delaware . . . . (800) 292-7826
Florida . . . . (800) 872-9909
Hawaii . . . . (800) 222-3229 (information)
(800) 222-7572 (forms)
Illinois . . . . (800) 732-8866 (information, forms)
(800) 624-2459 (forms during filing season)
Maine . . . . (800) 452-1903 (information)
(800) 338-5811 (forms)
Michigan . . . . (800) 877-MICH; (800) FORM-Z-ME
Minnesota . . . . (800) 652-1094 (personal)
(800) 657-3777 (corporate)
Nebraska . . . . (800) 422-4618 (personal)
(800) 742-7474 (corporate)
New Jersey . . . . (800) 323-4400
New York . . . . (800) 225-5829 (information)
(800) 443-3200 (refunds)
(800) 462-8100 (forms)
North Carolina . . . . (800) 222-9965 (information)
(800) 451-1404 (forms)
Ohio . . . . (800) 282-1780
West Virginia . . . . (800) 642-9016

Technology

National Small Flows Clearinghouse
Wastewater treatment technologies for small communities
(800) 624-8301

National Technical Information Service/U.S. Department of Commerce
To order publications on U.S. and foreign government technology, including medical technology
(800) 553-NTIS

Time

U.S. Naval Observatory
Recorded message giving the time (within milliseconds)
(202) 653-1800

Trade

Export-Import Bank
Export financing, marketing and insurance programs
(800) 424-5201; (202) 566-4423

Be patient. If any phone number is incorrect, call (area code) 555-1212 and request the new listing.

Hotlines

International Trade Commission
- To order ITC publications
- (202) 205-1807

International Trade Commission
- Petitions and complaints recording line
- (202) 205-2196

International Trade Commission
Trade Remedy Assistance Office
- Information regarding trade laws and help for small business with technical assistance
- (800) 343-9822

Overseas Private Investment Corporation
- Financing of overseas projects by U.S. investors
- (800) 424-6742

U.S. Department of Agriculture/Office of International Cooperation and Development
- Information/assistance/training for projects in developing countries and scientific exchanges with developed countries
- (202) 245-5796

U.S. Department of Commerce
- Leave message to have a trade specialist contact you
- (800) 343-4300

U.S. Department of Commerce
- Recorded message of Commerce Department news
- (202) 393-1847

U.S. Department of Commerce/Broadcast News Service
- Recorded message of information on foreign trade deficit, volume of imports, etc.
- (202) 393-4100

U.S. Department of Commerce/Bureau of Economic Analysis
- Recorded message of leading economic indicators with analysis and data for composite indexes
- (202) 898-2450

U.S. Department of Commerce/Bureau of Economic Analysis
- Recorded message of revised quarterly estimates of gross national products
- (202) 898-2451

U.S. Department of Commerce/Bureau of Economic Analysis
- Recorded message of personal income and outlays statistical information
- (202) 898-2452

U.S. Department of Commerce/Bureau of Economic Analysis
- Recorded message on merchandise trade, balance of payments basis or U.S. international transactions
- (202) 898-2453

U.S. Department of Commerce/Export Administration Bureau
- Information on export regulations, forms, commodity classifications and seminar program
- (202) 482-4811

U.S. Department of Commerce/International Trade Administration
- Small-to-medium sized businesses counseling number for assistance in export development
- (800) USA-TRADE

U.S. Department of the Treasury/Office of Foreign Assets Control
- Information on economic sanctions against Iraq, Libya, Nicaragua, Panama, South Africa, etc.
- (202) 622-2410

U.S. Trade Representative
- Recorded message on recent activities and regulation under section 301 of the Trade Act, 1974
- (202) 395-3871

Transportation

AMTRAK
- AMTRAK tickets or travel information
- (800) USA-RAIL

Transportation Network
- Transportation seminars, contracting information and transit services
- (800) 522-7786

U.S. Department of Transportation (DOT)
- Non-safety transportation complaints such as lost baggage
- (202) 366-2220

U.S. Department of Transportation (DOT)/Federal Aviation Administration
- To report possible safety or Federal Aviation Administration (FAA) Regulations violations
- (800) 255-1111

U.S. Department of Transportation (DOT)/Federal Aviation Administration
- Consumer complaints regarding carry-on baggage, aircraft security, child infant seat, aircraft and airmen verification and noise abatement
- (800) FAA-SURE

U.S. Department of Transportation (DOT)/National Highway Traffic Safety Administration
- Highway safety information and to report auto safety defects and recall information on autos manufactured in the past 10 years
- (800) 424-9393; 366-0123 in Washington, DC

Travel/Tourism

Nation's Capital Events Hotline
- Recorded message of activities at parks, embassies, etc.
- (202) PA4-0009

State Offices of Tourism; information about the following states:

State	Phone
Alabama	(800) ALABAMA
Connecticut	(800) 282-6863
Delaware	(800) 441-8846
Idaho	(800) 635-7820
Illinois	(800) ABE-0121
Louisiana	(800) 334-8626
Maryland	(800) MD-IS-FUN
Mississippi	(800) 647-2290
New Mexico	(800) 545-2040
North Dakota	(800) 437-2077
Ohio	(800) BUCKEYE
Oregon	(800) 547-7842
Rhode Island	(800) 556-2484
South Dakota	(800) 843-1930
West Virginia	(800) 225-5982

U.S. Congress
- Information on tours of the U.S. Capitol
- (202) 225-6827

U.S. Department of Health and Human Services/Centers for Disease Control
- Vaccination requirements, disease outbreaks, AIDS and the foreign traveler, etc., information
- (404) 332-4559

U.S. Department of State/Bureau of Consular Affairs (BCA/State)
- Citizens Emergency Center, which gives assistance to Americans traveling or arrested abroad
- (202) 647-5225

U.S. Department of State/Bureau of Consular Affairs (BCA/State)
- Information about visas
- (202) 647-0510

U.S. Department of State/Bureau of Consular Affairs (BCA/State)
- Information about passports
- (202) 647-0518

Be patient. If any phone number is incorrect, call (area code) 555-1212 and request the new listing.

Information Starting Places

Volunteerism

U.S. Geological Survey
Recorded message of information on "Volunteer for Science" program
(703) 648-7440

Weather

U.S. Department of Commerce/National Oceanic and Atmospheric Administration
National Climatic Data Center Archives on weather and data for the nation
(704) 259-0682

Whistleblower Hotlines

Unless otherwise noted, Whistleblower Hotlines are established as a means of reporting fraud, waste, abuse or mismanagement within a particular federal agency. The agencies with these hotlines are listed below:

Agency for International Development
(202) 875-4171

U.S. Department of Agriculture
(800) 424-9121; (202) 472-1388

Department of the Army
(800) 446-9000; (800) 572-9000 (VA); (202) 695-1578

U.S. Department of Commerce
(800) 424-5197

U.S. Department of Defense
To report fraud or corruption by employees of DOD contractors
(800) 424-9098

U.S. Department of Education
(800) 647-8733; (202) 755-2770

U.S. Department of Energy
(800) 541-1625; (202) 586-4073

Federal Bureau of Investigation
(202) 324-2901

U.S. Department of Health and Human Services
(800) 368-5779; (410) 965-5953

U.S. Department of Housing and Urban Development
(800) 347-3735; (202) 708-4200

U.S. Department of the Interior
(800) 424-5081

U.S. Department of Justice
(800) 869-4499; (202) 514-3435

U.S. Department of Labor
(800) 347-3756; (202) 219-5227

U.S. Department of State
(202) 647-3320

U.S. Department of Transportation
(800) 424-9071; (202) 366-1461

U.S. Department of Treasury
(800) 359-3898; (202) 622-1090

U.S. Department of Veterans Affairs
(202) 233-5394

Environmental Protection Agency
(202) 260-3000

Equal Employment Opportunity Commission
(202) 663-7020

General Accounting Office
To report fraud, waste, abuse or illegal acts within federal government
(202) 512-7470

General Services Administration
(800) 424-5210

Interstate Commerce Commission
(202) 275-7147

Merit Systems Protection Board
(800) 872-9855; (202) 653-7188

National Aeronautics and Space Administration
(800) 424-9183; (202) 755-3402

Navy Department
To report waste, fraud or abuse within Navy or by Navy contractors
(800) 522-3451

Office of Personnel Management
(202) 606-2423

Railroad Retirement Board
(800) 772-4258; (312) 751-4336

Social Security Administration
(800) 368-5779

Small Business Administration
(202) 205-6580

Tennessee Valley Authority
(800) 323-3835
(800) 423-3071 (Tennessee only); (615) 632-3550

Be patient. If any phone number is incorrect, call (area code) 555-1212 and request the new listing.

Recorded Messages

You'll find many other recorded messages in every chapter, particularly in Health and Medicine as well as Federal Jobs Banks in the Careers and Workplace Chapter. Dozens of taped information spots prepared by the Immigration and Naturalization Service are included in the Law and Social Justice Chapter.

Agriculture Department News	(202) 488-8358
Bicentennial Gold Coins	(800) 822-6500
Botanic Garden Upcoming Events	(202) 225-7099/8333
Career America Hotline	(912) 757-3000
Commerce Department News	(202) 393-1847
Consumer Price Index	(202) 606-7828
Consumer Product Safety Commission Investigations	(800) 638-CPSC
Current Labor Statistics	(202) 606-7828
Education Department Financial Aid	(800) 433-3243
Employment Lost Index	(202) 606-7828
Employment Situation Information	(202) 606-7828
Engraving and Printing	(202) 874-3188
Federal Communications Commission	(202) 632-7000
Federal Employees Retirement Information	(202) 606-0400
Federal Job Information Center	(202) 606-2700
Federal Trade Commission Meetings	(202) 326-2711
Geological Survey Volunteers	(703) 648-7440
Gross National Product	(202) 898-2451
Immigration and Naturalization	(202) 307-1501
Labor Department News	(202) 606-7828
Leading Economic Indicators	(202) 898-2450
Merchandise, Trade, and Equipment Transactions	(202) 898-2453
Nation's Capital Events Hotline	(202) PA 4-0009
Naval Academy	(800) 638-9156
Nuclear Regulatory Commission Rules	(301) 492-7424
Peace Corps	(800) 424-8580
Pension Plans and Interest Rates	(202) 778-8899
Personal Income and Outlays	(202) 898-2452
President's Daily Schedule	(202) 456-2343
President's Voice on Current Issues	(800) 424-9090
Producer Price Index	(202) 606-7828
Public Debt	(202) 874-4000
Public Health Corps Scholarships	(800) 638-0824
Radon Hotline	(800) SOS-RADON
Savings Bonds	(202) 447-1775
SBA Answer Desk	(800) 827-5722
Smithsonian Dial-A-Museum	(202) 357-2020
Smithsonian Skywatchers Report	(202) 357-2000
St. Lawrence Seaway Ship Arrival	(315) 769-2422
Time (within milliseconds)	(202) 653-1800
Thrift Supervision	(202) 906-6988
Treasury Bills	(202) 874-4000
US House of Representatives Floor Votes	
Democratic Cloakroom	(202) 225-7400
Republican Cloakroom	(202) 225-7430
US International Transactions Weekend Preview	(202) 393-4102
US Senate Floor Votes	
Democratic Cloakroom	(202) 224-8541
Republican Cloakroom	(202) 224-8601

Be patient. If any phone number is incorrect, call (area code) 555-1212 and request the new listing.

Consumer Power General Sources

* *See also Investments and Financial Services Chapter*
* *See also Agriculture and Farming Chapter*
* *See also Health and Medicine*

When you find yourself the victim of an unfair business practice, you don't have to sit there and feel helpless. This chapter includes a wide variety of programs that offer information and advice on consumer complaints such as mail fraud, deceptive advertising, and warrantee enforcement. You'll find answers to consumer questions on everything from tanning salons to funeral practices. You should also see the Expert Chapter for subject specific experts on all kinds of consumer issues.

★ Advertising Practices
Federal Trade Commission (FTC)
Advertising Practices
6th and Pennsylvania Ave., NW
Washington, DC 20580 (202) 326-3131

This division of the FTC promotes the distribution of truthful information to the public through law enforcement and oversight activities in the following areas: 1) General advertising for deceptive claims at the national and regional level. 2) Advertising claims for food and over-the-counter drugs, particularly claims relating to safety or effectiveness. 3) Tobacco advertising, which includes monitoring for unfair practices or deceptive claims, implementing cigarette and smokeless tobacco labeling laws, and reporting to Congress on cigarette and smokeless tobacco labeling, advertising, and promotion. 4) Performance and energy-savings claims for solar products, furnaces, window coverings, room heaters, wood burning products, gas-saving products and motor oils, and other products featuring energy conservation. For more information about any of these programs, contact this office.

★ Advocacy Program
Federal Trade Commission
Bureau of Economics
6th and Pennsylvania Ave., NW
Washington, DC 20580 (202) 326-3429

Under the Advocacy Program, the FTC's three bureaus--Economics, Competition, and Consumer Protection--present comments to other Federal agencies concerning the effect of regulation on competition and consumers. Some recent studies have analyzed the effect of state entry regulation on retail automobile markets, certificate of need regulation in the health care field, and consumer information regulations in the insurance industry. For more information on these and other advocacy program studies, contact this bureau.

★ Air Travelers' Rights and Complaints
Consumer Affairs Division
Intergovernmental and Consumer Affairs
Governmental Affairs
Office of the Secretary of Transportation
U.S. Department of Transportation
400 7th Street, SW
Washington, DC 20590-0001 (202) 366-2220

If your problem cannot be resolved directly with the airline, contact this office for information on air travelers' rights and for assistance in resolving problems with airlines and charter flights. Complaints about delayed or canceled flights, reservations, lost baggage, smoking, refunds, and overbooking can also be handled here.

★ Alcohol, Tobacco, and Firearms Information
Communications Center
Bureau of Alcohol, Tobacco, and Firearms
U.S. Department of the Treasury
650 Massachusetts Ave.

Washington, DC 20226 (202) 927-7777

This Center functions as a 24 hours a day, seven days a week clearinghouse for those seeking assistance from the Bureau of Alcohol, Tobacco, and Firearms.

★ Alcohol, Tobacco, and Firearms: Laws and Regulations
Superintendent of Documents
Government Printing Office
Washington, DC 20402 (202) 927-3238

The *Alcohol, Tobacco, and Firearms Quarterly Bulletin* announces all new laws, regulations, codes, and rulings or changes related to alcohol, tobacco, and firearms. The subscription price is $13 per year (S/N 748-001-00000-0).

★ Automobile Fuel Economy
Motor Vehicle Requirements Division
Office of Market Incentives
Rulemaking
National Highway Traffic Safety Administration (NHTSA)
U.S. Department of Transportation
400 7th Street, SW
Room 5320
Washington, DC 20590 (202) 366-0486

NHTSA issues fuel economy standards and collects information on the technological and economic capabilities of automobile manufacturers to maximize fuel efficiency. Contact this office for information and referrals.

★ Auto Safety Hotline
Office of Defects Investigation (NEF-10)
National Highway Traffic Safety Administration
U.S. Department of Transportation
400 7th Street, SW
Room 5326 (800) 424-9393
Washington, DC 20590 (202) 366-0123

This toll-free hotline is accessible in all 50 states, Puerto Rico, and the Virgin Islands. Consumers may call to report automobile safety problems or to request information on recalls, defects, investigations, child safety seats, tires, drunk driving, crash test results, seat belts, air bags, odometer tampering, and other related topics. Staff will also make referrals to state and other agencies. Also ask about the New Car Assessment Program (NCAP), which provides comparable data on the frontal crashworthiness of selected new vehicles.

★ Buying By Phone
Federal Trade Commission (FTC)
Enforcement Division
6th and Pennsylvania Ave., NW
Washington, DC 20580
Recording for orders or complaints (202) 326-3768

The FTC receives complaints indicating that businesses and other organizations have problems with some telephone solicitors who use illegal tactics to make sales or send unordered merchandise. For more information about these illegal

Be patient. If any phone number is incorrect, call (area code) 555-1212 and request the new listing.

solicitors, often called "WATS-line hustlers" because they use long-distance phone lines, contact your local FTC office, or the office above.

* Care Labeling

Federal Trade Commission (FTC)
Marketing Practices
6th and Pennsylvania Ave., NW
Washington, DC 20580 (202) 326-3034

Under the FTC's Care Labeling Rule concerning textile clothing, a care label must be attached to most clothing--except articles that are used to primarily to cover or protect the head and hands--giving care instructions. For more information on the Care Labeling Rule and your rights, or to report clothing you have purchased that has no care label attached, contact the FTC.

* Consumer Affairs

Office of Consumer Affairs (OCA)
U.S. Department of Health and Human Services
Washington, DC 20201 (202) 634-4140

The OCA is responsible for providing the President and federal agencies with advice and information regarding the interests of American consumers. The OCA encourages and assists in developing new consumer programs; makes recommendations to improve federal consumer programs; cooperates with state agencies and voluntary organizations in advancing consumer interests; promotes improved consumer education; recommends legislation and regulations to help consumers; and encourages the exchange of ideas among industry, government, and consumers. *The Consumer's Resource Handbook* and *Consumer Information Catalog* are available free from Consumer Information Center, P.O. Box 100, Department 635H, Pueblo, CO 81009, or by calling (719) 948-4000.

* Consumer Affairs - International

Commercial, Legislative and Business Affairs
Bureau of Economic and Business Affairs
U.S. Department of State
2201 C St., NW
Room 6822
Washington, DC 20520 (202) 647-1942

This office monitors developments in international consumer affairs and coordinates U.S. participation in international organizations dealing with consumer affairs policy.

* Consumer Complaint Letters to the FTC

Federal Trade Commission (FTC)
Correspondence Branch
6th and Pennsylvania Ave., NW
Washington, DC 20580

Letters from consumers are very important to the work of the FTC. They are often the first indication of a problem in the marketplace and may provide the initial evidence to begin an investigation. Although the FTC is not authorized to resolve individual consumer complaints, it can act when it sees a pattern of possible law violations. If you have witnessed an incidence of unfair trade practice, write a letter to the FTC to help them determine if any federal action is warranted.

* Consumer Information Catalog

Catalog
Pueblo, CO 81009

Published quarterly, *The Consumer Information Catalog* includes a descriptive listing of approximately 200 booklets from a variety of federal agencies. The publications cover health, federal benefits, money management, housing, child care, employment, small business, education, food and nutrition, consumer protection, and more. Some booklets are free and some are available at cost. The Center also has a list of over 100 booklets available free in Spanish. They include a variety of subjects such as health, money management, children, federal benefits, and more. To obtain a copy, write to LISTA, Pueblo, CO 81009. Here is a brief list of some of the subjects you will find:

Auto

Nine Ways to Lower Your Auto Insurance
Recycling Used Oil

Children

Becoming a Nation of Readers: What Parents Can Do
TV With Books Completes the Picture

Parenting

Growing Up Drug Free
When Parents Divorce

Employment

Tips for Finding the Right Job
What You Should Know About the Pension Law

Federal Programs

Guide to Health Insurance for People with Medicare
Medicare Q and A
Understanding Social Security

Food and Nutrition

Food Additives

Health

Getting the Lead Out
Rx to OTC
Getting a Second Opinion

Housing

A Home of Your Own
Homebuyer Guide to Environmental Hazards

Money

Consumer Credit Handbook
Managing Money Throughout Life
Investment Swindles...How They Work and How to Avoid Them
Fraud By Phone
Swindlers are Calling

Sources of Assistance

Getting Information from FDA
U.S. Government TDD Directory
Your Right to Federal Records

* Consumer Information Center

Pueblo, CO 81009 (202) 501-1794

The Consumer Information Center (CIC) was established in 1970 to help federal agencies and departments release consumer information they wish to bring to the public's attention and to help build public awareness and use of this information. CIC is a separately funded operation located in the General Services Administration, and it is under the policy guidance of the Special Adviser to the President for Consumer Affairs. CIC has a small staff of consumer information specialists available on a selected basis to speak at or participate in national conferences. CIC's exhibit, which includes free catalogs, is also available for major conferences.

* Consumer Information Media Hotline

Pueblo, CO 81009 (202) 501-1794

Members of the Consumer Information Center (CIC) media staff are ready to help reporters research consumer stories and can put reporters in touch with contacts who will answer questions directly.

* Consumer Publications

Federal Trade Commission (FTC)
Public Reference Branch
Room 130
6th and Pennsylvania Ave., NW
Washington, DC 20580 (202) 326-2222 - Recording

The following publications are available free of charge by visiting the FTC in person, but if that is not possible, the FTC will send you any of them free of charge except those marked with an asterisk (*), which are available for $.50 from the Consumer Information Center, Pueblo, CO 81009.

About Fine Jewelry*
Art Fraud
Bargain Jewelry

Be patient. If any phone number is incorrect, call (area code) 555-1212 and request the new listing.

Consumer Power

Buying By Phone
Buying Native American Jewelry
Care Labels: Caring For Your Clothes
Consumer Alert: Investing In Rare Coins
Consumer Guide to the FTC Funeral Rule
Consumer Quiz
Contest Cons
Dollars for Dancing
Door to Door Sales
Eye Care
Eyeglasses
Franchise and Business Opportunities
Generic Drugs
Health Claims: Separating Fact From Fiction
Health Questions: How To Talk To and Select Physicians, Pharmacists, Dentists, and Vision Care Specialists
Health Spas: Exercise Your Rights
How To Buy A Manufactured Home*
How To Write A Wrong: Complain Effectively And Get Results
Indoor Tanning*
Job-Hunting: Should You Pay?
Layaway Purchase Plans
Real Estate Brokers
Service Contracts
Shopping by Mail
Shopping by Phone and Mail
Smart Buying for Young Consumers
Telemarketing Travel Fraud*
Telephone Investment Fraud
Unordered Merchandise
Vacation Time Sharing Tips
Warranties
What's New About Care Labels
Work-At-Home Schemes
Your Home, Your Choice: A Workbook For Older People and Their Families*

Automobile
Automatic Transmission Repair*
Car Rental Guide
Car Ads: Low Interest Loans and Other Offers
Consumer Guide to Vehicle Leasing*
General Motors Consumer Mediation/Arbitration Program
New Car Buying Guide
Volkswagen Consumer Mediation/Arbitration Program

Consumer Financing
Escrow Accounts For Home Mortgages
Building A Better Credit Record: What To Do, What To Avoid*
Buying and Borrowing: Cash In On The Facts*
Consumer Handbook on Adjustable Rate Mortgages
Cosigning A Loan
Credit and Charge Card Fraud
Credit and Older Americans
Credit Billing Errors? Use FCBA
Credit Practices Rule
Electronic Banking
Equal Credit Opportunity
Fair Credit Reporting
Fair Credit Reporting Act
Fair Credit Billing
Fair Debt Collection
Fix Your Own Credit Problems and Save Money
Getting a Loan: Your Home As Security
Home Equity Credit Lines*
Income Tax Preparation Services
Lost or Stolen: Credit and ATM Cards
Money Matters: How To Talk To and Select Lawyers, Financial Planners, Tax Preparers, and Real Estate Brokers
Mortgage Money Guide*
Refinancing Your Home
Second Mortgage Financing
Scoring for Credit
Solving Credit Problems
Using Plastic: A Young Adult's Guide To Credit Cards
Women and Credit Histories

* Crashworthiness: Air Bags, Child Seats, Helmets, Seat Belts

Office of Crashworthiness Research (NRD-10)
Research and Development
National Highway Traffic Safety Administration
U.S. Department of Transportation
400 7th Street, SW
Washington, DC 20590 (202) 366-4862

Research is conducted on vehicle crashworthiness and crash avoidance. To determine how drivers and passengers fare in head-on collisions, information is collected on seat belts, air bags, child safety restraints, motorcycle helmets, fuel systems, rearview mirrors, tires, door locks, seats, bumpers, and school busses. The annual publication, *Federal Motor Vehicle Safety Standards and Regulations*, is available for $134 (S/N 950-031-00000-0) from the Government Printing Office, Superintendent of Documents, Washington, DC 20402; (202) 783-3238. New Car Assessment Program information on selected models is available from the Auto Safety Hotline: (800) 424-9393.

* Essential Air Service

Office of Aviation Analysis
Policy and International Affairs
Office of the Secretary of Transportation
U.S. Department of Transportation
400 7th Street, SW, Room 6401
Washington, DC 20590 (202) 366-5903

The Department's Essential Air Service Program ensures that certain cities will be served by air transportation. The program establishes subsidy levels, selects carriers, processes applications to change service levels, and reviews fitness of carriers. Contact the office listed for information about this program.

* Explosives/Stolen Weapons Hotline

Explosives Enforcement Branch
Bureau of Alcohol, Tobacco, and Firearms (ATF)
U.S. Department of the Treasury
650 Massachusetts Ave. (202) 927-7930
Washington, DC 20226 (202) 927-7777

Those with information on a major arson incident or bombing, or those aware of stolen/lost weapons or explosives, may call the above hotline. One of four national response teams will be rushed to the scene within 24 hours. A report will be taken by those answering the phone, and the information will be transferred to the nearest agent in the area. Each of the four response teams is composed of 10 special agents, a forensic chemist, and an explosive specialist from ATF's Explosives Technology Branch. A state or local law enforcement or fire service official can request the services of a National Response Team by contacting an ATF Special Agent in charge at one of 22 strategic office locations throughout the United States:

Atlanta, GA: (404) 331-6526
Birmingham, AL: (205) 731-1205
Boston, MA: (617) 565-7042
Brentwood, TN: (615) 736-5412
Charlotte, NC (704) 371-6125
Dallas, TX: (214) 767-2250
Detroit, MI: (313) 226-4830
Houston, TX: (713) 229-3511
Kansas City, MO: (816) 374-7188
Los Angeles, CA: (213) 894-4812
Louisville, KY: (502) 582-5211
Miami, FL: (305) 536-4368
Middleburg Heights, OH: (216) 522-7210
Nashville, TN: (615) 736-7879
New Orleans, LA: (504) 589-2048
New York, NY: (212) 264-4657
Oak Brook, IL: (312) 620-7824
Philadelphia, PA: (215) 597-7266
San Francisco, CA: (415) 974-9589
Seattle, WA: (206) 442-4485
St. Louis, MO: (314) 425-5560
St. Paul, MN: (612) 290-3092
Washington, DC: (703) 285-2543

Be patient. If any phone number is incorrect, call (area code) 555-1212 and request the new listing.

General Sources

* Eye Care

Federal Trade Commission (FTC)
Service Industry Practices
6th and Pennsylvania Ave., NW
Washington, DC 20580 (202) 326-3303

Under the FTC Rule, an eye care specialist is required to provide you with your eyeglass prescription, immediately after the examination, so that you can then comparison shop for eye glasses. The specialist, however, is not required to provide you with your contact lens fitting specifications. For more information on eye care products and services and your consumer rights, contact the FTC.

* Firearms and Explosives

Licensing Center
Bureau of Alcohol, Tobacco and Firearms
U.S. Department of the Treasury
650 Massachusetts Ave.
Washington, DC 20226 (800) 366-5423

This office provides license information.

* Firefighting, Prevention, and Forest Fires Bibliography

Superintendent of Documents
Government Printing Office
Washington, DC 20402 (202) 783-3238

Fire safety publications are listed, including improving the fire safety of cigarettes and the effect of cigarettes on the ignition of furnishings. Free.

* Funeral Rule

Federal Trade Commission (FTC)
Bureau of Consumer Protection
6th and Pennsylvania Ave., NW
Washington, DC 20580 (202) 326-3128

Each year Americans arrange more than two million funerals for family and friends, and the FTC has developed a trade regulation rule concerning funeral industry practices to enable consumers to obtain information about funeral arrangements. For a free brochure on the funeral rule, including price disclosures, embalming information, and cremation, contact this FTC office.

* Gangs, Guns, Drugs...Had Enough

Bureau of Alcohol, Tobacco and Firearms
U.S. Department of the Treasury
650 Massachusetts Ave.
Washington, DC 20226 (800) ATF-GUNS

Information is accepted at this office regarding illegal use, buying or selling of firearms. Any suspicious gang activity may also be reported here. If you wish, information may be given anonymously.

* General Motors Consumer Mediation Program

Federal Trade Commission (FTC)
Enforcement Division
6th and Pennsylvania Ave., NW
Washington, DC 20580 (202) 326-3027

Under the terms of a 1983 FTC order, all owners of General Motors (GM) cars and light trucks with engine or transmission problems have an opportunity to get money back spent on repairs, or to get repairs by GM at no charge. For a free handbook about this mediation/arbitration program, call (800) 824-5109, or contact the FTC for a free fact sheet outlining your rights.

* Geologic Hazards

Geologic Inquiries
U.S. Geological Survey
911 National Center
Reston, VA 22092 (703) 648-4380

This division evaluates environmental hazards which are associated with earthquakes, volcanoes, floods, droughts, toxic materials, landslides, subsidience, and other ground failures. Methods of hazards prediction are developed through the study of the Earth's internal structure. Engineering problems are identified and solved, including problems in the selection of sites for power stations, highways, bridges, dams, and hazardous waste disposal.

* Grape Wine Label Information

Distribution Center
Bureau of Alcohol, Tobacco, and Firearms
U.S. Department of the Treasury
7943 Angus Ct.
Springfield, VA 22153 (703) 455-7801

The free brochure, *What You Should Know About Grape Wine Labels*, describes the elements written on a label for grape wine and what can be learned from the label. These include brand, vintage date, varietal designations, alcohol content, appellation of origin, viticultural area, name or trade name, and estate bottled.

* Health and the Environment

American Council on Science and Health
1995 Broadway, 2nd Floor
New York, NY 10023-5860 (212) 362-7044

The American Council on Science and Health (ACSH) is a consumer education association providing the public with scientifically balanced evaluations of food, chemicals, the environment and health. Publications: *ACSH News and Views, Inside ACSH, ACSH Media Update.*

* Health Fraud

Federal Trade Commission (FTC)
Bureau of Consumer Protection
6th and Pennsylvania Ave., NW
Washington, DC 20580 (202) 326-3128

Each year billions of consumer dollars are wasted on useless remedies and devices. This FTC office can provide you with information on how to spot worthless, fraudulent claims involving products which "cure" arthritis, cancer, weight loss, cellulite, baldness, and much more.

* Health Spa Complaints

Federal Trade Commission
Bureau of Consumer Protection
6th and Pennsylvania Ave., NW
Washington, DC 20580 (202) 326-3319

The most frequent complaints about health spas concern high pressure sales tactics, misrepresentations about facilities and services, and spas that go out of business. This office can provide you with information about your rights or how to file a complaint.

* Interstate Bussing, Trucking, Railroad Complaints

The Interstate Commerce Commission has three regional offices which serve a variety of functions, one of which is to answer inquiries and assist the public with concerns regarding interstate bus, trucking, and railroad companies. The most frequent calls involve moving companies.

Eastern
Interstate Commerce Commission, 3535 Market St., Room 16400, Philadelphia, PA 19104; (215) 596-4040. States served: AL, CT, DE, DC, FL, GA, KY, MA, MD, ME, MS, OH, PA, NC, NH, NJ, NY, RI, SC, TN, VA, VT, WV.

Central
Interstate Commerce Commission, 55 W. Monroe, Suite 550, Chicago, IL 60603; (312) 353-6204. States served: AR, IA, IL, IN, KS, LA, MI, MO, MN, NE, ND, OK, SD, TX, WI.

Western
Interstate Commerce Commission, 211 Maine St., Suite 500, San Francisco, CA 94105; (415) 744-6520. States served: AK, AZ, CA, CO, ID, MT, NV, NM, OR, UT, WA, WY.

* Legal Action Against Companies

Federal Trade Commission (FTC)
Office of the General Counsel
6th and Pennsylvania Ave., NW
Washington, DC 20580 (202) 326-2481

During an investigation, the FTC staff may find reason to believe that an individual company has violated the law. If the case is not settled by a formal agreement with the company (a consent order), the FTC may decide to sue the company. Depending on the circumstances, the case will be tried before an administrative law judge or in federal court. The FTC may seek a cease and

Consumer Power

desist order, a preliminary or permanent injunction, consumer redress, or other appropriate relief.

* Loss and Damage of Cargo Claims

Office of Compliance and Consumer Assistance
Interstate Commerce Commission
12th St. and Constitution Ave., NW, Room 4412
Washington, DC 20423 (202) 927-5520

While the Commission does not have specific binding authority to adjudicate a dispute claim, it will render all possible assistance. There are several publications available to inform the consumer of his or her rights. *Loss and Damage Claims! Can You Collect?* provides the basic information on cargo claim problems. *Administrative Ruling 120* deals with concealed loss or damage claims. For a copy of these publications and further assistance, contact the Office of Compliance and Consumer Assistance.

* Marketing Practices

Federal Trade Commission (FTC)
Marketing Practices
6th and Pennsylvania Ave., NW
Washington, DC 20580 (202) 326-3128

This division of the FTC brings law enforcement actions with regard to unfair or deceptive marketing and warranty practices. Although the FTC is not authorized to resolve individual consumer complaints, it can act when it sees a pattern of possible law violations. Deceptive sales programs areas include the following: business opportunities, multi-level marketing plans, and pyramid sales schemes; business and office supply sales schemes; counterfeit goods; fraudulent health spa practices; health or safety risks or defects in major consumer products, such as cars; rebate coupon problems; travel clubs or coupons and vacation certificates; and vacation timesharing or campground plans. This division also enforces actions regarding warranties, franchising rules, and funeral rules. For more information on these or other advertising issues, contact this office.

* Maximum Speed Limit

Police Traffic Services Division
Office of Enforcement and Emergency Services
Traffic Safety Programs
National Highway Traffic Safety Administration
U.S. Department of Transportation
400 7th Street, SW, Room 6124
Washington, DC 20590 (202) 366-5440

The National Maximum Speed Limit is 65 miles per hour on certain interstate highways. This office processes annual certifications of maximum speed limit enforcement programs throughout the U.S. and assists states in developing and improving enforcement efforts.

* Meat and Poultry Hotline

Food Safety and Inspection Service
U.S. Department of Agriculture
Washington, DC 20250 (800) 535-4555

This service takes calls from consumers on cases of meat or poultry food poisoning or complaints about meat or poultry spoilage due to improper packaging or processing. They can also provide you with health-oriented information on safe handling and storage of meats and poultry.

* Moving

Office of the Secretary
Interstate Commerce Commission
12th St. and Constitution Ave., NW
Washington, DC 20423 (202) 927-5520

When You Move: Your Rights and Responsibilities is a pamphlet your mover gives you to provide information about your rights and responsibilities as a shipper of household goods. It includes information on estimates, contracts, weight of shipment, pick-up and delivery, notification of charges, and payments. Also included is a section on filing of loss or damage claims.

* Moving and Trucking Complaint and Performance Data

Office of Compliance and Consumer Assistance
Interstate Commerce Commission (ICC)
12th St. and Constitution Ave., NW

Washington, DC 20423 (202) 927-5520

Among the many consumer-oriented services of the ICC is a series of advisory bulletins alerting the public and prospective transportation users of the existence of certain transportation problems, and of a regulation requiring household goods carriers to furnish an information bulletin to each prospective customer. You may obtain these advisories by calling or writing this office.

* News Releases From FTC

Federal Trade Commission (FTC)
Office of Public Affairs (OPA)
6th and Pennsylvania Ave., NW
Washington, DC 20580 (202) 326-2178

This office provides information to the public through the media. It issues news releases on all significant Commission actions, responds to reporters' inquiries and arranges television, radio, and print interviews for FTC officials. OPA also issues a weekly calendar of Commission events and a weekly summary of press releases, called *News Notes*, which are available to the public. To be placed on the mailing list for *News Notes*, contact this office. Weekly Calendar: Call (202) 326-2711 on Monday mornings for current weeks' activities.

* Odometer Tampering

Odometer Fraud Staff
Office of Chief Counsel
National Highway Traffic Safety Administration (NHTSA)
U.S. Department of Transportation
400 7th Street, SW, Room 5219
Washington, DC 20590 (202) 366-9511

Federal law requires that the seller of a car sign a disclosure statement that the mileage on the odometer is accurate and has not been rolled back. NHTSA enforces the odometer law via inspections and criminal charges. Information on odometer tampering is also available from the Auto Safety Hotline: (800) 424-9393.

* Postal Inspection Service

Inspection Service Department
U.S. Postal Service
475 L'Enfant Plaza, SW
Washington, DC 20260-2100 (202) 268-4267

As the law enforcement arm of the Postal Service, The Postal Inspection Service protects the mails, postal funds, and property; investigates internal conditions and needs that may affect postal security and effectiveness; apprehends those who violate the postal laws; and audits financial and nonfinancial operations. Information on past and present schemes used to defraud the public is available as well. Help is available if you experience difficulty with a company or suspect that you have been the victim of mail fraud. There is a Regional Chief Inspector in each of the five postal regions. Information and complaints of postal violations should be presented to the nearest Postal Inspector in charge.

Central Region

Chicago
Main Post Office Bldg., Chicago, IL 60607-5401; (312) 765-4605
433 W. Van Buren St., Chicago, IL 60669-2201; (312) 765-4500

Denver
P.O. Box 329, Denver, CO 80201-0329; (303) 297-6220

Des Moines
P.O. Box 566, Des Moines, IA 50302-0566; (515) 253-9060

Detroit
P.O. Box 330119, Detroit, MI 48232-6119; (313) 226-8184

Indianapolis
7188 Lakeview Pkwy. W. Dr., Indianapolis, IN 46268-4101; (317) 327-2500

Kansas City
3101 Broadway, Suite 850, Kansas City, MO 64111-2416; (816) 932-0400

Milwaukee
P.O. Box 788, Milwaukee, WI 53201-0788; (414) 291-2475

St. Louis
1106 Walnut St., St. Louis, MO 63199-2201; (314) 539-9300

Be patient. If any phone number is incorrect, call (area code) 555-1212 and request the new listing.

General Sources

St. Paul
P.O. Box 64558, St. Paul, MN 55164-2201; (612) 293-3202/3200

Eastern Region
Cynwyd
1 Bala Cynwyd Plaza, Bala Cynwyd, PA 19004-3509; (215) 668-4500

Baltimore
P.O. Box 1856, Baltimore, MD 21203-1856; (301) 347-4380

Charlotte
2901 I-85 S., Charlotte, NC 28228-3000; (704) 329-9120

Cincinnati
P.O. Box 14487, Cincinnati, OH 45250-0487; (513) 684-5700

Cleveland
P.O. Box 5726, Cleveland, OH 44101-0726; (216) 443-4000

Harrisburg
P.O. Box 3535, Harrisburg, PA 17105-3535; (717) 257-2330

Philadelphia
P.O. Box 7500, Philadelphia, PA 19101-9000; (215) 895-8450

Pittsburgh
1001 California Ave., Pittsburgh, PA 15290-9000; (412) 359-7900

Richmond
P.O. Box 25009, Richmond, VA 23260-5009; (804) 775-6267

Washington, DC
P.O. Box 96096, Washington, DC 20066-6096; (202) 636-2339/2300

Northeast Region
Newark
Gateway No. 2, McCarter Hwy. and Market St., Newark, NJ 07175-0001; (201) 621
5500
P.O. Box 509, Newark, NJ 07101-5901; (201) 596-5450

Boston
P.O. Box 2217, Boston, MA 02202-2217; (617) 654-5840

Buffalo
685 Ellicott Sq., Buffalo, NY 14203-2545; (716) 856-3674

Hartford
P.O. Box 2169, Hartford, CT 06145-2169; (203) 524-6060

New York
P.O. Box 5555, James Farley Bldg., New York, NY 10116-0555; (212) 330-3844

San Juan
P.O. Box 3667, San Juan, PR 00936-9614; (809) 749-7600/1-2-3

Southern Region
Memphis
10th Fl., 1407 Union Ave., Memphis, TN 38161-0001; (901) 722-7700
P.O. Box 3180, Memphis, TN 38173-0180; (901) 576-2137

Atlanta
P.O. Box 16489, Atlanta, GA 30321-0489; (404) 765-7369

Birmingham
P.O. Box 2767, Birmingham, AL 35202-2767; (205) 521-0270

Fort Worth
P.O. Box 162929, Fort Worth, TX 76161-2929; (817) 625-3411

Houston
P.O. Box 1276, Houston, TX 77251-1276; (713) 238-4400

Miami
P.O. Box 520772, Miami, FL 33152-0772; (305) 470-0379

New Orleans
P.O. Box 51690, New Orleans, LA 70151-1690; (504) 589-1200

Tampa
P.O. Box 22526, Tampa, FL 33622-2526; (813) 281-5200

Western Region
San Bruno
850 Cherry Ave., San Bruno, CA 94098-0100; (415) 742-4411

Oakland
7717 Edgewater Dr., Oakland, CA 94621-3013; (415) 636-2600

Pasadena
P.O. Box 2000, Pasadena, CA 91102-2000; (818) 405-1200

Phoenix
P.O. Box 20666, Phoenix, AZ 85036-0666; (602) 223-3660

Portland
Suite 790, 921 SW Washington, Portland, OR 97205-2898; (503) 294-2263

San Diego
P.O. Box 2110, San Diego, CA 92112-2110; (619) 233-0610

San Francisco
P.O. Box 882000, San Francisco, CA 94188-2000; (415) 550-5602/5700

Seattle
P.O. Box 400, Seattle, WA 98111-4000; (206) 442-6300

* Radon

Public Information Center
Environmental Protection Agency
401 M St., SW, PM-211 B
Washington DC 20460 (202) 260-2080

A Citizen's Guide to Radon helps readers understand the radon problem and decide if they need to take action to reduce radon levels in their homes. It explains what radon is, how it is detected, and what the results mean. Contact this office for your free copy.

* Reference Guides on Consumer Concerns

Science and Technology Division
Reference Section
Library of Congress
Washington, DC 20540 (202) 707-5580

Informal series of reference guides are issued free from the Science and Technology Division under the general title, *LC Science Tracer Bullet.* These guides are designed to help readers locate published material on subjects about which they have only general knowledge. New titles in the series are announced in the weekly Library of Congress *Information Bulletin* that is distributed to many libraries including:

80-14 Automotive Maintenance and Repair
80-18 Health Foods
81-6 Pets and Pet Care
81-9 Cable Television (Cable TV)

* Service Industry Practices

Federal Trade Commission (FTC)
Service Industry Practices
6th and Pennsylvania Ave., NW
Washington, DC 20580 (202) 326-3303

This FTC division focuses on deception and misrepresentation in the advertising of professional services. Law enforcement activities are directed toward restrictions on advertising and other business practices of professionals that may impede competition and consumer choice. Other activities include investigating investment schemes; monitoring industry standards and certification programs and the Retail Food Advertising and Marketing Practices Rule. Program areas

Be patient. If any phone number is incorrect, call (area code) 555-1212 and request the new listing.

Consumer Power

include advertising, eyeglasses, employment counseling services, health care services, and legal services. This division's current investment fraud investigations focus on gemstones, cellular phone lotteries, rare coins, and art. Contact this division for more information on any of these programs or investigations.

* Shopping By Mail

Federal Trade Commission (FTC)
Marketing Practices
6th and Pennsylvania Ave., NW
Washington, DC 20580 (202) 326-3128

Ordering merchandise by mail can be a convenient way to save time, energy, and sometimes money, but if your merchandise arrives late or not at all, you need to know your rights. The FTC can furnish you with information concerning the Mail Order Merchandise Rule, but to resolve a complaint against a company, contact your local Postmaster, your local consumer protection agency, or the Direct Marketing Association at 6 East 43rd St., New York, NY 10017.

* State Motor Vehicle Inspections

Records and Motor Vehicle Services Division (NTS-43)
National Highway Traffic Safety Administration (NHTSA)
U.S. Department of Transportation
400 7th Street, SW
Washington, DC 20590 (202) 366-2676

NHTSA's Motor Vehicle Inspection Program is aimed at providing car owners with preventive information on what repairs are needed to achieve greater safety, lower pollution, and better mileage. The annual *Study of the State Motor Vehicle Inspection Program* is available from this office.

* Telemarketing Travel Fraud

Federal Trade Commission
Marketing Practices
6th and Pennsylvania Ave., NW
Washington, DC 20580 (202) 326-3128

Have you ever been tempted to buy one of those bargain-priced travel packages sold over the telephone? Be careful. Your dream vacation may turn into a misadventure if you fall victim to one of the many travel scams being sold over the phone which are defrauding consumers out of millions of dollars each month. If you feel you are a victim of just such a scam, or you want information on how to avoid them, contact this office for their free brochure.

* Trade Regulation Enforcement

Federal Trade Commission (FTC)
Enforcement Division
601 Pennsylvania Ave., NW
Washington, DC 20580 (202) 326-2996

This division of the FTC monitors compliance with Commission orders and, along with the Regional Offices, enforces a number of trade regulations and specific laws. What follows is a brief listing of some of the FTC laws and regulations, along with the respective FTC expert in that area:

Appliance Labeling Rule, which requires the disclosure of energy costs of home appliances. James Mills, (202) 326-3035.

Cooling-Off Rule, which requires sellers to give consumers notice of their three-day cancellation rights for sales made away from the seller's place of business. George Brent Mickum, (202) 326-3131.

Games of Chance in the Food Retailing and Gasoline Industries Rule, which requires disclosure of the odds of winning prizes, the random distribution of the winning prize pieces, and the publication of the winners' names. John Mendenhall, Cleveland Regional Office, (216) 522-4210.

Negative Option Rule, which requires sellers who use negative option purchase plans, such as book and record clubs, to give members at least 10 days to reject the monthly selection. Suzanne Patch, (202) 326-2981.

Octane Posting and Certification Rule, which requires the posting of octane ratings on gasoline dispensers. Neil Blickman, (202) 326-3038.

R-value Rule, which requires sellers to disclose the thermal efficiency of home insulation. Kent Howerton, (202) 326-3013.

Used Car Rule, which requires dealers to post on each used car a "Buyers Guide" that gives information about the warranty coverage, tells the meaning of an "as is" sale, and suggests that consumers ask about getting an independent inspection before buying the car. George Brent Mickum, (202326-3131.

Fair Packaging and Labeling Act, which requires consumer commodities to be accurately labeled to describe the product's identity and net quantity. Bret Smart, Los Angeles Regional Office, (301) 575-7975.

Hobby Protection Act, which requires imitation coins, medals, and other monetary items to be marked "copy," and imitation political items to be marked with the year of manufacture. Robert Easton, (202) 326-3029.

Textile, Wool, and Fur Acts, which protect consumers against mislabeling, false advertising, and false invoicing of textile, wool, and fur products. Bret Smart, Los Angeles Regional Office, (301) 575-7975.

Amended Wool Products Labeling and Textile Fiber Products Identification Acts, which require all wool and textile items, domestic or imported, to be labeled with the country of origin. Steve Ecklund, (202) 326-3034.

Unordered Merchandise Statute, which permits consumers to keep, as a free gift, merchandise they received through the U.S. mail but did not order. Vada Martin, (202) 326-3002.

Made in USA, requires labeling and advertising to state country of origin. Steve Ecklund, (202) 326-3034.

* Transportation Issues

Office of Public Interest Groups
Intergovernmental and Consumer Affairs
Governmental Affairs
Office of the Secretary of Transportation
U.S. Department of Transportation (DOT)
400 7th Street, SW
Washington, DC 20590 (202) 366-1524

This office acts as a liaison between Congress, state and local governments, business and industry, and public interest groups to ensure that their needs are considered when Department policy decisions are made. Public and private organizations can contact this office to communicate needs and comment on DOT programs and regulations.

* Transportation Safety Institute

Transportation Safety Institute (DMA-60)
Research and Special Programs Administration
U.S. Department of Transportation
6500 South MacArthur Blvd.
Oklahoma City, OK 73169 (405) 680-3153

The Institute supports the Department's efforts to reduce transportation accidents. It develops and conducts training programs for Federal, state, and local governments; industry; and foreign personnel. Courses are offered in aviation, highway, marine, pipeline, and railroad safety; materials analysis; transportation security; and other subjects. Mail: P.O. Box 25082, Oklahoma City, OK 73125-5050.

* Vehicle Importation

Public Information Division
U.S. Customs Service
U.S. Department of the Treasury
P.O. Box 7407
Washington, DC 20044 (202) 927-6724

The pamphlet, *Importing a Car*, outlines the provisions for dutiable entry or free entry of automobiles, trucks, and motorcycles. Prior arrangements, documentation, safety and emissions standards, and federal tax guidelines are also discussed.

* Vehicle Manufacturer Safety Compliance

Vehicle Manufacturer Safety Compliance (NEF-30)
Enforcement
National Highway Traffic Safety Administration
U.S. Department of Transportation
400 7th Street, SW

Be patient. If any phone number is incorrect, call (area code) 555-1212 and request the new listing.

Washington, DC 20590 (202) 366-2832
To ensure that foreign and domestic vehicle and equipment manufacturers comply with federal motor vehicle safety standards, this office performs compliance testing, inspections, and investigations involving about 150 performance requirements and nearly 3000 equipment items.

* Vehicle Research and Testing

Vehicle Research and Test Center
Research and Development
National Highway Traffic Safety Administration (NHTSA)
U.S. Department of Transportation
P.O. BOX 37
East Liberty, OH 43319 (513) 666-4511
NHTSA evaluates the effectiveness of Federal Motor Vehicle Safety Standards. This engineering facility performs tests to obtain basic data used to establish standards for safety and fuel efficiency of motor vehicles.

* Volkswagen Consumer Mediation Program

Federal Trade Commission (FTC)
Bureau of Consumer Protection
6th and Pennsylvania Ave., NW
Washington, DC 20580 (202) 326-3022
Under the terms of a 1988 FTC order, Volkswagen has established a mediation program for all owners of Volkswagen of America or Audi cars and light trucks with engine problems. To find out more about whether you qualify to receive a

settlement for reimbursement for repairs, contact either the FTC, your local Better Business Bureau, or Volkswagen of America, Inc.

* Warranties

Federal Trade Commission (FTC)
Division of Marketing Practices
6th and Pennsylvania Ave., NW
Washington, DC 20580 (202) 326-3128
Although the FTC cannot intervene in individual disputes and does not handle private cases, the FTC does want to know if companies are meeting their warranty obligations. To report violations of the Warranty Act or warranty-related problems, or to request information concerning warranties in general, contact this office.

* Work-At-Home Schemes

Division of Marketing Practices
Federal Trade Commission (FTC)
6th and Pennsylvania Ave., NW
Washington, DC 20580 (202) 326-3128
Be careful about work-at-home ads--stuffing envelopes, assembling work, and others--especially ones that promise you large profits in a short period of time. While some of these plans are legitimate, many are not, and if you feel you've been taking advantage of, or if you'd like to know precautions to take against fraudulent schemes, contact the Better Business Bureau, your local Postmaster, your state's Attorney General's office, or the FTC.

Be patient. If any phone number is incorrect, call (area code) 555-1212 and request the new listing.

State Consumer Protection Offices

You are interested in investing in a company that sells educational courses to the public, but you want to know if they are getting any complaints about their sales practices. How can you find out? Or perhaps you are the manufacturer of a potato peeler which is sold with a warning against using the product on anything other than potatoes. Are you protected from a law suit brought against you by a consumer who cut his finger while using your potato peeler on an orange? On the consumer side, you may have a problem with a product or service, and the retailer has ignored your complaints or given you the run around. What are your rights? In any of these cases, you will probably need consumer protection advice, and quickly. Instead of hiring a high-priced consumer lawyer to solve your problems, contact your state Consumer Affairs Office, which can give you as much, if not more, of the information and advice you may need as the lawyer can give you, but for free.

The kinds of information available from these offices varies from state-to-state; however, most of them can help you with your inquiry or complaint. Aside from just handling complaints, many states publish valuable consumer information on their in-state companies. For example, Alabama will provide you with a listing of all companies that have gone out of business; Arkansas publishes a Buyer Beware List of companies that have been brought to court; New York and Iowa publish yearly reports naming companies that have had complaints filed against them; and Oklahoma and New Mexico release periodic press releases to warn the public of companies that have had court actions taken against them.

If you have yet to purchase a product and want to make sure that you don't get a lemon, state Consumer Offices can help you, too. Most states will provide some information by phone about companies that have had complaints filed against them in the state. Some states, however, require that you speak directly with the investigator assigned to the case, while in others your request must be in writing. Currently, the following states will provide listings of all companies that have had complaints filed against them: Alabama, Arkansas, Delaware, Maine, Maryland, Michigan, Vermont. And 18 states have toll free numbers for in-state consumers to file complaints or to search out information about whether a company has had complaints filed against it. Only five states--Colorado, Illinois, Nevada, Missouri, and West Virginia--do not provide any consumer protection information at all.

Most offices will advise you to take the following steps when lodging a complaint of your own. First, contact the retailer in person or by phone and let them know the nature of the problem. If that doesn't yield the proper response, take step two: write an angry letter that clearly states the problem, the date of purchase, a copy of the receipt, canceled check, or itemized charge bill, and what you would consider a fair and equitable settlement. If you still get no satisfactory response, contact the Consumer Affairs Office.

If you purchased an offending product in another state, start with that state's Consumer Affairs Office. Most offices offer a wide selection of information and educational materials, and most will be glad to answer your questions or direct you toward someone who can. But before you even start, it is very important that you have copies of any relevant sales receipts, other sales documents, and all correspondence between yourself and the retailer and/or manufacturer.

State Consumer Protection Offices

Alabama

Office of Attorney General, Consumer Protection Division, 11 South Union St., Montgomery, AL 36130; (205) 242-7334, (800) 392-5658. Information on a specific company can be obtained by writing to this office. A listing of complaints filed against a company as well as a listing of companies that have gone out of business can be obtained.

Alaska

The Consumer Protection Section in the Office of the Attorney General has been closed. Consumers with complaints are being referred to the Better Business Bureau. 3380 C Street, Suite 103, Anchorage, AK, 99503, (907) 562-0704.

Arizona

Financial Fraud Division, Office of Attorney General, 1275 W. Washington St., Phoenix, AZ 85007; (602) 542-3702, 542-5763, (800) 352-8431. Information on complaints on a specific company can be given over the phone. A listing of companies in their files with complete name, address and zip code is also available.

Arkansas

Consumer Protection Division, Office of Attorney General 200 Tower Bldg., 323 Center St., Little Rock, AR 72201; (501) 682-2341/TDD, (800) 482-8982. Information can be given over the phone on current lawsuits pending, or the names of companies who have failed to respond to a complaint after it has been issued. A Buyer Beware List is distributed, which informs consumers which companies have been brought to court.

California

State Department of Consumer Protection, 400 R St., Suite 1040, Sacramento, CA 95814; consumer information, (916) 445-1254; complaint assistant (916) 445-0660. Data is computerized and available on computer readable formats. A disclosure policy prohibits the release of company information. This office will refer consumers to appropriate licensing boards if necessary. (916) 522-1700/TDD, (800) 344-9940.

Colorado

Consumer Protection Unit, Office of Attorney General, 110 16th St., 10th Floor, Denver, CO 80202; (303) 620-4500. A disclosure policy prohibits the release of any company information. No publications available.

Connecticut

Department of Consumer Protection, State Office Building, 165 Capitol Ave., Hartford, CT 06106; (203) 566-4999, (800) 842-2649, (800) 538-2277. Requests for specific information on a company must be made in writing. Information is given on the company's license, and complaint record over the last 2 years.

Delaware

Division of Consumer Affairs, Department of Community Affairs, 820 North French St., Wilmington, DE 19801; (302) 571-3250, (800) 443-2179, (800)

State Consumer Protection Offices

736-4000. A list of companies with registered complaints can be obtained from this office.

District of Columbia

Department of Consumer and Regulatory Affairs, 614 H. St., NW, Washington, DC 20001; (202) 727-7000. Specific information on some companies may be given over the phone, including the name of the company president or officer. For detailed information a request must be made in writing.

Florida

Department of Agriculture and Consumer Services, Division of Consumer Services, 218 Mayo Building, Tallahassee, FL 32399; (904) 488-2226, (800) 342-2176/TDD, (800) 342-2175, (800) 327-3382. Information on complaints of a specific company can be given over the phone. Some information is available on computer readable formats.

Georgia

Office of Consumer Affairs, 2 Martin Luther King, Jr. Dr., Plaza Level, East Tower, GA 30334; (404) 656-3790, (404) 651-8600, (800) 869-1123.

Hawaii

Office of Consumer Protection, Department of Commerce and Consumer Affairs, P.O. Box 3767, Honolulu, HI 96812; (808) 586-2630. Information on the number of complaints filed, date of complaints and a public review of a specific company can be given over the phone.

Idaho

Office of Consumer Protection, State House, Room 113A, Boise, ID 83720; (202) 334-2424, (800) 432-3545. Consumer brochures are available. Data is computerized but business status reports are not given to the general public.

Illinois

Consumer Protection Division, Office of Attorney General, 500 S. Second St., Springfield, IL 62706; (217) 782-0244, (800) 252-8666. Information on a specific company is not given over the phone. Data is computerized but not released. Mediation consumer brochures are available.

Indiana

Consumer Protection Division, Office of Attorney General, 219 State House, Indianapolis, IN 46204; (317) 232-6330, (800) 382-5516. All company information is available for public record but must have the permission of the specific company before it can be released to the public. Data files are computerized and available on computer readable formats with company consent.

Iowa

Consumer Protection Division, Office of Attorney General, 1300 E. Walnut, Cooper Building, Des Moines, IA 50319; (515) 281-5926. Information on the number of complaints filed on a specific company can be given over the phone by an assigned investigator. A yearly report is published and available to the public. No computer listings are available.

Kansas

Consumer Protection Division, Office of Attorney General, 301 West 10th, Kansas Judicial Center, 2nd Floor, Topeka, KS 66612; (913) 296-3751, (800) 432-2310. Complaint or information on a lawsuit for a specific company can be given over the phone by talking with the case attorney. Data files are computerized but a complete listing of companies in the file is considered confidential.

Kentucky

Consumer Protection Division, Office of Attorney General, 209 Saint Clair St., Frankfort, KY 40601; (502) 564-2200, (800) 432-9257. Information on complaints of a specific company can be given over the phone. Various consumer brochures are published.

Louisiana

Department of Urban and Community Affairs, P.O. Box 94005, Baton Rouge, LA 70804; (504) 342-7373. Litigation information on a specific company can be given over the phone.

Maine

Bureau of Consumer Credit Protection, State House Station # 35, Augusta, ME 04333-0035; (207) 582-8718, (207) 289-3716 (9 a.m.-1 p.m.), (800) 332-8529. Investigation results of a specific company can be given over the phone. Staff will also advise you on registration or license information for a specific company. Consumer purchasing brochures are available. Data is in the process of becoming computerized. A listing of all companies in their file including name, address and zip code is available in hand written form.

Maryland

Consumer Protection Division, Office of Attorney General, 7 North Calvert St., 200 St. Paul Place, Baltimore, MD 21202; (301) 528-8662 (9 a.m.-3 p.m.), (800) 969-5766. Information on the number of complaints within a 3 year period a company has received can be obtained over the phone. Data files are computerized, and are available on computer readable formats. A listing of all companies in their file is available to the public.

Massachusetts

Consumer Protection Division, Department of Attorney General, 131 Tremont St., 1st Floor, Boston, MA 02111; (617) 727-8400. Information on complaints and specific fees charged by a specific company can be obtained over the phone. Data files are computerized. For specific company requests, the name, address and zip code is provided.

Michigan

Consumer Protection Division, Office of Attorney General, P.O. Box 30213, Lansing, MI 48909; (517) 373-1140. Information on the number of complaints or written inquiries of a specific company can be given over the phone (limited to 2 requests at a time). Computer listings of companies and their addresses are available for a fee of $.20 per page.

Minnesota

Office of Consumer Services, Office of Attorney General, 117 University Avenue, St. Paul, MN 55155; (612) 296-2331. The status of legal action and information on complaints of a specific company can be given over the phone. No computer listings are available.

Mississippi

Consumer Protection Division, Office of Attorney General, P.O. Box 22947, Jackson, MS 39225-2947; (601) 354-6018. Information on complaints filed for a specific company can be given over the phone. Data files are not computerized.

Missouri

Department of Economic Development, P.O. Box 899, Jefferson City, MO 65102; (314) 751-3321. There is no Consumer Protection Agency in Missouri; for specific information contact this office.

Montana

Consumer Affairs Unit, Department of Commerce, 1424 Ninth Ave., Helena, MT 59620; (406) 444-4312, (800) 332-2272. Information on complaints on a specific company can be given over the phone. All investigative information is confidential. Data files are not computerized.

Nebraska

Consumer Protection Division, Department of Justice, 2115 State Capital, P.O. Box 98920, Lincoln, NE 68509; (402) 471-2682. A computer check detailing the nature of a complaint for a specific company, and if the complaint was resolved is available from this office. Data files are computerized.

Nevada

Consumer Affairs Office, Department of Commerce, State Mail Room Complex, Las Vegas, NV 89158; (702) 486-7355. A disclosure policy prohibits the release of any company information.

New Hampshire

Consumer Protection Bureau, Office of Attorney General, State House Annex, Concord, NH 03301; (603) 271-3641. Information on court actions for a specific company can be given over the phone. Some data is computerized, entire files are not available to the public.

New Jersey

Division of Consumer Affairs, P.O. Box 45027, Newark, NJ 07101; (201) 648-4010, (800) 242-5846. Information on the nature of complaints filed for a specific company can be given over the phone. Data files are computerized but an entire listing of all companies is not available.

New Mexico

Consumer and Economic Crime Division, Office of Attorney General, P.O.

Be patient. If any phone number is incorrect, call (area code) 555-1212 and request the new listing.

Consumer Power

Drawer 1508, Santa Fe, NM 87504; (505) 872-6060, (800) 432-2070. Information on complaints on a specific company can be given over the phone. A press release is published every two weeks warning consumers of current scams. Data files are not computerized.

New York

New York State Consumer Protection Board, 99 Washington Ave., Albany, NY 12210; (518) 474-8583. An annual report is available to the public. Data files are computerized in the complaint unit located in Buffalo and Rochester. Call this office for referral.

North Carolina

Consumer Protection Section, Office of Attorney General, Department of Justice Building, P.O. Box 629, Raleigh, NC 27602; (919) 733-7741. Information on the number of complaints filed for a specific company can be obtained from the specialist who handled the case. Published information is available on complaint laws. Data files are computerized, but a listing of all companies on file is not released.

North Dakota

Consumer Fraud Division, Office of Attorney General, State Capitol Building, Bismarck, ND 58505; (701) 224-2210, (800) 472-2600. Information on the complaint record of a specific company can be given over the phone. Various consumer brochures are published. Data files are not computerized.

Ohio

Consumer Frauds and Crimes Section, Office of Attorney General, 30 East Broad St., State Office Tower, Columbus, OH 43266; (614) 466-4986, (800) 282-0515, (614) 466-1393/TDD. Only information concerning a law suit against a specific company can be given over the phone. Various consumer brochures are published. Names of businesses with complaints filed against them are released with a written request.

Oklahoma

Consumer Affairs, Office of Attorney General, 420 W. Main, Suite 550, Oklahoma City, OK 73102; (405) 521-4274. Information on the number of complaints, and legal action taken against a specific company can be given over the phone. Consumer brochures and press releases are available. Data files are not computerized.

Oregon

Financial Fraud Section, Department of Justice, Justice Building, Salem, OR 97310; (503) 378-4320. Information on the number of complaints and a brief summary of the complaints against a specific company can be given over the phone. Various consumer brochures are available including the Unlawful Trade Practices Act. Data files are computerized, but no listings are available.

Pennsylvania

Bureau of Consumer Protection, Office of Attorney General, Strawberry Square, 14th Floor, Harrisburg, PA 17120; (717) 787-9707, (800) 441-2555. Only information concerning a court case of a specific company can be given over the phone. Data files are computerized, no listings are available.

Rhode Island

Consumer Protection Division, Department of Attorney General, 72 Pine St., Providence, RI 02903; (401) 277-2104, (401) 274-4400, ext. 354/TDD, (800) 852-7776. Information concerning cases of consumer fraud are available. Data is computerized and available on computer readable formats. A complete listing of all companies in their files with the name, address, zip code of each company is available.

South Carolina

Consumer Protection Office, Office of Attorney General, P.O. Box 5757, Columbia, SC 29250; (803) 734-9452, (803) 734-9455/TDD, (800) 922-1594. Information on complaints and the closing of a specific company can be obtained over the phone. Information is also available on the company's credit rating and certification (if it applies).

South Dakota

Division of Consumer Affairs, Office of Attorney General, 500 East Capital, State Capital Bldg., Pierre, SD 57501; (605) 773-4400. Information on complaints on a specific company can be given over the phone, including the firm's name and address. Data files are computerized but a complete listing of all businesses in the file is not available. A consumer handbook is published.

Tennessee

Antitrust and Consumer Protection Division, Office of Attorney General, 450 James Robertson Parkway, Nashville, TN 37243-0485; (615) 741-2672. Information on whether or not a complaint has been filed against a specific company is available over the phone. For more detailed information the investigator on the case must be contacted. A Consumer Survival Kit is distributed as well as various consumer brochures.

Texas

Consumer Protection Division, Office of Attorney General, 714 Jackson, Suite 700, Dallas, TX 75202; (214) 742-8944. Information on complaints on a specific company can be given over the phone. Some data is computerized. No lists are available.

Utah

Division of Consumer Protection, Department of Business Regulation, 160 E. South, P.O. Box 45802, Salt Lake City, UT 84145-0802; (801) 530-6601. Information on complaints taken to court are available over the phone. Various consumer information publications are available including the Unfair Practice Act, Lemon Law, and other brochures on fraud and pyramid schemes. Data files are not computerized.

Vermont

Public Protection Division, Office of Attorney General, 109 State St., Montpelier, VT 05609-1001; (802) 828-3171. A listing of complaints made, how many, a brief summary and how and if the complaint was resolved is available for a specific company. Data files are computerized; a computer listing can be generated. Various consumer brochures are available on housing, credit, mail order, auto, health, and money matters.

Virginia

Office of Consumer Affairs, P.O. Box 1163, Richmond, VA 23219; (804) 786-2042. Information on if a complaint exists, if it was resolved and how, is available for a specific company over the phone. Various brochures concerning Virginia consumer laws are published. Data files are computerized from 1986 to the present. No listings are available.

Washington

Attorney General's Office, Consumer and Business Fair Practices Division, 900 Fourth Ave., Suite 2000, Seattle, WA 98164; (206) 464-6431, (800) 551-4636. To have access to complaint files, a public disclosure agreement form must be filled out. The only information given out over the phone is if a company has been sued.

West Virginia

Consumer Protection Division, Office of Attorney General, 812 Quarrier St., Charleston, WV 25301; (304) 348-8986, (800) 368-8808. A disclosure policy prohibits the release of any information on a specific company.

Wisconsin

Office of Consumer Protection, Department of Justice, P.O. Box 7856, Madison, WI 53707; (608) 266-1852, (800) 362-8189. Information on complaints filed on a specific company can be given over the phone. Various consumer brochures are published. Some data are computerized.

Wyoming

Consumer Protection Office, Office of Attorney General, 123 State Capitol Building, Cheyenne, WY 82002; (307) 777-7874. Information on complaints on a specific company can be given over the phone. Some data are computerized. No listings are available.

Be patient. If any phone number is incorrect, call (area code) 555-1212 and request the new listing.

Money, Banking, and Credit

* Banking and Credit Problem Hotline

Office of Consumer Affairs
Federal Deposit Insurance Corporation (FDIC)
550 17th St., NW, Room F-130 (800) 934-3342
Washington, DC 20429 (202) 898-3535

This office answers questions and addresses complaints regarding FDIC-insured banks. A computerized system helps to track complaints from their initial filing to their resolution. A follow-up complaint satisfaction survey is also conducted periodically. Banking questions may be directed to the nearest regional FDIC office, or call the FDIC's toll-free customer service hotline between 9 a.m. and 4 p.m. EST, Monday through Friday.

* Consumer Banking and Finance Publications

Public Information Materials Directory. Catalogues most publications and audiovisual materials prepared by the 12 Federal Reserve Banks and the Board of Governors of the Federal Reserve System. This information is designed to increase public understanding of the functions and operations of the Federal Reserve System, monetary policy, financial markets and institutions, consumer finance and the economy. Copies of this directory can be obtained from the Federal Reserve Bank in your district.

What follows is a list of the Federal Reserve Banks across the U.S., along with their free consumer publications available:

Board of Governors of the Federal Reserve System
Publications Services, MS-138
20th St. and Constitution Ave., NW
Washington, DC 20551 (202) 452-3244

Consumer Handbook on Adjustable Rate Mortgages. Explains adjustable rate mortgages and some of the risks and advantages.

Consumer Handbook to Credit Protection Laws. Tells how consumer credit laws can help in shopping for and applying for credit and in keeping a good credit record.

Consumer's Guide to Mortgage Closings. Explains the mortgage closing process.

Consumer's Guide to Mortgage Lock-Ins. Describes various aspects of mortgage lock-ins.

Consumer's Guide to Mortgage Refinancing. Discusses the process and some of the risks and advantages to mortgage refinancing.

Guide to Business Credit and the Equal Credit Opportunity Act. Advises consumers of their rights under the Act when applying for a business loans and helps consumers prepare effective loan presentations.

Guide to Federal Reserve Regulations. Explains the goals and scope of Federal Reserve regulations.

How to File a Consumer Credit Complaint. Tells how to file a complaint against a bank.

Welcome to the Federal Reserve. Structure and function of the System.

What You Should Know About Home Equity Lines of Credit. Describes what the equity plan does, how it works and obtaining the credit. Also includes checklist and glossary.

Federal Reserve Bank of Atlanta
Public Affairs Department
104 Marietta St. NW
Atlanta, GA 30303-2713 (404) 521-8020

Bank Examiner Flimflam. Information on what to do if you are a victim of the "bank examiner" or "policeman" scam. Warns bank customer against possible theft by deception.

Economic Review. A bimonthly publication presenting new research and articles on the economy of the Southeast.

Federal Reserve Bank of Boston
Bank and Public Services Department
600 Atlantic Ave.
Boston, MA 02106 (617) 973-3459

Checkpoints. Explains how to write, deposit, and cash checks; also available in Spanish and Portuguese.

Home Improvement Credit: Avoiding Second Mortgage Fraud. Homeowners' rights when in need of credit for home improvement projects.

Massachusetts in the 1990's: The Role of the State Government. Focuses on expenditures and summarizes the recent revenue experience and outlook.

New England Economic Indicators. Monthly report of statistical data for the nation and New England states.

New England Economic Review. Publishes articles of broad economic interest bi-monthly.

Right Checks. Outlines the use of specialized checks. Certified, personal, travelers, government, cashier and postal money orders.

Wishes and Rainbows. Touches on the economic problem of scarce resources and society's reaction through a children's story.

Federal Reserve Bank of Chicago
Public Information Center
230 S. LaSalle St.
P.O. Box 834
Chicago, IL 60690-0834 (312) 322-5111

ABC's of Figuring Interest. Ways of calculating interest and how the dollar amount paid was affected.

Credit Guide. Basic guidelines for obtaining and using consumer credit.

Economic Perspectives. Bimonthly publication on banking, business, and agriculture.

Great Lakes Economy. Looking North and South. Economic trends, performances and linkage within the region through agriculture, energy, research and development.

Home Improvement Credit: Avoiding Second Mortgage Fraud. Homeowners' rights when in need of credit for home improvement projects.

Seventh District Economic Data. Provides statistical data on population, business, agriculture, foreign trade, and finance for the five states of the 7th Federal Reserve District.

Federal Reserve Bank of Cleveland
Public Information Department
P.O. Box 6387
Cleveland, OH 44101-1387 (216) 579-2047

Economic Review. Quarterly publication featuring monetary, economic, and banking topics of district and national interest.

Economic Trends (Chartbook). Charts latest economic statistics and briefly discusses the current economy. Monthly.

Federal Reserve Bank of Dallas
Public Affairs Department
2200 N. Pearl
Dallas, TX 75201 (214) 922-6000

Quarterly Survey of Agricultural Credit Conditions. Discusses regional agricultural developments.

Southwest Economy. Bimonthly publication of articles on economic and financial topics.

United States Savings Bonds. Basic information.

United States Treasury Securities. Basic information on investing in Treasury bills, notes and bonds.

Federal Reserve Bank of Kansas City
Public Affairs Department
925 Grand Ave.
Kansas City, MO 64198-0001 (816) 881-2683

Banking Regulation: Its Purposes, Implementation and Effect. A look at today's regulatory system and recent changes in banking.

Economic Review. Discusses a variety of economic and financial topics; quarterly.

Financial Market Volatility and Economy. How to cope with market volatility.

Federal Reserve Bank of Minneapolis
Public Affairs
250 Marquette Ave.
Minneapolis, MN 55401-0291 (612) 340-2446

Agricultural Credit Conditions. Quarterly survey of district farm economy.

Be patient. If any phone number is incorrect, call (area code) 555-1212 and request the new listing.

Consumer Power

Consumer Credit Protection: Do You Know Your Rights? Easy-to-understand summary of consumers' credit protection rights.

Fedgazette. Quarterly business and economics newspaper for the ninth district. Features include opinion survey results, current business news, economic indicators and commentary.

Quarterly Review. Includes feature articles on the district economy.

Federal Reserve Bank of New York
Public Information Department
33 Liberty Street
New York, NY 10045 (212) 720-6134

Consumer Credit Regulators (Fedpoints 17). Reviews the responsibilities of the 12 federal organizations charged with administering consumer regulations.

Debit and Deficits. Their size and impact and measures for bringing them under control.

Primer on Inflation. Process, causes, transmittion and alternatives for dealing with the problem.

Quarterly Review. Reports on business activities and the money and bond markets.

Story of Foreign Trade and Exchange. Explains basic principle. Comic-style booklet.

Federal Reserve Bank of Philadelphia
Public Information Department
P.O. Box 66
Philadelphia, PA 19105 (215) 574-6115

Applying for Credit and Charge Cards: What Consumers Should Know About the Cost and Terms of Credit. Explains the Fair Credit Act.

Business Outlook Survey. Reports on manufacturing in the district and provides forecasts for the next six months; monthly.

Business Review. Bimonthly articles for readers with a general interest in economics.

Buying Treasury Securities. Provides basic information on investing in Treasury bills, notes, and bonds.

Electronic Banking for Today's Consumer. Explains electronic services such as ATMs, direct deposit, bill-paying services, and point-of-sale terminals, as well as consumer protections of Regulation E.

Fair Debt Collection Practices Act. Summarizes the main provisions of the Act.

Frauds and Scams: Protect Yourself and Your Money. Protecting yourself against old and new scams.

Give Yourself Credit. Guides consumers through various credit protection laws.

How the New Equal Credit Opportunity Act Affects You. Outlines the Act's main provisions for consumers.

Plastic Fraud: Getting a Handle on Debit and Credit Cards. Discusses consumer awareness concerning credit and debit card fraud and the regulations protecting consumers.

Quarterly Regional Economic Report. Analyzes the economy of the district.

Your Credit Rating. Describes the importance of credit histories and consumers' rights when using credit, including ways to correct records.

Federal Reserve Bank of Richmond
Public Services Department
P.O. Box 27622
Richmond, VA 23261 (804) 697-8109

Black Banks. Profiles operating revenue and distribution by profit/loss size of black banks.

Community Affairs Officers at Federal Reserve Banks. Outlines the Community Affairs Officer's role, duties, and responsibilities, particularly those related to the Community Reinvestment Act.

Cross Sections. Quarterly reviews of business and economic developments.

Homeownership. Guidelines for buying and owning a home.

How Much Are You Worth. Monitoring the finances and economics of the household.

Where Banks Get Their Money. Information of banks' sources of funds.

Federal Reserve Bank of St. Louis
Public Information Office
P.O. Box 442
St. Louis, MO 63166 (314) 444-8444, ext. 545

Agriculture: an Eighth District Perspective. Quarterly summary of national and district agricultural developments.

Annual U.S. Economic Data. Provides selected economic statistics.

Pieces of Eight: An Economic Perspective on the Eighth District. Summarizes national and district business developments.

Review. Examines national and international economic developments; analyzes various sectors of the district; ten issues per year.

Federal Reserve Bank of San Francisco
Public Information Department
P.O. Box 7702
San Francisco, CA 94120 (415) 974-2163

Give Yourself Credit. Guides the consumer through various credit protection laws.

Economic Review. Discusses selected economic, banking, and financial topics; quarterly.

Weekly Letter. Highlights a major economic issue each week.

Teaching Materials. Audiovisual Materials. Films, filmstrips, slides and video cassettes, in most cases, may be borrowed from within the district of the issuing Bank and do require return postage. Exceptions include the educational filmstrips issued by the Federal Reserve Bank of New York which are sold at nominal cost. For a listing of titles and the issuing Bank, request the Public Information Materials directory from your districts' Bank.

* Consumer Expenditure and Family Budgets

Consumer Expenditure Surveys Division
Office of Prices and Living Conditions
Bureau of Labor Statistics
U.S. Department of Labor
2 Massachusetts Ave. NE, Room 3985
Washington, DC 20212 (202) 606-6872

The *Consumer Expenditure Studies,* a continuing annual survey of consumer expenditures and income, is the basic source of data for the revision of items and weights in the market basket of consumer purchases to be priced for the Consumer Price Index. Selected data is classified by income class, family size, and other demographic and economic characteristics of consumer units. Coverage includes the urban population of the U.S. through 1983, and the total population in 1984 and after.

* Consumer's Financial Guide

Publications Section
Printing Branch, Stop C-11
U.S. Securities and Exchange Commission
Washington, DC 20549 (202) 272-7040

The free publication, *Consumer's Financial Guide,* contains basic information on choosing investments and keeping them safe, trading securities, and the different protections guaranteed by law. To obtain this publication, contact this office.

* Consumer Price Index Within 24 hours

National Technical Information Service
U.S. Department of Commerce
5285 Port Royal Road
Springfield, VA 22161 (703) 487-4630

A Consumer Price Index data summary is available by mailgram within 24 hours of the CPI release. It provides unadjusted and seasonally adjusted U.S. City Average data for All Urban Consumers and for Urban Wage Earners and Clerical Workers. The cost of this service is $190 per year.

* Consumer Prices

Office of Prices and Living Conditions
Bureau of Labor Statistics
U.S. Department of Labor
2 Massachusetts Ave. NE, Room 3615
Washington, DC 20212 (202) 606-7000

The Labor Department measures consumer price changes for a predetermined market basket of consumer goods and services for two population groups: all urban consumers, and urban wage earners and clerical workers. The fixed market basket includes 382 entry level items representing all goods and services purchased for everyday living by all urban residents. Monthly and bimonthly indexes are available for various geographic regions.

* Consumer Purchasing Power Index

Superintendent of Documents
Government Printing Office
Washington, DC 20402 (202) 783-3238

Each monthly issue of the *Consumer Price Index Detailed Report* provides a comprehensive summary of price movements for the month, plus statistical tables, charts, and technical notes. The report covers two indexes, the Consumer

Be patient. If any phone number is incorrect, call (area code) 555-1212 and request the new listing.

Money, Banking, and Credit

Price Index for All Urban Consumers, and the Consumer Price Index for Wage Earners and Clerical Workers. The indexes reflect data for the U.S. city average and selected areas. An annual subscription is available for $23. (S/N 729-001-00000-3).

* Credit and ATM Cards

Federal Trade Commission
Credit Practices
6th and Pennsylvania Ave., NW
Washington, DC 20580 (202) 326-3175

Loss or theft of credit and ATM cards is a serious consumer problem; however, there are laws which establish procedures for you and your creditors to follow to resolve problems with these cards. This office investigates credit card fraud and can give you information on what to do if any of your cards are missing or stolen.

* Credit Card and Computer Fraud

Fraud Division
Office of Investigations
U.S. Secret Service
U.S. Department of the Treasury
1800 G St., NW
Washington, DC 20223 (202) 535-5850

The fraudulent use of credit and debit cards is a federal violation. Investigations are conducted by the Secret Service, including stolen or lost credit cards, the misuse of credit card account numbers, automated teller machine fraud, telephone fraud involving long distance calls, and other types of access device fraud. Computer fraud is a recent concern of the Secret Service. New law enforcement techniques are being pioneered in an effort to identify computer criminals.

* Credit Pamphlets

Office of Consumer Affairs
Federal Deposit Insurance Corporation (FDIC)
550 17th St., NW, Room F-130
Washington, DC 20429 (202) 898-3535

The following FDIC pamphlets are free and are available in English and Spanish.

Consumer Information. Provides an overview of the FDIC, its regional offices, and the major consumer and civil rights laws and regulations that protect bank customers.

Equal Credit Opportunity and Age. Describes Credit Law and age discrimination.

Equal Credit Opportunity and Women. Describes Credit Law and issues of sex and marital status.

Fair Credit Billing. Offers consumers advice on handling disputes regarding billing errors and defective merchandise in ways designed to protect their credit rating.

Fair Credit Reporting Act. Details consumers' rights to know what credit and personal information has been obtained about them by "Consumer Reporting Agencies" and what their rights are to challenge inaccurate information.

Truth in Lending. Explains how the Truth in Lending Law protects consumers from hidden finance charges when obtaining credit.

* Credit Practices

Federal Trade Commission (FTC)
Credit Practices Division
6th and Pennsylvania Ave., NW
Washington, DC 20580 (202) 326-3175

This division of the FTC works to ensure that creditors, credit counselors, certain mortgage lenders, and others who grant credit do not engage in unfair or deceptive acts or practices in providing credit or credit-related services. It also enforces the specific consumer protection statutes and rules listed below. Contact this division for more information about these topics. *Consumer Leasing Act*, which requires lessors to give consumers specific information on lease costs and terms. *Electronic Fund Transfer Act*, which requires institutions to disclose in writing important terms, such as charges for electronic fund transfers. *Equal Credit Opportunity Act*, which prohibits any creditor from denying credit to a consumer on the basis of sex, marital status, color, race, religion, national origin, age, or receipt of public assistance. *Truth in Lending Act*, which requires creditors to disclose in writing certain cost information, such as the annual percentage rate

(APR), before consumers enter into credit transactions. *Credit Practices Rule*, which prohibits certain security interests and collection remedies in consumer credit contracts--namely, confessions of judgment, wage assignments, waivers of exemption, and security interests in certain household goods. *Holder-in-Due Course Rule*, which preserves consumers' claims and defenses involving performance of merchandise bought on credit against a non-seller owner of the credit contract.

* Credit Problems

Federal Trade Commission
Bureau of Consumer Protection
Credit Practices Division
6th and Pennsylvania Ave., NW
Washington, DC 20580 (202) 326-3175

Before you pay a credit repair clinic to "fix" your credit record, learn what the law says and consider saving your money by making some phone calls yourself. This office can give you information on how to "fix" your own credit rating, along their free brochure.

* Credit Protection Laws

Publication Services
MS-138, Board of Governors
Federal Reserve System
Washington, DC 20551 (202) 452-3244

The *Consumer Handbook to Credit Protection Laws*, which can help you better understand how the credit protection laws can help you, is available free from this office.

* Damaged Currency Redemption

Office of Currency Standards
Bureau of Engraving and Printing
U.S. Department of the Treasury
Room 344A, BEPA
P.O. Box 37048
Washington, DC 20013 (202) 662-2361

All mutilated currency may be sent to the above address where trained personnel will determine if it can be exchanged at face value. All final decisions for redemption of this currency are made by the Treasurer of the United States. Currency should be sent by registered mail to the P.O. box address above.

* Direct Deposit of Social Security Payments

Office of the Assistant Commissioner Field Operations
Financial Management Service
U.S. Department of the Treasury
401 14th St., SW
Washington, DC 20227 (202) 874-7328

Presumed Direct Deposit is an approach of establishing Direct Deposit as the "normal" way to receive Social Security benefit payments. Sign-up techniques are simplified. Customer Service is being increased in over-the-counter and over-the-phone contacts. Beneficiaries may still choose to receive a check if they prefer or if they do not have a banking relationship.

* Donations to the Public Debt

Office of the Commissioner
Bureau of the Public Debt
U.S. Department of the Treasury
999-E St., NW
Washington, DC 20239 (202) 219-3300

Since the U.S. Government maintains a public debt of more than $1.9 trillion dollars, and is currently paying $176 billion in interest to pay off this debt, they are asking for donations from the general public to pay off the debt. The Treasury has an account into which money received as gifts is deposited. The money is used to pay at maturity, or to redeem or buy before maturity, an obligation of the Government included in the public debt. You can send donations to: Bureau of the Public Debt, Department G, Washington, DC 20239-0601.

* Fair Credit Billing

Federal Trade Commission
Division of Credit Practices

Be patient. If any phone number is incorrect, call (area code) 555-1212 and request the new listing.

Consumer Power

6th and Pennsylvania Ave., NW
Washington, DC 20580 (202) 326-3175

Credit card billing errors do occur, but they are simple to resolve if you know how to use the Fair Credit Billing Act, which protects your rights as a card user. For a free brochure on this Act or on credit billing laws in general, contact the FTC.

* Fair Credit Reporting

Federal Trade Commission
Credit Practices
6th and Pennsylvania Ave., NW
Washington, DC 20580 (202) 326-3175

If you've ever applied for a charge account, a personal loan, insurance, or a job, someone is probably keeping a file on you. This file might contain information on how you pay your bills, or whether you've been sued, arrested, or have filed for bankruptcy. Credit bureaus gather and sell this information as "consumer reports" to creditors, employers, and other businesses, but the Fair Credit Reporting Act protects you by requiring credit bureaus to furnish correct and complete information. This office can give you more information on your rights.

* Fair Debt Collection

Federal Trade Commission
Credit Practices
6th and Pennsylvania Ave., NW
Washington, DC 20580 (202) 326-3175

If you use credit cards, owe money on a loan, or are paying off a home mortgage, you are a "debtor." And although you may never come in contact with a debt collector, if you do, you should know the law to make sure you are treated fairly. This office can provide you with information about your rights as a debtor.

* Women and Credit Histories

Federal Trade Commission (FTC)
Bureau of Consumer Protection
6th and Pennsylvania Ave., NW
Washington, DC 20580 (202) 326-3175

Each year many women are denied credit because they cannot show how they have used it, but two federal laws, the Equal Credit Opportunity Act and the Fair Credit Reporting Act, give you specific rights that help protect your credit history and make it easier for you to obtain credit. For more information, including a brochure on how to establish your credit, contact the FTC.

Be patient. If any phone number is incorrect, call (area code) 555-1212 and request the new listing.

Product Safety

* Accident Investigations Data Base

National Injury Information Clearinghouse
U.S. Consumer Product Safety Commission (CPSC)
5401 Westbard Avenue
Room 625
Washington, DC 20207   (301) 504-0424

CPSC accident investigation reports provide information about an accident's sequence, human behavior, and role of the consumer product in the accident. Following is a description of the information in the CPSC's Accident Investigations database, which includes accidents occurring after mid-1972: the state in which the accident occurred; the victim's background, including age, race, sex, education, and number of days incapacitated; the injury diagnosis; the consumer product involved; the product manufacturer; and more. Most information requests are answered without charge within 10 working days, but there is a charge for costs in excess of $25.

* Consumer Commission Meetings and Reports

Office of the Secretary
U.S. Consumer Product Safety Commission (CPSC)
Washington, DC 20207   (301) 504-0800

Commission meetings and meetings of the commissioners or Commission staff with persons outside of government are generally open to the public. In addition, records of what was discussed at those meetings are available for public inspection. Notices of meetings are generally published in the Commission's Public Calendar at least seven days before the meetings take place. Contact this office for a free copy of the Public Calendar.

* Consumer Deputy Program

U.S. Consumer Product Safety Commission (CPSC)
5401 Westbard Avenue
Washington, DC 20207   (301) 504-0788

As an unpaid volunteer, you can work with district and regional Commission offices to visit retail stores to make sure that the stores are complying with CPSC guidelines. Volunteers identify themselves to the store, check the inventory, and then report their findings back to the CPSC. The most recent Deputy program involves monitoring stores for the illegal sale of lawn darts.

* Consumer Injury Surveillance System

National Injury Information Clearinghouse
U.S. Consumer Product Safety Commission (CPSC)
5401 Westbard Avenue, NW
Washington, DC 20207   (301) 504-0424

The National Electronic Injury Surveillance System (NEISS) collects injury data from a sample of hospitals with emergency rooms across the U.S. and its territories. This data provides national estimates of the number and severity of injuries associated with but not necessarily caused by consumer products and treated in hospital emergency rooms. Information gathered from these and other sources, such as death certificates and reported incidents, guides the Commission in setting priorities for selecting types of products for further investigation and action. NEISS data are available in various computer formats. Any of the standard reports may be requested from this office, while custom reports are available at variable rates.

* Consumer Outreach Programs

U.S. Consumer Product Safety Commission (CPSC)
5401 Westbard Avenue
Washington, DC 20207   (301) 504-0580

By contacting the Commission's main office in Washington, DC, or your local CPSC regional office, you can arrange to have a consumer education specialist visit your business, school, community group, or organization for a presentation on consumer product hazards and safety strategies.

* Consumer Product/Product-Related Injury Hotline

Office of Information and Public Affairs
U.S. Consumer Product Safety Commission (CPSC)
Washington, DC 20207   (800) 638-2772

To report a hazardous product or product-related injury, call this toll-free number. This hotline handles more than 200,000 calls each year. Operators are on duty from 10:30 a.m. to 4:00 p.m. Eastern Standard Time, Monday through Friday.

* Consumer Product Safety Commission Library

U.S. Consumer Product Safety Commission (CPSC)
5401 Westbard Avenue, NW
Room 546
Washington, DC 20207   (301) 504-0044

The CPSC library's collection includes reference materials on engineering, economics, and health sciences, which CPSC staff and other researchers may use for background on product safety issues. The library does not include CPSC documents and publications.

* Consumer Safety Databases

U.S. Consumer Product Safety Commission (CPSC)
5401 Westbard Avenue
Washington, DC 20207   (301) 504-0424

Although the Commission does not maintain databases which are accessible to outside users, specific requests for data are handled by the Commission's National Injury Information Clearinghouse or the Division of Automated Data Processing. Data may be provided to the requestor in the form of printouts, 9 track tapes, or 5 1/4 inch floppy diskettes. All information disclosed must first meet the disclosure requirements of the Consumer Product Safety Act. What follows is sampling of the Commission's databases.

- American Association of Poison Centers: Information on childhood poisoning incidents received annually and prepared on various substance categories.
- All Terrain Vehicle (ATV) Deaths: Information on ATV-related deaths, including investigation and injury reports, and death certificates.
- Chemicals in Products: Contains complete chemical and biological information on consumer products.
- Childhood Drowning Study: Contains information of swimming pool-related deaths of children.
- Death Certificates: Information on death certificates involving product-related deaths in the U.S.
- Establishment Inventory System: Maintains information on businesses which CPSC monitors or otherwise contacts, including data on firms, products, inspections, samples, and violations.
- Fire Incident Reporting System: Contains information on electrical and range/oven fires collected from fire departments throughout the U.S.
- Lawn Mower Special Survey: Maintains reports of lawn mower-related injuries over the last four years.
- PCAT Data Collection: Contains children poisoning information, including records of ingestion by product categories for children under 5 years of age.
- Product Defect Identification: contains manufacturer and retail reports to CPSC of product defects with injury risks, along with complaints and injuries of which the companies are aware.

* Consumer's Resource Handbook

Office of Information and Public Affairs
U.S. Consumer Product Safety Commission (CPSC)
Washington, DC 20207

This free *Consumer's Resource Handbook* shows you how to communicate more effectively with manufacturers, retailers, and service providers. The first section features tips on avoiding purchasing problems and getting the most for your money by giving steps for handling your own complaint and writing an effective complaint letter. The second section, the *Consumer Assistance Directory*, lists

Be patient. If any phone number is incorrect, call (area code) 555-1212 and request the new listing.

Consumer Power

consumer offices in both public and private sectors that provide assistance for consumer complaints. Available from the Consumer Information Center, Pueblo CO 81009.

* Explosives Hotline

Explosives Enforcement Branch
Bureau of Alcohol, Tobacco, and Firearms
U.S. Department of the Treasury
650 Massachusetts Ave.
Washington, DC 20226

(202) 927-7930
(202) 927-7777

Those with information on a major arson incident or bombing, or those aware of stolen explosives, may call the above hotline. One of four national response teams will be rushed to the scene within 24 hours. A report will be taken by those answering the phone, and the information will be transferred to the nearest agent in the area. Each of the four response teams is composed of 10 special agents, a forensic chemist, and an explosive specialist from ATF's Explosives Technology Branch. A state or local law enforcement or fire service official can request the services of a National Response Team by contacting an ATF Special Agent in charge at one of 22 strategic office locations throughout the United States:

Atlanta, GA: (404) 331-6526
Birmingham, AL: (205) 731-1205
Boston, MA: (617) 565-7042
Brentwood, TN: (615) 736-5412
Charlotte, NC (704) 371-6125
Dallas, TX: (214) 767-2250
Detroit, MI: (313) 226-4830
Houston, TX: (713) 229-3511
Kansas City, MO: (816) 374-7188
Los Angeles, CA: (213) 894-4812
Louisville, KY: (502) 582-5211
Miami, FL: (305) 536-4368
Middleburg Heights, OH: (216) 522-7210
New Orleans, LA: (504) 589-2048
New York, NY: (212) 264-4657
Oak Brook, IL: (312) 620-7824
Philadelphia, PA: (215) 597-7266
San Francisco, CA: (415) 974-9589
Seattle, WA: (206) 442-4485
St. Louis, MO: (314) 425-5560
St. Paul, MN: (612) 290-3092
Washington, DC: (703) 285-2543

* Explosives Incidents Statistics

Explosives Division
Office of Law Enforcement
Bureau of Alcohol, Tobacco, and Firearms
U.S. Department of the Treasury
650 Massachusetts Ave.
Washington, DC 20226
(202) 927-7930

The annual *Explosives Incidents Report* highlights statistics of explosive incidents and stolen explosives and recoveries. Tables include incidents by state, by target, and by types of explosives used. Significant explosives incidents during the year are also described. To obtain a copy of the report, contact Distribution Center, Bureau of Alcohol, Tobacco, and Firearms, U.S. Department of the Treasury, 7943 Angus Ct., Springfield, VA 22153.

* Firearms: Federal Regulations

Distribution Center
Bureau of Alcohol, Tobacco, and Firearms
U.S. Department of the Treasury
7943 Angus Ct.
Springfield, VA 22153
(703) 455-7801

Federal firearms laws are outlined in the free book, *Your Guide to Federal Firearms Regulation: 1988-1989*. Regulations concerning state firearms control assistance; machine guns, destructive devices, and certain other firearms; certain firearms administered by other federal agencies; commerce in firearms and ammunition, and the importation of arms, ammunition and implements of war are included. For questions on Federal Firearms Laws, regulations, procedures or policies - contact the ATF compliance operations office nearest you, seen in the list below (alphabetical by state).

Birmingham, AL 35209 (205) 731-0400
Little Rock, AR 72201 (501) 378-6457
Los Angeles, CA 90053 (213) 894-4817
Sacramento, CA 95814 (916) 551-1323
San Francisco, CA 94107 (415) 974-7778
San Jose, CA 95113 (408) 291-7464
Santa Ana, CA 92712 (714) 836-2946
Santa Rosa, CA 95404 (707) 576-0184
Denver, CO 80294 (303) 844-5027
Hartford, CT 06103 (203) 722-2037
Miami, FL 33166 (305) 592-9967
Tampa, FL 33602 (813) 228-2346
Atlanta, GA 30340 (404) 986-6075
Chicago, IL 60604 (312) 353-3797
Frankfort, KY 40601 (502) 223-3350
Louisville, KY 40202 (502) 582-5217
Baltimore, MD 21201 (301) 962-3200
Boston, MA 02222-1079 (617) 565-7073
Farmington Hills, MI 48331 (313) 226-4735
St. Paul, MN 55101 (612) 290-3496
Kansas City, MO 64106 (816) 426-2464
St. Louis, MO 63101 (314) 539-2251
Parsippany, NJ 07054 (201) 334-7058
Buffalo, NY 14202 (716) 846-4048
New York, NY 10008 (212) 264-4650
Charlotte, NC 28209 (704) 371-6127
Cincinnati, OH 45203 (513) 684-3351
Middleburg Hts.,OH 44130 (216) 522-3374
Portland, OR 97218 (503) 231-2331
Lansdale, PA 19446 (215) 248-5252
Pittsburgh, PA 15222 (412) 644-2919
Hato Rey, PR 00918 (809) 753-4082
Dallas, TX 75242 (214) 767-9461
Houston, TX 77024 (713) 220-2157
San Antonio, TX 78206 (512) 229-6168
Richmond, VA 23240 (804) 771-2877
Seattle, WA 98174 (206) 442-5900
Milwaukee, WI 53202 (414) 291-3991

* Firearms Identification

Distribution Center
Bureau of Alcohol, Tobacco, and Firearms
U.S. Department of the Treasury
7943 Angus Ct.
Springfield, VA 22153
(703) 455-7801

The free publication, *Identification of Firearms*, helps individuals in identifying weapons classified as firearms, including destructive devices. Pictures and descriptions are included of machine guns and machine pistols, shotguns, rifles, silencers, and other weapons and destructive devices.

* Fishery Products Grading and Inspection

Utilization Research and Services
National Marine Fisheries Service
National Oceanic and Atmospheric Administration
U.S. Department of Commerce
1335 East-West Hwy., Room 6142
Silver Spring, MD 20910
(301) 713-2245

The National Marine Fisheries Service conducts a voluntary seafood inspection program on a fee-for-service bases. A wide range of inspection services are available to any interested party, including harvesters, processors, food-service distributors, and importers and exporters. These services include vessel and plant sanitation inspection, product evaluation (in-plant and warehouse lot), product specification review, label review, laboratory analyses (microbiological tests, chemical contaminant/indices of decomposition, species identification), training, and education and information. This office has a great deal of information concerning inspections, grading of products, and regulations. They also publish a document listing fishery products that have been produced in fish establishments approved by the National Marine Fisheries Service.

* National Injury Information Clearinghouse

U.S. Consumer Protection Safety Commission (CPSC)
5401 Westbard Avenue, Room 625
Washington, DC 20207
(301) 504-0424

Be patient. If any phone number is incorrect, call (area code) 555-1212 and request the new listing.

Product Safety

This clearinghouse collects, investigates, analyzes, and distributes injury data and information relating to the causes and prevention of death, injury, and illness associated with consumer products. It maintains thousands of detailed investigative reports of injuries associated with consumer products and has access to automated databases with several million incidents of injuries that have been reported by a nationwide network of hospital emergency departments. Technical analysts prepare publications, such as hazard analyses, special studies, and data summaries, a catalog of which is available by contacting the clearinghouse.

* Publications

Office of Information and Public Affairs
U.S. Consumer Product Safety Commission (CPSC)
EXPA
Washington, DC 20207 (800) 638-2772

The following consumer publications describe some of the common hazards associated with the use of consumer products and recommend ways to avoid these hazards. They come in the form of fact sheets (F.S.), brochures, and materials developed especially for use by classroom teachers. Some of the publications listed here can also be requested from the Commission's Regional Offices. Direct your request to the above address on a post card.

General Information
- Who We Are and What We Do
- Compilation of Laws
- Consumer Resource Handbook (1988)
- CPSC Hotline Brochure
- Some Federal Consumer Oriented Agencies (F.S. 52)

Annual Reports
- Annual Report 1987
- Annual Report 1986
- Annual Report 1984 Part II
- Annual Report 1983 Part II
- Annual Report 1982
- Annual Report 1981 Parts I,II

Bicycle Safety
- Sprocketman (a comic book for high school age students)
- Mini Bikes (F.S. 38)

Children's Furniture
- Cribs (F.S. 43)
- High Chairs (F.S. 70)
- Bunk Beds (F.S. 71)
- Tips for Your Baby's Safety - Nursery Equipment Checklist (English and Spanish)
- The Safe Nursery - A Buyer's Guide to Nursery Equipment (English and Spanish)
- Be Sure It's Safe For Your Baby

Children's Safety
- Skateboards (F.S. 93)
- Protect Your Child
- Bumps Teachers Guide
- Super Sitter

Compliance Publications
- Retailers Guide (1/86)
- Guide for Manufacturers, Distributors, and Retailers
- Guide for Retailers (9/84)

Curriculum Guides and Lessons for Use By Educators
- It's No Accident - Consumer Product Safety
- Guide for Teachers of Grades 3-6
- Flammable Products: A Guide for Teachers of Secondary Grades
- Flammable Products: A Guide for Teachers of Elementary Grades (Spanish)
- Flammable Fabrics: Teacher's Guide (4T)
- Flammable Fabrics: Student Readings (4-S)
- Halloween Safety Teacher's Guide (9T)
- Holiday Safety Teacher's Guide (7T)
- Poison Prevention Teacher's Guide (6T)

Electric Safety
- Ranges and Ovens (F.S. 9)
- TV Fire and Shock (F.S. 11)
- Electric Blenders (F.S. 50)
- Clothes Dryers (F.S. 73)
- Ground Fault Circuit Interrupters (F.S. 99)
- CPSC Guide to Electrical Safety
- Consumer Product Safety Alert on Antennas
- Electrical Safety Room by Room Audit Checklist (English and Spanish)
- (This is also available on "slow play disc" for the blind.)

Final Reports
- Final Report of the National Conference on Product Safety (1982)
- Final Report of the National Conference on Product Safety (1984)
- Final Report of the National Consumer Product Safety Conference for Retailers
- Final Report of the National Conference on Fire Toxicity

Fire Safety
- Fireworks (F.S. 12)
- Upholstered Furniture (F.S. 53)
- Halloween Safety (F.S. 100)
- What You Should Know About Smoke Detectors
- Give a Gift--Give a Smoke Detector (poster)
- Home Fire Safety Checklist

Hazardous Substances
- School Science Laboratories: A Guide to Some Hazardous Products
- Asbestos in the Home
- List of Asbestos in Hair Dryers
- Methylene Chloride Safety Alert

Holiday Safety
- Merry Christmas With Safety

Home Heating Equipment
- Space Heaters (F.S. 34)
- Fireplaces (F.S. 44)
- Furnaces (F.S. 79)
- Wood Burning Stoves (F.S. 92)
- Kerosene Heaters (F.S. 97)
- Electric Space Heaters (F.S. 98)
- 464 Chimneys Safety Alert (1984)
- Caution: Choosing and Using Gas Space Heaters
- What You Should Know About Kerosene Heaters
- What You Should Know About Space Heaters

Home Insulation
- Installing Insulation Safety
- Insulation Installers Guide
- Q&A Urea Formaldehyde Foam Insulation

Indoor Air Quality
- The Inside Story: A Guide to Indoor Air Quality

Outdoor Power Equipment
- Power Mowers (F.S. 1)
- Chain Saws (F.S. 51)
- Chain Saw Safety Guide
- Consumer Product Safety Alert on Chain Saws
- Mower Hazards and Safe Practices (poster)
- Power Mower and Maintenance Storage Tips
- Safety, Sales, and Services
- Power Lawn Mower Safety Kit--Teachers Manual
- Power Mower Hazards and Safety Features (poster)

Older Consumers Safety
- Home Safety Checklist for Older Consumers (English and Spanish)

Playground Equipment
- Play Happy, Play Safely: Little Big Kids (4-6 years)
- Handbook for Playground Safety, Volume I, General Guidelines
- Handbook for Playground Safety, Volume II, Technical Guidelines

Poison Prevention
- First Aid Brochure
- Locked-up Poisons (English and Spanish)
- Poison Lookout Checklist
- Poison Prevention Packaging: A Text for Pharmacies and Physicians

Be patient. If any phone number is incorrect, call (area code) 555-1212 and request the new listing.

Consumer Power

Pool Safety
Children and Pool Safety Checklist
Backyard Pool--CPSC Safety Alert (5/87)

Spanish Fact Sheets
Power Mowers (F.S. 1)
Kitchen Ranges (F.S. 61)
Carbon Monoxide (F.S. 13)
Infant Falls (F.S. 20)
Mobile Homes (F.S. 39)
Older Consumers and Stairway Accidents (F.S. 48)
Kitchen Knives (F.S. 83)
Trampolines (F.S. 85)

Toys Safety
Toys (F.S. 47)
Electric Toys (F.S. 61)
Toy Chests (F.S. 74)
Baby Rattles (F.S. 86)
For Kids Sake, Think Toy Safety Pamphlet (English and Spanish)
Toy Safety Coloring Book (English and Spanish)

Which Toy For Which Child 0-5 Years
Which Toy For Which Child 6-12

Miscellaneous
All Terrain Vehicle (ATV) Safety Alert
How to Plan and Conduct Consumer Product Safety Information Programs
Ladders (F.S. 56)
Clothes Dryers (F.S. 73)
Publications Catalog
Refuse Bins (F.S. 81)

* Safety Standard Changes

U.S. Consumer Product Safety Commission (CPSC)
5401 Westbard Avenue
Washington, DC 20207 (301) 504-0580

If you think that the current safety specifications on a certain product, such as a toy or a kitchen appliance, aren't tough enough, you can petition the CPSC to make the changes and possibly have your recommendations used in the new specifications. Contact this office for more details.

Be patient. If any phone number is incorrect, call (area code) 555-1212 and request the new listing.

Post Office and Mailing

* **Administrative Support Manual**
Consumer Affairs
U.S. Postal Service
475 L'Enfant Plaza, SW
Washington, DC 20260-3121 (202) 268-2284
This subscription service consists of a basic manual and supplementary material for an indeterminate period. This manual describes matters of internal administration in the Postal Service. It includes functional statements as well as policies and requirements regarding security, communications (printing directives, forms, records, newsletters), government relations, procurement and supply, data processing systems, maintenance, and engineering. A subscription is available for $16 domestic, $20 foreign, S/N 039-000-00281-7, from: Superintendent of Documents, Government Printing Office, Washington, DC 20402-0001; (202) 783-3238.

* **A Consumer's Guide to Postal Crime Prevention**
Public Affairs Branch
The Postal Inspection Service
US Postal Service
475 L'Enfant Plaza, SW
Washington, DC 20260-2100 (202) 268-4293
The free booklet, *A Consumer's Guide to Postal Crime Prevention*, is full of tips and ideas on how to discourage mail thieves and how to help put mail fraud con artists out of business. Consumers who believe they are victims of mail fraud should write the nearest office of the Postal Inspection Service or refer the information through their local postmaster.

* **A Guide to Business Mail Preparation**
Marketing Department
Regular Mail Services Division
U.S. Postal Service
475 L'Enfant Plaza, SW
Room 5541
Washington, DC 20260-6336 (202) 268-2222
This free guide provides voluntary guidelines for postal customers and their suppliers regarding the preparation of letter mail for successful processing on the latest in high-speed automated mail sorting equipment. Computerized mail processing is faster, more efficient, economical, and accurate than older manual or mechanized sorting and mailing methods. Information on addressing for automation, postnet bar codes, and FIM patterns is covered.

* **Business Guide to Postal Crime Prevention**
Public Affairs Branch
The Postal Inspection Service
US Postal Service
475 L'Enfant Plaza, SW
Washington, DC 20260-2100 (202) 268-4293
The booklet, *Postal Crime Prevention: A Business Guide*, shows business owners how to protect themselves from con artists and thieves whose business is mail fraud and mail theft. It includes information on different types of mail fraud to watch for, check cashing precautions, guidelines for mailroom security, bombs in the mail, and additional information.

* **Business Mailer Information**
Communications Department
U.S. Postal Service
475 L'Enfant Plaza, SW
Washington, DC 20260 (202) 268-2158
The free monthly publication, *Memo to Mailers*, advises business mailers of all rate and classification changes as well as other postal news. It is available from *Memo to Mailers*, Post Office Box 999, Springfield, VA 22150-0999.

* **Business Reply Mail**
Rates and Classification Department
U.S. Postal Service
475 L'Enfant Plaza, SW
Washington, DC 20260 (202) 268-5311
Businesses and others who want to encourage responses to their mailings by paying the postage for those responses might consider using business reply mail. Under this service, all responses are returned to the sender from any U.S. post office to any valid address in the United States. Business reply mail must be prepaid according to a specified format, and a small annual fee is charged for each permit issued. The mailer guarantees to pay the postage for all replies returned to him or her at the regular first class rate plus a business reply fee. For additional information, contact this office.

* **Business Reply Mailgram**
Rates and Classification Department
U.S. Postal Service
475 L'Enfant Plaza, SW
Washington, DC 20260 (202) 268-5311
A Business Reply Mailgram is now available for customers who require a quick turnaround response. This mailgram provides all of the features of a regular Mailgram with the addition of a built-in response device using a Business Reply envelope. Contact this office for more information.

* **Carrier Alert Program**
Communications Department
U.S. Postal Service
475 L'Enfant Plaza, SW
Washington, DC 20260 (202) 268-2158
Pioneered by the Postal Service and the National Association of Letter Carriers, the Carrier Alert Program encourages letter carriers to watch participants' mailboxes for mail accumulations that might signal illness or injury. Accumulations of mail are reported by carriers to their supervisors who then notify a sponsoring agency, through locally developed procedures, for follow-up action. Since its founding in 1982, this lifeline has been cited for saving dozens of lives.

* **Consumer Advocate**
The Consumer Advocate
U.S. Postal Service
475 L'Enfant Plaza, SW, Room 5821
Washington, DC 20260-2202 (202) 268-2281
The Consumer Advocate, a postal ombudsman, represents the interest of the individual mail customer in matters involving the Postal Service by bringing complaints and suggestions to the attention of top postal management and solving the problems of individual customers. Contact your postmaster if your problem cannot be solved by your local post office.

* **Consumer's Directory of Postal Services and Products**
Consumer Advocate
U.S. Postal Service
475 L'Enfant Plaza West, SW
Washington, DC 20260-2202
This directory, which discusses the various services and products the Postal Service offers, will help you choose the right service to meet your individual needs and save time and money. Included is information on mail services, addressing and packaging, special services, stamp collecting and mail fraud. To obtain a copy, contact this office or your local post office.

* **Current Mail Rates, Fees and Services**
Rates and Classification Department
U.S. Postal Service

Be patient. If any phone number is incorrect, call (area code) 555-1212 and request the new listing.

Consumer Power

475 L'Enfant Plaza, SW
Washington, DC 20260 (202) 268-5169
This department can give you information on current mail rates, fees, and services.

* Customer Service Representatives

Marketing and Sales Group
U.S. Postal Service
475 L'Enfant Plaza, SW
Washington, DC 20260 (202) 268-2267
The U.S. Postal Service has a local sales staff of Customer Service Representatives found in main post offices. Their services include helping you get the most for your postage dollar; showing you how to set up a mail room; resolving your business mail problems and selling services. Contact this office for more information on getting these services.

* Customs

United States Customs Service
Treasury Department
PO Box 7407
Washington, DC 20229-7407 (202) 566-2957
All mail originating in foreign countries and most United States territories is subject to U.S. Customs Service examination upon entering the United States. Many imported goods are subject to U.S. customs duty. When goods enter by mail, the duty assessed by Customs is collected by the Postal Service, as is a customs clearance and delivery fee on each mail piece on which customs duty is paid.

* Design Licenses

Law Department
U.S. Postal Service
475 L'Enfant Plaza, SW
Washington, DC 20260 (202) 268-2329
Designs of postage stamps issued after January 1, 1978, are copyrighted and may not be reproduced except under license granted by the U.S. Postal Service. Earlier designs are in the public domain and may be reproduced without permission for philatelic, educational, historical, and newsworthy purposes.

* Directives and Forms Catalog

Document Control Division
Office of Information Services
Information Resource Management Department
U.S. Postal Service
Washington, DC 20260-1571
This document is a catalog of all national directives and forms currently used in the Postal Service. A complete edition of this publication is published three times a year. Interim changes appear regularly in the "Directives Update" and "Forms Update" in the *Postal Bulletin*. Also included is a list of directives which the public may obtain free of charge at main post offices.

* Domestic Mail Manual

Consumer Affairs Department
U.S. Postal Service
475 L'Enfant Plaza, SW, Room
Washington, DC 20260-6300 (202) 268-2281
The manual is designed to assist customers in obtaining maximum benefits from domestic postal services. It includes applicable regulations and information about rates and postage, classes of mail, special services, wrapping and mailing requirements, and collection and delivery services. The subscription service consists of four cumulative issues a year and is available for $36 domestic, $45.75 foreign, S/N 739-003-00000-8, from: Superintendent of Documents, Government Printing Office, Washington, DC 20402-0001; (202) 783-3238.

* Freedom of Information Requests

General Counsel
Postal Rate Commission
1333 H St., NW, Suite 300
Washington, DC 20268-0001 (202) 789-6820
For information requests under the Freedom of Information Act, contact the office above.

* Hazardous and Illegal Items

Postal Inspection Service
U.S. Postal Service
475 L'Enfant Plaza, SW
Washington, DC 20260-2186
It is illegal to send through the U.S. Mail any article, composition, or material which may kill or injure another person, or obstruct mail service or damage property. Harmful matter includes, but is not limited to poisons, poisonous animals, insects, and reptiles, including all types of snakes and spiders; all disease germs or scabs, and all explosives, flammable material, dangerous machines, and mechanical, chemical or other devices or compositions which may catch fire or explode. Contact this office for more information on the guidelines.

* History of Rural Post Offices

Administrative Office
Postal Rate Commission
1333 H St., NW, Suite 300
Washington, DC 20268-0001 (202) 789-6840
At the Crossroads: An Inquiry into Rural Post Offices and the Communities They Serve investigates the sociological implications and community effects resulting from the closing of a post office in a small rural community. The study shows the history and development of postal delivery and the Postal Service as it affects rural areas. Write or call for a free copy.

* International Mail Manual

International Postal Affairs Department
U.S. Postal Service
475 L'Enfant Plaza, SW
Washington, DC 20260 (202) 268-2445
This manual sets forth the policies, regulations, and procedures governing international mail services offered to the public by the Postal Service. It includes the postage rates, fees, and mail preparation information for Postal Union mail, parcel post, and International Express Mail, as they apply to each individual country. A subscription is available for $17 domestic, and $21 foreign, S/N 739-004-00000-4, from: Superintendent of Documents, Government Printing Office, Washington, DC 20402-0001; (202) 783-3238.

* International Surface Airlift

International Postal Affairs
U.S. Postal Service
475 L'Enfant Plaza, SW
Washington, DC 20260 (202) 268-2445
International Surface Air Lift service provides fast delivery, at a cost lower than airmail, for publications and printed matter sent overseas at surface rate. The postage rate is a per pound rate.

* Legal Restrictions

Postal Inspection Service
U.S. Postal Service
475 L'Enfant Plaza, SW
Washington, DC 20260-2186 (202) 268-4293
There are legal restrictions on the mailing of radioactive material, firearms, knives, and sharp instruments, drugs and narcotics, and other controlled substances as defined by Federal law and related Federal regulations. Certain potentially harmful or dangerous articles and substances may be mailed if special packaging and labeling requirements are met. Your local postmaster or account representative can provide more details.

* Library

Library
U.S. Postal Service
475 L'Enfant Plaza SW, Room 11800
Washington, DC 20260-1641 (202) 268-2904
Along with a working collection of materials in law, the social sciences, and technology, the Postal Library contains a unique collection of postal materials, legislative files from the 71st Congress to date, reports, pamphlets, clippings, photographs, general postal histories, periodicals of the national postal employee organizations, Universal Postal Union studies, and Postal laws and regulations handbooks and manuals. The library is open to the public weekdays from 9 a.m. to 4 p.m. Reading Rooms are located on the 11th Floor North.

Be patient. If any phone number is incorrect, call (area code) 555-1212 and request the new listing.

Post Office and Mailing

* Mail Fraud

Postal Inspection Service
U.S. Postal Service
475 L'Enfant Plaza, SW
Washington, DC 20260-2186 (202) 268-4293

Mail Fraud is a scheme to get money, or anything of value from the public by offering a product, service, or investment opportunity that does not live up to its claims. Prosecutors must prove the claims were intentionally misrepresented and that the mails were used to carry out the scheme. The Postal Inspection Service investigates violations of the mail fraud law. Consumer complaints are the primary basis for investigation by Postal Inspectors. Some of the more common mail fraud schemes include medical fraud, work-at-home-schemes, land fraud, charity fraud, insurance fraud, investment fraud, and home improvement fraud.

* Mailing Free Matter For Blind and Visually Handicapped Persons

Office of Consumer Affairs
US Postal Service
475 L'Enfant Plaza, SW
Washington, DC 20260 (202) 268-2281

The free pamphlet, *Mailing Free Matter For Blind and Visually Handicapped Persons,* is designed to answer the most often asked questions about mailing free matter for the visually handicapped. It discusses qualifying, eligibility, conditions and restrictions on mailings, and the steps to make special arrangements for delivery.

* Mailing Services for the Blind and Handicapped

Office of the Consumer Advocate
U.S. Postal Service
L'Enfant Plaza, SW
Washington, DC 20260-6320 (202) 268-2281

Persons who are blind or who cannot use or read conventionally-printed material due to a physical handicap may qualify to mail items free of postage. To be eligible, a competent authority must submit a statement to the post office where postage-free mailings will be made or received, certifying that the individual is unable to read conventional reading material. Certain conditions and restrictions apply. The same general rules apply to both domestic and international mail service. Special arrangements for delivery or pickup of free mail for eligible persons may be arranged through local post offices depending on the circumstances. Contact this office for more information.

* Mailing to the Soviet Union

International Postal Affairs Department
U.S. Postal Service
475 L'Enfant Plaza, SW
Washington, DC 20260-6500 (202) 245-4575

Of all countries of the world with which the U.S. Postal Service exchanges mail, none has created more problems for U.S. mailers than the Soviet Union. U.S. mailers can reduce many of their frustrations by getting clear information on how to send mail to the Soviet Union, and how to seek redress if problems are encountered. Contact this office for more information on prohibited items, restricted articles, and size and weight limits.

* National ZIP Code and Post Office Directory

Delivery Distribution Department
U.S. Postal Service
475 L'Enfant Plaza, SW
Washington, DC 20260 (202) 268-6990

Proper ZIP Code information is essential for speedy and economic delivery of your mail. The *ZIP Code Directory* is an up-to-date and comprehensive listing of ZIP Code information by state and post office. It includes instructions for quickly finding a ZIP Code number when an address is known. The ZIP Code Directory also includes official lists of post offices, named stations, named branches, and community post offices in the United States. The volume includes a wealth of handy information about ZIP Codes, postal abbreviations, and basic postal procedures, and is an indispensable aid that is worth its price many times over. Available for $15, foreign $18.75 from: Superintendent of Documents, Government Printing Office, Washington, DC 20402-0001; (202) 783-3238.

* Pornography

Postal Inspection Service
U.S. Postal Service
475 L'Enfant Plaza, SW
Washington, DC 20260-2186 (202) 636-2339

To stop the mailing of unsolicited sexually-oriented advertisements to yourself or your minor children, fill out *Application for Listing Pursuant of 39 USC 3010,* at your local post office. Thirty days after your name has been added to the Postal Service reference list, any mailer who sends you sexually oriented advertisements is subject to legal action by the U.S. Government. To stop the mailing of any further advertisements to yourself which you consider "erotically arousing or sexually provocative," fill out *Notice for Prohibitory Order Against Sender of Pandering Advertisement in the Mails,* at your local post office.

* Postal Bulletin

Consumer Affairs
U.S. Postal Service
475 L'Enfant Plaza, SW
Washington, DC 20260 (202) 268-2284

This weekly publication contains current orders, instructions and information relating to the Postal Service, including philatelic, airmail, money order, parcel post, etc. The subscription is available for $63 domestic, and $78.75 foreign per year, (S/N 739-001-0000-5) from: Superintendent of Documents, Government Printing Office, Washington, DC 20402-0001; (202) 783-3238.

* Postal Commission Procedures

Administrative Office
Postal Rate Commission
1333 H St., NW, Suite 300
Washington, DC 20268-0001 (202) 789-6840

The publication, *The Postal Rate Commission in Brief,* outlines the steps of various cases and decisions for which the Commission is responsible. The steps in a postal rate case and the decision procedure are outlined, as well as those of a mail classification case. Change in nationwide service, the appeal process for closing or consolidating a small post office, and the way in which rate or service complaints are handled are also described. Contact this office to receive a copy.

* Postal Financial Management Manual

Superintendent of Documents
Government Printing Office
Washington, DC 20402-0001 (202) 783-3238

The *Financial Management Manual* presents an overview of the financial activities of the Postal Service. It summarizes the following topics: general accounting, post office accounting, accounts receivable and accounts payable, budget and planning, payroll accounting and control of assets.

* Postal Inspection Service

Inspection Service Department
U.S. Postal Service
475 L'Enfant Plaza, SW
Washington, DC 20260-2100 (202) 268-4267

As the law enforcement arm of the Postal Service, The Postal Inspection Service protects the mails, postal funds, and property; investigates internal conditions and needs that may affect postal security and effectiveness; apprehends those who violate the postal laws; and audits financial and nonfinancial operations. Information on past and present schemes used to defraud the public is available as well. Help is available if you experience difficulty with a company or suspect that you have been the victim of mail fraud. There is a Regional Chief Inspector in each of the five postal regions. Information and complaints of postal violations should be presented to the nearest Postal Inspector in charge.

Central Region

Chicago
Main Post Office Bldg., Chicago, IL 60607-5401; (312) 765-4605
433 W. Van Buren St., Chicago, IL 60669-2201; (312) 765-4500

Denver
P.O. Box 329, Denver, CO 80201-0329; (303) 297-6220

Des Moines
P.O. Box 566, Des Moines, IA 50302-0566; (515) 253-9060

Be patient. If any phone number is incorrect, call (area code) 555-1212 and request the new listing.

Consumer Power

Detroit
P.O. Box 330119, Detroit, MI 48232-6119; (313) 226-8184

Indianapolis
7188 Lakeview Pkwy.W. Dr., Indianapolis, IN 46268-4101; (317) 328-2500

Kansas City
3101 Broadway, Suite 850, Kansas City, MO 64111-2416; (816) 932-0400

Milwaukee
P.O. Box 788, Milwaukee, WI 53201-0788; (414) 287-2200

St. Louis
1106 Walnut St., St. Louis, MO 63199-2201; (314) 539-9300

St. Paul
P.O. Box 64558, St. Paul, MN 55164-2201; (612) 293-3202/3200

Eastern Region
Cynwud
1 Bala Cynwyd Plaza, Bala Cynwyd, PA 19004-3509; (215) 668-4500

Baltimore
P.O. Box 1856, Baltimore, MD 21203-1856; (301) 347-4380

Charlotte
2901 I-85 S., Charlotte, NC 28228-3000; (704) 329-9120

Cincinnati
P.O. Box 14487, Cincinnati, OH 45250-0487; (513) 684-5700

Cleveland
P.O. Box 5726, Cleveland, OH 44101-0726; (216) 443-4000

Harrisburg
P.O. Box 3535, Harrisburg, PA 17105-3535; (717) 257-2330

Philadelphia
P.O. Box 7500, Philadelphia, PA 19101-9000; (215) 895-8450

Pittsburgh
1001 California Ave., Pittsburgh, PA 15290-9000; (412) 359-7900

Richmond
P.O. Box 25009, Richmond, VA 23260-5009; (804) 775-6267

Washington, DC
P.O. Box 96096, Washington, DC 20066-6096; (202) 636-2339/2300

Northeast Region
Newark
Gateway No. 2, McCarter Hwy. and Market St., Newark, NJ 07175-0001; (201) 621-5500
P.O. Box 509, Newark, NJ 07101-5901; (201) 596-5450

Boston
P.O. Box 2217, Boston, MA 02202-2217; (617) 654-5840

Buffalo
685 Ellicott Sq., Buffalo, NY 14203-2545; (716) 856-3674

Hartford
P.O. Box 2169, Hartford, CT 06145-2169; (203) 524-6060

New York
P.O. Box 5555, James Farley Bldg., New York, NY 10116-0555; (212) 330-3844

San Juan
P.O. Box 3667, San Juan, PR 00936-9614; (809) 749-7600/1-2-3

Southern Region
Memphis
10th Fl., 1407 Union Ave., Memphis, TN 38161-0001; (901) 722-7700
P.O. Box 3180, Memphis, TN 38173-0180; (901) 576-2137

Atlanta
P.O. Box 16489, Atlanta, GA 30321-0489; (404) 765-7369

Birmingham
P.O. Box 2767, Birmingham, AL 35202-2767; (205) 521-0270

Fort Worth
P.O. Box 162929, Fort Worth, TX 76161-2929; (817) 625-3411

Houston
P.O. Box 1276, Houston, TX 77251-1276; (713) 238-4400

Miami
P.O. Box 520772, Miami, FL 33152-0772; (305) 470-0379

New Orleans
P.O. Box 51690, New Orleans, LA 70151-1690; (504) 589-1200

Tampa
P.O. Box 22526, Tampa, FL 33622-2526; (813) 281-5200

Western Region
San Bruno
850 Cherry Ave., San Bruno, CA 94098-0100; (415) 742-4411

Oakland
7717 Edgewater Dr., Oakland, CA 94621-3013; (415) 636-2600

Pasadena
P.O. Box 2000, Pasadena, CA 91102-2000; (818) 405-1200

Phoenix
P.O. Box 20666, Phoenix, AZ 85036-0666; (602) 223-3660

Portland
Suite 790, 921 SW Washington, Portland, OR 97205-2898; (503) 294-2263

San Diego
P.O. Box 2110, San Diego, CA 92112-2110; (619) 233-0610

San Francisco
P.O. Box 882000, San Francisco, CA 94188-2000; (415) 550-5602/5700

Seattle
P.O. Box 400, Seattle, WA 98111-4000; (206) 442-6300

* Postal Life: The Magazine for Postal Employees

Consumer Affairs
U.S. Postal Service
475 L'Enfant Plaza, SW
Washington, DC 20260 (202) 268-2284

This bimonthly periodical contains articles, with illustrations, about new methods, techniques and programs of the U.S. Postal Service. Its purpose is to keep postal employees informed and abreast of developments in the U.S. Postal Service. The subscription is available for $11 domestic, and $13.75 foreign per year, S/N 739-002-00000-1, from: Superintendent of Documents, Government Printing Office, Washington, DC 20402-0001; (202) 783-3238.

* Postal Publications

Contact your local post office.

Introduction To Stamp Collecting. Offers advice on starting a collection, ideas for various types of collections, how to obtain and care for stamps, and philatelic resources, organizations, and publications.

INTELPOST EMS Express Mail. This brochure provides information on service, rates and benefits, and service destinations. Pick one up at your local post office.

How to Pack and Wrap Parcels for Mailing and *How to Prepare and Wrap Packages.* Contain helpful tips and guidelines for mailing packages, including minimum size standards, mailing nonstandard-size parcels, and selecting the proper container. They are available at your local post office.

Acceptance of Hazardous, Restricted or Perishable Matter. Contains detailed information on hazardous material. Your local postmaster or account representative can provide you with a copy of this publication.

Be patient. If any phone number is incorrect, call (area code) 555-1212 and request the new listing.

Post Office and Mailing

Express Mail Corporate Account and *Express Mail General Information*. Provides information on service options, preparing your package, rates and making payments, and how to protect your packages.

Selling to the Postal Service. Offers details on Postal Service procurement including specific supplies and services.

Customer Guide to Filing Indemnity Claims on Domestic Mail. Explains the specific procedures that must be followed when filing a claim for compensation including who can file, when to file, where to file, how to file, and information on claim forms. Copies are available at your local post office.

* Postal Publications and Handbooks

Data Information Center
Document Control Division
U.S. Postal Service
475 L'Enfant Plaza, SW
Washington, DC 20260 (202) 268-2852

Postal Service Publication No. 223 lists all technical publications available, including titles of publications and their supply source.

* Postal Rate Commission

Postal Rate Commission
1333 H St., NW, Suite 300
Washington, DC 20268-0001 (202) 789-6800

The Postal Rate Commission considers proposed changes in postal rates, fees, and mail classifications and issues recommendations to the Governors of the Postal Service. It also considers changes in the nature of available postal service. Postal Service decisions to close or consolidate post offices are also reviewed. The Commission also investigates complaints concerning postal rates and service on the national level. Five Commissioners serve a six-year term of office and are appointed by the President.

* Postal Rate Commission Open Meetings

General Counsel
Postal Rate Commission
1333 H St., NW, Suite 300
Washington, DC 20268-0001 (202) 789-6820

The Commission meetings are the forums where postal rates, fees, mail classifications, service changes, and post office closings and consolidations are discussed. They are open to the public, except in special circumstances, but public participation is not permitted. Documents from these meetings are also available to the public at the headquarters offices.

* Postal Rate Complaints

General Counsel
Postal Rate Commission
1333 H St., NW, Suite 300
Washington, DC 20268-0001 (202) 789-6820

Written complaints may be addressed to the above office if you feel changes are needed in the rate and classification structure of mail or if you believe the nationwide system of the Postal Service can be improved. Local problems must be addressed to the U.S. Postal Service directly.

* Postal Rate Consumer Information

Consumer Advocate
Postal Rate Commission
1333 H St., NW, Suite 300
Washington, DC 20268-0001 (202) 789-6830

Information on the activities of the Postal Rate Commission is distributed by the Consumer Advocate. If a postal rate case is pending, the newspapers and other media are alerted. Consumer groups are also notified.

* Postal Service Changes

Postal Rate Commission
1333 H St., NW, Suite 300
Washington, DC 20268-0001 (202) 789-6800

The Postal Service asks the Postal Commission for their advisory opinion on proposed changes in nationwide postal services, rates, and classifications. These formal requests are then published in the *Federal Register*.

* Postal Service Films

Communications Department
The U.S. Postal Service
475 L'Enfant Plaza, SW
Washington, DC 20260 (202) 268-2156

A few general films are available for loan to the public. One film, for example, traces the route of a letter as it goes through the postal service system, and another film demonstrates the importance of letters in people's lives.

* Postal Speakers Network

Assistant Postmaster General
Communications Department
U.S. Postal Service
475 L'Enfant Plaza, SW, Room 5300
Washington, DC 20260 (202) 268-2143

Speakers may be scheduled free of charge provided two to three months notice is given and provided those interested give preliminary information. It is also possible to coordinate Postal Service participation in meetings of national organizations and associations. Speakers for meetings that are regional or local in nature are scheduled by the appropriate Regional Postmaster General's office or the Regional Chief Inspector's office.

* Practice and Procedures

Administrative Office
Postal Rate Commission
1333 H St., NW, Suite 300
Washington, DC 20268-0001 (202) 789-6840

Rules of Practice and Procedure describes in detail the methods for handling the Postal Rate Commission's responsibilities. First is a listing of rules that apply to general business matters, including term definitions, the docket and hearing calendar, inquiries, and public attendance at Commission meetings. Rules are also written for rates or fees changes, for changing the mail classification schedule, for postal service changes, and for rate and service complaints. The method for filing testimony by those who wish to intervene in rate and classification proceedings is also included, as well as the procedure for an appeal to a decision to close or consolidate small post offices.

* Products and Services

The Marketing Department
The U.S. Postal Service
475 L'Enfant Plaza, SW, Room 5014
Washington, DC 20260 (202) 268-2222

For information on specific U.S. Postal Service products and services, contact this office.

* Regional and Field Division Offices

U.S. Postal Service
475 L'Enfant Plaza, SW
Washington, DC 20260-0010

In addition to the national headquarters, regional and field division offices supervise more than 40,000 post offices, branches, stations, and community post offices throughout the United States. Each of the five Regional Postmasters General manage postal activities in a geographical area as indicated below.

Central Region
433 W. Van Buren St., Chicago, IL 60699-0100; (312) 765-5000. Areas served: CO, IL, IN (except ZIP Codes 420, 423, 424, 470, 476, 477), IA, KS, MI, MN, MO, NE, ND, SD, WI, WY.

Eastern Region
P.O. Box 8601, Philadelphia, PA 19197-0100; (215) 931-5001. Areas served: DC, DE, IN (ZIP Codes 420, 423, 424, 470, 476, 477), KY, MD, NJ (ZIP Codes 080-084), NC, OH, PA, SC, VA, WV.

Northeast Region
6 Griffin Park Rd. N, Windsor, CT 06006-0100; (203) 285-7001. Areas served: CT, MA, ME, NH, NJ (ZIP Codes 070-079, 085-089), NY, Puerto Rico, RI, VT, Virgin Islands.

Southern Region
1407 Union Ave., Memphis, TN 38166-0100; (901) 722-7333. Areas served: AL, AR, FL, GA, LA, MS, OK, TN, TX (except ZIP Codes 797-799).

Be patient. If any phone number is incorrect, call (area code) 555-1212 and request the new listing.

Consumer Power

Western Region
850 Cherry Ave., San Bruno, CA 94099-0100; (415) 742-4922. Areas served: AK, AZ, CA, HI, ID, MT, NV, NM, OR, TX (ZIP Codes 797-799), UT, WA, Pacific Possessions and Trust Territories.

* Public Hearings on the Postal System

Docket Section
Postal Rate Commission
1333 H St., NW, Suite 300
Washington, DC 20268-0001 (202) 789-6845

When a proposed change in the national Postal Service is recommended before the Postal Rate Commission, public hearings are held. Testimony is given on the program, and those in attendance are given an opportunity to address questions. The records of these public hearings are used in making the final decisions on postal system changes. To be placed on the mailing list to receive notices of these hearings, contact the office above. A hearing calendar and a docket of all proceedings from the hearings is also available for public inspection. Office hours are 8 a.m. to 5 p.m., Monday through Friday. You must have the docket number of the proceeding you wish to examine.

* Rural or Highway Contract Route

Rural Delivery Division
Delivery and Distribution and Transportation Department
U.S. Postal Service
Washington, DC 20260 (202) 268-6990

General distribution of third class mail to each boxholder on a rural or highway contract route, or for each family on a rural route, or for all boxholders at a post office that does not have city or village carrier service, may have the mail addressed omitting the names of individuals and box or route numbers if the mailer uses this form of address: "Postal Customer," or, to be more specific: "Rural (or Highway Contract Route) Boxholder, City (or town), State." On request, a Postmaster will furnish mailers with the number of families and boxes served on each route.

* Small Post Office Closings

Delivery Distribution and Transportation Department
U.S. Postal Service
475 L'Enfant Plaza, SW
Washington, DC 20260 (202) 268-6990

Contact this office for information on small post office closings or consolidations.

* Third-Class Mail Preparation

Marketing and Sales
U.S. Postal Service
475 L'Enfant Plaza, SW
Washington, DC 20260-3121 (202) 268-2143

If you're planning to mail at the third-class bulk rates, this publication explains what bulk business mail is, and how to get the most out of it. If you already have the necessary permits to mail at the bulk third-class rates, this publication will serve as a valuable reference.

Be patient. If any phone number is incorrect, call (area code) 555-1212 and request the new listing.

Housing and Real Estate General Sources

* *See also Your Community Chapter*

This chapter provides good starting places for finding information in the housing and real estate industry. You'll find sources on such topics as surplus property, urban homesteading, construction standards, and even historic preservation. There's information here for anyone interested in housing and real estate, including first time home buyers, urban planners, and real estate speculators. Whether you're looking for mortgage counseling, foreclosed properties, or information on housing discrimination, you should be able to find what you're looking for.

* Accessible Housing Reports for the Handicapped

HUD USER
P.O. Box 6091 (800) 245-2691
Rockville, MD 20850 (301) 251-5154

HUD USER makes the following series of reports available on research performed to make buildings accessible to and usable by all Americans:

Access to the Built Environment: A Review of Literature (#660), $15. Describes the history of efforts to achieve a barrier-free environment and pertinent Federal, State, and municipal laws and regulations.

Accessible Buildings for People With Walking and Reaching Limitations (#661), $15. Discusses the research conducted in such areas as wheelchair maneuvers, ramps, toilet stalls, bathrooms, kitchens, doorways, elevators, and public phones and mailboxes.

Accessible Buildings for People With Severe Visual Impairments (#662), $15. Reports the results of a study of orientation and mobility problems that occur in visually impaired individuals in architectural settings, and solutions for dwellings to conform to American National Standards Institute specifications.

A Cost-Benefit Analysis of Accessibility (#664), $10. Presents a cost-benefit analysis for removing architectural barriers from residential and nonresidential buildings.

Adaptable Dwellings (#665), $10. Reviews the research completed to determine what parts of a dwelling should be designed for accessibility and to what extent special features are needed from a disabled person's viewpoint.

Adaptable Housing: Marketing Accessible Housing for Everyone (HUD #004981), $4. A primer of adaptable housing for designers and builders, as well as developers, managers, architects, product manufacturers, and government and building code officials.

* American Housing Survey for the United States

HUD User
P.O. Box 6091 (800) 245-2691
Rockville, MD 20850 (301) 251-5154

This survey is the result of personal and telephone interviews of approximately 190,000 households in 44 selected metropolitan areas conducted by the Census Bureau for HUD. Information is provided on the size and composition of the U.S. housing inventory, occupant characteristics, changes in the stock due to new construction, indicators of housing and neighborhood quality, and the characteristics of recent movers. The study contains hundreds of different kinds of information on such housing-related topics as age, race sex, and income of households; source of income--wages, pensions, dividends, welfare, Social Security; reasons for moving from last home; type and condition of housing; amount of rent or mortgage payment, value of property, purchase price, downpayment; number of rooms, bedrooms, baths; repairs, alterations, additions; plumbing, heating, cooling equipment, and other appliances; cost of fuel and utilities, type of fuel used; neighborhood quality--police protection, hospitals; neighborhood problems--crime, pollution, street noise.

The information from this survey can be used in many ways. Mortgage lenders, developers, marketing analysts, and demographers can use the survey information to examine economic and social trends for planning and decisionmaking. Manufacturers, housing analysts, financial institutions, and planners may study particular markets, which builders and real estate brokers can rely on to help them better understand their housing markets. Data is also available on magnetic tape or compact disc. If you need microdata, the survey is now available in CD-ROM (compact disc-read only memory) in two formats: ASCII and SAS internal format. The cost is $3 for the information in hard copy, and $125 for the data on CD-ROM.

* Builder and Developer Publications

HUD USER
P.O. Box 6091 (800) 245-2691
Rockville, MD 20850 (301) 251-5154

The following is a sampling of publications of interest to real estate developers, builders, and others in the housing construction industry. $3 is charged per document for handling.

Affordable Housing Challenge and Response, Vol.1: Affordable Residential Land Development (HUD 005961 $4)

Affordable Housing Challenge and Response, Vol.2: Affordable Residential Construction (HUD 00501 $4)

Home Builder's Guide for Earthquake Design (HUD 001621 $4)

Home Building Cost Cuts: Construction Methods and Materials for Affordable Housing (looseleaf bulletins) (HUD 002930 $4)

Noise Assessment Guidelines (HUD 001746 $20)

Rehabilitation Guidelines 1986: Includes guidelines on setting and adopting standards for building rehabilitation, approval of building rehabilitation, managing official liability associated with building rehabilitation, egress, electrical, plumbing, fire ratings, archaic materials and assemblies, structural assessment, walls, windows, roofs, and building systems. ($4 each or set for $20)

EER-2 Energy Efficient Residence: Research Results (HUD 003755 $4)

Reducing Energy Costs in Multifamily Housing (HUD 004609 $4)

Regional Guidelines for Building Passive Energy Conserving Homes (HUD 005082 $4)

Site Planning for Solar Access: A Guidebook for Residential Developers and Site Planners (HUD 002062 $4)

Cost of Lead Based Paint Abatement in Public Housing (HUD 004596 $4)

Survey of Passive Solar Homes (HUD 002083 $4)

Housing Special Populations: A Resource Guide - 1987 (HUD 005040 $4). Provides the housing specialist with resources on housing the elderly, disabled persons, and the homeless. Annotated references to reports, books, and articles provide access to pertinent up-to-date information. Photographs help illustrate the unique circumstances and real life situations faced by these special groups. Also included in the guide is a list of organizations - with names, addresses, and phone numbers - to allow networking opportunities with colleagues.

Environmental Hazards in Residential Construction (HUD 005056 $5). Indoor pollutants are an increasingly alarming health hazard. This is a guide to reports, articles, pamphlets, and books addressing four indoor environmental hazards: asbestos, radon gas, lead-based paint, and formaldehyde. A resource section lists organizations, government resources, and periodicals that can provide additional information.

Blueprint Catalog. Describes 48 full size working drawings of affordable and energy-efficient housing designs available from HUD USER (Free)(** Blue Cat).

Housing and Real Estate

Designing Affordable Houses (S/N 023-000-00702-9, $1.75). Various plans for building moderate cost homes.

House Construction: How to Reduce Costs (S/N 001-000-03729-3, $2.50)

Finishing Wood Exteriors (S/N 001-000-04450-8, $3.25). Provides information on the characteristics and proper application of finishes to solid and reconstituted wood products. Also discusses the different kinds of wood, the selection, application, and maintenance practices that affect surfaces to be finished.

* Community and Urban Planning Publications

HUD USER
P.O. Box 6091 (800) 245-2691
Rockville, MD 20850 (301) 251-5154

The following is a sampling of publications of interest to community and urban planners available for a $3 handling charge.

Local Property Urban Homesteading Demonstration (HUD 005176 $20)
Rental Housing: Condition and Outlook (HUD 002221 $4)
Affordable Housing: How Local Regulatory Improvements Can Help (HUD 002733 $5)
Affordable Housing: What States Can Do (HUD 002734 $5)
Housing Rehabilitation for Small Cities, Second Edition: The Community Development Approach (HUD 004684 $10)
How to Design a Rental Rehabilitation Program: Training Exercises for Program Operators (HUD 003763 $4)
Case Study of Local Control Over Housing Development: The Neighborhood Strategy Area (HUD 002896 $4)
Final Report of the Evaluation of the Urban Initiatives Anti-Crime Demonstration (HUD 0050930 $4)
Implementing Community Development: A Study of the Community Development Block Grant Program (HUD 00274 $4)
Insider's Guide to Managing Public Housing, Vol. 1, Diagnosing Management Problems (HUD 003952 $20)
Insider's Guide to Managing Public Housing, Vol. 2, Analysis Guide (HUD 003032 $15 and HUD 003033 $4)
Tools and Techniques for Housing Development: A Guidebook for Local Officials (HUD 003291 $15)
Effects of Tax Reform on Housing and Urban Development - 1987 (HUD 004843 $10). The articles and reports in this resource guide will help builders, architects, planners, local government officials, and other housing and urban development professionals analyze the effects of the new law on homebuilding and financing, real estate investment, municipal capital spending, and low-income housing construction and financing.
Housing Rehabilitation: Programs, Techniques, and Resources-1987 (HUD 004843 $10). This guide to publications offers an overview of housing rehabilitation in central cities in the U. S., covering rehabilitation technology, local approaches, Federal programs, and historic preservation. A list of relevant organizations, journal titles, and other resources is included.
Enterprise Zones in America: A Selected Resource Guide - 1986 (HUD 4646 $4, Vol. #2, HUD 005453 $4). The goal of enterprise zones is the stimulation of business--especially small enterprises--in depressed areas through the provision of tax and other incentives and through deregulation. This reference guide includes summaries and bibliographic information on 31 publications which focus in the historical background of the concept, discuss key issues involved in creating zones, and summarize reports based on State and local experiences with enterprise zones.
Affordable Housing: A Selected Resource Guide--1985 (HUD 004003 $2.50). This guide, with more than 50 annotated listings, is divided into five sections: Cost-Saving Design and Technology, Local Actions to Promote Affordable Housing, Financing, Case Studies, and Outreach Materials.
Multi-Family Homesteading: A Guide for Local Governments (HUD 005826 $4) Explains how conversion of underutilized or abandoned multi-family property to shared ownership by long-term residents can help a community. Discusses selection of developers, property selection, project planning and design, financing, marketing, and management of these developments.

* Counseling for Homebuyers, Homeowners, and Tenants

Single Family Servicing Branch
Secretary-Held and Counseling Services
Office of Insured Single Family Housing
U.S. Department of Housing and Urban Development
Washington, DC 20410-8000 (202) 708-3664

To help reduce delinquencies, defaults, and foreclosures, HUD provides free counseling to homeowners and tenants under its programs through HUD-approved counseling agencies. The counselors advise and assist homeowners with budgeting, money management, and buying and maintaining their homes. Contact this office or your local HUD office of information on the counseling agency nearest you.

* Consumer Housing Publications

Consumer Information Center
Pueblo, CO 81002

Write to the above address to order any of the following publications:

Consumer Handbook on Adjustable Rate Mortgages. Basic features, advantages and risks, and terminology associated with adjustable rate mortgages. (1984, Federal Reserve Board, 423 Y., $.50).

A Consumer's Guide to Mortgage Lock-ins. What they are and how you can lock-in interest rates and points when applying for a mortgage. (1988, Federal Reserve Board, 424 Y., $.50).

A Consumer's Guide to Mortgage Refinancing. What the costs are and how to tell if the time is right to refinance your home. (1988, Federal Reserve Board, 425 Y., $.50).

Guide to Single Family Home Mortgage Insurance. Protects lenders against losses on mortgages so they can offer you terms you might not have otherwise. Learn about these options and your responsibilities. (1990 Housing and Urban Development, 120 Y. $1)

Home Buyer's Vocabulary. Defines common words and terms used in the real estate world. Especially useful for the first time buyer. (1987 Housing and Urban Development, 121 Y. $1)

Home Mortgages: Understanding the Process and Your Right to Fair Lending. Describes your responsibilities and legal protections regarding application and credit evaluation (1990, Federal Reserve Board, 426 Y. $.50)

How to Buy a Manufactured (Mobile) Home. Helpful tips on selection, placement transportation warranties installation, and inspection. (1992, Federal Trade Commission, 427 Y., $.50).

Reverse Mortgages. Learn how to convert home equity into cash. Explains the three different types of reverse mortgages available, and how to get more information on home equity conversion plans. (1991 Federal Trade Commission, 475 Y., $.50)

When Your Home is On the Line. Your home serves as collateral for a home equity loan. Here are questions, terms, tips, and more - all to help you find the best deal. (1989, Federal Reserve Board, 428 Y. $.50)

Wise Home Buying. Here's help in finding the right house: when to use a broker, inspection, and shopping for a mortgage (1987, Housing and Urban Development, 123 Y. $1)

Simple Home Repairs Inside. Step-by-step directions with pictures on how to repair or replace doors, faucets, plugs, windows, screens, tiles, and more. (1986 U.S. Department of Agriculture, 125 Y. $1.50)

* Country Homes

USDA, Farmers Home Administration
Single Family Housing Division
14th and Independence Ave., SW
Washington, DC 20250 (202) 720-4323

The Farmers Home Administration makes low-interest loans to qualified applicants to purchase homes or farms in rural areas. They are also charged with disposing of properties that are foreclosed. First, the Farmers Home Administration makes any necessary repairs to the property, then offers them for sale to people who have the same qualifications as those applying for loans. Eligible applicants also qualify to purchase at special low interest rates (as low as 1%). If no eligible applicants purchase a property, it is then put up for sale to the general public at competitive prices. If the property is not sold within 10 days, it is reduced by 10%.

* Directory of Information Resources in Housing and Urban Development

HUD USER
P.O. Box 6091 (800) 245-2691
Rockville, MD 20850 (301) 251-5154

The most recent edition of this directory lists 150 trade and professional organizations, public agencies, advocacy groups, and research and educational institutes in housing and urban development. Each entry describes the organization's purpose and services and includes an address and telephone number. These contacts can provide current relevant information on today's key housing issues. The *Directory* also describes 54 online databases available in the field. This publication is available for $25.

General Sources

* Earth Sheltered Buildings

Science and Technology Division
Reference Section
Library of Congress
Washington, DC 20540 (202) 707-5580

An informal series of reference guides are issued free from the Science and Technology Division under the general title, *LC Science Tracer Bullet*. These guides are designed to help readers locate published material on subjects about which they have only general knowledge. New titles in the series are announced in the weekly *Library of Congress Information Bulletin* that is distributed to many libraries. The relevant study is No. 82-3 *Earth Sheltered Buildings*.

* Escrow Accounts For Home Mortgages

Federal Trade Commission (FTC)
Division of Credit Practices
6th and Pennsylvania Ave., NW
Washington, DC 20580 (202) 326-3175

Each month millions of homeowners pay money into escrow accounts to cover property taxes and hazard insurance through their lending institutions, but many don't even know what these escrow accounts really are. If you have questions about escrow practices, rates, and laws, contact your bank, your state banking agency, or the FTC.

* HUD Programs Investigation Division

Office of Fair Housing and Equal Opportunity
U.S. Department of Housing and Urban Development (HUD)
Washington, DC 20410-2000 (202) 708-0404

HUD determines the extent to which its programs comply with Federal laws forbidding discrimination in all federally funded activities. This office investigates complaints and reviews HUD programs to eliminate discrimination. Activities are made more responsive to minorities and promote their participation in HUD programs. Technical assistance is available to state and local agencies with civil rights problems.

* Fair Housing Complaints

Fair Housing Enforcement Division
Office of Fair Housing and Equal Opportunity
U.S. Department of Housing and Urban Development (HUD)
Washington, DC 20410-2000
For filing complaints: (202) 619-8041

HUD administers the law that prohibits discrimination in housing on the basis of race, color, religion, sex, and national origin; investigates complaints of housing discrimination; and attempts to resolve them through conciliation. Two common forms of discrimination are redlining and steering. Redlining is the illegal practice of refusing to originate mortgage loans in certain neighborhoods on the basis of race or ethnic origin. Steering is the illegal act of limiting the housing shown by a real estate agent to a certain ethnic group. If you have experienced housing discrimination, you should file a complaint with any HUD office in person, by mail, or by telephone at the numbers listed here. HUD refers complaints to state and local fair housing agencies.

* Fair Housing: Voluntary Compliance

Office of Voluntary Compliance
Office of Fair Housing and Equal Opportunity
U.S. Department of Housing and Urban Development (HUD)
Washington, DC 20410-2000 (202) 708-1992

HUD promotes voluntary compliance in the private sector and with other Federal agencies in the area of fair housing activities nationwide. HUD executes Voluntary Affirmative Marketing Agreements with housing industry groups, both locally and nationwide. Comprehensive fair housing plans are also developed with local units of government. HUD also organizes volunteer citizen groups to work with these plans and agreements. Trade and professional organizations in housing and related fields, including homebuilders, real estate brokers, mortgage lenders, and rental property managers are asked to comply.

* Federal National Mortgage Association (Fannie Mae)

Federal National Mortgage Association
3900 Wisconsin Ave., NW
Washington, DC 20016 (202) 752-7000

This governmental financial institution has been created to serve as a secondary source of mortgage funds. By purchasing loans from lenders, it serves as a conduit for funds from investors into the loan industry. Even though it is a privately-owned, profit-motivated corporation, the Secretary of HUD has regulatory authority over Fannie Mae's operations.

* Foreign Investments in the U.S.

Land Branch, ERS
U.S. Department of Agriculture
1301 New York Ave., NW
Washington, DC 20005-4788 (202) 219-0420

Foreign investment in U.S. agricultural land has been reported for 14.8 million acres in 1,918 of the 3,041 counties in the U.S. *Foreign Ownership of U.S. Agricultural Land through December 31, 1991* lists data for each county to show the number of acres, its value, country of origin, and use of the land. This publication is also available on tape from AFIDA Database (800-999-6779).

* Ginnie Mae Mortgage-Backed Securities

Government National Mortgage Association
U.S. Department of Housing and Urban Development (HUD)
Washington, DC 20410-9000 (202) 708-0926

The Government National Mortgage Association guarantees the timely payment of principal and interest on securities issued by lenders and backed by pools of Government-underwritten residential mortgages. The program's purpose is to attract non-traditional investors into the residential mortgage market by offering them a high-yield, risk-free, Government-guaranteed security which has none of the servicing obligation associated with a mortgage loan portfolio. GNMA II, which supplements the original program, has a central paying agent, Chemical Bank, which makes consolidated payments to investors. Larger, geographically-dispersed, multiple-issuer mortgage pools, as well as custom pools, are offered. A mix of interest rates is also provided among the mortgages within the pool. Securities under this program are privately issued and backed by pools of FHA or Veteran's Administration mortgages. Included in the mortgage pools are single-family level payment, graduated payment, growing equity, and manufactured housing loans. Lending institutions under this program must be in good standing and have adequate net worth, staffing, and experience.

* Handicapped Access to Buildings

Architectural and Transportation Barriers
Compliance Board
Suite 1000, 1331 F St., NW
Washington, DC 20004-1111 (800) USA-ABLE Ext 38 (202) 272-5434

This organization, affiliated with the U.S. Department of Education, provides information in compliance with standards for access to and use of buildings by handicapped persons.

Uniform Federal Assessibility Standards: Architectural requirements for access to federally funded facilities. Based on the ATBCB Minimum Guidelines and Requirements for Accessible Design.

* Handicapped Housing Information for Developers

Office of Elderly and Assisted Housing
U.S. Department of Housing and Urban Development (HUD)
Washington, DC 20410-8000 (202) 708-2866

This office can provide you with complete information on the procedure to obtain Section 202 funding for handicapped housing projects. An information packet, which outlines the program requirements and the specifications for the construction of the project to be funded, is available.

* Historic Preservation

Superintendent of Documents
Government Printing Office (GPO)
Washington, DC 20402 (202) 783-3238

The following publications on historic preservation are available from the GPO for $1 unless otherwise noted:

Architectural Character: Identifying the Visual Aspects of Historic Buildings as an Aid to Preserving Their Character Cleaning and Waterproof Coating of Masonry Buildings
Conserving Energy in Historic Buildings
Dangers of Abrasive Cleaning to Historic Buildings
Exterior Paint Problems on Historic Woodwork
Historic America: Buildings, Structures, and Sites ($29)

Be patient. If any phone number is incorrect, call (area code) 555-1212 and request the new listing.

Housing and Real Estate

Interior Building: Its Architecture and Its Art ($8.50)
Keeping It Clean: Removing Exterior Dirt, Paint, Stains, and Graffiti From Historic Masonry Buildings ($2.50)
Metals in America's Historic Buildings: Uses and Preservation Treatment ($6)
National Register of Historic Places
New Exterior Additions to Historic Buildings: Preservation Concerns
Preservation Briefs: Recognizing and Resolving Common Preservation Problems ($9)
Preservation of Historic Adobe Buildings
Preservation of Historic Concrete Problems and General Approaches
Preservation of Historic Glazed Architectural Terra-Cotta
Preservation of Historic Pigmented Structural Glass, Vitrolite and Carrara Glass
Preservation Tax Incentives for Historic Buildings
Rehabilitating Historic Storefronts
Rehabilitating Interiors in Historic Buildings: Identifying and Preserving Character, Defining Elements
Repair and Thermal Upgrading of Historic Steel Windows ($1.25)
Repair of Historic Wooden Windows
Repointing Mortar Joints in Historic Brick Buildings
Roofing for Historic Buildings
Secretary of the Interior's Standards for Rehabilitation and Guidelines for Rehabilitating Historic Buildings ($2)
Interpreting the Secretary of the Interior's Standards for Rehabilitation, Volume 3 ($9)
Technologies for Prehistoric and Historic Preservation ($10)
Use of Substitute Materials in Historic Buildings: Exterior Applications

* Home Ownership Publications

Veterans Assistance Office
U.S. Department of Veterans Affairs (VA)
810 Vermont Ave., NW
Washington, DC 20420 (202) 872-1151

The following publications are available to veterans from their VA regional office:

Pointers for the Veteran Homeowner. A guide for veterans whose home mortgage is guaranteed or insured under the GI Bill.
To the Home-Buying Veteran. A guide for veterans planning to buy or build homes with a VA loan.
VA-Guaranteed Home Loans for Veterans. To help you understand what the VA can and cannot do for the home purchaser.

* Houses From Failed Saving and Loans Companies

Resolution Trust Corporation (800) 431-0600
Washington, DC 20429 (202) 789-6316

As a result of the hundreds of failed US Savings and Loan institutions the US Government has had on over 30,000 real property assets, it is attempting to auction these assets off at the best available price. The inventory contains approximately 12,000 single family homes, 2,500 commercial properties and 800 parcels of undeveloped land.

* Housing Consumer Publications

Superintendent of Documents
Government Printing Office
Washington, DC 20402 (202) 783-3238

The following publications are geared toward home buyers, and prospective home buyers, who may not be familiar with such issues as consumer rights, mortgages, financing, and much more. Each publication is followed by the GPO order number and price.

Wise Home Buying (S/N 023-000-00752-5, $1). Instructs the first-time home buyer in selecting and financing a house. Discusses the relation of housing costs to income, new versus old houses, mortgage loans, real estate brokers, and more.

Home Buyer's Vocabulary (S/N 023-000-00751-7, $1). Provides general, nontechnical definitions of terms the potential home buyer will encounter in buying and financing a home.

* Housing Discrimination

Fair Housing Enforcement Division
Office of Fair Housing and Equal Opportunity
U.S. Department of Housing and Urban Development (HUD)

Washington, DC 20410-2000 (202) 708-2213

Technical assistance is available to state and local agencies, private and public groups, and profit or nonprofit organizations to help them prevent or eliminate discriminatory housing practices.

* Housing Finance Statistics

Financial Policy Division
Office of Housing
U.S. Department of Housing and Urban Development (HUD)
Washington, DC 20410 (202) 755-7270

Studies are conducted by the Financial Policy Division of HUD in areas relating to the mortgage market, securities, taxation, market trends, and interest rates, among others. If you are interested in receiving information about these subjects or want to be placed on the mailing list, contact this office.

* Housing Research and Policy

Assistant Secretary for Policy Development and Research
U.S. Department of Housing and Urban Development (HUD)
Washington, DC 20410-6000 (202) 708-1600

This office is responsible for economic and policy analyses, research, demonstrations, and evaluations of national housing and community development. All policy development data generated by HUD are made available to interested parties, such as state and local governments, financial institutions, builders, developers, neighborhood groups, and universities and colleges. The research addresses many issues, including the management, operation, and maintenance of the insured and assisted multi-family housing inventory; the stability of the nation's housing finance system; the design of sound mortgage instruments and improvements in FHA programs; the increase of housing affordability through technological and regulatory improvements; the improvement of public housing; the assurance of a supply of affordable rental housing units; the promotion of fair and nondiscriminatory housing; and the study of housing-related health problems.

* HUD Counseling Agency Program

Single Family Servicing Branch
Secretary-Held and Counseling Services
Office of Insured Single Family Housing
U.S. Department of Housing and Urban Development (HUD)
Washington, DC 20410-8000 (202) 708-3664

Housing counseling grants are awarded on a competitive basis to HUD-approved counseling agencies to reimburse them partially for costs. These agencies and private and public organizations must be competent and have knowledge and experience in housing counseling. The maximum grant available is $40,000 per agency.

* HUD's Major Publication Sources

HUD USER
P.O. Box 6091 (800) 245-2691
Rockville, MD 20850 (301) 251-5154

HUD USER, the research information service sponsored by HUD's Office of Policy Development and Research, distributes the latest research in the fields of housing and urban development in a variety of formats tailored to your needs. These include:

Document delivery - Printed copies of recently published reports and photocopies of unpublished and out-of-print materials.

Resource guides - illustrated collections of abstracts on topics of special interest, such as housing rehabilitation, enterprise zones, public housing, alternative housing arrangements, affordable housing, fair housing, elderly housing, homelessness, and accessible environments for the disabled.

Directory of Information Resources in Housing and Urban Development- a valuable reference tool providing descriptions of 114 organizations and 37 online databases in the housing, construction, and planning fields.

Searches on HUD USER ONLINE - performed by HUD USER reference specialists to help you locate documents containing information in your area of interest.

Microfiche - copies of any non-copyrighted documents in HUD USER ONLINE in an economical and space-saving format.

Be patient. If any phone number is incorrect, call (area code) 555-1212 and request the new listing.

Audiovisual programs - to stimulate discussion at group meetings on improving housing and neighborhoods.

* HUD Library and Information Service

Program Information Center
U.S. Department of Housing and Urban Development (HUD)
Washington, DC 20410 (202) 708-1420

If you need additional assistance and direction to particular programs within HUD, or have questions about how HUD can work for you, contact the Program Information Center, and they will gladly assist you.

* Land Sale Fraud

Federal Trade Commission
Marketing Practices
6th and Pennsylvania Ave., NW
Washington, DC 20580 (202) 326-3128

This office investigates fraud as it relates to the sale of land to the public, and can provide you with information about your rights and how to avoid fraudulent practices.

* Land Sales

Interstate Land Sales Registration
U.S. Department of Housing and Urban Development (HUD)
Washington, DC 20410-8000 (202) 708-0502

The registration of interstate land sales protects subdivision lot purchasers by prohibiting fraudulent practices requiring of land developers and promoters full financial disclosure. Before a lot can be sold or leased, two conditions must be met by developers: 1) A Statement of Record must be filed with HUD, containing full and current disclosure about the ownership of the land, the state of title, planned physical characteristics, planned availability of roads, services, utilities, and other matters; and 2) A printed Property Report must be delivered to each purchaser or lessee in advance of signing the contract or agreement. Anti-fraud provisions apply to subdivisions containing 25 or more lots. HUD may seek an injunction against any developer whom it can show is violating or about to violate the law, and may suspend the registration of a developer whose Statement of Record or Property Report contains misrepresentation or omits material facts.

* Lenders Offering FHA-Insured Mortgages

Office of Insured Single Family Housing
U.S. Department of Housing and Urban Development (HUD)
Washington, DC 20410-8000 (202) 708-2700

This HUD office maintains a listing of lenders who participate in FHA-insured mortgage programs. You can also get this information by contacting your local Field Office.

* Mobile Home Construction and Safety Standards

Office of Single Family Housing
Office of Manufactured Housing and Regulatory Functions
Manufactured Housing and Construction Standards Division
U.S. Department of Housing and Urban Development (HUD)
Washington, DC 20410-8000 (202) 708-2210

U.S. Department of Housing and Urban Development (HUD) issues Federal manufactured home construction and safety standards to reduce the number of personal injuries and deaths, and the amount of insurance costs and property damage resulting from manufactured home accidents. The program also strives to improve the quality and durability of manufactured homes. Standards are enforced by HUD directly or by various States which have established State administrative agencies that participate in the program. HUD inspects factories and obtains records needed to enforce the standards, and if standards are not met, the manufacturer is forced to notify the consumer and to correct any defects found.

* Multifamily Property Disposition

Multifamily Sales Division
Office of Multifamily Housing
U.S. Department of Housing and Urban Development (HUD)
Washington, DC 20410 (202) 708-3000

Multifamily properties are sold through sealed-bid auctions across the country. This office maintains a listing of the current available properties. To be placed on the mailing list for current and new properties that become available, contact this office.

* Multifamily Property Standards

Government Printing Office
Superintendent of Documents
Washington, DC 20402 (202) 783-3238

HUD publishes a subscription service entitled *Minimum Property Standards, Volume II, Multifamily Housing*. The services consist of a basic manual and quarterly revisions in looseleaf form. Standards in the areas of health and safety, durability, energy, the elderly, and the handicapped are included. The subscription price is $35/year. (S/N 923-001-00000-0).

* Native American Indians and Housing

Office of Public Affairs
Bureau of Indian Affairs
U.S. Department of the Interior
18th and C Sts., NW
Washington, DC 20240 (202) 208-3671

The free booklet, *American Indians Today: Answers to Your Questions, 1988*, contains useful information on the Native American Indians and their relationship to the Bureau of Indian Affairs. Programs within the Bureau, including education, health services, and housing are briefly outlined and contain recent statistics. Many questions are answered within the booklet, including the rights of the Indians to own land and have their own governments. A map locates the Indian lands and communities, showing Federal and State Indian Reservations and other Indian groups. An excellent bibliography, prepared by the Smithsonian Institution, is included.

* Real Estate Settlements

Real Estate Settlement Procedures Act (RESPA)
Office of Insured Single Family Housing
U.S. Department of Housing and Urban Development (HUD)
Washington, DC 20410-8000 (202) 708-4560

RESPA requires that lenders give all borrowers of federally-insured mortgage loans a HUD-prepared booklet with information about real estate transactions, settlement services, cost comparisons, and relevant consumer protection laws. When applying for a loan, borrowers must receive the booklet along with the lender's good faith estimate of the settlement costs they are likely to incur. One day before settlement, the borrower may request that the person conducting the settlement provide information on the actual settlement costs. At settlement, both the buyer and seller are entitled to a settlement statement that itemizes the costs they paid in connection with the transaction.

* Recent Research Results (RRR)

HUD USER
P.O. Box 6091 (800) 245-2691
Rockville, MD 20850 (301) 251-5154

This newsletter contains short summaries of reports recently published under the auspices of the HUD Office of Policy Development and Research. To be put on the mailing list, contact this office.

* Rental Rates

Technical Support Division
Office of Multifamily Housing
U.S. Department of Housing and Urban Development (HUD)
Washington, DC 20410 (202) 708-0035

The Federal Register contains a yearly listing of the fair market rental rates in 450 market areas around the country. The data show the rental rates for various types of dwellings

* Research in Assisted Housing

Assistant Secretary for Policy
Development and Research
U.S. Department of Housing and Urban Development (HUD)
Washington, DC 20410-6000 (202) 708-1600

This office conducts research and evaluations to develop more efficient, effective, and equitable ways to assist low-income households. HUD's assisted housing programs are monitored and evaluated, and alternatives are investigated. Data is collected and analyzed by the Department's staff and made available to

Be patient. If any phone number is incorrect, call (area code) 555-1212 and request the new listing.

Housing and Real Estate

interested parties, to federal agencies, and to Congress. Assisted housing research conducted includes the following areas: administrative costs of operating assisted housing programs, development costs of assisted housing programs, alternative assisted housing demonstrations, efficient, effective management of public housing projects, benefits to participants in assisted housing programs, and environmental hazards in assisted housing.

* Single Family Property Auctions

Sales Promotion Branch
Office of Single Family Housing
U.S. Department of Housing and Urban Development (HUD)
Washington, DC 20410 (202) 708-2700

Single-family homes are sold by sealed-bid auction in every city in the country. These properties are advertised in local newspapers.

* Surplus Property

Public Benefit Program
Division of Health Facilities Planning
PHS, Room 17A10
5600 Fishers Lane
Rockville, MD 20857 (301) 443-2265

The Public Health Service has real estate property available for use under two programs. The first program allows the property to be used for a public health purpose by local and state governments and private nonprofit organizations certified under the IRS code. The property can be used for such projects as nursing homes, clinics, or mental health centers. You are deeded the property with a thirty year period of restriction. The second program allows the property to be used by local government or private nonprofit organizations for homeless shelters.

* Surplus Veterans Homes

U.S. Department of Veterans Affairs
810 Vermont Ave, NW
Washington, DC 20420 (202) 872-1151

The U.S. Department of Veterans Affairs sells foreclosed properties through private real estate brokers. Properties are frequently advertised in local newspapers. Almost any real estate agent can show you the property. Local Veterans offices are the best sources of information on the procedures involved in purchasing these properties. Prices drop on those homes that are not sold in a certain period of time. Veterans financing is possible, but you get a 10% discount if you pay cash. See the Section on Computerized Electronic Bulletin Boards for getting this information online with your modem.

* Urban Homesteading

Urban Homesteading Office
Office of Urban Rehabilitation
Community Planning and Development

U.S. Department of Housing and Urban Development (HUD)
Washington, DC 20410-7000 (202) 708-1367

Urban homesteading is designed to revitalize declining neighborhoods and reduce the amount of federally-owned properties by transferring vacant and unrepaired single-family properties to new homeowners for rehabilitation. Federally-owned properties are transferred to local governments that have developed homesteading programs approved by HUD. Local governments then transfer the properties for a nominal sum to eligible individuals or families called homesteaders. Priority is given to lower-income persons. The homesteaders must occupy the property as a principal residence for at least five years, and must bring it up to local code standards within three years. Rehabilitation may be carried out by a contractor or by the homesteader.

* Urban Policy Report to Congress

Assistant Secretary for Policy
Development and Research
U.S. Department of Housing and Urban Development (HUD)
Washington, DC 20410-6000 (202) 708-1600

Under the Urban Growth and New Community Development Act of 1970, Congress is required to develop a national urban growth policy report every two years. This report summarizes trends, identifies significant problems, evaluates the effectiveness of federal efforts to deal with the problems, and makes recommendations for legislative and administrative actions.

* Urban Trees Money

Cooperative Forestry, FS
U.S. Department of Agriculture (USDA)
P.O. Box 96090
Washington, DC 20090-6090 (703) 235-1376
OR: Your regional Forest Service Office

The USDA will provide financial, technical, and related assistance in order to plant and protect trees, maintain and use wood from trees in open spaces, green belts, roadside screens, parks woodlands, curb areas, and residential developments in urban areas.

* Veterans Foreclosed Homes

U.S. Department of Veterans Affairs
810 Vermont Ave, NW
Washington, DC 20420 (202) 872-1151

The U.S. Department of Veterans Affairs sells foreclosed properties through private real estate brokers. Properties are frequently advertised in local newspapers, giving information such as address, number of bedrooms and bathrooms, particular defects in the property and price. Almost any real estate can show you the property. Local Veterans offices are the best source of information on the procedures involved in purchasing these properties. Many local offices maintain the information on local online bulletin boards. See the Chapter on Electronic Bulletin Boards.

Be patient. If any phone number is incorrect, call (area code) 555-1212 and request the new listing.

Federal Money for Housing and Real Estate

The following is a description of the federal funds available to renters, homeowners, developers, and real estate investors for housing in urban and rural areas. This information is derived from the *Catalog of Federal Domestic Assistance* which is published by the U.S. Government Printing Office in Washington, DC. The number next to the title description is the official reference for this federal program. Contact the office listed below the caption for further details.

* Water Bank Program 10.062
Agricultural Stabilization and Conservation Service
U.S. Department of Agriculture
P.O. 2415
Washington, DC 20013 (202) 720-6221
To conserve surface waters; preserve and improve the nation's wetlands; increase migratory waterfowl habitat in nesting, breeding, and feeding areas in the U.S.; and secure environmental benefits for the nation. Types of assistance: direct payment. Estimate of annual funds available: $ 11,395,000.

* Rural Clean Water Program (RWCP) 10.068
Conservation and Environmental Protection Division
Agricultural Stabilization and Conservation Service
U.S. Department of Agriculture
P.O. Box 2415
Washington, DC 20013 (202) 720-6221
To achieve improved water quality in the most cost-effective manner possible in keeping with the provisions of adequate supplies of food, fiber, and a quality environment. Types of assistance: direct payment. Estimate of annual funds available: $ 0.

* Emergency Loans 10.404
Administrator, Farmers Home Administration
U.S. Department of Agriculture
Washington, DC (202) 690-1533
To assist family farmers, ranchers and aquaculture operators with loans to cover losses resulting from major and/or natural disasters. Types of assistance: loan guarantee. Estimate of annual funds available: $ 100,000,000.

* Farm Operating Loans 10.406
Director, Farmer Programs Loan Making Division
Farmers Home Administration
U.S. Department of Agriculture
Washington, DC 20250 (202) 720-1632
To enable operators of not larger than family farms through the extension of credit and supervisory assistance, to make efficient use of their land, labor, and other resources. Types of assistance: loan guarantee. Estimate of annual funds available: $ 1,250,000,000.

* Farm Ownership Loans 10.407
Administrator, Farmers Home Administration
U.S. Department of Agriculture
Washington, DC 20250 (202) 382-1632
To assist eligible farmers, ranchers, and aquaculture operators, including farming cooperatives, corporations, partnerships, and joint operations through the extension of credit to become owner-operators of not larger than family farms. Types of assistance: loan guarantee. Estimate of annual funds available: $ 300,000,000.

* Very Low and Low Income Housing Loans (Section 502 Rural Housing Loans) 10.410
Administrator, Farmers Home Administration
U.S. Department of Agriculture
Washington, DC 20250 (202) 447-7967
To assist lower-income rural families to obtain decent, safe, and sanitary dwellings and related facilities. Subsidized funds are available only for low- and very low-income applicants. The funds are loans for new or existing construction not currently financed or owned by FMHA. Types of assistance: direct loans. Estimate of annual funds available: $ 650,000,000.

* Rural Housing Site Loans (Section 523 and 524 Site Loans) 10.411
Administrator, Farmers Home Administration
U.S. Department of Agriculture
Washington, DC 20250 (202) 720-1474
To assist public or private nonprofit organizations interested in providing sites for housing, to acquire and develop land in rural areas to be subdivided as adequate building sites. Types of assistance: direct loans. Estimate of annual funds available: $ 0.

* Rural Rental Housing Loans 10.415
Administrator, Farmers Home Administration
U.S. Department of Agriculture
Washington, DC 20250 (202) 382-1604
To provide economically designed and constructed rental and cooperative housing and related facilities suited for independent living for rural residents. Types of assistance: loan guarantee. Estimate of annual funds available: $ 341,000,000.

* Very Low-Income Housing Repair Loans and Grants (Section 504 Rural Housing Loans and Grants) 10.417
Administrator, Farmers Home Administration
U.S. Department of Agriculture
Washington, DC 20250 (202) 720-1474
To give very low-income rural homeowners an opportunity to make essential repairs to their homes to make them safe and to remove health hazards to the family or community. Types of assistance: loans, grants. Estimate of annual funds available: loans - $ 11,100,000. Grants - $5,000,000.

* Rural Rental Assistance Payments (Rental Assistance) 10.427
Administrator, Farmers Home Administration
U.S. Department of Agriculture
Washington, DC 20250 (202) 720-1599
To reduce the rents paid by low-income families occupying eligible Rural Rental Housing (RRH) Rural Cooperative Housing (RCH), and Farm Labor Housing (LH) projects financed by the Farmers Home Administration through its Sections 515, 514, and 516 loans and grants. Types of assistance: direct payment. Estimate of annual funds available: $ 342,000,000.

* Rural Housing Preservation Grants 10.433
Multiple Family Housing Loan Division
Farmers Home Administration
U.S. Department of Agriculture

Be patient. If any phone number is incorrect, call (area code) 555-1212 and request the new listing.

Housing and Real Estate

Washington, DC 20250 (202) 720-1606
To assist very low and low-income rural homeowners in obtaining adequate housing to meet their needs by providing the necessary assistance to repair or rehabilitate their housing. Types of assistance: grants. Estimate of annual funds available: $ 10,000,000.

To make homeownership more readily available to families displaced by a natural disaster, urban renewal, or other government actions and to increase homeownership opportunities for low-income and moderate-income families. Types of assistance: loan guarantee. Estimate of annual funds available: $ 87,551,000.

* Interest Reduction Payments-Rental and Cooperative Housing for Lower Income Families (236) 14.103
Director, Office of Multifamily Housing Management
U.S. Department of Housing and Urban Development
Washington, DC 20410 (202) 708-3730
To provide good quality rental and cooperative housing for persons of low- and moderate-income by providing interest reduction payments in order to lower their housing costs. Types of assistance: direct payments. Estimate of annual funds available: $ 634,159,000.

* Mortgage Insurance: Homes in Outlying Areas 203(i) 14.121
Director, Insured Single Family Development Division
Office of Single Family Housing
U.S. Department of Housing and Urban Development
Washington, DC 20410 (202) 708-2700
To help families purchase homes in outlying areas. Types of assistance: loan guarantee. Estimate of annual funds available: Funding included in 14.117.

* Rehabilitation Mortgage Insurance 203(k) 14.108
Director, Single Family Development Division
U.S. Department of Housing and Urban Development
Washington, DC 20410 (202) 708-2720
To help families repair or improve, purchase and improve, or refinance and improve existing residential structures more than one year old. Types of assistance: loan guarantee. Estimate of annual funds available: $ 98,507,000.

* Mortgage Insurance: Homes in Urban Renewal Areas (22 Homes) 14.122
Director, Insured Single Family Development Division
Office of Single Family Housing
U.S. Department of Housing and Urban Development
Washington, DC 20410 (202) 708-2700
To help families purchase or rehabilitate homes in urban renewal areas. Types of assistance: loan guarantee. Estimate of annual funds available: $ 393,000.

* Manufactured Home Loan Insurance-Financing Purchase of Manufactured Homes as Principal Residences of Borrowers (Title I) 14.110
Director, Title I Insurance Division
U.S. Department of Housing and Urban Development (800) 733-4663
Washington, DC 20410 (202) 708-2880
To make possible reasonable financing of manufactured home purchases. Types of assistance: loan guarantee. Estimate of annual funds available: (loan insured including funding for programs 14.142 and 14.162) $1,358,812,000.

* Mortgage Insurance-Housing in Older, Declining Areas 223(e) 14.123
Single Family Development Division
Office of Insured Single Family Housing
Washington, DC 20410 (202) 708-2700
To assist in the purchase or rehabilitation of housing in older, declining urban areas. Types of assistance: loan guarantee. Estimate of annual funds available: $ 19,881,000.

* Mortgage Insurance-Construction or Substantial Rehabilitation of Condominium Projects 234 (d) 14.112
Insurance Division
Office of Insured Multifamily Housing Development
U.S. Department of Housing and Urban Development
Washington, DC 20410 (202) 708-2556
To enable sponsors to develop condominium projects in which individual units will be sold to home buyers. Types of assistance: loan guarantee. Estimate of annual funds available: $ 10,254,000.

* Mortgage Insurance-Cooperative Projects (213 Cooperatives) 14.126
Insurance Division
Office of Insured Multifamily Housing Development
U.S. Department of Housing and Urban Development
Washington, DC 20410 (202) 708-2556
To make it possible for nonprofit cooperative ownership housing corporations or trusts to develop or sponsor the development of housing projects to be operated as cooperatives. Types of assistance: loan guarantee. Estimate of annual funds available: $ 0.

* Mortgage Insurance - Homes 203(b) 14.117
Director, Insured Family Development Division
Office of Single Family Housing, HUD
Washington, DC 20410 (202) 708-2700
To help families undertake home ownership. Types of assistance: loan guarantee. Estimate of annual funds available: (Mortgage Insured-including funding for 14.119, 14.121, 14.163, 14.175) $47,411,931,000.

* Mortgage Insurance-Manufactured Home Parks (207(m) Manufactured Home Parks) 14.127
Insurance Division
Office of Insured Multifamily Housing Development
U.S. Department of Housing and Urban Development
Washington, DC 20410 (202) 708-2556
To make possible the financing of construction or rehabilitation of manufactured home parks. Types of assistance: loan guarantee. Estimate of annual funds available: $ 0.

* Mortgage Insurance 203(h): Homes for Disaster Victims 14.119
Director, Single Family Development Division
Office of Insured Single Family Housing, HUD
Washington, DC 20410 (202) 708-2700
To help victims of a major disaster undertake home ownership on a sound basis. Types of assistance: loan guarantee. Estimate of annual funds available: Funding included in 14.117.

* Mortgage Insurance - Purchase by Homeowners of Fee Simple Title from Lessors (240) 14.130
Director, Single Family Development Division
Office of Insured Single Family Housing, HUD
Washington, DC 20410 (202) 708-2700
To help homeowners obtain fee-simple title to the property which they hold under long-term leases and on which their homes are located. Types of assistance: loan guarantee. Estimate of annual funds available: $ 0.

* Mortgage Insurance-Homes for Low and Moderate Income Families 221(d)(2) 14.120
Director, Single Family Development Division
Office of Insured Family Housing, HUD
Washington, DC 20410 (202) 708-2700

* Mortgage Insurance: Purchase of Sales-Type Cooperative Housing Units (213 Sales) 14.132
Director, Single Family Development Division
Office of Insured Family Housing, HUD

Federal Money for Housing and Real Estate

Washington, DC 20410 (202) 708-2700
To make available good quality, new housing for purchase by individual members of a housing cooperative. Types of assistance: loan guarantee. Estimate of annual funds available: $ 0.

* **Mortgage Insurance: Purchase of Units in Condominiums (234(c)) 14.133**
Director, Single Family Development Division
Office of Insured Single Family Housing, HUD
Washington, DC 20410 (202) 708-2700
To enable families to purchase units in condominium projects. Types of assistance: loan guarantee. Estimate of annual funds available: $ 2,856,274,000.

* **Mortgage Insurance: Rental Housing (207) 14.134**
Insurance Division
Office of Insured Multifamily Housing Development
U.S. Department of Housing and Urban Development
Washington, DC 20410 (202) 708-2556
To provide good quality rental housing for middle income families. Types of assistance: loan guarantee. Estimate of annual funds available: $ 0.

* **Mortgage Insurance: Rental Housing for Moderate Income Families and Elderly Market Interest Rate 221(d)(3) and (4) Multifamily 14.135**
Insurance Division
Office of Insured Multifamily Housing Development
U.S. Department of Housing and Urban Development
Washington, DC 20410 (202) 708-2556
To provide good quality rental or cooperative housing for moderate income families and the elderly. Types of assistance: loan guarantee. Estimate of annual funds available: $ 890,238,000.

* **Mortgage Insurance-Rental Housing for the Elderly (231) 14.138**
Insurance Division
Office of Insured Multifamily Housing Development
U.S. Department of Housing and Urban Development
Washington, DC 20410 (202) 708-2556
To provide good quality rental housing for the elderly. Types of assistance: loan guarantee. Estimate of annual funds available: $ 0.

* **Mortgage Insurance-Rental Housing in Urban Renewal Areas (220 Multifamily) 14.139**
Insurance Division
Office of Insured Multifamily Housing Development
U.S. Department of Housing and Urban Development
Washington, DC 20410 (202) 708-2556
To provide good quality rental housing in urban renewal areas, code enforcement areas, and other areas designated for overall revitalization. Types of assistance: loan guarantee. Estimate of annual funds available: $ 7,576,000.

* **Section 106(b) Nonprofit Sponsor Assistance Program (Nonprofit Sponsor Loan Fund) 14.141**
Director
Assisted Elderly and Handicapped Housing Division
Office of Elderly and Assisted Housing, HUD
Washington, DC 20410 (202) 708-2730
To assist and stimulate prospective private nonprofit sponsors/borrowers of Section 202 housing to develop sound housing projects for the elderly or handicapped. Types of assistance: loan. Estimate of annual funds available: $ 0.

* **Property Improvement Loan Insurance for Improving All Existing Structures and Building of New Nonresidential Structures (Title I) 14.142**
Director, Title I Insurance Division
U.S. Department of Housing and Urban Development (800) 733-4663
Washington, DC 20410 (202) 708-2880

To facilitate the financing of improvements to homes and other existing structures and the building of new nonresidential structures. Types of assistance: loan guarantee. Estimate of annual funds available: $ 1,358,812,000.

* **Supplemental Loan Insurance-Multifamily Rental Housing 14.151**
Insurance Division
Office of Insured Multifamily Housing Development
U.S. Department of Housing and Urban Development
Washington, DC 20411 (202) 708-2556
To finance repairs, additions and improvements to multifamily projects, group practice facilities, hospitals, or nursing homes already insured by HUD or held by HUD. Types of assistance: loan guarantee. Estimate of annual funds available: $ 246,206,000.

* **Mortgage Insurance for the Purchase or Refinancing of Existing Multifamily Housing Projects (Section 223(f) Insured Under Section 207) 14.155**
Office of Insured Multifamily Housing Development
Insurance Division, HUD
Washington, DC 20410 (202) 708-2556
To provide mortgage insurance to lenders for the purchase or refinancing of existing multifamily housing projects, whether conventionally financed or subject to federally insured mortgages. Types of assistance: loan guarantee. Estimate of annual funds available: $ 558,295,000.

* **Housing for the Elderly or Handicapped (202) 14.157 Assisted Elderly and Handicapped Housing Division**
Office of Elderly and Assisted Housing, HUD
Washington, DC 20410 (202) 708-2730
To provide for rental or cooperative housing and related facilities (such as central dining) for the elderly or handicapped. Types of assistance: loan. Estimate of annual funds available: $ 0.

* **Section 245 Graduated Payment Mortgage Program 14.159**
Director, Single Family Development Division
Office of Insured Single Family Housing, HUD
Washington, DC 20410 (202) 708-2700
To facilitate early home ownership for households that expect their incomes to rise. Types of assistance: loan guarantee. Estimate of annual funds available: $ 548,027,000.

* **Mortgage Insurance-Combination and Manufactured Home Lot Loans (Title I) 14.162**
Director, Title I Insurance Division, HUD (800) 733-4663
Washington, DC 20410 (202) 708-2880
To make possible reasonable financing of manufactured home purchases and lot to place it on. Types of assistance: loan guarantee. Estimate of annual funds available: Funding including in 14.110.

* **Mortgage Insurance-Cooperative Financing (203(n)) 14.163**
Director, Single Family Development Division
Office of Insured Single Family Housing, HUD
Washington, DC 20410 (202) 708-2700
To provide insured financing for the purchase of the Corporate Certificate and Occupancy Certificate. Types of assistance: loan guarantee. Estimate of annual funds available: Funding included in 14.117.

* **Operating Assistance for Troubled Multifamily Housing Projects (Flexible Subsidy Fund) (Troubled Projects) 14.164**
Chief, Program Support Branch
Management Operations Division
Office of Multifamily Housing Management, HUD

Be patient. If any phone number is incorrect, call (area code) 555-1212 and request the new listing.

Housing and Real Estate

Washington, DC 20410 (202) 708-3730

To provide assistance to restore or maintain the physical and financial soundness of certain projects assisted or approved for assistance under the National Housing Act or under the Housing and Urban Development Act of 1965. Types of assistance: grants, direct payments. Estimate of annual funds available: $ 0.

* Mortgage Insurance-Homes-Military Impacted Areas (238(c)) 14.165

Director, Single Family Development Division
Office of Insured Single Family Housing, HUD
Washington, DC 20410 (202) 708-2700

To help families undertake home ownership in military impacted areas. Types of assistance: loan guarantee. Estimate of annual funds available: $ 13,425,000.

* Mortgage Insurance-Homes for Members of the Armed Services (Section 222) 14.166

Director, Single Family Development Division
Office of Insured Single Family Housing, HUD
Washington, DC 20410 (202) 708-2700

To help members of the armed services on active duty to purchase a home. Types of assistance: loan guarantee. Estimate of annual funds available: $ 4,588,000.

* Mortgage Insurance-Two Year Operating Loss Loans, Section 223(d) 14.167

Office of Insured Multifamily Housing Development
Insurance Division Housing, HUD
Washington, DC 20410 (202) 755-2556

To insure a separate loan covering operating losses incurred during the first two years following the date of completion of a multifamily project with a HUD insured first mortgage. Types of assistance: loan guarantee. Estimate of annual funds available: $ 10,890,000.

* Mortgage Insurance-Growing Equity Mortgages (GEMs) 14.172

Director, Single Family Development Division
Office of Insured Single Family Housing, HUD
Washington, DC 20410 (202) 708-2700

To provide a rapid principal reduction and shorter mortgage term by increasing payments over a 10 year period, thereby expanding housing opportunities to the homebuying public. Types of assistance: loan guarantee. Estimate of annual funds available: Funding included in 14.159.

* Multifamily Coinsurance (Section 223(f); Section 221(d); Section 232) 14.173

Office of Insured Multifamily Housing Development
Coinsurance Division, HUD
Washington, DC 20410 (202) 708-3730

Under the coinsurance programs, HUD authorizes approved lenders to coinsure mortgage loans. In exchange for the authority to perform the required underwriting, servicing, management and property disposition functions, approved lenders assume responsibility for a portion of any insurance loss on the coinsured mortgage. Types of assistance: loan guarantee. Estimate of annual funds available: $ 0.

* Housing Development Grants 14.174

Director, Development Grants Division
Rm. 6110, Office of Elderly and Assisted Housing
U.S. Department of Housing and Urban Development
451 7th St., SW
Washington, DC 20410 (202) 755-4961

To support the construction or substantial rehabilitation of rental housing in areas experiencing severe shortages of decent rental housing opportunities for families and individuals without other reasonable and affordable housing alternatives in the private market. Types of assistance: grants. Estimate of annual funds available: $ 0.

* Adjustable Rate Mortgages (ARMS) 14.175

Director, Single Family Development Division
Office of Insured Single Family Housing, HUD
Washington, DC 20410 (202) 708-2700

To provide mortgage insurance for an adjustable rate mortgage which offers lenders more assurance of long term profitability than a fixed rate mortgage, while offering consumer protection. Types of assistance: loan guarantee. Estimate of annual funds available: Funding included in 14.117.

* Nehemiah Housing Opportunity Grant Program (Nehemiah Housing) 14.179

Morris E. Carter, Director
Single Family Housing Development Division
U.S. Department of Housing and Urban Development
451 7th St, SW
Washington, DC 20410 (202) 708-2700

To provide an opportunity for those families who otherwise would not be financially able to realize their dream of owning a home. Types of assistance: grant. Estimate of annual funds available: $ 18,834,000.

* Community Development Block Grants/Entitlement Grants 14.218

Entitlement Cities Division
Office of Block Grant Assistance
Community Planning and Development
451 7th St., SW
Washington, DC 20410 (202) 708-1577

To develop viable urban communities, by providing decent housing and a suitable living environment. Types of assistance: grants. Estimate of annual funds available: $ 1,958,529,000.

* Community Development Block Grants/Small Cities Program (Small Cities) 14.219

State and Small Cities Division
Office of Block Grant Assistance
Community Planning and Development, HUD
451 7th St., SW
Washington, DC 20410 (202) 708-1322

The primary objective of this program is the development of viable urban communities by providing decent housing, a suitable living environment, and expanding economic opportunities. Types of assistance: grants. Estimate of annual funds available: $ 36,539,000.

* Specially Adapted Housing for Disabled Veterans (Paraplegic Housing) 64.106

U.S. Department of Veterans Affairs
Washington, DC 20420

To assist certain severely disabled veterans in acquiring suitable housing units, with special fixtures and facilities made necessary by the nature of the veterans disabilities. Types of assistance: direct payment. Estimate of annual funds available: $ 14,815,000.

* Veterans Housing-Guaranteed and Insured Loans (VA Home Loans) 64.114

U.S. Department of Veterans Affairs
Washington, DC 20420

To assist veterans, certain service personnel, and certain unmarried surviving spouses of veterans, in obtaining credit for the purchase, construction or improvement of homes on more liberal terms than are generally available to non-veterans. Types of assistance: loan guarantee. Estimate of annual funds available: $ 121,594,141,000.

* Veterans Housing-Direct Loans for Disabled Veterans 64.118

U.S. Department of Veterans Affairs
Washington, DC 20420

To provide certain severely disabled veterans with direct housing credit in connection with grants for specially adaptable housing with special features or

Be patient. If any phone number is incorrect, call (area code) 555-1212 and request the new listing.

movable facilities made necessary by the nature of their disabilities. Types of assistance: direct loans. Estimate of annual funds available: $ 33,000.

* Veterans Housing-Manufactured Home Loans 64.119

U.S. Department of Veterans Affairs
Washington, DC 20420

To assist veterans, servicepersons, and certain unmarried surviving spouses of veterans in obtaining credit for the purchase of a manufactured home on more liberal terms than are available to non-veterans. Types of assistance: loan guarantee. Estimate of annual funds available: $ 9,633,000.

* Weatherization Assistance for Low-Income Persons 81.042

Mary E. Fowler, Chief
Weatherization Assistance Programs, Branch 232

Conservation and Renewable Energy, DOE
Forrestal Bldg.
Washington, DC 20585 (202) 586-2204

To insulate the dwellings of low income persons particularly the elderly and handicapped low income in order to conserve needed energy and to aid those persons least able to afford higher utility costs. Types of assistance: grants. Estimate of annual funds available: $ 80,000,000.

* Flood Insurance 83.100

David L. Cobb, Federal Insurance Administration
FEMA
Washington, DC 20472 (202) 646-2780

To enable persons to purchase insurance against losses from physical damage to or loss of buildings and or contents therein caused by floods, mudflow, or flood related erosion in the U.S. Types of assistance: Insurance. Estimate of annual funds available: $ 764,687,000.

Be patient. If any phone number is incorrect, call (area code) 555-1212 and request the new listing.

Housing and Real Estate

State Money For Housing and Real Estate

State Initiatives

While affordable housing has long held an important place on the federal government's policy agenda, budget cutbacks in recent years have forced the government to turn over many housing responsibilities to the states. Housing finance agencies (HFAs) have been created by states to issue tax-exempt bonds to finance mortgages for lower-income first-time home buyers and to build multi-family housing.

States are involved in a host of initiatives throughout the broad spectrum of housing finance and development. Interim construction financing programs which can reduce the basic costs of lower-income housing projects have been initiated in a number of states, together with innovative home ownership programs and programs directed toward rehabilitation and improved energy conservation.

States are also venturing into areas which have not received as much public sector attention until recently. By encouraging non-traditional types of housing, such as accessory units, shelters, and single room occupancy housing, states are addressing important elements of the housing market.

In Colorado, the state Housing and Finance Authority (CHFA) has issued more than $2 billions of bonds and notes since its establishment in 1973, providing housing for more than 33,000 families and individuals of low and moderate income; 19,000 first-time home buyers and over 14,500 rental housing units. In recent years the state has broadened CHFA's authority to allow it to develop finance programs to assist the growth of small business, help exports with insurance on goods sold overseas, and similar projects.

Colorado has done more than simply help its citizens find housing: the programs have resulted in construction employment of more than 20,000 jobs, with wages estimated at almost $20 million in new local real estate taxes and an indirect gain of $1.6 billion for the state.

Wisconsin, Maine and New York each have 20 programs including special ones for women and minorities, for disabled persons, and for environmental hazard removal.

Maryland operates 25 programs, including those to help people with closing costs and settlement expenses. It also has special funds available for the elderly and is developing an emergency mortgage fund to help people who have fallen behind in their payments. Non-profit developers can also tap the state for money to build low-cost rental units.

Among Michigan's 29 programs and Minnesota's 25 are several for neighborhood revitalization. Minnesota also offers programs targeting the needs of urban Indians and migrant farm workers. Alaska, Oregon and Vermont offer financing for tenant acquisition of mobile home parks.

Funds are also available for persons who take steps to make their homes more energy efficient, for home owners and landlords who remove lead paint from dwelling units, for houses without plumbing or those with plumbing that is dysfunctional, for handicapped persons, and to help landlords defray the costs of bringing low-income housing into compliance with state and local housing codes. There are also funds for non-profit organizations to acquire or renovate existing houses and apartments for use as group homes for special needs such as mentally retarded.

In many states, elderly home owners can look to the HFA to obtain financing and/or support services they need to remain in their homes and avoid institutionalization. Some of the states have more than one agency dedicated to housing and we have attempted to list them all here. Also, many cities and counties have quasi-federal/quasi-local "housing authorities" with additional programs. Check your local government listings for these.

The following is a complete listing of state housing programs.

State Housing Offices

Alabama

Alabama Housing Finance Authority, P.O. Box 230909, Montgomery; AL 36123-0909; (205) 242-4310.

1) Mortgage Revenue Bond Program: low-rate loans for income-eligible first-time home buyers.
2) Downpayment Assistance Program: matching funds for lower-income home buyers.
3) Mortgage Credit Certificate Program: provides a 20% federal tax credit on mortgage loan interest for lower-income home buyers.
4) Low-Income Housing Tax Credit Program: federal tax credits for owners of low-income rental housing.
5) Multi-Family Bond Program: tax-exempt bonds for financing multi-family projects with units affordable to low-income tenants.

Alaska

Alaska Housing Finance Corp., P.O. Box 101020, 235 East 8th Avenue, Anchorage, AK 99510; (907) 561-1900.

1) Home Ownership Assistance Program: interest subsidy to as low as 6%.
2) Mobile Home Loan Program: low downpayment.
3) Taxable Mortgage Program: for those other than first time home buyers and veterans.
4) Triplex/Fourplex Mortgage Program: up to $384,000 with 20% down.
5) Tax Exempt Mortgage Program: loans up to $157,190 for single family and $176,996 for duplexes.
6) Second Mortgage Program: up to $99,900 for single family homes and $127,800 for duplexes can be used for home purchase or home improvement.
7) Veterans Mortgage Program: low interest loans to veterans and members of the reserve and National Guard.
8) Refinance Program: reduce monthly payments on existing loans.
9) Non-Conforming Property Program: homes which cannot be financed through traditional financing.
10) Condominium Projects: loans for condominium owners.
11) Mobile Home Park Loans:
12) Home Owners' Assistance Program: lowers mortgage payments and assists home owners in financial difficulty.
13) Refinance Program of a Non-AHFC Loan: refinancing for a loan not held

State Money for Housing and Real Estate

by AHFC.

14) Second Mortgage Program for Health and Safety Repairs: for AHFC loan borrowers to bring property up to safety and health requirements.

15) Condo Association Loan Program: loans to home owners' associations for common area improvements necessary to health and safety.

16) Mortgage Guaranty Insurance Corporation: special financing for borrowers purchasing certain foreclosed condo and Planned Unit Development units.

Arizona

Arizona Department of Commerce, Office of Housing Development, 1700 West Washington, Phoenix, AZ 85007; (602) 280-1365.

1) Low-Income Housing Tax Credits: federal income tax credits for owners of low-income housing units.

2) Low Interest Mortgage Programs: typically below 9% interest loans for eligible Arizonans to purchase homes.

3) Arizona Housing Trust Fund: construction, housing rehabilitation, down payment, and closing cost assistance for low/moderate income home buyers.

4) Rental Rehabilitation Program: assists owners in rehabilitating rental housing for low/moderate income households.

Arkansas

Arkansas Development Finance Authority, P.O. Box 8023, 100 Main St., Suite 200, Little Rock, AR 72203; (501) 682-5900.

1) Affordable Housing Program: loans to developers to build houses in designated areas.

2) Single-Family: below market rate loans to first time home buyers for the purchase of a single-family home.

3) Low-Income Housing Tax Credit Program: federal tax credits for owners of low-income rental housing.

4) Home Energy Loan Program: low-rate loans for home owners making energy conservation repairs and improvements.

California

California Housing Finance Agency, 1121 L Street, 7th Floor, Sacramento, CA 95815; (916) 322-3991.

1) Multi-Family Program: permanent financing for builders and developers of multi-family unit, elderly and congregate rental housing.

2) Development Loan Program: 7% loans to small and minority developers.

3) Self-Help Housing Program: funds to non-profit developers in order to produce self-help housing.

4) Home Purchase Assistance Program: low interest loans for low/moderate income first-time home buyers.

5) Matching Downpayment Program: deferred payment second mortgage loans to assist with closing costs or reduce monthly payments on first mortgages of limited-income home buyers.

6) CHFA Resale Program: below market-rate loans to first-time home buyers who meet income limits and are purchasing previously-owned property within CHFA sales price limits.

7) Compensating Balance Program: construction financing to minority/women-owned business enterprises and self-help program developers.

8) Self-Help Builder Assistance Program: construction financing for self-help builders.

9) Self-Help Housing Program: finances self-help homes under supervision of non-profit organizations.

California Department of Housing and Community Development, P.O. Box 952050, Sacramento, CA 94252-2050; (916) 322-1560.

1) California Home Ownership Assistance Program (CHAP): loans for up to 49% of purchase price for low/moderate-income home buyers.

2) California Housing Rehabilitation Program-Owner Component: low-rate loans to bring homes up to code, make general improvements, or to make adaptations for handicapped.

3) Natural Disaster Assistance Program: rehabilitation loans for property damaged by natural disaster.

4) Self-Help Housing Program: technical assistance for low/moderate income households building or rehabilitating their own homes.

5) Mobile Home Park Assistance Program: loans and technical assistance to mobile home park resident organizations that are purchasing their park.

6) Rental Housing Construction Program: very low-rate loans for development and construction costs associated with new rental housing units for low-income households.

7) Family Housing Demonstration Program: very low-rate loans to develop new, or rehabilitate existing, rental or co-op housing that provides on-site support programs for low-income households.

8) Permanent Housing for the Handicapped Homeless Program: partial funding to acquire, rehabilitate, and operate housing for the disabled homeless.

9) State Rental Rehabilitation Program: partial funding to rehabilitate low/moderate-income rental housing in small rural communities.

10) California Energy Conservation Rehabilitation Program: grants of up to $5,000 per unit to assist energy conservation rehabilitation of low-income owner and renter farmworker housing, residential hotels, and rental housing for the elderly and handicapped.

11) Pre-Development Loan Program: low-rate, 3-year loans for pre-development costs of low-income housing projects.

12) PLP Natural Disaster Component: low-rate, 3-year loans for pre-development costs of reconstruction or rehabilitation of subsidized housing damaged by natural disaster.

13) Emergency Shelter Program: grants to provide emergency shelter for homeless households.

14) Farmworker Housing Grant Program: grants to provide owner-occupied and rental units for year-round, low-income agricultural workers and to rehabilitate those damaged by natural disaster.

15) Federal Emergency Shelter Grant Program: grants to provide emergency shelter to homeless households.

16) Section 8 Housing Assistance Program: rental assistance payments for very low-income households.

17) Office of Migrant Services: grants to provide housing and support services for migrant families during peak season.

18) Rental Security Deposit Guarantee Demonstration Program: provides landlords with rental deposit guarantees for homeless families transitioning to permanent rental housing.

19) Rural Communities Facilities Technical Assistance Program: grants and technical assistance to rural communities seeking federal and state water and wastewater project loans and grants.

20) Senior Citizen Shared Housing Program: grants to assist seniors in obtaining shared housing or for development of group residences.

Colorado

Colorado Housing and Finance Authority, 1981 Blake Street, Denver, CO 80202; (303) 297-7427.

1) Single-Family Program: lower-than-market interest rates available to first-time home owners.

2) Commercial Division Programs: financial assistance provided to assist small businesses with expansion of their facilities.

3) Rental Acquisition Program: offers affordable multi-family housing for low-income households.

4) Section 8 Moderate Rehabilitation Program: incentives to property owners who rehabilitate substandard rental housing for low-income tenants qualifying for rent subsidies.

5) Low-Income Housing Tax Credit Program: federal tax credits for owners of low-income rental housing.

6) Mortgage Credit Certificates: reduction of federal income tax for home buyers.

7) Tax-Exempt Bond Program: financing for acquisition and/or rehabilitation of low-income rental housing.

8) Special Needs Housing Fund: financing for housing for frail elderly, mentally ill, battered persons, runaways, etc.

9) Shelter Housing Assistance Program: financing for emergency or transitional housing.

10) Construction Loan Fund: Short-term loans to non-profits for acquisition, rehab, construction and development costs of low-income housing to be sold.

11) Housing Development Loan Fund: short-term loans to non-profits for pre-development costs or acquisition of property for low-income multi-family housing projects.

12) Special Projects Program: short-term loans to non-profits for acquisition, rehab, or construction of projects such as group homes, shelters, co-ops, mobile home parks.

13) Deferred-5 (D-5) Program: assistance with downpayment, repairs, and other costs associated with home purchase for participants in Colorado Single-Family Mortgage Program.

14) Rural Development Loan Program: loans for businesses in rural areas of Colorado.

Connecticut

Connecticut Housing Finance Authority, 40 Cold Spring Road, Rocky Hill, CT 06067; (203) 721-9501.

1) Home Mortgage Program: low-interest mortgages for low-and moderate-income persons and families.

2) Rehabilitation Mortgages: loans to protect or improve livability or energy efficiency of a home.

3) Reverse Annuity Mortgages (RAM): allows senior citizens to convert their home's equity into monthly tax-free cash payments.

Be patient. If any phone number is incorrect, call (area code) 555-1212 and request the new listing.

Housing and Real Estate

4) Market Rate Multi-Family Program: below conventional-rate financing to develop or rehabilitate multi-family housing with units affordable to low-income households.

5) Low-Income Housing Tax Credit Program: federal tax credits for owners of low-income rental housing.

6) Private Rental Investment Mortgage and Equity Program: financing for mixed-income rental developments.

7) Apartment Conversion for the Elderly: loans to home owners 62 years of age or older for additions or conversions to their homes to create income-producing rental units.

Delaware

Delaware State Housing Authority, Division of Housing and Community Development, 18 the Green, P.O. Box 1401, Dover, DE 19901; (302) 739-4263.

1) Single-Family Mortgage Program: low-interest loans to first-time home buyers.

2) Housing Development Funds: loans to developers of housing for low- and moderate-income persons and families.

3) Housing Rehabilitation Loan Program: $15,000 for ten years at 3% to fix up single-family homes.

4) Rent Subsidy Programs: money to provide subsidies for low- and moderate-income rental housing.

5) Public Housing Home Ownership Program: provides public housing tenants and families on the waiting list the opportunity to purchase affordable homes in residential neighborhoods.

6) Rental Rehabilitation Program: loans to cover up to 50% of rehab costs for low/moderate income housing.

7) Emergency Shelter Grants Program: to assist emergency housing shelters for the homeless.

8) Community Development Block Grants: funding to maintain or improve housing of low/moderate-income households.

9) Multi-Family Mortgage Revenue Bonds: financing for profit and non-profit developers of low-income housing.

10) Low-Income Housing Tax Credit Program: federal tax credits for owners of low-income rental housing.

District of Columbia

DC Housing Finance Agency, 1401 New York Avenue, NW, Suite 540, Washington, DC 20005; (202) 408-0415.

1) Single-Family Purchase Program: loans to first-time home buyers with 5% down and 8.5% interest.

2) Multi-Family Program: construction and permanent financing for developers of multi-family housing with at least 20% of the units designated for low-income households.

District of Columbia Department of Housing and Community Development, 51 N Street, NE, Washington, DC 20002; (202) 535-1353.

1) Home Purchase Assistance Program: low or no interest loans for low- and moderate-income home buyers.

2) First Right Purchase Assistance Program: low-cost loans for low- and moderate-income individuals and tenant groups to exercise their right to purchase their rental housing that is being offered for sale.

3) Homestead Housing Preservation Program: repossessed properties are sold to eligible District residents at low cost and with deferred payment loans.

4) Multi-Family Housing Rehabilitation Loan Program: low-rate financing for construction and rehabilitation of multi-family housing.

5) Direct Loan Rehabilitation Program: below-market financing (as low as 3%) for rehabilitation of single- and multi-family residential, mixed use, and commercial property.

6) Rental Rehabilitation Program: low or no interest deferred loans for rehabilitation and rent subsidies for property owners and tenants of low-income housing.

7) Distressed Properties Program: tax incentives to encourage the development of new rental housing or for the rehabilitation of vacant rental housing; similar benefits for occupied properties in economic difficulty.

8) Section 8 Moderate Rehabilitation Program: incentives for property owners to rehabilitate rental apartments for low-income households; rental income guaranteed via rent subsidies.

9) Low-Income Housing Tax Credit Program: tax credits for owners of low-income rental housing.

10) Single-Family Housing Rehabilitation Program: low-cost financing for the rehabilitation of one to four unit low-income housing in designated areas.

11) Home Improvements for the Handicapped: grants to remove barriers and improve accessibility; for home owners or landlords on behalf of handicapped tenants.

12) Weatherization Assistance Program: grants to low-income home owners and renters for weatherization of properties as determined by an energy audit.

13) Delinquent Home Mortgage Payments Program: low-cost, three-month loans to avoid foreclosure due to loss of employment or other crisis.

14) Housing Finance for Elderly, Dependent, and Disabled: loans for development of housing for special needs households.

Florida

Florida Housing Finance Agency, 2571 Executive Center Circle East, Tallahassee, FL 32399; (904) 488-4197.

1) First-Time Homebuyer Mortgage Revenue Bond Program: below-market rate financing for first-time home buyers with low/moderate income.

2) Home Ownership Assistance Program: $1700 zero interest, due-on-sale loan to defer closing costs.

3) Affordable Housing Loan Program: below market financing for developers/ home buyers of rental and for-sale housing.

4) State Apartment Incentive Loan Program: low-rate financing for developers who build or rehabilitate rental housing with 20% of units for low-income households and to eligible non-profit sponsors of housing projects.

5) Low-Income Housing Tax Credit Program: federal tax credits for owners of low-income rental housing.

6) Market-Rate Multi-Family Bond Loan Program: below-market financing to developers of rental housing with 20% for low-income households.

7) Section 8 Program: federal rent subsidies for low-income tenants.

Georgia

Georgia Residential Finance Authority, 60 Executive Parkway South, Suite 250, Atlanta, GA 30329; (404) 679-4840.

1) Single-Family Home Ownership Loan Program: 1.5% below prevailing interest rates for first-time home owners.

2) Mortgage Credit Certificate Program: 20% of mortgage interest can be used as a federal tax credit.

3) Payment of some or all of rental costs for low-income families or singles who are elderly, handicapped or disabled.

4) Multi-family Bond Program: below-market interest rate loans to develop or rehabilitate multi-family rental housing.

5) Low-Income Housing Credit Program: federal income tax credits to construct or rehabilitate low-income rental housing.

6) Section 8 Existing Housing Assistance: rental assistance subsidy payments to landlords of low-income individuals or families.

7) Rental Rehabilitation Program: loans and grants up to $5,000 per unit to rehabilitate rental housing.

8) Appalachian: grants and loans for site development, technical assistance and others for low-and moderate-income housing projects.

9) Development Advances for Non-Profit Sponsors: financial and technical assistance to qualified non-profit organizations engaged in the development of low- and moderate-income rental housing.

10) Georgia Energy Fund: loans and grants up to $3,00 for energy saving home improvements.

11) Homeless Shelter Programs: grants to shelter facilities for building improvements and renovation.

Hawaii

Hawaii Housing Authority, 1002 North School Street, P.O. Box 17907, Honolulu, HI 96817; (808) 848-3277.

1) Hula Mae Single-Family Program: low-interest loans to first-time home buyers.

2) State Rent Supplement Program: rent subsidies to tenants in approved projects.

3) Tax Reform: Multi-Family Program: tax credits to investors in qualified low-income rental housing projects.

4) Modernization and Maintenance: funds for the preservation and maintenance of existing housing.

5) Housing Finance Revolving Fund: long-term mortgage financing in geographic areas or for projects where private mortgage insurers will not insure.

6) Section 8 Certificate/Voucher Programs: rental housing subsidies.

7) Public Housing Projects: low rent housing for eligible families, elderly or disabled.

Idaho

Idaho Housing Agency, 760 W. Myrtle, Boise, ID 83702; (208) 336-0161.

1) Mortgage Credit Certificates: home buyers who have not owned a home in the last three years can claim 20% of their mortgage interest as a tax credit.

2) Single Family Mortgage Purchase Program: below-market rate loans for first-time and limited-income home buyers.

3) Section 8 New Construction/Substantial Rehab Program: financing of multi-family housing affordable to very low-income households via rent subsidies.

4) Section 8 Moderate Rehab Program: incentives for property owners to

Be patient. If any phone number is incorrect, call (area code) 555-1212 and request the new listing.

State Money for Housing and Real Estate

upgrade substandard rental units to be occupied by low-income tenants qualifying for rent subsidies.

5) Section 8 Existing Certificate and Voucher Program: assistance for low-income households to meet costs of rental housing.

6) Rental Rehabilitation Program: funding for private property owners to make improvements to rental units in eligible locations.

7) Low-Income Housing Tax Credit Program: tax credit for owners/developers of housing for low-income households.

8) Stewart B. McKinney Permanent Housing Program for Handicapped Homeless: grant funds for private non-profit project sponsors.

9) Multi-Family Housing Financing: loans for new construction or substantial rehab of multi-family housing with a percentage rented to low-income tenants.

Illinois

Illinois Housing Development Authority, 401 N. Michigan Ave., Suite 900, Chicago, IL 60611; (312) 836-5200 or (800) 942-8439.

1) Moderate Rehabilitation Program: low-interest loans to rehabilitate low-income housing.

2) Congregate Housing Finance Program: loans for congregate housing for the elderly.

3) Illinois Homebuyer Program: low-interest mortgages for first-time income-eligible home buyers.

4) Affordable Housing Trust Fund: grants and loans to profit and non-profit developers of low-income housing projects.

Indiana

Indiana Housing Finance Authority, One North Capitol, Suite 515, Indianapolis, IN 46204; (317) 232-7777.

1) Single-Family Program: loans to home buyers at 1 to 2 percentage points below the market rate.

2) Multi-Family Program: loans for developers of low- and moderate- income housing.

3) Mortgage Credit Certificate Program: tax credits to families purchasing mobile homes.

4) Low-Income Housing Tax Credit: federal tax credit to owners of low-income rental housing.

5) Low-Income Housing Trust Fund: matching funds for development of low-income housing, permanent or transitional.

Iowa

Iowa Finance Authority, 100 East Grand Avenue, Suite 250, Des Moines, IA 50309; (515) 281-4058.

1) Single-Family Mortgage Loans: low-interest loans to home buyers

2) Mortgage Credit Certificate Program: tax credits of up to 20% of the interest paid annually on home loans.

3) Small Business Loan Program: loans for small business.

4) Title Guaranty Program: to guaranty (insure) titles to Iowa real estate.

5) Economic Development Loan Program: for businesses exceeding the limitations of the Small Business Loan Program.

6) Targeted Area Assistance Program: assistance with origination fees and discount points.

7) Closing Cost Assistance: up to 3% or $1200 to help with closing costs of eligible buyers.

8) Low-Income Housing Tax Credit Program: federal tax credits for owners of low-income rental housing.

9) Housing Assistance Fund Program: funding for multi-family rehab and construction, rent subsidies, group homes, shelters, and other housing projects.

10) Homeless Shelter Assistance: funding for homeless shelters.

Kansas

Kansas Office of Housing, Department of Commerce, 400 S.W. 8th, 5th Floor, Topeka, KS 66603; (913) 296-3481.

1) Tax Credits for Low-Income Housing: tax credits for developers who rent to low-income families.

2) Rental Rehabilitation Loan Program: loans up to $5,000 per rental unit to bring unit up to city code standard.

3) Emergency Shelter Grant Program: grants to local government agencies to provide emergency shelters for homeless households.

4) Permanent Housing for Handicapped Homeless: grants for acquisition, rehabilitation, and operation of multi-unit and group home projects for disabled homeless.

Kentucky

Kentucky Housing Corporation, 1231 Louisville Road, Frankfort, KY 40601; (502) 564-7630 or (800) 633-8896.

1) Single-Family Home Ownership: low-interest loans to home buyers who currently do not own property.

2) Elderly Rural Rehabilitation Program: grants to elderly in rural areas for the installment of indoor plumbing facilities.

3) Grants to the Elderly for Energy Repairs (GEER): grants to elderly for home energy repairs.

4) Housing Trust: single-family loans for eligible low-income families.

5) EPIC (Equity Partners Investing in the Commonwealth) Program: financing for eligible Kentuckians for downpayment and closing costs.

6) KHC Urban Program: initiatives to produce affordable housing in designated urban areas.

7) KHC Rural Program: loans and administrative assistance to non-profit organizations for construction or rehab of low-income housing.

8) Kentucky Appalachian Housing Program: site development grants and loans for housing developments in 49 eastern KY counties.

9) Country Home Program: low-rate construction financing for families in 63 counties.

10) Field Services/Special Population Needs Emergency Fund: loans for emergency repairs for low-income Kentuckians.

11) Permanent Housing for Homeless Handicapped Persons: funds for acquisition/rehabilitation of housing for homeless handicapped persons.

12) Section 8 Programs: rent subsidies and other assistance to low-income households.

13) Rental Housing Finance Program: below-market financing for low-income rental housing.

14) Rental Deposits Surety Program: assistance with utility and security deposits for low-income households.

15) Residential Investment Program: fixed-rate mortgages for non-profit sponsors of new rental units in rural counties.

16) Low-Income Housing Tax Credits: federal tax credits for owners of low-income rental housing.

Louisiana

Louisiana Housing Finance Agency, 5615 Corporate, Suite 6A, Baton Rouge, LA 70808-2515; (504) 925-3675.

1) Single-Family: lower-interest rate (8.8%) 30 yr. FHA/VA financing for first-time home buyers.

2) Multi-Family: financing available for developers of low-moderate income housing development.

3) Tax Credit Programs: federal and state income tax credit provisions provided to developers of low-to-moderate multi-family development.

4) Housing Development Action Grants: financing for multi-family housing developments.

Maine

Maine State Housing Authority, P.O. Box 2669, 295 Water Street, Augusta, ME 04330; (207) 626-4600, (800) 452-4668.

1) Home Start Program: low-income loans for first-time home buyers.

2) Home Preservation Grant Program: grants for home improvements for very low-income home owners.

3) New Housing Initiatives Program: loans, grants, revolving funds, or administrative fees for developing non-traditional single family and rental housing initiatives to persons of low-income.

4) Home Purchase Program: low downpayment and low-rate financing for first-time income-eligible home buyers.

5) Purchase Plus Improvement: home improvement loans for borrowers in the Home Purchase or Home Start programs.

6) Underground Oil Storage Tank Removal Program: grants or interest-free loans to property owners for removal and disposal of environmentally hazardous underground oil storage tanks and pipes and installation of replacements.

7) Home Equity Conversion Mortgage: supplies elderly home owners with cash for some of the equity in their homes.

8) Home Improvement Program: low-rate home improvement loans.

9) Rental Loan Program: below market rate loans for new or rehabilitated rental housing affordable to low/moderate income households.

10) Rental Rehabilitation Program: low-interest deferred payment loans to repair substandard apartments.

11) Mental Health Facilities Fund: low-rate loans for housing the mentally ill.

12) MSHA 202 Start Program: up-front loans to non-profit developers of new rental housing for very low-income elderly or handicapped.

13) Land Acquisition Program: low-rate deferred payment loans to non-profit housing corporations to buy land for affordable housing.

14) Homeless Shelter Assistance: funding to operate or improve shelters.

15) Environmental Access Grants and Loans (EAGL): grants or 0% loans for disabled persons to make adaptations in their homes.

16) Supportive Housing Initiative Program (SHIP): low-rate, no/low down payment loans for non-profit organizations developing housing for special needs

Be patient. If any phone number is incorrect, call (area code) 555-1212 and request the new listing.

Housing and Real Estate

households.
17) Low-Income Housing Tax Credit: tax credits to developers of housing for low-income households.
18) Section 8 New Construction: rent subsidies for low-income households.
19) Section 8 Moderate Rehabilitation: rent subsidies for low-income households in rehabilitated rental units.
20) Section 8 Certificates and Vouchers: rental assistance for low-income tenants.

Maryland

Department of Housing and Community Development, 45 Calvert St., Annapolis, MD 21401; (301) 974-2176.
1) Rental Housing Production Program: loans to developers or non-profit organizations to cover the costs of construction, rehabilitation, acquisition or related development costs through interest rate writedowns or rent subsidies.
2) Mortgage Program: below-market interest rate mortgage financing for low- and moderate-income home buyers.
3) Home and Energy Loan Program: below-market interest rate loans for home and energy conservation improvements for single-family homes.
4) Multi-Family Home and Energy Loan Program: rehabilitation and energy conservation loans for multi-family rental projects and single scattered-site rental properties.
5) Housing Rehabilitation Program: loans to limited income homeowners, owners of multi-unit residential buildings and owners of small nonresidential properties.
6) Group Home Financing Program: low-interest, no interest deferred payment loans to non-profit organizations to purchase and modify housing for use as group homes and shelters.
7) Residential Lead Paint Abatement Program: loans to finance the abatement of lead paint in rental properties.
8) Elderly Rental Housing Program: new construction financing for rental housing for elderly citizens.
9) Rental Housing Allowance Pilot Program: subsidies to very low-income individuals with emergency needs.
10) Emergency Mortgage Assistance: assists home owners in imminent danger of losing homes to foreclosure after loss of income due to critical circumstances.
11) Reverse Equity Program: enables low-income elderly to access home equity to pay housing and other expenses that facilitate continued occupancy.
12) Settlement Expense Loan Program: low-rate loans up to $5000 toward settlement expenses for low-moderate income home buyers.
13) Multi-Family Bond Program: below-market financing for low-income multi-family rental housing development.
14) Non-Profit Rehabilitation Program: low-rate loans to non-profit organizations to rehabilitate low-income rental housing.
15) Partnership Rental Housing Program: loans for local governments and housing authorities for development or acquisition of low-income rental housing.
16) Construction Loan Program: low-rate financing for development of affordable single-family or multi-family housing.
17) Shelter One: loans and technical assistance to non-profit organizations undertaking their first housing project.
18) Housing Rehabilitation Program-Single Family: low-rate financing for rehabilitation of small residential properties for low-income households.
19) Accessory, Shared and Sheltered Housing Program: low-rate loans to finance additions and improvements to create accessory, shared or sheltered housing for low-income households.
20) Indoor Plumbing Program: low-rate loans to provide indoor plumbing.
21)Energy Bank Program: matching funds to low-income home owners for energy conservation improvements.
22) Section 8 Existing Certificate/Voucher Program: rent subsidies for low-income households.
23) Section 8 Moderate Rehabilitation Program: incentives to property owners for improvements to deteriorating housing units to be rented to households eligible for rent subsidies.
24) Section 8 Rental Rehabilitation Program: rehab funds for property owners renting to low-income households.
25) Low-Income Housing Tax Credit Program: federal tax credits to owners of low-income rental housing.

Massachusetts

Massachusetts Housing Finance Agency, 50 Milk Street, Boston, MA 02190; (617) 451-3480.
1) Home Ownership Opportunity Program: housing for purchase by first time low- and moderate-income home buyers at 30 to 40 percent below market rates.
2) General Lending: special loans for Vietnam Era Veterans, low-income and minority borrowers and physically handicapped.
3) Neighborhood Rehabilitation Programs: funds for people who buy and/or rehabilitate homes in locally designated neighborhoods.
4) New Construction Set-Aside: funds for purchasers of new homes and condominiums built by specific developers.
5) Home Improvement Program: loans for owner-occupied, 1- to 4-family homes.
6) State Housing Assistance for Rental Productions (SHARP): interest rate subsidies to developers for production of rental housing where at least 25% are available to low-income households.
7) Project TAP (Tenant Assistance Program): training for project residents for drug- and alcohol-related problems.
8) Low-Income Housing Tax Credit Program: federal tax credits for owners of low-income rental housing.
9) 80/20 Program: financing for developments with 20% of the units designated for low-income households.
10) Mortgage Credit Certificate Program: federal tax credits for eligible first-time home buyers.
11) Mortgage Insurance Program: lower premium private mortgage insurance available to HOP- and MHFA-assisted borrowers.
12) Rental Acquisition Development Initiative: low-rate financing for developers of rental properties with units affordable to low-income households.
13) Supportive Services in Elderly Housing: assists elderly residents in avoiding premature placement in nursing homes by delivering affordable homemaking, health care, and other services.
14) Acquisition Set-Aside Program: allows builders to offer lower interest mortgages to eligible home buyers as a sales incentive in return for reducing cost of units.

Executive Office of Communities and Development, Commonwealth of Massachusetts, 100 Cambridge Street, Room 1804, Boston, MA 02202; (617) 727-7765.
1) Section 8 Certificate/Voucher Programs: rent subsidies for low-income households.
2) Chapter 707 Scattered Site Certificate Program: rent subsidies similar to Section 8 Certificate Program.
3) Chapter 707 Transitional Housing Program: for battered women, pregnant teenagers, and homeless women and children.
4) Chapter 707 Residential Services Programs: provide long-term housing opportunities for the chronically mentally ill.

Michigan

Michigan State Housing Development Authority, Plaza One, Fourth Floor, 401 South Washington Square, P.O. Box 30044, Lansing, MI 48909; (517) 373-8370 or (800) 327-9158.
1) Single-Family Home Mortgage: low-interest loans for single-family homes and condominiums.
2) Michigan Mortgage Credit Certificates: federal income tax credits that give home buyers more income to qualify for a mortgage.
3) Home and Neighborhood Improvement Loans: home improvement loans for homes over 20 years old at interest rates from 1 to 9 percent.
4) Section 8 Existing Rental Allowance Program: rent subsidies for low-income persons who find their own housing in private homes and apartment buildings.
5) Moderate Rehabilitation Loans to Landlords: loans to landlords for rehabilitation of units.
6) Housing for the Handicapped: financing for group homes for the handicapped.
7) Housing for the Homeless: grants to organizations to operate shelters for the homeless.
8) High Risk Home Improvement Program: interest-free home repair loans to high-risk and low-income households in the City of Grand Rapids and in Buena Vista.
9) Low-Income Housing Tax Credit Program: federal tax credits for owners/developers of low-income rental housing.
10) 70/30 Rental Housing Program: low interest loans to construct or rehabilitate low-income rental housing.
11) 80/20 Direct Lending Program: low interest financing for development or renovation of low-income rental housing.
12) Community Development Block Grant (Small Cities) Program: for neighborhood revitalization and improvements to infrastructure and rental housing.
13) Comprehensive Neighborhood Rehabilitation Competition: for neighborhood revitalization projects.
14) Emergency Housing Apartment Program (EHAP): pilot project; loans and grants for purchase and renovation of a homeless shelter.
15) Home Improvement Loan Program (HIP/CHIP): low cost home improvement loans.
16) Homeless Children's Fund: funds raised for shelters and transitional housing.
17) HOPE (Housing Opportunities Providing Equity): low rate loans to developers of housing for families receiving public assistance.
18) Housing Assistance Program: targeted technical and financial assistance to

Be patient. If any phone number is incorrect, call (area code) 555-1212 and request the new listing.

State Money for Housing and Real Estate

local governments.

19) Loans to Non-Profits: for neighborhood revitalization of single-family and rental housing.

20) Neighborhood Builders Alliance: targeted technical and financial assistance to local governments and non-profits.

21) Neighborhood Housing Grant Program: assistance to non-profits for neighborhood revitalization of single-family and rental housing.

22) Neighborhood Preservation Program (NPP): targeted technical and financial assistance for local governments sponsoring neighborhood infrastructure improvements and building preservation.

23) Pass Through Program: loans for low-income rental housing development.

24) Set-Asides for Non-Profits: homebuyer assistance for low-income households participating in programs of non-profit organizations.

25) Special Housing Program: for handicapped group homes and other housing needs of the handicapped.

26) Supported Independent Living Program and Respite Program: for housing needs of the handicapped.

27) Taxable Bond Program: rental housing construction and renovation.

28) Urban Development Initiative: targeted technical assistance to local governments.

29) Freddie Mac/MSHDA Housing Initiative: low downpayment loans with liberal eligibility requirements; not restricted to first-time buyers.

Minnesota

Minnesota Housing Finance Agency, 400 Sibley Street, St. Paul, MN 55101; (612) 296-9951, (612) 296-7608, or (800) 652-9747.

1) Indian Housing Programs: mortgage and home improvement financing for tribal housing as well as home ownership loans at below-market interest rates.

2) Innovative Housing Loan Program: no-interest and low-interest loans to develop housing that is innovative in design, construction, marketing and/or financing.

3) Accessibility Deferred Loan Program: interest-free loans to households with a disabled member.

4) Rental Rehabilitation Grant Program: dollar-for-dollar grants to rental property owners.

5) Rental Rehabilitation Loan Program: low-interest loans to rental property owners.

6) Section 8 Housing Assistance: rents subsidies for low-income renters.

7) Elderly Home Sharing Program: grants to non-profits who assist elderly in sharing homes.

8) Purchase Plus Program: financing for both purchase and rehabilitation of existing housing for median income or below.

9) Minnesota Mortgage Program: below-market rate loans for low/moderate income first-time home buyers.

10) Home Ownership Assistance Fund: downpayment and monthly payment assistance to lower income MHFA mortgage recipients.

11) Urban Indian Housing Program: below-market financing for Indians in Duluth, Minneapolis and St. Paul.

12) Urban and Rural Homesteading Program: grants to organizations to acquire and rehabilitate vacant and condemned properties for sale to first-time "at risk" home buyers.

13) Deferred Loan Program: deferred payment loans to assist low-income home owners making home improvements.

14) Great Minnesota Fix-Up Fund: below-market home-improvement loans for low/moderate income credit-worthy home owners.

15) Home Energy Loan Program: low-rate loans for increasing energy-efficiency of homes; no maximum income limits.

16) Neighborhood Preservation Loan Program: property improvement loans for low/moderate income households or owners of low/moderate income rental housing in designated areas.

17) Revolving Loan Program: rehabilitation financing for low/moderate income home owners who don't qualify for other programs.

18) Housing Trust Fund: zero-interest deferred loans for development of low-income rental and co-op housing.

19) $1.00 Home Set-Aside Program: HUD lease program for non-profit use of repossessed HUD homes to house the homeless.

20) Intermediate Care Facilities for the Developmentally Disabled: below-market financing for non-profit sponsors to develop residential facilities for the developmentally disabled.

21) Low-Income Housing Tax Credit Program: federal tax credit for owners of low-income rental housing.

22) Low-Income Individuals and Small Family Rental Housing Program: zero-interest deferred loans to rehabilitate small family low-income housing.

23) Low-Income Large Family Rental Housing Program: financing for construction of large rental units for low-income families.

24) Migrant Housing Program: matching funds to eligible sponsors developing housing for migrant farm workers and their families.

25) New Construction Tax Credit Mortgage/Bridge Loan Program: for construction/rehabilitation of rental units for low-income households.

Mississippi

Mississippi Home Corporation, 510 George Street, Suite 107 Dickson Building, Jackson, MS 39201; (601) 359-6700.

1) Single-Family Home Ownership Program: low-rate financing for income-eligible first-time home buyers.

2) Low-Income Housing Tax Credit Program: tax credits for owners of low-income rental housing.

3) Downpayment Assistance Program: for buyers who can afford mortgage payments but not a downpayment.

4) Rental Rehabilitation Program: (under development).

5) Energy Conservation Revolving Loan Fund: (under development).

Missouri

Missouri Housing Development Commission, 3770 Broadway, Kansas City, MO 64111; (816) 756-3790.

1) Multi-Family Program: low-interest rate mortgages to developers of multi-family developments.

2) Single-Family Housing: below-market interest rate mortgages for first-time home buyers.

3) Neighborhood Loan Program: loans to neighborhood organizations and/or developers for acquiring and rehabilitating residential properties.

4) Home Improvements/Weatherization Loan Program: low-interest loans to assist qualified home owners in home improvements that will increase energy efficiency.

5) Blended Multi-Family Program: low-interest rates to developers to stimulate production of housing for low-and moderate-income families and individuals.

6) RTC Home Purchase Program: low-rate financing to purchase reduced cost housing.

7) HUD Repo Properties: HUD-insured low-rate loans for low-income households to purchase HUD-foreclosed properties.

8) Low-Income Housing Tax Credit Program: tax credits for owners of low-income rental housing.

9) Section 8 Programs: subsidies and financial assistance for low-income tenants.

10) Operation Homeless: provides homeless households with Section 8 certificates or vouchers to secure affordable subsidized rental housing.

11) Housing Trust Fund Program: non-Section 8 rental assistance payments for low-income households.

12) Housing Inventory Recycling Program: funds to facilitate purchase of foreclosed homes by lower income households.

13) FmHA Supplemental Subsidy Program: rent subsidies for low-income elderly in FmHA housing projects.

14) Missouri Low-Income Housing Tax Credit Program: supplements the federal Low-Income Housing Tax Credit Program.

Montana

Montana Board of Housing, 2001 Eleventh Avenue, Helena, MT 59620; (406) 444-3040.

1) Single-Family Programs: low-interest loans to low-income families.

2) Multi-Family Program: construction loans to developers of multi-family units for persons and families of lower income.

3) Mortgage Credit Certificate Program: federal tax credits for low/moderate income mortgage holders.

4) Low-Income Housing Tax Credit Program: federal tax credits for owners of low-income housing.

5) Reverse Annuity Mortgage Loans: home-equity loans for senior 68+) home owners.

6) Recycled Mortgage Purchase Program: assists lower income households who cannot purchase homes through the Single-Family Mortgage Program; grant funds help lower construction costs for developers, reduce home prices, create low-interest loans, and assist with downpayments and closing costs.

Nebraska

Nebraska Investment Finance Authority, 1033 O Street, Suite 218, Lincoln, NE 68508; (402) 434-3900.

1) Single-Family Mortgage Program: low-cost loans for single family homes, townhomes, condominiums, mobile homes, and up to 4-unit dwellings.

2) Multi-Family Loan Program: attractive interest rates for developers of rental housing for low- and moderate-income households.

3) Home Improvement Loan Program: low-interest loans to home owners to make needed home improvements.

4) Agricultural Finance Programs:

First-Time Farmer Loan: loans to purchase agricultural real estate.

FmHA: loans to refinance existing agricultural loans.

Be patient. If any phone number is incorrect, call (area code) 555-1212 and request the new listing.

Housing and Real Estate

5) Low-Income Housing Tax Credit Program: federal tax credits for owners of low-income housing.

Nevada

Department of Commerce, Housing Division, 1802 N. Carson St., Suite 154, Carson City, NV 89710; (702) 687-4258.

1) Single Family Mortgage Purchase Program: loans to moderate-income families with no previous home ownership interest within the last 3 years.

2) Industrial Development Bonds: low financing costs for new construction or expansion manufacturing projects.

3) Rural Area Housing Program: low-interest mortgage loans to developers to develop affordable rental units outside metropolitan areas.

Nevada Rural Housing Authority, 2100 California Street, Carson City, NV 89701; (702) 687-5797.

New Hampshire

Housing Finance Authority, P.O. Box 5087, Manchester, NH 03108; (603) 472-8623.

1) Rental Assistance: rental subsidies to eligible families, elderly, disabled or handicapped.

2) Single-Family Mortgage Program: low-interest mortgage funds to qualifying individuals and households.

3) Multi-Family Housing Program: construction loans for small rental projects for private for profit developers and non-profit organizations.

4) Special Needs Fund: funding for housing for individuals with special needs.

5) Affordable Housing Fund: financing primarily for non-profit or co-op multi-family projects.

6) Downpayment/Closing Cost Assistance Program: for borrowers who can afford mortgage payments but lack downpayment and closing costs.

7) Home Equity Conversion Program: loans to help seniors meet living and medical expenses while retaining ownership and residence in their own homes.

8) Section 8 Housing Programs: rental assistance for low-income households.

9) Low-Income Housing Tax Credit Program: tax credits for owners of low-income rental housing.

10) Supportive Services Program: funding for seniors to receive services they need to remain independent.

11) Mortgage Credit Certificate Program: federal tax credits for low/moderate income home buyers.

12) Mixed Income Rental Programs: funding for housing developments with some units affordable to lower income households.

13) Energy Improvements Program: matching grants and loans for low-income households to make energy conservation improvements.

14) Affordable Home Ownership Program: financing for developers of single family homes to be sold at below market cost.

New Jersey

New Jersey Housing Agency, 3625 Quakerbridge Road, Trenton, NJ 08650-2085; (609) 890-1300 or (800) NJ-HOUSE.

1) Home Buyers Program: low-interest loans to urban area first-time buyers with a 5% downpayment.

2) Rental Repair Loan Program: loans to finance the rehabilitation of occupied rental developments.

3) Continuing Care Retirement Communities: construction loans and lower-than-market mortgage interest rates for residential communities for senior citizens.

4) Home Buyers Program: low-rate financing and low downpayments for income-eligible first-time home buyers or home buyers in 41 targeted urban areas.

5) Home Buyers 100% Financing Program: for low/moderate-income first-time or urban buyers.

6) Home Ownership for Performing Employees (HOPE) Program: financial assistance from sponsoring employers to reduce downpayment, closing costs and monthly payments for their employees.

7) Development Set-Aside Program: mortgage funding for purchasers of housing units in Agency-approved housing developments.

8) Multi-Family Rental Housing Program: low-rate financing for developers of rental housing for low/moderate income households.

9) Low-Income Housing Tax Credit Program: federal tax credits for owners of low-income rental housing.

10) Revolving Loan Program: financing for the production of small and medium-sized rental housing projects with units affordable to low-income households.

11) Services for Independent Living Program: support services that enable senior citizens in Agency-financed housing to avoid institutionalization.

12) Boarding House Life Safety Improvement Loan Program: low-rate loans to finance safety improvements in boarding homes.

13) Transitional Housing Program: financing for the construction of transitional housing for the homeless.

14) Seed Money Loan Program: funding of pre-development costs for non-profits seeking to develop affordable housing.

New Mexico

Mortgage Finance Authority, P.O. Box 2047, Albuquerque, NM 87103; (505) 843-6880 or (800) 444-6880.

1) Single-Family Program: below-market loans to first-time home buyers.

2) Multi-Family Programs: financing of multi-family housing for low- and moderate-income tenants.

New Mexico State Housing Authority, 1100 St. Francis Drive, Santa Fe, NM 87503; (505) 827-0258.

1) Low-Income Housing Tax Credit Program: federal tax credits for owners of low-income rental housing.

2) State Housing Rehabilitation Program: rehabilitation grants for low-income elderly, handicapped and disabled home owners.

3) Section 8 Housing Assistance Payments Program (Voucher): rent subsidies for low-income households who locate their own housing.

4) HUD Rental Rehabilitation Program: grants to rehabilitate sub-standard rental units for rental to low-income tenants qualifying for rent subsidies.

New York

State of New York, Executive Department, Division of Housing and Community Renewal, One Fordham Plaza, Bronx, NY 10458; (212) 519-5700.

1) Special Needs Housing Program: grants to non-profit sponsors for single room occupancy dwellings units for low-income individuals.

2) Low-Income Housing Trust Fund: funds to non-profit sponsors to rehabilitate existing properties into affordable low-income housing.

3) Housing Development Fund: temporary financing to non-profit sponsors developing housing with private or government-aided mortgages

4) Rental Rehabilitation Program: up to $8,500 per unit to subsidize up to 50% of the cost of moderate rehabilitation of residential units in lower-income neighborhoods.

5) Rural Preservation Program: funds to local not-for-profit organizations engaging in a variety of activities for the benefit of low- and moderate-income persons.

6) Rural Rental Assistance Program: monthly rent subsidy payments to owners of multi-family projects on behalf of low-income tenants.

7) Turn Key/Enhanced Housing Trust Fund: financing for developers of low-income rental housing.

8) Infrastructure Development Demonstration Program: grant funds for infrastructure improvements (water lines, roads, sidewalks, utility lines) that serve affordable housing projects.

9) Urban Initiative Program: funding for community preservation and improvement in designated urban areas.

10) Rural Area Revitalization Program: funding for not-for-profit organizations to make housing improvements in designated areas.

11) Housing Opportunities Program for the Elderly-RESTORE: funds for not-for-profit organizations to make emergency home repairs for elderly home owners.

12) Shared Housing Development Program: funding for boarding houses, accessory apartments and "granny flats" in designated areas.

13) Clinton Preservation Program: financing to preserve and improve the Clinton neighborhood in NYC.

14) Low-Income Housing Tax Credit Program: federal tax credits for owners of low-income housing rental.

15) Neighborhood Preservation Program: funding to defray administrative costs of not-for-profit organizations performing neighborhood preservation activities.

16) Rural Home Ownership Assistance Program: funds to defray administrative costs of not-for-profit organizations assisting low-income households in the acquisition, financing, and rehabilitation of affordable housing.

17) Neighborhood Redevelopment Demonstration Program: funds for planning, administration and project costs for activities that promote affordable housing or improve neighborhoods.

18) Section 8 Moderate Rehabilitation Program: incentives for property owners to upgrade substandard rental housing for tenants qualifying for rent subsidies.

19) Section 8 Existing Housing Program: rent subsidies for low-income households.

20) Senior Citizen Rent Increase Exemption: exemption from rent increases for tenants 62 years of age or older who live in rent-controlled apartments in NYC and 15 other areas; landlords are compensated with certificates to pay real estate taxes or to convert to cash.

New York State Housing Authority, 250 Broadway, New York, NY 10007; (212) 306-3000.

Be patient. If any phone number is incorrect, call (area code) 555-1212 and request the new listing.

State Money for Housing and Real Estate

North Carolina

North Carolina Housing Finance Agency, 3300 Drake Circle, Suite 200, Raleigh, NC 27611; (919) 781-6115.

1) Single-Family Mortgage Loan Program: below-market, fixed-rate loans for first-time home buyers with low/moderate income.

2) Home Improvement Loan Program: rehabilitation loans of up to $15,000 at rates as low as 1% to improve owner occupied housing.

3) Governor's NCHFA/FmHA Elderly Subsidy Program: rental subsidy of up to $100 per month based on occupant's income.

4) Mortgage Credit Certificate Program: tax-credit for first-time home buyers paying mortgage interest.

5) Home Ownership Challenge Fund: funding to non-profits that create home ownership opportunities for low-income households.

6) Maxwell/Fuller Self-Help Housing Program: zero-interest loans to nonprofits managing self-help or owner-built housing projects for low-income households.

7) Multi-Family Loan Program: below-market financing for developers of low/moderate-income rental housing.

8) Multi-Family subsidized Program: rent subsidies for low-income tenants.

9) Low-Income Housing Tax Credit Program: federal tax credits for owners of low-income housing.

10) Catalyst Loan Program: funding for non-profits for front-end costs in the development of low-income rental housing.

11) Rental Rehabilitation Program: rehabilitation funds for privately-owned rental housing for low-income households.

12) Energy Conservation and Housing Rehab Incentive Program: deferred payment loans and grants for energy conservation and housing rehab improvements on low-income housing.

13) Energy-Efficient Housing Production Program: financing for new or rehabilitated housing for low-income households.

14) Non-Profit Development Program: funds for non-profits for pre-development costs, construction financing and administrative expenses associated with development of affordable housing.

15) Resolution Trust Corporation Clearinghouse: property information for purchasers, allowing qualified purchasers right of first refusal for single family and multi-family properties affordable to low/moderate income households.

North Dakota

Housing Finance Agency, P.O. Box 1535, Bismarck, ND 58502; (701) 224-3434.

1) Housing Assistance: rental assistance program for low-income renter households and mobile home space renters.

2) Single Family Program: low interest loans for low- to moderate-income first-time home buyers.

3) Housing Assistance Program: certificates and vouchers to assist low-income tenants with rent payments.

4) Moderate Rehabilitation Program: incentives for rehabilitation of substandard housing for rental to low-income tenants qualifying for rent-subsidies.

5) Low-Income Housing Tax Credit Program: federal tax credits for owners of low-income rental housing.

Ohio

Ohio Housing Finance Agency, 775 High St., 26th Floor, Columbus, OH 43266; (614) 466-7970.

1) Seed Money Loan Program: no-interest loans to non-profit, public and limited profit entities to arrange financing for low- and moderate-income rental housing developments.

2) First-Time Homebuyer Program: below-market financing for first-time home buyers.

3) Home Ownership Incentive Programs: low interest rates and downpayments for non-profit developers of housing to meet special needs (single parents, minorities, disabled, rural, inner city).

4) Development Loan Program: financing for construction and development costs of low/moderate income housing by non-profit and limited profit sponsors.

5) Low-Income Housing Tax Credit Program: federal tax credits for owners of low-income rental housing.

6) 403 Rental Housing Gap Financing Program: financial assistance to non-profit organizations for development of low-income rental housing.

7) Rental Housing Energy Conservation Program: funds to non-profits for energy-efficient rehabilitation or new construction of low-income rental housing.

8) Multi-Family Rental Development Program: financing for purchase, construction, and rehabilitation of multi-family rental housing for the elderly.

9) Section 8 Rental Assistance Program: rent subsidies.

Oklahoma

Oklahoma Housing Finance Agency, P.O. Box 26720, Oklahoma City, OK 73126-0720; (405) 848-1144 or (800) 256-1489.

1) Single-Family Mortgage Revenue Bond Program: low-rate loans to first-time home buyers.

2) Multi-Family Mortgage Revenue Bond Program: funds for the purchase, construction or rehabilitation of housing for low/moderate income families.

3) Homeless Program: support for homeless families while they await funds for housing.

4) Section 8 Existing Housing Assistance Program: rent subsidies for low-income tenants.

5) Section 8 Rental Rehabilitation Program: matching funds for property owners who renovate rental units for low/moderate-income households.

6) Section 8 Voucher Assistance Program: rent subsidies for low-income households who locate their own housing.

Oregon

Oregon Housing Agency, Housing Division, 1600 State St., Suite 100, Salem, OR 97310; (503) 378-4343.

1) Elderly and Disabled Housing Program: below-market interest rate mortgage loans for multi-family housing for elderly and disabled.

2) Family Rental Housing Program: financing for multi-unit rental housing for low-income families.

3) Seed Money Advance Program: no-interest advances to non-profits to cover pre-construction costs.

4) Low-Income Housing Tax Credit: federal income tax credits to developers who construct, rehabilitate, or acquire qualified low-income rental housing.

5) Single-Family Mortgage Program: below-market interest rate loans to low- and moderate-income Oregon home buyers.

6) Mortgage Credit Certificate Program: federal tax credit for low- and moderate-income Oregonians to purchase, improve or rehabilitate a single-family residence.

7) Oregon Lenders' Tax Credit Program: very low interest loans to non-profits from qualified Oregon financial institutions for low-income multi-family housing.

8) Low-Income Rental Housing Fund: rental assistance for low-income families.

9) Mobile Home Park Purchase Program: financial and technical assistance for tenants' associations to purchase their mobile home parks.

10) Partnership Housing Team: technical assistance to local governments and non-profits developing low-income housing.

11) Community Development Corporation Program: grants and technical assistance for local community development corporations to increase their skills in establishing low-income housing.

Pennsylvania

Pennsylvania Housing Finance Agency, 2101 North Front St. Harrisburg, PA 17105; (717) 780-3800.

1) Home Owners Emergency Mortgage Assistance Program: loans to keep delinquent home owners from losing their homes to foreclosure.

2) Rental Housing Development Program: low-interest financing for developers of low-income multi-family rental housing.

3) Low-Income Housing Tax Credit Program: federal tax credit for owners of low-income rental housing.

4) Rental Rehabilitation Program: financing for property owners who rehabilitate low-income rental units.

5) Statewide Home Ownership Program: low-interest financing for first-time home buyers or buyers of property in targeted areas.

6) HomeStart Program: financing for middle-income first-time home buyers, single-parent families, and certain veterans.

7) Lower-Income Home Ownership Program: low-interest financing, reduced fees and closing cost assistance for low-income first-time home buyers and handicapped persons.

8) Non-Profit Seed Fund Program: pre-development loans for non-profits constructing or rehabilitating multi-family low-income housing.

9) Supportive Services Program: to help elderly residents of subsidized senior citizen rental apartments meet routine needs that enable them to remain in their own homes.

Rhode Island

Rhode Island Housing and Mortgage Finance Corporation, 60 Eddy St., Providence, RI 02903; (401) 751-5566.

1) Home Repair: fixed rate-loans to make needed repairs on 1 to 6 unit dwellings owned or occupied by low- and moderate-income persons.

2) Rental Housing Production and Rehabilitation: tax-exempt and/or taxable bond financing for developers for projects where a minimum of 20% of the units are rented to low-income tenants.

3) First Homes Program: low-rate mortgages for income-eligible first-time home buyers.

4) Accessory Apartments: low-rate loans to create a separate apartment unit in the home.

5) Energy-Efficient Homes Program: additional assistance to FIRST HOMES

Be patient. If any phone number is incorrect, call (area code) 555-1212 and request the new listing.

Housing and Real Estate

mortgagees if their home receives a high energy-efficiency rating.

6) Buy-It/Fix-It Program: low-rate financing to buy or refinance an older home and make substantial repairs.

7) Home Equity Conversion Mortgage Program: reverse mortgages to enable older home owners to remain in and retain ownership of their homes.

8) Home Owner's Notes Program: helps first-time home buyers assemble funding from several sources.

9) Mortgage Credit Certificates: tax credit for first-time home buyers.

10) Construction Loan Program: below market rate loans to build/rehab affordable 1/4 family homes for low/moderate-income persons.

11) Cooperative Housing Demonstration Program: funding packages for non-profit organizations to develop cooperative housing.

12) Land Bank Program: below market rate loans for purchase or refinancing of undeveloped land to be used for low/moderate-income housing.

13) Lease-Purchase Program: financing for non-profit organizations to develop housing that will be leased to low/moderate-income households.

14) Low-Income Housing Tax Credit Program: tax credits for owners of rental housing for low-income households.

15) Pre-Development Loan Program: short-term loans to cover pre-development costs for non-profit developers.

16) Preservation Loan Fund: below-market rate loans to preserve affordability of existing subsidized rental housing.

17) Emergency Housing Assistance Program: assistance to qualified low-income households facing a temporary housing crisis.

18) Employer Assisted Housing: employer resources combine with existing programs to provide affordable housing for employees.

19) Supportive Services/Robert Wood Johnston Foundation: supportive services for residents of RI Housing-financed developments to enable them to remain independent.

South Carolina

South Carolina State Housing Financing and Development Authority, 1710 Gervais St., Suite 300, Columbia, SC 29201; (803) 734-8836.

1) Multi-Family Development Programs: construction loans to construct houses for rental to low and moderate-to-low income persons.

2) Moderate Rehabilitation Program: mortgage financing for the upgrade of substandard rental housing.

3) Home Ownership Mortgage Purchase Program: below market rate financing for income-eligible home buyers.

4) Community Home Ownership Opportunity Partnership (CHOP): below market rate financing for purchase of affordable homes by qualified borrowers in conjunction with local communities' contributions.

5) Low-Income Housing Tax Credit Program: tax credits for developers of low-income rental housing.

6) Section 8 Certificates and Vouchers: rental assistance for low-income households.

7) Section 8 Moderate Rehabilitation Program: rent subsidies for low-income households.

South Dakota

South Dakota Housing Development Authority, P.O. Box 1237, Pierre, SD 57501; (605) 773-3181.

1) Existing Housing Assistance Payments Program: money to assist lower-income families pay for modest rental housing.

2) Energy Efficiency Program - New Construction: new construction loans for homes complying with super-insulation standards.

3) Home Ownership Mortgage Program: low-rate financing for eligible single families to build, rehabilitate or buy homes.

4) Multi-Family Housing Trust Fund: permanent and temporary mortgage loans to finance the construction of multi-family housing.

5) Low-Income Housing Tax Credit Program: federal tax credits for developers/owners of low-income housing.

6) Emergency Shelter Grants Program: financing of shelters for homeless and special needs households.

7) Rental Rehab Program: financing for owners of rental properties occupied by low-income households.

Tennessee

Tennessee Housing Development Agency, 700 Landmark Center, 401 Church St., Nashville, TN 37219; (615) 741-4979.

1) Home Ownership Program: reduced interest rate loans to low- and moderate-income families.

2) Veterans: permanent mortgage financing available for disabled Veterans who need specially designed homes.

3) Rental Rehabilitation: lower-than-market loans to owners of rental property to rehabilitate units. This program also offers a grant of up to $5000 per unit to keep the cost of rehabilitation down.

4) Owner-Built Homes: permanent financing for homes built by the owners. Sweat equity serves as the downpayment.

5) Turn Key III: subsidized rent to bring economically viable residents into personal home ownership.

6) Section 8 Rental Assistance Program: subsidy funds to low-income households.

7) Technical Assistance Program: technical assistance to public and private sponsors of low- and moderate-income housing.

8) Low-Income Housing Tax Credit: tax credits for owners of low-income housing.

9) Moderate Rehabilitation Program: incentives for property owners to upgrade substandard rental units to be occupied by low-income tenants qualifying for rent subsidies.

10) HOUSE Program: funding for special needs housing projects.

Texas

Texas Housing Agency, PO Box 13941 Capitol Station, Austin, TX 78711; (512) 472-7500.

1) Mortgage Credit Certificate Program: up to $2,000 of federal tax credits for first-time home owners.

2) Low-Income Rental Housing Tax Credit: federal tax credits for those who wish to acquire, construct, or rehabilitate rental housing for low-income families.

3) Single-Family Bond Program: low-rate financing for low/moderate income first-time home buyers.

4) Section 8 Housing Assistance Program: rental assistance via subsidies for low-income households.

Utah

Utah Housing Finance Agency, 177 East 100 South, Salt Lake City, UT 84111; (801) 521-6950.

1) Single-Family Mortgage Program: money to first-time home buyers or home buyers in targeted areas with required downpayment.

Vermont

Vermont Housing Finance Agency, One Burlington Sq., PO Box 408, Burlington, VT 05402; (802) 864-5743, (800) 222-VFHA.

1) Mortgage Plus: federal income tax credit for up to 20% of interest on a home loan.

2) Mortgages for Vermonters: low-interest mortgages for first-time buyers.

3) Energy-Rated Homes of Vermont Mortgage Program: money to modify homes to make them energy efficient.

4) New Home Financing: low-rate financing for qualified borrowers purchasing new homes.

5) Mobile Home Financing: mortgage financing for modular or permanently fixed mobile homes; financing for non-profit or tenant acquisition of mobile home parks.

6) Perpetually Affordable Housing Program: low-rate financing for non-profit housing developers providing home ownership opportunities that will remain affordable over the long term.

7) Rural Vermont Mortgage: low-rate financing for low-income households in rural areas.

8) Home Energy/Improvement Loan Program: low-rate loans for low/moderate-income home owners to make energy improvements.

9) Multi-Family Financing: financing to eligible housing sponsors who wish to build or renovate low/moderate-income rental or cooperative housing.

10) Low-Income Housing Tax Credit Program: tax credits for developers/owners of rental housing for low-income households.

11) Vermont Housing Ventures: low-rate financing to cover pre-development costs of locally based non-profit housing.

12) Housing Foundation, Inc.: purchases and preserves housing units threatened with conversion to unsubsidized stock; aids in tenant acquisition of mobile home parks.

13) Housing Vermont: develops affordable housing in partnership with non-profit organizations throughout the state.

14) Vermont Home Mortgage Guarantee Board (VHMGB): low-cost mortgage insurance for low/moderately-priced housing.

15) Vermont Housing and Conservation Board: grants and loans to projects which meet both affordable housing and conservation goals.

16) ENABLE Program: low-rate loans to finance modifications designed to make housing more accessible for the elderly and disabled.

Vermont State Housing Authority, P.O. Box 397, Montpelier, VT 05601-0397; (802) 828-3295.

Be patient. If any phone number is incorrect, call (area code) 555-1212 and request the new listing.

State Money for Housing and Real Estate

Virginia

Virginia Housing Development Authority, 601 S. Belvedere Street, Richmond, VA 23220; (804) 782-1986.

1) Home Mortgage Loan Program: below-market loans to eligible home buyers with required downpayment.

2) Virginia Housing Fund: flexible, below-market rate loans for lower-income people.

3) Home Rehabilitation Loan Program: loans at 8% interest for 6 months to 8-year terms.

4) Targeted Area Program: below-market loans with low downpayments for purchasers of homes in designated areas.

5) Multi-Family Loan Program: below-market loans to developers of low/moderate-price rental housing.

6) Low-Income Housing Tax Credit Program: federal tax credits for owners of low-income rental housing.

7) Rental Rehabilitation Program: grants for up to 50% of rehab costs for low-income rental housing.

8) Section 8 Rent Subsidy Programs: subsidies to assist low-income households in meeting rental housing costs.

9) Joint Program for Housing Persons with Mental Disabilities and Recovering Substance Abusers: below-market loans to assist non-profit sponsors in developing supportive housing facilities.

Washington

Washington State Housing Finance Commission, 111 Third Ave., Suite 2240, Seattle, WA 98101-3202; (206) 464-7139.

1) Mortgage Credit Certificate Program: tax credits to prospective first-time home buyers purchasing manufactured, newly-constructed or existing homes.

2) Multi-Family Program: financing to developers of multi-family projects where at least 20% or more units will be rented to lower- to mid-income persons, the elderly or the handicapped.

3) Low-Income Housing Tax Credit Program: federal tax credits to developers/owners of low-income rental housing.

4) Single Family Mortgage Revenue Bond Program: below market rate loans for income-eligible first time home buyers and buyers of residences in targeted areas.

5) Non-Profit Owners Program: tax-exempt financing for group homes, congregate housing, and retirement housing (non-medical).

6) Multi-Family Tax Exempt Bond Financing Program: tax exempt financing for developers/owners of multi-family housing with a percentage set aside for low-income households; new construction, acquisition and rehabilitation.

West Virginia

West Virginia Housing Development Fund, 814 Virginia St., East, Charleston, WV 25301; (304) 345-6475.

1) Mortgage Credit Certificate Program: federal tax credit for home buyers.

2) Single Family Mortgage Program: financing for single family homes with deferred payment loans to pay downpayment and closing costs.

3) Multi-Family Construction Loan Incentive Program: construction financing for sponsors of low-income multi-family housing.

4) Building Revitalization/Reutilization Program: funds for rehabilitation of existing downtown residential and commercial buildings.

5) Emergency Shelters Program: financing for construction, rehabilitation, and acquisition of shelters.

6) Housing Development Fund/Army Corps of Engineers Flood Mitigation: includes flood-proofing of individual homes.

7) Community Provider Financing Program: low-interest loans to non-profits for financing the acquisition or construction of health facilities.

8) Home Rehab Program: low-cost loans to repair flooded homes.

9) Low-Income Housing Tax Credit Program: federal tax credits for developers/owners of low-income multi-family housing.

10) Land Development Program: low-rate financing for developers of raw land to support housing developments.

11) Rental Rehab Program: grants for upgrading rental units for low-income households.

12) ARC Program: funding of site development costs in the Appalachian region.

Wisconsin

Wisconsin Housing and Economic Development Authority, PO Box 1728, Madison, WI 53701; (608) 266-7884 or (800) 362-2767.

1) HOME Program: low interest, fixed rate, 30-year loans.

2) Home Energy Loan Program: low-interest loans to make energy conserving improvements on homes.

3) DEER Program: money to non-profits to acquire and rehabilitate older single-family and two-family homes with special emphasis on energy conservation. Restored homes are then sold.

4) Rental Housing Programs: financing of rental housing for low-and moderate-income individuals and families, elderly and disabled.

5) Community Housing Alternatives Program: loans for construction, purchase or rehabilitation of projects to house those who are chronically disabled due to mental illness, development disability, physical disability, or alcohol- or other drug-related dependence, or those over 60 years of age.

6) Rental Rehabilitation Program: money for rehabilitation of rental units for low-income households.

7) Low-Income Housing Tax Credits: federal tax credits for low-income rental housing in Wisconsin.

8) WHEDA Foundation Grants: grants to non-profit housing project sponsors.

9) Business Development Bond Program: financing for small- and medium-sized businesses.

10) Linked Deposit Loan Program: loans to businesses that are more than 50% owned by women or minorities.

11) Business Energy Fund Program: low-cost financing to small businesses for energy conservation improvements.

12) Credit Relief Outreach Program: agricultural related families can receive interest rate reduction and loan guarantees of up to $20,000.

13) Home Improvement Loan Program: below-market financing for low/moderate income home owners to make eligible home improvements such as energy-conserving improvements.

14) Blueprint Loan Program: low cost, short-term financing for pre-development costs associated with creating multi-family housing under government programs.

15) Section 8 Rent Subsidy Program: rent subsidies for low/moderate income rental households.

16) Small Business Loan Guarantee Program: funding necessary to guarantee conventional loans needed by businesses to fulfill awarded contracts.

17) Neighborhood Housing Program Fund: supports development and improvement of low-income housing and urban and rural neighborhood revitalization.

18) Elderly Housing Program Fund: supports development and improvement of non-institutional housing facilities for frail or low-income elderly persons.

19) Persons-in-Crisis Housing Program Fund: supports development and improvement of emergency shelters and group/transitional housing.

20) Wisconsin Partnership for Housing Development: development financing and technical assistance to community-based organizations providing housing to low-income households.

21) Rental Property Energy Efficiency Loan Fund: financing for purchase and installation of energy-saving measures in rental properties.

Wyoming

Wyoming Community Development Authority, 123 S. Durbin St., P.O. Box 634, Casper, WY 82602; (307) 265-0603.

Funding for single-family homes, multi-family projects, and economic development.

1) Single Family Mortgage Program: low-rate financing for first-time home buyers.

2) Section 8 Rental Assistance Program: certificates and vouchers to assist low-income rental households.

3) Rental Rehab Program: loans for owners of rental housing in targeted areas.

4) Urban Homesteading Program: sale of deteriorating government-owned residences to "urban homesteaders" who agree to restore and live in them.

5) WCDA CDBG Revolving Loan Fund: for housing rehabilitation that benefits low/moderate income households.

6) Low-Income Tax Credit Program: tax credits for owners of rental housing affordable to low-income households.

Be patient. If any phone number is incorrect, call (area code) 555-1212 and request the new listing.

Housing and Real Estate

Gardening

* Alternative Farming Systems

Alternative Farming Systems
U.S. Department of Agriculture
10301 Baltimore Blvd.
Beltsville, MD 20705 (301) 504-5204

This center covers organized farming or gardening that includes low-input, sustainable, or regenerative agriculture. Conservation tillage and other cultivation practices, such as intercropping, crop rotation, and use of green manures, are also covered.

* Botanic Garden: 10,000 Plant Species

U.S. Botanic Garden
Office of Director
2245 First St., SW
Washington, DC 20024 (202) 225-8333

The Botanic Garden is a living museum open daily, free of charge, containing noteworthy collections, including Economic Plants, Cycads, Orchids, Begonias, Cacti and Succulents, Carnivorous Plants, Bromeliads, Ferns, Roses, Palms, and other miscellaneous tropical and subtropical plants, many of which are rare species. There are special displays during most of the year, and in their proper seasons banana, papaya, orange, lemon, tangerine, kumquat, averrhoa, coffee, and surinam cherry are displayed in luxuriant fruiting. Included in its glasshouse collections are many of the plants brought to the U.S. Botanic Garden from the Wilkes Expedition to the South Seas in 1842. The entire collection of the Garden includes over 10,000 species and varieties of plant growth. The collection attracts many visitors annually, including botanists, horticulturists, students, and garden club members. The horticultural and botanical library is available by appointment only.

* Botanical Garden Tours

Public Programs Office
U.S. Botanic Garden
245 1st St., SW
Washington, DC 20024 (202) 226-4082

The Botanic Garden is open to the public from 9 a.m. to 9 p.m. daily June through August, and from 9 a.m. to 5 p.m. the rest of the year. Tours are given to interested groups, including garden clubs, professional organizations, and school children.

* Botanical Specimens for Plant Breeders

U.S. Botanic Garden
Office of Director
2245 First St., SW
Washington, DC 20024 (202) 225-8333

Though not operated as a scientific institution, the Botanic Garden does make educational facilities available for study to students, botanists, and floriculturists on many rare and interesting botanical specimens. Working with scientists, the Garden grows, displays, and keeps records on significant botanical collections for study and for exchange with other institutions. The Garden is a gene pool resource for plant breeders. It is also involved in the preservation of rare or endangered plants and is actively building and displaying economic plants. Every year botanical specimens are received from all over the world with requests for identification, and one of the services offered by the Garden to the public is the identification of such specimens and the furnishing of information relating to the proper care for them, and methods of growing them.

* Christmas Tree Diseases

Superintendent of Documents
Government Printing Office
Washington, DC 20402 (202) 783-3238

Tree publications are listed, including those of interest to tree growers and the lumber industry. Also featured is a guide to Christmas Tree diseases and books listing the tropical timbers of the world. Free.

* Compost and Improved Soil

Soil Microbial Systems
U.S. Department of Agriculture
Building 318, Room 108 BARC-E
Beltsville, MD 20705 (301) 504-8163

This office provides technical assistance on the production and use of compost, soil, and microbes.

* Desert and Tropical Plants Museum

The Conservatory
Maryland Avenue
1st to 2nd Sts., SW
Washington, DC 20024 (202) 225-6647

The Conservatory houses permanent collections of tropical, subtropical, and desert plants in an exhibition area of 38,000 square feet. Just across from the Conservatory on Independence Avenue, the Frederic Auguste Bartholdi Park features displays of bulbs, annuals, and perennials.

* Environmental Impact on Plant Species

U.S. Botanic Garden
Office of Director
2245 First St., SW
Washington, DC 20024 (202) 225-8333

In these times of global changes, with climate changes, the greenhouse effect, and the need for species diversity, strategically placed at the foot of our nation's Capitol, the Botanic Garden's spectacular displays of significant plant collections can have a strong impact on people's awareness of the environment.

* Gardening and Plant Propagation Workshops

Poplar Point
700 Howard Road, SE
Anacostia, DC 20020 (202) 225-6420

The Poplar Point Production Facility is a nursery and greenhouse range responsible for plant production for the U.S. Botanic Garden and the entire Capitol Hill Complex. The facility is open by appointment and occasionally tours of the facility are conducted for the public. Next year a new nursery will be built and many hands-on classes and workshops on gardening and plant propagation will be held there.

* Gypsy Moth Control

Printing and Distribution Management Branch, APHIS
U.S. Department of Agriculture
Federal Building, Room G-100
6505 Belcrest Rd.
Hyattsville, MD 20782 (301) 436-7176

The following publication is available free of charge from APHIS: *Don't Move the Gypsy Moth* (July 1985). This tells how to make sure outdoor household articles don't spread gypsy moths.

* Horticulture

Horticulture
U.S. Department of Agriculture
10301 Baltimore Blvd.
Beltsville, MD 20705 (301) 504-5204

This center covers technical horticultural or botanical questions, economic botany, wild plants of possible use, herbs, bonsai, and floriculture.

* Horticultural Classes: Medicinal Plants to Lawn Care

Public Programs Office
U.S. Botanic Garden

Be patient. If any phone number is incorrect, call (area code) 555-1212 and request the new listing.

Gardening

245 1st St., SW
Washington, DC 20024 (202) 226-4082

Horticultural classes are held throughout the year on timely subjects related to botanical, horticultural, and environmental interests. Many leading scientists are featured as lecturers and all classes are free of charge. Classes consist of a lecture incorporating slides or demonstrations, tours or workshops. Some examples of recent classes include Fall Lawn Care, Decorating With Exotics, Native Medicinal Plants, and The Dynamics of Horticultural Therapy. A calendar of all classes is available.

* Horticulture Clearinghouse

Horticulture
U.S. Department of Agriculture
10301 Baltimore Blvd.
Beltsville, MD 20705 (301) 504-5204

This center covers technical horticultural or botanical questions, economic botany, wild plants of possible use, herbs, bonsai, and floriculture.

* Indoor and Outdoor Insects Identification

Contact your local USDA
Extension Service Agent

Technical assistance is available to help you identify and eliminate any problems you may have which are caused by insects and bugs. You are encouraged to catch one of the insects causing the problem and send it in for analysis. Contact your local Extension Service for more information.

* Landscaping

Landscape Architect
Engineering Division
Soil Conservation Service
U.S. Department of Agriculture (USDA)
6129 South Building
Washington, DC 20250 (202) 720-8518

Assistance is available to help anyone with landscaping-related problems from your local USDA Extension Service agents. Help is also available to those having problems with larger projects involving conservation. Contact the above office.

* National Arboretum

U.S. National Arboretum
3501 New York Ave.
Educational Department
Washington, DC 20002 (202) 475-4815

Various woody ornamental and outdoor plants are grown and cared for on the 444 acres comprising the U.S. National Arboretum. Admission and parking are free, and guided tours for 10 or more are available with 3 weeks advance notice. Many free classes are offered, along with many special events and functions associated with gardening and growing plants. A free monthly newsletter lists the monthly calendar.

* Patents on Seeds

Plant Variety Protection Office
Commodities Scientific Support Division
AMS, NAL, Room 500
Beltsville, MD 20705 (301) 504-5518

Unique seeds, with few exceptions, that are sexually reproduced can be protected by patents. The protection, which extents for 18 years, provides owners with exclusive rights to sell, reproduce, export, and produce the seed.

* Plant and Flower Shows

Office of the Director
U.S. Botanic Garden
245 1st St., SW
Washington, DC 20024 (202) 225-8333

Spectacular seasonal plant and flower shows are scheduled throughout the year. The Annual Spring Flower Show features spring flowering plants and is held from Palm Sunday through Easter Sunday. The Summer Terrace Display is held on the patio in front of the Conservatory from late May through September. Hundreds of flowering and foliage plants in hanging baskets highlight this event. Mid-November through Thanksgiving Day features The Annual Chrysanthemum Show. The Annual Poinsettia Show takes place from mid-December through the

Christmas holidays. The Garden also hosts various plant and flower shows sponsored by area garden clubs and plant societies each year. Each show has a theme and offers excellent ideas for new plants, innovative garden designs, and uses state-of-the-art gardening techniques. Special exhibits are being prepared for The U.S. Botanic Garden's 150th Anniversary in 1992. Call (202) 225-7099 for more information about shows.

* Plant Care and Botanical Garden Calendar

Public Programs Office
U.S. Botanic Garden
245 1st St., SW
Washington, DC 20024 (202) 226-4082

Handouts are provided on plant culture, sources for plants and care for certain plants. A pamphlet offers a self-guided tour of the Garden. Brochures including schedules for shows and horticultural classes, and historical information about the Garden are also available.

* Plant Care Telephone Line and Information Service

Plant Information Service
U.S. Botanic Garden
245 1st St., SW
Washington, DC 20024 (202) 225-8333

The Garden serves as a center for plant information offering a telephone information service as well as responding to written inquiries Monday through Friday from 9:00 a.m. to 11:30 a.m.

* Plant Protection and Rescue Center

U.S. Botanic Garden
Office of Director
2245 First St., SW
Washington, DC 20024 (202) 225-8333

Serving as a Plant Rescue Center for the USDA's Animal and Plant Health Inspection Service, the Botanic Garden is legally obligated to care for and preserve the multitude of protected plants it receives that are illegally shipped into the U.S. Through this program, the Garden helps visitors recognize the value of preservation and protection of plants.

* Plants: Research and Reference

National Arboretum Library
3501 New York Ave., NE
Washington, DC 2000 (202) 475-4815

This library provides information on many aspects of indoor plants and gardening.

* Seed Quality and Inspection Labs

Federal Seed Lab
U.S. Department of Agriculture
Beltsville, MD 20705 (301) 504-8089

The federal government can test seeds to determine their quality and whether they are free from contamination. They will also prosecute any agent that transfers contaminated or mislabeled seeds from state to state. Seeds are examined by or at a state agent's request, and there may be some fee involved.

* Sick House Plants, Pets, Trees, and Lawns

Contact your local U.S. Department of Agriculture
Extension Service Agent

Free technical assistance is available to help diagnose and cure diseases of plants and animals. Services range from telephone consultations and free literature, to analyzing your pets' stools or your plants' leaves for disease.

* Tracer Bulletins to Gardening References

Science and Technology Division
Reference Section
Library of Congress
Washington, DC 20540 (202) 707-5580

An informal series of reference guides are issued free from the Science and Technology Division under the general title, *LC Science Tracer Bullet*. These guides are designed to help readers locate published material about subjects about

Be patient. If any phone number is incorrect, call (area code) 555-1212 and request the new listing.

Housing and Real Estate

which they have only general knowledge. New titles in the series are announced in the weekly Library of Congress *Information Bulletin* that is distributed to many libraries. The following is a list of *Tracer Bullets* currently available:

81-15 History of American Agriculture
82-2 Gardening
82-6 Biological Control of Insects
83-5 Plant Exploration and Introduction
85-1 Herbs and Herb Gardening
85-2 Landscape Gardening
85-10 Rose Culture
86-3 Jojoba and Other Oilseed Plants

86-4 Composite Materials
88-5 Soil Erosion

* Wood Pests

Forest Insect and Disease Research
U.S. Department of Agriculture (USDA)
FS, Room 609 RP-E
Arlington, VA 22209 (703) 453-9532
OR: Your local Forest Service or Extension Office

The USDA provides technical assistance for insects and diseases to wood, whether it is in use or stored, wood products, or urban trees. All insect and disease suppression projects must meet specific criteria for federal participation.

Be patient. If any phone number is incorrect, call (area code) 555-1212 and request the new listing.

Education School: Grades K-12

* *See also Careers and Workplace Chapter*
* *See also Drugs and Chemical Enforcement Chapter*
* *See also Current Events and Homework Chapter*
* *See also Weather and Maps Chapter*

Studies and new assessments of American education abound. Take advantage of the numerous clearinghouses which are excellent starting points for information. Resources on pre-school and early childhood development are sprinkled here. Vocational education is included in the next section on postsecondary education. Students and teachers alike will find very relevant information in the Current Events and Homework Chapter toward the end of the book. And, of course, additional classroom materials and lesson plans are identified throughout the book.

* Academic Affairs

Academic Affairs
Veterans Health Services and Research Administration
U.S. Department of Veterans Affairs (DVA)
810 Vermont Ave., NW, Room 876
Washington, DC 20420 (202) 535-7527

The DVA conducts the largest coordinated health professions education and training efforts of its kind in the U.S. Its purpose is to assure high quality health care for veterans and to develop a sufficient number of all categories of professional and other health personnel. For more information contact the office above.

* Alternative versus Traditional Schools

ERIC Clearinghouse on Educational Management
University of Oregon
1787 Agate St.
Eugene, OR 97403-5207 (503) 686-5043

Subject areas include all aspects of the administration, leadership, finance, governance, and structure of public and private education organizations at the elementary, middle, and secondary levels, including facility planning, design, construction, equipment and furnishing, and maintenance; and pre-service and in-service preparation of administrators. Topics covered include the social, technological, political, and legal contexts of education organizations, and of State and Federal programs and policies, and traditional and alternative schools.

* America 2000

America 2000
U.S. Department of Education (800) 872-5327
Washington, DC 20202 (202) 401-2000

In response to the growing concern that American schools were not producing graduates with sufficient skills to meet the challenges of the 21st century, President Bush kicked off America 2000. Goals of America 2000 include: increasing graduation rate to 90%, putting American students first in the world in science and math, and ensuring all schools are free of drugs and violence. America 2000 will be implemented at the Community level. Periodic Satellite Town Meetings are held on the goals of America 2000. Contact the America 2000 staff for information on America 2000 schools and meetings in your area.

* America 2000 Arts Partnership

America 2000
Office of Education Research and Improvement
U.S. Department of Education
Washington, DC 20202 (202) 219-2050

Arts have been incorporated into the larger America 2000 project through the joint cooperation of the U.S. Department of Education and the National Endowment for the Arts. Current plans include the seven following components: Developing World Class Standards in the Arts; Involving America 2000 Communities; Helping States Implement High National Standards; Creating a National Center for Arts Education; Expanding the National Assessment of Educational Progress (NAEP); Developing a Research Agenda in Arts Education; and Designing a National Arts Education Dissemination Network.

* American Educators Teaching Abroad

Superintendent of Documents
Government Printing Office (GPO)
Washington, DC 20402 (202) 783-3238

The United States Information Agency (USIA) publishes many teaching materials, including books, maps, complete teaching modules, and 14 magazines in 20 languages. By law most USIA publications may be distributed only in foreign countries. However, by congressional action, *English Teaching Forum*, a quarterly for English teachers worldwide, published by USIA's English Language Programs Division, is available in the United States through the GPO.

* American Studies for Foreigners

Division of Study of the U.S.
United States Information Agency
301 Fourth St., SW, Room 256
Washington, DC 20547 (202) 619-4562

The Division for the Study of the U.S. promotes foreign education through conferences, seminars, exchange programs for foreign educators, grants, and development of school resource materials. The Academic Specialist Branch provides grants for American teachers to instruct their peers at foreign educational institutions. Contact this office for more information.

* Army Reserve Community Projects: From Baseball to Language Training

Chief of U.S. Army Reserve
Public Affairs, The Pentagon
Washington, DC 20310 (703) 697-7369

The Army Reserve provides a variety of community services through their special programs. Requests are handled on a case by case basis based on their current ability to help. Projects might involve building a community playground or a baseball field. Through the Adopt-a-School Program, Corps people with special skills or training teach special courses, such as a foreign language or communications, or may be involved in extra-curricular activities. Contact your local Army Reserve headquarters or the above office for further information.

* Arts Education

National Arts Education Research Center
New York University School of Education, Health,
Nursing and Arts Profession
26 Washington Place, #21
New York, NY 10003 (212) 998-5050

Established in 1987 as a joint project of the U.S. Department of Education and the National Endowment for the Arts, the Center develops teaching strategies and curricula in arts education. The Center's research design is unique in that it comprises teacher-centered, classroom based collaborations among teachers,

Be patient. If any phone number is incorrect, call (area code) 555-1212 and request the new listing.

Education

university researchers, professional artists, aestheticians and critics. The Center has a network of more than 60 practicing arts educators in 23 states. Work in the Center focuses on secondary education in music, visual arts and theater arts with a special concentration on interdisciplinary and multicultural studies.

* Arts Education Research Publications

National Arts Education Research Center
School of Music
University of Illinois at Urbana-Champaign
1114 West Nevada Street
Urbana, IL 61801 (217) 333-1027

While the Center concluded its work in 1991, there are still ten publications available including: *Status of Arts Education in American Public Schools: Summary and Conclusions*; *Dance Education in American Public Schools* (case studies); *Guide to Curriculum Development in Elementary School Drama/Theatre Education*; and others.

* Arts in Education Initiatives

Arts-In-Education
National Endowment for the Arts
1100 Pennsylvania Ave., NW, Room 602
Washington, DC 20506 (202) 682-5426

The Arts-In-Education Program is a partnership through cooperative efforts of the Arts Endowment, state arts and education agencies, local communities, and other organizations. The Program's overall goal is to advance the arts as part of basic education. Grants are awarded to place practicing artists in a variety of educational settings and to support other projects designed to enhance arts education in schools. Arts in Education Partnership Grants encourage plans and projects that promote the arts in schools as a basic component of the curriculum in kindergarten through high school. The U.S. Department of Education plans to expand the National Assessment of Educational Progress to include an assessment of student's knowledge of the arts by the middle 1990s. The following publications are available from the AIE program at no charge: *Planning to Make the Arts Basic*; *Special Projects Handbook Editions I and II*; and *State Arts Agency Arts in Education Profiles*.

* Arts Plus Program

Arts in Education
National Endowment for the Arts
1100 Pennsylvania Ave., NW,
Washington, DC 20506 (202) 682-5400

The Arts Plus program awards cooperative agreements to support projects of three years duration. In FY 1992, the projects must focus on the disciplines of dance, opera, or theater. The intent of these collaborative projects is to secure the educational organization's commitment to include arts in its goals, programs, daily plans, curriculum and long range plans.

* Art Slides, Films, Video Loan Program

Department of Education Resources
National Gallery of Art
Constitution and 6th St., NW
Washington, DC 20565 (202) 842-6273

Color slide programs, films, and videocassettes are loaned at no cost to schools, libraries, community organizations, and individuals across the nation. The programs deal with a wide range of subjects drawn from the Gallery's permanent collections and special exhibitions. A free catalog listing all free-loan Extension Programs is available.

* Bilingual and Minority Languages Affairs Multifunctional Resource Centers (MRC)

Office of Bilingual Education and Minority
Languages Affairs
330 C St., SW
Washington, DC 20202 (202) 205-5463

These resource centers provide in-service training and technical assistance to parents and educational personnel participating in, or preparing to participate in, instructional programs for limited English proficient children. The centers work closely with state and federal programs in their regions to coordinate program improvement for language minority children. Their efforts include training in the theory and practice of second language acquisition; techniques for developing English language skills; methods for improving content area

instruction for language minority children; increasing parent involvement; the use of paraprofessionals in the classroom; dropout prevention; and the integration of multicultural materials in instructional programs. MRCs conduct local and regional workshops, participate in state, regional and federal training programs, and provide in-service and consultation support to individual schools and districts. The Office of Bilingual Education and Minority Languages Affairs can provide you with information on current programs.

Brown University, New England Multifunctional Resource Center, 345 Blackstone Blvd., Weld Building, Providence, RI 02906; (401) 274-9548. Serving: Maine, New Hampshire, Vermont, Massachusetts, Connecticut, and Rhode Island.

Hunter College and the Research Foundation of the City University of New York, 695 Park Ave., Box 367, New York, NY 10021; (212) 772-4764. Serving: New York.

COMSIS Corporation, 8737 Colesville Road, Suite 1100, Silver Spring, MD 20910; (301) 588-0800 or (800) 228-6723. Serving: Pennsylvania, Ohio, West Virginia, Virginia, Kentucky, New Jersey, Delaware, Maryland, and District of Columbia.

Florida Atlantic University College of Education, 500 N.W. 20th Street, Boca Raton, FL 33431; (407) 367-2301 or (800) 328-6721. Serving: Alabama, Florida, Georgia, Mississippi, North Carolina, South Carolina, and Tennessee.

InterAmerica Research Associates, Midwest Bilingual Education, MRC 2360 East Devon Ave., Suite 3011, Des Plaines, IL 60018; (708) 296-6070. Serving: Arkansas, Illinois, Indiana, Louisiana, and Missouri.

Upper Great Lakes MRC, Wisconsin Center for Education Research, University of Wisconsin, Madison, 1025 West Johnson St., Madison, WI 53706; (608) 263-4216. Serving: Iowa, Michigan, Minnesota, and Wisconsin.

Southwest Education Development Laboratory, 211 East 7th St., Austin, TX 78701; (512) 476-6861. Serving: Texas.

University of Oklahoma, Division of Continuing Education and Public Affairs, 555 Constitution Ave., Norman, OK 73037; (405) 325-1731 or (800) 523-7363. Serving: Oklahoma, Kansas, Nebraska, South Dakota, and North Dakota.

Interface Network, Inc., 4800 S.W. Griffith Drive, Suite 202, Beaverton, OR 97005; (503) 644-5741. Serving: Idaho, Oregon, Montana, Washington, and Wyoming.

Multifunctional Resource Center, Arizona State University, College of Education, Tempe, AZ 85287; (602) 965-5688. Serving: Arizona, New Mexico, Utah, Colorado, and Nevada.

San Diego State University Foundation, 6363 Alvarado Court, Suite 200, San Diego, CA 92120; (619) 594-5193. Serving: Southern California.

ARC Associates, Inc., 310 Eighth St., Suite 311, Oakland, CA 94607; (510) 834-9455. Serving: Northern California.

Metropolitan University, Apartado 21150, Rio Piedras, PR 00928; (809) 766-1717. Serving: Puerto Rico and Virgin Islands.

ARC Associates, Inc., 1314 South King St. Suite 1456, Honolulu, HI 96814; (808) 536-4494. Serving: Hawaii and America Samoa.

University of Guam, Project BEAM, College of Education, UOG Station, Mangilao, Guam 96913; (671) 734-4113. Serving: Guam, Wake Island, the Commonwealth of the Northern Marianas, the Republic of Palau, the Republic of the Marshall Islands, and the Federated States of Micronesia.

Interface Network, Inc., 4155 Tudor Centre Drive, Suite 103, Anchorage, AK 99501; (907) 563-7787. Serving: Alaska.

* Bilingual and Minority Languages Evaluation Assistance Centers

Office of Bilingual Education and Minority
Languages Affairs
330 C St., SW
Washington, DC 20202 (202) 205-5463

Be patient. If any phone number is incorrect, call (area code) 555-1212 and request the new listing.

School: Grades K-12

These evaluation assistance centers provide training and technical assistance, on request, to state and local education agencies serving limited English proficient students. The EAC-East and EAC-West present workshops and seminars at regional meetings, state education agency events, multi-local education agency conferences, and sponsored meetings under the office. In addition, they provide direct, on-site training and consultations to individual projects and respond to written and telephone requests for information and assistance.

Evaluation Assistance Centers - East:
1730 N. Lynn Street, Suite 401, Arlington, VA 22209; (703) 528-3588.

IDRA 5835 Callaghan Rd, Suite 350, San Antonio, TX 78228; (512) 684-8180.

Evaluation Assistance Centers - West:
121 Tijeras NE, Suite 2100, Albuquerque, NM 87102; (800) 247-4269.

Oakland Field Office, ARC Associates 310 Eighth Street, Suite 220, Oakland, CA 94607; (510) 834-9545.

* Bilingual Education Clearinghouse

National Clearinghouse for Bilingual Education (NCBE)
1118 22nd Street NW — (202) 467-0867
Washington, DC 20037 — (800) 321-6223

NCBE provides information to practitioners in the field on curriculum materials, program models, methodologies, and research findings on the education of limited English proficient (LEP) individuals. They also offer an electronic information system, free to users, where you may access a database of curriculum materials and literature related to the education of LEP persons. An electronic bulletin board is also available which contains news from federal, state, and local education agencies, conference announcements, and other current information. NCBE also develops and publishes three types of publications: a bimonthly newsletter, occasional papers, and program information guides. Their newsletter, *FORUM*, is available free of charge. Below is a sampling of other publications available through this organization:

Assessment and Placement of Language Minority Students: Procedures for Mainstreaming ($2.50)
Meeting the Needs of Gifted and Talented Minority Language Students: Issues and Practices ($2.50)
Using Computer Concepts as Problem Solving Tools in the Language Learning Classroom ($2.50)
Parent Involvement: A Resource for the Education of Limited English Students ($2.50)
Affective Considerations in Bilingual Education: Problems and Solutions ($4)
Program Development to Meet the Educational Needs of Limited English Proficient Students: A Bibliography of Capacity Building ($5)
Review of the State-of-the-Art of Educational Technologies Implemented in Programs Serving LEP Students ($10.50)
Application of Immersion Education in the United States ($2.25)

* Bill of Rights Information

Mini Page Books
PO Box 419150
Kansas City, MO 64141

Mini Page publishers have been producing reprints of the award winning series about the Constitution. In 1991, it also began publishing a series on the Bill of Rights. The Bill of Rights packet includes: a letter from former Chief Justice Warren E. Burger, the 12 issue Bill of Rights Series, and a 24 page guide to the Bill of Rights. The Bill of Rights Mini Page Packet is available for $8. The Mini Page Constitution Packet is available for $10.

* Books and Reading

Center for the Book
Library of Congress
Washington, DC 20540 — (202) 707-5221

A partnership between the federal government and private industry, the Center for the Book works closely with other organizations to explore important issues dealing with books and educational communities. The Center encourages reading and research about books and reading and serves as a catalyst by bringing together authors, publishers, librarians, booksellers, educators, scholars, and readers to discuss common concerns. In 1991 the Center promoted "The Year of the Lifetime Reader," while the 1992 theme was "Explore New Worlds - READ!" The 1993 theme will be "Books Change Lives." The Center also plans

to honor Thomas Jefferson for his dedication to education in the promotion of liberty. Four primary concerns are: television and the printed word, reading development, international role of the book, and publishing. The center is funded by tax-deductible contributions.

* Braille U.S. Constitution

National Braille Press, Inc.
88 St. Stephen St.
Boston, MA 02115

Individuals may request free copies of the U.S. Constitution in Braille at the above address.

* Captioned Movies and Videos for the Hearing Impaired

Modern Talking Pictures
500 Park St., North
St. Petersburg, FL 33709 — (813) 541-7571

This company's captioned film/video program provides a free loan service of educational and theatrical films and videos for various groups to assist deaf/hearing impaired persons in educational and recreational pursuits. Comprehensive, free catalogs list over 3,500 films and videocassettes. Language controlled open-captions (subtitles) appear on each film and video.

* Chapter 1 Education Grants

Office of Elementary and Secondary Education
U.S. Department of Education
Washington, DC 20022-6132 — (202) 401-1709

Chapter 1 provides financial assistance to local school districts to meet the special needs of educationally disadvantaged children who live in areas that have large concentrations of low-income families. Deprived children at the preschool, elementary, and secondary school level are eligible for assistance. In 1992-93 almost 6 million children will participate in the program. The estimated budget for the program is $6.7 billion.

* Children's Literature

Children's Literature Center
National Programs, Library of Congress
Washington, DC 20540 — (202) 707-5535

The Center prepares lists and scholarly bibliographies and provides other reference services for individuals who serve children, including scholars, writers, teachers, librarians, and illustrators. The center also has many publishers' catalogs that list titles to be published in the upcoming year, a wide range of periodicals about children's literature, and lists from rare and used book sellers. The Center can also provide you with reading lists for your children grouped by age and type of literature. *Books for Children*, a guide to reference sources for children's literature published annually for $1 per issue, is available from the Superintendent of Documents, Government Printing Office, Washington, DC 20402; (202) 783-3238.

* Christa McAuliffe Fellowship Program

Office of School Improvement Programs
Office of Elementary and Secondary Education
U.S. Department of Education
Washington, DC 20202 — (202) 401-1342

This program is designed to reward excellence in teaching by encouraging outstanding teachers to continue their education, to develop innovative programs, to consult with or assist local educational agencies, private schools or private school systems, and to engage in other educational activities. The Secretary of Education awards national fellowships to teachers who are citizens of the United States or permanent residents of the Commonwealth of Puerto Rico, Guam, the Virgin Islands, the Northern Marianas Islands, or Palau.

* Consumer Publications for Students and Teachers

Office of Information and Public Affairs
U.S. Consumer Product Safety Commission
Washington, DC 20207 — (800) 638-2772

The following consumer publications describe some of the common hazards associated with the use of consumer products and recommend ways to avoid these hazards. They come in the form of fact sheets (FS), brochures, and materials developed especially for use by classroom teachers. Some publications listed here can also be requested from the Commission's Regional Offices.

Be patient. If any phone number is incorrect, call (area code) 555-1212 and request the new listing.

Education

It's No Accident: A Guide for Teachers of Grades 3-6
Flammable Products: A Guide for Teachers of Secondary Grades
Flammable Products: A Guide for Teachers of Elementary Grades (Spanish)
Flammable Fabrics: Teacher's Guide (4T)
Flammable Fabrics: Student Readings (4-S)
Halloween Safety Teacher's Guide (9T)
Holiday Safety Teacher's Guide (7T)
Poison Prevention Teacher's Guide (6T)

* Curriculum and Student Standards

Consortium for Policy Research in Education
The Eagleton Institute of Politics Rutgers
The State University of New Jersey
90 Clifton Avenue
New Brunswick, NJ 08901 (908) 828-3872

Major research areas include curriculum and student standards, teacher policies, indicators and monitoring, new roles and responsibilities; and evolution of reform. Publications are available in the following areas: Curriculum and Standards, Educational Indicators, Evolution of the Reform Movement, New Roles and Responsibilities (for education), Teacher Policy. Also available from the Center are numerous publications on school finance.

* Counseling and Personnel Services Information

ERIC Clearinghouse on Counseling and Personnel Services
University of Michigan School of Education
Room 2108, 610 East University St.
Ann Arbor, MI 48109-1259 (313) 764-9492

Subject areas cover the preparation, practice, and supervision of counselors at all educational levels and in all settings; theoretical development of counseling and guidance; personnel procedures such as testing and interviewing and the analysis and distribution of the resulting information; group work and case work; nature of pupil, student, and adult characteristics; personnel workers and their relation to career planning, family consultations, and student orientation activities. The Center also publishes the quarterly newsletter *CAPS Capsule*. Also ask for the CAPS publication list. One of the most popular CAPS products is the *CounselorQuest*, a compilation of 165 ERIC digests designed to answer counselor's questions on a wide range of subjects. It is available for $19.95.

* Creative and Analytical Thinking Skills

Commissioner of Patents and Trademarks
Patent and Trademark Office
U.S. Department of Commerce
2121 Crystal Dr., Room 1101C
Arlington, VA 22202 (703) 305-8292

Project XL is a PTO outreach program designed to encourage the development of analytical and creative thinking and problem-solving skills among America's youth. The principal focus of this effort is on the promotion of educational programs that teach critical and creative thinking. They present national and regional conferences, and established an Education Roundtable, an open forum and nation discussion network. This office distributes an information guide called the *Inventive Thinking Project*, designed to channel students in grades K-12 into the inventive thinking process through the creation of their own unique inventions or innovations. They are also in the process of developing an educator's resource guide and a special curriculum. Contact this office for more information about Project XL and the assistance and products they have available.

* Current Education Information On-Line

OERI Electronic Bulletin Board
Office of Educational Research and Development
U.S. Department of Education (800) 424-1616
Washington, DC 20202 (202) 219-1513

This free service offers a means of obtaining current tables of education data, bulletins, and announcements of data tapes and reports. In operation 24 hours a day, this bulletin board can be accessed toll-free, using a modem and almost any type of microcomputer with communications software.

* Deaf Children's Education

Gallaudet University
800 Florida Avenue, NE
Washington, DC 20002

On agreement with the U.S. Department of Education, Gallaudet operates a model Secondary School for the Deaf for students from the District of Columbia, Maryland, Virginia, West Virginia, Pennsylvania, and Delaware. The University also operates the Kendall Elementary Demonstration School, which experiments in techniques and materials and disseminates information to educational facilities for deaf children. For more information, contact Gallaudet.

* Disabilities Information Clearinghouse

Clearinghouse on Disability Information Program
Information and Coordination Staff
U.S. Department of Education
Room 3132
Mary Switzer Building
Washington, DC 20202-2524 (202) 205-8241

The Clearinghouse responds to inquiries on a wide range of topics. Information is especially strong in the areas of Federal funding for programs serving individuals with disabilities, Federal legislation affecting the disability community, and Federal programs benefitting people with disabilities. Free publications from the Clearinghouse include the following:

OSERS News in Print - a newsletter focusing on OSERS programs and research.
A Summary of Existing Legislation Affecting Persons with Disabilities - a history of all relevant federal laws enacted through 1987. An update will be published in August 1992.

The Clearinghouse can also steer you to other publications on disabilities and federal programs. The following are some examples:

Adult Basic Education Programs for Disabled Adults.
Educating Students with Learning Problems: A Shared Responsibility.
Free Appropriate Public Education for Students with Handicaps: Requirements under Section 504 of the Rehabilitation Act of 1973.
EEO and Affirmative Action for Employment of Handicapped Persons by Federal Contractors.
Employers are Asking about Accommodating Workers with Disabilities. Identifies common barriers in the workplace and provides suggestions for accommodation.
Fact Sheet No. 7, Handicapped Assistance Loans. Explains the qualifications and conditions for loan approval to small business owners with physical handicaps.
Hiring the Mentally Restored Makes Dollars and Sense. Includes the following publications: Affirmative Action to Employ Mentally Restored People; Eight Questions Employers Ask about Hiring the Mentally Restored; and The Mentally Restored and Work: A Successful Partnership.
A Summary Guide to Social Security and Supplemental Income with Incentives for the Disabled and Blind. This booklet was designed to assist professionals who need to know the work incentive provisions for working with potential or actual SSI or SSDI beneficiaries.
Your Medicare Handbook: A Comprehensive Guide to Your Medicare Hospital and Medical Insurance Benefits.
Facts about Down Syndrome.
Caring about Kids: Helping the Hyperactive Child. Discusses the causes, diagnosis, and treatment of hyperactivity in children.
Periodontal Disease and Diabetes: A Guide for Patients.
Housing and Disabled People--Q and A's for the Disabled.
Statistics Related: SSA Research and Statistics Publications Catalog. Bibliography listing studies conducted or funded by the Social Security Administration. A number of the studies deal with disability related topics.

* Dropout Prevention Demonstrations

Office of School Improvement Programs
Office of Elementary and Secondary Education
U.S. Department of Education
Washington, DC 20202 (202) 401-0657

Under this program, discretionary grants are made to local educational agencies, educational partnerships, and community based organizations to demonstrate: effective programs to identify potential school dropouts; effective programs to encourage dropouts to return to school; effective programs to identify at risk students; and model systems of developing information about why children drop out of school. Approximately 80% of the funds are used under two priority areas: schoolwide restructuring and reform, and targeted programs for at-risk youth. The remaining 20% of the funds support field-initiated projects.

Be patient. If any phone number is incorrect, call (area code) 555-1212 and request the new listing.

School: Grades K-12

* Drug Prevention Videos

Office of Public Affairs
U.S. Department of Education
400 Maryland Ave., SW
Washington, DC 20202 (202) 401-1576

Eight productions, close-captioned for the hearing impaired, have been designed to inform students, attending kindergarten through 12th grade, about the dangers of drug use in an engaging and entertaining manner. Contact this office for further information on borrowing or purchasing these videos.

* Drug Free Schools and Communities Program

Drug Free Schools and Communities Staff
Office of Elementary and Secondary Education
U.S. Department of Education
Washington, DC 20202 (202) 401-1599

This program provides grant funds for several programs designed to promote drug free schools. State Formula Grants fund Governor's funds which go to local governments and non-profit groups drug prevention programs as well as funding teacher training in this area. The State Formula Grants also fund local and state agencies to operate drug education and rehabilitation activities in elementary and secondary schools. Several discretionary grants are also available for work at the local level. Contact the U.S. Department of Education for an application form for Grants, CFDA Number 84.184B.

* Early Start Program

Office of Migrant Education
Office of Elementary and Secondary Education
U.S. Department of Education
Washington, DC 20202 (202) 401-0740

This program is designed to provide assistance to States to establish and improve programs for meeting the special educational needs of children of migratory agricultural workers by integrating early childhood education and adult education into a unified program.

* Education Grant Programs Guide

1992 Guide to U.S. Department of Education Programs
Superintendent of Documents
U.S. Government Printing Office
Washington, DC 20402

Published annually, the *Guide* gives a brief description of the financial assistance programs available through the U.S. Department of Education. The cost of this publication is $3.50.

* Education Information and Assistance

Office of Public Affairs
U.S. Department of Education
400 Maryland Ave., SW
Washington, DC 20202 (202) 401-1576

If you need information about a particular educational issue, this is a useful starting place.

* Education Information Processing and Reference

ERIC Processing and Reference Facility
ORI, Inc. Information Systems
2440 Research Boulevard
Suite 550
Rockville, MD 20850-3238 (301) 590-1420

This centralized information processing unit serves all components that contribute to the ERIC system: Central ERIC, 16 clearinghouses, the ERIC Document Reproduction Service, Oryx Press (publisher of the *Current Index to Journals in Education),* and the Government Printing Office (publisher of *Resources in Education).* Their services include facility management and support; facility operations; reference and user services; and technical support for systems maintenance. From the ERIC database, this facility produces a variety of products and publications, including *Resources in Education* and its semi-annual indexes, ERIC Thesaurus and other system publications, and copies of the ERIC database tape that it provides to subscribers around the world.

* Education Publications

Superintendent of Documents
U.S. Government Printing Office
Washington, DC 20402-9371 (202) 783-3238

Becoming a Nation of Readers: Implications for Teachers. ($1.50 - S/N 065-000-00260-4).

Dealing with Dropouts: The Urban Superintendent's Call to Action. ($3.25 - S/N 065-000-00321-0).

Class Size and Public Policy: Politics and Panaceas ($2.75 S/N 065-000-00326-1). Describes the issues surrounding reduction in class size in the public schools.

Places Where Children Succeed: A Profile of Outstanding Public Elementary Schools. ($3.50, S/N 065-000-00323-6). Describes the national recognition program, the criteria, and processes that led to the selection of the schools and basic background information about the characteristics of the schools.

What Works: Research About Teaching and Learning, second edition ($3 - S/N 065-000-00304-0). Update of the original *What Works,* it contains 59 practical findings of ways to help educate children. A Spanish version is also available from ERIC in microfiche.

Alliance for Excellence: Librarians Respond to 'A Nation at Risk'. ($2.50, S/N 065-000-00207-8).

Assessment of Readiness for School: Implications for a Statistical Program, Report of a Planning Conference, 1/31/87. ($4.50, S/N 065-000-00316-3). Assesses readiness of students for kindergarten or the first grade.

Basic Educational Skills Project: Your Child and Language ($2.25 - S/N 017-092-00089-8). Describes how infants and young children learn to talk.

Your Child and Math ($3 - S/N 017-092-00081-2)

Your Child and Problem Solving ($2.25 - S/N 017-092-00085-5)

Beautiful Junk ($2.50 - S/N 017-092-0004-9). Consists of a list of 'found materials' or equipment and supplies which can be acquired at relatively low cost to supplement purchased program aids considered necessary for a preschool program.

Elementary School Aerospace Activities: A Resource for Teachers ($6.50, S/N 033-000-00693-4). Contains many suggestions for teaching children about space exploration which have been field tested in elementary schools.

Experiences in School Improvement: Story of 16 American Districts ($4.50, S/N 065-000-00343-1).

Good Secondary Schools: What Makes Them Tick? ($1, S/N 065-000-00273-6).

How to Help Your Child Achieve in School ($3.75, S/N 065-000-00176-4).

Living in Space: Books I and II ($4.75 each, S/Ns 033-000-01000-1 and 033-000-01001-0). Contains classroom and home activities designed to encourage student interest in space.

Safety in the Air: A Curriculum About Flight and Air Traffic Control Designed for Middle School Students ($3.50, S/N 050-007-00661-6).

Soozie and Katy: We're Teaming Up for Your Good Health: President's Drug Awareness Campaign ($1.25, S/N 027-004-00036-9). Study guide which promotes home and classroom discussions of medicine and use and misuse of drugs. Intended for very young children.

Watch Out, Storms Ahead! Owlie Skywarn's Weather Book ($1.50, S/N 003-017-00513-5). Prepared especially for elementary school children, this informational comic book tells what to do during hurricanes, tornados, flash floods, and lightning storms. Includes quizzes.

Directory of Academic Institutions and Organizations: Drug, Alcohol, and Employee Assistance Program Educational Resources (1988) ($4.50, S/N 017-024-01355-2).

Involvement in Learning: Realizing the Potential of American Higher Education ($4.50, S/N 065-000-00353-8).

Pocket Guide to Federal Help for Individuals With Disabilities ($1, S/N 065-000-00314-7).

Check This Out: Highlights of Model Library Programs ($2, S/N 065-000-00346).

Digest of Education Statistics, 1988 ($19, S/N 065-000-00351). Includes statistics on institutions, resources, faculty and students, outcomes, and public and private support.

* Education Savings Bonds

U.S. Savings Bonds Division
U.S. Department of the Treasury
1111 20th St., NW
Washington, DC 20226 (202) 377-7925

The new education savings bond program permits qualified taxpayers to exclude from their gross income all or a portion of the interest earned on eligible Series EE savings bonds issued after 1989. To qualify for this exclusion, tuition and other post-secondary educational expenses must be incurred by the taxpayer, the taxpayer's spouse, or the taxpayer's dependent at postsecondary educational

Education

institutions. These institutions are those that meet federal financial aid program standards. In addition, there are income limitations on participation in the program. Contact this office for more information on the program.

* Eisenhower Mathematics and Science Education

Improvement Program
U.S. Department of Education
555 New Jersey Ave, NW, Suite 522
Washington, DC 20208-5524 (202) 219-1496

The purpose of the Eisenhower program is to support innovative projects of national significance directed at improving the quality of teaching and instruction in mathematics and science in the schools and to increase the access of all students to that instruction. Programs focus on teacher training and curriculum change at the K-12 levels. Strong emphasis is placed on reaching students who have been relatively underrepresented in the past as well as those who are relatively more gifted and talented. At the elementary level, most projects incorporate an increased emphasis on practical hands on problem solving and higher order thinking skills. At the secondary level, a curriculum improvement project awarded to the National Science Teachers Association will have students study physics, chemistry, biology, and earth/space science every year for six years instead of the traditional year long segments in each area. The Office of Educational Research and Improvement can provide you with a booklet listing current projects under the Eisenhower program.

* Elementary and Early Childhood Education Information

ERIC Clearinghouse on Elementary and
Early Childhood Education
University of Illinois
805 West Pennsylvania Ave.
Urbana, IL 61801-4897 (217) 333-1386

Subject areas cover all aspects of the cognitive, emotional, social, and physical development and education of children from birth through early adolescence, excluding specific elementary school curriculum areas. Among the topics covered are prenatal and infant development and care; child care programs and community services for children at local, state, and federal levels; parent, child, and family relationships; home and school relationships; technology and children; preparation of early childhood teachers and caregivers; foster care and adoption; theoretical and philosophical issues related to children's development and education.

* Educators for Social Responsibility

475 Riverside Drive
Room 450
New York, NY 10115 (212) 870-3318

Educators for Social Responsibility (ESR) works to promote social responsibility and awareness through education in the hopes of developing people who can work effectively with others to help create a just, peaceful, ecologically sound world. Core components of the program include teacher training in conflict resolution and peer mediation of conflict. ESR also sponsors a Multicultural Education Project. Contact ESR for information on programs and for a list of the regional ESR chapters.

* Elementary Education

Center for the Learning and Teaching of
Elementary Subjects
Michigan State University
College of Education
East Lansing, MI 48824 (517) 353-6470

Major research areas include ideal curriculum, instruction, and assessment practices in elementary content areas; integrated studies of current practice; and improvement of existing practice.

* Environmental Education Materials

Public Information Center
Environmental Protection Agency (EPA)
401 M St., SW, PM-211 B
Washington DC 20460 (202) 260-2080

The EPA can provide you with a teacher package with materials for teachers of students in grades 1-12. In particular, *Environmental Education Materials For Teachers and Young People* is a free annotated list of educational materials on environmental issues. Entries include diverse materials ranging from workbooks

and lesson plans to newsletters, films, and computer software intended for young people. Educational materials available from sources other than EPA are listed alphabetically following the name of their sponsoring organization or group. A separate listing of selected EPA publications and other material available from EPA's Public Information Center is included in this pamphlet, as well as a short descriptive list of environmental education resource facilities. *Earth Notes* is an EPA publication aimed at grades 1-6 and contains information on Earth Day and trees. Also included in the package are posters you can put up in the classroom. Contact this office to order your free package.

* Evaluation, Standards, and Testing

Center for Research on Evaluation, Standards and Student Testing
CRESST
Regents of the University of California
Center for the Study of Evaluation
University of California at Los Angeles
10880 Wilshire Blvd. 7th Floor
Los Angeles, CA 90024-1522 (310) 206-1532

Major research areas include testing for the improvement of learning; systems for evaluating and improving educational quality; the impact of testing and evaluation on educational standards, policy, and practice; and school reform. CRESST publishes a quarterly newsletter, *CRESST Line* as well as a semi-annual research periodical entitled *Evaluation Comment*, which highlights a single theme in each issue.

* Follow Through Educational Program

Compensatory Education Programs
Office of Elementary and Secondary Education
U.S. Department of Education
Washington, DC 20202 (202) 401-1682

This program provides grants to local education agencies, private agencies and organizations for the purpose of developing and disseminating information and services to improve the school performance of children from low-income families in grades K-3. Research grants are also available to public and non-profit agencies, institutions, or organizations to conduct research directly related to the Follow Through Program.

* Foreign Languages Assistance Program

Office of School Improvement Programs
Office of Elementary and Secondary Education
U.S. Department of Education
Washington, DC 20202 (202) 401-1062

This program is designed to provide financial assistance to States for foreign language instruction at both the elementary and secondary education levels in Chinese, Japanese, Korean, Arabic, and Russian. These languages have been identified as important to the economic and security interests of the United States.

* Geography Education

American Geographical Society
156 Fifth Avenue
Room 600
New York, NY 10010 (212) 242-0214

The Society presents lectures, conferences and symposia, awards honors to scholars and explorers, conducts research on a wide range of geographical topics, and has amassed the largest geographical research library in the Western Hemisphere. It is also involved in improving geographical education, sponsors educational travel programs, and promotes better geographical education for grades K-12.

* Gifted and Talented National Clearinghouse

ERIC Clearinghouse on Handicapped and Gifted Children
Council for Exceptional Children
1920 Association Dr.
Reston, VA 22091-1589 (703) 620-3660

Subject areas include all aspects of the education and development of handicapped persons, including prevention of handicaps, identification and assessment of handicaps, and intervention and enrichment programs for the handicapped both in special settings and within the mainstream. All aspects of the education and development of gifted persons are also covered.

Be patient. If any phone number is incorrect, call (area code) 555-1212 and request the new listing.

School: Grades K-12

* Hawaiian Family Based Education Centers

Office of School Improvement Programs
Office of Elementary and Secondary Education
U.S. Department of Education
Washington, DC 20202 (202) 401-0657

This program is designed to develop and operate family based education centers throughout the Hawaiian Islands. These centers include parent, infant and preschool programs, as well as research, development and assessment of the activities.

* Head Start Development Program for Low-Income 3-5 Year Olds

Head Start Bureau
U.S. Department of Health and Human Services
P.O. Box 1182
Washington, DC 20013 (202) 205-8560

Project Head Start, a comprehensive child development program, was launched by the Federal Government in 1965 to help young children from low-income families get a better start in life. The education program is administered by the Administration for Children, Youth and Families. Grants are awarded by Health and Human Services Regional Offices to local public agencies and private non-profit organizations for the purpose of operating a Head Start program at the community level. There are special programs for Indian and migrant farmworker children. Head Start also publishes a pamphlet entitled *Easing the Transition from Preschool to Kindergarten*. Contact Head Start for more information about its programs.

* High School and Intercollegiate Debate Topics

Your Congressman's Office

A series of free reports are prepared by the Congressional Research Service of the Library of Congress that contain pertinent excerpts, bibliographic references, and other materials related to debate topics for that year. For high school debate teams, the topics are selected by the National University Extension Service Association, and for college, the topics are selected by the American Speech Association.

* High School Student Pages at U.S. Congress

Page Board
Room H-154, The Capitol
Washington, DC 20515 (202) 225-3505

Being a Page is an opportunity to live in the nation's capitol and see Congress at work. Pages are selected by Representatives and Senators whose seniority permits this privilege. Pages must be at least juniors in high school. They serve principally as messengers carrying documents, letters, and messages between the House and Senate, Members' offices, committees, and the Library of Congress. They also prepare the House and Senate Chambers for each day's business. Pages serve one or two terms of an academic year and also during the summer months. Their tenure depends on ability, conduct, academic performance, and their sponsor's term in office.

* High School Training

Veterans Assistance Office
U.S. Department of Veterans Affairs
810 Vermont Ave., NW
Washington, DC 20420 (202) 535-2044

A veteran may pursue high school training or training to pass the GED examination and may receive educational assistance allowance without a charge against basic entitlement. Additional secondary school training, such as refresher courses or deficiency courses, are permitted if needed to qualify for admission to an appropriate educational institution. Contact your VA regional office for more information.

* Homeless Children Education

Compensatory Education Programs
Office of Elementary and Secondary Education
U.S. Department of Education
Washington, DC 20202 (202) 401-1682

Through this program, grants for state activities are provided to State educational agencies to ensure that homeless children have access to free, appropriate public education.

* HOTS (High Order Thinking Skills)

University of Arizona
College of Education
Tucson, AZ 85721 (602) 621-1305

HOTS is a general thinking skills program designed primarily for Chapter 1 and mildly impaired Learning Disabled students in grades 4-7. The thinking skills are designed to enhance social interaction and basic skills. HOTS represents a new approach to compensatory education in that instead of reteaching the information the students did not previously learn, HOTS provides the types of thinking skills that students need to be able to learn the material the first time it is taught. Contact the University of Arizona for more information about the program.

* How Our Laws Are Made

Superintendent of Documents
Government Printing Office
Washington, DC 20402 (202) 275-3030

The booklet, *How Our Laws Are Made*, is prepared by the House of Representatives and provides a plain language explanation of how a legislative idea travels the complex passageways of the federal lawmaking process to become a statute. It is available for $2.50 from the Superintendent of Documents.

* Indian Education

Office of Indian Education
Bureau of Indian Affairs
U.S. Department of the Interior
18th and C Sts., NW
Washington, DC 20240 (202) 208-6123

The Office of Indian Education provides funding for both public and private Indian schools. Also sponsored are adult education classes and college scholarships. To receive information regarding Indian Education statistics and various programs sponsored by the Bureau of Indian Affairs, contact this office.

* International Youth Exchange

The Bureau of Educational and Cultural Affairs
Youth Exchange Programs Division
United States Information Agency (USIA)
301 Fourth St., SW, Room 357
Washington, DC 20547 (202) 619-6299

This office administers grants to non-profit organizations for international educational and cultural exchanges for youths 15 to 25 years of age. Organizations wishing to become sponsors, or individuals wishing to be put in contact with sponsoring organizations, can receive free information from this office. A list of prior fiscal year awards is also available. The Division also manages the Congress-Bundestag Youth Exchange Program which sends 400 American high school students to work in the German parliament and an equal number of Germans to work in the U.S. Congress. The Samantha Smith Memorial Exchange Program supports grants for exchanges with Eastern Europe and the former U.S.S.R. When contacting USIA, ask for the *Advisory List of International Educational Travel and Exchange Programs* which lists organizations that sponsor travel programs.

* Languages and Linguistics Education Information

ERIC Clearinghouse on Languages and Linguistics
Center for Applied Linguistics
1118 22nd St., NW
Washington, DC 20037-0037 (202) 429-9551

Subject areas cover languages and language sciences; theoretical and applied linguistics; all areas of foreign language, second language and linguistics pedagogy or methodology; psycholinguistics and the psychology of language learning; cultural and intercultural context of languages; application of linguistics in language teaching; bilingualism and bilingual education; sociolinguistics; study abroad and international exchanges; teacher training and qualifications specific to the teaching of a foreign language and second language; commonly and uncommonly taught languages, including English as a second language; and related curriculum developments and problems.

* Literature Education

Center for Learning and Teaching of Literature
State University of New York at Albany
School of Education

Education

1400 Washington Ave.
Albany, NY 12222 (518) 442-5026
Major research areas include current emphases in curriculum and instruction; teaching and learning processes; and assessment.

* Magnet Schools Assistance Program

Office of School Improvement Programs
Office of Elementary and Secondary Education
U.S. Department of Education
Washington, DC 20202 (202) 401-1358

This program is designed to provide grants to eligible local educational agencies to develop and operate magnet schools that are a part of an approved desegregation plan. The criteria used to define a magnet school in this program are the following: a distinctive school curriculum based on a special theme or method of instruction; a unique district role and purpose for voluntary desegregation; a voluntary choice of the school by student and parent; and open access to school enrollment beyond a regular attendance zone.

* Migrant Education Programs

Office of Migrant Education
Office of Elementary and Secondary Education
U.S. Department of Education
Washington, DC 20202 (202) 401-0740

This program is designed to provide financial assistance to State Educational Agencies to establish or improve programs designed to meet the special educational needs of children of migratory agricultural workers or fishers aged 3-21. The program includes a basic grant component, a record transfer system, and a coordination program for the state agencies.

* NASA Education Workshops for Elementary School Teachers (NEWEST)

Elementary and Secondary Programs Branch
Educational Affairs Division
Mail Code XEE
NASA Headquarters
Washington, DC 20546 (202) 358-1520

NEWEST is for elementary school teachers (grades 1-6) in all disciplines. Selected teachers are awarded a two-week, expense-paid workshop at a NASA field center, with each center hosting about 20 teachers. The workshops vary from center to center. Although all focus on current NASA programs, each center conducts activities unique to its work. During their stay, teachers meet with scientists, technicians, and educational specialists. Teachers are instructed how to apply their experiences to their elementary curriculum.

* NASA Minority Summer High School Apprentice Research Program (SHARP)

Elementary and Secondary Programs Branch
Educational Affairs Division
National Aeronautics and Space Administration
Mail Code XEE
Washington, DC 20546 (202) 358-1516

SHARP provides an opportunity for targeted underrepresented minority students in grades 10-12 who live within commuting distance of a participating NASA field center to take part in an eight-week, paid apprenticeship, where they work directly with NASA scientists or engineers. Interested students submit an application and references from a school administrator, teacher, or guidance counselor. Chosen students work with scientists or engineers whose work is related to his or her career aspirations, which may include computers, research, navigation, or guidance systems.

* National Center for Geographic Education

Indiana University of Pennsylvania
Geography Department
Leonard Hall, Room 16A
Indiana, PA 15705-1087 (412) 357-6290

The Council is overseeing the development of World Class Standards in geography. It encourages the training of teachers in geographic concepts, practices, and teaching methods and improves the teaching and learning of geography in schools as well as among adult groups outside schools. Publications include the *Journal of Geography*, the newsletter *Perspective*, and *Pathways in*

Geography, a series of publications for teachers, students, teacher trainers and curriculum planners.

* National Center for History in the Schools

University of California
Moore Hall 234
405 Hilgard Avenue
Los Angeles, CA 90024-1521 (310) 825-8388

This Center is leading a national effort to develop World Class Standards in American history and world history. It has also developed curricular units on subjects such as the ancient Near East, China under the Han dynasty, and America in colonial times. It is supported by the U.S. Department of Education and the National Endowment for the Arts.

* National Council for History Education

26915 Westwood Road
Suite B-2
Westlake, OH 44145-4656 (216) 835-1776

This is the successor organization to the Bradley Commission on History in Schools, which published *Building a History Curriculum: Guidelines for Teaching History in School*. It acts as a clearinghouse for information on history in education, provides a network for history educators as well as publishing a monthly newsletter for parents, educators, and policy makers.

* National Council for the Social Studies

3501 Newark Street, NW
Washington, DC 20016 (202) 966-7840

The Council promotes the teaching of social studies at all levels and provides information and resources to social studies teachers in all 50 states and more than 69 foreign countries.

* National Geographic Society Geography Education Program

17th and M Streets, NW
Washington, DC 20036 (202) 775-6701

The Society brings together academic geographers and K-12 teachers through a network of state geographic alliances based on university campuses across the country. Interested K-12 teachers may ask to be placed on the mailing list. All teachers on the mailing list will receive a packet of information during Geographic Awareness Week. It publishes the newsletter *Update*, which includes lesson plans. It also sponsors teacher workshops in Washington, DC, and in all states and territories.

* Native American Indians

Office of Public Affairs
Bureau of Indian Affairs (BIA)
U.S. Department of the Interior
18th and C Sts., NW
Washington, DC 20240 (202) 208-1711

The free booklet, *American Indians Today: Answers to Your Questions, 1988*, contains useful information on the Native American Indians and their relationship to the Bureau of Indian Affairs. Programs within the Bureau, including education, health services, and housing are briefly outlined and contain recent statistics. Many questions are answered within the booklet, including the rights of the Indians to own land and have their own governments. A map locates the Indian lands and communities, showing Federal and State Indian Reservations and other Indian groups. An excellent bibliography, prepared by the Smithsonian Institution, is included.

* Native American Indian Education Programs

Office of Indian Education Programs
Bureau of Indian Affairs
U.S. Department of the Interior
18th and C Sts., NW
Washington, DC 20240 (202) 208-1711

The Office of Indian Education Programs can provide you with information on efforts to improve Native American education. Part of this program has integrated Indian schools into the America 2000 education program. Numerous programs are also available for disadvantaged and handicapped Indian children.

Be patient. If any phone number is incorrect, call (area code) 555-1212 and request the new listing.

School: Grades K-12

Other BIA sponsored programs are the following: Solo Parent, for single parents to finish high school while living at school with their children; Close Up, for civic education; Junior Achievement, for applied economics; and Family and Child Education, a family literacy program for children 1-5 years old and their parents. The Bureau of Indian Affairs publishes an *Education Directory* which is an invaluable source for information on programs as well as for contacts in BIA.

* Natural History Museum Education Program

National Museum of Natural History
Office of Education
Room 212, Mail Stop 158
Washington, DC 20560 (202) 357-2747

The museum has an extensive educational school program with film and workshops available at your school or the museum, including museum lesson tours, the Discovery Room, the Naturalist Center, and instructional kits. A catalog of services can be sent to you. The Office also publishes a quarterly calendar of films and events at the Museum.

* Parent Pamphlets on Student Performance

Consumer Information Center
P.O. Box 100
Pueblo, Colorado 81002

AIDS and the Education of Our Children: A Guide for Parents and Teachers (Free; 507V).
Schools That Work: What Works in Educating Disadvantaged Children (Free, 509V).
Schools Without Drugs (Free;, 510V).
Help Your Child Become a Good Reader ($.50, 411V).
Help Your Child Do Better in School ($.50, 412V).
Help Your Child Improve in Test-Taking ($.50, 413V).
Help Your Child Learn to Write Well ($.50, 415V).

* Performing Arts Education

Kennedy Center for the Performing Arts
New Hampshire Avenue at Rock Creek Pkway
Washington, DC 20566 (202) 416-8800

The education department within the Kennedy Center is designed to transmit the vision of the Kennedy Center by fostering understanding of and participation in the performing arts through exemplary educational programs and performances.

* Physical/Recreational Education

ERIC Clearinghouse on Teacher Education
American Association of Colleges for Teacher
Education (AACTE)
One Dupont Circle, NW, Suite 610
Washington, DC 20036-2412 (202) 293-2450

This clearinghouse can provide you with information on all aspects of physical, health, and recreation education.

* Presidential Honor Students

White House Commission on Presidential Scholars
U.S. Department of Education
Room 2189
400 Maryland Ave., SW
Washington, DC 20202 (202) 401-0986

This annual program honors 141 students chosen among the nation's most outstanding graduating high school seniors. Those students who become Presidential Scholars are chosen on the basis of their accomplishments in many areas--academic and artistic success, demonstrated leadership, and involvement in school and community. Students may not apply individually to the program nor may their schools nominate them. The Scholars are given a medallion and are invited to Washington, DC where they are honored. There is no monetary award.

* President's Council on Physical Fitness

701 Pennsylvania Ave., NW, Suite 250
Washington, DC 20004 (202) 272-3432

The Council serves as a catalyst to promote, encourage, and motivate the development of physical fitness and sports programs for all Americans.

* Reading and Communication Skills Information

ERIC Clearinghouse on Reading and Communication Skills
Indiana University
Smith Research Center
2805 East 10th St., Suite 150
Bloomington, IN 47405-2373 (812) 335-5847

Subject areas include reading, English and communication skills (verbal and nonverbal) preschool through college; education research and development in reading, writing, speaking, and listening; identification, diagnosis, and remediation of reading problems; speech communication, mass communication, interpersonal and small group interaction, interpretation, rhetorical and communication theory, instructional development, speech sciences, and theater. Preparation of instructional staff and related personnel in these areas are also covered.

* Reading Is Fundamental

Reading Is Fundamental (RIF)
600 Maryland Ave., SW, Suite 500
Washington, DC 20024 (202) 287-3220

The RIF Guide to Encouraging Young Readers ($8.95). Hundreds of kid-tested activities designed to engage children from infancy to age 11 in the fun of reading; an annotated reading list of 200 children's books; resource listing of book clubs and magazines, parent's books and concerned organizations. RIF can also send you information on how to establish a RIF Center in your community or how to become a volunteer at a RIF center near you. Below is a list of publications that can be ordered from RIF.

Children's Bookshelf ($1). Annotated list of 106 books organized for four age ranges.
Reading is Fun! ($1). Tips for parents to prepare young children for reading.
Books to Grow On ($2). Magazine for parents including reading tips and games and puzzles for young readers.
Children Who Can Read, But Don't ($.50). How to help readers aged 9-12 discover the fun of reading.
Choosing Good Books for Children ($.50). Information and resources to help parents find appropriate books for children to age 12.
Encouraging Soon-to-Be Readers ($.50). How to excite preschoolers about books and help them to develop skills that lead to reading.
Magazines and Family Reading ($.50). Ways that magazines can get the whole family turning pages.
Reading Aloud to Your Children ($.50). The why's, when's, where's, what's and how's of reading aloud.
Reading: What's In It for Teenagers/Teenagers and Reading ($.50). Two brochures in one, perforated for parents to keep their half and give the other half to their teenager.
TV and Reading ($.50). Suggestions to help parents help their children achieve a healthy balance.
Upbeat and Offbeat Activities to Encourage Reading ($.50). Playful projects and activities to help preschoolers and beginning readers build skills.

* Reading Research Center

Center for the Study of Reading
University of Illinois
174 Children's Research Center
51 Gerty Drive Champaign, IL 61820 (217) 333-2552

Major research areas include acquisition of knowledge and skills, instruction in reading, text characteristics, and reading proficiency. The Center can send you a list of their technical reports and publications which are available for a fee. Publications from the Center include the following:

Beginning to Read: Thinking and Learning about Print - A Summary
Teaching Reading: Strategies from Successful Classrooms
Becoming a Nation of Readers: the Report of the Commission on Reading
A Guide to Selected Basal Reading Programs
10 Ways to Help Your Children Become Better Readers
Teachers and Independent Reading: Suggestions for the Classrooms

* Research on Teaching

Institute for Research on Teaching (IRT)
Michigan State University
252 Erickson Hall
College of Education
East Lansing, MI 48824-1034 (517) 353-0658

Be patient. If any phone number is incorrect, call (area code) 555-1212 and request the new listing.

Education

The Institute's goal is to study the whole teacher, i.e., teacher's role as related to society, the school district, and the students; the professional planning, thinking, and decision making involved in playing these roles; and the strategies for setting and reaching goals related to student needs. Current research at the IRT focuses on the relationship between teacher behavior and student achievement. IRT ongoing projects include the following: Elementary Subjects Center - focuses on effective elementary school teaching; Writing Strategies Instruction - teaches elementary school teachers how to teach effective writing skills; Science Achievement - this project is working to rewrite a commercial science textbook prototype unit; Responsive Reading Strategies - the focus here is on the relationship between responsive elaboration and student achievement; Reciprocal Teaching; Dilemma Management in Mathematics Teaching; and more. The IRT also publishes a newsletter entitled *Communications Quarterly*. A publications list and catalog are also available.

* Rural Education and Small Schools Clearinghouse

ERIC Clearinghouse on Rural Education and Small Schools
Appalachia Educational Laboratory, Inc.
1031 Quarrier St.
P.O. Box 1348
Charleston, WV 25325-1348 (304) 347-0400

Subject areas cover economic, cultural, social, or other factors related to education programs and practices for rural residents; American Indians/Alaska Natives, Mexican Americans, and migrants; education practices and programs in all small schools; and outdoor education. This includes programs, practices, and materials that provide learning experiences designed to meet the special needs of rural populations and schools where conditions of smallness are a factor.

* School Administrators and Management Clearinghouse

ERIC Clearinghouse on Educational Management
University of Oregon
1787 Agate St.
Eugene, OR 97403-5207 (503) 686-5043

Subject areas include all aspects of the administration, leadership, finance, governance, and structure of public and private education organizations at the elementary, middle, and secondary levels, including facility planning, design, construction, equipment and furnishing, and maintenance; and pre-service and in-service preparation of administrators. Topics covered include the social, technological, political, and legal contexts of education organizations, and of State and Federal programs and policies, and traditional and alternative schools.

* School Discipline, Phonics and Other Publications

U.S. Department of Education
Office of Educational Research and Improvement
555 New Jersey Ave., NW
Washington, DC 20208-5641 (800) 424-1616

Elementary School Recognition Program (brochure) (PIP 88-821): Describes the program, requirements, characteristics of successful schools, and information on how to apply.
Improving School Discipline (IS 88-161).
Students at Risk (IS 89-540).
Ten Steps to a Successful Magnet Program (OR 88-510).
Ten Ways to Help Your Children Become Better Readers.
What We Know About Phonics (IS 88-163).
Employment Outcomes of Recent Master's and Bachelor's Degree Recipients (CS 88-251).
Students Report Job Success More Important Than Making Money (CS 88-436).
Check This Out Fact Sheet: Literacy for Every Adult Project (LP 89-732).
Check This Out Fact Sheet: Read-Aloud Programs for the Elderly (LP 89-731).
Helping Your Child Use the Library (LP 89-712).
Approaches to Drug and Alcohol Abuse (PIP 89-857).
Drug Prevention Curricula: A Guide to Selection and Implementation (PIP 88-835).
Five Tips to Improving Teaching (IS 87-127).
The Impact on Children's Education: TV's Influence on Cognitive Development (OR 88-507).
School Climate and Reading Performance (CS 88-605).
Education Statistics - 1988 Pocket Digest (OERI # 88611, Series: PD-88). Selected key statistics from the Digest of Education.
Pocket Projections, 1977-78 to 1997-98. (OERI No. 88612, Series: PP-88). Pocket-sized pamphlet of projections of key elementary/secondary and higher education statistics.
American Education at a Glance (OERI No. 89618, Series: NA). A variety of charts and tables providing an overview of American education.

Young Adult Literacy and Schooling (OERI No. 88604).
Teacher Incentive Programs in Public Schools (OERI No. 89063, Series: PUP-85).

* Secondary Schools

Center on Organization and Restructuring of Schools
University of Wisconsin - Madison
1025 West Johnson St.
Madison, WI 53706 (608) 263-7575

Major research areas include a clearinghouse on academic achievement; non-instructional influences on adolescent engagement and achievement; the stratification of learning opportunities in middle and high schools; higher-order thinking in the high school curriculum; programs and policies to serve at risk students; and alternative structures and the quality of teacher worklife. The Center also publishes a quarterly newsletter entitled *Issues*, and also publishes occasional issues-oriented *Briefs*. A publications list is also available.

* Secondary School Teaching

Center for Research on the Context of Secondary School Teaching
Stanford University - School of Education
CERAS Building
Stanford, CA 94305 (415) 723-4972

Major research areas include conceptualization and development; the relationship of context to school workplace conditions, teaching and student outcomes; state reform and teacher contexts; inner city, high poverty schools; and alternative schools. While current projects are scheduled to end in late 1992, the Center has applied for a National Science Foundation Grant to continue research with specific application to math and science.

* Social Organization of Schools

Center for Social Organization of Schools
Johns Hopkins University
3505 North Charles St.
Baltimore, MD 21218-2498 (410) 516-0370

The purpose of the Center is to study how changes in the social organization of schools can make them more effective for all students in promoting academic achievement, development of potential, and later-life career success. A publications list is also available.

* Social Studies and Curriculum Kits

Sir S Documents
Education Branch
National Archives and Records Administration
8th St. and Pennsylvania Ave., NW, Room 505
Washington, DC 20408 (202) 724-0454

A catalog is available which contains supplemental teaching units with primary sources from the National Archives. Each unit is a package of materials that serves as a complete classroom set. A unit contains about 50 reproductions of documents, with some also including cassette tapes. The materials deal with certain key issues of the period, with governmental and political responses to these issues, and with public attitudes. Each unit includes a detailed teachers' guide containing developmental exercises to help students examine the documents. Each unit costs $40. The following 12 units are currently available.

The Constitution - Evolution of a Government.
The Bill of Rights - Evolution of Personal Liberties.
The United States Expands West, 1785-1842.
Westward Expansion, 1842-1912.
The Civil War - Soldiers and Civilians.
The Progressive Years, 1898-1917.
World War I - The Home Front.
The 1920s.
The Great Depression and the New Deal.
World War II - The Home Front.
The Truman Years, 1945-1953.
Peace and Prosperity, 1953-1961.
For ordering information you can also contact SIRS at (800) 374-SIRS.

* Social Studies/Social Science Education Information

ERIC Clearinghouse on Social Studies/Social Science Education
Social Studies Development Center
Indiana University

School: Grades K-12

Smith Research Center
2805 East Tenth St., Suite 120
Bloomington, IN 47405-2373 (812) 335-3838

Subject areas include all levels of social science education (history, geography, anthropology, economics, sociology, social psychology, and political science); applications of theory and research to social science education; values education; contribution of social science disciplines; comparative education (K-12); social studies content and curriculum materials on such subjects as law-related education, bias and discrimination, and aging. Subjects also include the humanities (music and art).

* Social Studies Teachers Workshops

Education Branch
National Archives and Records Administration
8th St. and Pennsylvania Ave., NW, Room 505
Washington, DC 20408 (202) 724-0454

This workshop, sponsored each summer, provides a varied program of lectures, demonstrations analysis of documents, independent research, and group work that introduces teachers to the holdings and organization of the National Archives. Participants learn how to use Archives materials to develop teaching units. The cost of the program for 1993 will be $100.

* Students with Handicaps National Clearinghouse

ERIC Clearinghouse on Handicapped and Gifted Children
Council for Exceptional Children
1920 Association Dr.
Reston, VA 22091-1589 (703) 620-3660

Subject areas include all aspects of the education and development of handicapped persons, including prevention of handicaps, identification and assessment of handicaps, and intervention and enrichment programs for the handicapped both in special settings and within the mainstream. All aspects of the education and development of gifted persons are also covered.

* Teacher Education Clearinghouse

ERIC Clearinghouse on Teacher Education
American Association of Colleges for Teacher
Education (AACTE)
One Dupont Circle, NW, Suite 610
Washington, DC 20036-2412 (202) 293-2450

Subject areas cover school personnel at all levels; teacher selection and training; pre-service and in-service preparation and retirement; the theory, philosophy, and practice of teaching; and curricula and general education not specifically covered by other clearinghouses. Also included are all aspects of physical education, health, dance, and recreation education.

* Teacher Education Research

National Center for Research on Teacher Learning
College of Education
Michigan State University
Erickson Hall
East Lansing, MI 48824-1034 (517) 355-9302

This Center focuses on the area of teacher learning. Currently, the Center is working on three projects that encompass 11 individual studies. Project A looks at the beliefs teachers acquire about teaching before they enter the profession. Project B is split into two studies. The first of these examines the subject matter teachers learn in college to gain insight into the substantive knowledge base of teachers. The second looks at programs designed to prepare teachers for work in multicultural learning environments. Project C, an amalgam of 8 studies, focuses on how teachers weave different kinds of knowledge together. The Center also puts out a publications list and publishes a quarterly magazine entitled *Colloquy*, which examines issues relevant to teaching different subjects.

* Teacher of the Arts Summer Fellowships

Council for Basic Education
725 15th Street, NW
Washington, DC 20005 (202) 347-4171

Fellowships under this program are awarded for four to eight weeks of independent study. Eligible teachers must be currently working with K-12 students. Teacher-Fellows use personally developed plans for serious independent study of the arts or related issues. Approximately 20 awards will be granted in 1992. Call for more information.

* Teaching Materials on the Constitution

Center for Research and Development
in Law-Related Education (CRADLE)
Wake Forest University School of Law
P.O. Box 7206, Reynolds Station (800) 437-1057
Winston-Salem, NC 27109 (919) 759-5435

The Commission on the Bicentennial of the U.S. Constitution, in conjunction with Wake Forest University, makes available a national repository of teaching materials about the Constitution. Primarily on the Law and the Constitution, the resources are written for use by teachers from pre-kindergarten through 12th grades. Lessons are also available on disk and can be downloaded from the electronic bulletin board network. Teachers can submit lessons to be included on the network. Pocket Constitutions are also available. Write for a free catalog.

* Teacher's Guide to Selective Service Registration

Public Affairs
Selective Service System
1023 31st St., NW
Washington, DC 20435 (202) 724-0790

A Teacher's Guide to Selective Service Registration is designed to assist teachers in their preparation of lessons covering the Selective Service System and describes the purpose, history, organization, and function of the System. With a summary of important teaching points, and questions and answers at the end of each chapter, this guide assists teachers in teaching their students about the Selective Service System. Also available is a fact pack that contains information on state laws relating to registration, student loans and registration, and job training benefits and registration. For additional information, contact this office.

* Testing Educational Achievement

National Assessment of Educational Progress
Educational Testing Service
P.O. Box 2923
Princeton, NJ 08541 (800) 223-0267

NAEP surveys the educational achievement of 9-year-olds, 13-year-olds, 17-year-olds, and at grades 4, 8, and 12, and periodically, young adults. The surveys are conducted in such areas as art, career and occupational development, citizenship, literature, mathematics, music, reading, science, social studies, and writing. Different learning areas are assessed every two years, and all areas are periodically reassessed to measure changes in educational achievement. A publications brochure is available through this office, and surveys may be purchased. Below is a sampling of other publications available through NAEP:

Reading Objectives: 1986 and 1988 ($5)
Writing Objectives: 1988 ($5)
Literature and U.S. History: The Instructional Experience and Factual Knowledge of High School Juniors ($8.50)
Who Reads Best? Factors Relating to Reading Achievements: Grades 3, 7 and 11. ($11)
Computer Competence: The First National Assessment ($12.50)
The Mathematics Report: Are We Measuring Up? (12.50)
The Science Report Card: Elements of Risk and Recovery ($14)
An Executive Summary to the Math Report Card (Free)
Science Learning Matters: An Interpretive Overview to the Science Report Card (Free)

* Tests, Measurement, and Evaluation Clearinghouse

ERIC Clearinghouse on Tests, Measurement, and Evaluation
American Institutes for Research
Washington Research Center
3333 K St., NW
Washington, DC 20007-3893 (202) 342-5060

Subject areas include the assessment and evaluation of education projects or programs; tests and other measurement devices; methodology of measurement and evaluation; research design and methodology; human development; and learning theory in general.

* Urban Community Enrichment Program (UCEP)

Elementary and Secondary Programs Branch
Educational Affairs Division
Mail Code XEE
NASA Headquarters
Washington, DC 20546 (202) 453-8386

Be patient. If any phone number is incorrect, call (area code) 555-1212 and request the new listing.

Education

UCEP is specifically targeted toward middle-school students in urban areas with high percentages of minorities. NASA specialists will meet with school representatives to formulate a custom-tailored program to fit the school's needs. Typically a program begins with teacher orientation workshops followed by assemblies, a series of student workshops, and classroom visits. In the classroom, NASA specialists work with students on various hands-on activities, such as building rockets or airplanes or learning about how information is transmitted from space back to Earth.

* Urban Education Clearinghouse

ERIC Clearinghouse on Urban Education
Teachers College
Columbia University Institute for Urban
and Minority Education
Main Hall, Room 303, Box 40
525 West 120th St.
New York, NY 10027-9998 (212) 678-3433

Subject areas include programs and practices in schools in urban areas and the education of racial/ethnic minority children and youth in various settings--local, national, and international; the theory and practice of education equity; urban and minority experiences; and urban and minority social institutions and services.

* Women's Educational Equity Program

Office of School Improvement Programs
Office of Elementary and Secondary Education

U.S. Department of Education
Washington, DC 20202 (202) 401-0355

This program is designed to provide educational equity for women who suffer discrimination based on sex and/or race, age, ethnic origin, or disability. Grant programs provide financial assistance to public agencies, private non-profit organizations and institutions and individuals for the development of educational materials and model programs that promote equity for women and girls.

* Writing Skills: Students and Instructors

Center for the Study of Writing and Literacy
School of Education
University of California at Berkeley
5531 Tolman Hall
Berkeley, CA 94720 (510) 643-7022

From 1990 to 1995 the Center is sponsoring twelve research projects. Through these projects it is seeking to understand more explicitly the diverse resources students have, how students from a variety of backgrounds acquire writing and literacy skills; the types of instructional practices that address the diverse needs of students, and ways in which schools and the teaching profession can be structured to support and sustain responsive approaches to education. In conjunction with the National Writing Project, the Center also publishes *The Quarterly*, a journal on the teaching and learning of writing. The Center also offers seminars and collaborates with researchers and research centers throughout the nation. A publications list is available upon request.

Be patient. If any phone number is incorrect, call (area code) 555-1212 and request the new listing.

College and Continuing Education

* Adult and Vocational Curriculum National Network

National Network for Curriculum Coordination
in Vocational and Technical Education
Office of Vocational and Adult Education

The six coordination centers provide leadership in curriculum coordination activities and offer a variety of curriculum-related activities, which include collecting and distributing curriculum information and products and assisting individuals, schools, and groups in addressing and resolving problems.

Western Curriculum Coordination Center, College of Education, University of Hawaii, 1776 University Ave., Wist. 216, Honolulu, HI 96822; (808) 948-7834. Serving: American Samoa, Arizona, California, Guam, Hawaii, Nevada, and Trust Territory Government of Northern Marianas.

East Central Curriculum Coordination Center, Sangamon State University, F-2, Springfield, IL 62708; (217) 786-6375. Serving: Delaware, District of Columbia, Indiana, Illinois, Maryland, Michigan, Minnesota, Ohio, Pennsylvania, Virginia, West Virginia, and Wisconsin.

Southeast Curriculum Coordination Center, Mississippi State University, Research and Curriculum Unit, P.O. Drawer DX, Mississippi State, MS 39762; (601) 325-2510. Serving: Alabama, Florida, Georgia, Kentucky, Mississippi, North Carolina, South Carolina, and Tennessee.

Northeast Curriculum Coordination Center, New Jersey Vocational Education Resource Center, Rutgers University, Crest Way, Aberdeen, NJ 07747; (201) 290-1900. Serving: Connecticut, Maine, Massachusetts, New Hampshire, New Jersey, New York, Puerto Rico, Rhode Island, Vermont, and Virgin Islands.

Mideast Curriculum Coordination Center, State Department of Vocational and Technical Education, 1500 West Seventh Ave., Stillwater, OK 74074-4364; (405) 377-2000, Ext. 252. Serving: Arkansas, Iowa, Kansas, Louisiana, Missouri, Nebraska, New Mexico, Oklahoma, and Texas.

Northwestern Curriculum Coordination Center, St. Martin's College Old Main, Room 478, Lacey, WA 98503; (206) 438-4456. Serving: Alaska, Colorado, Idaho, Montana, North Dakota, Oregon, South Dakota, Utah, Washington, and Wyoming.

* Adult Continuing Education Clearinghouse

ERIC Clearinghouse on Adult, Career and
Vocational Education
Ohio State University Center on Education and
Training for Employment
1900 Kenny Rd. (800) 848-4815
Columbus, OH 43210-1090 (614) 292-4353

Subject areas cover all levels of adult and continuing education from basic literacy training through professional skill upgrading; vocational and technical education covering all service areas for secondary, postsecondary, and adult education populations; and career education and career development programs for all ages and populations in educational, institutional, business, and industrial settings. The Clearinghouse also now has subprofessional fields in industrial arts, corrections education, entrepreneurship, and adult retraining.

* Adult Educators

Clearinghouse on Adult Education
U.S. Department of Education
Office of Vocational and Adult Education
330 C St., SW
Washington, DC 20202 (202) 205-9872

This clearinghouse links the adult education community with existing resources in adult education. The Bibliography of Resource Materials provides a complete list of materials available from the clearinghouse. Examples include a directory of adult education-related programs, fact sheets on such topics as literacy and disabled adults, and materials concerning English as a second language.

* American and Foreign Teachers Exchange Program

Office of Academic Programs
United States Information Agency
301 Fourth St., SW, Room 353
Washington, DC 20547 (202) 619-4360

The Advising, Teaching, and Specialized Programs Division serves overseas education advising centers, foreign exchange students in the U.S., and administers the International Student Exchange Program for one-to-one exchange of university students. Its Teacher Exchange Branch arranges one and two way exchanges of U.S. and foreign teachers, and summer seminars for U.S. teachers to study abroad. Free brochures and applications are available.

* American Educators Teaching Abroad

Superintendent of Documents
Government Printing Office
Washington, DC 20402 (202) 783-3238

The United States Information Agency (USIA) publishes many teaching materials, including books, maps, complete teaching modules, and 14 magazines in 20 languages. By law most USIA publications may be distributed only in foreign countries. However, by congressional action, two magazines are available in the United States. *English Teaching Forum*, a quarterly for English teachers worldwide, is published by USIA's English Language Programs Division. This magazine is available through the GPO.

* Black Universities and Agricultural Sciences

Special Advisor to the Deputy Secretary
Agricultural Stabilization and Conservation Service
P.O. Box 2415
Washington, DC 20013 (202) 720-4797

The USDA has a unique relationship with 17 historically black universities that began in 1890 when these schools were designated by Congress as Land-Grant Institutions. In 1988 a symposium was sponsored by USDA at one of these institutions to re-examine the partnership between USDA and the universities. Work is underway on a number of recommendations that came from this conference:

- Programs of financial assistance are being developed to help minorities through college.
- Liaison officers are working at each school to recruit students into the agricultural sciences and from there into careers at USDA.
- A marketing program is being developed for careers in agriculture and home economics and for educational opportunities at the 1990s.
- A K-12 career awareness initiative program is underway in food and agricultural sciences.
- More than 400 summer jobs were created around the country in the agricultural sciences for students.
- Partnerships are being developed between predominantly white land-grant institutions and the historically black schools.
- A program is being developed to work with the agricultural high schools in areas of higher education and career development.

* Career Education

ERIC Clearinghouse on Adult, Career and
Vocational Education
Ohio State University Center on Education and
Training for Employment
1900 Kenny Rd. (800) 848-4815
Columbus, OH 43210-1090 (614) 292-4353

Subject areas cover all levels of adult and continuing education from basic literacy training through professional skill upgrading; vocational and technical education covering all service areas for secondary, postsecondary, and adult education populations; and career education and career development programs for all ages and populations in educational, institutional, business, and industrial settings.

Be patient. If any phone number is incorrect, call (area code) 555-1212 and request the new listing.

Education

* College Environmental Curricula Grants

Office of Environmental Education
Environmental Protection Agency
401 M St., SW, Room A107
Washington DC 20460 (202) 260-4958

The Office of Environmental Education awards money to colleges to support the development of environment-related curriculum, allowing these colleges to then train State employees. The office also awards fellowships to State employees to continue their education concerning the environment. The fellowship applications are given out through the individual States. Other grants are awarded for a variety of environmentally related projects. These grants are coordinated by the EPA's regional offices. Contact this office for more information.

* College Courses

Information Office
U.S. Department of Agriculture Graduate School
Capital Gallery Building
600 Maryland Ave. S.W., Room 129
Washington, DC 20024 (202) 720-4419

The USDA Graduate School, which is open to the public, offers college courses on nonagricultural subjects at reasonable prices. Although the school does not grant degrees, college credits are awarded and can be transferred to other universities. Some lectures are available on film, videotape, and in manuscript form.

* College Library Technology Grants

Library Development Staff
Library Programs/OERI
U.S. Department of Education
555 New Jersey Ave., NW, Room 404
Washington, DC 20208-5571 (202) 219-1315

The purpose of these grants is to encourage resource-sharing projects among the libraries of institutions of higher education through the use of technology and networking; to improve resource sharing services provided with public and private non-profit organizations, and to conduct innovative research and demonstration projects which meet special needs in utilizing technology to enhance library services. The Department of Education can send you an application form and a list of past awardees.

* Congress-Bundestag Exchange Program

CDS International Inc.
330 Seventh Ave.
New York, NY 10001 (212) 760-1400

Through this program, Americans between the ages of 18 and 24 have the opportunity to live and work in Germany. The program lasts for one year and successful applicants will spend their year learning German, further developing skills at a German technical school or University, and working in an internship with a German company. Contact the program for more information and an application.

* Cooperative Education Program (CEP)

Personnel Policy and Work Force
Effectiveness Division
Mail Code NPM
NASA Headquarters
Washington, DC 20546 (202) 453-2603

CEP gives high school, college, and graduate students an opportunity to work at a NASA field center while completing their education. Participating students usually alternate working one semester with studying one semester. In addition to job experience, the program also serves as a recruitment tool. Interested students must be attending school, be enrolled in their school's co-op program, maintain at least a 2.0 overall grade point average, and be recommended by the school. Each NASA field center negotiates its own cooperative agreements with school in its geographic area, and it is usually the responsibility of a school to initiate the venture.

* Cultural and Educational International Exchange

Office of Public Liaison
United States Information Agency (USIA)
301 Fourth St., SW, Room 602
Washington, DC 20547 (202) 619-4355

The USIA can provide you with information on public and private organizations which sponsor international exchange activities. The book *Fulbright Grants and Other Grants for Graduate Study Abroad* contains a lot of valuable information both on the Fulbright program and on other organizations sponsoring exchanges.

* Exchange Programs with Eastern Europe

Office of Academic Programs
United States Information Agency (USIA)
301 4th Street, SW
Washington, DC 20547 (202) 619-6137

The Office of Academic Programs can provide you with information on several new programs to exchange scholars with and accept students from Eastern Europe and the former Soviet Union. Notable programs include the Benjamin Franklin Fellowship, the Samantha Smith Program, the Alexander Hamilton Program for business students, and the John Marshall program for students in law and political science. Contact USIA for the list of programs.

* Fellowships: Latin America

Inter-American Fellowship Programs
901 N. Jewett Street, 10th Fl.
Arlington, VA 22203 (703) 841-3800

This grant program stresses practical solutions to obstacles in grassroots development by fostering increased attention within the academic community on micro-level development in Latin America and the Caribbean. Part of the fellowships go to scholars and professionals from research and development institutions in Latin America and the Caribbean whose work would benefit from graduate-level study at U.S. universities, while other fellowships go to doctoral candidates and master's-level students enrolled in U.S. universities to conduct field research in Latin America or the Caribbean.

* Foreign Exchange Students and Agriculture

Office of International Cooperation,
International Training Division
U.S. Department of Agriculture
South Building, Room 3121
Washington, DC 20250-4300 (202) 690-2796

Students from developing countries can obtain assistance in identifying where to train in agriculture in the U.S. and in other countries.

* Foreign Language Materials Acquisition

Library Development Staff
Library Programs/OERI
U.S. Department of Education
555 New Jersey Ave., NW, Room 404
Washington, DC 20208-5571 (202) 219-1315

The Department of Education has grants available for state and local libraries for the acquisition of foreign language materials such as books, periodicals, newspapers, microforms, and various audio-visual materials. Contact the Library Development Staff for details.

* Foreign Language Training

Defense Language Institute
Foreign Language Center
Non-Resident Division
Presidio of Monterey, CA 93944 (408) 647-5000

The Defense Language Institute is one of the world's largest language training centers. The holdings of its library--over 100,000 books in 50 languages--are available through a national inter-library loan program. The non-resident division offers foreign language courses for sale. A catalog of the languages available may be obtained for $5.25. Write or call for brochures on the Institute and information regarding inter-library loans.

* Foreign Student Support Services

Advising, Teaching, and Specialized Programs Division
Office of Academic Programs
Bureau of Educational and Cultural Affairs
United States Information Agency (USIA)
301 Fourth St., SW, Room 349
Washington, DC 20547 (202) 619-5434

Be patient. If any phone number is incorrect, call (area code) 555-1212 and request the new listing.

College and Continuing Education

USIA develops a variety of programs to aid foreign students in the United States. Free information is available.

* Foreign Training for Veterans, Inservice Students and Eligible Dependents

Veterans Assistance Office
U.S. Department of Veterans Affairs
810 Vermont Ave., NW
Washington, DC 20420 (202) 535-2044

The pamphlet, *Foreign Training for Veterans, Inservice Students and Eligible Dependents*, provides general information about the approval of courses at foreign schools. It also provides specific information for veterans, inservice students and dependents planning to pursue training at a foreign school. This pamphlet lists those foreign schools which offer at least one course approved for training. Note, however, that not all the courses at a listed school are necessarily approved for training. Please read the pamphlet carefully. It is available from your regional VA office.

* Fulbright Foreign Studies Scholarships

Office of Academic Programs
The Bureau of Educational and Cultural Affairs
United States Information Agency (USIA)
301 Fourth St., SW, Room 234
Washington, DC 20547 (202) 619-7360

This office develops and runs all academic programs of USIA, including the best-known educational exchange, the Fulbright Scholarship program. About 5,000 Fulbright grants are awarded each year to American students, teachers, and scholars to work abroad and to foreign citizens to teach, study, and conduct research in the U.S. The book *Fullbright Scholar Program: Grants for Faculty and Professionals* contains information on the application process for grants, the fields of study necessary, and a directory of country programs/requirements. In addition to the Fulbright program, the Academic Exchange Programs Division of this office administers grants to private agencies conducting complementary programs to the Fulbright academic exchanges, and has responsibilities for foreign research centers, Fulbright commissions, and seminars for foreign Fulbright students. Contact this office for more information and application forms for the Fulbright program.

* Health Care Training Programs

Academic Affairs
Veterans Health Services and Research Administration
U.S. Department of Veterans Affairs (DVA)
810 Vermont Ave., NW, Room 876
Washington, DC 20420 (202) 535-5094

The DVA has over 2,000 training relationships between VA health care facilities and schools of medicines, dentistry, nursing, pharmacy, social work, and other allied health professions and occupations at the graduate and undergraduate levels. For more information, contact the office above.

* Health Professional Scholarship Program

Associated Health Professions
Education Programs Services
Veterans Health Services and Research Administration
U.S. Department of Veterans Affairs
810 Vermont Ave., NW, Room 878
Washington, DC 20420 (202) 535-3588

The VA Health Professional Scholarship Program assists in the recruitment of health professionals in the VA health care system. In return for scholarship support while in college, participants agree to serve a minimum of one year in VA medical centers in the discipline for which degree was awarded. For more information, contact the office above. Ask in particular about the Scholarship Awards and the Reserve Member Stipend Awards.

* Higher Education Clearinghouse

ERIC Clearinghouse on Higher Education
George Washington University
One Dupont Circle
Washington, DC 20036-1183 (202) 296-2597

Subject areas cover education beyond the secondary level that leads to a four-year, masters, doctoral, or professional degree and includes courses and programs designed to enhance or update skills obtained in these degree programs. Also included are student programs, conditions, and problems at colleges and universities. Other areas include academic advising, university and college faculty; graduate and professional education; professional continuing education; governance and management of higher education institutions; legal issues and legislation; financing; planning and evaluation; facilities--their structural design, management implications, curriculum and instructional problems, programs, and development; and business or industry education programs leading to a degree.

* Higher Education Partnerships

Higher Education Programs
Room 350 A, Administration Building
U.S. Department of Agriculture
Washington, DC 20250 (202) 720-7854

In order to maintain superior scientific and professional expertise in the food and agricultural sciences, higher education must make major shifts in such areas as instructional emphasis, faculty competencies, and scientific instrumentation. Working with colleges and universities, business, and industry, USDA's Higher Education Program (HEP) has initiated several national projects aimed at federal-state and public-private partnerships; assessing competencies needed by scientists; revitalizing curricula; improving faculty development programs; strengthening industry-academia networks to stimulate outstanding students; developing student recruitment programs; and gathering manpower supply-demand statistics and career information.

* Higher Education Programs

Higher Education Programs
Room 350 A, Administration Building
U.S. Department of Agriculture
Washington, DC 20250 (202) 720-7854

Although the USDA does not make individual loans or scholarships to students, it does makes grants to universities to carry out various programs. For information on individual monetary awards, contact your local cooperative extension agent. The USDA administers the following programs:

Morrill-Nelson Formula Grants: Land-grant institutions use Morrill-Nelson funds to support faculty salaries, curriculum development, and other instructional operating costs. All food and agricultural sciences resident instruction programs at land-grant institutions are eligible for this support. The current annual appropriation is $2.8 million--$50,000 per school.

Food and Agricultural Sciences National Needs Graduate Fellowship Grants: This program consists of competitive institutional grants to recruit and support new graduate students in areas with shortages of expertise in biotechnology, agricultural engineering, food and agricultural marketing, food science, and human nutrition. The fellowship program is a national investment strategy to attract outstanding students to pursue advanced degrees in food and agricultural sciences. Institutions with Master's or doctoral programs in these fields are eligible to participate.

National Needs Graduate Fellowship Grants: This program consists of competitive grants open to all colleges and universities to stimulate development of scientists and professionals in national need areas and to attract outstanding scholars to careers in food and agricultural sciences. Two year stipends for masters students are $10,000 annually, three year stipends for doctoral students are $17,000 annually.

Institution Challenge Grants: These competitive grants are open to all colleges and universities to ameliorate national problems affecting the quality of education, to foster university partnerships with industry and with other universities, and to stimulate non-Federal support for education. Awards are $50,000 to $80,000 for up to three years. Matching support is required.

Postdoctoral Research Associates Program: Each year the Agricultural Research Service employs up to 100 new Research Associates (postdoctorals) and, at any given time, as many as 350 may be on board across the U.S. The program provides an opportunity for new Ph.Ds to receive advanced specialized training unavailable elsewhere.

* Historically Black Colleges and Universities Program

Office of White House Initiatives on the HBCUs.
U.S. Department of Education
7th and D Sts. SW

Be patient. If any phone number is incorrect, call (area code) 555-1212 and request the new listing.

Education

Washington, DC 20202 (202) 708-8667

Through the Historically Black Colleges and Universities Program, the Department of Education is tasked to design a program to achieve an increase by the Historically Black Colleges and Universities (HBCU) in federally sponsored programs. The Department of Education can provide you with the annual Federal Performance Report on Executive Agency Actions to Assist HBCUs and answer any questions you may have about the program. Below is a list of contact numbers in the Federal Departments and agencies for the HBCU program.

Agency for International Development . . . . (703) 816-0249
U.S. Information Agency . . . . (202) 619-4574
U.S. Department of Agriculture . . . . (202) 720-2019
Central Intelligence Agency . . . . (703) 874-4456
U.S. Department of Commerce . . . . (202) 377-3007
U.S. Department of Defense . . . . (703) 694-1151
U.S. Department of Education . . . . (202) 708-5547
U.S. Department of Energy . . . . (202) 586-8393
U.S. Environmental Protection Agency . . . . (202) 260-4575
Equal Employment Opportunity Commission . . . . (202) 663-7038
U.S. Department of Health and Human Services . . . . (202) 245-3087
U.S. Department of Housing and Urban Development . . . . (202) 708-0030
U.S. Department of the Interior . . . . (202) 208-6403
U.S. Department of Justice . . . . (202) 501-8748
U.S. Department of Labor . . . . (202) 523-6151
National Aeronautics and Space Administration . . . . (202) 755-1089
National Endowment for the Arts . . . . (202) 682-5454
National Science Foundation . . . . (202) 357-7350
National Endowment for the Humanities . . . . (202) 786-0318
National Credit Union Administration . . . . (202) 682-9600
U.S. Nuclear Regulatory Commission . . . . (301) 492-8877
U.S. Department of State . . . . (202) 647-9438
U.S. Small Business Administration . . . . (202) 205-6410
U.S. Department of Transportation . . . . (202) 366-4648
U.S. Department of the Treasury . . . . (202) 622-1160
U.S. Department of Veterans Affairs . . . . (202) 233-2012

* International Auditor Fellowship Program

Director, Office of International Audit Organization Liaison
General Accounting Office (GAO)
441 G St., NW, Room 7806
Washington, DC 20548 (202) 275-4707

GAO attempts to share its knowledge and experience with other nations, particularly from the developing world. The most visible effort is the Comptroller General's International Auditor Fellowship Program, established in 1979, through which a small number of auditors from developing countries are selected annually to spend three to six months in an academic and on-the-job experience program in the U.S. Although GAO cannot pay travel and subsistence for the Fellows, it provides the training itself at no cost, and assists many participants in obtaining financial aid from the U.S. Agency for International Development, and the United Nations Development Program, and Fellows are increasingly receiving aid from their own governments. This is GAO's lead office in dealing with representatives of international audit organizations, and those of individual foreign governments.

* Junior Colleges Clearinghouse

ERIC Clearinghouse on Junior Colleges
University of California at Los Angeles
Mathematical Sciences Building, Room 8118
405 Hilgard Ave.
Los Angeles, CA 90024-1564 (310) 825-3931

Subject areas include the development, administration, and evaluation of two-year public and private community and junior colleges, technical institutes, and two-year branch university campuses. This covers the organization, administration, finance, governance, role and mission, and futures of such institutions; staff preparation, development, and evaluation; curricula and program; teaching methods; student services; libraries and learning resource centers; and methodologies of research applied to two-year colleges.

* Land-Grant Colleges

Extension Service Information Office
U.S. Department of Agriculture
Room 3328, South Building
Washington, DC 20250 (202) 720-3029

Congress originally mandated that federal funds be used to support a college or university in each state in 1862, which established the land-grant college network. In 1890 additional legislation was passed to include 17 traditionally black institutions. Today, a large variety of initiatives are taking place at these institutions aimed at building and improving programs to educate students in the agricultural sciences. Cooperative Extension Offices, which provide practical education and information to scientists, researchers, farmers, as well as the general public, are located at each land-grant institution. Liaison work with educational, research, government, business, and public and private organizations is conducted. The state agricultural experiment stations--located at the land grant institutions--conduct agricultural research geared at critical state, regional, and national issues. The Office of Higher Education Programs sponsors the 1890 Institution Capacity Building Grants for 1890 Land-Grant universities and Tuskegee university to advance university teaching and research capabilities. Grants range from $50,000 to $350,000 for up to three years.

* Lecturing Opportunities in Hungary

Office of Academic Programs
The Bureau of Educational and Cultural Affairs
United States Information Agency (USIA)
301 Fourth St., SW, Room 234
Washington, DC 20547 (202) 619-4420

USIA can provide you with information on the Hamilton and Marshall Chairs which provide for the sending of distinguished American scholars in Economics and Political Science, respectively, to lecture in Hungary.

* Library Career Training Grants

Library Development Staff
Library Programs/OERI
U.S. Department of Education
555 New Jersey Ave., NW, Room 404
Washington, DC 20208-5571 (202) 219-1315

The Department of Education awards grants for professional education or retraining in librarianship through fellowships, institutes, or traineeships in order to establish, develop, and expand programs of library and information science, including new techniques of information transfer and communication technology.

* Library Resources Program

Library Development Staff
Library Programs/OERI
U.S. Department of Education
555 New Jersey Ave., NW, Room 404
Washington, DC 20208-5571 (202) 219-1315

The Department of Education promotes high quality research and education nationwide by providing funds to major research libraries to preserve and strengthen their collections as well as expanding resources available to university researchers.

* Lunar Samples for University Educators

Johnson Space Center
Curator's Office, Code SN2
Houston, TX 77058 (713) 483-3274

Under the Thin Section Program a set of lunar thin sections is available for instructive and study purposes by college and university science instructors. The materials consist of twelve samples of lunar soils and rocks and a description booklet. Contact this office for information on participating in this program.

* Montgomery GI Bill for Education - Active Duty

Veterans Benefits Administration
U.S. Department of Veterans Affairs
810 Vermont Ave, NW
Washington, DC 20420 (202) 233-5154

You may be eligible for benefits under the Montgomery GI Bill if you are on active duty or have served three years in the active duty military or two years active plus four years in the reserve. You must have served in the military after June 30, 1985 and been honorably discharged if no longer in the service. Contact the Benefits Administration for the free booklet *Summary of Education Benefits Under the Montgomery GI Bill-Active Duty Educational Assistance Program, Chapter 30 of Title 38 U.S. Code.* This booklet contains information on eligibility and benefits.

Be patient. If any phone number is incorrect, call (area code) 555-1212 and request the new listing.

College and Continuing Education

* Montgomery GI Bill for Education - Selected Reserve Duty

Veterans Benefits Administration
U.S. Department of Veterans Affairs
810 Vermont Ave, NW
Washington, DC 20420 (202) 233-5154

Reservists who have or have had a 6 year obligation to serve in the Selected Reserve after June 30, 1985, have completed the Initial Active Duty Training, and are in good standing with their units may be eligible for educational benefits under the Montgomery GI Bill. Contact the Benefits Administration for the free booklet *Summary of Educational Benefits Under the Montgomery GI Bill-Selected Reserve Educational Assistance Program, Chapter 106 of Title 10 U.S. Code.* This booklet contains information on eligibility and benefits.

* NASA University Programs Branch

Educational Affairs Division
Mail Code XEU
NASA Headquarters
Washington, DC 20546 (202) 358-1531

This program awards grants to graduate students on a competitive basis whose research interests are compatible with NASA research programs. Fellowships are for one year and are renewable, based on progress reports, of up to three years. The fellowships also allow students to carry out a plan of study or research at their home university, but those awarded by NASA field centers require fellows to spend some time at the center, usually from a few weeks to a summer each year.

* National Center on Adult Literacy

University of Pennsylvania
3910 Chestnut Street
Philadelphia, PA 19104-3111 (215) 898-2100

NCAL heads a national initiative to focus research and development on adult literacy. The center sponsors innovative research, works with practitioners to improve instruction, and gives decision-makers the tools to form sound practices. Current project areas include: motivational factors in adult literacy participation, families and literacy learning, workplace literacy, and adult literacy and English as a second language. The Center publishes the quarterly newsletter *NCAL Connections.* Also ask for a publications list.

* Native American Programs

Office of Indian Education Programs
Bureau of Indian Affairs
U.S. Department of the Interior
18th and C Sts. NW
Washington, DC 20240 (202) 208-4871

The Bureau of Indian Affairs sponsors several programs to promote higher education for Native Americans. The Higher Education Grant Program provides grants to Indians to work toward an undergraduate degree. The Special Higher Education Grant Program provides funds for Indians to pursue a graduate degree. The Adult Education Program provides funds for Indian adults to pursue a GED. The Summer Law Program provides funding for 30 Indian Students who have been accepted into an accredited law school to participate in a summer institute which will prepare them for the first year of law school. A good source of information on Indian education in general is the annual *Office of Indian Education Programs Education Directory.*

* Postsecondary Education National Center

National Center for Research to
Improve Postsecondary Teaching and Learning
School of Education
University of Michigan
Ann Arbor, MI 48198-1259 (313) 936-2741

Major research areas include classroom teaching and learning strategies; curricular design: influences and impact; faculty as a key resource; organizational context for teaching and learning; learning, teaching and technology; research leadership, and design and integration. The following are titles are available from the "Accent" series:

Why Does it Take "Forever" to Revise the Curriculum?
Assessing Growth in Thinking in College Courses: A Caveat.
The Computer Revolution in Teaching.
Administrative Barriers to Improving Undergraduate Education.

Teaching Thinking in College.
What are Academic Administrators Doing to Improve Undergraduate Education?
Bridging the Gap Between Education Research and College Teaching?
Personal Growth as a Faculty Goal for Students.

* Postsecondary School Administration

Center for Higher Education Governance and Leadership
University of Maryland
College of Education, Room 4114
CSS Building
College Park, MD 20742-2435 (301) 405-5582

Major research areas cover the examination of postsecondary education finance and governance.

* Resident Research Associate Program

University Programs Branch
Educational Affairs Division
Mail Code XEU
NASA Headquarters
Washington, DC 20546 (202) 358-1531

This program gives postdoctoral scientists and engineers an opportunity to perform research at specified NASA field centers, working full time on the research that their award is based on. They must be in residence at the sponsoring field center during the entire associateship. Awardees must hold a PhD, ScD, or other earned research doctoral degree recognized in U.S. academic circles as equivalent to the PhD, and must also demonstrate superior ability for creative research.

* Sea-Grant Colleges

Office of Oceanic Research Programs
National Oceanic and Atmospheric Administration
U.S. Department of Commerce
1335 East-West Hwy.
Silver Spring, MD 20910 (301) 713-2427

The National Sea Grant College Program is a national network of over 300 colleges, universities, research institutions, and consortia working in partnership with industry and the federal government to support Great Lakes and marine research, education, and extension services. This program provides support for institutions engaged in comprehensive marine research, education, and advisory service programs, supports individual projects in marine research and development, and sponsors education of ocean scientists and engineers, marine technicians, and other specialists at selected colleges and universities.

* Service Academy Appointments

For those seeking appointments to the service academies, it is necessary to write your U.S. Senator or Representative for a recommendation. Call the Capitol switchboard to reach your Member of Congress at (202) 224-3121.

* State Clearinghouses for Adult Education

The following are sources of adult information at the state level:

Comprehensive Adult Student Assessment System, 2725 Congress St., Suite 1-M, San Diego, CA 92110; (619) 230-2975

Dissemination Network for Adult Educators, 1575 Old Bayshore Highway, Burlingame, CA 94010; (800) 672-2494 (in CA), (415) 692-2956. This network provides information, in-service training, and technical assistance to adult educators. A bi-monthly publication, *Network News,* is available free of charge.

Connecticut Adult Education Staff Development Center, 64 St. James St., West Hartford, CT 06119; (203) 233-8001. The center provides adult educators with comprehensive professional development services, access to the Adult Education Resource Library collection of over 8,500 materials, technical assistance, and information distribution.

ACE Staff Development Network of Delaware, International Reading Association, 800 Barksdale Rd., P.O. Box 8139, Newark, DE 19714-8139; (302) 731-1600.

Northern Area Adult Education Service Center, Northern Illinois University, Gabel Hall, Room 200, DeKalb, IL 60115; (815) 753-1441.

Be patient. If any phone number is incorrect, call (area code) 555-1212 and request the new listing.

Education

Central Illinois Adult Education Service Center, Regional Office of Education, 200 South Frederick St., Rantoul, IL 61866; (217) 893-9696.

Southern Illinois Adult Education Service Center, Southern Illinois University, Building 3, 0147, Edwardsville, IL 62026; (618) 692-2254.

Indiana Adult Education Resource Center, 3725 N. Mitthoeffer Rd., Indianapolis, IN 46236; (317) 899-0822.

Adult Resource Center, Independence Community College, 217 West Main, Independence, KS 67301; (316) 331-4420.

Central Kansas Resource Center, USD #373, 725 Main, Newton, KS 67114; (316) 283-0957.

Adult Education Center, 422 South Main, Ottawa, KS 66067; (913) 242-6719.

Adult Resource Center, 1201 First Ave., Dodge City, KS 67801; (316) 225-0186.

Kentucky Heartland Adult Resource Center, 110 South Main St., Elizabethtown, KY 42701; (502) 737-0452.

Adult Education Program Resource Center, Worcester State College, 486 Chandler St., Worcester, MA 01602; (617) 793-8157.

The Center for Adult Learning and Literacy, Ronan Hall, 251 Central, Michigan University, Mount Pleasant, MI 48859; (517) 774-6793.

University of Southern Mississippi, Adult Education Clearinghouse, Southern Station 5154, Hattiesburg, MS 39406; (601) 266-4621

Lifelong Learning Resource Network, College of Education, Montana State University, Bozeman, MT 59717; (406) 994-4731.

Adult Education Resource Center, Glassboro State College, 307 Girard Rd., Glassboro, NJ 08028; (609) 863-7131.

Adult Education Resource Center, Jersey City State College, Jersey City, NJ 07305; (201) 547-3101.

Community and Continuing Education Information Service, The New York State Education Department, Albany, NY 12234; (518) 474-3639.

Literacy Assistance Center, Inc., 15 Dutch St., 4th Floor, New York, NY 10038; (212) 267-5309.

Statewide Adult Education Resource Center, 222 West Bowen, Bismarck, ND 58504; (701) 221-3790.

Advance Pennsylvania Department of Education, Resource Center, 333 Market St., 11th Floor, Harrisburg, PA 17126-0333; (717) 783-9192.

Trends Austin Community College, P.O. Box 2285, Austin, TX 78768; (512) 472-1387.

Vermont Educational Resource Center, Department of Education, 120 State St., Montpelier, VT 05602; (802) 828-3352.

Virginia Adult Basic Education Resource Center, Room 4065, Oliver Hall, 1015 W. Main St., Box 2020, Richmond, VA 23284-2020; (800) 237-0178, or (804) 367-6521.

West Virginia Vocational Curriculum Laboratory, Cedar Lakes Conference Center, Ripley, WV 25271; (800) 982-5627.

* Veterans Continuing Education

Continuing Education Service
Academic Affairs
Veterans Health Services and Research Administration (VHS&RA)
U.S. Department of Veterans Affairs (DVA)
810 Vermont Ave., NW, Room 875E

Washington, DC 20420 (202) 535-5183

The DVA conducts system-wide continuing education programs to bring the latest in scientific, medical and management knowledge to VHS&RA employees. These programs include workshops, seminars and individual training, and all forms of audiovisual, print, and transmission media. Contact the office above for more information.

* Vocational Education Clearinghouse

ERIC Clearinghouse on Adult, Career and
Vocational Education
Ohio State University Center on Education and
Training for Employment
1900 Kenny Rd. (800) 848-4815
Columbus, OH 43210-1090 (614) 292-4353

Subject areas cover all levels of adult and continuing education from basic literacy training through professional skill upgrading; vocational and technical education covering all service areas for secondary, postsecondary, and adult education populations; and career education and career development programs for all ages and populations in educational, institutional, business, and industrial settings.

* Vocational Education Research

National Center Clearinghouse
National Center for Research in Vocational Education
1995 University Avenue, Suite 375
University of California (800) 762-4093
Berkeley, CA 94704 (510) 642-4004

This Center's mission is to find out what knowledge is needed for successful employment in both today's and tommorrow's workplace and then look into how our schools can better get this knowledge to students. The Center's research agenda is organized around the following themes: understanding how work is changing and what these changes imply for students; identifying better educational strategies for preparing students for work; strengthening the capacity of postsecondary vocational education to respond to an increasingly diverse student body; and improving assessment methods for secondary and postsecondary education. The Center provides several services including: dissemination of information through the ADVOCNET network and the RIVE and VECM databases and its newsletter *Change Agent*; collection of data on vocational education; Leadership development (University of Minnesota); Inservice Education (Virginia Polytechnic Institute and State University); and Technical Assistance for Special Populations (University of Illinois). The Center can provide you with an extensive publications catalog as well as a Human Resource directory for all members of the affiliated universities involved in the program.

* White House Fellowship Program

President's Commission on White House Fellowships
712 Jackson Place, NW
Washington, DC 20503 (202) 395-4522

The White House Fellowship program is a highly competitive opportunity to participate in and learn about the Federal government from a unique perspective. For one year, 11 to 19 Fellows are selected to work in the Executive Office of the President or in an Executive Branch department or agency. The qualities being sought are high levels of achievement, demonstrated leadership, commitment to serve others, and the skill which would make one a good special assistant in the short run and a national leader in the long run. Although there is no age limit, the program is designed to encourage future leaders rather than reward established leaders. For further information, contact the above office.

* Workplace Safety and Health Courses

Division of Training and Manpower Development
National Institute for Occupational Safety and health
4676 Columbia Parkway
Cincinnati, OH 45226 (513) 533-8221

This division offers courses for industry and health care professional on such topics as occupational safety, industrial hygiene, and safety in the laboratory. For a course listing and description, contact this office.

Be patient. If any phone number is incorrect, call (area code) 555-1212 and request the new listing.

Science Teachers and Students

* Aerospace Education

National Headquarters
Civil Air Patrol
Maxwell AFB, AL 36112-5572 (205) 293-5463

The Civil Air Patrol (CAP), the civilian auxiliary of the U.S. Air Force, offers workshops, materials, and programs for all grade levels, from kindergarten through the postgraduate level. Resources include activity books, posters, guides to aerospace education and careers, textbooks for one-year high school elective courses in aerospace, and a guide to additional educational resources available from the U.S. Department of Defense that includes resources available from military installations, the Air National Guard, Air Force Recruiting Services, military museums, and other sites.

* Aerospace Education Services Program (AESP)

Elementary and Secondary Programs Branch
Educational Affairs Division
Mail Code XEE, NASA Headquarters
Washington, DC 20546 (202) 453-8386

Under AESP, previously known as Spacemobile, specialists, all former teachers themselves, reach millions of students each year as they cross the county from September to June each year, assisting school so students and teachers can see first-hand what NASA is all about. Visits are scheduled by NASA field centers, and all cover the principles of rocketry, living and working in space, aeronautics, space science, and NASA's history and accomplishments. Schools are encouraged to arrange for an in-service workshop for teachers, which will be conducted at the school by an AESP specialist prior to the visit.

* Aerospace Software Directory

Educational Technology Branch
Educational Affairs Division
Mail Code XE
NASA Headquarters
Washington, DC 20546 (202) 453-8388

The *Aerospace Software Directory*, a survey of all commercially available aerospace-related software, is available for download via Spacelink and at NASA Teacher Resource Centers. The current directory contains information on more than 75 software packages and how to obtain them. An updated directory containing more than 200 packages will soon be available and updated regularly.

* Aviation and Space Science Instruction

Aviation Education Officer
Federal Aviation Administration (FAA)
U.S. Department of Transportation
800 Independence Ave., SW
Washington, DC 20591

The FAA's Aviation Education Program offers volunteer assistance to the nation's schools through the following programs: career guidance; tours of airports, control towers, and other facilities; classroom lectures and demonstrations; aviation safety information; aviation education resource materials; computerized clearinghouse of aviation and space information; aviation science instruction programs for home/school computers; "Partnerships-in-Education" activities; and teachers' workshops. Write to the above office for more information.

* Aviation Materials for Educators

Office of Public Affairs
Federal Aviation Administration
Aviation Education Program
800 Independence Ave., SW
Washington, DC 20591 (202) 366-4000

The Federal Aviation Administration (FAA), as part of its effort to promote better understanding of aviation and air transportation, offers educational materials and publications to both teachers and students. These include instructional materials, films, aviation career information, historical publications, and a guide to additional materials from other sources.

* Challenger Center for Space Science Education

Challenger Center for Space Science Education
1101 King Street, Suite 190
Alexandria, VA 22314 (703) 683-9740

The Challenger Center is a privately funded, nonprofit organization founded as a living memorial to the Challenger crew by stimulating space-related education. The center plans to construct a series of simulated space environment centers linked to museums, science centers, and school districts throughout the world through a comprehensive, international endowment campaign. The first center, the Challenger Center Space-Life Station, will be built in the Washington, DC, area, and will serve as headquarters for the network. An educator membership is available that includes a journal, newsletter, updates, and conference information.

* Community Involvement Program

Elementary and Secondary Programs Branch
Educational Affairs Division
Mail Code XEE
NASA Headquarters
Washington, DC 20546 (202) 453-8386

Through a series of meetings, NASA staff members and community educators custom-tailor each Community Involvement Program (CIP) to match the community where it is held. A typical CIP might include school assemblies, teacher workshops, a visit by an astronaut, exhibits in shopping centers and schools, presentations by NASA scientists, competitions for students, and public events.

* Cooperative Education Program (CEP)

Personnel Policy and Work Force Effectiveness Division
Mail Code NPM
NASA Headquarters
Washington, DC 20546 (202) 453-2603

CEP gives high school, college, and graduate students an opportunity to work at a NASA field center while completing their education. Participating students usually alternate working one semester with studying one semester. In addition to job experience, the program also serves as a recruitment tool. Interested students must be attending school, be enrolled in their school's coop program, maintain at least a 2.0 overall grade point average, and be recommended by the school. Each NASA field center negotiates its own cooperative agreements with school in its geographic area, and it is usually the responsibility of a school to initiate the venture.

* Educational Publications Directory

U.S. Government Printing Office
Washington, DC 20401 (202) 783-3238

The Educational Affairs Division of NASA produces an annual directory of educational and technical publications that can be purchased through the GPO. It contains ordering information and order forms, but does not include publications available from NASA field centers, a listing of which is available from the Teacher Resource Center serving your geographic area.

* Environmental/Energy Education

Environmental/Energy Education
Land Resources Division
Resource Development
Tennessee Valley Authority (TVA)
Norris, TN 37828 (615) 632-1640

Much of TVA's environmental education effort is accomplished through university-based environmental education centers. The TVA has worked with

Be patient. If any phone number is incorrect, call (area code) 555-1212 and request the new listing.

Education

several universities and colleges across the Valley and seven states to develop environmental education teaching aids and programs for schools, along with workshops for teachers. At the national level, the TVA has been involved in coordinating programs with the Environmental Protection Agency. In addition, TVA offers teacher workshops and interpretive programs for groups at Land Between the Lakes, an experimental area for schools and the public to study total resource management. Contact this office for more information on the TVA's environmental education programs.

* Graduate Student Researchers Program

University Programs Branch
Educational Affairs Division
Mail Code XEU
NASA Headquarters
Washington, DC 20546 (202) 453-8344

This program awards grants to graduate students on a competitive basis whose research interests are compatible with NASA research programs. Fellowships are for one year and are renewable, based on progress reports, of up to three years. The fellowships also allow students to carry out a plan of study or research at their home university, but those awarded by NASA field centers require fellows to spend some time at the center, usually from a few weeks to a summer each year.

* Lunar Rocks On Loan

Johnson Space Center
Educational Coordinator
Houston, TX 77058

Under the Educational Disk Program, NASA will loan teachers six samples of lunar material (three lunar soils and three lunar rocks) encapsulated in a six-inch diameter clear lucite disk, accompanied by written and graphic descriptions of each sample in the disk; a film; a sound and slide presentation; a teacher workbook; and additional printed material. Science teachers may qualify for the use of the disk by attending one of the many workshops sponsored by NASA's Space Science Education Specialists scheduled during the year at different locations throughout the U.S.

* Math Competition: MATHCOUNTS

Elementary and Secondary Programs Branch
Educational Affairs Division
Mail Code XEE
NASA Headquarters
Washington, DC 20546 (202) 453-8388

MATHCOUNTS is an annual math competition for 7th and 8th grade students that brings a number of organizations together, including NASA and the U.S. Department of Education, to promote and reward excellence in mathematics. Competition begins each September with a qualifying test, and those who qualify are then coached by their teachers for the regional competition in February, the State competition in April, and the national competition in May in Washington, DC.

* Mathematics Education

Center for the Learning and Teaching of Mathematics
Wisconsin Center for Education Research
University of Wisconsin at Madison
1025 West Johnson St.
Madison, WI 53706 (608) 263-4285

Major research areas include cognitively guided instruction in mathematics education; learning and instruction of algebra, early arithmetic, geometry, and rational numbers; mathematics curriculum study; and the assessment of mathematics.

* NASA Education Workshops for Elementary School Teachers (NEWEST)

Elementary and Secondary Programs Branch
Educational Affairs Division
Mail Code XEE
NASA Headquarters
Washington, DC 20546 (202) 453-8386

NEWEST is for elementary school teachers (grades 1-6) in all disciplines. Selected teachers are awarded a two-week, expense-paid workshop at a NASA field center, with each center hosting about 20 teachers. The workshops vary from center to center. Although all focus on current NASA programs, each center conducts activities unique to its work. During their stay, teachers meet with scientists, technicians, and educational specialists. Teachers are instructed how to apply their experiences to their elementary curriculum.

* NASA Education Workshop for Math and Science Teachers (NEWMAST)

Elementary and Secondary Programs Branch
Educational Affairs Division
Mail Code XEE, NASA Headquarters
Washington, DC 20546 (202) 453-8386

NEWMAST makes awards to math, science, and technology teachers in grades 7-12 with a two week, expense-paid workshop at a NASA field center each year. Applications must be submitted in the winter, and the winners are announced in the spring. Teachers are chosen on the basis of educational background, teaching experience, recommendations, personal and professional goals, and an essay explaining how selection for NEWMAST will benefit the applicant's students, colleagues, and community.

* NASA Report To Educators

Distribution Officer
Mail Code XEP
NASA Headquarters
Washington, DC 20546 (202) 453-8380

This report, a free quarterly prepared for more than 100,000 members of the educational community, contains educational information, including information on technology spinoffs, new publications and resource materials, conferences, and ongoing programs and competitions.

* Resident Environmental Education

Environmental/Energy Education
Land Between The Lakes
Resource and Development
Tennessee Valley Authority
Golden Pond, KY 42231 (502) 924-1606

The Youth Station and Brandon Spring at Land Between The Lakes operates the residential education program to promote better environmental understanding, aesthetic appreciation, and man's place in nature. These dorm-style activity areas are open year-round and accommodate kindergarten through college-level groups. Groups are welcome to carry out their own programs, or the staff can help in developing them. Activities include canoeing, pond studies, and nature walks. With Murray (Kentucky) State University Center for Environmental Education, the staff provides additional workshops for area teachers and in-service students.

* Resident Research Associate Program

University Programs Branch
Educational Affairs Division
Mail Code XEU
NASA Headquarters
Washington, DC 20546 (202) 453-8344

This program gives postdoctoral scientists and engineers an opportunity to perform research at specified NASA field centers, working full time on the research that their award is based on. They must be in residence at the sponsoring field center during the entire associateship. Awardees must hold a PhD, ScD, or other earned research doctoral degree recognized in U.S. academic circles as equivalent to the PhD, and must also demonstrate superior ability for creative research.

* Satellite Videoconferences

Video Conference Coordinator
NASA Aerospace Education Services Program
Oklahoma State University
300 N. Cordell
Stillwater, OK 74078 (405) 744-7015

or

Educational Technology Branch
Educational Affairs Division
Mail Code XE
NASA Headquarters
Washington, DC 20546 (202) 453-8388

Be patient. If any phone number is incorrect, call (area code) 555-1212 and request the new listing.

Science Teachers and Students

During the school year, a series of educational programs is delivered by satellite to teachers across the country. The content of each videoconference varies, but all cover aeronautics or space science topics of interest to the educational community. Past topics have included the Hubble Space Telescope, the Freedom Space Station, and the Space Shuttle program. The broadcasts are interactive; a number is flashed across the bottom of the screen, and viewers can call collect to ask questions or take part in a discussion.

* Science and Engineering Fairs

Elementary and Secondary Programs Branch
Educational Affairs Division
Mail Code XEE, NASA Headquarters
Washington, DC 20546 (202) 453-8386

NASA takes part in the International Science and Engineering Fair for high school students by awarding certificates of merit at the regional and state levels of competition, and sending a team of judges to the international fair, where they select up to 12 students to receive an expense-paid trip with their teachers to a NASA field center. Local science fairs that are not affiliated with the international fair can take part in NASA's award system by requesting information from the field center serving their geographical area.

* Science Education

National Center for Improving Science Education
The Network, Inc.
290 South Main St.
Andover, MA 01810 (508) 470-1080

or

Washington DC Office
1920 L St., NW, Suite 202
Washington, DC 20036 (202) 467-0652

Major research areas include the assessment of science; science curriculum study; and science instruction study.

* Science, Mathematics, and Environmental Education Information

ERIC Clearinghouse on Science, Mathematics,
and Environmental Education
Ohio State University
1200 Chambers Rd., Room 310
Columbus, OH 43212-1792 (614) 292-6717

Subject areas cover science, mathematics, environmental, and engineering education at all levels, and within these broad subject areas, the following topics: development of curriculum and instructional materials; teachers and teacher education; learning theory/outcomes (including the impact of such factors as interest level, intelligence, values, and concept development upon learning in these fields); education programs; research and evaluative studies; media applications; and computer applications.

* Science, Technology, and Social Science Data Base

General Reading Rooms
Library of Congress
Washington, DC 20540 (202) 707-5522

The *Science, Technology, and Social Science Database* is a computerized directory of more than 14,000 organizations or individuals who will provide information to the general public on topics primarily in science, technology, and the social sciences. Citations generally contain the name of the organization or person, mailing address, telephone number, areas of interest, special collections, publications, and special services.

* Space Camp

Space and Rocket Center
One Tranquility Base (800) 63-SPACE
Huntsville, AL 35807-0680 (205) 837-3400

Space Camp and Space Academy, sponsored by the Space and Rocket Center, give both children and adults an opportunity to take part in mission-oriented programs similar to an actual space mission. Participants spend from three to ten days learning about the principles of rocketry and living in space, and then go through a simulated mission. Prices range from $400 to $800, depending on the program and age of the participant.

* Space Education Resource Center

U.S. Space Foundation
1525 Vapor Trail
Colorado Springs, CO 80916 (719) 550-1000

The U.S. Space Foundation serves as a national resource for research and educational information on all aspects of space. The foundation has developed or assisted other organizations and individuals in developing space-related educational materials and offering teacher workshops. The staff is also available for classroom visits.

* Space-Exposed Experiment Developed for Students (SEEDS)

Elementary and Secondary Programs
Educational Affairs Division
Mail Code XEO, NASA Headquarters
Washington, DC 20546 (202) 453-2995

In 1984, 65 pounds of tomato seeds were put aboard a passive satellite launched aboard the Space Shuttle. The plan calls for the seeds to be retrieved in November 1989 and then made available, along with control seeds, to teachers who requested participation in the program. The students will then germinate the two groups of seeds and determine the effects, if any, of long-term exposure to radiation and other conditions in space. As the retrieval date nears, NASA plans to contact those on the list to receive seeds to verify that they still want to participate. But because of cancellations, teachers not on the original list are encouraged to continue to request the seeds.

* Spacelink

Spacelink Administrator
Marshall Space Flight Center
Mail Code CA-20
Huntsville, AL 35807 (205) 544-6527

Spacelink is an information access system that allows individuals to log on and receive news about current NASA programs and activities and other space-related information, including historical and astronaut data, lesson plans and classroom activities, and even entire publications, such as the *Aerospace Software Directory* and *Educational Publications Directory*. Although primarily intended as a resource for teachers, anyone with a personal computer and modem can access the network. The only charge is the cost of the long distance phone call. The first time you access the network, you identify yourself as a new user and are then given a hands-on guide to the use of the network. Spacelink is menu-driven and self-explanatory, so even novice computer users should experience no major difficulties.

* Space Museum Education Programs

Office of Education, P-700
National Air and Space Museum
Smithsonian Institution
Washington, DC 20560 (202) 786-2106

The National Air and Space Museum offers a wide variety of educational activities, including making personnel available for teacher workshops, assistance in preparing resource materials, and making many of its resource materials available in the museum's Education Resource Center. The museum also offers teacher workshops year-round and produces classroom activities and materials for use in conjunction with a planned trip to the museum or as enrichment materials.

* Space Orientation Course for Educators

Space and Rocket Center
One Tranquility Base (800) 63-SPACE
Huntsville, AL 35807-0680 (205) 837-3400

This orientation course for educators is a five-day program that introduces educators to space-related topics and shows them how to incorporate what they learn there into classroom activities.

* Space Science Student Involvement Program

Elementary and Secondary Programs Branch
Educational Affairs Division
Mail Code XEE
NASA Headquarters
Washington, DC 20546 (202) 453-8386

Be patient. If any phone number is incorrect, call (area code) 555-1212 and request the new listing.

Education

The Space Science Student Involvement Program (SSIP), an annual program that involves students in creating experiments, art, and newspaper articles in areas of interest to NASA, honors outstanding student work through awarding various prizes, but the awards are secondary to participation in classroom activities. Students complete in five categories, some of which are broken down into separate competitions for different grade levels. Depending on the category, winners receive expense-paid trips to NASA field centers or national science symposia, and cash awards. What follows is a listing of the different categories for competition:

Space Station Proposal: for students in grades 6-8 and 9-12. The entry must be a proposal for an experiment that theoretically can be performed on the Space Station. Although experiments do not have to be constructed or performed, they should demonstrate their value and applicability to space.

National Aerospace Internship: Zero-Gravity Research Facility Proposal: Open to students in grades 9-12. Students propose experiments that theoretically can be tested in the Zero-Gravity Research Facility at Lewis Research Center.

National Aerospace Internship: Wind Tunnel Proposal: Open to students in grades 10-12. Students propose experiments that theoretically can be tested in the Wind Tunnel at Langley Research Center.

School Newspaper Competition: Open to students in grades 6-8 and 9-12. Students submit a promotional advertisement or article about SSIP that was published in their school newspaper.

National Juried Art Competition: Mars Settlement: Open to students in grades 6-8 and 9-12. Students research and illustrate their concept of the first settlement on Mars which can accommodate 10 people, illustrate life support and transportation, and be accompanied by an explanatory paragraph.

* Summer Faculty Fellowship Program

University Programs Branch
Educational Affairs Division
Mail Code XEU, NASA Headquarters
Washington, DC 20546 (202) 453-8344

This fellowship program gives faculty fellows in various academic disciplines the opportunity to use NASA field centers to perform research. Those selected spend 10 weeks at a field center and received a stipend. The program is open to U.S. citizens with teaching or research appointments in universities or colleges; priority is given to applicants with two years of experience, and most have doctorate degrees and carry an academic title of assistant, associate, or full professor. About 200 fellowships are awarded each year.

* Summer High School Apprentice Research Program (SHARP)

Elementary and Secondary Programs Branch
Educational Affairs Division
National Aeronautics and Space Administration
Mail Code XEE
Washington, DC 20546 (202) 453-8386

SHARP provides an opportunity for targeted underrepresented minority students in grades 10-12 who live within commuting distance of a participating NASA field center to take part in an eight-week, paid apprenticeship, where they work directly with NASA scientists or engineers. Interested students submit an application and references from a school administrator, teacher, or guidance counselor. Chosen students work with scientists or engineers whose work is related to his or her career aspirations, which may include computers, research, navigation, or guidance systems.

* Teacher-In-Space Program

Elementary and Secondary Programs Branch
Educational Affairs Division
Mail Code XEE
NASA Headquarters
Washington, DC 20546 (202) 453-8386

As part of the Challenger Center for Space Science Education, 100 education ambassadors from the NASA space program travel across the country, spreading the word about the education opportunities and programs from NASA. This program does not, however, take applications from teachers who wish to travel in space. For more information on NASA ambassadors, contact this office.

* Teacher Resource Centers (TRC)

Educational Affairs Division
Office of External Relations
National Aeronautics and Space Administration
Washington, DC 20546 (202) 453-1110

These resource centers contain a wealth of information for educators interested in space- and science-related material: publications, reference books, slides, audio cassettes, video cassettes, telelecture programs, computer programs, lesson plans and activities, and lists of publications available from government and nongovernment sources. Much of the material is free. In the case of media such as videocassettes, however, educators are asked to supply their own media; copying facilities are available at all field centers. What follows is a list of the TRCs and the regions they serve:

Ames Research Center, Teacher Resource Center, Mail Stop 204-7, Moffett Field, CA 94035; (415) 694-6077. Areas served: Alaska, Arizona, California, Hawaii, Idaho, Montana, Nevada, Oregon, Utah, Washington, and Wyoming.

Jet Propulsion Laboratory, Teacher Resource Center, JPL Educational Outreach, Mail Stop CS-530, Pasadena, CA 91109; (818) 354-6916. Areas served: Same as Ames Research Center above.

John F. Kennedy Space Center, Educator Resource Library, Mail Stop ERL, Kennedy Space Center, FL 32899; (305) 867-4090. Areas served: Florida, Georgia, Puerto Rico, and Virgin Islands.

Langley Research Center, Teacher Resource Center, Mail Stop 146, Hampton, VA 23665-5225; (804) 865-4468/3017. Areas served: Kentucky, North Carolina, South Carolina, Virginia, and West Virginia.

Lyndon B. Johnson Space Center, Teacher Resource Center, Mail Stop AP-4, Houston, TX 77058; (513) 483-8696. Areas served: Colorado, Kansas, Nebraska, New Mexico, North Dakota, Oklahoma, South Dakota, and Texas.

John C. Stennis Space Center, Teacher Resource Center, Building 1200, Stennis Space Center, MS 39529; (601) 688-3338. Area served: Mississippi.

Goddard Space Flight Center, Teacher Resource Laboratory, Mail Stop 130.3, Greenbelt, MD 20771; (301) 286-8570. Area served: Connecticut, Delaware, District of Columbia, Maine, Maryland, Massachusetts, New Hampshire, New Jersey, New York, Pennsylvania, Rhode Island, and Vermont.

Lewis Research Center, Teacher Resource Center, Mail Stop 8-1, Cleveland, OH 44135; (216) 433-2016/2017. Areas served: Illinois, Indiana, Michigan, Minnesota, Ohio, and Wisconsin.

Marshall Space Flight Center, Alabama Space and Rocket Center, NASA Teacher Resource Center, Huntsville, AL 35807; (205) 544-5812. Areas served: Alabama, Arkansas, Iowa, Louisiana, Missouri, and Tennessee.

* Teacher Resource Network

Educational Affairs Division
Office of External Relations
National Aeronautics and Space Administration
Washington, DC 20546 (202) 453-1110

To make information available to the educational community, NASA has created the Teacher Resource Network made up of Teacher Resource Centers, Regional Teacher Resource Centers, and the Central Operation of Resources for Educators.

* Teacher Workshops

Elementary and Secondary Programs Branch
Educational Affairs Division
Mail Code XEE, NASA Headquarters
Washington, DC 20546 (202) 453-8386

Aerospace Education Services Program (AESP) specialists conduct workshops for teachers each summer at NASA field centers, elementary and secondary schools, and on college campuses. Workshops cover astronomy, aeronautics, life in space, principles of rocketry, Earth sciences, and remote sensing. A typical workshop includes how-to and hands-on activities to help teachers incorporate what they learn into classroom activities and programs to supplement existing curricula.

Be patient. If any phone number is incorrect, call (area code) 555-1212 and request the new listing.

Science Teachers and Students

* Teaching Materials for Geology

Geologic Inquiries Group
U.S. Geological Survey
907 National Center
Reston, VA 22092   (703) 648-4383

Packets of geological teaching aids for different grade levels and geographic location are available from the Geologic Inquiries Group and from the Earth Science Information Centers listed elsewhere in this book. These packets include lists of reference materials, various maps and map indexes, and a selection of general interest publications. Requests for teachers packets should be sent on school letterhead, indicating the grade level and subject of interest.

* Urban Community Enrichment Program (UCEP)

Elementary and Secondary Programs Branch
Educational Affairs Division
Mail Code XEE, NASA Headquarters
Washington, DC 20546   (202) 453-8386

UCEP is specifically targeted toward middle-school students in urban areas with high percentages of minorities. NASA specialists will meet with school representatives to formulate a custom-tailored program to fit the school's needs. Typically a program begins with teacher orientation workshops followed by assemblies, a series of student workshops, and classroom visits. In the classroom, NASA specialists work with students on various hands-on activities, such as building rockets or airplanes or learning about how information is transmitted from space back to Earth.

Education

Innovation and Trends

* Appalachia Education Research Center

Appalachia Educational Laboratory, Inc.
1030 Quarrier St.
P.O. Box 1348
Charleston, WV 25325 (304) 347-0400

Major activity areas include classroom instruction, school governance and administration, policy and planning, professional preparation and research, regional liaison center, school service center, and rural and small schools. States served: Kentucky, Tennessee, Virginia, and West Virginia.

* Arts Education Research and Testing

University of Illinois at Urbana - Champaign
College of Applied and Fine Arts
105 Davenport House
809 South Wright St.
Champaign, IL 61820-6219 (217) 333-2186

Major research areas include the development and validation of standardized achievement tests in the area of artistic processes and techniques in art history; national study on literacy and art education; role of music in general education; status surveys in art, visual, dance and drama in the elementary and secondary schools; drama/theatre, visual and dance; influence on culture condition on the learning of arts; development of computer assisted testing (music education); design of studies in dance; designs of studies in theatre; status survey of music education in elementary and secondary schools; and arts education field work: and observational studies.

* Congressional Technology Assessment Fellowships

Congressional Fellowships
Personnel Office
Office of Technology Assessment (OTA)
Congress of the United States
Washington, DC 20510

OTA awards up to six fellowships each year, providing an opportunity for individuals of demonstrated outstanding ability to gain a better understanding of science and technology issues facing Congress, along with the ways in which Congress establishes national policy related to these issues. Applications must be received by January 31. Stipends range from $28,000 to $55,000, depending upon background and experience. For further information, write this office.

* Document Reproduction of Education Research

ERIC Document Reproduction Service
Computer Microfilm Corporation
3900 Wheeler Ave. (703) 823-0500
Alexandria, VA 22304-5110 (800) 227-3742

This service is responsible for microfilming the ERIC documents announced in *Resources in Education*. Once microfilmed, the RIE documents can be purchased as either microfiche or paper reproductions by simply calling EDRS. You can expect to receive your requests within 3 to 5 working days. EDRS supplies more than 1 million microfiche each month to over 750 locations around the world.

* Educational Abstracts Journal

Resources in Education (RIE)
Superintendent of Documents
U.S. Government Printing Office
Washington, DC 20402-9371 (202) 783-3238

Published for the U.S. Department of Education in twelve monthly issues, *Resources in Education*, a monthly abstract journal of ERIC, covers the document literature of education. It is indexed by subject institution, personal author, and publication type. A year's subscription to the journal is $66, and the semi-annual index is $20 per year.

* Education and Employment

National Center on Education and Employment
Teachers College
Columbia University, Box 174
New York, NY 10027 (212) 678-3091

Major research areas include education and the labor market; the role of family background, school characteristics, and school curriculum in the link between education and labor market outcomes; youth participation in job training and labor market outcomes; knowledge acquisition at work; and community-based planning for work-related education.

* Educational Institutions Providing the ERIC System

ERIC Processing and Reference Facility
2440 Research Blvd., Suite 550
Rockville, MD 20850 (301) 590-1420

The free *Directory of ERIC Information Service Providers* lists all of the service providers, primarily colleges and universities, within the ERIC system according to geographical region. It includes organizations that provide computerized searches of the ERIC database, that have sizeable collections of ERIC microfiche, and that subscribe to and collect the various ERIC publications.

* Education Reform and Policy Research

Center for Policy Research in Education
The Eagleton Institute of Politics Rutgers
The State University of New Jersey
Wood Lawn--Neilson Campus
New Brunswick, NJ 08901 (201) 828-3872

Major research areas include curriculum and student standards, teacher policies, indicators and monitoring, new roles and responsibilities; and evolution of reform.

* Educational Research and Databases

Center for Electronic Records
National Archives and Records Administration
Room 20E
8th St. and Pennsylvania Ave., NW
Washington, DC 20408 (202) 523-3267

This center holds a variety of records pertaining to educational research, including data from the U.S. Department of Education, Office of Education, U.S. Department of Health, Education, and Welfare, as well as other government agencies. Some of the data consists of basic skills test scores, teacher questionnaires, and principal questionnaires.

* Educational Resources Information Center

(ERIC) Clearinghouses
Office of Educational Research and Improvement
555 New Jersey Ave., NW
Washington, DC 20208 (202) 357-6088

The Educational Resources Information Center (ERIC) is a national education information system responsible for developing, maintaining, and providing access to the world's largest education research database. The ERIC system includes a network of clearinghouses, each of which acquires and reviews documents and prepared indexes and abstracts, which are then entered into the ERIC database, which contains over 650,000 abstracts. ERIC is made available to a wide variety of users through multiple means, including microfiche collections (available in over 700 libraries around the world) and through vendor-provided online and compact disk-read only memory (CD-ROM) searching. Periodic reports, digests, and other documents are prepared by the clearinghouses, each of which covers education research and practice in an assigned topic area. Each clearinghouse also provides a variety of user services, including training, and responds to numerous requests for information. *A Pocket Guide to ERIC* and *All About ERIC* are available free of charge from this office to clarify the activities of the ERIC system.

Be patient. If any phone number is incorrect, call (area code) 555-1212 and request the new listing.

Innovation and Trends

* Educational Technology

Educational Technology Center
Harvard Graduate School of Education
337 Gutman Library
6 Appian Way
Cambridge, MA 02138 (617) 495-9373

Major research areas include mathematics, science, computer education, and new technologies.

Subject areas cover educational technology and library and information science at all levels. This includes instructional design, development and evaluation with emphasis on educational technology, along with the media of educational communication; computers and microcomputers, telecommunications (cable, broadcast, satellite); and audio and video recordings, film and other audiovisual materials, as they pertain to teaching and learning. Within library and information science, the focus is on the operation and management of information services for education-related organizations. All aspects of information technology related to education are considered within this scope.

* Education Technologies

Office of Technology Assessment (OTA)
600 Pennsylvania Ave., SE
Washington, DC 20510 (202) 228-6936

New curriculum requirements, shortages of qualified teachers in some subjects, sparse student enrollment in some regions, and rising costs for educational services contribute to an increasing need for effective methods for providing instruction. OTA is currently studying these problems and the various technological options, their costs, effectiveness, and tradeoffs, in the K-12 school setting. Contact Linda Roberts, the project director, for more information.

* Far West Educational Research and Development

Far West Laboratory for Educational Research
and Development
1855 Folsom St.
San Francisco, CA 94103 (415) 565-3000

Major activity areas include teaching and learning, improving organizational effectiveness, professional preparation and development, students at risk, Center for Educational Policy, Southern Service Center, rural and small schools, planning and evaluation, and publication services. States served: Arizona, California, Nevada, and Utah.

* Grants and Contracts Service

Office of Management
U.S. Department of Education
400 Maryland Ave.
Washington, DC 20202 (202) 732-2804

This office publishes the pamphlet, *GCMS: Grants and Contracts Management System*, which gives you over-all information about the on-line information system which monitors the educational grant and procurement contract awards of the U.S. Department of Education. It also contains a telephone list of contacts within the system to call for information and inquiries on the status of your application. For information concerning GCMS, contact the Director, Management Support Division, Grants and Contracts Service, (202) 732-2773.

* Guidelines for Publishing Educational Material with ERIC

ERIC Educational Resources Information Center
2440 Research Boulevard, Suite 550
Rockville, MD 20850-3238

This free pamphlet outlines the types of documents suitable for ERIC publication and the procedure for submitting the documents to ERIC.

* Guide to the Department of Education Office of Educational Research and Improvement

America's Education Fact Finder
Office of Educational Research and Improvement
U.S. Department of Education
555 New Jersey Ave., NW
Washington, DC 20208

The *Guide* is free pamphlet is an overview of the functions of the Office of Educational Research and Development. It also contains important phone numbers to call for specific projects within the department, including Research, Library Programs, and Information Services.

* Information Resources Clearinghouse

ERIC Clearinghouse on Information Resources
Syracuse University School of Education
030 Huntington Hall, 150 Marshall St.
Syracuse, NY 13244-2340 (315) 443-3640

* Language Education and Research

Center for Language Education and Research
University of California
1100 Glendon Ave., Suite 1740
Los Angeles, CA 90024 (213) 206-1486

Major research areas include academic knowledge base; professional development of the language educator; improvement of content of curricula and programs; linguistic and metalinguistic underpinnings of academic learning; second language instructional programs; language attrition; relations across linguistic minority and second language programs.

* Languages and Linguistics Education Information

ERIC Clearinghouse on Languages and Linguistics
Center for Applied Linguistics
1118 22nd St., NW
Washington, DC 20037-0037 (202) 429-9551

Subject areas cover languages and language sciences; theoretical and applied linguistics; all areas of foreign language, second language and linguistics pedagogy, or methodology; psycholinguistics and the psychology of language learning; cultural and intercultural context of languages; application of linguistics in language teaching; bilingualism and bilingual education; sociolinguistics; study abroad and international exchanges; teacher training and qualifications specific to the teaching of a foreign language and second language; commonly and uncommonly taught languages, including English as a second language; and related curriculum developments and problems.

* Leadership in Education

Center for School Leadership
Graduate School of Education
Harvard University
Monroe C. Gutman Library
Appian Way
Cambridge, MA 02138-3704 (617) 495-3575

Major research areas ask the following: What is good school leadership? How does good school leadership come about? What will good school leadership mean in the future?

* Learning Skills

Center for the Study of Learning
Learning, Research and Development Center
University of Pittsburgh
3939 O'Hara St.
Pittsburgh, PA 15260 (412) 624-7485

Major research areas include mathematics, science, social studies learning, and learning skills.

* Midwest Regional Education Research Lab

Mid-Continent Regional Educational Laboratory
Denver Office: 12500 East Iliff, Suite 201
Aurora, CO 80014 (303) 337-0990

or

Kansas City Office: 4709 Belleview Ave.
Kansas City, MO 64112 (816) 756-2401

Their major activities are to foster regional communication and networks; distribute information, and provide technical assistance to improve educational practice; strengthen the region's capacity to design and implement policies that support school improvement; develop databases on economic, social, political, and educational trends in the region; develop new resources aimed at improving education for students most in need; and rural and small schools. States served: Colorado, Kansas, Nebraska, Missouri, Wyoming, North Dakota, and South Dakota.

Be patient. If any phone number is incorrect, call (area code) 555-1212 and request the new listing.

Education

* National Longitudinal Study

National Educational Longitudinal Study of 1988 (NELS:88)
National Opinion Research Center
1155 East 60th St.
Chicago, IL 60637 (312) 702-8998

NELS:88 is a longitudinal study that begins with a survey in 1988 of eighth grade students, their schools, teachers, and their parents. This study will track the critical transitions experienced by young adults as they progress through junior high school, high school, and postsecondary education into the world of work. This study will yield policy-relevant information about such topics as high school effectiveness, discipline, homework, coursetaking patterns, cognitive ability, dropouts, private schools, vocational education, special education, instruction for limited-English-speaking students, postsecondary access and choice, student financial assistance, employment during high school and college, transfer behaviors, vocational training, on-the-job training, labor force participation, employment stability, family formation, and graduate/professional training. Conducted every two years, published information concerning the survey is available in June of the year following the actual survey. For information on how to obtain the results of the survey, contact the Center for Education Statistics, Elementary/Secondary Outcomes Division, (202) 357-6777.

* North Central Region Lab

North Central Regional Educational Laboratory
295 Emroy Ave.
Elmhurst, IL 60126 (312) 941-7677

Major activity areas include improving student performance, strengthening the quality of instruction, developing the education professions, and rural and small schools. States served: Illinois, Indiana, Iowa, Michigan, Minnesota, Ohio, and Wisconsin.

* Northeast Education Research Lab

Regional Laboratory for Educational Improvement of the Northeast and Islands
290 South Main St.
Andover, MA 01810 (508) 470-0098

Major activity areas include leadership for school improvement, teacher development, public policy for school improvement, at-risk youth, rural and small schools, and program governance and support. Areas served: Connecticut, Maine, Massachusetts, New Hampshire, New York, Rhode Island, Vermont, Puerto Rico, and the Virgin Islands.

* Northwest Regional Lab

Northwest Regional Educational Laboratory
101 S.W. Main St.
Suite 500
Portland, OR 97204 (503) 275-9500

Major activity areas include evaluation assessment, cultural understanding, and equity; business and human resource agencies; professional development, rural and small schools, school improvement; and technology. Other Laboratory Programs include education and work; evaluation and assessment; institutional development and communication; literacy and language; planning and service coordination; R&D for Indian education; school improvement program; technology program; and the Western Center for Drug-Free Schools and Communities. Areas served: Alaska, Idaho, Montana, Oregon, Washington, American Samoa, Guam, Hawaii, and the Northern Mariana Islands.

* Regional Educational Laboratories Programs For the Improvement of Practice

Educational Networks Division
Office of Educational Research and Improvement
555 New Jersey Ave., NW
Washington, DC 20208 (202) 357-6186

This office funds nine regional laboratories which carry out applied research, development, and technical assistance for educators, parents, and decisionmakers in the 50 states, the District of Columbia, Puerto Rico, the Virgin Islands, and the Pacific Basin Region. Each laboratory serves a geographic region and is governed by an independent board of directors. Those listed here are under a five-year contract through November 30, 1990. These laboratories plan programs through an ongoing assessment of regional needs, a knowledge of the current trends in research practice, and interaction with the many other agencies and institutions that assist communities and schools with educational improvement.

Improving schools and classrooms is the goal of the laboratories, a goal they carry out through a common set of five tasks or functions:

Working with other regional organizations to apply research and improve schools. Partner organizations include state departments of education, intermediate school districts and intradistrict collaboratives, universities, colleges, and state associations of educators and parents;

Assisting state-level policymakers on the implications of educational research and practice for policies and programs;

Conducting applied research and developing materials, programs, and publications that support the mission of school and classroom improvement;

Collaborating with other laboratories, research centers, and national associations to extend and enhance related research and development; and

Developing effective internal management, governance, planning, and self-evaluation, as well as reviewing regional needs and developments.

* Research and Development Centers Nationwide

National Research and Development Centers
Office of Educational Research and Development
555 New Jersey Ave., NW
Washington, DC 20208 (202) 357-6079

These university-based centers focus research on topics of national significance to educational policy and practice. Each center works in a defined field on a multi-year (and usually multi-disciplinary) program of research and development. Each center's role is to: 1) exercise leadership in its mission area; 2) conduct programmatic research and development; 3) attract the sustained attention of the best researchers to education problems; 4) create a long-term interaction between researchers and educators; 5) participate in a network for collaborative exchange in the education community; and 6) engage in an information distribution program.

* Research for Better Schools

Research for Better Schools
444 North Third St.
Philadelphia, PA 19123 (215) 574-9300

Major activity areas include institutional development, cooperative school improvement, state leadership assistance, applied research, products for special populations, national networking, and rural and small schools. Areas served: Delaware, District of Columbia, Maryland, Pennsylvania, and New Jersey.

* Southeastern Education Research Lab

Southeastern Educational Improvement Laboratory
P.O. Box 12746
200 Park Offices
Suite 204
Research Triangle Park, NC 27709-2746 (919) 549-8216

Major activity areas include improving writing, math, and leadership skills; making effective use of technology; state policy and educational reform; the teaching profession; dropout prevention; and rural and small schools. States served: Alabama, Florida, Georgia, Mississippi, North Carolina and South Carolina.

* Southwest Regional Education Research Lab

Southwest Educational Development Laboratory
211 East Seventh St.
Austin, TX 78701 (512) 476-6861

Major activity areas include improving teacher and administrator performance, improving school and classroom productivity, facilitating student achievement, information services for education decisionmakers, and rural and small schools. States served: Arkansas, Louisiana, New Mexico, Oklahoma, and Texas.

* Statistics and Information

Office of Educational Research and Improvement Information Services
555 New Jersey Ave., NW (800) 424-1616
Washington, DC 20208 (202) 626-9854

This office is staffed with statisticians and education information specialists who

Be patient. If any phone number is incorrect, call (area code) 555-1212 and request the new listing.

can answer your questions about education statistics, research, technology, and practice, particularly as they related to programs in OERI. Information Services sells education data on tape and runs special tabulations against OERI databases. A free pamphlet, *America's Education Fact Finder: Office of Educational Research and Improvement*, lists important phone numbers and describes the major areas of OERI services.

* Technology in Education

Center for Technology in Education
Bank St. College of Education
610 West 112th St.
New York, NY 10025 (212) 663-7200

Major research areas include integrating technology into learning and instruction; assessing learning; linking reform and restructuring to learning and technology; and adapting and designing advanced technologies.

Be patient. If any phone number is incorrect, call (area code) 555-1212 and request the new listing.

Education

Money for Teachers and Schools

Grants from the federal government are available not only to educators and faculty, but to universities and other educational institutions. In addition to the money programs identified here for medical school and other fields, more grants are listed in the Careers and Workplace Chapter. The information is taken from the *Catalog of Federal Domestic Assistance* which is published by the U.S. Government Printing Office in Washington, DC. The number next to the title description is the official reference number listed in this catalog. Contact the office listed below the title for details.

* Post-Baccalaureate Facility Fellowships (Faculty Fellowships) 13.147
Anastasia Buchanan, Division of Nursing
Health Resources and Services Administration, PHS
Room 5C-13, 5600 Fishers Lane
Rockville, MD 20857 (301) 443-5763
To provide grants to eligible schools of nursing to: investigate cost-effective alternatives to traditional health care modalities; examine nursing interventions that result in positive outcomes in health status; address other areas of nursing practice. Types of assistance: grants. Estimate of annual funds available: $ 1,079,000.

* Grants for Two Year Programs of Schools of Medicine or Osteopathy (Two Year Schools) 13.149
Dr. Donald Weaver, Director, Division of Medicine
Health Resources and Services Administration, PHS
Room 4C-25, 5600 Fishers Lane
Rockville, MD 20857 (301) 443-6190
To maintain and improve schools which provide the first or last two years of education leading to the degree of Doctor of Medicine or Osteopathy. Types of assistance: grants. Estimate of annual funds available: $ 211,600.

* Grants for Faculty Training Projects in Geriatric Medicine and Dentistry (Geriatric Fellowships) 13.156
Dr. Donald Weaver, Director, Division of Medicine
Health Resources and Services Administration, PHS
Room 4C-25, 5600 Fishers Lane
Rockville, MD 20857 (301) 443-6190
To assist in the operation of postdoctoral training preparing current and future faculty for leadership roles in geriatric medicine and dentistry. Types of assistance: grants. Estimate of annual funds available: $ 3,491,000.

* Excellence in Minority Health Education and Care (Centers for Excellence) 13.157
Grants Management Officer
Health Resources and Services Administration
Room 8C-22, 5600 Fishers Lane
Rockville, MD 20857 (301) 443-2100
To strengthen the national capacity to train minority students in the health professions; and to support the health professions schools which have trained a significant number of the nation's minority health professionals. Types of assistance: grants. Estimate of annual funds available: $ 9,459,000.

* Capitation Grants for Schools of Public Health (Capitation Grants) 13.339
John R. Westcott, Grants Management Officer
Health Resources and Services Administration
5600 Fishers Lane, Room 8C-22
Rockville, MD 20857 (301) 443-6880
To provide financial assistance to accredited schools of public health which meed requirements for sustaining total full-time equivalent student enrollment levels. Types of assistance: grants. Estimate of annual funds available: $ 4,698,000.

* Nurse Training Improvement - Special Projects (Special Projects, Grants and Contracts for Improvement in Nurse Training) 13.359
Dr. Mary Hill
Division of Nursing
Health Resources and Services Administration
Public Health Service
5600 Fishers Lane
Rockville, MD 20857 (301) 443-6193
To help schools of nursing and other institutions improve the quality and availability of nursing education through projects for specified purposes such as providing continuing education for nurses, demonstrating improved geriatric training, increasing nursing personnel in rural areas. Types of assistance: grants. Estimate of annual funds available: $ 11,970,000.

* Minority Biomedical Research Support (MBRS) 13.375
Director, Minority Biomedical Research Support
Program Branch
Division of Research Resources
National Institutes of Health
Bethesda, MD 20892 (301) 496-6745
To address the lack of representation of minorities in biomedical research by increasing the pool of minorities pursing research careers. Types of assistance: grants. Estimate of annual funds available: $ 28,147,000.

* Cancer Research Manpower 13.398
Dr. Vincent J. Cairoli, Chief
Cancer Training Branch
Division of Cancer Prevention and Control
National Cancer Institute EPN/232B
Bethesda, MD 20892 (301) 496-8580
To make available support for nonprofit institutions interested in providing biomedical training opportunities for individuals interested in careers in basic and clinical research to support important areas of the National Cancer Program. Types of assistance: grants. Estimate of annual funds available: $ 41,781,000.

* Administration on Developmental Disabilities - University Affiliated Programs 13.632
Program Development Division
Office of Human Development Services
U.S. Department of Health and Human Services
Washington, DC 20201 (301) 245-1961
To defray the cost of administration and operation of programs that provide interdisciplinary training for personnel concerned with developmental disabilities. Types of assistance: grants. Estimate of annual funds available: $ 12,570,000.

* Child Welfare Services Training Grants 13.648
Director, Program Support Division
Children's Bureau
Administration for Children, Youth, and Families
P.O. Box 1182
Washington, DC 20013 (202) 755-7820

Be patient. If any phone number is incorrect, call (area code) 555-1212 and request the new listing.

Money For Teachers and Schools

To develop and maintain an adequate supply of qualified and trained personnel for the field of services to children and their families, and to improve educational programs and resources for preparing personnel for this field. Types of assistance: grants. Estimate of annual funds available: $ 3,696,000.

* Special Programs for the Aging - Title IV - Training Research and Discretionary Projects and Programs 13.668

Mike Suzuki, Associate Commissioner
Office of Program Development
Administration on Aging
U.S.Department of Health and Human Services
Washington, DC 2021 (202) 245-0442

To provide adequately trained personnel in the field of aging, improve knowledge of the problems and needs of the elderly, and to demonstrate better ways of improving the quality of life for elderly. Types of assistance: grants. Estimate of annual funds available: $ 24,173,000.

* Health Careers Opportunity Program 13.822

Grants Management Officer
Health Resources and Services Administration
Room 8C-22
5600 Fishers Lane
Rockville, MD 20857 (301) 443-6857

To identify, recruit, and select individuals from disadvantaged backgrounds for education and training in a health or allied health professions school. Types of assistance: grants. Estimate of annual funds available: $ 18,692,037.

* Area Health Education Centers (AHEC) 13.824

Dr. Donald Weaver, Director
Division of Medicine HRSA
Public Health Service
5600 Fishers Lane
Rockville, MD 20857 (301) 443-6190

To improve the distribution, supply, quality, utilization, and efficiency of health personnel in the health service delivery system and for the purpose of increasing the regionalization of educational responsibilities of health professions schools. Types of assistance: grants. Estimate of annual funds available: $ 12,527,000.

* Medical Library Assistance 13.879

Dr. Jeanne Brand, Extramural Programs
National Library of Medicine
Bethesda, MD 20894 (301) 496-6131

To improve health information services by providing funds to train professional personnel, strengthen library and information services, support biomedical publication, and conduct research in information science and in medical information. Types of assistance: grants. Estimate of annual funds available: $ 13,551,000.

* Minority Access to Research Careers (MARC) 13.880

Edward Blynum, Program Director (MARC Program)
National Institute of General Medical Sciences
National Institutes of Health
Bethesda, MD 20892 (301) 496-7941

To assist minority institutions to train greater numbers of scientist and teachers in health related fields. Types of assistance: grants. Estimate of annual funds available: $ 9,053,000.

* Grants for Physician Assistant Training Program (Physical Assistant Training Program) 13.886

Dr.Donald Weaver, Director, Division of Medicine
Bureau of Health Professions, HRSA, PHS, DHHS
Parklawn Bldg., Room 4C-25
5600 Fishers Lane
Rockville, MD 20857 (301) 443-6190

To enable public or nonprofit private health or educational entities to meet the cost of projects to plan, develop and operate programs for the training of physicians assistants. Types of assistance: grants. Estimate of annual funds available: $ 452,000.

* Resource and Manpower Development in the Environmental Health Sciences (Core Centers and Research Training Program) 13.894

Director
Division of Extramural Research and Training
National Institute of Environmental Health Sciences
P.O. Box 12233
Research Triangle Park, NC 27709 (919) 541-7723

To provide long-term, stable support for broadly based multidisciplinary research and training on environmental health problems in Environmental Health Sciences Center. Types of assistance: grants. Estimate of annual funds available: $ 25,303,000.

* Grants for Faculty Development in Family Medicine 13.895

Dr. Donald Weaver, Director
Division of Medicine, HRSA, PHS
Room 4C-25, 5600 Fishers Lane
Rockville, MD 20857 (301) 443-6190

To increase the supply of physician faculty available to teach in family medicine programs and to enhance the pedagogical skills of faculty presently teaching in family medicine. Types of assistance: grants. Estimate of annual funds available: $ 4,757,000.

* Residency Training and Advanced Education in the General Practice of Dentistry 13.897

Richard G. Weaver, Dental Health Branch
Division of Assoc. and Dental Health Professions
HRSA, PHS, 5600 Fishers Lane
Rockville, MD 20857 (301) 443-6837

To assist schools of dentistry and institutions conducting post-graduate dental training in defraying the costs of projects to plan, develop, and operate an approved residency or advanced educational program in the general practice of dentistry. Types of assistance: grants. Estimate of annual funds available: $ 1,691,000.

* National Health Promotion 13.900

Deputy Director
Office of Disease Prevention and Health Promotion
U.S. Department of Health and Human Services
Room 2132, 330 C Street, SW
Washington, DC 20201 (202) 245-7611

To engage national membership organizations from various sectors as a means of expanding and coordinating health promotion efforts. Types of assistance: grants. Estimate of annual funds available: $ 363,080.

* Grants for Faculty Development in General Internal Medicine and/or General Pediatrics (GIM/GP Faculty Development) 13.900

Dr. Donald Weaver, Director
Division of Medicine, HRSA, PHS
Room 4C-25, 5600 Fishers Lane
Rockville, MD 20857 (301) 443-6190

To promote the development of faculty skills in physicians (full-time, part-time, volunteer, fellows and/or residents) who are currently teaching or who plan teaching careers in general internal medicine and/or general pediatrics training programs. Types of assistance: grants. Estimate of annual funds available: $ 3,633,703.

* Grants for the Training of Health Professions in Geriatrics 13.969

Mr. William Koenig
HRSA, PHS
U.S. Department of Health and Human Services
5600 Fishers Lane
Rockville, MD 20857 (301) 443-6887

To develop regional resource centers focused on strengthening multidisciplinary training of health professionals in geriatric health care. Types of assistance: grants. Estimate of annual funds available: $ 9,382,000.

Be patient. If any phone number is incorrect, call (area code) 555-1212 and request the new listing.

Education

* **Health Professions Recruitment Program for Indians (Recruitment Program) 13.970**
Division of Grants and Contracts
Grants Management Branch
Indian Health Service
PHS, DHHS
Room 6A-33, 5600 Fishers Lane
Rockville, MD 20857 (301) 443-5204
To identify Indians with a potential for education or training in the health professions and to encourage and assist them to enroll in health or allied health professional schools. Types of assistance: grants. Estimate of annual funds available: $ 600,000.

* **Grants for Establishment of Departments of Family Medicine (Family Medicine Departments) 13.984**
Dr. Donald Weaver, Director
Division of Medicine
BHPR, HRSA, PHS
Room 4C-25, 5600 Fishers Lane
Rockville, MD 20857 (301) 443-6190
To assist in establishing, maintaining or improving family medicine academic administrative units to provide clinical instruction in family medicine in order that these units are comparable in status, faculty and curriculum to those other clinical units at the applying school. Types of assistance: grants. Estimate of annual funds available: $ 2,235,000.

* **Airway Science (AWS) 20.107**
Office of Training and Higher Education, ANT 30
Federal Aviation Administration
400 7th St., SW, Plaza Room PL-10
Washington, DC 20591 (202) 366-7003
To assist recognized colleges and/or universities in the need for facilities and equipment for Airway Science (AWS) curriculum students. Types of assistance: grants. Estimate of annual funds available: $ 1,000,000.

* **State Marine Schools 20.806**
Bruce J. Carlton, Director
Office of Maritime Labor and Training
Maritime Administration
U.S. Department of Transportation
Washington, DC 20590 (202) 366-5755
To train merchant marine officers in state marine schools. Types of assistance: direct payments. Estimate of annual funds available: $ 27,576,000.

* **Promotion of the Arts - Arts in Education 45.003**
Dr. Warren Newman
Arts in Education Program
Room 602, National Endowment for the Arts
The Nancy Hanks Center
1100 Penn. Ave., NW
Washington, DC 20506 (202) 682-5797
To encourage state and local arts agencies to develop long-term strategies in assisting appropriate state and local education authorities to establish the arts as basic in education. Types of assistance: grants. Estimate of annual funds available: $ 5,600,000.

* **Promotion of the Humanities - Summer Seminars for College Teachers 45.116**
Summer Seminars for College Teachers
Division of Fellowships and Seminars
National Endowment for the Humanities, Room 316
Washington, DC 20506 (202) 786-0463
To provide opportunities for teachers in five, four, and two-year colleges; for scholars employed in libraries, museums, historical associations, and other humanities institution to work during the summer in their areas of interest under the direction of distinguished scholars at institutions with library resources suitable for advanced study and research. Types of assistance: grants. Estimate of annual funds available: $ 3,780,000.

* **Promotion of the Humanities - Summer Stipends 45.121**
Division of Fellowships and Seminars
Summer Stipends
National Endowment for the Humanities, Room 316
Washington, DC 20506 (202) 786-0466
To provide support for individual faculty and staff members at universities and two-year and four-year colleges and for others who have made or have demonstrated promise of making significant contributions to the humanities. Types of assistance: grants. Estimate of annual funds available: $ 800,000.

* **Promotion of the Humanities-Elementary and Secondary Education in the Humanities 45.127**
Elementary and Secondary Education in the Humanities
National Endowment for the Humanities
Room 302
Washington, DC 20506 (202) 786-0377
To increase the effectiveness of humanities teaching in our nation's elementary, middle, and secondary schools. Types of assistance: grants. Estimate of annual funds available: $ 7,344,000.

* **Promotion of the Humanities-Fellowships for University Teachers 45.142**
Fellowships for University Teachers
Division of Fellowships and Seminars
National Endowment for the Humanities, Room 316
Washington, DC 20506 (202) 786-0466
To provide time for uninterrupted study and research to university teachers, and faculty members of postgraduate professional schools who can make significant contributions to thought and knowledge in the humanities. Types of assistance: grants. Estimate of annual funds available: $ 3,165,000.

* **Promotion of the Humanities - Fellowships for College Teachers and Independent Scholars 45.143**
Fellowships for College Teachers and Independent Scholars
Division of Fellowships and Seminars, Room 316
National Endowment for the Humanities
Washington, DC 20506 (202) 786-0466
To provide opportunities for college teachers and independent scholars to pursue independent study and research that will enhance their capacities as teachers, scholars, or interpreters of the humanities. Types of assistance: grants. Estimate of annual funds available: $ 3,390,000.

* **Promotion of the Humanities-Reference Materials/Tools 45.145**
Division of Research Programs
Reference Materials/Tools
Room 318
National Endowment for the Humanities
Washington, DC 20506 (202) 786-0358
To fund, wholly or partially projects which create research tools important for scholarly research. Types of assistance: grants. Estimate of annual funds available: $ 2,615,000.

* **Promotion of the Humanities-Higher Education in the Humanities 45.150**
Higher Education in the Humanities
National Endowment for the Humanities, Room 302
Washington, DC 20506 (202) 786-0380
To assist institutions of higher education in their efforts to improve the teaching of the humanities. Types of assistance: grants. Estimate of annual funds available: $ 7,344,000.

* **Promotion of the Humanities-Summer Seminars for School Teachers 45.151**
Summer Seminars for School Teachers
Division of Fellowships and Seminars
National Endowment for the Humanities, Room 316
Washington, DC 20506 (202) 786-0463

Be patient. If any phone number is incorrect, call (area code) 555-1212 and request the new listing.

Money For Teachers and Schools

To provide opportunities for school teachers to work during the summer under the direction of a distinguished teacher and active scholar at colleges and universities throughout the country, studying seminal works in the humanities in a systematic and thorough way. Types of assistance: grants. Estimate of annual funds available: $ 3,725,000.

* Promotion of the Humanities - Travel to Collections (Travel to Collections) 45.152

Division of Fellowships and Seminars
Travel to Collections
Room 316
National Endowment for the Humanities
Washington, DC 20506 (202) 786-0463

To advance basic research in the humanities by enabling American scholars to travel to use the research collections of libraries, archives, museums or other research repositories to consult research materials which are of fundamental importance for the progress of scholarly work. Types of assistance: grants. Estimate of annual funds available: $ 300,000.

* NEH/Reader's Digest Teacher Scholar Program 45.154

Elementary and Secondary Education in the Humanities
National Endowment for the Humanities
Room 302
Washington, DC 20506 (202) 786-0377

To increase the effectiveness of humanities teaching in our nation's elementary, middle, and secondary schools. Types of assistance: grants. Estimate of annual funds available: $ 1,500,000.

* Teacher Preparation and Enhancement 47.066

Division of Teacher Preparation and Enhancement
National Science Foundation
1800 G. St., NW
Washington, DC 20550 (202) 573-7073

To attract highly talented men and women to elementary, middle/junior high and secondary school science and mathematics teaching careers, to improve preservice teacher preparation programs to develop teachers capabilities in these critical areas. Types of assistance: grants. Estimate of annual funds available: $ 63,525,000.

* Materials Development, Research, and Informal Science Education 47.067

Materials Development, Research, and Informal
Science Education
National Science Foundation
1800 G St., NW
Washington, DC 20550 (202) 357-7452

To expand the knowledge base and to provide new and improved models and materials resources needed to increase the quality of and continuously renew, the Nation's precollege education system in mathematics, science and technology. Types of assistance: grants. Estimate of annual funds available: $ 44,002,000.

* Studies and Program Assessment 47.068

Office of Studies and Program Assessment
National Science Foundation
1800 G. St., NW
Washington, DC 20500 (202) 357-7425

To serve a major role in policy formulation to improve and strengthen science and engineering education in the U.S. and to provide support for leadership efforts of the Foundation in science in engineering education activities. Types of assistance: grants. Estimate of annual funds available: $ 4,500,000.

* Research Initiation and Improvement 47.069

Division of Research Initiation and Improvement
National Science Foundation
1800 G St., NW
Washington, DC 20550 (202) 357-7552

Types of assistance: grants. Estimate of annual funds available: $ 23,043,000.

* Undergraduate Science, Engineering and Mathematics Education 47.071

Division of Undergraduate Science
Engineering and Mathematics Education
National Science Foundation
Room 6739
2800 G. St., NW
Washington, DC 20500 (202) 357-7051

To assist college and universities to achieve and maintain strong, high quality undergraduate science, engineering and mathematics instructional programs for all of their students. Types of assistance: grants. Estimate of annual funds available: $ 28,000,000.

* Air Pollution Control Manpower Training 66.003

Environmental Protection Agency
Grants Administration Division, PM 216
Washington, DC 20460

To develop career-oriented personnel qualified to work in pollution abatement and control. Types of assistance: grants. Estimate of annual funds available: $ 400,000.

* Air Pollution Control - Technical Training 66.006

Betsy Dodson
Air Pollution Training Institute, EPA
Research Triangle Park, NC 27711 (919) 541-2401

To provide technical training to personnel from state and local air pollution control agencies. Types of assistance: training. Estimate of annual funds available: $ 241,000.

* National Gallery of Art Extension Services 68.001

Department of Extension Programs
National Gallery of Art
Washington, DC 20565 (202) 737-4215

To provide educational material on the Gallery's collections and exhibitions free of charge except for transportation costs, to schools, colleges, and libraries across the Nation. Types of assistance: other. Estimate of annual funds available: $ 698,000.

* University-Laboratory Cooperative Program 81.004

Larry L. Barker
Division of University and Industry Programs
Office of Energy Research, DOE
Washington, DC 20585 (202) 586-8947

To provide college and university science and engineering faculty and students with energy-related training and research experience in areas of energy research at DOE facilities. Types of assistance: grants, other. Estimate of annual funds available: $ 8,000,000.

* Energy Policy, Planning and Development 81.080

Stephen F. Durbin
Resource Management Office
Policy Planning and Analysis
Forrestal Bldg., 1000 Independence Ave., SW
Washington, DC 20585 (202) 586-5325

To provide financial assistance for gathering outside experts for seminars, conferences and work groups to discuss specific energy policy issues and write recommendations and reports. Types of assistance: grants. Estimate of annual funds available: $ 150,000.

* Minority Educational Institution Research Travel Fund (MIRT) 81.083

Isiah O. Sewell
Office of Minority Economic Impact MI-2.2, DOE
Forrestal Bldg., Rm 5B-110
Washington, DC 20585 (202) 586-1953

To provide travel funds to faculty members and graduate students of minority postsecondary educational institutions to encourage and assist in initiating and improving energy related research. Types of assistance: direct payments. Estimate of annual funds available: $ 50,000.

Be patient. If any phone number is incorrect, call (area code) 555-1212 and request the new listing.

Education

* **Minority Educational Institution Assistance 81.094**
Isiah O. Sewell
Office of Minority Economic Impact, DOE
1000 Independence Ave., SW
Washington, DC 20585 (202) 586-1593
Types of assistance: grants. Estimate of annual funds available: $ 1,000,000.

* **Educational Exchange - University Lecturers (Professors) and Research Scholars (Fulbright-Hays Program) 82.002**
Council for International Exchange of Scholars
11 Dupont Circle, Suite 300
Washington, DC 20036
To improve and strengthen the international relations of the U.S. by promoting mutual understanding among the peoples of the world through educational exchanges. Types of assistance: grants. Estimate of annual funds available: $ 20,138,170.

* **Adult Education-State Administered Basic Grant Program 84.002**
D. Kay Wright
Division of Adult Education
Office of Assistant Secretary for Vocational and Adult Education
U.S. Department of Education
Washington, DC 20202-7320 (202) 732-2270
To improve educational opportunities for adults and to encourage the establishment of adult education programs. Types of assistance: grants. Estimate of annual funds available: $ 136,344,000.

* **Bilingual Education 84.003**
Rudolph Munis
Office of Bilingual Education and Minority Languages Affairs
U.S. Department of Education
330 C St., SW, Room 1086
Washington, DC 20202 (202) 732-5700
To develop and carry out programs of bilingual education in elementary and secondary schools. Types of assistance: grant, direct payments. Estimate of annual funds available: $151,946,000.

* **Civil Rights Technical Assistance and Training 84.004**
Division of Discretionary Grants
Steven L. Brockhouse
Office of Elementary and Secondary Education
400 Maryland Ave., SW
Washington, DC 20202-6438. (202) 732-4360
To provide technical assistance and training services to school districts to cope with educational problems occasioned by discrimination from race, sex, and national origin. Types of assistance: grants. Estimate of annual funds available: $ 23,443,000.

* **Education of Handicapped Children in State-Operated or Supported Schools (Chapter 1, ESEA Handicapped) 84.009**
Division of Assistance to States
Office of the Asst. Secretary for Special Education and Rehabilitative Services
U.S. Department of Education
Washington, DC 20202 (202) 732-1025
To extend and improve comprehensive educational programs for handicapped children enrolled in state-operated or state-supported schools. Types of assistance: grants. Estimate of annual funds available: $ 148,200,000.

* **Educationally Deprived Children - Local Educational Agencies (Chapter 1, of Title I, ESEA) 84.010**
Compensatory Education Programs
Office of Elementary and Secondary Education

U.S. Department of Education
400 Maryland Ave., SW, Room 2043
Washington, DC 20202 (202) 732-4682
To provide financial assistance to local educational agencies to meet the special needs of educationally deprived children selected in accordance with Section 1014 of Chapter 1. Types of assistance: grants. Estimate of annual funds available: $4,026,100,000.

* **Migrant Education-Basic State Formula Grant Program (State Migrant Education Program) 84.011**
Office of Migrant Education
Office of Elementary and Secondary Education
U.S. Department of Education
400 Maryland Ave., SW
Washington, DC 20202 (202) 732-4746
To establish and improve programs to meet the special educational needs of migratory children of migratory agricultural workers or migratory fishers. Types of assistance: grants. Estimate of annual funds available: $ 263,436,000.

* **Educationally Deprived Children - State Administration (Chapter 1, ESEA; State Administration) 84.012**
Compensatory Education Programs
Office of Elementary and Secondary Education
U.S. Department of Education
400 Maryland Ave. SW, Room 2043
Washington, DC 20202 (202) 732-4682
To provide financial assistance to enable state educational agencies to meet their administrative responsibilities under the Chapter 1 program. Types of assistance: grants. Estimate of annual funds available: $ 40,508,000.

* **Neglected and Delinquent Children (Chapter 1 ESEA; Neglected and Delinquent) 84.013**
Compensatory Education Programs
Office of Elementary and Secondary Education
U.S. Department of Education
400 Maryland Ave., SW, Room 2043
Washington, DC 20202 (202) 732-4682
To provide financial assistance to State agencies to meet the special needs of institutionalized neglected or delinquent children and children in community day programs for whom they have an educational responsibility. Types of assistance: grants. Estimate of annual funds available: $ 31,616,000.

* **Follow Through 84.014**
Compensatory Education Programs
Office of Elementary and Secondary Education
U.S. Department of Education
400 Maryland Ave., SW, Room 2043
Washington, DC 20202 (202) 732-4682
To sustain and augment in primary grades the gains that children from low income families make in Head Start and other quality preschool programs. Types of assistance: grants. Estimate of annual funds available: $ 7,262,000.

* **National Resource Centers and Fellowships Program for Language and Area or Language and International Studies 84.015**
Joseph F. Belmonte
Advanced Training and Research Branch
Center for International Education
7th and D St., SW
Washington, DC 20202 (202) 732-3283
To promote instruction in those modern foreign languages area and international studies critical to national needs by supporting the establishment, strengthening and operation of such programs at colleges and universities. Types of assistance: grants. Estimate of annual funds available: $ 11,234,000.

* **Undergraduate International Studies and Foreign Language Programs 84.016**
International Studies Branch

Be patient. If any phone number is incorrect, call (area code) 555-1212 and request the new listing.

Money For Teachers and Schools

Center for International Education
Office of Postsecondary Education
U.S. Department of Education
7 and S St., SW
Washington, DC 20220 (202) 732-3290
The Undergraduate International Studies and Foreign Language program issues awards to institutions of higher education and public and nonprofit private agencies and organizations. Types of assistance: grants. Estimate of annual funds available: $ 2,725,000.

* International Research and Studies (HEA Title VI Research and Studies) 84.017

Division of Advanced Training and Research
International Education Programs
U.S. Department of Education
7 and D St., SW
Washington, DC 20202 (202) 732-3297
To improve foreign language and area studies training through support of research and studies, experimentation and development of specialized instructional materials. Types of assistance: grants. Estimate of annual funds available: $ 1,480,000.

* Fulbright-Hays Seminars Abroad - Special Bilateral Projects (Fulbright Exchange) 84.018

International Studies Branch
Center for International Education
U.S. Department of Education
Room 3053
7 and D Sts., SW
Washington, DC 20202 (202) 732-3292
To increase mutual understanding and knowledge between the people of the U.S. and those in other countries by offering qualified U.S. educators opportunities to participate in short-term study seminars. Types of assistance: grants. Estimate of annual funds available: $ 775,000.

* Fulbright-Hays Training Grants - Faculty Research Abroad 84.019

Merian Kane
Center for International Education
U.S. Department of Education
Room 3053, 7 and D Sts.
Washington, DC 20202 (202) 732-3301
To help universities and colleges strengthen their language and area studies programs by enabling faculty members to conduct research abroad in order to improve their skill in languages. Types of assistance: grants. Estimate of annual funds available: $ 692,000.

* Fulbright-Hays Training Grants - Group Projects Abroad 84.021

Office of Asst Secretary for Postsecondary Education
U.S. Department of Education
7 and D Sts., SW
Washington, DC 20202 (202) 732-3294
To help educational institutions improve their programs in modern foreign language and area studies. Types of assistance: grants. Estimate of annual funds available: $ 2,013,000.

* Handicapped-Innovation and Development (Research in Education for the Handicapped) 84.023

Division of Innovation and Development
Office of Asst. Secretary for Special Education and
Rehabilitative Services
U.S. Department of Education
400 Maryland Ave., SW
Washington, DC 20202 (202) 205-8156
To improve the education of handicapped children through research and development projects and model programs (demonstrations). Types of assistance: grants. Estimate of annual funds available: $ 17,026,000.

* Handicapped Early Childhood Education (Early Education Program) 84.024

Nancy Safer
Division of Educational Services
Special Education Programs
U.S. Department of Education
400 Maryland Ave., SW
Washington, DC 20202 (202) 732-1109
To support demonstrations, dissemination and implementation of effective approaches to preschool and early childhood education handicapped children. Types of assistance: grants. Estimate of annual funds available: $ 23,147,000.

* Handicapped Education-Deaf-Blind Centers (Services for Deaf-Blind Children and Youth) 84.025

Nancy Safer
Division of Educational Services
Special Education Service
U.S. Department of Education
400 Maryland Ave., SW
Washington, DC 20202 (202) 723-1109
To provide technical assistance to state education agencies and to improve services to deaf-blind children and youth. Types of assistance: grants. Estimate of annual funds available: $ 14,189,000.

* Handicapped Media Services and Captioned Films (Media Materials; Technology for the Handicapped) 84.026

Nancy Safer
Division of Educational Services
Special Education Programs
U.S. Department of Education
Washington, DC 20202 (202) 732-1109
To maintain a free loan service of captioned films for the deaf and instruction media for the educational, cultural, and vocational enrichment of the handicapped. Types of assistance: direct payments. Estimate of annual funds available: $ 13,403,000.

* Handicapped-State Grants (Part B, Education of the Handicapped Act) 84.027

Division of Assistance to States
Office of Special Education
U.S. Department of Education
400 Maryland Ave., SW
Washington, DC 20202 (202) 732-1025
To provide grants to states to assist them in providing a free appropriate public education to all handicapped children. Types of assistance: grants. Estimate of annual funds available: $1,475,449,000.

* Handicapped Regional Resource and Federal Centers 84.028

Mary Gardner
Division of Assistance to States
Office of Special Education
U.S. Department of Education
400 Maryland Ave., SW
Washington, DC 20202 (202) 732-1026
To establish regional resource centers which provide advice and technical services to educators for improving education of handicapped children. Types of assistance: grants. Estimate of annual funds available: $ 6,338,000.

* Handicapped Education-Special Education Personnel Development (Training Personnel for the Education of the Handicapped) 84.029

Norm How
Division of Personnel Preparation
Special Education Programs
U.S. Department of Education
Washington, DC 20202 (202) 732-1070
To address identified shortages of special education teachers and related service

Be patient. If any phone number is incorrect, call (area code) 555-1212 and request the new listing.

Education

personnel. Types of assistance: grants. Estimate of annual funds available: $ 67,095,000.

* Clearinghouses for the Handicapped Program 84.030

Division of Educational Services
Office of Asst. Secretary for Special Education
and Rehabilitative Services
U.S. Department of Education
400 Maryland Ave, SW
Washington, DC 20202 (202) 205-5809

To disseminate information regarding education programs and services for handicapped children. Types of assistance: grants. Estimate of annual funds available: $ 1,135,000.

* Higher Education-Institutional Aid Special Needs Program 84.031

Institutional Aid Programs
Office of Postsecondary Education
U.S. Department of Education
400 Maryland Ave., SW
Washington, DC 20202 (202) 732-3308

To help eligible colleges and universities to strengthen their management and fiscal operations. Types of assistance: grants. Estimate of annual funds available: $ 77,459,000.

* Library Services (LSCA-Title I) 84.034

Robert Klaassen
Public Library Support Staff
Library Programs
U.S. Department of Education
Washington, DC 20208 (202) 357-6303

To assist in extending public library services to areas without service or with inadequate service. Types of assistance: grants. Estimate of annual funds available: $ 79,388,820.

* Interlibrary Cooperation and Resource Sharing (LSCA-Title III) 84.035

Robert Klaassen
Public Library Support Staff
Library Programs
Office of Educational Research and Improvement
U.S. Department of Education
Washington, DC 20208 (202) 357-6303

To plan and take steps leading to the development of cooperative networks. Types of assistance: grants. Estimate of annual funds available: $ 18,719,960.

* Library Career Training (HEA Title II-B) 84.036

Yvonne Carter
Library Development Staff, Library Programs
U.S. Department of Education
55 New Jersey Avenue, NW
Washington, DC 20208 (202) 357-6320

To assist institutions of higher education and library organizations and agencies in training or retraining persons in areas of library specialization where there are shortages. Types of assistance: grants. Estimate of annual funds available: $ 400,000.

* Library Research and Demonstration (HEA Title II-B) 84.039

Yvonne Carter
Library Development Staff
U.S. Department of Education
55 New Jersey Ave., NW
Washington, DC 20208-1430 (202) 357-6320

To award grants and contracts for research and/or demonstration projects in areas of specialized services intended to improve library and information science practices. Types of assistance: grants. Estimate of annual funds available: $ 308,000.

* Student Support Services 84.042

Division of Student Services
Office of Postsecondary Education
U.S. Department of Education
400 Maryland Ave., SW
Washington, DC 20202 (202) 732-4804

To provide supportive services to disadvantaged college students to enhance their potential for successfully completing the postsecondary education program in which they are enrolled. Types of assistance: grants. Estimate of annual funds available: $ 86,599,000.

* Vocational Education-Basic Grants to States 84.048

Division of Vocational Education
Winifred I. Warnat
U.S. Department of Education
400 Maryland Ave., SW
Washington, DC 20202 (202) 732-2441

To assist states in expanding, improving, modernizing, and developing quality vocational education programs. Types of assistance: grants. Estimate of annual funds available: $715,600,000.

* Vocational Education - Consumer and Homemaking Education 84.049

Winifred I. Warnat
Director, Division of Vocational Education
U.S. Department of Education
400 Maryland Ave., SW
Washington, DC 20202 (202) 732-2441

To assist states in conducting programs in consumer and homemaking education. Types of assistance: grants. Estimate of annual funds available: $ 33,118,000.

* National Vocational Education Research 84.051

Glenn C. Boerrigter
U.S. Department of Education
Division of National Programs
400 Maryland Ave., SW
Washington, DC 20202 (202) 732-2367

To provide support for the National Center for Research in Vocational Education and six curriculum coordination centers and special research projects. Types of assistance: grants. Estimate of annual funds available: $ 7,102,963.

* Higher Education-Cooperative Education (Cooperative Education Program) 84.055

Division of Higher Education Incentive Programs
Office of Postsecondary Education
U.S. Department of Education
Washington, DC 20202 (202) 732-4861

To provide federal support for planning, establishing, expanding, and carrying out projects of cooperative education in institutions of higher education. Types of assistance: grants. Estimate of annual funds available: $ 13,622,000.

* Indian Education-Special Programs and Projects (Indian Education Act-Subpart 2) 84.061

Indian Education Programs
Office of Elementary and Secondary Education
U.S. Department of Education
400 Maryland Ave., SW
Washington, DC 20202 (202) 732-1887

To plan, develop and implement programs and projects for the improvement of educational opportunities for Indian children, to prepare and improve the qualifications of persons serving Indian students in educational personnel positions. Types of assistance: grants. Estimate of annual funds available: $ 12,307,000.

* Indian Education-Adult Indian Education (Indian Education Act-Subpart 3) 84.062

Indian Education Programs
Office of Elementary and Secondary Education

Be patient. If any phone number is incorrect, call (area code) 555-1212 and request the new listing.

Money For Teachers and Schools

U.S. Department of Education
400 Maryland Ave., SW
Washington, DC 20202 (202) 732-1887

To plan develop and implement programs for Indian adults to decrease the rate of illiteracy, increase the mastery of basic skills, and increase the number who earn high school equivalency diplomas. Types of assistance: grants. Estimate of annual funds available: $ 4,000,000.

* Higher Education-Veterans Education Outreach Program (VEOP) 84.064

Neil McArthur, Division of Higher Education Incentive Programs
Office of Postsecondary Education
U.S. Department of Education
400 Maryland Ave., SW
Washington, DC 20202 (202) 732-4406

To encourage colleges and universities to service the special needs of veterans, especially the physically disabled or educationally disadvantaged veterans. Types of assistance: direct payments. Estimate of annual funds available: $ 2,838,000.

* Educational Opportunity Centers 84.066

Division of Student Services
Education Outreach Branch, U.S. Department of Education
400 Maryland Ave., SW
Washington, DC 20202 (202) 732-4804

To provide information on financial and academic assistance available for qualified adults desiring to pursue a program of postsecondary education, and to assist them in applying for admission to institution of postsecondary education. Types of assistance: grants. Estimate of annual funds available: $ 11,665,000.

* Indian Education-Grants to Indian Controlled Schools (Indian Education-Part A Set-Aside, NonLEAs) 84.072

Indian Education Programs, U.S. Department of Education
Office of Elementary and Secondary Education
400 Maryland Ave., SW
Washington, DC 20202 (202) 732-1887

To provide financial assistance to Indian controlled schools to develop and implement elementary and secondary school programs designed to meet the special educational needs of Indian children. Types of assistance: grants. Estimate of annual funds available: $ 3,500,000.

* National Diffusion Network (NDN: National Diffusion Network) 84.073

Lee Wickline
National Diffusion Network, Recognition Division
55 New Jersey Ave., NW
Washington, DC 20208 (202) 357-6134

To promote and accelerate the systematic, rapid dissemination and adopting by public and nonpublic educational institutions nationwide. Types of assistance: grants. Estimate of annual funds available: $ 11,066,000.

* Postsecondary Education Programs for Handicapped Persons (Postsecondary Programs) 84.078

Joseph Rosenstein, Division of Educational Services
Special Education Programs
U.S. Department of Education
400 Maryland Ave., SW
Washington, DC 20202 (202) 732-1176

To develop and operate specially designed model programs of vocational, technical, postsecondary or adult education for deaf or other handicapped persons. Types of assistance: grants. Estimate of annual funds available: $ 5,770,000.

* Women's Educational Equity (Women's Educational Equity Act Program) 84.083

Director, Division of Discretionary Grants
Office of Elementary and Secondary Education
U.S. Department of Education
400 Maryland Ave., SW

Washington, DC 20202 (202) 732-4351

To promote educational equity for women and girls at all levels of education and to provide financial assistance to local educational institutions to help them meet the requirements of Title IX. Types of assistance: grants. Estimate of annual funds available: $ 2,949,000.

* Handicapped Education-Severely Handicapped Program (Programs for Severely Handicapped Children and Youth) 84.086

Nancy Safer, Division of Educational Services
U.S. Department of Education
400 Maryland Ave., SW
Washington, DC 20202 (202) 732-1109

To improve and expand innovative educational/training services for severely handicapped children and youth. Types of assistance: grants. Estimate of annual funds available: $ 5,297,000.

* Strengthening Research Library Resources (HEA Title II-C) 84.091

Louise Sutherland, Library Development Staff
Library Programs
U.S. Department of Education
Washington, DC 20208-5571 (202) 357-6322

To promote research and education of high quality throughout the U.S. by providing financial assistance. Types of assistance: grants. Estimate of annual funds available: $ 5,675,000.

* Bilingual Vocational Instructor Training 84.099

Division of National Programs
Office of Vocational and Adult Education
U.S. Department of Education
400 Maryland Ave., SW
Washington, DC 20202 (202) 732-2365

To provide training for instructors and other ancillary personnel in bilingual vocational training programs. Types of assistance: grants, direct payments. Estimate of annual funds available: $ 565,650.

* Bilingual Vocational Materials, Methods, and Techniques 84.100

Laura Kar, Division of National Programs
Office of Vocational and Adult Education
U.S. Department of Education
400 Maryland Ave., SW
Washington, DC 20202 (202) 732-2365

To develop instructional materials, methods, techniques, to encourage research programs and demonstration projects and to overcome the shortage of instructional materials available for bilingual vocational training programs. Types of assistance: grants. Estimate of annual funds available: $ 377,100.

* Training for Special Programs Staff and Leadership Personnel 84.103

May Weaver, Division of Student Services
Office of Postsecondary Education
U.S. Department of Education
400 Maryland Ave., SW
Washington, DC 20202 (202) 732-4804

To provide training for staff and leadership personnel employed in, or preparing for employment in, projects funded under the Special Programs for Students from Disadvantaged Backgrounds. Types of assistance: grants. Estimate of annual funds available: $ 1,281,000.

* Fund for the Improvement of Postsecondary Education (FIPSE) 84.116

Fund for the Improvement of Postsecondary Education
Office of the Asst. Secretary for Postsecondary Education
7 and D Sts., SW, Rm 3100
Washington, DC 20202 (202) 732-5750

To provide assistance for innovative programs which improve the access to and

Education

the quality of postsecondary education. Types of assistance: grants. Estimate of annual funds available: $ 11,856,000.

* Educational Research and Development 84.117

U.S. Department of Education
Office of Educational Research and Improvement
55 New Jersey Ave., NW
Washington, DC 20208 (202) 357-6079

To provide grants, contracts and cooperative agreements to individuals and institutions seeking to advance knowledge about education policy and practice. Types of assistance: grants. Estimate of annual funds available: $ 18,794,000.

* Minority Science Improvement (MSIP) 84.120

Argelia Velez-Rodriguez
Division of Higher Education Incentive Programs
U.S. Department of Education
Washington, DC 20202 (202) 732-4396

To assist institutions to improve the quality of preparation of their students for graduate work or careers in science. Types of assistance: grants. Estimate of annual funds available: $ 5,307,000.

* Secretary's Discretionary 84.122

U.S. Department of Education, FIRST
Office of Educational, Research and Improvements
Washington, DC 20202 (202) 357-6496

To assist in research, dissemination, demonstration, improvement of training, and technical assistance activities, which address some national education priority as authorized by Section 583 of the Education Consolidation and Improvement Act. Types of assistance: grants. Estimate of annual funds available: $ 4,691,000.

* Law-Related Education 84.123

School Improvement Programs
Office of Elementary and Secondary Education
400 Maryland Ave., SW
Washington, DC 20202 (202) 732-4357

To support programs at the elementary and secondary school levels by developing and implementing model projects designed to institutionalize law-related. Types of assistance: grants. Estimate of annual funds available: $ 3,952,000.

* Territorial Teacher Training Assistance Program 84.124

Education Networks Division
Program for the Improvement of Practice
U.S. Department of Education
Washington, DC 20208 (202) 357-6616

To provide assistance for the training of teachers in elementary and secondary public and private schools in Guam, etc. Types of assistance: grants. Estimate of annual funds available: $ 1,976,000.

* Rehabilitation Services - Basic Support (Basic Support) 84.126

Office of Program Operations
Rehabilitation Services Administration
U.S. Department of Education
Washington, DC 20202 (202) 732-1406

To provide vocational rehabilitation services to persons with mental and/or physical handicaps. Types of assistance: grants. Estimate of annual funds available: $ 1,437,973,057.

* Rehabilitation Training 84.129

Rehabilitation Services Administration
Office of Special Education and Rehabilitative Services
U.S. Department of Education
Washington, DC 20202 (202) 732-1400

To support projects to increase the numbers and improve the skills of personnel trained in providing vocational rehabilitation services to handicapped individuals in areas targeted as having personnel shortages. Types of assistance: grants. Estimate of annual funds available: $ 30,134,000.

* Migrant Education-High School Equivalency Program (HEP) 84.141

Office of Migrant Education
Office of Elementary and Secondary Education
U.S. Department of Education
400 Maryland Ave., SW
Washington, DC 20202 (202) 732-4746

To assist students who are engaged or who whose families are engaged in migrant and other seasonal farm work to obtain the equivalent of a secondary school diploma. Types of assistance: grants. Estimate of annual funds available: $ 7,410,000.

* Federal State and Local Partnerships for Educational Improvement (Chapter 2, State Block Grants) 84.151

Division of Educational Support
State and Local Educational Programs
Office of Elementary and Secondary Education
U.S. Department of Education
Washington, DC (202) 732-4156

To assist state and local educational agencies to improve elementary and secondary education. Types of assistance: grants. Estimate of annual funds available: $ 462,977,000.

* Business and International Education 84.153

International Studies Branch
Center for International Education
U.S. Department of Education, Room 3053
Washington, DC 20202 (202) 732-3302

To promote innovation and improvement in international business education curricula at institutions of higher education and serve the needs of the business community. Types of assistance: grants. Estimate of annual funds available: $ 2,125,000.

* Secondary Education and Transitional Services for Handicapped Youth 84.158

Division of Educational Services
Office of Special Education Program
400 Maryland Ave., SW
Washington, DC 20202 (202) 732-1109

To strengthen and coordinate education, training, and related services for handicapped youth. Types of assistance: grants. Estimate of annual funds available: $ 7,284,000.

* Training Interpreters for Deaf Individuals 84.160

Office of Special Education and Rehabilitative Services
U.S. Department of Education
Washington, DC 20202 (202) 732-1322

To support projects, increase the numbers and improve the skills of manual and oral interpretors who provide services to deaf individuals. Types of assistance: grants. Estimate of annual funds available: $ 900,000.

* State Grants for Strengthening the Skills of Teachers and Instruction in Mathematics and Science 84.164

Dr. Allen A. Schmieder
Suite 2040
School Improvement Programs
400 Maryland Ave., SW
Washington, DC 20202 (202) 732-4336

To improve the skills of teachers and instruction in the areas of mathematics and science, also to increase the accessibility of such instruction to all students. Types of assistance: grants. Estimate of annual funds available: $ 128,440,000.

* National Programs For Strengthening, Teaching, and Administration in Mathematics and Science Programs 84.168

U.S. Department of Education, FIRST
Office of Educational Research and Improvement
Washington, DC 20208 (202) 357-6496

Be patient. If any phone number is incorrect, call (area code) 555-1212 and request the new listing.

Money For Teachers and Schools

To provide support for projects designed to improve the quality of instruction in mathematics and science. Types of assistance: grants. Estimate of annual funds available: $ 8,892,000.

* Construction, Reconstruction, and Renovation of Academic Facilities (Academic Facilities Program) 84.172

Division of Higher Education Incentive Programs
Office of Postsecondary Education
U.S. Department of Education
Washington, DC 20202 (202) 732-4389
To provide assistance to institutions of postsecondary education in order to construct reconstruct or renovate academic facilities. Types of assistance: grants. Estimate of annual funds available: $ 6,366,000.

* Leadership in Educational Administration Development (LEAD) 84.178

Hunter Moorman
Office of Educational Research and Improvement
U.S. Department of Education
Washington, DC 20208 (202) 357-6116
To provide assistance for eligible parties to establish and operate technical assistance centers that promote the development of leadership skills in school administrators. Types of assistance: grants. Estimate of annual funds available: $ 8,222,000.

* Technology, Educational Media and Materials for the Handicapped (Technical Development) 84.180

Division of Innovation and Development
Office of Assistant Secretary for Special Education
and Rehabilitative Services
U.S. Department of Education
400 Maryland Ave., NW
Washington, DC 20202 (202) 205-8123
To provide contracts, grants, or cooperative agreements for the purpose of advancing the use of new technology. Types of assistance: grants. Estimate of annual funds available: $ 4,730,000.

* Handicapped Infants and Toddlers (Early Intervention Grants) 84.181

Nancy Safer
Division of Educational Services
Office of Special Education Program
U.S. Department of Education
400 Maryland Ave., SW
Washington, DC 20202 (202) 732-1109
To assist each state and territory to develop a state-wide comprehensive, coordinated multidisciplinary, interagency system to provide early intervention services for handicapped infants and toddlers and their families. Types of assistance: grants. Estimate of annual funds available: $ 69,831,000.

* National Programs for Drug-Free Schools and Communities 84.184

U.S. Department of Education
Office of Elementary and Secondary Education
Room 4132
400 Maryland Ave., SW
Washington, DC 20202 (202) 732-4579
To assist in drug and alcohol abuse education and prevention, personnel training and curriculum demonstration activities, as authorized by the Drug Free Schools and Communities Act of 1986. Types of assistance: grants. Estimate of annual funds available: $ 59,770,000.

* Drug-Free Schools and Communities - State Grants (Drug-Free Schools and Communities) 84.186

Allen King
U.S. Department of Education
Office of Elementary and Secondary Education

400 Maryland Ave., SW
Washington, DC 20202 (202) 732-4599
To provide financial assistance to establish programs of alcohol and drug abuse education and prevention coordinated with related community efforts and resources. Types of assistance: grants. Estimate of annual funds available: $ 287,730,000.

* Supported Employment Services for Individuals with Severe Handicaps (Supported Employment Services Program) 84.187

Mark E. Shob
Office of Program Operations
Rehabilitation Services Administration
U.S. Department of Education
Washington, DC 20202-2574 (202) 732-1406
To provide grants for training and traditionally time limited post employment services leading to supported employment for individuals with severe handicaps. Types of assistance: grants. Estimate of annual funds available: $ 26,900,000.

* Christa McAuliffe Fellowships (CMFP) 84.190

U.S. Department of Education
Office of the Asst. Secretary for Elementary and
Secondary Education
400 Maryland Ave., SW
Washington, DC 20202 (202) 732-4342
To reward excellence in teaching by providing financial assistance to outstanding teachers to continue their education. Types of assistance: grants. Estimate of annual funds available: $ 1,892,000.

* National Adult Education Research 84.191

Richard F. DiColar
Division of National Programs
Office of Vocational and Adult Education
U.S. Department of Education
400 Maryland Ave., SW
Washington, DC 20202 (202) 732-2362
Types of assistance: grants. Estimate of annual funds available: $ 412,000.

* Adult Education for the Homeless 84.192

Division of Adult Education
Office of Vocational and Adult Education
U.S. Department of Education
400 Maryland Ave., SW
Washington, DC 20202 (202) 732-2390
To provide literacy training and basic skills remediation for adult homeless individuals, including a program of outreach activities. Types of assistance: grants. Estimate of annual funds available: $ 7,094,000.

* Bilingual Education Support Services 84.194

Office of Bilingual Education and Minority
Languages Affairs
Edward Fuentes
330 C St., SW, Room 5086
Washington, DC 20202 (202) 732-5972
To provide in-service training and technical assistance to parents and educational personnel participating in, or preparing to participate in bilingual education programs. Types of assistance: grants. Estimate of annual funds available: $ 20,772,000.

* Bilingual Education Training Grants 84.195

Division of National Programs
Office of Bilingual Education and Minority Languages Affairs
Dr. Mary T. Mahony
330 C St., SW, Room 50861
Washington, DC 20202 (202) 732-5722
To provide financial support for programs designed to meet the training needs for additional or better trained education personnel in Bilingual Education. Types of assistance: grants. Estimate of annual funds available: $ 30,413,000.

Be patient. If any phone number is incorrect, call (area code) 555-1212 and request the new listing.

Education

* College Library Technology and Cooperation Grants (HEA Title II-D) 84.197

Linda Loeb, Program Officer
Library Development Staff, Library Programs
U.S. Department of Education
Washington, DC 20202 (202) 357-6902

To encourage resource sharing activities among the libraries in institutions of higher education through the use of technology and networking. Types of assistance: grants. Estimate of annual funds available: $ 3,651,000.

* Workplace Literacy 84.198

Nancy Brooks, Division of National Programs
Office of Vocational and Adult Education
U.S. Department of Education
400 Maryland Ave., SW
Washington, DC 20202 (202) 732-2269

The Adult Education Act was amended to establish workplace literacy partnerships. Types of assistance: grants. Estimate of annual funds available: $ 11,856,000.

* Vocational Education-Cooperative Demonstration 84.199

Richard DiCola, Division of National Programs
Office of Vocational and Adult Education
U.S. Department of Education
400 Maryland Ave., SW
Washington, DC 20202 (202) 732-2362

To support exemplary cooperative demonstration programs for high technology training pertaining to vocational education. Types of assistance: grants. Estimate of annual funds available: $ 14,361,000.

* School Dropout Demonstration Assistance (Dropout Prevention Program) 84.201

John Fiegel
U.S. Department of Education
Division of Educational Support
Office of Elementary and Secondary Education
400 Maryland Ave., SW
Washington, DC 20202 (202) 732-4342

To provide financial assistance to local educational agencies, educational partnerships and community based organizations to establish and demonstrate effective dropout prevention and reentry programs. Types of assistance: grants. Estimate of annual funds available: $ 21,736,000.

* STAR Schools Program (Star Schools) 84.203

Frank Withrow
Office of Educational Research and Improvement
U.S. Department of Education
Washington, DC 20208-5644 (202) 357-6200

To provide demonstration grants to eligible telecommunications partnerships to develop, construct and acquire audio and visual facilities and equipment. Types of assistance: grants. Estimate of annual funds available: $ 14,399,000.

* School, College, and University Partnership (SCUP) 84.204

May J. Weaver
U.S. Department of Education
Division of Student Services
400 Maryland Ave., SW
Washington, DC 20202 (202) 732-4804

To encourage partnerships between institutions of higher education and secondary schools serving low-income students to support programs that improve the academic skills of public and private nonprofit secondary school students. Types of assistance: grants. Estimate of annual funds available: $ 2,760,000.

* Educational Personnel Training 84.207

Allen King, Director
Drug-Free Schools and Communities Program

U.S. Department of Education
400 Maryland Ave., SW
Washington, DC 20202 (202) 732-4599

To provide financial assistance to State Education Agencies and Institutions of Higher Education to establish, expand or enhance programs and activities for the training of teachers in drug abuse programs. Types of assistance: grants. Estimate of annual funds available: $ 7,000,000.

* Native Hawaiian Model Curriculum Implementation Project (Kamehameha Elementary Education Program (KEEP)) 84.208

Ramon Ruiz
U.S. Department of Education
400 Maryland Ave., SW
Washington, DC 20202 (202) 732-4153

To implement and increase the impact of the Kamehameha Elementary Education Program Model Demonstration Curriculum. Types of assistance: direct payments. Estimate of annual funds available: $ 395,200.

* Native Hawaiian Family Based Education Centers 84.209

Mr. Ramon Ruiz
U.S. Department of Education
School Improvement Programs
400 Maryland Ave., SW
Washington, DC 20202 (202) 732-4153

To develop and operate a minimum of eleven family based education centers throughout the Hawaiian Islands. Types of assistance: direct payments. Estimate of annual funds available: $ 1,778,400.

* First Schools and Teachers 84.211

Daniel Schecter
U.S. Department of Education, FIRST
Office of Educational Research and Improvement
Washington, DC 20208 (202) 357-6496

To support projects to improve educational opportunities for the performance of elementary and secondary school students and teachers. Types of assistance: grants. Estimate of annual funds available: $ 3,952,000.

* First Family School Partnerships 84.212

Daniel Schecter
U.S. Department of Education, FIRST
Office of Educational Research and Improvement
Washington, DC 20208 (202) 357-6496

To increase the involvement of families in improving the educational achievement of their children in preschool, elementary and secondary schools. Types of assistance: grants. Estimate of annual funds available: $ 1,976,000.

* Even Start - Local Education Agencies 84.213

Mary Jean LeTendre
U.S. Department of Education
Compensatory Education Programs
Office of Elementary and Secondary Education
400 Maryland Ave., SW
Washington, DC 20202 (202) 732-4682

To provide family centered education projects to help parents become full partners in the education of their children. Types of assistance: grants. Estimate of annual funds available: $ 14,375,400.

* Even Start - Migrant Education 84.214

John Staehle
Office of Elementary and Secondary Education
Migrant Education
U.S. Department of Education
400 Maryland Ave., SW, Room 2145
Washington, DC 20202 (202) 732-4746

To establish and improve programs to meet the special educational needs of the children of migratory agricultural workers. Types of assistance: grants. Estimate of annual funds available: $ 444,600.

Be patient. If any phone number is incorrect, call (area code) 555-1212 and request the new listing.

Money For Teachers and Schools

* The Secretary's Fund for Innovation in Education 84.215

Daniel Schecter
U.S. Department of Education, FIE
Office of Educational Research and Improvement
Washington, DC 20208 (202) 357-6496

To conduct projects that offer the promise of identifying and disseminating innovative educational approaches at the preschool, elementary and secondary level. Types of assistance: grants. Estimate of annual funds available: $ 15,678,000.

* Student Literacy Corps 84.219

U.S. Department of Education
Office of the Deputy Assistant Secretary for
Higher Education Programs
400 Maryland Ave., SW
Washington, DC 20202 (202) 708-6128

To promote student literary corps projects operated by institutions of higher education where volunteer undergraduates will serve as unpaid literacy tutors in public community agencies. Types of assistance: grants. Estimate of annual funds available: $ 4,940,000.

* Center for International Business Education 84.220

Susanna Easton
International Studies Branch
Center for International Education
U.S. Department of Education
Room 3052
400 Maryland Ave., SW
Washington, DC 20202 (202) 732-3302

To serve the international needs of the business community by promoting improved business strategies in international trade. Types of assistance: grants. Estimate of annual funds available: $ 741,000.

* Native Hawaiian Special Education 84.221

Dr. Martin J. Kaufman (202) 732-1107

To operate projects addressing the special education needs of Native Hawaiian Students. Types of assistance: grants. Estimate of annual funds available: $ 494,000.

* National School Volunteer Program 84.222

Daniel Schecter, FIRST Program
Office of Educational Research and Improvement
U.S. Department of Education
55 New Jersey Ave., NW
Washington, DC 20208 (202) 357-6496

To conduct volunteer programs nationally in schools. Types of assistance: grants. Estimate of annual funds available: $ 988,000.

* State-Administered English Literacy 84.223

Ronald Pugsley
Division of Adult Education
Office of Vocational and Adult Education
U.S. Department of Education
400 Maryland Ave., SW
Washington, DC 20202 (202) 732-2272

To provide grants to states to conduct English literacy projects for individuals of limited English proficiency. Types of assistance: grants.

* Bicentennial Educational Grant Program 90.001

Commission on the Bicentennial of the U.S. Constitution
Attn: Educational Programs
808 17th St., NW
Washington, DC 20006 (202) 653-5110

To help elementary and secondary school teachers develop a better understanding of the history and development of the U.S. Constitution and Bill of Rights so that they will become more able to teach the Constitution to young learners. Types of assistance: grants. Estimate of annual funds available: $ 3,600,000.

Education

Federal Money for Students

Both the federal government and state governments have student loan programs and other financial assistance to pursue higher education. And these programs are not limited to young adults, but include the elderly as well. The federal programs identified here are taken from the *Catalog of Federal Domestic Assistance* which is published by the U.S. Government Printing Office in Washington, DC. The number next to the title is the official reference. In the case of the federal agency, contact the office listed below the title for more details. Refer to the next section for a state-by-state listing of financial aid and scholarships for students.

* Minority Research and Teaching Grants (MRTP Small Grants Program) 10.140
Ezra Naughton
Minority Research and Teaching Programs
Office of Advocacy and Enterprise
U.S. Department of Agriculture
14th and Independence Ave., SW
Washington, DC 2025 (202) 447-2019
Types of assistance: grants. Estimate of annual funds available: $ 100,000.

* Minority Research and Teaching Grants (MRTP Small Grants Program) 10.140
Dr. Ezra Naughton
Minority Research and Teaching Programs
Office of Advocacy and Enterprise
U.S. Department of Agriculture
14th and Independence Ave., SW
Washington, DC 20250 (202) 447-2019
Types of assistance: grants. Estimate of annual funds available: $ 100,000.

* Food and Agricultural Sciences National Needs Graduate Fellowship Grants 10.210
Director, Higher Education Programs
U.S. Department of Agriculture
Administration Bldg., Room 350-A
14th and Independence Ave., SW
Washington, DC 20250 (202) 447-7854
To award grants to colleges and universities that have superior teaching and research competencies in the food and agricultural sciences to encourage outstanding students to pursue and complete a graduate degree in an area of food and agricultural sciences. Types of assistance: grants. Estimate of annual funds available: $ 2,766,440.

* Selected Reserve Educational Assistance Program (Montgomery GI Bill Act of 1984) 12.609
Assistant Secretary of Defense (Reserve Affairs)
Pentagon, Room 3E325
Washington, DC 20301-1500 (202) 695-7459/7429
To encourage and sustain membership in the National Guard and Reserves. Types of assistance: direct payment. Estimate of annual funds available: $ 116,000,000.

* Health Education Assistance Loans (HEAL) 13.108
Michael Heninburg
Division of Student Assistance
Bureau of Health Professions
HRSA, PHS, Room 8-39, 5600 Fishers Lane
Rockville, MD 20857 (302) 443-1173
To authorize Health Education Assistance Loans (HEAL) for educational expenses available from eligible lenders such as banks, credit unions, savings and loan associations, etc. Types of assistance: loan guarantee. Estimate of annual funds available: $ 200,000,000.

* Grants for Preventive Medicine Residency Training (Preventive Medicine Residency) 13.117
Donald Weaver
Director, Division of Medicine
Health Resources and Services Administration
5600 Fishers Lane
Rockville, MD 20857 (301) 443-6190
To promote the post-graduate education of physicians in preventive medicine Types of assistance: grants. Estimate of annual funds available: $ 1,503,000.

* Grants for Podiatric Medicine Training (Podiatric Medicine) 13.119
Dr. Donald Weaver, Director, Division of Medicine
Health Resources and Services Administration
5600 Fishers Lane
Rockville, MD 20857 (301) 443-6190
To provide clinical training for podiatry students recruited from areas that are currently under-served. Types of assistance: grants. Estimate of annual funds available: $ 350,000.

* Health Professions Pregraduate Scholarship Program for Indians 13.123
IHS Scholarship Program, Indian Health Services
Public Health Service, DHHS
5600 Fishers Lane, Room 6-12
Rockville, MD 20857 (301) 443-6197
Types of assistance: grants. Estimate of annual funds available: $ 1,451,440.

* Nurse Anesthetist Traineeships 13.124
Division of Nursing
Bureau of Health Professions
Health Resources and Services Administration, PHS
Room 5C-13, 5600 Fishers Lane
Rockville, MD 20857 (301) 443-6880
To provide traineeships for full-time study in accredited training programs for registered nurses who have completed 12 months of study in nurse anesthetist training programs. Types of assistance: grants. Estimate of annual funds available: $ 784,000.

* Financial Assistance for Disadvantaged Health Professions Students (FADHPS) 13.139
Division of Student Assistance
Health Resources and Services Administration, PHS
Parklawn Bldg. Room 8-23
5600 Fishers Lane
Rockville, MD 20857 (301) 443-1173
To assist disadvantaged health professions students who are of exceptional financial need to obtain a degree in medicine, osteopathic medicine, or dentistry by providing financial support to help pay for their costs of eduction. Types of assistance: grant. Estimate of annual funds available: $ 4,849,000.

Be patient. If any phone number is incorrect, call (area code) 555-1212 and request the new listing.

Federal Money For Students

* **Post-Baccalaureate Facility Fellowships (Faculty Fellowships) 13.147**
Anastasia Buchanan, Division of Nursing
Health Resources and Services Administration, PHS
Room 5C-13, 5600 Fishers Lane
Rockville, MD 20857 (301) 443-5763
To provide grants to eligible schools of nursing to: investigate cost-effective alternatives to traditional health care modalities, examine nursing interventions that result in positive outcomes in health status, address other ares of nursing practice. Types of assistance: grants. Estimate of annual funds available: $ 1,079,000.

* **Special International Postdoctoral Research Program in Acquired Immunodeficiency Syndrome 13.154**
Chief, International Research and Awards Branch
Fogarty International Center
Bethesda, MD 20892 (301) 496-6688
To support collaborative research between the U.S. and foreign scientists who wish to enhance their knowledge and skills in the epidemiology, diagnosis, prevention, and treatment of acquired immunodeficiency syndrome (AIDS). Types of assistance: grants. Estimate of annual funds available: $ 700,000.

* **National Health Service Corps Loan Repayment (NHSC Loan Repayment Program) 13.162**
Director, Division of Health Services Scholarships
Health Resources and Services Administration
Room 7-34, 5600 Fishers Lane
Rockville, MD 20857 (301) 443-3744
To help assure an adequate supply of trained health professionals for the National Health Service Corps by providing for the repayment of educational loans for participants who agree to serve an applicable period of time in a health manpower shortage. Types of assistance: grants. Estimate of annual funds available: $ 4,501,000.

* **Indian Health Service Educational Loan Repayment (IHS Loan Repayment Program) 13.164**
Hazel Black, Health Manpower Support Branch, IHS
Room 9A-22, Parklawn Bldg.
5600 Fishers Lane
Rockville, MD 20857 (301) 443-4242
To help insure an adequate supply of trained health professionals for Indian Health Service facilities by providing for the repayment of educational loans for participants who agree to serve an applicable period of time at a facility. Types of assistance: grants. Estimate of annual funds available: $ 2,000,000.

* **Grants for State Loan Repayment (State Loan Repayment Program) 13.165**
Director
Division of National Health Service Corps
Health Resources and Services Administration
Room 7A-39, 5600 Fishers Lane
Rockville, MD 20857 (301) 443-2900
To assist states in establishing loan repayment programs that will help to assure an adequate supply of trained health professionals in states by providing for the repayment of health professions educational loans for participants who agree to serve an applicable period of time in a health manpower shortage area in the state. Types of assistance: grant. Estimate of annual funds available: $ 4,501,000.

* **National Research Service Awards - Health Services Research Training 13.225**
National Center for Health Services Research and
Health Care Technology Assessment, PHS
U.S. Department of Health and Human Services
Room 18A-10, Parklawn Bldg.
Rockville, MD (301) 443-4033
To provide predoctoral and postdoctoral training opportunities in health services research. Types of assistance: grant. Estimate of annual funds available: $ 1,322,975.

* **Occupational Safety and Health-Training Grants (ERC; Educational Resource Centers) 13.263**
Procurement and Grants Office, CDC, DHHS
1600 Clifton Road, NE, Mail Stop E14
Atlanta, GA 30333 (404) 842-6575
To develop specialized professional personnel in occupational safety and health problems with training in occupational medicine. Types of assistance: grants. Estimate of annual funds available: $ 10,095,000.

* **Alcohol and Drug Abuse Clinical or Service-Related Trainingships for Registered Nurses) 13.274**
Frances Cotter
Division of Clinical and Prevention Research
National Institute on Alcohol Abuse and Alcoholism
5600 Fishers Lane
Rockville, MD 20857 (301) 443-1207
To provide specialized training of heath and allied health professions personnel to assure that the alcohol and drug abuse knowledge and skills of such personnel are appropriate to the needs of those they serve. Types of assistance: grants. Estimate of annual funds available: $ 1,100,000.

* **Mental Health National Research Service Awards for Research Training (NRSA Program) 13.282**
Dr. Lyle Bivens, Director
Division of Basic Sciences
Room 11-803, 5600 Fishers Lane
Rockville, MD 20857 (301) 443-3563
To assure a continuing and adequate supply of well-trained personnel who are able to conduct research on mental health problems. Types of assistance: grant. Estimate of annual funds available: $ 19,710,000.

* **National Health Service Corps Scholarship Program (NHSC Scholarship Program) 13.288**
National Health Service Corps Scholarship Program
Health Resources and Services Administration
PHS, DHHS, Parklawn Bldg., Room 7-16
5600 Fishers Lane
Rockville, MD (301) 443-1646
To support training of physicians, dentists, and other health professionals as requested for professional service as members of the National Health Service Corps in Health Manpower Shortage Areas of the United States. Types of assistance: grants. Estimate of annual funds available: $ 0.

* **Nurse Practitioner and Nurse Midwife Education and Traineeships 13.298**
Dr. Thomas P. Phillips
Division of Nursing
Health Resources and Services Administration, PHS
Room 5C-26, 5600 Fishers Lane
Rockville, MD 20857 (301) 443-6333
To educate registered nurses who will be qualified to provide primary health care. Types of assistance: grants. Estimate of annual funds available: $ 11,773,000.

* **Health Professions Student Loans (HPSL) 13.342**
Division of Student Assistance
Health Resources and Services Administration, PHS
Room 823, 5600 Fishers Lane
Rockville, MD 20857 (301) 443-1173
To increase educational opportunities for students in need of financial assistance to pursue a course of study in specified health professions by providing long term low interest loans. Types of assistance: loans. Estimate of annual funds available: $ 4,300,000.

* **Professional Nurse Traineeships (Nurse Traineeships; Trainee) 13.358**
Anastasia Buchanan, Division of Nursing
Health Resources and Services Administration
PHS, DHHS

Be patient. If any phone number is incorrect, call (area code) 555-1212 and request the new listing.

Education

5600 Fishers Lane
Room 5C-13
Rockville, MD 20857 (301) 443-5768
To prepare registered nurses as administrators, researchers, teachers, nursing specialist, nurse midwives, and nurse practitioners for positions in hospitals and related institutions in public health agencies. Types of assistance: grants. Estimate of annual funds available: $ 1,275,200.

* Nursing Student Loans (NSL) 13.364

Division of Student Assistance
Health Resources and Services Administration
PHS, DHHS
Parklawn Bldg. Room 8-23
5600 Fishers Lane
Rockville, MD 20857 (301) 443-1173
To assist students in need of financial assistance to pursue a course of study in professional nursing education by providing long-term, low interest loans, currently at the rate of 5 percent. Types of assistance: loans. Estimate of annual funds available: $ 6,000,000.

* Minority Biomedical Research Support (MBRS) 13.375

Director, Minority Biomedical Research Support
Program Branch
Division of Research Resources
National Institutes of Health
Bethesda, MD 20892 (301) 496-6745
To address the lack of representation of minorities in biomedical research by increasing the pool of minorities pursing research careers. Types of assistance: grants. Estimate of annual funds available: $ 28,147,000.

* Grants for Graduate Training in Family Medicine (Family Medicine Residency) 13.379

Dr. Donald Weaver
Director, Division of Medicine
Health Resources and Services Administration
Room 4C25, 5600 Fishers Lane
Rockville, MD 20857 (301) 443-6190
To increase the number of physicians practicing family medicine. Types of assistance: grants. Estimate of annual funds available: $ 11,827,000.

* Cancer Research Manpower 13.398

Dr. Vincent J. Cairoli, Chief
Cancer Training Branch
Division of Cancer Prevention and Control
National Cancer Institute EPN/232B
Bethesda, MD 20892 (301) 496-8580
To make available support for nonprofit institutions interested in providing biomedical training opportunities for individuals interested in careers in basic and clinical research to support important areas of the National Cancer Program. Types of assistance: grants. Estimate of annual funds available: $ 41,781,000.

* Child Development Associate Scholarships 13.614

Mrs. Dollie Wolverton, Head Start Bureau
400 6th St., SW
Washington, DC 20024 (202) 755-7710
To support the cost of assessing and providing credentials to candidates for certification as Child Development Associates (CDA). Types of assistance: grants. Estimate of annual funds available: $ 1,450,000.

* Child Welfare Services Training Grants 13.648

Director, Program Support Division
Children's Bureau
Administration for Children, Youth and Families
P.O. Box 1182
Washington, DC 20013 (202) 755-7820
To develop and maintain an adequate supply of qualified and trained personnel for the field of services to children and their families, and to improve educational programs and resources for preparing personnel for this field. Types of assistance: grant. Estimate of annual funds available: $ 3,696,000.

* Special Programs for the Aging-Title IV-Training, Research and Discretionary Projects and Programs 13.668

Mike Suzuki, Associate Commissioner
Office of Program Development
Administration on Aging, DHHS
Washington, DC 2021 (202) 245-0442
To provide adequately trained personnel in the field of aging, improve knowledge of the problems and needs of the elderly, and to demonstrate better ways of improving the quality of life for elderly. Types of assistance: grants. Estimate of annual funds available: $ 24,173,000.

* Scholarships for Students of Exceptional Financial Need (EFN Scholarship) 13.820

Michael Heninburg
Division of Student Assistance
Health Resources and Services Administration
Public Health Service
Room 8-23, 5600 Fishers Lane
Rockville, MD 20857 (301) 443-1173
To make funds available to authorized health professions schools to award scholarships to health professions students of exceptional financial need. Types of assistance: grant. Estimate of annual funds available: $ 6,578,000.

* Health Careers Opportunity Program 13.822

Grants Management Officer
Health Resources and Services Administration
Room 8C-22, 5600 Fishers Lane
Rockville, MD 20857 (301) 443-6857
To identify recruit, and select individuals from disadvantaged backgrounds for education and training in a health or allied health professions school. Types of assistance: grant. Estimate of annual funds available: $ 18,692,037.

* Medical Library Assistance 13.879

Dr. Jeanne Brand
Extramural Programs
National Library of Medicine
Bethesda, MD 20894 (301) 496-6131
To improve health information services by providing funds to train professional personnel, strengthen library and information services, support biomedical publication, and conduct research in information science and in medical information. Types of assistance: grants. Estimate of annual funds available: $ 13,551,000.

* Minority Access to Research Careers (MARC) 13.880

Edward Blynum
Program Director (MARC Program)
National Institute of General Medical Sciences, NIH
Bethesda, MD 20892 (301) 496-7941
To assist minority institutions to train greater numbers of scientists and teachers in health related fields. Types of assistance: grants. Estimate of annual funds available: $ 9,053,000.

* Grants for Residency Training in General Internal Medicine and/or General Pediatrics (Primary Care Training) 13.884

Dr. Donald Weaver, Director
Division of Medicine, HRSA, PHS
Room 4C25, 5600 Fishers Lane
Rockville, MD 20857 (301) 443-6190
To promote the graduate education of physicians who plan to enter the practice of general internal medicine or general pediatrics. Types of assistance: grants. Estimate of annual funds available: $ 13,749,297.

* Grants for Physician Assistant Training Program (Physical Assistant Training Program) 13.886

Dr. Donald Weaver, Director
Division of Medicine

Be patient. If any phone number is incorrect, call (area code) 555-1212 and request the new listing.

Federal Money For Students

Bureau of Health Professions
HRSA, PHS
U.S. Department of Health and Human Services
Parklawn Bldg., Room 4C-25
5600 Fishers Lane
Rockville, MD 20857 (301) 443-6190
To enable public or nonprofit private health or educational entities to meet the cost of projects to plan, develop and operate programs for the training of physicians assistants. Types of assistance: grants. Estimate of annual funds available: $ 452,000.

* Resource and Manpower Development in the Environmental Health Sciences (Core Centers and Research Training Program) 13.894

Director, Division of Extramural Research and Training
National Institute of Environmental Health Sciences
P.O. Box 12233
Research Triangle Park, NC 27709 (919) 541-7723
To provide long-term, stable support for broadly based multidisciplinary research and training on environmental health problems in Environmental Health Sciences Center. Types of assistance: grant. Estimate of annual funds available: $ 25,303,000.

* Grants for Predoctoral Training in Family Medicine (Predoctoral Training) 13.896

Dr. Donald Weaver, Director
Division of Medicine, HRSA, PHS
Room 4C-25, 5600 Fishers Lane
Rockville, MD 20857 (301) 443-6190
To assist schools of medicine and osteopathy in meeting the cost of projects to plan, develop, and operate professional predoctoral training programs in the field of family medicine. Types of assistance: grant. Estimate of annual funds available: $ 4,178,000.

* Residency Training and Advanced Education in the General Practice of Dentistry 13.897

Richard G. Weaver
Dental Health Branch
Division of Assoc. and Dental Health Professions
HRSA, PHS
5600 Fishers Lane
Rockville, MD 20857 (301) 443-6837
To assist schools of dentistry and institutions conducting post-graduate dental training in defraying the costs of projects to plan, develop, and operate an approved residency or advanced educational program in the general practice of dentistry. Types of assistance: grants. Estimate of annual funds available: $ 1,691,000.

* Health Administration Graduate Traineeships 13.962

John R. Westcott, Grants Management Officer
Bureau of Health Professions, HRSA
Room 8C-22, 5600 Fishers Lane
Rockville, MD 20857 (301) 443-6880
To support eligible students enrolled in accredited graduate programs in health administration, hospital administration of health policy analysis and planning. Types of assistance: grants. Estimate of annual funds available: $ 470,000.

* Traineeships for Students in Schools of Public Health and Other Graduate Public Health Programs (Public Health Traineeships) 13.964

John R. Westcott
Grants Management Officer, HRSA
Room 8C-22, 5600 Fishers Lane
Rockville, MD 20857 (301) 443-6880
To support traineeships for students in graduate educational programs in accredited schools of public health or other public or nonprofit educational entities (excluding programs eligible for support under Section 791A which offer graduate programs for training. Types of assistance: grants. Estimate of annual funds available: $ 2,819,000.

* Grants for the Training of Health Professions in Geriatrics 13.969

Mr. William Koenig
HRSA, PHS
U.S. Department of Health and Human Services
5600 Fishers Lane
Rockville, MD 20857 (301) 443-6887
To develop regional resource centers focused on strengthening multidisciplinary training of health professionals in geriatric health care. Types of assistance: grants. Estimate of annual funds available: $ 9,382,000.

* Health Professions Scholarship Program 13.972

Larry Thomas
IHS Scholarship Program
Indian Health Service, PHS, DHHS
Room 6-12, 5600 Fishers Lane
Rockville, MD 20857 (301) 443-6197
To provide scholarships to Indians and other students at health professions schools in order to obtain health professionals to serve Indians. Types of assistance: grants. Estimate of annual funds available: $ 4,058,000.

* Senior International Fellowships 13.989

Bettie J. Graham, Ph.D., Chief
International Research Awards Branch
Fogarty International Center
Bethesda, MD 20892 (301) 496-6688
To promote the exchange of ideas and information about the latest advances in the biomedical and behavioral sciences between U.S. biomedical scientists and those of other nations of the world and to bring to the foreign and U.S. institutions the knowledge and professional scientific background which will lead to improvement in the biomedical research potential of both institutions. Types of assistance: grants. Estimate of annual funds available: $ 922,000.

* Community Development Work-Study Program 14.234

U.S. Department of Housing and Urban Development
Community Planning and Development
Office of Program Policy Development
Technical Assistance Div.
451 7th St., SW
Washington, DC (202) 755-6092
Under the Community Development Work-Study Program (CSWSP), HUD will make grants to institutions of higher education, either directly or through area-wide planning organizations or states, for the purpose of providing assistance to economically disadvantaged and minority students who participate in community development work-study programs and are enrolled full-time graduate or undergraduate programs in community management. Types of assistance: grants. Estimate of annual funds available: $ 3,000,000.

* Urban Mass Transportation Managerial Training Grants (Mass Transit Technology and Technical Assistance Program) 20.503

Office of Technical Assistance and Safety
Urban Mass Transportation Administration
U.S. Department of Transportation
400 Seventh St., SW
Washington, DC 20590 (202) 366-0080
To provide fellowships for training of managerial, technical and professional personnel employed in the urban mass transportation field. Types of assistance: grants. Estimate of annual funds available: $ 1,953,000.

* U.S. Merchant Marine Academy (Kings Point) 20.807

Bruce J. Carlton, Director
Office of Maritime Labor and Training
Maritime Administration
U.S. Department of Transportation
Washington, DC 20590 (202) 366-5755
To train merchant marine officers. Types of assistance: training. Estimate of annual funds available: $ 20,587,000.

Be patient. If any phone number is incorrect, call (area code) 555-1212 and request the new listing.

Education

* **Federal Employment for Disadvantaged Youth - Part Time (Stay-in-School Program) 27.003**
Yolanda Wilson, Programs Division
Office of Affirmative Recruiting and Employment
Office of Personnel Management
1900 E St., NW
Washington, DC 20415 (202) 632-0601
To give disadvantaged young people, 16 years of age and older, an opportunity for part-time employment with federal agencies in order to allow them to continue their education without interruptions caused by financial pressures. Types of assistance: federal employment. Estimate of annual funds available: $ 0.

* **Federal Employment for Disadvantaged Youth - Summer (Summer Aids) 27.004**
Office of Affirmative Recruiting and Employment
Office of Personnel Management
1900 E St., NW
Washington, DC 20415 (202) 632-0601
To give disadvantaged young people, 16 years of age or older, meaningful summer employment with the federal Government. Types of assistance: federal employment. Estimate of annual funds available: $ 0.

* **Federal Summer Employment (Summer Jobs in Federal Agencies) 27.006**
Staffing Policy Division
Career Entry and Employee Development Group
Office of Personnel Management
1900 E St., NW
Washington, DC 20415 (202) 632-0728
To provide summer employment primarily for college students and high schools students with special skills. Types of assistance: federal employment. Estimate of annual funds available: $ 0.

* **Promotion of the Arts - Arts Administration Fellows Program (Fellowship Program) 45.021**
Arts Administration Fellows Program
National Endowment for the Arts
1100 Penn Ave., NW
Washington, DC 20506 (202) 682-5786
To provide a limited number of 13 week fellowships for professionals in arts management and related fields. Types of assistance: grants. Estimate of annual funds available: $ 200,000.

* **Promotion of the Humanities - Younger Scholars (High School and College Students) 45.115**
Division of Fellowships and Seminars
Younger Scholars Program
Room 316, National Endowment for the Humanities
Washington, DC 20506 (202) 786-0643
To support non-credit humanities projects during the summer by college students and advanced high school students. Types of assistance: grants. Estimate of annual funds available: $ 400,000.

* **Promotion of the Humanities-Fellowships for University Teachers 45.142**
Fellowships for University Teachers
Division of Fellowships and Seminars
National Endowment for the Humanities, Room 316
Washington, DC 20506 (202) 786-0466
To provide time for uninterrupted study and research to university teachers, and faculty members of postgraduate professional schools who can make significant contributions to thought and knowledge in the humanities. Types of assistance: grant. Estimate of annual funds available: $ 3,165,000.

* **Promotion of the Humanities - Fellowships for College Teachers and Independent Scholars 45.143**
Fellowships for College Teachers and Independent Scholars
Division of Fellowships and Seminars, Room 316

National Endowment for the Humanities
Washington, DC 20506 (202) 786-0466
To provide opportunities for college teachers and independent scholars to pursue independent study and research that will enhance their capacities as teachers, scholars, or interpreters of the humanities. Types of assistance: grants. Estimate of annual funds available: $ 3,390,000.

* **Promotion of the Humanities-Regrants Program/ Selected Areas 45.153**
National Endowment for the Humanities
Regrants Program/International Research
Room 318
Washington, DC 20506 (202) 786-0204
To award funds that will be regranted through fellowships and grants-in-aid to support individual American scholars pursuing research in all fields of the humanities. Types of assistance: grants. Estimate of annual funds available: $ 145,000.

* **Graduate Research Fellowships 47.009**
Dr. Douglas S. Chapin
Graduate Fellowships, Division of Research Career Development
National Science Foundation
1800 G. Street, NW
Washington, DC 20550 (202) 357-7856
To provide tangible federal encouragement to highly talented graduate students for advanced study in the sciences, mathematics and engineering. Types of assistance: grants. Estimate of annual funds available: $ 24,016,000.

* **Young Scholars (National Science Foundtion) 47.072**
Dr. Elmina D. Johnson
Division of Research Career Development
National Science Foundation
Room 6730
1800 G. St., NW
Washington, DC 20500 (202) 357-7538
To identify secondary school students with high potential, high ability in science mathematics and/or engineering and to facilitate their making of informed career choices. Types of assistance: grants. Estimate of annual funds available: $ 7,000,000.

* **Veterans Educational Assistance (Noncontributory GI Bill) 64.111**
U.S. Department of Veterans Affairs
Washington, DC 20420
To make service in the Armed Forces more attractive by extending benefits of a higher education to qualified persons who might not otherwise be able to afford such an education. Types of assistance: direct payment. Estimate of annual funds available: $ 333,026,000.

* **Post-Vietnam Era Veterans' Educational Assistance (Voluntary-Contributory Matching Program) 64.120**
U.S. Department of Veterans Affairs
Central Office
Washington, DC 20420
To provide educational assistance to persons entering the Armed Forces after December 31, 1976 and before July 1, 1985, to assist persons in obtaining an education they might otherwise not be able to afford. Types of assistance: direct payment. Estimate of annual funds available: $ 208,120,000.

* **All Volunteer Force Educational Assistance (Montgomery GI Bill Active Duty) 64.124**
U.S. Department of Veterans Affairs
Central Office
Washington, DC 20420
To help service persons readjust to civilian life after their separation from military service. Types of assistance: direct payment. Estimate of annual funds available: $ 46,091,000.

Be patient. If any phone number is incorrect, call (area code) 555-1212 and request the new listing.

Federal Money For Students

* **University-Laboratory Cooperative Program 81.004**
Larry L. Barker
Division of University and Industry Programs
Office of Energy Research, DOE
Washington, DC 20585 (202) 586-8947
To provide college and university science and engineering faculty and students with energy-related training and research experience in areas of energy research at DOE facilities. Types of assistance: grants, other. Estimate of annual funds available: $ 8,000,000.

* **Pre-Freshman Engineering (PREP) 81.047**
Division of University and Industry Programs
Office of Energy Research, DOE
Forrestal Bldg., 1000 Independence Ave., SW
Washington, DC 20585 (202) 586-1634
To alleviate manpower shortages in engineering by preparing and guiding minority and women high school students in the selection of college preparatory courses in science and mathematics. Types of assistance: grants. Estimate of annual funds available: $ 300,000.

* **Minority Educational Institution Research Travel Fund (MIRT) 81.083**
Isiah O. Sewell
Office of Minority Economic Impact MI-2.2, DOE
Forrestal Bldg., Room 5B-110
Washington, DC 20585 (202) 586-1953
To provide travel funds to faculty members and graduate students of minority postsecondary educational institutions to encourage and assist in initiating and improving energy related research. Types of assistance: direct payment. Estimate of annual funds available: $ 50,000.

* **Minority Honors Training and Industrial Assistance Program (Minority Honors Program) 81.084**
Isiah O. Sewell
Office of Minority Economic Impact, DOE
Forrestal Bldg., Room 5B-110
Washington, DC 20585 (202) 586-1593
To provide scholarship funding to financially needy minority honor students pursuing training in energy related technologies and to develop linkages with energy industries. Types of assistance: grants. Estimate of annual funds available: $ 402,000.

* **Science and Engineering Research Semester 81.097**
Donna J. Prokop
Division of University and Industry Programs
Office of Energy Research, DOE
Washington, DC 20585 (202) 586-8949
To give college juniors and seniors the opportunity to participate in hands-on research at the cutting edge of science at the DOE National laboratories. Types of assistance: training, direct payment. Estimate of annual funds available: $ 1,500,000.

* **Educational Exchange-Graduate Students (Fulbright Program) 82.001**
Institute of International Educational
809 United Nations Plaza
New York, NY 10017
To improve and strengthen international relations of the U.S. by promoting better mutual understanding among the peoples of the world through educational exchanges. Types of assistance: grants. Estimate of annual funds available: $ 5,518,581.

* **Educational Exchange-University Lecturers (Professors) and Research Scholars (Fulbright-Hays Program) 82.002**
Council for International Exchange of Scholars
11 Dupont Circle, Suite 300
Washington, DC 20036

To improve and strengthen the international relations of the U.S. by promoting mutual understanding among the peoples of the world through educational exchanges. Types of assistance: grants. Estimate of annual funds available: $ 20,138,170.

* **Adult Education-State Administered Basic Grant Program 84.002**
D. Kay Wright, Division of Adult Education
Office of Assistant Secretary for Vocational and Adult Education
U.S. Department of Education
Washington, DC 20202-7320 (202) 732-2270
To improve educational opportunities for adults and to encourage the establishment of adult education programs. Types of assistance: grants. Estimate of annual funds available: $ 136,344,000.

* **Supplemental Educational Opportunity Grants (SEOG) 84.007**
Division of Policy and Program Development
Student Financial Assistance Programs
U.S. Department of Education
400 Maryland Ave., SW
Washington, DC 20202 (202) 732-4490
To provide eligible undergraduate postsecondary students with demonstrated financial need with grant assistance to help meet educational expenses. Types of assistance: direct payments. Estimate of annual funds available: $ 440,739,000.

* **National Resource Centers and Fellowships Program for Language and Area or Language and International Studies 84.015**
Joseph F. Belmonte
Advanced Training and Research Branch
Center for International Education
7th and D St., SW
Washington, DC 20202 (202) 732-3283
To promote instruction in those modern foreign languages area and international studies critical to national needs by supporting the establishment, strengthening and operation of such programs at colleges and universities. Types of assistance: grant. Estimate of annual funds available: $ 11,234,000.

* **Fulbright-Hays Training Grants-Doctoral Dissertation Research Abroad 84.022**
Center for International Education
Office of Asst Secretary for Postsecondary Education
U.S. Department of Education
Room 3928, 7 and D Sts., SW
Washington, DC 20202 (202) 732-3298
To provide opportunities for graduate students to engage in full-time dissertation research abroad in modern foreign language and area studies. Types of assistance: grants. Estimate of annual funds available: $ 1,680,000.

* **Handicapped Education - Special Education Personnel Development (Training Personnel for the Education of the Handicapped) 84.029**
Norm How
Division of Personnel Preparation
Special Education Programs
U.S. Department of Education
Washington, DC 20202 (202) 732-1070
To address identified shortages of special education teachers and related service personnel. Types of assistance: grants. Estimate of annual funds available: $ 67,095,000.

* **Guaranteed Student Loans (Stafford Loans, PLUS Loans, Supplemental Loans for Students (SLS) and Consolidation Loans 84.032**
Division of Policy and Program Development
Student Financial Assistance Programs
U.S. Department of Education

Be patient. If any phone number is incorrect, call (area code) 555-1212 and request the new listing.

Education

Washington, DC 20202 (202) 732-4242

To authorize guaranteed loans for education expenses available from eligible lenders such as banks, credit unions, savings and loan associations, pension funds, insurance companies, and schools to vocational undergraduate and graduate students enrolled at eligible postsecondary institutions. Types of assistance: loan guarantee. Estimate of annual funds available: $ 12,591,000.

* College Work-Study Program (CWS) 84.033

G. Oren
Division of Policy and Program Development
Student Financial Assistance Programs
U.S. Department of Education
400 Maryland Ave., SW
Washington, DC 20202 (202) 732-4490

To provide part-time employment to eligible postsecondary students to help meet educational expenses. Types of assistance: direct payment. Estimate of annual funds available: $ 612,142,000.

* Library Career Training (HEA Title II-B) 84.036

Yvonne Carter
Library Development Staff
Library Programs
U.S. Department of Education
55 New Jersey Avenue, NW
Washington, DC 20208 (202) 357-6320

To assist institutions of higher education and library organizations and agencies in training or retraining persons in areas of library specialization where there are shortages. Types of assistance: grants. Estimate of annual funds available: $ 400,000.

* Perkins Loans 84.038

G. Orem
Division of Program and Policy Development
U.S. Department of Energy
400 Maryland Ave., SW
Washington, DC 20202 (202) 732-4490

To provide eligible postsecondary students with demonstrated financial need with low-interest loan funds to help meet educational expenses. Types of assistance: direct payment. Estimate of annual funds available: $ 184,956,000.

* Talent Search 84.044

Division of Student Services
Education Outreach Branch
U.S. Department of Education
400 Maryland Ave., SW, Room 3030
Regional Office Bldg. 3
Washington, DC 20202 (202) 732-4804

To identify disadvantaged youths with potential for postsecondary education to encourage them in continuing in and graduating from secondary school and in enrolling programs of postsecondary education. Types of assistance: grants. Estimate of annual funds available: $ 26,240,000.

* Upward Bound 84.047

Division of Student Services
Education Outreach Branch
U.S. Department of Education
400 Maryland Ave., SW
Room 3060, Regional Office Bldg. 3
Washington, DC 20202 (202) 732-4804

To generate skills and motivation necessary for success in education beyond high school among low income and potential first generation college students and veterans. Types of assistance: grants. Estimate of annual funds available: $ 91,990,000.

* Vocational Education-Basic Grants to States 84.048

Winifred I. Warnat
Division of Vocational Education
U.S. Department of Education
400 Maryland Ave., SW
Washington, DC 20202 (202) 732-2441

To assist states in expanding, improving, modernizing and developing quality vocational education programs. Types of assistance: grants. Estimate of annual funds available: $ 715,600,000.

* Pell Grant Program 84.063

Division of Policy and Program Development
Office of Postsecondary Education
U.S. Department of Education
400 Maryland Ave., SW
Washington, DC 20202 (800) 353-INFO

To provide eligible undergraduate postsecondary students with demonstrated financial need with grant assistance to help meed educational expenses. Types of assistance: direct payment. Estimate of annual funds available: $ 4,574,325,000.

* Educational Opportunity Centers 84.066

Division of Student Services
Education Outreach Branch
U.S. Department of Education
400 Maryland Ave., SW
Washington, DC 20202 (202) 732-4804

To provide information on financial and academic assistance available for qualified adults desiring to pursue a program of postsecondary education and to assist them in applying for admission to institution of postsecondary education. Types of assistance: grants. Estimate of annual funds available: $ 11,665,000.

* Grants to States for State Student Incentives (State Student Incentive Grants; SSIG) 84.069

Fred H. Sellers
Division of Policy and Program Development
Office of Student Financial Assistance
U.S. Department of Education
Washington, DC 20202 (202) 732-4507

To provide grants to the states for use in programs of financial assistance to eligible postsecondary students. Types of assistance: grants. Estimate of annual funds available: $ 71,895,000.

* Indian Education - Fellowships for Indian Students (Section 423 Fellowships) 84.087

Indian Education Programs
Office of Elementary and Secondary Education
U.S. Department of Education
400 Maryland Ave., SW
Washington, DC 20202 (202) 732-1887

To enable Indian students to pursue a course of study leading to a post-baccalaureate degree in medicine, psychology, clinical psychology, law, education and related fields. Types of assistance: grants. Estimate of annual funds available: $ 1,600,000.

* Patricia Roberts Harris Fellowships (Graduate Programs) 84.094

Charles H. Miller
Division of Higher Education Incentive Programs
Office of Postsecondary Education
U.S. Department of Education
Washington, DC 20202 (202) 732-4395

Provide grants to institutions of higher education to support fellowships for graduate and professional education to students demonstrating financial need. Types of assistance: grants. Estimate of annual funds available: $ 15,711,000.

* Law School Clinical Experience Program 84.097

Division of Higher Education Incentive Programs
Office of Postsecondary Education
U.S. Department of Education
Washington, DC 2022 (202) 732-4395

Establish and expand programs in law schools to provide clinical experience to students in the practice of law. Types of assistance: grants. Estimate of annual funds available: $ 3,952,000.

Be patient. If any phone number is incorrect, call (area code) 555-1212 and request the new listing.

Federal Money For Students

* Fund for the Improvement of Postsecondary Education (FIPSE) 84.116

Fund for the Improvement of Postsecondary Education
Office of the Assistant Secretary for
Postsecondary Education
7 and D Sts., SW
Room 3100
Washington, DC 20202 (202) 732-5750

To provide assistance for innovative programs which improve the access to and the quality of postsecondary education. Types of assistance: grants. Estimate of annual funds available: $ 11,856,000.

* Law-Related Education 84.123

School Improvement Programs
Office of Elementary and Secondary Education
400 Maryland Ave., SW
Washington, DC 20202 (202) 732-4357

To support programs at the elementary and secondary school levels by developing and implementing model projects designed to institutionalize law-related education. Types of assistance: grants. Estimate of annual funds available: $ 3,952,000.

* Rehabilitation Training 84.129

Rehabilitation Services Administration
Office of Special Education and
Rehabilitative Services
U.S. Department of Education
Washington, DC 20202 (202) 732-1400

To support projects to increase the numbers and improve the skills of personnel trained in providing vocational rehabilitation services to handicapped individuals in areas targeted as having personnel shortages. Types of assistance: grants. Estimate of annual funds available: $ 30,134,000.

* Legal Training for the Disadvantaged (The American Bar Association Fund for Public Education) 84.136

Division of Higher Education Incentive Programs
Office of Postsecondary Education
U.S. Department of Education
Washington, DC 20202 (202) 732-4393

To provide educationally and economically disadvantaged students many with marginal or less than traditional admissions credentials. Types of assistance: grants. Estimate of annual funds available: $ 1,892,000.

* Migrant Education-High School Equivalency Program (HEP) 84.141

Office of Migrant Education
Office of Elementary and Secondary Education
U.S. Department of Education
400 Maryland Ave., SW
Washington, DC 20202 (202) 732-4746

To assist students who are engaged or who whose families are engaged in migrant and other seasonal farm work to obtain the equivalent of a secondary school diploma. Types of assistance: grant. Estimate of annual funds available: $ 7,410,000.

* Migrant Education - College Assistance Migrant Program (CAMP) 84.149

Office of Migrant Education
Office of Elementary and Secondary Education
U.S. Department of Education
400 Maryland Ave., SW
Room 2145
Washington, DC 20202 (202) 732-4746

To assist students who are engaged, or whose families are engaged, in migrant and other seasonal farmwork who are enrolled or are admitted for enrollment on a full-time basis in the first academic year at an institution of higher education. Types of assistance: grants. Estimate of annual funds available: $ 1,482,000.

* Business and International Education 84.153

International Studies Branch
Center for International Education
U.S. Department of Education
Room 3053
Washington, DC 20202 (202) 732-3302

To promote innovation and improvement in international business education curricula at institution of higher education and serve the needs of business community. Types of assistance: grants. Estimate of annual funds available: $ 2,125,000.

* Training Interpreters for Deaf Individuals 84.160

Office of Special Education and Rehabilitative Services
U.S. Department of Education
Washington, DC 20202 (202) 732-1322

To support projects, increase the numbers and improve the skills of manual and oral interpretive who provide services to deaf individuals. Types of assistance: grants. Estimate of annual funds available: $ 900,000.

* State Grants for Strengthening the Skills of Teachers and Instruction in Mathematics and Science 84.164

Dr. Allen A. Schmieder, Suite 2040
School Improvement Programs
400 Maryland Ave., SW
Washington, DC 20202 (202) 732-4336

To improve the skills of teachers and instruction in the areas of mathematics and science, also to increase the accessibility of such instruction to all students. Types of assistance: grants. Estimate of annual funds available: $ 128,440,000.

* Jacob K. Javits Fellowships 84.170

Division of Higher Education Incentive Programs
Office of Postsecondary Education
U.S. Department of Education
Washington, DC 20202 (202) 732-4415

To provide fellowships to individuals for graduate study in the arts, humanities and social sciences to individuals of superior ability. Types of assistance: grants. Estimate of annual funds available: $ 7,904,000.

* Paul Douglas Teacher Scholarships 84.176

U.S. Department of Education
Office of Asst. Secretary for Postsecondary Education
Division of Policy and Program Development
Washington, DC 20202 (202) 732-4507

To provide scholarships through the states that enable and encourage outstanding high school graduates who demonstrate an interest in teaching. Types of assistance: grants. Estimate of annual funds available: $ 15,235,297.

* Robert C. Byrd Honors Scholarships (Byrd Scholarship Program) 84.185

Fred H. Sellers
U.S. Department of Education
Office of Student Financial Assistance
Division of Policy and Program Development
Washington, DC 20202 (202) 732-4507

To provide scholarships to promote student excellence and achievement to recognize exceptionally able students who show promise of continued academic achievement. Types of assistance: grants. Estimate of annual funds available: $ 8,200,000.

* Christa McAuliffe Fellowships (CMFP) 84.190

U.S. Department of Education
Office of the Asst. Secretary for Elementary and Secondary Education
400 Maryland Ave., SW
Washington, DC 20202 (202) 732-4342

To reward excellence in teaching by providing financial assistance to outstanding teachers to continue their education. Types of assistance: grants. Estimate of annual funds available: $ 1,892,000.

Be patient. If any phone number is incorrect, call (area code) 555-1212 and request the new listing.

Education

* Graduate Assistance in Areas of National Need (GAANN) 84.200

Allen P. Cissell
Division of Higher Education Incentive Programs
Office of Postsecondary Education
U.S. Department of Education
Washington, DC 20202 (202) 732-4415

To provide federal support to graduate academic departments, programs, and units of institutions of higher education for the purpose of sustaining and enhancing the capacity for teaching and research in academic areas of national need. Types of assistance: grants. Estimate of annual funds available: $ 12,844,000.

* Grants to Institutions to Encourage Minority Participation in Graduate Education (Minority Participation in Graduate Education) 84.202

Walter T. Lewis
Division of Higher Education Incentive Programs
Office of Postsecondary Education
U.S. Department of Education
Washington, DC 20202 (202) 732-4393

To provide grants to institutions of higher education to enable them to identify talented undergraduate students that demonstrate financial need and are from minority groups under-represented in graduate education. Types of assistance: grants. Estimate of annual funds available: $ 3,476,000.

* Jacob K. Javits Gifted and Talented Students (Gifted and Talented) 84.206

L. Ann Benjamin
Research Applications Division
Programs for the Improvement of Practice
U.S. Department of Education
55 New Jersey Ave., NW
Washington, DC 20202 (202) 357-6187

To provide financial assistance to state and local educational agencies, institutions of higher education and other public and private agencies and organizations to stimulate research, development training and similar activities designed to ensure that needs of elementary and secondary schools meet the special educational needs of gifted and talented students. Types of assistance: grants. Estimate of annual funds available: $ 7,904,000.

* Native Hawaiian Gifted and Talented 84.210

Ramon Ruiz
U.S. Department of Education
School Improvement Programs
400 Maryland Ave., SW
Washington, DC 20202 (202) 732-4153

To provide financial assistance to the University of Hawaii at Hilo to establish a native Hawaiian Gifted and Talented Center. Types of assistance: direct payment. Estimate of annual funds available: $ 790,400.

* Ronald E. McNair Post-Baccalaureate Achievement (McNair Programs) 84.217

May J. Weaver
U.S. Department of Education
Division of Student Services
400 Maryland Ave., SW
Washington, DC 20202 (202) 732-4804

To provide grants for higher education institutions to prepare low-income first generation college students for doctoral study. Types of assistance: grants. Estimate of annual funds available: $ 1,482,000.

* Harry S. Truman Scholarship Program 85.001

Malcolm C. McCormack, Executive Secretary
712 Jackson Place, NW
Washington, DC 20006 (202) 395-4831

To honor former President Harry S. Truman through the operation of an education scholarship program, financed by a permanent trust fund endowment to develop increased opportunities for young Americans to prepare for and pursue careers in public service. Types of assistance: direct payment. Estimate of annual funds available: $ 2,431,000.

Be patient. If any phone number is incorrect, call (area code) 555-1212 and request the new listing.

The World's Largest Educational Database

The Educational Resources Information Center (ERIC) is a nationwide information service set up to collect materials about current developments in education and make them available to the public. The system includes 16 clearinghouses, each of which is responsible for acquiring, processing, and disseminating information about a particular aspect of education. Policy makers, researchers, education practitioners, librarians, students, parents, and community members use ERIC to stay abreast of the most up-to-date developments in education.

ERIC's database is the world's largest source of education information, containing bibliographic information of more than 665,000 documents and journal articles on education research and practice. The ERIC database is available at more than 3,000 locations worldwide.

How to use Eric

ERIC clearinghouses offer a wide variety of services and products. Clearinghouses answer questions about their subject fields, run computer searches of the ERIC database, develop short bibliographies, newsletters, and other free or inexpensive materials; and publish handbooks of teaching and learning materials for use in the classroom.

ACCESS ERIC is the main center for the ERIC clearinghouses. Specific questions are referred to the appropriate clearinghouse best equipped to answer them. Contact: ACCESS ERIC, Aspen Systems Corporation, 1600 Research Blvd., Rockville, MD 20850, (800) USE-ERIC.

Elementary and Early Childhood

This Clearinghouse provides information on the development and education of children from birth through early adolescence. Among the topics covered are: prenatal and infant development and care; child care programs and community services for children at local, state, and federal levels; family relationships; home and school relationships; technology and children; preparation of early childhood teachers and caregivers; foster care and adoption; and theoretical and philosophical issues related to children's development and education.

The clearinghouse provided a couple with guides, publications and checklists to help them select a day care center. They also directed them on where to search for more information on day care centers, and provided a guide to assess their preschooler's development.

A reporter called the clearinghouse to obtain information for a news story on the quality of foster care. After conducting a database search, the clearinghouse sent articles, research reports, and statistics.

ERIC/EECE Digests and Resource Lists are free; publications and ReadySearches are individually priced. Contact: Eric Clearinghouse On Elementary And Early Childhood Education, University of Illinois, 804 West Pennsylvania Ave., Urbana, IL 61801-4897, (217) 333-1386.

Teacher Education

The ERIC Clearinghouse on Teacher Education provides comprehensive information on health, physical education, recreation, and dance and movement education.

Many administrators and researchers call the clearinghouse to get answers to questions on the reform movement in teacher certification: What are the requirements? How do they vary from state to state? What are the current objectives and priorities?

A math teacher wanted to expand his horizons in the classroom by introducing some computer games to help his students learn to multiply and divide. The Clearinghouse sent him a bibliography called *Simulations and Games* which has over 2,000 entries in 60 categories reflecting the growing interest in applying computer games to education.

Contact: Eric Clearinghouse On Teacher Education, American Association of Colleges for Teacher Education, One Dupont Circle, NW, Suite 610, Washington, DC 20036-2412, (202) 293-2450.

Handicapped and Gifted

This Clearinghouse provides information on the education and development of handicapped persons, including prevention of handicaps, identification and assessment of handicaps, and intervention and enrichment programs for the handicapped both in special settings and within the mainstream. All aspects of the education and development of gifted persons are covered as well.

A teacher was helped to mainstream a handicapped student in her vocational education classes. She obtained information on how to make the child feel more comfortable, and ways to adapt her teaching style to the child's needs. She received research briefs on being at ease with handicapped children, and managing stress for the learning disabled.

A graduate student needed information on the post-school status of learning disabled students. The clearinghouse provided research and resource summaries, a bibliography of selected publications, suggestions for database searching, and referrals to other sources of information.

Be patient. If any phone number is incorrect, call (area code) 555-1212 and request the new listing.

Education

For pricing information contact Information Services at (202) 357-6089. Contact: Eric Clearinghouse on Handicapped and Gifted Children, The Council for Exceptional Children, 1920 Association Dr., Reston, VA 22091-1589, (703) 620-3660.

Educational Management

This Clearinghouse distributes information on the leadership, management, and structure of public and private educational organizations, and many facets of administration and methods of organizational change. The Clearinghouse also provides information on sites and equipment and aspects of planning and operating an educational facility.

A policymaker formulating educational policy needed to understand the nature of teachers' work. The clearinghouse sent literature to answer questions such as How do teachers preserve the quality of instruction in the face of never-ending task demands? What benefits do teachers derive from their interactions with students? and What would a cooperative alliance between policymakers and teachers look like?

A high school principal was concerned about racism in school. The clearinghouse provided a bulletin explaining why racism is on the rise and reporting on effective programs to foster cultural acceptance.

Publications vary in price from $4 to $25. Database searches range from $7.50 to $30+ according to the type and length of search. Other short product series are available free. For a pricing list, contact Eric Clearinghouse On Educational Management, College of Education, University of Oregon, 1787 Agate Street, Eugene, OR 97403, (503) 346-5043.

Languages and Linguistics

This Clearinghouse provides information on language and language sciences and all areas of language instruction methodology and learning, including foreign language. Additionally it monitors bilingualism and bilingual education, study abroad and international exchanges, and teacher training.

A public policy maker obtained information on the problems facing illiterate adults who are not native English speakers, and what the most effective education strategies have been.

A business owner wanted information on teaching English as a second language for to improve communication in the workplace. He received an annotated bibliography with abstracts and call numbers of documents relative to the topic.

Minibibliographies and fact sheets are free. Ready-made computer search printouts are available for $10 each, prepaid. Prices vary for a tailor-made search. Contact Eric Clearinghouse On Languages and Linguistics, Center for Applied Linguistics, 1118 22nd St., NW, Washington, DC 20037-0037, (202) 429-9292.

Tests, Measurement and Evaluation

The Clearinghouse provides information on the assessment and evaluation of education projects or programs; tests and other measurement devices; methodology of measurement and evaluation; research design and methodology; human development; and learning theory in general.

Many researchers call the clearinghouse to obtain statistics on the various states that deal with testing for teachers. What percentage of would-be teachers certify? Which states have more stringent standards? and How do the standards for certification vary from state to state?

Many educators and researchers obtain information on the effectiveness of the Scholastic Aptitude Test to determine college entrance. Do statistics show that the tests discriminate against certain minority groups? Are the tests effective tools for measurement? The clearinghouse can provide this information.

For pricing information and a listing of publications contact Information Services at (202) 357-6088. Contact: Eric Clearinghouse On Tests, Measurement, And Evaluation, American Institutes for Research, Washington Research Center, 3333 K St., NW, Washington, DC 20007-3893, (202) 342-5060.

Urban Education

The Clearinghouse provides information on programs and practices in schools in urban areas and the education of racial/ethnic minority children and youth in various settings; theory and practice of education equity; and urban and minority experiences and social institutions and services.

Members of school boards of education obtain research and current studies from the clearinghouse on the most effective programs for reducing the dropout rates among inner city high school students.

Federal government employees and media personnel often call the clearinghouse to obtain data on how much money is spent on programs to reduce drop-out rates, especially around the time of appropriations.

For pricing information and a list of publications contact Information Services at (202) 357-6847. Contact: Eric Clearinghouse On Urban Education, Teachers College, Columbia University Institute for Urban and Minority Education, Main Hall, Room 303, Box 40, 525 West 120th St., New York, NY 10027-9998, (212) 678-3433.

Rural Education, Small Schools

The Clearinghouse provides information on economic, cultural, social, and other factors of education for rural residents, including American Indians/Alaska Natives, Mexican Americans, and migrants; and education in all small schools.

A policymaker obtained information about the emerging problem of maintaining and replacing school buildings in rural areas. The clearinghouse sent reports analyzing the available options, outlining implications for educators, and developing recommendations for possible consideration by state-level policymakers.

The World's Largest Educational Database

A teacher with several children whose immigration status placed them at risk in his classes contacted the clearinghouse to obtain publications describing the plight of these children in American schools, the legal issues and pertinent court rulings, and prohibited and recommended practices.

Contact: Eric Clearinghouse On Rural Education And Small Schools, Appalachia Educational Laboratory, Inc., 1031 Quarrier St., P.O. Box 1348, Charleston, WV 25325-1348, 800/624-9120 (outside WV), 800/344-6646 (in WV). For pricing information and a listing of publications contact Information Services at (202) 357-6286.

Adult, Career and Vocational Learning

The Clearinghouse provides materials covering all levels of adult and continuing education from basic literacy training through professional skill upgrading; vocational and technical education covering all service areas for secondary, post-secondary, and adult populations; and career education and career development programs for all ages and populations in educational, institutional, business, and industrial settings.

The clearinghouse conducted a database search for a businessman on the latest information in robotics and their applications.

An employer wanted to implement flex time, work share and several pre-retirement plans for his employees. The clearinghouse provided him with information on various experimental models, resources to help him set up and start the programs, and research on the effectiveness of the programs in other worksites.

Contact: Eric Clearinghouse On Adult, Career And Vocational Learning, Ohio State University Center on Education and Training for Employment, 1960 Kenny Rd., Columbus, OH 43210-1090, (800) 848-4815, (614) 292-4353. For pricing information contact Information Services at (202) 357-6089.

Higher Education

The Clearinghouse provides information covering education beyond the secondary level that leads to a four-year, masters, doctoral, or professional degree and that includes courses and programs designed to enhance or update skills obtained in these degree programs. It also covers business or industry education programs leading to a degree.

What research and assessments are available on the trends and issues in higher education? What are students really learning? The clearinghouse maintains up-to-date research and information on these issues.

A graduate student, interested in what percentage of state university faculty are minorities and women, obtained data on the diversity in state university faculties. Another student obtained figures on the number of female Hispanic school administrators in Ohio.

A basic bibliographic printout consists of up to 100 current citations. The cost varies: $80 corporate; $40 academic

institutions; $25 students. Contact Eric Clearinghouse On Higher Education, George Washington University, One Dupont Circle, Washington, DC 20036-1183, (202) 296-2597.

For further pricing information contact the User Services Specialist at (202) 357-6919.

Junior Colleges

This Clearinghouse provides information on the development, administration, and evaluation of two-year public and private community and junior colleges, technical institutes, and two-year branch university campuses. It also deals with linkages between two-year colleges and business/industrial organizations.

A researcher obtained information on the graduation rates of nursing students working on A.A. degrees from junior colleges. How many of these students are returning women and mothers?

Another researcher requested information on recruiting minorities and women, and efforts to retain them in junior colleges.

Contact: Eric Clearinghouse On Junior Colleges, University of California at Los Angeles, Mathematical Sciences Building, Room 8118, 405 Hilgard Ave., Los Angeles, CA 90024-1564, (213) 825-3931. For pricing information contact Information Services at (202) 357-6925.

Information Resources

This Clearinghouse provides information covering educational technology and library and information science at all levels. Within library and information science, the focus is on the operation and management of information services for education-related organizations. All aspects of information technology related to education are considered within this scope.

A school administrator called the clearinghouse to obtain the latest research on the value of using computers and applying video technology to enhance learning. He received some of the clearinghouse's own materials and learned how to access the database to obtain more specific information.

A software company needed information on the advantages of the CD-ROM over floppy disks. The clearinghouse sent the company various studies comparing the different types of computer base media.

ERIC digests and minibibliographies are free. More exhaustive database searches vary in cost. Contact Eric Clearinghouse On Information Resources, Syracuse University School of Education, 30 Huntington Hall, 150 Marshall Street, Syracuse, NY 13244-2340, (315) 443-3640. For pricing information contact Information Services at (202) 357-6846.

Science, Math and the Environment

The ERIC Clearinghouse for Science, Mathematics, and Environmental Education acquires educational literature on the

Education

following topics: development of curriculum and instructional materials; teachers and teacher education; learning theory/outcomes; educational programs; research and evaluative studies; media applications; and computer applications.

A sixth-grade teacher obtained information to help her teach a lesson on environmental education. She received a publication suggesting activities related to proper use and disposal of hazardous materials found in the home. She also received a list of suggested activities to involve her students in examining the nature and importance of recycling along with a list of films, readings, and organizations to contact for further information.

The clearinghouse can provide materials to answer questions such as How are microcomputers being used in laboratory activities? What are the recent developments in college mathematics? What are the common safety hazards in science classrooms? What resources are available for teaching mathematics in a bilingual classroom? What are the environmental education objectives, activities, accomplishments, and plans of the agencies of the Federal Government?

There is a minimal charge for certain publications and bibliographies. In-depth database searches range in cost from $10 to $25. Contact: Eric Clearinghouse For Science, Mathematics, And Environmental Education, 1200 Chambers Road - 3rd Floor, Columbus, OH 43212, (614) 292-6717.

Reading and Communication Skills

This Clearinghouse makes available hard-to-find educational materials such as research reports, literature reviews, curriculum guides, conference papers, projects or program reviews, and government reports. Each year ERIC/RCS helps thousands of people find useful information related to education in reading, English, journalism, theater, speech and mass communications.

The clearinghouse can provide materials to answer questions such as: How can newspapers, television and film be used as effective teaching tools? What strategies help Dyslexic students? What are specific problems in media ethics? How does bias affect the perception of journalists? and What models have been used to foster cognitive development in college students?

An English teacher wished to incorporate computers into her classroom at the elementary level. The clearinghouse provided guidelines on the sequential organization of word-processing skills, software selection, class organization, desktop publishing, and a variety of other lessons for the effective integration of computers into the instructional program.

ERIC/RCS Focused Access to Selected Topics Bibliographies, newsletters, and Digests with information and references on topics of current interest are free of charge. Multiple copies of publications for workshop distribution are available at no-cost. Question-answering is also a free service. Customized computer searches of the ERIC database are conducted for $20 for the first 50 citations. Contact Eric Clearinghouse On Reading And Communication Skills, Indiana University, Smith Research Center, Suite 150, 2805 East Tenth Street, Bloomington, IN 47408-2698.

Social Studies and Social Science

This Clearinghouse describes journal articles and documents at all levels of social studies and social science education, including anthropology, economics, geography, sociology, social psychology, civics, and political science. It also covers materials on history and on social topics such as law-related education, ethnic studies, bias and discrimination, aging, adoption, women's equity, and sex education.

A curriculum policy maker obtained information from the clearinghouse focusing on what is happening now in computer use and what might be expected in the future for social studies.

A middle school world geography teacher wished to supplement her lessons on Africa and African culture. The clearinghouse provided essays on what, why, and how to teach about people and places of Africa, provided teaching materials, and listed resources including a select bibliography on teaching about Africa and listings of national centers of African studies and other organizations with resources in Africa.

You can obtain a customized computer search of the ERIC database on a requested topic for $10 to $25 to yield an annotated bibliography of up to 50 documents and journal articles in the ERIC system. Call or write the ERIC/ChESS User Services Coordinator for more information. Contact Eric Clearinghouse For Social Studies/social Science Education, Social Studies Development Center, Indiana University, Smith Research Center, 2805 East Tenth St., Suite 120, Bloomington, IN 47405, (812) 855-3838.

Counseling and Personnel Services

This Clearinghouse provides documents covering all levels of counseling and personnel services including preparation, practice, and supervision of counselors at all education levels and in all settings; theoretical development of counseling and guidance; personnel procedures such as testing and interviewing and the analysis and dissemination of the resultant information; group work and case work; nature of pupil, student, and adult characteristics; personnel workers and their relation to career planning, family consultations, and student orientation activities.

The clearinghouse can provide materials to answer questions from the public and professionals such as How can I enhance a student's self-esteem through counseling? How can counselors effectively intervene in the problems of child abuse? What are the emerging priorities for counseling in the 1990's? What counseling relevant software programs are available and how can the software be used? and What dropout prevention programs have been effective?

Contact Eric Clearinghouse On Counseling And Personnel Services, 2108 School of Education, University of Michigan, Ann Arbor, MI 48109-1259, (313) 764-9492.

Be patient. If any phone number is incorrect, call (area code) 555-1212 and request the new listing.

State Money for Students

Alabama

Alabama Commission on Higher Education, One Court Square, Suite 221, Montgomery, Alabama 36197, (205) 269-2700. Alabama's programs are to encourage Alabama residents to attend in-state schools. The programs include the Student Assistance Program; the Student Grant Program; the Emergency Secondary Education Scholarship Program for Math and Science; and grants for children of deceased policemen/ firefighters.

Alaska

Alaska Commission on Postsecondary Education, Pouch FP, Juneau, AK 99811; (907) 465-2854. Alaska's programs include the Alaska Teacher Scholarship Loan Program.

Arizona

Arizona Commission for Postsecondary Education, 1937 West Jefferson Street, Phoenix, AZ 85009; (602) 255-3109. Scholarships are offered by many of Arizona's universities.

Arkansas

Arkansas Department of Higher Education, 1220 West Third Street, Little Rock, AR 72201; (501) 371-1441. Arkansas' programs include the Loan Emergency Program awarded to students from areas with poor education systems, and the Governor's Scholar Program awarded to the top students in the state.

California

California Student Aid Commission, P.O. Box 942845, Sacramento, CA 94245-0845; (916) 445-0880. California's programs include grants, loans, and scholarships. A workbook with information on these programs is available.

Colorado

Colorado Commission on Higher Education, 1300 Broadway, 2nd Floor, Denver, CO 80203; (303) 866-2723. Colorado administers eight programs in the areas of grants, scholarships, and work-study. It also offers a Diversity Grant Program for students from underrepresented groups.

Connecticut

Connecticut Board of Higher Education, 61 Woodland Street, Hartford, CT 06105-2391; (203) 566-2618. Need-based grants are one of the programs administered by the state of Connecticut.

Delaware

Delaware Postsecondary Education Commission, 820 French Street, Wilmington, DE 19801; (302) 571-3240. Delaware's programs include need- and merit-based scholarship programs. Scholarship loans can be repaid by one-year of service for each year of support.

District of Columbia

Office of State Education Affairs, 2100 Martin Luther King, Jr., Ave., SE, Suite 401, Washington, DC 20020; (202) 727-3688. The District of Columbia's programs include need-based grants for residents.

Florida

Florida Office of Student Financial Aid, State Programs Unit, Florida Education Center, Tallahassee, FL 32399; (904) 488-1034. Florida offers approximately twenty-six scholarships, grants, and loans. Some of its programs include A Critical Teacher Shortage Loan Program, the 'Chappie' James Scholarship awarded to the most promising student, and the Challenger Astronauts Memorial Scholarships. Fellowships and loans are also offered to graduate students.

Georgia

Georgia Department of Education, Division of General Instruction, 1952 Twin Towers East, Atlanta, GA 30334-5040; (404) 656-5812. Georgia's programs include scholarships and grants. A merit-based program includes the Georgia Scholar Program.

Hawaii

Hawaii Department of Education, Student Personnel Services, 1302 Queen Emma Street, Room A-207, Honolulu, HI 96813; (808) 548-4394. Hawaii's programs include scholarships and grants. *Bulletin 15* describes Hawaii's programs and includes other pertinent information.

Idaho

Office of the State Board of Education, 307 Len B. Jordan Building, 650 West State Street, Boise, ID 83720; (208) 334-2270. Idaho administers programs which include the Idaho Scholarship Program, the Education Incentive Program in Education and Nursing, and a Work-Study Program.

Illinois

Illinois Student Aid Commission, 106 Wilmort Road, Deerfield, IL 60015; (708) 948-8550. Illinois' programs include scholarships based on merit and need and are offered to Illinois residents attending a college or university within the state.

Indiana

State Student Assistance Commission of Indiana, 964 North Pennsylvania St., Indianapolis, IN 46204; (317) 232-2350. Indiana's programs include a need-based grant program and a merit-based Hoosier Scholar Program.

Iowa

Iowa College Aid Commission, 201 Jewett Building, Ninth and Grant Avenue, Des Moines, IA 50309; (515) 282-3501. Some of the programs Iowa offers include an Iowa Tuition Grant, a State of Iowa Scholarship, a Loan Reimbursement in Nursing, and Technical Grants to a two-year community college.

Kansas

Kansas Board of Regents, Capital Tower, 400 8th St., SW, Suite 609, Topeka, KS 66603; (913) 296-3517. Kansas administers approximately sixteen programs in grants and scholarships, including a Scholarship Program which awards a maximum of $1,000 per year. Nursing scholarships which meet certain criteria and graduate scholarships are also administered.

Kentucky

Kentucky Higher Education Assistance Authority, 1050 US 127 South, Frankfort, KY 40601; (502) 564-3553. Kentucky strives to keep its tuition at state colleges and universities affordable by using state monies. Scholarships and grants are offered to students.

Louisiana

Special Commission on Education Services, P.O. Box 91202, Baton Rouge, LA 70821-9202; (504) 922-1011. Louisiana's programs include grants and scholarships.

Maine

Maine Department of Higher Education, State House Station 119, Augusta, ME 04333; (207) 289-2183. Maine administers various scholarships, grants, and loans, including the Maine Student Incentive Program offered to a resident attending a college in Maine or in any other of the five New England states. Post-graduate scholarships in the medical field are also available.

Maryland

Maryland Higher Education Commission, The Jeffrey Building, 16 Francis Street, Suite 209, Annapolis, MD 21401; (301) 974-5370. Maryland offers scholarships, loans, and grants, in addition to Senatorial and House of Delegate scholarships which are awarded annually.

Massachusetts

Board of Regents of Higher Education, Scholarship Office, 330 Stuart Street, Boston, MA 02116; (617) 727-9420. Massachusetts administers approximately twelve scholarships programs and a Graduate Grant Program.

Michigan

Michigan Department of Education, Student Financial Assistance Services, P.O.

Be patient. If any phone number is incorrect, call (area code) 555-1212 and request the new listing.

Education

Box 3008, Lansing, MI 48909; (517) 373-3394. Michigan administers scholarships, grants, and loans.

Minnesota

Minnesota Higher Education Coordinating Board, Capitol Square Building, Suite 400, 550 Cedar Street, St. Paul, MN 55101, (612) 296-3974. Minnesota's programs include grants, loans, a State Grant Program, and a Child-Care Program.

Mississippi

Board of Trustees of State Institutions of Higher Learning, 3825 Ridgewood Rd., Jackson, MS 39211-6453; (601) 982-6570. Mississippi administers approximately fifteen programs, including scholarships, grants, and loans, all of which are need- and/or merit-based.

Missouri

Missouri Coordinating Board of Higher Education, P.O. Box 1438, Jefferson City, MO 65102; (314) 751-3940. Missouri's programs include the need-based Missouri Student Grant and the Missouri Higher Education Academic Scholarship awarded to those students who scores on the SAT or ACT fall within the top three percent (this award is revised annually).

Montana

Office of the Commissioner of Higher Education, 35 South Last Chance Gulch, Helena, MT 59620; (406) 444-6570. Montana's programs include need- and merit-based scholarships.

Nebraska

Nebraska Coordinating Commission for Postsecondary Education, 301 Centennial Mall, South, P.O. Box 95005, Lincoln, NE 68509-5505; (402) 471-2847. Nebraska administers a "decentralized" form of student aid in higher education. Monies are allocated based on a formula to postsecondary schools. Students should contact the financial aid office at the college they plan to attend for scholarship, grant, and loan information.

Nevada

Nevada Department of Education, 400 West King Street, Carson City, NV 89710; (702) 885-3104. Nevada administers financial programs through their colleges.

New Hampshire

New Hampshire Postsecondary Education Commission, 2 Industrial Park Drive, Concord, NH 03301; (603) 271-2550. New Hampshire administers approximately six programs in state scholarships and grants. Students must meet residency requirements.

New Jersey

New Jersey Department of Higher Education, Office of Student Assistance, 4 Quakerbridge Plaza, CN 540, Trenton, NJ 08625; (609) 588-3228. New Jersey administers approximately five programs in state scholarships and grants. Included in these five are the Distinguished State Scholar Program and the Tuition Aid Grant. Recipients must be New Jersey residents attending a college within the state.

New Mexico

New Mexico Education Assistance Foundation, P.O. Box 27020, Albuquerque, NM 81725; (505) 345-3391. New Mexico administers scholarships, grants, and loans.

New York

New York Higher Education Services Corporation, Student Information, Albany, NY 12255; (518) 474-5592. New York administers approximately twenty-one state programs, including two general Grant Programs for full- and part-time students and undergraduate Scholarship and Fellowship awards. New York also administers an Empire State Excellence Scholarship.

North Carolina

North Carolina State Education Assistance Authority, P.O. Box 2688, Chapel Hill, NC 27514; (919) 549-8614. North Carolina administers scholarship, grant, and loan programs.

North Dakota

North Dakota Student Financial Assistance Program, State Capitol, 600 East Boulevard, Bismarck, ND 58505; (701) 224-4114. North Dakota administers approximately three programs, including the merit-based North Dakota Scholars Program.

Ohio

Ohio Board of Regents, 30 East Broad Street, Columbus, OH 43215; (614) 466-7420. Ohio administers approximately five need- and merit-based program, plus an Instructional Grant Program. All of these programs are restricted to Ohio residents only.

Oklahoma

Oklahoma State Regents for Higher Education, 500 Education Building, State Capitol Complex, Oklahoma City, OK 73105; (405) 521-2444. Oklahoma administers approximately six programs, including the merit-based Chancellors Scholarship Program. These programs are restricted to Oklahoma residents attending a college in-state.

Oregon

Oregon State Scholarship Commission 1445 Willamette Street, Eugene, OR 97401; (503) 686-4166. Oregon administers programs for need-based grants, academic- and need-based cash awards, and private awards. These are available to Oregon residents only.

Pennsylvania

Pennsylvania Higher Education Assistance Agency, 660 Boas Street, Harrisburg, PA 17102; (717) 257-2550. Pennsylvania administers programs in the areas of grants, loans, and scholarships.

Rhode Island

Rhode Island Higher Education Assistance Authority, 560 Jefferson Boulevard, Warwick, RI 02886; (401) 277-2050. Rhode Island administers one Grant Program and three Scholarship Programs, including a Teacher Scholarship for "the best and the brightest." These programs are awarded on the basis of need and/or merit.

South Carolina

South Carolina Commission on Higher Education, 1333 Main Street, Suite 300, Columbia, SC 29201; (803) 253-6260. South Carolina administers scholarship and grant programs to approximately eighteen private colleges.

South Dakota

South Dakota Department of Education and Cultural Affairs, Office of the Secretary, 700 Governors Drive, Pierre, SD 57501; (605) 773-3134. South Dakota administers approximately five need- and merit-based programs in the areas of scholarships and grants.

Tennessee

Tennessee Student Assistance Corporation, 404 James Robertson Parkway, Suite 1250, Parkway Towers, Nashville, TN 37243-0820; (615) 741-1346. Tennessee administers state grants, loans, and scholarships.

Texas

Texas Coordinating Board on Higher Education, Box 12788, Capitol Station, Austin, TX 78711; (512) 462-6400. Texas is a decentralized state for programs. Students should contact the Financial Aid office at the college they plan to attend for grant, scholarship, and loan information

Utah

Utah System for Higher Education, 355 West North Temple, 3 Triad, Suite 550, Salt Lake City, UT 84180-1205; (801) 538-5247. Utah administers state funds using a decentralized system. Students should contact the Financial Aid Office at the college they plan to attend.

Vermont

Vermont Student Assistance Corporation, P.O. Box 2000, Champlain Mill, Winooski, VT 05404; (802) 655-9602. Vermont's programs include the need-based Vermont Incentive Program Grant and non-degree Grant Programs and Honors Scholarships.

Virginia

Virginia State Council of Higher Education, Office of Financial Aid, James Monroe Building, 101 North 14th Street, Richmond, VA 23219; (804) 225-3146. Virginia administers need- and merit-based programs for scholarships, grants, and work-study.

Washington

Council for Postsecondary Education, 917 Lakeridge Way, GV 11, Olympia, WA 98504; (206) 753-3571. Washington administers approximately five programs

Be patient. If any phone number is incorrect, call (area code) 555-1212 and request the new listing.

including the Washington State Need Grant and the Washington Scholars Program.

West Virginia

West Virginia Higher Education Program, P.O. Box 4007, Charleston, WV 25364-4007; (304) 347-1266. West Virginia's programs include scholarships (including a Teacher's Scholarship), grants, and college work-study.

Wisconsin

State of Wisconsin Higher Educational Aids Board, P.O. Box 7885, Madison, WI 53707-7885; (608) 267-2206. Wisconsin administers approximately eight need- and merit-based scholarships and grants. Programs are also available for Indians, minorities, and the handicap.

Wyoming

Wyoming Department of Higher Education, Hathaway Building, Cheyenne, WY 82002; (307) 777-6213. Wyoming administers scholarships and grants, including a First Generation American Scholarship to a qualifying high school senior in Wyoming.

Be patient. If any phone number is incorrect, call (area code) 555-1212 and request the new listing.

Education

State Money For College Students

Students seeking financial assistance should ask the State higher education agency in their home state for information about State aid — including aid from a program jointly funded by individual states and the U.S. Department of Education. Each State has its own name for this program, as well as its own award levels, eligibility criteria, and application procedures.

Your State can also give you information about the Paul Douglas Teacher Scholarship Program, which is a Federal program administered at the State level. These scholarships are for outstanding high school graduates who want to pursue teaching careers after they finish college. A Douglas scholarship provides up to $5,000 per year to students who graduate from high school in the top 10% of their class, and who meet other selection criteria their State may establish. Generally, students are required to teach two years for each year of scholarship assistance they receive.

The agency in your State responsible for public elementary and secondary schools can also give you information on the Robert C. Byrd Honors Scholarship Program and the National Science Scholars Program (NSSP). Under the Byrd Program, students who demonstrate outstanding academic achievement and show promise of continued excellence may receive $1,500 for their first year of postsecondary education. Under the NSSP, graduating high school seniors (or those who will obtain the equivalent of a certificate of graduation) who have demonstrated excellence and achievement in the physical, life, or computer sciences, mathematics, or engineering may receive funds to continue their studies at the postsecondary level. Scholarships of up to $5,000 per year of undergraduate study, or the cost of education, whichever is less, are awarded to two students from each Congressional district.

Federal loans, grants and work-study programs are also available. Contact your school's financial aid administrator to find out details and to determine which ones are available at your school. First-time undergraduates may receive all three types of financial aid. Graduate students may apply for loans or Work-Study, but not for Pell Grants or SEOG. The State aid totals below reflect State grant and scholarship amounts and do not include Federal funding.

The U.S. Department of Education offers the following major financial aid programs:

Loans:

1) Stafford Loans are low-interest loans made to students attending school at least half-time. Loans are made by a lender such as a bank, credit union, or savings and loan association. Sometimes a school acts as a lender. These loans are insured by the guarantee agency in each State and reinsured by the Federal Government. Students must repay this loan. To find out the name, address, and telephone number of the guarantee agency in your State, as well as information about borrowing, call the Federal Student Aid Information Center at (800) 4-FED AID.

2) PLUS loans are for parents who want to borrow to help pay for their children's education. Supplemental Loans for Students (SLS) are for student borrowers. Both loans provide additional funds for educational expenses, and, like Stafford Loans, are made by a lender such as a bank, credit union, or savings and loan association.

3) Perkins Loans: This low-interest (5 percent) loan is for first-time undergraduates and graduate students with exceptional financial need, as determined by the school. For undergraduate students, priority is given to Pell Grant recipients. Loans are made through a school's financial aid office; the school is the lender. These loans must be repaid. Students may borrow up to $4,500 if they have completed less than two years of a program leading to a first bachelor's degree, or if they are enrolled in a vocational program. Students may borrow up to $9,000 if they have already completed two years of study toward a first bachelor's degree and have achieved third-year status. Up to $18,000 may be borrowed for graduate or professional study. See your school's financial aid department for details.

Grants:

1) Pell Grant: This award helps first-time undergraduates pay for their education after high school. Eligibility for those who receive a Pell Grant for the first time is usually limited to five to six years of undergraduate study, not including remedial coursework. Awards for the 1992-93 academic year will depend upon program funding. The maximum award for the 1991-92 academic year was $2,400. Students must attend school at least half-time. Grants do not have to be paid back. For more information, contact the financial aid administrator of the college or university you are attending.

2) Supplemental Educational Opportunity Grant (SEOG): This award helps first-time undergraduates with exceptional financial need, as determined by the school. Priority is given to Pell Grant recipients. An SEOG does not have to be paid back. Students can get up to $4,000 a year, depending upon available funding.

Work-Study:

1) College Work-Study (CWS): This program provides jobs for first-time undergraduates and for graduate students who need financial aid. CWS lets you earn money to help pay your educational expenses. Students are paid at least the current Federal minimum wage, but the pay may also be related to the type of work done and the skills required. Schools set individual work schedules and must pay students directly at least once a month.

Be patient. If any phone number is incorrect, call (area code) 555-1212 and request the new listing.

State Money For College Students

State Money For Students

Alabama

Alabama Commission on Higher Education, One Court Square, Suite 221, Montgomery, Alabama 36197, (205) 269-2700. Alabama's programs encourage Alabama residents to attend in-State schools. Residency is required to participate in the programs listed below. In 1990-91, Alabama awarded $8,940,217 in State-supported student assistance.

1) Alabama Student Assistance Program: These need-based, State/Federal grants range from $300 to $2,500 per academic year. At most institutions, awards are limited to undergraduate study. Nearly 90 Alabama institutions participate in the program.

2) Alabama Student Grant Program: This award of grant assistance is open to undergraduates attending an eligible independent Alabama college or university. Up to $1,200 is available per academic year.

3) Alabama Guaranteed Student Loan Program (AGSLP): This need-based, low interest loan program provides up to $2,625 per academic year for the first and second years of undergraduate study, up to $4,000 per academic year for students who have completed the first two years of undergraduate study, and up to $7,500 per academic year for graduate or professional students. A maximum of $17,250 for undergraduate study is offered; $54,750 for graduate and undergraduate studies combined.

4) Alabama National Guard Assistance Program: Awards are used for tuition, educational fees and book/supplies for Alabama National Guard members to attend a State public postsecondary educational institution. Awards are limited to $500 per term, and no more than $1,000 per year and are not need-based.

5) Emergency Secondary Education Scholarship Program: This scholarship/loan program was created to attract capable students to the teaching profession in math and science education. Up to $3,996 is offered per academic year.

6) Alabama Nursing Scholarships: Scholarship/loans of varying amounts are awarded to students enrolled in eligible nursing programs at participating institutions.

7) Alabama GI Dependents Educational Benefit Program: Tuition, fees and book assistance is available to children and spouses of eligible Alabama veterans who attend State public postsecondary schools. This program is open to undergraduates only.

8) American Legion Scholarship and American Legion Auxiliary Scholarship Programs: Open to students who are the sons, daughters, grandsons or granddaughters of veterans of World War I, World War II, Korea or Vietnam. Grants are used for tuition, fees and board expenses to attend a public postsecondary school. Awards are restricted to students who attend institutions with on-campus housing.

9) Senior Adult Scholarships: This free tuition program is available to individuals, 60 years of age or older, who attend public two-year postsecondary education institutions.

10) Junior and Community College Athletic Scholarships: Awards are based on demonstrated athletic ability determined through try-outs. Awards fund total tuition. Students must attend State public junior and community colleges. Awards are not based on financial need.

11) Junior and Community College Performing Arts Scholarships: Awards are based on demonstrated talent determined through competitive auditions. Awards fund total tuition. Students must attend State public junior and community colleges. Awards are not based on financial need.

12) Alabama Scholarships for Dependents of Blind Parents: This award covers instructional fees and tuition for children from families in which the head of the family is blind and whose family income is insufficient to provide educational benefits.

13) Police Officer's and Firefighters Survivor's Educational Assistance Program: The grant covers fees, books and supplies for dependents and eligible spouses of Alabama police officers and firefighters killed in the line of duty. There is no limit on the amount awarded to recipients. Applicants must enroll in an undergraduate program at a State public postsecondary education institution.

14) Stafford Student Loans: These loans are available for undergraduate, graduate, vocational or professional students who demonstrate financial need. Students may borrow $2,625 for each of the first two undergraduate years, and up to $4,000 annually through the fifth year. Graduate students may borrow up to $7,500 a year.

15) Parent Loans for Undergraduate Students (PLUS) and Supplemental Loans for Students (SLS): Parents may borrow for a dependent student under the PLUS Program. Independent undergraduate students and graduate and professional students may apply for SLS. Up to $4,000 is offered per academic year for each program. The maximum amount for each program is $20,000.

16) Wallace-Folsom Prepaid College Tuition Program: Parents, grandparents, friends, or any other sponsor may purchase a contract to guarantee tuition payment for a determined number of credit hours for a baccalaureate degree.

Age limits apply to students enrolled in this program. Lump-sum or periodic payment plans may be selected.

17) Perkins Loans: This low-interest (5 percent) loan is for first-time undergraduates and graduate students with exceptional financial need, as determined by the school. For undergraduate students, priority is given to Pell Grant recipients. Loans are made through a school's financial aid office, the school is the lender. These loans must be repaid. Students may borrow up to $4,500 if they've completed less than two years of a program leading to a first bachelor's degree, or if they are enrolled in a vocational program. Students may borrow up to $9,000 if they've already completed two years of study toward a first bachelor's degree and have achieved third-year status. Up to $18,000 may be borrowed for graduate or professional study. See your school's financial aid department for details.

18) Pell Grant: This award helps first-time undergraduates pay for their education after high school. Eligibility for those who receive a Pell Grant for the first time is usually limited to five to six years of undergraduate study, not including remedial coursework. Awards for the 1992-93 academic year will depend upon program funding. The maximum award for the 1991-92 academic year was $2,400. Students must attend school at least half-time. Grants do not have to be paid back. For more information, contact the financial aid administrator of the college or university you are attending.

19) Supplemental Educational Opportunity Grant (SEOG): This award helps first-time undergraduates with exceptional financial need, as determined by the school. Priority is given to Pell Grant recipients. An SEOG doesn't have to be paid back. Students can get up to $4,000 a year, depending upon available funding.

20) College Work-Study (CWS): This program provides jobs for first-time undergraduates and for graduate students who need financial aid. CWS lets you earn money to help pay your educational expenses. Students are paid at least the current Federal minimum wage, but the pay may also be related to the type of work done and the skills required. Schools set individual work schedules and must pay students directly at least once a month.

Alaska

Alaska Commission on Postsecondary Education, Pouch FP, Juneau, AK 99811-0505; (907) 465-2962. The following programs are open to Alaskan residents, only. In 1990-91, $1,623,852 was awarded in funding.

1) Michael Murphy Memorial Scholarship Loan: Funds up to $1,000 per year for undergraduates are awarded to full-time students pursuing a degree program at an accredited college or university in law enforcement, law, probation and parole, penology, or closely related fields. Loans are non-interest bearing and, upon degree completion, the scholarship loan recipient receives forgiveness of 20% of total loan indebtedness for each period he or she is employed full-time in Alaska law enforcement or a related field.

2) Robert C. Thomas Memorial Scholarship Loan Fund: This scholarship provides loans to students who wish to pursue a degree at an accredited college or university that will lead to a career in education, public administration, or other closely related fields. Funds up to $1,000 per year are available for full-time study. Undergraduates and graduates are eligible to apply. Loans are non-interest bearing and, upon degree completion, the scholarship loan recipient receives forgiveness of 20% of total loan indebtedness for each period he or she is employed full time in an education or public administration field.

3) A.W. "Winn" Brindle Memorial Scholarship Loan: This program funds provide educational loans to Alaska full-time undergraduate or graduate study at accredited schools in the following degree or certificate programs: fisheries, fishery management, food technology, fishery science, seafood processing, and other related fields. Awards cover the cost of tuition and fees, books and supplies, room and board, and transportation costs for up to two round trips between the recipient's home and school each year. A loan may be made for up to five years of undergraduate study, five years of graduate study, or a combined maximum of eight years of study.

4) Alaska State Educational Incentive Grant Program: This program provides grants to eligible students enrolled in their first undergraduate program at in-State or out-of-State postsecondary educational institutions. Grants range from $100 to $1,500, depending upon financial need.

5) Teacher Scholarship Loan Program: This program encourages Alaska high school graduates to pursue teaching careers in rural elementary and secondary schools in the State. Students may borrow up to $7,500 per year for in-State or out-of-State study. Loans may be used for tuition, room and board, books, and supplies, and transportation costs of up to two round trips between the student's home community and the school of attendance. Loans are awarded for a maximum of five years of undergraduate study.

6) Stafford Student Loans: These loans are available for undergraduate, graduate, vocational or professional students who demonstrate financial need. Students may borrow $2,625 for each of the first two undergraduate years, and up to

Education

$4,000 annually through the fifth year. Graduate students may borrow up to $7,500 a year. Not more than $17,250 can be borrowed for all years of undergraduate study, $73,500 for all years of graduate study, or $54,750 for undergraduate and graduate study combined.

7) Supplemental Loans for Students: This program is available to graduate, professional and independent undergraduate students. The annual maximum SLS loan limit is $4,000 and depends on the student's educational program length. Borrowers cannot exceed a maximum of $20,000.

8) Parent Loans for Students (PLUS): The PLUS program is for parents who wish to borrow for their student dependents. The parent is responsible for the repayment of the loan even if the dependent's education is not completed. The annual maximum PLUS amount is $4,000 per eligible dependent student up to a cumulative maximum of $20,000.

Arizona

Arizona Commission for Postsecondary Education, 3030 North Central, Suite 1407, Phoenix, AZ 85012; (602) 229-2590. Arizona administers a "decentralized" form of student aid in higher education. Monies are allocated based on a formula to postsecondary schools and each college or university sets their own funding limits. Students should contact the financial aid office at the college they plan to attend for scholarship, grant, and loan information. State residency is required for the programs listed below.

1) Arizona State Student Incentive Grant Program: This program provides grants from $100 to $2,500 to needy students who attend participating postsecondary educational institutions in Arizona. It is available to both undergraduate and graduate students who are attending school on at least a half-time basis in an eligible program.

2) Vocational Rehabilitation Assistance: Persons with a physical or mental disability that substantially interferes with obtaining employment may be eligible for assistance from this program. Each qualified individual works with a counselor to develop an appropriate rehabilitative program. This program is tailored to the individual and may include classroom training as well as work experience. Depending upon need, support services such as day care and allowances for transportation and books and supplies are provided. Supplemental training stipends are available on a limited basis. Additional information may be obtained by contacting the Vocational Rehabilitation Division of the nearest office of the Arizona Department of Economic Security. In 1990-91, 332 students received funding through this program.

3) Student Exchange Program: The Western InterState Commission for Higher Education (WICHE) helps Arizona students obtain access to five fields of professional education not available in Arizona, but made available at participating institutions in other Western States at a reduced tuition rate. The reduced tuition usually amounts to the in-State rate at public schools and one-third the regular tuition rate at private schools.

4) Stafford Student Loans: These loans are available for undergraduate, graduate, vocational or professional students who demonstrate financial need. Students may borrow $2,625 for each of the first two undergraduate years, and up to $4,000 annually through the fifth year. Graduate students may borrow up to $7,500 a year. Not more than $17,250 can be borrowed for all years of undergraduate study, $73,500 for all years of graduate study, or $54,750 for undergraduate and graduate study combined.

5) Supplemental Loans for Students: This program is available to graduate, professional and independent undergraduate students. The annual maximum SLS loan limit is $4,000 and depends on the student's educational program length. Borrowers cannot exceed a maximum of $20,000.

6) Parent Loans for Students (PLUS): The PLUS program is for parents who wish to borrow for their student dependents. The parent is responsible for the repayment of the loan even if the dependent's education is not completed. The annual maximum PLUS amount is $4,000 per eligible dependent student up to a cumulative maximum of $20,000.

7) Perkins Loans: This low-interest (5 percent) loan is for first-time undergraduates and graduate students with exceptional financial need, as determined by the school. For undergraduate students, priority is given to Pell Grant recipients. Loans are made through a school's financial aid office, the school is the lender. These loans must be repaid. Students may borrow up to $4,500 if they've completed less than two years of a program leading to a first bachelor's degree, or if they are enrolled in a vocational program. Students may borrow up to $9,000 if they've already completed two years of study toward a first bachelor's degree and have achieved third-year status. Up to $18,000 may be borrowed for graduate or professional study. See your school's financial aid department for details.

8) Pell Grant: This award helps first-time undergraduates pay for their education after high school. Eligibility for those who receive a Pell Grant for the first time is usually limited to five to six years of undergraduate study, not including remedial coursework. Awards for the 1992-93 academic year will depend upon

program funding. The maximum award for the 1991-92 academic year was $2,400. Students must attend school at least half-time. Grants do not have to be paid back. For more information, contact the financial aid administrator of the college or university you are attending.

9) Supplemental Educational Opportunity Grant (SEOG): This award helps first-time undergraduates with exceptional financial need, as determined by the school. Priority is given to Pell Grant recipients. An SEOG doesn't have to be paid back. Students can get up to $4,000 a year, depending upon available funding.

10) College Work-Study (CWS): This program provides jobs for first-time undergraduates and for graduate students who need financial aid. CWS lets you earn money to help pay your educational expenses. Students are paid at least the current Federal minimum wage, but the pay may also be related to the type of work done and the skills required. Schools set individual work schedules and must pay students directly at least once a month.

Arkansas

Arkansas Department of Higher Education, 114 East Capitol, Little Rock, AR 72201; (501) 324-9300. Students must be Arkansas residents to qualify for the following programs. In 1990-91, $5,107,000 was awarded in State funding.

1) Student Assistance Grants: Full-time undergraduate and high school seniors may apply for grants of up to $624 per year. Grants are awarded on a first come, first served basis by financial need.

2) Governor's Scholars: Scholarships of $2,000 per academic year are awarded to 100 high school seniors in recognition of outstanding academic achievement and leadership. Students with at least an ACT score of 27 or a grade point average of 3.60 may apply.

3) Arkansas Academic Challenge Scholarship: Scholarships of $1,000 per academic year are awarded to high school seniors with financial need, an ACT score of 19 and a grade point average of 2.50 in the precollegiate core course curriculum.

4) Paul Douglas Teaching Scholarship: These scholarships are available to full-time undergraduate and high school seniors who graduated in the top 10% of their high school graduating class or scored at least 62 on the GED and are pursuing certification to teach at the pre-school, elementary, or secondary level. Scholarships are for $5,000 per academic year. After graduation, recipients are required to teach two years for each year of scholarship assistance to receive total loan forgiveness.

5) Emergency Secondary Education Loan: Loans of $2,500 are available to full-time undergraduates or graduate students pursuing a secondary education teaching certificate in the following categories: foreign language, math, science, special education, guidance/counseling or gifted/talented. Repayment of the loan is forgiven at 20% for each year taught in approved subject shortage areas in Arkansas secondary schools after graduation.

6) MIA/KIA Dependent's Scholarship: This scholarship is open to full-time undergraduate/graduate students and high school seniors who are dependents/spouses of person's who were declared Killed in Action, Missing in Action or were Prisoner's of War. The award provides a waiver of in-State tuition, on-campus room, board, and fees at State higher education institutions. Students must attend an approved two or four year State supported college, university or vocational/technical school. Graduate students must not have received their undergraduate education in Arkansas.

7) Law Enforcement Officer's Dependents Scholarship: This scholarship is available to full-time undergraduates and high school seniors who are dependents of persons who were killed or totally disabled in the line of duty as law enforcement officers. The award is limited to eight semesters and does not include board, books, materials and supplies, dues or extracurricular activity fees. Spouses lose eligibility, if they remarry.

8) Second Effort Scholarship: The Arkansas Department of Higher Education contacts the individuals with the top ten GED scores and offers this scholarship. Awards are for $1,000 per academic year.

9) Stafford Student Loans: These loans are available for undergraduate, graduate, vocational or professional students who demonstrate financial need. Students may borrow $2,625 for each of the first two undergraduate years, and up to $4,000 annually through the fifth year. Graduate students may borrow up to $7,500 a year. Not more than $17,250 can be borrowed for all years of undergraduate study, $73,500 for all years of graduate study, or $54,750 for undergraduate and graduate study combined.

10) Supplemental Loans for Students: This program is available to graduate, professional and independent undergraduate students. The annual maximum SLS loan limit is $4,000 and depends on the student's educational program length. Borrowers cannot exceed a maximum of $20,000.

11) Parent Loans for Students (PLUS): The PLUS program is for parents who wish to borrow for their student dependents. The parent is responsible for the repayment of the loan even if the dependent's education is not completed. The

State Money For College Students

annual maximum PLUS amount is $4,000 per eligible dependent student up to a cumulative maximum of $20,000.

12) Perkins Loans: This low-interest (5 percent) loan is for first-time undergraduates and graduate students with exceptional financial need, as determined by the school. For undergraduate students, priority is given to Pell Grant recipients. Loans are made through a school's financial aid office, the school is the lender. These loans must be repaid. Students may borrow up to $4,500 if they've completed less than two years of a program leading to a first bachelor's degree, or if they are enrolled in a vocational program. Students may borrow up to $9,000 if they've already completed two years of study toward a first bachelor's degree and have achieved third-year status. Up to $18,000 may be borrowed for graduate or professional study. See your school's financial aid department for details.

13) Pell Grant: This award helps first-time undergraduates pay for their education after high school. Eligibility for those who receive a Pell Grant for the first time is usually limited to five to six years of undergraduate study, not including remedial coursework. Awards for the 1992-93 academic year will depend upon program funding. The maximum award for the 1991-92 academic year was $2,400. Students must attend school at least half-time. Grants do not have to be paid back. For more information, contact the financial aid administrator of the college or university you are attending.

14) Supplemental Educational Opportunity Grant (SEOG): This award helps first-time undergraduates with exceptional financial need, as determined by the school. Priority is given to Pell Grant recipients. An SEOG doesn't have to be paid back. Students can get up to $4,000 a year, depending upon available funding.

15) College Work-Study (CWS): This program provides jobs for first-time undergraduates and for graduate students who need financial aid. CWS lets you earn money to help pay your educational expenses. Students are paid at least the current Federal minimum wage, but the pay may also be related to the type of work done and the skills required. Schools set individual work schedules and must pay students directly at least once a month.

California

California Student Aid Commission, P.O. Box 942845, Sacramento, CA 94245-0845; (916) 445-0880. In 1990-91, $161 million was awarded in new and renewable Cal Grants. Students must be California residents to be eligible to participate in the programs listed below.

1) Cal Grants, A,B, and C are available for undergraduate students. A: Cal Grants A: Helps low- and middle-income students with tuition/fee costs. Grant recipients are selected on the basis of financial need and grade point average. In 1991-92, new awards range from $700 to $5,250 at independent schools and colleges, from $700 to about $1,900 at the University of California, and from $700 to about $1,000 at California State University. The minimum course length is two academic years.

B) Cal Grants B: This grant provides a living allowance (and sometimes tuition/fee help) for very low-income students. In 1991-92, the living allowance for new awards, ranged from $700 to $1,410. The tuition/fee award ranged from $700 to about $1,000 at California State University, and from $700 to about $1,900 at the University of California, and from $700 to $5,250 at independent schools and colleges. The minimum course length is one academic year.

C) Cal Grant C: Helps vocational school students with tuition and training costs. For 1991-92, awards ranged from $700 to $2,360 for tuition and fees. In addition, students must show a $700 need in order to receive a $530 allowance for tools, books and equipment.

2) State Work-Study Program: This program offers eligible college and university students the opportunity to earn money to defray educational expenses. Jobs may be available with public institutions or non-profit or profit-making enterprises. Students will be paid at rates comparable to those paid for positions within the employing organization.

3) Assumption Program of Loans for Education (APLE): Teacher candidates may apply for up to $8,000 in loan-assumption benefits through this program. The Commission annually accepts up to 500 new APLE program applicants who are selected by participating postsecondary institutions with approved teacher preparation programs. To receive benefits, participants must provide three consecutive years of teaching in a California public school in a designated subject matter shortage area or in a school serving in a high proportion of low-income students.

4) Graduate Fellowship Program: Candidates must be pursuing recognized advanced or professional degrees on at least a half-time basis at an eligible California graduate or professional school. Applicants must demonstrate their intent to become college or university faculty members. Awards are made on the basis of grades, graduate admissions test scores and consideration of disadvantaged background.

5) Law Enforcement Personnel Dependents Scholarship: This program provides

educational grants to needy dependents and spouses of California peace officers, officers and employees of the Department of Corrections or Youth Authority, and permanent and full-time firefighters who have been killed or totally disabled in the line of duty. Grants at four year colleges range from $100 to $1,500 per year with a maximum of $6,000 in a six year period. Grants at community colleges range from $100 to $500 per year, up to four years.

6) Stafford Student Loans: These loans are available for undergraduate, graduate, vocational or professional students who demonstrate financial need. Students may borrow $2,625 for each of the first two undergraduate years, and up to $4,000 annually through the fifth year. Graduate students may borrow up to $7,500 a year. Not more than $17,250 can be borrowed for all years of undergraduate study, $73,500 for all years of graduate study, or $54,750 for undergraduate and graduate study combined.

7) Supplemental Loans for Students: This program is available to graduate, professional and independent undergraduate students. The annual maximum SLS loan limit is $4,000 and depends on the student's educational program length. Borrowers cannot exceed a maximum of $20,000.

8) Parent Loans for Students (PLUS): The PLUS program is for parents who wish to borrow for their student dependents. The parent is responsible for the repayment of the loan even if the dependent's education is not completed. The annual maximum PLUS amount is $4,000 per eligible dependent student up to a cumulative maximum of $20,000.

9) State Veterans Benefits: Dependents of California veterans who are current totally service-connected disabled or deceased, wives of totally disabled veterans, and widows of deceased veterans may be eligible to receive benefits from the California Department of Veteran's Affairs. The benefits include a $100 per month subsistence allowance and a waiver of registration and tuition fees at the University of California, California State University, and community colleges.

10) Perkins Loans: This low-interest (5 percent) loan is for first-time undergraduates and graduate students with exceptional financial need, as determined by the school. For undergraduate students, priority is given to Pell Grant recipients. Loans are made through a school's financial aid office, the school is the lender. These loans must be repaid. Students may borrow up to $4,500 if they've completed less than two years of a program leading to a first bachelor's degree, or if they are enrolled in a vocational program. Students may borrow up to $9,000 if they've already completed two years of study toward a first bachelor's degree and have achieved third-year status. Up to $18,000 may be borrowed for graduate or professional study. See your school's financial aid department for details.

11) Pell Grant: This award helps first-time undergraduates pay for their education after high school. Eligibility for those who receive a Pell Grant for the first time is usually limited to five to six years of undergraduate study, not including remedial coursework. Awards for the 1992-93 academic year will depend upon program funding. The maximum award for the 1991-92 academic year was $2,400. Students must attend school at least half-time. Grants do not have to be paid back. For more information, contact the financial aid administrator of the college or university you are attending.

12) Supplemental Educational Opportunity Grant (SEOG): This award helps first-time undergraduates with exceptional financial need, as determined by the school. Priority is given to Pell Grant recipients. An SEOG doesn't have to be paid back. Students can get up to $4,000 a year, depending upon available funding.

13) College Work-Study (CWS): This program provides jobs for first-time undergraduates and for graduate students who need financial aid. CWS lets you earn money to help pay your educational expenses. Students are paid at least the current Federal minimum wage, but the pay may also be related to the type of work done and the skills required. Schools set individual work schedules and must pay students directly at least once a month.

Colorado

Colorado Commission on Higher Education, 1300 Broadway, 2nd Floor, Denver, CO 80203; (303) 866-2723. Colorado administers programs in the areas of grants, scholarships, and work-study. Students must be Colorado residents in order to participate in the following programs. In 1991-92, State education appropriations totalled $32,954,064.

1) Colorado Diversity Grants: These grants are available as part of a State-wide effort to increase participation of underrepresented groups in the Colorado public higher education system.

2) Colorado Student Incentive Grants (CSIG): Grants are available to qualified undergraduates with substantial financial need. Student grants under this program are comprised of both Federal and State funds.

3) Colorado Student Grants (CSG): Grants are available to qualified undergraduates with documented financial need.

4) Colorado Part-time Grants: These need based grants are for less than full-time students attending eligible Colorado institutions.

Be patient. If any phone number is incorrect, call (area code) 555-1212 and request the new listing.

Education

5) Colorado Work-Study: This part-time employment program is designed to assist students with financial need as well as those who have a need for work experience.

6) Undergraduate Merit Awards: Awards are available to students who demonstrate superior scholarship or talent as defined by the Colorado college or university they attend.

7) Colorado Graduate Grants: Graduate students with financial need may apply for this program.

8) Colorado Graduate Fellowships: This program provides merit-based awards to graduate students.

9) Law Enforcement/POW-MIA Dependents Tuition Assistance: This award, of approximately $5,000, pays tuition for dependents of Colorado law enforcement offices, fire or national guard personnel killed or disabled in the line of duty, and for dependents of prisoners of war or service personnel listed as missing in action. Dependents of disabled personnel must have demonstrated financial need for assistance. Applications are available at the Commission on Higher Education.

10) Colorado Nursing Scholarship: These scholarships provide assistance to individuals who wish to pursue nursing education and who agree to practice in Colorado. Applications are available from the Commission on Higher Education in April of each year. Funding for $220,000 has been appropriated for the 1991-92 academic year.

11) Stafford Student Loans: These loans are available for undergraduate, graduate, vocational or professional students who demonstrate financial need. Students may borrow $2,625 for each of the first two undergraduate years, and up to $4,000 annually through the fifth year. Graduate students may borrow up to $7,500 a year. Not more than $17,250 can be borrowed for all years of undergraduate study, $73,500 for all years of graduate study, or $54,750 for undergraduate and graduate study combined.

12) Supplemental Loans for Students: This program is available to graduate, professional and independent undergraduate students. The annual maximum SLS loan limit is $4,000 and depends on the student's educational program length. Borrowers cannot exceed a maximum of $20,000.

13) Parent Loans for Students (PLUS): The PLUS program is for parents who wish to borrow for their student dependents. The parent is responsible for the repayment of the loan even if the dependent's education is not completed. The annual maximum PLUS amount is $4,000 per eligible dependent student up to a cumulative maximum of $20,000.

14) Perkins Loans: This low-interest (5 percent) loan is for first-time undergraduates and graduate students with exceptional financial need, as determined by the school. For undergraduate students, priority is given to Pell Grant recipients. Loans are made through a school's financial aid office, the school is the lender. These loans must be repaid. Students may borrow up to $4,500 if they've completed less than two years of a program leading to a first bachelor's degree, or if they are enrolled in a vocational program. Students may borrow up to $9,000 if they've already completed two years of study toward a first bachelor's degree and have achieved third-year status. Up to $18,000 may be borrowed for graduate or professional study. See your school's financial aid department for details.

15) Pell Grant: This award helps first-time undergraduates pay for their education after high school. Eligibility for those who receive a Pell Grant for the first time is usually limited to five to six years of undergraduate study, not including remedial coursework. Awards for the 1992-93 academic year will depend upon program funding. The maximum award for the 1991-92 academic year was $2,400. Students must attend school at least half-time. Grants do not have to be paid back. For more information, contact the financial aid administrator of the college or university you are attending.

16) Supplemental Educational Opportunity Grant (SEOG): This award helps first-time undergraduates with exceptional financial need, as determined by the school. Priority is given to Pell Grant recipients. An SEOG doesn't have to be paid back. Students can get up to $4,000 a year, depending upon available funding.

17) College Work-Study (CWS): This program provides jobs for first-time undergraduates and for graduate students who need financial aid. CWS lets you earn money to help pay your educational expenses. Students are paid at least the current Federal minimum wage, but the pay may also be related to the type of work done and the skills required. Schools set individual work schedules and must pay students directly at least once a month.

Connecticut

Connecticut Board of Higher Education, 61 Woodland Street, Hartford, CT 06105-2391; (203) 566-8118. Connecticut received a double appropriation of $19.4 million for 1990-1992 for State educational funding. To be eligible for the programs listed below, students must be State residents.

1) Scholastic Achievement Grant: Grants of up to $2,000 a year are awarded to Connecticut high school seniors who rank in the top 20% of their class or who achieve SAT scores of at least 1,100 (27 on the ACT test). Awards are based on financial need and are to be used at a Connecticut college or in States which have reciprocity agreements with Connecticut.

2) Connecticut Independent College Student Grant: Up to $6,384 a year is available in grants to State residents attending Connecticut independent colleges. Awards are based on financial needs.

3) Connecticut Aid for Public College Students: Awards of up to the amount of unmet financial need are available for students attending Connecticut public colleges.

4) Aid to Dependents of Deceased, Disabled MIA Veterans: This award is available to students whose parent was a Connecticut resident upon entry into the U.S. Armed Forces and served during the war; death must be service-related; disability rated permanent and 100% by the Veterans Administration. Awards of $400 a year are based on financial need.

5) Connecticut Nursing Scholarship: This scholarship is available to students enrolled full-time in a three-year hospital school of nursing in Connecticut, or in a two- or four-year nursing program at a Connecticut College. The amount of the award varies and is based on academic standing and financial need.

6) Family Education Loan Program (FELP): Loans that range from $2,000 to $20,000 a year at a fixed rate are available to students enrolled at least half-time in Connecticut non-profit colleges, or Connecticut residents enrolled at least half-time in a non-profit college anywhere in the U.S. Call 1(800) 252-FELP (in Connecticut) or (203) 522-0766 for information.

6) Tuition Waiver for Veterans: This program is available to veterans who are Connecticut residents when enrolling in college and upon entry in the U.S. Armed Forces or children of Vietnam veterans declared MIA/POW attending Connecticut public colleges. The waiver is equal to tuition only.

7) Tuition Waiver for Senior Citizens: This program is available to students, age 62 and over, attending Connecticut public colleges. The waiver is equal to tuition only.

8) Stafford Student Loans: These loans are available for undergraduate, graduate, vocational or professional students who demonstrate financial need. Students may borrow $2,625 for each of the first two undergraduate years, and up to $4,000 annually through the fifth year. Graduate students may borrow up to $7,500 a year. Not more than $17,250 can be borrowed for all years of undergraduate study, $73,500 for all years of graduate study, or $54,750 for undergraduate and graduate study combined.

9) Supplemental Loans for Students: This program is available to graduate, professional and independent undergraduate students. The annual maximum SLS loan limit is $4,000 and depends on the student's educational program length. Borrowers cannot exceed a maximum of $20,000.

10) Parent Loans for Students (PLUS): The PLUS program is for parents who wish to borrow for their student dependents. The parent is responsible for the repayment of the loan even if the dependent's education is not completed. The annual maximum PLUS amount is $4,000 per eligible dependent student up to a cumulative maximum of $20,000.

11) Perkins Loans: This low-interest (5 percent) loan is for first-time undergraduates and graduate students with exceptional financial need, as determined by the school. For undergraduate students, priority is given to Pell Grant recipients. Loans are made through a school's financial aid office, the school is the lender. These loans must be repaid. Students may borrow up to $4,500 if they've completed less than two years of a program leading to a first bachelor's degree, or if they are enrolled in a vocational program. Students may borrow up to $9,000 if they've already completed two years of study toward a first bachelor's degree and have achieved third-year status. Up to $18,000 may be borrowed for graduate or professional study. See your school's financial aid department for details.

12) Pell Grant: This award helps first-time undergraduates pay for their education after high school. Eligibility for those who receive a Pell Grant for the first time is usually limited to five to six years of undergraduate study, not including remedial coursework. Awards for the 1992-93 academic year will depend upon program funding. The maximum award for the 1991-92 academic year was $2,400. Students must attend school at least half-time. Grants do not have to be paid back. For more information, contact the financial aid administrator of the college or university you are attending.

13) Supplemental Educational Opportunity Grant (SEOG): This award helps first-time undergraduates with exceptional financial need, as determined by the school. Priority is given to Pell Grant recipients. An SEOG doesn't have to be paid back. Students can get up to $4,000 a year, depending upon available funding.

14) College Work-Study (CWS): This program provides jobs for first-time undergraduates and for graduate students who need financial aid. CWS lets you earn money to help pay your educational expenses. Students are paid at least the current Federal minimum wage, but the pay may also be related to the type of work done and the skills required. Schools set individual work schedules and must pay students directly at least once a month.

Be patient. If any phone number is incorrect, call (area code) 555-1212 and request the new listing.

State Money For College Students

Delaware

Delaware Postsecondary Education Commission, 820 N. French Street, Wilmington, DE 19801; (302) 577-3240. Students must be Delaware residents in order to qualify for the following programs. In 1992, Delaware appropriated $130 million in State funding. State appropriations per student for Delaware higher education rank 20th in the nation, 2% above average.

1) Delaware Postsecondary Scholarship Fund: This need-based grant program assists Delaware students in meeting college costs. Funds awarded are not repaid by the students or their parents. Grants may be used at Delaware colleges, and under certain conditions in States other than Delaware. The maximum grant is $1,000 per year. Reapplication is required each year are requested.

2) Christa McAuliffe Teacher Scholarship Loan: This scholarship loan awards scholarships to academically talented Delaware students who agree to pursue teaching careers at the elementary and secondary levels in Delaware public schools. This merit-based award of $1,000 minimum is renewable for up to four years, and must be repaid with teaching service.

3) Diamond State Scholarship: This program promotes academic achievement among Delaware students. The Diamond State Scholars are awarded scholarships of $1,000 which are renewable for four years of undergraduate study. Approximately 50 awards are made each year to graduating high school seniors.

4) B. Bradford Barnes Scholarship: This program was established by the State to honor the memory of a Speaker of the House who died while serving in the General Assembly. One merit-based, renewable scholarship is awarded annually to an outstanding high school senior who has accepted an offer of admission from the University of Delaware. The scholarship pays full tuition, fees, room and board at the University of Delaware.

5) Delaware Nursing Incentive Scholarship Loan: This scholarship loan program was established to encourage academically talented Delaware students to pursue education leading to certification as a Registered or Practical Nurse. Awards are up to $3,000 per year, renewable for up to four years of study, and must be repaid with nursing practice at a Delaware State-owned hospital.

6) Delaware Optometric Institutional Aid: This program maintains an agreement with the Pennsylvania College of Optometry (PCO) to assist Delawareans in obtaining a degree in optometry. Under this agreement the State provides $4,000 per year for up to four years for a limited number of Delaware residents who qualify for admission. PCO applies the entire $4,000 to the student's tuition. The student must repay 25% of the State support and practice optometry in Delaware for the same number of hears he/she received State support.

7) Stafford Student Loans: These loans are available for undergraduate, graduate, vocational or professional students who demonstrate financial need. Students may borrow $2,625 for each of the first two undergraduate years, and up to $4,000 annually through the fifth year. Graduate students may borrow up to $7,500 a year. Not more than $17,250 can be borrowed for all years of undergraduate study, $73,500 for all years of graduate study, or $54,750 for undergraduate and graduate study combined.

8) Supplemental Loans for Students: This program is available to graduate, professional and independent undergraduate students. The annual maximum SLS loan limit is $4,000 and depends on the student's educational program length. Borrowers cannot exceed a maximum of $20,000.

9) Parent Loans for Students (PLUS): The PLUS program is for parents who wish to borrow for their student dependents. The parent is responsible for the repayment of the loan even if the dependent's education is not completed. The annual maximum PLUS amount is $4,000 per eligible dependent student up to a cumulative maximum of $20,000.

10) Perkins Loans: This low-interest (5 percent) loan is for first-time undergraduates and graduate students with exceptional financial need, as determined by the school. For undergraduate students, priority is given to Pell Grant recipients. Loans are made through a school's financial aid office, the school is the lender. These loans must be repaid. Students may borrow up to $4,500 if they've completed less than two years of a program leading to a first bachelor's degree, or if they are enrolled in a vocational program. Students may borrow up to $9,000 if they've already completed two years of study toward a first bachelor's degree and have achieved third-year status. Up to $18,000 may be borrowed for graduate or professional study. See your school's financial aid department for details.

11) Pell Grant: This award helps first-time undergraduates pay for their education after high school. Eligibility for those who receive a Pell Grant for the first time is usually limited to five to six years of undergraduate study, not including remedial coursework. Awards for the 1992-93 academic year will depend upon program funding. The maximum award for the 1991-92 academic year was $2,400. Students must attend school at least half-time. Grants do not have to be paid back. For more information, contact the financial aid administrator of the college or university you are attending.

12) Supplemental Educational Opportunity Grant (SEOG): This award helps first-time undergraduates with exceptional financial need, as determined by the school. Priority is given to Pell Grant recipients. An SEOG doesn't have to be

District of Columbia

Office of State Education Affairs, 2100 Martin Luther King, Jr., Ave., SE, Suite 401, Washington, DC 20020; (202) 727-3685. In 1991-92, a total of $719,929 was awarded. The DC State Student Incentive Grant Program provided $548,106 in funding. The DC Nurses Training Corps Program awarded $171,823. District residency is required to participate in the following programs, unless specified.

1) DC State Student Incentive Program: Between $400 and $1,500 is available to students who have been permanent DC residents for at least 15 months, and attend school full-time at an accredited postsecondary institution in the U.S.

2) DC Nurses Training Corps Program: This renewable program is open to nursing students who plan to attend or are attending the University of DC, Catholic University of America, Howard University, Georgetown University, or the Margaret Murray Washington Career Development Center. Students must agree to work at DC General Hospital, DC Office on Aging or the Commission of Public Health. Up to $22,000 per year is available based on the cost of attendance at school. Students must work two years for every year of scholarship received.

3) TERI Supplemental Loan: This private loan provides funding from $2,000 to $20,000 a year at a fixed or variable rate. Undergraduate or graduate students attending a participating college or university in the U.S. may apply. Contact the financial aid office at a participating college or university for details or contact The Education Resources Institute (TERI) at 1(800) 255-TERI.

4) Stafford Student Loans: These loans are available for undergraduate, graduate, vocational or professional students who demonstrate financial need. Students may borrow $2,625 for each of the first two undergraduate years, and up to $4,000 annually through the fifth year. Graduate students may borrow up to $7,500 a year. Not more than $17,250 can be borrowed for all years of undergraduate study, $73,500 for all years of graduate study, or $54,750 for undergraduate and graduate study combined.

5) Supplemental Loans for Students: This program is available to graduate, professional and independent undergraduate students. The annual maximum SLS loan limit is $4,000 and depends on the student's educational program length. Borrowers cannot exceed a maximum of $20,000.

6) Parent Loans for Students (PLUS): The PLUS program is for parents who wish to borrow for their student dependents. The parent is responsible for the repayment of the loan even if the dependent's education is not completed. The annual maximum PLUS amount is $4,000 per eligible dependent student up to a cumulative maximum of $20,000.

7) Perkins Loans: This low-interest (5 percent) loan is for first-time undergraduates and graduate students with exceptional financial need, as determined by the school. For undergraduate students, priority is given to Pell Grant recipients. Loans are made through a school's financial aid office, the school is the lender. These loans must be repaid. Students may borrow up to $4,500 if they've completed less than two years of a program leading to a first bachelor's degree, or if they are enrolled in a vocational program. Students may borrow up to $9,000 if they've already completed two years of study toward a first bachelor's degree and have achieved third-year status. Up to $18,000 may be borrowed for graduate or professional study. See your school's financial aid department for details.

8) Pell Grant: This award helps first-time undergraduates pay for their education after high school. Eligibility for those who receive a Pell Grant for the first time is usually limited to five to six years of undergraduate study, not including remedial coursework. Awards for the 1992-93 academic year will depend upon program funding. The maximum award for the 1991-92 academic year was $2,400. Students must attend school at least half-time. Grants do not have to be paid back. For more information, contact the financial aid administrator of the college or university you are attending.

9) Supplemental Educational Opportunity Grant (SEOG): This award helps first-time undergraduates with exceptional financial need, as determined by the school. Priority is given to Pell Grant recipients. An SEOG doesn't have to be paid back. Students can get up to $4,000 a year, depending upon available funding.

10) College Work-Study (CWS): This program provides jobs for first-time undergraduates and for graduate students who need financial aid. CWS lets you earn money to help pay your educational expenses. Students are paid at least the current Federal minimum wage, but the pay may also be related to the type of

Education

work done and the skills required. Schools set individual work schedules and must pay students directly at least once a month.

Florida

Florida Office of Student Financial Assistance, State Programs Unit, Florida Education Center, Tallahassee, FL 32399-0400; (904) 488-1034. In 1991-92, approximately $86 million was appropriated for State educational funding. Students must be Florida residents to participate in the programs which are detailed below.

1) Florida Student Assistance Grants (FSAG): These need-based grants may range from $200 to $1,500 per academic year. The program is open to full-time undergraduate students with financial need who are attending an eligible public or private Florida institution.

2) State Tuition Voucher (STV): This undergraduate award is used for tuition and fees at an eligible independent Florida college or university. The award is not based on need and the amount depends on the number of eligible students and level of funding.

3) Florida Undergraduate Scholars' Fund: This merit scholarship program provides awards to outstanding Florida high school graduates. Initial awards are for $1,000, $1,500 or $2,500 depending on eligibility. Renewal awards are $2,500.

4) Public School Work Experience (PSWEP): This program supports employment for undergraduate students as teacher aides or science laboratory assistants in public schools; as reading tutors in adult basic skills education programs; or as tutors/counselors for educationally disadvantaged freshmen in public postsecondary schools.

5) College Career Work Experience Program (CCWEP): This need-based program is open to undergraduate students with financial need who are enrolled at least half-time at an eligible Florida institution. It provides jobs related to their declared major areas of study or career interest. The amount of award varies according to financial need.

6) "Chappie" James Most Promising Teacher Scholarship Loan Program: This scholarship loan program provides up to $4,000 per academic year to outstanding Florida high school seniors who intend to enter the public school teaching profession in Florida. The loan is repaid by teaching service or cash.

7) Critical Teacher Shortage Scholarship Loan Program: This scholarship loan program was created to attract capable students to the teaching profession in critical teacher shortage areas. Up to $4,000 per academic year is available for a maximum of two years. The loan is repaid by teaching service or cash.

8) Mary McLeod Bethune Scholarship Challenge Grant Fund: This need-based scholarship provides $3,000 per academic year to outstanding high school seniors who will attend Florida Agricultural and Mechanical University, Bethune-Cookman College, Edward Waters College or Florida Memorial College. Applicants must be enrolled as full-time undergraduate students.

9) Seminole/Miccosukee Indian Scholarship: This program provides scholarships for Seminole and Miccosukee Indians of Florida who are enrolled as full-time or part-time undergrade or graduate students. The amount of scholarship is determined by the respective tribe.

10) Confederate Memorial Scholarship: This scholarship for lineal descendants of Confederate soldiers and sailors provides $150 for an academic year.

11) Scholarships for Children of Deceased or Disabled Veterans: This scholarship provides funding for dependent children of deceased or 100% disabled veterans or servicemen officially classified as "Prisoners of War" or "Missing in Action." The amount equals tuition and fees for an academic year at a public Florida institution. Residency requirement varies.

12) Jose Marti Scholarship Challenge Grant Fund: This need based scholarship for Hispanic Americans provides $2,000 for an academic year. It is available for undergraduate or graduate study and the amount available is contingent upon matching contributions from private sources. Applicants may apply for the first year of undergraduate study or the first year of graduate study.

13) Vocational Gold Seal Endorsement Scholarship: This scholarship program is available to high school graduates who wish to pursue postsecondary vocational-technical education. Up to $2,000 per academic year is provided.

14) Florida Minority Medical Education Program: This program encourages minorities to enter the medical profession The maximum award is $10,000 per year for three students at each of the State's four participating medical schools: University of Florida, University of South Florida, University of Miami, Southeastern University of Health Sciences. The program requires two years' primary care service in a medically underserved area of Florida or repayment of all scholarship money with interest.

15) Masters' Fellowship Loan Program for Teachers: This fellowship loan program was created to attract liberal arts graduates, science graduates, and mid-career returning students to teaching in Florida public schools. Awards of $6,000 are provided in addition to an amount equal to the average tuition and fees at the State universities for up to two semesters or three quarters and one summer term.

16) Critical Teacher Shortage Tuition Reimbursement Program: This tuition reimbursement program encourages public school district employees certified to teach to become certified in, or gain a graduate degree in, a critical teacher shortage area. Up to $78 per credit hour is provided for up to nine credit hours per academic year. The maximum total is thirty-six credit hours.

17) Critical Teacher Shortage student Loan Forgiveness Program: This loan forgiveness program was created to attract qualified personnel to seek employment in Florida public schools in designated critical teacher areas. It provides repayment of educational loans in return for teaching in a critical teacher shortage area. Up to $2,500 per year is available for four years for teachers with undergraduate loans or $5,000 per academic year for up to two years for teachers with graduate loans.

18) Virgil Hawkins Fellowship: Fellowships are available for minority students attending Florida State University and the University of Florida Law School. An award of $5,000 is provided for a maximum of three years.

19) Exceptional Student Education Training Grant for Out of Field Teachers; This tuition reimbursement program is available to teachers holding a valid Florida teaching certificate but who are not fully certified in the areas of exceptionality in which they teach. Up to $200 per course for a maximum of three courses or nine semester hours per term is available.

20) Stafford Student Loans: These loans are available for undergraduate, graduate, vocational or professional students who demonstrate financial need. Students may borrow $2,625 for each of the first two undergraduate years, and up to $4,000 annually through the fifth year. Graduate students may borrow up to $7,500 a year. Not more than $17,250 can be borrowed for all years of undergraduate study, $73,500 for all years of graduate study, or $54,750 for undergraduate and graduate study combined.

21) Supplemental Loans for Students: This program is available to graduate, professional and independent undergraduate students. The annual maximum SLS loan limit is $4,000 and depends on the student's educational program length. Borrowers cannot exceed a maximum of $20,000.

22) Parent Loans for Students (PLUS): The PLUS program is for parents who wish to borrow for their student dependents. The parent is responsible for the repayment of the loan even if the dependent's education is not completed. The annual maximum PLUS amount is $4,000 per eligible dependent student up to a cumulative maximum of $20,000.

23) Perkins Loans: This low-interest (5 percent) loan is for first-time undergraduates and graduate students with exceptional financial need, as determined by the school. For undergraduate students, priority is given to Pell Grant recipients. Loans are made through a school's financial aid office, the school is the lender. These loans must be repaid. Students may borrow up to $4,500 if they've completed less than two years of a program leading to a first bachelor's degree, or if they are enrolled in a vocational program. Students may borrow up to $9,000 if they've already completed two years of study toward a first bachelor's degree and have achieved third-year status. Up to $18,000 may be borrowed for graduate or professional study. See your school's financial aid department for details.

24) Pell Grant: This award helps first-time undergraduates pay for their education after high school. Eligibility for those who receive a Pell Grant for the first time is usually limited to five to six years of undergraduate study, not including remedial coursework. Awards for the 1992-93 academic year will depend upon program funding. The maximum award for the 1991-92 academic year was $2,400. Students must attend school at least half-time. Grants do not have to be paid back. For more information, contact the financial aid administrator of the college or university you are attending.

25) Supplemental Educational Opportunity Grant (SEOG): This award helps first-time undergraduates with exceptional financial need, as determined by the school. Priority is given to Pell Grant recipients. An SEOG doesn't have to be paid back. Students can get up to $4,000 a year, depending upon available funding.

26) College Work-Study (CWS): This program provides jobs for first-time undergraduates and for graduate students who need financial aid. CWS lets you earn money to help pay your educational expenses. Students are paid at least the current Federal minimum wage, but the pay may also be related to the type of work done and the skills required. Schools set individual work schedules and must pay students directly at least once a month.

Georgia

Georgia Department of Education, Division of General Instruction, 1954 Twin Towers East, Atlanta, GA 30334-5050; (404) 656-5812. Georgia provides no State grants but does offer the merit-based Georgia Scholar Program. This program identifies and recognizes high school seniors who have achieved excellence in school and community life. Requirements include a minimum score of 1300 on the SAT test or a score of 31 on the ACT or a ranking in the upper 10% of his or her graduating class. As a recipient of the award, the student may receive a Governor's Scholarship if he or she continues their postsecondary education in

State Money For College Students

an approved public or private college or University in Georgia and meets other program requirements. The scholarship is used to defray the cost of tuition for a maximum of four years eligibility.

1) Stafford Student Loans: These loans are available for undergraduate, graduate, vocational or professional students who demonstrate financial need. Students may borrow $2,625 for each of the first two undergraduate years, and up to $4,000 annually through the fifth year. Graduate students may borrow up to $7,500 a year. Not more than $17,250 can be borrowed for all years of undergraduate study, $73,500 for all years of graduate study, or $54,750 for undergraduate and graduate study combined.

2) Supplemental Loans for Students: This program is available to graduate, professional and independent undergraduate students. The annual maximum SLS loan limit is $4,000 and depends on the student's educational program length. Borrowers cannot exceed a maximum of $20,000.

3) Parent Loans for Students (PLUS): The PLUS program is for parents who wish to borrow for their student dependents. The parent is responsible for the repayment of the loan even if the dependent's education is not completed. The annual maximum PLUS amount is $4,000 per eligible dependent student up to a cumulative maximum of $20,000.

4) Perkins Loans: This low-interest (5 percent) loan is for first-time undergraduates and graduate students with exceptional financial need, as determined by the school. For undergraduate students, priority is given to Pell Grant recipients. Loans are made through a school's financial aid office, the school is the lender. These loans must be repaid. Students may borrow up to $4,500 if they've completed less than two years of a program leading to a first bachelor's degree, or if they are enrolled in a vocational program. Students may borrow up to $9,000 if they've already completed two years of study toward a first bachelor's degree and have achieved third-year status. Up to $18,000 may be borrowed for graduate or professional study. See your school's financial aid department for details.

5) Pell Grant: This award helps first-time undergraduates pay for their education after high school. Eligibility for those who receive a Pell Grant for the first time is usually limited to five to six years of undergraduate study, not including remedial coursework. Awards for the 1992-93 academic year will depend upon program funding. The maximum award for the 1991-92 academic year was $2,400. Students must attend school at least half-time. Grants do not have to be paid back. For more information, contact the financial aid administrator of the college or university you are attending.

6) Supplemental Educational Opportunity Grant (SEOG): This award helps first-time undergraduates with exceptional financial need, as determined by the school. Priority is given to Pell Grant recipients. An SEOG doesn't have to be paid back. Students can get up to $4,000 a year, depending upon available funding.

7) College Work-Study (CWS): This program provides jobs for first-time undergraduates and for graduate students who need financial aid. CWS lets you earn money to help pay your educational expenses. Students are paid at least the current Federal minimum wage, but the pay may also be related to the type of work done and the skills required. Schools set individual work schedules and must pay students directly at least once a month.

Hawaii

Hawaii Department of Education, Student Personnel Services, 1302 Queen Emma Street, Room A-207, Honolulu, HI 96813; (808) 735-3981. Hawaii's programs of scholarships and grants are available to State residents. Bulletin 15, a 275-page financial aid guide, describes Hawaii's programs and includes other pertinent information. This book will be updated in October, 1992 and is available for $5, plus $2 for shipping and handling.

1) Hawaii Student Incentive Grants (HSIG): These grants provide tuition waivers for undergraduate students. A student must be eligible for a PELL Grant and be a Hawaii resident, as defined by the Board of Regents for tuition purposes.

2) Regents Scholarship for Academic Excellence: This scholarship of $4,000 per year and a full tuition waiver is provided to entering freshmen with combined SAT score of 1200 and high school grade point average of 3.5. The scholarship is renewable for four years if the student continues to meet eligibility requirements. This program also includes a one-time $2,000 grant that pays for an approved study abroad/exchange program during the student's junior year.

3) Presidential Achievement Scholarship: These scholarship provide $4,000 per year plus a full tuition waiver to juniors with a cumulative grade point average of 3.7 and who show superior academic achievement or creative efforts. They are renewable for one year if eligibility requirements are met. This program also includes a one-time $2,000 grant that pays for an approved study abroad/exchange program during the student's junior year.

4) Pacific Asian Scholarships: These scholarships are waivers of tuition to students for academic merit (3.5 cumulative grade point average or better), who are pursuing study relevant to the Pacific and Asian region.

5) Stafford Student Loans: These loans are available for undergraduate, graduate, vocational or professional students who demonstrate financial need. Students may borrow $2,625 for each of the first two undergraduate years, and up to $4,000 annually through the fifth year. Graduate students may borrow up to $7,500 a year. Not more than $17,250 can be borrowed for all years of undergraduate study, $73,500 for all years of graduate study, or $54,750 for undergraduate and graduate study combined.

6) Supplemental Loans for Students: This program is available to graduate, professional and independent undergraduate students. The annual maximum SLS loan limit is $4,000 and depends on the student's educational program length. Borrowers cannot exceed a maximum of $20,000.

7) Parent Loans for Students (PLUS): The PLUS program is for parents who wish to borrow for their student dependents. The parent is responsible for the repayment of the loan even if the dependent's education is not completed. The annual maximum PLUS amount is $4,000 per eligible dependent student up to a cumulative maximum of $20,000.

8) Perkins Loans: This low-interest (5 percent) loan is for first-time undergraduates and graduate students with exceptional financial need, as determined by the school. For undergraduate students, priority is given to Pell Grant recipients. Loans are made through a school's financial aid office, the school is the lender. These loans must be repaid. Students may borrow up to $4,500 if they've completed less than two years of a program leading to a first bachelor's degree, or if they are enrolled in a vocational program. Students may borrow up to $9,000 if they've already completed two years of study toward a first bachelor's degree and have achieved third-year status. Up to $18,000 may be borrowed for graduate or professional study. See your school's financial aid department for details.

9) Pell Grant: This award helps first-time undergraduates pay for their education after high school. Eligibility for those who receive a Pell Grant for the first time is usually limited to five to six years of undergraduate study, not including remedial coursework. Awards for the 1992-93 academic year will depend upon program funding. The maximum award for the 1991-92 academic year was $2,400. Students must attend school at least half-time. Grants do not have to be paid back. For more information, contact the financial aid administrator of the college or university you are attending.

10) Supplemental Educational Opportunity Grant (SEOG): This award helps first-time undergraduates with exceptional financial need, as determined by the school. Priority is given to Pell Grant recipients. An SEOG doesn't have to be paid back. Students can get up to $4,000 a year, depending upon available funding.

11) College Work-Study (CWS): This program provides jobs for first-time undergraduates and for graduate students who need financial aid. CWS lets you earn money to help pay your educational expenses. Students are paid at least the current Federal minimum wage, but the pay may also be related to the type of work done and the skills required. Schools set individual work schedules and must pay students directly at least once a month.

Idaho

Office of the State Board of Education, 307 Len B. Jordan Building, 650 West State Street, Boise, ID 83720-3650; (208) 334-2270. In 1991-92, Idaho received $251,600 in appropriations for State educational funding. Students must be State residents in order to participate in the programs listed below.

1) Idaho Scholarship Program: This program provides awards of $2,650 per year to graduating Idaho high school seniors who wish to pursue their postsecondary education at an Idaho college or university. The award is based on academic merit and is automatically renewed each year as long as the student maintains satisfactory grades. Twenty-five percent of the initial scholarships each year are given to vocational students. Students must be enrolled as a full-time student in an academic or vocational program at an Idaho college or university.

2) Paul L. Fowler Memorial Scholarship Program: This memorial scholarship provides assistance to outstanding students in Idaho, Washington and Oregon. There is no geographical limitation as to the location of the institutions of higher learning which recipients may attend. The one-year awards are for $2,830 and recipients are selected on the basis of rank in class and ACT scores.

The following scholarships are not administered by the State Board of Education, but are available to Idaho students Statewide.

1) Idaho Governor's Scholarship Program: Scholarships of $3,000 are awarded on the basis of scholastic achievement, leadership and community involvement. Students must have a cumulative grade point average of 3.5 or rank in the top 10% of his/her graduating class and score in the top 5% of the ACT. Recipients must enroll as a full-time student in an academic program at an Idaho college or university. For further information, call (208) 342-1663.

2) Idaho Minority and "At-Risk" Student Scholarship: Awards of $2,500 are

Be patient. If any phone number is incorrect, call (area code) 555-1212 and request the new listing.

Education

available to help talented students who may not be able to attend college because of their cultural, economic, or physical circumstances. Recipients must be full-time undergraduate students at one of the following eligible postsecondary institutions: Boise State University, Idaho State University, North Idaho College, Eastern ID Technical College, Lewis-Clark State College, University of Idaho, College of Southern Idaho and the College of Idaho. For further details, contact the financial aid office of the college or university you plan to attend.

3) Education Incentive Loan Forgiveness: This program provides loan forgiveness to Idaho students who wish to pursue a teaching career or professional nursing career within the State. Recipients must rank within the upper 15% of his/her graduating class or have earned a cumulative grade point average of 3.0 or higher. They must also pursue a teaching career or a nursing career within Idaho for a minimum of two years or pay back their loans with interest.

Loans, Grants and Work-Study Options

1) Stafford Student Loans: These loans are available for undergraduate, graduate, vocational or professional students who demonstrate financial need. Students may borrow $2,625 for each of the first two undergraduate years, and up to $4,000 annually through the fifth year. Graduate students may borrow up to $7,500 a year. Not more than $17,250 can be borrowed for all years of undergraduate study, $73,500 for all years of graduate study, or $54,750 for undergraduate and graduate study combined.

2) Supplemental Loans for Students: This program is available to graduate, professional and independent undergraduate students. The annual maximum SLS loan limit is $4,000 and depends on the student's educational program length. Borrowers cannot exceed a maximum of $20,000.

3) Parent Loans for Students (PLUS): The PLUS program is for parents who wish to borrow for their student dependents. The parent is responsible for the repayment of the loan even if the dependent's education is not completed. The annual maximum PLUS amount is $4,000 per eligible dependent student up to a cumulative maximum of $20,000.

4) Perkins Loans: This low-interest (5 percent) loan is for first-time undergraduates and graduate students with exceptional financial need, as determined by the school. For undergraduate students, priority is given to Pell Grant recipients. Loans are made through a school's financial aid office, the school is the lender. These loans must be repaid. Students may borrow up to $4,500 if they've completed less than two years of a program leading to a first bachelor's degree, or if they are enrolled in a vocational program. Students may borrow up to $9,000 if they've already completed two years of study toward a first bachelor's degree and have achieved third-year status. Up to $18,000 may be borrowed for graduate or professional study. See your school's financial aid department for details.

5) Pell Grant: This award helps first-time undergraduates pay for their education after high school. Eligibility for those who receive a Pell Grant for the first time is usually limited to five to six years of undergraduate study, not including remedial coursework. Awards for the 1992-93 academic year will depend upon program funding. The maximum award for the 1991-92 academic year was $2,400. Students must attend school at least half-time. Grants do not have to be paid back. For more information, contact the financial aid administrator of the college or university you are attending.

6) Supplemental Educational Opportunity Grant (SEOG): This award helps first-time undergraduates with exceptional financial need, as determined by the school. Priority is given to Pell Grant recipients. An SEOG doesn't have to be paid back. Students can get up to $4,000 a year, depending upon available funding.

7) College Work-Study (CWS): This program provides jobs for first-time undergraduates and for graduate students who need financial aid. CWS lets you earn money to help pay your educational expenses. Students are paid at least the current Federal minimum wage, but the pay may also be related to the type of work done and the skills required. Schools set individual work schedules and must pay students directly at least once a month.

Illinois

Illinois Student Aid Commission, 106 Wilmont Road, Deerfield, IL 60015; (708) 948-8550. Illinois administers the second largest financial aid program in the country. In 1990-91, $201,105,565 was awarded in State funding programs. The majority of that funding, $182,407,924, was distributed through their Monetary Award Program (MAP).

1) Monetary Award Program: The Monetary Award Program provides grants for students that demonstrate financial need. Students are not required to submit high school grades or test scores when applying for a MAP grant. Students must enroll at an approved Illinois MAP institution (more than 200 qualify) and enroll for at least six credit hours per term. MAP grants can only be applied toward

tuition and mandatory fees. For this reason, all awards are paid directly to the college or university. Grants are awarded up to $3,500.

2) Illinois Merit Recognition Scholarship Program: This program provides a one-time $1,000 award to Illinois high school students who rank in the top 5% of their class at the end of the seventh semester. Financial need is not a factor in determining recipients. The scholarship can be used for tuition, fees or other expenses at approved Illinois institutions. In 1990-91, this program awarded $4,232,000 to 4,390 students.

3) Stafford Student Loans: These loans are available for undergraduate, graduate, vocational or professional students who demonstrate financial need. Students may borrow $2,625 for each of the first two undergraduate years, and up to $4,000 annually through the fifth year. Graduate students may borrow up to $7,500 a year. Not more than $17,250 can be borrowed for all years of undergraduate study, $73,500 for all years of graduate study, or $54,750 for undergraduate and graduate study combined.

4) Illinois Opportunity Loan Program: This program is a loan program for middle-income Illinois families. The program provides loans to qualified dependent and independent undergraduate and graduate students. This loan is not based on financial need, but Pell Grant eligibility must be determined by the financial aid administrator before a student may apply. A Pell Grant is a Federally funded program that provides grants for undergraduate students attending school at least half-time. The maximum loan amounts through this program and the Stafford Loan Program combined are $2,625 for sophomore level undergraduate, $4,000 for junior and senior level undergraduate and $7,500 for graduate and professional students. The minimum loan amount is $1,000.

5) Supplemental Loans for Students: This program is available to graduate, professional and independent undergraduate students. The annual maximum SLS loan limit is $4,000 and depends on the student's educational program length. Borrowers cannot exceed a maximum of $20,000.

6) Parent Loans for Undergraduate Students (PLUS) and Supplemental Loans for Students (SLS): Parents may borrow for a dependent student under the PLUS Program. Independent undergraduate students, and graduate and professional students may apply for SLS. Up to $4,000 is offered per academic year for each program. The maximum amount for each program is $20,000.

7) Perkins Loans: This low-interest (5 percent) loan is for first-time undergraduates and graduate students with exceptional financial need, as determined by the school. For undergraduate students, priority is given to Pell Grant recipients. Loans are made through a school's financial aid office, the school is the lender. These loans must be repaid. Students may borrow up to $4,500 if they've completed less than two years of a program leading to a first bachelor's degree, or if they are enrolled in a vocational program. Students may borrow up to $9,000 if they've already completed two years of study toward a first bachelor's degree and have achieved third-year status. Up to $18,000 may be borrowed for graduate or professional study. See your school's financial aid department for details.

8) Pell Grant: This award helps first-time undergraduates pay for their education after high school. Eligibility for those who receive a Pell Grant for the first time is usually limited to five to six years of undergraduate study, not including remedial coursework. Awards for the 1992-93 academic year will depend upon program funding. The maximum award for the 1991-92 academic year was $2,400. Students must attend school at least half-time. Grants do not have to be paid back. For more information, contact the financial aid administrator of the college or university you are attending.

9) Supplemental Educational Opportunity Grant (SEOG): This award helps first-time undergraduates with exceptional financial need, as determined by the school. Priority is given to Pell Grant recipients. An SEOG doesn't have to be paid back. Students can get up to $4,000 a year, depending upon available funding.

10) College Work-Study (CWS): This program provides jobs for first-time undergraduates and for graduate students who need financial aid. CWS lets you earn money to help pay your educational expenses. Students are paid at least the current Federal minimum wage, but the pay may also be related to the type of work done and the skills required. Schools set individual work schedules and must pay students directly at least once a month.

Illinois residents who meet special requirements may be eligible for one of the following four financial assistance programs. These grant programs are not based on financial need and do not require repayment:

1) National Guard/Naval Militia Grant Program: members of the Illinois Naval Militia are eligible for payment of tuition and some fees for either undergraduate or graduate education. The individual must be registered as enlisted personnel or be an officer up to the rank of captain, be enrolled at an Illinois State-supported college or university and have one full year of service in the National Guard or Naval Militia.

2) Illinois Veteran Grant Program: The Illinois Veteran Grant (IVG) Program pays tuition and certain fees at all Illinois State-supported colleges, universities and community colleges for Illinois residents. Recipients may use their grant

Be patient. If any phone number is incorrect, call (area code) 555-1212 and request the new listing.

State Money For College Students

assistance for either undergraduate or graduate study for a period of up to 16 calendar years or a maximum of 120 eligibility points, whichever comes first.

3) Police Officer/Fire Officer Dependent's Grant Program: The spouse and children of Illinois police and fire personnel killed in the line of duty may be eligible for grant assistance to meet college tuition and mandatory fees at approved Illinois colleges and universities. Children who apply for this program must be 25 years old or younger, attend college in Illinois and meet several other eligibility requirements.

4) Correctional Officer's Survivor's Grant Program: The spouse and children of a State of Illinois Department of Corrections worker killed or at least 90% disabled in the line of duty may be eligible for grant assistance. The grant can only be used for tuition and mandatory fees at approved Illinois colleges and universities.

Indiana

State Student Assistance Commission of Indiana, 964 North Pennsylvania St., Indianapolis, IN 46204; (317) 232-2350.

1) Indiana Higher Education Grant: This award focuses on tuition and fees and is "need-based", with students with the least ability to finance a college education receiving the largest grants. In 1991-92, $14,784,660 was awarded to 49,000 recipients. Maximum Indiana Higher Education Grants for the 1991-92 academic year ranged from $950 at the lowest-cost State-supported college to $3,764 at many of the private colleges and universities. The average award was $1,390; the minimum grant is $200.

Loans, Grants and Work-Study Options

1) Stafford Student Loans: These loans are available for undergraduate, graduate, vocational or professional students who demonstrate financial need. Students may borrow $2,625 for each of the first two undergraduate years, and up to $4,000 annually through the fifth year. Graduate students may borrow up to $7,500 a year. Not more than $17,250 can be borrowed for all years of undergraduate study, $73,500 for all years of graduate study, or $54,750 for undergraduate and graduate study combined.

2) Supplemental Loans for Students: This program is available to graduate, professional and independent undergraduate students. The annual maximum SLS loan limit is $4,000 and depends on the student's educational program length. Borrowers cannot exceed a maximum of $20,000.

3) Parent Loans for Students (PLUS): The PLUS program is for parents who wish to borrow for their student dependents. The parent is responsible for the repayment of the loan even if the dependent's education is not completed. The annual maximum PLUS amount is $4,000 per eligible dependent student up to a cumulative maximum of $20,000.

4) Perkins Loans: This low-interest (5 percent) loan is for first-time undergraduates and graduate students with exceptional financial need, as determined by the school. For undergraduate students, priority is given to Pell Grant recipients. Loans are made through a school's financial aid office, the school is the lender. These loans must be repaid. Students may borrow up to $4,500 if they've completed less than two years of a program leading to a first bachelor's degree, or if they are enrolled in a vocational program. Students may borrow up to $9,000 if they've already completed two years of study toward a first bachelor's degree and have achieved third-year status. Up to $18,000 may be borrowed for graduate or professional study. See your school's financial aid department for details.

5) Pell Grant: This award helps first-time undergraduates pay for their education after high school. Eligibility for those who receive a Pell Grant for the first time is usually limited to five to six years of undergraduate study, not including remedial coursework. Awards for the 1992-93 academic year will depend upon program funding. The maximum award for the 1991-92 academic year was $2,400. Students must attend school at least half-time. Grants do not have to be paid back. For more information, contact the financial aid administrator of the college or university you are attending.

6) Supplemental Educational Opportunity Grant (SEOG): This award helps first-time undergraduates with exceptional financial need, as determined by the school. Priority is given to Pell Grant recipients. An SEOG doesn't have to be paid back. Students can get up to $4,000 a year, depending upon available funding.

7) College Work-Study (CWS): This program provides jobs for first-time undergraduates and for graduate students who need financial aid. CWS lets you earn money to help pay your educational expenses. Students are paid at least the current Federal minimum wage, but the pay may also be related to the type of work done and the skills required. Schools set individual work schedules and must pay students directly at least once a month.

Iowa

Iowa College Aid Commission, 201 Jewett Building, 914 Grant Avenue, Des Moines, IA 50309-2824; (515) 281-3501. Iowa has appropriated over $45 million for student aid and is providing over 30,000 awards through need-based scholarship, grant and work study programs. The Iowa Tuition Grant Program enables nearly 14,400 students to pay the cost of attending ap private college in Iowa. State residency is required in order to participate in these programs.

1) State of Iowa Scholarship Program: State Scholar applicants must rank in the top 15% of their class and take the ACT test by October of their senior year. Each scholar is eligible to receive an award ranging from $100 to $400 per year. Award amounts are determined by academic index and the number of units which each student takes in the subject of math, science, social studies, foreign language, and language arts. Awards may be used at eligible Iowa schools.

2) Iowa Tuition Grants: This grant provides students with the option of attending Iowa private colleges and universities. The grant is based on financial need with priority given to the neediest applicants. The maximum grant is $2,650 for each year of full-time undergraduate study. The award may also be pro-rated for less than full-time study.

3) Iowa Vocational-Technical Tuition Grants: This program provides need-based grants for Iowa students enrolled in career education courses at area community colleges. The maximum grant is $600 for a full year (four quarters or two semesters and a summer session).

4) Iowa Grants: This grant assists exceptional need students enrolled in an undergraduate program at an Iowa State university, independent college or university or area community college. The maximum grant is $1,000 for each year of full-time undergraduate study (12 or more semester hours). The award may also be prorated for less that full-time study.

5) Stafford Student Loans: These loans are available for undergraduate, graduate, vocational or professional students who demonstrate financial need. Students may borrow $2,625 for each of the first two undergraduate years, and up to $4,000 annually through the fifth year. Graduate students may borrow up to $7,500 a year. Not more than $17,250 can be borrowed for all years of undergraduate study, $73,500 for all years of graduate study, or $54,750 for undergraduate and graduate study combined.

6) Supplemental Loans for Students: This program is available to graduate, professional and independent undergraduate students. The annual maximum SLS loan limit is $4,000 and depends on the student's educational program length. Borrowers cannot exceed a maximum of $20,000.

7) Parent Loans for Students (PLUS): The PLUS program is for parents who wish to borrow for their student dependents. The parent is responsible for the repayment of the loan even if the dependent's education is not completed. The annual maximum PLUS amount is $4,000 per eligible dependent student up to a cumulative maximum of $20,000.

8) Perkins Loans: This low-interest (5 percent) loan is for first-time undergraduates and graduate students with exceptional financial need, as determined by the school. For undergraduate students, priority is given to Pell Grant recipients. Loans are made through a school's financial aid office, the school is the lender. These loans must be repaid. Students may borrow up to $4,500 if they've completed less than two years of a program leading to a first bachelor's degree, or if they are enrolled in a vocational program. Students may borrow up to $9,000 if they've already completed two years of study toward a first bachelor's degree and have achieved third-year status. Up to $18,000 may be borrowed for graduate or professional study. See your school's financial aid department for details.

9) Pell Grant: This award helps first-time undergraduates pay for their education after high school. Eligibility for those who receive a Pell Grant for the first time is usually limited to five to six years of undergraduate study, not including remedial coursework. Awards for the 1992-93 academic year will depend upon program funding. The maximum award for the 1991-92 academic year was $2,400. Students must attend school at least half-time. Grants do not have to be paid back. For more information, contact the financial aid administrator of the college or university you are attending.

10) Supplemental Educational Opportunity Grant (SEOG): This award helps first-time undergraduates with exceptional financial need, as determined by the school. Priority is given to Pell Grant recipients. An SEOG doesn't have to be paid back. Students can get up to $4,000 a year, depending upon available funding.

11) College Work-Study (CWS): This program provides jobs for first-time undergraduates and for graduate students who need financial aid. CWS lets you earn money to help pay your educational expenses. Students are paid at least the current Federal minimum wage, but the pay may also be related to the type of work done and the skills required. Schools set individual work schedules and must pay students directly at least once a month.

Be patient. If any phone number is incorrect, call (area code) 555-1212 and request the new listing.

Education

Kansas

Kansas Board of Regents, Capitol Tower, 400 8th St., SW, Suite 609, Topeka, KS 66603; (913) 296-3517. In 1991-92, approximately $8 million in State aid was administered through this office. Students must be Kansas residents to participate in the following programs.

1) Kansas Minority Scholarship: This program provides need-based awards to ethnic minority students attending Kansas two or four year institutions. Selection is based o academic performance, ethnic category and financial need. Up to $1,500 is available per academic year up to four years. Funding assists approximately 135 students.

2) Vocational Education Scholarship: This merit-only award assists students enrolling in eligible vocational programs. Applicants must take the vocational exam and be among the top 100 scorers. Up to $500 is available per academic year. Funding assists approximately 100 students.

3) Kansas Teacher Scholarship: This service-based award encourages high academic achievers to enter teaching, teach in Kansas, and teach in "hard-to-fill" disciplines. Undergraduates without prior teacher certification eligibility may be considered. Up to $5,000 per academic year is available and is limited to four years unless enrolled in a five year program. Funding assists approximately 100 students.

4) Kansas Nursing Scholarship: This service-based award encourages students to study nursing and then practice nursing in Kansas. The program is jointly sponsored with health care agencies. Students must secure sponsorship. After passing the licensing exam, a student must be employed by the sponsor for one year for each year of funding or repay the funds at 15% interest. $2,500 per academic year is available for LPN, $3,500 per academic year for RPN. Approximately 270 students are funded each year.

5) Kansas State Scholarship: This need-based award assists students designated during their high school senior year as State Scholars. Funding is provided by both Federal and State sources and ranges from $50 to $1,000 per academic year. Funding assists approximately 1,350 students and is limited to four academic years unless enrolled in a designated five year program.

Loans, Grants and Work-Study Options

1) Stafford Student Loans: These loans are available for undergraduate, graduate, vocational or professional students who demonstrate financial need. Students may borrow $2,625 for each of the first two undergraduate years, and up to $4,000 annually through the fifth year. Graduate students may borrow up to $7,500 a year. Not more than $17,250 can be borrowed for all years of undergraduate study, $73,500 for all years of graduate study, or $54,750 for undergraduate and graduate study combined.

2) Supplemental Loans for Students: This program is available to graduate, professional and independent undergraduate students. The annual maximum SLS loan limit is $4,000 and depends on the student's educational program length. Borrowers cannot exceed a maximum of $20,000.

3) Parent Loans for Students (PLUS): The PLUS program is for parents who wish to borrow for their student dependents. The parent is responsible for the repayment of the loan even if the dependent's education is not completed. The annual maximum PLUS amount is $4,000 per eligible dependent student up to a cumulative maximum of $20,000.

4) Perkins Loans: This low-interest (5 percent) loan is for first-time undergraduates and graduate students with exceptional financial need, as determined by the school. For undergraduate students, priority is given to Pell Grant recipients. Loans are made through a school's financial aid office, the school is the lender. These loans must be repaid. Students may borrow up to $4,500 if they've completed less than two years of a program leading to a first bachelor's degree, or if they are enrolled in a vocational program. Students may borrow up to $9,000 if they've already completed two years of study toward a first bachelor's degree and have achieved third-year status. Up to $18,000 may be borrowed for graduate or professional study. See your school's financial aid department for details.

5) Pell Grant: This award helps first-time undergraduates pay for their education after high school. Eligibility for those who receive a Pell Grant for the first time is usually limited to five to six years of undergraduate study, not including remedial coursework. Awards for the 1992-93 academic year will depend upon program funding. The maximum award for the 1991-92 academic year was $2,400. Students must attend school at least half-time. Grants do not have to be paid back. For more information, contact the financial aid administrator of the college or university you are attending.

6) Supplemental Educational Opportunity Grant (SEOG): This award helps first-time undergraduates with exceptional financial need, as determined by the school. Priority is given to Pell Grant recipients. An SEOG doesn't have to be paid back. Students can get up to $4,000 a year, depending upon available funding.

7) College Work-Study (CWS): This program provides jobs for first-time undergraduates and for graduate students who need financial aid. CWS lets you earn money to help pay your educational expenses. Students are paid at least the current Federal minimum wage, but the pay may also be related to the type of work done and the skills required. Schools set individual work schedules and must pay students directly at least once a month.

Kentucky

Kentucky Higher Education Assistance Authority, 1050 US 127 South, Frankfort, KY 40601-4323; (502) 564-7990. Kentucky strives to keep its tuition at State colleges and universities affordable by using State monies. In 1990-91, $19,041,000 was awarded in State aid. The Kentucky Higher Education Assistance Authority administers three programs: College Access Program (CAP) Grants and Kentucky Tuition Grants (KTG). Either of these grants or a combination is referred to as a KHEAA grant. Applicants must attend an eligible Kentucky college, be enrolled in an undergraduate degree program, be State residents, establish financial need, and meet program requirements. Funds are limited, so students who file by April 1 have the best chance of receiving awards.

1) College Access Program Grants (CAP): A CAP Grant is awarded to financially needy undergraduate students enrolled for a minimum of six semester hours at a two- or four-year public or private non-profit college or proprietary school. The grant amount each year is equal to the community college tuition rate. CAP recipients must have an expected family contribution of $3,000 or less.

2) Kentucky State Student Incentive Grant Program: Program requirements are the same as the CAP program listed above.

3) Kentucky Tuition Grants (KTG): This program provides need-based grants to qualified applicants to attend one of the Commonwealth's independent, non-profit colleges. The program assists full-time students with the higher tuition charges at these schools. The maximum KTG award is $1,200 per academic year.

4) Stafford Student Loans: These loans are available for undergraduate, graduate, vocational or professional students who demonstrate financial need. Students may borrow $2,625 for each of the first two undergraduate years, and up to $4,000 annually through the fifth year. Graduate students may borrow up to $7,500 a year. Not more than $17,250 can be borrowed for all years of undergraduate study, $73,500 for all years of graduate study, or $54,750 for undergraduate and graduate study combined.

5) Supplemental Loans for Students: This program is available to graduate, professional and independent undergraduate students. The annual maximum SLS loan limit is $4,000 and depends on the student's educational program length. Borrowers cannot exceed a maximum of $20,000.

6) Parent Loans for Students (PLUS): The PLUS program is for parents who wish to borrow for their student dependents. The parent is responsible for the repayment of the loan even if the dependent's education is not completed. The annual maximum PLUS amount is $4,000 per eligible dependent student up to a cumulative maximum of $20,000.

7) Perkins Loans: This low-interest (5 percent) loan is for first-time undergraduates and graduate students with exceptional financial need, as determined by the school. For undergraduate students, priority is given to Pell Grant recipients. Loans are made through a school's financial aid office, the school is the lender. These loans must be repaid. Students may borrow up to $4,500 if they've completed less than two years of a program leading to a first bachelor's degree, or if they are enrolled in a vocational program. Students may borrow up to $9,000 if they've already completed two years of study toward a first bachelor's degree and have achieved third-year status. Up to $18,000 may be borrowed for graduate or professional study. See your school's financial aid department for details.

8) Pell Grant: This award helps first-time undergraduates pay for their education after high school. Eligibility for those who receive a Pell Grant for the first time is usually limited to five to six years of undergraduate study, not including remedial coursework. Awards for the 1992-93 academic year will depend upon program funding. The maximum award for the 1991-92 academic year was $2,400. Students must attend school at least half-time. Grants do not have to be paid back. For more information, contact the financial aid administrator of the college or university you are attending.

9) Supplemental Educational Opportunity Grant (SEOG): This award helps first-time undergraduates with exceptional financial need, as determined by the school. Priority is given to Pell Grant recipients. An SEOG doesn't have to be paid back. Students can get up to $4,000 a year, depending upon available funding.

10) College Work-Study (CWS): This program provides jobs for first-time undergraduates and for graduate students who need financial aid. CWS lets you earn money to help pay your educational expenses. Students are paid at least the current Federal minimum wage, but the pay may also be related to the type of work done and the skills required. Schools set individual work schedules and must pay students directly at least once a month.

State Money For College Students

Louisiana

Office of Student Financial Assistance, P.O. Box 91202, Baton Rouge, LA 70821-9202; (504) 922-1011. Students must be State residents to be eligible for the programs listed below.

1) Louisiana Tuition Assistance Plan: This need-based award pays undergraduate tuition at a State public college or university. The recipient must have been a Louisiana resident for at least two years prior to application or have a parent or guardian who is a domiciliary of Louisiana. Approximately, 3,000 awards are presented annually.

2) Louisiana T.H. Harris Scholarship: This academic merit scholarship is awarded to Louisiana high school graduates who have achieved a 3.0 high school grade point average on a 4.0 scale. The award amount is $400 per year up to $2,000. Students must be enrolled as full-time undergraduates at a Louisiana public college or university. 3,750 awards are given out annually.

3) Louisiana Rockefeller State Wildlife Scholarship: This program was designed to attract graduates in Wildlife Forestry, or Marine Sciences to Louisiana. Grant amounts range from $1,000 per year up to $7,000 for undergraduates, or up to two years of graduate study. Students must attend a Louisiana public college or university full-time. They must also obtain a wildlife, forestry, or marine science degree or repay the scholarship plus interest. Sixty scholarships are awarded each year.

4) Louisiana Opportunity Loan: This loan assists students of middle income families in meeting rising education costs. Amounts range from $2,625 to $7,500 per year depending upon class standing. The maximum amount is $17,250 for undergraduate study and $54,750 for graduate study. Students must be enrolled full-time at a Louisiana public or private approved institution of higher education. Students must reapply annually for funds.

5) Stafford Student Loans: These loans are available for undergraduate, graduate, vocational or professional students who demonstrate financial need. Students may borrow $2,625 for each of the first two undergraduate years, and up to $4,000 annually through the fifth year. Graduate students may borrow up to $7,500 a year. Not more than $17,250 can be borrowed for all years of undergraduate study, $73,500 for all years of graduate study, or $54,750 for undergraduate and graduate study combined.

6) Supplemental Loans for Students: This program is available to graduate, professional and independent undergraduate students. The annual maximum SLS loan limit is $4,000 and depends on the student's educational program length. Borrowers cannot exceed a maximum of $20,000.

10) Parent Loans for Students (PLUS): The PLUS program is for parents who wish to borrow for their student dependents. The parent is responsible for the repayment of the loan even if the dependent's education is not completed. The annual maximum PLUS amount is $4,000 per eligible dependent student up to a cumulative maximum of $20,000.

7) Perkins Loans: This low-interest (5 percent) loan is for first-time undergraduates and graduate students with exceptional financial need, as determined by the school. For undergraduate students, priority is given to Pell Grant recipients. Loans are made through a school's financial aid office, the school is the lender. These loans must be repaid. Students may borrow up to $4,500 if they've completed less than two years of a program leading to a first bachelor's degree, or if they are enrolled in a vocational program. Students may borrow up to $9,000 if they've already completed two years of study toward a first bachelor's degree and have achieved third-year status. Up to $18,000 may be borrowed for graduate or professional study. See your school's financial aid department for details.

8) Pell Grant: This award helps first-time undergraduates pay for their education after high school. Eligibility for those who receive a Pell Grant for the first time is usually limited to five to six years of undergraduate study, not including remedial coursework. Awards for the 1992-93 academic year will depend upon program funding. The maximum award for the 1991-92 academic year was $2,400. Students must attend school at least half-time. Grants do not have to be paid back. For more information, contact the financial aid administrator of the college or university you are attending.

9) Supplemental Educational Opportunity Grant (SEOG): This award helps first-time undergraduates with exceptional financial need, as determined by the school. Priority is given to Pell Grant recipients. An SEOG doesn't have to be paid back. Students can get up to $4,000 a year, depending upon available funding.

10) College Work-Study (CWS): This program provides jobs for first-time undergraduates and for graduate students who need financial aid. CWS lets you earn money to help pay your educational expenses. Students are paid at least the current Federal minimum wage, but the pay may also be related to the type of work done and the skills required. Schools set individual work schedules and must pay students directly at least once a month.

Maine

Maine Department of Higher Education, State House Station 119, Augusta, ME 04333; (207) 289-2183. In 1990-91, $4.8 million in State funding was awarded. Applicants must be Maine residents to participate in the programs listed.

1) Maine Student Incentive Scholarship Program (MSISP): Applicants must be at least half-time undergraduate students and attend any eligible post-secondary institution in New England, Alaska, Delaware, the District of Columbia, Maryland and Pennsylvania. Full-time students may receive up to $500 at a public institution and up to $1,000 at a private institution. Part-time students will receive one half the full-time award. These awards are based on a student's financial needs.

2) Blaine Scholars Program: Any high school senior who will graduate from high school in the upper half of his class may apply. Scholar loans are competitive and based on academic achievement. The program also offers Teachers Loans for Maine teachers employed at least half-time by a Maine school. Students may borrow up to $1,500 per year, renewable, up to a $6,000 limit. Loans may be forgiven for teaching service.

3) Stafford Student Loans: These loans are available for undergraduate, graduate, vocational or professional students who demonstrate financial need. Students may borrow $2,625 for each of the first two undergraduate years, and up to $4,000 annually through the fifth year.

4) Parent Loans for Undergraduate Students (PLUS) and Supplemental Loans for Students (SLS): Parents may borrow for a dependent student under the PLUS Program. Independent undergraduate students and graduate and professional students may apply for SLS. Up to $4,000 is offered per academic year for each program. The maximum amount for each program is $20,000.

5) State Veterans Benefits: Spouses or children, widows or widowers, of veterans killed or permanently disabled as a result of military service may apply for a maximum of $300 per year for private schools. Free tuition is offered for State supported post-secondary schools.

6) Maine Educational Loan Authority (MELA) Supplemental Education Program: Qualified applicants may borrow from $2,000 to $20,000 a year to cover education related expenses with a supplemental loan from the Maine Education Loan Authority. The amount is determined by the school.

7) Indian Scholarships: Waivers covering tuition and fees are available through the University of Maine System for members of the Passamaquoddy and Penobscot Tribes. They are also available for others who have resided in Maine for at least one year and who have at least one parent or grandparent on the census of a North American Indian Tribe or with a band number of the Micmac or Maliseet Tribes. In addition, room and board charges are subsidized for those eligible students residing in university dormitories.

8) Tuition Waiver Program for Children of Fire fighters and Law Enforcement Officers Killed in the Line of Duty: This program provides a tuition waiver at schools in the University of Maine System for children of fire fighters and law enforcement officers who have been killed in the line of duty or injured during the performance of their duties which resulted in death.

9) Perkins Loans: This low-interest (5 percent) loan is for first-time undergraduates and graduate students with exceptional financial need, as determined by the school. For undergraduate students, priority is given to Pell Grant recipients. Loans are made through a school's financial aid office, the school is the lender. These loans must be repaid. Students may borrow up to $4,500 if they've completed less than two years of a program leading to a first bachelor's degree, or if they are enrolled in a vocational program. Students may borrow up to $9,000 if they've already completed two years of study toward a first bachelor's degree and have achieved third-year status. Up to $18,000 may be borrowed for graduate or professional study. See your school's financial aid department for details.

10) Pell Grant: This award helps first-time undergraduates pay for their education after high school. Eligibility for those who receive a Pell Grant for the first time is usually limited to five to six years of undergraduate study, not including remedial coursework. Awards for the 1992-93 academic year will depend upon program funding. The maximum award for the 1991-92 academic year was $2,400. Students must attend school at least half-time. Grants do not have to be paid back. For more information, contact the financial aid administrator of the college or university you are attending.

11) Supplemental Educational Opportunity Grant (SEOG): This award helps first-time undergraduates with exceptional financial need, as determined by the school. Priority is given to Pell Grant recipients. An SEOG doesn't have to be paid back. Students can get up to $4,000 a year, depending upon available funding.

12) College Work-Study (CWS): This program provides jobs for first-time undergraduates and for graduate students who need financial aid. CWS lets you earn money to help pay your educational expenses. Students are paid at least the current Federal minimum wage, but the pay may also be related to the type of work done and the skills required. Schools set individual work schedules and must pay students directly at least once a month.

Be patient. If any phone number is incorrect, call (area code) 555-1212 and request the new listing.

Education

Maryland

Maryland Higher Education Commission, State Scholarship Administration, The Jeffrey Building, 16 Francis Street, Suite 209, Annapolis, MD 21401-1781; (410) 974-5370. Maryland gives more than $22 million in financial assistance to more than 20,000 State residents each year.

1) Maryland State Scholarship Program: This award provides $200 to $2,500 per year, up to four years with a possible fifth year, to qualified undergraduates. Students must attend a Maryland degree-granting or nursing institution. Limited out-of-State awards are given to approximately 10% of applicants. Students must attend school full-time except for part-time nursing students.

2) Senatorial Scholarship Program: This program provides from $400 to $2,000 to full-time and part-time students enrolled in undergraduate, graduate and certain vocational programs. The awards are made by the State Senators to students in their districts and is automatically renewed until the degree is granted (up to four years maximum).

3) House of Delegates Award: These awards are made by State Delegates to students in their districts. The amount of the award varies, with a minimum of $200 offered. The program is open to full-time and part-time students in undergraduate, graduate and certain vocational programs. The renewable award is offered for one to four years. Students should apply directly to their Delegates for this program.

4) Tolbert Grant: This one year award of $200 to $1,500 is open to full-time students attending vocational programs in Maryland private career schools. Applicants may reapply up to a two year maximum.

5) Distinguished Scholar Program: This program is open to National Merit and Achievement Finalists and academically or artistically gifted and talented students. Awards of $3,000 are granted, up to a maximum of four years. Students must attend an accredited Maryland post secondary school on a full-time basis and maintain a 3.0 grade point average.

6) Teacher Education Distinguished Scholar Program: These $3,000 awards are open to students who have received a Distinguished Scholar Award. Awards of $3,000 are granted, up to a maximum of four years. Students must attend an accredited Maryland post secondary school on a full-time basis and maintain a 3.0 grade point average. Recipients must teach in a Maryland public school for one year for each year of the award.

7) Edward Conroy Grant: This program is open to disabled public safety employees, children of POW's, dependents of military and public safety personnel deceased or disabled in the line of duty. The award provides tuition and mandatory fees up to $2,400 for full-time and part-time undergraduate and graduate students. A maximum of eight years of funding is available. Maryland residency is not required for this program.

8) Maryland State Nursing Scholarship: This program provides up to $2,400, with a need-based additional grant of up to $2,400, to undergraduate and graduate nursing students. Recipients must serve in a Maryland shortage area one year for each year of the award.

9) Physical and Occupational Therapists and Assistants Scholarships: This program provides $2,000 per year, up to four years, for full-time undergraduate students pursuing a career in physical and occupational therapy. Recipients must provide one year of service in a State hospital, or to handicapped students for each year of the award.

10) Family Practice Medical Scholarship: This program provides $7,500 per year, up to four years, for full-time graduate students planning a career in family practice medicine. Two new awards are made each year. Students must attend the University of Maryland at Baltimore and be willing to practice medicine for three years in Maryland following graduation. A minimum of five years Maryland residency is required.

11) Professional Scholarship: Eligible applicants must be enrolled in a degree or diploma program in dentistry, law, medicine, nursing or pharmacy. This program provides $200 to $1,000 per year, up to four years, for full-time undergraduate, graduate and nursing students.

12) Sharon Christa McAuliffe Critical Shortage Teacher Scholarship: This program provides up to $,700 in tuition and fees, room and board for full-time undergraduate and graduate students planning to enter the teaching profession. Awards are offered up to five semesters. Recipients must teach in a Maryland public school for one year for each year of the award.

13) Child Care Provider Scholarship: Full-time and part-time undergraduates who are planning a career in child care are eligible for this program. Awards are renewable and range from $500 to $2,000 per year. Recipients must provide one year of child care service for each year of assistance.

14) Reimbursement of Fire Fighters and Rescue Squad Members: Tuition of up to $2,200 per year is provided for fire fighters and rescue squad members attending a Maryland degree-granting program. Applicants may be full-time or part-time undergraduate or graduate students. The award is renewable. Reimbursement is made one year after completion of course work and recipients must continue to be active in Maryland as a fire fighter or rescue squad member.

15) Loan Assistance Repayment Program (LARP): Applicants must be a graduate of a Maryland institution and be employed by the State or local government or a non-profit organization. Renewable loans of up to $7,500 per year are offered. Priority is given to critical shortage employment fields.

16) Stafford Student Loans: These loans are available for undergraduate, graduate, vocational or professional students who demonstrate financial need. Students may borrow $2,625 for each of the first two undergraduate years, and up to $4,000 annually through the fifth year. Graduate students may borrow up to $7,500 a year. Not more than $17,250 can be borrowed for all years of undergraduate study, $73,500 for all years of graduate study, or $54,750 for undergraduate and graduate study combined.

17) Supplemental Loans for Students: This program is available to graduate, professional and independent undergraduate students. The annual maximum SLS loan limit is $4,000 and depends on the student's educational program length. Borrowers cannot exceed a maximum of $20,000.

18) Parent Loans for Students (PLUS): The PLUS program is for parents who wish to borrow for their student dependents. The parent is responsible for repayment of the loan even if the dependent's education is not completed. The annual maximum PLUS amount is $4,000 per eligible dependent student up to a cumulative maximum of $20,000.

19) Perkins Loans: This low-interest (5 percent) loan is for first-time undergraduates and graduate students with exceptional financial need, as determined by the school. For undergraduate students, priority is given to Pell Grant recipients. Loans are made through a school's financial aid office, the school is the lender. These loans must be repaid. Students may borrow up to $4,500 if they've completed less than two years of a program leading to a first bachelor's degree, or if they are enrolled in a vocational program. Students may borrow up to $9,000 if they've already completed two years of study toward a first bachelor's degree and have achieved third-year status. Up to $18,000 may be borrowed for graduate or professional study. See your school's financial aid department for details.

20) Pell Grant: This award helps first-time undergraduates pay for their education after high school. Eligibility for those who receive a Pell Grant for the first time is usually limited to five to six years of undergraduate study, not including remedial coursework. Awards for the 1992-93 academic year will depend upon program funding. The maximum award for the 1991-92 academic year was $2,400. Students must attend school at least half-time. Grants do not have to be paid back. For more information, contact the financial aid administrator of the college or university you are attending.

21) Supplemental Educational Opportunity Grant (SEOG): This award helps first-time undergraduates with exceptional financial need, as determined by the school. Priority is given to Pell Grant recipients. An SEOG doesn't have to be paid back. Students can get up to $4,000 a year, depending upon available funding.

22) College Work-Study (CWS): This program provides jobs for first-time undergraduates and for graduate students who need financial aid. CWS lets you earn money to help pay your educational expenses. Students are paid at least the current Federal minimum wage, but the pay may also be related to the type of work done and the skills required. Schools set individual work schedules and must pay students directly at least once a month.

Massachusetts

Board of Regents of Higher Education, Scholarship Office, 330 Stuart Street, Boston, MA 02116; (617) 727-9420. Students must be State residents in order to participate in the programs listed below.

1) Massachusetts General Scholarship: This scholarship provides funding ranging from $200 to $1,900 to students attending full-time, State-approved Massachusetts postsecondary schools.

2) Gilbert Matching Scholarship: This scholarship is available to full-time students attending an independent regionally accredited Massachusetts school. The amount of the award is determined by the school's financial aid office.

3) Tuition Waiver Program: This program waives up to the cost of tuition for students enrolled in Massachusetts State-supported colleges or universities. The amount of the award varies and is determined by the institution's financial aid office.

4) Massachusetts Family Education Loan: This loan provides up to 100% of the cost of attendance at a Massachusetts State-approved post secondary school. Specific eligibility criteria is available at individual participating Massachusetts colleges and universities.

5) TERI Supplemental Loan (TERI): This private loan provides funding from $2,000 to $20,000 a year at a fixed or variable rate. Undergraduate or graduate students attending a participating college or university in the U.S. may apply. Contact the financial aid office at a participating college or university for details or contact The Education Resources Institute (TERI) at 1(800) 255-TERI.

6) Professional Education Plan (PEP): Graduate students may borrow up to $7,500 on their own signature, depending on cumulative education debt. Students

Be patient. If any phone number is incorrect, call (area code) 555-1212 and request the new listing.

State Money For College Students

with a credit-worthy co-borrower may borrow up to $20,000.

7) Stafford Student Loans: These loans are available for undergraduate, graduate, vocational or professional students who demonstrate financial need. Students may borrow $2,625 for each of the first two undergraduate years, and up to $4,000 annually through the fifth year. Graduate students may borrow up to $7,500 a year. Not more than $17,250 can be borrowed for all years of undergraduate study, $73,500 for all years of graduate study, or $54,750 for undergraduate and graduate study combined.

8) Supplemental Loans for Students: This program is available to graduate, professional and independent undergraduate students. The annual maximum SLS loan limit is $4,000 and depends on the student's educational program length. Borrowers cannot exceed a maximum of $20,000.

9) Parent Loans for Students (PLUS): The PLUS program is for parents who wish to borrow for their student dependents. The parent is responsible for the repayment of the loan even if the dependent's education is not completed. The annual maximum PLUS amount is $4,000 per eligible dependent student up to a cumulative maximum of $20,000.

10) Perkins Loans: This low-interest (5 percent) loan is for first-time undergraduates and graduate students with exceptional financial need, as determined by the school. For undergraduate students, priority is given to Pell Grant recipients. Loans are made through a school's financial aid office, the school is the lender. These loans must be repaid. Students may borrow up to $4,500 if they've completed less than two years of a program leading to a first bachelor's degree, or if they are enrolled in a vocational program. Students may borrow up to $9,000 if they've already completed two years of study toward a first bachelor's degree and have achieved third-year status. Up to $18,000 may be borrowed for graduate or professional study. See your school's financial aid department for details.

11) Pell Grant: This award helps first-time undergraduates pay for their education after high school. Eligibility for those who receive a Pell Grant for the first time is usually limited to five to six years of undergraduate study, not including remedial coursework. Awards for the 1992-93 academic year will depend upon program funding. The maximum award for the 1991-92 academic year was $2,400. Students must attend school at least half-time. Grants do not have to be paid back. For more information, contact the financial aid administrator of the college or university you are attending.

12) Supplemental Educational Opportunity Grant (SEOG): This award helps first-time undergraduates with exceptional financial need, as determined by the school. Priority is given to Pell Grant recipients. An SEOG doesn't have to be paid back. Students can get up to $4,000 a year, depending upon available funding.

13) College Work-Study (CWS): This program provides jobs for first-time undergraduates and for graduate students who need financial aid. CWS lets you earn money to help pay your educational expenses. Students are paid at least the current Federal minimum wage, but the pay may also be related to the type of work done and the skills required. Schools set individual work schedules and must pay students directly at least once a month.

Michigan

Michigan Department of Education, Student Financial Assistance Services, P.O. Box 30008, Lansing, MI 48909; (517) 373-3394. Competitive Scholarships and tuition Grants are provided to help meet the demonstrated financial need of eligible State residents. Awards range from $100 to a maximum of the amount of demonstrated financial need, school's tuition, or State annual maximum amount established by the Michigan Higher Education Assistance Authority. Demonstrated financial need is based on two factors: the cost of college attendance and available financial resources. The college budget includes tuition, fees, books, room, board, travel and miscellaneous costs. In 1990-91, the Competitive Scholarship Program awarded $30,122,285 to 24,279 students. The Tuition Grant Program awarded $42,220,816 to 26,872 students. State residency is required for the following programs:

1) Competitive Scholarships: This program is limited to high school graduates favorably recommended by an appropriate educational institution and who achieve a semifinalist score on the American College Test (ACT). Those who demonstrate financial need are eligible for monetary consideration. Awards are limited to undergraduates enrolled at least half-time at an eligible Michigan college. Students enrolled in a program leading to a degree in theology, divinity or religious education are ineligible for State scholarships or tuition grants. A student may not concurrently receive State scholarship and tuition grant assistance.

2) Tuition Grants: This program is open to students attending an independent non-profit Michigan college or university. Tuition grants are available to both undergraduates and graduates enrolled at least half-time and are based on financial need.

Minnesota

Minnesota Higher Education Coordinating Board, Capitol Square Building, Suite 400, 550 Cedar Street, St. Paul, MN 55101, (612) 296-3974. In 1991-92, Minnesota received $76.8 million in appropriations for State grants. Students must be Minnesota residents to be eligible for the following programs, unless otherwise specified.

Loans, Grants and Work-Study Options

1) Stafford Student Loans: These loans are available for undergraduate, graduate, vocational or professional students who demonstrate financial need. Students may borrow $2,625 for each of the first two undergraduate years, and up to $4,000 annually through the fifth year. Graduate students may borrow up to $7,500 a year. Not more than $17,250 can be borrowed for all years of undergraduate study, $73,500 for all years of graduate study, or $54,750 for undergraduate and graduate study combined.

2) Supplemental Loans for Students: This program is available to graduate, professional and independent undergraduate students. The annual maximum SLS loan limit is $4,000 and depends on the student's educational program length. Borrowers cannot exceed a maximum of $20,000.

3) Parent Loans for Students (PLUS): The PLUS program is for parents who wish to borrow for their student dependents. The parent is responsible for the repayment of the loan even if the dependent's education is not completed. The annual maximum PLUS amount is $4,000 per eligible dependent student up to a cumulative maximum of $20,000.

4) Perkins Loans: This low-interest (5 percent) loan is for first-time undergraduates and graduate students with exceptional financial need, as determined by the school. For undergraduate students, priority is given to Pell Grant recipients. Loans are made through a school's financial aid office, the school is the lender. These loans must be repaid. Students may borrow up to $4,500 if they've completed less than two years of a program leading to a first bachelor's degree, or if they are enrolled in a vocational program. Students may borrow up to $9,000 if they've already completed two years of study toward a first bachelor's degree and have achieved third-year status. Up to $18,000 may be borrowed for graduate or professional study. See your school's financial aid department for details.

5) Pell Grant: This award helps first-time undergraduates pay for their education after high school. Eligibility for those who receive a Pell Grant for the first time is usually limited to five to six years of undergraduate study, not including remedial coursework. Awards for the 1992-93 academic year will depend upon program funding. The maximum award for the 1991-92 academic year was $2,400. Students must attend school at least half-time. Grants do not have to be paid back. For more information, contact the financial aid administrator of the college or university you are attending.

6) Supplemental Educational Opportunity Grant (SEOG): This award helps first-time undergraduates with exceptional financial need, as determined by the school. Priority is given to Pell Grant recipients. An SEOG doesn't have to be paid back. Students can get up to $4,000 a year, depending upon available funding.

7) College Work-Study (CWS): This program provides jobs for first-time undergraduates and for graduate students who need financial aid. CWS lets you earn money to help pay your educational expenses. Students are paid at least the current Federal minimum wage, but the pay may also be related to the type of work done and the skills required. Schools set individual work schedules and must pay students directly at least once a month.

1) State Grant Program: This award is based on financial need and goes toward the cost of attendance at a postsecondary institution. All applicants must contribute at least 50% of their cost of education. The maximum award in 1991-92 ranges from $2,675 at a community college to $5,706 at a private four-year college. The average award is $1,200. Eligible students must be enrolled at least half-time in any year of undergraduate study and attend eligible Minnesota colleges.

2) State Part-Time Grant Program: This grant is awarded to students who are enrolled less than half-time and are pursuing a program or course of study that applies to a degree, diploma or certificate. The amount of the award is determined by the individual school's financial aid office.

3) Rural Nursing Grants: This award is available to students entering or enrolled in a registered or licensed practical nursing program who have no previous nursing training or education and agree to practice at least three of their first five years in a designated rural area. Awards are based upon financial need and proved 20% of an applicant's combined State and Federal Pell Grant awards. The minimum amount awarded is $100.

4) Minnesota Indian Scholarship Program: This scholarship is based on financial need and is awarded to students who are one-fourth or more Indian ancestry and is a resident of Minnesota and a member of a recognized Indian tribe. The student must be a high school graduate or have their GED and show an ability

Be patient. If any phone number is incorrect, call (area code) 555-1212 and request the new listing.

Education

to benefit from advanced education. Recipients must be accepted by an approved Minnesota institution and be approved by the Minnesota Indian Scholarship Committee. The average award is $1,450.

5) Dislocated Rural Workers Program: This program is open to rural Minnesotans enrolled in an adult farm management program or programs providing preparation for available employment, a person who has lost or is about to lose their job, a displaced homemaker or farmer with severe financial need. The program includes spouses. Awards are based on financial need and determined by the financial aid office of the individual school.

6) Non-AFDC Child Care Grant Program: Students who do not receive Aid to Families with Dependent Children who have children 12 and under and demonstrate financial need may receive assistance to help pay for child care from the financial aid administrator at the school they plan to attend. Assistance may cover the hours necessary for education and up to 20 hours of employment. Eligible institutions include all public post-secondary schools and private, baccalaureate degree granting colleges or universities in Minnesota. Students should apply to the financial aid office at their school.

7) Summer Scholarships for Academic Enrichment: This program provides financial assistance of up to $1,000 to Minnesota students grades 7-12 who attend eligible summer academic programs sponsored by Minnesota postsecondary schools. These include the University of Minnesota campuses, State universities, community colleges, private colleges and technical colleges. Awards are based on financial need. Students must have earned at least a B average for the most recently recorded school term, or have a B average in the subject area of the enrichment course.

8) State Veterans' Dependents Assistance Program: This program provides aid to dependents of POWs and MIAs. The award provides up to $250 per year for tuition and fee assistance at Minnesota private postsecondary institutions.

9) Safety Officers' Survivor Program: Dependent children less than 23 years of age and the surviving spouse of a public safety officer killed in the line of duty on or after January 1, 1973, are eligible to receive educational benefits. For students attending public institutions, the award is the actual tuition and fees charged by the institution or the highest tuition and fees charged by a public institution in Minnesota. Awards are renewable for a maximum of six semesters or nine quarters or their equivalent.

10) Rural Physicians Loan Forgiveness Program: Medical students who agree to serve at least three of their first five years in practice following residency in a designated rural areal are eligible to apply for this program. Up to eight applicants may participate each year. Participants may designate up to $10,000 as a qualified loan for each year of medical school, to a maximum of four years. For each year the physician serves in a designated rural area, an award will be paid that is equal to one year of qualified loans and the interest accrued on them.

Loans, Grants and Work-Study Options

1) Stafford Student Loans: These loans are available for undergraduate, graduate, vocational or professional students who demonstrate financial need. Students may borrow $2,625 for each of the first two undergraduate years, and up to $4,000 annually through the fifth year. Graduate students may borrow up to $7,500 a year. Not more than $17,250 can be borrowed for all years of undergraduate study, $73,500 for all years of graduate study, or $54,750 for undergraduate and graduate study combined.

2) Supplemental Loans for Students: This program is available to graduate, professional and independent undergraduate students. The annual maximum SLS loan limit is $4,000 and depends on the student's educational program length. Borrowers cannot exceed a maximum of $20,000.

3) Parent Loans for Students (PLUS): The PLUS program is for parents who wish to borrow for their student dependents. The parent is responsible for the repayment of the loan even if the dependent's education is not completed. The annual maximum PLUS amount is $4,000 per eligible dependent student up to a cumulative maximum of $20,000.

4) Perkins Loans: This low-interest (5 percent) loan is for first-time undergraduates and graduate students with exceptional financial need, as determined by the school. For undergraduate students, priority is given to Pell Grant recipients. Loans are made through a school's financial aid office, the school is the lender. These loans must be repaid. Students may borrow up to $4,500 if they've completed less than two years of a program leading to a first bachelor's degree, or if they are enrolled in a vocational program. Students may borrow up to $9,000 if they've already completed two years of study toward a first bachelor's degree and have achieved third-year status. Up to $18,000 may be borrowed for graduate or professional study. See your school's financial aid department for details.

5) Pell Grant: This award helps first-time undergraduates pay for their education after high school. Eligibility for those who receive a Pell Grant for the first time is usually limited to five to six years of undergraduate study, not including remedial coursework. Awards for the 1992-93 academic year will depend upon program funding. The maximum award for the 1991-92 academic year was $2,400.

Students must attend school at least half-time. Grants do not have to be paid back. For more information, contact the financial aid administrator of the college or university you are attending.

6) Supplemental Educational Opportunity Grant (SEOG): This award helps first-time undergraduates with exceptional financial need, as determined by the school. Priority is given to Pell Grant recipients, An SEOG doesn't have to be paid back. Students can get up to $4,000 a year, depending upon available funding.

7) College Work-Study (CWS): This program provides jobs for first-time undergraduates and for graduate students who need financial aid. CWS lets you earn money to help pay your educational expenses. Students are paid at least the current Federal minimum wage, but the pay may also be related to the type of work done and the skills required. Schools set individual work schedules and must pay students directly at least once a month.

Mississippi

Student Financial Aid Office, Mississippi Postsecondary Education, Financial Assistance Board, 3825 Ridgewood Rd., Jackson, MS 39211-6453; (601) 982-6570. Students must be Mississippi residents in order to participate in the programs listed below. In 1991-92, $2,952,015 was awarded in State funding.

1) Academic Common Market Program: This program is an interstate agreement among southern States for sharing academic programs. Participating States make arrangements for their residents who qualify to enroll in specific programs in other States on an in-State tuition basis. The waiver of out-of-State tuition is not granted to Mississippi residents pursuing degree programs that are available in Mississippi. There are no repayment requirements for assistance under this program.

2) State Student Incentive Grant Program SSIG): This program is administered by the financial aid office on the campus of each participating college/university. Each participating college/university recommends the recipients for this grant from the eligible students on its campus through the regular financial aid award process. Applicants must demonstrate financial need and be enrolled as a full-time undergraduate at a non-profit State college/university. Awards range from $200 to $1,500 per academic year. There are no repayment requirements for assistance under this program.

3) Mississippi Public Management Graduate Internship Program: This program offers assistance to United States residents or those possessing "green cards", enrolled at Jackson State University, Mississippi State University, University of Mississippi, or University of Southern Mississippi. Participants must have a grade point average of 3.0 or higher an have completed at least one semester of course work earning a "B" or higher in a quantitative research methods course. Participants are awarded a $1,000 stipend per month plus 1% fringe benefits, up to eight months. Approximately 10 participants are selected per year.

4) William Winter Teacher Scholar Loan Program: The program is open to Mississippi students enrolled full-time in any accredited program that leads to a baccalaureate degree and a Class A teaching certificate. Students intending to teach in a critical subject are will be given priority in selection. This merit-based program provides $1,000 per academic year for freshmen/sophomore participants, while junior/senior participants receive $3,000 per academic year. Approximately 50 participants per grade level are selected each year. The award is made on an annual basis with priority given to renewal students and a program participation limit of four years.

5) African-American Doctoral Teacher Loan/Scholarship Program: This program is open to full-time students who are pursuing a career in teaching at an accredited public Mississippi college or university. Participants must also meet the program's academic qualifications. Under the program, $10,000 is awarded per academic year. Approximately five participants are selected per year. The award is made on an annual basis with priority given to renewal students and a program participation limit of three years. Obligation can be discharged on the basis of one year's teaching service at an accredited public Mississippi college or university for one year's loan/scholarship.

6) Southern Regional Educational Board (SREB) Loan/Scholarship Program: This program offers assistance students enrolled in an approved accredited School of Optometry or Osteopathic Medicine and who meet the program's academic qualifications. The amount of the award is determined by the SREB Board and is dependent upon the availability of funds. The award is made on an annual basis with priority given to renewal students and a program participation limit of four years. The number of recipients is designated by the Board. Obligation can be discharged on the basis of one year's service in the field of approved training in Mississippi for one year's loan/scholarship.

7) Law Enforcement Officers and Firemen Scholarship Program: This program provides scholarships for the spouse and the children of full-time Mississippi law enforcement officers and firemen/firefighters who were fatally injured or totally disabled from injuries which occurred during the line of duty. The applicant must be enrolled or accepted for enrollment at a Mississippi State-supported

Be patient. If any phone number is incorrect, call (area code) 555-1212 and request the new listing.

State Money For College Students

college or university. Awards cover the cost of tuition and the average cost of a dormitory room plus required fees including applicable course fees. Recipients are entitled to eight semesters of scholarship assistance. Children are entitled to the scholarship until the age of 23. There are no repayment requirements.

8) Southeast Asia POW/MIA Scholarship Program: This program provides scholarships for children of Mississippi veterans presently or formerly listed as missing in action in Southeast Asia. Children of Mississippi veterans who have been prisoners of a foreign government as the result of a military action against the U.S. naval vessel Pueblo are also eligible. The applicant must be enrolled or accepted for enrollment at a Mississippi State-supported college or university. The scholarship covers the cost of tuition and the average cost of a dormitory room plus required fees including applicable course fees. Children are entitled to the scholarship until the age of 23.

Professional/Medical Scholarships:

Financial obligation can be discharged for the programs listed below on the basis of one year's service in the approved field of training for one year's loan/scholarship.

1) Graduate and Professional Degree Loan/Scholarship Program: This program is open to students seeking a professional degree not available at a Mississippi university and who, as a result, enroll in an accredited out-of-State institution. Participants must also meet the program's academic qualifications. The approved fields of study are limited to health-related professions including chiropractic medicine, orthotics/prosthetics and podiatric medicine. An average of $3,000 is awarded each year to each participant. Approximately ten participants per grade level are selected per academic year.

2) State Medical Education Loan/Scholarship Program: This program offers assistance to State students who have been accepted for admission to the University of Mississippi School of Medicine and who meet program academic qualifications. Acceptable fields of study, training and practice include family medicine, internal medicine, pediatrics, or obstetrics/gynecology. Awards of $6,000 per year are made to approximately five to ten recipients per grade level. This annual award is limited to four years. Obligation can be discharged on the basis of one year's service in a geographical area of critical need in Mississippi designated by the Mississippi State Department of Health or entry into full-time public health work at a State health institution or community health center for one year's loan/scholarship.

3) State Dental Education Loan/Scholarship Program: This program is available to students who have been accepted for admission to the University of Mississippi School of Dentistry and who meet program academic qualifications. Awards of $4,000 per year are made to three to five recipients. This annual award is limited to four years.

4) Career Ladder Nursing Loan/Scholarship Program: This program is available to students who have graduated from an accredited high school and an accredited school of nursing, and who are a Mississippi licensed registered nurse seeking a Bachelor's degree (BSN). Under the program, $1,500 is awarded per academic year. Participation is limited to two years.

5) Nursing Education Loan/Scholarship Program: This program offers assistance to students enrolled full- or part-time in a school of nursing approved by the Board of Trustees and who meet the program's academic qualifications. Those pursuing a BSN Degree are eligible to receive up to $2,000 per academic year, up to two years of full-time study. Those pursuing MSN Degree are eligible to receive up to $3,000 per year, up to one year of full-time study. Those pursuing a DSN degree ar eligible to receive up to $5,000 per academic year for two years of full-time study.

6) Special Nursing Education Loan/Scholarship for Study in Baccalaureate Nursing Education Program: This privately funded scholarship is funded by the Vicksburg Foundation. The program assists State residents studying toward a baccalaureate degree in nursing and is based on financial need and the Pre-Nursing Exam (NLN) score. The applicant must be a junior or senior enrolled full-time in an approved accredited Mississippi school of nursing. The total amount of assistance available is $4,000, payable $2,000 per academic year.

7) Health Care Professions Loan Scholarship Program: This program is available to full-time junior or senior students who are enrolled in an accredited training program of critical need in the State. Programs include: speech pathology, psychology, occupational therapy, physical therapy and other allied health programs in critical demand. Awards of $1,500 are made to one recipient per critical training program each year. Program participation in limited to two years.

8) Special Medical Education Loan/Scholarship Program: This privately funded scholarship is funded by the Vicksburg Foundation. The program offers assistance to junior and senior students enrolled at the University of Mississippi School of Medicine. Assistance of up to $12,000, payable $6,000 per academic year, is awarded based on class rank. Medical study, training and practice must be in specialty areas other than primary care.

Loans, Grants and Work-Study Options

1) Stafford Student Loans: These loans are available for undergraduate, graduate, vocational or professional students who demonstrate financial need. Students may borrow $2,625 for each of the first two undergraduate years, and up to $4,000 annually through the fifth year. Graduate students may borrow up to $7,500 a year. Not more than $17,250 can be borrowed for all years of undergraduate study, $73,500 for all years of graduate study, or $54,750 for undergraduate and graduate study combined.

2) Supplemental Loans for Students: This program is available to graduate, professional and independent undergraduate students. The annual maximum SLS loan limit is $4,000 and depends on the student's educational program length. Borrowers cannot exceed a maximum of $20,000.

3) Parent Loans for Students (PLUS): The PLUS program is for parents who wish to borrow for their student dependents. The parent is responsible for the repayment of the loan even if the dependent's education is not completed. The annual maximum PLUS amount is $4,000 per eligible dependent student up to a cumulative maximum of $20,000.

4) Perkins Loans: This low-interest (5 percent) loan is for first-time undergraduates and graduate students with exceptional financial need, as determined by the school. For undergraduate students, priority is given to Pell Grant recipients. Loans are made through a school's financial aid office, the school is the lender. These loans must be repaid. Students may borrow up to $4,500 if they've completed less than two years of a program leading to a first bachelor's degree, or if they are enrolled in a vocational program. Students may borrow up to $9,000 if they've already completed two years of study toward a first bachelor's degree and have achieved third-year status. Up to $18,000 may be borrowed for graduate or professional study. See your school's financial aid department for details.

5) Pell Grant: This award helps first-time undergraduates pay for their education after high school. Eligibility for those who receive a Pell Grant for the first time is usually limited to five to six years of undergraduate study, not including remedial coursework. Awards for the 1992-93 academic year will depend upon program funding. The maximum award for the 1991-92 academic year was $2,400. Students must attend school at least half-time. Grants do not have to be paid back. For more information, contact the financial aid administrator of the college or university you are attending.

6) Supplemental Educational Opportunity Grant (SEOG): This award helps first-time undergraduates with exceptional financial need, as determined by the school. Priority is given to Pell Grant recipients. An SEOG doesn't have to be paid back. Students can get up to $4,000 a year, depending upon available funding.

7) College Work-Study (CWS): This program provides jobs for first-time undergraduates and for graduate students who need financial aid. CWS lets you earn money to help pay your educational expenses. Students are paid at least the current Federal minimum wage, but the pay may also be related to the type of work done and the skills required. Schools set individual work schedules and must pay students directly at least once a month.

Missouri

Missouri Coordinating Board of Higher Education, P.O. Box 1438, Jefferson City, MO 65102; (314) 751-3940. State residency is required to participate in the following programs.

1) Missouri Parent Loans for Undergraduate Students (PLUS) and Missouri Supplemental Loans for Students (SLS): Parents may borrow for a dependent student under the PLUS Program. Independent undergraduate students and graduate and professional students may apply for SLS. Up to $4,000 is offered per academic year for each program. The maximum amount for each program is $20,000.

2) Missouri Stafford Student Loans: These loans are available for undergraduate, graduate, vocational or professional students who demonstrate financial need. Students may borrow $2,625 for each of the first two undergraduate years, and up to $4,000 annually through the fifth year. Graduate students may borrow up to $7,500 a year. Not more than $17,250 can be borrowed for all years of undergraduate study, $73,500 for all years of graduate study, or $54,750 for undergraduate and graduate study combined.

3) Missouri Higher Education Academic Scholarship Program: The Missouri Higher Education Academic Scholarship Program, also known as "Bright Flight," provides maximum scholarship awards of $2,000 per year to eligible students. In 1990-91, 4,544 students received $8,731,000 through this program. Recipients must attend a participating Missouri post secondary institution full-time and have a composite score on the American College Testing Program (ACT) in the top 3% of all Missouri students taking those tests. These scholarships may be renewed annually up to five years of study.

4) Missouri Student Grant Program: Missouri Student Grants are awarded to undergraduate students who demonstrate financial need and are enrolled full-time at an approved Missouri school. Missouri grants do not have to be paid back. The award amount will vary from school to school depending on the total

Education

cost of education. The minimum annual grant award is $1,500 and is divided equally into semester or quarter payments. In 1990-91, 9358 students were awarded $11,079,096 in funding through this program.

5) Public Service Officer or Employee's Child Survivor Grant Program: This program provides tuition grants to eligible undergraduate students enrolled in participating Missouri post secondary institutions. This program is open to dependent children of a public safety officer or employee of the Department of Highways and transportation (engaged in the construction or maintenance of the State's highways, roads and bridges) who was killed in the line of duty. The maximum tuition grant amount per academic year is the least of: the actual tuition charged at the institution where the student is enrolled full-time, or the amount of tuition charged a Missouri undergraduate resident enrolled full-time in the same class level and in the same academic major as an applicant at the University of Missouri.

Loans, Grants, and Work-Study Options

1) Stafford Student Loans: These loans are available for undergraduate, graduate, vocational or professional students who demonstrate financial need. Students may borrow $2,625 for each of the first two undergraduate years, and up to $4,000 annually through the fifth year. Graduate students may borrow up to $7,500 a year. Not more than $17,250 can be borrowed for all years of undergraduate study, $73,500 for all years of graduate study, or $54,750 for undergraduate and graduate study combined.

2) Supplemental Loans for Students: This program is available to graduate, professional and independent undergraduate students. The annual maximum SLS loan limit is $4,000 and depends on the student's educational program length. Borrowers cannot exceed a maximum of $20,000.

3) Parent Loans for Students (PLUS): The PLUS program is for parents who wish to borrow for their student dependents. The parent is responsible for the repayment of the loan even if the dependent's education is not completed. The annual maximum PLUS amount is $4,000 per eligible dependent student up to a cumulative maximum of $20,000.

4) Perkins Loans: This low-interest (5 percent) loan is for first-time undergraduates and graduate students with exceptional financial need, as determined by the school. For undergraduate students, priority is given to Pell Grant recipients. Loans are made through a school's financial aid office, the school is the lender. These loans must be repaid. Students may borrow up to $4,500 if they've completed less than two years of a program leading to a first bachelor's degree, or if they are enrolled in a vocational program. Students may borrow up to $9,000 if they've already completed two years of study toward a first bachelor's degree and have achieved third-year status. Up to $18,000 may be borrowed for graduate or professional study. See your school's financial aid department for details.

5) Pell Grant: This award helps first-time undergraduates pay for their education after high school. Eligibility for those who receive a Pell Grant for the first time is usually limited to five to six years of undergraduate study, not including remedial coursework. Awards for the 1992-93 academic year will depend upon program funding. The maximum award for the 1991-92 academic year was $2,400. Students must attend school at least half-time. Grants do not have to be paid back. For more information, contact the financial aid administrator of the college or university you are attending.

6) Supplemental Educational Opportunity Grant (SEOG): This award helps first-time undergraduates with exceptional financial need, as determined by the school. Priority is given to Pell Grant recipients. An SEOG doesn't have to be paid back. Students can get up to $4,000 a year, depending upon available funding.

7) College Work-Study (CWS): This program provides jobs for first-time undergraduates and for graduate students who need financial aid. CWS lets you earn money to help pay your educational expenses. Students are paid at least the current Federal minimum wage, but the pay may also be related to the type of work done and the skills required. Schools set individual work schedules and must pay students directly at least once a month.

Montana

Office of the Commissioner of Higher Education, 35 South Last Chance Gulch, Helena, MT 59620-3104; (406) 444-6594. Montana's programs include need- and merit-based scholarships. Montana administers a "decentralized" form of student aid in higher education. Monies are allocated based on a formula to postsecondary schools. Students should contact the financial aid office at the college they plan to attend for scholarship, grant, and loan information. State residency is required.

1) State Student Incentive Grants (SSIG): Awards are based on financial need. The maximum award is $900 per year. To be eligible, State residents must be full-time undergraduates and attending a participating Montana school. The Montana University system grants fee waivers to a limited number of students enrolled at Montana State University, the University of Montana, Eastern Montana College, Northern Montana College, Western Montana College, or Montana Tech. Fee waivers may be available to: Native Americans, senior citizens, some veterans, war orphans, dependents of prisoners of war, residents of Mountain View and Pine Hill schools, and similar public and private non-sectarian Montana charitable institutions, athletes, National Merit Scholarship semi-finalists, and recipients of High school and Community College Honor Scholarships. Fees waived vary and are granted on the basis of financial need and academic or athletic achievement. Contact the schools listed above for more information.

2) Stafford Student Loans: These loans are available for undergraduate, graduate, vocational or professional students who demonstrate financial need. Students may borrow $2,625 for each of the first two undergraduate years, and up to $4,000 annually through the fifth year. Graduate students may borrow up to $7,500 a year. Not more than $17,250 can be borrowed for all years of undergraduate study, $73,500 for all years of graduate study, or $54,750 for undergraduate and graduate study combined.

3) Supplemental Loans for Students: This program is available to graduate, professional and independent undergraduate students. The annual maximum SLS loan limit is $4,000 and depends on the student's educational program length. Borrowers cannot exceed a maximum of $20,000.

4) Parent Loans for Students (PLUS): The PLUS program is for parents who wish to borrow for their student dependents. The parent is responsible for the repayment of the loan even if the dependent's education is not completed. The annual maximum PLUS amount is $4,000 per eligible dependent student up to a cumulative maximum of $20,000.

5) Perkins Loans: This low-interest (5 percent) loan is for first-time undergraduates and graduate students with exceptional financial need, as determined by the school. For undergraduate students, priority is given to Pell Grant recipients. Loans are made through a school's financial aid office, the school is the lender. These loans must be repaid. Students may borrow up to $4,500 if they've completed less than two years of a program leading to a first bachelor's degree, or if they are enrolled in a vocational program. Students may borrow up to $9,000 if they've already completed two years of study toward a first bachelor's degree and have achieved third-year status. Up to $18,000 may be borrowed for graduate or professional study. See your school's financial aid department for details.

6) Pell Grant: This award helps first-time undergraduates pay for their education after high school. Eligibility for those who receive a Pell Grant for the first time is usually limited to five to six years of undergraduate study, not including remedial coursework. Awards for the 1992-93 academic year will depend upon program funding. The maximum award for the 1991-92 academic year was $2,400. Students must attend school at least half-time. Grants do not have to be paid back. For more information, contact the financial aid administrator of the college or university you are attending.

7) Supplemental Educational Opportunity Grant (SEOG): This award helps first-time undergraduates with exceptional financial need, as determined by the school. Priority is given to Pell Grant recipients. An SEOG doesn't have to be paid back. Students can get up to $4,000 a year, depending upon available funding.

8) College Work-Study (CWS): This program provides jobs for first-time undergraduates and for graduate students who need financial aid. CWS lets you earn money to help pay your educational expenses. Students are paid at least the current Federal minimum wage, but the pay may also be related to the type of work done and the skills required. Schools set individual work schedules and must pay students directly at least once a month.

Nebraska

Nebraska Coordinating Commission for Postsecondary Education, 301 Centennial Mall, South, P.O. Box 95005, Lincoln, NE 68509-5505; (402) 471-2847. Nebraska administers a "decentralized" form of student aid in higher education. Monies are allocated based on a formula to postsecondary schools. A limited number of State programs are administered directly through postsecondary schools. Students should contact the financial aid office at the college they plan to attend for scholarship, grant, and loan information. State residency is required.

Loans, Grants and Work-Study Options

1) Stafford Student Loans: These loans are available for undergraduate, graduate, vocational or professional students who demonstrate financial need. Students may borrow $2,625 for each of the first two undergraduate years, and up to $4,000 annually through the fifth year. Graduate students may borrow up to $7,500 a year. Not more than $17,250 can be borrowed for all years of undergraduate study, $73,500 for all years of graduate study, or $54,750 for undergraduate and graduate study combined.

2) Supplemental Loans for Students: This program is available to graduate, professional and independent undergraduate students. The annual maximum SLS

Be patient. If any phone number is incorrect, call (area code) 555-1212 and request the new listing.

State Money For College Students

loan limit is $4,000 and depends on the student's educational program length. Borrowers cannot exceed a maximum of $20,000.

3) Parent Loans for Students (PLUS): The PLUS program is for parents who wish to borrow for their student dependents. The parent is responsible for the repayment of the loan even if the dependent's education is not completed. The annual maximum PLUS amount is $4,000 per eligible dependent student up to a cumulative maximum of $20,000.

4) Perkins Loans: This low-interest (5 percent) loan is for first-time undergraduates and graduate students with exceptional financial need, as determined by the school. For undergraduate students, priority is given to Pell Grant recipients. Loans are made through a school's financial aid office, the school is the lender. These loans must be repaid. Students may borrow up to $4,500 if they've completed less than two years of a program leading to a first bachelor's degree, or if they are enrolled in a vocational program. Students may borrow up to $9,000 if they've already completed two years of study toward a first bachelor's degree and have achieved third-year status. Up to $18,000 may be borrowed for graduate or professional study. See your school's financial aid department for details.

5) Pell Grant: This award helps first-time undergraduates pay for their education after high school. Eligibility for those who receive a Pell Grant for the first time is usually limited to five to six years of undergraduate study, not including remedial coursework. Awards for the 1992-93 academic year will depend upon program funding. The maximum award for the 1991-92 academic year was $2,400. Students must attend school at least half-time. Grants do not have to be paid back. For more information, contact the financial aid administrator of the college or university you are attending.

6) Supplemental Educational Opportunity Grant (SEOG): This award helps first-time undergraduates with exceptional financial need, as determined by the school. Priority is given to Pell Grant recipients. An SEOG doesn't have to be paid back. Students can get up to $4,000 a year, depending upon available funding.

7) College Work-Study (CWS): This program provides jobs for first-time undergraduates and for graduate students who need financial aid. CWS lets you earn money to help pay your educational expenses. Students are paid at least the current Federal minimum wage, but the pay may also be related to the type of work done and the skills required. Schools set individual work schedules and must pay students directly at least once a month.

Nevada

Nevada Department of Education, 400 West King Street, Carson City, NV 89710; (702) 687-5915. Nevada administers a "decentralized" form of student aid in higher education. Monies are allocated based on a formula to eligible postsecondary institutions. The Nevada Student Incentive Grant Program administers renewable, need-based awards of up to $2,500 per year. In 1990-91, the program awarded $204,665 in funding. Students should contact the financial aid office at the college they plan to attend for further information. State residency is required.

Loans, Grants, and Work-Study Options

1) Stafford Student Loans: These loans are available for undergraduate, graduate, vocational or professional students who demonstrate financial need. Students may borrow $2,625 for each of the first two undergraduate years, and up to $4,000 annually through the fifth year. Graduate students may borrow up to $7,500 a year. Not more than $17,250 can be borrowed for all years of undergraduate study, $73,500 for all years of graduate study, or $54,750 for undergraduate and graduate study combined.

2) Supplemental Loans for Students: This program is available to graduate, professional and independent undergraduate students. The annual maximum SLS loan limit is $4,000 and depends on the student's educational program length. Borrowers cannot exceed a maximum of $20,000.

3) Parent Loans for Students (PLUS): The PLUS program is for parents who wish to borrow for their student dependents. The parent is responsible for the repayment of the loan even if the dependent's education is not completed. The annual maximum PLUS amount is $4,000 per eligible dependent student up to a cumulative maximum of $20,000.

4) Perkins Loans: This low-interest (5 percent) loan is for first-time undergraduates and graduate students with exceptional financial need, as determined by the school. For undergraduate students, priority is given to Pell Grant recipients. Loans are made through a school's financial aid office, the school is the lender. These loans must be repaid. Students may borrow up to $4,500 if they've completed less than two years of a program leading to a first bachelor's degree, or if they are enrolled in a vocational program. Students may borrow up to $9,000 if they've already completed two years of study toward a first bachelor's degree and have achieved third-year status. Up to $18,000 may be borrowed for graduate or professional study. See your school's financial aid department for details.

5) Pell Grant: This award helps first-time undergraduates pay for their education after high school. Eligibility for those who receive a Pell Grant for the first time is usually limited to five to six years of undergraduate study, not including remedial coursework. Awards for the 1992-93 academic year will depend upon program funding. The maximum award for the 1991-92 academic year was $2,400. Students must attend school at least half-time. Grants do not have to be paid back. For more information, contact the financial aid administrator of the college or university you are attending.

6) Supplemental Educational Opportunity Grant (SEOG): This award helps first-time undergraduates with exceptional financial need, as determined by the school. Priority is given to Pell Grant recipients. An SEOG doesn't have to be paid back. Students can get up to $4,000 a year, depending upon available funding.

7) College Work-Study (CWS): This program provides jobs for first-time undergraduates and for graduate students who need financial aid. CWS lets you earn money to help pay your educational expenses. Students are paid at least the current Federal minimum wage, but the pay may also be related to the type of work done and the skills required. Schools set individual work schedules and must pay students directly at least once a month.

New Hampshire

New Hampshire Postsecondary Education Commission, 2 Industrial Park Drive, Concord, NH 03301; (603) 271-2555. In 1990-91, the Commission awarded $1,323,251 in funding. Students must be New Hampshire residents in order to participate in the following programs.

1) New Hampshire Incentive Program: Grants from $100 to $2,000 are provided to New Hampshire undergraduate students attending eligible postsecondary institutions with the six New England States accredited by the New England Association for Schools and Colleges. Students must demonstrate financial need and academic ability. In 1990-91, $525,000 was awarded through this program.

2) Scholarships for Orphans of Veterans: Scholarships of $1,000 per year are offered to students whose parent(s) died as a result of service in World War I, World War II, the Korean conflict, or the Southeast Asian Conflict. The deceased parent(s) must have been residents of New Hampshire at the time of their death. Applicants must be between the ages of 16 and 25. Students are eligible for tuition waivers at New Hampshire public postsecondary institutions. In 1990-91, $10,000 in funding was awarded.

3) New Hampshire Nursing Grants: Grants are provided to students who agree to practice nursing in New Hampshire one year for every year in which they receive the grant following graduation from State approved nursing schools. The grant amount is dependent upon need and is awarded for a maximum of two years. In 1990-91, approximately $40,000 in grants was awarded through this program.

Loans, Grants and Work-Study Options

1) Stafford Student Loans: These loans are available for undergraduate, graduate, vocational or professional students who demonstrate financial need. Students may borrow $2,625 for each of the first two undergraduate years, and up to $4,000 annually through the fifth year. Graduate students may borrow up to $7,500 a year. Not more than $17,250 can be borrowed for all years of undergraduate study, $73,500 for all years of graduate study, or $54,750 for undergraduate and graduate study combined.

2) Supplemental Loans for Students: This program is available to graduate, professional and independent undergraduate students. The annual maximum SLS loan limit is $4,000 and depends on the student's educational program length. Borrowers cannot exceed a maximum of $20,000.

3) Parent Loans for Students (PLUS): The PLUS program is for parents who wish to borrow for their student dependents. The parent is responsible for the repayment of the loan even if the dependent's education is not completed. The annual maximum PLUS amount is $4,000 per eligible dependent student up to a cumulative maximum of $20,000.

4) Perkins Loans: This low-interest (5 percent) loan is for first-time undergraduates and graduate students with exceptional financial need, as determined by the school. For undergraduate students, priority is given to Pell Grant recipients. Loans are made through a school's financial aid office, the school is the lender. These loans must be repaid. Students may borrow up to $4,500 if they've completed less than two years of a program leading to a first bachelor's degree, or if they are enrolled in a vocational program. Students may borrow up to $9,000 if they've already completed two years of study toward a first bachelor's degree and have achieved third-year status. Up to $18,000 may be borrowed for graduate or professional study. See your school's financial aid department for details.

5) Pell Grant: This award helps first-time undergraduates pay for their education after high school. Eligibility for those who receive a Pell Grant for the first time is usually limited to five to six years of undergraduate study, not including

Education

remedial coursework. Awards for the 1992-93 academic year will depend upon program funding. The maximum award for the 1991-92 academic year was $2,400. Students must attend school at least half-time. Grants do not have to be paid back. For more information, contact the financial aid administrator of the college or university you are attending.

6) Supplemental Educational Opportunity Grant (SEOG): This award helps first-time undergraduates with exceptional financial need, as determined by the school. Priority is given to Pell Grant recipients. An SEOG doesn't have to be paid back. Students can get up to $4,000 a year, depending upon available funding.

7) College Work-Study (CWS): This program provides jobs for first-time undergraduates and for graduate students who need financial aid. CWS lets you earn money to help pay your educational expenses. Students are paid at least the current Federal minimum wage, but the pay may also be related to the type of work done and the skills required. Schools set individual work schedules and must pay students directly at least once a month.

New Jersey

New Jersey Department of Higher Education, Office of Student Assistance, 4 Quakerbridge Plaza, CN 540, Trenton, NJ 08625; (609) 588-3288. In 1990-91, $95.6 million was awarded in State funding.

1) Tuition Aid Grants: These grants are available to students who are or intend to be full-time undergraduates at an approved New Jersey college or university. For the 1991-92 academic year, grants range in value from $400 to $4,580 per year based upon the student's need and college choice. Grants are renewable annually.

2) Educational Opportunity Fund Grants (EOF): This program is available to students from educationally disadvantaged backgrounds with demonstrated financial need. Generally, family income for dependent students cannot exceed $15,320 for a two-person household. Single independent student income cannot exceed $9,450, and the income for independent students with a two-person household cannot exceed $11,780. Applicants must be full-time matriculated students in a New Jersey college or university. Undergraduate grants range from $200 to $1,950 per year and graduate grants are awarded up to $4,000 per year. Grants are renewable. Campus EOF programs include summer sessions, tutoring, counseling, and development courses.

3) Edward J. Bloustein Distinguished Scholar Program: Students demonstrating high academic achievement based upon their secondary school records and junior year SAT scores will be selected for consideration by their secondary schools. Additional scholarships are awarded to the State's urban and economically distressed areas based on class rank and grade point average. Recipients must enroll at a New Jersey college or university as full-time undergraduate students. Financial need is not a factor in determining eligibility. Awards are $1,000 per year. Students demonstrating financial need may receive up to an additional $1,000 per year.

4) Garden State Scholars Program: Students demonstrating high academic achievement based upon their secondary school records and junior year SAT scores will be selected for consideration by their secondary schools. Recipients must enroll at a New Jersey college or university as full-time undergraduate students. Awards are granted for $500 per year throughout their undergraduate program regardless of financial need. Students demonstrating financial need may receive an additional $500 per year.

5) Public Tuition Benefits Program: Eligible applicants include dependents of emergency service personnel and law enforcement officers killed in the line of duty, who are residents of New Jersey and attend a New Jersey college or university as full-time undergraduates. Grants pay the actual costs of tuition up to the highest tuition charged at a New Jersey college or university.

6) Veterans Tuition Credit Program: U.S. Veterans, who were, or are, eligible for Federal veteran's assistance, and served in the U.S. Armed Forces between December 31, 1960 and August 1, 1974, may apply. Applicants must have been New Jersey residents at the time of induction or discharge, or for at least two year prior to the time of application, excluding active duty. The maximum award is $400 per year for full-time attendance or $200 per year for half-time attendance at any eligible undergraduate, graduate or vocational institution in the U.S.

7) POW/MIA Program: Eligible applicants include child dependents of military service personnel, who were officially declared Prisoners of War or Missing in Action after January 1, 1960, and who are State residents attending a New Jersey college or university as an undergraduate on at least a half-time basis. Grants pay the actual cost of tuition charges incurred at any New Jersey college or university.

Loans, Grants, and Work-Study Options

1) Stafford Student Loans: These loans are available for undergraduate, graduate, vocational or professional students who demonstrate financial need. Students may borrow $2,625 for each of the first two undergraduate years, and up to $4,000 annually through the fifth year. Graduate students may borrow up to $7,500 a year. Not more than $17,250 can be borrowed for all years of undergraduate study, $73,500 for all years of graduate study, or $54,750 for undergraduate and graduate study combined.

2) Supplemental Loans for Students: This program is available to graduate, professional and independent undergraduate students. The annual maximum SLS loan limit is $4,000 and depends on the student's educational program length. Borrowers cannot exceed a maximum of $20,000.

3) Parent Loans for Students (PLUS): The PLUS program is for parents who wish to borrow for their student dependents. The parent is responsible for the repayment of the loan even if the dependent's education is not completed. The annual maximum PLUS amount is $4,000 per eligible dependent student up to a cumulative maximum of $20,000.

4) Perkins Loans: This low-interest (5 percent) loan is for first-time undergraduates and graduate students with exceptional financial need, as determined by the school. For undergraduate students, priority is given to Pell Grant recipients. Loans are made through a school's financial aid office, the school is the lender. These loans must be repaid. Students may borrow up to $4,500 if they've completed less than two years of a program leading to a first bachelor's degree, or if they are enrolled in a vocational program. Students may borrow up to $9,000 if they've already completed two years of study toward a first bachelor's degree and have achieved third-year status. Up to $18,000 may be borrowed for graduate or professional study. See your school's financial aid department for details.

5) Pell Grant: This award helps first-time undergraduates pay for their education after high school. Eligibility for those who receive a Pell Grant for the first time is usually limited to five to six years of undergraduate study, not including remedial coursework. Awards for the 1992-93 academic year will depend upon program funding. The maximum award for the 1991-92 academic year was $2,400. Students must attend school at least half-time. Grants do not have to be paid back. For more information, contact the financial aid administrator of the college or university you are attending.

6) Supplemental Educational Opportunity Grant (SEOG): This award helps first-time undergraduates with exceptional financial need, as determined by the school. Priority is given to Pell Grant recipients. An SEOG doesn't have to be paid back. Students can get up to $4,000 a year, depending upon available funding.

7) College Work-Study (CWS): This program provides jobs for first-time undergraduates and for graduate students who need financial aid. CWS lets you earn money to help pay your educational expenses. Students are paid at least the current Federal minimum wage, but the pay may also be related to the type of work done and the skills required. Schools set individual work schedules and must pay students directly at least once a month.

New Mexico

New Mexico Educational Assistance Foundation, 3900 Osuna NE, PO Box 27020, Albuquerque, NM 81725-7020; (505) 345-3371. In 1990-91, the Foundation awarded $11,198,000 is State funding. In 1991-92, funding totalled $13,210,000. State residency is required for the following programs:

1) New Mexico Student Incentive Grant: Grants ranging from $200 to $2,500 per year are awarded to students attending public and private State institutions. Grants are based on financial need. Students must be enrolled at least half-time as undergraduates.

2) Three Percent Scholarship Program: This program is a gratis scholarship that provides tuition and fee grants to undergraduate and graduate students who possess "good moral character, satisfactory initiative, scholastic standing and personality." Students must be enrolled at a public post-secondary institution in New Mexico. At least one-third of the scholarships must be based on financial need.

3) New Mexico Scholars Program: This program encourages New Mexico high school graduates to attend college in New Mexico by providing scholarships that pay for tuition, required student fees and books for an academic year at eligible post-secondary institutions. Eligible students must have graduated in the upper 5% of his/her high school class or obtained a composite score of at least 25 on the American College Test (ACT). Students may receive up to four annual awards based on academic progress. A combined family income may not exceed $30,000 per year.

4) New Mexico Work-Study Program: The New Mexico Work-Study Program provides employment opportunities for qualified undergraduate and graduate students. Employment is limited to post-secondary non-profit institutions, State political subdivisions, State agencies and Commission on Higher Education approved non-profit organizations. One-third of the awards are based on financial need.

5) Student Choice: Student Choice grants are made to residents attending private

Be patient. If any phone number is incorrect, call (area code) 555-1212 and request the new listing.

State Money For College Students

independent institutions of higher education. Students must be enrolled for at least six semester credit hours at the College of Sante Fe, St. John's College in Santa Fe or the College of the Southwest in Hobbs.

6) Vietnam Veterans' Scholarship Program: The Vietnam Veterans' Scholarship provides tuition payments, book allowance and required student fees to Vietnam Veterans. A student's eligibility must be certified by the New Mexico Veterans' Service Commission. Scholarships are awarded on a first-come, first-served basis. The program is open to undergraduate and graduate students.

7) Athlete Scholarship Program: The Athlete Scholarship Program provides a tuition and required student fee grant to eligible athletes at the University of New Mexico, New Mexico State University, Eastern New Mexico University, New Mexico Highlands University, Western New Mexico University and New Mexico Junior College. Eligibility includes New Mexico residents and non-residents. No more than 75% of the awards may go to out-of-State residents.

8) New Mexico Nursing Student Loan for Service Program: This is a loan-for-service program that is designed to increase the number of nurses in medically underserved areas in New Mexico. Loans may be forgiven through service or repaid. Undergraduates and graduates may borrow a maximum of $2,500 per year up to an aggregate total of $10,000. Students must be enrolled in an approved nursing education program preparing for a Licensed Practical Nursing degree (LPN), Associate Degree in Nursing (ADN) or a Baccalaureate of Science degree in Nursing (BSN).

9) Graduate Scholarship Program: This program's goal is to increase graduate enrollment, particularly for minorities and women, in academic fields in the State's public universities. Preference is given to students enrolled in business, engineering, computer science, mathematics and agriculture. The award pays a maximum of $7,200 per academic year which may be renewed annually. Recipients must serve ten hours per week in an unpaid internship or assistantship.

10) Osteopathic Medical Student Loan Program: This loan-for-service program works to increase the number of Osteopathic physicians in medically underserved areas in New Mexico. Loans may be forgiven through service or repaid. Students may borrow a maximum of $10,000 per year up to five years. Highest priority is given to students with financial need.

11) Professional Student Exchange Program: This exchange program provides New Mexico residents access to academic professional programs at out-of-State institutions at reduced tuition rates on a preferred admission basis. State support is provided for programs not offered at in-State colleges. Categories include: dentistry, veterinary medicine, occupational therapy, optometry, osteopathic medicine, podiatry, graduate library studies and public health.

12) New Mexico Physician and Physician Assistant Student Loan for Service Program: This loan-for-service program was created to increase the number of physicians and physician assistants in medically underserved rural areas in New Mexico. Students may borrow a maximum of $10,000 per academic year. Loans may be forgiven through service or may be repaid. Students must declare intent to practice as a physician or physician assistant in New Mexico and be enrolled and accepted by an accredited school. Highest priority is given to students with financial need.

13) Minority Doctoral Assistance Loan for Service Program: This loan-for-service program was created to increase the number of ethnic minorities and women available to teach engineering, physical or life sciences, mathematics and other academic disciplines in which they are underrepresented in New Mexico colleges and universities. Students must attend a sponsoring New Mexico four year institution and be approved by their academic committee.

Loan and Grant Options

1) Stafford Student Loans: These loans are available for undergraduate, graduate, vocational or professional students who demonstrate financial need. Students may borrow $2,625 for each of the first two undergraduate years, and up to $4,000 annually through the fifth year. Graduate students may borrow up to $7,500 a year. Not more than $17,250 can be borrowed for all years of undergraduate study, $73,500 for all years of graduate study, or $54,750 for undergraduate and graduate study combined.

2) Supplemental Loans for Students: This program is available to graduate, professional and independent undergraduate students. The annual maximum SLS loan limit is $4,000 and depends on the student's educational program length. Borrowers cannot exceed a maximum of $20,000.

3) Parent Loans for Students (PLUS): The PLUS program is for parents who wish to borrow for their student dependents. The parent is responsible for the repayment of the loan even if the dependent's education is not completed. The annual maximum PLUS amount is $4,000 per eligible dependent student up to a cumulative maximum of $20,000.

4) Perkins Loans: This low-interest (5 percent) loan is for first-time undergraduates and graduate students with exceptional financial need, as determined by the school. For undergraduate students, priority is given to Pell Grant recipients. Loans are made through a school's financial aid office, the school is the lender. These loans must be repaid. Students may borrow up to $4,500 if they've completed less than two years of a program leading to a first bachelor's degree, or if they are enrolled in a vocational program. Students may borrow up to $9,000 if they've already completed two years of study toward a first bachelor's degree and have achieved third-year status. Up to $18,000 may be borrowed for graduate or professional study. See your school's financial aid department for details.

5) Pell Grant: This award helps first-time undergraduates pay for their education after high school. Eligibility for those who receive a Pell Grant for the first time is usually limited to five to six years of undergraduate study, not including remedial coursework. Awards for the 1992-93 academic year will depend upon program funding. The maximum award for the 1991-92 academic year was $2,400. Students must attend school at least half-time. Grants do not have to be paid back. For more information, contact the financial aid administrator of the college or university you are attending.

6) Supplemental Educational Opportunity Grant (SEOG): This award helps first-time undergraduates with exceptional financial need, as determined by the school. Priority is given to Pell Grant recipients. An SEOG doesn't have to be paid back. Students can get up to $4,000 a year, depending upon available funding.

New York

New York Higher Education Services Corporation, Student Information, Albany, NY 12255; (518) 474-5592. In 1990-91, the Tuition Assistance Program appropriated $435 million in funding. Approximately $20.2 million was appropriated in scholarships. Students must be New York residents to participate in the following programs.

1) Tuition Assistance Program (TAP): This program offers awards up to $4,125, or tuition, whichever is less, to help students pay tuition at postsecondary institutions in the State. A TAP award is a grant that students do not have to repay. Undergraduate students may receive up to four years of assistance for full-time study or up to five years in certain programs. Graduate or professional students may also receive up to four years of TAP for full-time study for a combined undergraduate-graduate total of eight years.

2) Aid for Part-Time Study (APTS): These grants provide aid for part-time study up to $2,000 per year, but cannot exceed tuition. The amount of the award is established by the participating college.

3) New York Regents Professional Opportunity Scholarships: Full-time students pursuing one of twenty-one professional careers may be eligible for this scholarship. Professions range from accounting to veterinary medicine. Contact the New York Higher Education Services Corporation for a complete listing. Awards range from $1,000 to $5,000 per year for up to four years of study. If an approved program requires more than four years of study, a student will be eligible for payments for the required duration of study. Students must work one year for each annual payment received. Employment must be in the studied profession and be within New York State. If the student does not begin practice within one year of program completion, the student must repay twice the amount of all scholarship monies received plus interest.

4) New York Regents Health Care Opportunity Scholarships: This annual scholarship awards between $1,000 to $10,000 per year to students studying medicine and dentistry. Students must attend an approved program in New York State full-time. Awards are dependent upon family income and are available for up to four years. Upon completion of study, the student must work one year for each annual payment received. However, the minimum service requirement is two years, even if only one annual payment was received. Employment must be in the studied profession and must be in a designated physician-shortage area of New York State. The same penalties apply as above to those students who do not meet their service obligation.

5) New York State Health Service Corps Scholarships: This competitive scholarship provides up to $15,000 per year for two years of full-time study. The award is presented to students studying to become: dental hygienists, midwives, nurse practitioners, occupational therapists, pharmacists, physical therapists, physician assistants, registered nurses, or speech-language pathologists. Students must have been accepted or enrolled full-time in an approved professional program and be within two years of becoming eligible for New York State licensure in their chosen field. Students must agree to work 18 months in a State-operated facility or certain State-licensed voluntary agency for each year of scholarship support received. Selection is based upon academic achievement, previous work experience in the chosen health profession, and demonstrated interest in working with institutionalized populations.

6) Empire State Challenger Scholarship for Teachers: This program provides up to $3,000 per year to those planning a career in the teaching profession. Contact your high school guidance counselor, college financial aid administrator or the New York State Education Department for program details.

7) Regents Award for Children of Deceased or Disabled Veterans: Awards of $450 per year are provided to children whose parent(s) served during World War I, World War II, Korean War, or Vietnam War. Parents may also have served

Be patient. If any phone number is incorrect, call (area code) 555-1212 and request the new listing.

Education

as Merchant Seamen during World War II, or during military operations in Lebanon, Grenada, Panama or the Persian Gulf. Undergraduate work in all programs of study are funded.

8) Regents Awards for Children of Deceased Police Officers, Firefighters, and Correction Officers: Awards of $450 per year are provided to students in this category. Undergraduate work in all study programs are funded.

9) Memorial Scholarships for Children of Deceased Police Officers and Firefighters: Undergraduate students who qualify under this category are eligible to receive the actual tuition or tuition and fees at State University of New York, whichever is less, plus allowances for room, board, books, supplies and transportation.

10) Opportunity Programs: New York State provides financial aid for students who are both academically and economically disadvantaged. The financial aid is combined with programs of special counseling, tutoring, and remedial course work. Assistance is limited and is at the discretion of the college. Awards vary with financial need.

11) State Aid to Native Americans: Up to $1,350 may be awarded yearly to enrolled members of Indian tribes within New York State for half-time or full-time study in the State.

12) Vietnam Veterans Tuition Awards: This program provides tuition assistance to eligible Vietnam Veterans enrolled in an undergraduate program at a degree-granting institution or at an approved vocational school. Awards are $1,000 per semester for full-time study and $500 per semester for part-time study but cannot exceed tuition costs.

Loans, Grants and Work-Study Options

1) Stafford Student Loans: These loans are available for undergraduate, graduate, vocational or professional students who demonstrate financial need. Students may borrow $2,625 for each of the first two undergraduate years, and up to $4,000 annually through the fifth year. Graduate students may borrow up to $7,500 a year. Not more than $17,250 can be borrowed for all years of undergraduate study, $73,500 for all years of graduate study, or $54,750 for undergraduate and graduate study combined.

2) Supplemental Loans for Students (SLS): This program is available to graduate, professional, and independent undergraduate students. The annual maximum SLS loan limit is $4,000 and depends on the student's educational program length. Borrowers cannot exceed a maximum of $20,000.

3) Parent Loans for Students (PLUS): The PLUS program is for parents who wish to borrow for their student dependents. The parent is responsible for the repayment of the loan even if the dependent's education is not completed. The annual maximum PLUS amount is $4,000 per eligible dependent student up to a cumulative maximum of $20,000.

4) Perkins Loans: This low-interest (5 percent) loan is for first-time undergraduates and graduate students with exceptional financial need, as determined by the school. For undergraduate students, priority is given to Pell Grant recipients. Loans are made through a school's financial aid office; the school is the lender. These loans must be repaid. Students may borrow up to $4,500 if they've completed less than two years of a program leading to a first bachelor's degree, or if they are enrolled in a vocational program. Students may borrow up to $9,000 if they've already completed two years of study toward a first bachelor's degree and have achieved third-year status. Up to $18,000 may be borrowed for graduate or professional study. See your school's financial aid department for details.

5) Pell Grant: This award helps first-time undergraduates pay for their education after high school. Eligibility for those who receive a Pell Grant for the first time is usually limited to five to six years of undergraduate study, not including remedial coursework. Awards for the 1992-93 academic year will depend upon program funding. The maximum award for the 1991-92 academic year was $2,400. Students must attend school at least half-time. Grants do not have to be paid back. For more information, contact the financial aid administrator of the college or university you are attending.

6) Supplemental Educational Opportunity Grant (SEOG): This award helps first-time undergraduates with exceptional financial need, as determined by the school. Priority is given to Pell Grant recipients. An SEOG doesn't have to be paid back. Students can get up to $4,000 a year, depending upon available funding.

7) College Work-Study (CWS): This program provides jobs for first-time undergraduates and for graduate students who need financial aid. CWS lets you earn money to help pay your educational expenses. Students are paid at least the current Federal minimum wage, but the pay may also be related to the type of work done and the skills required. Schools set individual work schedules and must pay students directly at least once a month.

North Carolina

North Carolina State Education Assistance Authority, P.O. Box 2688, Chapel Hill, NC 27515-2688; (919) 549-8614. In 1991-92, scholarship/grant programs

totalled $80,912,693. This includes need-based as well as non-need based undergraduate and graduate programs. State residency is required for participation in the following programs:

1) Appropriated Grants: This category includes funds for both full-time and part-time undergraduates plus graduate and first year professional students attending the University of North Carolina (UNC). Awards are based on financial need and vary depending upon the cost of education at the institution, other available financial aid and the financial resources of the student or family.

2) Paul Douglas Teacher Scholarship Program (PDTS): Although this is a Federally funded scholarship, the program in this State is administered by the North Carolina State Education Assistance Authority. These scholarships are for outstanding high school graduates who want to pursue teaching careers after they finish college. A Douglas scholarship provides up to $5,000 a year to students who graduate from high school in the top 10% of their class, and have a cumulative GPA of 3.0 on a 4.0 scale. Students must express an interest in becoming a teacher at the preschool, elementary or secondary level, especially in North Carolina. Students are required to teach two years for each year of scholarship assistance they receive.

3) Incentive Scholarship Program: These renewable awards are open to undergraduate students who enroll at Elizabeth City State University, Fayetteville State University, North Carolina Agricultural and Technical State University, North Carolina Central University, Pembroke State University, and Winston-Salem University. Awards vary, but annual awards may not exceed $3,000 for any recipient. To be eligible, students must meet certain admissions standards, including specified grade-point averages, submit to standardized assessments and participate in required public service activities.

4) Minority Presence Grant Program:

A) General Program: Grants are available to North Carolina students taking at least three hours of degree-credit course work per semester at a UNC institution where their race is in the minority. The amount of the award depends upon the financial need of the recipient and the availability of funds.

B) Doctoral/Law/Veterinary Medicine Program: These grants are available to Black North Carolinians who are enrolled full-time in a doctoral degree program at East Carolina University, North Carolina State University, UNC-Chapel Hill and UNC-Greensboro, or the UNC-Chapel Hill Law School. Each recipient is awarded $4,000 (up to $4,000 for law) for the academic year, with an option of $500 in additional support for study during the summer.

5) North Carolina Community College Scholarship Program: North Carolina students enrolled at least part-time at one of the 58 State community colleges may apply. This renewable program awards 950 scholarships at $375 each annually. Priority is given to students enrolled in college transferable curriculum programs, those seeking new job skills, women in non-traditional curricula, and students who participated in an ABE, GED, or High School Diploma program.

6) North Carolina Student Incentive Grant: This program is open to full-time undergraduates who demonstrate substantial financial need and are enrolled in a State college or university. Awards range from $200 to $1,500 per year, dependent upon need. The average award is approximately $750.

7) North Carolina Legislative Tuition Grant Program: This program assists full-time undergraduates attending a North Carolina private college or university. The maximum award for 1991-92 is $1,150 per year or $575 per semester. This program is not based on financial need. Students must be eligible for in-State tuition rates under the terms and conditions of the current UNC residence manual and meet program conditions.

8) North Carolina Teaching Fellows Scholarship Program: Selection is based upon high school grades, class standing, SAT scores, writing samples, community service and references. Up to 400 Teaching Fellows are selected annually from area high schools. Scholarships of $5,000 per year are renewable for four years of college. Recipients must attend one of the following institutions: Appalachian State University East Carolina University, Elon College, Meredith College, North Carolina A&T University, North Carolina Central University, North Carolina State University, UNC campuses at Asheville, Chapel Hill, Charlotte, Greensboro, Wilmington and Western Carolina University.

9) North Carolina Veterans Scholarship: This award is available to children of certain deceased or disabled veterans or of veterans who were listed as POW/MIA. The veteran must have been a legal resident of North Carolina at time of entry into service, or the child must have been born in North Carolina and resided there continuously. Full scholarships are provided for four academic years of free tuition, room and board and fees at State-supported institutions. Limited scholarships provide free tuition and mandatory fees. The yearly value at private institutions is $3,000 (full) and $1,200 (limited). Awards may be used for undergraduate or graduate study.

10) American Indian Student Legislative Grant Program: This special program provides grants to needy resident North Carolina Indians. Grants up to $500 per academic year are provided for full-time undergraduate or graduate students and a reduced amount proportional to academic load for part-time students. Fellowships at the doctoral level award $4,000 annually to eligible students who

Be patient. If any phone number is incorrect, call (area code) 555-1212 and request the new listing.

State Money For College Students

study at one of the UNC constituent institutions. Awards may be renewed annually.

11) North Carolina Student Loan Program for Health, Science and Mathematics: Applicants must be accepted as full-time students in accredited associate, baccalaureate, master's or doctoral program leading to a degree. Maximum loans range from $2,500 to $7,500 a year depending on the degree level. Rewards are renewable and recipients are chosen according to major, academic capabilities and financial need.

12) Nurse Education Scholarship Loan Program: These awards range from $400 to $5,000, dependent upon financial need, for students studying for the Bachelor of Science Degree in Nursing. Awards range from $400 to $3,000 for students enrolled in the Associate Degree in Nursing and LPN programs.

13) Nursing Scholars Program: This new program is a competitive, renewable, merit-based scholarship/loan available to students planning a nursing career. Recipients are selected based on academic achievement, leadership potential and a desire to practice nursing on a full-time basis in North Carolina. Financial need is not a criterion. Candidates for the Associate degree in nursing receive $3,000 per year; for the diploma in nursing, $3,000; and for the Bachelor of Science in nursing, $5,000 or $3,000 per year. Up to 450 scholarship/loans are funded annually. An annual award of $6,000 is available for a second year of full-time study toward a masters degree in nursing.

14) Board of Governors Dental Scholarship: A student must be accepted for admission to the UNC School of Dentistry, have financial need and express an intent to practice dentistry in the State. This scholarship provides an annual stipend of $5,000 plus tuition, mandatory fees and approved costs for certain instruments and supplies. Awards are renewable annually for a period of four years, dependent upon program specifications.

15) Board of Governors Medical Scholarship Program: Students must be accepted for admission to one the following North Carolina medical schools: Bowman Gray of Wake Forest University, Duke University, East Carolina University and UNC-Chapel Hill. An applicant must demonstrate financial need and express an intent to practice medicine in the State. This scholarship provides an annual stipend of $5,000 plus tuition and mandatory fees. The student must be nominated for the award by one of the four medical schools. Twenty recipients are chosen annually, subject to budget restrictions.

16) Prospective Teacher Scholarship Loans: Recipients are selected on the basis of GAP, SAT scores, class rank, congressional district, recommendations, and certification areas of need. Students must attend one of the 45 public or private State colleges or universities with a North Carolina approved education program or enroll in a technical institute or community college with a transfer program. Awards are made of up to $2,000 per academic year for up to four years of undergraduate study and recipients in special services areas (i.e., school psychologists, counselors, speech language specialists and audiologists) receive up to $2,000 per academic year for the minimum number of years required to earn an entry level degree. One year of the loan will be forgiven for each full year the recipient teaches or works as a special services professional in a State public school.

17) State Contractual Scholarship Program: This program provides scholarship funds to private State colleges or universities for needy North Carolina full or part-time undergraduates. Each eligible school receives up to $450 per State resident undergraduate enrolled. Awards based on financial need are at the discretion of the financial aid office.

18) Vocational Rehabilitation Program: Persons with a physical or mental disability that substantially interferes with obtaining employment may be eligible for assistance from this program. Each qualified individual works with a counselor to develop an appropriate rehabilitative program. This program is tailored to the individual and may include classroom training as well as work experience. Depending upon need, support services such as day care and allowances for transportation and books and supplies are provided. Supplemental training stipends are available on a limited basis. Additional information may be obtained by contacting the Vocational Rehabilitation Division of the nearest student's home or the North Carolina Department of Rehabilitation Services at (919) 733-3364.

Federal Loans, Grants and Work-Study Options

1) Stafford Student Loans: These loans are available for undergraduate, graduate, vocational or professional students who demonstrate financial need. Students may borrow $2,625 for each of the first two undergraduate years, and up to $4,000 annually through the fifth year. Graduate students may borrow up to $7,500 a year. Not more than $17,250 can be borrowed for all years of undergraduate study, $73,500 for all years of graduate study, or $54,750 for undergraduate and graduate study combined.

2) Supplemental Loans for Students: This program is available to graduate, professional and independent undergraduate students. The annual maximum SLS loan limit is $4,000 and depends on the student's educational program length. Borrowers cannot exceed a maximum of $20,000.

3) Parent Loans for Students (PLUS): The PLUS program is for parents who wish to borrow for their student dependents. The parent is responsible for the repayment of the loan even if the dependent's education is not completed. The annual maximum PLUS amount is $4,000 per eligible dependent student up to a cumulative maximum of $20,000.

4) Perkins Loans: This low-interest (5 percent) loan is for first-time undergraduates and graduate students with exceptional financial need, as determined by the school. For undergraduate students, priority is given to Pell Grant recipients. Loans are made through a school's financial aid office, the school is the lender. These loans must be repaid. Students may borrow up to $4,500 if they've completed less than two years of a program leading to a first bachelor's degree, or if they are enrolled in a vocational program. Students may borrow up to $9,000 if they've already completed two years of study toward a first bachelor's degree and have achieved third-year status. Up to $18,000 may be borrowed for graduate or professional study. See your school's financial aid department for details.

5) Pell Grant: This award helps first-time undergraduates pay for their education after high school. Eligibility for those who receive a Pell Grant for the first time is usually limited to five to six years of undergraduate study, not including remedial coursework. Awards for the 1992-93 academic year will depend upon program funding. The maximum award for the 1991-92 academic year was $2,400. Students must attend school at least half-time. Grants do not have to be paid back. For more information, contact the financial aid administrator of the college or university you are attending.

6) Supplemental Educational Opportunity Grant (SEOG): This award helps first-time undergraduates with exceptional financial need, as determined by the school. Priority is given to Pell Grant recipients. An SEOG doesn't have to be paid back. Students can get up to $4,000 a year, depending upon available funding.

7) College Work-Study (CWS): This program provides jobs for first-time undergraduates and for graduate students who need financial aid. CWS lets you earn money to help pay your educational expenses. Students are paid at least the current Federal minimum wage, but the pay may also be related to the type of work done and the skills required. Schools set individual work schedules and must pay students directly at least once a month.

North Dakota

North Dakota Student Financial Assistance Program, State Capitol, 600 East Boulevard, Bismarck, ND 58505; (701) 224-4114. In 1990-91, $1,176,719 was awarded in in State grants to $2,100 students. State residency is required to participate in the following programs:

1) North Dakota Student Financial Assistance Program: Grants of up to $600 are available to students to attend any public or private, non-profit postsecondary training institution in North Dakota. To qualify, students must enroll in a course of study of at least nine months in duration with a minimum of 12 credits for each enrollment period.

2) North Dakota Scholars Program: This program provides approximately 50 tuition scholarships to high school seniors who rank in the top 5% of all North Dakota students taking the ACT assessment and ranking in the top 20% of their high school graduation class. The scholarship must be used at a North Dakota college or university.

3) North Dakota Nursing Scholarship/Loan Program: This scholarship provides funds for qualified students who express an interest in preparing a career in nursing and show financial need. Each recipient must sign and execute a note for each payment. The maximum amounts of the scholarships are: $5,000 to professional nurse graduates, $3,000 to professional nurse students and $2,000 to practical nurse students.

4) North Dakota Indian Scholarship: The North Dakota University System provides renewable grants ($2,000 maximum) for Indian students who have been admitted to a postsecondary institution in North Dakota. Awards are made for one academic year. The applicant must be either a resident of North Dakota with 1/4 degree Indian blood or an enrolled member of a tribe, now resident in North Dakota. Residency for each student is determined by the postsecondary institution that the student is attending.

Federal Loans, Grants and Work-Study Options

1) Stafford Student Loans: These loans are available for undergraduate, graduate, vocational or professional students who demonstrate financial need. Students may borrow $2,625 for each of the first two undergraduate years, and up to $4,000 annually through the fifth year. Graduate students may borrow up to $7,500 a year. Not more than $17,250 can be borrowed for all years of undergraduate study, $73,500 for all years of graduate study, or $54,750 for undergraduate and graduate study combined.

2) Supplemental Loans for Students: This program is available to graduate, professional and independent undergraduate students. The annual maximum SLS loan limit is $4,000 and depends on the student's educational program length.

Education

Borrowers cannot exceed a maximum of $20,000.

3) Parent Loans for Students (PLUS): The PLUS program is for parents who wish to borrow for their student dependents. The parent is responsible for the repayment of the loan even if the dependent's education is not completed. The annual maximum PLUS amount is $4,000 per eligible dependent student up to a cumulative maximum of $20,000.

4) Perkins Loans: This low-interest (5 percent) loan is for first-time undergraduates and graduate students with exceptional financial need, as determined by the school. For undergraduate students, priority is given to Pell Grant recipients. Loans are made through a school's financial aid office, the school is the lender. These loans must be repaid. Students may borrow up to $4,500 if they've completed less than two years of a program leading to a first bachelor's degree, or if they are enrolled in a vocational program. Students may borrow up to $9,000 if they've already completed two years of study toward a first bachelor's degree and have achieved third-year status. Up to $18,000 may be borrowed for graduate or professional study. See your school's financial aid department for details.

5) Pell Grant: This award helps first-time undergraduates pay for their education after high school. Eligibility for those who receive a Pell Grant for the first time is usually limited to five to six years of undergraduate study, not including remedial coursework. Awards for the 1992-93 academic year will depend upon program funding. The maximum award for the 1991-92 academic year was $2,400. Students must attend school at least half-time. Grants do not have to be paid back. For more information, contact the financial aid administrator of the college or university you are attending.

6) Supplemental Educational Opportunity Grant (SEOG): This award helps first-time undergraduates with exceptional financial need, as determined by the school. Priority is given to Pell Grant recipients. An SEOG doesn't have to be paid back. Students can get up to $4,000 a year, depending upon available funding.

7) College Work-Study (CWS): This program provides jobs for first-time undergraduates and for graduate students who need financial aid. CWS lets you earn money to help pay your educational expenses. Students are paid at least the current Federal minimum wage, but the pay may also be related to the type of work done and the skills required. Schools set individual work schedules and must pay students directly at least once a month.

Ohio

Ohio Board of Regents, 30 East Broad Street, Columbus, OH 43266-0417; (614) 466-7420. The Ohio Board of Regents offers student financial aid programs to assist Ohio's college-bound students in meeting educational costs. In 1990-91, approximately $80 million was awarded in scholarships and grants. Ohio residency is required to participate in the following programs.

1) Ohio Instructional Grants: This grant program assists low and middle income families in meeting tuition costs. The amount of each award is based on reported family income and number of dependent children. Grants range from $216 to $1,326 for full-time undergraduates attending public colleges and universities; $540 to $3,306 for students attending private institutions of higher education; and from $372 to $2,268 for students attending proprietary institutions. This grant pays instructional and general fees (tuition) only.

2) Ohio Student Choice Grant Program: This program provides tuition assistance to students attending Ohio non-profit colleges or universities to reduce the gap between tuition costs at public and private institutions. Eligible applicants include students enrolled full-time in a bachelor's degree program in an Ohio non-profit college or university. Award amounts vary from year to year. The award for the 1991-92 year was $494. This grant pays instructional and general fees (tuition) only.

3) Ohio War Orphans Scholarship Program: This program assists in meeting college costs of the children of deceased or disabled Ohio war veterans and children of Vietnam conflict MIAs or POWs. Students must be between the ages of 16 and 21, and enrolled or intend to enroll full-time at an Ohio public college or university or an eligible private non-profit institution of higher education. The scholarship provides general and instructional fees for students attending public colleges or universities. Children of Vietnam conflict MIAs or POWs also receive benefits for room, board and books. Students attending private non-profit institutions receive the average dollar equivalent of the public college costs. The scholarship may be used for instructional and general fees. Dependents of Vietnam conflict MIAs or POWs may use scholarship benefits for instructional and general fees, room and board, and books.

4) Ohio Academic Scholarship Program: This scholarship recognizes an outstanding senior scholar from each high school in Ohio and encourages enrollment in Ohio institutions of higher education. Scholars receive $1,000 per year for a maximum of four academic years. Scholarships of $1,000 are awarded annually to each participating chartered high school in Ohio.

5) Regents Graduate/Professional Fellowship Program: This program recognizes the outstanding academic achievement of Ohio's baccalaureate graduates and encourages their pursuit of graduate or professional degrees in Ohio. Eligible applicants include college or university seniors or baccalaureate degree candidates who will enroll as full-time graduate students in eligible Ohio graduate or graduate professional schools. Regents Fellows receive $3,500 per year for a maximum of two academic years.

6) Police and Firefighter Tuition Benefits: This program provides benefits for children of Ohio firefighters and peace officers killed in the line of duty. Eligible applicants include Ohio residents under 26 years, or under 30 years if honorably discharged from the armed services. The award covers instructional and general fees at a State college or university or the average equivalent at a participating private college. The maximum grant covers four years of undergraduate study.

7) Bureau of Indian Affairs Educational Assistance: This scholarship provides up to $1,500 per year to students of American Indian heritage. An applicant must be at least 1/4 blood American Indian or an enrolled member of a Federally recognized tribe. Preference is given to full-time students who live on or near a reservation. Individual tribes may set priorities for available funds.

8) Nursing Loans: This program provides financial assistance to nursing students based on financial need. Students must be enrolled at least half-time in participating schools of nursing. The loan maximum is $2,500 for years and two, and up to $4,000 for years three and four. A portion of the loan may be canceled for specified career service.

Federal Loans, Grants and Work-Study Programs

1) Stafford Student Loans: These loans are available for undergraduate, graduate, vocational or professional students who demonstrate financial need. Students may borrow $2,625 for each of the first two undergraduate years, and up to $4,000 annually through the fifth year. Graduate students may borrow up to $7,500 a year. Not more than $17,250 can be borrowed for all years of undergraduate study, $73,500 for all years of graduate study, or $54,750 for undergraduate and graduate study combined.

2) Supplemental Loans for Students: This program is available to graduate, professional and independent undergraduate students. The annual maximum SLS loan limit is $4,000 and depends on the student's educational program length. Borrowers cannot exceed a maximum of $20,000.

3) Parent Loans for Students (PLUS): The PLUS program is for parents who wish to borrow for their student dependents. The parent is responsible for the repayment of the loan even if the dependent's education is not completed. The annual maximum PLUS amount is $4,000 per eligible dependent student up to a cumulative maximum of $20,000.

4) Perkins Loans: This low-interest (5 percent) loan is for first-time undergraduates and graduate students with exceptional financial need, as determined by the school. For undergraduate students, priority is given to Pell Grant recipients. Loans are made through a school's financial aid office, the school is the lender. These loans must be repaid. Students may borrow up to $4,500 if they've completed less than two years of a program leading to a first bachelor's degree, or if they are enrolled in a vocational program. Students may borrow up to $9,000 if they've already completed two years of study toward a first bachelor's degree and have achieved third-year status. Up to $18,000 may be borrowed for graduate or professional study. See your school's financial aid department for details.

5) Pell Grant: This award helps first-time undergraduates pay for their education after high school. Eligibility for those who receive a Pell Grant for the first time is usually limited to five to six years of undergraduate study, not including remedial coursework. Awards for the 1992-93 academic year will depend upon program funding. The maximum award for the 1991-92 academic year was $2,400. Students must attend school at least half-time. Grants do not have to be paid back. For more information, contact the financial aid administrator of the college or university you are attending.

6) Supplemental Educational Opportunity Grant (SEOG): This award helps first-time undergraduates with exceptional financial need, as determined by the school. Priority is given to Pell Grant recipients. An SEOG doesn't have to be paid back. Students can get up to $4,000 a year, depending upon available funding.

7) College Work-Study (CWS): This program provides jobs for first-time undergraduates and for graduate students who need financial aid. CWS lets you earn money to help pay your educational expenses. Students are paid at least the current Federal minimum wage, but the pay may also be related to the type of work done and the skills required. Schools set individual work schedules and must pay students directly at least once a month.

Oklahoma

Oklahoma State Regents for Higher Education, 500 Education Building, State Capitol Complex, Oklahoma City, OK 73105-4503; (405) 840-8356. State residency is required to participate in the following programs. In 1991-92, total State funding figures were $13,282,967.

State Money For College Students

1) Oklahoma Tuition and Grant Program: This need-based grant program is open to Oklahoma students who attend approved colleges, universities, and vocational-technical schools in Oklahoma. Awards are approved for full-time or part-time students and undergraduate or graduate study. The maximum annual award is 75% of enrollment costs or $1,000, whichever is less.

2) William P. Willis Scholarship Program: Eligible applicants include low-income, full-time students attending one of Oklahoma public colleges or universities. Students are nominated by presidents of Oklahoma State System institutions of higher education. Scholarships are awarded on a yearly basis, renewable for up to three years, and covers general enrollment fees, books, materials and room and board.

3) Future Teachers Scholarship Program: This competitive scholarship is available to outstanding high school graduates who demonstrate an interest in teaching in fields where there is a teacher shortage in Oklahoma. Eligible applicants must rank in the top 15% of their high school graduating class. Scholarships are awarded for up to $1,500 per year for full-time students and up to $750 per year for half-time students. The scholarship may be renewed up to four years.

Loans, Grants and Work-Study Options

1) Stafford Student Loans: These loans are available for undergraduate, graduate, vocational or professional students who demonstrate financial need. Students may borrow $2,625 for each of the first two undergraduate years, and up to $4,000 annually through the fifth year. Graduate students may borrow up to $7,500 a year. Not more than $17,250 can be borrowed for all years of undergraduate study, $73,500 for all years of graduate study, or $54,750 for undergraduate and graduate study combined.

2) Supplemental Loans for Students: This program is available to graduate, professional and independent undergraduate students. The annual maximum SLS loan limit is $4,000 and depends on the student's educational program length. Borrowers cannot exceed a maximum of $20,000.

3) Parent Loans for Students (PLUS): The PLUS program is for parents who wish to borrow for their student dependents. The parent is responsible for the repayment of the loan even if the dependent's education is not completed. The annual maximum PLUS amount is $4,000 per eligible dependent student up to a cumulative maximum of $20,000.

4) Perkins Loans: This low-interest (5 percent) loan is for first-time undergraduates and graduate students with exceptional financial need, as determined by the school. For undergraduate students, priority is given to Pell Grant recipients. Loans are made through a school's financial aid office, the school is the lender. These loans must be repaid. Students may borrow up to $4,500 if they've completed less than two years of a program leading to a first bachelor's degree, or if they are enrolled in a vocational program. Students may borrow up to $9,000 if they've already completed two years of study toward a first bachelor's degree and have achieved third-year status. Up to $18,000 may be borrowed for graduate or professional study. See your school's financial aid department for details.

5) Pell Grant: This award helps first-time undergraduates pay for their education after high school. Eligibility for those who receive a Pell Grant for the first time is usually limited to five to six years of undergraduate study, not including remedial coursework. Awards for the 1992-93 academic year will depend upon program funding. The maximum award for the 1991-92 academic year was $2,400. Students must attend school at least half-time. Grants do not have to be paid back. For more information, contact the financial aid administrator of the college or university you are attending.

6) Supplemental Educational Opportunity Grant (SEOG): This award helps first-time undergraduates with exceptional financial need, as determined by the school. Priority is given to Pell Grant recipients. An SEOG doesn't have to be paid back. Students can get up to $4,000 a year, depending upon available funding.

7) College Work-Study (CWS): This program provides jobs for first-time undergraduates and for graduate students who need financial aid. CWS lets you earn money to help pay your educational expenses. Students are paid at least the current Federal minimum wage, but the pay may also be related to the type of work done and the skills required. Schools set individual work schedules and must pay students directly at least once a month.

Oregon

Oregon State Scholarship Commission, 1445 Willamette Street, Eugene, OR 97401; (503) 346-4166. The Commission administers private award scholarship programs and State grant programs to Oregon residents. Their largest programs, the Oregon Need Grant and Oregon Cash Award, receive approximately 90,000 applications annually and in 1990-91 disbursed $12 million in aid to 16,000 students.

1) Oregon State Grants: The commission awards State grants to Oregon resident undergraduate students who enroll full-time at a non-profit college or university in Oregon. Both State grants are awarded on the basis of financial need. Either grant may be received for twelve terms or eight semesters if a student maintains satisfactory academic progress and files a new need analysis form each year to demonstrate continued financial need.

A) Cash Awards: These grants are awarded to graduating high school seniors with high academic potential as well as financial need. Cash Awardees are selected on the basis of high school GPA, as well as SAT or ACT scores, reported by high schools for the top 10% of graduating seniors. During 1992-93, the amount of a Cash Award is $864.

B) Need Grants: Eligibility for this program is based only on financial need. The amount of the award depends on the level of need and the cost of education. For Oregon schools, the 1992-93 maximum award a community college is $4,828, the maximum at a public four-year school is $966, and at private schools the maximum ranges from $978 to $1,920.

The Oregon State Scholarship Commission administers a number of private award programs with very specific eligibility requirements. Scholarships are available to high school seniors, high school graduates, undergraduates and graduate students. Students may receive a listing of individual programs and their requirements directly from the Commission.

Loans, Grants, and Work-Study Options

1) Stafford Student Loans: These loans are available for undergraduate, graduate, vocational or professional students who demonstrate financial need. Students may borrow $2,625 for each of the first two undergraduate years, and up to $4,000 annually through the fifth year. Graduate students may borrow up to $7,500 a year. Not more than $17,250 can be borrowed for all years of undergraduate study, $73,500 for all years of graduate study, or $54,750 for undergraduate and graduate study combined.

2) Supplemental Loans for Students: This program is available to graduate, professional and independent undergraduate students. The annual maximum SLS loan limit is $4,000 and depends on the student's educational program length. Borrowers cannot exceed a maximum of $20,000.

3) Parent Loans for Students (PLUS): The PLUS program is for parents who wish to borrow for their student dependents. The parent is responsible for the repayment of the loan even if the dependent's education is not completed. The annual maximum PLUS amount is $4,000 per eligible dependent student up to a cumulative maximum of $20,000.

4) Perkins Loans: This low-interest (5 percent) loan is for first-time undergraduates and graduate students with exceptional financial need, as determined by the school. For undergraduate students, priority is given to Pell Grant recipients. Loans are made through a school's financial aid office, the school is the lender. These loans must be repaid. Students may borrow up to $4,500 if they've completed less than two years of a program leading to a first bachelor's degree, or if they are enrolled in a vocational program. Students may borrow up to $9,000 if they've already completed two years of study toward a first bachelor's degree and have achieved third-year status. Up to $18,000 may be borrowed for graduate or professional study. See your school's financial aid department for details.

5) Pell Grant: This award helps first-time undergraduates pay for their education after high school. Eligibility for those who receive a Pell Grant for the first time is usually limited to five to six years of undergraduate study, not including remedial coursework. Awards for the 1992-93 academic year will depend upon program funding. The maximum award for the 1991-92 academic year was $2,400. Students must attend school at least half-time. Grants do not have to be paid back. For more information, contact the financial aid administrator of the college or university you are attending.

6) Supplemental Educational Opportunity Grant (SEOG): This award helps first-time undergraduates with exceptional financial need, as determined by the school. Priority is given to Pell Grant recipients. An SEOG doesn't have to be paid back. Students can get up to $4,000 a year, depending upon available funding.

7) College Work-Study (CWS): This program provides jobs for first-time undergraduates and for graduate students who need financial aid. CWS lets you earn money to help pay your educational expenses. Students are paid at least the current Federal minimum wage, but the pay may also be related to the type of work done and the skills required. Schools set individual work schedules and must pay students directly at least once a month.

Pennsylvania

Pennsylvania Higher Education Assistance Agency, 660 Boas Street, Harrisburg, PA 17102; (717) 257-2550. Approximately $155 million in State grants was awarded to 120,000 students in 1990-1991. Students must be residents of Pennsylvania to participate in the following programs.

Education

1) Pennsylvania State Grants: Full-time undergraduate students who demonstrate financial need are eligible for these grants. Awards are limited to 80% of tuition and fees up to $2,300 at approved institutions in Pennsylvania. At approved institutions outside of the State, the grant limit is $600. Pennsylvania also requires that grant recipients file for aid in the Federal Pell Grant Program. The remainder of the costs are then met through borrowing, working or other aid programs. Awards are made for a maximum of one academic year at a time. Grants do not have to be repaid.

2) Grants for Veterans and POW/MIA Dependents: Qualified veterans of the U.S. Armed Services are eligible for consideration for State Grants while they are full-time undergraduate students. Grants are limited to 80% of tuition and fees up to a maximum of $2,300 at a Pennsylvania School or $800 at out-of-State schools.

Undergraduate State grants are also available to dependents of military service personnel, who were officially declared Prisoners of War or Missing in Action after January 31, 1955. Students must demonstrate financial need, be State residents, and attend a PHEAA approved Pennsylvania college or university on at least a half-time basis.

Loans, Grants and Work-Study Options

1) Stafford Student Loans: These loans are available for undergraduate, graduate, vocational or professional students who demonstrate financial need. Students may borrow $2,625 for each of the first two undergraduate years, and up to $4,000 annually through the fifth year. Graduate students may borrow up to $7,500 a year. Not more than $17,250 can be borrowed for all years of undergraduate study, $73,500 for all years of graduate study, or $54,750 for undergraduate and graduate study combined.

2) Supplemental Loans for Students: This program is available to graduate, professional and independent undergraduate students. The annual maximum SLS loan limit is $4,000 and depends on the student's educational program length. Borrowers cannot exceed a maximum of $20,000.

3) Parent Loans for Students (PLUS): The PLUS program is for parents who wish to borrow for their student dependents. The parent is responsible for the repayment of the loan even if the dependent's education is not completed. The annual maximum PLUS amount is $4,000 per eligible dependent student up to a cumulative maximum of $20,000.

4) Perkins Loans: This low-interest (5 percent) loan is for first-time undergraduates and graduate students with exceptional financial need, as determined by the school. For undergraduate students, priority is given to Pell Grant recipients. Loans are made through a school's financial aid office, the school is the lender. These loans must be repaid. Students may borrow up to $4,500 if they've completed less than two years of a program leading to a first bachelor's degree, or if they are enrolled in a vocational program. Students may borrow up to $9,000 if they've already completed two years of study toward a first bachelor's degree and have achieved third-year status. Up to $18,000 may be borrowed for graduate or professional study. See your school's financial aid department for details.

5) Pell Grant: This award helps first-time undergraduates pay for their education after high school. Eligibility for those who receive a Pell Grant for the first time is usually limited to five to six years of undergraduate study, not including remedial coursework. Awards for the 1992-93 academic year will depend upon program funding. The maximum award for the 1991-92 academic year was $2,400. Students must attend school at least half-time. Grants do not have to be paid back. For more information, contact the financial aid administrator of the college or university you are attending.

6) Supplemental Educational Opportunity Grant (SEOG): This award helps first-time undergraduates with exceptional financial need, as determined by the school. Priority is given to Pell Grant recipients. An SEOG doesn't have to be paid back. Students can get up to $4,000 a year, depending upon available funding.

7) College Work-Study (CWS): This program provides jobs for first-time undergraduates and for graduate students who need financial aid. CWS lets you earn money to help pay your educational expenses. Students are paid at least the current Federal minimum wage, but the pay may also be related to the type of work done and the skills required. Schools set individual work schedules and must pay students directly at least once a month.

Rhode Island

Rhode Island Higher Education Assistance Authority, 560 Jefferson Boulevard, Warwick, RI 02886; (401) 277-2050. In 1990-91, $10,068,000 was awarded in funding. Students must be Rhode Island residents in order to participate in the programs listed below.

1) State Scholarship: Scholarships are based on grades or test scores as well as financial need. Students must be enrolled or accepted in a college, university or technical school on at least a half-time basis. Awards range from $250 to $2,000 depending on State money provided and student need.

2) Best and Brightest Scholarship: This competitive academic scholarship is available to graduating seniors at Rhode Island high schools seniors who want to become teachers when they finish college. Recipients must have been accepted as full-time students at colleges or universities in a program leading to teacher certification. The maximum award amount given is $5,000 per year. Recipients must fulfill a teaching obligation of two years for each year of scholarship. If this is not met, the scholarship becomes a loan.

3) Paul Douglas Scholarship: Although this is a Federally funded scholarship, the program in this State is administered by the Rhode Island Higher Education Assistance Authority. These scholarships are for outstanding high school graduates who want to pursue teaching careers after they finish college. A Douglas scholarship provides up to $5,000 a year to students who graduate from high school in the top 10% of their class, and have a cumulative GPA of 3.0 on a 4.0 scale. Students must express an interest in becoming a teacher at the preschool, elementary or secondary level, especially in Rhode Island. Students are required to teach two years for each year of scholarship assistance they receive.

Loans, Grants and Work-Study Options

1) Stafford Student Loans: These loans are available for undergraduate, graduate, vocational or professional students who demonstrate financial need. Students may borrow $2,625 for each of the first two undergraduate years, and up to $4,000 annually through the fifth year. Graduate students may borrow up to $7,500 a year. Not more than $17,250 can be borrowed for all years of undergraduate study, $73,500 for all years of graduate study, or $54,750 for undergraduate and graduate study combined.

2) Supplemental Loans for Students: This program is available to graduate, professional and independent undergraduate students. The annual maximum SLS loan limit is $4,000 and depends on the student's educational program length. Borrowers cannot exceed a maximum of $20,000.

3) Parent Loans for Students (PLUS): The PLUS program is for parents who wish to borrow for their student dependents. The parent is responsible for the repayment of the loan even if the dependent's education is not completed. The annual maximum PLUS amount is $4,000 per eligible dependent student up to a cumulative maximum of $20,000.

4) Perkins Loans: This low-interest (5 percent) loan is for first-time undergraduates and graduate students with exceptional financial need, as determined by the school. For undergraduate students, priority is given to Pell Grant recipients. Loans are made through a school's financial aid office, the school is the lender. These loans must be repaid. Students may borrow up to $4,500 if they've completed less than two years of a program leading to a first bachelor's degree, or if they are enrolled in a vocational program. Students may borrow up to $9,000 if they've already completed two years of study toward a first bachelor's degree and have achieved third-year status. Up to $18,000 may be borrowed for graduate or professional study. See your school's financial aid department for details.

5) Pell Grant: This award helps first-time undergraduates pay for their education after high school. Eligibility for those who receive a Pell Grant for the first time is usually limited to five to six years of undergraduate study, not including remedial coursework. Awards for the 1992-93 academic year will depend upon program funding. The maximum award for the 1991-92 academic year was $2,400. Students must attend school at least half-time. Grants do not have to be paid back. For more information, contact the financial aid administrator of the college or university you are attending.

6) Supplemental Educational Opportunity Grant (SEOG): This award helps first-time undergraduates with exceptional financial need, as determined by the school. Priority is given to Pell Grant recipients. An SEOG doesn't have to be paid back. Students can get up to $4,000 a year, depending upon available funding.

7) College Work-Study (CWS): This program provides jobs for first-time undergraduates and for graduate students who need financial aid. CWS lets you earn money to help pay your educational expenses. Students are paid at least the current Federal minimum wage, but the pay may also be related to the type of work done and the skills required. Schools set individual work schedules and must pay students directly at least once a month.

South Carolina

South Carolina Commission on Higher Education, 1333 Main Street, Suite 300, Columbia, SC 29201; (803) 253-6260. In 1990-91, $400,000 was awarded through the Commission, although other State agencies also provide funding. The following programs are open to South Carolina residents only.

1) South Carolina Tuition Grants: This program is open to students accepted for full-time enrollment in eligible private institutions in the State. Grants are based upon financial need and range up to $3,320 per year depending upon tuition

State Money For College Students

cost. In 1990-91, $16 million was awarded through this program.

2) South Carolina Graduate Incentive Fellowship Program: This program is open to full-time graduate and first year professional students with strong academic records. To be eligible, the student must be a member of a minority race at the institution to be attended. South Carolina residency requirements do not apply to students enrolled in doctoral programs. Recipients may receive a maximum of $5,000 per year for masters and first professional studies, and a maximum of $10,000 per year for doctoral studies.

3) South Carolina *Other Race* Program: Eligible applicants include members of a minority race at the institution to be attended. Eligible institutions include all public senior colleges and Denmark Technical College. Students must meet certain academic requirements. The college selects recipients based on academic performance and related criteria. Awards are given up to $1,000 per year.

4) Palmetto Fellows Scholarship: Eligible applicants include students who have attained an established qualifying score on the PSAT and plan to attend in-State institutions. Students may apply in the fall of their senior year. Recipients may receive up to $5,000 per year. Awards are renewable for three years. In 1990-91, $400,000 was awarded in funding.

5) Vocational Rehabilitation Benefits: This program is available to students who have physical or mental handicaps that limit vocational opportunities. Awards up to $2,000 per year are given based on financial need and cover educational fees. Additional funds are available for special services.

6) South Carolina Medical and Dental Scholarship Fund: This program is available to students who are accepted for enrollment in an approved accredited medical or dental school in the U.S. Applicants must be willing to practice in manpower shortage areas. Loans are forgivable under certain conditions. Loans of $10,000 per academic year are awarded up to four years.

7) Tuition Waiver for Senior Citizens: Tuition waivers are available to students, age 60 and over, attending South Carolina public colleges. Students must meet institution admissions policies. The waiver is equal to tuition only in the public college to be attended.

8) Free Tuition for Children of Deceased or Disabled South Carolina Veterans: A waiver of tuition is available to students attending any public institution in South Carolina, if they are children of deceased or totally disabled veterans. This waiver is not based upon financial need.

9) Free Tuition for Children of Deceased or Disabled South Carolina Firemen, Law Officers, and Members of Civil Air Patrol or Organized Rescue Squad: A waiver of tuition is available to students attending any public postsecondary institution in South Carolina, if they are children of deceased or totally disabled personnel, as described above. This waiver is not based upon financial need.

Loans, Grants and Work-Study Options

1) Stafford Student Loans: These loans are available for undergraduate, graduate, vocational or professional students who demonstrate financial need. Students may borrow $2,625 for each of the first two undergraduate years, and up to $4,000 annually through the fifth year. Graduate students may borrow up to $7,500 a year. Not more than $17,250 can be borrowed for all years of undergraduate study, $73,500 for all years of graduate study, or $54,750 for undergraduate and graduate study combined.

2) Supplemental Loans for Students: This program is available to graduate, professional and independent undergraduate students. The annual maximum SLS loan limit is $4,000 and depends on the student's educational program length. Borrowers cannot exceed a maximum of $20,000.

3) Parent Loans for Students (PLUS): The PLUS program is for parents who wish to borrow for their student dependents. The parent is responsible for the repayment of the loan even if the dependent's education is not completed. The annual maximum PLUS amount is $4,000 per eligible dependent student up to a cumulative maximum of $20,000.

4) Perkins Loans: This low-interest (5 percent) loan is for first-time undergraduates and graduate students with exceptional financial need, as determined by the school. For undergraduate students, priority is given to Pell Grant recipients. Loans are made through a school's financial aid office, the school is the lender. These loans must be repaid. Students may borrow up to $4,500 if they've completed less than two years of a program leading to a first bachelor's degree, or if they are enrolled in a vocational program. Students may borrow up to $9,000 if they've already completed two years of study toward a first bachelor's degree and have achieved third-year status. Up to $18,000 may be borrowed for graduate or professional study. See your school's financial aid department for details.

5) Pell Grant: This award helps first-time undergraduates pay for their education after high school. Eligibility for those who receive a Pell Grant for the first time is usually limited to five to six years of undergraduate study, not including remedial coursework. Awards for the 1992-93 academic year will depend upon program funding. The maximum award for the 1991-92 academic year was $2,400. Students must attend school at least half-time. Grants do not have to be paid back. For more information, contact the financial aid administrator of the college or university you are attending.

6) Supplemental Educational Opportunity Grant (SEOG): This award helps first-time undergraduates with exceptional financial need, as determined by the school. Priority is given to Pell Grant recipients. An SEOG doesn't have to be paid back. Students can get up to $4,000 a year, depending upon available funding.

7) College Work-Study (CWS): This program provides jobs for first-time undergraduates and for graduate students who need financial aid. CWS lets you earn money to help pay your educational expenses. Students are paid at least the current Federal minimum wage, but the pay may also be related to the type of work done and the skills required. Schools set individual work schedules and must pay students directly at least once a month.

South Dakota

South Dakota Department of Education and Cultural Affairs, Office of the Secretary, 700 Governors Drive, Pierre, SD 57501; (605) 773-3134. State residency is required for the following programs. In 1990-91, $300,000 was awarded through the two programs below.

1) South Dakota State Student Incentive Grant Program: Grants ranging from $200 to $2,500 per year are awarded to students attending public and private State institutions. Grants are based on financial need. Students must be enrolled at least half-time as undergraduates.

2) South Dakota Tuition Equalization Grant Program: This program is available to financially needy students who are enrolled as full-time undergraduate students at an eligible South Dakota private college. The maximum grant is the total amount of tuition and mandatory fees charged by the institution for the academic year, or $250, whichever is less. Students may apply annually for the award for up to four years, or until they receive a baccalaureate degree.

Loans, Grants and Work-Study Options

1) Stafford Student Loans: These loans are available for undergraduate, graduate, vocational or professional students who demonstrate financial need. Students may borrow $2,625 for each of the first two undergraduate years, and up to $4,000 annually through the fifth year. Graduate students may borrow up to $7,500 a year. Not more than $17,250 can be borrowed for all years of undergraduate study, $73,500 for all years of graduate study, or $54,750 for undergraduate and graduate study combined.

2) Supplemental Loans for Students: This program is available to graduate, professional and independent undergraduate students. The annual maximum SLS loan limit is $4,000 and depends on the student's educational program length. Borrowers cannot exceed a maximum of $20,000.

3) Parent Loans for Students (PLUS): The PLUS program is for parents who wish to borrow for their student dependents. The parent is responsible for the repayment of the loan even if the dependent's education is not completed. The annual maximum PLUS amount is $4,000 per eligible dependent student up to a cumulative maximum of $20,000.

4) Perkins Loans: This low-interest (5 percent) loan is for first-time undergraduates and graduate students with exceptional financial need, as determined by the school. For undergraduate students, priority is given to Pell Grant recipients. Loans are made through a school's financial aid office, the school is the lender. These loans must be repaid. Students may borrow up to $4,500 if they've completed less than two years of a program leading to a first bachelor's degree, or if they are enrolled in a vocational program. Students may borrow up to $9,000 if they've already completed two years of study toward a first bachelor's degree and have achieved third-year status. Up to $18,000 may be borrowed for graduate or professional study. See your school's financial aid department for details.

5) Pell Grant: This award helps first-time undergraduates pay for their education after high school. Eligibility for those who receive a Pell Grant for the first time is usually limited to five to six years of undergraduate study, not including remedial coursework. Awards for the 1992-93 academic year will depend upon program funding. The maximum award for the 1991-92 academic year was $2,400. Students must attend school at least half-time. Grants do not have to be paid back. For more information, contact the financial aid administrator of the college or university you are attending.

6) Supplemental Educational Opportunity Grant (SEOG): This award helps first-time undergraduates with exceptional financial need, as determined by the school. Priority is given to Pell Grant recipients. An SEOG doesn't have to be paid back. Students can get up to $4,000 a year, depending upon available funding.

7) College Work-Study (CWS): This program provides jobs for first-time undergraduates and for graduate students who need financial aid. CWS lets you earn money to help pay your educational expenses. Students are paid at least the current Federal minimum wage, but the pay may also be related to the type of work done and the skills required. Schools set individual work schedules and must pay students directly at least once a month.

Be patient. If any phone number is incorrect, call (area code) 555-1212 and request the new listing.

Education

Tennessee

Tennessee Student Assistance Corporation, 404 James Robertson Parkway, Suite 1950, Parkway Towers, Nashville, TN 37243-0820; (615) 741-1346. Students must be residents of Tennessee in order to participate in the following programs. In 1990-91, the Tennessee Student Assistance Award (State grant) provided $13,086,000 in funding. The Teacher/Loan Scholarship awarded $330,000.

1) Tennessee Student Assistance Award: This need-based, nonrepayable grant provides up to $1,482 per year for undergraduate students attending eligible Tennessee postsecondary institutions. Students must also be eligible for a Pell Grant.

2) Tennessee Academic Scholars Program: This highly competitive scholarship is available to entering freshmen with a 3.5 high school GPA and who achieve an ACT or SAT score in the top 5% nationally. The award provides up to $4,000 annually for a maximum of four years to attend an eligible Tennessee institution.

3) Teacher Loan Program for Disadvantaged Areas of Tennessee: This program is available to students pursuing teacher certification at a kindergarten through twelfth grade level. Recipients must pledge to teach in a disadvantaged geographic area. Funds are awarded up to $1,500 per academic year with a maximum of $6,000 available for a four-year period.

4) Teacher Loan/Scholarship Program: This program is available to students pursuing teacher certification in art/music at the kindergarten through eighth grade level, math/science at the seventh through twelfth grade level, elementary education or special education. Recipients must pledge to teach in a Tennessee public school in one of the areas listed for a minimum of four years. Up to $1,500 per academic year is available for a maximum of four years to students attending an eligible Tennessee institution.

5) Community College Education Recruitment Scholarship for Minorities: This program is available to entering freshmen who are members of minorities and plan to enroll in a teacher education program at a Tennessee community college. Eligible high school students must have achieved a grade point average of 2.5 on a 4.0 scale, at least 20 on the ACT or SAT tests or have graduated in the top 25% of their graduating class. Awards of $2,000 per academic year are available ($1,000 for half-time enrollment).

6) Minority Teaching Fellows Program: This program is available to entering freshmen with a 2.5 high school GPA on a 4.0 scale. Applicants must achieve at least 18 on the ACT test or 780 on the SAT or be in the top 25% of their high school class. Recipients must agree to teach at a kindergarten through twelfth grade level in a Tennessee public school. Funds are awarded up to $5,000 per academic year with a maximum of $20,000 available.

Loans, Grants and Work-Study Options

1) Stafford Student Loans: These loans are available for undergraduate, graduate, vocational or professional students who demonstrate financial need. Students may borrow $2,625 for each of the first two undergraduate years, and up to $4,000 annually through the fifth year. Graduate students may borrow up to $7,500 a year. Not more than $17,250 can be borrowed for all years of undergraduate study, $73,500 for all years of graduate study, or $54,750 for undergraduate and graduate study combined.

2) Supplemental Loans for Students: This program is available to graduate, professional and independent undergraduate students. The annual maximum SLS loan limit is $4,000 and depends on the student's educational program length. Borrowers cannot exceed a maximum of $20,000.

3) Parent Loans for Students (PLUS): The PLUS program is for parents who wish to borrow for their student dependents. The parent is responsible for the repayment of the loan even if the dependent's education is not completed. The annual maximum PLUS amount is $4,000 per eligible dependent student up to a cumulative maximum of $20,000.

4) Perkins Loans: This low-interest (5 percent) loan is for first-time undergraduates and graduate students with exceptional financial need, as determined by the school. For undergraduate students, priority is given to Pell Grant recipients. Loans are made through a school's financial aid office, the school is the lender. These loans must be repaid. Students may borrow up to $4,500 if they've completed less than two years of a program leading to a first bachelor's degree, or if they are enrolled in a vocational program. Students may borrow up to $9,000 if they've already completed two years of study toward a first bachelor's degree and have achieved third-year status. Up to $18,000 may be borrowed for graduate or professional study. See your school's financial aid department for details.

5) Pell Grant: This award helps first-time undergraduates pay for their education after high school. Eligibility for those who receive a Pell Grant for the first time is usually limited to five to six years of undergraduate study, not including remedial coursework. Awards for the 1992-93 academic year will depend upon program funding. The maximum award for the 1991-92 academic year was $2,400. Students must attend school at least half-time. Grants do not have to be paid back. For more information, contact the financial aid administrator of the college or university you are attending.

6) Supplemental Educational Opportunity Grant (SEOG): This award helps first-time undergraduates with exceptional financial need, as determined by the school. Priority is given to Pell Grant recipients. An SEOG doesn't have to be paid back. Students can get up to $4,000 a year, depending upon available funding.

7) College Work-Study (CWS): This program provides jobs for first-time undergraduates and for graduate students who need financial aid. CWS lets you earn money to help pay your educational expenses. Students are paid at least the current Federal minimum wage, but the pay may also be related to the type of work done and the skills required. Schools set individual work schedules and must pay students directly at least once a month.

Texas

Texas Coordinating Board on Higher Education, Box 12788, Capitol Station, Austin, TX 78711-2788; (512) 483-6200. Texas is a decentralized State for programs. Students should contact the Financial Aid office at the college they plan to attend for grant, scholarship, and loan information. Texas residency is required for the programs listed below unless otherwise specified.

1) Texas Public Education Grant: This grant is available to State residents, nonresidents and foreign students attending public colleges in Texas. Grants are for undergraduate and graduate programs. The maximum award is based on individual financial need.

2) Tuition Equalization Grant: This program is available to Texas residents or National Merit Scholarship recipients. Eligible students are undergraduates or graduates enrolled at least half-time at independent Texas colleges. The maximum award is the lesser of the student's need or $1,900.

3) Student Incentive Grant: This grant is available to residents or nonresidents enrolled at least half-time in an undergraduate or graduate program a Texas public college. The maximum award is the lesser of the student's need or $1,250.

4) Texas Educational Opportunity Grant: This program provides grants to undergraduates enrolled at least half-time at a public or non-profit Texas independent college. Priority is given to minorities, first-generation college students, and students with high financial need. The maximum award is the lesser of the student's need or $1,500.

5) Texas Tuition Assistance Grant: This program is available for undergraduates enrolled on a full-time basis who attend public or non-profit independent Texas colleges. The initial award must be applied for within two years of high school graduation. To be eligible, a student's high school student's grade point average must be equal to 80 on a scale of 100. For continuation of the award, college grade point average must be 2.5 on a 4.0 scale. The maximum award is the lesser of the student financial need or the amount of tuition charged at a public senior level institution.

6) State Scholarship Program for Ethnic Recruitment: To be eligible, a student must be a member of an ethnic group comprising less than 40% of a college's enrollment. The maximum award is $1,000. The program is available to undergraduate and graduate students enrolled on a full-time basis at a public senior Texas college. Entering freshmen must have a minimum 800 SAT or 18 ACT score or new transfer students with a minimum of 2.75 college grade point averages.

7) State Scholarships are available for a number of nursing programs in Texas. Programs exist for ethnic minorities, rural professionals, vocational and graduate nursing students and for licensed vocational nurses working toward becoming professional nurses. Information may be obtained through the director of vocational or professional nursing or the director of financial aid at any non-profit institution in Texas offering an accredited program in nursing. Applications may be obtained through the relevant director of financial aid.

8) Blind or Deaf Students are exempted from tuition and fees at public colleges and universities in Texas. Students must provide certification of deafness or blindness from the appropriate State vocational or rehabilitation agency to the registrar's office of the institution to be attended.

9) Children of Disabled Firemen and Peace Officers are exempt from tuition and fees at public colleges and universities in Texas. To be eligible, the student must be the child of deceased or disabled firemen, peace officers, custodial employees of the Department of Corrections, or game wardens, whose death or disability was sustained in the line of duty while serving in Texas. The award must be applied for prior to the student's 21st birthday.

10) Children of Prisoners of War or Persons Missing in Action: A dependent child of a Texas resident who is either a prisoner of war or missing in action is exempt from tuition and fees at public colleges or universities in Texas. Students must provide proof of the parent's status from the Department of Defense.

11) Firefighters Enrolled in Fire Science Courses: This program is open to residents and nonresidents who are enrolled in fire science courses offered as part of a fire science curriculum. The program provides exemption from tuition and laboratory fees at public colleges or universities in Texas.

12) Veterans and Dependents (The Hazelwood Act): This program provides

Be patient. If any phone number is incorrect, call (area code) 555-1212 and request the new listing.

State Money For College Students

exemption from tuition and some fees at some Texas private colleges and universities to honorably discharged veterans who were residents of Texas when they entered the service. Exemptions may also apply to children whose parent(s) died while in the Armed Forces and to children of members of the Texas National Guard and Texas Air National Guard who died since Jan. 1, 1946, while on active duty.

13) Highest Ranking High School Graduate: To be eligible, the student must be the highest ranking graduate of an accredited high school in the State. The program provides exemption from tuition for two semesters only, of first regular session at public colleges and universities following high school graduation.

14) Students from Other Nations of the American Hemisphere (Good Neighbor Scholarship): The program provides exemption from tuition, only, at Texas public colleges and universities to native-born citizens and residents from another nation of the American (Western) Hemisphere. The student must be scholastically qualified for admission to a public college or university in Texas. A maximum of 235 students may participate in this program per year. Students should apply through the financial aid office or foreign student office of his or her university.

Loans, Grants and Work-Study Options

1) Stafford Student Loans: These loans are available for undergraduate, graduate, vocational or professional students who demonstrate financial need. Students may borrow $2,625 for each of the first two undergraduate years, and up to $4,000 annually through the fifth year. Graduate students may borrow up to $7,500 a year. Not more than $17,250 can be borrowed for all years of undergraduate study, $73,500 for all years of graduate study, or $54,750 for undergraduate and graduate study combined.

2) Supplemental Loans for Students: This program is available to graduate, professional and independent undergraduate students. The annual maximum SLS loan limit is $4,000 and depends on the student's educational program length. Borrowers cannot exceed a maximum of $20,000.

3) Parent Loans for Students (PLUS): The PLUS program is for parents who wish to borrow for their student dependents. The parent is responsible for the repayment of the loan even if the dependent's education is not completed. The annual maximum PLUS amount is $4,000 per eligible dependent student up to a cumulative maximum of $20,000.

4) Perkins Loans: This low-interest (5 percent) loan is for first-time undergraduates and graduate students with exceptional financial need, as determined by the school. For undergraduate students, priority is given to Pell Grant recipients. Loans are made through a school's financial aid office, the school is the lender. These loans must be repaid. Students may borrow up to $4,500 if they've completed less than two years of a program leading to a first bachelor's degree, or if they are enrolled in a vocational program. Students may borrow up to $9,000 if they've already completed two years of study toward a first bachelor's degree and have achieved third-year status. Up to $18,000 may be borrowed for graduate or professional study. See your school's financial aid department for details.

5) Pell Grant: This award helps first-time undergraduates pay for their education after high school. Eligibility for those who receive a Pell Grant for the first time is usually limited to five to six years of undergraduate study, not including remedial coursework. Awards for the 1992-93 academic year will depend upon program funding. The maximum award for the 1991-92 academic year was $2,400. Students must attend school at least half-time. Grants do not have to be paid back. For more information, contact the financial aid administrator of the college or university you are attending.

6) Supplemental Educational Opportunity Grant (SEOG): This award helps first-time undergraduates with exceptional financial need, as determined by the school. Priority is given to Pell Grant recipients. An SEOG doesn't have to be paid back. Students can get up to $4,000 a year, depending upon available funding.

7) College Work-Study (CWS): This program provides jobs for first-time undergraduates and for graduate students who need financial aid. CWS lets you earn money to help pay your educational expenses. Students are paid at least the current Federal minimum wage, but the pay may also be related to the type of work done and the skills required. Schools set individual work schedules and must pay students directly at least once a month.

Utah

Utah System for Higher Education, 355 West North Temple, 3 Triad, Suite 550, Salt Lake City, UT 84180-1205; (801) 538-5247. In 1991-92, Utah awarded $570,000 in State funding. Utah administers funding to State residents. The State use a decentralized system. Students should contact the financial aid office at the college they plan to attend.

1) State Student Incentive Grant Program: This program makes Federal and State funds available to students with substantial financial need. The Utah Board of Regents administers this program. A maximum of $2,500 per student per academic year may be awarded to students who meet eligibility criteria.

Loans, Grants, and Work-Study Options

1) Stafford Student Loans: These loans are available for undergraduate, graduate, vocational or professional students who demonstrate financial need. Students may borrow $2,625 for each of the first two undergraduate years, and up to $4,000 annually through the fifth year. Graduate students may borrow up to $7,500 a year. Not more than $17,250 can be borrowed for all years of undergraduate study, $73,500 for all years of graduate study, or $54,750 for undergraduate and graduate study combined.

2) Supplemental Loans for Students: This program is available to graduate, professional and independent undergraduate students. The annual maximum SLS loan limit is $4,000 and depends on the student's educational program length. Borrowers cannot exceed a maximum of $20,000.

3) Parent Loans for Students (PLUS): The PLUS program is for parents who wish to borrow for their student dependents. The parent is responsible for the repayment of the loan even if the dependent's education is not completed. The annual maximum PLUS amount is $4,000 per eligible dependent student up to a cumulative maximum of $20,000.

4) Perkins Loans: This low-interest (5 percent) loan is for first-time undergraduates and graduate students with exceptional financial need, as determined by the school. For undergraduate students, priority is given to Pell Grant recipients. Loans are made through a school's financial aid office, the school is the lender. These loans must be repaid. Students may borrow up to $4,500 if they've completed less than two years of a program leading to a first bachelor's degree, or if they are enrolled in a vocational program. Students may borrow up to $9,000 if they've already completed two years of study toward a first bachelor's degree and have achieved third-year status. Up to $18,000 may be borrowed for graduate or professional study. See your school's financial aid department for details.

5) Pell Grant: This award helps first-time undergraduates pay for their education after high school. Eligibility for those who receive a Pell Grant for the first time is usually limited to five to six years of undergraduate study, not including remedial coursework. Awards for the 1992-93 academic year will depend upon program funding. The maximum award for the 1991-92 academic year was $2,400. Students must attend school at least half-time. Grants do not have to be paid back. For more information, contact the financial aid administrator of the college or university you are attending.

6) Supplemental Educational Opportunity Grant (SEOG): This award helps first-time undergraduates with exceptional financial need, as determined by the school. Priority is given to Pell Grant recipients. An SEOG doesn't have to be paid back. Students can get up to $4,000 a year, depending upon available funding.

7) College Work-Study (CWS): This program provides jobs for first-time undergraduates and for graduate students who need financial aid. CWS lets you earn money to help pay your educational expenses. Students are paid at least the current Federal minimum wage, but the pay may also be related to the type of work done and the skills required. Schools set individual work schedules and must pay students directly at least once a month.

Vermont

Vermont Student Assistance Corporation, P.O. Box 2000, Champlain Mill, Winooski, VT 05404; (802) 655-9602. In 1990-91, VSAC awarded $21,635,000 in funding. Students must be Vermont residents to participate in the following programs.

1) Vermont Incentive Grants: Applicants may include any full-time undergraduate who attends or plans to attend an approved post-high school degree program and has not already received a bachelor's degree. Applicants may also include students enrolled at the University of Vermont College of Medicine or is enrolled in a Doctor of Veterinary Medicine program at an accredited school of veterinary medicine. During 1991-92, grants ranged from $300 to $5,150. Grants are based upon financial need.

2) Vermont Part-Time Student Grants: This need-based grant program is open to students accepted or enrolled in a degree, diploma, or certificate program at the undergraduate level. Applicants must take fewer than 12 credits per semester and have not received a bachelor's degree. Awards vary depending upon credit hours taken.

3) Vermont Non-Degree Student Grant Program: This program is open to students enrolled in any non-degree course that will improve employability or encourage further study. Awards are based upon financial need and are up to $325 for one course per semester. The award may be used for tuition and fees.

4) Vermont EXTRA Loans (Supplemental): This program is available to students enrolled in a Vermont postsecondary school or Vermont residents attending out-of-State schools. Borrowers and co-borrowers must meet

Be patient. If any phone number is incorrect, call (area code) 555-1212 and request the new listing.

Education

established credit standards. EXTRA borrowers must first apply for the maximum PLUS or SLS Loan. Loans do not exceed the student's estimated cost of attendance less the estimated financial assistance awarded.

Additional Federal Loans, Grants and Work-Study Options

1) Stafford Student Loans: These loans are available for undergraduate, graduate, vocational or professional students who demonstrate financial need. Students may borrow $2,625 for each of the first two undergraduate years, and up to $4,000 annually through the fifth year. Graduate students may borrow up to $7,500 a year. Not more than $17,250 can be borrowed for all years of undergraduate study, $73,500 for all years of graduate study, or $54,750 for undergraduate and graduate study combined.

2) Supplemental Loans for Students: This program is available to graduate, professional and independent undergraduate students. The annual maximum SLS loan limit is $4,000 and depends on the student's educational program length. Borrowers cannot exceed a maximum of $20,000.

3) Parent Loans for Students (PLUS): The PLUS program is for parents who wish to borrow for their student dependents. The parent is responsible for the repayment of the loan even if the dependent's education is not completed. The annual maximum PLUS amount is $4,000 per eligible dependent student up to a cumulative maximum of $20,000.

4) Perkins Loans: This low-interest (5 percent) loan is for first-time undergraduates and graduate students with exceptional financial need, as determined by the school. For undergraduate students, priority is given to Pell Grant recipients. Loans are made through a school's financial aid office, the school is the lender. These loans must be repaid. Students may borrow up to $4,500 if they've completed less than two years of a program leading to a first bachelor's degree, or if they are enrolled in a vocational program. Students may borrow up to $9,000 if they've already completed two years of study toward a first bachelor's degree and have achieved third-year status. Up to $18,000 may be borrowed for graduate or professional study. See your school's financial aid department for details.

5) Pell Grant: This award helps first-time undergraduates pay for their education after high school. Eligibility for those who receive a Pell Grant for the first time is usually limited to five to six years of undergraduate study, not including remedial coursework. Awards for the 1992-93 academic year will depend upon program funding. The maximum award for the 1991-92 academic year was $2,400. Students must attend school at least half-time. Grants do not have to be paid back. For more information, contact the financial aid administrator of the college or university you are attending.

6) Supplemental Educational Opportunity Grant (SEOG): This award helps first-time undergraduates with exceptional financial need, as determined by the school. Priority is given to Pell Grant recipients. An SEOG doesn't have to be paid back. Students can get up to $4,000 a year, depending upon available funding.

7) College Work-Study (CWS): This program provides jobs for first-time undergraduates and for graduate students who need financial aid. CWS lets you earn money to help pay your educational expenses. Students are paid at least the current Federal minimum wage, but the pay may also be related to the type of work done and the skills required. Schools set individual work schedules and must pay students directly at least once a month.

Virginia

Virginia State Council of Higher Education, Office of Financial Aid, James Monroe Building, 101 North 14th Street, Richmond, VA 23219; (804) 371-7941. In 1991-92, students received more than $71.6 million through student aid programs funded by the Commonwealth. Of that amount, approximately $36.9 million was awarded based on the financial need of the recipients. Students must be residents of Virginia to participate in the following programs.

1) Virginia College Assistance Program (CSAP): CSAP is available to undergraduate students who demonstrate financial need as determined by the institution. The amount of the award ranges from $400 to $2,000.

2) Virginia Scholars Program (VSP): VSP is a merit-based scholarship program designed to encourage Virginia's brightest high school seniors and two-year college students to attend school in Virginia. The maximum award amount is $3,000 per year.

3) Virginia Tuition Assistance Grant Program (TAGP): This program is available to undergraduate and graduate/professional students who are residents of Virginia and enrolled full-time in a degree seeking program at eligible private colleges or universities in Virginia. There is no financial need requirement for this grant. The award amount is determined yearly by the General Assembly.

4) Virginia Transfer Grant Program (VTGP): VTGP is available to "other race" students who are enrolled in a traditionally white or black four-year Virginia public college or university. Applicants must meet minimum criteria and qualify for entry as a first-time transfer student. The grant is administered by the

institution and provides up to full tuition and mandatory fees.

5) Virginia Work-Study Program: This need-based program allows undergraduate and graduate students to earn money to contribute toward their education expenses. The amount of the award varies with the hourly wage and the number of hours worked.

6) Last Dollar: The Last Dollar Program awards grants to Black undergraduate students enrolled for the first time in a State supported college or university in Virginia. Financial need must be demonstrated and the size of the award cannot exceed financial need.

7) Paul Douglas Teacher Scholarship: Although this is a Federally funded scholarship, the program in this State is administered by the Virginia State Council of Higher Education. This scholarship encourages outstanding high school graduates to pursue teaching careers. It awards scholarships on a competitive basis to qualified students who rank in the top 10% of their high school graduating class. Applicants must enroll for full-time study in a program which leads to teacher certification. The maximum award per year is $5,000.

8) Nursing Scholarship Program: This program assists students who agree to engage continuously in nursing work in Virginia for one month for each $100 of scholarship funds. Contact Department of Health at (804) 786-3554 for further details.

9) Medical Scholarship Program: This program provides funds to students at Virginia medical schools who are studying to be primary care physicians. Recipients must agree to practice in an area of need in Virginia or serve as an employee of State health, welfare, or corrections for a period of years equal to the number of years for which the scholarship is awarded. Contact the Department of Health at (804) 786-4891 for further details.

10) Rural Dental Scholarships: Ten scholarships are awarded at $2,500 per year to dental students. Recipients must agree to work in an area of need or for the State one year for every year of scholarship awarded. Contact the Director of Financial Aid, Medical College of Virginia at (804) 786-9196.

11) Virginia Teaching Scholarship: This program provides scholarships to college juniors and seniors to help increase the supply of properly endorsed teachers in special need teaching fields. The amount of the award is $2,000 per academic year, and the recipient must teach one year in public schools for each year of the award. Contact the Virginia Department of Education at (804) 225-2013 for information.

12) Traineeship for Special Education Personnel: This program provides $450 to encourage teachers to become endorsed in Special Education. Applicants must possess a teaching degree and endorsement and be recommended by their school board. Contact the number listed directly above for information.

13) State Law Enforcement Officers Educational Program: This program provides reimbursement for law enforcement officers who attend college. Contact the Criminal Justice Services Training Div., at (804) 786-7801 for details.

14) State Cadetships: This program provides tuition, required fees, room and board for qualified State cadets.

15) Virginia War Orphan Education Act: This program provides 100% of tuition and required fees for any child of a veteran who was killed in action or 100% permanently disabled as a result of a wartime service-related injury. Recipients must attend a public college or university in Virginia. Contact the Division of War Veterans Claims at (703) 857-7104 for information.

16) Soil Scientist Program: This award covers tuition and required fees for four soil students at Virginia Tech. Recipients must agree to work one year for each year of scholarship awarded. contact Dept. of Agronomy, VA Tech at (703) 231-9785 for details.

17) Senior Citizens Tuition Waiver: This program provides tuition waivers for credit courses for Virginia residents aged 60 and older who have individual taxable income from the previous year of $10,000 or less. Information is available from the admissions office at any public Virginia college or university.

Additional Loans, Grants and Work-Study Options

1) Stafford Student Loans: These loans are available for undergraduate, graduate, vocational or professional students who demonstrate financial need. Students may borrow $2,625 for each of the first two undergraduate years, and up to $4,000 annually through the fifth year. Graduate students may borrow up to $7,500 a year. Not more than $17,250 can be borrowed for all years of undergraduate study, $73,500 for all years of graduate study, or $54,750 for undergraduate and graduate study combined.

2) Supplemental Loans for Students: This program is available to graduate, professional and independent undergraduate students. The annual maximum SLS loan limit is $4,000 and depends on the student's educational program length. Borrowers cannot exceed a maximum of $20,000.

3) Parent Loans for Students (PLUS): The PLUS program is for parents who wish to borrow for their student dependents. The parent is responsible for the repayment of the loan even if the dependent's education is not completed. The annual maximum PLUS amount is $4,000 per eligible dependent student up to a cumulative maximum of $20,000.

4) Perkins Loans: This low-interest (5 percent) loan is for first-time

Be patient. If any phone number is incorrect, call (area code) 555-1212 and request the new listing.

State Money For College Students

undergraduates and graduate students with exceptional financial need, as determined by the school. For undergraduate students, priority is given to Pell Grant recipients. Loans are made through a school's financial aid office, the school is the lender. These loans must be repaid. Students may borrow up to $4,500 if they've completed less than two years of a program leading to a first bachelor's degree, or if they are enrolled in a vocational program. Students may borrow up to $9,000 if they've already completed two years of study toward a first bachelor's degree and have achieved third-year status. Up to $18,000 may be borrowed for graduate or professional study. See your school's financial aid department for details.

5) Pell Grant: This award helps first-time undergraduates pay for their education after high school. Eligibility for those who receive a Pell Grant for the first time is usually limited to five to six years of undergraduate study, not including remedial coursework. Awards for the 1992-93 academic year will depend upon program funding. The maximum award for the 1991-92 academic year was $2,400. Students must attend school at least half-time. Grants do not have to be paid back. For more information, contact the financial aid administrator of the college or university you are attending.

6) Supplemental Educational Opportunity Grant (SEOG): This award helps first-time undergraduates with exceptional financial need, as determined by the school. Priority is given to Pell Grant recipients. An SEOG doesn't have to be paid back. Students can get up to $4,000 a year, depending upon available funding.

7) ADVANTAGE: This long-term, educational loan program is designed for families who wish to supplement, or do not qualify for, other forms of financial assistance. Loans are made through banks, credit unions, and savings and loan associations, and the program is administered by the State Assistance Authority. Advantage loans are credit-based, and the interest rates are variable throughout the life of the loan. Loans are available from $1,000 to $15,000 per year up to $60,000 over the college career.

Washington

Higher Education Coordinating Board, 917 Lakeridge Way, GV-11, Olympia, WA 98504; (206) 753-3571. Students must have established State residency to participate in the following programs. In 1990-91, $30,057,000 was awarded in State funding.

1) Washington State Need Grant Program: This grant program provides educational assistance to needy or disadvantaged students who enroll at one of Washington's public or private, two-year, four-year or vocational-technical institutions; or selected proprietary schools. In the most recent year for which statistics are available, approximately 16,00 students received over $12.8 million in assistance from this program.

2) Washington State Work-Study Program: This program offers financial aid to needy students through part-time employment at Washington State public or private institutions of postsecondary education. The State reimburses the employer for a major share of the wages. Wherever possible, employment will be related to the student's academic pursuits or area of career interest. In the most recent for which statistics were available, 5,000 students earned $13 million (including the employers share) to help meet educational costs.

3) Washington Scholars Program: This program recognizes and honors three high school seniors from each legislative district. Eligible students representing the top 1% of the senior class are nominated by the high school principals based on academic accomplishments, leadership, and community service. Scholars attending a Washington public college or university receive a full tuition and fee waiver for undergraduate studies. Scholars attending a Washington independent college or university receive a grant that is matched by the school on a dollar for dollar basis.

4) Future Teachers Conditional Scholarship Program: This State scholarship was established to recruit future teachers from students who have distinguished themselves through academic achievement and students who act as role models for children, including targeted ethnic minorities. The $3,000 scholarships are renewable for up to five years and require a ten year Washington public school teaching commitment or repayment of the scholarship plus interest. This program isnot based on need.

5) Nurses Conditional Scholarship: This State scholarship encourages qualified individuals to serve in nursing shortage areas. Recipients agree to nurse in a State defined shortage area for five years or repay the scholarship plus interest. The renewable scholarship pays the cost of attendance for the nursing program, up to $3,000 per year. This is a non-need based program.

6) Teacher Incentive Loan for Mathematics and Science: The Math-Science Loan program provides need-based loans of up to $2,500 per year to students who intend to teach math or science at the middle or secondary level. Applicants must be declared majors in math or science who have been accepted into a program of teacher preparation. The loan is canceled for recipients who teach math or science for ten years in Washington's public middle or secondary

schools; otherwise it must be repaid with interest over a ten year period. This is a need-based program.

7) Western InterState Commission for Higher Education (WICHE) Professional Exchange Program: This is a program for optometry students providing State support to needy Washington residents enrolled in out-of-State optometry programs.

8) Western InterState Commission for Higher Education (WICHE) Regional Graduate Program: Under this category, qualified Washington residents may enroll at reduced tuition rates in out-of-State master's and doctoral programs not offered in Washington. Programs are primarily in the science and liberal arts rather than in the professional fields.

8) Tuition Waiver Program: This program enables public two- and four-year colleges and universities to waive all or part of the tuition and fees of needy or disadvantaged students from revenue generated by tuition and fees. Application is automatic when a student applies for financial aid from a public Washington State institution. In the most recent year for which statistics were available, more than 6,000 students received approximately $3.4 million in the program, with an average waiver being worth $523.

Loan and Grant Options

1) Stafford Student Loans: These loans are available for undergraduate, graduate, vocational or professional students who demonstrate financial need. Students may borrow $2,625 for each of the first two undergraduate years, and up to $4,000 annually through the fifth year. Graduate students may borrow up to $7,500 a year. Not more than $17,250 can be borrowed for all years of undergraduate study, $73,500 for all years of graduate study, or $54,750 for undergraduate and graduate study combined.

2) Supplemental Loans for Students: This program is available to graduate, professional and independent undergraduate students. The annual maximum SLS loan limit is $4,000 and depends on the student's educational program length. Borrowers cannot exceed a maximum of $20,000.

3) Parent Loans for Students (PLUS): The PLUS program is for parents who wish to borrow for their student dependents. The parent is responsible for the repayment of the loan even if the dependent's education is not completed. The annual maximum PLUS amount is $4,000 per eligible dependent student up to a cumulative maximum of $20,000.

4) Perkins Loans: This low-interest (5 percent) loan is for first-time undergraduates and graduate students with exceptional financial need, as determined by the school. For undergraduate students, priority is given to Pell Grant recipients. Loans are made through a school's financial aid office, the school is the lender. These loans must be repaid. Students may borrow up to $4,500 if they've completed less than two years of a program leading to a first bachelor's degree, or if they are enrolled in a vocational program. Students may borrow up to $9,000 if they've already completed two years of study toward a first bachelor's degree and have achieved third-year status. Up to $18,000 may be borrowed for graduate or professional study. See your school's financial aid department for details.

5) Pell Grant: This award helps first-time undergraduates pay for their education after high school. Eligibility for those who receive a Pell Grant for the first time is usually limited to five to six years of undergraduate study, not including remedial coursework. Awards for the 1992-93 academic year will depend upon program funding. The maximum award for the 1991-92 academic year was $2,400. Students must attend school at least half-time. Grants do not have to be paid back. For more information, contact the financial aid administrator of the college or university you are attending.

6) Supplemental Educational Opportunity Grant (SEOG): This award helps first-time undergraduates with exceptional financial need, as determined by the school. Priority is given to Pell Grant recipients. An SEOG doesn't have to be paid back. Students can get up to $4,000 a year, depending upon available funding.

West Virginia

West Virginia Higher Education Program, P.O. Box 4007, Charleston, WV 25364; (304) 347-1211. Students must be West Virginia residents to qualify for the programs listed below. In 1990-91, the State allocated $3,545,000 for awards.

1) West Virginia Higher Education Grant: This grant program is the primary State-funded financial aid program for West Virginia students at the post-secondary level. The program is designed to assist needy undergraduate West Virginia residents who require financial assistance in order to meet their educational goals. The amount of nonrepayable grants fluctuates from year to year according to available funding and number of applicants. For example, in 1991-92, the maximum grants were $600 at out-of-State colleges and universities, $1,814 at in-State private educational institutions, and from $554 to $1,326 at in-State public colleges and universities. The minimum grant for 1991-92 was $350.

2) Underwood-Smith Teacher Scholarship Program: In 1990-91, 137 recipients,

Be patient. If any phone number is incorrect, call (area code) 555-1212 and request the new listing.

Education

received $618,181.

A) Undergraduate Level: This State funded student aid program encourages outstanding high school graduates to pursue teaching careers and graduate scholarships. Scholarships do not exceed $5,000 and are awarded on the basis of academic qualifications and interest in teaching. A total of $750,000 in State funds was allocated for scholarship awards during the 1991-92 academic year. To qualify, students must graduate in the top 10% of his or her class, have a cumulative GPA of 3.25 after successfully completing two years of course work at an approved institution, or score in the top 10% Statewide of those students taking the ACT.

B) Graduate Level: To qualify, students must have or will be graduating in the top 10% of his or her college or university class and be enrolled or accepted at a West Virginia institution of higher education in a program which leads to teacher certification. Recipients must agree to teach at a public pre-school, elementary, or secondary school level in West Virginia for two years for each year of scholarship assistance unless entering a teacher shortage area, an exceptional children's program, or economically disadvantaged area or repay all scholarship money with interest.

3) Central Office of the State College and University Systems Medical Student Loan Program: This program provides loans to students who demonstrate financial need, meet academic standards, and are enrolled or accepted for enrollment at the West Virginia University School of Medicine, the Marshall University School of Medicine, or the West Virginia School of Osteopathic Medicine. Award amounts are determined annually and cannot exceed $5,000 per year.

Additional Loans, Grants and Work-Study Options

1) Stafford Student Loans: These loans are available for undergraduate, graduate, vocational or professional students who demonstrate financial need. Students may borrow $2,625 for each of the first two undergraduate years, and up to $4,000 annually through the fifth year. Graduate students may borrow up to $7,500 a year. Not more than $17,250 can be borrowed for all years of undergraduate study, $73,500 for all years of graduate study, or $54,750 for undergraduate and graduate study combined.

2) Supplemental Loans for Students: This program is available to graduate, professional and independent undergraduate students. The annual maximum SLS loan limit is $4,000 and depends on the student's educational program length. Borrowers cannot exceed a maximum of $20,000.

3) Parent Loans for Students (PLUS): The PLUS program is for parents who wish to borrow for their student dependents. The parent is responsible for the repayment of the loan even if the dependent's education is not completed. The annual maximum PLUS amount is $4,000 per eligible dependent student up to a cumulative maximum of $20,000.

4) Perkins Loans: This low-interest (5 percent) loan is for first-time undergraduates and graduate students with exceptional financial need, as determined by the school. For undergraduate students, priority is given to Pell Grant recipients. Loans are made through a school's financial aid office, the school is the lender. These loans must be repaid. Students may borrow up to $4,500 if they've completed less than two years of a program leading to a first bachelor's degree, or if they are enrolled in a vocational program. Students may borrow up to $9,000 if they've already completed two years of study toward a first bachelor's degree and have achieved third-year status. Up to $18,000 may be borrowed for graduate or professional study. See your school's financial aid department for details.

5) Pell Grant: This award helps first-time undergraduates pay for their education after high school. Eligibility for those who receive a Pell Grant for the first time is usually limited to five to six years of undergraduate study, not including remedial coursework. Awards for the 1992-93 academic year will depend upon program funding. The maximum award for the 1991-92 academic year was $2,400. Students must attend school at least half-time. Grants do not have to be paid back. For more information, contact the financial aid administrator of the college or university you are attending.

6) Supplemental Educational Opportunity Grant (SEOG): This award helps first-time undergraduates with exceptional financial need, as determined by the school. Priority is given to Pell Grant recipients. An SEOG doesn't have to be paid back. Students can get up to $4,000 a year, depending upon available funding.

7) College Work-Study (CWS): This program provides jobs for first-time undergraduates and for graduate students who need financial aid. CWS lets you earn money to help pay your educational expenses. Students are paid at least the current Federal minimum wage, but the pay may also be related to the type of work done and the skills required. Schools set individual work schedules and must pay students directly at least once a month.

Wisconsin

State of Wisconsin Higher Educational Aids Board, P.O. Box 7885, Madison, WI 53707-7885; (608) 267-2206. Students must be State residents to participate in the following programs. State grant programs in 1992-93 will award close to $4.5 million in funding.

1) Wisconsin Higher Education Grant: This undergraduate grant program is open to open to students enrolled at least half-time at the University of Wisconsin or vocational/technical institutions. The maximum award is $1,800 with ten semesters of eligibility. All awards are based on student financial need.

2) Talent Incentive Program: This program provides grants to severely needy nontraditional students. The maximum award is $1,800. The program is open to freshmen and upperclassmen who continue to be enrolled and have financial need. Eligibility cannot exceed ten semesters.

3) Wisconsin Tuition Grant: This undergraduate grant program is open to students enrolled in independent, non-profit Wisconsin institutions. All awards are based on financial need and the difference between the tuition actually paid by the student and the tuition which would have been paid if the student attended the University of Wisconsin at Madison. The maximum award is $2,172 with ten semesters of eligibility.

4) Visual and Hearing Impaired Program: This program provides grants for undergraduate study to students who are legally deaf and blind. To be eligible for the grant, the student must have financial need as determined by the institution the student attends. If the impairment prevents the student from studying in a Wisconsin institution, he or he may attend an out-of-State institution that specializes in teaching the blind or deaf and still receive a maximum grant of $1,800 per year. Eligibility cannot exceed ten semesters.

5) Minority Retention Grant: This program provides financial assistance to Black, Hispanic, and Native American students to improve their opportunities for retention and graduation. Eligible applicants also include students admitted to the U.S. after December 31, 1975 who are either a former citizen of Laos, Vietnam or Cambodia or whose ancestor was a citizen of those countries. Eligibility cannot exceed eight semesters. The University of Wisconsin has a similar program.

6) Wisconsin Native American Student Grant: Awards under this program are made to students who are at least 25% Native American heritage. Applicants must attend a Wisconsin institution, either public, independent, or proprietary. Awards are made to graduate students as well as undergraduates. Maximum award is $2,200 a year with a limit of ten semesters of eligibility.

7) Academic Scholarships: The graduate with the highest grade point average from each Wisconsin high school is eligible for a scholarship to attend any accredited Wisconsin public or private non-profit institution of higher education. High schools with over 1,000 students will have one or more additional scholars. Awards vary, but are at least $1,500. Scholars who continue to attend full-time with a 3.0 grade point average will have their awards renewed for up to three additional years.

8) Nursing Student Stipend Loans: State funded forgivable loans are available to students enrolled as full-time second year vocational or technical students or collegiate juniors and seniors in a program which provides an associate degree diploma, or bachelor's degree in nursing. Borrowers may receive up to $2,500 per year, based on financial need, for a total of $5,000. Funds are also available to masters candidates who intend to teach nursing. Recipients must provide one year of service in a Wisconsin hospital, nursing home or public agency for twelve months for each $1,000 in stipend they receive or repay the loan.

9) Minnesota-Wisconsin Reciprocity Program: Wisconsin residents may attend a Minnesota public college or university and pay the reciprocity tuition charged by that institution. All academic programs are eligible except for the doctoral programs in medicine, dentistry, and veterinary medicine.

Additional Loans, Grants and Work-Study Options

1) Stafford Student Loans: These loans are available for undergraduate, graduate, vocational or professional students who demonstrate financial need. Students may borrow $2,625 for each of the first two undergraduate years, and up to $4,000 annually through the fifth year. Graduate students may borrow up to $7,500 a year. Not more than $17,250 can be borrowed for all years of undergraduate study, $73,500 for all years of graduate study, or $54,750 for undergraduate and graduate study combined.

2) Supplemental Loans for Students: This program is available to graduate, professional and independent undergraduate students. The annual maximum SLS loan limit is $4,000 and depends on the student's educational program length. Borrowers cannot exceed a maximum of $20,000.

3) Parent Loans for Students (PLUS): The PLUS program is for parents who wish to borrow for their student dependents. The parent is responsible for the repayment of the loan even if the dependent's education is not completed. The annual maximum PLUS amount is $4,000 per eligible dependent student up to a cumulative maximum of $20,000.

4) Perkins Loans: This low-interest (5 percent) loan is for first-time undergraduates and graduate students with exceptional financial need, as determined by the school. For undergraduate students, priority is given to Pell Grant recipients. Loans are made through a school's financial aid office, the

Be patient. If any phone number is incorrect, call (area code) 555-1212 and request the new listing.

school is the lender. These loans must be repaid. Students may borrow up to $4,500 if they've completed less than two years of a program leading to a first bachelor's degree, or if they are enrolled in a vocational program. Students may borrow up to $9,000 if they've already completed two years of study toward a first bachelor's degree and have achieved third-year status. Up to $18,000 may be borrowed for graduate or professional study. See your school's financial aid department for details.

5) Pell Grant: This award helps first-time undergraduates pay for their education after high school. Eligibility for those who receive a Pell Grant for the first time is usually limited to five to six years of undergraduate study, not including remedial coursework. Awards for the 1992-93 academic year will depend upon program funding. The maximum award for the 1991-92 academic year was $2,400. Students must attend school at least half-time. Grants do not have to be paid back. For more information, contact the financial aid administrator of the college or university you are attending.

6) Supplemental Educational Opportunity Grant (SEOG): This award helps first-time undergraduates with exceptional financial need, as determined by the school. Priority is given to Pell Grant recipients. An SEOG doesn't have to be paid back. Students can get up to $4,000 a year, depending upon available funding.

7) College Work-Study (CWS): This program provides jobs for first-time undergraduates and for graduate students who need financial aid. CWS lets you earn money to help pay your educational expenses. Students are paid at least the current Federal minimum wage, but the pay may also be related to the type of work done and the skills required. Schools set individual work schedules and must pay students directly at least once a month.

Wyoming

Wyoming Department of Higher Education, Hathaway Building, Cheyenne, WY 82002; (307) 777-6213. In 1990-91, total State revenue was $271,221,976. Students must be Wyoming residents in order to participate in the following programs.

1) Scholarship/Loan Fund for Superior Students in Education: These scholarship/loans are available to high school graduates who have demonstrated high scholastic achievement and qualities of leadership and who plan to teach in Wyoming public schools. Each year 20 scholarships may be awarded to Wyoming high school graduates to attend the University or any community college in the State and major in education. Awards are available up to eight semesters, with no more than four at a community college.

2) President's Honor Scholarship: High school seniors who have demonstrated outstanding academic achievement and leadership potential are eligible for this scholarship. Nominations are made by high school officials and the number of awards is dependent upon the size of the high school graduating class. Scholarships may be used an any State community college as well as the University of Wyoming. Recipients must have a high school GPA of 3.01 out of 4.0 to qualify. The value of the scholarship generally equals full in-State tuition and fees. No more than eight semesters of scholarship is awarded.

3) County Commissioners Scholarship: These scholarships are available to students who are residents of Wyoming and who graduate from a Wyoming high school Funds are provided by appropriation from the Wyoming State Legislature. The awards are generally made for the amount of tuition and fees. Scholarships may be used at any public institution in Wyoming. Students should apply directly to the Board of County Commissioners in their county of residence.

4) Bureau of Indian Affairs Scholarship and Loan: This programs offers grants to students who are at least one fourth degree American Indian, Eskimo or Aleut, who are of tribes served by the Bureau for educational purposes, enrolled or accepted for enrollment and have a definite financial need.

5) Northern Arapaho Tribal Scholarship: These scholarships are available to high school graduates who are enrolled members of the Northern Arapaho Tribe. Scholarships may be used for full-time study at any public institution in Wyoming. Applications should be made to the Community Development Office, Wind River Indian Agency, Fort Washakie, WY 82514, six weeks prior to the beginning of the school year.

6) Shoshone Tribal Scholarship: These scholarships are available to high school graduates who are enrolled members of the Wind River Shoshone Tribe. Scholarships may be used at any public institution in Wyoming for full-time study. Applications should be made to the Community Development Office listed above.

Loans, Grants and Work-Study Options

1) Stafford Student Loans: These loans are available for undergraduate, graduate, vocational or professional students who demonstrate financial need. Students may borrow $2,625 for each of the first two undergraduate years, and up to $4,000 annually through the fifth year. Graduate students may borrow up to $7,500 a year. Not more than $17,250 can be borrowed for all years of undergraduate study, $73,500 for all years of graduate study, or $54,750 for undergraduate and graduate study combined.

2) Supplemental Loans for Students: This program is available to graduate, professional and independent undergraduate students. The annual maximum SLS loan limit is $4,000 and depends on the student's educational program length. Borrowers cannot exceed a maximum of $20,000.

3) Parent Loans for Students (PLUS): The PLUS program is for parents who wish to borrow for their student dependents. The parent is responsible for the repayment of the loan even if the dependent's education is not completed. The annual maximum PLUS amount is $4,000 per eligible dependent student up to a cumulative maximum of $20,000.

4) Perkins Loans: This low-interest (5 percent) loan is for first-time undergraduates and graduate students with exceptional financial need, as determined by the school. For undergraduate students, priority is given to Pell Grant recipients. Loans are made through a school's financial aid office, the school is the lender. These loans must be repaid. Students may borrow up to $4,500 if they've completed less than two years of a program leading to a first bachelor's degree, or if they are enrolled in a vocational program. Students may borrow up to $9,000 if they've already completed two years of study toward a first bachelor's degree and have achieved third-year status. Up to $18,000 may be borrowed for graduate or professional study. See your school's financial aid department for details.

5) Pell Grant: This award helps first-time undergraduates pay for their education after high school. Eligibility for those who receive a Pell Grant for the first time is usually limited to five to six years of undergraduate study, not including remedial coursework. Awards for the 1992-93 academic year will depend upon program funding. The maximum award for the 1991-92 academic year was $2,400. Students must attend school at least half-time. Grants do not have to be paid back. For more information, contact the financial aid administrator of the college or university you are attending.

6) Supplemental Educational Opportunity Grant (SEOG): This award helps first-time undergraduates with exceptional financial need, as determined by the school. Priority is given to Pell Grant recipients. An SEOG doesn't have to be paid back. Students can get up to $4,000 a year, depending upon available funding.

7) College Work-Study (CWS): This program provides jobs for first-time undergraduates and for graduate students who need financial aid. CWS lets you earn money to help pay your educational expenses. Students are paid at least the current Federal minimum wage, but the pay may also be related to the type of work done and the skills required. Schools set individual work schedules and must pay students directly at least once a month.

Education

State Education Information

A friend recently had the idea of marketing "Class of 2001" T-shirts to the parents of the kindergarten class of '88. Faced with the problem of estimating the size of the market, he did what any sharp young entrepreneur would do -- he turned to his state department of education for all of the little details...and a mailing list to boot.

It would probably take some effort to come up with a service or product that a school district doesn't buy short of military hardware (but that, too, might be changing). Like the federal government, schools purchase just about everything under the sun. Each state has a department of education or public instruction which collects and disseminates information on students, staff, school finances, and other related matters. And this data can help you sell a lot more than just T-shirts.

You can use the data to find the names and addresses of science teachers if you've got a great new product for demonstrating chemical reactions or cell osmosis; of math teachers if you've got 3-D geometry models or a novel new software idea; or PE teachers if you're designing football gear for the next century. Remember, teachers are usually the first to lobby for specific new textbooks and learning tools.

Information on the student population of a given school district can yield a pretty accurate picture of who lives where, what their parents earn and how they spend it -- priceless marketing information available at no or little cost to you. If you sell real estate or insurance, having accurate school district information may be essential in closing a sale or targeting new clients.

In addition, there is plenty of money to be made with accurate information on high school seniors. From yearbooks to class rings, prom gowns to SAT tutorials, the senior class is an industry unto itself. So, rather than wait for the "Class of 2001" to grow up, many businesses are already using state education information to get a edge over the competition.

Each state has a Department of Education or Public Instruction which collects and disseminates information pertaining to students, staff, finances and general matters. A representation of types of data collected and maintained is as follows:

Students:

- by grade
- by sex
- by ethnicity
- by special programs (special education, vocational education, bilingual and English as a second language, compensatory education, gifted and talented, migrant)
- by curriculum enrollment, graduates, dropouts, accidents, immunizations, projected enrollment and attendance, test scores.

Educators and Staff:

- Professional job assignments (teachers, administrators, support staff and aides, secretaries)
- sex
- ethnicity
- salaries
- program areas
- highest college degree attained
- months of contract
- days employed
- certification/permits granted
- tenure
- experience.

School District Finances:

- district budgeting and audited accounting data on revenues
- expenditures
- assets
- liabilities
- fund balances
- bond/loan requirements
- local school tax information
- district detailed state aid calculations
- total receipts and disbursements
- taxable property values.

General:

- number of districts
- demographic data
- address and telephone numbers of school campuses within district
- maps
- census.

By observing trends in statistical data, a school system can monitor school programs, improve data management, and address changing economic perspectives in education. In each state a statistical service department is responsible for the identification, implementation, and operation of data collection procedures. Within each state, various offices are responsible for:

* Analyzing, interpreting, and disseminating data relating to public and private elementary and secondary schools. Some offices also include data on colleges and universities of the state;

* Coordinating data collection procedures within the department;

* Recommending policies and procedures for processing statistics;

* Conducting special statistical studies; and

Be patient. If any phone number is incorrect, call (area code) 555-1212 and request the new listing.

State Education Information

* Preparing projections and estimates.

The information each education department needs is collected annually, and by using machine-readable forms and electronic data processing, various outputs are produced.

Descriptive Reports

These are the major sources of information that states regarding their school programs. Data include enrollment by grade and race, daily session data, distribution of graduating class, number of dropouts, special programs, availability of resources (videos, computers etc.), and a faculty listing.

Statistical Reports

A wide variety of statistical analyses of characteristics of public school professional staff are produced, including such factors as salary, degree status, certification status, experience, sex, and age. Summaries of various factors are usually available by school, school district, county, geographic region and for the total state. Also, a number of student statistics can be easily generated including: enrollment by grade, racial/ethnic characteristics, course registrations, student staff ratios, class size, and teacher load.

Special Requests

Requests for special data are handled in a variety of ways. Simple requests can be resolved by referencing a publication. Other more complex requests require custom searching of the databases and may require computer programming. In some cases there is a cost recovery fee, and in most cases a written request is preferred and will receive a higher priority.

List of State Department of Education Offices

Alabama

Alabama Department of Education, Montgomery, AL 36130; (205) 242-9590. The computer services department provides computer printouts, and information on magnetic tape or computer diskette. There is a basic charge of $50 per hour for searches. Printouts of information over 50 pages cost an additional $.05 per page. There is a charge of $10 per diskette and $25 per tape. The basic fee for mailing labels is $65 plus an additional $.05 per label for those that run over 1,300. The Department of Education also publishes an *Annual Report*.

Alaska

Alaska Department of Education, Data Processing, P.O.F, Juneau, AK; (907) 465-2808. This office provides computer searches and printouts. Specialized requests should be in writing. Publications include an *Annual Report*.

Arizona

Arizona Department of Education, 1535 West Jefferson, Phoenix, AZ 85007; (602) 542-5295. The data processing department provides services such as computer searches, printouts and magnetic tapes. Requests should be in writing, and the fee varies depending upon the extent of programming necessary. The office publishes an *Annual Report*.

Arkansas

Arkansas Department of Education, Office of Accountability, 4 State Capitol Mall, Little Rock, AR 72201; (501) 682-4229. The Office of Accountability provides computer searches and information via printouts and diskettes. Requests may be made directly over the telephone, but those of a complex nature should be put in writing. There is no fee for services. Publications include: *Affecting Basic Skills Achievement Through Technology - A Research Report*, *Arkansas Policy Statements*, *Federal Focus*, *Needs Assessment: Education for Economic Security Act - Title II, EESA*, *Networking Strategies: Community Education Proven Practice II*, *Private Schools in Arkansas*, *Statistical Summary for the Public Schools of Arkansas*.

California

California Department of Education, 721 Capitol Mall, P.O. Box 944272, Sacramento, CA 94244; (916) 657-2676. The Demographics Services Department provides computer searches and printouts. There is no charge for publications or small searches, but detailed requests require a fee. Requests should be in writing. The office's publications include: *Enrollment Data*, *Racial or Ethnic Distribution of Staff and Students in California Public Schools*, and *Language Census Report*.

Colorado

Colorado Department of Education, 201 E. Colfax, Denver, CO 80203; (303) 866-6837. This office provides computer searches if data are readily available on staff and student enrollment. Requests should be in writing. Publications include *Status of K-12 Public Education in Colorado*, *Certificated Personnel and Related Information*, and *Pupil Membership and Related Information*. A fee of $5 is charged for each report.

Connecticut

Connecticut Department of Education, Office of Research and Evaluation, Box 2219, Hartford, CT 06145; (203) 566-5866. This office provides information through computer searches, printouts and magnetic tapes. They very rarely charge for services and publish an *Annual Report*.

Delaware

Delaware Department of Public Instruction, John Townsend Building, P.O. Box 1402, Dover, DE 19903; (302) 739-4583. This office provides board approved reports listing statistics on school enrollments, number of teachers, educational statistics, and teacher personnel reports. They publish a *Report of Educational Statistics* for $7.50.

Florida

Florida Department of Education, 275 Knott Building, Tallahassee, FL 32399; (904) 487-2280. This service provides computer searches and printouts. If you send in a computer diskette they will transfer the information requested. Their publications include *MIS Statistical Brief* (monthly), *Profiles of Florida School Districts* and administrative support briefs.

Georgia

Georgia Department of Education, Twin Towers East, Atlanta, GA 30334; (404) 656-2400. The Statistical Services Department provides information such as basic attendance data and enrollment data, some financial information, types of enrollment, and the expenditure and cost per child. Computer searches and printouts of existing data are available. There is a charge of $.10 per page if the printout is over 20 pages long. Handouts of specific summaries are available.

Hawaii

Hawaii Department of Education, Office of Information Resource Management, P.O. Box 2360, Honolulu, HI 96804. Enrollment data can be obtained free of charge from this office in printout form. At present, computer diskettes and magnetic tapes are not available. Specialized requests should be in writing. Publications include *Education Today in Hawaii* and the *Annual Financial Report*.

Idaho

Idaho Department of Education, Len B. Jordan Office Building, 650 West State Street, Boise, ID 83720; (208) 334-3330. The Department of Statistical Services provides limited computer searches and free printouts if data exists. There is a base charge of $25 for labels. Their publications include *Financial Summaries*, and an *Annual Statistical Report of Public School Certified Personnel and Employees in Non-Certified Positions*. They also provide an *Educational Directory* for $5.

Illinois

Illinois State Board of Education, 100 North First St., Springfield, IL 62777; (217) 782-3950. The Department of Statistics provides computer searches and printouts free of charge. There is a charge for magnetic tapes. Their publications include *Annual Statistical Report of Illinois Public School Districts* and *Schools and School Directories*.

Be patient. If any phone number is incorrect, call (area code) 555-1212 and request the new listing.

Education

Indiana

Indiana Department of Education, Education Information Systems, Room 229, State House, Indianapolis, IN 46204; (317) 232-0808. This office provides computer searches, printouts and magnetic tapes. Types of information available include enrollment figures, graduation rate, average teacher, and teacher to pupil ratio. Their publications include the *Fall Enrollment Report, Indiana Public School Professional Personnel Data,* and *Non-Certified Personnel Data.* There is a $5 set up fee for computer printout information and a charge of $.15 per page for xeroxed pages.

Iowa

Iowa Department of Education, Grimes State Office Building, Des Moines, IA 50319; (515) 281-5294. This office provides computer searches, printouts and magnetic tapes. There is no charge for standard enrollment and staff reports, but individual reports may require a charge, depending upon the degree of difficulty it took to gather the information. Teachers' names and school addresses are released. Their publications include the *Commission of Education Annual Report* and the *Educational Directory.*

Kansas

Kansas State Department of Education, 120 East 10th St., Topeka, KS 66612; (913) 296-4961. This office provides free computer searches, and printouts. Requests should be in writing. Publications include: *A Strategic Plan for Kansas Public Education for the Year 2005, Annual Report, Profile of Kansas Schools, Profiles of Kansas Education Personnel: Superintendents, Teachers, Elementary Principals, Principals, AVTS Directors,* and *Community College Presidents, 125 Years of Kansas History: How Should Educators Approach It?*

Kentucky

Kentucky Department of Education, Frankfort, KY 40601; (502) 564-4813. Services: This office provides computer searches, printouts and bulletins. While the bulletins and most statistical searches are free, stylized reports require a charge. Their publications include: *Profiles of Kentucky Public Schools, Public School Financial Analysis, Local District Annual Financial Reports, Receipts and Expenditures, Public School Salaries.*

Louisiana

Louisiana Department of Education, P.O. Box 94064, Baton Rouge, LA 70804; (504) 342-3731. The Bureau of School Accountability provides computer searches, printouts and magnetic tapes. Publications include the *Annual Financial and Statistical Report.*

Maine

Maine Department of Educational and Cultural Services, Educational Building, Station No. 23, Augusta, ME 04333; (207) 289-5841. This office provides computer searches and printouts plus magnetic tapes upon special request. Requests should be in writing. The cost is $.02 per name, with a $3 minimum. The cost for labels is $.05 each. Information on grades kindergarten through the twelfth grade is available. Teacher names and school addresses are released. Publications include: *Maine School Statistics, Students Educated at Public Expense, Resident Per Pupil Operating Costs, Maine Educational Facts.* All publications are $3 and less.

Maryland

Maryland Department of Education, Office of Management and Information Systems, 200 West Baltimore St., Baltimore, MD 21201; (301) 333-2659. This office's services include computer searches and printouts from large databases only (enrollment, finance, staff). The information that was previously printed in the *Annual Report* is now distributed in specific smaller releases. There is no charge for printouts or reports.

Massachusetts

Massachusetts Department of Education, 1385 Hancock St., Quincy, MA 02169; (617) 770-7209. Computer searches and printouts are available throughout this office, free of charge. They are currently in the process of converting to an electronic access system. Information available includes: attendance data and drop out reports. Publications include: *Distribution of High School Graduates, Per Pupil Expenditure.*

Michigan

Michigan Department of Education, Information Center Data Services, P.O. Box 30008, Lansing, MI 48909; (517) 335-0422. This office provides computer searches and printouts on a limited basis., Diskettes are available. At present, there is no base charge for services, but this would depend upon the extent of the request. All information requests should be in writing. Publications include *Financial*

Data Statistics and *Fingertip Facts.*

Minnesota

Minnesota Department of Education, Data Management Information, 550 Cedar St., Capitol Square Bldg., St. Paul, MN 55101; (612) 296-2751. This office provides computer searches, printouts and diskettes, free of charge. Teachers' names and school addresses are available on labels from the Documents Division. Their publications include their *Annual Report.*

Mississippi

Mississippi Department of Education, P.O. Box 771, Jackson, MS 39205; (601) 359-3527. Management Information Services provides computer searches, printouts and magnetic tapes. Requests should be in writing. Fees vary depending upon the scope of the request and whether or not a program has to be specifically written. Their publications are $5 each and include the *Annual Report, Statistical Report,* and *School Dropouts by Reasons.*

Missouri

Missouri Department of Education School Data Section, P.O. Box 480, Jefferson City, MO 65102; (314) 751-2569. Computer searches and printout requests are evaluated individually. This office's publications include the *Report of the Public Schools of Missouri,* and *Missouri School Director,* which they sell for $6.

Montana

Montana Office of Public Instruction, State Capitol, Helena, MT 59620; (406) 444-3656. This office provides computer searches and printouts. Special requests should be in writing. They also publish a report on *Public Education in Montana.*

Nebraska

Nebraska Department of Education Management Information Systems, Box 94987, 301 Centennial Mall, South Lincoln, NE 68509; (402) 471-2367. This office's services include computer searches, printouts and magnetic tapes. Fees vary depending upon the scope of the project. The office prefers that requests be in writing. Labels and listings of names are also provided for a fee. Teachers' names and school addresses are released in the School Directories. The office's publications include an *Annual Report,* and a series of reports called *Information Tabs.*

Nevada

Nevada Department of Education, 400 W. King St., Carson City, NV 89710; (702) 687-3100. This office provides computer searches and printouts based upon aggregated student demographic data. Requests should be written. Their publications include a *Status Report,* and reports on *Student Dropout* and *Math and Science.*

New Hampshire

New Hampshire Department of Education, State Office Park South, 101 Pleasant St., Concord, NH 03301; (603) 271-2778. The office of Computer and Statistical Services provides computer searches and printouts. They prefer that requests be made in writing, although this is not required. Mailing labels are $.03 each. Teachers' names and school addresses are released under certain circumstances. The office's publications include their *Biennial Report* and a statistical brochure called the *Stat Handout.*

New Jersey

New Jersey Department of Education, 225 West State St., Trenton, NJ 08625; (609) 292-7629. Services include computer searches, printouts and magnetic tapes upon individual request. There is no set fee for services, since it varies according to the scope of the request. The office's major publications include reports on *Vital Education Statistics,* and *Enrollment Projections.*

New Mexico

New Mexico Department of Education, Education Building, Santa Fe, NM 87501; (505) 827-6524. This office provides computer searches and printouts, free of charge. Requests for computer information should be in writing. Teachers' names and school addresses released under certain circumstances. The office publishes the *New Mexico School District Profile.*

New York

New York Department of Education, Information Center on Education, Albany, NY 12234; (518) 474-8716. This office provides computer searches, printouts and magnetic tapes. Requests should be in writing. Teachers names and addresses are not released. Publications include: *Projections of Public and Non-public School Enrollment and High School Graduates, Public School Professional Personnel Report, Non-public School Enrollment and Staff, Distribution of High School*

State Education Information

Graduates and College-Going Rate, Racial/Ethnic Distribution of Public School Students and Staff, and *Education Statistics.*

North Carolina

North Carolina Department of Public Education, 116 W. Edenton St., Raleigh, NC 27603; (919) 733-9722. This office provides computer searches and printouts. Fees vary, depending upon the complexity of the request. The office's publications include the *Annual Data Plan* and *Selected Financial Data Report.*

North Dakota

North Dakota Department of Public Instruction, Bismarck, ND 58505; (701) 224-2268. This office provides computer searches, printouts and magnetic tapes. If the request involves a special computer program to be run, a minimum charge of $10 is required. Information requests can be given directly over the telephone. Teachers' names and school addresses are released. The office's publications include *Finance Facts* and a *Statewide Summary on Personnel.*

Ohio

Ohio Department of Education, Computer Services, Room 808, 65 Front St., Columbus, OH 43215; (614) 466-7000. This office provides computer searches, printouts and magnetic tapes. There is a $75 minimum charge for services. Requests should be in writing. Publications include a *Salary Study Guide* and *Cost Per Pupil Report.*

Oklahoma

Oklahoma State Department of Education, Data Research Services, 2500 N. Lincoln Blvd., Oklahoma City, OK 73105; (405) 521-3354. This office provides computer searches and printouts. The cost is $.05 per page, with a $10 minimum, plus shipping. The department will send you the material with an invoice in six to eight working days. Publications include an Educational Directory and Dropout Report. Nonprofit organizations can receive the information on diskette or magnetic tape for $15 per disk with a $50 minimum.

Oregon

Oregon Department of Education, Data Processing, 700 Pringle Parkway S.E., Salem, OR 97310; (503) 378-3581. This office provides computer searches and printouts. If you send in your own formatted 3.5 diskette, they will transfer the information to it for you. Requests should be in writing and services are free. Publications include: *Oregon School District Census by ESD Lines, School District Budget Summary, Status of School District Tax Bases, Oregon School Districts - Organization, Location and Size,* and *Oregon Public and Private High School Graduates - Actual and Projected.*

Pennsylvania

Pennsylvania Department of Education, Office of Data Services, 333 Market St., Harrisburg, PA 17126; (717) 787-2644. This office provides computer searches and printouts. In general, services are free, but a large request for a printout or mailing labels may require a fee. Requests should be in writing. They publish the *Status Report On Education In Pennsylvania* and numerous other reports.

Rhode Island

Rhode Island Department of Education, 22 Hayes St., Providence, RI 02908; (401) 277-2841. This office provides computer searches and printouts on a limited basis. Although there is no charge for services at the present time, a fee scale is being developed. Requests should be in writing and take two weeks to fulfill. Their major publications include the *Annual Report on Statistical Tables* and the *Report on Education Indicators.*

South Carolina

South Carolina Department of Education, Rutledge, Management Information Section, Office of Research, Room 605, Rutledge Building, Columbia, SC 29201; (803) 734-8262. This office provides computer searches and printouts. Special requests should be in writing. Fees vary for the use of computer time, and are dependent upon the complexity of the request. Their list of publications includes: *Pupils in South Carolina Schools, Supplemental Salary Study of Selected School, District, and County Personnel,* and an *Annual Salary Study.*

South Dakota

South Dakota Department of Education and Cultural Affairs, Richard F. Kneip Building, 700 Governors Dr., Pierre, SD 57501; (605) 773-3447. This office provides computer searches and printouts. Special requests should be in writing. They also publish the *Educational Statistics Digest.*

Tennessee

Tennessee Department of Education, Office of the Commissioner, Cordell Hull Building, Nashville, TN 37219; (615) 741-0728. This office does not normally provide computer searches but will provide you with a free copy of their *Annual Statistics Report* or *School Directory.*

Texas

Texas Department of Education, Division of Public Information, 1701 N. Congress, Austin, TX 78701; (512) 463-9000. This office provides computer searches, printouts and diskettes. Requests should be in writing. The charge is $10 per diskette, $16 per hour of programming and $.35 per second of computer time. Publications include *Public Education and You.*

Utah

Utah Board of Education, Department of Finance, 250 East 500 South, Salt Lake City, UT 84111; (801) 538-7500. Printouts of information are provided free of charge. The department prefers requests to be in writing. Publications available include the *Annual Report.*

Vermont

Vermont Department of Education, Statistics and Information Unit State Office Building, 120 State St., Montpelier, VT 05602; (802) 828-3151. This office provides information via printouts and diskettes. There is a $25 charge for diskettes unless the requestor is a non-profit organization. Requests should be in writing. They also publish an *Annual Statistical Report of Schools.*

Virginia

Virginia Department of Education, Division of Information Services, 101 N. 14th St., Richmond, VA 23219; (804) 225-2949. The Division of Information Services provides computer searches and distributes information via printouts and booklets. Requests must be in writing. Diskette and magnetic tapes are available through special, written requests. Service fees vary according to the complexity of the request. The office publishes the *Superintendent's Annual Report* which summarizes student, faculty and finance information. The current publication, which is free, contains information based on the 1989-90 school year.

Washington

Washington Superintendent of Public Instruction, Old Capitol Building, FG-11, Olympia, WA 98504; (206) 753-1700. Services: This office conducts computer searches and provides information via printouts, diskettes and computer tapes. There is a charge of $5 per diskette and $25 per tape. Special requests should be in writing. Publications include *Dropout and Graduation Statistics, Minority Enrollment Report,* and *Facts on Washington.*

West Virginia

West Virginia Department of Education, Department of Statistical Information, Capitol Complex, Charleston, WV 25305; (304) 558-6300. This office provides computer searches and printouts. Although they do not normally provide information on diskette or magnetic tape, they can do so if you specify your required format. Requests for information can be made directly over the phone as well as in writing. The office does charge a fee if they write an individual computer program to handle a request. Most information is provided through free printout reports. The office publishes an *Annual Report.*

Wisconsin

Wisconsin Department of Public Instruction, 125 S. Webster, P.O. Box 7841, Madison, WI 53707; (608) 266-3390. Printouts of information are provided free of charge. At present, diskettes and magnetic tapes are not available, but will be accessible at a later date. Specialized requests should be made in writing. Computer searches are run, if data exists. An *Annual Report* is published.

Wyoming

Wyoming Department of Education, Statistical Department, Hathaway Building, 2nd Floor, Cheyenne, WY 82002; (307) 777-7673. This office provides computer searches and printouts free of charge. A written request for information is required. Publications include the *Statistical Report Series I-III.* At present, information is not provided on diskette or magnetic tape.

Be patient. If any phone number is incorrect, call (area code) 555-1212 and request the new listing.

Careers and Workplace General Sources

* *See also Business and Industry Chapter*
* *See also Economics, Statistics and Demographics Chapter*
* *See also Your Community: Money for Communities and Non-Profits Chapter*

Each month, several federal and state agencies collect, analyze, and publish data which reflect the current employment and unemployment situation around the country. This information often reveals changing profiles of the U.S. work force, future trends, and even the impact of technological innovations on the work force. Besides employment statistics, you'll also find information on such hot topics as child care, foreign labor trends, genetic testing, and literacy in the workplace.

* 800 Labor Publications

Office of Information and Public Affairs
U.S. Department of Labor
200 Constitution Ave., NW, Room S1032
Washington, DC 20210 (202) 219-7316

This office can provide you with a free catalog of publications of the U.S. Department of Labor. It contains over 800 title listings in 26 labor categories, and provides ordering information.

* Affirmative Action: Successful Strategies

Superintendent of Documents
Government Printing Office
Washington, DC 20402 (202) 783-3238

Opportunity 2000: Creative Affirmative Action Strategies for a Changing Workforce is a study which profiles the strategies that companies use to ease the conflict between work and family responsibilities and to recruit, develop, and retain minority and economically disadvantaged workers, disabled workers, older workers, and veterans. This publication is available for $5. For more information contact: Information Office, Employment Standards Administration, U.S. Department of Labor, 200 Constitution Ave., NW, Room C4331, Washington, DC 20210; (202) 219-8743.

* American Workforce in the Year 2000

Superintendent of Documents
Government Printing Office
Washington, DC 20402 (202) 783-3238

Workforce 2000 is a U.S. Department of Labor funded study that looks into the workplace and workforce changes that will take place by the year 2000. The department is using this study to rethink their policies and programs in order to prepare the country for the changes ahead. The study looks at the forces shaping the American economy, scenarios for the year 2000, work and workers in the year 2000 and six challenges the country will face. This publication is available for $5.

* Caregiving for the Elderly

Women's Bureau
U.S. Department of Labor
200 Constitution Ave., NW, Room S3315 (800) 827-5335
Washington, DC 20210 (202) 219-6631

Caring for the dependent elderly will become a major issue for the 21st century labor force. The issue arises with the aging of the U.S. population and the restructuring of the American family as women, the traditional care-givers, move into the workforce in increasing numbers. The Women's Bureau can provide you with the factsheet *Eldercare: An Overview*, which discusses important issues related to eldercare in the next century.

* Caribbean Basin Employment and Trade

Bureau of International Economic Affairs
U.S. Department of Labor
200 Constitution Ave., NW, Room S5355
Washington, DC 20210 (202) 219-7597

The annual report, *Trade and Employment Effects of the Caribbean Basin Economic Recovery Act*, describes the provisions included in the CBERA, along with the benefits they provide to beneficiary countries. It also analyzes changes in U.S. trade with CBERA countries, and looks at trends in U.S. employment in those industries which have undergone the most significant changes in trade flows. Contact this office for more information on the report.

* Changing Workplace and Labor Force

Industry Injuries and Illnesses Data
Superintendent of Documents
Government Printing Office
Washington, DC 20402 (202) 783-3238

Many of the Bureau of Labor Statistics' major surveys and research studies are available in the BLS bulletin series, which include more than 100 area and industry wage studies each year and about 40 volumes dealing with a wide range of economic subjects. Here are examples of publications in this series.

New Worklife Estimates contains detailed working life tables and is widely used in liability litigations ($3.25).

Women at Work: A Chartbook focuses on women's economic activity: labor force trends; occupational and industrial employment patterns; and market work of women in a family context ($4).

Children of Working Mothers, part of the Special Labor Force Report series, discusses the increases in the number of children with working mothers and the two major reasons for this growth ($3).

Occupational Projections and Training Data serves as a statistical and research supplement to the *Occupational Outlook Handbook*. It provides detailed data on careers and projected occupational employment, replacement needs, and education and training program completions ($5.50).

* Child Care Survey and Trends

Information Office
U.S. Department of Labor
200 Constitution Ave., NW, Room S1032
Washington, DC 20210 (202) 219-9711

The free report, *Child Care: A Workforce Issue*, is a product of a U.S. Department of Labor internal task force on child care, and is the first step toward understanding child care as a workforce issue. It includes a survey of current activities on the government and private level, examines work-related trends and needs, and analyzes potential problems.

* Child Labor Laws

Child Labor Programs
Employment Standards Administration
200 Constitution Ave., NW, Room S3510
Washington, DC 20210 (202) 219-7640

The Fair Labor Standards Act protects young workers from employment that might interfere with their educational opportunities or be hazardous to their health or well-being. There are different standards for work allowed, depending

Be patient. If any phone number is incorrect, call (area code) 555-1212 and request the new listing.

General Sources

upon the age of the child. Contact the Child Labor Programs office for more information.

* Civil Service Employment

Superintendent of Documents
Government Printing Office
Washington, DC 20402 (202) 783-3238

The 1988 book *Civil Service 2000* outlines the expected demographic changes in the Federal workforce and the changes in skills that the Government will need between now and the year 2000. It includes an appendix which discusses Federal child care programs and policies. Cost - $2.

* Commission on Achieving Necessary Skills

Education and Training Administration (ETA)
U.S. Department of Labor
200 Constitution Ave, NW
Washington, DC 20402 (202) 219-6871

The Secretary's Commission on Achieving Necessary Skills has released its first report, which outlines the skills and skill levels necessary for entry level work in today's economy. For information on the report, contact the ETA.

* Commissions on Women

Women's Bureau
U.S. Department of Labor
200 Constitution Ave., NW, Room S3315
Washington, DC 20210 (202) 219-6631

This Bureau provides funds and other assistance to support regional conferences of women's commissions and the annual convention of The National Association of Commissions for Women, an umbrella organization. The women's commission movement continues to grow, and now 247 state, regional, and local commissions for women are reported.

* Competitiveness in the Workplace

Office of Technology Assessment
600 Pennsylvania Ave., SE
Washington, DC 20510 (202) 228-8996

The Office of Technology Assessment has numerous reports on issues related to competitiveness, employment, and training. The following is a list of reports completed in the last several years.

The Use of Integrity Tests for pre-employment screening. (SET-442) Sept. 1990.
Worker Training: Competing in the new international economy. (ITE 457) Sept. 1990.
Technology and structural unemployment: reemploying displaced adults. (ITE-250).
Plant Closing: advance notice and rapid response. (ITE-321) Sept. 1986.
Displaced homemakers: programs and policy. (ITE-292) Oct. 1985.
Demographic trends and the scientific and engineering workforce. (TM-SET-35)
Automation and the workplace: selected labor, education, and training issues. (TM-CIT-25) March 1983.

* Consumer Price Index and Labor Data on Computer Diskette

BLS Office of Publications
U.S. Department of Labor
441 G St., NW, Room 2831A
Washington, DC 20212 (202) 606-7827

Computer diskettes offer an easy-to-use way to manipulate data for economists, other social scientists, researchers, managers, and policymakers with an interest in measuring employment, prices, productivity, injuries and illnesses, and wages. BLS diskette users need an IBM-compatible microcomputer and Lotus 1-2-3 Version 1A or Version 2. Each diskette contains the named data series and a brief technical description that highlights regular revisions, if any, and typical uses for statistics. A flyer is available which describes the diskettes available and their cost.

* Current Employment Analyses

Office of Employment and Unemployment Statistics
Bureau of Labor Statistics
U.S. Department of Labor

441 G St., NW, Room 2486
Washington, DC 20212 (202) 606-6378

Labor force statistics from the *Current Population Survey* provide a comprehensive body of information on the employment and unemployment experience of the nation's population, classified by age, sex, race, and a variety of other characteristics. The data is published in a variety of sources, including the monthly news release, *The Employment Situation*, and the monthly periodical, *Employment and Earnings*. Data uses include economic indicators, measure of potential labor supply, and evaluation of wage rates and earnings trends for specific demographic groups.

* Current Wage Developments

Superintendent of Documents
Government Printing Office
Washington, DC 20402 (202) 783-3238

Each monthly issue of *Current Wage Developments* includes selected wage and benefit changes, work stoppages, major agreements that expire during the next month, calendar of features, and statistics on compensation changes. The cost is $15 per year. For more information on this data, contact Office of Compensation and Working Conditions, Bureau of Labor Statistics, U.S. Department of Labor, 441 G St., NW, Room 2021, Washington, DC 20212; (202) 606-1382.

* Employer Resource Kit on Employees' Family Needs

Work and Family Clearinghouse
Women's Bureau
U.S. Department of Labor
200 Constitution Ave., NW, Room S3306
Washington, DC 20210 (800) 827-5335

The *Work and Family Resource Kit* is designed to help employers understand the range of family needs emerging in the workplace and the numerous ways a company can respond. It provides a state-of-the-art review of these options as well as advantages and disadvantages. Also listed are references and resources to help employers select the most appropriate response for their employees' family needs. Two recent publications included in the Resource Kit are *Women Workers: Outlook to 2005* and *Women With Work Disabilities*.

* Employment and Earnings: Monthly Publication

Editors
Bureau of Labor Statistics
U.S. Department of Labor
441 G St., NW, Room 2089
Washington, DC 20212 (202) 606-6373

Employment and Earnings is a monthly publication prepared by the Office of Employment and Unemployment Statistics, with data collected by the Bureau of the Census and state employment security agencies. Detailed information is given according to employment status and characteristics of the employed and unemployed. The data are also categorized into employment setting, hours and earnings, and state and labor force data. Subscriptions can be ordered for $25 per year by contacting: Superintendent of Documents, Government Printing Office, Washington, DC 20402; (202) 783-3238.

* Employment and Training Administration Projects and Publications

Office of Worker Retraining and Adjustment Programs
Employment and Training Administration (ETA)
U.S. Department of Labor
200 Constitution Ave., NW, Room N4469
Washington, DC 20210 (202) 219-5577

ETA has recently completed several studies related to employment issues and worker training. In addition, it has also initiated several new studies. The publication *America and the New Economy* discusses a wide range of evolving forces that will affect industries, workers, and their occupations and the standing of the U.S. in world markets. ETA has also completed several studies of displaced workers and the implementation of assistance to them through the Economic Dislocation and Worker Adjustment Assistance Act. New studies initiated during the past year include the following:

- JTPA Title IV Migrant and Seasonal Farmworker Program.
- School to Work Transition Demonstration.
- Multi-State Job Bank Pilot Program.
- EDWAA Farmer/Rancher Demonstration Program.
- EDWAA Job Creation Program.

Be patient. If any phone number is incorrect, call (area code) 555-1212 and request the new listing.

Careers and Workplace

* Employment and Unemployment: Monthly Data and Estimates

Office of Employment and Unemployment Statistics
Bureau of Labor Statistics
441 G St., NW
Room 2919
Washington, DC 20212 (202) 606-6347

This office collects, analyzes, and publishes detailed industry data on employment, wages, hours, and earnings of workers on payrolls of non-agricultural business establishments. It also publishes monthly estimates of state and local area unemployment for use by federal agencies in allocating funds as required by various federal laws. In addition, the office provides current data on occupational employment for most industries for economic analysis and for vocational guidance and education planning.

* Employment Policy and Goals

National Commission for Employment Policy
1522 K St., NW, Suite 300
Washington, DC 20005 (202) 724-1545

This Commission is an independent federal agency with responsibility for examining broad issues of development, coordination, and administration of employment and training programs, as well as advising the President on national employment and training issues. Some of the major responsibilities of the Commission include identifying and examining the employment goals and needs of the nation, examining and evaluating the effectiveness of federally-assisted employment and training programs, and evaluating the impact of tax policies on needs of the nation. The Commission conducts and sponsors research, analyzes the findings, holds public hearings, and publishes an annual report of its findings and recommendations. A current listing of Commission publications is available.

* Employment Projections: 650 Occupations and 300 Industries

Office of Economic Growth and Employment Projections
U.S. Department of Labor
601 D St., NW, Room 4414
Washington, DC 20212 (202) 606-5720

This office produces national occupational employment projections for over 650 detailed occupations for all industries combined and within over 300 detailed industries.

* Employment Research and Evaluation Studies

Office of Policy-Research and
Evaluation Projects
U.S. Department of Labor
200 Constitution Ave., NW, Room S2006
Washington, DC 20210 (202) 219-6181

A free listing is available of all the employment research and evaluation projects completed since 1980 by the U.S. Department of Labor, along with information on how to obtain copies of the reports. The inventory is broken down into the following major topic areas and the reports are listed chronologically: Discrimination/Minorities; Drug Abuse and AIDS Issues in the Workplace; Labor Market Issues and Studies (includes mobility, minimum wage, and farmworker shortage); Labor Market Theory; Miscellaneous and Cross-Program Studies; Occupational Disease; Occupational Safety and Health; Pensions; Public Employment; Quality of Work Life (includes productivity, job satisfaction); Training; Unemployment (includes unemployment insurance); Unions/Labor Relations; Youth; and Price Schedule.

* Employment Statistics for 800 Occupations and 400 Industries

Office of Employment and Unemployment
Bureau of Labor Statistics
U.S. Department of Labor
441 G St., NW, Room 2913
Washington, DC 20212 (202) 606-6515

Available occupational employment statistics include data on employment by occupation and industry for about 800 occupations and 400 industries. Published in bulletins, such as *Occupational Employment* in (industries), data are used for evaluation of current and historical employment by industry and occupation and vocational planning.

* Foreign Economic Impact on U.S. Employment

Office of International Economic Affairs
Bureau of International Labor Affairs
200 Constitution Ave., NW
Room S5325
Washington, DC 20210 (202) 219-7610

The Labor Department's foreign economic research program evaluates the effects of foreign economic developments on the earnings and employment of U.S. workers. This includes quantitative analysis of the impact of policies on international trade, investment, and technology transfer. Often undertaken in response to congressionally-mandated studies or to requests from other executive branch agencies, research is conducted by staff economists and supplemented by outside research contractors. A complete list of the research is available by contacting this office.

* Foreign Labor Trends

Office of Foreign Relations
Bureau of International Labor Affairs
U.S. Department of Labor
200 Constitution Ave., NW, Room S5006
Washington, DC 20210 (202) 219-6257

The U.S. Department of State has 47 labor foreign service attaches placed in embassies all over the world. They monitor and report foreign labor developments, as well as educate other countries on U.S. labor developments. They submit annual reports, including an additional 70 embassy reports, to the U.S. Department of Labor, which then publishes the *Foreign Labor Trends Series*. Available through Superintendent of Documents, Government Printing Office, Washington DC 20402; (202) 783-3238; cost $36 per year. Country labor profiles for some 55 nations are also available.

* Foreign Visitor Program

Special Mediation Services
Federal Mediation and Conciliation Service (FMCS)
2100 K St., NW, Room 709
Washington, DC 20427 (202) 653-6271

Representatives of labor, management, and governments from around the world can see how arbitration, mediation, collective bargaining, and employee involvement programs function in the U.S. by participation in this visitor program. Industrial labor relations are targeted. For more information, contact the Special Mediation Services office listed.

* Future Jobs in 250 Industries

Office of Economic Growth
Bureau of Labor Statistics
U.S. Department of Labor
601 D St., NW, Room 4000
Washington, DC 20212 (202) 606-5700

This office has information on 250 industries regarding employment requirements, specifically on the demand for employment in the future. Industries covered follow the 1972 Standard Industrial Classification Manual. The November, 1989, issue of the *Monthly Labor Review* provides an overview of the data available.

* Government Contractors Employment Standards

Office of Federal Contract Compliance Program
Employment Standards Administration
U.S. Department of Labor
200 Constitution Ave., NW
Room C3325
Washington, DC 20210 (202) 219-9475

This office ensures that federal contractors and subcontractors or contractors with federally-assisted construction contracts do not discriminate against any employee or applicant for employment because of race, color, religion, or national origin, and that these contractors take affirmative action to hire and promote qualified handicapped people, Vietnam-era veterans, and disabled veterans of all wars. This office also investigates complaints to determine whether federal contractors are meeting these obligations.

* Government Labor Statistics Programs

Office of Publications
Bureau of Labor Statistics

General Sources

U.S. Department of Labor
441 G St., NW, Room 2421
Washington, DC 20212 (202) 606-7828
The free publication, *Major Programs of the Bureau of Labor Statistics*, presents in concentrated form the scope of the Bureau's major statistical programs, the data available, the form of publication, some of the uses of the data, and selected publications and data tapes.

* Handicapped Persons Affirmative Action

Office of Federal Compliance Programs
Employment Standards Administration
U.S. Department of Labor
200 Constitution Ave., NW, Room C3325
Washington, DC 20210 (202) 219-9475
The Rehabilitation Act of 1973 prohibits most employers doing business with the federal government from discriminating in employment against handicapped persons. Employers with contracts in excess of $2,500 must take affirmative action to hire and promote qualified handicapped persons.

* History of Labor in the U.S.

Assistant Secretary for Policy
U.S. Department of Labor
200 Constitution Ave., NW, Room S2109
Washington, DC 20210 (202) 219-6461
The Labor Historian can answer any historical inquiries regarding the Department. Questions usually come from Congressional offices, newspapers, and students. As well as conducting his own research on various aspects of Department history, the historian also assists those researching the Department of Labor. The Historian maintains a large photo collection which is open to the public.

* Home-Based Manufacturing Operations

Wage and Hour Division
Employment Standards Administration
U.S. Department of Labor
200 Constitution Ave., NW, Room S3516
Washington, DC 20210 (202) 219-7043
Home-based industry work has always been permitted except in seven industries: knitted outerwear, women's apparel, jewelry manufacturing, gloves and mittens, button and buckle manufacturing, handkerchief manufacturing, and embroidery. In 1984, the U.S. Labor Department lifted the total ban on home work in knitted outerwear, and is now considering a proposal to lift the ban on all industries except women's apparel and those jewelry manufacturing operations in the home that may be hazardous. Contact this office for more information on homework and FLSA enforcement.

* Hours and Earnings Monthly Survey

Office of Employment and Unemployment Statistics
Bureau of Labor Statistics
U.S. Department of Labor
441 G St., NW, Room 2919
Washington, DC 20212 (202) 606-6347
A monthly survey provides hours and earnings data collected from payroll records of business establishments. The data available includes gross hours and earnings of production or nonsupervisory workers in 454 industries, and overtime hours in 323 manufacturing industries. The data are published in a variety of sources, and are used as economic indicators, wage negotiations, and economic research and planning.

* Industry and Employment Projections

Office of Economic Growth and Employment Projections
Bureau of Labor Statistics
U.S. Department of Labor
601 D St., NW, Room 4414
Washington, DC 20212 (202) 606-5720
State and area employment data classified by industry division, and gross weekly hours and earnings for production and related workers in manufacturing is available, as is other data, including demographic employment/unemployment, monthly labor force and unemployment, occupational employment, and area wage surveys.

* Industry-Occupation Employment Matrix

Office of Economic Growth and Employment Projections
Bureau of Labor Statistics
U.S. Department of Labor
601 D St., NW, Room 4000
Washington, DC 20212 (202) 606-5730
The National Industry-Occupation Employment Matrix provides detailed information on the distribution of occupational employment by industry. Coverage is for over 650 detailed occupations--wage and salary, self-employed, and unpaid family workers, and wage and salary workers only for over 300 detailed industries.

* Industry Technological Trends

Industry Productivity Studies Division
Office of Productivity and Technology
U.S. Department of Labor
200 Constitution Ave., NW, Room S4320
Washington, DC 20210 (202) 606-5624
This office looks at a variety of technological trends. One study analyzes major impending changes in products, materials, and production methods in selected industries; their present and future applications; and their effect on output, productivity, employment, skill levels, training, and occupational requirements. Another study analyzes technological changes that have major effects on more than one industry. Coverage includes selected innovations such as computers and numerical control of machine tools, with an emphasis on innovations that will be important in the next five to 10 years.

* International Labor Affairs

International Labor Organization
Bureau of International Organization Affairs
U.S. Department of State
2201 C St., NW, Room 5336
Washington, DC 20520 (202) 647-4196
As a United Nations affiliate, the International Labor Organization (ILO) is comprised of three parts: government, worker, and employee delegations from 150 countries. Headquartered in Geneva, the ILO meets three times a year and holds an annual conference. The ILO serves as a multilateral technical assistance agency designed to promote free labor in a free market system, along with investigating international human rights complaints. They also take a major role in workers rights, such as the right to bargain collectively, and protection from discrimination.

* Job Counseling and Placement Fraud

Federal Trade Commission (FTC)
Bureau of Consumer Protection
6th and Pennsylvania Ave., NW
Washington, DC 20580 (202) 326-3650
The FTC often receives complaint letters about job counseling and placement services which charge large fees and misrepresent their services. The FTC publishes an Alert Sheet entitled *Job Ads, Job Scams, and "900" Numbers*. Other information is available in the FTC brochures *Job Hunting: Should You Pay and "900" Numbers*. For information on how to select a legitimate employment service or to complain about one which you feel has misrepresented itself, contact your local FTC office.

* Job Corps Statistics

Office of Job Corps
Employment and Training Administration
U.S. Department of Labor
500 C St. NW, Room 341
Washington, DC 20001 (202) 639-1654
Job Corps statistics are available, including cost statistics, enrollee demographics, and enrollee outcomes. Contact this office for further information.

* Job Search Booklet

Employment and Training Administration
U.S. Department of Labor
200 Constitution Ave, NW, Room S2322
Washington, DC 20210 (202) 219-6871
The Education and Training Administration publishes a booklet entitled *Tips for Finding the Right Job*. This booklet contains information on all aspects of the job

Be patient. If any phone number is incorrect, call (area code) 555-1212 and request the new listing.

Careers and Workplace

search including resume writing, interviewing, test taking, cover letters, post interview follow up, and time management. It is available free.

* Job Training for the Homeless

Employment and Training Administration
U.S. Department of Labor
200 Constitution Ave., NW, Room N4649
Washington, DC 20210 (202) 219-5577

This program is authorized by the Stewart B. McKinney Homeless Assistance Act and has the objective of providing training, support and housing programs to increase the employment opportunities, job retention, and the attainment of permanent housing for homeless persons.

* Labor Force: A National Profile

Office of Employment and Unemployment Statistics
Bureau of Labor Statistics
U.S. Department of Labor
441 G St., NW, Room 2486
Washington, DC 20212 (202) 606-6378

The labor force statistics available include employment status of the U.S. population 16 years and over by age, sex, race, hispanic ethnicity, martial status, family relationships, Vietnam-era Vietnam status, educational attainment, school enrollment, and residence in metropolitan/nonmetropolitan areas and poverty/nonpoverty areas. Also included is information concerning employed and unemployed persons by occupation, industry, and class of worker, as well as characteristics, work history, and job seeking intentions of persons not in the labor force. Special topics, such as the labor force status of particular groups of the population, occupational mobility and work experience, are also available.

* Labor Force Population Trends

Office of Employment and Unemployment Statistics
Bureau of Labor Statistics
U.S. Department of Labor
441 G St., NW, Room 2486
Washington, DC 20212 (202) 606-6378

This office analyzes and publishes data from the *Current Population Survey* on the labor force, employment, unemployment, as well as on persons not in the labor force. Studies based on the CPS data cover a broad range of topics, including annual analyses of labor market developments, occupational analyses, characteristics of special worker groups (such as minorities and women maintaining families), and employment-related economic hardship.

* Labor Statistics Availability

Division of Information Services
Bureau of Labor Statistics
U.S. Department of Labor
441 G St., NW, Room 2831A
Washington, DC 20212 (202) 606-7828

The Bureau of Labor Statistics can provide you with a tentative release schedule for BLS major economic indicators. The schedule lists the information available (i.e., employment situation, consumer price index, productivity and costs, etc.), as well as the date and time of the information release. The *BLS Update* also contains the release dates for the quarter.

* Labor Statistics Catalog

Office of Publications
Bureau of Labor Statistics
441 G St., NW
Washington, DC 20212 (202) 606-7828

The free quarterly publication, *BLS Update*, contains a complete list of new BLS publications, including a brief description and ordering information. Also included are BLS summaries, data services, telephone numbers for recorded summaries of BLS data, as well as general information concerning BLS.

* Labor Statistics Handbook

Publications
Bureau of Labor Statistics
U.S. Department of Labor
441 G St., NW
Washington, DC 20212 (202) 606-7828

The annual *Handbook of Labor Statistics* contains historical data for the major statistical series produced by the Bureau and is available for $9.50.

* Labor Statistics Monthly Review

Superintendent of Documents
Government Printing Office
Washington, DC 20402 (202) 783-3238

Each issue of the *Monthly Labor Review* includes analytical articles, 47 pages of current statistics, reports on industrial relations, book reviews, and other features for a cost of $20 per year.

* Labor Surplus Areas and Government Contracts

Superintendent of Documents
Government Printing Office
Washington, DC 20402 (202) 783-3238

Area Trends in Employment and Unemployment is a list of labor surplus areas, which are designated as such by the U.S. Department of Labor. This list is used to give priority in awarding government contracts. Once an area has been placed on the list, it remains there for one year. This monthly publication is available for $25. For more information on the labor surplus issues, contact: Employment Service, Employment and Training Administration, U.S. Department of Labor, 200 Constitution Ave., NW, Room N4456, Washington, DC 20210; (202) 535-0189.

* Library on Labor Movement and Occupational Evolution

U.S. Department of Labor
200 Constitution Ave., NW, Room N2439
Washington, DC 20210 (202) 219-6992

This library has a wealth of historical labor material, as well as collections of state labor department reports, documents, and trade union journals. The library is open to the public and staffed by reference librarians, who will assist you in locating materials. The library is open 8:15-4:45 Monday through Friday. Appointments are not necessary. The library also participates in the Inter-Library Loan system.

* Local Area Employment and Unemployment

Office of Employment and Unemployment Statistics
Bureau of Labor Statistics
U.S. Department of Labor
441 G St., NW, Room 2083
Washington, DC 20212 (202) 606-6390

This office provides laborforce, employment, and unemployment data estimated by state employment security agencies. These data are used primarily to allocate federal funds to local jurisdiction. The coverage includes annual average data with demographic detail for 50 states, the District of Columbia, 30 large metropolitan areas, and 11 of their central cities, and monthly data to include 50 states, 330 areas, 3,100 counties, and 500 cities of 50,000 or more. The data are published in a variety of sources, including the annual bulletin, *Geographic Profile of Employment and Unemployment*, and the monthly periodical, *Employment and Earnings*.

* Longitudinal Employment Surveys

Office of Economic Research
Bureau of Labor Statistics
U.S. Department of Labor
441 G St., NW, Room 2026
Washington, DC 20212 (202) 606-7631

Every couple of years, this office updates *The National Longitudinal Surveys*, which study employment profiles of certain age groups . The groups include young women who were 14-24 in 1968; mature women who were 30-44 in 1967; and youth who were 14-21 in 1979. Information available includes labor market activities, characteristics of jobs, earnings, unemployment, social and demographic characteristics, education, and training.

* Minimum Wage and Overtime Pay Standards

Office of Information and Consumer Affairs
Employment Standards Administration
U.S. Department of Labor
200 Constitution Ave., NW, Room C4331
Washington, DC 20210 (202) 219-8743

Be patient. If any phone number is incorrect, call (area code) 555-1212 and request the new listing.

General Sources

The Fair Labor Standards Act establishes minimum wages, overtime pay, recordkeeping, and child labor standards which affect some 73 million employees. It requires employers to pay at least the federally-standardized minimum wage per hour to all covered and nonexempt employees, and to pay one and one-half times their regular pay for all hours worked over 40 in the work week.

* Minimum Wage Exemptions

Special Employment Branch
Wage and Hour Division
Employment Standards Administration
U.S. Department of Labor
200 Constitution Ave., NW, Room S3516
Washington, DC 20210 (202) 219-8727

This office issues certificates allowing employers to pay subminimum wages to full-time students, trainees, and handicapped workers. Contact this office for more information regarding these certificates.

* Multifactor Productivity Trends

Industry Productivity Studies Division
Office of Productivity and Technology
U.S. Department of Labor
200 Constitution Ave., NW, Room S4320
Washington, DC 20210 (202) 606-5624

This program develops indexes of multifactor productivity-output per unit of combined labor and capital inputs-for major sectors of the economy and for manufacturing industries at the 2-digit Standard Industrial Classification level. Indexes are published in the publication *Multifactor Productivity Indexes for Private Business, Private Nonfarm Business, and Manufacturing Sectors.*

* Necessary Job Skills in Today's and Tomorrow's Labor Force

Information Office
Employment Training Administration
U.S. Department of Labor
200 Constitution Ave., NW, Room S2322
Washington, DC 20210 (202) 219-6871

Building A Quality Workforce is a joint initiative of the U.S. Departments of Labor, Education and Commerce. The first part of this free report describes research about entry level skills, business needs, current and projected skills gaps, and how well education is responding to the challenge. The second contains descriptive profiles of several communities working on closing the gap between workplace needs and workforce capabilities.

* Occupational and Economic Outlook Projections

Office of Economic Growth
Bureau of Labor Statistics
U.S. Department of Labor
601 D St., NW, Room 4000
Washington, DC 20212 (202) 606-5700

The BLS publication *Outlook: 1990 - 2005* contains projections for the following occupational and economic categories: Gross National Product; Labor Force Growth; Industry Employment; Occupational Employment; and other issues. The Bureau has detailed employment projections for more than 500 occupations.

* Occupational Outlook Handbook, 1992-93

Superintendent of Documents
Government Printing Office
Washington, DC 20402 (202) 783-3238

This set of 20 individual booklets includes all categories of occupations listed in the *Occupational Outlook Handbook*. Each booklet covers a specific occupational field or area. These reprints are especially useful for jobseekers who want to know about a single field or counselors who need to make the contents of a single book accessible to many jobseekers. Cost - $24 per set.

* Occupational Titles and Classifications Dictionary

Superintendent of Documents
Government Printing Office
Washington, DC 20402 (202) 783-3238

A compendium of approximately 12,000 occupations, the *Dictionary of Occupational Titles*, 4th Edition defines each occupation and provides a classification structure that groups them in terms of related duties and activities. It also includes sections on the purpose of the dictionary and how to use the data bank for job placement. All occupational titles are arranged alphabetically and by industry for easy reference. The cost is $32. A 1986 supplement is available for $5.50. A magnetic tape of the dictionary is available for $210 from: National Technical Information Service, 5285 Port Royal Rd., Springfield, VA 22161; (703) 487-4650.

* On-site Child Care

Women's Bureau
U.S. Department of Labor
200 Constitution Ave., NW
Room S3309
Washington, DC 20210 (202) 219-6652

The free publication, *Employers and Child Care: Benefiting Work and Family*, is designed for employers and employees concerned with developing programs and policies to assist in quality and cost-efficient child care programs while parents are at work. Created to help in a vast array of situations, it provides guidance to those who wish to improve employee productivity and business' ability to recruit and retain the best workers. It is designed for people who are concerned about fulfilling two essential and often conflicting responsibilities--working and caring for their families. The Women's Bureau can also provide you with the fact-sheet entitled *Child Care: An Overview*, which can provide you with more general information on issues related to child care and the workplace.

* Pension Benefit Guaranty Corporation

Public Affairs
Pension Benefit Guaranty Corporation (PBGC)
2020 K St., NW, Room 7100
Washington, DC 20006-1860 (202) 778-8840

The PBGC works to ensure the solvency and viability of company sponsored pension plans. It directly pays the benefits of some 142,000 retirees from terminated pension plans. The corporation is financed from premiums charged to companies that sponsor insured pension plans. The PBGC also works to ensure that underfunded programs are brought up to full funding within a reasonable time period. For more information, contact the PBGC.

* Plant Closings and Permanent Layoffs

Office of Labor-Management Programs
Bureau of Labor-Management Relations
U.S. Department of Labor
200 Constitution Ave., NW, Room N5416
Washington, DC 20210 (202) 219-4473

The Industrial Adjustment Service was created to help address the problems of workers affected by plant closings or major lay-offs. IAS provides a broad array of services and information to help lessen the impact of dislocation and speed up the transfer of dislocated workers to new jobs. IAS works directly with a particular enterprise, with a particular industry, and/or with state and local government officials and private sector representatives to help them develop the knowledge and skills necessary to deal with plant closings and lay-offs, and to assist dislocated workers. Available information includes workshops, technical assistance, publications, and information regarding the Canadian response to permanent lay-offs.

* Plant Closings Notifications

Notification (WARN)
Office of Employment and Training Programs
Employment and Training Administration
U.S. Department of Labor
200 Constitution Ave., NW, Room N4703
Washington, DC 20210 (202) 219-5577

WARN requires that employers with 100 or more employees provide 60 days advance notice of a plant closing or mass layoff. A plant closing is a permanent or temporary shutdown of a single site of employment or one or more facilities or operating unit within a single site or employment, resulting in an employment loss at the site during any 30-day period for 50 or more employees. A mass layoff is a reduction in force at a single site during any 30 day period which results in the employment loss of at least 1/3 of the employees and at least 50 employees or at least 500 employees.

Be patient. If any phone number is incorrect, call (area code) 555-1212 and request the new listing.

Careers and Workplace

* Productivity and Technology Statistics

Office of Productivity and Technology Studies
Bureau of Labor Statistics
U.S. Department of Labor
200 Constitution Ave., NW, Room S4320
Washington, DC 20210 (202) 606-6222

This office is responsible for three major research programs. The productivity program compiles and analyzes productivity and related statistics on the U.S. business economy and its major sectors, and on individual industries and government. The technological studies program investigates trends in technology and their impact on employment and productivity. And the international labor statistics program compiles and analyzes data on productivity and related factors in foreign countries for comparison with the U.S. experience. The free directory, *BLS Publications on Productivity and Technology*, lists all the publications of each program.

* Roadmap to All Labor Data

Superintendent of Documents
Government Printing Office
Washington, DC 20402 (202) 783-3238

The *BLS Handbook of Methods* provides comprehensive information for each major program of the Bureau of Labor Statistics on sources of data, statistical procedures, where the data are published, and their uses and limitations. It includes descriptions for labor force statistics, occupational pay surveys, Employment Cost Index, productivity measures, Consumer Price Index, and for much more. The cost is $11.

* Self Employment Demonstration Projects

Employment and Training Administration (ETA)
U.S. Department of Labor
200 Constitution Ave., NW, Room N4643
Washington, DC 20210 (202) 219-5577

The U.S. Department of Labor has been exploring the viability of self-employment for people receiving unemployment insurance. In two demonstration projects the Department provided eligible UI claimants interested in self-employment with a package of assistance designed to help them start their own businesses. Call ETA for more information on and results from this project.

* Trade-Related Employment Issues

Bureau of International Labor Affairs
U.S. Department of Labor
200 Constitution Ave., NW, Room S2235
Washington, DC 20210 (202) 219-6043

The Bureau of International Labor Affairs represents the U.S. Department of Labor in the development of international economic and trade policies that affect the welfare of U.S. workers. This role includes conducting research on trade-related employment issues, coordinating advice received from Labor Advisory Committees on Trade authorized by the Trade Agreements Act of 1979, and acting as a liaison between other federal departments, agencies, and organized labor. The Bureau is also a member of various interagency committees charged with trade policy functions, and continues to participate in the formulation of U.S. immigration policy.

* Trade Adjustment Assistance

Employment and Training Administration (ETA)
Office of Trade Adjustment Assistance
U.S. Department of Labor
200 Constitution Ave, NW, Room C-4318
Washington, DC 20210 (202) 219-4756

Trade Adjustment Assistance is available to workers who lose their jobs or whose hours and wages are reduced as a result of increased imports. Workers may be eligible for training, a job search allowance, a relocation allowance, and other reemployment services. Weekly trade readjustment allowances may be payable to workers following their exhaustion of unemployment benefits. Information on the program is available from the U.S. Department of Labor in Washington or at any of the 10 ETA regional offices around the country.

* Unemployment Insurance for Lost Wages

Office of Employment and Unemployment Statistics
Bureau of Labor Statistics (BLS)
U.S. Department of Labor

441 G St., NW, Room 2919
Washington, DC 20212 (202) 606-6347

Insured Employment and Wages data are collected quarterly by state employment security agencies in cooperation with BLS. The data available include monthly employment, total quarterly wages, taxable wages, employer contributions, and reporting units, by industry, county, and state, for workers covered by state unemployment insurance laws and by the Unemployment Compensation for Federal Employees program.

* Union Contracts Database

Bureau of Labor Statistics
U.S. Department of Labor
441 G St., NW, Room 2919
Washington, DC 20212 (202) 606-5886

The BLS maintains a database of union contracts searchable by company name and dating back one year. Call or write for more information on the database. This database was formerly handled by the Federal Mediation and Conciliation Service.

* Veterans and Federal Contracts

Veterans Employment and Training
U.S. Department of Labor
200 Constitution Ave., NW, Room S1313
Washington, DC 20210 (202) 219-9116

Federal government contractors and subcontractors (with government contracts of $10,000 or more) are required by law to take affirmative action to employ and to advance in employment qualified special disabled and Vietnam-era Veterans. All suitable employment openings must be given to the nearest local State Employment Office. A Veterans Employment and Training Representative is located in each office to provide employment advice and assistance to veterans. Contact the Office of Federal Contract Compliance Programs if it appears that a contractor has failed to comply. Complaints can be made to: Office of Federal Contract Compliance Programs, U.S. Department of Labor, 200 Constitution Ave., NW, Room C3325, Washington, DC 20210; (202) 219-9475.

* Veterans Employment Program

Assistant Secretary for Veterans
Employment and Training
U.S. Department of Labor
200 Constitution Ave., NW, Room S1313
Washington, DC 20210 (202) 219-9116

Employment-related services designed to aid veterans include counseling, testing, and skills training; unemployment compensation for newly separated ex-service members while they look for civilian employment; tax credits for private employers who hire certain target groups of veterans; placement in private and public sector jobs; and reemployment rights assistance. For more information, contact the Veterans' Employment and Training Office.

* Wage and Hour Investigations

Employment Standards Administration
U.S. Department of Labor
200 Constitution Ave., NW, Room S3028
Washington, DC 20210 (202) 219-8353

This division administers the Fair Labor Standards Act, which includes minimum wage, overtime pay, and child labor provisions. Its responsibilities also have grown to include other laws and regulations which protect worker's wages and working conditions. Wage and Hour Division compliance officers across the country conduct investigations of employers covered by the various laws which the division administers, to determine whether workers are being paid in compliance with the laws. They are also responsible for investigating complaints filed by employees who allege that their employers discriminated against them for actions they took to further the purposes of various environmental protection laws, and for improving conditions for migrant farm workers.

* Wage and Industrial Relations Information

Office of Compensation and Working Conditions
Bureau of Labor Statistics
U.S. Department of Labor
441 G St., NW, Room 2021
Washington, DC 20210 (202) 606-6220

The Bureau of Labor Statistics conducts three major types of occupational wage

General Sources

surveys: 1) area surveys, 2) industry surveys, and 3) a national white-collar salary survey. Non-wage compensation is covered in a comprehensive survey of the incidence and characteristics of employee benefit plans. They also develop measures of trends in employee compensation. The office's program of studies in labor-management relations includes analyses of wage and benefit changes in major collective bargaining agreements, statistics on work stop pages, and reports on pending labor-management negotiations in major bargaining units.

* Wage and Price Indexes on Computer Tape

Bureau of Labor Statistics (BLS)
U.S. Department of Labor
441 G St., NW, Room 1077
Washington, DC 20212 (202) 606-5888

BLS major data series are available on magnetic tape. The standard format is 9-track, 6250 BPI. In addition to the data files listed, BLS makes some microdata tapes and also prepares customized data files on a cost-for-service basis. Available data files include consumer expenditures, consumer price index, export-import price indexes, and labor force, as well as many others. A brochure is available which describes the tapes, ordering information, and the cost of each tape.

* Wage Surveys: Area, Industry and White Collar Earnings

Office of Compensation and Working Conditions
Bureau of Labor Statistics
U.S. Department of Labor
441 G St. NW, Room 2021
Washington, DC 20210 (202) 606-6220

This office conducts three different types of wage surveys. The area and industry surveys provide annual data on averages and distributions of earnings for selected occupations in major industry groups in metropolitan areas. The white-collar salary survey is the annual *Professional, Administrative, Technical, and Clerical Survey* which is used in the Federal pay-setting process and provides data on salaries in white-collar occupations from a national sample of establishments.

* White-Collar Salaries

Benefit Levels Division
Office of Compensation Levels and Trends
Bureau of Labor Statistics
U.S. Department of Labor
441 G St., NW, Room 2025
Washington, DC 20210 (202) 606-6225

The annual white-collar salary survey provides data on salaries in white-collar occupations from a national sample of establishments. The data available includes averages and distributions of salary rates for about 100 professional, administrative, technical, and clerical work levels. The results are published in the annual news release, *White-Collar Salaries*, and the annual bulletin, *National Survey of Professional, Administrative, Technical, and Clerical Pay*.

* Women and Office Automation

Women's Bureau
U.S. Department of Labor
200 Constitution Ave., NW, Room S3309
Washington, DC 20210 (202) 219-6652

The impact of automation on the quality of worklife as well as on the economic well-being of clerical workers and their families is a matter of priority for the Women's Bureau. The free publication, *Women and Office Automation: Issues for the Decade Ahead*, discusses the quality of work, training and retraining, home-based clerical work, and health and safety issues.

* Women in the Workforce Clearinghouse

Women's Bureau
U.S. Department of Labor
200 Constitution Ave., NW, Room S3315 (800) 827-5335
Washington, DC 20210 (202) 219-6665

The Women's Bureau offers a free listing of publications they have available. They have eighteen fact sheets on women workers, as well as information on women in technology, careers/job options, child care, and standards and legislation affecting women. The Bureau has a variety of program models available dealing with employment of women and several conference models. Currently, the staff is focusing on identifying the characteristics of cities presently

experiencing labor shortages and other economic stresses expected to be more widespread by the year 2000, the impact of trade competition on women's jobs, child care for women workers, and many other women's issues. *There's No Such Thing As Women's Work* is a video which reviews the history of women in the workforce and provides information about meeting present day work and family challenges.

* Women Worker Data

Office of Publications
Bureau of Labor Statistics
U.S. Department of Labor
441 G St., NW, Room 2421
Washington, DC 20212 (202) 606-7828

This office publishes a wide array of information about women in the labor force. This information is presented to the public through a variety of publications, including news releases, periodicals, bulletins, reports, tapes, and diskettes. The pamphlet, *Where to Find BLS Statistics on Women*, identifies the particular publications in which specific data services may be found, along with information on how to obtain BLS publications. The data includes information labor force status, employment, and unemployment, earnings and hours of work, education, occupational injuries and illness, and unpublished data.

* Work and Family Clearinghouse

Women's Bureau
U.S. Department of Labor
200 Constitution Ave., NW, Room S3306
Washington, DC 20210 (800) 827-5335

The Work and Family Clearinghouse was designed and established to assist employers in identifying the most appropriate policies for responding to the dependent care (child and/or elder care) needs of employees who are seeking to balance their dual responsibilities. Information and guidance are available in five broad areas: direct services, information services, financial assistance, flexible policies, and public-private partnership. Technical assistance includes national and state information sources, bibliographic references, conference information, research and statistics. *Program Profiles* are available which describe employer-related child and elder care systems already in place.

* Work Based Learning Programs

Office of Work Based Learning
Employment and Training Administration
U.S. Department of Labor
200 Constitution Ave., NW, Room N4703
Washington, DC 20210 (202) 219-5577

In September 1990 six seed money grants were awarded to test innovative approaches to improve the school-to-work transition for youth. During fiscal year 1991 the grantees developed models to redesign school curriculum so students learn job-related subjects. Major findings from this study have been summarized and published in the report entitled *Formula for Success*. Contact ETA for information on how to obtain the report.

* Work Permits for Foreigners

Labor Certification Division
Employment Service
Employment and Training Administration
U.S. Department of Labor
200 Constitution Ave., NW
Room N4456
Washington, DC 20210 (202) 219-0163

If an employer wishes to hire foreign workers, he must first obtain a foreign labor certificate, which is a statement from the U.S. Department of Labor stating that there is no U.S. citizen available to fill the job. The Department investigates to make sure that the wages and working conditions of the foreign workers will not seriously affect the wages and working conditions of U.S. workers. An employer applies for a foreign labor certificate through the local state employment service office, which then conducts a job hunt before sending the application form to the area regional office for approval or disapproval.

* Worker Training

Superintendent of Documents
Government Printing Office
Washington, DC 20402 (202) 783-3238

Be patient. If any phone number is incorrect, call (area code) 555-1212 and request the new listing.

Careers and Workplace

The publication *Worker Training: Competing in the New International Economy* focuses on ways in which public and private firms can develop and tap their employees skills, making them and America more competitive. It compares education and training offered by foreign countries and discusses new training organizations, support structures, and training approaches that can enhance the scope and quality of training at all levels of the workplace. Cost - $12.

* Workplace Literacy, Youth Training and Other Projects

Office of Strategic Planning and Policy Development
Employment and Training Administration
U.S. Department of Labor
200 Constitution Ave., NW
Room N5637
Washington, DC 20210 (202) 219-0677

Research, Demonstration, and Evaluation Projects summarizes the projects funded by the Employment and Training Administration. The most recent focus has been on workplace literacy, youth, worker adjustment, women-families-welfare, and improving employment and training programs. This free catalog provides several indexes and ordering information.

* Work Stoppages and Strikes

Office of Compensation and Working Conditions
Bureau of Labor Statistics
U.S. Department of Labor
441 G St., NW, Room 2032
Washington, DC 20212 (202) 606-6275

This office generates monthly and annual data on major strikes and lock outs. The coverage includes all strikes and lock outs involving 1,000 workers or more and lasting more than one shift. This information measures collective bargaining and economic effects of work stoppages.

* Youth Opportunities Unlimited (YOU)

Employment and Training Administration
U.S. Department of Labor
200 Constitution Ave., NW, Room N4649
Washington, DC 20210 (202) 219-5577

The YOU projects provide intensive comprehensive training, employment and related services to youth in high-poverty target areas in six cities and one rural area. The primary goals were to achieve substantial gains in the rate of high school completions and significant declines in teen pregnancy, crime, and substance abuse.

Be patient. If any phone number is incorrect, call (area code) 555-1212 and request the new listing.

Career and Job Training Opportunities

For anyone looking for help choosing a career, changing jobs, or finding a job, there is plenty of help at little or no cost. Not only can you find where the job opportunities are, you can also see what the job market will be for any profession next year, or even five years from now. If you want to know what part of the country is the best market for, say nurses or engineers, you can find out in one phone call. If you want to choose a major in college that will be marketable when you graduate, that's available too. There are even national computerized job banks and job matching programs listed here that will help match your background and abilities with available jobs. Besides help in finding a job, you'll also find job training and retraining vocational programs, along with plenty of assistance for such special groups as the disabled, displaced homemakers, the elderly, veterans, and those suffering lay-offs from large industries.

* Airline Jobs Bank
Office of Labor-Management Programs
Bureau of Labor-Management Relations
U.S. Department of Labor
200 Constitution Ave., NW
Room N5416
Washington, DC 20210 (202) 219-4473

The Airline Rehire Program gives displaced airline workers first-right-of-hire preference for jobs with pre-deregulation air carriers if the workers were dislocated between 1978 and 1988. One of the key features of this program is a national listing of airline vacancies compiled and kept at the New York State employment service. All carriers are required to list openings with the Job Bank, and anyone may use the list to obtain information about airline vacancies.

* Art Conservation and Museum Careers
Office of Museum Programs
Smithsonian Institution
900 Jefferson Dr., S.W.
Washington, DC 20560 (202) 357-3101

The Audiovisual department of the Office of Museum Programs has a forty slide program as well as a bibliography covering topics such as museum careers, museum environments, and conservation and preservation. You can obtain more information on these resources at the Office of Museum Programs.

* Aviation Careers
Aviation Education Officer
Federal Aviation Administration
U.S. Department of Transportation
800 Independence Ave., SW
Washington, DC 20591 (202) 267-3469

The FAA's Aviation Education Program offers volunteer assistance to the nation's schools through the following programs: career guidance; tours of airports, control towers, and other facilities; classroom lectures and demonstrations; aviation safety information; aviation education resource materials; computerized clearinghouse of aviation and space information; aviation science instruction programs for home/school computers; "Partnerships-in-Education" activities; and teachers' workshops. Write to the above office for more information.

* Basic Skills for Employment
Superintendent of Documents
Government Printing Office
Washington, DC 20402 (202) 783-3238

To improve the quality of the American workforce, the country needs to find better ways of teaching literacy and basic skills to workers who lack them. The U.S. Departments of Labor and Education teamed up to study the problem of workers lacking basic reading skills and to propose remedies to the problem. The results of the study are summarized in the publication *The Bottom Line: Basic Skills in the Workplace.*

* Career Encyclopedia and Prospects
Office of Information
Bureau of Labor Statistics
U.S. Department of Labor, 441 G St., NW
Washington, DC 20212 (202) 606-7828

The *Occupational Outlook Handbook* is an encyclopedia of careers covering 225 occupations. For each of these, information is included on what the work is like, 1986 employment figures, educational and training requirements, advancement possibilities, job prospects through the year 2000, earnings-related occupations, and where to find additional information. The cost of the handbook is $22. The *Occupational Outlook Quarterly* can help students, guidance counselors, and employment counselors keep abreast of current occupational and employment developments between editions of the *Occupational Outlook Handbook.* The quarterly supplement provides you with advice on how to get a job, articles on new occupations, addresses and phone numbers for more information on apprenticeships and training, and information on special scholarships for talented students. The cost of the *Quarterly* is $5 per year. Both books can be ordered by contacting: Superintendent of Document, Government Printing Office, Washington, DC 20402; (202) 783-3238. Both of these books are available at public libraries.

* Careers in Dozens of Fields
Superintendent of Documents
Government Printing Office
Washington, DC 20402 (202) 783-3238

The following reprints are available from the *Occupational Outlook Handbook:*

Business, Managerial, and Legal Occupations. $2.50
Clerical and Other Administrative Support Occupations. $1.75
Communications, Design, Performing Arts, and Related Occupations. $1.50
Computer and Mathematics-Related Occupations. $1.50
Construction and Extractive Occupations. $1.75
Dietetics, Nursing, Pharmacy and Therapy Occupations. $1.50
Education, Social Service, and Related Occupations. $2
Engineering, Scientific, and Related Occupations. $1.75
Health Technologists and Technicians. $1.50
Mechanics, Equipment Installers, and Repairers. $2
Medical and Dental Practitioners and Assistants. $1.25
Metalworking and Woodworking Occupations. $1.50
Production and Transportation Occupations. $2
Protective Service Occupations and Compliance Inspectors. $1
Sales Occupations. $1.25
Service Occupations: Food, Cleaning, Health and Personal. $1.50
Technologists and Technicians, Except Health. $1.25
Tomorrow's Jobs: Overview. $1.25

* Career Options: Art Museums to Zoos
Superintendent of Documents
Government Printing Office
Washington, DC 20402 (202) 783-3238

The U.S. Department of Labor publishes a $7 book titled *Career Opportunities in Art Museums, Zoos and Other Interesting Places.*

Be patient. If any phone number is incorrect, call (area code) 555-1212 and request the new listing.

Careers and Workplace

* Coast Guard Training

U.S. Coast Guard
U.S. Department of Transportation
Aeronautical Center
MPB 237, P.O. Substation 18
Oklahoma City, OK 73169-6999 (405) 680-4265

Coast Guard personnel are trained for advancement through a nonresident course program developed by this Institute. For more information about Guard training or for referral to Institute staff members, contact the number listed.

* Creative Writers Publishing Grants

Literature Program
National Endowment for the Arts
1100 Pennsylvania Ave., NW, Room 723
Washington, DC 20506 (202) 682-5451

The Literature Program assists individual creative writers and literature translators, encourages wider audiences for contemporary literature, and assists non-profit literary organizations. Fellowships enable writers and translators to set aside time for writing and research. Publishing grants provide assistance to literary magazines, small presses, and various distribution projects. Grants are also available to support residencies for writers to allow them to interact with their public. Literary centers may request funds but must offer a regular format of readings, workshops, and technical assistance for writers. Grants can be made to individuals or to non-profit organizations if such donations qualify as charitable deductions under Section 170(c) of the Internal Revenue Code of 1954. Grants range from $2,000 to $50,000.

* Criminal Justice Career Opportunities

Superintendent of Documents
Government Printing Office
Washington, DC 20402 (202) 783-3238

The *Criminal Justice Careers Guidebook* provides detailed information on criminal justice occupations in the areas of law enforcement, corrections and rehabilitation, and the judiciary. Duties, job requirements, and opportunities are described for each occupation and sources of further information are identified. It can be purchased from GPO for $7.

* Dictionary of 20,000 Occupational Titles

Superintendent of Documents
Government Printing Office
Washington, DC 20402 (202) 783-3238

A compendium of approximately 20,000 occupations, the *Dictionary of Occupational Titles* defines each occupation and provides a classification structure that groups them in terms of related duties and activities. It also includes sections on the purpose of the dictionary and how to use the data bank for job placement. All occupational titles are arranged alphabetically and by industry for easy reference. The cost is $32. A 1986 supplement is available for $5.50. A magnetic tape of the dictionary is available for $210 from: National Technical Information Service, 5285 Port Royal Rd., Springfield, VA 22161; (703) 487-4650.

* Disabilities Program

Employment and Training Administration (ETA)
U.S. Department of Labor
200 Constitution Ave, NW
Washington, DC 20210

The ETA funds several projects to increase the number and quality of job opportunities for disabled individuals under the Job Training Partnership Act. These projects provide services which address each of the major conditions which constitute barriers to labor market participation - sight, hearing, epilepsy, mental retardation and other physical and emotional impairments.

* Disabled Veterans: Job Matching Service

Veterans Employment and Training
U.S. Department of Labor
200 Constitution Ave., NW, Room S1313
Washington, DC 20210 (202) 219-9116

Located in most employment service offices, the Disabled Veterans' Outreach Program is staffed by veterans who provide special assistance to other veterans and help them obtain employment and training services. The DVOP staff develop networks of employer contacts and work with community groups and veterans organizations in their effort to find jobs for their clients. Unique to this program is the emphasis to seek out and help disabled and Vietnam-era veterans.

* Dental Health Professions

Division of Associated and Dental Health Professions
Health Resources and Services Administration
5600 Fishers Lane, Room 8-101
Rockville, MD 20857 (301) 443-6854

This division serves as a principle focus with regard to health professions education, practice, and service research, in the fields of dentistry, optometry, pharmacy, veterinary medicine, public health, and allied health professions. It supports and conducts programs, surveys, and studies to analyze and improve the quality, development, organization, utilization, and credentialing of personnel in these fields. It also supports and conducts special educational initiatives. A publications list for professionals is available.

* Disease Control and Environmental Health Training

Training and Laboratory Program Office
Centers for Disease Control
1600 Clifton Rd.
Atlanta, GA 30333 (404) 639-2142

The Centers for Disease Control offers course work on such topics as environmental health sciences, communicable disease control, and vector-born disease control. Anyone can take these courses; however, they are designed for hospital personnel and health care providers. These classes are offered at a variety of locations, as well as many being available as self-study training courses.

* Displaced Homemakers Job Network

Job Network for Displaced Homemakers
1625 K St., NW
Suite 300
Washington, DC 20006 (202) 467-6346

Supported by the Women's Bureau at the U.S. Department of Labor, the Displaced Homemakers Network is the only national organization which addresses the specific concerns of displaced homemakers. Through its Washington, DC, office, it works to increase displaced homemakers' options for economic self-sufficiency, to provide information about the public policy issues which affect displaced homemakers, to provide technical assistance resources for service providers, and to help program staff around the country locate the information and expertise they need to develop programs that work for displaced homemakers. There are many publications and newsletters available, and the staff can assist you in locating a displaced homemakers program near you.

* Employment in Transportation

Central Employment Office
Office of Personnel
U.S. Department of Transportation
400 7th St., SW, Room 9113
Washington, DC 20590 (202) 366-9417

Employment inquiries for positions in Washington, DC, should be submitted to this office. Regional and district offices handle employment in their areas. Civil Service positions include air traffic controller; electronics maintenance technicians; civil, aeronautical, automotive, electronic, and highway engineers; and administrative, management, and clerical positions.

* Employment Search Strategies

Superintendent of Documents
Washington, DC 20402 (202) 783-3238

A new ETA publication, *Tips for Finding the Right Job*, can help you take advantage of successful job-hunting strategies and find out what you need to know before your job interview. It can be ordered from GPO for $1.25.

* Employee Training Technologies and Competitiveness

Office of Technology Assessment (OTA)
600 Pennsylvania Ave., SE
Washington, DC 20510 (202) 228-6352

Currently, OTA is exploring the connections between new workplace technologies, employee training, and competitiveness. The study will examine such topics as national investment in training; demographic changes in the work

Be patient. If any phone number is incorrect, call (area code) 555-1212 and request the new listing.

Career and Job Training Opportunities

force; employee training in countries that are major industrial competitors of the U.S.; and policy questions concerning existing federal programs. Contact Wendell Fletcher, the project director, for more information.

* Environmental Protection Job Opportunities

Superintendent of Documents
Government Printing Office
Washington, DC 20402 (202) 783-3238

The U.S. Department of Labor publishes the *Environmental Protection Careers Guidebook* which is sold by the Government Printing Office for $7.50.

* Epidemic Intelligence Service

Epidemiology Program Office
Centers for Disease Control
Atlanta, GA 30333 (404) 639-3588

The Epidemic Intelligence Service is a two-year program of service and on-the-job training for health professionals, most of whom are physicians, in the practice of epidemiology. The officers have opportunities to investigate disease outbreaks, conduct epidemiologic studies, teach, travel, and present and publish their work. The class begins with a training course, and then the class responds to inquiries, monitors reports of disease, investigates outbreaks, and analyzes epidemiologic data.

* Experimental Job Training Opportunities

Office of Strategic Planning and Policy Development
Employment and Training Administration
U.S. Department of Labor
200 Constitution Ave., NW, Room N5637
Washington, DC 20210 (202) 219-7674

This office plans and implements Pilot and Demonstration Programs to provide job training, employment opportunities, and related services for individuals with specific disadvantages. These programs address industry-wide skill shortages and offer technical expertise to particular client groups. They also develop information networks among organizations with similar Job Training Partnership Act-related objectives. Administered at the National level and operated at the state and local level, these programs cover disadvantaged groups in the labor market, including offenders, individuals with limited English language proficiency, handicapped person, women, single parents, displaced homemakers, youth, older workers, those who lack educational credentials and public assistance recipients.

* Federal Aviation Administration Academy

Federal Aviation Administration
U.S. Department of Transportation
P.O. Box 25082, AAC-900
Oklahoma, OK 73125 (405) 680-7904

The Academy is the principal source of technical information on U.S. civil aviation. It conducts training for FAA personnel through resident or correspondence courses and occasional on-site training. Air traffic training is available for specialists who man the FAA airport traffic control towers, air route traffic control center, and flight service stations. Electronic training is also available for engineers and technicians who install and maintain navigation and traffic control communications facilities. Initial and recurrent training is also conducted for air carrier and general operations inspectors. The Academy provides air navigation facilities and flight procedures analysis to flight inspection personnel.

* Financial and Other Service Sector Jobs

Superintendent of Documents
Government Printing Office
Washington, DC 20402 (202) 783-3238

The U.S. Department of Labor publishes a book for $7 titled *Occupational Employment in Mining, Construction, Finance, and Services* which can be purchased from the Government Printing Office.

* Fish Husbandry Training Academy

National Fisheries Center
U.S. Fish and Wildlife Service
Box 700
Kearneysville, WV 25430 (304) 725-8461, ext. 5333

The National Fisheries Center and its five field stations are world-renowned as a focal point for fish health research and fisheries development. Studies include nutrition, genetics, diseases, management technology, and technical services. The facility contains a training academy of fish husbandry.

* Foreign Service Career Counseling

Personnel Office
Special Services Branch
United States Information Agency
301 Fourth St., SW, Room 525
Washington, DC 20547 (202) 619-3732

Information on career opportunities in the Foreign Service is available from this office. This office can also send you an application for the Foreign Service Exam.

* Future Job Trends by Occupation

Superintendent of Documents
Government Printing Office
Washington, DC 20402 (202) 783-3238

A supplement to the latest edition of the *Occupational Outlook Handbook, Occupational Projections and Training Data* provides detailed, comprehensive statistics and technical data supporting the information presented in the *Handbook*. It also presents a broad overview of expected trends in employment in the mid 1990's and provides employment data for approximately 200 occupations profiled in the *Handbook*. This supplement is a key reference source for training officials, education planners, and vocational and employment counselors. The cost is $5.50.

* Health Careers

Superintendent of Documents
Government Printing Office
Washington, DC 20402 (202) 783-3238

The Labor Department publishes a reference book on employment opportunities and trends titled *Health Careers Guidebook* which can be purchased for $7.50 from the Government Printing Office.

* Health Professions and Training Programs

Division of Public Health Professions
Health Resources and Services Administration
5600 Fishers Lane, Room 8-101
Rockville, MD 20857 (301) 443-6854

This division supports programs and provides grants for the following areas: Geriatric Education Centers; Rural Areas Health Care; Dentistry; Schools of Public Health; Preventive Medicine Residency Training; and Graduate Programs in Health Administration. Call for more information on programs.

* Highly Skilled Jobs Apprenticeship

Bureau of Apprenticeship and Training
Employment and Training Administration
U.S. Department of Labor
200 Constitution Ave., NW, Room N4649
Washington, DC 20210 (202) 219-5540

Apprenticeship is a combination of on-the-job training and related classroom instruction in which workers learn the practical and theoretical aspects of a highly skilled occupation. Apprenticeship programs are operated on a voluntary basis by employers, employer associations, or management and labor groups. The role of the federal government is to encourage and promote the establishment of apprenticeship programs and provide technical assistance to program sponsors. The related classroom instruction is given in the program sponsor's training facility or a local technical school or junior college.

* Indians and Job Training

Office of Tribal Services
Bureau of Indian Affairs
U.S. Department of the Interior
18th and C Sts., NW
Washington, DC 20240 (202) 208-2570

This office serves as a cross between the Health and Human Services, Labor, Justice, and Housing and Urban Development Departments for the Indian population. The needy are paid welfare subsidies and provided job training. This office also operates 19 special federal courts and funds 127 tribal courts, along

Be patient. If any phone number is incorrect, call (area code) 555-1212 and request the new listing.

Careers and Workplace

with administering the police force for Indian reservations, and a rehabilitation program for Indian homes.

* Information and Records Management Training

Records Administration Information Center
National Archives and Records Administration
8th St. and Pennsylvania Ave., NW
Washington, DC 20408   (202) 501-6015

The Directory of Records Administration Training Programs in the Washington, DC Area lists classes available from government, academic, and private sources in such subject areas as records management, Information Resource Management, micrographics, and optical disks. Basic courses currently being offered include: Introduction to Records Management; Files Improvement; and Records Disposition. Contact this office for a copy.

* International Trade Commission Jobs

Office of Personnel
U.S. International Trade Commission
500 E St., SW, Room 314
Washington, DC 20436   (202) 205-2651

Information on employment can be obtained from the Personnel Director. Personnel employed include international economists, attorneys, accountants, commodity and industry specialists and analysts, and clerical and other support personnel.

* Job Corps Conservation Centers

Office of Historically Black College
and University Programs and Job Corps
U.S. Department of the Interior
18th and C Sts., NW
Washington, DC 20240   (202) 208-6403

This residential program provides job training for disadvantaged youth throughout the country. You must be between the ages of 16 and 22 to participate. Twelve conservation centers are located throughout the country for training purposes.

* Job Corps for Youths

Office of Job Corps
Employment and Training Administration
U.S. Department of Labor
500 C St., NW
Washington, DC 20001   (202) 639-1654

The Job Corps, a Federally administered national employment and training program, is designed to serve severely disadvantaged youth 16-21 years old. Enrollees are provided food, housing, education, vocational training, medical care, counseling, and other support services. The program prepares youth for stable, productive employment and entrance into vocational/technical schools or other institutions for further education or training. Job Corps centers range in capacity from 175 to 2,600 enrollees. Some of the centers are operated by the U.S. Departments of Interior and Agriculture (civilian conservation centers), while the remaining centers are operated under contracts with the U.S. Department of Labor primarily by major corporations. Vocational training is given in such occupations as auto repair, carpentry, painting, nursing, business and clerical skills, as well as preparation for the General Education Development (GED) high school equivalency examination. To apply, contact and Job Service office, or call the Job Corps Alumni Association's toll-free number: (800) 424-2866.

* Jobs For Seniors 55 Years and Up

Office of Special Targeted Programs
Employment and Training Administration
U.S. Department of Labor
200 Constitution Ave., NW, Room N4643
Washington, DC 20210   (202) 219-5904

Sponsored by state and territorial governments and ten national organizations, the Senior Community Service Employment Program promotes the creation of part-time jobs in community service activities for jobless, low-income persons who are at least 55 years of age and have poor employment prospects. Individuals work in part-time jobs at senior citizens centers, in schools or hospitals, in programs for the handicapped, in fire prevention programs, and on beautification and restoration projects. This program makes possible and array

of community services to the elderly. SCSEP participants must be at least 55 years of age, have family income of not more than 25% above the Federal poverty level, and be capable of performing the tasks to which they are assigned. For more information, contact state offices for the aging, area agencies on aging, or local job service offices.

* Job Training and Employment Publications

Superintendent of Documents
Government Printing Office
Washington, DC 20402   (202) 783-3238

The GPO sells hundreds of publications on employment and occupations. Call GPO and ask for Subject Bibliographies 044 and 202, which contain lists of available publications and their prices. The Subject Bibliographies are free.

* Job Training and Employment Services

Office of the Assistant Secretary for Employment and Training
U.S. Department of Labor
200 Constitution Ave., NW, Room S2321
Washington, DC 20210   (202) 219-6236

The Job Training Partnership Act provides job training and employment services for economically disadvantaged adults and youth, dislocated workers, and others who face significant employment barriers. The goal of this Act is to move the jobless into permanent, unsubsidized, self-sustaining employment. State and local governments have primary responsibility for the management and administration of job training programs. In addition, a new public/private partnership has been created to plan and design training programs as well as to deliver training and other services.

* Job Training and Workplace Research and Development

Office of Strategic Planning and Policy Development
Employment and Training Administration
U.S. Department of Labor
200 Constitution Ave., NW, Room N5637
Washington, DC 20210   (202) 219-5677

Research, Demonstration, and Evaluation Projects summarizes the projects funded by the Employment and Training Administration. The most recent focus has been on workplace literacy, youth, worker adjustment, women-families-welfare, and improving employment and training programs. This free catalog provides several indexes and ordering information.

* Job Training for Ex-Offenders

Office of the Assistant Secretary for Employment and Training
U.S. Department of Labor
200 Constitution Ave., NW, Room S2321
Washington, DC 20210   (202) 219-6236

The ETA has several programs and services available that can help ex-offenders find employment. Programs include the following: Job Training Partnership Act programs, U.S. Employment Service, Targeted Jobs Tax Credit Program, Apprenticeship programs, Job Corps, Federal Bonding Program, and Tips for Finding the Right Job. Call ETA for more information.

* Junior Foreign Service Officer Trainee Program

Personnel Office
Special Services Branch
United States Information Agency
301 Fourth St., SW, Room 525
Washington, DC 20547   (202) 619-3117

Each December the Foreign Service Officer Examination is held at many locations in this country and overseas to screen candidates for the Junior Officer Trainee Program. Date, locations, and other information is available from this office.

* Literature Translators Opportunities

Literature Program
National Endowment for the Arts
1100 Pennsylvania Ave., NW, Room 723
Washington, DC 20506   (202) 682-5451

The Literature Program assists individual creative writers and literature

Be patient. If any phone number is incorrect, call (area code) 555-1212 and request the new listing.

Career and Job Training Opportunities

translators, encourages wider audiences for contemporary literature, and assists non-profit literary organizations. Fellowships enable writers and translators to set aside time for writing and research. Publishing grants provide assistance to literary magazines, small presses, and various distribution projects. Grants are also available to support residencies for writers to allow them to interact with their public. Literary centers may request funds but must offer a regular format of readings, workshops, and technical assistance for writers. Grants can be made to individuals or to non-profit organizations if such donations qualify as charitable deductions under Section 170(c) of the Internal Revenue Code of 1954. Grants range from $2,000 to $50,000.

* Local Help for Job Seekers

Employment and Training Administration
U.S. Department of Labor
200 Constitution Ave., NW, Room N4470
Washington, DC 20210 (202) 219-0157

The U.S. Employment Service, through affiliated state employment agencies, operates almost 2,000 local employment service (job service) offices. They assist job seekers in finding employment and assist employers in filling job vacancies. They administer occupational aptitude tests and circulate information about jobs and training opportunities.

* Marketing Your Job Talents

Superintendent of Documents
Government Printing Office
Washington, DC 20402 (202) 783-3238

The best selling book, *Merchandising Your Job Talents*, shows job hunters how to sell their knowledge, skills, and experience effectively in today's competitive marketplace. It covers everything from self-appraisal and resume preparation to testing and interviewing. Sample resumes and a sample letter of application are included as guidelines in this $2.75 publication.

* Matching Yourself with the Workworld

Superintendent of Documents
Government Printing Office
Washington, DC 20402 (202) 783-3238

Designed to assist you in comparing job characteristics with your skills and interests, the publication, *Matching Yourself with the World of Work*, lists and defines 17 occupational characteristics and requirements, and matches these characteristics with 200 occupations chosen from the 1988-89 *Occupational Outlook Handbook*. It is available for $1.

* Medical/Scientist Training

Medical Scientist Training Program (MSTP)
National Institute of General Medical Sciences
Westwood Building, Room 905
Bethesda, MD 20892 (301) 496-7301

The MSTP provides assistance to students attempting to receive the dual degree of MD-PHD. Candidates must show evidence of high academic performance and significant prior research experience. Up to six years of support is given, and candidates must attend MSTP support institutions.

* Migrant and Seasonal Farmworker Opportunities

Employment and Training Administration
U.S. Department of Labor
200 Constitution Ave., NW, Room N4641
Washington, DC 20210 (202) 219-5500

This office administers a national program to help combat chronic unemployment, underemployment, and substandard living conditions among migrant and seasonal farm workers and their families. Supportive services are available to farm workers who seek alternative job opportunities that will enable them to secure stable employment at an income above the poverty level, and improve the living standard of those who remain in the agricultural labor market. Through grants to public and private non-profit institutions, economically disadvantaged farmworker families are furnished training and other employment-related services, including classroom training, on-the-job training, work experience, and supportive services. Supportive services include day care, health care, legal aid, transportation assistance and food and housing in emergency situations. You can contact this office for help in finding a local sponsor.

* Mining and Construction Jobs

Superintendent of Documents
Government Printing Office
Washington, DC 20402 (202) 783-3238

The U.S. Department of Labor publishes a book for $7 titled *Occupational Employment in Mining, Construction, Finance, and Services*.

* Minority Access to Biomedical Research Careers

Minority Access to Research Careers Program
National Institute of General Medical Sciences
Westwood Buildings, Room 9A18
Bethesda, MD 20892 (301) 496-7301

This program provides special training opportunities in biomedical science for students and faculty at institutions with substantial minority enrollments. There are four types of support: 1) Honors Undergraduate Research Training Program, which provides support to institutions to teach and provide research training to honors students in their junior or senior year who plan biomedical research careers. 2) The Predoctoral Fellowship provides support for graduates of the MARC honors undergraduate program to pursue a graduate degree in the biomedical sciences (not medical school). 3) The Faculty Fellowship Program provides opportunities for research training for faculty members of colleges with high minority enrollment. 4) The Visiting Scientist Fellowship provides support for outstanding scientists-teachers to serve as visiting scientists at colleges with substantial minority enrollments.

* Modern Archives Management Training

Office of Public Programs
National Archives and Records Administration
8th St. and Pennsylvania Ave., NW, Room 505
Washington, DC 20408 (202) 501-6017

The "Modern Archives Institute: Introduction to Modern Archives Administration," is a two-week archival training course that offers an introduction to archival theory and practice for participants. It is sponsored by the National Archives Trust Fund Board, and includes lectures, discussions, workshops, and visits to the Manuscript Division of the Library of Congress and various units of the National Archives. The Institute is offered twice a year.

* National Computerized Job Bank

United States Employment Service
Employment and Training Administration
U.S. Department of Labor
200 Constitution Ave., NW, Room N4456
Washington, DC 20210 (202) 219-4389

A computerized network connecting more than 2,000 Job Service (Employment Service) Offices, the Interstate Job Bank is your opportunity to explore available jobs listed in all 50 states. During any given week there are over 20,000 job openings available in the IJB. During a year approximately 42,000 job orders containing 97,000 job openings are distributed through the IJB. When an employer cannot fill a job with local talent, the job than gets listed with the Interstate Job Bank. Jobs are listed three ways; as a detailed job description, and on two indexes, one listed by State and one by occupation. You may have access to any one of these listings through the Job Service Office. After you have selected the jobs you are interested in, a review with your local Job Service representative is in order. A proper plan is developed which may include sending your resume directly to an employer or to a Job Service office in another State. The Interstate Job Bank is a free service.

* Native Americans and Museum Professions

Office of Museum Programs
Smithsonian Institution
900 Jefferson Dr., SW
Washington, DC 20560 (202) 357-3101

The Native American Museums Program provides information services and educational opportunities for employees of tribal and urban native American museums and cultural centers. The Program offers workshops, short-term residencies, technical assistance, publications, and audio-visual materials on museums.

* Native Americans: Job Training

Office of Special Targeted Programs
Employment and Training Administration

Be patient. If any phone number is incorrect, call (area code) 555-1212 and request the new listing.

Careers and Workplace

U.S. Department of Labor
200 Constitution Ave., NW, Room N4643
Washington, DC 20210 (202) 219-5502
The U.S. Department of Labor sponsors special employment and training programs designed to help jobless Native Americans. Those eligible include Indians, Eskimos, Aleuts, Hawaiians, and other persons of native American descent who are economically disadvantaged, unemployed, or underemployed. In addition to job referrals, these programs offer job training, counseling, and other employment-related services to help Native Americans prepare for and hold productive jobs. To make participation easier, child care, transportation, and training allowances are included as part of the programs. You can apply by contacting tribal or other grantees representing the reservations or villages who receive Labor Department grants, or you can get further information by contacting the office above.

* Non-Manufacturing Industries Job Outlook

Superintendent of Documents
Government Printing Office
Washington, DC 20402 (202) 783-3238
The Labor Department publishes a book titled *Occupational Employment in Selected Nonmanufacturing Industries* which can be purchased for $5 from the Government Printing Office.

* Nursing Research Training

National Center for Nursing Research
National Institutes of Health
Building 31, Room 5B25
9000 Rockville Pike
Bethesda, MD 20892 (301) 496-0207
The National Center for Nursing Research (NCNR) supports nursing research and research training related to patient care, the promotion of health, and the prevention of disease. NCNR also supports studies of nursing interventions, procedures, and delivery methods, as well as the ethics of patient care. Publications are available regarding NCNR and its research grant process.

* Occupational Exploration Encyclopedia

Superintendent of Documents
Government Printing Office
Washington, DC 20402 (202) 783-3238
The *Guide For Occupational Exploration* is an invaluable reference source which provides detailed occupational and labor market information you can use to assist job seekers in getting and keeping a job. The *Guide* groups thousands of occupations in the world of work by the interests, traits, and abilities required for successful performance. It also gives descriptive summaries for each work group and assists individuals in reviewing, understanding, and evaluating their own interests and relating them to pertinent career fields. It is available at many public libraries. Another complementary resource, *Selection Workbook for Use with Guide for Occupational Exploration*, is available for $4.25.

* Occupational Safety and Health Courses

Division of Training and Manpower Development
National Institute for Occupational Safety and Health
4676 Columbia Parkway
Cincinnati, OH 45226 (513) 533-8221
This division offers courses for industry and health care professionals on such topics as occupational safety, industrial hygiene, and safety in the laboratory. For a course listing and description, contact this office.

* Oceanographic Corps Jobs

Commission Personnel Division
NOAA Corps
National Oceanic and Atmospheric Administration
U.S. Department of Commerce
11400 Rockville Pike
Rockville, MD 20852 (301) 443-8905
The NOAA Corps is the uniformed service of the U.S. Department of Commerce responsible for operating and managing NOAA's fleet of hydrographic, oceanographic, and fisheries-research ships and for supporting NOAA scientific programs. Engineering, computer science, mathematics, and science baccalaureate or higher degree graduates are sought for positions in the Corps.

* Office Automation Impact on Women

Women's Bureau
U.S. Department of Labor
200 Constitution Ave., NW, Room S3309 (800) 827-5335
Washington, DC 20210 (202) 219-6652
The impact of automation on the quality of worklife as well as on the economic well-being of clerical workers and their families is a matter of priority for the Women's Bureau. The free publication, *Women and Office Automation: Issues for the Decade Ahead*, discusses the quality of work, training and retraining, home-based clerical work, and health and safety issues.

* Pilot Schools

U.S. Government Printing Office
Superintendent of Documents
Washington, DC 20402 (202) 783-3238
The *List of Certified Pilot Schools* is an up-to-date directory of pilot training schools in the U.S. It is available for $1.75 from the GPO (#050-007-00763-9).

* Reemployment Help for the Jobless

Office of Employment and Training Programs
Employment and Training Administration
U.S. Department of Labor
200 Constitution Ave., NW, Room N4703
Washington, DC 20210 (202) 535-0577
The Economic Dislocation and Worker Adjustment Assistance Act (EDWAA) provides assistance to dislocated workers whose employment loss means they are unlikely to return to their previous industries or occupations. This includes workers who lose their jobs because of plant closings or mass lay-offs; long-term unemployed persons with limited local opportunities; and farmers, ranchers, and other self-employed persons who become jobless due to general economic conditions or national disasters. EDWAA has a local service-delivery system through which sub-state areas and grantees provide assistance to workers. Major activities and services under EDWAA include: 1) rapid response: the state's Dislocated Worker Unit (DWU) must be alerted to plant closings and mass lay-offs, and responds with on-site services to assist workers facing job losses; 2) retraining services, including basic education, occupational skills and/or on-the-job training; 3) needs-related payments: dislocated workers may receive payments to complete their training once their unemployment insurance is exhausted; and 4) reemployment services, such as job search and placement, and relocation assistance. Contact this office for further information.

* Securities and Exchange Commission Jobs

The Director of Personnel
U.S. Securities and Exchange Commission
450 5th St., NW
Washington, DC 20549 (202) 272-2550
With the exception of the attorney category, positions are in the competitive civil service and are filled generally by selection from lists of eligibles who have taken civil service examinations. The Commission operates a college and law school recruitment program, including on-campus visitations for interview purposes. Inquiries should be directed to this office.

* Skills Needed For Specific Jobs

Superintendent of Documents
Government Printing Office
Washington, DC 20402 (202) 783-3238
Selected Characteristics of Occupations Defined in the Dictionary of Occupational Titles is a supplement to the *Dictionary of Occupational Titles* which can save you time in matching individual skills and qualifications to available positions. It provides information on the training time, the physical demands, and environmental conditions for particular jobs. For more information regarding this publication and other career and occupation publications contact: Office of Public Affairs, Employment and Training Administration, 200 Constitution Ave., NW, Room S2322, Washington, DC 20210; (202) 219-6871.

* Special Help To Workers Laid Off

Office of Trade Adjustment Assistance
Employment and Training Administration
U.S. Department of Labor
601 D St., NW, Room 6434
Washington, DC 20210 (202) 219-5555

Be patient. If any phone number is incorrect, call (area code) 555-1212 and request the new listing.

Career and Job Training Opportunities

The Trade Act of 1974 provides assistance to workers who become totally or partially separated from employment because of increased import competition. Such assistance may consist of training, job search and relocation allowances, special help in finding a new job, and weekly cash benefits equal to the level of regular unemployment compensation payable in the separated worker's state (A worker must exhaust all unemployment insurance benefits available in his state before collecting weekly cash benefits under the Trade Act). Petitioning worker groups may be certified eligible to apply for worker adjustment assistance if the department determines that increased imports of articles like or directly competitive with those produced by the petitioning worker's firm contributed importantly to decreased sales or production and to worker separations.

* State Employment Services for the Unemployed

Employment and Training Administration
U.S. Department of Labor
200 Constitution Ave., NW, Room S2307
Washington, DC 20210 (202) 219-6050

This administration's threefold responsibilities cover: 1) training programs, including the Job Training Partnership Act (JTPA), which prepares unskilled and dislocated workers for productive employment; 2) the network of state employment service offices, which helps place people in jobs; and 3) income maintenance for those who lose their jobs through no fault of their own. Under JTPA alone, more than two million persons are provided employment and training services each year. Federal funds are apportioned to the states, which provide the training and other services, working with local governments, business and industry, labor, education, and nonprofit groups. About 2,200 state employment service offices across the country make over three million job placements annually. For those out of work, state unemployment insurance offices, operating under federal guidelines, provide weekly cash benefits which become an important revenue source in local communities.

* Tomorrow's Jobs in 250 Industries

Office of Economic Growth
Bureau of Labor Statistics
U.S. Department of Labor
601 D St., NW, Room 4000
Washington, DC 20212 (202) 606-5700

This office has information on 250 industries regarding employment requirements, specifically on the demand for employment in the future. Industries covered follow the *1972 Standard Industrial Classification Manual*. The November, 1989, issue of the *Monthly Labor Review* provides an overview of the data available.

* U.S. Merchant Marine Academy

Maritime Administration
U.S. Department of Transportation-Kings Point
Long Island, NY 11024 (516) 773-5000

Future merchant marine officers are trained here in navigation instrumentation, ship maneuvering, ship management, and communications. The Academy also administers a Federal assistance program for maritime academies in California, Maine, Massachusetts, Michigan, New York, and Texas.

* Veterans' Employment and Training Help

Veterans' Employment and Training Service (VETS)
U.S. Department of Labor
200 Constitution Ave., NW, Room S1315
Washington, DC 20210 (202) 219-9116

The Veterans' Employment and Training Service is responsible for administering veterans' employment and training programs and activities through VETS to ensure that legislative and regulatory mandates are accomplished. The field staff of VETS works closely with and provides technical assistance to State Employment Security Agencies and Job Training Partnership Act grant recipients to ensure that veterans are provided the priority services required by law. They also coordinate with employers, labor unions, veterans, service organizations, and community organizations through planned public information and outreach activities.

* Veterans' Reemployment Rights

Veterans' Employment and Training
U.S. Department of Labor
200 Constitution Ave., NW

Room S1313
Washington, DC 20210 (202) 219-9116

The law provides that any employee enlisting in or inducted into the Armed Services, who leaves a position in order to perform military service, will be given back his or her position that he or she otherwise would have achieved had it not been for his or her military service. For more information on qualifications and eligibility, or if you need to register a complaint, contact this office.

* Veterans' Transition Assistance Program

Veterans' Employment and Training
U.S. Department of Labor
200 Constitution Ave., NW
Room S1313
Washington, DC 20210 (202) 219-9116

The veterans Transition Assistance Program was established to meet the needs of active duty servicemembers scheduled for separation by offering them job search assistance. The TAP has been increased due to the downsizing of America's standing forces with the end of the Cold War. TAP workshops provide servicemembers with information on conducting a successful job search, information on career decision-making, a realistic evaluation of employability, current occupational and labor market information, and information on veterans benefits.

* Vocational Job Preparation and Opportunities

Superintendent of Documents
Government Printing Office
Washington, DC 20402 (202) 783-3238

The book, *Vocational Preparation and Occupations*, can help job seekers to apply what they've learned in the classroom to office practices in the workplace. It provides comprehensive and reliable information for approximately 570 vocational programs, describing the physical demands, environmental conditions, and preparation and study time required for a wide variety of occupations. The cost is $21. For more information on career publications contact: Office of Public Affairs, Employment and Training Administration, 200 Constitution Ave., NW, Room S2322, Washington, DC 20210; (202) 219-6871.

* Welfare Recipients: Job Training Programs

Employment and Training Administration
U.S. Department of Labor
200 Constitution Ave., NW, Room N4470
Washington, DC 20210 (202) 535-0174

Under the Work Incentive Program, employment, training, and social supportive services such as child care, housing assistance, medical services, etc., are available to public welfare applicants and recipients in order to enable them to become self-supporting and independent of welfare assistance. All welfare applicants and recipients must register with the WIN program.

* Women in Non-Traditional Careers

Superintendent of Documents
Government Printing Office
Washington, DC 20402 (202) 783-3238

For use by career counselors and educators, *Women in Non-traditional Careers: Journal and Curriculum Guide*, contains a comprehensive selection of ideas, activities, and resources. It can help women to learn more about careers in carpentry, mechanics, printing, engineering, architecture, and other non-traditional fields. Included with the *Guide* is a sample journal which can be used in the classroom to allow women to record their thoughts in diary format. The journal contains questions, facts, and quotes intended to enhance self-understanding with regard to non-traditional roles. The cost is $47.

* Women's Jobs in Highway Construction

Women's Bureau
U.S. Department of Labor
200 Constitution Ave., NW, Room S3309
Washington, DC 20210 (202) 219-6652

Women in Highway Construction, a jointly-funded project of the Women's Bureau, the Employment and Training Administration, and the Federal Highway Administration, will identify the barriers women face in the construction trades and develop a model program to be used by State Highway Departments and highway construction contractors in recruiting and hiring women.

Be patient. If any phone number is incorrect, call (area code) 555-1212 and request the new listing.

Careers and Workplace

* Work-Based Learning

Employment and Training Administration
U.S. Department of Labor
200 Constitution Ave, NW, Room S2322
Washington, DC 20210 (202) 219-6871

America's economic future will increasingly depend on highly skilled workers. In 1987 the U.S. Department of Labor launched an initiative to determine what role the apprenticeship concept might play in raising the skill levels of American workers. The results are summarized in the report *Work Based Learning: Training America's Workers*. It is available free from the U.S. Dept. of Labor.

* Youth Conservation Corps: Conservation

United States Youth Conservation Corps
U.S. Fish and Wildlife Service
National Park Service
Washington, DC 20240 (202) 343-5951

The Park Service's Youth Conservation Corps is a summer employment program for young men and women, ages 15 through 18, who work, learn, and earn wages accomplishing needed conservation work on public lands. The program is also administered by the Forest Service of the U.S. Department of Agriculture. Projects include constructing trails, building campground facilities, planting trees, collecting litter, clearing streams, improving wildlife habitats, and office work. Limited positions are available.

* Youth Conservation Corps: Health Professions

National Health Service Corps Scholarship Program
5600 Fishers Lane, Room 637
Rockville, MD 20857 (301) 443-6354

The National Health Service Corps helps alleviate the shortage of health professionals in geographically isolated or rural areas by offering a loan repayment program. The program pays the participants' lenders up to $20,000 a year toward their qualified health professions education loans during their contracted service periods.

* Youth Conservation Corps Regional Offices

Youth Program Officer
National Park Service
U.S. Department of the Interior
Room 4415, P.O. Box 37127
1100 L St., NW
Washington, DC 20013-7127 (202) 343-5514

Alaska
National Park Service, 2525 Gambell St., Room 107, Anchorage, AK 99503; (907) 257-2698. Serving: Alaska

Mid-Atlantic Region
National Park Service, 143 S. Third St., Philadelphia, PA 19106; (215) 597-5375. Serving: Delaware, Maryland, Pennsylvania, Virginia, and West Virginia

Midwest Region
National Park Service, 1709 Jackson St., Omaha, NE 68102; (402) 221-3995. Serving: Illinois, Indiana, Iowa, Kansas, Minnesota, Michigan, Missouri, Nebraska, Ohio, and Wisconsin

Washington, DC
National Park Service, 1100 Ohio Dr., SW, Washington, DC 20242; (202) 485-9855. Serving: DC, Maryland, and Virginia

North Atlantic Region
National Park Service, 15 State St., Boston, MA 02109; (617) 565-8860. Serving: Maine, Massachusetts, New Hampshire, New Jersey, New York, Rhode Island, Vermont, and Connecticut

Pacific Northwest Region
National Park Service, 83 S. King St., Suite 212, Seattle, WA 98104; (206) 442-1006. Serving: Washington, Oregon, and Idaho

Rocky Mountain Region
National Park Service, 12795 West Alameda Parkway, P.O. Box 25287, Lakewood, CO 80225; (303) 969-2605. Serving: Colorado, Montana, North Dakota, South Dakota, Utah, and Wyoming

Southeast Region
National Park Service, 75 Spring St., SW, Atlanta, GA 30303; (404) 331-4290. Serving: Alabama, Florida, Georgia, Tennessee, Mississippi, Kentucky, North Carolina, South Carolina, Puerto Rico, and the Virgin Islands

Southwest Region
National Park Service, P.O. Box 728, Santa Fe, NM 87504; (505) 988-6371. Serving: Arkansas, Louisiana, New Mexico, Oklahoma, and Texas

Western Region
National Park Service, 450 Golden Gate Ave., Box 3603, San Francisco, CA 94102; (415) 556-1866. Serving: Arizona, California, Nevada, and Guam

Be patient. If any phone number is incorrect, call (area code) 555-1212 and request the new listing.

Employee Benefits and Rights

Pension plans, lie detector tests, affirmative action, and many other issues of worker protection are covered here. With these sources you'll be able to find out how your employee benefits compare with thousands of others across the country, how to protect your pension, or even how to contest the findings of a lie detector test. Additional sources on union grievance procedures and rights are included in the next section on Labor-Management Cooperation.

* Affirmative Action of Handicapped Persons

Office of Federal Compliance Programs
Employment Standards Administration
U.S. Department of Labor
200 Constitution Ave., NW, Room C3325
Washington, DC 20210 (202) 219-9475

The Rehabilitation Act of 1973 prohibits most employers doing business with the federal government from discriminating in employment against handicapped persons. Employers with contracts in excess of $2,500 must take affirmative action to hire and promote qualified handicapped persons.

* Age or Pay Discrimination

Equal Employment Opportunity Commission
1801 L Street, NW (800) 669-EEOC
Washington, DC 20507 (202) 663-4395

Discrimination on the basis of age is illegal under the 1964 Civil Rights Act. In addition, it is illegal to differentiate pay scales on the basis of sex for the same work. For information or to file a complaint, contact the EEOC.

* Child Labor Laws

Child Labor Programs
Employment Standards Administration
200 Constitution Ave., NW, Room S3510
Washington, DC 20210 (202) 219-7640

The Fair Labor Standards Act protects young workers from employment that might interfere with their educational opportunities or be hazardous to their health or well-being. There are different standards for work allowed, depending upon the age of the child. Contact the Child Labor Programs office for more information.

* Coal Miners' Benefits

Coal Mine Workers' Compensation Division
Employment Standards Administration
U.S. Department of Labor
200 Constitution Ave., NW, Room C3526
Washington, DC 20210 (202) 219-6795

Benefits are available for medical treatment and monthly payments to coal miners totally disabled from pneumoconiosis (black lung) arising from employment in the nation's coal mines. There are also benefits for the miner's dependents and to certain survivors of miners who died while totally disabled from pneumoconiosis. A copy of the *Black Lung Benefits Act* is available by contacting this office.

* Disabilities Discrimination

Equal Employment Opportunity Commission
1801 L Street, NW (800) 669-EEOC
Washington, DC 20507 (202) 663-4395

Title I of the Americans with Disabilities Act of 1990, prohibits private employers, state and local governments, employment agencies and labor unions from discriminating against qualified individuals with disabilities in job application procedures, hiring, firing, advancement, compensation, job training, and other terms, conditions and privileges of employment. For more information or to file a complaint, contact the EEOC.

* Employee Benefits National Survey

Office of Compensation Levels and Trends
Bureau of Labor Statistics
U.S. Department of Labor
441 G Street, NW
Room 2021
Washington, DC 20212 (202) 606-6300

This office conducts an annual survey of employers in the private sector and sample data on the incidence and characteristics of employee benefit plans. Data available include incidence and detailed characteristics of 11 private sector employee benefits paid for, at least in part, by the employer. The data are presented separately for three occupational groups: professional-administrative; technical-clerical; and production workers.

* Employee Pay and Benefits Cost Index

Office of Compensation and Working Conditions
Bureau of Labor Statistics
U.S. Department of Labor
441 G St., NW, Room 2026
Washington, DC 20212 (202) 606-6200

The quarterly *Employment Cost Index* measures changes in total compensation (wages, salaries, and employer costs for employee benefits) in wages and salaries only. Coverage includes all private industry and state and local government workers, but excludes Federal government, farm, household, self-employed, proprietors, and unpaid family workers.

* Employee Protection on Garnishing Wages

Wage-Hour Division
Employment Standards Administration
U.S. Department of Labor
200 Constitution Ave., NW
Room 3502
Washington, DC 20210 (202) 219-8305

The Federal Wage Garnishment Law limits the amount of an employee's disposable earnings which may be withheld in any one week by an employer to satisfy creditors. "Disposable Earnings" means that part of an employee's earnings remaining after deduction of any amount required by law. This law does not apply to bankruptcy court orders and debts for state and federal taxes. This law also prohibits an employer from discharging an employee whose earnings have been subjected to garnishment for any one indebtedness. Contact this office for more information on wage garnishments.

* Employee Whistleblower Abuse and Waste Hotline

Inspector General's Office
U.S. Department of Commerce
14th St. and Constitution Ave., NW
Room 7898C (800) 424-5197
Washington DC 20230 (202) 377-2495

This hotline was established so that consumers and employees could report fraud, abuse, or waste within any office in the U.S. Department of Commerce. All reports are investigated and reports can be made anonymously. The Pentagon, HUD, and other government departments also have whistleblower hotlines.

Be patient. If any phone number is incorrect, call (area code) 555-1212 and request the new listing.

Careers and Workplace

* Employer's and Employee's Pension Guides

Public Affairs
Pension Benefit Guaranty Corporation
2020 K Street, NW
Room 7100
Washington, DC 20006-1860 (202) 778-8840

This office will provide you with the following publications free of charge:

Employer's Pension Guide. This is a cooperative project of the Pension and Welfare Benefits Administration of the U.S. Department of Labor, the Internal Revenue Service, and the Pension Benefit Guaranty Corporation to provide a general overview of the responsibilities under federal law of employers who sponsor single-employer defined benefit pension plans. It describes federal pension law effective as of 1989. However, it is not intended to be, nor is it, all-inclusive; for specific legal or technical information, consult these federal agencies or a private sector employee benefits specialist.

Your Guaranteed Pension. This booklet answers some of the most frequently asked questions about the Pension Benefit Guaranty Corporation and its termination insurance program for single-employer defined benefit pension plans. The answers in it apply to pension plan terminations taking place in 1989. For terminations that occurred in previous years, different rules may apply.

Your Pension: Things You Should Know About Your Pension Plan. This publication is intended to serve as a handy explanation of pension plans; what they are, how they operate, and the rights and options of participants. It should not be relied upon for information about your specific pension plan. That information should be obtained from your Plan Administrator or the Summary Plan Description of your pension plan.

* Equal Employment Opportunity

Office of Federal Contract Compliance Programs
Employment Standards Administration
U.S. Department of Labor
200 Constitution Ave., NW
Room N3424
Washington, DC 20210 (202) 219-9428

Executive Order 11246 requires that equal opportunity be provided for all persons without regard to race, color, religion, sex or national origin, employed or seeking employment with Government contractors or subcontractors. It also applies to construction contractors who are performing on construction projects being built with Federal financial assistance. Contact the above office for more information.

* Farm Worker Protection and Rights

Farm Labor Programs
Employment Standards Administration
U.S. Department of Labor
200 Constitution Ave., NW, Room S3510
Washington, DC 20210 (202) 219-7605

The Migrant and Seasonal Agricultural Workers Protection Act requires agricultural employers, agricultural associations, and farm labor contractors to observe certain labor standards when employing migrant and seasonal agricultural workers, unless exemptions apply. Certain persons and organizations, such as family businesses, small businesses, some seed and tobacco operations, labor unions, and their employees, are exempt. MSPA requires farm labor contractors to register with the U.S. Department of Labor. Contact this office for more information about the Act and for a list of workers' rights.

* Federal Wage-Hour Standards

Program Development and Research Division
Employment Standards Administration
U.S. Department of Labor
200 Constitution Ave., NW, Room 3319
Washington, DC 20210 (202) 219-8288

This division conducts research on the major programs within the Employment Standards Administration. Within the Wage-Hour Division, research is conducted on the provisions of the Fair Labor Standards Act and the Davis-Bacon Act. Within the Workers' Compensation Programs, they look into the provisions of the Federal Employees' Compensation Act, and publish annual reports concerning the Longshoremen and Black Lung Benefits Acts. They also conduct research on federal contract compliance.

* Foreigners and Work Permits

Labor Certification Division
Employment Service
Employment and Training Administration
U.S. Department of Labor
200 Constitution Ave., NW, Room N4456
Washington, DC 20210 (202) 219-0163

If an employer wishes to hire foreign workers, he must first obtain a foreign labor certificate, which is a statement from the U.S. Department of Labor stating that there is no U.S. citizen available to fill the job. The U.S. Department investigates to make sure that the wages and working conditions of the foreign workers will not seriously affect the wages and working conditions of U.S. workers. An employer applies for a foreign labor certificate through the local state employment service office, which then conducts a job hunt before sending the application form to the area regional office for approval or disapproval.

* Formal Labor Complaints

Office of the General Counsel
National Labor Relations Board
1717 Pennsylvania Ave., NW, Room 1001
Washington, DC 20570 (202) 254-9150

The General Counsel issues and prosecutes formal complaints before the National Labor Relations Board.

* Freedom on Information Act Requests

Disclosure Officer
Pension Benefit Guaranty Corporation
2020 K St., NW
Washington, DC 20006-1860 (202) 778-8839

Contact the office above for Freedom of Information Act requests.

* Garnishment of Wages

Wage-Hour Division
U.S. Department of Labor
200 Constitution Ave., NW, Room S3014
Washington, DC 20210 (202) 219-7451

The Federal Wage Garnishment Law limits the amount of an employee's disposable earnings which may be withheld in any one week by an employer to satisfy creditors. The law also prohibits an employer from discharging an employee whose earnings have been subjected to garnishment for any one indebtedness.

* Handicapped Workers

Office of Federal Contract Compliance Programs
Employment Standards Administration
U.S. Department of Labor
200 Constitution Ave., NW, Room N3424
Washington, DC 20210 (202) 219-9428

Under the Rehabilitation Act of 1973 Government Contractors and subcontractors are required to take affirmative action to employ and advance employment of qualified handicapped individuals.

* Job Counseling and Placement Fraud

Federal Trade Commission
Bureau of Consumer Protection
6th and Pennsylvania Ave., NW
Washington, DC 20580 (202) 326-3650

The FTC often receives complaint letters about job counseling and placement services which charge large fees and misrepresent their services. For information on how to select a legitimate employment service or to complain about one which you feel has misrepresented itself, contact your local FTC office.

* Lie Detector Testing

Wage and Hour Division
Employment Standards Administration
U.S. Department of Labor
200 Constitution Ave., NW, Room S3502
Washington, DC 20210 (202) 219-8305

The Employee Polygraph Protection Act prohibits most private employers from

Be patient. If any phone number is incorrect, call (area code) 555-1212 and request the new listing.

Employee Benefits and Rights

using lie detector tests either for pre-employment screening or during the course of employment. Federal, State, and local government employers are exempted for the Act. The law provides several limited exemptions which permit the use of polygraph tests. For more information on the law and the use of polygraphs, contact this office.

* Longshore and Harbor Workers Benefits

Longshore and Harbor Worker's
Compensation Division
U.S. Department of Labor
200 Constitution Ave., NW, Room C4315
Washington, DC 20210 (202) 219-8572

The Longshore and Harbor Worker's Compensation Act covers all maritime workers for job-related injury, illness, or death on the navigable waters of the U.S., as well as employees working on adjoining piers, docks, and terminals. Compensation is paid by insurance carriers or by employers who are self-insured.

* Minorities/Women in Management

Program Development and Research Division
Employment Standards Administration
U.S. Department of Labor
200 Constitution Ave., NW, Room 3319
Washington, DC 20210 (202) 219-8288

The *Report on the Glass Ceiling Initiative* was released in August 1991. This study sought to identify artificial barriers that prevent women and minorities from advancing to mid and upper level management positions in the corporate world and to determine how such barriers could be removed. Information on the study and its findings are available from the Employment Standards Administration.

* National Origin or Religious Discrimination

Equal Employment Opportunity Commission
1801 L Street, NW (800) 669-EEOC
Washington, DC 20507 (202) 663-4395

Discrimination on the basis of national origin or religious orientation is illegal under the 1964 Civil Rights Act. For information or to file a complaint, contact the EEOC.

* Pension and Retirement Audits

Office of the Chief Accountant
Pension and Welfare Benefits Administration
U.S. Department of Labor
200 Constitution Ave., NW, Room N5677
Washington, DC 20210 (202) 219-8951

This office serves as the U.S. Department of Labor's primary advisor on accounting, auditing, and actuarial issues stemming from its responsibilities under the Employee Retirement Income Security Act and the Federal Employees' Retirement System Act. It serves as the primary agency contact with accounting and actuarial organizations, as well as with federal and state agencies on accounting matters. It also administers a comprehensive system of compliance audits under FERSA and reviews annual financial reports.

* Pension Benefit Annual Report

Public Affairs
Pension Benefit Guaranty Corporation (PBGC)
2020 K St., NW, Room 7100
Washington, DC 20006-1860 (202) 778-8840

This publication contains information on PBGC, including financial statements and an actuarial report. To obtain a copy contact the office above.

* Pension Benefits

Office of Research and Economic Analysis
Pension and Welfare Benefits Administration
U.S. Department of Labor
200 Constitution Ave., NW, Room N5647
Washington, DC 20210 (202) 219-9421

This office can provide you with a list of reports prepared under contract to the U.S. Department of Labor concerning pensions. Some of the more recent studies include pension plan terminations with asset reversions, study of the investment performance of ERISA plans, and the effect of job mobility on pension plans.

* Pension Failure Early Warning

Coverage and Inquiries Branch
Insurance Operations U.S. Department
Pension Benefit Guaranty Corporation
2020 K St., NW
Washington, DC 20006-1860 (202) 778-8800

An "early warning system" is provided under the Employee Retirement Income Security Act (ERISA) of 1974, which requires that PBGC be notified within 30 days if an insured pension plan or plan sponsor is experiencing certain problems. Contact this office for more information. This notice is intended to provide PBGC with an opportunity to determine whether action is necessary to protect the interests of either the plan participants or the pension insurance program. PBGC may assess a penalty of up to $1,000 a day for failure to provide such required information. Contact the office above for more information including information on filing reportable events.

* Pension Insurance Premiums

Coverage and Inquiries Branch
Insurance Operations U.S. Department
Pension Benefit Guaranty Corporation
2020 K St., NW
Washington, DC 20006-1860 (202) 778-8800

PBGC's insurance is financed by premiums paid by covered plans or employers sponsoring these plans, and employer liability owed to PBGC when underfunded plans terminate. The PBGC administers two pension insurance programs: the single-employer program and the multiemployer program. Under the single-employer program, a company can voluntarily terminate its plan using either a standard termination procedure or a distress termination procedure. In addition, the PBGC may seek termination of a plan when necessary to protect the interests of the plan participants, of the plan, or of the PBGC. The PBGC must seek plan termination when a plan cannot pay current benefits. Multiemployer pension plans are maintained under collectively-bargained agreements between employee representatives and two or more unrelated employers. If a PBGC-insured multiemployer plan becomes insolvent, it receives financial assistance from the PBGC, thus enabling the plan to pay participants their guaranteed benefits. Contact the office above for more information.

* Pension Plan Financial Statements

Financial Operations U.S. Department
Pension Benefit Guaranty Corporation
2020 K St., NW, Room 6000
Washington, DC 20006-1860 (202) 778-8801

Contact the office above to obtain information on the PBGC combined financial statements which include the assets and liabilities of all defined benefit pension plans for which the Corporation is trustee.

* Pension Plan Insurance Coverage

Coverage and Inquiries Branch
Insurance Operations U.S. Department
Pension Benefit Guaranty Corporation
2020 K St., NW
Washington, DC 20006-1860 (202) 778-8800

For additional information or assistance on the single-employer defined benefit pension plan insurance program, or on defined benefit plan terminations, contact the office above.

* Pension Plans: Disclosure Requirements

Public Disclosure Room
Pension and Welfare Benefits Administration
U.S. Department of Labor
200 Constitution Ave., NW, Room N5507
Washington, DC 20210 (202) 219-8771

If you are covered by a pension plan and/or a welfare benefit plan, the administrator of your plan must give you a summary plan description (SPD), written in a manner easily understood, which provides information about eligibility, benefits, and procedures. Plan administrators also are required to provide you with a summary of any important changes in the SPD; a summary of the annual report that is filed with the Internal Revenue Service; a statement of accrued and vested benefits when you leave employment or have a break in service; and a written explanation if your claim for benefits has been denied. Administrators file copies of the SPD and certain other reports with the U.S. Department of Labor and are available to the public.

Be patient. If any phone number is incorrect, call (area code) 555-1212 and request the new listing.

Careers and Workplace

* Pension Plans Publications

Division of Public Information
Pension and Welfare Benefits Administration
U.S. Department of Labor
200 Constitution Ave., NW, Room N5666
Washington, DC 20210 (202) 219-8921

The publications listed below are available free of charge from this office:

What You Should Know About the Pension Law
How to File a Claim for Your Benefit
Your Pension
Often-Asked Questions About Employee Retirement Benefits
Trouble-Shooter's Guide to Filing the ERISA Annual Reports
Know Your Pension Plan
How to Obtain Employee Benefit Documents From the Labor U.S. Department
Reporting and Disclosure Guide for Employee Benefit Plans
Summary Plan Description Requirements Under ERISA
The Prudence Rule and Pension Plan Investments Under ERISA
Fiduciary Standards: Employee Retirement Income Security Act
Exemptions From ERISA Prohibited Transactions Provision
ERISA Reports to Congress
U.S. Department of Labor Highlights
PWBA Fact Sheets
PWBA: Administering The Pension and Welfare Law
A Brief Look at Pension Plan Charges Under the Tax Reform Act of 1986

* Pension Protection and Retirement Equity

Pension and Welfare Administration
U.S. Department of Labor
200 Constitution Ave., NW, Room N5666
Washington, DC 20210 (202) 219-8921

The Retirement Equity Act of 1984 was designed to provide greater pension equity for women and for all workers and their spouses by taking into account changes in work patterns and marriage as an economic partnership. The new provisions lower the age for earning pension credits, provides for leaves of absences from work, and allow for greater benefits relating to marriage. Contact this office for further information.

* Pension Public Records

Disclosure Officer
Pension Benefit Guaranty Corporation
2020 K St., NW, Room 7100
Washington, DC 20006-1860 (202) 778-8839

Trusteeship plans, opinion letters, opinion manuals, litigation, termination case data sheets, and case log terminating plans updated quarterly are available for inspection from the office above. Also, *Annual Premium Reports* on microfilm filed by pension plans may be inspected. Contact the office above.

* Pension Terminations

Coverage and Inquiries Branch
Insurance Operations U.S. Department
Pension Benefit Guaranty Corporation
2020 K St., NW
Washington, DC 20006-1860 (202) 778-8800

Employers may end ("terminate") a defined benefit pension plan, but only if they meet safeguards designed to protect the plan participants. This can be accomplished either through a standard termination or a distress termination. In addition, PBGC may take action to terminate a plan if certain statutory criteria are met. PBGC encourages employers who are considering plan termination to explore alternatives that may enable them to preserve the plan and avoid benefit losses for their employees. Such alternatives may include "freezing" a plan or continuing to maintain and fund a plan although the facility has been shut down and its employees laid off. Employers should consult with private employee benefit specialists, the IRS, or PBGC for more information on these and other alternatives.

* Pension Trusteeships

Coverage and Inquiries Branch
Insurance Operations U.S. Department
Pension Benefit Guaranty Corporation
2020 K St., NW
Washington, DC 20006-1860 (202) 778-8800

If a plan qualifies for distress termination and can pay all of its benefit liabilities, PBGC will authorize the plan administrator to distribute the assets and complete the termination as in a standard termination. If the plan cannot pay all of its benefit liabilities, the plan administrator may be authorized to distribute the assets or PBGC may become trustee of the plan, either by agreement with the plan administrator or by order of a U.S. District Court. As trustee, PBGC will acquire the plan's records and assets, if any, as well as responsibility for benefit payments. PBGC will use its insurance funds to the extent necessary to pay the plan participants their guaranteed benefits. The plan's sponsor and its controlled group then become liable to PBGC for unpaid contributions and for unfunded benefit liabilities. Contact the office above for further information.

* Pregnancy Discrimination

Equal Employment Opportunity Commission
1801 L Street, NW
Washington, DC 20507 (202) 663-4395

Discrimination on the basis of pregnancy, childbirth or related medical conditions constitutes unlawful sex discrimination under Title VII of the 1964 Civil Rights Act. Women affected by pregnancy or related conditions must be treated in the same manner as other applicants or employees with similar limitations or abilities. For more information or to file a complaint, contact the EEOC.

* Private Pension and Welfare Protection

Pension and Welfare Benefits Administration
U.S. Department of Labor
200 Constitution Ave., NW, Room N5666
Washington, DC 20210 (202) 219-8921

The Retirement Equity Act (1984) is designed to provide greater pension equity for women and for all workers and their spouses. It liberalizes such rules as those affecting participation, vesting, break in service, joint-and-survivor annuity, and alienation and assignment of benefits. This new law also protects the benefits of millions of workers and their beneficiaries in private pension plans and sets minimum standards to protect the interest of participant and their beneficiaries. Contact this office for more information.

* Railroad Retirement

Railroad Retirement Board
844 North Rush Street
Chicago, IL 60611-2092 (312) 751-4777

The Railroad Retirement Board (RRB) is an independent federal agency whose primary function is to administer comprehensive retirement-survivor and unemployment-sickness benefit programs for the nation's railroad workers and their families, under the Railroad Retirement and Railroad Unemployment and Insurance Acts. RRB publications include: *Annual Reports, Pocket Guide to Railroad Retirement Benefits; Federal Income Tax and Railroad Retirement Benefits; Medicare for Railroad Workers and Their Families; Railroad Unemployment and Sickness Insurance Benefits; Railroad Retirement Handbook; Monthly Benefits Statistics; RRB News;* and *Railroad Retirement Information.* For further information or publications, contact the RRB.

* Sexual Harassment

Equal Employment Opportunity Commission
1801 L Street, NW (800) 669-EEOC
Washington, DC 20507 (202) 663-4395

Unwelcome sexual advances, requests for sexual favors, and other verbal or physical conduct of a sexual nature constitute sexual harassment when submission to or rejection of this conduct explicitly or implicitly affects an individual's employment, unreasonably interferes with an individual's work performance or creates an intimidating, hostile or offensive work environment. This type of behavior violates Title VII of the Civil Rights Act of 1964. For more information or to file a complaint, contact the EEOC.

* Statistical History of Pension Claims

Corporate Policy and Research U.S. Department
Pension Benefit Guaranty Corporation
2020 K St., NW, Room 7300
Washington, DC 20006-1860 (202) 778-8851

Contact the office above to obtain information on pension liabilities guaranteed by the PBGC which includes assets of terminated plans, statutory employer liability, and the resulting net claims.

Be patient. If any phone number is incorrect, call (area code) 555-1212 and request the new listing.

Employee Benefits and Rights

* Transit System Employee Protection

Office of Labor-Management Programs
Bureau of Labor-Management Relations
U.S. Department of Labor
200 Constitution Ave., NW, Room N5416
Washington, DC 20210   (202) 219-4473

Federal law requires that arrangements be made to protect the rights of transit system employees when a state or local body uses federal funds to acquire or improve that system. This requirement is one of several laws administered by the U.S. Department of Labor to protect specific employees who might be adversely affected by a federal program. The protective arrangements must include preservation of rights, privileges, and benefits under existing collective bargaining agreements, continuation of collective bargaining rights, protection of individual employees against a worsening of their positions, assurances of employment and priority of reemployment, and paid training or retraining programs. An employee who believes he or she has been adversely affected as a result of federal transit assistance can make a claim with the U.S. Department of Labor.

* Unemployment Insurance and Reemployment

Demonstration Project
Unemployment Insurance Service
Employment and Training Administration
U.S. Department of Labor
200 Constitution Ave., NW, Room S4231
Washington, DC 20210   (202) 219-7831

The Employment and Training Administration has begun to review a number of nontraditional approaches to the Unemployment Insurance system. These alternative approaches involve several demonstration projects and include the following reemployment services: job search assistance, referral to training, relocation assistance, monetary incentives to search for work faster, and grants for self-employment. For more information about these projects, contact this office.

* Unemployment Insurance Help

Employment and Training Administration
U.S. Department of Labor
200 Constitution Ave., NW, Room S4231
Washington, DC 20210   (202) 219-7831

Unemployment Insurance programs provide limited compensation to workers who lose their jobs through no fault of their own. The Federal government establishes guidelines and pays state administrative costs from funds collected under the Federal Unemployment Tax Act, and the states operate the program under these guidelines. Claimants must be able to work, available to work, and seeking work.

* Unemployment Insurance Laws: State Comparisons

Superintendent of Documents
Government Printing Office
Washington, DC 20402   (202) 783-3238

The Comparison of State Unemployment Insurance Laws analyzes State unemployment insurance statutes. It provides text and tables on coverage, taxation, benefits, eligibility, administration of program, and temporary disability benefits. A three year subscription is available for $32. For more information on the laws contact: Unemployment Insurance, Employment and Training Administration, U.S. Department of Labor, 200 Constitution Ave., NW, Room C4512, Washington, DC 20210; (202) 219-0200.

* Unemployment Insurance Surveys

Office of Legislation and Actuarial Services
Employment and Training Administration
U.S. Department of Labor
200 Constitution Ave., NW, Room S4519
Washington, DC 20210   (202) 219-0630

The *UI Data Summary* is produced quarterly from state-reported data contained in the Unemployment Insurance Data Base, as well as UI-related data from outside sources. This report is intended to provide the user with a quick overview of the status of the unemployment insurance system at the national and state levels. Tables are provided for each state, and many data items are repeated on summary tables.

* Veteran Reemployment Rights

Veterans Employment and Training
U.S. Department of Labor
200 Constitution Ave., NW, Room S1313
Washington, DC 20210   (202) 219-9116

The law provides that any employee enlisting in or inducted into the Armed Services, who leaves a position in order to perform military service, will be given back his or her position that he or she otherwise would have achieved had it not been for his or her military service. For more information on qualifications and eligibility, or if you need to register a complaint, contact this office.

* Veteran Job Training Program

Assistant Secretary For Veterans
Employment and Training
U.S. Department of Labor
200 Constitution Ave., NW, Room S1313
Washington, DC 20210   (202) 219-9110

Employment-related services designed to aid veterans include counseling, testing, and skills training; unemployment compensation for newly separated ex-service members while they look for civilian employment; tax credits for private employers who hire certain target groups of veterans; placement in private and public sector jobs; and reemployment rights assistance. For more information, contact the Veterans Employment and Training Office.

* Vietnam and Disabled Vets Job Placement

Veterans Employment and Training
U.S. Department of Labor
200 Constitution Ave., NW, Room S1313
Washington, DC 20210   (202) 219-9110

Federal government contractors and subcontractors (with government contracts of $10,000 or more) are required by law to take affirmative action to employ and to advance in employment qualified special disabled and Vietnam-era Veterans. All suitable employment openings must be given to the nearest local State Employment Office. A Veterans Employment and Training Representative is located in each office to provide employment advice and assistance to veterans. Contact the Office of Federal Contract Compliance Programs if it appears that a contractor has failed to comply. Complaints can be made to: Office of Federal Contract Compliance Programs, U.S. Department of Labor, 200 Constitution Ave., NW, Room C3325, Washington, DC 20210; (202) 219-9475.

* Workers' Compensation for Federal Employees

Federal Employees' Compensation Division
Office of Workers' Compensation Programs
Employment Standards Administration
U.S. Department of Labor
200 Constitution Ave., NW, Room S3229
Washington, DC 20210   (202) 219-7552

This office can provide you with a variety of free publications which explain the Federal Employees' Compensation Act, claim forms for work-related disabilities or deaths, as well as checklists for evidence required in support of claims for occupational diseases, such as work-related coronary illness, pulmonary disease, and hearing loss. *Federal Injury Compensation* is a free publication which lists questions and answers regarding the Federal Employees' Compensation Act. Contact this office for a list of publications, and further information.

Be patient. If any phone number is incorrect, call (area code) 555-1212 and request the new listing.

Careers and Workplace

Labor-Management Relations

Reducing tensions between management and workers and improving the quality of worklife are emerging issues for companies nationwide. Here you will find all kinds of information on such issues as collective bargaining agreements, union contracts, cooperative workshops, and pending legislation. You can find additional sources on productivity, one of the underlying goals of labor-management cooperation, in the Business and Industry chapter.

* Alternative Dispute Resolution

Federal Mediation and Conciliation Service (FMCS)
2100 K St., NW
Washington, DC 20427 (202) 653-5300

The term "Alternative Dispute Resolution" is used to describe a variety of approaches that are alternatives to courtroom or agency adjudication and rulemaking. Under the Administrative Disputes Resolution Act of 1990 (PL 101-552), FMCS was officially authorized to share its expertise in all aspects of dispute resolution with federal agencies, including third-party dispute resolution assistance; dispute resolution training for agency personnel; and consultation systems design. A one day "awareness" workshop which explores the various ADR techniques of negotiation, mediation, fact finding, settlement, judges, facilitation, mini-trials, arbitration, negotiated rule-making, and consensual decision-making. This workshop includes a combination of lecture, discussions, exercises, and mock mediations. Call the FMCS for more information.

* Arbitrators and Mediators

Federal Mediation and Conciliation Service (FMCS)
2100 K St., NW
Washington, DC 20427 (202) 653-5300

Through its regional offices and suboffices, FMCS assists federal agencies, private sector employers, and labor organizations in resolving labor-management disputes. When there is no local or state resource available, the parties involved may contact the regional FMCS office to be assigned a qualified mediator or arbitrator, on call 24 hours a day. Upon request, mediators will assist the parties in resolving disputes, and arbitrators will make a final decision. Technical assistance includes training for one or both parties in developing constructive methods of dispute resolution, help in forming committees, and collective bargaining workshops. Contact your local FMCS office for any of these services.

* Case Processing of Worker Grievances

Management and Information Systems Branch
National Labor Relations Board (NLRB)
1717 Pennsylvania Ave, NW
Room 393
Washington, DC 20570 (202) 634-4124

This service monitors all NLRB cases from their initial filing to their final resolution. Information regarding regional cases is tabulated and detailed in reports issued periodically to Board members for their use only. Summaries and statistical tables regarding these cases are published in the Annual Report available from the U.S. Government Printing Office.

* Collective Bargaining Agreements and Case Files

Office of Research and Information Management
National Mediation Board
1425 K Street, NW
Room 910
Washington, DC 20572 (202) 357-0466

The public may inspect copies of collective bargaining agreements between labor and management of rail and air carriers at this office. Copies of awards and interpretations issued by the National Railroad Adjustment Board are also available. Write or visit the office listed above to access copies of collective bargaining agreements. Some National Railroad Adjustment Board documents may require a Freedom of Information Act request. Submit FOIA requests to the National Mediation Board at above address, telephone (202) 523-5996.

* Collective Bargaining Annual Report

Office of Public Affairs
Federal Mediation and Conciliation Service (FMCS)
2100 K St., NW, Room 909
Washington, DC 20427 (202) 653-5290

Booklets about collective bargaining, arbitration, and mediation in the private, federal, State, and local sectors are available from this office. The *FMCS Annual Report* summarizes major negotiations and important developments of the year. To obtain these publications and for further information, contact Public Affairs.

* Collective Bargaining Units

Division of Information
National Labor Relations Board (NLRB)
1717 Pennsylvania Ave., NW, Room 710
Washington, DC 20570 (202) 632-4950

A bargaining unit, in general, is a group of two or more employees whose mutual interests form a reasonable basis for collective bargaining. The National Labor Relations Board is responsible for determining units appropriate for collective bargaining purposes. Questions concerning bargaining units should be directed to this office, or to the regional office in the area where the employee unit is located.

* Cooperative and Employee Involvement Programs

Information Office
Bureau of Labor-Management Relations
U.S. Department of Labor
200 Constitution Ave., NW, Room N5419
Washington, DC 20210 (202) 219-6098

Film/Video Sourcebook for Cooperative and Employee Involvement Programs covers films and videotapes which deal directly with cooperative and employee involvement programs. It does not include films on motivation, behavior, supervision, or self-training. Description and distribution information accompanies each listing. Contact this office for your free copy.

* Cooperative Labor-Management Clearinghouse

Information Office
Bureau of Labor-Management Relations
U.S. Department of Labor
200 Constitution Ave., NW, Room N5402
Washington, DC 20210 (202) 219-6481

The Bureau has developed a national information clearinghouse to help with the exchange of information among employers, unions, and others interested to joint labor-management programs, and innovative workplace practices. A computerized database contains basic information on programs operating in a variety of firms and organizations in the private and public sectors, including the names of individuals in these organizations who can provide additional information. Listings from the clearinghouse are available to all interested parties upon request. Database information can be accessed easily according to type of industry and employer size, geographic area, program type/features, program scope and workplace issues addressed, union involvement and year program began.

* Employer/Union Cooperative Efforts

Superintendent of Documents
Government Printing Office
Washington, DC 20402 (202) 783-3238

Be patient. If any phone number is incorrect, call (area code) 555-1212 and request the new listing.

Labor-Management Relations

The Bureau of Labor Statistics publishes *Labor-Management Cooperation: Recent Efforts and Results* describes the kinds of problems employers and unions face and illustrates some of the cooperative strategies adopted in seeking solutions ($6).

This program provides grants to support the establishment and operation of joint labor-management committees in public and private sectors. Labor-management committees operate at the plant level, on a community or area wide basis, within a particular industry, and in public sector organizations at various levels. Contact the FMCS for more information on getting involved in this program.

* Employers Register with OLMS

Office of Labor-Management Standards
U.S. Department of Labor
200 Constitution Ave., NW, Room S2203
Washington, DC 20210 — (202) 219-8174

This register contains the names of companies and individuals which have filed employer reports with OLMS from 159 to 1986. It includes the city and state in which the employer is located, the file number assigned by OLMS, and last fiscal year for which the employer filed an LM-10 report.

* Labor Practices in Federal Service

Public Information Office
Federal Labor Relations Authority (FLRA)
500 C St., SW
Washington, DC 20424 — (202) 382-0711

Contact this office to obtain a copy of the *FLRA Annual Report*, which describes significant decisions of the FLRA and case processing statistics of the General Counsel of the Authority. Cases of alleged unfair labor practices in federal service are investigated and prosecuted by the General Counsel and are heard by the FLRA's Office of Administrative Law Judges.

* Federal Labor Relations Documents

Office of Case Control
Federal Labor Relations Authority (FLRA)
500 C St., SW
Washington, DC 20424 — (202) 382-0748

Case file information is maintained on FLRA hearings and cases prosecuted to ensure compliance with the rights and obligations of federal employees to organize, bargain collectively, and participate in labor organizations. To view FLRA case dockets and decisions, call ahead to this office to arrange for a visit.

* Labor Union Regulations

Office of Labor-Management Standards
U.S. Department of Labor
200 Constitution Ave., NW, Room S1032
Washington, DC 20210 — (202) 219-7343

Labor-Management Standard is a newsletter sent to approximately 200 international unions, informing the union presidents about OLMS compliance assistance and enforcement programs. As part of the publication, OLMS includes *Labor-Management Reporting and Disclosure Act Compliance Tips*, which are detachable sheets that can be distributed to affiliated locals to assist them in complying with various LMRDA provisions.

* Federal Labor Relations Authority Publications

Public Information Office
Federal Labor Relations Authority (FLRA)
500 C St., SW
Washington, DC 20424 — (202) 382-0711

The Federal Labor Relations Authority has several free publications available including the following: *Federal Service Labor-Management Statute; A Guide to the Federal Service Labor-Management Relations Statute;* and the *Annual Report of the Federal Labor Relations Authority* and the *Federal Services Impasses Panel.*

* Mediation Board Publications

Office of Executive Secretary
National Mediation Board
1425 K St., NW, Room 910
Washington, DC 20572 — (202) 523-5920

There are three annual subscription mailing lists available from the Board. Costs may be reduced or waived when it is in the public interest to do so.

Subscription List #1, $175: *Annual Reports of the NMB; Certifications and Dismissals; Determination of Craft or Class; Findings Upon Investigation; Emergency Board Reports*

Subscription List #2, $ 50: *Annual Reports of the NMB; Emergency Board Reports; Determination of Craft or Class*

Subscription List #3, $ 35: *The Representation Manual* and amendments

* Federal Labor Relations Freedom of Information

Public Information Office
Federal Labor Relations Authority (FLRA)
500 C St., SW
Washington, DC 20424 — (202) 382-0711

The Public Information Office listed above is the Freedom of Information Act contact for the Authority.

* Mediation Cases

Legal Services Office
Federal Mediation and Conciliation Service (FMCS)
2100 K St., NW, Room 712
Washington, DC 20427 — (202) 653-5305

This office represents FMCS in legal cases. In unusually complex and technical mediation efforts, Legal Services staff participate as part of the mediation team. Contact this office for more information on labor-management conciliation cases.

* Federal Labor Relations Library

Library
Federal Labor Relations Authority (FLRA)
500 C St., SW, Room 235
Washington, DC 20424 — (202) 382-0765

A small specialized collection is housed here. Material covers federal service labor-management relations and the Federal Labor Relations Authority. The library is open to the public, but due to tight security in the building, you are advised to call ahead for an appointment.

* Mediation National Board Freedom of Information

National Mediation Board
1425 K St., NW
Washington, DC 20572 — (202) 523-5996

This office handles Freedom of Information Act requests regarding the National Mediation Board.

* Foreign Visitor Program

Special Mediation Services
Federal Mediation and Conciliation Service (FMCS)
2100 K St., NW, Room 709
Washington, DC 20427 — (202) 653-6271

Representatives of labor, management, and governments from around the world can see how arbitration, mediation, collective bargaining, and employee involvement programs function in the U.S. by participation in this visitor program. Industrial labor relations are targeted. For more information, contact the Special Mediation Services office listed.

* Mediation Programs

Federal Mediation and Conciliation Service (FMCS)
2100 K St., NW
Washington, DC 20427 — (202) 653-5305

The FMCS sponsors a variety of workshops in labor-management dispute resolution. Workshops focus on two principal themes: the development of effective labor-management committees and the promotion of effective labor-management communication. FMCS programs include:

* Labor-Management Cooperation Program

Federal Mediation and Conciliation Service (FMCS)
2100 K St., NW
Washington, DC 20427 — (202) 653-5300

Be patient. If any phone number is incorrect, call (area code) 555-1212 and request the new listing.

Careers and Workplace

Labor-Management Committee (LMC) - The LMC represents an ongoing forum for dealing provocatively with common problems ranging from attitudes to productivity improvements. FMCS can assist the parties to not only design the framework for an effective LMC, but can provide training in the application of proven problem solving processes necessary to promote the success of Labor-Management Committee Operations.

* Mediation Service Freedom of Information

Legal Services Office
Federal Mediation and Conciliation Service (FMCS)
2100 K St., NW, Room 712
Washington, DC 20427 (202) 653-5305

This office handles FMCS Freedom on Information Act requests.

* National Labor Relations Act

National Labor Relations Board (NLRB)
1717 Pennsylvania Ave., NW, Room 393
Washington, DC 20570 (202) 632-4950

The National Labor Relations Act states and defines the rights of employees to organize and to bargain collectively with their employers through representatives of their own choosing. The Act ensures that labor representatives are chosen by secret ballot and also defines certain practices of employers and unions as unfair labor practices. The NLRB can provide you with a free guide to the National Labor Relations Act that explains its provisions in detail.

* Negotiation Impasses

Federal Services Impasses Board
Federal Labor Relations Authority (FLRA)
500 C St., SW, Room 215
Washington, DC 20424 (202) 382-0981

When negotiation impasses develop between Federal agencies and employee representatives, this panel provides assistance in resolving the stalemate. The following publications are available: *Guide to Hearing Procedures of the Federal Services; Impasses Panel; Subject Matter Index; Table of Cases;* and the *Annual Report.*

* NLRB Annual Report

Division of Information
National Labor Relations Board (NLRB)
1717 Pennsylvania Ave., NW, Room 710
Washington, DC 20570 (202) 632-4950

The National Labor Relations Board's activities and its significant case decisions for the previous fiscal year are highlighted in its Annual Report. Included are summaries of unique and/or precedent setting unfair labor practice decisions and representation elections. Statistical tables break down case information into such categories as geographic location, type of industry involved, actions taken, and final case disposition. Questions regarding the report should be directed to this office, and to purchase the report, contact the Superintendent of Documents, Government Printing Office, Washington, DC 20402; (202) 783-3238.

* NLRB Cases

Office of the Executive Secretary
National Labor Relations Board (NLRB)
1717 Pennsylvania Ave., NW, Room 701
Washington, DC 20570 (202) 254-9118

All pertinent information regarding current cases before the NLRB is tracked by this service. Summaries include such information as the type of allegation, industries involved, location of the incident, and actions already taken. This document is for internal National Labor Relations Board use only. The office also communicates on behalf of the board with employees, employers, members of Congress, labor organizations, other agencies, and the general public.

* NLRB Elections

Division of Information
National Labor Relations Board (NLRB)
1717 Pennsylvania Ave., NW, Room 710
Washington, DC 20570 (202) 632-4950

Secret ballot elections, conducted by the National Labor Relations Board, are held by employees to determine whether union representation is desired for the purpose of collective bargaining. The Board publishes a monthly update,

National Labor Relations Board Monthly Election Report, available for $17 per year from Superintendent of Documents, Government Printing Office, Washington, DC 20402; (202) 783-3238. Contact this office for more information regarding petitioning for an election as well as Certification of Representative, Decertification, Withdrawal of Union-Shop Authority, Employer Petition, Unit Clarification, and Amendment of Certification.

* NLRB Freedom of Information

Division of Advice
National Labor Relations Board (NLRB)
1717 Pennsylvania Ave., NW
Washington, DC 20570 (202) 254-9128

The Regional Advice Branch advises the general counsel and regional directors on special issues of law and policy and performs legal research. This branch prepares the general counsel's quarterly reports and guideline memoranda on important legal issues for regional directors and for the public. It also coordinates compliance with the Freedom of Information Act.

* NLRB Legal Advisor

Office of the Solicitor
National Labor Relations Board (NLRB)
1717 Pennsylvania Ave., NW
Washington, DC 20570 (202) 254-9110

The solicitor is the chief legal officer for the board. The office advises the board on questions of law and procedure, on intervention in court proceedings to protect the board's jurisdiction, on the board's exercise of its discretion regarding injunctive relief and on the enforcement of the boards orders. The office also serves as the boards liaison with members of Congress, the White House, state officials or other agencies and members of the bar.

* NLRB Meetings

Division of Information
National Labor Relations Board (NLRB)
1717 Pennsylvania Ave., NW, Room 710
Washington, DC 20570 (202) 632-4950

The public is usually allowed to attend National Labor Relations Board meetings. Information regarding upcoming meetings is published in the *Federal Register* or can be attained through this office.

* NLRB Publications

Division of Information
National Labor Relations Board (NLRB)
1717 Pennsylvania Ave, NW, Room 710
Washington, DC 20570 (202) 632-4950

Contact this office to obtain a free list of the National Labor Relations Board publications. The list includes information regarding the documents' frequency of publication, stock numbers, and cost. The following pamphlets are available free in limited quantity:

A Career in Labor: Management Relations as an Attorney.
A Career in Labor: Management Relations as a Field Examiner.
The National Labor Relations Board and You. (Representation Cases)
The National Labor Relations Board and You. (Unfair Labor Practices)
The National Labor Relations Board: What It Is, What It Does.
Your Government Conducts an Election for You on the Job.

* NLRB Public Information Room

Records Management
National Labor Relations Board (NLRB)
1717 Pennsylvania Ave., NW, Room 260
Washington, DC 20570 (202) 254-9488

This facility provides for public inspection of the Board's decisions, appeals, and advice papers.

* NLRB Speakers

Division of Information
National Labor Relations Board (NLRB)
1717 Pennsylvania Ave., NW, Room 710
Washington, DC 20570 (202) 632-4950

Personnel from Washington headquarters and the regional offices serve as

Be patient. If any phone number is incorrect, call (area code) 555-1212 and request the new listing.

Labor-Management Relations

speakers and panelists before bar associations, labor and management organizations, as well as education and civic groups. For more information regarding the speaker program, contact this office or your nearest National Labor Relations Board regional office.

* NLRB Weekly Summary

Superintendent of Documents
Government Printing Office
Washington, DC 20402 (202) 783-3238

The NLRB's publication, *Weekly Summary of National Labor Relations Board Cases,* is available through the Government Printing Office for $84 per year.

* Office of Labor Management Standards Publications

Office of Labor-Management Standards
U.S. Department of Labor
200 Constitution Ave, NW, Room S2203
Washington, DC 20210 (202) 219-8174

The OLMS publishes a variety of pamphlets explaining the rights and obligations of employers, employees, unions, and union officers under the under the Labor-Management Reporting and Disclosure Act of 1959. Available publications include: *All About OLMS; Bonding Requirements Under the LMRDA and the CSRA; Completing Your LM-3; Electing Union Officers; Reports Required Under the LMRDA and the CSRA; Rights and Responsibilities Under the LMRDA and the CSRA; Trusteeship Requirements Under the LMRDA and the CSRA;* and *Union Investigations Under the LMRDA.* Contact the OLMS for copies of these publications.

* President's Advisory Committee on Mediation and Conciliation

Federal Mediation and Conciliation Service (FMCS)
2100 K St., NW
Washington, DC 20427 (202) 653-5300

Between 1985 and 1987 this committee heard testimony from business, labor, and the public sector regarding the health of their relationship, the role of mediation and arbitration in sustaining that relationship, and the future of collective bargaining in America. The report is available free from the FMCS.

* Preventive Mediation

Federal Mediation and Conciliation Service (FMCS)
2100 K St., NW
Washington, DC 20427 (202) 653-5300

FMCS preventive mediation is increasingly used by business and labor to anticipate problems before they obstruct the collective bargaining process from functioning as it should. Mediators use a variety of preventive mediation activities, including, among others, Labor-Management committees, a diversity of training programs, and for serious cases, Relationship by Objective Programs. Entire industries are addressed through conferences and seminars designed to raise the consciousness of the participants of the consequences of the failing relationship. Contact the FMCS for more information.

* Quality-of-Worklife

National Audiovisual Center
8700 Edgeworth Dr.
Capitol Heights, MD 20743 (301) 763-1891

Work Worth Doing is a two-part news documentary which describes how six progressive companies and their unions are using a variety of cooperative labor relations practices and quality-of-work-life programs not only to survive in the market place, but to thrive. *Part I* is an overview of several types of programs instituted in various organizations, and *Part II* provides more detailed information about how these programs were implemented and are maintained. Each part costs $110.

* Railroad Carrier Employee Grievances

National Railroad Adjustment Board
National Mediation Board
175 W. Jackson Blvd., Room A931
Chicago, IL 60604 (312) 886-7303

The Railroad Adjustment Board handles carrier employee grievances and disputes related to the interpretation and application of existing contracts which cannot be resolved in the usual manner. Disputes may concern rates of pay or working conditions, for example. Disputes are referred by petition of either or both parties to the appropriate Adjustment Board division.

- First Division: Train and yard service employees including engineers, firemen, hostlers, conductors, and trainmen.

- Second Division: Machinists, boilermakers, blacksmiths, sheetmetal workers, carmen, coach cleaners, powerhouse employees, and railroad shop laborers.

- Third Division: Clerical employees, station and tower employees, telegraph employees, dispatchers, maintenance of way men, freight handlers, store employees, signalmen, sleeping car conductors, porters, maids, and dining car employees.

- Fourth Division: Employees of carriers directly or indirectly engaged in transportation of passengers or cargo by water and employees not coming under the jurisdiction of the other three divisions.

For further information, contact the office listed.

* Statistics on Dispute Mediation

Federal Mediation and Conciliation Service (FMCS)
2100 K St., NW, Room 712
Washington, DC 20427 (202) 653-5305

The FMCS can provide you with statistics on dispute mediation, preventive mediation, work stoppages, and contract mediation analysis for calendar years 1985-1990.

* Unfair Labor Practice Charges

Office of Appeals
National Labor Relations Board (NLRB)
1717 Pennsylvania Ave., NW, Room 1154
Washington, DC 20570 (202) 254-9316

Unfair labor practice charges may be filed by employees, employers, and unions against businesses and\or labor organizations at the nearest National Labor Relations Board regional office. If the regional office refuses to issue a complaint, contact this main office..

* Unfair Labor Practice Hearings

Division of Administrative Law Judges
National Labor Relations Board (NLRB)
1375 K St., NW, Room 1121
Washington, DC 20005 (202) 633-0500

Administrative law judges conduct formal hearings regarding unfair labor practices. In addition to ruling on these cases, the judges assign hearing dates and maintain the calendar of upcoming cases.

* Union Bylaws and Public Information

Disclosure Room
Office of Labor-Management Standards
U.S. Department of Labor
200 Constitution Ave., NW, Room N5620
Washington, DC 20210 (202) 219-8861

Unions must file information reports, constitutions and bylaws, and annual financial reports with the Secretary of Labor. Officers and employees of labor unions must report any loans and gifts received from, or certain financial interests in, employers whose employees the union represents. Employers who engage in certain financial dealings with their employees, unions, and labor-relations consultants must file reports, as well as labor-relations consultants who enter into agreements with employers to persuade employees as to the manner of exercising their rights. All reports are public information, and may be examined at the OLMS national and regional offices. The publication, *Reports Required,* gives detailed information on who needs to file reports, and general rules relating to these reports.

* Union Contracts Bargaining Calendar

Superintendent of Documents
Government Printing Office
Washington, DC 20402 (202) 783-3238

The Bureau of Labor Statistics' publishes *Bargaining Calendar,* a yearly schedule

Be patient. If any phone number is incorrect, call (area code) 555-1212 and request the new listing.

Careers and Workplace

of information on anticipated contract adjustments between labor and management negotiators. Major situations by company and union are identified in which contracts will terminate, deferred wage increases will become due, changes in the Consumer Price Indexes will be reviewed, and contracts will be renewed ($5).

* Union Contracts Clearinghouse

Public File of Collective Bargaining Agreements
Labor-Management Relations
Bureau of Labor Statistics
U.S. Department of Labor
441 G St., NW, Room 2032
Washington, DC 20212 (202) 606-6289

The Bureau of Labor Statistics maintains for public examination and use a file of collective bargaining agreements, including an annual and monthly calendar of contract expirations. The file covers 5,000 agreements in private industry and government, including virtually all those covering bargaining units with 1,000 employees or more, exclusive of railroads and airlines. Negotiators for both labor and management use this data.

* Union Contracts Database

Legal Services Office
Federal Mediation and Conciliation Service (FMCS)
2100 K Street, NW
Room 712
Washington, DC 20427 (202) 653-5305

The office also maintains a database of union contracts searchable by company name and dating back one year. Information can be obtained by written request.

* Union Contracts: Help Getting Copies

Office of Labor-Management Standards
U.S. Department of Labor
200 Constitution Ave., NW, Room S2203
Washington, DC 20210 (202) 219-8174

Every employee (whether or not a union member) is entitled, on request, to receive from a local union a copy of each collective bargaining agreement made by the local which directly affects that person's rights as an employee. OLMS should be notified if the union fails to furnish copies of the agreements.

* Union Information

Office of Labor-Management Standards
U.S. Department of Labor
200 Constitution Ave., NW, Room S2203
Washington, DC 20210 (202) 219-8174

The OLMS keeps a registry by location and name, each of the unions that files reports under the LMRDA or the CSRA. It also contains addresses of national unions and a series of statistical appendices such as the number of reporting affiliates per national union. This publication is available from the Government Printing Office.

* Union Investigations

Office of Labor-Management Standards
U.S. Department of Labor
200 Constitution Ave., NW, Room S2203
Washington, DC 20210 (202) 219-8174

The Labor-Management Reporting and Disclosure Act authorizes the Secretary of Labor to investigate any union to determine whether a violation has occurred. The investigation can be prompted by an analysis of reports a union files or in response to specific complaints. If the investigation is based on a complaint, information such as the complainant's name and the specific details of the complaint will not be disclosed, and the union will not be allowed to review the complaint or obtain a copy of it. Criminal violations will be referred to the Justice Department.

* Union Members' Bill of Rights

Office of Labor-Management Standards
U.S. Department of Labor
200 Constitution Ave., NW, Room S2203
Washington, DC 20210 (202) 219-8174

The Labor-Management Reporting and Disclosure Act grants certain rights to union members and protects their interests by promoting democratic procedures within labor organizations. The Act establishes a Bill of Rights for union members; reporting requirements for labor organizations, union officers, and employees, employers, labor-relations consultants, and surety companies; standards for the regular election of union officers; and certain safe guards for labor organization funds. Copies of the law and additional information are available from this office.

* Union Officer Elections Case Digest

Office of Labor-Management Standards
U.S. Department of Labor
200 Constitution Ave., NW, Room S2203
Washington, DC 20210 (202) 219-8174

The Digest and supplements present summaries of LMRDA and CSRA union officer election cases and trusteeship cases. Entries are excerpted from reported and unreported judicial opinions and court documents, and OLMS case records and deal with the legal aspects of the cases. The first 2 volumes of the digest, which cover from 1959-1982 are out of print, but information on them may be available from OLMS. The third volume, covering 1983 through 1986 is available from GPO for $23.

Be patient. If any phone number is incorrect, call (area code) 555-1212 and request the new listing.

Occupational Health and Safety

* *See also Drug and Chemical Dependence Chapter*

All sorts of work-related health and safety issues are covered here, including radiation from computer screens, high blood pressure screening, smoking restrictions, and exposure to hazardous materials. These sources can tell you whom to contact for the latest scientific data on work-related injuries and safety, and can assist businesses in helping them follow federal and state safety guidelines. You'll find additional sources mentioned in the Health and Medicine Chapter in the section on Hazards: Chemicals and Toxins.

* Accident Reporting Network

Office of Field Programs
Occupational Safety and Health Administration
U.S. Department of Labor
200 Constitution Ave., NW, Room N3603
Washington, DC 20210 (202) 219-7725

All employers are required to report all accidents which result in a work-related death or five or more hospitalizations to the nearest OSHA office within 48 hours. You can not be discriminated against, fired, demoted, or otherwise penalized for complaining about a hazard to your employer, requesting an OSHA inspection, or participating in union safety and health activities. OSHA can take action, including going to court if necessary, to force your employer to restore your job, earnings, and benefits. You will not have to pay and legal fees.

* Airline Pilots Medical Certification

Civil Aeromedical Institute
Federal Aviation Administration
U.S. Department of Transportation
Mike Monroney Aeronautical Center
P.O. Box 25082
Oklahoma, OK 73125 (405) 680-4806

CAMI operates a program for the medical certification of airmen, and educates pilots and physicians in matters related to aviation safety. It is also responsible for developing and producing brochures, slides, and training films for distribution to aviation groups and organizations. Contact CAMI for more information on certification or these education programs.

* Appealing an OSHA Standard

Office of the Assistant Secretary
Occupational Safety and Health Administration
U.S. Department of Labor
200 Constitution Ave, NW, Room S2315
Washington, DC 20210 (202) 219-7162

No decision on a permanent standard is ever reached without due consideration of the arguments and data received from the public in written submissions and at hearings. However, any person who may be adversely affected by a final or emergency standard may file a petition within 60 days for judicial review of the standard with the U.S. Court of Appeals for the circuit in which the objector lives or has his business.

* Appealing OSHA Citations

Office of Information
Occupational Safety and Health Review Commission
1825 K St., 4th Floor
Washington, DC 20006-1246 (202) 634-7943

If an employer disagrees with any aspect of an Occupational Safety and Health Administration citation, issued by an inspector in the workplace, the employer must notify OSHA of that disagreement within 15 working days of receiving the citation. The employer is then entitled to have its dispute resolved by this Commission. A case that comes before the Commission is first heard and decided by an Administrative Law Judge. The judge's decision may be reviewed at the discretion of the Commission members, who have the authority to change that decision. Commission decisions and Judges' decisions not reviewed by the Commission can be appealed to the United States Court of Appeals.

* Audiovisuals on Occupational Safety and Health

Audiovisual Training Programs
National Audiovisual Center
Customer Services Section
8700 Edgeworth Dr.
Capitol Heights, MD 20743 (301) 763-1896

The *Occupational Safety and Health Audiovisual Training Programs* catalog lists over 65 high quality, low-cost hazard training programs from the safety experts at OSHA, NIOSH, and other federal agencies. It features OSHA's popular *Hazard Recognition Series* that teaches people what they need to know to work safety in a variety of situations. Contact this office for your free catalog.

* Aviation Medicine

Biomedical and Behavioral Science Division
Office of Aviation Administration
Federal Aviation Administration
U.S. Department of Transportation
800 Independence Ave., SW, Room 325
Washington, DC 20591 (202) 267-3535

The FAA conducts aeromedical research on in the following areas:

- *Psychology:* evaluates spatial disorientation and visual perception in the aviation environment;
- *Physiology:* performance and health of aircrew and air traffic controllers under diverse environmental conditions;
- *Toxicology:* toxic hazards such as pesticides used in aerial application, products of combustion and ionizing radiation from air shipment of radioactive cargo in the high-altitude environment;
- *Protection and survival:* studies of techniques for lessening or preventing crash injuries, developing concepts and evaluating survival equipment used under adverse physical conditions, establishing human physical limitations of civil aviation operations, and evaluating emergency procedures for downed aircraft.

* Businesses Promoting Health

National Health Information Clearinghouse
P.O. Box 1133 (800) 336-4797
Washington, DC 20013 (301) 565-4167 (MD and DC)

Health Promotion and Business Coalitions: Current Activities and Prospects for the Future provides an overview of the health education and promotion activities of 105 business health coalitions and includes five detailed case studies. This 78 page manual (Order No. W0003) is available for $2.

* Chemical Hazards

Clearinghouse for Occupational Safety and Health Information
NIOSH
4676 Columbia Parkway
Cincinnati, OH 45226 (513) 533-8287

This clearinghouse can answer a wide range of questions regarding chemical hazards in the workplace and occupational safety by using their databases (National Occupational Hazard Survey and NIOSH Technical Information Center) to research your questions. They have many publications, such as *Prevention of Leading Work-Related Diseases* and *NIOSH Recommendations for Occupational Safety*, including a free catalog.

Be patient. If any phone number is incorrect, call (area code) 555-1212 and request the new listing.

Careers and Workplace

* College Courses

Division of Training and Manpower Development
National Institute for Occupational Safety and Health
4676 Columbia Parkway
Cincinnati, OH 45226 (513) 533-8221

This division offers courses for industry and health care professionals on such topics as occupational safety, industrial hygiene, and safety in the laboratory. For a course listing and description, contact this office.

* Companies Inspected by OSHA

Office of Management Data Systems
Directorate of Administrative Programs
Occupational Safety and Health Administration (OSHA)
U.S. Department of Labor
200 Constitution Ave, NW, Room N3661
Washington, DC 20210 (202) 523-7008

This office can provide you with the entire range of inspection data, including who, what, when, where, and why companies were inspected, and the violations that were found.

* Educational Resource Centers for Health/Safety Training

4676 Columbia Parkway
Cincinnati, OH 45226-1998 (513) 533-8241

NIOSH supports Educational Resource Centers (ERCs) at 14 American universities to help ensure an adequate supply of trained occupational safety and health professionals.

* Employee Health Promotion Efforts

National Health Information Clearinghouse
P.O. Box 1133 (800) 336-4797
Washington, DC 20013 (301) 565-4167 (MD and DC)

Worksite Health Promotion: A Bibliography of Selected Books and Resources lists and describes resources for employee health promotion programs. This 22 page pamphlet (Order No. W0005) is available for $3.

* Employee Safety Program

Consumer Product Safety Commission
5401 Westbard Avenue
Bethesda, MD 20207 (301) 504-0580

Through one of its regional offices, the Commission will send you information on safety hazards and accident prevention on-the-job.

* Equipment for Determining Hazards in the Workplace

Occupational Safety and Health Administration (OSHA)
U.S. Department of Labor
U.S. Post Office Bldg.
Fifth and Walnut Sts.
Cincinnati, OH 45202 (513) 684-3721

The OSHA Cincinnati Laboratory develops, evaluates, calibrates, and repairs hazard measurement instrumentation and equipment. They can provide you with information on all aspects of this equipment.

* Environmental and Occupational Health

Society for Occupational and Environmental Health (SOEH)
P.O. Box 42360
Washington, DC 20015-0360 (202) 762-9319

This society's members include physicians, hygienists, economists, laboratory scientists, academics, and labor and industry representatives.

* Fatal Accident Investigations

National Institute for Occupational Safety and Health (NIOSH)
944 Chestnut Ridge Road
Morgantown, WV 26505-2888 (304) 291-4575

NIOSH identifies risk factors for work-related fatalities and injuries through its Fatal Accident Circumstances and Epidemiology project (FACE).

* Hazards Detection

National Institute for Occupational Safety and Health (NIOSH)
4676 Columbia Parkway
Cincinnati, OH 45226 (800) 356-4674

NIOSH is responsible for conducting research to make the nation's workplaces healthier and safer by responding to urgent requests for assistance from employers, employees, and their representatives where imminent hazards are suspected. They conduct inspections, laboratory and epidemiologic research, publish their findings, and make recommendations for improved working conditions to regulatory agencies. NIOSH trains occupational health and safety workers and communicates research results to those concerned.

* Hazards Outreach Program

Office of Field Programs
U.S. Department of Labor
200 Constitution Ave., NW, Room N3603
Washington, DC 20210 (202) 219-7925

Local offices of the Occupational Safety and Health Administration carry out many different programs: enforcement, voluntary compliance programs, and training and education. OSHA personnel are available to speak at civic clubs, union meetings, and trade association gatherings to explain new OSHA standards, encourage participation in OSHA rule makings, and answer questions about the agency's approach to workplace safety and health. OSHA also demonstrates, to the extent possible, technical equipment and materials. Prepackaged training programs are available to unions or trade groups. Contact you local OSHA office for more information.

* Health Hazard Evaluation

(800) 35-NIOSH

Employers, employees, or their representatives who suspect a health problem in the workplace can request a National Institute of Occupation Safety and Health (NIOSH) Health Hazard Evaluation to assess the problem.

* Health Initiatives in the Workplace

National Institute on Drug Abuse, Room 10A53
5600 Fishers Lane
Rockville, MD 20857 (301) 443-6710

This office develops policies and provides leadership for the implementation and administration of a national program to eliminate illegal drug use in the workplace. Its programs include research, treatment, training, and prevention activities as well as projects related to the development of a comprehensive Drug-Free Workplace program. OWI has developed mandatory guidelines for federal workplace drug testing programs, which include scientific and technical requirements and certification standards for laboratories engaged in urine drug testing for federal agencies. OWI analyzes and recommends Employee Assistance Programs and distributes a four-part videotape series on drugs at work.

* Health Hazard Evaluations

200 Independence Ave, SW
Washington, DC 20201 (800) 35-NIOSH

Employers, employees, or their representatives who suspect a health problem in the workplace can request a NIOSH Health Hazard Evaluation (HHE) to assess the problem.

* Health On-the-Job and Future Strategies

National Health Information Clearinghouse
P.O. Box 1133 (800) 336-4797
Washington, DC 20013 (301) 565-4167 (MD and DC)

The Future of Work and Health: Implications for Health Strategies summarizes emerging trends in work and health and explores issues concerning the development of health care strategies for worksites in the future. Copies of this 46-page booklet (Order No. W0013) is available for $2 to cover postage/handling.

* Health Promotion in the Workplace

Office of Disease Prevention and Health Promotion
Public Health Service
330 C St., SW, Room 2132
Washington, DC 20201 (202) 205-8583

Be patient. If any phone number is incorrect, call (area code) 555-1212 and request the new listing.

Occupational Health and Safety

This office works on developing policies for the Year 2000 objectives for health promotion. Their Preventive Services Task Force is developing recommendations for clinical practice, in addition to a worksite Health Promotion Task Force and a Nutrition Branch. This office also operates the Health Promotion Clearinghouse which offers many publications.

* High Blood Pressure Screening

High Blood Pressure Information Center
4733 Bethesda Ave, Suite 530
Bethesda, MD 20814 (301) 951-3260

The High Blood Pressure Information Center can send you information on setting up a screening program in the workplace.

* Industrial Hygiene

National Institute for Occupational Safety and Health (NIOSH)
4676 Columbia Parkway
Cincinnati, OH 45226 (800) 356-4674

NIOSH is responsible for conducting research to make the nation's workplaces healthier and safer by responding to urgent requests for assistance from employers, employees, and their representatives where imminent hazards are suspected. They conduct inspections, laboratory and epidemiologic research, publish their findings, and make recommendations for improved working conditions to regulatory agencies. NIOSH trains occupational health and safety workers and communicates research results to those concerned.

* Industry Health Studies

Division of Surveillance
Hazard Evaluation and Field Studies
National Institute for Occupational Safety and Health (NIOSH)
4676 Columbia Parkway
Cincinnati, OH 46226 (800) 356-4674

NIOSH conducts a wide range of studies regarding occupational health. They look at exposure to chemicals, PCB, and asbestos in the workplace, as well as other occupational health hazards. This information is made public to companies, unions, and private citizens.

* Industry Injuries and Illnesses Data

Superintendent of Documents
Government Printing Office
Washington, DC 20402 (202) 783-3238

Many of the Bureau of Labor Statistics' major surveys and research studies are available in the BLS *Bulletin Series,* which include more than 100 area and industry wage studies each year and about 40 volumes dealing with a wide range of economic subjects. For example, *Occupational Injuries and Illnesses in the United States by Industry* is an annual report with detailed tables showing the job-related injury and illness experience of employees in a wide range of industries. Contact this office for more information on available publications on occupational injury and illness statistics.

* Information Clearinghouse

Information Office
Occupational Safety and Health Administration (OSHA)
U.S. Department of Labor
200 Constitution Ave., NW, Room S2315
Washington, DC 20210 (202) 219-8151

This office can provide you with information regarding the various OSHA programs, and can direct your inquiries to the appropriate office. The staff also schedules and coordinates public hearings and supports advisory committees in their development of recommendations to the Assistant Secretary of OSHA. A good starting place for information on OSHA is the booklet *All About OSHA.* It is available free of charge from OSHA.

* Injured Workers Statistics

Office of Safety, Health and Working Conditions
Bureau of Labor Statistics
U.S. Department of Labor
601 D St., NW, Room 4014
Washington, DC 20210 (202) 606-6167

This office maintains the nationwide employer record keeping system on job-related injuries and illnesses, conducts the annual survey based on these records and analyzes the results, and compiles supplementary statistics from other sources. States provide additional information on occupational accidents and exposures from workers' compensation records which give a sharper definition of occupational safety and health problems, associated characteristics, and possible action indicators. The *Work Injury Report* examines selected types of work injures to develop a detailed profile of characteristics associated with the injuries data from questionnaires completed by injured workers.

* Injuries and Illnesses On-the-Job

Office of Safety, Health and Working Conditions
Bureau of Labor Statistics
U.S. Department of Labor
601 D St., NW
Washington, DC 20210 (202) 606-6167

An annual survey, conducted by State employment security agencies on a cooperative basis with Bureau of Labor Statistics, provides data on the incidence of occupational injuries and illnesses by industry and State. Data available include incidence votes by private industry for injuries and illnesses, with estimates of numbers of fatal and nonfatal cases, and lost workday cases. *Work Injury Report Surveys* provide data collected from employees on characteristics of selected types of injuries. Data available include type of equipment involved, availability and use of protective devices, worker activity at time of accident, amount of training worker received, and presence of hazardous conditions.

* Job Safety and Health Information Clearinghouse

Technical Data Center
Occupational Safety and Health Administration (OSHA)
U.S. Department of Labor
200 Constitution Ave, NW, Room N2634
Washington, DC 20210 (202) 219-7500

This center houses technical information on all industries covered by OSHA. They maintain a library of 8,000 volumes and 250 journals, as well as an extensive microform collection of industry standards and OSHA rule making records. They have access to a wide variety of databases, including Dialog and two of their own. The Center is also the docket office and holds the hearing records on standards, the comments, and final rules, and can provide certified copies. The center is open to the public 8:15 a.m. to 4:45 p.m., Monday through Friday.

* Manufacturing Plants and Chemical Registry

National Institute of Occupational Safety and Health (NIOSH)
Division of Surveillance Hazard Evaluation
4676 Columbia Parkway
Cincinnati, OH 45226 (513) 841-4491

NIOSH maintains two databases, the National Occupational Hazard Survey Databases I & II, which contain surveys of 5,000 manufacturing plants each. NIOSH administers a questionnaire, investigates health and safety programs, and conducts an inventory of chemicals. Through the databases, NIOSH can identify potential exposure agents, describe health and safety programs, and by chemical can develop estimates of number of people exposed.

* Mine Accident Prevention Training

Division of Policy and Program Coordination
Education and Training
Mine Safety and Health Administration
U.S. Department of Labor
4015 Wilson Blvd., Room 576
Arlington, VA 22203 (703) 235-1400

Training is an important tool for preventing accidents and avoiding unsafe and unhealthful working conditions. Training specialists coordinate their districts various training and miners to tailer programs specifically to individual needs. Training specialists conduct examinations to certify miners for certain specialized work, review training plans submitted by the mine operators, conduct various accident prevention programs, and assist at regional mine rescue contests.

* Miner Health and Safety Training Academy

Continuing Education Department
P.O. Box 1166
Beckley, WV 25801 (304) 255-6451

The National Mine Health and Safety Academy is the world's largest educational institution devoted solely to safety and health in mining. The academy serves as

Be patient. If any phone number is incorrect, call (area code) 555-1212 and request the new listing.

Careers and Workplace

the central training facility for federal mine inspectors and mine safety professionals from other government agencies, the mining industry, and labor. Courses are offered on safety and inspection procedures, accident prevention, investigations, industrial hygiene, mine emergency procedures, mining technology, and management theory and techniques. The academy also provides field training and serves as a technical resource to help meet the mining community's instructional needs.

* Mine Safety and Health Case Files

Docket Office
Federal Mine Safety and Health Review Commission
1730 K St., NW, 6th Floor
Washington, DC 20006 (202) 653-5629

Transcripts of hearings and written decisions on mine safety and health cases brought before the Commission are housed here. Cases may involve mine closure orders, citations, or violations of mandatory safety and health standards, for example. Records may be freely accessed on a walk-in basis, but if a case is not recent, call ahead as old files are archived and may require a couple of weeks to retrieve.

* Mine Safety and Robotics

Health, Safety, and Mining Technology
Bureau of Mines
U.S. Department of the Interior
2401 E St., NW
Washington, DC 20241 (292) 501-9321

The Bureau is studying ways to improve mine safety and to eliminate the health risks of mining. One of the areas of emphasis is finding ways to reduce a miner's exposure to respirable dust, which causes black lung and other respiratory diseases. Studies in safety precautions help companies build more stable mines with better roof support systems and more efficiently detect flammable gases and ignition sources. Research on automation and robotics to do the more hazardous jobs is also being done.

* Mine Safety Clearinghouse

Office of Information and Public Affairs
Mine Safety and Health Administration
U.S. Department of Labor
4015 Wilson Blvd.
Arlington, VA 22203 (703) 235-1452

This office can provide you with general information regarding the Mine Safety and Health Administration, as well as brochures, manuals, and other publications regarding mine safety and health.

* Mine Safety Reviews

Acting Chairman
Federal Mine Safety and Health Review Commission
1730 K St., NW, 6th Floor
Washington, DC 20006 (202) 653-5644

Cases are brought before this commission and its Administrative Law Judges by the Mine Safety and Health Administration, mine operators, and miners or their representatives. Cases reviewed usually revolve around actions of the Mine Safety and Health Administration, which enforces occupational safety standards in U.S. surface and underground mines. Hearings are held as close as practical to locations of the mines involved. The Office of Administrative Law Judges operates from the following locations: 2 Skyline Plaza, 5203 Leesburg Pike, Falls Church, VA 22041, (703) 756-6200; and at the Colonnade Center, Room 280, 1244 Speer Blvd., Denver, CO 80204; (303) 844-5266. For further information on Commission activities, contact the Chairman's office listed above.

* Miners X-Rays

944 Chestnut Ridge Road
Morgantown, WV 26505-2888 (304) 291-4301

NIOSH administers periodic chest X-rays to coal miners to facilitate early detection of coal workers pneumoconiosis.

* Mining Hazards: Safety and Prevention Assistance

Office of Information
Mine Safety and Health Administration (MSHA)
U.S. Department of Labor

4015 Wilson Blvd
Arlington, VA 22203 (703) 234-1452

Specialists from MSHA's technical support facilities can provide technical and engineering assistance in helping to reduce hazards in their operations' mining systems. MSHA's engineers, scientists, and industrial hygienists often suggest possible solutions to difficult problems dealing with the safe design or maintenance of mining equipment and machinery, roof support or ventilation systems and mine waste facilities, and with the regular measurement and control of miners' exposure to health hazards such as nose, radiation, or harmful dust.

* Mining Industry Training Products

National Mine Health and Safety Academy
Attention: Business Office
P.O. Box 1166
Beckley, WV 25802 (304) 256-3257

The free catalog, *Training Products for the Mining Industry*, is divided into three major sections: films and videotapes; training materials such as instructional programs and safety manuals; and a complete listing of available MSHA informational reports. Each item includes a brief description, ordering information, and cost.

* Mining Injury and Illness Registry

MSHA Safety and Health Technology Center
Mine Safety and Health Administration (MSHA)
U.S. Department of Labor
P.O. Box 25367
Denver, CO 80225 (303) 236-2716

MSHA specialists collect, analyze, and publish data obtained from mine operators on the prevalence of work-related injuries and illnesses in the mining industry. This information helps MSHA's own staff, mining companies, and labor organizations gauge the effectiveness of their safety programs and to make needed improvements. MSHA specialists also publish a number of analytical studies and reports each year for use by the mining industry and the general public.

* NIOSH Databases

4676 Columbia Parkway
Cincinnati, OH 45226-1998 (513) 533-8326

NIOSH maintains an extensive database of occupational safety and health information from around the world.

* NIOSH Publications

4676 Columbia Parkway
Cincinnati, OH 45226-1998 (513) 533-8573

The *NIOSH Bookshelf* lists the publications available from NIOSH. It contains listings for publications containing recommendations for chemical, physical and other hazards in the workplace. it also lists NIOSH bibliographies as well as technical publications available. It is free.

* Occupational Health and Safety TVA Investigations

Human Resources
Tennessee Valley Authority
MPB 1E 215B-M
Muscle Shoals, AL 35660

This office formulate and oversees the implementation of TVA's occupational health and safety policies and plans. It develops and issues standards for control of hazards in the workplace, supports the investigation of serious accidents, and ensures appropriate follow-through. The staff coordinates TVA review of regulatory requirements and industry trends relating to safety practices, and develops agency comments on proposed regulations. Staff develops and delivers management and employee safety orientation and training in health and safety. The program provides industrial hygiene services for the agency, including surveys to measure employee exposure to toxic chemicals and physical agents, and recommends appropriate administrative and engineering control methods. It is responsible for handling workplace and community noise prevention programs, and by-product material licensing support and radiation safety services.

* Occupational Safety and Health Publications

Superintendent of Documents
Government Printing Office
Washington, DC 20402 (202) 783-3238

Be patient. If any phone number is incorrect, call (area code) 555-1212 and request the new listing.

Occupational Health and Safety

The Government Printing Office can provide you with a bibliography that lists hundreds of source materials on occupational safety and health issues. Call the GPO and ask for *Subject Bibliography 213*. It's free.

* Occupational Safety and Health Review Regional Offices

Atlanta
Peachtree St., NE, Room 587, Atlanta, GA 30367; (404) 347-3573

Boston
133 Portland St, 1st Floor, Boston, MA 02114; (617) 565-7164

Chicago
230 South Dearborn Street, Room 3244, Chicago, IL 60604; (312) 353-2220.

Dallas
525 Griffin Street, Room 602, Dallas, TX 75202; (214) 767-4731

Denver
Federal Building, Room 1576, 1961 Stout Street, Denver, CO 80294; (303) 844-3061

Kansas City
911 Walnut Street, Kansas City, MO 64106; (816) 426-5861.

New York
201 Varick Street, Room 670, New York, NY 10014; (212) 337-2378.

Philadelphia
Gateway Building, Suite 2100, 3535 Market Street, Philadelphia, PA 19104; (215) 596-1201.

San Francisco
71 Stevenson Street, Room 415, San Francisco, CA 94105; (415) 744-6670.

Seattle
1111 Third Avenue, Suite 715, Seattle, WA 98174; (206) 553-5930.

* OSHA Certificate of Service

Executive Secretary
Occupational Safety and Health Review Commission
1825 K St., 4th Floor
Washington, DC 20006-1246 (202) 219-8148

Documents that have been filed with the Commission or an Administrative Law Judge of the Commission must be copied and given to all parties in a case, either by first-class mail or by hand. A statement must also be submitted showing the date and manner of the delivery and the names of the persons receiving copies of the documents.

* OSHA Commission Decisions Index

Executive Secretary
Occupational Safety and Health Review Commission
1825 K St., 4th Floor
Washington, DC 20006-1246 (202) 219-8148

The *Index to Decisions of the OSHRC*, which lists company names and OSHRC docket numbers, is sold based on the number of pages and the years requested. For a price quote, contact the above office. Subscriptions to microfiche copies of OSHRC decisions, called *OSHRC Reports*, are available from the Superintendent of Documents, Government Printing Office, Washington, DC

* OSHA Commission Docket

Office of Information
Occupational Safety and Health Review Commission
1825 K St., NW, 4th Floor
Washington, DC 20006-1246 (202) 219-8148

Copies of the proceedings of any of the cases decided by the Commission and Administrative Law Judges are available for public inspection. An appointment in advance is needed with the office above.

* OSHA Commission Publications

Office of Information
Occupational Safety and Health Review Commission
1825 K St., NW, 4th Floor
Washington, DC 20006-1246 (202) 219-8148

The following information booklets are free upon request describing the function of the Commission: *Simplified Proceedings, Rules of Procedure, A Guide to Procedures of the OSHRC*, and the *Annual Report to the President*.

* OSHA Complaint and Response

Executive Secretary
Occupational Safety and Health Review Commission
1825 K St., 4th Floor
Washington, DC 20006-1246 (202) 219-8148

Within 30 calendar days of the date on which the Commission receives an employer's Notice of Contest, the Secretary of Labor must file a written complaint with the Commission. A copy must be sent to the employer and any other parties in the case. The complaint sets forth in detail the alleged violation for which the employer received the citation. The employer must then file a written answer to the complaint with the Commission within 30 calendar days after receipt of the complaint. This answer must admit or deny each paragraph and subparagraph of the complaint. The answer is filed by mailing it to the address above.

* OSHA Employer Notice of Contest

Office of Information
Occupational Safety and Health Review Commission
1825 K St., 4th Floor
Washington, DC 20006-1246 (202) 219-8148

There are two steps that must be taken by an employer who wishes to contest all or part of a citation received from the Occupational Safety and Health Administration. Within 15 working days from receipt of the proposed penalty, the employer must notify the Labor Department of the employer's intent to contest all or part of the citation, the penalty proposed, or the time allowed for the correction of the alleged violation. This notification is called a *Notice of Contest*. After the U.S. Department of Labor notifies the Review Commission that the citation has been contested, the employer will receive a notice from the Review Commission that the case has been filed. Forms will also be supplied to notify affected employees and their union that a notice of contest has been filed.

* OSHA Freedom of Information Act Requests

Freedom of Information Act Officer
Occupational Safety and Health Review Commission
1825 K St., NW, 4th Floor
Washington, DC 20006-1246 (202) 219-8148

Freedom of Information requests should be sent to the officer above.

* OSHA Publications

Information Office
Occupational Safety and Health Administration (OSHA)
U.S. Department of Labor
200 Constitution Ave., NW, Room S2315
Washington, DC 20210 (202) 219-8151

OSHA can provide you with a list of publications related to safety and health issues free of charge. GPO and NTIS publications are also listed in this publication.

* OSHA Simplified Appeals Process

Executive Secretary
Occupational Safety and Health Review Commission
1825 K St., 4th Floor
Washington, DC 20006-1246 (202) 219-8148

Simplified proceedings are designed to expedite the resolution of cases, to make it easier for those appearing before the Commission to proceed without an attorney, to reduce paperwork, and to reduce the expense of litigation. This process is used in cases where the issues are less involved and a formal procedure is not needed for a fair hearing. Contact this office for more information.

Careers and Workplace

* Petition for Modification of Abatement

Executive Secretary
Occupational Safety and Health Review Commission
1825 K St., 4th Floor
Washington, DC 20006-1246 (202) 219-8148

If an employer has made a good faith effort to correct an OSHA violation within the given abatement period but has not been able to do so because of reasons beyond his/her control, he/she may file a petition for modification of abatement. This petition is filed with the Occupational Safety and Health Administration Area Director no later than the end of the next working day following the day on which abatement was to have been completed.

* Petitioning the Government on Safe Working Conditions

Office of the Assistant Secretary
Occupational Health and Safety Administration (OSHA)
U.S. Department of Labor
200 Constitution Ave., NW, Room S2315
Washington, DC 20210 (202) 219-7162

OSHA can begin standards-setting procedures on its own initiative, or in response to petitions from other parties, including the Secretary of Health and Human Services, the National Institute for Occupational Safety and Health, State and local governments, any nationally-recognized standards-producing organization, employer or labor representative, or any other interested party. Contact this office for more information on the standard setting procedure.

* Publications and Training Materials

OSHA Publications
Occupational Safety and Health Administration (OSHA)
U.S. Department of Labor
200 Constitution Ave., NW, Room N4101
Washington, DC 20210 (202) 219-4667

Contact this office for a list of OSHA free publications and *Federal Register* reprints pertaining to OSHA. These publications are available at no charge.

* Regulations

Subscription Service
Superintendent of Documents
Government Printing Office
Washington, DC 20402 (202) 783-3238

The OSHA subscription service was developed to assist the public in keeping current with OSHA standards. This service provides all standards, interpretations, regulations, and procedures in easy to use loose-leaf form, punched for use in a three-ring binder. All changes and additions are issued for and indefinite period of time. The following volumes are available:

General Standards and Interpretations (includes agriculture)
Maritime Standards and Interpretations
Construction Standards and Interpretations
Other Regulations and Procedures
Field Operations Manual
Industrial Hygiene Field Operations Manual

* Review Commission

Occupational Safety and Health Review Commission
1825 K St., 4th Floor
Washington, DC 20006-1246 (202) 634-7960

The Occupational Safety and Health Review Commission serves as a court to resolve disputes that arise under the Occupational Safety and Health Act of 1970, which involves workplace inspections. The Commission is not connected in any way with the U.S. Department of Labor or the Occupational Safety and Health Administration.

* Safety and Health Training Institute

Occupational Safety and Health Administration (OSHA)
U.S. Department of Labor
1555 Times Dr.
Des Plaines, IL 60018 (312) 297-4810

The OSHA Training Institute in Des Plaines, Illinois, provides basic and advanced training and education in safety and health for federal and state compliance officers; state consultants; other federal agency personnel; private sector employers; and employees and their representatives. Institute courses cover such areas as electrical hazards, machine guarding, ventilation, and ergonomics. Many courses are available for personnel in the private sector dealing with such subjects as safety and health in the construction industry and methods of voluntary compliance with OSHA standards.

* Safety and the Workplace: Onsite Consultation

OSHA Publications
Occupational Safety and Health Administration (OSHA)
U.S. Department of Labor
200 Constitution Ave., NW, Room N4101
Washington, DC 20210 (202) 219-4667

Using a free consultation service, employers can find out about potential hazards at their worksites, improve their safety management systems, and even qualify for a one-year exemption from routine OSHA inspections. Primarily targeted for smaller businesses, this safety and health consultation program is completely separate from the OSHA inspection effort. In addition, no citations are issued or penalties proposed. These consultations are carried out through State OSHA consultation programs. Contact this OSHA office for a listing of these state programs.

* Scientific and Medical Issues

Directorate of Technical Support
U.S. Department of Labor
200 Constitution Ave., NW, Room N3653
Washington, DC 20210 (202) 523-7031

This office serves as the principal source of agency expertise with respect to scientific, engineering, and medical issues involved in the overall occupational safety and health field. The Directorate manages a centralized program to provide technical interpretations and clarifications of OSHA standards, rule making and related matters.

* Small Business and Employee Health

National Health Information Clearinghouse
P.O. Box 1133 (800) 336-4797
Washington, DC 20013 (301) 565-4167 (MD and DC)

Small Business and Health Promotion: The Prospects Look Good. A Guide for Providers of Health Promotion Programs presents small business owners' views on health promotion, suggesting ways that community-based programs can work effectively with small businesses. This 35-page booklet (Order No. W0004) is available for $2.

* Small Business Health and Safety

National Institute for Occupational Safety and Health
4676 Columbia Parkway
Cincinnati, OH 45226 (513) 533-8287

Many publications are available through this office regarding safety, occupational hazards, and occupational safety and health programs for a variety of business settings. Contact this office for a free catalog of publications.

* Smoking Restrictions and Bans

Office of Smoking and Health
5600 Fishers Lane, Room 1-10
Rockville, MD 20857 (301) 443-1690

No Smoking: A Decision Maker's Guide to Reducing Smoking at the Workplace discusses the impact of smoking on employees and businesses and describes programs companies have used to restrict or ban smoking at work. This 42-page manual (Order No. W0001) is available, $2 handling fee.

* Speakers from OSHA

Occupational Safety and Health Review Commission
1825 K St., NW, 4th Floor
Washington, DC 20006-1246 (202) 219-8148

The Chairman, General Counsel, and members of the Commission have participated as speakers for various industry and civic organizations. A written request to the individual is necessary for a confirmation of availability and attendance.

Be patient. If any phone number is incorrect, call (area code) 555-1212 and request the new listing.

Occupational Health and Safety

* Standards on Occupational Safety and Health

Superintendent of Documents
Government Printing Office
Washington, DC 20402 (202) 783-3238

The *Federal Register* is one of the best sources of information on standards, since all OSHA standards are published there when adopted, as are all amendments, corrections, insertions, or deletions. Annual subscriptions are available from the Government Printing Office. Each year the office of the *Federal Register* publishes all current regulations and standards in the *Code of Federal Regulations*, available at many libraries and from the Government Printing Office. OSHA's regulations are collected in Title 29 of the CFR, Part 1900-1999.

* Toxic Hazards in the Workplace

Salt Lake City Laboratory
Occupational Safety and Health Administration (OSHA)
U.S. Department of Labor
P.O. Box 15200
Salt Lake City, UT 84115 (801) 524-5287

The OSHA Analytical Laboratory conducts extensive analyses, tests, and studies of all samples submitted by safety and health compliance officers and others to evaluate toxicity and the existence of health hazards.

* Worker Health and Safety Standards

Directorate of Health Standards Programs
Occupational Safety and Health Administration (OSHA)
U.S. Department of Labor
200 Constitution Ave., NW, Room N3718
Washington, DC 20210 (202) 219-7075

OSHA develops mandatory health standards for such varied fields as manufacturing, construction, longshoring, agriculture, law and medicine, charity and disaster relief, organized labor, and private education. Contact this office about these standards.

* Workplace Safety and Health Awards

Occupational Safety and Health Administration (OSHA)
U.S. Department of Labor
200 Constitution Ave., NW, Room N3700
Washington, DC 20210 (202) 219-7266

Designed to augment OSHA's enforcement efforts, the Star, Merit, and Demonstration Programs encourage and recognize excellence in occupational safety and health. Only those companies which demonstrate commitments to workplace safety and health beyond the requirements of the OSHA standards are eligible. Participation in the programs exempts a worksite from OSHA's programmed inspections. Companies must have strong safety and health programs, along with employee participation. Contact this office for an application, information, and complete details regarding the various programs.

* Worksite Health Promotion Survey

National Health Information Clearinghouse
P.O. Box 1133 (800) 336-4797
Washington, DC 20013-1133 (301) 565-4167 (MD and DC)

National Survey of Worksite Health Promotion Activities: A Summary provides the findings of this 1985 telephone survey of a representative sampling of worksites with 50 or more employees. This monograph (Order No. M0005) is available for $2.

* Worksite Health Programs

National Health Information Clearinghouse
P.O. Box 1133 (800) 336-4797
Washington, DC 20013-1133 (301) 565-4167 (MD and DC)

Worksite Wellness Media Reports illustrate examples of worksite health promotion programs and also present comprehensive reports on health facts. These reports are designed for the media covering the business community. The latest report totaling 318 pages (Order No. W0015) is available for $3.

Be patient. If any phone number is incorrect, call (area code) 555-1212 and request the new listing.

Careers and Workplace

Federal Employment

As the largest single employer in the country, the federal government has plenty of benefits, programs, and services for its employees, many of whom may not know all that's available to them. Here federal employees will find information sources on pensions, compensation, new job opportunities, health benefits, merit pay, and countless other programs.

* Affirmative Employment
Office of Affirmative Employment Programs
Office of Personnel Management
1900 E St., NW, Room 6355
Washington, DC 20415 (202) 606-1059

The Office of Personnel Management (OPM) seeks to eliminate nonmerit considerations such as race, color, religion, sex, national origin, or age from all aspects of federal employment through its affirmative employment efforts. OPM also operates selective placement programs for physically and mentally handicapped persons, and programs for other groups including veterans, youths, and women. Contact this office for more information.

* Alcoholic and Drug Treatment Programs
Employee Health Services
Personnel Systems and Oversight Group
Office of Personnel Management
1900 E St., NW, Room 7300
Washington, DC 20415 (202) 606-2900

All government employee health and alcoholism/drug abuse programs are overseen by this office. Contact this office for more information.

* Annuities
Retirement and Insurance Group
Annuitant Services Division
Office of Retirement Programs
Office of Personnel Management
1900 E St., NW, Room 3321
Washington, DC 20415 (202) 606-2039

This office has free pamphlets describing annuity benefits under the civil service retirement system. Contact this office for more information.

* Appeals Process
Office of the Appeals Counsel
Merit Systems Protection Board
1120 Vermont Ave., NW
Room 864
Washington, DC 20419 (202) 653-8888

The Office of Appeals Counsel assists the Board in judicially settling petitions for review from initial decisions issued by administrative judges in the regional offices. The office receives and analyzes the petitions, researches applicable laws, rules, and precedents, and submits proposed opinions to the board members for their final settlement. When an agency issues a decision notice to an employee on a matter that is appealable to the Board, the agency must provide the employee with a notice of the time limits for the appeal and the address for filing the appeal, a copy of or access to a copy of the Board's regulations, a copy of the appeal form, and a notice of any right the employee has to file a grievance.

* Appeals Regional Offices
Office of Public Affairs
Merit Systems Protection Board
1120 Vermont Ave., NW
Room 800
Washington, DC 20419 (202) 653-8900

The MSPB Regional Offices are located in 11 major metropolitan areas throughout the United States: Atlanta, Boston, Chicago, Dallas, Denver, New York, Philadelphia, St. Louis, San Francisco, Seattle, and Washington, DC. These offices receive and process the initial appeals filed with the Board. Administrative judges in the regional offices have the primary function of issuing fair, timely, and well-reasoned decisions on all appeals. Contact this office for a listing of these offices and more information.

* Aviation Careers
Aviation Education Officer
Federal Aviation Administration (FAA)
U.S. Department of Transportation
800 Independence Ave., SW
Washington, DC 20591 (202) 267-3469

The FAA's Aviation Education Program offers volunteer assistance to the nation's schools through the following programs: career guidance; tours of airports, control towers, and other facilities; classroom lectures and demonstrations; aviation safety information; aviation education resource materials; computerized clearinghouse of aviation and space information; aviation science instruction programs for home/school computers; "Partnerships-in-Education" activities; and teachers' workshops. Write to the above office for more information.

* Civil Service Exams
Federal Job Information Center
General Information
Office of Personnel Management
1900 E St., NW, Room 1416
Washington, DC 20415 (202) 606-2700

Information on Civil Service Exams is contained in the pamphlet, *Current Federal Examination Announcements* (AN-2279). This free pamphlet is available from any Federal Job Information Center.

* Compensation Benefits
Office of Worker's Compensation Programs
Employment Standards Administration
U.S. Department of Labor
200 Constitution Ave., NW
Room S3524
Washington, DC 20210 (202) 219-7503

The Federal Employees' Compensation Act (FECA) provides compensation benefits to civilian employees of the U.S. for disability due to personal injury sustained while in the performance of duty. The Act also provides compensation for employment-related disease. Benefits also available to injured employees include rehabilitation, medical, surgical, and hospital services and supplies, and necessary transportation expenses. FECA provides compensation to dependents if the injury or disease causes the employees's death.

* Employee and Annuitant Information Center
Retirement Information Branch
Retirement Programs
Retirement and Insurance Group
Office of Personnel Management
1900 E St., NW, Room 1323B
Washington, DC 20415 (202) 606-0500

This clearinghouse offers guidance on federal retirees' annuities.

Be patient. If any phone number is incorrect, call (area code) 555-1212 and request the new listing.

Federal Employment

* Employee Conduct Regulations

Office of Government Ethics
Office of Personnel Management
1201 New York Ave., Suite 500
Washington, DC 20005 (202) 523-5757

Ethics in Government, federal regulations, and a digest of opinions since 1979 is outlined in the *Agency Relations Packet*, which is available free from the above office.

* Environmental Protection Agency Job Hotline

Recruitment, Environmental Protection Agency (EPA)
401 M Street, SW
Washington, DC 20460 (800) 338-1350

This EPA National Recruitment Program Number enables potential hirees to contact the Agency for employment information and assists EPA managers in locating and hiring qualified employees to fill vacant positions. The number operates Monday through Friday, 8:30 a.m. to 4:30 p.m. (EST).

* Ethics in Federal Workplace

Office of Government Ethics
Office of Personnel Management
1201 New York Ave., Suite 500
Washington, DC 20005 (202) 523-5757

To prevent conflicts of interest on the part of officers and employees of any executive agency, overall direction of executive branch policies is provided by this office. Rules and regulations are developed here pertaining to employee conduct and post-employment conflicts of interest, and public financial disclosure is monitored. Contact this office for more information.

* Executive Development Center

Federal Executive Institute
Office of Personnel Management
1301 Emmet St.
Charlottesville, VA 22901 (804) 980-6200

The Federal Executive Institute (FEI) is an interagency executive development center which responds to the training and development needs of federal executives. FEI programs schedule courses that are designed to facilitate executive improvement. Programs in four categories are conducted: The Executive leadership and Management Program, the Senior Executive Education program, FEI alumni Follow-up Conferences, and Special Programs.

* Executive Management Training

Washington Management Institute
Executive Personnel and Management Development
Office of Personnel Management
1121 Vermont Ave., NW, Room 308
Washington, DC 20415 (202) 606-0889

Executive and managerial training and development services to support government agencies in their efforts to achieve greater efficiency and effectiveness in managing federal programs is provided by the Institute. Send mail to P.O. Box 988, Washington, DC 20044.

* Exemption from Competitive Service

Examination Services Division
Office of Personnel Management
1900 E St., NW, Room 6303
Washington, DC 20415 (202) 606-2525

Information and advice on "exemption" from competitive service is available from this office.

* Ex-Railroad Workers Placement Service

Unemployment and Sickness Insurance
Railroad Retirement Board
844 Rush St.
Chicago, IL 60611 (312) 751-4800

The Board operates a free job placement service for experienced railroad workers who have lost their jobs. It is available to those claiming unemployment benefits. Contact this office or the nearest Railroad Retirement Board Office for more information.

* Federal Contracts

Procurement and Administrative Services
Administrative Group
Office of Personnel Management
1900 E Street, NW
Room 1452
Washington, DC 20415 (202) 606-2240

Information on contracts can be obtained by contacting one of the regional offices listed below.

Atlanta Region
Richard B. Russell Federal Building, 75 Spring Street, SW, Atlanta, GA 30303-3019; (404) 331-3459. Serving: Alabama, Florida, North Carolina, South Carolina, Georgia, Mississippi, Tennessee, and Virginia

Chicago Region
John C. Kluczynski Federal Building, 230 South Dearborn Street, Chicago, IL 60604; (312) 353-2901. Serving: Illinois, Indiana, Iowa, Kansas, Kentucky, Michigan, Minnesota, Missouri, Nebraska, North Dakota, Ohio, South Dakota, West Virginia, and Wisconsin

Dallas Region
1100 Commerce Street, Dallas, TX 75242; (214) 767-8235. Serving: Arkansas, Arizona, Colorado, Louisiana, Montana, New Mexico, Oklahoma, Texas, Utah, and Wyoming

Philadelphia Region
William J. Green, Jr., Federal Building, 600 Arch Street, Philadelphia, PA 19106-1596; (215) 597-4431. Serving: Connecticut, Delaware, Maine, Maryland, Massachusetts, New Hampshire, New Jersey, New York, Pennsylvania, Puerto Rico, Rhode Island, Vermont, and Virgin Islands

San Francisco Region
211 Main Street, 7th Floor, San Francisco, CA 94105; (415) 974-9662. Serving: Alaska, California, Hawaii, Idaho, Nevada, Oregon, Pacific Ocean Area, and Washington

* Federal Employees' Attitudes Surveys

Center for Electronic Records
National Archives and Records Administration
8th St. and Pennsylvania Ave., NW
Room 20E
Washington, DC 20408 (202) 501-5402

This center has data pertaining to federal employees' attitudes on a variety of topics, and can provide you with a complete list of the survey samples.

* Federal Employees Current Attitudes

Office of Evaluation and Personnel Management
Office of Personnel Management
1900 E St., NW
Washington, DC 20415 (202) 606-1212

A government-wide attitude survey of federal employees was administered to establish a baseline of employee attitudes about their jobs and work environment. Groupings include federal agencies, pay levels, pay systems, and supervisory and non-supervisory personnel. *Federal Employee Attitudes: Phase 2--Follow Up*, a report, can be purchased from the Superintendent of Documents, Government Printing Office, Washington, DC 20402; (202) 783-3238.

* Federal Job Information Centers

Federal Job Information Center
General Information
Office of Personnel Management
1900 E Street, NW
Room 1416
Washington, DC 20415 (202) 606-2700

Federal Job Information Centers are located in major metropolitan areas. This network of centers provides information on summer employment, necessary application forms, exams, and all other aspects pertaining to federal employment. *Federal Job Information Centers*, a free directory, is available from the above office. By using the government pages of your local phone directory, you will be able to locate the center nearest you.

Be patient. If any phone number is incorrect, call (area code) 555-1212 and request the new listing.

Careers and Workplace

* Federal Labor Relations Authority Freedom of Information

Public Information Office
Federal Labor Relations Authority (FLRA)
500 C St., SW
Washington, DC 20424 (202) 382-0711

The Public Information Office listed above is the Freedom of Information Act contact for the Authority.

* FED Fact Pamphlets

Office of Public Affairs
Office of Personnel Management
1900 E St., NW, Room 5F12
Washington, DC 20415 (202) 606-1212

Pamphlets that cover a variety of subjects related to government employees are issued by the Office of Personnel Management. Single copies are available free, and multiple copies of *FED Facts* must be purchased from the Superintendent of Documents, Government Printing Office, Washington, DC 20402; (202) 783-3238.

*Incentive Awards Program
Political Activity of Federal Employees
The Federal Retirement System
Financial Protection for Federal Employees
The Federal Merit Promotion Policy
Serving the Public: The Extra Step
The Federal Wage System
Meeting Your Financial Obligations
Maternity Leave
Employee Appeals from Actions
The Displaced Employee Program
Reductions in Force in Federal Agencies
Reemployment Rights of Federal Employees Who Perform Duty in the Armed Forces
Federal Labor Relations
Pay Under the General Schedule
The Cost of Living Allowance for Federal Employees
The Intergovernmental Mobility Program
How Your GS Job is Classified
Merit System Principles and Prohibited Personnel Practices
Furlough*

* Forest Ranger Jobs

Forest Service
U.S. Department of Agriculture
Recruitment
P.O. Box 2417
Washington, DC 20013 (703) 235-2730

Contact this office for information on a career as a forest ranger.

* General Schedule Classification

Office of Public Affairs
Office of Personnel Management
1900 E St., NW, Room 5F12
Washington, DC 20415 (202) 606-1212

A variety of publications on government service classifications are available. Single copies are free, including *A Report on Study of Position Classification Accuracy in Executive Branch on Occupation Under the General Schedule* and *FED Facts* on *How Your GS Job is Classified.* The *Handbook of Occupational Groups and Series of Classes* ($120) is sold by the Superintendent of Documents, Government Printing Office, Washington, DC 20402; (202) 783-3238.

* Government Affairs Institute

Executive Personnel and Management
Development Division
Office of Personnel Management
1121 Vermont Ave., NW, Room 200
Washington, DC 20415 (202) 606-0889

This office offers the following services: interagency seminars, conducted on Capitol Hill to provide on-site experience with Congress; single-agency or single-program projects, tailored to meet the specific needs of an agency or clusters of agencies with related missions; courses offered by the Government Affairs Institute designed to meet developmental needs of current and future executives and managers. Seminars for support staff personnel are also offered. Contact this office for more information.

* Health Benefits

Insurance Programs
Retirement and Insurance Programs
Office of Personnel Management
1900 E St., NW, Room 3415
Washington, DC 20415 (202) 606-3821

This office oversees the federal employees health benefits program which includes various types of hospital, surgical and medical benefits for federal employees. Numerous free publications are available on this subject: *Federal Employee Health Benefits Program* (biweekly and monthly health benefits rates), and *Information to Consider in Choosing a Health Plan.* Contact this office for more information.

* Health Professions in U.S. Public Health Corps

Office of Data Analyses and Management
Bureau of Health Professions
5600 Fishers Lane, Room 8-43
Rockville, MD 20857 (301) 443-6936

The Bureau of Health Professions supports the development of human resources needed to staff the U.S. health care system. It is concerned with health professions education, credentialing of health care personnel, and analysis of data to project needs for health care personnel. They also support student assistance and analyze current and future personnel supply, requirements and distribution. This office can supply you with data regarding health profession supply distribution on the level of nursing training in any area of the country. This information is often used by consultants, corporations involved with medical technology, and other government agencies.

* Incentive Awards

Personnel Systems and Oversight Group
Office of Personnel Management
1900 E St., NW, Room 7316
Washington, DC 20415 (202) 606-2828

Cash and honor awards are available under the incentive award program to employees for effecting improvements in government operations or services through their suggestions, inventions, and superior performance. The following publications are available for free: *Federal Incentive Awards Program-Annual Report;* and *Limited Resources-Unlimited Ideas.* Contact this office for more information.

* Index To OPM Information

Publishing Management Branch
Administration Group
Internal Distribution
Office of Personnel Management (OPM)
1900 E St., NW, Room B430
Washington, DC 20415 (202) 606-1212

The annual OPM index with quarterly supplements is available at no cost from this office. This index lists all Office of Personnel Management publications, including information required to be available under the Freedom of Information Act. Requests must be submitted in writing.

* Insurance Programs

Insurance Programs
Retirement and Insurance Group
Office of Personnel Management
1717 H St., NW, Room 3415
Washington, DC 20415 (202) 606-3821

The free pamphlet, *Federal Employees Group Life Insurance Program,* provides information on regular and optional life insurance programs. Contact this office for more information.

* Interagency Training Courses

Office of Washington Training and Development Services
Washington Area Service Center
Office of Personnel Management

Be patient. If any phone number is incorrect, call (area code) 555-1212 and request the new listing.

Federal Employment

1121 Vermont Ave., NW, Room 1216TC
Washington, DC 20415 (202) 632-4410

The *Interagency Training Catalog of Courses* contains a variety of training programs offered by various federal agencies. These courses are available to federal, State, and local government employees. The following is a sample listing of courses: automated data processing, communications and office skills, general management, labor relations, management sciences, personnel management, and records management. Contact this office for more information.

* Job Grading System

Standard Development Staff
Office of Classifications
Personnel Systems and Oversight Group
Office of Personnel Management
1900 E St., NW, Room 7H29
Washington, DC 20415 (202) 606-2970

The publication, *Job Grading System for Trades and Labor Occupations*, is available on a subscription basis ($100) from the Superintendent of Documents, Government Printing Office, Washington, DC 20402; (202) 783-3238. For additional information contact the office above.

* Labor Agreement Information Retrieval System (LAIRS)

Labor Agreement Information Retrieval System
Office of Labor Relations and Workforce Performance
Personnel Systems and Oversight Group
Office of Personnel Management
1900 E St., NW, Room 7431
Washington, DC 20415 (202) 606-2940

The LAIRS system provides current and historic information about the federal labor relations program. The information is provided in the form of computer searches, microfiche of full text decisions, published analytic reports, current periodicals, and variety of audio-visual training aids. The file contains negotiated agreements, arbitration awards, and significant Federal labor relations decisions. A fee schedule is included. This system publishes labor-management reports, surveys, digests, and other related publications. A publications list and additional information can be obtained from the above office.

* Labor Management Information

Labor Agreement Information Retrieval Systems
Office of Personnel Management
1900 E St., NW, Room 7429
Washington, DC 20415 (202) 606-2940

This public reference room has labor-management reports, surveys, and analyses available for public viewing. An appointment is suggested.

* Labor-Management Relations

Employee Labor and Agency Relations
Personnel Systems and Oversight Group
Office of Personnel Management
1900 E St., NW, Room 7412
Washington, DC 20415 (202) 606-2930

This office provides information, guidance, and assistance to agencies, unions, and the public on federal labor-management relations. Eligible labor organizations are consulted in the development and revision of government-wide personnel policies.

* Labor Management Surveys

Labor Agreement Information Retrieval System (LAIRS)
Office of Personnel Management
1900 E St., NW, Room 7431
Washington, DC 20415 (202) 606-2940

The LAIRS (Labor Agreement Information Retrieval System) generates numerous surveys and analytical studies, including:

A Survey of Unfair Labor Practice Complaints in The Federal Government
Maternity/Sick Leave Provisions in Federal Agreements
Productivity Clauses in Federal Agreements

Single copies of these publications are available free of charge.

* Labor Practices in Federal Service

Public Information Office
Federal Labor Relations Authority (FLRA)
500 C St., SW
Washington, DC 20424 (202) 382-0711

Contact this office to obtain a copy of the *FLRA Annual Report*, which describes significant decisions of the FLRA and case processing statistics of the General Counsel of the Authority. Cases of alleged unfair labor practices in federal service are investigated and prosecuted by the General Counsel and are heard by the FLRA's Office of Administrative Law Judges.

* Labor Relations Documents

Office of Case Control
Federal Labor Relations Authority (FLRA)
500 C St., SW
Washington, DC 20424 (202) 382-0748

Case file information is maintained on FLRA hearings and cases prosecuted to ensure compliance with the rights and obligations of federal employees to organize, bargain collectively, and participate in labor organizations. To view FLRA case dockets and decisions, call ahead to this office to arrange for a visit.

* Labor Relations Reading

Library
Federal Labor Relations Authority (FLRA)
500 C St., SW, Room 235
Washington, DC 20424 (202) 382-0765

A small specialized collection is housed here. Material covers federal service labor-management relations and the Federal Labor Relations Authority. The library is open to the public, but due to tight security in the building, you are advised to call ahead for an appointment.

* Loans Available to Federal Retirees

External Affairs
Federal Retirement Thrift Investment Board
1250 H St., NW
Washington, DC 20005 (202) 523-5660

Federal Employee's Retirement System and Civil Service Retirement System employees may borrow their own contributions and earnings from the Thrift Savings Plan account for the purchase of a primary residence, medical expenses, educational expenses, and financial hardships. The minimum loan is $1,000, and the loan is repaid through regular payroll allotments. For more information about loans, federal employees should ask their employing agency for copies of the *Thrift Savings Plan* loan program materials.

* Merit Systems Protection Board (MSPB)

Office of Public Affairs
1120 Vermont Ave., NW, Room 800
Washington, DC 20419 (202) 653-8900

The Merit Systems Protection Board is an independent agency in the Executive branch of the Federal Government whose job it is to see that Federal employees are protected against abuses by agency management, that Executive branch agencies make employment decisions in accordance with the merit system principles, and that Federal merit systems are kept free of prohibited personnel practices. The booklet *An Introduction to the MSPB* describes its basic functions. A publications list is also available.

* Merit Systems Protection Personnel Practices

Office of Policy and Evaluation
Merit Systems Protection Board (MSPB)
1120 Vermont Ave., NW, Room 884
Washington, DC 20419 (202) 653-8900

The Merit Systems Protection Board conducts special studies on the civil service and other executive branch merit systems and reports to the President and the Congress on whether the federal work force is being adequately protected against political abuses and prohibited personnel practices. You can receive a list and free copies of MSPB reports by contacting the office. Some recently released reports include *First-Line Supervisory Selection in the Federal Government*, and *U.S. Office of Personnel Management and the Merit System: A Retrospective Assessment*.

Be patient. If any phone number is incorrect, call (area code) 555-1212 and request the new listing.

Careers and Workplace

* Occupational Health Facilities

Office of Labor Relations and Workforce Performance
Employee Relations Division
Office of Personnel Management
1900 E St., NW
Washington, DC 20415 (202) 606-1269

A directory of Federal Occupational Health Facilities is available from this office for free.

* Office of Personnel Management Library

Finance and Administrative Services
Administration Group
Office of Personnel Management (OPM)
1900 E Street, NW
Room 5L44
Washington, DC 20415 (202) 606-1432

The OPM Library contains a comprehensive collection of materials on personnel management and the federal civil service. The library also issues *Personnel Literature,* a monthly with an annual index ($18) which is available from the Superintendent of Documents, Government Printing Office, Washington, DC 20402; (202) 783-3238.

* Office of Personnel Management Publications

Superintendent of Documents
Government Printing Office (GPO)
Washington, DC 20402 (202) 783-3238

The GPO has a list of OPM publications available for a fee. The list is free. Ask for *Subject Bibliography 300.*

* Merit Pay

Office of Public Affairs
Office of Personnel Management
1900 E St., NW
Washington, DC 20415 (202) 606-1212

Information on the merit pay system for supervisors and management officials in grades below Senior Executive Schedules is available in the publication, *FED Facts on Merit System Principles and Prohibited Personnel Practices,* which are available from the above office.

* Military Personnel Records Archives Center

National Personnel Records Center
National Archives and Records Administration
9700 Page Blvd
St. Louis, MO 63132 (314) 263-7247

The National Personnel Records Center stores the personnel records of former federal employees. The Center can answer requests for information, most of which are inquiries relating to claims for benefits. Service numbers are as follows:

Army: .... (314) 538-4261
Navy and Marines: .... (314) 538-4141
Air Force: .... (314) 538-4243

* Negotiation Impasses

Federal Services Impasses Board
Federal Labor Relations Authority (FLRA)
500 C St., SW, Room 215
Washington, DC 20424 (202) 382-0981

When negotiation impasses develop between Federal agencies and employee representatives, this panel provides assistance in resolving the stalemate. The following publications are available: *Guide to Hearing Procedures of the Federal Services; Impasses Panel; Subject Matter Index; Table of Cases;* and the *Annual Report.*

* Pay and Benefits Inquiries

Office of Retirement and Insurance Policy
Office of Personnel Management
1900 E St., NW, Room 4330
Washington, DC 20415 (202) 606-0788

Questions about federal holidays, salary schedules, group life insurance, health benefits, occupational health insurance, sick leave, retirement, and so on, can be answered by this office.

* Pension and Retirement Audits

Office of the Chief Accountant
Pension and Welfare Benefits Administration
U.S. Department of Labor
200 Constitution Ave., NW
Room N5677
Washington, DC 20210 (202) 219-8951

This office serves as the U.S. Department of Labor's primary advisor on accounting, auditing, and actuarial issues stemming from its responsibilities under the Employee Retirement Income Security Act and the Federal Employees' Retirement System Act (FERSA). It serves as the primary agency contact with accounting and actuarial organizations, as well as with federal and state agencies on accounting matters. It also administers a comprehensive system of compliance audits under FERSA and reviews annual financial reports filed under ERISA.

* Personnel Investigations

Office of Federal Investigations
Investigation Group
Office of Personnel Management
PO Box 886
Washington, DC 20044 (202) 376-3800

Used in support of the selection and appointment processes, these investigations serve several purposes: to determine the suitability of applicants under consideration for appointment; to check on applicants or employees under consideration for appointment to positions having either national security or special professional or administrative qualifications requirements, or both; and to enforce civil service regulations. The Office of Personnel Management also makes loyalty determinations of United States citizens employed or under consideration for employment by international organizations of which the United States is a member. Contact this office for more information.

* Personnel Investigator

Office of the Special Counsel
1120 Vermont Ave (202) 653-7188
Washington, DC 20419 (800) 872-9855

The Office of the Special Counsel is an independent investigative and prosecuting agency that litigates before the Merit Systems Protection Board. The office is responsible for investigating allegations of prohibited personnel practices, prohibited political activities by federal and certain state and local employees, arbitrary or capricious withholding of information in violation of the Freedom of Information Act, prohibited discrimination when found by appropriate authority, and other activities prohibited by any civil service law, rule, or regulation. The office is also responsible for receiving and referring to the appropriate agency information that indicates a violation of any law, rule, or regulation, mismanagement, a gross waste of funds, an abuse of authority, or a substantial and specific danger to public health or safety. The Special Counsel may request the Merit Systems Protection Board to order disciplinary action against any employee who violates civil service laws, rules, and regulations. Any federal employee may file a complaint with the office.

* Personnel Management

Personnel and EEO Division
Office of Personnel Management
1900 E St., NW, Room 1469
Washington, DC 20415 (202) 606-1402

This office manages the following personnel management responsibilities: government-wide classification system, administration of government pay systems; development and operation of information systems to support and improve federal personnel management decisionmaking; and independent evaluation of agency personnel management systems. Contact this office for more information.

* Personnel Management Manual

Inventory Management
Office of Personnel Management
1900 E St., NW, Room E453
Washington, DC 20415 (202) 606-2440

The *Federal Personnel Manual* covers all aspects of personnel management and includes letters, bulletins, and supplements. This publication is prepared by the

Federal Employment

various units within the Office of Personnel Management and is available on a subscription basis from the Superintendent of Documents, Government Printing Office, Washington, DC 20402; (202) 783-3238.

* Personnel Publications

Library
Finance and Administrative Services
Administration Group
1900 E Street, NW
Room 5L44
Washington, DC 20415 (202) 606-1432

Personnel Literature is a monthly publication that includes about 200 or so personnel management subjects, such as performance evaluation, productivity, executives, employee training and development, and labor management relations. It includes federal, state, and local governments, foreign governments, and private organizations. It is sold for $18 per year by the Superintendent of Documents, Government Printing Office, Washington, DC 20402; (202) 783-3238.

* Personnel Records Archives

National Personnel Records Center
National Archives and Records Administration
111 Winnebago Street
St. Louis, MO 63118 (314) 425-5761

Federal employees' personnel records are transferred and stored in the National Personnel Records Center. The Center can answer questions regarding the information available, and can provide copies of documents. Only civilian records are stored here. Contact the Center for more information.

* Personnel Records System

Personnel Records and Systems Division
Office of Personnel Management
1900 E St., NW, Room 5305
Washington, DC 20415 (202) 606-2868

Basic Personnel Records and Files System describes the personnel records system of the Office of Personnel Management. This publication is available by subscription for $65 from the Superintendent of Documents, Government Printing Office, Washington, DC 20402; (202) 783-3238.

* Postal Career Executive Service

Employee Relations Department
U.S. Postal Service
475 L'Enfant Plaza, SW
Washington, DC 20260 (202) 268-3643

The postal career executive program develops qualified managers and supervisors through training, educational and work experiences. Contact this office for more information about this program.

* Postal Inspector Jobs

Chief Postal Inspector
U.S. Postal Service
475 L'Enfant Plaza, SW
Washington, DC 20260 (202) 268-4267

Information about Inspection Service employment may be obtained from the Chief Postal Inspector.

* Postal Service Employee/Labor Relations Manual

Employee Relations Department
U.S. Postal Service
475 L'Enfant Plaza, SW
Washington, DC 20260 (202) 268-3643

This subscription service consists of a basic manual and updated transmittal letters for an indeterminate period. This manual sets forth the personnel policies and regulations governing employment with the Postal Service. Topics covered include organization management, job evaluation, employment and placement, pay administration, employee benefits, employee relations, training, safety and health, and labor relations. The subscription is available for $29 domestic, and $36.25 foreign per year from: Superintendent of Documents, Government Printing Office, Washington, DC 20402-0001; (202) 783-3238

* Postal Service Employment

Employee Relations Department
U.S. Postal Service
475 L'Enfant Plaza, SW
Washington, DC 20260 (202) 268-3643

General information about jobs such as clerk, letter carrier, etc., including information about programs for veterans, may be obtained by contacting the nearest post office. Individuals, generally college graduates interested in engineering, management, finance, personnel work, or in employment as physicists, mathematicians, and operations research analysts, may obtain information by contacting the above office.

* Postal Service Handicapped Employment

Employee Relations Department
U.S. Postal Service
475 L'Enfant Plaza, SW
Washington, DC 20260 (202) 268-3643

The Postal Service created a noncompetitive hiring process for severely handicapped applicants. This program allows the Veterans Administration and State agencies for the disabled (once certified by the Postal Service as having appropriate screening and development capabilities) to refer severely handicapped individuals for direct career appointments.

* Postal Service Union Negotiations

Human Resources Group
U.S. Postal Service
475 L'Enfant Plaza, SW Room 9021
Washington, DC 20260 (202) 268-3619

The Postal Service is the only Federal agency whose employment policies are governed by a process of collective bargaining. Labor contract negotiations, affecting all bargaining unit personnel, as well as personnel matters involving employees not covered by collective bargaining agreements, are administered by the Human Resources Group.

* Presidential and Vice-Presidential Financial Reporting

Office of Government Ethics
Office of Personnel Management
1201 New York Ave., NW, Suite 500
Washington, DC 20005 (202) 523-5757

This office is responsible for the financial statements of top personnel in the Executive Branch, including the President, Vice President, and anyone with a basic rate of pay equal to or above a General Schedule-16. All appointees file with the agency in which they are employed. The financial statements of the U.S. President and the Vice President are available.

* Presidential Management Intern Programs

Office of Personnel Management
1900 E St., NW, Room 7H34
Washington, DC 20415 (202) 606-1212

Two-year internships in the federal service are available for recipients of graduate degrees in general management with a public sector focus. Contact this office for more information about the Presidential Management Intern Program.

* Productivity Among Civil Servants

Industry Productivity Studies Division
Office of Productivity and Technology
Bureau of Labor Statistics
U.S. Department of Labor
200 Constitution Ave., NW, Room S4320
Washington, DC 20210 (202) 606-6222

Productivity measures are developed annually for various functional levels within the Federal government. The information available includes annual indexes of output per employee year, unit labor costs, compensation per employee year, and out put and employee years. Data come from 455 organizations within 48 Federal departments and agencies.

* Public Policy Training

Executive Seminar Center
Office of Training

Be patient. If any phone number is incorrect, call (area code) 555-1212 and request the new listing.

Careers and Workplace

Office of Personnel Management
1121 Vermont Ave., NW
Room 1200
Washington, DC 20044 (202) 632-4410

The following Centers are residential interagency training facilities to aid government agencies in meeting programmatic and managerial training needs. Federal, State, and local governments may take advantage of the programs. The curriculum includes seminars on administration of public policy; public program management; science, technology and public policy; national economy and public policy; intergovernmental relations; domestic policies and programs; management and executive development; energy policies and programs. Locations of the centers are as follows:

Eastern Executive Seminar Center, c/o U.S. Merchant Marine Academy, Kings Point, NY 11024; (516) 487-4500 or 482-8200, ext 343

Central Executive Seminar Center, Broadway and Kentucky Ave., Oak Ridge, TN 37831-3515; (615) 576-1730

Western Executive Seminar Center, 1405 Curtis, Denver, CO 80202

* Railroad Certificate of Service Months and Compensation

Research and Employment Accounts
Railroad Retirement Board
844 Rush St.
Chicago, IL 60611 (312) 751-4968

Each year railroad employees receive a Certificate of Service Months and Compensation (Form BA-6) from their employers or from the Board, which provides a current record of service and compensation. Contact the above listed office to report incorrect information.

* Railroad Employees Benefit Statistics

Office of Public Affairs
Railroad Retirement Board
844 Rush St.
Chicago, IL 60611 (312) 751-4777

Information on Board operations and on the laws it administers is available. Publications include *Annual Report, Statistical Supplement, Monthly Benefit Statistics,* and several informational pamphlets. The *Annual Report* can be ordered from the Superintendent of Documents, Government Printing Office, Washington, DC 20402; (202) 783-3238.

* Railroad Retirement and Survivor Benefits

Bureau of Retirement Claims
Railroad Retirement Board
844 Rush St.
Chicago, IL 60611 (312) 751-4600

Railroad retirement benefits include regular employee retirement annuities after 10 year of service, supplemental annuities, spouse annuities, cost-of-living increases in employee and spouse retirement benefits, and other survivor benefits. *Railroad Retirement and Survivor Benefits* describes these benefits and provides practical information on how to claim them. It also includes relevant tax information.

* Railroad Retirement Appeals Process

Bureau of Hearings and Appeal
Railroad Retirement Board
844 Rush St.
Chicago, IL 60611 (312) 751-4790

Railroad employees can demand an official review of any determination to deny their benefits. If the review still denies the benefits, the employee can appeal.

* Railroad Retirement Benefit Conferences

Labor Member
Railroad Retirement Board
844 Rush St.
Chicago, IL 60611 (312) 751-4905

The Board conducts conferences to describe the benefits available under its retirement-survivor, unemployment-sickness, and Medicare programs. Attendants receive a copy of the *Informational Conference Handbook*--a comprehensive

source of information on Board programs--plus pamphlets and other materials highlighting Board programs.

* Railroad Retirement Board Field Offices

Railroad Retirement Board
844 Rush St.
Chicago, IL 60611 (312) 751-4777

Railroad Retirement Board offices are located across the country in localities accessible to large numbers of railroad workers. Personnel are on hand to explain benefit rights and responsibilities, assist employees in applying for benefits, and to answer questions related to the Board's programs. To locate the nearest Board office check the telephone directory under "United States Government", your Post Office, or a Federal Information Center. If there is no Board office nearby, call the nearest district office to set up an appointment to meet with a traveling Board representative.

* Railroad Retirement Board Freedom of Information

Office of Information Resources Management
Railroad Retirement Board
844 Rush St.
Chicago, IL 60611 (312) 751-4692

For Freedom of Information Act requests, contact the above office.

* Railroad Employee Service and Earnings Records

Research and Employment Accounts
Railroad Retirement Board
844 Rush St.
Chicago, IL 60611 (312) 751-4980

Records of service and earnings are kept on all railroad employees since 1936. The records are kept under the employee's Social Security number. Businesses covered by this program include railroads engaged in interstate commerce and some of their subsidiaries, railroad associations, and national railway labor organizations. Contact this office for more information on the records and how to access them.

* Railroad Workers Sickness and Unemployment Benefits

Bureau of Unemployment and Sickness Insurance
Railroad Retirement Board
844 Rush St.
Chicago, IL 60611 (312) 751-4800

Railroad unemployment insurance provides cash benefits in the form of unemployment benefits and sickness benefits. Under the Railroad Unemployment Insurance Act, an employee's eligibility is generally based on railroad service and earnings in the previous calendar year. Contact this office or your nearest Railroad Retirement Board regional office for more information on benefits.

* Retiree Interfund Transfers

External Affairs
Federal Retirement Thrift Investment Board
1250 H St., NW
Washington, DC 20005 (202) 523-5660

Open seasons for Federal employees provide the opportunity for Federal Employees' Retirement System employees to transfer a portion of their previously invested contributions and all earnings on their own contributions among three investment Plans: the Government Securities Investment Fund, the Common Stock Index Investment Fund, and the Fixed Income Index Investment Fund. Contact the above office or your employing Federal agency for further information.

* Retirees Health and Life Insurance

Office of Insurance Programs
Office of Personnel Management
1900 E Street, NW
Room 3H37
Washington, DC 20415 (202) 606-0770

Comparisons of various types of medical benefits and life insurance for retired federal employees are available from this office.

Be patient. If any phone number is incorrect, call (area code) 555-1212 and request the new listing.

Federal Employment

* Retirement Benefits

Office of Retirement Programs
Retirement and Insurance Group
Adjudication Division
Retirement Information Office
Office of Personnel Management
1900 E St., NW, Room 1323
Washington, DC 20415 (202) 606-0500

All claims for benefits under the retirement system must be adjudicated. Benefits are not paid automatically. Information on how to apply for retirement benefits, death benefits, and refunds is available from this office.

* Retirement Programs

Retirement Information Office
Office of Retirement Programs
Retirement and Insurance Group
Office of Personnel Management
1900 E St., NW, Room 1323
Washington, DC 20415 (202) 606-0500

You can get a variety of free publications on government retirement programs from this office. Some of these include *Federal Retirement Facts; Your Retirement System* (questions and answers on the federal civil service retirement law); *Information for Annuitants; Retirement Benefits When You Leave the Government Early;* and *Federal Fringe Benefits Facts.*

* Retirement Thrift Personnel Training Program

Federal Retirement Thrift Investment Board
1250 H St., NW
Washington, DC 20005 (202) 523-4511

The Board annually trains personnel in Federal agencies, particularly benefits officers, on the summary of the Thrift Benefits Plan. These persons are then prepared to explain the plan to other Federal employees and to answer questions concerning the options under the plan.

* Retirement Thrift Savings Plan

External Affairs
Federal Retirement Thrift Investment Board
1250 H St., NW
Washington, DC 20005 (202) 523-5660

Federal employees may benefit from this retirement savings and investment plan, which provides tax deferral on up to 5 percent for Civil Service Retirement System employees and 10 percent for Federal Employees' Retirement System employees from their basic pay. It also provides secure investments in the Government Securities Investment Fund, immediate vesting in one's own contributions and their earnings, a loan program, portability if leaving Government service, and a choice of withdrawal options. For further information, contact the above office for the brochure, *Thrift Savings Plan for Federal Employees.*

* Salary Schedules

Advisory Services Division
Office of Pay and Benefits
Office of Personnel Management
1900 E St., NW, Room 7434
Washington, DC 20415 (202) 606-2848

Salary and grade rates are available for General Schedule, Executive Schedule, and Senior Executive Schedule employees. Contact this office for more information.

* Senior Executive Candidates

Office of Executive and Management Policy
Office of Personnel Management
1900 E. Street, NW
Room 6R48
Washington, DC 20415 (202) 606-1610

This program prepares senior federal managers and other employees at a certain level to enter the Senior Executive Service by providing opportunities to improve upon and/or acquire the management and executive competencies required for the SES. Details about the program are available from the office listed above.

* Senior Executive Service

Senior Executive Service Division (SES)
Office of Personnel Management
1900 E Street, NW
Room 6R58
Washington, DC 20415 (202) 606-1728

SES provides every eligible senior manager the chance to shift top career managers around to meet the senior executive's needs. Additional information on the service is available from this office.

* Speakers About Public Service

Office of Public Affairs
Office of Personnel Management
1900 E St., NW
Washington, DC 20415 (202) 606-1212

Professional societies, business and labor groups, and other organizations can contact this office to arrange for representatives of the Office of Personnel Management to speak on federal personnel policies and changes.

* Special Benefits

Advisory Service Division
Office of Retirement Benefits and Policy
Retirement and Insurance Policy
Office of Personnel Management
1900 E St., NW, Room 4351
Washington, DC 20415 (202) 606-0777

Information on special civil service benefits is available from the Advisory Service. This is a recorded message.

* Standards for Federal Employment

Office of Classifications
Standards Development Staff
Career Entry and Employee Development Group
Office of Personnel Management
199 E St., NW, Room 6515
Washington, DC 20415 (202) 606-2970

Standards for evaluating employment requirements for most government occupations are developed by this office. Minimum qualification standards are provided to individual agencies, and they can then add more qualifications of their own if necessary. Contact this office for more information.

* Summer Job Announcements

Federal Job Information Center
General Information
Office of Personnel Management
1900 E Street, NW
Room 1416
Washington, DC 20415 (202) 606-2700

Announcements and information on summer employment opportunities with federal agencies is available.

* Tax Savings and the Retirement Thrift Savings Plan

External Affairs
Federal Retirement Thrift Investment Board
1250 H St., NW
Washington, DC 20005 (202) 523-5660

Thrift Savings Plan contributions are deducted from Federal pay before Federal and, in most cases, State income taxes are calculated. Until you withdraw your TSP account, you pay no income tax on the money you contribute, the money your agency contributes (if you are a Federal Employees' Retirement System employee), or the earnings on your account. For further information, contact your Federal employing agency or the above office for a copy of *Summary of the Thrift Savings Plan for Federal Employees.*

* Thrift Plan Investment Options

External Affairs
Federal Retirement Thrift Investment Board
1250 H St., NW
Washington, DC 20005 (202) 523-5660

Be patient. If any phone number is incorrect, call (area code) 555-1212 and request the new listing.

Careers and Workplace

Under present law, most Plan assets in the early years of investing, including some contributions (all of them if you are a Civil Service Retirement System employee) and all agency contributions, must be invested in a fund consisting of short-term, nonmarketable U.S. Treasury securities specially issued to the Thrift Savings Plan. This is the Government Securities Investment Fund or the G Fund. Federal Employee' Retirement System employees may make some of their own contributions, and beginning in 1993, may allocate some of their agency's contributions, to either the Common Stock Index Investment Fund or the Fixed Income Index Investment Fund or both. For a description of the advantages and risks of these investment options, contact your federal agency or the office above for a copy of the *Summary of the Thrift Savings Plan for Federal Employees*.

* Thrift Savings Annuities

External Affairs
Federal Retirement Thrift Investment Board
1250 H St., NW
Washington, DC 20005 (202) 523-5660

The Thrift Savings Plan provides a number of life annuity choices for Federal employees. A life annuity is a monthly benefit paid to you for life. You may choose to receive equal monthly payments or choose initially lower payments that increase each year. Some choices also provide your surviving spouse or other designated survivor with a monthly benefit for life after you die. The joint life annuities provide either a 100 percent or 50 percent survivor benefit. Contact the benefit officer at your employing Federal agency for more details.

* Thrift Savings Plan Investment Management

External Affairs
Federal Retirement Thrift Investment Board
1250 H St., NW
Washington, DC 20005 (202) 523-5660

The five member Board of the Federal Retirement Thrift Investment Board establishes the Plan's investment policies. The actual management of the money in the Plan is handled differently for each of the three investment funds. The Government Securities Investment Fund is managed directly by experienced financial/investment analysts on the Board staff following the policies adopted by the Board. The other two funds, the Common Stock Index Investment Fund and the Fixed Income Index Investment Fund, are handled by private sector investment managers. The firms are selected by the Executive Director of the Board through the competitive procurement process.

* Whistleblower Abuse and Waste Hotlines

Inspector General's Office
U.S. Department of Commerce
14th St. and Constitution Ave., NW
Room 7898C (800) 424-5197
Washington, DC 20230 (202) 377-2495

This hotline was established so that consumers and employees could report fraud, abuse, or waste within any office in the U.S. Department of Commerce. All reports are investigated and reports can be made anonymously. The Pentagon, HUD, and other government departments also have whistleblower hotlines.

* Withdrawing Money under the Thrift Savings Plan

External Affairs
Federal Retirement Thrift Investment Board
1250 H St., NW
Washington, DC 20005 (202) 523-5660

You cannot withdraw any portion of your Thrift Savings Plan account while you are still employed by the Federal government. The basic purpose of the plan is to provide a retirement income. For further information, contact the above office.

* Work Force Analysis and Statistics

Superintendent of Documents
Government Printing Office
Washington, DC 20402 (202) 783-3238

Statistics and analyses are available on the Federal Civilian Work Force. A bi-monthly publication, *Federal Civilian Work Force Statistics*, contains information on current employment by branch, agency, and area; trends of employment and payroll, and accessions and separations. Summary tables and narrative analyses are given. This can be purchased for $8 a year from GPO.

* Working for the U.S.A.

Federal Job Information Center
General Information
Office of Personnel Management
1900 E St., NW, Room 1416
Washington, DC 20415 (202) 606-2700

This free pamphlet is available from any Federal Job Information Center.

Be patient. If any phone number is incorrect, call (area code) 555-1212 and request the new listing.

Federal Job Banks

Here you will find the offices within each of the government agencies and departments which have responsibility for personnel. Dial-a-Job recorded messages inform callers about immediate job openings. Future employment prospects, the interview process, and other questions about the civil service can be directed to these offices which are staffed with knowledgeable federal employees. In the cases of those agencies which are not listed here, or only have a recorded message, refer to the Federal Public Information Offices section in the Information Starting Places Chapter. If you run into any difficulties with a particular federal office, contact either of your U.S. Senators or Representatives.

ACTION
Room 5101, 1100 Vermont Avenue, NW
Washington, DC 20525
(202) 606-5135
(202) 606-5000 recorded message

Administrative Conference of the U.S.
2120 L Street, NW, Suite 500
Washington, DC 20037
(202) 254-7020

African Development Foundation
1400 I Street, NW
Washington, DC 20005
(202) 673-3916

Agency for International Development
515 22nd Street, NW
Washington, DC 20523-0222
(202) 663-2400

Agriculture, U.S. Department of
14th St. and Independence Ave., SW
Washington, DC 20250
(202) 720-5625
(202) 720-2436
(202) 720-2108

Agricultural Research Job Line
Beltsville, MD
(301) 344-2288 recorded message

Air Force, U.S. Department of the
The Pentagon
Civilian Personnel
Arlington, VA 20310
(703) 695-4389
(703) 693-6550 DIAL-A-JOB recorded message

Alcohol Tobacco and Firearms Bureau
Employment Branch 1216
650 Massachusetts Ave., NW
Washington, DC 20226
(202) 566-7321

American Battle Monument Commission
Pulaski Building
20 Massachusetts Ave., NW, Room 5127
Washington, DC 20314
(202) 272-0534

Appalachian Regional Commission
1666 Connecticut Ave., Suite 721 NW
Washington, DC 20235
(202) 673-7896

Arms Control and Disarmament Agency
320 21st Street, NW
Washington, DC 20451
(202) 647-2034

Army, U.S. Department of
Personnel and Employment Service
The Pentagon
Arlington, VA 20310-6800
(703) 545-6700

Board for International Broadcasting
Administrative Management Assistant
1201 Connecticut Ave., NW
Suite 400
Washington, DC 20036
(202) 254-8040

Bureau of Public Debt
U.S. Department of the Treasury
999 E Street, NW
Washington, DC 20239
(202) 874-4000 recorded message

Census Bureau
14th St. and Constitution Ave., NW
Washington, DC 20230
(301) 763-5537

Central Intelligence Agency
Arlington, VA 20505
(703) 351-2028

Civil Rights Commission
5401 Westbard Avenue
Washington, DC 20207
(202) 376-8330

Commission of Fine Arts
441 F Street, NW, Suite 312
Pension Bldg.
Washington, DC 20001
(202) 504-2700

Commodity Futures Trading Commission
2033 K St., Suite 202, NW
Washington, DC 20581
(202) 254-6387
(202) 254-3346 recorded message

Consumer Product Safety Commission
5401 Westbard Ave.
Bethesda, MD 20207
(301) 504-0100

Be patient. If any phone number is incorrect, call (area code) 555-1212 and request the new listing.

Careers and Workplace

Defense, U.S. Department of
The Pentagon
Civilian Personnel
Arlington, VA 20310-6800
(703) 545-6700

Defense Logistics Agency
Bldg. 6, Room 214
Cameron Station
Alexandria, VA 22304-6100
(703) 274-7087
(703) 274-7372 recorded message

Education, U.S. Department of
400 Maryland Avenue, SW
Washington, DC 20202
(202) 708-5366
(202) 401-0559 recorded message

Equal Employment Opportunity Commission
1801 L St., NW
Washington, DC 20507
(202) 663-4337
(202) 663-4306

Employment Standards Administration
Bureau of Labor Statistics
U.S. Department of Labor
200 Constitution Ave., NW
Washington, DC 20210
(202) 219-8743

Energy, U.S. Department of
1000 Independence Ave., SW
Washington, DC 20585
(202) 586-4333 recorded message
(202) 586-8839

Environmental Protection Agency
401 M Street, SW
Washington, DC
(202) 260-2090
(202) 260-3285
(202) 260-5055 recorded message

Executive Office of the President
725 17th Street, NW
Washington, DC 20503
(202) 395-3000

Export-Import Bank of the U.S.
811 Vermont Avenue, NW
Washington, DC 20571
(202) 566-8834

Farm Credit Administration
Human Resources Division
1501 Farm Credit Drive
Mclean, VA 22102-5090
(703) 883-4135
(703) 883-4139 recorded message.

Federal Aviation Administration
800 Independence Avenue, NW
Washington, DC 20591
(202) 267-3229

Federal Bureau of Investigation
7799 Leesburg Pike
Falls Church, VA 22045
(202) 324-6223

Federal Communications Commission
1919 M Street, NW, Room 212

Washington, DC 20554
(202) 632-7120

Federal Deposit Insurance Corporation
Personnel Officer
550 17th Street, NW
Washington, DC 20429
(202) 393-8400

Federal Election Commission
Personnel Officer
999 E St., NW, Suite 812
Washington, DC 20463
(202) 219-4290

Federal Emergency Management Agency
Office of Personnel
500 C St., SW, Room 810
Washington, DC 20472
(202) 646-4041 vacancy hotline number

Federal Home Loan Bank Board
1700 G Street, NW
Washington, DC 20552
(202) 906-6060

Federal Labor Relations Authority
607 14th Street, NW
Washington, DC 20424-0001
(202) 482-6660

Federal Maritime Commission
800 N. Capitol, NW
Washington, DC 20573
(202) 523-5773

Federal Mediation and Conciliation Service
2100 K St., NW, Room 718
Washington, DC 20427
(202) 653-5260

Federal Mine Safety and Health Review Commission
Administrative Officer
1730 K St., NW
Washington, DC 20006
(202) 653-5615

Federal Reserve System
Human Resources Management
20th and C Street, NW, MS 156
Washington, DC 20551
(202) 452-3880
(202) 452-3038 recorded message

Federal Retirement Thrift Investment Board
Personnel Officer
1250 H Street, NW
Washington, DC 20005
(202) 942-1680

Federal Trade Commission
Pennsylvania Ave. at 6th Street, NW
Washington, DC 20591
(202) 326-2020

Forest Service
General Employment
Room 913 RP-E
Rosslyn, VA 22209
(703) 235-2730

General Accounting Office
Office of Recruitment
441 G Street, NW

Be patient. If any phone number is incorrect, call (area code) 555-1212 and request the new listing.

Federal Job Banks

Washington, DC 20536
(202) 512-8361 GS 2-12
(202) 275-6017 GS 13 & Up

General Services Administration
Office of Personnel
General Services Building
18th and F St., NW, Room 1100
Washington, DC 20405
(202) 501-0398

Government Printing Office
North Capitol and H Street, NW
Washington, DC 20401
(202) 512-0000

Health and Human Services, U.S. Department of
5600 Fishers Lane
Rockville, MD 20857
(301) 443-6900

Health and Human Services, U.S. Department of
Alcohol Drug Abuse and Mental Health
Administration PHS-HHE
5600 Fishers Lane
Rockville, MD
(301) 443-5407
(301) 443-2282

Health and Human Services, U.S. Department of
Health Resources and Services Administration
5600 Fishers Lane
Rockville, MD 20857
(301) 443-1230 recorded message

Health and Human Services, U.S. Department of
National Institutes of Health
9000 Rockville Pike
Bethesda, MD 20205
(301) 402-4111
(301) 496-2403 recorded message

House of Representative
U.S. Capitol Placement Office
Ford House Office Building
Room 219
Washington, DC 20515
(202) 226-6731

Housing and Urban Development, U.S. Department of
451 7th Street, S.W.
Washington, DC 20410
(202) 708-5408
(202) 708-0381
(202) 708-3203 recorded message

Immigration and Naturalization Service
U.S. Department of Justice
425 Eye Street, NW
Washington, DC 20536
(202) 514-2000

Inter-American Foundation
901 N. Stuart Street, 10th Floor
Arlington, VA 22203
(703) 841-3866

Interior, U.S. Department of
18th and C Streets, NW
Washington, DC 20240
(202) 208-5701
(202) 501-9630 Bureau of Mines
(703) 358-1743 Fish and Wildlife
(202) 208-7581 Indian Affairs

(202) 208-4649 Park Service (national)
(202) 619-9259 Park Service (metro)

Internal Revenue Service (IRS)
U.S. Department of the Treasury
1111 Constitution Ave., NW
Washington, DC 20224
(202) 622-5000

International Development
2401 E Street, NW
Washington, DC 20523
(202) 663-1512

International Trade Commission
500 E Street, SW
Washington, DC 20436
(202) 205-2000

Interstate Commerce Commission
12th and Constitution Ave., NW
Washington, DC 20423
(202) 927-7119

Justice, U.S. Department of
10th St. and Constitution Ave., NW
Washington, DC 20530
(202) 514-6818 recorded message

Labor, U.S. Department of
200 Constitution Avenue, NW
Washington, DC
(202) 219-6666
(202) 219-6646 recorded message

Library of Congress
101 Independence Avenue, NW
Washington, DC 20594
(202) 707-5000

Merit Systems Protection Board
Personnel Division
1120 Vermont Ave., NW
Washington, DC 20419
(202) 653-5916

National Aeronautics and Space Administration
Human Resources Management Division
Code DP
400 Maryland Ave., SW
Washington, DC 20546
(202) 358-0000

National Archives and Records Administration
Personnel Services Division
7th and Pennsylvania Ave., NW
Washington, DC 20408
(202) 501-6100

National Art Gallery
Washington, DC 20594
(202) 842-6282
(202) 842-6298 recorded message

National Capitol Planning Commission
Office of Administration
801 Pennsylvania Ave., NW
Suite 301
Washington, DC 20576
(202) 724-0170

National Credit Union Administration
Office of Personnel
1776 G St., NW, 7th Floor

Be patient. If any phone number is incorrect, call (area code) 555-1212 and request the new listing.

Careers and Workplace

Washington, DC 20456
(202) 682-9720

National Endowment for the Arts
1100 Pennsylvania Ave., NW, Room 208
Washington, DC 20506
(202) 682-5405

National Endowment for the Humanities
100 Pennsylvania Ave., NW, Room 417
Washington, DC 20506
(202) 786-0415

National Labor Relations Board
1717 Pennsylvania Ave., NW
Washington, DC 20750
(202) 254-9168

National Mediation Board
1301 K St., Suite 250 East, NW
Washington, DC 20572
(202) 523-5950

National Oceanic and Atmospheric Administration
U.S. Department of Commerce
Washington, DC 20230
(301) 443-8274/8275

National Science Foundation
1800 G St., Room 208, NW
Washington, DC 20550
(202) 357-5000

National Security Agency
ATT: M 322
Fort Meade, MD 20755-6000
(410) 859-6444

National Technical Information Service
8001 Forbes Pl.
Springfield, VA 22161
(703) 487-4680

National Transportation Safety Board
490 L'Enfant Plaza
Washington, DC 20594
(202) 382-6717
(202) 382-6542 recorded message

Navy, U.S. Department of
Civilian Personnel
HRO-CC, Room 436, CM #2
Washington, DC 20376-5006
(703) 607-2302 Placement
(703) 607-1751/1752 Vacancies

Nuclear Regulatory Commission
Office of Personnel
Washington, DC 20555
(301) 492-4661

Occupational Safety and Health Administration
Personnel
200 Constitution Ave., NW
Washington, DC 20210
(202) 219-8013

Occupational Safety and Health Review Commission
1120 20th Street, NW, 9th Floor
Washington, DC 20036-3419
(202) 606-5390

Office of Personnel Management
Congressional Liaison Of OPM

Rayburn House Office Building
Washington, DC 20515
(202) 225-4955 recorded message

Overseas Private Investment Corporation
Personnel
1100 New York Ave., NW
Washington, DC 20527
(202) 336-8529

Panama Canal Commission
2000 L St., Room 550, NW
Washington, DC 20036
(202) 634-6441

Peace Corps
1890 K Street, NW, Suite 4100
Washington, DC 20526
(202) 606-3120
(800) 424-8580 toll-free job info
(202) 606-3214 recorded message

Pennsylvania Avenue Development Corporation
1331 Pennsylvania Ave., NW, Suite 1220 North
Washington, DC 20004-1703
(202) 724-9091.

Pension Benefit Guaranty Corporation
2020 K St., NW, Room 3700
Washington, DC 20006
(202) 778-8808

Postal Rate Commission
Administrative Office
1333 H St., Suite 300, NW
Washington, DC 20268-0001
(202) 789-6840

Railroad Retirement Board
Director of Personnel
844 Rush Street
Chicago, IL 60611
(312) 751-4580

Securities and Exchange Commission
450 5th Street, NW
Washington, DC 20549
(202) 272-2550
(202) 272-3100 Recorded message

Selective Service System
1023 31st Street, NW
Washington, DC 20435
(202) 724-0820

Senate
Hart Senate Office Building
Room S H 142 B
Washington, DC 20510
(202) 224-9167

Small Business Administration
409 3rd Street, SW
Washington, DC 20416
(202) 205-6780

Smithsonian Institution
955 L'Enfant Plaza, SW
Washington, DC 20560
(202) 287-3100

State, U.S. Department of
2201 C Street, NW
Washington, DC 20520

or
Personnel
P.O. Box 18657
Washington, DC 20036-8657
(202) 647-7284 recorded message
(703) 875-7490 Foreign Service
(202) 647-7280 #2 Civil Service

Tennessee Valley Authority
400 West Summit Hill Drive
ET - 5P - K
Knoxville, TN 37902
(615) 632-7746

Treasury, U.S. Department of
15th St. and Pennsylvania Ave.,NW
Washington, DC 20220
(202) 622-1470

U.S. Information Agency
301 4th St., SW, Room 518
Washington, DC 20547
(202) 619-4659

U.S. Agency For International Development
Washington, DC 20523-0111
(202) 663-1310

U.S. International Trade Commission
Office of Personnel
500 E St., Room 314, SW
Washington, DC 20436
(202) 205-2651

U.S. Postal Service
475 L'Enfant Plaza
Room 1813, SW
Washington, DC 20260-0010
(202) 268-3646
(202) 268-3218 recorded message.

U.S. Tax Court
400 2nd St., NW, Room 146
Washington, DC 20217
(202) 606-8724

U.S. Trade and Development Program
Agency for International Development
5A16 Room 309
Washington, DC 20523-1602
(202) 875-4357

Veterans Affairs, U.S. Department of
810 Vermont Avenue, NW
Washington, DC 20420
(202) 233-4000

Be patient. If any phone number is incorrect, call (area code) 555-1212 and request the new listing.

Careers and Workplace

Research Grants in Every Field

You'll discover from this list of federal grants that research opportunities exist in almost every occupational field from forestry to injury prevention to library development. The following is a description of the federal dollars available to researchers, organizations, and universities. Grants to teachers and those involved in education are listed separately in the Education Chapter. This information is taken from the *Catalog of Federal Domestic Assistance* which is published by the U.S. Government Printing Office in Washington, DC. The number next to the title description is the official reference number listed in this catalog. Contact the office listed below the title for more details.

* Special Emphasis Outreach Programs Grants 10.140
Obie Patterson, Special Emphasis Outreach Programs
Office of Advocacy and Enterprise
U.S. Department of Agriculture
14th and Independence Ave., SW
Washington, DC 20250 (202) 447-2019

* Grants for Agricultural Research, Special Research Grants (Special Research Grants) 10.200
Administrator, Cooperative State Research Service
U.S. Department of Agriculture
Washington, DC 20250 (202) 720-4423

* Cooperative Forestry Research (McIntire-Stennis Act) 10.202
Administrator, Cooperative State Research Service
U.S. Department of Agriculture
Washington, DC 20250 (202) 720-4423

* Payments to 1890 Land-Grant Colleges and Tuskegee University 10.205
Administrator, Cooperative State Research Service
U.S. Department of Agriculture
Washington, DC 20250 (202) 720-4423

* Grants for Agricultural Research-Competitive Research Grants 10.206
Chief Scientist, Competitive Research Grants Office
U.S. Department of Agriculture, Aerospace Bldg.
Room 323, 14th and Independence Ave, SW
Washington, DC 20250 (202) 401-5022

* Animal Health and Disease Research 10.207
Administrator, Cooperative State Research Service
U.S. Department of Agriculture
Washington, DC 20250 (202) 720-4423

* Higher Education Strengthening Grants 10.211
Administrator, Cooperative State Research Service
U.S. Department of Agriculture
Washington, DC 20250 (202) 720-4423

* Morrill-Nelson Funds for Food and Agricultural Higher Education 10.214
Deputy Administrator
Office of Higher Education Programs
Administration Bldg., Room 350-A

U.S. Department of Agriculture
Washington, DC 20250 (202) 720-7854

* Sustainable Agriculture Research & Education 10.215
Administrator
Cooperative State Research Service
U.S. Department of Agriculture
Washington, DC 20250 (202) 720-4423

* Technical Agricultural Assistance 10.960
Mr. Harry Mattox
Office of International Cooperation and Development
Technical Assistance Division
U.S. Department of Agriculture
Washington, DC 20250 (202) 690-1924

* International Agricultural Research (International Research) 10.961
L. Whetten Reed
Office of International Cooperation and Development
Research & Scientific Exchange Division
U.S. Department of Agriculture
Washington, DC 20250 (202) 690-4872

* International Training-Foreign Participant 10.962
Dr. Frank A. Fender
Office of International Cooperation and Development
Food Industries Division
U.S. Department of Agriculture
Washington, DC 20250 (202) 690-1339

* Research and Evaluation Program 11.312
David H. Geddes, Room H-7319
EDA, U.S. Department of Commerce
Washington, DC 20230 (202) 377-4085

* Anadromous Fish Conservation Act Program 11.405
Director, Office of Fisheries Conservation and Management
National Marine Fisheries Service
1335 East-West Highway
Silver Spring, MD 29010 (301) 713-2334

* Interjurisdictional Fisheries Act of 1986 11.407
Director, Office of Fisheries Conservation and Management
National Marine Fisheries Service
1335 East-West Hwy
Silver Spring, MD 20910 (301) 713-2347

Be patient. If any phone number is incorrect, call (area code) 555-1212 and request the new listing.

Research Grants in Every Field

* **Sea Grant Support 11.417**
Director, National Sea Grant College Program
National Oceanic and Atmospheric Administration
1335 East West Hwy
Silver Spring, MD 20920 (301) 713-2448

* **Financial Assistance for Ocean Resources Conservation and Assessment Program 11.426**
NOAA, National Ocean Service
Office of Ocean Resources Conservation & Marine Assessment
(N/ORCA), Room 212, 6001 Executive Ave.
Rockville, MD 20852

* **Fisheries Development and Utilization Research and Development Grants and Cooperative Agreements Program 11.427**
Office of Trade and Industry Services
National Marine Fisheries Service
NOAA, U.S. Department of Commerce
1335 East-West Hwy.
Silver Spring, MD 20910 (301) 713-2358

* **Marine Sanctuary Program 11.429**
Chief, Sanctuaries and Reserves Division
Office of Ocean and Coastal Resource Management
National Ocean Service, NOAA
1825 Conn. Ave, N.W., Room 714
Washington, DC (202) 606-4122

* **Undersea Research 11.430**
Director, Office of Undersea Research
National Oceanic and Atmospheric Administration
1335 East-West Hwy
Silver Spring, MD 20910 (302) 713-2427

* **Climate and Atmospheric Research 11.431**
Director, Office of Global Programs
National Oceanic and Atmospheric Administration
1335 East-West Hwy
Silver Spring, MD 20910 (303) 427-2089

* **Measurement and Engineering Research and Standards 11.609**
National Institute of Standards & Technology
Gaithersburg, MD 20899

* **Regional Centers for the Transfer of Manufacturing Technology 11.611**
Dr. Philip N. Nanzetta, Director
NIST MTC Program, Room B112
Chemistry Bldg, NIST
Gaithersburg, MD 20899 (301) 975-3414

* **Minority Business Development Centers (MBDC) 11.800**
Assistant Director, Office of Operations
Room 5063, Minority Business Development Agency
U.S. Department of Commerce
14th & Constitution Ave., NW
Washington, DC 20230 (202) 377-8015

* **American Indian Program (AIP) 11.801**
Assistant Director, Office of Operations
Room 5096, Minority Business Development Agency

U.S. Department of Commerce
14th & Constitution Ave., NW
Washington, DC 20230 (202) 377-8015

* **Procurement Technical Assistance for Business Firms (Procurement Technical Assistance (PTA)) 12.002**
Defense Logistics Agency, Cameron Station
Office of Small and Disadvantaged
Business Utilization (DLA-U)
Room 4C112
Alexandria, VA 22304-6100 (202) 274-6471

* **Food and Drug Administration-Research 93.103**
Robert L. Robins, Chief
Grants and Assistance Agreements Section
Div. of Contracts and Grants
Food and Drug Administration
HFA-520, Room 3-20
Parklawn Bldg., 5600 Fishers Lane
Rockville, MD (301) 443-6170

* **Maternal and Child Health Federal Consolidated Programs (Special Projects of Regional and National Significance (SPRANS) 93.110**
Maternal and Child Health Bureau
HRSA, Public Health Service
Room 9-11, 5600 Fishers Lane
Rockville, MD 20852 (301) 443-2170

* **Adolescent Family Life Research Grants 93.111**
Eugenia Eckard
Office of Adolescent Pregnancy Programs
Office of Population Affairs
Office of the Assistant Secretary of Health
Hubert Humphrey Bldg.
200 Independence Ave., SW, 736E
Washington, DC 20201 (202) 245-1181

* **Biological Response to Environmental Health Hazards 93.113**
Director
Division of Extramural Research and Training
National Institute of Environmental Health Sciences
Public Health Service
Department of Health and Human Services
P.O. Box 12233
Research Triangle Park, NC 27709 (919) 541-7643

* **Applied Toxicological Research and Testing (Bioassay of Chemicals and Test Development) 93.114**
Director
Division of Extramural Research and Training
National Institute of Environmental Health Sciences
Public Health Service
Department of Health and Human Services
P.O. Box 12233
Research Triangle Park, NC 27709 (919) 541-7643

* **Biometry and Risk Estimation-Health Risks From Environmental Exposures 93.115**
Director, Division of Extramural Research and Training
National Institute of Environmental Health Sciences
Public Health Service
U.S. Department of Health and Human Services
P.O. Box 12233
Research Triangle Park, NC 27709 (919) 541-7643

Be patient. If any phone number is incorrect, call (area code) 555-1212 and request the new listing.

Careers and Workplace

* **Project Grants and Cooperative Agreements for Tuberculosis Control Programs 93.116**
Chief, Grants Management Branch
CDC, PHS, DHHS
1600 Clifton Road, NE
Atlanta, GA 30333 (404) 639-2508

* **Acquired Immunodeficiency Syndrome (AIDS) Activity (AIDS) 93.118 Grants Management Branch**
Procurement and Grants Office
Centers for Disease Control
U.S. Department of Health and Human Services
255 E. Paces Ferry Rd., NE
Atlanta, GA 30305 (404) 842-6575

* **Oral Diseases and Disorders Research 93.121**
Extramural Program
National Institute of Dental Research
National Institutes of Health
Bethesda, MD 20892 (301) 496-7884

* **Centers for Research and Demonstration for Health Promotion and Disease Prevention (Prevention Centers) 93.135**
Diane Jones, Project Officer
NCCDPHP, CDC, PHS
Atlanta, GA 30333 (404) 488-5395

* **Injury Prevention and Control Research Projects 93.136**
Division of Injury Epidemiology and Control
Center for Environmental Health and Injury Control
Center for Disease Control
Public Health Service
Atlanta, GA 30333 (404) 488-4265

* **Intramural Research Training Award (IRTA Program) 93.140**
Associate Director for Intramural Affairs
National Institutes of Health
Shannon Bldg. Room 140
Rockville, MD 20892 (301) 496-4920

* **NIEHS Hazardous Waste Worker Health and Safety Training (Superfund Worker Training Program) 93.142**
Director, Division of Extramural Research and Training
National Institute of Environmental Health Sciences
P.O. Box 12233
Research Triangle Park, NC 27709 (919) 541-0752

* **NIEHS Superfund Hazardous Substances-Basic Research and Education 93.143**
Director, Division of Extramural Research and Training
National Institutes of Environmental Health Sciences
P.O. Box 12233
Research Triangle Park, NC 27709 (919) 541-0797

* **AIDS Education and Training Centers 93.145**
Marc Rivo, MD, Director
Division of Medicine
Bureau of Health Professions
Health Resources and Services Admin, Room 4C05
5600 Fishers Lane
Rockville, MD 20857 (301) 443-6190

* **Human Genome Research 93.172**
Mark Guyer, MD
National Center for Human Genome Research
NIH, PHS, DHHS
Bethesda, MD 20892 (301) 496-0844

* **Biological Research Related to Deafness and Communicative Disorders 93.173**
Dr. Ralph F. Naunton
National Institute of Deafness
and Other Communicative Disorders
Executive Plaza South, Room 400-B
Bethesda, MD 20892 (301) 496-1804

* **Conference Grant (Substance Abuse) 93.174**
Office for Substance Abuse Prevention (OSAP)
Alcohol, Drug Abuse and Mental Health Administration
Rockwall II Bldg.
5600 Fishers Lane
Rockville, MD 20857 (301) 443-6980

* **ADAMHA Small Instrumentation Program Grants (ASIP) 93.176**
Mr. James Moynihan
Division of Basic Science
NIMH, 5600 Fishers Lane, Room 11-95
Rockville, MD 20857 (301) 443-3107

* **Health Services Research and Development Grants 93.226**
Agency for Health Care Policy and Research
PHS, DHHS, Suite 601, Executive Office Center
2101 E. Jefferson St.
Rockville, MD 20852 (301) 227-8447

* **Mental Health Research Grants 93.242**
Dr. Stephen Koslow, Director
Division of Basic Brain & Behavioral Sciences
National Institute of Mental Health
5600 Fishers Lane
Rockville, MD 20857 (301) 443-3563

* **Occupational Safety and Health Research Grants 93.262**
Henry Cassell, Procurement and Grants Office, CDC
DHHS, 255 E. Paces Ferry Rd., NE, MS-E14
Atlanta, GA 30333 (404) 842-6630

* **Alcohol Scientist Development Award and Research Scientist Development Award for Clinicians (Research Center ("K") Awards) 93.271**
Dr. William Lands, Director
Division of Basic Research
National Institute on Alcohol Abuse and Alcoholism
PHS, 5600 Fishers Lane
Rockville, MD
(301) 443-1206

* **Alcohol National Research Service Awards for Research Training (NRSA Program) 93.272**
Dr. William Lands, Director
Division of Basic Research
National Institute on Alcohol Abuse and Alcoholism
PHS, 5600 Fishers Lane
Rockville, MD (301) 443-1206

Be patient. If any phone number is incorrect, call (area code) 555-1212 and request the new listing.

Research Grants in Every Field

* **Alcohol Research Programs 93.273**
Dr. William Lands, Director
Division of Basic Research
National Institute on Alcohol Abuse and Alcoholism
PHS, 5600 Fishers Lane
Rockville, MD (301) 443-1206

* **Drug Abuse National Research Service Awards for Research Training (NRSA Program) 93.278**
Dr. James Dingell, Director
Division of Preclinical Research
National Institute on Drug Abuse
5600 Fishers Lane
Rockville, MD 20857 (301) 443-1887

* **Drug Abuse Research Programs 93.279**
Dr. James Dingell, Director
Division of Preclinical Research
National Institute on Drug Abuse
5600 Fishers Lane
Rockville, MD 20857 (301) 443-1887

* **Mental Research Scientist Development Award and Research Scientist Development Award for Clinicians (Career Development ("K") Awards) 93.281**
Dr. Stephen Koslow, Director
Division of Basic Brain & Behavioral Sciences
National Institute of Mental Health
Parklawn Building
5600 Fishers Lane, Room 11-103
Rockville, MD 20857 (301) 443-3563

* **General Clinical Research Centers 93.333**
General Clinical Research Centers Program
National Center for Research Resources
National Institutes of Health
Bethesda, MD 20892 (301) 496-6595

* **Biomedical Research Support 93.337**
Marjorie Tingle, MD
National Center for Research Resources
National Institutes of Health
Bethesda, MD 20892 (301) 496-6743

* **Nursing Research - Health Promotion and Disease Prevention 93.361**
National Center for Nursing Research
National Institutes of Health
Public Health Service
Bldg. 31, Room 5B03
Bethesda, MD 20892 (301) 496-0523

* **Biomedical Research Technology 93.371**
Biomedical Research Technology Program
National Center for Research Resources
National Institutes of Health
Bethesda, MD 20892 (301) 496-5411

* **Research Centers in Minority Institutions (RCMI) 93.389**
Dr. Sidney A. McNairy, Director
RCMI
National Center for Research Resources
Bethesda, MD 20205 (301) 496-6341

* **Academic Research Enhancement Award (AREA) 93.390**
Office of Research Training & Special Programs
Office of Extramural Research
National Institutes of Health
Bethesda, MD 20892 (301) 496-1968

* **Cancer Cause and Prevention Research 93.393**
Dr. Richard H. Adamson, Director
Division of Cancer Etiology
National Cancer Institute
Bethesda, MD 20892 (301) 496-6618

* **Cancer Detection and Diagnosis Research 93.394**
Dr. Faye Austin, Acting Associate Director
Extramural Research Program
National Cancer Institute
Bethesda, MD 20892 (301) 496-7815

* **Cancer Treatment Research 93.395**
Dr. Bruce Chabner
Division of Cancer Treatment
National Cancer Institute
Bethesda, MD 20892 (301) 496-4291

* **Cancer Biology Research 93.396**
Dr. Faye Austin, Acting Associate Director
Extramural Research Program
National Cancer Institute
Bethesda, MD 20892 (301) 496-8636

* **Cancer Centers Support 93.397**
Dr. Brian Kimes
Training & Resources Program
Division of Cancer Biology and Diagnosis
National Cancer Institute, EPN/308C
Bethesda, MD 20892 (301) 496-8537

* **Cancer Control 93.399**
Dr. Edward Sondick, Deputy Director
Division of Cancer Prevention and Control
National Cancer Institute
Bethesda, MD 20892 (301) 496-9569

* **Head Start 93.600**
Administration for Children, Youth and Families
Head Start
U.S. Department of Health and Human Services
P.O. Box 1182
Washington, DC 20013 (202) 245-0569

* **Child Welfare Research and Demonstration 93.608**
Penny Maza
Child Welfare Services
Children's Bureau
Administration for Children and Families
P.O. Box 1182
Washington, DC 20013 (202) 245-0712

* **Social Services Research and Demonstration 93.647**
Paul Bordes, Director
Division of Research and Evaluation
Office of Policy & Evaluationi
Administration of Children and Families
Room 334-C, 370 L'Enfant Promenade SW
Washington, DC 20201 (202) 401-9224

Be patient. If any phone number is incorrect, call (area code) 555-1212 and request the new listing.

Careers and Workplace

* Adoption Opportunities 93.652
Delmar Weathers, Children's Bureau
Administration for Children, Youth and Families
P.O. Box 1182
Washington, DC 20013 (202) 245-0671

* Child Abuse and Neglect Discretionary Activities 93.670
Director
National Center on Child Abuse and Neglect (NCCAN)
P.O. Box 1182
Washington, DC 20013 (202) 245-0347

* Social Security-Research and Demonstration (SSA Research and Demonstration) 93.812
Lawrence H. Pullen, Chief, Grants Management Staff
Office of Acquisition and Grants, ODCM
Social Security Administration, 1-E-4
1710 Gwynn Oak Ave.
Baltimore, MD 21207 (401) 965-9502

* Biophysics and Physiological Sciences 93.821
Dr. James Cassatt, Director
Biophysics and Physiological Sciences
National Institutes of Health
Bethesda, MD 20892 (301) 496-7463

* Heart and Vascular Diseases Research 93.837
Director, Division of Heart and Vascular Diseases
National Heart, Lung, and Blood Institute
Bethesda, MD 20892 (301) 496-2553

* Lung Diseases Research 93.838
Director, Division of Lung Diseases
National Heart, Lung, and Blood Institute
Bethesda, MD 20892 (301) 496-7208

* Blood Diseases and Resources Research 93.839
Director, Division of Blood, Diseases, and Resources
National Heart, Lung, and Blood Institute
Bethesda, MD 20892 (301) 496-4868

* Arthritis, Musculoskeletal and Skin Diseases Research 93.846
Dr. M. Lockshin, Director
Extramural Activities Program
National Institute of Arthritis and
Musculoskeletal and Skin Diseases
Bldg. 31, Room 4C32, NIH
Bethesda, MD 20892 (301) 496-0802

* Diabetes, Endocrinology and Metabolism Research 93.847
Dr. E. Johnson, Director
Division of Diabetes, Endocrinology and Metabolic Diseases
Room 9A16, Bldg. 31
National Institute of Diabetes and Kidney Diseases
National Institutes of Health
Bethesda, MD 20892 (301) 496-7348

* Digestive Diseases and Nutrition Research 93.848
Dr. Jay Hoofnagle, Director
Division of Digestive Diseases and Nutrition
Room 9A23, Bldg. 31, NIH
Bethesda, MD 20892 (301) 496-1333

* Kidney Diseases, Urology and Hematology Research 93.849
Dr. G. Striker, Director
Division of Kidney, Urologic and Hematologic Diseases
Room 9A17, Bldg. 31
National Institutes of Health
Bethesda, MD 20892 (301) 496-6325

* Biological Basis Research in the Neurosciences 93.854
Mr. Edward Donohue
Division of Extramural Activities
NINDS, NIH
Federal Bldg. Room 1016
Bethesda, MD 20892 (301) 496-4188

* Allergy, Immunology and Transplantation Research 93.855
Gary Thompson, Grants Management Branch
National Institute of Allergy and Infectious Diseases
National Institutes of Health
Bethesda, MD 20892 (301) 496-7075

* Microbiology and Infectious Diseases Research 93.856
Gary Thompson, Grants Management Branch
National Institute of Allergy and Infectious Diseases
National Institutes of Health
Bethesda, MD 20892 (301) 496-7075

* Pharmacological Sciences 93.859
Dr. Christine Carrico, Program Director
National Institute of General Medical Sciences
National Institutes of Health
Bethesda, MD 20892 (301) 496-7707

* Genetics Research 93.862
Dr. Judith H. Greenberg, Program Director
National Institute of General Medical Sciences, NIH
Bethesda, MD 20892 (301) 496-7175

* Cellular and Molecular Basis of Disease Research 93.863
Dr. Charles Miller, Program Director
Cellular and Molecular Basis of Disease
National Institute of General Medical Sciences, NIH
Bethesda, MD 20892 (301) 496-7021

* Population Research 93.864
Donald E. Clark, Chief
Office of Grants and Contracts
National Institute of Child Health and Human Development
National Institutes of Health
Bethesda, MD 20892 (301) 496-5001

* Research for Mothers and Children 93.865
Donald E. Clark, Chief
Office of Grants and Contracts
National Institute of Child Health and Human Development
National Institutes of Health
Bethesda, MD 20892 (301) 496-5001

* Aging Research 93.866
Dr. Richard L. Sprott
National Institute of Aging, NIH
Bethesda, MD 20892 (301) 496-4996

Be patient. If any phone number is incorrect, call (area code) 555-1212 and request the new listing.

Research Grants in Every Field

* **Retinal and Choroidal Diseases Research 93.867**
Carolyn Grimes
Extramural Services Branch
National Eye Institute
National Institutes of Health
Bethesda, MD 20892 (301) 496-5884

* **Anterior Segment Diseases Research 93.868**
Carolyn Grimes
Extramural Services Branch
National Eye Institute, NIH
Bethesda, MD 20892 (301) 496-5884

* **Strabismus, Amblyopia and Visual Processing 93.871**
Carolyn Grimes
Extramural Services Branch
National Eye Institute, NIH
Bethesda, MD 20892 (301) 496-5884

* **Alcohol Research Center Grants 93.891**
Dr. William Lands, Acting Director
Division of Basic Research
National Institute on Alcohol Abuse and Alcoholism
PHS, 5600 Fishers Lane
Rockville, MD 20857 (301) 443-2530

* **Resource and Manpower Development in the Environmental Health Sciences 93.894**
Director, Division of Extramural Research and Training
National Institute of Environmental Health Sciences
P.O. Box 12233
Research Triangle Park, NC 27709 (919) 541-7634

* **Family Planning-Services Delivery Improvement Research Grants (SDI) 93.974**
Eugenia Eckard
Office of Population Affairs
Office of the Asst Secretary for Health, DHHS
Room 736E, Hubert Humphrey Bldg.
200 Independence Ave, SW
Washington, DC (202) 245-1181

* **Preventive Health Services - Sexually Transmitted Diseases Research, Demonstrations, and Public Information and Education Grants 93.978**
Chief, Grants Management Branch, Procurement and Grants Office
CDC, PHS, DHHS
255 E. Paces Ferry Rd., NE
Atlanta, GA 30333 (404) 842-6804

* **Corrections-Research and Evaluation and Policy Formulation 16.602**
Chief, Community Services Division
National Institute of Corrections
320 First St., NW, Room 200
Washington, DC 20534 (202) 724-3106

* **Employment and Training Research and Development Projects 17.248**
Chief, Division of Research and Demonstration
Employment and Training Administration
U.S. Department of Labor
Washington, DC 20210 (202) 535-0677

* **Occupational Safety and Health (OSHA) 17.500**
Assistant Secretary
Occupational Safety and Health Administration
U.S. Department of Labor
Washington, DC 20210 (202) 523-9361

* **Urban Mass Transportation Grants for University Research and Training 20.502**
Office of Technical Assistance and Safety
Office of Training
Research and Rural Transportation (TTS-31)
Urban Mass Transit Administration
400 7th St., SW, Room 6100
Washington, DC 20590 (202) 366-0201

* **Urban Mass Transportation Technical Studies Grants (Technical Planning Studies) 20.505**
Director, Office of Planning (TGM 20)
Office of Grants Management
Federal Transit Administration, DOT
400 7th St., SW
Washington, DC 20590 (202) 366-2360

* **Promotion of the Humanities-Regrants/Centers for Advanced Study 45.122**
Division of Research Programs
Centers for Advanced Study, Room 318
National Endowment for the Humanities
Washington, DC 20506 (202) 786-0210

* **Promotion of the Humanities-Interpretive Research/ Humanities, Science and Technology 45.133**
Humanities, Science and Technology
Division of Research Programs
National Endowment for the Humanities
Room 318
Washington, DC 20506 (202) 786-0120

* **Promotion of the Humanities - Regrants Program/ International Research 45.148**
National Endowment for the Humanities
International Research, Room 318
Washington, DC 20506 (202) 786-0210

* **Promotion of the Humanities-Division of Preservation and Access 45.149**
Division of Preservation & Access
National Endowment for the Humanities, Room 802
Washington, DC 20506 (202) 786-0570

* **Promotion of the Humanities-Travel to Collections (Travel to Collections) 45.152**
Division of Fellowships and Seminars
Travel to Collections, Room 316
National Endowment for the Humanities
Washington, DC 20506 (202) 786-0463

* **Engineering Grants 47.041**
Glen Larsen, Program Analyst
Directorate for Engineering
National Science Foundation, Room 1126e
1800 G St., NW
Washington, DC 20500 (202) 357-9774

Be patient. If any phone number is incorrect, call (area code) 555-1212 and request the new listing.

Careers and Workplace

* Mathematical and Physical Sciences 47.049
Assistant Director
Mathematical and Physical Sciences
National Science Foundation
1800 G. St, NW
Washington, DC 20550 (202) 357-9742

* Geosciences 47.050
Dr. Eugene W. Bierly, Atmospheric Sciences
National Science Foundation
1800 G. St., NW
Washington, DC 20550 (202) 357-9874

* Computer and Information Science and Engineering (SISE) 47.070
Asst Director
Computer and Information Science and Engineering
National Science Foundation
1800 G St., NW, Room 306
Washington, DC 20550 (202) 357-7936

* Science and Technology Centers 47.073
Director
Office of Science and Technology Infrastructure
National Science Foundation
1800 G St., NW
Washington, DC 20550 (202) 357-9808

* Environmental Protection-Consolidated Research 66.500
Director, Research Grants Staff
RD-675, EPA
Washington, DC 20460 (202) 260-7473

* Solid Waste Disposal Research 66.504
Director, Research Grants Staff
RD-675, EPA
Washington, DC 20460 (202) 260-7473

* Water Pollution Control-Research, Development, and Demonstration 66.505
Director, Research Grants Staff
RD 675, EPA
Washington, DC 20460 (202) 260-7473

* Safe Drinking Water Research and Demonstration 66.506
Director, Office of Research Grants
RD-675, EPA
Washington, DC 20460 (202) 260-7473

* Toxic Substances Research 66.507
Director, Research Grants Staff
RD-675, EPA
Washington, DC 20460 (202) 260-7473

* Superfund Technical Assistance Grants for Citizen Groups at Priority Sites 66.806
Office of Emergency and Remedial Response
OS-220-N, EPA
401 M St., SW
Washington, DC 20460 (703) 308-8380

* University-Laboratory Cooperative Program 81.004
Larry L. Barker
Division of University and Industry Programs
Office of Energy Research, DOE
Washington, DC 20585 (202) 586-8947

* Energy-Related Inventions 81.036
George Lewitt, Director
Office of Technology Evaluation and Assessment
National Institute of Standards and Technology
Gaithersburg, MD 20899 (301) 975-5500

* Basic Energy Sciences--University and Science Education 81.049
William Burrier
Division of Acquisition and Assistance Management
Office of Energy Research, DOE
Mail Stop G-236
Washington, DC 20545 (301) 353-5544

* Energy Conservation for Institutional Buildings 81.052
Robert Volk, Director
Institutional Conservation Programs Division
Office of Conservation and Renewable Energy
CE-231, 5G-063, DOE
Washington, DC 20585 (202) 586-8034

* University Coal Research 81.057
Jack Jennings
Office of Technical Coordination
Assistant Secretary of Fossil Energy
Washington, DC 20545 (301) 903-4251

* University Research Instrumentation 81.077
Michael Wolfe
Postsecondary Programs Division
Office of University and Science Education (ER-82)
Office of Energy Research, DOE
Washington, DC 20585 (202) 586-8910

* Industrial Energy Conservation 81.078
Marsha Quinn
Office of Industrial Technologies, CE-14, DOE
Washington, DC 20585 (202) 586-2097

* Regional Biomass Programs 81.079
Mike Voorhies
Office of National Programs, CE-52, DOE
Washington, DC 20585 (202) 586-1480

* Domestic and International Energy Policy Development 81.080
Stephen F. Durbin, Resource Management Office
Office of Domestic and International Energy Policy (EP-3)
7B-098, Forrestal Bldg.
1000 Independence Ave., SW
Washington, DC 20585 (202) 586-5325

* Minority Educational Institution Research Travel Fund (MIRT) 81.083
Isiah O. Sewell, Office of Minority Economic Impact
MI-2.2, DOE
Forrestal Bldg. Room 5B-110
Washington, DC 20585 (202) 586-1953

Be patient. If any phone number is incorrect, call (area code) 555-1212 and request the new listing.

Research Grants in Every Field

* Conservation Research and Development 81.086
Barbara Twigg
Office of Management and Resources
Conservation and Renewable Energy
Washington, DC 20585 (202) 586-8714

* Renewable Energy Research and Development 81.087
Barbara Twigg
Office of Management and Resources
Conservation and Renewable Energy
Washington, DC 20585 (202) 586-8714

* Fossil Energy Research and Development 81.089
Dwight Mottet
Department of Energy
Fossil Energy Program, FE-122
Germantown, MD 20545 (202) 903-3008

* Socioeconomic and Demographic Research, Data and Other Information 81.091
Georgia R. Johnson
U.S. Department of Energy
Forrestal Bldg. Room 5B-110
Washington, DC 20585 (202) 586-1593

* Environmental Restoration 81.092
Office of Environmental Restoration
Office of Restoration & Waste Management
Department of Energy
Washington, DC 20545 (202) 586-6363

* Nuclear Energy, Reactor Systems, Development, and Technology 81.095
H. Rohm
Office of Nuclear Energy (NE-40)
Germantown Bldg.
Washington, DC 20545 (301) 353-6590

* Innovative Clean Coal Technology 81.096
C. Lowell Miller
U.S. Department of Energy
Fossil Energy Program
Clean Coal Technology
Washington, DC 20585 (703) 235-2450

* International Research and Studies (HEA Title VI Research and Studies) 84.017
Division of Advanced Training and Research
International Education Programs
U.S. Department of Education, ROB-3
7 & D St., SW
Washington, DC 20202-5331 (202) 708-7283

* Disabled--Innovation and Development 84.023
Division of Innovation and Development
Office of Asst. Secretary for Special Education
and Rehabilitative Services
U.S. Department of Education
400 Maryland Ave., SW
Washington, DC 20202 (202) 732-1107

* Library Research and Demonstration 84.039
Yvonne Carter
Library Development Staff
Library Programs
Office of Educational Research & Improvement
U.S. Department of Education
555 New Jersey Ave., NW
Washington, DC 20208-5571 (202) 219-1315

* National Vocational Education Research 84.051
Howard Hjelm
U.S. Department of Education
Division of National Programs
Office of Vocational and Adult Education
400 Maryland Ave., SW
Washington, DC 20202-7242 (202) 732-2350

* Educational Research and Development 84.117
Jackie Jenkins
U.S. Department of Education
Office of Educational Research and Improvement
555 New Jersey Ave., NW
Washington, DC 20208 (202) 219-2079

* National Institute on Disability and Rehabilitation Research 84.133
Director, National Institute on Disability
and Rehabilitation Research
Office of Assistant Secretary for Special
Education & Rehabilitation Services
U.S. Department of Education
400 Maryland Ave., SW
Washington, DC 20202-2572 (202) 732-4532

* Disabled--Special Studies and Evaluations 84.159
Marty Kaufman
Division of Innovation and Development
Office of Special Education Programs
400 Maryland Ave., SW
Washington, DC 20202 (202) 732-1106

* National Adult Education Discretionary Program 84.191
Richard F. DiColar
Division of National Programs
Office of Vocational and Adult Education
U.S. Department of Education
400 Maryland Ave., SW
Washington, DC 20202-7242 (202) 732-2362

Be patient. If any phone number is incorrect, call (area code) 555-1212 and request the new listing.

Arts and Humanities
Artists, Designers, Performers

* *See also Careers and Workplace; Research Grants in Every Field Chapter*

Here is a sampling of the opportunities for dancers, fashion designers, sculptors, theater companies, musicians, and other artists. A complete list of federal grants for artists is outlined in "Money for the Arts" in this chapter. The Performing Arts Library listed below serves as a clearinghouse for information and reference assistance on dance, theater, opera, music as well as film and broadcasting.

* Actors, Mimes, and Playwrights Grants

Theater Program, National Endowment for the Arts
1100 Pennsylvania Ave., NW, Room 608
Washington, DC 20506 (202) 682-5425

The Theater Program provides financial assistance for the creation and presentation of work by professional artists, primarily in companies, and to bring the work to locales where theater is generally not available. There are fellowships for mimes and solo performance artists, as well as for playwrights. The Professional Theater Training category is designed to encourage efforts to raise professional standards by assisting professional training of theater artists. Grants are also available to organizations and publishers for projects and services that address the needs of the theater. Grants can be made to individuals and non-profit organizations if such donations qualify as charitable deductions under Section 170(c) of the Internal Revenue Code of 1954.

* American Culture and Folk Art Grants

Folk Arts Program, National Endowment for the Arts
1100 Pennsylvania Ave., NW, Room 725
Washington, DC 20506 (202) 682-5449

The Folk Arts Program supports the traditional arts that have grown through time within the many groups that make up the United States. The Program's objectives are to present and enhance this multi-cultural artistic heritage and to make it more available to a wider public audience. The Program offers grants for the presentation and documentation of traditional arts and artists, as well as for supporting the development of state- or regionally-based folk arts programs. Fellowships are given to master folk artists to provide national recognition.

* Art Grant Application Guide

Public Information Offices
National Endowment for the Arts
1100 Pennsylvania Ave., NW, Room 617
Washington, DC 20506 (202) 682-5400

The National Endowment for the Arts offers a free publication, the *Guide to the National Endowment for the Arts*, which outlines its various programs and grants, and provides a calendar of deadlines, as well as application information for the grants. Regional offices and other related agencies are also listed.

* Arts Education and Successful Teaching

National Arts Education Research Center
New York University School of Education, Health,
Nursing and Arts Profession
32 Washington Place, #42
New York, NY 10003 (212) 998-5050

Major research areas include the processes of successful teaching and curriculum in arts education; videotape documentation of successful teaching in arts education; and educational relationships among the schools and cultural institutions.

* Artists as Teachers Grants

Arts-In-Education
National Endowment for the Arts
1100 Pennsylvania Ave., NW, Room 602
Washington, DC 20506 (220) 682-5426

The Arts-In-Education Program is a partnership program through cooperative efforts of the Arts Endowment, state arts and education agencies, local communities, and other organizations. The Program's overall goal is to advance the arts as part of basic education. Grants are awarded to place practicing artists in a variety of educational settings and to support other projects designed to enhance arts education in schools. Arts in Schools Basic Education Grants encourage plans and projects that promote the arts in schools as a basic component of the curriculum in kindergarten through high school.

* Classical Music Concerts

Public Affairs Office
Library of Congress
Washington, DC 20540 (202) 707-2905

A variety of cultural programs takes place each year in the Library, including poetry and other literary readings, lectures, and musical presentations. Among the most popular musical events are the Julliard String Quartet concerts featuring five Stradivari instruments given to the Library in the 1930s. Other gifts have brought the Library a variety of musical pieces including two Bach cantatas and sketches for portions of two Beethoven quartets. Recordings of Julliard concerts and many other programs are played on radio stations across the country, and lectures are often published for distribution. Also prints and photographs, maps and musical scores, rare books, and manuscripts are drawn from the collections and displayed in the Library in continually changing exhibitions. Many exhibits are sent on tour to libraries and museums across the nation. A free monthly calendar of events is available by written request.

* Dance and Choreography Grants

Dance Program, National Endowment for the Arts
1100 Pennsylvania Ave., NW, Room 621
Washington, DC 20506 (202) 682-5435

The Dance Program focuses on American dance, and offers grants to dance companies, choreographers, and dance organizations to allow for the improvement of their staffs, as well as supporting performers and performances and the commissioning of new work. The program also offers grants to organizations and individuals who provide services to dancers, choreographers and companies, such as those that provide performance space or communication within the dance world. A Choreographers Fellowship has been established which provides financial assistance for an individual's artistic growth, and the funds can be used for any project which aids in creative development. Grants can be made to individuals or to non-profit organizations if such donations qualify as charitable deductions under Section 170(c) of the Internal Revenue Code of 1954.

* Distinguished Designer Fellowships

Design Arts Program, National Endowment for the Arts
1100 Pennsylvania Ave., NW, Room 625
Washington, DC 20506 (202) 682-5437

Distinguished Designer Fellowships are awarded to people who have made lifetime contributions to the field of design, so as to allow them time to explore new concepts and ideas in design. Grants are also made to organizations that award design fellowships to broaden the base of support for the field. The Design Arts Program supports projects in the fields of architecture, landscape architecture, urban design, historic preservation, urban planning, interior design, industrial design, graphic design, and fashion design. Grants can be made to

Be patient. If any phone number is incorrect, call (area code) 555-1212 and request the new listing.

Artists, Designers, Performers

individual, or to non-profit organizations, including arts groups and local and state governments if such donations qualify as charitable deductions under Section 170(c) of the Internal Revenue Code of 1954. Grants can range from $5,000 to $40,000.

* Duck Stamp Design Competition

Federal Duck Stamp Office
U.S. Fish and Wildlife Service
1849 C St.
Washington DC 20240 (202) 208-4354

Each year, a Duck Stamp Design Competition is held, with the winning design chosen by a panel of waterfowl and art experts. Any artist can enter the contest by submitting a 7 X 10 inch waterfowl design and paying an entry fee. The winner receives a pane of stamps bearing his or her design. Winning artists also sell prints of their prize entries which are eagerly sought by collectors.

* Fashion, Graphic, Industrial Designers Grants

Design Arts Program
National Endowment for the Arts
1100 Pennsylvania Ave., NW, Room 625
Washington, DC 20506 (202) 682-5437

The Design Arts Program supports projects in the fields of architecture, landscape architecture, urban design, historic preservation, urban planning, interior design, industrial design, graphic design, and fashion design. Grants are given to projects that advance design through practice, theory and research, media, and education concerning design. Some examples may be to produce a new graphic system, to study the theory of landscape architecture, or to produce a film on design issues. Grants are also made to organizations that award design fellowships to broaden the base of support for the field.

Grants can be made to individual, or to non-profit organizations, including arts groups and local and state governments if such donations qualify as charitable deductions under Section 170(c) of the Internal Revenue Code of 1954. Grants can range from $5,000 to $40,000.

* Folklife Crafts and American Traditions

Center for Folklife Programs and Cultural Studies
Smithsonian Institution
955 L'Enfant Plaza
Washington, DC 20590 (202) 287-3424

Through its annual Festival of American Folklife, the Smithsonian created a program of folklife presentations for the general public for two weeks each summer. The Office also carries on research in folklife traditions, publishes documentary and analytical studies, develops and organizes exhibitions with folklife themes, and cooperates with Universities and other institutions in presentation projects involving traditional craftsman and performing artists.

* Free National Gallery Concerts

National Gallery of Art
Constitution and 6th St., NW
Washington, DC 20565 (202) 842-6247

Free concerts are presented in the East Garden Court every Sunday evening, September to June. The National Gallery Orchestra performs and features guest musicians as well. Concerts are announced in the Calendar of Events.

* Jazz Performers, Choruses and Grants for Other Musicians

Music Program
National Endowment for the Arts
1100 Pennsylvania Ave., NW, Room 702
Washington, DC 20506 (202) 682-5445

The Music Program provides support for the creation and performance of music, with an emphasis on assisting the growth of American music and musicians. Fellowships for composers and collaborators, jazz performers and composers are designed to help create or complete new work. Jazz study apprenticeships are available to aspiring performers and professionals. Grants are awarded to solo recitalists to assist with study, rehearsal, and preparation costs. Support is available for single-music and multi-music presenters and for music festivals. Grants help jazz organizations hire professional management personnel and assist organizations with innovative projects that benefit the field of jazz. Music ensembles, choruses, and orchestras can receive grants to help pay a variety of expenses, such as salaries, touring, or collaboration with other groups. Music professional training supports music and advanced training on programs leading to professional careers in music. Grants also assist non-profit organizations and individuals in recording and distributing American music, and to establish a variety of residencies for composers or ensembles.

* Museum Artistic Initiative Grants

Museum Program
National Endowment for the Arts
1100 Pennsylvania Ave., NW, Room 624
Washington, DC 20506 (202) 682-5442

The Museum Program is designed to meet the needs of the museum field by providing funding for a variety of projects. The first is Professional Development, where they award grants for formal museum training programs, internships, and apprenticeships, as well as providing fellowships to museum professionals for independent study. The second category is Utilization of Museum Resources, which is designed to help organizations make greater use of museum collections and other resources. Grants help with reinstallation, exhibitions, and collection sharing. Grants can be used to develop related programs and events that enrich these presentations, including the preparation and publication of exhibition catalogs. The Education category provides for educational programs for the community, which can include outside specialists, and the Catalog category supports the cataloging of a permanent museum collection and the publication of materials related to the collection. Special Artistic Initiatives is designed to encourage long-term programming by museums and should include a unifying, thematic framework. The Museum Program helps museums conserve collections by providing grants for planning, conservation, and training. Grants also aid in collection maintenance through solving problems in climate control, security, and storage. Museums are encouraged to purchase works by living American artists, as well as to mount or participate in special exhibitions.

* Musicians Overseas Concert Tours

Artistic Ambassador Program
Office of Private Sector Programs
Bureau of Educational and Cultural Affairs
United States Information Agency
301 Fourth St., SW, Room 224
Washington, DC 20547 (202) 619-5338

This program, begun in 1983, sends gifted American musicians who are not under professional management on overseas tours, where they give public concerts and work with music students and faculties. The program began with pianists, and now also includes piano-violin-cello trios. Contact this office for information on the selection process and tour itineraries.

* Opera and Musical Theater Funding

Opera-Musical Theater Program
National Endowment for the Arts
1100 Pennsylvania Ave., NW, Room 703
Washington, DC 20506 (202) 682-5447

The Opera-Musical Theater Program assists all forms of music theater generally involving voice. Grants support professional opera and musical theater production organizations, and the creation, development, rehearsal, and production of new American or seldom-produced works. Funds are available to bring performances to areas where they generally do not take place. Independent producers can also receive support for the development of new works. National service organizations and special projects. Individual and non-profit organizations can apply for grants, if such donations qualify as charitable deduction under Section 170(c) of the Internal Revenue Code of 1954.

* Overseas Speaking Opportunities for Artists

American Participants (AmParts)
Office of Program Coordination and Development
United States Information Agency (USIA)
301 Fourth St., SW, Room 550
Washington, DC 20547 (202) 619-4720

AmParts are experts in a field--usually economics, international affairs, literature, the arts, U.S. political and social processes, sports, science, or technology--sent abroad by USIA to meet with groups or individual professional counterparts. Recruited on the basis of requests of USIA staff in other countries, AmParts often engage in informal lecture/discussions with small groups, grant media interviews, or speak before larger audiences. Those interested in the American Participant program are invited to submit a brief letter indicating times of

Be patient. If any phone number is incorrect, call (area code) 555-1212 and request the new listing.

Arts and Humanities

availability, along with a curriculum vitae and at least two lecture topics with brief talking points.

* Performing Artists International Tours

National Endowment for the Arts
1100 Pennsylvania Ave., NW, Room 517
Washington, DC 20506 (202) 682-5562

The Rockefeller Foundation, the United States Information Agency, and the Arts Endowment jointly fund performing artists invited to international festivals abroad and fund U.S. representation at major international exhibitions of visual art. Fellowships are also available to artists in various disciplines to work and study in Japan and France.

* Performing Arts and Visual Arts Copyright

Entries Catalogs
Superintendent of Documents
Government Printing Office
Washington, DC 20402 (202) 783-3238

The following copyright catalogs, which list materials registered only during the period covered by each issue, are available on microfiche only and are sold as individual subscriptions:

Part 1: Nondramatic Literary Works (quarterly) $14 per year.
Part 2: Serials and Periodicals (semi-annually) $5 per year.
Part 3: Performing Arts (quarterly) $13 per year.
Part 4: Motion Pictures and Filmstrips (semi-annually) $5 per year.
Part 5: Visual Arts (excluding maps) (semi-annually) $5 per year.

* Performing Arts Clearinghouse

John F. Kennedy Center for the Performing Arts
2700 F St. N.W.
Washington, DC 20566 (202) 416-8780

The Performing Arts Library is a joint project of the Library of Congress and the Kennedy Center, and offers information and reference assistance on dance, theater, opera, music, film, and broadcasting.

* Performing Arts Resource Center

Performing Arts Reading Room
Room LM113
Library of Congress
Washington, DC 20540 (202) 707-5507

The Performing Arts Reading Room houses the Library of Congress's non-book collections in the performing arts area: music, dance, sound recordings, motion pictures, and television. The collection includes more than 4,000,000 pieces of music and manuscripts, some 300,000 books and pamphlets, and about 350,000 sound recordings reflecting the development of music in Western civilization from earliest times to the present. Reference services are available. Adjacent to the reading room is the Recorded Sound Reference Center for users primarily interested in sound recordings and radio materials. Listening facilities are available in the reading room, but their use is limited of those doing research of a specific nature leading to publication or production. Musicians who wish to play music drawn from the Library's collection may use the piano available in an adjacent sound proof room.

* Polar Expeditions for Artists and Photographers

Ice Operations Division
Office of Navigation Safety and Waterways Services
U.S. Coast Guard
U.S. Department of Transportation
2100 2nd St., SW, Room 1202 A
Washington, DC 20593-0001 (202) 267-1450

The Coast Guard furnishes vessels to other agencies, such as the National Science Foundation, U.S. Geological Survey, and the Navy, to conduct research and ice operations in Arctic and Antarctic waters. The agencies sponsoring the missions select scientists, researchers, students, and in some cases, journalists, photographers, and artists to accompany the mission when space is available. This office is a good starting point for obtaining information on the pertinence of a mission to your field, to be directed to the appropriate agency sponsors, and for information about the data collected during missions.

* Surveys of Educational Schooling

University of Illinois at Urbana - Champaign
Grants and Contracts
109 Coble Hall
801 South Wright St.
Champaign, IL 61820-6242 (217) 333-2186

Major research areas include the development and validation of standardized achievement tests in the area of artistic processes and techniques in art history; national study on literacy and art education; role of music in general education; status surveys in art, visual, dance and drama in the elementary and secondary schools; drama/theater, visual and dance; influence on culture condition on the learning of arts; development of computer assisted testing (music education); design of studies in dance; designs of studies in theater; status survey of music education in elementary and secondary schools; and arts education field work: observational studies.

* Studios, Exhibits, and Funding for Artists

Presenting and Commissioning Program
National Endowment for the Arts
1100 Pennsylvania Ave., NW, Room 726
Washington, DC 20506 (202) 682-5444

The Inter-Arts Program supports projects which emphasize the creation, production, and exhibition of new works that cross the lines of individual disciplines of arts. The program funds presenting organizations, artists' colonies, and service organizations, as well as interdisciplinary projects involving original work by artists in a variety of disciplines. Grants help professional presenters improve their ability to present diverse arts programming in their community, and assist arts agencies that help presenters strengthen their skills in presenting artists. Grants can also be made to artists' colonies that provide studios, living space, and uninterrupted time to creative artists.

* Theater Company Funding

Theater Program
National Endowment for the Arts
1100 Pennsylvania Ave., NW, Room 608
Washington, DC 20506 (202) 682-5425

The Theater Program provides financial assistance for the creation and presentation of work by professional artists, primarily in companies, and to bring the work to locales where theater is generally not available. There are fellowships for mimes and solo performance artists, as well as for playwrights. The Professional Theater Training category is designed to encourage efforts to raise professional standards by assisting professional training of theater artists. Grants are also available to organizations and publishers for projects and services that address the needs of the theater. Grants can be made to individuals and non-profit organizations if such donations qualify as charitable deductions under Section 170(c) of the Internal Revenue Code of 1954.

* Theater Playbills and Rare Books Collection

Rare Book and Special Collections Division
Library of Congress, Deck B
Washington, DC 20540 (202) 707-5434

The Rare Books Division contains about 300,000 volumes and 200,000 pamphlets, broadsides, theater playbills, title pages, manuscripts, posters, and photographs. The collection includes documents of the first fourteen congresses of the United States, the personal libraries of Thomas Jefferson and Harry Houdini, incunabula; miniature books and dime novels, and the Russian Imperial collection. The division has its own central card catalog plus special card files that describe individual collections or special aspects of books from many collections.

* Transportation Architecture and Beautification

Environment Division
Policy and International Affairs
Office of the Secretary of Transportation
U.S. Department of Transportation (DOT)
400 7th Street, SW, Room 9217
Washington, DC 20590 (202) 366-4366

This is the DOT contact point for environmental issues. Staff can provide you with information and referrals on such subjects as highway beautification, transportation architecture, bicycle paths, historic preservation activities, and environmental impact statements.

Be patient. If any phone number is incorrect, call (area code) 555-1212 and request the new listing.

Artists, Designers, Performers

* Travel Abroad for Artists and Performers

Office of Arts America
The Bureau of Educational and Cultural Affairs
United States Information Agency (USIA)
301 Fourth St., SW, Room 567
Washington, DC 20547 (202) 619-4779

Arts America recruits artists and performers to visit other countries and provides some assistance to artists traveling privately. The USIA sends some 15 large fine arts exhibitions and 25 performing arts groups overseas annually. Panels set up by the National Endowment for the Arts recommends a group of candidates, from which the USIA selects the programs participants. A Speakers Program recruits artists from the fields of literature, film, and the plastic and performing arts, on the basis of requests from overseas posts. AculSpecs are American specialists, in one of the plastic or performing arts, who visit a foreign country for two to six weeks with a local host institution for a program of master classes, workshops, and demonstrations. Arts America sponsors about 30 of these programs a year. This office also provides support materials for major fine and performing arts projects; publishes a quarterly list of privately traveling artists; and tries to assist overseas posts in programming these performers.

* Visual Media Grants to Artists

Visual Arts Program
National Endowment for the Arts
1100 Pennsylvania Ave., NW
Room 729
Washington, DC 20506 (202) 682-5448

The Visual Arts Program awards fellowships to artists in a wide variety of visual media, enabling them to set aside time to pursue their work. It also awards grants to organizations that assist visual artists and support public art projects, such as art in parks, plazas, and airports. Funding is available for a variety of projects that enable visual artists to communicate with their peers and the public, and for a variety of on-going visual arts programs, including exhibitions and access to working facilities. Grants can be made to individuals or to non-profit organizations if such donations qualify as a charitable deduction under Section 170(c) of the Internal Revenue Code of 1954.

Be patient. If any phone number is incorrect, call (area code) 555-1212 and request the new listing.

Arts and Humanities

Film, Photography, and Media Arts

Numerous archives on broadcast and film are readily available not only to researchers but to the public at large. The government produces new audiovisuals every year on virtually every field of interest. These films, slide shows, video and audio tapes can be purchased and often rented. Grants available to the media arts community are listed in "Money for the Arts" in this chapter.

* 8,000 Government Films, Videos and Other Audiovisuals

National Audiovisual Center
National Archives and Records Administration
Customer Services Section P2
8700 Edgeworth Dr.
Capitol Heights, MD 20743 (301) 763-1896

The National Audiovisual Center was established to serve as the central source for all federally-produced audiovisual materials and to make them available to the public through information and distribution services. Through the Center's distribution programs, the public has access to more than 8,000 titles covering a wide range of subjects. Major subject concentrations in the Center's collection include history, medicine, dentistry and the allied health sciences, safety, aviation and space technology, vocational and management training, and the environmental sciences. The audiovisual materials are available for sale, rental, or preview. A *Media Resources Catalog* is available at no charge and lists the materials by subject and title.

* Aerial Photographs and Surveys

Cartographic and Architectural Branch
Non-Textual Division
National Archives and Records Administration
8th St. and Pennsylvania Ave., NW
Washington, DC 20408 (703) 756-6700

The Cartographic and Architectural Branch has over 11 million maps, charts, aerial photographs, architectural drawings, patents, and ship plans, which constitute one of the world's largest accumulations of such documents. Some of the holdings are grouped under subject areas such as Mapping, which contains exploration and scientific surveys (as from the Lewis and Clark Expedition), public land surveys, Indian affairs, topography and natural resources, navigation, census mapping, and maps of foreign countries. All the holdings can be examined in the research room at 841 South Pickett St., Alexandria, VA, from 8:00 a.m. to 4:30 p.m., Monday through Friday. Reproductions can be furnished for a fee.

* African Art and Culture Photographic Archives

National Museum of African Art
950 Independence Ave., SW
Washington, DC 20560 (202) 357-4654

The Eliot Elisofon Photographic Archives is devoted to the collection, preservation, and management of visual resources of sub-Saharan African Art. It conducts picture research and collaborates with art historians, anthropologists, filmmakers, and other interested specialists in the publication and exhibition of its images. In addition, it serves as an international clearinghouse for information about African art and cultural history. The collection is divided into two major categories: art, which includes photographs of art objects in the permanent collection, as well as in public and private collections; and field, which contains images of African life. An overall guide to the collection and a price list are available upon request.

* Air and Space Archival Videodiscs

Smithsonian Institution Press
c/o Order Dept. 900
Blue Ridge Summit, PA 17214 (800) 782-4612

The National Air and Space Museum is reproducing its entire photo archives on videodiscs. Ten discs are planned, featuring color and black and white photographs of the U.S. and foreign aircraft, as well as of the artifacts and people associated with the development of aviation and space flight.

* American Slides and Photographs Databases

Office of Research Support
National Museum of American Art
9th and G Sts. N.W.
Washington, DC 20560 (202) 357-1626

The Office of Research Support maintains seven research projects totaling over 530,000 art data records and over 250,000 photographic images. Each of the projects uses automation in cataloging information and images, thus providing the user with access to art information and reproductions in a variety of ways. The Peter A. Juley and Son Collection of more than 127,000 photographic negatives documenting American art and artists photographed between 1896 and 1975 by this New York City firm; and the Slide and Photograph Archives, a collection of over 90,000 slides and 200,000 photographs available for study and 20,000 slides available for loan. Please call in advance for an appointment.

* Art Slides, Films, Video Loan Program

Education Resources Programs
National Gallery of Art
Extension Services
Constitution and 6th St., NW
Washington, DC 20565 (202) 842-6273

Color slide programs, films, and videocassettes are loaned at no cost to schools, libraries, community organizations, and individuals across the nation. The programs deal with a wide range of subjects drawn from the Gallery's permanent collections and special exhibitions. A free catalog listing all free-loan Extension Programs is available.

* Film and Broadcast Resource Center

John F. Kennedy Center for the Performing Arts
2700 F St. N.W.
Washington, DC 20566-0001 (202) 416-8780

The Performing Arts Library is a joint project of the Library of Congress and the Kennedy Center, and offers information and reference assistance on dance, theater, opera, music, film, and broadcasting.

* Film and Sound Recordings Archives

Motion Picture and Video and Sound Branch
National Archives and Records Administration
8th St. and Pennsylvania Ave., NW
Room 2W
Washington, DC 20408 (202) 501-5449

The Motion Picture, Sound, and Video Branch has 150,000 reels of motion picture film and several thousand videotapes from government sources as well as private individuals and organizations. The films consist of edited and nonedited footage, documentaries, newsreels, news films, combat films, and research and development test films. The collection generally covers 1914 to the present. The Archives also hold a collection of more than 115,000 sound recordings received from federal and private agencies, and commercial and foreign sources. There are several card catalogs to assist you in research, and copies can be made upon request. It is best to call ahead for an appointment to reserve a viewing room.

Be patient. If any phone number is incorrect, call (area code) 555-1212 and request the new listing.

Film, Photography, and Media Arts

* Filming on Public Lands

Land and Renewable Resources
Bureau of Land Management
U.S. Department of the Interior
18th and C Sts., NW
Washington, DC 20240   (202) 208-4896

The Bureau of Land Management issues leases, rights-of-way, and use permits for a wide variety of public lands including parks; power transmission and distribution lines; petroleum products collection and transmission systems; advertising and motion picture filming; and recreational events.

* Fish and Wildlife Photographs

Audio Visuals
U.S. Fish and Wildlife Service
18th and C Sts., NW
Washington, DC 20240   (202) 208-5611

The Audio Visual Department of the U.S. Fish and Wildlife Service has an extensive collection of both black and white pictures and color slides of fish and wildlife. There is no charge for their lending service, which extends 30 or 90 days. If the photographs or slides are used in publications, the photographer and the U.S. Fish and Wildlife Service must be given credit.

* Folkways Musical Recordings Archive

Office of Folklife Programs
955 L'Enfant Plaza, SW. Suite 2600
Washington, DC 20560   (202) 287-3251

The Folkways Records Archive, comprising the Moses and Frances Asch Collection, contains material related to the 2,200 published recordings of Folkways Records. The Folkways collection documents world-wide musical traditions, the spoken words of significant American figures, historical events, and nonmusical sounds of technology and nature. A catalog of the archives holdings is available which includes information on how to purchase recordings of the music.

* Government Videotapes and Film Archives

Motion Picture and Video and Sound Branch
National Archives and Records Administration
8th St. and Pennsylvania Ave., NW, Room 2W
Washington, DC 20408   (202) 501-5449

The Motion Picture, Sound, and Video Branch has 150,000 reels of motion picture film and several thousand videotapes from government sources and from private individuals and organizations. The films consist of edited and nonedited footage, documentaries, newsreels, news films, combat films, and research and development test films. The collection generally covers 1914 to the present. The Archives also holds a collection of more than 115,000 sound recordings received from federal and private agencies, and commercial and foreign sources. There are several card catalogs to assist you in research, and copies can be made upon request. It is best to call ahead for an appointment to reserve a viewing room.

* Historical Sound Recordings

Motion Picture, Broadcasting, and Recorded Sound Division
3rd Floor, Room 338
Library of Congress
Washington, DC 20540   (202) 707-5840

The sound recording collection reflects the entire spectrum of history of sound from wax cylinders to quadraphonic discs and includes such diverse media as wire recordings, aluminum discs, zinc discs, acetate-covered glass discs, rubber compound discs, and translucent plastic discs. The division has also recently made all of its materials recorded prior to 1909 available on 8-inch compressed audio discs for individual users in the Recorded Sound Reading Room using a micro computer. Included are the Berliner collection, from the company which invented and introduced disc recording, radio news commentaries from 1944 to 1946, eyewitness descriptions of marine combat and House of Representatives debates. For purchase by researchers, the Division's laboratory is prepared to make taped copies of recordings in good physical condition, when not restricted by copyright, performance rights, or provisions of gift or transfer. The requester is responsible for any necessary search--by mail or in person--of Copyright Office records to determine the copyright status of specific recordings. The Division also offers copies of some of its holdings for sale in disc form. These include a number of LP records of folk music, poetry, and other literature.

* Interactive Video Project

National Demonstration Laboratory for Interactive
Educational Technologies
Library of Congress
Madison Building
1st and Independence SE
Smithsonian Institution
Washington, DC 20540   (202) 707-4157

The National Demonstration Laboratory is a testing center for educational applications of interactive technologies and a clearinghouse of information about the technologies. It was established as a joint effort of the Smithsonian Institution and the Interactive Video Consortium, a group of public television stations actively involved with interactive technologies. The NDL clearinghouse database eventually will be accessible electronically. This online database will be available free of charge to all NDL Affiliates and to the public through paid subscription. The database will include information about basic attributes of interactive technologies, specific educational applications, bibliographic references, and equipment and software options. The coupling of interactive computer programs with multimedia materials offers educators the ability to maximize scarce resources, to address curriculum problems, and to reach new groups of learners. NDL conducts seminars and workshops which bring together educators, public broadcasters, and developers of software and hardware. They also identify elements of educational curricula that would be suitable for interactive video applications and distributes an assessment of interactive video user training and funding needs. Call or write for more information.

* Media Arts and Filmmaker Grants

National Endowment for the Arts
1100 Pennsylvania Ave., NW, Room 720
Washington, DC 20506   (202) 682-5452

This program provides support to individual artists working in these media and to non-profit organizations that help artists carry out their projects. The program also offers funding for a limited number of major public television and radio series that bring other art forms to a wide public. Grants are available to support productions in film and video that emphasize the use of these media as art forms. The American Film Institute Independent Filmmaker Program supports media artists working in animated, documentary, experimental, and narrative film and video. Fellowships are available through regional media arts centers, with funds also available to these centers to help make the arts of film and video more widely appreciated and practice. Grants assist organizations that distribute significant films and videotapes, and sponsor conferences, workshops, and publications. Grants can be made to individuals, or non-profit organizations, including arts centers, if such donations qualify as charitable deductions under Section 170(c) of the Internal Revenue Code of 1954.

* Motion Picture and Broadcasting Collection

Motion Picture, Broadcasting, and Recorded
Sound Division, 3rd Floor Room 338
Library of Congress
Washington, DC 20540   (202) 707-5840

The Library's film and television collections contain more than 100,000 titles and more than 1,000 titles are added each month through copyright deposit, purchase, gift, or exchange. Items selected from copyright deposits include feature films and short works of all sorts, fiction and documentary, exemplifying the range of current film and video production. The collections also include some 90,000 stills. The film and television collections are maintained for research purposes. Limited viewing and listening facilities for individual users are provided in the reading rooms.

* Motion Picture and Sound Recordings Copyright Entries Catalogs

Superintendent of Documents
Government Printing Office
Washington, DC 20402   (202) 783-3238

The following copyright catalogs, which list materials registered only during the period covered by each issue, are available on microfiche only and are sold as individual subscriptions:

Part 4: Motion Pictures and Filmstrips (semi-annually) $5 per year.
Part 5: Visual Arts (excluding maps) (semi-annually) $5 per year.
Part 6: Maps (semi-annually) $5 per year.
Part 7: Sound Recordings (semi-annually) $7.50 per year.
Part 8: Renewals (semi-annually) $5 per year.

Be patient. If any phone number is incorrect, call (area code) 555-1212 and request the new listing.

Arts and Humanities

* Motion Picture Archives

National Museum of Natural History
10th St. and Constitution Ave., N.W.
Washington, DC 20560 (202) 357-3349

This Archives was established to collect and preserve Motion picture film and video recordings of Western and nonwestern cultures. The growing collection consists of over three million feet of ethnographic film and video records of diverse cultures from every major geographical region in the world. Access to the holdings is available though SIBIS. The HSFA performs a full range of archival functions, including locating and collecting ethnographic footage, conducting film preservation work, refining techniques for storing and maintaining archival film collections, and developing a system for cataloging ethnographic film and video materials. The HSFA sponsors public screenings and lectures, and serves as a national clearinghouse for information about ethnographic film. Researchers must make appointments forty-eight hours in advance.

* Panama Canal Photographs

Office of Public Affairs
Panama Canal Commission
APO Miami, FL 34011-5000 (507) 52-3165

8 x 10 glossy, black and white photographs are available free of charge showing the Locks towing locomotives helping ease container ships into locks of the Panama Canal. Contact this office for more information.

* Park System Photographs

Photo Library
Office of Public Affairs
National Park Service
U.S. Department of the Interior
18th and C Sts., NW
Washington, DC 20240 (202) 208-7394

This library contains photos and transparencies of the National Park Service that can be borrowed free of charge. Geologic features, living history, and natural history subjects are available.

* Photographic and Microform Archives

National Gallery of Art
Constitution and 6th St., NW
Washington, DC 20565-0046 (202) 842-6039

The Photographic Archives is a study and research collection of black-and-white photographs, negatives, microforms and reproductive prints, which documents works of art and architecture and consists of over 1,232,000 photographs and negatives and 4,183,000 microform images. A summary listing of the current holdings is available. The Archives is open to all Gallery library users.

* Photographs from the U.S. Geological Survey

Photographic Library, MS 914
U.S. Geological Survey
Box 25046, Federal Center
Denver, CO 80225 (303) 236-1010

The Photographic Library of the U.S. Geological Survey contains a special collection of approximately 250,000 photographs. The Library may be used by the public as well as by personnel of other government agencies. Persons who wish to obtain prints, copy negatives, and duplicate transparencies from the collection are encouraged to visit the library. If this is not possible, the staff will prepare lists of specific photographs in response to requests. Many photographs are selected by searching U.S. Geological Survey publications and are identified by title and number of the publication as well as the number of the page and plate of the figure found. To obtain information on purchasing prints, negatives, or transparencies, contact the library directly.

* Photographs of Masterpieces

National Gallery of Art
Office of Photographic Services
Constitution and 6th St., NW
Washington, DC 20565 (202) 842-6231

Black and white, 8 x 10 photographs of works from the National Gallery of Art's permanent collections are available for purchase, either by visiting the Office of Photographic Services or by mail. Color transparencies of works from the Gallery, to be used for publication, are available for rental only and must be requested in writing.

* Photographic Views of the U.S. Capitol

The Curator's Office
Architect of the Capitol
The Capitol Building
Room SB15
Washington, DC 20515 (202) 225-1222

Views of the U.S. Capitol, a collection of seven popular views of the United States Capitol, are compiled from the Capitol collection maintained by the Architect of the Capitol. Reproductions may be purchased from the following office, but no photographs from this collection may be used for commercial purposes: Photoduplication Service, Library of Congress, Washington, DC 20540.

* Prints and Photographs Archives

Prints and Photographs Division
Library of Congress, LM 337
Washington, DC 20540 (202) 707-6394

More than 10 million items in the Library of Congress chronicle American life and society from its earliest days to the present through its prints and photographs. Items include architectural plans, posters, cartoons, drawings, and advertising labels. Reference librarians will assist those doing their own research, and they can furnish names of freelance picture researchers for individuals who cannot get to the Library.

* Public Lands Photos

Office of Public Affairs
Bureau of Land Management
U.S. Department of the Interior
18th and C Sts., NW
Washington, DC 20240 (202) 208-5717

Thousands of black and white photographs and color slides are available, including forestry, realty, minerals, and range subjects.

* Smithsonian Collection Slides and Photographs

Photographic Services
Smithsonian Institution
14th and Constitution Ave.
Washington, DC 20560 (202) 357-1487

Slides, transparencies, and prints (black and white and color) are available of photographs in the Smithsonian's collections. You can also order their seven slide series on a variety of topics, and most include a booklet and cassette tape. For a slide series catalog or ordering information, contact Photographic Services.

* Slide Lending Series on Art

National Gallery of Art
Constitution and 6th St., NW
Washington, DC 20565 (202) 842-6100

The National Gallery maintains a lending slide collection of over 50,000 images, which are loaned to the public free of charge. There is no list of the slide lending collection, but selections for National Gallery objects can be made from Gallery catalogs. Up to 50 slides can be borrowed at one time and may be kept for a period of two weeks. The slide library is open to the public.

* Six Million Still Pictures

Still Pictures Branch
National Archives and Records Administration
8th St. and Pennsylvania Ave., NW, Room 18N
Washington, DC 20408 (202) 501-5455

There are approximately six million still pictures in the Archives, including posters and photographs of artwork. Among the photographers represented in the Archives holdings are Matthew Brady, Carleton Watkins, William Henry Jackson, and Ansel Adams. There are leaflets which describe available selected photographs and slides in a variety of areas. Copies of still photographs are available as copy negatives and color and black-and-white prints and slides. Contact the office for information about photographs and a current price list.

* Sound Recordings of Poetry and Other Literature

Motion Picture, Broadcasting,
and Recorded Sound Division
Library of Congress

Be patient. If any phone number is incorrect, call (area code) 555-1212 and request the new listing.

Film, Photography, and Media Arts

Washington, DC 20540 (202) 707-5840

The Library of Congress offers copies of some of its poetry and literature holdings for sale in disc form. Contact this office for information on what's available, along with prices.

* Space Photographs

Customer Services
Earth Resources Observation System Data Center (EROS)
U.S. Geological Survey
Sioux Falls, SD 57198 (605) 594-6546

The EROS Data Center maintains photographs from many of the space missions, including those of the space shuttle, Apollo, and Gemini. Contact the center directly for information concerning specific topics.

* TV and Radio Production Funding

Humanities Projects in Media
Division of General Programs
National Endowment for the Humanities
1100 Pennsylvania Ave., NW, Room 420
Washington, DC 20506 (202) 606-8278

The Humanities Projects in Media supports the planning, writing, or production of television and radio programs in the humanities, which are intended for general audiences. Awards are made for both adult and children's programming. The collaboration of scholars in the humanities with experienced writers, producers, and directors is required.Non-profit institutions, organizations and groups, including public television and radio stations may apply for grants.

* Washington Architecture Photographs

United States Commission of Fine Arts (CFA)
441 F St., Suite 312
Washington, DC 20001 (202) 504-2200

CFA maintains a file of photographs of past and present Washington, DC, architectural projects which involve the CFA. Reproductions are available to the public for a processing fee upon written request. Call this office for information on what photographs are available in their files.

* Worldwide Film and Video Collection

Human Studies Film Archives (HSFA)
National Museum of Natural History
10th St. and Constitution Ave., N.W.
Washington, DC 20560 (202) 357-3349

This Archives was established to collect and preserve motion picture film and video recordings of Western and nonwestern cultures. The growing collection consists of over three million feet of ethnographic film and video records of diverse cultures from every major geographical region in the world. Access to the holdings is available though the Smithsonian Institute Bibliographical Information (SIBIS). The HSFA performs a full range of archival functions, including locating and collecting ethnographic footage, conducting film preservation work, refining techniques for storing and maintaining archival film collections, and developing a system for cataloging ethnographic film and video materials. The HSFA sponsors public screenings and lectures, and serves as a national clearinghouse for information about ethnographic film. Researchers must make appointments forty-eight hours in advance.

Be patient. If any phone number is incorrect, call (area code) 555-1212 and request the new listing.

Arts and Humanities

Money for the Arts

The following is a description of money programs available to artists and other interested parties from the federal government. The information is taken from the *Catalog of Federal Domestic Assistance* which is published by the U.S. Government Printing Office in Washington, DC. The number next to the title description is the reference number listed in this *Catalog*. Contact the office listed below the title for more information about any of these programs.

* Promotion of the Arts-Design Arts 45.001
Director, Design Arts Program
National Endowment for the Arts
1100 Pennsylvania Ave., NW
Washington, DC 20506 (202) 682-5437
To promote excellence in design by funding activities in architecture, landscape architecture, urban design, historic preservation, planning, interior design, graphic design, industrial design and fashion design. Types of assistance: grants, direct payment. Estimate of annual funds available: $ 4,200,000.

* Promotion of the Arts-Dance 45.002
Dance Program
National Endowment for the Arts
1100 Pennsylvania Ave., NW.
Washington, DC 20506 (202) 682-5435
The Dance Program provides support for professional choreographers, dance companies, and organizations that present or serve dance. Types of assistance: grants, direct payments. Estimate of annual funds available: $ 9,152,000.

* Promotion of the Arts - Arts in Education 45.003
Dr. Warren Newman, Arts in Education Program
Room 602, National Endowment for the Arts
The Nancy Hanks Center
1100 Pennsylvania Ave., NW
Washington, DC 20506 (202) 682-5797
To encourage state and local arts agencies to develop long-term strategies in assisting appropriate state and local education authorities to establish the arts as basic in education. Types of assistance: grants. Estimate of annual funds available: $ 600,000.

* Promotion of the Arts - Literature 45.004
Director, Literature Program
National Endowment for the Arts
1100 Pennsylvania Ave., NW
Washington, DC 20506 (202) 682-5451
To aid creative writers of fiction and non-fiction, poets, and translators of literary works through fellowships, funding of residencies for writers and support for noncommercial literary magazines and small presses. Types of assistance: grants. Estimate of annual funds available: $ 5,000,000.

* Promotion of the Arts - Music 45.005
Director, Music Program
National Endowment for the Arts
1100 Pennsylvania Ave., NW
Washington, DC 20506 (202) 682-5445
To support excellence in music performance and creativity and to develop informed audiences for music; throughout the country. Types of assistance: grants. Estimate of annual funds available: $ 15,650,000.

* Promotion of the Arts - Media Arts: Film/Radio/Television 45.006
Clara Welsh, Media Arts Program
National Endowment for the Arts
1100 Pennsylvania Ave., NW
Washington, DC 20506 (202) 682-5452
To provide grants in support of projects designed to assist individuals and groups to produce films, radio and video of high aesthetic quality, to exhibit and disseminate media arts. Types of assistance: grants. Estimate of annual funds available: $ 13,100,000.

* Promotion of the Arts - State Programs 45.007
Director, State Program
National Endowment for the Arts
1100 Pennsylvania Ave., NW
Washington, DC 20506 (202) 682-5429
To assist state and regional public arts agencies in the development of programs for the encouragement of the arts and artists, and to assist organizations providing services at a national level to state or local arts agencies. Types of assistance: grants. Estimate of annual funds available: $ 25,526,000.

* Promotion of the Arts - Theater 45.008
Director, Theater Program
National Endowment for the Arts
1100 Pennsylvania Ave., NW
Washington, DC 20506 (202) 682-5425
To provide grants to aid professional theater companies and theater artists, national theater service, organizations, professional theater training institutions, and professional theater presenters, including festivals. Types of assistance: grants. Estimate of annual funds available: $ 10,750,000.

* Promotion of the Arts - Visual Arts 45.009
Director, Visual Arts Program
National Endowment for the Arts
1100 Pennsylvania Ave., NW
Washington, DC 20506 (202) 682-5448
To provide grants to assist visual artists including painters, sculptors, photographers, crafts artists, printmakers, artists specializing in drawing, artists creating books, video artists, performance artists, conceptual artists. Types of assistance: grants. Estimate of annual funds available: $ 6,100,000.

* Promotion of the Arts-Expansion Arts 45.010
E'Vonne C. Rorie
Expansion Arts Program
National Endowment for the Arts
1100 Pennsylvania Ave., NW
Washington, DC 20560 (202) 682-5443
To provide grants to professionally directed arts organizations of high artistic quality which are deeply rooted in and reflective of the culture of a minority. Types of assistance: grants. Estimate of annual funds available: $ 6,700,000.

* Promotion of the Arts - Inter-Arts 45.011
Director
Presenting and Commissioning Program
National Endowment for the Arts
1100 Pennsylvania Ave., NW
Washington, DC 20506 (202) 682-5444

Be patient. If any phone number is incorrect, call (area code) 555-1212 and request the new listing.

Money for the Arts

To provide grants for projects that potentially have national or regional impact. Types of assistance: grants. Estimate of annual funds available: $ 4,300,000.

* Promotion of the Arts - Museum 45.012

Director, Museum Program
National Endowment for the Arts
1100 Pennsylvania Ave., NW
Washington, DC 20506 (202) 682-5442

To provide grants in support of American museum's essential activities and the evolving needs of the museum field. Types of assistance: grants. Estimate of annual funds available: $ 12,740,000.

* Promotion of the Arts - Challenge Grants 45.013

Challenge and Advancement Grant Programs
Room 617
National Endowment for the Arts
1100 Pennsylvania Ave., NW
Washington, DC 20506 (202) 682-5436

To assist on a one-time basis projects designed to have a lasting impact that can help move the nation forward in achieving excellence in the arts, access to, and/or appreciation of such excellence. Types of assistance: grants. Estimate of annual funds available: $ 18,500,000.

* Promotion of the Arts - Opera-Musical Theater 45.014

Director, Opera-Musical Theater Program
National Endowment for the Arts
1100 Pennsylvania Ave., NW
Washington, DC 20506 (202) 682-5447

To support excellence in the performance and creation of professional opera and musical theater throughout the Nation. Types of assistance: grants. Estimate of annual funds available: $ 6,517,000.

* Promotion of the Arts - Folk Arts 45.015

Director, Folk Arts Program
National Endowment for the Arts
1100 Pennsylvania Ave., NW
Washington, DC 20506 (202) 682-5449

To provide grants to assist, foster, and make publicly available the diverse traditional American folk arts throughout the country. Types of assistance: grants. Estimate of annual funds available: $ 3,100,000.

* Promotion of the Arts - Arts Administration Fellows

Program (Fellowship Program) 45.021
Arts Administration Fellows Program
National Endowment for the Arts
1100 Pennsylvania Ave., NW
Washington, DC 20506 (202) 682-5786

To provide a limited number of 13 week fellowships for professionals in arts management and related fields. Types of assistance: grants. Estimate of annual funds available: $ 200,000.

* Promotion of the Arts - Advancement Grants 45.022

Challenge and Advancement Grant Programs
Room 617
National Endowment for the Arts
1100 Pennsylvania Ave., NW
Washington, DC 20506 (202) 682-5436

To assist arts organizations develop specific strategies to eliminate deficiencies in organizational management practice and to take carefully planned steps toward achievement of long range goals. Types of assistance: grants. Estimate of annual funds available: $ 1,300,000.

* Promotion of the Arts - Local Programs (Local Programs) 45.023

Local Programs
National Endowment for the Arts
Nancy Hawks Center
1100 Pennsylvania Ave., NW
Washington, DC 20506 (202) 682-5431

To enhance to the quality and availability of the arts by fostering expansion of public support for the arts at the local level and to strengthen the local arts agency as a mechanism for arts planning, financial support and development and to encourage joint planning for the arts by federal, state, and local art agencies, community leaders, public officials, art organizations, and artists. Types of assistance: grants. Estimate of annual funds available: $ 2,566,000.

* Promotion of the Humanities - Humanities Projects in Media 45.104

Division of General Programs
Humanities Projects in Media
National Endowment for the Humanities, Room 420
Washington, DC 20506 (202) 606-8278

To encourage and support radio and television production that advances public understanding and appreciation of the humanities by adults and young people of junior high and high school age. Types of assistance: grants. Estimate of annual funds available: $ 11,084,000.

* Arts and Artifacts Indemnity 45.201

Alice M. Whelihan, Indemnity Administrator
Museum Program
National Endowment for the Arts
Washington, DC 20506 (202) 682-5442

To provide for indemnification against loss or damage for eligible art works, artifacts and objects. Types of assistance: Insurance. Estimate of annual funds available: $ 0.

Be patient. If any phone number is incorrect, call (area code) 555-1212 and request the new listing.

Arts and Humanities

Money for the Humanities

The following is a description of the money programs available to those interested in the humanities. The information is taken from the *Catalog of Federal Domestic Assistance* which is published by the U.S. Government Printing Office in Washington, DC. The number next to the title description is the reference number listed in this *Catalog*. Contact the office listed below the title for more information about any of the programs listed.

* Promotion of the Humanities - Humanities Projects in Media 45.104

Division of General Programs
Humanities Projects in Media
National Endowment for the Humanities, Room 420
Washington, DC 20506 (202) 606-8278

To encourage and support radio and television production that advances public understanding and appreciation of the humanities by adults and young people of junior high and high school age. Types of assistance: grants. Estimate of annual funds available: $ 11,084,000.

* Promotion of the Humanities - Public Humanities Projects 45.113

Public Humanities Projects
Division of General Programs
National Endowment for the Humanities, Room 426
Washington, DC 20506 (202) 606-8271

To support humanities projects addressed to out-of-school audiences. All projects must draw upon resources and scholars in the fields of the humanities. Types of assistance: grants. Estimate of annual funds available: $ 2,330,000.

* Promotion of the Humanities - Younger Scholars 45.115

Division of Fellowships and Seminars
Younger Scholars Program, Room 316
National Endowment for the Humanities
Washington, DC 20506 (202) 606-8643

To support non-credit humanities projects during the summer by college students and advanced high school students. Types of assistance: grants. Estimate of annual funds available: $ 372,000.

* Promotion of the Humanities - Summer Seminars for College Teachers 45.116

Summer Seminars for College Teachers
Division of Fellowships and Seminars
National Endowment for the Humanities, Room 316
Washington, DC 20506 (202) 606-8463

To provide opportunities for teachers in five, four, and two-year colleges; for scholars employed in libraries, museums, historical associations, and other humanities institution to work during the summer in their areas of interest under the direction of distinguished scholars at institutions with library resources suitable for advanced study and research. Types of assistance: grants. Estimate of annual funds available: $ 4,575,000.

* Promotion of the Humanities - Summer Stipends 45.121

Division of Fellowships and Seminars, Summer Stipends
National Endowment for the Humanities, Room 316
Washington, DC 20506 (202) 606-8466

To provide support for individual faculty and staff members at universities and two-year and four-year colleges and for others who have made or have demonstrated promise of making significant contributions to the humanities. Types of assistance: grants. Estimate of annual funds available: $ 892,000.

* Promotion of the Humanities - Regrants/Centers for Advanced Study 45.122

Division of Research Programs
Regrants/Centers for Advanced Study, Room 318
National Endowment for the Humanities
Washington, DC 20506 (202) 606-8210

To support interrelated research in well-defined subject areas at independent centers for advanced study, American research centers overseas, and independent research libraries and museums. Types of assistance: grants. Estimate of annual funds available: $ 1,050,000.

* Promotion of the Humanities - Reference Materials/Access 45.124

Reference Materials/Access
Division of Research Programs, Room 318
National Endowment for the Humanities
Washington, DC 25006 (202) 606-8570

To fund, wholly or partially, projects which will improve and facilitate scholarly access to significant research resources in order to contribute to greater knowledge and understanding of the humanities. Types of assistance: grants. Estimate of annual funds available: $ 2,565,000.

* Promotion of the Humanities - Humanities Projects in Museums and Historical Organizations 45.125

Humanities Projects in Museums and Historical Organizations
Division of General Programs, Room 420
National Endowment for the Humanities
Washington, DC 20506 (202) 606-8284

To assist museums, historical organizations, and other similar cultural institutions to plan and implement effective and imaginative programs which use material culture to convey and interpret the humanities to the general public. Types of assistance: grants. Estimate of annual funds available: $ 9,217,000.

* Promotion of the Humanities - Elementary and Secondary Education in the Humanities 45.127

Elementary and Secondary Education in the Humanities
National Endowment for the Humanities, Room 302
Washington, DC 20506 (202) 606-8377

To increase the effectiveness of humanities teaching in our Nation's elementary, middle, and secondary schools. Types of assistance: grants. Estimate of annual funds available: $ 7,100,000.

* Promotion of the Humanities - State Programs 45.129

Division of State Programs
National Endowment for the Humanities, Room 411
Washington, DC 20506 (202) 606-8254

To promote local humanities programming through renewable program grants to humanities councils within each of the 50 states, the District of Columbia, Puerto Rico, and the U.S. Virgin Islands for the purpose of regranting funds to local non-profit organizations. Types of assistance: grants. Estimate of annual funds available: $ 28,258,000.

Be patient. If any phone number is incorrect, call (area code) 555-1212 and request the new listing.

Money for the Humanities

* Promotion of the Humanities - Challenge Grants 45.130

Office of Challenge Grants, Room 429
National Endowment for the Humanities
Washington, DC 20506 (202) 606-8361

To support educational and cultural institutions and organizations in order to increase their financial stability and to sustain or improve the quality of humanities programs. Types of assistance: grants. Estimate of annual funds available: $ 14,228,000.

* Promotion of the Humanities - Texts/Publication Subvention 45.132

Division of Research Programs Texts/Publication
Subvention, Room 318
National Endowment for the Humanities
Washington, DC 20506 (202) 606-8207

To ensure through grants to publishing entities the dissemination of works of scholarly distinction in the humanities. Types of assistance: grants. Estimate of annual funds available: $ 350,000.

* Promotion of the Humanities - Interpretive Research/ Humanities, Science and Technology 45.133

Humanities, Science and Technology
Division of Research Programs
National Endowment for the Humanities, Room 318
Washington, DC 20506 (202) 606-8210

To support humanities research designed to deepen our understanding of science and technology and its role in our culture. Types of assistance: grants. Estimate of annual funds available: $ 600,000.

* Promotion of the Humanities - Regrants/Conferences 45.134

Division of Research Programs
Regrants, Room 318
National Endowment for the Humanities
Washington, DC 20506 (202) 606-8204

To support conferences, symposia and workshops which enable scholars to discuss and advance the current state of research on a particular topic or to consider directions in which research in a given field should move. Types of assistance: grants. Estimate of annual funds available: $ 400,000.

* Promotion of the Humanities - Humanities Projects in Libraries and Archives 45.137

Division of General Programs
Humanities Projects in Libraries
National Endowment for the Humanities, Room 429
Washington, DC 20506 (202) 606-8271

To encourage public understanding o the humanities and an interest in academic and public libraries' humanities resources through thematic programs, exhibitions, publications, and other library activities to stimulate use of the resources. Types of assistance: grants. Estimate of annual funds available: $ 2,727,000.

* Promotion of the Humanities - Interpretive Research/ Projects 45.140

Interpretive Research/Projects
Division of Research Programs, Room 318
National Endowment for the Humanities
Washington, DC 20506 (202) 606-8210

To advance important original researching all fields of the humanities. Types of assistance: grants. Estimate of annual funds available: $ 2,800,000.

* Promotion of the Humanities - Fellowships for University Teachers 45.142

Fellowships for University Teachers
Division of Fellowships and Seminars
National Endowment for the Humanities, Room 316
Washington, DC 20506 (202) 606-8466

To provide time for uninterrupted study and research to university teachers, and faculty members of postgraduate professional schools who can make significant contributions to thought and knowledge in the humanities. Types of assistance: grant. Estimate of annual funds available: $ 3,173,000.

* Promotion of the Humanities - Fellowships for College Teachers and Independent Scholars 45.143

Fellowships for College Teachers and Independent Scholars
Division of Fellowships and Seminars
Room 316
National Endowment for the Humanities
Washington, DC 20506 (202) 606-8466

To provide opportunities for college teachers and independent scholars to pursue independent study and research that will enhance their capacities as teachers, scholars, or interpreters of the humanities. Types of assistance: grants. Estimate of annual funds available: $ 3,173,000.

* Promotion of the Humanities - Reference Materials/ Tools 45.145

Division of Research Programs
Reference Materials/Tools, Room 318
National Endowment for the Humanities
Washington, DC 20506 (202) 606-8358

To fund, wholly or partially projects which create research tools important for scholarly research. Types of assistance: grants. Estimate of annual funds available: $ 2,615,000.

* Promotion of the Humanities - Texts/Editions 45.146

Division of Research Programs
Texts/Editions, Room 318
National Endowment for the Humanities
Washington, DC 20506 (202) 606-8207

To fund, wholly or partially, projects that create editions of materials important for scholarly research in the humanities and of interest to general audiences. Types of assistance: grants. Estimate of annual funds available: $ 2,700,000.

* Promotion of the Humanities - Texts Translations 45.147

Division of Research Programs
Texts/Translations, Room 318
National Endowment for the Humanities
Washington, DC 20506 (202) 606-8207

To support translations into English of texts and documents that will make major contributions to research in the humanities and lead to greater public awareness of the traditions and achievements of other cultures. Types of assistance: grants. Estimate of annual funds available: $ 1,100,000.

* Promotion of the Humanities - Regrants Program/ International Research 45.148

National Endowment for the Humanities
Regrants Program/International Research, Room 318
Washington, DC 20506 (202) 606-8204

To foster understanding by Americans of the history, culture and traditions of other nations. Types of assistance: grants. Estimate of annual funds available: $ 1,950,000.

* Promotion of the Humanities - Office of Preservation 45.149

Office of Preservation
National Endowment for the Humanities
Room 802
Washington, DC 20506 (202) 606-8570

To fund, wholly or partially, projects which will promote the preservation of research resources (library, archival, and other collections) relating to the humanities in the U.S. Types of assistance: grants. Estimate of annual funds available: $ 12,330,000.

Be patient. If any phone number is incorrect, call (area code) 555-1212 and request the new listing.

Arts and Humanities

* Promotion of the Humanities - Higher Education in the Humanities 45.150
Higher Education in the Humanities
National Endowment for the Humanities, Room 302
Washington, DC 20506 (202) 606-8380
To assist institutions of higher education in their efforts to improve the teaching of the humanities. Types of assistance: grants. Estimate of annual funds available: $ 7,100,000.

* Promotion of the Humanities - Summer Seminars for School Teachers 45.151
Summer Seminars for School Teachers
Division of Fellowships and Seminars
National Endowment for the Humanities, Room 316
Washington, DC 20506 (202) 606-8463
To provide opportunities for school teachers to work during the summer under the direction of a distinguished teacher and active scholar at colleges and universities throughout the country, studying seminal works in the humanities in a systematic and thorough way. Types of assistance: grant. Estimate of annual funds available: $ 5,172,000.

* Promotion of the Humanities - Travel to Collections (Travel to Collections) 45.152
Division of Fellowships and Seminars/Travel
to Collections, Room 316
National Endowment for the Humanities
Washington, DC 20506 (202) 606-8463
To advance basic research in the humanities by enabling American scholars to travel to use the research collections of libraries, archives, museums, or other research repositories to consult research materials which are of fundamental importance for the progress of scholarly work. Types of assistance: grants. Estimate of annual funds available: $ 99,000.

* Promotion of the Humanities - Regrants Program/ Selected Areas 45.153
National Endowment for the Humanities
Regrants Program/International Research, Room 318
Washington, DC 20506 (202) 606-8204
To award funds that will be regranted through fellowships and grants-in-aid to support individual American scholars pursuing research in all fields of the humanities. Types of assistance: grants. Estimate of annual funds available: $ 145,000.

* NEH/Reader's Digest Teacher Scholar Program 45.154
Elementary and Secondary Education in the Humanities
National Endowment for the Humanities, Room 302
Washington, DC 20506 (202) 606-8377
To increase the effectiveness of humanities teaching in our nation's elementary, middle, and secondary schools. Types of assistance: grants. Estimate of annual funds available: $ 1,500,000.

* Promotion of the Humanities - Dissertations
Dissertation Grants
Division of Fellowships and Seminars
National Endowment for the Humanities, Room 316
Washington, DC 20506 (202) 606-8463
To offer support for doctoral candidates in the writing of their dissertations in the humanities. All requirements for a Ph.D must be completed except for their dissertation. Types of assistance: grants. Estimate of annual funds available: $987,000.

* Promotion of the Humanities - Study Grants for College and University Teachers
Division of Fellowships and Seminars
National Endowment for the Humanities, Room 316
Washington, DC 20506 (202) 606-8463
To encourage college and university teachers with a heavy teaching responsibilities to undertake independent study to increase their knowledge, enrich understanding of the humanities and to pursue projects that will inform their teaching. Types of assistance: grants. Estimated annual funds available: $297,000.

* Promotion of the Humanities - Special Opportunity in Foreign Language Education
Division of Education Programs
National Endowment for the Humanities, Room 302
Washington, DC 20506 (202) 606-8373
To improve and strengthen foreign language education in the nation's schools, colleges and universities. All foreign language application with attention directed to less commonly taught languages as Russian, Arabic, Japanese and Chinese. Types of assistance: grants. Estimated annual funds available: $3,417,000.

* Institute of Museum Services 45.301
Institute of Museum Services
1100 Pennsylvania Ave, NW, Room 510
Washington, DC 20506 (202) 606-8536
To support the efforts of museums to conserve the nation's historic, scientific and cultural heritage. Types of assistance: grants, direct payments. Estimate of annual funds available: $ 27,000,000.

* National Historical Publications and Records Grants 89.003
National Archives and Records Administration
National Historical Publications and Records
Commission
National Archives Bldg.
Washington, DC 20408 (202) 501-5600
To carry out the National Historical Documents Program which will help preserve important historical documents. Types of assistance: grants. Estimate of annual funds available: $ 4,339,000.

Be patient. If any phone number is incorrect, call (area code) 555-1212 and request the new listing.

Historians, Scholars and Writers

In addition to source documents and other materials available to researchers, courses in historical editing and works of archivists are included in the listings below. The section, "Money for the Humanities," in this chapter identifies additional funding and scholarship opportunities.

* Advertising Labels, Cartoons, Posters, Prints Archives
Prints and Photographs Division
Library of Congress, LM 337
Washington, DC 20540 (202) 707-6394

More than 10 million items in the Library of Congress chronicle American life and society from its earliest days to the present through its prints and photographs. Items include architectural plans, posters, cartoons, drawings, and advertising labels. Reference librarians will assist those doing their own research, and they can furnish names of freelance picture researchers for individuals who cannot get to the Library.

* Air and Space History Archives
Archives
National Air and Space Museum
7th St. and Independence Ave. S.W.
Washington, DC 20590 (202) 357-3133

The National Air and Space Archives assembles and preserves documentary materials that chronicle the history and development of aerospace technology and exploration. Collection-level descriptions are available to researchers through SIBIS and will also be available soon in a published preliminary guide. The Archives also includes the U.S. Air Force Pre-1954 Still Photograph Collection and videodisc viewing facilities. Direct mail to: Smithsonian Institution, MRC 3222, Washington, DC 20506.

* Alexander Graham Bell and History of American Science
Joseph Henry Papers
Arts and Industries Building, 2188
900 Jefferson Dr. S.W.
Washington, DC 20560 (202) 357-2787

The Joseph Henry Papers conducts research on the life of Joseph Henry (1797-1878), first secretary of the Smithsonian Institution, the early history of the Smithsonian, and the development of American science during the mid-nineteenth century. It has over ninety thousand manuscripts, as well as research aids and reference guides. In addition, the Joseph Henry Papers curates the Bell-Henry Library, which contains the scientific library of Alexander Graham Bell and the personal library of Henry. Appointments should be made in advance.

* American Civilization Studies
American Studies Program
Barney Studio House
Smithsonian Institution.
Washington, DC 20560 (202) 673-4872

This office conducts a program in the material aspects of American civilization for graduate students enrolled in cooperating Universities. Interested students should apply to the American Studies department of the George Washington University or the University of Maryland, or the Office of American Studies.

* American Ethnology Archive of Historical Manuscripts
National Museum of Natural History
10th St. and Constitution Ave. N.W.
Washington, DC 20560 (202) 357-1986

The NAA holds the Bureau of American Ethnology's collection of historical manuscripts that relates to the linguistics, ethnology, archeology, physical anthropology, and history of North American Natives. It also has the administrative records of the Department of Anthropology. The photograph collection incorporates 150,000 original negatives and prints made by photographers who worked with American Indian subjects. Other pictorial materials are available through SIBIS.

* American History and Advertising History Archives
National Museum of American History
12th St. and Constitution Ave. N.W.
Washington, DC 20560 (202) 357-3270

The Archives Center provides research materials for museum staff, scholars, students, writers and other researchers. The collections are organized in four areas: Manuscripts (personal papers and records of businesses and other organizations); Advertising history; Historical photographs; and Films, audiotapes, and videotapes covering a number of subject areas. Holdings are described through SIBIS. Researchers are urged to call in advance.

* American History Branch Library
National Museum of American History
Room 5016
12th and Constitution Ave. N.W.
Washington, DC 20560 (202) 357-2414

The Library houses a collection of 165,000 volumes of book and bound journals on engineering, transportation, military history, science, applied science, decorative arts, and domestic and community life in addition to American history and the history of science and technology. They have special collections of trade literature and materials about world fairs. The Library is open to the public by appointment.

* American Portraits Research Center
National Portrait Gallery
8th and F Sts. N.W.
Washington, DC 20560 (202) 357-2578

The *Catalog of American Portraits*, administered by the National Portrait Gallery, is a national reference center whose files contain photographs and documentation for more than eighty thousand likenesses of historically important Americans. Arranged alphabetically by subject, the files are extensively cross-referenced by artist. A continuing Automated National Portrait Survey has made its holdings more readily accessible to researchers. Computerized indices by subject, artist, occupation, location, and medium make the catalog a valuable resource.

* Anthropology, Archeology, Bibliography and Other Interpretative Research Funding
Division of Research Programs
National Endowment for the Humanities
1100 Pennsylvania Ave., NW, Room 318
Washington, DC 20506 (202) 606-8200

The purpose of this Program is to support scholarly research and interpretation that will advance knowledge and deepen or broaden understanding of major topics in the humanities. Projects supported in this program include biographies, research in various humanities disciplines, cultural anthropology, and archeology.

* Archeological Assistance
Archeological Assistance Division (AAD)
National Park Service (NPS)
U.S. Department of the Interior

Be patient. If any phone number is incorrect, call (area code) 555-1212 and request the new listing.

Arts and Humanities

800 N. Capital St. NW
Suite 210
Washington, DC 20002 (202) 343-4101

This division of NPS provides technical assistance to federal and state agencies on the identification, evaluation, and preservation of archeological properties. AAD is developing a series of technical publications, including *Archeological Assistance Program Technical Briefs*. The National Archeological Database is maintained, along with other archeological clearinghouses.

* Architectural Drawings and Cartographic Archives

Cartographic and Architectural Branch
Non-Textual Division
National Archives and Records Administration
8th St. and Pennsylvania Ave., NW
Washington, DC 20408 (703) 756-6700

The Cartographic and Architectural Branch has over 11 million maps, charts, aerial photographs, architectural drawings, patents, and ship plans, which constitute one of the world's largest accumulations of such documents. The Branch holds architectural and engineering drawings created by civilian and military agencies. All the holdings can be examined in the research room at 841 South Pickett St., Alexandria, VA, from 8:00 a.m. to 4:30 p.m., Monday through Friday. Reproductions can be furnished for a fee.

* Architecture in the National Parks

Park Historic Architecture Division
National Park Service
U.S. Department of the Interior
800 N. Capital St. NW
Suite 360
Washington, DC 20002 (202) 343-8146

Activities related to the preservation of historic and prehistoric structures and cultural landscapes within the National Park System are administered by this office. *A List of Classified Structures* is maintained, which is an inventory of all historic and prehistoric structures in the System. A bibliography of Cultural Resources Management is also administered, listing all reports that address cultural resources in the Park System.

* Archives Center

National Museum of American History
12th St. and Constitution Ave. N.W.
Washington, DC 20560 (202) 357-3270

The Archives Center provides research materials for museum staff, scholars, students, writers and other researchers. The collections are organized in four areas: Manuscripts (personal papers and records of businesses and other organizations); Advertising history; Historical photographs; and Films, audiotapes, and videotapes covering a number of subject areas. Holdings are described through SIBIS. Researchers are urged to call in advance.

* Book Promotion Overseas of American Authors

Book Programs Division
Office of Cultural Centers and Resources
Bureau of Educational and Cultural Affairs
United States Information Agency
301 Fourth St., SW, Room 320
Washington, DC 20547 (202) 619-4896

USIA helps in the translation, publication, and promotion of American books overseas. The Promotion Branch organizes traveling book exhibits and supports an American presence at international book fairs. The Field Operations Branch supports the translation and publication of a broad range of titles, mostly in the social sciences and humanities.

* Comic Books and Cartoon History

Smithsonian Books and Recordings
P.O. Box 2061
Colchester, VT 05449-2061 (800) 927-7377

A *Smithsonian Book of Comic-Book Comics* ($21.96 non-member, $19.95 member) is the definitive collection from the Golden Age of 1938-1955. A *Smithsonian Collection of Newspaper Comics* ($29.97 non-member, 27.96 member) brings you more than 750 comic sequences from 1896 to the present day. For Smithsonian Magazine membership information please call 1-800-533-7901.

* Continental Congress and Other Diplomatic Papers

Civil Reference Branch
National Archives and Records Administration
8th St. and Pennsylvania Ave., NW, Room 11
Washington, DC 20408 (202) 501-5395

The Civil Reference Branch holds the records of all government civilian agencies, including records of the Continental Congress and other diplomatic records.

* Creative Writers Publishing Grants

Literature Program
National Endowment for the Arts
1100 Pennsylvania Ave., NW, Room 723
Washington, DC 20506 (202) 682-5451

The Literature Program assists individual creative writers and literature translators, encourages wider audiences for contemporary literature, and assists non-profit literary organizations. Fellowships enable writers and translators to set aside time for writing and research. Publishing grants provide assistance to literary magazines, small presses, and various distribution projects. Grants are also available to support residencies for writers to allow them to interact with their public. Literary centers may request funds but must offer a regular format of readings, workshops, and technical assistance for writers. Grants can be made to individuals or to non-profit organizations if such donations qualify as charitable deductions under Section 170(c) of the Internal Revenue Code of 1954. Grants range from $2,000 to $50,000.

* Declassified Government Documents

Records Declassification Division
Office of the National Archives
National Archives and Records Administration
8th St. and Pennsylvania Ave., NW, Room 18W
Washington, DC 20408 (202) 501-5345

This office performs systematic review and research-initiated review of security-classified records using guidelines prepared by federal agencies having jurisdiction over the information. These guidelines provide the National Archives with the authority to systematically review and declassify most records more than 30 years old. With research-initiated review, requests are submitted under the provisions of the Freedom of Information Act. The Archives then refers the classified document to the responsible agency for possible release.

* Decorative and Interior Arts Research Center

Doris and Henry Dreyfuss Study Center and Library
Cooper-Hewitt Museum
Smithsonian Institution's National Museum of Design
2 East 91st St. 3rd Floor
New York, NY 10128 (212) 860-6887

The Study Center and Library serve as a resource for scholars, researchers, designers, and students for the study of design. The library contains fifty thousand volumes, with specialized holdings in decorative arts, textiles, and needlework, wallcoverings, architecture, pattern and ornament, landscape design, industrial design, interior design, theater design, and graphic design. Researchers are asked to call or write in advance. Photographs may be ordered through the museum's Photographic Services Department.

* Every Book Published Since 1454

Catalog Management and Publications Division
LA 2004
Library of Congress
Washington, DC 20540 (202) 707-5965

The *National Union Catalog* lists the world's books published since 1454 and held in approximately 1,100 North American libraries and other union catalogs that record the location of books in Slavic, Hebraic, Japanese, and Chinese languages (if Romanized). The catalog is produced on microfiche, and many libraries have it.

* Federal Government's Watchdog History

Information Handling and Support Facilities
General Accounting Office
P.O. Box 6015
Gaithersburg, MD 20877 (202) 275-6241

The free book, *GAO: An Administrative History 1966-1981*, describes the role and

Be patient. If any phone number is incorrect, call (area code) 555-1212 and request the new listing.

operations of the GAO, and its evolution over the past fifteen years. The activities of the GAO offices and divisions are detailed, and their functions and accomplishments are described.

* Fellowship Program for Researchers and Scholars

Woodrow Wilson International Center for Scholars
Smithsonian Institution
1000 Jefferson Dr. S.W.
Washington, DC 20560 (202) 357-2763

The Center conducts a fellowship program for advanced research, and awards 40 residential fellowships annually in an international competition to individuals with outstanding project proposals representing the entire range of scholarship, with strong emphasis on the humanities and social sciences. Where appropriate, Fellows may be associated with one of the Center's eight programs: the American Society and Politics Program; the Asia Program; the East European Program; the History, Culture, and Society Program; the International Security Studies Program; the Kennan Institute for Advanced Russian Studies; the Latin American Program; or the West European Program. The Center sponsors an extensive series of meetings, information discussions, and formal colloquia on special topics. They also publish the *Wilson Quarterly*.

* Folk Culture Archive

American Folklife Center
Library of Congress
Washington, DC 20540 (202) 707-6590

This Center collects and maintains archives, conducts scholarly research, and coordinates the development of field projects, performances, exhibitions, festivals, workshops, publications, and audiovisual programs on American folklife. *Folk Life Center News* is a free quarterly newsletter on folklife activities and programs. The Center maintains and administers an extensive collection of folk music, folk culture, ethnomusicology, and grass-roots oral history--both American and international--in published and unpublished forms. The Archive houses more than 30,000 hours of folk-related recordings, manuscripts, and raw materials. The Archive Reading Room, (202) 707-5510, contains more than 4,000 books and periodicals, plus unpublished theses, and dissertations, field notes, and many textual and some musical transcriptions and recordings. A free listing of the Archive's publications is available.

* Folklife Studies Worldwide

Office of Folklife Programs Archive
Folkways Records Archive
Office of Folklife Programs
955 L'Enfant Plaza, SW, Suite 2600
Washington, DC 20560 (202) 287-3251

The Office of Folklife Programs Archive contains folkloristic materials generated through research for and documentation of the Festival of American Folklife Studies Monograph/Film Series. These materials document hundreds of folk culture traditions from the United States and forty-five other countries. Researchers should call for an appointment.

* Fulbright Foreign Exchange Scholarships

Office of Academic Programs
Bureau of Educational and Cultural Affairs
United States Information Agency
301 Fourth St., SW, Room 234
Washington, DC 20547 (202) 619-6409

This office develops and runs all academic programs of USIA, including the best-known educational exchange, the Fulbright Scholarship program. About 5,000 Fulbright grants are awarded each year to American students, teachers, and scholars to work abroad and to foreign citizens to teach, study, and conduct research in the U.S. In addition to the Fulbright program, the Academic Exchange Programs Division, (202) 619-4360, of this office administers grants to private agencies conducting complementary programs to the Fulbright academic exchanges, and has responsibilities for foreign research centers, Fulbright commissions, and seminars for foreign Fulbright students. Contact this office for more information and application forms for the Fulbright program.

* Gettysburg Address and Other Manuscripts

Manuscript Division
LH 101, Library of Congress
Washington, DC 20540 (202) 707-5387

More than 40 million pieces of manuscript material are housed in the Manuscript Division, including the letters, diaries, speech drafts (including the copy of the Gettysburg Address), scrapbooks, telegrams, and so forth of influential people. For instance, the Library owns the papers of 23 of the presidents from George Washington to Calvin Coolidge, as well as materials of Clara Barton, Sigmund Freud, and Benjamin Franklin. The Manuscript is open to persons engaged in serious research who present proper identification. Hours of operation are 8:30 a.m. to 5:00 p.m., Monday through Friday (except national holidays).

* Government Agencies' Significant Records

Office of the National Archives
National Archives and Records Administration
8th St. and Pennsylvania Ave., NW
Room 20E
Washington, DC 20408 (202) 501-5575

The Center for Electronic Records administers computer files having enduring value that have been transferred to the National Archives from other federal agencies. A free copy of the *Center for Electronic Records Title List (A Partial and Preliminary List of the Datasets in Custody of the National Archives)* is available, as is information regarding their reference services and charges.

* Government Humanities Grants News

Public Information Office
National Endowment for the Humanities
1100 Pennsylvania Ave., NW
Room 410
Washington, DC 20506 (202) 606-8443

Humanities is a bimonthly magazine published by NEH features articles by nationally known scholars and writers on current humanities topics, listings of recent grants by discipline, calendars of grant application deadlines, guide sections for those who are thinking of applying for an NEH grant, and essays about noteworthy NEH-supported projects. A subscription for $11 per year is available from the Superintendent of Documents, Government Printing Office, Washington, DC 20402; (202) 783-3238.

* Government Record Management News

Records Administration Information Center
Agency Services Division
National Archives and Records Administration
8th St. and Pennsylvania Ave., NW
Washington, DC 20408 (202) 501-6000

The Records Administration Information Center is a valuable resource for all records managers. This Center can answer your specific records management questions and direct you to useful publications and other sources of assistance, along with arranging for individual assistance with planning for training, electronic records systems, developing records schedules, and other projects. *Recordfacts Update* is published by the Records Administration Information Center to share news about records administration throughout the federal records community. The newsletter provides information on National Archives programs and initiatives, agency records management programs, and available resources. This free publication is directed mostly to federal records managers, but is an excellent resource for any records managers.

* Grants for Archival History and Preservation

National Archives and Records Administration
8th St. and Pennsylvania Ave., NW
Room 300
Washington, DC 20408 (202) 501-5200

The Commission awards grants to promote a variety of historically-oriented projects, such as archival programs, documentary publications projects, and archival and editorial education. The Publications Program provides grant money for printed and microfilm publications of the papers of famous American diplomats, politicians, reformers, scientists, labor figures, as well as corporate and organizational records. A subsidy program provides grants to non-profit presses to help support publication costs of sponsored editions. The Records Program makes grants to state and local governments, historical societies, archives, libraries, and associations for the preservation, arrangement, and description of historical records. Education programs include an institute to train scholars in documentary editing and fellowships in the fields of documentary editing and archival administration.

Be patient. If any phone number is incorrect, call (area code) 555-1212 and request the new listing.

Arts and Humanities

* Guides to Scholarly Sources

Smithsonian Institution Press
c/o Order Dept. 900 (800) 782-4612
Blue Ridge Summit, PA 17214 (717) 794-2148

Produced by the Woodrow Wilson International Center for Scholars, these guides are designed to be descriptive, evaluative surveys of source materials. Each guide is divided into two parts. Part I examines area collections - libraries; archives and manuscript depositories; art, film, music, and map collections; and data banks. Part II focuses on pertinent activities of Washington-based organizations, public and private. Given for each are its related functions, materials and products. The series includes:

Cartography and Remote Sensing
African Studies
East Asian Studies
South Asian Studies
Southeast Asian Studies
Central and East European Studies
Northwest European Studies
Latin American and Caribbean Studies
Middle Eastern Studies
Russian/Soviet Studies
Film and Video Collections
Audio Resources

* Handbook of North American Indians

Smithsonian Institution Press
c/o Order Dept 900 (800) 782-4612
Blue Ridge Summit, PA 17214 (717) 794-2148

This twenty-volume encyclopedia summarizes knowledge about all Native peoples north of Mesoamerica, including cultures, languages, history, prehistory, and human biology. This bound series is a standard reference work for anthropologists, historians, students, and the general public. It contains chapters by authorities on each topic, including one on each tribe.

* Historical Documents Editing Classes

National Historical Publications and
Records Commission
National Archives and Records Administration
8th St. and Pennsylvania Ave., NW, Room 607
Washington, DC 20408 (202) 501-5600

The NHPRC Institute for the Editing of Historical Documents is held for two weeks each summer at the University of Wisconsin, Madison. Admission is competitive and applicants should hold a Masters degree in American History or American Studies or have equivalent training. Tuition is $250.

* Historical Grants for Humanities Disciplines Study

Division of Research Programs
National Endowment for the Humanities
1100 Pennsylvania Ave., NW, Room 318
Washington, DC 20506 (202) 606-8200

In this category, the Endowment supports research that employs the theories and methods of humanities disciplines to study science, technology, and medicine. Historical studies and studies of the fundamental concerns that lie behind current issues are eligible for funding. An example would be an historian studying the history of the Islamic hospital to better understand the development of Western medicine.

* Historical Handbook Series Bibliography

Superintendent of Documents
Government Printing Office
Washington, DC 20402 (202) 783-3238

Historical landmarks are described in the historical handbooks featured in this listing. Sites include Antietam Battlefield, Devil's Tower in Wyoming, Ford's Theater, Glacier Bay, Lincoln Memorial, and Nez Perce National Historical Park in Idaho, among others. Free.

* Historic American Buildings Survey

Historic American Buildings Survey
National Park Service
U.S. Department of the Interior

P.O. Box 37127
Washington, DC 20013-7127 (202) 343-9625

The *Historic American Buildings Survey* has led the approach of preservation through the documentation of historic buildings, and landscape architectural and streetscape recording. Priority is given to those buildings administered by the National Park Service, to nationally significant structures (including National Historic Landmarks), and to historic buildings that are threatened by demolition. Collections of the *Survey* are accessible to the public in the Library of Congress' Prints and Photographs Division in Room 339 of the James Madison Building, First and Independence, SE, Washington, DC All records can be reproduced.

* Historic American Engineering Record

Historic American Engineering Record
National Park Service
U.S. Department of the Interior
P.O. Box 37127
Washington, DC 20013-7127 (202) 343-9625

Historic American Engineering Record was established to document historic engineering, industrial, and technological works throughout the country. It is conducted by the Park Service in cooperation with the American Society of Civil Engineers and the Library of Congress. The records take the form of measured drawings, professional photographs, historical reports, technical analyses, and motion pictures. This collection, like the *Historic American Building Survey*, is also accessible to the public at the Library of Congress' Prints and Photographs Division, Room 339, James Madison Building, First and Independence Ave., SE, Washington, DC.

* Historic Landmarks

The National Historic Landmarks Program
National Park Service
U.S. Department of the Interior
800 N. Capital St. NW
Washington, DC 20002 (202) 343-8167

Under the National Historic Landmarks Program, historic sites are identified for their national significance. Sites and structures found nationally significant by the Secretary are eligible for designation as National Historic Landmarks and are included in the *National Register* and listed monthly in the *Federal Register*. Upon the owner's agreement to adhere to accepted preservation precepts, landmark designation is recognized by the award of a bronze plaque and a certificate.

* Historic Preservation Assistance

Preservation Assistance Division
National Park Service
U.S. Department of the Interior
800 N. Capital St. NW
Washington, DC 20002 (202) 343-9573

The Preservation Assistance Division guides Federal and state agencies and the general public in historic preservation project work. Standards and guidelines are established, information on technical preservation is distributed, and training is given on technical preservation approaches and treatments. This office also administers the Preservation Tax Incentives program, the status of National Historic Landmarks, and the Historic Preservation Fund grant-in-aid program.

* Historic Preservation Council

Advisory Council on Historic Preservation
1100 Pennsylvania Ave., NW
Suite 809
Washington, DC 20004 (202) 606-8503

Affiliated with the U.S. Department of the Interior, this council advises Congress and the President on matters of historic preservation. The Council is composed of the Secretaries of the Interior, Housing and Urban Development, Commerce, Treasury, Transportation, and Agriculture; the Attorney General; the Administrator of the General Services Administration; the Chairman of the National Trust for Historic Preservation; the Secretary of the Smithsonian Institution; and 10 non-federal members appointed by the President.

* Historic Preservation Publications

Cultural Resources Programs
National Park Service
U.S. Department of the Interior

Be patient. If any phone number is incorrect, call (area code) 555-1212 and request the new listing.

Historians, Scholars and Writers

800 N.Capital St. NW
Washington, DC 20002 (202) 343-9596

The *Catalog of Historic Preservation Publications* is a valuable listing of books on the subject of historic preservation. Books on the actual preservation of old buildings are included, as well as the procedures to follow to register buildings in the National Register. Archeological research, architecture, historic landmarks, and anthropology are also featured subjects.

* Historic Sites of the United States

Superintendent of Documents
Government Printing Office
Washington, DC 20402 (202) 783-3238

The GPO bibliography of public buildings, landmarks, and historic Sites of the United States is divided into the categories of historic sites, posters, preservation methods for historic buildings, and descriptions of public buildings. Highlights include a poster of the Statue of Liberty and an historic guide to the White House. Free.

* History of the U.S. Capitol

Superintendent of Documents
Government Printing Office
Washington, DC 20402 (202) 783-3238

The Capitol provides a pictorial and narrative history of the U.S. Capitol building and the Congresses that have served there. Included are sections devoted to the Architects of the Capitol, the Speaker of the House, House and Senate Leadership, pages of the U.S. Congress, Congress in international affairs, elected officers of the Senate, a profile of the 100th Congress, women in American politics, and related information. The cost is $10 from the Government Printing office, S/H 052-071-00687-7, but if you contact your congressman's office, you can get a complimentary copy.

* Humanities Publication Funding

Division of Research Programs
National Endowment for the Humanities
1100 Pennsylvania Ave., NW, Room 318
Washington, DC 20506 (202) 606-8200

This Program provides support for the preparation for publication of texts that promise to make major contributions to the study of the humanities. Support is available for editions of works and documents, for translation of works into English, and for the publication and distribution of scholarly books in all fields of the humanities.

* Indian Ancestry

Branch of Tribal Enrollment
Bureau of Indian Affairs
U.S. Department of the Interior
18th and C Sts., NW
Washington, DC 20240 (202) 208-3702

Tracing your Indian ancestry requires that you first do basic genealogical research to obtain following information: the names of your Indian ancestors; dates of birth, marriages, and death; where they lived; their brothers and sisters; and very importantly, their tribal affiliations. To verify that your ancestors are on official tribal rolls or censuses, contact the National Archives and Records Administration, Civil Resources Division, 8th and Pennsylvania Ave., NW, Washington, DC 20408, (please do not call). You may also receive assistance from the office above. The requirements of the particular tribe of your Indian ancestors will determine whether you are eligible for membership.

* Information On Demand

Humanities and Social Services
Library of Congress, LJ 109
Washington, DC 20540 (202) 707-5530

If you need information that is contained in the material in the Library of Congress collections, the reference staff will find it for you and relay it over the phone. If the information you require is too extensive, however, the reference staff will refer you to private researchers who work on a fee basis.

* International Scholars Exchange Programs

International Activities
3123 S. Dillon Ripley Center

1100 Jefferson Dr. S.W.
Smithsonian Institution
Washington, DC 20560 (202) 357-4282

Handbook on International Research and Exchanges serves as a basic reference document for Smithsonian staff who travel abroad on official business or who engage in international scholarly or museum exchanges. Although directed toward Smithsonian staff, this publication can give others helpful tips for conducting research and exchanges abroad, including visas, research permits and money concerns, and also covers issues surrounding immigration and international visitors.

* International Peace Fellowships

Jennings Randolph Program for International Peace
United States Institute of Peace
1550 M St., NW
Washington, DC 20005-1708 (202) 429-3886

This Program provides fellowships to scholars and leaders in peace to undertake research and other appropriate forms of communication on issues of international peace and the management of international conflict. The Fellowship Program has three levels: Jennings Randolph Distinguished Fellows are individuals whose careers show extraordinary accomplishment concerning questions of international peace; United States Institute of Peace Fellows are individuals also of accomplishment, but of somewhat less eminence; and United States Institute of Peace Scholars are individuals working on doctoral dissertations in the field.

* International Research and Advanced Study Grants

Division of Research Programs
National Endowment for the Humanities
1100 Pennsylvania Ave., NW
Room 318
Washington, DC 20506 (202) 606-8200

Grants in the Centers for Advanced Study category support interrelated research efforts at independent research libraries and museums, American research centers overseas, and centers for advanced study. Grants awarded by the centers enable individual scholars to pursue their own research and to participate in the interchange of ideas among the Centers' scholars. Grants in the International Research category provide funds to national organizations and learned societies to enable scholars to pursue research abroad, to attend or participate in international conferences, and to engage in collaborative work with foreign colleagues.

* Korean War Data Files

Center for Electronic Records
National Archives and Records Administration
8th St. and Pennsylvania Ave., NW
Room 20E
Washington, DC 20408 (202) 501-5575

The Center for Electronic Records maintains military data files for all branches of the military and a variety of records on Korean War.

* Laws and How They Are Made

Superintendent of Documents
U.S. Government Printing Office
Washington, DC 20402 (202) 783-3238

The handbook, *How Our Laws Are Made*, is designed to enable every citizen to gain a greater understanding of the Federal legislative process. It discusses the various steps of the Federal lawmaking process from the origin of an idea for a legislative proposal through its publication as a statute. It is $2.50 from GPO. S/N 052-071-00893-4.

* Library of Congress Reading Rooms

Main Reading Room
Library of Congress
Washington, DC 20540 (202) 707-5521

Located on the first floor of the Thomas Jefferson Building, the main reading room contains material on American history, economics, fiction, language and literature, political science, government documents, and sociology. A reference collection for these materials is also housed there. These reading rooms are not equipped to answer reference questions over the telephone, but will provide information on their collections, hours of operation, and the like.

Be patient. If any phone number is incorrect, call (area code) 555-1212 and request the new listing.

Arts and Humanities

Social Science . . . . (202) 707-5522
Microform . . . . (202) 707-5471
Local History and Genealogy . . . . (202) 707-5537
Newspapers and Current Periodicals . . . . (202) 707-5690
Science . . . . (202) 707-5639
Law Library . . . . (202) 707-5079
Performing Arts . . . . (202) 707-5507
Performing Arts Library at the Kennedy Center . . . . (202) 707-6245
Motion Picture, Broadcasting, and Recorded Sound . . . . . . (202) 707-5840
Archive of Folk Culture . . . . (202) 707-6590
Prints and Photographs . . . . (202) 707-6394
Manuscripts . . . . (202) 707-5387
Rare Book and Special Collections . . . . (202) 707-5434
Geography and Map . . . . (202) 707-6277
Hispanic . . . . (202) 707-5400
European . . . . (202) 707-5858
Asian . . . . (202) 707-5428
African and Middle Eastern Division . . . . (202) 707-5528
Music . . . . (202) 707-5504

* Literary Works Copyright Entries Catalogs

Superintendent of Documents
Government Printing Office
Washington, DC 20402 (202) 783-3238

The following copyright catalogs, which list materials registered only during the period covered by each issue, are available on microfiche only and are sold as individual subscriptions:

Part 1: Nondramatic Literary Works (quarterly) $14 per year.
Part 2: Serials and Periodicals (semi-annually) $5 per year.

* Literature Translators Funding

Literature Program
National Endowment for the Arts
1100 Pennsylvania Ave., NW
Room 723
Washington, DC 20506 (202) 682-5451

The Literature Program assists individual creative writers and literature translators, encourages wider audiences for contemporary literature, and assists non-profit literary organizations. Fellowships enable writers and translators to set aside time for writing and research. Publishing grants provide assistance to literary magazines, small presses, and various distribution projects. Grants are also available to support residencies for writers to allow them to interact with their public. Literary centers may request funds but must offer a regular format of readings, workshops, and technical assistance for writers. Grants can be made to individuals or to non-profit organizations if such donations qualify as charitable deductions under Section 170(c) of the Internal Revenue Code of 1954. Grants range from $2,000 to $50,000.

* Manuscript and Archives Repositories

Repositories in the United States
National Historical Publications
and Records Commission
Oryx Press
2214 North Central at Encanto (800) 279-ORYX
Phoenix, AZ 85004 (602) 265-2651

The Directory of Archives and Manuscripts provides in-depth information on over 4,500 archives and manuscript repositories. Each entry describes contents of holdings, physical size of the collection, dates covered by materials, materials solicited, and bibliographic references to selected guides. This *Directory* is available for $55.

* Manuscript Preservation Archive

National Endowment for the Humanities
1100 Pennsylvania Ave., NW
Room 802
Washington, DC 20506 (202) 606-8570

Vast numbers of source documents are in danger of destruction due to the disintegration of the paper on which they are written. This program provides support to projects that deal with this problem, such as those that save informational content, improve collection maintenance, and develop preventive care practices. Non-profit institutions and organizations may apply.

* Minority Research Grants

Fellowships and Grants
Smithsonian Institution
Washington, DC 20560 (202) 287-3271

The Smithsonian offers fellowships and internships for research and study in fields which are actively pursued by the museums and research organizations of the Institution. Both predoctoral and postdoctoral fellowships are available, as well as Minority Faculty Fellowships. The length of the term and size of the stipend vary. The Minority and Native American Internship Programs are performed under direct supervision of Smithsonian staff, as tutorial situations.

* Modern Archives Management Training Course

Office of Public Programs
National Archives and Records Administration
8th St. and Pennsylvania Ave., NW, Room 505
Washington, DC 20408 (202) 501-5200

The "Modern Archives Institute: Introduction to Modern Archives Administration," is a two-week archival training course that offers an introduction to archival theory and practice for participants. It is sponsored by the National Archives Trust Fund Board, and includes lectures, discussions, workshops, and visits to the Manuscript Division of the Library of Congress and various units of the National Archives. The Institute is offered twice a year.

* National Air and Space Museum Branch Library

National Air and Space Museum
7th and Independence Ave. S.W.
Room 3100
Washington, DC 20590 (202) 357-3133

This library houses more than 30,000 books, 4700 periodical titles, 6,000,000 technical reports, and is enriched by a documentary archival collection which includes 900,000 photographs, drawings, and other documents. The scope of the collection covers history of aviation and space, flight technology, aerospace industry, biography, lighter-than-air technology and history, rocketry, earth and planetary sciences, and astronomy. The Library is open to the public by appointment.

* National Anthropological Archives

National Museum of Natural History
10th St. and Constitution Ave. N.W.
Washington, DC 20560 (202) 357-1986

The NAA holds the Bureau of American Ethnology's collection of historical manuscripts that relates to the linguistics, ethnology, archeology, physical anthropology, and history of North American Natives. It also has the administrative records of the Department of Anthropology. The photograph collection incorporates 150,000 original negatives and prints made by photographers who worked with American Indian subjects. Other pictorial materials are available through SIBIS.

* National Archives Conferences and Workshops

Office of Public Affairs
National Archives and Records Administration
8th St. and Pennsylvania Ave., NW
Washington, DC 20408 (202) 501-5525

A free, monthly Calendar of Events is available which includes information on free films and lectures, as well as information on workshops, exhibitions, and tours.

* National Archives Posters and Publications

Publications Sales
National Archives and Records Administration
8th St. and Pennsylvania Ave., NW
Washington, DC 20408 (202) 724-0086

There are several brochures which list publications available from the National Archives and Records Administration. *Select List of Publications of the National Archives and Records Administration* includes publications of several finding aids to records held by NARA that are currently in print. Also included are professional archival papers and books, and other materials of interest to researchers. *Publications from the National Archives* includes guide and indices to collections in specific areas and publications that will be useful to archivists, historians and researchers, as well as general-interest books concerning U.S. history of the National Archives. The *Celebrating the Constitution* booklet

Be patient. If any phone number is incorrect, call (area code) 555-1212 and request the new listing.

Historians, Scholars and Writers

describes more than 50 publications, gifts, and audiovisual programs that relate to the Constitution. *Full-Color High Quality Posters from Your National Archives* illustrates 29 popular historical and contemporary posters and postcards.

* National Register of Historic Places

Interagency Resources Division
National Park Service
U.S. Department of the Interior
800 N. Capital St. NW
Suite 250
Washington, DC 20002 (202) 343-9500

The National Register of Historic Places is administered by the Interagency Resources Division of NPS. Along with the Preservation Assistance Division, this office administers the Historic Preservation Fund grants-in-aid to states and the National Trust for Historic Preservation. Technical workshops and other assistance is provided on preservation planning, and a database of historic information is maintained.

* Native Americans and Other Minorities Bibliography

Superintendent of Documents
Government Printing Office
Washington, DC 20402 (202) 783-3238

The publications describing the Native American Indian are listed in this bibliography. Also included are a selection of books discussing the Black, Hispanic, and other minority populations. Free.

* Native American Indian Publications

Office of Public Affairs
Bureau of Indian Affairs
U.S. Department of the Interior
18th and C Sts., NW
Washington, DC 20240 (202) 343-1711

The following is a listing of free publications from the Bureau of Indian Affairs Public Affairs office. Due to the limited supply and small staff only one copy of each publication may be requested.

Booklists:
Book List for Young Readers
General Reading List for Adults
Languages
Legends and Myths
Music
Religions and Ceremonials
Wars and Local Disturbances
Origin

* Natural History Library

Natural History Library
10th and Constitution Ave. N.W.
Washington, DC 20560 (202) 357-4696

This library houses 330,000 books and bound journals and receives 1,963 journal subscriptions. The library consists of a main location and several subject-based locations. Topics covered include biology, geology, paleontology, ecology, anthropology, botany, entomology, and mineral sciences. Call to make an appointment or for information on the location of the subject-based libraries.

* National Registry of Natural Landmarks

National Registry Branch
National Park Service
U.S. Department of the Interior
800 N. Capital St. NW
Suite 250
Washington, DC 20002 (202) 343-9536

The Park Service conducts natural region studies to identify areas that are of potential national significance. These areas are then studied in the field by scientists. Natural areas considered of national significance are cited by the Secretary of the Interior as eligible for recognition as Registered Natural Landmarks. The owner may apply for a certificate and bronze plaque designating the site.

* Newspapers and Periodicals From Around the World

Library of Congress
Washington, DC 20540 (202) 707-5650

Hundreds of different newspapers and periodicals from all fifty states and countries around the world are available on microfilm for $30 for domestic and $35 for foreign publications. Subscriptions are available or single issues can be ordered. Orders must be prepaid or charged to a standing account at the Library of Congress.

* North American Indian Handbook

Superintendent of Documents
Government Printing Office
Washington, DC 20402 (202) 783-3238

Handbook of North American Indians is the first to be published of a set of volumes that will give a summary of the prehistory, history, and cultures of the native peoples of America who lived north of central Mexico.

Arctic. Vol.5, 1984 (S/N 047-000-00398-9, $29)
Subarctic. Vol. 6, 1981 (S/N 047-000-00374-1, $25)
California. Vol. 8, 1981. (S/N 047-000-00347-4, $25)
Southwest. Vol. 9, 1979. Covers Puebloan peoples and general Southwest prehistory and history. (S/N 047-000-00361-0, $23)
Southwest. Vol. 10, 1983. Contains 56 articles about the non-Puebloan peoples of the Southwest and some surveys on the entire Southwest. (S/N 047-000-00390-3, $25)
Great Basin. Vol. 11, 1986. Surveys the Shoshone, Bannock, Ute, Paiute, Washoe, and Kawaiisu peoples who once inhabited the entire Great Basin region of western North America.(S/N 047-000-00401-2, $27)
Northeast. Vol. 15, 1978. (S/N 047-000-00351-2, $27)

* Overseas Research Grants

Fellowships and Grants
Smithsonian Institution
Washington, DC 20560 (202) 287-3271

The office also administers a Special Foreign Currency Program, a nationally competitive grants program for research carried out by U.S. institutions in countries where the United States owns local currencies deemed by the Treasury Department to be in excess of normal U.S. needs. Write or call for more information or applications.

* Overseas Tour for Scholars

American Participants (AmParts)
Office of Program Coordination and Development
United States Information Agency
301 Fourth St., SW
Room 550
Washington, DC 20547 (202) 619-4720

AmParts are experts in a field -- usually economics, international affairs, literature, the arts, U.S. political and social processes, sports, science, or technology -- sent abroad by USIA to meet with groups or individual professional counterparts. Recruited on the basis of requests of USIA staff in other countries, AmParts often engage in informal lecture/discussions with small groups, grant media interviews, or speak before larger audiences. Those interested in the American Participant program are invited to submit a brief letter indicating times of availability, along with a curriculum vitae and at least two lecture topics with brief talking points. A free brochure on the program is available from this office.

* Peace and International Relations Research Studies

United States Institute of Peace
1550 M Street, NW
Suite 700
Washington, DC 20005-1708 (202) 457-1700

The Institute of Peace designs and directs research and studies projects carried out through a process which includes the production of working papers on selected topics and their discussion by experts in public session. Working-group projects proceed through four or more public sessions involving a core group of experts. Studies are conceived on the same scale, but with a changing cast of experts. Public workshops are three-hour, monthly events designed for group discussion around a discrete topic of current concern.

Be patient. If any phone number is incorrect, call (area code) 555-1212 and request the new listing.

Arts and Humanities

* Peale Family Papers (1735-1885)

Peale Family Papers
National Portrait Gallery
8th and F Sts. N.W.
Washington, DC 20560 (202) 357-2565

The Peale Family Papers is a project that carries on research in eighteenth and early nineteenth century art and cultural history, with particular attention to Maryland and Philadelphia from 1735 to 1885. The project's files contain documents, correspondence, diaries, manuscripts, writings, secondary literature and some photographs of Charles Wilson Peale, his children and his relatives. The files may be consulted by appointment.

* Political Science Fellowships

United States Institute of Peace
1550 M St. N.W.
Washington, DC 20005 (202) 457-1700

The Grants Program provides financial support to nonprofit organizations, official public institutions, and individuals to fund projects on various themes and topics of interest. Past projects have included the role of third-party negotiators in the resolution of regional conflicts, religious and ethical questions in war and peace, and the use of non-violent sanctions in confronting political violence. Call or write for more information regarding grant application procedures.

* Preservation of Library Materials

National Preservation Program Office
Library of Congress, LMG 21
Washington, DC 20540 (202) 707-1840

The Preservation Office is involved in a constant race against time to preserve its millions of items from disintegration. Newspapers are immediately microfilmed, motion pictures are rushed to refrigerated vaults, manuscripts are put in fumigating vaults, and maps are encased in polyester envelopes. But the main problem for preservationists is acid and its affect on paper. Recently the Library's chemists developed a technique whereby wood pulp books are placed in huge vacuum tanks which are flooded with diethyl zinc gas, thus deacidifying them for another hundred years. Research continues on longstanding preservation problems. A series of leaflets on various preservation and conservation topics is available from the office.

* Presidential Documents and Public Papers

Office of the Federal Register
National Archives and Records Administration
8th St. and Pennsylvania Ave., NW, Room 8401
Washington, DC 20408 (202) 523-5230

The *Weekly Compilation of Presidential Documents* is published each week and contains all of the President's statements, nominations, acts he approves, weekly schedules, transcripts of speeches; basically all of his actions. A subscription for $58 a year is available by contacting the Superintendent of Documents, Government Printing Office, Washington, DC, 20402; (202) 783-3238.

* Presidential Papers

Superintendent of Documents
U.S. Government Printing Office
Washington, DC 20402 (202) 783-3238

The following volumes are part of *Public Papers of the Presidents*, a series containing documents from certain periods of the Presidency. Public messages, nominations, appointments, Executive orders, speeches, and statements of the President as issued by the Press Secretary can be found within these volumes. The volumes available from GPO include the following:

Ronald Reagan, 1983, Book I, $31
Ronald Reagan, 1983, Book II, $32
Ronald Reagan, 1984, Book I, $36
Ronald Reagan, 1984, Book II, $36
Ronald Reagan, 1985, Book I, $34
Ronald Reagan, 1985, Book II, $30
Ronald Reagan, 1986, Book I, $37
Ronald Reagan, 1986, Book II, $35
Ronald Reagan, 1987, Book I, $33
Ronald Reagan, 1987, Book II, $35
Ronald Reagan, 1988, Book I, $39
Ronald Reagan, 1988-89, Book II, $38 Book II

* Presidential Libraries

National Archives and Records Administration
8th St. and Pennsylvania Ave., NW
Room 104
Washington, DC 20408 (202) 501-5700

Through the Presidential Libraries, which are located on sites selected by the presidents and built with private funds, the National Archives preserves and makes available for use the Presidential records and personal papers that document the actions of a particular president's administration. In addition to providing reference services on Presidential documents, each library prepares documentary and descriptive publications and operates a museum to exhibit documents, historic objects, and other memorabilia of interest to the public. Each library provides research grants to scholars and graduate students for the encouragement of research in Presidential libraries' holdings and of publication or works based on such research. Public programs of the libraries include conferences, lectures, films, tours, commemorative events, and seminars. For further information, contact the Presidential library of your choice.

Herbert Hoover Library, West Branch, IA, 52358, (319) 643-5301
Franklin D. Roosevelt Library, Hyde Park, NY, 12538, (914) 229-8114
Harry S. Truman Library, Independence, MO, 64050; (816) 833-1400
Dwight D. Eisenhower Library, Abilene, KS, 67410; (913) 263-4751
John F. Kennedy Library, Boston, MA, 02125; (617) 929-4577
Lyndon B. Johnson Library, Austin, TX, 78705; (512) 482-5137
Gerald R. Ford Library, Ann Arbor, MI, 48109; (313) 668-2218
Gerald R. Ford Museum, Grand Rapids, MI, 49504; (616) 456-2675
Nixon Presidential Materials Staff, Washington, DC, 20408; (703) 756-6498
Jimmy Carter Library, Atlanta, GA, 30307; (404) 331-3942
Ronald Reagan Library, Simi Valley, CA; (805) 522-8511

* Private Library Space for Researchers

Research Facilities Section
General Reading Rooms
Library of Congress
Washington, DC 20540 (202) 707-5211

For increased convenience, full-time scholars and researchers may apply for study desks in semi-private areas within the Library of Congress.

* Reproductions and Help for Researchers

National Archives and Records Administration
8th St. and Pennsylvania Ave., NW
Room 205
Washington, DC 20408 (202) 501-5403

Staff members provide reference service on records by responding in person, over the telephone, and in writing to requests for information from or about records, making original records available to researchers in research rooms, providing researchers with copies of records for a fee, and preparing microform publications of heavily used series of records. The Reference Services Branch refers requests to the branch in the National Archives that has custody of the relevant records. *Ordering Reproductions From the National Archives* is a helpful brochure which outlines the information needed to fill your request. Contact the References Services Branch for more information.

* Regional Archive Centers Nationwide

Regional Archives System
National Archives and Records Administration
8th St. and Pennsylvania Ave., NW
Washington, DC 20408 (202) 501-5510

This periodic newsletter includes information regarding activities at the various regional archives centers, including workshops, exhibits, publications, and networking information.

* Smithsonian Archives Guide

Smithsonian Archives
Smithsonian Institution
900 Jefferson Dr. S.W.
Washington, DC 20560 (202) 357-1420

This free *Guide to Smithsonian Archives* is a reference resource to the holdings of the Archives, giving a detailed listing of the records, papers, and projects the Archives has, as well as information regarding their use.

Be patient. If any phone number is incorrect, call (area code) 555-1212 and request the new listing.

Historians, Scholars and Writers

* Smithsonian Institution Library Services

Smithsonian Institution Libraries
10th St. and Constitution Ave., NW
Washington, DC 20560 (202) 357-2139

The libraries of the Smithsonian Institution include approximately 950,000 volumes, with strengths in natural history, museology, history of science, and the humanities. Inquiries on special subjects or special collections should be addressed to the appropriate branch library or to the Central Reference and Loan.

* State Historical Records

National Historical Publications and Records Commission
National Archives and Records Administration
8th St. and Pennsylvania Ave., NW
Room 607
Washington, DC 20408 (202) 501-5600

The governor of each state appoints a State Historical Records Coordinator, who is in charge of either the state archival agency of the state-funded historical agency. The governor also appoints a State Historical Records Advisory Board, which is the central advisory body for state projects and records planning. The Board makes funding recommendations to the National Historical Publications and Records Commission concerning records grant applications from institutions and organizations in the state. The Board may also undertake projects and studies of its own, solicit or develop proposals for Commission-funded projects, and review the progress of State Category Grants funded by the Commission. The grants fund projects for the preservation, arrangement, and description of historical records.

* Status of Presidential Documents

Executive Clerks Office
The White House
Washington, DC 20500 (202) 456-2226

The Executive Clerks Office reviews, processes, and records all documents signed by the President. To find out the status of any official Presidential proclamation, Executive order, nomination, appointment or legislation, contact the office above.

* Telephone Reference Service at Library of Congress

Library of Congress
Washington, DC 20540 (202) 707-5522

This service provides information to callers about the collections within the Library of Congress and how they can be used. In planning your research, remember that the Library of Congress is the library of last resort -- all other inter-library loan avenues must be exhausted before you may borrow a book from the Library of Congress. Always begin your research with your local library.

* Thomas Jefferson's Library and Other Rare Books Collection

Rare Book and Special Collections Division
Library of Congress, LJ 256
Washington, DC 20540 (202) 707-5434

The Rare Books Division contains about 300,000 volumes and 200,000 pamphlets, broadsides, theater playbills, title pages, manuscripts, posters, and photographs. The collection includes documents of the first fourteen congresses of the United States, the personal libraries of Thomas Jefferson and Harry Houdini, incunabula; miniature books and dime novels, and the Russian Imperial collection. The division has its own central card catalog plus special card files that describe individual collections or special aspects of books from many collections.

* Vice-Presidential Papers

Office of Presidential Libraries
National Archives and Records Administration
8th St. and Pennsylvania Ave., NW
Room 104
Washington, DC 20408 (202) 501-5700

Vice-Presidential records are subject to the same provisions as Presidential records and become property of the United States Government.

* Vietnam War Records

Center for Electronic Records
National Archives and Records Administration
8th St. and Pennsylvania Ave., NW, Room 20E
Washington, DC 20408 (202) 523-3267

The Center has records created between 1954 and 1975 by U.S. Army- Vietnam, U.S. Military Assistance Command-Thailand, and U.S. Military Assistance Command-Vietnam. Together they constitute the central documentary record on the war in Southeast Asia. They have divisional and brigade records, as well as records of combat units, which include those performing infantry, armor, aviation, artillery, and calvary functions, and those support units performing engineering signal, maintenance, and medical functions.

* Visual Arts Fellowships

National Gallery of Art
Center for Advanced Study in the Visual Arts
Constitution and 6th St., NW
Washington, DC 20565 (202) 842-6480

The Center has a four-part program of fellowships, meetings, publications, and research in the field of visual arts. The Center offers a series of discussions, symposia, and lectures. Nine pre-doctoral fellowships are available for productive scholarly work in the history of art, architecture, and urban form, as well as senior fellowships and visiting senior fellowships for post-doctoral studies. Center 8 is a publication which contains research reports by members of the Center, as well as a record of the activities of the Center. The Center also publishes an annual listing of research in the history of art sponsored by a number of granting institutions.

* Washington DC Historic Street Plans

Public Information Office
Pennsylvania Avenue Development Corporation
1311 Pennsylvania Ave., NW
Suite 1220 North
Washington, DC 20004 (202) 724-9059

The following publications are available:

Pennsylvania Avenue Development Corporation, Annual Report, 1988
The Pennsylvania Avenue Plan, 1974
Amendments to the Pennsylvania Avenue Plan
The Avenue Report (a quarterly newsletter)

* Weekly Presidential Documents

Superintendent of Documents
U.S. Government Printing Office
Washington, DC 20402 (202) 783-3238

The *Weekly Compilation of Presidential Documents,* compiles transcripts of the President's news conferences, messages to Congress, public speeches and statements, and other presidential materials released by the White House. The *Compilation* carries a *Monthly Dateline* and covers materials released during the preceding week. Each issue carries an index of contents and a cumulative index to prior issues. Separate indexes are published quarterly, semiannually, and annually. Other finding aids include lists of laws approved by the President and of nominations submitted to the Senate, and a checklist of White House releases. Subscriptions are $58 per year S/N-769-007-00000-8, and single copies are $2.

* White House Publications Listing

National Tech Information Service
5185 Port Royal Rd.
Springfield, VA 22161 (703) 487-4650

Publications of the Executive Office of the President is listing of the documents issued from EOP, including where to obtain them. Contact the office above to get your free copy.

* White House Watergate Tapes and Transcripts

Nixon Presidential Materials Project
Office of Presidential Libraries
National Archives and Records Administration
8th St. and Pennsylvania Ave., NW
Washington, DC 20408 (703) 756-6498

The White House Watergate tapes are available for public listening and consist of 31 conversations that were played to the juries as evidence in *United States v.*

Be patient. If any phone number is incorrect, call (area code) 555-1212 and request the new listing.

Arts and Humanities

John B. Connally and *United States v. John D. Ehrlichman, Harry R. Haldeman, Robert Mardian, John N. Mitchell, and Kenneth W. Parkinson.* This is a total of 12½ hours of conversation. You can order transcripts of the conversations for a small fee, and can make an appointment to listen to the tapes at the Archives Annex at 845 South Pickett Street, Alexandria, Virginia. The remaining White House tapes are currently undergoing archival processing.

* World War II Military Data Files

Center for Electronic Records National Archives and Records Administration 8th St. and Pennsylvania Ave., NW, Room 20E

Washington, DC 20408 (202) 501-5565 The Center for Electronic Records maintains military data files for all branches of the military and a variety of records from World War II.

* World War II Nazi Records

National Archives and Records Administration 8th St. and Pennsylvania Ave., NW Room 8N Washington, DC 20408 (202) 501-5383 This office holds all the records of the German Army that were captured during World War II, and can direct you to guides to the collection.

Be patient. If any phone number is incorrect, call (area code) 555-1212 and request the new listing.

Museums and Cultural Resources

The national museums and libraries span geographical and cultural boundaries to allow anyone to tap into arts, ethnography, anthropology, craft, architecture, archeology, history, oral tradition and folklore as well as natural history. The Museological Clearinghouse may serve as a good point of departure to locate the collections and experts in a particular time in history as well as to learn about trends in the museum world. Also refer to the section on Money for the Arts in this chapter which includes federal funding for exhibits and promotion of the arts.

* African Art National Museum

National Museum of African Art
Smithsonian Institution
950 Independence Ave. S.W.
Washington, DC 20590 (202) 357-4600 ext.200

The National Museum of African Art is dedicated to the collection, exhibition, and study of traditional arts of sub-Saharan Africa. Included in the collection are sculptures, textiles, jewelry, architectural elements, decorative arts, and utilitarian objects. They have an extensive education program, in addition to gallery lectures, programs for families and films for children. A free calendar of exhibitions and programs is available.

* African Art and Culture Photographic Archives

National Museum of African Art
950 Independence Ave. S.W.
Washington, DC 20560 (202) 357-4600 ext.280

The Eliot Elisofon Photographic Archives is devoted to the collection, preservation, and management of visual resources of sub-Saharan African Art. It conducts picture research and collaborates with art historians, anthropologists, filmmakers, and other interested specialists in the publication and exhibition of its images. In addition, it serves as an international clearinghouse for information about African art and cultural history. The collection is divided into two major categories: art, which includes photographs of art objects in the permanent collection, as well as in public and private collections; and field, which contains images of African life. An overall guide to the collection and a price list are available upon request.

* African Art Library

Smithsonian Institution
950 Independence Ave. S.W.
Washington, DC 20560 (202) 357-4600 ext.285

The Library maintains a collection of 15,000 books and 280 periodical titles on traditional and contemporary arts of Africa, including sculptural and decorative arts, ethnography, anthropology, craft, architecture, archeology, history, oral tradition and folklore, and African retentions in the New World. The Library is open to the public by appointment.

* Afro-American History and Cultures Exhibit

Anacostia Neighborhood Museum
Smithsonian Institution
1901 Fort Place S.E.
Washington, DC 20020 (202) 287-3306

This museum presents exhibitions on the history and cultures of Afro-Americans. The Research Department, open for use by scholars, conducts independent studies in the areas of Afro-American history, minority and ethnic studies, and history of Washington, DC. The Education Department develops independent programs and activities to serve the needs and interests of the local school community. These activities include a traveling puppet troupe, teacher workshops and seminars, and a circulating library of children's books for use by teachers.

* Air Force Art Collection

Secretary of the Air Force
Art and Museum Branch
The Pentagon, Room 4A120
Washington, DC 20330 (703) 697-6629

The Air Force Museum has available 8 x 10 reproduction photographs of the Air Force art collection. They will accept written requests.

* American Art Collections Nationwide

Archives of American Art
Smithsonian Institution
8th and G Sts. N.W.
Washington, DC 20560 (202) 357-2781

The Archives of American Art publishes a quarterly *Journal* that contains articles based on its collections and features reports from the regional centers. Separate publications include: *The Card Catalog of the Manuscript Collections of the Archives of American Art; Archives of American Art Collection of Exhibition Catalogs; Archives of American Art, A Directory of Resources;* and *Archives of American Art, A Checklist of the Collection.*

* American Art Museum

Barney Studio House
National Museum of American History
Smithsonian Institution
Washington, DC

The house, a curatorial department of the National Museum of American Art, was built by artist Alice Pike Barney in 1902 to be her home, studio and salon. Now being renovated, this unique showplace is filled with paintings by Mrs. Barney and her friends, ornate furniture, oriental rugs and decorative bibelots. It is open by reservation for guided visits, and an annual series of programs is presented in the spirit of the salons given by Mrs. Barney. Closed until further notice.

* American Arts and Industries Museum

Discovery Theater
Smithsonian Institution
Arts and Industries Building
900 Jefferson Dr., SW
Washington, DC 20560 (202) 357-1500

Currently, the Arts and Industries Building houses "1876: A Centennial Exhibition", which recalls the ambiance of the Victorian era by recreating the United States Centennial Exhibition held in Philadelphia in 1876. The building also houses the Smithsonian's Discovery Theater, which, from October to June, offers a changing series of live performances designed for young people and their families, including presentations by puppeteers, dancers, actors, mimes, and singers. Hours of operation - 10 a.m. to 4 p.m.

* American Crafts and Designers

Renwick Gallery
17th and Pennsylvania Ave., NW
Washington, DC 20560 (202) 357-2531

The Renwick Gallery of the National Museum of American Art exhibits the creative achievements of designers and craftspeople in the United States. The programs include lunchtime films, concerts, and other musical events, lectures and craft demonstrations, and children's programs related to current exhibitions. A free monthly calendar is available.

Be patient. If any phone number is incorrect, call (area code) 555-1212 and request the new listing.

Arts and Humanities

* American Culture and Folk Art Grants

Folk Arts Program
National Endowment for the Arts
1100 Pennsylvania Ave., NW, Room 725
Washington, DC 20506
(202) 682-5449

The Folk Arts Program supports the traditional arts that have grown through time within the many groups that make up the United States. The Program's objectives are to present and enhance this multi-cultural artistic heritage and to make it more available to a wider public audience. The Program offers grants for the presentation and documentation of traditional arts and artists, as well as for supporting the development of state- or regionally-based folk arts programs. Fellowships are given to master folk artists to provide national recognition.

* American History Branch Library

National Museum of American History
Room 5016
12th and Constitution Ave. N.W.
Washington, DC 20560
(202) 357-2414

The Library houses a collection of 165,000 volumes of book and bound journals on engineering, transportation, military history, science, applied science, decorative arts, and domestic and community life in addition to American history and the history of science and technology. They have special collections of trade literature and materials about world fairs. The Library is open to the public by appointment.

* American History National Museum

National Museum of American History
Directors Office
Smithsonian Institution
12th Sts. and Constitution Ave. N.W.
Washington, DC 20560
(202) 357-2510

The museum's mission is to illuminate through collections, exhibitions, research, publications, and educational programs, the entire history of the United States, including the external influences that have helped to shape the national character. From the patent model Eli Whitney's cotton gin to a Ford Model T, objects on display at the Museum embody the nation's scientific, technological, and cultural heritage. Recent major reinstallations treat everyday life in America just after the Revolutionary War, the American Industrial Revolution, and the diverse origins of the American people. You will find exhibits on agriculture, medicine, armed forces history, graphic arts, ceramics, glass, political history, and many other areas. Educational activities are directed toward both children and adults. Musical programs are offered regularly. Demonstration Centers offer participatory educational experiences where visitors may touch and handle objects.

* American Painting and Sculpture Databases

Office of Research Support
National Museum of American Art
9th and G Sts. N.W.
Washington, DC 20560
(202) 357-1626

The Office of Research Support maintains seven research projects totaling over 530,000 art data records and over 250,000 photographic images. Each of the projects uses automation in cataloging information and images, thus providing the user with access to art information and reproductions in a variety of ways. The research databases are: the Inventory of American Paintings Executed before 1914, a computerized index to over 250,000 paintings; the Inventory of American Sculpture, an on-line interactive database accessible through SIBIS, containing information on sculpture and outdoor monuments; the Pre-1877 Art Exhibition Catalog Index, recording works of art listed in catalogs of art exhibitions held in the U.S. and Canada; the Smithsonian Art Index, which lists drawings, prints, paintings, and sculptures located in Smithsonian scientific, technical, and historical collections; the Permanent Collection Database, comprising over 32,000 objects in the museum's collection; the Peter A. Juley and Son Collection of more than 127,000 photographic negatives documenting American art and artists photographed between 1896 and 1975 by this New York City firm; and the Slide and Photograph Archives, a collection of over 90,000 slides and 200,000 photographs available for study and 20,000 slides available for loan. Please call in advance for an appointment.

* American Portraits Research Center

National Portrait Gallery
8th and F Sts. N.W.

Washington, DC 20560
(202) 357-2578

The Catalog of American Portraits, administered by the National Portrait Gallery, is a national reference center whose files contain photographs and documentation for more than eighty thousand likenesses of historically important Americans. Arranged alphabetically by subject, the files are extensively cross-referenced by artist. A continuing Automated National Portrait Survey has made its holdings more readily accessible to researchers. Computerized indices by subject, artist, occupation, location, and medium make the catalog a valuable resource.

* Antiques and Historical Design

National Cooper-Hewitt Museum of Design
Smithsonian Institution
2 E. 91st St.
New York, NY 10128
(212) 860-6868

The Cooper-Hewitt Museum is the only museum in the United States devoted exclusively the study and exhibition of historical and contemporary design. The collection contains textiles, wallpaper, furniture, ceramics, glass, architectural ornaments, metalwork, woodwork, drawings and prints. A joint venture with the Book-of-the-Month Club offers a 15-page series entitled *The Smithsonian Illustrated Library of Antiques*. A continuing series of handbooks surveying each of the collections now numbers 20 titles. Educational programs offered include lectures, craft workshops, repair clinics, seminars, young people's classes, and performing arts demonstrations.

* Archeological Policies for National Parks

Anthropology Division
National Park Service
U.S. Department of the Interior
800 N. Capital St. NW
Washington, DC 20002
(202) 343-8161

The Anthropology Division of NPS is responsible for developing service-wide archeological and ethnographic program policies, guidelines, and standards. This function is concerned with preservation, protection, and visitor use activities related to the archeological aspects of the cultural resources of the Park System.

* Architectural and Engineering Drawings

Cartographic and Architectural Branch
Special Archives Division
National Archives and Records Administration
8th St. and Pennsylvania Ave., NW
Washington, DC 20408
(703) 756-6700

The Cartographic and Architectural Branch has over 11 million maps, charts, aerial photographs, architectural drawings, patents, and ship plans, which constitute one of the world's largest accumulations of such documents. The Branch holds architectural and engineering drawings created by civilian and military agencies. All the holdings can be examined in the research room at 841 South Pickett St., Alexandria, VA, from 8:00 a.m. to 4:30 p.m., Monday through Friday. Reproductions can be furnished for a fee.

* Architecture of the U.S. Capitol

The Curator's Office
Architect of the Capitol
The Capitol Building
Room SB15
Washington, DC 20515
(202) 225-1222

A packet of fact sheets on the various features and artifacts of the Capitol is available free of charge. It includes information on the Statue of Freedom; the tile floor of the Capitol; the history of the old subway transportation system connecting the Capitol and the Russell Office Building; the Rotunda Frieze; the "cornstalk" or "corncob" columns and capitals; the dome; the historic catafalque; Washington's tomb; those who have lain in state in the rotunda; the flags over the east and west central fronts; and the architects and architecture of the Capitol.

* Army and Air Force 1.2 Million Photographs

Still Media Records Center
U.S. Dept. of Defense
Bldg. 168, Anacostia Code SMRC
2701 S. Capital St. SW
Washington, DC 20374-5080
(202) 433-2166

Be patient. If any phone number is incorrect, call (area code) 555-1212 and request the new listing.

Museums and Cultural Resources

This center maintains a collection of over 1.2 million photographs and views on the Air Force and Army from 1954 to the present, and on the Navy and Marine Corps from 1959 to the present. Reprints can be purchased for a nominal fee. Write or call for a general information sheet and current price list.

* Army Art and Photograph Archive

U.S. Army Center of Military History
Attn: DAMH-HSA
20 Massachusetts Ave., NW (703) 274-8290
Washington, DC 20314 (202) 475-2716

The Center maintains a photographic library and archives of all paintings in the Army art collection. They have a catalog of negatives, and you can order prints for a small fee. Write or call for their free brochure describing their collection.

* Art Donations and Bequests

Development Department
National Gallery of Art
Constitution and 6th St., NW
Washington, DC 20565 (202) 842-6372

The Gallery seeks gifts-in-kind of American and Western European works of art. All donations should be discussed with the Development Department.

* Art Exhibits for American Embassies

Bureau of Administration
U.S. Department of State
21st and Virginia Ave., NW
Room B-258
Washington, DC 20520 (202) 647-5723

The State Department is responsible for placing original American art in U.S. Embassies. Based on cooperation between the government and the private sector, museums, corporate and private collectors, commercial galleries, and artists donate or lend American art representing all styles, periods, and media. Currently, more than 3,000 works of art valued at more than $35.2 million are being circulated in 123 countries. Write for an information brochure.

* Art Exhibits Insurance Coverage

Arts and Artifacts Indemnity Museum
National Endowment for the Arts
1100 Pennsylvania Ave., NW
Room 624
Washington, DC 20506 (202) 682-5442

This program provides grants for insurance against loss or damage for art works borrowed for international exhibitions. Individuals, non-profit institutions, and government agencies may apply. The art works can be insured for up to $50 million.

* Art Exhibits in the Halls of Congress

Secretary of the Senate
U.S. Capitol
Washington, DC 20510 (202) 224-3121

Most people tour the Capitol and admire its art work, but miss the works of art throughout all the buildings in the Capitol complex. The Rayburn House Office Building displays a statue of Sam Rayburn. The basement rotunda in the Cannon House Office Building displays a large model of the Capitol. The Hart Senate Office Building has an impressive Alexander Calder sculpture which fills the entire atrium courtyard space. Large, stately, richly detailed caucus rooms are historic places where major public hearings over the past three quarters of a century have taken place. The subway tunnel between the Cannon House Office Building and the Capitol is the site for a display of paintings done by high school artists who enter their works in congressional district competitions sponsored by the Congressional Arts Caucus.

* Art Exhibits Overseas

Office of Arts America
The Bureau of Educational and Cultural Affairs
United States Information Agency
301 Fourth St., SW
Room 567
Washington, DC 20547 (202) 485-2779

Arts America recruits artists and performers to visit other countries and provides some assistance to artists traveling privately. The USIA sends some 15 large fine arts exhibitions and 25 performing arts groups overseas annually. Panels set up by the National Endowment for the Arts recommends a group of candidates, from which the USIA selects the programs participants. A Speakers Program recruits artists from the fields of literature, film, and the performing arts, on the basis of requests from overseas posts. AculSpecs are American specialists, in one of the plastic or performing arts, who visit a foreign country for two to six weeks with a local host institution for a program of master classes, workshops, and demonstrations. Arts America sponsors about 30 of these programs a year. This office also provides support materials for major fine and performing arts projects; publishes a quarterly list of privately traveling artists; and tries to assist overseas posts in programming these performers.

* Art History Archive from 18th Century On

Archives of American Art
American Art and Portrait Gallery
8th and F Sts., NW
Washington, DC 20560 (202) 357-2781

The Archives of American Art is dedicated to the collection, preservation, and study of papers and other primary records of the history of the visual arts in America. Its collections, comprising more than eight million items, are the world's largest single source for such information. The collections include correspondence, journals, business papers, and other documentation of artists, dealers, critics, art historians, and art institutions from the eighteenth century to the present. Microfilm copies of many of the collections are available through interlibrary loan. Holdings of the Archives are described in a published card catalog (1980 -) and on SIBIS. In addition to its headquarters in Washington DC, the Archives of American Art maintains offices in four cities: Boston: (617) 565-8444; Detroit: (313) 226-7544; New York City: (212) 399-5015; and Los Angeles: (818) 405-7847, all of which serve as regional collecting and research centers, and provide microfilm of the collections to researchers. The Archives publishes the Archives of American Art Journal quarterly and sponsors symposia and lectures on art history subjects. Subscription 1 yr. - $35, 2 yr. - $65, 3 yr. - $90, single copy - $10.

* Art in the Capitol

The Curator's Office
Architect of the Capitol
The Capitol Building, Room SB15
Washington, DC 20515 (202) 225-1222

The U.S. Capitol is a recognized work of art. The classical architecture and the interior embellishments set the backdrop for the variety and scope of American history and culture. Much of the Capitol's art collection is catalogued in *Art in the Capitol*, published by the Architect of the Capitol under the direction of the Joint Committee on the Library.

* Arts in Education Initiatives

Arts-In-Education
National Endowment for the Arts
1100 Pennsylvania Ave., NW, Room 602
Washington, DC 20506 (220) 682-5426

The Arts-In-Education Program is a partnership program through cooperative efforts of the Arts Endowment, state arts and education agencies, local communities, and other organizations. The Program's overall goal is to advance the arts as part of basic education. Grants are awarded to place practicing artists in a variety of educational settings and to support other projects designed to enhance arts education in schools. Arts in Schools Basic Education Grants encourage plans and projects that promote the arts in schools as a basic component of the curriculum in kindergarten through high school.

* Art Slides, Films, Video Loan Program

Education Resources Programs
National Gallery of Art
Extension Services
Constitution and 6th St., NW
Washington, DC 20565 (202) 842-6273

Color slide programs, films, and videocassettes are loaned at no cost to schools, libraries, community organizations, and individuals across the nation. The programs deal with a wide range of subjects drawn from the Gallery's permanent collections and special exhibitions. A free catalog listing all free-loan Extension Programs is available. For booking a program call (202) 842-6263

Be patient. If any phone number is incorrect, call (area code) 555-1212 and request the new listing.

Arts and Humanities

* Asia and Near East Art National Collection

Sackler Gallery
Smithsonian Institution
1050 Independence Ave. SW
Washington, DC 20560
(202) 357-1924

Opened in 1987, the Sackler Gallery has over 1000 art objects from China, South and Southeast Asia, and the ancient Near East given to the museum by the late Arthur M. Sackler. Future programs at the gallery include major international shows offering both surveys of distinctive traditions and comparative exhibitions showing the art of different centuries, geographic areas, and types of patronage. Most exhibitions will be accompanied by public programs and scholarly symposia. The Sackler has a library and a slide study room which are open to the public. *Asian Art* is a quarterly journal published by Oxford University Press in association with the Sackler Gallery *Scholar's Guides to Washington DC.*

* Asian and Near Eastern Art Museum

Freer Gallery of Art
Smithsonian Institution
1050 Independence Ave. SW
Washington, DC 20560
(202) 357-1924

The Freer Gallery of Art is a museum of Asian and Near Eastern Art from the third millennium B.C. to the early 20th century. It also houses a group of works by late 19th and early 20th century American artists. The building, the original collection, and an endowment fund were the gift of Charles Lang Freer. The 26,800 Art works now in the Freer's Asian and Near Eastern collections include paintings, ceramics, manuscripts, metalwork, and sculpture. The Freer and the Sackler Gallery have joined together to share staff and research facilities, as well as a library housed at the Sackler. The Technical Laboratory conducts research and conservation of objects from the Freer and Sackler collections. It undertakes technical analyses of Asian art, investigates and rectifies conservation problems, and ensures that art works are in stable condition for exhibition. A free public lecture series is held where scholars present illustrated lectures on Asian and Near Eastern Art. The Freer is currently undergoing a major construction and renovation project and will be closed until May 1993.

* Attracting Wider Audience to Smithsonian Museums

Wider Audience Development Programs
Arts and Industries Building
Suite 2472
Smithsonian Institution
Washington, DC 20560
(202) 786-2403

The role of this Office is to extend the reach of Smithsonian programs to segments of the public that traditionally have been under-represented in the institution's audience. The office helps museums, offices, and bureaus throughout the institution in their outreach efforts. The OCWA systematically ensures participation in minority groups at receptions and special events.

* Audiovisual Materials for Art Exhibits

National Gallery of Art
Audiovisual Department
Constitution and 6th St., NW
Washington, DC 20565
(202) 842-6565

This office produces multi-image programs which accompany major exhibitions, as well as archival videotaping of exhibitions, special events, and lectures.

* Central Museological Clearinghouse

Office of Museum Programs
A and I Building 2235
900 Jefferson Dr. S.W.
Washington, DC 20560
(202) 357-3101

This information center and library has a working collection of resources on all aspects of museum operations. The Center, as the only central source of museological information in the United States, also contains evaluation studies, visitor surveys, volunteer manuals, long-range development plans, sample by-laws, and characters and museum collection management records. The Center is open to the public by appointment.

* Color Reproductions of National Collection

National Gallery of Art
Constitution and 6th St., NW
Washington, DC 20565
(202) 842-6466

The Publications Sales Department offers a large selection of color reproductions and scholarly publications related to the collections, exhibits, and other activities of the Gallery. Additional offerings include books and videocassettes on fine art and architecture, slide sets from the permanent collection, framed and matted reproductions and games. A free color reproductions mail order catalog is available. Mail order No. (301) 322-5906.

* Conservators and Archaeometry Training

Conservation-Analytical Laboratory
Smithsonian Institution
Museum Support Center
4210 Silver Hill Rd.
Suitland, MD 20560
(301) 287-3700

The Conservation-Analytical Laboratory engages in research in the conservation, technical study, and analysis of museum objects and related materials. Conservation-related information is made available to museum professionals nationwide and to the general public. In the archaeometry program, physical scientists engage in analytical and technical studies of artifacts. The laboratory performs conservation treatments on objects from the Smithsonian collections that present special problems. The conservation training program provides internship training for conservation students and organizes advanced specialist training courses for practicing conservators.

* Conservation and Preservation Survey

National Institute for the Conservation
of Cultural Property, Inc (NIC)
3299 K St. NW, Suite 403
Smithsonian Institution
Washington, DC 20007
(202) 625-1495

This clearinghouse for museums and conservationists is currently undertaking several projects, including the Conservation Assessment Survey Program, which is designed to help museums organize and weed out their collections; and the Save Outdoor Sculpture (SOS) project, which catalogs, inventories, and ensures that outdoor sculptures are treated properly.

* Contemporary and Historical Design

National Cooper-Hewitt Museum of Design
Smithsonian Institution
2 E. 91st St.
New York, NY 10128
(212) 860-6868

The Cooper-Hewitt Museum is the only museum in the United States devoted exclusively the study and exhibition of historical and contemporary design. The collection contains textiles, wallpaper, furniture, ceramics, glass, architectural ornaments, metalwork, woodwork, drawings and prints. A continuing series of handbooks surveying each of the collections now numbers 20 titles. Educational programs offered include lectures, craft workshops, repair clinics, seminars, young people's classes, and performing arts demonstrations.

* Dial-A-Museum

Visitor Information Center
Smithsonian Institution
1000 Jefferson Dr., SW
Washington, DC 20560
(202) 357-2020

By calling this number, you will hear a taped telephone message with daily announcements on new exhibits and special events.

* Disabled Smithsonian Visitors

Visitor Information and Associates' Reception Center
Smithsonian Institution
1000 Jefferson Dr. S.W.
Washington, DC 20560
(202) 357-2700

A free guide book to the Smithsonian is available for disabled visitors, which includes information on parking, transportation, wheelchair access, bathrooms, and telephones. Sign language and oral interpreter services may be arranged three days in advance. Several museums have large-print brochures available. Hours 9AM-4PM.

* Elderly and Disabled Access to the Arts

Office for Special Constituencies
National Endowment for the Arts

Be patient. If any phone number is incorrect, call (area code) 555-1212 and request the new listing.

Museums and Cultural Resources

1100 Pennsylvania Ave., NW
Room 605
Washington, DC 20506
(202) 682-5532
(202) 682-5496 TDD

The Office for Special Constituencies assists individuals and organizations in making arts activities accessible to older adults, disabled people, and those in institutions. Contact this Office for assistance and materials, including examples of how other arts groups have made their programs available to special groups, along with model project guidelines.

* Endowment for the Arts Grant Application Guide

Public Information Offices
National Endowment for the Arts
1100 Pennsylvania Ave., NW
Room 617
Washington, DC 20506
(202) 682-5400

The National Endowment for the Arts offers a free publication, the *Guide to the National Endowment for the Arts*, which outlines its various programs and grants, and provides a calendar of deadlines, as well as application information for the grants. Regional offices and other related agencies are also listed.

* Family Art Programs in Washington

National Gallery of Art
Education Division
Constitution and 6th St., NW
Washington, DC 20565
(202) 842-6246

Family programs are offered on Saturday mornings for families with children ages 6 to 12. These events usually include a film or special activity and a tour and lasts about 1 1/2 hours. Advance registration is required.

* Famous American Portraits

National Portrait Gallery
Publications Office
Smithsonian Institution
8th and G Sts. N.W.
Washington, DC 20560
(202) 357-2995

The National Portrait Gallery's collection consists of paintings, sculpture, prints, drawings, and photographs of figures significant to the history of the United States. At any given time, any number of research projects may be in progress on topics in American history, biography, and portraiture. This unique reference facility contains documentation on nearly 70,000 portraits of noted Americans. The Gallery provides a full range of educational services both within the museum and out in the community, including a Speakers' Bureau, a Lunchtime Lectures Series, and "Portraits in Motion" performance series, which presents actors and musicians in readings, concerts, and plays. Education office (202) 357-2920.

* Films and Lectures on Art

National Gallery of Art
Adult Programs
Constitution and 6th St., NW
Washington, DC 20565
(202) 842-6247

Free films on art, along with feature films, are presented at the Gallery. The *Calendar of Events* lists the titles and times of the showings. Free lectures are given by distinguished scholars on Sundays. No reservations are needed, but seating is limited. Andrew W. Mellon Lectures in the Fine Arts, a six-lecture series given at the Gallery, encompasses the history, criticisms, and theory of the visual and performing arts. All lectures also are announced in the Gallery's *Calendar*.

* Folklife Crafts and American Traditions

Center for Folklife Programs and Cultural Studies
Smithsonian Institution
955 L'Enfant Plaza
Washington, DC 20590
(202) 287-3424

Through its annual Festival of American Folklife, the Smithsonian created a program of folklife presentations for the general public for two weeks each summer. The Office also carries on research in folklife traditions, publishes documentary and analytical studies, develops and organizes exhibitions with folklife themes, and cooperates with Universities and other institutions in presentation projects involving traditional craftsman and performing artists.

* Folklife Studies Worldwide

Office of Folklife Programs Archive/
Folkways Records Archive
Office of Folklife Programs
955 L'Enfant Plaza S.W.
Suite 2600
Washington, DC 20560
(202) 287-3251

The Office of Folklife Programs Archive contains folkloristic materials generated through research for and documentation of the Festival of American Folklife Studies Monograph/Film Series. These materials document hundreds of folk culture traditions from the United States and forty-five other countries. Researchers should call for an appointment.

* Folkways Musical Recordings Archive

Office of Folklife Programs Archives
955 L'Enfant Plaza, SW
Suite 2600
Washington, DC 20560
(202) 287-3251

The Folkways Records Archive, comprising the Moses and Frances Asch Collection, contains material related to the 2,200 published recordings of Folkways Records. The Folkways collection documents world-wide musical traditions, the spoken words of significant American figures, historical events, and nonmusical sounds of technology and nature. A catalog of the archives holdings is available which includes information on how to purchase recordings of the music.

* Hirshhorn Museum and Sculpture Garden

Smithsonian Institution
7th St. and Independence Ave. S.W.
Washington, DC 20560
(202) 357-3091

The Hirshhorn Museum and Sculpture Garden is devoted to the exhibition, interpretation, and study of modern and contemporary art. The Collection consists of 19th and 20th century sculpture, paintings, prints and drawings. Children's events and a supplementary program of lectures, documentary films, art films, and performing arts are offered. Outreach programs provide on-site classroom preparation, lecture services for adult community groups, and a teachers' workshop course.

* Historic Architecture in the National Parks

Park Historic Architecture Division
National Park Service
U.S. Department of the Interior
800 N.Capital St. NW
Suite 360
Washington, DC 20002
(202) 343-8146

Activities related to the preservation of historic and prehistoric structures and cultural landscapes within the National Park System are administered by this office. *A List of Classified Structures* is maintained, which is an inventory of all historic and prehistoric structures in the System. A bibliography of Cultural Resources Management is also administered, listing all reports that address cultural resources in the Park System.

* Humanities Exhibits at Museums and Historical Organizations Grants

Division of General Programs
National Endowment for the Humanities
1100 Pennsylvania Ave., NW, Room 420
Washington, DC 20506
(202) 606-8284

This Program provides support for the planning and implementation of temporary and permanent exhibitions, historic site interpretations, publications, lectures and other educational programs, which engage the public in a greater appreciation and understanding of the humanities. Grants allow institutions to plan projects that interpret collections and to carry out permanent or temporary projects. Grants can support the cataloguing of a collection to make possible their use in programs on the humanities, as well as allowing for planning of computerized documentation. Self-study grants allow an organization to evaluate its humanities resources and develop long-range plans. Grants can be made to non-profit organizations, including local and state governments, if such donations qualify as charitable deductions under Section 170(c) of the Internal Revenue Code of 1954.

Be patient. If any phone number is incorrect, call (area code) 555-1212 and request the new listing.

Arts and Humanities

* Import Controls on Cultural Property

Cultural Property Advisory Committee
Bureau of Educational and Cultural Affairs
United States Information Agency
301 Fourth St., SW, Room 247
Washington, DC 20547 (202) 619-6612

This Presidential committee, comprised private citizens who are archaeologists, art dealers, representatives of the museum community, or the general public, advises the deputy USIA director, who determines whether the U.S. should impose import controls on endangered archaeological and ethnological materials at the request of foreign countries. The Cultural Property staff investigates and reports to the committee, and serves as liaison to federal agencies and to the archaeological, art dealer, museum, and preservation communities affected by U.S. actions under the 1983 Cultural Property Act.

* Indian Arts and Crafts Development

Indian Arts and Crafts Board
Bureau of Indian Affairs
U.S. Department of the Interior
18th and C Sts., NW
Washington, DC 20240 (202) 208-3773

The Indian Arts and Crafts Board promotes the development of Native Indian arts and crafts so that the artists will achieve economic stability. Three museums are operated by the Board: the Sioux Indian Museum in Rapid City, South Dakota; the Museum of the Plains Indian in Browning, Montana; and the Southern Plains Indian Museum in Anadarko, Oklahoma. These museums contain historic artifacts of these Indian tribes, but primarily function as contemporary showcases of Indian art. The Board also provides advisory services for Indian artists and craftsmen. To obtain a free *Source Directory* listing some 250 locations where Indian art can be seen and purchased, contact the office above.

* Indian Arts and Crafts Directory

Indian Arts and Crafts Board
Bureau of Indian Affairs, Room 4004
U.S. Department of the Interior
Washington, DC 20240 (202) 208-3773

The Indian Arts and Crafts Board has compiled a source directory of arts and crafts businesses owned and operated by Indians, Eskimos and Aleuts. The free directory lists the name, address, and phone number of each business and the types of products sold. The Indian Arts and Crafts Board's goal is to make the Indian populations more economically independent through their native arts and crafts.

* Indian Craft Shops

Indian Craft Shop
Bureau of Indian Affairs
U.S. Department of the Interior
18th and C Sts., NW
Washington, DC 20240 (202) 208-4056

Indian Craft Shop
Bureau of Indian Affairs
U.S. Department of the Interior
1050 Wisconsin Ave., NW
Washington, DC 20007 (202) 342-3918

These shops contain Indian crafts that can be purchased by the public. The hours at the Main Building location are 8:30 a.m. to 4:30 p.m., Monday through Friday. At the Wisconsin Avenue location, the hours are 10:00 a.m. to 7:00 p.m., Monday through Saturday, and 12:00 noon to 6:00 p.m., Sunday.

* Indian Museums

Southern Plains Indian Museum
P.O. Box 749
Anadarko, OK 73005 (405) 247-6221

Museum of the Plains Indian
P.O. Box 400
Browning, MT 59417 (406) 338-2230

Sioux Indian Museum
P.O. Box 1504

Rapid City, SD 57709 (605) 348-0557

These three Indian museums are administered by the Indian Arts and Crafts Board of the Bureau of Indian Affairs, U.S. Department of the Interior. The museums issue free informational pamphlets and brochures about their respective programs and exhibition activities. Contact the museums directly to be placed on their mailing lists.

* Indian Publications and Audiovisuals

Indian Arts and Crafts Board
Bureau of Indian Affairs
Room 4004
U.S. Department of the Interior
Washington, DC 20240 (202) 208-3773

The Indian Arts and Crafts Board has compiled a listing of their publications and audiovisuals available to the public. Titles include *Contemporary Southern Plains Indian Metalwork, Painted Tipis by Contemporary Plains Indian Artists, Coyote Tales of the Montana Salish, Contemporary Indian Artists - Montana/Wyoming,* and *Contemporary Southern Plains Indian Painting.* Two slide lecture kits are available for purchase at $50 each: *Contemporary Indian and Eskimo Crafts of the United States* and *Contemporary Sioux Painting.*

* International Museum Scholars Exchange

International Activities
3123 S. Dillon Ripley Center
1100 Jefferson Dr. S.W.
Smithsonian Institution
Washington, DC 20560 (202) 357-4282

Handbook on International Research and Exchanges serves as a basic reference document for Smithsonian staff who travel abroad on official business or who engage in international scholarly or museum exchanges. Although directed toward Smithsonian staff, this publication can give others helpful tips for conducting research and exchanges abroad, including visas, research permits and money concerns, and also covers issues surrounding immigration and international visitors.

* Military Photographic Archives

Still Picture Branch (NNSP)
National Archives Records Administration
Eighth and Pennsylvania Ave., NW
Room 18N
Washington, DC 20408 (202) 501-5455

The archives holds the official photographic collection for the Army, Navy, and Marine Corps dating 1955 back to the founding of the country. Patrons can order photographic reproductions and posters for a small fee. Write or call for a price sheet, a "Select List" of period topics--including The Civil War, World War II, the Old West, the American Revolution, and American Cities--and a catalog entitled *War and Conflict.*

* Museum Artistic Initiative Grants

Museum Program
National Endowment for the Arts
1100 Pennsylvania Ave., NW, Room 624
Washington, DC 20506 (202) 682-5442

The Museum Program is designed to meet the needs of the museum field by providing funding for a variety of projects. The first is Professional Development, where they award grants for formal museum training programs, internships, and apprenticeships, as well as providing fellowships to museum professionals for independent study. The second category is Utilization of Museum Resources, which is designed to help organizations make greater use of museum collections and other resources. Grants help with reinstallation, exhibitions, and collection sharing. Grants can be used to develop related programs and events that enrich these presentations, including the preparation and publication of exhibition catalogs. The Education category provides for educational programs for the community, which can include outside specialists, and the Catalog category supports the cataloging of a permanent museum collection and the publication of materials related to the collection. Special Artistic Initiatives is designed to encourage long-term programming by museums and should include a unifying, thematic framework. The Museum Program helps museums conserve collections by providing grants for planning, conservation, and training. Grants also aid in collection maintenance through solving problems in climate control, security, and storage. Museums are encouraged to purchase works by living American artists, as well as to mount or participate in special exhibitions. Grants can be made to

Be patient. If any phone number is incorrect, call (area code) 555-1212 and request the new listing.

Museums and Cultural Resources

non-profit institutions if such donations qualify as charitable deductions under Section 170(c) of the Internal Revenue Code of 1954. Some of the grants are matching grants, and the range goes up to $125,000.

* Museum Careers and Conservators Audiovisuals

Office of Museum Programs
Smithsonian Institution
900 Jefferson Dr. S.W.
Washington, DC 20560 (202) 357-3101

The Audiovisual department of the Office of Museum Programs has forty slide and video programs, covering topics such as museum careers, museum environments, and conservation and preservation. You can view the slides and videotapes at the Office of Museum Programs.

* Museum Career Training Grants

National Museum Act
Smithsonian Institution
Arts and Industries Building
900 Jefferson Dr.S.W.
Washington, DC 20560 (202) 357-2987

The National Museum Act authorizes the Smithsonian to make grants that would enhance professionalism in museums. Awards are made for training career employees in museum practices, for research on museum-related problems and for projects involving the distribution of technical information. Grants are made to museums, museum-related organizations, academic institutions, and sponsored individuals pursuing careers in conservation practices.

* Museum Collections in National Parks

Curatorial Services Division
National Park Service (NPS)
U.S. Department of the Interior
800 N. Capital St. NW
Washington, DC 20002 (202) 343-8138

National Park Service museum collections are managed by this branch of NPS. The office's *NPS Museum Handbook* provides guidelines on the acquisition, documentation, cataloging, conservation, storage, use, and disposition of museum objects. The Automated National Catalog System maintains the centralized records of museum pieces belonging to the Park System.

* Museum Conservation Science Center

Museum Support Center Library
Smithsonian Institution
4210 Silver Hill Rd.
Suitland, MD 20746 (301) 287-3666

This library provides information about conservation of materials and museum objects, conservation science, which includes archaeometry, the study of museum environments, and the analysis of materials by such means as X-ray, diffraction, and gas chromatography. This library is open to the public by appointment.

* Museum Contracts and Small Business

Office of Procurement Property Management
Smithsonian Institution
Washington, DC 20560 (202) 287-3238

This office provides information regarding contract application for services such as supplies, construction, equipment, and research. They can answer questions regarding the application process, and can direct you to offices possibly in need of your services.

* Museum of the U.S. Department of the Interior

Departmental Museum
U.S. Department of the Interior
18th and C Sts., NW, Room 1240
Washington, DC 20240 (202) 208-4743

The highlights of this museum's exhibit include Native American artifacts and dioramas depicting the history of each of DOI's Bureaus. Of particular interest to children is a collection of fossils and a display of fragments from the moon's surface. The display is oriented to children in the fourth grade and older, but younger children are welcome. The hours of operation are 8 a.m. to 4 p.m., Monday through Friday.

* Museum Programs Clearinghouse

Smithsonian Institution
Office of Museum Programs
900 Jefferson Dr. S.W. Room 2235
Washington, DC 20560 (202) 357-3101

The Office of Museum Programs provides professional development training, advisory assistance, and research services to the national and international museum community and the Smithsonian staff through sponsorship of workshops, internships, and professional visitor programs, an audiovisual production and loan program, a museum reference center, a native American training program, and publications. The Audio-visual Program distributions slide-cassette and video-tape programs on conservation, exhibitions, museum education, security, museum careers, and folklife. The Native American Museums Program provides information services and educational opportunities for employees of tribal and urban native American museums and cultural Centers. The Program offers workshops, short-term residencies, technical assistance, publications, and audio-visual materials on museums.

* National Air and Space Museum

Public Affairs Office
Smithsonian Institution
7th St. and Independence Ave. S.W.
Washington, DC 20560 (202) 357-1552

The National Air and Space Museum was established to memorialize the development of air and space flight, and to collect, display, and preserve aeronautical and space flight artifacts. The 23 galleries contain items ranging from the Wright 1903 Flyer to Apollo 11. The Langley Theater, with a giant screen presentation, shows a variety of films every half hour, as does the Albert Einstein Planetarium. Both charge a small fee. There are live, free presentations concerning the current night sky, and there are monthly sky lectures by staff and guest speakers. A summer concert series is presented on the terrace. The Museum's Education Resource Center provides air-and-space-related materials for teachers. The Office of Education produces three new publications: *Discovery*, a curriculum package for kindergarten through third grade; 5, 4, 3, 2, 1, a guide for the very young visitor; and *Skylines*, a quarterly newsletter for educators.

* National American Art Collection

National Museum of American Art
Smithsonian Institution
8th and G Sts. N.W.
Washington, DC 20560 (202) 357-3095

The National Museum of American Art's collections of American paintings, sculptures, graphics, folk art, and photographs exhibit a broad range of artistic achievement in America from the 18th century to the present. The museum holds extensive public programs which include lectures, symposia, concerts, poetry readings, and other special events. A free calendar of events is available. NMAA conducts extensive research on American Art and has implemented seven discrete research databases totalling over 530,000 records (see Office of Research Support). They also publish a scholarly journal, *Smithsonian Studies in American Art*, with articles ranging from interviews with artists to discussions of artistry in films.

* National Gallery of Art Extension Services 68.001

Education Resources
National Gallery of Art
Washington, DC 20565 (202) 737-6273

To provide educational material on the Gallery's collections and exhibitions free of charge except for transportation costs, to schools, colleges, and libraries across the nation. Free catalog available. Types of assistance: other. Estimate of annual funds available: $ 698,000.

* National Gallery Collection Catalogs

Division of Records and Loans
National Gallery of Art
Constitution and 6th St., NW
Washington, DC 20565 (202) 842-6234

The Gallery is publishing a systematic catalog of its entire collection of paintings, sculpture, decorative arts, and Steiglitz photographs. Twenty-five volumes are planned, and the first volume, *Early Netherlandish Paintings*, is available now at the Museum for $14.95.

Be patient. If any phone number is incorrect, call (area code) 555-1212 and request the new listing.

Arts and Humanities

* National Gallery's Permanent Collection Catalog Museum Shop
National Portrait Gallery
Smithsonian Institution
8th and F Sts. N.W.
Washington, DC 20560 (202) 357-1447
This book contains photographs of the entire collection of the National Portrait Gallery, including the sculptures. Cost: $24.95 ($3.95 shipping and handling).

* Native American Internship Opportunities
Fellowships and Grants
Smithsonian Institution
Washington, DC 20560 (202) 287-3271
The Smithsonian offers fellowships and internships for research and study in fields which are actively pursued by the museums and research organizations of the Institution. Both predoctoral and postdoctoral fellowships are available, as well as Minority Faculty Fellowships. The length of the term and size of the stipend vary. The Minority and Native American Internship Programs are performed under direct supervision of Smithsonian staff, as tutorial situations.

* Natural History Collection: Anthropology to Zoology
Museum of Natural History, Directors Office
Smithsonian Institution
10th and Constitution Ave., NW
Washington, DC 20560 (202) 357-2664
The Museum of Natural History is responsible for the largest natural history collections in the world. The collections are organized into eight major research and curatorial units: the departments of Anthropology, Botany, Entomology, Invertebrate Zoology, Mineral Sciences, Paleobiology, and Vertebrate Zoology and the Smithsonian Oceanographic Sorting Center. Some of the objects and specimens include minerals and gems, meteoritic geology, sea life, insects, ice age mammals, origins and traditions of Western Civilization, and the splendors of nature. The size of the collection increases by up to a million new specimens annually. The museum conducts research on a wide variety of topics, and more than 2,000 scholars visit the museum each year. A free calendar of events is available outlining programs, symposia, lectures, and films available.

* Natural History Library
Natural History Library
10th and Constitution Ave. N.W.
Washington, DC 20560 (202) 357-4696
This library houses 330,000 books and bound journals and receives 1,963 journal subscriptions. The library consists of a main location and several subject-based locations. Topics covered include biology, geology, paleontology, ecology, anthropology, botany, entomology, and mineral sciences. Call to make an appointment or for information on the location of the subject-based libraries.

* Natural History Museum Education Program
National Museum of Natural History
Office of Education
Room 212, Mail Stop 158
Washington, DC 20560 (202) 357-2747
The museum has an extensive educational school program with film and workshops available at your school or the museum, including museum lesson tours, the Discovery Room, the Naturalist Center, and instructional kits. A catalog of services can be sent to you. The Office also publishes a quarterly calendar of films and events at the Museum.

* Numismatic Collection: Coins, Medals, Paper Money
National Museum of American History
Smithsonian Institution
12th and Constitution Ave. N.W.
Washington, DC 20560 (202) 357-1798
The Numismatic Collection contains 900,000 coins, medals, and paper money from ancient times to the present day.

* Outdoor Sculpture (SOS) Project
National Institute for the Conservation
of Cultural Property, Inc (NIC)

3299 K St. NW
Suite 403
Smithsonian Institution
Washington, DC 20007 (202) 625-1495
This clearinghouse for museums and conservationists is currently undertaking several projects, including the Conservation Assessment Survey Program, which is designed to help museums organize and weed out their collections; and the Save Outdoor Sculpture (SOS) project, which catalogs, inventories, and ensures that outdoor sculptures are treated properly.

* Post-Byzantine Art to Present Library
National Gallery of Art
Reference Desk
Constitution and 6th St., NW
Washington, DC 20565 (202) 842-6511
The Gallery's library has over 150,000 volumes with a specialty in Renaissance and Baroque art. The collection covers the period from Post-Byzantine to the present, focusing on the history and criticism of art. The stacks themselves are closed; however, the library is open to the public, but you should call for the hours and to make an appointment.

* Philatelic Collection: Stamps and Postal Memorabilia
National Museum of American History
12th and Constitution Ave. N.W.
Washington, DC 20560 (202) 357-1796
This is the largest and most extensive collection of postage stamps and postal memorabilia in the world, and is the third most valuable collection in the Smithsonian. It comprises 16 million objects, including a pair of confederate stamps, Amelia Earhardt's flight jacket, and the mail wrapper the Hope Diamond was sent in when it was donated to the Smithsonian. The museum has slide programs available free of charge to civic groups, postal unions, and philatelic organizations.

* Photographs of Masterpieces
National Gallery of Art
Office of Visual Services
Constitution and 6th St., NW
Washington, DC 20565 (202) 842-6231
Black and white, 8 x 10 photographs of works from the National Gallery of Art's permanent collections are available for purchase, either by visiting the Office of Photographic Services or by mail. Color transparencies of works from the Gallery, to be used for publication, are available for rental only and must be requested in writing.

* Slide Lending Series on Art Slide Library
National Gallery of Art
Constitution and 6th St., NW
Washington, DC 20565 (202) 842-6100
The National Gallery maintains a lending slide collection of over 50,000 images, which are loaned to the public free of charge. There is no list of the slide lending collection, but selections for National Gallery objects can be made from Gallery catalogs. Up to 50 slides can be borrowed at one time and may be kept for a period of two weeks. The slide library is open to the public.

* Smithsonian Archives Guide
Smithsonian Archives
Smithsonian Institution
900 Jefferson Dr. S.W.
Washington, DC 20560 (202) 357-1420
This free *Guide to Smithsonian Archives* is a reference resource to the holdings of the Archives, giving a detailed listing of the records, papers, and projects the Archives has, as well as information regarding their use.

* Smithsonian Central Exhibits Office
Smithsonian Institution
1111 N. Capitol St.
Washington, DC 20560 (202) 357-3118
The Office provides design, editorial production, installation and other

Be patient. If any phone number is incorrect, call (area code) 555-1212 and request the new listing.

Museums and Cultural Resources

specialized exhibition services for a variety of Smithsonian programs. For instance, they recently completed a life-size model of the jaw of a prehistoric shark, and also provided texts, graphic panels, maps, and time lines for a traveling exhibit on Ancient Syria.

* Smithsonian Institution Library Services

Smithsonian Institution Libraries
10th St. and Constitution Ave. N.W.
Washington, DC 20560 (202) 357-2139

The libraries of the Smithsonian Institution include approximately 950,000 volumes, with strengths in natural history, museology, history of science, and the humanities. Inquiries on special subjects or special collections should be addressed to the appropriate branch library or to the Central Reference and Loan.

* Smithsonian Institution Press

Smithsonian Institution
1111 North Capitol St.
Washington, DC 20560 (202) 287-3738

The Smithsonian has been publishing books since its foundation and functions like a university press. It publishes 70 scholarly books each year, in addition to several hundred popular books on topics such as science, art, American history and architecture. Call for a free catalog. To place an order call (800) 927-7377.

* Smithsonian Museum Internships

Office of Museum Programs
Arts and Industries Building
Room 2235
Smithsonian Institution
Washington, DC 20560 (202) 357-3101

Three publications are available for interns: *Internships and Fellowships* describes the majority of internship and fellowship programs at the Smithsonian. The *Handbook for Smithsonian Interns* provides information about Smithsonian procedures, facilities, services and activities available to interns. *Housing Information for Interns and Fellows* is a guide to short-term housing in the Washington metropolitan area. A new publication, *Internship Opportunities at the Smithsonian*, is a comprehensive listing of all the internships available at each of the museums.

* Smithsonian Museum Merchandise

Capital Gallery Building
600 Maryland Ave. S.W
Suite 295B (202) 287-3563
Washington, DC 20560 mail order catalog (202) 287-3566

Many of the Smithsonian museums run shops which sell books, crafts, games, toys, posters, and cards. They also have a mail-order service which publishes three merchandise catalogs each year.

* Smithsonian Slides and Photographs

Photographic Services
Smithsonian Institution
14th and Constitution Ave.
Washington, DC 20560 (202) 357-1487

Slides, transparencies, and prints (black and white and color) are available of photographs in the Smithsonian's collections. You can also order their seven slide series on a variety of topics, and most include a booklet and cassette tape. For a slide series listing or ordering information, contact Photographic Services.

* Smithsonian Records and Books

Smithsonian Institution
P.O. Box 2061
Colchester, VT 05449-2061 (800) 927-7377 (PRESS)

The Smithsonian Institution produces and markets recordings of both modern and classical works, illustrating research in music history developed by Smithsonian staff and, in many cases, performed on instruments from the Institute's extensive collection. The Recordings include a wide range of music from country and western, to jazz to Bach. The Smithsonian also publishes quality illustrated books and a free catalog. For information on the Smithsonian Magazine membership programs call 1-800-533-7901.

* Traveling National Gallery Exhibits

Exhibit Lending Service
National Gallery of Art
Constitution and 6th St., NW
Washington, DC 20565 (202) 842-6083

The National Lending Service was established to make the collections of the Gallery accessible to museums throughout the U.S. This is accomplished through two programs: the Extended Loan Program which allows a museum to borrow up to five works of art for a year; and the Special Exhibition Program which provides exhibitions of up to 50 works in groups of 10, for periods of 4 to 6 weeks. Call or write for information on qualifications and costs.

* Visual Arts Fellowships

National Gallery of Art
Center for Advanced Study in the Visual Arts
Constitution and 6th St., NW
Washington, DC 20565 (202) 842-6480

The Center has a four-part program of fellowships, meetings, publications, and research in the field of visual arts. The Center offers a series of discussions, symposia, and lectures. Nine pre-doctoral fellowships are available for productive scholarly work in the history of art, architecture, and urban form, as well as senior fellowships and visiting senior fellowships for post-doctoral studies. *Center 8* is a publication which contains research reports by members of the Center, as well as a record of the activities of the Center. The Center also publishes an annual listing of research in the history of art sponsored by a number of granting institutions.

Be patient. If any phone number is incorrect, call (area code) 555-1212 and request the new listing.

Arts and Humanities

State Arts Programs

Alabama

Alabama Arts Council, 1 Dexter Ave., Montgomery, AL 36130; (205) 242-4075. Alabama administers twelve Fellowship Programs in the Arts. These Fellowships are in increments of $2,500 and $5,000.

Alaska

Alaska Arts Council, Juneau, AK 99811; (907) 279-1558. Alaska administers several grant Programs and Project grants for artists. Monetary grant monies range from $800 for Project Grants to approximately $24,000 to a non-profit organization in 1989. The Artists in Schools program employs visual artists, dancers, musicians, actors, puppeteers, poets, writers, and traditional Native artists to conduct in-depth residencies, workshops and performances in schools throughout the state.

Arizona

Arizona Arts Commission, 417 W Roosevelt St. Phoenix, AZ 85003; (602) 279-1558. Arizona administers Arts Programs to individual Artists and non-profit organizations within the state. They have the Artists in Education Program, Artists Fellowship Programs, and general grant fund monies.

Arkansas

Arkansas Arts Council, 225 East Markeham St., Little Rock, AR 72201; (501) 371-2539. Arkansas administers Fellowships to individuals ranging from $5,000 to $10,000. Grants are given to organizations ranging from $500 to $60,000. Program support grants are also given to organizations. Monies are given yearly in visual arts and literature and every third year in music and dance.

California

California Arts Council, Public Information Council, 1901 Broadway Suite A, Sacramento, CA 95818; (916) 322-9900. California administers Grants to individuals and organizations ranging from $1,000 to $100,000. Fellowships are given to individuals only in increments of $5,000.

Colorado

Colorado Council on the arts, 750 Pennsylvania, Denver, CO 80203; (303) 894-2517. Colorado administered one million dollars in grants to approximately two hundred Arts organizations and individuals in 1989. Grants are in increments from $1,000 to $5,000 and are given to Colorado residents only. Creative Fellowships are given in such areas as visual arts, poetry, and folk art. These are administered on a rotating schedule.

Connecticut

Connecticut Commission on Arts, 227 Lawrence St., Hartford, CT 06106; (203) 566-4770. Connecticut administers Grant Programs to increase the quality of Art to the public. The maximum grants given are $25,000. Recipients must meet certain criteria along with meeting residency requirements.

Delaware

Delaware Division of the Arts, 820 North French St., Wilmington, DE 19801; (302) 736-5304. Delaware administers Fellowships in the Arts including poets and writers. Project Support Grants are offered for non-profit organizations as well as Operating Support Grants. Project Grants range from $500 to $3,000.

District of Columbia

District of Columbia Council of Arts, 410 8th St., NW, 5th Floor, Stables Art Center, Washington, DC 20004; (202) 724-5613. The District of Columbia administers approximately eight programs in the Arts. Training Projects for Professional Artists along with Project Support for groups and individuals are given. These projects range from $5,000 to $40,000 for major institutions.

Florida

Florida Arts Council, Division of Cultural Affairs, Department of State, Tallahassee, FL 32399-0250; (904) 487-2980. Florida administers Artists Fellowships and Grants to non-profit organizations. Awards in amounts of $5,000 are given to professional artists. They also sponsor the Arts in Education Program.

Georgia

Georgia Council for Arts, 2982 East Exchange Pl., Suite 100, Tucker, GA 30084; (404) 493-5780. Georgia administers Grants to non-profit organizations and Grants to individuals to complete projects. The maximum award that can be requested for individuals is $5,000 and $150,000 for organizations.

Hawaii

Hawaii State Foundation On Culture and Arts, 335 Merchant St., Room 202, Honolulu, HI 96813; (808) 548-4145. Hawaii administers programs in the areas of Grants to it's residents. They have a Purchases of Services Program. Funding is divided among eight different categories in the Arts.

Idaho

Idaho Commission on Arts, 304 West State St., Boise, ID 83720; (206) 334-2119. Idaho administers Grants and Fellowships to artists and organizations within the State ranging from $3,000 to $25,000 for organizations and $3,000 for individuals. Also available are Apprenticeship Programs. Idaho has grants available for Folk Art and Arts in Rural Towns Program.

Illinois

Illinois Arts Commission, State Of Illinois Center, 100 West Randolph Suite 10-500, Chicago, IL 60601; (312) 814-6750. Illinois administers Grant Programs to non-profit organizations and Fellowships to individuals only. Special Assistance Grants are also available to non-profit organizations.

Indiana

Indiana Arts Commission, 46 South Pennsylvania, 6th Floor, Indianapolis, IN 46204; (317) 232-1288. Indiana administers Grants and Fellowships to Artists and non-profit organizations within the State.

Iowa

Iowa Council On Arts, Capitol Complex, Des Moines, IA 50319; (515) 281-4451. Iowa administers approximately sixty programs to Artists and non-profit organizations. Grants range from $70 to $25,000. A Directory of Programs and Services can be obtained from the above address.

Kansas

Kansas Arts Commission, Jayhawk Tower, 700 Jackson, Suite 1004, Topeka, KS 66603; (913) 296-3335. Kansas administers the Artists Fellowship Program. Four awards are given yearly by application based on need and talent. Professional Development Grant Workshops are also held. Grants are given to developing professionals, as well as students. These programs are for Kansas residents only.

Kentucky

Kentucky Arts Council, Berryhill, Frankfort, KY 40601; (502) 564-3757. Kentucky administers The Artists Fellowship Program with ten awards being given in the amount of $5,000 each on a yearly basis. Awards are given to working professional artists meeting residency requirements.

Louisiana

Louisiana State Division Of Arts, PO Box 44247, Baton Rouge, LA 70804; (504) 342-8180. Louisiana administers Grants to organizations and Fellowships to individuals. Grant amounts are up to $350,000 or 5% of the organization's budget, whichever is less. Fellowship amounts are $5,000.

Maine

Maine Arts Commission, State House, Station 25, Augusta, ME 04333; (207) 289-2724. Maine administers Grants and Fellowships to organizations and individuals in the amount of $2,000. An Artist in Residence Program is also awarded.

Maryland

Maryland Arts Council, 15 W Mulberry St., Baltimore, MD 21202; (301) 333-8232. Maryland administers Grants to individuals and organizations under nine different disciplines. For fiscal year 1990, individuals can be awarded amounts ranging from $2,500 to $6,000.

Be patient. If any phone number is incorrect, call (area code) 555-1212 and request the new listing.

State Arts Programs

Massachusetts

Massachusetts Cultural Council, 80 Boylston St., Boston, MA 02116; (617) 727-3668. This 24 year old agency traditionally funds individuals and non-profit groups incorporated in Massachusetts in 20 different programs. Areas of funding include fellowships, education, community art, minority artists, and contemporary arts. Guidelines for this state's programs will soon be available from the Council.

Michigan

Michigan Council for the Arts, 1200 Sixth St., Detroit, MI 48226-2461; (313) 256-3731. Grant programs are arranged in three general funding programs: Arts Organizations, Arts Projects, and Individual Artists. To request program guidelines, contact the specific Client Service Unit listed for each category. Any nonprofit organization or institution , artist, local government, school or community group in Michigan is eligible to apply for MCA grant funds. All funded activities must take place within the state and comply with equal opportunity standards.

Minnesota

Minnesota State Arts Board, 432 Summit Ave, St. Paul, MN 55102; (612) 297-4211. Minnesota administers several grants to individuals and organizations. Grants to individuals include Artist Assistance Fellowships ($6,00 for time, materials, and living expenses), Career Opportunity Grants, the Headlands Project Residency Project, and the Folk Arts Apprenticeships ($100 to $4,000 for the study of traditional artform with master fold artist).

Mississippi

Mississippi Arts Commission, 239 North Lanar St., Suite 207, Jackson, MS 39201; (601) 359-1000. Mississippi administers six Granting Programs and General Operating support grants for Arts in Cultural Organizations that fund up to 10% of the organization's income. Local arts organizations are funded up to 25% of their income. Project Support Grants range up to $5,000. Arts in Education Special Projects and Artists in Residence Program range up to $7,000. There are $5,000 Grants for Artist Fellowships that are on a three year rotating cycle for each discipline. Fifty percent of an Artist's fees are covered from the Touring Arts Roasters program.

Missouri

Missouri State Council on the Arts, Wainwright Office Complex, 111 N. 7th St., Suite 105, St. Louis, MO; (314) 444-6845. Missouri's State Council on the Arts is intended to increase the arts. It funds art programs and individuals (individuals must be a resident and must have 50% matching funds.

Montana

Montana Arts Council, 48 N. Last Chance Gulch, Helena, MT 59620; (406) 444-6430. This state agency promotes the state's diverse arts, artists, and cultural organizations. Programs which are administered include grants to organizations, fellowships for individuals, artists in schools programs, and a writers program (to help get first book published). A free newsletter for artists is available.

Nebraska

Nebraska Arts Council, 1313 Farman On The Mall, Omaha, NE 69102-1873; (402) 471-2211. Nebraska Arts Council is funded by the state of Nebraska and the National Endowment of the Arts. Funds are provided for non-profit Arts and non-Art organizations incorporated into the state. Grant categories for Arts organizations include: Year-Long Program, Projects, Artists in School-Communities, Learning through the Arts, Community challenge, Local partnership Incentive Program, Mini-grants, Dance on Tour, Professional Development Grants, and the Nebraska Touring Program. Depending upon the category, grants range from $500 to a maximum of $50,000. Non-Arts organizations include: Artists in Schools/Communities, Learning through the Arts, Mini grants, Nebraska Touring Program, and Project Grants. Most grants require a cash match.

Nevada

Nevada State Council on the Arts, 329 Flint St., Reno, NV 89501; (702) 789-0225. Nevada provides a variety of grant and fellowship programs for artists and non-profit organizations in the state and for those bringing their artistic talents to Nevada. The Artist in Residence program provides an opportunity for artists around the country to spend one month in a work/instruction arrangement within elementary and high schools, community centers, and other organizations. Direct assistance grants are available for Nevada residents up to $1,000 for organizational projects and for individual artists for their work or travel. Grants of up to $7,500 are given to organizations in Nevada for performing arts and visual arts productions brought into the state from outside the area. Artist fellowships are available for Nevada residents that provide living expenses during

the artist's career. Fellowships from $2,000 to $8,000 are offered. Slide or documentation of the artist's work must be submitted, and exhibition records must be shown as evidence of artistic activity and contributions to the community. Folk arts apprenticeships, with grants totaling $2,000, are also provided where folk artists have the opportunity to work with master craftsmen in order to learn skills to be passed down through generations.

New Hampshire

New Hampshire Division of Arts, Council of the Arts, 40 North Main St., Concord, NH 03301; (603) 271-2789. New Hampshire administers Grants in four categories: 1) Umbrella Grants, 2) Touring Program, 3) Arts in Education, and 4) Percent for Art Program. Monies vary depending upon the individual category , ranging from $50 to $15,000. The Percent for Art Program is a slide registry for commissioning for new pieces of art for new State buildings being built.

New Jersey

New Jersey State Council on the Arts, 4 n Broad St., CN 306, Trenton, NJ 08625; (609) 292-6130. The New Jersey State Council on the Arts awards matching grants to organizations incorporated in New Jersey in the following funding categories: general operating support, special project support, state/county partnership block grants, challenge and endowment grants, and Arts Basic to Education grants. Challenge grants are offered to leverage increased contributions from corporate, foundation, and other private and public sources. Arts Basic to Education Grants provide funds to those groups whose mission is to provide art education to children in grades k-12. Non-profit organizations in the state may also apply for non-matching grants in the areas of technical assistance, development. artistic focus, and fellowship support. Technical assistance grants, awarded to strengthen the effectiveness of arts management skills, have ranged from $5,000 to $15,000. Emerging and developing New Jersey arts organizations may apply for development grants, traditionally between $5,000 and $40,000. Fellowship support is available for individual artists of New Jersey traditionally in amounts from $5,000 to $15,000. Applications must be received by February of each year. Areas of artistic talent that are eligible include literature, dance, music, composition, opera/music theater composition, interdisciplinary work, visual arts, such as sculpture, painting, graphics, and experimental design arts, crafts, photography, and media arts.

New Mexico

New Mexico Cultural Affairs Arts Division, 224 East Palace Ave, Sante Fe, NM 87506; (505) 827-6490. New Mexico administers Grants to non-profit organizations in the areas of Arts in Education, Teacher training and Artists Residencies, and Public Art Programs. One percent of the cost of the project for Art in public places is granted to eligible candidates.

New York

New York State Council on the Arts, 915 Broadway, New York, NY 10010; (212) 614-2904. Non-profit arts organizations in New York may receive grants from the Council. Arts and education, dance groups, museums, theater, and folk arts are among the categories eligible. Individual artists are funded through sponsoring organizations. These individual grants are available in five areas; film production, media production, visual artist sponsored projects, theater commissions, and music commissions. The amount of funding available is dependent of the project being proposed.

North Carolina

North Carolina Cultural Resources Arts Council, 109 East Jones St., Raleigh, NC 27611; (919) 733-2821. North Carolina administers Grants and Awards to Artist and non-profit organizations, as well as operating support to eligible major institutions. Program and salary assistance, Fellowships and Project Grants, and Summer Intern Programs are available to residents of the state.

North Dakota

North Dakota Council On Arts, Black Building #606, 118 Broad Way, Fargo, ND 58102; (701) 237-8959. North Dakota administers Grants and Scholarships in various categories: Institutional Grants, Artists in Resident by duration , Training Arts, In ACCESS Program, and Fellowship Programs. Monies vary depending upon the individual program awarded. These monies range from $100 up $20,000. In the training Arts, sponsors apply for up to 40% of the Artist fee.

Ohio

Ohio Council on Arts, 727 East Main St., Columbus, OH 43205; (614) 466-2613. Individual Fellowships are granted to residents with at least one year residency prior to the January 15 deadline imposed. No student may apply. These Fellowships range from $5,000 to $10,000. Work may have been previously created. No project proposals are considered, nor are the awards based upon

Be patient. If any phone number is incorrect, call (area code) 555-1212 and request the new listing.

Arts and Humanities

need. Awards are given also for good work. There is a Peer Panel review. Ohio has Artist in Public Institutions and Artist in Public Education Awards. Funding varies. There are numerous other services available to the residents of Ohio.

Oklahoma

State Arts Council of Oklahoma, 640 Jim Thorpe Bldg., Oklahoma City, OK 73105; (405) 521-2931. Projects undertaken by non-profit art organizations within Oklahoma can receive matching grants from this Council for individual projects. There is no limit to the amount of the grants; however, they are dependent on the appropriations available. Applications must be filed 18 months prior to funding. Grants of over $2,000 and under $2,000 are offered for arts projects making a request within a shorter time frame. Those grants for under $2,000 are usually given to smaller organizations or towns sponsoring special performances or exhibits. A matching grant program whereby identified artists tour and perform on behalf of the Council is sponsored in cooperation with interested organizations. Minority grants of up to $5,000, particularly focused on the Indian population of Oklahoma, are offered to promote artistic efforts. Sixty grants of $500 each are being given to interested cities, towns, and schools who participate in Oklahoma's Homecoming '90 program. An artist in residence matching grant program is also available for elementary and high schools.

Oregon

Oregon Arts Commission, 835 Summer St., NE, Salem, OR 97301; (503) 378-3131. Oregon administers Grants and Fellowships to non-profit organizations within the state of Oregon. There is one dead line per year. Some of the categories are: Program Grants-Operating, Special Project-one of a kind, Oregon Arts Challenge-major institutions receiving a percent of the groups budget, Arts in Education Project Grants, Presenting Grants, Development of Cultural facilities, and Professional Development Grants. Monies range from $500 to $225,000, depending upon the individual program. Eight individual artists fellowships of $3,000 are awarded per year. There are two $10,000 Masters fellowship awards for film video awarded per year.

Pennsylvania

Pennsylvania Council on the Arts, Room 216, Finance Bldg., Harrisburg, PA 17120; (717) 787-6883. Fellowships are provided to qualified artists in Pennsylvania from this state Council. Non-profit organizations in the state may receive general operating and specific support grants. Funding is given to some organizations requesting assistance with summer programs, including music, presenting organizations, cross disciplinary programs, and theater. Local arts festivals may also receive financial aid. Bussing grants are provided to non-profit organizations if they are transporting groups to art activities. Consultant fees of $1,000 can be obtained by organizations requiring outside technical assistance.

Rhode Island

Rhode Island State Council On The Arts, 95 Cedar ST., Suite 103, Providence, RI 02903; (401) 277-3880. Grants are available from this organization to non-profit organizations and artists in Rhode Island. Organizational grants fall into three categories; access, arts programs, and residencies in elementary and high schools. The amount of money granted varies, depending on the operating budget of the organization applying for the funding. Individual fellowships are available for artists in 12 areas of practice. Artist project grants and folk art apprenticeships are also sponsored. An artist development fund has also been established to enhance artistic experience and to provide contingency funding.

South Carolina

South Carolina Art Commission, 1800 Gervais St., Columbia, SC 29201; (803) 734-8696. South Carolina offers Artist Development, Community Arts Development , Arts Education Grants, Fellowships, and a variety of direct programs for state residents. These categories require matching funds. At the same time Teacher Incentive Programs are offered which do not require matching funds.

South Dakota

South Dakota Arts Council, 108 W 11th St., Sioux Falls, SD 57102-0788; (605) 339-6646. Organization grants are offered by this Council whereby 10 percent of the operating expenses are funded to state and community arts councils in South Dakota. Matching project grants are available for state arts organizations and for other organizations with work related to South Dakota. The Arts Bank underwrites performances in South Dakota up to $500. Technical assistance, with a maximum amount of $500, is provided to State arts organizations. An excursion program offers up to $500 for an individual artist to participate in a learning experience through the Council's professional development program. Touring groups may receive a grant of up to 50% of tour costs that provides additional opportunities for performances. Schools may apply for the Artists in Schools residence program for grades K-12 in order to benefit from working with well-

known artists from both in and out of state. South Dakota artists may apply for fellowships of $5,000 each. Emerging artists are also offered fellowships in the amount of $1,000, and projects of artists can be funded for up to 50% of the total cost. Artists from around the country interested in the Artists in Schools residency may apply to be a participant. Awards are $700 for one week, $2,800 for one month, and $9,600 for one semester. Individual artists matching grants are also available for state residents wishing to tour additional locations. South Dakota teachers may also apply for art educator grants of up to $1,000.

Tennessee

Tennessee Art Commission, 320-6th Ave North, Suite 100, Nashville, TN 37243-0780; (615) 741-1701. Tennessee administers Grants to residents which are members of non-profit organizations and individuals ranging from $500 to $50,000 depending on the size of the organization or the program which the individual applies for. Special opportunities are available for the residents of the state of Tennessee.

Texas

Texas Commission on the Arts,Box 13406, Capitol Station, Austin, TX 78711-3406; (512) 463-5535. Texas administers Grants in three categories: Organization, Project, and Touring. There are fourteen separate programs such as Arts in Education, Rural Arts Programming, Exhibits Support, Special Events, Planning Grants, and many others. Texas supports non-profit organizational arts and does Arts related Programming.

Utah

Utah Council of Arts, 617 E S Temple, Salt Lake City, UT 84102; (801) 538-3000. The Utah Arts Council administers several grants to non-profit organizations. Grants range from $300 to $140,000 and includes general support grants, Challenger grants (to $2,500), and Community Arts Development grants (to $3,000). The Arts Council also administers community-state partnerships, performing art tours, an arts-in-education program, folk arts apprenticeships, and design arts programs.

Vermont

Vermont Council on Arts, 136 State St., Montpelier, VT 05602; (802) 828-3291. The mission of the Vermont Council on Arts is to foster a vital Artistic Community and Excellence in the Arts, and to make available the richness and diversity of the arts to all. Grants and fellowships for non-profit organizations range from $3,500 for individual artists fellowships, $40 for touring programs, to $10,000 for organizations. The Vermont Council on Arts is not part of the State Government. They are an independent non-profit organization and therefore offer memberships to its residents, produces a publication, and elects its Board of Trustees from its membership.

Virginia

Virginia Commission for the Arts, James Monroe Bldg. 17th Floor, 101 N 14th St., Richmond, VA 23219-3683; (804) 225-3132. Virginia Commission for the Arts is the State Agency which supports the arts through distributing grants annually to Artists and Arts organizations. It provides technical assistance and arts management. Through various programs monies are distributed totaling up to $5,000,000 at times. Grants are awarded to individuals in such areas as playwriting and literature.

Washington

Washington State Arts Commission, 110 9th and Columbia Bldg., MS-GH11, Olympia, WA 98504-4111; (206) 753-3860. Five fellowships of $5,000 each are given annually to Washington artists. Grants are also provided to non-profit organizations for program projects and operating support. These matching grants range from $1,000 to $79,000. The Artist in Residence is sponsored in public schools and institutions with grants totaling $1,500. Cultural enrichment programs are supported within the school systems. The Arts in Public Places Program provides that 1/2 of 1% of the money for each government financed building is to be allocated for the purchase of art.

West Virginia

Department of Culture and History, Arts and Humanities Division, Capital Complex Cultural Center, Charleston, WV 25305; (304) 348-0240. This department supports and promotes the arts of West Virginia. Grants are administered to artists, craft people, and organizations. They range from $250 to $80,00 and usually fund 50% of projects. The department has approximately $1 million a year to grant.

Wisconsin

Wisconsin Arts Board, 131 W. Wilson St., Suite 301, Madison, WI 53703; (608)

Be patient. If any phone number is incorrect, call (area code) 555-1212 and request the new listing.

266-0190. Wisconsin administers approximately fifteen programs in the Arts. Programs are awarded in apprenticeships, development, fellowships, new work awards, and Educational Opportunity Grants. An Arts in Education Residency Program is also awarded to schools and community agencies. Preference is given to Wisconsin residents, but these programs are open to all US residents.

Wyoming

Wyoming Arts Council, 2320 Capitol Ave., Cheyenne, WY 82002; (307) 777-7742. Wyoming administers such programs in Individual Artists Grants for specific projects. Arts and Education programs fund school or community non-profit organizations and provide project or technical support to non-profit organizations.

Arts and Humanities

State Money for the Arts and Artists

Listed below are the money programs available from each state for the arts and artists. Although every state has different requirements for their programs, certain guidelines hold true for every state arts program. Individuals applying for fellowships must meet state residency requirements. Fellowships are granted to professional artists, not students. Organizations must be non-profit and tax exempt and provide arts programming and/or services.

Matching grants are often required for organizations requesting funding. Matching grants require that the recipient of the grant raise funds in some proportion to the amount awarded. In some instances, in-kind goods and services may be used in place of matching grants. An in-kind contribution of goods is a contribution of any tangible, useable item that the organization would have otherwise had to purchase to obtain. An in-kind contribution of a service includes intangible contributions such as donations of volunteer time, or the use of facilities or equipment.

Individuals or organizations interested in applying for a grant should determine their basic eligibility through the information in the *Guide to the National Endowment for the Arts* which is available from the Public Information Office, National Endowment for the Arts, Nancy Hanks Center, 1100 Pennsylvania Ave., NW, Washington, DC 20506.

Potential applicants should then request application guidelines from the appropriate state program office. These guidelines contain application forms and instructions as well as more detailed information on grants. Most organizations have seen severe budget cutbacks since the 1990-91 fiscal year. As a result, the figures listed below for overall funding are often higher than what is now available.

State Arts Programs

Alabama

Alabama Arts Council, 1 Dexter Ave., Montgomery, AL 36130-5810; (205) 242-4076.

Individual Artists Programs:

1) Fellowship in Arts Administration: Awards of $5,000 are given to any administrator or artist who has been employed by an Alabama Arts organization in a full time paid position for at least two years prior to application.

2) Artists Fellowships: Grants of $5,000 or $10,000 are available for individual artists in the following disciplines: design, literature, media/photography, music, theater, visual arts, and crafts.

3) Technical Assistance: Limited funds are available up to $1,000 to help arts organizations develop specific administrative and technical skills. To be eligible for this, as well as the artists fellowship program mentioned above, an artist must be a legal resident of Alabama and have lived in the state for two years prior to application.

4) Artist Residences: In-state and out-of-state practicing artists are reviewed for school and community residencies. Residency length varies from two weeks to ten months. Alabama residency requirements are not applicable under this program.

5) Folk Art Apprenticeships: Cash awards of up to $5,000 are given to master folk artists willing to take students and teach them their craft. Students who have entered into an agreement with a master folk artist may also apply.

Organizational Funding:

Alabama also offers grant funding to non-profit organizations and public and private educational institutions. All grants, with the exception of Artist Fellowships, must be matched by at least an equal amount from other sources by the applicant.

1) Advanced Institutional Assistance: Applies to the state's larger cultural organizations. Grants are based on the organization's actual cash income for three years prior to application.

2) Arts in Education Projects: Provides support for projects and residencies in private and public elementary and secondary schools. Minimum support is $500. Grants provide up to 50% of the total project budget or 60% of the total cost of an artist residency.

3) Design Arts Projects: Provides state support for projects that increase public awareness of the role of design. Minimum support is $500 and funding is available for up to 50% of the total project budget.

4) Folklife Program: Designed to help preserve and present Alabama folklife culture. Includes the annual Alabama Folk Heritage Award to a Master folk artist and an apprenticeship program. Applications requesting at least $500 and not more than 50% of the total project budget will be eligible for consideration.

5) Local Arts Councils: Provides specialized support and structure for local arts councils. Grants range from $2,500 for technical assistance and planning funds to $7,500 for special projects.

6) Presenter Program: Grants are available to offset the costs of presenting performances and exhibitions. For basic presenter activities, applicants may request up to 25% of the engagement fee of a performance event or 25% of the combined cost of the shipping fee and insurance for an exhibition.

7) Project Assistance Programs: Offers financial assistance for a wide range of community-oriented arts projects. Minimum funding is $1,000. Up to 50% of the total cost for a project or service is eligible for funding.

Alaska

Alaska State Council on the Arts, 411 W. 4th Ave. Suite 1E, Anchorage, AK 99501-2343; (907) 279-1558. In 1991, Alaska provided $1,537,575 in grant funding. Except for artist grants, the Council awards funds only to Alaskan non-profit organizations, schools or government agencies.

Individual Artists Programs:

1) Individual Artist Fellowships: Non-matching $5,000 awards are given to experienced, professional artists to aid them in creating new works and/or in the development of their careers. In 1991, $30,000 in grants was awarded.

2) Travel Grant Program: Assists professional artists to attend in-state, national or international events. Pays two-thirds of travel up to a maximum of $600. In 1991, 24 out of 35 travel grants were awarded.

3) Master Arts and Apprentice Grants in Traditional Native Arts: Grants of up to $2,000 are awarded for study with a master craftsman, musician, dancer or storyteller. These grants pay the fee of the master artist and other essential costs of the apprenticeship. Ten out of twenty apprenticeship applications were funded in 1991.

Organizational Funding:

1) Grants to Local Arts Agencies: Encourages arts development at the local level for primarily community oriented projects. In 1991, grants were awarded ranging from $2000 to $74,000.

2) Season Support: Grants assist with a portion of an organization's ongoing artistic and administrative functions. In 1991, grants ranged from $1,000 to $183,200.

3) Project Grants: Provides matching funds twice a year to non-profit organizations, schools and government agencies for specific local arts projects and programs. In 1991, 38 projects were funded.

4) Workshop Grants: Provides an opportunity to hold short-term workshops using artists and other professional resources as instructors. Grants provide all but $50 of the instructor's fee and in-state travel costs.

Be patient. If any phone number is incorrect, call (area code) 555-1212 and request the new listing.

State Money for the Arts and Artists

Educational Funding:

1) Artist Residency Grants: Provides matching funds to Alaskan schools to support artists' residencies. Offers artists an opportunity to work with students in on-site residency situations for extended periods of up to four months in time. $117,800 was awarded in 1991 to the Arts in Education program.

Arizona

Arizona Arts Commission, 417 W. Roosevelt St. Phoenix, AZ 85003; (602) 255-5882. In 1991, the Commission awarded $3,224,116 to state arts organizations and artists.

Individual Artists Programs:

1) Fellowships: Awards between $5,000 and $7,500 are given in creative writing, performing arts and visual arts.

2) Artist Projects: Supports individual artists in all disciplines and collaborations between artists. Awards up to $5,000 are granted to provide assistance such as travel funds or research and development time.

Organizational Funding:

Funding priority has been given to projects in rural areas of the state and to projects coordinated by ethnic-run organizations or those serving ethnic communities.

1) Project Support: A flexible category designed to respond to the changing needs of the arts within the state. Artists in residence, consultant services and festivals are included in this group. A funding scale can be obtained directly from the Arts Commission.

2) Administrative/General Operating Support: Provides grants which assist with administrative expenses of arts organizations. The program is divided into three levels based upon the size of the organization's operating budget and amount of assistance needed. Grants can range between 10% of an organization's operating budget to 50% of a professional director's salary.

Educational Funding:

1) Artists in Residence: Provides the opportunity for artists, educators and students to work together on in-depth creative projects. Residences usually range from two weeks to a month. Artists participating in this program are jured onto the Commission's Artist Roster. Schools and other community organizations use the Artist Roster to select artists for residencies. Different residencies include: individual artist, performing company, folklorist, teacher resource, and interdisciplinary (two or more artists in different disciplines).

2) Education Initiatives: Schools or organizations may apply for assistance to sponsor projects that include new initiatives, new elements of an existing program, or ones that expand current work in arts education. Some initiatives may take multiple years to implement.

3) Project Support: Project support is available to sponsors to contract with artists who are not on the Artist Roster in educational settings.

Arkansas

Arkansas Arts Council, 225 East Markeham St., Little Rock, AR 72201; (501) 324-9337. Arkansas Arts Council administers grants on a yearly basis to individuals, educational institutions and non-profit organizations. Funds for all categories, with the exception of individual artists programs, must be at least equally matched by the applicant organization with cash from sources other than the Council or National Endowment for the Arts (NEA). In 1991, $1,062,521 was awarded in grants to non-profit arts organizations.

Individual Artists Programs:

1) Fellowships: The Individual Artist Fellowship Program makes unconditional awards to professional artists in recognition of their artistic accomplishments. It is a non-matching cash award. In recognition of 1993 as the Year of American Craft, a maximum of ten $5,000 fellowships in the categories of crafts and three-dimensional visual arts will be funded.

Organizational Funding:

1) General Operating Support Grants: Provide support for non-profit agencies that produce/promote the performing, visual or literary arts. Applicants may apply for up to 20% of their preceding year's actual income.

2) Program Support Grants: Assists non-profit organizations in producing, presenting and promoting public arts events or activities that meet specific needs of the organization or artists.

3) Professional and Organizational Development Grant: Aids emerging Arkansas arts organizations in obtaining professional assistance. Awards are for a one year period, although recipients may reapply the following year for new services.

Educational Funding:

1) Arts-in-Education: Funding is used to place professional artists in school and community residences. Funds may also support educational projects to help make the arts basic in grades kindergarten through twelve. Applicants must provide an equal cash match the first year with increased cash match in subsequent years.

2) Mini-Grants: Provides funding throughout the year for unanticipated or emergency situations. Generally, grants will be less than $1,000 with most falling in the range of $500 or less.

Community Programs:

1) Artists In Residence: Includes several categories of grants as well as assistance for developmental activities on the local level. This program places professional artists in elementary, middle and high schools for residencies varying in length from one week to one semester.

2) Community Arts Development Grants: Local arts councils may apply for project support for arts service activities. Regional organizations may also be eligible.

California

California Arts Council, Public Information Council, 2411 Alhambra Blvd., Sacramento, CA 95817; (916) 739-3186. In 1991-92, the Council administered $12,916,000 in funding to non-profit arts organizations and artists. Individual artist fellowships totalled $255,000.

Individual Artists Programs:

1) Artists Fellowship Program: Each year, fellowships of $5,000 each are awarded to exemplary California resident artists. These are not project grants, but are given to recognize and honor the work and careers of artists. Thus, choreographers may, but dancers may not apply; playwrights but not actors, etc. At present, artists may apply only once in a four-year cycle. Categories include: 1992-93, literature; 1993-94, visual arts; 1994-95, performing arts.

2) Artists in Residence Program: Offer long-term interaction between professional artists and the public, in workshops sponsored by schools, government units, non-profit arts organizations, and tribal councils. The Arts Council does not maintain rosters of eligible artists or sponsors. Projects are locally developed by the artist and sponsor organization and last at least three months; most are for nine to eleven months. An artist may be funded for three consecutive years, then must take a year off before reapplying. The Council funds two types of residencies. In an individual Residency, one or two artists work with a sponsor on a project. In a Multi-Residency, eligible non-profit arts organizations coordinate the work of several artists at one or more sites. The individual artist earns $1,300 a month for 80 hours of project time; multi-residency artists have varied fees and hours.

3) Traditional Folk Arts Program: Identifies, assists, encourages and honors folk artists.

A) Apprenticeships: Non-matching grants are available to individuals who share membership in the same cultural community -- family, ethnic, tribal, relations -- where the art form originates.

B) Sponsor Organizations: Matching grants are available to non-profit tax-exempt groups, such as community and cultural organizations, tribal councils or other Native American cultural organizations, libraries, etc. Generally, funds are for projects that present folk arts and artists in events such as festivals or concerts and projects that provide services and technical assistance to the field.

Organizational Funding:

1) Organizational Support Program: Awards grants form general operations or for projects that aid artistic or administrative development. Applicants must show two consecutive years of arts programming in California. A non-arts organization may apply if arts programming is integral to its activities. This program supports small to mid-size organizations as well as large budget organizations with budgets over $1,000,000.

2) Multi-Cultural Arts Development: Aids the development of ethnic arts groups and organizations. Provides two-year grants of up to $80,000 to eligible organizations. Categories include multi-cultural entry and multi-cultural advancement programs.

3) Performing Arts Touring and Presenting Program: Helps bring performances of high artistic quality to California audiences. Qualified non-profit organizations and government agencies may request fee support when hiring artists included in the Touring Artists directory. Fee support consists of partial reimbursement for fees paid to the artists.

4) California Challenge Program: Encourages opportunities for innovation in the arts, and requires the raising of new private sector contributions. Organizations must have annual incomes over $200,000 to be eligible to compete. Awards generally range from $25,000 to $75,000 and must be matched two or three times the award amount in new, private contributions.

Arts and Humanities

Colorado

Colorado Council on the Arts, 750 Pennsylvania, Denver, CO 80203; (303) 894-2617. Colorado's Arts Organizations Program awarded $821,000 in 1991-92 to approximately 150 programs. Individual Artist Programs awarded $114,000 in direct financial support.

Individual Artists Programs:

1) Creative Fellowships: Recognizes outstanding accomplishment among Colorado creative artists. Fellowships in media and performing arts, visual arts and literature are made directly to the individual artist on the basis of sample work submitted for review. In 1990-91, 16 Fellowships were awarded totalling $64,000.

2) Colorado Visions Project Grants: Provide direct financial support for projects grants for individual artists. In 1990-91, ten awards totalling $19,980 were given to those who competed with others in their own geographic region.

3) Folk Arts Master/Apprentice Program: Provides direct financial support for a master artist to train a practicing artist in a traditional folk art form. Seventeen grants totalling $28,032 were awarded in 1990-91.

Organizational Grants:

1) Entry Grants: Supports organizations that represent minorities, under served constituencies, rural communities and emerging organizations. In 1990-91, ten grants were awarded that ranged from $1,000 to $3,500.

2) Institutional Partnership Program: Funds support Colorado based major institutions. Awards are for annual operating support. Participants must have a budget of $250,000 or more for at least a three year period prior to application.

3) Project Grants: Provides support for projects designed to enhance artistic achievement, improve management or provide the public with accessible arts experiences.

4) Rural Arts Initiatives: This program serves rural areas of the state and projects coordinated by ethnic-run organizations or serving ethnic communities. In 1990-91, 18 grants were awarded. Contact CCAH staff for grants details at (303) 894-2673 or (303) 894-2670.

5) Summer Activities Programs: Eligible organizations are those that produce their programming between May 15 and September 15 of each year.

6) Organizational Assistance Program: Supplies a variety of technical and management assistance services to Colorado nonprofit cultural organizations. Services areas range from grassroots fund raising to programmatic cost accounting. This is a referral program handled by CCAH staff.

7) Community Arts Development Grants: Local arts councils may apply for project support for arts service activity or for community based activities. Local arts councils may apply for collaborative projects with individual artists or other organizations.

Educational Funding:

1) Artists in Residence Program: Places professional Colorado artists in elementary, middle and high schools for residencies varying in length from one week to one semester. Residencies are available in all disciplines from architecture to performing and visual arts to film/video and literature.

Connecticut

Connecticut Commission on Arts, 227 Lawrence St., Hartford, CT 06106; (203) 566-4770. In 1991, the Commission awarded 392 grants totalling $1,941,128. $100,000 was awarded in individual artist grants.

Individual Artists Programs:

1) Artist Grants: Provides direct support to resident artists who have lived and worked in Connecticut for a minimum of four years at the time of application. Twenty awards of $5,000 each are distributed based on a professional peer review selection process. In 1992, artist grants will be devoted to choreography, creative writing, film and video, and music composition. In 1993, grants will be devoted to the visual arts.

2) Artists Residencies: The resource directory at the back of Artsbook lists "Brokers of Arts-in-Education Services," organizations which provide artists for residencies. Through the Arts in Education program, residencies are supported with Commission funding. Schools, senior centers, correctional institutions, non-profit sites and community arts centers may apply for matching funds to hire artists.

Organizational Funding:

1) Multi-Year Funding: Designed to assist the long term development of organizations through better strategic planning, improved programs and more stable funding. Operates on a three-year funding cycle.

2) Professional Development Funding: Assists smaller arts organizations in obtaining professional assistance. Awards are for a one year period, although the program will attempt to provide assistance for a maximum of three years on an annually decreasing basis, beginning with up to 50% of the position's salary for the first year, 33% for the second and 25% for the third.

3) Arts Project Grants: Grants are available to organizations to produce exhibitions, festivals, literary publications an dance, music, theater or film productions. Grants are also available to pay consultant fees for professional assistance in areas such as promotion or budgeting. The maximum award is $10,000, the minimum award is $500.

Delaware

Delaware Division of the Arts, 820 North French St., Wilmington, DE 19801; (302) 577-3540. In 1991-92, the Division awarded $1,195,286 in funding. This included $39,000 in individual artist fellowships and $135,500 to arts education programming.

Individual Artists Programs:

1) Individual Artist Fellowships: Funds grants for professional development based on demonstrated creativity and skills in an art form. Grants are divided into two categories: A) Emerging Professionals with grants of $2,000 and B) Established Professionals with grants of $5,000. Recipients in the Emerging Artist category may apply in the Established Professional category after a three-year period.

Organizational Funding:

1) Project Support Grants: Provides funding on a matching basis for specific arts projects. Grants may fund up to 50% of the total cash expense of each project, although awards are often less. Matching funds must be in cash and may not come form the NEA.

2) General Operating Support Grants: Support overall activities of established arts institutions. Each organization is eligible to receive a single General Operating Grant in lieu of several project grants. The two categories of General Operating Support are Primary Institutions and Program Support.

3) Emergency Grants: Grants of up to $500 can be obtained in response to an emergency situation which requires financial assistance. Annual events or other recurring events do not qualify in this category.

4) Grants to Emerging Organizations: Organizations may apply for matching grants of up to 50% of their budget for arts projects and/or administrative costs such as marketing, membership development or management.

Educational Funding:

1) Arts in Education Residencies: Provides matching funds to place professional literary, visual and performing artists in educational settings for residencies of ten days to one year. A five day residency may be approved for first-time sites, and for special populations.

District of Columbia

District of Columbia Council of Arts, 410 Eight St., NW, 5th Floor, Stables Art Center, Washington, DC 20004; (202) 724-5613. The Commission awards grants to individual artists and to arts and community-based organizations through its Grants-in-Aid Program. Grants are not project related. Individuals and arts organizations may apply in one of the following disciplines: crafts, dance, interdisciplinary/performance art (individuals only), literature, media, multi-disciplinary, music, theater and the visual arts.

Individual Artists Programs:

To be eligible, an artist must be a resident of the District of Columbia for at least one year prior to application deadline and maintain residence during the grant period. Individuals are awarded grants which range from $1,000 to $5,000. There is no matching fund requirement.

Organizational Funding:

Organizations are eligible to apply for grant amounts up to $40,000. Grants in this category are usually awarded in the $5,000 to $20,000 range. These funds must be matched dollar for dollar, i.e., an organization requesting $15,000 must document $30,000 in expenses. In-kind services may not be used to satisfy the matching requirement.

Florida

Florida Arts Council, Division of Cultural Affairs, Department of State, Tallahassee, FL 32399-0250; (904) 487-2980. In 1991-92, Florida funded $2,173,800 in grants to statewide arts organizations.

Individual Artists Programs:

1) Individual Artist Fellowship Program: Fellowships of $5,000 each are awarded

Be patient. If any phone number is incorrect, call (area code) 555-1212 and request the new listing.

State Money for the Arts and Artists

to Florida professional creative artists who have demonstrated exceptional talent and ability. In 1991-92, the Division received 525 applications and awarded 34 fellowships. Fellowships may be awarded in: dance, folk art, interdisciplinary arts, literature, media arts, music, theater, and visual arts and crafts.

Organizational Funding:

Grants are funded in the following disciplines: dance, folk arts, interdisciplinary arts, literature, media arts, multi-disciplinary arts, music, sponsor/presenter, theater, and visual arts. Arts organizations must meet specific discipline requirements. Grants range from $25,000 to $40,000.

1) General Program Support: Funds the day to day operations and programs. This type of funding is broad in scope.

2) Specific Project Support: Funds a particular project, program, or series within the applicant organization's total operations. No more than one application may be submitted in any grant cycle. Non-arts organizations may also request funding of up to $20,000. Non-profit organizations are those whose primary mission, or more than half of the operating budget, is not dedicated to activity in the arts. Specific projects are also funded under this category.

3) Challenge Grant Program: Provides funding incentives to cultural institutions or groups of institutions. Challenge grants range from $10,000 to more than $100,000 and must be matched by the applicant institution(s) on at least a three-to-one basis.

4) Technical Assistance Grants: Promotes professional development for arts organizations within five funding categories including: mini-grants, staff exchange grants, consultant grants, in-service training grants and special grants. Grants are funded up to $1,000 and generally require a dollar-for-dollar match. However, as a general policy, funding is only given for up to one-third of the project cost.

Educational Funding:

1) Artist Residency: Places practicing professional artists in educational settings (school or non-school) to work with students in on-site residency situations. Residencies last from ten days to two months or longer. Grants range up to $20,000.

2) Arts Education Project Support: Designed to develop or strengthen arts curricula for pre-kindergarten through twelfth grade students. Grants range up to $20,000.

3) Special Projects: Grants fund projects addressing areas of educational significance and those with potential statewide impact. Projects may involve artist-teacher collaborations, or special populations (such as mentally or physically challenged students or the elderly) in school or non-school settings. Funding is available up to $20,000.

Georgia

Georgia Council for Arts, 530 Means St., N.W., Suite 115, Atlanta, GA 30318; (404) 651-7920. The total amount of organizational funding in 1991-92 was $2,740,809. Grants for individuals totalled $122,500. In general, grant categories include: architecture/environmental arts, dance, arts-related education, film-making, folk arts/heritage arts and crafts, arts-related historic preservation, literary arts, multi-media, museums, music, photography, public radio and television, theater and visual arts.

Individual Artists Programs:

Individual Artist Grants: Georgia offers individual artist grants only for the creative not the performing arts. Thus, choreographers may, but dancers may not apply; playwrights but not actors, etc. This grant category provides support for individual Georgia artists on the basis of artistic merit. Funded artists must complete the specific projects funded. Grants range from $500 to $5,000.

Organizational Funding:

1) Major Arts Organization Grants: This grant category provides general or project support to arts organizations which have been certified as major arts organizations, based on factors such as budget size and leadership. Maximum grant request is $150,000 and organizations must apply for funding on at least a four-to-one cash matching basis.

2) Arts Organization Grants: These grants provide general or project support to arts organizations and community arts councils/agencies. Grants are available in amounts of $5,000, $22,500 and $55,000, dependent upon the size of the non-profit organization and the length it has been in operation. Organizations which apply for amounts up to the $22,500 maximum must match the request on a one-to-one basis, and organizations which apply for amounts above $22,500 up to the $55,000 maximum must match the request on a three-to-one basis. At least 75% of the match must be cash. The match also may include in-kind income-donated materials, space or services.

3) Civic/Education Government/Other Grants: This grant category provides support for arts programming offered by civic, education, government, and other organizations, including educational institutions and units of local/state government. Grants fund project support for arts-related programming. Grant categories and matching requirements are the same as those listed above for arts organizations grants.

4) Arts Council/Agency Development Grants: This three-year program develops community arts councils/agencies state-wide which strengthen and encourage arts activities at the local level. Two options are available, depending upon the level of Council funding and local support. Option One provides for employment of a full-time local director/coordinator, assisted by a part-time secretary. Option Two provides for employment of a part-time director/coordinator. The Council provides in-service training and continuing consultation for the local director/coordinator, who administers a budget developed by the Council. Funding ranges from $5,000 to $15,000. This is a matching fund program.

5) Georgia Touring Grants: This grant category provides fee support to presenters to promote touring by groups/individuals on the Georgia Touring Roster. Presenters may request up to 25% of the fee.

6) Technical Assistance Grants: These grants provide support to improve artistic quality or managerial effectiveness through employment or consultants. Consultants may then give intensive, short-term professional advice in specific problem or growth areas. The maximum grant request is $500.

7) Georgia Folklife Program: This program brings the public into contact with Georgia's indigenous, ethnic and immigrant traditional arts through documentation and programming. During 1992-93, the Folklife Advisory Panel will assist the Council in developing a three-year plan to establish funding and programming priorities. Technical assistance is currently available to artists, arts organizations and the general public. For information, call (404) 493-5780.

Educational Funding:

1) Artist-in-Education Program: Hires artists for residencies lasting from three to 18 weeks, and as consultants for shorter periods. The program engages the services of creative artists and places them in schools or all grade levels throughout the state. Disciplines include: architecture/environmental design, dance, literature, media arts, music theater, folk arts and visual arts. The artist spends four half of the time working with students and teacher and the remaining time working on his or her own creative projects in a studio on-site, open to observers by invitation. Artists-in-residence become temporary employees of the State of Georgia. Depending upon length and relocation needs, salaries range from $500 to $600 per week.

Hawaii

Hawaii State Foundation On Culture and Arts (SFCA), 335 Merchant St., Room 202, Honolulu, HI 96813; (808) 548-4145. In 1990-91, Hawaii led the nation in per capita state support for the arts. More than $8,700,000 was appropriated. Allocations were disbursed to 88 non-profit organizations and were used to support 152 projects.

Individual Artists Programs:

In 1990, the SFCA began establishing the foundations for an artist fellowship program which recognizes Hawaii's visual and performing artists of exceptional talent. An award of $500 was granted.

Organizational Funding:

Grants are provided to organizations that provide services and carry out activities such as concerts, performances, workshops, lectures, exhibits, etc. Proposals are considered in eight program areas: Arts in Education, Community Arts, Ethnic Heritage and Folk Arts, Humanities, Literary Arts, Media Arts, Performing Arts (Dance/Theater and Music/Opera), and Visual and Environmental Arts. The folk arts program provides Apprenticeship Awards, ranging from $1,600 to $2,700, that provide funding for one-to-one instruction between a master traditional artist and experiences apprentice.

Idaho

Idaho Commission on Arts, 304 West State St., Boise, ID 83720; (208) 334-2119.

Individual Artists Programs:

1) Fellowship Awards: Fellowships of $5,000 are awarded in literature, music, theater, dance, media, visual arts, crafts and design.

2) Worksites Awards: Worksites are awarded to artists to work with a master, either in a small group, a studio, in workshops, seminars, or in a one-to-one arrangement. They are also awarded for artist residencies. Awards range up to $5,000.

3) Sudden Opportunity Awards: Grants of up to $1,000 are awarded to support an artist's work and/or career, and special, time-limited opportunities.

4) Traditional Native Arts Apprenticeship Program: Supports master/apprenticeship opportunities. The usual amount awarded is $1,500. This

Be patient. If any phone number is incorrect, call (area code) 555-1212 and request the new listing.

Arts and Humanities

includes approximately $10 per hour for 100 hours of instruction plus travel and materials expenses.

5) Writer-in-Residence: This $10,000 award provides recognition and financial support to a distinguished Idaho writer. The award is distributed over a two-year term.

Organizational Funding:

1) General Operating Support: Applicants may apply for single year funding of up to $15,000 or multi-year funding of up to $25,000.

2) Project Support: Encourages a variety of high-quality arts activities in Idaho communities. Applicants may request up to one-half of the project costs with a minimum of $1,500 and a maximum of $10,000.

3) Performing Arts Touring: Supports performances of exceptional quality in Idaho communities. The maximum grant under this category is $5,000. There is no minimum.

4) Arts in Rural Towns: This three-year grant encourages the creation and growth of local arts councils and presenters in rural communities. Funding is non-competitive once the organization has been accepted into the program.

5) Local Arts Council Salary Assistance: Strengthens local arts councils by supporting paid management positions. This is a three year grant. Personnel costs will be funded on declining percentages.

6) Arts in Rural Towns (ARTs): Encourages the creation and growth of local arts councils and presenters in Idaho's rural communities. This three year funding commitment totals $3,700.

7) FastFunds: Provide timely assistance to meet unanticipated opportunities for presenting or producing the arts. Grants are available for up to one-half of the project costs up to $1,500.

8) Cultural Facilities Grants: Encourage local support, both public and private, for feasibility studies, renovation, or construction of performance, exhibition or artist spaces. Organizations may apply for up to $10,000. Grant funds must be matched with an equal amount of cash.

9) Technical Assistance: This flexible program provides grants from $100 to $500 to artists, (including folk artists), arts educators, arts organizations, and school administrators to improve their effectiveness in the arts or arts education.

Educational Funding:

1) Artists-in-Residence: Provides opportunities for artists to work in school and community residencies. Artists and companies are selected for inclusion in Idaho's roster of arts in education and touring artists. Artists are then contacted directly by the sponsoring organization to sponsor residencies. Minimum residency length is ten days. Generally, grants range from $850 to $2,400 and pay up to 50% of the project's total costs.

2) Master Teacher Awards: Grants of up to $600 are awarded to assist Idaho teachers in the development of innovative arts education curriculum.

3) Special Projects Awards: Grants from $700 to $3,500 are awarded to encourage innovative efforts in arts education. Grants cover up to 50% of the total project costs.

Illinois

Illinois Arts Commission, State Of Illinois Center, 100 West Randolph, Suite 10-500, Chicago, IL 60601; (312) 814-6750. In 1990-91, the Commission awarded over $11,300,000 in funding to non-profits arts organizations. In addition to the programs detailed below, grants are funded for choral music and opera, dance, ethnic and folk arts, symphonies and ensemble, theater and visual arts programs.

Individual Artists Programs:

1) Fellowships: Non-matching fellowships in fixed amounts of $5,000 and $10,000 and Finalist Awards of $500 are awarded to exceptional Illinois artists. Fellowships are awarded in: choreography, crafts, ethnic and folk arts, interdisciplinary/performance arts, media arts, music composition, photography, playwriting/screenwriting, poetry, prose and the visual arts.

2) Apprenticeship Program: Provides grants which recognize and foster the master/artist apprenticeship relationship.

3) Literacy Awards: Awards of $1,000 are given each year for the publication of quality new writing by Illinois writers in non-profit magazines.

Organizational Funding:

1) Access Program: Supports projects designed to explore new strategies that enrich the artistic pluralism of the state and involve the culture of under-represented populations.

2) Literature Programs: Support organizations which promote the creation, publication and distribution of creative writing.

3) Media Program: Funds organizations engaged in the production of film, video and audio art, as well as exhibition and service organizations that promote the creation, distribution and public awareness of the media arts.

4) Multi-Disciplinary Programs: Support and assist projects and institutions whose activities combine or involve two or more arts disciplines.

5) Presenters Development Programs: Offers programming/ operation support to presenters of quality performing arts activities.

6) Artstour: Provides fee support to presenting organizations for Illinois performing groups/artists.

7) Special Assistance Grants: These grants are available throughout the year to address specific artistic, programming, administrative or technical needs.

Educational Funding:

1) Artists-in-Residence: Supports artist residences in school and community-based organizations.

2) ArtsResource: Assists schools with their efforts to develop curriculum for comprehensive arts programs.

Indiana

Indiana Arts Commission, 402 W. Washington St., Room 072, Indianapolis, IN 46204-2741; (317) 232-1268. The Indiana Arts Commission (IAC) awards grants in 16 categories: dance, design arts, education, expansion arts, folk arts, literature, local arts agencies, media arts, multi-arts, museums, music, presenters, statewide arts service organizations, theater and visual arts. In 1990-91, the Commission awarded $2,485,941 in grants awards and services and $118,000 in Individual Artist Fellowships to 25 Indiana artists.

Individual Artists Programs:

1) Individual Artist Fellowships: Non-matching cash grants are awarded to help develop the careers of visual, performing, media, literary and folk artists. Artists use the grants for specific projects or to purchase supplies or develop new techniques.

Organizational Funding:

1) General Operating Support: Assists arts organizations that create, produce, present or service the arts. The program helps established institutions support their overall activities, and grants are awarded to organizations for a complete organization plan rather than a specific project. The grant is awarded to organizations that have received at least two previous IAC Arts Projects and Series grants in at least two of the last three fiscal years.

2) State and Local Partnership: Provides grants that assist local arts or community agencies throughout Indiana. The grant is awarded to organizations that have received at least two previous IAC Arts Projects and Series grants in at least two of the last three fiscal years.

3) Arts Projects and Series: Funds arts organizations and other non-profit organizations that conduct high-quality arts activities. Funding is provided for a single activity or a series of activities. Individual artists seeking funding must have the sponsorship of a non-profit applicant organization that is responsible for the project and will administer the funds. Up to 50% of a project's cost may be funded.

Educational Funding:

1) Arts in Education Grants: Place professional artists in educational settings throughout Indiana. During the program, artists spend one-half of their time as practicing artists in educational settings and the other half in independent, creative work. Residencies range from one to eight months and artists are paid on a per diem basis. Individual artist stipends increased 42% in 1990-91.

2) Visiting Arts Program: Brings artists into Indiana sites with ongoing educational programming for short-term residencies, student or teacher workshops, or educational performances. The IAC offers grants of up to $2,000 for educational programs.

3) Arts: Rural and Multi-cultural (ARM) Program: Encourages the development of ongoing commitment to the arts in Indiana's rural and multi-cultural communities. Grants are available to target communities for touring, technical assistance and arts projects. The IAC covers 75% of an activity's fees; applicants provide the remaining portion.

4) Technical Assistance: Grants in this category fund consultant services for organizations on technical matters, administrative functions, and problem-solving techniques. Arts professionals can get financial assistance through these grants to attend conferences and workshops.

5) Presenter Touring Program: Encourages the presentation of high-quality art throughout the state. Grants of up to $4,000 are given to presenters to assist with the fees for sponsoring and presenting the groups and exhibitions listed in the IAC's adjudicated Artist Directory.

Iowa

Iowa Council On Arts, Capitol Complex, Des Moines, IA 50319; (515) 281-4451. In 1991-92, 581 non-profit institutions received $911,868 in funding. Individual

Be patient. If any phone number is incorrect, call (area code) 555-1212 and request the new listing.

State Money for the Arts and Artists

fellowships were awarded to 46 artists totalling $34,221. Iowa administers approximately sixty programs to Artists and non-profit organizations. Grants range from $70 to $25,000. A Directory of Programs and Services can be obtained from the above address.

Individual Artists Programs:

Artist Mini Grants provide direct financial assistance to Iowa artists to support opportunities in the grants listed below. Project Mini Grants, professional development Mini Grants and arts education Mini Grants are limited to $500. Training grants are limited to $200.

1) Artist Project Grants: Grants support projects that are designed and managed by artists. The type of projects funded in this category are intentionally broad so artists may develop projects which meet their individual needs. Projects may include research and development or the completion or presentation of a work in progress.

2) Artist Professional Development Grants: Grants support individual artists seeking professional development opportunities. Examples may include career planning, financial management, legal aspects, marketing, professional presentations and technical assistance.

3) Artist Training Grants: Support individual artists to attend training opportunities such as seminars, workshops, and conferences. Out-of-state travel is an allowable expense.

4) Artist Arts Education Grants: These awards support opportunities for artists to develop, enhance, or expand their knowledge and materials of their art form for use in educational settings. Projects may include research, development and/or implementation of arts education projects.

5) Community Folk Arts Residency Program: Allows apprentice and master artists the opportunity to showcase their skills in their local community or region of Iowa. Residencies should take place at a public location such as a local arts council, school, local museum, library or city/county historical society. Residency costs should be kept between $500 and $1,000.

6) Iowa Scholarship for the Arts: This annual award encourages the development of high school seniors and college students who excel in the arts and who have enrolled in educational programs leading to careers in the arts. Up to five scholarships of $1,000 each may be awarded. Awards are for undergraduate study only and must be used for tuition at the institution where recipients are enrolled.

7) Iowa Literary Awards Prospectus: This competition recognizes outstanding Iowa poets and fiction writers. There are two awards in each category. First Prize is a $1,000 cash award and Second Prize is a $500 cash award.

8) Special Constituencies Program: This program supports arts residencies for the traditionally unserved and underserved audiences, e.g., the elderly, institutionalized, disadvantaged and at-risk populations, including youth, and projects for people with physical and/or mental disabilities. Residencies vary in length from one day to one year and in frequency (daily, monthly, etc.). A two hour minimum project is required. Artist fees are $650 per week, $150 per day, and $30 per hour.

Organizational Funding:

1) Arts to Go Presenter Program: Provides Iowa non-profit organizations financial assistance in presenting high quality music, theater, and dance performance or literary readings in their communities. The presenter should contact one or more artists/companies on the Arts to Go Roster and confirm contractual arrangements. Presenters may request up to 50%, or $3,000, whichever is less, for each artist/company booked.

2) Training Grants: Up to $200 in non-matching funds is available to organizations wanting to strengthen the administrative skills of staff or volunteers.

3) Technical Assistance: Matching grants of up to $500 are available to assist organizations in strengthening the effectiveness of their structure, programs, or services.

4) Operational Support Grants: A limited number of grants are awarded for general operating support to large-budgeted and mid-sized organizations that provide cultural and managerial excellence on a continuing basis. Large-budgeted organizations are funded on a two year cycle. Mid-sized organizations may receive up to $10,000 annually and must demonstrate the ability to cash match the award.

5) Project Support: Grants provide financial incentives for non-profit organizations to develop and maintain art projects that make the arts accessible to Iowans at the grassroots level. The funding average in this matching grant category is $1,600.

6) Emergency Project Support: Provide up to $500 in emergency support for projects unforeseen at the time of deadline for Project Support Grants.

Educational Funding:

1) Area Education Agencies Grants: The Council provides matching grants of up to $1,000 per project to agencies to fund arts education opportunities within their area. Projects must provide professional staff development or in-service training in one or more of the major arts disciplines.

2) Artists in Schools/Communities Residencies: Encourages work in collaborations with schools and local organizations in developing educational experiences in the arts. Projects must be at least five days in length and no more than four-and-a-half hours per day. Artists are available in the following disciplines: literature, theater, music, folk arts, dance, visual arts, opera/music theater, design arts, crafts, photography/holography/media art or interdisciplinary. The applicant organization must contact an artist for the project from the residency roster available prior to submitting an application. The standard artist's fee, $750 for a one week project, must be matched in cash by the applicant organization.

3) Arts Education Mini Grants: Matching grants are available to organizations to develop and implement arts education programs or projects. Funding may be used for conferences, in-service training or innovative projects. Grants must be matched dollar-for-dollar in cash.

Kansas

Kansas Arts Commission, Jayhawk Tower, 700 Jackson, Suite 1004, Topeka, KS 66603-3714; (913) 296-3335. The Commission provides direct or indirect funding to artists, schools, government units, and cultural, social and educational organizations and institutions across Kansas. In 1992, approximately $1,200,000 was awarded in funding.

Individual Artists Programs:

1) Fellowships in the Performing Arts: The Commission awards up to four fellowships to outstanding Kansas artists. Fellowships are $5,000 each. A rotating cycle has been established to offer fellowships in a different field each year. In 1993, fellowships will be awarded in the visual arts and in 1994, in literature.

2) Professional Development Grant Program: Grants of up to $500 each are awarded to individual creative artists from a $5,000 funding pool. Awards encourage the development of Kansas-resident artists who are creating original work in any discipline. Grants are designed to help cover up to 50% of project expenses. These expenses must clearly demonstrate the next step of the artist's development.

3) Folk Arts Apprenticeship Program: Preserves traditional, folk and ethnic crafts, trades, music, and dance by bringing together qualified apprentices with recognized master artists living in Kansas. Each approved apprenticeship is eligible for grant support to help cover expenses.

Organizational Funding:

Major grants are awarded each May for the following fiscal year. Grants of matching funds are offered in the following categories:

1) Local Arts Agency Support: Provides up to 50% of basic operating expenses to a publicly accountable community organization or city or county government agency that provides cultural planning and development.

2) Basic Program Support: Provides 50% of the operating costs for arts agencies, and for arts programs at non-arts agencies with a structure similar to a separate non-profit agency, with a governing board or advisory group and a separate budget.

3) Project Support: Grants provide up to 50% of the expenses for one-time or stand-alone arts events. These may include workshops, exhibitions, publications, performances, and lectures or demonstrations.

4) Statewide Arts Service Organizations: Provides up to 50% of basic operating and programming expenses for organizations that provide professional development, networking, and educational services to a specific arts constituency that is intrastate or statewide.

Educational Funding:

1) Planning Education in the Arts in Kansas (PEAK): Offers grants of up to $2,000 to schools or school districts that express a commitment to improve education opportunities for children.

2) Artist in Residency and Visiting Artist Grants: Provide schools, organizations and institutions with matching funds and a roster of professional artists in most disciplines for symbiotic residencies of varying lengths. Residencies vary in length from one day to a full academic year. The Visiting Artist component offers residencies of one to five days.

Kentucky

Kentucky Arts Council, 31 Fountain Place, Frankfort, KY 40601; (502) 564-3757. Matching grants from the Council are available to Kentucky non-profit organizations committed to providing arts programs and services to the public. Grant amounts vary from year to year and depend upon the availability of funds. Non-matching fellowships are available to Kentucky artists. In 1990-91, non-profit organizations received $3,040,788 in funding. Individual artists received $87,026

Be patient. If any phone number is incorrect, call (area code) 555-1212 and request the new listing.

Arts and Humanities

in fellowships. Kentucky administers The Artists Fellowship Program with ten awards being given in the amount of $5,000 each on a yearly basis. Awards are given to working professional artists meeting residency requirements.

Organizational Funding:
1) Project and Touring Grants: Provide opportunities to enhance or complement an arts organization's artistic development.
2) Consultant Grants: Provide technical assistance for artistic and management improvements.
3) Challenge Grants: Acts as incentives for broad-based, ongoing private support of arts organizations.
4) Arts Development Grants: Grants are designed for long-term organizational and artistic improvements and salary assistance supplements for top-level professional artistic and management positions.

Grants are also available for community arts development. They include:
1) Project and Touring Grants: Funding is provided for community and folk art projects that strengthen and stimulate local and neighborhood arts activity or share local arts with other Kentucky communities.
2) Special Initiatives: Funding is provided for specific issues such as rural arts development.
3) Consultant Grants: Funding encourages ongoing arts programming to communities where little exists.
4) Community Artist Residencies: Residencies support outstanding artists.

Educational Funding:
In 1990-91, this program provided $388,194 in artist residencies and $87,026 in general arts in education funding.
1) Artists in Residence Grants: Place outstanding professional artists in educational and community settings.
2) Teacher Incentive Project Grants: Funds projects, designed by teachers in collaboration with professional artists, which use artists residencies to integrate the arts into the regular classroom or to strengthen and enrich teaching in the arts.
3) Project and Touring Grants: fund projects which demonstrate the value of arts in education.

Interim Grants are available in all program areas to provide one-time funding for emergencies or for unexpected and outstanding opportunities in the arts.

Louisiana

Louisiana State Division Of Arts, PO Box 44247, Baton Rouge, LA 70804; (504) 342-8180. In 1990-91, Louisiana administered $772,197 in grants to non-profit organizations. Individual fellowships totalled $50,000, with $21,500 awarded in apprenticeships. Louisiana administers Grants to organizations and Fellowships to individuals. Grant amounts are up to $350,000 or 5% of the organization's budget, whichever is less. Fellowship amounts are $5,000 to each discipline, three in visual arts, two in literature.

Individual Artists Programs:
1) Artist Fellowships: Non-matching Artist Fellowships of $5,000 are awarded to artists of exceptional talent from the following disciplines: crafts, dance, design arts, folklife, literature, media, music, theater, and visual arts.
2) Folklife Apprenticeships: Non-matching apprenticeship grants of up to $5,000 are available to master folk artists and apprentices who will work together during an apprenticeship period.

Organizational Funding:
1) Project Assistance Program: This program provides project support for specific activities or services, growth and administrative development, increased arts services for the community, opportunities for involvement of individual professional artists, and contributions to the cultural enrichment of the general public. Grants are available in the following disciplines: dance, design arts, folklife, literature, media, multi-discipline, music, theater and visual arts and crafts. Grants do not exceed $15,000 and must be matched at least dollar for dollar in either cash or in a combination of cash and in-kind contributions. At least 50% of the amount requested must be matched with cash.
2) Technical Assistance: This pilot project promotes professional development in emerging arts organizations. Grants are available to assist organizations to obtain artistic or management consultation or training. Grants are offered up to $1,000 and must be matched on a one to one basis in cash.
3) Local Arts Agency Program: This program is divided into two categories:
A) Local Arts Agency Level One: Designed for established arts agencies that provide diverse programs and services in their communities or region. Organizations must have had annual operating revenues of $100,000 or more for the preceding fiscal year and have at least one full-time, paid professional staff

member. Grants do not exceed $350,000 or 50% of the projected year's cash budget excluding Division of the Arts Grants.
B) Local Arts Agency Level Two: Supports local arts agencies in early stages of development. Grants may be used for planning, operations, special projects, or organizational and professional staff development. Grants do not exceed $10,000 or 505 of the projected year's budget. Grants must be matched dollar-for-dollar in either cash or a combination of cash and in-kind services. At least 50% of the amount requested must be matched with cash.
4) General Operating Support: This program provides support for organizations whose programming has major impact on their communities and on the state's cultural environment. There are two funding levels:
A) Level One: Provides support for organizations whose annual budget is $500,000 or more. Grants do not exceed $350,000, or 50% of the projected year's cash budget excluding Division of the Arts grants.
B) Level Two: Provides support for organizations whose budget is at least $100,000, but less than $500,000. Funding does not exceed $75,000, or 50% of the projected year's cash budget excluding Division of the Arts Grants.

Educational Funding:
Louisiana's Arts in Education Programming provides support for Arts Basic, Residencies, and Projects. Grants may be requested for up to 50% of the total cost of a project or artist residency. Grants must be matched at least dollar for dollar in cash or a combination of cash and in-kind contributions. At least 50% of the amount requested must be matched with cash.
1) Arts Basic: Supports planning or programming grants which assist in making the arts basic to the kindergarten through twelfth grade curriculum in Louisiana schools.
2) Arts in Education Residencies: Places professional artists or folklorists in public and private, elementary and secondary schools to work and demonstrate their art forms. Visiting Artists (1-10 days per site or school), Short-Term Residencies (11-40 days per semester), and Long-Term Residencies (41 or more days per semester) are funded.
3) Arts in Education Projects: Support specific arts related activities which relate to the artistic educational development of elementary and secondary school students.

Maine

Maine Arts Commission, State House Station 25, Augusta, ME 04333; (207) 289-2724. In 1991-92, $654,644 was awarded to Maine non-profit organizations. Individual artists were awarded $18,000 in fellowships.

Individual Artists Programs:
1) Individual Artists Fellowship: Provides a limited number of fellowships to Maine artists in recognition of artistic excellence. Up to six awards of $3,000 may be awarded annually.
2) Traditional Arts Apprenticeships: Up to seven awards of $1,200 each will be given to master artists to teach their respective apprentices.
3) Regional Arts Program: Designed to generate interest and participation in the arts at the community level. The Commission selects seven non-profit arts organizations from seven regions of the state as regranting sites. Grants do not exceed $650. All grants must be matched on a one-to-one cash basis.

Organizational Funding:
Maine offers an Institutional Support Program which provides two year funding for established professional, non-profit cultural organizations, schools, and other organizations for specific local arts projects and programs. Categories include:
1) Operating Support: This multi-year grant supports the ongoing work of the state's leading cultural institutions. The grant amount requested is determined by a formula that takes a base dollar amount plus a percentage of the applicant's operating budget. For 1992-93 this amount will be $3,000 plus 1% of the applicant's total revenues.
2) Project Support: This highly competitive grant funds innovative projects in the arts and creative projects within the ongoing work of the organization. Grants do not exceed $20,000 for the two-year grant period, or go over 30% of an organization's annual operating budget.

Educational Organizations:
1) Special Projects in Arts Education: This pilot program encourages non-cultural institutions and schools to collaborate with one another. Applicants may request up to $2,500. A 50/50 cash match is required. Both collaborators must show a cash commitment to the project.
2) Professional Development for Teachers: Provides opportunities for teachers to increase their knowledge about or through the arts. Funding is available for conferences, seminars, workshops and long term summer institutes. Applicants may request up to $2,000. A 50/50 cash match is required. Requests in the $500 - $1,000 range are encouraged.

Be patient. If any phone number is incorrect, call (area code) 555-1212 and request the new listing.

State Money for the Arts and Artists

Maryland

Maryland Arts Council, 15 W Mulberry St., Baltimore, MD 21201; (301) 333-8232. In 1991-92, Maryland provided over $2,000,000 in grants to county arts organizations and artists.

Individual Artists Programs:

The Council provides direct grants to individual artists, offers professional advice, and initiates projects that provide services and opportunities for Maryland artists.

1) Individual Artist Awards: Awards range from $1,000 to $6,000 and are based solely on the basis of creative excellence. Fellowships are intended for use toward professional career development. Awards are granted annually in all disciplines. For further information, on Individual Artists Awards, write or call MSAC offices (P.O. Box 1515, Baltimore, MD 21203-1515 (410) 333-8232) and request a copy of the current guidelines for grants to individual artists.

Organizational Funding:

The Community Arts Development program supports county arts council organizations in each of the 23 counties of Maryland Baltimore City. Funds are used in each county to regrant to local arts organizations, support various arts programs, assist local arts groups with fundraising, publicity, promotion and planning, and to support the operating expenses of the county arts council.

1) Grants to Major Institutions: Offer general operating support to established non-profit, tax exempt Maryland cultural institutions which offer high quality arts programming and services. Organizations must have had an independent board of directors and professional staff and an operating budget of at least $1,000,000 for the two most recently completed fiscal years.

2) General Operating Grants: Designed for arts organizations whose programming is recognized to have substantial impact on their communities. Grants are awarded in: children's events, dance, folk arts/heritage, literature, media, multi-discipline, music, theater and visual arts. Eligible organizations are those that produce or present the arts through public programs or services. All grants must be matched at least three-to-one. Up to 10% of an arts organization's operating cash expenses may be funded.

3) Special Project Grants: Open to arts organizations that request funding for an arts activity that represents a clear and innovative change from its current and recent activities. The minimum grant request is $1,000 and funding cannot exceed more than 50% of the project's total cost. All Special Project Grants must be matched at least dollar for dollar with funds from non-Maryland state sources.

4) Grants to Non-Arts Organizations: The Council offers Program and Project grant assistance to non-arts organizations that provide arts programming to the general public in community settings such as colleges, libraries, churches, and community services. For additional information about grants to non-arts organizations, call (410) 333-8232.

5) Maryland Folklife Program: Provides research and technical support to individuals and organizations engaged in the study and interpretation of Maryland's folk culture. Activities include public talks, film screenings to community groups and advice in the design of exhibitions, festivals, concerts and other main events.

Educational Funding:

1) Artists-in-Education Program: Provides funds, augmented by a grant from the National Endowment for the Arts, for residencies and visits in schools and other educational settings by poets, artists, and performers. Schools and other sponsoring organizations provide partial funding for projects that vary from one-day visits to three month residencies. Disciplines include: poetry, visual arts, and performing arts.

2) Arts Advancement Program: Provides technical assistance and management support services to producing and presenting arts organizations throughout the state. The program includes workshops, organizational analysis, management audits, and long-term planning and development constituencies.

Massachusetts

Massachusetts Cultural Council, 80 Boylston St., 10th Floor, Boston, MA 02116; (617) 727-3668. The Massachusetts Cultural Council (MCC) offers grants and services to 2,500 schools, 335 local arts lottery councils in 348 communities, 1,500 non-profit cultural organizations and individual practitioners. The Commission's 1991-92 budget is $3,500,000. Individual artists were awarded $60,000 in individual fellowships. The Commission has requested $6,100,000 in funding for 1993.

Individual Artists Programs:

1) Individual Project Support: Provides an opportunity for individual artists, humanists, and interpretive scientists to apply directly to the council for support of creative and innovative projects. Categories for fiscal year 1993 include crafts and new approaches to science literacy. Awards range from $2,000 to $5,000.

Projects must culminate in a formal public presentation in cooperation with a cultural organization, community center, government agency or corporation.

Organizational Funding

1) General Project Support: Designed to support cultural programs and services of excellence for the general public. A project can be a single event or a series of activities. The Council encourages collaborations. Organizations must have completed one year of cultural programming prior to application deadline and have a minimum operating budget of $2,500. Applicants can request up to 50% of the total project cost. Grants range from $2,000 to $15,000 and must be matched on a one-to-one basis with cash and in-kind goods and services.

Educational Funding:

1) Education Project Support: Provides direct services to children, particularly inner-city youth, those in rural areas, and those in low-income communities, as well as those with differing abilities and bilingual students. Organizations must have completed one year of cultural programming prior to application deadline and have a minimum operating budget of $2,500. The Council will fund up to 50% of the total project cost. Grants range from $2,000 to $15,000 and must be matched on a one-to-one basis with cash and in-kind goods and services.

2) Residency Program: Provides the opportunity for students and teachers to work with an artist from five to forty or more days. The artist must spend a minimum of two days per week in the school throughout the length of the residency. The Council will pay from 40% to 70% of an artist's fee of $150 per day depending on the length of the residency.

Michigan

Michigan Council for the Arts, 1200 Sixth St., Detroit, MI 48226-2461; (313) 256-3731. The Council for the Arts is in the process of being restructured. By Fall, 1992 the Council will have reshaped its programs for 1993 and thoroughly developed a new agenda of arts support for 1994. In 1992-93, $4,200,000 has been marked for state funding of arts programming. Grant programs are arranged in three general funding programs: Arts Organizations, Arts Projects, and Individual Artists. To request program guidelines, contact the specific Client Service Unit listed for each category. Any nonprofit organization or institution, artist, local government, school or community group in Michigan is eligible to apply for MCA grant funds. All funded activities must take place within the state and comply with equal opportunity standards.

Minnesota

Minnesota State Arts Board, 432 Summit Ave, St. Paul, MN 55102; (612) 297-2603. In 1990-91, the Board administered $4,869,495 in funding to non-profit organizations. Thirty-five individual fellowships were awarded totalling $210,000.

Individual Artists Programs:

1) Fellowships: These year-long fellowships recognize outstanding professional artists working in visual, literary and performing arts. All fellowships are $6,000.

2) Career Opportunity Grants: These awards help artists take advantage of impending, concrete opportunities that will significantly advance their work or careers. Projects must be unique short-term opportunities. Grants are available in variable amounts from $100 to $1,000. A total of $5,500 is available during each review cycle.

3) Headlands Residency Project: This residency program for Minnesota creative artists is at Headlands Center for the Arts in Sausalito, CA, near San Francisco. Artists receive a travel allowance, living stipend, housing, and studio space for three to five months to live and work with other artists.

4) Folk Arts Apprenticeship Grants: These non-matching grants are given for the serious study of traditional arts between a master artist and apprentice. Grant awards range from $100 to $4,000.

5) Folk Arts Sponsorship Grants: Provide annual matching grants for research and presentation of Minnesota folk arts events. Grants range from $100 to $4,000.

6) Minnesota Touring Arts: This three-year program promotes increased touring by state professional performing arts within the state and 60 miles or more from their home base. Selected groups will receive up to 30% of artistic fees for touring performances. Maximum grant for each performance is $3,000. Selected groups may also receive up to $1,000 for technical assistance.

7) Operating Support Program: Provides unrestricted operating support to arts organizations that produce or exhibit works of art or offer a broad range of services to artists. Grant amounts are up to 10% of cash income budget. Minimum grants range between $5,000 and $10,000.

8) Series Presenters Programs: Funds nonprofit, tax exempt groups which present five or more professional artists or artistic companies in a community during an annual season. Grants are awarded up to 20% of cash expenses. The minimum grant is $5,000.

Be patient. If any phone number is incorrect, call (area code) 555-1212 and request the new listing.

Arts and Humanities

Educational Support:
1) Organizational Support Grants: Encourages and expands the delivery of cost efficient quality arts programs to Minnesota schools. Grants are awarded to Minnesota arts organizations that offer school residencies of at least five days in length. Matching grants are available in variable amounts and do not exceed one-half of residency expenses.
2) School Support Grants: Awards matching grants to elementary and secondary schools to sponsor individual arts residencies which range from five days to one year in length. Schools may request up to one-half of residency expenses.

Mississippi

Mississippi Arts Commission, 239 North Lamar St., Suite 207, Jackson, MS 39201; (601) 359-6030.

Individual Artists Programs:
1) Artist Fellowships: Non-matching fellowships of up to $5,000 are awarded to individual artists in the disciplines designated each year. Awards are based on the quality of past work. For 1993, categories are creative writing, music composition and the folk arts. For 1994, categories include the visual arts, choreography and film, video and media.

Organizational Funding:
1) General Operating Support: Provides funds for ongoing activities for arts and cultural organizations (not local arts agencies) or major arts division of non-profit organizations. Grant awards average between $10,000 and $30,000. Organizations are encouraged to apply for 10% of actual cash revenues received the previous fiscal year.
2) Local Arts Agencies: Applicants are encouraged to apply for 25% their income. Grants average between $5,000 and $25,000.
3) Organizational Development: Provides support for ongoing activities of new arts and cultural organizations , incorporated for seven years or less. Organizations with a full-time professional director working at least 35 hours per week may apply for up to $9,000. Organizations with part-time or volunteer staff may apply up to $5,000.
4) Project Support: Fund a wide variety of arts projects and/or arts components of larger projects. Organizations may apply for funding for more than one project; however, the total for all projects may not exceed $5,000 in any fiscal year.
5) Mississippi Touring Arts: Fifty percent of an Artist's fees, up to $2,000, are covered from the Touring Arts Rosters program.

Educational Organizations:
1) Arts in Education: Advances basic arts education for all students, not only the gifted and talented, in kindergarten through twelfth grade. Up to $7,000 in matching funds are awarded.

Missouri

Missouri State Council on the Arts, Wainwright Office Complex, 111 N. 7th St., Suite 105, St. Louis, MO 63101-2188; (314) 340-6845. In 1991-92, Missouri granted $4,129,895 to non-profit, tax exempt state-based arts organizations. The Council is unable to fund fellowships to individuals.

Organizational Funding:
The Council offers financial assistance through seven art areas: dance, literature, media, multi-discipline, music, theater, and visual arts. A program administrator supervises applications in each area.
1) Community Arts Program (CAP): Helps non-metropolitan community arts councils and other local arts coordinating agencies sponsor projects in more than one art form. It also helps arts agencies upgrade their management abilities. Financial assistance is available for up to 50% of project support, arts agency administration salary support and office support. See Council guidelines for geographic restrictions.
2) Community Arts Special Projects: Organizations may apply for up to $2,000 for new projects not covered in its Community Arts Program application. Priority is given to new CAP applicants.
3) Statewide Arts Service Organizations: Provides financial assistance to organizations in the delivery of service to their statewide (or multi-state) arts constituency. Eligible organizations must be governed by a board of directors that has representation throughout the state and/or from a multi-state area.
3) Technical Assistance: Designed to help arts organizations develop specific administrative and technical skills. Eligible activities include: contracting with a consultant to assist the organization in a particular area, or defraying the cost of attending a workshop or conference that will help the organization develop needed skills and expertise. Funding of up to $2,000 may be requested. Applicants must provide at least 25% of the project's cost.

Educational Funding:
1) Artist Residency Program: Offers Missouri students and adults the opportunity to participate in artist residencies which promote and enrich existing arts curricula. Offers artists an opportunity to work with students in on-site residency situations for extended periods of time. Artists are paid on a per diem basis. For information, call (314) 727-4422.
2) Traditional Arts Apprenticeship Program: Provides opportunities for qualified apprentices to learn style, technique, and repertoire from recognized folk art masters. This program is administered by the University of Missouri Cultural Heritage Center in Columbia. Funding is provided by the Council and the NEA. For information, call (314) 882-6296.

Montana

Montana Arts Council, 48 N. Last Chance Gulch, Helena, MT 59620; (406) 444-6430. This state agency promotes the state's arts, artists, and cultural organizations. In the 1992-93 biennium, $1,300,000 was awarded for 101 projects in 32 communities. Grants ranged from $1,000 to $73,400. The average grant was approximately $13,000. It is estimated that $670,000 may be available for each year of the 1994-95 grant period.

Individual Artists Programs:
1) Individual Artist Fellowships: Awards of $2,000 are presented annually to artists of merit. Decisions are based on the quality of an artist's work and are awarded in a variety of disciplines.

Organizational Funding:
Each dollar in grant funds must be matched by the applicant with one dollar in cash or in-kind goods and services. At least one-third of the amount requested must be matched in cash. Grants seldom exceed $6,000 and the average grant is $1,500.
1) Cultural and Aesthetic Project Grants: These grants are awarded by the legislature for a two-year period. Grants are awarded in: visual, performing, literary and media arts, history, archaeology, folklore, archives, collections, research, historic preservation and the construction or renovation of cultural facilities. Categories include:
A) Special Project Grants: Awarded for specific activities, services or events of limited duration, the expansion of on-going programs to meet defined needs and to support projects which generate new sources of revenue.
B) Operational Support Grants: These grants are available for cultural organizations which have been in existence for at least two years. Generally, each grant dollar must be matched with one dollar in cash or in-kind goods and services.
C) Capital Expenditure Grants: Grants are available for additions to a collection or acquisition of works of art, artifacts or historical documents; historic preservation, and the renovation of construction of cultural facilities. Each grant dollar generally must be matched with three dollars in cash or in-kind goods and services.
D) Challenge Grants: Grants are awarded for the expansion of permanent endowments to support non-profit cultural organizations and activities. Each grant dollar must be matched with three dollars in cash, irrevocable planned or deferred gifts or life insurance, devises and bequests.
E) Immediate Action Grants: These grants are awarded throughout the year to enable the Council to respond to unanticipated opportunities or emergencies which occurred after the regular grant request deadline. Grants generally do not exceed $500.
2) Underwriting Assistance Grants: Grants are given as "courage money" to sponsors of professional performing arts touring companies and artists. Grants are awarded on a first-come, first-serve basis and preference is given to small communities. Grants are limited to a maximum of $300.
3) Folklife and traditional Arts Grant Program: Matching grants are available to non-profit groups such as community and cultural organizations, tribes, professional societies, local arts agencies and libraries for projects designed to support folklife and traditional arts.

Educational Funding:
1) Artists in Schools/Communities: These grants allow professional artists to work in residencies in schools or community settings. Nationally selected poets and writers, musicians, dancers, visual artists, theater artists, folk artists and video artists are available. Artists are paid on a per diem basis.

Nebraska

Nebraska Arts Council, 1313 Farman On The Mall, Omaha, NE 69102-1873; (402) 595-2122. In 1991-92, the Council awarded $1,108,975 in grants to non-profit organizations. Individual artists received a total of $30,000.

Be patient. If any phone number is incorrect, call (area code) 555-1212 and request the new listing.

State Money for the Arts and Artists

Individual Artists Programs:

1) Individual Artist Fellowships: Fellowships operate on a two-year alternating cycle. The award pool is equally divided each year between visual arts and one other discipline area. Literature and performing arts are eligible in alternating years. Dollar amounts depend on federal funds available. In 1991-92, each discipline was allocated $16,000 for awards.

Organizational Funding:

1) Basic Support Grant: Provides general operating support throughout the year to arts organizations. Applicants are divided into four categories, based on their previous year's fiscal budget. Minimum basic level funding is $500.

2) Community Challenge Grant: Provides a year of activities to new and emerging arts organizations. Applicants may request up to $1,000 during the first year; $1,500 during the second year; and $2,000 in the third year. All grants require matching funds.

3) Director's Fund: Grants are available to arts and non-arts organizations for emergency or contingency funds, high-risk ventures, professional development, pilot projects, and collaborative new work/projects between Nebraska arts organizations and individual artists. Grants may cover up to one-half of the total project. Grants range from $100 to $1,000.

4) Special Projects: Supports a wide variety of specific arts projects such as exhibitions, festivals or poetry readings. One-half of the total cost of the project may be funded. Grants range from $500 to $10,000.

5) Nebraska Touring Program/Exhibits Nebraska: Provides grants to sponsors of performances or exhibits selected from a roster of eligible artists or organizations.

6) Arts as Basic in the Curriculum/Community: Supports fees for projects sponsored by arts or non-arts organizations which integrate the arts into the basic curriculum of as a school district or emphasize collaborations with an arts education focus.

7) Nebraska Touring Program/Exhibits Nebraska (NTP) Technical Assistance Program: Provides up to $500 per year for non-performance production/exhibit expenses to artists, groups, or non-profit arts organizations.

8) Artists in Schools/Communities: Supports fees for artists' residencies sponsored by non-arts organizations in school or community settings. Residencies can be short-term, long-term or extended-term.

Nevada

Nevada State Council on the Arts, 329 Flint St., Reno, NV 89501; (702) 688-1225. In 1991-92, the Council awarded $1,200,000 in funding to non-profit arts organizations and artists. Individual artists fellowships totalled $20,000.

Individual Artists Programs:

1) Artists Fellowships: Assists in the creation of new works and supports artists' efforts to advance their careers. Fellowships range from $2,000 to $10,000 and are available to artists with one-year Nevada residency at time of application.

2) Folk Arts Apprenticeships: Supports master-apprentice learning relationships that continue Nevada's traditional arts and cultures. Awards of $2,500 are available to master folk artists and one or two apprentices, with at least one a Nevada resident.

Organizational Funding:

1) Grants to Organizations: Provides funding to strengthen and improve arts organizations. Grants range from $1,000 to $22,500 dependent upon the size of the non-profit organization. Public institutions are eligible for project support only.

2) Grants to Presenters: These grants are awarded to presenting organizations to support the presentation of performing or visual arts seasons. Grants are awarded on a competitive basis. Grants range from $1,001 to $7,500 for non-profit organizations and from $1,001 to $5,000 for public institutions.

3) Rural Arts Development: Provides support to develop stronger arts in Nevada's rural communities. Non-matching grants of up to $5,000 are awarded to non-profit, tax exempt community organizations or local government entities. Grants of up to $15,000 are awarded to developing arts organizations. Funds require a one-to-two local match to state/federal dollars and should be used to undertake new or expanded community initiatives, or assist in programming.

4) Challenge Grant Program: Established tax exempt, non-profit organizations may apply for grants up to $30,000 that may be used to strengthen long-term operations and financial stability. Funds may be used for creating a new, or adding to an existing, endowment or cash reserve; capital expenditures for building acquisition or renovation; land acquisition directly related to the organization's mission; major equipment (over $1,000); or collections acquisition.

5) Mini-Grants: Grants of up to $1,000 are provided for specific, short-term assistance which fills an immediate need. New or established tax exempt, non-profit organizations, public institutions, individual artists, administrators, art educators and board members may apply for funding.

Educational Funding:

1) Artist in Residence Program: Provides an opportunity for artists around the country to spend one month in a work/instruction arrangement within elementary and high schools, community centers, and other organizations. Artists' fees for 1991-92 are $2,200 per residency month (20 days). Applicant sites must match Council funds on at least a one-to-one basis.

New Hampshire

New Hampshire Division of Arts, Council of the Arts, 40 North Main St., Concord, NH 03301-4974; (603) 271-2789. New Hampshire provided approximately $600,000 in funding in 1990-1991. Nine fellowships of $3,000 each were given to individual artists.

Individual Artists Programs:

1) Individual Artist Fellowships: Fellowships are awarded to professional artists in recognition of excellence and range from $1,500 to $3,000.

2) Artist Opportunity Grants: These awards are open only to artists designated as finalists for the current fellowship year. Grants up to $500 are awarded.

3) Discovery Award: Designed to find artists who may "fall through the gaps" of the Council's grants. The first award will be announced in October, 1993. The maximum amount awarded is $500.

Organizational Funding:

Matching funds are often required under this category.

1) Operating Grants: Provide funds for ongoing administrative and arts programming needs of nonprofit community arts organizations. Funding is for 20% of the organization's annual operating income or $8,000, whichever is less.

2) Program Grant: Cash match grants of up to $4,000 are open to community arts organizations without paid staff and to non-arts organizations.

3) Salary Assistance Grants: These grants are open to incorporated community arts councils seeking administrative staff for the first time or securing additional staff or staff hours. Maximum funding is $5,000 with a minimum match of $2,500. An arts council may apply for second-year funding up to $3,000 with a minimum match of $1,500. By year three, the organization must be able to assume full payment of the salary.

4) Special Project Grants: Matching grants of up to $4,000 are awarded to support specific arts programming activities.

5) Rural Residency Grants: Grants of up to 50% of total residency costs or $2,000, whichever is less, are available for three to ten day community-based artist residencies. Full-time residency applicants are eligible for up to 75% or $3,000, whichever is less.

6) Technical Assistance Grants: Three types of grants are offered: Consultancies ($500), Scholarship Aid/Travel Fund ($250), and Grants to New Arts Organizations ($750).

7) Arts Institution (A1) Grants: Consists of A-1 Development and Operating Grants. While both grants can be used to help with operating expenses, Development Grants incorporate a challenge grant to help organizations raise funds from new or established donors. Funding ranges from $9,000 to $16,000.

8) Project Grants: Supports specific arts programming for the general public. May be a single event or a thematically linked set of events. Up to $4,500 is available in funding.

Educational Organizations:

Three basic types of grants are offered:

1) Artist in Residence Grants: Supports the costs of bringing artists to sites where they will work with students and teachers, kindergarten through twelfth grade, over time from three to sixty days. Depending upon the length of residency, grants range from $400 to $4,000.

2) AIE Initiatives: Provides arts education programs for students pre-kindergarten through twelfth grade and to education professionals who serve this group. Grants range from $2,000 to $5,000.

3) Teacher/Artist Curriculum Collaborations: Designed for a two-year cycle, these provide incentives for teachers to integrate new arts curricula with educational programs. Funding is available up to $1,000 in the first year; up to $1,490 in the second.

New Jersey

New Jersey State Council on the Arts, CN 306, Trenton, NJ 08625; (609) 292-6130. In 1991-92, the Council awarded $9,172,034 in grants to non-profit organizations. Out of 1,052 applicants, 74 individual fellowships were awarded totalling $474,000.

Individual Artists Programs:

1) Fellowships: Fellowships are awarded to professional New Jersey artists. No

Be patient. If any phone number is incorrect, call (area code) 555-1212 and request the new listing.

Arts and Humanities

students are eligible. Categories include: choreography, music composition, opera/music theater composition, theater (mime), experimental art, graphics, painting, sculpture, design arts, crafts, photography, media arts (film/video), prose, play writing, poetry and interdisciplinary arts. An artist may only apply in one discipline and only in one category. In 1991-92 fellowships were awarded in $12,000, $7,000 and $5,000 amounts.

Organizational Funding:

Open to non-profit, tax exempt organizations that have been in existence and active for at least two years at the time of application. All organizations applying for support must apply for either a general operating support grant or special project grant. All grants offered through this program are matching grants. All matches must be cash matches. Categories include:

1) General Operating Support: Includes discretionary, non-project oriented funding to support overall administrative as well as artistic operations. Organizations must be multi-regional or statewide in public impact. Awards generally do not exceed 20% of total projected expenditures.

2) Special Project Support: Grants are awarded specifically for an arts project/event of an eligible non-profit organization, agency or local government institution. Projects must be multi-regional or statewide in public impact.

3) Arts Basic to Education Awards: Support offered to arts education organizations and agencies that provide art-in-education services to children in grades kindergarten through twelfth.

4) Major Impact Arts Organizations: Funding is granted to a limited number of arts organizations which meet the highest standards of excellence and administrative and fiscal responsibility. Designations are made for a three-year period.

5) Challenge Grants: May be offered to help the arts organization leverage increased contributed support from corporations, foundations and other public and private sources. Funds must be matched and may be applied to general operations.

6) Technical Assistance; Grants are offered that assist organizations in obtaining needed expertise and management skills. These grants usually do not require a match.

Educational Organizations:

Arts in Education Programs (AIE) are available to public, private and parochial schools, school districts, non-profit community organizations, non-profit local arts center, and organizations that sponsor non-for-profit community projects. The NJSCA awards sponsors matching funds to pay for artists' fees only.

1) Artists-in-Education Programs: Residencies range from five-day short-term residencies to long-term residencies lasting 100 days. Disciplines include: architecture, dance, folk arts, jazz, media arts, theater/drama, visual arts/crafts and writing.

2) Artist/Teacher/Institute: Is a ten-day summer program that offers educators the same opportunities for artistic growth that students experience in AIE residencies. Workshops and in-depth arts experiences are available in all disciplines.

New Mexico

New Mexico Cultural Affairs Arts Division, 224 East Palace Ave, Sante Fe, NM 87501; (505) 827-6490. The New Mexico Art Division is unable to fund fellowships to individuals. It encourages applicant organizations to involve resident New Mexico artists. However, the Division will support local sponsorship of out-of-state artists or organizations to enrich a resident group or when the services fill a need that cannot be met locally. In 1990-91, the Division awarded $1,200,000 in grant funding to non-profit organizations.

Organizational Funding:

New Mexico administers grants to non-profit organizations. Generally, grant applicants must provide at least a one-to-one cash match. Categories include:

1) Established Arts Organizations: This category purchases art services on behalf of New Mexico residents from established professional organizations. Applicants fall into three categories: those whose cash operating incomes for the preceding year were greater than $500,000, less than $500,000 and less than $100,000. Grants range from $10,000 to $120,000 dependent upon category.

2) Civic and Community Arts Organizations: Supports those organizations that promote, produce, and/or present quality arts experiences but do not meet the requirements to apply as Professional Arts Organizations. The maximum grant available is 50% of cash operating income, excluding grants from the Arts Division, or $15,000, whichever is less.

3) Culturally Diverse Organizations: Designed to develop stronger ethnic arts organizations on a long-term basis. The maximum grant available is 50% of cash operating income, excluding grants from the Arts Division, or $15,000, whichever is less.

4) Arts Projects: Purchases short-term arts services on behalf of New Mexico

residents. Maximum request is $5,000 for Folk Arts, Culturally Diverse Arts, and other Arts Projects.

5) Incentives to Present New Mexico Touring Artists: Assists presenters in obtaining the services of New Mexico touring performing artist on behalf of their communities. Presenters may be awarded up to 50% of any given fee on the application.

Educational Programs:

1) Artists Residencies: Places qualified artists in various community, rural, and institutional settings through grants for collaborative residencies or rural and institutional residencies. There is a ten-day minimum residency length. Artists are paid a minimum of $110 per working day.

New York

New York State Council on the Arts, 915 Broadway, New York, NY 10010; (212) 387-7000. In 1991, New York awarded $46,327,400 in grants to non-profit arts organizations.

Individual Artists Programs:

The Council and local regrant agencies are unable to make grants directly to individuals. All applications must be sponsored by nonprofit organizations. Grants are awarded through Cultural Service Contracts with the non-profit organizations which direct the funds to the individual's project. In 1991-92, the Program received $1,159,020 in support. Funding categories include: composers' commissions, film production, media production, visual arts, and theater. Up to $25,000 may be granted.

Organizational Funding:

Non-profit arts organizations in New York may receive grants from the Council. The Council has 17 program areas of support including: architecture, planning and design, arts in education, capital funding initiative, dance, electronic media and film, folk arts, individual artists, literature, museum, music, musical instrument revolving loan fund, presenting operations, special arts services, state local partnership, theater and the visual arts. Funding is available through two categories:

1) General Operating Support: Provides unrestricted support for ongoing institutional activities. Each program has its particular criteria and restrictions. In general, a group must have at least three years prior support from the program in order to be eligible.

2) Multi-Year Support: Many programs offer multi-year support in areas other than General Operating Support. In these instance, organizations do have the option of applying for more than one year of support.

In addition to providing support to nonprofit arts organizations through its own funding process, the Council also supports a statewide local regranting system called Decentralization. Grants up to $5,000 are funded to support professional and avocational arts activities in all artistic disciplines within local communities.

Educational Programs:

Arts in Education: Is a collaboration between the Council and the State Education Department. Non-profit cultural and environmental organizations based in New York may submit applications. In 1991-92, $3,074,850 was awarded in grants. Funding categories include general operating support, planning grants, implementation grants, special projects, evaluation/research and long-term projects. Arts and education, dance groups, museums, theater, and folk arts are among the categories eligible. Individual artists are funded through sponsoring organizations. These individual grants are available in five areas; film production, media production, visual artist sponsored projects, theater commissions, and music commissions. The amount of funding available is dependent of the project being proposed.

North Carolina

North Carolina Arts Council, Department of Cultural Resources, Raleigh, NC 27601-2807; (919) 733-2821. The Council provides over 1,700 grants each year to artists and non-profit organizations for arts programming throughout the state. In 1990-91, the Council awarded $4,531,761 in grants to non-profit organizations. Individual artists received $113,100 in fellowships.

Individual Artists Programs:

1) Fellowships: Awards recognize the contribution of exemplary artists and provide funds for continued creative development. Fellowships of $8,000 are available in dance, literature, music, theater and the visual arts.

2) Artist Project Grants: Support professional artists for specific artistic projects. Grants are available in dance, folklife, literature and visual arts and range from

Be patient. If any phone number is incorrect, call (area code) 555-1212 and request the new listing.

State Money for the Arts and Artists

$5,000 to $8,000.

3) Residencies: Residencies provide opportunities for artists to work in schools and community colleges. Residency opportunities at out-of-state arts centers are also available in some categories.

4) Folk Heritage Awards: These awards recognize the lifetime achievement of folk artists who have made outstanding contributions to the state's cultural heritage. A non-matching cash amount of $3,000 is awarded.

5) Folklife Documentary Project Grants: Grants provide support for the preservation of the state's traditional culture through the use of modern documentary technology. Grants rarely exceed $10,000.

6) Touring Artists Roster: Contains a list of selected performing artists receiving fee support for touring performances in the state. Current artists on the roster and recent alumni may also apply for scholarship and project assistance.

7) Writers Scholarships provide support to writers to attend workshops, conferences, book fairs or other educational events. Grants do not exceed $500.

8) Internships: Programs are available to individuals for training in arts administration.

Organizational Funding:

The Council's grant programs are available in eight categories: community development, dance, folklife, literature, music, theater, touring/presenting and the visual arts. Support includes funding for includes program support, interdisciplinary/special projects, and organizational development grants as well as the general support grants listed below:

1) Major Organization Support: Provides funding for the artistic programs and administration of the state's major dance, music and visual arts organizations.

2) General Support: Provides funding for the artistic programs and administration of established theater and literary organizations.

3) Local Government Challenge: These grants match new allocations provided by country and municipal governments for local arts council programming.

4) Management Service Organization: Grants support statewide organizations serving community arts programming.

Educational Organizations:

1) Arts in Education: Supports the arts in education and assists the Basic Education Program through artist residencies, program development grants, and Arts-in-Education project grants. The Council plans to hold a statewide conference on arts education. It also plans to publish a directory on model projects, as well as develop an audiovisual program to encourage arts in education and work with the North Carolina Association of Arts Councils to establish a network of local contacts in the field of education.

North Dakota

North Dakota Council On Arts, Black Building #606, 118 Broad Way, Fargo, ND 58102; (701) 239-7150. In 1990-91, the Council awarded $462,500 to non-profit organizations. Individuals received $25,000 in fellowship grants.

Individual Artists Programs:

1) Artists Fellowships Program: Assists North Dakota artists in furthering their professional artistic careers. Fellowship funds come from individual and business donations and interest from the state's Cultural Endowment. Fellowships are awarded in the following disciplines: dance, music, opera/musical theater, theater, visual arts, architecture/design, crafts, photography, media arts, literature, interdisciplinary arts, and folk arts.

2) Professional Development Program: Provides financial assistance for informational/educational opportunities relating to the arts and arts development, or to benefit arts organizations by providing support for consultants and technical or artistic advisors. Only one grant of up to $300 will be provided per artist or organization per year. Grants do not require matching funds.

Organizational Funding:

1) ACCESS Grant Program: Provides state funds to non-profit organizations for general operating as well as special projects.l Generally it serves small, rural or emerging groups, or those making special efforts to provide arts experiences to previously underserved audiences.

2) Institutional Support: Supports non-profit organizations for general operating as well as for performances, exhibitions, workshops and other special projects in all arts disciplines. Mini-grant requests of $500 are accepted throughout the year.

3) Rural Arts Initiative: Combines federal, state, and local funding to assist the significant organizational, programmatic, and artistic growth of selected local arts organizations in small, rural towns.

4) Touring Arts Program: Provides a roster of high quality, low cost touring events, and grants state funds to non-profit organizations sponsoring these events in North Dakota communities.

Educational Funding:

1) Artists-in-Residence: Provides a roster of qualified artists who can work with students in elementary and secondary schools for sustained periods of time, and provides federal funds to non-profit organizations and local school districts for sponsoring these artists.

2) Local Education in the Arts Planning: (LEAP) Program regrants federal funds to assist local school districts in developing five-year education plans.

Ohio

Ohio Council on Arts, 727 East Main St., Columbus, OH 43205-1797; (614) 466-2613. New Guidelines will be available in June, 1992. In 1991-92 Ohio awarded $9,896,213 in grants to non-profit organizations and artists.

Individual Artists Programs:

1) Individual Artist Program: Offers fellowships of $5,000 and $10,000 and artist residency opportunities. Individual Fellowships are granted to residents with at least one year residency prior to the January 15 deadline imposed. No student may apply. Artist in residency opportunities at P.S.I. in Long Island, NY and Headlands Center for the Arts in Sausalito, CA are open to artists who have received Individual Artists Fellowships.

2) Major Fellowships: This program offers a two-year fellowship of $50,000 ($25,000 per year) to outstanding Ohio artists. The Program is open to choreographers, music composers, performance artists, interdisciplinary and media artists, creative writers, craftspersons, designers, photographers and visual artists.

3) Individual Artist Program: Provides Professional Development Assistance of up to $1,000 to help the artist pay for a variety of activities.

4) Traditional and Ethnic Arts Apprenticeship Program: Offers grants up to $2,000. A traditional master artist an apprentice artist apply together for a one-year apprenticeship.

Organizational Funding:

Support for organizations include funding for: art in public places, dance, design arts, interdisciplinary arts, literature, media arts, multi-arts, music, theater, traditional and ethnic arts, and visual arts and crafts.

1) Major Institution Support: Helps fund operational expenses for Ohio institutions with operating incomes over $500,000.

2) Project Support: Provides partial funding toward year-long projects or short-term projects sponsored by arts and non-arts organizations.

3) Operating Support: Funds the ongoing artistic and administrative functions of arts organizations with operating incomes under $500,000 for a full year of services, July 1 - June 30.

4) Sudden Opportunity Grants: Provides money for an unforeseen arts opportunity that may occur between council Board meetings. Grants are limited to $2,000 and fund a wide variety of activities.

Oklahoma

State Arts Council of Oklahoma, 640 Jim Thorpe Bldg., Oklahoma City, OK 73105-4987; (405) 521-2931. Financial assistance is available to qualified organizations for a wide variety of arts projects which fall with the Council's guidelines. Applications are accepted from nonreligious, non-profit, tax-exempt organizations. The Council is unable to fund individuals. In 1990-91, Oklahoma provided $2,904,043 in grant funding to non-profit organizations. Colleges, schools and universities which receive funding through the State Regents for Higher Education, or substantial private sources, are a lower funding priority except in areas where the university or college is the sole source of arts events in a community. The Council will fund personnel or administrative costs associated with a project. The Council does not fund general administrative expenses or general organizational support.

Organizational Funding:

All funding for the Advanced Request, Over $2,000 and Under $2,000 Project Assistance categories must be matched dollar-for-dollar by the applicant. Fifty percent of the matching funds must be cash.

1) Advanced Request Funding: This category encourages project planning 16 months in advance of the fiscal year in which activities will occur. It allows for the inclusion of Advanced Request Category recommendations in the State Arts Council's budget request to the Governor and Legislature in Sept. of each year.

2) Project Assistance Over $2,000: Supports programs or projects for which the total financial assistance requested form the Council exceeds $2,000. Applicants are reviewed by advisory panels which make funding recommendations to the Council. Projects must be submitted no later than December 10.

3) Project Assistance Under $2,000: Provides assistance for smaller or low-cost projects. Applications are reviewed monthly on a first-come, first-served basis by

Be patient. If any phone number is incorrect, call (area code) 555-1212 and request the new listing.

Arts and Humanities

the Executive Committee of the State Arts Council. Applications must be submitted no later than 60 days prior to the project beginning date.

4) Minority Arts: This category is for requests of under $5,000 to be used primarily for technical assistance to minority arts organizations or for special projects designed for audience development, community participation or projects directed toward youth. The match for the projects may be in-kind. Limited funds are available. The deadline for submission is 60 days prior to project start date.

5) Fairs and Festivals: Are defined as one-day indoor or outdoor community celebrations of the arts. Financial assistance for a one-day fair or festival is generally under $500. Applications for one-day fair and festival events should be submitted under the Under $2,000 category. Applications for fairs and festivals lasting two or more days should be submitted in the Under $2,000, Over $2,000 or Advanced Request categories depending upon the amount of funding requested. Applications will be judged on an individual basis.

6) Artists-in Residences Program: Applications are accepted from local education agencies and non-profit, tax exempt community organizations. A residency's structure is determined by the on-site arts planning team and consists mostly of class sessions. Teachers or adult workshops, lecture, and mini-performances are some of the other possible activities. A school or community residency may last up to 36 weeks and is based on a 40-hour work week. Half of that time is spent with residency participants, the remaining time is designated as studio time for the artist. The artist's compensation for an approved residency is $520 per week. There is a set relocation fee for travel to residencies outside the artist's home town. Artists are responsible for their own transportation, board and lodging.

7) Oklahoma Touring Program: Enables the Council to share the cost of quality Oklahoma performing events with local community organizations. Producers of dance, music, opera and theater, along with storytellers and folk artists are chosen on the basis of artistic quality. Any nonreligious, nonprofit, tax-exempt organization, governmental unit, tribal government or educational institution is eligible for assistance. Touring costs are shared by the council and the presenter. Funding is available for 50% of the contracted performance or exhibition fee.

Oregon

Oregon Arts Commission, 550 Airport Road SE, Salem, OR 97301; (503) 378-3625. In 1991-92, the Commission awarded $1,476,608 in grants to non-profit arts organizations. Individuals received $54,000 in fellowships.

Individual Artists Programs:

1) Artist Fellowships: Individual artists may apply for either a $3,000 Individual Artist Fellowship or a $10,000 Masters Fellowship, but not both. Categories include: visual arts and crafts, literary arts, media arts, design arts, photography, performing arts and interdisciplinary work. Masters applications must have been residents of the state for five years previous to application deadline date.

2) Western States Regional Media Arts Fellowships: Available to artists living in the thirteen western states, including Oregon, and the Pacific territories. Project grants up to $7,000 are available for production expenses for proposed new work or work in progress.

Organizational Funding:

1) Program Grants: Non-profit arts organizations which have been in existence at least two years may apply. Grants contribute to an organization's entire year's programming. Grants are intended primarily for mid-sized arts organizations and generally do not exceed $5,000.

2) Oregon Arts Challenge: Open to private non-profit, tax exempt arts organizations. An organization must have been in existence in substantially its current form for at least five years and have experienced, professional management on a full-time basis. The maximum grant is $225,000. All grants must be matched at least one-to-one within certain Council regulations.

3) Special Project Grants: Support initiatives which are not a part of an arts organization's regular programming. Projects are generally one-time initiatives, and will not be supported more than two years. Grants generally do not exceed $3,000. Funding includes special constituencies, art in public places, new works services to the arts and folk arts.

4) Presenting Grants: Support performances of traveling artists in Oregon. First priority goes to support Oregon performing arts groups, however, sponsors may apply for funds to support out-of-state companies when their services fulfill a need not met within the state. Grants are made to non-profit organizations which sponsor performing artists, not directly to touring artists. Maximum amount of funding is $200.

5) Professional Development Grants: This program includes local arts agencies. Grants are available in two categories:

A) Training: Funds for arts administrators to attend workshops and seminars that develop administrative skills.

B) Consultants: Funds for consultants to conduct training workshops, work with board or staff members, or assist in activities such as marketing and facilities

planning.

6) Emergency Grants: Funding for opportunities that may arise during the year for which an organization needs support, but for a legitimate reason could not apply at the spring deadline. Maximum funding is $500.

Educational Programs:

1) Artist Residencies: Introduces practicing professional artists into community settings to engage students, teachers and the public in the arts. Residencies are offered in all arts disciplines: visual arts, crafts, design, architecture, creative writing, dance, music, film and video, folk arts, theater, and interdisciplinary projects. Short-term and long-term residencies are available. Artists are paid on a per diem basis.

2) Arts Education Project Grants: Supports projects that make the arts basic to education within the schools and extends arts education opportunities for Oregon students beyond the schools. Grants of up to $3,000 are awarded for one-time projects or as seed money to develop a program.

Pennsylvania

Pennsylvania Council on the Arts, Room 216, Finance Bldg., Harrisburg, PA 17120; (717) 787-6883. In 1991-92, 1001 non-profit organizations received $19,007,611 in funding. Fellowships were awarded to 75 individual artists totalling $475,548.

Individual Artists Programs:

Applicants must have lived in Pennsylvania for two years prior to applying for funding and should have had a minimum of three years professional experience in their field.

1) Fellowships: Limited fellowships are available to established or emerging artists. Categories include: crafts, dance, folklife, literature, media arts (audio/radio), music (composers, jazz composers and performers, and solo recitalists), inter-disciplinary arts, theater and screenwriters and visual arts. Awards are made directly to the individual primarily on the basis of the creative excellence of the work submitted for review.

Organizational Funding:

Organizations must be non-profit, tax exempt corporations providing arts programming and/or services to Pennsylvania. Categories include: broadcast of the arts, crafts, inter-disciplinary arts, dance, literature, local arts services, local government, media arts, museums, music, presenting organizations, theater and visual arts. Non-profit organizations may apply on behalf of an unincorporated arts group. In this capacity, the organization becomes a "conduit" for grant funds and is financially, administratively and programmatically responsible. Unless otherwise specified, grants must be matched on a dollar for dollar basis. The Council will support no more than 50% of a project. If necessary, a reasonable portion of the acquired matching funds may be in-kind contributions of facilities, goods and services. Funding includes:

1) General Support: Assists arts organizations which have been regularly receiving Council support for the costs of their annual activities. First-time applicants should not apply for General Support. Organizations must have been in operation for at least three prior to application and be under professional artistic and managerial leadership on a year-round basis.

2) Technical Assistance: Non-matching grants are available to engage consultants to review programs and operations and advise and assist in organization planning and development. Maximum funding is $1,000. Conference grants of up to $250 are also available.

3) Busing Program: Busing grants are provided to non-profit organizations if they are transporting groups to art activities. Non-matching grants are awarded up to $250 per trip.

Educational Programs:

1) Residencies: The Arts in Education Program (AIE) places practicing artists in schools and community settings, particularly where quality arts experiences are not readily available. AIE covers all disciplines. Priority is given to Pennsylvania artists. In cases where extreme financial needs can be demonstrated, the normal 50% matching requirements may be waived. Residencies last from a minimum of ten days in length to a maximum of 80 days. The cost of a residency is 4150 per day for the resident artist's fees. Applicants may also apply for funds for travel and daily expenses.

Rhode Island

Rhode Island State Council On The Arts, 95 Cedar St., Suite 103, Providence, RI 02903; (401) 277-3880. In 1991-92, the Council awarded $1,469,857 to non-profit arts organizations. Out of 225 applicants, 24 individual artists received $42,000 in fellowships.

Be patient. If any phone number is incorrect, call (area code) 555-1212 and request the new listing.

State Money for the Arts and Artists

Individual Artists Programs:

Applicants must be eighteen years of age or older and have lived in the state for at least one year prior application. Grants fall into four categories:

1) Artist Projects: Enables an artist to create new work and/or complete works-in-progress by providing direct financial assistance. Grants range from $2,000 to $5,000.

2) Fellowships: Fellowships are offered in: choreography, crafts, design, drawing and printmaking, film and video, folk arts, literature, music composition, new genres, painting, photography and three-dimensional art. Grant recipients each receive $3,000. A runner-up in each category, if awarded, will receive a $500 honorarium.

3) Folk Arts Apprenticeships: This program fosters the sharing of traditional (folk) artistic skills between a master and an apprentice who is already familiar with the genre. Grants range from $100 to $2,000. For exceptional projects, higher amounts may be awarded. Most of the support is for the master's fee.

Organizational Funding:

Minimum grant awards are $100 and funds must be expended during the fiscal year of the award. Program grants, with the exception of general operating support, are divided into two categories. Level I grants range from $100 to $2,000. Level II grants range from $2,001 to $5,000. A dollar-for-dollar cash match is required.

1) Access Initiatives: Provides funds for projects that assure equal opportunity and access for underserved groups and individuals.

2) Arts Programming: Provides matching funds for a wide variety of arts-related projects planned and executed by eligible nonprofit organizations.

3) Organizational Development: Supplies funds to advance an organization's artistic, management, and technical capabilities.

4) General Operating Support: Provides partial operating costs for the state's established arts producing/exhibiting organizations. Organizations are eligible for single year funding if they have had a three-year grant history with the Council. Organizations that have made a statewide impact may apply for multi-year funding if their budget is over $100,000 and have had a five-year grant history with the Council.

All grants require a dollar-for-dollar match. The Council will fund up to 50% of the organization's budget. Funding is not available to local arts councils, service organizations, amateur organizations, or all volunteer organizations.

Educational Funding:

1) Artist Residency Grants: Grants sponsor both professional and folk artists for residencies in educational settings. Residencies are carried out by artists from the Arts in Education Artist Roster and are long-term (15 to 100 days for professional artists; minimum of five days for folk artists). Grants are funded up to $12,000.

2) Arts as Basic in Curriculum (ABC) Grants: Supports funding to help make the arts a basic part of kindergarten through twelfth grade education. Grants are funded up to $2,500.

3) Rhode Island Comprehensive Arts Planning Grants (RICAP) Grants: Open to Rhode Island public school districts with a need to coordinate and improve educational programs in dance, theater, music, visual arts and creative writing for its students. $2,000 will be awarded to each year's chosen districts. Special training, resources, workshops, and professional leadership is built into the award.

South Carolina

South Carolina Art Commission, 1800 Gervais St., Columbia, SC 29201; (803) 734-8696. New grant guidelines are due out in mid-summer, 1992. Grants to non-profit arts organizations totalled $2,000,000. Six individual artist fellowships of $7,500 each were awarded in 1991-92.

Individual Artists Programs:

1) Fellowships: Five fellowships are available annually in the following disciplines: visual arts, crafts, literature and music performance. These non-matching awards are for $5000.

2) Special Projects: Funds specific, planned activities such as the production of new work, marketing and professional development. These matching grants generally do not exceed $7,500.

3) Small Grants: Provide funding for short-term, small budget projects which arise during the current year. Grants do not exceed $1,000.

Organizational Funding:

Organizations apply either as Professional Arts Organizations or Other Organizations. Funding options include matching programs such as advancement grants, challenge grants, endowment development grants, local government challenge grants, subgranting, small grants and ticket subsidy grants. All options are not available to all organizations. Within both categories, there are three groups:

1) Professional Arts Organizations:

A) Established Organizations: Applicants in this group must be invited to apply. Organizations must have distinguished themselves as among the state's major cultural institutions and leading arts councils. Funding generally does not exceed $75,000 annually.

B) Developing Organizations: Assists the planned development of already stable, professional arts organizations. Funding rarely exceeds $40,000.

C) Emerging Organizations: Assists arts organizations whose objective is to become fully professional, but have not yet attained organizational stability. Funds rarely exceed $15,000.

2) Other Organizations:

A) Non-Arts Institutions: Supports major arts projects with significant statewide impact sponsored by colleges, universities, and other types of institutions. Funds generally do not exceed $20,000.

B) Community Presenters of Series, Exhibitions and Readings: Encourages innovative programming by supporting high quality offerings. These highly competitive grants rarely exceed $10,000.

C) Community Events, Projects and Arts Organizations: Established to enhance the quality and encourage risk taking in community-based arts programming. Grants rarely exceed $10,000.

Educational Funding:

1) Artists-in-Residence: This program places artists in the literary, performing, and visual arts and crafts in a school setting for residencies for one to thirty-two weeks. Teacher workshops are also conducted. A participating artist must be on the South Carolina Arts Commission's Approved Artist Roster. Short-term, long-term and extended residencies are available with the Commission providing forty to sixty percent of funding.

2) Artists Visits: This new offering allows Roster Artists to make one or two day visits to provide a variety of services such as classes, workshops for teachers, specific arts projects, etc. The Commission provides 40% of funding.

3) Special Projects Option: Encourages new arts education projects that are well outside the realm of the residency options and which make a qualitative difference in a site's program. Creative and innovative projects compete in this option. The Commission provides 40% of funding.

South Dakota

South Dakota Arts Council, 108 W. 11th St., Sioux Falls, SD 57102-0788; (605) 339-6646. All grants (except Emerging Artist Grants and Fellowships) are intended to be seed money. Applicant organizations and individuals are funded up to 50% of projected costs. Funding is available in the following arts disciplines: dance, music, opera/music theater, theater, visual arts, design arts, crafts, photography, media arts, literature and folk arts. In 1991-92, the Council distributed $551,800 in grants to non-profit arts organizations. Individual fellowships totalled $30,000.

Individual Artists Programs:

1) Artist Fellowship Grants: Recognize South Dakota artists of exceptional talent in any arts discipline with $5,000 non-matching grants.

2) Emerging Artists Grants: Recognizes artists for their potential for growth and contribution to the arts. This non-matching grant of $1,000 can only be awarded to an individual artist once every three years.

3) Project Grants: Assist individual artists in the presentation of a project for the general public or an activity which meets specific needs of the applicant artist. Awards up to 50% of the total project costs. Grants must be matched at least dollar for dollar in cash or in combination with an in-kind service.

Organizational Funding:

1) General Operating Support: Provides operating assistance to South Dakota non-profit presenting or producing arts institutions and community arts councils. Grants are funded up to 10% of the applicant's annual eligible cash operating expenses.

2) Project Grants: Assist non-profit organizations in the presentation of an activity or series of activities for the general public which meet specific needs of the applicant organization.

Awards up to 50% of the total project costs. Grants must be matched at least dollar for dollar in cash or in combination with an in-kind service.

3) Interim Project Grants: Open to organizations that have not received a General Operating Support or Project Grant. Up to $500 in matching funds may be awarded in special cases involving new sites, new events or new organizations.

4) Emergency Grants: Up to $500 in funds may be awarded to organizations which need emergency support, but for a legitimate reason, could not apply on the February 1 deadline.

5) Arts Bank: Provides an underwriting to remove fear of financial loss in

Be patient. If any phone number is incorrect, call (area code) 555-1212 and request the new listing.

Arts and Humanities

producing and sponsoring performances, workshops and other arts events for local audiences without removing the community effort required to support the event. An organization cannot receive more than $1,000 from the Arts bank within a fiscal year.

6) Technical Assistance: Provides matching funds for professional advice on technical matters, specific programs, projects, and/or administrative functions of non-profit arts organizations. Grants up to $500 are provided to match 50% of the consultant's negotiated fee and travel/lodging/meals at state government rates.

7) Professional Development: Assists individuals associated with arts organizations with in improving their ability to work for arts in South Dakota. Grants up to $500 are provided to match 50% of the consultant's negotiated fee and travel/lodging/ meals at state government rates. Funds are awarded to the applicant organization.

8) Touring Arts: Help make the arts available in all regions of the state. Provides matching funds to individuals for touring in any arts discipline.

Educational Funding:

1) Artists-in-Schools: Places practicing artists of quality work in residences of one week or longer in schools. Preference is given to public and private elementary and secondary schools in South Dakota. Artist fees are supported on a matching funds basis between the sponsoring organization and the Council.

2) Art Educator Grants: Assist teachers from all arts disciplines in the development of arts education curricula for students in grades kindergarten through twelfth.

Tennessee

Tennessee Art Commission, 320-6th Ave North, Suite 100, Nashville, TN 37243-0780; (615) 741-1701. In 1991-92, the Commission awarded $2,456,525 in matching grants to non-profit arts organizations. Nine individual fellowships were awarded totalling $22,500.

Individual Artists Programs:

1) Individual Artists Fellowships: Provides as many as eight awards to outstanding Tennessee artists in each of the following disciplines: crafts, dance, literature, media, music, opera, theater, and visual arts. Each fellowship will be at least $2,500 or more. Honorable mention grants, if given, usually are for less than $2,500.

Organizational Funding:

1) Arts Build Communities: This pilot project works in direct partnership with one or more designated agencies in each of Tennessee's nine developmental districts to increase arts awareness and involvement throughout the state. Each designated agency receives a "block grant" of a per capita share of 41 million appropriated to the Arts commission for community grants. All funds received by a designated agency must be matched on a one-to-one basis. See the Commission's Guideline to Grants for complete details.

2) Arts Projects: Provides funds for a wide variety of quality arts projects and programs. Grants range from $500 to $6,000. Funds are available to those counties not being served by a designated agency under Arts Build Communities. Non-profit organizations in the following counties only may apply for an Arts Project matching grant: Cheatham, Dickson, Giles, Hickman, Houston, Humphreys, Lawrence, Lewis, Maury, Montgomery, Perry, Robertson, Rutherford, Stewart, Wayne, Williamson and Wilson.

3) Community Orchestra Challenge Grants: Provides matching funds for Tennessee's community orchestras in amounts ranging from $1,000 to $15,000. To be eligible, an orchestra must have an annual operating income of under $500,000 (excluding all in-kind contributions).

4) General Operating Support: Provides general, non-project support to established non-profit, tax exempt organizations exclusively involved in on-going, continuous arts activities or services. Funding is divided into organizations with operating expenses under $499,999, and over $500,000. Funding is available for up to 10% of an organization's total operating expenses for their last year's income.

5) Partnerships for Access and Appreciation: Provides matching funding for underserved and under-represented art disciplines and forms. Each funded project must involve at least two non-profit Tennessee organizations or at least one artist and one non-profit Tennessee organization. Grants generally range from $10,000 to $25,000.

6) Special Opportunity Grants: Provides funds for unexpected but important arts activities. Matching grants of up to $500 are offered for activities of modest size.

7) Technical Assistance Program: Provides funds for special technical assistance, often by out-of-state consultants. Grants range from $500 to $2,500 and may require a cash and/or in-kind match.

8) Touring Arts Program: Brings professional performers to communities by providing financial assistance to qualified presenters/sponsors. Performers are

available for one or two-day residencies. Grants range from $1,000 to $5,000. Matching funds are required.

Educational Funding:

1) Artists Residencies: Places professional artists in educational settings. They serve primarily as a resource to existing teaching staff. Grants range between $500 and $10,000, depending upon the arts discipline and length of residency. Organizations must supply matching funds. Residences are available in architecture/ environment, dance/movement, film/video, folk arts, multi-arts, music, poetry/creative writing, theater, and visual arts/crafts. Individual elementary, middle, and secondary schools may apply. Community arts councils, museums, statewide arts organizations, and other Tennessee chartered non-profit organizations may apply as a coordinating agency.

Texas

Texas Commission on the Arts, 920 Colorado, P.O. Box 13406 Capitol Station, Austin, TX 78711-3406; (512) 463-5535. In 1991-92, the Commission awarded $3,832,679 in funding to non-profits arts organizations. Texas does not offer direct funding to individuals. Individual artists are funded indirectly through the Arts in Education and the Touring Programs. In addition, individual artists may apply to the Commission under the umbrella of a non-profit organization or government entity.

Organizational Funding:

There are three types of financial assistance with no maximum or minimum funding levels. Funding for an application is determined by the review process and the amount of funds available to the Commission at a given time.

1) Organizational Assistance: Provides financial assistance for operational support for a 12-month period. This program is available to: major institutions, cultural and artistic organizations, local arts agencies, cultural/arts service organizations, regional organizations, and private non-profit education organizations. Matching requirements are one-to-one with the exception of major institutions, which must provide a two-to-one match. All match funds must be in cash.

2) Project Assistance: Provides support for a specific event, project, or activity, either programmatic or administrative. This program is available to all groups. Applicant matching funds must be a minimum of 50% of the cost. Half of these funds may be in-kind contributions, which are the value of goods and services directly donated to a project, where no dollars are exchanged.

3) Touring Assistance: Provides up to 50% artist fee support to presenters who present companies/artists for both visual and performing events. Performers are chosen from the Texas Touring Program Company/Artist Roster. Presenters are approved for a two-year period.

Educational Funding:

1) Arts in Education Program: Available to professionally staffed organizations for up to 50% of project costs for an artist-in residence. Priority is given to programs involving students in grades kindergarten through twelfth, teacher training, and that show evidence of community involvement. Artists are required to provide 20 hours of service of artist development time during a normal 40-hour week and are paid on per diem basis.

Utah

Utah Council of Arts, 617 E. South Temple, Salt Lake City, UT 84102-1177; (801) 553-5895. In 1991-92, 181 grants were awarded to organizations totalling $921,255.

Individual Artists Programs:

1) Visual Artist Fellowships: The Council awards two $5,000 visual artists fellowships annually through the Visual Arts Program. Fellowships are available for individual artists practicing crafts, painting, drawing, printmaking, photography, sculpture, artist's bookmaking, and working in new genres, performance arts, conceptual arts and video. These grants do not require matching funds.

2) Folk Arts Apprenticeship Program: Assists traditional artists and their communities by providing up to $2,500 to support one-on-one teaching between master artists and qualified apprentices. In 1991-92, 11 new apprenticeships were funded.

Organizational Funding:

1) Grants Program: The Council supports non-profit organizations through grants awarded on the basis of program quality. Annual grants are awarded to a wide variety of recipients, ranging from the Utah Symphony to the smallest community arts council. Grants range from $300 to $130,000 and includes general

Be patient. If any phone number is incorrect, call (area code) 555-1212 and request the new listing.

State Money for the Arts and Artists

support grants, Challenger grants (to $2,500), and Community Arts Development grants. Currently, total grants program funds are matched approximately 24-to-1 by funds from other sources.

2) Community/State Partnership Program (C/SP): Assists community arts councils in incorporating, fundraising, presenting arts events and initiating board development.

3) Utah Performing Arts Tour: Encourages and supports professional residency activities that otherwise might not take place. Each winter a roster of performing artists and companies is selected through applications and auditions. While Utah artists are highly encouraged to apply, out-of-state-artists are included on the tour each season. Technical assistance is provided in such areas as audience development, ticket-pricing, publicity and program development.

Educational Funding:

1) Arts in Education: Encourages the recognition of the arts as part of basic education, primarily through school and community residencies and project grants in arts education. Residencies range from 10 days to a year in length. Artists receive $25 per hour and work four hours per day. In 1991-92, 126 residencies were funded totalling $211,114. Sixty artists were employed.

Vermont

Vermont Council on Arts, 133 State St., Montpelier, VT 05633-6001; (802) 828-3291. The Vermont Council on Arts is an independent non-profit organization and not part of the State Government. In 1990-91, the Council awarded $512,000 in grants to non-profit organizations. Individuals received $78,500 in funding.

Individual Artists Programs:

1) Artist Development Grants: Assists artists' professional development by supporting master classes, workshops, project development, documentation and more. Awards range from $100 to $500 for individual submissions and up to $1,000 for collaborative applications.

2) Fellowships: The Council awards $3,500 for Fellowships; $500 for Finalist awards in recognition of artistic accomplishment. The program is highly competitive with only 5% to 8% of all applicants receiving awards.

3) Project Grants: Funds specific arts projects within the general scope of arts organizations or non-arts organizations. Individual artists may apply for Project Grants in cooperation with an organization serving as Fiscal Agent. See Organizational Funding for details.

Organizational Funding:

1) Operating Grants: Provide general support for Vermont non-profit, tax exempt organizations for one year. Based on their most recently completed fiscal year, eligible organizations with an annual cash income of at least $15,000 and less than $125,000 may apply for a maximum of 10% of its annual operating budget. Grants rarely exceed $6,000. Eligible organizations with an annual cash income of more than $125,000 may apply for a maximum of 5% of its annual operating budget. Grants rarely exceed $15,000. Applications must be for at least $1,500 a year.

2) Project Grants: Awarded for specific arts projects within the general scope of arts organizations, non-arts organizations or for the projects of artists working individually, in collaboration, or in partnership with an organization. Matching grants fund up to 50% of the project's cash cost or $3,000, whichever is less.

3) Service Organization Grants: Supports non-profit organizations by providing resources and developmental opportunities. Grants range from $500 to $5,000, but are limited to half of the applicant's total operating budget based on the applicant's most recently completed fiscal year.

4) Options Programs: Provides partial support to arts presenters and schools which hire culturally diverse artists not on the current Vermont Council on the Arts (VCA) Touring or Art in Education rosters. Sponsors may request up to $100 a day for performances, workshops and residencies, up to $750 per year.

5) Touring Artists Program: Offers partial support to local non-profit sponsors, including schools and municipalities, for performances of artists who are on the VCA Artists Register.

Educational Funding:

1) Residency Program: Brings working professional artists, including architects, craftsmen, dancers, musicians, poets, writers, media, theater and visual artists into schools and other educational settings for residencies of a week to several months. Artists are paid a minimum of $160 per day, plus materials, mileage and hospitality, as negotiated with sponsor.

2) Development Grants: Supports projects that advance the goal of the arts becoming a basic part of education in Vermont public schools. Non-profit arts organizations, Vermont public schools, and professional organizations may apply.

3) Residency Grants for Sponsors: Provides support for schools and non-profit educational organizations which host residencies by practicing artists from the Vermont Council on the Arts Register.

Virginia

Virginia Commission for the Arts, Lewis House, 223 Governor St., Richmond, VA 23219-2010; (804) 225-3132. The Commission distributes grants to artists, arts and other non-profit organizations, educational institutions, educators, and local governments, as well as providing technical assistance in arts management. In 1990-91, $3,396,410 was awarded in grants to non-profit organizations. Individual artists were awarded $101,110 in fellowships.

Individual Artists Programs:

1) Project Grants: A limited number of non-matching grants of $5,000 each are available to professional artists to support projects that will advance their art form or careers. One arts discipline will be eligible for support each year on a rotating basis. Grants will be awarded to visual artists in 1992-93 and to poets and fiction writers in 1993-94.

2) Writers in Virginia: This grant program provides subsidy for readings and workshops by Virginia writers in a wide variety of settings. Funding is available up to 50% of the writer's fee, with a maximum of $250 available. Sponsors may receive a total of $500 in any year. Grants are awarded on a first-come, first-served basis.

Organizational Funding:

Maximum grants do not exceed more than 30% of an organization's income for the previous year. Most applicants receive much less than 30% of their income in Commission grants.

1) General Operating Support: Provides funding to non-profit arts organizations to maintain stability and encourage advancement. Eligible activities include general operating expenses, special projects, construction or renovation costs and reserve funds. Applicants may apply for 10% of their previous year's cash income for each year of the grant period, less Commission support and money raised for capital purposes in the previous year. Grants range from $500 to $150,000 per year.

2) Technical Assistance Grants: Non-matching grants provide outside help for organizations on particular problems. Organizations with annual incomes of $50,000 or more can apply for up to $1,000 in grants. Organizations with incomes of less than $50,000 can apply for up to $1,500 in grants.

3) Performing Arts Endowment Matching Program: This pilot program matches the interest earned by performing arts organizations on their endowment funds. It is open to organizations which produce music, opera, theater and dance and pay its performers professional-level salaries. Funds may either be used for performers' salaries or be placed in the principal of the endowment fund.

4) Local Government Challenge Grants: The competitive program will match up to $5,000 in tax monies given by independent town, city and county governments to arts organizations in their jurisdictions.

5) Touring Assistance Programs: This grant program supports touring by Virginia performing artists and arts organizations within the state. The Commission will fund up to 50% of the fee for any touring program listed in the Virginia Commission for Arts Tour Directory.

Educational Funding:

1) Artist-in-Education Residency Program: Places professional artists of various disciplines in residencies directed toward elementary and secondary students and their teachers. Generally, the Commission will award no more than 50% of the total cash cost of the residency program. First-time applicants, however, may request up to two-thirds of the total cash cost of the residency.

2) Community College Artist Residency Program: Places professional artists of a variety of disciplines in long-term residencies in community colleges of six to nine months. Eligible sponsors include Virginia Community Colleges. Any professional artist in the discipline selected each year may apply to be included on the roster of eligible artists. Funding is tied to current faculty salary levels.

3) Arts-in-Education Development Grants: This program is available to all Virginia public schools and private schools. The program promotes the planning and development of sequential arts instruction in schools that do not currently offer arts education in the curriculum. Up to 50 of a project's cash cost can be funded. Funding can be used for projects such as workshops, consultants, or in-service training.

4) Teacher Incentive Grant Program: Provides financial assistance, up to $300, to classroom teachers (pre-kindergarten through twelfth grade) to develop innovative ways of integrating the arts into the basic curriculum. The program is available to certified elementary and secondary classroom teachers, in any discipline, currently employed by Virginia educational institutions.

5) AIE Technical Assistance: Provides arts education associations, educators, arts administrators, etc., with opportunities for training, assistance, and services in the area of arts education. Grants of up to $1,000 are available for activities such as short-term consultancies by arts education specialists or attendance at arts education conferences or seminars.

Be patient. If any phone number is incorrect, call (area code) 555-1212 and request the new listing.

Arts and Humanities

Washington

Washington State Arts Commission, 110-9th and Columbia Bldg., MS-GH11, Olympia, WA 98504-2675; (206) 753-3860. The total budget for 1991-92 is $8,000,000.

Individual Artists Programs:

1) Artist Fellowship Awards: Awards of $5,000 are given to nine Washington practicing professional artists. Awards are made in the two-dimensional arts and literary arts in even-numbered years, and in the three-dimensional and performing arts (choreography, composition, and playwrighting) in odd-numbered years. The tenth fellowship is awarded in the media arts.

2) Governor's Arts Awards: Honors the state's outstanding artists, arts supporters and arts organizations.

3) Governor's Ethnic Heritage Awards: Honors individuals who have enhanced the state's cultures.

Organizational Funding:

1) Project Support Program: Provides smaller arts organizations an opportunity to apply for as much as $2,000 for short-term endeavors.

2) Organizational Support Program: Provides mid-sized arts organizations grants of up to $10,000. Funding is made in three categories:

A) Arts Organizations: This category includes arts producing, arts service and arts education organizations such as theater orchestras, museums, dance companies, professional arts schools, cultural heritage associations, media arts center, etc.

B) Arts Series Presenters: Rather than producing a single artistic event for their community, a "presenter" organizes, selects, and presents works by producing arts organizations and artists in a season, or series of events. A series presenter must sponsor three, or more, arts events during the year which are promoted as a series rather than as separate events.

C) Local Arts Agencies: Provides support to a non-profit local arts agency, arts council, arts commission or entity.

3) Institutional Support Program: Helps fund 19 of Washington's major music, dance, theater and visual arts organizations which annually bring some 2,500 artists before audiences of more than 2,000,000.

Educational Funding:

1) Cultural Enhancement Program (CEP): During the 1991-92 school year, CEP will bring approximately 50 performing artists and ensembles to most of the state's 296 school districts. CEP offers elementary and secondary schools performances in music, dance and drama. A school may hire an artist to do follow-up workshops for a class or school or apply for an AIR grant (see below).

2) Artists in Residence Program (AIR): In a typical year, 90 AIR artists and art critics will complete approximately 275 two-week residencies in schools, prisons, hospitals, community centers, and for special populations. Longer residencies of four weeks are also available. This is a cost-sharing (matching) program between the Commission and a sponsor. It is a competitive program, and successful applicants will receive a grant for 50% of the artist/scholar fees. A sponsor will spend approximately $608 per week per residency with an out-of-town artist/scholar and approximately $400 per residency week for an artist/scholar local to the site. The sponsor will also spend approximately $50 on artist's mileage and fees for the residency pre-planning meeting.

West Virginia

Department of Culture and History, Arts and Humanities Division, Capital Complex Cultural Center, Charleston, WV 25305; (304) 558-0220. In 1991-92, the Division awarded just over $1,000,000 in grants to non-profit arts organizations and individuals. The majority of programs offer award grants to local sponsors for a project involving an individual artist. Artists arrange the proposed project with a sponsor who then applies for the grant.

Individual Artists Programs:

The Division has just begun a pilot program for individual fellowships based on artistic merit. In 1991, $40,000 was awarded in the media arts. If this program proves successful, fellowships of $2,500 each will also be available in literature, music composition, crafts and the visual arts. At present, the following programs do not provide direct financial assistance to individual artists, they provide opportunities for sponsors to present artists in alternative ways. Artists are encouraged to contact potential sponsors about applying to present these programs.

1) Support for Artists Program: Designed to assist artists with professional development through exhibitions, performances, commissions and other projects.

2) West Virginia Artists List and Register: Contains a comprehensive listing of performing, visual and literary artists. Interested artists and organizations should call (304) 558-0220 for more information.

3) West Virginia Jured Exhibition: Is a biennial statewide exhibition for visual artists and craftsmen which provides direct awards to artists through competitive juring. Nationally recognized jurors select artists whose works receive purchase awards and merit awards totalling $33,000.

4) Presenting West Virginia Artists Program: Museums and galleries may select a West Virginia artist who has been accepted in a minimum of three jured exhibitions or who has documentation of significant professional accomplishment and present the artist in a one person exhibition. A maximum of $15,000 per exhibition is available for two projects each year.

5) Showcase of Visual Arts Program: Museums and galleries may request assistance to present a showcase exhibition of West Virginia artists who have been award winners in jured exhibitions or have documentation of significant professional accomplishment. Three to five artists, each of who agree to exhibit up to six recently created works, can be eligible. A maximum of $15,000 per exhibition is available for these projects.

Organizational Funding:

1) Major Institutions Support Grant Program (MIS): Supports and stabilizes existing non-profit organizations by providing financial assistance toward their overall programming budget. Organizations must have a minimum operating base of at least $500,000, been in existence for five years and serve a large audience that represents a broad cross-section of citizens. Up to $125,000 is available in funding.

2) Support for Arts Institutions/Arts Organizations: Performing arts institutions, galleries, museums and other arts organizations with boards of directors are eligible for this program. Funds may be used to support programming and exhibition costs. Maximum funding is $25,000.

3) Residencies for Performing Arts Organizations and Institutions: Open to organizations such as orchestras, chamber groups, dance groups and theater companies that include guest artists who are presented on their season of programs. Up to $10,000, or 50% of the contract fees for each artist, will be awarded.

4) Arts in the Community (AIC) assists public schools and communities with up to 50% ($1,000 maximum) of the contractual fees and expenses of West Virginia performing, literary, media, and visual arts. This program is designed for individual schools or communities that present a single arts event for the year. A maximum of $12,000 in bookings is available for each individual artist and $30,000 for each touring company in a fiscal year.

5) Touring Program: Enables sponsors to present performing, literary and visual artists or exhibitions in their communities and schools. Sponsors of national touring companies can request up to 50% of the contract fee involved.

6) Media Arts Projects: Supports media arts projects (film, video and audio) in the areas of artist's fees, production and post-production costs and presentation costs. Arts organizations may apply for 50% of the costs mentioned above, up to $10,000 per project. Non-matching grants up to $5,000 are available to individual artists.

7) Performing Arts: Includes competitive commissions of new works and support for new productions. Encourages the creation of new works by American composers, playwrights, writers and choreographers. Applicants are strongly encouraged to work with West Virginia artists. Organizations may request up to 50% of funding.

8) Travel Fund: Provides artists and arts administrators of all volunteer or professionally staffed arts organizations with financial assistance to attend professional events outside the state. Expenses up to $200 are funded.

9) Project 20/21: Encourages individual arts organizations and communities to develop long-range plans to strengthen and advance their administrative and technical development. Non-profit arts organizations, city or council governments or similar organizations are eligible to apply. Typically, grants are awarded for up to 50% of fees and expenses.

Educational Funding:

1) Arts in Education provides assistance with the planning and development of various projects involving schools and the community. Performances, demonstrations, artist residencies, teacher training and other innovative arts education projects are eligible for support. Artist in Residences projects range from a minimum of one week to one year.

Wisconsin

Wisconsin Arts Board, 131 W. Wilson St., Suite 301, Madison, WI 53703; (608) 266-0190. For most programs, recipients must match state awards with cash or donated services. In 1992-93, $3,561,571 was awarded to non-profit arts institutions. Individual fellowships of $5,000 each are awarded to ten artists per year.

Individual Artists Programs:

1) Fellowships: Awards of $5,000 each are granted in the following disciplines:

Be patient. If any phone number is incorrect, call (area code) 555-1212 and request the new listing.

State Money for the Arts and Artists

dance, music, opera/musical theater, theater, visual arts, design arts, crafts, photography, media arts, literature, interdisciplinary arts and folk arts.

2) New Work Awards: Funds the creation of new artistic works through awards of $3,500 each. In 1992-93, $52,500 was awarded under this category.

3) Development Grants: Provides awards of $1,000 each to support the artist's professional development.

4) Folk Art Apprenticeships: Provide funding for master artists to pass skills to apprentices.

Organizational Funding:

1) Artistic Program Support I: Promotes artistic quality, organizational and financial stability and long-range planning for producing arts organizations which have state-wide impact and budgets of $400,000 or more.

2) Artistic Program Support II: Supports same goals as above for organizations with budgets of $50,000 to $400,000. State and private universities may also apply to this category for specific project support.

3) Small Organization Support: Provides project funding of up to $3,000 to organizations with budgets of less than $50,000. Individual artists engaged in entrepreneurial activities may also be eligible.

4) Community Arts Program: Provides matching grants to local arts agencies and arts service organizations for community projects. The Arts Board will support up to 50% of the total expense of the project. Applicants must show at least one-half of the match as a cash contribution.

5) Performing Arts Network (PAN)-Wisconsin: Provides support to arts organizations that sponsor a series of four or more performances engaging professional touring artists.

6) Wisconsin Touring Program: Provides support for organizations to sponsor a performance by a Wisconsin professional touring artist.

7) Folk Arts Opportunity Grants: Supports projects that help preserve and present Wisconsin folklife culture. Generally, grants range from $1,000 to $5,000. Applicants must provide support that matches the Arts Board's funding.

8) Cultural Diversity Initiative: Provides funds to strengthen and stabilize cultural diverse arts organizations with annual budgets under $300,000, based in underserved communities.

9) Salary Assistance Grants: Provides partial support for new, permanent artistic or administrative personnel for non-profit arts organizations.

Educational Funding:

1) Artists-in-Education Residency: Provides funds to schools and community agencies to cover expenses of five-day to year-long artist residencies. Artists are selected form the AIE Artists Directory.

2) Educational Opportunity Grants: Supports funding for schools to use individuals listed in AIE Artists Directory to provide hands-on service for kindergarten through twelfth grade teacher training.

Wyoming

Wyoming Arts Council, 2320 Capitol Ave., Cheyenne, WY 82002; (307) 777-7742.

Individual Artists Programming:

1) Performing Arts: This program incorporates music, theater, dance, stage, light and costume design, mime, opera and many other disciplines. It includes the Performing Arts Fellowships, with up to four $2,500 awards given, Individual Artist grants and supports the block-booking efforts of Wyoming's presenters.

2) Visual Arts: Sponsors six exhibits annually in the Council gallery as well as the biennial fellowship exhibition with tours throughout the Rocky Mountain West. The program coordinates the Visual Arts Fellowships, which award up to four

$2,500 awards. It also provides specialized training opportunities, such as the 1991-92 Professional Development Series for visual artists and maintains a registry of over 400 Wyoming artists for review by galleries, corporations and other seeking commissioned works.

3) Literature: Offers support through fellowships and individual artist grants and brings nationally known writers to the state as well as sponsoring readings for Wyoming writers. Sponsors both the Literary Fellowship Program, with up to four $2,500 awards given, and the Blanchan/Doubleday Memorial Awards of $1,000 each.

Organizational Funding:

Wyoming's Community Service Program provides direct grants, training, technical assistance, and information to non-profit arts organizations. In 1991, the council awarded $232,411 to 80 groups in 19 of 23 counties. All grants requests must be matched a minimum of one-to-one with foundation, corporate or local cash funding. Generally, no more than 20% of an organizations' total cash expenses is awarded.

1) General Operating Support Grant: Covers the cost of administration and operation of the organization, as well as its artistic programming, excluding touring. Eligible organizations must have an annual budget greater than $100,000 and have at least one paid, full-time staff member.

2) Project Grants: Funds a specific, one-time arts project, event or a limited series of events. Projects may involve performing, visual, literary, media, folk or multi-disciplinary arts.

3) Touring: Presenting and Producing Grants: Supports organizations and presenting groups taking productions out of the local area and/or presenting events of regional, state and national interest.

4) Technical Assistance: Assists with program and board development or any area that may prove to be helpful in strengthening the organization. Maximum funding is 50% of the project's total cash expense.

Educational Funding:

Grants require a one-to-one cash match. In 1991, the Arts in Education Program granted $53,751 to communities, with 70 artists spending 1,829 days with students, educators and community members.

1) Art is Essential Grant: Encourages schools and organizations to plan for an entire year of arts in education. Applicants may apply at one deadline only for year-long projects, multiple projects or projects that occur yearly and require constant planning. Generally, no more than 30% of an organization's total cash budget is funded.

2) Artist-In-Residence Grants: Places professional artists in schools, institutions and communities for projects ranging from one week to one year. The Council sets a minimum artist fee of $100 per day for residences up to three weeks in length, and $1,600 per month for long-term residencies. Sponsors pay the artists' travel fees and per diem costs for the length of the residency.

3) Project Grants: Offers funding assistance to schools and organizations to strengthen their on-going curriculum or develop new curriculum with the assistance of roster artists and/or consultants.

4) Technical Assistance/Inservice Grants: Helps schools and organizations provide training for teachers and administrators. The program brings scholars and experts in to provide specific training and sends school or organization personnel to workshops and classes where they learn skills to train others.

5) Trailblazer Projects: Arts programs which demonstrate an exciting, replicable activity, as determined by the grants review panels, may receive a special Trailblazer award to provide additional funding to document the project. This additional funding does not require a match and is an option for the applicant to accept.

Be patient. If any phone number is incorrect, call (area code) 555-1212 and request the new listing.

Your Community Urban and Rural Resources

* *See also Auctions and Surplus Property Chapter*
* *See also Careers and Workplace Chapter*
* *See also Drugs and Chemical Dependence Chapter*
* *See also Education Chapter*
* *See also Government Financial Aid to Individuals Chapter*
* *See also Housing and Real Estate Chapter*

On nearly every page of this book there are numerous resources mentioned that can benefit your community. Non-profit and service organizations are eligible to apply for federal loans and grants which are intended for education, job training, housing and economic development. The most relevant money programs for cities and towns are identified in this chapter but others appear throughout this book. Regional offices which dot the country bring the resources and experts of the federal government closer as well. Also browse through the index and discover thousands of films and other audiovisuals which are available for community groups.

* Arson Prevention Traveling Exhibit

U. S. Fire Administration
Office of Fire Prevention and Arson Control
Federal Emergency Management Agency
16825 South Seton Ave.
Emmitsburg, MD 21727 (301) 447-1200

Arson Trailers tour the country to provide technical and educational assistance to State, local, and national fire service and community groups. Their public educations demonstrations include fire safety issues, local fire problems, and smoke detector usage and maintenance.

* Appalachian Communities Aid

Appalachian Regional Commission
News and Public Affairs
1666 Connecticut Avenue, NW
Room 624
Washington, DC 20235 (202) 673-7968

The Commission provides various grants and loans for economic, physical, and social development of the 13-state Appalachian region, which includes parts of Alabama, Georgia, Kentucky, Maryland, Mississippi, New York, North Carolina, Ohio, Pennsylvania, South Carolina, Tennessee, Virginia, and all of West Virginia. The Commission publishes the *Appalachian Regional Commission Annual Report* which provides financial statistics, activities and programs over the past year.

* County Cooperative Extension Service

Executive Officer
U.S. Department of Agriculture (USDA)
Room 340A Administration Building
Washington, DC 20250 (202) 720-0987

The USDA operates an extension program in 3,050 counties located in all of the 50 states and the U.S. territories. Federal, state, and local governments share in financing and conducting cooperative extension educational programs to help farmers, processors, handlers, farm families, communities, and consumers apply the results of food and agricultural research. The Extension Service has targeted 7 national initiatives to provide a new focus for educational efforts.

1) Improving Nutrition, Diet, and Health: Extension offers up-to-date information about the relationship of dietary practices to lifestyle factors; the safety, quality, and composition of foods; and consumers' needs and perceptions about the food industry.

2) International Marketing:

3) Revitalizing Rural America: In cooperation with local governments, Extension programs emphasize how to increase competitiveness and efficiency of rural programs, explore methods to diversify local economies and attract new business, adjust to impact of change, develop ways to finance and deliver services, and train leaders to make sound policy decisions for rural communities.

4) Substainable Agricultrue:

5) Waste Management:

6) Water Quality: Work with consumers, producers and local government to learn more about the importance of high-quality ground water and the conservation of water resources. Emphasis is also on the effects of agricultural chemicals and contaminants on water quality.

7) Youth at Risk: Extension is helping expand youth outreach resources to meet the needs of youth, develop programs for the most susceptible youth populations, provide leadership and job skills, and increase training of professionals and volunteers to work in communities to prevent and treat problems.

* Community and Rural Economic Development

Valley Resource Center
Resource Group
Tennessee Valley Authority
600 W. Summit Hill Dr.
Knoxville, TN 37902-2801 (615) 632-3215

The Valley Resource Center can be contacted for information on community and rural economic development programs.

* Community Health Services Grants

Bureau of Health Care Delivery and Assistance
Health Resources and Services Administration
5600 Fishers Lane, Room 7-05, Parklawn Bldg.
Rockville, MD 20857 (301) 443-2320
Publications (301) 443-1050

The Bureau of Health Care Delivery and Assistance Services focuses nationally on efforts to ensure the availability and delivery of health care services in health manpower shortage areas, to medically undeserved populations, and to special services populations, such as migrants or the homeless. The Bureau provides project grants to community-based organizations to meet the health needs of the undeserved or special needs populations.

* County Governments Environmental Activities

National Association of Counties (NACo)
440 1st St., NW
8th Floor
Washington, DC 20001 (202) 393-6226

Be patient. If any phone number is incorrect, call (area code) 555-1212 and request the new listing.

Urban and Rural Resources

NACo serves as a forum for improving the nation's county governments and to communicate the county viewpoint to national officials. NACo acts as a liaison with other levels of government, serves as a national advocate for counties, and achieves a public understanding of the role of counties in the intergovernmental system. *County News* is published bi-weekly, $75 a year.

* Dredging Permits

Regulatory Branch
U.S. Army Corps of Engineers
20 Massachusetts Ave., NW, Room 6235
Washington, DC 20314 (202) 272-0199

You must obtain a Corps permit if you plan to locate a structure, excavate, or discharge dredged or fill material in waters of the United States, including wetlands, or if you plan to transport dredged material for the purpose of dumping it into ocean waters. Contact the appropriate District Engineer office for current information and to apply for a permit. You may contact the above office for addresses and telephone numbers of the District offices.

* Economic Research Studies

Public Affairs
Economic Development Administration
U.S. Department of Commerce
14th St. and Constitution Ave., NW
Washington, DC 20230 (202) 377-5113

Economic Research Studies of the Economic Development Administration is an annotated bibliography listing economic research reports published by the Economic Development Administration. Each of the 210 entries includes an abstract and ordering information. The reports cover a broad range of topics and concentrate on the causes of economic distress and of economic growth, the basic remedy for distress. Contact EDA for your free copy.

* Election Assistance

Federal Election Commission (FEC)
Information Services
999 E Street, NW
Washington, DC 20463 (202) 219-3420

In an effort to promote voluntary compliance with the law, this office provides technical assistance to candidates and committees and others involved in elections. Staff will research and answer questions on the Federal Election Campaign Act and FEC regulations, procedures, and advisory opinions; direct workshops on the law; and publish a wide range of materials.

* Fair Lending Practices

Fair Lending Analyst
Office of Consumer Affairs
Federal Deposit Insurance Corporation (FDIC)
550 17th St., NW, Room F-130
Washington, DC 20429 (202) 898-3535

The Community Reinvestment Act of 1977 empowers the FDIC to monitor FDIC-insured, state-chartered banks to make sure that the banks are meeting the credit needs of the communities they serve, including low- and middle-income areas. Questions regarding community reinvestment should be directed to the nearest FDIC regional office or to the Fair Lending Analyst at the above office.

* Free Experts on Loan to Community Organizations

Pearson Program
Bureau of Personnel
U.S. Department of State
2101 C St NW, Room 2807
Washington, DC 20520 (202) 647-3308

The two objectives of this program are to allow State and local governments and related organizations to utilize the experience and expertise of Foreign Service Officers and to permit Foreign Service Officers to be assigned to positions with substantial program management responsibilities. Frequently officers are assigned to serve as special assistants to governors, mayors, city managers, and county commissioners. They have been assigned to a State department of social services, a regional local government innovation group, and to the Pan American Games organizing group. Interested organizations should discuss requests with the Office of Training and Liaison, and then submit a proposal. The U.S. Department of State will then attempt to identify an interested officer for the position.

* Free Food For Non-Profit Institutions

Food Distribution Division
Food and Nutrition Service
3101 Park Center Dr.
Room 503
Alexandria, VA 22302 (703) 305-2680

Charitable and rehabilitation institutions are usually eligible to receive surplus commodities stored by USDA. The commodities available are dairy products, grain oil, and peanuts.

* Geographic Names Information

Branch of Geographic Names
U.S. Geological Survey (USGS)
National Center, MS 523
Reston, VA 22092 (703) 648-4547

The USGS Branch of Geographic Names maintains a national research, coordinating, and information center to which all problems and inquiries concerning domestic geographic names can be directed. This office compiles name information, manages a names data repository, maintains information files, and publishes materials on domestic geographic names. The USGS, in cooperation with the Board on Geographic Names, maintains the *National Geographic Names Data Base* and compiles *The National Gazetteer of the United States of America* on a state-by-state basis.

* Health Services for Indigents

Bureau of Health Care Delivery and Assistance
Health Resources and Services Administration
5600 Fishers Lane
Room 7-05
Rockville, MD 20857 (301) 443-2320

The Bureau of Health Care Delivery and Assistance Services focuses nationally on efforts to ensure the availability and delivery of health care services in health manpower shortage areas, to medically underserved populations, and to special services populations, such as migrants or the homeless. It also administers the National Health Service Corps Program which recruits health care practitioners and places them in areas having shortages of people trained in health-related fields.

* Historic Places National Register

Interagency Resources Division
National Park Service
U.S. Department of the Interior
1100 L St., NW
Washington, DC 20005 (202) 343-9500

The National Register of Historic Places is administered by the Interagency Resources Division of NPS. Along with the Preservation Assistance Division, this office administers the Historic Preservation Fund grants-in-aid to states and the National Trust for Historic Preservation. Technical workshops and other assistance is provided on preservation planning, and a database of historic information is maintained.

* Local Environmental Health Managers

National Conference of Local
Environmental Health Administrators (NCLEHA)
Summit County Health Department
1100 Graham Circle
Cuyahoga Falls, OH 44224 (216) 923-4891

The National Conference of Local Environmental Health Administrators promotes efficient and effective local environmental health programs. NCLEHA is affiliated with the National Environmental Health Association.

* Local Government Environmental Activities

International City Managers Association (ICMA)
77 N. Capital, NE
Suite 500
Washington, DC 20002 (202) 289-4262

The purposes of ICMA are to enhance the quality of local government and to nurture and assist professional local government administrators in the U.S. and other countries.

Be patient. If any phone number is incorrect, call (area code) 555-1212 and request the new listing.

Your Community

* Mayors of Large Cities

U.S. Conference of Mayors
1620 I St., NW
4th Floor
Washington, DC 20006 (202) 293-7330

The United States Conference of Mayors is the official nonpartisan organization of cities with populations of 30,000 or more. It has taken the lead in calling national attention to the problems and the potential of urban America.

* Medical Services and Personnel Shortages Survey

National Clearinghouse for Primary Care Information
8201 Greensboro Dr., Suite 600
McLean, VA 22102 (703) 821-8955

This clearinghouse provides information services to support the planning, development, and delivery of ambulatory health care to urban and rural areas where shortages of medical personnel and services exist. Its primary audience is health care providers who work in community health centers. They have a list of publications and can make referrals to other health-related organizations. This clearinghouse also publishes a newsletter, *Primary Care Perspectives.*

* Military Base Closures: Community Adjustment

Office of Economic Adjustment
U.S. Department of Defense
The Pentagon, Room 4C767
Washington, DC 20301-4000 (703) 545-6700

The Office of Economic Adjustment assists local communities, areas or states affected by U.S. Department of Defense actions, such as base closures, establishment of new installations, and cutbacks or expansion of activities. It publishes a number of free publications on these issues, including *Communities in Transition, Economic Recovery,* and *Twenty-five Years of Civilian Re-use.* Write or call for more information.

* National Governor's Association

National Governor's Association (NGA)
444 North Capitol St., NW
Suite 250
Washington, DC 20001 (202) 624-5300

NGA serves as a vehicle through which governors influence the development and implementation of national policy and apply creative leadership to state problems.

* National League of Cities

National League of Cities (NLC)
1301 Pennsylvania Ave., NW
Suite 600
Washington, DC 20004 (202) 626-3000

NLC is dedicated to making cities efficient and improving the delivery of municipal services by providing answers to questions about the day-to-day realities of running a city or town including refuse collection, employment practices, police management, cable television, hazardous waste management and international trade.

* Non-Profits and Foreign Exchange Programs

Bureau of Education and Cultural Affairs
United States Information Agency (USIA)
301 Fourth St., SW, Room 216
Washington, DC 20547 (202) 619-4700

Grants and assistance are given to private non-profit organizations for exchange programs which further USIA goals of promoting mutual understanding between Americans and others. Any non-profit organization can submit proposals for partial funding.

* Place and Feature Names: State-by-State Dictionary

U.S. Geological Survey (USGS)
Books and Open File Reports
Box 25425, Federal Center
Denver, CO 80225 (303) 236-7476

The National Gazetteer of the United States of America is a geographic dictionary of place and feature names, published on a state-by-state basis. It includes a glossary of terms and abbreviations, a map of counties in a state, and an alphabetical listing of USGS topographic quadrangle maps of the state, in addition to the information contained in the *National Geographic Names Data Base.* Also listed are names of features from other historical sources. Variant names are listed and cross-referenced to their official names. A variant name is any other known name or spelling applied to a feature other than the official name. Also available at USGS, Branch of Distribution, P.O. Box 25286, Denver, CO 80225.

* Planned Approach to Community Health (PATCH)

Centers for Chronic Disease Prevention and Health Promotion
Centers for Disease Control
1600 Clifton Rd., NE
Bldg 3, Room 117
Atlanta, GA 30333 (404) 488-5401

CCDPHP staff work with State and local health departments and community members to organize local intervention programs. The center provides materials and technical assistance, and the communities invest their time and resources and make the program work. Programs have focused on cholesterol screening and nutrition, smoking cessation, alcohol misuse, and prevention of injuries from falls. The PATCH program also conducts international training conferences.

* Public Works Engineering

American Public Works Association (APWA)
1313 East 60th St.
Chicago, IL 60637 (312) 667-2200

The American Public Works Association consists of government officials, engineers, administrators and others engaged in the various aspects of public works and published *APWA Reporter* and *APWA Directory.*

* Resource Development

Resource Development
Tennessee Valley Authority (TVA)
P.O. Box 1010, Reservation Rd.
Muscle Shoals, AL 35660 (205) 386-2601

The TVA plans to fund several future development programs. These include the stewardship of TVA facilities and landholdings; the improvement of water resources; the development of the Land Between the Lakes to reach its potential as a national demonstration model; and the production of fertilizer technology that supports a profitable and competitive agriculture. Group economic and rural development programs will also be funded in the Valley Resource Center to expand the Valley's service sector, upgrade literacy and job skills, promote a competitive manufacturing section, and expand employment in natural resource-based industries.

* Rural Agricultural Processing Industries

Science and Education
Agricultural Research Service (ARS)
U.S. Department of Agriculture
Washington, DC 20250 (202) 720-5923

The ARS administers fundamental and applied research to solve problems in animal and plant protection and production; the conservation and improvement of soil, water and air; the processing, storage, and distribution of farm products; and human nutrition. The research applies to a wide range of goals, commodities, natural resources, fields of science and geographic, climatic, and environmental conditions.

Research activities are carried out at 138 domestic locations, including Puerto Rico, the Virgin Islands, and in 8 foreign countries. Much of this research is conducted in cooperation with State partners in the universities and experiment stations, other Federal agencies, and private organizations. A national program staff, headquartered at Beltsville, MD, is the focal point in the overall planning and coordination of the Service's national research programs. Day-to-day management of the various national research programs for specific field locations is assigned to 8 area offices.

* Rural Communities Clearinghouse

Rural Information Center
U.S. Department of Agriculture
10301 Baltimore Blvd., Room 304
Beltsville, MD 20705 (301) 504-5719

Be patient. If any phone number is incorrect, call (area code) 555-1212 and request the new listing.

Urban and Rural Resources

This center handles matters of economic competitiveness, economic development, local government, rural communities, community leadership, and natural resources. This center is a joint project of USDA's Extension Service and NAL.

* Rural Communities Financial Assistance

Farmers Home Administration (RDA)
U.S. Department of Agriculture
Washington, DC 20250 (202) 720-4323

RDA provides financial assistance to rural people and communities that cannot obtain commercial credit at affordable terms. Applicants must be unable to obtain credit from usual commercial sources. Examples of the types of loans available are Emergency Loans, Youth Project Loans, Housing Repair Loans and Grants, Business and Industry Loan Guarantees, Community Facilities Loans and Loan Guarantees, and Farm Operating Loans.

* State Legislatures Coordination

National Conference of State Legislatures (NCSL)
444 North Capitol St., NW
Suite 500
Washington, DC 20001 (202) 624-5400

NCSL is a national organization of state legislators and legislative staff whose aims are to improve the quality and effectiveness of state legislators, to ensure states a strong, cohesive voice in the federal decision-making process and to foster interstate communication and cooperation.

* Telecommunications and Computing Technology

Office of Technology Assessment
600 Pennsylvania Ave., SE
Washington, DC 20003 (202) 228-6760

Recent advances in information storage and transmission technologies, occurring in a new deregulated and intensely competitive economic climate, are rapidly changing the Nation's communication networks. OTA is studying the role of the Federal government in this area, along with how to coordinate them, resolve potential conflicts between them, and examine new communication systems abroad and their potential relationships to the U.S. systems. Contact Linda Garcia, the project director, for more information.

* Telecommunications Expertise for Libraries, Schools, Fire Departments

Public Telecommunications Facilities Program
National Telecommunications and Information Administration
U.S. Department of Commerce
14th St. and Constitution Ave., NW
Room 4625
Washington, DC 20230 (202) 377-5802

By identifying public service telecommunications needs, NTIA assists schools, hospitals, libraries, policy, fire departments, and government agencies in using advanced telecommunications systems and technology to achieve their goals.

* Towns and Townships Advocacy

National Association of Towns and Townships (NATT)
1522 K St., NW
Suite 600
Washington, DC 20005 (202) 737-5200

NATT is a federation of state organizations and individual communities which provide technical assistance, educational services and public policy support to local government officials of small communities across the country.

Be patient. If any phone number is incorrect, call (area code) 555-1212 and request the new listing.

Your Community

Neighborhood Improvements

* Aerial Photographs of Your Neighborhood

Customer User Services
Earth Resources Observation System Data Center (EROS)
U.S. Geological Survey
Mundt Federal Bldg.
Sioux Falls, SD 57198 (605) 594-6511

Aerial photographs are available from this center for most geographical regions of the country. Prices range from $6 to $65, depending on whether they are black and white or color photographs. Contact this office for ordering information.

* Afro-American and Minority Health Projects

Office of Minority Health
U.S. Department of Health and Human Services
200 Independence Ave., SW
Room 118F
Washington, DC 20201 (202) 245-0020

This office serves as the focal point for the implementation of the recommendations and findings from the Report of the Secretary's Task Force on Black and Minority Health. Community-based projects are being designed to reduce the more than 60,000 excess deaths each year among minority Americans. Major activities include conferences, grants for innovative community health strategies developed by minority coalitions, and research on risk factors affecting minority health. The Report may be obtained from Minority Health Resource Center, (301) 589-1938.

* Aircraft Noise

Noise Abatement Division
Office of Environment and Energy
Federal Aviation Administration
U.S. Department of Transportation
800 Independence Ave., SW, Room 432
Washington, DC 20591 (202) 267-3553

This FAA division conducts research on reducing noise levels of new aircraft, and retrofitting older aircraft to reduce noise levels.

* Air Force Bands

U.S. Air Force
Bands and Music Branch
The Pentagon, SAF/PAG
Washington, DC 20330-1000 (202) 767-5658

If there is an Air Force band stationed near you, you can request a public performance in your town. For information on where the bands are located and who to contact to schedule a performance, call the above coordinating office.

* Air Shows

Headquarters, U.S. Marine Corps
Community Relations
Washington, DC 20380-0001 (703) 614-1054

The Marine Corps can provide aviation demonstrations for community events. Contact your local Marine Corps headquarters or the above office for a referral.

* Anti-Drug Abuse Community Grants

Drug Abuse Prevention Oversight Staff
Office of the Secretary
U.S. Department of Education
400 Maryland Ave., SW, Room 1073
Washington, DC 20202-0100 (202) 401-1599

State and Local Grants Program: This is a formula grant program which allocates funds to States based on school-age enrollment. Funds are to be used for anti-drug abuse efforts in schools and community-based organizations. Contact Allen King, (202) 401-1599.

* Army Band and Chorus

Community Relations Division
U.S. Army Public Affairs
The Pentagon, Room 2E631
Washington, DC 20310 (703) 614-0739

To arrange for a performance in your community by the Army Field Band and Soldiers Chorus, the Golden Knights paratrooper unit, color guards, and other marching units, contact your nearest Army installation, or the above office for a referral.

* Army Paratroopers and Color Guards

Community Relations Division
U.S. Army Public Affairs
The Pentagon, Room 2E631
Washington, DC 20310 (703) 614-0739

To arrange for a performance in your community by the Golden Knights paratrooper unit, color guards, and other marching units, contact your nearest Army installation, or the above office for a referral.

* Army Reserve Band and Color Guard

Chief of U.S. Army Reserve
Public Affairs
Washington, DC 20310 (703) 696-3963

To request an Army Reserve band performance in your town, or to arrange for a color guard at a former military person's funeral, contact your local Army Reserve headquarters or the above office for a referral.

* Army Reserve Community Projects: Baseball to Language Training

Chief of U.S. Army Reserve
Public Affairs, The Pentagon
Washington, DC 20310 (703) 696-3962/3

The Army Reserve provides a variety of community services through their special programs. Requests are handled on a case by case basis based on their current ability to help. Projects might involve building a community playground or a baseball field. Through the Adopt-a-School Program, Corps people with special skills or training teach special courses, such as a foreign language or communications, or may be involved in extra-curricular activities. Contact your local Army Reserve.

* Art Exhibits: Parks, Plazas, Airports

Visual Arts Program
National Endowment for the Arts
1100 Pennsylvania Ave., NW, Room 729
Washington, DC 20506 (202) 682-5448

The Visual Arts Program awards fellowships to artists in a wide variety of visual media, enabling them to set aside time to pursue their work. It also awards grants to organizations that assist visual artists and support public art projects, such as art in parks, plazas, and airports. Funding is available for a variety of projects that enable visual artists to communicate with their peers and the public, and for a variety of on-going visual arts programs, including exhibitions and access to working facilities.

* Bank Loans and Community Reinvestment

Community Affairs Officer
Federal Reserve System
20th St. and Constitution Ave., NW
Washington, DC 20551 (202) 452-3000

The Community Reinvestment Act encourages banks and other institutions to help meet the credit needs for housing and other purposes in their communities. In accordance with this Act, the Community Affairs Officer and staff at each of

Be patient. If any phone number is incorrect, call (area code) 555-1212 and request the new listing.

Neighborhood Improvements

the 12 Federal Reserve Banks are responsible for advising depository institutions of private and public resources for community development. The officers also facilitate communications between borrowers, lending institutions, local government agencies, and others involved with community development financing. A pamphlet outlining the Community Reinvestment Act responsibilities of the Community Affairs Officers may be requested from the Federal Reserve Bank of Richmond, or the Community Affairs Officer at any Federal Reserve Bank.

* Cities in Schools: Truancy, Dropouts, Violence

Office of Juvenile Justice and Delinquency Prevention
U.S. Department of Justice
633 Indiana Ave., NW
Washington, DC 20531 (202) 307-0751

Cities in Schools, a public-private partnership that addresses the problems of dropouts and school violence, is designed to reduce school absenteeism and dropout rates by coordinating services for at-risk youngsters. Five regional offices help serve the 26 operating programs throughout the country and assist other local communities to initiate new Cities in Schools programs.

* Community Action Against Alcohol and Drug Addiction

National Clearinghouse on Alcohol and Drug Information
PO Box 2345
Rockville, MD 20847 (301) 468-2600

Communities: What You Can Do About Drug and Alcohol Abuse discusses various strategies for parent groups, schools, and workplaces and details various educational materials available. Single copies of this booklet (No.84-1310) are available free.

* Community Anti-Drug Alliance

ACTION
Drug Alliance Office
1100 Vermont Ave., NW, Suite 8200
Washington, DC 20525 (202) 606-4857

ACTION supports community-based prevention and education efforts with grants, contracts, conferences, and technical assistance. Nonprofit organizations and state and local governments are eligible to receive grants from ACTION. An announcement is made in the Federal Register regarding the type of activities that the ACTION grant is available for and organizations are encouraged to apply. ACTION also maintains a mailing list which sends copies of the notices appearing in the Federal Register directly to those on the list. To get the name of your organization on this list, call the number above.

* Community Business Development

Public Affairs
Economic Development Administration
U.S. Department of Commerce
14th St. and Constitution Ave., NW
Room 7810
Washington, DC 20230 (202) 377-5113

The Economic Development Administration provides loan guarantees to industrial and commercial firms, and technical assistance and grants to enable communities and firms to find solutions to problems that stifle economic growth. Contact this office for more information.

* Community Drug Abuse Situation

Information Systems Unit
Office of Diversion Control
Drug Enforcement Administration
U.S. Department of Justice
1405 Eye St. NW, Room 719
Washington, DC 20537 (202) 307-1000

For those who want to understand and evaluate the scope and magnitude of drug abuse in the United States, this network is an invaluable information source. Whether you are a local public administrator considering programs, a reporter on the heels of a story, or just a concerned parent, the Drug Abuse Warning Network can provide you with needed information. More than 900 hospital emergency rooms and medical examiner facilities supply data to the program. DAWN identifies drugs currently in vogue, determines existing patterns and profiles of abuse/abuser in Standard Metropolitan Statistical Areas, monitors systemwide abuse trends, detects new abuse entities and polydrug

combinations, and provides data needed for rational control and scheduling of drugs being abused. It is the full-information source on the drug problem in America.

* Community Involvement with Workplace Drug Abuse

National Audiovisual Center
Customer Service Section
8700 Edgeworth Drive
Capitol Heights, MD 20743-3701 (301) 763-1896

National Clearinghouse for Alcohol and Drug Information
P.O. Box 2345
Rockville, MD 20847 (301) 468-2600

Finding Solutions portrays drug abuse in the workplace as a community-wide problem; thus the solutions offered through education and prevention are presented as personal, workplace, and community responsibilities. Specific emphasis is placed on the need to effectively deliver accurate and credible information to the workforce, to promote workplace peer involvement and build community partnerships. It is available for sale and rental.

* Crime Insurance for Homeowners and Business

Federal Crime Insurance
P.O. Box 6301 (800) 638-8780
Rockville, MD 20849-6301 (301) 251-1660 in DC

The Federal Crime Insurance Program is a federally subsidized program sponsored by the Federal Emergency Management Administration for homeowners and commercial businesses to insure against burglary and robbery. To find out if your state is eligible and for further information, contact the office above. Those living in Maryland outside DC should call collect: (301) 251-1660.

* Ethnic or Racial Tensions Resolution

Community Relations Service (CRS)
U.S. Department of Justice
5550 Friendship Blvd., Suite 330
Chevy Chase, MD 20815 (301) 492-5929

If your community is being torn apart by ethnic disputes or police-citizen conflicts, you may need help from this special service, set up by the Civil Rights Act of 1964. The Community Relations Service exists to resolve such disputes. The agency provides direct conciliation and mediation assistance to communities to facilitate the peaceful, voluntary resolution of racial and ethnic disputes or conflicts, and the peaceful co-existence of police and citizens' groups in the rapidly changing neighborhoods of today's cities. The CRS regularly provides conferences, training workshops, and publications to any and all communities in an attempt to forestall such disputes. However, when tensions do break out, the CRS will initiate whatever steps are necessary to begin making progress toward bringing about a resolution. They normally begin with extensive informal discussions with public or police officials and local community leaders, but if the agency and the parties determine that formal negotiations offer the best hope for a settlement, the agency arranges and mediates the negotiations.

* Fire Prevention and Education

Office of Fire Prevention and Arson Control
U.S. Fire Administration
16825 South Seton Ave.
Emmitsburg, MD 21727 (301) 447-1122

For information on technical and educational assistance to State, local, and national fire services and community groups, contact the office above. Information on fire safety, residential sprinkler trailers and smoke detector usage and maintenance can be obtained from this office. Various forms of educational assistance (pamphlets, books, tapes) can be obtained. Call the office above to receive the following publications, and to find out how to receive the monthly newsletter, *Operation Life Safety.*

After the Fire: Returning (#5-0027)
America's Burning (#5-0025)
Check Your Hotspots Kit (#5-0101)
Home Fire Protection Fire Sprinkler (#5-0007)
It's Alarming (#5-0035) poster
Fire in the U.S. (#5-0135)
Organizing Your Community (#5-0068)
Public Fire Education Today (#5-0139)
Safety and Your Christmas Tree (#5-0029)

Be patient. If any phone number is incorrect, call (area code) 555-1212 and request the new listing.

Your Community

Smoke Detector and Fire Safety Guide (#5-0039)
Smoke Detector Kit (#5-0051)
Smoke Detectors: Don't Stay at Home (#5-0104)
U.S. Fire Administration Brochure (#5-0067)
Winter Fires (#5-0031)

* Fire Safety for Children

U.S. Fire Administration
16825 South Seton Ave.
Emmitsburg, MD 21727 (301) 447-1122

Contact the office above to obtain materials on fire safety for children. The following materials are available, in addition to Sesame Street education materials on fire safety education:

Adolescent Firesetter Handbook, ages 14 - 18 (#5-0091) FA-80
Child Firesetter Handbook, ages 7 - 13 (#5-0107) FA-82
Child Firesetter Handbook, ages 0 - 7 (#5-0106) FA-83
Curious Kids Kit (#5-0121) K-71
Juvenile Firesetter Handbook - Dealing with Children Ages 7-14 (FA-63)
Fire Safety Book (#5-0069) cass. (#5-0090)

* Free Christmas Trees

Division of Forestry
Bureau of Land Management (BLM)
U.S. Department of the Interior
1849 C. St., NW
Washington, DC 20240 (202) 208-5717

The BLM officials issue permits to cut Christmas trees for a nominal fee on Bureau of Land Management-administered lands in the 11 Western states and Alaska. Free-use permits are available from the Bureau to non-profit organizations for timber and trees to be used exclusively by that organization. This excludes the resale of any free timber or trees by those organizations.

* Historic Preservation Assistance

Preservation Assistance Division
National Park Service
U.S. Department of the Interior
1100 L St., NW
Washington, DC 20005 (202) 208-7394

The Preservation Assistance Division guides Federal and state agencies and the general public in historic preservation project work. Standards and guidelines are established, information on technical preservation is distributed, and training is given on technical preservation approaches and treatments. This office also administers the Preservation Tax Incentives program, the status of National Historic Landmarks, and the Historic Preservation Fund grant-in-aid program.

* Homeless, Migrants, Refugees: Health Services

Bureau of Health Care Delivery and Assistance
Health Resources and Services Administration
5600 Fishers Lane, Room 7-05
Rockville, MD 20857 (301) 443-2320

The Bureau of Health Care Delivery and Assistance Services focuses nationally on efforts to ensure the availability and delivery of health care services in health manpower shortage areas, to medically underserved populations, and to special services populations, such as migrants or the homeless. It also administers the National Health Service Corps Program which recruits health care practitioners and places them in areas having shortages of people trained in health-related fields.

* Job Creation Assistance

Technical Assistance Division
Economic Development Administration (EDA)
U.S. Department of Commerce
14th St. and Constitution Ave., NW
Washington, DC 20230 (202) 377-2127

The Technical Assistance Division of EDA sponsors programs of technical assistance to local communities which are designed to discover new ways to generate jobs. Local governments, non-profit organizations, and private firms can apply. Contact this office for more information.

* Marine Corps Air Show

Commandant of the Marine Corps (OLAC)
Headquarters Marine Corps, Community Relations
Washington, DC 20380 (703) 614-1034

Watch the AV8 Harrier jump jet (it shoots straight up and turns around in mid-air), the Drum and Bugle Corps, and Marine bands perform. You may write to the above address or your nearest Corp installation for their brochure explaining Marine Corps programs and how to complete the forms to arrange for these units' performance in your community. They can also provide you with a patriotic speaker for Veterans Day and Memorial Day events.

* Marine Corps Bands and Color Guards

Headquarters, U.S. Marine Corps
Code P.A.C.
Washington, DC 20380 (703) 614-1034

The Marine Corps can provide bands and color guards for community events. The Corps supports the Devil Pup program. Contact your local Marine Corps headquarters or the above office for a referral.

* Marine Corps Summer Camp

Headquarters, U.S. Marine Corps
Code P.A.C.
Washington, DC 20380-0001 (703) 614-1034

The Marine Corps sponsor a summer camp for high school youth. Contact your local Marine Corps headquarters or the above office for a referral.

* National Guard Community Participation

National Guard Bureau
Attn: NGB-PAC
Skyline #6
5109 Leesburg Pike, Suite 4013
Falls Church, VA 22041-3201 (703) 756-1923

Local National Guard units provide bands, color guards, and flight demonstrations for community events upon request of civic groups. The Guard also sponsors annual open houses and conducts tours of the local bases. A Speakers Bureau will provide experts to speak on defense and local issues, and the Guard sponsors orientation trips for civic leaders. Call or write for more information on the Guard's varied community assistance programs, including the loan of equipment to civic groups.

* Navy Bands and Concerts

U.S. Navy Band
Public Affairs Office
Washington Navy Yard
Washington, DC 20374-5054 (202) 433-2394

The U.S. Navy Concert Band and its specialty units--including the Topside Quartet (jazz, rock), Brass Navy Band, Saxaphone Quartet, Fairwinds Quartet (vocal), Windjammers, Tuba-Euphonium Quartet, Sea Chanters, Country Current, and the Commodores--are available to perform at community events nationwide. Units of the band perform a wide range of musical styles, from jazz, folk, and blue grass to classical chamber and cocktail music. Write or call for information on how to request the Band.

* Neighborhood Crime Comparison Information

Uniform Crime Reporting Section
Federal Bureau of Investigation
U.S. Department of Justice
9th and Pennsylvania Ave., NW, GRB
Washington, DC 20535 (202) 324-5015

If you'd like to know how safe your prospective new neighborhood is, contact the Uniform Crime Reporting Section. This annual report, *Crime In the United States* contains an exact reading of the crime rates of any city in America (down to the types of crimes committed most frequently in which neighborhoods). Also, local police departments of most major cities have neighborhood crime reports available and will actually rate the safety factor of your new address for you.

* Neighborhood Safety Videos and Publications

National Institute of Justice (NIJ)
NCJRS, Box 6000

Neighborhood Improvements

Dept. AID (800) 851-3420
Rockville, MD 20850 (301) 251-5500 in DC

NIJ has these and other publications and videos on crime prevention and the law. Many of the documents are free of charge, while others are available for a modest fee. When ordering or inquiring about an NIJ publication, refer to its NCJ number.

Crime Stoppers: A National Evaluation (RIB). 1986, 5 pp. (NCJ 102292).
The Growing Role of Private Security (RIB). 1984, 5 pp. (NCJ 94703).
Guardian Angels: An Assessment of Citizen Response to Crime: Executive Summary. 1986, 31 pp. (NCJ 1009111).
Improving the Use and Effectiveness of Neighborhood Watch Programs (RIA). 1988, 4 pp. (NCJ 108618).
Neighborhood Safety (Crime file videotape). 1985 (NCJ 97227). VHS, Beta, or 3/4-inch.
Taking a Bite Out of Crime: The Impact of a Mass Media Crime Prevention Campaign. 1984, 78 pp. (NCJ 93350). N.C.P. Council (202) 466-6272

* Neighborhood Watch Programs

Office of Crime Prevention
National Institute of Justice
U.S. Department of Justice
633 Indiana Ave. NW
Washington, DC 20531 (202) 307-2942

If you're interested in starting a Neighborhood Watch Program in your town, or want to know how you can make yours better, contact the Neighborhood Watch Specialists at the National Institute of Justice. They will be glad to help you make your neighborhood a safer place.

* Recycling Efforts

Public Information Center
Environmental Protection Agency
401 M St., SW, PM-211 B
Washington DC 20460 (202) 260-2080

Recycling Works! is a free booklet that provides information about successful recycling programs initiated by state and local agencies. It also describes private recycling efforts and joint recycling ventures of government and businesses. Publications are available through Resource Conservation and Recovery Act, (202) 260-9327.

* Residential Fire Sprinklers

Federal Emergency Management Agency (FEMA)
16825 South Seton Ave.
Emmitsburg, MD 21727 (301) 447-1021

Through its regional offices, FEMA conducts demonstrations of how residential fire sprinklers operate. Contact your regional FEMA office or the office above for more information.

* Telecommunications Expertise for Libraries, Schools, Fire Departments

Public Telecommunications Facilities Program
National Telecommunications and
Information Administration (NTIA)
U.S. Department of Commerce
14th St. and Constitution Ave., NW
Room 4625
Washington, DC 20230 (202) 377-5802

By identifying public service telecommunications needs, NTIA assists schools, hospitals, libraries, policy, fire departments, and government agencies in using advanced telecommunications systems and technology to achieve their goals.

* Toys for Tots

Commanding General (PAO)
4th Marine Division (Rein.), FMF
U.S. Marine Corps Reserve
4400 Dauphine St.
New Orleans, LA 70146-5400 (504) 948-1457

The Marine Corps Reserve sponsors an annual Christmas "Toys for Tots" project, which collects toys for needy children. To learn how to donate or provide a collection point at your place of business, contact your local Marine Corps Reserve office or the above office for more information.

* Waste Management Policy

Association of Metropolitan Sewerage Agencies (AMSA)
1000 Connecticut Ave., NW
Suite 1006
Washington, DC 20036 (202) 833-2672

The Association of Metropolitan Sewerage Agencies consists of sewerage agencies in areas with more than 250,000 people. It serves to exchange technical data and deals with the federal government on environmental and regulatory matters.

* Woodsy Owl: Litter Cleanup

U.S. Department of Agriculture
Forest Service
P.O. Box 96090
Washington, DC 20090-6090 (202) 205-1760

To increase children's awareness of our delicate environment, the Forest Service's Woodsy Owl campaign has a variety of free materials available, including coloring sheets, detective sheets, song sheets, patches, *Woodsy Owl on Camping* (brochure), and stickers. A Woodsy Owl costume is available to some community groups to compliment "Give A Hoot! Don't Pollute" campaign.

Be patient. If any phone number is incorrect, call (area code) 555-1212 and request the new listing.

Your Community

Traffic and Transportation

* Commuter and Air Taxi Services

Commuter and Air Taxi Branch
Transportation Division
Office of Federal Aviation Administration
800 Independence Ave., SW, Room 303
Washington, DC 20591 (202) 267-8086

Contact this office for information regarding policy, regulations, and directives for commuter and air taxi aircraft. A list is available of air taxi operators and commercial operators of small aircraft. This list available in Oklahoma City through F.V.N., (405) 680-4391.

* Essential Air Passenger Service

Aviation Analysis
U.S. Department of Transportation
400 7th St., SW, Room 6401
Washington, DC 20591 (202) 366-5903

This office guarantees that certain cities will be served by airlines. It also represents community views. Contact this office for more information on airport service.

* Funded Traffic Safety Projects

Evaluation Staff (NTS-31)
Traffic Safety Programs
National Highway Traffic Safety Administration
U.S. Department of Transportation
400 7th Street, SW
Washington, DC 20590 (202) 366-2759

Once known as the National Project Reporting System, funded project information collected by this office from each state is stored in a database. Projects are funded in areas such as occupant safety and alcohol. Findings are assembled annually in a published report providing an overview of the projects, their status, and how funding is apportioned, such as amounts to each project and within each project, amount to education, to enforcement, and to other areas. Contact the Evaluation Staff for details.

* Handicapped Assistance and Mass Transit

Office of Research, Training, and Rural Transportation
Urban Mass Transit Administration
400 7th St., SW, Room 6102
Washington, DC 20590 (202) 366-4995

UMTA is involved in a Congressionally-mandated project with the National Easter Seals Committee to study accessibility problems faced by the handicapped who use mass transit. The office runs a series of demonstrations on improved arrangements to help the handicapped.

* Highway Safety Accident Prevention

Office of Highway Safety (HHS-21)
Associate Administrator for Safety and Operations
Federal Highway Administration
U.S. Department of Transportation
400 7th St., SW
Washington, DC 20590 (202) 366-1153

Highway construction safety programs are funded to remove, relocate, or shield roadside obstacles; to identify and correct hazards at railroad crossings; and to improve signing, pavement markings, and signalization. For information and referral, contact the Office of Highway Safety. The following publications are also available:

Highway Safety Improvement Programs, Annual Report.
Status Report of Federal Funds Used for Highway Safety Programs.

Several other reports prepared by this office are available from National Technical Information Service, 5285 Port Royal Road, Springfield, VA 22161;

(703) 487-4650. A sampling of titles follows:

Inexpensive Accident Countermeasures at Narrow Bridges
Legibility and Driver Response to Selected Lane and Road Closure Barricades
Rollover Potential of Vehicles on Embankments, Sideslopes, and Other Roadside Features; Final Report
Constant Warning Time Devices for Railroad-Highway Crossings: Technical Summary
Studies of the Road Marking Code

* Highway Traffic Safety Records

U.S. Department of Transportation
National Highway Traffic Safety Administration (NHTSA)
Technical Reference Division (NAD-52)
Office of Administrative Operations
400 7th Street, SW
Washington, DC 20590 (202) 366-2768

NHTSA reports and records are available for public inspection at this location, and database searches can be requested for a fee. Holdings include vehicle research and test reports; investigation reports on accidents and defects; recall information; compliance reports; consumer complaints; consumer advisories; filmed records of research and tests; NHTSA *Technical Reports*; engineering specifications; and certification information. Both light and heavy highway vehicles are covered. Call ahead to ensure that the records you need will be on hand.

* Mass Transit Program Evaluation

Program Evaluation Division
Federal Transit Administration (FTA)
U.S. Department of Transportation
400 7th St., SW, Room 9306
Washington, DC 20590 (202) 366-1727

This office can provide you with information on its recent and on-going evaluations of projects and programs implemented by FTA. For information on earlier evaluations regarding bus, subway, and other modes of urban transit.

* Maximum Speed Limit

U.S. Department of Transportation
National Highway Traffic Safety Administration,
Police Traffic Services Division
Office of Enforcement and Emergency Services
Traffic Safety Programs
400 7th Street, SW, Room 5119
Washington, DC 20590 (202) 366-5440

The National Maximum Speed Limit is 65 miles per hour on certain interstate highways. This office processes annual certifications of maximum speed limit enforcement programs throughout the U.S. and assists states in developing and improving enforcement efforts.

* National Driver Register

National Driver Register (NTS-24)
Traffic Safety Programs
National Highway Traffic Safety Administration
U.S. Department of Transportation
400 7th Street, SW, Room 6124
Washington, DC 20590 (202) 366-4800

The *National Driver Register* is a central, computerized index of state records on drivers whose operator licenses have been revoked, denied, or suspended for more than 6 months. Data includes name, birthdate, height, weight, eye color, date and reason for action, and date of reinstatement. Applications for driver licenses are routinely checked against the register, and states exchange information via an electronic system.

Be patient. If any phone number is incorrect, call (area code) 555-1212 and request the new listing.

Traffic and Transportation

* Occupants Displaced by Highway Construction

Office of Right-of-Way (HRW-22)
Office of Right-of-Way and Environment
Federal Highway Administration (FHWA)
U.S. Department of Transportation
400 7th St., SW, Room 3219
Washington, DC 20590 (202) 366-0342

This office administers FHWA's lead role in implementing the Uniform Relocation Assistance and Real Property Acquisition Policies Act. When Federally funded highway construction projects involve displacing residents from acquired property, this Act sets policies for purchase of the land and relocating the people on it. The publication, *Your Rights and Benefits as Displaced Under the Federal Relocation Assistance Program,* is available from this office.

* Pedestrian and Driver Research

Office of Program Development and Evaluation (NTS-30)
National Highway Traffic Safety Administration
U.S. Department of Transportation
400 7th Street, SW, Room 6240
Washington, DC 20590 (202) 366-9591

This office studies factors affecting the safety of drivers and pedestrians. Research areas include determining the causes of unsafe driving and developing countermeasures; the effectiveness of vehicle occupant safety restraints; the effect of alcohol and drugs; the safety concerns of bicycles, motorcycles, and mopeds; driver license standards; and young drivers. This office can refer you to staff researching the topic of your interest.

* Pedestrian Safety

Geometric and Roadside Design Branch
Engineering Division
Office of Engineering Program Development
Federal Highway Administration
U.S. Department of Transportation
400 7th St., SW, Room 3128
Washington, DC 20590 (202) 366-1315

Highway design and roadside facilities are studied by this office to determine their impact on pedestrians and bicyclists. The publication, *Pedestrian and Bicycle Facilities* provides you with information about the roadside designs and structures used in safety-related applications.

* Private Sector Initiatives in Mass Transit

Office of Private Sector Initiatives
Office of Budget and Policy
Federal Transit Administration
U.S. Department of Transportation
400 7th St., SW, Room 9300
Washington, DC 20590 (202) 366-1666

This office encourages private sector involvement in mass transit throughout the United States. Specifically, they work through the following four areas:

1) Competitive Contracting: Local transit authorities are encouraged to open the provisioning of services up to private sector competition.

2) Entrepreneurial Services: Groups in the private sector are encouraged to start self-sustaining transit services (such as taxi and bus) in cooperation with local transit authorities.

3) Joint Development: Federal assistance is available to help plan public/private sector joint ventures at transit facilities.

4) Demand Management Program: Federal funds are available to encourage local employers and merchants to develop techniques to help manage transportation and mobility problems in their areas.

* Public Private Transportation Network (PPTN)

8737 Colesville Rd, Suite 1100
Silver Spring, MD 20910 (800) 522-7786

The *Transis Information Exchange* is a free technical assistance program sponsored by the Federal Transit Administration. PPTN assists public transit agencies, private transit operators, federal, state, and local officials, and others seeking guidance on transportation issues, especially concerning identification and fostering of public/private partnerships. Assistance includes site visits by a

network of industry professionals; speakers and facilitators for seminars, conferences, and workshops; and a library of technical assistance materials.

* Road Signs

Traffic Control Development Applications
Division (HTO-21)
Traffic Operations Division
Office of Safety and Operations
Federal Highway Administration
U.S. Department of Transportation
400 7th St., SW, Room 3419
Washington, DC 20590 (202) 366-2184

Efforts by this division improve the effectiveness and uniformity of such traffic control devices as road signs, signal lamps, and highway markings throughout the country. Standards are developed for designing signs and using other traffic control devices. The meanings of road signs and markings are described in *Road Symbol Signs,* which can be obtained by contacting the office listed above. Two other publications on the subject, listed below, are available from the Superintendent of Documents, U.S. Government Printing Office, Washington, DC 20402; (202) 783-3238: *Manual on Uniform Traffic Control Devices,* ($22) *Standard Highway Signs Book,* ($30).

* Roadway Beautification

Special Programs and Evaluation Branch (HRW-12)
Program Requirements Division
Office of Right-of-Way and Environment
Federal Highway Administration
U.S. Department of Transportation
400 7th St., SW, Room 3221
Washington, DC 20590 (202) 366-2017

Junkyards and outdoor advertising along federally aided and interstate highways are regulated under a program conducted through this office. The publication, *Junkyards, the Highway, and Visual Quality,* offers information on this program. To obtain a copy, or to request further details on highway beautification programs, contact the branch listed.

* Traffic Accident Data

Information Management and Anaylsis Branch
Office of Highway Safety
Federal Highway Administration
U.S. Department of Transportation
400 7th St., SW, Room 3407
Washington, DC 20590 (202) 366-2159

Statistics are kept here on fatal and injury accident rates for the Nation's highways. An extensive list of publications related to accidents and highway safety is also maintained. Call or write this office to request the data you need.

* Urban Mass Transportation Research

Manager, UMTRIS
Transportation Research Board
National Research Council
PO Box 289
Washington, DC 20055 (202) 334-3214

The Urban Mass Transportation Research Information Service is a computerized database on worldwide transportation research. Administered by the Transportation Research Board (TRB), it covers all phases of conventional, new, and automated public transportation. UMTRIS features database storage/ retrieval of abstracts of technical papers, journal articles, research reports, computer program descriptions, and statistical sources, as well as state-of-the-art bibliographies. Descriptions of ongoing research, especially that sponsored by UMTA, are also included. UMTRIS offers the public nearly 20,000 information references to ongoing and completed research activities, and adds 2,000 new references annually to the database. In addition to serving as the central source of technical information to the public and private sectors, UMTRIS also serves as an institutional memory for UMTA projects and project reports. The database can be searched online by any computer with a modem through DIALOG Information Services File 63. UMTRIS is supported by a National Network of Transportation Libraries (18), and they serve both as repositories that house and make UMTA documents available to the general public, as well as document delivery centers that provide UMTRIS users with full text copies of citations retrieved from the database.

Be patient. If any phone number is incorrect, call (area code) 555-1212 and request the new listing.

Your Community

Fires, Floods, and Disaster Relief

* Arson Control and Clearinghouse

U.S. Fire Administration
Federal Emergency Management Agency (FEMA)
16825 South Seton Ave.
Emmitsburg, MD 21727 (301) 447-1122

The Arson Resource Center is available to help answer your questions and locate resources related to arson. It was established several years ago by the U.S. Fire Administration, and has developed an impressive collection of arson-related materials. FEMA personnel and NETC students can borrow materials from the Center, and books and research reports are available to the general public through area libraries (interlibrary loan). Audio-visual and general references are stored in the Center for in-house use. The following publications and source materials on arson are available from the USFA free of charge:

Arson Victims: Suggestions (#5-0034)
Arson Resource Directory (#5-0087)
Arson Prosecution Issues (#5-0086)
Rural Arson Control (#5-0110)
Establishing an Arson Strike Force (#5-0111)

* Bomb Shelters Designs

Federal Emergency Management Agency (FEMA)
P.O. Box 70274
Washington, DC 20024 (202) 646-3484

The following free publications will show you the ins and outs of bomb shelters and their construction:

Shelters in New Homes (TR-60). Shows how any home builder or owner can provide an area that protects against fallout radiation and windstorm without sacrificing its day-to-day usefulness. It includes examples of multi-purpose areas, shelter designs and details, and radiation shielding principles.

Cost Benefits in Shelters (TR-69). Explores various areas of cost savings resulting from the incorporation of basic fallout shelter design techniques in new buildings.

Home Fallout Shelter--Snack Bar--Basement Location Plan D (H-12D). A snack bar built of brick and concrete block can be converted into shelter.

Home Fallout Shelter: Outside Concrete Shelter (H-12-1).
Home Fallout Shelter: Aboveground Home Shelter (H-12-2).
Home Blast Shelter: Underground Concrete Shelter (H-12-3).
Technical Standards for Fallout Shelter Designs (TM 72-1). Shows the technical architectural and environmental standards for fallout shelter design.

* Dam Safety and Hazards

Federal Emergency Management Agency (FEMA)
P.O. Box 70274
Washington, DC 20024 (202) 646-3484

The following publications are available from the office above and contain information on dam safety:

Civil Preparedness Guide: National Dam Safety Program for S & L (CPG 1-39) #8-0709
Dam Safety: An Owner's Guidance Manual (FEMA 145) #8-0648
Dam Safety: Know the Potential Hazard (L-152) #8-0607
Federal Guidelines for Dam Safety (FEMA-93) #8-0047
Financial Assistance Guidelines (CPG 1-32) #8-0404
Glossary of Terms for Dam Safety (FEMA-148) #8-0676

* Disaster Relief Grants and Loans

Federal Emergency Management Agency (FEMA)
P.O. Box 70274
Washington, DC 20024 (202) 646-3484

The following free publications will help you through the application process for Federal disaster relief grants and loans:

Handbook for Applicants (DR&R-1) #8-0056. Prescribes policy and procedures for requesting, obtaining, and administering FEMA grants for public assistance under the Disaster Relief Act of 1974.

Community Disaster Loan Handbook (DAP-5). For local governments and state and federal officials outlying FEMA Community Disaster Loan Program.

Financial Assistance Guidelines (CPG 1-32) #8-0404.

* Disaster Relief and Recovery Help

Federal Emergency Management Agency (FEMA)
P.O. Box 70274
Washington, DC 20024 (202) 646-3484

The *Digest of Federal Assistance Programs* (DAP-21) #8-0729, is designed to serve as an initial source of information for private citizens and public officials who need disaster assistance. It is a compendium of Federal programs specifically designed to supplement State and local relief and recovery efforts, as well as programs that may serve to lessen the effects of civil disasters or emergencies. It includes programs that either require a Presidential declaration of a major disaster or emergency and those which do not.

* Earthquakes and Small Businesses

Federal Emergency Management Agency (FEMA)
P.O. Box 70247
Washington, DC 20024 (202) 646-3484

Guidelines for Local Small Businesses in Meeting the Earthquake Threat is a booklet designed to help small businesses prepare for and respond to a catastrophic earthquake. It contains information on assessing earthquake risks and provides a planning framework for preparation, response, and long-term recovery for a small business. (FEMA-87) #8-0500

* Earthquake Hazard Reduction Program

Federal Emergency Management Agency (FEMA)
P.O. Box 70274
Washington, DC 20024 (202) 646-3484

The publication, *National Earthquake Hazard Reduction Program Five Year Plan*, presents an overview of FY 1985-89 program plans for the National Earthquake Hazard Reduction Program (NEHRP). It emphasizes the goals, objectives, and funding requirements for each of the participating major program elements. It also provides a comprehensive and coherent presentation of the activities projected by each participating agency for 5 fiscal years. It is available from the office above.

* Earthquake Safety Checklist

Federal Emergency Management Agency (FEMA)
P.O. Box 70274
Washington, DC 20024 (202) 646-3484

The following publications provide information on earthquake preparedness and safety:

Family Earthquake Safety Home Hazard Hunt and Drill (FEMA-113) #8-0871. Discusses how to identify and correct hazards in the home and practice what to do if an earthquake occurs.

Coping With Children's Reactions to Earthquakes and Other Disasters (FEMA-48) #8-0750. Deals with children's fears and anxieties following a disaster. In Spanish (FEMA-184) #8-0849

Earthquake Safety Checklist (FEMA-46) #8-0820. Safety tips for preparation, response to, and immediate aftermath of an earthquake.

Earthquakes (L-111) #8-0821. Offers safety tips for potential victims of earthquakes.

* Emergency and Fire Professionals Protection

Federal Emergency Management Agency (FEMA)
P.O. Box 700274

Be patient. If any phone number is incorrect, call (area code) 555-1212 and request the new listing.

Fires, Floods, and Disaster Relief

Washington, DC 20024 (202) 646-3484

The *U.S. Fire Administration Brochure* (L-160) #5-0067, describes the programs offered by the U.S. Fire Administration, including those that help fire service professionals manage fire data that gets the public involved, educates fire and emergency professionals, helps protect firefighters, promotes life-saving technology.

* Emergency Broadcast System

Federal Emergency Management Agency (FEMA)
P.O. Box 70274
Washington, DC 20024 (202) 646-3484

The leaflet, *Emergency Broadcast System* (L-93), cites the EBS as a method of communicating with the American public in the event of war, threat of war, or grave national crisis.

* Emergency Education Network

Emergency Education Network (EENET)
National Emergency Training Center
16825 South Seton Ave.
Emmitsburg, MD 21727 (301) 447-1068

EENET is owned and operated by FEMA to provide State and local emergency management personnel with quality education and training. Several shows per year are produced to be shown to live audiences via satellite or by cable. Contact the office above for further information.

* Emergency Management Institute

Emergency Management Institute
National Emergency Training Center
16825 South Seton Ave,
Emmitsburg, MD 21727 (301) 447-6771

This Institute provides courses on several different topics in emergency management and civil defense. For more information on these courses, contact the office above.

* Emergency Management Materials

Federal Emergency Management Agency (FEMA)
P.O. Box 70274
Washington, DC 20024 (202) 646-3484

Publications on emergency management which are available from the above office are listed below:

Emergency Management in Public Administration Education (FEMA-106) #6-0009
Emergency Management, USA (HS-2) #6-0141
In Time of Emergency - A Citizen's Handbook on Emergency Management (H-14) #8-0819
This is The Federal Emergency Management Agency #0-0058

* Emergency Medical Services

Federal Emergency Management Agency (FEMA)
P.O. Box 70274
Washington, DC 20024 (202) 646-3484

Introduction to Emergency Medical Services (SM 220) is a student manual which includes lectures, discussions, slide/tape presentations, case studies, and an optional workshop. Lessons cover topics on the historical perspective, system design, resources, medical control, EMS councils, legal and medical issues, communications, and mutual aid.

* Emergency Planning Educational Teleconferences

U.S. Fire Administration
Federal Emergency Management Agency (FEMA)
16825 South Seton Ave.
Emmitsburg, MD 21727 (301) 447-1122

FEMA holds an annual series of educational teleconferences for fire service and emergency management audiences on such topics as stress management, public affairs, residential sprinklers, flammable gases and liquids, AIDS, and radiation transportation accidents, and hazardous materials training. Copies of previous 52 shows are available for a charge, or could be borrowed from the State Emergency Management Offices, or one of the 10 FEMA Regional Offices.

* Emergency Plans for Acutely Toxic Chemicals

Emergency Planning and Community
Right to Know
U.S. Environmental Protection Agency (EPA)
401 M St., SW (800) 535-0202
Washington, DC 20460 (703) 920-9877

This EPA hotline provides communities with help in preparing for accidental releases of toxic chemicals. Communities can call to obtain interim guidelines regarding *Acutely Toxic Chemicals*. These guidelines cover Organizing a Community, Developing a Chemical Contingency Plan, and gathering site-specific information. The hotline also provides a list of more than 400 acutely toxic chemicals.

* Emergency Preparedness Offices Nationwide

The Federal Emergency Management Administration (FEMA) has regional offices throughout the country.

Region I
FEMA, J.W. McCormack Post Office and Courthouse Building, Room 442, Boston, MA 02109; (617) 223-9540. Serving: Connecticut, Maine, Massachusetts, New Hampshire, Rhode Island, and Vermont.

Region II
FEMA, 26 Federal Plaza, Room 1338, New York, NY 10278. Serving: New Jersey, New York, Puerto Rico, and Virgin Islands.

Region III
FEMA, Liberty Square Building (Second Floor), 105 South Seventh St., Philadelphia, PA 19106; (215) 931-5500. Serving: Delaware, District of Columbia, Maryland, Pennsylvania, Virginia, and West Virginia.

Region IV
FEMA, 1371 Peachtree Street, NE, Suite 700, Atlanta, GA 30309; (404) 853-4200. Serving: Alabama, Florida, Georgia, Kentucky, Mississippi, North Carolina, South Carolina, and Tennessee.

Region V
FEMA, 175 Jackson Blvd, 4th Floor, Chicago, IL 60604; (312) 408-5500. Serving: Illinois, Michigan, Minnesota, Ohio, and Wisconsin

Region VI
FEMA, Federal Regional Center, Room 206, 800 North Loop 288, Denton, TX 76201; (817) 898-9399. Serving: Arkansas, Louisiana, New Mexico, Oklahoma, and Texas.

Region VII
FEMA, Federal Official Building, 911 Walnut Street, Room 200, Kansas City, MO 64106; (816) 283-7061. Iowa, Kansas, Missouri, and Nebraska.

Region VIII
FEMA, Denver Federal Center Building 710, PO Box 25267, Denver, CO 80225; (303) 235-4800. Serving: Colorado, Montana, North Dakota, South Dakota, Utah, and Wyoming.

Region IX
FEMA, Presidio of San Francisco, Building 105, San Francisco, CA 94129; (415) 923-7100. Serving: Arizona, California, Hawaii, and Nevada. (Pacific Commonwealth and Territories)

Region X
FEMA, Federal Regional Center, 130 228th Street, SW, Bothell, WA 98021-9796; (206) 481-8800. Serving: Alaska, Idaho, Oregon, and Washington.

* Emergency Preparedness Publications

Federal Emergency Management Agency (FEMA)
P.O. Box 70274
Washington, DC 20024 (202) 646-3484

The *FEMA Publications Catalog* (FEMA-20) lists FEMA publications which are available to help meet the needs of citizens in emergency management matters. These publications are on subjects such as civil defense, earthquakes, floods, hurricanes, tornadoes, fire, nuclear accidents, acts of terrorism, dam safety, and hazardous materials incidents.

Be patient. If any phone number is incorrect, call (area code) 555-1212 and request the new listing.

Your Community

* Emergency Preparedness Responsibilities

Federal Emergency Management Agency (FEMA)
P.O. Box 70274
Washington, DC 20024 (202) 646-3484

The *Data Base Guide* (FPG 47.101) #07281, is a complete inventory of the automated data files used in support of the FEMA program offices. Included are data files which are the result of a cooperative effort between FEMA and other federal departments and agencies having delegated emergency preparedness responsibilities. These files have detailed information on virtually all of the resources important to the defense of, or--in the event of enemy attack--the survival and recovery of, the United States.

* Emergency Relief and Excess Food

Commodity Operations Division
U.S. Department of Agriculture
ASCS, Room 6745, South Building
Washington, DC 20250 (202) 720-4785

The Commodity Credit Corporation buys, stores, and distributes such commodities as dry milk, wheat, rice, and corn, which are acquired through price support programs. The commodities are sent overseas as donations, distributed to domestic food programs, or given to relief agencies in times of emergencies.

* Emergency Training National Center

National Emergency Training Center (NETC)
Federal Emergency Management Agency (FEMA)
The Learning Resource Center
16825 South Seton Ave. (800) 638-1821
Emmitsburg, MD 21727 (301) 447-1032

The Learning Resource Center is the NETC campus library for students in all areas of training at the National Emergency Training Center, and for the U.S. Fire Administration. Services include all types of reference work and interlibrary loans. Contact the office above for further information.

* Firefighters Safety and Health

Office of Firefighter Health and Safety
U.S. Fire Administration
16825 South Seton Ave.
Emmitsburg, MD 21727 (301) 447-6771

This office develops national standards for firefighter's health and safety and also researches and analyzes data concerning the well-being of firefighters while exposed to such hazards as fire, heat, toxic chemicals. Research on firefighters protective clothing and equipment and a hazardous chemical materials response suit is also being studied. Contact the office above for more information.

* Fire Incident Reporting System

National Fire Data Center
U.S. Fire Administration
16825 South Seton Ave.
Emmitsburg, MD 21727 (301) 447-1313

This office quantifies and analyzes fire loss experienced at the local, State, and federal levels. Data are available on standard fire incidents. This office offers participants both mainframe and microcomputer applications for data collection and analysis. For more information and information on the Management Application Project (MAP) and the National Fire Incident Reporting System (NFIRS), contact the office above.

* Flood Damage Prevention

Flood Protection Branch, Air and Water Resources
Tennessee Valley Authority (TVA)
River Basin Operations
Resource Development
Liberty Bldg.
524 Union Ave., Room 1A-37902
Knoxville, TN 37902 (615) 632-4455

TVA's local flood damage prevention program helps communities avoid flood damages through a variety of measures, including floodplain zoning, flood proofing, and flood insurance. To assess flood risks, a field staff of engineers gathers data which is used when considering community development proposals. The TVA promotes the wise use of flood hazard areas with information, guidance, and assistance for individuals and businesses to avoid and adjust to flood areas. Staff works with local officials to assess community flood situations, and evaluate and install prevention and warning programs. A great emphasis is placed on environmental aspects as the program tries to maintain the natural benefits of flood plains and meet community needs through use and management of river corridors.

* Flood Insurance for Property Owners

Federal Emergency Management Agency (FEMA)
Federal Insurance Administration
500 C Street, SW
Washington, DC 20472 (800) 638-6620

The National Flood Insurance Program (NFIP) helps property owners to purchase flood insurance. This insurance is designed to provide an insurance alternative to disaster assistance to meet the escalating costs of repairing damage. Contact the office above for information about the laws, regulations, or administrative policies related to the NFIP. Maryland residents outside of DC should call: (800) 492-6605, and those in Alaska, Guam, Hawaii, Puerto Rico, and Virgin Islands residents should call: (800) 638-6831.

Questions and Answers on the National Flood Insurance Program (FIA-2) #30002 contains questions and answers about the National Flood Insurance Program. There are six regional offices.

* Flood Plain Management Assistance

U.S. Army Corps of Engineers
Attn: CECW-PF
20 Massachusetts Ave., NW
Washington, DC 20314 (202) 272-0169

The Army Corps of Engineers provides information, guidance, and technical assistance to civic groups and organizations in developing regulations for flood plain use. These services help communities understand the extent and magnitude of flood hazards in their areas. For information, contact the above office.

* Flood Preparedness Publications

Federal Emergency Management Agency (FEMA)
P.O. Box 70274
Washington, DC 20024 (202) 646-3484

The Flood Insurance Administration series of publications provide information on specific topics within the National Flood Insurance Program. The following publication can be obtained from the office above:

Flood Emergency and Residential Repair Handbook (FIA-13) #3-0123. Provides homeowners, residential contractors, and local government officials with procedures for dealing with flood hazards and damages to homes and their contents.

* Flood-Prone Areas

Federal Emergency Management Agency (FEMA)
P.O. Box 70274
Washington, DC 20024 (202) 646-3484
(800) 333-1363

The Federal Emergency Management Agency publishes the *Flood Hazard Boundary Map* which shows the flood-prone areas within the community. Each map consists of one Map Index Page and one or more map sheets for all of the areas within the community's corporate limits subject to flooding. Call the number above for more information and map requests. *Guide To Flood Insurance Rate Map* (FIA-14) #3-0138 is a guide to help identify and understand key features of the Flood Insurance Rate Map.

* General Hazard Insurance

Federal Emergency Management Agency (FEMA)
P.O. Box 70274
Washington, DC 20024 (202) 646-3484

The *Insurance Handbook for Public Assistance* (DR&R-3) #8-0075, is a policy and procedural handbook for local, State, and Federal officials concerned with administering general hazard insurance and flood insurance requirements under the Disaster Relief Act of 1974.

* Hazardous Materials and Emergency Response

Toxicology Information Program (TIP)
National Library of Medicine
8600 Rockville Pike

Be patient. If any phone number is incorrect, call (area code) 555-1212 and request the new listing.

Fires, Floods, and Disaster Relief

Bethesda, MD 20894 (301) 496-6308

TIP was established to provide national access to information on toxicology. The program is charged with setting up computerized databases of information from the literature of toxicology and from the files of both governmental and non-governmental organizations. Among the databases are TOXLINE (Toxicology Information Online) and CHEMLINE, a chemical dictionary file. TIP implemented the TOXNET (Toxicology Data Network) system of toxicologically-oriented data banks, including the HSDB (Hazardous Substances Data Bank), which is useful in chemical emergency response. TIP also supports the Toxicology Information Response Center, which provides reference services to the scientific community.

* Hazardous Material Transportation Accidents

Office of Hazardous Materials and Planning and Analysis (DHM-63)
Research and Special Programs Administration
U.S. Department of Transportation
400 7th Street, SW, Room 8112
Washington, DC 20590 (202) 366-4555

This division collects and analyzes accident data from transporters of hazardous materials by highway, rail, air, and water and from container manufacturers. Information stored in the database includes the hazardous material involved, transporter name and mode, packaging used, cause of accident, and results. Contact the above office for searches. There may be a charge.

* Hurricane Safety for Kids

Children's Television Workshop
One Lincoln Plaza, Dept. CES/NH
New York, NY 10023 (212) 595-3456

The Federal Emergency Management Agency (FEMA) funded the creation of the *Big Bird Gets Ready for Hurricanes* kit, which is intended to help teachers and parents teach kids about hurricanes in a non-frightening way. The kit contains a 16-page booklet, a record of "The Hurricane Blues," and a board game (K-68) #8-0647. There is a charge.

* Legal Services for Disaster Victims

Federal Emergency Management Agency (FEMA)
P.O. Box 70274
Washington, DC 20024 (202) 646-3484

The *Manual for Disaster Legal Services* has been prepared by FEMA and the Young Lawyers Division (YLD) of the American Bar Association. Its purpose is to orient new and potential volunteers to the FEMA-YLD Program for offering legal services to victims following major disasters. In order to facilitate this orientation, the *Manual* emphasizes schematic diagram, paraphases statutes and regulations, and simplifies many issues relating to the program.

* Mental Health Services Response to Emergencies, Disasters and Crises

Emergency Services Branch, Violence and Tramatic Stress
National Institutes of Health
National Institute of Mental Health
5600 Fishers Lane, Room 18105
Rockville, MD 20857 (301) 443-3728

The Emergency Services Branch oversees three programs: 1) The Emergency Research Program studies the psychosocial response to mass emergencies; 2) The Crisis Counseling Program administers crisis counseling grants to states in which there has been a Presidentially-declared disaster; 3) The Emergency Preparedness Program plans for alcohol, drug abuse, and mental health disaster-related services nationwide. The program provides technical assistance and public education materials to states and local agencies in times of emergencies, and has three publications designed for non-mental health emergency workers (police, fire, emergency medical personnel) which focus on mental health issues.

* Natural Disaster and Nuclear Attack Planning for Families

Federal Emergency Management Agency (FEMA)
P.O. Box 70274
Washington, DC 20024 (202) 646-3484

In Time of Emergency: A Citizen's Handbook on Emergency Management (H-14) #8-0819, is addressed directly to the individual and the family to provide information and guidance on what can and should be done to prepare for a major natural disaster or nuclear attack.

* Natural Disaster Relief

Office of Government and Public Affairs
U.S. Department of Agriculture (USDA)
Washington, DC 20250 (202) 720-8732

This free publication provides an overview of USDA's disaster assistance programs. It describes types of assistance available and where to apply for assistance. Local extension agents in each county can approve disaster applications for the following: conservation structures (when located on eligible lands); rehabilitation of farm lands destroyed by disaster; crop payment subsidies for disruption caused by disaster to regular crop schedules; sale of animal feed at below market price in emergency situations; animal grazing on reserve or conservation lands in emergency situations; donation of animal feed to Indian reservations when needed; and donation of grain to migratory wildfowl domains. The federal government will also remove debris from a major disaster from publicly- or privately-owned lands or waters.

* Nuclear Crisis Planning

Federal Emergency Management Agency (FEMA)
P.O. Box 70274
Washington, DC 20024 (202) 646-3484

Preparedness Planning for a Nuclear Crisis (HS-4) #6-0178, is a FEMA home-study course that will help you better prepare for a nuclear attack by providing information on the following: the effects of nuclear weapons; evacuation and sheltering; preparation of stocking of fallout shelters; and development of emergency plans to improve the chance of survival for individuals and families.

* Nuclear Fallout Shelters

Federal Emergency Management Agency (FEMA)
P.O. Box 70274
Washington, DC 20024 (202) 646-3484

The free booklet, *HUD Aids for Fallout Shelter Development* (TR-58), describes the principal programs of the U.S. Department of Housing and Urban Development (HUD) which can be used to promote and develop fallout shelters when the requirements of the specific programs are met. Call HUD, (202) 275-0635.

* Posters: Natural and Civil Disasters

Federal Emergency Management Agency (FEMA)
P.O. Box 70274
Washington, DC 20024 (202) 646-3484

The following natural disaster informational posters are from FEMA:

Flood Insurance
Winter Watch for Kids
Earthquake
Emergency Poster
Accidental Launch Warning Message Threat Areas
NEW *Civil Defense* #8-0839
NEW *Flood Safety Rules* #0-0054.

* Temporary Housing

Federal Emergency Management Agency (FEMA)
P.O. Box 70274
Washington, DC 20024 (202) 646-3484

The Mobile Home Sales Handbook (DAP-20) #8-0376, establishes the Federal Emergency Management Agency policy regarding the sale of mobile homes, under Section 404 of the Disaster Relief Act of 1974, to eligible temporary housing occupants. It prescribes the methods, techniques, and procedures utilized in the sales transaction.

* Tornadoes, Hurricanes, and Flash Floods

Federal Emergency Management Agency (FEMA)
P.O. Box 70274
Washington, DC 20024 (202) 646-3484

The following FEMA publications will better help you prepare for severe weather disasters:

Be patient. If any phone number is incorrect, call (area code) 555-1212 and request the new listing.

Your Community

Hurricane Safety: Tips for Hurricanes (L-105) #0-0017
Tornado Safety Tips (L-148) #0-0164
Survival in a Hurricane Wallet Card
Tips for Tornado Safety Wallet Card #0-0117
Big Bird Gets Ready for Hurricane Kit (K-68) #8-0647

Washington, DC 20024 (202) 646-3484
hese FEMA publications will help you prepare for the winter storm season:

Safety Tips for Winter Storms (L-96) #0-0172
Winter Survival Coloring Book (FEMA-26). Includes safety tips on winter for children.
Winter Survival Test #0-0179. A test about safety precautions to be taken around the home before winter storms strike, including heating systems, room heaters and fireplaces, kitchen pipes, and emergency supplies.

* Winter Storm Safety

Federal Emergency Management Agency (FEMA)
P.O. Box 70274

Be patient. If any phone number is incorrect, call (area code) 555-1212 and request the new listing.

Money For Communities and Non-Profits

The federal money programs outlined here are designed to help communities solve many of today's difficult problems. Economic development opportunities such as job training funds are identified. Community improvement programs for emergency shelters, rural housing, senior centers, and mass transit services are described as well as airport modernization loans and grants. You will discover various services such as school lunch and nutrition programs, runaway halfway houses and health clinics. This information is derived from the *Catalog of Federal Domestic Assistance* which is published by the U.S. Government Printing Office in Washington, DC. The number next to the title description is the reference number listed in this *Catalog*. Contact the office listed below the title for more details.

* Resource Conservation and Development Loans 10.414

Director, Community Facilities Division
Farmers Home Administration
U.S. Department of Agriculture
Washington, DC 20250 (202) 382-1490

To provide loan assistance to local sponsoring agencies in authorized areas where acceleration of program of resource conservation, development, and utilization will increase economic opportunities for local people. Types of assistance: direct loan. Estimate of annual funds available: $ 1,207,000.

* Water and Waste Disposal Systems for Rural Communities 10.418

Administrator, Farmers Home Administration
U.S. Department of Agriculture
Washington, DC 20250 (202) 447-7967

To provide basic human amenities, alleviate health hazards and promote the orderly growth of the rural areas of the nation by meeting the need for new and improved rural water and waste disposal facilities. Types of assistance: loans, grants. Estimate of annual funds available: $ 330,380,000.

* Watershed Protection and Flood Prevention Loans 10.419

Director, Community Facilities Division
Farmers Home Administration
U.S. Department of Agriculture
Washington, DC 20250 (202) 382-1490

To provide loan assistance to sponsoring local organizations in authorized watershed areas for share of costs for works of improvements. Types of assistance: loan. Estimate of annual funds available: $ 7,949,000.

* Rural Self-Help Housing Technical Assistance (Section 523 Technical Assistance) 10.420

Administrator, Farmers Home Administration
U.S. Department of Agriculture
Washington, DC 20250 (202) 382-1474

To provide financial support for the promotion of a program of technical and supervisory assistance that will aid needy very low and low-income individuals and their families in carrying out mutual self-help housing efforts in rural areas. Types of assistance: grants. Estimate of annual funds available: $ 16,542,509.

* Community Facilities Loans 10.423

Director, Community Facilities Division
Farmers Home Administration
U.S. Department of Agriculture
Washington, DC 20250 (202) 382-1490

To construct, enlarge, extend, or otherwise improve community facilities providing essential services to rural residents. Types of assistance: loans. Estimate of annual funds available: $ 95,700,000.

* Technical Assistance and Training Grants 10.436

Administrator, Farmers Home Administration
U.S. Department of Agriculture
Washington, DC 20250 (202) 447-7967

To identify and evaluate solutions; to assist applicants in preparing applications made in accordance with Subparts A and H of 1942; and to improve operation and maintenance of water and waste disposal facilities in rural areas. Types of assistance: grants. Estimate of annual funds available: $ 1,094,000.

* Intermediary Relending Program 10.439

Farmers Home Administration
Room 6321, South Agriculture Building
Washington, DC 20250 (202) 475-4100

To finance business facilities and community development. Types of assistance: loans. Estimate of annual funds available: $ 14,000,000.

* Cooperative Extension Service 10.500

Extension Service
U.S. Department of Agriculture
Washington, DC 20250 (202) 447-3377

To help people and communities identify and solve their farm, home, and community problems through the practical application of research findings of USDA and the Land-Grant Colleges and Universities. Types of assistance: grants. Estimate of annual funds available: $ 346,465,000.

* Child Nutrition: State Administrative Expenses 10.560

Director, Child Nutrition Division
Food and Nutrition Service
U.S. Department of Agriculture
Alexandria, VA 22302 (703) 756-3590

To provide each state agency with funds for its administrative expenses in supervising and giving technical assistance to local schools, school districts and institutions in their conduct of child nutrition programs. Types of assistance: grants. Estimate of annual funds available: $ 56,754,000.

* Nutrition Education and Training Program (NET Program) 10.564

Nutrition and Technical Services Division
Food and Nutrition Service
U.S. Department of Agriculture
Alexandria, VA 22302 (703) 756-3554

To help subsidize State and local programs that encourage the dissemination of nutrition information to children participating, or eligible to participate in the school lunch and related child nutrition programs. Types of assistance: grants. Estimate of annual funds available: $ 5,000,000.

* Temporary Emergency Food Assistance (Administrative Costs) 10.568

Food Distribution Division, FNS, USDA

Be patient. If any phone number is incorrect, call (area code) 555-1212 and request the new listing.

Your Community

Room 502, Park Office Center
3101 Park Center Drive
Alexandria, VA 22302 (703) 756-3680
To make funds available to States for storage and distribution costs incurred by nonprofit eligible recipient agencies in providing food assistance to needy persons. Types of assistance: grants. Estimate of annual funds available: $ 50,000,000.

* Temporary Emergency Food Assistance (Food Commodities) 10.569

Food Distribution Division, FNS, USDA
Room 502, Park Office Center
3101 Park Center Drive
Alexandria, VA 22302 (703) 756-3680
To make food commodities available to States for distribution to the needy. Types of assistance: grants. Estimate of annual funds available: $ 120,000,000.

* Food Commodities for Soup Kitchens 10.571

Food Distribution Division
Food and Nutrition Service
U.S. Department of Agriculture
Alexandria, VA 22302 (703) 756-3680
To improve the diets of the homeless. Types of assistance: grants. Estimate of annual funds available: $ 40,000,000.

* Cooperative Forestry Assistance 10.664

Deputy Chief, State and Private Forestry
Forest Service
U.S. Department of Agriculture
P.O. Box 96090
Washington, DC 20090-6090 (202) 447-3332
With respect to nonfederal forest and other rural lands to assist in the advancement of forest resources management; the encouragement of the production of timber; the control of insects and diseases affecting trees and forests. Types of assistance: grants. Estimate of annual funds available: $ 43,731,000.

* Schools and Roads - Grants to States (25 Percent Payments to States) 10.665

James Turner
Acting Director of Fiscal and Public Safety
Forest Service, USDA, Room 701 RPE
P.O. Box 96090
Washington, DC 20090-6090 (703) 235-8159
To share receipts from the National Forests with the States in which the National Forests are situated. To be used for the benefit of the public schools and public roads of the county or counties in which the National Forest is situated. Types of assistance: grants. Estimate of annual funds available: $ 338,825,000.

* Schools and Roads - Grants to Counties (Payments to Counties) 10.666

James Turner
Acting Director of Fiscal and Public Safety
Forest Service, USDA, Room 701 RPE
P.O. Box 96090
Washington, DC 20090-6090 (703) 235-8159
To share receipts from National Grasslands and Land Utilization Projects with the counties in which the National Grasslands and Land Utilization Projects are situated. To be used for school or road purposes or both. Types of assistance: grants. Estimate of annual funds available: $ 16,413,000.

* Additional Lands - Grants to Minnesota (Minnesota Special) 10.668

James Turner
Acting Director of Fiscal and Public Safety
Forest Service, USDA, Room 701 RPE
P.O. Box 96090
Washington, DC 20090-6090 (703) 235-8159
To share National Forest receipts with the State of Minnesota in connection with lands situated in the counties of Cook, Lake, and St. Louis which are withdrawn from entry and appropriation under the public land laws of the United States. Types of assistance: grants. Estimate of annual funds available: $ 716,000.

* Accelerated Cooperative Assistance for Forest Programs on Certain Lands Adjacent to the Boundary Waters Canoe Area (BWCA) 10.669

Christopher Holmes, Deputy Chief
State and Private Forestry
Forest Service, U.S. Department of Agriculture
P.O. Box 2417
Washington, DC 20013 (703) 235-1537
To provide a system of grants in cooperation with the State of Minnesota, Division of Forestry, for the intensive management of forest resources on state, county, and private lands adjacent to the Boundary Waters Canoe Area Wilderness. Types of assistance: grants. Estimate of annual funds available: $ 2,800,000.

* Great Plains Conservation 10.900

Deputy Chief for Programs
Soil Conservation Service
U.S. Department of Agriculture
P.O. Box 2890
Washington, DC 20013 (202) 447-4527
To conserve and develop the Great Plains soil and water resources by providing technical and financial assistance to farmers, ranchers, and others in planning and implementing conservation practices. Types of assistance: direct payment. Estimate of annual funds available: $ 12,286,000.

* Resource Conservation and Development 10.901

Deputy Chief for Programs
Soil Conservation Service
U.S. Department of Agriculture
P.O. Box 2890
Washington, DC 20013 (202) 447-4527
To encourage and improve the capability of state and local units of government and local nonprofit organizations in rural areas to plan, develop and carry out programs for resource conservation and development. Types of assistance: grants. Estimate of annual funds available: $ 7,500,000.

* Watershed Protection and Flood Prevention (Small Watershed Program; PL-566 Program) 10.904

Deputy Chief for Programs
Soil Conservation Service
U.S. Department of Agriculture
P.O. Box 2890
Washington, DC 20013 (202) 447-4527
To provide technical and financial assistance in planning and carrying out works of improvement to protect, develop, and utilize the land and water resources in small watersheds. Types of assistance: grants. Estimate of annual funds available: $ 92,703,000.

* Rural Abandoned Mine Program (RAMP) 10.910

Deputy Chief for Programs
Soil Conservation Service
U.S. Department of Agriculture
P.O. Box 2890
Washington, DC 20013 (202) 447-4527
To protect people and the environment from the adverse effects of past coal mining practices, and to promote the development of soil and water resources of unreclaimed mined lands. Types of assistance: direct payments. Estimate of annual funds available: $ 4,594,000.

* Economic Development - Grants for Public Works and Development Facilities 11.300

David L. McIlwain, Director, Public Works Division
Economic Development Administration
Room H7326, Herbert Hoover Bldg.
U.S. Department of Commerce

Be patient. If any phone number is incorrect, call (area code) 555-1212 and request the new listing.

Money For Communities and Non-Profits

Washington, DC (202) 377-5265

To promote long-term economic development and assist in the construction of public works and development facilities needed to initiate and encourage the creation or retention of permanent jobs in the private sector in areas experiencing severe economic distress. Types of assistance: grants. Estimate of annual funds available: $ 139,266,000.

* Economic Development - Business Development Assistance 11.301

Deputy Assistant Secretary for Loan Programs
Economic Development Administration
Room H7844, Herbert Hoover Bldg.
U.S. Department of Commerce
Washington, DC (202) 377-5067

To sustain industrial and commercial viability in designated areas by providing financial assistance to businesses that create or retain permanent jobs, expand or establish plants in redevelopment areas for projects where financial assistance is not available from other sources on terms and conditions that would permit accomplishment of the project and further economic development in the area. Types of assistance: loan guarantee, grants. Estimate of annual funds available: $ 20,000,000.

* Economic Development-Support for Planning Organizations (Development District Program; Redevelopment Area Program; and Indian Program) 11.302

Luis F. Bueso, Director Planning Division
Economic Development Administration
Room H7023, Herbert Hoover Bldg.
Washington, DC 20230 (202) 377-2873

To assist in providing administrative aid to multi-county district and redevelopment area (primarily Indian reservations and lands) economic development planning and implementation capability and thereby promote effective utilization of resources in the creation of full-time permanent jobs for the unemployed and the underemployed in high distress areas. Types of assistance: grants. Estimate of annual funds available: $ 18,205,000.

* Economic Development-Technical Assistance 11.303

Richard E. Hage, Technical Assistance Programs
Economic Development Administration
Room H7319, Herbert Hoover Bldg.
U.S. Department of Commerce
Washington, DC (202) 377-2127

To promote economic development and alleviate under-employment and unemployment in distressed areas, EDA operates a technical assistance program. Types of assistance: grants. Estimate of annual funds available: $ 6,706,000.

* Economic Development-Public Works Impact Projects 11.304

David L. McIlwain, Director, Public Works Division
Economic Development Administration
Room H7326, Herbert Hoover Bldg.
Washington, DC (202) 377-5265

To promote long-term economic development and assist in providing immediate useful work (i.e., construction jobs) to unemployed and underemployed persons in designated project areas. Types of assistance: grants. Estimate of annual funds available: $ 139,266,000.

* Economic Development-State and Local Economic Development Planning (302(a) Grants-State and Urban Planning Programs) 11.305

Luis F. Bueso, Director Planning Division
Economic Development Administration
Room H7023, Herbert Hoover Bldg.
U.S. Department of Commerce
Washington, DC 20230 (202) 377-3027

To help state and/or local governments formulate and implement economic development plans designed to reduce unemployment and increase incomes. Types of assistance: grants. Estimate of annual funds available: $ 4,790,000.

* Special Economic Development and Adjustment Assistance Program-Sudden and Severe Economic Dislocation and Long-term Economic Deterioration (SSED and LTED) 11.307

Paul J. Dempsey, Director
Economic Adjustment Division
Economic Development Administration
Room H7327, Herbert Hoover Bldg.
U.S. Department of Commerce
Washington, DC (202) 377-2659

To assist state and local areas develop and/or implement strategies designed to address adjustment problems resulting from sudden and severe economic dislocation such as plant closings (SSED), or from long-term economic deterioration in the area's economy (LTED). Types of assistance: grants. Estimate of annual funds available: $ 24,657,000.

* Research and Evaluation Program 11.312

David H. Geddes
Room H-7319, EDA
U.S. Department of Commerce
Washington, DC 20230 (202) 377-4085

To assist in the determination of causes of unemployment, under-employment, underdevelopment, and chronic depression in various areas and regions of the nation. Types of assistance: grants. Estimate of annual funds available: $ 1,210,000.

* Anadromous and Great Lakes Fisheries Conservation 11.405

Director, Office of Fisheries Conservation and Management
National Marine Fisheries Service
1335 East-West Hwy
Silver Spring, MD 29910 (202) 673-5272

To cooperate with the states and other nonfederal interests in the conservation, development, and enhancement of the nation's anadromous fish and the fish in the Great Lakes and Lake Champlain that ascent streams to spawn, and for the control of sea lamprey. Types of assistance: grants. Estimate of annual funds available: $ 2,343,000.

* Interjurisdictional Fisheries Act of 1986 11.407

Director, Office of Fisheries Conservation and Management
National Marine Fisheries Service
1335 East-West Hwy
Silver Spring, MD 20910 (301) 427-2347

To assist states in managing interjurisdictional fisheries resources. Types of assistance: grants. Estimate of annual funds available: $ 0.

* Coastal Zone Management Program Administration Grants 11.419

Chief, Coastal Programs Division
Office of Ocean Coastal Resource Management
National Ocean Service, NOAA
U.S. Department of Commerce
1825 Connecticut Ave., NW
Washington, DC (202) 673-2515

To assist states in implementing and administering Coastal Zone Management programs that have been approved by the Secretary of Commerce. Types of assistance: grants. Estimate of annual funds available: $ 33,000,000.

* Coastal Zone Management Estuarine Research Reserves 11.420

Chief, Marine and Estuarine Management Div.
Office of Ocean and Coastal Resource Management
National Ocean Service, NOAA
U.S. Department of Commerce
1825 Connecticut, Ave., NW
Washington, DC (202) 673-5126

To assist states in the acquisition, research, development and operation of national estuarine research reserves for the purpose of creating natural field laboratories to gather data and make studies of the natural and human processes

Be patient. If any phone number is incorrect, call (area code) 555-1212 and request the new listing.

Your Community

occurring within the estuaries of the coastal zone. Types of assistance: grants. Estimate of annual funds available: $ 2,790,000.

* Fisheries Development and Utilization Research and Development Grants and Cooperative Agreements Program 11.427

Office of Trade and Industry Services
National Marine Fisheries Service, NOAA
U.S. Department of Commerce
Silver Spring, MD 20910 (301) 427-2358

To foster the development and strengthening of the fishing industry of the United States and increase the supply of wholesome, nutritious fish and fish products available to consumers. Types of assistance: grants. Estimate of annual funds available: $ 5,000,000.

* Intergovernmental Climate-Programs 11.428

National Climate Program Office, NOAA
U.S. Department of Commerce
11400 Rockville Pike
Rockville, MD 20852 (301) 443-8981

To aid states in the initiation of regional climate centers which will supply guidance, information and climate data to users in the private and public sectors. Types of assistance: grants. Estimate of annual funds available: $ 1,500,000.

* Marine Sanctuary Program 11.429

Chief, Marine and Estuarine Management Division
Office of Ocean and Coastal Resource Management
National Ocean Service, NOAA
U.S. Department of Commerce
1825 Connecticut Ave., NW
Washington, DC (202) 673-5126

To identify areas of the marine environment of special national significance due to their resource or human-use values; to provide authority for comprehensive and coordinated conservation and management of these marine areas that will complement existing regulatory authorities. Types of assistance: grants. Estimate of annual funds available: $ 766,000.

* Regional Centers for the Transfer of Manufacturing Technology 11.611

Dr. Philip N. Nanzetta
Director, NIST MTC Program
Room B112, Metrology Bldg, NIST
Gaithersburg, MD 20899 (301) 975-3414

To establish regional centers, the functions of which are to accelerate the transfer of advanced manufacturing technology from the NIST automated manufacturing research facility and similar research and development laboratories to small and medium sized U.S. based manufacturing firms. Types of assistance: grants. Estimate of annual funds available: $ 1,000,000.

* Minority Business and Industry Association - Minority Chambers 11.802

Asst. Director, Office of Program Development
Room 5096, Minority Business Development Agency
U.S. Department of Commerce (MB and IA/C of C)
14th and Constitution Ave, NW
Washington, DC 20230 (202) 377-5770

To provide financial assistance for Minority Business and Industry Association/Minority Chambers of Commerce (MB and IA/C of C) which act as advocates for their members and the minority community. Types of assistance: grants. Estimate of annual funds available: $ 1,420,000.

* Payments to States in Lieu of Real Estate Taxes 12.112

HQ, U.S. Army Corps of Engineers, Attn: CERM-F
20 Massachusetts Ave., NW
Washington, DC 20314-1000 (202) 272-1925

To compensate local taxing units for the loss of taxes from federally acquired lands, 75 percent of all monies received or deposited in the Treasury during any fiscal year for the account of leasing of lands acquired by the United States for flood control, navigation and allied purposes. Types of assistance: grants. Estimate of annual funds available: $ 5000000.

* Military Construction, Army National Guard 12.400

Chief, Army Installations Division
National Guard Bureau, Pentagon
Washington, DC 20310 (202) 697-1732

To provide a combat-ready reserve force and facilities for training and administering the Army National Guard units in the 50 states, District of Columbia, Commonwealth of Puerto Rico, Virgin Islands, and Guam. Types of assistance: grants. Estimate of annual funds available: $ 113,867,000.

* Impact Assistance for Areas Affected by the East Coast Trident Program (Community Impact Assistance) 12.608

Director, Office of Economic Adjustment, OASD
(FM&P), Pentagon, Room 4C767
Washington, DC 20301-4000 (202) 697-9155

To assist communities located near the Naval Submarine Base in Kings Bay, Georgia. Types of assistance: grants. Estimate of annual funds available: $ 5,000,000.

* Joint Military/Community Comprehensive Land Use Plans 12.610

Director, Office of Economic Adjustment, OASD
(FM&P), Pentagon, Room 4C767
Washington, DC 20301-4000 (202) 697-9155

To enable the Army, Navy, Air Force, and Marine Corps to participate in development and implementation of *Joint Military/Community Comprehensive Land Use Plans*. Types of assistance: grants. Estimate of annual funds available: $ 350,000.

* Mental Health Planning and Demonstration Projects 13.125

Mr. James Stockdill, Director
Division of Education and Service Systems Liaison
NIMH, Parklawn Bldg., Room 11C-26
5600 Fishers Lane
Rockville, MD 20857 (301) 443-3606

To promote the development of community support systems for the long-term mentally ill, including inappropriately institutionalized individuals, mentally disturbed children and youth, and homeless individuals in communities. Types of assistance: grants. Estimate of annual funds available: $ 25,920,000.

* Emergency Medical Services Children (EMS for Children) 13.127

Div. of Maternal, Child and Infant Health
Bureau of Health Care Delivery and Assistance
Health Resources and Services Admin.
Room 9-11, 5600 Fishers Lane
Rockville, MD 20857 (301) 443-2170

To support demonstration projects for the expansion and improvement of emergency medical services for children who need treatment for trauma or critical care. Types of assistance: grants. Estimate of annual funds available: $ 2,964,000.

* Technical and Non-Financial Assistance to Community and Migrant Health Centers 13.129

Director, Division of Primary Care Services
Bureau of Health Care Delivery and Assistance
Health Resources and Services Admin., Room 7A-55
5600 Fishers Lane
Rockville, MD 20857 (301) 443-2260

To provide assistance to community health centers (CHCs) in the following areas: the initiation of new shared services activities involving specific CHCs within a state or region; and the enhancement of the clinical capability of centers within a state or region including assistance in retention and recruitment of

Be patient. If any phone number is incorrect, call (area code) 555-1212 and request the new listing.

Money For Communities and Non-Profits

providers. Types of assistance: grants. Estimate of annual funds available: $3,000,000.

* Primary Care Services-Resource Coordination and Development Cooperative Agreements (Primary Care Services Cooperative Agreements) 13.130

Director, Div. of Primary Care Services
Bureau of Health Care Delivery and Assistance
Health Resources and Services Admin., Room 7A-55
5600 Fishers Lane
Rockville, MD 20857 (301) 443-3476

To coordinate local, state, and federal resources contributing to primary care service delivery in the state to meet the needs of medically under-served populations through community and migrant health centers, and the retention, recruitment and oversight of the National Health Service Corps and other health professions. Types of assistance: grants. Estimate of annual funds available: $4,140,000.

* Health Services Delivery to Persons with AIDS - Demonstration Grants (AIDS Service Demonstration Projects) 13.133

Office of AIDS Program
Bureau of Maternal and Child Health
and Resources Development
Health Resources and Services Admin., Room 9A-05
5600 Fishers Lane
Rockville, MD 20857 (301) 443-0652

To observe demonstration projects in Standard Metropolitan Statistical Areas (SMSAs) for the development and improvement of ambulatory and community-based medical and social services for persons with acquired immune deficiency syndrome (AIDS) and AIDS-related conditions. Types of assistance: grants. Estimate of annual funds available: $10,756,000.

* Assistance for Organ Procurement Organizations 13.134

Director, Division of Organ Transplantation
BMCH & RD
Health Resources and Services Admin.
Room 9-31, 5600 Fishers Lane
Rockville, MD 20857 (301) 443-7577

To provide for the planning, establishment, initial operation, and expansion of qualified organ procurement organizations. Types of assistance: grants. Estimate of annual funds available: $1,314,373.

* Minority Community Health Coalition Demonstration 13.137

Betty Lee Hawks, Room 118F
Hubert Humphrey Bldg.
200 Independence Ave., SW
Washington, DC 20201 (202) 245-0020

To demonstrate that coalitions of local community agencies can be formed to effectively impact on the disease risk factors and related health problems of minority groups, through unique and innovative methods of modifying behavioral and environmental factors involved. Types of assistance: grants. Estimate of annual funds available: $1,400,000.

* Protection and Advocacy for Mentally Ill Individuals (Mentally Ill P and A Services) 13.138

Mr. James Stockdill, Director
Division of Education and Service System Liaison
NIMH, Parklawn Bldg., Room 11C-26
5600 Fishers Lane
Rockville, MD 20857 (301) 443-3606

To enable the establishment and administration of a new system in each state to: protect and advocate the rights of mentally ill individuals and investigate incidents of abuse and neglect of mentally ill individuals. Types of assistance: grants. Estimate of annual funds available: $8,000,000.

* Drug and Alcohol Abuse Prevention - High-Risk Youth Demonstration Grants 13.144

Dr. Stephen Gardner, Chief
Demonstration Operations Branch
Div. of Demonstrations and Eval.
Alcohol, Drug Abuse and Mental Health Admin.
Room 13A45
Rockville, MD (301) 468-2600

To support prevention demonstration programs that will develop client and/or service systems targeted toward: decreasing the incidence and prevalence of drug and alcohol use among high-risk youth. Types of assistance: grant. Estimate of annual funds available: $24,540,000.

* AIDS Education and Training Centers 13.145

Director, Division of Medicine
Bureau of Health Professions
Health Resources and Services Admin.
Room 4C03, 5600 Fishers Lane
Rockville, MD 20857 (301) 443-6190

To provide education and training to primary care providers and others on the treatment and prevention of acquired immune deficiency syndrome (AIDS) in collaboration with health professions schools, local hospitals and health departments. Types of assistance: grants. Estimate of annual funds available: $13,751,000.

* AIDS Drug Reimbursements 13.146

Director, Bureau of Maternal and Child Health
Health Resources and Services Admin., Room 9-03
Parklawn Bldg.
5600 Fishers Lane
Rockville, MD 20857 (301) 443-0652

To cover the cost of the drug azidothymidine (AZT) and any other drug which proves to prolong the life of a person with AIDS who is a low-income individual no covered under the state Medicaid program or third party payors. Types of assistance: grants. Estimate of annual funds available: $15,000,000.

* Mental Health Services for the Homeless Block Grant (MHSH) 13.150

Mr. Thomas Reynolds, Grants Management Officer
Block Grant Programs, ADAMHA, Room 13C-20
Parklawn Bldg.
5600 Fishers Lane
Rockville, MD 20857 (301) 443-3334

To provide financial assistance to states to support services to chronically mentally ill individuals who are homeless or who are subject to a significant probability of becoming homeless. Types of assistance: grants. Estimate of annual funds available: $14,128,000.

* Project Grants for Health Services to the Homeless (Homeless Assistance Program) 13.151

Harold Dame, Director
Health Care Services for the Homeless Program
Health Resources and Services Admin.
Room 7-15, Parklawn Bldg.
5600 Fishers Lane
Rockville, MD 20857 (301) 443-8134

To provide health care services to homeless persons. Types of assistance: grants. Estimate of annual funds available: $14,820,000.

* Community Demonstration Grant Projects for Alcohol and Drug Abuse Treatment of Homeless Individuals (NIAAA Homeless Demonstration Grants) 13.152

Barbara Lubran, Homeless Initiative
NIAAA, Room 16C-02
5600 Fishers Lane
Rockville, MD 20857 (301) 443-0786

To provide, document and evaluate successful and replicable approaches to community-based alcohol and/or drug abuse treatment and rehabilitation services for individuals with alcohol or drug-related problems who are homeless

Be patient. If any phone number is incorrect, call (area code) 555-1212 and request the new listing.

Your Community

or at imminent risk of becoming homeless. Types of assistance: grants. Estimate of annual funds available: $ 4,545,000.

* Pediatric AIDS Health Care Demonstration Program 13.153

Division of Services for Children with Special Health Needs
Health Resources and Services Admin
Room 9A-11, Parklawn Bldg.
5600 Fishers Lane
Rockville, MD 20857 (301) 443-2170

To support demonstration projects for strategies and innovative models for intervention in pediatric AIDS and coordination of services for childbearing women and children with AIDS. Types of assistance: grants. Estimate of annual funds available: $ 7,901,000.

* Rural Health Research Centers 13.155

Ms. Arlene Granderson
Office of Rural Health Policy
Health Resources and Services Admin.
Parklawn Bldg., Room 14-22
5600 Fishers Lane
Rockville, MD 20857 (301) 443-2720

To support the development of rural health research centers to provide an information base and policy analysis capacity on the full range of rural health issues. Types of assistance: grants. Estimate of annual funds available: $ 1,500,000.

* State Comprehensive Mental Health Service Planning Development Grants 13.158

Maury Lieberman, Director
State Comprehensive Mental Health Planning Program
NIMH, Room 7-103
5600 Fishers Lane
Rockville, MD 20857 (301) 443-4257

To initiate or enhance a planning process at the state level that will lead to the design and implementation of a community-based system of comprehensive mental health services for adults with severe and persistent mental illness and child and adolescent populations with severe emotional disorders. Types of assistance: grants. Estimate of annual funds available: $ 4,787,000.

* Health Care Services in the Home 13.159

Bureau of Health Care Delivery and Assistance
Health Resources and Services Admin., Room 8A-17
Parklawn Bldg.
5600 Fishers Lane
Rockville, MD 20857 (301) 443-3476

To provide grants to the states for assisting grantees in carrying out demonstrations projects; to identify low-income individuals who can avoid institutionalized or prolonged hospitalization if skilled medical services or related health services are provided in the home. Types of assistance: grants. Estimate of annual funds available: $ 2,470,000.

* Minority AIDS Education/Prevention Grants 13.160

Jacqueline Bowles, M.D., Room 118F
Hubert Humphrey Bldg.
200 Independence Ave., SW
Washington, DC 20201 (202) 245-0020

To demonstrate that minority community-based organizations and national organizations can effectively develop and implement human HIV infection education and prevention strategies, using innovative approaches to prevent and reduce HIV transmission among minority populations. Types of assistance: grants. Estimate of annual funds available: $ 1,400,000.

* Health Program for Toxic Substances and Disease Registry 13.161

Dr. Barry Johnson, Assoc. Administrator, CDC, PHS
1600 Clifton Rd., NE
Atlanta, GA 30333 (404) 488-4590

To work closely with state, local, and other federal agencies to reduce or eliminate illness, disability and death resulting from exposure to the public and workers to toxic substances at spill and waste disposal sites. Types of assistance: grants. Estimate of annual funds available: $ 32,243,000.

* Health Services in the Pacific Basin 13.163

Howard Lerner
Bureau of Health Care Delivery and Assistance, PHS
Room 7A-55, 5600 Fishers Lane
Rockville, MD 20857 (301) 443-8134

To develop projects to build capacity and improve health services and systems, particularly preventive health services in the Commonwealth of the Northern Mariana Islands, American Samoa, Guam, Federated States of Micronesia, and Republic of Palau, and to provide technical assistance in support of such projects. Types of assistance: grants. Estimate of annual funds available: $ 741,000.

* Indian Health Service Health Promotion and Disease Prevention Demonstration Projects (HP/DP Demonstration Projects) 13.166

Kay Carpenter, Grants Management Branch
Indian Health Service
PHS, Room 6A-33
5600 Fishers Lane
Rockville, MD 20857 (301) 443-5204

To develop demonstration projects to determine the most effective and cost-efficient means of providing health promotion and disease prevention services, encouraging Indians to adopt good health habits, and reducing health risks to Indians, particularly the risks of heart disease, cancer, stroke, diabetes, depression and lifestyle-related accidents. Types of assistance: grants. Estimate of annual funds available: $ 500,000.

* Human Immunodeficiency Virus (HIV) Services

Planning Program Grants (HIV Services
Planning Program) 13.168
Office of Special Projects
Health Resources and Services Admin.
Room 9-13, 5600 Fishers Lane
Rockville, MD 20857 (301) 443-6775

To assist cities and states which have not been affected by the human immunodeficiency virus (HIV) epidemic to the same extent as high incidence cities in developing a coordinated strategy for the delivery of services to persons with HIV infection. Types of assistance: grants. Estimate of annual funds available: $ 3,600,000.

* Model Projects for Pregnant and Postpartum Women and Their Infants (Substance Abuse) 13.169

Bernard McColgan, Director
Division of Demonstrations and Evaluation
Alcohol, Drug Abuse and Mental Health Admin.
Room 13A-54, 5600 Fishers Lane
Rockville, MD (301) 443-4564

To promote the involvement and coordinated participation of multiple organizations in the delivery of comprehensive services for substance-abusing pregnant and postpartum women. Types of assistance: grants. Estimate of annual funds available: $ 4,000,000.

* Community Youth Activity Demonstration Grants 13.170

Office for Substance Abuse
Alcohol, Drug Abuse and Mental Health Administration
Room 9A-40, 5600 Fishers Lane
Rockville, MD 20857 (301) 443-0369

To provide assistance to states for the purpose of establishing and evaluating innovative alcohol and other drug abuse prevention services for youth and to encourage organizations in contact with these youth-at-risk to form partnerships for the purpose of carrying out activities and projects to prevent alcohol and other drug use among this population. Types of assistance: grants. Estimate of annual funds available: $ 1,061,600.

Be patient. If any phone number is incorrect, call (area code) 555-1212 and request the new listing.

Money For Communities and Non-Profits

* Community Youth Activity Program Block Grants (CYAP) 13.171
Mr. Thomas Reynolds, Grants Management Officer
Alcohol, Drug Abuse and Mental Health Administration
Room 13C-20, Parklawn Bldg.
5600 Fishers Lane
Rockville, MD 20857 (301) 443-3334
To provide financial assistance for the support of prevention services and partnerships designed to develop community activities targeted toward alcohol and other drug abuse prevention through education, training and recreation projects. Types of assistance: grants. Estimate of annual funds available: $ 3,633,750.

* Drug Abuse Treatment Waiting List Reduction Grants 13.175
Mr. Glenn Kamber
Office of Communications and External Affairs
Alcohol, Drug Abuse and Mental Health Admin., PHS
Room 12-C-15, 5600 Fishers Lane
Rockville, MD 20857 (301) 443-3783
To make one-time grants available to public and non-profit private entities to reduce drug abuse treatment waiting lists by expanding the capacity of existing programs. Types of assistance: grants. Estimate of annual funds available: $ 75,000,000.

* Family Planning-Services (Umbrella Councils) 13.217
Deputy Asst. Secretary for Population Affairs
U.S. Department of Health and Human Services
Room 736E, Hubert Humphrey Bldg.
200 Independence Ave., SW
Washington, DC (202) 245-0151
To provide educational, counseling, comprehensive medical and social services necessary to enable individuals to freely determine the number and spacing of their children, and by doing so helping to reduce maternal and infant mortality and promote the health of mothers and children. Types of assistance: grants. Estimate of annual funds available: $ 128,440,000.

* Community Health Centers 13.224
Director, Division Primary Care Services
Health Resources and Services Admin., Room 7A-55
Parklawn Bldg.
5600 Fishers Lane
Rockville, MD 20857 (301) 443-2260
To support the development and operation of community health centers which provide primary health services, supplemental health services and environmental health services to medically under-served populations. Types of assistance: grants. Estimate of annual funds available: $ 411,812,000.

* Indian Health Service-Health Management Development Program Indian Health) 13.228
Division of Grants and Contracts
Indian Health Service, PHS, Room 6A-33
5600 Fishers Lane
Rockville, MD 20857 (301) 443-5204
To improve the quality of the health of American Indians and Native Alaskans by providing a full range of curative, preventative and rehabilitative health services. Types of assistance: grants. Estimate of annual funds available: $ 12,500,000.

* Mental Health Clinical or Service Related Training Grants 13.244
Mr. James Stockdill, Director
Division of Education and Service Systems Liaison
NIMH, Parklawn Bldg., Room 11C-26
5600 Fishers Lane
Rockville, MD 20857 (301) 443-3606
To encourage mental health specialists to work in areas and settings where severe shortages exist; to increase the number of qualified minority personnel in the mental health professions. Types of assistance: grants. Estimate of annual funds available: $ 12,844,000.

* Migrant Health Centers Grants 13.246
Director, Migrant Health Program
Health Resources and Services Administration
Room 7A55
5600 Fishers Lane
Rockville, MD 20857 (301) 443-1153
To support the development and operation of migrant health centers and projects which provide primary health care services, supplemental health services and environmental health services which are accessible to migrant and seasonal agricultural farm workers and their families. Types of assistance: grants. Estimate of annual funds available: $45,646,000.

* National Health Service Corps 13.258
Dr. Audrey Manley, Director
National Health Service Corps
Health Resources and Services Admin.
Room 7A-39, Parklawn Bldg.
5600 Fishers Lane
Rockville, MD 20857 (301) 443-2900
To improve the delivery of health care services to residents in areas critically short of health personnel by the assignment of additional medical personnel. Types of assistance: loans. Estimate of annual funds available: $ 39,866,000.

* Family Planning-Personnel Training 13.260
Office of the Assistant Secretary for Health
U.S. Department of Health and Human Services
Room 736E, Hubert Humphrey Bldg.
200 Independence Ave., SW
Washington, DC 20201 (202) 245-0151
To provide job specific training for personnel to improve the delivery of family planning services. Types of assistance: grants. Estimate of annual funds available: $ 3,232,000.

* Childhood Immunization Grants (Section 317, Public Health Service Act; Immunization Program) 13.268
Dr. Walter Dowdle, Acting Director
Centers for Disease Control, PHS
U.S. Department of Health and Human Services
1600 Clifton Rd., NE
Atlanta, GA 30333 (404) 639-3291
To assist states and communities in establishing and maintaining preventive health service programs to immunize individuals against vaccine-preventable diseases. Types of assistance: grants. Estimate of annual funds available: $ 126,797,000.

* Centers for Disease Control - Investigations and Technical Assistance 13.283
Dr. Walter Dowdle, Acting Director
Centers for Disease Control, PHS
U.S. Department of Health and Human Services
1600 Clifton Rd., NE
Atlanta, GA 30333 (404) 639-3291
To assist state and local health authorities and other health related organizations in controlling communicable disease, chronic diseases, and other preventable health conditions. Types of assistance: grants. Estimate of annual funds available: $ 270,743,179.

* Native American Programs - Financial Assistance Grants 13.612
Administration for Native Americans
U.S. Department of Health and Human Services
Room 344-F, 200 Independence Ave., SW
Washington, DC 20201 (301) 245-7730
To provide financial assistance to public and private nonprofit organizations including Indian Tribes, urban Indian centers, Native Alaskan villages, Native Hawaiian organizations, rural off-reservation groups, and Native American Pacific Island groups for the development and implementation of social and economic development strategies that promote self-sufficiency. Types of assistance: grants. Estimate of annual funds available: $ 27,351,000.

Be patient. If any phone number is incorrect, call (area code) 555-1212 and request the new listing.

Your Community

* Administration for Children, Youth and Families - Runaway and Homeless Youth 13.623
Associate Commissioner
Family and Youth Services Bureau
U.S. Department of Health and Human Services
P.O. Box 1182
Washington, DC 20013 (202) 755-7800
To develop local facilities to address the immediate needs of runaway and homeless youth and their families. Types of assistance: grants. Estimate of annual funds available: $ 26,923,000.

* Administration on Developmental Disabilities - Basic Support and Advocacy Grants 13.630
Director
Program Operations Division
U.S. Department of Health and Human Services
Washington, DC 20201 (202) 245-2897
To assist states in the development of a comprehensive system and a coordinated array of services in order to support the developmentally disabled to achieve their maximum potential and ensure the protection of their legal and human rights. Types of assistance: grants. Estimate of annual funds available: $ 79,534,000.

* Administration on Developmental Disabilities - Projects of National Significance 13.631
Program Development Division
Administration on Developmental Disabilities
U.S. Department of Health and Human Services
Washington, DC 20201 (202) 245-1961
To provide grants and contracts for projects of national significance to increase and support the independence, productivity, and integration into the community of persons with developmental disabilities. Types of assistance: grants. Estimate of annual funds available: $ 2,901,000.

* Special Programs for the Aging - Title III, Part B Grants for Supportive Services and Senior Centers 13.633
Dr. Joyce Berry, Associate Commissioner
Office of Human Development Services
U.S. Department of Health and Human Services
Washington, DC 20201 (202) 245-0011
To assist state agencies on aging and their area agencies to foster the development of community-based systems of service for older persons via statewide planning and area planning and provision of supportive services, including multi-purpose senior centers. Types of assistance: grants. Estimate of annual funds available: $ 276,640,000.

* Children's Justice Grants to States 13.643
Josephine Reisnyder
National Center on Child Abuse and Neglect
Administration for Children, Youth and Families
P.O. Box 1182, SW
Washington, DC 20013 (202) 245-2860
To encourage states to enact child protective reforms which are designed to improve the handling of child abuse cases and the investigation and prosecution of cases of child abuse. Types of assistance: grants. Estimate of annual funds available: $ 6,297,873.

* Child Welfare Services - State Grants 13.645
Betty Stewart, Associate Commissioner
Children's Bureau
Administration for Children, Youth and Families
P.O. Box 1182
Washington, DC 20013 (202) 755-7600
To establish, extend, and strengthen child welfare services provided by state and local public welfare agencies to enable children to remain in their own homes. Types of assistance: grants. Estimate of annual funds available: $ 246,679,000.

* Social Services Research and Demonstration 13.647
Ann Queen, Director
Division of Research and Demonstration
U.S. Department of Health and Human Services
Room 334-F, Hubert Humphrey Bldg.
200 Independence Ave., SW
Washington, DC (202) 472-3026
To promote effective social services for dependent and vulnerable populations such as the poor, the aged, children and youth, Native Americans, and the handicapped. Types of assistance: grants. Estimate of annual funds available: $ 3,550,000.

* Adoption Opportunities: Administration for Children, and Families 13.652
Delmar Weathers
Children's Bureau
Administration for Children, Youth and Families
P.O. Box 1182
Washington, DC 20013 (202) 426-2822
To provide financial support for demonstration projects to improve adoption practices; to gather information on adoptions; and to provide training and technical assistance to improve adoption services. Types of assistance: grants. Estimate of annual funds available: $ 6,027,000.

* Grants to Indian Tribes: Special Programs for the Aging (Title VI, Part A Indian Programs) 13.655
Dr. Joyce Berry
Associate Commissioner
Office of State and Tribal Programs
Administration on Aging
U.S. Department of Health and Human Services
Washington, DC 20201 (202) 245-0011
To promote the delivery of supportive services, including nutrition services to older Indians and Alaskan Natives. Types of assistance: grants. Estimate of annual funds available: $ 7,410,000.

* Drug Abuse Prevention and Education for Runaway and Homeless Youth (Runaway Youth Drug Abuse Prevention and Education) 13.657
Frank Fuentes
Family and Youth Services Bureau
Administration for Children, Youth and Families
330 C St., SW
Washington, DC 20201 (202) 755-8888
To expand and improve existing drug abuse and prevention services to runaway and homeless youth and their families. Types of assistance: grants. Estimate of annual funds available: $ 12,000,000.

* Foster Care - Title IV-E 13.658
Betty Stewart, Associate Commissioner
Children's Bureau
P.O. Box 1182
Washington, DC 20013 (202) 755-7600
To provide Federal Financial Participation (FFP) in assistance on behalf of eligible children needing care away from their families (in foster care) who are in the placement and care of the state agency administering the program. Types of assistance: grant. Estimate of annual funds available: $ 1,363,971,000.

* Adoption Assistance 13.659
Betty Stewart, Associate Commissioner
Children's Bureau
P.O. Box 1182
Washington, DC 20013 (202) 755-7600
To provide Federal Financial Participation (FFP) to states which meet certain eligibility tests, in the adoption subsidy costs for the adoption of children with special needs. Types of assistance: grants. Estimate of annual funds available: $ 133,936,000.

Be patient. If any phone number is incorrect, call (area code) 555-1212 and request the new listing.

Money For Communities and Non-Profits

* **Drug Abuse Prevention and Education Relating to Youth and Gangs 13.660**

Frank Fuentes, Family and Youth Services Bureau
Administration for Children, Youth and Families
330 C St., SW
Washington, DC 20201 (202) 755-7800

To prevent and reduce the participation of youth in gangs that engage in illicit drug-related activities. Types of assistance: grants. Estimate of annual funds available: $ 12,500,000.

* **Native American Programs - Training and Technical Assistance 13.662**

Administration for Native Americans
U.S. Department of Health and Human Services, Room 344-F
200 Independence Ave., SW
Washington, DC 20201 (202) 245-7714

To promote the goal of economic and social self-sufficiency for American Indians, Native Hawaiians, Native Alaskans, and Native American Pacific Island groups. Types of assistance: grants. Estimate of annual funds available: $ 1,000,000.

* **Comprehensive Child Development Centers 13.666**

Allen Smith
Administration for Children, Youth and Families
P.O. Box 1182
Washington, DC 20013 (202) 755-7782

To plan for and carry out projects for intensive, comprehensive, integrated and continuous supportive services for infants, toddlers, and pre-schoolers from low-income families to enhance their intellectual, social, emotional and physical development. Types of assistance: grants. Estimate of annual funds available: $ 19,160,000.

* **Social Services Block Grant (Social Services) 13.667**

Director, Office of Policy, Planning and Legislation
Office of Human Dev. Services
200 Independence Ave., SW
Washington, DC 20201 (202) 245-2892

To enable each State to furnish social services best suited to the needs of the individuals residing in the State. Types of assistance: grant. Estimate of annual funds available: $ 2,700,000,000.

* **Administration for Children, Youth and Families - Child Abuse and Neglect State Grants 13.669**

Mary McKeough
National Center on Child Abuse and Neglect
Children's Bureau
P.O. Box 1182
Washington, DC 20013 (202) 245-2856

To assist states in improving and increasing activities for the prevention and treatment of child abuse, and to develop, strengthen, and carry out the program objectives through State grants. Types of assistance: grants. Estimate of annual funds available: $ 11,647,500.

* **Family Violence Prevention and Services 13.671**

Office of Policy, Planning and Legislation
Office of Human Development Services
200 Independence Ave., SW
Washington, DC 20201 (202) 245-2892

To demonstrate the effectiveness of assisting states and Indian Tribes in the prevention of family violence and to provide immediate shelter and related assistance for victims of family violence and their dependents. Types of assistance: grants. Estimate of annual funds available: $ 8,219,000.

* **Child Abuse Challenge Grants 13.672**

Josephine Reifsnyder
Administration for Children, Youth and Families
P.O. Box 1182
Washington, DC 20013 (202) 245-2860

To encourage states to establish and maintain trust funds or other funding mechanisms, including direct state appropriations to support child abuse and neglect prevention activities. Types of assistance: grants. Estimate of annual funds available: $ 4,834,000.

* **Grants to States for Planning and Development of Dependent Care Programs (Dependent Care Planning and Development) 13.673**

Family and Youth Services Bureau
Administration for Children, Youth and Families
400 6th St., SW
Washington, DC 20201 (202) 755-8888

To assist states in the planning, development, establishment, expansion or improvement of services related to dependent care resource and referral and services related to school age child care before and after school. Types of assistance: grants. Estimate of annual funds available: $ 11,856,000.

* **Independent Living 13.674**

Beverly Stubber, Director
Program Operation Division, Children's Bureau
Administration for Children, Youth and Families
P.O. Box 1182
Washington, DC 20014 (202) 755-7447

To assist states and localities in establishing and carrying out programs designed to assist children, with respect to whom foster care maintenance payments are being made by the state and who have attained age 16, in making the transition from foster care to independent living. Types of assistance: grants. Estimate of annual funds available: $ 45,000,000.

* **State Medicaid Fraud Control Units 13.775**

Jim Shields, Director
State Fraud Branch, Office of the Secretary, DHHS
Room 5449, North Bldg.
330 Independence Ave., SW
Washington, DC 20201 (202) 475-6520

To control provider fraud in the states Medicaid program. Types of assistance: grants. Estimate of annual funds available: $ 48,455,000.

* **State Survey and Certification of Health Care Providers and Suppliers 13.777**

Wayne Smith, Ph.D., Director
Office of Survey and Certification
Health Standards and Quality Bureau
Health Care Financing Administration
6325 Security Blvd.
Baltimore, MD 21207 (301) 966-6763

To provide financial assistance to any state which is able and willing to determine through its state health agency or other appropriate state agency that providers and suppliers of health care services are in compliance with federal regulatory health and safety standards. Types of assistance: grants. Estimate of annual funds available: $ 121,538,000.

* **Child Support Enforcement (Title IV-D) 13.783**

Wayne Stanton, Director
Office of Child Support Enforcement
Family Support Administration, 6th Floor
370 L'Enfant Promenade, SW
Washington, DC 20447 (202) 252-4500

To enforce the support obligations owed by absent parents to their children, locate absent parents, establish paternity and obtain child, spousal and medical support. Types of assistance: grants. Estimate of annual funds available: $ 941,000,000.

* **Child Support Enforcement Research (OCSE Research) 13.784**

David Arnaudo, Acting Chief
Planning and Evaluation Branch
Office of Child Support Enforcement, 4th Floor
370 L'Enfant Promenade, SW
Washington, DC 20447 (202) 252-5364

Be patient. If any phone number is incorrect, call (area code) 555-1212 and request the new listing.

Your Community

To discover, test, demonstrate, and promote utilization of new concepts which will increase cost effectiveness, reduce welfare dependency, and increase child support collections form absent parents. Types of assistance: grants. Estimate of annual funds available: $ 250,000.

* Refugee and Entrant Assistance-State Administered Programs 13.787

Bill F. Gee, Director
Office of Refugee Resettlement
Family Support Administration, 6th Floor
370 L'Enfant Promenade, SW
Washington, DC 20447 (202) 252-4545

To subsidize states for assistance provided to refugees, including Cuban and Haitian entrants for resettlement throughout the country, by funding maintenance and medical assistance, social services, and targeted assistance for eligible refugees and Cuban and Haitian entrants. Types of assistance: direct payment. Estimate of annual funds available: $ 326,726,000.

* Refugee Assistance-Voluntary Agency Programs 13.788

Bill F. Gee, Director
Office of Refugee Resettlement
Family Support Administration, 6th Floor
370 L'Enfant Promenade, SW
Washington, DC 20447 (202) 252-4545

To assist refugees in becoming self-supporting and independent members of American society, by providing grant funds to voluntary resettlement agencies currently resettling these refugees in the United States. Types of assistance: grants. Estimate of annual funds available: $ 15,808,000.

* Community Services Block Grant 13.792

James C. Checkan, Chief
Division of Block Grants
Office of Community Services
Family Support Administration
U.S. Department of Health and Human Services
370 L'Enfant Promenade, SW
Washington, DC 20447 (202) 252-5255

To provide services and activities having a measurable and potential major impact on causes of poverty in the community or those areas of the community where poverty is a particularly acute problem. Types of assistance: grant. Estimate of annual funds available: $ 318,630,000.

* Community Services Block Grant-Discretionary Awards 13.793

Ms. Jacqueline G. Lemire, Acting Director
Office of State and Project Assistance
Family Support Administration
370 L'Enfant Promenade, SW
Washington, DC 20447 (202) 252-5248

To support program activities of national or regional significance to alleviate the causes of poverty in distressed communities which promote full-time permanent jobs for poverty level project area residents. Types of assistance: direct payment. Estimate of annual funds available: $ 37,120,000.

* Community Services Block Grant Discretionary Awards-Community Food and Nutrition 13.795

Mr. Jim Hearn, Chief
Community Food and Nutrition Program (CFNP)
Family Support Administration
370 L'Enfant Promenade, SW
Washington, DC 20447 (202) 252-5252

To provide for community-based, local, and stateside programs which coordinate existing private and public food assistance resources to better serve low-income populations and to assist low-income communities to identify potential sponsors of child nutrition programs and initiate new programs in under-served areas. Types of assistance: grants, direct payment. Estimate of annual funds available: $ 2,418,000.

* Emergency Community Services for the Homeless 13.796

Janet Fox
Office of Community Services
Family Support Administration
370 L'Enfant Promenade, SW
Washington, DC 20447 (202) 252-5254

To use public resources and programs in a coordinated manner to meet the critically urgent needs of the homeless of the nation; and to provide funds for programs to assist the homeless with special emphasis on elderly persons, handicapped persons, families with children, Native Americans and veterans. Types of assistance: grants. Estimate of annual funds available: $ 18,918,000.

* Community Services Block Grant Discretionary Awards-Demonstration Partnerships 13.797

Marshall Borman, Office of the Director
Office of Community Services
370 L'Enfant Promenade, SW
Washington, DC 20447 (202) 252-5251

To stimulate eligible entities to develop new approaches to provide for greater self-sufficiency of the poor; test and evaluate the new approaches, disseminate project results and strengthen the ability of eligible entities to integrate, coordinate and redirect activities to promote maximum self-sufficiency. Types of assistance: grant. Estimate of annual funds available: $ 3,512,000.

* Project Grants for Non-Acute Care, Intermediate and Long-Term Care Facilities (1610(b) Program) 13.887

Ms. Katharine Buckner, Office of Health Facilities
Bureau of Maternal and Child Health and
Resources Development
Room 11A-10, 5600 Fishers Lane
Rockville, MD 20857 (301) 443-0271

To renovate, expand, repair, equip, or modernize non-acute care intermediate and long-term care facilities for patients with AIDS. Types of assistance: grants. Estimate of annual funds available: $ 3,952,000.

* National Health Promotion 13.900

Deputy Director
Office of Disease Prevention and Health Promotion
DHHS, Room 2132
330 C Street, SW
Washington, DC 20201 (202) 245-7611

To engage national membership organizations from various sectors as a means of expanding and coordinating health promotion efforts. Types of assistance: grants. Estimate of annual funds available: $ 363,080.

* Graduate Programs in Health Administration 13.963

Mr. John Westcott, Grants Management Officer
Bureau of Health Professions
Health Resources and Services Administration
Room 8C-22, 5600 Fishers Lane
Rockville, MD 20857 (301) 443-6880

To support accredited graduate education programs in health administration, hospital administration, and health planning. Types of assistance: grants. Estimate of annual funds available: $ 1,410,000.

* Coal Miners Respiratory Impairment Treatment Clinics and Services (Black Lung Clinics) 13.965

Director, Div. of Primary Care Services
Health Resources and Services Administration
Room 7A-55, 5600 Fishers Lane
Rockville, MD 20857 (301) 443-2260

To develop high quality, patient oriented, integrated systems of care which assure access to and continuity of appropriate primary, secondary and tertiary care with maximum use of existing resources. Types of assistance: grants. Estimate of annual funds available: $ 3,216,000.

Be patient. If any phone number is incorrect, call (area code) 555-1212 and request the new listing.

Money For Communities and Non-Profits

* **Preventive Health Services - Sexually Transmitted Diseases Control Grants 13.977**
Dr. Walter R. Dowdle, Acting Director, CDC
PHS, DHHS
1600 Clifton Road, NE
Atlanta, GA 30333 (404) 639-3291
To reduce morbidity and mortality by preventing cases and complications of sexually transmitted diseases (STD). Types of assistance: grants. Estimate of annual funds available: $ 61,354,800.

* **Mental Health Disaster Assistance and Emergency Mental Health 13.982**
Dr. Mary Lystad, Chief
Disaster Assistance and Emergency Mental Health Section
National Institute of Mental Health
5600 Fishers Lane
Rockville, MD 20857 (301) 443-4735
Provision of supplemental emergency mental health counseling to individuals affected by major disasters, including the training of volunteers to provide such counseling. Types of assistance: grants. Estimate of annual funds available: $ 397,614.

* **Health Programs for Refugees (Immigration and Nationality Act) 13.987**
Dr. Walter R. Dowdle, Acting Director
CDC, PHS, DHHS
Atlanta, GA 30333 (404) 639-1286
To assist states and localities in providing health assessment and follow-up activities to new refugees and in addressing refugee health problems of public health concern. Types of assistance: grants. Estimate of annual funds available: $ 4,138,000.

* **Cooperative Agreements for State-Based Diabetes Control Programs 13.988**
Chief, Grants Management Office
Procurement and Grants Office
CDC, PHS, DHHS
Atlanta, GA 30333 (404) 842-6575
To implement comprehensive programs which will ensure that persons with diabetes who are at high risk for certain complications of diabetes are identified, entered into the health are system and receive on going state-of-the-art preventive care and treatment. Types of assistance: grants. Estimate of annual funds available: $ 4,861,000.

* **National Health Promotion 13.990**
Deputy Director
Office of Disease Prevention and Health Promotion
DHHS, Room 2132
330 C St, SW
Washington, DC 20201 (202) 245-7611
To engage national membership organizations from various sectors as a means of expanding and coordinating health promotion efforts. Types of assistance: grants. Estimate of annual funds available: $ 1,325,000.

* **Preventive Health and Health Services Block Grant (PHS Block Grants) 13.991**
Chief, Grants Management Branch
Centers for Disease Control
Atlanta, GA 30333 (404) 842-6575
To provide states with resources for comprehensive preventive health services including: emergency medical services, health incentive activities, hypertension programs, rodent control, etc. Types of assistance: grant. Estimate of annual funds available: $ 85,259,000.

* **Alcohol and Drug Abuse and Mental Health Services Block Grant (ADMS Block Grant) 13.992**
Mr. Thomas Reynolds, Grants Management Officer
Block Grant Programs, ADAMHA

Room 13C-20, Parklawn Bldg.
5600 Fishers Lane
Rockville, MD 20857 (301) 443-3334
To provide financial assistance to States and Territories to support projects for the development of more effective prevention, treatment and rehabilitating programs and activities to deal with alcohol and drug abuse. Types of assistance: grants. Estimate of annual funds available: $ 765,314,000.

* **Maternal and Child Health Services Block Grant 13.994**
Office of Maternal and Child Health
Health Resources and Services Administration, PHS
Room 9A-11, 5600 Fishers Lane
Rockville, MD 20857 (301) 443-2170
To enable states to maintain and strengthen their leadership in planning, promoting, coordinating and evaluating health care for mothers and children and in providing health services for mothers and children who do not have access to adequate health care. Types of assistance: grants. Estimate of annual funds available: $ 46,293,300.

* **Adolescent Family Life-Demonstration Projects 13.995**
Office of Adolescent Pregnancy Programs
Office of the Assistant Secretary for Health, DHHS
Room 736E, HHH Bldg.
200 Independence Ave., SW
Washington, DC (301) 245-6335
To promote adoption as an alternative for adolescent parents. Types of assistance: grants. Estimate of annual funds available: $ 6,114,000.

* **Mortgage Insurance-Hospitals (242 Hospitals) 14.128**
Insurance Division
Office of Insured Multifamily Housing Development
U.S. Department of Housing and Urban Development
Washington, DC 20410 (202) 755-6223
To make possible the financing of hospitals. Types of assistance: loan guarantee. Estimate of annual funds available: $ 217,858,000.

* **Mortgage Insurance-Nursing Homes, Intermediate Care Facilities and Board and Care Homes (232 Nursing Homes) 14.129**
Insurance Division
Office of Insured Multifamily Housing Development
U.S. Department of Housing and Urban Development
Washington, DC 20412 (202) 755-6223
Types of assistance: loan guarantee. Estimate of annual funds available: $ 233,419,000.

* **Section 106(b) Nonprofit Sponsor Assistance Program (Nonprofit Sponsor Loan Fund) 14.141**
Director
Assisted Elderly and Handicapped Housing Division
Office of Elderly and Assisted Housing, HUD
Washington, DC 20410 (202) 426-8730
To assist and stimulate prospective private nonprofit sponsors/borrowers of Section 202 housing to develop sound housing projects for the elderly or handicapped. Types of assistance: loan. Estimate of annual funds available: $ 960,000.

* **Congregate Housing Services Program (CHSP) 14.170**
Assisted Elderly and Handicapped Housing Division
Office of Elderly and Assisted Housing
U.S. Department of Housing and Urban Development
Washington, DC 20410 (202) 755-5866
To prevent premature or unnecessary institutionalization of elderly-handicapped, non-elderly handicapped, and temporarily disabled, to provide a variety of innovative approaches for the delivery of meals and non-medical supportive services while utilizing existing service programs and to fill gaps existing service

Your Community

systems. Types of assistance: grants. Estimate of annual funds available: $ 6,400,000.

* Housing Development Grants 14.174
Director, Development Grants Division, Room 6110
Office of Elderly and Assisted Housing, HUD
451 7th St., SW
Washington, DC 20410 (202) 755-6142
To support the construction or substantial rehabilitation of rental housing in areas experiencing severe shortages of decent rental housing opportunities for families and individuals without other reasonable and affordable housing alternatives in the private market. Types of assistance: grants. Estimate of annual funds available: $ 20,000,000.

* Nehemiah Housing Opportunity Grant Program (Nehemiah Housing) 14.179
Morris E. Carter, Director
Single Family Housing Development Division, HUD
451 7th St., SW
Washington, DC 20410 (202) 755-6700
To provide an opportunity for those families who otherwise would not be financially able to realize their dream of owning a home. Types of assistance: grant. Estimate of annual funds available: $ 20,000,000.

* Community Development Block Grants/Entitlement Grants 14.218
Entitlement Cities Division
Office of Block Grant Assistance
Community Planning and Development
451 7th St., SW
Washington, DC 20410 (202) 755-5977
To develop viable urban communities, by providing decent housing and a suitable living environment. Types of assistance: grants. Estimate of annual funds available: $ 2,053,100,000.

* Community Development Block Grants/Small Cities Program (Small Cities) 14.219
State and Small Cities Division
Office of Block Grant Assistance Community Planning and Development, HUD
451 7th St., SW
Washington, DC 20410 (202) 755-6223
The primary objective of this program is the development of viable urban communities by providing decent housing, a suitable living environment, and expanding economic opportunities. Types of assistance: grants. Estimate of annual funds available: $ 38,395,000.

* Section 312 Rehabilitation Loans 14.220
Community Planning and Development
Office of Urban Rehabilitation, HUD
451 7th St., SW
Washington, DC 20410 (202) 755-0367
To promote the revitalization of neighborhoods by providing funds for rehabilitation of residential, non-residential and mixed use property in areas determined to be eligible by local governments for activities under either the Community Development Block Grant, Urban Development Action Grant, or Section 810 Urban Homesteading areas. Types of assistance: loans. Estimate of annual funds available: $ 19,510,000.

* Urban Development Action Grants 14.221
Office of Urban Development Action Grants
Community Planning and Development, HUD
451 7th St., SW
Washington, DC 20410 (202) 755-6290
To assist severely distressed large and small cities, urban counties, Guam, the Virgin Islands, Indian Tribes and non-distressed cities containing pockets of poverty in alleviating economic deterioration by means of increased public and private investment in order to aid in economic recovery. Types of assistance: grants. Estimate of annual funds available: $ 49,337,000.

* Urban Homesteading 14.222
Director, Urban Homesteading Program
Office of Urban Rehabilitation, HUD
Washington, DC 20410 (202) 755-5324
To provide homeownership opportunities to credit-worthy individuals and families primarily of lower income, utilizing federally-owned housing stock. Types of assistance: other. Estimate of annual funds available: $ 13,831,000.

* Indian Community Development Block Grant Program 14.223
Office of Program Policy Development
Community Planning and Development, HUD
451 7th St., SW
Washington, DC 20410 (202) 755-6092
To provide assistance to Indian Tribes and Alaska Native Villages in the development of viable Indian Communities. Types of assistance: grants. Estimate of annual funds available: $ 27,000,000.

* Community Development Block Grants/Secretary's Discretionary Fund/Insular Area 14.225
Office of Program Policy Development
Community Planning and Development, HUD
451 7th St., SW
Washington, DC 20410 (202) 755-6092
To provide community development assistance to American Samoa, Guam, the Northern Mariana Islands, Palau and the Virgin Islands. Types of assistance: grants. Estimate of annual funds available: $ 7,000,000.

* Community Development Block Grants/Secretary's Discretionary Fund/Technical Assistance Program 14.227
Office of Program Policy Development
Community Planning and Development, HUD
451 7th St., SW
Washington, DC 20410 (202) 755-6876
To help states, units of general local government, Indian tribes and area wide planing organizations to plan, develop and administer local Community Development Block Grant and Urban Development Action Grant programs. Types of assistance: grants, direct payments. Estimate of annual funds available: $ 10,750,000.

* Community Development Block Grants/State's Program 14.228
State and Small Cities Division
Office of Block Grant Assistance
Community Planning and Development, HUD
451 7th St., SW
Washington, DC 20410 (202) 755-6876
The primary objective of this program is the development of viable urban communities by providing decent housing, a suitable living environment and expanding economic opportunities principally for persons of low and moderate income. Types of assistance: grants. Estimate of annual funds available: $ 841,505,000.

* Rental Housing Rehabilitation (Rental Rehabilitation) 14.230
David M. Cohen, Office of Urban Rehabilitation
Community Planning and Development, HUD
451 7th St., SW
Washington, DC 20410 (202) 755-5685
To increase the supply of standard rental housing units affordable to lower income families. Types of assistance: grants. Estimate of annual funds available: $ 177,418,000.

* Emergency Shelter Grants Program (ESGP) 14.231
James Broughman, Director
Entitlement Cities Division
U.S. Department of Housing and Urban Development (HUD)

Be patient. If any phone number is incorrect, call (area code) 555-1212 and request the new listing.

Money For Communities and Non-Profits

451 7th St., SW, Room 7282
Washington, DC 20410 (202) 755-5977
The program is designed to help improve the quality of existing emergency shelters for the homeless, to help make available additional emergency shelters, and to help pay the costs of operating emergency shelters. Types of assistance: grants. Estimate of annual funds available: $ 47,302,000.

* **Community Development Block Grant/Secretary's Discretionary Fund Special Projects (Special Projects Program) 14.232**
Office of Program Policy Development
Community Planning and Development, HUD
451 7th St., SW
Washington, DC 20410 (202) 755-6090
To award grants to states and units of general local government for special projects that address community development activities. Types of assistance: grants. Estimate of annual funds available: $ 12,250,000.

* **Fair Housing Assistance Program-State and Local (FHAP) 14.401**
Assistant Secretary for Fair Housing and Equal Opportunity
U.S. Department of Housing and Urban Development (HUD)
451 7th St., SW
Washington, DC 20410 (202) 755-0455
To provide to those agencies to whom HUD must refer Title VIII complaints both the incentives and resources required to develop an effective work force to handle complaints and provide technical assistance and training. Types of assistance: grants. Estimate of annual funds available: $ 4,300,000.

* **Community Housing Resource Board Program (CHRB) 14.403**
Florence L. Maultsby, Director
HUD, Office of Fair Housing and Equal Opportunity
Office of Voluntary Compliance
Washington, DC 20410 (202) 755-7007
To provide funding to Community Housing Resource Boards (CHRBs) that have the responsibility of providing program implementation assistance to housing industry groups that have signed Voluntary Affirmative Marketing Agreements (VAMAs) with HUD. Types of assistance: grants. Estimate of annual funds available: $ 1,000,000.

* **Mariel-Cubans 16.572**
Louise Lucas, Bureau of Justice Assistance
Office of Justice Programs
633 Indiana Avenue, NW
Washington, DC 20531 (202) 724-8374
To provide financial reimbursements to states for their expenses by reason of Mariel-Cubans having to be incarcerated in state facilities for terms requiring incarceration for the period of October 1, 1988 through September 30, 1989, following their conviction of a felony committed after having been paroled into the U.S. by the Attorney General during the 1980 influx of Mariel-Cubans. Types of assistance: grant. Estimate of annual funds available: $ 5,000,000.

* **Criminal Justice Block Grants 16.573**
Office of Justice Program
Bureau of Justice Assistance
U.S. Department of Justice
Washington, DC 20531 (202) 272-6838
To provide financial assistance to states and units of local government in carrying out programs to improve the criminal justice system with emphasis on projects to assist in the drug control problem. Types of assistance: grants. Estimate of annual funds available: $ 2,463,000.

* **Emergency Federal Law Enforcement Assistance 16.577**
Louise Lucas, Bureau of Justice Assistance
Office of Justice Programs
U.S. Department of Justice

633 Indiana Ave., NW
Washington, DC 20531 (202) 724-8374
To provide necessary assistance to and through a state government to provide an adequate response to an uncommon situation which requires law enforcement, which is or threatens to become of serious or epidemic proportions and with respect to which state and local resources are inadequate to protect the lives and property of citizens or to enforce the criminal law. Types of assistance: grants. Estimate of annual funds available: $ 1,148,000.

* **Narcotics Control Discretionary Grant Program (Discretionary Program) 16.580**
Office of Justice Programs
Bureau of Justice Assistance
U.S. Department of Justice
633 Indiana Ave., NW
Washington, DC 20531 (202) 272-4606
To enhance the capacity of each state to define the drug problem and to focus on program development on areas of greatest need. Types of assistance: grant. Estimate of annual funds available: $ 30,071,000.

* **Drug Law Enforcement Program-Prison Capacity (Prison Capacity Program) 16.581**
Nicholas L. Demos, Office of Justice Programs
Bureau of Justice Assistance
U.S. Department of Justice
Washington, DC 20531 (202) 272-4605
To provide technical assistance, training and financial support to state, local and private nonprofit organizations dealing with state prison capacities and their alternatives. Types of assistance: grants. Estimate of annual funds available: $ 3,000.

* **Crime Victim Assistance/Discretionary Grants 16.582**
Marti Speights, Division Director
Office for Victims of Crime
Office of Justice Programs
U.S. Department of Justice
633 Indiana Ave., NW
Washington, DC 20531 (202) 272-6500
One percent of the Crime Victims Fund is statutorily reserved by the Office for Victims of Crime for grants to provide training and technical assistance services to eligible crime victims assistance programs and for financial support of services to victims of federal crime by eligible crime victims assistance programs. Types of assistance: grants, direct payments. Estimate of annual funds available: $ 935,000.

* **Children's Justice Act Discretionary Grants for Native American Indian Tribes (Children's Justice Act for Native American Indian Tribes) 16.583**
Marti Speights, Division Director
Office for Victims of Crime
Office of Justice Programs
U.S. Department of Justice
633 Indiana Ave., NW
Washington, DC 20531 (202) 272-6500
Fifteen percent of the funds from the Crime Victims Services that are transferred to the U.S. Department of Health and Human Services as part of the Children's Justice Act are to be statutorily reserved by the Office for Victims of Crime to make grants for the purpose of assisting native American Indian tribes in developing, establishing and operating programs. Types of assistance: grants, direct payments. Estimate of annual funds available: $ 631,000.

* **Corrections-Training and Staff Development 16.601**
National Institute of Corrections
320 First St., NW, Room 200
Washington, DC 20534 (202) 724-3106
To devise and conduct in various geographical locations, seminars, workshops and training programs for law enforcement officers, judges and judicial personnel, probation and parole personnel, correctional personnel, welfare workers and other personnel, including lay ex-offenders and paraprofessionals,

Be patient. If any phone number is incorrect, call (area code) 555-1212 and request the new listing.

Your Community

connected with the treatment and rehabilitation of criminal and juvenile offenders. Types of assistance: grants. Estimate of annual funds available: $2,273,544.

* Corrections-Technical Assistance/Clearinghouse 16.603

Technical Assistance Coordinator
National Institute of Corrections
320 First St., NW, Room 200
Washington, DC 20534 (202) 724-3106

To encourage and assist federal, state, and local government programs and services, and programs and services of other public and private agencies, institutions, in their efforts to develop and implement improved corrections programs. Types of assistance: grants. Estimate of annual funds available: $2,895,000.

* Labor Force Statistics 17.002

Thomas J. Plewes
Bureau of Labor Statistics
U.S. Department of Labor
Washington, DC 20212 (202) 523-1180

To provide statistical data on labor force activities. Types of assistance: grants. Estimate of annual funds available: $ 110,264,000.

* Employment Service 17.207

Robert A. Schaerfl
Director, United States Employment Service
Employment and Training Administration
U.S. Department of Labor
Washington, DC 20210 (202) 535-0157

To place persons in employment by providing a variety of placement-related services without charge to job seekers and to employers seeking qualified individuals to fill job openings. Types of assistance: grants. Estimate of annual funds available: $ 763,752,000.

* Dislocated Workers: Employment and Training Assistance 17.246

Robert N. Columbo
Employment and Training Administration
U.S. Department of Labor
200 Constitution Ave., NW
Washington, DC 20210 (202) 535-0577

To assist dislocated workers obtain unsubsidized employment through training and related employment services using a decentralized system of state programs. Types of assistance: grants. Estimate of annual funds available: $ 284,626,000.

* Migrant and Seasonal Farmworkers (Migrant and Other Seasonally Employed Farmworker Programs) 17.247

Office of Special Targeted Programs
Division of Seasonal Farmworker Programs
Employment and Training Administration
U.S. Dept. of Labor, Room 4641
200 Constitution Ave., NW
Washington, DC (202) 535-0500

To provide job training, job search assistance, and other supportive services for those individuals who suffer chronic seasonal unemployment and underemployment in the agricultural industry. Types of assistance: grants. Estimate of annual funds available: $ 68,522,000.

* Employment Services and Job Training-Pilot and Demonstration Programs 17.249

Administrator, Office of Strategic Planning
and Policy Development
Employment and Training Administration
U.S. Department of Labor
200 Constitution Ave., NW
Washington, DC (202) 535-0677

To provide, foster, and promote job training and other services which are most appropriately administered at the national level and which are operated in more than one state to groups with particular disadvantage in the labor market. Types of assistance: grants. Estimate of annual funds available: $ 38,964,000.

* Job Training Partnership Act (JTPA) 17.250

Robert N. Colombo
Employment and Training Administration
U.S. Department of Labor
200 Constitution Ave., NW
Washington, DC 20210 (202) 535-0577

To provide job training and related assistance to economically disadvantaged individuals and others who face significant employment barriers. Types of assistance: grants. Estimate of annual funds available: $ 1,788,772,000.

* Native American Employment and Training Programs 17.251

Division of Indian and Native American Programs
Employment and Training Administration
U.S. Department of Labor
Room N4641
200 Constitution Ave., NW
Washington, DC (202) 535-0502

To afford job training to Native Americans facing serious barriers to employment, who are in special need of such training to obtain productive employment. Types of assistance: grants. Estimate of annual funds available: $ 59,713,000.

* Mine Health and Safety Grants 17.600

Assistant Secretary of Labor for Mine Safety and Health
Mine Safety and Health Administration
U.S. Dept. of Labor,
Ballston Towers No. 3
Arlington, VA 22203 (703) 235-8264

To assist states in developing and enforcing effective mine health and safety laws and regulations. Types of assistance: grants. Estimate of annual funds available: $ 4,988,000.

* Disabled Veterans Outreach Program 17.801

Veterans Employment and Training Service
Office of the Assistant Secretary for Veterans
Employment and Training
U.S. Department of Labor
Room S-1316
200 Constitution Ave., NW
Washington, DC (202) 523-9110

To provide funds to states to provide job and job training opportunities for disabled and other veterans through contacts with employers. Types of assistance: grants. Estimate of annual funds available: $ 72,962,000.

* Local Veterans Employment Representative Program (LVER Program) 17.804

Veterans Employment and Training Service
Office of the Asst. Secretary for Veterans
Employment and Training
U.S. Dept. of Labor, Room S1316
200 Constitution Ave., NW
Washington, DC 20210 (202) 523-9110

To provide funds to State Employment Service/Job Service Agencies to ensure that there is local supervision of compliance with federal regulations, performance standards, and grant agreement provisions in carrying out requirements of 38 USC 2004 in providing veterans with maximum employment and training opportunities. Types of assistance: grants. Estimate of annual funds available: $ 66,998,000.

* Boating Safety Financial Assistance 20.005

Commandant
U.S. Coast Guard
Washington, DC 20593-0001 (202) 267-0978

To encourage greater state participation and uniformity in boating safety, particularly to permit the states to assume the greater share of boating safety

Be patient. If any phone number is incorrect, call (area code) 555-1212 and request the new listing.

Money For Communities and Non-Profits

education , assistance, and enforcement activities. Types of assistance: grants. Estimate of annual funds available: $ 60,000,000.

* Airport Improvement Program (AIP) 20.106

FAA, Office of Airport Planning and Programming
Grants-in-Aid Division, APP-500
800 Independence Ave., SW
Washington, DC 20591 (202) 267-3831

To assist sponsors, owners, or operators of public-use airports in the development of a nationwide system of airports adequate to meet the needs of civil aeronautics. Types of assistance: grants. Estimate of annual funds available: $ 1,400,000,000.

* Highway Planning and Construction (Federal-Aid Highway Program) 20.205

Thomas O. Willete, Director
Office of Engineering, FHA
400 7th St., SW
Washington, DC 20590 (202) 366-4853

To assist state highway agencies (SHA) in the development of an integrated, interconnected network of highways by constructing and rehabilitating the interstate highway system and building or improving primary, secondary and urban systems roads, and streets. Types of assistance: grants. Estimate of annual funds available: $ 1,371,300.

* Motor Carrier Safety Assistance Program (MCSAP) 20.218

Associate Administrator for Motor Carriers
FHA
Washington, DC 20590 (202) 366-2519

To reduce the number and severity of accidents and hazardous materials incidents involving commercial motor vehicles by substantially increasing the level of enforcement activity and the likelihood that safety defects, driver deficiencies, and unsafe carrier practices will be detected and corrected. Types of assistance: grants. Estimate of annual funds available: $ 46,700,000.

* Grants-In-Aid for Railroad Safety-State Participation (State Participation in Railroad Safety) 20.303

Associate Administrator for Safety
Federal Railroad Administration
Room 8320A
400 7th St., SW
Washington, DC 20590 (202) 366-0895

To promote safety in all areas of railroad operations; reduce railroad related accidents and casualties; and to reduce damage to property caused by accidents involving any carrier of hazardous materials by providing State participation in the enforcement and promotion of safety practices. Types of assistance: grants. Estimate of annual funds available: $ 950,000.

* Local Rail Service Assistance (National Rail Service Continuation Grants) 20.308

Office of Passenger and Freight Services
Federal Railroad Administration, Room 5410
400 7th St., SW
Washington, DC 20590 (202) 366-1677

To maintain efficient local rail freight services. Types of assistance: Grant. Estimate of annual funds available: $ 10,996,000.

* Urban Mass Transportation Capital Improvement Grants (Capital Grants) 20.500

Urban Mass Transportation Administration
U.S. Department of Transportation
400 7th St., SW
Washington, DC 20590

To assist in financing the acquisition, construction, reconstruction and improvement of facilities and equipment for use, by operation, lease, or otherwise in mass transportation service in urban areas. Types of assistance: grants. Estimate of annual funds available: $ 825,208,000.

* Urban Mass Transportation Managerial Training Grants (Mass Transit Technology and Technical Assistance Program) 20.503

Office of Technical Assistance and Safety
Urban Mass Transportation Administration
U.S. Department of Transportation
400 Seventh St., SW
Washington, DC 20590 (202) 366-0080

To provide fellowships for training of managerial, technical and professional personnel employed in the urban mass transportation field. Types of assistance: grants. Estimate of annual funds available: $ 1,953,000.

* Urban Mass Transportation Technical Studies Grants (Technical Planning Studies) 20.505

Director, Office of Planning Assistance
Office of Grants Management
Urban Mass Transportation Administration, DOT
400 7th St., SW
Washington, DC 20590 (202) 366-1662

To assist in planning, engineering and designing of urban mass transportation projects, and other technical studies in a program for a united or officially coordinated urban transportation system. Types of assistance: grants. Estimate of annual funds available: $ 47,687,000.

* Urban Mass Transportation Capital and Operating Assistance Formula Grants 20.507

Director, Office of Planning Assistance
Office of Grants Management
Urban Mass Transportation Administration, DOT
400 7th St., SW
Washington, DC 20590 (202) 366-1662

To assist in financing the acquisition, construction, cost effective leasing, planning and improvement of facilities and equipment for use by operation or lease or otherwise in mass transportation service. Types of assistance: grants. Estimate of annual funds available: $ 1,904,730,000.

* Public Transportation for Nonurbanized Areas (Section 18) 20.509

Urban Mass Transportation Administration
Office of Grants Management
Office of Capital and Formula Assistance
400 7th St., SW
Washington, DC 20590 (202) 366-2053

To improve, initiate, or continue public transportation services in nonurbanized areas by providing financial assistance for the acquisition, construction and improvement of facilities and equipment and the payment of operating expenses by operating contract, lease or otherwise. Types of assistance: grants. Estimate of annual funds available: $ 87,318,000.

* Urban Mass Transportation Technical Assistance 20.512

Associate Administrator for Technical
Assistance and Safety (UTS-1)
Urban Mass Transportation Administration, DOT
400 7th St., SW, Room 6431
Washington, DC 20590 (202) 366-4052

To improve mass transportation service, to contribute toward meeting total urban transportation needs at a minimum cost, and to assist in the reduction of urban transportation needs by improving the ability of transit industry operating officials to plan, manage, and operate their systems more effectively and safely. Types of assistance: grants. Estimate of annual funds available: $ 7,133,000.

* Capital Assistance Program for Elderly and Handicapped Persons (Section (b)(2)) 20.513

Urban Mass Transportation Administration
Office of Grants Management
Office of Capital and Formula Assistance
400 7th St., SW
Washington, DC 20590 (202) 366-2053

Be patient. If any phone number is incorrect, call (area code) 555-1212 and request the new listing.

Your Community

To provide financial assistance in meeting the transportation needs of elderly and handicapped persons where public transportation services are unavailable. Types of assistance: grants. Estimate of annual funds available: $ 35,057,000.

★ State and Community Highway Safety 20.600
Brian McLaughlin
Coordinator of Regional Operations
National Highway Traffic Safety Administration
Washington, DC 20590 (202) 366-2121
To provide a coordinated national highway safety program to reduce traffic accidents, deaths, injuries, and property damage. Types of assistance: grants. Estimate of annual funds available: $ 124,400,000.

★ Pipeline Safety 20.700
William Gute
Research and Special Programs Administration
U.S. Department of Transportation
400 7th St., SW
Washington, DC 20590 (202) 366-4046
To develop and maintain state natural gas, liquified natural gas, and hazardous liquid pipeline safety programs. Types of assistance: grants. Estimate of annual funds available: $ 4,400,000.

★ Tax Counseling for the Elderly 21.006
Marion L. Butler, Tax Counseling for the Elderly
Taxpayer Service Division
Internal Revenue Services
1111 Constitution Ave., NW
Washington, DC 20224 (202) 566-4904
To authorize the Internal Revenue Service to enter into agreement with private or public nonprofit agencies or organizations to establish a network of trained volunteers to provide free income tax information and return preparation assistance to elderly taxpayers. Types of assistance: direct payment. Estimate of annual funds available: $ 2,789,000.

★ Appalachian Supplements to Federal Grant-In-Aid Community Development 23.002
Executive Director
Appalachian Regional Commission
1666 Connecticut Avenue, NW
Washington DC 20235 (202) 673-7874
To meet the basic needs of local areas and assist in improving creation of jobs and private sector involvement and investment by funding development facilities such as water and sewage systems, sewage treatment plants, industrial sites and providing basic water and sewer facilities. Types of assistance: grants. Estimate of annual funds available: $ 17500.

★ Appalachian Development Highway System (Appalachian Corridor) 23.003
Executive Director
Appalachian Regional Commission
1666 Connecticut Ave., NW
Washington, DC 20235 (202) 673-7874
To provide a highway system which, in conjunction with other federally-aided highways, will open u areas with development potential within the Appalachian region where commerce an d communication have been inhibited by lack of adequate access. Types of assistance: grants. Estimate of annual funds available: $ 52,924,000.

★ Appalachian Health Programs (Appalachian 202 Health Programs) 23.004
Executive Director
Appalachian Regional Commission
1666 Connecticut Avenue, NW
Washington DC 20235 (202) 673-7874
To make primary health care accessible, reduce infant mortality and recruit needed health manpower in designed "health-shortage" areas. Types of assistance: grants. Estimate of annual funds available: $ 763,100.

★ Appalachian Housing Project Planning Loan, Technical Assistance Grant and Site Development and Off-Site Improvement Grant 23.005
Executive Director
Appalachian Regional Commission
1666 Connecticut Ave., NW
Washington, DC 20235 (202) 673-7874
To stimulate the creation of jobs and private sector investment through low and moderate income housing construction and rehabilitation, and to assist in developing site and off-site improvements for low and moderate income housing in the Appalachian Region. Types of assistance: grant. Estimate of annual funds available: $ 1,500,000.

★ Appalachian Local Access Roads 23.008
Executive Director
Appalachian Regional Commission
1666 Connecticut Ave., NW
Washington, DC 20235 (202) 673-7874
To provide access to industrial, commercial, educational, recreational, residential and related transportation facilities which directly or indirectly relate to the improvement of the areas determined by the states to have significant development potential. Types of assistance: grant. Estimate of annual funds available: $ 5,000,000.

★ Appalachian Local Development District Assistance (LDD) 23.009
Executive Director
Appalachian Regional Commission
1666 Connecticut Ave., NW
Washington, DC 20235 (202) 673-7874
To provide planning and development resources in multicounty areas; to help develop the technical competence essential to sound development assistance. Types of assistance: grant. Estimate of annual funds available: $ 3,200,000.

★ Appalachian Mine Area Restoration 23.010
Executive Director, Appalachian Regional Commission
1666 Connecticut Ave., NW
Washington, DC 20235 (202) 673-7874
To further the creation of jobs by rehabilitating areas presently damaged by deleterious mining practices and by controlling or abating mine drainage pollution. Types of assistance: Grant. Estimate of annual funds available: $ 0.

★ Appalachian State Research, Technical Assistance, and Demonstration Projects (State Research) 23.011
Executive Director, Appalachian Regional Commission
1666 Connecticut Ave., NW
Washington, DC 20235 (202) 673-7874
To expand the knowledge of the region to the fullest extent possible by means of state-sponsored research studies, technical assistance and demonstration projects in order to assist the Commission in accomplishing the objectives of the Act. Types of assistance: grant. Estimate of annual funds available: $ 1,000,000.

★ Appalachian Vocational and Other Education Facilities and Operations 23.012
Executive Director
Appalachian Regional Commission
1666 Connecticut Ave., NW
Washington DC 20235 (202) 673-7874
To provide the people of the region with the equipment, renovation and operating funds for training and education necessary to obtain employment at their best capability for available job opportunities. Types of assistance: grants. Estimate of annual funds available: $ 3,000,000.

★ Appalachian Child Development 23.013
Executive Director, Appalachian Regional Commission
1666 Connecticut Ave., NW
Washington, DC 20235 (202) 673-7874
To provide child development services throughout the region which meet the

Money For Communities and Non-Profits

needs of industry and its employees. Types of assistance: grants. Estimate of annual funds available: $ 318,635.

* Training Assistance to State and Local Government 27.009

Assistant Director
Office of Employee and Executive Development
Office of Personnel Management
P.O. Box 7230
Washington, DC 20044 (202) 632-6802

To assist state and local governments and Indian tribal governments in training professional, administrative, and technical personnel to increase their capability for mission accomplishment. Types of assistance: training. Estimate of annual funds available: $ 0.

* Presidential Management Intern Program 27.013

Programs Division
Office of Affirmative Recruiting and Employment
Career Entry and Employee Development Group
Office of Personnel Management
1900 E St., NW
Washington, DC (202) 632-0496

To attract to the federal service graduate students of exceptional potential who are receiving advanced degrees in a variety of academic disciplines and who have a clear interest in and commitment to a career in the analysis and management of public programs and policies. Types of assistance: federal employment. Estimate of annual funds available: $ 203000.

* Employment Discrimination-State and Local Anti-Discrimination Agency Contracts 30.002

Robert L. Walker
Program Development and Coordination Division
Systemic Investigation and Individual Compliance Programs
EEOC, Room 433
2403 E St., NW
Washington, DC (202) 634-6806

To assist EEOC in the enforcement of Title VII of the Civil Rights Act of 1964, as amended and of the age discrimination in employment act of 1967 by investigating and resolving charges of employment discrimination based on race, color, religion, sex, national origin, etc. Types of assistance: direct payment. Estimate of annual funds available: $ 20,000,000.

* Employment Discrimination Project Contracts - Indian Tribes 30.009

Robert L. Walker, Director
Program Development and Coordination Division
Systemic Investigation and Individual Compliance Program
EEOC, 2403 E St., NW
Washington, DC (202) 634-6806

To insure the protection of employment rights of Indians working on reservation. Types of assistance: grants. Estimate of annual funds available: $ 20,000,000.

* Labor-Management Cooperation 34.002

Division of Labor Management Grant Programs
Federal Mediation and Conciliation Service
2100 K St., NW
Washington, DC 20247 (202) 653-5320

Types of assistance: grants. Estimate of annual funds available: $ 11,900,000.

* Community Development Revolving Loan Program for Credit Unions (CDCU) 44.002

Mr. Floyd Lancaster
Community Development Revolving Loan Program for Credit Unions
National Credit Union Administration
1776 G St., NW
Washington, DC 20456 (202) 682-9780

To support community based credit unions in their efforts to stimulate economic development activities which result in increased income, ownership and employment opportunities for low-income residents and to provide basic

financial and related services to residents of their communities. Types of assistance: direct loans. Estimate of annual funds available: $ 0.

* Promotion of the Arts-State Programs 45.007

Directors, State Program
National Endowment for the Arts
100 Pennsylvania Ave., NW
Washington, DC 20506 (202) 682-5429

To assist state and regional public arts agencies in the development of programs for the encouragement of the arts and artists, and to assist organizations providing services at a national level to state or local arts agencies. Types of assistance: grants. Estimate of annual funds available: $ 25,526,000.

* Promotion of the Arts-Expansion Arts 45.010

E'Vonne C. Rorie
Expansion Arts Program
National Endowment for the Arts
1100 Pennsylvania Ave., NW
Washington, DC 20560 (202) 682-5443

To provide grants to professionally directed arts organizations of high artistic quality which are deeply rooted in and reflective of the culture of a minority. Types of assistance: grants. Estimate of annual funds available: $ 6,700,000.

* Promotion of the Arts: Inter-Arts 45.011

Director, Inter-Arts Program
National Endowment for the Arts
1100 Pennsylvania Ave., NW
Washington, DC 20506 (202) 682-5444

To provide grants for projects that potentially have national or regional impact. Types of assistance: grants. Estimate of annual funds available: $ 4,300,000.

* Promotion of the Arts - Challenge Grants 45.013

Challenge and Advancement Grant Programs
Room 617, National Endowment for the Arts
1100 Pennsylvania Ave., NW
Washington, DC 20506 (202) 682-5436

To assist on a one-time basis, projects designed to have a lasting impact that can help move the National forward in achieving excellence in the arts, access to, and/or appreciation of such excellence. Types of assistance: grants. Estimate of annual funds available: $ 18,500,000.

* Promotion of the Arts-Folk Arts 45.015

Director, Folk Arts Program
National Endowment for the Arts
1100 Pennsylvania Ave., NW
Washington, DC 20506 (202) 682-5449

To provide grants to assist, foster, and make publicly available the diverse traditional American folk arts throughout the country. Types of assistance: grants. Estimate of annual funds available: $ 3,100,000.

* Promotion of the Arts (Local Programs) 45.023

Local Programs, National Endowment for the Arts
Nancy Hawks Center
1100 Pennsylvania Ave., NW
Washington, DC 20506 (202) 682-5431

To enhance to the quality and availability of the arts by fostering expansion of public support for the arts at the local level and to strengthen the local arts agency as a mechanism for arts planning, financial support and development and to encourage joint planning for the arts by Federal, state, and local art agencies, community leaders, public officials, art organizations, and artists. Types of assistance: grants. Estimate of annual funds available: $ 2,566,000.

* Management and Technical Assistance for Socially and Economically Disadvantaged Businesses: 7(j) Development Assistance Program 59.007

Associate Administrator for Minority Small Business
1441 L St., NW, Room 602
Washington, DC 20416 (202) 653-6475

Be patient. If any phone number is incorrect, call (area code) 555-1212 and request the new listing.

Your Community

To provide management and technical assistance through qualified individuals, public or private organizations to existing or potential businesses which are economically and socially disadvantaged or which are located in areas of high concentration of unemployment. Types of assistance: grants. Estimate of annual funds available: $ 8,080,000.

* Physical Disaster Loans (7(b) Loans (DL)) 59.008
Disaster Assistance Division, SBA
1441 L St., NW
Washington, DC 20416 (202) 653-6879
To provide loans to the victims of designated physical-type disasters for uninsured loans. Types of assistance: loans, loan guarantee. Estimate of annual funds available: $ 280,000,000.

* Service Corps of Retired Executives Association (SCORE) 59.026
National SCORE Office
1129 20th St., NW
Washington, DC 20036 (202) 653-6279
To utilize the management experience of retired and active business executives to counsel and train potential in existing small businesses. Types of assistance: grants, other. Estimate of annual funds available: $ 900,000.

* Small Business Development Center (SBDC) 59.037
Small Business Administration
Office of Small Business Development Center
1441 L St., NW, Room 317
Washington, DC 20416 (202) 653-6768
To provide management counseling, training and technical assistance to the small business community through Small Business Development Centers (SBDCs). Types of assistance: grants. Estimate of annual funds available: $ 45,000,000.

* Veterans State Domiciliary Care 64.014
Asst. Chief
Medical Director for Geriatrics and Extended Care
U.S. Department of Veterans Affairs
Washington, DC 20420 (202) 233-3679
To provide financial assistance to states furnishing domiciliary care to eligible veterans in State Veterans Homes which meet the standards prescribed by the Secretary of Veterans Affairs. Types of assistance: grants. Estimate of annual funds available: $ 13,188,000.

* Veterans State Nursing Home Care 64.015
Asst. Chief
Medical Director of Geriatrics and Extended Care
U.S. Department of Veterans Affairs
Washington, DC 20420 (202) 233-3679
To provide financial assistance to states furnishing nursing home care to eligible veterans in State Veterans Homes which meet the standards prescribed by the Secretary of Veterans Affairs. Types of assistance: grants. Estimate of annual funds available: $ 69,100,000.

* Veterans State Hospital Care 64.016
Asst. Chief Medical Director for Geriatrics
and Extended Care
U.S. Department of Veterans Affairs
Washington, DC 20420 (202) 233-3679
To provide financial assistance to states furnishing hospital care to eligible veterans in State Veterans Homes which meet the standards prescribed by the Secretary of Veterans Affairs. Types of assistance: grants. Estimate of annual funds available: $ 3,669,000.

* State Cemetery Grants 64.203
Director, State Cemetery Grant Program
National Cemetery System
U.S. Department of Veterans Affairs
810 Vermont Ave., NW
Washington, DC 20420 (202) 233-2313

To assist states in the establishment, expansion and improvement of veterans cemeteries. Types of assistance: grants. Estimate of annual funds available: $ 9,000,000.

* Air Pollution Control Program Support 66.001
Steve Hitte, Air Quality Management Division
Office of Air and Radiation, EPA
Research Triangle Park, NC 27711 (919) 541-0886
To assist state, municipal, intermunicipal, and interstate agencies in planning developing, establishing, improving and maintaining adequate programs for prevention and control of air quality standards. Types of assistance: grants. Estimate of annual funds available: $ 101,500,000.

* Air Pollution Control-Technical Training 66.006
Betsy Dodson
Air Pollution Training Institute, EPA
Research Triangle Park, NC 27711 (919) 541-2401
To provide technical training to personnel from state and local air pollution control agencies. Types of assistance: training. Estimate of annual funds available: $ 241,000.

* Construction Grants for Wastewater Treatment Works 66.418
James Hanlon, Director
Municipal Construction Division, WH-547
Office of Municipal Pollution Control, EPA
Washington, DC 20460 (202) 382-5859
To assist and serve as an incentive in construction of municipal wastewater treatment works which are required to meet state and/or federal water quality standards. Types of assistance: grants. Estimate of annual funds available: $ 1,166,000,000.

* Water Pollution Control-State and Interstate Program Support (106 Grants) 66.419
Edmund M. Notzon, Director
Analysis and Evaluation Division
Office of Water Regulations and Standards
Office of Water, EPA
Washington, DC 20460 (202) 382-5389
To assist states, territorial Indian Tribes and interstate agencies in establishing and maintaining adequate measures for prevention and control of surface and ground water pollution. Types of assistance: grants. Estimate of annual funds available: $ 67,100,000.

* Water Quality Control Training Seminars, Data and Monitoring Publications (STORET-Storage and Retrieval System) 66.423
Phillip H. Lindenstruth, Chief
Client Services Branch
Office of Information Resources Management
Washington, DC 20460 (202) 382-7220
To provide state, interstate and other water pollution control and water resource management agencies orientation and where requested training in the use of the storage and retrieval system used by EPA. Types of assistance: Training. Estimate of annual funds available: $ 0.

* State Public Water System Supervision 66.432
Ray Enyeart, Office of Drinking Water
Office of Water, EPA
Washington, DC 20460 (202) 382-5551
To foster development and maintenance of state programs which implement the Safe Drinking Water Act. Types of assistance: Grant. Estimate of annual funds available: $ 33,450,000.

* State Underground Water Source Protection 66.433
Francoise Brasier, Chief
Underground Injection Control Branch

Be patient. If any phone number is incorrect, call (area code) 555-1212 and request the new listing.

Office of Drinking Water
Office of Water, EPA
401 M St., SW
Washington, DC 20460 (202) 382-5530
To foster development and implementation of underground injection control (UIC) programs under the Safe Drinking Water Act. Types of assistance: grants. Estimate of annual funds available: $ 10,500,000.

* **Water Pollution Control-Lake Restoration Cooperative Agreements (Clean Lakes Program) 66.435**
Environmental Protection Agency
Grants Administration Division (PM-216)
Washington, DC 20460
To provide financial assistance to states for assessing the water quality of publicly-owned freshwater lakes, diagnosing the causes of degradation in publicly owned lakes, developing lake restoration and protection plans. Types of assistance: grants. Estimate of annual funds available: $ 12,500,000.

* **Construction Management Assistance (Construction Grants Delegation to States) 66.438**
Robert Lee, Delegation Management Branch
Municipal Construction Division, WH-547
Environmental Protection Agency
Washington, DC 20460 (202) 382-7359
To assist and serve as an incentive in the process of delegating the states a maximum amount of authority for conducting day-to-day matters related the management of the construction grant program. Types of assistance: Grant. Estimate of annual funds available: $ 60,531,000.

* **Water Quality Management Planning (205(j)) 66.454**
Edmund M. Notzon, Director
Analysis and Evaluation Division
Office of Water Regulations and Standards, EPA
401 M St., SW
Washington, DC 20460 (202) 382-5389
To assist states (including territories and the District), public comprehensive planning organizations, and interstate organizations in carrying out water quality management planning. Types of assistance: grants. Estimate of annual funds available: $ 23,000,000.

* **Construction Grants for Abatement of Combined Sewer Overflow Pollution in Marine Bays and Estuaries (Marine CSO Reserve) 66.455**
Municipal Facilities Division
Office of Municipal Pollution Control
Office of Water
Environmental Protection Agency
Washington, DC 20460
To award grants to Combined Sewer Overflow projects which are designed to restore uses of the receiving waters in Bays and Estuaries which have been impaired by the impact of CSOs. Types of assistance: grants. Estimate of annual funds available: $ 10,000,000.

* **National Estuary Program 66.456**
Louise Wise, Chief
Technical Support Division
Office of Marine and Estuarine Protection, EPA
Washington, DC 20460 (202) 475-7102
To authorize the Agency to convene Management Conferences with participants from states, legislatures, etc., to develop programs to protect and restore coastal resources in estuaries of national significance. Types of assistance: grants. Estimate of annual funds available: $ 9,677,837.

* **Capitalization Grants for State Revolving Funds (State Revolving Fund) 66.458**
Robert Lee, Delegation Management Branch
Municipal Construction Division
Office of Municipal Control, EPA

Washington, DC 20460 (202) 382-7359
To create State Revolving Funds through a program of capitalization grants to states which will provide a feasible transition to state and local financing of municipal wastewater treatment facilities. Types of assistance: grants. Estimate of annual funds available: $ 1,361,000,000.

* **Nonpoint Source Reservation (205(j)(5)) 66.459**
James Meck, Chief, Nonpoint Sources Branch
Criteria and Standards Division
Office of Water Regulations and Standards, EPA
401 M St., SW
Washington, DC 20460 (202) 382-7100
To assist states in developing and implementing non-point source management programs. Types of assistance: grants. Estimate of annual funds available: $ 12,500,000.

* **Air Pollution Control Research 66.501**
Environmental Protection Agency
Grants Administration, PM 216
Washington, DC 20460
Types of assistance: grants. Estimate of annual funds available: $ 15,469,300.

* **Environmental Protection Consolidated Grants - Program Support (Consolidated Program Support Grants) 66.600**
Richard Mitchell, Grants Administration Division
PM 216f, Environmental Protection Agency
Washington, DC 20460 (202) 382-5297
The consolidated program support grant is an alternative assistance delivery mechanism which allows a state or local agency responsible for continuing pollution control programs to develop an integrated approach to pollution control. Types of assistance: grants. Estimate of annual funds available: $ 30,000,000.

* **Pesticides Enforcement Program 66.700**
A.E. Conroy II, Director
Office of Compliance Monitoring
Office of Pesticides and Toxic Substances, EPA
Washington, DC 20460 (202) 382-7003
To assist states in developing and maintaining comprehensive pesticide enforcement programs. Types of assistance: grants. Estimate of annual funds available: $ 8,803,400.

* **Toxic Substances Compliance Monitoring Cooperative Agreements 66.701**
A.E. Conroy II, Director
Office of Compliance Monitoring
Office of Pesticides and Toxic Substances, EPA
Washington, DC 20460 (202) 382-3807
To assist states in developing and maintaining comprehensive Toxic Substance enforcement programs. Types of assistance: grants. Estimate of annual funds available: $ 2,200,000.

* **Asbestos Hazards Abatement (Schools) Assistance (Hazard Abatement Assistance Branch HAAB) 66.702**
Regina Busong
Environmental Protection Agency
401 M St., SW
Washington, DC 20460 (202) 382-3949
To create a program information distribution, technical and scientific assistance and financial support Local Education Agencies. Types of assistance: grants, direct loans. Estimate of annual funds available: $ 13,005,000.

* **Pesticides Certification Program 66.704**
Stephen Johnson
Field Operations Division, OPP
Office of Pesticides and Toxic Substances, EPA

Be patient. If any phone number is incorrect, call (area code) 555-1212 and request the new listing.

Your Community

Washington, DC 20460 (703) 557-7410
To assist states, territories and possessions of the U.S., including the District of Columbia and Indian Tribes, in developing and maintaining comprehensive programs to certify applicators to apply restricted use pesticides. Types of assistance: grants. Estimate of annual funds available: $ 1,680,000.

* Hazardous Waste Management State Program Support 66.801
Grants Administration Division, EPA
Washington, DC 20460
To assist state governments in the development and implementation of an authorized hazardous waste management program for the purpose of controlling the generation, transportation, treatment, storage and disposal of hazardous waste. Types of assistance: grants. Estimate of annual funds available: $ 66,000,000.

* Hazardous Substance Response Trust Fund (Superfund) 66.802
Jon Baker Wine, Chief
State Involvement Section
Office of Emergency and Remedial Response, EPA
Washington, DC 20460 (202) 382-2443
To determine level of hazard at sites listed in the CERCLA Information System. Types of assistance: grants. Estimate of annual funds available: $ 195,529,167.

* State Underground Storage Tanks Program (UST Program) 66.804
Joseph Retzer, Director
Implementation Division
Underground Storage Tank Program (OSWER), EPA
401 M St., SW
Washington, DC 20460 (202) 382-7601
To assist states in Development and implementation of their own underground storage tank programs to operate in lieu of the federal Program. Types of assistance: grants. Estimate of annual funds available: $ 9,000,000.

* Underground Storage Tank Trust Fund Program 66.805
Joseph Retzer, Director
Implementation Division
Office of the Underground Storage Tanks, EPA
Waterside Mall, 401 M St., SW
Washington, DC 20460 (202) 382-7601
To support the development of state corrective action and enforcement programs that address releases from underground storage tanks containing petroleum. Types of assistance: grants. Estimate of annual funds available: $ 42,500,000.

* Superfund Technical Assistance Grants for Citizen Groups at Priority Sites 66.806
Murray Newton
Office of Emergency and Remedial Response, EPA
401 M St., SW
Washington, DC 20460 (202) 382-2443
To provide resources for community groups to hire technical advisors who can assist them in interpreting technical information concerning the assessment of potential hazards and the selection and design of appropriate remedies. Types of assistance: grants. Estimate of annual funds available: $ 5,540,000.

* Foster Grandparent Program (FGP) 72.001
Program Officer, Foster Grandparent Program
Senior Companion Program, ACTION
806 Connecticut Ave., NW
Washington, DC 20525 (202) 634-9349
To provide part-time volunteer service opportunities for low income persons age 60 and over and to give supportive person-to-person service in health, education welfare and related settings to help alleviate the physical mental and emotional problems of infants, children or youth having special or exceptional needs. Types of assistance: grants. Estimate of annual funds available: $ 58,928,000.

* Retired Senior Volunteer Program (RSVP) 72.002
Program Officer
Retired Senior Volunteer Program, ACTION
1100 Vermont Ave., NW
Washington, DC 20525 (202) 634-9353
To provide a variety of opportunities for retired persons, aged 60 or over to serve their community through significant volunteer service. Types of assistance: grants. Estimate of annual funds available: $ 30,862,000.

* Service-Learning Programs 72.005
ACTION, Student Community Service Programs
1100 Vermont Ave., NW
Washington, DC 20525 (202) 634-9424
To encourage and enable students in secondary, vocational and post-secondary schools to participate in community service projects addressing poverty related problems. Types of assistance: grants. Estimate of annual funds available: $ 1,352,000.

* Senior Companion Program 72.008
Program Officer
Foster Grandparent Senior Companion Program
Development and Planning Branch, ACTION
1100 Vermont Ave., NW
Washington, DC 20525 (202) 634-9351
To provide volunteer opportunities for low income people aged 60 and older which enhance their ability to remain active and provide critically needed community services. Types of assistance: grants. Estimate of annual funds available: $ 25,135,000.

* Volunteerism: Minigrants Program 72.010
Technical Assistance Officer
Program Demonstration and Development Division
Room M513, ACTION
1100 Vermont Ave., NW
Washington, DC 20525 (202) 634-975
To initiate, strengthen and/or supplement volunteer efforts and to encourage broad-based volunteer citizen participation. Types of assistance: grants. Estimate of annual funds available: $ 150,000.

* State Office of Voluntarism (SOV) 72.011
National SOV Program Manager
Program Development and Demonstration Division
ACTION, Room M513
1100 Vermont Ave., NW
Washington, DC 20525 (202) 634-9749
To promote and coordinate voluntary participation in state and local government and public and private nonprofit organizations by fostering developing creating and/or supporting Offices of Voluntarism at the state level to stimulate new active citizen initiatives. Types of assistance: grants. Estimate of annual funds available: $ 100,000.

* Volunteer Demonstration Program (Demonstration Grants) 72.012
Asst. Director
Program Demonstration and Development Division
ACTION
1100 Vermont Ave., NW
Washington, DC 20525 (202) 634-9757
To explore areas of human and social concern where citizens, as volunteers can contribute toward individual self-reliance and community self-sufficiency. Types of assistance: grants. Estimate of annual funds available: $ 754,000.

* Technical Assistance Program (TAP) 72.013
Technical Assistance Officer
Technical Assistance Program, ACTION
1100 Vermont Ave., NW
Washington, DC 20525 (202) 634-9757
To help voluntary and nonprofit organizations respond to the training, technical assistance and management needs of volunteers and organizations undertaking

Be patient. If any phone number is incorrect, call (area code) 555-1212 and request the new listing.

Money For Communities and Non-Profits

voluntary efforts. Types of assistance: grants. Estimate of annual funds available: $ 46,000.

* Drug Alliance 72.014
Director, Drug Alliance
Program Demonstration and Development Division
ACTION
1100 Vermont Ave., NW
Washington, DC 20525 (202) 634-9759
To strengthen and expand the efforts of community-based volunteer groups working to prevent drug abuse. Types of assistance: grants. Estimate of annual funds available: $ 313,000.

* Energy Extension Service 81.050
Ronald W. Bowes, Chief
Energy Management and Extension Branch
U.S. Department of Energy
(CE-221), Forrestal Bldg.
1000 Independence Ave., SW
Washington, DC 20585 (202) 586-8288
To encourage individuals and small establishments to reduce energy consumption and convert to alternative energy sources. Types of assistance: grants. Estimate of annual funds available: $ 3,844,000.

* Energy Conservation for Institutional Buildings 81.052
Elmer Lee
Institutional Conservation Programs Division
Office of Conservation and Renewable Energy, CE-231
U.S. Department of Energy
Washington, DC 20585 (202) 586-8034
Types of assistance: grants. Estimate of annual funds available: $ 36,600,000.

* Nuclear Waste Disposal Siting (Consultation and Cooperation Financial Assistance) 81.065
James C. Bresee
Office of Civilian Radioactive Waste Management
Washington, DC (202) 586-9173
To provide for the development of a repository for the disposal of high level radioactive waste and spent nuclear fuel. Types of assistance: direct payment. Estimate of annual funds available: $ 16,000,000.

* Energy Task Force for the Urban Consortium 81.081
Linda J. DelaCroix, Project Manager
Building Services Division
Office of Conservation and Renewable Energy, DOE
1000 Independence Ave., SW
Washington, DC 20585 (202) 586-1851
To develop the capability to address energy related problems and to evaluate and test community energy supply and conservation techniques. Types of assistance: grants. Estimate of annual funds available: $ 1,960,000.

* Reimbursement for Firefighting on Federal Property 83.007
Clyde A. Bragdon, Jr., Administrator,
U.S. Fire Administration
500 C St., SW
Federal Center Plaza
Washington, DC 20472 (301) 447-1080
To provide that each fire service organization which engages in firefighting operations on Federal property may be reimbursed for their direct expenses and direct losses incurred in firefighting Types of assistance: direct payment. Estimate of annual funds available: $ 0.

* Community-Based Anti-Arson Program 83.008
Office of Acquisition Management
Attn: Cathy Green, Room 732
500 C St., SW

Washington, DC 20472
To assist local community based anti-arson organizations increase and intensify arson mitigation efforts. Types of assistance: grants. Estimate of annual funds available: $ 300,000.

* Emergency Management Institute-Training Assistance (Student Stipend Reimbursement Program (SEP)) 83.400
National Emergency Training Center
Student Services Branch
16825 S. Seton Ave.
Emmitsburg, MD 21727 (301) 447-1000
To defray travel and per diem expenses of state and local emergency management personnel who attend training courses conducted by the Emergency Management Institute. Types of assistance: direct payment. Estimate of annual funds available: $ 700,000.

* Emergency Management Institute-Architect/Engineer Student Program 83.401
Linda Whitaker
Engineering and Survey Branch, FEMA
Washington, DC 20472 (202) 646-3061
To train architectural or engineering students to survey buildings to determine the degree to which they provide protection against nuclear disaster effects. Types of assistance: Training. Estimate of annual funds available: $ 0.

* Emergency Management Institute-Field Training Program (Comprehensive Cooperative Agreements (CCA)) 83.403
Emergency Management Institute
16825 S. Seton Ave.
Emmittsburg, MD 21227 (301) 447-1000
To provide FEMA support to state-based training programs. Types of assistance: grants, Training. Estimate of annual funds available: $ 4,500,000.

* National Fire Academy-Training Assistance (State Stipend Reimbursement Program) 83.405
National Emergency Training Center
Student Services Branch
16825 S. Seton Ave.
Emmitsburg, MD 21727 (301) 447-1000
To provide travel stipends to students attending Academy courses, train the trainer, and in-service instructor training. Types of assistance: direct payment. Estimate of annual funds available: $ 1,102,163.

* Civil Defense - State and Local Emergency Management Assistance (Emergency Management Assistance) 83.503
Marilyn Barton, Office of Civil Defense
State and Local Programs and Support Directorate
FEMA
Washington, DC 20472 (202) 646-3510
To develop civil defense organizations in the states and their political subdivisions in order to plan for and coordinate emergency activities in the event of attack or natural disaster. Types of assistance: grants. Estimate of annual funds available: $ 58,123,000.

* Other State and Local Direction, Control and Warning 83.504
Earl Tildon
Direction and Control Branch, FEMA
Washington, DC 20472 (202) 646-3094
To assist state and local governments in preventive maintenance and corrective maintenance management planning and repair and replacement costs of emergency communications and warning systems and emergency operating center equipment and facilities. Types of assistance: grants. Estimate of annual funds available: $ 1,543,000.

Be patient. If any phone number is incorrect, call (area code) 555-1212 and request the new listing.

Your Community

* State Disaster Preparedness Grants (Disaster Preparedness Improvement Grant) 83.505
Gregory Jones
Office of Disaster Assistance Programs
State and Local Programs and Support, FEMA
Washington, DC 20472 (202) 646-3668
To assist states in developing and improving state and local plans, programs, and capabilities for disaster preparedness and prevention. Types of assistance: grants. Estimate of annual funds available: $ 2,800,000.

* State and Local Emergency Operating Centers (EOC) 83.512
Earl T. Tildon
Direction and Control Branch
Emergency Management Systems Support Division
FEMA
Washington, DC 20472 (202) 646-3094
To enhance effective, reliable and survivable direction and control capabilities of state and local government. Types of assistance: grant. Estimate of annual funds available: $ 5,000,000.

* State and Local Warning and Communications Systems 83.513
Joseph H. Massa
Communications Management Officer, FEMA
Washington, DC 20472 (202) 646-3083
To maintain the civil defense readiness of state and local governments by furnishing matching funds for the purchase of equipment and supporting materials for state and local direction and control. Types of assistance: grants. Estimate of annual funds available: $ 500,000.

* Population Protection Planning 83.514
C. Dwight Poe
State and Local Programs and Support Directorate
FEMA
Washington, DC 20472 (202) 646-3492
To assist states and localities to develop multi-hazard emergency operations plans that detail the planning provisions that are necessary to ensure the protection of people from the effects of nuclear attack. Types of assistance: grants. Estimate of annual funds available: $ 8,400,000.

* Disaster Assistance 83.516
Deborah Hard, FEMA
Office of Disaster Assistance Programs
Washington, DC 20472 (202) 646-3612
To provide supplemental assistance to states, local government, certain private nonprofit organizations and individuals in alleviating suffering and hardship resulting from major disasters or emergencies declared by the President. Types of assistance: grants, direct payment. Estimate of annual funds available: $ 220,000,000.

* Hazard Mitigation Assistance 83.519
Karen Helbrecht, Hazard Mitigation Branch
Disaster Assistance Programs, FEMA
500 C St., SW
Washington, DC 20472 (202) 646-3358
To assist states or local units of government in preparing a hazard mitigation plan. Types of assistance: grants. Estimate of annual funds available: $ 200,000.

* Hurricane Preparedness Grants (Hurricane Preparedness) 83.520
Frederick H. Sharrocks, Jr.
Earthquakes and Natural Hazards Programs Division
State and Local Programs and Support, FEMA
Washington, DC 20472 (202) 646-2796
Major objectives of the Hurricane Preparedness Program are to provide technical and financial assistance to state and local governments to conduct a Hurricane Preparedness Study that addresses the unique consequences of hurricanes in high-risk, high-population areas, reduce hurricane-caused injuries and save lives by assisting in the preparation of a hurricane evacuation plan, and reduce property damage caused by hurricanes. Types of assistance: grants. Estimate of annual funds available: $ 50,000.

* Earthquake Hazards Reduction Grants (Earthquake Hazards Reduction) 83.521
Gary D. Johnson
Earthquakes and Natural Hazards Programs Division
State and Local Programs and Support, FEMA
Washington, DC 20472 (202) 646-2799
To reduce, abate and mitigate the potential loss of life and property as the result of the occurrence of an earthquake by fostering the increase in public awareness. Types of assistance: Grant. Estimate of annual funds available: $ 1,565,000.

* Radiological Defense (Radiological Defense (RADEF)) 83.522
Michael S. Pawlowski, Chief
Radiological Defense Branch
Office of Civil Defense
Systems Support Division, FEMA
Washington, DC 20472 (202) 646-3080
To develop and implement Radiological Defense capabilities to minimize the effects of war-related radiological hazards. Types of assistance: grants. Estimate of annual funds available: $ 8,122,000.

* Federal Emergency Management Food and Shelter Program (Emergency Food and Shelter) 83.523
Fran McCarthy, FEMA
Office of Disaster Assistance Programs
Washington, DC 20472 (202) 646-3648
To supplement and expand on-going efforts to provide shelter, food and supportive services for needy families and individuals. Types of assistance: grants. Estimate of annual funds available: $ 114,000,000.

* National Defense/National Direct/Perkins Loan Cancellations (formerly National Direct Student Loan (NDSL) 84.037
Robert R. Coates
Division of Program Operations
Student Financial Assistance Programs
400 Maryland Ave., SW
Washington, DC 20202 (202) 732-3715
To reimburse institutions for their share of loans cancelled for National Defense Student Loan recipients who become teachers or who perform active military service in the U.S. Armed Forces. Types of assistance: direct payment. Estimate of annual funds available: $ 32,306,000.

* Impact Aid-Construction (Impact Aid; Construction) 84.040
Charles E. Hansen
Program Operations, Impact Aid Program
U.S. Department of Education
400 Maryland Ave., SW
Washington, DC 20202-6244 (202) 732-4651
To provide assistance for the construction of urgently needed minimum school facilities in school districts which have had substantial increases in school membership as a result of new or increased Federal Activities. Types of assistance: grants. Estimate of annual funds available: $ 24,700,000.

* Impact Aid-Maintenance and Operation (Impact Aid/Disaster Aid) 84.041
Charles Hansen
Impact Aid Program
Office of Elementary and Secondary Education
U.S. Department of Education
400 Maryland Ave., SW
Washington, DC 20202 (202) 732-4651

Be patient. If any phone number is incorrect, call (area code) 555-1212 and request the new listing.

Money For Communities and Non-Profits

To provide financial assistance to local educational agencies when enrollments or availability of revenue are adversely affected by federal activities. Types of assistance: direct payment. Estimate of annual funds available: $ 708,396,000.

* Vocational Education-State Councils 84.053

Division of Vocational Education
Office of Asst Secretary for Vocational
and Adult Education
U.S. Dept. of Education
400 Maryland Ave., SW
Washington, DC 20202 (202) 732-2441

To advise the State Board for Vocational Education on the development and administration of the State Plan. Types of assistance: grants. Estimate of annual funds available: $ 7,904,000.

* Indian Education-Formula Grants to Local Educational Agencies (Indian Education Act - Subpart 1) 84.060

Office of Indian Educations
U.S. Department of Education
400 Maryland Ave., SW
Washington, DC 20202 (202) 732-1887

To develop and carry out elementary and secondary school programs designed to meet the special educational and culturally related academic needs of Indian children. Types of assistance: grants. Estimate of annual funds available: $ 49,248,000.

* Rehabilitation Services-Basic Support (Basic Support) 84.126

Office of Program Operations
Rehabilitation Services Administration
U.S. Department of Education
Washington, DC 20202 (202) 732-1406

To provide vocational rehabilitation services to persons with mental and/or physical handicaps. Types of assistance: grants. Estimate of annual funds available: $ 1,437,973,057.

* Rehabilitation Services-Service Projects (Rehabilitation Service Projects) 84.128

Rehabilitation Services Administration
Office of Asst. Secretary for Special Education
and Rehabilitative Services
U.S. Department of Education
Washington, DC 20202 (202) 732-1347

To provide funds to state vocational rehabilitation agencies and public nonprofit organizations for projects and demonstration which hold promise of expanding and otherwise improving services for groups of mentally and physically handicapped individuals over and above those provided by the Basic Support Program. Types of assistance: grants. Estimate of annual funds available: $ 47,687,000.

* Migrant Education - Interstate and Intrastate Coordination Program 84.144

Office of Migrant Education
Office of Elementary and Secondary Education
U.S. Department of Education
400 Maryland Ave., SW, Room 2145
Washington, DC 20202 (202) 732-4746

To carry out activities to improve the interstate and intrastate coordination of migrant education between state and local education agencies. Types of assistance: grants. Estimate of annual funds available: $ 8,264,000.

* Transition Program for Refugee Children 84.146

Office of Bilingual Education and Minority Languages Affairs
U.S. Department of Education
330 C St., SW, Room 5086
Washington DC 20202 (202) 732-5708

To provide financial assistance to state and local educational agencies to meet the special educational needs of eligible refugee children enrolled in elementary and secondary schools. Types of assistance: grants. Estimate of annual funds available: $ 15,808,000.

* Public Library Construction (LSCA Title II) 84.154

Public Library Support Staff
Library Programs
U.S. Department of Education
Washington, DC 20208 (202) 357-6303

To assist with public library construction. Types of assistance: grants. Estimate of annual funds available: $ 21,877,520.

* Removal of Architectural Barriers to the Handicapped 84.155

Special Education Programs
U.S. Department of Education
400 Maryland Ave., SW
Washington, DC 20202 (202) 732-1025

To provide financial assistance to state educational agencies an through them local educational agencies and intermediate educational units to pay all or part of the costs of altering existing buildings and equipment to remove architectural barriers to the handicapped. Types of assistance: grants. Estimate of annual funds available: $ 0.

* Client Assistance For Handicapped Individuals (CAP) 84.161

U.S. Department of Education
Associate Commissioner for Program Operations
Office of Special Education and Rehabilitative Services
Washington, DC 20202 (202) 732-1406

To provide assistance in informing and advising clients and client applicants of available benefits under the Rehabilitation Act. Types of assistance: grants. Estimate of annual funds available: $ 7,682,000.

* Library Services for Indian Tribes and Hawaiian Natives 84.163

Library Development Staff, Library Programs
Office of Educational Research and Improvement
U.S. Department of Education
Washington, DC 20208 (202) 357-6323

To promote the extension of public library services to Indian people living on or near reservations; for Indian tribes and Indian in Oklahoma. Types of assistance: grants. Estimate of annual funds available: $ 2,448,700.

* Magnet Schools Assistance 84.165

Division of Discretionary Grants, Room 2040
400 Maryland Ave., SW
Washington, DC 20202 (202) 732-4360

To provide grants to eligible local educational agencies for use in magnet schools that are part of approved desegregation plans. Types of assistance: grants. Estimate of annual funds available: $ 113,620,000.

* Library Literacy (LSCA Title VI) 84.167

Library Development Staff, Library Programs
Office of Educational Research and Improvement
U.S. Department of Education
Washington, DC 20208 (202) 357-6321

To provide support to state public libraries for coordinating and planning library literacy programs and making arrangements for training librarians and volunteers to carry out such programs. Types of assistance: grants. Estimate of annual funds available: $ 4,730,000.

* Handicapped-Preschool Grants 84.173

Division of Educational Services
Office of the Asst. Secretary for Special Education
and Rehabilitative Services
U.S. Department of Education
Washington, DC 20202 (202) 732-1109

Be patient. If any phone number is incorrect, call (area code) 555-1212 and request the new listing.

Your Community

To provide grants to states to assist them in providing a free appropriate public education to preschool age handicapped children. Types of assistance: grants. Estimate of annual funds available: $ 247,000,000.

* Vocational Education-Community Based Organizations 84.174

U.S. Department of Education
Office of Asst. Secretary for Vocational and Adult Education
400 Maryland Ave., SW
Washington, DC 20202 (202) 732-2441

To provide educational assistance to severely disadvantaged youth, through the collaboration of public agencies, community based organizations and business concerns to enable them to succeed in vocational education. Types of assistance: grant. Estimate of annual funds available: $ 8,892,000.

* Leadership in Educational Administration Development (LEAD) 84.178

Hunter Moorman
Office of Educational Research and Improvement
U.S. Department of Education
Washington, DC 20208 (202) 357-6116

To provide assistance for eligible parties to establish and operate technical assistance centers that promote the development of leadership skills in school administrators. Types of assistance: grants. Estimate of annual funds available: $ 8,222,000.

* Drug Free Schools and Communities-Regional Centers 84.188

Alan King
Drug-Free Schools and Communities Staff
Office of Elementary and Secondary Education
400 Maryland Ave., SW
Washington, DC 20202 (202) 732-4599

To provide financial assistance to maintain five regional centers to train school teams and assist local education agencies in developing and strengthening programs of alcohol and drug abuse education and prevention. Types of assistance: grants. Estimate of annual funds available: $ 15,638,000.

* Demonstration Centers for the Retraining of Dislocated Workers 84.193

Paul Geib
Division of National Programs
Office of Vocational and Adult Education
U.S. Department of Education
400 Maryland Ave., SW
Washington, DC 20202 (202) 732-2364

To establish one or more demonstration centers for the retraining of dislocated workers in order to demonstrate the application of general theories of vocational education to the specific problems of retraining displaced workers. Types of assistance: grants. Estimate of annual funds available: $ 212,420.

* State Activities - Education of Homeless Children and Youth 84.196

Compensatory Education Programs
Office of Elementary and Secondary Education
U.S. Department of Education
400 Maryland Ave., SW, Room 2043
Washington, DC 20202 (202) 732-4682

To establish or designate an office in each state educational agency and Outlying Area for the coordination of education for homeless children and youth. Types of assistance: grants. Estimate of annual funds available: $ 4,834,000.

* Native Hawaiian Family Based Education Centers 84.209

U.S. Department of Education
Mr. Ramon Ruiz
School Improvement Programs
400 Maryland Ave., SW
Washington, DC 20202 (202) 732-4153

To develop and operate a minimum of eleven family based education centers throughout the Hawaiian Islands. Types of assistance: direct payment. Estimate of annual funds available: $ 1,778,400.

* Capital Expenses (Chapter 1 - Capital Expenses) 84.216

U.S. Department of Education
Mary Jean LeTendre
Compensatory Education Programs
400 Maryland Ave., SW, Room 2043
Washington, DC 20202 (202) 732-4682

To provide payments to local educational agencies for increases in capital expenses paid from Chapter 1 funds for the purpose of regaining levels of instructional services to eligible private school children. Types of assistance: grants. Estimate of annual funds available: $ 19,760,000.

* State Improvement (Chapter 1 State Improvement Program Grants) 84.218

U.S. Department of Education
Compensatory Education Programs
Office of Elementary and Secondary Education
400 Maryland Ave., SW
Washington, DC 20202 (202) 732-4682

To provide payments to state and local educational agencies to operate Chapter 1 program improvement plans. Types of assistance: grants. Estimate of annual funds available: $ 5,686,000.

* Native Hawaiian Special Education 84.221

Dr. Martin J. Kaufman (202) 732-1107

To operate projects addressing the special education needs of Native Hawaiian Students. Types of assistance: grants. Estimate of annual funds available: $ 494,000.

Be patient. If any phone number is incorrect, call (area code) 555-1212 and request the new listing.

Volunteerism

* ACTION/VISTA Activities

ACTION
1100 Vermont Ave., NW
Room 1100
Washington, DC 20525 (202) 606-4857

ACTION Update contains articles on the latest ACTION programs and projects, along with notices of upcoming volunteer-related events and publications of interest.

* Anti-Drug Programs in Your Community

ACTION
Drug Alliance Office
1100 Vermont Ave., NW
Washington, DC 20525 (202) 606-5108

Created in response to the Anti-Drug Act of 1986, ACTION's anti-drug effort encourages and promotes volunteer, community-based programs for the nation's at-risk youth and the elderly. The free booklet, *Take Action Against Drug Abuse: How to Start a Volunteer Anti-Drug Program in Your Community*, outlines the "how to" strategies of getting started, fundraising, grantsmanship, long-term fundraising, volunteer recruitment and management, and publicity. Contact this office to receive a free booklet and for more information on setting up an anti-drug program in your community.

* Community Volunteer Service Programs

ACTION
Drug Alliance Office
1100 Vermont Ave., NW
Washington, DC 20525 (202) 606-5108

ACTION is the principal agency in the Federal Government for administering volunteer service programs. Many of the various components of ACTION, such as Foster Grandparents and VISTA, are involved in community drug abuse education, prevention or treatment programs. The Drug Alliance Office coordinates the agency's drug abuse activities, awards grants that strengthen and expand local volunteer activities combatting illegal drug use among youth and the misuse of prescription and over-the-counter drugs by the elderly, provides training and technical assistance, and conducts public awareness and education efforts.

* Fish and Wildlife Service

U.S. Fish and Wildlife Service
4401 N. Fairfax Dr.
Arlington, VA 22203 (703) 358-1700

Would you like to spend some time banding birds at a national wildlife refuge, feeding fish at a national fish hatchery, or doing research in a laboratory? Then consider volunteering with the U.S. Fish and Wildlife Service. There are no age requirements; however, anyone under 18 must have written parental approval. Young people under 16 years of age are encouraged to volunteer as part of a supervised group, such as a Boy Scout troop, Girl Scout troop, or 4H Club. Contact one of the U.S. Fish and Wildlife regional offices for possible volunteer programs in your area.

* Forest Service Volunteers

Public Affairs Office
U.S. Department of Agriculture
P.O. Box 96090
Washington, DC 20090-6090 (202) 205-1760

The Forest Service has a volunteer program for almost everyone--retirees, professionals, housewives, students, teenagers, and youngsters. Typical jobs include working with specialists in resource protection and management, cooperative forestry, or research. You may also work at a Visitor Information Center by conducting interpretive natural history walks.

* Foster Grandparents Volunteers

Foster Grandparent Program
ACTION
1100 Vermont Ave., NW
Washington, DC 20525 (202) 606-4857

As Foster Grandparents, low-income persons 60 and over provide companionship and guidance to mentally, physically, or emotionally handicapped children who are abused, neglected, in the juvenile justice system, or who have other special needs. Foster Grandparents are assigned to individual children on a one- to-one basis. Most Grandparents serve in "volunteer stations" such as public schools, day care centers, residential facilities and hospitals for mentally retarded, emotionally disturbed and physically handicapped children; in correctional facilities and in homes of abused/neglected children. Typically, Foster Grandparents devote two hours daily to each of two children during a 20-hour service week. Volunteers receive a modest tax-free stipend to cover the cost of volunteering; transportation, a meal while in service, accident and liability insurance, and an annual physical examination. For more information on becoming a foster grandparent, or on having a foster grandparent program in your community, contact this office.

* Health Research Volunteers

Normal Volunteer Program
Clinical Center
Building 10, Room 1C-121B
Bethesda, MD 20892 (301) 496-4763

Many of the research programs at National Institutes of Health require normal volunteers who can provide clinicians with indices of normal body functions. There is a small compensation for their participation.

* National Archives and Geneaology

National Archives and Records Administration
8th St. and Pennsylvania Ave., NW, Room G-8
Washington, DC 20408 (202) 501-5402

Volunteers are needed to lead tours, welcome visitors at the information desk, assist staff with information and administrative services, and to become genealogical staff aides to assist new genealogical researchers.

* National Park Service

Office of Public Affairs
National Park Service
U.S. Department of the Interior
18th and C Sts., NW
Washington, DC 20240 (202) 208-6843

The National Park Service provides many opportunities for volunteers to help at their many parks and historic sites. Contact the National Park nearest you for more information.

* National Volunteer Week

Office of National Service
Old Executive Office Building, Room 100
The White House
Washington, DC 20500 (202) 456-6266

Each spring, the President sets aside a week for the special recognition of volunteers and their achievements. ACTION promotes National Volunteer Week among federal agencies, state and local governments, and private organizations that use volunteers nationwide.

* Retired Business Executives

Service Corps of Retired Executives (SCORE)
National SCORE Office
U.S. Small Business Administration

Be patient. If any phone number is incorrect, call (area code) 555-1212 and request the new listing.

Your Community

1129 20th Street, NW, Room 410 (800) 827-5722
Washington, DC 20416 (202) 634-1500, ext. 287

Retired business executives volunteer their time and services to help small business solve their operating and management problems. Assigned SCORE counselors visit the owners in their places of business to analyze the problems and offer guidance. In addition to learning more about the SCORE program by calling the toll-free SBA Answer Desk, also refer to your local telephone directory to contact the community-based SCORE center.

★ Retired Peace Corps Volunteers
Office of Private Sector Relations
Peace Corps
1990 K. St., NW, Room 8400
Washington, DC 20526 (202) 606-3406

This office serves as the link between the corporate community and the Peace Corps' Office of Returned Volunteer Services.

★ Retired Senior Volunteers (RSVP)
ACTION
1100 Vermont Ave., NW
Washington, DC 20525 (202) 606-4857

RSVP offers opportunities for older citizens to use their talents and experience in community service, ranging from first aid to tutoring. RSVP operates through grants to public and private non-profit organizations in local communities. Anyone retired and aged 60 or over is eligible to be an RSVP volunteer. Volunteers services include adult basic education, guardians ad litum, tax aides, consultancy services, Meals on Wheels, museum tour guides, low-cost weatherization and home repair, classroom aides, health care and substance abuse counseling, home visitation and long term care, telephone reassurance and many others. Contact this office for more information on becoming a retired senior volunteer, or if you would like to set up a program in your community.

★ Senior Companions
ACTION
1100 Vermont Ave., NW
Washington, DC 20525 (202) 606-4857

Senior Companions, all low-income persons 60 or over, provide care and companionship to other adults, especially the elderly, in an effort to help them maintain their highest level of independent living. The supportive services given by Senior Companions helps prevent the inappropriate institutionalization of homebound persons. Special emphasis areas include acute care discharge planning, mental health, substance abuse, and care of the terminally ill. Applicants must be at least 60 years old, physically able, and willing to serve 20 hours per week and meet income eligibility guidelines, which vary from state to state. Contact this office for more information on becoming a senior companion, or if you would like to set up a program in your community.

★ Smithsonian Curatorial-Aides
Visitor Information and Associates' Reception Center
Smithsonian Institution
1000 Jefferson Drive S.W.
Washington, DC 20560 (202) 357-2627

Volunteers can participate in an independent program in which their educational and professional backgrounds are matched with curatorial or research requests from within the Smithsonian Institution.

★ Smithsonian Museums Tour Guides
Visitor Information and Associates' Reception Center
Smithsonian Institution
1000 Jefferson Drive S.W.
Washington, DC 20560 (202) 357-2627

Volunteers are needed and welcomed at the Smithsonian Institution to serves as information volunteers or tour guides at many of the museums and Smithsonian programs and activities.

★ Smithsonian Research Expeditions
Smithsonian National Associates
Smithsonian Institution
490 L'Enfant Plaza SW
Room 4210
Washington, DC 20560 (202) 357-4800

The Smithsonian Research Expeditions Program gives volunteers an opportunity to provide assistance to Smithsonian researchers and scholars. Expedition participants contribute their labor and financial support to projects led by Smithsonian scientists, curators, and research associates that result in exhibitions, publications, and collections for the Smithsonian Institution. Collaborating with staff, expedition volunteers work in field settings, laboratories, and archives to collect, organize, and interpret data. Expeditions cover a range of topics from archaeological digs to photographing radios. Financial Support contributed by participants is used for direct project expenses and follow-up work related to these projects.

★ Speakers for Community Groups
See all other Chapters.

Every federal department and many government agencies have a speakers bureau to inform interested organizations and citizen groups about many of the major community concerns. Many resources are available on medical issues such as health fairs and cholesterol screening. Public education, space programs, housing programs, weapons systems are some of the other areas where federal experts might be available to come to speak.

★ Student Community Service
Student Service Learning Program
ACTION
1100 Vermont Ave., NW
Washington, DC 20525 (202) 606-4857

Student Community Service projects are designed to encourage students to undertake volunteer service in their communities to enhance the educational value of the service experience and to serve the needs of the low-income community. Volunteers are non-stipended and must be enrolled in secondary, secondary vocational, or post-secondary schools on an in-school or out-of-school basis. Contact this office for more information on becoming a student volunteer, or if you would like student volunteers assigned to your community.

★ Veterans Voluntary Service
Chief of Voluntary Services
Veterans Administration Medical Center

Refer to your local telephone directory for the nearest VA hospital or medical center. Many opportunities exist for volunteers to help veterans.

★ Volunteers In Service To America (VISTA)
ACTION
1100 Vermont Ave., NW (800) 424-8580
Washington, DC 20525 (202) 606-4857

VISTA volunteers work to alleviate poverty in the United States. They are assigned to serve on a full-time, full-year basis at the request of public or private non-profit organizations. Volunteers live and work among the poor, serving in urban areas, rural areas, or on Indian reservations, and share their skills and experience in such fields as literacy, employment training, food distribution, shelter for the homeless, and neighborhood revitalization. Volunteers must be citizens or permanent residents of the U.S. and at least 18 years of age. They receive a basic subsistence allowance covering housing, food and incidentals. An additional $75 a month is paid as a stipend upon completion of service. Also, while in service, VISTA volunteers may be eligible for deferment of repayment of certain types of student loans, or under certain circumstances cancellation of a portion of National Direct Student loans. Contact this office for more information on becoming a VISTA volunteer or getting VISTA volunteers to help out in your community.

Government Financial Help To Individuals Poor, Elderly, Disabled, and Unemployed

* *See also Your Community Chapter*
* *See also Housing and Real Estate Chapter*

Besides the well-known federal programs like food stamps and job training for dislocated workers, there are many other financial assistance plans such as compensation to crime victims, health benefits for refugees, temporary child care and crisis nurseries. The following is a description of these money programs available along with community organizations which in turn distribute government assistance to needy Americans. The information is taken from the *Catalog of Federal Domestic Assistance* which is published by the U.S. Government Printing Office in Washington, DC. The number next to the title description is a reference number listed in this *Catalog*. Contact the office listed below the title for more details.

* Food Stamps 10.551
Andrew P. Hornsby, Jr., Deputy Administrator
Food Stamp Programs
Food and Nutrition Service
U.S. Department of Agriculture
Alexandria, VA 22302 (703) 305-2062
To improve diets of low-income households by increasing their food purchasing ability. Types of assistance: direct payment. Estimate of annual funds available: $ 21,028,289,000.

* School Breakfast Program 10.553
Director, Child Nutrition Division
Food and Nutrition Service
U.S. Department of Agriculture
Alexandria, VA 22302 (703) 305-2590
To assist states in providing a nutritious nonprofit breakfast service for school students, through cash grants and food donations. Types of assistance: grants. Estimate of annual funds available: $ 813,540,000.

* National School Lunch Program 10.555
Director, Child Nutrition Division
Food and Nutrition Service
U.S. Department of Agriculture
Alexandria, VA 22302 (703) 305-2590
To assist states, through cash grants and food donations, in making the school lunch program available to school students of all incomes and to encourage the domestic consumption of nutrition agricultural commodities. Types of assistance: grants. Estimate of annual funds available: $3,969,373,722.

* Special Milk Program for Children 10.556
Stanley C. Garnett, Acting Director
Child Nutrition Division
Food and Nutrition Service
U.S. Department of Agriculture
Alexandria, VA 22302 (703) 305-2590
To provide subsidies to schools and institutions to encourage the consumption of fluid milk by children of high school grade and under. Types of assistance: grants. Estimate of annual funds available: $ 21,917,623.

* Special Supplemental Food Program for Women, Infants, and Children (WIC Program) 10.557
Ronald Vogel, Director
Supplemental Food Programs Division
Food and Nutrition Service
U.S. Department of Agriculture
Alexandria, VA 22302 (703) 305-2746
To supply, at no cost, supplemental nutrition foods and nutrition eduction as an adjunct to good health care to low-income pregnant and postpartum women, infants and children identified to be at nutritional risk. Types of assistance: grants. Estimate of annual funds available: $ 2,153,286,000.

* Child Care Food Program 10.558
Stanley C. Garnett, Acting Director
Director, Child Nutrition Division
Food and Nutrition Service
U.S. Department of Agriculture
Alexandria, VA 22302 (703) 305-2590
To assist states, through grants-in-aid and other means, to maintain nonprofit food service programs for children in public and private nonprofit non-residential institutions providing child care; family day care homes and private for-profit centers that receive compensation under title XX for at least 25 persons. Types of assistance: grants. Estimate of annual funds available: $ 1,187,747,000.

* Summer Food Service Program for Children 10.559
Stanley C. Garnett, Acting Director
Director, Child Nutrition Division
Food and Nutrition Service
U.S. Department of Agriculture
Alexandria, VA 22302 (703) 305-2590
To assist states, through grants-in-aid and other means, to conduct nonprofit food service programs for needy children during the summer months. Types of assistance: grants. Estimate of annual funds available: $ 203,200,000.

* State Administrative Matching Grants for Food 10.561
Stamp Program
Andrew P. Hornsby, Jr.
Deputy Administrator
Food Stamp Programs
Food and Nutrition Service
U.S. Department of Agriculture
Alexandria, VA 22302 (703) 365-2062
To provide federal financial aid to state agencies for costs incurred to operate the Food Stamp Program. Types of assistance: grants. Estimate of annual funds available: $1,588,976,000.

* Nutrition Assistance for Puerto Rico (NAP) 10.566
Andrew P. Hornsby, Jr.
Deputy Administrator
Food Stamp Programs
Food and Nutrition Service
U.S. Department of Agriculture
Alexandria, VA 22303 (703) 365-2062
A cash grant alternative to the food stamp program to improve diets of needy persons residing in the Commonwealth of Puerto Rico. Types of assistance: direct payment. Estimate of annual funds available: $ 1,051,000,000.

Be patient. If any phone number is incorrect, call (area code) 555-1212 and request the new listing.

Government Financial Help to Individuals

* Food Distribution Program on Indian Reservations 10.567

Alberta C. Frost, Director
Food Distribution Division
Food and Nutrition Service
U.S. Department of Agriculture
Alexandria, VA 22302 (703) 305-2680

To improve the diets of needy persons in households on or near Indian reservations and to increase the market for domestically produced foods acquired under surplus removal or price support operations. Types of assistance: grants. Estimate of annual funds available: $ 18,444,000.

* Nutrition Program for the Elderly (Commodities) (NPE) 10.570

Food Distribution Division
Food and Nutrition Service
U.S. Department of Agriculture
Alexandria, VA 22302 (703) 305-2680

To improve the diets of the elderly and to increase the market for domestically produced foods acquired under surplus removal or price support operations. Types of assistance: grants. Estimate of annual funds available: $ 142,912,000.

* Temporary Child Care and Crisis Nurseries 13.656

Joan Goffney
Children's Bureau
Program Support Division
400 6th St., SW
Washington, DC 20201 (202) 755-7730

To provide temporary, non-medical care for handicapped children and children with chronic or terminal illnesses to alleviate social, emotional and financial stress among the families of such children. Types of assistance: grants. Estimate of annual funds available: $ 4,949,000.

* Adoption Assistance 13.659

Betty Stewart
Associate Commissioner
Children's Bureau
P.O. Box 1182
Washington, DC 20013 (202) 755-7600

To provide Federal Financial Participation (FFP) to states which meet certain eligibility tests, in the adoption subsidy costs for the adoption of children with special needs. Types of assistance: grants. Estimate of annual funds available: $ 133,936,000.

* Medical Assistance Program (Medicaid; Title XIX) 13.714

Fred Schutzman, Director
Health Care Financing Administration
U.S. Department of Health and Human Services
Room 233
E. High Rise Bldg.
6325 Security Blvd.
Baltimore, MD 21207 (301) 966-3229

To provide financial assistance to states for payments of medical assistance on behalf of cash assistance recipients, children, pregnant women, and the aged who meet income and resource requirements, and other categorically eligible groups. Types of assistance: grants. Estimate of annual funds available: $ 34,290,000.

* Medicare-Hospital Insurance (Medicare) 13.773

Barbara Gagel, Director
Bureau of Program Operations
Room 300
Meadows East Building
Health Care Financing Administration
Baltimore, MD 21207 (301) 966-5874

To provide hospital insurance protection for covered services to persons age 65 or above, to certain disabled persons and to individuals with chronic renal disease. Types of assistance: direct payment. Estimate of annual funds available: $ 57,100,000

* Medicare-Supplemental Medical Insurance (Medicare) 13.774

Barbara Gagel, Director
Bureau of Program Operation, Room 300
Meadows East Bldg.
Health Care Financing Administration
Baltimore, MD 21207 (301) 966-5874

To provide medical insurance protection for covered services to persons age 65 or over, to certain disabled persons and to individuals with chronic renal disease who elect this coverage. Types of assistance: direct payment. Estimate of annual funds available: $ 46,145,000,000.

* Family Support Payments to States Assistance Payments 13.780

Office of the Director
Office of Family Assistance
U.S. Department of Health and Human Services
5th Flr, Aerospace Bldg
370 L'Enfant Promenade, SW
Washington, DC 20447 (202) 252-4950

To set general standards for state administration; provide the federal financial share to states for Aid to Families with Dependent Children (AFDC). Types of assistance: grants. Estimate of annual funds available: $ .1016E+11.

* Job Opportunities and Basic Skills Training (JOBS) 13.781

Office of the Director
Family Support Administration
5th Floor, Aerospace Bldg.
370 L'Enfant Promenade, SW
Washington, DC 20447 (202) 252-4950

To assure that needy families with children obtain the education, training, and employment that will help them avoid long-term welfare dependence. Types of assistance: grants. Estimate of annual funds available: $ 39,000,000.

* State Legalization Impact Assistance Grants (SLIAG) 13.786

Norman Thompson, Director
Division of State Legalization Assistance
Family Support Administration
370 L'Enfant Promenade, SW
Washington, DC 20447 (202) 252-4571

To offset part of the costs state and local governments incur in providing public subsistence assistance, public health assistance, and educational services to eligible legalized aliens. Types of assistance: grants. Estimate of annual funds available: $ 643,500,000.

* Low-Income Home Energy Assistance 13.789

Floyd D. Brandon, Director
Office of Energy Assistance
Family Support Administration
370 L'Enfant Promenade, SW
Washington, DC 20447 (202) 252-5296

To make grants available to states and other jurisdictions to assist eligible households to meet the costs of home energy. Types of assistance: grants. Estimate of annual funds available: $1,383,200,000.

* Work Incentive Program/Win Demonstration Program (WIN/WIN Demo) 13.790

Ronald E. Putz, Exec. Director
National Coordination Committee, WIN
U.S. Department of Labor
Washington, DC 20210 (202) 535-0174

To move men, women, and out-of-school youth, age 16 or older from dependency on Aid to Families with Dependent Children (AFDC) grants to economic independence through permanent, productive employment by providing appropriate education, job training, job placement and other related services. Types of assistance: grants. Estimate of annual funds available: $91,440,000.

Be patient. If any phone number is incorrect, call (area code) 555-1212 and request the new listing.

Poor, Elderly, Disabled, and Unemployed

* Social Security-Disability Insurance 13.802
Office of Public Inquiries
Room 4100, Annex
Social Security Administration
Baltimore, MD 21235 (301) 965-2736
To replace part of the earning lost because of a physical or mental impairment severe enough to prevent a person from working. Types of assistance: direct payment. Estimate of annual funds available: $ .2232E+11.

* Social Security - Retirement Insurance 13.803
Office of Public Inquiries
Room 4100, Annex
Social Security Administration
Baltimore, MD 21235 (301) 965-2736
To replace part of the earnings lost due to retirement. Types of assistance: direct payment. Estimate of annual funds available: $ .1577E+12.

* Social Security - Special Benefits for Persons Aged 72 and Over 13.804
Office of Public Inquiries
Room 4100, Annex
Social Security Administration
Baltimore, MD 21235 (301) 965-2736
To assure some regular income to certain persons age 72 and over who had little or no opportunity to earn Social Security protection during their working years. Types of assistance: direct payment. Estimate of annual funds available: $ 24,000,000.

* Social Security - Survivors Insurance 13.805
Office of Public Inquiries
Room 4100, Annex
Social Security Administration
Baltimore, MD 21235 (301) 965-2736
To replace part of the earnings lost to dependents because of the worker's death. Types of assistance: direct payment. Estimate of annual funds available: Not specified.

* Special Benefits for Disabled Coal Miners (Black Lung) 13.806
Office of Public Inquiries
Room 4100, Annex
Social Security Administration
6401 Security Blvd. (800) 772-1213
Baltimore, MD 21235 (410) 965-7700
To pay benefits to coal miners who have become disabled due to pneumoconiosis (black lung disease) or other chronic lung disease arising from coal mine employment and their dependents or survivors. Types of assistance: direct payment. Estimate of annual funds available: $ 892,000,000.

* Supplemental Security Income 13.807
Office of Public Inquiries
Room 4100, Annex
Social Security Administration
Baltimore, MD 21235 (301) 965-2736
To assure a minimum level of income to persons who have attained age 65 or are blind or disabled, whose income and resources are below specified levels. Types of assistance: direct payment. Estimate of annual funds available: $ .1134E+11.

* Health Programs for Refugees (Immigration and Nationality Act) 13.987
Dr. Walter R. Dowdle, Acting Director
CDC, PHS, DHHS
Atlanta, GA 30333 (404) 639-1286
To assist states and localities in providing health assessment and follow-up activities to new refugees and in addressing refugee health problems of public health concern. Types of assistance: grants. Estimate of annual funds available: $ 4,138,000.

* Cooperative Agreements for State-Based Diabetes Control Programs 13.988
Chief, Grants Management Office
Procurement and Grants Office
CDC, PHS, DHHS
Atlanta, GA 30333 (404) 842-6575
To implement comprehensive programs which will ensure that persons with diabetes who are at high risk for certain complications of diabetes are identified, entered into the health are system and receive on going state-of the-art preventive care and treatment. Types of assistance: grants. Estimate of annual funds available: $ 4,861,000.

* Congregate Housing Services Program (CHSP) 14.170
Assisted Elderly and Handicapped Housing Division
Office of Elderly and Assisted Housing
U.S. Department of Housing and Urban Development
Washington, DC 20410 (202) 708-3291
To prevent premature or unnecessary institutionalization of elderly-handicapped, non-elderly handicapped, and temporarily disabled, to provide a variety of innovative approaches for the delivery of meals and non-medical supportive services while utilizing existing service programs and to fill gaps in existing service systems. Types of assistance: grants. Estimate of annual funds available: $ 6,400,000.

* Public Safety Officers Benefits Program 16.571
William F. Powers, Director
or Richard J. Condon
Public Safety Officers Benefits Program
Bureau of Justice Assistance
Washington, DC 20531 (202) 307-0635
To provide a $100,000 death benefit to the eligible survivors of federal, state or local public safety officers whose death is the direct and proximate result of a personal injury sustained in the line of duty. Types of assistance: direct payment. Estimate of annual funds available: $ 30,148,000.

* Crime Victim Assistance 16.575
State Compensation and Assistance Division
Office for Victims of Crime
Office of Justice Programs
U.S. Department of Justice
633 Indiana Ave., NW
Washington, DC (202) 307-5947
Each year provide up to 45 percent of the Crime Victims Fund generated through federal criminal fines, penalty assessments, forfeited appearance bonds to be distributed to the states to support crime victim assistance programs. Types of assistance: grants. Estimate of annual funds available: $ 65,650,000.

* Crime Victim Compensation 16.576
State Compensation and Assistance Division
Office for Victims of Crime
Office of Justice Programs
U.S. Department of Justice
Washington, DC 20531 (202) 307-5947
To provide up to 49.5 percent per year of the Crime Victims fund generated through federal criminal fines, penalty assessment, forfeited appearance bonds, bail bonds, etc., to be distributed among the states to the direct benefit derived by victims from the program. Types of assistance: grants. Estimate of annual funds available: $ 65,650,000.

* Unemployment Insurance 17.225
Jeanette Rozzero, Director
Unemployment Insurance Service
Employment and Training Administration
U.S. Department of Labor
Washington, DC 20210 (202) 523-7831
To administer program of unemployment insurance for eligible workers through federal and state cooperation; to administer payment of Trade Adjustment Assistance Types of assistance: grant, direct payment. Estimate of annual funds available: $ 2,322,913,000.

Be patient. If any phone number is incorrect, call (area code) 555-1212 and request the new listing.

Government Financial Help to Individuals

* Senior Community Service Employment Program (SCSEP) (Older Worker Program) 17.235

Office of Special Targeted Programs
Employment and Training Administration
U.S. Department of Labor, Room N4641
200 Constitution Ave., NW
Washington, DC 20210 (202) 535-0500

To provide foster and promote useful part-time work opportunities in community service activities for low income persons who are 55 years old and older. Types of assistance: grant. Estimate of annual funds available: $ 342,814,000.

* Trade Adjustment Assistance - Workers 17.245

Marvin Fooks, Director
Office of Trade Adjustment Assistance
Employment and Training Administration
U.S. Department of Labor
601 D St., NW, Room 6434
Washington, DC (202) 523-0555

To provide adjustment assistance to workers adversely affected by increased imports of articles like or directly competitive with articles produced by such workers firm. Types of assistance: direct payment. Estimate of annual funds available: $ 42,300,000.

* Dislocated Workers: Employment and Training Assistance 17.246

Employment and Training Administration
U.S. Department of Labor
200 Constitution Ave., NW
Washington, DC 20210 (202) 535-0577

To assist dislocated workers obtain unsubsidized employment through training and related employment services using a decentralized system of State programs. Types of assistance: grants. Estimate of annual funds available: $ 571,117,000.

* Migrant and Seasonal Farmworkers (and Other Seasonally Employed Farmworkers) 17.247

Office of Special Targeted Programs
Division of Seasonal Farmworker Programs
Employment and Training Administration
U.S. Dept. of Labor, Room 4641
200 Constitution Ave., NW
Washington, DC (202) 535-0500

To provide job training, job search assistance, and other supportive services for those individuals who suffer chronic seasonal unemployment and underemployment in the agricultural industry. Types of assistance: grants. Estimate of annual funds available: $ 56,690,000.

* Employment Services and Job Training - Pilot and Demonstration Programs 17.249

Administrator, Office of Strategic Planning
and Policy Development
Employment and Training Administration
U.S. Department of Labor
200 Constitution Ave., NW
Washington, DC (202) 535-0677

To provide foster, and promote job training and other services which are most appropriately administered at the national level and which are operated in more than one State to groups with particular disadvantage in the labor market. Types of assistance: grants. Estimate of annual funds available: $ 37,000,000.

* Job Training Partnership Act (JTPA) 17.250

Hugh Davies
Employment and Training Administration
U.S. Department of Labor
200 Constitution Ave., NW
Washington, DC 20210 (202) 535-0580

To provide job training and related assistance to economically disadvantaged individuals and others who face significant employment barriers. Types of assistance: grants. Estimate of annual funds available: $ 1,771,550,000.

* Native American Employment and Training Programs 17.251

Division of Indian and Native American Programs
Employment and Training Administration
U.S. Department of Labor
Room N4641
200 Constitution Ave., NW
Washington, DC (202) 535-0500

To afford job training to Native Americans facing serious barriers to employment, who are in special need of such training to obtain productive employment. Types of assistance: grants. Estimate of annual funds available: $ 58,461,000.

* Longshore and Harbor Workers' Compensation 17.302

Office of Workers' Compensation Programs
Division of Longshore and Harbor
Workers' Compensation
Washington, DC 20210 (202) 523-8721

To provide compensation for disability or death resulting from injury, including occupational disease, to eligible private employees. Types of assistance: direct payment. Estimate of annual funds available: $ 4,000,000.

* Coal Mine Workers Compensation (Black Lung) 17.307

Division of Coal Mine Workers Compensation
Office of Workers Compensation Programs
Employment Standards Administration
U.S. Dept. of Labor
Washington, DC 20210 (202) 523-6692

To provide benefits to coal miners who have become totally disabled due to coal workers pneumoconiosis (CWP) and to widows and other surviving dependents of miners who have died of this disease, or who were totally disabled from the disease at the time of death. Types of assistance: direct payment. Estimate of annual funds available: $ 526,468,000.

* Tax Counseling for the Elderly 21.006

Marion L. Butler
Tax Counseling for the Elderly
Taxpayer Service Division
Internal Revenue Service
1111 Constitution Ave., NW
Washington, DC 20224 (202) 566-6603

To authorize the Internal Revenue Service to enter into agreement with private or public nonprofit agencies or organizations to establish a network of trained volunteers to provide free income tax information and return preparation assistance to elderly taxpayers. Types of assistance: direct payment. Estimate of annual funds available: $ 3,000,000.

* Appalachian Vocational and Other Education Facilities and Operations 23.012

Executive Director
Appalachian Regional Commission
1666 Connecticut Ave., NW
Washington, DC 20235 (202) 673-7874

To provide the people of the region with the equipment, renovation and operating funds for training and education necessary to obtain employment at their best capability for available job opportunities. Types of assistance: grants. Estimate of annual funds available: $ 7,500,000.

* Federal Employment Assistance For Veterans 27.002

Edward P. McHugh
Office of Affirmative Recruiting and Employment
Office of Personnel Management
1900 E St., NW, Room 6332
Washington, DC 20415 (202) 606-0960

To provide assistance to veterans in obtaining federal employment. Types of assistance: employment. Estimate of annual funds available: $ 172,000.

Be patient. If any phone number is incorrect, call (area code) 555-1212 and request the new listing.

Poor, Elderly, Disabled, and Unemployed

*** Federal Employment for Individuals with Disabilities (Selective Placement Program) 27.005**
Office of Affirmative Recruiting and Employment
Office of Personnel Management
1900 E St., NW
Washington, DC 20414 (202) 606-0870
To encourage federal agencies to provide assistance to persons with disabilities in obtaining and retaining federal employment. Types of assistance: federal employment. Estimate of annual funds available: $ 110,000.

*** Social Insurance for Railroad Workers 57.001**
Public Affairs Railroad Retirement Board
844 Rush St.
Chicago, IL 60611 (312) 751-4777
To pay rail social security, rail industry pensions, special windfalls, supplemental annuities, permanent and occupational disability and sickness and unemployment benefits to workers and their families. Types of assistance: direct payment. Estimate of annual funds available: $8,037,000,000.

*** Pension to Veterans' Surviving Spouse and Children (Death Pension) 64.105**
U.S. Department of Veterans Affairs
Washington, DC 20420
To assist needy surviving spouses, and children of deceased war-time veterans whose deaths were not due to service. Types of assistance: direct payment. Estimate of annual funds available: $ 1,292,772,000.

*** Senior Environmental Employment Program (SEE) 66.508**
Environmental Protection Agency
Office of Research and Development of Exploratory Research
Washington, DC 20460
To use the talents of older Americans to provide technical assistance to federal, state and local environment agencies for projects of pollution prevention abatement and control. Types of assistance: grants. Estimate of annual funds available: $ 30,000,000.

*** Weatherization Assistance for Low-Income Persons 81.042**
James Gardner, Jr., Chief
Weatherization Assistance Programs, Branch 232
Conservation and Renewable Energy
U.S. Department of Energy
Forrestal Bldg.
Washington, DC 20585 (202) 586-2204
To insulate the dwellings of low income persons, particularly the elderly and handicapped low income, in order to conserve needed energy and to aid those persons least able to afford higher utility costs. Types of assistance: grants. Estimate of annual funds available: $ 80,000,000.

*** Centers for Independent Living 84.132**
Office of Developmental Programs
Rehabilitation Services Administration, OSERS
U.S. Department of Education
400 Maryland Ave., SW
Washington, DC 20202 (202) 732-1292
To provide independent living services to individuals with severe handicaps to assist them to function more independent in family and community settings or secure and maintain appropriate employment. Types of assistance: grants. Estimate of annual funds available: $ 29,000,000.

*** Comprehensive Services for Independent Living (Comprehensive Services Part A) 84.169**
Mark Shoob, Associate Commissioner
Office of Asst. Secretary for Special Education

and Rehabilitative Services
U.S. Department of Education
Washington, DC 20202 (202) 732-1406
To provide independent living services for individuals with severe handicaps in assisting them to function independently in family and community settings or to secure and maintain appropriate employment. Types of assistance: grants. Estimate of annual funds available: $ 14,654,000.

*** Rehabilitation Services - Independent Living Services for Older Blind Individuals 84.177**
Ann Queen
Rehabilitation Services Administration
OSERS
U.S. Department of Education
MES Building, Room 3328
330 C St., NW
Washington, DC 20202 (202) 732-1341
To provide independent living services to older blind individuals. Types of assistance: grants. Estimate of annual funds available: $ 6,505,000.

*** Supported Employment Services for Individuals with Severe Handicaps (Supported Employment Services Program) 84.187**
Mark E. Shoob
Office of Program Operations
Rehabilitation Services Administration
U.S. Department of Education
Washington, DC 20202-2574 (202) 732-1406
To provide grants for training and traditionally time limited post employment services leading to supported employment for individuals with severe handicaps. Types of assistance: grants. Estimate of annual funds available: $ 32,059,000.

*** Demonstration Centers for the Retraining of Dislocated Workers 84.193**
Paul Geib
Division of National Programs
Office of Vocational and Adult Education
U.S. Department of Eduction
400 Maryland Ave., SW
Washington, DC 20202 (202) 732-2364
To establish one or more demonstration centers for the retraining of dislocated workers in order to demonstrate the application of general theories of vocational education to the specific problems of retraining displaced workers. Types of assistance: grants. Estimate of annual funds available: $ 0.

*** State Grants for Technology and Related Assistance to Individuals with Disabilities (Technology Assistance Program) 84.224**
NIDRR
400 Maryland Ave., SW
Washington, DC 20202 (202) 732-1134
To provide grants to states to assist them in developing and implementing comprehensive consumer responsive state-wide programs of technology related assistance for individuals with disabilities. Types of assistance: grants. Estimate of annual funds available: $31,848,000.

*** Pension Plan Termination Insurance (ERISA) 86.001**
Pension Benefit Guaranty Corporation
2020 K St., NW
Washington, DC 20006 (202) 778-8800
To encourage the continuation and maintenance of voluntary private pension plans for the benefit of their participants. Types of assistance: Insurance of annual funds available: $ 894,318,000.

Be patient. If any phone number is incorrect, call (area code) 555-1212 and request the new listing.

Government Financial Help to Individuals

Veterans and Dependents

* *See also International Relations and Defense*

This section identifies the offices, mostly at the U.S. Department of Veterans Affairs, which compensate Americans who have served in the U.S. Armed Forces and their dependents. A number appears by some of the caption headings which is the official reference from the U.S. Government Printing Office's *Catalog of Federal Domestic Assistance*. Contact the office listed below the title for more details.

* Agent Orange or Nuclear Radiation Exposure

Veterans Assistance Office
U.S. Department of Veterans Affairs (VA)
810 Vermont Ave., NW
Washington, DC 20420 (202) 872-1151

The U.S. Department of Veteran Affairs is authorized by law to provide certain health care services to any veteran of the Vietnam Ear (August 5, 1964 through May 7, 1975) who, while serving in Vietnam, may have been exposed to dioxin or to a toxic substance in a herbicide or defoliant used for military purposes. VA has an onging program for examining veterans concerned about the possible health effects of Agent Orange exposure. Vietnam veterans are encouraged to request an examination at their nearest VA healthcare facility. A veteran who participates will receive a comprehensive physical examination and be asked to complete a questionnaire about service experience in Vietnam. The veteran is advised, through personal consultation, of the results of that examination. The examination determines the current health status of the veteran and assists in detecting any illnes or injury the veteran may have, regardless of origin, which may serve as the basis for follow-up. The finding of these examinations are entered into a registry. The same process is available for any veteran who exposed while serving on active duty to ionizing radiation from the detonation of a nuclear device in connection with the veteran's participation in the test of a nuclear device or with the American occupation of Hiroshima and Nagasaki, Japan during the period beginning on September 11, 1945, and ending on July 1, 1946. The veteran should contact the nearest VA medical center for an examination.

* Alcohol and Drug Dependence Treatment

Veterans Assistance Office
U.S. Department of Veterans Affairs (VA)
810 Vermont Ave., NW
Washington, DC 20420 (202) 872-1151

After hospitalization for alcohol or drug treatment, veterans may be eligible for outpatient care, or may be authorized to continue treatment or rehabilitation in facilities such as halfway houses or therapeutic communities at VA expense. For more information contact your VA medical center.

* Appealing Veterans Benfit Claims

Veterans Assistance Office
U.S. Department of Veterans Affairs (VA)
810 Vermont Ave., NW
Washington, DC 20420 (202) 872-1151

Veterans who believe they have VA benefits coming to them but have been denied those benefits have the right to appeal. Not all VA findings are appealable, but those dealing with compensation or pension benefits, education benefits, waiver of recovery of overpayments, and reimbursement of unauthorized medical services are typical issues which may be appealed to the Board of Veterans Appeals. Additional information on appeals may be found in VA pamphlet 1-1, *Board of Veterans Appeals, Appeals Regulations and Rules of Practice*, available from the office above.

* Automobiles and Adaptive Equipment for Certain Disabled Veterans and Members of the Armed Forces 64.100

U.S. Department of Veterans Affairs (VA)
Washington, DC 20420

To provide financial assistance to certain disabled servicepersons and veterans toward the purchase price of an automobile or other conveyance and an additional amount for adaptive equipment. Types of assistance: direct payment. Estimate of annual funds available: $ 21,589,000.

* Benefits Assistance Service

Veterans Assistance Office
U.S. Department of Veterans Affairs (VA)
810 Vermont Ave., NW
Washington, DC 20420 (202) 872-1151

This office provides veterans on their first visit with information about and assistance is applying for various federal benefits. The information provided can also be found in the VA regional offices.

* Benefits Information

Veterans Assistance Office
U.S. Department of Veterans Affairs (VA)
810 Vermont Ave., NW
Washington, DC 20420 (202) 872-1151

The U.S. Department of Veterans Affairs provides a full range of benefits for eligible veterans and dependents. Toll-free benefits information is available to all veterans at VA regional offices. Check your local telephone directory under United States Government, Department of Veterans Affairs, for the benefits information in your area--or ask your directory assistance operator. Other sources that provide information about benefits are service organizations and state and local offices of veterans affairs.

* Board of Veterans Appeals Decisions

Board of Veterans Appeals (BVA)
U.S. Department of Veterans Affairs (VA)
Washington, DC 20420 (202) 233-3336

The appellate decisions of the Board of Veterans Appeals have been indexed to facilitate access to the contents of decisions (BVA Index 1-01-1). The index is published quaterly in microfiche form with an annual cumulation. It is organized to provide citations to BVA decisions under subject terms chosen to describe the issues adjudicated in the appeals. For information on obtaining the index or purchasing a microfiche copy, contact your regional VA office or the office above.

* Burial Expenses

Veterans Assistance Office
U.S. Department of Veterans Affairs (VA)
810 Vermont Ave., NW
Washington, DC 20420 (202) 872-1151

Benefits are available to help with the burial expensies of veterans and certain dependents or survivors. Assistance for burial of dependents and survivors is limited to interment in a national cemetery. For more information contact your regional VA office.

* Burial Expenses Allowance for Veterans 64.101

U.S. Department of Veterans Affairs (VA)
Washington, DC 20420

To provide a monetary allowance not to exceed $150 toward the plot or interment expense for certain veterans not buried in a national cemetery. Types of assistance: direct payment. Estimate of annual funds available: $ 129,818,000.

Be patient. If any phone number is incorrect, call (area code) 555-1212 and request the new listing.

Veterans and Dependents

* Burial Flags

Veterans Assistance Office
U.S. Department of Veterans Affairs (VA)
810 Vermont Ave., NW
Washington, DC 20420 (202) 872-1151

An American flag is available to drape the casket of an eligible veteran, after which it may be given to the next of kin, a close friend, or an associate of the deceased. The VA may also issue a flag for a veteran who is missing in action and is later presumed dead. Apply at any VA regional office or most local post offices.

* Burial in Arlington National Cemetery

Superintendent
Arlington National Cemetery
Arlington, VA 22211 (703) 697-2131

The Arlington National Cemetery is under the jurisdiction of the Department of the Army, and burial is limited to specific categories of military personnel and veterans except in the case of cremated remains to be placed in the columbarium. For more information contact the office above.

* Burial in National Cemeteries

Veterans Assistance Office
U.S. Department of Veterans Affairs (VA)
810 Vermont Ave., NW
Washington, DC 20420 (202) 872-1151

Burial in a VA national cemetery is available to any eligible veteran, spouse, unremarried widow/widower, minor children, and under certain conditions, unmarried adult children. Detailed information regarding eligibility and interments is contained in the VA pamphlet, *Interments in National Cemeteries*. Contact your regional VA office for this pamphlet and for more information and assistance in filing burial benefit claims.

* Chaplain Service

Chaplain Service (125)
U.S. Department of Veterans Affairs (VA)
810 Vermont Ave., NW
Washington, DC 20420 (202) 535-7594

The Chaplain Service provides for the spiritual welfare of the patients at VA facilities. The program includes opportunities for religious worship in the appropriate setting, pastoral ministry to individual patients and administration in crises situations, opportunities for sacramental ministry and pastoral counseling and other supportive suervices to aid in the total care and treatment of veteran patients. For more information, contact the office above.

* Compensation

Veterans Assistance Office
U.S. Department of Veterans Affairs (VA)
810 Vermont Ave., NW (800) 827-1000
Washington, DC 20420 (202) 872-1151

Veterans who are disabled by injury or disease incurred or aggravated during active service in the line of duty during wartime or peacetime service and discharged or separated under other than dishonorable conditions are eligible for VA compensation. Eligible veterans are entitled to monthly disability payments. For more information on eligibility and benefits, contact your regional VA office.

* Compensation for Service-Connected Deaths for Veterans Dependents (Death Compensation) 64.102

U.S. Department of Veterans Affairs (VA)
Washington, DC 20420

To compensate surviving spouses, children, and dependent parents for the death of any veteran who died before January 1, 1957, because of a service-connected disability. Types of assistance: direct payment. Estimate of annual funds available: $ 19,888,000.

* Dental Treatment

Veterans Assistance Office
U.S. Department of Veterans Affairs (VA)

810 Vermont Ave., NW
Washington, DC 20420 (202) 827-1151

The VA provides dental services to eligible veterans on an outpatient basis. Outpatient dental treatment begins with an intraoral examinations and may include the full spectrum of modern diagnostic, surgical, restorative, and preventive techniques. In some instances, the dental care may be comprehensive in nature, while in other cases, the type and extent of treatment may be limited. The measure of treatment is determined by specific eligibilities, service-connection, and/or correlation of the dental conditions with the veteran's medical problems. For more information, including eligibility, contact the nearest VA medical center.

* Dietetic Service

Dietetic Service
Veterans Health Services and Research Administration
U.S. Department of Veterans Affairs (VA)
810 Vermont Ave., NW, Room 927
Washington, DC 20420 (202) 535-7485

VA dietitians direct nutritional care veterans in all settings by providing active programs which encompass the entire range of nutrition services. There are 13 VA sponsored Dietetic Internships which graduate registration eligible dietitians each year. For more information, contact the office above.

* Disabled Veterans Outreach Program 17.801

Veterans Employment and Training Service
Office of the Assistant Secretary for
Veterans Employment and Training
U.S. Dept. of Labor, Room 5-1316
200 Constitution Ave., NW
Washington, DC 20210 (202) 523-9110

To provide funds to states to provide job and job training opportunities for disabled and other veterans through contacts with employers. Types of assistance: grants. Estimate of annual funds available: $ 77,901,000.

* Domiciliary Care

Veterans Assistance Office
U.S. Department of Veterans Affairs (VA)
810 Vermont Ave., NW
Washington, DC 20420 (202) 872-1151

The VA provides care on an ambulatory self-care basis for veterans disabled by age or disease who are not in need of acute hospitalization and who do not need the skilled nursing services provided in nursing homes. For information on eligibility and general information, contact any VA office.

* Domiciliary Care (VA Domiciliary Care) 64.008

Asst. Chief, Medical Director for Geriatrics
and Extended Care (181)
U.S. Department of Veterans Affairs (VA)
Washington, DC 20420 (202) 535-7530

To provide the least intensive level of VA inpatient care for ambulatory veterans disabled by age or illness who are not in need of more acute hospitalization and who do not need the skilled nursing provided in nursing homes. Types of assistance: other. Estimate of annual funds available: $ 218,569,000.

* Driver Training for the Handicapped

Rehabilitation Medicine Service
U.S. Department of Veterans Affairs (VA)
810 Vermont Ave., NW
Washington, DC 20420 (202) 535-7273

The VA provides driver education and training for all eligible handicapped veterans and certain military personnel. The DVA has established 40 driver training centers for the handicapped throughout the U.S. For more information, contact the office above.

* Education and Training

Veterans Assistance Office
U.S. Department of Veterans Affairs (VA)
810 Vermont Ave., NW
Washington, DC 20420 (202) 872-1151

VA administers basic programs for veterans and servicepersons seeking

Be patient. If any phone number is incorrect, call (area code) 555-1212 and request the new listing.

Government Financial Help to Individuals

assistance for education and training. For eligible persons with service between February 1, 1955, and December 31, 1976, such assistance is available under the noncontributory GI Bill. Veterans and servicepersons who entered the military from January 1, 1977, through June 30, 1985, may receive educational assistance under a contributory plan. Individuals entering on active duty after June 30, 1985, may receive benefits under the Montgomery GI Bill. Contact your regional VA office for specific information on eligibility and benefits.

* Employment and Training Program 17.802

Veterans Employment and Training Service
Office of the Assistant Secretary for
Veterans Employment and Training
Room 51316
200 Constitution Ave., NW
Washington, DC 20210 (202) 523-9110

To develop programs to meet the employment and training needs of service-connected disabled veterans, veterans of the Vietnam era and veterans who were recently separated from the military service. Types of assistance: grants. Estimate of annual funds available: $ 8,792,000.

* Fee-Basis Medical Program

Veterans Assistance Office
U.S. Department of Veterans Affairs (VA)
810 Vermont Ave., NW
Washington, DC 20420 (202) 872-1151

The VA authorizes veterans to receive medical services from other individuals or organizations by compensating participating members for services performed and paying the veteran for travel expenses incurred for the visit. For more information, contact the nearest VA Medical Center or regional VA office.

* Federal Benefits for Veterans and Dependents

Superintendent of Documents
U.S. Government Printing Office
Washington, DC 20402 (202) 783-3238

The booklet, *Federal Benefits for Veterans and Dependents*, stock #051-000-00198-2, provides information on the many benefits made available to veterans and dependents. It is available from GPO for $2.75.

* Fiduciary and Field Examinations

Veterans Assistance Office
U.S. Department of Veterans Affairs (VA)
810 Vermont Ave., NW
Washington, DC 20420 (202) 872-1151

For information on payment of VA benefits on behalf of adult beneficiaries who are incompetent or under some other legal disability, contact the VA regional office. Information on payments of benefits to minor beneficiaries who are not in care of a natural or adoptive parent can also be obtained from the VA regional office.

* Headstone or Grave Marker

Director
Monument Service (42)
National Cemetery System
U.S. Department of Veterans Affairs (VA)
Washington, DC 20420 (202) 275-1480

Headstones and markers are provided for the gravesites of eligible veterans buried in private or national cemeteries. Eligibility is the same as for burial in a national cemetery. The headstone or grave marker is provided without charge and shipped at government expense to the consignee designated. The cost of placing the marker in a private cemetery must be borne by the applicant. Forward applications (VA Form 40-1330) to the address above. VA regional offices will provide information and other assistance. For more information contact the office above.

* Health Care Product Support

Director
U.S. Department of Veterans Affairs (VA)
Marketing Center
P.O. Box 76
Hines, IL 60141 (708) 216-2479

The Marketing Center (MKC) is the largest combined contracting activity within the U.S. Department of Veterans Affairs. It is responsible for supporting the health care delivery systems of the DVA and other government agencies by providing and validating a centralized acquisition program for health care products in a cost effective manner. The primary responsibility of the MKC is assuring contracts are in place to support the DVA's Central Distribution System. Contact the office above for more information.

* Health Care System

Veterans Assistance Office
U.S. Department of Veterans Affairs (VA)
810 Vermont Ave., NW
Washington, DC 20420 (202) 872-1151

Perhaps the most visible of all VA benefits and services are its hospitals and medical care services, which make up the largest health care system in the free world. More than 90 percent of VA employees are associated with medical care. Of VA's 172 medical centers, some 140 are affiliated with 104 medical schools. More than half of America's practicing physicians receive training in VA medical centers. In addition to medical centers, the health care system includes nursing homes, domiciliaries, and readjustment counseling Vet centers. Contact the nearest VA medical center for specific information.

* High School Training

Veterans Assistance Office
U.S. Department of Veterans Affairs (VA)
810 Vermont Ave., NW
Washington, DC 20420 (202) 872-1151

A veteran may pursue high school training or training to pass the GED examination and may receive educational assistance allowance without a charge against basic entitlement. Additional secondary school training, such as refresher courses or deficiency courses, are permitted if needed to qualify for admission to an appropriate educational institution. Contact your VA regional office for more information.

* Home Ownership Publications

Veterans Assistance Office
U.S. Department of Veterans Affairs (VA)
810 Vermont Ave., NW
Washington, DC 20420 (202) 872-1151

The following publications are available to veterans from their VA regional office:

Pointers for the Veteran Homeowner. A guide for veterans whose home mortgage is guaranteed or insured under the GI Bill.

To the Home-Buying Veteran. A guide for veterans planning to buy or build homes with a VA loan.

VA-Guaranteed Home Loans for Veterans. To help you understand what the VA can and cannot do for the home purchaser.

* Insurance

Veterans Assistance Office
U.S. Department of Veterans Affairs (VA)
810 Vermont Ave., NW
Washington, DC 20420 (202) 872-1151

Low cost insurance is available for veterans with service-connected disabilities. Veterans who are totally disabled may apply for a waiver of premiums on these policies. For more information on GI life insurance and Servicemen's Group Life Insurance (SGLI), Veterans Group Life Insurance (VGLI), and Veterans Mortgage Life Insurance (VMLI), contact the nearest VA office. The Insurance Information Toll-Free Number, (800) 669-8477, is a nationwide source for insurance inquiries and requests for service. It is also useful for policyholders and beneficiaries who are covered by a VA administered life insurance policy. Calls can be made to the number above from 8:00 a.m. to 5:30 p.m. EST.

* Job-Finding Assistance

Veterans Assistance Office
U.S. Department of Veterans Affairs (VA)
810 Vermont Ave., NW
Washington, DC 20420 (202) 872-1151

Assistance in finding jobs is provided to veterans through state employment/job service local offices throughout the country. The Local Veterans Employment

Veterans and Dependents

Representatives provide functional supervision of job counseling, testing, and employment referral and placement services provided to veterans. Priority in referral to job openings and training opportunities is given to eligible veterans, with preferential treatment for disabled veterans. In addition, the job service assists veterans who are seeking employment by providing information about job markets on-the-job and apprenticeship training opportunities in cooperation with VA Regional Offices and Vet Centers. Veterans should apply for this kind of help at their nearest local state employment service/job service office, not VA.

* Life Insurance (GI Insurance 64.103)

U.S. Department of Veterans Affairs (VA)
Regional Office and Insurance Center
P.O. Box 8079
Philadelphia, PA 19101 (800) 669-8477

To provide life insurance protection for veterans of World War I, World War II, Korean conflict and service-disabled veterans separated from active duty on or after April 25, 1951, and to provide mortgage protection life insurance for those disabled veterans who are given a VA grant to secure specially adapted housing under Chapter 21, Title 38, USC. Types of assistance: direct loan, insurance. Estimate of annual funds available: $ 85,233,000.

* Loans

Veterans Assistance Office
U.S. Department of Veterans Affairs (VA)
810 Vermont Ave., NW
Washington, DC 20420 (202) 233-2044

Certain veterans and dependents are eligible for GI loans for homes, condiminiums, and manufactured homes. Also, certain disabled veterans of military service may be entitled under certain conditions to a grant from VA for a home specially adapted to their needs. For more information on these loans and grants, contact the nearest VA regional office.

* Medical Care for Dependents or Survivors

CHAMPVA Registration Center
U.S. Department of Veterans Affairs Medical Center
1055 Clermont St.
Denver, CO 80220 (303) 782-3800

The Civilian Health and Medical Program is a medical benefits program through which VA helps pay for medical services and supplies that eligible dependents and survivors of certain veterans obtain from civilian, non-VA sources. Normally, care under this program will be provided in non-VA facilities. VA facilities may be utilized for treatment when (1 they are equipped to provide the care, and (2 use of these facilities does not interfere with care and treatment of veterans. For more information, including eligibility, contact the office above.

* Medical Service

Medical Service
Veterans Health Services and Research Administration
U.S. Department of Veterans Affairs (VA)
810 Vermont Ave., NW
Washington, DC 20420 (202) 535-7577

This office is the representative, advocate, and monitoring office of Internal Medicine which constitutes the major bed and clinic service in the VA. It includes Cardiology, Pulmonary Disease, Gastroenterology, Hematology, Oncology, Endocrinology, Infectious Disease, Nephrology, Rheumatology, Dermatology, General Internal Medicine, Nutrition, Geriatrics, and Clinical Pharmacology. As such, this Service is responsible for a variety of important functions designed to maintain high standards of patient care, education, research, and administration. Contact the office above for further information.

* Memorial Markers and Memorial Plots

Veterans Assistance Office
U.S. Department of Veterans Affairs (VA)
810 Vermont Ave., NW
Washington, DC 20420 (202) 872-1151

A memorial headstone or marker may be furnished on application by a close relative recognized as the next of kin to commemorate any eligible veteran, including a person who died in active military service, whose remains have not been recovered or identified; who was buried at sea; who was donated to science; or who who cremated and the ashes scattered without interment of any portion of the ashes. The memorial may be erected in a private cemetery in a plot provided by the applicant or in a memorial section of a national cemetery. Contact the nearest VA regional office for more information.

* National Cemeteries 64.201

Director, Field Operations (401)
National Cemetery System
U.S. Department of Veterans Affairs (VA)
Washington, DC 20420 (202) 275-9163

To provide for interment in national cemeteries of veterans and members of the Armed Forces of the United States whose service terminated other than dishonorably and certain eligible dependents. Types of assistance: other. Estimate of annual funds available: $ 67,515,000.

* Nursing Home Care

Veterans Assistance Office
U.S. Department of Veterans Affairs (VA)
810 Vermont Ave., NW
Washington, DC 20420 (202) 872-1151

For admission or transfer to VA Nursing Home Care Units, it is essentially the same as for hospitalization. Direct admission to private nursing homes at VA expense is limited to (1 veterans who require nursing care for a service-connected disability after medical determination by VA; (2 any person in an Armed Forces hospital who required a protracted period of nursing care and who will become a veteran upon discharge from the Armed Forces; and (3 a veteran who had been discharged from a VA medical center and is receiving VA medical center based home health services. VA may transfer veterans who need nursing home care to private nursing homes at VA expense from VA medical centers, nuring homes or domiciliaries. For more information, contact and VA medical facility.

* Office of Systems Planning, Policy, and Acquisition Control (004M)

U.S. Department of Veterans Affairs (VA)
810 Vermont Ave., NW
Washington, DC 20420 (202) 872-1151

Contact the office above to obtain a copy of *Veterans Affairs Information Systems Plan: Fiscal year 1987-1993.*

* Overseas Medical Benefits

Veterans Assistance Office
U.S. Department of Veterans Affairs (VA)
810 Vermont Ave., NW
Washington, DC 20420 (202) 872-1151

Reimbursed fee-basis medical care is available outside of the U.S. to veterans for treatment of service-connected disabilities and conditions adjunct to the rated disabilities. Prior to treatment, an authorization must be obtained from the nearest American embassy or consulate. In Canada, veterans should contact the local office of the Canadian Department of Veterans Affairs. In emergency situations, treatment should be reported within 72 hours. Nursing care is not available in foreign jurisdiction.

* Patient Treatment File

Reports and Statistics (10A4Z)
Veterans Health Services and Research Administration
U.S. Department of Veterans Affairs (VA)
810 Vermont Ave., NW
Washington, DC 20420 (202) 233-2424

The *Patient Treatment File* is a discharge oriented database which contains medical and administrative data for the following types of care provided or paid for by the U.S. Department of Veterans Affairs: VA and non-VA hospitals, VA and non-VA nursing homes, and VA domiciliaries. The file is maintained in fiscal year segments so that complete data for a particular year is not available until some months after the end of the fiscal year. For more information, including the types of data collected, contact the office above.

* Paraplegic Housing - Specially Adapted Housing for Disabled Veterans 64.106

U.S. Department of Veterans Affairs (VA)
Washington, DC 20420

Be patient. If any phone number is incorrect, call (area code) 555-1212 and request the new listing.

Government Financial Help to Individuals

To assist certain severely disabled veterans in acquiring suitable housing units, with special fixtures and facilities made necessary by the nature of the veterans disabilities. Types of assistance: direct payment. Estimate of annual funds available: $ 14,815,000.

* Pensions

Veterans Assistance Office
U.S. Department of Veterans Affairs (VA)
810 Vermont Ave., NW
Washington, DC 20420 (202) 872-1151

Those eligibile for VA pensions include wartime veterans with limited income discharged under other than dishonorable conditions after 90 or more days service who are permanently and totally disabled for reasons not traceable to service, nor due to willful misconduct or vicious habits. Veterans 65 years of age or older and not working are considered permanently and totally disabled. A pension is not payable to those who have estates that can provide adequate maintenance. For more information on eligibility and benefits, contact your regional VA office.

* Pension for Non-Service-Connected Disability for Veterans (Pension) 64.104

U.S. Department of Veterans Affairs (VA)
Washington, DC 20420

To assist wartime veterans in need whose non-service connected disabilities are permanent and total, preventing them from following a substantially gainful occupation. Types of assistance: direct payment. Estimate of annual funds available: $ 2,535,363,000.

* Pension to Veterans, Surviving Spouses, and Children (Death Pension) 64.105

U.S. Department of Veterans Affairs (VA)
Washington, DC 20420

To assist needy surviving spouses, and children of deceased war-time veterans whose deaths were not due to service. Types of assistance: direct payment. Estimate of annual funds available: $ 1,292,772,000.

* Presidential Memorial Certificates

Veterans Assistance Office
U.S. Department of Veterans Affairs (VA)
810 Vermont Ave., NW
Washington, DC 20420 (202) 872-1151

Presidential Memorial Certificates expressing the country's grateful recognition of the person's service in the armed forces and bearing the signature of the President are made available to the next of kin of deceased eligible veterans or of persons who were members of the Armed Forces at time of death. Eligible recipients include the next of kin, a relative or friend upon request, or an authorized representative acting on behalf of such relative or friend. Notice of a veteran's death is normally received in one of VA's regional offices, and that facility identifies the next of kin from the veteran's records and requests the certificates from Washington, DC. Next of kin of veterans need not apply. Others should apply to a VA regional office.

* Procurement of Headstones and Markers 64.202

Director, Monument Service
U.S. Department of Veterans Affairs (VA)
810 Vermont Ave., NW
Washington, DC 20420 (202) 275-1480

To provide headstones or markers for all unmarked graves in national, post and state Veterans cemeteries and upon receipt of application for the unmarked graves of eligible veterans interred in private cemeteries. Types of assistance: direct payments. Estimate of annual funds available: $ 29,350,000.

* Prosthetic Devices

Veterans Assistance Office
U.S. Department of Veterans Affairs (VA)
810 Vermont Ave., NW
Washington, DC 20420 (202) 872-1151

Veterans may be provided prosthetic appliances necessary for treatment of any condition when receiving hospital, domiciliary, or nursing home care in a facility under the direct jurisdiction of the VA. For more information, contact the Prosthetic Activity at VA medical center.

* Readjustment Counseling Service

Readjustment Counseling Service (10B/RC)
U.S. Department of Veterans Affairs (VA)
810 Vermont Ave., NW, Room 851
Washington, DC 20420 (202) 535-7554

The Readjustment Counseling Service Vietnam Era Veterans Outreach Centers (Vet Centers) are community-based, Department of Veterans Affairs (VA) services which were established following a recognition of the special readjustment needs of veterans who served during the Vietnam War, and from a desire to provide needed readjustment assistance to both top combat veterans and to support personnel of the Vietnam Era. The mission of the Readjustment Counseling Service (RCS) is to provide a wide range of outreach and direct psychosocial counseling services through storefront operations to veterans of the Vietnam era in order to help them make a satisfactory post-war readjustment to civilian life. For more information, including obtaining the address of your nearest Vet Center, contact the office above.

* Recreation Service

Recreation Service (11K)
Veterans Health Services and Research Administration
U.S. Department of Veterans Affairs (VA)
Washington, DC 20420 (202) 233-2424

The VA's recreational programs attempt to improve the quality of patient's lives and facilitate their reentry into the community. For more information, contact the office above.

* Rehabilitation Research

Rehabilitation Research and Development (110)
U.S. Department of Veterans Affairs (VA)
810 Vermont Ave., NW
Washington, DC 20420 (202) 535-7152

This program focuses directly on the needs of the veteran who is functionally impaired as a result of amputation, paralysis, or the loss or impairment of his or her vision, hearing, or speech. The latest computer and other technological advances are used to develop devices, techniques, and concepts in rehabilitation that will minimize the disability and promote functional independence among disabled veterans. Information and technology transfer is distributed through interagency agreements and collaborative efforts with the private sector. Contact the office above for more information.

* Social Work

Social Work Service (122)
U.S. Department of Veterans Affairs (VA)
810 Vermont Ave., NW
Washington, DC 20420 (202) 535-7588

Social Work Service is an integral part of the overall VA health-care program and operates in close concert with all medical services. Its purpose is to provide help to veterans and their families in resolving the psychosocial, emotional, and economic problems in dealing with the stresses of illness and disability. Social workers furnish psychosocial, diagnostic, and treatment services to the comprehensive treatment of veteran patients moving through admission, hospitalization, and post-hospital care back into the community. Social workers are also actively involved in outreach, readmission, and aftercare phases of the Department of Veterans Affairs' health care programs. For further information, contact the office above.

* Survivors and Dependents Educational Assistance 64.117

U.S. Department of Veterans Affairs (VA)
Central Office
Washington, DC 20420

To provide partial support to those seeking to advance their education who are qualifying spouses, surviving spouses, or children of deceased or disabled veterans, or of service personnel who have been listed for a total of more than 90 days as missing in action, or as prisoners of war. Types of assistance: direct payment. Estimate of annual funds available: $ 99,416,000.

Be patient. If any phone number is incorrect, call (area code) 555-1212 and request the new listing.

Veterans and Dependents

* Veterans' Court of Appeals
Court of Veterans Appeals
1625 K St., NW, Suite 400
Washington DC 20006 (202) 501-5970
A Court of Veterans Appeals reviews benefit claims that are appealed on or after November 18, 1988. The Court has exclusive jurisdiction to review decisions of the Board of Veterans Appeals.

* Veterans Compensation for Service-Connected Disability (Compensation) 64.109
U.S. Department of Veterans Affairs (VA)
Washington, DC 20420
To compensate veterans for disabilities incurred or aggravated during military service according to the average impairment in earning capacity such disability would case in civilian occupations. Types of assistance: direct payment. Estimate of annual funds available: $ 9,893,084,000.

* Veterans Dependency and Indemnity Compensation for Service-Connected Death (DIC) 64.110
U.S. Department of Veterans Affairs (VA)
Washington, DC 20420
To compensate surviving spouses, children, and parents for the death of any veteran who died on or after January 1, 1957, because of a service-connected disability, or while in the active military, naval or air service. Types of assistance: direct payment. Estimate of annual funds available: $ 2,609,751,000.

* Veterans Hospital Based Home Care 64.022
Asst. Chief, Medical Director for Geriatrics and Extended Care
U.S. Department of Veterans Affairs (VA)
Washington, DC 20420 (202) 535-7530
To provide individual medical, nursing, social and rehabilitative services to eligible veterans in their home environment by VA hospital staff. Types of assistance: other. Estimate of annual funds available: $ 30,600,000.

* Veterans Nursing Home Care (VA Nursing Home Care) 64.010
Asst. Chief Medical Director for Geriatrics and Extended Care (114A)
U.S. Department of Veterans
Washington, DC 20402 (202) 535-7179
To accommodate eligible veterans who are not acutely ill and not in need of hospital care, but who require skilled nursing care, related medical services, supportive personal care and individual adjustment services. Types of assistance: other. Estimate of annual funds available: $ 1,016,864,000.

* Veterans Outpatient Care 64.011
Director for Administration (161B2)
U.S. Department of Veterans Affairs (VA)
Washington, DC 20420 (202) 535-7384
To provide medical and dental services, medicines and medical supplies to eligible veterans on an outpatient basis. Types of assistance: other. Estimate of annual funds available: $ 3,778,816,000.

* Veterans Prescription Service (Medicine for Veterans) 64.012
Asst. Chief, Medical Director for Clinical Affairs (111H)
U.S. Department of Veterans Affairs (VA)
Washington, DC 20420 (202) 535-7302
To provide eligible veterans and certain dependents and survivors of veterans with prescription drugs and expendable prosthetic medical supplies from VA pharmacies upon presentation of prescriptions from a licensed physician. Types of assistance: Other. Estimate of annual funds available: $ 1,007,000.

* Veterans Prosthetic Appliances (Prosthetics Services) 64.013
Director
Prosthetic and Sensory Aids (117C)
U.S. Department of Veterans Affairs (VA)
Washington, DC 20420 (202) 535-7293
To provide through purchase and/or fabrication, prosthetic and related appliances, equipment and services to disabled veterans so that they may live and work as productive citizens. Types of assistance: other. Estimate of annual funds available: $ 185,111,100.

* Veterans Rehabilitation - Alcohol and Drug Dependence (Alcohol and Drug Dependence Treatment Program, Mental Health and Behavioral Sciences Service) 64.019
Director, Mental Health and Behavioral Sciences Services (111C)
U.S. Department of Veterans Affairs (VA)
Washington, DC 20420 (202) 535-7316
To provide medical, social and vocational rehabilitation to eligible alcohol and drug dependent veterans. Types of assistance: other. Estimate of annual funds available: $ 515,433,000.

* Vocational Rehabilitation for Disabled Veterans (Vocational Rehabilitation) 64.116
U.S. Department of Veterans Affairs (VA)
Central Office
Washington, DC 20420
To provide all services and assistance necessary to enable service-disabled veterans and service persons hospitalized pending discharge to achieve maximum independence in daily living and, to the maximum extent feasible to become employable and to obtain and maintain suitable employment. Types of assistance: direct payment. Estimate of annual funds available: $ 107,010,000.

* Vocational Training for Certain Veterans Receiving VA Pension 64.123
U.S. Department of Veterans Affairs (VA)
Central Office
Washington, DC 20420
To assist new pension recipients to resume and maintain gainful employment by providing vocational training and other services. Types of assistance: direct payment. Estimate of annual funds available: $ 475,000.

* Voluntary Service
Veterans Assistance Office
U.S. Department of Veterans Affairs (VA)
810 Vermont Ave., NW
Washington, DC 20420 (202) 872-1151
The U.S. Department of Veterans Affairs encourages and trains volunteers to work at VA facilities in a variety of assignments beneficial to veterans and rewarding to volunteers. For complete information on voluntary service, contact the Chief of Voluntary Service at the nearest VA Medical Center.

* Work-Study Program
Veterans Assistance Office
U.S. Department of Veterans Affairs (VA)
810 Vermont Ave., NW
Washington, DC 20420 (202) 872-1151
Veteran-students enrolled as full-time students may agree to perform VA-related services and receive an additional allowance. The veterans who are 30 percent or more disabled from service-connected disabilities will be given preference. Contact your regional VA office for more information.

Vacations and Business Travel Tourist Adventures

* *See also the Arts and Humanities Chapter, Museums and Cultural Resources*
* *See also Weather and Geography Chapter for long-range weather forecasts and maps.*
* *See also the International Trade Chapter for overseas promotion opportunities.*

Here you'll find new ideas for your vacations that you'll probably never get from a travel agent. What about a polar expedition on an icebreaker? If you plan to travel to Europe, what about seeing if the U.S. Information Agency has any interest in paying you to give a lecture? Even if you don't have the energy to visit campgrounds or glaciers, you can still travel to those places simply by writing away for brochures, posters, and other publications available from the National Park Service. Boaters will find all sorts of information about rules, regulations, and safety, including coloring books for the youngsters. You'll also find handy tips for airborne travelers, on both domestic and international flights. We've also compiled a complete listing of each state's travel and tourism hotlines, which can help you map out any trip you want to take in the U.S.

* Agricultural Research Center Tours

Tour Coordinator, Agricultural Research Center
U.S. Department of Agriculture
Building 302
Beltsville, MD 20705 (301) 504-9403
Tour Reservations (301) 504-8483

Visitors to the Beltsville Agricultural Research Center can arrange for guided tours. The center is closed to the public on Saturdays, Sundays, and holidays.

* Air Force Base Tours

Secretary of the Air Force
Office of Public Affairs
The Pentagon, Room 4A120
Washington, DC 20330 (703) 697-4100

Attend an annual open house on your local Air Force base, where you will tour the base, view aircraft on display, and watch an air show. Contact the Air Force installation nearest you, or the above office for a referral.

* Air Force Test Flight Center Tours

Air Force Flight Test Center
Public Affairs Office AFFTC/PA
SE Mojave
Edwards Air Force Base, CA 93524-1225 (805) 277-3510

The Test Center sponsors an annual open house, usually in October, when the public is invited on a six-hour tour of the base. You can view the aircraft up close, watch a demonstration of the military "working" dogs, and view historical films of the base. Write or call the Public Affairs Office for more information.

* Airport and Control Tower Tours

Aviation Education Officer
Federal Aviation Administration (FAA)
U.S. Department of Transportation
800 Independence Ave., SW (202) 267-3476
Washington, DC 20591 (202) 267-3469

The FAA's Aviation Education Program offers volunteer assistance to the nation's schools through these programs: career guidance; tours of airports, control towers, and other facilities; classroom lectures and demonstrations; aviation safety information; aviation education resource materials; computerized clearinghouse of aviation and space information; aviation science instruction programs for home/school computers; "Partnerships-in-Education" activities; and teachers' workshops. Write to the above office for more information.

* American War Memorials

The American Battle Monuments Commission
Casimir Pulaski Building
20 Massachusetts Avenue, NW
Washington, DC 20314-0001 (202) 272-0533

Presently 124,921 U.S. War Dead are interred in U.S. administered cemeteries around the world, including 24 military burial grounds on foreign soil, and 15 separate monuments, 4 memorials, and 2 tablets in the United States. Each year the Commission publishes attractive, free pamphlets which highlight individual memorials, and include locations, site descriptions and photographs, brief histories of the battles in which the deceased fought, and directions from the nearest major airports. Back issues covering specific memorials are also available at no charge.

* Army Facilities Tours

Community Relations Division
U.S. Army Public Affairs
The Pentagon, Room 2E637
Washington, DC 20310 (703) 695-4462
Public Inquiries (703) 614-0739
Community Relations (703) 697-5081

The Army arranges tours of its facilities and special exhibits for the public. You may watch paratroopers jump, rangers train, tanks and artillery fire, and personally talk to soldiers about their jobs. Contact your nearest army installation for more information, or the above office which will refer you to the appropriate contact.

* Botanical Garden Tours

Public Programs Office
U.S. Botanic Garden
245 1st St., SW
Washington, DC 20024 (202) 226-4082

The Botanic Garden is open to the public from 9 a.m. to 9 p.m. daily June through August, and from 9 a.m. to 5 p.m. the rest of the year. Tours are given to interested groups, including garden clubs, professional organizations, and school children. The gardens are located at 1st and Maryland Avenue, SW, Washington, DC; (202) 225-7099.

* Buffalo and Cattle Refuges

Division of Refuges
U.S. Fish and Wildlife Service
4401 N. Fairfax Dr., Room 670
Arlington, VA 22203 (703) 358-1744

Buffalo and Texas longhorn cattle, as well as deer and elk, can be enjoyed at wildlife refuges maintained by the U.S. Department of the Interior. Wichita Mountains in Oklahoma and Fort Niobrara in Nebraska preserve these animals in their natural habitat. The government periodically auctions these animals to the public at these locations. For more information, contact the refuge managers directly: Fort Niobrara National Wildlife Refuge, Hidden Timber Route, HC 14, Box 67, Valentine, NE 69201; (402) 376-3789. Witchita Mountains Wildlife Refuge, Rt. 1, Box 448, Indiahoma, OK 73552; (405) 429-3221. You can see

Be patient. If any phone number is incorrect, call (area code) 555-1212 and request the new listing.

Tourist Adventures

Buffalo also at the National Bison Range in Moiese, Montana. For more information on this refuge, contact National Bison Range, Moiese, MT 59824; (406) 644-2211.

* Capitol Hill Guided Tours

Capitol Guide Service
The Capitol
Washington, DC 20510 (202) 225-6827

Before leaving home for vacation, write your Representative and/or Senator--as far in advance as possible--for tickets to the morning VIP congressional tour specifying the date you wish to visit. Tickets are limited, but it's worth a try. Also request a Visitor's Pass for each member of your party to view a session of the House and/or Senate. House and Senate passes are not interchangeable, and they do not admit the bearer to special events and to a joint session of the Congress. House Gallery passes are good for both sessions of Congress. Senate Gallery passes are good for only one session. Sometimes visitors get a chance to speak with their elected representatives or their staff. Foreigners wishing to enter need only to come to the door.

The Capitol is located between Constitution and Independence Avenues at First Street. The East Front entrance at East Capitol Street is open daily, 9:00-4:30, except Thanksgiving, Christmas, and New Year's. Free 35-minute guided tours for the public leave from the Rotunda every 10 minutes (more frequently in the summer) between 9 a.m. and 3:45 p.m. You'll view the National Statuary Hall, the House and Senate Chambers, and the Rotunda. The Capitol Rotunda and Statuary Hall are open in the summer until 10 p.m. The House and Senate Wings are also open when either of those legislative bodies is in night session.

* Currency Engraving and Printing Tours

Bureau of Engraving and Printing
U.S. Department of the Treasury
14th and C Streets, SW
Washington, DC 20228 Recorded Messages: (202) 874-3188

A continuous self-guided tour at the Bureau features actual currency production. Visitors are able to view the various production steps, and tour guides are available to answer questions and assist visitors. Visitors may purchase uncut sheets of currency, engraved prints, small bags of shredded currency, and souvenir cards at the Visitor's Center. Tours may be taken Monday through Friday from 9 a.m. to 2 a.m., and admission is free.

* Diplomatic Reception Rooms

Tour Office
U.S. Department of State
2201 C St., NW (202) 647-3241
Washington, DC 20520 FAX: (202) 736-4232

Diplomatic reception rooms, which showcase American cultural heritage of the 18th and 29th centuries, are furnished with priceless antiques that have been donated or loaned to the State Department. These rooms are used for official functions by the President, the Vice President, the Secretary of State, and other governmental officials. The tour office can arrange public tours upon request by reservation only, for up to 50 people.

* Engineering Inventions and Tours

Tours
National Institute of Standards and Technology
Gaithersburg, MD 20899 Recorded Message: (301) 975-3585

Free tours of the various facilities at NIST are given on Thursdays at 9:30 a.m. They generally last for two hours, and the public is welcome, but should schedule reservations in advance through Jan Hauber at the office above.

* Federal Reserve Visitors

Office of Protocol
Board of Governors Office
Federal Reserve System
Room B2217-B
20th St. and Constitution Ave., NW
Washington, DC 20551 (202) 452-3149

Those interested in visiting the Federal Reserve Board in Washington, DC, should contact this office. At least one tour is conducted every Thursday at 2:30 p.m., and special arrangements may be made to accommodate groups of 10 or more.

* Glacier Bay and Other Historical Landmarks

Superintendent of Documents
Government Printing Office
Washington, DC 20402 (202) 783-3238

Historical landmarks are described in the historical handbooks featured in this listing. Sites include Antietam Battlefield, Devil's Tower in Wyoming, Ford's Theatre, Glacier Bay, Lincoln Memorial, and Nez Perce National Historical Park in Idaho, among others. Free.

* House of Representatives Passes

Your Member of Congress
U.S. House of Representatives
Washington, DC 20515 (202) 224-3121

The U.S. House of Representatives meets in the House Chamber in the south wing of the Capitol. The public is seated in the side and rear galleries; seats are available to those who secure passes from their Representative on a first come, first served basis.

* Indian Museums

Southern Plains Indian Museum
P.O. Box 749
Anadarko, OK 73005 (405) 247-6221

Museum of the Plains Indian
P.O. Box 400
Browning, MT 59417 (406) 338-2230

Sioux Indian Museum
P.O. Box 1504
Rapid City, SD 57709 (605) 348-0557

These three Indian museums are administered by the Indian Arts and Crafts Board of the Bureau of Indian Affairs, U.S. Department of the Interior. The museums issue free informational pamphlets and brochures about their respective programs and exhibition activities. Contact the museums directly to be placed on their mailing lists.

* Indian Reservations

If you are interested in visiting an Indian reservation on your vacation, or even if you are just interested in finding out more firsthand information about a particular tribe or reservation, you should contact any of the following offices listed below. Since not every Indian reservation allows public tours, you'll have to contact each individually to find out any tourism programs.

Field Offices

Anadarko Agency
P.O. Box 309, Anadarko, OK 73005; (405) 247-6673

Anchorage Agency
1675 C Street, Anchorage, AK 99501; (907) 271-4088

Ardmore Agency
P.O. Box 997, Ardmore, OK 73402; (405) 223-6767

Bethel Agency
P.O. Box 347, Bethel, AK 99559; (907) 543-2726

Blackfeet Agency
Browning, MT 59417; (406) 338-7686

Central California Agency
1800 Tribute Road, Suite 111, Sacramento, CA 95815; (916) 978-4337

Cherokee Agency
Cherokee, NC 28719; (704) 497-9131

Cheyenne River Agency
P.O. Box 325, Eagle Butte, SD 57625; (605) 964-6611

Chinle Agency
P.O. Box 7, Chinle, AZ 86503; (602) 674-5201

Chickasaw Agency
P.O. Box 2240, Ada, OK 74821; (405) 436-0784

Be patient. If any phone number is incorrect, call (area code) 555-1212 and request the new listing.

Vacations and Business Travel

Choctaw Agency
421 Powell, Philadelphia, MS 39350; (601) 656-1523

Colorado River Agency
Rt. 1, Box 9-C, Parker, AZ 85344; (602) 669-7111

Colville Agency
P.O. Box 111, Nespelem, WA 99155; (509) 634-4901

Concho Agency
1635 E. Highway 66, El Reno, OK 73036-5769; (405) 262-7481

Crow Agency
Crow Agency, MT 59022; (406) 638-2672

Crow Creek Agency
P.O. Box 616, Ft. Thompson, SD 57339; (605) 245-2311

Eastern Navajo Agency
P.O. Box 32, Crownpoint, NM 87313; (505) 786-6100

Eastern Nevada Agency
P.O. Box 28, Elkon, NV 89801; (702) 738-5165

Fairbanks Agency
Federal Building and Courthouse, 101 12th Avenue, Box 16, Fairbanks, AK 99701; (907) 456-0222

Flathead Agency
Box A, Pablo, MT 59855; (406) 675-2700

Fort Apache Agency
P.O. Box 560, Whiteriver, AZ 85941; (602) 338-5354

Fort Belknap Agency
P.O. Box 98, Harlem, MT 59526; (406) 353-2901 ext. 23

Fort Berthold Agency
P.O. Box 370, New Town, ND 58763; (701) 627-4707

Fort Defiance Agency
P.O. Box 619, Fort Defiance, AZ 86504; (602) 729-5041

Fort Hall Agency
Fort Hall, ID 83203; (208) 238-2301

Fort Peck Agency
P.O. Box 637, Poplar, MT 59255; (406) 768-5312

Fort Totten Agency
P.O. Box 270, Fort Totten, ND 58335; (701) 766-4545

Fort Yuma Agency
P.O. Box 1591, Yuma, AZ 85364; (619) 572-0248

Great Lakes Agency
Ashland, WI 54806; (715) 682-4527/8

Hopi Agency
P.O. Box 158, Keams Canyon, AZ 86034; (602) 738-2228

Horton Agency
P.O. Box 31, Horton, KS 66439; (913) 486-2161

Jicarilla Agency
P.O. Box 167, Dulce, NM 87528; (505) 759-3651

Laguna Agency
P.O. Box 1448, Laguna, NM 87026; (505) 522-6001

Lower Brule Agency
P.O. Box 190, Lower Brule, SD 57548; (605) 473-5512

Makah Agency
P.O. Box 116, Neah Bay, WA 98357; (206) 645-2229

Menominee Area Rep
Minneapolis Area Office, 331 2nd Avenue, Minneapolis, MN 55401-2241; (612) 373-1000

Mescalero Agency
P.O. Box 189, Mescalero, NM 88340; (505) 671-4423

Metlakatla Field Station
P.O. Box 458, Metlakatla Field Station, Metlakatla, AK 99926; (907) 886-3791

Miami Agency
P.O. Box 391, Miami, OK 74355; (918) 542-3396

Michigan Agency
Federal Square Office Plaza, P.O. Box 884, Sault Ste. Marie, MI 49783; (906) 632-6809

Minnesota Agency
Route 3, P.O. Box 112, Cass Lake, MN 56633; (218) 335-2350

Minnesota Sioux Field Rep
Minneapolis Area Office, 331 2nd Avenue E, 6th Floor, Minneapolis, MN 55402; (612) 349-3382

Muskogee Area Office
Old Federal Bldg., Muskogee, OK 74401; (918) 687-2296

New York Liaison Office
P.O. Box 7366, Syracuse, NY 13261-7366; (315) 423-5476

Nome Agency
P.O. Box 1108, Nome, AK 99762; (907) 443-2284

Northern California Agency
P.O. Box 494879, Redding, CA 96049-4879; (916) 246-5141

Northern Cheyenne Agency
Lame Deer, MT 59043; (406) 477-8242

Northern Idaho Agency
P.O. Box 277, Lapwai, ID 83540; (208) 843-2267

Northern Pueblos Agency
1570 Pachaco Street, Building D6, Santa Fe, NM 87501; (505) 753-1400

Okmulgee Agency
P.O. Box 370, Okmulgee, OK 74447; (918) 756-3950

Olympic Peninsula Agency
P.O. Box 120, Office Building, Hoquiam, WA 98550; (206) 533-9100

Osage Agency
Pawhuska, OK 74056; (918) 287-1032

Papago Agency
P.O. Box 578, Sells, AZ 85634; (602) 383-3286

Palm Springs Agency
P.O. Box 2245, Palm Springs, CA 92262; (619) 322-2086

Pawnee Agency
P.O. Box 440, Pawnee, OK 74058; (918) 762-2585

Pima Agency
P.O. Box 8, Sacaton, AZ 85247; (602) 562-3326

Pine Ridge Agency
P.O. Box 1203, Pine Ridge, SD 57770; (605) 867-5121

Puget Sound Agency
3006 Colby St., Federal Bldg., Everett, WA 98201; (206) 258-2651

Ramah-Navajo Agency
Ramah, NM 87321; (505) 775-3235

Red Lake Agency
Red Lake, MN 56671; (218) 679-3361

Be patient. If any phone number is incorrect, call (area code) 555-1212 and request the new listing.

Tourist Adventures

Rocky Boy's Agency
Box Elder, MT 59521; (406) 395-4476

Rosebud Agency
P.O. Box 550, Rosebud, SD 57570; (605) 747-2224

Sac & Fox Area
Tama, IA 56671; (515) 484-4041

Salt River Agency
Rt. 1, P.O. Box 117, Scottsdale, AZ 85256; (602) 640-2842

San Carlos Agency
P.O. Box 209, San Carlos, AZ 85550; (602) 475-2321

Seattle Support Center
P.O. Box 80947, Seattle, WA 98104; (206) 764-3328

Seminole Agency
6075 Stirling Rd., Hollywood, FL 33024; (305) 581-7050, Extension 356-7288

Shawnee Agency
Route 5, Box 148, Shawnee, OK 74801; (405) 273-0317

Shiprock Agency
P.O. Box 966, Shiprock, NM 87420; (505) 368-4427

Siletz Agency
P.O. Box 539, Siletz, OR 97380; (503) 444-2679

Sisseton Agency
P.O. Box 688, Agency Village, SD 57262; (605) 698-7676

Southeast Agency
P.O. Box 3-8000, Juneau, AK 99802; (907) 586-7304

Southern California Agency
3600 Lime Street, Suite 722, Riverside, CA 92501; (714) 276-6624

Southern Paiute Field Station
Box 986, Cedar City, UT 84720; (801) 586-1121

Southern Pueblos Agency
P.O. Box 1667, Albuquerque, NM 87103; (505) 766-3021

Southern Ute Agency
P.O. Box 315, Ignacio, CO 81137; (303) 563-4511

Spokane Agency
P.O. Box 389, Wellpinit, WA 99040; (509) 258-4561

Standing Rock Agency
P.O. Box E, Ft. Yates, ND 58538; (701) 854-3431

Tahlequah Agency
P.O. Box 828, Tahlequah, OK 74465; (918) 456-6146

Talihina Agency
P.O. Drawer H, Talihina, OK 74571; (918) 567-2207

Truxton Canon Agency
Valentine, AZ 86437; (602) 769-2286

Turtle Mountain Agency
P.O. Box 60, Belcourt, ND 58316; (701) 477-3191

Uintah & Ouray Agency
Fort Duchesne, UT 84026; (801) 722-2406

Umatilla Agency
P.O. Box 520, Pendleton, OR 97801; (503) 276-3811

Ute Mountain Agency
General Delivery, Towaoc, CO 81334; (303) 565-8471

Wahpeton Indian School
Wahpeton Indian School, Wahpeton, ND 58075; (701) 642-3796

Wapato Irrigation Project
P.O. Box 220, Wapato, WA 98951; (509) 877-3155

Warm Springs Agency
P.O. Box 1239, Warm Springs, OR 97761; (503) 553-2411

Western Navajo Agency
P.O. Box 127, Tuba City, AZ 86045; (602) 283-4531

Western Nevada Agency
1300 S. Curry Street, Carson City, NV 89701; (702) 887-3500

Wewoka Agency
P.O. Box 1060, Wewoka, OK 74884; (405) 257-6257

Wind River Agency
Ft. Washakie, WY 82514; (307) 332-7812

Winnebago Agency
Winnebago, NE, 68071; (402) 878-2502

Yakima Agency
P.O. Box 632, Toppenish, WA 98948; (509) 865-2255

Yankton Agency
Wagner, SD 57380; (605) 384-3651

Zuni Agency
P.O. Box 369, Zuni, NM 87327; (505) 782-5591

Area Offices

Aberdeen Area Director
Bureau of Indian Affairs, 115 4th Avenue, SE, Aberdeen, SD 57401-4382; (605) 226-7343. Serving Nebraska, North Dakota, South Dakota.

Albuquerque Area Director
Bureau of Indian Affairs, 615 1st Street, NW, Box 26567, Albuquerque, NM 87125-6567; (505) 766-3170. Serving Colorado, New Mexico, Texas.

Anadarko Area Director
Bureau of Indian Affairs, WCD Office Complex, Box 368, Anadarko, OK 73005-0368; (405) 247-6673. Serving Kansas, Western Oklahoma, Texas.

Billings Area Director
Bureau of Indian Affairs, 316 North 26th Street, Billings, MT 58101-1397; (406) 657-6315. Serving Montana, Wyoming.

Eastern Area Director
Bureau of Indian Affairs, Mail Stop 260 - VA SQ, 1951 Constitution Avenue, NW, Washington, DC 20245; (703) 235-2571. Serving New York, Maine, Florida, North Carolina, Louisiana, Mississippi, Rhode Island, Connecticut, Alabama, Massachusetts.

Juneau Area Director
Bureau of Indian Affairs, Federal Building, P.O. Box 3-8000, Juneau, AK 99802-1219; (907) 586-7177. Serving Alaska.

Minneapolis Area Director
Bureau of Indian Affairs, 15 South 5th Street, 10th Floor, Minneapolis, MN 55401-1020; (612) 373-1010. Serving Minnesota, Iowa, Michigan, Wisconsin.

Muskogee Area Director
Bureau of Indian Affairs, 5th and West Okmulgee, Muskogee, OK 74401-4898; (918) 687-2296. Serving Eastern Oklahoma, Missouri.

Navajo Area Director
Bureau of Indian Affairs, P.O. Box M, Window Rock, AZ 86515-0714; (602) 871-5151. Serving Navajo Reservation only--Arizona, Utah, New Mexico.

Phoenix Area Director
Bureau of Indian Affairs, 1 North First Street, P.O. Box 10, Phoenix, AZ 85001-0010; (602) 379-6600. Serving Arizona, Nevada, Utah, California.

Portland Area Director
Bureau of Indian Affairs, 911 Eleventh Avenue, NE, Portland, OR 97232-4169; (503) 231-6702. Serving Oregon, Idaho, Washington, Montana, Alaska (Metlakatla).

Be patient. If any phone number is incorrect, call (area code) 555-1212 and request the new listing.

Vacations and Business Travel

Sacramento Area Director
Bureau of Indian Affairs, 2800 Cottage Way, Sacramento, CA 95825-1884; (916) 978-4691. Serving California.

* Korean War Veterans Memorial

The American Battle Monuments Commission (ABMC)
Casimir Pulaski Building
20 Massachusetts Avenue, NW
Room 5127
Washington, DC 20314-0001 (202) 272-0533

In 1986 a new law authorized the ABMC to erect a memorial in the Washington, DC, area to honor all servicemen and women of the Armed Forces of the United States who served during the Korean War, particularly those who were killed in action, are still listed as Missing in Action, or were held as prisoners of war. For information on its concept, construction, and fund raising efforts, contact the ABMC.

* Lawrence Livermore Computer Facility Tours

Visitors Center
Lawrence Livermore National Laboratory
Greenville Road
P.O. Box 808
Livermore, CA 94550 (510) 422-9797

The National Laboratory conducts public tours of its facility center, highlighting the NOVA Laser, by reservation only. You must, however, be 18 years of age or older. For information, contact the Visitors Center. The facility is closed weekends.

* Missile Testing Center Tours

U.S. Department of the Army
Public Affairs Office
Building 122
White Sands Missile Range, NM 88002-5047 (505) 678-1134

This research and missile testing center invites the public to an open house twice a year, which includes a visit to the "Trinity Site" where the first atomic detonation took place. The center publishes a brochure and fact sheets on its history, mission, and wide range of programs. The test range also functions as a wildlife preserve. Write or call for their free publications and information on open house days.

* Museum of the U.S. Department of the Interior

Departmental Museum
U.S. Department of the Interior (DOI)
1849 C St., NW, Mail Stop 4512
Washington, DC 20240 (202) 208-4743

The highlights of this museum's exhibit include Native American artifacts and dioramas depicting the history of each of DOI's Bureaus. Of particular interest o children is a collection of fossils and a display of fragments from the moon's surface. The display is oriented to children in the fourth grade and older, but younger children are welcome. The hours of operation are 8 a.m. to 5 p.m., Monday through Friday. You must have a photo ID to enter the building.

* Music at the Capitol

Architect's Office
Room SB-15
U.S. Capitol Building
Washington, DC 20515 (202) 225-1200

The Capitol and the House and Senate office buildings resound, especially during the spring and summer months, with all types of music. The American Festival/Concerts at the Capitol are sponsored by the Congress and the Secretary of the Interior. They are performed by the National Symphony and have been conducted by various maestros. The Service bands and choral groups of the Air Force, Army, Marine Corps, and Navy provide summer night entertainment for the public in concerts that have become a Capitol tradition. Concerts are free and seating on the lawn and picnics are in order. In addition, the Capitol and its various office buildings are filled throughout the year, but especially during the winter holiday season, with the joyous voices of choral groups. These appearances are arranged well in advance by the Senators or Representatives through the Architect of the Capitol.

* NASA Tours

Dryden Flight Research Facility
POB 273, TR-42
Edwards, CA 93523 (805) 258-3460

NASA offers its own base tours with a 25 minute film showing Dryden's current project testings and concluding with a 45 minute walking tour of two active hangers. Tours are Monday-Friday, 10:15 and 1:15. The tours are free, but reservations are required.

* National Aquarium

U.S. Department of Commerce Building
14th St. and Constitution Ave., NW (202) 482-2826
Washington, DC 20230 Recorded Information: (202) 482-2825

This public aquarium houses both fresh water and marine animals. Exhibits are representations of our natural environment and demonstrate basic biological concepts and principles. The admission fee is $2 for adults and $.75 for senior citizens (over 62) and children ages 4-12. Children 3 and under are admitted free. The hours are 9-5.

* National Arboretum Tours

U.S. National Arboretum
3501 New York Ave.
Educational Department
Washington, DC 20002 Recorded Information: (202) 475-4815

Various woody ornamental and outdoor plants are grown and cared for on the 444 acres comprising the U.S. National Arboretum. Admission and parking are free, and guided tours for 10 or more are available with 3 weeks advance notice. Many free classes are offered, along with many special events and functions associated with gardening and growing plants. A free quarterly newsletter lists the monthly calendar.

* National Park Service Folders Bibliography

Superintendent of Documents
Government Printing Office
Washington, DC 20402 Recorded Information: (202) 783-3238

National Park Service brochures are featured, including the lesser-known areas of the national parks and a Washington, DC, guide. Also included are books on the preservation of historic structures. Free.

* Nation's Capitol Walker's Guide

Public Information Office
Pennsylvania Avenue Development Corporation
1331 Pennsylvania Ave., NW
Suite 1220 North
Washington, DC 20004-1703 (202) 724-9091

A Walker's Guide to Pennsylvania Avenue provides the locations and architects of the PADC projects on Pennsylvania Avenue. This guide is free.

* Natural Landmarks Registry

National Registry of Natural Landmarks
Wildlife and Vegetation Division
National Park Service
U.S. Department of the Interior
P.O. Box 37127
Washington, DC 20013-7127 (202) 343-8129

The Park Service conducts natural region studies to identify areas that are of potential national significance. These areas are then studied in the field by scientists. Natural areas considered of national significance are cited by the Secretary of the Interior as eligible for recognition as Registered Natural Landmarks. The owner may apply for a certificate and bronze plaque designating the site.

* Panama Canal Tours

Orientation Services
The Office of Public Affairs
c/o Panama Canal Commission
Unit 2300 APOAA 34011 (800) 622-2625, ext. 52-5463

The Canal Guide Service, operated by the Panama Canal Commission, offers free tours of the Panama Canal to the public. Tours are given seven days a week

Be patient. If any phone number is incorrect, call (area code) 555-1212 and request the new listing.

Tourist Adventures

from 9:00 a.m. to 5:00 p.m. The tour takes less than an hour and include a slight briefing, a topographical model of the Canal to view, and a film. Visitors are welcome at the Miraflores Locks on the Pacific side of the Isthmus where a pavilion provides a vantage point for viewing transiting ships. Interested members of the public should call two days in advance to make a reservation. Another attraction is the high doomed ceiling, the dramatic murals, and the marble columns and floor make the rotunda the main attraction of the Administration Building at Balboa Heights. The murals depict the digging of Gaillard Cut at Gold Hill, the erection of a lock gate, and the construction of the Gatun Dam spillway and Miraflores Locks. For more information, contact this office.

* Pentagon Art Tours

Director, Pentagon Tours
OASD-PA(DCR)
The Pentagon
Room 1E776
Washington, DC 20301 (703) 695-1776

Free tours of the Pentagon art collection are conducted Monday through Friday, except holidays, every half hour from 9:30 a.m. to 3:30 p.m. All you need is a valid I.D. to sign up; children under 10 must be accompanied by an adult. Go to the ticket window at the main concourse by the Metro entrance. Only if you have a group of 30 or more do you need to write for a reservation; otherwise, just come, first come, first served.

* Polar Expeditions with Civilians

Ice Operations Division
Office of Navigation Safety and Waterways Services
U.S. Coast Guard
U.S. Department of Transportation
2100 2nd Street, SW
Room 1202 A
Washington, DC 20593-0001 (202) 267-1450

The Coast Guard furnishes vessels to other agencies, such as the National Science Foundation, U.S. Geological Survey, and the Navy, to conduct research and ice operations in Arctic and Antarctic waters. The agencies sponsoring the missions select scientists, researchers, students, and in some cases, journalists, photographers, and artists to accompany the mission when space is available. This office is a good starting point for obtaining information on the pertinence of a mission to your field, to be directed to the appropriate agency sponsors, and for information about the data collected during missions.

* Public Buildings and Historic Sites of the United States

Superintendent of Documents
Government Printing Office (GPO)
Washington, DC 20402 (202) 783-3238

The GPO bibliography of public buildings, landmarks, and historic Sites of the United States is divided into the categories of historic sites, posters, preservation methods for historic buildings, and descriptions of public buildings. Highlights include a poster of the Statue of Liberty and an historic guide to the White House. Free.

* Statue of Liberty

Superintendent of Documents
Government Printing Office
Washington, DC 20402 Recorded Message: (202) 783-3238

The Statue of Liberty Exhibit is a full-color pamphlet describing the museum of the Statue of Liberty. It recounts the history of the Statue, describes the intricacies of its architecture and design, and provides information on its French designers and its massive refurbishing. 1988 (S/N 024-005-01025-4, $2.50).

* U.S. Congress Memorial and Historic Trees

Architect of the Capitol
U.S. Capitol Building
Washington, DC 20515 (202) 224-6645

Since the early 1900s, ninety-four memorial and historic trees have been planted. Seventy-three are still living on the Capitol grounds. Trees have been planted to memorialize different senators and congressman as well as such people as mothers of America and Vietnam veterans. To obtain a chart which will help you locate various dedicatory trees, contact the Architect's office.

* Voice of America Radio Public Tours

Office of External Affairs
Voice of America (VOA)
United States Information Agency
330 Independence Ave., SW
Washington, DC 20547 Recorded Message: (202) 619-4700

Tours of the main headquarters of the VOA, which produces radio programming in 43 languages heard all over the world, are given each weekday except legal holidays. A guide shows visitors the technical operations center, the newsroom, several studios, where either live broadcasts or recordings are being sent out, and a film on the VOA. The 45 minute free tours are scheduled for 8:40, 9:40 and 10:40 a.m., and 1:40 and 2:40 p.m. Reservations are preferred.

* Washington DC Art Museums

For tour information, contact the appropriate office listed below, or call (202) 357-1300 (switchboard) or (202) 357-2700 for tour information.

Anacostia Museum
Education Department, Anacostia Museum, 1901 Fort Place S.E., Washington, DC 20020; (202) 287-3369.

Cooper-Hewitt Museum
Membership Department, Cooper-Hewitt Museum, 2 East 91st St., New York, NY 10128; (212) 860-6868.

Freer Gallery of Art
Tour Information, Freer Gallery of Art, 12th St. and Jefferson Drive SW, Washington, DC 20560; (202) 357-2104.

Hirshom Museum and Sculpture Garden
Office of Education, Hirshom Museum and Sculpture Garden, 8th St. and Independence Ave. S.W., Washington, DC 20560; (202) 357-3235.

Kennedy Center
Tour Information, Friends of the Kennedy Center, Washington, DC 20566; (202) 416-8340.

National Air and Space Museum
Office of Volunteer Service, National Air and Space Museum, 7th St. and Independence Ave., S.W., Washington, DC 20560; (202) 357-1400.

National Gallery of Art
Education Office, National Gallery of Art, Washington, DC 20565; (202) 842-6246.

National Museum of African Art
Department of Education, National Museum of African Art, 950 Independence Ave., S.W., Washington, DC 20560; (202) 357-4600, ext 221 or 222.

National Museum of American Art
Division of Museum Programs, Office of Educational Programs, National Museum of American Art, Smithsonian Institution, 8th and G St., NW, Room 181, Washington, DC 20560; (202) 357-3095 or Tour Coordinator, (202) 357-3111.

National Museum of American History
Office of Public Programs, National Museum of American History, 14th St. and Constitution Ave. NW, Washington, DC 20560; (202) 357-1481; 357-1563 TDD.

National Museum of Natural History
Office of Education, National Museum of Natural History, 10th St. and Constitution Ave. N.W., Washington, DC 20560; (202) 357-2747.

National Portrait Gallery
Curator of Education, National Portrait Gallery, Eighth and F Sts. N.W., Washington, DC 20560; (202) 357-2920.

National Zoological Park
Friends of the National Zoo, National Zoological Park, 3000 Connecticut Ave., N.W., Washington, DC 20008; (202) 673-4960. Visitor Information (202) 357-2700.

Smithsonian Environmental Research Center
Department of Education, Smithsonian Environmental Research Center, P.O. Box 28, Edgewater, MD 21037; (301) 261-4190, Ext 241.

Be patient. If any phone number is incorrect, call (area code) 555-1212 and request the new listing.

Vacations and Business Travel

Dial A Museum
800 Jefferson Drive SW, Washington, DC; (202) 357-2020.

Smithsonian Institutions
1000 Jefferson Drive SW, Washington, DC 20560; (202) 357-2700. Visitor Center and Assoc. Reception Center. Info for the Deaf, TDD (202) 357-1729.

* Washington, DC Landmarks and Points of Interest

Superintendent of Documents
Government Printing Office
Washington, DC 20402 (202) 783-3238

Washington, DC: Official National Park Guidebook is a colorful descriptive handbook of the Nation's Capitol and nearby Maryland, Virginia and West Virginia. It includes full-color photographs of Washington's landmarks, guide maps, and descriptive histories of all points of interest. 1989 (S/N 024-005-01034-3, $5).

* Washington, DC Pennsylvania Avenue Events

Public Information Office
Pennsylvania Avenue Development Corporation
1331 Pennsylvania Ave., NW
Suite 1220 North
Washington, DC 20004-1703 (202) 724-9091

Throughout the year, various events are held on Pennsylvania Avenue. Dial (202) 724-0009 to hear a recorded message providing daily information about events on Pennsylvania Avenue.

* White House Tours

The White House Office
1600 Pennsylvania Ave., NW (202) 456-1414
Washington, DC 20500 Recording: (202) 456-7041

Tours of the White House are held every Tuesday through Saturday from 10:00 a.m. to 12:00 noon, unless the White House is closed due to an official function. No tickets or reservations are required. For more information call the number above.

* Witness Congressional Committee Hearings and Meetings

Contact your Congressman or Senator, or
Senate or House Press Galleries (202) 224-3121

Most House and Senate committee hearings and meetings are open to the public. Your Representative or Senator's office should be able to brief you on the subject matter of the hearing and give you a copy of the bill which will be discussed, or a summary of the previous testimony they have heard. By attending committee meetings, you can gain an understanding of the issues gaining the attention of lawmakers and see the legislative process at work. Another type of committee hearing is an "oversight" or investigative session. Members examine the operations of a government agency or search some area of public life that may require future legislation. Hearings are conducted for a variety of reasons; principal among them are to gather information, generate publicity, and assess the level of support. Informed and interested witnesses may appear before the committee, including Federal officials, interest group representatives, academic experts, and private citizens. A civics lesson in action, the committee "mark-up session" occurs after all the testimony has been received and when the drafting of the legislation and voting on provisions actually takes place. This is the heart of the legislative process, where all the political pressures collide with policy questions. It is at this stage when the language of the bill is determined by the committee. Contact your Senator and Representative or call the Senate or House Press Galleries at (202) 224-3121 for news about the schedule for committee activities. When in the DC area, check the Washington Post front section (Today in Congress) for House/Senate committee activities.

Be patient. If any phone number is incorrect, call (area code) 555-1212 and request the new listing.

Parks and Camping

* Architecture in the Parks

Historic Architectural Division
National Park Service
U.S. Department of the Interior
800 N. Capitol Street NW
Washington, DC 20002 (202) 343-8146

Activities related to the preservation of historic and prehistoric structures and cultural landscapes within the National Park System are administered by this office. *A List of Classified Structures* is maintained, which is an inventory of all historic and prehistoric structures in the System. A bibliography of Cultural Resources Management is also administered, listing all reports that address cultural resources in the Park System.

* Apostle Islands

Superintendent of Documents
Government Printing Office
Washington, DC 20402 (202) 783-3238

Apostle Islands: A Guide to Apostle Islands Lakeshore, Wisconsin recounts the history of these islands, describes the geographical features, and looks at the inland sea. It provides tips on where to visit, wild animal life, and plant life. Full-color photographs are included. (S/N 024-005-01023-8, $2.25).

* Bicycle Paths and Other Transit Environments

Environment Division
Office of Regulatory Affairs
U.S. Department of Transportation (DOT)
400 7th Street, SW, Room 9217
Washington, DC 20590 (202) 366-4366

This is the DOT contact point for environmental issues. Staff can provide you with information and referrals on such subjects as highway beautification, transportation architecture, bicycle paths, historic preservation activities, and environmental impact statements.

* Campgrounds on Public Lands

Office of Public Affairs
Bureau of Land Management
U.S. Department of the Interior
18th and C Sts., NW
Washington, DC 20240 (202) 208-5717

The Recreation Guide to BLM Public Lands features a map outlining all of the public lands used as recreational areas. Designations on the map include campgrounds, visitors centers, national wild and scenic rivers, national wilderness areas, and national historic and scenic trails. Also included are the states that contain public lands, and state and district offices to contact for additional information. Alaska, Arizona, California, Colorado, Idaho, Montana, Nevada, New Mexico, Oregon, Utah, Washington, and Wyoming are the key states described. To obtain this free guide, call (202) 653-8828, Office of Public Affairs, 1620 L Street NW, Washington, DC 20036.

* Camping and Hiking East of the Mississippi

Land Between the Lakes
Resource and Development
Tennessee Valley Authority
100 Van Morgan Drive
Golden Pond, KY 42211-9001 (502) 924-5602

Land Between the Lakes offers recreation for tourists on over 300 miles of undeveloped shoreline. The Woodlands Nature Center offers animal exhibits both animals and special programs for the public, including over 200 miles of hiking trails. Wrangler's Camp offers horseback riding on its 26 miles of trails, along with barns, tethers, and posts for riders. Turkey Bay offers an area reserved for off-road vehicle recreation. Three primary campgrounds offer over 1,000 sites and numerous informal shoreline campgrounds. Land Between the Lakes also boasts their own resident buffalo herd--the largest publicly-owned

herd east of the Mississippi River. For more information on recreation opportunities at Land Between the Lakes, contact this office.

* Camping Guide to the National Parks

Superintendent of Documents
Government Printing Office
Washington, DC 20402 (202) 783-3238

The National Parks: Camping Guide 1991-92 contains basic information about the facilities and recreational opportunities available to users of the National Park System camping areas. It also provides an alphabetical list of camping areas by state. 1988 (S/N 024-005-01080-7, $4).

* Camping Reservations

Campsite reservations (800) 283-CAMP

Call Ahead for Happy Camping is a Forest Service program that makes it easier for you to use the 156 National Forests, where you can hike, fish, camp, ski, or just relax. There are over 100,000 miles of trails and 10,000 recreation sites. Call this toll-free number to make reservations at any of the National Forests across the U.S.

* Federal Recreation Passport Program

National Park Service Information Office
Office of Public Affairs
National Park Service
P.O. Box 37127
Washington, DC 20013-7127 (202) 208-6843

The following fee options are available for entrance into federal recreation areas (national parks, and national wildlife refuges). Reservations may be made by contacting: Mistix, P.O. Box 85705, San Diego, CA 92138-5705, (800) 365-2267 (camp). For more information on fees and programs, contact your regional national park office.

Single Visit Entrance Fee
Fees range from $1 per person to $10 per vehicle as set by the individual areas. At national park units, fees are charged of visitors 17 through 61 years of age; at national wildlife refuges, visitors 16 through 61 years of age. This fee allows entry to the specific national park or national wildlife unit (where fees are paid). It is good daily or other term, as posted.

Golden Eagle Passport
$25 annually. At national park units, fees are charged of visitors 17 through 61 years of age; at national wildlife refuges, visitors 16 through 61 years of age. This fee allows entry to all federal entrance fee areas, from January 1 through December 31.

Golden Age Passport
Free, for visitors 62 years or older. This allows entry to all federal entrance fee areas plus 50 percent discount on recreation use fees, and is good for the bearer's lifetime.

Golden Access Passport
Free, for visitors who are blind or permanently disabled. This allows entry to all federal entrance fee areas plus 50 percent discount on recreation use fees, and is good for the bearer's lifetime.

Park Pass
$10-$15 annually, for visitors 17 through 61 years of age. This allows entry to the national park unit at which the pass is purchased, from January 1 through December 31.

Duck Stamp
$12.50 annually, for visitors 16 through 61 years of age. This allows entry to all national wildlife refuges which charge entrance fees, from July 1 through June 30.

Be patient. If any phone number is incorrect, call (area code) 555-1212 and request the new listing.

Vacations and Business Travel

* Lesser-Known Parks

Superintendent of Documents
Government Printing Office
Washington, DC 20402 (202) 783-3238
This publication of the National Park Service is *The National Parks: Lesser-Known Areas* (024-005-00911-6, $1.50).

* National and Historical Parks, Monuments and Preserves

Alabama
Horseshoe Bend National Military Park, Route 1, Box 103, Daviston, AL 36256
Russell Cave National Monument, Route 1, Box 175, Bridgeport, AL 35740

Alaska
Aniakchak National Monument and Preserve, P.O. Box 7, King Salmon, AK 99613
Bering Land Bridge National Preserve, P.O. Box 220, Nome, AK 99762
Cape Krusenstern National Monument, P.O. Box 1029, Kotzebue, AK 99752
Denali National Park and Preserve, P.O. Box 9, McKinley Park, AK 99755
Gates of the Arctic National Park and Preserve, P.O. Box 74680, Fairbanks, AK 99707
Glacier Bay National Park and Preserve, Gustavus, AK 99826
Katmai National Park and Preserve, P.O. Box 7, King Salmon, AK 99613
Kenai Fjords National Park, P.O. Box 1727, Seward, AK 99664
Klondike Gold Rush National Historical Park, P.O. Box 517, Skagway, AK 99840
Kobuk Valley National Park, P.O. Box 1029, Kotzebue, AK 99752
Lake Clark National Park and Preserve, 701 C St., P.O. Box 61, Anchorage, AK 99513
Noatak National Preserve, P.O. Box 1029, Kotzebue, AK 99752
Sitka National Historical Park, P.O. Box 738, Sitka, AK 99835
Wrangell-St. Elias National, Park and Preserve, P.O. Box 29, Glenallen, AK 99588
Yukon-Charley Rivers, National Preserve, P.O. Box 64, Eagle, AK 99738

Arizona
Coronado National Memorial, Rural Route 2, P.O. Box 126, Hereford, AZ 85615
Grand Canyon National Park, P.O. Box 129, Grand Canyon, AZ 86023
Hot Springs National Park, P.O. Box 1860, Hot Springs, AZ 71902
Petrified Forest National Park, Petrified Forest National Park, AZ 86028
Saguaro National Monument, 36933 Old Spanish Trail, Tucson, AZ 85730
Tumacacori National Historic Park, P.O. Box 67, Tumacacori, AZ 85640

Arkansas
Arkansas Post National Memorial, Route 1, P.O. Box 16, Gillett, AR 72055
Buffalo National River, P.O. Box 1173, Harrison, AR 72601
Hot Springs National Park, P.O. Box 1860, Hot Springs, AR 71902
Pea Ridge National Military Park, Pea Ridge, AR 72751

California
Channel Islands National Park, 1901 Spinnaker Drive, Ventura, CA 93001
Death Valley National Monument, Death Valley, CA 92328
Golden Gate National Recreation Area, Fort Mason, Bldg. 201, San Francisco, CA 94123
Joshua Tree National Monument, 74485 National Monument Drive, Twenty Nine Palms, CA 92277
Kings Canyon National Park, Three Rivers, CA 93271
Lassen Volcanic National Park, P.O. Box 100, Mineral, CA 96063
Pinnacles National Monument, Paicines, CA 95043
Point Reyes National, Seashore, Point Reyes, CA 94956
Redwood National Park, 1111 Second St., Crescent City, CA 95531
San Francisco Maritime National Historical Park, Fort Mason, Bldg. 201, San Francisco, CA 94123
Santa Monica Mountains, National Recreation Area, 22900 Ventura Blvd, Suite 140, Woodland Hills, CA 91364
Sequoia National Park, Three Rivers, CA 93271
Whiskeytown-Shasta-Trinity, National Recreation Area, P.O. Box 188, Whiskeytown, CA 96095
Yosemite National Park, P.O. Box 577, Yosemite National Park, CA 95389

Colorado
Colorado National Monument, Fruita, CO 81521
Curecanti National Recreation Area, 102 Elk Creek, Gunnison, CO 81230
Dinosaur National Monument, P.O. Box 210, Dinosaur, CO 81610

Florissant Fossil Beds National Monument, P.O. Box 185, Florissant, CO 80816
Great Sand Dunes National Monument, Mosca, CO 81146
Mesa Verde National Park, Mesa Verde National Park, CO 81330
Rocky Mountain National Park, Estes Park, CO 80517

District of Columbia
Constitution Gardens, 900 Ohio Dr., SW, Washington, DC 20242
John F.Kennedy Center for the Performing Arts, National Park Service, 2700 F St., NW, Washington, DC 20566
Lyndon B.Johnson Memorial, Grove on the Potomac, c/o NCP - George Washington Memorial Pkwy, Turkey Run Park, McLean, VA 22101
National Capital Parks, National Capitol Region, 1100 Ohio Drive SW, Washington, DC 20242
Rock Creek Park, 5000 Glover Rd., NW, Washington, DC 20015
Theodore Roosevelt Island, c/o George Washington Memorial Pkwy, Turkey Run Park, McLean, VA 22101
Thomas Jefferson Memorial and Tidal Basin, c/o NCP - Central, 900 Ohio Dr., SW, Washington, DC 20242
Vietnam Veterans Memorial, c/o National Capitol Parks, Central, 900 Ohio Drive SW, Washington, DC 20242

Florida
Big Cypress National Preserve, Star Route, P.O. Box 110, Ochopee, FL 33943
Biscayne National Park, P.O. Box 1369, Homestead, FL 33090
Canaveral National Seashore, P.O. Box 6447, Titusville, FL 32782
DeSoto National Memorial, 75th St., NW, Bradenton, FL 33529
Everglades National Park, P.O. Box 279, Homestead, FL 33030
Fort Caroline National Memorial, 12713 Fort Caroline Rd., Jacksonville, FL 32225
Fort Jefferson National Monument, c/o Everglades National Park, P.O. Box 279, Homestead, FL 33030
Fort Matanzas National Monument, c/o Castillo de San Marcos, 1 Castillo Drive, St. Augustine, FL 32084
Gulf Islands National Seashore, 1801 Gulf Breeze Pkwy, Gulf Breeze, FL 32561
Timucuan Ecological and Historic Preserve, 12713 Fort Caroline Road, Jacksonville, FL 32225

Georgia
Chattahoochee River National Recreation Area, 1978 Island Ford Pkwy, Dunwoody, GA 30350
Chickamauga and Chattanooga National Military Park, P.O. Box 2128, Fort Oglethorpe, GA 30742
Cumberland Island National Seashore, P.O. Box 806, St. Marys, GA 31558
Kennesaw Mountain National, Battlefield Park, P.O. Box 1167, Marietta, GA 30061
Ocmulgee National Monument, 1207 Emery Highway, Macon, GA 31201

Guam
War in the Pacific National Historic Park, P.O. Box FA, Agana, GU 96910

Hawaii
Haleakala National Park, P.O. Box 369, Makawao, HI 96768
Hawaii Volcanoes National Park, Hawaii National Park, HI 96718
Kalaupapa National Historical Park, Kalaupapa, HI 96742
National Park of American Samoa, c/o Pacific Area Office, P.O. Box 50165, Honolulu, HI 96850
Pu'uhonua o Honaunau National Historical Park, P.O. Box 128, Honaunau Kona, HI 96726
USS Arizona Memorial, 1 Arizona Memorial Place, Honolulu, HI 96818

Idaho
City of Rocks National Reserve, 963 Blue Lake Blvd., Suite 1, Twin Falls, ID 83301
Craters of the Moon National Monument, P.O. Box 29, Arco, ID 83213

Indiana
George Rogers Clark National Historical Park, 401 S. Second St., Vincennes, IN 47591
Indiana Dunes National Lakeshore, 1100 N. Mineral Springs Rd., Porter, IN 46304

Iowa
Effigy Mounds National Monument, RR 1, Box 25A, Harpers Ferry, IA 52146

Kansas
Fort Larned National Historic Site, Route 3, Larned, KS 67550

Parks and Camping

Kentucky
Cumberland Gap National Historical Park, P.O. Box 1848, Middlesboro, KY 40965
Mammoth Cave National Park, Mammoth Cave, KY 42259

Louisiana
Jean Lafitte National Historical Park and Preserve, 423 Canal St., Room 210, New Orleans, LA 70130-2341

Maine
Acadia National Park, P.O. Box 177, Bar Harbor, MED 04609

Maryland
Antietam National Battlefield, P.O. Box 158, Sharpsburg, MD 21782
Assateague Island National Seashore, Rt. 2, P.O. Box 294, Berlin, MD 21811
Catoctin Mountain Park, 6602 Foxville Rd., Thurmont, MD 21788
Chesapeake and Ohio Canal Historical Park, P.O. Box 4, Sharpsburg, Md. 21782
Fort Washington Park, NCP - East, 1900 Anacostia Dr., SE, Washington, DC 20020
Greenbelt Park, 6565 Greenbelt Rd., Greenbelt, MD 20770
Piscataway Park, c/o NCP - East, 1900 Anacostia Dr. SE, Washington, DC 20019

Massachusetts
Boston National Historical Park, Charlestown Navy Yard, Boston, MA 02129
Cape Cod National Seashore, South Wellfleet, MA 02663
Lowell National Historical Park, 169 Merrimack St., Lowell, MA 01852
Minute Man National Historical Park, P.O. Box 160, 174 Liberty St., Concord, MA 01742

Michigan
Isle Royale National Park, 87 N. Ripley St., Houghton, MI 49931
Pictured Rocks National Lakeshore, P.O. Box 40, Munising, MI 49862
Sleeping Bear Dunes National Lakeshore, P.O. Box 277, 9922 Front St., Empire, MI 49630

Minnesota
Pipestone National Monument, P.O. Box 727, Pipestone, MN 56164
Voyageurs National Park, P.O. Box 50, International Falls, MN 56649

Mississippi
Brices Cross Roads National Battlefield Site, c/o Natchez Trace Pkwy, Rural Route 1, NT-143, Tupelo, MS 38801
Gulf Islands National Seashore, 3500 Park Rd., Ocean Springs, MS 39564
Natchez Trace Parkway, Rural Route 1, NT-143, Tupelo, MS 38801
Tupelo National Battlefield, c/o Natchez Trace Pkwy, Rural Route 1, NT-143, Tupelo, MS 38801
Vicksburg National Military Park, 3201 Clay St., Vicksburg, MS 39180

Missouri
Jefferson National Expansion Memorial, 11 North 4th St., St. Louis, MO 63102
Ozark National Scenic Riverways, P.O. Box 490, Van Buren, MO 63965
Wilson's Creek National Battlefield, Postal Drawer C, Republic, MO 65738

Montana
Big Hole National Battlefield, P.O. Box 237, Wisdom, MT 59761
Bighorn Canyon National Recreation Area, P.O. Box 458, Fort Smith, MT 59035
Custer Battlefield National Monument, P.O. Box 39, Crow Agency, MT 59022
Glacier National Park, West Glacier, MT 59936
Grant-Kohrs Ranch National Historic Site, P.O. Box 790, Deer Lodge, MT 59722

Nebraska
Agate Fossil Beds National Monument, P.O. Box 27, Gering, NE 69341

Nevada
Great Basin National Park, Baker, NV 89311
Lake Mead National Recreation Area, 601 Nevada Hwy, Boulder City, NV 89005-2426

New Jersey
Edison National Historic Site, Main Street and Lakeside Avenue, West Orange, NJ 07052
Morristown National Historical Park, Washington Place, Morristown, NJ 07960

New Mexico
Carlsbad Caverns National Park, 3225 National Parks Hwy, Carlsbad, NM 88220
Chaco Culture National Historical Park, Star Route 4, P.O. Box 6500, Bloomfield, NM 87413

El Malpais National Monument, P.O. Box 939, Grants, NM 87020
Pecos National Historical Park, P.O. Box Drawer 418, Pecos, NM 87522

New York
Federal Hall National Memorial, Manhattan Sites, 26 Wall St., New York, NY 10005
Fire Island National Seashore, 120 Laurel St., Patchogue, NY 11772
Gateway National Recreation Area, Floyd Bennett Field, Bldg. 69, Brooklyn, NY 11234
General Grant National Memorial, 122nd St. and Riverside Dr., New York, NY 10027
Hamilton Grange National Memorial, 287 Convent Ave., New York, NY 10031
Saratoga National Historical Park, R.D. 2, P.O. Box 33, Stillwater, NY 12170
Women's Rights National Historical Park, P.O. Box 70, Seneca Falls, NY 13148

North Carolina
Blue Ridge Parkway, 700 Northwestern Plaza, Asheville, NC 28801
Cape Hatteras National Seashore, Rt. 1, P.O. Box 675, Manteo, NC 27954
Cape Lookout National Seashore, P.O. Box 690, Beaufort, NC 28516
Guilford Courthouse National Military Park, P.O. Box 9806, Greensboro, NC 27429
Moores Creek National Battlefield, P.O. Box 69, Currie, NC 28435
Wright Brothers National Memorial, Cape Hatteras Group, Rt. 1, P.O. Box 675, Manteo, NC 27954

North Dakota
Knife River Indian Village National Historic Park, RR 1, Box 168, Stanton, ND 58571
Theodore Roosevelt National Park, P.O. Box 7, Medora, ND 58645

Ohio
Cuyahoga Valley National Recreation Area, 15610 Vaughn Rd., Brecksville, OH 44141
Mound City Group National Monument, 16062 State Route 104, Chillicothe, OH 45601
Perry's Victory and International Peace Memorial, P.O. Box 549, 93 Delaware Ave., Put-in-Bay, OH 43456

Oklahoma
Chicksaw National Recreation Area, P.O. Box 201, Sulphur, OK 73086

Oregon
Crater Lake National Park, P.O. Box 7, Crater Lake, OR 97604
Fort Clatsop National Memorial, Rt. 3, P.O. Box 604-FC, Astoria, OR 97103
Oregon Caves National Monument, 19000 Caves Highway, Cave Junction, OR 97523

Pennsylvania
Delaware Water Gap National Recreation Area, Bushkill, PA 18324
Fort Necessity National Battlefield, The National Pike, R.D. 2, P.O. Box 528, Farmington, PA 51437
Gettysburg National Military Park, Gettysburg, PA 17325
Independence National Historical Park, 313 Walnut St., Philadelphia, PA 19106
Johnstown Flood National Memorial, c/o Allegheny Portage Railroad NHS, P.O. Box 247, Cresson, PA 16630
Thaddeus Kosciuszko National Memorial, c/o Independence NHP, 313 Walnut St., Philadelphia, PA 19106
Upper Delaware Scenic and Recreational River, P.O. Box C, Narrowsburg, NY 12764
Valley Forge National Historical Park, Valley Forge, PA 19481

Rhode Island
Roger Williams National Memorial, P.O. Box 367, Annex Station, Providence, RI 02901

South Carolina
Cowpens National Battlefield, P.O. Box 308, Chesnee, SC 29323
Kings Mountain National Military Park, P.O. Box 40, Kings Mountain, NC 28086

South Dakota
Badlands National Park, P.O. Box 6, Interior, SD 57750
Jewel Cave National Monument, RR 1, Box 60AA, Custer, SD 57730
Mount Rushmore National Memorial, P.O. Box 268, Keystone, SD 57751
Wind Cave National Park, Hot Springs, SD 57747

Tennessee
Big South Fork National River and Recreation Area, P.O. Drawer 630, Oneida,

Be patient. If any phone number is incorrect, call (area code) 555-1212 and request the new listing.

TN 37841
Fort Donelson National Battlefield, P.O. Box 434, Dover, TN 37058-0434
Great Smoky Mountains National Park, Gatlinburg, TN 37738
Obed Wild and Scenic River, P.O. Box 429, Wartburg, TN 37887
Shiloh National Military Park, P.O. Box 61, Shiloh, TN 38376
Stones River National Battlefield, Rt. 10, P.O. Box 495, Old Nashville Hwy, Murfreesboro, TN 37130

Texas
Amistad Recreation Area, P.O. Box 420367, Del Rio, TX 78842-0367
Big Bend National Park, Big Bend National Park, TX 79834
Big Thicket National Preserve, 3785 Milam, Beaumont, TX 77701
Chamizal National Memorial, c/o Federal Bldg., 700 E. San Antonio, Suite D-301, El Paso, TX 79901
Guadalupe Mountains National Park, H.C. 60, P.O. Box 400, Salt Flat, TX 79847-9400
Lake Meredith Recreation Area, P.O. Box 1438, Fritch, TX 79036
Lyndon B. Johnson National Historical Park, P.O. Box 329, Johnson City, TX 78636
Padre Island National Seashore, 9405 S. Padre Island Dr., Corpus Christi, TX 78482-5597
San Antonio Missions National Historical Park, 2202 Roosevelt Ave., San Antonio, TX 78210-4919

Utah
Arches National Park, P.O. Box 907, Moab, UT 84532
Bryce Canyon National Park, Bryce Canyon, UT 84717
Canyonlands National Park, 125 W. 200 South, Moab, UT 84532
Capital Reef National Park, Torrey, UT 84775
Glen Canyon Recreation Area, P.O. Box 1507, Page, UT 86040
Natural Bridges National Monument, Box 1, Lake Powell, UT 84533
Zion National Park, Springdale, UT 84767-1099

Virginia
Appomattox Court House National Historical Park, P.O. Box 218, Appomattox, VA 24522
Arlington House, The Robert E. Lee Memorial, c/o George Washington Memorial Pkwy, Turkey Run Park, McLean, VA 22101
Colonial National Historical Park, P.O. Box 210, Yorktown, VA 23690
Fredericksburg and Spotsylvania National Military Park, P.O. Box 679, Fredericksburg, VA 22404
George Washington Memorial Parkway, Turkey Run Prk, McLean, VA 22101
Great Falls Park, 9200 Old Dominion Dr., Great Falls, VA 22066
Jamestown National Historic Site, c/o Colonial Park, P.O. Box 210, Yorktown, VA 23690
Manassas National Battlefield Park, P.O. Box 1830, Manassas, VA 22110
Petersburg National Battlefield, P.O. Box 549, Rt. 36 East, Petersburg, VA 23804
Prince William Forest Park, P.O. Box 209, Triangle, VA 22172
Richmond National Battlefield Park, 3215 E. Broad St., Richmond, VA 23223
Shenandoah National Park, Rt. 4, P.O. Box 348, Luray, VA 22835
Wolf Trap Farm Park for the Performing Arts, 1551 Trap Rd., Vienna, VA 22180

Virgin Islands
Buck Island Reef National Monument, P.O. Box 160, Christiansted, St. Croix, VI 00820
Virgin Islands National Park, P.O. Box 7789, Charlotte Amalie, St. Thomas, VI 00801

Washington
Coulee Dam National Recreation Area, P.O. Box 37, Coulee Dam, WA 99116
Ebey's Landing National Historical Reserve, P.O. Box 774, 23 Front St., Coupeville, WA 98239
Klondike Gold Rush National Historical Park, 117 S. Main St., Seattle, WA 98104
Lake Chelan National Recreation Area, 2105 Hwy 20, Sedro Woolley, WA 98284
Mount Ranier National Park, Tahoma Woods Star Route, Ashord, WA 98304
North Cascades National Park, 2105 Hwy 20, Sedro Woolley, WA 98284
Olympic National Park, 600 E. Park Ave., Port Angeles, WA 98362
Ross Lake National Recreation Area, 2105 Hwy 20, Sedro Woolley, WA 98284
San Juan Island National Historical Park, P.O. Box 429, Friday Harbor, WA 98250

West Virginia
Appalachian National Scenic Trail, P.O. Box 807, Harpers Ferry, WV 25425
Harpers Ferry National Historical Park, P.O. Box 65, Harpers Ferry, WV 25425
New River Gorge National River, P.O. Box 2289, Oak Hill WV 25901

Wisconsin
Apostle Islands National Lakeshore, Rt. 1, P.O. Box 4, Bayfield, WI 54814
St. Croix and Lower St. Croix, National Scenic Riverways, P.O. Box 708, St. Croix Falls, WI 54024

Wyoming
Devils Tower National Monument, Devils Tower, WY 82212
Fossil Butte National Monument, P.O. Box 527, Kemmerer, WY 83101
Grand Teton National Park, P.O. Drawer 170, Moose, WY 83012
John D. Rockefeller Memorial Parkway, c/o Grand Teton National Park, P.O. Drawer 170, Moose, WY 83012
Yellowstone National Park, P.O. Box 168, Yellowstone National Park, WY 82190

* National Parks Exhibits and Programs

Division of Interpretation
National Park Service
U.S. Department of the Interior
800 N. Capitol, NW, Room 560
Washington, DC 20002 (202) 523-5270

The National Park Service assists its facilities in planning and carrying out their exhibits and visitor programs. Their future plans include more involvement in environmental education programs to be offered at the Park Service sites.

* National Park Service Clearinghouse

Technical Information Center
National Park Service, Denver Service Center
12795 W. Alameda Parkway
P.O. Box 25287
Denver, CO 80225-0287 (303) 969-2130

The Technical Information Center has been designated by the National Park Service as the central repository for all National Park Service-generated planning, design, and construction maps, drawings, and reports as well as related cultural, environmental, and other technical documents. Bibliographic data on aerial photography is also maintained. The Center reproduces and delivers copies of the available materials for the Service, other agencies, and the public, both here and abroad. Today, the system has a holding of 100,000 data records, which represent about 500,000 microfilm aperture cards of maps, plans, and drawings; 1,000 records of resource and site aerial photography; and 25,000 planning, design, environmental, cultural resource, and natural resource documents. There is a fee depending on the material requested.

* National Park Service Films

National Audiovisual Center
8700 Edgeworth Dr.
Capitol Heights, MD 20743-3701 (301) 763-1896

The National Audiovisual Center contains more than 2,700 titles of videocassettes, films and slide/sound programs. Among them are some wonderful presentations produced by the National Park Service and the U.S. Fish and Wildlife Service. Materials may be rented or purchased. Contact the AV Center for specific information. Some titles include:

Everglades: Seeking a Balance
Gulf Island Beaches, Bays, Sands, and Bayous
California Gray Whale
Environmental Awareness
Giant Sequoia
One Man's Alaska
Sanctuary: The Great Smoky Mountains
Crater Lake
Yellowstone
Washington, DC: Fancy Free
Glacier Bay
Bighorn Canyon Experience
Cape Cod
What is a Mountain?
Living Waters of the Big Cypress
National Parks: Our Treasured Lands
Mt. McKinley
America's Wetlands
Parrots of Luquillo
Where the Fish Will Be
Patuxent Wildlife Research Center
Minnesota Valley National Wildlife Refuge

Be patient. If any phone number is incorrect, call (area code) 555-1212 and request the new listing.

Parks and Camping

* National Park Service Management and Programming

Park Practice Program
National Park Service
Technical Publications Program
U.S. Department of the Interior
P.O. Box 37127
Washington, DC 20013-7127 (202) 343-7067

The Park Practice Program is a cooperative effort between the National Park Service and the National Recreation and Park Association. Three publications are produced quarterly in an effort to instruct recreational and park directors on the latest information in the field:

TRENDS. Discusses topics of general interest in park and recreation management and programming. $35.

GRIST. Contains practical solutions to everyday problems in park and recreation operations including energy conservation, cost reduction, safety, and maintenance and designs for small structures.

DESIGN. Offers plans for park and recreation structures which demonstrate quality design and intelligent use of materials. $35.

These publications are available as a set in an annual subscription of $55. *GRIST* is also available separately for a yearly price of $30. Subscription inquiries should be addressed to: National Recreation and Park Association, 2775 S. Quincy Street, Suite 300, Arlington, VA 22206; (703) 820-4940.

* National Parks Service Posters and Charts

Superintendent of Documents
Government Printing Office (GPO)
Washington, DC 20402 (202) 783-3238

The following National Park Service posters and charts are available from GPO. Several titles can be purchased at special discounts when buying 100-count lots.

The Alpine Northwest
The Atlantic Barrier
The Canyon Country
The Desert
Edgar Allan Poe
Everglades
George Washington Carver
Glacier Bay
Greater Yellowstone Panorama
Hawaii Volcanoes
North Cascades Panorama
The Rocky Mountains
The Sierra Range
Statue of Liberty
Yosemite Panorama
National Park Service
American/British Charts

Six charts were produced jointly with the Sunday Times of London to commemorate the American bicentennial. Each poster is illustrated in full color and presents many facts about life during the Revolutionary War era and the war itself. They may be purchased individually, in a set of one each, or in cartons of 100 per subject.

The American Navies 1775-1783
The Continental Soldier
Philadelphia 1776
The British Navy 1775-1783
The British Redcoat
London 1776

* National Park Service Regional Offices

Alaska
2525 Gambell St., Room 107, Anchorage, AK 99503; (907) 257-2696

Mid-Atlantic
143 S. 3rd Street, Philadelphia, PA 19106; (215) 597-3679. Serving: PA, VA, WV, DE, MD

Midwest
1709 Jackson St., Omaha, NE 68102; (402) 221-3448. Serving: NE, MO, KS, IA,

IL, IN, WI, MI, MN, OH

Washington, DC
1100 Ohio Dr., SW, Washington, DC 20242; (202) 619-7222

North-Atlantic
15 State St., Boston, MA 02109-3572; (617) 223-5001. Serving: NY, NJ, CT, RI, MA, NH, VT, ME

Pacific Northwest
83 South King St., Suite 212, Seattle, WA 98104; (206) 553-5565. Serving: WA, OR, ID

Rocky Mountain
12795 W. Alameda Pkwy, Denver, CO 80225; (303) 969-2503. Serving: MT, ND, SD, WY, UT, CO

Southeast
75 Spring St., Atlanta, GA 30303; (404) 331-5186. Serving: MS, TN, AL, GA, FL, SC, NC, KY, Virgin Is., PR

Southwest
P.O. Box 728, Santa FE, NM 87504-0728; (505) 988-6388. Serving: NM, TX, LA, OK, AR

Western
600 Harrison Street, Suite 600, San Francisco, CA 94107; (415) 744-3876. Serving: CA, AZ, NV, HI, Guam, Northern Marianas Is., Am Samoa, Micronesia, Marshall Is., Palau

* National Park Service Reservations

Ticketron
Department R
401 Hackensack Ave.
Hackensack, NJ 07601

or

Nationwide Reservations
1849 C Street, NW
Room 1013
Washington, DC 20240 (202) 208-4747

Reservations to the following national park sites are available from the agent listed above. Advanced notice of eights weeks is needed for individual campsites. Phone reservations must be made directly with those parks accepting them; this information is listed in the Ticketron brochure. The parks include: Acadia National Park, Maine; Assateague Island National Seashore, Maryland/Virginia; Cape Hatteras National Seashore, North Carolina; Grand Canyon National Park, Arizona; Great Smoky Mountains National Park, North Carolina/Tennessee; Joshua Tree National Monument, California; Rocky Mountain National Park, Colorado; Sequoia-Kings Canyon National Park, California; Shenandoah National Park, Virginia; Whiskeytown National Recreation Area, California; Yellowstone National Park, Idaho/Montana/Wyoming; Yosemite National Park, California.

* National Park Service Statistical Abstract

Statistical Office
Denver Service Center - TNT
National Park Service
U.S. Department of the Interior
P.O. Box 25287 (303) 969-6977
Denver, CO 80225 Main Office: (303) 969-2503

National Park Service statistics from 1982-1988 are included in the *Park Service Statistical Abstract*. Recreation visits in the Service are summarized in information tables, such as visitor use, total visits, visits by region and state, visits by urban-rural location, overnight stays, and number of tour buses.

* National Park Service Videos and Literature

Harpers Ferry Historical Association, Inc.
P.O. Box 197
High St.
Harpers Ferry, WV 25425 (800) 821-5206

This historical society serves as a distributing agency for the sale and rental of materials produced for the National Park Service. A catalog is available listing videos and handbooks, and another 80 historic films are available from the

Be patient. If any phone number is incorrect, call (area code) 555-1212 and request the new listing.

Vacations and Business Travel

Association for purchase or three-day rental. Some video titles include: *Challenge of Yellowstone, Great Sand Dunes, Shenandoah: The Gift, Cape Cod Treasury, Gulf Islands, Antietam Visit, Civil War Artillery, A Lasting Victory (Robert E. Lee)*, and *Blessings of Liberty* (produced for the 200th birthday of the U.S. Constitution). The handbooks describe historical events and different locations within the Park Service. Inquire about a current listing of materials.

* National Parks Index

Superintendent of Documents
Government Printing Office
Washington, DC 20402 (202) 783-3238

Published yearly, *The National Parks: Index* describes the National Park System and provides information on the available facilities. (S/N 024-005-01094-7, $3.75)

* National Parks Visitor Facilities and Services

National Park Hospitality Association
P.O. Box 27
Mammoth Cave, KY 42259 (502) 773-2191

The publication, *National Park Visitor Facilities and Services*, lists all concessioner lodging and service information for the National Parks. To obtain a copy, send $4.15 to the office above.

* National Wildlife Refuges Guide

Superintendent of Documents
Government Printing Office
Washington, DC 20402 (202) 783-3238

National Wildlife Refuges: A Visitor's Guide is a foldout map of the United States including locations of all national wildlife refuges, a list of their names and addresses, and a description of available activities. 1991 (S/N 024-010-00690-1, $1).

* Recreation and Outdoor Activities Bibliography

Superintendent of Documents
Government Printing Office
Washington, DC 20402 (202) 783-3238

This bibliography is divided into the categories of boating and water activities, camping and hiking, fishing and hunting, national recreation areas, winter activities, and general information. Free.

* Recreation Guide to BLM Public Lands

Office of Public Affairs
Bureau of Land Management (BLM)
U.S. Department of the Interior
18th and C Sts., NW
Washington, DC 20240 (202) 208-5717

The *Recreation Guide to BLM Public Lands* features a map outlining all of the public lands used as recreational areas. Designations on the map include campgrounds, visitors centers, national wild and scenic rivers, national wilderness areas, and national historic and scenic trails. Also included are the states that contain public lands, and state and district offices to contact for additional information. Alaska, Arizona, California, Colorado, Idaho, Montana, Nevada, New Mexico, Oregon, Utah, Washington, and Wyoming are the key states described.

* Recreation Market Study

Recreation Resources Assistance Division
National Park Service
National Trails and Recreational Branch
U.S. Department of the Interior
P.O. Box 37127, Code 782
800 N. Capitol Street NW
Washington, DC 20013-7127 (202) 343-3780

The *National Recreation Survey* provides current information on what Americans do for recreation in the outdoors and their expectations of recreational opportunities. The survey contains valuable market data on such topics as favorite activities, importance of recreation areas and their distance from home, characteristics of trips and outings, characteristics of respondents who spend money on outdoor recreation, and reasons for discontinuing a recreation activity.

Various tables that relate to the National Park System and its participants are included.

* State Parks, Forest Camping Areas and Other Recreation Areas

Publication Relations
Tennessee Valley Authority (TVA)
400 W. Summit Hill Dr.
Knoxville, TN 37902 (615) 632-4402

Contact this office for all generic information on the TVA Agency, including the history behind the agency. A brochure is available with questions and answers most frequently asked about the TVA agency, lakes and dams.

Recreation on TVA Lakes
TVA
Natural Resources Building
Ridgeway Road
Norris, TN 37828 (615) 632-1600

This office can provide you with a free pamphlet which describes recreation areas on the Tennessee Valley Authority lakeshores, including boat docks, resorts, state parks, U.S. Forest Service camp areas, and those county, national, city, state, and municipal parks which have docks or camping areas. Maps are also available.

* Tourism Programs on Public Lands

Office of Public Affairs
Bureau of Land Management
U.S. Department of the Interior
1849 C St., NW
Washington, DC 20240 (202) 208-5717

In recognition of the importance of outdoor recreation to Americans, *Recreation 2000 Executive Summary* sets forth the commitment of the Bureau of Land Management to the management of outdoor recreation resources in the public lands. The plan highlights the areas in which the Bureau intends to concentrate future efforts, such as visitor information, resource protection, land ownerships, partnerships, volunteers, tourism programs, facilities, and permits, fees, and concessions. This publication also features a map outlining all of the public lands used as recreational areas. Designations on the map include campgrounds, visitors centers, national wild and scenic rivers, national wilderness areas, and national historic and scenic trails. Also included are the states that contain public lands, and state and district offices to contact for additional information. Alaska, Arizona, California, Colorado, Idaho, Montana, Nevada, New Mexico, Oregon, Utah, Washington, and Wyoming are the key states described.

* United States Service Police

National Capital Region
National Park Service
U.S. Department of the Interior
1100 Ohio Dr., SW
Washington, DC 20242 (202) 619-7310

The U.S. Park Police have the same authority and powers as the Washington, DC metropolitan police. They also act as hosts to park visitors.

* Whale Watching

Office of Protected Resources
National Marine Fisheries Service
National Oceanic and Atmospheric Administration
U.S. Department of Commerce
1335 East-West Hwy.
Silver Spring, MD 20910 (301) 713-2332

The Marine Mammal Protection Act commits the United States to long-term management and research programs to conserve and protect these animals. The National Marine Fisheries Service grants or denies requests for exemptions, issues permits, carries out research and management programs, enforces the Act, participates in international programs, and issues rules and regulations to carry out its mission to conserve and protect marine mammals. An annual report is available for the Office of Protected Resources, which gives detailed information regarding the activities of the Office. This office can also provide you with copies of the Act, and two publications: *First Aid For Stranded Marine Mammals*, and *Proceedings of the Workshop to Review and Evaluate Whale Watching Programs and Management Needs*.

Be patient. If any phone number is incorrect, call (area code) 555-1212 and request the new listing.

Parks and Camping

* Wild and Scenic Rivers

Land and Renewable Resources
Bureau of Land Management
U.S. Department of the Interior
1849 C St., NW, W0200
Washington, DC 20240
(202) 208-4896

The Bureau of Land Management manages about 2,200 miles of the Wild and Scenic River System, primarily in the western United States. These areas are located in the directory, *Recreation Guide to BLM Public Lands*, available from the Office of Public Affairs, Bureau of Land Management, U.S. Department of the Interior, Washington, DC 20240.

* Woodsy Owl and Children's Materials

U.S. Department of Agriculture
Forest Service
P.O. Box 96090
Washington, DC 20090-6090
(202) 205-1785

To increase children's awareness of our delicate environment, the Forest Service's Woodsy Owl campaign has a variety of free materials available, including coloring sheets, detective sheets, song sheets, patches, "Woodsy Owl on Camping" (brochure), and stickers.

Be patient. If any phone number is incorrect, call (area code) 555-1212 and request the new listing.

Vacations and Business Travel

Boating and Fishing

* Advanced Marine Vehicles

Planning Branch
Research and Development Staff
Office of Engineering and Development
U.S. Coast Guard
U.S. Department of Transportation
2100 2nd St., SW, Room 6208
Washington, DC 20593-0001 (202) 267-1030

Information can be obtained here about research conducted by the Coast Guard in support of its operations and responsibilities. Areas of study include ice operations, ocean dumping, law enforcement, environmental protection, port safety and security, navigation aids, search and rescue procedures, recreational boating, energy, and advanced marine vehicles. For referral to specific personnel working in these areas, contact the Planning Branch.

* Aids to Navigation

Office of Navigation Safety and Waterways Services
U.S. Coast Guard
U.S. Department of Transportation
2100 2nd St., SW, Room 1116
Washington, DC 20593-0001 (202) 267-1965

The Coast Guard maintains aids to navigation such as lighthouses and lights, buoys, beacons, fog signals, and long-range radionavigation aids like LORAN-C and OMEGA. The aids are established to assist navigators in plotting safe courses on waters under U.S. jurisdiction and in certain international areas. The seven volumes of *Light Lists*, which detail the navigation aids in seven geographic areas, are available at varying cost ($16-$25 per volume) from the Superintendent of Documents, Government Printing Office, Washington, DC 20402; (202) 783-3238. The *LORAN-C User Handbook*, which explains the radionavigation system and how to use it, is also available from GPO for $4.75.

* Army Corps of Engineers Recreational Facilities Films

U.S. Army Corps of Engineers
Directorate of Information Management
Visual Information Branch
CEHEC-IM-V
20 Massachusetts Ave., NW
Washington, DC 20314 (202) 272-0717

This office maintains a still photographic library and offers a free film loan and video distribution program. The Corps has educational and public relations films on their recreational facilities, navigation, flood control, hydro-electric power, and environmental systems. Write for information on the how to participate in the program.

* Boating Correspondence Course

U.S. Government Bookstore
Norwest Banks Building
201 W. 8th Street
Pueblo, CO 81003-3091 (719) 544-3142

Designed for boaters who can't attend a boating class, *The Skipper's Course* covers basic navigation, legal requirements, anchoring, weather, emergency procedures, boat handling, and safety. A certificate of completion is awarded. Stock No: 050012002258. Price: $6.50.

* Coast Guard Courses and Textbooks

Coast Guard Auxiliary National Board, Inc.
9949 Watson Industrial Park
St. Louis, MO 63126

The following are textbooks used in Coast Guard Auxiliary public education courses. They can be ordered by writing to the above address, or you can get each textbook by taking the course of the same title through the Coast Guard. To find out where courses are offered near you, call the Courseline at (800) 336-BOAT; or (800) 245-BOAT in VA.

Boating Skills and Seamanship. Boating laws and regulations, boat handling, and navigation ($8).
Sailing and Seamanship. Same basic text as above, geared to sailboats ($8).
Advanced Coastal Piloting. How to read charts, plot courses, predict tides, and use navigation aids ($8).

* Coast Guard Rescue Service

SAR Database Manager
Search and Rescue Division
Commandant (G-NRS-1)
Office of Navigation Safety and Waterways Services
U.S. Coast Guard
U.S. Department of Transportation
2100 2nd Street, SW
Room 1422
Washington, DC 20593-0001 (202) 267-1579

The Search and Rescue (SAR) program maintains a comprehensive system of resources to save lives and prevent personal injury and property damage on the navigable waters of the U.S. This system includes rescue vessels, aircraft, and communication facilities. A cooperative international distress response system is also maintained for incidents on the high seas. For more information about the Guard's SAR program, contact the branch listed above.

* Free Boat Inspection

Courtesy Marine Examination (CME)
BOAT/U.S. Foundation
880 S. Pickett St. (800) 336-BOAT
Alexandria, VA 22304 (800) 245-BOAT (in VA)

The U.S. Coast Guard Auxiliary offers a free safety inspection called a Courtesy Marine Examination. A specially trained Coast Guard Auxiliarist will examine your craft to determine if it has all the necessary and recommended equipment. If properly equipped, you'll be awarded a CME decal. To arrange for your CME, call the toll-free number or contact your local Coast Guard Auxiliary.

* Land Between the Lakes

Land Between The Lakes
Natural Resources
Resource and Development
Tennessee Valley Authority (TVA)
Golden Pond, KY 42211-9001 (502) 924-5602

Land Between The Lakes is a 40-mile-long peninsula located between Kentucky and Barkley Lakes in west Kentucky and Tennessee. In its 25th year of operation, Land Between The Lakes is managed by TVA to provide an outstanding outdoor recreation experience. A living history farm exhibit called "Homeplace-1850," recreates life as it existed on a typical farmstead in the area before the Civil War. Exhibitors tend crops and animals, prepare meals, and perform hundreds of other farm chores in the same manner as their forebears did. Recreation programs at Land Between the Lakes are for everyone, but many programs are tailored to groups with special needs.

* Marine Advisory Service

National Sea-Grant College Program
National Oceanic and Atmospheric Administration
U.S. Department of Commerce
1335 East-West Hwy. (301) 713-2483 (Maryland)
Silver Spring, MD 20910 (202) 482-6090 (DC)

Operated through the Sea-Grant Colleges, the marine advisory service consists of agents and specialists who are experts in areas such as seafood technology, marine economics, coastal engineering, commercial fishing, recreation, and communications. These specialists provide a link between the people who live and work in coastal areas and researchers in the universities. They sponsor workshops, conferences, and seminars on marine issues for the public and representatives of industry and government agencies. They talk to high school

Boating and Fishing

science classes, as well as publish bulletins, fact sheets, newsletters, technical papers, and audio-visual materials concerning marine affairs. The following is a list of Sea-Grant Colleges, and people you can contact for more information.

Sea Grant Colleges

Alabama
See Mississippi

Alaska
Alaska Sea Grant College Program
University of Alaska Fairbanks
138 Irving II
Fairbanks, AK 99775-5040 (907) 474-7086

Arizona
Environmental Research Laboratory
University of Arizona
2601 E. Airport Drive
Tucson, AZ 85706-6985 (602) 741-1990

California
California Sea Grant
University of California/San Diego
9500 Gilman Drive
La Jolla, CA 92093-0232 (619) 534-4444

Sea Grant Program
University of Southern California
University Park
Los Angeles, CA 90089-1231 (213) 740-1961

Connecticut
Connecticut Sea Grant
Marine Sciences Institute
University of Connecticut
Building 24, Avery Point
Groton, CT 06340 (203) 445-8664

Delaware
University of Delaware Sea Grant
Marine Communications Office
263 E. Main Street
Newark, DE 19716 (302) 831-8083

Florida
Florida Sea Grant
Building 803
University of Florida
Gainesville, FL 32611-0341 (904) 392-2802

Georgia
Georgia Sea Grant
Ecology Building
University of Georgia
Athens, GA 30602 (404) 542-7671

Hawaii
University of Hawaii
Sea Grant College Program
1000 Pope Road, MSB 200
Honolulu, HI 96822 (808) 956-7410

Illinois
Illinois-Indiana Sea Grant
University of Illinois
65 Mumford Hall
1301 W. Gregory Drive
Urbana, IL 61801 (217) 333-9448

Indiana
See Illinois

Louisiana
Louisiana Sea Grant
Center for Wetland Resources

Louisiana State University
Baton Rouge, LA 70803 (504) 388-6449

Maine
Maine Sea Grant Communications
30 Coburn Hall
University of Maine
Orono, ME 04469 (207) 581-1440

Marine Law Institute
University of Maine School of Law
246 Deering Avenue
Portland, ME 04102 (207) 780-4474

Maryland
Maryland Sea Grant
1123 Taliaferro Hall
University of Maryland
College Park, MD 20742 (301) 405-6371

National Sea Grant College Program
NOAA, SSMB-1/5206
1335 East-West Hwy.
Silver Spring, MD 20910 (301) 713-2431

Massachusetts
MIT Sea Grant
Building E-38, Room 300
Massachusetts Inst. of Technology
292 Main Street
Cambridge, MA 02139 (617) 253-7041

Sea Grant Program
Woods Hole Oceanographic Institution
Woods Hole, MA 02543 (508) 548-1400

Michigan
Michigan Sea Grant Publications
University of Michigan
2200 Bonisteel Blvd.
Ann Arbor, MI 48109-2099 (313) 764-1138

Minnesota
Minnesota Sea Grant
University of Minnesota
1518 Cleveland Ave. N, Room 302
St. Paul, MN 55108 (612) 625-9288

Mississippi
Mississippi-Alabama Sea Grant Consortium
P.O. Box 7000
Ocean Springs, MS 39564-7000 (601) 875-9341

New Hampshire
New Hampshire Sea Grant
Kingman Farm
University of New Hampshire
Durham, NH 03824 (603) 749-1565

New Jersey
Sea Grant Program
New Jersey Marine Sciences Consortium
Building No. 22
Fort Hancock, NJ 07732 (908) 872-1300

New York
New York Sea Grant Institute
Dutchess Hall Room 137
SUNY at Stony Brook
Stony Brook, NY 11794-5001 (516) 632-6905

North Carolina
North Carolina Sea Grant
North Carolina State University
Box 8605
Raleigh, NC 27695 (919) 515-2454

Be patient. If any phone number is incorrect, call (area code) 555-1212 and request the new listing.

Vacations and Business Travel

Ohio
Ohio Sea Grant
Ohio State University
1314 Kinnear Road
Columbus, OH 43212 (614) 292-8949

Oklahoma
Department of Chemistry
Attn. F. Schmitz
University of Oklahoma
620 Parrington Oval, Room 208
Norman, OK 73019 (405) 325-5581

Oregon
National Coastal Resources Research and Development Inst.
528 SW Mill, Suite 222
P.O. Box 751
Portland, OR 97207 (503) 725-5725

Oregon Sea Grant
Oregon State University
AdS 402
Corvallis, OR 97331-2134 (503) 737-2716

Publications Orders
Agricultural Communications
Oregon State University
AdS 422
Corvallis, OR 97331-2119 (503) 737-2513

Puerto Rico
Puerto Rico Sea Grant Program
Communications Office
RUM-UPR P.O. Box 5000
Mayaguez, PR 00709-5000 (809) 834-4726

Rhode Island
National Sea Grant Depository
Pell Library Building
Bay Campus
University of Rhode Island
Narragansett, RI 02882 (401) 792-6114

Rhode Island Sea Grant
Publications Unit
University of Rhode Island
Bay Campus
Narragansett, RI 02882-1197 (401) 792-6842

South Carolina
South Carolina Sea Grant Consortium
287 Meeting Street
Charleston, SC 29401 (803) 727-2078

Texas
Texas Sea Grant
Texas A&M-Galveston
P.O. Box 1675
Galveston, TX 77553-1675 (409) 762-9800

Virginia
Virginia Sea Grant
Madison House
University of Virginia
170 Rugby Road
Charlottesville, VA 22903 (804) 924-5965

Washington
Washington Sea Grant, HG-30
University of Washington
3716 Brooklyn Avenue, NE
Seattle, WA 98105 (206) 543-6600

Wisconsin
Sea Grant Institute
University of Wisconsin

1800 University Avenue
Madison, WI 53705 (608) 263-3259

* Marine Environmental Information

Pollution Response Branch
Marine Environmental Response Division
Office of Marine Safety, Security,
and Environmental Protection
U.S. Coast Guard
U.S. Department of Transportation
2100 2nd Street, SW
Room 2104 (202) 267-0518
Washington, DC 20593-0001 (202) 267-2611

This office responds to requests for marine environmental protection information from Congress and other federal agencies, state agencies, schools, industries, and the general public. Data is available on laws relating to the protection of the marine environment, incidents involving releases of oil or other hazardous substances, and federally funded spill response operations.

* Marine Fire and Rescue Technology

Library
Coast Guard Research and Development Center
U.S. Coast Guard
U.S. Department of Transportation
1082 Shennecossett Road
Groton, CT 06340-6096 (203) 441-2648

Marine research is conducted here in areas such as ice technology, navigation instrumentation technology, ocean dumping surveillance, pollution, search and rescue techniques, and marine fire and safety technology. This library is a good starting point for obtaining specific information about what research is done by the Center and for referrals to appropriate experts.

* Mariners Weather Log

National Oceanographic Data Center
National Oceanic and Atmospheric Administration
Universal South Building
Room 406
Washington, DC 20235 (202) 606-4594

The Mariners Weather Log is a unique source of information on marine weather and climate and their effects on operations at sea. Published quarterly by the National Oceanographic Data Center, the *Mariners Weather Log* provides comprehensive coverage of major storms of the North Atlantic and North Pacific, reports and annual summaries on tropical cyclones, information on the National Weather Service's Marine Observation Program, selected shipboard gale and wave observations, and general articles about weather and climate, hazards and safety precautions, and related marine lore. An annual subscription is available for $12 from the Superintendent of Documents, Government Printing Office, Washington, DC 20402; (202)783-3238.

* Navigation Regulations

Navigation Rules and Information Branch
Short-Range Aids to Navigation Division
Office of Navigation and Waterways Services
U.S. Coast Guard
U.S. Department of Transportation
2100 2nd Street, SW
Room 1416E
Washington, DC 20593-0001 (202) 267-0357

The Coast Guard establishes regulations for waterways safety that must be followed by U.S. vessels on the high seas and inland waters. These include rules on maneuvering and requirements for lights, sound signals, and radio telephones. For information on the rules, contact the above office or obtain a copy of *Navigation Rules, International and Inland,* available for $12 from the Superintendent of Documents, Government Printing Office, Washington, DC 20402; (202) 783-3238. This rulebook is required by law to be carried on all vessels 39.4 feet or more in length.

* Pleasure Boating on the St. Lawrence Seaway

Public Affairs Office
Saint Lawrence Seaway Development Corporation
U.S. Department of Transportation

Be patient. If any phone number is incorrect, call (area code) 555-1212 and request the new listing.

Boating and Fishing

P.O. Box 520
Massena, NY 13662-0520 (315) 764-3261
The publication, *Pleasure Craft Guide: The Seaway*, provides you with information on boating in the St. Lawrence River. Contact this office to obtain your free copy.

* Recreational Fishing

Public Affairs
National Marine Fisheries Service
National Oceanic and Atmospheric Administration
U.S. Department of Commerce
1335 East-West Highway, Room 9272
Silver Spring, MD 20910 (301) 713-2245
The National Marine Fisheries Service manages the country's stocks of saltwater fish and shellfish for both commercial and recreational interests. NMFS administers and enforces the Magnuson Fishery Conservation and Management Act to assure that fishing stays within sound biological limits, and that U.S. commercial and recreational fishermen have the opportunity to harvest all the available fish within these limits. Several hundred Fisheries Service scientists conduct research relating to these management responsibilities in science and research centers in 15 states and the District of Columbia. Many of these laboratories have evolved a major field of interest, and have special knowledge of the fish in their geographical area that leads to predictions of abundance, economic forecasts, and direct assistance to sport fishermen and commercial fishing businesses.

* Recreational Maps and Navigational Charts

TVA Maps and Surveys
Tennessee Valley Authority (TVA)
HB1A, 1101 Market Street
Chattanooga, TN 37402-2801 (615) 751-MAPS
Many recreational maps and navigational charts of TVA lakes are available to the public for a small fee. Detailed routes to shoreline recreation areas. The maps show water depths, the location of and detailed routes to the public recreation areas, boat docks, resorts, and roads. The navigational charts for the main lakes show navigation channels, buoys, lights, and other navigational aids, while maps for tributary lakes show the numbered signs TVA has installed at strategic locations on shore to aid fishermen and recreation boaters in locating their position. A map showing TVA dams and steam plants, including important facts about each of them, is available, along with cadastral and topographic maps, aerial photographs, and survey control data. Each request should specify the lake(s) of interest.

* Recreation Market Study

Recreation Resources Assistance Division
National Park Service
Trails, Rivers, and Conservation Assistance Branch
U.S. Department of the Interior
800 N. Capitol Street, NW
Washington, DC 20001 (202) 343-3780
The *National Recreation Survey* provides current information on what Americans do for recreation in the outdoors and their expectations of recreational opportunities. The survey contains valuable market data on such topics as favorite activities, importance of recreation areas and their distance from home, characteristics of trips and outings, characteristics of respondents who spend money on outdoor recreation, and reasons for discontinuing a recreation activity. Various tables that relate to the National Park System and its participants are included.

* Recreation on Public Lands

Office of Public Affairs
Bureau of Land Management
U.S. Department of the Interior
1849 C St., NW
Washington, DC 20240 (202) 208-5717
In recognition of the importance of outdoor recreation to Americans, *Recreation 2000 Executive Summary* sets forth the commitment of the Bureau of Land Management to the management of outdoor recreation resources in the public lands. The plan highlights the areas in which the Bureau intends to concentrate future efforts, such as visitor information, resource protection, land ownerships, partnerships, volunteers, tourism programs, facilities, and permits, fees, and concessions.

* Resort Guides

National Oceanographic Data Center
National Environmental Satellite, Data, and Information Service
National Oceanic And Atmospheric Administration
U.S. Department of Commerce
1825 Connecticut Ave., NW, Room 406
Washington, DC 20235 (202) 606-4549
The National Oceanographic Data Center and the Sea Grant Programs in various coastal states have produced a series of climate guides to coastal recreation areas. The guides include useful information about winds, waves, and air and water temperatures, as well as tips on sportfish species, tourist attractions, weather hazards, and safety precautions. Single copies of these publications are available for a $3 mailing/handling charge per order (not per publication). The following is a list of the resort guides available:

Hawaii: The Big Island
Recreation and Weather Guide to the Minnesota Shore of Lake Superior
Western Lake Erie Recreational Climate Guide
Central Lake Erie Recreational Climate Guide
Lake Huron Recreation and Weather
Massachusetts Saltwater Fishing and Weather Guide
Nassau County (Long, Island, NY) Recreation and Climate Guide

* Safety Information for Marine Dealers

Marine Dealer Visitation Program
Office of Navigation Safety and Waterway Services
U.S. Coast Guard
U.S. Department of Transportation
2100 2nd St., SW (800) 368-5647
Washington, DC 20593-0001 (202) 267-0780 (in DC)
Through the Marine Dealer Visitation Program, boating equipment dealers can receive updates on regulations, information on Courtesy Marine Examinations, and details about boating safety education courses. Participating dealers will be visited quarterly by a local Coast Guard Auxiliarist, be given a literature rack with boating brochures and pamphlets for customers, and will receive a "Cooperating Marine Dealer" decal for shop door or window. Marine dealers can participate by calling the Boating Safety Hotline listed above.

* Safety on Small Passenger Vessels

Marine Inspection Office
Your Local Coast Guard Office
Most small passenger vessels (less than 100 tons and carrying more than 6 people) are required to adhere to certain Coast Guard safety regulations. These include having a safety orientation procedure for passengers (announcement or placard), posting of emergency instructions, a life preserver for every person on board, and a Coast Guard safety certification. Marine Inspection Offices around the country issue the certificates. To find an Inspection Office near you, or to report a violation or complaint, call the Boating Safety Hotline (800) 368-5647; or (202) 267-0780 in DC.

* Scenic River Study

Recreation Program
Lands, River Basin Operations
Tennessee Valley Authority (TVA)
Norris, TN 37828 (615) 632-1606
The recreation staff completed a TVA river system evaluation, which identifies streams with recreation and aesthetic values, such as the French Broad River in western North Carolina, the eastern Tennessee River, and the Bear Creek streams in northern Alabama. This study also addresses one of the major problems which inhibits full enjoyment of these resources by Valley residents: a lack of easy access to the rivers. Contact this office for more information on this study and its findings.

* Swimming Areas and Aquatic Plants

Aquatic Biology Department
Resource Development
River Basin Operations
Water Resources
Tennessee Valley Authority (TVA)
311 Broad St.
Chattanooga, TN 37402-2801 (615) 751-0011
TVA's two major weapons for controlling the spread of pesky aquatic plants,

Be patient. If any phone number is incorrect, call (area code) 555-1212 and request the new listing.

Vacations and Business Travel

such as Eurasian watermilfoil, spiney-leaf naiad, and hydrilla in its reservoirs, is the winter and summer draw downs and the selective spraying of herbicides. Reservoir levels may be lowered several feet in the late summer to dry out and kill the roots of these plants embedded in shallow areas of the reservoirs; while at other times, lake levels may be held higher than normal to prevent sunshine from penetrating to the bottom and thus prevent germination and growth of new colonies. Selective use of approved herbicides in high priority use areas, such as swimming beaches, developed shoreline, and marinas, is another effective control method. Several experimental control strategies also are being tested on TVA lakes. One of the most promising is a cooperative effort between TVA and the U.S. Army Corps of Engineers. TVA proposes to conduct large scale demonstrations on Guntersville reservoir on the use of Grass Carp, hydrilla fly, a fungus to control watermilfoil, and other methods being currently tested on a smaller scale by the Corps Waterways Experiment Station.

* Toll-Free Help for Boaters

Boating Safety Hotline
Consumer and Regulatory Affairs Branch (G-NAB-5)
Auxiliary, Boating, and
Consumer Affairs Division
Office of Navigation Safety and
Waterways Services
U.S. Coast Guard
U.S. Department of Transportation
2100 2nd Street, SW
Room 1109 (800) 368-5647
Washington, DC 20593-0001 (202) 267-0780 (in DC)

This service is toll-free throughout the U.S., including Alaska, Hawaii, Puerto Rico, and the Virgin Islands. Staff can provide you with information on such topics of interest to boaters as safety recalls, publications, Coast Guard department contacts and addresses, public education courses, and free Coast Guard services. If hotline operators cannot answer your question directly, you'll get a call back from someone who can. Ask for a consumer information packet, and you'll receive a group of publications and consumer *Fact Sheets* on topics like safe boating, getting help on the water, floatation devices, federal regulations, sanitation devices, and sources of boating education. The *Boater's Source Directory*, included in the packet, is a guide to a wide variety of federal, state, private, and non-profit agencies that provide literature, technical information, free services, and other assistance to recreational boaters. Among the freebies you can request is the *Water 'N Kids* coloring book for 4-8 year olds, which explains basic concepts of water safety. The hotline also takes consumer complaints about safety defects and violations. Operators answer between 8 a.m. and 4 p.m. Eastern Time, and an answering machine takes messages after hours.

* Updates for Mariners

Local Notice to Mariners
District Commander
Your local Coast Guard Office (800) 368-5647

The free *Local Notice to Mariners* is issued weekly by each Coast Guard District. Intended for small craft owners, it advises you of changes in the status of aids to navigation (buoys, radiobeacons, etc.); chart updates; drawbridge operations; and safety warnings for particular areas. This *Local Notice* often includes temporary changes not included in the Defense Mapping Agency's *Notice to Mariners*. To order a subscription for the *Local Notice*, send a written request to the District Commander of your local Coast Guard office. For referral to the correct address, call the Boating Safety Hotline (800) 368-5647; or (202) 267-0780 in DC.

* Water Recreation Areas

U.S. Army Corps of Engineers
Directorate of Civil Works
Natural Resources Management Branch, CECW-ON
20 Massachusetts Ave., NW
Washington, DC 20314 (202) 272-0247

The Corps has a brochure and map showing the extensive recreational facilities available at U.S. Army Corps of Engineers lakes throughout the country. They offer camp sites, picnic areas, swimming beaches, hiking trails, boating, canoeing, fishing, ice fishing, hunting, and snowmobiling. The Corps also offers safety training classes in water-related sports. To arrange for a speaker to come to your school or to order the brochure entitled *Lakeside Recreation*, write or call the above office.

* Wild Rivers and Other Public Lands

Office of Public Affairs
Bureau of Land Management (BLM)
U.S. Department of the Interior
1849 C St., NW
Washington, DC 20240 (202) 208-5717

The *Recreation Guide to BLM Public Lands* features a map outlining all of the public lands used as recreational areas. Designations on the map include campgrounds, visitors centers, national wild and scenic rivers, national wilderness areas, and national historic and scenic trails. Also included are the states that contain public lands, and state and district offices to contact for additional information. Alaska, Arizona, California, Colorado, Idaho, Montana, Nevada, New Mexico, Oregon, Utah, Washington, and Wyoming are the key states described.

Be patient. If any phone number is incorrect, call (area code) 555-1212 and request the new listing.

International Travel

* American Experts Overseas Lecture Tour

Office of Program Coordination and Development
United States Information Agency (USIA)
301 Fourth St., SW, Room 550
Washington, DC 20547 (202) 619-4764

AmParts are experts in a field--usually economics, international affairs, literature, the arts, U.S. political and social processes, sports, science, or technology--sent abroad by USIA to meet with groups or individual professional counterparts. Recruited on the basis of requests of USIA staff in other countries, AmParts often engage in informal lecture/discussions with small groups, grant media interviews, or speak before larger audiences. Those interested in the American Participant program are invited to submit a brief letter indicating times of availability, along with a curriculum vitae and at least two lecture topics with brief talking points. A free brochure on the program is available from this office.

* Animals and Plants Quarantine

APHIS
U.S. Department of Agriculture
Room G-110 Federal Building
6505 Belcrest Rd.
Hyattsville, MD 20782 (301) 436-7279

This office will advise travelers about what agriculture and related products may be brought into the U.S. from foreign countries.

* Arctic and Antarctic Polar Expeditions with Civilians

Ice Operations Division
Office of Navigation Safety and Waterways Services
U.S. Coast Guard
U.S. Department of Transportation
2100 2nd St., SW, Room 1202 A
Washington, DC 20593-0001 (202) 267-1450

The Coast Guard furnishes vessels to other agencies, such as the National Science Foundation, U.S. Geological Survey, and the Navy, to conduct research and ice operations in Arctic and Antarctic waters. The agencies sponsoring the missions select scientists, researchers, students, and in some cases, journalists, photographers, and artists to accompany the mission when space is available. This office is a good starting point for obtaining information on the pertinence of a mission to your field, to be directed to the appropriate agency sponsors, and for information about the data collected during missions.

* Binational Libraries and Cultural Centers Worldwide

Library Programs Division
Bureau of Educational and Cultural Affairs
United States Information Agency (USIA)
301 Fourth St., SW, Room 314
Washington, DC 20547 (202) 619-4915

USIA maintains or supports 156 libraries and reading rooms in 95 countries, as well as library programs at 111 binational centers in 24 countries. Collections focus on fostering foreign understanding of U.S. people, history, and culture. A bi-weekly bibliography, listing 80-100 titles on international relations and developments in the U.S., is one of many library services provided for the overseas posts, including reference and research assistance.

* Booklets for Travelers

Government Printing Office
Superintendent of Documents
Washington, DC 20402 (202) 783-3238

The U.S. Department of State offers several brochures and pamphlets regarding traveling abroad ($1 each):

A Safe Trip Abroad. Provides suggestions for avoiding and coping with potential problems and crises abroad.

Tips for Americans Residing Abroad. Includes basic travel information and suggestions, as well as health, insurance, and assistance information of interest to senior citizens traveling abroad.

Your Trip Abroad. Provides basic information on such matters as passport applications, visas, and other documents; obtaining services and help overseas from U.S. consuls; and foreign legal requirements.

Tips for Travelers to the Caribbean.
Tips for Travelers to the People's Republic of China.
Tips for Travelers to Eastern Europe and Yugoslavia.
Tips for Travelers to the USSR.
Tips for Travelers to South Africa.

* Certification for Travel Abroad

Authentications
Foreign Affairs Center
Bureau of Administration
2400 M Street, NW, Room 101
Washington, DC 20520 (202) 647-5002
Executive Office (202) 647-9415

Several steps are necessary in order to get a document authenticated for a use by a foreign government. For legal papers to do business in a foreign government (such as a power of attorney), the papers must be notarized, signed by the Clerk of Court, and then sent to the Secretary of State for the State seal. This Office authenticates the State seal, verifying that it is a legal document. Foreign governments often require that any legal document, whether personal, educational or business related, be authenticated. This includes birth certificates, marriage licenses, divorce papers, or school transcripts.

* CIA World and Country Maps

National Technical Information Service (NTIS)
U.S. Department of Commerce
5285 Port Royal Road
Springfield, VA 22161 (703) 487-4650

Hundreds of maps generated by the Central Intelligence Agency are sold through NTIS. There are country maps as well as maps of continents are available. smaller geographical areas and city maps such as Moscow and Vicinity; Middle East Area Oilfields and Facilities; Israeli Settlement in the Gaza Strip; South Africa: Industrial Activity and Production; Africa Ethnolinguistic Groups; and street maps for Moscow, Shanghai and many other cities.

* Citizens Arrested Overseas

Citizens Emergency Center
Overseas Citizens Service
Bureau of Consular Affairs
2201 C St., NW, Room 4800
Washington, DC 20520 (202) 647-5225

The Citizens Emergency Center monitors the cases of Americans arrested abroad and acts as a liaison between the prisoner's family and consular officers overseas. A consular officer visits the American as soon as possible, provides information regarding the foreign legal system and a list of attorneys, and offers other assistance such as contacting family or friends. The consular officer's role in arrest cases is one of observation and support, regularly visiting the prisoner and checking his or her welfare, monitoring human rights, and the status of the case. The Center assists in transferring of funds, and when a prisoner's health or life is endangered by inadequate diet or medical care provided by the local prison, dietary food supplements and/or medical care may be arranged through a U.S. Government loan authorized under the Emergency Medical and Dietary Assistance Program.

* Citizens Emergency Center

Overseas Citizens Service
Bureau of Consular Affairs
2201 C St., NW, Room 4800
Washington, DC 20520 (202) 647-5225

Be patient. If any phone number is incorrect, call (area code) 555-1212 and request the new listing.

Vacations and Business Travel

This center provides assistance to and protects the welfare of U.S. citizens abroad in the following Ways:

Arrests - See "Citizens Arrested Overseas"

Financial Assistance - Assists Americans overseas who find themselves in financial trouble. They first attempt to locate private sources of funds from family or friends, and then assist with the transfer of funds to the individual. If none can be found, the Center will approve a repatriation loan which will pay for the individual's direct return to the nearest port of entry in the U.S.

Medical Assistance - Assists with handling the problems of Americans who become physically or mentally ill while traveling or living abroad. Locates and notifies family or friends, and transmits private funds. When necessary they will assist in the return of the ill or injured person to the U.S. with appropriate medical escort. Full expenses must be borne by citizen.

Deaths - The consular officer reports the death of a U.S. citizen to the next of kin, and will assist in making arrangements for local burial or for return of the body to the U.S. Cost must be borne by family members.

Welfare/Whereabouts - The Center relays the request for assistance and all pertinent data available on the individual to the U.S. Embassy or consulate responsible for the area where the individual is believed to be traveling or residing, and the consular officer then attempts to locate these individuals. In cases of disasters such as earthquakes, or plane crashes, the Center ascertains the names of U.S. citizens involved and informs their families.

Travel Advisories - The Center gives advice to the public and U.S. Foreign Service posts on the advisability of travel to certain countries or areas.

Search and Rescue - The Center monitors the search and rescue efforts outside the U.S., such as attempting to locate missing planes or boats that might be carrying Americans.

* Commercial Library Program Publications List

Foreign Affairs Information Management Center
U.S. Department of State
2201 C St., NW, Room 3239
Washington, DC 20520 (202) 647-1062

This list provides a wide-ranging selection of publications useful to commercial reference facilities. It contains annotated bibliographies of directories, buyers' guides, yearbooks, atlases, etc., in general and in special product areas. State manufacturing and industrial directories are included, as are telex directories.

* Country and Territory Info Pamphlets

Superintendent of Documents
Government Printing Office
Washington, DC 20402 (202) 783-3238

Background Notes, a series of short, factual pamphlets about various countries and territories of the world, plus selected international organizations, contain up-to-date information on each country's people, culture, geography, history, government, political conditions, economy, defense, and foreign relations with other countries, including the United States. A reading list provides additional sources of information about the country, and travel notes, maps, and occasional photographs are often included. A complete set can be purchased from the Government Printing Office for $63.

* Cruise the Panama Canal

The Panama Canal Commission
2000 L St, NW, Suite 550
Washington, DC 20036-4996 (202) 634-6441

Office of Public Affairs
Panama Canal Commission
Unit 2300, APOAA 34011 (800) 622-2625, ext. 52-5463

Information on cruises of the Panama Canal is available through the above offices. At the Panama Canal you don't have to leave the ship to see the sights. Passengers can watch as their northbound cruise ship enters Pedro Miguel Locks on a northbound transit. In the distance they can see Gaillard Cut where the Canal passes through the Continental Divide. For more information, contact either of the above offices.

* Customs Information for Travelers

Public Information Office
U.S. Customs Service
U.S. Department of the Treasury
P.O. Box 7407
Washington, DC 20044 (202) 927-6724

Know Before You Go contains Customs hints for residents returning to the U.S. from abroad. Topics include declaration of articles acquired abroad, Customs exemptions, gifts, dutiable articles and those free of duty, rates of duty, prohibited and restricted articles, and other pointers.

* Customs Rules for Government Personnel: Civilian and Military

Public Information Office
U.S. Customs Service
U.S. Department of the Treasury
P.O. Box 7407
Washington, DC 20044 (202) 927-6724

The free leaflet, *U.S. Customs Highlights for Government Personnel,* provides customs information for civilian employees and military personnel of the U.S. Government when returning to the States with personal and household effects after an extended tour of duty abroad and when returning on leave or TDY. Subjects include customs declarations and limitations, gifts, automobiles, and prohibited and restricted importations.

* Customs Rules for Private Flyers

Smuggling Investigations Division
Office of Enforcement Regulations
U.S. Customs Service
U.S. Department of the Treasury
1301 Constitution Ave., NW
Washington, DC 20229 (202) 927-0650

Private, corporate, and charter pilots on business or pleasure flights to and from foreign countries should become acquainted with the booklet, *Customs Rules for Private Flyers,* available from the Public Information Office, U.S. Customs Service, P.O. Box 7407, Washington, DC 20044. It sets forth basic Customs requirements, provides a list of airports at which Customs processing may be obtained, and explains overtime charges.

* Customs Tips for Visitors

Information Services Division
Office of Logistics Management
U.S. Customs Service
U.S. Department of the Treasury
1301 Constitution Ave., NW
Washington, DC 20229 (202) 927-5980

The free flyer, *Customs Tips for Visitors,* briefly describes the customs regulations for foreign visitors to the United States. Personal exemptions and a list of items that must meet certain requirements are featured. For further information on customs requirements for foreign visitors, the free pamphlet, *Customs Hints for Visitors,* is also helpful in outlining declarations, exemptions, gifts, duty, and prohibited and restricted articles. To obtain a copies of these publications, write to Public Information Office, U.S. Customs Service, P.O. Box 7407, Washington, DC 20044.

* Executive-Diplomat Seminars

Office of Public Programs
U.S. Department of State
Bureau of Public Affairs
2201 C St., NW, Room 5831
Washington, DC 20520-6810 (202) 647-1433

The State Department holds seminars designed for corporate vice-presidents who do business abroad. These two day seminars, offered twice yearly, begin with a discussion of global foreign policy objectives, and then focus on economic topics and business opportunities. Contact this office for information on scheduling.

* Hostage Taking: Preparation, Avoidance and Survival

Superintendent of Documents
Government Printing Office
Washington, DC 20402 (202) 783-3238

Be patient. If any phone number is incorrect, call (area code) 555-1212 and request the new listing.

International Travel

The State Department's Bureau of Diplomatic Security publishes this pamphlet which explains what you can do to make yourself less susceptible to terrorist violence and how to improve your chances of survival should your efforts fail. Information includes personal preparations, security measures, and tips on hostage survival. Fee $1.50.

* Importing of Articles from Developing Countries

Public Information Office
U.S. Customs Service
U.S. Department of the Treasury
P.O. Box 7407
Washington, DC 20044 (202) 927-6724

Generalized System of Preferences (GSP) is a system used by many developed countries to help developing nations improve their financial or economic condition through export trade. It provides for the duty-free importation of a wide range of products from certain countries which would otherwise be subject to customs duty. The free pamphlet, *GSP and the Traveler*, lists popular tourist items eligible for duty-free treatment under GSP and the beneficiary countries.

* Importing Pleasure Boats

Carrier Rulings Branch
Office of Regulations and Rulings
U.S. Customs Service
U.S. Department of the Treasury
Franklin Court
1099 14th Street NW
Washington, DC 20005 (202) 482-6940

When a pleasure boat or yacht arrives in the United States, the first landing must be at a Customs port or designated place where Customs service is available. The pamphlet, *Pleasure Boats*, explains the Customs formalities involving pleasure boats to help you plan your importation and reporting requirements, overtime charges, and provides other information relating strictly to pleasure boats. You can get a copy of *Pleasure Boats* from the Public Information Office, U.S. Customs Service, P.O. Box 7407, Washington, DC 20044.

* Overseas Citizens Services

U.S. Department of State
2201 C Street, NW
Room 4800
Washington, DC 20520 (202) 647-3816

Overseas Citizens Services is responsible for administering laws, formulating regulations, and implementing policies relating to the broad range of consular services provided to U.S. citizens abroad. These services include providing assistance to and protecting the welfare of U.S. citizens abroad, overseeing the payment of Federal benefits overseas, documenting U.S. citizens born abroad, and making determinations concerning acquisition and nationality abroad. Overseas Citizens Services serves as a liaison between concerned family members, friends, and members of Congress in the United States and consular posts and citizens abroad.

* Overseas Security Advisory Council (OSAC)

Bureau of Diplomatic Security
DA/OSAC
U.S. Department of State
2216 Gallows Road
Dunn Loring, VA 22027 (703) 204-6185

Overseas Security Advisory Council was established to promote security for American business interests abroad. In 1987, OSAC was extended overseas through the establishment of "mini-councils" in some of the world's most important business centers. Business representatives in these areas meet locally with Diplomatic Security Officers to promote security for Americans and American interests. Besides regular meetings to plan and exchange information, OSAC also produced a number of well-received publications, such as *Security Guidelines for American Families Living Abroad* and distributed the Diplomatic Security-produced children's security video, *Are You A-OK*. OSAC also sends threat advisories and general security information to more than 700 companies, and is now providing this information through a computer information database.

* Panama Canal Tours

Orientation Services
The Office of Public Affairs

c/o Panama Canal Commission
Unit 2300
APOAA 34011 (800) 622-2625, ext. 52-5463

The Canal Guide Service, operated by the Panama Canal Commission, offers free tours of the Panama Canal to the public. Tours are given seven days a week from 9:00 a.m. to 5:00 p.m. The tour takes less than an hour and include a slight briefing, a topographical model of the Canal to view, and a film. Visitors are welcome at the Miraflores Locks on the Pacific side of the Isthmus where a pavilion provides a vantage point for viewing transiting ships. Interested members of the public should call two days in advance to make a reservation. Another attraction is the high doomed ceiling, the dramatic murals, and the marble columns and floor make the rotunda the main attraction of the Administration Building at Balboa Heights. The murals depict the digging of Gaillard Cut at Gold Hill, the erection of a lock gate, and the construction of the Gatun Dam spillway and Miraflores Locks. For more information, contact this office. The history of the Panama Railroad has been closely linked with that of the Panama Canal since long before the waterway was opened to traffic. The first railroad built through the tropical jungles of the New World served for almost 60 years as the only means of transportation across the narrow Isthmus of Panama. Before the Canal was opened in 1914, the Panama Railroad was reported to have the heaviest traffic per mile of all the railroads in the world. The railroad makes five trips per day across the Isthmus, Monday through Friday, and three trips per day on Saturday and Sunday. The train takes an hour and a half to cross the Isthmus. For more information, contact this office.

* Passport Agent's Manual

Passport Services
Bureau of Consular Affairs
U.S. Department of State
2201 C Street, NW
Room 5813
Washington, DC 20520 (202) 647-6633

The material in this manual is furnished for the passport agent's guidance and is intended to cover the most frequently encountered situations. It has information on evidence of citizenship, names allowed on passports, evidence of identity, and application procedures. A list of travel-related forms and brochures is also included.

* Passport Information

Passport Services
Bureau of Consular Affairs
U.S. Department of State
2201 C Street, NW
Room 5813
Washington, DC 20520 (202) 647-0518

Passport Services provides a recorded message at (202) 647-0518 which explains the documents you need and application process for obtaining a passport, as well as reporting the loss or theft of your passport. It also explains how you can obtain a copy of the report of a birth or death of a U.S. citizen abroad. The message will direct you to the proper agencies for information regarding naturalization, travel advisories, customs regulations, and shots required by various countries.

* Passport Offices Throughout America

You may apply for a passport at any passport agency and at many Clerks of Court Offices or Post Offices designated to accept passport applications. The regional offices are as follows:

Boston
Thomas P. O'Neill Federal Building, 10 Causeway Street, Suite 247, Boston, MA 02202-1094; (617) 565-6990.

Chicago
Kluczynski Office Building, 230 S. Dearborn St., Room 380, Chicago, IL 60604; (312) 353-7155.

Honolulu
New Federal Building, 300 Ala Moana Blvd., Room C-106, Honolulu, HI 96850-0001; (808) 541-1918.

Houston
Mickey Leland Federal Building, 1919 Smith Street, Suite 1100, Houston, TX 77002-8049; (713) 653-3153.

Be patient. If any phone number is incorrect, call (area code) 555-1212 and request the new listing.

Vacations and Business Travel

Los Angeles
Federal Bldg., 11000 Wilshire Blvd., Los Angeles, CA 90024-3615; (310) 575-7070.

Miami
Claude Pepper Federal Office Building, 51 Southwest 1st Ave., 3rd Floor, Miami, FL 33130-1680; (305) 536-4681.

New Orleans
701 Loyal Ave., Postal Services Bldg., T-12005, New Orleans, LA 70113-1931; (504) 589-6728/29.

New York
Rockefeller Center, International Bldg., 630 5th Ave., Room 270, New York, NY 10111-0031; (212) 541-7710/399-5290.

Philadelphia
Federal Building, 600 Arch St., Room 4426, Philadelphia, PA 19106-1685; (215) 597-7480.

San Francisco
Tishman Speyer Building, 525 Market St., Room 200, San Francisco, CA 94105-2773; (415) 744-4019 or (415) 744-4444 (recording).

Seattle
Federal Building, 915 2nd Ave., Room 992, Seattle, WA 98174-1091; (206) 220-7777/7788.

Stamford
One Landmark Square, Broad and Atlantic Sts., Stamford, CT 06901-2767; (203) 325-3538/3539/3530/4401 (recording).

Washington, DC
Room G62, 1425 K St., NW, Room 214, Washington, DC 20522-1705; (202) 326-6060 or (202) 647-0518 (recording).

* Pet and Wildlife Importation

Public Information Office
U.S. Customs Service
U.S. Department of the Treasury
P.O. Box 7407
Washington, DC 20044 (202) 927-6724

The Public Health Service, U.S. Department of Agriculture, U.S. Fish and Wildlife Service, and the U.S. Department of the Treasury have combined efforts to describe the regulations on the importing of pets and wildlife into the United States. Pets, particularly dogs, cats, and turtles, brought into this country must be examined for possible evidence of disease that can be transmitted to humans. Certain animals are prohibited from entry that have been exposed to foot and mouth disease. Endangered species, both plant and animal, may not be imported without special permits. *Pets, Wildlife* explains these regulations in further detail.

* Returning U.S. Residents and Customs

Public Information Office
U.S. Customs Service
U.S. Department of the Treasury
P.O. Box 7407
Washington, DC 20044 (202) 927-6724

Pocket Hints is a brief outline of customs responsibilities of returning residents. Duty free exemptions, restricted or prohibited articles, and customs declarations are summarized.

* Security Guidelines for American Enterprises

Bureau of Diplomatic Security
Overseas Security Advisory Council (OSAC)
U.S. Department of State, SA-11
2216 Gallows Road
Dunn Loring, VA 22027 (202) 663-0549

This publication provides security guidelines for American private sector and personnel abroad. This is the third OSAC publication printed and distributed by the State Department. The implementation of security guidelines contained in this publication could reduce the vulnerability of American private sector enterprises abroad to criminal or terrorist acts, and emphasize site selection and operational security. Previous publications include *Crisis Management Guidelines* and *Security Guidelines for American Families Living Abroad.*

* Terrorism and Diplomatic Security

Public Information
Bureau of Diplomatic Security
DS/SA
U.S. Department of State
2121 Virginia Ave., NW, SA-10
Washington, DC 20520 (202) 663-0549

The Bureau of Diplomatic Security was created in 1985 in an effort to deal with terrorist attacks against overseas missions. All but the smallest of American overseas missions have a Regional Security Officer (RSO) on staff to manage security and keep employees safe on the job and at home. The bureau is responsible for the physical security of the mission, as well as construction and information security. Diplomatic Security Analysts study and analyze intelligence information from a variety of sources, including specific terrorist groups to better understand their tactics and anticipate their actions. They have also developed public service announcements and related security awareness materials for the American tourist, business traveler, and Foreign Service family. DS has produced educational videotapes and instructional materials that teach the basics of security to Americans living and working abroad. Other videos focus on professional conduct in foreign cultures. The pamphlet, Countering Terrorism, lists several suggestions for security measures for your home, family, and business, as well as what to do in the event of a kidnapping.

* Travel Advisories on Civil Unrest Around-the-World

Citizens Emergency Center (CEC)
Overseas Citizens Services
U.S. Department of State
2201 C Street, NW
Room 4800
Washington, DC 20520 (202) 647-5225

CEC is responsible for issuing travel advisories when events abroad are likely to adversely affect traveling Americans. Travel advisories often concern international conflict, civil unrest within individual countries, natural disasters, or disease outbreaks. Many of the advisories refer to temporary conditions and are cancelled when the problem no longer poses a threat to travelers.

* Travel Tips for Senior Citizens

Overseas Citizens Services
U.S. Department of State
2201 C Street, NW
Room 4800
Washington, DC 20520 (202) 647-5226

This publication includes information on insurance, medication, travel advisories, and passports. They include a list of relevant publications, some practical travel tips, as well as the assistance you can expect from U.S. Embassies and consulates.

* Vessel Owners and Masters: Customs Rules

Public Information Office
U.S. Customs Service
U.S. Department of the Treasury
P.O. Box 7407
Washington, DC 20044 (202) 927-6724

Masters or vessel owners may incur penalties for violations of United States Customs laws, including violations committed by members of their crews. The brochure, *Notice to Masters of Vessels*, notifies the masters of proper precautions in the areas of arrival and entry, and merchandise in order to avoid penalties for violations.

* Visa Information for U.S. Citizens Wishing to Travel to Foreign Countries

Overseas Citizens Services
U.S. Department of State
2201 C St., NW, Room 4800
Washington, DC 20520 (202) 647-5225

This office can provide you with visa requirements for U.S. citizens wishing to travel to foreign countries. They stress that this information is subject to change and that the definitive information regarding visas can come only from the foreign embassies. This taped message lists all the countries, their current visa requirements, travel advisories for the countries, as well as the embassies' phone numbers.

Be patient. If any phone number is incorrect, call (area code) 555-1212 and request the new listing.

International Travel

* Visiting and Living Abroad

Office of Citizens Consular Services
Bureau of Consular Affairs
U.S. Department of State
2201 C St., NW, Room 4817
Washington, DC 20520 (202) 647-3444

This office provides services to U.S. citizens abroad in a variety of ways:

Acquisition and Loss of Citizenship: Determination of an individual's citizenship status is a function of the office if the person is not in the United States.

Passport and Registration Services Abroad: Issues passports, as well as Cards of Identity and Registration as proof of U.S. citizenship. This office officially records a person's U.S. citizenship and/or makes his/her residence a matter of record.

Consular Report of Birth: This official record is considered a basic citizenship document setting forth detailed information regarding the facts of birth and parentage, as basis for child's claim to citizenship.

Child Custody Disputes: Helps parents locate children abroad, monitors their welfare upon request, and provides general information about child custody laws and procedures.

Federal Benefits: Assists in processing claims and distributing checks.

International Adoption: Provides general information on adoptions, makes inquiries regarding status of cases, and assists in clarifying documentary requirements.

Judicial Services: Provides advice on the assistance which consular officers can render to U.S. citizens overseas engaged in private legal suits and maintains lists of attorneys. They also administer notarial and authentication functions.

Estates and Property Claims: Consular Officer has statutory responsibility for the personal estates of U.S. citizens who die abroad if the deceased has no legal representative in the country where the death occurred. The Office gives general information regarding property claims and provides a list of attorneys.

Selective Service Registration: Registers people for selective service.

Shipping and Seamen: This office has statutory responsibility to protect the interests of American seamen, vessels, and shipping firms abroad.

Voting: Provides non-partisan voting information and assists in requesting absentee ballots.

Vacations and Business Travel

Domestic Tourism and Trends

* Airline Passenger Safety

Community and Consumer Liaison Division
Office of Public Affairs
Federal Aviation Administration
U.S. Department of Transportation
800 Independence Ave., SW
Washington, DC 20591 (202) 267-3481

Airline passengers who have inquiries or complaints regarding airplane safety should contact this office.

* Air Travelers' Rights and Complaints

Consumer Affairs Division, I-25
Intergovernmental and Consumer Affairs
Governmental Affairs
Office of the Secretary of Transportation
U.S. Department of Transportation
400 7th Street, SW
Washington, DC 20590-0001 (202) 366-2220

If your problem cannot be resolved directly with the airline, contact this office for information on air travelers' rights and for assistance in resolving problems with airlines and charter flights. Complaints about delayed or canceled flights, reservations, lost baggage, smoking, refunds, and overbooking can also be handled here.

* AMTRAK Passenger Services

AMTRAK
60 Massachusetts Ave., N.E.
Washington, DC 20002 (202) 906-2733

The Passenger Services Department handles all of the onboard service aspects of AMTRAK, including all of its employees across the country.

* AMTRAK Customer Relations

AMTRAK
Customer Relations
60 Massachusetts Ave. N.E.
Washington, DC 20002 (202) 906-2121

You may call or write the Customer Relations Office concerning any comments or problems with AMTRAK service. Please include your ticket receipt and dates of travel to help with the resolution of your problem.

* Auto Safety Hotline

Office of Defects Investigation (NEF-10)
National Highway Traffic Safety Administration
U.S. Department of Transportation
400 7th Street, SW, Room 5319 Recording: (202) 366-0123
Washington, DC 20590-0001 Recording: (800) 424-9393

This toll-free hotline is accessible in all 50 states, Puerto Rico, and the Virgin Islands. Consumers may call to report automobile safety problems or to request information on recalls, defects, investigations, child safety seats, tires, drunk driving, crash test results, seat belts, air bags, odometer tampering, and other related topics. Staff will also make referrals to state and other agencies. Also ask about the New Car Assessment Program (NCAP), which provides comparable data on the frontal crashworthiness of selected new vehicles.

* Charting a Course for International Tourism in the Nineties

U.S. Travel and Tourism Administration (USTTA)
U.S. Department of Commerce
Room 1868
Washington, DC 20230 (202) 482-4752

Charting a Course for International Tourism in the Nineties: A handbook for managers and executives dealing with international tourism as it relates to commercial and economic activity, political and foreign policy implications, socio-cultural and environmental aspects and implications through the year 2000. Available free from USTTA, Office of Research. (1990, 50 pages).

* Consumer Rights on Airlines

Government Printing Office
Superintendent of Documents
Washington DC 20402 (202) 783-3238

Fly Rights is an easy-to-read booklet that explains the rights and responsibilities of air travellers. It is available at nominal cost from the GPO.

* Handicapped Visitors

Office of Research
United States Travel and Tourism Administration
U.S. Department of Commerce
14th St. and Constitution Ave., NW
Room 1868
Washington DC 20230 (202) 482-4028

The United States Welcomes Handicapped Visitors is a publication designed to give advice and guidance to handicapped visitors wishing to travel to and within the United States. It explains Federal regulations and policies of the various modes of transportation, as well as offering information regarding destinations, resources, publications, organizations, and some practical advice. Contact this office for your free copy.

* Multilingual Receptionists

United States Travel and Tourism Administration (USTTA)
Office for Tourism Marketing
U.S. Department of Commerce
14th St. and Constitution Ave., NW
Room 1860
Washington, DC 20230 (202) 482-0137

To ensure that international visitors enter the U.S. with minimal difficulty, USTTA sponsors a uniformed corps of multilingual receptionists at 12 gateway airports who provide interpreter and allied services required for U.S. entry formalities. International gateways offering this service include New York (Kennedy); Seattle; San Juan; Philadelphia; Miami; Boston; Los Angeles; Honolulu; Bangor; Atlanta; New Orleans and Baltimore-Washington International.

* Rail Tickets or Travel Information

AMTRAK
60 Massachusetts Ave., N.E.
Washington, DC 20002 1-800-USA-RAIL

For information regarding tickets or travel on AMTRAK, call 1-800-USA-RAIL. AMTRAK also publishes a travel planner which provides travel tips and services, as well as a listing AMTRAK's vacation packages.

* Tourism in the U.S.A.

United States Travel and Tourism Administration
Office for Tourism Marketing
U.S. Department of Commerce
14th St. and Constitution Ave. NW
Room 1860 (202) 482-4752
Washington, DC 20230 (202) 482-0137

Tourism USA is a book produced as an aid to communities interested in initiating or developing tourism as a part of their economic development plan, and has been revised and expanded to also include international marketing and visitor services for special populations. Statistical data has been revised to reflect the most current facts available. This publication covers guidelines for tourism development, including appraising tourism potential, planning for tourism,

Be patient. If any phone number is incorrect, call (area code) 555-1212 and request the new listing.

Domestic Tourism and Trends

assessing product and market, marketing tourism, visitor services, and sources of assistance. The first book is free; additional copies are $5 each.

* Tourism Offices

United States Travel and Tourism Administration
Office of Tourism Marketing
U.S. Department of Commerce
14th St. and Constitution Ave., NW
Room 1860
Washington, DC 20230 (202) 482-4003

The following is a complete listing of addresses and phone numbers for all state and territorial tourism offices. Contact the office listed above for your free copy.

* Tourism Revenue

Office for Tourism Marketing
United States Travel and Tourism Administration (USTTA)
U.S. Department of Commerce
14th St. And Constitution Ave. NW
Room 1860
Washington, DC 20230 (202) 482-4003

This office's goal is to increase the U.S. share of international visitors. This is accomplished through several means, one of which is cooperative marketing and advertising overseas. This office often puts together special advertising sections designed for foreign countries. A free publication, *Marketing U.S. Tourism Abroad: A Manual of Cooperative Marketing Programs In USTTA Markets,* lists cooperative advertising opportunities, travel shows, seminars, and travel missions. *The Manual* includes costs, formats, and deadlines. This Office also assists State and local travel organizations, and private industry around issues such as marketing tourism and visitor services.

* Travel Industry Market Research

Office of Research
United States Travel and Tourism Administration (USTTA)
U.S. Department of Commerce
14th St. and Constitution Ave., NW
Room 1868
Washington, DC 20230 (202) 482-4028

USTTA gathers, analyzes and published international travel statistics, which define the direction and impact of foreign trends, determine foreign market potential, and guide marketing efforts. USTTA's *Inflight Survey* gathers essential marketing information on international travelers to and within the United States, as well as Americans traveling abroad. Conducted with public and private sector tourism organizations and 35 major international air carriers, the *Survey* provides data on travel patterns and preference of foreign visitors. The *Bibliography of Selected USTTA Research Publications and Marketing Manuals* is available at no charge, and includes a description and ordering information for the following USTTA publications:

Recap of International Travel To and From the United States. Summarizes annual developments in inbound/outbound tourism (free).

Summary and Analysis of International Travel to the United States. Provides monthly foreign visitor arrival statistics by region and for 90 different countries. Tables include a variety of travel data (price varies depending on year).

Outlook for International Travel To and From the United States. Provides one-year forecast of international travel to/from the U.S. (free).

Canadian Travel to the United States: 1988. Details Canadian tourism to the U.S. (free).

Impact of Foreign Visitors' Spending on State Economies 1985-1986. (free)

In-Flight Survey of International Air Travelers. Overseas and Mexican Visitors to the United States and (2) *U.S. Travelers to Mexico and Overseas Countries.* Provides survey data on travel characteristics and spending patterns of international air travelers to and from the U.S. Free inbound and outbound profile sheets are available, along with an informational brochure and order form (prices range from $100 to $1000).

Analysis of International Air Travel To and From the United States on U.S./Foreign Flag Carriers (free).

Pleasure Travel Markets to North America. The studies of travel behavior provide information on past travel characteristics, trip planning information, attitudes toward overseas travel, the image of the U.S., and travel market segments. An information packet and free *Highlights* publication for each years study is available (prices range from $25 to $1000).

Sectorial Analyses Reports on International Travel. Reports commissioned on four key sectors of the travel industry: Lodging; Air Travel; Inter-City Bus; and Rental Car. The analyses look at the economic impact of international travel on each sector of the U.S. economy, as well as at other issues ($10 for each report).

USTTA Country Travel Market Surveys. Consumer Surveys of Eight Individual Country Markets. Surveys of potential international travelers in the United Kingdom, Germany, France, Japan, Australia, Italy, Netherlands, and Mexico.

Marketing Tourism Abroad: USTTA's International Cooperative Marketing Manual. Provides information concerning the cooperative marketing programs offered by USTTA (free).

Developing A U.S. Regional Approach for Promoting Travel from Foreign Markets. Provides guidelines for developing regional organizational structures for planning and operating international tourism promotional programs ($25).

The United States Welcomes Handicapped Visitors- Designed to give advice and guidance to handicapped visitors wishing to travel to and within the United States (free).

* Traveling to the United States

Tourism Marketing
United States Travel and Tourism Administration (USTTA)
U.S. Department of Commerce
14th St. and Constitution Ave., NW
Washington, DC 20230 (202) 482-4003

Headquartered in Washington, DC, USTTA has six regional tourism offices in Toronto, Mexico City, Tokyo, London, Paris, and Frankfurt. These offices deal with foreign travel agents and tour operators and facilitate familiarization programs for foreign travel writers and tour operators seeking information on American travel destinations.

Be patient. If any phone number is incorrect, call (area code) 555-1212 and request the new listing.

State Travel Hotlines

If you are interested in travel related industries, planning a dramatic coast-to-coast sightseeing trip, or scouting out possible areas for relocation, your efforts can be made somewhat easier with the help of state offices of tourism. These offices will provide you with maps, brochures, and other valuable information. If you are planning to visit a particular city--say Sioux Falls--someone in the South Dakota state tourist office might send you a booklet of fascinating historical attractions in the areas. If you want to know where to find the hotels, motels or restaurants, cafes, diners, movie theaters, supermarkets, drug stores or churches, this is the place to start.

If you are interested in a specific activity, not just travel advice and information on tourist attractions, these offices can help you as well. Say, you want to pan for gold or visit an authentic western ghost town. By checking with the state tourism office you can get information on these sites, and perhaps also the name of a good book to prepare you for your visit. They might even be able to provide you with the name of a special guide or tour once you are in the area.

Other information from state tourism offices might include highway conditions, weather advice, local hotel/motel rates, and the best places to eat. In general, each state will provide information packages containing a travel guide, a calendar of events, state maps, and brochures from private, state, and regional tourist attractions.

State Travel and Tourism Hotlines

Alabama
(205) 242-4169

Alaska
(907) 465-2012

American Samoa
(684) 633-1091-2-3

Arizona
(602) 542-4764

Arkansas
(501) 682-1088

California
(916) 322-2881

Colorado
(303) 592-5510

Connecticut
(203) 258-4286

Delaware
(800) 441-8846 (302) 739-5749

District of Columbia
(202) 789-7000

Florida
(904) 488-5607/9187

Georgia
(404) 656-3553

Guam
(671) 646-5278-79

Hawaii
(808) 586-2550

Idaho
(208) 334-2470

Illinois
(312) 814-4732

Indiana
(317) 232-8860

Iowa
(515) 242-4705

Kansas
(913) 296-2009

Kentucky
(502) 564-4930

Louisiana
(504) 242-8110

Maine
(207) 289-5710

Marianas
(670) 234-8327

Maryland
(410) 333-6643

Massachusetts
(617) 727-3201

Michigan
(517) 373-0670

Minnesota
(612) 296-2755

Mississippi
(800) 647-2290 (601) 359-3297

Missouri
(314) 751-3051

Montana
(406) 444-2654

Be patient. If any phone number is incorrect, call (area code) 555-1212 and request the new listing.

State Travel Hotlines

Nebraska
(402) 471-3794

Nevada
(702) 687-4322

New Hampshire
(603) 271-2665

New Jersey
(609) 292-6963

New Mexico
(800) 545-2040 (505) 827-7400

New York
(518) 474-4116

North Carolina
(919) 733-4171

North Dakota
(800) 437-2077 (701) 224-2525

Ohio
(614) 466-8844

Oklahoma
(405) 521-3981

Oregon
(800) 547-7842; (503) 378-3451

Pennsylvania
(717) 787-5453

Puerto Rico
(809) 721-1576-2402

Rhode Island
(800) 556-2484 (401) 277-2601

South Carolina
(803) 734-0136

South Dakota
(800) 843-1930 (605) 773-3301

Tennessee
(615) 741-7225

Texas
(512) 462-9191

Utah
(801) 538-1030

Vermont
(802) 828-3236

Virginia
(804) 786-2051

Virgin Islands
(809) 774-8784

Washington
(206) 753-5600

West Virginia
(304) 348-2286/2200

Wisconsin
(608) 266-2345

Wyoming
(307) 777-7777

Be patient. If any phone number is incorrect, call (area code) 555-1212 and request the new listing.

Investments and Financial Services General Sources

See also Experts Chapter
See also Information on People, Companies, and Mailing Lists Chapter

This section contains more information about those companies which offer investments rather than investments themselves. More information about specific investments can be found in the Information on People, Companies and Mailing Lists Chapter as well as the Experts Chapter. A great starting place for any information is the Consumer Information Hotline in this chapter's Banking section. Elsewhere in this chapter are answers to numerous other questions about financial institutions such as the viability of your savings and loan or guides to establishing a credit union. You'll also find the names and addresses of appropriate offices which can help you with such nightmares as lost government bonds or stolen government checks. And, what about that $20 bill that barely survived getting washed along with your pants? You probably can redeem the damaged money by sending it to the federal office identified in the Money section.

* Credit Card and Computer Fraud

Fraud Division
Office of Investigations
U.S. Secret Service
U.S. Department of the Treasury
1800 G St., NW
Washington, DC 20223 (202) 435-6100

The fraudulent use of credit and debit cards is a federal violation. Investigations are conducted by the Secret Service, including stolen or lost credit cards, the misuse of credit card account numbers, automated teller machine fraud, telephone fraud involving long distance calls, and other types of access device fraud. Computer fraud is a recent concern of the Secret Service. New law enforcement techniques are being pioneered in an effort to identify computer criminals.

* Credit Card Collections

Office of the Assistant Commissioner Federal Finance
Financial Management Service
U.S. Department of the Treasury
401 14th St., SW
Washington, DC 20227 (202) 874-6720

Under the Credit Card Collection Network, Federal agencies are able to accept MasterCard and VISA from the public for payment of sales, services, fees, fines, and certain types of debts. By 1995, the annual volume via credit cards is expected to reach $150 billion.

* Direct Deposit of Federal Payments

Office of the Assistant Commissioner Regional Operations
Financial Management Service
U.S. Department of the Treasury
401 14th St., SW
Washington, DC 20227 (202) 874-6780

This system electronically deposits Federal payments into the beneficiary's checking or savings account. It does away with the costs associated with checks, reducing the cost to 6 cents versus 36 cents for check processing.

* Electronic Benefit Services

Office of the Assistant Commissioner Federal Finance
Financial Management Service
U.S. Department of the Treasury
401 14th St., SW
Washington, DC 20227 (202) 874-6720

The Financial Management Service is developing a coordinated government-wide plan to electronically deliver benefits to recipients, such as Social Security, welfare payments, and disability payments, through automated teller machines and point-of-sale terminals. The recipient will not need to have an account with the bank that operates the ATM or point-of-sale terminal.

* Electronic Data Interchange

Office of the Assistant Commissioner Regional Operations
Financial Management Service (FMS)
U.S. Department of the Treasury
401 14th St., SW
Washington, DC 20227 (202) 874-6780

The Financial Management Service is establishing an electronic funds transfer system, which would fully automate purchase, delivery, and payment cycles with agencies and businesses. As the Federal agencies expand, the number of automated trading partnerships would increase, and reductions in paperwork and delays in processing should significantly decrease.

* Electronic Federal Tax Deposit System

Office of the Assistant Commissioner Federal Finance
Financial Management Service (FMS)
U.S. Department of the Treasury
401 14th St., SW
Washington, DC 20227 (202) 874-6720

Plans have been initiated by FMS for the design, development, and implementation of a new electronic-oriented system to replace the outmoded, paper-based, error-prone Federal Tax Deposit System. Employers would use this system to remit withholding and other payroll payments to the government.

* Federal Reserve System Resource Materials

Publication Services
MS-138, Board of Governors
Federal Reserve System
Washington, DC 20551 (202) 452-3244

The free guide, *Public Information Materials of the Federal Reserve System*, describes publications and audiovisual materials available from the Federal Reserve System. It lists materials appropriate for students, consumer groups, economists, bankers, and the general public. Copies of the booklet may be obtained from any Federal Reserve Bank or from the office above.

* Fedwire Deposit System

Office of the Assistant Commissioner Federal Finance
Financial Management Service
U.S. Department of the Treasury
401 14th St., SW
Washington, DC 20227 (202) 874-6720

This system electronically processes 200,000 transactions and $90 billion in receipts annually, providing same-day information to the Treasury and the agencies about these deposits. Continuous access to the system is available through terminals linked to the computer.

Be patient. If any phone number is incorrect, call (area code) 555-1212 and request the new listing.

* Thrift Institutions Supervision

Office of Thrift Supervision (OTS)
U.S. Department of the Treasury
1700 G St., NW
Washington, DC 20552   (202) 906-6677

OTS is the regulatory successor to the Federal Home Loan Bank Board. It oversees the supervision of savings institutions by regulatory staff in its district offices. Regulations, directives, and policies are developed for the safe and sound operation of savings institutions and their compliance with federal law and regulations.

Investments and Financial Services

Banking

* Automated Clearinghouse Returns Compliance

Office of the Assistant Commissioner Regional Operations
Financial Management Service
U.S. Department of the Treasury
401 14th St., SW
Washington, DC 20227 (202) 874-6780

The Automated Clearinghouse program was developed to assure the return of Direct Deposit funds if they cannot be properly posted to the accounts of recipients by financial institutions. This could involve the funds of either the Federal Government and its agencies, or the public, depending on the Direct Deposit program being used.

* Bank Customer and Financial Industry Affairs

Customer and Industry Affairs
Comptroller of the Currency (OCC)
U.S. Department of the Treasury
250 E. Street, SW
Washington, DC 20219 (202) 874-4930

Consumer banking groups and other industries involved in the financial market are assisted by this office. It acts as a liaison as well as a provider of technical expertise in an effort to inform these groups of OCC policies and to foster a working relationship.

* Bank Education Programs

Consumer Activities
Bank Supervision
Comptroller of the Currency (OCC)
U.S. Department of the Treasury
250 E. Street, SW
Washington, DC 20219 (202) 874-4700

This office coordinates educational activities with banks, trade associations within the banking industry, and local consumer groups. Training professionals address issues relevant to the banking industry and OCC guidelines and assist in the development of compliance programs.

* Bank Examiners District Offices

Legislative and Public Affairs
Comptroller of the Currency
U.S. Department of the Treasury
250 E. Street, SW
Washington, DC 20219 (202) 874-5000

Northeastern District: 1114 Avenue of the Americas, Suite 3900, New York, NY 10036; (212) 819-9860

Southeastern: 245 Peachtree Center Ave., Marquis One Tower, Suite 600, Atlanta, GA 30303; (404) 659-8855

Central: 440 S. LaSalle St., One Financial Place, Suite 2700, Chicago, IL 60605; (312) 663-8000

Midwestern: 2345 Grand Ave., Suite 700, Kansas City, MO 64108; (816) 556-1800

Southwestern: 1600 Lincoln Plaza, 500 N. Akard, Suite 1600 Dallas, TX 75201-3394; (214) 720-0656

Western: 50 Fremont St., Suite 3900, San Francisco, CA 94105; (415) 545-5900

* Bank Holding Companies

Division of Bank Supervision and Regulation
Federal Reserve System
Room 3172, MS-174
20th St. and Constitution Ave., NW

Washington, DC 20551 (202) 452-2638

Bank holding companies must register with and report to the Federal Reserve System. A registered bank holding company must obtain the approval of the Board of Governors before acquiring more than 5% of the shares of either additional banks or permissible nonbanking companies. For more information on bank holding companies, contact this office.

* Banking Industry Research

Division of Research and Statistics
Federal Deposit Insurance Corporation (FDIC)
550 17th Street, NW
Room 2024I
Washington, DC 20429 (202) 898-3741

The FDIC continually researches and monitors trends in the economy and banking industry. Existing and proposed legislation is studied, as are banking reforms and the effect of interest and inflation rates.

* Banking Law Library

Federal Reserve System (FRS)
Room B1066
20th St. and Constitution Ave. NW
Washington, DC 20551 (202) 452-3284

For information on specific banking laws, contact the FRS Banking Law Library.

* Bank Liquidation

Division of Liquidation
Federal Deposit Insurance Corporation (FDIC)
1776 F Street, NW
8th Floor
Washington, DC 20429 (202) 898-7825

This office oversees the liquidation of failed banks which are insured by the FDIC, and cases are documented and maintained on file. For more information on accessing these files, contact this office.

* Bank Mergers

Division of Bank Supervision and Regulation
Federal Reserve System
Room 3172, MS-174
20th St. and Constitution Ave., NW
Washington, DC 20551 (202) 452-2638

The Federal Reserve Board must give prior approval to all proposed bank mergers between insured state-chartered member banks. Contact this office for more information on bank mergers.

* Banks in Developing Countries

Office of the Assistant Secretary of the Treasury
for International Affairs
Deputy Assistant Secretary for International
Development and Debt Policy
U.S. Department of the Treasury
1500 Pennsylvania Ave., NW, Room 3221
Washington, DC 20220 (202) 566-8243

This office assists in the development and operation of multinational banks in developing countries. These include the World Bank, Inter-American Development Bank, Asian Development Bank, and the African Development Bank.

* Bank Supervision and Regulation

Federal Reserve System
20th St. and Constitution Ave., NW
Washington, DC 20551 (202) 452-2773

Be patient. If any phone number is incorrect, call (area code) 555-1212 and request the new listing.

Banking

The Federal Reserve Board (FRS) supervises and regulates member banks and holding companies. Under the Depository Institutions Deregulation and Monetary Control Act of 1980, the FRS sets reserve requirements for, and provides services to, all U.S. depository institutions, not just to national banks and state-chartered member banks. The Board authorizes the acquisition of banks and closely related nonbanking activities by bank holding companies and other changes of control and mergers of banks and bank holding companies. Its responsibilities extend to many foreign activities of U.S. banking institutions and to foreign banking organizations operating in this country.

* Board of Governors

Federal Reserve System
20th St. and Constitution Ave., NW
Washington, DC 20551   (202) 452-2773

The responsibilities of the Board of Governors include supervising state member banks and all bank holding companies, overseeing Reserve Bank activities, writing consumer credit regulations, approving changes in the discount rate, setting reserve requirements, and establishing margin requirements. The seven members of the Board are appointed for 14-year terms by the U.S. President with the advice and consent of the Senate.

* Call Reports

Financial Disclosure Group
Federal Deposit Insurance Corporation (FDIC)
550 17th Street, NW
Room F-518
Washington, DC 20429   (800) 843-1669

Prepared quarterly by all FDIC-insured banks and mutual savings banks, Report of Condition and Income Statements of Banks, or Call Reports, include balance sheets, income statements, and supporting statements. Banks can call the toll-free number listed above for assistance in filling out Call Reports. When requesting a previously filed call report (currently available from March 1984 to June 1989), include the name of the bank and the quarter desired. Send requests to this office.

* Community Reinvestment

Fair Lending Analyst
Office of Consumer Affairs
Federal Deposit Insurance Corporation (FDIC)
550 17th Street, NW
Room F-130
Washington, DC 20429   (202) 898-3535

The Community Reinvestment Act of 1977 empowers the FDIC to monitor FDIC-insured, state-chartered banks to make sure that the banks are meeting the credit needs of the communities they serve, including low- and middle-income areas. Questions regarding community reinvestment should be directed to the nearest FDIC regional office or to the Fair Lending Analyst at the above office.

* Compliance Information

Office of Consumer Affairs
Federal Deposit Insurance Corporation (FDIC)
550 17th Street, NW
Room F-130
Washington, DC 20429   (202) 898-6777

For information regarding FDIC-insured, state-chartered banks complying with consumer laws and the Truth-in-Lending Act, contact any FDIC-insured bank, FDIC regional office, or the office above.

* Consumer Information

Office of Consumer Affairs
Federal Deposit Insurance Corporation (FDIC)
550 17th Street, NW
Room F-130
Washington, DC 20429   (202) 898-6777
                                        (800) 424-5488

This office answers questions and addresses complaints regarding FDIC-insured banks. A computerized system helps track complaints from their initial filing to their resolution. A follow-up complaint satisfaction survey is also conducted periodically. Banking questions may be directed to the nearest regional FDIC office, or call the FDIC's toll-free customer service hotline between 9 a.m. and 4 p.m. EST, Monday through Friday.

* Comptroller of the Currency Publications

Information Office
Comptroller of the Currency (OCC)
U.S. Department of the Treasury
250 E. Street, SW
Washington, DC 20219   (202) 874-5000

The Comptroller of the Currency's Information Office requires that all requests for a publications listing or other information be in writing to the Washington address above. All publications must be ordered from the Washington address, (202) 874-4960. Selected publications include the following:

Comptroller's Manual for Corporate Activities. This book makes available, in one place, OCC policies and procedures for processing applications for forming a new national bank. The manual can also be used by other institutions entering the national banking system, and by existing national banks expanding and restructuring. ($90)

Comptroller's Manual for National Banks. This looseleaf legal reference contains laws applicable to national banks with sections dealing with regulations and interpretive rulings issued by the OCC. ($50)

Comptroller's Manual for Consumer Examinations. This looseleaf publication is intended to assist the examiner in understanding consumer laws and regulations pertinent to national bank examinations. Examination procedures are also included. ($90)

Comptroller's Handbook for National Bank Examiners. Policies and procedures for the commercial examination of national banks are included in this looseleaf publication. ($90)

Comptroller's Handbook for Five Fiduciary. Policies and procedures are outlined for the examination of fiduciary activities of national banks. The handbook also assists the examiner in the preparation of examination reports of national bank trust departments, subsidiaries, and affiliates of national banks and their holding companies engaging in fiduciary activities. ($25)

Comptroller's Handbook for Compliance. Written for compliance examinations, this handbook is intended for use by examiners as a supervisory tool in performing compliance examinations, and by bankers as a self-assessment tool for analyzing bank compliance systems. ($25)

Fair Housing Home Loan Data System. This booklet is published for mortgage lending departments and officials of national banks, containing the final regulation for the system, instruction forms, and examples. ($1.50)

The Director's Book. Provides guidance to directors of national banks, outlining responsibilities of the board, highlighting areas of particular concern, and addressing in broad terms the duties and liabilities of the individual director. ($10)

Banking Bulletins and Circulars. Circulars provide information of continuing concern to national banks regarding OCC or OCC-supported policies and guidelines. Bulletins inform readers of pending regulation changes and other general information. ($25 each)

Microcomputer Applications for Consumer Activities. A guide to calculating Annual Percentage Rates. The package includes instructions and a 5 1/4" diskette (MS-DOS) for use in IBM-compatible microcomputers. ($20)

Interpretations. This subscription provides legal staff interpretations, trust interpretive letters, and investment securities letters. This monthly package represents the informal views of the Comptroller's staff concerning the applications of banking law to contemplated activities or transactions. ($125)

Weekly Bulletin. Contains all corporate decisions made by the Comptroller's office nationwide each week. Applications, approvals or denials, and consummations are noted for new banks, mergers, consolidations, and purchases and assumptions that result in national banks. This publication also carries branch and title changes, changes in controlling ownership, and other corporate changes for national banks. ($250)

Quarterly Journal. Serves as a journal of record for the most significant actions and policies of the OCC. It is published in March, June, September, and December. The journal includes policy statements, decisions on banking structure, selected speeches, testimony, material released in the interpretive letter series, summaries of enforcement actions, statistical data, and other information of interest to the administration of national banks. ($60 annually or $15 per single copy)

Be patient. If any phone number is incorrect, call (area code) 555-1212 and request the new listing.

Investments and Financial Services

* Deposit Data

Financial Disclosure Group
Federal Deposit Insurance Corporation (FDIC)
550 17th St., NW, Room F-518
Washington, DC 20429 (800) 843-1669

Summary of Deposits is an survey conducted among all FDIC-insured banks every June 30, the results of which are published annually. The *Annual Report of Trust Assets*, a similar survey, is conducted every December 31, among all financial institutions with trust departments. Computer printouts of both surveys are available for all banking offices within a given county, Metropolitan Statistical Area (MSA), or state. Magnetic tapes of *Summary of Deposit* data and the *Annual Report of Trust Assets* data for all U.S. banks for a given year are available for $75 each. Requests for computer printouts and magnetic tapes are handled by this office, which offers a toll-free number for customer assistance.

* Enforcement and Supervision

Office of Supervision and Applications
Division of Bank Supervision
Federal Deposit Insurance Corporation (FDIC)
550 17th St., NW, Room 5025
Washington, DC 20429 (202) 898-6915

This office monitors insured banks for compliance with FDIC regulations and has authority to approve bank applications for deposit insurance and branch formation. This office also initiates cease-and-desist orders against insured banks in the event they fail to correct violations of laws, regulations, or agreements with the FDIC.

* Farm Credit Publications

Office of Congressional and Public Affairs
Farm Credit Administration
1501 Farm Credit Drive
McLean, VA 22102 (703) 883-4056

Information on obtaining publications and documents can be obtained from the office above. Some of the documents available include the following:

New releases issued since January 1, 1990
Biographies of Farm Credit Administration officials
Speeches by FCA officials
FCA Handbook - Statutes and Regulations (Set fee charged)
FCA Examination Manual (Set fee Charged)
FCA Bulletin (Published 10 days after FCA Board meetings; 10 per year)
FCA Orders
FCA Organization Chart
FCA Board Policies
FCA Annual Report

* Farm Credit System

Office of Congressional and Public Affairs
Farm Credit Administration
1501 Farm Credit Drive
McLean, VA 22102 (703) 883-4056

The Farm Credit System is a network of farmer-owned lending institutions and specialized service organizations. More than 70 years ago Congress created the System to provide American agriculture with a dependable source of credit at competitive rates. Today the System provides about one-third of the total credit used by America's farmers, ranchers, and their cooperatives. The *Farm Credit System 1989 Information Guide*, which provides information on the Farm Credit System, including a list of the System's banks, is available free from the office above.

* Federal Cash Concentration System

Office of the Assistant Commissioner Federal Finance
Financial Management Service (FMS)
U.S. Department of the Treasury
401 14th St., SW
Washington, DC 20227 (202) 874-6720

CASH-LINK is FMS's effort to transform the Government's worldwide banking and cash operations. Through the resources of the banking community, the new system will electronically capture and report activity for government-wide collections. The new system will encompass seven collection systems: Treasury General Account Cash Concentration System; Financial Management Service Lockbox Network; Credit Card Collection Network; Fedwire Deposit System;

Federal Reserve System; Farmers Home Administration Cash Concentration System; and Commodity Credit Corporation Cash Concentration System.

* Federal Information Change Notification

Office of the Assistant Commissioner Regional Operations
Financial Management Service
U.S. Department of the Treasury
401 14th St., SW
Washington, DC 20227 (202) 874-6740

This is an automated procedure that financial institutions can use to notify Federal agencies that an error or change has occurred in the depositor's account number, the routing/transit number of the financial institution (small numbers on the bottom of checks), or the type of account (checking or savings) of an Automated Clearinghouse Payment.

* Federal Lockbox Network

Office of the Assistant Commissioner Federal Finance
Financial Management Service
U.S. Department of the Treasury
401 14th St., SW
Washington, DC 20227 (202) 874-6720

Office of the Assistant Commissioner Regional Operations
Financial Management Service
U.S. Department of the Treasury
401 14th St., SW
Washington, DC 20227 (202) 874-6740

The above offices oversee the Lockbox Network which consists of seven banks in nine cities: Atlanta, Chicago, Dallas, Los Angeles, Newark, Philadelphia, Pittsburgh, San Francisco, and St. Louis. Lockboxes, actually post office boxes, are used to collect and deposit mailed payments. More than 363 agency accounts are involved, and $95 billion is collected and processed annually. All 10 Internal Revenue Service centers utilized the lockbox network in 1989.

* Federal Reserve Banks and Treasury Servicing Offices

This is a list of every Treasury Direct servicing office in the U.S. Contact the servicing office closest to you to make transactions on your account, or to receive information about your Treasury security investments.

Federal Reserve Bank Atlanta, 104 Marietta St., NW, Atlanta, GA 30303; (404) 521-8657 (Recording)/(404) 521-8653

Federal Reserve Bank Baltimore, 502 S. Sharp St., P.O. Box 1378, Baltimore, MD 21203; (301) 576-3300

Federal Reserve Bank Birmingham, 1801 Fifth Ave., N., P.O. Box 830447, Birmingham, AL 35283; (205) 731-8500, Ext. 215 (Recording)/(205) 731-8702 (Ext 264)

Federal Reserve Bank Boston, 600 Atlantic Ave., P.O. Box 2076, Boston, MA 02106; (617) 973-3805 (Recording)/(617) 973-3810

Federal Reserve Bank Buffalo, 160 Delaware Ave., P.O. Box 961, Buffalo, NY 14240-0961; (716) 849-5046 (Recording)/(716) 849-5000

Federal Reserve Bank Charlotte, 530 E. Tryon St., P.O. Box 30248, Charlotte, NC 28202; (704) 358-2100

Federal Reserve Bank Chicago, 230 South LaSalle St., P.O. Box 834, Chicago, IL 60690; (312) 786-1110 (Recording)/(312) 322-5369

Federal Reserve Bank Cincinnati, 150 East Fourth St., Cincinnati, OH 45202 or P.O. Box 999, Cincinnati, OH 45201; (513) 721-4787, Ext. 334

Federal Reserve Bank Cleveland, 1455 East Sixth St., P.O. Box 6387, Cleveland, OH 44101; (216) 579-2490

Federal Reserve Bank Dallas, 400 South Akard St., Dallas, TX 75222; (214) 651-6362

Federal Reserve Bank Denver, 1020 16th St., P.O. Box 5228, Terminal Annex, Denver, CO 80217; (303) 572-2475 (Recording)/(303) 572-2470

Be patient. If any phone number is incorrect, call (area code) 555-1212 and request the new listing.

Banking

Federal Reserve Bank Detroit, 160 W. Fort St., P.O. Box 1059, Detroit, MI 48231; (313) 964-6153 (Recording)/(313) 964-6157

Federal Reserve Bank Houston, 1701 San Jacinto St., P.O. Box 2578, Houston, TX 77002; (713) 659-4433

Federal Reserve Bank Jacksonville, 800 West Water St., P.O. Box 2499, Jacksonville, FL 32231-2499; (904) 632-1179

Federal Reserve Bank Kansas City, 925 Grand Ave., P.O. Box 440, Kansas City, MO 64198; (816) 881-2767 (Recording)/(816) 881-2409

Federal Reserve Bank Little Rock, 325 West Capitol Ave., P.O. Box 1261, Little Rock, AR 72203; (501) 324-8275

Federal Reserve Bank Los Angeles, 950 S. Grand Ave., P.O. Box 2077, Terminal Annex, Los Angeles, CA 90051; (213) 624-7398

Federal Reserve Bank Louisville, 410 South Fifth St., P.O. Box 32710, Louisville, KY 40232; (502) 568-9232 (Recording)/(502) 568-9236

Federal Reserve Bank Memphis, 200 N. Main St., P.O. Box 407, Memphis, TN 38101; (901) 523-7171 Ext. 225 or 641

Federal Reserve Bank Miami, 9100 NW Thirty-Sixth St., P.O. Box 520847, Miami, FL 33152; (305) 593-9923 (Recording)/(305) 591-2065

Federal Reserve Bank Minneapolis, 250 Marquette Ave., Minneapolis, MN 55480; (612) 340-2075

Federal Reserve Bank Nashville, 301 Eighth Ave., N., Nashville, TN 37203; (615) 251-7100

Federal Reserve Bank New Orleans, 525 St. Charles Ave., P.O. Box 61630, New Orleans, LA 70161; (504) 593-3290 (Recording)/(504) 593-3200

Federal Reserve Bank New York, 33 Liberty St., Federal Reserve P.O. Station, New York, NY 10045; (212) 720-5823 (Recording)/(212) 720-6619

Federal Reserve Bank Oklahoma City, 226 Dean A. McGee Ave., P.O. Box 25129, Oklahoma City, OK 73125; (405) 270-8660 (Recording)/(405) 270-8652

Federal Reserve Bank Omaha, 2201 Farnam St., Omaha, NE 68102; (402) 221-5638 (Recording)/(402) 221-5633

Federal Reserve Bank Philadelphia, 100 N. 6th Street, P.O. Box 90, Philadelphia, PA 19105; (215) 574-6580 (Recording)/(215) 574-6680

Federal Reserve Bank Pittsburgh, 717 Grant St., P.O. Box 867, Pittsburgh, PA 15230-0867; (412) 261-7988 (Recording)/(412) 261-7863

Federal Reserve Bank Portland, 915 SW Stark St., P.O. Box 3436, Portland, OR 97208; (503) 221-5931 (Recording)/(503) 221-5932

Federal Reserve Bank Richmond, 701 East Byrd St., P.O. Box 27622, Richmond, VA 23261; (804) 697-8000

Federal Reserve Bank Salt Lake City, 120 South State St.,P.O. Box 30780, Salt Lake City, UT 84130; (801) 322-7911 (Recording); (801) 355-3131

Federal Reserve Bank San Antonio, 126 E. Nueva St.,P.O. Box 1471, San Antonio, TX 78295, (512) 224-2141, Ext. 311 (Recording)/(512) 224-2141 ext. 303 or 305

Federal Reserve Bank San Francisco, 101 Market St., P.O. Box 7702, San Francisco, CA 94120; (415) 882-9798 (Recording)/ (415) 974-2330

Federal Reserve Bank Seattle, 1015 Second Ave., P.O. Box 3567, Terminal Annex, Seattle, WA 98124; (206) 343-3615 (Recording)/(206) 343-3600

Federal Reserve Bank St. Louis, 411 Locust St., P.O. Box 14915, St. Louis, MO 63178; (314) 444-8602 (Recording)/(314) 444-8665

* FDIC Publications

Office of Corporate Communications
Federal Deposit Insurance Corporation (FDIC)

550 17th St., NW, Room 7118
Washington, DC 20429 (202) 898-6996

This office distributes the following free publications:

Annual Report. Summarizes the FDIC's operations, regulatory activities, and financial statements. Also included are statistical tables summarizing FDIC assistance to problem and failed banks.

Data Book. This six-volume set contains deposit information for all commercial and mutual savings banks, including U.S.-based branches of foreign banks. Each volume focuses on a different geographic area and includes a national summary with tables on bank structure, class, and size.

Merger Decisions. An annual summary of the FDIC's approvals and denials of bank mergers.

Statistics on Banking. This annual report details bank statistical data, including the total number of banks and branches, and information on incomes, assets, and liabilities of insured banks.

Symbol of Confidence. Provides an overview of the FDIC's history, responsibilities, and operations.

Trust Assets of Financial Institutions. Summarizes trust department data collected from all insured commercial banks. Data is presented by type of account, asset distribution, and size of account.

Your Insured Deposit. Provides examples of the FDIC's insurance coverage for common types of bank accounts.

* International Banking

Analysis Section
Division of Bank Supervision
Federal Deposit Insurance Corporation (FDIC)
550 17th St., NW, Room 5053
Washington, DC 20429 (202) 898-6821

FDIC-insured banks must first obtain FDIC approval before they establish, operate, or relocate a branch in a foreign country. FDIC approval is also needed before these banks acquire any ownership interest in a foreign bank. Insured branches of foreign banks located in the U.S. are also monitored by the FDIC. For more information, contact the nearest regional FDIC office or the office above.

* International Finance

Office of Development Finance
Bureau of Economic and Business Affairs
U.S. Department of State
2201 C St., NW, Room 2529
Washington, DC 20520 (202) 647-9426

As the liaison with multilateral development banks, such as the World Bank, African Development Bank, Asian Development Bank, and InterAmerican Bank, this office works on such development issues as coordinating official U.S. Government assistance to promote economic security in developing countries. This office also coordinates with the Export-Import Bank on trade issues.

* Law, Regulations, and Related Acts

Office of Corporate Communications
Federal Deposit Insurance Corporation (FDIC)
550 17th St., NW, Room 7118
Washington, DC 20429 (202) 898-6996

FDIC Law, Regulations, and Related Acts is a three-volume, loose-leaf bound publication containing the FDI Act, FDIC rules and regulations, advisory opinions, pertinent statutes, and consumer protection material, among other information. Revisions and updates are published bimonthly. For $225 subscribers receive the three-volume set and updates through December of that year, and they are billed $225 each December to renew the update service.

* Legislation on Financial Institutions

Office of Financial Institutions
Office of the Assistant Secretary of the Treasury
for Domestic Finance
U.S. Department of the Treasury

Be patient. If any phone number is incorrect, call (area code) 555-1212 and request the new listing.

Investments and Financial Services

1500 Pennsylvania Ave., NW
Washington, DC 20220 (202) 566-2103

Policy and legislation on the development and administration of banks and other financial institutions is handled by this office. A recent effort involved the study of the ailing thrift institutions, resulting in the formation of the Office of Thrift Supervision.

* Liquidation Litigation

Office of Corporate Communications
Federal Deposit Insurance Corporation (FDIC)
550 17th St., NW, Room 7118
Washington, DC 20429 (202) 898-6996

This office oversees liquidation litigation among FDIC-insured banks, as well as liquidation and insurance activities for the Federal Savings and Loan Insurance Corporation (FSLIC). Outside counsel is hired to help litigate an estimated 40,000 cases annually. Contact this office for more information on liquidation litigation issues.

* Office of Thrift Supervision District Offices

One Financial Ct., Boston, MA 02111 or P.O. Box 9106 GMF, Boston, MA 02205-9106; (617) 542-0150

One World Trade Center, FL 103, New York, NY 10048; (212) 912-4600

One Riverfront Center, 20 Stanwix St., Pittsburgh, PA 15222-4893; (412) 288-3400

P.O. Box 105217, Atlanta, GA 30348-5217; (404) 888-0771

P.O. Box 598, Cincinnati, OH 45201-0598; (513) 852-7500

P.O. Box 60, Indianapolis, IN 46206-0060; (317) 465-1600

111 E. Wacker Dr., Suite 700, Chicago, IL 60601-4360; (312) 565-5700

907 Walnut St., Des Moines, IA 50309; (515) 281-1100

P.O. Box 619026, Dallas/Fort Worth, TX 75261-9026; (214) 714-8500

P.O. Box 828, Topeka, KS 66601-0828; (913) 233-5300

P.O. Box 7165, San Francisco, CA 94120; (415) 616-1500

1501 Fourth Ave., FL 19, Seattle, WA 98101-1693; (206) 340-2300

* Office of Thrift Supervision Publications

Office of Thrift Supervision
U.S. Department of the Treasury
1700 G. Street, NW
Washington, DC 20552 (202) 906-6682

Thrift Activities Regulatory Handbook. Addresses all of the major areas of concern to examiners and supervisors regarding the safety and soundness of regulated institutions. (Price: $50 - members; $75 - non-members)

Compliance Activities Regulatory Handbook. Addresses compliance examination matters related to consumer protection laws and regulations, such as the Truth in Lending Act, and those related to the public interest, such as the Community Reinvestment and Bank Secrecy Acts. (Price: $25 - members; $25 - non-members)

Service Corporations Regulatory Handbook. Addresses issues that primarily arise in dealing with service corporations and discusses relationships between those entities and the parent thrift. (Price: $50 - members; $75 - non-members)

Holding Companies Regulatory Handbook. Addresses areas of particular interest when reviewing holding company operations. (Price: $50 - members; $75 - non-members)

Trust Activities Regulatory Handbook. Designed to assist in the examination of those thrift institutions and their subsidiaries that engage in trust activities. (Price: $50 - members; $75 - non-members)

Application Processing Regulatory Handbook. Contains guidance on how to process and analyze thrift and holding company applications. (Price: $50 - members; $75 - non-members)

Federal Financial Institutions Examination Council (FFIEC) EDP Handbook. This handbook is published by the FFIEC and is currently used by all financial regulatory agencies as a guide for conducting EDP examinations. (Price: $75)

Membership Directory of Institutions. Published during the first quarter of each year, this free directory lists all savings institutions insured by the Savings Association Insurance Fund (SAIF) and the Federal Deposit Insurance Corporation (FDIC), as well as those institutions that are members of the Federal Home Finance Board but are not federally insured. For a copy, call (202) 898-8909.

Compliance: A Self-Assessment Guide. This guide will help thrift institutions develop or improve internal policies and programs to ensure compliance with consumer and public interest laws. ($20)

CEBA Guide: Questions and Answers. The questions answered in this guide are those most commonly asked by examination and supervisory staff during the Comprehensive Equality Banking Act of 1987 (CEBA) training programs. ($3)

Bulletin Subscription Series. Thrift Bulletins provide national guidance to alert regulated institutions to practices or events of concern to the thrift industry. The annual subscription price is $175.

* Problem Banks

Office of Corporate Communications
Federal Deposit Insurance Corporation (FDIC)
550 17th Street, NW
Room 7118
Washington, DC 20429 (202) 898-6996

The FDIC uses the Uniform Interagency Bank Rating System to evaluate a bank's performance with respect to capital adequacy, asset quality, management/administration, earnings, and liquidity (known by the acronym CAMEL). Banks are rated on a scale from 1 to 5, with 1 indicating a very sound banking institution. Banks with ratings of 4 or 5 are considered to be problem banks, possibly requiring FDIC intervention and payoff. Individual bank ratings are not available to the public. Contact this office for more information about the rating system.

* Registration and Reporting

Public Files Registration and Disclosure
Federal Deposit Insurance Corporation (FDIC)
1776 F Street
Room 250
Washington, DC 20006 (202) 898-8909

The FDIC enforces the registration and reporting provisions of the 1934 Securities Exchange Act among FDIC-insured, nonmember banks. Banks with assets totalling more than $1 million and 500 or more security holders are required to file an initial registration statement which summarizes the bank's history, business operations, and overall financial condition. These banks are also required to file periodic reports which include Reports of Condition and Income Statements. The registration statements and periodic reports are filed and maintained in this office.

Be patient. If any phone number is incorrect, call (area code) 555-1212 and request the new listing.

Money

* Congressional Coins

Customer Service Center
U.S. Mint
U.S. Department of the Treasury
10001 Aerospace Dr.
Lanham, MD 20706 (301) 436-7400

The following Congressional coins can be purchased from the U.S. Mint:

Gold Five Dollar Congressional Coin. Features a rendition of the U.S. Capitol Dome and the spread eagle design from the Old Senate Chamber. Available as a proof for $215 and uncirculated for $200.

Olympics Half Dollar Coins. $9.50 and $7.50.

U.S. Mint proof coin sets and uncirculated sets can also be purchased. Contact this Center for more information.

* Counterfeit and Forgery Statistics

Public Affairs
U.S. Secret Service
U.S. Department of the Treasury
1800 G St., NW
Washington, DC 20223 (202) 435-5708

A statistical summary of activity within the Secret Service investigative area is available, including information on counterfeiting, check forgery, bond forgery, fraud, protective intelligence, and other criminal and noncriminal acts. Data includes investigative activity by fiscal year; counterfeiting trends of notes and coins; trends of counterfeit plant operations, including the production of counterfeit notes, office machine copies, food coupons, false IDs, and domestic and foreign currency; counterfeit notes received by major city and dollar amount; arrests; and forged checks and bonds received.

* Counterfeiting Investigations

Counterfeit Division
Office of Investigations
U.S. Secret Service
U.S. Department of the Treasury
1800 G St., NW
Washington, DC 20223 (202) 435-5756

Information may be obtained concerning facts about paper currency and recognizing counterfeit bills and coins. Guidelines are also available on what to do when you receive a counterfeit bill. For additional information, contact Public Affairs at (202) 435-5708.

* Counterfeit Money and Forged Checks

Superintendent of Documents
Government Printing Office
Washington, DC 20402 (202) 783-3238

Know Your Money describes and illustrates ways to recognize counterfeit bills and forged U.S. government checks. Price $1.75; order number S/N 048-006-00010-8.

* Currency and Stamp Production

Associate Director, Chief Operations Director, Operations
Bureau of Engraving and Printing
U.S. Department of the Treasury
14th and C Sts., SW
Washington, DC 20228 (202) 874-2002

The Bureau of Engraving and Printing designs, engraves, and prints United States paper currency; United States postage and revenue stamps; and miscellaneous engraved items for approximately 75 departments and independent agencies of the Federal Government. White house invitations, commissions, diplomas, certificates, identification cards, and liquor strip stamps are some of the approximately 700 miscellaneous products printed by the Bureau.

* Daily Treasury Statement

Superintendent of Documents
Government Printing Office
Washington, DC 20402 (202) 783-3238

Published daily except Saturdays, Sundays, and holidays, the subscription service, *Daily Treasury Statement,* outlines the cash and debt operations of the United States Treasury. The annual price is $204. (S/N 748-003-00000-2)

* Damaged Money Redemption

Office of Currency Standards
Bureau of Engraving and Printing
U.S. Department of the Treasury
Room 344A, BEPA
P.O. Box 37048
Washington, DC 20013 (202) 874-2194

All mutilated currency may be sent to the above address where trained personnel will determine if it can be exchanged at face value. All final decisions for redemption of this currency are made by the Treasurer of the United States. Currency should be sent by registered mail to the P.O. box address above.

* Federal Check Cashing Period

Office of the Assistant Commissioner Headquarters Operations
Financial Information
U.S. Department of the Treasury
3700 East West Highway, Room 509 A
Hyattsville, MD 20782 (202) 874-8800

Effective October 1, 1989, all Treasury checks must be cashed or deposited within 12 months of issuance for payment to be valid. If this time lapses, the holder of the check must contact the agency from where the check was drawn and ask to have another check issued. Entitlement of the funds never ceases. This program within the FMS is called Limited Payability.

* Federal Collections

Office of the Assistant Commissioner Federal Finance
Financial Management Service
U.S. Department of the Treasury
401 14th St., SW, Room 504
Washington, DC 20227 (202) 874-6720

The Financial Management Service (FMS) is responsible for the largest collection system in the world--approximately $1 trillion annually. These collections include tax deposits, custom duties, loan repayments, fines, services, and proceeds from leases. FMS provides transaction processing to Federal agencies, manages the systems by which Government collections are made, and sets policy for the use of the collection systems.

* Federal Open Market Committee

Division of Monetary Affairs
Federal Reserve System, Room B3022
20th St. and Constitution Ave., NW
Washington, DC 20551 (202) 452-3761

The Federal Open Market Committee exercises broad control over the growth of the nation's money supply and is in charge of the System's operations in both domestic securities markets and in foreign exchange markets. The Committee is composed of the seven members of the Board of Governors and five Reserve Bank presidents, including the president of the New York Reserve Bank, which conducts foreign and domestic operations for the Committee. For information on the nation's money supply and securities markets, contact this office.

* Federal Payments

Office of the Assistant Commissioner Regional Operations
Financial Management Service

Be patient. If any phone number is incorrect, call (area code) 555-1212 and request the new listing.

Investments and Financial Institutions

U.S. Department of the Treasury
401 14th St., SW
Washington, DC 20227 (202) 874-6740

The issuance of payments is a central financial operation of the Financial Management Service. The Service disburses approximately 800 million payments annually, and issues payments for virtually all Federal civilian agencies, or approximately 85 percent of total Government payments. Payments are issued from seven Regional Financial Center locations on the basis of payment vouchers certified by Federal agencies.

* Forgery Investigations

Forgery Division
Office of Investigations
U.S. Secret Service
U.S. Department of the Treasury
1800 G St., NW
Washington, DC 20223 (202) 435-5708

Since there are more than 800 million U.S. Government checks issued each year, they are attractive to criminals who specialize in stealing and forging them. Retail merchants often unknowingly aid the forger by failing to request proper identification. For additional information on precautions to take, contact Public Affairs at (202) 435-5708.

* Gold and Silver Bullion Coins

Public Information Office
U.S. Mint
U.S. Department of the Treasury
633-3rd St., NW
Washington, DC 20220 (202) 874-6450

The American Eagle Gold and Silver Bullion Coins are being minted to purchase as investments. The gold coins are available in one ounce, half-ounce, quarter-ounce and tenth-ounce weights. The silver coins are minted only in the one ounce size. To determine their worth, simply check listings in your daily newspaper. The coins may be purchased from various brokerage companies, participating banks, coin dealers, and precious metal dealers. To obtain a listing of sales locations in your area, contact the office above.

* Lost Government Checks

Office of the Assistant Commissioner
Headquarters Operations
Financial Information
U.S. Department of the Treasury
3700 East West Highway (202) 874-8800
Hyattsville, MD 20782 (301) 436-6349

To make a claim against Treasury for a lost check or one you believe has been cashed with a forged endorsement, you first must contact the agency that issued the check and obtain a copy of it along with a claim form. The agency will then contact Treasury to handle your claim. The office above ultimately handles the claim, but requests that it be contacted only when all else fails.

* Monetary Policy

Division of Monetary Affairs
Federal Reserve System (FRS)
Room B3022
20th St. and Constitution Ave., NW
Washington, DC 20551 (202) 452-3761

This FRS division analyzes issues in monetary policy, including open market operations, member bank discount borrowing at Federal Reserve Banks, and changes in reserve requirements.

* The Center for Applied Financial Management

The Center for Applied Financial Management
1411 K Street
Washington, DC 20227 (202) 376-1300

This center is part of the Financial Management Service (FMS). The center provides specialized financial training to federal financial and non-financial staffs and industry partners through on-site training courses, seminars, conferences and carefully designed on the job training. This training is designed to teach the use of current and future financial management tools, techniques and policies to improve financial management government-wide.

Be patient. If any phone number is incorrect, call (area code) 555-1212 and request the new listing.

Credit Unions

* CAMEL Rating System

Office of Examination and Insurance
National Credit Union Administration
1776 G Street, NW
Room 6601C
Washington, DC 20456 (202) 682-9640

Assigned following an examination of a credit union's safety and soundness, a CAMEL rating is a reliable indicator of future success or failure. The CAMEL rating looks at the key areas of a credit union's operations--capital adequacy, asset quality, management, earnings, and liquidity. Ratings range from Code 1, which is good, to Code 5, which is poor. For more information, contact the Office of Examination and Insurance.

* Central Liquidity Facility

National Credit Union Administration (NCUA)
1776 G Street, NW, Room 818
Washington, DC 20456 (202) 682-9600

The Central Liquidity Facility (CLF) is a mixed-ownership government corporation governed by the NCUA Board. CLF is a central source of short-term funds for the credit union system. It has a loan portfolio of $120.4 million and provides lines of credit totalling $13.5 million. To become a CLF member, a credit union or its designated agent must purchase stocks equal to one-half of one percent of the credit union's unimpaired capital and surplus.

* Chartering

Department of Insurance
National Credit Union Administration (NCUA)
1776 G Street, NW, Room 6601C
Washington, DC 20456 (202) 682-9640

The NCUA Board grants Federal Credit Union charters to groups sharing a common bond of occupation or association, or to groups within a well-defined neighborhood, community, or rural district. A preliminary investigation is made to determine if certain minimum standards are met before granting a federal charter. Call or write to the office listed above for more information on the chartering process.

* Consumer Complaints

National Credit Union Administration
1776 G St., NW
Washington, DC 20456 (202) 682-9650

The Administration investigates the complaints of members who are unable to resolve problems with their federal credit union where these problems relate to a possible violation of the Federal Credit Union Act or to consumer protection regulations. Complaints should be sent directly to the appropriate office.

* Credit Union Information

Public Information
National Credit Union Administration (NCUA)
1776 G St., NW
Washington, DC 20456 (202) 682-9650

Several publications are available to assist you in starting a federal credit union. *Chartering and Organizing of Federal Credit Unions* provides basic information about credit unions and their membership policies. The *Federal Credit Union Handbook* is intended to assist the board of directors in conducting the credit union's affairs. Contact the regional NCUA office near you for further information.

* Credit Union Supervision

Department of Supervision
National Credit Union Administration
1776 G St., NW, Room 6611

Washington, DC 20456 (202) 682-9640

Supervisory activities are carried out through annual examiner contacts and through periodic policy and regulatory releases from the Administration. The Administration also maintains a warning system designed to identify emerging problems as well as to monitor operations between examinations.

* Examiner Training Programs

National Credit Union Administration
1776 G St., NW
Washington, DC 20456 (202) 682-9600

This office offers classroom, as well as on-the-job training for new examiners, and offers technical seminars for senior examiners. These seminars cover such topics as consumer lending, investments, and dealing with problem case credit unions. The training programs are open to state supervisory personnel without charge.

* Liquidation

Office and Examination
Department of Insurance
National Credit Union Administration
1776 G Street, NW
Room 6601C
Washington, DC 20456 (202) 682-9640

Liquidation of federal credit unions is conducted according to the manual *Voluntary Liquidation Procedure for Insured Federal Credit Unions*. The major responsibility of the board is to conduct the liquidations in such a manner that the interest of the members, the insurance fund, and the creditors of the credit union are safeguarded. For information regarding liquidations, contact the Department of Insurance.

* Financial Performance Report

Public Information
National Credit Union Administration
1776 G St., NW
Washington, DC 20456 (202) 682-9650

The *Financial Performance Report* (FPR), an analytical tool created for management and supervisory purposes, is designed to provide a long-term picture of the financial trends and operating results of the credit union. The *FPR* is updated twice a year, with the December *FPR* providing percentile rankings that show where the credit union stands in relation to all other credit unions in key areas of financial performance. This publication breaks down the *FPR* and explains what each category means. A member has the right to inspect a federal credit union's books and records, including the board of directors' minutes.

* Insured Funds

Department of Insurance
National Credit Union Administration (NCUA)
1776 G Street, NW
Room 6601C
Washington, DC 20456 (202) 682-9640

Share insurance is mandatory for federal credit unions and for state-chartered credit unions in many states, while optional for other state-chartered credit unions that meet NCUA standards. Credit union members' accounts are insured up to $100,000. The National Credit Union Share Insurance Fund (NCUSIF) requires each insured credit union to place and maintain a one-percent deposit of its insured savings with the NCUSIF. The publication, *Your Insured Funds*, offers further explanation concerning insurance.

* Listing of Federal Credit Unions

Freedom of Information Officer
National Credit Union Administration (NCUA)
1776 G Street, NW

Be patient. If any phone number is incorrect, call (area code) 555-1212 and request the new listing.

Investments and Financial Services

Room 7355
Washington, DC 20456 (202) 682-9700

A master list of the names and addresses of all federally insured credit unions is available for public inspection in the Washington and regional offices. Copies of the list may be obtained at a nominal cost by writing to the Freedom of Information Officer. You may also receive a free list of National Credit Union Administration (NCUA) regional offices.

* Publications

National Credit Union Administration (NCUA)
1776 G St., NW, Room 7261
Washington, DC 20456 (202) 682-9700

A listing of NCUA publications is available from the Administrative office. These publications include the annual report, the credit union directory, as well as technical reports, such as *Chartering and Organizing of a Federal Credit Union*. There is a nominal charge for each publication.

Be patient. If any phone number is incorrect, call (area code) 555-1212 and request the new listing.

Stocks and Bonds

* Accounting

Office of the Chief Accountant
U.S. Securities and Exchange Commission
450 5th St., NW
Washington, DC 20549   (202) 272-2050

The SEC's Chief Accountant consults with representatives of the accounting profession and other standard-setting bodies that promote new or revised accounting and auditing standards. One of the Securities and Exchange Commission's major objectives is to improve accounting and auditing standards and to maintain high standards of professional conduct by the independent accountants. This office also drafts rules and regulations that dictate the requirements for financial statements, and rules which require that accountants examining financial statements filed with the SEC be independent of their clients. For more information accounting procedures, contact this office.

* American Depository Receipts

Office of International Corporate Finance
U.S. Securities and Exchange Commission
450 5th St., NW
Washington, DC 20549   (202) 272-3246

U.S. investors who are interested in foreign securities may purchase American Depository Receipts. These are negotiable receipts, registered in the name of a U.S. citizen, which represent a specific number of shares of a foreign corporation. For more information about American Depository Receipts, contact this office.

* Annual Reports to Shareholders

Public Reference Branch
U.S. Securities and Exchange Commission
450 5th St., NW, Room 1024   (202) 272-7450
Washington, DC 20549-1002   (202) 272-7459 (TTD)

Although not a required SEC filing, the *Annual Report to Shareholders* is the main document most public companies use to give information about corporations to shareholders. It is usually a state-of-the-company report which includes an opening letter from the Chief Executive Officer, financial data, results of continuing operations, market segment information, new product plans, subsidiary activities and research and development activities on future programs. Some filings are available in printed form, but all are available on microfiche.

* Annual (10-K) Reports: Investment Information

Public Reference Room
U.S. Securities and Exchange Commission
450 5th St., NW
Washington, DC 20549   (202) 272-7450

Many companies whose stock is traded over the counter or on a stock exchange must file "full disclosure" reports on a regular basis with the SEC. The annual report, or *Form 10-K,* is the most comprehensive of these. It describes and contains statistical information on the company's business operations, properties, parents, and subsidiaries; its management, including their salaries and their security ownership in the company; any matters which have been submitted to a vote of shareholders; and significant legal proceedings which involve the company. *Form 10-K* also contains the audited financial statements of the company, including a balance sheet, an income statement, and a statement of where funds come from and how they are used. The public may obtain copies for a small fee by visiting or writing the office above.

* Arbitration Procedures

Publications Section
Printing Branch, Stop C-11
U.S. Securities and Exchange Commission
Washington, DC 20549   (202) 272-7040

Arbitration Procedures is a free publication available from this office which discusses procedures for disputes with brokerage firms involving financial claims.

* Broker/Dealer Registration

Registration
U.S. Securities and Exchange Commission (SEC)
450 5th Street, NW
Washington, DC 20549   (202) 272-3900

The registration of brokers and dealers who solicit and execute securities transactions is an important part of the work of the SEC. Broker-dealers must abide by the securities laws, the rules of the self-regulatory organization of which they are members, and SEC rules. Registrations must be kept up to date and must reflect any changes in financial conditions over time. The registration form shows: form of organization; if it is a corporation, the date and state of incorporation, and class of equity security; if it is a sole proprietorship, the person's residence and Social Security number; if it is a successor to a previous broker or dealer, the SEC file number of the predecessor; persons with controlling interests; how the business is financed; the firm's or person's standing with the SEC and other regulatory agencies, including disclosure of having made false statements to the SEC in the past, been convicted in the last 10 years of a related felony, been prohibited in the last 10 years from financial activities, aided anyone in violating related laws or rules, been barred or suspended as a broker-dealer, been the subject of a cease and desist order, been associated with a similar firm that went bankrupt, information about the person or business that maintains the applicant's records and holds funds of the applicant or its customers; details about companies which control or are controlled by the applicant; whether the applicant is an investment adviser; types of business done (such as floor activity, underwriting or mutual fund retailing); descriptions of any nonsecurity business; and information about principals, including positions, securities held, Social Security numbers, education and background. Customers have the right to expect that trades will be executed promptly and that the broker will try to secure the best price, for example. They should expect to receive written confirmation of trading, with information including the date of the transaction, the identity of the security bought or sold, and the number of shares, units, or principal amount of the security. Customers can expect information on the cost of the transaction, including commissions charged, from the broker.

* Broker-Dealer Revocations

Office of Chief Counsel
Division of Market Regulation
U.S. Securities and Exchange Commission
450 5th Street, NW
Washington, DC 20549   (202) 272-3000

In the case members of an exchange or association, registered brokers or dealers, or individuals associated with any such firm, the Commission can issue an order specifying alleged illegal acts or practices and can direct that a hearing take place. If the Commission finds that the law has been violated, it may impose sanctions or bar a firm from conducting a securities business in interstate commerce or on exchanges, or an individual from association with a registered firm.

* Capital Formation for Small Businesses

The Office of Small Business Policy
Division of Corporation Finance
U.S. Securities and Exchange Commission
450 5th Street, NW
Washington, DC 20549   (202) 272-2644

The Securities and Exchange Commission's main responsibility under the securities laws is to protect investors and to make sure the capital markets operate fairly and orderly. However, the Commission is careful not to let its regulations impair capital formation by small businesses. Therefore, the SEC has taken a number of steps to help small businesses raise capital and to ease the burden of undue regulations under the federal securities laws. The Commission is continually examining other ways to meet these goals. For more information, contact this office.

Be patient. If any phone number is incorrect, call (area code) 555-1212 and request the new listing.

Investments and Financial Services

* Commission Meetings

Office of the Secretary
U.S. Securities and Exchange Commission
450 5th St., NW
Washington, DC 20549 (202) 272-2600

The Commission meets several times each month to debate and decide on regulatory issues. Like other regulatory agencies, the Commission has two types of meetings. Under the Government in the Sunshine Act, meetings may be open to the public and to members of the press; however, if it is necessary to protect the Commission's ability to conduct investigations and/or protect the rights of individuals and entities which may be the subject of Commission inquiries, meetings may be closed. Commission meetings are generally held to discuss and resolve issues the staff brings before the Commissioners. Issues may be interpretations of federal securities laws, amendments to existing rules under the laws, new rules (often to reflect changed conditions in the marketplace), actions to enforce the laws or to discipline those subject to direct regulation, legislation to be proposed by the Commission, and matters concerning administration of the Commission itself. Issues may be resolved in the form of new rules or amendments to existing ones, enforcement actions, or disciplinary actions. Notices of open and closed Commission meetings and the agendas of open meetings are published the preceding week in the *SEC News Digest*. For more information on weekly meetings, contact this office.

* Confirmation of Transaction

Office of Consumer Affairs
U.S. Securities and Exchange Commission
450 5th St., NW
Washington, DC 20549 (202) 272-7440
Consumer Telecommunications for the deaf (TTY-Voice) (202) 272-7065

There is a fundamental distinction between a broker and a dealer. The broker is the customers' agent who buys or sells securities for them. The broker owes the customer the highest fiduciary responsibility and can charge only the agency commission that the customer agreed to. On the other hand, a dealer acts as a principal and buys securities from or sells securities to customers. The dealer's profit is the difference between the prices for which the securities are bought and sold. The dealer normally will not disclose the fee or commission charged for services rendered. The law requires that the customer receive a written "confirmation" of each securities transaction. This confirmation discloses whether the securities firm is acting as a dealer (a principal for its own account) or as a broker (an agent for the customer). If the firm is acting as a broker, the confirmation must also disclose the broker's compensation from all sources, as well as other information about the transaction. For more information contact your regional office or contact the above SEC office.

* Consumer Complaints

Office of Consumer Affairs and Information Services
Investor Services Branch
U.S. Securities and Exchange Commission
450 5th St., NW
Washington, DC 20549 (202) 272-7440
Consumer Telecommunications for the deaf (TTY-Voice) (202) 272-7065

The Investor Services Branch reviews complaints from the investing public nationwide concerning their dealings with the securities industry and typically obtains written responses from firms mentioned in the complaint. Complaints regarding banks, broker-dealers, investors, junk bonds, investment advisers, and so on are all available for review by the general public. This office strives to improve and upgrade the SEC's complaint processing effort, analyze trends that surface as a result of complaints received, and increase the Commissions' activities in consumer education. Information suggesting a possible violation of federal securities laws is referred to appropriate Commission staff. When complaints entail private disputes between parties, Commission staff attempt informally to assist the parties in resolving the problem. The SEC also welcomes inquiries and reports about questionable securities practices. Investors should remember, however, that the SEC cannot function as a collection agency or directly represent them in a dispute. Direct investor complaints and grievances to the office above.

* Consumer's Financial Guide

Publications Section
Printing Branch, Stop C-11
U.S. Securities and Exchange Commission
Washington, DC 20549 (202) 272-7040

The free publication, *Consumer's Financial Guide*, contains basic information on choosing investments and keeping them safe, trading securities, and the different protections guaranteed by law. To obtain this publication contact this office.

* Corporate Finance Policy

Office of Corporate Finance
Office of the Assistant Secretary of the Treasury
for Domestic Finance
U.S. Department of the Treasury
1500 Pennsylvania Ave., NW
Washington, DC 20220 (202) 535-6334

This office is the Department of the Treasury's effort to influence the financial policy directives of corporations. The staff can help answer questions on the Treasury's guidelines on anything from leverage buyouts to junk bonds.

* Corporate Reorganization

Division of Corporation Finance
U.S. Securities and Exchange Commission (SEC)
450 5th St., NW
Washington, DC 20549 (202) 272-2800

Reorganization proceedings in the U.S. Courts are begun by a debtor, voluntarily, or by its creditors. Federal bankruptcy law allows a debtor in reorganization to continue operating under the court's protection while it attempts to rehabilitate its business and work out a plan to pay its debts. If a debtor corporation has publicly issued securities outstanding, the reorganization process may raise many issues that will directly affect the rights of public investors. The SEC is authorized to appear in any reorganization case and to present its views on any issue. However, the Commission gets involved only in proceedings which involve significant public investor interest--protecting public investors holding the debtor's securities, and participating in legal and policy issues concerning public investors. The SEC also continues to address matters of traditional Commission expertise and interest relating to securities. Where appropriate, it reviews reorganization plan disclosure statements and participates in some aspects of law enforcement. The court can confirm a reorganization plan if it is accepted by creditors for at least two-thirds of the amounts of allowed claims, more than one-half the number of allowed claims, and at least two-thirds in amount of the allowed shareholder interest. The biggest protection for public investors is the required disclosure statement issued by the debtor to seek votes on the reorganization plan. In addition, plans involving publicly held debtors usually provide for issuing new securities to creditors and shareholders which may be exempt from registration. For more information on reorganization, contact this office.

* Corporate Reporting

Public Reference Room
U.S. Securities and Exchange Commission (SEC)
450 5th St., NW
Washington, DC 20549 (202) 272-7450

Companies that want their securities registered and listed for public trading on an exchange have to file a registration application with both the exchange and the SEC. Companies that meet a specific size test, whose equity securities are traded over-the-counter, must file a similar registration form. Commission rules dictate the content and nature of these registration statements and require certified financial statements. Once their securities are registered, companies must file annual and other periodic reports to keep the file updated. Also, issuers must send certain reports to shareholders if they request them. Reports may be read at the public reference rooms, and copied there for a small fee, or obtained at reasonable rates from a copying service under contract to the Commission. For more information on registration, contact this office.

* Directory of Companies

Public Reference Branch
U.S. Securities and Exchange Commission
450 5th St., NW, Room 1024 (202) 272-7450
Washington, DC 20549-1002 (202) 272-7459 (TTD)

The annual *Directory of Companies* is a compendium of all companies which are required to file annual reports with the Securities and Exchange Commission under the Securities Exchange Act of 1934. It lists companies alphabetically and classifies them by industry group according to the *Standard Industrial Classification Manual of the Budget* (1992). It is available for $28 from: Superintendent of Documents, Government Printing Office, Washington, DC 20402; (202) 783-3238.

Be patient. If any phone number is incorrect, call (area code) 555-1212 and request the new listing.

Stocks and Bonds

* EDGAR User Manual

The Office of EDGAR Management
U.S. Securities and Exchange Commission, Operations Center
6432 General Green Way
Alexandria, VA 22312-2413 (202) 272-3806

Investors, securities analysts, and other members of the public have access to EDGAR information through a variety of subscriptions and services. A copy of the *EDGAR Filing Manual*, which provides detailed information and directions for making filings on EDGAR, is available by contacting this office.

* Electronic Security Processing

The Office of EDGAR Management
U.S. Securities and Exchange Commission (SEC)
Operations Center
6432 General Green Way
Alexandria, VA 2231202413 (202) 272-3806

The EDGAR management system permits corporations to make their required filings electronically via direct transmission, diskettes, or tapes to the Commission. EDGAR will help to speed up the processing and handling of the 11 million pages of disclosure information that are currently filed with the SEC each year. Private companies are encouraged to offer filer training and support on a competitive basis. The public portions of these filings are available in hardcopy printouts and on microfiche. For more information on the EDGAR Management system, contact this office.

* Enforcement Activities

Division of Enforcement
U.S. Securities and Exchange Commission (SEC)
450 5th St., NW
Washington, DC 20549 (202) 272-2900

The SEC's enforcement activities are designed to make sure that the Federal securities laws administered by the Commission are obeyed. These activities include measures to:

- Compel obedience to the disclosure requirements of the registration and other conditions of the act;
- Stop fraud and dishonesty in buying and selling securities;
- Obtain court orders prohibiting acts and practices that operate as a fraud upon investors or otherwise violate the laws;
- Suspend or revoke the registrations of brokers, dealers, and investment companies and investment advisers who willingly engage in fraudulent acts and practices;
- Suspend or bar from association persons associated with brokers, dealers, investment companies, and investment advisers who have violated any conditions of the Federal securities laws; and
- Prosecute persons who have engaged in fraudulent activities or other willful violations of those laws.

In addition, attorneys, accountants, and other professionals who violate the securities laws can loose their right to practice before the Commission. To this end, private investigations are conducted into complaints or other suspected securities violations. Evidence of law violations is used to revoke registration or used in Federal courts to control dishonest activities. If the evidence points to criminal fraud or some other type of intentional violation of the securities laws, the facts are referred to the Attorney General for criminal prosecution of the offenders. The Commission may assist in such prosecutions. For more information on enforcement contact this office.

* Exchange Registration

Registration
U.S. Securities and Exchange Commission (SEC)
450 5th St., NW
Washington, DC 20549 (202) 272-7250

Registration with the Commission is required of National securities exchanges with a substantial securities trading volume, brokers and dealers who conduct securities business in interstate commerce, transfer agents, clearing agencies, government and municipal brokers and dealers, and securities information processors. To register, exchanges must show that they are organized to comply with the provisions of the statute as well as the rules and regulations of the Commission. The registering exchanges must also show that their rules ensure fair dealing and protect investors. Each exchange is a self-regulatory organization. Its rules must provide for the expulsion, suspension, or other disciplining of member broker-dealers for unjust and unfair trading conduct.

Exchanges shall have full opportunity to establish self-regulatory measures ensuring fair dealing and investor protection. However, the SEC approves--by order, rule, or regulation--any rule changes of exchanges concerning various activities and trading practices if necessary. Exchange rules and revisions, proposed by exchanges or by the Commission, generally reach their final form after discussions between representatives of both bodies. For more information, contact this office.

* Fair and Orderly Markets

Division of Market Regulation
U.S. Securities and Exchange Commission (SEC)
450 5th St., NW
Washington, DC 20549 (202) 272-3000

The SEC supervises the securities markets and the conduct of securities professionals. It also serves as a watchdog to protect against fraud in the sale of securities, illegal sales practices, market manipulation, and other violations of investors' trust by broker/dealers. Generally, individuals who buy and sell securities professionally must register with a self-regulatory organization (SRO), meet certain qualifications requirements, and obey the rules of conduct adopted by the SRO. The broker/dealer firms for which they work must in turn register with the SEC and obey its rules relating to financial conditions and sales practices. They also must obey the rules of the exchange they belong to, and the rules of the National Association of Securities Dealers.

* Foreign Securities

Office of International Corporate Finance
U.S. Securities and Exchange Commission (SEC)
450 5th St., NW
Washington, DC 20549 (202) 272-3246

Foreign corporations that want to sell securities in the U.S. must register those securities with the SEC. They are generally subject to the same rules and regulations that apply to securities of U.S. companies, although the nature of information which foreign companies make available to investors may be somewhat different.

* Form 10-Q: Financial Background on Companies

Public Reference Room
U.S. Securities and Exchange Commission (SEC)
450 5th St., NW
Washington, DC 20549 (202) 272-7450

The *Form 10-Q* is a report filed quarterly by most public companies, containing information that is important for investors to know. It includes unaudited financial statements and provides a continuing view of the company's financial position during the year. The information includes the income statement; balance sheet; description of important changes since the previous quarter; legal processing; changes in securities; default upon senior securities; and other important events. The report must be filed for each of the first three fiscal quarters and is due within 45 days of the close of the quarter. For more information on these reports, contact this office.

* Fraudulent Securities Schemes

Publications Section
Printing Branch, Stop C-11
U.S. Securities and Exchange Commission (SEC)
Washington, DC 20549 (202) 272-7040

Several free publications are available through the Securities and Exchange Commission that warn investors against various fraudulent schemes. These include *How to Avoid Ponzi and Pyramid Schemes*, and *Warning to Investors About Get-Rich-Quick Schemes*. To obtain copies of these publications contact the above office.

* Help in Choosing an Investment

Office of Public Affairs
U.S. Securities and Exchange Commission (SEC)
450 5th St., NW
Washington, DC 20549 (202) 272-2650

If you are thinking about investing your money, you might need assistance in making the most suitable choices for your needs. The SEC is a good source of information on securities with many publications, a public reference room, disclosure reports, and ready information on how to protect yourself.

Be patient. If any phone number is incorrect, call (area code) 555-1212 and request the new listing.

Investments and Financial Services

* Holding Companies Acquisitions

Division of Investment Management
Office of Public Utility Regulation
U.S. Securities and Exchange Commission (SEC)
450 5th Street, NW
MS 10-16
Washington, DC 20549 (202) 272-3018

To be authorized by the SEC, holding companies and their subsidiaries that acquire securities and utility assets must meet the following standards: 1) The acquisition must not tend toward interlocking relations or concentrating control to the point that it is harmful to investors or the public interest; 2) Any fees, commissions, or other payments for the acquisition must be reasonable; 3) The acquisition must not complicate the capital structure of the holding company system or harm system functions; and 4) The acquisition must help develop an integrated public utility system that is economical and efficient. Contact this office for more information on these standards.

* Holding Companies Issuance and Sales of Securities

Division of Investment Management
Office of Public Utility Regulation
U.S. Securities and Exchange Commission (SEC)
450 5th Street, NW
MS 10-16
Washington, DC 20549 (202) 272-3018

Proposed security issues by any holding company must be analyzed, evaluated, and approved by the SEC staff to make sure that the security issues meet the following tests: 1) They conform to the security structure of the issuer and of other companies in the same holding company system; 2) They be proportionate to the earning power of the company; 3) They must be fitting and needed to help the company's business operate economically and efficiently; 4) The fees, commissions, and other payments in connection with the issue must be reasonable; and 5) The terms and conditions of the issue or sale of the security must not damage public or investor interest.

Other regulatory provisions regulate dividend payments (in circumstances where payments might result in corporate abuses); inter-company loans; solicitation of proxies, consents, and other authorizations; and insider trading. "Upstream" loans from subsidiaries to their parents and "upstream" or "cross-stream" loans from public utility companies to any holding company in the same holding company system require Commission approval. All services performed for any company in a holding company system by a service company in that system must be rendered at a fair cost. Contact this office for more information.

* Inquiry Processing

Office of Consumer Affairs and Information Services
Investor Services Branch
U.S. Securities and Exchange Commission (SEC)
450 5th St., NW
Washington, DC 20549 (202) 272-7440
Consumer Telecommunications for the deaf (TTY-Voice) (202) 272-7065

The Commission's consumer affairs staff received approximately 49,000 investor complaints and inquiries last year. These written or telephone complaints and inquiries are routinely tracked and analyzed through a computer program. In addition to tracking basic information about the specific entity named, investor information, and dates of correspondence, special codes are used to identify the type of entity and the nature of the complaint. Consumer affairs specialists research reference materials and/or databases in order to respond to inquiries. An investor must submit a complaint in writing if he or she wants Commission assistance in obtaining an explanation or resolution. In processing the majority of written complaints, the consumer affairs specialist requests a review of the complaint by the compliance or legal department of the appropriate broker-dealer, mutual fund, or issuer, along with a report of that department's findings. This report is then reviewed to determine whether it responds to the issues raised in the complainant's letter. In many cases, the firm will take action to resolve the problem. In others, the investor's claims or allegations are disputed. Since the Commission is not authorized to serve as a judge or arbitrator, the specialist advises the investor of his or her general rights of private recourse.

* Insider Securities Trading

Superintendent of Documents
Government Printing Office
Washington, DC 20402 (202) 783-3238

The *Official Summary* is a monthly report of securities transactions and holdings reported by "insiders" (officers, directors, and certain others) under clauses and agreements in the Federal securities laws. The *Summary* sells for $10 a copy, or $78 per year for a subscription in the U.S.; and $12.50 a copy, or $87.75 per year subscription foreign.

* Insider Trading

Office of Disclosure Policy
Division of Corporation Finance
450 5th St., NW
Washington, DC 20549 (202) 272-2589

Insider trading controls curb misuse of important confidential information which is not available to the general public. Examples of such misuse are buying or selling securities to make a profit or to avoid losses based on nonpublic information--or by telling others of the information so that they may buy or sell securities--before such information is generally available to all shareholders. Fines are imposed up to three times the profit gained, or loss avoided, through the use of nonpublic information. To further control the misuse of nonpublic information, the SEC requires all company officers and directors to file an initial report with them, and with the exchange on which the stock may be listed, which shows their holdings. Thereafter, they must file reports for any month during which there was any change in those holdings. Also, profits gained from purchases and sales (or sales and purchases) of such equity securities within any six-month period may be recovered by the company or by any security holder on its behalf in U.S. District Court. Such "insiders" are also not allowed to make short sales of their company's equity securities.

* Internationalization of Capital Markets

Office of International Corporate Finance
U.S. Securities and Exchange Commission (SEC)
450 5th St., NW
Washington, DC 20549 (202) 272-3246

The SEC has made special efforts to get a wide range of viewpoints on issues that affect investors and the securities industry. One of the issues Commissioners and industry and investor representatives discuss is internationalization. The Commission has worked out agreements with several nations and is in the process of discussing the need for greater coordination among the international capital markets. For more information, contact this office.

* Interstate Holding Companies

Division of Investment Management
Office of Public Utility Regulation
U.S. Securities and Exchange Commission (SEC)
450 5th Street, NW
MS 10-16
Washington, DC 20549 (202) 272-3018

Interstate holding companies engaged, through subsidiaries, in the electric utility business or those that sell natural or manufactured gas are subject to SEC regulations on matters such as structure of the system, acquisitions, combinations, and issue and sales of securities. These systems must register with the Commission and file initial and periodic reports containing detailed information about their organization, financial structure, and operations. For more information on these reports, contact this office.

* Investment Advisers Registration

Division of Investment Management
Office of Disclosure and Investment Adviser Regulation
U.S. Securities and Exchange Commission (SEC)
450 5th Street, NW
Washington, DC 20549 (202) 272-2107

Persons or firms who make money advising others about securities investment must register with the SEC and conform to standards designed to protect investors. The Commission may deny, suspend, or revoke investment adviser registrations if, after notice and hearing, it finds that a statutory disqualification exists and that the action is in the public interest. Persons or firms can be disqualified if they are convicted for financial crimes or securities violations, mail fraud, knowingly filing false reports with the Commission, and willfully violating the Advisers Act, the Securities Act, the Securities Exchange Act, the Investment Company Act, or the rules of the Municipal Securities Rulemaking Board. In these cases, registrations are denied, suspended, or revoked. The Commission may obtain injunctions to prevent these violations of the law from happening again in the future. The SEC may also recommend prosecution by the U.S. Department of Justice for fraudulent misconduct or willful violation of the law

Be patient. If any phone number is incorrect, call (area code) 555-1212 and request the new listing.

Stocks and Bonds

or Commission rules. The Commission has adopted rules that define fraudulent, deceptive, or manipulative acts and practices. Investment advisers are required to:

- Make known the reason they are selling securities to their clients;
- Maintain books and records according to Commission rules, and
- Make books and records available to the Commission for inspections.

* Investment Company Registration

Public Reference Room
U.S. Securities and Exchange Commission (SEC)
450 5th St., NW
Washington, DC 20549 (202) 272-7450

Activities of companies who invest, reinvest, and trade in securities, and who offer their securities to the public, are subject to the following SEC regulations: 1) They must disclose their financial condition and investment policies to provide investors complete information about their activities; 2) They cannot substantially change the nature of their business or investment policies without stockholder approval; 3) They may not have officers or directors who are guilty of securities fraud; 4) Underwriters, investment bankers, or brokers must constitute only a minority of the directors; 5) They must submit management contracts (and any material changes) to security holders for their approval; 6) They may not perform transactions with their directors, officers, or affiliated companies or persons without SEC approval; 7) They are forbidden to issue senior securities except under specified conditions and terms; and 8) They are prohibited from pyramiding and cross-ownership of their securities. Other provisions involve the following: advisory fees that don't conform to an adviser's fiduciary duty; sales and repurchases of securities issued by investment companies; exchange offers; and other activities of investment companies, including special provisions for periodic payment plans and face-amount certificate companies. Investment companies must not only be registered, but must also file periodic reports and are subject to the SEC's proxy and "insider" trading rules. For more information, contact this office.

* Legal Interpretation and Guidance

Office of the Chief Counsel
Division of Corporation Finance
U.S. Securities and Exchange Commission (SEC)
450 5th St., NW
Washington, DC 20549 (202) 272-2573

The Securities and Exchange Commission is willing to help the public, prospective registrants, and others, interpret the securities laws and regulations. In this way they can help answer legal questions about how laws apply and are regulated in certain situations, and to aid them in following the laws. For example, this advice might include an informal opinion about whether the offering of a particular security is subject to registration requirements and, if it is, advice on the type of information that must go on the registration form. By interpreting the rules and laws, the SEC makes sure registrants conform to them. For help with interpreting laws, or guidance, contact this office.

* Lost and Stolen Securities

Securities Information Center, Inc.
P.O. Box 9121
Wellesley Hills, MA 02181 (617) 235-8270

Every insured bank, broker, and registered transfer agent must be registered with the Securities Information Center. The Center maintains a computerized reporting and inquiry system for lost, stolen, counterfeit, and forged securities. All FDIC-insured banks are required to contact the Securities Information Center when they take custody of stocks or bonds valued in excess of $10,000 in order to verify their validity.

* Lost and Stolen Securities Database

Division of Market Regulation
U.S. Securities and Exchange Commission (SEC)
450 5th St., NW
Washington, DC 20549 (202) 272-3000

The SEC has a computer-assisted reporting and inquiry system for lost, stolen, counterfeit, and forged securities. All insured banks and brokers, members of the federal reserve, dealers, and other securities firms are required to register with the Securities Information Center, Inc., P.O. Box 421, Wellesley Hills, MA 02181; (617) 235-8270, where a central database records reported thefts and losses. Contact this office for more information.

* Margin Trading

Office of Legal Policy and Trading Practices
Division of Market Regulation
U.S. Securities and Exchange Commission (SEC)
450 5th Street, NW
Washington, DC 20549 (202) 272-2836

The Board of Governors of the Federal Reserve System sets limits on the amount of credit available to purchase or carry securities, and then periodically reviews them. This is to make sure that to much of the nation's credit isn't used in the securities markets. While the credit restrictions are set by the Board, the SEC handles investigations and enforcement.

* Market Investigations

Division of Market Regulation
Office of Inspections and Financial Responsibility
U.S. Security and Exchange Commission (SEC)
450 5th Street, NW
Washington, DC 20549 (202) 272-2830

SEC regional offices and its Division of Market Regulation conduct surprise investigations to check the books and records of regulated people and organizations to make sure their business practices are legal. Inquiries are also conducted into changes in the market, especially stocks which don't appear to result from general market trends or from known developments affecting the issuing company. For more information, contact your regional office or contact or the office above.

* Market Surveillance

Market Surveillance
Division of Enforcement
U.S. Securities and Exchange Commission (SEC)
450 5th St., NW
Washington, DC 20549 (202) 272-2230

Securities and Exchange Commission regulates securities trading practices in the exchange and the over-the-counter markets, and it has adopted regulations which, among other things, 1) define acts or practices which constitute a "manipulative or deceptive device or contrivance" prohibited by the statute; 2) regulate short selling, stabilizing transactions, and similar matters; 3) regulate the hypothecation of customers' securities; and 4) provide safeguards with respect to the financial responsibility of brokers and dealers. For more information on market surveillance, contact this office.

* Meeting Notes

Office of the Secretary
U.S. Securities and Exchange Commission (SEC)
450 5th St., NW
Washington, DC 20549 (202) 272-2600

For audiovisual tapes of the open meeting minutes, send your request in writing to this office.

* New Rules: Securities

Publications Unit
U.S. Securities and Exchange Commission (SEC)
450 5th Street, NW
C3-38
Washington, DC 20549 (202) 272-7460

For copies of recently adopted rules contact this office.

* Opening An Account

Public Reference Room
U.S. Securities and Exchange Commission (SEC)
450 5th St., NW
Washington, DC 20549 (202) 272-7450

Before opening an account with a broker, talk with registered representatives at several firms to find the person who best suits your needs. It is added protection to know that most broker/dealers registered with the SEC are members of the Securities Investor Protection Corporation, a nonprofit membership corporation which administers laws to help protect investors securities and funds held in brokerage accounts. Also, before choosing a broker, to get more factual information about the firm itself, you may order a copy of the firm's registration statement (Form BD) from the office above.

Be patient. If any phone number is incorrect, call (area code) 555-1212 and request the new listing.

Investments and Financial Services

* Opinions and Orders

The Office of Administrative Law Judges
U.S. Securities and Exchange Commission (SEC)
450 5th St., NW
Washington, DC 20549 (202) 272-7636

Associate of Adjudication, General Council
U.S. Securities and Exchange Commission (SEC)
450 5th St., NW
Washington, DC 20549 (202) 272-7400

The administrative law judges are responsible for scheduling and conducting hearings on administrative proceedings instituted by others. Opinions and orders resulting from these hearings are prepared by the Office of Opinions and Review. For more information on these hearings contact either of the offices above.

* Ponzi or Pyramid Schemes

Office of Consumer Affairs and Information Services
Investor Services Branch
U.S. Securities and Exchange Commission (SEC)
450 5th St., NW
Washington, DC 20549 (202) 272-7440
Consumer Telecommunications for the deaf (TTY-Voice) (202) 272-7065

The Securities and Exchange Commission will provide warnings against investing in a Ponzi or pyramid scheme. These schemes are varied, but usually promise very high yield, quick return, a "once in a lifetime" opportunity, and the chance to "get in on the ground floor." To notify the Securities and Exchange Commission of a fraudulent scheme and for further information, contact this office.

* Proxy Filings

Public Reference Branch
U.S. Securities and Exchange Commission (SEC)
450 5th Street, NW
Room 1024 (202) 272-7450
Washington, DC 20549-1002 (202) 272-7459 (TTD)

A proxy statement is a document which lets people know who holds stock in a company so they can cast educated votes on matters which are brought up at company meetings. Typically, a security holder is also given a "proxy" who can vote his or her securities if the holder does not attend the meeting. Definitive (final) copies of proxy statements and proxies are filed with the Commission at the time they are sent to security holders. Preliminary proxy filings are nonpublic upon filing, but may be obtained under FOIA once the definitive proxy has been filed and released. Some definitive filings are available in printed copy and on microfiche.

* Proxy Solicitations

Office of Chief Counsel
Division of Corporation Finance
U.S. Securities and Exchange Commission (SEC)
Washington, DC 20549 (202) 272-2573

The SEC administers laws which check the votes from holders of registered securities, both listed and over-the-counter, to elect directors and/or to approve corporate action. Solicitations, whether by management or minority groups, must give all important information needed for holders to vote. Holders also must be given an opportunity to vote "yes" or "no" on each matter. In a contest for control of corporate management, the rules require the names and interests of all "participants" in the proxy contest be made known so that holders can vote intelligently on corporate actions that require their approval. The Commission's rules require that proposed proxy material be filed early so the Commission can examine it to be sure all the information needed is given. In addition, the rules allow shareholders vote at the annual meetings. For more information on proxy solicitations, contact this office.

* Publications Listing

Publications
U.S. Securities and Exchange Commission (SEC)
450 5th Street, NW
Mail Stop C-11
Washington, DC 20549 (202) 272-7040

You can obtain a listing of current SEC publications by visiting Publications in Room 3C38 or writing to the office above.

* Reference Microfiche

Public Reference Branch
U.S. Securities and Exchange Commission
450 5th Street, NW, Room 1024 (202) 272-7450
Washington, DC 20549-1002 (202) 272-7459 (TTD)

The public may use the following reference microfiche in the Public Reference Room:

Workload List by File Name. Includes cumulative history and a quarterly supplement.
Workload List by File Number. Includes a cumulative history and a quarterly supplement.
SEC Public Reference. An alphabetical list of all registrants since 1934, including numbers of all files for each named registrant.
Ownership Report System: Cumulative. Contains the cumulative data in the *Official Summary of Security Transactions and Holdings* of corporate affiliates and "insiders."

* Registered Company Disclosure Statements (Prospectus)

Public Reference Room
U.S. Securities and Exchange Commission
450 5th St., NW
Washington, DC 20549 (202) 272-7450

Before any company offers its securities for sale to the general public, (with certain exceptions) it must file with the SEC a registration statement known as a "prospectus." The prospectus contains the basic business and financial information on an issuer dealing with a particular security that's being offered to help investors evaluate an investment and thereby helps them make an educated investment decision. In its registration statement, the company must provide information on the nature of its business, the company's management, the type of security it offers and its relation to other securities the company may have on the market, and the company's financial statements as certified by independent public accountants. Many companies must continue to update this information periodically, even if no new securities are being offered, and copies of the prospectus must be provided to investors. The SEC reviews registration statements for accuracy and completeness. Investors who purchase securities and suffer losses have important recovery rights under the law if they can prove that there was incomplete or inaccurate disclosure of important facts in the registration statement or prospectus. Investors may sue to recover losses through the courts if false or misleading statements were made in the prospectus. Some filings are available in paper form, and all filings are available on microfiche from the above office.

* Registration Exemptions for Securities

Registration
U.S. Securities and Exchange Commission
450 5th St., NW
Washington, DC 20549 (202) 272-3900

In general, registration requirements apply to securities of both domestic and foreign issuers, and to securities of foreign governments (or their instrumentalities) sold in domestic securities markets. However, some securities and transactions are exempt from registration provisions. Among these are:

- Private offerings to a limited number of persons or institutions who already have access to the information that registration would disclose and who do not propose to redistribute the securities;
- Offerings restricted to residents of the state in which the issuing company is organized and doing business;
- Securities of municipal, state, federal, and other governmental instrumentalities as well as charitable institutions, banks, and carriers subject to the Interstate Commerce Act;
- Offerings not exceeding certain specified amounts according to regulations of the Commission; and
- Offerings of "small business investment companies" made in accordance with rules and regulations of the Commission.

Whether or not the securities are exempt from registration, antifraud provisions apply to all sales of securities involving interstate commerce or the mails. For more information, contact this office.

* Regulations: Securities, Public Holding Companies

Publications Section

Be patient. If any phone number is incorrect, call (area code) 555-1212 and request the new listing.

Stocks and Bonds

Printing Branch, Stop C-11
U.S. Securities and Exchange Commission
Washington, DC 20549 (202) 272-7040

Regulation S-X is a basic accounting regulation which along with a number of opinions issued as *Accounting Series Releases*, governs the form and content of most of the financial statements filed with the Commission. *Regulation S-X* contains a form and requirements for financial statements of the Securities Act of 1933, the Securities Exchange Act of 1934, the Public Utility Holding Company Act of 1935, the Investment Company Act, and the Energy Policy and Conservation Act. There is no charge for copies of these statutes, but a 9" x 12" self-addressed envelope with $1.58 postage must be enclosed with each order.

* Reviewing a Prospectus

Public Reference Room
U.S. Securities and Exchange Commission (SEC)
450 5th St., NW
Washington, DC 20549 (202) 272-7450

If you are considering an investment in an open-end investment company, unit investment trust, or variable annuity, you should obtain and read a current prospectus before looking at other sales literature. Do not hesitate to seek advice if there is anything in the prospectus you do not understand. And if you do buy shares in the company, save the prospectus to refer to in the future. Some of the things the prospectus will tell you are the company's investment objectives--in other words, how it is designed to provide income, protect capital, minimize taxes, and so forth, the amount of any sales charges and the procedures for redeeming shares, and what risks may be involved in placing your money in that particular company. Registration is there to give you the facts about the company you're dealing with, and to thereby help you to make an informed decision. Keep in mind, however, that the Commission does not supervise the investment activities of these companies and that regulation by the Commission does not imply safety of investment. To obtain a current prospectus, contact this office.

* Revocations of Securities Registration

Office of Chief Counsel
Division of Market Regulation
U.S. Securities and Exchange Commission (SEC)
450 5th St., NW
Washington, DC 20549 (202) 272-3000

The SEC can deny registration to securities firms and, in some cases, may impose sanctions against a firm and/or individual in a firm for violation of Federal securities laws (such as manipulation of the market price of a stock, misappropriation of customer funds or securities, or other abuse of customer trust). The Commission polices the securities industry through its own inspections and by working with other securities groups. Brokers and dealers who violate regulations risk suspension or loss of registration with the Commission (and thus the right to continue conducting an interstate securities business) or suspension or expulsion from a self-regulatory organization. For more information, contact this SEC office.

* Rulemaking

Office of Public Affairs
U.S. Securities and Exchange Commission (SEC)
450 Fifth Street NW
Washington, DC 20549 (202) 272-2650

Rulemaking is one of the most common activities the divisions perform. The rules and registration forms that the SEC uses must constantly be evaluated and reviewed to make sure they are as practical and efficient as possible. If a particular rule appears to be burdensome or isn't achieving its objective, a staff members can recommend changes to the Commissioners. Many suggestions for rule changes follow consultation with industry representatives and others who are affected. The Commission normally gives advance public notice when they are planning to adopt new rules or registration forms, or to amend forms so that interested members of the public can comment on them. For information on rulemaking contact the individual divisions at the SEC.

* Section 13F Securities

Public Reference Branch
U.S. Securities and Exchange Commission (SEC)
450 5th Street, NW
Room 1024 (202) 272-7450
Washington, DC 20549-1002 (202) 272-7459 (TTD)

The quarterly publication, *13F Securities*, is a list of all current Section 13(f)

securities, that is, securities of a class described in Section 13(d)(1) of the Exchange Act.

* Securities and Exchange Docket

The Commerce Clearing House, Inc.
4025 West Peterson Avenue
Chicago, IL 60646 (312) 583-8500

Sorg Inc.
11 Eighth Ave.
New York, NY 10011 (212) 741-6600

The *SEC Docket* is a weekly collection of the full text of SEC releases, including the full texts of *Accounting Series* releases, corporate reorganization releases, and litigation releases. It is sold for $245 per year or $225 per year for two years. Subscriptions may be ordered from either of the companies listed above.

* Securities and Exchange Annual Reports

Superintendent of Documents
Government Printing Office (GPO)
Washington, DC 20402 (202) 783-3238

The First through Fiftieth SEC annual reports to Congress are out of print and available only for reference purposes in the SEC and Regional Offices. The *Fifty-First Annual Report (1985)* sells for $3.50, the *Fifty-Second (1986)* sells for $4.75, the *Fifty-Third (1987)* sells for $4.50, and the *Fifty-Fourth (1988)* sells for $5. These most recent annual reports are available at from the GPO.

* Securities and Exchange: How It Works

Publications Section
Printing Branch
Stop C-11
U.S. Securities and Exchange Commission (SEC)
Washington, DC 20549 (202) 272-7040

The Work of the SEC discusses the laws administered by the Commission, its organization, and public information about it. To obtain a copy contact this office.

* Securities and Exchange Information Line

SEC Information Line
U.S. Securities and Exchange Commission (SEC)
450 5th St., NW
Washington, DC 20549 (202) 272-5624

The Security and Exchange Commission's Information Line provides general information about the SEC 24 hours a day, 7 days a week. Different digit codes correspond to messages that callers might be interested in. The directory of messages and digit codes is as follows:

General Information
SEC Information Line Directory (10)
SEC Address and Business Hours (15)
SEC Organizational Structure (20)
Public Affairs (25)
Public Reference Room (30)
Publications (33)

Office of Consumer Affairs and Information Services
Investor Inquiries (35)
Investor Complaints (40)
Freedom of Information Act Requests (45)
Privacy Act Requests (50)

Division of Corporation Finance
Small Business Filers (55)
International Corporate Finance (60)

Division of Investment Management
Investment Adviser Registration (65)
Investment Company Registration (70)
Applications for Exemptive Relief (75)
Electronic Filing of Form N-SAR (80)

Division of Market Regulation
Broker-Dealer Registration (85)

Be patient. If any phone number is incorrect, call (area code) 555-1212 and request the new listing.

Investments and Financial Services

Lost and Stolen Securities (90)
Trading Suspensions (95)

For operator assistance, press zero. Note that callers using rotary dial telephones cannot access messages in the system. These callers will automatically be switched to an operator for assistance.

* Securities and Exchange Monthly Statistical Review

The Office of Economic Analysis
U.S. Securities and Exchange Commission (SEC)
450 5th St., NW
Washington, DC 20549 (202) 272-7104

Superintendent of Documents
Government Printing Office
Washington, DC 20402 (202) 783-3238

The *SEC Monthly Statistical Review* contains data on odd lot and round lot transactions, block distributions, working capital of U.S. corporations, assets of noninsured pension funds, Rule 144 filings, and 8K reports. The Office of Economic Analysis collects, processes, and publishes data on the financial condition of the securities industry, registered securities issues, and the trading volume and value of exchange-listed securities in its *SEC Monthly Statistical Review*. It is available for $19 per year from the Superintendent of Documents, Government Printing Office, Washington, DC 20402, and for more information on its contents, contact the SEC Public Reference Room.

* Securities and Exchange News Digest

Washington Service Bureau
655 15th Street, NW #1
Washington, DC 20005 (202) 508-0600

Mead Data Central - LEXIS
1850 18th Street, NW
Washington, DC 20036 (202) 785-3550

The *News Digest* is a daily summary of important SEC developments, including listings of registration, acquisition, and 8-K filings received by the Commission. It also lists certain no-action letters issued by the Commission, and time, date, place, and subject of Commission Open Meetings. The private firms listed above offer subscriptions to the *SEC News Digest*.

* Securities and Exchange Publications on Audio Cassettes

Publications Section
Printing Branch, Stop C-11
U.S. Securities and Exchange Commission (SEC)
Washington, DC 20549 (202) 272-7040

SEC publications may be taped on audio cassette at the request of individuals with handicaps. Orders should allow time for taping and processing.

* Securities and Exchange Public Reference Room

Public Reference Branch
U.S. Securities and Exchange Commission (SEC)
450 5th St., NW, Room 1024 (202) 272-7450
Washington, DC 20549-1002 (202) 272-7459 (TTD)

The SEC ordinarily makes public most of the information filed with it, including registration statements, proxy material, quarterly and annual reports, applications, and similar documents filed by corporations, mutual funds, or broker-dealers. Public Reference Rooms are located in Chicago, New York, and Washington, DC, regional offices where individuals can review and copy all public documents. In addition, copies may be ordered by writing or phoning the Commission. This information filed with the Commission is available for inspection weekdays from 9:00 a.m. to 5:00 p.m., and copies of the text of this material can be obtained from a private contractor. For a cost estimate or to order materials, contact this office.

* Securities and Public Offerings

Center for Electronic Records (NNX)
National Archives and Records Administration
Washington, DC 20208 (202) 501-5579

The National Archives maintains wide variety of archival information regarding the Securities and Exchange Commission, such as a broker-dealer directory, a corporation index system, and an investment company datafile. These datafiles, which are often continuously updated, are for sale on 9 track computer tape on a cost recovery basis. For a complete list of the data available, along with a current price list, contact the Center for Electronic Records.

* Securities Databases

Public Reference Branch
U.S. Securities and Exchange Commission (SEC)
450 5th St., NW, Room 1024 (202) 272-7450
Washington, DC 20549-1002 (202) 272-7459 (TTD)

Computer terminals which access certain SEC databases are located in the Reference Room for use by the public. You are welcome to use the terminals at any time during the business hours of the Public Reference Room. The databases are as follows:

Workload Teleprocessing Display System (WRKD). Provides an up-to-date listing of filings made by registrants. Filings are maintained on this index for approximately 40 months. Information on earlier filings may be found by using the history microfiche.

Securities Reporting System (SIRS). Provides information on securities transactions by company officers, directors, and beneficial owners. For each transaction, SIRS will list the trading date, name of the owner, number of shares involved, price per share, SEC received date, and the type of transaction (stock dividend, acquisition by gift, private purchase, open market purchase, stock split, etc.).

Proposed Sale of Securities Inquiry System (PSSI). An online retrieval system which lets the public access information filed on Forms 144. The system contains six months of historical data. Monthly updates are done around the 10th of each month. Searching by either the Issuer's Name or the Seller's Name or both, you will receive information such as the name of the issuer, the seller, the class of security being sold, date acquired and acquisition codes, number of securities to be sold, market value, shares outstanding, and more.

Proceedings and Litigation Action Display System (PLAD). An online, public system capable of reviewing public litigation data. The data displayed includes the type of action, name, address, jurisdiction, action date, violation, and disposition. The types of actions are federal, state and Canadian, National Association of Securities Dealers, and Stock Exchange.

* Securities Laws: Legal Assistance

The Office of Small Business Policy
Division of Corporation Finance
U.S. Securities and Exchange Commission (SEC)
450 5th St., NW
Washington, DC 20549 (202) 272-2644

The staff of the Office of Small Business Policy, as well as the personnel of the SEC Regional Offices, will assist you with any questions you may have regarding federal securities laws. For information about state securities laws, contact the appropriate state securities commissioner, whose office is usually located in each capital city.

* Securities Markets and Information Technology

Office of Technology Assessment (OTA)
600 Pennsylvania Ave., SE
Washington, DC 20510 (202) 228-6772

Fundamental changes are taking place in the securities and related financial markets that will affect the structure and operations of the exchanges, the links between markets, the nature of the products traded, and the strategies by which they are traded. OTA is currently studying the role that new information technologies--computers and telecommunications--play in these accelerating changes. Contact Vary Coates, the project director, for more information.

* Securities Rules and Regulations

Superintendent of Documents
Government Printing office
Washington, DC 20402-9325 (202) 783-3238

The entire text of the Commissions's rules and regulations is available from several private publishers of legal information, and many books on this subject are available at public libraries. Volumes of *Title 17 of the Code of Federal Regulations of April 1988* are available to the public. Rules (forms and interpretive releases also) under the securities laws are available as follows:

Be patient. If any phone number is incorrect, call (area code) 555-1212 and request the new listing.

Stocks and Bonds

Chapter I - Parts 1 to 199. These regulations administered by the Commodity Futures Trading Commission are $14.

Chapter II - Parts 200 to 239. This includes the SEC organization, conduct and ethics, information and requests, rules of practice, Regulation S-X and S-K and the Securities Exchange Act of 1933 for $14.

Chapter III - Parts 240 to End. This includes the Securities Exchange Act of 1934, the Public Utility Holding Company, and the Trust Indenture Investor Protection Corporation Acts for $21.

All three volumes for $54.

* Securities Violations: Litigation, Actions, and Proceedings

Public Reference Branch
U.S. Securities and Exchange Commission (SEC)
450 5th Street, NW
Room 1024   (202) 272-7450
Washington, DC 20549-1002   (202) 272-7459 (TTD)

The quarterly *Litigation, Actions and Proceedings Bulletin* contains information of official actions with respect to securities violations reported to the Commission. In addition, the *Bulletin* contains a supplement which lists the names of individuals reported as being wanted on charges of violations of law in connection with securities transactions. Contact this office for more information on obtaining copies.

* Small Business and the SEC

Publications Section
Printing Branch
Stop C-11
U.S. Securities and Exchange Commission (SEC)
Washington, DC 20549   (202) 272-7040

The free booklet, *Q&A: Small Business and the SEC,* discusses capital formation and the federal securities laws and is designed to help you understand some of the basis, necessary requirements that apply when you wish to raise capital by selling securities. It answers such questions as:

What are the federal securities laws?
Is any special help available for a small business that wants to sell its securities?
Should my company "go public"?
How does my small business "go public"?
If my company becomes "public," what are its disclosure obligations?
Are there legal ways to sell securities without registering with the SEC?
Are there state law requirements in addition to those under the federal securities laws?
Where can I go for more information?

* Small Business Policy

The Office of Small Business Policy
Division of Corporation Finance
U.S. Securities and Exchange Commission (SEC)
450 5th St., NW
Washington, DC 20549   (202) 272-2644

This office directs the SEC's small business rulemaking goals, reviews and comments on the impact the SEC rule proposals have on small issuers, and serves as a liaison with Congressional committees, government agencies, and other groups concerned with small business. Information on security laws that pertain to small business offerings may be obtained from this office.

* Standards for Securities Registration

Registration
U.S. Securities and Exchange Commission (SEC)
450 5th St., NW
Washington, DC 20549   (202) 272-3900

Registering securities with the SEC does not stop the sale of stock in risky, poorly managed, or unprofitable companies. Nor does the Commission approve or disapprove securities on their merits. The only standard which must be met when registering securities is adequate and accurate disclosure of required information on the company and its securities it wants to sell. The fairness of the terms, the issuing company's chances of successful operation, and other factors affecting the merits of investing in the securities have no bearing on the question of whether or not securities may be registered. Contact this office for more information on SEC securities standards.

* Statutes

Publications Section
Printing Branch
Stop C-11
U.S. Securities and Exchange Commission (SEC)
Washington, DC 20549   (202) 272-7040

The U.S. Securities and Exchange Commissions's mission is to administer federal securities laws to try to protect investors. The purpose of these laws is to make sure that the securities markets are fair and honest and to provide the means to enforce the securities laws through sanctions where necessary. Free copies of the following laws administered by the Commission are available from the above office:

Securities Act of 1933
Securities Exchange Act of 1934
Public Utility Holding Company Act of 1935
Trust Indenture Act of 1939
Investment Company Act of 1940
Investment Advisers Act of 1940

* Statutory Sanctions

Division of Enforcement
U.S. Securities and Exchange Commission (SEC)
450 5th St., NW
Washington, DC 20549   (202) 272-2900

Commission investigations are conducted privately to determine whether there is valid evidence of a law violation; whether action should begin to determine if a violation actually occurred; and, if so, whether some sanction should be imposed. The following provisions of the law, along with disclosure requirements, tend to inhibit fraudulent stock promotions and operations to help build the public's confidence in securities investments. When facts show possible fraud or other law violations, the laws provide several courses of action the Commission may take:

- Civil injunction: where the SEC may apply to a U.S. District Court for an order forbidding the acts or practices claimed to violate the law or Commission rules
- Administrative remedy, where the Commission may take specific action after hearings. It may issue orders to suspend or expel members from exchanges or over-the-counter dealers association; deny, suspend, or revoke broker-dealer registrations; or censure for misconduct or bar individuals from employment with a registered firm temporarily or permanently.

* Stop Orders

Office of Chief Counsel
Division of Corporation Finance
U.S. Securities and Exchange Commission (SEC)
450 5th St., NW
Washington, DC 20549   (202) 272-2573

The SEC may conclude that the lack of important information in some registration statements appears to be deliberate attempts to conceal or mislead. They may also conclude there is an attempt to conceal or mislead if the deficiencies are not corrected through the informal letter process. In these cases, the Commission may decide that it is in the public interest to conduct a hearing to develop the facts by evidence which determines if a "stop order" should be issued to refuse or suspend the statement. Although losses which may have been suffered in the purchase of securities are not restored to investors by the stop order, the Commissions's order stops future public sales. Also, the decision and the evidence on which it is based may help notify investors of their rights and aid them in their own recovery suits. For more information on stop orders, contact this SEC office.

* Tender Offer Solicitations

Office of Tender Offers
Division of Corporation Finance
U.S. Securities and Exchange Commission (SEC)
450 5th St., NW
Washington, DC 20549   (202) 272-3097

The Commission requires that important information be made known by anyone seeking to acquire over five percent of a company's securities by direct purchase or by tender offer. This information must also be given by anyone seeking shareholders to accept or reject a tender offer. Thus, as with the proxy rules, public investors holding stock in these corporations may make more informed

Be patient. If any phone number is incorrect, call (area code) 555-1212 and request the new listing.

Investments and Financial Services

decisions on takeover bids. These disclosure provisions are supported by certain other controls which help ensure investor protection in tender offers.

* The October 1987 Market Break

The Office of Consumer Affairs
U.S. Securities and Exchange Commission (SEC)
450 5th St., NW
Washington, DC 20549 (202) 272-7440

The Office of Consumer Affairs participated with other SEC organizations in developing the staff report on the October 1987 market break. The office analyzed the "market break complaints" that the SEC and Self-regulatory organizations received from October 14th through the 30th in 1987. Over 1,500 written complaints resulted from the market break. An additional 9,300 telephone complaints and questions were received during a six-week period, beginning October 19. Findings resulting from the consumer complaint analysis are contained in Chapter 12 of the staff report entitled, *The October 1987 Market Break*. The report is available for $38 from the Superintendent of Documents, Government Printing Office, Washington, DC 20402; (202) 783-3238.

* Transaction Complaint Investigations

Division of Enforcement
U.S. Securities and Exchange Commission (SEC)
450 5th St., NW
Washington, DC 20549 (202) 272-2900

Under the laws it administers, the SEC investigates complaints and other suspected law violations in securities transactions. Most of the Commission's investigations are private and are often about selling securities without registration or distorting facts about securities for sale are distorted or left out. Other types of inquiries relate to manipulating market prices of securities, misappropriating or illegally hypothecating customers' funds, conducting a securities business while bankrupt, broker-dealers buying or selling securities from or to customers at unfair prices, and broker-dealers who don't treat customers fairly. Inquiries and complaints by investors and the general public are the main sources of leads for detecting law violations in securities transactions. For more information on securities violations, contact this office.

* Treasury Securities

Federal Reserve Bank of Richmond
Public Services Department
P.O. Box 27622
Richmond, VA 23261 (804) 697-8000

On behalf of the U.S. Treasury, the Federal Reserve Banks handle public sales, transfers, and redemptions of U.S. government securities. *Investing In Govern-*

ment Securities outlines procedures for purchasing marketable U.S. government securities and is available free from the Federal Reserve Bank of Richmond, or by contacting any Federal Reserve Bank for additional information.

* Treasury Securities Booklet

Federal Reserve Bank of Richmond
Public Services Department
P.O. Box 27622
Richmond, VA 23261 (804) 697-8000

The booklet, *Buying Treasury Securities at Federal Reserve Banks*, which provides detailed information on buying treasury bills, notes, and bonds, can be purchased for $4.50 from this office. (Book only at this PO Box)

* Trust Indentures

Division of Corporation Finance
U.S. Securities and Exchange Commission (SEC)
450 5th St., NW
Washington, DC 20549 (202) 272-2800

The SEC ensures that bonds, debentures, notes, and similar debt securities offered for public sale and issued under trust indentures with more than $7.5 million of securities outstanding at any one time, conform to certain statutory standards. In an effort to protect the rights and interests of purchasers, the SEC works to:

- Prohibit the indenture trustee from conflicting interests which might affect its duties on behalf of the securities purchasers,
- Require the trustee to be a corporation with as little combined capital and surplus as possible,
- Impose high standards of conduct and responsibility on the trustee,
- Stop special collection of certain claims the issuer owes the trustee if there is default,
- Assure that the issuer supply the trustee with evidence of following indenture terms and conditions (such as those relating to the release or substitution of mortgaged property, issue of new securities, or satisfaction of the indenture), and
- Require the trustee to provide reports and notices to security holders.

They also work to make sure that the security holder's have a right to sue individually for principal and interest, except under certain circumstances. To help security holders communicate with each other on their rights as security holders, a list must be maintained. The SEC examines applications to qualify for trust indenture for compliance with the law and the Commission's rules. For more information on trust indentures, contact this office.

Be patient. If any phone number is incorrect, call (area code) 555-1212 and request the new listing.

Government Bonds, Bills and Notes

* Education Savings Bonds

U.S. Savings Bonds Division
U.S. Department of the Treasury
1800 K. St., NW
Washington, DC 20226 (202) 377-7925

The new education savings bond program permits qualified taxpayers to exclude from their gross income all or a portion of the interest earned on eligible Series EE savings bonds issued after 1989. To qualify for this exclusion, tuition and other post-secondary educational expenses must be incurred by the taxpayer, the taxpayer's spouse, or the taxpayer's dependent at postsecondary educational institutions. These institutions are those that meet federal financial aid program standards. In addition, there are income limitations on participation in the program. Contact this office for more information on the program.

* Federal Debt Management

Federal Finance
Office of the Assistant Secretary of the Treasury
for Domestic Finance
U.S. Department of the Treasury
1500 Pennsylvania Ave., NW
Room 2334
Washington, DC 20220 (202) 566-5806

Federal debt instruments are administered by this office, including public debt securities, nonmarketable public issues, federal agency securities, and government-sponsored agency securities.

* Government Securities Claims

Claims Section
Office of Securities and Accounting Services
Bureau of the Public Debt
U.S. Department of the Treasury
300 13th St., SW
Washington, DC 20239 (202) 874-4000

This office handles claims for lost, stolen, mutilated, or destroyed government securities.

* Retirement Bonds

Bureau of the Public Debt
U.S. Department of the Treasury
200 Third St.
Parkersburg, WV 26106-1328 (304) 420-6516

Retirement plan bonds and individual retirement bonds are no longer being issued. Redemption tables with the current value of the bonds, beginning with those issued in 1963, are available.

* Savings Bond Buyer's Guide

Office of Public Affairs
Marketing and Communications Branch
U.S. Savings Bonds Division
U.S. Department of the Treasury
1800 K. St., NW
Washington, DC 20226 (202) 377-7925

Building Security, Fulfilling Dreams: U.S. Savings Bonds Buyer's Guide describes the information you need to purchase savings bonds, such as available series and denominations, interest rates, where to buy, registration, annual limitation on purchases, redemption, tax status, exchange of series HH bonds, and safety features.

* Savings Bonds Information Guide

Consumer Information Center
P.O. Box 100

Pueblo, CO 81002

The *Savings Bonds Question and Answer Book* explains everything about the savings bond program, including information on purchase, interest, maturity, replacement, redemption, exchange, and taxes. (451V - $.50)

* Savings Bonds: Lost, Stolen or Destroyed

Bond Consultant Branch
Bureau of the Public Debt
U.S. Department of the Treasury
200 Third St.
Parkersburg, WV 26106-1328 (304) 420-6112

If your Savings Bonds are lost, stolen, or destroyed, you can apply for free replacement to the address above.

* Savings Bonds Rate Information

U.S. Savings Bonds Division
U.S. Department of the Treasury
1800 K. St., NW
Washington, DC 20226 (800) US-BONDS

For the current market rate of U.S. Savings Bonds, call the above number 24 hours a day, seven days a week.

* Savings Bonds Statistics

Market Analysis Office
Planning and Product Development Branch
U.S. Savings Bonds Division
U.S. Department of the Treasury
1800 K. St., NW
Washington, DC 20226 (202) 377-7925

To obtain statistics on sales, redemption, and retention of U.S. Savings Bonds, contact the office above.

* Savings Bonds Volunteer Activities

Office of Banking and Volunteer Activities
U.S. Savings Bonds Division
U.S. Department of the Treasury
1800 K. St., NW
Washington, DC 20226 (202) 377-7925

Volunteers within the Savings Bond marketing effort are the chief executive officers within industry who promote the purchase of bonds through payroll deductions. Contact the above office for additional information.

* Savings Bonds: Where to Buy

Savings Bonds Operations
Bureau of the Public Debt
U.S. Department of the Treasury
200 Third St.
Parkersburg, WV 26106-1328 (304) 420-6112

Series EE Bonds may be purchased over the counter from or through most commercial banks, as well as many savings and loans and other financial institutions qualified as issuing agents. They may also be purchased in person or by mail from Federal Reserve Banks and the Treasury Department, Bureau of the Public Debt. EE Bonds may also be purchased through payroll savings plans offered by employers and through Bond-a-Month plans offered by some financial institutions. Series HH Bonds are available only on exchange for eligible Series EE/E Bonds, and U.S. Savings Notes, with total redemption values of $500 or more, and through the authorized reinvestment of the redemption proceeds of matured Series H Bonds. They are issued only by Federal Reserve Banks and the Bureau of the Public Debt.

Be patient. If any phone number is incorrect, call (area code) 555-1212 and request the new listing.

Investments and Financial Services

* Savings Notes

Bureau of the Public Debt
U.S. Department of the Treasury
200 Third St.
Parkersburg, WV 26106-1328 (304) 420-6516

If you are a holder of savings notes, you may obtain information concerning their value and redemption from the office above.

* Treasury Direct

Securities Transactions Branch
Bureau of Public Debt
U.S. Department of the Treasury
300 13th St.
Washington, DC 20239-0001 (202) 874-4000, ext. 3
Hearing Impaired TTD Line: (202) 287-4097

Treasury Direct is the book-entry system within the Bureau of the Public Debt whereby new issues of bills, notes, and bonds are maintained as accounting records in a nationwide computer system with the Treasury and Federal Reserve, rather than in definitive form as engraved certificates. This involves only securities issued since July, 1986. The entire investment portfolio is maintained in a single master account. Direct access to your account is available nationwide from Federal Reserve Banks. Direct deposit of the refund, interest, and principal interest payments is also available. Multiple automatic reinvestment options can be used, enabling you to request reinvestment for up to two years after the first maturity date without having to complete and mail a reinvestment request. To mail tenders, address to: Bureau of the Public Debt, Department N, Washington, DC 20239-1500.

* Treasury Information Line

Customer Services
Bureau of Public Debt
U.S. Department of the Treasury
300 13th St.
Washington, DC 20239-0001 (202) 874-4000

This phone number is the path to discovering all the information you need to know concerning Treasury bills, notes, bonds, securities, savings Bonds, and other related topics. The following is a guide to finding the information you need on this electronic recorded message system:

- 3 - Securities Analyst Assistance
- 4 - Savings Bond Information
- 211 - Treasury Bill Offerings
- 212 - Treasury Note and Bond Offerings
- 221 - Treasury Bill Auction Results
- 222 - Treasury Note and Bond Auction Results
- 231 - Treasury Bill General Information
- 232 - Treasury Notes and Bonds General Information
- 233 - Treasury Direct System General Information
- 241 - Forms, Statement of Account, or IRS Form 1099 (Interest Earned)
- 251 - Treasury Securities Information
- 252 - Non-Receipt of Payment: Discount, Semi-Annual Interest, or Principal
- 253 - How to Report Change of Address
- 254 - Redeem Matured Registered and Bearer Treasury Securities
- 255 - Claim for Relief: Lost, Stolen, or Destroyed Registered and Bearer Treasury Securities
- 260 - Mail Gift to Reduce Public Debt

Be patient. If any phone number is incorrect, call (area code) 555-1212 and request the new listing.

State Banking Information

With bank failures increasing and a major savings and loan crisis in progress, it makes good sense to know as much as possible about your bank and its officers. If the security of your hard-earned nest egg concerns you, it might not be a bad idea to investigate your bank through the state banking department. Each state maintains records on banks under its jurisdiction, and often this information is available to the public, as long as you know how to go about getting it.

State banking offices are the best source of information on the financial status of all state chartered banks. They will provide information on the number and location of banks in your state, their assets, and recent corporate changes (new board members, new branches). In addition, requesting a fiduciary statement can provide you with a full list of bank officers and stockholders. States also maintain information on other lending institutions, such as savings and loans and credit unions.

For whatever reasons, not all states are as forthcoming as others when it comes to providing information on specific banks and lenders. Georgia is the only state that does not provide any information on banks within its borders, while the District of Columbia began doing so in mid-1989. Colorado, North Dakota, and Washington state will only answer written requests for banking data.

The following are examples of the types of information state banking departments provide.

Reports

Most state banking departments provide some type of financial information on the institutions that they regulate. Alaska and Maine will provide performance and status reports on specific institutions, while twenty-one states provide annual reports to the public. Louisiana and Missouri provide quarterly reports containing the names and addresses of all regulated banks and savings and loan institutions. Only Alaska provides daily earnings statements on its banks.

Connecticut's annual report contains the following information:

- consolidated Call Reports for all financial institutions.
- comparative, consolidated report of conditions of financial institutions.
- listing of all banks with the names of officers and directors
- addresses of all financial institutions, including motor vehicle finance companies, licensed dealers, sale of check companies, transportation of money and valuables companies, and pre-need funeral contract companies
- number and location of branch offices.

Phone Information

Information on regulated financial institutions is available by phone in fifteen states (see specific state).

Audits

In most states, bank audits are performed every 12 to 18 months. Louisiana, Oklahoma, Oregon and Vermont perform audits every two years; Maine and Tennessee every three years; and South Dakota and Vermont vary their audits between six months and five years. Texas is the only state that performs audits every six months. Audit information is confidential in most states, but Washington and Delaware will provide such information to the public. North Dakota, California, and Maryland provide limited audit information.

Directories

The following states have directories of financial institutions available for a fee: Alaska, California, Iowa, Kansas, Missouri, and Texas.

Call Reports

Sixteen states allow public review of banking call reports -- simply a balance sheet and an income statement. Institutions must submit this information on a quarterly basis. Some states will give you this information over the telephone.

Mailing Lists

Twenty-four states provide mailing lists -- the following states at no charge: Florida, Idaho, Nevada, New Hampshire, New Jersey, North Carolina, and West Virginia.

List Of State Banking Departments

Alabama

Zack Thompson, Superintendent of Banks, State Banking Department, 101 South Union Street, Montgomery, AL 36130 (205) 242-3452. Regulates: 167 banks, 1 state chartered trust company, and national banks; 1 savings and loan. An audit of each institution is done once a year. All information is sent to the Federal Reserve in Atlanta FDIC and not made public through this agency. General information on a specific institution can be given over the phone. Information is sent to the Federal Reserve in Atlanta. A mailing list of chartered banks is available for a fee.

Alaska

Willis F. Kirkpatrick, Director, Banking Securities and Corporations, P.O. Box 110807, Juneau, AK 99811 (907) 465-2521. Regulates: 15 banks, 1 savings and loan, 2 small loan companies, 15 premium financing companies and 2 credit unions. An audit of each institution is done once a year. All information is confidential. Only quarterly earnings statements are available. All information is sent to the FDIC. A directory of all financial institutions is available for $10.

Arizona

State Banking Department, 3225 North Central Avenue, Suite 800, Phoenix, AZ 85012 (602) 255-4421. Regulates: 37 banks, 8 savings and loans, 400 mortgage brokers, 29 credit unions, 600 used car dealers. An audit of each institution is done once a year. All information on the audit is confidential. Call Reports can be reviewed in the office. All information is sent to FDIC, Federal Bank Board,

Be patient. If any phone number is incorrect, call (area code) 555-1212 and request the new listing.

Investments and Financial Services

National Credit Union Administration. A mailing list of financial institutions is available for a fee.

Arkansas

Don Clark, Assistant Bank Commissioner, State Banking Department, Tower Bldg., 323 Center St., Suite 500, Little Rock, AR 72201-2613 (501) 324-9019. Regulates 181 state chartered banks. Each institution is audited every 2 years, information is confidential. Performance reports of each bank are available for a fee. Annual reports are available as well as a mailing list of financial institutions. Some data available on magnetic tape.

California

James E. Gilleran, Superintendent of Banks, State Banking Department, 111 Pine St., Ste. 1100, San Francisco, CA 94101; (415) 557-3535. Regulates: 256 state chartered banks, 24 trust companies, 101 foreign bank departments. Each institution is audited annually to every 18 months. Information concerning a bank's assets can be given over the phone. A statistical table is available free, as well as a directory of financial institutions for a small fee.

Colorado

Barbara M.A. Walker, State Banking Commission, 1560 Broadway, Suite 1175, Denver, CO 80204; (303) 894-7575. Regulates: 161 state chartered banks, 12 industrial banks and 12 money order companies. Most information is confidential. For specific information on a bank, a written request is required.

Connecticut

Ralph M. Shulanski, Jr., Banking Commissioner, Department of Banking, 44 Capitol Ave., Hartford, CT 06106; (203) 566-4560. Regulates: state banks, and savings and loans. Each institution is audited once a year, all information is confidential. Information from Call Reports is available over the phone, or can be inspected at the office. A mailing list of all financial institutions is available.

Delaware

Keith H. Ellis, Office of the State Bank Commissioner, State Bank Commissioner, State Banking Commission, 55 E. Loockerman St., Suite 210, Dover, DE 19901; P.O. Box 1401, Dover, DE 19903; (302) 739-4235. Regulates: state chartered commercial banks, savings and loan institutions. Audits are done annually and information is made available to the public. Annual Reports are available from this office, as well as a free mailing list of all financial institutions.

District of Columbia

Office of Banking and Financial Institutions, 1250 I. St., NW, Suite 1003, Washington, DC 20005; (202) 727-1566. Regulates: all depository institutions. No information available to the public until Spring, 1993.

Florida

Department of Banking and Finance, Division of Banking, Capitol Building, Suite 1401, Tallahassee, FL 32301; (904) 488-0370. Regulates: banks, savings and loans, credit unions and international agencies. Institutions are audited once every 18 months and data is kept confidential. Information is sent to FDIC. Call Report information can be given over the phone. A mailing list of all financial institutions is available at no charge.

Georgia

Department of Banking and Finance, 2990 Brandywine Rd., Suite 200, Atlanta, GA 30341; (404) 986-1633. Regulates: state chartered banks, sellers holding companies, credit unions and international banking offices. Institutions are audited between 12 and 18 months depending on size and age. Data files are kept confidential. For specific information on a bank, you must contact the bank individually. Data files are computerized but not available to the public.

Hawaii

Clifford Hisa, Commissioner, Department of Commerce and Consumer Affairs, Division of Financial Institutions, P.O. Box 2054, Honolulu, HI 96805; (808) 548-5855. Regulates: 7 banks, 2 saving and loans, 3 trust companies and 2 escrow companies. Each institution is audited once a year and data files are kept confidential. General comparative information on banks can be given over the phone. Information is sent to FDIC. A mailing list of financial institutions is available for $.25 per page.

Idaho

Belton J. Patty, Director, Department of Finance, 700 West State St., Boise, ID 83720; (208) 334-3319. Regulates: 14 banks with 87 branches, 99 finance companies, and 52 credit unions. Audits are done between 18 months and 2 years depending on type of institution. All data files are kept confidential. Information is sent to FDIC, Federal Reserve, Federal Home Loan Bank, and the National Credit Union Administration. Annual Reports are available to the public as well as a mailing list of all financial institutions. There is no charge for the list.

Illinois

Commissioner of Bank and Trust Companies, 117 South 5th St., Reische Building, Room 100, Springfield, IL 62701; (217) 785-2837. Regulates: 825 state chartered banks. Banks are audited once a year and data files are kept confidential. Data files are sent to FDIC. A mailing list of financial institutions is available in alphabetical order, or by county order for a fee of $25.

Indiana

Charles Phillips, Director of Financial Institutions, 402 W. Washington Street, Room WO66, Indianapolis, IN 46204; (317) 232-3956. Regulates: 208 banks, 64 credit unions, 13 savings and loans and 232 consumer credit loan companies. Each institution is audited once a year, all data files are kept confidential. Data files are sent to FDIC. Annual reports are made public as well as a mailing list of all the financial institutions. The mailing list is $100. Computerized data files includes banks opened, closed, or those with a new credit license. Data files are available to the public.

Iowa

Department of Banking, 200 E. Grand St., Suite 300, Des Moines, IA 50309; (515) 281-4014. Regulates: 458 state chartered banks, 117 loan companies, and 321 holding companies. Institutions are audited every 18 months. Data files are not made public; it is sent to FDIC in Kansas City. Information from Call Reports can be obtained for a fee of $5 each. Corporate files and stockholder lists are available for public inspection at the office.

Kansas

Frank D. Dunnick, State Bank Commissioner, State Banking Department, 700 Jackson St., Topeka, KS 66603; (913) 296-2266. Regulates: 373 state banks. Each bank is audited every 18 months. Call Report information is available over the phone. A Kansas International Bank Directory is available for a fee. Call (816) 421-7941.

Kentucky

Edward B. Hatchett Jr., Commissioner, Department of Financial Institutions, 911 Leawood Dr., Frankfort, KY 40601; (502) 564-3390. Regulates: state chartered banks, credit unions, finance companies selling and registering securities, mortgage companies. Financial institutions are audited once a year. All information is kept confidential. An annual report which gives bank locations and licenses received is available for free. Some financial information and mailing list information is available in computer readable formats.

Louisiana

Larry L. Murray, Commissioner of Financial Institutions, Office of Financial Institutions, P.O. Box 94095, Baton Rouge, LA 70804; (504) 925-4660. Regulates: 208 state chartered banks, 50 savings and loans, 85 credit unions, and 1200 consumer loan companies. Institutions are audited every two years, all data files are kept confidential. A quarterly report is available for $10.

Maine

H. Donald DeMatteis, Superintendent, Bureau of Banking, Department of Professional and Financial Regulations, State House Station #36, Augusta, ME 04333; (207) 582-8713. Regulates: 19 state chartered banks, 4 savings and loans, 12 credit unions and 14 trust companies. Institutions are audited every 3 years,

Be patient. If any phone number is incorrect, call (area code) 555-1212 and request the new listing.

State Banking Information

all data files are kept confidential. Data files are sent to FDIC. Call Report and balance sheet information is available over the phone. A status report is done on an annual basis for the state legislature and is available to the public. A mailing list of all financial institutions is available as well as information in computer readable formats.

Maryland

Margie Muller, State Bank Commissioner, Department of Licensing and Regulation, 501 St. Paul Place, 13th Floor, Baltimore, MD 21202; (301) 333-6808. Regulates: 78 state chartered banks, and 18 credit unions. Institutions are audited once a year. All data files are kept confidential. Call Report information and balance sheet data can be obtained over the phone.

Massachusetts

Michael C. Hanson, Commissioner, Division of Banks, 100 Cambridge St., 20th Floor, Boston, MA 02202; (617) 727-3120. Regulates: state chartered trust companies and credit unions. Audits are done once a year and all data files are kept confidential. Call reports are available for a fee of $8 per report. A mailing list of executives is available for a fee.

Michigan

Russell S. Kropschot, Commissioner, Financial Institutions Bureau, P.O. Box 30224, Lansing, MI 48909; (517) 373-3460. Regulates: 171 banks, 372 credit unions and 3 savings and loans. Institutions are audited annually and data files are kept confidential. An annual report is available to the public as well as a mailing list and computer readable formats of the financial institutions they regulate.

Minnesota

James G. Miller, Deputy Commissioner of Commerce, Financial Examinations Division, Department of Commerce, 133 E. 7th St., St. Paul, MN 55101; (612) 296-2135. Regulates: state chartered banks, mortgage companies, small loan companies and loan and thrifts (total of 5000). Each institution is audited every 18 months and data files are kept confidential. Data files are sent to FDIC. An annual report is available as well as Call Reports for $.50 per copy.

Mississippi

Department of Banking and Consumer Finance, P.O. Drawer 23729, Jackson, MS 39205-3729; (601) 359-1031. Regulates: 100 banks, 750 small loan companies, 80 credit unions. Institutions are audited once a year and data files are kept confidential. Information from a branch application can be inspected at this office.

Missouri

Earl L Manning, Commissioner's Office, Division of Finance, Department of Ecomonic Development, Regulation and Licensing, P.O. Box 716, Jefferson City, MO 65102; (314) 751-2545. Regulates: 450 banks and 500 small loan companies. Quarterly reports are available to the public.

Montana

Financial Division, Department of Commerce, Lee Metcalf Bldg., 1520 E. 6th Ave., Room 50, Helena, MT 59620; (406) 444-2091. Regulates: 106 state banks. Each bank is audited once a year, data files are reported to FDIC. Call Report information, assets,and liability statements can be given over the phone. A mailing list is available from the Montana Bankers Association for $15, (406) 443-4121.

Nebraska

Director, Department of Banking and Finance, 1200 N. Street, Suite 311, Atrium Bldg., Lincoln, NE 68508; (402) 471-2171. Regulates: 309 commercial banks and 6 industrial banks. Each bank is audited once a year. All data files are confidential. Information is sent to FDIC. Financial information from Call Reports is available over the phone.

Nevada

L. Scott Walshaw, Department of Commerce, Financial Institutions Division, 406 E. 2nd St., Carson City, NV 89710; (702) 687-4259. Regulates: banks, savings and loans, credit unions, thrift and loan companies, consumer finance companies and debt collection organizations. Institutions are audited once a year, data files are sent to FDIC. Some financial information is available over the phone. A mailing list of all financial institutions is available for a fee. Some data files are available in computer readable formats.

New Hampshire

A. Rolland Roberge, Bank Commissioner, Department of Banking, 169 Manchester St., Concord, NH 03301; (603) 271-3561. Regulates: state chartered banks, trust companies and savings and loans. Institutions are audited every 18 months. All data files are kept confidential. An annual report and monthly bulletin is available to the public, as well as a list of pending applications. A mailing list of financial institutions is available at no cost.

New Jersey

Jeff Connor, Commissioner, Department of Banking, 20 W. State St., P.O. Box CN-040, Trenton, NJ 08625; (609) 292-3420. Regulates: commercial and savings banks, credit unions, mortgage companies and small loan companies (6,000 total). Institutions are audited once a year and data files are kept confidential. An annual report and press releases are available. A mailing list of all financial institutions can be obtained at no charge. Some data may be available on computer magnetic tape.

New Mexico

Ray Adamik, Chief Bank Examiner, Financial Institution Division, 725 St. Michaels Dr., Santa Fe, NM 87503; (505) 827-7100. Regulates: 52 state banks, 35 state credit unions, 2 savings and loans, 24 escrow companies, 63 small loan companies and 10 mortgage companies. Institutions are audited once a year, data files are kept confidential. Information regarding the total asset of an institution can be given over the phone. An annual report is available to the public.

New York

Superintendent of Banks, State Banking Department, 2 Rector St., New York, NY 10006; (212) 618-6642. Regulates: state chartered banks, commercial banks, savings and loans, credit unions, and branches of foreign banks. Audits are done on an annual basis. Most data files are confidential. Brochures are available from the consumer division.

North Carolina

William T. Graham, Commissioner of Banks, Banking Commission, Department of Economic and Community Development, P.O. Box 29512, Raleigh, NC 27626; (919) 733-3016. Regulates: 65 state chartered banks, and finance companies. Institutions are audited once a year. Data files are kept confidential and sent to FDIC. Profit/loss statements are public information. A mailing list of all financial institutions is available at no charge.

North Dakota

Gary D. Preszler, Commissioner of Banking, State Capitol, 600 E. Blvd. Ave., 13th Floor, Bismarck, ND 58505; (701) 224-2253. Regulates: 117 state chartered banks, 54 credit unions and money brokers. Institutions are audited every 3 years. Some data files are available to the public with a written request to the Commissioner. Data files are sent to FDIC. Information from a bank's Call Report is available over the phone. A mailing list of all financial institutions is available for a fee.

Ohio

John Burns, Deputy Superintendent of Banks, Division of Banks, Department of Commerce, 77 S. High St. 21st Floor, Columbus, OH 43266; (614) 466-2932. Regulates: state chartered banks. Banks are audited every 18 months. All data files are kept confidential. A copy of data is sent to FDIC. No mailing lists available.

Oklahoma

Banking Department, Oklahoma Banking Association, 4100 N. Lincoln Blvd., Oklahoma City, OK 73105; (405) 521-2783. Regulates: state chartered banks, credit unions, savings and loans, and trust companies (total 296). Institutions are

Investments and Financial Services

audited every 2 years, all data files are kept confidential. Financial information and letters of correspondence can be reviewed by the public.

Oregon

Cecil R. Monroe, Administrator, Department of Insurance and Finance, Division of Finance and Capital Securities, 21 Labor and Industry Building, Salem, OR 97310; (503) 378-4140. Regulates: banks, trust companies, pawn brokers. Audits are performed every 2 years or when needed. All data files are confidential and sent to FDIC. Annual reports are available to the public. A mailing list of all financial institutions is available.

Pennsylvania

Sarah W. Hargrove, Secretary of Banking, 333 Market St., 16th Floor, Harrisburg, PA 17101; (717) 787-6991. Regulates: state chartered savings and loans, commercial banks, and foreign banks. Audits are done on a yearly basis, all data files are confidential. Data files are sent to FDIC. An annual report is available to the public.

Rhode Island

Edward D. Tare Jr., Associate Director, Superintendent of Banking, Banking Insurance and Securities Administration, Department of Business Regulation, 233 Richmond St., Suite 231, Providence, RI 02903; (401) 277-2405. Regulates: 5 saving banks and 11 trust companies, 1 savings and loans, 46 credit unions, and 450 finance companies. Audits are done once a year. All data files are kept confidential. Data files are sent to FDIC. An annual report is available for $25. Information from a Call Report is available from the office. Balance sheet data is computerized and available in various reports.

South Carolina

Louie A Jacobs, Commissioner of Banking, Bank Examining Division, 1015 Sumter St., Room 309, Columbia, SC 29201; (803) 734-1050. Regulates: 54 state chartered banks, 2 trust companies, 30 credit unions, and 6 savings and loans. Institutions are audited once a year. All data files are confidential and sent to FDIC. Information from a Call Report is available over the phone. An annual report is available which contains a list of all financial institutions and their addresses.

South Dakota

Richard A. Duncan, Director, Division of Banking, State Capitol Building, 500 E. Capital St., Pierre, SD 57501; (605) 773-3421. Regulates: 103 banks, 3 savings and loans, 22 mortgage companies, and 19 finance companies. Audits are done annually. All data files are confidential. An annual report is available to the public.

Tennessee

Talmadge Gilly, Commissioner, Department of Financial Institutions, John Sevier Bldg., 4th Floor, Nashville, TN 37243-0705 (615) 741-2236. Regulates: state banks, credit unions, savings and loans and money orders. Audits are done every 3 years. All data files are confidential. An annual report and information on a bank's total assets are available by visiting the office.

Texas

Catherine Ghiglieri, Banking Commissioner, Department of Banking, 2601 N. Lamar Ave., Austin, TX 78705 (512) 475-1300. Regulates: 542 banks, 2 banks (uninsured), 24 foreign bank agencies. Audits are done every 6 months. All data files are confidential. Information is sent to the Federal Reserve and FDIC. Information on a Call Report is available by visiting the office. A directory of all financial institutions is available for a fee of $15.

Utah

George Sutton, Commissioner, Department of Financial Institutions, P.O. Box 89, Salt Lake City, UT 84110 (801) 538-8830. Regulates: 37 banks. Audits are done between 6 months and 5 years. All data files are kept confidential. Data files are sent to FDIC and the Federal Reserve. Information on a report of condition can be given over the phone. Annual reports are available to the public.

Vermont

Jeffery Johnson, Commissioner, Department of Banking and Insurance, 120 State Street, Montpelier, VT 05620 (802) 828-3301. Regulates: 16 banks, 3 savings and loans, 49 credit unions, 1 trust company, 119 license lenders. Audits are done every 2 years and data files are available to the public. Information is sent to FDIC. An annual report is available to the public.

Virginia

Sidney A. Bailey, Commissioner, Bureau of Financial Institutions, State Corporation Commission, P.O. Box 2AE, Richmond, VA 23205 (804) 786-3657 Regulates: state chartered banks, credit unions, industrial loans, savings and loans, and mortgage brokers. (total of 500). Audits are done once a year. Data files are kept confidential. An annual report is available containing a list of financial institutions and the proper addresses.

Washington

John L. Bley, Supervisor of Banking, Division of Banking, Department of General Administration, 1400 S. Evergreen Park Dr., SW, Suite 120, PO Box 41026, Olympia, WA 98504 (206) 753-6520. Regulates: 99 state banks. Audits are done once a year. Data can be obtained with a written request. Data files are sent to FDIC. An annual report is available to the public.

West Virginia

Sharon G. Bias, Commissioner, West Virginia Division of Banking, State Capital Complex #3, Suite 311, 1900 Kanowha Blvd., E., Charleston, WV 25305-0240 (304) 348-2294. Regulates: 167 banks, 15 industrial loans, 16 credit unions, 55 small loan companies, 12 mortgage companies. Audits are done once a year. All data files are confidential. Information from Call Reports and correspondence is available for public inspection at this office. A mailing list of all financial institutions is available for free. Some financial information and Call Reports are computerized and information is released upon request.

Wisconsin

Toby E. Sherry, Office of the Commissioner of Banking, P.O. Box 7876, Madison, WI 53707 (608) 266-1621. Regulates: finance companies, loan companies, insurance companies, adjustment services, and state chartered banks licensed as finance companies. All data files from an audit are confidential. Information available to the public includes complaints registered, rate charges and an annual report. A mailing list of all financial institutions is available for a fee. Some data is available in computer readable formats.

Wyoming

Rodger Dewey, Director, Dept. of Audit, Herschler Bldg. 3rd Floor E, Cheyenne, WY 82002 (307) 777-6600. Regulates: 33 state chartered banks with 35 total branches, 1 savings and loan, and 2 trust companies. Audits are done annually and data files are kept confidential. Information is sent to regulatory agencies. An annual report and balance sheet information is available for public inspection at this office. A mailing list of all state and national banks is available.

Be patient. If any phone number is incorrect, call (area code) 555-1212 and request the new listing.

Commodities

See also Agriculture and Farming Chapter.

* Commission-Registered Traders

Registration Unit
Commodity Futures Trading Commission
2033 K Street, NW
Room 701
Washington, DC 20581
(202) 254-3688

Futures Commission brokers, commodity trading advisors, commodity pool operators, and other companies and individuals involved in futures trading register with the CFTC. To determine is a specific company or individual is registered call the Registration Unit. For a directory listing all firms involved in futures trading contact the National Futures Association, P.O. Box 98383, Chicago, IL 60693-0001, Attention: Business Systems Group, (312) 781-1300. Send check or money order for $25 and include your telephone number on the payment.

* Commodities Futures Trading Reference Books

Library
Commodity Futures Trading Commission
2033 K Street, NW
5th Floor
Washington, DC 20581
(202) 254-5901

A collection of commodity futures trading-related materials emphasizing law, economics, business, and commodities is maintained at the library. With approval and by pre-arranged appointment, limited public use of the facility is permitted. Contact the Library for details.

* Commodity Exchange Regulation

Division of Trading and Markets
Commodity Futures Trading Commission
2033 K St., NW, Room 640
Washington, DC 20581
(202) 254-8955

Regulation of the exchanges on which commodities futures are traded is the responsibility of this division. Approval of all futures contracts traded or exchanged must also be obtained from this office. For further information, contact the Division of Trading and Markets.

* Commodity Trading Complaints

Office of Proceedings
Complaint Section
Commodity Futures Trading Commission
2033 K St., NW
Washington, DC 20581
(202) 254-3067

This unit directs proceedings to determine if reparations are to be made to persons who claim damages as a result of violations of the Commodity Exchange Act. If you believe you may have been cheated or defrauded in trading transactions, the Commission should be advised. Staff here can also confirm if there are any pending or prior legal actions involving an individual or firm registered with the Commission.

* Company Information: FOIA Requests

Freedom of Information Act Office (FOIA)
Commodity Futures Trading Commission
2033 K St., NW, Room 211
Washington, DC 20581
(202) 254-3382

Information is collected by the Commission on futures commissions brokers, dealers, commodity futures exchanges, commodities trading advisors, and other individuals and companies involved in futures trading of commodities such as agricultural products, metals, and lumber. A FOIA request must be filed to obtain information that may be disclosed from registration applications, hearing and appeal transcripts, and other records on specific individuals and firms. Contact the FOIA office listed for details.

* Futures Markets Publications and Reports

Office of Communication and Education Services
Commodity Futures Trading Commission (CFTC)
2033 K St., NW
Washington, DC 20581
(202) 254-8630

Information from the Commission's studies of the functioning of futures markets can be obtained from this office. Reports and publications about the Commission and explaining commodities futures trading include background on Commodity Futures Trading Commission (information provided when requested).

CFTC Annual Report
Economic Purposes of Futures Trading
Reading Commodity Futures Price Tables

Contact the office listed to obtain reports, publications, and information.

* International Mineral Data

Superintendent of Documents
Government Printing Office
Washington, DC 20402
(202) 783-3238

The *Minerals Yearbook, 1988: Volume 111 (Area Reports: International)* contains the latest available mineral data from more than 150 foreign countries and discusses the importance of minerals to the economies of these nations. It reviews the international minerals industry in general and its relationship to the world economy (S/N 024-004-02217-5, 1988: $44).

* Mineral Commodity Summaries 1989

Minerals Information Office
Bureau of Mines/U.S. Geological Survey
U.S. Department of the Interior
1849 C St., NW, MS 2647-MIB
Washington, DC 20240
(202) 208-5520

Mineral Commodity Summaries 1992 lists the statistics available for 90 commodities, including domestic production and uses; salient statistics - United States; recycling; import sources; tariff; depletion allowance; government stockpile; events and trends; world mine production, reserves and reserve base; world resources; and substitutes. The expert's name and phone number of each report is also listed.

* Mineral Commodity Information

Minerals Information Office
U.S. Department of the Interior
1849 C St., NW, MS 2647-MIB
Washington, DC 20240
(202) 208-5520

The Minerals Information Office is staffed by mineral experts who distribute a wide variety of mineral-related information and publications to meet and support the needs of the public, as well as government agencies and the scientific and industrial sectors. The staff provides information on the most current as well as past published reports pertaining to minerals, mining, processing, and research, as well as updated listings of current reports.

* Mineral Deposits Database

Minerals Information Office
U.S. Department of the Interior
1849 C St., MS 2647-MIB
Washington, DC 20240
(202) 208-5520

The *Personal Computer Advanced Deposit Information Tracking System Mineral Deposit Data Base* contains information on 3,000 domestic and foreign (market economy countries) mining operations, including operation data (name, company, locations, etc.) and operation status (operation type, processing and

Be patient. If any phone number is incorrect, call (area code) 555-1212 and request the new listing.

Investments and Financial Services

milling methods, capacity, etc.). The database covers 34 critical and strategic commodities, representing those deposits most significant in terms of value and tonnage.

* Mineral Production and Consumption

Information and Analysis Division
Bureau of Mines
U.S. Department of the Interior
2401 E St., NW
Washington, DC 20241 (202) 634-7131

The Bureau of Mines collects information about minerals from U.S. mining companies and mineral processing plants. Mineral production and consumption is monitored throughout the world through contacts with foreign governments, U.S. embassies, international publications, and visits to mines overseas. The Bureau employs 11 state mineral specialists through cooperative data collection agreements with the states. Three regional field offices and nine research centers also gather information. The data is then made available to the public via reports, books, and computer disks.

* Minerals: Data, Industries, and Technology

Publication Distribution, Bureau of Mines
U.S. Department of the Interior
Cochrans Mills Rd.
P.O. Box 18070
Pittsburgh, PA 15236 (412) 892-4338

The Bureau of Mines publishes several reports of investigations and information circulars that are free of charge to those interested in mineral research. *Mineral Industry Surveys* are published monthly, quarterly, and annually, presenting data on various minerals and metals. Reprints from *Minerals Yearbook 1987* are available and report on the mineral industry in the United States and abroad. *Minerals Facts and Problems* covers the technology used in the extraction and processing of minerals.

* Minerals Yearbooks Bibliography

Superintendent of Documents
Government Printing Office
Washington, DC 20402 (202) 783-3238

Yearbooks on metals and minerals are listed, as well as reports on the domestic and international industry. Free.

* Monitoring Commodity Trading

Division of Economics and Analysis
Commodity Futures Trading Commission (CFTC)
2033 K St., NW
Washington, DC 20581 (202) 254-6990

Proposed futures trading contracts are reviewed for validity by this division. It also analyzes the economic implications of CFTC regulations and policies and watchdogs trading to detect manipulations, price distortions, and congestion in the markets. For further details, contact the division listed.

Be patient. If any phone number is incorrect, call (area code) 555-1212 and request the new listing.

Taxes Federal Tax Help

Federal Tax Help

Why pay money to expensive tax preparers, accountants, and attorneys when you can get better services and information directly from the government? The government has dozens of free tax help programs very few people know about. There is a special section at the end of this chapter for state tax assistance.

Interesting Facts

Gross internal revenue collections reached $1.01 trillion in 1989 (up 8.4%) and there were 199.6 million federal tax returns and supporting documents filed. IRS issued 82.6 million refunds totaling $93.6 billion, compared to $94.5 billion last year. Last year was the seventh year taxpayers were invited to make voluntary contributions to reduce the public debt. There were 529 contributions, totaling $204,000. For tax years beginning after 1990, unnecessary cosmetic surgery will not qualify as a deductible medical expense. Cosmetic surgery is any procedure that is directed at improving the patient's appearance and does not meaningfully promote the proper function of the body or prevent or treat illness or disease.

Taxpayers Affected by Operation Desert Shield

New Publication 945, *Tax Information for Those Affected by Operation Desert Shield*, contains answers to commonly asked questions that primarily apply to newly activated reservists, as well as all other active duty U.S. military personnel and their families, citizens who had been detained by Iraq, and citizens who had to leave the Middle East because of the adverse conditions. This publication covers many issues, such as available tax relief measures for suspending examinations or collection of back taxes, extending due dates for filing an income tax return, meeting the requirements for the foreign earned income exclusion, and seeking other tax assistance.

* Actuaries Enrollment Board

Joint Board for the Enrollment of Actuaries
Internal Revenue Service (IRS)
U.S. Department of the Treasury
1111 Constitution Ave., NW
Washington, DC 20220 (202) 523-8787

Individuals who wish to perform actuarial services must enroll with this Board within the IRS. The Board is also responsible for the supervision of actuaries and their enrollment revocation after fair hearings.

* Amending Your Tax Return

Service Center Directors
Deputy Commissioner, Operations
Internal Revenue Service (IRS)
1111 Constitution Ave., NW
Washington, DC 20224 (202) 622-4255

If you find that you did not report income on your tax form, did not claim deductions or credit you could have claimed, or you claimed deductions or credits that you should not have claimed, you can correct your return by filing a Form 1040X, Amended U.S. Individual Income Tax Return. Generally, this form must be filed within three years from the date of your original return or within two years from the date you paid your taxes, whichever is later. File Form 1040X with the IRS Service Center in your area, listed elsewhere in this book.

* Collection

Office of the Assistant Commissioner
Internal Revenue Service (IRS)
1111 Constitution Ave., NW, Room 7238
Washington, DC 20224 (202) 622-5430

Collection is responsible for securing delinquent Federal tax returns and for collecting taxes where the amount owed is not in dispute, but remains unpaid. The Service Center Collection Branch (SCCB) is Collection's first point of contact with taxpayers who are delinquent in filing returns and paying taxes. They send notices to taxpayers and act on the replies. The SCCB also reviews selected Forms W-4, Employee's Withholding Allowance Certificate, to determine whether employees have the correct amount of tax withheld from their wages and directs employers to increase the amount withheld when appropriate.

* Corporation Tax Statistics

Statistics of Income Division
Internal Revenue Service (IRS)
P.O. Box 2608
Washington, DC 20013 (202) 874-0360

The following Statistics of Income reports and tapes can be purchased from the Statistics of Income Division. Prepayment is required, with checks made payable to the IRS Accounting section:

Corporation Source Book, 1987, Publication 1053, $175. This 480-page document presents detailed income statement, balance sheet, tax and investment credit items by major and minor industries and size of total assets. A magnetic tape containing the tabular statistics for 1986 can be purchased for $1,500.

Partnership Source Book, 1957-1983, Publication 1289, $30. This 291-page document shows key partnership data for 1957 through 1983, at the minor, major and division industry levels. It includes a historical definition of terms section and a summary of legislative changes affecting the comparability of partnership data during that period. A magnetic tape containing the tabular statistics for partnerships can be purchased for $300 from the National Technical Information Service, Springfield, VA 22161.

Sole Proprietorship Source Book, 1957-1984, Publication 1323, $95. This source book is a companion to that for partnerships, described above. It is a 244-page document showing key proprietorship data for 1957 through 1984. Each page contains statistics for a particular industry. A magnetic tape containing the tabular statistics can be purchased for $245.

Studies of International Income and Taxes, 1979-1983, Publication 1267, $45. This report presents information from 13 Statistics of Income studies in the international area.

Partnership Returns, 1978-1982, Publication 369, $22. This report presents previously unpublished Statistics of Income data for 1980, 1981, and 1982, as well as data previously issued in the SOI Bulletin and in other publications.

* Earned Income Credit

Taxpayer Service Division
Internal Revenue Service (IRS)
1111 Constitution Ave., NW
Washington, DC 20224 (202) 874-1460

Be patient. If any phone number is incorrect, call (area code) 555-1212 and request the new listing.

Taxes

Low income taxpayers who keep a home for themselves and at least one child may claim the Earned Income Credit (EIC). Your earned income and adjusted gross income must each be less than $22,370. You may be entitled to a refundable credit of up to $2,211. Contact the toll-free hotline in your area for more information.

* Electronic Tax Filing

Electronic Filing Division
Internal Revenue Service (IRS)
1111 Constitution Ave., NW
Washington, DC 20224 (202) 927-2400

Electronic returns take a much shorter time to process because there are fewer steps in electronic processing, and that saves time. Electronic returns have a much higher accuracy rate than paper returns. This is because electronic returns are verified by electronic filing software before they are accepted. Usually, only people who expect a refund can file electronically, but this year, the service will conduct a pilot test for accepting and processing Balance Due returns. The test is limited to taxpayers who reside in the states of Georgia, Iowa, Indiana, Kentucky, Michigan, Ohio, Utah, Washington, and West Virginia. You must file you taxes electronically through a qualified electronic filer. This office can provide you with information on how to become an electronic filer, including the procedures, tests, and applications necessary. The following publications set the procedures for the electronic filing of tax year 1990 individual income tax returns and Direct Deposit. They also provide procedures for balance due returns.

1345 - *Procedures for Electronic Filing of Individual Income Tax Returns (Tax Year 1990).*

1346 - *Electronic Return File Specifications and Record Layouts for Individual Income Tax Returns.*

* Employee Plans and Exempt Organizations

Office of the Assistant Commissioner
Internal Revenue Service (IRS)
1111 Constitution Ave., NW
Washington, DC 20224 (202) 622-6710

The Employee Plans function administers the tax laws governing pension plans by issuing letters determining whether a plan qualifies under the law, examining returns to ensure that plans are complying with the law, and publishing rulings to clarify the law. Speakers address various practitioner groups across the country to highlight new Employee Plans developments and receive insights first-hand from practitioners. This office also handles exempt organizations, and administers the tax laws governing these organizations and private foundations. The IRS monitors whether sponsors of charitable fundraising events are providing accurate information on the extent to which contributions are deductible. The IRS educates the soliciting organizations and conducts a special examination program to decrease the abusive and misleading fundraising practices of some charities. Publication 1391, *Deductibility of Payments made to Charities Conducting Fundraising Events,* is part of an on-going educational program that includes speeches, taxpayer assistance workshops, and revisions to forms and publications. IRS has established a telephone hotline to help charities make a determination of the value of premiums offered in fundraising activities and to help charities answer questions from donors on the deductibility of contributions made. Charitable organizations engaging in misleading or abusive practices are referred for examination.

* Estate and Gift Tax

Office of Passthroughs and Special Industries
Internal Revenue Service (IRS)
1111 Constitution Ave., NW, Room 5427
Washington, DC 20224 (202) 622-3000

This office will help you on matters pertaining to the regulations of estate and gift tax. This office is most often used by lawyers who are helping people manage estates, but they will answer people's questions or direct them to appropriate sources for more information.

* Federal Tax Guide for Older Americans

Committee on Aging
U.S. House of Representatives
Washington, DC 20515 (202) 226-3375

The *Federal Income Tax Guide for Older Americans* is a free publication, which presents an introduction to the basic provisions of the Tax code benefiting older Americans. It is designed to address the needs of older Americans with moderate income. In addition to emphasizing issues directly affecting senior citizens, the Tax Guide also discusses this year's tax forms to better help taxpayers fully understand the entire process. It also identifies numerous Internal Revenue service publications and prerecorded telephone messages which give more detailed information on the subjects discussed.

* Foreign Language Assistance in Tax Preparation

Taxpayer Services, International
Internal Revenue Service (IRS)
U.S. Department of the Treasury
950 L'Enfant Plaza
Washington, DC 20024 (202) 874-1470

Interpreters are available at the IRS in the major foreign languages to assist taxpayers who do not speak English. Written requests for help may be sent to the above office, and IRS interpreters will respond to the questions, but only in English. Sometimes the State Department assists in the interpretation of letters. Requests are received only for obtaining solutions to specific tax problems and not for the preparation of tax returns.

Volunteer Income Tax Assistance (VITA) centers in local area often have foreign interpreters if the population in that area warrants them. Contact your local IRS office in the white pages of your phone directory or your area's Taxpayer Education Coordinator, listed elsewhere in this book, for information.

Many of the IRS forms are also available in Spanish. They are:

1S *Derechos del contribuyente (Your Rights as a Taxpayer),* 179 *Circular PR, Guia Contributiva Federal Para Patronos Puertoriquenos (Federal Tax Guide for Employers in Puerto Rico)*

556S *Revision de las Declaraciones de Impuesto, Derecho de Apelacion y Reclamaciones de Reembolsos (Examination of Returns, Appeal Rights, and Claims for Refund)*

579S *Como Preparar la Declaracion de Impuesto Federal (How to Prepare the Federal Income Tax Return)*

596SP *Credito por Ingroso del Trabajo*

594S *Proceso de cobro (Deudas del impuesto por razon del empleo) (The Collection Process: Employment Tax Accounts)*

850 *English-Spanish Glossary of Words and Phrases Used in Publications Issued by the Internal Revenue Service.*

* Foreign Tax Credits

Assistant Commissioner (International)
Internal Revenue Service (IRS)
U.S. Department of the Treasury
950 L'Enfant Plaza South, SW
Attn: IN:C:TPS
Washington, DC 20024 (202) 874-1470

If you need information or assistance in the guidelines for foreign tax credit allowed for income taxes paid to foreign governments, contact this office. Income in this situation is taxed by both the United States and the foreign country. Publication 514 from the IRS describes in detail the tax credit, who is eligible, and how to calculate the credit.

* Free Courses on How To Prepare Taxes

Volunteer and Education Branch
Taxpayer Service Division
Internal Revenue Service (IRS)
U.S. Department of the Treasury
1111 Constitution Ave., NW, Room 2706
Washington, DC 20224 (202) 622-7827

The Volunteer Income Tax Assistance (VITA) is a program within the IRS where training is provided to volunteers to help people prepare basic tax returns for older, handicapped and non-English speaking taxpayers. The volunteers serve in the community at neighborhood centers, libraries, churches and shopping malls. The IRS provides free instruction and materials and trains volunteers to prepare Forms 1040 EZ, 1040A, and the basic 1040. New volunteers generally receive four-to-five days instruction; experienced individuals, a one-to-two day

Be patient. If any phone number is incorrect, call (area code) 555-1212 and request the new listing.

Federal Tax Help

refresher. There is also self-instruction. Training is usually available December through January at convenient locations. In exchange for the free training, VITA asks that you spend several hours a week on VITA from January 1 through April 15. To join VITA in your area, just call the Taxpayer Education Coordinator at the number listed below.

Taxpayer Education Coordinators

550 22nd St., S, Stop 117, Birmingham, AL 35233; (205) 731-0403
P.O. Box 101500, Anchorage, AK 99510; (907) 261-4458
2120 N. Central Ave., Stop 6610-PX, Phoenix, AZ 85004; (602) 261-3861
P.O. Box 3778, Stop 25, Little Rock, AR 72203; (501) 378-5685
300 N. Los Angeles St., Room 5205, Los Angeles, CA 90012; (213) 894-4574
1221 Broadway, 4th Fl. Oakland, CA 94612; (415) 273-4233
Chet Holifield Federal Bldg., P.O. Box C-10, Laguna Niguel, CA 92677; (714) 643-4060
P.O. Box 2900, Stop SA5650, Sacramento, CA 95812; (916) 978-4083
55 S. Market St., Stop 77-01-6400, San Jose, CA 95113; (408) 291-7114
600 17th St.,Stop 6610-DEN, Denver, CO 80202-2490; (303) 844-3340
135 High St., Stop 115, Hartford, CT 06103; (203) 240-4154
P.O. Box 28, Wilmington, DE 19899; (302) 573-6270
(DC Office) P.O. Box 1076, Baltimore, MD 21203; (202) 488-3100, ext. 2222
P.O. Box 292590, Stop 6030, Building B, Fort Lauderdale, FL 33329-2590; (305) 424-2439
400 W. Bay St.,Stop 6250, Jacksonville, FL 32202 (904) 791-2514
P.O. Box 1037, Room 110, Federal Office Bldg., Atlanta, GA 30370; (404) 331-3808
PJKK Federal Building, P.O. Box 50089, Honolulu, HI 96850; (808) 541-3300
550 W. Fort St., Box 041, Boise, ID 83724; (208) 554-9183
P.O. Box 1193, Stop 32-1, Chicago, IL 60690; (312) 886-4609
P.O. Box 19201, Stop 8, Springfield, IL 62701; (217) 492-4386
P.O. Box 44211, Stop 60, Indianapolis, IN 46244; (317) 269-6216
P.O. Box 1337, Stop 30, Des Moines, IA 50305; (515) 284-4870
412 S. Main, Stop 6610-WIC, Wichita, KS 67202; (316) 291-6610
P.O. Box 1216, Stop 531, Louisville, KY 40201; (502) 582-6259
501 Magazine St., Room 605, New Orleans, LA 70130; (504) 589-2801
P.O. Box 1020, Augusta, ME 04330; (207) 622-8328
31 Hopkins Plaza, Room 615A, Baltimore, MD 21201; (301) 962-2222
JFK Federal Bldg., P.O. Box 9088, Boston, MA 02203; (617) 565-1645
P.O. Box 330400, Room 2442, Detroit, MI 48232-6500; (313) 226-3674
316 Robert St., Stop 26, St. Paul, MN 55101; (612) 290-3320
100 W. Capitol St., Suite 504, Stop 30, Jackson, MS 39269; (601) 965-4142
P.O. Box 1147, H.W. Wheeler Station, St. Louis, MO 63188; (314) 539-5660
Federal Building, 301 S. Park Ave., Drawer 10016, Helena, MT 59626-0016; (406) 449-5375
106 S. 15th St., Stop 27, Omaha, NE 68102; (402) 221-3501
4750 Oakey Blvd., Las Vegas, NV 89102; (702) 455-1029
80 Daniel St. Portsmouth, NH 03801; (603) 436-7386
425 Raritan Center Pkwy., Edison, NJ 08818; (201) 417-4071
517 Gold Ave, SW, Stop 6610-ALB, P.O. Box 1967, Albuquerque, NM 87103; (505) 766-2537
Leo O'Brien Federal Bldg., Clinton Ave., and N. Pearl St., Room 614, Albany, NY 12207; (518) 472-2886
P.O. Box 606, RM G-5D, Brooklyn, NY 11202; (718) 780-6020
P.O. Box 1040, Niagara Sq. Station, Buffalo, NY 14201; (716) 846-4007
P.O. Box 34036, Church St. Station, New York, NY 10008; (212) 264-3310
320 Federal Pl., Room 128, Greensboro, NC 27401; (919) 333-5620
P.O. Box 2461, Fargo, ND 58108; (701) 239-5213
P.O. Box 3459, Cincinnati, OH 45201; (513) 684-2828
P.O. Box 99184, Cleveland, OH 44199; (216) 522-3414
200 Northwest 4th St., Stop 6610, Oklahoma City, OK 73102; (405) 231-4989
P.O. Box 2709, Portland, OR 97208; (503) 221-6565
600 Arch St., Room 6424, Philadelphia, PA 19106; (215) 597-0512
P.O. Box 2488, Room 123, Pittsburgh, PA 15230; (412) 644-6504
P.O. Box 6627, Providence, RI 02940; (401) 528-4276
Strom Thurmond Federal Bldg., 1835 Assembly St., Room 408, Columbia, SC 29201; (803) 253-3031
P.O. Box 370, Aberdeen, SD 57402-0370; (605) 226-7230
P.O. Box 1107, MDP 46, Nashville, TN 37202; (615) 251-2247
300 E. 8th St., Stop 6610-AUS, Austin, TX 78701; (512) 499-5439
7839 Churchill Way, Stop 6610-DAL, Dallas, TX 75242; (214) 767-1428
4100 Westheimer, Stop 6610H-SW, Suite 280, Houston, TX 77027; (713) 541-7610
465 South 400 East, Stop 6610-SLC, Salt Lake City, UT 84111; (801) 524-6095
Courthouse Plaza, 199 Main St., Burlington, VT 05401; (802) 951-6473
P.O. Box 10049, Room 5223, Richmond, VA 23240; (804) 771-2289
915 Second Ave., MS-425, Seattle, WA 98174; (206) 443-4230
P.O. Box 1138, Stop 2108, Parkersburg, WV 26102; (304) 420-6612
P.O. Box 493, Milwaukee, WI 53201; (414) 291-3302
308 W. 21st St., Stop 6610-CHE, Cheyenne, WY 82001; (307) 772-2325
Mercantile Plaza Bldg., 10th Fl., Ave. Ponce De Leon, Stop 271/2, Hato Rey, PR 00917; (809) 498-5946

* Free Legal Help If You Get Audited

Volunteer and Education Branch
Taxpayer Service Division
Internal Revenue Service (IRS)
U.S. Department of the Treasury
1111 Constitution Ave., NW, Room 2706
Washington, DC 20224 (202) 622-7827

Under this program, law and graduate accounting school students are given special permission to practice before the IRS on behalf of taxpayers who cannot afford professional help. Volunteers are needed to help with the clinic operations or to serve as Student Tax Clinic Directors. Students work under the direction of their professors to handle legal and technical problems. Your local taxpayer education coordinator will inform you of tax clinics in your area.

* Free Tax Forms At Your Library

Volunteer and Education Branch
Taxpayer Service Division
Internal Revenue Service (IRS)
1111 Constitution Ave., NW, Room 1315
Washington, DC 20224 (202) 622-7827

The IRS supplies over 30,000 libraries, technical schools, prisons, and other facilities with free tax forms, audiovisual aids, and reference materials. These facilities are in need of volunteers to assist in distribution and use of these aids. Contact your local library or center and volunteer to help.

* Future Tax Legislation

Director, Legislative Affairs
Internal Revenue Service (IRS)
U.S. Department of the Treasury
1111 Constitution Ave., NW
Washington, DC 20224 (202) 622-3700

The Legislative Affairs Division is responsible for developing IRS legislative proposals, tracking pending legislation, analyzing and implementing new legislation, and preparing responses to General Accounting Office reports.

For further information regarding tax laws that have been introduced, or for an assessment of future laws, contact the following offices. Ask to speak with the person monitoring changes in the tax provision you are calling about.

U.S. Department of the Treasury, Legislative Affairs, 1500 Pennsylvania, Ave., Room 3134, Washington, DC 20224; (202) 566-2037
Senate Committee on Finance, 205 Dirksen Senate Office Building, Washington, DC 20510; (202) 224-4515
House Committee on Ways and Means, 1102 Longworth House Office Building, Washington, DC 20515; (202) 225-3625
Joint Committee on Taxation, 1015 Longworth House Office Building, Washington, DC 20515; (202) 225-3621

* Historian

Internal Revenue Service (IRS)
1111 Constitution Ave., NW
Washington, DC 20224 (202) 377-6456

The IRS decision to create this position follows a growing trend in both the government and corporate worlds to establish history offices, archives, and historic preservation efforts. This new function will help the IRS move into the future with an understanding and appreciation of its past. The historian will develop an archival collection of the most important historical documents created by the IRS, will research and write policy and management-related historical reports, prepare a full-length history of taxation in the U.S., establish a collection of oral history interviews, and assist IRS staff members in answering historical research questions.

* Hotline for Tax Aspects of Retirement Plans

Employee Plans Technical and Actuarial Division
Internal Revenue Service (IRS)
U.S. Department of the Treasury
1111 Constitution Ave., NW

Be patient. If any phone number is incorrect, call (area code) 555-1212 and request the new listing.

Taxes

Washington, DC 20224 (202) 566-6783/6784
The above numbers are hotlines to attorneys within this division that are there to discuss tax questions relating to retirement and pension plans, such as 401(k) and 501(c3). The hours are 1:30 to 4:00 p.m., Monday through Thursday.

* How to Protect Older Americans From Overpayment

Special Committee on Aging
U.S. Senate
Washington, DC 20510 (202) 224-5364
This is a free information paper updated yearly, which is designed to assure that older Americans claim every legitimate income tax deduction, exemption, and tax credit. This publication is very easy to understand and provides many examples and checklists. Also included is a section of income tax items which will change in the following year.

* Individual Income Tax Statistics

Statistics of Income Division
Internal Revenue Service (IRS)
P.O. Box 2608
Washington, DC 20013 (202) 874-0300
Statistics of Income - 1987, Individual Income Tax Returns, Publication 1304, is a report that presents information on sources of income, exemptions, itemized deductions, and tax computations, with the data presented by size of adjusted gross income and marital status. This publication is available from the Superintendent of Documents, Government Printing Office, Washington, DC 20402; (202) 783-3238 (S/N 048-004-02296-6).

* Individual Tax Model

Statistics of Income Division
Internal Revenue Service (IRS)
U.S. Department of the Treasury
1111 Constitution Ave., NW
Attn: R:S:P
Washington, DC 20224 (202) 874-0700
State tax officials determine rate structure and revenue yields through the use of *Individual Tax Model*. Public use tape files are available from the office above that include this tax model.

* Information for Tax Practitioners

Forms Distribution Centers
Internal Revenue Service (IRS)
U.S. Department of the Treasury
P.O. Box 85074, Richmond, VA 23261-5074
P.O. Box 8903, Bloomington, IN 61702
Rancho Cordova, CA 95743-0001 (800) 829-3676
Tax practitioners can benefit from the following information made available to them from the IRS. Publication 1045, *Information for Tax Practitioners*, contains orders blanks for ordering bulk supplies of federal income tax forms. Also within the publication is a form that allows one to be placed on a mailing list in his IRS district to receive a tax practitioner's newsletter. Package X is also available to practitioners with the most popular tax forms and instructions on how to prepare them.

* In-House IRS Audit Manuals

Freedom of Information Reading Room
Internal Revenue Service (IRS)
U.S. Department of the Treasury
1111 Constitution Ave., NW
Room 1569
Washington, DC 20224 (202) 622-5164
Tax audit manuals use by IRS staff and other in-house manuals are available to the public. Contact the office above for arrangements to use particular materials. For copies of manuals and written requests, write to: Internal Revenue Service, c/o Ben Franklin Station, P.O. Box 388, Washington, DC 20044, Attn: Freedom of Information Request.

Available IRS Technical Manuals:
Organization and Staffing (1100), $36.45
Policies of the Internal Revenue Service (1218), $14.55
Delegation Orders (1229), $17.10
Internal Management Document System (1230), $21.90

Disclosure of Official Information (1272), $63.15
Travel (1763), $29.85
General (4000), $20.10
Income Tax Examinations (4200), $74.85
Tax Audit Guidelines for Internal Revenue Examiners (4231), $27.20
Techniques Handbook for Specialized Industries (4232)

1. Insurance, $15.45
2. Auto Dealers, $2.55
3. Textiles, $4.80
4. Timber, $6.15
5. Brokerage Firms, $11.90
6. Railroads, $13.65
7. Construction, $4.65
8. Oil and Gas, $47.85
9. Financial Institution, $6.45
10. Public Utilities, $10.05
11. Barter Exchanges, -0-

Tax Audit Guidelines, Partnerships, Estates and Trusts, and Corporations (4233), $22.55
Techniques Handbook for In-Depth Examinations (4235), $25.65
Examination Tax Shelters (4236), $10.65
Report Writing Guide for Income Tax Examiners (4237), $21.30
Examination Techniques Handbook for Estate Tax Examiners (4350), $27.15
Handbook for Quality Review (4419), $11.40
Employment Tax Procedures (4600), $12.90
Excise Tax Procedure (4700), $17.55
Handbook for Examination Group Managers (4(10)20), $15.75
Classification (41(12)0), $8.10
General Procedural Guides (5100), $24.45
Collection Quality Review System (CQRS) (5190), $4.05
Delinquent Return Procedures (5200), $10.05
Balance Due Account Procedures (5300), $23.55
Service Center Collection Branch Procedures (5400), $93.90
Service Center Collection Branch Managers (5415), $9.90
Automated Collection Function Procedures (5500), $18.60
Automated Collection System Managers (5512), $21.30
Collection Field Function Techniques and Other Assignments (5600), $32.25
Employment Tax Examinations (5(10)00), $12.60
Collection Technical Review Handbook for Employment Tax Examination (5(10)20)), $2.25
Group Managers Handbook (5620)0), $8.40
Field Branch Chief's Handbook (5630)0), $3.75
Special Procedures (5700), $57
Special Procedures Function Managers (57(15)0), $3.90
Legal Reference Guide for Revenue Officers (57(16)0), $37.50
Records and Reports (5800), $9.60
Collection Reports for Field Managers (5890), $4.35
Collection Support Function (5900), $19.50
Taxpayer Service (6810), $51.45
Exempt Organizations (7751), $60.90
Private Foundations (7752), $40.05
Employee Plans Master File (7810), $10.50
Exempt Organizations Business Master File (7820), $26.70
Examination Procedures (7(10)00), $49.95
Employee Plans Examination Guidelines (7(10)54), $15
Exempt Organizations Exam. Guides Handbook (7(10)69), $13.80
Actuarial Guidelines (7(10)5(10)), $5.70
Appeals (Part VIII), $51
Handbook for Special Agents (9781), $84.15
Criminal Investigation (Part IX) $67.50
Technical (Part XI), $49.35
Employee Plans Training Program Phase I, Revised 10/87 (4210-01), $60.45
Employee Plans EP/EO CPE Operational Topics for 1989, Revised 12/88 (4213-002), $12.15
Employee Plans EP/EO CPE Technical Topics for 1989, Revised 12/88 (4213-003), $18.75
Employee Plans EP/EO CPE Technical Topics for 1989, Revised 3/89

(4213-005), $4.05
Employee Plans Training Program Phase II, Revised 01/87 (4220-01), $51.60
Exempt Organizations Continuing Professional Education Technical Instruction Program for 1986, Revised 01/86 (4277-20), $43.80
Exempt Organizations Continuing Professional Education Technical Instruction Program for 1987, Revised 01/87 (4277-25), $44.70
Exempt Organizations Continuing Professional Education Technical Instruction Program for 1988, Revised 01/88 (4277-28), $37.65
Exempt Organizations EP/EO CPE Operational Topics for 1989, Revised 01/89 (4277-31), $10.05
.*Exempt Organizations Continuing Professional Education Technical Instruction Program for 1989*, Revised 01/89 (4277-32), $43.35
Exempt Organization Continuing Professional Education Technical Instruction Program for 1989 Index, Revised 01/89 (4277-33), $9
Exempt Organization Continuing Professional Education Technical Instruction Program for 1990, Revised 1/90 (4277-039), $68.85
Exempt Organization Continuing Professional Education Technical Instruction Program for 1990 Index, Revised 1/90 (4277-040), $9.

* Internal Revenue Bulletin

Superintendent of Documents
Government Printing Office
Washington, DC 20402 (202) 783-3238

The *Internal Revenue Bulletin* announces official Internal Revenue Service rulings, Treasury decisions, Executive Orders, legislation, and court decisions pertaining to Internal Revenue matters. The price is $104 per year (S/N 748-004-00000-9). Twice yearly, the weekly issues of the *Internal Revenue Bulletin* are consolidated into the *Cumulative Bulletins* (Jan-June and July-Dec). These *Bulletins* are not included as part of this subscription, but are sold as separate subscriptions. The subject bibliography, *Internal Revenue Cumulative Bulletins*, lists the bulletins available, dating back to 1940. Prices range from $8 to $42, depending on the year.

* International Tax Assistance

Office of the Associate Chief Counsel, International
Internal Revenue Service (IRS)
950 L'Enfant Plaza, SW, IN:C:TPS
Washington, DC 20224 (202) 287-4311

The International Office plays the lead role in devising strategies to assure that worldwide revenues due the United States are assessed and collected. International maintains a high number of taxpayer service visits to U.S. embassies and consulates to help U.S. taxpayers living abroad and in U.S. territories and possessions. Year-round taxpayer assistance by IRS staff at 13 overseas posts is supplemented by these visits. International publicized worldwide undelivered refunds, attempting to reach 800 taxpayers owed over $1 million in refunds returned as undeliverable by the world's postal authorities. The specialists in this office will offer technical assistance concerning questions relating to foreign taxes and tax credits. Refer also to Publications 54, *Tax Guide for U.S. Citizens and Resident Aliens Abroad*, and 514, *Foreign Tax Credits for Individuals*. International's Office of International programs administers 35 income tax treaties, 16 estate tax treaties and 7 gift tax treaties worldwide. These treaties provide for relief from double taxation, exchanges of information, routine sharing of information, and simultaneous examinations. During the past year, this office successfully completed negotiations in 122 cases for U.S. taxpayers who requested relief from double taxation.

Overseas Posts:

Location	Phone
Bonn, West Germany	339-2119
Caracas, Venezuela	285-4641
London, England	408-8076 or 408-8077
Mexico City, Mexico	211-0042, ext. 3559
Nassau, Bahamas	809-322-1181
Ottawa, Canada	613-238-5335
Paris, France	4296-1202, ext. 2214
Riyadh, Saudi Arabia	488-3800, ext. 210
Rome, Italy	4674-2560
Sao Paulo, Brazil	881-6511, ext. 287
Singapore	338-0251, ext. 247
Sydney, Australia	261-9275
Tokyo, Japan	3224-5466

* IRS Assistance Through the Media

Audio/Visual Branch
Public Affairs Division, Internal Revenue Service (IRS)
U.S. Department of the Treasury
1111 Constitution Ave., NW
Washington, DC 20224 (202) 622-7541

To provide specialized tax information to targeted audiences, the IRS developed an alliance with various industry groups and Public Broadcasting Service stations to produce and market *Tax Tips on Tape*, a series of 27 videos. The programs were shown on 240 public broadcasting stations and coordinated with special Outreach Program events across the country. IRS also joined with Financial News Network to produce a weekly half-hour live show, *IRS Tax Beat*. Topics ranged from tax-exempt organizations to estate taxes and featured IRS executives and specialists answering call-in questions. As part of the continuing efforts to use the most efficient means to distribute information, the IRS began a weekly satellite transmission of tax programs, which were made available to cable outlets and television stations free of charge. Watch for these broadcasts in your local listings.

* IRS Collection of Delinquent Child Support Payments

Chief Operations Officer
Internal Revenue Service (IRS)
U.S. Department of the Treasury
1111 Constitution Ave, NW
Washington, DC 20224 (202) 622-6600

If a taxpayer fails to make support payments to a child or spouse who receives public assistance, Congress requires the IRS to withhold all or part of the taxpayer's income tax refund to cover the delinquent payments. Since 1986, the IRS has also been required to apply individual income tax refunds to child support payments for individuals who are not on welfare and to non-tax debts owed to some Federal agencies, such as student loans, military enlistment bonuses, and home mortgage loans, etc. Through an agreement with the U.S. Department of Health and Human Services, IRS acts as a collection agent for the state welfare agencies in all child or spousal support cases. The refund amounts are used to reimburse the agencies for the support they furnish through Aid to Families with Dependent Children, or are turned over to the parents having custody of the child or children in non-welfare cases. Other agreements with the U.S. Departments of Housing and Urban Development, Agriculture, Energy, Interior, Education, Defense, Treasury, Justice, Health and Human Services, and the Veterans Affairs, Railroad Retirement Board and Small Business Administration require the IRS to act as a collection agent for delinquent non-tax Federal debts.

* IRS Collections and Returns

Returns Processing and Accounting
Office of the Assistant Commissioner
Taxpayer Service and Returns Processing
Internal Revenue Service (IRS)
U.S. Department of the Treasury
1111 Constitution Ave., NW
Washington, DC 20224 (202) 622-6860

This office is responsible for the processing of collection and returns within the IRS tax system. Statistics generated from this office are available in the *Commissioner's Annual Report*, available from the Government Printing Office, Washington, DC 20402, for $3.50 (S/N 048-004-02280-9).

* IRS Community Outreach Assistance

Volunteer and Education Branch
Taxpayer Service Division
Internal Revenue Service (IRS)
U.S. Department of the Treasury
1111 Constitution Ave., NW, Room 2706
Washington, DC 20224 (202) 622-7827

IRS employees and volunteers provide free tax help in coordination with local groups. The help is offered at places of business, community or neighborhood centers, libraries, colleges, and other popular locations. Within the Community Outreach program, line-by-line help with your income tax forms is provided. Tax information seminars are also held, including discussions, films or videotapes, and a question and answer period. The programs are aimed at particular interest groups, such as low-to-middle income people interested in preparing their own returns, or small business owners needing free tax assistance. Contact the taxpayer education coordinator in your area for additional information.

Be patient. If any phone number is incorrect, call (area code) 555-1212 and request the new listing.

Taxes

* IRS Criminal Investigation

Assistant Commissioner, Criminal Investigation
Internal Revenue Service (IRS)
U.S. Department of the Treasury
1111 Constitution Ave., NW
Washington, DC 20224 (202) 622-6190

The mission of criminal investigation within the IRS is to encourage and achieve the highest possible level of voluntary compliance with the law by conducting investigations and recommending criminal prosecutions when warranted. Special agents target their efforts in the areas such as organized crime, narcotics trafficking, money laundering, questionable refund schemes, and tax shelters, of both domestic and international scope.

* IRS Private Letter Rulings and Information Letters

Technical Branch, Communications
Internal Revenue Service (IRS)
U.S. Department of the Treasury
1111 Constitution Ave., NW
Washington, DC 20224 (202) 622-7270

If your tax situation warrants special interpretation on a particular tax deduction you would like to take, you can ask the IRS for a private letter ruling. The tax laws are applied to your case which can make this procedure time-consuming. To apply for a private-letter ruling, pertinent information must be sent, including names, addresses, taxpayer identification numbers, your IRS district office, a statement on why you qualify for the deduction, and legal documents pertaining to the case. Contact the above office on the procedure to follow. Someone from the IRS will be assigned to your case, and a notification will be sent to you on how to check the status of your ruling. Publication 91-1 explains the private letter ruling process. There is now a user fee, usually $2500, for each ruling.

Determination letters are also issued by the IRS to businesses and organizations concerning questions related to employee pension plans and tax-exempt status. The procedure for submitting information for a determination letter is similar to filing for a private-letter ruling; however, both the IRS district offices and the national office receive these requests and make the determinations.

General information letters are frequently issued by the IRS, and the request for the information is not as formal as the above mentioned letters. Simply write a letter or postcard to either the IRS district office in your area or to the national office with your question or situation on which you would like advice.

If making an inquiry to the national office, all of the above letters should be addressed to: Internal Revenue Service (Attn: CC:CORP:T:U), P.O. Box 7604, Ben Franklin Station, Washington, DC 20224.

* IRS Research Efforts

Research Division
Assistant Commissioner, Planning, Finance, and Research
Internal Revenue Service (IRS)
U.S. Department of the Treasury
1111 Constitution Ave., NW
Washington, DC 20224 (202) 874-0100

IRS research efforts emphasize voluntary compliance, trend identification, and analysis. The IRS published estimates and projections of gross income owed but not voluntarily paid for individuals and corporations for selected years from 1973 through 1992. An analysis is also being completed on the net tax gap, the amount of income tax owed but not paid either voluntarily or involuntarily.

One of the primary objectives is to provide high quality service to taxpayers. IRS began conducting taxpayer opinion surveys in its functions that have direct contact with taxpayers to get initial or baseline measurements of taxpayer perceptions about the quality level of IRS service. A report has also been released on a new method for estimating taxpayer paperwork burden associated with preparation, recordkeeping, obtaining and learning materials, and filing forms associated with tax preparation.

IRS completed a second major study of the effects of refund offsets for non-tax debts on subsequent taxpayer behavior. IRS learned that taxpayers are more likely to file balance-due returns or not to file in the subsequent year.

* IRS Service Centers

Service Center Directors
Deputy Commissioner, Operations
Internal Revenue Service (IRS)

U.S. Department of the Treasury
1111 Constitution Ave, NW
Washington, DC 20224 (202) 622-4255

The following is a listing of the Internal Revenue Service Centers where taxpayers must mail their tax forms. If an addressed envelope comes with your return, the IRS asks that you use it. If you do not have one, or if you have moved during the year, mail your return to the Internal Revenue Service Center for the place where you live. No street address is needed.

Service Center Offices:

Andover, MA	(617) 474-5549
Atlanta, GA	(404) 455-2049
Austin, TX	(512) 462-7025
Austin Compliance Center	(512) 326-0816
Brookhaven (Holtsville), NY	(516) 654-6886
Cincinnati, OH	(606) 292-5316
Fresno, CA	(209) 488-6437
Kansas City, MO	(816) 926-6828
Memphis, TN	(901) 365-5419
Ogden, UT	(801) 625-6374
Philadelphia, PA	(215) 969-2499

Regional Offices:

North Atlantic	(212) 264-0839
Mid-Atlantic	(215) 597-3991
Southeast	(404) 331-4506
Central	(513) 684-2587
Midwest	(312) 886-4291
Southwest	(214) 767-5762
Western	(415) 556-3035

* IRS Speakers and Customized Seminars

District Offices
Internal Revenue Service (IRS)
1111 Constitution Ave., NW
Washington, DC 20224 (800) 829-1040

The Internal Revenue Service provides trained speakers for area civic organizations and other interested groups. Tax clinics are often organized for special interest groups. The IRS has also sponsored call-in radio programs where you may inquire about specific tax information. Contact the district offices of the IRS listed in this publication and inquire through the Public Affairs Director if these programs are of interest to you.

* IRS Special Enrollment Agents

Office of the Director of Practice
Internal Revenue Service (IRS)
U.S. Department of the Treasury
1111 Constitution Ave, NW
Washington, DC 20224 (202) 376-1421

IRS has designed a special enrollment of persons, other than attorneys and certified public accountants, who wish to represent clients before the IRS. This includes all matters connected with presentations to the Service, relating to a client's rights, privileges, and liabilities under laws or regulations administered by the Service. Such presentations include the preparation and filing of documents, all communications with the Service, and the representation of a client at conferences, hearings, and meetings. Candidates should be able to answer income tax accounting questions on the intermediate college course level. The following IRS publications, listed elsewhere in this book, will assist you in preparing for the examination:

- 17 *Your Federal Income Tax*
- 216 *Conference and Practice Requirements*
- 334 *Tax Guide for Small Business*
- 541 *Tax Information on Partnerships*
- 542 *Tax Information on Corporations*
- 553 *Highlights of the 1989 Changes*
- 560 *Self-Employed Retirement Plans*
- 589 *Tax Information on S Corporations*
- 590 *Individual Retirement Arrangements (IRAs)*

Answers to the previous year's examination may be obtained from the above address to assist you in preparing for the exam. Publication 1470, available from this office, includes an application for the test, as well as a copy of last year's exam. The two-day exam is given once a year in the fall.

Be patient. If any phone number is incorrect, call (area code) 555-1212 and request the new listing.

Federal Tax Help

* IRS Tax Compliance Program

Assistant Commissioner, Collection
Internal Revenue Service (IRS)
U.S. Department of the Treasury
1111 Constitution Ave., NW
Washington, DC 20224 (202) 622-5100

The Information Returns Program (IRP) is a largely computerized compliance program used by the IRS to match third party information on items, such as wages, interest, dividends, and certain deductions, with the amounts reported by taxpayers on their income tax returns. The IRS also uses the information to identify people who are reported to have received income, but did not file returns. In 1988, the IRS sent out 3.8 million notices reflecting discrepancies, and 3 million notices were sent to taxpayers for failure to file a tax return based upon information returns filed.

* IRS Technical-Advice Memorandums

Technical Branch, Communications
Internal Revenue Service (IRS)
U.S. Department of the Treasury
1111 Constitution Ave., NW
Washington, DC 20224 (202) 622-7270

If you are audited by the IRS and are in disagreement with the IRS agent over interpretation of a tax law, you can ask the agent to request a technical-advice memorandum for you. These memorandums must be requested through the IRS district offices. The national office then makes the final determination. Dollar amounts cannot be disputed through these memorandums, only the interpretation of the tax laws and procedures.

* IRS Walk-In Service Centers

Taxpayer Services
Internal Revenue Service (IRS)
U.S. Department of the Treasury
1111 Constitution Ave., NW, Room 2422
Washington, DC 20224 (202) 566-6352

Assisters are available in most IRS offices throughout the country to help you prepare your own return. In this way you will be given the opportunity to learn how to research and prepare your own tax return. An assister will "walk through" a return with you and a number of other taxpayers in a group setting. If you want help with your tax return, you should bring in your tax package, forms W-2 and 1099, and any other information (such as a copy of last year's return) that will help the assister to help you. At most IRS offices you can also get tax forms, publications, and help with questions about IRS notices or bills.

* Learn What's New In Taxes

Volunteer and Education Branch
Taxpayer Service Division
Internal Revenue Service (IRS)
U.S. Department of the Treasury
1111 Constitution Ave., NW, Room 2706
Washington, DC 20224 (202) 622-7827

Tax professionals can learn recent tax law changes at Practitioner Institutes, which will enhance the professional quality of the services they provide. These institutes are sponsored by qualified educational institutions, state and local governments, and professional and other non-profit organizations. Contact your local Taxpayer Education Coordinator regarding these institutes.

* Let the IRS Compute Your Taxes

District Offices
Internal Revenue Service (IRS)
U.S. Department of the Treasury
1111 Constitution Ave., NW
Washington, DC 20224 (800) 829-1040

If you use Form 1040A to compute your taxes, the IRS will complete the calculation for your taxes. You must complete the tax return through Line 20. All income must be from wages and interest. Other minor stipulations also apply. Contact the above number for specific details on completing your taxes in this way.

* Money Waiting for You: Unclaimed Refunds

Accounting Branch
Internal Revenue Service (IRS)
801 Pennsylvania Ave., NW

Washington, DC 20004 (301) 492-5400

This office processes returned refund checks. After an attempt has been made by the Post Office to track the taxpayer fails, the IRS computer checks names against W2 forms, employer records and Social Security records for a correct address. Regional Offices use the media to advertise names of taxpayers who are due refunds. If after three years the IRS has been unsuccessful in finding the taxpayer, the money is deposited into an unclaimed refund account where it remains until it is claimed. Should a taxpayer discover at any time that they did not receive their refund they should contact the Internal Revenue Service Center where they filed their claim, or the office listed above.

* Obtaining Prior Year Tax Returns

Service Center Directors
Chief Operations Officer
Internal Revenue Service (IRS)
U.S. Department of the Treasury
1111 Constitution Ave., NW
Washington, DC 20224 (202) 622-4255

It is possible to obtain a copy of your prior year tax return by completing Form 4506, *Request for Copy of Tax Form*, and mailing it to the Service Center where you filed the return. The charge is $4.25 for each year's return and must accompany this request. If a taxpayer's authorized representative wishes to request a copy of a taxpayer's prior year return, he or she must attach a signed copy of Form 2848, *Power of Attorney and Declaration of Representative*, or other document authorizing him or her to act for the taxpayer. In lieu of Form 4506, you can send a written request to the Service Center including the following information: your name, your social security number, and if you filed a joint return, the name and social security number of your spouse, the form number, the tax period, and your current address. You must sign this request, and if a joint return was filed, only one signature is needed. Allow 45 days to process the request. However, you often only need certain information, such as the amount of your reported income, the number of your exemptions, and tax shown on the return. You can get this information free if you write or visit an IRS office or call the toll-free number for your area.

* Penalties and Interest

Taxpayer Services
Internal Revenue Service (IRS)
1111 Constitution Ave., NW
Washington, DC 20224 (202) 566-6352

The law requires that IRS charge penalties for failure to file returns, late payments, payments with bad checks, negligence, false withholding statements, fraud, and other violations. The Penalty and Interest Notice Explanation (PINEX) notices are available upon request. These information notices show exactly how assessed penalties and interest have been computed on specific taxpayer accounts. The explanatory PINEX notices can be quickly computer-generated in response to taxpayer inquiries received by district offices and service centers. Taxpayer Service representatives are trained to answer taxpayer questions about these notices.

* Practitioner Services

Volunteer and Education Branch
Taxpayer Service Division
Internal Revenue Service (IRS)
1111 Constitution Ave., NW
Washington, DC 20224 (202) 622-7827

Each District Office puts out a newsletter (the frequency varies) designed for practitioners that provides information on a wide variety of tax topics. The district offices also have practitioner hotlines, which can answer questions regarding account questions their clients have.

* Small Business Tax Education Course

Volunteer and Education Branch
Taxpayer Service Division
Internal Revenue Service (IRS)
U.S. Department of the Treasury
1111 Constitution Ave., NW, Room 2706
Washington, DC 20224 (202) 622-7827

Approximately 1,000 junior colleges and universities are now offering a new course designed by the IRS for tax education of those in small businesses. Course materials are designed by the IRS, and the college may present the material as either a credit or non-credit course. Nine areas are covered in the

Be patient. If any phone number is incorrect, call (area code) 555-1212 and request the new listing.

Taxes

course, including business assets; use of the home for business; employment taxes; excise taxes; starting a business and recordkeeping; *Schedules C (Profit or Loss from a Business), SE (Social Security Self-Employment Tax),* and *1040-ES (Estimated Tax for Individuals);* self-employment retirement plans; partnerships; and tip reporting and allocation rules. Contact a taxpayer education coordinator in your area, listed in this publication, for information on courses in your area.

* Statistics of Income Bulletin

Statistics of Income Division
Internal Revenue Service (IRS)
U.S. Department of the Treasury
P.O. Box 2608
Washington, DC 20013 (202) 874-0700

The *Statistics of Income Bulletin* provides the earliest published annual financial statistics from the various types of tax and information returns filed with the Internal Revenue Service. The *Bulletin* also includes information from periodic or special analytical studies of particular interest to tax administrators. In addition, historical data is provided for selected types of taxpayers, as well as State data and gross internal revenue collections. The *SOI Bulletin* is published quarterly and is available from the Superintendent of Documents, Government Printing Office, Washington, DC 20402; (202) 783-3238. The subscription service is $20 annually, $7.50 for single copies.

* Tax Analysis

Office of Tax Analysis
Office of the Assistant Secretary
of the Treasury for Tax Policy
U.S. Department of the Treasury
1500 Pennsylvania Ave., NW
Washington, DC 20220 (202) 622-0050

This departmental office within Treasury analyzes tax programs and legislation and looks for alternative programs depending on the current economic climate. Advisors are available in many areas, such as economic modeling, revenue estimating, international taxation, individual taxation, business taxation, and depreciation analysis.

* Tax Assistance for the Military

Taxpayer Services, International
Internal Revenue Service (IRS)
U.S. Department of the Treasury
950 L'Enfant Plaza
Washington, DC 20024 (202) 287-4311

The IRS sends trained instructors to military bases here and overseas to train personnel on tax procedures. Through the VITA program, these military personnel then organize internal training sessions to assist others in the preparation of their tax returns. Those chosen to be instructors often have experience in taxation or accounting. If your tax situation is complex, the Legal Assistance offices at military bases can assist you. United States embassies and consulates are also accessible for those in need of their services.

The following international telephone numbers are the local numbers of the 14 U.S. Embassies and consulates with full-time permanent staff from the IRS. Please check with your telephone company for any country or city codes required if you are outside the local dialing area. The Nassau and Ottawa numbers include the United States area codes.

Bonn, West Germany	339-2119
Caracas, Venezuela	285-4641
London, England	408-8076 or 408-8077
Mexico City, Mexico	525-211-0042, ext. 3559
Nassau, Bahamas	809-322-1181
Ottawa, Canada	613-238-5335
Paris, France	4296-1202
Riyadh, Saudi Arabia	488-3800, ext. 210
Rome, Italy	4674-2560
Sao Paulo, Brazil	881-6511, ext. 287
Singapore	338-0251, ext. 245
Sydney, Australia	261-9275
Tokyo, Japan	3224-5466

Publication 3, *Tax Information for Military Personnel,* may also be useful to you. Write to your area's IRS forms and publications distribution center, listed elsewhere, for a copy or call (800) 424-3676.

* Tax Audits

Taxpayer Services
Internal Revenue Service (IRS)
U.S. Department of the Treasury
1111 Constitution Ave., NW
Washington, DC 20224 (202) 874-1460

If the IRS selects your return for examination, you may be asked to produce records such as canceled checks, receipts or other supporting documents to verify entries on your return. Not all examinations result in changes in tax liability. If the examination of your return shows that you overpaid your tax, you will receive a refund. If the examination of your return shows that you owe additional tax, payment is expected. If you don't agree with the Examiner's findings, you have the right to appeal them. During the examination process, you will be given information about your appeal rights. Publication 5, *Appeal Rights and Preparation of Protests for Unagreed Cases,* explains your appeal rights in detail and tells you exactly what to do if you want to appeal. You can appeal the findings of an examination with the IRS through their Appeals Office. Most differences can be settled through this appeals system without expensive and time-consuming court trials. If the matter cannot be settled to your satisfaction in appeals, you can take your case to court. Depending on whether you first pay the disputed tax, you can take your case to the U.S. Tax Court, the U.S. Claims Court, or your U.S. District Court. These courts are entirely independent of the IRS. As always, you can represent yourself or have someone admitted to practice before the court represent you. If you disagree about whether you owe additional tax, you generally have the right to take your case to the U.S. Tax Court if you have not yet paid the tax. Ordinarily, you have 90 days from the time the IRS mails you a formal notice telling you that you owe additional tax, to file a petition with the U.S. Tax Court. You can request simplified small tax case procedures if your case is $10,000 or less for any period or year. A case settled under these procedures cannot be appealed. If you have already paid the disputed tax in full, you may file a claim for a refund. If the IRS disallows the claim or you do not take action within 6 months, then you may take your case to the U.S. Claims Court or your U.S. District Court. If the court agrees with you on most issues in your case, and finds that the IRS position was largely unjustified, you may be able to recover some of your administrative and litigation costs. To do this, you must have used all the administrative remedies available to you within the IRS. This includes going through the Appeals system and giving the IRS all the information necessary to resolve the case. Publication 556, *Examination of Returns, Appeal Rights, and Claims for Refund,* will help you more fully understand your appeal rights.

Internal Revenue Service Regional Offices

Central: 550 Main St., Cincinnati, OH 45202. Serving: IN, KY, MI, OH, WV.

Mid-Atlantic: 841 Chestnut St., Philadelphia, PA 19107. Serving: DE, MD, NJ, PA, VA.

Midwest: One N. Wacker St., Chicago, IL 60606. Serving: IL, IA, MN, MO, MT, NE, ND, SD, WI.

North-Atlantic: 90 Church St., New York, NY 10007. Serving: CT, ME, MA, NH, NY, RI, VT.

Southeast: 275 Peachtree St., NE, Atlanta, GA 30043. Serving: AL, AR, GA, FL, LA, MS, NC, SC, TN.

Southwest: LB-70 Stop 1000 SWRO, 7839 Churchill Way, Dallas, TX 75251. Serving: AZ, CO, KS, NM, OK, TX, UT, WY.

Western: 1650 Mission St., 5th Fl., San Francisco, CA 94103. Serving: AK, CA, HI, ID, NV, OR, WA.

IRS Regional Directors of Appeals

Room 7514, 550 Main St., Cincinnati, OH 45202

841 Chestnut St., Philadelphia, PA 19107

230 N. Dearborn, 29th Fl., Room 2972, Chicago, IL 60604

90 Church St., New York, NY 10007

Room 625, 275 Peachtree St., NE, Atlanta, GA 30043

LB-70, Stop 8000 SWRO, 7839 Churchill Way, Dallas, TX 75251

1650 Mission St., 5th Fl., San Francisco, CA 94103

Be patient. If any phone number is incorrect, call (area code) 555-1212 and request the new listing.

Federal Tax Help

* Tax Counseling for the Elderly

Volunteer and Education Branch
Taxpayer Service Division
Internal Revenue Service (IRS)
U.S. Department of the Treasury
1111 Constitution Ave., NW
Room 2706
Washington, DC 20224 (202) 622-7827

Tax Counseling for the Elderly (TCE) provides free tax help to people aged 60 or older, especially those who are disabled or who have special needs. Volunteers who provide tax counseling are often retired individuals who are associated with non-profit organizations that receive grants from the IRS. The grants are used to help pay out-of-pocket expenses for the volunteers to travel wherever there are elderly who need help, whether they are homebound, in retirement homes, or at special TCE sites. Sites are located conveniently in neighborhood centers, libraries, churches and other places in the community. Contact your local taxpayer education coordinator for programs in your area.

The following IRS Publications, available free from the IRS ((800) TAX-FORM), may be useful for the elderly.

Publication 524, *Credit for the Elderly or the Disabled*
Publication 554, *Tax Information for Older Americans*

* Tax Court

United States Tax Court
400 Second St., NW
Washington, DC 20217 (202) 376-2751

If your taxes are delinquent, the Internal Revenue Service will issue you a delinquency notice, whether you are a consumer or a corporation. If you wish to contest the delinquency, a petition for a hearing can be filed with the U.S. Tax Court. This court is an independent court and not part of the IRS. The court's decision is final and cannot be appealed.

* Tax Data

Statistics of Income Division
Internal Revenue Service (IRS)
P.O. Box 2608
Washington, DC 20013 (202) 874-0700

The Statistics of Income Division has Public Use Magnetic Tape Microdata Files from which specific information requests can be filled on a cost reimbursable basis. These files include individual income tax returns for 1978-1986. (Individual income tax returns for 1966-1977 are available from the Center for Electronic Records of the National Archives and Records Administration, Washington, DC, 20408.) Files containing more limited data for each State are also available for 1985. All of these files have been edited to protect the confidentiality of individual taxpayers. Private foundations for 1982, 1983 and 1985 and non-profit charitable organizations for 1983 and 1985 are also available. The individual private foundation and charitable organization files are the only microdata files that can be released to the public. This office also has Migration Data, with compilations showing migration patterns, from where to where, by State and county, based on year-to-year changes in the tax return address. Data are available for selected time periods (according to the years in which returns were filed) between 1978 and 1988 and include counts of the number of individual income tax returns and personal exemptions. In addition, county income totals are available for Income Years 1982 and 1984 through 1987.

* Tax Education for High School Students

Volunteer and Education Branch
Taxpayer Service Division
Internal Revenue Service (IRS)
U.S. Department of the Treasury
1111 Constitution Ave., NW
Room 2706
Washington, DC 20224 (202) 622-7827

The IRS sponsors an introductory tax education program, *Understanding Taxes*, for high school students. Since many of the students have part-time jobs, the material that is learned can be practiced immediately. Instructional materials include computer software and video programs. Volunteer instructors are those who enjoy teaching and helping others, and who are knowledgeable about taxation. Your local taxpayer education coordinator will assist you in organizing these courses.

* Tax Exempt Organizations

Exempt Organizations Technical Division
Internal Revenue Service (IRS)
U.S. Department of the Treasury
1111 Constitution Ave., NW, Room 6411
Washington, DC 20224 (202) 622-8100

This office within the IRS sets the qualifications of organizations seeking a tax exempt status. Compliance with the law is also monitored. For a listing of the names of exempt organizations through October 31, 1988, subscribe to *Cumulative List of Organizations*, as legislated through Section 170(c) of the Internal Revenue Code of 1954. The subscription is $41 annually and includes three cumulative quarterly supplements. Available from the Superintendent of Documents, Government Printing Office, Washington, DC 20402, (202) 783-3238.

* Tax Help for the Hearing Impaired

Taxpayer Services Division
Internal Revenue Service (IRS)
U.S. Department of the Treasury
1111 Constitution Ave, NW
Washington, DC 20224
Teletypewriter Number (TTN) (800) 829-4059

Telephone tax service by way of a teletypewriter is available from the IRS to assist hearing impaired taxpayers. During the IRS filing season, the hours of operation are 8am to 6:45 pm EST. In the non-filing season, the hours are 8am to 4:30pm EST.

* Tax Help on Audio and Video Cassettes

Audio/Visual Branch
Public Affairs Division
Internal Revenue Service (IRS)
U.S. Department of the Treasury
1111 Constitution Ave., NW
Washington, DC 20224 (202) 622-7541

The IRS provides local libraries with audio cassettes and videocassettes, for loan to the public, on how to fill out Forms 1040EZ, 1040A, 1040, and Schedules A and B. These tax tapes contain simple, step-by-step instructions to the forms and tax tips. Contact this office or your local library for more information.

* Tax Information in Braille

National Library Service for the Blind
and Physically Handicapped
1291 Taylor St.
Washington, DC 20542 (202) 707-5100

IRS materials are available in Braille. They include Publications 17, *Your Federal Income Tax*, and 334, *Tax Guide for Small Business*, and Forms 1040, 1040A, and 1040EZ and instructions. They may be obtained at Regional Libraries for the Blind and Physically Handicapped. For a regional library in your area, contact the National Library Service for a listing.

* Tax Matters Digest System

Superintendent of Documents
Government Printing Office
Washington, DC 20402 (202) 783-3238

The *Bulletin Index - Digest System* contains the *Finding List* and *Digests* of all permanent tax matters published in the Internal Revenue System. Each subscription service consists of a basic manual and cumulative supplements for an indefinite period.

Service No. 1 - Income Taxes, 1953-1987. ($42) (S/N 948-001-00000-4)
Service No. 2 - Estate and Gift Taxes, 1953-1986. ($17) (S/N 948-002-00000-1)
Service No. 3 - Employment Taxes, 1953-1986. ($17) (S/N 948-003-00000-7)
Service No. 4 - Excise Taxes, 1953-1986. ($17) (S/N 948-004-00000-3)

* Tax Returns Prepared Free for Low Income, Elderly and Handicapped

Volunteer and Education Branch
Taxpayer Service Division
Internal Revenue Service (IRS)
U.S. Department of the Treasury
1111 Constitution Ave., NW

Taxes

Room 2706
Washington, DC 20224 (202) 622-7827

The Volunteer Income Tax Assistance (VITA) Program offers free tax help to people who cannot afford professional assistance. Volunteers help prepare basic tax returns for older, handicapped, and non-English-speaking taxpayers. Assistance is provided in the community at libraries, schools, shopping malls, and at other convenient locations.

Volunteers may take part in various VITA program activities, such as directly preparing returns, teaching taxpayers to prepare their own returns, managing a VITA site, or arranging publicity. Volunteers generally include college students, law students, members of professional business and accounting organizations, and members of retirement, religious, military, and community groups. The IRS provides VITA training materials and instructors. Training is conducted at a time and location convenient to volunteers and instructors. Generally, these sessions are offered in December through January each year.

The emphasis in VITA is to teach taxpayers to complete their own tax returns. A volunteer's role becomes that of an instructor rather than a preparer. VITA volunteers will teach taxpayers to prepare their own Forms 1040EZ, 1040A, 1040, and W-4. Assistance with state and local returns can also be provided. If complicated questions or returns are introduced, professional assistance will be provided or the taxpayer will be referred to one of the IRS publications for guidance. Contact your local taxpayer education coordinator for additional information on programs in your district.

Contact your local library or IRS office for locations near you.

* Tax Workshops for Small Businesses

Volunteer and Education Branch
Taxpayer Service Division
Internal Revenue Service (IRS)
U.S. Department of the Treasury
1111 Constitution Ave., NW
Room 2706
Washington, DC 20224 (202) 622-7827

Small businesses usually need help getting started and taxes are one important aspect of successful entrepreneurship. Small Business Tax Workshops help people understand their federal tax obligations. Free workshops explain withholding tax responsibilities and the completion of employment tax returns. Contact the Taxpayer Education Coordinator in your area for information regarding the meeting time and place. The following IRS publications are particularly useful to small business and are free by calling the IRS at (800) TAX-FORM:

Publication 334, *Tax Guide for Small Business*
Publication 583, *Taxpayers Starting a Business*

* Taxpayer Publications

Taxpayer Services
Internal Revenue Service (IRS)
1111 Constitution Ave., NW
Washington, DC 20224 (800) 829-3676

The IRS publishes over 100 free taxpayer information publications on various subjects. One of these, Publication 910, *Guide to Free Tax Services*, is a catalog of the free services and publications they offer.

* The Buck Stops Here

Problem Resolution Staff
Assistant to the Commissioner
Taxpayer Ombudsman
Internal Revenue Service (IRS)
U.S. Department of the Treasury
1111 Constitution Ave., NW
Washington, DC 20224 (202) 622-4300

A major goal of the Problem Resolution Program (PRP) is to solve tax problems that have not been resolved through normal procedures. PRP represents the interests and concerns of taxpayers within the IRS and seeks to prevent future problems by identifying the root causes of such problems. Each IRS district, service center and regional office has a Problem Resolution Officer (PRO). In resolving problems and protecting taxpayer rights, PROs have authority to intervene to assure IRS actions are correct and appropriate. Effective January 1, 1989, authority to issue Taxpayer Assistance Orders (TAOs) was granted to the

Taxpayer Ombudsman. This authority was delegated to the Problem Resolution Officers, as field representatives of the Ombudsman. TAOs may be issued when, in the judgement of the Ombudsman or PRO, a taxpayer is suffering, or is about to suffer a significant hardship as a result of an IRS action or inaction. A TAO can order the function that is handling the taxpayer's case to take appropriate steps to relieve the hardship. The order can also suggest alternative actions to resolve the case. Requests for such relief may be made by taxpayers, their representatives, or by IRS employees on behalf of taxpayers. Contact the IRS toll-free information number regarding tax questions, and ask for Problem Resolution assistance.

* Videos and Films on IRS Topics

Audio/Visual Branch
Public Affairs Division
Internal Revenue Service (IRS)
U.S. Department of the Treasury
1111 Constitution Ave., NW
Washington, DC 20224 (202) 622-7541

The IRS provides audio cassettes and video cassettes for loan to the public on how to fill out Forms 1040EX, 1040A, 1040, and schedules A and B. These tax tapes contain simple step-by-step instructions to the forms and tax tips. Other titles include:

Hey, We're Being Audited! - light-hearted film of an average family after being called in for an IRS tax audit.

A Sensible Approach for the Future of Your Business? - explains what electronic filing is, how to register with the IRS to offer electronic filing, and how it will benefit business.

You've Got To Do This - explains how electronic filing works and how you may get quick refunds.

Form 8300: Why You Should File - informs businesses about their reporting requirements to the IRS for cast transactions over $10,000.

A Video Guide to Taxes-1992 - quick update of tax law changes and general tax information for individual tax returns.

Por Que Nosotros, Los Garcia? - Spanish language film explains taxpayers' examination and appeal rights.

Por Que Los Impuestos? - reporter uncovers the history of taxation, how taxes are used, the rights and responsibilities of taxpayers, and the different kinds of IRS assistance available.

The IRS has distributed these tapes to many local libraries, as well as IRS district offices. Contact an IRS office near you for more information regarding these videos.

* Voicing Opinions of IRS Tax Laws

Office of Chief Counsel, Corporate
Internal Revenue Service (IRS)
U.S. Department of the Treasury
1111 Constitution Ave., NW
Attn: CC:CORP:T:R
Washington, DC 20224 (202) 622-7700

If you have a personal recommendation for changing a federal tax law, you may send written comments to the address above. The letter must include the section within the Internal Revenue Code in which the portion of the law appears. Please send an original and eight copies of the correspondence.

If you wish to comment on how to improve a tax form or instruction booklet, you may address correspondence to the Tax Forms Coordinating Committee, Internal Revenue Service, 1111 Constitution Avenue, NW, Washington, DC 20224.

Senators and members of the House of Representatives can also be contacted if you wish to voice your opinions of tax laws and procedures. Write to: The Honorable (the senator's name), U.S. Senate, Washington, DC 20510; or The Honorable (your representative's name), U.S. House of Representatives, Washington, DC 20515.

Be patient. If any phone number is incorrect, call (area code) 555-1212 and request the new listing.

Federal Tax Help

* Wage Reporting

Returns, Processing, and Accounting
Internal Revenue Service (IRS)
U.S. Department of the Treasury
1111 Constitution Ave., NW
Room 7009
Washington, DC 20224 (202) 622-6860

The combined annual wage reporting system was designed to assist employers in the reporting of taxes. For more assistance in this area, contact your local field office listed in your phone directory or the office above.

* Where To File: Mailing Address

If an addressed envelope came with your return, please use it. If you do not have one, or if you moved during the year, mail your return to the Internal Revenue Service Center for the place where you live. No street address is needed.

Florida, Georgia, South Carolina
Use this address: Atlanta, GA 39901

New Jersey, New York (New York City and counties of Nassau, Rockland, Suffolk, and Westchester)
Use this address: Holtsville, NY 00501

New York (all other counties), Connecticut, Maine, Massachusetts, New Hampshire, Rhode Island, Vermont
Use this address: Andover, MA 05501

Illinois, Iowa, Minnesota, Missouri, Wisconsin
Use this address: Kansas City, MO 64999

Delaware, District of Columbia, Maryland, Pennsylvania, Virginia
Use this address: Philadelphia, PA 19255

Indiana, Kentucky, Michigan, Ohio, West Virginia
Use this address: Cincinnati, OH 45999

Kansas, New Mexico, Oklahoma, Texas
Use this address: Austin, TX 73301

Alaska, Arizona, California (counties of Alpine, Amador, Butte, Calaveras, Colusa, Contra Costa, Del Norte, El Dorado, Glenn, Humboldt, Lake, Lassen, Mendocino, Modoc, Napa, Nevada, Placer, Plumas, Sacramento, San Joaquin, Shasta, Sierra, Siskiyou, Solano, Sonoma, Sutter, Tehama, Trinity, Yolo, and Yuba), Colorado, Idaho, Montana, Nebraska, Nevada, North Dakota, Oregon, South Dakota, Utah, Washington, Wyoming
Use this address: Ogden, UT 84201

California (all other counties), Hawaii
Use this address: Fresno, CA 93888

Alabama, Arkansas, Louisiana, Mississippi, North Carolina, Tennessee
Use this address: Memphis, TN 37501

American Samoa
Use this address: Philadelphia, PA 19255

Guam
Use this address: Commissioner of Revenue and Taxation
855 West Marine Dr
Agana, GU 96910

Puerto Rico (or if excluding income under section 933), Virgin Islands (Nonpermanent residents)
Use this address: Philadelphia, PA 19255

Virgin Islands (Permanent residents)
Use this address: V.I. Bureau of Internal Revenue
Lockharts Garden No. 1A
Charlotte Amalie,
St. Thomas, VI 00802

Foreign country: U.S. citizens and those filing Form 2555 or Form 4563
Use this address: Philadelphia, PA 19255

All A.P.O. or F.P.O. addresses
Use this address: Philadelphia, PA 19255

Be patient. If any phone number is incorrect, call (area code) 555-1212 and request the new listing.

Taxes

Tax Hotlines

Toll-free telephone tax assistance is available in all 50 states, the District of Columbia, Puerto Rico, and the Virgin Islands. There is no long distance charge for your call. It is best to call early in the morning or later in the week for prompt service. The IRS offers these suggestions for using its services.

Call IRS With Your Tax Question:
If the instructions to the tax forms and our free tax publications have not answered your question, please call us Toll-Free. Toll-Free is a telephone call for which you pay only local charges.

Choosing the Right Number:
Use only the number listed below for your area. Use a local city number only if it is not a long distance call for you. Please do not dial 1-800 when using a local city number.

Before You Call:
Remember that good communication is a two-way process. IRS representatives care about the quality of the service we provide to you, our customer. You can help us provide accurate, complete answers to your tax questions by having the following information available.

1. The tax form, schedule, or notice to which your question relates.
2. The facts about your particular situation (the answer to the same question often varies from one taxpayer to another because of differences in their age, income, whether they can be claimed as a dependent, etc.).
3. The name of any IRS publication or other source of information that you used to look for the answer.

Before You Hang Up:
If you do not fully understand the answer you receive, or you feel our representative may not fully understand your question, our representative needs to know this. He or she will be happy to take the additional time required to be sure we have answered your question fully and in the manner which is most helpful to you.

By law, you are responsible for paying your fair share of Federal income tax. If the IRS should make an error in answering your question, you are still responsible for the payment of the correct tax. Should this occur, however, you will not be charged any penalty. To make sure that IRS representatives give accurate and courteous answers, a second IRS representative sometimes listens in on telephone calls. No record is kept of any taxpayer's identity.

Alabama
(800) 829-1040

Alaska
Anchorage, 561-7484
Elsewhere, (800) 829-1040

Arizona
Phoenix, 640-3900
Elsewhere, (800) 829-1040

Arkansas
(800) 829-1040

California
Oakland, 839-1040
Elsewhere, (800) 829-1040

Colorado
Denver, 825-7041
Elsewhere, (800) 829-1040

Connecticut
(800) 829-1040

Delaware
(800) 829-1040

District of Columbia
(800) 829-1040

Florida
Jacksonville, 354-1760
Elsewhere, (800) 829-1040

Georgia
Atlanta, 522-0050
Elsewhere, (800) 829-1040

Hawaii
Oahu, 541-1040
Elsewhere, (800) 829-1040

Idaho
(800) 829-1040

Illinois
Chicago, 435-1040
In area code 708, 312-435-1040
Elsewhere, (800) 829-1040

Indiana
Indianapolis, 226-5477
Elsewhere, (800) 829-1040

Iowa
Des Moines, 283-0523
Elsewhere, (800) 829-1040

Kansas
(800) 829-1040

Kentucky
(800) 829-1040

Louisiana
(800) 829-1040

Maine
(800) 829-1040

Be patient. If any phone number is incorrect, call (area code) 555-1212 and request the new listing.

Tax Hotlines

Maryland
Baltimore, 962-2590
Elsewhere, (800) 829-1040

Massachusetts
Boston, 536-1040
Elsewhere, (800) 829-1040

Michigan
Detroit, 237-0800
Elsewhere, (800) 829-1040

Minnesota
Minneapolis, 644-7515
St. Paul, 644-7515
Elsewhere, (800) 829-1040

Mississippi
(800) 829-1040

Missouri
St. Louis, 342-1040
Elsewhere, (800) 829-1040

Montana
(800) 829-1040

Nebraska
Omaha, 422-1500
Elsewhere, (800) 829-1040

Nevada
(800) 829-1040

New Hampshire
(800) 829-1040

New Jersey
(800) 829-1040

New Mexico
(800) 829-1040

New York
Bronx, 488-9150
Brooklyn, 488-9150
Buffalo, 685-5432
Manhattan, 732-0100
Nassau, 222-1131
Queens, 488-9150
Staten Island, 488-9150
Suffolk, 724-5000
Elsewhere, (800) 829-1040

North Carolina
(800) 829-1040

North Dakota
(800) 829-1040

Ohio
Cincinnati, 621-6281
Cleveland, 522-3000
Elsewhere, (800) 829-1040

Oklahoma
(800) 829-1040

Oregon
Portland, 221-3960
Elsewhere, (800) 829-1040

Pennsylvania
Philadelphia, 574-9900
Pittsburgh, 281-0112
Elsewhere, (800) 829-1040

Puerto Rico
San Juan Metro area, 766-5040
Isla, 766-5549

Rhode Island
(800) 829-1040

South Carolina
(800) 829-1040

South Dakota
(800) 829-1040

Tennessee
Nashville, 259-4601
Elsewhere, (800) 829-1040

Texas
Dallas, 742-2440
Houston, 541-0440
Elsewhere. (800) 829-1040

Utah
(800) 829-1040

Vermont
(800) 829-1040

Virginia
Richmond, 649-2361
Elsewhere, (800) 829-1040

Washington
Seattle, 442-1040
Elsewhere, (800) 829-1040

West Virginia
(800) 829-1040

Wisconsin
Milwaukee, 271-3780
Elsewhere, (800) 829-1040

Wyoming
(800) 829-1040

Telephone Assistance Services for Hearing Impaired Taxpayers Who Have Access to TDD Equipment

Hours of Operation:

8:00 am to 6:30 pm EST — 9:00 am to 7:30 pm EST
(January 1 - April 4) — (April 5 - April 15)

9:00 am to 5:30 pm EST — 8:00 am to 4:30 pm EST
(April 16 to October 31) — (November 1 to December 31)

All locations in U.S., including Alaska, Hawaii,
Virgin Islands, and Puerto Rico — (800) 829-4059

Be patient. If any phone number is incorrect, call (area code) 555-1212 and request the new listing.

Taxes

Recorded Messages

What is Tele-Tax?

Recorded Tax Information has about 140 topics of tax information that answer many Federal tax questions. You can hear up to three topics on each call you make.

Automated Refund Information is available so you can check the status of your refund.

To Call Tele-Tax Toll-Free, Use Only the Numbers Listed Below for Your Area

Long-distance charges apply if you call from outside the local dialing area of the numbers listed below. Do not dial "1-800" when using a local number. However, when dialing from an area that does not have a local number, be sure to dial "1-800" before calling the toll-free number. A complete list of these topics follows this section.

How Do I Use Tele-Tax?

Recorded Tax Information

Topic numbers are effective January 1, 1991. Push-button (tone signaling) service is available 24 hours a day, 7 days a week. Rotary (dial)/Push-button (pulse dial) service is available Monday through Friday during regular office hours. (In Hawaii, from 6:30 am to 1:00 pm).

Select, by number, the topic you want to hear.

Have paper and pencil handy to take notes.

Call the appropriate phone number listed below. If you have a push-button (tone signaling) phone, immediately follow the recorded instructions. If you have a rotary (dial) or push-button (pulse dial) phone, wait for further recorded instructions.

Automated Refund Information

Be sure to have a copy of your tax return available since you will need to know the first social security number shown on your return, the filing status, and the exact amount of your refund.

Then, call the appropriate phone number listed below and follow the recorded instructions.

IRS updates refund information every 7 days. If you call to find out about the status of your refund and do not receive a refund mailing date, please wait 7 days before calling back.

Push-button (tone signaling) service is available Monday through Friday from 7:00 am to 11:30 pm. (Hours may vary in your area).

Rotary (dial)/push-button (pulse dial) service is available Monday through Friday during regular office hours. (In Hawaii, from 6:30 am to 1:00 pm.)

Alabama
(800) 829-4477

Alaska
(800) 829-4477

Arizona
Phoenix, 640-3933
Elsewhere, (800) 829-4477

Arkansas
(800) 829-4477

California
Counties of Alpine, Amador, Butte, Calaveras, Colusa, Contra Costa, Del Norte, El Dorado, Glenn, Humboldt, Lake, Lassen, Marin, Mendocino, Modoc, Napa, Nevada, Placer, Plumas, Sacramento, San Joaquin, Shasta, Sierra, Siskiyou, Solano, Sonoma, Sutter, Tehama, Trinity, Yolo, Yuba, (800) 829-4032
Oakland, 839-4245
Elsewhere, (800) 829-4477

Colorado
Denver, 592-1118
Elsewhere, (800) 829-4477

Connecticut
(800) 829-4477

Delaware
(800) 829-4477

District of Columbia
628-2929

Florida
(800) 829-4477

Georgia
Atlanta, 331-6572
Elsewhere, (800) 829-4477

Hawaii
(800) 829-4477

Idaho
(800) 829-4477

Illinois
Chicago, 886-9614
In area code 708, 312-886-9614
Springfield, 789-0489
Elsewhere, (800) 829-4477

Indiana
Indianapolis, 631-1010
Elsewhere, (800) 829-4477

Iowa
Des Moines, 284-7454
Elsewhere, (800) 829-4477

Kansas
(800) 829-4477

Kentucky
(800) 829-4477

Be patient. If any phone number is incorrect, call (area code) 555-1212 and request the new listing.

Recorded Messages

Louisiana
(800) 829-4477

Maine
(800) 829-4477

Maryland
Baltimore, 244-7306
Elsewhere, (800) 829-4477

Massachusetts
Boston, 536-0709
Elsewhere, (800) 829-4477

Michigan
Detroit, 961-4282
Elsewhere, (800) 829-4477

Minnesota
St. Paul, 644-7748
Elsewhere, (800) 829-4477

Mississippi
(800) 829-4477

Missouri
St. Louis, 241-4700
Elsewhere, (800) 829-4477

Montana
(800) 829-4477

Nebraska
Omaha, 221-3324
Elsewhere, (800) 829-4477

Nevada
(800) 829-4477

New Hampshire
(800) 829-4477

New Jersey
(800) 829-4477

New Mexico
(800) 829-4477

New York
Bronx, 488-8432
Brooklyn, 488-8432
Buffalo, 685-5533
Manhattan, 406-4080
Queens, 488-8432
Staten Island, 488-8432
Elsewhere, (800) 829-4477

North Carolina
(800) 829-4477

North Dakota
(800) 829-4477

Ohio
Cincinnati, 421-0329
Cleveland, 522-3037
Elsewhere, (800) 829-4477

Oklahoma
(800) 829-4477

Oregon
Portland, 294-5363
Elsewhere, (800) 829-4477

Pennsylvania
Philadelphia, 627-1040
Pittsburgh, 261-1040
Elsewhere, (800) 829-4477

Puerto Rico
(800) 829-4477

Rhode Island
(800) 829-4477

South Carolina
(800) 829-4477

South Dakota
(800) 829-4477

Tennessee
(800) 829-4477

Texas
Dallas, 767-1792
Houston, 541-3400
Elsewhere, (800) 829-4477

Utah
(800) 829-4477

Vermont
(800) 829-4477

Virginia
Richmond, 783-1569
Elsewhere, (800) 829-4477

Washington
Seattle, 343-7221
Elsewhere, (800) 829-4477

West Virginia
(800) 829-4477

Wisconsin
Milwaukee, 273-8100
Elsewhere, (800) 829-4477

Wyoming
(800) 829-4477

Tele-Tax Topic Numbers and Subjects

IRS Procedures and Services

- 101 IRS help available: Volunteer tax assistance programs, toll-free telephone, walk-in assistance, and outreach program
- 102 Tax assistance for individuals with disabilities and the hearing impaired
- 103 Small business tax educations: Tax help for small businesses
- 104 Problem resolution program: Special help for problem situations
- 105 Public libraries: Tax information tapes and reproducible tax forms.
- 106 1040 PC tax return
- 107 The collection process
- 108 Tax fraud: How to report
- 109 Types of organizations that qualify for tax-exempt status
- 110 Organizations: How to apply for exempt status
- 111 Examination appeal rights
- 112 Electronic filing
- 113 Power of attorney information
- 114 Change of address: How to notify IRS
- 911 Hardship assistance applications

Be patient. If any phone number is incorrect, call (area code) 555-1212 and request the new listing.

Taxes

999 Local information

Filing Requirements, Filing Status, Exemptions

- 151 Who must file?
- 152 Which form: 1040, 1040A, or 1040EZ?
- 153 When, where, and how to file
- 154 What is your filing status?
- 155 Dependents
- 156 Estimated tax
- 157 Amended returns
- 158 Decedents

Types of Income

- 201 Wages and salaries
- 202 Tips
- 203 Interest received
- 204 Dividends
- 205 Refund of state and local taxes
- 206 Alimony received
- 207 Business income
- 208 Sole proprietorship
- 209 Capital gains and losses
- 210 Pensions and annuities
- 211 Pensions: The general rule and the simplified general rule
- 212 Lump-sum distributions
- 213 Rental income and expenses
- 214 Renting vacation property/Renting to relatives
- 215 Royalties
- 216 Farming and fishing income
- 217 Earnings for clergy
- 218 Unemployment and compensation
- 219 Gambling income and expenses
- 220 Bartering income
- 221 Scholarships, fellowships and grants
- 222 Nontaxable income
- 223 Social Security and equivalent railroad retirement benefits
- 224 401(k) plans
- 225 Passive activities: Losses/Credits

Adjustments to Income

- 251 Individual retirement arrangements (IRAs)
- 252 Alimony paid
- 253 Bad debt reduction
- 254 Tax shelters

Itemized Deductions

- 301 Should I itemize?
- 302 Medical and dental expenses
- 303 Deductible taxes
- 304 Moving expenses
- 305 Interest expense
- 306 Contributions
- 307 Casualty losses
- 308 Miscellaneous expenses
- 309 Business use of home
- 310 Business use of car
- 311 Business travel expenses
- 312 Business entertainment expenses
- 313 Educational expenses
- 314 Employee business expenses

Tax Computation

- 351 Tax and credits figured by IRS
- 352 Self-employment tax
- 353 Five-year averaging for lump-sum distributions
- 354 Alternative minimum tax
- 355 Gift tax
- 357 Standard deduction
- 358 Tax on a child's investment income

Tax Credits

- 401 Child care credit
- 402 Earned income credit
- 403 Credit for the elderly or the disabled

General Information

- 451 Substitute tax forms
- 452 Highlights of 1992 tax changes
- 453 Refunds: How long they should take
- 454 Copy of your tax return: How to get one
- 455 Forms/Publications: How to order
- 456 Offers in compromise
- 457 Extensions for time to file your tax return
- 458 Form W-2: What to do if not received
- 459 Penalty for underpayment of estimated tax
- 460 Recordkeeping
- 461 How to choose a tax preparer
- 462 Failure to pay child/spousal support and other Federal obligations
- 463 Withholding on interest and dividends
- 464 What to do if you haven't filed your tax return
- 465 Checklist/Common errors when preparing your tax return
- 466 Withholding on pensions and annuities
- 467 What to do if you can't pay your tax
- 468 Desert Storm

IRS Notices and Letters

- 501 Notices: What to do
- 502 Notice of under-reported income - CP2000
- 503 IRS notices and bills/Penalty and interest charges

Basis of Assets, Depreciation, Sale of Assets

- 551 Sale of your home: General
- 552 Sale of your home: How to report gain
- 553 Sale of your home: Exclusion of gain, age 55 and over
- 554 Basis of assets
- 555 Depreciation
- 556 Installment sales

Employer Tax Information

- 601 Social security withholding rates
- 602 Form W-2: Where, when and how to file
- 603 Form W-4: Employee's Withholding Allowance Certificate
- 604 Employer identification number: How to apply
- 605 Form 942: Employer's Quarterly Tax Return for Household Employees
- 606 Form 941: Deposit requirements
- 607 Form 941: Employer's Quarterly Federal tax return
- 608 Form 940: Deposit requirements
- 609 Form 940/940EZ: Employer's Annual Federal Unemployment Tax Return
- 610 Targeted jobs credit
- 611 Tips: Withholding and reporting

Magnetic Media Information

- 651 Who must file/originals and corrections?
- 652 Acceptable media/Locating a third party to prepare your files
- 653 Applications, forms and information
- 654 Waivers, extensions, and format deviations
- 655 Test files and combined Federal/State filing
- 656 Electronic filing of information returns
- 657 Information returns bulletin board system

Tax Information for Aliens and U.S. Citizens Living Abroad

- 701 Resident and nonresident aliens
- 702 Dual-status alien
- 703 Foreign earned income exclusion: General
- 704 Foreign earned income exclusion: Who qualifies?
- 705 Foreign earned income exclusion: What qualifies?
- 706 Foreign tax credit

The following topics are in Spanish

- 751 Who must file?
- 752 Which form to use?
- 753 What is your filing status?
- 754 Earned income credit
- 755 Highlights of 1992 tax changes
- 756 Forms and publications: How to order
- 757 Alien tax clearance
- 758 Refunds: How long they should take
- 759 IRS help available: Volunteer tax assistance programs, toll-free telephone, walk-in assistance, and outreach program

Be patient. If any phone number is incorrect, call (area code) 555-1212 and request the new listing.

760 Social security and equivalent railroad retirement benefits

Tax Information for Puerto Rico Residents

851 Who must file a U.S. Income Tax Return in Puerto Rico

852 Deductions and Credits for Puerto Rico filers
853 Federal Employment Taxes in Puerto Rico
854 Tax Assistance for Residents of Puerto Rico

Be patient. If any phone number is incorrect, call (area code) 555-1212 and request the new listing.

Taxes

IRS Tax Forms

All Federal Income Tax Forms are listed in numerical order after this state-by-state roster. To order any of the IRS forms, publications and instruction packets which are listed in the next section, call the toll-free IRS hotline at (800) 424-3676. To send for forms through the mail, write to the approriate state address below. Two copies of each form and one copy of each set of instructions will be sent.

Forms Distribution Centers

Alabama
P.O. Box 8903
Bloomington, IL 61703

Alaska
Rancho Cordova, CA 95743-0001

Arizona
Rancho Cordova, CA 95743-0001

Arkansas
P.O. Box 8903
Bloomington, IL 61703

California
Rancho Cordova, CA 95743-0001

Colorado
Rancho Cordova, CA 95743-0001

Connecticut
P.O. Box 85074
Richmond, VA 23261-5074

Delaware
P.O. Box 85074
Richmond, VA 23261-5074

District of Columbia
P.O. Box 85074
Richmond, VA 23261-5074

Florida
P.O. Box 85074
Richmond, VA 23261-5074

Georgia
P.O. Box 85074
Richmond, VA 23261-5074

Hawaii
Rancho Cordova, CA 95743-0001

Idaho
Rancho Cordova, CA 95743-0001

Illinois
P.O. Box 8903
Bloomington, IL 61703

Indiana
P.O. Box 8903
Bloomington, IL 61703

Iowa
P.O. Box 8903
Bloomington, IL 61703

Kansas
P.O. Box 8903
Bloomington, IL 61703

Kentucky
P.O. Box 8903
Bloomington, IL 61703

Louisiana
P.O. Box 8903
Bloomington, IL 61703

Maine
P.O. Box 85074
Richmond, VA 23261-5074

Maryland
P.O. Box 85074
Richmond, VA 23261-5074

Massachusetts
P.O. Box 85074
Richmond, VA 23261-5074

Michigan
P.O. Box 8903
Bloomington, IL 61703

Minnesota
P.O. Box 8903
Bloomington, IL 61703

Mississippi
P.O. Box 8903
Bloomington, IL 61703

Missouri
P.O. Box 8903
Bloomington, IL 61703

Montana
Rancho Cordova, CA 95743-0001

Nebraska
P.O. Box 8903
Bloomington, IL 61703

Nevada
Rancho Cordova, CA 95743-0001

Be patient. If any phone number is incorrect, call (area code) 555-1212 and request the new listing.

IRS Tax Forms

New Hampshire
P.O. Box 85074
Richmond, VA 23261-5074

New Jersey
P.O. Box 85074
Richmond, VA 23261-5074

New Mexico
Rancho Cordova, CA 95743-0001

New York
P.O. Box 85074
Richmond, VA 23261-5074

North Carolina
P.O. Box 85074
Richmond, VA 23261-5074

North Dakota
P.O. Box 8903
Bloomington, IL 61703

Ohio
P.O. Box 8903
Bloomington, IL 61703

Oklahoma
P.O. Box 8903
Bloomington, IL 61703

Oregon
Rancho Cordova, CA 95743-0001

Pennsylvania
P.O. Box 85074
Richmond, VA 23261-5074

Puerto Rico
P.O. Box 85074
Richmond, VA 23261-5074

Rhode Island
P.O. Box 85074
Richmond, VA 23261-5074

South Carolina
P.O. Box 85074
Richmond, VA 23261-5074

South Dakota
P.O. Box 8903
Bloomington, IL 61703

Tennessee
P.O. Box 8903
Bloomington, IL 61703

Texas
P.O. Box 8903
Bloomington, IL 61703

Utah
Rancho Cordova, CA 95743-0001

Vermont
P.O. Box 85074
Richmond, VA 23261-5074

Virgin Islands
V.I. Bureau of Internal Revenue
Lockharts Garden No. 1A

Charlotte Amalie
St. Thomas, VI 00802

Virginia
P.O. Box 85074
Richmond, VA 23261-5074

Washington
Rancho Cordova, CA 95743-0001

West Virginia
P.O. Box 85074
Richmond, VA 23261-5074

Wisconsin
P.O. Box 8903
Bloomington, IL 61703

Wyoming
Rancho Cordova, CA 95743-0001

Foreign Addresses

Forms Distribution Center
P.O. Box 85074
Richmond, VA 23261-5074

Forms Distribution Center
Rancho Cordova, CA 95743-0001

Taxpayers with mailing addresses in foreign countries should send the order blank to either address. Send letter requests for other forms and publications to: Forms Distribution Center, P.O. Box 85074, Richmond, VA 23261-5074.

Numerical List of Federal Tax Return Forms and Related Forms

Timber/Forest Industries Schedules

Supplement to income tax return for taxpayers claiming a deduction for depletion of timber and for depreciation of plant and other timber improvements. IT-IRC sec. 631; Regs. sec. 1.611-3: IT-IRC sec. 6012; Pub. 17

Tax Forms Package 1 Federal Income Tax Forms

A package of income tax forms for nonbusiness and nonfarm taxpayers. Contains one copy of instructions for Form 1040 and two copies of the following: Form 1040, Schedule A, and Schedule B. IT-IRC sec. 6012; Pub. 17

Tax Forms Package 1-X Federal Income Tax Forms

A package of income tax forms for nonbusiness and nonfarm taxpayers. Contains one copy of instructions for Form 1040 and two copies of the following: Form 1040, Schedule A, Schedule B, Form 2106 and instructions, and Form 2441 and instructions. IT-IRC sec. 6012; Pub. 17

Tax Forms Package 2 Federal Income Tax Forms

A package of income tax forms for nonbusiness and nonfarm taxpayers. Contains one copy of instructions for Form 1040 and two copies of the following: Form 1040, Schedule A, Schedule B, Schedule D, Schedule E, Form 2441 and instructions, and Form 4562 and instructions. IT-IRC sec. 6012; Pub. 17

Tax Forms Package 2-R Federal Income Tax Forms

A package of income tax forms for nonbusiness and nonfarm taxpayers. Contains one copy of instructions for Form 1040 and two copies of the following: Form 1040, Schedule A, Schedule B, Schedule D, Schedule E, Schedule R and instructions, and Form 4562 and instructions. IT-IRC sec. 6012; Pub. 17

Be patient. If any phone number is incorrect, call (area code) 555-1212 and request the new listing.

Taxes

Tax Forms Package 3
Federal Income Tax Forms

A package of income tax forms for business taxpayers. Contains one copy of instructions for Form 1040 and two copies of the following: Form 1040, Schedule A, Schedule B, Schedule C, Schedule D, Schedule E, Schedule SE, Form 2441 and instructions, and Form 4562 and instructions. IT-IRC sec. 6012; Pub. 17

Tax Forms Package 3-E
Federal Income Tax Forms

A package of income tax forms for business taxpayers. Contains one copy of instructions for Form 1040 and two copies of the following: Forms 1040, Schedule A, Schedule B, Schedule C, Schedule D, Schedule E, Schedule SE, and Form 4562 and instructions. IT-IRC sec. 6012; Pub. 17

Tax Forms Package 4
Federal Income Tax Forms

A package of income tax forms for farm taxpayers. Contains one copy of instructions for Form 1040 and two copies of the following: Form 1040, Schedule A, Schedule B, Schedule C, Schedule D, Schedule E, Schedule F, Schedule SE, Form 2441 and instructions, Form 4136, and Form 4562 and instructions. IT-IRC sec. 6012; Pub. 17

Tax Forms Package 5
Federal Income Tax Forms

A package of income tax forms for individual taxpayers. Contains one copy of instructions for Form 1040A and two copies each of Form 1040EZ, Form 1040A, and Schedule 1 (Form 1040A).

Package X
Informational Copies of Federal Tax Forms

A two-volume set of income tax and information return forms, substitute forms information, and other information needed by tax practitioners to service their clients.

CT-1
Employer's Annual Railroad Retirement and Unemployment Repayment Tax Return

Used to report employees' and employers' taxes under the RRTA and RURT. Emp-IRC secs. 3201, 3202, 3221, 3321, 3322, and 6011; Regs. secs. 31.6011(a)-2, 31.6011(a)-3AT, and 31.6302(c)-2; Separate instructions

CT-2
Employee Representative's Quarterly Railroad Tax Return

Used to report employee representative's tax under the RRTA and RURT. Emp-IRC secs. 3211, 3321, and 6011; Regs. secs. 31.6011(a)-2 and 31.6011(a)-3AT

W-2
Wage and Tax Statement (For Use in Cities and States Authorizing Combined Form)

Used to report wages, tips and other compensation, allocated tips, employee social security tax, income tax, state or city income tax withheld; and to support credit shown on individual income tax return.
Emp-IRC sec 6051; Regs secs 1.6041-2 and 31.6051-1; Circular E; Separate instructions

W-2AS
American Samoa Wage and Tax Statement

Used to report wages, tips, and other compensation, employee social security tax, Samoan income tax withheld, and to support credit shown on American Samoa individual income tax return.
Emp-IRC sec. 6051; Regs. sec. 31.6051-1, Circular SS

W-2c
Statement of Corrected Income and Tax Amounts

Used to correct previously filed Forms W-2, W-2P, W-2AS, W-2CNMI, W-2GU, and W-2VI. Emp-IRC sec. 6051; Reg. sec. 1.6041-2 and 31.6051-1

499R-2/W-2PR
Puerto Rico Withholding Statement

Used to report social security wages, tips, and social security tax withheld for employees in Puerto Rico. Emp-IRC sec. 6051; Regs. sec. 31.6051-1; Circular PR

W-2G
Statement for Recipients of Certain Gambling Winnings

Used to report gambling winnings and any taxes withheld.
IT-IRC sec 3402(q) and 6041; Temp Regs sec 7.6041-1 and Regs sec 31.3402(q)-1(f); See separate Instructions for Forms 1099, 1098, 5498, 1096, and W-2G.

W-2GU
Guam Wage and Tax Statement

Used to report wages, tips and other compensation, employee social security tax, Guam income tax withheld, and to support credit shown on individual income tax return. Emp-IRC sec. 6051; Regs. sec. 31.6051-1; Circular SS

W-2CNMI
Commonwealth of Northern Mariana Islands Wage and Tax Statement

Used to report wages, tips and other compensation, employee social security tax, CNMI income tax withheld, and to support credit shown on individual income tax return. Emp-IRC sec. 6051; Regs. sec. 31.6050-1; Circular SS

W-2VI
U.S. Virgin Islands Wage and Tax Statement

Used to report wages, tips and other compensation, employee social security tax, VI income tax withheld, and to support credit shown on individual income tax return. Emp-IRC sec. 6051; Regs. secs. 1.6041-2 and 31.6051-1; Circular SS

W-2P
Statement For Recipients of Annuities, Pensions, Retired Pay, or IRA Payments

Used to report periodic distributions from annuities, pensions, retirement pay, and payments from an IRA; Federal and state income tax withheld.
Emp-IRC sec. 3402(o); Regs. sec. 32.1-1; Circular E; Separate instructions

W-3
Transmittal of Income and Tax Statements

Used by employers and other payers to transmit Forms W-2 and W-2P to the Social Security Administration. Emp-IRC sec. 6011; Reg. sec. 31.6051-2

W-3c
Transmittal of Corrected Income and Tax Statements

Used by employers and other payers to transmit corrected income and tax statements (Forms W-2c). Emp-IRC sec. 6011; Reg. 31.6051-2

W-3PR
Transmittal of Withholding Statements

Used by employers to transmit Forms 499R-2/W-2PR.
Emp-IRC sec. 6011; Reg. sec. 31.6051-2; Circular PR

W-3SS
Transmittal of Wage and Tax Statements

Used by employers to transmit Forms W-2AS, W-2CNMI, W-2GU, and W-2VI.
Emp-IRC sec. 6011; Reg. sec. 31.6051-2; Circular SS

W-4
Employee's Withholding Allowance Certificate

Completed by employee and given to employer so that proper amount of income tax can be withheld from wages. Also used by employee to claim exemption from withholding by certifying that he or she had no liability for income tax for preceding tax year and anticipates that no liability will be incurred for current tax year.
Emp-IRC secs. 3402(f), 3402(m) and 3402(n); Regs. secs. 31.3402(f)5)-1 and 31.3402(n)-1; Circular E

W-4P
Withholding Certificate for Pension or Annuity Payments

Used to figure amount of Federal income tax to withhold from periodic pension or annuity payments or to claim additional withholding or exemption from withholding for periodic or nonperiodic payments. Emp-IRC sec. 3405

W-4S
Request for Federal Income Tax Withholding from Sick Pay

Filed with a third party payer of sick pay to request Federal income tax

IRS Tax Forms

withholding. Emp-IRC sec. 3402(o); Regs. sec. 31.3402(o)-3

W-5
Earned Income Credit Advance Payment Certificate
Used by employee to request employer to furnish advance payment of earned income credit with the employee's pay. IRC sec. 3507

W-8
Certificate of Foreign Status
Used by foreign persons to notify payers of interest, mortgage interest recipients, or middlemen, brokers, or barter exchanges not to withhold or report on payments of interest, or on broker transactions or barter exchanges.
IRC secs. 3406, 6042, 6044, 6045, and 6049

W-9
Request for Taxpayer Identification Number and Certification
Used by a person required to file certain information returns with IRS to obtain the correct taxpayer identification number (TIN) of the person for whom a return is filed. Also used to claim exemption from backup withholding and to certify that the person whose TIN is provided is not subject to backup withholding because of failure to report interest and dividends as income.

W-10
Dependent Care Provider's Identification and Certification
Used by taxpayers to certify that the name, address, and taxpayer identification number of their dependent care provider is correct. IRS secs. 21, 129, 501(c)3)

SS-4
Application for Employer Identification Number
Used by employers and other entities to apply for an identification number.
Emp-IRC Regs. sec. 31.6011(b)-1; Circulars A and E

SS-4 PR
Solicitud de Numero de Identificacion Patronal
Used by employers and other entities in Puerto Rico to apply for an identification number. A variation of Form SS-4.
Emp-IR Regs. sec. 31.6011(b)-1; Circular PR

SS-5
Application for a Social Security Card
Used by an individual to obtain a social security number and card.
Emp-IR Regs. sec. 31.6011(b)-2; Circulars A and E

SS-8
Information for Use in Determining Whether a Worker Is an Employee for Federal Employment Taxes and Income Tax Withholding
Used to furnish information about services of an individual, generally selected as representative of a class of workers, to get written determination on status.
Emp-IRC sec. 3121; Regs. sec. 31.3121(d)-1

SS-16
Certificate of Election of Coverage Under the Federal Insurance Contributions Act
Used by religious orders, whose members are required to take a vow of poverty, to elect social security coverage.
Emp-IRC sec. 3121(r); Regs. sec. 31.3121(r)-1

11-C
Stamp Tax and Registration Return for Wagering
Used to report taxes due under IRC sections 4401 and 4411, and as an application for registry and wagering activity. Upon approval of the return, the Service will issue a Special Tax Stamp.
Ex-IRC secs. 4411 and 4412; Regs. secs. 44.4412 and 44.4901

56
Notice Concerning Fiduciary Relationship
Used by persons to notify IRS that they are acting in fiduciary capacity for other persons.
IT-IRC sec. 6903; Regs. sec. 301.6903-1

637
Registration for Tax-Free Transactions Under Chapters 31, 32, and 38 of the Internal Revenue Code
Used as an application and certificate; by manufacturers, refiners or importers who buy taxable articles tax-free for further manufacture of taxable articles, or for resale direct to a manufacturer for such purpose. The original of the application is validated and returned as the Certificate of Registry by the District Director. Ex-IRC secs. 4052, 4064(b)(1)(c), 4101, 4221, and 4661; Regs. secs. 48.4101-1, 48.4222(a)-1, and 48.4222(d)-1

637A
Registration for Tax-Free Sales and Purchases of Fuel Used in Aircraft
Used to register for tax-free sales under IRC section 4041(c). Filed by a seller who is a manufacturer, producer, importer, wholesaler, jobber, or retailer; or by a seller that is a commercial airline, nonprofit educational organization, or other exempt user that wishes to sell or purchase tax-free fuel for use in aircraft. The original of the application is validated by the District Director and returned as the Certificate of Registry.
Ex-IRC sec. 4041(c); Regs. sec. 48.4041-11

706
United States Estate (and Generation-Skipping Transfer) Tax Return
Used for the estate of a deceased United States resident or citizen.
E&G-IRC sec. 6018; Regs. sec. 20.6018-1; Separate instructions

706-A
United States Additional Estate Tax Return
Used to report recapture tax under special use valuation.
E&G-IRC sec. 2032A; Separate instructions

706CE
Certificate of Payment of Foreign Death Tax
Used to report credit against United States estate tax for estate inheritance, legacy, or succession tax paid to a foreign government.
E&G-IRC sec. 2014; Regs. sec. 20.2014-5

706GS(D)
Generation-Skipping Transfer Tax Return for Distributions
Used by distributees to report generation-skipping transfer tax on taxable distributions from trusts subject to the tax.
E&G-IRC sec. 2601; Temp Regs. sec. 26.2662-1(b)(1); Separate instructions

706GS(D-1)
Notification of Distribution from a Generation-Skipping Trust
Used by trustees to report certain information to distributees regarding taxable distributions from a trust subject to the generation-skipping transfer tax.
E&G-IRC sec. 2601; Temp. Regs. sec. 26.2662-1(b)(1)

706GS(T)
Generation-Skipping Transfer Tax Return for Terminations
Used by trustees to report generation-skipping transfer tax on taxable terminations of trusts subject to the tax.
E&G-IRC sec. 2601; Temp. Regs. sec. 26.2662-1(b)2); Separate instructions

706NA
United States Estate (and Generation-Skipping Transfer) Tax Return, Estate of nonresident not a citizen of the United States
Used for United States nonresident alien decedent's estate to be filed within 9 months after date of death.
E&G-IRC sec. 6018; Regs. sec. 20.6018-1(b); Separate instructions

Schedule S (Form 706)
Increased Estate Tax on Excess Retirement Accumulations
Used to pay the section 4980A increased estate tax on excess retirement accumulations. E&G-IRC sec. 4980A(d)

Be patient. If any phone number is incorrect, call (area code) 555-1212 and request the new listing.

Taxes

709

United States Gift (and Generation-Skipping Transfer) Tax Return

Used to report gifts of more than $10,000 (or, regardless of value, gifts of a future interest in property).
E&G-IRC sec. 6019; Regs. sec. 25.6019-1; Separate instructions

709-A

United States Short Form Gift Tax Return

Used to report gifts of more than $10,000 but less than $20,000 if the gifts are nontaxable by reason of gift splitting.
E&G-IRC secs. 6019, 6075; Regs. sec. 25.6019-1

712

Life Insurance Statement

Used with Form 706 or Form 709.
E&G-IRC secs 6001 and 6018; Regs secs 20.6001-1, 20.6018-4(d), 25.6001-1(b)

720

Quarterly Federal Excise Tax Return

Used to report excise taxes due from retailers and manufacturers on sale or manufacture of various articles; taxes on facilities and services; taxes on certain products and commodities (gasoline, coal, etc); windfall profits and Inland waterways taxes. Ex-IRC sec. 6011; Separate instructions

730

Tax on Wagering

Used to report taxes due under IRC section 4401.
Ex-IRC sec. 4401; Regs. sec. 44.6011(a)-1

843

Claim

Used to claim refund of taxes (other than income taxes) which were illegally, erroneously or excessively collected; or to claim amount paid for stamps unused or used in error or excess; and for a refund or abatement of interest or penalties assessed.
Misc-IRC secs. 6402, 6404, 6511, 6404(e), and 6404(f); Regs. secs. 31.6413(c)-1, 301.6402-2, and 301.6404-1

851

Affiliations Schedule

Used with Form 1120 by parent corporation for affiliated corporations included in consolidated tax return. IT-IRC sec. 1502; Regs. sec. 1.1502-75(h)

872-C

Consent Fixing Period of Limitation Upon Assessment of Tax Under Section 4940 of the Internal Revenue Code

Used only with Form 1023, Application for Recognition of Exemption, by an organization described in Internal Revenue Code section 170(b)(1)(A)(vi) or section 509(a)2), to request the organization be treated as a publicly supported organization during an advance ruling period. IT-IRC sec. 6501(c)4)

926

Return by a Transferor of Property to a Foreign Corporation, Foreign Trust or Estate, or Foreign Partnership

Used to report transfers of property by a U.S. person to a foreign partnership, trust or estate, or corporation, and pay any excise tax due on the transfer.
IT-IRC sec. 1491; Regs. sec. 1.1491-2

928

Gasoline Bond

Used to post bond for excise tax on fuel.
Ex-IRC sec. 4101

940

Employer's Annual Federal Unemployment (FUTA) Tax Return

Used by employers to report Federal unemployment (FUTA) tax. Emp-IRC sec 6011; IRC Chapter 23; Regs sec 31.6011(a)-3; Circular E; Circular SS

940-EZ

Employer's Annual Federal Unemployment (FUTA) Tax Return

Used by employers to report Federal unemployment (FUTA) tax. This form is a simplified version of Form 940.
EMP-IRC sec. 6011; IRC Chapter 23; Regs. sec. 31.6011(a)-3; Circular E; Circular SS

940PR

Planilla Para La Declaracion Anual Del Patrono-La Contribucion Federal Para el Desempleo (FUTA)

Used by employers in Puerto Rico. A variation of Form 940.
Emp-IRC sec. 6011; IRC Chapter 23; Regs. sec. 31.6011(a)-3; Circular PR

941

Employer's Quarterly Federal Tax Return

Used by employer to report social security taxes and income taxes withheld, advance earned income credit (EIC), and back up withholding.
Emp-IRC secs. 3101, 3111, 3402, 3405 and 3406; Regs. secs. 31.6011(a)-1 and 31.6011(a)-4; Circular E

Sch. A (Form 941)

Record of Federal Backup Withholding Tax Liability

Used to report backup withholding liability when treated as a separate tax for depositing purposes.
Emp-IRC secs. 3406, 6302; Regs. secs. 31.6302 and 35a.9999-3

941c

Statement to Correct Information Previously Reported on the Employer's Federal Tax Return

Used by employers to correct wages, tips, and tax previously reported.
Emp-IRC secs. 6205 and 6402; Regs. secs. 31.6011(a)-1, 31.6205-1, and 31.6402(a)-2; Circulars A, E, and SS

941c PR

Planilla Para La Correccion De Informacion Facilitada Anteriormente En Complimiento Con La Ley Del Seguro Social

Used by employers in Puerto Rico. A variation of Form 941c.
Emp-IRC Chapter 21; Regs secs 31.6011(a)-1 and 31.6205-1, 31.6402(a)-2; Circular PR

941E

Quarterly Return of Withheld Federal Income Tax and Hospital Insurance (Medicare) Tax

Used by State and local government employers and by other organizations that are not liable for social security taxes. A variation of Form 941.
Emp-IRC secs. 3121(u) and 3402

941-M

Employer's Monthly Federal Tax Return

Used by employers to report withheld income tax and social security taxes (because they have not complied with the requirements for filing quarterly returns, or for paying or depositing taxes reported on quarterly returns).
Emp-IRC sec. 7512; Regs. sec. 31.6011(a)-5

941 PR

Planilla Para La Declaracion Trimestral Del Patrono-La Contribucion Federal al Seguro Social

Used by employers in Puerto Rico. A variation of Form 941.
Emp-IRC secs. 3101 and 3111; Regs. sec. 31.6011(a)-1; Circular PR

941SS

Employer's Quarterly Federal Tax Return

Used by employers in Virgin Islands, Guam, the Northern Mariana Islands, and American Samoa. A variation of Form 941.
Emp-IRC secs. 3101 and 3111; Regs. sec. 31.6011(a)-1; Circular SS

Be patient. If any phone number is incorrect, call (area code) 555-1212 and request the new listing.

IRS Tax Forms

942
Employer's Quarterly Tax Return for Household Employees
Used by household employers quarterly to report social security and income taxes withheld from wages of household employees.
Emp-IRC secs. 3101 and 3111; Regs. sec. 31.6011(a)-1(a)(3)

942PR
Planilla Para La Declaracion Trimestral Del Patrono De Empleados Domesticos
Used by household employers in Puerto Rico to report social security taxes withheld from wages of household employees. A variation of Form 942.
Emp-IRC secs. 3101 and 3111; Regs. sec. 31.6011(a)-1(a)(3)

943
Employer's Annual Tax Return for Agricultural Employees
Used by Agricultural employers to report social security and income taxes withheld.
Emp-IRC secs. 3101, 3111 and 3402; Regs. sec. 31.6011(a)-1 and 31.6011(a)-4; Circular A

943A
Agricultural Employer's Record of Federal Tax Liability
Used by agricultural employers who have a tax liability of $3,000 or more during any month. Emp-IRC sec. 6302; Regs. sec. 6302(c)-1; Circular A

943 PR
Planilla Para La Declaracion Anual De La Contribucion Del Patrono De Empleados Agricolas
Used by agricultural employers in Puerto Rico. A variation of Form 943.
Emp-IRC secs 3101 and 3111; Regs sec 31.6011(a)-1, 31.6011(a)-4; Circular PR

943A-PR
Registro De La Obligacion Contributiva Del Patrono Agricola
Used by agricultural employers in Puerto Rico. A variation of Form 943A.
Emp-IRC sec. 6302; Regs. sec. 31.6302(c)-1; Circular PR

952
Consent to Fix Period of Limitation on Assessment of Income Taxes
Used when complete liquidation of a subsidiary is not accomplished within the tax year in which the first liquidating distribution is made. The receiving corporation is required to file this consent with its return for each tax year which falls wholly or partly within the period of liquidation.
IT-IRC sec. 332; Regs. sec. 1.332-4

966
Corporate Dissolution or Liquidation
Used (under IRC section 6043(a)) by corporations within 30 days after adoption of resolution or plan of dissolution, or complete or partial liquidation. (An information return.)
IT-IRC sec. 6043(a)

970
Application to Use LIFO Inventory Method
Used to change to the LIFO inventory method provided by section 472.
IT-IRC sec. 472; Regs. sec. 1.472-3

972
Consent of Shareholder to Include Specific Amount in Gross Income
Used by shareholders of a corporation who agree to include in their gross income for their taxable year a specific amount as a tax dividend.
IT-IRC sec. 565

973
Corporation Claim for Deduction for Consent Dividends
Used by corporations that claim a consent dividends deduction. Accompanied by filed consents of shareholders on Form 972. IT-IRC sec. 561

976
Claim for Deficiency Dividends Deduction by a Personal Holding Company, Regulated Investment Company, or Real Estate Investment Trust
Used by a personal holding company, regulated investment company, or real estate investment trust to claim a deficiency dividends deduction.
IT-IRC sec. 547 and 860; Regs. sec. 1.547-2(b)(2) and 1.860-2(b)(2)

982
Reduction of Tax Attributes Due to Discharge of Indebtedness
Used by a taxpayer who excludes from gross income under section 108 any amount of income attributable to discharge of indebtedness, in whole or in part, in the tax year, for which it is liable or subject. Also used as a consent of a corporation to adjustment of basis of its property under regulations prescribed under IRC section 1082(a)(2).
IT-IRC secs. 108, 1017, and 1082

990
Return of Organization Exempt From Income Tax (Except Private Foundation)
Used by organizations exempt under IRC section 501(a) and described in Code section 501(c), other than private foundations. (An information return.)
IT-IRC sec. 6033; Regs. sec. 1.6033-1(a)(2); Separate instructions

Package 990-1
Organizations Exempt from Income Tax under section 501(c) (other than sections 501(c)(3), (c)(4), (c)(6), and (c)(7), of the Internal Revenue Code)
A package of information forms for exempt organizations. Contains one copy each of Instructions for Forms 990, 990-EZ, and 990-T; two copies each of Forms 990, 990-EZ, and 990-T.
IT-IRC sec. 6033, one copy of Form 990-W, Form 1120-W, and instructions.

Package 990-2
Organizations Exempt from Income Tax under Section 501(c)(3) (other than Private Foundations as defined in Section 509(a), of the Internal Revenue Code)
A package of information forms for exempt organizations. Contains one copy each of Instructions for Forms 990, Schedule A (Form 990), 990-EZ, and 990-T; two copies each of Forms 990, Schedule A (Form 990), 990-EZ, and 990-T, one copy of Form 990-W, Form 1120-W, and instructions; one copy of Supplemental Instructions, and a sample filled-in Form 990 and Schedule A (Form 990).
IT-IRC sec. 6033

Package 990-3
Organizations Exempt from Income Tax under section 501(c)(4) of the Internal Revenue Code
A package of information forms for exempt organizations. Contains one copy each of Instructions for Forms 990, 990-EX, and 990-T; two copies each of Forms 990, 990-EX, and 990-T, one copy of Form 990-W, Form 1120-W, and instructions; one copy of Supplemental Instructions, and sample filled-in Forms 990-EZ and 990-T.
IT-IRC sec. 6033

Sch. A (Form 990)
Organization Exempt Under 501 (c)(3) (Supplementary Information)
Used by organizations described in IRC section 501(c)(3) (other than private foundations filing Form 990-PF).
IT-IRC sec. 6033; Separate instructions

990-BL
Information and Initial Excise Tax Return for Black Lung Benefit Trusts and Certain Related Persons
Used by Black Lung Benefit Trusts exempt under Section 501(c)(21) as an information return. Also used by these trusts and certain related persons for attaching Schedule A (Form 990-BL) when taxes under sections 4951 or 4952 are due.
IT/EX-IRC sec. 501 (c)(21); Chapter 42; Separate instructions

Taxes

990-C
Farmers' Cooperative Association Income Tax Return
Used by Farmers' Cooperative Marketing and Purchasing Association.
IT-IRC secs. 521, 1381, 1382, 1383, 1385, 1388, and 6012; Regs. secs. 1.522-1, 1.1381-1, 2, 1.1382-1, 2, 3, 4, 5, 6, 7, 1.1383-1, 1.1385-1, 1.388-1, and 1.6012-2(f); Separate instructions

990-EZ
Short Form Return of Organization Exempt Form Income Tax
Used by organizations of gross receipts less than $100,000 and total assets of less than $250,000 at end of year.
IT-IRC sec. 6033; Regs. sec. 1.6033-1(a)(2); Separate instructions

990-PF
Return of Private Foundation or Section 4947(a)(1)Trust Treated as a Private Foundation
Used by private foundations and Section 4947(a)(1)trusts. (An information return.) IT/Ex-IRC sec. 6033; IRC Chapter 42; Separate instructions

Package 990-PF
Returns for Private Foundations or Section 4947(a)(1) Trusts Treated as Private Foundations
A package of information forms used by private foundations and Sections 4947(a)(1)trusts. In addition to Form 990-PF, this package includes Form 990-T and Form 4720, Form 990-W, Form 1120-W and instructions for each form, and filled-in samples of Form 990-PF. IT-IRC sec. 6033

990-T
Exempt Organization Business Income Tax Return
Used by exempt organization with unrelated business income (under IRC section 511). IT-IRC secs. 511 and 6012; Regs. secs. 1.6012-2(e) and 1.6012-3(a)(5); Separate instructions

990-W
Estimated Tax on Unrelated Business Taxable Income for Tax-Exempt Organization
Used as a worksheet by tax-exempt trusts and tax-exempt corporations to figure their estimated tax liability. Tax-exempt trusts and corporations should keep it for their records. IT-IRC sec. 6154

1000
Ownership Certificate
Used by a citizen, resident individual, fiduciary, partnership, or nonresident partnership all of whose members are citizens or residents who have interest in bonds of a domestic or resident corporation (containing a tax-free covenant and issued before January 1, 1934). IT-IRC sec. 1461; Regs. sec. 1.1461-1(h)

1001
Ownership, Exemption, or Reduced Rate Certificate
Used by a nonresident alien individual or fiduciary, foreign partnership, foreign corporation or other foreign entity, nonresident foreign partnership composed in whole or in part of nonresident aliens (applies to IRC section 1451 only), or nonresident foreign corporation (applies to Code section 1451 only), receiving income subject to withholding under Code section 1441, 1442, or 1451. IT-IRC sec. 1461; Regs. sec. 1.1461-1(i)

Package 1023
Application for Recognition of Exemption Under Section 501(c)3-of the Internal Revenue Code
Used to apply for exemption under section 501(a) IRC as organizations described in section 501(c)3-(also sections 501(e) and (f)). Includes 3 copies of Form 872-C. IT-IRC sec. 501; Regs. sec. 1.501(a)-1(a)3)

Package 1024
Application for Recognition of Exemption Under Section 501(a) or Determination Under Section 120
Used by organizations to apply for exemption under IRC section 501(a) (as described in Code sections 501(c)2), 4), 5), 6), 7), 8), 9), (10), (12), (13), (15), (17), (19), 20) and 25). (Also used to apply for a determination as a qualified plan under section 120.) IT-IRC secs. 501, 120; Regs. sec. 1.501(a)-1(a)3)

1028
Application for Recognition of Exemption Under Section 521 of the Internal Revenue Code
Used by farmers, fruit growers, or similar associations to claim exemption under IRC section 521. IT-IRC sec. 521; Regs. sec. 1.521-1, Separate instructions

1040
U.S. Individual Income Tax Return
Used by citizens or residents of the United States to report income tax. (Also see Form 1040A, and 1040EZ.) IT-IRC secs. 6012 and 6017; Regs. secs. 1.6012-1 and 1.6017-1; Pub. 17; Separate instructions

Sch. A (Form 1040)
Itemized Deductions
Used to report itemized deductions (medical and dental expense, taxes, contributions, interest, casualty and theft losses, moving expenses, miscellaneous deductions subject to the 2% AGI limit, and other miscellaneous deductions). IT-IRC secs. 67, 163, 164, 165, 166, 170, 211, 212, 213, and 217; Pub. 17; See the separate instructions for Form 1040.

Sch. B (Form 1040)
Interest and Dividend Income
Used to list gross dividends received (if more than $400) and interest income (if more than $400), and to ask questions about foreign accounts and foreign trusts. IT-IRC secs. 6012, 61, and 116; Pub. 17; See the separate Instructions for Form 1040.

Sch. C (Form 1040)
Profit or Loss From Business
Used to figure profit or (loss) from business or professions. IT-IRC sec. 6017; Regs. sec. 1.6017-1; Pubs. 17 and 334; See separate Instructions for Form 1040.

Sch. D (Form 1040)
Capital Gains and Losses
Used to report details of gain (or loss) from sales or exchanges of capital assets; to figure capital loss carry-overs from 1989 to 1990, and to reconcile Forms 1099-B with tax return. IT-IRC secs. 1202-1223, 6045; Pubs. 17 and 334; See the separate Instructions for Form 1040.

Sch. D-1 (Form 1040)
Continuation Sheet for Schedule D (Form 1040)
Used to attach to Schedule D (Form 1040) to list additional transactions in Parts 2a and 9a.

Sch. E (Form 1040)
Supplemental Income and Loss
Used to report income from rents, royalties, partnerships, S corporations, estates, trusts, REMICs, etc. IT-IRC secs. 6012 and 6017; Regs. secs. 1.6012-1 and 1.6017-1; Pub. 17; See the separate Instructions for Form 1040.

Sch. F (Form 1040)
Farm Income and Expenses
Used to figure profit or (loss) from farming. IT-IRC sec. 6012; Regs. sec. 1.61-4; Pub. 225; See the separate Instructions for Form 1040.

Sch. R (Form 1040)
Credit for the Elderly or the Disabled
Used to figure credit for the elderly and for persons under 65 who retired on permanent and total disability and received taxable disability benefits. IT-IRC sec. 22; Pub. 17 and 524; Separate instructions

Sch. SE (Form 1040)
Social Security Self-Employment Tax
Used to figure self-employment income and self-employment tax. IT-IRC secs. 1401 and 1402; See the separate Instructions for Form 1040.

1040A
U.S. Individual Income Tax Return
Used by citizens and residents of the United States to report income tax. (Also see Form 1040 and 1040EZ.) IT-IRC sec. 6012; Regs. sec. 1.6012-1; Pub. 17; Separate instructions

Be patient. If any phone number is incorrect, call (area code) 555-1212 and request the new listing.

IRS Tax Forms

1040C

U.S. Departing Alien Income Tax Return

Used by aliens who intend to depart from the U.S., to report income received, or expected to be received for the entire taxable year, determined as nearly as possible by the date of intended departure. (Also see Form 2063.) IT-IRC sec. 6851; Regs. sec. 1.6851-2; Pub. 519; Separate instructions

1040-ES

Estimated Tax for Individuals

Used to pay income tax (including self-employment tax and alternative minimum tax) due (the tax that is more than the tax withheld from wages, salaries, and other payments for personal services). It is not required unless the total tax is more than withholding (if any) by $500 or more. IT-IRC sec. 6654

1040-ES (Espanol)

Contribucion Federal Estimada Del Trabajo Por Cuenta Propia-Puerto Rico

Used in Puerto Rico. The payment vouchers are provided for payment of self-employment tax on a current basis. IT-IRC sec. 6654

1040-ES (NR)

U.S. Estimated Tax for Nonresident Alien Individuals

Used by nonresident aliens to pay any income tax due in excess of the tax withheld. It is not required unless the total tax exceeds withholding (if any) by $500 or more. IT-IRC sec. 6654

1040EZ

Income Tax Return for Single Filers With No Dependents

Used by citizens and residents of the United States to report income tax. (Also see Form 1040 and Form 1040A.) IT-IRC sec. 6012; Reg. sec. 1.6012-1; Pub. 17; Separate instructions

1040NR

U.S. Nonresident Alien Income Tax Return

Used by all nonresident alien individuals, whether or not engaged in a trade or business within the United States, who file a U.S. tax return. Also used as required for filing nonresident alien fiduciary (estate and trusts) returns. IT-IRC secs. 871 and 6012; Pub. 519; Separate instructions

1040 PR

Planilla Para La Declaracion De La Contribucion Federal Sobre El Trabajo Por Cuenta Propia-Puerto Rico

Used in Puerto Rico to compute self-employment tax in accordance with IRC Chapter 2 of Subtitle A, and to provide proper credit to taxpayer's social security account. IT-IRC secs. 6017 and 7651; Regs. sec. 1.6017-1; Circular PR

1040SS

U.S. Self-Employment Tax Return-Virgin Islands, Guam, and American Samoa

Used to compute self-employment tax in accordance with IRC Chapter 2 of Subtitle A, and to provide proper credit to taxpayer's social security account. IT-IRC secs. 6017 and 7651; Regs. sec. 1.6017-1; Circular SS

1040X

Amended U.S. Individual Income Tax Return

Used to claim refund of income taxes, pay additional income taxes, or designate dollar(s) to a Presidential election campaign fund. IT-IRC secs. 6402, 6404, 6511, and 6096; Separate instructions

1041

U.S. Fiduciary Income Tax Return

Used by a fiduciary of a domestic estate or domestic trust to report income tax. IT-IRC sec. 6012; Regs. secs. 1.671-4, 1.6012-3(a), and 1.6041-1; Separate instructions

Sch. D (Form 1041)

Capital Gains and Losses

Used to report details of gain (or loss) from sales or exchanges of capital assets. IT-IRC sec. 6012; Regs. sec. 1.6012-3(a); Separate instructions

Sch. J. (Form 1041)

Information Return Trust Allocation of an Accumulation Distribution (IRC section 665)

Used by domestic complex trusts to report accumulation distributions. IT-IRC secs. 665, 666, and 667

Sch. K-1 (Form 1041)

Beneficiary's Share of Income, Deductions, Credits, etc.

Used to report each beneficiary's share of the income, deductions, credits, and distributable net alternative minimum taxable income form the estate or trust. IT-IRC sec. 6012; Regs. secs. 1.6012-3(a)

1041-A

U.S. Information Return-Trust Accumulation of Charitable Amounts

Used by a trust that claims a contribution deduction under IRC section 642(c), or by a trust described in Code section 4947(a)2). (An information return.) IT-IRC secs. 6034 and 6104; Regs. sec. 1.6034-1

1041-ES

Estimated Income Tax for Fiduciaries

Used to figure and pay estimated tax for fiduciaries. IT-IRC sec. 6654

1041-T

Transmittal of Estimated Taxes Credited to Beneficiaries

Used by a trust to make an election under section 643(g) to credit an overpayment of estimated tax to beneficiaries. IT-IRC sec. 643(g)

1042

Annual Withholding Tax Return for U.S. Source Income of Foreign Persons

Used by withholding agents to report tax withheld at source on certain income paid to nonresident aliens, foreign partnerships, or foreign corporations not engaged in a trade or business in the U.S. IT-IRC secs. 1441, 1442, and 1461; Regs. secs. 1.1441-1 and 1.1461-2(b); Separate instructions

1042S

Foreign Person's U.S. Source Income Subject to Withholding

Used by a withholding agent to report certain income and tax withheld at source for foreign payees. (An information return.) IT-IRC sec. 1461; Regs. sec. 1.1461-2(c); Separate instructions

1045

Application for Tentative Refund

Used by taxpayers (other than corporations) to apply for a tentative refund from the carryback of a net operating loss, unused general business credit, or overpayment of tax due to a claim of right adjustment under section 1341(b)(1). T-IRC sec. 6411; Regs. sec. 1.6411-1

1065

U.S. Partnership Return of Income

Used by partnerships as an information return. IT-IRC sec. 6031 and 6698; Regs. secs. 1.761-1(a), 1.6031-1, and 1.6033-1(a)5); Separate instructions

Package 1065

Federal Income Tax Forms

A package of income tax forms for partnerships. Contains one copy of instructions for Form 1065, two copies of Form 1065, six copies of Schedule K-1 (Form 1065) and two copies of instructions, two copies of Form 4562 and one copy of instructions. T-IRC sec. 6031

Sch. D (Form 1065)

Capital Gains and Losses

Used to show partnership's capital gains and losses. IT-IRC 6031

Sch. K-1 (Form 1065)

Partner's Share of Income, Credits, Deductions, Etc.

Used to show partner's share of income, credits, deductions, etc. IT-IRC secs. 702 and 703; Separate instructions

Be patient. If any phone number is incorrect, call (area code) 555-1212 and request the new listing.

Taxes

1066

U.S. Real Estate Mortgage Investment Conduit Income Tax Return

Used to report income, deductions, gains and losses, and the tax on net income from prohibited transactions, of a real estate mortgage investment conduit. IT-IRC secs. 860D and 860F(e); Separate instructions

Sch. Q (Form 1066)

Quarterly Notice to Residual Interest Holder of REMIC Taxable Income or Net Loss Allocation

Used to show residual interest holder's share of taxable income (or net loss), excess inclusion, and section 212 expenses. IT-IRC sec. 860G(c)

1078

Certificate of Alien Claiming Residence in the United States

Used by an alien claiming residence in the U.S., for income tax purposes. Filed with the withholding agent.

IT-IRC secs. 871 and 1441; Regs. secs. 1.1441-5 and 1.871-3,4

1090

Statement of Income, and Profit and Loss Accounts

Used by a railroad company with Form 1120. IT-Instruction for Form 1120

1096

Annual Summary and Transmittal of U.S. Information Returns

Used to summarize and transmit Forms W-2G, 1098, 1099-A, 1099-B, 1099-DIV, 1099-G, 1099-INT, 1099-MISC, 1099-OID, 1099-PATR, 1099-R, 1099-S, and 5498. IT-IRC secs. 408(i), 6041, 6041A, 6042, 6043, 6044, 6045, 6047, 6049, 6050A, 6050B, 6050D, 6050E, 6050H, and 6050J

1098

Mortgage Interest Statement

Used to report $600 or more of mortgage interest from an individual in the course of a trade or business.

IT-IRC sec. 6050H; Regs. sec. 1.6050H-2; See the separate Instructions for Forms 1099, 1098, 5498, 1096, and W-2G

1099-A

Information Return for Acquisition or Abandonment of Secured Property

Used by lenders to report acquisitions by such lenders or abandonments of property that secures a loan.

IT-IRC sec. 6050J; Temp. Regs. sec. 1.6050J-1T; See the separate Instructions for Forms 1099, 1098, 5498, 1096, and W-2G

1099-B

Statement for Recipients of Proceeds From Broker and Barter Exchange Transactions

Used by a broker to report gross proceeds from the sale or redemption of securities, commodities or regulated futures contracts, or by a barter exchange to report the exchange of goods or services. IT-IRC sec. 6045; Regs. sec. 1.6045-1; See the separate instructions for Forms 1099, 1098, 5498, 1096, and W-2G

1099-DIV

Statement for Recipients of Dividends and Distributions

Used to report dividends and distributions. IT-IRC secs. 6042 and 6043; Regs. secs. 1.6042-2 and 1.6043-2; See the separate instructions for Forms 1099, 1098, 5498, 1096, and W-2G

1099-G

Statement for Recipients of Certain Government Payments

Used to report government payments such as unemployment compensation, state and local income tax refunds, credits, or offsets, discharges of indebtedness by the Federal Government, taxable grants, and subsidy payments from the U.S. Department of Agriculture.

IT-IRC secs. 6041, 6050B, 6050D, and 6050E; Regs. secs. 1.6041-1, 1.6050B-1, 1.6050D-1, and 1.6050E-1; See the separate Instructions for Forms 1099, 1098, 5498, 1096, and W-2G

1099-INT

Statement for Recipients of Interest Income

Used to report interest income. IT-IRC secs. 6041 and 6049; Regs. secs. 1.6041-1, 1.6049-4, and Temp. Regs. sec. 1.6049-7T; See the separate Instructions for Forms 1099, 1098, 5498, 1096, and W-2G

1099-MISC

Statement for Recipients of Miscellaneous Income

Used to report rents, royalties, prizes and awards, fishing boat proceeds, payments by health, accident and sickness insurers to physicians or other health service providers, fees, commissions or other compensation for services rendered in the course of the payer's business when the recipient is not treated as an employee, direct sales of $5,000 or more of consumer products for resale, substitute payments by brokers in lieu of dividends or tax-exempt interest, and crop insurance proceeds. IT-IRC secs. 6041, 6041A, 6045(d), and 6050A; Regs. secs. 1.6045-2, and 1.6050A-1; See the separate Instructions for Forms 1099, 1098, 5498, 1096, and W-2G

1099-OID

Statement for Recipients of Original Issue Discount

Used to report original issue discount. IT-IRC sec. 6049; Regs. sec. 1.6049-4; Temp. Regs. secs. 1.6049-4, 1.6049-5T, and 1.6049-7T; See the separate Instructions for Forms 1099, 1098, 5498, 1096, and W-2G

1099-PATR

Statement for Recipients (Patrons) of Taxable Distributions Received From Cooperatives

Used to report patronage dividends.

IT-IRC sec. 6044; Regs. sec. 1.6044-2; See the separate instructions for Forms 1099, 1098, 5498, 1096, and W-2G

1099-R

Statement for Recipients of Total Distributions From Profit-Sharing, Retirement Plans, Individual Retirement Arrangements, Insurance Contracts, Etc.

Used to report total distributions from profit-sharing, retirement plans and individual retirement arrangements, and certain surrenders of insurance contracts.

IT-IRC sec. 402, 408, and 6047; Temp Regs. sec. 35.3405-1; Regs. secs. 1.408-7 and 1.6047-1; See the separate Instructions for Forms 1099, 1098, 5498, 1096, and W-2G

1099-S

Statement for Recipients of Proceeds From Real Estate Transactions

Used by the person required to report gross proceeds from real estate transactions.

IT-IRC sec. 6045(e); Temp Regs. sec. 1.6045-3T; See the separate Instructions for Forms 1099, 1098, 5498, 1096, and W-2G

1116

Computation of Foreign Tax Credit (Individual, Fiduciary, or Nonresident Alien Individual)

Used to figure the foreign tax credit claimed for the amount of any income, war profits, and excess profits tax paid or accrued during the taxable year to any foreign country or U.S. possession. IT-IRC secs. 27, 901, and 904; Pub. 514; Separate instructions

1118

Computation of Foreign Tax Credit-Corporations

Used to support the amount of foreign tax credit claimed on corporation income tax returns.

IT-IRC secs. 901 through 906; Separate instructions

I (Form 1118)

Computation of Reduction of Oil and Gas Extraction Taxes

Used to compute the section 907(a) reduction for a corporation that is claiming a foreign tax credit with respect to any income taxes paid, accrued, or deemed to have been paid during the tax year with respect to foreign oil and gas extraction income.

IT-IRC sec. 907

Be patient. If any phone number is incorrect, call (area code) 555-1212 and request the new listing.

Sch. J (Form 1118)

Separate Limitation Loss Allocations and Other Adjustments Necessary to Determine Numerators of Limitation Fractions, Year-End Recharacterization Balances and Overall Foreign Loss Account Balances

Used to show the adjustments to separate limitation income or losses in determining the numerators of the limitation fractions for each separate limitation; the year-end balances of separate limitation losses that were allocated among other separate limitations (in the current year or in prior years) that have yet to be recharacterized; and the balances in the overall foreign loss accounts at the beginning of the tax year, any adjustments to the account balances, and the balances, in the overall foreign loss accounts at the end of the tax year. IT-IRC sec. 904(f)

1120

U.S. Corporation Income Tax Return

Used by a corporation to report income tax. (Also see Form 1120-A.) IT-IRC sec. 6012; Regs. secs. 1.1502-75(h), and 1.6012-2; Separate instructions

Package 1120

Federal Income Tax Forms

A package of income tax forms for corporations. Contains one copy of instructions for Forms 1120 and 1120-A, two copies of Form 1120, two copies of Form 1120-A, two copies of Schedule D, one copy of Form 1120-W, two copies of Form 3468, two copies of Form 7004, and two copies of Form 4562. IT-IRC sec. 6012

Sch. D (Form 1120)

Capital Gains and Losses

Used with Forms 1120, 1120-A, 1120-DF, 1120-IC-DISC, 1120-F, 1120-FSC, 1120-H, 1120L, 1120-ND, 1120-PC, 1120-POL, 1120-REIT, 1120-RIC, 990-C and certain Forms 990-T to report details of gain (or loss) from sales or exchanges of capital assets, and to figure alternative tax. IT-IRC secs. 1201 and 1231

Sch. PH (Form 1120)

Computation of U.S. Personal Holding Company Tax

Used to figure personal holding company tax; filed with the income tax return of every personal holding company. IT-IRC secs. 541, 6012, and 6501(f); Separate instructions

1120-A

U.S. Corporation Short-Form Income Tax Return

Used by a corporation to report income tax. IT-IRC sec. 6012; Regs. sec. 1.6012-2; Separate instructions

1120-DF

U.S. Income Tax Return for Designated Settlement Funds (Under Section 468B)

Used by designated settlement funds to report contributions received, income earned, the administration expenses of operating the fund, and the tax on its investment income. IT-IRC secs. 468B and 6012; Separate instructions

1120F

U.S. Income Tax Return of a Foreign Corporation

Used by foreign corporations to report income tax. IT-IRC secs. 881, 882, 884, 887, and 6012; Separate instructions

1120-FSC

U.S. Income Tax Return of a Foreign Sales Corporation

Used by foreign sales corporations to report income tax. IT-IRC secs. 922, 6011(c), and 6012; Separate instructions

Sch. P (Form 1120-FSC)

Computation of Transfer Price or Commission

Used to compute transfer price or commission under IRC sections 925(a)(1) and 2). IT-IRC sec. 6011(c)

1120-H

U.S. Income Tax Return for Homeowners Associations

Used by homeowner associations to report income tax. (An annual return.) IT-IRC sec. 528 and Reg. sec. 1.528-8

1120-IC-DISC

Interest Charge Domestic International Sales Corporation Return

Used by domestic corporations that make the election under IRC section 992(b) to be a domestic international sales corporation. IT-IRC secs. 6011(c) and 6072(b); Separate instructions

Sch. K (Form 1120-IC-DISC)

Shareholder's Statement of IC-DISC Distributions

Used to report deemed and actual distributions from an IC-DISC to shareholders and to report deferred DISC income and certain other information to shareholders. IT-IRC secs. 6011(c)

Sch. P (Form 1120-IC-DISC)

Computation of Inter-company Transfer Price or Commission

Used to compute inter-company transfer prices or commissions under IRC sections 994(a)(1) and (2). IT-IRC secs. 6011(c)

Sch. Q (Form 1120-IC-DISC)

Borrower's Certificate of Compliance with the Rules for Producer's Loans

Used by an IC-DISC to establish that the borrower is in compliance with the rules for producer's loans. IT-Regs. sec. 1.993-4(d)

1120L

U.S. Life Insurance Company Income Tax Return

Used by life insurance companies to report income tax. IT-IRC secs. 801 and 6012; Reg. sec. 1.6012-2; Separate instructions

1120-ND

Return for Nuclear Decommissioning Funds and Certain Related Persons

Used by nuclear decommissioning funds to report income, expenses, transfers of funds to the public utility that created it and to figure the taxes on income plus penalty taxes on trustees and certain disqualified persons. IT-IRC sec. 468A; Separate instructions

1120-PC

U.S. Property and Casualty Insurance Company Income Tax Return

Used by nonlife insurance companies to report income tax. IT-IRC secs. 831 and 6012; Separate instructions

1120-POL

U.S. Income Tax Return for Certain Political Organizations

Used by certain political organizations to report income tax. IT-IRC secs. 856 and 6012; Separate instructions

1120-REIT

U.S. Income Tax Return for Real Estate Investment Trusts

Used by real estate investment trusts to report income tax. IT-IRC secs. 856 and 6012; Separate instructions

1120-RIC

U.S. Income Tax Return for Regulated Investment Companies

Used by regulated investment companies to report income tax. IT-IRC secs. 851 and 6012; Separate instructions

1120S

U.S. Income Tax Return for an S Corporation

Used by S corporations that have made the election prescribed by IRC section 1362. IT-IRC sec. 6037; IRC Subchapter S; Regs. sec. 1.6037-1; Separate instructions

Package 1120S Federal Income Tax Forms

A package of income tax forms for S Corporations. Contains one copy of instructions for Form 1120S, two copies of Form 1120S, two copies of Schedule D (Form 1120S), two copies of Schedule K-1 (Form 1120S), two copies of shareholder's instructions for Schedule K-1 (Form 1120S), and two copies of Form 4562. IT-IRC sec. 6037

Sch. D (Form 1120S) Capital Gains and Losses and Built-in Gains

Used by S corporations that have made the election prescribed by IRC section 1362. Sch. D is used to report details of gains (and losses) from sales, exchanges or distribution of capital assets and to figure the tax imposed on certain capital gains and certain built-in gains.

IT-IRC secs. 1201 and 1231; and IRC Subchapter S; Separate instructions

Sch. K-1 (Form 1120S) Shareholder's Share of Income, Credits, Deductions, Etc.

Used to show shareholder's share of income, credits, deductions, etc. A four-part assembly: A copy is filed with Form 1120S, a copy is for S corporation records, and a copy is given to each shareholder along with the separate instructions. IT-IRC sec. 6037

1120-W Corporation Estimated Tax

Used as a worksheet by corporations to figure estimated tax liability; not to be filed. Corporations should keep it for their records. IT-IRC sec. 6655

1120X Amended U.S. Corporation Income Tax Return

Used by corporations to amend a previously filed Form 1120 or Form 1120-A. IT-Regs. sec. 301.6402-3

1122 Authorization and Consent of Subsidiary Corporation to be Included in a Consolidated Income Tax Return

Used as the authorization and consent of a subsidiary corporation to be included in a consolidated income tax return. IT-IRC sec. 1502; Regs. sec. 1.1502-75(h)

1128 Application for Change in Accounting Period

Used to obtain approval of a change, adoption or retention of an accounting period. IT-IRC sec. 442; Regs. secs. 1.442-1(b) and 1.1502-76; Separate instructions

1138 Extension of Time for Payment of Taxes by a Corporation Expecting a Net Operating Loss Carryback

Used by a corporation expecting a net operating loss carryback to request an extension of time for payment of taxes. IT-IRC sec. 6164

1139 Corporation Application for Tentative Refund

Used by corporations to apply for a tentative refund from the carryback of a net operating loss, net capital loss, unused general business credit, or overpayment of tax due to a claim or right adjustment under section 1341(b)(1). IT-IRC sec. 6411

1310 Statement of Person Claiming Refund Due a Deceased Taxpayer

Used by claimant to secure payment of refund on behalf of a deceased taxpayer. IT-IRC sec. 6402; Regs. sec. 301.6402-2(e); Pubs. 17 and 559

1363 Export Exemption Certificate

Used by shipper or other person to suspend liability for the payment of the tax for a period of 6 months from the date of shipment from the point of origin. The original is filed with the carrier at time of payment of the transportation charges and the duplicate is retained with the shipping papers for a period of 3 years from the last day of the month during which the shipment was made from the point of origin. May also be used as a blanket exemption certificate, with approval of District Director. Ex-IRC secs. 4271 and 4272; Temp Regs. Part 154.2-1

2032 Contract Coverage Under Title II of the Social Security Act

Used to make an agreement pursuant to IRC section 3121(l). Emp-IRC sec. 3121(l); Regs. sec. 36.3121(l)(1)-1

2063 U.S. Departing Alien Income Tax Statement

Used by a resident alien who has not received a termination assessment, or a nonresident alien who has no taxable income from United States sources. IT-IRC sec. 6851(d); Regs. sec. 1.6851-2; Rev. Rul. 55-468; C.B.1955-2, 501; Pub. 519

2106 Employee Business Expenses

Used by employees to support deductions for business expenses. IT-IRC secs. 62, 162, and 274; Instructions for Form 1040, Pub. 463; Separate instructions

2119 Sale of Your Home

Used by individuals who sold their principal residence whether or not they bought another one. Also used by individuals 55 or over who elect to exclude gain on the sale of their principal residence. IT-IRC secs. 121 and 1034; Pub. 17; Separate instructions

2120 Multiple Support Declaration

Used as a statement disclaiming as an income tax exemption an individual to whose support the taxpayer and others have contributed. IT-IRC sec. 152(c); Regs. sec. 1.152-3(c); Pub. 17

2210 Underpayment of Estimated Tax by Individuals and Fiduciaries

Used by individuals and fiduciaries to determine if they paid enough estimated tax. The form is also used to compute the penalty for underpayment of estimated tax.

IT-IRC sec. 6654; Regs. secs. 1.6654-1 and 1.6654-2; Separate instructions

2210F Underpayment of Estimated Tax by Farmers and Fishermen

Used by qualified farmers and fishermen to determine if they paid enough estimated tax. Used only by individuals whose gross income from farming or fishing is at least two-thirds of their gross annual income. (All other individuals should use Form 2210.) The form is also used to compute the penalty for underpayment of estimated tax. IT-IRC sec. 6654; Reg. secs. 1.6654-1 and 1.6654-2

2220 Underpayment of Estimated Tax by Corporations

Used by corporations to determine if they paid enough estimated tax. The form is also used to compute the penalty for underpayment of estimated tax. IT-IRC sec. 6655; Separate instructions

2290 Heavy Vehicle Use Tax Return

Used to report tax due on use of any highway motor vehicle which falls within one of the categories shown in the tax computation schedule on the form or meets certain weight limitations. Ex-IRC sec. 4481; Regs. sec. 41.6011(a)-1(a)

2350 Application for Extension of Time to File U.S. Income Tax Return

Used by U.S. citizens and certain resident aliens abroad, who expect to qualify for special tax treatment to obtain an extension of time for filing an income tax return.

IT-IRC secs. 911 and 6081; Regs. sec. temporary 5b.911-6(b), 1.911-7(c), and 1.6081-2; Pub. 54

Be patient. If any phone number is incorrect, call (area code) 555-1212 and request the new listing.

2438
Regulated Investment Company Undistributed Capital Gains Tax Return
Used to report tax payable on or before 30th day after close of company's taxable year. A copy is filed with Form 1120-RIC. (An annual return.) IT-IRC sec. 852(b)3); Regs. sec. 1.852-9

2439
Notice to Shareholder of Undistributed Long-Term Capital Gains
Used as an annual statement to be distributed to shareholders of a regulated investment company. (Copy to be attached to Form 1120-RIC.) IT-IRC sec. 852(b)(3)(D)(i); Regs. sec. 1.852-9

2441
Child and Dependent Care Expenses
Used to figure the credit for child and dependent care expenses and/or the exclusion of employer-provided dependent care benefits. (To be attached to Form 1040.) IT-IRC sec. 21 and 129; Regs. sec. 1.44A-1; Pubs. 17 and 503

2553
Election by A Small Business Corporation
Used by qualifying small business corporations to make the election prescribed by IRC section 1362. IT-IRC sec. 1362; Separate instructions

2555
Foreign Earned Income
Used by U.S. citizens and resident aliens who qualify for the foreign earned income exclusion and/or the housing exclusion or deduction. (To be filed with Form 1040.) IT-IRC secs. 911 and 6012(c); Regs. secs. 1.911-1 and 1.6012-1; Pub. 54; Separate instructions

2670
Credit or Refund-Exemption Certificate for Use by a Nonprofit Educational Organization
Used by certain nonprofit educational organizations to support a claim for credit or refund to the person who paid the manufacturers excise tax, or the exemption of these sales from the special fuels tax under IRC Chapter 31. Ex-IRC secs. 4041, 4221, and 6416; Regs. sec. 48.4221-6

2688
Application for Additional Extension of Time To File U.S. Individual Income Tax Return
Used to apply for an extension of time to file Form 1040. IT-IRC sec. 6081; Regs. sec. 1.6081-1(b)(5); T.D.6436

2758
Application for Extension of Time To File Certain Excise, Income, Information, and Other Returns
Used to apply for an extension of time to file Form 1041 and certain other returns. A separate Form 2758 must be filed for each return. IT-IRC sec. 6081; Regs. sec. 1.6081-1(b)

2848
Power of Attorney and Declaration of Representative
Used as an authorization for one person to act for another in any tax matter (except alcohol and tobacco taxes and firearms activities). IT-Title 26, CFR, Part 601; Separate instructions

2848-D
Tax Information Authorization and Declaration of Representative
Used by one person to authorize another to receive or inspect confidential tax information (except alcohol and tobacco taxes and firearms activities) when power of attorney is not filed. IT-Title 26, CFR, Part 601; Separate instructions

3115
Application for Change in Accounting Method
Used to secure approval for change in accounting method. IT-IRC sec. 446(e); Regs. sec. 1.446-1(e); Separate instructions

3206
Information Statement by United Kingdom Withholding Agents Paying Dividends From United States Corporations to Residents of the U.S. and Certain Treaty Countries
Used to report dividends paid by U.S. corporations to beneficial owners of dividends paid through United Kingdom Nominees. Used when the beneficial owners are residents of countries other than United Kingdom with which the U.S. has a tax treaty providing for reduced withholding rates on dividends. IT secs. 7.507 and 7.508 of T.D. 5532

3468
Computation of Investment Credit
Used by individuals, estates, trusts, and corporations claiming an investment credit or business energy investment credit. Also see Form 3800. IT-IRC secs. 38, 46, 47, 48, and 49; Separate instructions

3491
Consumer Cooperative Exemption Application
Used by certain consumer cooperatives that are primarily engaged in retail sales of goods or services generally for personal, living or family use to apply for exemption from filing Forms 1096 and 1099-PATR. IT-IRC sec. 6044(c); Regs. sec. 1.6044-4

3520
U.S. Information Return-Creation of or Transfers to Certain Foreign Trusts
Used by a grantor in the case of an inter vivos trust, a fiduciary of an estate in the case of a testamentary trust, or a transferor to report the creation of any foreign trust by a U.S. person or the transfer of any money or property to a foreign trust by a U.S. person. IT-IRC sec. 6048; Regs. secs. 16.3-1 and 301.6048-1

3520-A
Annual Return of Foreign Trust with U.S. Beneficiaries
Used to report the operation of foreign trust that has U.S. beneficiaries. IT-IRC sec. 6048

3800
General Business Credit
Used to summarize investment credit (Form 3468), jobs credit (Form 5884), credit for alcohol used as fuel (Form 6478), credit for increasing research activities (Form 6765), and low-income housing credit (Form 8586). IT-IRC secs. 38 and 39; Separate instructions

3903
Moving Expenses
Used to support itemized deductions for expenses of travel, transportation and certain expenses attributable to disposition of an old residence and acquisition of a new residence for employees and self-employed individuals moving to a new job location. IT-IRC sec. 217; Regs. sec. 1.217; Pub. 521; Separate instructions

3903F
Foreign Moving Expenses
Used by U.S. citizens or resident aliens moving to a new principal workplace outside the United States or its possessions. IT-IRC 217(h); Pub. 521; Separate instructions

4029
Application for Exemption from Social Security Taxes and Waiver of Benefits
Used by members of qualified religious groups to claim exemption from social security taxes. IT-IRC sec. 1402(g)

4070
Employee's Report of Tips to Employer
Used by employees to report tips to employers. Emp-IRC sec. 3102(c); Regs. sec. 31.6053-1(b)(2)

Be patient. If any phone number is incorrect, call (area code) 555-1212 and request the new listing.

070-A
Employee's Daily Record of Tips
Used by employees to keep a daily record of tips received.
Emp-IRC sec. 3102(c); Regs. sec. 31.6053-4

4070PR
Informe al Patrono de Propinas Recibidas por el Empleado
Used by employees in Puerto Rico. A variation of Form 4070.
Emp-IRC sec. 3102(c); Regs sec. 31.6053-1(b)(2)

4070A-PR
Registro Diario de Propinas Recibidas por el Empleado
Used by employees in Puerto Rico. A variation of Form 4070-A.
Emp-IRC sec. 3102(c); Regs. sec. 31.6053-4

4136
Computation of Credit for Federal Tax on Gasoline and Special Fuels
Used by individuals, estates, trusts, or corporations, including S corporations and domestic international sales corporations, to claim credit for Federal excise tax on the number of gallons of gasoline and special fuels used for business. Also used to claim the one-time credit allowed owners of qualified diesel-powered highway vehicles.
Ex-IRC secs. 34, 4041, 4081, 4091, 6420, 6421, and 6427

4137
Computation of Social Security Tax on Unreported Tip Income
Used by an employee who received tips subject to FICA tax but failed to report them to his or her employer.
IT/Emp-IRC sec. 3102; Regs. sec. 31.3102-3(d) and 31.6011(a)-1(d)

4224
Exemption From Withholding of Tax on Income Effectively Connected With the Conduct of a Trade or Business in the United States
Used to secure, at the time of payment, the benefit of exemption from withholding of the tax on certain income for nonresident alien individuals and fiduciaries, foreign partnerships, and foreign corporations.
IT-IRC secs. 1441 and 1442; Regs. sec. 1.1441-4

4255
Recapture of Investment Credit
Used by individuals, estates, trusts, or corporations to figure the increase in tax if regular or energy property was disposed of or ceased to qualify before the end of the property class life or life years used to figure the credit.
IT-IRC sec. 47

4361
Application for Exemption from Self-Employment Tax for Use by Ministers, Members of Religious Orders and Christian Science Practitioners
Used by members of qualified religious groups to claim exemption from tax on self-employment income.
IT-IRC sec. 1402(e)

4461
Application for Approval of Master or Prototype Defined Contribution Plan
Used by employers who want an opinion letter for approval of form of a master or prototype plan.
IT-IRC secs. 401(a), and 501(a)

4461-A
Application for Approval of Master or Prototype Defined Benefit Plan
Used by employers who want an opinion letter for approval of form of a master or prototype plan.
IT-IRC secs. 401(a) and 501(a)

4461-B
Application of Master or Prototype Plan, or Regional Prototype Plan Mass Submitter Adopting Sponsor
Used by mass submitters who want approval on a plan of adopting sponsoring organization or sponsor. IT-IRC secs. 401(a) and 501(a)

4466
Corporation Application for Quick Refund of Overpayment of Estimated Tax
Used to apply for a "quick" refund of overpaid estimated tax. (Must be filed before the regular tax return is filed.) IT-IRC sec. 6425; Regs. sec. 1.6425-1(b)

4469
Computation of Excess Medicare Tax Credit
Used by railroad employee representatives and medicare qualified Government employees to figure their credit of excess medicare (hospital insurance benefits) tax. IT-IRC sec. 6413(c)(3); P.L.80-248

4506
Request for Copy of Tax Form
Used by a taxpayer or authorized representative to request a copy of a tax return or Forms W-2 that were filed with the return. IT-Regs. sec. 601.702

4506-A
Request for Public-Inspection Copy of Exempt Organization Tax Form
Used by a third-party for a copy of an exempt organization tax form which may be inspected at an IRS office. IT-IRC sec. 6104(b)

4562
Depreciation and Amortization
Used by individuals, estates, trusts, partnerships, and corporations claiming depreciation and amortization. Also used to substantiate depreciation deductions for automobiles and other listed property.
IT-IRC secs. 167, 168, 179 and 280F; Separate instructions

4563
Exclusion of Income for Bona Fide Residents of American Samoa
Used by bona fide residents of American Samoa to exclude income from sources in American Samoa, Guam, and the Commonwealth of the Northern Mariana Islands, to the extent specified in IRC section 931.
IT-IRC sec. 931; Regs. sec. 1.931-1; Pub. 570

4626
Alternative Minimum Tax-Corporations
Used by corporations to figure their alternative minimum tax and their environmental tax.
IT-IRC secs. 55, 56, 57, 58, 59, and 291; Separate instructions

4684
Casualties and Thefts
Used by all taxpayers to figure gains (or losses) resulting from casualties and thefts. IT-IRC sec. 165; Separate instructions

4720
Return of Certain Excise Taxes on Charities and Other Persons Under Chapters 41 and 42 of the Internal Revenue Code
Used by charities and other persons to compute certain excise taxes which may be due under IRC Chapters 41 and 42.
Ex-IRC secs. 4911, 4912, 4941, 4942, 4943, 4944, 4945, and 4955; Separate instructions

4768
Application for Extension of Time To File U.S. Estate (and Generation-Skipping Transfer) Tax Return and/or Pay Estate (and Generation-Skipping Transfer) Tax(es)
Used to apply for estate tax extensions in certain cases.
E&G-IRC secs. 6081 and 6161; Regs. sec. 20.6081-1 and 20.6161-1

Be patient. If any phone number is incorrect, call (area code) 555-1212 and request the new listing.

IRS Tax Forms

4782

Employee Moving Expense Information

Used by employers to show the amount of any reimbursement or payment made to an employee, a third party for the employee's benefit, or the value of services furnished in-kind, for moving expenses during the calendar year. IT-IRC secs. 82 and 217; Regs. sec. 31.6051-1(e)

4789

Currency Transaction Report

Used by financial institutions to report deposit, withdrawal, exchange of currency, or other payment or transfer, by, through, or to such financial institution which involves currency transactions of more than $10,000. P.L.92-508; Treasury Regs. 31CFR103)

4797

Sales of Business Property

Used to report details of gain (or loss) from sales, exchanges, or involuntary conversions (from other than casualty and theft) of noncapital assets and involuntary conversions (other than casualty and theft) of capital assets, held in connection with a trade or business or a transaction entered into for profit. Also used to compute recapture amounts under sections 179 and 280F when the business use of section 179 or 280F property drops to 50% or less. IT-IRC secs. 1231, 1245, 1250, 1252, 1254, and 1255; IT-IRC secs. 1202, 1211, and 1212; Separate instructions

4835

Farm Rental Income and Expenses

Used by landowner (or sublessor) to report farm rental income based on crops or livestock produced by the tenant where the landowner (or sublessor) does not materially participate in the operation or management of the farm. (Also see Schedule F (Form 1040).) IT-IRC sec. 61

4868

Application for Automatic Extension of Time to File U.S. Individual Income Tax Return

Used to apply for an automatic 4-month extension of time to file Form 1040. IT-IRC sec. 6081; Regs. sec. 1.6081-4; TD 7885

4876-A

Election To Be Treated as an Interest Charge DISC

Used by a qualifying corporation that wishes to be treated as an Interest Charge Domestic International Sales Corporation (Interest Charge DISC). IT-Regs. sec. 1.921

4952

Investment Interest Expense Deduction

Used by an individual, estate, or trust to figure the deduction limitation for interest expense on funds borrowed that is allocable to property held for investment. IT-IRC sec. 163(d)

4970

Tax on Accumulation Distribution of Trusts

Used by a beneficiary of a domestic or foreign trust to figure the tax attributable to an accumulation distribution. IT-IRC sec. 667

4972

Tax on Lump-Sum Distributions

Used to determine the income tax on the income portion of lump-sum distributions. IT-IRC sec. 402(e); Separate instructions

5074

Allocation of Individual Income Tax to Guam or the Commonwealth of the Northern Mariana Islands (CNMI)

Used as an attachment to Form 1040 filed by an individual who reports adjusted gross income of $50,000 or more, with gross income of $5,000 or more from Guam or CNMI sources. IT-IRC sec. 935; Regs. sec. 301.7654-1(d)

5213

Election to Postpone Determination as to Whether the Presumption that an Activity is Engaged in for Profit Applies

Used by individuals, trusts, estates, and S corporations to postpone a determination as to whether an activity is engaged in for profit. IT-IRC sec. 183(e)

5227

Split-Interest Trust Information Return

Used by section 4947(a)(2) trusts treated as private foundations. Ex-IRC sec. 6011; Separate instructions

5300

Application for Determination for Defined Benefit Plan

Used to request a determination letter as to the qualification of a defined benefit plan (other than a collectively-bargained plan). IT-IRC sec. 401(a); Separate instructions

Sch. T (Form 5300)

Supplemental Application for Approval of Employee Benefit Plans

Used as an attachment to Forms 5300, 5301, 5303, 5307, and 6406 to provide information on how the applicant meets the requirements of the Tax Equity and Fiscal Responsibility Act of 1982, the Tax Reform Act of 1984, and the Retirement Equity Act of 1984, and the Tax Reform Act of 1986. IT-IRC 401(a); Separate instructions

5301

Application for Determination for Defined Contribution Plan

Used to request a determination letter as to the qualification of a defined contribution plan (other than a collectively-bargained plan). IT-IRC sec. 401(a); Separate instructions

5302

Employee Census

Used as a schedule of the 25 highest paid participants of a deferred compensation plan, which is attached to Forms 5300, 5301, 5303, and 5307 (where applicable). IT-IRC sec. 401(a)

5303

Application for Determination for Collectively-Bargained Plan

Used to request a determination letter as to the qualification of a collectively-bargained plan. Also used by multi-employer plans covered by PBGC insurance to request a determination letter regarding termination. IT-IRC sec. 401(a); Separate instructions

5305

Individual Retirement Trust Account

Used as an agreement between an individual and the individual's trustee for the establishment of an individual retirement account. IT-IRC sec. 408(a)

5305-A

Individual Retirement Custodial Account

Used as an agreement between an individual and the individual's custodian for the establishment of an individual retirement account. IT-IRC sec. 408(a)

5305-SEP

Simplified Employee Pension-Individual Retirement Accounts Contribution Agreement

Used as an agreement between an employer and his or her employees to establish a Simplified Employee Pension. IT-IRC 408(k)

5305-A-SEP

Salary Reduction and Other Elective Simplified Employee Pension - Individual Retirement Accounts Contribution Agreement

Used as an agreement between an employer and his or her employees to

Be patient. If any phone number is incorrect, call (area code) 555-1212 and request the new listing.

Taxes

establish a Simplified Employee Pension with an elective deferral. IT-IRC sec. 408(k)(6)

5306

Application for Approval of Prototype or Employer Sponsored Individual Retirement Account

Used by banks, savings and loan associations, federally insured credit unions, and such other persons approved by the Internal Revenue Service to act as trustee or custodian, insurance companies, regulated investment companies and trade or professional societies or associations, to get the approval as to form of a trust or annuity contract which is to be used for individual retirement accounts or annuities. Also to be used by employees, labor unions and other employee associations that want approval of a trust which is to be used for individual retirement accounts. IT-IRC sec. 408(a), (b), or (c)

5306-SEP

Application for Approval of Prototype Simplified Employee Pension-SEP

Used by program sponsors who want to get IRS approval of their prototype simplified employee pension (SEP) agreements. IT-IRC sec. 408

5307

Application for Determination for Adopters of Master or Prototype, Regional Prototype or Volume Submitter Plans

Used to request a determination letter as to the qualification of any defined benefit or defined contribution plan (the form of which has been previously approved) other than a collectively bargained plan. IT-IRC sec. 401(a); Separate instructions

5308

Request for Change in Plan/Trust Year

Used by employer or plan administrators to request approval of change in a plan year or a trust year. IT-IRC sec. 412(c)(5), sec. 442

5309

Application for Determination of Employee Stock Ownership Plan

Used by corporate employers who wish to get a determination letter regarding the qualification of an Employee Stock Ownership Plan under IRC 409 or 4975(e)(7). IT-IRC 409-4975(e)(7)

5310

Application for Determination Upon Termination; Notice of Merger, Consolidation or Transfer of Plan Assets or Liabilities; Notice of Intent to Terminate

Used by an employer who wishes a determination letter as to the effect of termination of a plan on its prior qualification under IRC section 401(a); by every employer or plan administrator (if designated) for any plan merger or consolidation; or to give notice to PBGC of intent, for any transfer of plan assets or liabilities to another plan to terminate a defined benefit pension plan. IT-IRC secs. 401(a), 6058(b), ERISA sec. 4041(a); Separate instructions

5329

Return for Additional Taxes Attributable to Qualified Retirement Plans (Including IRAs), Annuities, and Modified Endowment Contracts

Used to report excise taxes or additional income tax owed in connection with individual retirement arrangements, annuities, and qualified retirement plans. IT-IRC secs. 72, 4973, 4974, and 4980A; Separate instructions

5330

Return of Excise Taxes Related to Employee Benefits Plans

Used to report and pay the excise tax imposed by IRC section 4791 on a minimum funding deficiency, by Code section 4973(a)(2) on excess contributions to a section 403(b)(7)(A) custodial account, by section 4975 on prohibited transactions, by section 4976 on disqualified benefits from welfare plans, by 4977 on certain fringe benefits, and by 4978 on certain ESOP transactions. Ex-IRC sec. 6011; Separate instructions

5452

Corporate Report of Nondividend Distributions

Used by corporations to report their nontaxable distributions. IT-CFR 1.301-1, 1.316-1, 1.333-1, and 1.6042-2

5471

Information Return With Respect to a Foreign Corporation

Used by U.S. persons to report their activities with related foreign corporations. IT-IRC secs. 951-972, 6035, 6038 and 6046; Separate instructions

Sch. M (Form 5471)

Foreign Corporation Controlled by a U.S. Person

Used by a U.S. person who controls a foreign corporation to report the activities between the U.S. person and the foreign corporation. IT-IRC sec. 6038

Sch. N (Form 5471)

Foreign Personal Holding Company

Used by officers, directors, and shareholders of foreign personal holding companies to report information concerning the foreign personal holding company. IT-IRC sec. 6035

Sch. O (Form 5471)

Organization or Reorganization of Foreign Corporation, and Acquisitions and Dispositions of its Stock

Used by U.S. persons to report acquisitions or dispositions of interests in foreign corporations. IT-IRC sec. 6046

5472

Information Return of a Foreign Owned Corporation

Used for reporting the activities between foreign owned corporations and persons related to transactions made by the corporations. IT-IRC sec. 6038A

5498

Individual Retirement Arrangement Information

Used to report contributions to individual retirement arrangements (IRAs) and the value of the account. IT-IRC sec. 408(i)(o); Prop. Regs. sec. 1.408-5; See the separate Instructions for Forms 1099, 1098, 5498, 1096, and W-2G

5500

Annual Return/Report of Employee Benefit Plan (with 100 or more participants)

Used to report on deferred compensation plans and welfare plans that have at least 100 participants. IT-IRC sec. 6058(a); ERISA section 103; Separate instructions

Sch. A (Form 5500)

Insurance Information

Used as an attachment to Forms 5500, 5500-C, or 5500-R to report information about insurance contracts that are part of a qualified deferred compensation plan. ERISA section 103(e)

Sch. B (Form 5500)

Actuarial Information

Used to report actuarial information for a defined benefit plan. (Attached to Forms 5500, 5500-C, or 5500-R.) IT-IRC sec. 6059; ERISA section 103(a); Separate instructions

Sch. C (Form 5500)

Service Provider Information

Used as an attachment to Form 5500 to report information about service providers and trustees of qualified deferred compensation plans. ERISA section 103.

Sch. P (Form 5500)

Annual Return of Fiduciary of Employee Benefit Trust

Used as an annual return for employee benefit trusts which qualify under section 401(a) and are exempt from tax under section 501(a). (Attach to Forms 5500, 5500-C or 5500-R.) IT-IRC secs. 6033(a) and 6501(a)

Be patient. If any phone number is incorrect, call (area code) 555-1212 and request the new listing.

IRS Tax Forms

Sch. SSA (Form 5500)
Annual Registration Statement Identifying Separated Participants with Deferred Vested Benefits
Used to list employees who separated from employment and have a deferred vested benefit in the employer's plan of deferred compensation. (Attached to Forms 5500, 5500-C, or 5500-R.) IT-IRC sec. 6057

5500-C/R
Return/Report of Employee Benefit Plan (with fewer than 100 participants)
Used to report on deferred compensation plans and welfare plans that have fewer than 100 participants.
IT-IRC sec. 6058(a); ERISA section 103; Separate instructions

5500EZ
Annual Return of One-Participant Owners and Their Spouses Pension Benefit Plan
Used to report on pension profit-sharing, etc. plans that cover only an individual or an individual and the individual's spouse who wholly own a business.
IT-IRC sec. 6058(a); Separate instructions

5558
Application for Extension of Time to File Certain Employee Plan Returns
Used to provide a means by which a person may request an extension of time to file Forms 5500, 5500-C, 5500-R, or 5330.

5578
Annual Certification of Racial Nondiscrimination for a Private School Exempt from Federal Income Tax
Used by certain organizations exempt or claiming to be exempt under IRC section 501(c)(3) and operating, supervising, or controlling a private school (or schools) to certify to a policy of racial nondiscrimination.
IT-IRC sec. 6001; Rev. Proc. 75-50, 1975-2; C.B.587

5712
Election to be Treated as a Possessions Corporation Under Section 936
Used by a corporation to elect to be treated as a possessions corporation for the tax credit allowed under IRC section 936. IT-IRC sec. 936(e)

5712-A
Cost Sharing or Profit Split Method Under Section 936(h)(5): Election and Verification
Used by a domestic corporation if it elects to compute its taxable income under either the cost sharing method or the profit split method. IT-IRC sec. 936(h)(5)

5713
International Boycott Report
Used by persons with operations in or related to any country associated in carrying out an international boycott.
IT-IRC sec. 999; Separate instructions

Sch. A (Form 5713)
Computation of the International Boycott Factor
Used by taxpayers in computing the loss of tax benefits under the international boycott factor method.
IT-IRC sec. 999

Sch. B (Form 5713)
Specifically Attributable Taxes and Income
Used by taxpayers in computing the loss of tax benefits under the specifically attributable taxes and income method.
IT-IRC sec. 999

Sch. C (Form 5713)
Tax Effect of the International Boycott Provisions
Used to summarize the loss of tax benefits resulting from the application of the international boycott provisions.
IT-IRC sec. 999

5735
Computation of Possessions Corporation Tax Credit Under Section 936
Used by qualified possessions corporations to compute credit allowed by IRC section 936.
IT-IRC sec. 936

Sch. P (Form 5735)
Allocation of Income and Expenses Under Section 936(h)(5)
Used by corporations that have elected the cost sharing or profit split method of computing taxable income. The form is attached to Form 5735.
IT-IRC sec. 935(h)(5)

5754
Statement By Person(s) Receiving Gambling Winnings
Used to list multiple winners of certain gambling proceeds.
IT-IRC sec. 3402(q); Regs. secs. 31.3402(q)-1(e) and 1.6011-3; See the separate Instructions for Forms 1099, 1098, 5498, 1096, and W-2G

5768
Election/Revocation of Election by an Eligible Section 501(c)3-Organization to Make Expenditures to Influence Legislation
Used by certain eligible IRC section 501(c)3-organizations to elect or revoke election to apply the lobbying expenditures provisions of code section 501(h).
IT-IRC secs. 501 and 4911

5884
Jobs Credit
Used by individuals, estates, trusts, and corporations claiming a jobs credit and any S corporation, partnership, estate or trust which apportion the jobs credit among their shareholders, partners, or beneficiaries. See also Form 3800.
IT-IRC secs. 38, 51, 52, and 53

6008
Fee Deposit for Outer Continental Shelf Oil
Used to deposit fees on oil that is produced on the Outer Continental Shelf.
IRC sec. 7805, sec. 302(d) of P.L.95-372

6009
Quarterly Report of Fees Due on Oil Production
Used to compute fees due on oil that is produced on the Outer Continental Shelf. IRC sec. 7805, sec. 302(d) of P.L.95-372

6069
Return of Excise Tax on Excess Contributions to Black Lung Benefit Trust Under Section 4953 and Computation of Section 192 Deduction
Used by exempt Black Lung Benefit Trusts as a worksheet to determine deduction under section 192 and to report tax under section 4953.
IT/Ex-IRC secs. 192 and 4953

6088
Distributable Benefits from Employee Pension Benefit Plans
Used to report the 25 highest paid participants of a deferred compensation plan, which is attached to Form 5310.
IT-IRC sec. 401(a)

6118
Credit for Income Tax Return Preparers
Used by income tax return preparers to file for refund of penalties paid.
IT-IRC sec. 6696

6177
General Assistance Program Determination
Used by a General Assistance Program of a state or political subdivision of a state in order to be designated as a Qualified General Assistance Program for purposes of certifying individual recipients of the program for the jobs credit.
IT-IRC sec. 51(d)(6)(B)

Taxes

6197
Gas Guzzler Tax
Used by automobile manufacturers and importers to report the tax on "gas guzzler" types of automobiles. The form is filed as an attachment to Form 720. Ex-IRC sec. 4064

6198
At-Risk Limitations
Used by individuals, partners, S corporation shareholders, and certain closely-held corporations to figure the overall profit (loss) from an at-risk activity for the tax year, the amount at-risk, and the deductible loss for the tax year. IT-IRC sec. 465; Separate instructions

6199
Certification of Youth Participating in a Qualified Cooperative Education Program
Used by a qualified school to certify that a student meets the requirements of Sec. 51(d)8-as a member of a targeted group eligible for the jobs credit. IT-IRC sec. 51

6251
Alternative Minimum Tax-Individuals
Used by individuals to figure their alternative minimum tax. IT-IRC secs. 55, 56, 57, 58, and 59; Separate instructions

6252
Installment Sale Income
Used by taxpayers other than dealers, who sell real or personal property, and receive a payment in a tax year after the year of sale. IT-IRC sec. 453; Pub. 537; Separate instructions

6406
Short Form Application for Determination for Amendment of Employee Benefit Plan
Used for amending a plan on which a favorable determination letter has been issued under ERISA. IRC secs. 401(a) and 501(a); Separate instructions

6478
Credit for Alcohol Used as Fuel
Used by taxpayers to figure their credit for alcohol used as fuel. The credit is allowed for alcohol mixed with other fuels and for straight alcohol fuel. See also Form 3800. IT-IRC sec. 38 and 40

6497
Information Return of Nontaxable Energy Grants or Subsidized Energy Financing
Used by every person who administers a government program for a Federal, state, or local governmental entity or agent thereof, that provides grants or subsidized financing under programs a principal purpose of which is energy production or conservation if the grant or financing is not taxable to the recipient. IT-IRC sec. 6050D; Regs. sec. 1.6050D-1

6627
Environmental Taxes
Used to report environmental taxes on petroleum and certain chemicals. Ex-IRC secs. 4611, 4661, and 4671

6765
Credit for Increasing Research Activities (or for claiming the orphan drug credit)
Used by individuals, estates, trusts, and corporations claiming a research credit for increasing the research activities of a trade or business. Also used to claim the orphan drug credit. See also Form 3800. IT-IRC secs. 28 and 41; Separate instructions

6781
Gains and Losses From Section 1256 Contracts and Straddles
Used by all taxpayers that held section 1256 contracts or straddles during the tax year. IT-IRC secs. 1092 and 1256

7004
Application for Automatic Extension of Time to File Corporation Income Tax Return
Used by corporations and certain exempt organizations to request an automatic extension of 6 months to file corporate income tax return. IT-IRC sec. 6081(b); Regs. sec. 1.6081-3

8023
Corporate Qualified Stock Purchase Election
Used by a purchasing corporation to elect section 338 treatment for the purchase of another corporation. IT-IRC sec. 338(g); Temp. Regs. sec. sf 338-1

8027
Employer's Annual Information Return of Tip Income and Allocated Tips
Used by large food or beverage employers to report each establishment's gross receipts, charge receipts and charge tips, and allocated tips of employees. IT-IRC sec. 6053(c); Regs. sec. 31.6053-3; Separate instructions

8027-T
Transmittal of Employer's Annual Information Return of Tip Income and Allocated Tips
Used by large food or beverage employers with more than one establishment to transmit Forms 8027. IT-IRC sec. 6053(c); Regs. sec. 31.6053-3

8038
Information Return for Tax-Exempt Private Activity Bond Issues
Used by issuers of tax-exempt private activity bonds to provide IRS with information required by section 149(e). IT-IRC sec. 149(e); Temp. Regs. sec. 1.149(e)-1T; Separate instructions

8038-G
Information Return for Tax-Exempt Governmental Bond Issues
Used by the issuers of tax-exempt governmental bonds (with issue prices of $100,000 or more) to provide IRS with information required by section 149(e). IT-IRC sec. 149(e); Temp. Regs. sec. 1.149(e)-1T; Separate instructions

8038-GC
Consolidated Information Return for Small Tax-Exempt Governmental Bond Issues, Leases and Installment Sales
Used by the issuers of tax-exempt governmental bonds (with issue prices of less than $100,000) to provide IRS with information required by section 149(e). IT-IRC sec. 149(e); Temp. Regs. sec. 1.149(e)-IT

8082
Notice of Inconsistent Treatment or Amended Return
Used by partners, S corporation shareholders and residual holders of an interest in a REMIC to report inconsistent treatment of partnership, S corporation or REMIC items or to report amendment of partnership, S corporation or REMIC items. Form 8082 is also used by the TMP (tax matters partner or tax matters person) to make an administrative adjustment request (AAR) on behalf of the partnership, S corporation, or REMIC. IT-IRC sec. 6222 and 6227(c); Separate instructions

8109
Federal Tax Deposit Coupon
Twenty-three preprinted deposit coupons for making deposits of Federal taxes (such as social security, Federal unemployment, and excise taxes) are contained in a coupon book. Instructions are in the coupon book, along with a reorder form (Form 8109A, FTD Reorder Form). IT/Emp/Ex-IRC sec. 6302; Regs. secs. 1.6302-1, 1.6302-2, 31.6302(c)-1, 31.6302(c)-2, 31.6302(c)-3, 46.6302(c)-1, 48.6302(c)-1, 49.6302(c)-1, 51.4995-3, and 52.6302-1

8109-B
Federal Tax Deposit Coupon
An over-the-counter Federal tax deposit coupon for making Federal tax deposits when Form 8109 deposit coupons have been reordered but not yet received or

Be patient. If any phone number is incorrect, call (area code) 555-1212 and request the new listing.

IRS Tax Forms

when a new entity has received its employer identification number but has not yet received its initial order of Forms 8109.

IT/Emp/Ex-IRC sec. 6302; Regs. secs. 1.6302-1, 1.6302-2, 31.6302(c)-1, 31.6302(c)-2, 31.6302(c)-3, 46.6302(c)-1, 48.6302(c)-1, 49.6302(c)-1, 51.4995-3 and 52.6302-1

8210

Self-Assessed Penalties Return

Used by payers of certain interest and dividends to figure and pay penalties imposed with regard to the filing of certain information returns and the furnishing of certain payee statements.

PA-IRC secs. 6676(b), 6721, 6722, 6723, and 6724; Temp. Regs. sec. 301.6723-1T

8233

Exemption From Withholding on Compensation for Independent Personal Services of a Nonresident Alien Individual

Used by nonresident alien individuals to claim exemption from withholding on compensation for independent personal services because of an income tax treaty or the personal exemption amount. Also used by nonresident alien students, teachers, and researchers to claim exemption from withholding under a U.S. tax treaty on compensation for services.

IT-IRC sec. 1441; Reg. sec. 1.1441-4

8264

Application for Registration of a Tax Shelter

Used by tax shelter organizers to register certain tax shelters with the IRS, for purposes of receiving a tax shelter registration number.

IT-IRC sec. 6111; Regs. secs. 301.6111-1T; Separate instructions

8271

Investor Reporting of Tax Shelter Registration Number

Used by persons who have purchased or otherwise acquired an interest in a tax shelter required to be registered to report the tax shelter registration number. Form is attached to any tax return on which a deduction, credit, loss, or other tax benefit is claimed, or any income reported, from a tax shelter required to be registered. IT-IRC sec. 6111; Regs. secs. 301.6111-1T

8274

Certification by Churches and Qualified Church-Controlled Organizations Electing Exemption from Employer Social Security Taxes

Used by churches and certain church-controlled organizations to elect exemption from social security taxes by certifying the organization is opposed to these taxes for religious purposes.

Emp-IRC sec. 3121(w)

8275

Disclosure Statement Under Section 6661

Used to disclose items which could cause a substantial understatement of income and is filed to avoid the penalty imposed by section 6661; Separate instructions PA-IRC sec. 6661; Regs. sec. 1.6661; Separate instructions

8279

Election To Be Treated as a FSC or as a Small FSC

Used by qualifying corporations that wish to be treated as a Foreign Sales Corporation (FSC) or Small Foreign Sales Corporation (Small FSC). IT-IRC sec. 927

8281

Information Return for Publicly Offered Original Issue Discount Instruments

Used by issuers of publicly offered debt instruments having OID to provide the information required by section 1275(c).

IT-IRC sec. 1275(c); Temp. Regs. sec. 1.1275-3T

8282

Donee Information Return

Used by exempt organizations who sells, exchanges, transfers, or otherwise disposes of the charitable property within 2 years after the date of the receipt of the contribution. The return is filed with the IRS and a copy is given to the donor. IT-IRC sec. 6050L

8283

Noncash Charitable Contributions

Used by individuals, closely held corporations, personal service corporations, partnerships, and S corporations to report contributions of property other than cash in which the total claimed value of all property exceeds $500. IT-IRC secs. 170; 1.170A-13 and 1.170A-13T; Separate instructions

8288

U.S. Withholding Tax Return for Dispositions by Foreign Persons of U.S. Real Property Interests

Used to transmit the withholding on the sale of U.S. real property by foreign persons. IT-IRC sec. 1445; Regs. secs. 1.1445-1 through 1.1445-7; Temp. Regs. secs. 1.1445-9T through 1.1445-11T

8288-A

Statement of Withholding on Dispositions by Foreign Persons of U.S. Real Property Interests

Anyone filing Form 8288 must attach copies A and B of Form 8288-A for each person subject to withholding. IT-IRC sec. 1445; Regs. secs. 1.1445-1 through 1.1445-7, Temp. Regs. secs. 1.1445-9T through 1.1445-11T

8288-B

Application for Withholding Certificate for Dispositions by Foreign Persons of U.S. Real Property Interests

Used to apply for a withholding certificate based upon certain criteria to reduce or eliminate withholding under section 1445.

IT-IRC sec. 1445; Regs. secs. 1.1445-3 and 1.1445-6 and Rev. Proc. 88-23

8300

Report of Cash Payments Over $10,000 Received in a Trade or Business

Used by a trade or business to report receipt of more than $10,000 cash in a transaction in the course of such trade or business.

IT-IRC sec. 6050I; Regs. 1.6050I-1

8308

Report of a Sale or Exchange of Certain Partnership Interests

Used by partnerships to report the sale or exchange of a partnership interest where a portion of any money or other property given in exchange for the interest is attributable to unrealized receivables or substantially appreciated inventory items (section 751(a) exchange). IT-IRC sec. 6050K

8328

Carryforward Election of Unused Private Activity Bond Volume Cap

Used by the issuing authority of tax-exempt private activity bonds to elect under section 146(f) to carryforward the unused volume cap for specific projects. IT-IRC sec. 146(f)

8329

Lender's Information Return for Mortgage Credit Certificates

Used by lenders of certified indebtedness amounts to report information regarding the issuance of mortgage credit certificates under section 25. IT-IRC sec. 25; Regs. sec. 1.25-8T

8330

Issuer's Quarterly Information Return for Mortgage Credit Certificates

Used by issuers of mortgage credit certificates to report information required under section 25. IT-IRC sec. 25; Regs. secs. 1.25-8T

8332

Release of Claim to Exemption for Child of Divorced or Separated Parents

Used to release claim to a child's exemption by a parent who has custody of his or her child and is given to the parent who will claim the exemption. The parent who claims the child's exemption attaches this form to his or her tax return. IT-IRC sec. 152(e)(2); Temp. Regs. sec. 1.152-4T; Pub. 504

Be patient. If any phone number is incorrect, call (area code) 555-1212 and request the new listing.

Taxes

8362
Currency Transaction Reported by Casinos
Used by casinos licensed by a state or local government having annual gaming revenues in excess of $1 million to report each deposit, withdrawal, exchange of currency or gambling tokens or chips or other payment or transfer, by, through, or to such casino, involving currency of more than $10,000.
P.L.91-508; Treasury Regs. secs. 31 CFR 103.22; 31 CFR 103.26; and 31 CFR 103.36

8390
Information Return for Determination of Life Insurance Company Earnings Rate Under Section 809
Used by certain life insurance companies to gather information to compute various earnings rates required by section 809.
IT-IRC sec. 809; Separate instructions

8396
Mortgage Interest Credit
Used by qualified mortgage credit certificate holders to figure their mortgage interest credit and any carryover to a subsequent year.
IT-IRC sec. 25

8404
Computation of Interest Charge on DISC-Related Deferred Tax Liability
Used by shareholders of Interest Charge Domestic International Sales Corporations (IC-DISCs) to figure and report their interest on DISC-related deferred tax liability. ITC 995(f); Treasury Regs. 1.995(f)

8453
U.S. Individual Income Tax Declaration for Electronic Filing
Used by qualified filers who file Forms 1040 and certain related schedules, 1040A and 1040EZ via electronic transmission on magnetic media. These filers must file Form 8453 to transmit the individual taxpayer's and return preparer's signature(s) for the return.
IT-IRC secs. 6012 and 6017

8453-E
Annual Return/Report of Employee Benefit Plan Magnetic Media/Electronic Filing
Used by qualified filers who file Forms 5500, 5500-C or 5500-R via electronic transmission.
IT-IRC sec. 6058

8453-F
U.S. Fiduciary Income Tax Declaration for Magnetic Tape/Electronic Filing
Used by qualified filers who file Form 1041 and related schedules via electronic transmission.
IT-IRC sec. 6012

8453-P
U.S. Partnership Declaration for Magnetic Tape/Electronic Filing
Used by qualified filers who file Form 1065 and related schedules via electronic transmission.
IT-IRC sec. 6031

8582
Passive Activity Loss Limitations
Used by individuals, estates, and trusts to figure the amount of any passive activity loss for the current tax year for all activities and the amount of the passive activity loss allowed on their tax returns.
IT-IRC sec. 469; Separate instructions

8582-CR
Passive Activity Credit Limitations
Used by individuals, estates, and trusts to figure the amount of any passive activity credit for the current year and the amount allowed on their tax returns.
IT-IRC sec. 469; Separate instructions

8586
Low-Income Housing Credit
Used by owners of residential rental projects providing low-income housing to claim the low-income housing credit. IT-IRC sec. 42

8594
Asset Acquisition Statement
Used by the buyer and seller of assets used in a trade or business involving goodwill or a going concern value.
IT-IRC 1060, Temp. Regs. sec. 1.1060-IT

8606
Nondeductible IRA Contributions, IRA Basis, and Nontaxable IRA Distributions
Used by individuals to report the amount of IRA contributions they choose to be nondeductible and to figure their basis in their IRA(s) at the end of the calendar year and the nontaxable part of any distributions they received.
IT-IRC sec. 408(o)

8609
Low-Income Housing Credit Allocation Certification
Used by housing credit agencies to allocate a low-income housing credit dollar amount. Also, used by low-income housing building owners to make elections and certify certain necessary information.
IT-IRC sec. 42

8610
Annual Low-Income Housing Credit Agencies Report
Used by housing credit agencies to transmit Forms 8609 and to report the dollar amount of housing credit allocations issued during the calendar year.
IT-IRC sec. 42

8611
Recapture of Low-Income Housing Credit
Used by taxpayers to recapture low-income housing credit taken in a prior year because there is a decrease in the qualified basis of a residential low-income housing building from one year to the next.
IT-IRC sec. 42(j)

8612
Return of Excise Tax on Undistributed Income of Real Estate Investment Trusts
Used by real estate investment trusts to report the excise tax on undistributed income. EX-IRC sec. 4981

8613
Return of Excise Tax on Undistributed Income of Regulated Investment Companies
Used by regulated investment companies to report the excise tax on undistributed income.
EX-IRC sec. 4982

8615
Computation of Tax for Children Under Age 14 Who Have Investment Income of More Than $1,000
Used to see if any of a child's investment income in excess of $1,000 is taxed at his or her parent's rate and, if so, to figure the child's tax.

8621
Return by a Shareholder of a Passive Foreign Investment Company or Qualified Electing Fund
Used by U.S. persons who own an interest in a foreign investment company to report elections, terminations of elections, and amounts to be included in gross income.
IT-IRC secs. 1291, 1293, and 1294

8645
Soil and Water Conservation Plan Certification
Used by taxpayers to certify that the plan under which they are claiming conservation expenses is an approved plan.
IT-IRC sec. 175(c)(3)

Be patient. If any phone number is incorrect, call (area code) 555-1212 and request the new listing.

IRS Tax Forms

8656
Alternative Minimum Tax-Fiduciaries
Used by a fiduciary of an estate or trust to compute the alternative minimum taxable income, distributable net alternative minimum taxable income, and to report any alternative minimum tax due.
IT-IRC secs. 55 - 59; Separate instructions

8689
Allocation of Individual Income Tax to the Virgin Islands
Used as an attachment to Form 1040 filed by an individual who reports adjusted gross income from Virgin Islands sources.
IT-IRC sec. 932

8693
Low-Income Housing Credit Disposition Bond
Used to post a bond to avoid recapture of the low-income housing credit under section 42(j)(6). IT-IRC secs. 42 and 42(j)(6)

8697
Interest Computation Under the Look-Back Method for Completed Long-Term Contracts
Used by taxpayers to figure the interest due or to be refunded under the look-back method of section 460(b)3-on certain long-term contracts entered into after February 28, 1986, that are accounted for under either the percentage of completion-capitalized cost method or the percentage of completion method.
IT-IRC secs. 460(a) and 460(b)(2)(B); Separate instructions

8703
Annual Certification by Operator of a Residential Rental Project
Used by operators of residential rental projects to provide annual information the IRS will use to determine whether the projects continue to meet the requirements of section 142(d). Operators indicate on the form the specific test the bond issuer elected for the project period and also indicate the percentage of low-income units in the residential rental project.
IT-IRC secs. 142

8709
Exemption From Withholding on Investment Income of Foreign Governments
Used by foreign governments or international organizations to claim exemption from withholding under sections 1441 and 1442 on items of income qualifying for tax exemption under section 892.
IT-IRC secs. 892

8716
Election To Have a Tax Year Other Than a Required Tax Year
Used by partnerships, S corporations, and personal service corporations to elect to have a tax year other than a required tax year.
IT-IRC sec. 444

Sch. H (Form 8716)
Section 280H Limitations for a Personal Service Corporation (PSC)
Used by personal service corporations to determine their compliance with the distribution requirements of Section 280H.
IRC secs. 280H and 444

8717
User Fee for Employee Plan Determination Letter Request
Used by applicants for Employee Plan determination letters to transmit the appropriate user fee. Rev. Proc. 89-4, 1983-3 I.R.B. 18

8718
User Fee for Exempt Organization Determination Letter Request
Used by applicants for Exempt Organization determination letters to transmit the appropriate user fee.
Rev. Proc. 89-4. 1989-3 I.R.B. 18

8736
Application for Automatic Extension of Time to File Returns for a Partnership, a REMIC, or for Certain Trusts
Used to apply for an automatic three-month extension of time to file Form 1041 (trust), Form 1041S, or Form 1065.
IT-IRC sec. 6081; Regs. secs. 1.6081-2T and 1.6081-3T

8743
Information on Fuel Inventories and Sales
Used by refiners and importers to report information on fuel inventories and sales. The form is filed as an attachment to Form 720.
EX-IRC secs. 4041, 4081, and 4091

8800
Application for Additional Extension of Time to File Return for a U.S. Partnership, REMIC, or for Certain Trusts
Used to apply for an additional extension of up to three months of time to file Form 1041 (trust), Forms 1041S, or Form 1065. A separate Form 8800 must be filed for each return.
IT-IRC sec. 6081; Regs. secs. 1.6081-2T and 1.6081-3T

8801
Credit for Prior Year Minimum Tax
Used by taxpayers to figure the minimum tax credit allowed for tax year.
IT-IRC sec. 53; Separate instructions

8802
Annual Summary of Capital Construction Fund Activity
Used by taxpayers who maintain a capital construction fund under section 607 of the Merchant Marine Act of 1936, to report deposits to and withdrawals from the fund and to report the balances of the memorandum accounts required by Internal Revenue Code section 7518(d).
IT-IRC sec. 7518; Separate instructions

8803
Limit on Alternative Minimum Tax For Children Under Age 14
Used by children under age 14 to see if the alternative minimum tax figured on Form 6251 can be reduced.
IT-IRC sec. 59(j)

8804
Annual Return for Partnership Withholding Tax (Section 1446)
Used to report the total liability under section 1446 for the partnership's tax year. Form 8804 is also a transmittal form for Form 8805.
IT-IRC sec. 1446; Rev. Proc. 89-31; Separate instructions

8805
Foreign Partner's Information Statement of Section 1446 Withholding Tax
Used to show the amount of effectively connected taxable income and the tax payments allocable to the foreign partner for the partnership's tax year.
IT-IRC sec. 1446; Rev. Proc. 89-31; Separate instructions

8807
Computation of Certain Manufacturers and Retailers Excise Taxes
Used by manufacturers, producers, and importers to figure the tax on the sale of fishing equipment, bows and arrows, pistols and revolvers, firearms, and shells and cartridges. And, used by retailers to figure the excise tax on the sale of truck, trailer, and semitrailer chassis and bodies, and tractors.
EX-IRC secs. 4161, 4181, and 4051

8809
Request for Extension of Time To File Information Returns
Used to request an extension of time to file Forms W-2, W-2G, W-2P, 1098, 1099, or 5498.
PA-IRC sec. 6081; Regs. sec. 1.6081-1

Be patient. If any phone number is incorrect, call (area code) 555-1212 and request the new listing.

Taxes

8810

Corporate Passive Activity Loss and Credit Limitations

Used by closely held C corporations and personal service corporations that have passive activity losses and/or credits. IT-IRC sec. 469; Separate instructions

8811

Information Return for Real Estate Mortgage Investment Conduits (REMICs) and Issuers of Collateralized Debt Obligations

Used by REMICs and issuers of Collateralized Debt Obligations to report entity information needed to compile Publication 938, *Real Estate Mortgage Investment Conduit (REMIC) Reporting Information.*

IT-IRC secs. 860A-G and 1272(a)(6)(C)(ii)

8813

Partnership Withholding Tax Payment (Section 1446)

Used to make payment to the Internal Revenue Service of withholding tax under section 1446. Each payment of section 1446 taxes made during the partnership's tax year must be accompanied by Form 8813.

IT-IRC sec. 1446; Rev. Proc. 89-31; Separate instructions

8814

Parent's Election to Report Child's Interest and Dividends

Used by parents who elect to report the interest and dividends of their child under age 14 on their own tax return. The form is used to figure the amount of the child's income to report on the parent's return and the amount of additional tax that must be added to the parent's tax.

IT-IRC 1(i)(7)

8816

Special Loss Discount Account and Special Estimated Tax Payments for Insurance Companies

Used by insurance companies that elect to take an additional deduction under section 847.

IT-IRC sec. 847

8817

Allocation of Patronage and Nonpatronage Income and Dividends

Used by taxable farmers cooperatives to show income and deductions by patronage and nonpatronage sources.

TD F 90-22.1

Report of Foreign Bank and Financial Accounts

Used by individuals, trusts, partnerships or corporations having a financial interest in, or signature authority or other authority over, bank, securities, or other financial accounts in a foreign country, when the accounts were more than $10,000 in aggregate value at any time during the calendar year.

P.L.91-508; Treasury Regs. 31CFR103)

Be patient. If any phone number is incorrect, call (area code) 555-1212 and request the new listing.

Free Tax Publications

The Internal Revenue Service publishes many free publications to help you "make your taxes less taxing." The publications listed in this section give general information about taxes for individuals, small businesses, farming, fishing, and recent tax law changes. (Forms and schedules related to the subject matter of each publication are indicated after each listing.) You may want to order one of these publications, and then, if you need more detailed information on any subject, order the specific publication about it.

IRS Forms and Publications Distribution

Taxpayer Services
Internal Revenue Service
U.S. Department of the Treasury
1111 Constitution Ave., NW, Room 2422
Washington, DC 20224 (800) 829-3676

Tax forms and publications can be obtained by calling the toll-free number. To send for forms through the mail, write to the state IRS address listed below. Two copies of each form and one copy of each set of instructions will be sent.

Alabama
P.O. Box 8903
Bloomington, IL 61703

Alaska
Rancho Cordova, CA 95743-0001

Arizona
Rancho Cordova, CA 95743-0001

Arkansas
P.O. Box 8903
Bloomington, IL 61703

California
Rancho Cordova, CA 95743-0001

Colorado
Rancho Cordova, CA 95743-0001

Connecticut
P.O. Box 85074
Richmond, VA 23261-5074

Delaware
P.O. Box 85074
Richmond, VA 23261-5074

District of Columbia
P.O. Box 85074
Richmond, VA 23261-5074

Florida
P.O. Box 85074
Richmond, VA 23261-5074

Georgia
P.O. Box 85074
Richmond, VA 23261-5074

Hawaii
Rancho Cordova, CA 95743-0001

Idaho
Rancho Cordova, CA 95743-0001

Illinois
P.O. Box 8903
Bloomington, IL 61703

Indiana
P.O. Box 8903
Bloomington, IL 61703

Iowa
P.O. Box 8903
Bloomington, IL 61703

Kansas
P.O. Box 8903
Bloomington, IL 61703

Kentucky
P.O. Box 8903
Bloomington, IL 61703

Louisiana
P.O. Box 8903
Bloomington, IL 61703

Maine
P.O. Box 85074
Richmond, VA 23261-5074

Maryland
P.O. Box 85074
Richmond, VA 23261-5074

Massachusetts
P.O. Box 85074
Richmond, VA 23261-5074

Michigan
P.O. Box 8903
Bloomington, IL 61703

Minnesota
P.O. Box 8903
Bloomington, IL 61703

Mississippi
P.O. Box 8903
Bloomington, IL 61703

Missouri
P.O. Box 8903
Bloomington, IL 61703

Montana
Rancho Cordova, CA 95743-0001

Be patient. If any phone number is incorrect, call (area code) 555-1212 and request the new listing.

Taxes

Nebraska
P.O. Box 8903
Bloomington, IL 61703

Nevada
Rancho Cordova, CA 95743-0001

New Hampshire
P.O. Box 85074
Richmond, VA 23261-5074

New Jersey
P.O. Box 85074
Richmond, VA 23261-5074

New Mexico
Rancho Cordova, CA 95743-0001

New York
P.O. Box 85074
Richmond, VA 23261-5074

North Carolina
P.O. Box 85074
Richmond, VA 23261-5074

North Dakota
P.O. Box 8903
Bloomington, IL 61703

Ohio
P.O. Box 8903
Bloomington, IL 61703

Oklahoma
P.O. Box 8903
Bloomington, IL 61703

Oregon
Rancho Cordova, CA 95743-0001

Pennsylvania
P.O. Box 85074
Richmond, VA 23261-5074

Puerto Rico
P.O. Box 85074
Richmond, VA 23261-5074

Rhode Island
P.O. Box 85074
Richmond, VA 23261-5074

South Carolina
P.O. Box 85074
Richmond, VA 23261-5074

South Dakota
P.O. Box 8903
Bloomington, IL 61703

Tennessee
P.O. Box 8903
Bloomington, IL 61703

Texas
P.O. Box 8903
Bloomington, IL 61703

Utah
Rancho Cordova, CA 95743-0001

Vermont
P.O. Box 85074
Richmond, VA 23261-5074

Virgin Islands
V.I. Bureau of Internal Revenue
Lockharts Garden No. 1A
Charlotte Amalie
St. Thomas, VI 00802

Virginia
P.O. Box 85074
Richmond, VA 23261-5074

Washington
Rancho Cordova, CA 95743-0001

West Virginia
P.O. Box 85074
Richmond, VA 23261-5074

Wisconsin
P.O. Box 8903
Bloomington, IL 61703

Wyoming
Rancho Cordova, CA 95743-0001

Foreign Addresses

Forms Distribution Center
P.O. Box 85074
Richmond, VA 23261

Forms Distribution Center
Rancho Cordova, CA 95743-0001

Taxpayers with mailing addresses in foreign countries should send requests or the order blank to whichever address is closer. Send letter requests for other forms and publications to: Forms Distribution Center, P.O. Box 85074, Richmond, VA 23261.

Free IRS Publications and Forms

The forms and schedules related to the subject matter of each publication are indicated after each listing.

1 Your Rights as a Taxpayer
To ensure that you always receive fair treatment in tax matters, you should know your rights. This publication clarifies your rights at each step in the tax process.

1S Derechos del Contribuyente (Your Rights as a Taxpayer)
Spanish version of Publication 1.

2 The ABC's of Income Tax
This publication gives the basic tax rules that can help you prepare your individual tax return. It explains who must file a return, which tax form to use, when the return is due, and other general information. It will help you decide which filing status you qualify for, whether you can claim any dependents, and whether the income you are receiving is taxable. The publication goes on to explain the kinds of expenses you may be able to deduct and the various kinds of credits you may be able to take to reduce your tax.
Forms 1040, 1040A, 1040EZ, Schedules A, B, D, E, R, SE, Forms W-2. 2106. 2119, 2441, and 3903.

3 Tax Information for Military Personnel
This publication gives information about the special tax situations of active members of the Armed Forces. It includes information on items that are includible in and excludable from gross income, alien status, dependency exemptions, sale of residence, itemized deductions, tax liability, and filing returns.
Forms 1040, 1040A, 1040EZ, 1040NR, 1040X, 1310, 2106, 2688, 2848, 3903, 3903F, 4868 and W-2.

Be patient. If any phone number is incorrect, call (area code) 555-1212 and request the new listing.

Free Tax Publications

4 Student's Guide to Federal Income Tax
This publication explains the federal tax laws that apply to high school and college students. It describes the student's responsibilities to file and pay taxes, how to file, and how to get help. Forms 1040EZ, W-2 and W-4.

17 Your Federal Income Tax
This publication can help you prepare your individual tax return. It takes you through the individual tax return and explains the tax laws that cover salaries and wages, interest and dividends, rental income, gains and losses, adjustments to income (such as alimony, and IRA contributions), and itemized deductions. Forms 1040, 1040A, 1040EZ, Schedules A, B, D, E, R, SE, Forms W-2, 2106, 2119, 2441, 3903.

225 Farmer's Tax Guide
This publication explains the federal tax laws that apply to farming. It gives examples of typical farming situations and discusses the kinds of farm income you must report and the different deductions you can take. Schedules A, D, F, SE (Form 1040), and Forms 1040, 4136, 4255, 4562, 4684, 4797, 6251.

334 Tax Guide for Small Business
This book explains some federal tax laws that apply to businesses. It describes the four major forms of business organizations: sole proprietorship, partnership, corporation, and S corporation: and explains the tax responsibilities of each. Schedule C (Form 1040), Schedule K-1 (Form 1065 and 1120S), Forms 1065, 1120, 1120-A, 1120S, 4562.

595 Tax Guide for Commercial Fishermen
This publication will familiarize you with the federal tax laws as they apply to the fishing industry. It is intended for sole proprietors who use Schedule C (Form 1040) to report profit or loss from fishing. This guide does not cover corporations or partnerships.
Schedule C (Form 1040), Forms 1099-MISC, 4562, 4797.

15 Circular E, Employer's Tax Guide
Every employer automatically receives this publication on its revision and every person who applies for an employer identification number receives a copy. Forms 940, 941, and 941E.

51 Circular A, Agricultural Employer's Tax Guide
Form 943.

54 Tax Guide for U.S. Citizens and Resident Aliens Abroad
This publication discusses the tax situations of U.S. citizens and resident aliens who live and work abroad. In particular, it explains the rules for excluding income and excluding or deducting certain housing costs. Answers are provided to questions that taxpayers abroad most often ask.
Forms 2555, 1116, and 1040, Schedule SE (Form 1040).

80 Circular SS, Federal Tax Guide for Employers in the Virgin Islands, Guam, American Samoa, and the Commonwealth of the Northern Mariana Islands
Forms 940, 941SS, and 943.

179 Circular PR, Guia Contributiva Federal Para Patronos Puertorriquenos (Federal Tax Guide for Employers in Puerto Rico)
Forms W-3PR, 940PR, 941PR, 942PR, and 943PR.

349 Federal Highway Use Tax on Heavy Vehicles
This publication explains which trucks, truck-tractors, and buses are subject to the federal use tax on heavy motor vehicles, which is one source of funds for the national highway construction program. The tax is due from the person in whose name the vehicle is either registered or required to be registered. The publication tells how to figure and pay the tax due. Form 2290.

378 Fuel Tax Credits and Refunds
This publication explains the credit or refund allowed for the federal excise taxes paid on certain fuels, and the income tax credit available when alcohol is used as a fuel. Forms 843, 4136 and 6478.

448 Federal Estate and Gift Taxes
This publication explains federal estate and gift taxes. Forms 706 and 709.

463 Travel, Entertainment, and Gift Expenses
This publication explains what expenses you may deduct for business-related travel, meals, entertainment, and gifts and it discusses the reporting and recordkeeping requirements for these expenses. The publication also summarizes the deduction and substantiation rules for employees, self-employed persons (including independent contractors), and employers (including corporations and partnerships). Form 2106.

501 Exemptions, Standard Deduction, and Filing Information
This publication provides answers to some basic tax questions: who must file; what filing status to choose; how many exemptions to claim; and how to figure the amount of the standard deduction. It also covers rules for foster care providers. Form 2120 and 8332.

502 Medical and Dental Expenses
This publication tells you how to figure your deduction for medical and dental expenses. You may take this deduction only if you itemize your deductions on Schedule A (Form 1040).
Schedule A (Form 1040).

503 Child and Dependent Care Expenses
This publication explains the credit you may be able to take if you pay someone to care for your dependent who is under 13, your disabled dependent, or your disabled spouse. For purposes of the credit, "disabled" refers to a person physically or mentally unable to care for himself or herself.
Schedule 1 (Form 1040A), and Form 2441.

504 Tax Information for Divorced or Separated Individuals
This publication explains tax rules of interest to divorced or separated individuals. It covers filing status, dependency exemptions, and the treatment of alimony and property settlements.

505 Tax Withholding and Estimated Tax
This publication explains the two methods of paying tax under our pay-as-you-go system. They are (1) Withholding. Your employer will withhold income tax from your pay. Tax is also withheld from certain other types of income. You can have more or less withheld, depending on your circumstances. (2) Estimated tax. If you do not pay your tax through withholding, or do not pay enough tax that way, you might have to pay estimated tax.
Forms W-4, W-4P, W-4S, 1040-ES, 2210, and 2210F.

508 Educational Expenses
This publication explains what work-related educational expenses qualify for deduction, how to report your expenses and any reimbursement you receive, and which forms and schedules to use.
Form 2106 and Schedule A (Form 1040).

509 Tax Calendars for 1993

510 Excise Taxes for 1993
This publication covers in detail the various federal excise taxes reported on Form 720. These include the following groupings: environmental taxes; facilities and service taxes on communication and air transportation; fuel taxes; manufacturers taxes; vaccines; and heavy trucks, trailers and tractors. In addition, it briefly describes other excise taxes and tells which forms to use in reporting and paying the taxes.
Forms 720, 8743, and 8807.

513 Tax Information for Visitors to the United States
This publication briefly reviews the general requirements of U.S. income tax laws for foreign visitors. You may have to file a U.S. income tax return during your visit. Most visitors who come to the United States are not allowed to work in this country. Please check with the Immigration and Naturalization Service before you take a job.
Forms 1040C, 1040NR, 2063, and 1040-ES (NR).

514 Foreign Tax Credit for Individuals
This publication may help you if you paid foreign income tax. You may be able to take a foreign tax credit or deduction to avoid the burden of double taxation. The publication explains which foreign taxes qualify and how to figure your credit or deduction. Form 1116.

Be patient. If any phone number is incorrect, call (area code) 555-1212 and request the new listing.

Taxes

515 Withholding of Tax on Nonresident Aliens and Foreign Corporations

This publication provides information for withholding agents who are required to withhold and report tax on payments to nonresident aliens and foreign corporations. Included are three tables listing U.S. tax treaties and some of the treaty provisions that provide for reduction of or exemption from withholding for certain types of income.

Forms 1042 and 1042S, 1001, 4224, 8233, 1078, 8288, 8288-B, 8804, 8805, 8288-A and W-8, 8813, and 8709.

516 Tax Information for U.S. Government Civilian Employees Stationed Abroad

This publication covers the tax treatment of allowances, reimbursements, and business expenses that U.S. government employees, including foreign service employees, are likely to receive or incur.

517 Social Security for Members of the Clergy and Religious Workers

This publication discusses social security coverage and the self-employment tax for the clergy. It also tells you how, as a member of the clergy (minister, member of a religious order, or Christian Science practitioner), you may apply for an exemption from the self-employment tax that would otherwise be due for the services you perform in the exercise of your ministry. Net earnings from self-employment are explained and sample forms are shown.

Form 2106, Form 1040, Schedule SE (Form 1040), and Schedule C (Form 1040).

519 U.S. Tax Guide for Aliens

This comprehensive publication gives guidelines on how to determine your U.S. tax status and figure your U.S. tax.

Forms 1040, 1040C, 1040NR, 2063, and Schedule A (Form 1040).

520 Scholarships and Fellowships

This publication explains the tax laws that apply to U.S. citizens and resident aliens who study, teach or conduct research in the United States or abroad under scholarships and fellowship grants.

521 Moving Expenses

This publication explains how, if you changed job locations last year or started a new job, you may be able to deduct your moving expenses. You may qualify for a deduction whether you are self-employed or an employee. The expenses must be connected with starting work at your new job location. You must meet a distance test and a time test. You also may be able to deduct expenses of moving to the United States if you retire while living and working overseas or if you are a survivor or dependent of a person who died while living and working overseas.

Forms 3903, 3903F, 4782.

523 Tax Information on Selling Your Home

This publication explains how you report gain from selling your home, how you may postpone the tax on part or all of the gain, and how you may exclude part or all of the gain from your gross income if you are 55 or older. Form 2119.

524 Credit for the Elderly or the Disabled

This publication explains how to figure the credit for the elderly or the disabled. You may be able to claim this credit if you are 65 or older, or if you are retired on disability and were permanently and totally disabled when you retired. Figure the credit on Schedule R (Form 1040), Credit for the Elderly or the Disabled. To take the credit you must file a Form 1040.

Schedule R (Form 1040).

525 Taxable and Nontaxable Income

This publication discusses wages, salaries, fringe benefits, and other compensation received for services as an employee. In addition, it discusses items of miscellaneous taxable income as well as items that are exempt from tax.

526 Charitable Contributions

If you make a charitable contribution or gift to, or for the use of, a qualified organization, you may be able to claim a deduction on your tax return. This publication explains how the deduction is claimed, and the limits that apply.

Schedule A (Form 1040), Form 2106.

527 Residential Rental Property

This publication defines rental income, discusses rental expenses, and explains how to report them on your return. It also discusses casualty losses on rental property, passive activity limits, at-risk rules pertaining to rental property, and the sale of rental property.

Schedule E (Form 1040), and Forms 4562 and 4797.

529 Miscellaneous Deductions

This publication discusses expenses you generally may take as miscellaneous deductions on Schedule A (Form 1040), such as unreimbursed employee expenses and expenses of producing income. It does not discuss other itemized deductions, such as the ones for charitable contributions, moving expenses, interest, taxes, or medical and dental expenses.

Schedule A (Form 1040), Form 2106.

530 Tax Information for Homeowners (Including Owners of Condominiums and Cooperative Apartments)

This publication gives information about home ownership and federal taxes. It explains how to determine basis, how to treat settlement and closing costs, and how to treat repairs and improvements you make. The publication discusses itemized deductions for mortgage interest, real estate taxes, and casualty and theft losses. It also explains the mortgage interest credit.

531 Reporting Income From Tips

This publication gives advice about keeping track of cash and charge tips and explains that all tips received are subject to federal income tax. The publication also explains the rules about the information that employers must report to the Internal Revenue Service about their employees' tip income.

Forms 4070 and 4070A.

533 Self-Employment Tax

This publication explains the self-employment tax, which is a social security tax for people who work for themselves. It is similar to the social security tax withheld from the pay of wage earners.

Schedule SE (Form 1040).

534 Depreciation

This publication discusses the various methods of depreciation, including the modified accelerated cost recovery system (MACRS).

Form 4562.

535 Business Expenses

This publication discusses business expenses such as: fringe benefits; rent; interest; taxes; insurance; and employee benefit plans. It also outlines the choice to capitalize certain business expenses; discusses amortization and depletion; covers some business expenses that may be deductible in some circumstances and not deductible in others; and points out some expenses that are not deductible.

536 Net Operating Losses

537 Installment Sales

This publication discusses sales arrangements that provide for part or all of the selling price to be paid in a later year. These arrangements are "installment sales." If you finance the buyer's purchase of your property, instead of having the buyer get a loan or mortgage from a bank, you probably have an installment sale. Form 6252.

538 Accounting Periods and Methods

This publication explains which accounting periods and methods can be used for figuring federal taxes, and how to apply for approval to change from one period or method to another. Most individual taxpayers use the calendar year for their accounting period and the cash method of accounting. Forms 1128 and 3115.

541 Tax Information on Partnerships

Forms 1065 and Schedules D, K, and K-1 (Form 1065).

542 Tax Information on Corporations

Forms 1120 and 1120-A

544 Sales and Other Dispositions of Assets

This publication explains how to figure gain and loss on various transactions, such as trading or selling an asset used in a trade or business, and it explains the tax results of different types of gains and losses. Not all transactions result in taxable gains or deductible losses, and not all gains are taxed the same way.

Schedule D (Form 1040) and Form 4797.

Be patient. If any phone number is incorrect, call (area code) 555-1212 and request the new listing.

Free Tax Publications

545 Interest Expense
This publication explains what items may and may not be deducted as interest. (Interest is an amount paid for the use of borrowed money.) This publication also explains how much interest you may deduct and how to figure this amount. Where you deduct interest expense depends on why you borrowed the money. Schedule A (Form 1040).

547 Nonbusiness Disasters, Casualties, and Thefts
This publication explains when you can deduct a disaster, casualty, or theft loss. Casualties are events such as hurricanes, earthquakes, tornadoes, fire, floods, vandalism, loss of deposits in a bankrupt or insolvent financial institution, and car accidents. The publication also explains how to treat the reimbursement you receive from insurance or other sources. Form 4684.

550 Investment Income and Expenses
This publication explains which types of investment income are and are not taxable, when the income is taxed, and how to report it on your tax return. The publication discusses the treatment of tax shelters and investment-related expenses. The publication also explains how to figure your gain and loss when you sell or trade your investment property.
Forms 1099-INT and 1099-DIV, Schedules B and D (Form 1040).

551 Basis of Assets
This publication explains how to determine the basis of property. The basis of property you buy is usually its cost. If you received property in some other way, such as by gift or inheritance, you normally must use a basis other than cost.

552 Recordkeeping for Individuals
This publication can help you decide what records to keep and how long to keep them for tax purposes. These records will help you prepare your income tax returns so that you will pay only your correct tax. If you keep a record of your expenses during the year, you may find that you can reduce your taxes by itemizing your deductions. Deductible expenses include medical and dental bills, interest, contributions, and taxes.

553 Highlights of 1992 Tax Changes
This publication discusses the more important changes in the tax rules brought about by recent legislation, rulings, and administrative decisions. It does not discuss all new tax rules or detail all changes. It highlights the important recent changes that taxpayers should know about when filing their 1989 tax forms and when planning for 1990.

554 Tax Information for Older Americans
This publication gives tax information of special interest to older Americans. An example takes you through completing a tax return and explains such items as the sale of a home, the credit for the elderly or the disabled, the supplemental Medicare premium, and pension and annuity income. The publication includes filled-in forms and schedules that show how these and other items are reported. Schedules B, D, and R (Form 1040), and Forms 1040 and 2119.

555 Community Property and the Federal Income Tax
This publication may help married taxpayers who are domiciled in one of the following community property states: Arizona, California, Idaho, Louisiana, Nevada, New Mexico, Texas, Washington or Wisconsin. If you wish to file a separate tax return, you should understand how community property laws affect the way you figure your tax before completing your federal income tax return.

556 Examination of Returns, Appeal Rights, and Claims for Refund
This publication may be helpful if your return is examined by the Internal Revenue Service. It explains that returns are normally examined to verify the correctness of reported income, exemptions, or deductions, and it describes what appeal rights you have if you disagree with the results of the examination. This publication also explains the procedures for the examination of items of partnership income, deduction, gain, loss, and credit. Information is given on how to file a claim for refund, the time for filing a claim for refund, and any limit on the amount of refund. Forms 1040X and 1120X

556S Revision de las Declaraciones de Impuesto, Derecho de Apelacion y Reclamaciones de Reembolsos (Examination of Returns, Appeal Rights, and Claims for Refund)
(Spanish version of Publication 556) Forms 1040X and 1120X

557 Tax-Exempt Status for Your Organization
This publication discusses how organizations become recognized as exempt from federal income tax under section 501(a) of the Internal Revenue Code. (These include organizations described in Code section 501(c).) The publication explains how to get a ruling or determination letter recognizing the exemption, and it gives other information that applies generally to all exempt organizations.
Forms 990, 990PF, 1023, and 1024.

559 Tax Information for Survivors, Executors, and Administrators
This publication can help you report and pay the proper federal income and estate taxes if you are responsible for settling a decedent's estate. The publication also answers many questions that a spouse or other survivor faces when a person dies.
Form 1040, Form 1041, Form 706, and Form 4810.

560 Self-Employed Retirement Plans
This publication discusses retirement plans for self-employed persons and certain partners in partnerships. These retirement plans are sometimes called Keogh plans or HR-10 plans.

561 Determining the Value of Donated Property
This publication can help donors and appraisers determine the value of property (other than cash) that is given to qualified organizations. It explains what kind of information you need to support a charitable deduction you claim on your return.
Form 8283.

564 Mutual Fund Distributions
This publication discusses the federal income tax treatment of distributions paid or allocated to you as an individual shareholder of a mutual fund. A comprehensive example shows distributions made by a mutual fund and an illustration of Form 1040.
Forms 1040, Schedule B (Form 1040), and Form 1099-DIV.

570 Tax Guide for Individuals in U.S. Possessions
This publication is for individuals with income from American Samoa, Guam, the Commonwealth of the Northern Mariana Islands, Puerto Rico, and the U.S. Virgin Islands.
Forms 4563, 5074, and 8689.

571 Tax-Sheltered Annuity Programs for Employees of Public Schools and Certain Tax-Exempt Organizations
This publication explains the rules concerning employers qualified to buy tax-sheltered annuities, eligible employees who may participate in the program, and the amounts that may be excluded from income. Form 5330.

575 Pension and Annuity Income (Including Simplified General Rule)
This publication explains how to report pension and annuity income on your federal income tax return. It also explains the special tax treatment for lump-sum distributions from pension, stock bonus, or profit-sharing plans.
Forms 1040, 1099-R and 4972.

578 Tax Information for Private Foundations and Foundation Managers
This publication covers tax matters of interest to private foundations and their managers, including the tax classification of the foundations, filing requirements, the tax on net investment income, and various excise taxes on transactions that violate the foundation rules. Form 990-F

579S Como Preparar la Declaracion de Impuesto Federal (How to Prepare the Federal Income Tax Return)
Forms 1040, 1040A, 1040EZ.

583 Taxpayers Starting a Business
This publication shows sample records that a small business can use if it operates as a sole proprietorship. Records like these will help you prepare complete and accurate tax returns and make sure you pay only the tax you owe. This publication also discusses the taxpayer identification number businesses must use, information returns businesses may have to file, and the kinds of business taxes businesses may have to pay.
Schedule C (Form 1040), and Form 4562.

Be patient. If any phone number is incorrect, call (area code) 555-1212 and request the new listing.

Taxes

584 Nonbusiness Disaster, Casualty, and Theft Loss Workbook

This workbook can help you to figure your loss from a disaster, casualty or theft. It will help you most if you list your possessions before any losses occur. The workbook has schedules to help you figure the loss on your home and its contents. There is also a schedule to help you figure the loss on your car, truck, or motorcycle.

586A The Collection Process (Income Tax Accounts)

This publication explains your rights and duties as a taxpayer who owes tax. It also explains the legal obligation of the Internal Revenue Service to collect overdue taxes, and the way we fulfill this obligation. It is not intended to be a precise and technical analysis of the law in this area.

586S Proceso de cobro (Deudas del impuesto sobre ingreso)

(Spanish version of Publication 586A)

587 Business Use of Your Home

This publication can help you decide if you qualify to deduct certain expenses for using part of your home in your business. You must meet specific tests and your deduction is limited. Deductions for the business use of a home computer are also discussed. Schedule C (Form 1040), and Form 4562.

589 Tax Information on S Corporations

This publication discusses the way corporations are taxed under subchapter S of the Internal Revenue Code. In general, an "S" corporation does not pay tax on its income. Instead, it passes through its income and expenses to its shareholders, who then report them on their own tax returns. Forms 1120S and Schedule K-1 (Form 1120S)

590 Individual Retirement Arrangements (IRAs)

This publication explains the rules for and the tax benefits of having an individual retirement arrangement (IRA). An IRA is a savings plan that lets you set aside money for your retirement. Generally, your contributions to an IRA are tax deductible in part or in full and the earnings in your IRA are not taxed until they are distributed to you. Forms 1040, 5329 and 8606.

593 Tax Highlights for U.S. Citizens and Residents Going Abroad

This publication briefly reviews various U.S. tax provisions that apply to U.S. citizens or resident aliens who live or work abroad and expect to receive income from foreign sources.

594 The Collection Process (Employment Tax Accounts)

This booklet explains your rights and duties as a taxpayer who owes employer's quarterly federal taxes. It also explains how we fulfill the legal obligation of the Internal Revenue Service to collect these taxes. It is not intended as a precise and technical analysis of the law.

594S Proceso de cobro (Deudas del impuesto por razon del empleo)

(Spanish version of Publication 594.)

596 Earned Income Credit

This publication discusses who may receive the earned income credit, and how to figure and claim the credit. It also discusses how to receive advance payments of the earned income credit. Forms W-5, 1040, and 1040A.

597 Information on the United States-Canada Income Tax Treaty

This publication reproduces the entire text of the U.S.-Canada income tax treaty, and also gives an explanation of provisions that often apply to U.S. citizens or residents who have Canadian source income. There is also a discussion that deals with certain tax problems that may be encountered by Canadian residents who temporarily work in the United States.

598 Tax on Unrelated Business Income of Exempt Organizations

This publication explains the unrelated business income tax provisions that apply to most tax-exempt organizations. An organization that regularly operates a trade or business that is not substantially related to its exempt purpose may be taxed on the income from this business. Generally, a tax-exempt organization with gross income of $1,000 or more from an unrelated trade or business must file a return. Form 990-T.

686 Certification for Reduced Tax Rates in Tax Treaty Countries

This publication explains how U.S. citizens, residents, and domestic corporations may certify to a foreign treaty country that they are entitled to treaty benefits.

721 Tax Guide to U.S. Civil Service Retirement Benefits

This publication explains how the federal income tax rules apply to the benefits that retired federal employees or their survivors receive under the U.S. Civil Service Retirement System or Federal Employees Retirement System. There is also information on estate taxes. Form 1040.

850 English-Spanish Glossary of Words and Phrases Used in Publications Issued by the Internal Revenue Service

901 U.S. Tax Treaties

This publication includes information about the reduced tax rates and exemptions from U.S. taxes provided under U.S. tax treaties with other countries. This publication is intended for residents of those countries who receive income from U.S. sources. Information for foreign workers and students is emphasized. Form 1040NR

904 Interrelated Computations for Estate and Gift Taxes

Forms 706 and 709.

907 Tax Information for Handicapped and Disabled Individuals

This publication explains tax rules of interest to handicapped and disabled people and to taxpayers with disabled dependents. For example, you may be able to take a tax credit for certain disability payments, you may be able to deduct medical expenses, and you may be able to take a credit for expenses of care for disabled dependents.

Schedule A (Form 1040), Schedule R (1040), and Form 2441.

908 Bankruptcy and Other Debt Cancellation

This publication explains the income tax aspects of bankruptcy and discharge of debt for individuals and small businesses. Forms 982, 1040, 1041, 1120.

909 Alternative Minimum Tax for Individuals

This publication discusses the alternative minimum tax, which applies to individuals. Forms 6251, 8801, and 8803.

911 Tax Information for Direct Sellers

This publication may help you if you are a "direct seller," a person who sells consumer products to others on a person-to-person basis. Many direct sellers sell door-to-door, at sales parties, or by appointment in someone's home. Information on figuring your income from direct sales as well as the kinds of expenses you may be entitled to deduct is also provided. Schedules C and SE (Form 1040).

915 Social Security Benefits and Equivalent Railroad Retirement Benefits

This publication explains when you have to include part of your social security or equivalent railroad retirement benefits in income on Form 1040. It also explains how to figure the amount to include. Forms SSA-1099 and RRB-1099, Social Security Benefits Worksheet, Notice 703, Forms SSA-1042S and RRB-1042S.

917 Business Use of a Car

This publication explains the expenses that you may deduct for the business use of your car. Car expenses that are deductible do not include the cost of commuting expenses (driving from your home to your workplace). The publication also discusses the taxability of the use of a car provided by an employer and rules on leasing a car for business. Form 2106

Be patient. If any phone number is incorrect, call (area code) 555-1212 and request the new listing.

Free Tax Publications

919 Is My Withholding Correct for 1991?
To help employees check their withholding, this publication has worksheets that will help them estimate both their 1990 tax and their total 1990 withholding. The employees can then compare the two amounts. The publication tells employees what to do if too much or too little tax is being withheld.
Form W-4.

924 Reporting of Real Estate Transactions to IRS
This publication informs sellers of certain real estate about the information they must provide to the real estate reporting person in order that the reporting person can complete the Form 1099-S that must be filed with the IRS.

925 Passive Activity and At-Risk Rules
This publication covers the rules that limit passive activity losses and credits and the at-risk limits. Form 8582.

926 Employment Taxes for Household Employers
This publication shows how a household employer reports federal income tax withholding, social security (FICA), and unemployment taxes (FUTA). You may be a household employer if you have a babysitter, maid, or other employee who works in your house. The publication also shows what records you must keep.
Forms W-2, W-3, 940, 940EZ, and 942.

929 Tax Rules for Children and Dependents
This publication describes the tax law affecting certain children and dependents. No personal exemption is allowed to a taxpayer who can be claimed as a dependent by another taxpayer. The standard deduction for dependents may be limited. Minor children may have to pay tax at their parent's tax rate.
Form 8615, Form 8814, and Form 8803.

936 Limits on Home Mortgage Interest Deduction
This publication covers the rules governing the deduction of home mortgage interest if your acquisition cost exceeds $1 million ($500,000 if you are married filing separately) or your home equity debt exceeds $100,000 ($50,000 if you are married filing separately). Worksheets are provided to determine what interest expenses qualify as home mortgage interest.

937 Business Reporting
The first part of this publication explains your responsibilities, if you have employees, to withhold federal income taxes and social security taxes (FICA) from their wages, and to pay social security taxes and federal unemployment taxes (FUTA). It also discusses the rules for advance payment of the earned income credit, and for reporting and allocating tips.
The second part provides general information about the rules for reporting payments to nonemployees and transactions with other persons. It also provides information on taxpayer identification numbers, backup withholding, and penalties relating to information returns.
Forms W-2, W-2G, W-4, 940, 941, 1098, 1099 series, 4789, 5498, 8300, and 8308.

938 Real Estate Mortgage Investment Conduits (REMICS) Reporting Information (And Other Collateralized Debt Obligations (CDOs))
This new publication discusses reporting requirements for issuers of real estate mortgage investment conduits (REMICS) and collateralized debt obligations (CDOs). This publication also contains a directory of REMICS and CDOs to assist brokers and middlemen in fulfilling reporting requirements.

939 Pension General Rule (Nonsimplified Method)
This publication covers the nonsimplified General Rule for the taxation of pensions or annuities, which must be used if the Simplified General Rule is not applicable or is not chosen. For example, the nonsimplified method must be used for payments under commercial annuities. The publication also contains the necessary actuarial tables for this method.

945 Tax Information for Those Affected by Operation Desert Shield
This publication covers many issues, such as available tax relief measures for suspending examinations or collection of back taxes, extending due dates for filing an income tax return, meeting the requirements for the foreign earned income exclusion, and seeking other tax assistance. This publication applies to newly activated reservists, as well as all other active duty U.S. military personnel and their families, citizens who had been detained by Iraq, and citizens who had to leave the Middle East because of the adverse conditions.

946 How to Begin Depreciating your Property
Publication for people who are depreciating property for the first time.

953 International Tax information for Businesses
Covers topics of interest to U.S. citizens and resident aliens with foreign investments and nonresident aliens who want to invest in U.S. businesses.

1004 Identification Numbers Under ERISA

1045 Information for Tax Practitioners

1212 List of Original Discount Instruments
This publication explains the tax treatment of original issue discount (OID). It describes how (1) Brokers and other middlemen, who may hold the debt instruments as nominees for the owners, should report OID to IRS and to the owners on Forms 1099-OID or 1099-INT, and (2) Owners of OID debt instruments should report OID on their income tax returns. The publication gives rules for figuring the discount amount to report each year, if required. It also gives tables showing OID amounts for certain publicly-traded OID debt instruments, including short-term U.S. Government securities.
Schedule B (Form 1040) and Forms 1099-OID and 1099-INT.

1244 Employee's Daily Record of Tips (Form 4070-A) and Employee's Report of Tips to Employer (Form 4070)
This publication explains how you must report tips if you are an employee who receives tips. Copies of the monthly tip report you must give your employer are included, as well as a daily list you can use for your own records.
Forms 4070 and 4070-A.

1544 Reporting Cash Payments of Over $10,000 (Received in a Trade or Business)
This new publication was developed to assist the government in the war against drugs. It contains information for filing Form 8300 and includes an example with a filled-in Form 8300.

Be patient. If any phone number is incorrect, call (area code) 555-1212 and request the new listing.

Taxes

State Tax Assistance

These state taxpayer service departments are the basic starting place for free assistance and guidance pertaining to your state taxes.

Alabama

Taxpayer Assistance
Alabama Income Tax Division
P.O. Box 327465
Montgomery, AL 36132-7465 (205) 242-1000

Alaska

(No individual income tax; corporation tax only)
Alaska Department of Revenue
Income and Excise Audit Division
Attn: Corporations Unit
P.O. Box SA
Juneau, AK 99801 (907) 465-2370

Arizona

Personal Income Tax
Arizona Department of Revenue
P.O. Box 29002
Phoenix, AZ 85038

Corporation Tax
Arizona Department of Revenue
P.O. Box 29079
Phoenix, AZ 85038
Information and fewer than 6 forms (602) 255-3381
6 or more forms (602) 542-4260

Arkansas

Arkansas Department of Finance Administration
Attn: Income Tax
P.O. Box 3628
Little Rock, AR 72203
General Information (501) 682-7250
Refund Information (501) 682-7280
Forms (501) 682-7255

California

Personal
Franchise Tax Board
P.O. Box 942840
Sacramento, CA 942857-0000 (800) 852-5711

Corporate
Franchise Tax Board
P.O. Box 942857
Sacramento, CA 94257-0500 (916) 369-0500

Colorado

Taxpayer Services
Department of Revenue
1375 Sherman Street
Denver, CO 80261
Personal (303) 534-1209
Corporate (303) 534-1209

Connecticut

Department of Revenue Services
92 Farmington Avenue
Hartford, CT 06105
Information and Forms (800) 321-7829
Information (203) 566-8520
Forms (203) 297-5773

Delaware

Delaware Division of Revenue
820 North French Street
Wilmington, DE 19899 (800) 292-7826
(302) 577-3300

Florida

Florida Taxpayer Assistance (800) 872-9909
P.O. Box 5139 (904) 488-6800
Tallahassee, FL 32314-5139
Bulk form orders (904) 488-8422

Georgia

Income Tax Division
P.O. Box 38007
Atlanta, GA 30334
Personal (404) 656-4293
Corporate (404) 656-4165

Hawaii

Taxpayer Services Branch
Hawaii State Tax Collector
P.O. Box 259
Honolulu, HI 96809-02559 (808) 548-4242
Information (800) 222-3229
Forms (800) 222-7572

Idaho

Idaho Department of Revenue and Taxation
P.O. Box 36
Boise, ID 83722 (208) 334-7787

Illinois

Illinois Department of Revenue
P.O. Box 19015
Springfield, IL 62794-9015 (217) 785-6760
Information all year, Forms July - December (800) 732-8866
Forms January - June (800) 624-2459

Indiana

Indiana Department of Revenue
Taxpayer Services Division
Room 104-B, 100 North Senate Street
Indianapolis, IN 46204 (317) 232-2240

Be patient. If any phone number is incorrect, call (area code) 555-1212 and request the new listing.

State Tax Assistance

Iowa

Iowa Department of Revenue and Finance
Hoover State Office Building
Des Moines, IA 50319

Information and forms	(515) 218-3114
Bulk form orders	(515) 281-5370

Kansas

Kansas Department of Revenue
Box 12001
Topeka, KS 66612-2001

Personal	(913) 296-0222
Business	(913) 296-1711

Kentucky

Kentucky Revenue Cabinet
Frankfort, KY 40618

Information	(502) 564-4580
Forms	(502) 564-3658

Louisiana

Louisiana Department of Revenue and Taxation
P.O. Box 201
Baton Rouge, LA 70821

Information	(504) 925-4611
Forms	(504) 925-7532
Refund information	(504) 925-4611

Maine

State of Maine
Department of Taxation
Station 24
Augusta, ME 04333

Information	(207) 626-8475
Information	(800) 452-1983
Forms	(800) 338-5811

Maryland

Comptroller of the Treasury
Income Tax Information
301 W. Preston St.
Baltimore, MD 21201

	(410) 974-3951

Massachusetts

Massachusetts Department of Revenue
100 Cambridge Street
Boston, MA 02204
Attention: Correspondence Unit

	(617) 727-4392

Michigan

Department of Treasury
430 West Allegan Street
Lansing, MI 48922

Information	(800) 877-MICH
Information	(517) 373-2910
Information	(517) 373-3386
Forms	(800) FORM-2-ME
Forms	(517) 373-6598
Forms	(517) 335-1144

Minnesota

Minnesota Taxpayer Assistance
10 River Park Plaza
St. Paul, MN 55146

Personal	(800) 652-9094
Personal	(612) 296-3781
Corporate	(800) 657-3777
Corporate	(612) 296-6181

Mississippi

Mississippi State Tax Commission
P.O. Box 1033
Jackson, MS 39215

	(601) 359-1141

Missouri

Taxpayer Assistance
Missouri Department of Revenue
P.O. Box 2200
Jefferson City, MO 65105-2200

Information	(314) 751-3503
Forms	(314) 751-4695

Montana

Montana Department of Revenue
Income Tax Division
P.O. Box 5803
Helena, MT 59604

Personal	(406) 444-2837
Corporate	(406) 444-3388

Nebraska

Nebraska Department of Revenue
Taxpayer Assistance
P.O. Box 94818
Lincoln, NE 68509

Personal Income Tax information, in season	(800) 422-4618
Personal Information, all year	(402) 471-5729
Corporate Information, all year	(800) 742-7474

Nevada

No Income Tax	(702) 687-4820

New Hampshire

No Income Tax	(603) 271-2191

New Jersey

New Jersey Division of Taxation
50 Barrack Street
CN 269
Trenton, NJ 08646

	(800) 323-4400
	(609) 292-6400

New Mexico

New Mexico Taxation and Revenue
P.O. Box 630
Santa Fe, NM 87509-0630

	(505) 827-0909

New York

New York State Department of Taxation and Finance
Taxpayer Assistance Bureau
W. A. Harriman Campus
Albany, NY 12227

General Information	(800) 225-5829
Refund Information	(800) 443-3200
Forms	(800) 462-8100
All	(518) 438-6777

North Carolina

Information:
North Carolina Department of Revenue
P.O. Box 25000
Raleigh, NC 27640

Refund Information:
North Carolina Department of Revenue

Be patient. If any phone number is incorrect, call (area code) 555-1212 and request the new listing.

Taxes

P.O. Box R
Raleigh, NC 27634

Information	(800) 222-9965
Forms	(800) 451-1404
All	(919) 733-3450

North Dakota

Office of State Tax Commissioner
600 East Boulevard Avenue
Bismarck, ND 58505-0599 (701) 224-3017

Ohio

Taxpayer Services
Ohio Department of Taxation
P.O. Box 2476 (800) 282-1782
Columbus, Ohio 43266-0076 (614) 846-6712

Oklahoma

Oklahoma Tax Commission
2501 Lincoln Boulevard (800) 522-8165
Oklahoma City, OK 73194 (405) 521-4321

Oregon

Oregon Department of Revenue
Tax Help Section
955 Center Street, NE
Salem, OR 97310 (503) 378-4988

Pennsylvania

Personal:
Pennsylvania Department of Revenue
Taxpayer Services
Department 280101
Harrisburg, PA 17128-0101 (717) 986-4621

Corporate:
Pennsylvania Department of Revenue
Business Trust Fund Taxes
Department 280904
Harrisburg, PA 17128-0904 (717) 787-2416

Rhode Island

Rhode Island Division of Taxation
1 Capitol Hill
Providence, RI 02908

Information	(401) 277-2905
Forms	(401) 277-3934

South Carolina

South Carolina Department of Revenue
P.O. Box 125
Columbia, SC 29214

Information	(803) 737-4709
Forms	(803) 737-5084

South Dakota

No Income Tax (605) 773-3311

Tennessee

Tennessee Taxpayer Services
504 Andrew Jackson Building
Nashville, TN 37242

Information	(615) 741-3581
Forms	(615) 741-2481

Texas

No Income Tax (512) 463-4600

Utah

Utah State Tax Commission
160 East 3rd South
Salt Lake City, UT 84134 (801) 530-4848

Vermont

Personal:
Vermont Department of Taxes
Pavillion Office Building
Montpelier, VT 05602 (802) 828-2515

Corporate:
Vermont Department of Taxes
P.O. Box 547
Montpelier, VT 05602 (802) 828-2865

Virginia

Virginia Department of Taxation
P.O. Box 6L
Richmond, VA 23282

* Place attention notation to what it concerns

Personal	(804) 367-8031
Corporate	(804) 367-8038
Forms	(804) 367-8055

Washington

No Income Tax (800) 233-6349

West Virginia

West Virginia Department of Revenue
P.O. Box 3784 (800) 642-9016
Charleston, WV 25337-3784 (304) 344-2068

Wisconsin

Taxpayer Services
Wisconsin Department of Revenue
P.O. Box 8906
Madison, WI 53708

Personal, information and forms	(608) 266-2486
Corporate, information and forms	(608) 266-2772
Bulk form orders	(608) 267-2025

Wyoming

No Income Tax (307) 777-7961

Be patient. If any phone number is incorrect, call (area code) 555-1212 and request the new listing.

Health and Medicine Clearinghouses and Starting Points

* *See also Experts Chapter*
* *See also Drugs and Chemical Dependence Chapter*
* *See also Careers and Workplace Chapter*
* *See also Economics, Demographics, and Statistics Chapter*
* *See also Environment and Nature Chapter*
* *See also Consumer Power Chapter*

Unlike any other chapter in this book, this chapter contains one information clearinghouse after another. Some of these national resource centers provide telephone help on many concerns; for example, the Family Life Information Exchange and Project Share. Other offices, like the Diabetic Information Clearinghouse, have a more concentrated focus. The Public Health Service of the U.S. Department of Health and Human Services is the primary arm of the federal government which disseminates information about promoting health and preventing disease. It sponsors the National Health Information Center which is accessible by a toll-free number. The Center will answer questions, send out medical journal abstracts, fact sheets and other materials, and refer callers to more specialized clearinghouses, government offices, city and county health departments, national associations, health advocacy groups, private organizations and foundations that focus on your health concern. Other government agencies, including the U.S. Department of Agriculture, the U.S. Environmental Protection Agency, and the Food and Drug Administration, also serve both as watchdogs and information providers on the safety of pharmaceuticals, drinking water, hazardous wastes, and food inspection.

Suppose your doctor has recommended a CAT scan or you've just gotten worrisome lab test results. Your first step is to call the National Health Information Center. The center can refer you to numerous organizations and one of the National Institutes of Health which specializes in this type of health problem. Do you have an appointment with a surgeon in a few weeks and want to be prepared to discuss the pros and cons of the operation? Look through this section for published resources, databases, medical libraries, and information clearinghouses that will give you powerful research tools. But, don't stop there. Consider contacting those universities and research centers identified in both the Medical Research Section as well as the Careers and Workplace Chapter, specifically the section titled Research Grants in Any Field, to learn about new experimental medical procedures, tests, and treatments. And, don't forget the hundreds of medical specialists whose phone numbers are listed in the Experts Chapter.

* Access to All Medical and Scientific Studies

National Library of Medicine
8600 Rockville Pike
Bethesda, MD 20894 (301) 496-6095

The National Library of Medicine (NLM) is the world's largest research library in a single scientific and professional field. The collection today stands at four million books, journals, technical reports, manuscripts, microfilms, and pictorial materials. The Library may be used by health professionals and health science students, and books and journals may also be requested on interlibrary loan (there is a fee for loan transactions). The Library's computer-based Medical Literature Analysis and Retrieval System (MEDLARS) has bibliographic access to NLM's vast store of biomedical information. All of the MEDLARS databases are available through NLM's online network of more than 20,000 institutions and individuals. NLM charges a user fee for access to the system. The Regional Medical Library Program is intended to provide health science practitioners, investigators, and educators convenient access to health care and biomedical information resources. The Regional Libraries provide reference service, referral service, and online access to MEDLARS.

* Adolescent Health

National Maternal and Child Health
Clearinghouse
38th and R Sts., NW
Washington, DC 20057 (202) 625-8410

This Clearinghouse has an extensive list of free publications concerned with adolescent health. Some of the titles include: *Adolescent Fathers: Directory of Services* (programs available state by state), *Adolescent Health: Catalog of Products* (journal articles, videotapes, curricula materials and patient education materials which focus on adolescent health), *Adolescent Substance Abuse,* and

Promoting the Health of Adolescents: Proceedings from the 1990 Adolescent Health Coordinators Conference.

* AIDS National Information Clearinghouse

National AIDS Information Clearinghouse
P.O. Box 6003 (301) 762-5111
Rockville, MD 20850 (800) 458-5231 (bulk orders)

A Centers for Disease Control service, this clearinghouse has publications, posters, and videos dealing with AIDS which are free of charge. The publications include a fact sheet, guidelines for the prevention of the spread of AIDS in schools and the workplace, and the Surgeon General's report on AIDS. They have two online databases; one dealing with organization, and the other lists unpublished educational materials (no journals).

* Alcohol and Drug Information Center

National Clearinghouse for Alcohol and Drug Information
P.O. Box 2345 (800) 729-6686
Rockville, MD 20852 (301) 468-2600

This clearinghouse makes referrals to local AA chapters and other self-help organizations as well as national associations as well as providing callers with materials about preventing or curing substance abuse.

* Almanac to National Institutes of Health

Division of Public Information
National Institutes of Health
Building 31, Room 2B03

Health and Medicine

Bethesda, MD 20892 (301) 496-4143

Published annually, the *NIH Almanac* presents pertinent facts about the National Institutes of Health. All the various institutes are listed, including information about their respective research and staffs. Historical data about NIH, as well as tables describing appropriations, staff and facilities, are also included. Information regarding lectures, Nobel Laureates, and the field units can also be found in this free sourcebook. Free database searches, publications and videos are available.

* America's Health Advisor: Surgeon General

Surgeon General
200 Independence Ave., SW
Room 716-G
Washington, DC 20201 (202) 245-6467

The Surgeon General provides leadership and direction for the Public Health Service Commissioned Corps. He serves as principal federal health advisor to the nation on public health matters and serves as the focal point for dialogue with professional societies, representing PHS at national and international meetings. The Surgeon General releases many reports such as *Smoking and Health* and *Healthy People*, and issues warnings to the public on health hazards. The Surgeon General also reviews plans for transportation, open testing, and disposal of lethal chemicals and biological agents.

* Arthritis Clearinghouse

National Arthritis and Musculoskeletal and Skin Diseases
Box AMS
Bethesda, MD 20892 (301) 495-4484

This clearinghouse responds to requests for information on arthritis, and musculoskeletal and skin diseases from health professionals and the general public. AMS uses the online database CHID (Combined Health Information Database) from which they can reference health information. Their bulletin, *MEMO*, published on an as-needed basis, contains current topics of interest. They can provide you with many brochures, reports, and other publications, along with a free publications listing.

* Asthma Clearinghouse

National Asthma Education Program
4733 Bethesda Ave.
Suite 530
Bethesda, MD 20814 (301) 951-3260

The Asthma Clearinghouse is a new clearinghouse, providing publications, reports, resources, and referrals to experts in the field of asthma. One report, the *Executive Summary: Guidelines for the Diagnosis and Management of Asthma*, explains the diagnosis, therapy, and other considerations for those that suffer from asthma. They can answer your questions or can direct you to those that can. Contact the Clearinghouse for more information. Other free publications include:

General Public

Check Your Asthma "I.Q." - true-or-false quiz.
Facts About Asthma - presents basic information on asthma.

Professionals

*Air Power - basics of asthma management in four 1-hour sessions for children ages 9-13 and their parents ($10).
*Air Wise - one-on-one sessions for hard to manage children ($16).
*Living With Asthma - contains eight sessions for children ages 8-13 and their parents ($40).
*Open Airways - seven sessions for inner-city children ages 4-12 and their parents and is designed for low-income, low-education families ($25).

*Available from: Superintendent of Documents, Government Printing Office, Washington, DC 20402; (202) 783-3238.

* Biotechnology Information Center

National Agriculture Library Building
Beltsville, MD 20705 (301) 504-6875

This Information Center covers genetic engineering and recombinant DNA techniques, tissue culture of plant and animal systems, single cell protein, immobilized enzymes, embryo transplants, and much more. They have access to a database, bibliographies, and other publications. Contact this Center for more information.

* Blood Resource

National Blood Resource Education Program
4733 Bethesda Ave., Suite 530
Bethesda, MD 20814 (301) 951-3260

This Program was established to ensure an adequate supply of safe blood and blood components to meet the Nation's needs and to ensure that blood and blood components are transfused only when therapeutically appropriate. This Program helps health professional understand the risks and benefits of blood transfusions, and ensures that patients receive appropriate information regarding transfusions. They also work to increase awareness that donating blood is a safe process. Contact this office for more information regarding blood donations and transfusions. Free publications include:

General Public

Check Your Blood "I.Q." - true-false quiz designed to educate public about blood donation and transfusion.
Your Operation- Your Blood - describes autologous transfusion options.

Professionals

Transfusion Alert: Indications for the Use of Red Blood Cells, Platelets, and Fresh Frozen Plasma - summarizes the indications for the use of these blood components.
Transfusion Alert: Use of Autologous Blood - discusses preoperative autologous blood donation, perioperative blood salvage, and acute normovolemic hemodilution.

* Cancer Hotline

Cancer Information Service
National Cancer Institute (800) 4-CANCER
Building 31, Room 10A18 (800) 638-6070 Alaska
9000 Rockville Pike (800) 524-1234 Hawaii
Bethesda, MD 20892 (301) 427-8656 Maryland

The Cancer Information Service assists cancer patients, families, and medical personnel on all aspects of cancer. They have information on treatment, rehab, and detection, as well as on financial assistance. Through their databases (see Automated Information Systems-Cancer), they have access to current research and physician referrals. Pamphlets, reports, and assistance in locating community resources is also available.

* Cancer Information Regional Offices

Cancer Information Service
National Cancer Institute
Building 31, Room 10A2A (800) 4-CANCER
9000 Rockville Pike (800) 524-1234 in Oahu, HI
Bethesda, MD 20892 (800) 638-6070 in AK

The National Cancer Institute has set up offices across the U.S. through which they route the Cancer Information Service calls for those particular areas. These offices offer the same services as the Cancer Information Service (see above). Contact this office for a list of offices and more information.

Cheap Health Publications

R. Woods
Consumer Information Center-2A
P.O. Box 100
Pueblo, CO 81002

The Consumer Information Center has many free or inexpensive publications dealing with a variety of health topics from various Federal Agencies. A new Consumer Information Catalog comes out each quarter. Write for your free copy. The following publications are available:

Contact Lenses: The Better the Care the Safer the Wear (539Y)
The Controversial Pap Test (540Y)
Facing Forward: A Guide for Cancer Survivors (541Y)
FDA Consumer - 10 issues (252Y-$1200)
Good News For Blacks About Cancer (542Y)
Smart Advice for Women 40 and Over: Have a Mammogram (543Y)
Who Donates Better Blood for You Than You? (544Y)
Why Do You Smoke? (545Y)
Why Women Don't Get Mammogram (And Why They Should) (546Y)
Antihistamines: How to Take Your Medicine (547Y)
Condoms and Sexually Transmitted Disease...Especially AIDS (548Y)
Estrogens - How To Take Your Medicine (549Y)
Nonsteroidal Anti-Inflammatory Drugs (550Y)

Be patient. If any phone number is incorrect, call (area code) 555-1212 and request the new listing.

Clearinghouses and Starting Points

Acne: Taming that Age-Old Adolescent Affliction (551Y)
AIDS (552Y)
Allergies (553Y)
Breast Lumps: Questions and Answers (554Y)
Chew Or Snuff is Real Bad Stuff (555Y)
Chronic Fatigue Syndrome (422Y)
Contact Dermatitis: Solutions to Rash Mysteries (556Y)
Dizziness (116Y, $1)
Getting a Second Opinion (557Y)
Headaches (117Y, $2)
The Menopause Time of Life (118Y, $1)
More Than Snuffles: Childhood Asthma (558Y)
So You Have High Blood Cholesterol (119Y. $1)
Toxic Shock Syndrome (559Y)
Ulcers: Screaming or Silent, Watch Them with Care (560Y)
Useful Information on Alzheimer's Disease (561Y)

* Child Health and Development

Office of Research Reporting
National Institute of Child Health and Human Development
Building 31, Room 2A-32
9000 Rockville Pike
Bethesda, MD 20892 (301) 496-5133

This Institute disseminates information on fetal, maternal and child development, as well as materials on reproductive biology, contraception, mental retardation, and a host of other related fields. Some of the publications include:

Facts About Childhood Hyperactivity
Facts About Down Syndrome
Facts About Dyslexia
Facts About Dysmenorrhea and Premenstrual Syndrome
Facts About Endometriosis
Facts About Oral Contraceptives
Facts About Precocious Puberty
Facts About Premature birth
Facts About Vasectomy Safety
Pregnancy Basics
Understanding Gestational Diabetes
Cesarean Childbirth
Learning Disabilities: A Report to the U.S. Congress
Centers of Excellence: The Mental Retardation Centers

* Child, Spouse, and Elder Abuse Clearinghouse

Clearinghouse on Family Violence Information
P.O. Box 1182
Washington, DC 20013 (703) 385-7565

This clearinghouse has information on spouse and elder abuse including brochures, audiovisual materials, and an in-house database from which they can retrieve reference materials and organizations involved with family violence. The publications they have available include:

Calendar of Conferences on Child Protection and Family Violence Issues ($1)
Child Abuse Prevention, Adoption, and Family Services Act of 1988
Child Abuse and Neglect and Family Violence Audiovisual Catalog ($20)
Family Violence Public Awareness Materials for Adults and Children ($3)
Child Abuse and Neglect and Family Violence Thesaurus ($25)
Classic Literature in Family Violence: Annotated Bibliography ($1)
Databases Containing Family Violence Information: Annotated Bibliography ($1)
State Legislative Solutions to the Problem of Family Violence: Annotated Bibliography ($1.80)
Family Violence: An Overview
Organizations Concerned with Child Abuse and Neglect and Family Violence Issues ($5.50)
Family Violence Research Instruments With Bibliography ($1.50)

Bibliographies
Abuse of the Elderly ($7)
Adult Protective Services ($1)
Battered Woman Syndrome ($1)
Causes and Definitions ($2.50)
Characteristics of Abusers ($4.50)
Characteristics of Victims ($3)
Child Witnesses of Family Violence ($2)

Conjugal Homicide ($1)
Crisis Intervention ($1)
Curricula/Training Materials ($4.50)
Effects of Family Violence ($5)
Family Violence and the Clergy ($1)
Family Violence Prevention ($3)
Family Violence Research ($7.50)
Government Policy and Legislation ($2.50)
Intervention with Children From Violent Homes ($2.50)
Legal Issues in Family Violence ($7.50)
Marital Rape and Sexual Assault ($1.50)
Medical Aspects of Family Violence ($2.50)
Multidisciplinary Approaches ($1)
Police Procedures for Domestic Calls ($5)
Resources for Assisting Ethnic Populations ($2)
Shelter Programs for Victims ($1.50)
Statistical Studies in Family Violence ($3)
Substance Abuse and Family Violence ($2)
Therapeutic Alternatives for Victims ($3)
Therapy for Batterers ($3)

* Communicative and Learning Disabilities

Office of Deafness and Communicative Disorders
Rehabilitation Services Administration
U.S. Department of Education
330 C St., SW, Room 3033 (202) 732-1401
Washington, DC 20201 (202) 732-1298 TDD

This office promotes improved and expanded rehabilitation services for deaf, hard of hearing, speech impaired, and language disordered individuals. As the liaison to national organizations and agencies concerned with deafness and communicative disorders, this office provides the following services: 1) they develop policies and standards for state rehabilitation agencies' work with these clients; 2) they review services to these clients by the agencies; 3) they provide technical assistance to Rehabilitation Services Administration staff; and 4) they provide information on the State-Federal rehabilitation program for communicatively impaired persons to public and private agencies, consumers and the general public.

* Consumer Affairs Center

Director of Information
Office of Consumer Affairs
U.S. Department of Health and Human Services
Washington, DC 20201 (202) 634-4140

This bureau coordinates new consumer programs, promotes improved consumer education, and serves as the catalyst for new laws and regulations protecting the interests of American health care consumers. It publishes a useful catalog titled *Consumer's Resource Handbook* which is available free from the Consumer Information Center, P.O. Box 100, Dept. 635H, Pueblo, CO 81009. This office can refer you to the appropriate office or agency for answers to your questions.

* Deafness Clearinghouse

National Institute on Deafness and Other
Communication Disorders Clearinghouse (NIDCD)
NIDCD Clearinghouse
P.O. Box 37777 (301) 496-7243
Washington, DC 20013 (301) 402-0252 (TDD)

The NIDCD has established a national clearinghouse of information and resources on the normal and disordered mechanisms of hearing, balance, smell, taste, voice, speech, and language. The Clearinghouse collects information on these seven research areas and disseminates it to health professional, patients, industry, and the public. They have access to the Combined Health Information Database (CHID), and have an extensive list of publications, including fact sheets, bibliographies, information packets, catalogs, and directories of information sources. They also publish a biannual newsletter. One of their newest directories is a directory of associations and organizations with an interest in deafness and other communication disorders. Contact the clearinghouse for more information.

* Dental Research

National Institute of Dental Research (NIDR)
National Institutes of Health
Bldg. 31, Room 2C35

Health and Medicine

Bethesda, MD 20892 (301) 496-4261

NIDR conducts research into the causes, prevention, diagnosis, and treatment of oral and dental diseases and conditions. They can answer questions regarding current research, and have publications, posters, and reports on a variety of dental topics. Some of the publications cover canker sores, fluoride treatment, periodontal disease, and tooth decay.

* Diabetes Information Clearinghouse

National Diabetes Information Clearinghouse (NDIC)
Box NDIC
Bethesda, MD 20892 (301) 468-2162

NDIC responds to requests for information about diabetes and its complications and distributes information appropriate to health professionals, people with diabetes and their families, and the general public. They have many publications and bibliographies, as well as *Diabetes Dateline*, a free quarterly current awareness newsletter that features news about diabetes research, upcoming meetings and events, and new publications. NDIC uses the online database CHID (Combined Health Information Database) from which they can reference health information. Contact this office for a free listing of their publications or further information.

* Digestive Diseases Information Clearinghouse

National Digestive Diseases Information Clearinghouse (NDDIC)
Box NDDIC
Bethesda, MD 20892 (301) 468-6344

NDDIC responds to requests for information about digestive diseases and distributes information to health professionals, people with digestive diseases, and the general public. They have many publications, as well as a news bulletin. NDDIC uses the online database CHID (Combined Health Information Database) from which they can access health information and organizations. Contact this office for a free listing of publications.

* Disease Information

Centers for Disease Control (CDC)
Information Resources Management Office
Mail Stop C-15
1600 Clifton Rd., NE
Atlanta, GA 30333 (404) 332-4555

The CDC and the Agency for Toxic Substances and Disease Registry have developed a Voice Information System that allows anyone using a touchtone phone, to obtain prerecorded information on particular health issue. The materials include information about certain diseases or health areas, symptoms and prevention methods, immunization requirements, current statistics, recent disease outbreak, and available printed materials. Currently information is available on AIDS, Chronic fatigue syndrome, cytomegalovirus, encephalitis, enteric diseases, Epstein-Barr, hepatitis, Lyme disease, malaria, rabies, Vaccine-preventable disease, and yellow fever. The most complex system is for international travelers' health. The system can also transfer the caller to a public health professional for additional information. The system is available 24 hours a day, although the health professionals are available Monday-Friday 8-4:30.

* Eye and Vision Clearinghouse

National Eye Institute (NEI)
National Institute of Health
Building 31, Room 6A32
9000 Rockville Pike
Bethesda, MD 20892 (301) 496-5248

NEI conducts, fosters and supports basic and applied research, including clinical trials, related to the cause, natural history, prevention, diagnosis, and treatment of disorders of the eye and visual system. Several brochures and reports are available for the general public and health professionals on a wide variety of related topics.

* Family Information Center

Family Information Center
U.S. Department of Agriculture
National Agricultural Library Building, Room 304
Beltsville, MD 20705 (301) 504-5204

This center offers expertise and materials beyond home economics with a focus on family adjustment to change and the management of stress, family and individual adjustment to midlife, and the aging process.

* Food Additives, RX and Medical Devices Consumer Info

Office of Public Affairs
Food and Drug Administration (FDA)
5600 Fishers Lane, HFE88
Rockville, MD 20857 (301) 443-3170

The FDA distributes many brochures and publications which cover a variety of topics, such as cosmetics, drugs, and foods. This office will gladly send you publications on topics that interest you. The *FDA Consumer*, which contains the latest developments at FDA, can be ordered for $12 per year from the Superintendent of Documents, Government Printing Office, Washington DC 20402, (202) 783-3238.

* General Medical Sciences

National Institute of General Medical Sciences (NIGMS)
National Institutes of Health
Building 31, Room 4A52
Bethesda, MD 20892 (301) 496-7301

NIGMS has five main program areas. Four of them - Cellular and Molecular Basis of Disease, Genetics, Pharmacological Sciences, and Biophysics and Physiological Sciences - fund grants for research projects and research training. The fifth program, Minority Access to Research Careers aims to increase the number and capabilities of minority individuals engaged in biomedical research and teaching by funding research training at colleges and universities with substantial minority enrollments as well as fellowships for faculty and students from such institutions. The Institute has no laboratories on the NIH campus. They publish an annual report which describes the research they have funded, and can refer you to the researcher in charge of a particular project.

* Health and Science Journals: Computerized Databases

National Library of Medicine (NLM)
8600 Rockville Pike
Bethesda, MD 20894 (301) 496-6095

MEDLARS is the computerized system of databases at the National Library of Medicine (NLM). The databases may be accessed by more than 20,000 universities, medical schools, commercial and non-profit organizations, and private individuals. MEDLARS contains 11,500,000 references to journal articles and books in the health sciences published after 1965. Some of the databases are:

MEDLINE: 700,000 references to biomedical journal articles published in the current and two preceding years.

CATLINE: 630,000 references to books and serials cataloged at NLM.

SERLINE: Bibliographic and preservation information for 70,000 serials titles.
AVLINE: Citations to 17,000 audiovisual teaching packages covering subject areas in the health sciences.

AIDSLINE: Bibliographic file of published literature on AIDS, focusing on the clinical and research aspects of the disease.

HISTLINE: 83,000 citations to monographs, journal articles, symposia, congresses, and similar composite publications as published annually in the Bibliography of the History of Medicine.

TOXLINE: Bibliographic references covering pharmacological, biochemical, physiological, environmental, and toxicological effects of drugs and other chemicals.

CHEMLINE: An online chemical dictionary with over 790,000 records.

HEALTH: Contains 400,000 references to literature on health planning, organization, financing, management, and manpower.

CANCERLIT: 580,000 references dealing with various aspects of cancer.

CLINPROT: Contains summaries of clinical investigations of new anti-cancer agents and treatment modalities.

PDQ: Provides state-of-the-art cancer treatment and referral information.

DIRLINE: A directory of organizations providing information in specific subject areas.

SDILINE: Contains current month's input to MEDLINE.

Be patient. If any phone number is incorrect, call (area code) 555-1212 and request the new listing.

Clearinghouses and Starting Points

BIOETHICSLINE: Contains citations to documents which discuss ethical and related public policy questions arising in health care or biomedical research.

POPLINE: Provides bibliographic citations to literature on population and family planning.

DOCUSER: Contains descriptive information about libraries and other organizations which use NLM's interlibrary loan services.

NAME AUTHORITY FILE: List of 300,000 personal names, corporate names, and decisions on how monographic series are classed.

MeSH VOCABULARY FILE: Information on 15,000 medical subject headings and 50,000 chemical substances used for indexing and retrieving references.

TOXNET: Provides information on potentially toxic or otherwise hazardous chemicals.

HSDB: Contains toxicological information strengthened with additional data related to the environment, emergency situations, and regulatory issues.

CCRIS: Contains evaluated data and information derived from both short- and long-term bioassays on 1200 chemical substances.

RTECS: Contains basic acute and chronic toxicity data on more than 92,000 potentially toxic chemicals.

The National Library of Medicine has developed GRATEFUL MED which is software program that allows you to track down information in the NLM databases via a personal computer. GRATEFUL MED is available for both IBM and Macintosh computers for only $29.95. For more information about GRATEFUL MED call (800) 638-8480.

* Health Assessments of Hazardous Substances

Agency for Toxic Substances and Disease Registry
1600 Clifton Rd., NE
Atlanta, GA 30333 (404) 639-0600

The Division of Health Assessment and Consultation conducts health assessments, which are written evaluations of the public health impact of hazardous substances that have been released into the environment in a specific geographic area. The general public can request that a health assessment be conducted. This Division also sponsors Citizens' Roundtables, designed to provide communities with the opportunity to express their needs and concerns. This Division also develops, implements and evaluates simulated emergencies involving hazardous substances.

* Health Care Delivery

Bureau of Health Care Delivery and Assistance
Health Resources and Services Administration
5600 Fishers Lane, Room 7-05
Rockville, MD 29857 (301) 443-2320

The Bureau of Health Care Delivery and Assistance helps assure that health care services are provided to medically underserved populations and to persons with special health care needs. The Bureau serves as a national focus for the development of primary health care delivery capacity, and for placement of health care professionals in Health Professional Shortage Areas to promote sustained sources of health services. Support for primary health care is provided primarily through Community Health Centers, Migrant Health Centers, Service for Special Populations, Services for Residents of Public Housing and the national Health Service Corps. For more information on these programs contact the office listed above.

* Health Data and Indexes

Clearinghouse on Health Indexes
Division of Analysis
National Center for Health Statistics
3700 East-West Highway, Room 2-27
Hyattsville, MD 20782 (301) 436-7035

This clearinghouse maintains a database which purports to reflect the health status of an individual or defined group. This data are designed to help planners, researchers, and administrators develop and improve health programs and strategies.

* Health Education on Toxic Substances

Agency for Toxic Substances and Disease Registry
1600 Clifton Rd., NE
Atlanta, GA 30333 (404) 639-0730

The Division of Health Education provides health professionals with appropriate educational materials on the health effects and medical surveillance of persons exposed to hazardous substances. Target audiences include medical associations, academic medical centers, medical schools, and schools of public health. A series of self-instructional documents called *Case Studies in Environmental Medicine* are published by this Division. Contact this office for more information.

* Healthfinder Series: Child Health to Long-term Care

ODPHP National Health Information Center
P.O. Box 1133 (800) 336-4797
Washington, DC 20013 (301) 565-4167 (in Maryland)

Healthfinder is a series of publications, each on a specific health topic. Each issue includes some general information, a list of publications available, and resources relevant to the topic. Health topics include Family Care, Women's Health, and Long-term Care.

* Health Hotlines

Specialized Information Services
National Library of Medicine (NLM)
Building 38A, Room 3N305
Bethesda, MD 20894

Health Hotlines is a compilation of organizations with toll-free telephone numbers. Most are listed in DIRLINE, NLM's Directory of Information Resources OnLINE. DIRLINE is an online database containing information on approximately 15,000 organizations. These organizations will provide information services directly to requestors. This free 50 page book lists organizations alphabetically, and by health topic.

* Health Profession Videotapes

Division of Disadvantaged Assistance
Bureau of Health Professions
5600 Fishers Lane
Room 8-20
Rockville, MD 20857 (301) 443-3843

The Bureau of Health Professions has produced fourteen videos appropriate for recruitment of minorities and disadvantaged students into the health professions. The minority focus includes Blacks, American Indians, Alaskan Natives, and Hispanics, and covers a wide variety of medical professions. Contact the Bureau for more information regarding these free videos.

* Health Resource Guide

National Heart, Lung, and Blood Institute (NHLBI)
Information Center
4733 Bethesda Ave., Suite 530
Bethesda, MD 20814 (301) 951-3260

The free NHLBI Kit '90, designed for use by program planners, includes information, resources, and ideas on high blood cholesterol, cigarette smoking, asthma, and blood resources. It can be used to support patient or public education programs, Manual A contains several elements to help the professional with program development and implementation, including examples of creative community programs, data and graphics, and a comprehensive listing of print and audiovisual materials. Manual B, Information for consumers, contains reproducible materials that can be easily duplicated on a copying machine.

* Health Services Publications Catalog

Office of Public Affairs
Health Resources and Services Administration (HRSA)
5600 Fishers Lane, Room 1443
Rockville, MD 20857 (301) 443-2086

The Health Resources and Services Administration offers a free catalog, *Current Publications*, which lists all the publications films, and videos produced by HRSA's three bureaus: Bureau of Health Care Delivery and Assistance, Bureau of Maternal and Child Health and Resources Development and Bureau of Health Professions. Also available is *HRSA: A Profile*, describing HRSA Bureaus, projects, issues, and initiatives.

Be patient. If any phone number is incorrect, call (area code) 555-1212 and request the new listing.

Health and Medicine

* Health Studies of Toxic Substances

Agency for Toxic Substances and Disease Registry
1600 Clifton Rd., NE
Atlanta, GA 30333 (404) 630-0550

The Division of Health Studies conducts health studies which evaluate the heath effects of human exposure to hazardous substances. This Division maintains the National Exposure Registry is comprised of chemical-specific subregistries designed to aid in assessing the long-term health consequences of low-level, long-term exposures to hazardous chemicals identifies at Superfund sites. A National Disease Registry is in the works.

* Healthy People

ODPH National Health Information Center
P.O. Box 1133 (800) 336-4797
Washington, DC 20013 (301) 565-4167

Healthy People 2000: National Health Promotion and Disease Prevention Objectives ($4) is a report which sets national goals for the decade to increase the span of healthy life for Americans, reduce health disparities, and achieve access to preventive services for all Americans. Goals are supported by 300 specific health objectives, in 22 priority areas, to be achieved by the year 2000.

Healthy Older People: The Report of the National Health Promotion Program ($2) provides a comprehensive look at what was learned from the first national public education effort aimed at reaching older adults with health promotion information. It examines how educational messages and programs on multiple risk factors were tailored for this age group, and how coalitions of health and aging groups were formed to disseminated these messages.

Healthy Children 2000: National Health Promotion and Disease Prevention Objectives Related to Mothers, Infants, Children, Adolescents, and Youth ($4) is a compilation of the Health People 2000 objectives related to maternal and child health.

* Healthy Start

Health Resources and Services Administration
5600 Fishers Lane, Room 1443
Rockville, MD 20857 (301) 443-2086

The Healthy Start Program is a Presidential initiative to reduce infant mortality through additional support for comprehensive service delivery in 15 high-risk communities, with the goal of reducing infant mortality by 50% over five years. The Public Affairs Office has put together an information packet, which includes some background information and a listing of grantees (including a breakdown of features and contact people).

* Heart, Lung, and Blood Disease Clearinghouse

National Heart, Lung and Blood Institute
Building 31, Room 4A-21
9000 Rockville Pike
Bethesda, MD 20892 (301) 496-4236

The Institute oversees the scientific investigation, prevention, and control of heart, blood vessel, lung, and blood diseases. The program emphasizes education concerning these diseases through a more rapid transfer of information into the mainstream of clinical medicine and personal health practices. Many publications are available for professionals and the general public on a wide variety of topics.

* Home Health Care and Hospice Resources

National Health Information Center
P.O. Box 1133 (800) 336-4797
Washington, DC 20013 (301) 565-4167 in MD

In its series called "Healthfinder", the center publishes a 6-page bulletin titled *Family Care* which lists organizations, self-help and support groups, as well as books about home care for the chronically or terminally ill or the disabled child or aging parent. Suggested resources for preparing for death such as living wills and organ or tissue donation are included in this "Healthfinder."

* Injury Information Clearinghouse

National Injury Information Clearinghouse
Consumer Product Safety Commission
5401 Westbard Avenue, Room 625
Washington, DC 20207 (301) 504-0424

This clearinghouse gathers, investigates, analyzes, and disseminates injury data relating to the causes and prevention of death, injury, and illness associated with consumer products. Use this information center to tap into the National Electronic Injury Surveillance System (NEISS) which selected hospital emergency rooms contribute case reports on product-related injuries.

* Laser Surgery Referral Network

National Health Information Center
P.O. Box 1133 (800) 336-4797
Washington, DC 20013 (301) 565-4167 in DC

This center can provide you with names of organizations and agencies involved with laser surgery, which can then refer you to experts in the field.

* Lead Poisoning Prevention

National Maternal and Child Health Clearinghouse
38th and R Sts., NW
Washington, DC 20057 (202) 625-8410

The Clearinghouse has four free publications concerned with lead poisoning, ranging from historical information to current resources. The titles include: *Childhood Lead Poisoning: Current Perspectives*, *Childhood Lead Poisoning Prevention - A Resource Guide*, *Historical Perspective on Health Effects of Lead*, and *Manual for the Identification and Abatement of Environmental Lead Hazards*.

* Medical Films and Videos

National Library of Medicine (NLM)
8600 Rockville Pike
Bethesda, MD 20894 (301) 496-6095

The National Library of Medicine's audiovisual collection consists of approximately 18,000 titles in a variety of formats including videocassettes, audiocassettes, 16mm films, filmstrips and slides, and some 1,200 motion pictures of historical interest. Most audiovisuals are in core biomedical subjects and are in English. The audiovisual titles in the NLM collection are available online through AVLINE, and in printed catalogue form in the NLM Audiovisuals Catalog. AVLINE is one of a number of databases on NLM's MEDLARS computer system. MEDLARS is accessed by universities, medical schools, hospitals, government agencies, and private individuals. NLM's Audiovisual Catalogue is produced quarterly with an annual cumulation issued in lieu of a fourth quarterly. This is available by contacting: Superintendent of Documents, U.S. Government Printing Office, Washington DC 20402/(202) 783-3238. Audiovisuals may be borrowed through the interlibrary loan service by requesting items through your local libraries. Libraries should send requests to local sources, and send requests to NLM only for those titles not held in their regions. Contact NLM for more information regarding their audiovisual services.

* Medicine for the Layman

Office of Clinical Center Communications
National Institutes of Health
Building 10, Room 1C255
Bethesda, MD 20892 (301) 496-2563

The Clinical Center has developed a Medicine for the Layman series which is designed to provide information to facilitate intelligent decisions, and includes free booklets and videotapes on a variety of topics. The booklets and videos include:

Booklets

Allergic Diseases
Alzheimer's Disease
Arthritis
Behavior Patterns and Health
Brain in Aging and Dementia
Cancer Treatment
Chronic Fatigue Syndrome
Diabetes in Adults
Drugs and the Brain
Epilepsy
Genetics of Cancer
Herpes
Multiple Sclerosis
Obesity and Energy Metabolism
Osteoporosis
Radiation Risks and Radiation Therapy
Risks of Heart Disease
Sickle Cell Anemia
Stroke Update

Be patient. If any phone number is incorrect, call (area code) 555-1212 and request the new listing.

Clearinghouses and Starting Points

Videos
Allergic Diseases
Arthritis Today
Bronchial Asthma
Cancer and the Environment
Cancer: What Is It?
Control and Therapy of Genetic Diseases
Coping with Aging Parents
Coping with the Changing Seasons
Diet and Cancer Prevention
Hearing Impairment: The Invisible Handicap
Lyme Disease
Parkinson's Disease: Natural and Drug-Induced Causes
Periodontal Disease
Phobias and Panic Disorder
Relief of Chronic Pain
Sleep and Its' Disorders
Ulcerative Colitis and Crohn's Disease
Understanding Seizure Disorders
Your Problem Feet: Care and Management

* Mental Health Clearinghouse

National Institute of Mental Health (NIMH)
Alcohol, Drug Abuse and Mental Health Administration
5600 Fishers Lane, Room 15C05
Rockville, MD 20857 (301) 443-4513

NIMH conducts research on mental disorders and mental health services, distributes information, conducts demonstration programs for the prevention, treatment, and rehabilitation of the mentally ill. Research focuses on the biological, psychological, epidemiological, and social science aspects of mental health and illness. NIMH collaborates with other organizations to promote effective mental health programs and provides technical assistance.

* Mental Retardation

President's Committee on Mental Retardation
330 Independence Ave., SW
Washington, DC 20201 (202) 619-0634

More than six million Americans of all ages experience mental retardation. The President's Committee on Mental Retardation was established to focus on a single area of national concern- mental retardation. Some of the areas covered include full citizenship, prevention, family and community services, and public awareness. The Committee also conducts public forums and publishes numerous documents in the field.

* Minorities and Blacks Health Coordinator

Office of Minority Health
U.S. Department of Health and Human Services
200 Independence Avenue SW, Room 118F
Washington, DC 20201 (202) 245-0020

This office monitors community-based projects designed to reduce over 60,000 excess deaths each year among minority Americans and develops recommendations for health strategies and research on risk factors affecting these populations.

* Minority Health Care

ODPHP National Health Information Center
P.O. Box 1133 (800) 336-4797
Washington, DC 20013 (301) 565-4167

Minority Health Care is part of the free *Healthfinder* series, and is designed as a resource list of materials that can be used in support of the health education process. Providing information about the symptoms of diseases, the link between lifestyle and diseases, and the importance of early detection and treatment is a necessary component of any health communication program. The *Healthfinder* includes materials aimed specifically at minority audiences, with some in other languages. They cover the six minority health areas and AIDS.

* Minority Health Clearinghouse

Office of Minority Health Resource Center (OMH)
P.O. Box 37337
Washington, DC 20013 (800) 444-6472

The OMH mission is to improve the health status of Asians, Pacific Islanders, Blacks, Hispanics, and Native Americans. Major activities include the dissemination of accurate and timely information regarding health care issues and status through conferences and workshops, awarding of grants for innovative community health strategies developed by minority coalitions, and research on risk factors affecting minority health. The Resource Center has information on minority health-related data and information resources available at the Federal, State, and local levels and provides assistance and information to people interested in minority health and minority health programs. A strategy guide was developed on methods of achieving the minority health goals. They have prepared "Closing the Gap," a series of fact sheets on the priority areas that describe the extent to which specific minority groups are affected, detail avenues for prevention, and offer resources for additional information. They have a database of minority health-related publications, organizations and programs that concentrate on minority health. The Resource Persons Network consists of more than 2200 physicians, nurses, social workers, and health educators who provide expert technical assistance to minority community-based organizations, voluntary groups, and individuals needing assistance. Publications available include:

Program/Project Description
Report of the Secretary's Task Force on Black and Minority Health
Violence and Homicide in Hispanic Communities: Conference Proceedings
Grants Fact Sheets

* National Health Information Center

National Health Information Center
P.O. Box 1133 (301) 565-4167 in MD
Washington, DC 20013 (800) 336-4797

This center should be the initial phone call because it can direct you to more specialized clearinghouses as well as health organizations and foundations. The National Health Information Center, through its resource files and database (DIRLINE), responds to questions regarding health concerns and can send publications, bibliographies, and other material. A library focusing on health topics is open to the public, and the Center also produces many different directories, and resource guides, which are available for a minimal cost. A publications catalog is free of charge. Two of the publications include a list of Selected Federal Health Information Clearinghouses and Information Centers and Toll-free Numbers for Health Information.

* Native Americans Health Services

Indian Health Service
Office of Communications
5600 Fishers Lane, Room 6-35
Rockville, MD 20857 (301) 443-3593

The goal of the Indian Health Service is to raise the health level of American Indians and Alaskan Natives to the highest possible level. IHS accomplishes this by providing a comprehensive health services delivery system, which includes hospital and ambulatory medical care, preventive and rehabilitative services, and community environmental health programs, among them the construction of water and sanitation facilities for more than one million American Indians and Alaskan Natives. The program offers maximum opportunity for tribal involvement in developing these and other programs to meet their health needs. IHS operates 43 hospitals, 71 health centers, and more than 100 smaller health stations and satellite clinics. Indian tribes may contract with IHS to operate their own health care facilities and programs.

* Neighborhood Medical Libraries throughout the U.S.

Greater Northeastern Regional Medical Library Program, The New York Academy of Medicine, 2 East 103rd Street New York, NY 10029; (212) 876-8763. States served: Connecticut, Delaware, Maine, Massachusetts, New Hampshire, New Jersey, New York, Pennsylvania, Rhode Island, Vermont, and Puerto Rico.

Southeastern Regional Medical Library Service, University of Maryland Health Sciences Library, 111 South Greene St., Baltimore, MD 21201; (301) 328-2855 or (800) 638-6093. States served: Alabama, Florida, Georgia, Maryland, Mississippi, North Carolina, South Carolina, Tennessee, Virginia, West Virginia, District of Columbia, and Virgin Islands.

Greater Midwest Regional Medical Library Network, University of Chicago, Library of Health Sciences, P.O. Box 7509, Chicago, IL 60680; (312) 996-2464. States served: Iowa, Illinois, Indiana, Kentucky, Michigan, Minnesota, North Dakota, Ohio, South Dakota, and Wisconsin.

Be patient. If any phone number is incorrect, call (area code) 555-1212 and request the new listing.

Health and Medicine

Midcontinental Regional Medical Library Program, University of Nebraska, Medical Center Library, 42nd and Dewey Avenue, Omaha, NE 68105; (402) 559-4326 or (800) MED-RMLA. States served: Colorado, Kansas, Missouri, Nebraska, Utah, and Wyoming.

South Central Regional Medical Library Program, University of Texas, Southwestern Medical Center at Dallas, 5323 Harry Hines Blvd., Dallas, TX 75235; (214) 688-2085. States served: Arkansas, Louisiana, New Mexico, Oklahoma, and Texas.

Pacific Northwest Regional Health Sciences Library Service, Health Sciences Library and Information Center, University of Washington Seattle, WA 98195; (206) 543-8262. States served: Alaska, Idaho, Montana, Oregon, and Washington.

Pacific Southwest Regional Medical Library Service, Louise Darling Biomedical Library, University of California, 10833 Le Conte Ave., Los Angeles, CA 90024; (213) 825-1200. States served: Arizona, California, Hawaii, Nevada, and U.S. Territories in the Pacific Basin.

South Central Regional Medical Library Service, Houston Academy of Medicine, Texas Medical Center Library, 1133 M.D. Anderson Blvd., Houston, TX 77030; (713) 790-7053. States served: Arkansas, Louisiana, New Mexico, Oklahoma, and Texas.

New England Regional Medical Library, University of Connecticut Health Center, Lyman Maynard Stowe Library, 263 Farmington Ave., Farmington, CT 06034; (203) 679-4500. States served: Connecticut, Maine, Massachusetts, New Hampshire, Rhode Island, and Vermont.

* Nursing Research

National Center for Nursing Research
National Institutes of Health
Bldg. 31, Room 5B25
Bethesda, MD 20892 (301) 496-0207

This Center supports research and research training related to promoting health and preventing disease, understanding and mitigating the effects of acute and chronic illnesses and disabilities, and improving patient care as well as the environment in which it is delivered.

* Occupational Health Clearinghouse

Technical Information Branch
National Institute for Occupational Safety and Health Information
4676 Columbia Parkway
Cincinnati, OH 45226
Technical Info: (800) 35-NIOSH; (513) 533-8328
Publications: (513) 841-4287
Library: (513) 533-8321

This center serves as a clearinghouse on occupational health, hazardous substances, and safety. Much of their information is available through interlibrary loans and online databases.

* Organ Transplantation

Division of Organ Transplantation
Bureau of Health Resources Development
Health Resources and Services Administration
5600 Fishers Lane, Room 11A-22
Rockville, MD 20857 (301) 443-7577

This Division conducts a program to foster relationships with public and private organizations to promote the concepts of organ donation and transplantation. The program provides information to professional associations, health providers, consumers and insurers, medical societies, State health departments, and the general public. The Program also supports the National Organ Procurement and Transplantation Network, designed to ensure equitable distribution of available organs to patients and transplant centers, and a Scientific Registry of demographic and clinical information on transplant recipients. An annual report, information on the Transplantation Network, a fact sheet on organ transplantation, and a Q&A publication are available.

* Patient Education Material

National Maternal and Child Health Clearinghouse
38th and R Sts., NW

Washington, DC 20057 (202) 625-8410

Patient Education Materials: A Resource Guide has been developed to help health professionals identify and locate materials on maternal and child health topics that are clear, concise, easy to read, and appropriate for the general public. Publications listed in this guide are national in scope and, with a few exceptions, currently available. This includes an annotated listing of source books, directories, and resource guides that describe patient education materials, and is arranged by the subject of format of materials included.

* Practitioner Helpline

Bureau of Health Professions
Health Resources and Services Administration
5600 Fishers Lane, Room 8-05
Rockville, MD 20857 (800) 767-6732

The National Practitioners Data Bank (NPDB) is a federally sponsored data bank containing information on all disciplinary actions and malpractice claims or actions against licensed health practitioners. The purpose of the NPDB is to contribute to the improvement of the quality of health care by restricting the ability of incompetent and unethical practitioners to move from State to State without disclosure or discovery of their previous poor performance. Insurance companies and other entities must report to the NPDB any payment they make on medical malpractice actions or claims. State medical and dental boards must report any disciplinary actions taken. Health Care entities must report decisions which adversely affect, for more than 30 days, the clinical privileges of the physician or dentist. Professional societies must report adverse actions regarding membership of physicians and dentists. This information is available to State licensing agencies, hospitals, and health care entities.

* Primary Care Information

Project Director
National Clearinghouse for Primary Care Information
8201 Greensboro Drive, Suite 600
McLean, VA 22102 (703) 821-8955

This center distributes materials on ambulatory care, financial management, primary health care, medical personnel and services primarily to health professionals as well as publications on community health centers, migrant health centers, childhood injury prevention efforts, clinical care and many other health concerns.

* Publications and Resource Catalog

National Health Information Center
P.O. Box 1133 (800) 336-4797
Washington, DC 20013 (301) 565-4167 in MD

This government clearinghouse publishes a 51-page catalog titled *Staying Healthy: A Bibliography of Health Promotion Materials*, which lists various Department of Health and Human Services clearinghouses and information centers as well as numerous health promotion and disease prevention booklets, fact sheets, program guides, films, videotapes, slides, and posters. The Office of Disease Prevention and Health Promotion of the U.S. Public Health Service also makes available single copies free of *Publications List* with an order form which describes publications under nine broad categories: Federal Programs and Policies; ODPHP Monograph Series; Community Health Promotion Programs; School Health Programs; Worksite Health Promotion Programs; Nutrition; Professional Education; Educational Materials; and Miscellaneous.

* Publications from all NIH Institutes

Public Information Division
National Institute of Health (NIH), Room 305
Bethesda, MD 20892 (301) 496-4143

The NIH Publications List (#91-7) is a free catalog which lists the publications available from each of the Institutes, as well as their addresses and phone numbers.

* Rehabilitation and Prosthetics

National Center for Medical Rehabilitation Research
National Institutes of Health
Building 31, Room 2A03
Bethesda, MD 20892 (301) 496-3454

This new Center will support and conduct research in restoring, replacing, or improving functional capability lost as a consequence of injury, disease, or congenital disorder; support research training programs; and foster research in

Be patient. If any phone number is incorrect, call (area code) 555-1212 and request the new listing.

Clearinghouses and Starting Points

assistive devices such as prosthetics and orthotics. Currently the Center is assessing the current status of medical rehabilitation, identifying medical rehabilitation research issues and opportunities, and recommending program priorities.

* Rehabilitation Resource Center

National Rehabilitation Information Center
8455 Colesville Road, Suite 935 (301) 588-9284 (MD only)
Silver Spring, MD 20910 (800) 346-2742 (voice and TDD)

This clearinghouse provides information on disability-related research,resources, and products for independent living as well as facts sheets, resource guides, and research and technical publications, newsletter, and a data base.

* Research Resources

Office of Science and Health Reports
National Center for Research Resources
National Institutes of Health
Bethesda, MD 20892 (301) 496-5545

The National Center for Research Resources provides to scientists the resources and services essential to studies of the treatment, cure and prevention of human diseases. It awards grants to develop and maintain shared research resources, and maintains General Clinical Research Centers where scientist study patients in order to diagnose and treat disease. Its Animal Resources Program supports a variety of animal research facilities and resources. They publish several research resources directories and guidelines, as well as information regarding the research centers. Some of their publications include:

Research Resources Reporter - monthly newsletter.

NCRR Program Highlights - annual report.

NCRR General Clinical Research Centers Directory - contains information about the centers, staffs, resources and major areas of investigation.

NCRR Biomedical Research Technology Resources Directory - lists resource center, staffs, resources, and major areas of investigation.

NCRR Resources for Comparative Biomedical Research Directory - contains information about specialized animal research and supply facilities, staffs, types of resources, and major areas of research.

* School Health

ODPHP National Health Information Center
P.O. Box 1133 (800) 336-4797
Washington, DC 20013 (301) 565-4167

The Clearinghouse has many publications dealing with health issues in schools, including the following:

Healthy Schools: A Directory of Federal Activities Related to Health Promotion through the Schools ($4) - presents information on activities of all Federal departments including contact information and brief program descriptions.

Healthy Kids For the Year 2000: An Action Plan for Schools ($6) - booklet presents a 12-step action plan that school leaders can use to attack the health problems facing youth by implementing a comprehensive school health program.

Achieving the 1990 Health Objectives For The Nation: Agenda for the Nation's Schools ($25) - contains a step-by-step description of strategies that schools and communities can implement in 14 key health areas.

National Adolescent Student Health Survey ($17.95) - reports on results of the first national survey in more than 20 years on teens' behavior, knowledge, and attitudes on health and sex-related issues.

Coalition Index: A Guide to School Health Education Materials ($10) - pulls together materials from nearly 20 national health-related organizations and categorizes the materials by content area.

Delber Oberteuffer Symposia which examine issues that make school health education important. Symposia series includes:
Administrative Aspects of School Health Education ($2).
Comprehensive School Health Education Programs: Issues of Quality ($2).

How Healthy Is Your School? ($12)- provides blueprint for assessing, planning, and implementing quality school health services, environment, and health education programs.

Promoting Health Education in Schools: Problems and Solutions ($13.95)- presents an informative overview of the critical issues involved in providing health education and health promotion through the schools.

* Second Opinion Hotline

National Second Surgical Opinion Program
Health Care Financing Administration
330 Independence Ave., SW (800) 492-6603 in Maryland only
Washington, DC 20201 (800) 638-6833

The National Second Surgical Opinion Program is an information resource for people faced with the possibility of non-emergency surgery. By calling its toll-free number, the staff will help you locate a surgeon or other specialist enrolled in the program who can offer you a second opinion. Pamphlets are available containing questions that patients looking for second opinions should ask.

* Spanish Language Health Information Materials

ODPHP National Health Information Center
P.O. Box 20013 (800) 336-4797
Washington, DC 20013 (301) 565-4167

Spanish Language Health Information Materials is part of the free Healthfinder series and is a guide to a number of public and private agencies and organizations that produce or distribute free or low-cost Spanish language health promotion materials. Entries are arranged alphabetically by health topics.

* Speech and Language Disorders Clearinghouse

National Institute on Deafness and
Other Communicative Disorders
NIH, Building 31, Room 1B62,
9000 Rockville Pike
Bethesda, MD 20892 (301) 496-7243

This--the newest Institute at NIH--funds intramural and extramural research on communicative disorders. Brochures and reports are available for professionals and the general public, covering a wide range of related topics.

* Sports Medicine and Orthopedics Clearinghouse

Musculoskeletal Diseases Program
National Institute of Arthritis and Musculoskeletal
and Skin Diseases
Westwood Building, Room 407
Bethesda, MD 20205 (301) 468-3235

This program focuses on orthopedic research, which includes sports medicine, growth and development of bone and bone cells, as well as head injury. Staff can answer questions regarding current research and treatment issues. Brochures and pamphlets are available through the National Institute of Arthritis and Musculoskeletal and Skin Diseases.

* Stroke and Brain Disorders Resource Center

National Institute of Neurological Disorders and Stroke (NINDS)
National Institutes of Health
9000 Rockville Pike
Building 31, Room 8A06
Bethesda, MD 20892 (301) 496-4697

NINDS conducts and guides research on the causes, prevention, diagnosis, and treatment of fundamental neurological disorders and stroke and trauma. The Institute gives grants for extramural research, as well as providing fellowships. Other areas of research include cerebral palsy, autism, dyslexia, multiple sclerosis, Parkinson's and Huntington's diseases, and epilepsy. Brochures and pamphlets are available.

* Toll-Free Health Hotlines

Public Health Service AIDS Information Hotline
(800) 342-AIDS
(800) 342-SIDA for information in Spanish
(800) 243-7889 (TTY/TDD)

Be patient. If any phone number is incorrect, call (area code) 555-1212 and request the new listing.

Health and Medicine

National AIDS Information Clearinghouse
(800) 458-5231

National Gay Lesbian Crisisline
(800) 221-7044
(212) 529-1604 in NY, AK, and HI

Al-Anon Family Group Headquarters
(800) 356-9996
(212) 245-3151 in NY and Canada

Alcoholism and Drug Addiction Treatment Center
(800) 382-4357

National Council on Alcoholism
(800) NCA-CALL

Alzheimer's Disease and Related Disorders Association
(800) 621-0379
(800) 572-6037 in IL

Brookdale Center on Aging Alzheimer's Respite Line
(800) 648-COPE for placing orders

AMC Cancer Information
(800) 525-3777

Cancer Information Service (CIS)
(800) 4-CANCER
(808) 524-1234 in Oahu, HI (Neighbor Islands call collect)
(800) 638-6070 in AK

Y-Me Breast Cancer Support Group
(800) 221-2141
(312) 799-8228 in IL

Chemical Referral Center
(800) CMA-8200 in continental US and Hawaii
(202) 887-1315 in DC and for collect calls from AK

National Pesticide Telecommunications Network
(800) 858-7378

National Child Abuse Hotline
(800) 422-4453

Parents Anonymous Hotline
(800) 421-0353
(800) 352-0386 in CA

National Child Safety Council Childwatch
(800) 222-1464

National Hotline for Missing Children
(800) 843-5678
(202) 644-9836 in DC

National Runaway Switchboard
(800) 621-4000

Cystic Fibrosis Foundation
(800) 344-4823
(301) 951-4422 in MD

American Diabetes Association
(800) ADA-DISC
(703) 549-1500 in VA and DC metro area

Juvenile Diabetes Foundation International Hotline
(800) 223-1138
(212) 889-7575 in NY

National Down Syndrome Congress
(800) 232-6372
(312) 823-7550 in IL

National Down Syndrome Society Hotline
(800) 221-4602
(212) 460-9330 in NY

Safe Drinking Water Hotline
(800) 426-4791
(202) 382-5533 in DC

Just Say No Kids Club
(800) 258-2766
(415) 939-6666 in CA

National Cocaine Hotline
(800) COC-AINE

Bulimia Anorexia Self-Help
(800) 227-4785

Aerobics and Fitness Foundation
(800) BE FIT 86

ODPHP National Health Information Center
(800) 336-4797
(301) 565-4167 in MD

The Epilepsy Foundation of America
(800) EFA-1000
(301) 459-1000 in MD
(800) 492-2523 Baltimore affiliate

HEATH Resource Center
(800) 544-3284
(202) 939-9320 in DC

Job Accommodation Network
(800) 526-7234
(800) 526-4698 in WV

Library of Congress National Library Services for the Blind and Physically Handicapped
(800) 424-8567
(202) 287-5100 in DC

National Information System for Health Related Services (NIS)
(800) 922-9234
(800) 922-1107 in SC

National Rehabilitation Information Center
(800) 34-NARIC
(301) 588-9284 in MD

National Headache Foundation
(800) 843-2256
(800) 523-8858 in IL

American Cleft Palate Association
(800) 24-CLEFT
(800) 23-CLEFT in PA

Dial a Hearing Test
(800) 222-EARS
(800) 345-EARS in PA

Grapevine
(800) 352-8888 Voice and TDD
(800) 346-8888 in CA, Voice and TDD

Be patient. If any phone number is incorrect, call (area code) 555-1212 and request the new listing.

Clearinghouses and Starting Points

Hearing Helpline
(800) 424-8576
(800) EAR-WELL
(703) 642-0580 in VA

National Association for Hearing and Speech Action Line
(800) 638-8255
(301) 897-0039 in HI, AK, and MD call collect

National Hearing Aid Helpline
(800) 521-5247
(313) 478-2610 in MI

Children's Hospice International
(800) 242-4453
(703) 684-0330 in VA

Hospice Education Institute Hospicelink
(800) 331-1620
(203) 767-1620 in CT

Hill Burton Hospital Free Care
(800) 638-0742
(800) 492-0359 in MD

Shriners Hospital Referral Line
(800) 237-5055
(800) 282-9161 in FL

Huntington's Disease Society of America
(800) 345-4372
(212) 242-1968 in NY

Recovery of Male Potency
(800) 835-7667
(313) 966-3219 in MI

Federal Internal Revenue Service for TDD Users
(800) 428-4732 TDD
(800) 382-4059 in IN; TDD
(800) 424-1040 Voice

The Orton Dyslexia Society
(800) ABCD-123
(301) 296-0232 in MD

American Liver Foundation
(800) 223-0179
(201) 857-2626 in NJ

Asthma Information Line
(800) 822-ASMA

Lung Line National Asthma Center
(800) 222-5864
(303) 355-LUNG in Denver

Lupus Foundation of America
(800) 558-0121
(202) 328-4550 in DC

Terri Gotthelf Lupus Research Institute
(800) 82-LUPUS
(203) 852-0120 in CT

DHHS Inspector General's Hotline
(800) 368-5779
(301) 597-0724 in MD

American Mental Health Fund
(800) 433-5959
(800) 826-2336 in IL

National Foundation for Depressive Illness
(800) 248-4344

Office of Minority Health Resource Center
(800) 444-6472

National Multiple Sclerosis Society
(800) 624-8236

The Living Bank
(800) 528-2971
(713) 528-2971 in TX

Organ Donor Hotline
(800) 24-DONOR

American Paralysis Association
(800) 225-0292
(201) 379-2690 in NJ

APA Spinal Cord Injury Hotline
(800) 526-3456
(800) 638-1733 in MD

National Spinal Cord Injury Association
(800) 962-9629
(617) 935-2722 in MA

National Parkinson Foundation
(800) 327-4545
(800) 433-7022 in FL
(305) 547-6666 in Miami

Parkinson's Education Program
(800) 344-7872
(714) 640-0218 in CA

American Society of Plastic and Reconstructive Surgeons
(800) 635-0635

Practitioner Reporting System
(800) 638-6725
(301) 881-0256 in MD (call collect)

ASPO/Lamaze (American Society for Psychoprophylaxis in Obstetrics)
(800) 368-4404
(703) 524-7802 in VA

National Pregnancy Hotline
(800) 852-5683
(800) 831-5881 in CA
(213) 380-8750 in Los Angeles

Pregnancy Counseling Services
(800) 368-3336
(804) 384-3043 in VA

American Leprosy Missions (Hansen's Disease)
(800) 543-3131
(201) 794-8650 in NJ

Cooley's Anemia Foundation
(800) 221-3571
(212) 598-0911 in NY

Cornelia de Lange Syndrome Foundation
(800) 223-8355
(203) 693-0159 in CT

Be patient. If any phone number is incorrect, call (area code) 555-1212 and request the new listing.

Health and Medicine

National Information Center for Orphan Drugs and Rare Diseases
(800) 456-3505

National Lymphedema Network
(800) 541-3259

National Neurofibromatosis Foundation
(800) 323-7938
(212) 460-8980 in NY

National Organization for Rare Disorders
(800) 999-6673
(203) 746-6518 in CT

National Tuberous Sclerosis Association
(800) 225-6872
(301) 459-9888 in MD

Tourette Syndrome Association
(800) 237-0717
(718) 224-2999 in NY

United Scleroderma Foundation
(800) 722-HOPE
(408) 728-2202 in CA

National Retinitis Pigmentosa Foundation
(800) 638-2300
(301) 225-9400 in MD

National Reye's Syndrome Foundation
(800) 233-7393
(800) 231-7393 in OH

Consumer Product Safety Commission
(800) 638-CPSC
(800) 638-8270 TDD
(800) 492-8104 TDD in MD

National Highway Traffic Safety Administration
(800) 424-9393
(202) 366-0123 in DC

National Safety Council
(800) 621-7619 for placing orders
(312) 527-4800 in IL

National Association for Sickle Cell Disease
(800) 421-8453
(213) 936-7205 in CA

Spina Bifida Information and Referral
(800) 621-3141
(301) 770-7222 in MD

American SIDS Institute
(800) 232-SIDS
(800) 847-7437 in GA

National SIDS Foundation
(800) 221-SIDS
(301) 459-3388 or 3389 in MD

Second Surgical Opinion Hotline
(800) 638-6833
(800) 492-6603 in MD

American Trauma Society (ATS)
(800) 556-7890
(301) 925-8811 in MD

American Kidney Fund
(800) 638-8299
(800) 492-8361 in MD

Simon Foundation
(800) 23-SIMON

VD Hotline (Operation Venus)
(800) 227-8922

American Council of the Blind
(800) 424-8666
(202) 393-3666 in DC

American Foundation for the Blind (AFB)
(800) 232-5463
(212) 620-2147

National Eye Care Project Helpline
(800) 222-EYES

Endometriosis Association
(800) 992-ENDO
(414) 962-8972 in WI

PMS Access
(800) 222-4767
(608) 833-4767 in WI

Women's Sports Foundation
(800) 227-3988
(212) 972-9170 in AK, HI, and CA

AIDS Clinical Trials Information Service
(800) TRIALS-A
(800) 243-7012 TTY/TDD

National Criminal Justice Reference Services/NIJ AIDS Clearinghouse
(800) 851-3420
(301) 251-5500

National Indian AIDS Hotline
(800) 283-AIDS

National Council on Aging
(800) 424-9046

National Clearinghouse for Alcohol and Drug Information
(800) 729-6686
(301) 468-2600

Recovering Network American Council on Alcoholism
(800) 527-5344

American Academy of Allergy and Immunology
(800) 822-2762
(414) 272-6071

Arthritis Foundation Information Line
(800) 283-7800

Asthma and Allergy Foundation of America
(800) 7-ASTHMA

National Audiovisual Center
(800) 638-1300
(301) 763-1896

American Cancer Society Cancer Response Line
(800) ACS-2345

Be patient. If any phone number is incorrect, call (area code) 555-1212 and request the new listing.

Clearinghouses and Starting Points

United Cerebral Palsy Association
(800) USA-1UCP
(212) 268-6655

National Resource Center on Child Abuse and Neglect
(800) 2-ASK-AHA

Human Growth Foundation
(800) 451-6434
(703) 883-1773

National Association for the Education of Young Children
(800) 424-2460
(202) 232-8777

National Youth Crisis Hotline
(800) HIT-HOME

Runaway Hotline
(800) 231-6946

National Foundation for Ileitis and Colitis
(800) 343-3637
(212) 679-1570

Drug-Free Workplace Helpline
(800) 843-4971

HUD Drug Information and Strategy Clearinghouse
(800) 245-2691
(301) 251-5154

National Institute on Drug Abuse Hotline
(800) 662-HELP

Target Resource Center
(800) 366-6667
(816) 464-5400 (MO)

Joseph and Rose Kennedy Institute of Ethics
National Reference Center for Bioethics Literature
(800) MED-ETHX
(202) 687-3885

National Fire Protection Association
(800) 344-3555
(617) 770-3000, ext. 416

YMCA of the USA
(800) USA-YMCA

Meat and Poultry Hotline
(800) 535-4555

Medic Alert Foundation
(800) ID-ALERT

Grief Recovery Institute
(800) 445-4808

IBM National Support Center for Persons with Disabilities
(800) IBM-2133 (voice/TDD)

National Center for Youth With Disabilities
Adolescent Health Program
(800) 333-NCYD
(612) 626-2825

National Easter Seals Society
(800) 221-6827
(312) 726-6200
(312) 726-4258 TDD

National Head Injury Foundation Family Helpline
(800) 444-6443

National Information Center for Children and Youth with Handicaps
(800) 999-5599
(703) 893-6061

National Information Systems For Health Related Services
(800) 922-9234
(800) 922-1107 (SC)

Deafness Research Foundation
(800) 535-3323
(212) 684-6556
(212) 684-6559 (TTY)

Ear Foundation
(800) 545-4327

Tele-Consumer Hotline
(800) 332-1124 (Voice/TDD)
(202) 223-4371

HUD User (Housing)
(800) 245-2691
(301) 251-5154

Impotence Information Center
(800) 843-4315

Health Insurance Association of America
(800) 635-1271

Medicare Telephone Hotline
(800) 638-6833

National Insurance Consumer Helpline
(800) 942-4242

National Criminal Justice Reference Service
(800) 851-3420

National Library of Medicine
(800) 272-4787
(301) 496-6308

American Lupus Society
(800) 331-1802

La Leche League International
(800) 525-3243

National Mental Health Association
(800) 969-6642

National Resource Center on Homelessness and Mental Illness
(800) 444-7415

National Multiple Sclerosis Society
(800) 624-8236

Myathenia Gravis Foundation
(800) 541-5454

American Narcolepsy Association
(800) 222-6085
(415) 591-7979

Be patient. If any phone number is incorrect, call (area code) 555-1212 and request the new listing.

Health and Medicine

American Institute for Cancer Research
(800) 843-8114

National Dairy Council
(800) 426-8271

Lifesavers Foundation
(800) 999-8822
(800) 950-1050

National Kidney Foundation
(800) ACT-GIVE

National Rehabilitation Information Clearinghouse
(800) 34-NARIC

National Stroke Association
(800) 367-1990

American Parkinson Disease Association
(800) 223-2732

American Board of Medical Specialties
(800) 776-2378

American Academy of Facial Plastic and Reconstructive Surgery
(800) 332-3223

International Childbirth Education Association
(800) 624-4934
(612) 854-8660

Amyotrophic Lateral Sclerosis Association
(800) 782-4747

Ankylosing Spondylitis Association
(800) 777-8189

Batten Disease Support
(800) 448-4570

Histiocytosis-X Association of America
(800) 548-2758
(609) 881-4911 (NJ)

Sarcoidosis Family Aid and Research Foundation
(800) 223-6429 (answering machine)
(201) 676-7901 (to speak with staff)

Sturge-Weber Disease Foundation
(800) 627-5482

National Highway Traffic Safety Administration Auto Safety Hotline
(800) 424-9393
(202) 366-0123

National Institute of Occupational Safety and Health, Technical Information Branch
(800) 35-NIOSH

Office of Navigation Safety and Waterway Services Auxiliary
(800) 368-5647 Boating Safety Hotline
(202) 267-0780

Courage Stroke Network
(800) 553-6321

American Society for Dermatologic Surgery, Inc.
(800) 441-2737

National Kidney Foundation
(800) 622-9010

Guide Dog Foundation for the Blind
(800) 548-4337
(516) 265-2121

The Lighthouse National Center for Vision and Aging
(800) 334-5497

National Association for Parents of the Visually Impaired
(800) 562-6265

National Center for Sight
(800) 221-3004

National Eye Research Foundation
(800) 621-2258

* Technology Assessment Reports

Office of Technology Assessment (OTA)
Publications Order
U.S. Congress
Washington, DC 20510-8025   (202) 224-8996

These OTA publications are available through the office above, the Government Printing Office, and the National Technical Information Service. To find out correct ordering information and prices, along with brief summaries of the following studies, contact the OTA office above and request their current publications catalog.

OTA has hundreds of reports dealing with health topics. These titles include:
AIDS and Health Insurance: An OTA Survey
Artificial Insemination: Practicing in the United States
Confused Minds, Burdened Families: Finding Help for People With Alzheimer's and Other Dementias
Contact Lenses
How Effective is AIDS Education
Indian Health Care
Losing a Million Minds: Confronting the Tragedy of Alzheimer's Disease and Other Dementias
Neonatal Intensive Care for Low Birthweight Infants: Costs and Effectiveness
Passive Smoking in the Workplace: Selected Issues
Preventing Illness and Injury in the Workplace
Reproductive Health Hazards in the Workplace
Technology and Aging in America
The Use of Preventive Services by the Elderly
Unconventional Cancer Treatments

Biological Applications
Alternatives to Animal Use In Research, Testing, and Education (BA-273)
Artificial Insemination: Practice in the United States (BP-BA-48)
Assessment of Technologies for Determining Cancer Risk From the Environment (H-138)
Commercial Development of Tests for Human Genetic Disorders (Staff Paper)
Commercial Biotechnology: An International Analysis (BA-218)
Federal Regulation and Animal Patents (Staff Paper)
Hearing Impairment and Elderly People (BP-BA-30)
Humane Gene Therapy (BP-BA-32)
Impacts of Applied Genetics: Micro-Organisms, Plants, and Animals (HR-132)
Impacts of Neuroscience (BP-BA-24)
Infertility: Medical and Social Choices (BA-358)
Innovative Biological Technologies for Lesser Developed Countries (BP-F-29)
Institutional Protocols for Decisions About Life-Sustaining Treatments (BA-389)
Life-Sustaining Technologies and the Elderly (BA-306)
Loosing a Million Minds: Confronting the Tragedy of Alzheimer's Disease and Other Dementias (BA-323)
Mapping Our Genes: Genome Projects - How Big, How Fast? (BA-373)
Reproductive Health Hazards in the Workplace (BA-266)
The Role of Genetic Testing in the Prevention of Occupational Disease (BA-194)
Status of Biomedical Research and Related Technology for Tropical Diseases (H-258)

Be patient. If any phone number is incorrect, call (area code) 555-1212 and request the new listing.

Technologies for Detecting Heritable Mutations in Human Beings (H-298)
Technologies for Managing Urinary Incontinence (HCS-33)
Technology and Aging in America (BA-264)
Transgenic Animals (Staff Paper)
World Population and Fertility Planning Technologies: The Next 20 Years (HR-157)

* Toxic Substances

Agency for Toxic Substances and Disease Registry
1600 Clifton Rd., NE
Atlanta, GA 30333 (404) 639-6000

The Division of Toxicology identifies priority hazardous substances, develops toxicological profiles, and implements health effects research. Contact this Division for more information.

* Tracer Bulletins: Asthma to Edible Wild Plants

Science and Technology Division
Reference Section
Library of Congress
Washington, DC 20540 (202) 707-5580

Informal series of reference guides are issued free from the Science and Technology Division under the general title, *LC Science Tracer Bullet.* These guides are designed to help readers locate published material on subjects about which they have only general knowledge. New titles in the series are announced in the weekly Library of Congress *Information Bulletin* that is distributed to many libraries including the following health-related Tracer Bulletins:

81-3	*Alcoholism*
81-17	*Epilepsy*
82-1	*Food Additives*
82-9	*Sickle Cell Anemia*
83-1	*Biofeedback*
83-6	*Mental Retardation*
85-6	*Acupuncture*
85-8	*Anorexia Nervosa/Bulimia*
85-10	*Rose Culture*
85-11	*Acquired Immune Deficiency Syndrome (AIDS)*
86-6	*Diabetes Mellitus*
86-8	*Indoor Air Pollution*
87-1	*Asbestos*
87-2	*Alzheimer's Disease*
87-6	*Stress: Physiological and Psychological Aspects*
87-7	*Osteoporosis*
89-5	*Human Diet and Nutrition*
89-7	*Allergy and Asthma*
90-10	*The Brain: An Overview*
91-3	*Dyslexia*
91-7	*Breast Cancer*
91-8	*Medicinal Plants*
91-9	*AIDS*
91-11	*Chemical Exposures: Toxicology, Safety, and Risk Assessment*

* Uniformed Service of the Health Sciences Video

Admissions Office
Uniformed Service of the Health Sciences
4301 Jones Bridge Rd.
Bethesda, MD 20814 (301) 295-3101

This sixteen minute video is available for free loan and describes the Uniformed Service of the Health Sciences school and the curriculum they have to offer. It is a great way for high school students to learn about this college. Contact the Admissions office for more information.

* Women's Health Resources

National Health Information Center
P.O. Box 1133 (800) 336-4797
Washington, DC 20013 (301) 565-4167 in MD

In its series, *Healthfinder*, the center publishes *Women's Health* which lists many organizations that provide information on a broad range of topics including pregnancy, gynecological, domestic violence, sports and fitness, and occupational health. This 6-page reference also lists books of particular relevance to women and their health. PHS Action Plan for Women's Health ($3) provides a comprehensive framework for improving the status of women's health in the areas of research, prevention, treatment, service, information, education and policy. The Plan identifies specific goals and action steps being pursued by PHS agencies and offices in an effort to meet the priority health needs of women across age, biological, and sociocultural contexts.

Health and Medicine

Healthy Lifestyle and Physical Fitness

Health professionals, community health centers, organizations, businesses, and individuals all can take advantage of the multitude of resources available to promote good health and prevent disease. Several federal agencies and departments, as well as numerous national organizations, offer bulletins, reference manuals, publications and expertise to encourage maintaining a healthy lifestyle and proper medical care. The National Health Information Center, a clearinghouse sponsored by the U.S. government, can direct you to a helpful agency such as the President's Council on Physical Fitness as well as to private organizations.

* Adolescent Health
Office of Technology Assessment
U.S. Congress
Washington, DC 20510 (202) 228-6590
This project will assess the health status of adolescents 10 to 18 years old and identify factors that put adolescents at risk for health problems or protect them from such problems. These factors include racial and ethnic backgrounds, socioeconomic status, gender, and developmental stage. This project will also address the special needs of rural youth and racial and ethnic minorities. Contact Denise Dougherty, project director.

* Adolescent Health Risk Assessment
Office of Technology Assessment (OTA)
600 Pennsylvania Ave., SE
Washington, DC 20510 (202) 224-8996
OTA has worked on a project to assess the health status of adolescents 10 to 18 years old and identify factors that put adolescents at risk for health problems, including racial and ethnic backgrounds, socioeconomic status, gender, and developmental stage. Particular attention is paid to the availability, effectiveness, and accessibility of health services for adolescents. *Adolescent Health: Time For a Change* is the resulting publication.

* Behavior Patterns and Health
Office of Clinical Center Communications
Warren G. Magnuson Clinical Center
NIH, Building 10, Room 5C-305
9000 Rockville Pike
Bethesda, MD 20892 (301) 496-2563
A 36-page report titled *Behavior Patterns and Health* (No. 85-2682) discusses the scientific evidence linking behavior to disease and suggests ways to reduce the risks of heart attack, lung cancer, and stroke by changing our lifestyle.

* Cancer Prevention Awareness
Office of Cancer Communications
National Cancer Institute
Building 31, Room 10A-24
9000 Rockville Pike (800) 4-CANCER
Bethesda, MD 20892 (800) 492-6000 in MD
Over 100 programs are described in this free *Cancer Prevention Resource Directory* which gives names, addresses, and telephone numbers of many national associations and health departments which encourage cancer prevention activities. Single copies of this manual are available free.

* Cancer: Testicular Self-Exam
Office of Communications
National Cancer Institute
Building 31, Room 10A18
9000 Rockville Pike
Bethesda, MD 20892 (301) 496-5583
A free pamphlet, *Testicular Self-Examination* (No. 86-2636), provides information about risks and symptoms of testicular cancer and suggestions effective self-examinations.

* Children: Risk Factors
National Technical Information Service (NTIS)
5285 Port Royal Road
Springfield, VA 22162 (703) 487-4650
This Center offers research findings including *Determinants of Children's Health* (NTIS PB-80-163603) which summarizes six closely related studies on the determinants of child health, with particular emphasis on home and local environmental factors, parents' schooling, and family income.

* Elderly and Exercise
National Institute on Aging Information Center
2209 Distribution Circle
Silver Spring, MD 20910 (301) 495-3455
Don't Take It Easy - Exercise! is a free two-page fact sheet which suggests ways for older Americans to remain active and healthy.

* Exercise and Arthritis
National Arthritis and Musculoskeletal
and Skin Diseases Information Clearinghouse
Box AMS
Bethesda, MD 20892 (301) 495-4484
A 20-page resource catalog titled *Exercise and Arthritis: An Annotated Bibliography, 1986* contains 37 references with abstracts, books, reports, and audiovisuals along with resources for developing an aquatic exercise regime, a home maintenance program, and exercises specifically for children.

* Exercise and Physical Fitness Programs
President's Council on Physical Fitness and Sports
450 5th St., NW, Suite 7103
Washington, DC 20001 (202) 272-3421
This executive branch office provides free single copies of many of its publications which range from swimming to walking: *Fitness Fundamentals, Fitness in the Workplace, One Step At A Time (An Introduction to Running); Physical Education: A Performance Checklist*. Several other pamphlets including *An Introduction to Physical Fitness* and *Aqua Dynamics: Physical Conditioning Through Water Exercises* can be purchased from the Government Printing Office.

* Exercising Your Heart
National Heart, Lung, and Blood Institute (NHLBI)
NIH, Building 31, Room 4A-21
9000 Rockville Pike
Bethesda, MD 20892 (301) 496-4236
Single copies are available at no charge on the following publications: *Exercise and Your Heart* (No. 81-1677), *NHLBI Facts About Exercise: How To Get Started, NHLBI Facts About Exercise: Sample Exercise Programs; NHLBI Facts About Exercise: What Is Fact and What Is Fiction?*

* Family Relationships and Lifecycles
Family Branch
U.S. Department of Agriculture
10301 Baltimore Blvd.
Beltsville, MD 20705 (301) 504-5204

Be patient. If any phone number is incorrect, call (area code) 555-1212 and request the new listing.

Healthy Lifestyle and Physical Fitness

This center answers questions about families throughout the lifecycle, from marital relationships and childbearing families to empty nest families and retirement, and deals with matters concerning social environment and family economics education.

* Federal Health Information Catalog

ODPHP National Health Information Center
P.O. Box 1133 (800) 336-4797
Washington, DC 20013 (301) 565-4167 (in Maryland)

Health Information Resources in the Federal Government identifies Federal agencies and projects that can provide information to health professionals and the general public. It includes major services and activities, publications and databases. Check with the Center to learn about the latest edition. A $2 fee covers the handling for this catalog.

* Genetic Screening in the Workplace

Office of Technology Assessment (OTA)
600 Pennsylvania Ave., SE
Washington, DC 20510 (202) 224-8996

OTA has studied the state-of-the-art technologies used by employers for genetic screening and monitoring, which includes a survey of the 500 largest U.S. industries, to largest utilities, and 11 major unions to determine the current nature and extent of employer testing. Also examined is the impact of genetic testing; relevant ethical issues; and legal issues, including employment discrimination. The title of the report is *Genetic Monitoring and Screening in the Workplace.*

* Health Observances

ODPHP National Health Information Center
P.O. Box 1133 (800) 336-4797
Washington, DC 20013 (301) 565-4167

National Health Observances are special months, weeks, or days devoted to promoting particular health concerns. This Healthfinder lists selected health observances for the year. Health professionals, teachers, and community groups can use these special events to launch health promotion activities, stimulate awareness of health risks, or focus on disease eradication. Materials available from sponsoring organizations range from a single flyer to packets of promotional materials.

* Health Promotion in the Workplace

Office of Disease Prevention and Health Promotion
Public Health Service
330 C St., SW, Room 2132
Washington, DC 20201 (202) 472-5660

As a policy arm of the Public Health Service, this office works on developing policies for the Year 2000 objectives for health promotion. Their Preventive Services Task Force is developing recommendations for clinical practice, in addition to a worksite Health Promotion Task Force and a Nutrition Branch. This office also operates the Health Promotion Clearinghouse which offers many publications.

* Health Promotion Project Funding

ODPHP National Health Information Center
P.O. Box 1133 (800) 336-4797
Washington, DC 20013 (301) 565-4167 in Maryland

The guide, *Locating Resources for Healthy People 2000 Health Promotion Projects,* is designed to assist newcomers on their search for health promotion funding by introducing them to the major tasks involved and information services available. This publication is divided into four major sections. Section I discusses basic principles of fundseeking. Sections II and III discuss where and how to look for health promotion funds, focusing on both private and public sectors. Major foundations and Federal agencies interested in health promotion, as well as local sources are listed. Section IV lists resources--organizations, foundations, publications, and databases--that can be useful to those seeking funds. Also included is an appendix, which includes a glossary, a list of acronyms, a bibliography, and a sample grant application form.

* Health Risk Appraisal Tests

ODPHP National Health Information Center
P.O. Box 1133 (800) 336-4797

Washington, DC 20013 (301) 565-4167 (in Maryland)

In its "Healthfinder" series, the Center publishes a resource list on *Health Risk Appraisals* which identifies computer-scored, microcomputer-based, and self-scored tests that analyze an individual's health history and current lifestyle to determine his or her risk for preventable death or chronic illness. This "Healthfinder" contains a vendor list of many corporate health promotion center, medical research institutions, and private organizations that offer such tests and the costs of each. *Health Risk Appraisals* is available for a $1 handling fee.

* Healthy Teeth

National Institute of Dental Research
NIH, Building 31, Room 2C35
9000 Rockville Pike
Bethesda, MD 20892 (301) 496-4261

The mission of the National Institute of Dental Research (NIDR) is to support studies to establish the causes, develop better treatments, and ultimately find ways to prevent or substantially lower the risk of developing oral disease. NIDR has extramural and intramural research programs, and supports the Epidemiology and Oral Disease Prevention Program, which sponsors studies of oral disease and engages in controlled clinical trials of potential preventive agents. NIDR grants fellowships and career development awards and sponsors many conferences and workshops. They distribute a wide range of brochures, reports, and posters for both the general public and professionals (many of which are also in Spanish). Some of the topics covered are tooth decay, fluoride use, and the oral health of U.S. adults.

* Immunizations and Disease Prevention

Office of Consumer Affairs
Public Inquiries
Food and Drug Administration
5600 Fishers Lane (HFE-88)
Rockville, MD 20857 (301) 443-3170

This office has many free publications pertaining to vaccinations including *New Vaccine Protects Against Serious "Day Care" Disease, Shots Adults Shouldn't Do Without, Vaccines: Precious Ounces of Prevention,* and *Whooping Cough Still threatens U.S. Children.*

* Lifestyle and Occupational Health Risk Scorecard

Health Risk Appraisal Activity
Centers for Disease Control
1600 Clifton Rd., NE
Building 3, A-11
Atlanta, GA 30333 (404) 329-3177

The Health Risk Appraisal Activity program works to develop computerized health risk appraisals (HRS); to provide technical assistance in their use through state and regional contacts; and to distribute general background information on HRA's. Current activities include supporting the development of a state-of-the-art, public domain HRA at the Carter Center, Emory University; integrating occupational risk appraisal with lifestyle risk appraisal; evaluating the effect on communities of HRA use; and supporting the development of HRA programs for specific populations.

* Mental Retardation Prevention

President's Committee on Mental Retardation
330 Independence Avenue SW
Room 4061
Washington, DC 20201 (202) 619-0634

A Guide for State Planning for the *Prevention of Mental Retardation and Related Developmental Disabilities* is a resource tool not intended solely for state-level health planners but also for city and county health departments, advocacy groups, organizations and others. Single copies of this 20-page manual are available free.

* Physical Fitness

President's Council on Physical Fitness and Sports
450 5th St., NW, Suite 7103
Washington, DC 20001 (202) 272-3421

The President's Council on Physical Fitness and Sports was established to serve as a catalyst to promote, encourage and motivate the development of physical fitness and sports programs for all Americans. These programs help focus public awareness on the importance of staying physically active by encouraging schools,

Be patient. If any phone number is incorrect, call (area code) 555-1212 and request the new listing.

Health and Medicine

business and industry, government, recreation agencies, sports and youth-serving organizations to step up their emphasis on developing and maintaining physical fitness and sports programs. Some activities include establishing a nationwide Local Councils on Physical Fitness and Sports, Older Adult Seminars and various awards programs. The Council also conducts a continuous public service advertising program. A free quarterly newsletter is available, which includes information on physical fitness, books, conferences, and relevant articles. The Council also has the following publications available:

Adult Physical Fitness - explains benefits of regular, vigorous exercise ($4.50)

Aqua Dynamics - comprehensive program of strength, flexibility and endurance exercises for the water ($3.75).

Fitness Fundamentals - outlines basic guidelines to follow to begin and maintain a personal exercise program ($25/100).

Introduction to Running: One Step At A Time - a handbook for beginning runners ($1).

Promoting Health, Preventing Disease: Objectives for the Nation - description of the national objectives in health and fitness for 1990 ($5).

Physical Fitness/Sports Medicine - quarterly bibliographic listing of references in more than 300 subject areas ($9/yr).

Walking For Exercise and Pleasure - an overview of walking as a means to physical fitness and recreational pleasure ($1).

1985 PCPFS Youth Fitness Survey - complete report on the 1985 School Population Fitness Survey, conducted by the University of Michigan ($5).

All of the above publications are available by contacting: Superintendent of Documents, Government Printing Office, Washington, DC 20402; (202) 783-3238.

* Physical Fitness Awards for Adults

President's Council on Physical Fitness and Sports
450 5th St., NW, Suite 7103
Washington, DC 20001 (202) 272-3421

The Presidential Sports Award recognizes adult participation in a regular program of exercise. Men and women 10 years of age and older can qualify for the award in one or more of 58 different sports and fitness activities. Specific requirements for each activity have been established for a four-month period. Upon meeting the qualifying standards, participants receive a personalized Presidential certificate of achievement and a sports award lapel pin. The Amateur Athletic Union administers the program.

The categories are: Aerobic Dance, Archery, Back Packing, Badminton, Baseball, Basketball, Bicycling, Bowling, Canoe-Kayak, Equitation, Fencing, Field Hockey, Figure Skating, Football, Golf, Gymnastics, Handball, Team Handball, Ice Hockey, Jogging, Judo, Karate, Marathon, Orienteering, Racquetball, Roller Skating, Rowing, Rugby, Running, Sailing, Scuba-Skiing, Skeet-Trap, Skiing (Alpine), Skiing (Nordic), Soccer, Softball, Sports/Fitness, Squash, Swimming, Table Tennis, Tae Kwon Do, Tennis, Volleyball, Endurance Walking, Fitness Walking, Race Walking, Water Skiing, Weight Training, Wrestling.

For additional information and logs contact: Tom Leix, Presidential Sports Award, P.O. Box 68207, Indianapolis, IN 46268; (317) 872-2900.

* Physical Fitness Awards for Youngsters

President's Council on Physical Fitness and Sports
450 5th St., NW, Suite 7103
Washington, DC 20001 (202) 272-3421

The President's Council on Physical Fitness and Sports conducts two award programs for young people ages 6-17 which are offered through the school system. The Presidential Physical Fitness Award is given for scoring at or above the 85th percentile on all five physical fitness tests. The Council also awards other award programs and fitness clinics. Contact this office for more information and a list of their publications.

* Preventive Health Goals

ODPHP National Health Information Center
P.O. Box 1133 (800) 336-4797

Washington, DC 20013 (301) 565-4167 (in Maryland)

The proceedings of an international symposium on preventive services in primary care held in 1987 are available which address recommendations and goals in a variety of fields ranging from dentistry, medicine, public health, and behavioral sciences. *Implementing Preventive Services* (No. F0022) discusses specific services such as immunizations, screening tests such as Pap Smears and mammography, and patient education. It is available for $3 handling fee. *Guide to Clinical Preventive Services: An Assessment of the Effectiveness of 169 Interventions* details the U.S. Preventive Task Force's age- and gender-specific guidelines for preventive services, establishing priorities for medical care.

* Preventive Health National Programs

Centers for Disease Control
1600 Clifton Rd., NE, E06
Atlanta, GA 30333 (404) 639-1800

This center plans, directs, and coordinates national programs of assistance involving preventive health services to State and local health agencies. CDC provides leadership to the health community, especially State and local agencies, in the development and implementation of improved preventive health services programs. It assists States and localities in specifying major health problems in the community and formulating intervention strategies, and through grants, assists them in establishing and maintaining prevention and control programs directed toward health problems. Some of the preventive health services covered include dental disease, immunizations, sexually transmitted diseases and tuberculosis.

* Rural Health Care

Office of Technology Assessment (OTA)
600 Pennsylvania Ave., SE
Washington, DC 20510 (202) 224-8996

OTA has reviewed and evaluated past and current rural health care efforts; examining how medical technologies have been and might be diffused into rural areas; and identifying policies that might improve the quality, affordability, and accessibility of rural health care. *Defining Rural Areas: Impact on Health Care Policy and Research* is the resulting publication.

* Safe Exercise, Nutrition, Medicines for Seniors

ODPHP Health Information Center
P. O. Box 1133 (800) 336-4797
Washington, DC 20013 (301) 565-4167 in MD

Healthy Older People, a public education program on health promotion and aging conducted by the Office of Disease Prevention and Health Promotion (ODPHP), encourages older people to adopt good health habits, concentrating on such areas as exercise, nutrition, injury prevention, smoking, and medicines. A list of broadcast and print materials is available to State and local groups, along with a list of State contacts, who are responsible for coordinating statewide activities. The program includes consumer education, professional education, and technical assistance. A Program Memo information on activities and regional workshops.

* Surgeon General's Reports on Health Promotion

ODPHP Health Information Center
P. O. Box 1133 (800) 336-4797
Washington, DC 20013 (301) 565-4167 in MD

The nation's priorities are outlined in a 177-page report titled *Healthy People: The Surgeon General's Report on Health Promotion and Disease Prevention* (No. F0005) which identifies specific goals in five stages of human development. Single copy is available for $1 handling fee. A companion version titled *Promoting Health/Preventing Disease: Objectives for the Nation* (No. F0009) discusses 15 priority areas. This 102-page report is available for $3 handling fee. The *1990 Health Objectives for the Nation: A Midcourse Review* (No. F0013) is available for $3.

* Walking and Fitness

President's Council on Physical Fitness and Sports
450 5th St., NW, Suite 7103
Washington, DC 20001 (202) 272-3421

The President's Council serves as a clearinghouse for information on all types of exercise programs including making available free a 16-page manual titled *Everybody's Walking For Fitness* and *Walking for Exercise and Pleasure*.

Be patient. If any phone number is incorrect, call (area code) 555-1212 and request the new listing.

Healthy Lifestyle and Physical Fitness

* Worksite Health Promotion

ODPHP Health Information Center
P. O. Box 1133 (800) 336-4797
Washington, DC 20013 (301) 565-4167 in MD

The Clearinghouse has the following publications dealing with worksite health promotion programs:

Worksite Nutrition Guide: Health Menu Program ($3) - provides practical information about developing worksite nutrition education programs.

Achieving the Year 2000 Health Objectives for the Nation: Strategies for Business and Labor ($20) - a discussion of what employers can do to promote good health among their employees and to meet the goals for a healthier Nation.

Financial Incentives for Health Lifestyles: Potential and Pitfalls ($30) - a critical discussion of monetary incentives for promoting healthier lifestyles among employees. Covers practical, legal, ethical, and medical aspects of such plans.

Health Promoting Policies and Programs for Small Business ($25) - a discussion of the critical challenges facing managers of small businesses who want to improve the health of their employees.

Directory of Federal Worksite Health Promotion Initiatives ($3) - compilation of projects and research sponsored by the Federal Government to stimulate and improve worksite health promotion in public and private sectors.

The Future of Work and Health: Implications for Health Strategies ($7) - summarizes emerging trends in work and health and explores issues concerning the development of health care strategies for worksites in the future.

National Survey of Worksite Health Promotion Activities: A Summary ($2) - reviews the findings of this 1985 telephone survey of a representative sample of worksites with 50 or more employees.

Worksite Wellness Media Reports ($3) - presents in one volume comprehensive reports on health facts and examples of worksite wellness programs in areas of health especially important to employers and employees.

Worksite Wellness Reports ($15)- background papers on which some of the reports appearing in the volume cited above are based.

Worksite Nutrition: A Decision Maker's Guide ($2) - presents rationale for implementing nutrition programs in the workplace and describes what resources employers need to conduct worksite nutrition programs.

* Worksite Health Promotion

National Resource Center on Worksite Health Promotion
777 North Capitol St., NE, #800 (202) 408-9320
Washington, DC 20002 (202) 408-9333 (TDD)

The Resource Center provides information about currently operating worksite health promotion programs in American corporations. The center also provides bibliographies of low-cost and free worksite health promotion materials available to businesses and develops lists of vendors offering health promotion services. The Center's database contains information on descriptions of health promotion programs, information on organizations that can help employers, and abstracts of program evaluations, cost-effectiveness studies, research-based guidelines, and other information. Some of the publications available include:

Healthy People 2000 at Work: Strategies for Employers ($20)
Working for Good Health: Small Business and Health Promotion ($25)
Financial Incentives for Healthy Lifestyles ($30)
Directory of Worksite Health Promotion Resources ($5)
Directory of State Health Promotion Resources for Employers ($15)
Worksite Health Promotion Sourcebook (TBA)

* Worksite Safety and Health

National Institute for Occupational Safety and Health (NIOSH)
4676 Columbia Parkway
Cincinnati, OH 45226 (800) 35-NIOSH

Healthy People 2000: National Health Promotion and Disease Prevention Objectives - Occupational Safety and Health is a free publication which is part of Healthy People 2000. It includes over 15 objectives for health promotion and disease prevention related to occupational safety and health.

Be patient. If any phone number is incorrect, call (area code) 555-1212 and request the new listing.

Health and Medicine

Food Facts, Nutrition, and Diets

* *See also Consumer Chapter*
* *See also Agriculture and Farming; Food Quality and Distribution Chapter*

Menu plans and recipes,as well as very technical information about the nutritional value of every conceivable food product, is available for the asking. Surplus commodities and donations to non-profits are contained here as well as in the Government Auctions and Surplus Property Chapter. Surveys of food expenditures and eating habits as well as eating disorders are just a phone call away.

* Agricola Database

Family Information Center
National Agricultural Library
U.S. Department of Agriculture
Room 304
Beltsville, MD 20705 (301) 504-5204

A computerized database called AGRICOLA contains information primarily on the agricultural sciences but includes a substantial number of citations to nutrition literature such as journal articles, government reports, serials, monographs, and pamphlets. The print counterpart to this online database is titled *Food and Nutrition Bibliography*. The database is accessible through two commercial vendors, BRS and DIALOG.

* Allergies: Special Recipes

Superintendent of Documents
U.S. Government Printing Office
Washington, DC 20402 (202) 783-3238

Cooking for People with Food Allergies is a 39-page booklet that provides information for those who need help managing food allergies or intolerances. It provides help selecting and preparing foods containing no wheat, milk, eggs, corn, or gluten. Recipes are included. ($1.50; 001-000-04512-1).

* American Diet Surveys

Superintendent of Documents
U.S. Government Printing Office
Washington, DC 20402 (202) 782-3238

A survey to measure the food intake of individuals, the quality of the diet, and the response of American diets to short-term changes in food supplies is being conducted. This survey and other HNIS findings support research in agricultural planning, the formation of agricultural and food policy, food quality and regulation, and nutrition education. The survey is published in several parts:

Women 19-50 and Their Children 1-5, 1 Day 1985 (85-1) $4.25
Low Income Women 19-50 and Their Children 1-5, 1 Day 1985 (85-2) $18.95
Men 19-50 Years, 1 Day, 1985 (85-3) $4.75
Women 19-50 and Their Children 1-5, 1 Day, 1986 (86-1) $4.75

* Anorexia Nervosa and Bulimia

National Institute of Child Health
and Human Development
National Institutes of Health (NIH)
Building 31, Room 2A-32
Bethesda, MD 20892 (301) 496-5133

Facts About Anorexia Nervosa explains the causes, symptoms and treatments for anorexia and bulimia as well as ongoing research efforts at NIH. This 8-page pamphlet is available free.

* Basic Four Food Groups: Dietary Guidelines

ODPHP Health Information Center
PO Box 1133 (800) 336-4797
Washington, DC 20013-1133 (301) 565-4167 in MD

The recent edition of the government's recommendations about starch, fiber, fat, sodium, sugar, alcohol and food intake titled *Nutrition and Your Health Dietary Guidelines for Americans* is available for $2. The Government Printing Office also sells this 20-page pamphlet in bulk (100 copies for $44).

* Budget to Stretch Food Dollars or Food Stamps

Food and Nutrition Information Center
National Agricultural Library Building
Room 304
Beltsville, MD 20705 (301) 504-5719

A manual titled *Making Your Food Dollars Count: A Project Guide*, suggests ways to spend money and food stamps on nutritious foods and explains how to setup such a education campaign within a community. This reference is available on loan or can be borrowed through an interlibrary loan.

* Calcium and Other Special Needs of Women

Office of Public Affairs
Food and Drug Administration
5600 Fishers Lane, HFE88
Rockville, MD 20857 (301) 443-3170

Several publications are available free which address the special nutrition needs of females including *Please Pass That Woman Some More Calcium and Iron* (No. 85-2198), *Osteoporosis: Calcium, and Estrogens* (No. 85-1117), and *The Nutritional Gender Gap at the Dinner Table* (No. 84-2197).

* Cancer Prevention and Nutrition

Office of Cancer Communications
National Cancer Institute
Building 31, Room 10A-24
9000 Rockville Pike (800) 4-CANCER
Bethesda, MD 20892 (800) 492-6000 in MD

This institute offers the latest findings and scientific studies about nutrition and cancer including a free 51-page pamphlet titled *Diet, Nutrition and Cancer Prevention: A Guide to Food Choices* (No. 85-2711) which describes what is known about the interrelationships of diet and certain cancers.

* Cellulite Removal Gimmicks

Office of Public Affairs
Food and Drug Administration
5600 Fishers Lane, HFE88
Rockville, MD 20857 (301) 443-3170

The FDA monitors many weight loss related-products and warns consumers about gimmicks sold which promise to get rid of fat on the hips and thighs.

* Cheap Nutrition Publications

R. Woods
Consumer Information Center
P.O. Box 100
Pueblo, CO 81002

The Consumer Information Catalog is a catalog of free and low-cost federal publications of consumer interest. A new catalog is published quarterly, and is available free of charge. The publications dealing with nutrition include:

Be patient. If any phone number is incorrect, call (area code) 555-1212 and request the new listing.

Food Facts, Nutrition, and Diets

Anabolic Steroids: Losing at Winning (516Y)
Calories and Weight (108Y)
Getting Fit Your Way (109Y)
Modified Fast: A Sometime Solution to a Weighty Problem (517Y)
Diet, Nutrition and Cancer Prevention: The Good News (526Y)
Dietary Guidelines for Americans (527Y)
Eating for Life (113Y, $1)
Eating to Lower Your High Blood Cholesterol (114Y, $2)
Fat Substitutes (528Y)
Fish and Seafood Made Easy (421Y, 50 cents)
Food Irradiation- Toxic to Bacteria, Safe for Humans (529Y)
Food News for Consumers- 4 issues (251Y, $5)
The Grazing of America: A Guide to Healthy Snacking (530Y)
Is That Newfangled Cookware Safe? (531Y)
Keeping Up with the Microwave Revolution (532Y)
Nutrition and the Elderly (533Y)
Preventing Food-Borne Illness (534Y)
Quick Consumer Guide to Safe Food Handling (535Y)
A Simple Guide to Complex Carbohydrates (536Y)
Thrifty Meals for Two (115Y, $2.50)
Weighing Food Safety Risks (537Y)
A Word About Low Sodium Diets (538Y)

* Cholesterol Facts

National Cholesterol Education
Program Information Center
4733 Bethesda Avenue
Room 530
Bethesda, MD 20814 (301) 951-3260

The Cholesterol Information Center has specialists on staff and provides printed information on cholesterol, diet, and high blood pressure to the public and health professionals. Some of the brochures which they distribute includes *NHLBI Facts About Blood Cholesterol.*

* Community Nutrition Services

National Clearinghouse for Primary Care Information
8201 Greensboro Drive #600
McLean, VA 22102 (703) 821-8955

This center offers manuals for community health centers, primary care providers, home health services, HMOs, and outpatient clinics on approaches for a nutrition program, such as counseling and referral. Single copies of a 96-page *Guide for Developing Nutrition Services in Community Health Programs* is available free.

* Diabetes, Digestive and Kidney Diseases

Clinical Nutrition Research Units (CNRU)
National Institute of Diabetes and
Digestive and Kidney Diseases
National Institutes of Health (NIH)
Building 31, Room 9A04
9000 Rockville Pike
Bethesda, MD 20892 (301) 496-1540

The CNRU is an integrated array of research, educational, and service activities focused on human nutrition in health and disease. It serves as the focal point for an interdisciplinary approach to clinical nutrition research. The findings are published in journals.

* Dietary Analysis for the Individual

National Technical Information Service (NTIS)
5285 Port Royal Rd.
Springfield, VA 22261 (703) 487-4650

NTIS sells a simple software program for IBM PC-compatible computers which will give you a dietary analysis of the foods you eat in a meal or for each day. Just by entering the names of the foods you have eaten, this program, developed by the USDA's Human Nutrition Information Service, will give you nutrient data information, calories, and recommended daily allowances on over 850 foods. The Dietary Analysis Program software is available for $60.

* Dietary Essentials

Grand Forks Human Nutrition Research Center
P.O. Box 7166, University Station

Grand Forks, ND 58202-7166 (701) 795-8456

This center focuses on defining human requirements for trace elements and the physiological and biochemical factors which influence those requirements.

* Dietary Guidelines

Superintendent of Documents
Government Printing Office
Washington, DC 20402 (202) 783-3238

The Government Printing Office has several publications designed to improve your eating habits. They include the following:

Shopping for Food and Making Meals in Minutes Using the Dietary Guidelines - describes quick meal hints, tips on reading food labels, an aisle-by-aisle shopping guide, and 18 timesaving recipe ideas (S/N 001-000-04529-6, $3).

Preparing Foods and Planning Menus Using the Dietary Guidelines - contains tips for cooking with less sugar, fat, and sodium; a daily guide to food choices; making the menu fit the family; and 10 recipe ideas (S/N 001-000-04527-0, $2.50).

Making Bag Lunches, Snacks, and Desserts Using the Dietary Guidelines - provides a muncher's guide; great-tasting desserts with less fat and sugar; the best in bag lunches, hot or cold; and 27 recipe ideas (S/N 001-000-04528-8, $2.50).

Eating Better When Eating Out Using the Dietary Guidelines - discusses ordering foods "your way," how to read menus, and fact and fiction about fast foods (S/N 001-000-04530-0, $1.50).

The Healthy Heart Cookbook - an enjoyable and exciting new way of cooking to keep your heart healthy and diet wise. Suggests ways to shop wisely, discusses good and bad cooking oils, and provides numerous tasty menu suggestions (S/N 008-070-00632-4, $3).

* Drugs and Food Interactions

Office of Public Affairs
Food and Drug Administration
5600 Fishers Lane
HFE88
Rockville, MD 20857 (301) 443-3170

A free report titled *Food and Drug Interactions* (No. 94-3070) explains why some foods and medicines may interfere with each other, and suggests ways to avoid the problem.

* Eating Disorders

Office of Public Affairs
Food and Drug Administration
5600 Fishers Lane
HFE88
Rockville, MD 20857 (301) 443-3170

Bulimia and anorexia nervosa are discussed in a short pamphlet, *Eating Disorders: When Thinness Becomes an Obsession* (No. 86-2211), available free.

* Eating Habits National Survey

Division of Health Examination Statistics
National Center for Health Statistics
3700 East-West Highway
Room 2-58
Hyattsville, MD 20782 (301) 436-7068

This division collects data on health-related matters and administers the National Health and Nutrition Survey, which assesses the health and nutritional status of the general population through direct physical examination.

* Elderly and Menu Ideas

National Institute on Aging Information Center
2209 Distribution Circle
Silver Spring, MD 20910 (301) 495-3455

The Institute makes available free several "Age Pages" which offer tips for seniors including *Food: Staying Healthy After 65*, *Be Sensible About Salt*, *Hints for Shopping, Cooking and Enjoying Meals*, and *Dietary Supplements: More Is Not Always Better.*

Be patient. If any phone number is incorrect, call (area code) 555-1212 and request the new listing.

Health and Medicine

* Emergency Food and Shelter

Emergency Food and Shelter National Board Program
601 North Fairfax St., Suite 225
Alexandria, VA 22314 (703) 683-1166

This Federal emergency program begun in 1983, and currently part of the Stewart B. McKinney Homeless Assistance Act, continues to provide funds for basic food and shelter. Local boards are established to select agencies that will receive monies to provide the food and shelter services. A quarterly newsletter and *Checklist for Success*, featuring exemplary local programs, are available free.

* Fad Diets and Diet Books

Office of Public Affairs
Food and Drug Administration
5600 Fishers Lane, HFE88
Rockville, MD 20857 (301) 443-3170

How to Take Weight Off Without Getting Ripped Off (No. 85-1116) discusses weight reduction products, fad diets, and other diet aids. Another free publication titled *Diet Books Sell Well But...* (No. 84-1093) reviews and evaluates some of the popular diet plans.

* Fast Foods and Nutrition

Office of Public Affairs
Food and Drug Administration
5600 Fishers Lane, HFE88
Rockville, MD 20857 (301) 443-3170

A free pamphlet titled *What About Nutrients In Fast Foods?* examines the pros and cons of "fast foods" and analyses the nutritional value of various menus.

* Fiber and Roughage

Office of Public Affairs
Food and Drug Administration
5600 Fishers Lane, HFE88
Rockville, MD 20857 (301) 443-3170

Single copies of the booklet, *Fiber: Something Healthy to Chew On* (No. 85-2206) discusses the role of fiber in nutrition.

* Food and Nutrition Service Publications

Food and Nutrition Service (FNS)
U.S. Department of Agriculture
Public Affairs Staff
3101 Park Center Dr.
Alexandria, VA 22302 (703) 305-2554

FNS publishes a variety of brochures explaining the various food assistance programs it operates both for those eligible for the programs and for those who administer them. Programs include the Child Nutrition Program; Food Distribution Program; Women, Infants, and Children (WIC) Program; Food Stamp Program; and various nutrition education materials. Requests for the Publications List are available from the above office, or from the Food and Nutrition Service Regional Offices listed below. Most publications are available free; those for sale are sold through the Government Printing Office.

* Food and Nutrition Services Regional Offices

Contact the regional office nearest you for getting answers to questions over the phone as well as data and information materials.

Northeast Region, 10 Causeway St., Room 501, Boston, MA 02222-1068; (617) 565-6370.

Southeast Region, 77 Forsyth St. SW, Atlanta, GA 30302; (404) 730-2565.

Southwest Region, 1100 Commerce St., Room 5-C-30, Dallas, TX 75242; (214) 767-0222.

Western Region, 550 Kearny St., Room 400, San Francisco, CA 94108; (415) 705-1310.

Mid-Atlantic Region, Mercer Corporate Park, Corporate Blvd., Trenton, NJ 08650; (609) 259-5100.

Midwest Region, 50 E. Washington St., 4th Floor, Chicago, IL 60602; (312) 353-6664.

Northwest Region, 1244 Speer Blvd., Denver, CO 80204; (303) 844-0300.

* Food Assistance to the Poor

Food and Nutrition Service (FNS)
Public Information Office
3101 Park Center Dr.
Park Office Bldg.
Alexandria, VA 22302 (703) 305-2554

FNS administers many federal-state programs to provide food assistance to those in need. The agency cooperates with state and local welfare agencies to administer the Food Stamp Program, which enables low-income families to purchase a greater variety of food to improve their diets. Additional agency programs help reduce agricultural surpluses by providing commodities and other foodstuffs to schools and other institutions for their use in special nutrition programs. These programs are designed to help needy children achieve nutritionally balanced diets. The Special Supplemental Food Program for Women, Infants, and Children (WIC) provides specific nutritious food supplements to pregnant and nursing women, as well as to children up to 5 years of age who are found to be "at nutritional risk" because of poor diet or low income. The Food Distribution Program donates food to various outlets: schools, charitable institutions, nutrition programs for the elderly, summer camps, disaster relief agencies, and programs for needy families on some Indian reservations. A publications list is available.

* Food Consumption Research

U.S. Department of Agriculture
6505 Belcrest Road, Room 368
Hyattsville, MD 20782 (301) 436-8498

Data have been collected and is being compiled for the *1987-88 Nationwide Food Consumption Survey* (NFCS 1987-88). This survey, conducted every 10 years, provides comprehensive information on the consumption of foods and nutrients and on the dietary status of U.S. households and individuals. For a summary of survey results, contact the above office.

* Food Contamination Inspection

Center for Food Safety and Applied Nutrition
Food and Drug Administration
200 C Street, SW, Room 6815
Washington, DC 20204 (202) 245-1144

The Center for Food Safety and Applied Nutrition conducts research and develops standards on the composition, quality, nutrition, and safety of food, food additives, colors, and cosmetics. The Center has cooperative arrangements with industries, such as milk and shellfish, where representatives from FDA, the state, and the industry meet to develop model codes and standards for the food product. The Center is responsible for food labeling, requiring ingredients to be listed in order of composition, as well as other nutritional information, such as fat and sodium content. They regulate the infant formula industry, ensuring that basic nutrients be included in the formula. The Center also administers a program of sampling food for possible contamination. Radiation from the Chernobyl accident and the Chilean Grape embargo are two recent examples studied under this program.

* Food Expenditures and Consumer Attitudes

Food Marketing and Economics Branch
Economics Research Service
1301 New York Ave., NW
Washington, DC 20005-4788 (202) 786-1862

Studies and expertise on such topics as the convenience food market, food purchases away from home, the fast food industry, the relationship between consumer attitudes about nutrition and actual food expenditures, and the economic effects of food safety regulations are available from this office.

* Food Preparation and Refrigeration

Office of Public Affairs
Food and Drug Administration
5600 Fishers Lane
HFE88
Rockville, MD 20857 (301) 443-3170

Enfermedades Causadas Por Alimentos Contaminados (No. 80-2044S) is available only in Spanish and recommends proper food preparation and refrigeration of various types of foods and also discusses some common foodborne organisms.

Be patient. If any phone number is incorrect, call (area code) 555-1212 and request the new listing.

Food Facts, Nutrition, and Diets

* Food Safety and Additives Info

Office of Public Affairs
Food and Drug Administration (FDA)
5600 Fishers Lane, HFE88
Rockville, MD 20857 (301) 443-3170

The FDA distributes many brochures and publications including *More Than You Ever Thought You Would Know About Food Additives* (No. 82-2160), *Consumer's Guide to Food Labels* (No. 85-2083), and *Sweetness Minus Calories = Controversy* (No. 85-2205). The *FDA Consumer*, which contains the latest developments at FDA, can be ordered for $12 per year from the Superintendent of Documents, Government Printing Office, Washington DC 20402, (202) 783-3238.

* Food Safety and Inspection

Office of Public Awareness
Food Safety and Inspection Service
U.S. Department of Agriculture (202) 447-9351
Room 1165-S (202) 447-3333 in DC
Washington, DC 20205 (800) 535-4555 Meat and Poultry Hotline

This office inspects and analyzes domestic and imported meat and poultry and establishes standards for processed meat and poultry products. Questions can be answered about the proper handling, preparation, and refrigeration, food poisoning, food additives, food labeling, sodium, and herbs.

* Food Tampering and Foreign Objects

Emergency Services
Food and Drug Administration (FDA)
5600 Fishers Lane
HFC-162, Room 1362
Rockville, MD 20857 (301) 443-1240

FDA has a 24-hour answering service at (202) 737-0448. If you find foreign objects or evidence of tampering with any food, drug (both human and animal), or cosmetic, you should report it to the Food and Drug Administration. This office deals with consumer complaints and recalls. You can also report the tampering to any of the FDA regional offices.

* Free Food For Non-Profit Institutions

Food Distribution Program, Food and Nutrition Service
U.S. Department of Agriculture (USDA)
3101 Park Center Dr., Room 502
Alexandria, VA 22302 (703) 756-3680

Charitable and rehabilitation institutions are usually eligible to receive surplus commodities stored by USDA. The commodities available are dairy products, grain oil, and peanuts.

* Government Dietary Guidelines

Human Nutrition Information Service (HNIS)
U.S. Department of Agriculture
Room 325 A, Federal Building
Hyattsville, MD 20782 (301) 436-8614

HNIS has developed seven basic eating principals, the Dietary Guidelines, that encourage variety, balance, moderation in food consumption. The first two guidelines recommend people eat a variety of foods that provide enough essential nutrients and calories to maintain a desirable weight; the other five suggest eating an adequate amount of starch and fiber and avoiding too much fat, sugar, sodium, and alcohol. Contact HNIS for a series of seven bulletins outlining the program.

* Healthy Menus

Food and Nutrition Information Center
U.S. Department of Agriculture
National Agricultural Library, Room 304
Beltsville, MD 20705 (301) 504-5719

Cartoons fill the pages of this booklet titled *Eating For Better Health* which contains nutrition and weight loss information as well as inexpensive recipes and menus. Other information and scientific findings are available from this agency.

* Health Promotion and Nutrition

Nutrition Branch
Office of Disease Prevention and Health Promotion

Public Health Service
330 C St., SW, Room 2132
Washington, DC 20201 (202) 472-5370

As a policy arm of the Public Health Service, this office works on developing policies for the Year 2000 objectives for health promotion. Their Preventive Services Task Force is developing recommendations for clinical practice, in addition to a worksite Health Promotion Task Force and a Nutrition Branch. This office also operates the Health Promotion Clearinghouse which offers many publications.

* Healthy Heart Menus

National Heart, Lung, and Blood Institute
National Institutes of Health (NIH)
Building 31, Room 42-21
9000 Rockville Pike
Bethesda, MD 20892 (301) 496-4236

The relationship between diet and heart disease is studied by this institute so it is an excellent place to learn the latest findings about reducing cholesterol and other risk factors. A lengthy 224-page report titled *Foods For Health: Report of the Pilot Program* (No. 83-2036) shares the results of a one-year experiment to increase consumer awareness and knowledge about nutrition as it relates to cardiovascular risk factors. Single copies of this report are available free as well as other pilot projects. Some of the free publications include:

Dietary Guidelines for Americans: Avoid Too Much Fat, Saturated Fat and Cholesterol
Eat Right to Lower Your High Blood Cholesterol
Eating to Lower Your Blood Cholesterol, and Nutrition and Your Health: Dietary Guidelines for Americans
Home and Garden Bulletin

* Low-Income Families and Nutrition Awareness

Food and Nutrition Information Center
National Agricultural Library Building
Room 304
Beltsville, MD 20705 (301) 344-3719

The Idea Book: Sharing Nutrition Education Experiences is designed for WIC (Women, Infants, and Children) nutrition educators and contains chapters covering motivation, planning, lesson plans, etc. This 89-page resource is available on loan from the Center and also is available through interlibrary loan.

* Malnutrition and Nutrition Research

Western Human Nutrition Research Center
P.O. Box 29997
Presidio of San Francisco
San Francisco, CA 94129 (415) 556-9699

This center develops improved methods for monitoring and evaluating nutritional status and investigates factors that lead to malnutrition. It also conducts studies on human nutritional requirements.

* Nutrient Data Tapes

National Technical Information Service
5285 Port Royal Rd.
Springfield, VA 22261 (703) 487-4650

The Human Nutrition Information Service collects and publishes information on disc and magnetic tape on the nutritive composition of foods. The agency gathers data from the scientific literature and from government, university, and food industry laboratories and directs laboratory studies to produce information. HNIS also compiles information on yield and nutrient retention of food items at different stages in production. Complete ordering information is available from the above address. See Human Nutrition Information Service Reports to order print versions of this information.

* Nutrient Values and Food Groups

Public Information Officer
Human Nutrition Information Service
U.S. Department of Agriculture
Federal Building
6505 Belcrest Road, Room 363
Hyattsville, MD 20782 (301) 436-8617

This office shares its research in nutritive value of foods and of the nutritional

Be patient. If any phone number is incorrect, call (area code) 555-1212 and request the new listing.

Health and Medicine

adequacy of diets and food supplies. It also maintains the Nutrient Data Bank which contains surveys and data on the nutrient values in foods and descriptions of foods. Various consumer materials are available as well as a publications list, including over 20 publications on the nutrient composition of foods. HNIS has several publications dealing with dietary guidelines for Americans, which are seven basic principles for developing and maintaining a healthier diet and are the basis for all Federal nutrition information and education programs for health Americans. Some of the publications available include:

Nutrition and Your Health: Dietary Guidelines for Americans (free, also in Spanish)
Dietary Guidelines and Your Diet ($4.50)
Preparing Foods and Planning Menus Using the Dietary Guidelines ($2.50)
Making Bag Lunches, Snacks, and Desserts Using the Dietary Guidelines ($2.50)
Shopping for Food and Making Meals in Minutes Using the Dietary Guidelines ($3)
Eating Better When Eating Out Using the Dietary Guidelines ($1.50)
Calories and Weight: The USDA Pocket Guide ($1.75)
Nutritive Value of Foods ($3.75)
Your Money's Worth in Foods ($2.25)
The Sodium Content of Your Food ($2.25)
Thrifty Meals for Two: Making Your Food Dollars Count ($2.50)
Cooking for People with Food Allergies ($1.50)
Good Sources of Nutrients ($5)

* Nutritionally-Related Chronic Diseases

Beltsville Human Nutrition Research Center
BARC-East, Building 308
Beltsville, MD 20705 (301) 344-2157

This center conducts research on nutrient composition and nutritional qualities of food; performs studies on energy metabolism and nutritional requirements; and develops dietary strategies that can delay the onset of nutritionally-related chronic diseases.

* Nutrition Education

Food and Nutrition Information Center
U.S. Department of Agriculture
National Agricultural Library, Room 304
Beltsville, MD 20705 (301) 504-5719

Nutrition Education Printed Materials and Audiovisuals: Grades Preschool through 6, and *Nutrition Education Printed Materials and Audiovisuals: Grades 7-12* both provide annotated listing of audiovisual and printed nutrition education materials for children. Topics include general nutrition, substance abuse, adolescent pregnancy nutrition guidelines, nutrition education programs, and fitness decisions. *Nutrition Education Resource Guide: An Annotated Bibliography of Educational Materials for the WIC and CSF Programs* focuses on client education materials within the subject areas of nutrition for pregnant, postpartum, and breastfeeding women, and nutrition for children from infancy through preschool. *Adult/Patient Nutrition Education Materials* is an annotated bibliography contains 130 citations on nutrition education materials for adults on a variety of topics including weight control, anorexia/bulimia, diabetes, heart disease, oral health and food quackery. *Sources of Free or Low-cost Food and Nutrition Materials* is a list of organizations that provide free or low-cost food and nutrition materials for consumers.

* Nutrition Labels and U.S. RDA

Office of Public Affairs
Food and Drug Administration
5600 Fishers Lane, HFE88
Rockville, MD 20857 (301) 443-3170

A short fact sheet titled *Nutrition Labels and U.S. RDA* explains the evolution of the Recommended Daily Allowances (RDAs) and the intention of nutritional labeling information.

* Nutrition Needs of Mothers and Infants

Children's Nutrition Research Center
at Baylor College of Medicine
1100 Bates St.
Houston, TX 77030 (713) 798-7000

This center focuses on determining the unique nutrient needs of pregnant and lactating women, and of children from conception through early years of development.

* Nutrition: Technical Assistance

National Center for Chronic Disease Prevention and Health Promotion
Centers for Disease Control
1600 Clifton Rd., NW, Room 1113C
Atlanta, GA 30333 (404) 488-5080

Through its divisions--chronic disease control, community intervention, health education, nutrition, and reproductive health--this center offers technical assistance and expertise in these categories, as well as in health promotion and health education. Primary recipients of technical assistance are official state and local health agencies, schools, and health care delivery settings. The Center maintains a database of health education programs and methods in schools and rural and urban communities, which is part of the Combined Health Information Database (CHID).

* Nutri-Topics

Food and Nutrition Information Center
U.S. Department of Agriculture
National Agricultural Library, Room 304
Beltsville, MD 20705 (301) 504-5719

Nutri-Topics are free brief reading lists designed to help locate information or resources on a given topic. They are available as separate lists of resources appropriate for one or more user levels: consumer, educator, and health professional. Included are print materials and lists of contacts for further information. Topics include:

Adolescent Pregnancy and Nutrition
Anorexia Nervosa and Bulimia
Children's Literature on Food and Nutrition
Diet and Cancer
Food Allergy, Intolerance, and Sensitivity
Food Safety: Ready-Prepared Foods
Food Safety, Teacher's Guide
Nutrition and Cardiovascular Disease
Nutrition and Diabetes
Nutrition and the Elderly
Nutrition and the Handicapped
Nutrition, Learning and Behavior
Sensible Nutrition
Sports Nutrition
Vegetarian Nutrition
Weight Control

Quick Biographies are lists of current references on a given topic. The topics covered include:

Adult/Patient Nutrition Education Materials
Childhood Obesity and Cardiovascular Disease
Cultural Perspectives on Food and Nutrition
Fish Oil: Role of Omega-3s in Health and Nutrition
Food Service: Printed Materials and Audiovisuals
Infant Nutrition
Nutrient Composition of Selected Grains as Food
Nutrition and AIDS
Nutrition and the Elderly
Nutrition Education Materials and Audiovisuals: Grades Preschool-6
Nutrition Education Printed Materials and Audiovisuals: Grades 7-12
Pesticide Residues in Food

* Obesity and Energy Metabolism

Office of Clinical Center Communications
Warren G. Magnuson Clinical Center
NIH, Building 10, Room 5C-305
9000 Rockville Pike
Bethesda, MD 20892 (301) 496-2563

Single copies are available free of a 23-page booklet titled *Obesity and Energy Metabolism* (No. 86-1805) which explains the relationship between too much food and too little exercise. A videotape based on this publication is available and can be purchased or available on a free loan basis.

* Older Adults and Nutrition

Human Nutrition Research Center on
Aging at Tufts University
711 Washington, St.

Be patient. If any phone number is incorrect, call (area code) 555-1212 and request the new listing.

Food Facts, Nutrition, and Diets

Boston, MA 02111 (617) 556-3330

This center researches the special nutritional needs of persons as they age, with a view toward enhancing the quality of later life through improved nutrition and health.

* Organic and Natural Foods

Office of Public Affairs
Food and Drug Administration
5600 Fishers Lane, HFE88
Rockville, MD 20857 (301) 443-3170

A short pamphlet titled *The Confusing World of Health Foods* (No. 84-2108) provides general information about foods sold as health foods and about such terms as "organic". *The Consumer's Guide to Food Labels* (No. 85-2083) translates the nutrition information which appears on food labels.

* Pesticide Residues

Office of Pesticide Programs
Environmental Protection Agency (EPA)
401 M St., SW
Washington DC 20460 (202) 557-7090

The Environmental Protection Agency (EPA) administers two Congressionally mandated statutes to control the more than 45,000 pesticide products registered for use in the United States. The EPA monitors the distribution and use of these pesticides, issuing civil or criminal penalties for violations. EPA also sets tolerances or maximum legal limits for pesticide residues on food commodities and feed grains to prevent consumer exposure to unsafe pesticide levels.

* Pick Your Own Fruits and Vegetables

Contact your local USDA Extension Service agent

Many farmers allow consumers to pick produce directly from their fields at substantial savings.

* Saccharin, Cyclamate and Aspartame

Office of Public Affairs
Food and Drug Administration (FDA)

5600 Fishers Lane
HFE88
Rockville, MD 20857 (301) 443-3170

The FDA offers information on food additives including free pamphlets such as *Sweetness Minus Calories = Controversy* (No. 85-2205) which gives the legal and scientific histories of these sugar substitutes and other sweeteners.

* Salt and Low-Sodium Diets

Office of Public Affairs
Food and Drug Administration
5600 Fishers Lane
HFE88
Rockville, MD 20857 (301) 443-3170

Free pamphlets about consumption of salt in one's daily diet are available, including *A Word About Low-Sodium Diets* (No. 87-2179) which suggests ways consumers can lower sodium intake and lists foods that are naturally low in sodium. A slide set titled "Good Sense About Sodium" (also available in Spanish), is obtainable through Consumer Affairs Officers in FDA district offices.

* Vitamins and Recommended Dietary Allowances

Office of Public Affairs
Food and Drug Administration
5600 Fishers Lane
HFE88
Rockville, MD 20857 (301) 443-3170

Single copies are available free of the government's recommended dietary allowances in a pamphlet titled *Some Facts and Myths of Vitamins* (No. 82-2164).

* Worksite Nutrition Programs

ODPHP Health Information Center
PO Box 1133 (800) 336-4797
Washington, DC 20013-1133 (301) 565-4167 in MD

A 58-page program for implementing nutrition programs in the workplace, this describes what resources employers need to conduct such a health initiative. *Worksite Nutrition: A Decision Maker's Guide* (No. U-0010) can be purchased for $2.

Be patient. If any phone number is incorrect, call (area code) 555-1212 and request the new listing.

Health and Medicine

Contraception and Pregnancy

Several government-sponsored clearinghouses listed below, such as the National Center for Maternal and Child Health and the Family Life Information Exchange, offer materials published by both federal and state health agencies as well as private organizations such as the March of Dimes Birth Defects Foundation. These information centers work in close coordination with many government and private groups and research hubs so they are in a position to refer callers to experts and organizations who can answer questions and concerns.

* Adolescent Fathers
National Maternal and Child Health Clearinghouse
38th and R Sts., NW
Washington, DC 20057 (202) 625-8410
Recent public policy efforts have been directed toward increasing paternal responsibility among young unwed fathers. This publication sought to determine what services were currently available to adolescent fathers. This free 140 page directory is broken down into programs offered in each state, and described services provided, funding, population, and outreach.

* Adolescent Pregnancy
National Clearinghouse on Maternal and Child Health
38th and R Sts., NW
Washington, DC 20057 (202) 625-8410
This Clearinghouse has free publications focusing on adolescent pregnancy concerns. Some of the titles include: *Adolescent Pregnancy - Resource Guide, Health Foods, Healthy Baby, Nutrition Management of the Pregnant Adolescent, Pregnancy and Childbearing Among Homeless Adolescents: Report of a Workshop,* and *Adolescent Fathers: Directory of Services.*

* Adolescent Pregnancy Programs
Office of Adolescent Pregnancy Programs
U.S. Department of Health and Human Services
200 Independence Avenue, SW, Room 736E
Washington, DC 20201 (202) 245-7473
This office promotes adoption as an alternative to early parenting and focuses on teenagers under 18 years of age. Pregnancy prevention strategies and information resources are coordinated by this office.

* Adoption: Decision and Resources
Family Life Information Exchange
P.O. Box 30146
Bethesda, MD 20814 (301) 585-6636
This clearinghouse offers numerous resources on the issue of putting up a child for adoption, including such free publications as *The Adoption Option: A Guidebook for Pregnancy Counselors* (No FP-10000).

* Birth Control and Sterilization Posters
Family Life Information Exchange
P.O. Box 30146
Bethesda, MD 20814 (301) 585-6636
This clearinghouse offers single free copies of several posters including "Spacing Pregnancy Means" (FP-100068) and "Sterilization is Permanent" (FP-100059).

* Birth Control Methods
National Institute of Child Health and Human Development
NIH, Building 31, Room 2A32
9000 Rockville Pike
Bethesda, MD 20892 (301) 496-5133
The National Institute of Child Health and Human Development distributes pamphlets and reports on the various methods of contraception, as well as medical updates on the risks and/or effectiveness of new forms of birth control. The 19-page booklet, *Facts About Oral Contraceptives,* is available free.

* Birth Defects and Developmental Disabilities Research
Birth Defects and Developmental Disabilities Division
National Center For Environmental Health and Injury Control
Centers for Disease Control
1600 Clifton Rd., NE
Atlanta, GA 30333 (404) 488-4706
Birth defects are the leading cause of infant mortality in the U.S., accounting for more than 20% of the infant deaths each year. This division conducts surveillance on birth defects and developmental disabilities, and assists states with programs to prevent both. They examine data to identify new risk factors for birth defects and developmental disabilities. They are now beginning to focus on three specific disease areas: spina bifida, fetal alcohol syndrome, and mild mental retardation, because research suggests that these diseases can be prevented. An annual program summary, and a bibliography of the division research reports are available.

* Breastfeeding Information
National Clearinghouse for Maternal and Child Health
38th and R St., NW
Washington, DC 20057 (202) 625-8410
This Clearinghouse has several free publications dealing with breast feeding, including:

Art and Science of Breastfeeding Manual

Breastfeeding Catalog of Products - include a listing of videotapes, posters, brochures, journal articles, data bases, curricula and training aids.

Nutrition during Lactation

Surgeon General's Workshop on Breastfeeding and Human Lactation - covers the physiology of breastfeeding, the unique values of human milk, current trends, and cultural factors relating to breastfeeding.

* Cesarean Childbirth
National Institute of Child Health and Human Development
NIH, Building 31, Room 2A32
9000 Rockville Pike
Bethesda, MD 20892 (301) 496-5133
This institute can provide data and medical information about this health issue. A 13-page booklet, *Facts About Cesarean Childbirth* (No. 431P), discusses cesarean delivery, types of incisions, current thinking about repeat cesarean, and the pros and cons of this method of birth.

* Child Health Info for Prospective and New Parents
National Center for Education in Maternal
and Child Health (NCEMCH)
38th and R St., NW
Washington, DC 20057 (202) 625-8400
The Center responds to information requests from prospective and new parents, consumers, and professionals. This clearinghouse provides technical assistance, and develops educational and reference materials. The NCEMCH Resource Center contains professional literature, patient education materials, curricula, audiovisuals, and information about organizations and programs. Major content areas include pregnancy, child and adolescent health, and human genetics.

Be patient. If any phone number is incorrect, call (area code) 555-1212 and request the new listing.

Contraception and Pregnancy

* Child Safety: CPR, Infant and Child Car Seats

National Health Information Center
P. O. Box 1133
(800) 336-4797
Washington, DC 20013
(301) 565-4167 (in MD)

Child Safety Resource Guide describes currently available publications that offer information for individuals responsible for the care and safety of young people. It is designed for educators looking for materials to support program activities, as well as for the general public. The materials listed focus on injury prevention and give tips and suggestions on protecting children against potential hazards in the home, in cars, on bicycles, and in the water. A short list of coloring and activities books is included, as well as sources of information on cardiopulmonary resuscitation.

* Cigarettes and the Unborn

Office on Smoking and Health
Mail Stop K-50
Centers for Disease Control
1600 Clifton Rd., NE
Atlanta, GA 30333
(404) 488-5705

This Office can provide you with information on smoking as it effects pregnancy and newborns. Some of the free pamphlets available include *Is Your Baby Smoking?* which explains the dangers of passive smoke on the baby; and "Baby In The House" Stickers which remind pregnant women that when they smoke, they smoke for two.

* Condoms and Effectiveness of other Contraception

Contraception Evaluation Branch
EPN 607, 9000 Rockville Pike
Bethesda, MD 20892
(301) 496-4924

The Contraception Evaluation Branch designs and supports a program of studies to clarify the safety and effectiveness of fertility control. They also provide ongoing surveillance of the effectiveness of fertility regulating products and surgical procedures. A major emphasis now is to demonstrate the degree to which barrier contraceptives reduce the risk of sexually transmitted diseases, including AIDS. Staff can refer you to researchers examining a particular birth control method, with most of their research being published in journals.

* Comparing Contraceptives

Office of Consumer Affairs
Food and Drug Administration
Public Inquiries
5600 Fishers Lane (HFE-88)
Rockville, MD 20857
(301) 443-3170

This agency publishes *Comparing Contraceptives* (No. 85-1123), which discusses the possible side effects and effectiveness of nine different types of birth control and also contains a chart.

* Diabetes and Pregnancy

National Institute of Child Health and Human Development
National Institutes of Health
Building 31, Room 2A32
9000 Rockville Pike
Bethesda, MD 20892
(301) 496-5133

Understanding Gestational Diabetes: A Practical Guide to a Healthy Pregnancy addresses questions about diet, exercise, measurement of blood sugar levels, and general medical and obstetric care of women with gestational diabetes. It answers such questions as: Will my baby have diabetes?, What can I do to control gestational diabetes?, and Will I have diabetes in the future? This is a free booklet.

* Down's Syndrome Information

National Institute of Child Health and Human Development
NIH, Building 31, Room 2A32
9000 Rockville Pike
Bethesda, MD 20892
(301) 496-5133

Facts About Down's Syndrome and *Facts About Down's Syndrome for Women Over 35* (No. 82-536), discuss genetic counseling, and the outlook for a child born with Down's syndrome. This institute can provide more technical and statistical information about this birth defect.

* Drinking When Pregnant

National Clearinghouse for Alcohol and Drug Information
P.O. Box 2345
Rockville, MD 20852
(301) 468-2600

The Clearinghouse has several free publications dealing with drinking and drug use during pregnancy. Some of the titles include:

Alcohol, Tobacco, and Other Drugs May Harm the Unborn - presents the most recent finding of basic research and clinical studies (PH291).

Drug Abuse and Pregnancy - provides an overview of the scope of the problem and effects of maternal drug use on the mother, fetus, and infant (CAP33).

How To Take Care of Your Baby Before Birth - a low-literacy brochure aimed at pregnant women that describes what they should and should not do during their pregnancy, emphasizing a no use of alcohol and other drugs message (PH239, also in Spanish).

An Inner Voice Tells You Not to Drink or Use Other Drugs - poster depicts an artistic rendition of a pregnant American Indian Woman (AV161).

Prenatal Drug Exposure: Kinetics and Dynamics - NIDA Research Monograph 60 - presents research studies on the effects of maternal use of dugs on the fetus (M60).

Prevention Resource Guide: Pregnant/Postpartum Women and Their Infants - Resource Guide targets pregnant and postpartum women, women between the ages of 15-44, counselors, health care providers, and prevention program planners. It provides a high-demand, comprehensive resource for information concerning alcohol and other drug prevention among pregnant and postpartum women and their infants (MS420).

Women and Alcohol - discussion of women and alcohol (RPO716).

* Drugs (Legal and Illegal) and Pregnancy

Office of Consumer Affairs
Food and Drug Administration
Public Inquiries
5600 Fishers Lane (HFE-88)
Rockville, MD 20857
(301) 443-3170

Single copies are available free of *Drugs and Pregnancy,* (No. 80-3083), which explains how medications, drugs, alcohol and tobacco are shared with the unborn baby. Other related hazards to the fetus are also discussed.

* Eating for Two

Office of Consumer Affairs
Food and Drug Administration
Public Inquiries
5600 Fishers Lane (HFE-88)
Rockville, MD 20857
(301) 443-3170

A free booklet, *All About Eating for Two* (No. 84-2183), discusses how pregnancy and breastfeeding affect a woman's nutritional needs.

* Environmental Exposures and Pregnancy

National Clearinghouse for Maternal and Child Health
38th and R St., NW
Washington, DC 20057
(202) 625-8410

Once thought to be a filter of harmful agents, the placenta is now known to be capable of transferring not only nutrients but harmful chemicals to the developing fetus. *Resource Guide - Environmental Exposures and Pregnancy* is a booklet which includes an annotated list of current publications and journal articles, a list of organizations that can provide additional information, and a list of teratogen information services. Federal and state government maternal and child health agencies may also be able to provide further assistance.

* Family Planning Promotion

Family Life Information Exchange
P.O. Box 30146
Bethesda, MD 20814
(301) 585-6636

The Family Life Information Exchange has information on family planning, adolescent pregnancy, and adoption. The have brochures and pamphlets, as well as catalogs containing family planning publications. A free newsletter on health

Be patient. If any phone number is incorrect, call (area code) 555-1212 and request the new listing.

Health and Medicine

education and family planning is also available. A free publications list is available which includes:

Information for Men---Your Sterilization Operation
Information for Women---Your Sterilization Operation
Program Guidelines for Project Grants for FP Services
The Adoption Option, Guidebook for Pregnancy Counselors
Many Teens are Saying "NO"
OAPP Funded Curricula
Trends in Adolescent Pregnancy and Childbearing
AFL Research Projects Summary
FP Grantees, Delegates, and Clinics 1991/1992 Directory
Title X National Family Planning Program Fact Sheet
Recommendations for Prevention of HIV in Health Care Settings
PHS Guidelines for Counseling and Testing to Prevent HIV and AIDS
Teenage Pregnancy and Fertility in the US
OPA Program Instructions: AIDS Education in Title X
BCRR Manual
Family and Adolescent Pregnancy
Human Immunodeficiency Virus Infection in the United States
Adolescent Abstinence: A Guide for FP Professionals
Your Contraceptive Choices: For Now, For Later
Improving the Quality of Clinician Pap Smear
AFL Demonstration Projects: Program and Evaluation Summaries
Sexually Transmitted Diseases Treatment Guidelines
OPA Program Instructions: Norplant Education in Title X

* Federal Resource Directory

National Maternal and Child Clearinghouse
38th and R Sts., NW
Washington, DC 20057 (202) 625-8410

This free resource directory includes a description of more than 500 publications and audiovisual materials related to maternal and child health, an annotated listing of over 80 federal agencies and information centers, and a directory of federal, regional, and state maternal and child health programs.

* Fetal and Newborn Development and Child Health

National Institute of Child Health and Human Development
National Institutes of Health
9000 Rockville Pike
Bethesda, MD 20892 (301) 496-3454

The National Institute of Child Health and Human Development (NICHHD) conducts and supports research on the reproductive, developmental, and behavioral process that determine the health of children, adults, families, and populations. Research for mothers, children, and families is designed to advance knowledge of fetal development, pregnancy, and birth; to identify the prerequisites of optional growth through infancy to adulthood; and to contribute to the prevention and treatment of mental retardation.

* Genetics

National Maternal and Child Health Clearinghouse
38th and R St., NW
Washington, DC 20057 (202) 625-8410

This Clearinghouse has an extensive list of free publications dealing with genetics. Some of the titles include: *Genetics: Abstract of Active Projects FY 1991, Genetics Support Groups, Human Genetics - Resource Guide,* and *Resources for Clergy in Human Genetic Problems.*

* Genetics Research

National Institute of General Medical Sciences (NIGMS)
National Institutes of Health
Building 31, Room 4A52
9000 Rockville Pike
Bethesda, MD 20892 (301) 496-7301

NIGMS supports research and research training in the basic biomedical sciences that form the foundation needed to make advances in the understanding of disease. Research focuses on the cellular basis of disease, genetics, pharmacological sciences, physiology and biomedical engineering. For instance, they look at how DNA is replicated or how drugs are metabolized in your body. They have brochures and reports for the general public and professionals on such topics as medicines and genetic diseases.

* Gynecological Health

National Health Information Center
P.O. Box 1133 (800) 336-4797
Washington, DC 20013 (301) 565-4167 in MD

In its series, "Healthfinder", the center publishes *Women's Health* which lists many organizations that provide information on a broad range of topics including gynecological, mitral valve prolapse, osteoporosis. This 6-page reference illustrates the array of organizations which offer expertise and information.

* Healthy Mothers, Healthy Babies

Office of Public Affairs
Health Resources and Services Administration
5600 Fishers Lane, Room 1443
Rockville, MD 20857 (301) 443-2086

The Health Resources and Services Administration offers a free catalog, *Current Publications,* which lists all the publications, films, and videos produced by HRSA's three bureaus: Bureau of Health Care Delivery and Assistance, Bureau of Maternal and Child Health and Resources Development and Bureau of Health Professions.

* Healthy Mothers, Healthy Babies

National Clearinghouse for Primary Care Information
8201 Greensboro Dr., Suite 600
McLean, VA 22102 (703) 821-8955

Healthy Mothers, Healthy Babies - A Compendium of Program Ideas for Servicing Low-Income Women provides useful suggestions to health care providers who work with low income populations, and suggests program planning and policy directions for State and national organizations concerned with maternal and infant health.

* Immunizations

Immunization Division
Centers for Disease Control
1600 Tullie Circle
Atlanta, GA 30333 (404) 639-1830

This Office responds to inquiries and provides information and publications regarding immunization against vaccine-preventable diseases of young children. They can provide you with reports of the recommendations of the Immunization Practices Advisory Committee, as well as informational pamphlets on the various vaccines all of our children should receive.

* Infants at Risk

National Center for Clinical Infant Programs
P.O. Box 25494 (800) 544-0155
Richmond, VA 23260 (703) 528-4300

The Center supports professional initiatives in infant health, mental health and development. Project Zero to Three, funded by the Bureau of Maternal and Child Health and Resources Development, focuses on infants who are disabled or at risk. Publications are available on clinical issues targeted at disciplines concerned with infants, toddlers, and their families.

* Infant Care

Superintendent of Documents
Government Printing Office
Washington, DC 20402 (202) 783-3238

Infant Care has been updated and rewritten especially for today's new parents. It presents the latest information on caring for a new baby from birth through the first year. Special attention is given to the all-important first few weeks of life, including advice on feeding and bathing a newborn and the minor illnesses and injuries that are common to infants. Topics covered include: before your baby arrives, caring for your baby, understanding baby's growth and development, your baby's health, keeping baby safe, emergencies and first aid, and changes you and your family face (S/N 017-091-00241-0, $4).

* Infertility and Population Research

Reproductive Sciences Branch
Center for Population Research
6130 Executive Blvd., Room 603

Be patient. If any phone number is incorrect, call (area code) 555-1212 and request the new listing.

Contraception and Pregnancy

Bethesda, MD 20892 (301) 496-6515

The Reproductive Sciences Branch supports basic research in reproductive sciences, such as the alleviation of human infertility, curing human reproductive diseases and disorders, development of healthy embryos, and the discovery of safe methods of contraception. Institutional Programs in Reproductive Sciences Research awards grants to leading institutions in the U.S. to help them to establish Program Projects and Research Centers to support research on reproductive sciences. They also support postdoctoral fellowships, institutional training grants, and other awards to facilitate the development and maintenance of reproductive sciences research programs. This Branch also organizes workshops and symposiums in the U.S. and abroad on various topics in the reproductive sciences.

* Infertility and Treatments

Office of Consumer Affairs
Food and Drug Administration
Public Inquiries
5600 Fishers Lane (HFE-88)
Rockville, MD 20857 (301) 443-3170

Single copies are available free of the two-page pamphlet, *Infertility and How It's Treated* (No. 83-3136).

* Maternal and Child Health Clearinghouse

National Clearinghouse for Maternal and
Child Health
38th and R St., NW
Washington, DC 20057 (202) 625-8410

This clearinghouse is a centralized source of materials and information in the areas of human genetics and maternal and child health. The clearinghouse responds to inquiries, distributes publications, bibliographies, and referral lists, which are compiled on an in-house, online database for related materials.

* Norplant

Center for Drug Evaluation and Research
HFD-8, Food and Drug Administration
5600 Fishers Lane
Rockville, MD 20857 (301) 295-8012

This Center can provide you with free reports and information regarding the new contraception called Norplant. Reports include information on patient labeling, prescribing, usage, warnings, and FDA statements regarding Norplant. The Contraceptive Development Branch of the Center for Population Research is beginning to conduct research regarding who chooses to use Norplant, and who chooses to discontinue it. They can be contacted at 9000 Rockville Pike, Bethesda, MD 20892; (301) 496-1661.

* Nutrition During Pregnancy

National Clearinghouse for Maternal and
Child Health
38th and R St., NW
Washington, DC 20057 (202) 625-8410

Nutrition During Pregnancy: Weight Gain, Nutrient Supplements summarizes the nutritional recommendations during pregnancy.

* Nutrition in Early Childhood

National Maternal and Child Health Clearinghouse
38th and R Sts., NW
Washington, DC 20057 (202) 625-8410

This Clearinghouse has two free publications concerned with childhood nutrition. *Nutritional Disorders of Children: Prevention, Screening, and Follow-up*, and *Nutrition Resources for Early Childhood - Resource Guide*, which is an annotated list of current nutrition education publication for children ages 1-5 years, their parents, caregivers, and teachers.

* Pediatric and Maternal AIDS

Pediatric, Adolescent, and Maternal AIDS Branch
Center for Research for Mothers and Children
National Institute of Child Health and Human Development
National Institutes of Health
9000 Rockville Pike
Bethesda, MD 20892 (301) 496-7339

This new Branch conducts research on AIDS and AIDS related viruses in pregnant women, mothers, infants, children, adolescents and the family unit as a whole and works towards providing a more precise understanding of the modes of transmission. This Branch strives to address areas which are unique to the maternal-child dyad, to the at-risk and infected adolescent, and to groups traditionally of special concern to pediatricians (hemophiliac children). A report to Council is available describing research efforts and goals. This office can provide you with current research, refer you to experts or provide you with information regarding clinical trials.

* Population Research: Fertility, Contraception

Center for Population Research (CPR)
Executive Plaza North
Room 604
Bethesda, MD 20892 (301) 496-1101

The Center for Population Research, as part of the National Institute of Child Health and Human Development, is responsible for the extramural effort in population research. It funds research through grants and contracts for studies on fertility, contraception, and population structure and change. The Interagency Committee on Population Research, a committee of Federal Agencies, facilitates the exchange of information on population research, which includes producing two free publications: *The Inventory and Analysis of Federal Population Research* which lists all the federally supported population research projects; and *The Inventory of Private Agency Population Research* which lists research projects by private organizations. CPR also advances international cooperation in population research and collaborates with the World Health Organization regarding the development of safe methods of contraception.

* Pregnancy and Childbirth Health Resources

National Health Information Center
P.O. Box 1133 (800) 336-4797
Washington, DC 20013 (301) 565-4167 in MD

In its series, "Healthfinder", the center publishes *Women's Health* which lists many organizations that provide information on a broad range of topics including pregnancy and childbirth. This 6-page reference illustrates the array of organizations which offer expertise and information.

* Pregnancy and Infancy Resources

Pregnancy and Perinatology Branch
National Institute of Child Health and Human Development
Room 643, EPN Building
9000 Rockville Pike
Bethesda, MD 20892 (301) 496-5575

Information on pregnancy, birth, and infant development and disorders is available through the Pregnancy and Perinatology Branch. They have brochures, pamphlets, reports, and information on current research. The research in this branch focuses on high-risk pregnancies, fetal pathophysiology, premature birth and labor, disorders of the newborn, sudden infant death syndrome, and AIDS. A report to Council is available which describes the research conducted.

* Pregnancy Basics

National Institutes of Child Health and Human Development
National Institutes of Health
Building 31, Room 2A32
9000 Rockville Pike
Bethesda, MD 20892 (301) 496-5133

Pregnancy Basics: What you need to know and do to have a good healthy baby is a free booklet which examines weight gain, vitamins, nutrition, exercise, smoking, drinking, drugs, and X-rays.

* Pregnancy-Related Deaths Investigation

Center for Chronic Disease Prevention and Health Promotion
Centers for Disease Control
1600 Clifton Rd, NE
Bldg 3, Room 117
Atlanta, GA 30333 (404) 488-5188

The National Maternal Mortality Surveillance System is maintained as an avenue for reporting pregnancy-related deaths in the United States. All reported deaths are investigated, and a liaison has been established with local and national organizations of obstetricians and gynecologists to improve obstetric practices.

Be patient. If any phone number is incorrect, call (area code) 555-1212 and request the new listing.

Health and Medicine

* Premature Birth

National Institute of Child Health and Human Development
National Institutes of Health
9000 Rockville Pike
Bethesda, MD 20892 (301) 496-5133

This institute has much information about premature labor and birth including two free booklets: *Little Babies Born Too Soon, Born Too Small* (No. 77-1079) and *Facts About Premature Birth*.

* Prenatal Care

National Clearinghouse for Maternal and Child Health
38th and R Sts. NW
Washington, DC 20057 (202) 625-8410

The Clearinghouse has an extensive list of free publications dealing with prenatal care, including:

Advances in the Prevention of Low Birthweight: An International Symposium
Caring for Our Future: The Content of Prenatal Care
Prenatal Care
Prenatal Care - Resource Guide
Prevention of Hemolytic Disease of the Fetus and Newborn due to RH Isoimmunization

* Prenatal Care: Government's Bestseller

National Clearinghouse for Maternal and Child Health
38th and R St., NW
Washington, DC 20057 (202) 625-8410

This clearinghouse makes available free single copies of *Prenatal Care* (Pub. No. H50), the federal government's popular 98-page "Dr. Spock" which provides basic information to pregnant women on caring for herself and her unborn baby. This booklet (No. 186P) is also available for $2.50 from the Consumer Information Center, Dept. Z, Pueblo, CO 81009. The Spanish version, *Cuidado Prenatal* (Stock No. 017-091-00209-6) is available for $4.50 from the Superintendent of Documents, Government Printing Office, Washington, DC 20402, (202) 783-3238.

* Prenatal Care: Technical Assistance

National Center for Chronic Disease Prevention
and Health Promotion
Centers for Disease Control (CDC)
1600 Clifton Rd., NW
Room 1113C
Atlanta, GA 30333 (404) 488-5086

This CDC center offers technical assistance and expertise on reproductive health as well as in health promotion and health education. Primary recipients of technical assistance are official state and local health agencies, schools, and health care delivery settings. The Center maintains a database of health education programs and methods in schools and rural and urban communities, which is part of the Combined Health Information Database (CHID).

* Preterm and Low Birth Weight Infants

National Clearinghouse on Maternal and Child Health
38th and R Sts., NW
Washington, DC 20057 (202) 625-8410

Each year in the United States, nearly seven percent of all babies are born weighing less than five and one-half pounds. *Preterm and Low Birthweight Infants - Resource Guide* includes an annotated listing of selected educational materials and a list of genetic services providers and voluntary and professional organizations, which may be able to provide additional information. Federal and state government maternal and child health agencies may also be able to provide further information.

* Sonograms and Its Effects on Pregnancy

National Institute of Child Health and
Human Development (NICHHD)
Office of Research Reporting, Building 31, Room 2A-32
9000 Rockville Pike
Bethesda, MD 20892 (301) 496-5133

This office distributes a 1984 NICHHD conference report entitled, *Diagnostic Ultrasound Imaging in Pregnancy*, which discusses the biophysics and bioeffects of sonograms, clinical applications, epidemiological studies, and the psychological, legal, and ethical dimensions of ultrasound imaging. A brief pamphlet, *The Unknowns of Ultrasound* (No. 83-8201) is also available free.

* Sterilization Operations

Family Life Information Exchange
P.O. Box 30146
Bethesda, MD 20814 (301) 585-6636

Information for Men-Your Sterilization Operation (FP-100014) is available in English and Spanish and includes 3-part consent form used for all federally funded vasectomies. *Information for Women-Your Sterilization Operation* (No 10015) provides information on tubal ligation and other methods of birth control. It is also available in Spanish.

* Sudden Infant Death Syndrome (SIDS)

National Sudden Infant Death Syndrome Clearinghouse
8201 Greensboro Dr., Suite 600
McLean, VA 22102 (703) 821-8955

This clearinghouse was established to provide information and educational materials on SIDS, apnea, and other related issues. The staff responds to information requests from professionals, families with SIDS-related deaths, and the general public by sending written materials and making referrals. The clearinghouse maintains a library of reference materials and mailing lists of state programs, groups, and individuals concerned with SIDS. Their many publications include bibliographies on SIDS and self-help support groups, a publications catalogue, and a newsletter. The free publications include:

Crib Death - explains SIDS in easy to read booklet form.

Directory of State Title V Maternal and Child Health Directors and SIDS Program Coordinators - lists MCH directors and SIDS coordinators by state; Federal and Federally supported programs; and private SIDS and SIDS-related programs.

Examination of the SIDS Infant: Investigative and Autopsy Protocols - reports the results of a 1975 national conference.

Fact Sheet: Facts about Apnea and Other Apparent Life-Threatening Events.

Fact Sheet: Grief of Children - discusses some of the common expressions of children's grief and offers way in which adults can help during the grieving process.

Fact Sheet: Parents and The Grieving Process - defines grief, presents common reactions and emotions expressed by people who are bereaved, and highlights the process by which resolution and recovery may be achieved.

Fact Sheet: SIDS Information for the EMT - provides suggestions for first response of EMTs and others at the time of sudden infant death.

Fact Sheet: What Is SIDS? - provides basic facts about SIDS and discusses reactions of the surviving family members and ways they can be helped.

FDA Safety Alert: Important Tips for Apnea Monitor Users - lists important tips to help parents and caregivers understand the limitations of infant apnea monitors and offers guidelines for their proper use.

A Guide to Resources in Perinatal Bereavement - offers selected resources for professionals working with parents who have lost a child.

Infantile Apnea and Home Monitoring-Consensus Statement - Statement form the October 1986 National Institutes of Health Consensus Development Conference on Infantile Apnea and Home Monitoring.

Information Exchange - Quarterly newsletter of SIDS Clearinghouse.

Joint Hearing on SIDS Before the Committees on Post Office and Civil Service, Committee on Energy and Commerce, and the Select Committee on Children, Youth, and Families, 99th Congress - Testimony to bring the issue of SIDS into the public domain, to generate support for educating the public and professionals about SIDS, and to encourage further research.

Los Hechos Sobre El Sindrome De La Muerte Infantil Repentina - Spanish translation of a basic brochure containing information about SIDS.

Muerte En La Cuna - Spanish translation of Crib Death.

Be patient. If any phone number is incorrect, call (area code) 555-1212 and request the new listing.

Contraception and Pregnancy

Nosology Guideline - supplement to the medical examiner's cause-of-death coding manual describing death certificate coding information for SIDS.

Sudden Infant Death Syndrome and Other Infant Losses Among Adolescent Parents: An Annotated Bibliography and Resource Guide - presents an overview of adolescent bereavement, abstract of articles, and resources for adolescents.

Sudden Unexplained Infant Death 1970-1975: An Evolution of Understanding - examines changes in understanding of sudden, unexpected, and unexplained infant death.

Talking to Children About Death - booklet helps prepare parents and other adults to talk to children about death.

* Teenage Pregnancy Prevention Grants

Adolescent Pregnancy Programs
PHS, Room 736E
200 Independence Ave., SW
Washington, DC 20201   (202) 245-7473

This office awards grants to private and public non-profit organizations to establish and operate voluntary family planning services. The Adolescent Family Life Program supports research projects and innovative family-centered, community-based demonstration projects to provide either care or prevention services for adolescents and their families.

* Toxoplasmosis and Birth Defects

National Institute of Allergy and Infectious Diseases
National Institutes of Health
Building 31, Room 7A-32
9000 Rockville Pike,
Bethesda, MD 20892   (301) 496-5717

A five-page booklet, *Toxoplasmosis*, (Pub. No. 83-308) discusses the hazards to the fetus of the toxoplasma parasites and suggests precautions to prevent the disease. Single copy available free from the institute.

* Workplace Hazards: Fetal Development and Pregnancy

National Institute for Occupational Safety
and Health (NIOSH)
4676 Columbia Parkway
Cincinnati, OH 45226   (800) 356-4674

NIOSH is responsible for conducting research to make the nation's workplaces healthier and safer by responding to urgent requests for assistance from employers, employees, and their representatives where imminent hazards are suspected. They conduct inspections, laboratory and epidemiologic research, publish their findings, and make recommendations for improved working conditions to regulatory agencies. NIOSH trains occupational health and safety workers and communicates research results to those concerned.

Health and Medicine

Stress, Mental Illness, and Family Violence

The National Institute of Mental Health of the National Institutes of Health is a useful starting place for discovering other information resources. Local and state chapters of the National Mental Health Association provide assistance to the mentally ill and their families, and provide help to school systems and local governments. Many county and state governments offer counseling and other services.

* Adolescent Violence and Death

National Technical Information Service
U.S. Department of Commerce
Springfield, VA 22161

Focal Points provides information on violence as a public health problem, particularly in the area of reducing the deaths of those in the 15-24 age group. Stress reduction and other programs that prevent violence are described. This publication (Order No.PB84-158385) is available for $7.

* Anger and Aggression

Public Inquiries Branch
National Institute of Mental Health
Parklawn Building
5600 Fishers Lane Room 15C-05
Rockville, MD 20857 (301) 443-4513

This Institute publishes several free pamphlets including *Plain Talk About Adolescence.*

* Biofeedback and Stress Reduction

Public Inquiries Branch
National Institute of Mental Health
Parklawn Building
5600 Fishers Lane Room 15C-05
Rockville, MD 20857 (301) 443-4513

Plain Talk About Handling Stress discusses the stages of physical and mental stress, describes the symptoms and offers suggestions for stress reduction. This is available free from the Institute, as is *Plain Talk About the Art of Relaxation.*

* Charla Franca: Como Tratar Al Nino Enojado

Public Inquiries Branch
National Institute of Mental Health
Parklawn Building
5600 Fishers Lane Room 15C-05
Rockville, MD 20857 (301) 443-4513

The Spanish version of *Plain Talk About Dealing With The Angry Child* (Pub No. 81-78 SP) is available free. The Institute publishes other pamphlets in Spanish.

* Cheap Mental Health Publications

R. Woods
Consumer Information Center-2A
P.O. Box 100
Pueblo, CO 81002

The Consumer Information Catalog is a catalog of free and low-cost federal publications of consumer interest. A new catalog is published each quarter, and is available free of charge. The publications they have available dealing with mental health include:

A Consumer's Guide to Mental Health Services (562Y)
Plain Talk About Depression (563Y)
Plain Talk About the Stigma of Mental Illness (565Y)
Plain Talk About Stress (566Y)
Plain Talk About Wife Abuse (567Y)
Schizophrenia: Questions and Answers (568Y)
What to Do When a Friend is Depressed (569Y)

* Child Abuse Prevention Programs

Clearinghouse on Child Abuse and Neglect
Administration for Children, Youth, and Families
P.O. Box 1182
Washington, DC 20013 (800) FYI-3366

The National Center on Child Abuse and Neglect (NCCAN) awards grants to states for a variety of programs dealing with child abuse and neglect; conducts research into the causes, prevention, and treatment of child abuse and neglect; funds demonstration programs to identify the best means of preventing maltreatment and treating troubled families; and funds the development and implementation of training programs. It distributes information through the Clearinghouse on Child Abuse and Neglect Information.

* Child Abuse and Neglect Clearinghouse

Clearinghouse on Child Abuse and Neglect Information
P.O. Box 1182
Washington, DC 20013 (800) FYI-3366

The Clearinghouse on Child Abuse and Neglect Information is a major resource for both professionals and the general public interested in child maltreatment issues. Publications distributed include bibliographies, training materials, and research reviews. The clearinghouse maintains a database (Dialogue File 64) from which they can retrieve information on specific topics. Contact this office for a free listing of their publications and other resources.

* Child Abuse Resources for Professionals

National Child Abuse and Neglect
Clinical Resource Center
1205 Oneida St.
Denver, CO 80220 (303) 321-3963

This center focuses on clinical issues by providing training and consultation on a fee-for-service basis and through networking of streamlining resources and referrals. Program and case consultation is provided at the Center or by phone (they have a WATS line) for a fee. An annual symposium and a scholars-in-residence program provides professionals and lay persons the opportunity to observe and participate in the Center's activities, which include workshops, seminars, and professional education. The Center's resource library offers audiovisual rentals and a free publications catalog.

* Child Abuse Signs and Symptoms

Clearinghouse on Child Abuse and Neglect Information
P.O. Box 1182
Washington, DC 20013 (800) FYI-3366

Child Abuse and Neglect: An Informed Approach To A Shared Concern is a free pamphlet providing information about detecting child abuse and how to obtain help.

* Child Adoption, Foster Care and Welfare

Children's Bureau
Administration for Children, Youth, and Families
Office of Human Development Services
P.O. Box 1182
Washington, DC 20013 (202) 245-0656

The Children's Bureau funds a range of state-run programs combatting child abuse and neglect, strengthening foster care and adoption services, and supporting other child welfare services.

Be patient. If any phone number is incorrect, call (area code) 555-1212 and request the new listing.

Stress, Mental Illness, and Family Violence

* Children of Alcoholic Families

National Clearinghouse on Alcohol Information
PO Box 2345 (800) 729-6686
Rockville, MD 20852 (301) 468-2600

A Growing Concern: How to Provide Services for Children of Alcoholic Families discusses issues and strategies for providing help to youngsters from homes with alcoholism. This 52-page booklet (Order No. PH196) is geared more to professionals and caregivers and is free.

* Child Sexual Abuse Info Center

National Resource Center on Child Sexual Abuse
Information Service
106 Lincoln St. (205) 533-KIDS
Huntsville, AL 35801 (800) KIDS-0006

The NRCCSA is an information, training, and technical assistance center designed for all professionals working in the field of child sexual abuse. They provide an array of services to help professionals better to investigate and manage child sexual victimization cases. The Information Service handles requests for information, and for a quarterly publication, *Roundtable*, which offers information, updates, and new developments on child abuse. This office also sponsors comprehensive training with national experts and leading professionals. Some of the publications available include:

National Directory of Child Sexual Abuse Treatment Programs - annotated listing of treatment programs ($25).

Think Tank Reports ($12 each)

Allegations of Sexual Abuse in Child Custody and Visitation Situations
Child Protective Services: A System in Crisis
A Judicial Response to Child Sexual Abuse
Enhancing Child Sexual Abuse Services to Minority Cultures
Investigation of Ritualistic Abuse Allegations
Sibling Incest
Professionals and Volunteers with a History of Abuse
Traditional Native American Healing and Child Sexual Abuse
A Coordinated Community Approach to Child Sexual Abuse: Assessing a Model

Building Blocks - history of National Children's Advocacy Center and explanation of current procedures ($12).

Best Practices: A Guidebook to Establishing a Children's Advocacy Center Program - designed to provide technical assistance ($50).

* Child Victimization and Exploitation

Paul and Lisa, Inc.
P.O. Box 348
Westbrook, CT 06498

Child victimization and exploitation are staggering problems in the United States. Paul and Lisa, Inc., is working to eliminate child prostitution, child pornography, exploitation, and abuse. The program has five components: intervention/ education, streetwork outreach, counseling/referral, rehabilitation, and reunification of children with their families or alternate placements, if necessary. This is funded in part by the Office of Juvenile Justice and Delinquency Prevention of the U.S. Department of Justice, (202) 307-5914.

* Community Mental Health Help

Consumer Information Center
Dept. Z
Pueblo, CO 81009

A Consumer's Guide to Mental Health Services describes the services available from community mental health centers, details different kinds of therapy and mental health professionals, and provides a list of warning signals and tells what to do in a crisis situation. This 21-page booklet is available free.

* Crisis Counseling Grants and Materials

Emergency Services Branch
National Institute of Mental Health
5600 Fishers Lane, Room 11C25
Rockville, MD 20857 (301) 443-4735

The Emergency Services Branch oversees three programs: 1) The Emergency Research Program studies the psychosocial response to mass emergencies; 2) The Crisis Counseling Program administers crisis counseling grants to states in which there has been a Presidentially-declared disaster; 3) The Emergency Preparedness Program plans for alcohol, drug abuse, and mental health disaster-related services nationwide. The program provides technical assistance and public education materials to states and local agencies in times of emergencies, and has three publications designed for non-mental health emergency workers (police, fire, emergency medical personnel) which focus on mental health issues. The following free publications are available:

Crisis Intervention Programs for Disaster Victims in Smaller Communities
Disaster Work and Mental Health: Prevention and Control of Stress Among Workers
Field Manual for Human Service Workers in Major Disasters
Human Problems in Major Disasters: A Training Curriculum for Emergency Medical Personnel
Innovations in Mental Health Services to Disaster Victims
Manual for Child Health Workers in Major Disasters
Prevention and Control of Stress Among Emergency Workers: A Pamphlet for Team Managers
Prevention and Control of Stress Among Emergency Workers: A Pamphlet for Workers
Role Stressors and Supports for Emergency Workers
Training Manual for Human Service Workers in Major Disasters

* Death and Grieving

National Sudden Infant Death Syndrome Clearinghouse
8201 Greensboro Drive
Suite 600
McLean, VA 22102 (703) 821-8955

The Grief of Children discusses some of the ways that children express grief and that adults can help. Two other short pamphlets available free are *Parents and the Grieving Process* and *Talking to Children About Death*.

* Depression: Diagnosis and Treatments

National Institute of Mental Health (NIMH)
Alcohol, Drug Abuse and Mental Health Administration
5600 Fishers Lane, Room 15C05
Rockville, MD 20857 (301) 443-4515

NIMH conducts research on depression and other mental disorders, distributes information, conducts demonstration programs for the prevention, treatment, and rehabilitation of the mentally ill. A major media campaign on depression, called Project D/ART (Depression/Awareness, Recognition, Treatment), is being developed by NIMH in collaboration with other organizations to provide information on symptoms, causes, and treatments of various depressive disorders. Many publications and reports are available on various topics for professionals and the general public. Some of the publications available include:

Affective Disorders: Recent Research and Related Developments
Beating Depression: New Treatments Bring Success
Bipolar Disorder: Manic-Depressive Illness
D/ART Fact Sheet
Depression: It's a Disease and It Can Be Treated
Depressive Illnesses: Treatments Bring New Hope
Helpful Facts About Depressive Disorders
Helping the Depressed Person Get Treatment
If You're Over 65 and Feeling Depressed...Treatment Brings New Hope
Let's Talk About Depression
Plain Talk About Depression
What to do When A Friend is Depressed: A Guide for Teenagers

* Elderly Alcohol Abuse

Information Center
National Institute on Aging
2209 Distribution Circle
Silver Spring, MD 20910 (301) 495-3455

Aging and Alcohol Abuse is a one-page information sheet available free from the National Institute on Aging.

* Emotional Problems and Self-Help

National Technical Information Service
U.S. Department of Commerce
Springfield, VA 22161

Health and Medicine

Self-help Groups As a Vehicle for Helping Individuals Cope with Emotional Problems discusses the potential for helping emotionally troubled individuals. This publication is available for $6.

* Family Adjustment and Crisis

Family Information Center
U.S. Department of Agriculture
National Agricultural Library Building,
Room 304
Beltsville, MD 20705 (301) 344-3719

This Center has information for the public on family adjustment to change and management of stress, as well as family and individual anxieties concerning midlife crisis and the aging process. Publications for professionals include *Special Reference Briefs* on critical aspects and stages of family life.

* Family Violence Treatment

Superintendent of Documents
Government Printing Office
Washington, DC 20402 (202) 783-3238

Treating Family Violence in a Pediatric Hospital: A Program of Training, Research, and Services describes a training program at Children's Hospital in Boston that provides services for the treatment of family violence in a pediatric hospital setting. It is intended for program directors, clinical practitioners, clinical researchers and trainers, and graduate schools of nursing psychiatry, psychology, and social work in connection with training in the area of family violence.

* Mental Health Databases

National Institute of Mental Health
Parklawn Building, Room 15C-05
5600 Fishers Lane
Rockville, MD 20857 (301) 443-4515

This Institute maintains databases which index and abstract documents from the worldwide literature pertaining to mental health. In addition to scientific journals, there are references to audiovisuals, dissertations, government documents and reports. Mental Health Abstracts is available on DIALOG and another commerical vendor, BRS, offers the National Institute of Mental Health database.

* Mental Health Directory

Superintendent of Documents
Washington, DC 20402 (202) 783-3238

Mental Health Directory 1990 is a comprehensive listing, by State, of outpatient mental health clinics, psychiatric hospitals, Veterans Administration medical centers, residential treatment centers for emotionally disturbed children, mental health day/night facilities, community mental health centers, and general hospitals with separate psychiatric services (017-024-01419-2, $23).

* Mental Health Publications

National Institute of Mental Health (NIMH)
5600 Fishers Lane, Room 15C-05
Rockville, MD 20857 (301) 443-4515

NIMH has a catalogue of free publications available dealing with a wide range of mental health issues. Some of the general publications available include:

A Consumer's Guide to Mental Health Services
Obsessive-Compulsive Disorder: Useful Information from the NIMH
Plain Talk About Aging
Plain Talk About Handling Stress
Plain Talk About Physical Fitness and Mental Health
Plain Talk About Mutual Help Groups
Plain Talk About the Art of Relaxation
Plain Talk About Wife Abuse
Useful Information on Anorexia Nervosa and Bulimia
Useful Information on Medications for Mental Illness
Useful Information on Paranoia
Useful Information on Sleep Disorders
You Are Not Alone: Facts About Mental Health and Mental Illness
Information Packet on Use of Mental Health Services by Children and Adolescents
National Plan for Research on Child and Adolescent Mental Disorders
Working Bibliography on Behavioral and Emotional Disorders and Assessment Instruments in Mental Retardation

Caring for People with Severe Mental Disorders: A National Plan of Research to Improve Services

Subscriptions

ADAMHA News ($6/yr) - Monthly newsletter of the Alcohol, Drug Abuse, and Mental Health Administration which provides coverage of events, research findings, budget, legislation, etc.

Psychopharmacology Bulletin ($18/yr) - disseminates research findings, with some issues focusing on the New Clinical Drug Evaluation Unit meeting.

Both subscriptions available from: Superintendent of Documents, Government Printing Office, Washington, DC 20402; (202) 7834-3238.

* Mental Health Videos

National Institute of Mental Health (NIMH)
Technical Services Branch
5600 Fishers Lane
Room 14-105
Rockville, MD 20857 (301) 443-4183

NIMH maintains a collection of videotapes, including public service announcements. If you want to order audiovisual materials, include in your order a blank videocassette with enough minutes on it to tape the materials you request.

Just Like You and Me (32 minutes) - features former mental patients who have made transition from hospitalization back to the community through the Transitional Employment Program.

Making the Numbers Work for You (35 minutes) - points out the need for timely, accurate statistical information from each State. Such information assists the Federal Government to compile figures on the needs and opportunities in promoting better mental health.

More Than A Grant (19 minutes) - describes some of the institute's programs and should encourage Historically Black Colleges and Universities faculties and students to explore ways of obtaining support for research projects in the field of mental health.

More Than A Passing Acquaintance (24 minutes) - story of how one community support program meets the challenge in providing services and opportunities for person who have made the transition from hospitalization back into the community.

Windows Into the Brain (19 minutes) - tells the story of three decades of scientific advances in brain imaging techniques.

Public Service Announcements (60 second and 30 second) - developed as part of the Anti-Stigma campaign, these announcements describe why people should not be "labeled" as former mental patients.

* Mental Illness and Attitudes

National Institute of Mental Health (NIMH)
5600 Fishers Lane, Room 15C05
Rockville, MD 20857 (301) 443-4515

NIMH has several free publications dealing with the stigma of mental illness and attitudes towards it. Some of the publications include:

Affirmative Action to Employ Mentally Restored People
Eight Questions Employers Ask About Hiring the Mentally Restored
Plain Talk About the Stigma of Mental Illness
The 14 Worst Myths About Recovered Mental Patients
The Mentally Restored and Work: A Successful Partnership
You Are Not Alone: Facts About Mental Health and Mental Illness

* Mental Illness and Medications

National Institute of Mental Health
5600 Fishers Lane, Room 15C-05
Rockville, MD 20857 (301) 443-4515

Medications for Mental Illness: What You Should Know About the Drugs Doctors Prescribe for Anxiety, Depression, Schizophrenia and Other Mental Disorders is a free booklet designed to help people understand how and why drugs can be used as part of the treatment for mental health problems. It includes questions you

Stress, Mental Illness, and Family Violence

should ask your doctor, and provides information on different classes of drugs, and things needing special consideration.

* Mental Retardation Services

President's Committee on Mental Retardation
330 Independence Ave., SW
Room 4262, North Building
Washington, DC 20201 (202) 619-0634

The President's Committee on Mental Retardation has information on prevention of biomedical and environmental causes of retardation, and family and community support services. Materials are also available on the legal rights of the mentally retarded and employment programs.

* Mental Retardation Research and Clearinghouse

Mental Retardation Research Centers
National Institute of Child Health and Human Development
Executive Plaza North, Room 631
6130 Executive Blvd.
Bethesda, MD 20897 (301) 496-1383

The Mental Retardation Research Centers are designed to further the understanding, treatment, and prevention of mental retardation. They are a combination of organized research and medical service programs, bringing the mentally retarded in contact with medical and behavioral specialists. The Centers offer programs to train medical students and postdoctoral fellows. Contact this office for a list of the Centers and information on current research.

* Physical Fitness and Mental Health

National Institute of Mental Health
5600 Fishers Lane, Room 15C05
Rockville, MD 20857 (301) 443-4515

Plain Talk About Physical Fitness and Mental Health presents ideas about exercise and its connection to mental stability, particularly for special groups of people. Single copies of this brief brochure (Order No. 84-1364) is available free.

* Runaway Hotline for Parents and Youngsters

(800) 621-4000

The National Runaway Hotline provides information and resources to parents and runaways. It will deliver messages to parents from their children and offer advice to runaways regarding places to go for help. The Hotline operates 24 hours a day, and all information is confidential.

* Runaway and Homeless Youth Shelters

Division of Runaway Youth Programs
Administration for Children, Youth and Families
P.O. Box 1182
Washington, DC 20013 (202) 245-0102

The Division of Runaway Youth Programs provides federal grants to states, communities, and public and private organizations to establish and operate runaway and homeless youth shelters. This year's budget is for $26 million. An annual report is available which lists all the grantees.

* Schizophrenia

National Institute of Mental Health (NIMH)
5600 Fishers Lane, Room 15C-05
Rockville, MD 20857 (301) 443-4515

NIMH supports research on the causes and new treatments of schizophrenia. They have produced several free publications dealing with schizophrenia, including:

A National Plan for Schizophrenia Research: Panel Recommendations
A National Plan for Schizophrenia Research: Report of the National Advisory Mental Health Council
Schizophrenia: Questions and Answers
Special Report: Schizophrenia 1987

Schizophrenia Bulletin (four issues, $19/yr) - publishes articles on all facets of schizophrenia research and treatment (available from: Superintendent of Documents, Government Printing Office, Washington, DC 20402; (202) 783-3238).

* Schizophrenia Research

Schizophrenia Research Branch
Division of Clinical Research
National Institute of Mental Health
Parklawn Building, Room 10C-16
5600 Fishers Lane
Rockville, MD 20857 (301) 443-4707

This research bureau has news of the latest medical research into schizophrenia, however, access to this information is limited to mental health professionals and researchers.

* State Mental Institutions Survey

Surveys and Reports Branch
National Institute of Mental Health
Parklawn Building, Room 18C-07
5600 Fishers Lane
Rockville, MD 20857 (301) 443-4707

This office has data on mental health facilities and generates the annual Census of State Mental Health Hospitals, which provides characteristics of patients.

* Stress in the Workplace

Superintendent of Documents
Government Printing Office
Washington, DC 20402 (202) 783-3238

Stress Management in Work Settings summarizes and reviews scientific evidence and practical issues relating to worksite stress management. It contains a collection of resources for training materials, products, and equipment (S/N 017-033-00428-5, $9.50).

* Stress Management Publications

Superintendent of Documents
US Government Printing Office
Washington, DC 20402

Stress Management in Work Settings summarizes scientific evidence and reviews conceptual and practical issues relating to worksite stress management. (Order No. 017-033-00428-5; $9.50)

An Evaluation Handbook for Health Education Programs in Stress Management (Order No. PB84-171735; $31) gives information on how to examine and evaluate stress management programs.

* Wife Beating and Elder Abuse Help Center

Clearinghouse on Family Violence Information
P.O. Box 1182
Washington, DC 20013 (703) 385-7565

This clearinghouse has information on spouse and elder abuse. They have brochures and audiovisual materials available, and an in-house database from which they can retrieve reference materials and organizations involved with family violence. The publications available include:

Calendar of Conferences on Child Protection and Family Violence Issues ($1)
Child Abuse Prevention, Adoption, and Family Services Act of 1988
Child Abuse and Neglect and Family Violence Audiovisual Catalog ($20)
Family Violence Public Awareness Materials for Adults and Children ($3)
Child Abuse and Neglect and Family Violence Thesaurus ($25)
Classic Literature in Family Violence: Annotated Bibliography ($1)
Databases Containing Family Violence Information: Annotated Bibliography ($1)
State Legislative Solutions to the Problem of Family Violence: Annotated Bibliography ($1.80)
Family Violence: An Overview
Organizations Concerned with Child Abuse and Neglect and Family Violence Issues ($5.50)
Family Violence Research Instruments With Bibliography ($1.50)

Bibliographies
Abuse of the Elderly ($7)
Adult Protective Services ($1)
Battered Woman Syndrome ($1)
Causes and Definitions ($2.50)
Characteristics of Abusers ($4.50)
Characteristics of Victims ($3)

Be patient. If any phone number is incorrect, call (area code) 555-1212 and request the new listing.

Health and Medicine

Child Witnesses of Family Violence ($2)
Conjugal Homicide ($1)
Crisis Intervention ($1)
Curricula/Training Materials ($4.50)
Effects of Family Violence ($5)
Family Violence and the Clergy ($1)
Family Violence Prevention ($3)
Family Violence Research ($7.50)
Government Policy and Legislation ($2.50)
Intervention with Children From Violent Homes ($2.50)
Legal Issues in Family Violence ($7.50)

Marital Rape and Sexual Assault ($1.50)
Medical Aspects of Family Violence ($2.50)
Multidisciplinary Approaches ($1)
Police Procedures for Domestic Calls ($5)
Resources for Assisting Ethnic Populations ($2)
Shelter Programs for Victims ($1.50)
Statistical Studies in Family Violence ($3)
Substance Abuse and Family Violence ($2)
Therapeutic Alternatives for Victims ($3)
Therapy for Batterers ($3)

Be patient. If any phone number is incorrect, call (area code) 555-1212 and request the new listing.

AIDS, Cancer and Other Diseases

Many of the offices and publications listed here will direct you to numerous non-profit and private organizations which also offer information and expertise. The National Health Information Center, for example, suggests interested individuals contact the American Red Cross for a series of brochures on the *Latest Facts About AIDS* which are produced jointly with the U.S. Public Health Service. Similarly, the National Cancer Institute will refer callers to such national groups as the American Lung Association and the American Heart Association.

* Acne and Skin Disease Prevention and Treatment

National Institute of Arthritis and Musculoskeletal and Skin Diseases (NIAMS)
National Institutes of Health
Building 31, Room 4C05
9000 Rockville Pike
Bethesda, MD 20892 (301) 496-8188

The NIAMS conducts and supports basic and clinical research concerning the causes, prevention, diagnosis, and treatment of a large number of diseases, including acne and skin problems. Reports and brochures for professionals and the general public are available, along with an information specialist who can provide in-depth information on a variety of related topics.

* AIDS (Acquired Immune Deficiency Syndrome) Hotline

AIDS Hotline (800) 342-2437
(800) 344-7432 (Servicia en Espanol)
(800) 243-7889 (TTY Deaf Access)

For information, pamphlets, and reports about AIDS (Acquired Immune Deficiency Syndrome), call above toll-free number.

* AIDS and Criminal Justice Workers

National Institute of Justice Clearinghouse (301) 251-5500

NIJ AIDS Clearinghouse is the only centralized source of information on how AIDS affects criminal justice professionals and their work. Staff specialists with a broad knowledge of AIDS issues are available to answer questions, make referrals, and suggest publications pertaining to AIDS as it relates to the criminal justice system.

* AIDS and Dentistry

Dental Disease Prevention Activity
Center for Prevention Services
Centers for Disease Control
1600 Clifton Road NE
Atlanta, GA 30333 (404) 693-3534

Preventing the Transmission of Hepatitis B, AIDS, and Herpes in Dentistry offers 13 pages of advice on preventive measures for dental health care workers to minimize their risk of the transmission of these diseases to themselves, their families, and patients. Single copies are free.

* AIDS and Runaways

Research and Program Development Division
Office of Juvenile Justice and Delinquency Prevention
U.S. Department of Justice
633 Indiana Ave., NW
Washington, DC 20531 (202) 307-0586

Often runaways resort to supporting themselves through prostitution and selling illegal drugs, which they frequently use as well. Young people who engage in sexual activity with multiple partners and use intravenous drugs place themselves at great risk of contracting AIDS and spreading the disease to others. The Runaways Risk Reduction Project is documenting the obstacles faced by programs serving this population; the project is also identifying the most promising prevention and intervention strategies at each stage of contact with youth: outreach, crisis intervention, intermediate care, transitional living, and aftercare.

* AIDS and Sexually Transmitted Diseases Resource Center

(800) 227-8922

The Sexually Transmitted Diseases Hotline provides information and referrals for treatment of sexually transmitted diseases. They can refer callers to clinics, support groups, and other services, and offer brochures and pamphlets. Their hours are 8 am to 8 pm (Pacific Standard Time).

* AIDS and the Workplace

(800) 458-5231

The National AIDS Information Clearinghouse has just established a special resources center for businesses, called Business Response to AIDS Resource Services. They have information on workplace policy, as well as materials kits for employers, CEOs, managers and shop stewards. These kits will contain brochures, fact sheets, labor issues, and other helpful information (the CEOs kits will contain a video). This service can also refer you to resources in your State and locality, as well as nationally. Contact the number listed above for more information on there free services.

* AIDS Clinical Trials

(800) 874-2572

The AIDS Clinical Trials Information Services puts callers in touch with experienced health specialists who provide information about AIDS clinical trials. These specialists access a database featuring up-to-date, accurate information on AIDS studies currently underway. The Service's health specialists are available to answer questions from individuals infected with HIV and their families, as well as from health professionals. They provide information on the purpose of the study, studies that are open, study locations, eligibility requirements and exclusion criteria, and names and telephone numbers of contact persons. They provide information on what Clinical Trials are, and distribute two publications, *AIDS/HIV Clinical Trial Handbook,* and *AIDS/HIV Treatment Directory,* for the American Foundation for AIDS Research.

* AIDS Films and Videos

National AIDS Information Clearinghouse
P.O. Box 6003
Rockville, MD 20850 (800) 458-5231

The National AIDS Information Clearinghouse has access to information on over 300 AIDS films and videotapes, and can provide you with a printout of films and videos designed to target a specific audience, ranging from teenagers to physicians. Each listing includes information on the producer, year, source, audience, and availability, as well as an abstract. Contact the Clearinghouse for more information.

* AIDS Information Online

National AIDS Clearinghouse
P.O. Box 6003
Rockville, MD 20849 (800) 458-5231

NAC ONLINE is the clearinghouse's computerized information network through which users can gain direct access to Clearinghouse resources and services. NAC ONLINE provides the latest news and announcements about many critical HIV- and AIDS-related issues, including prevention and education campaigns, treatment and clinical trials, legislation and regulation, and upcoming events. To find out more about NAC ONLINE, ask for the Systems Coordinator.

Be patient. If any phone number is incorrect, call (area code) 555-1212 and request the new listing.

Health and Medicine

* AIDS Parent Guide

National AIDS Clearinghouse
P.O. Box 6003
Rockville, MD 20849 (800) 342-2437

AIDS Prevention Guide is written for parents and other adults concerned about young people. It provides ideas to help adults start a conversation about AIDS. It presents the facts about AIDS - geared to elementary and junior and senior high school students - and offers common questions and accurate answers. It includes handouts for young people aged 10 to 20 years.

* AIDS Prevention National Clearinghouse

Posters, Publications, Databases, Videos
National AIDS Information Clearinghouse
PO Box 6003 (301) 762-5111
Rockville, MD 20850 (800) 458-5231 (bulk orders)

A Center for Disease Control service, this clearinghouse has publications, posters, and videos dealing with AIDS which are free of charge. The publications include a fact sheet, guidelines for the prevention of the spread of AIDS in schools and the workplace, and the Surgeon General's report on AIDS. They have two online databases; one deals with organization, and the other lists unpublished educational materials (no journals). Publications and brochures available include:

HIV Infection and AIDS: Are You At Risk?
Voluntary HIV Counseling and Testing: Facts, Issues, and Answers
Women, Sex, and AIDS
The Connection Between TB and HIV
Condoms and Sexually Transmitted Diseases...Especially AIDS
Surgeon General's Report on Acquired Immune Deficiency Syndrome

An extensive list of posters, public service announcements (print, radio, VHS), and displays are also available. The Clearinghouse has a catalog of HIV/AIDS Materials for Professionals, which contains directories, reports, brochures, videotapes, and other resources.

* AIDS Prevention and Control National Program

Office of Public Affairs
Centers for Disease Control
1600 Clifton Rd.
Atlanta, GA 30333 (404) 693-3534

This government agency, Centers for Disease Control (CDC), is responsible for the prevention and control of AIDS, Acquired Immune Deficiency Syndrome. The CDC provides leadership to the national HIV prevention program by providing technical and financial assistance for HIV prevention activities to state and local health and education agencies and other organizations. They conduct surveillance of HIV infection, associated diseases, and death. The CDC conducts and supports epidemiology and laboratory studies and provides HIV prevention guidelines, recommendations, and training. The CDC performs national public information activities and evaluates programs. For an HIV operation plan and AIDS packet contact this office.

* AIDS Research Worldwide

National Institute of Allergy and
Infectious Diseases (NIAID)
National Institutes of Health
Building 31
Room 7A32
9000 Rockville Pike
Bethesda, MD 20892 (301) 496-5717

The NIAID conducts and supports research to study the causes of allergic, immunologic, and infectious diseases, and to develop better means of preventing, diagnosing, and treating illness. Some of the studies look at the role of the immune system in chronic diseases, such as arthritis, and at disorders of the immune system, as in asthma. NIAID has become the lead component at NIH for coordinating and conducting AIDS research. Brochures and reports are available on a wide variety of topics. Some of the publications available include:

NIAID AIDS Research
Where do AIDS Drugs Come From?
NIAID AIDS Research: Opportunistic Infections
AIDS Clinical Trials: Talking It Over

* AIDS Resource Center

National AIDS Clearinghouse
P.O. Box 6003
Rockville, MD 20849 (800) 458-5231

In the Resource Center, visitors can examine all items listed in the Clearinghouse's databases. Materials cover a wide range of AIDS-related subjects: counseling and support groups, drug therapy and other treatments, HIV-prevention education, insurance, AIDS in the workplace, legal issues, and special populations. The collection includes reference sources, brochures, posters, audiocassettes, and videotapes. The Center also houses a unique collection of 400 HIV/AIDS newsletters produced by community-based organizations, State and local government agencies, and national associations. For more information or to make an appointment, call the Clearinghouse and ask to speak with the Librarian.

* AIDS: Surgeon General's Report

AIDS
PO Box 14252
Washington, DC 20044

This detailed 30-page report titled *Surgeon General's Report on Acquired Immune Deficiency Syndrome* discusses the facts about this disease, how it is transmitted, the relative risks of infection, and how to protect yourself against the disease.

* AIDS Videotapes

National Audiovisual Center
8700 Edgeworth Drive
Capitol Heights, MD 20743 (301) 763-1896

A 28-minute video titled "AIDS: Fears and Facts" answers questions most often asked by the general public about this disease. A short 13-minute videotape, "AIDS and Your Job--What You Should Know" outlines precautions that can be taken to reduce the risk of exposure to the AIDS virus by police, firefighters and other public safety professionals. Another video, "What If The Patient Has AIDS?" describes precautions for health care professionals. Each of these videos costs $55.

* Allergies: Home, School, and Work

National Audiovisual Center
8700 Edgeworth Drive
Capitol Heights, MD 20743 (301) 763-1896

A slide set, "Coping With Your Allergies At Home, At School, and on the Job", is available for $33, which includes 40 color slides, an audiocassette, and script.

* Allergies and Infectious Diseases Research

National Institute of Allergy and
Infectious Diseases (NIAID)
National Institutes of Health
Building 31, Room 7A32
9000 Rockville Pike
Bethesda, MD 20892 (301) 496-5717

The NIAID conducts and supports research to study the causes of allergic, immunologic, and infectious diseases, and to develop better means of preventing, diagnosing, and treating illness. Some of the studies look at the role of the immune system in chronic diseases, such as arthritis, and at disorders of the immune system, as in asthma. NIAID has become the lead component at NIH for coordinating and conducting AIDS research. Brochures and reports are available on a wide variety of topics.

* Allergies Dust and Drugs to Pollen

National Institute of Allergy
and Infectious Diseases
National Institutes of Health
Building 31, Room 7A32
9000 Rockville Pike
Bethesda, MD 20892 (301) 496-5717

A free copy of a 7-page pamphlet, *Allergies: Questions and Answers*, (No. 81-189) answers many general questions about allergies and offers information on their symptoms, prevention, diagnosis, and treatment. This institute offers single copies free of the following publications: *Drug Allergy* (No. 82-703), *Dust Allergy* (No. 83-490); *Mold Allergy* (No. 84-797); *Poison Ivy Allergy* (No. 82-897); *Pollen Allergy* (No. 76-493).

Be patient. If any phone number is incorrect, call (area code) 555-1212 and request the new listing.

AIDS, Cancer and Other Diseases

* Alzheimer's and Dementia

Office of Clinical Center Communications
Warren G. Magnuson Clinical Center
NIH, Building 10, Room 5C-305
9000 Rockville Pike
Bethesda, MD 20892 (301) 496-2563

The Brain in "Aging" and Dementia (No. 83-2625) discusses brain anatomy and physiology, the normal process of brain aging, and senility. Vascular dementia and Alzheimer's disease are described as well as research on the causes and treatment.

* Alzheimer's: Long-Term Care

Office of Technology Assessment (OTA)
600 Pennsylvania Ave., SE
Washington, DC 20510 (202) 224-8996

OTA has assessed existing methods of locating and arranging health and long-term care services for Alzheimer's and dementia patients. The study identifies methods that are successful in some communities and may serve as models for others. *Losing a Million Minds: Confronting the Tragedy of Alzheimer's Disease and Other Dementias* is the resulting publication.

* Alzheimer's Q & A

National Institute on Aging Information Center
2209 Distribution Circle
Silver Spring, MD 20910 (301) 495-3455

A 12-page free pamphlet, *Q & A: Alzheimer's Disease* (No. 81-1646), addresses fundamental issues related to the causes, symptoms, and treatment of this disease as well as research efforts surrounding it.

* Amyotrophic Lateral Sclerosis

National Institute of Neurological Disorders and Stroke
National Institutes of Health
9000 Rockville Pike
Building 31, Room 8A06
Bethesda, MD 20892 (301) 496-5751

This institute offers information on neurological and communicative disorders including a free 26-page pamphlet titled *Amyotrophic Lateral Sclerosis* (No. 84-916) which discusses the physiology and symptoms of this progressively crippling and fatal disease.

* Apnea and SIDS

National Sudden Infant Death Syndrome Clearinghouse
8201 Greensboro Drive
Suite 600
McLean, VA 22102 (703) 821-8955

This clearinghouse can provide many materials about infantile apnea, sudden infant death syndrome (SIDS), crib death including *Current Research in Sudden Infant Death* and *SIDS Information for the EMT*.

* Arteriosclerosis

National Heart, Lung, and Blood Institute
NIH, Building 31, Room 42-21
9000 Rockville Pike
Bethesda, MD 20892 (301) 496-4236

Cardiovascular diseases including arteriosclerosis are studied by this institute. Free pamphlets are available on a variety of heart problems.

* Arthritis and Treatments

Office of Clinical Center Communications
Warren G. Magnuson Clinical Center
NIH, Building 10, Room 5C-305
9000 Rockville Pike
Bethesda, MD 20892 (301) 496-2563

A free 27-page booklet, *Arthritis Today*, (No. 83-1945) explains gout, rheumatoid arthritis, and osteoarthritis, and discusses treatment. A videotape, "Arthritis Today", which covers the same material in the booklet is available on free loan to educators and institutions from the Modern Talking Picture Service, Inc., Film Scheduling Center, 5000 Park Street North, St.Petersburg, FL 33709, (813) 541-5763.

* Arthritis Information Clearinghouse

National Arthritis and Musculoskeletal and Skin Disease Information Clearinghouse
Box AMS
Bethesda, MD 20892 (301) 495-4484

This clearinghouse makes available many publications and offers telephone assistance. Many bibliographies are provided: *Directory of Information Sources, 1986* ($4); *Arthritis in Children: An Annotated Bibliography, 1986* ($3); *Arthritis and Employment: A Selected Bibliography, 1984* ($3); *Diet and Arthritis: An Annotated Bibliography, 1986* ($2); *Exercise and Arthritis, 1986* ($4); *Osteoarthritis Patient Education Materials: An Annotated Bibliography* ($3); *Psychosocial Aspects of Rheumatic Diseases: An Annotated Bibliography, 1985* ($3); *Rheumatoid Arthritis Patient Education Materials: An Annotated Bibliography* ($4); and *Sexuality and the Rheumatic Diseases: An Annotated Bibliography* ($3).

* Arthritis, Lyme and other Musculoskeletal Diseases

National Institute of Arthritis and Musculoskeletal and Skin Diseases (NIAMS)
National Institutes of Health
Building 31, Room 4C05
9000 Rockville Pike
Bethesda, MD 20892 (301) 496-8188

The NIAMS conducts and supports basic and clinical research concerning the causes, prevention, diagnosis, and treatment of a large number of diverse diseases, including arthritis, muscle diseases, Lyme disease, and acne. They fund Multipurpose Arthritis Centers which conduct research on various types of arthritis. Reports and brochures for professionals and the general public are available, along with an information specialist who can provide in-depth information on a variety of related topics. Contact this office for a free listing of the Arthritis Centers or for more information. The publications include:

Advances in Treatment of the Marfan Syndrome
Arthritis, Rheumatic Diseases, and Related Disorders - NIAMS 1989
Arthritis, Rheumatic Diseases, and Related Disorders - NIAMS 1990
Arthritis, Rheumatic Diseases, and Related Disorders - NIAMS 1991
Conference Report: Education Strategies for Improving the Outcome of Lupus in High Risk Populations
Executive Summary of Conference Report: Education Strategies for Improving the Outcome of Lupus in High Risk Populations
Living with Epidermolysis Bullosa
Medicine for the Layman - Arthritis
NIAMS Establishes Specialized Research Centers in Rheumatoid Arthritis, Osteoarthritis, and Osteoporosis
Osteoporosis: A Growing National Problem
Osteoporosis - Consensus Development Conference Statement
Researchers Seek Causes of Enigmatic Blistering Disorders
Researching the Cause and Treatment of Paget's Disease of Bone
Scientific Workshop: Research Directions in Osteoporosis
Synopsis: Workshop on Idiopathic Low-Back Pain
Therapies for People with Arthritis
Understanding Paget's Disease
Update: Lupus Erythematosus Research
What Black Women Should Know About Lupus
What You Should Know About Vitiligo
Workshop on Etiopathogenesis of Osteoarthritis
Osteoporosis - Cause, Treatment, Prevention (SASE with 45 cents postage)

* Asthma and Other Respiratory Disorders

National Institute of Allergy and Infectious Diseases
National Institutes of Health
Building 31, Room 7A32
9000 Rockville Pike
Bethesda, MD 20892 (301) 496-5717

A free 11-page report titled *Asthma* (No. 83-525) describes the triggers of asthma attacks and treatment and research on this respiratory disorder. This institute can offer information on sinusitis, tuberculosis and other respiratory problems.

* Blindness and Vision Problems

National Eye Institute (NEI)
Building 31, Room 6A32
9000 Rockville Pike
Bethesda, MD 20892 (301) 496-5248

NEI conducts, fosters and supports basic and applied research, including clinical

Health and Medicine

trials, related to the cause, natural history, prevention, diagnosis, and treatment of disorders of the eye and visual system. Several brochures and reports are available for the general public and health professionals on a wide variety of related topics as well as more specific concerns such as *Diabetes and Your Eyes.*

* Blood Donation

Office of Consumer Affairs
Food and Drug Administration
5600 Fishers Lane
Rockville, MD 20857 (301) 443-3170

Who Donates Better Blood For You Than You? is a free pamphlet which discusses the advantages of donating blood for yourself before undergoing surgery.

* Bone and Orthopedics Research

Musculoskeletal Diseases Program
National Institute of Arthritis and Musculoskeletal and Skin Diseases
Westwood Building, Room 407
Bethesda, MD 20205 (301) 496-7236

This program focuses on orthopedic research, which includes sports medicine, growth and development of bone and bone cells, as well as head injury. Staff can answer questions regarding current research and treatment issues and brochures and pamphlets are available through the National Institute of Arthritis and Musculoskeletal and Skin Diseases.

* Bowel Disease and Syndrome

National Digestive Diseases Information Clearinghouse
Box NDDIC
Bethesda, MD 20892 (301) 468-6344

This clearinghouse offers information and publications including *IBD and IBS: Two Very Different Problems* which compares inflammatory bowel disease and irritable bowel syndrome.

* Brain Tumors

National Institute of Neurological Disorders and Stroke
National Institutes of Health
9000 Rockville Pike
Building 31, Room 8A06
Bethesda, MD 20892 (301) 496-4697

Brain Tumors: Hope Through Research (No. 82-504) explains types of tumors, warning symptoms, and treatment including chemotherapy. This is a central information starting place for information on the brain.

* Breast Cancer Prevention and Treatment Clearinghouse

Cancer Information Service (CIS)
National Cancer Institute
Building 31, Room 10A24, NIH
9000 Rockville Pike (800) 4-CANCER
Bethesda, MD 20892 (800) 492-6600 in MD

Contact CIS for pamphlets, medical updates, organizations, and support groups dealing with breast cancer. *Breast Cancer: We're Making Progress Every Day* (No. 96-2409) summarizes the latest information about breast cancer including surgery, breast reconstruction, and rehabilitation. Single copies of this 12-page pamphlet are available free. *Breast Cancer: What You Should Know* (No. 85-2000) discusses X-ray mammography and other breast cancer screening methods.

* Breast Cancer Videotapes

National Audiovisual Center
8700 Edgeworth Drive
Capitol Heights, MD 20743 (301) 763-1896

Several videotapes can be purchased from the Center including: "Breast Cancer" and "Breast Cancer: We're Making Progress Everyday" as well as "BSE In Hospitals" which is an instructional program designed to help nurses teach hospitalized women how to perform breast self-examinations.

* Breast Exams and Breast Lumps

Cancer Information Service
National Cancer Institute
Building 31, Room 10A24, NIH

9000 Rockville Pike (800) 4-CANCER
Bethesda, MD 20892 (800) 492-6600 in MD

An illustrated guide for breast self-examination is included in a free 12-page pamphlet titled *Breast Cancer: We're Making Progress* (No. 96-8409). *Questions and Answers About Breast Lumps* (No. 86-2401) describes some of the most common noncancerous breast lumps and what can be done about them.

* Breast Implants

Division of Consumer Affairs (HFZ-210)
Center for Devices and Radiological Health
Food and Drug Administration (FDA)
Rockville, MD 20857 (301) 443-4190

The FDA has put together an information packet to answer questions regarding breast implants. It answers questions regarding the FDA's moratorium on silicone gel-filled breast implants, as well as providing general information on breast implants and who to contact for more information.

* Cancer and Afro-Americans

Cancer Information Service
National Cancer Institute
Building 31, Room 10A24, NIH
9000 Rockville Pike (800) 4-CANCER
Bethesda, MD 20892 (800) 492-6600 in MD

What Black Americans Should Know About Cancer (No. 82-1635) is a free 28-page booklet explaining the rates and risks of cancer among Blacks and answers the most often asked questions as well as prevention, detection, treatment, and rehabilitation.

* Cancer-Causing Products

Clearinghouse of Occupational Safety
and Health Information
National Institute of Occupational Safety and Health (NIOSH)
4676 Columbia Pkwy. (513) 533-8326
Cincinnati, OH 45226 (800) 35-NIOSH

NIOSH distributes a publication that lists the trade name products containing one or more of 16 carcinogens (substances for which evidence indicates a causal relationship between exposure to that substance and cancer). They can also provide you with other reports and information on carcinogens.

* Cancer: Chemotherapy, Radiation, Surgery

Office of Clinical Center Communications
Warren G. Magnuson Clinical Center
NIH, Building 10, Room 5C-305
9000 Rockville Pike
Bethesda, MD 20892 (301) 496-2563

This clinical center which experiments with unproven therapies on cancer patients shares its findings and offers several relevant publications including *Cancer Treatment* (No. 82-1807) and *Radiation Risks and Radiation Therapy* (No. 83-2367).

* Cancer Clearinghouse: AZT to Radon

Office of Cancer Communications
National Cancer Institute (NCI)
Building 31, Room 10A18
9000 Rockville Pike
Bethesda, MD 20892 (301) 496-5583

The NCI's overall mission is to conduct and support research, training, health information distribution, and other programs with respect to the cause, diagnosis, prevention, and treatment of cancer, and the continuing care of cancer patients and their families. Some of their current research is looking at Azidothymidine (AZT) in relation to AIDS, and the possible link between radon and lung cancer risk. NCI supports an information and education center, an International Cancer Research Databank, as well as national cancer research and demonstration centers.

* Cancer Detection and Diagnostic Imaging

Diagnostic Imaging Research Program
National Cancer Institute
Executive Plaza North, Room 800
Rockville, MD 20892 (301) 496-9531

Be patient. If any phone number is incorrect, call (area code) 555-1212 and request the new listing.

AIDS, Cancer and Other Diseases

The Diagnostic Imaging Program supports and administers grants and contracts for extramural research in the field of Diagnostic Imaging. The staff can also answer your questions regarding this medical technology.

* Cancer Information Regional Offices

Cancer Information Service
National Cancer Institute
Building 31, Room 10A18
9000 Rockville Pike
Bethesda, MD 20892 (800) 4-CANCER

The National Cancer Institute has set up offices across the U.S. through which they route the Cancer Information Service calls for those particular areas. These offices offer the same services as the Cancer Question and Answer Hotline (see above). Contact this office for a list of offices and more information.

* Cancer Journal

Superintendent of Documents
Government Printing Office
Washington, DC 20402 (202) 783-3238

The Journal of the National Cancer Institute covers basic and clinical oncology. Published twice monthly, it contains peer-reviewed scientific articles and reports, reviews of technical areas and issues, commentaries and editorials, and a news section. Also included are book reviews and listings, upcoming events, employment opportunities, and grants and fellowships. The cost is $60 per year. For back issues, contact: National Technical Information Service at (800) 336-4700.

* Cancer Literature: Bulletins and Bibliographies

Superintendent of Documents
Government Printing Office
Washington, DC 20402 (202) 783-3238

In addition to *The Journal*, the National Cancer Institute has several other publications. *Cancergrams* are monthly current awareness bulletins in 66 cancer-related subject areas and each issue contains abstracts of recent publications. Cost is between $7.50-$9 for a year depending upon subject area. *Oncology Overviews* are specialized bibliographies with abstracts, each referencing up to 500 recent publications. Some of the abstracts include editorial commentary which provides historical background and current research directions. Cost varies between $2.50-$10, depending upon topic. *Recent Reviews* are fully indexed and categorized collections of abstracts of 250-400 reviewed articles published during the year. The three volumes cover cancer diagnosis and treatment, carcinogenesis and cancer virology, immunology and biology. Cost varies between $4-$22 per volume. For back issues, contact: National Technical Information Service, 5285 Port Royal Rd., Springfield, VA 22161, (800) 336-4700.

* Cancer Pamphlets and Publications List

Cancer Information Service
National Cancer Institute
Building 31, Room 10A18
9000 Rockville Pike
Bethesda, MD 20892 (800) 4-CANCER

The National Cancer Institute has over one hundred publications available to the general public and health professionals (many are also in Spanish). Topics range from information on smoking to radiation therapy. Contact this office for a list of publications.

* Cancer Prevention Awareness

Office of Cancer Communications
National Cancer Institute
Building 31, Room 10A-18
9000 Rockville Pike
Bethesda, MD 20892 (301) 496-5583

The National Cancer Institute launched the Cancer Prevention Awareness Program which is a national public education effort aimed at reducing the cancer morality rate by 50 percent by the year 2000. The Program provides information through mass media and intermediary organizations to improve public knowledge and attitudes related to cancer and its prevention, and encourages individuals to adopt lifestyles which reduce their risk of developing cancer. NCI is collaborating with Giant Food Inc., a supermarket chain, in a consumer education program entitled "Eat for Health." The study is designed to inform consumers about nutrition, health promotion, and cancer risk reduction, and to test the effectiveness of supermarket nutrition education programs. One of the free pamphlets titled *Everything Doesn't Cause Cancer* (No. 84-2039) answers some common questions about the causes and prevention of cancer as well as methods for testing chemicals and test results. *Good News, Better News, Best News: Cancer Prevention* (No. 84-2671) discusses avoidable cancer risks and gives steps that one can take every day to prevent it.

* Cancer Q & A International Clearinghouse

Service Desk
International Cancer Information Center
National Cancer Institute, NIH
Building 82, Room 103 (301) 496-7403
Bethesda, MD 20892 (800) 4-CANCER

The International Cancer Information Center develops and applies state-of-the-art technology to collect the results of the latest information on cancer research, diagnosis, and treatment. Distributed through online databases, technical journals, and specialized publications (see Cancer Journal and Literature), the information services provide a resource to the most recent cancer information available. Updated monthly, the databases include PDQ, CANCERLIT, and CLINPROT. PDQ's database includes a file that summarizes the most current approaches to cancer treatment, a file of research treatment protocols that are open to patient entry, and a directory of physicians who provide cancer treatment, and health care organizations the have programs of cancer care. CANCERLIT is a comprehensive bibliographic database containing over 650,000 citations and abstracts of published cancer literature. CLINPROT database provides detailed summaries of about 1500 active, experimental cancer therapy protocols from the U.S. and other countries.

* Cancer Research on Causes and Biology

Frederick Cancer Research Facility
P.O. Box B
Frederick, MD 21701 (301) 846-5096

The Frederick Cancer Research Facility, as part of the National Cancer Institute, (NCI) is the leading center for cancer research. They support research on the causes and biology of cancer, the regulation of given expression, and chemical carcinogenesis. All research information is distributed through NCI.

* Cancer: Spanish Publications

Office of Communications
National Cancer Institute
Building 31, Room 10A18
9000 Rockville Pike
Bethesda, MD 20892 (301) 496-5583

The institute has numerous pamphlets published in Spanish that are available free including: *Los Examenes de Los Senos, Que Debe Saber Sobre Ellos* (No. 82-2138) on breast cancer and *Lo Que Usted Debe Saber Sobre El Cancer* (No. 83-1828) which is a bilingual booklet that answers questions about the causes, prevention, detection and treatment of cancer.

* Cancer: Speakers

Office of Communications
National Cancer Institute
Building 31, Room 10A18
9000 Rockville Pike
Bethesda, MD 20892 (301) 496-5583

This office can give you information on speakers who are available to talk on a variety of topics to the general public, as well as health professionals. The topics can range from current research to environmental risks. Contact this office for more information on scheduling.

* Cancer Unconventional Treatments

Office of Technology Assessment (OTA)
600 Pennsylvania Ave., SE
Washington, DC 20510 (202) 224-8996

OTA has worked on a study that summarizes available information on the major types of unconventional cancer treatments; describes the legal constraints on their availability; and examines the potential for evaluating these new treatments for safety and effectiveness. The title of the resulting publication is *Unconventional Cancer Treatments.*

Be patient. If any phone number is incorrect, call (area code) 555-1212 and request the new listing.

Health and Medicine

* Cancer: Videotapes

National Audiovisual Center
8700 Edgeworth Drive
Capitol Heights, MD 20743 (301) 763-1896

Several videos can be purchased including "Cancer and the Environment" which looks at such factors as chemical and industrial pollution, auto emissions, diet, estrogen, and tobacco. "Cancer: What Is It?" provides an overview of cancer and compares the behavior of malignant cells with normal cells. A 27-minute video, "Control and Prevention of Malignant Melanoma: A Program for Melanoma-Prone Families" discusses danger signs, skin self-examination, and prevention techniques of this potentially fatal skin cancer.

* Cancer Videotapes

Modern Talking Picture Service
5000 Park Street North
St. Petersburg, FL 33709 (800) 243-MTPS

The National Cancer Institute is making three videotapes available, without charge, to concerned health professionals. The videos deal with a specific type of mole, called the dysplastic nevus, which is an easily identifiable precursor of most familial melanomas. The video series, *Managing Dysplastic Nevi*, include "Control and Prevention of Malignant Melanoma: A Program for Melanoma-Prone Families", "Dysplastic Nevi and Melanoma: A Program for Pathologists", and "Dysplastic Nevi and Melanoma: A Program for Clinicians". Contact the Cancer Hotline at (800) 4-CANCER for more information.

* Carcinogens: Annual Report

Public Information Office
National Toxicology Program MD B2-04
P.O. Box 12233
Research Triangle Park, NC 27709 (919) 541-3991

Single copies of an abridged version of the *Annual Report on Carcinogens* is available. It identifies some 150 substances and processes and gives summaries of the evidence for their link with cancer in humans and laboratory animals. It also provides information on production, use, population exposed, cities, and federal regulations to safeguard the public.

* Cardiovascular Disease Contact List

Alabama
Hypertension Branch
Alabama Department of Public Health
434 Monroe St.
Montgomery, AL 36130 (205) 261-5128

Alaska
Chief Nutritionist
Division of Public Health
Alaska Department of Health and Social Services
Pouch H-06C
Juneau, AK 99811 (907) 465-3103

Arizona
Chief, Office of Health Promotion and Education
Arizona Department of Health Services
3008 N. 3rd. St.
Phoenix, AZ 85012 (602) 255-1292

Arkansas
Chronic Disease Program
Section of Health Maintenance
Arkansas Department of Health
4815 W. Markham
Little Rock, AR 77205 (501) 661-2602

California
Health Section
Department of Health Services
714 P St., Room 499
P.O. Box 942732
Sacramento, CA 94234 (916) 322-4787

Colorado
Cardiovascular Disease Control Program

Division of Prevention Programs
Colorado Department of Health
4210 E. 11th Ave.
Denver, CO 80220 (303) 331-8303

Connecticut
Center for Chronic Disease Control
Connecticut Department of Health Services
150 Washington St.
Hartford, CT 06106 (203) 566-7867

Delaware
Cardiovascular Disease Program
Bureau of Disease Prevention
Division of Public Health
Robbins Building
802 Silver Lake Blvd.
Dover, DE 19901 (302) 736-4745

District Of Columbia
Prevention Health Services Administration
DC Commission of Public Health
1660 L St., NW
Washington, DC 20036 (202) 673-6719

Florida
Nursing Consultant
Florida Department of Health and Rehabilitative Services
1317 Winewood Blvd.
Tallahassee, FL 32399 (904) 488-2901

Georgia
Program Manager
Stroke and Heart Attack Prevention Program
Georgia Department of Human Resources
878 Peachtree St., NE
Room 102
Atlanta, GA 30309 (404) 894-6640

Hawaii
Chief
Preventive Health Services Branch
Hawaii State Department of Health
P.O. Box 3378
Honolulu, HI 96801 (808) 548-5835

Idaho
Health Education Program Manager
Health Promotion/Disease Prevention Section
Bureau of Preventive Health
Division of Health
Idaho Department of Health and Welfare
Statehouse Mail
Boise, ID 83720 (208) 334-5933

Illinois
Community Chronic Disease Programs Section
Division of Chronic Diseases
Illinois Department of Public Health
535 W. Jefferson St.
Springfield, IL 62761 (217) 782-3300

Indiana
Director
Division of Chronic Disease
Indiana State Board of Health
1330 W. Michigan St.
P.O. Box 1964
Indianapolis, IN 46206 (317) 633-0399

Iowa
Community Nutritionist
Iowa Department of Public Health
Nutrition Bureau
Lucas State Office Building
Des Moines, IA 50319 (515) 281-7097

Be patient. If any phone number is incorrect, call (area code) 555-1212 and request the new listing.

AIDS, Cancer and Other Diseases

Kansas
Director
Office of Health and Environmental Education
Division of Health Information Systems
Landon State Office Building
10th Floor
Topeka, KS 66620 (913) 296-1216

Kentucky
Division of Epidemiology
Department for Health Services
Cabinet of Human Resources
275 E. Main St.
Frankfort, KY 40621 (502) 564-3418

Louisiana
Director of Adult Services
Louisiana Department of Health and Hospitals
Office of Public Health
P.O. Box 60630
New Orleans, LA 70160 (504) 568-7210

Maine
Division of Health Promotion and Education
Maine Department of Human Services
Bureau of Health
State House Station 11
Augusta, ME 04333 (207) 289-5180

Maryland
Division of Chronic Disease Prevention
Maryland Department of Health and Mental Hygiene
P.O. Box 13528
Baltimore, MD 21203 (301) 225-6778

Massachusetts
Bureau of Adult and Elderly Health
Massachusetts Department of Public Health
150 Tremont St.
Boston, MA 02111 (617) 727-2662

Michigan
Center for Health Promotion
Michigan Department of Public Health
3423 N. Logan St.
P.O. Box 30195
Lansing, MI 48909 (517) 335-8368

Minnesota
Health Promotion and Education
Minnesota Department of Health
717 S.E. Delaware St.
P.O. Box 9441
Minneapolis, MN 55440 (612) 623-5699

Mississippi
Mississippi Department of Health
Office of Health Promotion and Disease Prevention
P.O. Box 1700
Jackson, MS 39215 (601) 960-7946

Missouri
Division of Chronic Disease Prevention and Health Promotion
Missouri Department of Health
201 Business Loop/70 West
Columbia, MO 65203 (314) 876-8100

Montana
Consultant
Health Promotion and Chronic disease
Montana Department of Health
Cogswell Building
Helena, MT 59620 (406) 444-4740

Nebraska
Health Promotion and Education
Nebraska Department of Health

301 Centennial Mall S.
P. O. Box 95007
Lincoln, NE 68509 (402) 471-2101

Nevada
State Health Officer
Nevada State Health Division
505 E. King St.
Room 201
Carson City, NV 89710 (702) 885-4740

New Hampshire
Health Promotion Advisor
Bureau of Health Promotion
New Hampshire Division of Public Health Services
6 Hazen Dr.
Concord, NH 03301 (603) 271-4623

New Jersey
Assistant Director
Chronic Disease Prevention and Control
Chronic Disease Services
Division of Epidemiology and Disease Control
New Jersey State Department of Health
CN #369
Trenton, NJ 08625 (609) 588-7504

New Mexico
Chief
Adult Health Section
Public Health Division
New Mexico Health and Environment Department
Santa Fe, NM 87503 (505) 827-2501

New York
Bureau of Adult and Gerontological Health
New York State Department of Health
Nelson A. Rockefeller Empire State Plaza Tower Building
Albany, NY 12237 (518) 474-0512

North Carolina
Division Coordinator
Adult Health Services
North Carolina Department of Environment, Health,
and Natural Resources
P.O. Box 2091
1330 St. Mary St.
Raleigh, NC 27602 (919) 733-7081

North Dakota
Health Risk Reduction Project
Division of Community Health Nursing
North Dakota State Department of Health
and Consolidated Laboratories
Judicial Wing-2nd Floor
600 E. Boulevard Ave.
Bismarck, ND 58505 (701) 224-2494

Ohio
Chief
Division of Chronic Diseases
Ohio Department of Health
246 N. High St.
Columbus, OH 43266 (614) 466-2144

Oklahoma
Chief
Chronic Disease Section
Oklahoma State Department of Health
1000 NE 10th St.
P.O. Box 53551
Oklahoma City, OK 73152 (405) 271-4072

Oregon
Health Education Consultant
State of Oregon Department of Human Resources
Health Division

Be patient. If any phone number is incorrect, call (area code) 555-1212 and request the new listing.

Health and Medicine

1400 S.W. 5th Ave.
Portland, OR 97201 (503) 229-5691

Pennsylvania
Cardiovascular Disease Risk Reduction Program
Pennsylvania Department of health
P.O. Box 90
Harrisburg, PA 17108 (717) 787-7073

Rhode Island
Community Health Evaluation Coordinator
Rhode Island Department of Health
103 Cannon Building
3 Capitol Hill
Providence, RI 02908 (401) 277-6949

South Carolina
Center for Health Promotion
South Carolina Department of Health
and Environmental Control
2600 Bull St.
Columbia, SC 29201 (803) 737-4120

South Dakota
Health Education/Promotion Program
Division of Health Services
South Dakota Department of Health
523 E. Capitol
Pierre, SD 57501 (605) 773-3737

Tennessee
Director of Health Promotion/Disease Control
Tennessee Department of Health and Environment
100 Ninth Ave. N
Nashville, TN 37219 (615) 741-7366

Texas
Division of Public Health Promotion
Texas Department of Health
1100 W. 49th St.
Austin, TX 78756 (512) 458-7405

Utah
Division of Community Health Services
Utah Department of Health
P.O. Box 16660
Salt Lake City, UT 84116 (801) 538-6129

Vermont
Health Promotion
Vermont Department of Health
P.O. Box 70
Burlington, VT 05402 (802) 863-7330

Virginia
Office of Health Education and Information
Virginia Department of Health
James Madison Building
Room 515
109 Governor St.
Richmond, VA 23219 (804) 786-3551

Washington
Cardiovascular Risk Reduction Program
Chronic Disease Control
Section LK-13
Department of Social and Health Services
Division of Health
Olympia, WA 98504 (206) 586-6082

West Virginia
Cardiovascular Educator
Division of Health Promotion
West Virginia Department of Health
Boulevard Building
1411 Virginia St., E
Charleston, WV 25301 (304) 348-0644

Wisconsin
Chronic Disease Unit
Wisconsin Division of Health
Room 318, P.O. Box 309
Madison, WI 53701 (608) 266-7457

Wyoming
Health Risk Reduction Program
Wyoming Division of Health and Medical Services
Hathaway Building, 4th Floor
Cheyenne, WY 82002 (307) 777-6011

* Cerebral Palsy

National Institute of Neurological Disorders and Stroke
National Institutes of Health
9000 Rockville Pike
Building 31, Room 8A06
Bethesda, MD 20892 (301) 496-5751

This center for medical research has information about the latest developments on this disease as well as a free 26-page pamphlet titled *Cerebral Palsy: Hope Through Research* (No. 84-158).

* Children and Mental Health

National Institute of Mental Health (NIMH)
5600 Fishers Lane, Room 15C05
Rockville, MD 20857 (301) 443-4515

NIMH has several publications which deal with mental health in children. These publications are available at no charge. Titles include:

Helping the Hyperactive Child
Importance of Play
Learning While Growing: Cognitive Development
National Plan for Research on Child and Adolescent Mental Disorders
Plain Talk about Adolescence
Plain Talk About Raising Children
Pre-Term Babies
Research on Children and Adolescents with Mental, Behavioral and Development Disorders
Stimulating Baby Senses
When Parents Divorce

* Children with AIDS

National Clearinghouse on Maternal and Child Health
38th and R Sts., NW
Washington, DC 20057 (202) 625-8410

This Clearinghouse has four free publications concerned with AIDS and Children. The titles include: *Building Systems of Care for Children with HIV Infection and Their Families, Children with HIV/AIDS: A Sourcebook for Caring, Pediatric AIDS: Abstracts of Active Projects FY 1990 and FY 1991,* and *Surgeon General's Workshop on Children with HIV Infection and Their Families Report.*

* Cholesterol and Coronary Heart Disease

National Cholesterol Education Program
NIH, Building 31, Room 4A-21
9000 Rockville Pike
Bethesda, MD 20892 (301) 951-3260

This clearinghouse of the National Heart, Lung and Blood Institute (NHLBI) works to inform the public about cardiovascular disease. One of many publications available free is *NHLBI Facts About Blood Cholesterol* (No. 90-2696). The Program works to increase the general public's awareness about the importance of having their blood cholesterol levels checked, knowing what their cholesterol levels are, and taking steps to lower elevated levels. The Program also develops materials for the worksite and the schools. Some of the free publications include:

General Public
Dietary Guideline for Americans: Avoid Too Much Fat, Saturated Fat, and Cholesterol - tips for choosing and preparing foods.

Report of the Expert Panel on Detection, Evaluation, and Treatment of High Blood Cholesterol in Adults - provides practical guidelines for high blood cholesterol patients from detection to treatment.

Be patient. If any phone number is incorrect, call (area code) 555-1212 and request the new listing.

AIDS, Cancer and Other Diseases

Facts About...Blood Cholesterol - Q&A on lowering high blood cholesterol.

Eating to Lower Your High Blood Cholesterol - how-to booklet gives all the information needed to change eating habits and lower high blood cholesterol.

So You Have High Blood Cholesterol - easy to read pamphlet designed for patients diagnosed as having high blood cholesterol.

Professionals

Cholesterol: Current Concepts for Clinicians - for physicians, provides current perspectives and information and is designed for independent study.

Community Guide to Cholesterol Resources - lists vital education materials on the medical and scientific aspects of cholesterol and heart disease.

Executive Summary: Current Status of Blood Cholesterol Measurement in Clinical Laboratories in the U.S. - examines the accuracy of cholesterol measurements.

Recommendations Regarding Public Screening for Measuring Blood Cholesterol: Summary of a National Heart, Lung, and Blood Institute Workshop - discusses methods that could make public screening more effective.

Report of the Expert Panel on Population Strategies for Blood Cholesterol Reduction - reviews the scientific base for making recommendation to the general public.

Highlights of the NCEP Report on Blood Cholesterol Levels in Children and Adolescents - presents an overview of the recommendation in the Report.

* Cholesterol, High Blood Pressure, Smoking, and the Workplace

National Heart, Lung, And Blood Institute (NHLBI) Information Center 4733 Bethesda Ave., Suite 530 Bethesda, MD 20814 (301) 951-3260

The NHLBI Workplace Initiative promotes research and educational projects and materials that promote the reduction of cardiopulmonary morbidity and mortality among workers and their families. The Workplace Initiative kit contains materials for professionals and workers related to risk factors for cardiovascular and pulmonary disease, especially the three major modifiable risk factors: high blood pressure, high blood cholesterol, and cigarette smoking. Materials include: technical documents for health professionals, guides for workplace program planners, brochures and materials for workers, order forms for additional publications, and audiovisual materials. Some of the free publications include:

It's Your Business... Smoking Policies for the Workplace
Make Workplace Wellness Programs Work for Your Company
NHLBI Demonstration Projects in Workplace High Blood Pressure Control: Summary Report
1988 Methodological Issues in Worksite Research - Proceedings
Program Summary of a Conference on Worksite Health Promotion and Human Resources: A Hard Look at the Data
A Reading List for Heart and Lung Health at the Workplace
A Resource Guide for Heart and Lung Health at the Workplace
Small Business Basics: Guidelines for Heart and Lung Health at the Workplace
Workplace Facts on Heart Disease and Stroke: A Data Fact Sheet
Directory of Cardiovascular Resources for Minority Populations
Highlights of the 1987 Report of the Expert Panel on Detection, Evaluation, and Treatment of High Blood Cholesterol in Adults
NHLBI Kit '90
Patient Tracking for High Blood Pressure Control
The Physician's Guide: Improving Adherence Among Hypertensive Patients
Recommendations for Improving Cholesterol Measurement: Executive Summary
Recommendations Regarding Public Screening for Measuring Blood Cholesterol: Summary of a NHLBI Workshop
Report of the Expert Panel on Detection, Evaluation, and Treatment of High Blood Cholesterol in Adults
Report of the Expert Panel on Population Strategies for Blood Cholesterol Reduction
1988 Report of the Joint National Committee on Detection, Evaluation, and Treatment of High Blood Pressure
Reproducible Fact Sheets from NHLBI Kit '89
Three Community Programs Change Heart Health Across the Nation
With Every Beat of Your Heart: An Ideabook for Community Heart Health Programs

Posters

Even If You're Feeling Like Superman, You Need to Know Your Cholesterol Number
Their Future is in Your Hands. Treat Your High Blood Pressure Every Day (Spanish Only)
Quit to Win
Stanley Spencer Had a Stroke
Step to the Beat of a Health Heart
Stop! Do You Know Your Cholesterol Number?
Three Good Reasons to Control Your High Blood Pressure
You Can Shape Your Future

* Chronic Disease Prevention

Center for Chronic Disease Prevention and Health Promotion (CCDPHP) Centers for Disease Control (CDC) 1600 Clifton Rd., NE Building 3, Room 117 Atlanta, GA 30333 (404) 488-5080

Begun in 1988, this center was established in the belief that more emphasis was needed on chronic disease prevention if CDC was to accomplish its mission of preventing unnecessary illness, disability, and death. CCDPHP stresses translating research findings into effective community-based programs, strengthening the delivery of preventive health services, and designing programs to meet the needs of minority groups. Units within the center cover smoking and health, nutrition, school health, chronic disease control, reproductive health, diabetes, and surveillance and analysis. The center works with State health departments on breast cancer control projects that promote screening mammography, advanced training for technicians, equipment testing, and peer review. The Preventive Health and Health Services Block Grant helps fund states' efforts to combat chronic diseases and to offer health education. Some interventions are designed to serve the dual purpose of meeting local health needs and providing a model for other programs. The Center has established a newsletter, *Chronic Disease Notes and Reports,* to provide a regular forum for communication.

* Chronic Fatigue Syndrome

National Institute of Allergy and Infectious Diseases National Institutes of Health Building 31, Room 7A32 Bethesda, MD 20892 (301) 496-5717

Chronic Fatigue Syndrome is a fatigue that come on suddenly and is relentless or relapsing, causing debilitating tiredness or easy fatigability in someone who has no apparent reason for feeling this way. NIAID has a Backgrounder, which explains CFS, including current research, treatment, and causes. They also have compiled a list of support groups and resources, as well as other relevant articles. *Chronic Fatigue Syndrome,* part of the Medicine for the Layman Series, describes possible causes and treatment for CFS, and is available free from: Clinical Center Communications, National Institutes of Health, Building 10, Room 1C255, Bethesda, MD 20892; (301) 496-2563. The Centers for Disease Control also offers a background article and provides information about CDC research, including surveillance of community health department to determine the incidence of CFS and studies of blood samples from CFS patients to detect evidence of viral infection. For more information contact, Centers for Disease Control, Division of Viral Diseases, Bldg. 6, Room 120, Atlanta, GA 30333; (404) 639-1338.

* Chronic Pain Research and Therapies

National Institute of Neurological Disorders and Stroke National Institutes of Health 9000 Rockville Pike Building 31, Room 8A06 Bethesda, MD 20892 (301) 496-4697

This Institute conducts research on persistent pain and various therapies including drugs, acupuncture, surgery, electrical stimulation, and also psychological techniques.

* Cirrhosis of the Liver

National Digestive Diseases Information Clearinghouse Box NDDIC Bethesda, MD 20892 (301) 468-6344

A free four-page pamphlet titled *Cirrhosis of the Liver* (No. 84-1134) explains

Be patient. If any phone number is incorrect, call (area code) 555-1212 and request the new listing.

Health and Medicine

preventive measures including alcohol abstinence and other causes, symptoms, diagnosis and treatment.

* Colon Colitis, Diverticulitis, and Cancer

Office of Consumer Affairs, Public Inquiries
Food and Drug Administration
5600 Fishers Lane (HFE-88)
Rockville, MD 20857 (301) 443-3170

The Colon Goes Up, Over, Down, and Out (DHHS Pub. No. 84-1111) discusses how the colon works and is the site of many problems such as colon colitis, diverticulitis, and cancer.

* Condoms and Sexually Transmitted Diseases

National Clearinghouse for Primary Care Information
8201 Greensboro Dr., Suite 600
McLean, VA 22102 (703) 821-8955

Condoms and Sexually Transmitted Diseases... Especially AIDS is an easily understood brochure which answers 17 frequently asked questions about purchasing and using condoms. Facts about sexually transmitted diseases are listed.

* Cooley's Anemia

National Heart, Lung, and Blood Institute
NIH, Building 31, Room 42-21
9000 Rockville Pike
Bethesda, MD 20892 (301) 496-4236

This Institute offers information on many aspects of cardiovascular disease including a free pamphlet titled *Cooley's Anemia: Prevention Through Understanding* (No. 80-1269) which discusses prevention through testing and genetic counseling.

* Crohn's Disease

National Digestive Diseases Information Clearinghouse
Box NDDIC
Bethesda, MD 20892 (301) 468-6344

Information about ulcerative colitis and Crohn's Disease, clinical symptoms, epidemiological patterns, treatment strategies and experimental therapies are provided by this clearinghouse.

* Dementia Disorders

National Institute of Neurological Disorders and Stroke
National Institutes of Health
9000 Rockville Pike
Building 31, Room 8A06
Bethesda, MD 20892 (301) 496-5751

Alzheimer's Disease: A Scientific Guide for Health Practitioners (No. 84-2251) is a booklet which describes Alzheimer's, possible causes of the disease, diagnosis and treatment.

* Depression: Diagnosis and Treatments

National Institute of Mental Health (NIMH)
Alcohol, Drug Abuse and Mental Health Administration
5600 Fishers Lane, Room 15C05
Rockville, MD 20857 (301) 443-4515

NIMH conducts research on depression and other mental disorders, distributes information, conducts demonstration programs for the prevention, treatment, and rehabilitation of the mentally ill. A major media campaign on depression, called Project D/ART (Depression/Awareness, Recognition, Treatment), is being developed by NIMH in collaboration with other organizations to provide information on symptoms, causes, and treatments of various depressive disorders. Many publications and reports are available on various topics for professionals and the general public.

* Diabetes Control Programs

Division of Diabetes Translation
Office of Chronic Disease
Prevention and Health Promotion
CDC, 1600 Clifton Rd., E08

Atlanta, GA 30333 (404) 488-5000

This division has cooperative agreements with 30 states to establish Diabetes Control Programs. Through each state's health department, with the Center for Disease Control providing matching funds, these programs are designed for specific interventions for diabetics. They examine for eye disease complications and make appropriate referrals, as well as assist with diabetic pregnancy and lower limb circulation problems. Contact this office for referral to local states of for more information.

* Diabetes Information Center

National Diabetes Information Clearinghouse (NDIC)
Box NDIC
Bethesda, MD 20892 (301) 468-2162

NDIC responds to requests for information about diabetes and its complications and distributes information appropriate to health professionals, people with diabetes and their families, and the general public. They have many publications and bibliographies, as well as *Diabetes Dateline*, a free quarterly current awareness newsletter that features news about diabetes research, upcoming meetings and events, and new publications. NDIC uses the online database CHID (Combined Health Information Database) from which they can reference health information. Some other publications include:

Age Page: Dealing with Diabetes
Dental Tips for Diabetics
The Diabetes Dictionary
Diabetic Retinopathy
Insulin-Dependent Diabetes
Monitoring Your Blood Sugar
Noninsulin-Dependent Diabetes
Periodontal Disease and Diabetes, A Guide for Patients
The Prevention and Treatment of Five Complications of Diabetes, A Guide for Patients with an Introduction to Day-to-Day Management of Diabetes
Understanding Gestational Diabetes

Professional Materials
CHID Factsheet
CHID Search Reference Guide
CHID Word List
Detection and Prevention of Periodontal Disease in Diabetes
Diabetes in America, Diabetes Data Compiled 1984
Diabetes Dateline
Diabetes Fact Sheets: State-Specific Estimates of Diabetes Disease Burden
Diabetes Mellitus, Tans-NIH Research
Diabetes-Related Programs for Black Americans: A Resource Guide
Diet and Exercise in Noninsulin-Dependent Diabetes Mellitus
Educational Materials Assessment Worksheet
The National Long-Range Plan to Combat Diabetes
NDIC Brochure
NDIC Compendium - contains information about diabetes educational programs, materials, and selected pilot and feasibility studies supported by major diabetes organizations ($15).
NDIC Thesaurus

Bibliographies
Cookbooks for People with Diabetes
Diabetes and Kidney Disease
Foot Care and Diabetes
Pregnancy and Diabetes
Sports and Exercise for People with Diabetes

Fact Sheets
Diabetes in Blacks
Diabetes in Hispanics
Diabetes Education
Diabetic Neuropathy

* Diarrhea Prevention and Control

National Digestive Diseases Information Clearinghouse
Box NDDIC
Bethesda, MD 20892 (301) 468-6344

This clearinghouse offers information on this digestive tract disorder including *Diarrhea, Infectious and Other Causes* (No. 86-2749) and a free 12-page pamphlet *Traveler's Diarrhea*.

AIDS, Cancer and Other Diseases

* Digestive Health and Disease Clearinghouse

National Digestive Diseases Information Clearinghouse (NDDIC)
Box NDDIC
Bethesda, MD 20892 (301) 468-6344

NDDIC responds to requests for information about digestive diseases and distributes information to health professionals, people with digestive diseases, and the general public. They have many publications, as well as a news bulletin. NDDIC uses the online database CHID (Combined Health Information Database) from which they can access health information and organizations. Some of their free publications include:

Digestive Health and Disease: A Glossary (DD-01)
Facts and Fallacies About Digestive Diseases (DD-02)
Your Digestive System and How It Works (DD-03)
Diagnostic Tests for Digestive Diseases: X-rays and Ultrasound (DD-07)
IBD and IBS: Two Very Different Problems (DD-13)
Age Page: Constipation (DD-36)
Smoking and Your Digestive System (DD-52)

Fact Sheets
Inflammatory Bowel Disease
What is Irritable Bowel Syndrome?
Ulcerative Colitis
Heartburn
Diverticulosis and Diverticulitis
Diarrhea: Infectious and Other Causes
Bleeding In the Digestive Tract
Gas in the Digestive Tract
Hiatal Hernia
What Is Constipation?
Lactose Intolerance
What Is Dyspepsia?
Hemorrhoids
Stomach Ulcers
Pancreatitis
Cirrhosis of the Liver
Pamphlets
Peptic Ulcer
Gallstones

Information Packets
Crohn's Disease and Ulcerative Colitis
Diverticular Disease
Gallstones
Irritable Bowl Syndrome
Ulcers
Esophageal Reflux
Lactose Intolerance

Catalogues and Guides
Digestive Diseases Organizations: Lay and Voluntary
Digestive Diseases Organizations: Professional
NDDIC Brochure
DD Notes
CHID
Therapeutic Endoscopy and Bleeding Ulcers
CHID Search Reference Guide
CHID Word List
Hepatitis B Prevention: A Resource Guide
Research Opportunities and Programs in the Division of Digestive Diseases and Nutrition

* Dyslexia and Other Learning Disorders

Human Learning and Behavior Branch
National Institute of Child Health and Human Development
National Institutes of Health
9000 Rockville Pike
Bethesda, MD 20892 (301) 496-6591

The Human Learning and Behavior Branch is concerned with the development of human behavior, from infancy, through childhood and adolescence, into early maturity. Studies are supported in developmental psychobiology, behavioral pediatrics, cognitive and communicative processes, social and affective development, and health related behaviors, as well as learning disabilities, dyslexia and language disorders. A free booklet, *Developmental Dyslexia and Related Reading Disorders,* provides an overview of what is known and what remains to be learned about dyslexia. For information regarding current research, contact the office listed above.

* Eating Disorders

National Institute of Diabetes and Digestive and Kidney Diseases
National Institutes of Health
Bldg. 31, Room 3A18B
Bethesda, MD 20892 (301) 496-7823

The Obesity, Eating Disorders, and Energy Regulation Program of the Nutritional Sciences Branch emphasizes research on the biomedical and behavioral aspects of obesity, anorexia nervosa, bulimia and other eating disorders. The goals are to understand the etiology, prevention, and treatment of these conditions.

* Epilepsy and Convulsions

Office of Clinical Center Communications
Warren G. Magnuson Clinical Center
NIH, Building 10, Room 5C-305
9000 Rockville Pike
Bethesda, MD 20892 (301) 496-2563

This clinical center offers a free 24-page report titled *Epilepsy* (No. 82-2369) which discusses types of seizures and medical and surgical therapies.

* Eye Research Experiments Nationwide

National Eye Institute
National Institute of Health
Bldg 31, Room 6A-32
9000 Rockville Pike
Bethesda, MD 20892 (301) 492-5248

Intended for the practitioner, *Clinical Trials Supported by the National Eye Institute* briefly describes 20 ongoing research studies. Included is the current status of the study, the results, any publications that result from the studies, as well as a list of the participating clinical centers.

* Gallstone Disease

National Digestive Diseases Information Clearinghouse
Box NDDIC
Bethesda, MD 20892 (301) 468-6344

Questions about surgery and complications as well as the reasons for the formation of gallstones are addressed in this free 4-page pamphlet titled *Gallstone Disease* (No. 85-2752).

* Head Injury

Musculoskeletal Diseases Program
National Institute of Arthritis and Musculoskeletal and Skin Diseases
Westwood Building, Room 407
Bethesda, MD 20205 (301) 496-5717

This program focuses on orthopedic research, which includes sports medicine, growth and development of bone and bone cells, as well as head injury. Staff can answer questions regarding current research and treatment issues. Brochures and pamphlets are available through the National Institute of Arthritis and Musculoskeletal and Skin Diseases.

* Head Trauma and Rehab

National Institute of Neurological Disorders and Stroke
National Institutes of Health
9000 Rockville Pike
Building 31, Room 8A06
Bethesda, MD 20892 (301) 496-5751

Head Injury: Hope through Research (No. 84-2478) discusses ways to prevent head injuries and the resulting damage from different types of injuries, as well as rehabilitation techniques.

* Heart Attacks

National Heart, Lung, and Blood Institute
NIH, Building 31, Room 42-21
9000 Rockville Pike

Be patient. If any phone number is incorrect, call (area code) 555-1212 and request the new listing.

Health and Medicine

Bethesda, MD 20892 (301) 496-4236

A free 20-page booklet, *Heart Attacks* (No. 86-2700) discusses risk factors, symptoms, and treatment. A videotape based on this publication which offers encouraging evidence that cardiovascular disease death rates have decreased due to changes in diet and lifestyle is available for sale through the National Audiovisual Center, or on free loan to educators and institutions from the Modern Talking Service, Film Scheduling Center, 5000 Park Street North, St Petersburg, FL 33709, (813) 541-5763. *Test Your Healthy Heart I.Q.!* (No. 85-2724) offers over a dozen questions and answers about cardiovascular and pulmonary risk factors. There are many other publications available regarding the heart and heart problems. Contact this office for a publication list. Some of the publications available include:

The Heathy Heart Handbook for Women - self-help guide answers many questions about women and cardiovascular disease.

With Every Beat of Your Heart: An Ideabook for Community Heart Health Programs - provides basic information for use in starting or expanding a heart health program.

Test Your Healthy Heart "I.Q." - true-false test of heart disease.

Professionals

Directory of Cardiovascular Resources for Minority Population - describes available materials on cardiovascular disease.

Small Business Basics: Guidelines for Heart and Lung Health at the Workplace - pamphlet provides guidelines for establishing heart and lung health programs and practices at the workplace.

Play Your Cards Right...Stay Young at Heart: A Heart Health Nutrition Education Program - kit designed to help program planners implement a heart healthy eating program at their worksite cafeteria, restaurant, school, or other eating establishment.

* Heart Disease: Diagnosis and Treatment

Office of Clinical Center Communications
Warren G. Magnuson Clinical Center
NIH, Building 10, Room 5C-305
9000 Rockville Pike
Bethesda, MD 20892 (301) 496-2563

A free pamphlet, *Risk of Heart Disease*, discusses new findings in clinical cardiology, new techniques to diagnose abnormalities in the pumping function of the heart, and new concepts in treating people who come to the hospital with an acute heart attack.

* Heart Disease Videotapes

National Audiovisual Center
8700 Edgeworth Drive
Capitol Heights, MD 20743 (301) 763-1896

Several videos can be purchased from the Center and some can be rented free from the Modern Talking Picture Service Film Scheduling Center (5000 Park Street North, St. Petersburg, FL 33709, 813-5431-5763) including "Cholesterol, Diet and Heart Disease", "Heart Attacks", and "Coronary Heart Disease: Roles of Surgery and Balloon Dilatation".

* Hepatitis

National Digestive Diseases Information Clearinghouse
Box NDDIC
Bethesda, MD 20892 (301) 468-6344

Hepatitis B Prevention: A Resource Guide 1990 is a directory of 64 national, state, and local organizations that provide hepatitis B prevention services. It also includes a bibliography with 347 citations to professional and patient literature about hepatitis B prevention.

* Herpes Type I and Type II

National Institute of Allergy
and Infectious Diseases
National Institutes of Health
Building 31, Room 7A32
9000 Rockville Pike
Bethesda, MD 20892 (301) 496-5717

This institute offers information and various publications on sexually transmitted diseases including *Genital Herpes* (No. 84-2005) which is also available in Spanish (No. 854-656); and *Sexually Transmitted Diseases* (STDs).

* High Blood Pressure

High Blood Pressure Information Center
4733 Bethesda Avenue
Suite 530
Bethesda, MD 20814 (301) 951-3260

The Center is a source of information and educational materials for consumers, providers, and planners of high blood pressure control services. Print and audiovisual materials (for professionals and the public), as well as information on locations and services of community programs and activities are available. The Center can access material through the CHID database. A free newsletter, Info Memo, covers topics of interest concerning blood pressure, cholesterol and smoking and is published as needed. Several free publications available include:

Community Guide to High Blood Pressure (No. 82-2333)

High Blood Pressure: Things You and Your Family Should Know (No. 86-2025; also published in Spanish)

High Blood Pressure and What You Can Do About It

High Blood Pressure Control Programs at the Worksite (No. 83-1125)

Blacks and High Blood Pressure - pamphlet offers information on prevalence, and need for treatment.

General Public

Heart Attacks - contains facts about the leading cause of death in the U.S.

High Blood Pressure and What You Can Do About It - booklet provides an overview of high blood pressure.

High Blood Pressure: Things You and Your Family Should Know - basic leaflet about high blood pressure (Spanish).

Living With Hypertension - series of five pamphlets lets patients know they are in control of their hypertension.

Professionals

Hypertension Prevalence and the Status of Awareness, Treatment, and Control in the U.S. - present methodology and conclusions of a current estimation.

Measuring Progress in High Blood Pressure Control: An Evaluation Handbook - discusses reasons to evaluate your high blood pressure program.

Nonpharmacologic Approaches to the Control of High Blood Pressure - summary of current knowledge on a variety on nondrug approaches to reduce blood pressure.

Physician's Guide: How To Help Your Hypertensive Patients Stop Smoking - guide show what every physician con do within a busy office practice.

The Physician's Guide: Improving Adherence Among Hypertensive Patients - presents ways physicians can improve patient education, adherence to treatment, and control of high blood pressure.

1988 Report of the Joint National Committee on Detection, Evaluation, and Treatment of High Blood Pressure - reports latest consensus recommendations.

Statement on Hypertension in the Elderly - review finding from clinical trials, and presents new guidelines.

Working Group Report on Ambulatory Blood Pressure Monitoring - examines state of the technology of ambulatory blood pressure monitoring.

Working Group Report on High Blood Pressure in Pregnancy - provides guidance to physician in managing hypertensive patients who become pregnant and managing pregnant patients who become hypertensive.

Working Group Report on Hypertension and Chronic Renal Failure - reviews the current knowledge of the interaction.

Working Group Report on the Management of Patients with Hypertension and High Blood Cholesterol - designed to guide the clinician in managing patients with multiple cardiovascular risk factors.

Be patient. If any phone number is incorrect, call (area code) 555-1212 and request the new listing.

AIDS, Cancer and Other Diseases

* Homeless Mentally Ill Programs

Office of Programs for the Homeless Mentally Ill
National Institute of Mental Health (NIMH)
5600 Fishers Lane, Room 7C-08
Rockville, MD 20857 (301) 443-3706

This Office is the focal point for NIMH research, research demonstrations, and technical assistance activities concerning the housing and service needs of the homeless mentally ill population. The office sponsors a national program of research demonstration projects studying the coordination of housing and services for homeless mentally ill adults.

* Homeless Council

Interagency Council on the Homeless
451 Seventh St., SW, Suite 7274
Washington, DC 20410 (202) 708-1480

The Council was created by the Stewart B. McKinney Homeless Assistance Act to provide Federal leadership in the development of urgently needed assistance to protect and improve the lives and safety of homeless persons. The Council is comprised of 17 Federal agencies with jurisdiction over various aspects of Federal homelessness efforts. The Council provides technical assistance and publishes information concerning McKinney and other Federal homeless assistance programs in the Council Communique (a free, bi-monthly newsletter), funding bulletins, an annual report, and periodic legislative updates. The Council maintains a list of official state contacts for homeless issues.

* Homeless Veterans

Homeless Chronically Mentally Ill Veterans Program
U.S. Department of Veterans Affairs
810 Vermont Ave., NW
Washington, DC 20420 (202) 535-7303

The Homeless Chronically Mentally Ill Veterans Program provides outreach, VA case management services, and psychiatric residential treatment for homeless mentally ill veterans, when appropriate, in community-based facilities. A total of 45 sites in 26 states and the District of Columbia provide an integrated network of treatment programs for homeless veterans with chronic mental illness. The VA developed the Domiciliary Care for Homeless Veterans Program to address the unmet clinical needs of homeless veterans. More than 90% of the veterans served by this program, which operates in 27 sites, have psychiatric illness of alcohol or other drug dependency problems. Services include outreach and referral, screening and assessment, medical and psychiatric evaluation, treatment and rehabilitation, and post-discharge community support. Staff help veterans secure employment and housing. For more information on this program contact: Richard Olson, Domiciliary Care for Homeless Veterans Program, U.S. Department of Veterans Affairs, 810 Vermont Ave., NW, Washington, DC 20420; (202) 535-7530.

* Homelessness

National Resource Center On Homelessness and Mental Illness
Policy Research Associates, Inc.
262 Delaware Ave.
Delmar, NY 12054 (800) 444-7415

Under contract with the National Institute of Mental Illness, the Policy Research Associates develops and disseminates new knowledge about the coordination of housing and services for homeless mentally ill persons. Supported in part by the U.S. Department of Housing and Urban Development, this contract features an increased emphasis on the development, financing, and operation of housing for homeless mentally ill persons. This Center publishes *Access*, a bi-monthly newsletter, and has free information packets and database searches. They also have an organizational referral list, *Organizations Concerned with Homelessness and Mental Illness*, which includes information on more than 100 federal programs and national and state organizations working in the fields of homelessness and/or mental health. The Center has the following free information:

Information Packets
Financing Services for Homeless Mentally Ill Persons
Training Staff and Volunteers
Outreach Services for Homeless Mentally Ill Persons
Case Management with Homeless Mentally Ill Persons
Self-Help Programs
Working with Dually Diagnosed Homeless Persons
Working with Homeless Children at Risk for Severe Emotional Disturbance

Database Searches
General Information
Housing
Treatment/Clinical Issues
Health/Health Care
Legal Issues
Epidemiology
Research Methods/Program Evaluation

* Huntington's Disease Research Center

Department of Medical Genetics
Indiana University Medical School
Medical Research Building
975 W. Walnut St.
Indianapolis, IN 46202-5251 (317) 274-2245

The National Institutes of Health and Indiana University Medical Center, Indianapolis, maintain a roster of Huntington's Disease patients and families. Each of the families complete a family history questionnaire, and the statistics are used for research. IUMC also acts as a broker between families and researchers, who can request subjects for a particular project from IUMC's database of patients and families.

* Infectious Diseases

National Institute of Allergy and Infectious Diseases
National Institutes of Health
Building 31, Room 7A32
9000 Rockville Pike
Bethesda, MD 20892 (301) 496-5717

This institute offers many publications and expertise about diarrhea, bacterial meningitis, the common cold, mononucleosis, herpes, rabies, Rocky Mountain Spotted Fever, schistosomiasis, and other infectious diseases. *Understanding the Immune System* (No. 84-529) is a free 22-page report that discusses antigens, the immune system, disorders (including AIDS), the immunology of transplants, and new diagnostic methods.

* Infectious Diseases

Center for Infectious Diseases (CID)
Centers for Disease Control
1600 Clifton Rd., NE
Atlanta, GA 30333 (404) 639-3534

The CID surveys AIDS cases, epidemiologic studies, laboratory investigations, prevention strategies, and technology transfer concerning the HIV infection. They also examine vaccines and other strategies against bacterial, viral, and parasitic pathogens, such as rabies, hepatitis B, Hemophilis influenzae b, and malaria. They also develop and evaluate prevention and control methods for foodborne pathogens, such as Salmonella. This office can refer you to publications and researchers concerning your particular topic of interest.

* Kidney and Urological Diseases

National Kidney and Urological Diseases
Information Clearinghouse
Box NKUDIC
Bethesda, MD 20892 (301) 468-6345

This clearinghouse responds to inquiries regarding kidney and urological diseases. They can access the CHID (Combined Health Information Database) database to get further information. They have pamphlets, brochures, and reports for the public and professionals, and can refer people to voluntary and professional organizations. The free publications they have available include:

Understanding Urinary Tract Infections - patient and public education booklet.

Prevention and Treatment of Kidney Stones - describes diagnosis, treatment, and types of urinary incontinence.

Urinary Incontinence- describes diagnosis, treatment, and types of urinary incontinence.

Prostate Problems - describes common prostate problems such as prostatitis, benign prostatic hypertrophy, and prostate cancer.

National Kidney and Urologic Diseases Information Clearinghouse

Be patient. If any phone number is incorrect, call (area code) 555-1212 and request the new listing.

Health and Medicine

Extracorporeal Shock-Wave Lithotripsy - describes the removal of kidney and urinary tract stones.

Combined Health Information Database - describes subfiles in the database.

National Kidney and Urologic Diseases Information Clearinghouse Thesaurus - searching tool for the subfile on CHID.

Directory of Kidney and Urologic Disease-Related Organizations - lists professional, patient, and voluntary organizations.

Prostate Enlargement: Benign Prostatic Hyperplasia - gives basic information about the prostate gland and prostate enlargement.

Urinary Incontinence in Adults - summary statement of NIH Consensus Development Conference.

Diabetes and Kidney Disease: A Selected Annotated Bibliography

End-Stage Renal Disease: Choosing a Treatment That's Right for You

Bibliographies

Impotence

Dialysis - Professional Materials

Dialysis - Patient Materials

Urinary Incontinence - Professional Materials

Urinary Incontinence - Patient Materials

Prostate Disorders - Professional Materials

Prostate Disorders - Patient Materials

Urinary Stones - Professional Materials

Urinary Stones - Patient Materials

Urinary Tract Infections

Renal Nutrition

Transplantation - Professional Materials

Transplantation - Patient Materials

* Kidney Stones

National Institute of Diabetes and Digestive and Kidney Diseases

NIH, Building 31, Room 9A-04

9000 Rockville Pike

Bethesda, MD 20892 (301) 496-3583

This institute offers several publications free including: *Prevention and Treatment of Kidney Stones* (No. 83-2495) and *Extracorporeal Shock Wave Lithotripsy* (No. 84-859) as well as experts on staff who can answer questions.

* Kidney Transplants

National Institute of Diabetes and Digestive and Kidney Diseases

NIH, Building 31, Room 9A-04

9000 Rockville Pike

Bethesda, MD 20892 (301) 496-3583

This Institute conducts research regarding kidney transplants. The staff can refer you to current researchers, as well as sending you brochures and reports on this procedure.

* Lead Poisoning

Lead Poisoning Prevention Branch

National Center for Environmental Health and Injury Control

Centers for Disease Control (CDC)

1600 Clifton Rd., NE

Atlanta, GA 3033 (404) 488-4880

Childhood lead poisoning is one of the most common pediatric health problems in the United States today, and it is entirely preventable. New data indicate significant adverse effects of lead exposure in children at blood lead levels previously believed to be safe. For more information on lead poisoning, and a free copy of CDC's *Preventing Lead Poisoning in Young Children*, contact the office listed above.

* Lead Studies

Agency for Toxic Substances and Disease Registry

1600 Clifton Rd., NE

Atlanta, GA 30333 (404) 639-0700

ATSDR has developed a Lead Initiative to evaluate completed health assessments for sites that have lead as a contaminant of concern. This project stems from a report, *The Nature and Extent of Lead Poisoning in Children in the United States*, published by ATSDR. The goal of this project is to prevent lead toxicity in young children who are exposed to lead released from Superfund sites and facilities.

* Leprosy: Free Treatment

Gillis W. Long Hansen's Disease Center

Carville, LA 70721 (504) 642-4706

The Gillis W. Long Hansen's Disease Center primarily provides Hansen's Disease (leprosy) patients a place to receive a complete evaluation and treatment. Any person with a confirmed diagnosis of leprosy is eligible for admission. The Center conducts an extensive patient care and rehabilitation program, as well as research, training and education activities.

* Medical Devices Information

Division of Consumer Affairs

Center for Devices and Radiological Health

5600 Fishers Lane, HFZ-210

Rockville, MD 20857 (301) 443-4190

The Consumer Affairs Office can provide you with a publication list which contains information on a wide variety of medical and consumer products. Topics covered include: AIDS, air cleaners, apnea monitors, blankets, condoms, contraception, cordless phones, dental, dialysis, ECT, endometriosis, eyes, fluorescent lamps, gastric bubble, hair removal, handicapped, health fraud, hearing, home test kits, hyperthermia, investigational, lasers, mammography, medical devices, mercury vapor lamps, microwaves, MRI, nuclear medicine, osteoporosis, pacemakers, pain relief, product problem reporting program, scoliosis, silicone/collagen, sunlamps, sunscreens, tanning, toxic shock syndrome and tampons, ultraviolet radiation, ultrasound, video display terminals, and x-rays.

* Mitral Valve Prolapse

National Heart, Lung, and Blood Institute (NHLBI)

National Institutes of Health

Building 31, Room 42-21

9000 Rockville Pike

Bethesda, MD 20892 (301) 496-4236

This institute offers much information to enhance the public's understanding of cardiovascular disease and prevention. One of its free publications is *NHLBI Facts About...Mitral Valve Prolapse*.

* Nerve Regeneration and Brain Transplants

Office of Technology Assessment (OTA)

600 Pennsylvania Ave., SE

Washington, DC 20510 (202) 224-8996

Recent advances in neuroscience research have enormous potential to improve the lives of millions of Americans. OTA has studied the following neuroscience-associated topics: neural transplants and nerve regeneration, including related ethical and legal issues; biological rhythms and shift work; neurotoxicity testing by private and public organizations; and biochemical bases of mental illness. Contact Mark Schaefer, the project director, for more information. The resulting publication is titled *Impacts of Neuroscience*.

* Parkinson's Disease

National Institute of Neurological Disorders and Stroke

National Institutes of Health

9000 Rockville Pike

Building 31, Room 8A06

Bethesda, MD 20892 (301) 496-4697

Parkinson's Disease: Hope Through Research (No. 83-139) outlines the possible causes and treatments for Parkinson's disease and summarizes both research efforts and therapies.

* Periodontal Gum Disease

Periodontal Disease Centers

National Institute of Dental Research

Westwood Building, Room 559

Be patient. If any phone number is incorrect, call (area code) 555-1212 and request the new listing.

AIDS, Cancer and Other Diseases

533 Westbard Ave.
Bethesda, MD 20892 (301) 496-7784

This Institute funds the Periodontal Disease Centers which conduct research on the causes, treatment and prevention of periodontal disease. One of the centers focuses on the identification of risk factors. The staff can answer general questions regarding periodontal disease. Several free publications include: *Periodontal (Gum) Disease, Detection and Prevention of Periodontal Disease in Diabetes* (No. 86-1148) *Tooth Decay* (No. 82-1146), *Preventing Tooth Decay: A Guide to Implementing Self-Applied Fluoride Programs in School Settings;* and *Seal Out Dental Decay* (No. 80-1140) which discusses plastic sealants.

* Rare Diseases and Orphan Drugs Clearinghouse

National Information Center for Orphan Drugs and Rare Diseases
450 5th Street NW Room 7103
Washington, DC 20001 (800) 456-3505

This center (NICODARD) responds to inquiries on diseases with a prevalence of 200,000 or fewer cases in the United States. This clearinghouse, sponsored by the Food and Drug Administration, also gathers and disseminates information on medicines not widely researched or available.

* Rheumatic Disease

National Institute of Arthritis and Musculoskeletal Diseases
NIH,Building 31, Room 9A-04
Bethesda, MD 20892 (301) 496-5717

A 43-page reference titled *Rheumatic Diseases and the Older Adult: An Annotated Bibliography, 1986,* contains 86 references with abstracts to the medical literature for physicians, allied health professionals, and others interested in geriatric medicine and rheumatology. It is available for $4.

* Sickle Cell Centers

National Sickle Cell Disease Program
7550 Wisconsin Ave., Room 504
Bethesda, MD 20892 (301) 496-6931

This program funds centers to coordinate manpower, research, and facilities by offering a combination of research and demonstration services, screening and education clinics, public and professional education, and counseling and rehabilitation for sickle cell disease.

* Sickle Cell Disease

Superintendent of Documents
Government Printing Office
Washington, DC 20402 (202) 783-3238

Management and Therapy of Sickle Cell Disease presents articles on the treatment and management of sickle cell diseases. It covers laboratory diagnosis and newborn screening, sickle cell trait, nursing management, and psychosocial management. It serves as a working document for clinicians and physicians who may see only a limited number of patients with sickle cell disorder (S/N 017-043-00120-6, $3.25).

* Skin Diseases

National Arthritis and Musculoskeletal
and Skin Disease Information Clearinghouse
Box AMS
Bethesda, MD 20892 (301) 495-4484

Living with Epidermolysis Bullosa (No. 84-663), and *What You Should Know About Vitiligo* (No. 80-2088) are a sampling of materials available free from this clearinghouse.

* Spina Bifida

National Institute of Neurological Disorders and Stroke
National Institutes of Health
9000 Rockville Pike
Building 31, Room 8A06
Bethesda, MD 20892 (301) 496-4697

Spina Bifida: Hope through Research (No. 86-309) discusses the prevailing views about the causes, diagnosis, and medical care of this congenital spinal cord defect.

* Spinal Cord Injury

National Institute of Neurological Disorders and Stroke
National Institutes of Health
9000 Rockville Pike
Building 31, Room 8A06
Bethesda, MD 20892 (301) 496-4697

This institute offers information about the causes, implications,and outlook for spinal cord injuries and drug therapy, neural prostheses, and rehabilitation.

* Spinal Cord Injury

National Rehabilitation Information Center (NARIC)
8455 Colesville, Rd, Suite 935 (301) 588-9284
Silver Spring, MD 20910 (800) 346-2742 (Voice and TDD)

NARIC has put together a free resource guide for people with spinal cord injury and their families. Included in the guide is information about SCI-related magazines and newsletters you can read for knowledge and enjoyment; SCI organizations that assist people with SCI from point of injury onward, and organizations that focus on specific aspects of SCI; SCI membership organizations, and the names and addresses of their chapters; and a short listing of some of the documents available from the NARIC library that discuss topics of interest of people with SCI.

* Stroke and Brain Disorders Resource Center

National Institute of Neurological Disorders and Stroke (NINDS)
National Institutes of Health
9000 Rockville Pike
Building 31, Room 8A06
Bethesda, MD 20892 (301) 496-4697

NINDS conducts and guides research on the causes, prevention, diagnosis, and treatment of fundamental neurological disorders and stroke and trauma. The Institute gives grants for extramural research, as well as providing fellowships. Other areas of research include cerebral palsy, autism, dyslexia, multiple sclerosis, Parkinson's and Huntington's diseases, and epilepsy. Brochures and pamphlets available free include: *What You Should Know About Stroke and Stroke Prevention* (No. 81-1909) and *Stroke: Hope through Research* (No. 83-2222).

* Tooth Decay Prevention and Treatment

Dental Disease Prevention Activity
Centers for Disease Control
1600 Clifton Rd., NE
Atlanta, GA 30333 (404) 639-1830

The Dental Disease Prevention Activity is a resource for information on prevention activities in the field of dental health. It can provide you with information on fluoridation, periodontal disease, and baby-bottle tooth decay. A list of educational materials is also available including the following free publications: *Fluoridation...Nature's Way To Prevent Tooth Decay* (No. 81-8321) and *Fluoridation is for Everyone* (No. 77-8334).

* Toxic Shock Syndrome

Office of Consumer Affairs
Public Inquiries
Food and Drug Administration
5600 Fishers Lane (HFE-88)
Rockville, MD 20857 (301) 443-3170

A short brochure titled *Toxic Shock Syndrome and Tampons* (No. 85-4169) explains the symptoms and causes of this syndrome.

* Traumatic Brain Injury

National Rehabilitation Information Center (NARIC)
8455 Colesville, Rd, Suite 935 (301) 588-9284
Silver Spring, MD 20910 (800) 346-2742 (Voice and TDD)

NARIC has put together a free resource guide for people with traumatic brain injury and their families. This guide has information regarding national organizations, associations, and programs; support groups and state associations of the National Head Injury Foundation, periodicals, catalogs, directories and other sourcebooks, information resources, regional medical libraries, and rehabilitation research and training centers, and lists of books and articles in the NARIC collection that may be of interest to the newly injured person or family member.

Be patient. If any phone number is incorrect, call (area code) 555-1212 and request the new listing.

Health and Medicine

*** Ulcers: Gastric and Duodenal**

National Digestive Diseases Information Clearinghouse
Box NDDIC

Bethesda, MD 20892   (301) 468-6344

This clearinghouse can offer information on this disease and makes available free single copies of such publications as *Peptic Ulcer* (No. 85-3800).

Be patient. If any phone number is incorrect, call (area code) 555-1212 and request the new listing.

Cigarettes and Chewing Tobacco

* Cholesterol and Smoking Connection

Information Services
Cholesterol/Smoking Information Center
Building 31-A, Room 4A-21
Bethesda, MD 20892 (301) 951-3260

This center maintains a database and materials on blood cholesterol and smoking geared to the public, health professionals and issues pertaining to the workplace.

* Cigarettes: Self Test for Smokers

Office on Smoking and Health
Technical Information Center
Centers for Disease Control
1600 Clifton Rd. NE, Mail Stop K-50
Atlanta, GA 30333 (404) 488-5705

Smoking, Tobacco and Health (No. 87-8397) discusses the health risks and prevalence of smoking as well as tobacco growing, cigarette manufacturing, and marketing. *Out of the Ashes: Choosing a Method to Quit Smoking* is a guide to assist smokers in selecting a quitting program. Each of these publications are available free.

* Clearing the Air

Office of Cancer Communications
National Cancer Institute (NCI)
Building 31, Room 10A-18
9000 Rockville Pike (800) 4-CANCER
Bethesda, MD 20892 (301) 496-5583

Clearing the Air: A Guide to Quitting Smoking (No.86-1647) suggests various approaches to quit smoking. This 32 page pamphlet is also available in Spanish. Single copies are available free.

* Helping Smokers to Quit

Office of Cancer Communications
National Cancer Institute (NCI)
Building 31, Room 10A-18
9000 Rockville Pike
Bethesda, MD 20892 (800) 4-CANCER

NCI can provide you with free publications to assist smokers in the efforts to quit. Some of the publications include:

How To Help Your Patients Stop Smoking: A National Cancer Institute Manual for Physicians
How To Help Your Patients Stop Using Tobacco: A National Cancer Institute Manual For The Oral Health Team
Pharmacists Helping Smokers Quit Kit
Quit for Good Kit - packet designed for health professionals to assist their smoking patients to quit.

* No Smoking in Schools

Office of Cancer Communications
National Cancer Institute (NCI)
Building 31, Room 10A018
9000 Rockville Pike
Bethesda, MD 20892 (800) 4-CANCER

School Programs to Prevent Smoking: The National Cancer Institute Guide to Strategies That Succeed is designed to assist administrators in developing a successful no smoking policy in schools.

* Smoking And Health

Office on Smoking and Health
Centers for Disease Control
1600 Clifton Rd., NE
Mail Stop K-50
Atlanta, GA 30333 (404) 488-5705

The following are free publications dealing with smoking and health.

At A Glance - The Health Benefits Of Smoking Cessation: A Report Of the Surgeon General is a pamphlet highlighting the benefits of quitting smoking.

Smoking And Health: A National Status Report is a report to Congress discussing the status of smoking programs in the Nation.

Bibliography on Smoking and Health is a compilation of 1989 scientific information on tobacco and tobacco use.

* Smoking Cessation Methods

Office on Smoking and Health
Centers for Disease Control
1600 Clifton Rd., NE, Mail Stop K-50
Atlanta, GA 30333 (404) 488-5705

Review and Evaluation of Smoking Cessation Methods is an in-depth analysis of the variety of methods available to help smokers quit, including the effectiveness, benefits, and drawbacks of each method.

* Smoking Info Specifically for Parents

Office on Smoking and Health
Technical Information Center
Centers for Disease Control
1600 Clifton Road NE, Mail Stop K-50
Atlanta, GA 30333 (404) 488-5705

If Your Kids Think Everybody Smokes, They Don't Know Everybody. A Parent's Guide to Smoking and Teenagers (No. 83-50199) explains why some teenagers become smokers. This four page guide is available free.

* Smoking in the Workplace

Office of Cancer Communications
National Cancer Institute (NCI)
Building 31, Room 10A-18
9000 Rockville Pike
Bethesda, MD 20892 (800) 4-CANCER

NCI has put together a smoking policy package which examines the various questions and issues regarding smoking in the workplace. This information is free for the asking.

* Smokeless Tobacco and Dangers of Chewing

Dental Disease Prevention Activity
Centers for Disease Control
1600 Clifton Road NE
Atlanta, GA 30333 (404) 693-1830

Smokeless Tobacco Education Resources is an annotated list which includes educational materials on snuff and chewing tobacco available from federal, state and local agencies and from private sources. This 6-page bibliography is free.

* Smoking and High Blood Pressure

High Blood Pressure Information Center
120/80 National Institutes of Health
Bethesda, MD 20892 (301) 951-3260

A free 24-page reference titled *The Physician's Guide: How to Help Your Hypertensive Patients Stop Smoking* (NIH No. 84-1271) shows what doctors can do within a busy office practice to persuade hypertensive patients to stop smoking.

Be patient. If any phone number is incorrect, call (area code) 555-1212 and request the new listing.

Health and Medicine

* Smoking Cessation and Cancer Prevention

Office of Cancer Communications
National Cancer Institute (NCI)
Building 31, Room 10A-18
9000 Rockville Pike (800) 4-CANCER
Bethesda, MD 20892 (301) 496-5583

The National Cancer Institute carries out a multi-disciplinary program in smoking and tobacco research and control through the Smoking, Tobacco and Cancer Program. It conducts research in epidemiology and carcinogenesis and carry out interventions to reduce smoking and tobacco use. The program is now supporting large-scale intervention trials in eight areas, some of which are adolescent smoking prevention, mass media approach to smoking prevention, and cessation and smoking among minorities. NCI has begun a multicenter Community Intervention Trial for Smoking Cessation (COMMIT) to test strategies to produce long-term cessation among all cigarette smokers within a community, with particular emphasis on heavy smokers. One of their many publications includes *Smoking Programs for Youth* (No. 81-2156) which describes activities that can be pursued through schools and community groups.

* Smoking Risks and Prevention Clearinghouse

Information Center
National Heart, Lung, and Blood Institute
4733 Westbard Avenue, Suite 530
Bethesda, MD 20814 (301) 951-3260

The National Heart, Lung, and Blood Institute sponsors a Smoking Education Information Center which provides services to health professionals and the general public on smoking issues. They provide pamphlets, fact sheets, posters, and other publications, as well as information in response to inquiries. The center can access information on the Combined Health Information Database (CHID). A library and reading room are open to the public, and librarians are available to assist you. The *Infomemo* contains information on disease prevention, education and control. For a publications list or more information, contact this office. Some of the publications available include:

Clinical Opportunities for Smoking Intervention: A Guide for the Busy Physician
Nurses: Help Your Patients Stop Smoking
It's Your Business: Smoking Policies for the Workplace

* Smoking Technical Information Center

Office on Smoking and Health
Centers for Disease Control
1600 Clifton Road NE, Mail Stop K-50
Atlanta, GA 30333 (404) 488-5705

This office offers bibliographic and reference services to researchers through its Technical Information Center (TIC). The TIC publishes and distributes a number of titles in the field of smoking and health, and through its database can provide you with further bibliographic information. TIC's Smoking Studies Section designs and conducts national surveys on smoking behavior, attitude, knowledge, and beliefs regarding tobacco use. Visitors may use the collection between 8:30 am and 5:00 pm EST (call ahead), but reference services are also provided by phone. A free publications listing is also available. The free publications include:

Smoking, Tobacco and Health: A Fact Book
Clearing the Air
Guia Para Dejar De Fumar
Chew or Snuff is Real Bad Stuff
If Your Kid Thinks Everyone Smokes. . .
Nicotine Addiction and Cigarettes
is Your Baby Smoking?
Baby in the House Stickers
?Embarazada? He Aqui dos Buenas Razones Para Dejar De Fumar
Performance Edge
Out of the Ashes: Choosing a Method To Quit Smoking
At A Glance - The Health Benefits of Smoking Cessation: A Report of the Surgeon General, 1990
Good News For Smokers 50 and Older
Smoking and Health: A National Status Report
Highlights of State Tobacco and Health Data
Making Health Communication Programs Work: A Planner's Guide
Media Strategies for Smoking Control Guidelines
Review and Evaluation of Smoking Cessation Methods
Three JAMA Articles on Trends
Major Local Smoking Ordinances in the United States

Guide to Public Health Practice: State Health Agency Tobacco Prevention and Control Plans
HHS Model Sale of Tobacco Products to Minors Control Act
Inspector General's Report on Minors' Access to Cigarettes
Bibliography on Smoking and Health

* Smoking: Videotapes and Slides

National Audiovisual Center
8700 Edgeworth Drive
Capitol Heights, MD 20743-3701 (301) 763-1896

Numerous videotapes aimed at all ages groups are available can be purchased or rented including "Pressures to Smoke" and "Resisting Pressures to Smoke". "We Can't Go On Like This" (film and videotape) consists of the following seven vignettes that are designed to motivate a group to explore why they smoke, recognize the obstacles to quitting, and extinguish the habit: "Crisis"; "Digging Cigarettes"; "The Drag Race"; "Escalation"; "Gambling" "The Ordeal of Arnold Hertz"; "We Can't Go On Like This". "Everyone Can Do Something About Smoking" consists of 127 color slides which explain how organizations can help reduce the smoking problem. Another slide set available is "A Physician Talks About Smoking" which presents the latest information on the health effects so as to better equip health professionals who are asked to speak about the effects of smoking on health.

* Snuff and Chewing Tobacco Risks

Office of Cancer Communications
National Cancer Institute (NCI)
Building 31, Room 10A-18
9000 Rockville Pike (800) 4-CANCER
Bethesda, MD 20892 (301) 496-5583

In Answer To Your Questions on Smokeless Tobacco discusses the risks of snuff and chewing tobacco. Single copies are free.

* Stop Smoking Posters

Office of Smoking and Health
Technical Information Center
Centers for Disease Control
1600 Clifton Road NE, Mail Stop K-50
Atlanta, GA 30333 (404) 488-5705

"Don't Get Hooked!" (15" x 21", color) shows a fish smoking a cigarette caught by a fishing hook. It is also available in Spanish. Other posters include:

Fashion's In/Smoking Out
Performance Edge
Butt Out
History Posters:
Alexander
Columbus
Ross

* Stop Smoking: State and Local Programs

Office on Smoking and Health
Technical Information Center
Centers for Disease Control
1600 Clifton Road NE
Mail Stop K-50
Atlanta, GA 30333 (404) 488-5705

State and Local Programs on Smoking and Health: A Catalog of Local Programs Throughout the Country on Smoking and Health (No. 82-50189) is packed with descriptions of cessation clinics, prevention efforts, school programs, community and patient education programs, mass media campaigns, and individual self-help strategies. Single copies of this 151-page catalog are available free.

* Teaching Materials

National Technical Information Service
5285 Port Royal Rd.
Springfield, VA 22161 (703) 487-4650

I Don't! I Won't! Chew Tobacco Curriculum Kit contains teacher's flip chart and manual, and comic books and stickers for students. It is geared for grades K-3 and cost $40 (PB90-780677FAA).

Be patient. If any phone number is incorrect, call (area code) 555-1212 and request the new listing.

Cigarettes and Chewing Tobacco

* Teenage Cigarette Smoking Test
Office of Smoking and Health
Centers for Disease Control
1600 Clifton Road NE, Mail Stop K-50
Atlanta, GA 30333   (404) 488-5705

Teenage Cigarette Smoking Self Test is a quiz designed to help teens understand their feelings about smoking. This free 12-page booklet consists of a leader's guide followed by eight duplicating masters. *Chew of Snuff is Real Bad Stuff* is a pamphlet (folds out to a poster) for teenagers on the harmful effects of smokeless tobacco.

Health and Medicine

Aging and America's Elderly

With the dramatic demographic changes occurring, a wider array of government agencies and private organizations are focusing on some aspect of the "graying of America". This section introduces a sampling of resources available which target the special health needs and problems that go hand-in-hand with the aging process. Also, don't overlook the House and Senate Aging Committees because they study many health issues.

* Accidental Hypothermia

National Institute on Aging Information Center
2209 Distribution Circle
Silver Spring, MD 20910 (301) 495-3455

A free 12-page booklet, *A Winter Hazard for Older People: Accidental Hypothermia* (No. 81-1464), warns elderly persons to protect themselves against a progressive drop in deep body temperature that can be fatal if not detected in time and properly treated.

* Age Pages: Info on Health Concerns

National Institute on Aging Information Center
2209 Distribution Circle
Silver Spring, MD 20910 (301) 495-3455

This NIH Institute publishes dozens of fact sheets, printed on two sides in large type, for the lay audience. This series is termed "Age Pages" and a list for most of the fact sheets titled *Age Page Compilation*, is available free. Some of the "Age Pages" which are free include: *Be Sensible About Salt; Can Life Be Extended?; Considering Surgery?; Health Quackery; Hints for Shopping, Cooking and Enjoying Meals; Osteoporosis: The Bone Thinner; Prostate Problems: Safety Belt Sense; Senility: Myth or Madness?; Sexuality in Later Life; Stroke;* and *Urinary Incontinence.*

* Aging Administration

Administration on Aging
U.S. Department of Health and Human Services
330 Independence Ave., SW, Room 4646
Washington, DC 20201 (202) 619-0641

Administration On Aging's primary goals are to support a national network of State and area agencies on aging and Indian tribes in their efforts to reach out to older persons residing in communities; develop and oversee a comprehensive and coordinated system of supportive services and opportunities to meet the social and human service needs of the elderly; and service as an advocate on behalf of older people. AoA supports improvements in quality of life and services for older people through research and training grants. Results of these studies are made available to the public.

* Aging Issues

General Accounting Office
P.O. Box 6015
Gaithersburg, MD 20877 (202) 275-6241

Aging Issues is a free report which is a compilation of all 1991 reports and ongoing work conducted by GAO regarding older Americans. It covers a broad range of issues, including federal government activities in health care, housing, income security, and social and community services. This compilation provides a summary of reports for the given year.

* Aging Magazine

Administration on Aging
U.S. Department of Health and Human Services
Room 4643
330 Independence Ave., SW
Washington, DC 20201 (202) 619-1352

Aging Magazine, published quarterly for $6.50 per year, focuses on innovative programs and book reviews in the field of aging. This publication is primarily designed for professionals and service providers for the elderly.

* Alzheimer's Clearinghouse

Alzheimer's Disease Education and Referral Center
P.O. Box 8250
Silver Spring, MD 20907 (301) 495-3311

The National Institute on Aging established the Alzheimer's Disease Education and Referral Center as part of a broad program to conduct research and distribute information about Alzheimer's disease. Services include: information and referral on research efforts, diagnosis and treatment issues, and services to patients and family members, including referrals to resources at the national and state levels; distributes brochures, factsheets publication and reports; maintains the Alzheimer's disease subfile on the online Combined Health Information Database; develops collaborative relationships with Federal and state agencies with an interest in Alzheimer's disease; and maintains a library which includes books, reprints, and reference works, as well as videotapes. The publications are free and include;

*General Information Packet on Alzheimer's Disease
Alzheimer's Disease: Q&A
Differential Diagnosis of Dementing Diseases
Age Page - Confusion and Memory Loss in Old Age
Alzheimer's Disease Centers Program
Special Reports on Alzheimer's Disease
Fact Sheet: Alzheimer's Disease Database
ADEAR Center Brochure
Report of the DHHS Advisory Panel on Alzheimer's Disease
Family Reading List: Caring for Memory-Impaired Elders*

* Alzheimer's Q & A

National Institute on Aging Information Center
2209 Distribution Circle
Silver Spring, MD 20910 (301) 495-3455

A 12-page free pamphlet, *Q & A: Alzheimer's Disease* (No. 81-1646), addresses fundamental issues related to the causes, symptoms, and treatment of this disease as well as research efforts surrounding it.

* Alzheimer's Research

National Institute of Mental Health (NIMH)
5600 Fishers Lane, Room 15C05
Rockville, MD 20857 (301) 443-4515

NIMH supports intramural research on the causes and new treatment of Alzheimer's disease. Some of the free publications available include:

*Report of the Advisory Panel on Alzheimer's Disease, 1988-1989
Second Report of the Advisory Panel on Alzheimer's Disease, 1990
There Were Times, Dear. . . Living With Alzheimer's Disease
Useful Information on Alzheimer's Disease
Differential Diagnosis of Dementing Diseases*

* Alzheimer's Treatment

Superintendent of Documents
Government Printing Office
Washington, DC 20402 (202) 783-3238

Alzheimer's Disease Treatment and Family Stress: Directions for Research presents a collection of papers giving current information on research investigations that increase understanding of the nature and consequences of family caregiving (017-024-01365-0, $14).

Be patient. If any phone number is incorrect, call (area code) 555-1212 and request the new listing.

Aging and America's Elderly

* Brain and Dementia

Office of Clinical Center Communications
Warren G. Magnuson Clinical Center
NIH, Building 10, Room 5C-305
9000 Rockville Pike
Bethesda, MD 20892 (301) 496-2563

The Brain in "Aging" and Dementia (No. 83-2625) discusses brain anatomy and physiology, the normal process of brain aging, and senility. Vascular dementia and Alzheimer's disease are described as well as research on the causes and treatment.

* Brittle Bones

Osteoporosis Booklet
National Institute of Arthritis and Musculoskeletal Diseases
NIH, Building 31, Room 9A-04
Bethesda, MD 20892 (301) 496-5717

Osteoporosis: Cause, Treatment, Prevention (No. 86-2226) discusses this bone-thinning condition. Single copy free with a business-sized self-addressed envelope with $.44 postage.

* Cataracts and Glaucoma

National Eye Institute (NEI)
National Institutes of Health
Bldg. 31, Room 6A32
Bethesda, MD 20892 (301) 496-5248

NEI conducts research aimed at the prevention and nonsurgical treatment of cataracts. They also support research to understand the basis of optic nerve damage in glaucoma and at preventing loss of vision. They have publications on these topics and can answer your questions regarding current research.

* Central Clearinghouse

National Institute on Aging
National Institutes of Health
Federal Building, Room 6C12
Bethesda, MD 20892 (301) 496-1752

The National Institute on Aging (NIA) has responsibility for biomedical, social, and behavioral research and training related to the aging process and diseases and other special problems and needs of the aged. NIA continues to work on the Baltimore Longitudinal Study of Aging, which has followed the same 650 men since 1958 to measure the changes with age. NIA encourages and supports research on aging at universities, hospital, medical centers, and other organizations. Funds are made available for these investigations through a variety of grant and contract mechanisms.

* Chinese Publications for the Elderly

National Institute on Aging Information Center
2209 Distribution Circle
Silver Spring, MD 20910 (301) 495-3455

Several fact sheets, printed on two sides in large type, are published in Chinese including: *Arthritis Advice; Cancer Facts for People Over 50; Dealing with Diabetes; Dietary Supplements; Heat, Cold, and Being Old; Minorities and How They Grow Old; Foot Care for Older People; Safe Use of Medicines by Older People;* and *What To Do About the Flu.* Individual copies of these fact sheets are available free.

* Depression in the Elderly

National Institute of Mental Health
5600 Fishers Lane, Room 15C05
Rockville, MD 20857 (301) 443-4515

If You're Over 65 and Feeling Depressed...Treatment Brings New Hope is a free publication, which explains depression, provides a depression checklist, and describes causes and treatment for depression.

* Depression: Prevention and Intervention

National Institute of Mental Health
Public Inquiries Branch
Parklawn Building, Room 15C-05
5600 Fishers Lane
Rockville, MD 20857 (301) 443-4513

A free 8 page booklet, *If You're Over 65 and Feeling Depressed...Treatment Brings New Hope,* discusses depression in the elderly and various treatment options to consider.

* Eating for the Elderly

National Clearinghouse for Primary Care Information
8201 Greensboro Dr., Suite 600
McLean, VA 22102 (703) 821-8955

Easy Eating for Well-Seasoned Adults is a free collection of recipes submitted by older adults. It provides an excellent resource for older adult health center clients.

* Elder Abuse and Family Violence

Clearinghouse on Family Violence Information
P.O. Box 1182
Washington, DC 20013 (703) 385-7565

This clearinghouse has information on spouse and elder abuse. They have brochures and audiovisual materials available, and an in-house database from which they can retrieve reference materials and organizations involved with family violence.

* Geriatrics Career Training and Education Grants

Administration on Aging
Office of Program Development
330 Independence Ave., SW
Washington, DC 20201 (202) 619-0641

The Administration on Aging funds continuing education programs in the field of aging by giving grants to institutions of higher education and professional organizations. For a list of these institutions and organizations, contact this office.

* Geriatric Education Centers

Bureau of Health Professions
Health Resources and Services Administration (HRSA)
5600 Fishers Lane, Room 81-03
Rockville, MD 20857 (301) 443-6887

HRSA is supporting Geriatric Education Centers to facilitate the training of health professions faculty, students, and practitioners within specific geographical areas. These centers provide a nationwide network offering education and training opportunities for health professionals, including physicians, nurses, dentists, social workers, pharmacists, occupational therapists, physical therapists, optometrist, podiatrists, dieticians, health administrators, clinical psychologists, and other allied and public health personnel. The centers also develop new curricula, training materials, and clinical training sites. There are currently 33 centers. A 3 day "Geriatric Training Curriculum for Public Health Professionals" has been developed, and is intended to be a training resource useful in employment and educational settings, state and local governments, community-based organizations, and academic programs. A listing of the centers is available, as is information and publications available from each center.

* Gerontology Research: Physical, Mental, Emotional Changes

Gerontology Research Center
Francis Scott Key Medical Center
4940 Eastern Ave.
Baltimore, MD 21224 (301) 558-8114

The bulk of the National Institute on Aging intramural research is conducted at the Gerontology Research Center. In 1958 the Center began the Baltimore Longitudinal Study of Aging which involves 1,000 men and women, who, every two years, spend 2 1/2 days undergoing rigorous testing of their physical, mental, and emotional functions. The Center has laboratories to investigate a broad spectrum of human functions. They, as well as NIA, offer a wide range of pamphlets and reports on aging for professionals and the general public.

* Glaucoma Treatment

Office of Consumer Affairs
Food and Drug Administration (FDA)
5600 Fishers Lane
Rockville, MD 20857 (301) 443-3170

Be patient. If any phone number is incorrect, call (area code) 555-1212 and request the new listing.

Health and Medicine

A free 4-page pamphlet, *Keeping An Eye on Glaucoma,* (No. 80-3105) discusses the control of glaucoma with drugs and surgery.

* Hearing Aids

Office of Consumer Affairs
Food and Drug Administration (FDA)
5600 Fishers Lane
Rockville, MD 20857 (301) 443-3170

Contact this office for the free FDA publication, *Facts about Hearing and Hearing Aids* and other information about these medical devices. This free 32 page pamphlet (No. 79-4016) discusses the causes of and treatment for hearing loss and the selection, use, and care of hearing aids.

* Healthy Older People: Exercise, Nutrition, Medicines

ODPHP Health Information Center
P. O. Box 1133 (800) 336-4797
Washington, DC 20013 (301) 565-4167

Healthy Older People, a public education program on health promotion and aging conducted by the Office of Disease Prevention and Health Promotion (ODPHP), encourages older people to adopt good health habits, concentrating on such areas as exercise, nutrition, injury prevention, smoking, and medicines. A list of broadcast and print materials is available to State and local groups, along with a list of State contacts, who are responsible for coordinating statewide activities. The program includes consumer education, professional education, and technical assistance. A Program Memo maintains information on activities and regional workshops.

* Home IV Drug Therapies and Medicare

Office of Technology Assessment
U.S. Congress
Washington, DC 20510 (202) 228-6590

The development of new technologies that permit increasingly sophisticated health care to be provided at home has presented some perplexing issues for the Medicare program. At present, Medicare payment for Intravenous (IV) drug therapy is limited to hospital-based care, but new devices, new drugs, and new treatment protocols are available to patients in the home. This study will examine the potential impact of coverage for Medicare. Contact Elaine Power, the project director.

* Long-Term Care

ODPHP Health Information Center
P.O. Box 1133 (800) 336-4797
Washington, DC 20013 (301) 565-4167

In its series called "Healthfinder", this clearinghouse publishes *Long-Term Care* which explains issues and concerns regarding long-term care, as well as a list of publications and audiovisuals available from government agencies, community organizations, foundations and many other health groups.

* Medicare Claims

Attn: Larry Beasley
Health Care Financing Administration
Room 577, East High Rise Building
6325 Security Boulevard
Baltimore, MD 21207 (Written requests only)

A free 8-page pamphlet, *How To Fill Out A Medicare Claim Form,* provides a step by step explanation of how to fill out this basic form in order to get reimbursed for medical bills.

* Medicare Handbook, 1990

Superintendent of Documents
Government Printing Office
Washington, DC 20402 (202) 783-3238

As a result of the repeal of the Medicare Catastrophic Coverage Act of 1988, benefits for hospital, skilled nursing care, and hospice services under Medicare are different from those that were available in 1989. The Medicare Handbook, 1990 describes Medicare benefits available and premium, deductible, and coinsurance amounts that will have to be paid this year (S/N 017-060-00313-8, $2.25).

* Medicare Health Insurance

Medicare Hotline
Health Care Financing Administration
330 Independence Avenue SW (800) 638-6833
Washington, DC 20201 (800) 492-6603 in Maryland
or
Local Social Security Office

Several handy pamphlets are available free from local Social Security offices including *A Brief Explanation of Medicare* and *A Guide to Health Insurance for People with Medicare.* Both of these publications discuss what Medicare does and does not cover and discusses Medi-gap and other supplementary private health insurance plans.

* Medicare Videotapes

National Audiovisual Center
8700 Edgeworth Drive
Capitol Heights, MD 20743 (301) 763-1896

Several videotapes are sold by the Audiovisual Center including: "Medicare Magazine"; "Mr. Medicare" and "One Measure of Freedom." "Meet Medicare" is an audiocassette which can also be purchased.

* Medicine for the Layman

Office of Clinical Center Communications
National Institutes of Health
Building 10, Room 1C255
Bethesda, MD 20892 (301) 496-2563

The Clinical Center has developed a *Medicine for the Layman* series to educate consumers, allowing them to make informed medical decisions. Free booklets and videos are available on a variety of topics. Those related to the elderly include:

Arthritis
Alzheimer's
Coping with Aging Parents
Hearing Impairment
Parkinson's Disease
Brain in Aging and Dementia.

* Nursing Home Abuse

Superintendent of Documents
Government Printing Office
Washington, DC 20402 (202) 783-3238

Resident Abuse in Nursing Homes: Understanding and Preventing Abuse contains results of a study to promote a better understanding of abuse in nursing homes. It examines the nature of abuse and ways to prevent it, existing processes for resolving physical abuse complaints involving nursing home residents (S/N 017-022-01-12-3, $3.25).

* Older Americans Policies and Programs Review

Federal Council on the Aging
Room 4280, Cohen Building
330 Independence Ave., SW
Washington, DC 202021 (202) 619-2451

The Federal Council on the Aging reviews and evaluates Federal aging policies and programs for the purpose of appraising their value and their impact on the lives of older Americans. They serve as spokesperson on behalf of older Americans by making recommendations about Federal policies and programs. They inform the public about the problems and needs of the aging by collecting and distributing information, conducting or commissioning studies, and publishing their results and issuing reports. The Council provides public forums for discussing problems by sponsoring conferences, workshops, and other meetings.

* Osteoporosis

Office of Technology Assessment (OTA)
U. S. Congress
Washington, DC 20510 (202) 228-6590

It is estimated that 15 to 24 million Americans have osteoporosis- a condition in which bone mass, density, and quality are diminished, causing a person's bones to be fragile and highly susceptible to fracture. The capacity of existing technologies to detect bone loss early in the disease process and the cost of the technologies are key questions that will be examined in this OTA report. Contact Katie Maslow, project director.

Be patient. If any phone number is incorrect, call (area code) 555-1212 and request the new listing.

Aging and America's Elderly

* Osteoporosis and Older Women

Office of Consumer Affairs
Food and Drug Administration (FDA)
5600 Fishers Lane
Rockville, MD 20857 (301) 443-3170

Osteoporosis: Calcium and Estrogens (No. 85-1117) discusses the causes of this weakening of the bones, especially in older women, and how diet and estrogen treatment can help. Single copies of this 8-page brochure are available free.

* Osteoporosis Reports

National Arthritis and Musculoskeletal and Skin Diseases Information Clearinghouse
Box AMS
9000 Rockville Pike
Bethesda, MD 20892 (301) 495-4484

Osteoporosis, a condition in which the bone mass is low, represents a major public health problem and affects some 24 million Americans. The Clearinghouse has information for both the patient and physician regarding the cause, treatment and prevention of osteoporosis. Some of the publications include:

Osteoporosis
Osteoporosis: Cause, Treatment, Prevention
Osteoporosis: Patient Education Materials
Osteoporosis: Professional Education Materials
Osteoporosis: A Growing National Problem
Osteoporosis - Consensus Development Conference Statement
Scientific Workshop: Research Directions in Osteoporosis
Medicine for the Layman - Osteoporosis
Osteoporosis Research, Education and Health Promotion

* Paget's Bone Disease

National Institute of Arthritis and Musculoskeletal Diseases
NIH, Building 31, Room 9A-04
Bethesda, MD 20892 (301) 496-5717

A free 11-page booklet, *Understanding Paget's Disease* (No. 85-2241), describes this disease of the bone, which occurs most frequently between the ages of 50 and 70.

* Positive Approach to Aging

National Institute of Mental Health
Public Inquiries Branch
Parklawn Building, Room 15C-05
5600 Fishers Lane
Rockville, MD 20857 (301) 443-4513

A free four-page pamphlet, *Plain Talk About Aging*, describes the experience of growing old and suggests ways to plan carefully in order to have aging be a positive experience.

* Resource Directory

Superintendent of Documents
Government Printing Office
Washington, DC 20402 (202) 783-3238

The Resource Directory for Older People contains information on 215 organizations that deal specifically with the elderly, including Federal Government agencies, professional societies, private groups, and voluntary programs. Each listing provides the organization's address, telephone number, its mission, services, and free publications available. It answers many questions on the treatment for the elderly, and is useful to their families, students and health professionals, librarians, legal professionals, providers of social services, and others who have a special interest in the fields of aging (S/N 017-062-00143-0, $10).

* Rheumatic Disease

National Institute of Arthritis and Musculoskeletal Diseases
NIH, Building 31, Room 9A-04
Bethesda, MD 20892 (301) 496-5717

A 43-page reference titled *Rheumatic Diseases and the Older Adult: An Annotated Bibliography, 1986,* contains 86 references with abstracts to the medical literature for physicians, allied health professionals, and others interested in geriatric medicine and rheumatology. It is available for $4.

* Sexuality in Later Life

National Institute on Aging Information Center
2209 Distribution Circle
Silver Spring, MD 20910 (301) 495-3455

This double-sided fact sheet titled *Sexuality in Later Life* is one of many "Age Pages" available free from the center.

* Smoking and the Elderly

Office on Smoking and Health
Mail Stop K-50
Centers for Disease Control
1600 Clifton Rd., NE
Atlanta, GA 30333 (404) 488-5705

Good News for Smokers 50 and Older is a free fact sheet for older smokers outlining the health benefits of quitting smoking at any age.

* Spanish Publications for Elderly

National Institute on Aging Information Center
2209 Distribution Circle
Silver Spring, MD 20910 (301) 495-3455

Several fact sheets, printed on two sides in large type, are published in Spanish including: *Accidents and the Elderly; Crime and the Elderly; Foot Care for Older People;* and *Skin: Getting the Wrinkles Out of Aging.* Individual copies of these fact sheets are available free. A listing of all fact sheets published in various languages titled *Age Pages Compilation* is also available free.

* You and Your Aging Parents

Modern Talking Picture Service
Film Scheduling Center
5000 Park Street North
St. Petersburg, FL 33709 (813) 541-5763

A 58-minute videotape is available on free loan to educators and institutions titled "You and Your Aging Parents". It describes the stresses associated with growing old and addresses the challenge to the "sandwich generation". This video, part of the *Medicine for the Layman* series, is also for sale by the National Audiovisual Center, 8700 Edgeworth Drive, Capitol Heights, MD 20743; (301) 763-1896.

* Vision Impairment

National Eye Institute
NIH, Building 31
Room 6A-32, 9000 Rockville Pike
Bethesda, MD 20892 (301) 496-5248

Age-Related Macular Degeneration (No. 85-2294) explains how the eye works and how the degeneration occurs with the aging process. It tells how patients can check their own eyes and describes laser photocoagulation for treating this disease. Single copies available free. Also available are publications on cataracts and glaucoma.

* Volunteering

ACTION
1100 Vermont Ave., NW
Washington, DC 20525 (202) 606-5108

The ACTION agency supports the development of creative, effective, and lasting solutions to the challenges of crime, hunger, poverty, illiteracy, drug abuse, and homelessness. ACTION opens up rewarding opportunities for volunteers from all age groups and backgrounds to help their communities. The programs designed for older volunteers include the Foster Grandparents Program, Retired Senior Volunteer Program, and the Senior Companion Program. For more information about these programs contact the office listed above.

State Agencies on Aging

The offices listed in this section coordinate services for older Americans. They provide information on services, programs, and opportunities for these consumers and can refer you to local agencies.

Alabama
Dr. Oscar D. Tucker

Be patient. If any phone number is incorrect, call (area code) 555-1212 and request the new listing.

Health and Medicine

Executive Director
Commission on Aging
136 Catoma St. (205) 242-5743
Montgomery, AL 36130 (800) 243-5463 (AL)

Alaska
Ms. Connie Sipe
Executive Director
Older Alaskans Commission
P.O. Box C
Juneau, AK 99811 (907) 465-3250

American Samoa
Mr. Luavasa Tauala
Territorial Administration on Aging
Government of American Samoa
Pago Pago, AS 96799 011 (684) 633-1251

Arizona
Mr. Richard Littler, Administrator
Aging and Adult Administration
1400 West Washington, 950A
Phoenix, AZ 85007 (602) 542-4446

Arkansas
Mr. Herb Sanderson, Director
Office of Aging and Adult Services
Department of Human Services
P.O. Box 1437 (501) 682-2441
Little Rock, AR 72203 (800) 482-8049 (AR)

California
Ms. Chris Arnold, Director
Department of Aging (916) 322-5290
1600 K St. (916) 323-8913 (TDD)
Sacramento, CA 95814 (800) 231-4024 (CA)

Colorado
Ms. Irene Ibarra
Executive Director
Colorado Department of Social Services
1575 Sherman St.
Denver, CO 80203 (303) 866-5700

Connecticut
Ms. Edith Prague, Commissioner
Department of Aging
175 Main St. (203) 566-3238
Hartford, CT 06106 (800) 443-9946 (CT)

Delaware
Ms. Eleanor Cain, Director
Department of Health and Social Services
Division of Aging
1901 North DuPont Highway (302) 421-6791
New Castle, DE 19720 (800) 223-9074 (DE)

District Of Columbia
Ms. E. Veronica Pace
Executive Director
DC Office on Aging
1424 K St., NW, 2nd Floor
Washington, DC 20005 (202) 724-5622

Florida
Dr. Larry Polivka
Assistant Secretary
Aging and Adult Services
1321 Winewood Blvd., Room 323
Tallahassee, FL 32399 (904) 488-8922

Georgia
Mr. Fred McGinnis, Director
Office of Aging
878 Peachtree St., NE
Suite 632
Atlanta, GA 30309 (404) 894-5333

Guam
Mr. Robert Kelley
Acting Administrator
Office of Aging
Government of Guam
P.O. Box 2816
Agana, GU 96910 011 (671) 734-2942

Hawaii
Ms. Jeanette Takamura, Directory
Executive Office on Aging
335 Merchant St., Room 241 (808) 548-2593
Honolulu, HI 96813 (800) 468-4644 (HI)

Idaho
Ms. Charlene Martindale
Director, Idaho Office on Aging
Statehouse, Room 108
Boise, ID 83720 (208) 334-3833

Illinois
Mr. Victor Wirth, Director
Department of Aging
421 East Capitol Ave. (217) 785-2870
Springfield, IL 62701 (800) 252-8966 (IL/TDD)

Indiana
Ms. Geneva Shedd, Director
Aging/In-Home Care
Services Division
Department of Human Services
P.O. Box 7083 (317) 232-7020
Indianapolis, IN 46207 (800) 622-4972 (IN)

Iowa
Ms. Betty Grandquist
Executive Director
Department of Elder Affairs
914 Grand Ave., Suite 236 (515) 281-5187
Des Moines, IA 50319 (800) 532-3213 (IA)

Kansas
Ms. Joanne Hurst, Secretary
Department on Aging
Docking State Office Building
Room 122 South
915 Southwest Harrison St. (913) 296-4986
Topeka, KS 66612 (800) 432-3535 (KS)

Kentucky
Ms. Sue N. Tuttle, Director
Division for Aging Services
Department for Social Services
275 East Main St. (502) 564-6930
6th Floor West (800) 372-2991 (KY)
Frankfort, KY 40621 (800) 372-2973 (TDD in KY)

Louisiana
Ms. Vicky Hunt, Director
Governors Office of Elder Affairs
P.O. Box 80374
Baton Rouge, LA 70890 (504) 925-1700

Maine
Ms. Christine Gianopoulos
Director
Bureau of Elder and Adult Service
35 Anthony Ave.
Statehouse Station 11
Augusta, ME 04333 (207) 626-5335

Maryland
Ms. Rosalie Abrams, Director
Office on Aging
301 West Preston St. (301) 225-1100
10th Floor (301) 383-7555 (TDD)
Baltimore, MD 21201 (800) 243-3425 (MD)

Be patient. If any phone number is incorrect, call (area code) 555-1212 and request the new listing.

Aging and America's Elderly

Massachusetts
Mr. Franklin Ollivierre, Secretary
Executive Office of Elder Affairs — (617) 727-7750
38 Chauncy St. — (800) 882-2003 9MA0
Boston, MA 02111 — (800) 872-0166 (TDD in MA)
(800) 922-2275 (voice/TDD in MA - Elder Abuse Hotline)

Michigan
Ms. Nancy Crandall, Director
Office of Services to the Aging
P.O. Box 30026
Lansing, MI 48909 — (517) 373-8230

Minnesota
Mr. Gerald Bloedow
Executive Secretary
Minnesota Board on Aging
444 Lafayette Rd. — (612) 296-2544
St. Paul, MN 55155 — (800) 652-9747 (MN)

Mississippi
Ms. Billie Marshall
Director, Council on Aging
Division of Aging and Adult Services
421 West Pascagoula St. — (601) 949-2070
Jackson, MS 39203 — (800) 345-6347 (MS)

Missouri
Mr. Edwin Walker
Director, Division of Aging
P.O. Box 1337 — (314) 751-8535
Jefferson City, MO 65102 — (800) 392-0210 (MO)

Montana
Mr. Hank Hudson
Coordinator of Aging Services
Governor's Office State Capitol — (406) 444-4204
Helena, MT 59620 — (800) 332-2272 (MT)

Nebraska
Ms. Connie Bratka
Acting Director
Nebraska Department on Aging
State Office Building
P.O. Box 95044
Lincoln, NE 68509 — (402) 471-2306

Nevada
Ms. Suzanne Ernst, Administrator
Division for Aging Services
Department of Human Resources
340 North 11th St.
Las Vegas, NV 89158 — (702) 486-3545

New Hampshire
Mr. Richard Chevrefils, Director
Division of Elderly and Adult Services
6 Hazen Dr. — (603) 271-4680
Concord, NH 03301 — (800) 351-1888 (NH)

New Jersey
Ms. Lois Hull, Director
Division on Aging
Department of Community Affairs
101 South Broad St., CN 807 — (609) 292-4833
Trenton, NJ 08625 — (800) 792-8820 (NJ)

New Mexico
Ms. Michelle Grisham
Director, State Agency on Aging
224 East Palace Ave.
4th Floor — (505) 827-7640 (voice/TDD)
Santa Fe, NM 87501 — (800) 432-2080 (NM)

New York
Ms. Jane Gould, Director
New York State Office for the Aging

Agency Building 2, ESP — (518) 474-5731
Albany, NY 12223 — (800) 342-9871 (NY)

North Carolina
Ms. Bonnie Cramer, Director
Division of Aging
Department of Human Resources
Caller Box No. 2953
693 Palmer Dr. — (919) 733-3983
Raleigh, NC 27626 — (800) 662-7030 (voice/TDD in NC)

North Dakota
Mr. Larry Brewster, Administrator
Aging Services, Department of Human Service
600 East Boulevard — (701) 224-2310
Bismarck, ND 58505 — (800) 472-2622 (ND)

Ohio
Ms. Judith Brachman, Director
Ohio Department of Aging
50 West Broad St., 9th Floor — (614) 466-5500
Columbus, OH 43266 — (614) 466-6191 (TDD)
(800) 282-1206 (OH-nursing home information)

Oklahoma
Mr. Roy Keen
Division Administrator
Special Unit on Aging
P.O. Box 25352 — (405) 521-2281
Oklahoma City, OK 73125 — (405) 521-2827 (TDD)

Oregon
Mr. Richard Ladd, Administrator
Senior Services Division
Department of Human Resources
State of Oregon
313 Public Service Building — (503) 378-4728
Salem, OR 97310 — (800) 232-3020 (voice/TDD in OR)

Pennsylvania
Ms. Linda Rhodes, Secretary
Department of Aging
231 State St.
Harrisburg, PA 17101 — (717) 783-1549

Puerto Rico
Dr. Celia Cintron
Executive Director
Office of Elder Affairs
Call Box 563
Old San Juan Station, PR 00902 — (809) 721-4560

Rhode Island
Ms. Maureen Maigret, Director
Department of Elderly Affairs
160 Pine St. — (401) 277-2880 (voice/TDD)
Providence, RI 02903 — (800) 322-2880 (RI)

South Carolina
Ms. Ruth Seigler
Executive Director
South Carolina Commission on Aging
400 Arbor Lake Dr.
Suite B-500 — (803) 735-0210
Columbia, SC 29223 — (800) 868-9095

South Dakota
Ms. Gail Ferris, Administrator
Office of Adult Services and Aging
700 Governors Dr.
Pierre, SD 57501 — (605) 773-3656

Tennessee
Ms. Emily Wiseman, Director
Commission on Aging
706 Church St., Suite 201
Nashville, TN 37243 — (615) 741-2056

Be patient. If any phone number is incorrect, call (area code) 555-1212 and request the new listing.

Health and Medicine

Texas
Ms. Polly Owell
Executive Director
Texas Department on Aging
P.O. Box 12786, Capitol Station
Austin, TX 78711

(512) 444-2727 (voice/TDD)
(800) 252-9240 (TX)

Utah
Mr. Percy Devine, Director
Division of Aging and Adult Services
P.O. Box 45500
Salt Lake City, UT 84145

(801) 538-3910

Vermont
Mr. Lawrence Crist, Commissioner
Department of Aging and Disabilities
103 South Main St.
Waterbury, VT 05671

(802) 241-2400 (voice/TDD)

Virgin Islands
Ms. Juel Rhymer Molloy
Commissioner
Department of Human Services
Barbel Plaza South Charlotte Amalie
St. Thomas, VI 00802

(809) 774-0930

Virginia
Ms. Thelma Bland, Commissioner
Department for the Aging

700 East Franklin St.
10th Floor
Richmond, VA 23219

(804) 225-2271 (voice/TDD)
(800) 552-4464 (VA)
(800) 552-3402 (VA Ombudsman Hotline)

Washington
Mr. Charles Reed Assistant Secretary
Aging and Adult Services Administration
OB-44A
Olympia, WA 98504

(206) 493-2509
(800) 422-3263 (WA)

West Virginia
Dr. David Brown
Executive Director
Commission on Aging
State Capitol
Charleston, WV 25305

(304) 348-3317

Wisconsin
Ms. Donna McDowell, Director
Bureau on Aging
P.O. Box 7851
Madison, WI 53707

(608) 266-2536

Wyoming
Mr. Scott Sessions, Director
Division on Aging
139 Hathaway Building
Cheyenne, WY 82002

(307) 777-7986
(800) 442-2766 (WY)

Be patient. If any phone number is incorrect, call (area code) 555-1212 and request the new listing.

Handicapped/Disabled Resources

* *See also Law and Social Justice Chapter*

* Associations and Foundations Resource List

National Health Information Center
P.O. Box 1133 (800) 336-4797
Washington, DC 20013-1133 (301) 565-4167 (in MD)

This center provides information and support services offered by national organizations and foundations as well as government services available to individuals with handicaps or disabilities including its free six-page bulletin titled *Healthfinder: Family Care.*

* Braille Books and Computers for Blind

American Printing House for the Blind
1839 Frankfurt Ave.
Louisville, KY 40206 (502) 895-2405

American Printing House for the Blind produces a variety of material for the blind, including books, textbooks, and music in Braille, large type and talking books, flexible records, and cassettes. They also have computer hardware and software and free catalogs both in print and Braille.

* Captioned Movies and Videos for the Hearing Impaired

Modern Talking Pictures
500 Park St., North
St. Petersburg, FL 33709 (813) 541-7571

This company's captioned film/video program provides a free loan service of educational and theatrical films and videos for various groups to assist deaf/hearing impaired persons in educational and recreational pursuits. Comprehensive, free catalogs list over 3,500 films and videocassettes. Language controlled open-captions (subtitles) appear on each film and video.

* Clearinghouse on the Handicapped

Clearinghouse on the Handicapped
Switzer Building, Room 3132
330 C Street SW
Washington, DC 20202 (202) 732-1250

This center, sponsored by the U.S. Department of Health and Human Services, responds to inquiries by referrals to organizations that supply information to and about handicapped individuals. This government clearinghouse also provides material on federal benefits, funding, and legislation for the handicapped.

* Communicative and Deafness Disorders Rehabilitation

Office of Deafness and Communicative Disorders
Rehabilitation Services Administration
330 C St., SW, Room 303 (202) 732-1401
Washington, DC 20201 (202) 732-1298 TDD

The goal of this branch is to promote improved and expanded rehabilitation services for deaf, hard of hearing, speech impaired, and language disordered individuals. This office, as the liaison to national organizations and agencies concerned with deafness and communicative disorders, provide the following services: 1) they develop policies and standards for state rehabilitation agencies' work with these clients; 2) they review services to these clients by the agencies; and 3) they provide technical assistance to Rehabilitation Services Administration staff.

* Council on Disability

National Council on Disability
800 Independence Ave., SW
Suite 814 (202) 267-3846
Washington, DC 20591 (202) 267-3232 (TDD)

The fifteen Council members appointed by the President and confirmed by Congress review all laws, programs, and policies of the Federal Government that affect individuals with disabilities. The council then makes recommendations to the President, Congress, and Federal agencies on these issues. In addition, the council is studying the availability of health insurance coverage for persons with disabilities and sponsors conferences for families caring for the disabled. They publish *FOCUS*, a quarterly newsletter, an annual report, and *Education of Students with Disabilities: Where Do We Stand?*

* Deafness Clearinghouse

National Institute on Deafness and Other Communication
Disorders Clearinghouse (NIDCD)
P.O. Box 37777 (301) 496-7243
Washington, DC 20013 (301) 402-0252 (TDD)

The NIDCD has established a national clearinghouse of information and resources on the normal and disordered mechanisms of hearing, balance, smell, taste, voice, speech, and language. The Clearinghouse collects information on these seven research areas and disseminates it to health professional, patients, industry, and the public. They have access to the Combined Health Information Database (CHID), and have an extensive list of publications, including fact sheets, bibliographies, information packets, catalogs, and directories of information sources. They also publish a biannual newsletter. One of their newest directories is a directory of associations and organizations with an interest in deafness and other communication disorders. Contact the clearinghouse for more information.

* Development Disabilities and Mental Retardation Research

Office of Research Reporting
National Institute of Child Health and Human Development
National Institutes of Health (NIH)
Building 31, Room 2A-32
9000 Rockville Pike
Bethesda, MD 20892 (301) 496-5133

This NIH department can share scientific research and consumer information about various development disabilities, birth defects and related issues.

* Developmental Disabilities Resource Center

National Information System for Health Related Services
Center for Developmental Disabilities
Benson Building, First Floor (800) 922-9234
Columbia, SC 29208 (800) 922-1107 in SC

This clearinghouse offers information and makes referrals for parents and professionals concerned with children ages 0-21 with development disabilities or special health care needs. It also can identify federal, state and non-profit agencies in every state in the country.

* Disabilities Information Clearinghouse

Clearinghouse on Disability Information Program
Information and Coordination Staff
U.S Department of Education
Room 3132, Mary Switzer Building (202) 732-1723
Washington, DC 20202-2524 (202) 732-1241

This Clearinghouse responds to inquiries, provides referrals, and disseminates information about services for individuals with disabilities at the national, state, and local levels. Information is especially strong in the areas of Federal funding for programs services individuals with disabilities, Federal legislation affecting the disability community, and Federal programs benefiting people with disabilities. The following publications are available free:

Be patient. If any phone number is incorrect, call (area code) 555-1212 and request the new listing.

Health and Medicine

OSERS News in Print - newsletter focusing on Office of Special Education and Rehabilitative Services programs, innovative research, and topical information.

A Summary of Existing Legislation Affecting Persons with Disabilities.

A Pocket Guide to Federal Help for Individuals with Disabilities.

* Employment of the Handicapped

President's Committee on Employment of People with Disabilities
1331 F St., NW (202) 376-6200
Washington, DC 20004 (202) 376-6205 (TDD)

This committee provides information, training and technical assistance to America's business leaders, organized labor, rehabilitation and other service providers, advocacy organizations, families and individuals with disabilities. *Worklife* is a quarterly magazine with information that is vital to both employers and persons with disabilities seeking employment. A monthly newsletter, *Tips and Trends,* keeps people informed of meetings, happenings, and new developments. The Job Accommodation Network, (800) 526-7234, is a resource and consultation service to help firms make individualized accommodations for employees with disabilities. They offer technical help for specific accommodation solutions. The Committee has other helpful free publications available dealing with disabilities.

* Employment Research and Development

Administration Officer
Office of Research and Publications
President's Committee on Employment of the Handicapped
1111 20th Street NW, Room 660
Washington, DC 20036 (202) 653-2087

This advisory committee advocates the elimination of environmental and attitudinal barriers impeding the opportunities of handicapped persons. It offers materials on employment of disabled people, affirmative action, disabled veterans, taxes and disability, youth development. The committee publishes a quarterly information bulletin, *Disabled USA,* and sponsors exhibits, a speakers bureau, and public service advertising.

* Free Library Services for Physically Handicapped

National Library Service for the Blind and Physically Handicapped
Library of Congress (800) 424-8567
Washington, DC 20542 (202) 707-9287

This center works through local and regional libraries to provide free library service to persons unable to read or use standard printed materials because of visual or physical impairment. A bibliography of Braille and recorded materials on health topics is available as well as *Talking Book Topics.*

* Handicapped and Gifted Children

ERIC Clearinghouse on Handicapped and Gifted Children
Council for Exceptional Children
1920 Association Dr.
Reston, VA 22091 (703) 264-9474

ERIC (Educational Resources Information Center) is a federally funded information system, and has a database of over 400,0000 journal annotations and 300,000 education related documents abstracts. ERIC is also a source of publication about all aspects of education. ERIC Clearinghouse on Handicapped and Gifted Children gathers and disseminated educational information on all disabilities and giftedness across all age levels. They have publications, digests (2-4 page summaries of current topics), Research Briefs, Issue Briefs, Directories of currently funded research, topical INFO packets and Flyer Files, as well as a catalog of products and services available to the Special Educator. They also have database searches and reprints. For more information contact the Clearinghouse.

* Handicapped Rehabilitation Resources

Superintendent of Documents
Government Printing Office
Washington, DC 20402 (202) 783-3238

Designed for professionals and consumer groups, *The American Rehabilitation,* a quarterly publication from the Rehabilitation Services Administration, covers all aspects of life for handicapped individuals. A subscription is $5 per year.

* Infants with Disabilities Clearinghouse

National Information Clearinghouse for Infants with Disabilities and Life-Threatening Conditions
Benson Building, First Floor (800) 922-9234
Columbia, SC 29208 (800) 922-1107 in SC

This resource center offers help on legal and advocacy issues, financial assistance, community services, parent support and parent education, child protective services, home health services and other assistance to parents and professionals concerned about infants with disabilities.

* Learning Disabilities Clearinghouse

National Information Center for Handicapped Children and Youth
PO Box 1492 (703) 893-6061
Washington, DC 20013 (800) 999-5599

This clearinghouse helps parents of handicapped children, disabled adults, and professionals locate services for the handicapped and information on learning disabilities. Newsletters, parent guides, and other helpful publications are available at no charge.

* Parents of Disabled Referral Center

National Information Center for Children and Youth with Handicaps
PO Box 1492 (703) 893-6061
Washington, DC 20013 (800) 999-5599

This clearinghouse helps parents of handicapped children, disabled adults locate services and parent support groups. It also focuses on the needs of rural areas, culturally diverse populations, and severely handicapped people. This center also provides information on vocational/transitional issues, special education, and legal rights and advocacy. It provides fact sheets on specific disabilities including autism, cerebral palsy, hearing impairments, Down's syndrome, epilepsy, learning disabilities, mental retardation, physical disabilities, speech and language impairments, spina bifida, visual impairments. They have materials designed especially for parents including:

Parents' Guide to Accessing Programs for Infants, Toddlers, Preschoolers with Handicaps

Parents' Guide to Accessing Parent Programs, Community Services, and Record Keeping

Life After School for Children with Disabilities: Answers to Questions Parents Ask about Employment and Financial Assistance

A Parent's Guide: Accessing the ERIC Resource Collection

A Parent's Guide to Doctors, Disabilities, and the Family

A Parent's Guide: Planning a Move; Mapping Your Strategy

A Parent's Guide: Special Education and Related Services: Communicating Through Letter Writing

They also have listing of National Resources, as well as State Resources and National Toll Free Numbers.

* Rehabilitation Clearinghouse and Databases

National Rehabilitation Information Center
8455 Colesville Road, Suite 935 (301) 588-9284 (MD only)
Silver Spring, MD 20910 (800) 346-2742 (voice and TDD)

This clearinghouse provides information on disability-related research, resources, and products for independent living. It provides fact sheets, resource guides, and technical publications. It produces two bibliographic databases, ABLEDATA and REHABDATA which cover rehabilitation products and technical aids for disabled persons along with generic and brand names, manufacturers, distributors, uses, and costs. The publications available include:

Rehabdata Thesaurus ($25)
Guide to Periodicals in Disability and Rehabilitation ($15)
Directory of Librarians and Information Professionals ($5)
NARIC Quarterly Newsletter
Resource Guides:
Traumatic Brain Injury
Spinal Cord Injury
NARIC Mailing List ($50/1000 labels)

* Rehabilitation Research and Development

Director
National Institute on Disability and Rehabilitation Research
U.S. Department of Education

Be patient. If any phone number is incorrect, call (area code) 555-1212 and request the new listing.

Handicapped/Disabled Resources

Mary E. Switzer Building, Mail Stop 2305
330 C Street SW
Washington, DC 20202 (202) 732-6151

This institute disseminates information concerning developments in rehabilitation procedures, methods, and devices for people of all ages with physical and mental handicaps, especially those who are severely disabled. Statistical data on disabilities and research funding information are also available. A program directory is available which includes information on projects funded for the year.

* Special Health Care Needs

National Maternal and Child Health Clearinghouse
38th and R Sts., NW
Washington, DC 20057 (202) 625-8410

The Clearinghouse has an extensive list of free publications concerned with children with special health care needs. Two of the publications are resource guides: *1990 Resource Guide to Organizations Concerned with Developmental Handicaps*, and *Children with Special Health Care Needs- Resource Guide*.

* Speech and Language Disorders Clearinghouse

National Institute on Deafness and
Other Communicative Disorders
NIH, Building 31, Room 1B62,
9000 Rockville Pike
Bethesda, MD 20892 (301) 496-7243

This--the newest Institute at NIH--funds intramural and extramural research on communicative disorders. Brochures and reports are available for professionals and the general public, covering a wide range of related topics.

* TDD Directory

R. Woods
Consumer Information Center- 2A
P.O. Box 100
Pueblo, CO 81002

The U.S. Government TDD Directory lists federal agencies with Telecommunications Devices for the Deaf and how to reach hearing or speech-impaired federal employees if you don't use a TDD. This publication is free.

* Telephone Hotlines

The following clearinghouses are equipped to send information, make referrals to organizations as well as state and federal government agencies, and also provide telephone information.

Center for Handicapped Children and Teenagers	(415) 923-3549
Clearinghouse on the Handicapped	(404) 639-3534
Coordinating Council for the Handicapped	(312) 939-3513
Federation of the Handicapped	(212) 206-4250
Information Center for Individuals with Disabilities	(617) 727-5540
Information, Protection and Advocacy Center for Handicapped Individuals	(202) 547-8081
March of Dimes Birth Defects Foundation	(914) 428-7100
National Center for Youth with Disabilities	(800) 333-NCYD
National Information Clearinghouse for Infants with Disabilities and Life-Threatening Conditions	(800) 922-9234
National Institute on Disability and Rehabilitation Research	(202) 732-1134
National Information System for Health Related Services	(800) 922-9234

Be patient. If any phone number is incorrect, call (area code) 555-1212 and request the new listing.

Health and Medicine

Medical Devices, RX and Surgery

Contemplating a new treatment for back pain, wondering about donating blood, considering elective surgery? There are many specialists and agencies available to offer their expert opinions to help you make informed decisions with your medical team. A few phone calls can boost your ability to weigh the pros and cons of various medical tests and procedures and learn about the reputation of a hospital or health clinic. Several agencies can provide the latest information on specific medications, their generic equivalents and other therapeutic drugs. Even offices that are established to collect and disseminate data for health professionals on adverse drug reactions and experimental drugs can be accessible to individual consumers.

* Anesthesia and Therapeutic Drug Findings

Pharmacological Sciences Program
National Institute of General Medical Sciences (NIGMS)
Building 31, Room 4A52
9000 Rockville Pike
Bethesda, MD 20892 (301) 496-7707

This program supports research aimed at providing an improved understanding of biological phenomena and related chemical and molecular processes involved in the actions of therapeutic drugs, anesthetic agents, and their metabolites. This program supports research ranging from synthetic chemistry and basic biological and biochemical studies in molecular pharmacology to comparative studies in cell cultures and laboratory animals, as well as controlled clinical investigations in patients and normal volunteers. Grants are available. The *Biennial Report* describes the current research awards. The *Annual Report of NIGMS* lists all the various programs and their research highlights.

* Approval of All New Drugs

Center for Drug Evaluation and Research
Food and Drug Administration (FDA)
HFD 100, Room 14B45
5600 Fishers Lane
Rockville, MD 20857 (301) 295-8012; or

Office of Consumer Affairs
HFD 365, 5600 Fishers Lane
Rockville, MD 20857 (301) 443-3170

The Center for Drug Evaluation and Research develops policy with regard to the safety, effectiveness, and labeling of all drug products and evaluates new drug applications. It develops and implements standards for the safety and effectiveness of all over-the-counter drugs. It also conducts research and develops scientific standards on the composition, quality, safety, and effectiveness of drugs. A list of guidelines is available to help manufacturers comply with the requirements of the regulations. The staff will respond to requests from information regarding the laws, regulations, policies, and functions of the FDA as it pertains to drugs. Many FDA Consumer Report articles, as well as an FDA Consumer Special Report on drugs, are available to the public.

* Blood Banks and Supply

Information Center
Blood Resource Education Program
4733 Bethesda Ave., Suite 530
Bethesda, MD 20814 (301) 951-3260

The Blood Resource Education Program, supported by the National Heart, Lung, and Blood Institute, is designed to assure accessibility of an adequate supply of high-quality blood and blood products through studies of resource management, the establishment of a national blood data system, and recommendations concerning the structure and function of the national blood resource system. Contact this office for more information regarding the nation's blood supply.

* Brand Name Drug Directory

Superintendent of Documents
Government Printing Office

Washington, DC 20402 (202) 783-3238

The *National Drug Code Directory* is divided into four sections which alphabetically lists drugs by product trade name, chemical ingredient, short name, and the National Drug Codes which are specific numbers, assigned to the drugs by the Food and Drug Administration, used for insurance billing purposes. The cost of the directory is $76.

* CAT Scans and Safety of Other Technology

Office of Health Technology Assessment
U.S. Department of Health and Human Services
2101 E. Jefferson St., Suite 400
Rockville, MD 20852 (301) 227-8337

National Technical Information Service
5285 Port Royal Rd.
Springfield, VA 22161 (800) 336-4700

This office advises the Secretary of Health and Human Services regarding health care technology issues and makes recommendations with respect to whether specific health care technologies should be reimbursable under federally-financed health programs. The office also considers the safety and effectiveness of the technology. Impending assessments are announced in the Federal Register, and input is sought from appropriate Federal agencies. The final reports are made available to the public through the National Technical Information Service. Reports and abstracts published by the Office of Health Technology Assessment are available individually or in annual volume compilations. For copies of assessments or ordering information call: Agency for Health Care Policy and Research, 5600 Fishers Lane, Room 18-12, Rockville, MD 20857; (301) 443-4100.

* Construction of Hospitals and Health Facilities

Loan Division
Health Resources and Services Administration
5600 Fishers Lane, Room 11-A17
Rockville, MD 20857 (301) 443-5317

This office serves as the federal focus for examining capital and financial issues involved in health facilities, and administering insured and guaranteed loan programs for health facilities to determine compliance with assurances made during application for federal construction assistance. Materials are available on a variety of topics, including capital formation in health care facilities and cost containment in hospitals through energy conservation.

* Drug Reactions and Pharmaceutical News

Drug Bulletin
Food and Drug Administration
HFI 42, 5600 Fishers Lane
Rockville, MD 20857 (301) 443-3220

Published on an as-needed basis, the *Drug Bulletin* is free to professionals and the general public interested in learning the latest developments in the drug field, such drug reactions and new medical devices.

* Effective Health Care

Office of the Forum for Quality and Effectiveness in Health Care
Agency for Health Care Policy and Research

Be patient. If any phone number is incorrect, call (area code) 555-1212 and request the new listing.

Medical Devices, RX and Surgery

2101 E. Jefferson, Room 327
Rockville, MD 20852 (301) 443-8754

The Office of the Forum for Quality and Effectiveness in Health Care promotes the quality, appropriateness, and effectiveness of health care by facilitating the development of clinically relevant guidelines for specific conditions and treatments. Health care providers, educators, and consumers may use these guidelines to help determine how to prevent, diagnose, treat, and manage health conditions most effectively. Panels for seven conditions and treatments are meeting to produce the first group of guidelines. The seven conditions for guidelines are pressure sore management, depression treated in outpatient community-based settings, urinary incontinence, cataracts in otherwise healthy eyes, sickle cell anemia management, and benign prostatic hypertrophy. For more information contact the office listed above.

* Elderly Chinese and Medications

National Institute on Aging Information Center
2209 Distribution Circle
Silver Spring, MD 20910 (301) 495-3455

Safe Use of Medicines by Older People is a free fact sheet, printed on two sides in large type, and it is published in English and Chinese.

* Electrical Stimulation Medical Devices

Electrophysics Branch
Center for Devices and Radiological Health
12721 Twinbrook Parkway
Rockville, MD 20857 (301) 443-3840

The Electrophysics Branch of conducts research on medical devices involving electrical stimulation to evaluate and examine their safety at the cellular level. They also examine the calibration of microwave ovens. The staff can respond to written requests for information.

* Experimental Drugs for Cancer Treatment

Developmental Therapeutics Program
National Cancer Institute (NCI)
Executive Plaza North, Room 818
Bethesda, MD 20892 (301) 496-8747

The National Cancer Institute distributes two pharmaceutical publications free of charge: 1) NCI Investigational Drugs (89-2141) is an annual publication which encompasses most of the drugs in clinical trial under NCI auspices. It provides necessary product information to health care providers who utilize investigational drug products. 2) NCI Investigational Drugs-Chemical Information (86-2654) is designed to provide selected relevant chemical and physical data to investigators involved in various multi-disciplinary studies of drugs which were developed or are being developed by the Developmental Therapeutics Program. The staff is also available to answer your questions related to pharmaceuticals.

* Fraudulent Medical Devices

Office of Consumer Affairs
Food and Drug Administration
Public Inquiries
5600 Fishers Lane
Rockville, MD 20857 (301) 443-3170

The Food and Drug Administration does not have the authority to regulate all medical products but it monitors the marketplace and publishes several pamphlets designed to help consumers spot bogus remedies for arthritis, cancer and medical devices including: *The Big Quack Attack: Medical Devices* (No. 84-3147); *Quackery -- The Billion Dollar "Miracle" Business* (No. 85-4200), as well as *Back Pain: Ubiquitous, Controversial* (No. 84-3147).

* Freedom on Information: Medical Devices

Device Monitoring Branch
Bureau of Medical Devices
8757 Georgia Ave., Room 1222
Silver Spring, MD 20910 (301) 427-1134

The Bureau of Medical Devices reviews medical devices for particular specialties (neurology, cardiovascular, ophthalmic, radiology), and then compiles the reactions and malfunctions into a computer database. Through a Freedom of Information request at the following address, you can receive information regarding a specific medical device. FDA, Freedom of Information, 5600 Fishers Lane, HFI35, Rockville, MD 20857.

* Health Care Policy Research Publications

Center for Research Dissemination and Liaison
Agency for Health Care Policy and Research (AHCPR)
5600 Fishers Lane, Room 18-12
Rockville, MD 20857 (301) 227-8372

The Center links AHCPR with the health services community and the general public, and disseminates a wide variety of AHCPR publications, including intramural and extramural studies, technology assessments, conference proceedings, and research bibliographies. AHCPR's monthly newsletter, Research Activities, summarizes the findings of studies and announces publication of new research resources materials and upcoming conferences. Publications in Print highlights publications that are available.

* Health Services Cost

Center for General Health Services Extramural Research
Agency for Health Care Policy and Research
2101 E. Jefferson, Room 618
Rockville, MD 20852 (301) 443-2345

The Center focuses on the effects of market forces on the costs and performance of the health care system; the impact of technology on the quality of care; and the content, attributes and practices of primary care. Current research in investigating health care services for people with HIV or AIDS; the health of low-income groups; the elderly; delivery of health services in rural areas; conditions common to primary care; technology assessment; and medical liability. The Division of Cost and Finance studies the economic problems involved in making more cost-effective decisions in the health care sector, productivity in health care, and the effect of third-party reimbursement. They study alternative delivery systems such as health maintenance organizations. For more information contact the office listed above.

* Hospitalization and Treatment at Government's Expense

The Clinical Center
National Institutes of Health
Building 10, Room 2C-146
9000 Rockville Pike
Bethesda, MD 20892 (301) 496-4891

The Clinical Center, as part of the National Institutes of Health, is specially designed to place patient care facilities close to research laboratories to promote the quick transfer of new scientific findings to the treatment of patients. Institutes admit to their units only those patients (upon referral by personal physicians) who have the precise kind or stage of illness under investigation by scientist-clinicians. Contact the Clinic with questions regarding current research.

* Hospital Patients Complaints

Office of Health Facilities (OHF)
Health Resources and Services Administration
5600 Fishers Lane, Room 11-03 (800) 638-0742
Rockville, MD 20857 (800) 492-0359 (in MD)

The OHF answers questions on the Hill-Burton Free Health Care Program and responds to patient complaints on Hill-Burton facilities via a toll-free hotline. The OHF also maintains an in-house database on Hill-Burton facilities.

* Hospital Procedures and Discharge National Survey

Division of Health Care Statistics
NCHS
3700 East-West Highway, Room 2-63
Hyattsville, MD 20782 (301) 436-8522

This division has three branches which conduct research on long-term, hospital, and ambulatory care.

* Hospitals and Energy Conservation

Design and Energy Branch
Division of Facilities Assistance and Recovery
Room 11A19
5600 Fishers Lane
Rockville, MD 20857 (301) 443-5410

The Energy and Health Facilities Branch provides information on design and construction criteria and guidelines for health care facilities and provides guidelines on energy conservation of health care facilities. This Branch mostly

Be patient. If any phone number is incorrect, call (area code) 555-1212 and request the new listing.

Health and Medicine

provides technical assistance to health care facilities with government insured mortgages, though they do have a limited ability to assist those outside this loan portfolio.

* Hospitals Providing Free Care

Office of Health Facilities
Health Resources and Services Administration
5600 Fishers Lane, Room 11-03 (800) 638-0742
Rockville, MD 20857 (800) 492-0359 (in MD)

This hotline is a service of the Bureau of Resources Development, U.S. Department of Health and Human Services. It distributes information on applying for Hill-Burton assistance, which provides free or low-cost health care. They can answer questions regarding eligibility guidelines and facilities obligated to provide medical services.

* Inventions and New Medical Treatments

Office of Medical Applications of Research (OMAR)
National Institutes of Health
Building 1, Room 260
Bethesda, MD 20892 (301) 496-1143

OMAR is the focal point within the National Institutes of Health (NIH) for technology assessment and transfer activities. These activities are aimed at facilitating the transfer of results of publicly-funded biomedical research into clinical applications and evaluating these research findings for safety and effectiveness. OMAR co-sponsors Consensus Development Conferences which bring together representatives from various fields to assess the clinical applications of specific medical technologies, and then develop a consensus statement. Past topics include cesarean childbirth and Reye's Syndrome. OMAR also administers the NIH patent program, which promotes the transfer and commercialization of federally funded inventions by the private sector. OMAR disseminates information on new treatment methods and new technology.

* Laser Surgery Information

Consumer Information Center
Pueblo, CO 81009

The FDA's publication entitled *The Surgeon's Newest Scalpel is a Laser*, is designed for the general public and explains the medical applications of the laser and how it works.

* Laser Surgery Referral Network

National Health Information Center
P.O. Box 1133 (301) 565-4167
Washington, DC 20013 (800) 336-4797 outside Washington, DC

This center can provide you with names of organizations and agencies involved with laser surgery, which can then refer you to experts in the field.

* Lower-Cost Generic Drugs Information

Superintendent of Documents
Government Printing Office
Washington, DC 20402 (202) 783-3238

The publication, *Approved Drug Product with Therapeutic Equivalent Evaluation*, is designed for public education of prescription drugs and lower-cost substitutes in an effort to help the public and health care agencies control health care costs. The price of the manual is $87.

* Medical Data

Office of Science and Data Development
Agency for Health Care Policy and Research
6001 Montrose Rd., Room 704
Rockville, MD 20852 (301) 443-9386

The Office of Science and Data Development is responsible for increasing the quality and quantity of data available for health services research, specifically for Medical Treatment Effectiveness Program and patient outcomes research. There are many sources of data on the care provided to patients. However, the usefulness of those data for outcomes research may be limited by lack of access to the data and lack of comparability and uniformity among data bases. The Office investigates the feasibility of linking research-related data from different sources to improve the quality and quantity of data available for research. The Office develops uniform definition of data, especially data and describe patient

clinical and functional status, common reporting formats and linkages for those data. The Office evaluates existing data bases, their quality, and their availability, and then disseminates these findings. Contact the office listed above for more information.

* Medical Devices: Technical Assistance for Small Businesses

Division of Small Manufacturer's Assistance
Center for Devices and Radiological Health
Food and Drug Administration (FDA)
5600 Fishers Lane, HF2-220
Rockville, MD 20857 (301) 443-6597

The FDA provides information to small businesses regarding device regulations and what is needed to get approval. The FDA often holds meetings and workshops to offer further assistance. The handbook, *A Small Business Guide to FDA*, explains how the FDA works and the approval process. This Center provides copies of device regulations and FDA documents, as well as guidelines and aids that simplify manufacturer requirements. The *SMA MEMO* contains articles and tips on medical device regulations and reports on Center activities.

* Medical Devices Updates

Center for Devices and Radiological Health
Food and Drug Administration
5600 Fishers Lane
Rockville, MD 20857 (301) 443-4690

This center conducts research relating to medical devices, reviews and evaluates medical devices approval application, and develops regulations relating to these devices. They publish two bulletins, the *Medical Devices Bulletin* and the *Radiological Health Bulletin*, both of which cover safety alerts, upcoming research, meetings, and new FDA regulations. These bulletins are designed for the medical industry community. To order the bulletins, write the center or call the editors. Radiological Health Bulletin Editor: (301) 443-5860; Medical Devices Bulletin Editor: (301) 443-5807.

* Medical Effectiveness

Center for Medical Effectiveness Research
Agency for Health Care Policy and Research
6001 Montrose Rd., Room 704
Rockville, MD 20852 (301) 443-0782

The Center for Medical Effectiveness Research has primary responsibility for the health services research supported by grants and contracts under the Medical Treatment Effectiveness Program (MEDTEP). The goal of MEDTEP activities is improved effectiveness of clinical practice. The Center concentrates on studies of specific clinical conditions for which alternative treatments are widely used and for which data are available or can be readily developed. Conditions are emphasized that affect large numbers of people, involve relatively expensive treatment, and are priorities in the Medicare program. Patient Outcomes Research Team (PORT) projects focus on variations in clinical practice and outcomes for a particular medical condition. Each PORT project is designed to identify and analyze the outcomes and costs of alternative practice patterns for a specific condition, determine the best strategy for treatment or clinical management, and develop and test methods for reducing inappropriate variations. Contact the office listed above for more information.

* Medical Expenditures

Center for General Health Services Intramural Research
Agency for Health Care Policy and Research
5600 Fishers Lane, Room 18A-31
Rockville, MD 20857 (301) 443-4108

The National Medical Expenditure Survey was designed to meet the need for analyzing how Americans use medical services, what they pay for care, and how these expenditures are finances. A publications list is available which lists the publications from the Survey. For more information, contact the Office listed above.

* Medicare's Prescription Drug Benefit

Office of Technology Assessment (OTA)
600 Pennsylvania Ave., SE
Washington, DC 20510 (202) 228-6590

OTA will study the experience of public and private payers of prescription drugs, including how they set payment rates, promote appropriate use, and control total

Be patient. If any phone number is incorrect, call (area code) 555-1212 and request the new listing.

Medical Devices, RX and Surgery

expenditures. The study will apply this experience to develop methods that the Medicare program might use to pay for multiple- and single-source drugs, and pharmaceutical services. Contact Jane Sisk, the project director, for more information.

* Medicines Affected by Age, Genes, and Diet

National Institute of General Medical Sciences
Building 31, Room 4A52
9000 Rockville Pike
Bethesda, MD 20892 (301) 496-7301

A 62-page booklet titled *Medicines and You* (No.81-2140) describes how your age, your genes, and your diet can affect the way medicines will work in your body. This report describes ongoing research on biological reactions to drugs.

* Medicines and the Elderly

National Audiovisual Center
8700 Edgeworth Drive
Capitol Heights, MD 20743 (301) 763-1896

A film or videotape titled "Wise Use of Drugs: A Program for Older Americans" is available for sale and rental. This 30 minute program suggests ways to prevent drug dependence and gives suggestions for productive visits to the doctor to insure the patient is given complete information about prescribed drugs.

* Medicines: Bad Reactions and Complaints

Practitioner Reporting System
Food and Drug Administration
12601 Twinbrook Parkway (800) 638-6725
Rockville, MD 20852 (301) 881-0256 (in MD)

The Practitioner Reporting System offers a service for health professionals to report problems with drugs or medical devices. A copy of the report goes to the manufacturer, as well as to the Food and Drug Administration.

* Orphan Drugs and Rare Diseases

National Information Center on Orphan Drugs
and Rare Diseases (NICODARD)
P.O. Box 1133 (202) 429-9091
Washington, DC 20013 (800) 456-3505 outside DC

NICODARD staff, a component of the National Health Information Center, can answer questions on rare diseases and on orphan drugs. The Center is a service of the Office of Disease Prevention and Health Promotion, DHHS, and is sponsored by the Orphan Products Development Board of the Food and Drug Administration. A directory of organizations and educational materials is available from the National Technical Information Service.

* Over-the-Counter Drugs and RX Consumer Info

Office of Public Affairs
Food and Drug Administration
5600 Fishers Lane, HFE88
Rockville, MD 20857 (301) 443-3170

The FDA distributes many brochures and publications which cover a variety of topics, such as drugs, cosmetics, and foods safety and additives. This office will gladly send publications on topics that interest you. The *FDA Consumer*, which contains the latest developments at FDA, can be ordered for $12 per year from the Superintendent of Documents, Government Printing Office, Washington DC 20402, (202) 783-3238.

* Over-the-Counter and RX Drugs Safety

Center for Drug Evaluation and Research
HFD 100, Room 14B45
5600 Fishers Lane
Rockville, MD 20857 (301) 295-8012; or

Office of Consumer Affairs
HFD 365, 5600 Fishers Lane
Rockville, MD 20857 (301) 443-3170

The Center for Drug Evaluation and Research develops policy with regard to the safety, effectiveness, and labeling of all drug products and evaluates new drug applications. It develops and implements standards for the safety and effectiveness of all over-the-counter drugs. It also conducts research and develops scientific standards on the composition, quality, safety, and effectiveness of drugs.

A list of guidelines is available to help manufacturers comply with the requirements of the regulations. The staff will respond to requests from information regarding the laws, regulations, policies, and functions of the FDA as it pertains to drugs. Many FDA Consumer Report articles, as well as an FDA Consumer Special Report on drugs, are available to the public.

* Pharmaceutical Companies Intelligence

Drug Listing Branch
Food and Drug Administration
5600 Fishers Lane, HFO 334
Rockville, MD 20857 (301) 295-8083

This Food and Drug Administration office compiles many different types of drug-related lists, which can be obtained by writing the Freedom of Information Office listed below. Available lists include drug establishments, private label distributors, prescription drug establishments, over-the-counter and bulk drugs, drug products, and import products. The fee varies, depending upon the list. Freedom of Information, FDA, 5600 Fishers Lane, HFI 35, Rockville, MD 20857, (301) 443-6310.

* Pharmaceutical Exports and Mislabeling

Office of Technology Assessment (OTA)
600 Pennsylvania Ave., SE
Washington, DC 20510 (202) 224-8996

The U.S. pharmaceutical industry is a major supplier of pharmaceuticals to developing countries, but the industry has been criticized for mislabeling certain drugs sold in those countries. OTA has studied whether inappropriate labeling is occurring today to allow health workers in those developing countries to use drugs safely and effectively. The resulting publication is titled *Drug Labeling in Developing Countries.*

* Pharmaceutical Research and Development

Office of Technology Assessment (OTA)
600 Pennsylvania Ave., SE
Washington, DC 20510 (202) 228-6590

OTA is working on a project to examine trends in the structure, process, and products of pharmaceutical R&D in the U.S., with the goal of developing and implementing a system for estimating and tracking R&D costs over time. The study will also describe the organization of the pharmaceutical R&D enterprise, identifying how costs differ by therapeutic class or biological research area. Contact Judith Wagner, the project director, for more information.

* Pharmacology Experiments and Research

Pharmacological Sciences Program
National Institute of General Medical Sciences
Building 31, Room 4A52
9000 Rockville Pike
Bethesda, MD 20892 (301) 496-7707

This program supports research aimed at providing an improved understanding of biological phenomena and related chemical and molecular processes involved in the actions of therapeutic drugs, anesthetic agents, and their metabolites. This program supports research ranging from synthetic chemistry and basic biological and biochemical studies in molecular pharmacology to comparative studies in cell cultures and laboratory animals, as well as controlled clinical investigations in patients and normal volunteers. Grants are available, including pre- and postdoctoral fellowships. The *Biennial Report* describes the current research awards. The *Annual Report of NIGMS* lists all the various programs and their research highlights.

* Radiation Dose Information

Radiopharmaceutical Internal Dose Information Center
P.O.Box 117
Oak Ridge Associated Universities
Oak Ridge, TN 37821-0117 (615) 576-3450

This center primarily serves researchers at government agencies and nuclear medicine centers as well as private physicians having questions about internal radiation dose calculations, especially those involving radiopharmaceuticals.

* Radiation Safety Alerts

Medical Devices and Radiation
Food and Drug Administration

Be patient. If any phone number is incorrect, call (area code) 555-1212 and request the new listing.

Health and Medicine

5600 Fishers Lane
Rockville, MD 20857 (301) 443-4690

This center conducts research relating to medical devices, reviews and evaluates medical devices approval application, and develops regulations relating to these devices. They publish two bulletins, the *Medical Devices Bulletin* and the *Radiological Health Bulletin*, both of which cover safety alerts, upcoming research, meetings, and new FDA regulations. These bulletins are designed for the medical industry community. To order the bulletins, write the center or call the editors. Radiological Health Bulletin Editor: (301) 443-5860; Medical Devices Bulletin Editor: (301) 443-5807.

* Second Opinion Surgical Hotline

National Second Surgical Opinion Program
Health Care Financing Administration
330 Independence Ave., SW (800) 638-6833
Washington, DC 20201 (800) 492-6603 in Maryland only

The National Second Surgical Opinion Program is an information resource for people faced with the possibility of non-emergency or elective surgery. By calling its toll-free number, the staff will help you locate a surgeon or other specialist enrolled in the program who can offer you a second opinion. Pamphlets are available with questions that patients looking for second opinions should ask.

* Tranquilizer Warnings

Office of Public Affairs
Food and Drug Administration
5600 Fishers Lane
HFE88
Rockville, MD 20857 (301) 443-3170

A Guide to the Proper Use of Tranquilizers (No. 86-3158) is a free 4-page booklet available on the safe use of this medicines used for treating intense anxiety disorders.

* X-rays and Safety

Office of Consumer Affairs
Food and Drug Administration
Public Inquiries
5600 Fishers Lane
Rockville, MD 20857 (301) 443-3170

Several free pamphlets on radiation are available including: *Primer on Radiation* (No. 79-8099); *Seeking the Safest X-ray Picture* (No. 79-8091); *X-ray Record Card* (No. 80-8024); and *X-rays: Get the Picture on Protection* (No. 80-8088).

Be patient. If any phone number is incorrect, call (area code) 555-1212 and request the new listing.

Chemicals, Toxins, and Other Health Hazards

* *See also Careers and Workplace Chapter*
* *See also Environment and Nature Chapter*

Online databases can be accessed to obtain the latest information on potential health hazards as well as known carcinogens and other dangerous chemicals and substances. In addition, several directories and printouts are available to determine environmental risks to our health in the home, school, and at work.

* Access to Computerized Toxicology Databases

Toxicology Information Program (TIP)
National Library of Medicine
8600 Rockville Pike
Bethesda, MD 20894 (301) 496-6308

TIP was established to provide national access to information on toxicology. The program is charged with setting up computerized databases of information from the literature of toxicology and from the files of both governmental and non-governmental organizations. Among the databases are TOXLINE (Toxicology Information Online) and CHEMLINE, a chemical dictionary file. TIP implemented the TOXNET (Toxicology Data Network) system of toxicologically-oriented data banks, including the HSDB (Hazardous Substances Data Bank), which is useful in chemical emergency response. TIP also supports the Toxicology Information Response Center, which provides reference services to the scientific community.

* Birth Defects and Cancer: Harmful Chemicals

National Institute of Environmental Health Sciences
National Institutes of Health (NIH)
Public Affairs Office
Research Triangle Park, NC 27709 (919) 541-3345

This NIH institute can share the latest scientific findings on cancer-causing agents.

* Chemicals, Pesticides and Prevention

National Center for Environmental Health and Injury Control
Centers for Disease Control
1600 Clifton Road, F29
Atlanta, GA 30333 (404) 488-4102

This center offers free publications on such topics as injury prevention, recreational safety, rodent control, and toxic agent control. You may request a copy of their publications list.

* Dangerous Exposure to Toxins: Experiments

Clinical Biochemistry Branch
Division of Environmental Health Laboratory Sciences
Centers for Disease Control (CDC)
1600 Clifton Rd.
Atlanta, GA 30333 (404) 488-4132

This research branch of CDC develops, validates and applies laboratory technology which improves the detection, treatment, and prevention of human toxicant exposures and resulting adverse health effects. Contact this office for more information regarding toxicant exposures.

* Environmental Toxicology Training and Research

National Institute of Environmental Health Sciences
National Institutes of Health
P.O. Box 12233
Research Triangle Park, NC 27709 (919) 541-3345

The National Institute of Environmental Health Sciences supports the National Toxicology Program, as well as research on how living organisms react and adapt to the environment. Some of the research encompasses neuroscience, biophysics, and genetics. They offer training programs for scientists and cooperate with many international organizations.

* Harmful Environment Factors

National Institute of Environmental Health Sciences (NIEHS)
P.O. Box 12233
Research Triangle Park, NC 27709 (919) 541-3345

The National Institute of Environmental Health Sciences supports nd conducts research focusing on the interaction between humans and potentially toxic agents in their environment. The research concentrates on recognizing, identifying and investigating environmental factors that may be harmful and quantifying those factors. NIEHS research also focuses on developing an understanding of the mechanisms of action of toxic agents on biological systems. Information based on research is transmitted to regulatory agencies, other government agencies, the Congress, industry and the public.

* Latest Findings about Toxics

National Toxicology Program
National Institute of Environmental Health Sciences
B2-04
P.O. Box 12233
Research Triangle, NC 27709 (919) 541-3991

The National Toxicology Program's main objectives are to increase the depth of knowledge about the toxicology of chemicals, to evaluate the full range of toxic effects of chemicals, to develop and validate new more effective and efficient assays for toxicity, and to distribute toxicological information resulting from its studies. The *Environmental Health Perspectives* is a scientific journal on the biological effects of environmental agents and the mechanisms through which these agents interact with living systems. The journal can be ordered from Superintendent of Documents, U.S. Government Printing Office, Washington, DC 20402, (202) 783-3238.

* Lead-Based Paint

Reference Supervisor
HUD User
Box 280
Germantown, MD 20874 (800) 245-2691 (301) 251-5154 in DC

This computer-based information service offer personalized literature searches by reference staff on such concerns about housing safety and lead-based paint.

* On-the-Job Hazards: Registry of 40,000 Chemicals

Toxicological Information Program
Specialized Information Services
National Library of Medicine
8600 Rockville Pike
Bethesda, MD 20894 (301) 496-1131

The Registry of Toxic Effects of Chemical Substances (RTECS) is a database of toxicological information compiled, maintained and updated by the National Institute for Occupational Safety and Health. The RTECS now lists over 40,000 chemicals and the concentrations at which toxicity is known to occur. The printed version is available from Superintendent of Documents, Government Printing Office, Washington, DC 20402, (202) 783-3238. The magnetic computer tape is available from National Technical Information Service, 5285 Port Royal Road, Springfield, VA 22161, (703) 487-4650. The on-line database is available from RTECS, Toxicological Information Program, Specialized Information Services, National Library of Medicine, Bethesda, MD 20894, (301) 496-1131. For additional information, contact: The Editor, RTECS, 4676 Columbia Parkway, Cincinnati, OH 45226, (513) 533-8317.

Be patient. If any phone number is incorrect, call (area code) 555-1212 and request the new listing.

Health and Medicine

* Risk Reduction of Toxic Chemicals Exposures

National Center for Toxicological Research
Jefferson, AR 72079 (501) 541-4517

This center focuses on the need for increased research to develop better ways of assessing the risk of toxic chemicals to humans, and to help reduce those risks. This center also provides the FDA and other regulatory agencies with the knowledge to make regulatory decisions concerning toxic substances. Research is undertaken by a variety of disciplines, including biochemical and comparative toxicology.

* Toxic and Pesticide Information Hotline

National Pesticide Telecommunications Network (800) 858-7378

This service of the U.S. Environmental Protection Agency and Texas Tech University is open 24 hours, 7 days a week. It responds to non-emergency questions about the effects of pesticides, toxicology and symptoms, environmental effects, disposal and cleanup, and safe use of pesticides.

* Toxicological Information Program

Specialized Information Services
National Library of Medicine
8600 Rockville Pike
Bethesda, MD 20894 (301) 496-1131

The Registry of Toxic Effects of Chemical Substances (RTECS) is a database of toxicological information compiled, maintained and updated by the National Institute for Occupational Safety and Health. The RTECS now lists over 40,000 chemicals and the concentrations at which toxicity is known to occur. The printed version is available from Superintendent of Documents, Government Printing Office, Washington, DC 20402, (202) 783-3238. The magnetic computer tape is available from National Technical Information Service, 5285 Port Royal Road, Springfield, VA 22161, (703) 487-4650. The on-line database is available from RTECS, Toxicological Information Program, Specialized Information Services, National Library of Medicine, Bethesda, MD 20894, (301) 496-1131. For additional information, contact: The Editor, RTECS, 4676 Columbia Parkway, Cincinnati, OH 45226, (513) 533-8317.

* Workplace Hazards Detection

National Institute for Occupational Safety and Health (NIOSH)
4676 Columbia Parkway
Cincinnati, OH 45226 (800) 356-4674

NIOSH is responsible for conducting research to make the nation's workplaces healthier and safer by responding to urgent requests for assistance from employers, employees, and their representatives where imminent hazards are suspected. They conduct inspections, laboratory and epidemiologic research, publish their findings, and make recommendations for improved working conditions to regulatory agencies. NIOSH trains occupational health and safety workers and communicates research results to those concerned.

Be patient. If any phone number is incorrect, call (area code) 555-1212 and request the new listing.

Medical Research: Clues and Answers

Knowledge about breakthroughs in medical research is not confined to the scientific community. Anyone should look upon organizations and centers engaged in clinical studies and experiments as important information resources to learn about the latest theories which explain the complexities of medicine and health.

* Applications and Answers about NIH Grants

Division of Research Grants (DRG)
National Institutes of Health
3333 Westbard Ave., Room 449
Bethesda, MD 20892 (301) 496-7441

The Division of Research Grants provides for review of National Institutes of Health grant applications. They collect, store, analyze, and evaluate management and program data needed in the administration of extramural programs. This office disseminated information on the various extramural programs and now have the information on the DRG online system. For guidelines and proposal application, contact this office.

* Biomedical Research Projects Underway

Research Resources Information Center
1601 Research Blvd.
Rockville, MD 20850 (301) 984-2870

You may write for the free directory, *Biomedical Research Technology Resources*, which lists all the current biomedical research projects funded through National Institutes of Health and the services available to other researchers (see Biomedical Research Technology Program).

* Biomedical Computing, Engineering and Technologies

Biomedical Research Technology Program
Westwood Building, Room 8A11
National Institutes of Health (NIH)
5333 Westbard Avenue
Bethesda, MD 20892 (301) 496-5545

NIH's Biomedical Research Technology Program focuses on biomedical computing, biomedical engineering, and technologies for the study of bimolecular and cellular structure and function. Most of the Program's budget is directed to the support of research center grants. Grants are also available for projects of advanced technology related to biomedical research. The research centers are open to outside investigators. Contact this office for a free *Biomedical Research Technology Resources Directory* or grant applications.

* Blacks and Minority Scientists Research Grants

Minority Investigator Research Enhancement Award (MIREA)
Deputy Director, Extramural Activities Program
National Institute of Arthritis and
Musculoskeletal and Skin Diseases
Westwood Building, Room 403
Bethesda, MD 20892 (301) 496-7495

Deputy Director, Division of Extramural Activities
National Institute of Diabetes and Digestive
and Kidney Diseases
Westwood Building, Room 406
Bethesda, MD 20892 (301) 496-7083

The MIREA provides support for faculty members of minority institutions to allow them to collaborate with principal investigators of active research grants funded by the National Institute of Arthritis and Musculoskeletal and Skin Diseases (NIAMS) or the National Institute of Diabetes and Digestive and Kidney Diseases (NIDDK). MIREA is part of an effort to strengthen biomedical research and training in institutions with significant commitments to minorities and thereby to increase the participation of minority scientists in biomedical research.

* Blood and Biological Products Standards

Center for Biologics Evaluation and Research
Food and Drug Administration
Building 29, Room 129
8800 Rockville Pike
Bethesda, MD 20205 (301) 496-8228

The Center for Biologics Evaluation and Research, a regulatory agency for biological products, and conducts research related to the development, manufacture, testing, and use of both new and old biological products. It also conducts research on the preparation, preservation, and safety of blood and blood products. The Center cooperates with other agencies, organizations, universities and, scientists regarding biological products. The information they have is technical in nature.

* Brain Tissue Banks for Neurological and Psychiatric Diseases Research

Dr. Edward D. Bird
Professor of Neuropathology
Mclean Hospital
115 Mill St.
Belmont, MA 02178 (617) 855-3426

Human Specimen Bank
Dr. Wallace W. Tourtellotte
Chief of Neurology Service
V.A.- Wadsworth Medical Center
Building 212, Room 31
Los Angeles, CA 90073 (213) 824-4307

The National Institute of Mental Health and National Institute of Neurological Disorders and Stroke support the Brain Tissue Bank at the Mclean Hospital, Belmont, Massachusetts. Both Institutes also support the Human Specimen Bank at the V.A.- Wadsworth Medical Center, Los Angeles, California. These tissue banking resource collects brain tissues obtained at autopsy, blood serum, and spinal fluid, stores them cryogenically and in formalin, and distributes these materials to research scientists.

* Birth Control: Researching New Contraceptive Methods

Contraception Development Branch
EPN 600, 6130 Executive Blvd.
Rockville, MD 20892 (301) 496-1661

The Contraception Development Branch supports research on the development of new fertility regulating methods with emphasis on improving both effectiveness and acceptability. Some of the research focuses on biological evaluation of new compounds, development of improved vaginal and uterine contraception based on chemical or physical methods, and clinical trials of sex steroids. They collaborate with other national and international organizations, such as The World Health Organization and the Population Council and its International Committee for Contraceptive Research. This Branch also holds workshops on various topics.

* Computer-Assisted Medical Instruction R&D

Lister Hill Center for Biomedical Communications
8600 Rockville Pike
Bethesda, MD 20894 (301) 496-4441

This center is responsible for conducting research and development in computer-assisted instruction, distributed information systems, artificial intelligence and expert systems, and electronic document storage and retrieval. The Center's programs cover six areas: communications engineering, information

Be patient. If any phone number is incorrect, call (area code) 555-1212 and request the new listing.

Health and Medicine

technology, computer science, audiovisual program development, educational technology, and training and consultation. A publications list is available.

* Genetics and Basic Science Research

National Institute of General Medical Sciences (NIGMS)
National Institutes of Health
Building 31, Room 4A52
9000 Rockville Pike
Bethesda, MD 20892 (301) 496-7301

NIGMS supports research and research training in the basic biomedical sciences that form the foundation needed to make advances in the understanding of disease. Research focuses on the cellular basis of disease, genetics, pharmacological sciences, physiology and biomedical engineering. For instance, they look at how DNA is replicated or how drugs are metabolized in your body. They have brochures and reports for the general public and professionals on such topics as medicines and genetic diseases.

* Grants from National Institutes of Health

Office of Grants Inquiries
National Institutes of Health (NIH)
5333 Westbard Ave., Room 449
Bethesda, MD 20892 (301) 496-7441

This office can answer your questions regarding policies, applications, procedures, and other information concerning NIH grants.

* Health Sciences International Collaboration

Fogarty International Center (FIC)
for Advanced Studies in Health Sciences
National Institutes of Health
Building 16, Room 306
Bethesda, MD 20852 (301) 496-2075

This international research center assembles scientists and others in the biomedical, behavioral and related fields for discussion, study, and research relating to the international development of the health science. It also sponsors research programs, conferences, and seminars to further international cooperation and collaboration in the life sciences. FIC oversees the Scholars-in-Residence program and awards fellowships to foreign scientists. Publications are available covering international health care concerns.

* Heart and Lung Transplants

National Heart, Lung, and Blood Institute
National Institutes of Health
Building 31, Room 5A-52
9000 Rockville Pike
Bethesda, MD 20892 (301) 496-4236

This Institute is involved with both intra- and extramural, experimental research regarding transplantation of the heart and lungs. Current research focuses on immune modulation and organ rejection, as well as on long-term preservation of the heart to allow for transplantation. The staff can refer you to current researchers, and can send you brochures and reports on this procedure.

* Laboratory Animals for Medical Research

Veterinary Resources Program
National Center for Research Resources
National Institutes of Health
Westwood Building, Room 857
Bethesda, MD 20892 (301) 496-2527

The Animal Resources Program helps meet the needs of biomedical researchers for high quality, disease-free animals and specialized animal research facilities. The program supports, via grants and contracts, primate research centers and their field stations, primate breeding and supply projects, animal diagnostic laboratories, and a variety of other research projects. The program comprises three subprograms: The Regional Primate Research Centers, Laboratory Animal Sciences, and Biological Models and Materials Resources. Contact this office for

more information and a free directory which informs researchers of the resources provided and how to access them.

* Mental Health Grants for Hispanic and Other Minorities

Associate Director for Special Populations
National Institute of Mental Health
5600 Fishers Lane, Room 11-95
Rockville, MD 20857 (301) 443-2847

The Minority Group Mental Health Program has two funding components. 1) It funds research and development centers to provide minorities (Hispanic, Asia and Native Americans) an opportunity to conduct research on specific minority concerns. And 2) It funds minority students through the MARC, Minority Fellowship, and Minority Institution Research Development Programs, which are designed to give minorities grants for mental health research.

* Neurophysiology and Computer Systems

Research Services Branch
National Institute of Mental Health
Building 36, Room 2A03
Bethesda, MD 20892 (301) 496-4957

The scientists and engineers of this research branch of NIMH develop experimental design, data processing, and computer programs to help with research in neurophysiology, neurogenetics, and neurochemistry. The researchers can provide consultation in statistical analysis and experimental design, along with information on image processing programs which are available to the public.

* Ongoing NIH Scientific Research Database

Research Documentation Section
Division of Research Grants
National Institutes of Health
5333 Westbard Avenue
Westwood Building, Room 148B
Bethesda, MD 20892 (301) 496-7543

The Computer Retrieval of Information on Scientific Projects (CRISPS) system is designed to provide scientific and associated grant identification information on research currently being done at the National Institute of Health.

* Pharmacology Research

Pharmacology Research Associate Program (PRAP)
National Institute of General Medical Sciences
Westwood Building, Room 919
Bethesda, MD 20892 (301) 496-7301

The PRAP is a small, highly selective intramural activity supported by the National Institute of General Medical Sciences. Each year 11 recently trained scientists are selected for a 2-year period of postdoctoral research in laboratories at NIH and the Alcohol, Drug Abuse, and Mental Health Administration. Associates conduct research under the direction of senior scientists and take course work.

* Research Money: Comprehensive List of Grantees

Health-Related Research and Development
Office of Extramural Research
NIH, Building 1, Room 144
9000 Rockville Pike
Bethesda, MD 20892 (301) 496-5126

This office can answer your questions regarding grants and contracts and direct you to the appropriate office for your research needs. This office also formulates grant award policies and procedures and publishes the *Research Award Index*, a directory of the research awards for each year, available for $92 from the Superintendent of Documents, Government Printing Office, Washington, DC 20402, (202) 783-3238.

Be patient. If any phone number is incorrect, call (area code) 555-1212 and request the new listing.

Health Care Costs and Services

Health policy and the health care delivery systems are evaluated and reassessed every day. Numerous sources for data and statistics are readily available which can help reveal information on particular medical procedures, hospitals and other aspects of health care.

* Births, Abortions, Deaths Statistics
Division of Vital Statistics
National Center for Health Statistics
3700 East-West Highway
Room 1-44
Hyattsville, MD 20782 (301) 436-8952
This division collects data on births, deaths, abortions, marriages, and divorces, and produces annual data for the U.S., states, countries, and local areas.

* Community Health Services for Homeless, Migrant Farmworkers and Other Populations
Bureau of Health Care Delivery and Assistance
Health Resources and Services Administration
5600 Fishers Lane, Room 7-05
Rockville, MD 20857 (301) 443-2320
The Bureau of Health Care Delivery and Assistance Services focuses nationally on efforts to ensure the availability and delivery of health care services in health manpower shortage areas, to medically underserved populations, and to special services populations, such as migrants or the homeless. The Bureau provides project grants to community-based organizations to meet the health needs of the undeserved or special needs populations.

* Cost of Health Care: Statistics
Office of Public Affairs
Health Care Financing Administration
200 Independence Ave., SW
Room 423-H
Washington, DC 20201 (202) 245-8056; or

Office of Research and Statistics
Social Security Administration
1875 Connecticut Ave., NW
Washington, DC 20009 (202) 965-1234
These offices collect statistics regarding health, health care, and health care financing. They compile and distribute data on a wide variety of topics, such as spending on health care services, the age of recipients of services, and health problems.

* Cost of Medicaid and Medicare
Health Care Financing Administration (HCFA)
6325 Security Blvd.
Baltimore, MD 21207 (301) 597-3933
This office compiles statistics on Medicaid, health coverage for low-income, and Medicare, health coverage for the elderly. The data are broken down many ways such as populations, expenditures, and utilization. Each year they publish a HCFA statistics booklet which provides significant summary information about health expenditures and HCFA programs.

* Cradle to Grave Health Statistics
National Center for Health Care Statistics
Scientific and Technical Information Branch
3700 East West Highway
Room 1-57
Hyattsville, MD 20782 (301) 436-8500
The National Center for Health Statistics (NCHS) is the Federal Government's principal vital and health statistics agency. It collects, analyzes, and distributes data, conducts research in statistical and survey methodology, and provides technical assistance in the U.S., foreign countries, and for other organizations. They conducted several population-based surveys, such as the National Health Interview Survey and the National Health and Nutrition Examination Survey; and several record-based surveys, such as the National Hospital Discharge Survey and The National Nursing Home Survey. NCHS cooperates with states and other countries to improve the quality and availability of data. A central component of NCHS is to distribute its data, which is done through a series of publications, public use data files, and unpublished tabulations, as well as through journals, conferences, and workshops.

* Doctor Visits National Survey
Division of Health Examination Statistics
National Center for Health Statistics
3700 East-West Highway
Room 2-58
Hyattsville, MD 20782 (301) 436-7068
This division collects data on health-related matters and administers the National Health and Nutrition Survey, which assesses the health and nutritional status of the general population through direct physical examination.

* Federal Health Policy Evaluations
Information Specialist
DHHS Policy Information Center
U.S. Department of Health and Human Services
200 Independence Avenue SW
Room 438-F
Washington, DC 20201 (202) 245-6445
This center identifies, collects, and indexes all program evaluations, studies, and reports of government health programs from such agencies as the General Accounting Office, the Congressional Budget Office,the Office of Technology Assessment. Abstracts of these evaluations are available as well as the annual publication, *Compendium of HHS Evaluation Studies.*

* Health Care Delivery and Health Professions
Office of Public Affairs
Health Resources and Services Administration
5600 Fishers Lane
Room 1443
Rockville, MD 20857 (301) 443-2086
The Health Resources and Services Administration offers a free catalog, *Current Publications*, which lists all the publications films, and videos produced by HRSA's three bureaus: Bureau of Health Care Delivery and Assistance, Bureau of Maternal and Child Health and Resources Development and Bureau of Health Professions.

* Illness and Wellness Status of 50,000 Families
Division of Health Interview Statistics
National Center for Health Statistics
3700 East-West Highway
Room 2-44
Hyattsville, MD 20782 (301) 436-7085
This division administers the National Health Interview Survey, which is the principal source of information on the health, illness, and disability status of non-institutionalized population. The survey focuses on current health topics and is conducted continually in 50,000 households.

Be patient. If any phone number is incorrect, call (area code) 555-1212 and request the new listing.

Health and Medicine

* Government Health Programs Report Card

Policy Information Center
U.S. Department of Health and Human Services
200 Independence Ave., SW, Room 438-F
Washington, DC 20201 (202) 245-6445

This center has identified, collected, and indexed the U.S. Department of Health and Human Services' program evaluations and evaluative research reports. Also collected are reports from the DHHS Office of the Assistant Secretary for Planning and Evaluation, the DHHS Inspector General's Office, and the General Accounting Office, the Congressional Budget Office, and the Office of Technology Assessment. A one-page description sheet, including an abstract, is prepared for each study. Copies may be purchased through the National Technical Information Service. Inquiries are answered by telephone, by mail, or by personal assistance. An in-house, online database provides access to the reports by subject and/or sponsoring agency, with custom printouts, including abstracts, available upon request. An annual publication, Compendium of HHS Evaluation Studies, is also available.

* Grants for Health Promotion Projects

ODPHP National Health Information Center
P.O. Box 1133 (800) 336-4797
Washington, DC 20013 (301) 565-4167 (in MD)

The guide, *Locating Resources for Healthy People 2000 Health Promotion Projects*, is designed to assist newcomers on their search for health promotion funding by introducing them to the major tasks involved and information services available. This publication is divided into four major sections. Section I discusses basic principles of fundseeking. Sections II and III discuss where and how to look for health promotion funds, focusing on both private and public sectors. Major foundations and Federal agencies interested in health promotion, as well as local sources are listed. Section IV lists resources--organizations, foundations, publications, and databases--that can be useful to those seeking funds. Also included is an appendix, which includes a glossary, a list of acronyms, a bibliography, and a sample grant application form.

* Marriage and Divorce Statistics

Division of Vital Statistics
National Center for Health Statistics
3700 East-West Highway, Room 1-44
Hyattsville, MD 20782 (301) 436-8952

This division collects data on the number of marriages and divorces as well as statistics of births, abortions, and deaths. It produces annual data for the U.S., states, countries, and local areas.

* Medical Services and Personnel Shortages

National Clearinghouse for Primary Care Information
8201 Greensboro Dr., Suite 600
McLean, VA 22102 (703) 821-8955

This clearinghouse provides information services to support the planning, development, and delivery of ambulatory health care to urban and rural areas where shortages of medical personnel and services exist. Its primary audience is health care providers who work in community health centers. They have a list of publications and can make referrals to other health-related organizations. This clearinghouse also publishes a newsletter, *Primary Care Perspectives*.

* Nurses, Doctors, and Services Availability

Bureau of Health Care Delivery and Assistance
Health Resources and Services Administration
5600 Fishers Lane, Room 7-05
Rockville, MD 20857 (301) 443-2320

The Bureau of Health Care Delivery and Assistance Services focuses nationally on efforts to ensure the availability and delivery of health care services in health manpower shortage areas, to medically underserved populations, and to special services populations. It also administers the National Health Service Corps Program which recruits health care practitioners and places them in areas having shortages of people trained in health-related fields.

* Planned Approach to Community Health (PATCH) Program

Center for Chronic Disease Prevention
and Health Promotion (CCDPHP)
Centers for Disease Control
1600 Clifton Rd., NE
Bldg 3, Room 117
Atlanta, GA 30333 (404) 639-2838

CCDPHP staff work with State and local health departments and community members to organize local intervention programs. The center provides materials and technical assistance, and the communities invest their time and resources and make the program work. Programs have focused on cholesterol screening and nutrition, smoking cessation, alcohol misuse, and prevention of injuries from falls. The PATCH program also conducts international training conferences.

* Prepaid Medicare Health Care

Deputy Director
Office of Prepaid Health Care
Health Care Financing Administration
Parklawn Building, Room 9-11
330 Independence Avenue SW, Room 436
Washington, DC 20201 (202) 619-0815

This office offers materials on health maintenance organizations (HMOs), specifically the capitation concept under Medicare designed to control health costs. Since this bureau monitors qualified plans, it can serve as an information resource on Medicare prepaid health care plans.

* World Health Policies

Office of International Health (OIH)
U.S. Department of Health and Human Services
5600 Fishers Lane, Room 18-87
Rockville, MD 20857 (301) 443-1774

This office supports the Assistant Secretary for Health in developing policy, and also coordinates activities of the Public Health Service in the field of international health. It works closely with the World Health Organization and other international organizations and oversees PHS participation in over 25 bi-national health agreements. The OIH will respond to questions regarding U.S. participation in international health agreements and programs. A publications list is available.

Be patient. If any phone number is incorrect, call (area code) 555-1212 and request the new listing.

Drugs and Chemical Dependence General Sources

* *See also Education Chapter*
* *See also Information from Lawmakers Chapter*
* *See also Health and Medicine Chapter*
* *See also Law and Social Justice Chapter*

This chapter includes information sources which deal primarily with alcohol and illegal drugs. The first section identifies several different government agencies, private organizations, clearinghouses, and databases which track chemical dependence in the U.S., as well as international trends. Drug-related crime, traffic accidents, and other statistics are also included. The Education and Prevention Section offers all sorts of publications and audiovisuals for teachers, counselors, health professionals, parents, and students. Comic books and coloring books for youngsters also are noted, as well as free posters which carry the drug-free message. Many organizations experimenting with different strategies for prevention and detection of drug abuse in schools, communities and workplaces are listed. Under the Treatment and Rehabilitation section you'll find several resources which can provide you with counseling, referrals, and printed materials on the problems of addiction. Al-Anon Family Group Headquarters, for example, with its round-the-clock toll-free number, offers help to families dealing with alcoholism. The Psychiatric Institute runs the National Cocaine Hotline and answers questions and provides referrals to drug rehab centers. Both the National Health Information Center and the National Clearinghouse on Alcohol and Drug Information are excellent places to learn about the array of private resources, new organizations, hotlines, and self-help programs for those who need them. Dozens of federal and state government law enforcement agencies, as well as those involved with international drug trafficking enforcement and prosecution, are listed in the last section of this chapter.

* Academic Institutions and Strategies for Substance Prevention

Office for Substance and Alcohol Abuse (OSAP)
5600 Fishers Lane
Rockville, MD 20847-2345 (301) 443-6480

Single publications are free of charge, including a publications catalog. Many are available in Spanish. Examples are: *Alcohol Practices, Policies, and Potentials of American Colleges and Universities: A White Paper* (CS02) and *Strategies for Preventing Alcohol and Other Drug Problems on College Campuses: Program Administrators Guide* (CS03). Both of these are designed to help colleges deal with alcohol and drugs on campuses.

* Alcohol and AIDS

National Clearinghouse for Alcohol and Drug Information
P.O. Box 2345
Rockville, MD 20847 (301) 468-2600

The following are available publications that are free:

Preventing HIV Infection Among Youth (BK193)

NIDA-Capsule: Facts Supporting NIDA's Drug Abuse and AIDS Prevention Campaign for Teens (CP36). This pamphlet explains how alcohol can change a person's judgement about having unsafe sex.

* Alcohol, Drug Abuse and Mental Health Administration

Alcohol, Drug Abuse and Mental Health
Administration (ADAMHA)
5600 Fishers Lane
Rockville, MD 20857 (301) 443-8956

ADAMHA conducts and supports research on the biological, psychological, behavioral and epidemiological aspects of alcoholism, drug abuse, and mental health and illness; supports the training of scientists to conduct research in the alcoholism, drug abuse and mental heath fields; gathers and analyzes data about the extent of alcohol, drug abuse and mental health problems and the national response to these needs; encourages groups to facilitate and expand programs for the prevention and treatment; and provides information on alcoholism, drug abuse, and mental health to the public and to the scientific community. A new pamphlet is available: *Update September 1992*, and will be sent upon request.

* Alcoholism and Health Insurance Coverage

National Institute on Alcohol Abuse and Alcoholism (NIAAA)
Parklawn Building
5600 Fishers Lane, Room 16C141
Rockville, MD 20857 (301) 443-3860

The NIAAA looks at trends relating to treatment of alcoholism and insurance financing issues. It advocates adequate health insurance coverage for alcoholism treatment, and conducts studies on this topic, which are available to the public. Call the Clearinghouse at (800) 729-6686. Catalog is free upon request.

* Alcohol in the Workplace

National Clearinghouse
P.O. Box 2345
Rockville, MD 20847-2345 (301) 468-2600

An Employers Guide to Dealing with Substance Abuse (PHD543), *Research on Drugs and the Workplace* (CAP24), and *Workers at Risk: Drugs and Alcohol on the Job* (PHD521) discuss all aspects of alcohol and the workplace. These are available free, as well as a catalog of other publications.

* Alcoholism Magazine for Professionals

Superintendent of Documents
U.S. Government Printing Office
Washington, DC 20402 (202) 783-3238

Alcohol Health and Research World, a magazine published quarterly and available for $11 per year, provides professionals with information regarding current research, prevention, and treatment of alcoholism, and includes comment and opinion section, along with information about upcoming events.

* American Alliance for Rights and Responsibilities

AARR
Suite 1112, 1725 K St. NW
Washington, DC 20006 (202) 785-7844

This is a national non-profit membership organization which is trying to help restore civic duty to the American public. It is working on drug and alcohol abuse and the rights and responsibilities of families. Publications are available free. One of them is *The Winnable War: A Community Guide to Eradicating Street Drug Markets.*

Be patient. If any phone number is incorrect, call (area code) 555-1212 and request the new listing.

Drugs and Chemical Dependence

* Alcohol Resources and Bibliographies

National Clearinghouse for Alcohol Information
P.O. Box 2345 (800) 729-6686
Rockville, MD 20847-2345 (301) 468-2600

Single copies of each of these resource bulletins are available free: *Self Help Groups for Professionals and Special Populations* (No. MS330); *Publishers of Books on Alcohol Topics* (No. MS313); *What You Can do About Drug Use in America* (PHD587); *You Can Help Your Community Get Rid of Drugs* (PHD577); *Training Drug Treatment Staff in the Age of Aids.* You can also order the latest copy of their catalog. The following Prevention Resource Guides are available free, and contain facts, figures, resources, and other information relevant to the specific guide:

Prevention Resource Guide: American Indians/Native Alaskans
Prevention Resource Guide: Asian and Pacific Islander Americans
Prevention Resource Guide: Children of Alcoholics
Prevention Resource Guide: College Youth
Prevention Resource Guide: Elementary Youth
Prevention Resource Guide: Pregnant/Postpartum Women and Their Infants
Prevention Resource Guide: Preschool Children
Prevention Resource Guide: Rural Communities
Prevention Resource Guide: Secondary School Students

* Alcohol and Drug Awareness

National Clearinghouse for Alcohol and Drug Information
P.O. Box 2345
Rockville, MD 20847-2345 (301) 468-2600

RADAR (The regional alcohol and drug awareness resource) network provides information centers across the country and in Canada. These centers provide the public with a variety of local services. State and Canadian locations are available through this office.

* Alcoholism and Pregnancy

National Clearinghouse
P.O. Box 2345
Rockville, MD 20847-2345 (301) 468-2600

These are two publications available on what happens when you drink when you are pregnant: *How to Take Care of Your Baby Before Birth* (PH239), *Alcohol Alert #13: Fetal Alcohol Syndrome* (PH297), and *Alcohol, Tobacco, and Other Drugs May Harm the Unborn* (PH291) are excellent sources on fetal risk of abnormalities. Also discussed are complications in labor and custodial rights after birth.

* Careers in Psychological and Epidemiological Aspects of Chemical Dependence

Chemical Dependence
National Institute on Drug Abuse (NIDA)
5600 Fishers Lane
Rockville, MD 20857 (301) 443-6480

It also supports research training of individuals and institutions who are training individuals in the biological and psychological sciences and epidemiological aspects of drug abuse to enable them to pursue careers in research. For free information call the National Clearinghouse, (301) 468-2600.

* Children of Alcoholics

National Clearinghouse for Alcohol Information
P.O. Box 2345 (800) 729-6686
Rockville, MD 20852 (301) 468-2600

Prevention Resource Guide: Children of Alcoholics (MS417) and *Alcohol Alert #9: Children of Alcoholics: Are They Different?* (PH288) are two free publications. *The Typical Alcoholic American* (AV195) is a poster that is of particular interest to children of alcoholics.

* Cocaine: Pharmacology, Prevention, and Treatment

National Clearinghouse for Alcohol and
Drug Information
P.O. Box 2345 (800) 729-6686
Rockville, MD 20852 (301) 468-2600

These publications are available from the Clearinghouse:

Crack Cocaine: A Challenge for Prevention. OSAP Prevention, Monograph 9(1991)
The Epidemiology of Cocaine Use and Abuse. NIDA Research, Monograph 110(1991)
Cocaine Abuse (CAP05)
Cocaine Freebase (CAP05)
Use and Consequences of Cocaine (CAP07)

* Community Action Against Addiction

National Clearinghouse on Alcohol and Drug Information
P.O. Box 2345 (800) 729-6686
Rockville, MD 20892 (301) 468-2600

The Clearinghouse has many free publications dealing with drug abuse and the community. Some of the titles include:

Citizen's Alcohol and Other Drug Prevention Directory. Resources for Getting Involved.
Connections.
The Door to Recovery: Community Drug Abuse Treatment.
The Fact Is...Communications Programs Can Help to Prevent Alcohol and Other Drug Problems.
Communities Creating Change: 1990 Exemplary Alcohol and Other Drug Prevention Programs.
Evaluating Faculty Development and Clinical Training Programs in Substance Abuse: A Guidebook.
Handbook for Evaluating Drug and Alcohol Prevention Programs.
How to Start and Run an Alcohol and Other Drug Information Center: A Guide.
Little League Drug Education Program (video).
Making Health Communication Programs Work: A Planner's Guide.
Message and Material Review Process.
Parent Training Is Prevention.
Prevention Plus II: Tools for Creating and Sustaining a Drug-Free Community.
Turning Awareness Into Action.
What You Can Do About Drug Use in America.
Prevention: From Knowledge to Action.
The Primary Prevention of Alcohol Problems: A Critical Review of the Research Literature.
The Fact Is...Resources Are Available for Disabled Persons With Alcohol and Other Drug Problems.
The Fact Is...Reaching Hispanic/Latino Audiences Requires Cultural Sensitivity.
Safer Streets Ahead.
Substance Abuse Prevention Within Inner-City Communities.
Surgeon General's Workshop on Drunk Driving Proceedings.
Surgeon General's Workshop on Drunk Driving: Background Papers.
The Fact Is...Training Is Available for Professionals in the Field of Alcohol and Other Drug Abuse.
Twenty Exemplary Prevention Programs: Helping Communities to Help Themselves.
The Fact Is...You Can Effectively Launch Media Campaigns.
The Fact Is...You Can Start a Student Assistance Program.
Youth at High Risk for Substance Abuse.
A Community Solution, Drug Abuse Treatment.
Overcoming Barriers to Drug Abuse Treatment in the Community.

* Community Prevention and Education Grants

ACTION
Drug Alliance Office
1100 Vermont Ave., NW, Suite 8200
Washington, DC 20525 (202) 606-5212

ACTION supports community-based prevention and education efforts with grants, contracts, conferences, and technical assistance. Nonprofit organizations and state and local governments are eligible to receive grants from ACTION. An announcement is made in the Federal Register regarding the type of activities that the ACTION grant is available for and organizations are encouraged to apply. ACTION also maintains a mailing list which sends copies of the notices appearing in the Federal Register directly to those on the list. To get the name of your organization on this list, call the number above.

* Community Volunteer Service Programs

ACTION
Drug Alliance Office
1100 Vermont Ave., NW, Suite 8200
Washington, DC 20525 (202) 606-5212

Be patient. If any phone number is incorrect, call (area code) 555-1212 and request the new listing.

General Sources

ACTION is the principal agency in the Federal Government for administering volunteer service programs. Many of the various components of ACTION, such as Foster Grandparents and VISTA, are involved in community drug abuse education, prevention or treatment programs. The Drug Alliance Office coordinates the agency's drug abuse activities, awards grants that strengthen and expand local volunteer activities combatting illegal drug use among youth and the misuse of prescription and over-the-counter drugs by the elderly, provides training and technical assistance, and conducts public awareness and education efforts.

interagency agreement (with the U.S. Department of Education) enables State vocational rehabilitation agencies to receive training through the development, implementation, and evaluation of a comprehensive drug rehabilitation training and information program. The ultimate goal of this program is to secure employment for eligible youth ages 14-18 who have been drug dependent.

* Driving-While-Intoxicated Statistics

Transportation Department
National Highway Traffic Safety Administration
400 7th Street SW
Washington, DC 20590 (202) 366-0123

The National Center tabulates data on highway traffic accidents and maintains statistics on accidents and fatalities due to alcohol or drug use. They have extensive data on drunk driving, seat belts and alcohol, as well as much more. One free information pamphlet is *Drunk Driving Facts*.

* Drug Abuse and AIDS

National Clearinghouse for Alcohol and Drug Information
P.O. Box 2345
Rockville, MD 20852 (800) 729-6686

Publications available on Drug Abuse and Aids include:
Drug Abuse and AIDS (CAP04)
How Getting High Can Get You AIDS (PHD573)
Training Drug Treatment Staff in the Age of AIDS (PHD571).

Posters available include:
AIDS. Another Way Drugs Can Kill (AV187). This poster explains the drugs/sex/AIDS connection. It includes a quiz on drugs and AIDS.
Fatal Accident (AV60). This poster shows how drugs can cause two kinds of car "accidents", crashes and HIV/AIDS transmissions.

* Drug Abuse and AIDS Helpline

National Institute of Drug Abuse (NIDA) (800) 662-HELP

NIDA Helpline provides general phone information on drug abuse and on AIDS as it relates to intravenous drug users. This hotline offers referrals to drug rehab centers. Hours: 9 a.m. - 3 a.m. Monday through Friday; 12 p.m. - 3 a.m. on weekends.

* Drug Abuse and Pregnancy

National Clearinghouse for Alcohol and Drug Information
P.O. Box 2345
Rockville, MD 20852 (800) 729-6686

Publications about pregnant women and drug abuse include:

Guess Who Else Can Get AIDS If You Shoot Drugs? Your Baby (AVD23)
How to Take Care of Your Baby Before Birth (PH239)
Drug Abuse and Pregnancy (CAP33)
Alcohol, Tobacco, and Other Drugs May Harm the Unborn (PH291).

* Drug Abuse Research

National Institute on Drug Abuse (NIDA)
5600 Fishers Lane
Rockville, MD 20857 (301) 443-6480

NIDA conducts and supports research on the biological, psychological, psychosocial, and epidemiological aspects of drug abuse. It also collaborates with and provides technical assistance to State drug abuse authorities, and encourages State and community efforts in planning, establishing, maintaining, coordinating, and evaluating more effective drug abuse programs.

* Drug Dependent Youth and Jobs

Office of Juvenile Justice and Delinquency Prevention
U.S. Department of Justice
633 Indiana Ave., NW
Washington, DC 20531 (202) 307-5940

Drug-dependent youth who receive vocational rehabilitation services present unique challenges to State vocational rehabilitation service delivery systems. An

* Drug Rehabilitation Services

Office of Public Affairs
Administration for Children and Families (ACE)
902 9th and D Sts.
Washington, DC 20047 (202) 673-3331

This office provides leadership and direction to human services programs for the elderly, children and youth, families, Native Americans, persons living in rural areas, and handicapped persons. HDS administers rehabilitation services for these groups.

* Drugs and the Workplace

National Clearinghouse for Alcohol and Drug Information
P.O. Box 2345
Rockville, MD 20852 (800) 729-6686

These publications are available through the Clearinghouse Catalog:

An Employer's Guide to Dealing with Substance Abuse (PHD5430)
How Drug Abuse Takes Profit out of Business, How Drug Treatment Helps Put It Back (PHD574).

* Drug-Related Highway Accidents Research

National Highway Traffic Safety Administration (NHTSA)
400 Seventh St., SW
Washington, DC 20590 (202) 366-9550

NHTSA is the Federal focal point for the national effort to eliminate driving while intoxicated,, including research on drug-related highway problems. Call (202) 366-9588 for free information.

* Drug Reports

General Accounting Office (GAO)
P.O. Box 6015
Gaithersburg, MD 20877 (202) 275-6241

The GAO conducts reports on various topics including various issues regarding drugs. *Nonprescription Drugs: Over the Counter and Underemphasized* examines the FDA's procedures for approving and monitoring over-the-counter drugs in order to identify potential vulnerabilities in the procedures that could result in the approval and marketing of unsafe and ineffective drugs. *Adolescent Drug Use Prevention: Common Features of Promising Community Programs* examines the design, implementation, and results of promising comprehensive, community-based drug use prevention programs for young adolescents, regardless of their funding sources. These reports are free.

* Drug Testing to Identify High-Risk Youths

Office of Juvenile Justice and Delinquency Prevention (OJJDP)
Office of Justice Programs
U.S. Department of Justice
633 Indiana Ave., NW
Washington, DC 20531 (202) 307-0751

The OJJDP funds programs such as Urine Testing of Juvenile Detainees to Identify High-Risk Youths, and Drug Testing Guidelines for Juvenile Justice agencies. Program goals include developing a comprehensive drug identification, screening, and testing program to be included in training curriculums for juvenile justice policymakers, administrators, and direct service professionals. Call 1-800-638-8736 for free information.

* Effective Anti-Drug Strategies

Office of Juvenile Justice and Delinquency Prevention (OJJDP)
U.S. Department of Justice
633 Indiana Ave., NW
Washington, DC 20531 (202) 307-5914

To effectively combat youth drug and alcohol abuse and coordinated juvenile substance abuse prevention and treatment programs, further knowledge must be gained on strategies and approaches that communities are using nationwide. OJJDP funded the Introduction of Effective Systemwide Strategies To Combat

Be patient. If any phone number is incorrect, call (area code) 555-1212 and request the new listing.

Drugs and Chemical Dependence

Youth Drug and Alcohol Abuse project to help communities assess their resources and capabilities, and use a coordinated systemwide approach to address drug- and alcohol-related problems. A three-volume assessment report was produced containing a review of literature, information describing 10 promising approaches, and a model for community action against drug and alcohol abuse.

* Effective Parenting Skills with High-Risk Youth

Office of Juvenile Justice and Delinquency Prevention (OJJDP)
Office of Justice Programs
U.S. Department of Justice
633 Indiana Ave., NW (800) 638-8736
Washington, DC 20531 (202) 307-0751

The purpose of Identification and Transfer of Effective Juvenile Justice Projects and Services: Effective Parenting Strategies for Families of High Risk Youth is to reduce delinquency and drug abuse in youth by providing community agencies with information and skills to implement special programs for families of high-risk youth. This project currently is assessing existing family-oriented programs that have demonstrated success in decreasing delinquency, drug use, or associated risk factors.

* Employee Assistance for Drug and Alcohol Abuse

National Clearinghouse for Alcohol and Drug Information
P.O. Box 2345
Rockville, MD 20852 (800) 729-6686

The Fact Is...Employee Assistance Contacts Are Available In Every State is a free publication, which explains that an Employee Assistance Program is a professional assessment/referral and/or short term counseling service for motivating and helping employees with alcohol, drug, or mental health problems to seek and accept appropriate help. EAPs are particularly concerned with problems that adversely affect job performance. These programs can serve as part of a comprehensive approach to combat alcohol and other drug abuse in the workplace. The following is a list of State EAP contacts who are available for providing technical assistance to private sector CEOs, managers, supervisors, and union representatives who are establishing or managing employee assistance programs.

Alabama
Phillip Johnson
Alabama Department of Mental Health
P.O. Box 3710
Montgomery, AL 36193 (205) 271-9285

Alaska
Matthew Feliz/George Mundel
Office of Alcoholism and Drug Abuse
Department of Health and Social Services
BY H-05-F (907) 586-6201 (Juneau)
Juneau, AK 99811 (907) 561-4213 (Anchorage)

Arizona
Russ Binicki
Maricopa County EAP
Luhrs Building
11 W. Jefferson, Suite 14
Phoenix, AZ 85003 (602) 261-7030

Arkansas
Ray Stephens
Assistant Deputy Director
Office on Alcohol and Drug Abuse Prevention
400 Donaghey Plaza North
P.O. Box 1437
7th and Main St.
Little Rock, AR 72203 (501) 682-6652

California
Cliff Coleman
Department of Alcohol and Drug Programs
111 Capitol Mall
Sacramento, CA 95814 (916) 323-1860

Colorado
Ed Kraft

OPC Position
Alcohol and Drug Abuse Division
Department of Health
4210 East 11th Ave.
Denver, CO 80220 (303) 331-8201

Connecticut
Margaret Perla
Deputy Director
Connecticut Alcohol and Drug Abuse Commission
999 Asylum Ave.
Hartford, CT 06105 (203) 566-3075

Delaware
Paul Poplawski
Division of Alcoholism, Drug Abuse, and Mental Health
1901 North Dupont Highway
New Castle, DE 19720 (302) 421-6109

District Of Columbia
Charles W. Avery
Office of Health Planning and Development
Commission of Public Health
425 Eye St., NW, Room 3210
Washington, DC 20001 (202) 724-5637

Florida
Linda Lewis
HRS-Department of Personnel Management
1317 Winewood Blvd.
Building 3, Room 216
Tallahassee, FL 32399 (904) 488-0900

Georgia
Ed Pierce
Substance Abuse Service
878 Peachtree St., NE
Suite 319
Atlanta, GA 30309 (404) 728-4033

Hawaii
John McCarthy
Department of Health
c/o Alcohol and Drug Abuse Branch
P.O. Box 3378
Honolulu, HI 96801 (808) 548-4280

Idaho
Tina Klampt
Substance Abuse Program
Department of Health and Welfare
450 West State St.
Boise, ID 83720 (208) 334-5935

Illinois
Marie Apke
State of Illinois Center
100 West Randolph, Suite 3-300
Chicago, IL 60601 (312) 917-6983

Indiana
Johnie Underwood, Director
Division of Addiction Services
Department of Mental Health
117 E. Washington St.
Indianapolis, IN 46204 (317) 232-7816

Iowa
Janet Zwick, Director
Iowa Division of Substance Abuse and Health Promotions
Lucas State Office Building
321 E. Twelfth St.
Des Moines, IA 50319 (515) 281-8021

Kansas
Suzanne Milburn
Health and Environment

Be patient. If any phone number is incorrect, call (area code) 555-1212 and request the new listing.

General Sources

Landon State Office Building
10th Floor
900 Southwest Jackson St.
Topeka, KS 66620 (913) 296-1224

Kentucky
Michael Townsend
Substance Abuse Division
275 East Main St.
Frankfort, KY 40621 (502) 564-2880

Louisiana
Sanford Hawkins
Office of Prevention and Recovery
2744B Wooddale Blvd.
Baton Rouge, LA 70805 (504) 922-0728

Maine
Kevin Parker, Director
State Employee Assistance Program
P.O. Box 112
Hallowell, ME 04347 (207) 289-5752

Maryland
Sharon Dow
Alcohol and Drug Abuse Administration
201 West Preston St., 4th Floor
Baltimore, MD 21201 (301) 225-6548

Massachusetts
David Mulligan
Division of Alcoholism and Drugs
150 Tremont St., 6th Floor
Boston, MA 02111 (617) 727-8614

Michigan
Barry Mintzes
Programs Administrator, OSAS-MDPH
3423 North Logan
P.O. Box 30195
Lansing, MI 48909 (517) 335-8810

Minnesota
Keith Tweenen
Summit Bank Building, Suite 200
205 Aurora Ave.
St. Paul, MN 55103 (612) 296-0765

Mississippi
Anne Robertson, Director
Division of Alcohol and Drug Abuse
Department of Mental Health
1500 Woolfolk Building
Jackson, MS 39201 (601) 359-1297

Missouri
Lois Olson, Director
Division of Alcohol and Drug Abuse
Department of Mental Health
1915 South Ridge Dr.
P.O. Box 687
Jefferson City, MO 65102 (314) 751-4942

Montana
Daryl Bruno
Alcohol and Drug Abuse Division
Department of Institutions
1539 11th Ave.
Helena, MT 59620 (406) 444-2827

Nebraska
Malcolm Herd
Division of Alcoholism and Drug Abuse
Department of Public Institutions
P.O. Box 94728
Lincoln, NE 68509 (402) 471-2851, ext. 5583

Nevada
Sharyn Peal
Bureau of Alcohol and Drug Abuse
505 East King St., Room 500
Carson City, NV 89710 (702) 885-4790

New Hampshire
Carol Gregory
Employee Assistance Program
Health and Human Services Building
6 Hazen Dr.
Concord, NH 03301 (6303) 271-4628

New Jersey
Larry Ganges/ Mark Brown
Department of Health
129 East Hanover St., CN 362
Trenton, NJ 08625 (609) 292-0729

New Mexico
Carol Ross, Director
New Mexico State EAP
825 Topeka St.
Santa Fe, NM 87501 (505) 827-9920

New York
Dan Forget
Bureau of Occupational Industrial Services
New York Division of Alcoholism and Alcohol Abuse
194 Washington Ave.
Albany, NY 12210 (518) 474-6422

Jim Sipe
Program Manager
State EAP
Governor's Office of Employee Relations
1 Commerce Plaza
Suite 706
Albany, NY 12260 (518) 473-3414

North Carolina
Roy Sonovick
Alcohol and Drug Abuse
Department of Human Services
State Capitol Building
Bismarck, ND 58505 (701) 224-2769

Ohio
Phil Flench
Industrial Commission of Ohio
4th Floor
246 North High St.
Columbus, OH 43215 (614) 644-8968

Oklahoma
Steve West
Alcohol and Drug Abuse Division
Department of Mental Health
p.O. Box 53277, Capitol Station
Oklahoma City, OK 73152 (405) 271-7474

Oregon
Jeffrey N. Kushner
Office of Alcohol and Drug Abuse Programs
1178 Chemeketa St., NE
Salem, OR 97310 (503) 378-2163

Pennsylvania
Jeff Johnston, Director
Bureau of Program Services
H&W Building, Room 929
P.O. Box 90
Harrisburg, PA 17109 (717) 783-8200

Puerto Rico
Isabel Sullveres de Martinez
Employee Assistance Program Department of Service Against Addiction

Be patient. If any phone number is incorrect, call (area code) 555-1212 and request the new listing.

Drugs and Chemical Dependence

Box 21414
Rio Piedras Station
Rio Piedras, PR 00928 (809) 758-7330

Rhode Island
Robert MacDonald
Rhode Island Employee Assistance Program
33 College Hill Rd.
Warwick, RI 02886 (401) 828-9560

South Carolina
Robert R. Charles
South Carolina Commission on Alcohol and Drug Abuse
3700 Forest Dr.
Suite 300
Columbia, SC 29204 (803) 734-9547

South Dakota
Barry Pillen, EAP Coordinator
Division of Alcohol and Drug Abuse
Joe Foss Building
523 East Capital
Pierre, SD 57501 (605) 773-3123

Tennessee
Carole M. Boone, Ed.D.
Doctors Building, 4th Floor
706 Church St.
Nashville, TN 37219 (615) 741-1925

Texas
Robby Duffield
Commission on Alcohol and Drug Abuse
1705 Guadalupe St.
Austin, TX 78701 (512) 463-5510

Utah
Jeano Campanaro
Department of Social Services
Human Resources/Organizational Development
120 North, 200 West, Human Resources
3rd. Floor
Salt Lake City, UT 84103 (801) 538-4216

Vermont
Buell Mitchell and John Taylor
EAP Coordinators
Office of Alcohol and Drug Abuse Programs
103 South Main St.
Waterbury, VT 05676 (802) 241-2170

Virginia
Wayne Thacker
Division of Mental Health/Mental Retardation/Substance Abuse Services
109 Governor St.
Richmond, VA 23219 (804) 786-3906

Washington
Dwight Bond
907 North West Ballard Way
Seattle, WA 98107 (206) 545-7782

West Virginia
Jack Clohan/Gary Koontz
Department of Health and Human Services
Division of Alcohol and Drug Abuse
State Office Complex, Building 3
1800 Washington St., E
Room 402
Charleston, WV 25305 (304) 348-2276

Wisconsin
Steve Ojibway
Department of Health and Social Services
P.O. Box 7851
1 West Wilson St., Room 434
Madison, WI 53707 (608) 267-9281

Wyoming
Jean DeFratis, Director
Alcohol and Drug Abuse Programs
Hathaway Building
Cheyenne, WY 82002 (307) 777-7115, ext. 7118

* Gangs and Drugs

Office of Juvenile Justice and Delinquency Prevention
U.S. Department of Justice
633 Indiana Ave., NW
Washington, DC 20531 (202) 307-5940

A crucial issue in addressing gang and drug problems is the need for close cooperation and sharing of information among all key juvenile justice policymakers within a jurisdiction. The Gang and Drug POLICY Training Program provides assistance to personnel from all arenas of the local juvenile justice system in confronting drug activity by gangs. The objectives of this training program are to present to key policymakers a cooperative interagency process that leads to improved public and private gang and drug prevention, intervention, and suppression strategies.

* Homelessness and Alcohol and Drug Abuse

Homeless Demonstration and Evaluation Branch
National Institute on Alcohol Abuse and Alcoholism
5600 Fishers Lane
Room 13C-02
Rockville, MD 20857 (301) 443-9334

This Branch supports a variety of contracts and cooperative agreements, including a research demonstration program authorized by the Stewart B. McKinney Homeless Assistance Act. The research demonstration program contributes to scientific knowledge regarding effective interventions for homeless individuals with alcohol and other drug problems. The HDEB also supports technical assistance papers on the housing and service needs of this population. Information about the research demonstration program and other documents about homelessness, alcohol and other drug problems are available through the National Clearinghouse for Alcohol and Drug Information (800-729-6686).

* House of Representatives Narcotics Committee

U.S. Congress
House Select Committee on Narcotics Abuse and Control
Ford House Office Building
Washington, DC 20515 (202) 226-3040

This special committee investigates drug abuse, conducts hearings in Washington and throughout the country, and publishes numerous studies which are available to the public. The caller must request specific information for specific hearings.

* Illegal Drug Use in Youth

Office of Juvenile Justice and Delinquency Prevention
P. O. Box 6000
Rockville, MD 20850 (800) 638-8736

The Coordinating Council is a group of 16 Federal agencies who held a workshop to develop interagency initiatives to combat the juvenile drug problem. *The 1990 Action Plan to Prevent Illegal Drug Use Among High-Risk Youth* provides details of the 19 interagency projects. They also produced *Juvenile Alcohol and Other Drug Abuse: A Guide to Federal Initiatives for Prevention, Treatment, and Control* which will serve as a resource for State, local, and private agencies and individuals working to combat juvenile drug and alcohol abuse.

* Indian Housing Programs

Headstart Public and Indian Housing Program
U.S. Department of Housing and Urban Development
451 7th Street, SW
Room 4112
Washington, DC 20410 (202) 708-4214

This non-profit organization provides information for establishing child day care centers.

* Innovative Approaches in Criminal Justice

National Institute of Justice
U.S. Department of Justice
P.O. Box 6000 (800) 851-3420

Be patient. If any phone number is incorrect, call (area code) 555-1212 and request the new listing.

General Sources

Rockville, MD 20850 (301) 251-5500

National Institute of Justice (NIJ) publishes:

A Criminal Justice System Strategy for Treating Cocaine-Heroin Abusing Offenders in Custody

Issues and Practices in Criminal Justice

Arresting the Demand for Drugs; Characteristics of Different Types of Drug Involved Offenders.

Searching for Answers: Second Annual Evaluation Report on Drugs and Crime, Report to the President, the Attorney General, and the Congress

A Comparison of Urinalysis Technologies for Drug Testing in Criminal Justice

Drug Use Forecasting

Mandatory and Random Drug Testing in the Honolulu Police Department

Prison Programs for Drug-Involved Offenders

Urine Testing of Detained Juveniles To Identify High-Risk Youth

In-Prison Programs for Drug-Involved Offenders

Multijurisdictional Drug Law Enforcement Strategies: Reducing Supply and Demand

* International Criminal Justice Clearinghouse

National Institute of Justice
U.S. Department of Justice
633 Indiana Ave., NW
Washington, DC 20531 (202) 307-0751

The Institute operates an international information center, the National Criminal Justice Reference Service. Subscribers receive the bimonthly *NIJ Reports*, which includes feature articles on major research developments and abstracts of the latest additions to the NCJRS database, which now numbers more than 100,000 documents.

* Juvenile Justice Clearinghouse

Office of Juvenile Justice and Delinquency Prevention (OJJDP)
P.O. Box 6000
Rockville, MD 20850 (800) 638-8736

Publications, research findings, and program evaluations are available as well as specific services including database searches, referrals, conference support, and other juvenile justice products. Free publications dealing with juveniles and alcohol and drug use include:

OJJDP Update on Statistics: *Juvenile Court Drug and Alcohol Cases: 1985-1988.*

OJJDP Update on Programs: *Drug Recognition Techniques for Juvenile Justice Professionals.*

OJJDP Update on Statistics: *Growth In Minority Detentions Attributed to Drug Law Violators.*

1990 Action Plan to Prevent Illegal Drug Use Among High-Risk Youth.

Juvenile Alcohol and Other Drug Abuse: A Guide to Federal Initiatives for Prevention, Treatment, and Control.

* Local Drug Treatment Centers Incentives

Susan Lachter David or Audrey Yorrell
National Institute on Drug Abuse
5600 Fishers Lane
Room 10a-39
Rockville, MD 20857 (301) 443-1124

Overcoming Barriers to Drug Abuse Treatment in the Community is a flexible education model for use by communities which have funding and want to establish drug treatment facilities. This model is used in communities to educate people about drug treatment with the goal of countering resistance to the establishment of new treatment facilities. Materials are available to help local providers site facilities (How-to Resource Manual and Media package), as well as materials to assist communities groups in educating the public (Resource manual and media materials). These materials are free. This Office can also provide technical assistance.

* "McGruff" Crime Prevention Campaign

Bureau of Justice Assistance
U.S. Department of Justice
633 Indiana Ave., NW
Washington, DC 20531 (202) 307-0751

National Crime Prevention (McGruff) Campaign, supported by BJA, develops and disseminates crime prevention materials, provides technical assistance and training, and operates a clearinghouse for information on crime prevention programs, publications, and workshops.

* Mental Health and Chemical Dependence

National Institute of Mental Health (NIMH)
5600 Fishers Lane
Rockville, MD 20857 (301) 443-3877/4513

NIMH supports research on the relationships between mental health and drug or alcohol abuse.

* Minorities and Prevention Grants

Attie Key
Minority Substance Abuse Prevention
U.S. Department of Health and Human Services
Security Lane, Rockwall II
Rockville, MD 20857 (301) 443-0365

This government agencies awards grants for minority substance abuse prevention programs.

* Mutual-Help Groups

National Clearinghouse for Alcohol and Drug Information
P.O. Box 2345
Rockville, MD 20852 (800) 729-6686

The Fact Is...There Are Specialized Mutual-Help Groups For Those With Alcohol and Drug Problems (MS330) is a free publication which discusses self-help groups that have emerged in response to special concerns expressed by those seeking recovery for alcohol and other drug problem. The publication lists the self-help groups, providing general information about the group and a central phone number.

* Narcotic Drugs and Psychotropic Substances

International Regulations
Food and Drug Administration (FDA)
5600 Fishers Lane
Rockville, MD 20857 (301) 443-4480

FDA works with the DEA as a drug regulatory agency. Together, they are responsible for working with the international community (the U.N. and WHO) to ensure appropriate scheduling of narcotic drugs and psychotropic substances.

* National Criminal Survey and Other Statistics

Bureau of Justice Statistics
U.S. Department of Justice
633 Indiana Ave., NW
Washington, DC 20531 (202) 307-0751

The Bureau of Justice Statistics (BJS) maintains statistics about crime, its perpetrators and victims, and the operation of the criminal justice system at the Federal, State and local level. The National Institute of Justice sponsors research on crime and its control and is a central federal resource for information on innovative approaches in criminal justice. BJS publishes *Report to the Nation on Crime and Justice: Second Edition, Profile of State Prison Inmates, 1986, Drug Law Violators, 1980-86: Federal Offenses and Offenders, Drug Use and Crime: State Prison Inmate Survey, 1986, and Survey of Youth in Custody, 1987.*

* National Drug Enforcement Data Clearinghouse

Drugs and Crime Data Center and Clearinghouse
Bureau of Justice Statistics
U.S. Department of Justice
633 Indiana Ave., NW
Washington, DC 20531 (202) 307-0751

This clearinghouse gathers existing data on drugs and the justice system, identifies drug enforcement data gaps, and prepares special reports and tabulations of existing drug data. The clearinghouse will respond to your requests for drugs and crime data, let you know about new drugs and crime data reports, send you reports on drugs and crime, conduct special bibliographic searches for you, refer you to data on epidemiology, prevention and treatment of substance abuse, publish special reports, and prepare a comprehensive, concise report. Some of the reports available include:

BJS Sourcebook of Criminal Justice Statistics

Drugs and Crime Facts, 1990

Felony Case Processing in State Courts, 1986

Profile of Felons Convicted in State Courts, 1986

Felony Defendants in Large Urban Counties, 1988

Federal Criminal Case Process, 1980-87

Be patient. If any phone number is incorrect, call (area code) 555-1212 and request the new listing.

Drugs and Chemical Dependence

Violent State Prisoners and Their Victims
State Drug Resources: A National Directory
Federal Drug Data for National Policy
Drugs and Crime Facts, 1989
Catalog of Selected Federal Publications On Illegal Drug and Alcohol Abuse

* President's Drug Czar

Office of National Drug Control Policy
Executive Office of the President
Washington, DC 20500 (202) 467-9800

The President's White House staff, specifically the Drug Policy Office, focuses on proposed legislation and other efforts in the "War on Drugs." The written information includes: *Understanding Drug Treatment, National Drug Control Safety,* and monthly bulletins. A free annual report is available, titled *National Drug Control Strategy: A Nation Responds to Drug Use.* It sets forth a unified attack against illegal drugs. It examines, goals, objectives, current use, treatment, organizations, suppliers, recommendations, and much more. Call for your free copy.

* Prevention, Intervention and Treatment for Juveniles

Office of Juvenile Justice and Delinquency Prevention (OJJDP)
Office of Justice Programs
U.S. Department of Justice
633 Indiana Ave., NW
Washington, DC 20531 (202) 307-0751

Joint projects between The Research and Program Development Division and the Special Emphasis Division of OJJDP include:

Promising Approaches for the Prevention, Intervention, and Treatment of Illegal Drug and Alcohol Use Among Juveniles is designed to help communities with high rates of adolescent drug and alcohol abuse. The project will identify and review promising juvenile drug programs, develop and test program prototypes and provide training.

* Public Health Services and Resources

Health Resources and Services Administration (HRSA)
5600 Fishers Lane
Rockville, MD 20857 (301) 443-2086

HRSA has leadership responsibility in the Public Health Service for general health services and resource issues relating to access, equity, quality and cost of care. This treatment includes AIDS patients as well as drug or alcohol dependent persons.

* Public Housing Drug Strategy Clearinghouse

Drug Information and Strategy Clearinghouse
U.S. Department of Housing and Urban Development (HUD)
P.O. Box 6424
Rockville, MD 20850 (800) 955-2232

Sponsored by HUD, the clearinghouse provides housing officials, residents, and community leaders with information and assistance on drug abuse prevention and drug trafficking control techniques. They have created a database containing information on improving resident screening procedures, strengthening eviction policies, increasing cooperation with local law enforcement, implementing drug tip hotlines, forming resident patrols, starting child care centers, and organizing drug education/prevention activities. The clearinghouse also provides information packages, resource lists, HUD regulations, referrals, and a newsletter, Home Front. A community guide called *The Winnable War: A Community Guide to Eradicating Street Drug Markets,* is also available. The clearinghouse assists PHAs and IHAs applying for PHDEP grant funds. Publications include:

Funding Resource List
Information Resources List
State Contact List
Model Programs Information Package
Grantsmanship Information Package
Needs Assessment Information Package
Risk Factor Approach to Drug Abuse Prevention Programs
Drugs in Housing: What Managers Can Do
Drug Information and Strategy Clearinghouse Brochure
Home Front

* Public Housing Modernization Anti-Drug Project

Bill Flood and Janice Rattley
U.S. Department of Housing and Urban Development
Room 4122
7th and D Sts.
Washington, DC 20047 (202) 708-1422

The Comprehensive Improvement Assistance Program provides incentives for comprehensive modernization improvements, some of which may serve to prevent drug activity.

* Public Housing Resident Management Grants

U.S. Department of Housing and Urban Development (HUD)
820 1st St. NE
Washington, DC 20002 (202) 275-7965

This HUD program funds the establishment of resident management groups in public housing.

* Senate Committee

U.S. Senate
Subcommittee on Children
Committee on Labor and Human Resources
Washington, DC 20510 (202) 224-5630

This is one of several subcommittees in the U.S. Senate which focus on some aspect of chemical dependence.

* State Drug Abuse Authorities

The following is a list of the drug abuse agencies in each state responsible for drug abuse prevention and treatment services:

Department of Health and Social Services
Office of Alcoholism and Drug Abuse
P.O. Box 110607
Juneau, AK 99811-0607 (907) 586-6201

Department of Mental Health Community Programs
Div. of Mental Illness and Substance Abuse
200 Interstate Park Dr.
P.O. Box 3710
Montgomery, AL 36109 (205) 271-9209

Arkansas Office of Alcohol and Drug Abuse Prevention
P.O. Box 329
Little Rock, AR 72203
Director (501) 371-2603
Program Implementation Development (501) 371-2604

Arizona Department of Health Services
Office of Community Behavioral Health
1740 W. Adam
Phoenix, AZ 85007 (602) 220-6506

Department of Alcohol and Drug Abuse
1700 K St.
Sacramento, CA 95814 (916) 445-0834

Colorado Department of Health
Alcohol and Drug Abuse Division
4210 E. 11th Ave.
Denver, CO 80220 (303) 331-8201

Connecticut Alcohol and Drug Abuse Commission
999 Asylum Ave.
Hartford, CT 06105 (203) 566-4145

Department of Human Services
Office of Health Planning and Development
1660 L St. NW, Suite 1117
Washington, DC 20036 (202) 673-7481

Bureau of Alcoholism and Drug Abuse
1901 N. Dupont Hwy.
New Castle, DE 19720 (302) 577-4460

Be patient. If any phone number is incorrect, call (area code) 555-1212 and request the new listing.

General Sources

Department of Health and Rehabilitative Services
Alcohol and Drug Abuse Program
1317 Winewood Blvd.
Tallahassee, FL 32301 (904) 488-8304

Georgia Department of Human Resources
Div. of Mental Health and Mental Retardation
Alcohol and Drug Section
878 Peachtree St., NE, Suite 319
Atlanta, GA 30309 (404) 894-4200

Government of Guam
Dept. of Mental Health and Substance Abuse
P.O. Box 9400
Tamuning, GU 96931 (671) 646-9260

Department of Health
Mental Health Div.
Alcohol and Drug Abuse Branch
1270 Emma St.
Queen Emma Building, Room 706
Honolulu, HI 96813 (808) 586-4007

Iowa Department of Public Health
Div. of Substance Abuse and Health Promotion
321 E. 12th St.
Lucas State Office Bldg., Fourth Floor
Des Moines, IA 50319 (515) 281-4417

Department of Health and Welfare
Bureau of Substance Abuse and Social Services
450 W. State, 3rd Floor
Boise, ID 83720-5450 (208) 334-5935

Illinois Department of Alcoholism and Substance Abuse
100 W. Randolph St., Suite 5-600
Chicago, IL 60601 (312) 814-3840

State of Indiana Department of Mental Health
Division of Addiction Services
402 W. Washington St., Room 353
Indianapolis, IN 46204 (317) 232-7837

Alcohol and Drug Abuse Services
300 S.W. Oakley
Biddle Bldg., 6th Floor
Topeka, KS 66606 (913) 296-3925

Department for Mental Health/Mental Retardation Services
Div. of Substance Abuse
275 E. Main St.
Health Services Bldg, 1st Floor
Frankfort, KY 40621 (502) 564-2880

Office of Prevention and Recovery from Alcohol and Drug Abuse
1201 Capitol Access Rd.
P.O. Box 3868
Baton Rouge, LA 70821 (504) 342-9352

Massachusetts Divisions of Substance Abuse Services
150 Tremont St.
Boston, MA 02111 (617) 727-1960

Alcohol and Drug Abuse Administration
201 W. Preston St.
Herbert O'Conor Bldg.
Baltimore, MD 21201 (410) 225-6910

Office of Alcohol and Drug Abuse Prevention
Bureau of Rehabilitation
State House
Station 11
Augusta, ME 04333 (207) 287-2781

Michigan Department of Public Health
Office of Substance Abuse Services
3423 N. Logan St.

P.O. Box 30195
Lansing, MI 48909 (517) 335-8810

Department of Human Services
Chemical Dependency Program Division
444 Lafayette Road
Space Center Bldg., 2nd Floor
St. Paul, MN 55155-3823 (612) 296-4610

Mental Health Department
Alcohol and Drug Abuse Services
239 N. Lamar Street
Jackson, MS 39201 (601) 359-1288

Missouri Department of Mental Health
Div. of Alcohol and Drug Abuse
1706 E. Elm St.
P.O. Box 687
Jefferson City, MO 65102 (314) 751-4942

State of Montana Department of Institutions
Alcohol and Drug Abuse Div.
1539 11th Ave.
Helena, MT 59620 (406) 444-4927

Division of Mental Health/Mental Retardation Services
Alcohol and Drug Abuse Section
325 N. Salisbury St.
Albemarle Bldg., Room 1168
Raleigh, NC 27603 (919) 733-4670

North Dakota Department of Human Services
Division of Alcoholism and Drug Abuse
State Capitol/Judicial Wing
1839 E. Capitol Ave.
Bismarck, ND 58501 (701) 224-2769

Nebraska Department of Public Institutions
Div. of Alcoholism and Drug Abuse
P.O. Box 94728
Lincoln, NE 68509-4728 (402) 471-2851 or 5583

New Hampshire Office of Alcohol and Drug Abuse Prevention
State Office Park
105 Pleasant St.
Concord, NH 03301 (603) 271-6100

Alcoholism, Drug Abuse and Addiction Services Division
129 E. Hanover St.
CN 362
Trenton, NJ 08625 (609) 292-0362

Behavioral Health Services Division
Substance Abuse Bureau
1190 St. Francis Dr.
P.O. Box 968
Santa Fe, NM 87502 (505) 827-2601

Department of Human Resources
Bureau of Alcohol and Drug Abuse
505 E. King St.
Carson City, NV 89710 (702) 687-4790

Office of Alcoholism and Substance Abuse Services (OASAS)
Executive Park South, Box 8200
Albany, NY 12203 (518) 457-7629

Alcohol and Drug Abuse
181 Washington Blvd.
Columbus, OH 43215 (614) 645-7306

Oklahoma Department of Mental Health
Alcohol and Drug Programs
1200 NE 13th St.
P.O. Box 53277
Oklahoma City, OK 73152-3277 (405) 271-8653

Be patient. If any phone number is incorrect, call (area code) 555-1212 and request the new listing.

Drugs and Chemical Dependence

Office of Alcohol and Drug Abuse Programs
1178 Chemeketa NE
Salem, OR 97310 (503) 378-2163

Pennsylvania Department of Health
Drug and Alcohol Programs
Commonwealth and Forster Sts.
P.O. Box 90
Harrisburg, PA 17108 (717) 787-9857

Puerto Rico Department of Addiction Control Services
P.O. Box 21414
Rio Piedras, PR 00928 (809) 764-3795

Department of Mental Health/
Mental Retardation and Hospitals
Division of Substance Abuse
Substance Abuse Administration Bldg.
P.O. Box 20363
Cranston, RI 02920 (401) 464-2091

South Carolina Commission on Alcohol and Drug Abuse
3700 Forest Dr.
Landmark East, Suite 300
Columbia, SC 29204 (803) 734-9520

South Dakota Division of Alcohol and Drug Abuse
Hill View Plaza
500 E. Capital
Pierre, SD 57501 (605) 773-3123

Tennessee Department of Mental Health/Mental Retardation
Alcohol and Drug Abuse Services
255 Court of Hull Building
Nashville, TN 37247 (615) 741-1921

Department of Health Services
P.O. Box 409CK
HICOM
Saipan, Mariana Islands, TT 96950 (670) 234-8950

Texas Commission on Alcohol and Drug Abuse
1720 Brazof St.
Austin, TX 78701 (512) 867-8700

Utah State Division of Alcoholism and Drugs
120 N. 200 West
4th Floor
Salt Lake City, UT 84103 (801) 538-3939

Virginia Department of Mental Health/Mental Retardation
Office of Substance Abuse Services
109 Governor St.
P.O. Box 1797
Richmond, VA 23214 (804) 786-3906

Virgin Islands Division of Mental Health
St. Thomas, VI 00801 (809) 775-3302

Office of Alcohol and Drug Abuse Programs
103 S. Main St.
State Office Bldg.
Waterbury, VT 05676 (802) 241-2170

Washington Department of Social and Health Services
Bureau of Alcoholism and Substance Abuse
7th Ave. SE, Building C, Room 4408
Olympia, WA 98504-5330 (206) 438-8200

Office of Alcohol and Other Drug Abuse
1 W. Wilson St.
P.O. Box 7851
Madison, WI 53707 (608) 266-3442

Department of Health
Div. of Alcoholism and Drug Abuse
State Capital Complex

Building 6, Room 738
Charleston, WV 25305 (304) 558-2276

Alcohol and Drug Abuse Programs
Hathaway Bldg.
Room 451, 4th Floor
Cheyenne, WY 82003-0480 (307) 777-7116

* Steroids Abuse

Drug Planning and Outreach Staff
Office of Elementary and Secondary Education
400 Maryland Ave. SW
Washington, DC 20202-6123 (202) 401-3030

This office provides materials to schools and communities in developing a comprehensive program to prevent the use of alcohol and other drugs. Revised recently to include statistics and information on alcohol, tobacco, and steroids.

Steroids Mean Trouble (AVD16). A poster which shows a football player with facts about steroids.

Anabolic Steroids: A Threat to Body and Mind (PHD561) Reports on steroid abuse in the United States, most users being under age 18

Anabolic Steroid Abuse. NIDA Research Monograph 102 (M102) is a 248 page publication which discusses the abuse of steroids, as well as the history and development of this drug.

* TeamSpirit

Pacific Institute for Research and Evaluation
7315 Wisconsin Ave., Number 900 East
Bethesda, MD 20814

TeamSpirit is designed to empower high school youth to take an active role in preventing drug and alcohol use and impaired driving by their peers. It is based on the belief that youth can become a potent force in combating substance abuse among their peers. The TeamSpirit model consists of two phases: a residential leadership training conference at which youth develop action plans for local program activities, and the delivery of extensive technical assistance and support services to nurture individual school and community team activities. This program is sponsored by the Office of Juvenile Justice and Delinquency Prevention of the U.S. Department of Justice (202) 307-5914.

* Toll-free Hotlines

Here are some of the primary hotlines:

* Child Help - National Child Abuse Hotline (800) 422-4453
A recorded phone system directs you to the pertinent area of information that you desire. Information can be received. A list of booklets, pamphlets, etc. are read through the system. The price and address is given for you to mail the information.

* Cocaine Helpline (800) 944-4860

* Humanistic Foundation (800) 999-4572
(800) 944-4860

This is a national 24 hour service which provides a recorded phone system to help you with various psychological problems. The menu includes depression, anxiety, AIDS, drug and chemical dependence. There is also health care information. Referrals to other agencies and services are given as they apply to your problem.

* Just Say No Foundation (800) 258-2766
A person will answer the phone if you call Monday through Friday between 7AM-5PM Pacific time. He or she will answer your questions and send you free information.

* CDC National AIDS Clearinghouse (800) 458-5231
This is a national service which operates Monday through Friday from 9AM-7PM. During these hours you can get information sent to you from the phone system or speak to a counselor. During off hours you can receive information only. It also speaks in Spanish.

* CDC National AIDS Hotline (800) 342-2437
This service is available 24 hours a day, 7 days a week. A person will answer the

Be patient. If any phone number is incorrect, call (area code) 555-1212 and request the new listing.

General Sources

phone and answer questions about AIDS, give counseling, refer you to a support group, or help you in whatever way is possible.

* MADD - Mothers Against Drunk Driving (800) 438-6233
This is the national headquarters in Texas. Most states have their own 800 number and offices. They are there Monday through Friday from 8:30-5:00 Central time. On off hours there is an answering service. Some great pamphlets you can receive free are *One Drink Can Be Too Many* and *Every Drop Counts* which both explain how just one alcoholic drink can affect your driving ability and increase your risk of being in a car crash. Other booklets will tell you exactly what MADD is, programs in your area, statistics, and legislative goals. This is a reliable service available by phone.

* National Council of Child Abuse and Family Violence (800) 222-2000
This Monday-Friday, 8AM-5PM Pacific time service will answer your questions concerning referrals, services, etc. by phone or mail. On off days there is a recording telling you the days and hours to reach them. You can receive information by mail or phone on child abuse, family violence, and child sexual abuse. Printed information gives you current support programs and prevention/treatment programs.

* National Institute on Drug Abuse (800) 662-HELP
This service operates Monday through Friday, 9AM-3AM, and weekends, 12PM-3AM. You will be referred to appropriate agencies and sources in your area. They will direct you to information in your area and give you numbers to call. There is often a long wait to speak with someone.

* National Runaway Switchboard and Suicide Hotline (800) 621-4000
Hearing Impaired-TDD (800) 621-0394
This national hotline is open 24 hours per day, 365 days a year. The services it can provide are crisis intervention, referrals and youth advocacy. A pamphlet is available which explains the service and gives advice for parents of runaways.

* National Sexually Transmitted Disease Hotline (800) 227-8922
This service operates Monday through Friday, 8AM-11PM Eastern time. During off hours a recording will tell you the hours to call back. If you call during their hours of operation, a person will answer information on the phone, provide counseling and give you referrals. They will send you free information on specific diseases.

* Parents Anonymous National Office (800) 421-0353
This non-profit service operates Monday through Friday, 8AM-4:30PM Pacific time. You will receive referrals to services in your state. During off hours you are directed to free support groups in the LA area.

* National Council on Alcoholism and Drug Dependence (800) 322-2255
This recording operates Monday through Friday, 24 hours per day. You give it your zip code and receive local offices. You can also give it your name and

number to get free information. The recording reassures you that your call is kept confidential.

* TARGET National Resource Bank (800) 366-6667
This national service is located in Kansas City, Missouri. During off hours you can leave a message or call (800) 999-9999 which is an emergency service. During their hours of operation, you can receive information on drugs. You can also receive a catalog with different sources on information on alcohol, tobacco, and other drugs.

* Emergency Service Hotline (800) 999-9999
This is a 24 hour per day, Monday through Friday emergency service. It is available for runaways, pregnant women who need help, and those who need help with drug and/or alcohol related problems in an emergency situation.

* Workplace and Drug and Alcohol Use

National Clearinghouse for Alcohol and Drug Information
P.O. Box 2345
Rockville, MD 20852 (800) 729-6686

The Clearinghouse has several free publications and videos dealing with drugs and the workplace. Some of the titles include:

AIDS/HIV Infection and the Workplace: NIDA Workgroup Report
Assessment of Laboratory Quality in Urine Drug Testing.
Comprehensive Procedures for Drug Testing in the Workplace.
Drug Abuse Curriculum for Employee Assistance Program Professionals.
Drug Abuse in the Workplace Videotape Series.
Drug-Free Federal Workplace: Executive Order 12564 of September 15, 1988.
Drug-Free Workplace Requirements; Notice and Interim Final Rules.
Drugs in the Workplace, Research and Evaluation Data.
The Fact is...Employee Assistance Contacts Are Available in Every State.
An Employer's Guide to Dealing with Substance Abuse.
Listing of Drug Testing Laboratories Certified by the U.S. Department of Health and Human Services
Mandatory Guidelines for Federal Drug Testing.
Mandatory Guidelines for Federal Workplace Drug Testing Programs; Final Guidelines.
Model Plan for a Comprehensive Drug-Free Workplace Program.
NIDA Capsule: Resources to Address Drugs in the Workplace.
NIDA's Drug-Free Workplace Helpline.
Public Law 100-690. Subtitle D-Drug-Free Workplace Act of 1988.
Drug-Free Workplace Act.
Research on Drugs and the Workplace.
Technical, Scientific, and Procedural Issues of Employee Drug Testing.
What Works: Workplaces Without Drugs.
Workers at Risk: Drugs and Alcohol on the Job.

Be patient. If any phone number is incorrect, call (area code) 555-1212 and request the new listing.

Drugs and Chemical Dependence

Education and Prevention

* Academic Institutions and Educational Resources

National Clearinghouse for Alcohol and Drug Information
Office for Substance and Alcohol Prevention (OSAP)
P.O. Box 2345
Rockville, MD 20847 (301) 468-2600

Single copies of publications are sent free of charge and a publications catalog is available. Examples include the *Directory of Academic Institutions and Organizations: Drug, Alcohol, and Employee Assistance Program Educational Resources*, which include educational opportunities on subjects relevant to employee assistance, covering academic institutions, national organizations, and State alcohol and drug abuse agencies.

* ACTION Drug Abuse Prevention Nationwide

ACTION
Drug Alliance Office
1100 Vermont Avenue NW (800) 424-8867
Washington, DC 20525 (202) 606-4902

ACTION sponsors educational prevention programs in the community geared to youth drug abuse prevention. The Regional Offices are:

Region I
10 Causeway Street, Room #473, Boston, MA 02222; (617) 565-7000. Services Connecticut, Maine, Massachusetts, New Hampshire, Vermont and Rhode Island.

Region II
6 World Trade Center, Room 758, New York, NY 10048-0206; (212) 466-3858. Services New Jersey, New York, Puerto Rico and the Virgin Islands.

Region III
U.S. Customs House, 2nd and Chestnut Sts., Room 108, Philadelphia, PA 19106-2912; (215) 597-3495. Services Kentucky, Maryland, Delaware, Ohio, Pennsylvania, Virginia, West Virginia and Washington, DC.

Region IV
101 Marietta St., NW, Suite 1003, Atlanta, GA 30323-2301; (404) 331-2058. Services Alabama, Florida, Georgia, Mississippi, North Carolina, South Carolina and Tennessee.

Region V
175 West Jackson Blvd., Suite 1207, Chicago, IL 60604-3964; (312) 353-5107. Services Illinois, Indiana, Iowa, Michigan, Minnesota and Wisconsin.

Region VI
1100 Commerce, Room 6B11, Dallas, TX 75242-9494; (214) 767-9494. Services Arkansas, Kansas, Louisiana, Missouri, New Mexico, Oklahoma and Texas

Region VIII (There is no Region VII)
Executive Tower Bldg., Suite 2930, 1405 Curtis St., Denver, CO 80202; (303) 844-2671. Services Colorado, Wyoming, Montana, Nebraska, North Dakota, South Dakota and Utah.

Region IX
211 Main St., Room 530, San Francisco, CA 94105-1914; (415) 744-3016. Services Arizona, California, Hawaii, Nevada.

Region X
915 Second Avenue, Suite 3190 Federal Office Building, Seattle, WA 98174-1103; (206) 553-4975. Services Alaska, Idaho, Oregon and Washington.

* Adolescent Peer Pressure and Prevention Study

National Clearinghouse for Alcohol and Drug Information
P.O. Box 2345 (800) 729-6686
Rockville, MD 20852 (301) 468-2600

The Clearinghouse has several free publications, posters, and videos dealing with teenagers and drug use. Some of the titles include:

The Adolescent Assessment/Referral System Manual.
Preventing Adolescent Drug Use: From Theory to Practice.
Prevention Resource Guide: Secondary School Students.
Facts About Teenagers and Drug Abuse.
High School Senior Drug Use: 1975-1990.
News Release: High School Senior Drug Use, 1990.
Steroids Mean Trouble (poster).
Alcohol and Youth: Fact Sheet.
Treatment for Adolescent Substance Abusers.
Adolescent Drug Abuse: Analyses of Treatment Research - NIDA Research Monograph.
Quick List: 10 Steps to Help Your Child Say No (PH230) is a poster that parents can use to help their child stay away from drugs.
Too Many Young People Drink and Know Too Little About the Consequences (PH305) provides answers to questions such as why teenagers drink, and why young drinkers turn to drugs; as well as up to date statistics about teenagers and drugs.

* After-School High Risk Youth

Federal Bureau of Investigation (FBI)
9th St. and Pennsylvania Ave., NW
Washington, DC 20535 (202) 324-2080

High Risk Youth Program is an FBI effort to establish an after school drug abuse prevention program in conjunction with the Office of Juvenile Justice and Delinquency Prevention (OJJDP), and the Boys and Girls Clubs of America. This program targets high risk youth in the area of drug prevention and education. The program goal is to channel the energies of youth into positive activities which will prepare them to live a drug free life. Activities will be developed which teach or reinforce youth life skills (self esteem, decision making, etc.), drug education, and drug refusal skills. This information will also be incorporated into existing programs, such as vocational training. Information on the High Risk Youth Program can be obtained from your local chapter of Boys and Girls Clubs of America.

* AIDS and IV Drug Users Educational Materials

Office of Substance Abuse Prevention (OSAP)
National Institute on Alcohol Abuse and Alcoholism
5600 Fishers Lane
Rockville, MD 20857 (301) 443-3860

OSAP, in cooperation with the Centers for Disease Control, develops educational materials to reduce the risks of AIDS among IV drug users. Publications to call and request are: *Psychological, Neurological, and Substance Aspects of AIDS* (OMOO-4044) and *When Someone Close Has AIDS: Acquired Immunodeficiency Syndrome* (ADM89-1515).

* Alcohol Abuse, Prevention and Education

National Clearinghouse for Alcohol Information
P.O. Box 2345 (800) 729-6686
Rockville, MD 20847 (301) 468-2600

The National Clearinghouse for Alcohol and Drug Information (NCADI) is a centralized source for information about the causes and treatment of alcoholism and other drug addiction. They have the latest research results, articles, videos and other print materials. A sampling of free fact sheets available includes: *Alcohol and Safety* (No. MS 311), *Legal Drinking Age Summary 1986* (No. MS308); *Treatment for Alcohol Problems: How to Find Help* (No. MS 299); *Sex-Related Alcohol Effects* (No. MS 247); *Prevention of Alcohol Problems* (No. MS 305). For a $15 annual handling fee, the bimonthly bulletin, *Prevention Pipeline*, can be sent to keep you informed of the latest research, programs, or events. NCADI offers technical support to organizations through use of resource lists, direct mail and materials, as well as outreach to groups.

Be patient. If any phone number is incorrect, call (area code) 555-1212 and request the new listing.

Education and Prevention

* Americans For a Drug Free America

Federal Bureau of Investigation (FBI)
9th St. and Pennsylvania Ave., NW
Washington, DC 20536 (202) 324-3000

This booklet is available through the F.B.I. It discusses the widespread drug abuse in our country. It explains different kinds of drugs, as well as the problems that are the result of them, such as suicide, child abuse, and other violence.

* Anti-Drug Effort in Workplace

Occupational Safety and Health Administration (OSHA)
200 Constitution Ave., NW
Washington, DC 20210 (202) 523-7162

OSHA aids the anti-drug effort by ensuring safe and healthful working conditions in the Nation's 4.5 million workplaces.

* Audiovisuals Videotapes Center

Drug Planning and Outreach Staff
Office of Elementary and Secondary Education
400 Maryland Ave., SW
Washington, DC 20202-6123 (202) 401-3030

During 1987, awards were made to develop and distribute audiovisual materials to elementary and secondary schools for drug abuse education and prevention activities. These materials are close-captioned videotapes with brief teacher guides. Copies of the tapes have been sent to all the Nation's school districts and are also available from the National Clearinghouse for Alcohol and Drug Information (301-468-2600), the National Audio-Visual Center (301-763-1896), and from each of the Regional Centers (Eileen Nicosia, 202-732-2311).

* Close-Captioned Hearing Impaired Videos

Office of Public Affairs
U.S. Department of Education
400 Maryland Ave., SW
Washington, DC 20202 (202) 401-3030

Eight productions, close-captioned for the hearing impaired, have been designed to inform students, attending kindergarten through 12th grade, about the dangers of drug use in an engaging and entertaining manner. Contact this office for further information on borrowing or purchasing these videos. Will send information upon request.

* College and University Drug-Free Network

Vonnie Clement
Office of Educational Research and Improvement (OERI)
555 NJ Ave., Room 5026
Washington, DC 20208-5644 (202) 401-3030

OERI continues to support development of a national network of colleges committed to eliminating drug and alcohol abuse on their campuses. Initial networking efforts focused on four year residential colleges so that information on comparable problems could be shared; however, the focus has expanded to address the concerns of the two-year degree student and the commuter population. Over 1300 colleges and universities have joined the Network. They have the following publications: *Network Directory;* a collection of presentations titled *Approaches to Drug Abuse Prevention at Colleges and Universities; Network Update* newsletter; *What Works: Schools Without Drugs; A Guide for College Presidents and Governing Boards;* and *Success Stories From Drug-Free Schools.*

* College Students and Drug Use

National Clearinghouse for Alcohol and Drug Information
P.O. Box 2345
Rockville, MD 20852 (800) 729-6686

The Clearinghouse has several free publications, dealing with alcohol and drug use and college students. Some of the titles include:

Alcohol Practices, Policies, and Potentials of American Colleges and Universities: A White Paper.
Strategies for Preventing Alcohol and Other Drug Problems on College Campuses: Faculty Members' Handbook.
Strategies for Preventing Alcohol and Other Drug Problems on College Campuses: Program Administrators' Handbook.
Prevention Resource Guide: College Youth.

* Community Involvement with Workplace Drug Abuse Video

National Audiovisual Center
Customer Service Section
8700 Edgeworth Drive
Capitol Heights, MD 20743-3701 (301) 763-1896

National Clearinghouse for Alcohol and Drug Information
P.O. Box 2345 (800) 729-6686
Rockville, MD 20847 (301) 468-8200

Finding Solutions portrays drug abuse in the workplace as a community-wide problem; thus the solutions offered through education and prevention are presented as personal, workplace, and community responsibilities. Specific emphasis is placed on the need to effectively deliver accurate and credible information to the workforce, to promote workplace peer involvement and build community partnerships. It is available for sale and rental.

* Community Prevention and Education Grants

ACTION
Drug Alliance Office
1100 Vermont Ave., NW (800) 424-8867
Washington, DC 20525 (202) 606-4920

ACTION supports community-based prevention and education efforts with grants, contracts, conferences, and technical assistance. Nonprofit organizations and state and local governments are eligible to receive grants from ACTION. An announcement is made in the Federal Register regarding the type of activities that the ACTION grant is available for and organizations are encouraged to apply. ACTION also maintains a mailing list which sends copies of the notices appearing in the Federal Register directly to those on the list. To get the name of your organization on this list, call the number above.

* Don't Drink Posters

National Clearinghouse for Alcohol and Drug Information
P.O. Box 2345 (800) 729-6686
Rockville, MD 20847 (301) 468-2600

Single copies of these posters are free:

The Herschel Walker Poster. (AVD45)
An Inner Voice Tells You Not to Drink or Use Other Drugs (AV161)
The Typical Alcoholic American (AV195)

* Drug Abuse Curricula

National Clearinghouse for Alcohol and Drug Information
P.O. Box 2345
Rockville, MD 20852 (800) 729-6686

The Office of Educational Research and Improvement of the U.S. Department of Education has developed several publications dealing with substance abuse curriculum. *Learning to Live Drug Free: A Curriculum Model for Prevention* provides a framework for classroom-based prevention efforts in kindergarten through grade 12. The model includes lessons, activities, background for teachers and suggestions for involving parents and the community in drug prevention. *Drug Abuse Curricula Criteria* is a guide to help schools and school district staff select and implement substance abuse curricula in elementary and secondary schools. Other publications developed by NCADI include *The National Commission on Drug-Free Schools: Final Report* which outlines goals for achieving drug-free schools by the year 2000. *Performance Edge Kit* is for teenagers and focuses on the effects smoking and drinking have on physical performance (includes video, magazine, poster and guide for coaches and teachers). *Teaching About Substance Abuse: A Resource Manual for Faculty Development* includes materials, information and resources to assist faculty members to learn more about alcohol and other drug abuse. Other publications include:

The Fact is...The Use of Steroids in Sports Can Be Dangerous.
The Fact Is...You Can Prevent Alcohol and Other Drug Problems Among Elementary School Children.
The Fact Is...You Can Prevent Alcohol and Other Drug Use Among Secondary High School Students.
The Fact Is...You can Start a Student Assistance Program.
What Works: Schools Without Drugs.

Be patient. If any phone number is incorrect, call (area code) 555-1212 and request the new listing.

Drugs and Chemical Dependence

* Drug Abuse Publications and Coloring Books

Office of Public Affairs
Drug Enforcement Administration
U.S. Department of Justice
1405 I Street, NW
Washington, DC 20537 (202) 307-7977

Soozie and Katy is a coloring and activity book for youngsters that describes the appropriate use of legal drugs and the dangers accompanying misuse of medicines. Other free publications include:

Drugs of Abuse - a reference for a consensus of current scientific findings.
Time to Focus On The User.
Anabolic Steroids and You.
DEA's Demand Reduction Program.
No Magic Bullet: A Look at Drug Legalization.
Pumping Trouble; The Problem of Steroid Use.
Guidelines for a Drug Free Workplace.
Drug Abuse Prevention for Explorers: A Guidebook.
Healthy Bodies Don't Need Drugs!
Coca Cultivation and Cocaine Processing: An Overview.

* Drug Abuse Posters

National Clearinghouse for Alcohol and Drug Information
P.O. Box 2345 (800) 729-6686
Rockville, MD 20847 (301) 468-2600

The clearinghouse has the following free posters dealing with drug abuse as well as AIDS and drugs:

AIDS. Another Way Drugs Can Kill
Drug Busters. Don't Let Drugs Win
Get Your Kids Addicted to Something That Costs Just 35 Cents an Ounce - (books)
Get Your Kids Hooked on Something Before Someone Else Does
Guess Who Else Can Get AIDS If you Shoot Drugs/ Your Baby Can
Guia Practica: 10 pasos que ayudan a sus hijos a decir "No"
The Herschel Walker Poster
If You Ever Shot Drugs, Get Tested Before you Get Pregnant
An Inner Voice Tells You Not to Drink or Use Other Drugs Poster
The Jets poster
Live the Dream, Say No To Alcohol and Drug Abuse Poster
A Man Who Shoots Up Can Be Very Giving. He Can Give You and Your Baby AIDS
McGruff: Say 'No' to Crack and Other Drugs
Most Babies with AIDS Are Born to Mothers of Fathers Who Have Shot Drugs
Performance Edge Poster
Quick List: Ten Steps to Help Your Child Say "No"
Steroids Mean Trouble Poster
Stopping Teenage Drug Abuse Will Take Two Generations
Studies Prove Children Can't Smoke Pot While Swimming Underwater
When You Share Needles You Could Be Shooting Up AIDS Poster

* Drug Abuse Resistance Education Project

Federal Bureau of Investigation
9th St. and Pennsylvania Ave., NW
Washington, DC 20535 (202) 324-2080

Drug Abuse Resistance Education (DARE) targets children before they are likely to experiment with drugs, alcohol, and tobacco. This approach attempts to prevent drug use and to reduce drug trafficking by eliminating the demand for drugs. Veteran uniformed law enforcement officers are trained to teach a structured curriculum in school classrooms, an effort that also enhances the image of police officers within the community.

* Drug and Substance Abuse Prevention

National Clearinghouse for Alcohol and Drug Information
P.O. Box 2345 (800) 729-6686
Rockville, MD 20847 (301) 468-2600

The office, created by the Anti-Drug Abuse Act, promotes and distributes prevention materials (posters, kits, resource lists) throughout the country. It develops materials and distributes information from its database on prevention, intervention, and treatment for a wide variety of audiences. OSAP supports community-based prevention programs through grant programs and on-site consultation, as well as the National Clearinghouse for Alcohol and Drug Information.

* Drug Alliance Coalitions and Networks Grants

ACTION
Drug Alliance Office
1100 Vermont Ave., NW (800) 424-8867
Washington, DC 20525 (202) 606-4902

ACTION awards grants to develop coalitions and partnerships working together to prevent and combat chemical dependence at the community level.

* Drug Experts International Speakers Bureau

U.S. Information Agency (USIA)
301 Fourth St., SW
Washington, DC 20547 (202) 619-4700

USIA provides public affairs support through its posts in U.S. embassies in countries where illicit drug production and/or trafficking has been identified as a priority issue. USIA selects key people in the international drug field for professional exchange programs in the U.S.; and schedules seminars, conferences, and other activities for U.S. specialists in drug-related fields before selected audiences in key countries.

* Drug-Free School Recognition Program

James Better
Office of Educational Research and Improvement
U.S. Department of Education
555 NJ Ave.
Washington, DC 20208 (202) 708-5366

Under the Drug-Free School Recognition Program, applications from nominated schools are reviewed by experts in the area of drug and alcohol prevention. The schools or programs selected for recognition are honored at ceremonies in Washington, DC.

* Drug-Free Schools and Communities Coordination

Office of Substance Abuse Prevention (OSAP)
National Institute on Alcohol Abuse and Alcoholism
5600 Fishers Lane
Rockville, MD 20857 (301) 443-3860

OSAP conducts training, technical assistance, data collection, and evaluation activities of programs supported under the Drug Free Schools and Communities Act of 1986. It also supports the development of model, innovative, community-based programs to discourage alcohol and drug abuse among young people.

* Drug-Free Schools Manual

Information Office
U.S. Department of Education
555 New Jersey Avenue, NW (800) 624-0100
Washington, DC 20208 (202) 659-4854

Schools Without Drugs suggests ways that students, parents, schools and communities can fight drugs and describes working programs. This free 87-page booklet also discusses legal issues faced by educational institutions. It also explains how different drugs are used, what they look like and the physical side effects that a user experiences.

* Drug-Free Workplace Helpline

National Information on Drug Abuse (NIDA) (800) 843-4971
(301) 443-6780 (in MD)

The Workplace Helpline answers questions and provides technical assistance to business, industry, and unions about developing and implementing comprehensive drug-free workplace programs. Corporate executive officers, managers, and union representatives are encouraged to call for assistance. The Helpline provides telephone consultation, resource referrals, networking services, and publications to assist in planning, policy development, and program implementation. They have a four-part videotape series for loan on drugs in the workplace. The hotline operates from 9 am to 8 pm EST (Monday-Friday).

* Drug Information for Community Groups

ACTION
1100 Vermont Ave., NW (800) 424-8867
Washington, DC 20525 (202) 606-4902

Some of the publications currently available include: *Meeting the Challenge,* a guide for service clubs; *Take Action Against Drug Abuse: How To Start A*

Be patient. If any phone number is incorrect, call (area code) 555-1212 and request the new listing.

Education and Prevention

Volunteer Anti-Drug Program in Your Community; Just Say No Guide for Older American Volunteers.

* Drugs At Work Videotapes:

Employee and Employer Versions
National Audiovisual Center
Customer Service Section
8700 Edgeworth Drive
Capitol Heights, MD 20743-3701 (301) 763-1896

National Clearinghouse for Alcohol and
Drug Information
P.O. Box 2345 (800) 729-6686
Rockville, MD 20852 (301) 468-2600

"Drugs at Work" is a 23 minute educational documentary which describes costs of drug use for the workplace, the individual, and the public; and examines action being taken by government and private companies. Interviews with drug users who have sought treatment and with experts on drugs in the workplace are included; and government and industry representatives describe federal and corporate programs currently underway. This video is available in both employer and employee versions. It is available for sale and rental.

* Drugs: Fact Sheets

National Clearinghouse for Alcohol and Drug Information
P.O. Box 2345 (800) 729-6686
Rockville, MD 20852 (301) 468-2600

The clearinghouse offers a series of fact sheets giving basic information about the psychological and physiological effects of various drugs. Single copies of these booklets are available free; many are printed in Spanish:

Alcohol Alert #7, Alcohol Use and Abuse: Where Do the Numbers Come From? (PH278)
Drug Abuse Statistics, 1990 Population Estimates (CAP22)

* Drunk Driving Films and Videotapes

National Audiovisual Center
8700 Edgeworth Drive
Capitol Heights, MD 20743-3701 (301) 763-1896

The National Audiovisual Center sells several videotapes: "Under The Influence" and "Until I Get Caught." "Spirits of America," available for rent and sale, deals with issues, attitudes and standards of American drinking patterns and the historical and cultural aspects associated with them.

* Effective School Programs Newsletter

Drug Planning and Outreach Staff
Office of Elementary and Secondary Education
400 Maryland Ave. SW
Washington, DC 20202-6123 (202) 401-3030

Challenge Newsletter: bi-monthly, highlights successful programs, provides the latest research on effective prevention measures, and answers questions about school-based efforts. The newsletter is distributed to superintendents, principals, and parent groups across the country. Contact Charlotte Gillespie, (202) 401-3030.

* Elementary School Drug Prevention Videos

National Audiovisual Center
8700 Edgeworth Drive
Capitol Heights, MD 20743 (800) 638-1300

The following drug prevention videos are available for loan through one of the above Regional Centers or the National Clearinghouse:

The Drug Avengers. Ten 5-minute animated adventures that urge caution about ingesting unfamiliar substances; encourages students to trust their instincts when they think something is wrong; and show that drugs make things worse, not better. Grades 1-6.

Fast Forward Future. A magical device allows youngsters to peer into the future and see on a TV screen what will happen if they use drugs and what will happen if they remain drug free. Grades 1-6.

Straight Up. A fantasy adventure that features information on the effects of drugs,

developing refusal skills, building self-esteem, and resisting peer pressure. Grades 4-6.

Additional videos to purchase for Drug Abuse Prevention:
Straight At Ya'. Kirk Cameron talks with students about peer pressure and drugs. Grades 7-9.

Lookin' Good. Shows kids how to build a peer support group to resist drugs. Grades 7-9.

Downfall: Sports and Drugs. Shows athletes who took drugs, mainly steroids, and how their careers suffered. Grades 7-12.

Hard Facts. Three stories about drugs in high school. Grades 10-12.

Private Victories. Four stories on how drugs affect different aspects of a person's life. Grades 10-12.

* Elementary School Education Resources

National Clearinghouse for Alcohol and Drug Information
P.O. Box 2345 (800) 729-6686
Rockville, MD 20852 (301) 468-2600

Learning to Live Drug Free: A Curriculum Model for Prevention (BKD51) and *Performance Edge Kit* (PEO1-4) are teaching aids for kindergarten through grade 12.

* Employee Assistance Programs Videotape

National Audiovisual Center
Customer Service Section
8700 Edgeworth Drive
Capitol Heights, MD 20743-3701 (301) 763-1896

National Clearinghouse for Alcohol and Drug Information
P.O. Box 2345 (800) 729-6686
Rockville, MD 20852 (301) 468-8200

Getting Help presents detailed information about the use of Employee Assistance Programs (EAPs) in addressing drug use in the workplace. The film describes the value of EAPs to employees and employers through comments by business, labor, and government leaders, and EAP professionals; presentation of three model programs; and EAP client interviews. It encourages employers to consider EAPs as a tool in combatting drugs at work, and provides employees with reassuring information about the confidentiality and effectiveness of an EAP program. This video is available in both employer and employee versions. It is available for sale and rental.

* Ethnic Minorities and Alcoholism and Drug Prevention

National Clearinghouse on Alcohol Information
P.O. Box 2345 (800) 729-6686
Rockville, MD 20852 (301) 468-2600

Substance Abuse Among Blacks in the U.S. (CAP34)
Substance Abuse Among Hispanic Americans. (CAP30)
Minority Substance Abuse Prevention Project: Ad Hoc Task Force General Recommendations (RPO705)

The Clearinghouse catalog has other sources about this subject.

* FBI Substance Abuse Prevention Education

Federal Bureau of Investigation (FBI)
9th St. and Pennsylvania Ave., NW
Washington, DC 20535 (202) 324-2080

Each FBI field office has a Special Agent Drug Demand Reduction Coordinator who provides substance abuse prevention education to youth between the ages of 5 and 18 years. The FBI Coordinator gets involved in existing drug prevention initiatives in schools and may also assist in implementing new programs. The Research/Drug Demand Reduction Unit has the following free publications available:

Americans for a Drug-Free America.
Children and Drugs: What Can A Parent Do?
Captain America Goes to War Against Drugs (Marvel Comics).
Archie and His Pals In..The Peer Helping Program!
Drugs In The Workplace.

Be patient. If any phone number is incorrect, call (area code) 555-1212 and request the new listing.

Drugs and Chemical Dependence

* Federal Employees Drug-Free Workplace Effort

Office of Personnel Management
1900 E St., NW
Washington, DC 20415 (202) 606-2424

The Office of Personnel Management (OPM) administers a merit system for Federal employment that includes recruiting, examining, training and promoting people on the basis of their knowledge and skills. The Office's role is to ensure that the Federal Government provides an array of personnel services to applicants and employees. This office, with the U.S. Department of Health and Human Services, has developed drug-free workplace plans for Federal agencies.

* Handbooks: Schools Without Drugs

Drug Planning and Outreach Staff
Office of Elementary and Secondary Education
400 Maryland Ave., SW
Washington, DC 20202-6123 (202) 401-3030

This office provides materials to schools and communities in developing a comprehensive program to prevent the use of alcohol and other drugs. Revised recently to include statistics and information on alcohol, tobacco, and steroids. *Growing Up Drug Free: A Parent's Guide to Prevention,* a handbook for parents to help families take an active role in drug prevention before a problem occurs. Copies are available free of charge. Call (800) 624-0100 or in the Washington metropolitan area call (202) 401-3030. Books also can be ordered from the National Clearinghouse for Alcohol and Drug Information.

* Hawaiian Natives Education Program Grants

Drug Planning and Outreach Staff
Office of Elementary and Secondary Education
400 Maryland Ave., SW
Washington, DC 20202-6123 (202) 401-3030

Organizations, primarily those that serve and represent Hawaiian natives, can receive funds for drug prevention and education activities. Contact Allen King, (202) 401-1599.

* High School Drug Prevention Videos

National Audiovisual Center
8700 Edgeworth Drive
Capitol Heights, MD 20743 (800) 638-1300

Hard Facts About Alcohol, Marijuana, and Crack. Offers factual information about the dangers of drug use in a series of dramatic vignettes.

Speak Up, Speak Out: Learning to Say No to Drugs. Gives students specific techniques they can use to resist peer pressure and say no to drug use.

Dare to be Different. Uses the friendship of two athletes in their last year of high school to illustrate the importance of goals and values in resisting pressures to use drugs.

Downfall: Sports and Drugs. Shows how drugs affect athletic performance and examines the consequences of drug use, including steroid use, on every aspect of an athlete's life - career, family, friends, sense of accomplishment, and self-esteem.

Private Victories. Illustrates the effects of drug and alcohol use on students and the value of positive peer influences in resisting peer pressure to use drugs.

* High School Student Attitudes and Trends

National Clearinghouse for Alcohol
and Drug Information
P.O. Box 2345
Rockville, MD 20852 (301) 468-2600

High School Senior Drug Use: 1975-1990 provides tables on the prevalence and incidence of drug use among students (free).

* Indian Elementary and Secondary School Children

Drug Planning and Outreach Staff
Office of Elementary and Secondary Education
400 Maryland Ave., SW
Washington, DC 20202-6123 (202) 401-3030

Programs for Indian Youth: Anti-alcohol and drug abuse education and prevention services will be provided to Indian children attending elementary and secondary schools on reservations which are operated by the Bureau of Indian Affairs. Contact Allen King, (202) 401-1599.

* Indian Tribes and Tribal Schools Education

Bureau of Indian Affairs (BIA)
U.S. Department of Interior
Washington, DC 20240 (202) 208-3710

The BIA funds drug education and prevention efforts aimed at American Indian youth as well as tribes and tribal schools. The purpose of the program is to heighten awareness of problems of alcohol and drug abuse among American Indians and to make BIA-funded schools drug-free. BIA also administers a program for Indian children on reservations who attend elementary and secondary schools through a memorandum of agreement with the U.S. Department of Education.

* Junior High School Drug Prevention Videos

National Audiovisual Center
8700 Edgeworth Drive
Capitol Heights, MD 20743 (800) 638-1300

The following drug prevention videos are available for loan through one of the above Regional Centers or the National Clearinghouse:

Straight at Ya. Tips on peer pressure, saying no and building self-esteem.

Lookin' Good. A two-part series based on actual incidents that convey the dangers of drug use and promote the use of peer support groups.

* Law Enforcement Officials Speakers Bureau

Executive Office for United States Attorneys
U.S. Department of Justice
Tenth Street and Pennsylvania Avenue NW
Washington, DC 20530 (202) 514-2121

The Department of Justice drug education effort emphasizes the importance of citizen involvement and the participation of local business and industry, law enforcement officials and schools. Public service announcements, lectures, and speeches by US Attorneys on the drug issue and prevention, are common.

* On-the-Job Drug Testing Videos

National Audiovisual Center
Customer Service Section
8700 Edgeworth Drive
Capitol Heights, MD 20743-3701 (301) 763-1896

National Clearinghouse for Alcohol and Drug Information
P.O. Box 2345 (800) 729-6686
Rockville, MD 20852 (301) 468-8200

Drug Testing: Handle with Care describes the options available in designing a drug testing component as part of a comprehensive drug-free workplace program. Procedures addressing the needs of both the employer and the employee, to ensure the accuracy and reliability of test results, for specimen collection and laboratory analysis, and a discussion of the critical role of the Medical Review Officer (MRO) are highlighted. Case studies of public/private, unionized/nonunionized work environments with testing components are presented. This video is available in both employer and employee versions. It is available for sale and rental.

* Parent Group Grants

ACTION
Drug Alliance Office
1100 Vermont Ave., NW, Suite 8300 (800) 424-8867
Washington, DC 20525 (202) 606-4902

The Drug Alliance Grants from ACTION are intended to strengthen and expand the efforts of community-based volunteer groups working to prevent drug abuse. These grants support innovative volunteer projects including organization of parent groups.

* Parent Guides for Alcohol and Drug Information

National Clearinghouse for Alcohol and Drug Information
P.O. Box 2345
Rockville, MD 20852 (800) 729-6686

Be patient. If any phone number is incorrect, call (area code) 555-1212 and request the new listing.

Education and Prevention

The clearinghouse has the following free publications available, dealing with drug and alcohol use:

Growing Up Drug Free: A Parent's Guide to Prevention.
Guia Practica: 10 pasos que ayudan a sus hijos a decir "No" (Quick List: 10 Steps to Helps Your Child Say "No").
Parent Training Is Prevention.
Pointers for Parents Card.
Quick List: 10 Steps to Help Your Child Say "No".
10 Steps to Help Your Child Say "No". A Parent's Guide.

* Positive Peer Prevention Youth Groups Funding

Drug Alliance Office
ACTION
1100 Vermont Ave., NW
Suite 8200 (800) 424-8867
Washington, DC 20525 (202) 606-4902

Drug Alliance Grants from ACTION have supported positive peer prevention activities for youth; the development of technical assistance materials; organization of youth groups.

* Postsecondary Education and Prevention Grants

Drug Planning and Outreach Staff
Office of Elementary and Secondary Education
400 Maryland Ave., SW
Washington, DC 20202-6123 (202) 401-3030

Grants for Institutions of Higher Education (IHEs): This program is divided between two groups. First, the Fund for the Improvement of Postsecondary Education has awarded 297 grants since fiscal year 1987 to institutions of higher education to develop and operate drug education and prevention programs. Second, the Drug-Free Schools and Communities Staff in the Office of Elementary and Secondary Education (OESE) has awarded 138 grants to support preservice or inservice personnel training or demonstration programs in drug and alcohol abuse education and prevention for use in elementary and secondary schools. Discretionary grant program.

* Prevention Programs That Work

National Clearinghouse for Alcohol and Drug Information
P.O. Box 2345 (800) 729-6686
Rockville, MD 20852 (301) 468-2600

Single copies are free: *How to Start and Run an Alcohol and Other Drug Information Center: A Guide* (BK169).

* Public Service Announcements Available

National Institute on Drug Abuse (NIDA)
5600 Fishers La.
Rockville, MD 20857 (301) 443-1124

Radio, print and television public service announcements are available through NIDA which focus on high school and college students on crack and cocaine and a specially designed message for family members of cocaine users. NIDA also offers two booklets *Cocaine/Crack. The Big Lie*, and *When Cocaine Affects Someone You Love*, designed for family members of cocaine users.

* RADAR: Alcohol and Drug Awareness Centers

National Clearinghouse for Alcohol and Drug Information (NCADI)
P.O. Box 2345 (800) 729-6686
Rockville, MD 20852 (301) 468-2600

NCADI works with and through Regional Alcohol and Drug Awareness Resource (RADAR) Network Centers located in almost every state. NCADI and the RADAR Network have become the national resource system for information on the latest research results, popular press and scholarly journal articles, videos, prevention curricula, print materials, and program descriptions. Most of the materials are provided free.

* Respect for Laws and Legal System Curricula

Office of Juvenile Justice and Delinquency Prevention (OJJDP)
U.S. Department of Justice
633 Indiana Ave., NW
Washington, DC 20531 (202) 307-0751

Law-Related Education (LRE) is a program of instruction designed to provide students with a conceptual as well as a practical understanding of the law and legal processes. Its goal is to equip students with knowledge of both their rights and responsibilities under the law and to foster law-abiding behavior and respect for law enforcement and the justice system. In addition, law student chapters of LRE in 10 states are initiating LRE substance abuse prevention programs in their areas. (TDTAD)

* Roles and Responsibilities for a Drug Free School and Community

National Commission on Drug Free Schools
U.S. Department of Education
400 Maryland Ave. SW
Washington, DC 20201-0110 (202) 401-1599

This is a large poster with different aspects of drug awareness and prevention. The chart shows how students, families, the media, businesses, etc. deal with drug problems and prevention.

* Satellite Broadcasting on Chemical Dependence

U.S. Information Agency (USIA)
301 Fourth St., SW
Washington, DC 20547 (202) 619-4700

USIA uses satellite broadcasting and the full range of its communications resources, including the Voice of America, a world-wide press service and television production, to carry its message to foreign audiences. It also supports local programs by acquiring and adapting U.S. materials on drug abuse prevention and control for overseas use.

* School and Community Grants

Drug Planning and Outreach Staff
Office of Elementary and Secondary Education
400 Maryland Ave., SW
Washington, DC 20202-6123 (202) 401-3030

State and Local Grants Program: This is a formula grant program which allocates funds to States based on school-age enrollment. Funds are to be used for anti-drug abuse efforts in schools and community-based organizations. Contact Allen King, (202) 401-1599.

* Safe Schools Program

National Institute of Justice
633 Indiana Ave. NW, Room 805
Washington, DC 20531 (202) 514-6235

Assists school administrators in developing and maintaining safe environments.

* Spanish Drug Abuse Information Hotline

For Spanish speaking callers: (800) 66-AYUNDA

The National Drug Abuse Information and Treatment Hotline helps drug users find and use local treatment programs, and acquaints those affected by the drug use of a significant other with much needed support groups and/or services. Referrals are also made to local crisis or information hotlines and support groups. Many pamphlets and brochures on a variety of drug topics are available. The hotline is in service 9 am to 3 am EST (Monday-Friday) and 12 pm to 3 am EST (Saturday-Sunday).

* Substance Abuse Counselors and Health Professionals

Office of Substance Abuse Prevention (OSAP)
National Institute on Alcohol Abuse and Alcoholism
5600 Fishers Lane
Rockville, MD 20857 (301) 443-0365

OSAP supports clinical training programs for substance abuse counselors and other health professionals involved in drug abuse education, prevention, and intervention.

* TARGET: Health Lifestyles for High School Students

National Federation of State High School Associations
P.O. Box 20626 (800) 366-6667
Kansas City, MO 64195 (816) 464-5400

The TARGET service is designed to cultivate healthy lifestyles among America's

Be patient. If any phone number is incorrect, call (area code) 555-1212 and request the new listing.

Drugs and Chemical Dependence

youth. The program offers workshops, training seminars, and an information bank on chemical use and prevention. It has a computerized referral service for substance abuse literature and prevention programs. A catalog is available with pamphlets, posters, videos, and course guides for teachers about steroids, crack, and alcohol as well as tobacco. Other information includes monthly newsletters and other publications.

* Teenagers and Alcoholism

National Clearinghouse for Alcohol and Drug Information
P.O. Box 2345
Rockville, MD 20847 (301) 468-2600

This clearinghouse provides many materials geared to adolescents including:

Too Many Young People Drink and Know Too Little About the Consequences (PH305) answers questions about frequency among teen drinking

Prevention Resource Guide: Impaired Driving (MS434) is a 20 page booklet that gives information about the effects of impaired driving

Safer Streets Ahead (PH292) discusses drinking and driving.

* Teachers, Counselors and Educational Personnel Training

Drug Planning and Outreach Staff
Office of Elementary and Secondary Education
400 Maryland Ave., SW
Washington, DC 20202-6123 (202) 401-3030

Educational Personnel Training Program is a discretionary grant program designed to provide financial assistance to State educational agencies, local educational agencies, and institutions of higher education for programs and activities used to train teachers, administrators, guidance counselors, and other educational personnel on drug and alcohol abuse education and prevention. Contact Allen King, (202) 401-1599.

* U.S. Department of Education Regional Centers

Drug Planning and Outreach Staff
Office of Elementary and Secondary Education
400 Maryland Ave., SW
Washington, DC 20202-6123 (202) 401-3030

Regional Centers are authorized to: 1) train school teams to assess and combat drug and alcohol abuse problems, 2) assist State educational agencies in coordinating and strengthening alcohol and drug abuse education and prevention programs, 3) assist local educational agencies and institutions of higher education in developing training programs for educational personnel, and 4) evaluate and disseminate information on effective substance abuse, education prevention programs and strategies.

Northeast
12 Overton Ave., Sayville, NY 11782-0403; (516) 589-7022. Serving: Connecticut, Delaware, Maine, Maryland, Massachusetts, New Hampshire, New Jersey, New York, Ohio, Pennsylvania, Rhode Island, and Vermont.

Midwest
1900 Spring Rd., Oak Brook, IL 60521; (708) 571-4710. Serving: Indiana, Illinois, Iowa, Michigan, Minnesota, Missouri, Nebraska, North Dakota, South Dakota, and Wisconsin.

Southeast
Spencerian Office Plaza, University of Louisville, Louisville, KY 40292; (502) 588-0052. Serving: Alabama, District of Columbia, Florida, Georgia, Kentucky,

North Carolina, South Carolina, Tennessee, Virginia, West Virginia, Virgin Islands, and Puerto Rico.

Southwest
555 Constitution Ave., Norman, OK 73037; (405) 325-1454, or (800) 234-7972 (outside Oklahoma). Serving: Arizona, Arkansas, Colorado, Kansas, Louisiana, Mississippi, New Mexico, Oklahoma, Texas and Utah.

Western
101 SW Main St., Suite 500, Portland, OR 97204; (503) 275-9480, or (800) 547-6339 (outside Oregon). Serving: Alaska, California, Hawaii, Idaho, Montana, Nevada, Oregon, Washington, Wyoming, American Samoa, Guam, Northern Mariana Islands, and Republic of Palau.

* Women and Alcoholism

National Clearinghouse for Alcohol and Drug Information
P.O. Box 2345
Rockville, MD 20852 (800) 729-6686 (301) 468-2600

Information geared for women is available through the Clearinghouse. Some examples of their latest publications are:

Alcohol Alert #10- Alcohol and Women (PH290) examines physical and emotional side effects on women, as well as prevention and treatment.

Prevention Resource Guide: Women (MS433)

Prevention Resource Guide: Pregnant/Postpartum Women and Their Infants (MS420)

The Fact is...Education Can Help Prevent AIDS and Drug Abuse Among Women (MS395).

* Workplace Drug Awareness

American Council For Drug Education
204 Monroe St.
Rockville, MD 20850

A catalog is available with pamphlets and posters designed to give employers and employees information about drugs in the workplace.

* Workplace Initiatives Research Grants

Grants Management Office
National Institute on Drug Abuse (NIDA)
Room 10-25, 5600 Fishers Lane
Rockville, MD 20857 (301) 443-6480

NIDA supports research on the prevalence, impact, and treatment of drug abuse in the workplace through its research grant programs. Information on the grant application process can be obtained from Information and consultation on specific research topics can be obtained from the Office of Workplace Initiatives, NIDA, Room 10-A-53, 5600 Fishers Lane, Rockville, MD 20857.

* Young Athletes and Drug Prevention

Drug Enforcement Administration (DEA)
U.S. Department of Justice
700 Army Navy Dr.
Arlington, VA 22202 (202) 307-1000

Team Up for Drug Prevention With America's Young Athletes is a free booklet for coaches that includes information about alcohol and other drugs, reasons why athletes use drugs, suggested activities for coaches, a prevention program, a survey for athletes and coaches, and sample letters to parents.

Be patient. If any phone number is incorrect, call (area code) 555-1212 and request the new listing.

Treatment and Rehabilitation

* **Alaskan Natives Prevention and Treatment Services**
Indian Health Service
U.S. Department of Health and Human Services
5600 Fishers Lane
Rockville, MD 20857 (301) 443-1087
The Indian Health Service (IHS) coordinates agency resources and services for alcohol and drug abuse prevention, intervention, treatment and aftercare of American Indians as well as Alaska Natives with opportunity for maximum tribal involvement in developing and managing programs to meet their health needs.

* **Drug and Alcohol Treatment for Disabled**
Social Security Administration (SSA) (800) 722-1213
6401 Security Blvd. (800) 325-0778 for hearing impaired
Baltimore, MD 21235 (301) 965-7700
The SSA administers a national program of contributory social insurance, and provides extensive services for the disabled, including drug and alcohol treatment.

* **Drug Abusers Treatment and Rehab Advocacy**
National Institute on Drug Abuse (NIDA)
5600 Fishers Lane
Rockville, MD 20857 (301) 443-6480
NIDA encourages other Federal agencies, national, foreign, State and local organizations, hospitals and volunteer groups to enable them to facilitate and extend programs for the prevention of drug abuse, and for the care, treatment and rehabilitation of drug abusers.

* **Drug and Alcohol Treatment Referrals**
National Clearinghouse for Alcohol and Drug Information
Box 2345
Rockville, MD 20852 (800) 729-6686
The National Directory of Drug Abuse and Alcoholism Treatment and Prevention Programs is a free directory published by the National Institute on Alcohol Abuse and Alcoholism and the National Institute on Drug Abuse. It contains referral information about treatment and prevention programs (408 pp.).

* **Drug Rehabilitation Services**
Office For Children and Families (ACYF)
U.S. Department of Health and Human Services
200 Independence Ave., SW
Washington, DC 20201 (202) 205-8347
This office provides leadership and direction to human services programs for the elderly, children and youth, families, Native Americans, persons living in rural areas, and handicapped persons. ACYF administers rehabilitation services for these groups.

* **Family-Based Approach and Adolescent Drug Treatment**
National Clearinghouse for Alcohol and Drug Information
P.O. Box 2345 (800) 729-6686
Rockville, MD 20852 (301) 468-2600
Single copies of publications are sent free of charge and a publications catalog is available, including *Adolescent Drug Abuse: Analyses of Treatment Research*, which assesses the adolescent drug user and offers theories, techniques, and findings about treatment and prevention. It also discusses family-based approaches.

* **Federal Employees with HIV/AIDS**
Office of Personnel Management (OPM)
1900 E St., NW
Washington, DC 20415 (202) 606-2424
OPM has also developed guidelines for the Federal government in dealing with employees with HIV/AIDS.

* **Local Drug Treatment Centers Incentives**
Susan David or Audrey Yowell
National Institute on Drug Abuse
5600 Fishers Lane, Room 10A-39
Rockville, MD 20857 (301) 443-1124
Overcoming Barriers to Drug Abuse Treatment in the Community is a flexible education model for use by communities which have funding and want to establish drug treatment facilities. This model is used in communities to educate people about drug treatment with the goal of countering resistance to the establishment of new treatment facilities. Materials are available to help local providers site facilities (How-to resource Manual and Media package), as well as materials to assist communities groups in educating the public (Resource manual and media materials). These materials are free. This Office can also provide technical assistance.

* **Local Treatment Program Referrals**
National Institute on Drug Abuse (800) 662-HELP
Provides drug related information to the general public, helps drug users find and use local treatment programs, and acquaints those affected by the drug use of a significant other with much needed support groups and/or services. Referrals are also made to local crisis or information hotlines and support groups, such as Cocaine Anonymous and Narcotics Anonymous. They provide many pamphlets and brochures on a variety of drug topics. The hotline is in service 9am to 3am EST (Monday-Friday) and 12pm to 3am EST (Sat.-Sun.).

* **Methadone and Anti-Addiction Drugs**
Food and Drug Administration (FDA)
5600 Fishers Lane
Rockville, MD 20857 (301) 295-8029
The FDA's activities are directed toward protecting the health of the Nation against impure and unsafe foods, drugs, and cosmetics, and other potential hazards. The FDA directs educational efforts at the proper use of prescription and over-the-counter drugs. FDA is also responsible for the regulatory restrictions on the dispensing of drugs for treatment, including methadone to treat opiate addiction.

* **Native Americans Intervention and Treatment**
Bureau of Indian Affairs (BIA)
U.S. Department of Interior
Washington, DC 20240 (202) 208-3710
Through an agreement between BIA and the Indian Health Service, these organizations coordinate agency resources and services for alcohol and drug abuse prevention, intervention, treatment and aftercare of American Indians.

* **Substance Abuse Treatment and Rehab**
Health Care Financing Administration (HCFA)
200 Independence Ave., SW
Washington, DC 20201 (202) 690-6113
The financing of the national drug abuse treatment rehabilitation and prevention programs has been a joint effort of Federal and state government and the private sector. Medicare and medicaid will not pay for certain types of treatment for alcohol and/or drug dependency.

* **Veterans Alcohol Dependent Treatment Programs**
U.S. Department of Veterans Affairs
810 Vermont Ave., NW

Be patient. If any phone number is incorrect, call (area code) 555-1212 and request the new listing.

Drugs and Chemical Dependence

Washington, DC 20420 (202) 233-4000

The Veteran's Administration offers treatment to veterans for alcohol and drug abuse. The Veteran's Administration currently operates 149 alcohol dependent treatment programs nationwide which provide diagnosis and treatment on both an inpatient and an outpatient basis.

* Veteran's Drug and Alcohol Treatment

U.S. Department of Veterans Affairs
810 Vermont Ave., NW
Washington, DC 20420 (202) 233-4000

The Veteran's Administration operates diverse programs to benefit veterans and members of their families. These benefits include education and rehabilitation, including drug or alcohol treatment. Call or write for booklet describing benefits available for veterans and their dependents.

* Veteran's Drug Abusers Halfway Houses and VA Hospitals

U.S. Department of Veterans Affairs
810 Vermont Ave., NW
Washington, DC 20420 (202) 233-4000

Additionally, the VA operates 52 specialized drug dependence programs which offer care and treatment for drug abusers in VA hospitals. They also have many contracts with half-way houses in local communities to place veterans with either alcohol or drug dependencies. Information on any of these programs can be obtained by contacting the Veteran's Administration office nearest you.

* Veteran's Hospitals Substance Abuse Research

U.S. Department of Veterans Affairs
810 Vermont Ave., NW
Washington, DC 20420 (202) 233-4000

The Veteran's Administration conducts extensive research in the field of substance abuse in the 172 VA hospitals nationwide. They also opened the Clinical Alcoholism Research Center in San Diego in 1985. No grants for research are offered by the Veteran's Administration in the field of alcohol and drug abuse.

* Veteran's Outpatient Treatment

U.S. Department of Veterans Affairs
810 Vermont Ave., NW
Washington, DC 20420 (202) 233-4000

After hospitalization for alcohol or drug treatment, veterans may be eligible for outpatient care, or may be authorized to continue treatment or rehabilitation in facilities such as halfway houses or therapeutic communities at the expense of the Department of Veterans Affairs.

* VA Medical Centers Inpatient and Outpatient Care

U.S. Department of Veterans Affairs
810 Vermont Ave., NW
Washington, DC 20420 (202) 233-4000

Patients may be admitted to any VA medical center for inpatient care. However, there are specialized VA Alcohol Dependence Treatment Programs and Drug Dependence Treatment Programs for inpatient and/or outpatient care in VA medical centers in the following states:

A denotes Alcoholism Program
D denotes Drug Dependence Program
A & D denote both Alcohol and Drug Dependence Programs

Alabama
700 S. 19th St., Birmingham, AL 35233 (A); (205) 933-8101
Loop Rd., Tuscaloosa, AL 35404 (A); (205) 554-2000
Tuskegee, AL 36803; (205) 727-0550

Alaska
2925 DeBanrd, Anchorage, AK 99508-2989; (907) 257-4700

Arizona
7th St. and Indian School Rd., Phoenix, AZ 85012 (A); (602) 277-5551
500 Hwy. 89 N., Prescott, AZ 86313 (A); (602) 445-4860
3601 6th Ave., Tucson, AZ 85723 (A & D); (602) 792-1450

Arkansas
4300 W. 7th St., Little Rock, AR 72205 (A & D); (501) 661-1202

California
2615 E. Clinton Ave., Fresno, CA 93703 (A); (209) 225-5323
11201 Benton St., Loma Linda, CA 92357 (A); (714) 825-7084
5901 E. 7th St., Long Beach, CA 90822 (A & D); (213) 494-2611
11301 Wilshire Blvd., West Los Angeles, CA 90073 (A & D); (213) 478-3711
425 S. Hill St., Los Angeles, CA 90013 (A & D); (213) 894-3902
150 Muir Rd., Martinez, CA 94553 (A & D); (415) 372-2000
3801 Miranda Ave., Palo Alto, CA 94304 (A & D); (415) 493-5000
3350 LaJolla Village Dr., San Diego, CA 92161 (A & D); (619) 552-8585
4150 Clement St., San Francisco, CA 94121 (A & D); (415) 221-4810
16111 Plummer St., Sepulveda, CA 91343 (A & D); (818) 895-9346
125 N. Jackson St., San Jose, CA 95116; (408) 275-7600
4951 Arroyo Rd., Livermore, CA 94550; (415) 447-2560

Colorado
1055 Clermont St., Denver, CO 80220 (A & D); (303) 393-2882
Hwy. 183 off Hwy. 50, Fort Lyon, CO 81038 (A); (303) 456-1260
2121 North Ave., Grand Junction, CO 81501; (303) 242-0731

Connecticut
W. Spring St., West Haven, CT 06516 (A); (203) 932-5711
555 Willard Ave., Newington, CT 06111 (A & D); (203) 666-6951

Delaware
1601 Kirkwood Hwy., Wilmington, DE 19805; (302) 994-2511

District of Columbia
50 Irving St., NW, Washington, DC 20422 (A & D); (202) 745-8000

Florida
1000 Bay Pines Blvd., N. Bay Pines, FL 33504 (A); (813) 398-6661
Archer Rd., Gainesville, FL 32602 (A); (904) 374-6089
1201 N.W. 16th St., Miami, FL 33125 (A & D); (305) 324-4455
801 S. Marion St., Lake City, FL 32055; (904) 755-3016
13000 Bruce B. Downs Blvd., Tampa, FL 33612; (813) 972-2000

Georgia
1670 Clairmont Rd., Atlanta (Decatur), GA 30033 (A & D); (404) 321-6111
1 Freedom Way, Augusta, GA 30910 (A); (706) 733-0188
1826 Veterans Blvd., Dublin GA 31021; (912) 272-1210

Hawaii
300 Ala Moana Blvd., Honolulu, HI 96850; (808) 541-1600

Idaho
500 W. Fort St., Boise, ID 83702; (208) 336-5100

Illinois
820 S. Damen Ave., Chicago, IL 60680 (A & D); (312) 666-6500
1900 E. Main St., Danville, IL 61832 (A); (217) 442-8000
Roosevelt Rd. and 5th Ave., Hines, IL 60141 (A & D); (708) 343-7200
333 E. Huron St., North Chicago, IL 60611 (A & D); (312) 943-6600
2401 W. Main St., Marion, IL 62959 (A & D); (618) 997-5311

Indiana
1481 W. 10th St., Indianapolis, IN 46202 (A & D); (317) 635-7401
E. 38th St., Marion, IN 46952 (A); (317) 674-3321
2121 Lake Ave., Fort Wayne, IN 46805; (219) 436-5431

Iowa
30th and Euclid, Des Moines, IA 50310 (A); (515) 271-5805
1515 W. Pleasant St., Knoxville, IA 50138; (515) 842-3101

Kansas
4101 S. 4th St. Trafficway, Leavenworth, KS 66048 (A); (913) 682-2000
2200 Gage Blvd., Topeka, KS 66622 (A); (913) 272-3111
5500 E. Kellogg, Wichita, KS 67218; (316) 685-2221

Kentucky
Leestown Rd., Lexington, KY 40511 (A); (606) 233-4511
800 Zorn Ave., Louisville, KY 40206; (502) 895-3401

Be patient. If any phone number is incorrect, call (area code) 555-1212 and request the new listing.

Treatment and Rehabilitation

Louisiana
1601 Perdido St., New Orleans, LA 70146 (A & D); (504) 568-0811
510 E. Stoner Ave., Shreveport, LA 71101 (A); (318) 424-6012
Shreveport Highway, Alexandria, LA 71301 (A & D); (318) 473-0010

Maine
Rt. 17, Togus, ME 04330 (A); (207) 623-8411

Maryland
3900 Loch Raven Blvd., Baltimore, MD 21218 (A & D); (301) 467-9932
31 Hopkins Plaza, Baltimore, MD 21201; (301) 467-9932
9600 North Point Rd., Fort Howard, MD 21052; (410) 477-1800
Perry Point, MD 21902 (A & D); (410) 642-2411

Massachusetts
200 Springs Rd., Bedford, MA 01730 (A & D); (617) 275-7500
150 S. Huntington Ave., Boston, MA 02130 (A & D); (617) 232-9500
940 Belmont St., Brockton, MA 02401 (A); (508) 583-4500
421 N. Main, Northampton, MA 01060 (A); (413) 584-4040

Michigan
Southfield and Outer Dr., Allen Park, MI 48101 (A & D); (313) 562-6000
5500 Armstrong Rd., Battle Creek, MI 49015 (A & D); (616) 966-5600
H Street, Iron Mountain, MI 49801 (A & D); (906) 774-3300
2215 Fuller Rd., Ann Arbor, MI 48105 (A & D); (313) 769-7100

Minnesota
One Veterans Dr., Minneapolis, MN 55417 (A & D); (612) 725-2000
8th St., St. Cloud, MN 56303 (A); (612) 255-6395

Mississippi
400 Veterans Ave., Biloxi, MS 39531 (A); (601) 388-5541
1500 E. Woodrow Wilson Dr., Jackson, MS 39216 (A); (601) 362-4471

Missouri
1 270, St. Louis, MO 63125 (A & D); (314) 894-6653
4801 Linwood Blvd., Kansas City, MO 64128; (816) 861-4700
800 Hospital St., Columbia, MO 65201; (314) 443-2511
1500 N. Westwood Blvd. Poplar Bluff, MO 63901; (314) 686-4151

Montana
William St., Fort Harrison, MT 59636 (A & D); (406) 442-6410

Nebraska
2201 N. Broad Well, Grand Island, NE 68803 (A & D); (308) 382-3660
600 S. 70th St., Lincoln, NE 68510 (A); (402) 489-3802
4101 Woolworth Ave., Omaha, NE 68105 (A); (402) 346-8800

Nevada
1000 Locust St., Reno, NV 89520 (A & D); (702) 786-7200
1703 W. Charleston Blvd., Las Vegas, NV 89102; (702) 385-3700

New Hampshire
718 Smyth Rd., Manchester, NH 03104 (A); (603) 624-4366

New Jersey
Tremont Ave., East Orange, NJ 07019 (A & D); (201) 676-1000
Knoll Croft Rd., Lyons, NJ 07939 (A); (201) 647-0180

New Mexico
2100 Ridgecrest Dr., SE, Albuquerque, NM 87108 (A); (505) 265-1711

New York
113 Holland Ave., Albany, NY 12208 (A & D); (518) 462-3311
130 W. Kingsbridge Rd., Bronx, NY 10468 (A & D); (212) 584-9000
800 Poly Place, Brooklyn, NY 11209 (A & D); (718) 630-3500
3495 Bailey Ave., Buffalo, NY 14215 (A); (716) 834-9200
Fort Hill Ave., Canandaigua, NY 14424 (A); (716) 394-2000
Old Albany Post Rd., Montrose, NY 10548 (A & D); (914) 737-4400
1st Ave. at E. 24th St., New York, NY 10010 (D); (212) 686-7500
Middleville Rd., North Port, NY 11678; (516) 261-4400
100 State St., Rochester, NY 14614; (716) 263-6710
800 Irving Ave., Syracuse, NY 13210 (A & D); (315) 476-7461
Bath, NY 14810; (607) 776-2111

North Carolina
1601 Brenner Ave., Salisbury, NC 28144 (A); (704) 638-9000

508 Fulton St., Durham, NC 27705; (919) 286-0411
2300 Ramsey St., Fayetteville, NC 28301; (919) 488-2120
1100 Tunnel Rd., Asheville, NC 28805 (A & D); (704) 298-7911

North Dakota
2101 Elm St., Fargo, ND 58102; (701) 232-3241

Ohio
3200 Vine St., Cincinnati, OH 45220 (A & D); (513) 861-3100
1000 Brecksville Rd., Brecksville, OH 44141 (A & D); (216) 526-3030
17273 State Route 104, Chillicothe, OH 45601; (614) 773-1141
4100 W. 3rd St., Dayton, OH 45428; (513) 268-6511
2090 Kenny Rd., Columbus, OH 43221; (614) 469-5916
10701 East Blvd., Cleveland, OH 44106 (A); (216) 791-3800

Oklahoma
921 N.E. 13th St., Oklahoma City, OK 73104 (A & D); (405) 270-0501
635 W. 11th St., Tulsa, OK 74127 (D); (918) 581-7161

Oregon
New Garden Valley Blvd., Roseburg, OR 97470 (A); (503) 440-1000
Hwy. 62, White City, OR 97503 (A); (503) 826-2111
3710 SW US Veterans Hospital Rd., Portland, OR 97207 (A & D); (503) 257-2500

Pennsylvania
Blackhorse Rd., Coatesville, PA 19320 (A & D); (215) 384-7711
University and Woodland Ave., Philadelphia, PA 19104 (A & D); (215) 823-5809
Highland Dr., Pittsburgh, PA 15206 (A); (412) 363-4900
1111 East End Blvd., Wilkes-Barre, PA 18711; (717) 824-3521
1700 S. Lincoln Ave., Lebanon, PA 17042; (717) 272-6621
325 New Castle Rd., Butler, PA 16001; (412) 287-4781

Puerto Rico
GPO Box 5800, San Juan, PR 00927 (A & D), (809) 758-7575

Rhode Island
Davis Park, Providence, RI 02908 (A & D); (401) 273-7100

South Carolina
109 Bee St., Charleston, SC 29401 (A); (803) 577-5011
Garners Ferry Rd., Columbia, SC 29209 (A); (803) 774-4000

South Dakota
I 90/Hwy. 34, Fort Meade, SD 57741 (A); (605) 347-2511
5th St., Hot Springs, SD 57747 (A); (605) 745-2000
601 S. Cliff Ave., Suite C, Sioux Falls, SD 57117 (A & D); (605) 336-3230

Tennessee
1030 Jefferson Ave., Memphis, TN 38104 (A & D); (901) 523-8990
Sidney and Lamont St., Johnson City, Mountain Home, TN 37684 (A); (615) 926-1171
3400 Lebanon Rd., Murfreesboro, TN 37129 (A); (615) 893-1360
1310 24th Ave. S, Nashville, TN 37212; (615) 327-4751

Texas
2400 Gregg St., Big Spring, TX 79720 (A); (915) 263-7361
4500 S. Lancaster Rd., Dallas, TX 75216 (A & D); (214) 376-5451
2002 Holcombe Blvd., Houston, TX 77030 (A & D); (713) 791-1414
7400 Merton Minter Blvd., San Antonio, TX 78284 (A); (512) 617-5300
1901 S. First, Temple, TX 76504 (A); (817) 778-4811
Memorial Dr., Waco, TX 76711 (A); (803) 752-6581
5919 Brook Hollow Dr., El Paso, TX 79925 (A & D); (915) 540-7892
1201 E. Ninth St., Bonham, TX 75418 (A & D); (903) 583-2111
3600 Memorial Blvd. Kerrville, TX 78028 (A & D); (512) 896-2020
6010 Amarillo Blvd., West, Amarillo, TX 79106 (A & D); (806) 355-9703

Utah
500 Foothill Blvd., Salt Lake City, UT 84148 (A & D); (801) 582-1565

Vermont
N. Hartland Rd., White River Junction, VT 05001 (A); (802) 295-9363

Virginia
Emancipation Dr., Hampton, VA 23667 (A); (804) 722-9961
1201 Broadrock Rd., Richmond, VA 23249 (D); (804) 230-0001
1970 Roanoke Blvd., Salem, VA 24153 (A); (703) 982-2585

Be patient. If any phone number is incorrect, call (area code) 555-1212 and request the new listing.

Drugs and Chemical Dependence

Washington
Gravely Lake Dr. and Veterans Dr., American Lake, Tacoma, WA 98493 (A & D); (206) 582-8440
1660 S. Columbian Way, Seattle, WA 98108 (A & D); (206) 762-1010
77 Wainwright Dr., Walla Walla, WA 99362 (A & D); (509) 525-5200
North 4815 Assembly St., Spokane, WA 99208 (A & D); (509) 328-4521

West Virginia
Rt 9, Martinsburg, WV 25410 (A); (304) 263-0811
Milford/Chestnut Sts., Clarksburg, WV 26301 (A & D); (304) 623-3461

Wisconsin
County Trunk E., Tomah, WI 54660 (A); (608) 372-3971
5000 W. National Ave., Milwaukee, WI 53295 (A & D); (414) 384-2000
2500 Overlook Terrace, Madison, WI 53705 (A & D); (608) 256-1901

Wyoming
Fort Rd., Sheridan, WY 82801 (A); (307) 672-3473
2360 E. Pershing Blvd., Cheyenne, WY 82001 (A & D); (307) 778-7550

Be patient. If any phone number is incorrect, call (area code) 555-1212 and request the new listing.

Law Enforcement and Prosecution

* **Airborne Drug Smugglers Interdiction**
Federal Aviation Administration (FAA)
800 Independence Ave., SW
Washington, DC 20591 (202) 267-3484
The Federal Aviation Administration (FAA) assists the anti-drug effort in pinpointing and intercepting airborne drug smugglers by enhanced use of radar, posting aircraft lookouts and tracking the movement of suspect aircraft through air traffic control centers.

* **Campaign Against Marijuana Planting**
Bureau of Land Management (BLM)
U.S. Department of Interior
Washington, DC 20240 (202) 208-5717
The Campaign Against Marijuana Planting (CAMP) attempts to eliminate the planting of marijuana on public land as well as drug labs that are operated on public land. Information should be called in to either your local office of the Bureau of Land Management, local officials in your area, or the national office listed above.

* **Chronic Juvenile Offenders, Victimization of Children**
Office of Juvenile Justice and
Delinquency Prevention
U.S. Department of Justice
633 Indiana Ave., NW
Washington, DC 20531 (202) 724-7782
The Special Emphasis Division provides technical assistance for Federal, State and local governments, as well as for public and private agencies and individuals in planning, establishing, funding, operating, or evaluating juvenile delinquency prevention programs.

* **Counternarcotics Intelligence Center**
Central Intelligence Agency (CIA)
McLean, VA (703) 482-1100
The DCI Counterintelligence Center at CIA headquarters pools intelligence information to help in the search of drug traffickers, in conjunction with FBI, DEA, and other government agencies. The DCI Counternarcotics Center includes representatives from the intelligence community including DEA, FBI, Customs, Coast Guard, NSA and DOD. The Center combines CIA and operations officers who have full access to intelligence on international drug trafficking. Its mission is to use intelligence better to help the policy community address the national security problems caused by narcotics and to help the U.S. government fight international narcotics trafficking.

* **Court Security**
U.S. Marshals Service
U.S. Department of Justice
Washington, DC 20531 (202) 307-9100
The Service protects members of the Federal judiciary and court facilities against all forms of terrorism and violent tactics which are routinely encountered. Cases generating broad media and public interest, as well as violent threats to the presiding trial judge, will intensify as law enforcement agencies focus on dangerous drug related investigations.

* **Crime Victimization and Compensation**
Office for Victims of Crime (OVC)
U.S. Department of Justice
633 Indiana Ave., NW
Washington, DC 20531 (202) 514-6444
This national office provides technical assistance and grants to states to enhance victim compensation and assistance programs.

* **Criminal Justice Database and Reference Service**
National Criminal Justice Reference Service
P.O. Box 6000 (800) 851-3420
Rockville, MD 20850 (301) 251-5000
The National Criminal Justice Reference System is a computerized database of more than 90,000 criminal-justice-related information sources. Information specialists are available to search the database or to use other research techniques to answer questions.

* **Customs Service Air and Marine Interdiction Efforts**
U.S. Customs Service (USCS)
1301 Constitution Ave., NW
Washington, DC 20229 (202) 927-6724
The Service is responsible for the processing and regulation of people, carriers, cargo, currency and mail which pass into and out of the United States. Customs has developed innovative inspection, air and marine interdiction programs and works closely with DEA in the development of intelligence and other cooperative drug enforcement efforts.

* **Diplomatic Initiatives on Crop Control and Interdiction**
Bureau of International Narcotics Matters
U.S. Department of State
2201 C St., NW
Washington, DC 20520 (202) 647-8464
The Bureau of International Narcotics Matters (INM) has overall responsibility for international drug policy development, program management, and diplomatic initiatives. Its major programs are concerned with bi- and multi-lateral assistance for crop control, interdiction, and related enforcement activities in producer and transit nations. INM also provides narcotics-related development assistance, technical assistance for demand reduction programs, and training for foreign personnel in narcotics enforcement and related procedures to strengthen interdiction and enforcement efforts.

* **Drivers Under-the-Influence Detection**
National Highway Traffic Safety Administration
400 Seventh St., SW
Washington, DC 20590 (202) 366-0123
The Drug Recognition Program is a program being conducted by the National Highway Traffic Safety Administration (NHTSA) and the Bureau of Justice Assistance. It is a means of improving enforcement of drug-impaired driving violations. The program trains police officers as Drug Recognition Experts (DREs), enabling the officers to develop skills in evaluating the drivers condition and securing evidence for conviction. Site selection criteria for this program are outline in a monograph available from the above address.

* **Drug Dealer Evictions from Public Housing**
U.S. Department of Housing and Urban Development (HUD)
451 Seventh Ave., SW
Washington, DC 20410 (202) 708-1422
HUD is working with the Attorney General, and the Secretary of HHS as well as local public housing authorities, State and Federal law enforcement officers, and local agencies to achieve drug-free public housing.

* **Drug-Free Federal Prisons**
Bureau of Prisons
320 First St., NW
Washington, DC 20534 (202) 514-2000
The Bureau of Prisons provides psychological and drug abuse treatment services and places increased emphasis creating drug-free prisons so as to break the link between drug use and crime.

Be patient. If any phone number is incorrect, call (area code) 555-1212 and request the new listing.

Drugs and Chemical Dependence

* Drug Labs on Public Lands Investigations

Bureau of Land Management (BLM)
U.S. Department of Interior
Washington, DC 20240 (202) 208-5717

The Campaign Against Marijuana Planting (CAMP) attempts to eliminate the planting of marijuana on public land as well as drug labs that are operated on public land. Information regarding Brochures regarding the Bureau's efforts are available as well as copies of the annual report are available through the Washington, DC office.

* Drug-Related Crime Data

Data Center and Clearinghouse for Drugs and Crime
1600 Research Boulevard
Rockville, MD 20850 (800) 666-3332

Drug enforcement data, information on drug trafficking and illicit drug-related aspects of crime are available from this clearinghouse.

* Drug Seizures and Prosecution

Drug Enforcement Administration (DEA)
U.S. Department of Justice
1405 I St., NW
Washington, DC 20537 (202) 401-7834

DEA investigates and prosecutes suspects connected with illicit drug trafficking. It regulates the legitimate manufacture and distribution of controlled substances. It maintains statistics regarding all Federal illicit drug seizures. It trains narcotics officers in other Federal, State, and local agencies as well as foreign police. DEA operates the El Paso Intelligence Center (EPIC), 24 hour daily national center for operational drug enforcement information. The regional offices are:

Atlanta
Richard B. Russell Federal Building, 75 Spring St. SW, Room 740, Atlanta, GA 30303; (404) 331-4401

Boston
Room G-64 JFK Federal Building, Boston, MA 02203; (617) 565-2800

Chicago
500 Dirksen Federal Building, 219 S. Dearborn St., Chicago, IL 60604 (312) 353-7875

Dallas
1880 Regal Row, Dallas, TX 75235; (214) 767-7151

Denver
721 19th St., Room 316, Denver, CO 80201; (303) 844-3951

Detroit
357 Federal Building, 231 W. Lafayette, Detroit, MI 48226; (313) 226-7290

Houston
333 W. Loop North, Suite 300, Houston, TX 77024; (713) 681-1771

Los Angeles
350 S. Figueroa St., Suite 800, Los Angeles, CA 90071; (213) 894-2650

Miami
8400 NW 53rd St., Miami, FL 33166; (305) 591-4870

Newark
806 Federal Office Building, Newark, NJ 07102; (201) 645-6060

New Orleans
1661 Canal St., Suite 2200, New Orleans, LA 70112; (504) 589-3894

New York
555 W. 57th St., Suite 1900, New York, NY 10019; (212) 399-5151

Philadelphia
10224 William J. Green Federal Building, Philadelphia, PA 19106; (215) 597-9530

Phoenix
One N. First St., Suite 201, Phoenix, AZ 85004; (602) 261-4866

San Diego
402 W. 35th St., National City, CA 92050; (619) 585-4200

San Francisco
450 Golden Gate Ave., Room 12215, P.O. Box 36035, San Francisco, CA 94102; (415) 556-6771

Seattle
220 W. Mercer, Suite 301, Seattle, WA 98119; (206) 442-5443

St. Louis
7911 Forsythe Blvd., Suite 500, United Missouri Bank Bldg. St. Louis, MO 63015; (314) 425-3241

Washington, DC
400 Sixth St., SW, Room 2558, Washington, DC 20024; (202) 724-7834

* Drugs-in-the Workplace

Federal Bureau of Investigation
U.S. Department of Justice
9th St. and Pennsylvania Ave., NW
Washington, DC 20535 (202) 324-3000

Each of the 58 Federal Bureau of Investigation (FBI) field offices have a Special Agent (SA) Drug Demand Reduction Coordinator to the FBI's drugs-in-the-workplace efforts. The FBI coordinator may assist drug prevention efforts, for example, educational programs; employee assistance programs; supervisory training; and drug testing.

* Drug Smuggling Hotline

Interdiction Committee
U.S. Customs Service
U.S. Department of the Treasury
1301 Constitution Ave., NW
Washington, DC 20229 (800) BE-ALERT

The Zero Tolerance program helps you notify authorities if you witness drug smuggling activities in your area. By calling the number above, authorities will be contacted, and the network will contact your local federal officials.

* Drug Sniffing Dogs

Canine Training Center
U.S. Customs Service
U.S. Department of the Treasury
HCR Box 7
Front Royal, VA 22630 (202) 566-8188

The Customs Canine Enforcement Training Center is about 70 miles west of Washington, DC, in Front Royal, VA. The dogs and officers are trained by Customs canine enforcement officers with professional experience in the field. The dogs are taught to detect concealed narcotics and dangerous drugs, while the officer is instructed in law enforcement and in detecting the dog's alert signals when contraband is discovered. Dogs are obtained from animal shelters around the country or from individual owners. Canine enforcement teams assigned to seaports and airports alternate between examining aircraft, vessels, baggage, cargo, and mail. Teams stationed at land border crossings devote their time to examining vehicles and merchandise entering the United States.

* Extraditions

U.S. Marshals Service
U.S. Department of Justice
600 Army Navy Dr.
Arlington, VA 22202 (202) 307-9100

The Marshals Service acts as the government's arm for reaching out and returning fugitives to the United States to face charges and put an end to their illegal activities.

* FBI Special Agent Drug Demand Reduction

Federal Bureau of Investigation (FBI)
9th St. and Pennsylvania Ave., NW
Washington, DC 20535 (202) 324-3000

The primary responsibility of the FBI is its cooperative efforts with the Drug Enforcement Agency to investigate drug matters and drug trafficking involvement by organized crime. The FBI conducts court authorized electronic surveillance and drug-related financial and public corruption investigations. Each of the 56 FBI field offices have a Special Agent (SA) Drug Demand Reduction Coordinator to carry forward the FBI's Drug Demand Reduction Program and

Be patient. If any phone number is incorrect, call (area code) 555-1212 and request the new listing.

Law Enforcement and Prosecution

the FBI's drugs-in-the-workplace efforts. These FBI Drug Demand Reduction Coordinators are also listed in the Experts Chapter.

F.B.I. SA James Caverly
U.S. Post Office and Courthouse
5th Floor, 45 Broadway
Albany, NY 12201-1219
(518) 465-7551

F.B.I. SA James Garay
301 Grand Ave., NE
Albuquerque, NM 87192
(505) 247-1555

F.B.I. SA Billy G. Andrews
Suite 6
222 W. 7th Ave.
Anchorage, AK 99513-7598
(907) 276-4441

F.B.I. SA Frank Pickens
2635 Century Center Parkway
Atlanta, GA 30345
(404) 679-9000

F.B.I. SA Joseph Monroe
7142 Ambassador Rd.
Baltimore, MD 21207
(301) 265-8080

(2) F.B.I. SA Ashley C. Curry and G. Wray Morse
Room 1400
2121 Building
Birmingham, AL 35203
(205) 252-7705

F.B.I. SA Matthew J. Cronin
J.F.K. Federal Office Bldg.
Boston, MA 02203
(617) 742-5533

F.B.I. SA Bernard Walsh
Room 1400
Federal Office Bldg.
111 W. Huron St.
Buffalo, NY 14202
(716) 856-7800

F.B.I. SA Gerard D. Sullivan
6010 Kenley Lane
Charlotte, NC 28217
(704) 529-1030

F.B.I. SA Terri Beck
Room 905
E.M. Dirksen Federal Office Bldg.
219 S. Dearborn St.
Chicago, IL 60604
(312) 431-1333

F.B.I. SA David L. Lichtenfeld
Room 9023
Federal Office Bldg.
550 Main St.
Cincinnati, OH 45202
(513) 421-4310

F.B.I. SA Robert L. Hawk
Room 3005
Federal Office Bldg.
1240 E. 9th St.
Cleveland, OH 44199
(216) 522-1400

F.B.I. SA James H. Davis
Suite 1357
Strom Thurmond Federal Bldg.

1835 Assembly St.
Columbia, SC 29201
(803) 254-3011

F.B.I. SA Thomas Westberg
Suite 300
1801 N. Lamar
Dallas, TX 75202
(214) 720-2200

F.B.I. SA Alison King
Room 1823
Federal Office Bldg.
Denver, CO 80202
(303) 629-7171

F.B.I. SA Henry W. Glaspie, III
P.V. McNamara Federal Office Bldg.
477 Michigan Ave.
Detroit, MI 48226
(313) 965-2323

F.B.I. SA Hector Armijo
Suite C-600
700 E. San Antonio Ave.
El Paso, TX 79901
(915) 533-7451

F.B.I. SA Vincent John McNally
Room 4307
Kalanianaole Federal Office Bldg.
300 Ala Moana Blvd.
Honolulu, HI 96850
(808) 521-1411

F.B.I. SA Charles Kearney, Jr.
Suite 200
2500 East T.C. Jester
Houston, TX 77008
(713) 868-2266

F.B.I. SA Walter L. Setmeyer, Jr.
Room 679
Federal Office Bldg.
575 N. Pennsylvania St.
Indianapolis, IN 46204
(317) 639-3301

F.B.I. SA Laura Lee Henry
Suite 1553
Federal Office Bldg.
100 W. Capitol St.
Jackson, MS 39269
(601) 948-5000

F.B.I. SA James Stanton
4th Floor Oaks V
7820 Arlington Expressway
Jacksonville, FL 32211
(904) 721-1211

F.B.I. SA Dennis J. Glenn
Room 300
U.S. Courthouse
Kansas City, MO 64106
(816) 221-6100

F.B.I. SA A. Wayne Baker
6th Floor
710 Locust St.
Knoxville, TN 37901
(615) 544-0751

F.B.I. SA Debbie Calhoun
700 E. Charleston Blvd.
Las Vegas, NV 89104
(702) 385-1281

Be patient. If any phone number is incorrect, call (area code) 555-1212 and request the new listing.

Drugs and Chemical Dependence

F.B.I. SA Phyllis Cournan
Suite 200
2 Financial Centre
10825 Financial Pkwy.
Little Rock, AR 72201
(501) 221-9100

F.B.I. SA Brent Braun
Federal Office Bldg.
11000 Wilshire Blvd.
Los Angeles, CA 90024
(213) 477-6565

F.B.I. SA William S. Cheek, Jr.
Room 500
Federal Office Bldg.
600 Martin Luther King Pl.
Louisville, KY 40202
(502) 583-3941

F.B.I. SA Joseph F. DeBiaggio
Room 841
Clifford Davis Federal Office Bldg.
167 N. Main St.
Memphis, TN 38103
(901) 525-7373

F.B.I. SA Gordon McNeill
16320 NW Second Ave.
N. Miami Beach, FL 33169
(305) 944-9101

F.B.I. SA Dale G. Mueller
Room 700
Federal Office Bldg. and
U.S. Courthouse
517 E. Wisconsin Ave.
Milwaukee, WI 53202
(414) 276-4684

F.B.I. SA Dag Sohlberg
5-1100, 111 Washington Ave. S,
Minneapolis, MN 55401
(612) 376-3200

F.B.I. SA David A. Chaney
One St. Louis Centre
1 St. Louis St.
Mobile, AL 36602
(205) 438-3674

F.B.I. SA James Kyle
Gateway 1
Market St.
Newark, NJ 07102
(201) 622-5613

F.B.I. SA Joseph W. Butchka
Federal Office Bldg.
150 Court St.
New Haven, CT 06510
(203) 777-6311

F.B.I. SA Ronald R. Travis
Suite 2200
1250 Poydras St.
New Orleans, LA 70112
(504) 522-4671

F.B.I. SA Louis Stith
26 Federal Plaza
New York, NY 10278
(212) 553-2700

F.B.I. SA Joseph G. O'Brien
Room 839
200 Granby St.

Norfolk, VA 23510
(804) 623-3111

F.B.I. SA Dan L. Vogel
Suite 1600
50 Penn Plaza
Oklahoma City, OK 73118
(405) 842-7471

F.B.I. SA Jim W. Isom
Room 7401
Federal Office Bldg. and
U.S. Courthouse
215 N. 17th St.
Omaha, NE 68102
(402) 348-1210

F.B.I. SA James T. McAleer
William J. Green, Jr. Federal
Office Bldg.
600 Arch St.
Philadelphia, PA 19106
(215) 629-0800

F.B.I. SA John J. Callahan
Suite 400
210 E. Indiaola
Phoenix, AZ 85012
(602) 279-5511

F.B.I. SA David J. Kwait
Room 1300
Federal Office Bldg.
1000 Liberty Ave.
Pittsburgh, PA 15222
(412) 471-2000

F.B.I. SA C. Ronald J. Makinson
Crown Plaza Bldg.
1500 SW 1st Ave.
Portland, OR 97201
(503) 224-4181

F.B.I. SA Wayne Smith
111 Greencourt Rd.
Richmond, VA 23228
(804) 261-1044

F.B.I. SA Thomas P. Griffin
Federal Office Bldg.
2800 Cottage Way
Sacramento, CA 95825
(916) 481-9110

F.B.I. SA John M. Mauzey
Room 2704
Federal Office Bldg.
1520 Market St.
St. Louis, MO 63103
(314) 241-5357

F.B.I. SA E. Ronald J. Van Vranken
Room 3203
Federal Office Bldg.
125 S. State St.
Salt Lake City, UT 84138
(801) 355-7521

F.B.I. SA April Hall
Room 433
Old Post Office Bldg.
615 E. Houston
San Antonio, TX 78205
(512) 225-6741

F.B.I. SA Ronald G. Orrantia
Room 6S-31

Be patient. If any phone number is incorrect, call (area code) 555-1212 and request the new listing.

Law Enforcement and Prosecution

Federal Office Bldg.
880 Front St.
San Diego, CA 92188
(619) 231-1122

F.B.I. SA Thomas Anderson
450 Golden Gate Ave.
San Francisco, CA 94102
(415) 553-7400

F.B.I. SA Jesus Marti
Room 526
U.S. Courthouse and Federal
Office Bldg.
Hato Rey, PR 00918
(809) 754-6000

F.B.I. SA Richard Thurston
Room 710
Federal Office Bldg.
915 Second Ave.
Seattle, WA 98174
(206) 622-0460

F.B.I. SA DeWayne Wright
400 W. Monroe St., Suite 400
Springfield, IL 62704
(217) 522-9675

F.B.I. SA Maria Vazquez
Room 610
Federal Office Bldg.
500 Zack St.
Tampa, FL 33602
(813) 228-7661

F.B.I. SA Samuel Feemster
Washington Metropolitan Field Office
1900 Half St.
Washington, DC 20535
(202) 324-3000

* Federal Prosecutors

Executive Office for United States Attorneys
U.S. Department of Justice
Tenth Street and Pennsylvania Avenue NW
Washington, DC 20530 (202) 514-2000

The U.S. Attorneys conduct the prosecution in Federal court of drug trafficking and connected illegal activities. They provide coordination of major drug investigations to ensure that the court cases produced will be successfully prosecuted.

* Federal and Local Law Enforcement Prosecutors Coordination

Executive Office for United States Attorneys
U.S. Department of Justice
Tenth Street and Constitution Avenue NW
Washington, DC 20530 (202) 514-2000

Established Law Enforcement Coordinating Committees (LECCs) are composed of the heads of Federal, state and local law enforcement and prosecutorial agencies who collectively assess the crime problems in each district and determine how best to use available resources to attach those problems. Cross-designation of local prosecutors as Federal prosecutors is now a frequent occurrence in cooperative investigations and prosecutions.

* Firearms and Drug Trafficking

Bureau of Alcohol, Tobacco, and Firearms (ATF)
650 Massachusetts Ave., NW
Washington, DC 20226 (202) 927-7777

ATF is pursuing drug-related violations of Federal law concerning firearms, destructive devices and explosives. ATF's resources include undercover agents, national response bomb scene investigation teams, an international firearms identification and tracking system, a worldwide explosives incident data bank and

tracking capability, auditors, and agents with experience in investigating complex RICO and conspiracy cases.

* Forest Service Anonymous Witness Reporting System

U.S. Forest Service
701-RP-E
P.O. Box 96090
Washington, DC 20090 (800) 782-7463

"Forest Service National Anonymous Witness Reporting System" is toll free nationwide "hotline" telephone number for the purpose of receiving confidential information related to drug and other criminal law violations occurring in the National Forest System, and providing this information to key contacts in the Forest Service. Rewards of up to $5000 may be given witnesses who report information leading to the seizure of controlled substances and/or for apprehension of suspects.

* Fugitive Apprehension

U.S. Marshals Service
U.S. Department of Justice
600 Army Navy Dr.
Arlington, VA 22202 (202) 307-9100

As the U.S. Department of Justice agency with primary investigative responsibility for most Federal fugitives, the Marshals Service devotes considerable resources toward apprehending those fugitives with drug-related charges and backgrounds. The Drug Enforcement Administration has transferred all its fugitive cases to the Service.

* Grants for Public Agencies and Non-Profits

Bureau of Justice Assistance
U.S. Department of Justice
633 Indiana Ave., NW
Washington, DC 20531 (202) 514-6278

The Bureau of Justice Assistance has a Discretionary Grant Program which provides assistance to public agencies and private nonprofit organizations for: 1) demonstration programs that, in view of previous research or experience, are likely to be successful in more than one jurisdiction. 2) Educational and training programs for criminal justice personnel and technical assistance to States and units of local government. 3) Projects that are national or multistate in scope, and that address the 18 authorized purposes of the Anti-Drug Abuse Act of 1986.

* Herbicides for Narcotic Plants International Eradication

USDA Agricultural Research Service (ARS)
Building 302
BARC-E
10300 Baltimore Ave.
Beltsville, MD 20705-2350 (301) 504-9403

ARS works with the State Department's Bureau of International Narcotics Matters and the Drug Enforcement Agency to determine the efficacy as well as the environmental impact of using herbicides in eradicating narcotic plants. The Agricultural Attaches posted in some drug producing countries are involved directly with local narcotic plant eradication programs.

* High-Level Drug Traffickers

Narcotics and Dangerous Drugs Section
Criminal Division
U.S. Department of Justice
700 Army Navy Drive
Arlington, VA 22202 (202) 307-4132

This section investigates and prosecutes high-level drug traffickers and members of criminal organizations involved in the importation, manufacture, shipment or distribution of illicit narcotics and dangerous drugs, with particular emphasis on litigation attacking the financial bases of those criminal organizations.

* Highway Safety and Enforcement Nationwide

National Highway Traffic Safety Administration (NHTSA)
400 Seventh St., SW
Washington, DC 20590 (202) 366-9550

The Drug Recognition Program is a program being conducted by National Highway Traffic Safety Administration (NHTSA) and the Bureau of Justice

Be patient. If any phone number is incorrect, call (area code) 555-1212 and request the new listing.

Drugs and Chemical Dependence

Assistance. It is a means of improving enforcement of drug-impaired driving violations. The program trains police officers as Drug Recognition Experts (DREs), enabling the officers to develop skills in evaluating the drivers condition and securing evidence for conviction. The Governors' Highway Safety Representatives and Coordinators may be contacted for those who are interested in exploring the possibilities of implementing this program.

Alabama
Representative: Gene Anderson, Director, Dept. of Economic and Community Affairs, 401 Adams Ave., P.O. Box 5690, Montgomery, AL 36103-5690; (205) 242-8672
Coordinator: Kater Williams and James Quinn, Highway and Traffic Safety, Law Enforcement and Planning Division, 401 Adams Ave., P.O. Box 5690, Montgomery, AL 36103-5690; (205) 242-5897

Alaska
Representative and Coordinator: Gayle Horetski, Director, Highway Safety and Planning Agency, Department of Public Safety, 450 Whittier St., P.O. Box N, Juneau, AK 99811; (907) 465-4322

Arizona
Representative: R.J. "Rick" Ayers, Office of Highway Safety, 3010 N. Second St., Suite 105, Phoenix, AZ 85012; (602) 223-2359
Coordinator: Howard Adams, Office of Highway Safety, 3010 N. Second St., Suite 105, Phoenix, AZ 85012; (602) 223-2359

Arkansas
Representative: Maurice Smith, Director, Arkansas State Highway and Transportation Department, P.O. Box 2261, Little Rock, AK 72203, (501) 569-2648
Coordinator: Mike Selig, Manager, Traffic Safety Division; (501) 569-2231

California
Representative: Peter O'Rourke, Director, Office of Traffic Safety, Business and Transportation Agency, 700 Franklin Blvd., Suite 330, Sacramento, CA 95823; (916) 445-0527
Coordinator: Ray Biancalana, Office of Traffic Safety, Business and Transportation Agency, 700 Franklin Blvd., Suite 330, Sacramento, CA 95823; (916) 445-0527

Colorado
Representative: Dr. A. Ray Chamberlain, (303) 757-9201
Coordinator: John Conger, Director, Division of Highway Safety, 4201 E. Arkansas Ave., Denver, CO 80222; (303) 757-9440

Connecticut
Representative and Coordinator: Susan C. Maloney, Governor's Representative, Bureau of Highways, 24 Wolcott Hill Road, P.O. Box Drawer A, Wethersfield, CT 06109; (203) 666-4343

Delaware
Representative: Colonel Clifford M. Graviet, Rt. 13, P.O. Box 430, Dover, DE 19901; (302) 739-5911
Coordinator: Lt. Paul Stafford, Rt. 13, P.O. Box 430, Dover, DE 19901; (302) 739-5613

District of Columbia
Representative: Esther Hager Francis, Director, Department of Public Works, 2000 14th St., NW, 6th Floor, Washington, DC 20009; (202) 939-8000
Coordinator: Carole A. Lewis, Highway Safety Program; (202) 939-8018

Florida
Representative: Frank Carlile, Department of Transportation, 605 Suwanne St., MS-57, Tallahassee, FL 32399-0450; (904) 922-5820
Coordinator: Billy G. Morris, Department of Transportation, 605 Suwanne St., MS-53; (904) 488-3546

Georgia
Representative and Coordinator: Dr. Thomas L. Coleman, Governor's Office of Highway Safety, 100 Peachtree St., Suite 2000, Atlanta, GA 30303; (404) 656-6996

Hawaii
Representative: Rex D. Johnson, Department of Transportation, 869 Punchbowl St., Honolulu, HI 96813; (808) 587-2150
Coordinator: Lawrence Hao, Director, Motor Vehicle Safety Office, 1505 Dillingham Blvd., Room 214, Honolulu, HI 96817; (808) 832-5820

Idaho
Representative: Marc Johnson, Governor's Highway Safety Representative, Governor's Office, State House Mail, Boise, ID, (208) 344-2100
Coordinator: Marie Bishop, Transportation Department, P.O. Box 7129, 3311 W. State St., Boise ID; (208) 334-8101

Illinois
Representative: Melvin H. Smith, Division of Traffic Safety, Department of Transportation, P.O. Box 19245, 3215 Executive Park Dr., Springfield, IL 62794; (217) 782-4972
Coordinator: Larry Wort, Bureau of Safety Programs; (217) 782-4974

Indiana
Representative: Bobby Small, State House, Room 206, Indianapolis, Indiana 46204; (317) 232-2588
Coordinator: J. Thomas Koutsoumpas, Director, Office of Traffic Safety, ISTA Building, Suite 330, 150 West Market, Indianapolis, Indiana 46204; (317) 232-4220

Iowa
Representative: Paul H. Wieck, Iowa Department of Public Safety, Wallace State Office Bldg., Des Moines, IA 50319; (515) 281-5104
Coordinator: J. Michael Laski, Governor's Traffic Safety Bureau; (515) 281-8400

Kansas
Representative: Michael Johnston, Department of Transportation, Docking St. Office Building, 7th Floor, Topeka, KS 66612; (913) 296-3461
Coordinator: Rosalie Thornburgh, Transportation Safety Administrator; (913) 296-3756

Kentucky
Representative: Billy G. Wellman, State Police Headquarters, 919 Versailles Rd., Frankfort, KY 40601-9980; (502) 695-6300
Coordinator: David H. Salyers, Highway Safety Standards Branch; (502) 695-6356

Louisiana
Representative: Betty Theis, Highway Safety Commission, P.O. Box 66336, Baton Rouge, LA 70896; (504) 925-6991
Coordinator: Sue Dixon (504) 925-6846

Maine
Representative and Coordinator: Richard Perkins, Department of Public Safety, 36 Hospital St., Augusta, ME 04330; (207) 582-8776

Maryland
Representative: O. James Lighthizer, Secretary of Transportation, P.O. Box 8755, BWI International Airport, Baltimore, MD 21240-0755; (410) 859-7397
Coordinator: Dennis Atkins, Division of Transportation Safety; (410) 584-7697

Massachusetts
Representative and Coordinator: Nancy J. Luther, Governor's Highway Safety Bureau, 100 Cambridge Street, Room 2104, Boston, MA 02202; (617) 727-5073

Michigan
Representative and Coordinator: Thomas Krycinski, Office of Highway Safety Planning, 300 S. Washington Square, Suite 300, Lansing, MI 48913; (517) 334-5210

Minnesota
Representative: Thomas Frost, Department of Public Safety, Transportation Bldg., St. Paul, MN 55155; (612) 296-6642
Coordinator: Thomas A. Boerner, Director of Traffic Safety; (612) 296-3804

Mississippi
Representative and Coordinator: Donald O'Cain, 301 W. Pearl St., Jackson, MI 39203-3085; (601) 949-2225

Missouri
Representative: Arvid E. West, Jr., Department of Public Safety, P.O. Box 104808, 311 Ellis Boulevard, Jefferson City, Missouri 65101-4808; (314) 751-7643
Coordinator: Richard Echols, Deputy Director; (314) 751-4161

Montana
Representative and Coordinator: Albert E. Goke, Highway Traffic Safety Division, Department of Justice, 303 N. Roberts, Helena, MT 59620; (406) 444-3412

Be patient. If any phone number is incorrect, call (area code) 555-1212 and request the new listing.

Law Enforcement and Prosecution

Nebraska
Representative: Jack C. Conrad, Department of Motor Vehicles, P.O. Box 94612, Lincoln, NE 68509; (402) 471-2281
Coordinator: Fred E. Zwonechek, Highway Safety Program Office, State House Station 94612; (402) 471-2515

Nevada
Representative: James P. Weller, Department of Motor Vehicles, 555 Wright Way, Carson City, NV 89711-0990; (702) 687-5375
Coordinator: Marlen Schultz, Traffic Safety Division; (702) 687-5720

New Hampshire
Representative and Coordinator: John B. McDuffee, Highway Safety Agency, 117 Manchester St., Concord, NH 03301; (603) 271-2131

New Jersey
Representative and Coordinator: James Arena, Office of Highway Traffic Safety, Department of Law and Public Safety, CN048, Trenton, NJ 08625; (609) 588-3750

New Mexico
Representative: Louis J. Medrano, Highway and Transportation Dept., P.O. Box 1149, Santa Fe, NM 87504-1149; (505) 827-5109
Coordinator: John D. Fenner, Traffic Safety Bureau; (505) 827-0427

New York
Representative: Patricia B. Adduci, Department of Motor Vehicles, Empire State Plaza, Swan St. Bldg., Albany, NY 12228; (508) 474-0841
Coordinator: William G. Rourke, Traffic Safety Committee; (518) 474-3135

North Carolina
Representative and Coordinator: Paul B. Jones, Governor's Highway Safety Program, 215 E. Lane St., Raleigh, NC 27601; (919) 733-3083

North Dakota
Representative: Richard J. Backes, Director, Highway Department, 608 E. Boulevard Ave., Bismarck, ND 58505-0178; (701) 224-2581
Coordinator: Mylo J. Hehloff, Driver License and Traffic Safety; (701) 224-2600

Ohio
Representative: Charles Shipley, Department of Highway Safety, P.O. Box 7167, Columbus, OH 42366-0563; (614) 466-3383
Coordinator: Laura Ludwig, Office of the Governor's, Highway Safety Representative; (614) 466-3250

Oklahoma
Representative and Coordinator: Dr. Tim W. Mauldin, Jr., Highway Safety Office, 3223 N. Lincoln, Oklahoma City, OK 73105; (405) 521-3314

Oregon
Representative: Donald E. Forbes, Oregon Traffic Safety Commission, 135 Transportation Bldg., Salem, OR 97310; (503) 378-6388
Coordinator: Edward Marqes, (503) 378-3669

Pennsylvania
Representative: Mario D. Pirritano, Deputy Secretary for Safety Administration, 1200 Transportation and Safety Building, Harrisburg, PA 17120; (717) 787-3928
Coordinator: Thomas E. Bryer, Center for Highway Safety, 215 Transportation and Safety Bldg; (717) 787-7350

Puerto Rico
Representative: Dr. Hermenegildo Ortiz-Quinones, Secretary of Transportation and Public Works, Box 41269, Minillas Station, Santurce, PR 00940; (809) 726-6670
Coordinator: Lenidas Ramirez, Traffic Safety Commission, Box 41289, Minillas Station; (809) 723-3590

Rhode Island
Representative: Daniel P. Fanning, Department of Transportation, State Office Bldg., Smith St., Providence, RI 02903; (401) 277-2481
Coordinator: Edward J. Walsh, Gov's Office of Highway Safety, 345 Harris Ave., Providence, RI 02909; (401) 277-3024

South Carolina
Representative and Coordinator: Perry Brown, Office of Highway Safety Programs, 1205 Pendleton Street, Room 453, Columbia, SC 29201; (803) 734-0421

South Dakota
Representative: Jeff Stingley, Department of Commerce and Regulation, 910 E. Sioux Ave., Pierre, SD 57501; (605) 773-3178
Coordinator: Jeff Holden, State and Community Programs, Dept. of Commerce and Regulation, 118 West Capitol Avenue, Pierre, SD 57501; (605) 773-3675

Tennessee
Representative: James Evans, Department of Transportation, 505 Deaderick St., Suite 700, Nashville, TN 37243-0341; (615) 741-2848
Coordinator: Clarence Elkins, Governor's Highway Safety Program; (615) 741-2589

Texas
Representative: Arnold W. Oliver, State Dept. of Highways and Public Transportation, 125 E. 11 St., Austin, TX 78701; (512) 465-6751
Coordinator: Gary Trietsch, Traffic Safety Section (D-18STO); (512) 465-6751

Utah
Representative: D. Douglas Bodrero, Department of Public Safety, 4501 S. 2700 West, Salt Lake City, UT 84119; (801) 965-4463
Coordinator: Dick Howard, Highway Safety Division; (801) 965-4409

Vermont
Representative: Michael D. Griffes, Secretary of Transportation, 133 State St., Montpelier, VT 05603-001; (802) 828-2011
Coordinator: Jean Johnson, Exec. Asst. to the Secretary of Transportation, Vermont Highway Safety Program; (802) 828-2665

Virginia
Representative: Donald E. Williams, Department of Motor Vehicles, P.O. Box 27412, Richmond, VA 23269; (804) 357-6602
Coordinator: William Leighty, Deputy Commissioner for Transportation Safety; (804) 357-6614

Washington
Representative: Chuck Hayes, Traffic Safety Commission, 1000 S. Cherry St., MS/PD-11, Olympia, WA 98504; (206) 753-6197
Coordinator: Steve Lind, Traffic Safety Commission; (206) 753-6197

West Virginia
Representative: James Albert, Criminal Justice and Highway Safety Office, 1204 Kanawha Blvd., Charleston, WV 25301; (304) 558-8814
Coordinator: James R. Grate

Wisconsin
Representative: Charles Thompson, Department of Transportation, Office of Highway Safety, P.O. Box 7910, 4802 Sheboygan Ave., Madison, WI 53707; (608) 266-1113
Coordinator: David Manning; (608) 267-3710

Wyoming
Representative: Donald G. Pruter, State Highway Safety Engineer, Wyoming Highway Safety Department, P.O. Box 1708, Cheyenne, WY 82002-9019; (307) 777-4450

Virgin Islands
Representative and Coordinator: Enrique Richards, Lagoon St. Complex, Frediksted, St. Croix, Virgin Islands 08840; (809) 772-5820

* Immigration and Naturalization Service (INS)

Immigration and Naturalization Service
425 I St., NW
Washington, DC 20536 (202) 514-2000

The Immigration and Naturalization Service (INS) is responsible for control of illegal entry of persons along our borders, and assists in apprehending smugglers. The Border Patrol is active in drug abuse education and prevention, conducting demonstrations with "drug sniffing dogs" in classrooms and providing drug education information to students.

* Interagency Law Enforcement Training Center

Federal Law Enforcement Training Center
Glynco, GA 31524 (912) 267-2100

The Center is the interagency training facility serving 63 Federal law enforcement organizations. The major training effort is in the area of basic programs to teach common areas of law enforcement skills to police and investigative personnel.

Drugs and Chemical Dependence

The Center offers selective, highly specialized training programs to State and local officers.

* International Fugitives and International Police

International Criminal Police Organization
U.S. National Central Bureau
Washington, DC 20530 (202) 272-8383

This Bureau serves as the communications link among more than 20,000 state and local law enforcement organizations and as the U.S. liaison to INTERPOL. It investigates large-scale narcotics offenses and apprehends international fugitives often involving arrests and extraditions to the countries where the crimes were committed.

* Justice Department Anti-Drug Coordination

Office of Justice Programs (OJP)
U.S. Department of Justice
633 Indiana Ave., NW
Washington, DC 20531 (202) 307-5933

This office is responsible for policy coordination and general management responsibilities for five OJP bureaus or offices. The Bureau of Justice Assistance (BJA) offers technical assistance to State and local units of government to control crime and drug abuse and to improve the criminal justice system. The Bureau of Justice Statistics (BJS) maintains statistics about crime, its perpetrators and victims, and the operation of the criminal justice system at the Federal, State and local level. The Office of Juvenile Justice and Delinquency Prevention attempts to prevent drug abuse among youth at high risk. The Office for Victims of Crime oversees the Crime Victims Fund which is money comes from fines of Federal criminals. These funds are made available to each State, the District of Columbia, and six Territories to support expanded and improved State victim assistance and compensation programs. The National Victims Resource Center maintains a data base that describes more than 2,000 victim assistance and family violence programs throughout the country.

* Juvenile Delinquency National Trends

Office of Juvenile Justice and Delinquency Prevention (OJJDP)
Office of Justice Programs, U.S. Department of Justice
633 Indiana Ave., NW
Washington, DC 20531 (202) 307-0751

The Research and Program Development Division sponsors research on national trends in juvenile delinquency and serious juvenile crime, prevention strategies, and the juvenile justice system.

* Juvenile Justice Professionals Training

Office of Juvenile Justice and Delinquency Prevention (OJJDP)
Office of Justice Programs, U.S. Department of Justice
633 Indiana Ave., NW
Washington, DC 20531 (202) 307-0751

The Training, Dissemination, and Technical Assistance Division (TDTAD) is responsible for programs that train personnel who work with juvenile offenders and their families.

* Law Enforcement Explorer Programs

Office of Juvenile Justice and Delinquency Prevention (OJJDP)
Office of Justice Programs, U.S. Department of Justice
633 Indiana Ave., NW
Washington, DC 20531 (202) 307-0751

The Training, Dissemination, and Technical Assistance Division (TDTAD) oversees the Exploring Careers in Law Enforcement and Criminal Justice. About 42,000 youths, both male and female, are involved in Law Enforcement Explorer programs, which recently initiated an anti-substance abuse program.

* Law Enforcement Policy Resource Center

Law Enforcement Policy Resource Center
U.S. Department of Justice
633 Indiana Ave., NW
Washington, DC 20531 (202) 307-5933

The Center develops model policies for law enforcement agencies, as well as program briefs and model legislation regarding issues of interest to law enforcement policy makers.

* Mafia and Organized Crime Investigations

U.S. Marshals Service
U.S. Department of Justice
600 Army Navy Drive
Arlington VA 22202 (202) 307-9100

The Marshals Service is a charter member of the Organized Crime Drug Enforcement (OCDE) Task Force with full-time investigators assigned to all 13 task force locations.

* Maritime Drug Smuggling Interdiction

U.S. Coast Guard (USCG)
2100 Second St., SW
Washington, DC 20593 (202) 267-2229

The Coast Guard is the only Federal agency with jurisdiction on the high seas as well as territorial waters and has greatly expanded efforts directed against maritime drug smugglers. USCG ships, boats, planes and helicopters conduct routine drug law enforcement patrols and special operations through the maritime arena. Coast Guard emphasis is on detecting and boarding vessels smuggling illicit drugs while still in transit to the United States. In support of its expansive role in interdiction, the Coast Guard maintains an extensive intelligence organization with heavy emphasis on drug trafficking.

* Military Drug Testing Program

Health Affairs
U.S. Department of Defense
Washington, DC OSD 20301-1155 (703) 545-6700

Health Affairs is responsible for drug testing programs for the military services. It is also responsible for conducting periodic surveys of illegal drug use among the military.

* Money Laundering Investigations

Internal Revenue Service (IRS)
U.S. Department of Treasury
1111 Constitution Ave., NW
Washington, DC 20224 (800) 829-1040

IRS supports drug law enforcement by pursuing income tax violations and money laundering related to the financial aspects of illegal drug trafficking. IRS agents trace the movement of funds to document the acquisition of forfeitable assets by drug traffickers. Using search warrants, IRS seizes various financial reports, including travel records, money orders, and cashier check receipts, which can reveal the concealment or illegal transfer of financial assets. The information gained through the warrants can lead to assets seizable under statutory forfeiture provisions.

* Narcotics Cultivation in Developing Countries

Agency for International Development
320 21st St., NW
Washington, DC 20523 (202) 647-4000

The Agency for International Development (AID) works with the International Narcotics Matters Bureau at the U.S. Department of State in designing and implementing foreign assistance programs related directly and indirectly to drug problems in developing nations. AID assistance is particularly focused on rural development programs in traditional growing regions. The alternative agricultural and other economic pursuits made possible by AID funds are, in many countries, the key to gaining their cooperation towards eliminating cultivation of illicit narcotics.

* Narcotics Identification Manual

Superintendent of Documents
Government Printing Office
Washington, DC 20402 (202) 783-3238

The manual, *Narcotics Identification Manual*, provides descriptions and color photographs to help you identify narcotics, depressants, stimulants, cannabis, hallucinogens, and crack. Included is a chart listing controlled substances, their uses, and effects. This manual sells for $4.25 (S/N 048-002-00101-0).

* Narcotic Plants Detection and Eradication

National Park Service
U.S. Department of Interior
Washington, DC (202) 619-7222

Be patient. If any phone number is incorrect, call (area code) 555-1212 and request the new listing.

Law Enforcement and Prosecution

The Service is responsible for enforcing the laws on Federal lands which prohibit cultivation of narcotic plants.

* National Forests Marijuana Eradication Program

U.S. Forest Service
14th St. and Independence Ave., SW
Washington, DC 20250 (202) 205-1760

The Forest Service assists the Drug Enforcement Agency in the national Domestic Marijuana Eradication and Suppression Program which promotes information sharing and provides training, equipment, investigative and aircraft support to state and local enforcement officers. Some 150 special agents are involved in the Forest Service's Law Enforcement Staff, which consists of 650 armed, uniformed law enforcement officers, who since passage of National Forest Drug Control Act in 1986, have authority under Title 21 arrest drug traffickers and producers.

* National Victims Resource Center

Office for Victims of Crime (OVC)
U.S. Department of Justice
633 Indiana Ave., NW
Washington, DC 20531 (202) 307-5983

A National Victims Resource Center at the National Criminal Justice Reference Service that provides victim-related publications, statistics, research, program referrals, and other information from its computerized data base. The Center collects and maintains information on programs throughout the United States that provide services to victims, on State victim/witness programs that receive funds under VOCA, and on Federal victim/witness programs.

* NOAA Drug Interdiction Efforts

National Oceanic and Atmospheric Administration (NOAA)
U.S. Department of Commerce
Washington, DC 20230 (202) 377-8090

Through the course of their regular activities, NOAA provides detection assistance for drug interdiction efforts.

* On-the-Job Drug Testing Videos

National Audiovisual Center
Customer Service Section
8700 Edgeworth Drive
Capitol Heights, MD 20743-3701 (301) 763-1896

National Clearinghouse for Alcohol and Drug Information
P.O. Box 2345
Rockville, MD 20847 (301) 468-8200

Drug Testing: Handle with Care describes the options available in designing a drug testing component as part of a comprehensive drug-free workplace program. Procedures addressing the needs of both the employer and the employee to ensure the accuracy and reliability of test results, for specimen collection and laboratory analysis, and a discussion of the critical role of the Medical Review Officer (MRO) are highlighted. Case studies of public/private, and unionized/nonunionized work environments with testing components are presented. This video is available in both employer and employee versions for sale and rental.

* Parole and Recidivism Rate

U.S. Parole Commission
5550 Friendship Blvd.
Chevy Chase, MD 20815 (301) 492-5990

The Parole Commission is investigating ways in which they may help break the link between crime and drug use in hopes of both reducing drug use and crime, but also of reducing the recidivism rate.

* Pentagon Drug Policy and Enforcement

U.S. Department of Defense
Office of Drug Policy and Enforcement
Washington, DC 20301-1155 (703) 545-6700

Drug policy and enforcement, including coordination of all DOD activities related to Federal drug abuse eradication; provision of Department resources and support to other agencies for drug law enforcement efforts; military and civilian drug testing policy; advice and assistance to the Secretary of Defense and other officials of the Department on anti-drug abuse aspects of departmental policy, plans and programs.

* Public Lands Special Drug Agents

Bureau of Land Management (BLM)
U.S. Department of Interior
Washington, DC 20240 (202) 208-5717

The Special Agents of BLM are responsible for enforcing Federal laws and regulations relating to the public lands and resources. This includes conducting criminal investigations and the ability to arrest violators. State Offices include:

Alaska
222 W. 7th Ave., #13, Anchorage, AK 99513-7599, Ed Spang, State Director (907) 271-5076; David Vickery, Public Affairs, (907) 271-5555

Arizona
3707 N. 7th St., P.O. Box 16563, Phoenix, AZ 85011, Les Rosenkrance, State Director, (602) 640-5501; Joanie Redfield, Public Affairs, (602)640-5504

BIFC
Boise Interagency Fire Center, 3905 Vista Ave., Boise, ID 83705, Jack Wilson, BLM Director, (208) 389-2446; Arnold Hartigan, Public Affairs, (208) 389-2457

California
2800 Cottage Way, E-2841, Sacramento, CA 95825, Ed Hastey, State Director, (916) 978-4743; Tony Staed, Public Affairs, (916) 978-4746

Colorado
2850 Youngfield St., Lakewood, CO 80215-7076, Bob Moore, State Director, (303) 239-3700; Marta Witt, Public Affairs, (303) 239-3667

Eastern States
7450 Boston Blvd., Springfield, VA 22153, Denise Meridith, State Director, (703) 440-1700; Terry Lewis, Public Affairs, (703) 440-1713

Idaho
3380 Americana Terrace, Boise, ID 83706, Del Vail, State Director, (208) 384-3001; Jack Sept, Public Affairs, (208) 384-3014

Montana
222 N. 32nd St., P.O. Box 36800, Billings, MT 59107, Bob Lawton, State Director, (406) 255-2904; Trudie Olson, Public Affairs, (406) 255-2913

Nevada
850 Harvard Way, P.O. Box 12000, Reno, NV 89520-0006, Billy Templeton, State Director, (702) 785-6590; Robert Stewart, Public Affairs, (702) 785-6586

New Mexico
1474 Rodeo Rd., P.O. Box 27115, Santa Fe, NM 87505-7115, Larry Woodard, State Director, (505) 438-7501; Lee Keesling, Public Affairs, (505) 438-7514

Oregon
1300 N.E. 44th Ave., P.O. Box 2965, Portland OR 97213, Dean Bibles, State Director, (503) 280-7024; Lauri Hennessey, Public Affairs, (503) 280-7287

PTC
Phoenix Training Center, 5050 N. 19th Ave., Suite 300, Phoenix, AR 85015, Lynn Engdahl, Manager, (602) 640-2651

Utah
324 South State St., CFS Finance Center Bldg., Suite 301, Salt Lake City, UT 84111-2303, James M. Parker, State Director, (801) 539-4010; Jerry Meredith, Public Affairs, (801) 539-4021

Wyoming
2515 Warren Ave., P.O. Box 1828, Cheyenne, WY 82001, Ray Brubaker, State Director, (307) 775-6001; Jay Guerin, Public Affairs, (307) 775-6011

* Public Housing Drug Eradication Grants

Howard Mortman
U.S. Department of Housing and Urban Development
Room 4114, P.O. Box 6424
Rockville, MD 20850 (202) 708-1197

HUD's Public Housing Drug Elimination Program - grant program for community-wide drug prevention programs

Be patient. If any phone number is incorrect, call (area code) 555-1212 and request the new listing.

Drugs and Chemical Dependence

* Prisoner Detention and Transportation System

U.S. Marshals Service
U.S. Department of Justice
600 Army Navy Drive
Arlington, VA 22202 (202) 307-9100

All persons arrested and detained by order of the Federal courts for prosecution on violations of Federal laws are placed into the custody of the Marshals Service. The Service's National Prisoner Transportation System is continually required to provide extraordinary security for the movement of major drug dealers to and from scheduled court appearances.

* Prisoners, Paroles, Sentencing Data

Data Center and Clearinghouse for Drugs and Crime
Office of Justice Programs, U.S. Department of Justice
633 Indiana Ave., NW (800) 666-3332
Washington, DC 20531 (202) 724-7782

The Data Center and Clearinghouse for Drugs and Crime was established by the Justice Department's Bureau of Justice Statistics and the Bureau of Justice Assistance to provide access to existing data on drug law enforcement and the justice system's treatment of drug offenders and nondrug offenders who are drug users. They will send a free 1992 directory. Free publications include:

Order Number / Title and Release Date
86223 Prisoners and Alcohol - 1/83
87575 Prisoners and Drugs - 3/83
87068 Report to the Nation - 1st Edition - 83
96501 Examining Recidivism - 85
96132 Pretrial Release and Misconduct - 1/85
97681 Felony Sentencing in 18 Local Jurisdictions - 5/85
99175 Jail Inmates, 1983 - 11/85
100582 Prison Admissions and Releases, 1983 - 86
101043 Sentencing and Time Served - 87
104916 Recidivism of Young Parolees - 5/87
105506 Report to the Nation - 2nd Edition - 88
105743 Sentencing Outcomes in 28 Felony Courts, 1985 - 87
108544 Time Served in Prison and on Parole, 1984 - 12/87
109686 Tracking Offenders, 1984 - 1/88
109926 Profile of State Prison Inmates - 1/88
109929 Pretrial Release and Detention: The Bail Reform Act of 1984 - 2/88
109945 Drunk Driving - 88
110643 Bureau of Justice Statistics Data Report 1987 - 88
111612 Sourcebook of Criminal Justice Statistics, 1987 - 88
111763 Drug Law Violators 1980-1986 - 6/88
111940 Drug Use and Crime - 7/88
113365 Survey of Youth in Custody - 9/88
114746 The Redesigned National Crime Survey: Selected New Data - 1/89
115210 Felony Sentences in State Courts, 1986 - 2/89
115749 Bureau of Justice Statistics Annual Report 1988 - 89
116261 Recidivism of Prisoners Released in 1983 - 3/89
116262 Bureau of Justice Statistics Data Report 1988 - 89
116315 Prisoners in 1988 - 4/89
118311 Federal Criminal Cases, 1980-87 - 7/89
94073 Drug Use and Pretrial Crime in the District of Columbia - 6/84
96668 Probing the Links Between Drugs and Crime - 2/85
98259 Use of Forfeiture Sanctions in Drug Cases - 85
98902 Interpol: Global Help in Fight Against Drugs - 9/85
100737 Drinking and Crime - 86
100741 Heroin - 87
100756 Project DARE: Teaching Kids to Say "No" - 3/86
102632 Employee Drug Testing Policies in Police Departments - 10/86
102668 Drugs and Crime: Controlling Use and Reducing Risk through Testing - 11/86
104555 Drug Trafficking - 87
104556 Drug Testing - 87
104557 Drug Education - 87
104865 Controlling Drug Abuse and Crime: A Research Update - 3/87
106992 Drugs and Crime: Current Federal Research - 8/88
107272 Drug Use Forecasting: New York 1984-1986 - 87
108560 Characteristics of Different Types of Drug Involved Offenders - 88
109957 Attorney General Announces NIJ DUF - 3/88

110423 Drug Use Forecasting Packet - 11/86
113915 A Criminal Justice System Strategy for Treating Cocaine-Heroin Abusing Offenders in Custody - 3/88
114730 Identifying Drug Users and Monitoring Them During Conditional Release - 2/88
115403 Street Level Drug Enforcement - 9/88
117999 In-Prison Programs for Drug-Involved Offenders - 7/89
106663 Intensive Supervision Probation and Parole - 88
113110 Reducing Crime by Reducing Drug Abuse - 6/88
114801 Implementing Project Dare: Drug Abuse Resistance Education - 6/88
116317 Drug Control and System Improvement Discretionary Grant Program - 1/89
116322 TASC: Implementing the Model - 9/88
116323 Treatment Alternatives to Street Crime - 1/88
117432 Drug Recognition Program - 89
117435 Report on Drug Control, 1988 - 89
118317 Estimating the Costs of Drug Testing - Pretrial Testing Program - 6/89
115416 Urinalysis as Part of a Treatment Alternatives to Street Crime Program - 7/88
999092 Data Center and Clearinghouse for Drugs and Crime brochure
999100 Drugs and Crime rolodex card

* Rewards for Information on Drug Traffickers Tax Evasion

Internal Revenue Service (IRS)
U.S. Department of Treasury
1111 Constitution Ave., NW
Washington, DC 20224 (800) 829-1040

Individuals who have information regarding drug traffickers that is of a financial nature can contact the Internal Revenue Service. If the information leads to a successful trial and unpaid taxes are received by the Internal Revenue Service, the informant is eligible to receive a reward (if the information given to the IRS was not obtainable elsewhere and was instrumental in the conviction). The reward varies and is based upon a percentage of assets retrieved. This is not an anonymous information tip system or reward system, but the IRS maintains that confidentiality is strictly enforced.

* Seized and Forfeited Assets

U.S. Marshals Service
U.S. Department of Justice
600 Army Navy Drive
Arlington, VA 22202 (202) 307-9100

The Marshal Service is responsible for the centralized management of the National Asset Seizure and Forfeiture Fund which includes uniform management procedures in the care, maintenance and disposal of seized and forfeited assets.

* U.S. Secret Service Involvement

U.S. Secret Service (USSS)
1800 G St., NW
Washington, DC 20223 (202) 435-7575

The USSS is involved in drug law enforcement investigations as a result of their following responsibilities including: any offense against the laws of the U.S. relating to currency, coins, obligations, and securities of the U.S. or of foreign governments; forgery and fraudulent negotiation or redemption of Federal Government checks, bonds, and other obligations or securities of the U.S.; offenders of laws pertaining to electronic funds transfer frauds, credit and debit card frauds, false identification documents or devices, computer access fraud, and U.S. Department of Agriculture food coupons, including authority to participate cares.

* Witness Security Protection

U.S. Marshals Service
U.S. Department of Justice
600 Army Navy Drive
Arlington, VA 22202 (202) 307-9100

The Federal Government's witness security program entails relocation, identity change and a range of other sophisticated services, including personal protection, in order for witnesses to contribute important testimony in drug court cases.

Be patient. If any phone number is incorrect, call (area code) 555-1212 and request the new listing.

Law and Social Justice General Sources

* *See also Drug and Chemical Dependence Chapter*
* *See also Careers and Workplace; Research Grants in Every Field Chapter*
* *See also Your Community; Money for Communities and Non-Profits Chapter*
* *See also Health and Medicine Chapter; Stress, Mental Illness and Family Violence Chapter*
* *See also Government Financial Help for Individuals Chapter*
* *See also Patents, Trademarks and Copyrights Chapter*

The U.S. Department of Justice is the most well-known law enforcement organization of the federal government, particularly with the much-publicized activities of the Antitrust Division, the FBI and the Drug Enforcement Agency. The department is the central collector of local and state crime statistics. Also housed within this large department is the Immigration and Naturalization Service. But there are many other resources including state and federal agencies which provide free legal assistance.

* Adjudication, Arrests and National Statistics

Bureau of Justice Statistics
U.S. Department of Justice
633 Indiana Ave., NW
Washington, DC 20531 (202) 307-0765

The U.S. is one of only a few developed countries that has no national court statistics. There are police statistics compiled annually that show the number of persons arrested in the U.S., and there are national prison statistics compiled annually on the number sent to prison. But there are no nationwide statistics that show what happens between arrest and imprisonment. The BJS National Judicial Reporting Program is a statistical series designed to close this gap in American criminal justice statistics. This program will make it possible to answer numerous questions about felony courts that cannot now be answered, such as:

Nationwide, how many persons were convicted of felonies last year?
How many convicted felons received a jury trial?
What percent of convicted felons were sentenced to prison?
What was the average prison sentence for drug trafficking?

Contact this office to find out more information about the status and availability of new national adjudication statistics.

* Administrative Law and Government Procedures

Administrative Conference of the United States
1220 L St., NW, Suite 500
Washington, DC 20037 (202) 254-7020

This government think tank explores ways to improve federal agencies administer regulations, entitlements, and other programs. The Conference studies adjudication, administrative law, governmental processes, judicial review, regulation, and rulemaking. It publishes *1988 Annual Report* and their newsletter, *Administrative Conference News*, which are available free to the public. Also available is the *Administrative Conference of the United States: A Bibliography 1968-1986.*

* AIDS and the Law

National Institute of Justice (NIJ)
NCJRS, Box 6000
Dept. AID (800) 851-3420
Rockville, MD 20850 (301) 251-5500 in DC

NIJ has the following publications and others on AIDS and legal issues available. Many of the documents are free of charge, while others are available for a modest fee. When ordering or inquiring about an NIJ publication, refer to its NCJ number.

HIV Infection and AIDS: Are You at Risk? 1992
AIDS and the Law Enforcement Officer (RIA). 1987, 6 pp. (NCJ 107541).
Voluntary HIV Counseling and Testing: Facts, Issues, and Answers, 1991.
The Cause, Transmission, and Incidence of AIDS (AIDS Bulletin). 1987, 4 pp. (NCJ 106678).
AIDS Prevention Guide. 1991.

Update on AIDS in Prisons and Jails 1991.
AIDS in Probation and Parole 1989.

* Antitrust Violations and Company Investigations

Legal Policy
Antitrust Division
U.S. Department of Justice
10th St. and Constitution Ave. NW
Room 3233
Washington, DC 20530 (202) 514-2512

A total case history of all antitrust investigations is available to the public. If you wish to know if a particular company is being, or ever has been, investigated for antitrust violations, and what the formal complaints were, you are welcome to thumb through the files. In addition, these files can tell you what types of violations have been investigated and what rulings have been brought down in each case. A complete transcript of pleadings, depositions, and summaries of legal procedures in all cases are available. These files are an invaluable source of legal history and precedents, and a perfect guide to business practices. For a photocopy of any portion of the Antitrust Case files, contact the Legal Procedure Unit at the above address.

* Antitrust Enforcement and the Consumer

Public Affairs
Antitrust Division
U.S. Department of Justice
10th St. and Constitution Ave., NW
Room 3107
Washington, DC 20530 (202) 324-2464

The free publication, *Antitrust Enforcement and the Consumer*, details general information on the how antitrust law helps the consumer, as well as specific descriptions of the Sherman and Clayton Acts, various cases the Justice Department has prosecuted and an explanation of how these violators cheated the consumer. The pamphlet also includes the addresses of all of the regional Antitrust Division offices and all of the Federal Trade Commission's regional offices throughout the country.

* Antitrust and Export Trading

Foreign Commerce Section
Antitrust Division
U.S. Department of Justice
10th St. and Constitution Ave., NW
Room 3264
Washington, DC 20530 (202) 514-2464

The United States' policy on foreign trade is developed and preserved by this office. Their staff and files are an incomparable source of information for anyone interested in United States trade and commerce, or the effect of foreign markets on our economy. Investors and bond salesmen, bankers and businessmen--

Be patient. If any phone number is incorrect, call (area code) 555-1212 and request the new listing.

Law and Social Justice

anyone who needs up-to-the-minute knowledge, even high-school students reporting on inflation--should start here. Congressmen are constantly in touch with the Foreign Commerce Section before voting on trade bills. Rising politicians who want to stand on their economic platform get their data here; voters should, too. In addition, this Section administers the Export Trading Act and works with the Commerce Department to issue all Export Trading Certificates.

* Antitrust Law and Joint Research Ventures

Superintendent of Documents
U.S. Government Printing Office
Washington, DC 20402 (202) 783-3238

The publication, *Antitrust Guide Concerning Research Joint Ventures*, describes the ways that corporate cooperation on research (joint ventures) can be pursued without violating antitrust laws. The *Guide* is available for $5.50 from the GPO.

* Arson, Burglary, and Other Crime Trends

Uniform Crime Reporting Section
Federal Bureau of Investigation
U.S. Department of Justice
9th and Pennsylvania Ave., NW, GRB
Washington, DC 20535 (202) 324-2614

Crime in the United States, an annual report, taken from over 17,000 law enforcement agencies and 98% of the country, is the ultimate information source on crime. Breaking crime down into 8 basic categories (arson, larceny, burglary, aggravated assault, forgery fraud, drugs, prostitution, gambling) the report gives an exact reading of the criminal trends in our country. It lists the crime rates by state, in rural and urban areas, by gender, race, and age. Police find it an invaluable source for crime analysis and lean on it heavily when projecting the year's budget or discussing allocation of manpower. Public policy makers refer to it when debating new programs or community services. This report is fundamental for making better laws, for helping sociologists chart trends, for journalists writing articles. It can even tell prospective homebuyers how safe their future neighborhood will be. The report includes complete listings of types of weapons used in crimes, motives, victim/offender relationships. Anything you could ever want to know about crime in this country is in this report.

* Arson Control and Clearinghouse

U.S. Fire Administration
16825 South Seton Ave.
Emmitsburg, MD 21727 (301) 447-1122

The Arson Resource Center is available to help answer your questions and locate resources related to arson. It was established several years ago by the U.S. Fire Administration, and has developed an impressive collection of arson-related materials. FEMA personnel and NETC students can borrow materials from the Center, and books and research reports are available to the general public through area libraries (interlibrary loan). Audio-visual and general references are stored in the Center for in-house use. The following publications and source materials on arson are available from the USFA free of charge:

Arson Resource Directory (#5-0087)
Rural Arson Control (#5-0110)
Establishing an Arson Strike Force (#5-0111)
Arson Prosecution: Issues and Strategies
America Burning Revisited
Fire and Arson Investigator's Field Index Directory

* Arson Incidents National Database

Arson Information Management Systems (AIMS)
Office of Fire Prevention and Arson Control
U.S. Fire Administration
16825 South Seton Ave.
Emmitsburg, MD 21727 (301) 447-1200

The Arson Information Management Systems (AIMS) is a computerized database for the recording of data from reported arson cases, and used to facilitate analysis of such data for use by investigators, emergency personnel, law enforcers, and others. For more information on AIMS, contact the office above.

* Arson Prevention Traveling Exhibit

Office of Fire Prevention and Arson Control
Federal Emergency Management Agency

16825 South Seton Ave.
Emmitsburg, MD 21727 (301) 447-1200

Arson Trailers tour the country to provide technical and educational assistance to State, local, and national fire service and community groups. Their public educations demonstrations include fire safety issues, local fire problems, and smoke detector usage and maintenance.

* Art Theft FBI Database

Laboratory Division
Federal Bureau of Investigation
U.S. Department of Justice
9th St. and Pennsylvania Ave., NW
Washington, DC 20535 (202) 324-4545

The *National Stolen Art File* is a database which lists all currently missing works of art reported as stolen from either public or private collections in the United States. Contact this office for obtaining information from the file.

* Attorney Training

Attorney General's Advocacy Institute
Executive Office for US Attorneys
U.S. Department of Justice
10th St. and Constitution Ave., NW
Room 1342
Washington, DC 20530 (202) 514-2121

The Advocacy Institute trains Assistant U.S. Attorneys and all U.S. Department of Justice attorneys in trial advocacy. The Institute offers courses on civil, criminal and appellate advocacy, and seminars on such specialized topics as white-collar crime, narcotics, conspiracy, environmental litigation, bankruptcy, land condemnations, public corruption and fraud, civil rights, witness security, and computer fraud.

* Child Abuse Prosecution

National Center for the Prosecution of Child Abuse
1033 N. Fairfax St., Suite 200
Alexandria, VA 22314 (703) 739-0321

The National Center for the Prosecution of Child Abuse provides technical assistance, training, and clearinghouse services to improve the investigation and prosecution of child abuse cases and the procedures for dealing with children who have been victims of physical and sexual abuse. It is designed to help prosecutors dealing with the particular complexities of child abuse cases to safeguard child victims against further trauma during a criminal justice process designed for adults. The Center has produced a manual on the investigation and prosecution of child abuse cases. Contact this Center for more information.

* Child Victimization and the Law

National Institute of Justice (NIJ)
NCJRS, Box 6000
Dept. AID (800) 851-3420
Rockville, MD 20850 (301) 251-5500 in DC

NIJ has the following publications and others on child victimization and the law. Many of the documents are free of charge, while others are available for a modest fee. When ordering or inquiring about an NIJ publication, refer to its NCJ number.

Guardians Ad Litem in the Criminal Courts. 1988, 64 pp. (NCJ 110006).
Prosecution of Child Sexual Abuse: Innovations in Practice (RIB). 1985, 7 pp. (NCJ 99317).
Prosecuting Child Sexual Abuse: New Approaches (RIA). 1985, 5 pp. (NCJ 102994).
Using Dolls to Interview Child Victims: Legal Concerns and Procedures (RIA). 1988, 6 pp. (NCJ 108470).
When the Victim Is a Child. 1985, 134 pp. (NCJ 97664).

* Cities in Schools: Truancy, Dropouts, Violence

Office of Juvenile Justice and Delinquency Prevention
U.S. Department of Justice
633 Indiana Ave., NW
Washington, DC 20531 (202) 307-0751

Cities in Schools, a public-private partnership that addresses the problems of dropouts and school violence, is designed to reduce school absenteeism and

Be patient. If any phone number is incorrect, call (area code) 555-1212 and request the new listing.

General Sources

dropout rates by coordinating services for at-risk youngsters. Five regional offices help serve the 26 operating programs throughout the country and assist other local communities to initiate new Cities in Schools programs.

* Coast Guard Law Books

Law Library
U.S. Coast Guard
U.S. Department of Transportation
2100 2nd St., SW, Room 4407
Washington, DC 20593-0001 (202) 267-2536

This library supports the Coast Guard's enforcement division. Books housed here cover case law, statutory law, and other reference works specific to the Coast Guard's role as enforcer of Federal laws on the high seas and U.S. waters. The library is open to the public.

* Coast Guard Law Enforcement Planning

Planning Branch
Research and Development Staff
Office of Engineering and Development
U.S. Coast Guard
U.S. Department of Transportation
2100 2nd St., SW, Room 6208
Washington, DC 20593-0001 (202) 267-1030

Information can be obtained here about research conducted by the Coast Guard in support of its operations and responsibilities. Areas of study include ice operations, ocean dumping, law enforcement, environmental protection, port safety and security, navigation aids, search and rescue procedures, recreational boating, energy, and advanced marine vehicles. For referral to specific personnel working in these areas, contact the Planning Branch.

* Company Antitrust Compliance or Violation

Antitrust Division
U.S. Department of Justice
10th St. and Constitution Ave., NW
Room 3233
Washington, DC 20530 (202) 633-2481

Under the Business Review procedure, any firm may submit a proposed business activity to the Antitrust Division and receive a statement as to whether the Division would challenge the action as a violation of the federal antitrust laws. In addition, you can obtain copies of all such letters and replies in the *Digest of Business Reviews*, an annual publication of the U.S. Department of Justice. The indexes to the *Digest*, updated yearly, allow easy research of all the letters issued since 1968 according to topic, commodity, or service involved, and name of the requesting party. The *Digest*, annual supplements, and revised indexes are available from the Legal Procedure Unit.

* Conservation Law Enforcement Training

Law Enforcement Division
U.S. Fish and Wildlife Service
4401 N. Fairfax Dr. Room 500
Arlington, VA 22203 (703) 358-1949

Through this division, state conservation officers are trained in the area of criminal law as it applies to the enforcement of wildlife protection.

* Consumer Antitrust Complaint

Litigation Section
Antitrust Division
U.S. Department of Justice
10th St. and Constitution Ave. NW
Room 910
Washington, DC 20530 (202) 514-2464

If you wish to register a consumer complaint, call the Litigation Section of the Antitrust Division. The Litigation Section can tell you exactly who to get in touch with to lodge your complaint. They can also tell you if litigation is called for and are responsible for bringing such litigation to bear.

* Corrections and Prisons Clearinghouse

National Institute of Corrections
Bureau of Prisons
U.S. Department of Justice

320 1st St., NW
Washington, DC 20534 (202) 307-1304

This office provides several types of technical assistance to correctional agencies and institutes themselves. They can offer advice on managerial procedures or suggest security improvements. Agencies can seek the NIC's help for any nature of problem they may be having with policy and procedure. If an institution has had a rash of successful escapes, they will send people to investigate the problem and suggest potential solutions. The NIC also trains some state and local managerial or executive officials. Anyone interested in a career in corrections management should also contact them.

* Crime Insurance for Homeowners and Business

Federal Crime Insurance
P.O. Box 6301
Rockville, MD 20850 (800) 638-8780
(301) 251-1660 in DC

The Federal Crime Insurance Program is a federally subsidized program sponsored by the Federal Emergency Management Administration for homeowners and commercial businesses to insure against burglary and robbery. To find out if your state is eligible and for further information, contact the office above. Those living in Maryland outside DC should call collect: (301) 251-1660.

* Crime Victims Publications

National Victims Resource Center (NVRC)
Box 6000-AIQ (800) 627-6872
Rockville, MD 20850 (301) 251-5525 in DC area

The following crime victim-related publications are available free of charge from NVRC:

Crime of Rape
Domestic Violence
Drunk Driving
Economic Cost of Crime
Elderly Victims
Handgun Crime Victims
Hate Crimes
Missing, Abducted, Runaway, and Thrownaway Children in America
Neighborhood Safety
Police and Child Abuse
Risk of Violent Crimes
Robbery Victims
Sexual Assault: An Overview
Teenage Victims
Violence in Schools
Violent Crime By Strangers and Non-strangers
Violent Crime Trends

* Criminal Justice Bibliographies

National Criminal Justice Reference Service (NCJRS)
National Institute of Justice (NIJ)
U.S. Department of Justice
Box 6000 (800) 851-3420
Rockville, MD 20850 (301) 251-5500

The NCJRS acts as an international clearinghouse and reference center on subjects as diverse as Affirmative Action and Jail-Based Inmate Programs. The NCJRS has a bibliography of hundreds of publications. Contact the NCJRS Distribution Service at the above address, or contact the National Institute of Justice, 633 Indiana Ave., NW, Washington, DC 20531; (202) 724-2956.

* Criminal Justice Database

National Crime Information Center
Technical Services Division
Federal Bureau of Investigation
JEH Bldg. NW
Washington, DC 20535 (202) 324-2711

On written request, the National Crime Information Center can provide you with information, on-line, concerning wanted persons, missing persons, stolen property, and computerized criminal histories. Searches and printouts are free.

* Criminal Justice Research

Office of Communication and Research Utilization
National Institute of Justice (NIJ)

Be patient. If any phone number is incorrect, call (area code) 555-1212 and request the new listing.

Law and Social Justice

U.S. Department of Justice
633 Indiana Ave. NW
Washington, DC 20531 (202) 514-6203

The National Institute of Justice has experts on nearly every field of criminal justice to help you find whatever information you're looking for. If you'd like to set up a Neighborhood Watch in your area, talk to Richard Titus or Lois Mock at (202) 724-7684. Do you want to know about environmental security? The NIJ has a specialist for you. Child abuse, DWI's, incidents of family violence, drug prevention education? They have an expert. The NIJ even has a specialist who can tell you anything you want to know about insanity as a defense in a criminal case.

* Criminal Justice: Schools, TV, Families

National Institute of Justice (NIJ)
NCJRS, Box 6000
Dept. AID (800) 851-3420
Rockville, MD 20850 (301) 251-5500 in DC

NIJ has these and other videos and publications on crime and the law. Many of the documents are free of charge, while others are available for a modest fee. When ordering or inquiring about an NIJ publication, refer to its NCJ number.

Biology and Crime (Crime File videotape). 1985 (NCJ 97216).
Crime and Mental Disorder (RIB). 1984, 6 pp. (NCJ 94074).
Families and Crime (Crime File videotape). 1986 (NCJ 104208).
The Nature and Patterns of American Homicide. 1985, 73 pp. (NCJ 97964).
Safer Schools--Better Students (videotape). 1985 (NCJ 98687).
TV and Violence (Crime File videotape). 1985 (NCJ 97234).
Acquaintance Rape: The Hidden Crime. 1991, 423 pp. (NCJ 132446).
Crimes of the Middle Classes: White-Collar Offenders in the Federal Courts. 1991, 229 pp. (NCJ 132842).

* DNA Fingerprinting

National Institute of Justice (NIJ)
U.S. Department of Justice
Box 6000
Rockville, MD 20850 (301) 251-5500

NIJ-funded research has produced a new technique for identifying a criminal suspect by analyzing DNA in hair, blood, and other body fluids. The FBI is currently using this technology, which is expected to dramatically increase success in investigating violent crimes such as rape and murder. Another important breakthrough has shown that it is possible to determine blood group types from bone fragments left at the scene of a crime or accident. The research is working on a reliable procedure for grouping ABO antigens in bone. This research will eventually expand into testing for DNA in skeletal remains. Contact NIJ for more information on this new technology.

* Domestic Violence Resource Center

National Victims Resource Center
Box 6000-AIQ (800) 627-6872
Rockville, MD 20850 (301) 251-5525 in DC

The National Victims Resource Center works as an information clearinghouse for the U.S. Department of Justice's Office of Victims of Crime. Family violence experts can assist callers in finding shelters for beaten women or local support groups. The NVRC also distributes a wide array of free publications. They also administer a library of more than 7,000 victim-related books and articles covering child physical and sexual abuse, victims services, domestic violence, victim-witness programs, and violent crime.

* Drug Abuse Warning Network (DAWN)

National Institute on Drug Abuse (NIDA)
5600 Fishers Lane
Rockville, Md 20857 (301) 443-6504

For those who want to understand and evaluate the scope and magnitude of drug abuse in the United States, this network is an invaluable information source. Whether you are a local public administrator considering programs, a reporter on the heels of a story, or just a concerned parent, the Drug Abuse Warning Network can provide you with needed information. More than 900 hospital emergency rooms and medical examiner facilities supply data to the program. DAWN identifies drugs currently in vogue, determines existing patterns and profiles of abuse/abuser in Standard Metropolitan Statistical Areas, monitors systemwide abuse trends, detects new abuse entities and polydrug combinations, and provides data needed for rational control and scheduling of

drugs being abused. It is the full-information source on the drug problem in America.

* Drug Testing and the Law

National Institute of Justice (NIJ)
NCJRS, Box 6000
Dept. AID (800) 851-3420
Rockville, MD 20850 (301) 251-5500 in DC

NIJ has these and other videos and publications on drug testing and the law. Many of the documents are free of charge, while others are available for a modest fee. When ordering or inquiring about an NIJ publication, refer to its NCJ number.

Drug Surveillance Through Urinalysis (videotape). 1986 (NCJ 100130). VHS, Beta, or 3/4-inch.
Drug Testing (Crime File videotape). 1986 (NCJ 104213). VHS, Beta, or 3/4-inch.
Drug Testing (Crime File study guide). 1986, 4 pp. (NCJ 104556).
Drugs and Crime: Controlling Use and Reducing Risk Through Testing (RIA). 1986, 6 pp. (NCJ 102668).
Police Drug Testing. 1987, 109 pp. (NCJ 105191).
Testing to Detect Drug Abuse (TAP publication). 1986, 2 pp. (NCJ 104282).

* Ethnic Tensions Resolution and Assistance

Community Relations Service (CRS)
U.S. Department of Justice
5550 Friendship Boulevard
Suite 300
Chevy Chase, MD 20815 (301) 492-5929

If your community is being torn apart by ethnic disputes or police-citizen conflicts, you may need help from this special service, set up by the Civil Rights Act of 1964. The Community Relations Service exists to resolve such disputes. The agency provides direct conciliation and mediation assistance to communities to facilitate the peaceful, voluntary resolution of racial and ethnic disputes or conflicts, and the peaceful co-existence of police and citizens' groups in the rapidly changing neighborhoods of today's cities. The CRS regularly provides conferences, training workshops, and publications to any and all communities in an attempt to forestall such disputes. However, when tensions do break out, the CRS will initiate whatever steps are necessary to begin making progress toward bringing about a resolution. They normally begin with extensive informal discussions with public or police officials and local community leaders, but if the agency and the parties determine that formal negotiations offer the best hope for a settlement, the agency arranges and mediates the negotiations.

* Explosives and Firearms Tracing Guidebook

Distribution Center
Bureau of Alcohol, Tobacco, and Firearms
U.S. Department of the Treasury
7943 Angus Ct.
Springfield, VA 22153 (703) 455-7801

The free book, *Firearms and Explosives Tracing Guidebook* is designed to assist law enforcement officials in preparing trace requests and determining whether or not firearms or explosives can be traced. Additional materials relating to firearms and explosives identification are included as a reference guide.

* FBI Academy and Careers

Federal Bureau of Investigation
Washington Metropolitan Field Office
Washington, DC 20535 (202) 324-3000

Federal Bureau of Investigation Academy
Quantico, VA 22135 (703) 640-6131

If you're interested in making a career out of the FBI, here's your chance. Contact the Academy or the FBI directly to obtain information on agent, special agent, or nonagent and managerial positions.

* Federal Law Enforcement Training

Federal Law Enforcement Training Center
U.S. Department of the Treasury
Glynco, GA 31524 (912) 267-2100

Be patient. If any phone number is incorrect, call (area code) 555-1212 and request the new listing.

General Sources

Federal Law Enforcement Training Center
Office of Artesia and Marana Operation
U.S. Department of the Treasury
1300 West Richey St.
Artesia, NM 88210 (505) 748-8000

The Centers above are the Federal Government's principal resources for conducting interagency law enforcement training. There are 62 Federal organizations that participate in training at Glynco. Since many individual agencies conduct very specific advanced programs for their own employees, approximately 20 participating organizations have training offices at Glynco, GA, or at the facilities at Marana, AZ and Artesia, NM.

Basic training programs provide training to entry-level Federal uniformed officers in basic law enforcement skills, such as firearms, arrest techniques, principles of law, and driver training. Programs include Immigration and Naturalization Service's Detention Officer Training, U.S. Customs Service Inspector Training, Basic Law Enforcement for Land Management Agencies, Basic Law Enforcement for Indian Police, Border Patrol Training, and Park Police Training, among others. Examples of advanced training for experienced law enforcement officers include Officer Safety and Survival Training, Antiterrorism Management and Contingency Training, National Wildfire Investigation Training, White Collar Crime Training, and Marine Law Enforcement.

* Firearms: State Laws and Published Ordinances

Distribution Center
Bureau of Alcohol, Tobacco, and Firearms
U.S. Department of the Treasury
7943 Angus Ct.
Springfield, VA 22153 (703) 455-7801

The free book, *Firearms: State Laws and Published Ordinances*, outlines the state and local laws and ordinances for firearms of all states, commonwealths, and possessions of the United States. A ready reference table for use with the publication lists key elements of state laws, such as purchaser waiting period, purchaser requirements, license/permit to purchase, license as dealer manufacturer, licensee record-keeping requirements, and local government limits, and where they can be located in the laws and ordinances. State attorneys are also listed if you have state-related questions or problems regarding firearms.

* Forensics Computerized Database

Laboratory Division
Federal Bureau of Investigation
U.S. Department of Justice
9th St. and Pennsylvania Ave., NW
Washington, DC 20535 (202) 324-4545

The Forensics Information System is computerized database used to identify all types of forensic evidence. It includes a Rifling Characteristics File which can identify the manufacturer and type of weapon that may have been used to fire a bullet. Other files can be used to identify tire tracks or shoe prints left at the scene of a crime.

* Funding for Criminal Justice Research

Office on Justice Programs
U.S. Department of Justice
633 Indiana Ave. NW
Room 900
Washington, DC 20531 (202) 307-0652

Anyone interested in conducting advanced research in any Criminal Justice related fields can apply for funding from this office. Past projects to receive support from this office include studies investigating the impact of the latest technologies on conviction rates.

* Guns and Criminals Videos and Publications

National Institute of Justice (NIJ)
NCJRS, Box 6000
Dept. AID (800) 851-3420
Rockville, MD 20850 (301) 251-5500 in DC

NIJ has these and other videos and publications on weapons, crime, and the law. Many of the documents are free of charge, while others are available for a modest fee. When ordering or inquiring about an NIJ publication, refer to its NCJ number.

The Armed Criminal in America (RIB). 1986, 5 pp. (NCJ 102827).

The Armed Criminal in America: A Survey of Incarcerated Felons. 1985, 52 pp. (NCJ 97099).

Gun Control (Crime File videotape). 1985 (NCJ 97224). VHS, Beta, 3/4-inch.

Gun Control (Crime File study guide). 1985, 4 pp. (NCJ 100740).

* Guns and Firearms Tracing Center

National Tracing Center
Bureau of Alcohol, Tobacco, and Firearms
U.S. Department of the Treasury
3361-F 75th Ave.
Landover, MD 20785 (800) 424-5057

The National Tracing Center provides firearms tracing services to duly authorized law enforcement agencies in the United States and those in many foreign countries. Tracing is the systematic tracking of firearms from manufacturer to purchaser (and/or possessor) for the purpose of aiding law enforcement in identifying suspects involved in criminal violations, establishing stolen status, and proving ownership.

24 Hour Number: (301) 436-8159
Out of Business Records: (800) 424-8201
Special Agent in Charge: (301) 436-8230

* Habitual Juvenile Offenders

Office of Juvenile Justice and Delinquency Prevention
U.S. Department of Justice
633 Indiana Ave., NW
Washington, DC 20531 (202) 307-5914

The Serious Habitual Juvenile Offenders Comprehensive Action Program is providing intensive training and technical assistance to 20 communities to help their juvenile justice systems more efficiently identify, adjudicate, supervise, and incarcerate serious habitual juvenile offenders. Contact this office for more information on this program and how its successes might be applied to other communities.

* Heroin Situation Indicators

Office of Intelligence
Drug Enforcement Administration
U.S. Department of Justice
1405 Eye St., NW, Room 1013
Washington, DC 20537 (202) 307-1000

A retail and wholesale heroin price/purity index is available based upon data from the analysis of drug evidence samples submitted to the Drug Enforcement Administration. In addition, reports are available on heroin-related emergency room admissions and deaths from 21 major metropolitan areas scattered throughout the country. These reports are published on a quarterly basis.

* High Seas Law Enforcement

Navigation Safety and Waterway Services
U.S. Coast Guard
U.S. Department of Transportation
2100 2nd St., SW, Room 3110
Washington, DC 20593-0001 (202) 267-2267

As the primary maritime law enforcement agency for the U.S., the Coast Guard enforces Federal laws, treaties, and international agreements to which the U.S. is a party. The Coast Guard may conduct investigations when violations are suspected, such as smuggling, drug trafficking, or polluting. Empowered to board and inspect vessels routinely as well, the Guard also conducts :"suspicionless" boardings to prevent violations. To report suspicious or questionable activity on boats, or to complain about an improperly conducted boarding, call the Boating Safety Hotline, (800) 368-5647; or (202) 267-0780 in DC, or contact your local Coast Guard commander. The office listed above can provide you with information about the Coast Guard's law enforcement role and the National Narcotics Border Interdiction System, which coordinates multi-agency and international operations with other countries to suppress narcotics trafficking.

* Hypnosis: Forensic Tool

National Victims Resource Center
Box 6000-AIQ (800) 627-6872
Rockville, MD 20850 (301) 251-5525 in DC area

Contact this Center for the free publication, *Forensic Use of Hypnosis*, which details how evidence revealed through hypnosis is used in court cases.

Be patient. If any phone number is incorrect, call (area code) 555-1212 and request the new listing.

Law and Social Justice

* Identifying Victims of Catastrophic Accidents

FBI Disaster Squad
Laboratory Division
Federal Bureau of Investigation
U.S. Department of Justice
J. Edgar Hoover Bldg., Room 11255
Washington, DC 20537 (202) 324-4410

The Disaster Squad is expert at identifying victims of catastrophic accidents. Government agencies rely upon them whenever victim identification is a problem. For local law enforcement, private investigators, transportation companies, or even families of the missing, the Disaster Squad can make a thorough analysis through fingerprints, dental records, and other physical evidence, and lay the mystery to rest. Contact this office for more information on the Squads services.

* Inmate Locator Line

Public Information
Bureau of Prisons
U.S. Department of Justice
320 1st St., NW, Room 640
Washington, DC 20536 (202) 307-3198

A special phone service hotline is available for people trying to locate family members or loved ones believed to be incarcerated in local, state, or federal correctional institutions. Call the Inmate Locater Line: (202) 724-3126 between 10 a.m. and 4:30 p.m. EST.

* Inside the FBI

Office of Public Affairs and Congressional Services
Federal Bureau of Investigation
U.S. Department of Justice
J. Edgar Hoover Bldg., Room 7116
Washington, DC 20535 (202) 324-5352

If you have a group planning on visiting Washington, DC, and would like to make the FBI Headquarters a part of that trip, contact the Office of Public Affairs. Guided tours are offered Mondays through Fridays (except holidays) from 9:00 a.m. to 4:00 p.m. No appointments are necessary for groups numbering fifteen or less.

* Jail Overcrowding

National Institute of Justice (NIJ)
NCJRS, Box 6000
Dept. AID (800) 851-3420
Rockville, MD 20850 (301) 251-5500 in DC

NIJ has videos and publications on prison and jail overcrowding. Many of the documents are free of charge, while others are available for a modest fee. When ordering or inquiring about an NIJ publication, refer to its NCJ number.

* Juvenile Delinquency Risk Factors

Office of Juvenile Justice and Delinquency Prevention
Research and Program Development Division
U.S. Department of Justice
633 Indiana Ave., NW
Washington, DC 20531 (202) 307-5929

This research division assesses a wide range of risk factors faced by children between the ages of six and 17. Researchers are looking beyond established delinquency correlates--such as age, race, and sex--to investigate more practical factors, such as personality characteristics, drug use, family relationships, school experience, the community environment, peer/gang associations, and juvenile justice sanctions. Contact this division for more information on this research.

* Juvenile Drug Abuse Risk Factors

Office of Juvenile Justice and Delinquency Prevention
Research and Program Development Division
U.S. Department of Justice
633 Indiana Ave., NW
Washington, DC 20531 (202) 724-7560

This division has researched drug use among juveniles to develop information on high-risk factors for drug use among youth, and on the effectiveness of interventions for preventing or controlling illegal drug use. These studies include recommendations for promising prevention and rehabilitation strategies. Contact this division for more information.

* Law Enforcement Officers: Deaths and Assaults

Uniform Crime Reporting Section
Federal Bureau of Investigation (FBI)
U.S. Department of Justice
9th and Pennsylvania Ave., NW, GRB
Washington, DC 20535 (202) 324-2614

The publication, *Law Enforcement Officers Killed or Assaulted*, is available from the FBI Crime Reporting Section in three yearly forms: the six-month report, preliminary annual, and annual. Write to the above address for a free copy.

* Law Enforcement Training for State and Local Officers

Federal Law Enforcement Training Center (FLETC)
U.S. Department of the Treasury
Glynco, GA 31524 (912) 267-2100

FLETC's Office of State and Local Law Enforcement conducts over 25 specialized programs both at Glynco and at various sites around the country. Some of these programs include: Child Abuse and Exploitation Investigative Techniques, Managing Juvenile Operations, Schools Are For Effective Police Operations Leading to Improved Children and Youth Services, Cargo Theft Investigations, Fraud and Financial Investigations, Hazardous Waste Investigations, Prison/Jail Crisis Response Training, Criminal Investigations in an Automated Environment, Fugitive Investigations Training, Advanced Arson for Profit Investigations, and Narcotics Officer Training.

* Lie Detector Tests: Reliability

National Institute of Justice (NIJ)
U.S. Department of Justice
Box 6000
Rockville, MD 20850 (800) 851-3420

To investigate the validity of polygraph examinations in criminal investigations, an NIJ study compared the accuracy of human examiners to that of a computer program in assessing the truth of answers to specific questions. The computer program was found to be just as reliable as that of the human examiners. Contact this Institute for more information on this study and the use of polygraphs in criminal justice.

* Maximum Speed Limit Enforcement

Police Traffic Services Division
Office of Enforcement and Emergency Services
Traffic Safety Programs
National Highway Traffic Safety Administration
U.S. Department of Transportation
400 7th Street, SW, Room 6124
Washington, DC 20590 (202) 366-5440

The National Maximum Speed Limit is 65 miles per hour on certain interstate highways. This office processes annual certifications of maximum speed limit enforcement programs throughout the U.S. and assists states in developing and improving enforcement efforts.

* Missing and Exploited Children Clearinghouse

National Center for Missing and Exploited Children
Publications Department
2101 Wilson Blvd. Suite 550
Arlington, VA 22201-3052 (703) 235-3900

This Center serves as a clearinghouse of information on missing or exploited children; provides technical assistance to citizens and law-enforcement agencies; offers training programs to law-enforcement and social service professionals; distributes photos and descriptions of missing children nationwide; coordinates child protection efforts with the private sector; networks with nonprofit organizations and state clearinghouses; and provides information on effective state legislation to ensure the protection of children. The following publications are available free of charge:

Books:
Child Molesters: A Behavioral Analysis
Child Sex Rings: A Behavioral Analysis
Children Traumatized in Sex Rings
Interviewing Child Victims of Sexual Exploitation
Nonprofit Service Provider's Handbook
Parental Kidnapping
Selected State Legislation
Youth at Risk

Be patient. If any phone number is incorrect, call (area code) 555-1212 and request the new listing.

General Sources

Brochures:
Child Protection
Child Protection Priorities
For Camp Counselors
Just in Case...You are Considering Daycare
Just in Case...You Are Considering Family Separation
Just in Case...You Are Dealing with Grief Following the Loss of a Child
Just in Case...You Are Using the Federal Parent Locator Service
Just in Case...You Need a Babysitter
Just in Case...Your Child Is a Runaway
Just in Case...Your Child is Testifying in Court
Just in Case...Your Child is the Victim of Sexual Abuse or Exploitation
Just in Case...Your Child Is Missing

Taking a Bite Out of Crime: The Impact of a Mass Media Crime Prevention Campaign. 1984, 78 pp. (NCJ 93350).

* Neighborhood Watch Programs

National Crime Prevention Council
17 K St. N.W.
2nd Floor
Washington, DC 20036 (202) 466-NCPC

If you're interested in starting a Neighborhood Watch Program in your town, or want to know how you can make yours better, contact the Neighborhood Watch Specialists at the National Institute of Justice. They will be glad to help you make your neighborhood a safer place.

* National Emergencies

FEMA
P.O. Box 70274
Washington, DC 20024 (202) 646-2500

Federal Emergency Management Agency (FEMA) is part of our government which deals with planning for and/or coordinating relief in various national emergencies. FEMA plans for nuclear attacks, security emergencies, disaster recovery aid, and helps to coordinate food, shelter, and financial aid in the event of any natural or manmade disasters. There are ten regional offices across the country. They are:

Region I - 442 J.W. McCormack, POCH, Boston, MA 02109; (617) 223-9540
Region II - 26 Federal Plaza, N.Y.C., NY 10278; (212) 264-8980
Region III - 105 S. 7th St., Philadelphia, PA 19106; (215) 597-9416
Region IV - 1371 Peachtree St. N.E., Suite 700, Atlanta, GA 30309; (404) 347-2400
Region V - 175 W. Jackson Blvd., 4th Floor, Chicago, IL 60604; (312) 431-5501
Region VI - Federal Regional Center, Room 206, Denton, TX 76201; (807) 898-9104
Region VII - 911 Walnut St., Room 300, Kansas City, MO 64106; (816) 374-5912
Region VIII - Federal Regional Center, Building 710, Box 25267, Denver, CO 80225-0267; (303) 235-4811
Region IX - Building 105, Presidio of San Francisco, San Francisco, CA 94129 (415) 923-7100
Region X - Federal Region Center, 130 228th St., S.W., Bothell, WA 98021-9796 (206) 487-4604

* New Federal Laws

Office of the Federal Register
National Archives and Records Administration
8th St. and Pennsylvania Ave., NW, Room 8401
Washington, DC 20408 (202) 523-5230

This office receives all the laws enacted by Congress for publication in the *Federal Register* and can provide information regarding these laws. They also publish *United States at Large*, a compilation of laws enacted during a particular year.

* Odometer Tampering

Odometer Fraud Staff
Office of Chief Counsel
National Highway Traffic Safety Administration (NHTSA)
U.S. Department of Transportation
400 7th Street, SW, Room 5219
Washington, DC 20590 (202) 366-9511

Federal law requires that the seller of a car sign a disclosure statement that the mileage on the odometer is accurate and has not been rolled back. NHTSA enforces the odometer law via inspections and criminal charges. Information on odometer tampering is also available from the Auto Safety Hotline: (800) 424-9393.

* Neighborhood Crime Comparison Information

Uniform Crime Reporting Section
Federal Bureau of Investigation
U.S. Department of Justice
9th and Pennsylvania Ave., NW, GRB
Washington, DC 20535 (202) 324-2614

If you'd like to know how safe your prospective new neighborhood is, contact the Uniform Crime Reporting Section. This annual report, *Crime In the United States* contains an exact reading of the crime rates of any city in America (down to the types of crimes committed most frequently in which neighborhoods). Also, local police departments of most major cities have neighborhood crime reports available and will actually rate the safety factor of your new address for you.

* Police-Citizen Conflict Resolution

Community Relations Service (CRS)
U.S. Department of Justice
5550 Friendship Blvd., Suite 300
Chevy Chase, MD 20815 (301) 492-5929

The agency provides direct conciliation and mediation assistance to communities to facilitate the peaceful, voluntary resolution of racial and ethnic disputes or conflicts, and the peaceful co-existence of police and citizens' groups in the rapidly changing neighborhoods of today's cities. They normally begin with extensive informal discussions with public or police officials and local community leaders, but if the agency and the parties determine that formal negotiations offer the best hope for a settlement, the agency arranges and mediates the negotiations.

* Neighborhood Safety Videos and Publications

National Institute of Justice (NIJ)
NCJRS
Box 6000
Dept. AID (800) 851-3420
Rockville, MD 20850 (301) 251-5500 in DC

NIJ has these and other publications and videos on crime prevention and the law. Many of the documents are free of charge, while others are available for a modest fee. When ordering or inquiring about an NIJ publication, refer to its NCJ number.

Crime Stoppers: A National Evaluation (RIB). 1986, 5 pp. (NCJ 102292).
The Growing Role of Private Security (RIB). 1984, 5 pp. (NCJ 94703).
Guardian Angels: An Assessment of Citizen Response to Crime: Executive Summary. 1986, 31 pp. (NCJ 1009111).
Improving the Use and Effectiveness of Neighborhood Watch Programs (RIA). 1988, 4 pp. (NCJ 108618).
Neighborhood Safety (Crime file videotape). 1985 (NCJ 97227). VHS, Beta, or 3/4-inch.

* Police Use of Deadly Force

Community Relations Service
5550 Friendship Blvd., Room 330
Chevy Chase, MD 20815 (301) 492-5929

There has been a steady increase in cases of community disruption due to minority groups' belief that the police have used deadly force--or a severe degree of non-lethal force-- when it was unwarranted. Two booklets, *Police Use of Deadly Force*, and *Principles of Good Policing*, provides information that will be useful to citizens and police looking for constructive alternatives to continued hostility and suspicion.

* Prisons and Correctional Institutions Clearinghouse

National Institute of Corrections Information Center
Bureau of Prisons
U.S. Department of Justice
1860 Industrial Circle, Suite A
Long Mont, CO 80501 (303) 682-0213

This center is the complete source of information on correctional institutions. They have the data to answer any and all questions. Public policy makers who are considering the economics and potential benefits of a proposed new prison

Law and Social Justice

would be wise to get in touch with the NIC, as would construction companies thinking of making a bid on a new site. Politicians, correctional officials, reporters, or even inmates who want to investigate possible reforms should contact this office.

* Prisons: History, Statistics

Public Affairs
Bureau of Prisons
U.S. Department of Justice
320 1st St., NW, Room 640
Washington, DC 20536   (202) 307-3198

The Bureau of Prisons has many publications available to the public. They release an annual *State of the Bureau* report, as well as publications describing new and existing facilities, a history of the development of the federal bureau, and an annual statistical report of the Nation's correctional facilities.

* Protection of the President

Personnel Division
U.S. Secret Service
U.S. Department of the Treasury
1800 G St., NW
Washington, DC 20223   (202) 435-5800

Protection is the key mission of the Uniformed Division of the Secret Service. They are responsible for the White House Complex; the Main Treasury Building and Annex and other Presidential offices; the President and immediate family; the official residence of the Vice President and his immediate family; and foreign diplomatic missions as prescribed by statute.

* Racial Disputes Resolution

Community Relations Service (CRS)
U.S. Department of Justice
5550 Friendship Blvd., Suite 300
Chevy Chase, MD 20815   (301) 492-5929

If your community is being torn apart by ethnic disputes or police-citizen conflicts, you may need help from this special service, set up by the Civil Rights Act of 1964. The Community Relations Service exists to resolve such disputes. The agency provides direct conciliation and mediation assistance to communities to facilitate the peaceful, voluntary resolution of racial and ethnic disputes or conflicts, and the peaceful co-existence of police and citizens' groups in the rapidly changing neighborhoods of today's cities. The CRS regularly provides conferences, training workshops, and publications to any and all communities in an attempt to forestall such disputes. However, when tensions do break out, the CRS will initiate whatever steps are necessary to begin making progress toward bringing about a resolution. They normally begin with extensive informal discussions with public or police officials and local community leaders, but if the agency and the parties determine that formal negotiations offer the best hope for a settlement, the agency arranges and mediates the negotiations.

* Recidivism Statistics

Bureau of Justice Statistics
U.S. Department of Justice
633 Indiana Ave., NW
Washington, DC 20531   (202) 307-0765

The National Recidivism Data Base links Bureau of Justice Statistics corrections data with State and FBI criminal history information to derive representative samples of individuals released from State prisons, follow these samples for several years, and produce estimates on the incidence, prevalence, and seriousness of later arrests and dispositions. For information on available statistics on prison recidivism, contact this office.

* RX Drug and Controlled Substances Registration

Registration Section
Office of Compliance and Regulatory Affairs
Drug Enforcement Administration
U.S. Department of Justice
666 11th St., NW, Room 920
Washington, DC 20001   (202) 307-1000

Information is available about registration under the Controlled Substances Act. Every person who manufactures, distributes, or dispenses any controlled substance, or who proposes to engage in the manufacture, distribution, or dispensing of any controlled substance, must register annually with the

Registration Branch of the DEA. The names of all registrants are available to the public. A schedule of all controlled substances is also available. In addition, the DEA will investigate any registrant to ensure that they are accountable for the controlled substances handled if presented with requests or evidence which would seem to warrant such investigation.

* Secret Service Special Agents

Personnel Division
U.S. Secret Service
U.S. Department of the Treasury
1800 G St., NW
Washington, DC 20223   (202) 435-5800

Special agents for the Secret Service are charged with two missions: protection and investigation. In addition to those protected by the Uniformed Division, the Special Agents guard former Presidents and their spouses, children of former Presidents, visiting heads of foreign states and governments and their spouses, and major Presidential and Vice Presidential candidates. Counterfeiting, forgery, and fraud investigations are also performed by Special Agents. Candidates interested in applying may contact local Secret Service field offices.

* Settlement of Claims Against the Government

Claims Group General Government Division
General Accounting Office (GAO)
441 G St., NW
Washington, DC 20548   (202) 275-3102

In addition to helping settle claims of one government agency against another, this GAO office also settles claims by and against the United States. Claims may involve individuals, businesses, or foreign, state, and municipal governments. Claims are settled by GAO when the departments and agencies have not been given specific authority to handle their own claims and when they involve 1) doubtful questions of law or fact; 2) appeals of agency actions; 3) certain debts which agencies are unable to collect; and 4) waivers of certain erroneous payments for pay. Contact GAO for more information.

* Stolen Pharmaceuticals and Other Drug Theft Office of Intelligence

Drug Enforcement Administration (DEA)
U.S. Department of Justice
1405 Eye St., NW, Room 1013
Washington, DC 20537   (202) 307-1000

All legal drug handlers registered with the Drug Enforcement Administration are required to report thefts or losses on controlled substances. Stolen supplies from legitimate drug handlers comprise a substantial portion of the illicit drug distribution network. The DEA has a fully updated list of all reports of drug theft. For information contact the Office of Intelligence at the above address or phone number.

* Supreme Court Library

Supreme Court of the United States Library
1 1st St., NE
Washington, DC 20543   (202) 479-3175

A complete working collection of American, English, and Canadian statutes, records and briefs dating back to 1832 are contained in this library. Historical and constitutional documents along with the federal tax laws and legislative histories of selected federal acts are also available here. The library is open to the public, Monday through Friday, 9am-4:15pm, to use the records and briefs department.

* U.S. Park Police

National Capital Region
National Park Service
U.S. Department of the Interior
1100 Ohio Dr., SW
Washington, DC 20242   (202) 208-4747

The U.S. Park Police have the same authority and powers as the Washington, DC metropolitan police. They also act as hosts to park visitors.

* Victimization Statistics

National Victims Resource Center

Be patient. If any phone number is incorrect, call (area code) 555-1212 and request the new listing.

Box 6000-AIQ . . . . (800) 627-6872
Rockville, MD 20850 . . . . (301) 251-5525 in DC
This Center can provide you with nationwide statistics on the victims of crime.

* Violent Criminal Behavior

National Institute of Justice (NIJ)
U.S. Department of Justice
Box 6000
Rockville, MD 20850 . . . . (301) 251-5500
NIJ research has examined the relation between early child abuse, neglect, and subsequent violent criminal behavior. Criminal records of substantiated cases of individuals abused as children were compared with criminal records of a matched group of non-abused individuals. The results to date suggest that those who were abused as children did commit more violent offenses as adults than those not abused as children. Contact this office for more information on this topic.

* Whistleblower Hotlines and Government Inspector Generals

Many federal departments and agencies have hotlines, some toll-free numbers, into the office of the Inspector General. The responsibility of the IG is chiefly an in-house auditor looking for fraud, mismanagement, and government waste. These whistleblower hotlines exist to encourage federal employees, state employees, contractors, and citizens to report any allegations.

U.S. Department of Agriculture
Office of Inspector General
P.O. Box 23399 . . . . (800) 424-9121
Washington, DC 20026 . . . . (202) 727-2540

U.S. Department of the Army
The Pentagon . . . . (800) 572-9000
Washington, DC 20310 . . . . (703) 545-6700

U.S. Department of Commerce
14th and Constitution Ave., NW
Room 7898-C . . . . (800) 424-5197
Washington, DC 20230 . . . . (202) 377-2495

U.S. Department of Defense
Defense Hotline
The Pentagon . . . . (800) 424-9098
Washington, DC 20301-1900 . . . . (703) 545-6700

U.S. Department of Education
Inspector General Hotline
P.O. Box 23458 . . . . (800) 647-8733
Washington, DC 20026 . . . . (202) 205-5770

U.S. Department of Energy
1000 Independence Ave., SW
Room 5D039, Forrestal Building
Washington, DC 20585 . . . . (202) 586-5000

U.S. Department of Health and Human Services
OIG Hotline
P.O. Box 17303 . . . . (800) 368-5779
Baltimore, MD 21203-7303 . . . . (202) 619-0257

U.S. Department of Housing and Urban Development
451 7th St., SW, Room 8254
Washington, DC 20410 . . . . (202) 708-1422

U.S. Department of the Interior
18th and C Sts., NW, Room 5359 . . . . (800) 424-5081
Washington, DC 20240 . . . . (202) 208-3424

U.S. Department of Justice
Office of Professional Responsibility
10th and Constitution Ave., NW, Room 4304 . . . . (800) 869-4499
Washington, DC 20530 . . . . (202) 514-3435

U.S. Department of Labor
200 Constitution Ave., NW

Room S1303 . . . . (800) 424-5409
Washington, DC 20210 . . . . (202) 357-0227

U.S. Department of State
2201 C St., NW
New State Building, Room 6821
Washington, DC 20520 . . . . (202) 647-3320

U.S. Department of Transportation
400 7th St., NW, Room 9210 . . . . (800) 424-9071
Washington, DC 20590 . . . . (202) 366-1461

U.S. Department of Treasury
15th and Pennsylvania Ave., NW, Room 2412 . . . . (800) 826-0407
Washington, DC 20220 . . . . (202) 622-1090

U.S. Department of Veterans Affairs
1425 K St., NW
McPherson Building, Room 1100
Washington, DC 20420 . . . . (202) 233-5394

Environmental Protection Agency
401 M St., SW
Room 307 NE Mall . . . . (800) 424-4000
Washington, DC 20460 . . . . (202) 260-4977

Federal Bureau of Investigation
Inspections Division
Washington, DC 20535 . . . . (202) 324-2901

General Accounting Office
441 G St., NW . . . . (202) 272-5557
Washington, DC 20548 . . . . (800) 424-5454

General Services Administration
18th and F Sts., NW, Room 5340 . . . . (800) 424-5210
Washington, DC 20405 . . . . (202) 501-0450

Merit Systems Protection Board
Office of the Special Counsel
1120 Vermont Ave., NW, Suite 1100 . . . . (800) 872-9855
Washington, DC 20005 . . . . (202) 653-9125

National Aeronautics and Space Administration
Inspector General
P.O. Box 23089
L'Enfant Station . . . . (800) 424-9183
Washington, DC 20026 . . . . (202) 755-3402

Office of Personnel Management
1900 E St., NW, Room 6831
Washington, DC 20415 . . . . (202) 606-1200

Railroad Retirement Board
Office of Inspector General
Office of Investigation
844 N. Rush St., Room 450 . . . . (800) 772-4258
Chicago, IL 60611 . . . . (312) 751-4336

Small Business Administration
1441 L St., NW, Room 203
Washington, DC 20416 . . . . (202) 653-7557

Tennessee Valley Authority
400 West Summit Hill Drive . . . . (800) 323-3835
Knoxville, TN 37902 . . . . (615) 632-3550

U.S. Agency for International Development
21st and Virginia Ave.
Room 5644, New State Building
Washington, DC 20523 . . . . (202) 647-7844

U.S. Information Agency
Donohoe Building, Room 1100
400 6th St., SW
Washington, DC 20547 . . . . (202) 401-7931

Be patient. If any phone number is incorrect, call (area code) 555-1212 and request the new listing.

Law and Social Justice

* World's Largest Law Library

Law Library
Library of Congress
Washington, DC 20540 (202) 707-5000

As the world's largest and most comprehensive library of foreign, international, and comparative law, the Law Library provides information for all known legal systems including common law, civil law, Roman law, canon law, Chinese law, Jewish and Islamic law, and ancient and medieval law. Specialists with knowledge of more than fifty languages provide reference and research service in all known legal systems. U.S. legislative documents housed here include the *Congressional Record* (and its predecessors), the serial set, a nearly complete set of bills and resolutions, current documents, committee prints, reports, hearings, etc. plus a complete set of U.S. Supreme Court records and briefs and collections of U.S. Court of Appeals records and briefs. It is open to the public Monday-Friday 8:30 AM-9:30 PM, Saturday 8:30 AM-5 PM, and Sunday 1-5 PM. The law library has five major divisions:

American-British Law: United States, Australia, Canada, Great Britain, India, New Zealand, Pakistan, certain other countries of the British Commonwealth and their dependent territories, and Eire: (202) 707-5077.

European Law: Nations of Europe and their possessions, except Spain and Portugal: (202) 707-5088.

Hispanic Law: Spain and Portugal, Latin America, Puerto Rico, the Philippines, and Spanish- and Portuguese-language states of Africa: (202) 707-5070.

Far Eastern Law: Nations of East and Southeast Asia including China, Indonesia, Japan, Korea, Thailand, and former British and French possessions in the area: (202) 707-5085.

Near Eastern and African Law: Middle Eastern countries, including the Arab states, Turkey, Iran, and Afghanistan, and all African countries, except Spanish- and Portuguese-language states and possessions: (202) 707-5073.

Be patient. If any phone number is incorrect, call (area code) 555-1212 and request the new listing.

Courts and Legal Help

* Administration of U.S. Courts

Administrative Office of the United States Courts
1 Columbus Circle, N.E.
Washington, DC 20002 (202) 273-3000

This Office is responsible for supervision of administrative matters in all courts except the Supreme Court, supervising accounts and practices of the Federal probation offices, certain administrative matters within the Bankruptcy court, and exercises general supervision over administrative matters in offices of the United States magistrates. Information may be obtained from the following offices:

Bankruptcy Division:	(202) 273-1900
Court Administration Division:	(202) 273-1530
Defender Services Division:	(202) 273-1670
General Counsel:	(202) 273-1100
Magistrates Division:	(202) 273-1830
Personnel Division:	(202) 273-2777
Probation Division:	(202) 273-1600
Human Resources	(202) 273-1200

* Arbitrators and Mediators

Federal Mediation and Conciliation Service (FMCS)
2100 K St., NW
Washington, DC 20427 (202) 653-5300

Through its regional offices and suboffices, FMCS assists federal agencies, private sector employers, and labor organizations in resolving labor-management disputes. When there is no local or state resource available, the parties involved may contact the regional FMCS office to be assigned a qualified mediator or arbitrator, on call 24 hours a day. Upon request, mediators will assist the parties in resolving disputes, and arbitrators will make a final decision. Technical assistance includes training for one or both parties in developing constructive methods of dispute resolution, help in forming committees, and collective bargaining workshops. Contact your local FMCS office for any of these services.

* Bankruptcy Clearinghouse

Administrative Office of the United States Courts
Bankruptcy Division
1 Columbus Circle N.E.
Washington, DC 20002 (202) 273-1900

Since the Administrative Office has general supervision for the bankruptcy courts, information on bankruptcy forms, fees, and explanations of the Bankruptcy Act is available.

* Bench Book for District Court Judges

Information Service Division
Federal Judicial Center
1 Columbus Circle NE
Washington, DC 20002 (202) 273-4153

The *Bench Book for United States District Court Judges* is available to judicial personnel only. This book contains statutes, suggestions, recommendations, and reference materials for judicial proceedings. The book is prepared by the Judicial Center from the guidance of experienced district judges.

* Civil and Criminal District Court Procedures

Superintendent of Documents
Government Printing Office
Washington, DC 20402 (202) 783-3238

Rules of Civil Procedure for the United States District Courts, With Forms. Contains the Rules of Civil Procedure for United States District Courts as promulgated and amended by the Supreme Court to October 1, 1977. $3.75

Federal Rules of Evidence. Sets forth Rules of Evidence for use in proceedings in the courts of the United States and before United States magistrates. $1.75

Federal Rules of Appellate Procedure. Contains the Federal Rules of Appellate Procedure as promulgates and amended by the United States Supreme Court to October 1, 1979, along with the forms adopted by the Court. $2

A publications catalog is available free upon request.

* Constitution and Supreme Court Decisions

Supreme Court of the United States
1 1st St., NE
Washington, DC 20543 (202) 252-3000

The *Constitution of the United States of America: Analysis and Interpretation* includes the text of the Constitution, along with its amendments prefacing annotations of the Supreme Court decisions that are relevant to the way the Constitution is interpreted. The cost is $70 and is available from the Superintendent of Documents, Government Printing Office, Washington, DC 20402; (202) 783-3238.

* Disabled and Handicapped Persons: Legal Aid

National Association of Protection and Advocacy System (NAPAS)
220 Eye Street, NW
Suite 150
Washington, DC 20002 (202) 408-9514

Every state and the territories provide legal assistance for the handicapped and developmentally disabled. This national organization also coordinates state agencies for the mentally ill and client assistance program. NAPAS publishes a newsletter titled *Annual Report.* The following is a list of the state protection and advocacy agencies for those with developmental disabilities.

Alabama Disabilities Advocacy Program	(205) 348-4928
Alaska Advocacy Services	(800) 478-1234
	(907) 344-1002
American Samoa Client Assistance P&A Program	(684) 633-2441
Arizona Center for Law in the Public Interest	(602) 274-6287
Arkansas Advocacy Services	(501) 324-9215
	(800) 482-1174
California Protection and Advocacy Inc.	(800) 776-5746
	(916) 488-9950
	(818) 546-1631
	(510) 839-0811
Colorado Legal Center	(303) 722-0300
Connecticut Office of P&A	(800) 842-7303
	(203) 297-4300
	(203) 566-2101
Delaware Disabilities Law Program	(302) 856-0038
	(302) 764-2400
District of Columbia Information, Protection, and Advocacy	(202) 727-0977
	(202) 966-8081
Florida Advocacy Center for Persons with Disabilities	(904) 488-9071
	(800) 342-0823
Georgia Advocacy Office, Inc.	(800) 282-4538
	(404) 885-1234
Guam Advocacy Office	(671) 646-9026
Hawaii Protection and Advocacy Agency	(808) 949-2922
Idaho's Coalition of Advocates for the Disabled	(208) 336-5353
Illinois Protection and Advocacy Inc.	(312) 341-0022
	(217) 782-5374
Indiana Advocacy Services	(800) 622-4845
	(317) 232-1150
Iowa Protection and Advocacy Service, Inc.	(515) 278-2502
Kansas Advocacy and Protection Services	(800) 432-8276
	(913) 776-1541
Kentucky Office for Public Advocacy Division	(800) 372-2988
	(502) 564-2967
Louisiana Advocacy Center for the Elderly and Disabled	(800) 662-7705
	(504) 5522-2337

Be patient. If any phone number is incorrect, call (area code) 555-1212 and request the new listing.

Law and Social Justice

Maine Advocacy Services . . . . (800) 452-1948
(207) 377-6202

Maryland Disability Law Center . . . . (800) 233-7201
(410) 333-7251

Massachusetts Disability Law Center . . . . (617) 723-8455

Michigan Protection and Advocacy Service . . . . (517) 487-1755

Minnesota Legal Aid Society of Minneapolis . . . . (612) 332-1441

Mississippi Protection and Advocacy System . . . . (601) 981-8207

Missouri Protection and Advocacy System . . . . (800) 392-8667
(314) 893-3333

Montana Advocacy Program . . . . (800) 245-4743
(406) 444-3889

Nebraska Advocacy Services . . . . (402) 474-3183

Nevada Office of Protection and Advocacy . . . . (800) 992-5715
(702) 575-5912

New Hampshire Disabilities Rights Center . . . . (603) 228-0432

New Jersey Office of Advocacy . . . . (800) 792-8600
(609) 292-9742

New Mexico Protection and Advocacy System . . . . (800) 432-4682
(505) 256-3100

New York Commission on Quality of Care for the
Mentally Disabled . . . . (518) 473-7378

North Carolina Governor's Advocacy Council for Persons
with Disabilities . . . . (919) 733-9250

North Dakota Protection and Advocacy Project . . . . (800) 474-2670
(701) 224-2972

Northern Mariana Islands Catholic Social Services . . . . (670) 234-6981

Ohio Legal Rights Service . . . . (800) 282-9181
(614) 466-7264

Oklahoma Protection and Advocacy Agency . . . . (918) 664-5883

Oregon Advocacy Center . . . . (503) 243-2081

Pennsylvania Protection and Advocacy . . . . (800) 692-7443
(412) 363-7223
. . . . (215) 557-7112

Puerto Rico Governor's Office Ombudsman for the Disabled . (809) 766-2333

Rhode Island Protection and Advocacy System . . . . (401) 831-3150

South Carolina Protection and Advocacy System . . . . (800) 922-5225
(803) 782-0639

South Dakota Advocacy Project, Inc. . . . . (800) 658-4782
(605) 224-8294

Tennessee E.A.C.H. Inc. . . . . (800) 342-1660
(615) 298-1080

Texas Advocacy, Inc. . . . . (800) 252-9108
(512) 454-4816

Utah Legal Center for the Handicapped . . . . (800) 662-9080
(801) 363-1347

Vermont Developmental Disability Law Project . . . . (802) 863-2881

Virginia Department for Rights of the Disabled . . . . (800) 552-3962
(804) 225-2042

Virgin Islands Committee on Advocacy for the
Developmentally Disabled . . . . (809) 772-1200

Washington Protection and Advocacy System . . . . (206) 324-1521

West Virginia Advocates . . . . (800) 950-5250
(304) 346-0847

Wisconsin Coalition for Advocacy . . . . (608) 267-0214

Wyoming Protection and Advocacy System . . . . (800) 624-7648
(307) 638-7668

* Disaster Victims Legal Services

Federal Emergency Management Agency (FEMA)
P.O. Box 70274
Washington, DC 20024 (202) 646-2500

The *Manual for Disaster Legal Services* has been prepared by FEMA and the Young Lawyers Division (YLD) of the American Bar Association. Its purpose is to orient new and potential volunteers to the FEMA-YLD Program for offering legal services to victims following major disasters. In order to facilitate this orientation, the *Manual* emphasizes schematic diagram, paraphrases statutes and regulations, and simplifies many issues relating to the program.

* Federal Courts Office Procedure

Judicial Center
1 Columbus Circle, N.E.
Washington, DC 20002 (202) 273-4153

Office procedures relating to organization and process of the federal courts is defined in a free handbook available only to certain judicial personnel from this office.

* Federal Courts Report

Administrative Office of the United States Courts
811 Vermont Ave., NW
Washington, DC 20544 (202) 273-3000

The business of all the federal courts (except the United States Court of Military Appeals and United States Tax Courts) is included in the *Reports of the Proceedings of the Judicial Conference of the United States, 1991.* It is available for $13 from the Superintendent of Documents, Government Printing Office, Washington, DC 20402; (202) 783-3238.

* Federal Judicial Resource Center

Federal Judicial Center
1 Columbus Circle N.E.
Washington, DC 20002 (202) 273-4153

The subjects in this service cover civil and criminal procedure, constitutional law and probabilities, and court management. Material on all areas of the federal judicial administration can be obtained by writing the Federal Judicial Center.

* Federal Magistrates

Administrative Office of the United States Courts
Magistrates Division
1 Columbus Circle N.E.
Washington, DC 20002 (202) 273-1830

Information and statistics on the offices of the United States magistrates is provided annually to Congress and can be obtained by contacting this Administrative Office of the United States Courts, Magistrates Division.

* Federal Public Defenders

Administrative Office of the United States Courts
1 Columbus Circle N.E.
Washington, DC 20002 (202) 273-3000

Under the Criminal Justice Act, the *Federal Public Defenders and Federal Community Defender Organizations by the Districts Courts* is made available to the public. *Annual Reports* are provided by Defender organizations listing their activities.

* Foreigners Visiting Judicial Branch

Federal Judicial Center
Information Services Division
1 Columbus Circle N.E.
Washington, DC 20002 (202) 273-4153

Arrangements for official visitors from abroad, along with conducting briefings and assembling materials are conducted in this division.

* Judicial Branch Answer Desk

Federal Judicial Center
Dolly Madison House
1 Columbus Circle N.E.
Washington, DC 20002 (202) 273-4153

Call this center to determine how this branch of government can help you or can refer you to the appropriate office, agency, or court.

* Judicial Conference Update

Federal Judicial Center
Center Information Services Office
1 Columbus Circle N.E.
Washington, DC 20002 (202) 273-4153

The Third Branch is a monthly bulletin that reports to the federal judicial community and other parties on the endeavors of the Judicial Conference. It also provides a monthly update of changes in federal judicial personnel.

* Judicial Education and Training

Federal Judicial Center
1 Columbus Circle, NE

Be patient. If any phone number is incorrect, call (area code) 555-1212 and request the new listing.

Courts and Legal Help

Washington, DC 20002 (202) 273-4153
This Center provides continuing education for federal judicial personnel. It also conducts research, development, and training for the judicial system.

* Judicial Research Reports

Federal Judicial Center
1 Columbus Circle, NE
Washington, DC 20002 (202) 273-4153
Research reports, staff papers, manuals, handbooks, and catalogs are publications that are available containing the results of research and analysis done for or by the Center. A publications catalog and other information can be obtained from the Federal Judicial Center.

* Law School Free Legal Clinics

Office of Public Affairs
Legal Services Corporation
750 1st St., NE, 11th Floor
Washington, DC 20002 (202) 336-8896
The Law School Clinic Program is an additional source of legal assistance for the poor. A significant achievement of these clinics is their ability to educate students in substantive and procedural law, while providing a service to clients in their local communities.

* Legal Aid and Services Clearinghouse

National Clearinghouse on Legal Services
407 S. Dearborn St.
Chicago, IL 60605 (312) 939-3830
As a grantee of the Legal Services Corporation, this clearinghouse conducts research on computerized databases for LSC funded organizations. They maintain a brief bank and publish two newsletters each month with information on legal briefs. Copies of the briefs are free to LSC organizations, and for a slight fee to the public. Each month they publish Clearinghouse Review, which contains relevant articles and briefs (free to LSC organizations, a yearly fee to all others). The clearinghouse also has manuals on public law.

* Legal Services and Problems

Office of Public Affairs
Legal Services Corporation
750 1st St. NE
11th Floor
Washington, DC 20002 (202) 336-8896
If you are in need of legal services, the Office of Public Affairs can direct you to the LSC field office that serves your area. If you feel that you are eligible for services but are denied by the field office, LSC's Public Affairs Office will help you have your complaints investigated.

* Legal Services Corporation Grantees and Contracts

Office of Field Services
Legal Services Corporation
750 1st St. NE, 11th Floor
Washington, DC 20002 (202) 336-8800
A Fact Book, published yearly by LSC for $30, contains information regarding LSC funding data, program expenditures, and program characteristics, as well as information on national support centers and program services to clients. The Corporation's objective in compiling and issuing this *Fact Book* is to provide a complete and objective profile of legal services programs, which can serve as a reliable reference tool for policy decision-making and further quantitative analysis. A directory of the Legal Services Corporation's contract and grantee agencies is available for $8.

* Legal Services Corporation Opinions

General Counsel's Office
Legal Services Corporation
750 1st St. NE
Washington, DC 20002 (202) 336-8800
This office contains the final opinions, briefs, and orders for all cases adjudicated by Legal Services Corporation. All of these documents can be examined during business hours.

* Legal Services Corporation Newsletter

Legal Services Corporation
750 1st St. NE.
Washington, DC 20002 (202) 336-8800
Legal Services Board is a quarterly publication which contains information on LSC regulations and activities, as well as articles by Board members. Information is also included on LSC funded organizations.

* Legal Services National Support Centers

Office of Public Affairs
Legal Services Corporation
750 1st St. NE
Washington, DC 20002 (202) 336-8896
The Corporation currently funds sixteen National Support Centers that specialize in various aspects of "poverty law" or in the problems of particular classes of individuals, such as migrants or the elderly. The centers produce publications and provide information relating to their respective areas. In addition they lobby Congress and federal agencies and monitor legislation and regulations of interest to their purported constituencies. The Support Centers, however, provide little or no actual representation of poor clients. Contact this office for more information regarding the individual Support Centers and their areas of interest.

* Mediation Board Publications

Office of Executive Secretary
National Mediation Board
1301 K St., NW,
Washington, DC 20572 (202) 523-5920
There are three annual subscription mailing lists available from the Board. Costs may be reduced or waived when it is in the public interest to do so.

Subscription List #1, $175: *Annual Reports of the NMB; Certifications and Dismissals; Determination of Craft or Class; Findings Upon Investigation; Emergency Board Reports.*

Subscription List #2, $ 50: *Annual Reports of the NMB; Emergency Board Reports; Determination of Craft or Class.*

Subscription List #3, $ 35: *The Representation Manual and Amendments.*

* Mediation Cases

Legal Services Office
Federal Mediation and Conciliation Service (FMCS)
2100 K St., NW, Room 712
Washington, DC 20427 (202) 653-5305
This office represents FMCS in legal cases. In unusually complex and technical mediation efforts, Legal Services staff participate as part of the mediation team. Contact this office for more information on labor-management conciliation cases.

* Mediation National Board Freedom of Information

National Mediation Board
1301 K St., NW
Washington, DC 20572 (202) 523-5996
This office handles Freedom of Information Act requests regarding the National Mediation Board.

* Native Americans with Disabilities Legal Aid

Native American DNA-People's Legal Services
P.O. Box 306
Window Rock, AZ 86515 (602) 871-4151
This advocacy group provides legal help to Indians with handicaps and developmental disabilities.

* Probation Practices

Administrative Office of the United States Courts
Probation Division
Washington, DC 20002 (202) 273-1600
The quarterly journal, *Federal Probation*, contains correctional philosophy and practices. The Administrative Office supervises the accounts and practices of the federal probation offices. Contact this office to obtain a copy.

Be patient. If any phone number is incorrect, call (area code) 555-1212 and request the new listing.

Law and Social Justice

* Public Defenders of U.S. Courts

Administrative Office of the United States Courts
1 Columbus Circle NW
Washington, DC 20002 (202) 273-3000

Under the Criminal Justice Act, the *Federal Public Defenders and Federal Community Defender Organizations by the Districts Courts* is made available to the public. *Annual Reports* are provided by Defender organizations listing their activities.

* State Justice Free Newsletter

State Justice Institute News
120 South Fairfax St.
Alexandria, VA 22314 (703) 684-6100

This free quarterly newsletter, *State Justice Institute News*, provides information about SJI grant programs, upcoming conferences, and the grant application process.

* State Justice Grant Categories

State Justice Institute
120 South Fairfax St.
Alexandria, VA 22314 (703) 684-6100

The Institute provides grants, contracts and cooperative agreements to State courts and organizations that can help improve the judicial administration of the State courts. To accomplish this goal, the Institute funds education projects in five categories: 1) Programs of proven merit which support established, exemplary, direct training to State trial and appellate court judges and other court personnel; 2) State initiatives which support state-based training projects developed or endorsed by the State courts for the benefit of judges and other court personnel in a particular state. This would include pre-bench orientation, development of bench books and model plans for career-long education for the judiciary; 3) National and regional training programs which fund projects addressing SJI Special Interest categories, which include seminars on topics that transcend state lines, regional training programs sponsored by national organizations, or specialized training programs for trial court judges; 4) Technical assistance which provides coordination, support services, information distribution, and other activities necessary for the development of effective education programs for judges, such as the development of educational curriculum or distribution of information about continuing judicial education programs; 5) Conferences which fund regional or national conferences that address topics of major concern to state judiciary.

* Supreme Court Document Copies

Library
Supreme Court of the United States
1 1st St., NE
Washington, DC 20543 (202) 479-3175

Supreme Court documents may be copied at the Library, Supreme Court of the United States, or by mail at the cost of $.10 per page by contacting the Photoduplication Service, Library of Congress, Washington, DC 20540; (202) 479-3011.

* Supreme Court Information

Supreme Court
Clerk's Office
1 1st St., NE
Washington, DC 20543 (202) 479-3011

The status of pending cases, docket sheet information, and admissions to the Supreme Court bar can be obtained from the Clerk's Office. This office also distributes court opinions.

* Supreme Court Publications

Supreme Court of the United States
Information
Supreme Court Building
1 1st St., NE
Washington, DC 20543 (202) 479-3000

Individual Slip Opinions include all of the Supreme Court's opinions as announced from the bench. They are issued periodically and cost $140 a term of Court. *Preliminary Prints* (advance parts) are official United States Reports containing all the opinions with syllabi, indices, tables of cases, and other editorial additions. They are issued periodically and cost $56 a term of Court.

* Supreme Court Records

Supreme Court
Clerk's Office
1 1st St., NE
Washington, DC 20543 (202) 479-3011

Supreme Court records are housed in over 20 regional depositories. Contact this office for a list of their locations.

* Tax Court Decisions

United States Tax Court
400 2nd St., NW
Washington, DC 20217 (202) 376-2754

United States Tax Court Reports contain a consolidation of the tax decisions for a month. The yearly subscription cost is $26 and is available from the Superintendent of Documents, Government Printing Office, Washington, DC 20402; (202) 783-3238.

* Tribal Courts for Native Americans

Office of Tribal Services
Bureau of Indian Affairs
U.S. Department of the Interior
18th and C Sts., NW
Washington, DC 20240 (202) 208-3710

This office serves as a cross between the Health and Human Services, Labor, Justice, and Housing and Urban Development Departments for the Indian population. The needy are paid welfare subsidies and provided job training. This office also operates 19 special federal courts and funds 127 tribal courts, along with administering the police force for Indian reservations, and a rehabilitation program for Indian homes.

Be patient. If any phone number is incorrect, call (area code) 555-1212 and request the new listing.

Immigration and Naturalization

* "Ask Immigration" Center

Central Office
Immigration and Naturalization Service (INS)
425 I Street, NW
Washington, DC 20536 (202) 514-4316

The "Ask Immigration" telephone service system provides pre-recorded information on a wide range of immigration- and citizenship-related topics. This Service is available 24 hours a day, 7 days a week. If you are calling from a location outside the local calling area of the INS office, you will be charged long distance telephone costs. Immigration Information Officers are available to provide personal assistance at the local INS offices listed below during different times of the day. To find out the exact times such assistance is available and the regular business hours for each office, listen carefully to the initial answer message when you call the office in your area and follow the instructions provided. If all you need is an INS form and want it mailed to your address, the initial message will tell you which number on your telephone to press. Leave your name, address, INS form(s) needed, and/or information materials you require. For the Immigration Service to respond promptly to your request, be sure to state your name clearly, spelling it if necessary, and provide your current, complete address. After calling the appropriate state INS office (refer to separate listing of INS state offices), enter one of the number codes below which corresponds to the information about immigration and naturalization that you need.

Information About INS, Special Policies and How to Report Illegal Aliens:
101 the Immigration and Naturalization Service
102 how to report aliens illegally in the U.S. and companies that hire them
103 PRC Nationals
104 the INS Outreach Program
105 where to mail applications
106 reporting your change of address to INS
107 how to obtain copies of documents
108 immigrant visa availability list
109 filing Appeals and Motions

Information About Legalization and Employer Sanctions:
201 who is eligible for legalization
202 employer sanctions
203 family fairness program for legalized aliens
204 anti-discrimination protection under immigration law
205 how to apply for permanent resident status if you resided in the U.S. since January 1972
206 special agricultural worker program
207 systematic alien verification for entitlements program

Information About Immigrant Visas, Adoptions, Asylum and Permanent Residency:
301 filing petition to sponsor an immediate relative
302 filing petitions to sponsor prospective immigrant employees
303 how an alien in the U.S. may request to change their status to become a permanent resident
304 when a U.S. citizen marries a foreign national outside the U.S.A.
305 how to file a joint petition for a spouse to remove conditional basis of permanent resident status
306 immigration benefits for adoption before 16th birthday
307 orphan petitions
308 application for asylum in the U.S.A.
309 permanent residence for recipients of approved asylum applications

Information About Obtaining or Replacing an Alien Residency (or Green) Card:
401 how to obtain an alien residency card
402 applying for a replacement alien residency card
403 if you never received your alien residency card

Information About Temporary Nonimmigrant Visas and Status:
501 nonimmigrant or temporary visas
502 how to request an extension of temporary stay

503 change of status from one nonimmigrant classification to another for work purposes
504 applying for a replacement I-94 arrival-departure document
505 temporary visitors' visa
506 a fiance/fiancee visa
507 requirements for classification as a nonimmigrant temporary worker or trainee H-1, H-2 and H-3
508 requirements for classification as a J-1 nonimmigrant exchange alien
509 L-1 visa status for intracompany transfers
510 requirements for classification as an E-1 or E-2 nonimmigrant treaty trader or investor

Information About Foreign Student Visas:
601 permission to go to school
602 student visa extension
603 permission for foreign student to work
604 visas for spouse and dependent children of foreign students
606 how to maintain your student status

Permission For Travel Outside the United States:
701 departure from the U.S.A. by permanent residents
702 student travel outside the U.S.A.
703 travel authorization for refugees - refugee travel documents
704 how to request emergency travel
705 travel by an alien whose application for permanent resident status is still pending

Information About Citizenship and Naturalization:
801 citizenship and naturalization requirements
802 citizenship for children born outside the U.S.
803 naturalization bases upon military service
804 derivative citizenship for children of U.S. citizens
805 residency requirements for naturalization
806 how to file for naturalization in behalf of a child
807 replacement of certification of citizenship or naturalization
808 how to renounce or forfeit U.S. citizenship

* Citizenship Education Videos

Immigration and Naturalization Service (INS)
U.S. Department of Justice
425 Eye St., NW
Room 7228
Washington, DC 20536 (202) 514-4316

Schools, community service organizations, churches, or others who wish to run citizenship education programs may borrow any of the several videocassettes available from the INS free of charge. The INS currently has twelve videocassettes available covering topics ranging from a focus on specific articles of the Constitution to the story of the American Flag, from an examination of the electoral process to biographies of George Washington and Abraham Lincoln. All videocassettes will be shipped postage free. A complete list of the available videocassettes and a synopsis of each can also be obtained by writing or calling the INS. In addition, a series of textbooks are available for school districts wishing to include citizenship education in their curriculum. These textbooks come in elementary or secondary reading levels.

* Employers Hotline on Immigrant Employees

Immigration and Naturalization Service (INS)
U.S. Department of Justice
425 Eye St., NW
Room 7116
Washington, DC 20536 (202) 514-4316

If you are unsure how the Immigration Reform and Control Act affects you as employer, call this number. Information is available in both English and Spanish, on employee and employer responsibilities and punishments. You can also receive information on legalization requirements and other general information.

Be patient. If any phone number is incorrect, call (area code) 555-1212 and request the new listing.

Law and Social Justice

It will tell you exactly what your responsibilities are both to those workers who are eligible for legalization and those who are not, as well as explain your rights as an employer.

* Farmworkers: English and Spanish Immigration Information

Immigration and Naturalization Service (INS)
U.S. Department of Justice
425 Eye St., NW
Room 7116
Washington, DC 20536 (202) 514-4316

If you are unsure how the Immigration Reform and Control Act affects you as a farmworker, call this number. It contains important information, in both English and Spanish, on employee and employer responsibilities and punishments. It can tell you whether or not your employer has treated you fairly and what you can do about it. You can also receive information on alien benefits, legalization requirements, and other general information.

* Immigration and Naturalization State Offices

Each of these state offices operate "Ask Immigration". In addition to these tape recorded messages, staff is available to provide information and send literature in response to telephone requests.

Alaska
Anchorage: .... (907) 343-7820

Arizona
Phoenix: .... (602) 379-3122
Tucson: .... (602) 670-6229

California
Fresno: .... (209) 487-5091
Los Angeles: .... (213) 894-2119
Sacramento: .... (916) 551-2785
San Diego: .... (619) 557-5570
San Francisco: .... (415) 705-4411
San Jose: .... (408) 291-7876

Colorado
Denver: .... (303) 371-3041

Connecticut
Hartford: .... (203) 240-3171

District of Columbia
Washington, (Arlington, VA): .... (703) 307-1501
Washington, (INS Central Office): .... (202) 514-4316

Florida
Jacksonville: .... (904) 791-2624
Miami: .... (305) 536-5741
Tampa: .... (813) 228-2131

Georgia
Atlanta: .... (404) 331-5158

Hawaii
Honolulu: .... (808) 541-1379

Illinois
Chicago: .... (312) 353-7334

Indiana
Indianapolis: .... (317) 331-6009

Kentucky
Louisville: .... (502) 582-6375

Louisiana
New Orleans: .... (504) 589-6533

Maine
Portland: .... (207) 780-3352

Maryland
Baltimore: .... (301) 962-2065

Massachusetts
Boston: .... (617) 565-3879

Michigan
Detroit: .... (313) 226-3240

Minnesota
St. Paul: .... (612) 854-7754

Missouri
Kansas City: .... (816) 891-0603
St. Louis: .... (314) 539-2532

Montana
Helena: .... (406) 449-5288

Nebraska
Omaha: .... (402) 697-9155

Nevada
Las Vegas: .... (702) 384-3696
Reno: .... (702) 784-5427

New Jersey
Newark: .... (201) 645-4400

New Mexico
Albuquerque: .... (505) 766-2378

New York
Albany: .... (518) 472-4621
Buffalo: .... (716) 849-6760
New York: .... (212) 206-6500

North Carolina
Charlotte: .... (704) 523-1704

Ohio
Cincinnati: .... (513) 684-3781
Cleveland: .... (216) 522-4770

Oklahoma
Oklahoma City: .... (405) 231-4121

Oregon
Portland: .... (503) 326-3006

Pennsylvania
Philadelphia: .... (215) 597-3961
Pittsburgh: .... (412) 644-3356

Puerto Rico
San Juan: .... (809) 766-5280

Tennessee
Memphis: .... (901) 544-3301

Texas
Dallas: .... (214) 655-5384
El Paso: .... (915) 532-0273
Harlingen: .... (512) 425-7333
Houston: .... (713) 847-7900
San Antonio: .... (512) 229-6350

Utah
Salt Lake City: .... (801) 524-5771

Virginia
Norfolk: .... (804) 441-3081

Washington
Seattle: .... (206) 442-5956
Spokane: .... (509) 353-2129

Be patient. If any phone number is incorrect, call (area code) 555-1212 and request the new listing.

Immigration and Naturalization

* Political Asylum

Office of Asylum Affairs
Bureau of Human Rights and
Humanitarian Affairs
U.S. Department of State
SA-17, Room 520
Washington, DC 20520   (202) 326-6110

This office handles the U.S. Department of State's responsibilities regarding political asylum by providing advisory opinions on the cases to the Immigration and Naturalization Service.

* Work Permits for Foreigners

Labor Certification Division
Employment and Training Administration
U.S. Department of Labor
200 Constitution Ave., NW, Room N4456
Washington, DC 20210   (202) 535-0163

If an employer wishes to hire foreign workers, he must first obtain a foreign labor certificate, which is a statement from the U.S. Department of Labor stating that there is no U.S. citizen available to fill the job. The Department investigates to make sure the wages and working conditions of the foreign workers will not seriously affect U.S. workers. An employer applies for a foreign labor certificate through the local state employment service office, which then conducts a job hunt before sending the application form to the area regional office for approval or disapproval.

Be patient. If any phone number is incorrect, call (area code) 555-1212 and request the new listing.

Law and Social Justice

Discrimination and Civil Rights

* *See also Health and Medicine Chapter, Handicapped/Disabled Resources*
* *See also Information from Lawmakers Chapter*

* Advocates for the Handicapped Clearinghouse

National Information Center for Handicapped Children and Youth
PO Box 1492 (703) 893-6061
Washington, DC 20013 (800) 999-5599

This clearinghouse helps parents of handicapped children, disabled adults, and professionals locate services for the handicapped and information on disabilities.

* Affirmative Action and Hiring the Handicapped

Office of Federal Compliance Programs
Employment Standards Administration
U.S. Department of Labor
200 Constitution Ave., NW, Room C3325
Washington, DC 20210 (202) 523-9475

The Rehabilitation Act of 1973 prohibits most employers doing business with the federal government from discriminating in employment against handicapped persons. Employers with contracts in excess of $2,500 must take affirmative action to hire and promote qualified handicapped persons.

* Age Discrimination

U.S. Equal Employment Opportunity Commission (EEOC)
1400 L Street, NW (800) 669-3362
Washington, DC 20005 (202) 663-4264

Persons 40 years of age or older are protected by the Age Discrimination in Employment Act, which prohibits arbitrary age discrimination in hiring, discharge, pay, promotions, fringe benefits, and other aspects of employment. Retaliation against a person who files a charge of age discrimination, participates in an investigation, or opposes an unlawful practice is also illegal. Contact this office for their free fact sheet and more information on age discrimination.

* Alaskan Natives

Office of Public Affairs
Bureau of Indian Affairs
U.S. Department of the Interior
18th and C Sts., NW
Washington, DC 20240 (202) 208-3710

Some free publications available from the Bureau of Indian Affairs Public Affairs office. Due to the limited supply and small staff, only one copy of each publication may be requested:

Federal Acknowledgment Process
Alaska Natives
American Indian and Alaskan Native Education
Bureau of Indian Affairs Social Services Program
1980 Census Count of American Indians
Employment with BIA
Housing Program for Indians
List of Tribal Entities Recognized and Eligible to Receive Services from the U.S. Bureau of Indian Affairs Federal/Indian Relationship

* American Indians Rights

Office of Public Affairs
Bureau of Indian Affairs
U.S. Department of the Interior
18th and C Sts., NW
Washington, DC 20240 (202) 208-3710

The free booklet, *American Indians Today: Answers to Your Questions, 1991*, contains useful information on the Native American Indians and their relationship to the Bureau of Indian Affairs. Programs within the Bureau,

including education, health services, and housing are briefly outlined and contain recent statistics. Many questions are answered within the booklet, including the rights of the Indians to own land and have their own governments. A map locates the Indian lands and communities, showing Federal and State Indian Reservations and other Indian groups. An excellent bibliography, prepared by the Smithsonian Institution, is included. It will also provide sources for audio-visual materials.

* Asian Americans and Immigrants Discrimination

U.S. Commission on Civil Rights
Clearinghouse Division, Room 700
1121 Vermont Ave., NW
Washington, DC 20425 (202) 376-8105

The Commission is a primary source for civil rights laws and regulations. Numerous publications are available at no charge from the Commission on Civil Rights and they may also be available at depository libraries including:

Recent Activities Against Citizens and Residents of Asian Descent. Discusses historical discrimination against Asian immigrants and Asian Americans, factors in anti-Asian activity, and specific incidents since 1920 of violence, harassment, and intimidation against persons of Asian descent.

* Business EEOC Assistance Program

Office of Program Operations
U.S. Equal Employment Opportunity Commission (EEOC)
1400 L Street, NW (800) 669-3362
Washington, DC 20005 (202) 663-4264

The EEOC offers access to equal employment information and provides educational and technical assistance to small and mid-size employers and unions regarding their rights and obligations under federal laws prohibiting discrimination in the workplace. The program stresses such topics as sex and discrimination, sexual harassment, employee selection procedures, recordkeeping requirements, and layoffs. Contact this office for more information on assistance programs.

* Civil Rights Commission Clearinghouse

Robert S. Rankin Civil Rights Library
U.S. Commission on Civil Rights
1121 Vermont Ave., NW, Room 709
Washington, DC 20425 (202) 376-8810

The Civil Rights Memorial Library, located at the Civil Rights Commission's headquarters in Washington, DC, is a clearinghouse of civil rights information and contains 50,000 reference works, including 400 civil rights and minority issues journals, periodicals, legal journals, 3,500 reels of microfilm, and a comprehensive collection of reports, transcripts, and civil rights texts. It also maintains two online database systems: Ohio College Library Center (OCLC), and Dialog.

* Civil Rights Commission Regional Offices

Eastern Regional Division, 1121 Vermont Ave., NW, Washington, DC 20425; (202) 523-5264

Central Regional Division, Old Federal Office Building, 911 Walnut Street, Room 3103, Kansas City, MO 64106; (816) 374-5253

Western Regional Division, 3660 Wilshire Boulevard, Suite 810, Los Angeles, CA 90010; (213) 894-3437

Be patient. If any phone number is incorrect, call (area code) 555-1212 and request the new listing.

Discrimination and Civil Rights

* Civil Rights Complaints

U.S. Commission on Civil Rights
Complaint Referral
1121 Vermont Ave., NW
Washington, DC 20425 (202) 376-8376

Contact this office or a regional office of the CCR if you have complaints about discrimination and/or the abuse of civil rights.

* Civil Rights Directories and Publications

U.S. Commission on Civil Rights
Clearinghouse Division, Room 700
1121 Vermont Ave., NW
Washington, DC 20425 (202) 376-8105

The following publications are a sampling of those available at no charge from the Commission on Civil Rights. These publications are designed to provide reliable information about civil rights problems and about the laws, procedures, and approaches available for resolving them. A complete *Catalog of Publications* is available free of charge, and those publications that are out of print may be available at depository libraries across the U.S.

Civil Rights Directory. Lists private and public individuals and organizations concerned with civil rights at local, State, Federal, and national levels.

The Economic Progress of Black Men in America. Examines earnings and employment of black men from 1940 to 1980, sources of the earning gap with white men and effects of civil rights policies.

Police Practices and the Preservation of Civil Rights. A statement expressing concern that violation of civil rights by some police officers is a serious national problem. Includes recommendations for remedy.

* Civil Rights Enforcement

Civil Rights Division
U.S. Department of Justice
10th St. and Constitution Ave., NW
Room 5643
Washington, DC 20530 (202) 514-2007

If you have any questions as to the enforcement of 1964 Civil Rights Act, contact the Civil Rights Division. Information on the history of Civil Rights enforcement, as well as actual case history may be obtained by calling or writing the above address. Note: This office will not have information on the Civil Rights movement or on Dr. Martin Luther King, Jr., except insofar as they pertain to federal investigations or prosecutions.

* Civil Rights Hearings

U.S. Commission on Civil Rights
Clearinghouse Division, Room 700
1121 Vermont Ave., NW
Washington, DC 20425 (202) 376-8376

Transcripts of discussions at conferences, consultations sponsored by the Commission on Civil Rights, and testimony at Commission hearings are available to the public. Commission hearings focus government and public attention on civil rights problems and examine the manner in which Federal authorities discharge their civil rights responsibilities.

* Civil Rights: Proposed Legislation

U.S. Commission on Civil Rights
Office of Staff Director
1121 Vermont Ave., NW
Washington, DC 20425 (202) 523-5571

This office can provide you with current information on civil rights legislation and other relevant issues of civil rights law.

* Civil Rights Updates and Newsletter

U.S. Commission on Civil Rights
1121 Vermont Ave., NW
Washington, DC 20425 (202) 376-8177

Update, a monthly summary of the Civil Rights Commission's projects and activities, is available to the public free of charge. Another free publication, *Perspectives*, is published quarterly to provide varied views and information on civil rights issues.

* Employment Discrimination and Affirmative Action

Equal Opportunity Programs Staff
Justice Management Division
U.S. Department of Justice
10th St. and Constitution Ave., NW
Room 1230
Washington, DC 20530 (202) 514-6734

Do you feel you've been unjustly discriminated against in the workplace? Contact this office and the U.S. Department of Justice will tell you exactly how the annual affirmative action plan affects equal employment opportunity.

* Employment Discrimination: Filing A Complaint

U.S. Equal Employment Opportunity Commission (EEOC)
1400 L Street, NW
Washington, DC 20005 (800) 669-3362

If you believe you have been discriminated against by an employer, labor union, or employment agency when applying for a job or on the job because of race, color, sex, religion, national origin, or age, you may file a charge of discrimination with the EEOC. Charges may be filed in person, by mail, or telephone by contacting the nearest EEOC field office or the national office listed above.

* Equal Employment Opportunity Hotline

U.S. Equal Employment Opportunity Commission (EEOC)
1400 L Street, NW (800) 669-3362
Washington, DC 20005 (202) 663-4264

This toll-free hotline receives and investigates employment discrimination charges against private employers and state and local governments. The EEOC Attorney-of-the-Day can offer telephone guidance to callers with their questions about alleged discrimination.

* Equal Employment Opportunity Offices Nationwide

Albuquerque Area Office, 505 Marquette, NW, Suite 900, Albuquerque, NM 87102-2189, (505) 766-2061

Atlanta District Office, 75 Piedmont Avenue, NE, Suite 1100, Atlanta, GA 30335; (404) 331-6093

Baltimore District Office, 111 Market Place, Suite 4000, Baltimore, MD 21202; (301) 962-3932

Birmingham District Office, 2121 Eighth Avenue, North, Suite 824, Birmingham, AL 35203; (205) 731-0082

Boston Area Office, 1 Congress St., Boston, MA 02114; (617) 565-3200

Buffalo Local Office, 28 Church Street, Room 301, Buffalo, NY 14202; (716) 846-4441

Charlotte District Office, 5500 Central Avenue, Charlotte, NC 28212; (704) 567-7100

Chicago District Office, 536 South Clark Street, Room 930-A Chicago, IL 60605; (312) 353-2713

Cincinnati Area Office, The Ameritrust Building, 525 Vine St., Suite 801, Cincinnati, OH 45202; (513) 684-2851

Cleveland District Office, 1375 Euclid Avenue, Room 600, Cleveland, OH 44115; (216) 522-2001

Dallas District Office, 8303 Elmbrook Drive, Dallas, TX 75247; (214) 767-7015

Denver District Office, 1845 Sherman Street, 2nd Floor, Denver, CO 80203; (303) 866-1300

Detroit District Office, 477 Michigan Avenue, Room 1540, Detroit, MI 48226; (313) 226-7636

El Paso Area Office, The Commons Building C., 4171 N.Mesa St., Suite 103, El Paso, TX 79901; (915) 534-6550

Be patient. If any phone number is incorrect, call (area code) 555-1212 and request the new listing.

Law and Social Justice

Fresno Local Office, 1313 P Street, Suite 103, Fresno, CA 93721; (209) 487-5793

Greensboro Local Office, 324 West Market Street, Room B-27, P.O. Box 3363, Greensboro, NC 27401; (919) 333-5174

Greenville Local Office, 15 S. Main St., Suite 530, Greenville, SC 29601; (803) 241-4400

Honolulu Local Office, 677 Ala Moana Blvd., Suite 404, P.O. Box 50082, Honolulu, HI 96813; (808) 541-3120

Houston District Office, 1919 Smith St., 7th Floor, Houston, TX 77002; (713) 653-3320

Indianapolis District Office, 46 East Ohio Street, Room 456, Indianapolis, IN 46204; (317) 226-7212

Jackson Area Office, 207 W. Amite St., Jackson, MS 39201; (601) 965-4537

Kansas City Area Office, 911 Walnut, 10th Floor, Kansas City, MO 64106; (816) 426-5773

Little Rock Area Office, 320 West Capitol Avenue, Suite 621, Little Rock, AR 72201; (501) 378-5060

Los Angeles District Office, 3660 Wilshire Boulevard, 5th Floor, Los Angeles, CA 90010; (213) 251-7278

Louisville Area Office, 600 Martin Luther King Jr. Place, Room 268, Louisville, KY 40202; (502) 582-6082

Memphis District Office, 1407 Union Avenue, Suite 621, Memphis, TN 38104; (901) 722-2617

Miami District Office, Federal Building, One Northeast First Street, 6th Floor, Miami, FL 33132; (305) 536-4491

Milwaukee District Office, 310 West Wisconsin Avenue, Suite 800, Milwaukee, WI 53203; (414) 297-1111

Minneapolis Local Office, 220 Second Street South, Room 108, Minneapolis MN 55401-2141; (612) 370-3330

Nashville Area Office, 50 Vantage Way, Suite 202, Nashville, TN 37228; (615) 736-5820

Newark Area Office, 60 Park Place, Room 301, Newark, NJ 07102; (201) 645-6383

New Orleans District Office, 701 Loyola Avenue, Suite 600, New Orleans, LA 70113; (504) 589-2329

New York District Office, 90 Church Street, Room 1501, New York, NY 10007; (212) 264-7161

Norfolk Area Office, 252 Monticello Ave., 1st Floor, Norfolk, VA 23510; (804) 441-3470

Oakland Local Office; 1333 Broadway, Room 430, Oakland, CA 94612; (415) 273-7588

Oklahoma Area Office, 531 Couch Drive, Oklahoma City, OK 73102; (405) 231-4911

Philadelphia District Office, 1421 Cherry Street, 10th Floor, Philadelphia, PA 19102; (215) 592-9350

Phoenix District Office, 4520 N. Central Avenue, Suite 300, Phoenix, AZ 85012-1848; (602) 640-5000

Pittsburgh Area Office, 1000 Liberty Ave., Room 2038 A, Pittsburgh, PA 15222, (412) 644-3444

Raleigh Area Office, 1309 Annapolis Dr., Raleigh, NC 27608; (919) 856-4064

Richmond Area Office, 3600 W. Broad St., Room 229, Richmond, VA 23240; (804) 771-2692

San Antonio District Office, 5410 Fredericksburg Road, Suite 200, San Antonio, TX 78229; (512) 229-4810

San Diego Local Office, 401 B St., Suite 1550, San Diego, CA 92101; (619) 557-7235

San Francisco District Office, 901 Market Street, Suite 500, San Francisco, CA 94103; (415) 744-6500

San Jose Local Office, 96 N. 3rd St., Suite 200, San Jose, CA 95112; (408) 291-7352

Savannah Local Office, 10 Whitaker Street, Suite B, Savannah, GA 31401; (912) 944-4234

Seattle District Office, 2815 Second Avenue, Suite 500, Seattle, WA 98121; (206) 553-0968

St. Louis District Office, 625 N. Euclid Street, 5th Floor, St. Louis, MO 63108; (314) 425-6585

Tampa Area Office, 501 E. Polk St., Suite 1020, Tampa, FL 33602; (813) 228-2310

Washington Field Office, 1400 L St. NW, Suite 200, Washington, DC 20005; (202) 663-4264

* Equal Opportunity and Non-Discrimination

Information Handling and Support Facilities
General Accounting Office
P.O. Box 6015
Gaithersburg, MD 20877 (202) 275-6241

A Compilation of Federal Laws and Executive Orders for Nondiscrimination and Equal Opportunity Programs (#HRD-78-138) is a free 72-page book that can help companies avoid employment discrimination problems. It cites 87 laws and orders relating to equal rights in employment practices, as well as in the provision of services. Each citation briefly describes the law or order, identifies what type of discrimination it prohibits and to whom it applies, and which agencies enforce it.

* Equal Work Equal Pay

U.S. Equal Employment Opportunity Commission (EEOC)
1400 L Street, NW (800) 669-3362
Washington, DC 20005 (202) 663-4264

Women and men who perform substantially equal work in the same establishment are covered by the Equal Pay Act, which prohibits employers from discriminating in pay because of sex and from reducing the wages of either sex to comply with the law. A violation may exist where a different wage is paid to a predecessor or successor employee of the opposite sex. Retaliation against a person who files a charge of equal pay discrimination, participates in an investigation, or opposes an unlawful employment practice also is illegal. Contact this office for a free fact sheet or to file a complaint.

* Fair Housing Local and State Agencies

U.S. Commission on Civil Rights
Clearinghouse Division, Room 700
1121 Vermont Ave., NW
Washington, DC 20425 (202) 376-8105

The Commission is a primary source for civil rights laws and regulations. Numerous publications are available at no charge from the Commission on Civil Rights and they may also be available at depository libraries including:

Directory of State and Local Fair Housing Agencies. For 91 State and local governmental agencies, describes classes protected under the pertinent fair housing law and unlawful discriminatory housing practices.

* Housing Discrimination

Housing and Civil Enforcement Section
Civil Rights Division
U.S. Department of Justice
10th St. and Constitution Ave., NW, Room 7525
Washington, DC 20530 (202) 514-2007

Be patient. If any phone number is incorrect, call (area code) 555-1212 and request the new listing.

Discrimination and Civil Rights

If you feel you've been denied housing due to racial, sexual, or religious discrimination, contact the Housing and Civil Enforcement Section of the U.S. Department of Justice. Their advisers can tell you if and what action is warranted in your case, and they can also refer you to local agencies for the help you need. This office is also responsible for bringing civil actions in federal courts whenever there is reasonable cause to believe that a person or group is denying housing unjustly due to discrimination.

* Minorities and Women: Last Hired, First Fired

U.S. Commission on Civil Rights
Clearinghouse Division
Room 700
1121 Vermont Ave., NW
Washington, DC 20425 (202) 376-8105

The Commission is a primary source for civil rights laws and regulations. Numerous publications are available at no charge from the Commission on Civil Rights and they may also be available at depository libraries including:

Last Hired, First Fired: Layoffs and Civil Rights. Examines the effects of seniority as applied to layoffs of minority and female workers.

* Minority Hiring Statistics

U.S. Equal Employment Opportunity Commission (EEOC)
Survey Division, 9th Floor
1400 L Street, NW
Washington, DC 20005 (202) 363-4948

EEOC compiles minority employment statistics for the following groups: private employment; unions; state and local governments; elementary and secondary education; health services; clericals; service-oriented industries; and skilled and craft industries. The database is searchable by occupation, industry, and region–state, county, or city. Searches and printouts are available free of charge. A publications catalog is free upon request.

* Native Americans with Disabilities Legal Aid

Native American DNA-People's Legal Services
P.O. Box 306
Window Rock, AZ 86515 (602) 871-4151

This advocacy group provides legal help to Indians with handicaps and developmental disabilities. * Native

* Native Americans Rights

Office of Public Affairs
Bureau of Indian Affairs
U.S. Department of the Interior
18th and C Sts., NW
Washington, DC 20240 (202) 208-3710

The free booklet, *American Indians Today: Answers to Your Questions, 1988,* contains useful information on the Native American Indians and their relationship to the Bureau of Indian Affairs. Programs within the Bureau, including education, health services, and housing are briefly outlined and contain recent statistics. Many questions are answered within the booklet, including the rights of the Indians to own land and have their own governments. A map locates the Indian lands and communities, showing Federal and State Indian Reservations and other Indian groups. An excellent bibliography, prepared by the Smithsonian Institution, is included.

* Pregnancy Discrimination

U.S. Equal Employment Opportunity Commission (EEOC)
1400 L Street, NW (800) 669-3362
Washington, DC 20005 (202) 663-4264

Discrimination on the basis of pregnancy, childbirth, or related medical conditions constitutes unlawful sex discrimination. Women affect by pregnancy or related conditions must be treated in the same manner as other applicants or employees with similar abilities or limitations. Contact EEOC for more information on hiring, pregnancy and maternity leave, child care, health insurance, fringe benefits, and filing charges of discrimination.

* Religious Discrimination

U.S. Commission on Civil Rights
Clearinghouse Division, Room 700
1121 Vermont Ave., NW
Washington, DC 20425 (202) 376-8105

The Commission is a primary source for civil rights laws and regulations. Numerous publications are available at no charge from the Commission on Civil Rights and they may also be available at depository libraries including:

Religion in the Constitution: A Delicate Balance. Addresses the issues of religious discrimination.

* School Desegregation and Textbooks

U.S. Commission on Civil Rights
Clearinghouse Division, Room 700
1121 Vermont Ave., NW
Washington, DC 20425 (202) 376-8105

The Commission is a primary source for civil rights laws and regulations. Numerous publications are available at no charge from the Commission on Civil Rights and they may also be available at depository libraries including:

Fair Textbooks: A Resource Guide. Lists materials aimed at reducing biases in textbooks, organizations, publishers, and their guidelines.

New Evidence on School Desegregation. This report analyzes data from 125 school districts for 1967 to 1985 to see the extent of racial imbalance in schools.

* Sex Discrimination and Filing Complaints

U.S. Commission on Civil Rights
Clearinghouse Division, Room 700
1121 Vermont Ave., NW
Washington, DC 20425 (202) 376-8105

The Commission is a primary source for civil rights laws and regulations. Numerous publications are available at no charge from the Commission on Civil Rights and they may also be available at depository libraries including:

Guide to Federal Laws and Regulations Prohibiting Sex Discrimination. Summarizes Federal laws, policies, and regulations banning sex discrimination and tells how to file complaints.

* Voting Rights

U.S. Commission on Civil Rights
Clearinghouse Division, Room 700
1121 Vermont Ave., NW
Washington, DC 20425 (202) 376-8105

The Commission is a primary source for civil rights laws and regulations. Numerous publications are available at no charge from the Commission on Civil Rights and they may also be available at depository libraries including:

Citizen's Guide to Understanding the Voting Rights Act. Explains the provisions of the 1965 Voting Rights Act, and how individuals may make complaints and comments.

The Voting Rights Act: Unfulfilled Goals. An evaluation of the status of minority voting rights in jurisdictions covered by the original provision of the 1965 act.

Information on People, Companies, and Mailing Lists Who Owes Money To Whom

Any public or private company, organization, and for that matter, individual, that borrows money and offers an asset as collateral, must file with the state at the Office of Uniform Commercial Code (UCC). A filing is made for each loan and each of the documents is available to the public. To obtain these documents is a two-step process. The first step is to request a search to see if there are any filings for a certain company. The fee for such a search usually is under $10. You will next want to request copies of each of these documents. The cost for each document averages only a few dollars. This Office of Uniform Commercial Code is part of the state government and usually is located near or in the same office as the Office of Corporations which falls under the Secretary of State.

The initial search of records will provide:

- the number of listings under one name;
- the file number for each of the listings;
- the date and time of filing; and
- the name and address of the debtor.

Each UCC filing will disclose:

- a description of the asset placed as collateral; and
- the name and address of the secured party.

This disclosure not only provides insights into the financial security of an individual or organization, but it can also give a picture of their assets. Remember, this information is available on any public or private company or individual. The next time your brother-in-law asks you for money for a new business venture, it probably is worth the investment of a few dollars for a UCC search to see whether your relative owes money to others.

Most states will ask if you would like certified or non-certified information. Certification means that they will stand by the accuracy of the information if it is used in a court or other legal proceeding. For most cases, business researchers will not need the extra procedure of certification.

Farm Loan Filings

The Food and Security Act of 1986 is a law that involves filings on crop and livestock loans. Not all states have adopted this law. However, those which have must set up an automated central filing system under the Office of Uniform Commercial Code. Many states have not adopted the law because of the expense involved in setting up the system. Under this system the office must be able to provide information on filings in 24 hours. The purpose of the system is to notify those who purchase crops from growers if the farmer has already offered that crop as collateral.

UCC Request Forms

Some states provide you with current information about recent filings over the telephone, but others will only accept your request on a standard UCC Form. Still others will respond if you send your request in writing but will give you a discount if your query is on an official UCC Form. Most states use UCC Form 11 for requesting information. Copies of UCC Forms for all 50 states are available by calling Forms, Inc. (800-854-1080). The cost for any amount under 100 is sixty cents a form.

Online Access

With online capabilities you can usually search by such categories as: personal or commercial debtor, type of amendments, name of secured party, name of assigned party, and type of collateral. The following states offer online access to their files: Alabama, Colorado, Florida, Illinois, Iowa, Kansas, Massachusetts, Mississippi, New Mexico, Oregon, South Dakota, Texas, Utah, Washington, and Wyoming.

Exceptions

Louisiana is the only state that has not adopted the Uniform Commercial Code. Some parishes (counties) require filings. In Georgia these filings are maintained by the Clerk of the Superior Court.

Uniform Commercial Code Offices

Alabama

Uniform Commercial Code Division, Secretary of State, 4121 Carmichael Rd. Suite 200, Montgomery, AL 36106; (205) 242-5231 (mailing address: P.O. Box 5616, Montgomery, AL 36103). Searches: Requests must be submitted in writing. The charge is $5 for name searches submitted on Alabama Form UCC-11, $7 for searches submitted by letter and $1 for each additional listing. Copies of Documents: Available for $1 per page. Farm Filings: Call (205) 242-5231. List of new farm filings published every month. Regular printed listing is $25 per year for each collateral code. Microfiche listing is $15 per year for each collateral code. Online Access: Pilot Dial Up Program. Free. Does not show collateral. Contact: Robina Jenkins, (205) 242-5136.

Alaska

Uniform Commercial Code Division, Central Filing System, 3601 C St., Ste 1140-A, Anchorage, AK 99503; (907) 762-2104. Searches: Requests must be submitted in writing on an Alaska Form UCC-11. The charge is $15 per listing for copy search, $5 for information search. Information search only states whether an encumbrance exists and when it was filed. Copies of Documents: Available for $15 for all documents in a file (includes search fee.). File does not include lapsed documents. Farm Filings: Maintained by the District Recorder's Office.

Arizona

Uniform Commercial Code Department, Secretary of State, 7th Floor, 1700 W. Washington, Phoenix, AZ 85007; (602) 542-6178. Searches: Requests must be submitted in writing on Arizona Form UCC-3 or UCC-11. The charge is $8 per

Be patient. If any phone number is incorrect, call (area code) 555-1212 and request the new listing.

Who Owes Money To Whom

name plus 50 cents per listing for copying fee. Fees must be paid in advance. Send blank check with stated limit or $8 and they will call you with the additional amount. When they receive it they will release the documents. Copies of Documents: Available for 50 cents a page. Farm Filings: Maintained by the County Recorder.

Arkansas

Uniform Commercial Code, Secretary of State, State Capitol Building, Room 25, Little Rock, AR 72201; (501) 682-5078. Searches: Requests must be submitted in writing in a letter or on a Arkansas Form UCC-11. The charge is $5 per debtor name. Copies of Documents: Available for $5 for the first three pages. Each additional page is $1. They will bill you for copies. Farm Filings: Maintained in this office. Same price and search request structure.

California

Uniform Commercial Code Division, Secretary of State, P.O. Box 1738, Sacramento, CA 95812 (street address: 1230 J Street, Sacramento, CA 95814); (916) 445-8061. Searches: Request must be submitted in writing in a letter, on a California Form UCC-3 or Form UCC-11. Charge is $11 per name. One name per request only. For $30 a one name search will be conducted and all documents copied. Additional charges will be billed by invoice. Copies of Documents: Available for $1 for the first page and 50 cents for every additional page. All documents are certified. For additional gold seal certification, or to certify a file number, the fee is an additional $5. Farm Filings: If you do not find them at the state level, remember some are filed with the county government (there is no standard procedure in California).

Colorado

Uniform Commercial Code Division, Secretary of State, 1560 Broadway, Suite 200, Denver, CO 80202; (303) 894-2200. Searches: A telephone information searches of two debtor's names (last four filings of each) is available at no cost. These searches are not certified. Written requests must be on a Form UCC-11 or it will not be processed. They prefer you send no money in and let them bill you. The charge is $25 for a search of one debtor name. A computer printout will be sent to verify the search if you do not want a copy search. Copies of Documents: Available for $1.25 per page. Farm Filings: Maintained at the County Court Recorder. Online Access: Call Patti Webb at (303) 894-2200 ext. 300 for information on orientation classes for new accounts. They offer several subscription packages: 3 months for $300, or 1 year for $1000 with 15 minute access time each call; 1 year for $5000 with private telephone number, and 1 year for $10,000 with direct computer hookup, which allows user to connect as many as 8 computer terminals to the system.

Connecticut

Uniform Commercial Code Division, Secretary of State, 30 Trinity Street, Hartford, CT 06106; (203) 566-4021. Searches: Request must be submitted in writing. The charge is $18 for request submitted on a Connecticut Form UCC-11. The charge for requests submitted by letter is $22. Copies of Documents: The charge for the first three pages is $5, each additional page is $3. Farm Filings: Maintained in this office. Use Connecticut Form UCC-a.

Delaware

Uniform Commercial Code Section, P.O. Box 793, John G. Townsend Building, Dover, DE 19903 (Street Address: Federal and Duke of York Street, Dover, DE 19901); (302) 739-4279 (Choose 8 for UCC recorded message, choose 0 for a UCC service representative). Searches: Requests must be submitted in writing on UCC-11 Form. $10 per each debtor's name search. Copies of Documents: Available for $2 per page. They will bill you. Farm Filings: Maintained by this office. This office is in the middle of being computerized. List of new filings in a particular category can be provided upon special request.

District of Columbia

Recorder of Deeds, 515 D Street NW, Washington, DC 20001; (202) 727-5374. Searches: Requests must be submitted in writing. No special form required. The charge is $30 for each secured party. Must be paid in advance. Copies of Documents: Available for $2.25 per page, plus $2.25 for certification. Farm Filings: Maintained in this office. This office is computerized.

Florida

Uniform Commercial Code Division, Department of State, P.O. Box 5588, Tallahassee, FL 32314 (Street Address: 409 Gaines Street, Tallahassee, FL 32301); (904) 487-6845. Searches: (904) 487-6063. For printed verification a written request must be submitted on Florida Form UCC-11. Copies of Documents: Available for $2.75 per page. Farm Filings: Filings are maintained by the County Circuit Court. Online Access: UCC Division, 409 E. Gaines Street, Tallahassee, FL 32399; (904) 487-6866. Write or call and they will send you an information booklet that describes the service they have available through CompuServe, (800) 848-8199. The cost for online service is $24 per hour, plus $2 per month flat fee and other small fees charged by CompuServe.

Georgia

The State of Georgia does not maintain Uniform Commercial Code Filings. Contact the Clerk of Superior Court at the County level for these filings.

Hawaii

Uniform Commercial Code, Bureau of Conveyance, P.O. Box 2867, Honolulu, HI 96803; (808) 548-3108. Searches: Requests must be submitted in writing on a Hawaii Form UCC-3 or any state's UCC-11. The search charge is $25 per debtor name, plus an additional 50 cents per listing. They will call you if there will be more charges for additional names found. Copies of Documents: Available for 50 cents per page. Farm Filings: Maintained by this office. Online Access: No.

Idaho

Secretary of State, Uniform Commercial Code Division, State House, Boise, ID 83720; (208) 334-3191. Searches: Information may be requested by phone or in writing. The charge is $13 for phone requests and for written requests. An additional $1 is charged if the request is not submitted on an Idaho UCC-4 Form. Charge for written requests submitted on UCC Form is $12. Copies of Documents: The charge for copying all documents involved in a search is $1. Farm Filings: A 24-hour Expedite Service is available for these filings. The charge is $17 for info search and $23 for copies. Online Access: Hopefully will be available in the future.

Illinois

Uniform Commercial Code Division, Secretary of State, Centennial Building, Room 30, 2nd and Edwards Street, Springfield, IL 62756; (217) 782-7518. Searches: All requests must be in writing. Requests on non-standard forms will not be processed. Requests submitted on a Illinois Form UCC-11.7 are $10. Copies of Documents: The charge is 50 cents per page. Farm Filings: If you do not find them at the state level, remember, some are filed with the county government. (There is no standard procedure in Illinois.) Payment for searches and copies may be charged to VISA or Master Charge. Microfilm: Copies of all documents filed within the month are available on a subscription basis for $250 per month. Daily Computer Printout Listing: Available for $250 per month. Online Access: For information write the above office, or contact: Louise Blakley, (217) 785-2235. A brochure explaining the system will be sent to you.

Indiana

Uniform Commercial Code Division, Secretary of State, 302 West Washington Street, Room E 018, Indianapolis, IN 46204; (317) 232-6393. Searches: All searches must be requested in writing. An Indiana Form UCC-11 is preferred. The charge is $1 per debtor's name and 50 cents for each filing, and 50 cents per statement on the listing. All requests for searches received by Federal Express or Express Mail with return envelope are given a priority. Copies of Documents: The charge is 50 cents per page and $1 for certification. Farm Filings: If incorporated they are filed both at this office and the county recorder where the land is located. If the farm is not incorporated the filing is placed at the county recorder's office only. Online Access: Not available. This office has one of the quickest turnaround times in the nation but is not computerized.

Iowa

Uniform Commercial Code Division, Secretary of State, Second Floor, Hoover Building, Des Moines, IA 50319; (515) 281-5204. Searches: Information may be requested by phone if you already have an established account, or in writing. The cost of a phone search is $5, plus $1 for a printout. The charge for a non-standard request is $6 and $5 for a request submitted on an Iowa Form UCC-11. Copies of Documents: The fee is $1 for each copy requested. All copies of liens are certified. Farm Filings: Maintained by this office. (Monthly updating may be obtained from Iowa Public Record Service, (515) 223-1153.) Online Access: Available. Contact Allen Welsh, (515) 281-8363. Cost is $150 per year, 30 cents per minute, plus telephone charges for dialup program.

Kansas

Uniform Commercial Code Division, Secretary of State, Second Floor, State Capitol, Topeka, KS 66612; (913) 296-3650. Searches: Phone requests are accepted with VISA or MC or from those holding a prepaid account with the UCC. The charge for phone requests is $15 per name for verbal information and $5 for an order. The charge for written requests is $5. If staffing permits, all requests are filled within 24 hours. Copies of Documents: The charge is $1 per

Be patient. If any phone number is incorrect, call (area code) 555-1212 and request the new listing.

Information On People, Companies, and Mailing Lists

page. There is no additional charge for certification of name searches. They are always sent out certified. For file number searches, certification must be requested. Fee is 50 cents. Farm Filings: This office has handled farm filings since 1984. Filings prior to that year are maintained by the County Register of Deeds. Online Access: Will be available in the future from Kansas Information Network with imaging capacity. Contact: Cathy. Other: Microfilm cost $25 per roll plus $7.50 for postage and handling, for up to 50 rolls. Total file has 42 rolls. New rolls, 4-5 monthly can be sent. Magnetic Tape: Master file costs $2,000. Updates are $15 weekly or $75 monthly.

Kentucky

Uniform Commercial Code Division, Office of Secretary of State, State Capitol Bldg., Capitol Avenue, Frankfort, KY 40601; (502) 564-2848 Ext. 441. Searches: All searches of UCC filings must be conducted in person by requester or by outside agencies. Law firms or Kentucky Lender's Assistance, (606) 278-6586 may do it for you. In addition to their fee, the UCC charges 10 cents per page for plain copies; $5 for certification and 50 cents for every page thereafter. Farm Filings: Filings are maintained by the County Circuit Court. Online Access: No.

Louisiana

The state of Louisiana has not adopted the Uniform Commercial Code. Filings may be maintained at the Parish (county) level.

Maine

Uniform Commercial Code Division, Secretary of State, State House Station 101, Augusta, ME 04333; (207) 289-4177. Searches: All requests must be submitted in writing in a letter or on a Form UCC-11. State whether plain or certified copies are desired. Cost is $2 per page plus $10 for certification. Will bill. For expedited service an additional $5 fee guarantees a 24 hour turnaround time. Farm Filings: Maintained by this office. Online Access: No.

Maryland

Uniform Commercial Code Division, State Department of Assessments and Taxation, 301 West Preston Street, Baltimore, MD 21201; (301) 225-1340. Searches: The State of Maryland does not conduct searches. They will provide a list of title companies that do provide that service. Some are: Hylinf Infoquest, (301) 728-4990 and Harbor City Research, (301) 539-0400. Copies cost $1 per page. Cost to certify a document is $6. Farm Filings: Maintained by this office. Online Access: No.

Massachusetts

Uniform Commercial Code Division, Secretary of State, Room 1711, 1 Ashburton Place, Boston, MA 02108; (617) 727-2860. Searches: Requests must be submitted in writing on a Form UCC-11 (any state's form is acceptable). The charge is $5 for an information computer printout and $10 for computer printout with face page and up to 15 pages. They will call you if pages exceed this limit. All fees must be paid in advance. Requests sent by Federal Express or Express Mail will be sent out same way with Air Bill, but all requests are processed in order received. No expediting service available. Copies of Documents: Charge is $2 per page and $3 for certification. Farm Filings: Maintained in Town Clerk's Office. Online Access: Available for $149 per year plus 40 cents per minute. Also carried by commercial services. Contact Richard Shipley, (617) 729-5412.

Michigan

Uniform Commercial Code Section, P.O. Box 30197, Lansing, MI 48909-7697 (Mailing Address: 7064 Crowner Dr., Lansing, MI 48909); (517) 322-1495. Searches: Telephone requests are handled on an expedite basis for already established accounts. The charge is an additional $25. You must have an account number with the UCC Section to obtain this service. The charge for requests submitted on non-standard forms are $6. Requests submitted on a Michigan Form UCC-11 is $3. Requests sent out by Federal Express or Express Mail are given priority, but all requests are processed in the order received. Copies of Documents: The charge is $1 per page and $1 for certification. Farm Filings: Filings are maintained by the County Recorder of Deeds. Online Access: No. Other: Microfilm available in contract basis for $50 per month. Format is not computer indexed. Write above address for details and contract.

Minnesota

Uniform Commercial Code Division, Secretary of State, 180 State Office Building, St. Paul, MN 55155; (612) 296-2434. Searches: Requests must be submitted in writing and include a SASE. The charge for a request submitted on a Minnesota Form UCC-11 is $11. The charge for a request submitted on a non-standard form is $14. These charges include information on 5 listings and/or 5 copies. You will be billed if there are additional copies in excess of five. The charge for additional listings is 50 cents/listing. Copies of Documents: Available for 50 cents/page. Charge for certified copies is a $5 plus 50 cents for each page. Farm Filings: Available from the County Recorder of Deeds unless the debtor is a non-resident or a corporation and then they are filed with the UCC Division.

Mississippi

Uniform Commercial Code Division, Secretary of State, 202 N. Congress St., #601, Jackson, MS 39201; (601) 359-1614. Searches: Phone information is available at no cost. Information available by phone is: approximate number of filings, secured party, file numbers, and date and time of filing. The charge for written requests submitted on Mississippi Form UCC-11 is $5. The charge for written requests submitted on non-standard forms is $10. Copies of Documents: Available for $2 a pages. Send initial $5 or $10 fee only. They will bill you for the exact amount of copies made. Farm Filings: Farm Filings are maintained by the above office. Other: Master list of all farm registrations available for $2040. Master list by type is $500 per crop. Online Access: Contact Cheryl Crawford, (601) 359-1548. The cost is $250 per month plus 50 cents per transaction with minimum of 100 transactions. Service will be available as of 1/92. Will display name, address and collateral. Complete file microfilm available for $50 per roll.

Missouri

Uniform Commercial Code Division, Secretary of State, P.O. Box 1159, Jefferson City, MO 65102; (314) 751-2360. Searches: Information searches will be given over the phone. These searches are not certified and are free of charge. (This service is not available on Mondays or the day after a holiday.) The charge for written requests is $8. Copies of Documents: Available for $8 per listing. The $8 fee covers the first 10 pages. Additional pages are 50 cents each. Farm Filings: Maintained by the County Recorder.

Montana

Uniform Commercial Code Bureau, Secretary of State, Capitol Station, Helena, MT 59620; (406) 444-3665, FAX: (406) 444-3926. Searches: Requests for searches will be accepted by phone. The charge if you have a prepaid account is $7, the same as for a written request. There are no restrictions on form in which you put written requests. Searches are conducted the day of the request for a $5 fee. Regular requests processed in 48 hours. Copies of Documents: Available for 50 cents a page. The charge for certification is $2. Farm Filings: Maintained in this office. For total listing of crop you are interested in, fill out a Buyer's Registration Form for crops you want on the list. Results can be done on paper or microfiche. Service is done on a cost recovery basis. Online Access: Contact Florence, (406) 444-3665. She will send you an information brochure. The charge is $25 per month for unlimited use. Printed copies cost 50 cents each and are statutorily accepted documents.

Nebraska

Uniform Commercial Code Division, P.O. Box 95104, 301 Centennial Mall S., Lincoln, NE 68509; (402) 471-4080. Searches: The charge for requests by phone is $1 per debtor's name. No verification is sent unless requested. If requested the charge for the printout is $3. The charge for written requests is $3. A computer printout containing a list of the filings is sent to the requester. Copies of Documents: Available for 50 cents per page. They will bill. Farm Filings: Maintained by the county government, but the above office will hooked up to all 93 countries and will do a search for you. The county will bill you directly for its service. Magnetic Tape: Available to large companies for $250 per month. Online Access: Available. Charge is $2 per inquiry. Contact Debbie Pester.

Nevada

Uniform Commercial Code Division, Secretary of State, Capitol Complex, Carson City, NV 89710; (702) 687-5298. Searches: Only written requests for information will be accepted. The charge is $6 for a request submitted on a Nevada Form UCC-3, Form UCC-11 or any type of letter. For an additional $10 your request will be expedited. This fee must be paid with a separate check. Copies of Documents: Available for $1 per page and an additional $6 for certified copies. Farm Filings: Maintained at the office of the County Recorder. Online Access: No.

New Hampshire

Uniform Commercial Code Division, Secretary of State, State House, Room 204, Concord, NH 03301; (603) 271-3276 or 271-3277. Searches: Requests must be submitted in writing by letter or on a Form UCC-11, and must contain a SASE in which requested documents will be mailed. Requests will not be processed without SASE enclosed. The charge for a request submitted on a New Hampshire Form UCC-11 is $5. The charge for a request submitted on a letter or non-standard form is $7. Copies of Documents: Available for 75 cents per file. Farm Filings: Maintained by this office. Microfiche: Available from New England Micrographics. Contact Nick Brattan, (603) 625-1171. Online Access: No. This office is not computerized.

Who Owes Money To Whom

New Jersey

Uniform Commercial Code Division, State Department, State Capitol Building, CN303, Trenton, NJ 08625; (609) 530-6426. Searches: Requests must be submitted in writing with exact name and address of debtor or on a New Jersey Form UCC-11 or a security agreement signed by the debtor. Payment must accompany request unless prepaid UCC account, Visa or MasterCard is used. Request may be Faxed, (609) 530-0688. The charge is $25. Document is certified. Expedite Service is available for $5. The requester pays the express mail expense. Copies of Documents: Available for $1 per page. Farm Filings: Maintained by the county and the state. At the county level you will want to check with the County Recorder. Online Access: No.

New Mexico

Uniform Commercial Code Division, Bureau of Operations, Secretary of State, Executive Legislative Building, Room 400, Santa Fe, NM 87503; (505) 827-3600. Searches: Certification is $8. Copies cost $1 per page. The State of New Mexico does not do searches, but they will provide you with a list of abstract companies that are authorized to do so. Call Bureau of Operations for list, (505) 827-3608. Farm Filings: This office located at the same address with conduct a search for an Agricultural Eddective Financing Statement for $15. Contact Ben Vegil, (505) 827-3609. They will follow-up the verbal report with a written statement. Online Access: Available through local services: Federal Abstracts, (505) 982-5537, Lawyer's Title, (505) 988-2333 and Capitol Documents, (505) 984-2696. Also available from Dun and Bradstreet.

New York

Uniform Commercial Code Division, Secretary of State, P.O. Box 7021, Albany, NY 12225; (518) 474-4763. Searches: Requests must be submitted in writing. For requests submitted on a New York Form UCC-11 the charge is $7. For requests submitted on non-standard forms the charge is $12. Copies of Documents: Available for $1.50 per page. Farm Filings: Maintained by both the state and the County Recorder. Online Access: No. Other: Microfiche available for $300 per month. Contact Virginia Cellery at (518) 432-2733.

North Carolina

Uniform Commercial Code Division, Secretary of State, 300 N. Salisbury Street, Raleigh, NC 27611; (919) 733-4205. Searches: Requests must be submitted in writing. Signature for the requester is required, therefore make request on Form UCC-11 or North Carolina Form UCC-11. The charge is $8 per name. Search fee must be sent with request. All requests are handled within 24 hours of receipt. Copies of Documents: Available for $1 per page. Will bill. Farm Filings: Maintained by this office and County Recorder. Online Access: No, but will be available in the future. Other: Microfilm can be purchased for $50 per roll. New monthly listings generate about 2 rolls per month. Contact Judy Chapman.

North Dakota

Uniform Commercial Code Division, Secretary of State, Main Capitol Building, 600 Boulevard Avenue East, Bismarck, ND 58505; (701) 224-3662. Searches: Requests may be phoned in or be submitted in writing preferably on a North Dakota UCC-11. Letters and nonstandard forms also accepted. The charge is $5. Copies of Documents: Available for $5 for the first three pages and $1 a page for additional pages. Farm Filings: The Central Notice staff will take requests for searches over the phone for crop and livestock filings. The charge is the same as above. Written requests are the same as stated above. Farm equipment and real estate filings are optional and may be maintained by the state or the County Register of Deeds until 1/92. As of 1/92 the UCC and County Register of Deeds will be hooked up to the same system. Online Access: No, but will be available in the future.

Ohio

Uniform Commercial Code Division, Secretary of State, 30 E. Broad Street, 14th Floor, Columbus, OH 43266-0418; (614) 466-9316. Searches: Phone requests for information are not certified and are free of charge. Call (614) 466-3623/3126. Limit is 3 requests per phone call. Written requests may be submitted on a non-standard letter form, Form UCC-11 or on an Ohio Form UCC-11. The charge is $9. It takes 6 months for these searches to be conducted. Expedite service is available for an additional $9. These requests are processed in 5 working days. Copies of Documents: Available for $1 per page. Farm Filings: Maintained by the County Recorder. Online Access: No.

Oklahoma

Uniform Commercial Code Office, Oklahoma County Clerk, 320 Robert S. Kerr, Room 105, Oklahoma City, OK 73102; (405) 278-1521. Searches: Requests must be submitted in writing. The charge is $5. Copies of Documents: Available for $1 per page. Send $5 search fee with request. They will bill you for copies and call if amount is over $25. The charge for certification is $1. Farm Filings: Maintained by Secretary of State's Office, (405) 521-2474. Online Access: No.

Oregon

Uniform Commercial Code Division, Secretary of State, Room 41, State Capitol, Salem, OR 97310; (503) 378-4146. Searches: Requests must be phoned in using Visa or MasterCard, charged to an established prepaid UCC account or submitted in writing by letter, or on Form UCC-11 or preferably on a Oregon Form UCC-25R. The charge is $5 per debtor's name. Copies of Documents: Available for $1 per page. Farm Filings: Maintained by this office. The charge for a search is $5 per name. Monthly reports by agricultural product code are available on microfilm or paper copy. For microfilm contact Micelle. Cost is $10 per reel weekly. Online Access: Available for $25 per month, plus 20 cents a minute for online use. Contact Michelle. Commercially available from Prentice Hall, (800) 452-7856.

Pennsylvania

Uniform Commercial Code Division, Corporation Bureau, State Department, 308 N. Office Building, Harrisburg, PA 17120; (717) 787-8712. Searches: Requests for searches must be paid in advance by check or money order only and submitted in writing on a Pennsylvania Form UCC-11. The charge is $12 per name search. $28 to certify. Must may in advance by check or money order. Copies of Documents: Available for $2 per page. Farm Filings: Maintained by this office. Online Access: Information America, (404) 892-1800.

Rhode Island

Uniform Commercial Code Division, Secretary of State, 100 North Main Street, Providence, RI 02903; (401) 277-2521. Searches: Requests must be submitted in writing. Same charge for request in letter form or on Form UCC-11. Call for number of pages. Requests will not be processed without payment in full. The charge is $5. Copies of Documents: Available for 50 cents per copy. Farm Filings: Maintained by the City Recorder of Deeds. Online Access: No.

South Carolina

Uniform Commercial Code Division, Secretary of State, P.O. Box 11350, Columbia, SC 29211; (803) 734-2175. Searches: Requests must be submitted in writing on Form UCC-11, or preferably South Carolina Form UCC-4. Letters are not accepted. The charge is $5 per debtor name. No priority or expediting service. All requests done in the order received. Copies of Documents: Available for $2 for the first page, $1 for each page thereafter. Farm Filings: Maintained by County Recorder. Online Access: No. Other: Microfilm from Archives is purchased by Dun and Bradstreet and may be purchased from the UCC division directly. Contact Thresha Southerland, (803) 734-2176. One tape costs $50.

South Dakota

Central Filing System, Secretary of State, 500 E. Capitol, Pierre, SD 57501; (605) 773-4422. Searches: Telephone information provided for no charge. Requests for searches are accepted from those with prepaid deposit accounts. Written requests are accepted on any UCC standard request form. The charge is $4. Fee for certification is $5. Copies of Documents: Available for 50 cents per page. They will bill you. Farm Filings: Maintained by this office. Online access at no charge is available. Online Access: Available by subscription. The system can be used by those with IBM compatible computers and Hayes compatible modems. Cost is $240 per year for 200 transactions and 10 cents per transaction thereafter.

Tennessee

Uniform Commercial Code Section, Secretary of State, J.K. Polk Building, 505 Deaderick St., Suite 1800, Nashville, TN 37219; (615) 741-3276. Searches: Requests must be submitted in writing, preferably on a Tennessee Form UCC-11. Indicate if you want information or information plus copies. The charge is $10 even if the search shows no listing. Send the $10 fee with request. Copies of Documents: Available for $1 per copy. Do not send money with request. They will bill you. Requests sent with Express Mail envelopes will be sent the next day. All other requests take 3-4 days to process. Farm Filings: Maintained by this office and County Recorder. It is necessary to check with both offices. Online Access: No.

Texas

Uniform Commercial Code, Secretary of State, P.O. Box 13193, Austin, TX 78711-3193; (512) 475-2705. Searches: The charge for a search requested by phone is $25. The charge for written requests submitted on Texas Form UCC-11 is $10. May FAX: (512) 475-2812. The charge for written requests submitted on a letterhead or non-standard form is $25. Copies of Documents: Available for $1.50 per page with a $5 minimum charge. The charge for certification is an additional $5. Farm Filings: Maintained by the above office. Online Access:

Information On People, Companies, and Mailing Lists

Available by Dialup Service. Cost is $3 per search, deducted from prepaid account. Contact Tina Whiteley, (512) 475-2700.

Utah

Uniform Commercial Code Division, Business Regulation Department, 300 South Street, Second Floor, Salt Lake City, UT 84110; (801) 530-6020. Searches: Written request may be on letter, UCC-11 or Utah Form UCC-2. The charge is $10 per debtor name. Copies of Documents: Available for 30 cents per page. Will bill. Certification: No additional charge. Document already certified. Farm Filings: Central Filings maintained these files. Phone requests are accepted. The charge is $10. Online Access: Available through Data-Share program on a subscription basis. The charge is $10 per month plus 10 cents per minute and telephone charges. Contact Mary Ann Saddler or Ted Wiggin at (801) 530-6643.

Vermont

Uniform Commercial Code, Secretary of State, Montpelier, VT 05609 (Regular mail to: 109 State Street, Montpelier, VT 05609-1104; Fed Ex to: 94 Main Street, Montpelier, VT 05609); (802) 828-2388. Searches: Requests for searches may be phoned in or submitted in writing. They will bill for phone requests. The charge is $5 per debtor name, plus 50 cents for an information sheet containing debtor's name, secured party, file number, and date and time filed. Copies of Documents: Available for $2 for 5" x 8" or $5 for 8 1/2" x 11" copies. Certification fee is $5. Farm Filings: Central Filings Section maintains these files. Contact the above address. The charges for searches is the same. Online Access: No.

Virginia

Uniform Commercial Code Division, State Corporation Commission, P.O. Box 1197, Richmond, VA 23209 (Street Address: 1220 Bank Street, Richmond, VA 23209); (804) 786-3689. Searches: Requests for searches must be submitted in writing in a letter or Form UCC-11. The charge is $6 per debtor name. Copies of Documents: Available for $1 per page. There is an additional charge of $6 for certification. Farm Filings: Maintained by this office and the County Recorder. Online Access: No.

Washington

Uniform Commercial Code Division, Department of Licensing, 405 Black Lake Blvd., Olympia, WA 98502 (Mailing Address: PO Box 9660, Olympia, WA 98507); (206) 753-2523. Searches: Requests must be submitted in writing. Indicate if you want information or information and copies. The charge is $7 for all the listings of one debtor. Copies of Documents: Available for $12. This includes search fee, plus copies of all documents for one debtor. Farm Filings: Maintained in this office. Microfilm: Copies of each days filings are available for $6.50 per day plus shipping and handling fees. Online Access: Contact Darla Gehrke at (206) 752-2523 for information on how to set up a prepaid account. Monthly minimum deposit is $200 from which $1 per minute online time and other fees are deducted.

West Virginia

Uniform Commercial Code Division, Secretary of State, 1900 Kanawha, Bldg. 1, Room 131W, Charleston, WV 25305-0770; (304) 345-4000. Searches: Phone requests for information are accepted. The charge is $5. They will bill you. Written requests are preferred. The charge is $3 if Form UCC-11 is used, $5 for all others. Copies of Documents: Available for 50 cents per page. The charge for certification is $5. Farm Filings: Maintained by this office. Online Access: No.

Wisconsin

Uniform Commercial Code Division, Secretary of State, 30 West Mifflin St., Madison, WI 53703 (Mailing Address: P.O. Box 7847, Madison, WI 53707); (608) 266-3087. Searches: Phone requests for information are accepted. The charge is $5 per filing. The charge for written requests is $5 per debtor name. Copies of Documents: Available for $1 per document. Certification certificate must be requested in writing and is an additional 50 cents. Farm Filings: Maintained by the County Register of Deeds. Other: Microfiche is available on a monthly basis. Contact Bonnie Fredrick at (608) 266-3087.

Wyoming

Uniform Commercial Code, Secretary of State, State Capitol Building, Cheyenne, WY 82002; (307) 777-5372. Searches: Phone requests for information are accepted for 2 debtor names. Requests may be Faxed to (307) 777-5339. The charge is $5 for each name. The charge for written requests is the same. Copies of Documents: Available for 50 cents per page. Farm Filings: Maintained by this office and the County Recorder. Check both. Online Access: Available for $50 per month, plus telephone charges and usage fee. Minimum usage fee is $26 per month. Contact Jeanie Sawyer.

Be patient. If any phone number is incorrect, call (area code) 555-1212 and request the new listing.

Professional People and Local Businesses

State Licensing Offices

Buried within each state government are several, and sometimes dozens, of offices where individuals as well as business establishments must register in order to perform certain types of services and commercial activities. State laws require accountants, architects, concert promoters, employment agencies, podiatrists and numerous other professionals to register. The data derived from these regulatory boards provide unique opportunities for researchers and marketing executives to obtain demographic data, mailing lists and even competitive information.

Mailing Lists

Mailing lists offer the biggest potential from these offices. The unusual as well as the mundane are available in a variety of formats. Many of these lists are not accessible commercially, but you can get them from the states inexpensively and usually without restrictions. In other words, you can purchase a state list once, and use it over and over again. Commercial list brokers will never let you do this. Here is a sampling of available mailing lists:

- 1 cent per name for all dentists in Kentucky;
- Free directory of real estate agents in Arizona;
- $40 for a list of all nurses in Colorado;
- A mailing list of all contractors in Arkansas for $10;
- 2 cents per name for all swimming pool dealers in Florida;
- A listing of librarians in Georgia;
- 4 cents a name for all the psychologists in California;
- $100 for a computer tape of all accountants in Florida;
- $1.45 per 1,000 names for all medical practices in Illinois;
- Free list of all attorneys in Maine.

Almost every state provides mailing labels in the form of cheshire or pressure sensitive labels. In many cases, the charge is nominal.

Common Lists and Specialized Rosters

Every state maintains a variety of standard rosters. Some states keep as few as 20 lists and others have over 100. Names of licensed professionals and business establishments available from most every state include:

- medical professionals
- accountants
- real estate agents and brokers
- veterinarians
- barbers
- insurance agents
- architects
- nursing homes
- cosmetologists
- hearing aid dealers
- social workers
- lawyers

After reviewing the rundown of all 50 states and District of Columbia licensing boards, you will be amazed at the variety of lists that are within easy reach. In most cases you can obtain printouts for such licensed services as:

- burglar alarm contractors in Maine
- tow truck operations in Minnesota
- hat cleaners in Ohio
- ski areas in Michigan
- day care centers in New York
- security guards in New Hampshire
- outfitters in Colorado

Computer Tapes and Diskettes: Selections and Sorting Options

Many states can provide the information on magnetic tape and some are beginning to offer data on IBM PC compatible diskettes. Almost every state will allow you to select names by zip code or county whether the licensee is active or inactive. Some states will allow you to select certain demographic characteristics, such as years of formal education.

Markets and Demographics

With a little creativity and resourcefulness, the information at licensing boards can provide pertinent clues in formulating a market profile. For example, you can determine:

- which counties have the highest concentration of psychologists;
- what is the average number of years of schooling for real estate agents in certain zip codes;
- which zip codes have experienced the fastest growth for accountants for the past 10 years;
- the number of out-of-state licensed paralegals;
- which counties have the most podiatrists or veterinarians
- how many insurance agents there are in a given county.

Some states have the capability of performing historical analysis, while others will supply you with the raw data.

Competitive Intelligence

Depending upon the type of business you are investigating, pertinent competitive information may be ferreted from state

Information on People, Companies, and Mailing Lists

licensing boards. For example, if you are a dentist, mobile home dealer, nursing home administrator or real estate broker, you could plot how many competitors you are up against in a given zip code or county. Or, you may be able to determine how many opticians work for an eye care chain, or tax consultants for a given tax preparer.

Organization of Licensing Boards

Approximately half of the states have a central office which is responsible for all licensed professions. For such states it is a relatively easy process to obtain information because it is all generated from a single source. However, the other states make this task difficult. Typically, each separate independent board maintains information for one profession. The only connection these agencies have to the state government is that their board members are appointed by the governor.

States With Restrictions

Six states have laws that place certain stipulations on the use of their lists of licensed professionals. In these cases the data may not be used for commercial purposes. Iowa, Montana, New York, North Dakota, Rhode Island and Washington have such restrictions. The District of Columbia, Hawaii and Kansas do not release addresses but will provide names.

Licensing Boards

Besides issuing licenses to professionals so they can do business, the following offices act as consumer watchdogs to make sure that those with licenses do business fairly and ethically. Not only will these offices investigate complaints against licensed professionals, they also have the ability to revoke or suspend the licenses if the professional repeatedly acts unprofessionally or unethically. Each state listing includes the professionals licensed in that state, including health professionals, along with their different licensing offices where noted.

Alabama

State Occupational Information Coordinating Community (SOICC), 401 Adams Ave., P.O. Box 5690, Montgomery, AL 36103-5690; (205) 242-2990. Licensing boards and professions: accountants, aircraft personnel, architects, auctioneers, audiologists, speech pathologists, bar pilots, water transportation personnel, boxer and wrestler trainers, classroom teachers, coal mine foremen/mine electricians, cosmetologists, counselors, dentists, dental hygienists, chiropractors, doctors of medicine, physician's assistants, surgeon's assistants, school bus drivers, embalmer/funeral directors, engineer-in-training and professional engineers, land surveyors, fire fighters, foresters, general contractors, hearing aid specialists, heating and air conditioning contractors, insurance agents, interior designers, landscape architects, landscape horticulturist/planters, lawyers, pest control operators and fumigators, tree surgeons, law enforcement personnel, nurses, nursing home administrators, optometrists, pharmacists, physical therapists, physical therapist assistants, plumbers, podiatrists, polygraph examiners, psychologists, real estate brokers, security salespersons, social workers, veterinarians.

Alaska

Division of Occupational Licensing, Department of Commerce and Economic Development, State of Alaska, P.O. Box 110806, Juneau, AK 99811-0806; (907) 465-2534. Licensing boards and professions: architects, engineers, land surveyors, audiologists, barbers and hairdressers, chiropractors, collection agencies, construction contractors, concert promoters, dental professionals, dispensing opticians, electrical administrators, geologists, guides, hearing aid dealers, marine pilots, physicians, morticians, naturopaths, nursing, nursing home administrators, optometrists, pharmacists, physical therapists, psychologists, public accountants, veterinarians.

Arizona

Arizona Department of Revenue, 1600 West Monroe, Phoenix, AZ 85007; (602) 542-4576. Licensing boards and professions: pharmacists, physical therapists, podiatrists, psychologists, chiropractors, dentists, teachers, homeopathic specialists, veterinarians, medical examiners, radiologic technicians, naturopathic physicians, nurses, opticians, optometrists, osteopaths, barbers, cosmetologists, real estate brokers, contractors, technical registrators, insurance agents, physician assistants, nursing care administrators.

Arkansas

Governor's Office, State Capitol Building, Little Rock, AR 72201; (501) 682-2345. Licensing boards and professions: architects, abstracters, accountants, barber examiners, funeral directors, contractors, cosmetologists, dental examiners, electricians, speech pathologists, audiologists, nurses, pharmacists, real estate brokers, veterinary engineers, land surveyors, athletic trainers, chiropractors, collection agencies, counselors, embalmers, foresters, landscape architects, manufactured home builders, physicians, opticians, optometrists, podiatrists, psychologists, sanitarians, social workers, soil classifiers, therapy technologists.

California

State of California, Department of Consumer Affairs, 400 R Street, Sacramento, CA 95814; (916) 323-2191, or (800) 344-9940 (toll-free in CA). Licensing boards professions: professional engineers, cosmetologists, fabric care technicians, physical therapists, medical quality assurance, physician's assistants, chiropractors, acupuncture specialists, accountants, psychologists, registered nurses, pharmacists, architects, funeral directors, embalmers, landscape architects, veterinarians, animal health technicians, home Furnishings decorators, collection and investigative agents, dentists, dental auxiliaries, barbers, behavioral scientists, optometrists, shorthand reporters, structural pest control operators, athletic trainers, vocational nurses, psychiatric technicians, osteopaths, electronic repair dealers, personnel services, geologists and geophysicists, dispensing opticians/contact lens examiners, respiratory care specialists, nursing home administrators, podiatrists, hearing aid dispensers, speech pathologists, audiologists, tax preparers.

Colorado

Department of Regulatory Agencies, State Services Building, 1560 Broadway, Suite 1550, Denver, CO 80202; (303) 894-7855. Licensing Board/Professions: accountants, architects, barbers, cosmetologists, chiropractors, dentists, electricians, engineers, hearing aid dealers, insurance agents, land surveyors, mobile home dealers, nurses, nursing home administrators, optometrists, outfitters, pharmacists and pharmacies, physical therapists, physicians, plumbers, psychologists, realtors, ski lift operators, social workers, veterinarians.

Connecticut

Occupational Licensing Division, Department of Consumer Products, 165 Capitol Avenue, Hartford, CT 06106; (203) 566-1107, or (800) 842-2649 (toll-free in CT). Licensed Occupations: electricians, plumbers, heating and cooling specialists, well drillers, elevator installers, home improvement contractors, arborists, TV and radio repair specialists. Licensed Health Professions: Department of Health Services, 150 Washington St., Hartford, CT 06106; (203) 566-7398. Physicians, dentists, optometrists, osteopaths, naturopaths, homeopaths, chiropractors, psychologists, registered nurses, licensed practical nurses, dental hygienists, registered physical therapists, hypertrichologists, audiologists, speech pathologists, podiatrists, hairdressers, barbers, embalmers, funeral directors, sewer installers/ cleaners, registered sanitarians, nursing home administrators, hearing aid dealers, opticians, veterinarians, occupational therapists. Other Licensed Professions: Contact Professional Licensing Division, 165 Capitol Avenue, Room G1, Hartford, CT 06106, (203) 566-1814: architects, landscape architects, engineers, engineers-in-training, land surveyors, pharmacists, patent medicine distributors, mobile manufactured home parks.

Delaware

Division of Professional Regulation, P.O. Box 1401, O'Neil Building, Dover, DE 19903; (302) 739-4522. Complaints in writing only. Licensed Professionals: architects, accountants, landscape architects, cosmetologists, barbers, podiatrists, chiropractors, dentists, electricians, adult entertainment, physicians, nurses, real

Professional People and Local Businesses

estate brokers, land surveyors, private employment agencies, athletic (wrestling and boxing), deadly weapons dealers, nursing home administrators, funeral directors, social workers, speech pathologists, hearing aid dealers, audiologists, psychologists, veterinarians, optometrists, occupational therapists, pharmacists, river boat pilots.

District of Columbia

Department of Consumer and Regulatory Affairs, 614 H Street NW, Room 108, Washington, DC 20001; (202) 727-7080. Licensing Board/Professions: accountants, architects, barbers, cosmetologists, dentists, dieticians, electricians, funeral directors, physicians, nurses, nursing home administrators, occupational therapists, optometrists, pharmacists, physical therapists, plumbers, podiatrists, engineers, psychologists, real estate agents, refrigeration and air conditioning specialists, social workers, steam and other operating engineers, veterinarians.

Florida

Florida Department of Professional Regulation, 1940 N. Monroe St., Tallahassee, FL 32399-075; (904) 488-6602. Licensing boards and professions: accountants, architects, barbers, chiropractors, cosmetologists, dentists, dispensing opticians, electrical contractors, professional engineers and land surveyors, landscape architects, funeral directors and embalmers, medical examiners, hearing aid dispensers, naturopathics, nursing home administrators, nurses, optometrists, osteopaths, pharmacists, pilot commissioners, podiatrists, psychologists, real estate brokers, veterinarians, acupuncture technicians, radiological health technicians, laboratory services, entomology specialists, emergency medical personnel.

Georgia

Examining Board Division, Secretary of State, 166 Pryor Street, SW, Atlanta, GA 30303; (404) 656-3900. Licensing boards and professions: accountants, architects, athletic trainers, auctioneers, barbers, chiropractors, construction industry, cosmetologists, professional counselors, social workers, marriage and family therapists, dietitians, dentists, engineers, land surveyors, foresters, funeral directors/embalmers, geologists, hearing aid dealers and dispensers, landscape architects, librarians, physicians, nurses, nursing home administrators, occupational therapists, dispensing opticians, optometrists, pharmacists, physical therapists, podiatrists, polygraph testers, practical nurses, private detectives and security agencies, psychologists, recreation specialists, sanitarians, speech pathologists, audiologists, used car dealers, used motor vehicle dismantlers, rebuilders, and salvage dealers, veterinarians, water and wastewater treatment plant operators and laboratory analysts.

Hawaii

Office of the Director, Department of Commerce and Consumer Affairs, P.O. Box 3469, Honolulu, HI 96801; (808) 548-7462. Licensing boards and professions: accountants, acupuncture specialists, barbers, boxers, chiropractors, contractors, cosmetologists, dental examiners, detectives and guards, electricians and plumbers, elevator mechanics, engineers, architects, land surveyors, landscape architects, hearing aid dealers and fitters, massage specialists, physicians, motor vehicle Industry, motor vehicle repair technicians, naturopaths, nurses, nursing home administrators, dispensing opticians, optometrists, osteopaths, pest control operators, pharmacists, physical therapists, psychologists, real estate brokers, speech pathologists, audiologists, veterinarians, embalmers/funeral directors, collection agencies, commercial employment agencies, mortgage and collection servicing agents, mortgage brokers and solicitors, port pilots, time sharing and travel agents.

Idaho

State of Idaho, Department of Self-Governing Agencies, Bureau of Occupational Licenses, Owyhee Plaza, 1109 Main, #220, Boise, ID 83702; (208) 334-3233. Licensing boards and professions: accountants, athletic directors, bartenders, engineers, land surveyors, dentists, geologists, physicians, architects, barbers, chiropractors, cosmetologists, counselors, dentists, environmental health specialists, hearing aid dealers and fitters, landscape architects, morticians, nursing home administrators, optometrists, podiatrists, psychologists, social workers, outfitters and guides, pharmacists, public works contractors, real estate brokers.

Illinois

State of Illinois, Department of Professional Regulations, 320 W. Washington, Third Floor, Springfield, IL 62786; (217) 785-0800. Licensed professions: athletic trainers, architects, barbers, cosmetologists, chiropractors, collection agencies, controlled substance specialists, dentists and dental auxiliaries, polygraph testers, detectives, embalmers, funeral directors, land sales, land surveyors, physicians, nurses, nursing home administrators, occupational therapists, optometrists, pharmacists, physical therapists, podiatrists, boxing and wrestling, engineers, psychologists, accountants, real estate brokers and salespersons, roofing contractors, shorthand reporters, social workers, structural engineers, veterinarians.

Indiana

Indiana Professional Licensing Agency, Indiana Government Center S., 302 W. Washington Street, Room E-034, Indianapolis, IN 46204; (317) 232-3997. Licensing boards and professions: accountants, architects, auctioneers, barbers, beauticians, boxers, engineers and land surveyors, funeral directors, plumbers, real estate agents, TV-radio and watch repair technicians. Licensed health professionals: Indiana Health Professional Bureau, One America Square #1020, Indianapolis, IN 46282; (317) 232-2960 for the following medical specialties: chiropractors, dentists, health facility administrators, nurses, optometrists, pharmacists, sanitarians, speech pathologists, audiologists, psychologists, veterinarians, hearing aid dealers, podiatrists, physical therapists.

Iowa

Bureau of Professional Licensing, Iowa Department of Health, Lucas State Office Building, Des Moines, IA 50319; (515) 281-4401. Licensed professionals: dietitians, funeral directors and embalmers, hearing aid dealers, nursing home administrators, optometrists, ophthalmology dispensers, podiatrists, psychologists, physical and occupational therapists, occupational therapist assistants, social workers, speech pathologists and audiologists, respiratory care therapists, barbers, cosmetologists, chiropractors, nurses, physicians, dentists, pharmacists, veterinarians. Other licensed professionals: Professional Licensing Regulation Division, Department of Commerce, 1918 SE Hulsizer, Ankeny, IA 50021: accountants, engineers and land surveyors, landscape architects, architects, real estate agents.

Kansas

Secretary of State, State Capitol, 2nd Floor, Topeka, KS 66612; (913) 296-3489. Licensing boards: abstracters, accountants, adult home administrators, operating engineers, plumbers and pipefitters, carpenters, electrical workers, attorneys, barbers, cosmetologists, court reporters, dentists and dental auxiliaries, educators, emergency medical services, healing arts specialists, hearing aid dispensers, insurance agents, land surveyors, embalmers/funeral directors, nurses, optometrists, pharmacists, physical therapists, podiatrists, private schools, real estate agents, engineers, architects, landscape architects, veterinarians.

Kentucky

Division of Occupations and Professions, P.O. Box 456, Frankfort, KY 40602-0456; (502) 564-3296. Licensing boards and professions: hearing aid dealers, nurses, private schools, psychologists, social workers, speech and audiologists. Other licensed professionals: Kentucky Occupational Information Coordinating Committee, 275 E. Main St., Two Center, Frankfort, KY 40621; (502) 564-4258: accountants, agriculture specialists, architects, auctioneers, bar examiners, barbers, chiropractors, dentists, hairdressers, cosmetologists, emergency medical technicians Services, radiation and product safety specialists, insurance agents, medical licensure supervisors, natural resources and environmental protection specialists, nursing home administrators, ophthalmic dispensers, optometric examiners, pharmacists, physical therapists, podiatrists, polygraph examiners, professional engineers and land surveyors, real estate agents, veterinarians.

Louisiana

Department of Economic Development, 101 France St., Baton Rouge, LA 70802; (504) 342-5361. Licensing boards and professions: acupuncture assistants, adoption agencies, adult day care administrators, agricultural consultants, alcoholic beverages solicitors, ambulatory surgical centers, arborists, archaeological investigators, architects, auctioneers, barbers, beauticians, bedding and furniture upholsterers, beer distributors, blind business enterprise operators, blood alcohol analysts, embalmers/funeral directors, accountants, shorthand reporters, chiropractors, pesticide applicators, driving school instructors, sewage/construction contractors, cotton buyers, waste-salvage oil operators, cut flower dealers, dairy product retailers, day care centers, fuels dealers, dentists, drug manufacturers, egg marketers, electrolysis technicians, embalmers, emergency medical technicians, employment service agencies, family support counselors, grain dealers, hearing aid dealers, hemodialysis clinics, home health centers, horticulturists, independent laboratories, sewage system installers, insurance, landscape architects, nurses, lime manufacturers, liquefied gas distributors, livestock dealers, maternity homes, mental and substance abuse clinics, midwives, nursing home administrators, nursery stock dealers, occupational therapists, optometrists, pesticide dealers, pharmacists, physical therapists, physicians, physicians, plant breeders, plumbers, podiatrists, solid waste processors, seafood distributors, psychologists, radiation therapists, radio and television repair technicians, radiologic technologists, real estate brokers, sanitarians, social workers, speech pathologists and audiologists, veterinarians, voice stress analysts.

Maine

Department of Professional and Financial Regulation, State House Station 35, Augusta, ME 04333; (207) 582-8700. Licensing boards and professions: veterinarians, itinerant vendors, consumer credit protection services, insurance agents, athletic trainers, real estate agents, geologists and soil scientists, solar energy auditors, hearing aid dealers and fitters, accountants, arborists, barbers, commercial drivers, education instructors, speech pathologists and audiologists, auctioneers, electricians, funeral directors, foresters, dietitians, nursing home administrators, oil and solid fuel installers, substance abuse counselors, mobile home parks, river pilots, physical therapists, plumbers, psychologists, social workers, radiological technicians, occupational therapists, respiratory care therapists, nurses, dentists, chiropractors, osteopaths, podiatrists, physicians, engineers, attorneys.

Maryland

Division of Maryland Occupational and Professional Licensing, 501 St. Paul Pl., 9th Floor, Baltimore, MD 21202; (410) 333-6209. Licensed professionals: architects, master electricians, engineers, foresters, hearing aid dealers, landscape architects, pilots, plumbers, land surveyors, public accountants, second hand dealers, precious metal and gem dealers, pawnbrokers, real estate agents and brokers, home improvement contractors, barbers and cosmetologists. Referral to the licensing agency for collection agencies, mortgage brokers and insurance agents can be provided by the office listed above. Other licensed professions: Boards and Commissions, Department of Health and Dental Hygiene, 4201 Patterson Ave., Baltimore, MD 21215; (410) 764-4747: audiologists, chiropractors, dentists, dietitians, electrologists, medical examiners, morticians, nurses, nursing home administrators, optometrists, occupational therapists, pharmacists, physical therapists, podiatrists, professional counselors, psychologists, environmental sanitarians, speech pathologists, social workers, well drillers, water work and waste system operators.

Massachusetts

Division of Registration, 100 Cambridge St., Boston, MA 02202; (617) 727-3074. Licensing boards and professions: electrologists, gas fitters, hairdressers, health officers, landscape architects, licensed practical nurses, nursing home administrators, optometrists, physician's assistants, podiatrists, pharmacists, plumbers, psychologists, real estate brokers, registered nurses, sanitarians, speech pathologists, audiologists, social workers, tv-repair technicians, physical therapists, occupational therapists, athletic trainers, architects, barbers, barber shops, certified public accountants, chiropractors, dental hygienists, dentists, dispensing opticians, pharmacies, electricians, embalmers, engineers, veterinarians.

Michigan

Michigan Department of License and Regulation, P.O. Box 30018, Lansing, MI 48909; (517) 373-1870. Licensing board and professions: accountants, architects, barbers, athletic control (wrestlers and boxers), builders, carnival amusement rides, cosmetologists.

Minnesota

Office of Consumer Services, Office of Attorney General, 1400 NCL Tower, 445 Minnesota Street, St. Paul, MN 55101; (612) 296-2331. Licensing boards and professions: abstracters, accountants, adjusters, alarm and communications contractors, architects, assessors, attorneys, auctioneers, bailbondsmen, barbers, beauticians, boiler operators, boxing related occupations, brokers, building officials, burglar installers, chiropractors, clergy, cosmetologists, dentists, dental assistants, dental hygienists, private detectives, electricians, energy auditors, engineers, financial counselors/financial planners, funeral directors/embalmers/morticians, hearing aid dispensers, insurance agents, investment advisors, landscape architects, land surveyors, midwives, notary publics, nursing home administrators, optometrists, osteopathic physicians, pawnbrokers, peace officers, pharmacists, physical therapists, physicians, surgeons, physician's assistants, high pressure pipefitters, plumbers, podiatrists, practical nurses,

precious metal dealers, process servers, psychologists, real estate brokers, registered nurses, rehabilitation consultants, sanitarians, securities brokers, tax preparers, teachers, tow truck operators, transient merchants, veterinarians, water conditioning contractors and installers, water and waste treatment operators, water well contractors/explorers/engineers.

Mississippi

Secretary of State, P.O. Box 136, Jackson, MS 39205; (601) 359-3123. Licensing boards and professions: agricultural aviation pilots, architects, landscape architects, athletic trainers, funeral directors, chiropractors, dentists, physicians, nurses, nursing home administrators, optometrists, pharmacists, physical therapists, psychologists, veterinarians, barbers, cosmetologists, engineers and land surveyors, foresters, polygraph examiners, public accountants, public contractors, real estate agents.

Missouri

Division of Professional Registration, Department of Economic Development, 3605 Missouri Blvd., Jefferson City, MO 65109; (314) 751-0293. Licensing boards and professions: accountants, architects/engineers/land surveyors, athletic trainers, barbers, chiropractors, cosmetologists, professional counselors, dentists, embalmers/funeral directors, healing arts specialists, employment agencies, hearing aid dealers/fitters, nurses, optometrists, podiatrists, pharmacists, real estate agents, veterinarians, insurance agents, nursing home administrators, lawyers, dental hygienists, physicians, physical therapists, speech pathologists and audiologists, psychologists.

Montana

Professional and Occupational Licensing, Business Regulation, Department of Commerce, 111 N. Jackson St., Helena, MT 59620; (406) 444-3737. Licensing boards and professions: accountants, acupuncturists, architects, athletic trainers, barbers, beer distributors, chiropractors, cosmetologists, dental hygienists, dentists, denturists, electricians, electrologists, employment Agencies, engineers and land surveyors, hearing aid dispensers, insurance, landscape architects, lawyers, librarians, medical doctors, morticians, nurses, nursing home administrators, occupational therapists, operating engineers (boiler), optometrists, osteopathic physicians, pawnbrokers, physical therapists, plumbers, podiatrists, polygraph examiners, private investigators, psychologists, contractors, radiologic technologists, real estate brokers and salesmen, sanitarians, securities brokers and salesmen, social workers and counselors, speech pathologists and audiologists, taxidermists, tourist campground and trailer courts, veterinarians, water well drillers.

Nebraska

Bureau of Examining Boards, Nebraska Department of Health, P.O. Box 95007, Lincoln, NE 68509; (402) 471-2115. Licensing boards and health professions: athletic trainers, advanced emergency medical technicians, audiologist/speech pathologists, cosmetologists, chiropractors, dentists/dental hygienists, embalmers/funeral directors, hearing aid dealers and fitters, pharmacists, podiatrists, optometrists, physical therapists, nurses, nursing home administrators, massage specialists, occupational therapists, professional counselors, psychologists, respiratory care specialists, social workers, sanitarians, veterinarians. For other licensing boards and professions, contact the NE state operator at (402) 471-2311 to be connected with the board that licenses the following professions: accountants, engineers/architects, barbers, abstracters, appraisers, land surveyors, landscape architects.

Nevada

State of Nevada Executive Chamber, Capitol Complex, 1 E. Liberty Street, #311, Reno, NV 89501; (702) 786-0231. Licensing boards and professions: accountants, architects, athletic trainers, audiologists and speech pathologists, barbers, chiropractors, contractors, cosmetologists, dentists, engineers and land surveyors, funeral directors and embalmers, hearing aid specialists, homeopaths, landscape architects, liquefied petroleum gas distributors, marriage and family counselors, physicians, naturopathic healing arts specialists, nurses, dispensing opticians, optometrists, oriental medicine, osteopaths, pharmacists, physical therapists, podiatrists, private investigators, psychologists, shorthand reporters, taxicab drivers, veterinarians.

New Hampshire

SOICC of New Hampshire, 64 B Old Sun Cook Rd., Concord, NH 03301; (603) 228-9500. Licensing boards and professions: accountants, emergency medical

Be patient. If any phone number is incorrect, call (area code) 555-1212 and request the new listing.

Professional People and Local Businesses

technicians, engineers/architects/land surveyors, attorneys, auctioneers, insurance (bailbondsmen), barbers, cosmetologists, chiropractors, court reporters, dentists, drivers education Instructors, electricians, funeral directors/embalmers, engineers, physicians, private security guards, lobbyists, nurses, nursing home administrators, occupational therapists, optometrists, psychologists, pesticide control operators, pharmacists, plumbers, podiatrists, real estate agents, teacher agents, veterinarians, water supply and pollution control operators.

New Jersey

Director, Centralized Licensing for the Licensing Boards, Division of Consumer Affairs, 375 West State Street, Trenton, NJ 08625; (609) 292-4670. Licensing boards and professions: accountants, architects, barbers, beauticians, dentists, electrical contractors, marriage counselors, plumbers, morticians, nurses, ophthalmic dispensing technicians, optometrists, pharmacists, physical therapists, professional engineers and landscape surveyors, professional planners, psychological examiners, shorthand reporters, veterinarians, public movers and warehousemen, acupuncture specialists, landscape architects, athletic trainers, hearing aid dispensers, chiropractors, opthomologists.

New Mexico

Regulation and Licensing Department, 725 St. Michael's Drive, P.O. Box 25101, Santa Fe, NM 87504; (505) 827-7000. Licensing boards and professions: accountants, architects, athletic promoters, barbers, chiropractors, cosmetologists, dentists, engineers and land surveyors, landscape architects, physicians, nurses, nursing home administrators, occupational therapists, optometrists, osteopaths, pharmacists, physical therapists, podiatrists, polygraphers, private investigators, psychologists, realtors, thanatopractice, veterinarians.

New York

New York State Education Department, Division of Professional Licensing, Cultural Education Center, Empire State Plaza, Albany, NY 12230; (518) 474-3852, or (800) 342-3729 (toll-free in NY). Licensed professionals: acupuncturists, architects, audiologists, certified shorthand reporters, chiropractors, dentists, landscape architects, land surveyors, massage therapists, physicians, osteopaths, nurses, occupational therapists, ophthalmic dispensers, optometrists, pharmacists, physical therapists, podiatrists, engineers, psychologists, public accountants, social workers, speech pathologists, veterinarians.

North Carolina

North Carolina Center for Public Policy Research, P.O. Box 430, Raleigh, NC 27602; (919) 832-2839. Licensing boards and professions: architects, auctioneers, barbers, boiler operators, accountants, chiropractors, cosmetologists, registered counselors, dental, electrical contractors, foresters, general contractors, hearing aid dealers and fitters, landscape architects, landscape contractors, marital and family therapists, physicians, navigators and pilots, morticians, nurses, nursing home administrators, opticians, optometrists, osteopaths, pesticide operators, pharmacists, physical therapists, plumbers and heating specialists, podiatrists, practicing psychologists, private protective services, professional engineers and land surveyors, public librarians, real estate, refrigeration technicians, sanitarians, social workers, speech and language pathologists, structural pest control operators, veterinarians, waste water treatment operators, water treatment facility operators.

North Dakota

North Dakota Legislative Council Library, 600 East Boulevard Avenue, Bismarck, ND 58505; (701) 224-2916. Licensing boards and professions: abstracters, accountants, architects, athletic trainers, audiologists and speech pathologists, barbers, chiropractors, cosmetologists, dentists, dietitians, electricians, embalmers, emergency medical services, engineers and land surveyors, hearing aid dealers and fitters, massage therapists, physicians, nurses, nursing home administrators, occupational therapists, optometrists, pharmacists, physical therapists, plumbers, podiatrists, private investigators, private police security, psychologists, real estate agents, respiratory care specialists, social workers, soil classifiers, veterinarians, water well contractors.

Ohio

State of Ohio, Department of Administrative Services, Division of Computer Services, 30 East Broad St., 40th Floor, Columbus, OH 43215-0409; (614) 466-8029. Licensed professionals: wholesale distributors of dangerous drugs, terminal distributors of dangerous drugs, pharmacists, accountants, barbers, barber shops, beauty shops, managing cosmetologists, cosmetologists, manicurists, architects, landscape architects, practical nurses, registered nurses, surveyors, engineers, surveyors, dentists, dental hygienists, osteopaths, physicians, podiatrists, chiropractors, midwives, embalmers, funeral directors, embalmer and funeral directors, hat cleaners, dry cleaners, public employment agencies, auctioneers, private investigators, auctioneers.

Oklahoma

Governor's Office, State Capitol, Oklahoma City, OK 73105; (405) 521-2342 or State Information Operator, (405) 521-1601. Licensing board and professions: accountants, real estate agents, physicians, foresters, medico-legals, nursing homes, nurses, optometrists, osteopaths, physicians, pharmacists, polygraph examiners, psychologists, shorthand reporters, social workers, speech pathologists, veterinarians, landscape architects, architects, chiropractors, cosmetologists, dentists, embalmers and funeral directors. For other licensed professionals, contact Occupational Licensing, OK State Health Department, 1000 North East, 10th Street, Oklahoma City, OK 73117; (405) 271-5217: barbers, hearing aid dealers, electricians, water and waste treatment plant operators.

Oregon

Department of Economic Development, Small Business Advocates, 595 Cottage St. NE, Salem, OR 97310; (800) 547-7842 or (800) 233-3306 (toll-free in OR). Licensing boards and professions: accountants, architects, barbers and hairdressers, builders, contractors, collection agencies, debt consolidators, geologists, landscape architects, landscape contractors, and TV/radio service dealers, engineering examiners, fire marshals, insurance agents, maritime pilots, real estate agents, tax practitioners.

Pennsylvania

Bureau of Professional and Occupational Affairs, 618 Transportation and Safety Building, Harrisburg, PA 17120-2649; (717) 787-8503, or (800) 822-2113 (toll-free in PA). Licensing boards and professions: accountants, architects, auctioneers, barbers, cosmetology, funeral directors, landscape architects, professional engineers, real estate agents. For licensed health professions, contact Bureau of Professional and Occupational Affairs, Secretary of State, 618 Transportation and Safety Building, Harrisburg, PA 17120; (717) 783-1400: dentists, physicians, nurses, nursing home administrators, occupational therapists, optometrists, osteopaths, pharmacists, physical therapists, podiatrists, psychologists, speech--language and hearing specialists, veterinarians, navigators.

Rhode Island

Rhode Island Occupational Information Coordinating Commission, 22 Hayes Street, Providence, RI 02908; (401) 272-0830. Licensing boards and professions: nurses aides, psychologists, respiratory therapists, sanitarians, speech pathologists, veterinarians, physical therapists, plumbers, podiatrists, prosthetists, nurses, nursing home administrators, occupational therapists, opticians, optometrists, osteopaths, physician assistants, embalmers/funeral directors, hairdressers, cosmetologists, manicurists, massage therapists, physicians, midwives, acupuncturists, athletic trainers, audiologists, barbers, barber shops, chiropractors, dentists, dental hygienists, electrologist, architects, coastal resource management, engineers and land surveyors.

South Carolina

South Carolina State Library, 1500 Senate St., Columbia, SC 29201; (803) 734-8666. Licensing boards and professions: accountants, architects, auctioneers, barbers, morticians, chiropractors, contractors, cosmetologists, dentists, engineers, environmental systems (well diggers), foresters, funeral services, landscape architects, physicians, nurses, nursing home administrators, occupational therapists, opticians, optometrists, pharmacists, physical therapists, professional counselors, marriage and family therapists, psychologists, real estate agents, sanitarians, home builder, social workers, speech pathologist/audiologists, veterinarians, athletic trainers (boxing and wrestling), geologists.

South Dakota

Department of Commerce and Regulation, 500 E. Capitol Ave., Pierre, SD 57501-5070; (605) 773-3178. South Dakota Medical and Osteopath Examiners, 1323 S. Minnesota Avenue, Sioux Falls, SD 57105; (605) 336-1965. Licensing boards and professions: physicians, osteopaths, physician's assistants, physical therapists, medical corporations, emergency technicians, abstracters, accountants, barbers, chiropractors, cosmetologists, electricians, engineers/architects, funeral

Be patient. If any phone number is incorrect, call (area code) 555-1212 and request the new listing.

directors, hearing aid dispensers, medical/osteopaths, nurses, nursing home administrators, optometrists, pharmacists, plumbers, podiatrists, psychologists, real estate agents, social workers, veterinarians.

Tennessee

Division of Regulatory Boards, Department of Commerce and Insurance, 500 James Robertson Parkway, Nashville, TN 37243; (615) 741-3449. Licensing boards and professions: accountants, architects and engineers, auctioneers, barbers, collection services, contractors, cosmetologists, funeral directors and embalmers, land surveyors, motor vehicle salesmen and dealers, personnel recruiters, pharmacists, polygraph examiners, real estate. For other licensed health professionals, contact Division of Health Related Professions, Department of Health and Environment, 283 or 287 Plus Park Blvd Complex, Nashville, TN 37247-1010; (615) 367-6220: dentists, dental hygienists, podiatrists, physicians, physician's assistants, osteopaths, optometrists, veterinarians, nursing home administrators, dispensing opticians, chiropractors, social workers, hearing aid dispensers, registered professional environmentalists, marital and family counselors, speech pathology/audiologists, occupational and physical therapists, x-ray technicians, registered nurses, licensed practical nurses.

Texas

Texas Department of Commerce, 410 E. 5th Street, P.O. Box 12047, Austin, TX 78711-2728; (512) 320-0110, or (800) 888-0511 (toll-free in TX). Licensing boards and professions: accountants, architects, barbers, cosmetologists, morticians, educators, public safety, chiropractors, psychologists, dentists, real estate agents, engineers, veterinarians, insurance agents, land surveyors, landscape architects, fitting and dispensing of hearing aids, private investigators and private security agencies, polygraph, Vocational nurses, nursing home administrators, physicians, optometrists, structural pest control operators, pharmacists, physical therapists, plumbers, podiatrists, professional counselors, dietitians, speech-language pathology and audiology.

Utah

Division of Occupational and Professional Licensing, Department of Business Regulation, Heber M. Wells Building, 160 East 300 South, P.O. Box 45805, Salt Lake City, UT 84145-0805; (801) 530-6628. Licensing boards and professions: accountants, architects, barbers, cosmetologists, electrologists, chiropractors, podiatrists, dentists, dental hygienists, embalmers, funeral directors, pre-need sellers, engineers, land surveyors, physicians, surgeons, Naturopaths, registered nurses, licensed practical nurses, nurse midwives, nurse anesthetists, nurse specialists, prescriptive practice specialist, IV therapists, optometrists, osteopaths, pharmacists, pharmacies, manufacturing pharmacies, shorthand reporters, veterinarians, health facility administrators, sanitarians, morticians, physical therapists, psychologists, clinical social workers, conduct research on controlled substance, marriage and family therapists, master therapeutic recreational specialists, speech pathologists, audiologists, occupational therapists, hearing aid specialists, massage therapists, massage establishments, acupuncture practitioners, physician assistants, dieticians, contractors.

Vermont

Division of Licensing and Registration, Secretary of State, Pavilion Office Building, Montpelier, VT 05609; (802) 828-2363. Licensing boards and professions: accountants, architects, barbers, boxing control, chiropractors, cosmetologists, dentists, engineers, funeral directors/embalmers, land surveyors, medical board (physicians, podiatrists, real estate brokers, veterinarians, physical therapists, social workers, physician assistants, motor vehicle racing, nurses, nursing home administrators, opticians, optometrists, osteopaths, pharmacies, pharmacist, psychologists, private detectives, security Guards, radiological technicians.

Virginia

Virginia Department of Commerce, 3600 W. Broad St., Richmond, VA 23230; (804) 367-8500. Licensed professions: accountants, architects, auctioneers, audiologists, barbers, boxers, contractors, commercial driver training schools, employment agencies, professional engineers, geologists, hairdressers, harbor pilots, hearing aid dealers and fitters, landscape architects, nursing home administrators, librarians, opticians, polygraph examiners, private security services, real estate brokers, speech pathologists, land surveyors, water and wastewater works operators, wrestlers. For licensed health professions, contact Health Professionals: (804) 662-9900. The office listed above can provide you with phone numbers for the following licensing boards: dentists, funeral directors/embalmers, physicians, medical/legal assistants, nurses, optometrists, pharmacists, psychologists, professional counselors, social workers, veterinarians.

Washington

Department of Health, P.O. Box 47860, Olympia, WA 98504-7860; (206) 586-4561. Licensed professions: acupuncturists, auctioneers, architects, barbers, camp club registration/salespersons, chiropractors, cosmetology schools/instructors, cosmetologists, manicurists, collection agencies, debt adjusters/agencies, dentists, dental hygienists, drugless therapeutic-naturopaths, employment agencies/managers, professional engineers, engineers-in-training, land surveyors, engineering corporations/partnerships, escrow officers/agents, firearms dealers, embalmers, apprentice embalmers, funeral directors, funeral establishments, hearing aid dispensers/trainees, land development registration, landscape architects, massage operators, midwives, notary publics, nursing home administrators, occularists, occupational therapists, dispensing opticians, optometrists, osteopaths, osteopathic physician/surgeon, osteopathic physician assistants, physicians, surgeons, physician's assistants, limited physician, podiatrists, practical nurses, psychologists, physical therapists, real estate (brokers, salespersons, corporations, partnerships, branch offices), land development representatives, registered nurses, timeshare registration and salespersons, veterinarians, animal technicians.

West Virginia

Administrative Law Division, Secretary of State, State Capitol, Charleston, WV 25305; (304) 345-4000. Licensing boards and professions: accountants, architects, barbers, beauticians, chiropractors, dentists, and dental hygienists, embalmers and funeral directors, engineers, foresters, hearing-aid dealers, landscape architects, land surveyors, law examiners, physicians, practical nurses, registered nurses, nursing home administrators, occupational therapists, optometrists, osteopaths, pharmacists, physical therapists, psychologists, radiologic technicians, real estate agents, sanitarians, state water resources, veterinarians.

Wisconsin

Department of Regulation and Licensing, P.O. Box 8935, Madison, WI 53708; (608) 266-7482. Licensed professions: accountants, animal technicians, architects, architects, engineers, barbers, bingo organizations, morticians, chiropractors, cosmetologists, distributors of dangerous drugs, dental hygienists, dentists, interior designers, private detectives, drug manufacturers, electrologists, professional engineers, funeral directors, hearing aid dealers/fitters, land surveyors, manicurists, physicians, surgeons, nurse midwives, registered nurses, licensed practical nurses, nursing home administrators, optometrists, pharmacists, physical therapists, physician's assistants, podiatrists, psychologists, raffle organizations, real estate brokers, beauty salons, electrolysis salons, veterinarians.

Wyoming

Governor's Office, State Capitol, Cheyenne, WY 82002; (307) 777-7434. Licensing boards and professions: funeral directors and embalmers, health service administrators, buyers and purchasing agents, shorthand reporters, medical record technicians, accountants and auditors, claims adjusters, appraisers, engineers, architects, surveyors, interior designers and decorators, medical laboratory workers, dental laboratory technicians, opticians, radiological technicians, respiratory technicians, quality control inspectors, security salespeople, insurance agents, real estate agents, physicians, physician's assistants, chiropractors, pharmacists, occupational therapists, activity therapists, physical therapists, speech pathologist and audiologist, veterinarian, optometrist, dietitians, dentists, dental hygienists, registered nurses, licensed practical nurses, emergency medical technicians, nurse's aides, medical assistants, counselors, lawyers, legal assistants, cosmetologists and barbers.

Be patient. If any phone number is incorrect, call (area code) 555-1212 and request the new listing.

Driver's Licenses and Motor Vehicles

State Division of Motor Vehicles

Mailing lists galore and plentiful market research data derived from state motor vehicle departments offer the potential for increasing your bottom line. Did you ever want to know how many 40-year-old males in Boston wear contact lenses, or perhaps obtain the names and addresses of all Arizonians who own Cadillacs? Well, it is within the realm of possibility.

Believe it or not, those long lines that drive us crazy when registering a car or renewing a driver's license have a bright side. Each person in line turns over a wealth of information about himself or herself to the state. This data -- name, address, age, physical characteristics, and buying patterns -- are the stuff of which customer lists, market studies, and demographic analyses are made. While states charge you for this information, it will cost a fraction of what you would spend if you hired some sharp marketing consultant to unearth the data.

Take the example of my friend, Ron, a mechanic for expensive foreign cars in Wilmington, Delaware. One day Ron got tired of watching his boss laugh all the way to the bank and decided he wanted to open a shop of his own. Through the state he was able to obtain printouts of all owners of Audis, BMWs, and Mercedes in his area. Armed with this information, Ron ultimately was able to obtain a small business loan, open a shop, and now is making more than I'd care to admit.

Many states maintain files not only on autos, but also on boats and recreational vehicles. This data can be of further help in targeting potential customers. It doesn't take business brilliance to deduce that a person living in Palm Beach, who owns several high-ticket imported cars and has a 37-foot Hatteras yacht, is a potential customer for a home security company.

Many states will sort through their driver's license database by age and sex for an additional charge and provide a listing, for example, of all females between the ages of 18 and 45 years living in a particular district. If you are launching a magazine aimed at working women, this is priceless marketing intelligence. The same holds true for older persons who have special senior citizen identifiers and for young males who are eligible for the Selective Service.

This data is used in countless ways by researchers for compiling statistics on health issues, and used by the government for manufacturer recalls or warranty programs and emission studies. Insurance companies, financial institutions, and other businesses thrive on this cross-sectioning of the body public.

Information derived from a state's automobile owner registration master file is usually available in two formats -- magnetic tape or computer printouts. Most states prefer sending a tape for larger files, but will send printouts for shorter sorts. Some states also offer mailing labels for an additional charge.

The most likely sorting options include: an entire state file; all vehicles within a county; vehicle type (two-door, four-door, four-wheel drive) by state or county; and vehicle make by year, state or county.

Driver's license information can usually be extracted to provide: name and license number (only); name, license number, and address; and a variety of other factors regarding age or sex. All states charge for this information, usually per 1,000 entries plus a set-up fee, but the potential for increasing your profits by using this valuable data will far outweigh the costs.

There are a few states which do not allow access to this data. These are Connecticut, South Dakota, Rhode Island, New Jersey, Indiana, Hawaii, Georgia, and Arkansas. Utah, North Carolina, and Montana are the three states which will not divulge driver's license information but will turn over vehicle registration files. And three states, Pennsylvania, New Mexico and Kansas, will only give you the information under very specific circumstances. That leaves 38 states which are wide open.

Motor Vehicle Offices

Alabama

Drivers: Alabama Department of Public Safety, Drivers License Division, P.O. Box 1471, Montgomery, AL 36192; (205) 242-4400. Services: Individual records can be retrieved for $5.75 per record.

Arizona

Drivers: Arizona Motor Vehicles Division, 1801 W. Jefferson St., Phoenix, AZ 85007; (602) 255-7567. Request must be in writing with complete name, license number and date of birth. The cost is $3 for a 39 month check, $5 for a 5 year check.

Owners: Arizona Motor Vehicles Division, 1801 W. Jefferson St., Room 230M, Phoenix, AZ 85007; (602) 255-7567. Database: Arizona Drivers - contains owner's name and address plus make, model, year, tag and license numbers for 1,655,833 cars and 875,000 other vehicles. Services: A mailing list is available for $3,300, or a computer tape can be purchased and data sorted by name and address. Tape cost is $30 per 1,000 names received.

Arkansas

Drivers: Arkansas Office of Motor Vehicle Registration, P.O. Box 1272, Little Rock, AR 72203; (501) 682-7060. Services: license information is protected under the Privacy Act. A release must be signed by a driver before that data can be released.

Owners: Arkansas Office of Motor Vehicle Registration, P.O. Box 1272, Little Rock, AR 72203; (501) 682-4603. Database: Arkansas Automobile Owners - contains owner's name and address plus make, model, year and license number for over 15 million automobiles and approximately 300,000 million other vehicles including motorcycles and boats. Services: No data tapes released. Records are open for public inspection at the office only.

California

Drivers: Department of Motor Vehicles, P.O. Box 944247, Sacramento, CA 94269; (916) 657-6555. Services: Individual records can be requested; must identify the name, license number and date of birth of the driver.

Be patient. If any phone number is incorrect, call (area code) 555-1212 and request the new listing.

Information on People, Companies, and Mailing Lists

Owners: Department of Motor Vehicles, P.O. Box 944247, MS-D-146, Sacramento, CA 94244-2470; (916) 657-7669. Database: California Automobile Owners - contains owner's name and address as well as make, model, year, tag and license numbers of 16.5 million automobiles and 631,000 motorcycles. Services: This file must be purchased in its entirety (i.e., information of all motorcycles and registration records for automobiles costs approximately $100 per 1,000 names).

Colorado

Drivers: Colorado Motor Vehicle Division, Traffic Records, 140 W. 6th Ave., #104, Denver, CO 80204; (303) 572-5601. Database: Colorado Drivers - contains name, address, license number of 3,167,570 drivers. It is available in three files: minor, provisional and adult permits. Services: One time single run only of name, address and license number only. The cost of $25 per 1,000 names with a $1,000 minimum plus set-up fee.

Owners: Colorado Motor Vehicle Division, Traffic Records, 140 W. 6th Ave., #103, Denver, CO 80204; (303) 623-9463. Database: Colorado Owners - contains name and address. Services: One time single run only of name, address and license number only. The cost of $25 per 1,000 names with a $1,000 minimum.

Connecticut

Drivers and Owners: Connecticut State Department of Motor Vehicles, 60 State Street, Wethersfield, CT 06109; (203) 566-3830. Data is not released.

Delaware

Drivers: Delaware Motor Vehicles Division, P.O. Box 698, Dover, DE 19903; (302) 739-4461. Database: Delaware Drivers - provides name, address, height, weight and other drivers license information except hair color of 494,035 drivers. Services: Some ready-made programs available. Any additional programming requires additional charges.

Owners: Delaware Motor Vehicle Division, P.O. Box 698, Dover DE 19903; (302) 739-4421. Database: Delaware Drivers - provides owner's name and address along with make, model, year, title number, expiration date of 580,849 registration cars, motorcycles or trucks. Services: A data tape can be purchased with sorting of reportable variables for $375 plus $11 per 1,000 names.

District of Columbia

Drivers: District of Columbia, Department of Public Works Information Office, 301 C St., NW, Room 1025, Washington, DC 20001; (202) 727-6761. Database: District of Columbia Drivers - contains name, address, suspensions, sex, Social Security number, height, type of permit, license number, expiration dates, and restrictions of 800,000 drivers. Services: Computer tapes and printouts available. Data can be sorted by categories but not recommended. Cost is $1,700.

Owners: District of Columbia, Department of Public Works Information Office, 301 C St., NW, Room 1025, Washington, DC 20001; (202) 727-1159. Database: District of Columbia Owners - contains owner's name, address, make, model, year, tag number, and registration number of 263,290 vehicles. Services: Computer tape available, data can be sorted by category. Cost is $900.

Florida

Drivers: Florida Highway Safety and Motor Vehicles Department, Neil Kirkman Building, Tallahassee, FL 32301; (904) 488-6710. Database: Florida Drivers - contains name, address, and date of birth of over 12 million drivers. Services: No sorting is available. A computer tape or printout can be obtained for $.45 per second.

Owners: Florida Highway Safety and Motor Vehicles Department, Neil Kirkman Building, Tallahassee, FL 32301; (904) 488-6710. Database: Florida Automobile Owners - provides owner's name and address plus make, model, year, tag number and class code for 7 million cars and 5 million other vehicles. Services: No sorting is available, data available on a computer tape or printout. Cost is $1.60 per second.

Georgia

Drivers: Motor Vehicle Records, 959 E. Confederate Ave., Atlanta, GA 30316; (404) 624-7487. Data is not released.

Owners: Motor Vehicle Division, Trinity Washington Bldg., Atlanta, GA 30334; (404) 656-4156. Data is not released.

Hawaii

Drivers and Owners: Division of Motor Vehicles and Licenses, 1455 S. Beretania St., Honolulu, HI 96814; (808) 973-2700. Data is not released.

Idaho

Drivers: Idaho Transportation Department, Economics and Research Section, P.O. Box 7129, Boise, ID 83707-1129; (208) 334-8741. Database: Idaho Drivers - provides name, address, sex, date of birth, license type, expiration date, and county of residence of approximately 1,000,000 drivers. Services: Data may be selected by sex, age or range of ages, and county of residence. Cost: $75 plus computer charges (varies depending on size of the file, sorts, etc.) and shipping.

Owners: Idaho Transportation Department, Economics and Research Section, P.O. Box 7129, Boise, ID 83707-1129; (208) 334-8741. Database: Idaho Owners - provides registered owner, address, make, model, year, issue and expiration date. Approximately 1,300,000 records. Services: Data can be selected by registration type, and/or county of residence. The cost is $75 plus computer charges (this varies depending on the size of the file, sorts, etc.) and shipping charges. Computer tape or printouts are available.

Illinois

Drivers: Illinois Secretary of State, Drivers Services Division, 2701 S. Dirksen Parkway, Springfield, IL 62723; (217) 782-1978. Database: Illinois Drivers - contains name, address, sex, date of birth, license issue and expiration date of 8 million drivers. Services: Data can be sorted by various categories and provided on a computer tape for $200 plus $20 per 1,000 names, or on a printout for $.50 per page (15,000 names or less).

Owners: Illinois Secretary of State, Centennial Building, Room 114, Springfield, IL 62756; (217) 782-0029. Database: Illinois Automobile Owners - provides owner's name and address, make, model and year of over 6 million passenger cars and over 2 million other vehicles. Services: Complete records are available. Data can be sorted by various categories. Computer tapes available for $200 plus $20 per 1,000; computer printouts for $.50 per pate (15,000 names or less).

Indiana

Drivers and Owners: Indiana Bureau of Motor Vehicles, 100 N. Senate Ave., Indianapolis, IN 46204; (317) 232-2798. Data is not released.

Iowa

Drivers: Iowa Department of Transportation, Drivers Services, Lucas State Office Building, Des Moines, IA 50319; (515) 244-8725. Database: Iowa Drivers - provides name, address, date of birth, height, weight, restrictions, issue and expiration dates, license number, and restrictions of 2.5 million drivers. Services: Data is listed in order by license number. Data cannot be sorted. Computer tapes available, $370 (Tapes must be provided by requester).

Owners: Iowa Department of Transportation, Office of Vehicle Registration, P.O. Box 9204, Des Moines, IA 50306-9204; (515) 237-3182. Database: Iowa Automobile Owners - provides complete description of vehicle for 4.2 million cars and other vehicles. Services: Data tapes available for $.39 per thousand names plus $14 for each tape, computer time charge for sorts and $20 set up fee.

Kansas

Drivers: Topeka Drivers Licenses Bureau, 37th and Burlingame, Topeka, KS 66609; (913) 266-7380. Data tapes not released for commercial purposes.

Owners: Kansas Titles and Registration Bureau, Room 123 S. Docking State Office Building, 915 Harrison, Topeka, KS 66626; (913) 296-3621. Data tapes not released for commercial purposes.

Kentucky

Drivers: Kentucky Transportation Cabinet, Division of Driver Licensing, State Office Building, 501 High Street, Frankfort, KY 40622; (502) 564-4864. Database: Kentucky Drivers - provides name, address, and date of birth of over 2.4 million

Be patient. If any phone number is incorrect, call (area code) 555-1212 and request the new listing.

Driver's Licenses and Motor Vehicles

drivers. Services: Data can be sorted by various categories. Computer tapes or printouts are available for $.01 per name plus $510 for programming and computer costs. Mailing labels are available for $2.45 per 1,000 plus above charges.

Owners: Kentucky Transportation Cabinet, Division of Motor Vehicle Licensing, State Office Building, Room 205, Frankfort, KY 40622; (502) 564-4864. Database: Kentucky Automobile Owners - provides owner's name and address along with make, model and year for over 2 million vehicles. Services: Data can be sorted by various categories. Computer tapes and printouts available for $.02 per name plus programming costs. Mailing labels can be purchased for $3.50 per 1,000 plus programming costs.

Louisiana

Drivers: Louisiana Department of Public Safety and Corrections, P.O. Box 66614, Baton Rouge, LA 70896; (504) 925-6146. Database: Louisiana Drivers - provides name, address, height, weight, sex, date of birth of 2.7 million drivers. Services: Computer tape and printout available. Data can be sorted by variables. Cost is $.03 per name plus $500.

Owners: Louisiana Department of Public Safety and Corrections, P.O. Box 66614, Baton Rouge, LA 70896; (504) 925-6146. Database: Louisiana Owners - provides owner's name, address, make, model and year, date of acquisition, color, new or used for 4.5 million vehicles. Services: Computer tape and printout available for $.03 per record and $500.

Maine

Drivers: Maine Motor Vehicle Division, 101 Hospital Street, Station 29, Augusta, ME 04333; (207) 289-5553. Database: Maine Drivers - provides name, address, date of birth, and sex of 800,000 drivers. Services: Data available on computer tape, printout available for $.25 per name. Mailing labels are available for an extra charge.

Owners: Maine Motor Vehicles Division, 101 Hospital Street, Station 29, Augusta, ME 04333; (207) 289-5553. Database: Maine Automobile Owners - contains owner's name and address, date of birth as well as make, model, year, identification number for 700,000 registered vehicles. Services: Data can be sorted by variables and can be purchased on computer tape, printout or mailing labels. Cost available on request.

Maryland

Drivers: Maryland Motor Vehicle Administration, 6601 Ritchie Highway, Room 200, Glen Burnie, MD 21062; (410) 768-7665. Database: Maryland Drivers - contains name, address, date of birth, height, weight, and identification number of over 2 million drivers. Services: Data can be sorted by variables and is available on computer tape for $500 (non-refundable charge) plus $.05 for each record.

Owners: Maryland Motor Vehicle Administration, 6601 Ritchie Highway, Room 200, Glen Burnie, MD 21062; (410) 768-7665. Database: Maryland Automobile Owners - provides owner's name and address along with make, model and year for nearly 3,000,000 passenger cars and 3 million other vehicles. Some insurance information is included.

Massachusetts

Drivers: Massachusetts Registry of Motor Vehicles, 100 Nashua Street, Boston, MA 02114; (617) 727-3716. Database: Massachusetts Automobile Drivers - provides name, address, and Social Security number of 4 million drivers. Services: Data can be sorted by all variables except sex. The cost is $1,000 for the first 1,000 names and $40 per 1,000 records thereafter. Data is available on computer tape or printout (for less than 30,000 names).

Owners: Massachusetts Registry of Motor Vehicles, 100 Nashua Street, Boston, MA 02114; (617) 727-3716. Database: Massachusetts Automobile Owners - contains owner's name and address along with make, model and year of 5 million vehicles. Services: Sorting of data is available, for instance, by particular insurance company the owner carries. The cost is $1,000 for the first 1,000 names and $40 per 1,000 records thereafter. Data is available on computer tape or printout (for less than 30,000 names).

Michigan

Drivers: Michigan Systems Programming Division, 7064 Crowners Drive, Lansing, MI 48918; (517) 322-1584. Database: Michigan Drivers - provides names, address, date of birth, and sex of 6,447,174 drivers. Services: Data may be selected by sex, date of birth, county, state, city, and zip code at a cost of $64 per 1,000 names versus $16 per 1,000 names unsorted. There is a $500 minimum charge. Data can be purchased on computer tape or printout. Limited amounts are also available on disc.

Owners: Michigan Department of State, Data Processing Division, 7064 Crowners Drive, Lansing, MI 48918; (517) 322-1584. Database: Michigan Automobile Owners - provides owner's name and address with year, license number, make and model of 5,234,916 passenger cars and 2,261,688 other vehicles. Services: The cost for sorting is $64 per 1,000 names versus $16 per 1,000 unsorted names. There is a $500 minimum charge. Data can be purchased on computer tape or printout. Limited amounts are also available on disc.

Minnesota

Drivers: Minnesota Department of Public Safety, Driver/Vehicle Services Division, Transportation Building, 395 John Ireland Blvd., St. Paul, MN 55155; (612) 297-2442. Database: Minnesota Drivers - provides name, address, and sex of 3.3 million drivers. Services: Data can be sorted; there is an extra fee if more information is required. Data is available on printout or computer tape or mailing labels for $8 to $10 per name with a $500 minimum. Custom programming cost varies depending on complexity of request.

Owners: Minnesota Department of Public Safety, Driver/Vehicle Services Division, Transportation Building, 395 John Ireland Boulevard, St. Paul, MN 55155; (612) 296-6911. Database: Minnesota Automobile Owners - contains owner's name and address along with make, model and year for 3.2 million cars and 1.2 million other vehicles. Services: Certain data can be sorted. Data is available on computer tape or printout. There is a $500 minimum plus $8 per 1,000 names.

Mississippi

Drivers: Mississippi Department of Public Safety/Data Processing, P.O. Box 958, Jackson, MS 39205; (601) 987-1212. Database: Mississippi Drivers - contains name, address, date of birth, race and sex of over 1,924,696 drivers. Services: Data cannot be sorted. The entire file must be purchased for $250 plus $20/reel.

Owners: Mississippi State Tax Commission Network, P.O. Box 960, Room 220, Jackson, MS 39205; (601) 359-1117. Database: Mississippi Automobile Owners - provides a complete file, including owner's name and address, make, model, year of 1.6 million registered vehicles. Services: Data can be sorted and made available on computer tape or printout. Fees range from $1,000 - $2,000. Mailing labels available for an extra charge.

Missouri

Drivers: Missouri Department of Revenue, Information Services Bureau, P.O. Box 41, Jefferson City, MO 65105; (314) 751-5486. Database: Missouri Drivers - contains name, address, sex, date of birth, height, weight, eye color, restrictions, license number, class, and county of 3.4 million drivers. Services: Data available on computer tape or printouts for $.018 per 50,000 records. Process fee is $85.26 and programming fee is $28.75 per hour. Mailing labels available for an extra charge $2 per 1,000.

Owners: Missouri Department of Revenue, Information Services Bureau, P.O. Box 41, Jefferson City, MO 65105; (314) 751-5486. Database: Missouri Owners - provides name and address of registered owners plus make, model, year, number of cylinders, type of fuel, license ID number, license expiration date, and year for over 4.2 million cars and 3.4 million other vehicles. Services: Data available on computer tape or printout. Cost: $.018 per 50,000 records. Process fee is $85.26 and programming fee is $28.75 per hour. Mailing labels available for an extra fee of $2 per 1,000.

Montana

Drivers: Drivers Services, 303 North Roberts, Helena, MT 59620; (406) 444-3275. Data is not released.

Owners: Montana Motor Vehicle Division, 925 Main St., Deer Lodge, MT 59722; (406) 846-1423. Database: Montana Automobile Owners - provides owner's name and address along with year, make, model, body, color, serial number, second

Information on People, Companies, and Mailing Lists

owner for over one million registered vehicles. Services: Data available on computer tape and printout. The cost is $300 for the first 10,000 names and $30 per 1,000 names thereafter on tape or disc. Cost for each additional 1,000 names on printout is $40.

Nebraska

Drivers: Nebraska Department of Motor Vehicles, P.O. Box 94789, Lincoln, NE 68509; (402) 471-3909. To receive information you must provide the correct name, date of birth, or license number for each record requested. The cost is $1.75 per record.

Owners: Nebraska Department of Motor Vehicles, P.O. Box 94789, Lincoln, NE 68509; (402) 471-3909. Database: Nebraska Automobile Owners - provides a listing by make, model, and year which includes owner's name and address for 856,000 passenger cars and 650,000 other vehicle owners. Services: Data can be provided on computer tape and printout for $12 per 1,000 names with a $300 minimum.

Nevada

Drivers: Nevada Department of Motor Vehicles, 555 Wright Way, Carson City, NV 89711; (702) 687-5370. Database: Nevada Drivers - provides name, address, date of birth, height, weight, for more than one million drivers. Services: Data can be sorted by county, zip code, date of birth and make of car. Data available on computer tape or printout (up to 1,000,000 names). Mailing labels available for an extra fee. Cost is $2,500 for the entire file or $15 per 1,000 for a partial listing.

Owners: Nevada Department of Motor Vehicles, 555 Wright Way, Carson City, NV 89711; (702) 687-5370. Database: Contains owner's name, address along with make, model and year for one million registered vehicles. Data may also be selected by county, zip code and make of car. Services: Computer tape is available for $2,500 or portions prorated $15 per thousand. A printout is available up to 1,000,000 records. Also available on mailing labels. (Prices are subject to change.)

New Hampshire

Drivers: New Hampshire Department of Safety, Data Processing, 10 Hazen Drive, Concord, NH 03305; (603) 271-2314. Database: New Hampshire Drivers - consists of name, address, physical characteristics, Social Security number, class of license, issue and expiration date, and restriction of 843,000 drivers. Services: Data can be sorted by sex or age. Data provided on computer tape or printout. Prices vary, depending on data requested and size of the file.

Owners: New Hampshire Department of Safety, Data Processing, 10 Hazen Dr., Concord, NH 03305; (603) 271-2314. Database: New Hampshire Owners - contains owner's name and address as well as make, model and year for 815,628 passenger cars and 517,606 other vehicles. Services: Data can be sorted by zip code, model or make. Data available on computer tape or printout (extra charge). Fees vary depending on request. Entire file available on microfiche for $50.

New Jersey

Drivers and Owners: Data is not available for purchase. Must write in for individual records. New Jersey Division of Motor Vehicles, 25 S. Montgomery St., Trenton, NJ 08660; (609) 588-2424.

New Mexico

Drivers and Owners: Data cannot be sold for commercial purposes. New Mexico Taxation and Revenue Department, Motor Vehicle Division, P.O. Box 1028, Santa Fe, NM 87504-1028; (505) 827-2294.

New York

Drivers: NY State Department of Motor Vehicles, Data Preparation, Empire State Plaza, Albany, NY 12202. Printouts available by written request. Cost for individual record is $5 per search.

Owners: State Department of Motor Vehicles, Empire State Plaza, P.O. Box 2650, Room 433, Albany, NY 12202; (518) 473-5595. Data tapes are not available for purchase. Must write in for individual records at $5 per record.

North Carolina

Drivers: No records released.

Owners: Transportation Data Service Center, Century Center, Bldg. B, 1020 Birchridge Rd., Raleigh, NC 27610; (919) 250-4204. Database: North Carolina Automobile Owners - provides owner's name and address, second owner's name, make, model, year, plate classification, license number and weight of vehicle for 5.5 million registered vehicles. Services: Data can be sorted by model, year, make, county, zip code and other variables. The cost is $250 for the first 12,500 records and $20 per 1,000 records thereafter.

North Dakota

Drivers: North Dakota Drivers License and Traffic Safety Division, 608 East Boulevard Avenue, Bismarck, ND 58505-0700; (701) 224-2601. Database: North Dakota Drivers - provides name, address, date of birth, and license number of 450,000 drivers. Services: Special sort and/or extraction is available. The cost is $9 per 1,000 names with a $250 minimum. Mailing labels are available for an extra fee.

Owners: North Dakota Department of Transportation, Motor Vehicle Service Division, 608 E. Boulevard, Bismarck, ND 58505; (701) 224-2725. Database: North Dakota Automobile Owners - contains owner's name and address along with make, model and year of 369,010 passenger cars and 391,968 other vehicles. Services: Data can be sorted by variables and provided on computer printout tape for $50 plus $40 per 1,000 names. Mailing labels are available for an extra fee.

Ohio

Drivers: Ohio Bureau of Motor Vehicles, Data Services, P.O. Box 16520, Columbus, OH 43266-0020; (614) 752-7695. Database: Ohio Drivers - includes name, address, sex, date of birth, height, weight, hair color, eye color, zip code, and some restrictions for over 7.4 million registered drivers. Services: Data can be sorted by variables. Data is available on computer tape for $.075 per record. Mailing labels are $.08 each.

Owners: Ohio Bureau of Motor Vehicles, Data Services, P.O. Box 16520, Columbus, OH 43266-0020; (614) 752-7695. Database: Ohio Automobile Owners - provides owner's name and address along with make, model, year, license number, and expiration date for over 9 million registered vehicles. Services: Data can be sorted by variables. Available on computer tape or printout at $.075 per record. Mailing labels provided for $.08 each.

Oklahoma

Drivers and Owners: Data tapes are not sold. Individual records available for $1 each. Oklahoma Tax Commission, Motor Vehicle Division, 2501 N. Lincoln Blvd., Oklahoma City, OK 73194; (405) 521-3217.

Oregon

Drivers: Oregon Department of Transportation, Motor Vehicles Division, 1905 Lana Ave., NE, Salem, OR 97314; (503) 378-6995. Database: Oregon Drivers - contains name, address, sex, age, and year of birth for over 2 million drivers. Services: Data can be sorted and provided on computer tape for $180 or printout for $180 for full file.

Owners: Oregon Department of Transportation, Motor Vehicles Division, 1905 Lana Ave., NE, Salem, OR 97314; (503) 378-6995. Database: Oregon Automobile Owners - contains owner's name and address along with make, model and year for over two million registered vehicles. Services: Data can be selected by variables, data available on computer tape or printout for $180.

Pennsylvania

Drivers and Owners: Data only available with a special request. Not available for commercial purposes. Bureau of Drivers Licenses Information, Box 58691, Harrisburg, PA 17106; (717) 787-2158.

Rhode Island

Drivers and Owners: Data not available to the public. Department of Motor Vehicles, State Office Building, Providence, RI 02903; (401) 277-2970.

Be patient. If any phone number is incorrect, call (area code) 555-1212 and request the new listing.

Driver's Licenses and Motor Vehicles

South Carolina

Drivers: South Carolina Highway Department, Public Transportation, P.O. Box 1498, Columbia, SC 29216-0028; (803) 251-2940. Database: South Carolina Drivers - provides name, address, date of birth, license number, and restrictions for 1.8 million drivers. Services: Data may be sorted by last name, zip code, tag number as well as automobiles and/or motorcycles for 100,000 records. Computer tapes or printouts are available for $1,200.

Owners: South Carolina Highway Department, Public Transportation, P.O. Box 1498, Columbia, SC 29216-0019; (803) 251-2960. Database: South Carolina Automobile Owners - contains name and address of 700,000 registered vehicle owners along with make, year and serial number. Services: Data may be sorted by last name, county, city, state, insurance information and tag number as well as automobile and/or motorcycles. Requests must be mailed in. Prices are available upon written request.

South Dakota

Drivers and Owners: Data is not released. Division of Motor Vehicles, 118 W. Capitol St., Pierre, SD 57501; (605) 773-3545.

Tennessee

Drivers: Department of Safety Information System, 150 Foster Ave., Nashville, TN 37210; (615) 251-5322. Database: Tennessee Drivers - contains name, address, date of birth, sex and physical characteristics of approximately 3.5 million drivers. Services: Data can be sorted by category. Computer tapes, printouts and mailing labels are available for a minimum $500 plus $.10 per record.

Owners: Department of Safety Information Systems, 1150 Foster Ave., Nashville, TN 37210; (615) 251-5322. Database: Tennessee Automobile Owners - contains owner's name, address, model, make, year and tag number of approximately 4 million vehicles. Services: Computer tapes, printouts and mailing labels available for $300 minimum, plus $100 set up fee plus $20.05 per 1,000 names. (Prices subject to change.)

Texas

Drivers: Texas Department of Public Safety, Attn: L.I. and V.I., P.O. Box 4087, Austin, TX 78773; (512) 465-2000. Database: Texas Drivers - provides name, address, date of birth, and license number for over 1.3 million drivers. Services: Data can be sorted by category. Data provided on computer tape for $30,000 for the entire file, or $2.25 per 1,000.

Owners: Texas Department of Transportation, Division of Motor Vehicles, 40th and Jackson, Austin, TX 78779-0001; (512) 465-7531. Database: Texas Automobile Owners - contains owner's name and address along with make, model, year, previous owner, and lien holder for 14 million vehicles. Services: Sorting is not available. Data available on computer tape for $4,000 plus $.30 per 1,000 written records.

Utah

Drivers: Department of Public Safety, Drivers License Division, 4501 S. 2700 West, 3rd Floor, P.O. Box 30560, Salt Lake City, UT 84130-0560; (801) 965-4437. Data is not released.

Owners: Utah State Tax Commission, Data Processing, 160 E. 300 South St., Salt Lake City, UT 84134; (801) 530-4848. Database: Utah Automobile Owners - provides owner's name and address along with make, model and year for 1.9 million vehicles. Services: Data can be sorted and made available on computer tape for $300 to $400.

Vermont

Drivers: Vermont Department of Motor Vehicles, 120 State St., Montpelier, VT 05603; (802) 828-2020. Database: Vermont Drivers - contains name, address, physical characteristics, license number and date of birth for 427,512 drivers. Services: Full identification must be provided in order to obtain information. Cost is $4 for each record up to 4 records.

Owners: Vermont Department of Motor Vehicles, 120 State Street, Montpelier, VT 05603; (802) 828-2020. Database: Vermont Automobile Owners - provides owner's name and address along with make, model and year for 327,016 passenger cars and 207,684 other vehicles. Services: Must provide vehicle identification to obtain information. Cost is $4 for each record up to 4 records.

Virginia

Drivers: Data is not released.

Owners: Dealer and Information, P.O. Box 7412, Richmond, VA 23269.; (804) 367-0455. If you provide the license number, they will provide the information. Initial fee of $3,000 plus $5 per record.

Washington

Drivers: Department of Licensing, Highways/Licensing Building, P.O. Box 3090, Olympia, WA 98507; (206) 753-6961. Database: Washington Drivers - provides driver's name, date of birth and address of registered drivers. Services: Sorting is available. A written request is required and an agreement must be signed. Each program is custom made. The charge is $3,680 plus tax.

Owners: Department of Licensing, Highways/Licenses Building, Olympia, WA 98507; (206) 753-6950. Database: Washington Automobile Owners - contains owner's name, address, make, model, year and class of vehicle. Services: Data can be sorted alphabetically by owner's name, address, make, model, year and class of vehicle. It can be sorted alphabetically by owner's name, address, make, model, year and class of vehicle. It can be sorted alphabetically by owner's name, state or county. A written request is required and an agreement must be signed. Each program is custom made. The charge is $3,680 plus tax.

West Virginia

Drivers: West Virginia Department of Motor Vehicles, Bldg. #3, Room 113, Charleston, WV 25317; (304) 348-2723. Database: West Virginia Drivers - provides name, address, height, weight, race, sex, and date of birth for 1.4 million drivers. Services: Data can be sorted and provided on computer tape or printout. Cost is $5,040.

Owners: West Virginia Department of Motor Vehicles, Bldg. #3, Room 113, Charleston, WV 25317; (304) 348-2723. Database: West Virginia Automobile Owners - contains owner's name and address along with make, model and year of 1.4 million passenger cars and 246,000 other vehicles. Services: Data can be sorted and provided on computer tape or printout for $5,040.

Wisconsin

Drivers: Wisconsin Department of Transportation, 4802 Sheybogan Ave., P.O. Box 7918, Madison, WI 53711; (608) 266-2237. Database: Wisconsin Drivers - provides an alphabetical list of name, address, date of birth, sex and driver's record for 4.5 million drivers. Services: Data available on computer tape for $2,200.

Owners: Wisconsin Department of Transportation, 4802 Sheybogan Ave., P.O. Box 7911, Madison, WI 53707-7911; (608) 266-1951. Database: Wisconsin Owners- provides owner's name and address plus make, model and year of 2.3 million passenger cars and 1.7 million other vehicles. Services: Data cannot be sorted. Entire file must be purchased on computer tape for $2,200.

Wyoming

Drivers: Wyoming Department of Transportation, Attn: Driver Control, P.O. Box 1708, Cheyenne, WY 82003; (307) 777-5259. Database: Wyoming Driver - provides name, address, date of birth, Social Security number, status, expiration, and issuance date for 500,000 drivers. Services: Cost for magnetic tape: $1 per record with a $100 minimum. All requests must be approved by the Commission.

Owners: Wyoming Department of Transportation, Licensing Station, 5300 Bishop Blvd., Cheyenne, WY 82009; (307) 777-6511. Individual record searches with a written request. Cost $5 per search.

Be patient. If any phone number is incorrect, call (area code) 555-1212 and request the new listing.

Information on People, Companies, and Mailing Lists

Other Info Sources On People

Here are trail guides for genealogy research as well as all the major federal government sources for locating individuals. Also refer to the other sections in this chapter, specifically Who Owes Money to Whom and Driver's Licenses and Motor Vehicles which identify other sources for gathering information on the family clan or next door neighbors.

* Army Active Personnel Locator

U.S. Department of the Army
Worldwide Locator, EREC (800) 444-3333
Ft. Benjamin Harrison, IN 46249-5301 (317) 542-4211

To locate a missing relative in the active army, contact this service. There is a small fee for the search.

* Army Discharged Personnel Locator Service

National Personnel Records Center
9700 Page Blvd.
St. Louis, MO 63132-5200 (314) 538-4201

To locate a relative or friend who is has been discharged from the Army, or who is deceased, contact the above office. The locator service's records go back to 1912; you may be able to find out what your great, great grandfather did in the Army. There is a small fee for the search.

* Army Personnel Locator

U.S. Army Worldwide Locator, ELREC
Fort Benjamin Harrison, IN 46249 (317) 542-4211 (recording)

To locate a long lost relative who is still on active duty in the Army, contact this office by letter. There is a small fee for their services. The telephone recording will give you information on the procedure and the data they need from you to initiate their search.

* Army Reserve and Retiree Locator

Army Reserve Personnel Center
U.S. Department of the Army
9700 Page Blvd.
St. Louis, MO 63132-5200 (314) 538-3828

To locate a missing relative in the Army reserve (who is not assigned to a unit), or to locate a living Army retiree, contact this office. There is a small fee.

* Biographical Directory of the U.S. Congress 1774-1989

Superintendent of Documents
Government Printing Office
Washington, DC 20402 (202) 783-3238

The Biographical Directory of the U.S. Congress 1774-1989, contains authoritative biographies of the more than 11,000 men and women who have served in the U.S. Congress from 1789 to 1989, and in the Continental Congress between 1774 and 1789. Many features include a listing of all chairmen of standing committees, all major formal leadership positions, bibliographic citations, and major revisions of political party affiliations reflecting the latest scholarship. You'll also find complete rosters of State congressional delegations for the First through 100th Congresses. This bicentennial edition is the most comprehensive *Biographical Directory of the United States Congress* ever issued. The latest edition published at the beginning of the 101st Congress is available through the Government Printing Office for $82.

* Congressional Directory

Superintendent of Documents
Government Printing Office
Washington, DC 20402 (202) 783-3238

The *Congressional Directory* has been the official handbook for the Congress since 1821 and is also widely used by Federal agency officials and the general public. Its contents include lists of addresses, rooms, and phone numbers of Members, biographical sketches of Members, Capitol officers and officials, committees, departments, and information on diplomatic offices and statistics. It also includes lists of members of the press admitted to the House and Senate galleries. The *1991-1992 Official Congressional Directory of the 101st Congress* is available for $16 in paperback, $20 in hardback, and $27 for a hardback copy with a thumb index.

* Family and Military Genealogy

Military Reference Branch
National Archives and Records Administration
8th St. and Pennsylvania Ave., NW
Washington, DC 20408 (202) 501-5385

The National Archives holds military service records and veterans' benefits records (pensions and bounty-land application files) for service performed from the Revolution (1775) through the early 20th century. The Archives does not have Confederate pension records, which were authorized by some southern states. To order photocopies of military service records, you must use National Archives Trust Fund Form 80 and submit a separate form for each file requested. You can obtain copies of this form and additional information about military service records from the Reference Services Branch at (202) 523-3218. Your order must contain the following information: soldier's full name; period/war in which he/she served; state from which he/she served; branch of service; and whether the service was with the Union or Confederate forces.

* Federal Campaign Finance Law Complaints

Federal Election Commission
999 E Street, NW (800) 424-9530
Washington, DC 20463 (202) 219-3420

If you believe a violation of the Federal campaign finance law has taken place, you may file a complaint with the Federal Election Commission. Send the Commission a letter explaining why you believe the law may have been violated, describe the specific facts and circumstances, and name the individuals or organizations responsible. The letter must be sworn to, signed, and notarized. Complaints of alleged violations receive case numbers and are called MURs, Matters Under Review.

* Federal Elections Clearinghouse

Federal Election Commission
999 E Street, NW
Washington, DC 20463 (202) 219-3670

The Election Clearinghouse assists election officials and the general public by responding to inquiries concerning the electoral process, publishing research, and conducting workshops on all matters related to Federal election administration.

* Federal Elections Library

Federal Election Commission (FEC) Library
999 E Street, NW, Room 801
Washington, DC 20463 (202) 219-3312

The FEC Library's collection includes basic legal research tools and materials dealing with political campaign finance, corporate and labor political activity, and campaign finance reform. The Library staff prepares indexes to Advisory Opinions and Matters Under Review (MURs), as well as a *Campaign Finance and Federal Election Law Bibliography*, which are available for purchase from the FEC's Public Records Office.

Be patient. If any phone number is incorrect, call (area code) 555-1212 and request the new listing.

Other Info Sources On People

* Federal Employees' Personnel Records

National Personnel Records Center
National Archives and Records Administration
111 Winnebago Street
St. Louis, MO 63118   (314) 219-3312

Federal employees' personnel records are transferred and stored in the National Personnel Records Center. The Center can answer questions regarding the information available, and can provide copies of documents. Contact the Center for more information.

* Financial Disclosure Database on Federal Candidates

Federal Election Commission (FEC)
Data Systems Development Division
999 E Street, NW
Washington, DC 20463   (202) 219-4140

The FEC maintains a computer database of information from all reports filed by political committees, individuals, and other entities since 1972. The data is sorted into indexes which permit a detailed analysis of campaign finance activity and, additionally, provide a tool for monitoring contribution limitations. The data can be searched by specific candidate or contributor. By contacting this office, individuals can have searches done on twenty names or less free. For searches of more than 20 names, cost varies depending on computer time needed.

* Genealogy Reference

Main Reading Room
Library of Congress
Washington, DC 20540   (202) 707-5521

Located on the first floor of the Thomas Jefferson Building, the main reading room contains material on American history, economics, fiction, language and literature, political science, government documents, and sociology. A reference collection for these materials is also housed there. These reading rooms are not equipped to answer reference questions over the telephone, but will provide information on their collections, hours of operation, and the like.
Local History and Genealogy, (202) 707-5537.

* Genealogy Research

Reference Services Branch
8th St. and Pennsylvania Ave., NW, Room 205
Washington, DC 20408   (202) 501-5400

Using Records in the National Archives for Genealogical Research is a free, 25-page brochure which explains a little about genealogical research in general, and then outlines the genealogical records in the National Archives. It includes the necessary information in order to research your request.

Guide to Genealogical Research in the National Archives is available for $25 and contains information about individuals whose names appear in census records, military service and pension files, ship passenger and arrival lists, land records, and many other types of records. This Guide shows how to tap this rich resource, explaining what types of records are preserved in the National Archives and what specific information about individuals is included in each type of record. For more information on genealogical research, contact the Reference Services Branch.

* Genealogical Workshops

Education Branch
National Archives and Records Administration
8th St. and Pennsylvania Ave., NW, Room 505
Washington, DC 20408   (202) 724-0456

Genealogical workshops are offered quite frequently by the Education Branch of the National Archives. The topics covered include census records, passenger lists, naturalization records, military service records, as well as many other genealogical topics. Each workshop lasts three hours and costs $10. Call or write for a complete workshop schedule.

* Historical Documentary Editions 1988

National Historical Publications and Records Commission
National Archives and Records Administration
8th St. and Pennsylvania Ave., NW, Room 300
Washington, DC 20408   (202) 501-5605

This free catalog lists and describes all the documentary editions supported by the Commission with funds or by formal endorsement. These editions represent a major, long-term effort to make the nation's important documents widely available for study and research. Each title includes a brief description, as well as ordering information.

* Inmate Locator Line

Public Information, Bureau of Prisons
U.S. Department of Justice
320 1st St., NW, Room 640
Washington, DC 20536   (202) 307-3198

A special phone service hotline is available for people trying to locate family members or loved ones believed to be incarcerated in local, state, or federal correctional institutions. Call the Inmate Locator Line: (202) 724-3126 between 10 a.m. and 4:30 p.m. EST.

* Military and Civilian Employment Records

National Personnel Center
9700 Page Blvd.
St. Louis, MO 63232   (314) 538-5201

This Center holds both military and civilian Federal personnel records dating from 1900 to the present. The Center prefers written requests for reference assistance.

* Military Pension Genealogy Searches

General Reference Branch
National Archives and Records Administration
Washington, DC 20408   (202) 501-5430

This office holds military service and pension records of people who served prior to 1900. The office accepts written requests only. Ask for *Form NATF 80*.

* Military Records 19th Century On

Suitland Reference Branch
National Archives and Records Administration
Washington, DC 20409   (202) 763-7410

This office holds historical material, including Land Office records, military personnel records dating prior to 1900, State Department personnel overseas post records since 1935, the Japanese war relocation records, records of the U.S. military government of Germany and Japan, as well as records of all military actions dating from the Revolutionary War through 1963. The office provides reference assistance in locating historical material, and will accept reference questions both in writing and by phone.

* Military Reference

Office of the National Archives
National Archives and Records Administration
8th St. and Pennsylvania Ave., NW, Room 13W
Washington, DC 20408   (202) 501-5385

The Military Reference Branch maintains records of military personnel separated from the U.S. Air Force, Army, Coast Guard, Marine Corps, Navy, Confederate States, volunteers, as well as veterans records. The publication, *Military Service Records in the National Archives of the United States*, provides a detailed list of the holdings and pertinent details about the records.

* Military Service Genealogy Searches

General Reference Branch
National Archives and Records Administration
Washington, DC 20408   (202) 501-5430

This office holds military service and pension records of people who served prior to 1900. The office accepts written requests only. Ask for *Form NATF 80*.

* National Driver Register

National Driver Register (NTS-24)
Traffic Safety Programs
National Highway Traffic Safety Administration
U.S. Department of Transportation
400 7th Street, SW, Room 5119
Washington, DC 20590   (202) 366-4800

The *National Driver Register* is a central, computerized index of state records on drivers whose operator licenses have been revoked, denied, or suspended for

Be patient. If any phone number is incorrect, call (area code) 555-1212 and request the new listing.

more than 6 months. Data includes name, birthdate, height, weight, eye color, date and reason for action, and date of reinstatement. Applications for driver licenses are routinely checked against the register, and states exchange information via an electronic system.

* Personal Census Records Service

The Census History Staff
Data User Services Division
Bureau of the Census
U.S. Department of Commerce
Washington, DC 20233 (301) 763-7936

The Bureau of the Census employs a staff to search the Federal censuses of population from 1900 on, stored at Pittsburgh, Kansas, and provide, for a fee, official transcripts of personal data from these records to individuals who lack other birth or citizenship documents. Government agencies and employers often accept these transcripts as evidence of age and place of birth for obtaining employment, social security benefits, old age assistance, passports, naturalization papers, or delayed birth certificates, and for other purposes. The personal information recorded in these censuses may be furnished only upon the written request of the named individual or his or her legal representative. Application forms, with detailed information, can be obtained by contacting either office above.

* Photographs of Every Member of Congress

The Superintendent of Documents
Government Printing Office
Washington, DC 20402 (202) 275-3030

The *Congressional Pictorial Directory* contains photographs of the President, Vice President, members of the Senate and House, Officers of the Senate and House, Officials of the Capitol, and a list of the Senate delegations and an alphabetical list of senators and representatives. The paperback edition is $4.24, and the hardback copy is $14.

* Presidential Political Appointments: The "Plum" Book

Senate Government Affairs Committee
Dirksen Office Building
Room S-340
Washington, DC 20510 (202) 224-3791

Superintendent of Documents
Government Printing Office
Washington, DC 20402 (202) 275-3030

U.S. Policy and Supporting Positions, more commonly known as the *Plum Book,* lists some 3,000 political appointment jobs and describes the type of appointment, tenure, grade, and salary. It is available for sale at the Superintendent of Documents for $14 per copy.

* Prisoners of War and Reclassification

U.S. Department of Defense
Force Management and Personnel
The Pentagon
Room 3E767
Washington, DC 20301-4000 (703) 695-7402

For information on conscientious objectors and POW's, including reclassification and discharge data, contact the above office.

* Prisoner-of-War Records

Military Services Branch
National Archives and Records Administration
8th St. and Pennsylvania Ave., NW
Room 13W
Washington, DC 20408 (202) 501-5385

This Branch has information regarding Prisoner-of-War records through the Civil War, and can also direct you to the proper office for information regarding prisoners-of-war through the Vietnam War.

* Salaries and Expenses of Congressmen, Congresswomen, and Their Employees

House Document Room
H-226 Capitol Bldg.
Washington, DC 20515 (202) 225-3456

The *Report of the Clerk of the House* includes the salaries of House members' staffs, committee staffs, and House officers and employees. This quarterly report includes a listing of House expenditures.

* Salaries and Expenses of U.S. Senators and Their Staff

Senate Document Room
B-04 Senate Hart Office Building
Washington, DC 20510 (202) 224-7860

The biannual *Report of the Secretary of the Senate* lists Senate expenditures and details the salaries of senators' staff, members, committee staff members, and officers and employees of the Senate.

* Selective Service Registration Status

Registration Information Office
P.O. Box 4638
North Suburban, IL 60197-4638 (708) 688-6888

If you have any questions regarding an individual's status and the requirement to register, call or write this office.

* Ship Passenger Arrival Lists

Reference Services Branch
National Archives and Records Administration
8th St. and Pennsylvania Ave., NW
Washington, DC 20408 (202) 501-5400

The National Archives compiles ship passenger arrival records dating from 1820 for most east and gulf coast ports, a few lists dating from 1800 for Philadelphia, and from the 1890's for San Francisco and Seattle. Archives staff can conduct searches if you know the full name of the passenger, the port of entry, and the approximate date of arrival.

* State Access to Financial Disclosure Database

Federal Election Commission
Public Records Office
999 E Street, NW
Washington, DC 20463 (202) 219-4140

Under the State Access Program, individuals and organizations in 15 states now have immediate online access to several standard FEC computer indexes which provide descriptive information on all registered political committees, the total receipts and disbursements of committees, and a listing of all PAC contributions to federal candidates. Participating states with operational terminals within their State Election Offices include: Arizona, Colorado, Connecticut, Georgia, Illinois, Iowa, Massachusetts, Michigan, New Jersey, New Mexico, Ohio, Tennessee, Vermont, Washington, and Wisconsin.

* State Election Finance Records

Federal Election Commission (FEC)
Public Records Office
999 E Street, NW
Washington, DC 20463 (202) 219-3420
(800) 424-9530

Researchers can obtain campaign finance reports from the records office in each state. Contact this FEC office to order a list of the names, addresses, and phone numbers of national and state disclosure offices.

* Vietnam Casualty Computer Printout

Center for Electronic Records
National Archives and Records Administration
Washington, DC 20408 (202) 501-5575

This office holds all Federal records on computer disk, which include all recent Department of Defense records and the casualty lists from the Vietnam War. Copies may be purchased.

Be patient. If any phone number is incorrect, call (area code) 555-1212 and request the new listing.

Information On Any Company

When many researchers are doing investigations on companies they often rely only on two major information sources:

Public Companies = U.S. Securities and Exchange Commission Filings

Privately Held Companies = Dun & Bradstreet Reports

Although many people still depend heavily on the Securities and Exchange Commission (SEC) and Dun & Bradstreet (D & B), these two resources have severe limitations. The Securities and Exchange Commission has information on approximately only 10,000 public companies in the United States. However, according to the IRS and the U.S. Bureau of the Census (both agencies count differently), there are between 5,000,000 and 12,000,000 companies in the country. So you can see that the SEC represents only a small fraction of the universe. Also, if you are interested in a division or a subsidiary of a public corporation and that division does not represent a substantial portion of the company's business, there will be no information on their activities on file at the SEC. This means that for thousands of corporate divisions and subsidiaries, it is necessary to look beyond the SEC.

D & B Won't Jail You For Not Telling The Truth But The Government Will

The problems with Dun & Bradstreet reports are more significant than the shortcomings of company filings at the SEC. The main drawback is that D & B reports have been established primarily for credit purposes and are supposed to indicate the company's ability to pay its bills. Therefore, you will find information from current creditors about whether a business is late in its payments, which may or may not be a useful barometer to evaluate the company.

If there is additional financial information in these reports, you should also be aware of who in the company provides D & B with information and their motives. The information contained in these reports does not carry the legal weight of the company information registered with the Securities and Exchange Commission. If a company lies about any of the information it turns over to the SEC, a corporate officer could wind up in jail. Dun & Bradstreet, however, collects its information by telephoning a company and asking it to provide certain information voluntarily. The company is under no obligation to comply and, equally important, is under no obligation to D & B to be honest. Unlike the government, Dun & Bradstreet cannot prosecute.

If a competitor or someone was interested in acquiring Information USA, Inc., for example, the first likely step would be to obtain any financial data about this privately held company. In this hypothetical case, Information USA, Inc. might be interested in such a sale or perhaps want to impress the competition. Consequently, the information supplied to Dun & Bradstreet most likely would be the sanitized version which I would want outsiders to see. My only dilemma would be in remembering what half truths we told D & B last year so that our track record would appear consistent. However, Information USA, Inc. would not, and does not, play such games with its financial information filed with the Maryland Secretary of State.

This is why resourceful researchers are starting to appreciate the value of the thousands of non-traditional information sources such as public documents and industry experts.

Starting At The Securities And Exchange Commission

First find out whether the company you are gathering intelligence about is a public corporation. If it is, you should get your hands on copies of the company's SEC filings. The fastest way to make this determination is to call:

Disclosure Inc.
5161 River Road Building 60 — (301) 951-1300
Bethesda, MD 20816 — (800) 638-8241/231-3282

The price depends on which document you wish to have retrieved. The range is between $13 to $30 per document. If the company in question files with the Securities and Exchange Commission, the least you should do is to obtain a copy of the Annual Report, known as 10-K. This disclosure form will give you the most current description of the company's activities along with their annual financial statement.

Financial Statements In Addition To The Annual Report

In addition to the 10-K you may also want to see the company's most current financial statements by obtaining copies of all 10-Q's filed since their last 10-K. 10-Q's are basically quarterly financial statements which will bring you up-to-date since the last annual report.

The two other documents which may be of immediate interest are the 8-K's and the Annual Report to Stockholders. An 8-K will disclose any major developments that have occurred since the last annual report, such as information about a takeover or major lawsuit. The Annual Report to Stockholders, the glossy quasi-public relations tool that is sent to all those who own stock in the company, can provide another component in assembling a company's profile. The most interesting item in this report, which is not included in the 10-K Annual Report, is the message from the president. This message often provides insights about the company's future plans.

Be patient. If any phone number is incorrect, call (area code) 555-1212 and request the new listing.

Information on People, Companies, and Mailing Lists

Obtaining Copies of SEC Documents

The fastest way to get SEC documents is through one of the many document retrieval companies which provide this service. In addition to the firm mentioned above, other companies that specialize in quickly obtaining corporate SEC filings include:

1) FACS Info Service, Inc.
157 Fisher Avenue
Eastchester, NY 10709
(800) 303-6901
FAX: (914) 779-7038

2) Federal Document Retrieval, Inc.
SEC Building, 450 5th St. NW
Washington, DC 20001
(202) 347-2824

3) Meredith Hurt & Associates
11526 Maple Ridge Road
Reston, VA 22090
(202) 628-9628

4) Research Information Services
717 D Street, NW
Washington, DC 20004
(202) 737-7111
FAX: (202) 737-3324

5) Prentice Hall Legal and Financial Services
1090 Vermont Ave., NW, Suite 430
Washington, DC 20005
(202) 408-3120
FAX: (202) 408-3142

6) Washington Service Bureau
655 15th Street NW, Room 275
Washington, DC 20005
(202) 508-0600
FAX: (202) 508-0694

7) Washington Document Service
450 5th Street NW, Suite 1C45
Washington, DC 20001
(202) 628-5200
FAX: (202) 626-7628

8) Vickers Stock Research Corp.
600 S Street NW, Suite 504
Washington, DC 20004
(202) 626-4951

You can also go to one of the four major SEC Document Rooms to see any public filing. These reference rooms are located in Washington, DC, New York City, Chicago, and Los Angeles.

If the company headquarters or main office is located in the area served either by the Atlanta, Boston, Denver, Fort Worth, or Seattle regional offices, the 10-K and other documents can be examined at the appropriate SEC office. For the exact location of any of the regional offices mentioned contact:

Office of Public Affairs
U.S. Securities and Exchange Commission
450 5th Street NW, Stop 1-2
Washington, DC 20549
(202) 272-2650

One way to obtain free copies of these reports is to call the company and tell them you are a potential investor. Many public corporations are set up to respond to these inquiry.

Before you order any of these SEC filings, it is wise to ask for the total number of pages contained in each of the documents you want to obtain. Most of these document retrieval firms charge by the page, and no doubt, you don't want to be surprised if a company's amendment to its 10-K happens to run 500 pages in length.

Once you have obtained the SEC documents you can then explore the additional sources described below.

Clues At The State Level About Privately Held Companies Plus Divisions And Subsidiaries Of Public Corporations

The following sources are designed primarily to help you gather information on privately held companies or those divisions and subsidiaries of public corporations which are not contained in documents filed with the U.S. Securities and Exchange Commission. However, the sources described here will enhance your work in collecting data on all types of companies. If the company in question is not publicly owned, the next step is to turn your attention to the appropriate state government offices. All companies doing business in any state leave a trail of documentation there. The number of documents and the amount of detail vary widely depending upon the state regulations and the type of company.

One of the main reasons you should begin your search with the state government is that it may take longer to retrieve information from the state offices than from other checkpoints which are described in this Section.

Puzzling Together Bits of Information

Remember that only the U.S. Securities and Exchange Commission documents provide you with information on your competitor or acquisition candidate. All other government documents are generated to comply with some law or policy, such as pollution control, consumer protection, or tax collection. Because of this, government bureaucrats who collect and analyze these documents have no idea just how valuable the information can be to you. Do not expect that the data contained in other government documents will be presented in a way that automatically will suit your particular needs. Furthermore, no single document will provide all the information about a corporate entity that you are seeking.

The strategy is to get any information you can because each piece might contribute to your overall information mosaic. Although a full profit and loss statement will be out of reach, the office of uniform commercial code can tell you to whom the company owes money and provide a description of the corporation's assets. The state office of corporations may not give you the total sales figure, but if the company's headquarter is out of state, it may tell you the corporation's total sales in that state and what percentage this is of its total. With a little bit of algebra you can estimate the total sales.

If it were as easy as making one phone call and getting complete financial information on any company, everyone would be doing it. Your competitive advantage lies in getting information that other people don't know about, or are too lazy to get.

In the event you intend to dig around at the state level, the following three offices are a must. They offer the biggest potential for the least amount of effort:

Be patient. If any phone number is incorrect, call (area code) 555-1212 and request the new listing.

Information on Any Company

1) Office of Corporations
Every corporation, whether it is headquartered or has an office in a state, must file some information with a state agency. The corporations division or office of corporations usually is part of the office of the Secretary of State. When a company incorporates or sets up an office in the state, it must file incorporation papers, or something similar. This provides, at a minimum, the nature of the business, the names and addresses of officers and agents, and the amount of capital stock in the company. In addition to this registration, every company must file some kind of annual report. These annual reports may or may not contain financial data. Some states require sales figures, and others ask just for asset figures.

2) Office of Uniform Commercial Code
Any organization, and for that matter, any individual, which borrows money and offers an asset as collateral, must file within the state at the office of uniform commercial code. A filing is made for each loan and each of the documents is available to the public. To obtain these documents is a two step process. First, one must request a search to see if there are any filings for a certain company. The fee for a search is usually under $10. Such a search will identify the number of documents filed against the company. You then will have to request copies of each of these documents. The cost for each document averages only a few dollars. This office of uniform commercial code usually is located in, or near to, the same office of corporations.

3) State Securities Office
The U.S. Securities and Exchange Commission in Washington, DC regulates only those corporations which sell stock in their company across state lines. There is another universe of corporations which sells stock in their companies only within state lines. For such stock offerings, complete financial information is filed with the state securities regulator. These documents are similar to a those filed at the U.S. Securities and Exchange Commission. But, remember, that the documents vary from one state to the next and, equally important, the requirement of filing an annual report differs from state to state. Usually a telephone call to the office in charge can tell you whether a particular company has ever offered stock intrastate. If so, you are then in a position of getting copies of these filings. Usually the Secretary of State's office can refer you to the state's securities regulator.

Finding The Right State Office

Because of the multitude of differences between the 50 state governments, expect to make half a dozen calls before you locate the right office. Several starting places are described below with the simplest ones listed first.

1) State Government Operator
The AT&T information operator can give you the telephone number for the state government operator, and then in turn you can ask for the phone number of the specific government office.

2) State Department of Commerce
Now that every state is aggressively trying to get companies to expand or relocate to their state, these departments can serve as excellent starting points, because they are familiar with other government offices which regulate business. Many times these departments have established a "one-stop office" with a separate staff on call to help a business find whatever information it needs.

3) State Capital Library
By asking the state government operator to connect you to the state capital library, a reference librarian can identify the state agency which can best respond to your queries.

4) Directories
If you intend to dig around various state government offices on more than just an infrequent basis, you might consider purchasing a state government directory. Usually the state office of Administrative Services will sell you a directory, or you might want to contact the state bookstore. If you want to purchase a directory that covers all 50 states, consider:

State Executive Directory
Carroll Publishing Company
1058 Thomas Jefferson Street NW
Washington, DC 20007 (202) 333-8620
(Price is $135 per year plus shipping and handling.)

Tracking The Trail of Company Information In Other State Offices

The three offices described earlier are only the starting places for information on companies. There are dozens of other state agencies that are brimming with valuable bits of data about individual corporations; however, these sources require a bit more care because they can be used only under certain circumstances or require extra resourcefulness.

1) Utility and Cable TV Regulators
Utility companies are heavily regulated by state agencies, and as a result, there is a lot of financial and operational information that is accessible. Most people know that gas and electric companies fall into this category, but you may not be aware that this also applies to water companies, bus companies, rail systems, telephone companies, telecommunication companies, and cable TV operators.

2) Other State Regulators
State government is very similar to the federal government in that its function is to regulate many of the activities of the business community. In those states where state laws and enforcement are very effective, Uncle Sam relies on those states to enforce the federal laws. For example, the U.S. Food and Drug Administration will use the records from the state of New Jersey for information on pharmaceutical manufacturers instead of sending out its own team of federal data collectors. The U.S. Environmental Protection Administration will use state records in those states that have strict environmental statutes rather than using its own resources.

3) Financial Institutions
Banks, savings and loans, credit unions and other financial institutions all file information with the state bank regulator. Many of these organizations are also regulated by federal agencies so what you get from the state office often will be a copy of the form filed with the federal government.

Information on People, Companies, and Mailing Lists

4) Environment Regulators
Almost every state has an office which regulates pollutants in the air, water and ground. Such departments are similar to the U.S. Environmental Protection Agency in Washington, DC and monitor whether any new or old business is polluting the environment. If the company you are investigating has plans to build a new plant in the state, get ready to collect some valuable information. Before construction can begin, the company must file information with the state environmental protection agency. These documents will detail the size of the plant, what kind of equipment it will use, and how much this equipment will be used. With such information, other manufacturers in the same business can tell exactly what the capacity and estimated volume of the plant will be. Sometimes there will be three separate offices with authority over air, water or solid waste. Each will collect basically the same information, and they can be used, one against each other, to ensure that you get all the information you need.

5) Department of Commerce/Economic Development
As mentioned earlier, each state is now actively trying to attract and develop business development within the state. The state's office of economic development or department of commerce is normally charged with this responsibility. To attract business to the state, this agency has to know all about existing business throughout the state, which all translates into who is doing what, how successful they are, and how large the company is. At a minimum, the economic development office can probably provide you with information on the number of employees for a given company. They will also be aware what other government offices in the state keep records about the industry or company which interests you. The experts at this state agency are similar to the 100 industry analysts at the U.S. Department of Commerce and can serve as excellent resources for collecting government information on an industry.

6) State Government Contractors
Although many states are not accustomed to sharing information with researchers, you should be able to obtain details about any purchase the state makes. If the company in question sells to the state, you should get copies of their contracts. Just like the federal government which makes all this procurement information available, the state which spends public funds guarantees that the public has a right to know how the money is being spent. You may have to enforce your rights under the state law which is equivalent to the federal Freedom of Information Act.

7) Minority and Small Business
Many states maintain special offices which track minority firms and other small companies. These offices can be helpful by identifying these businesses and may also be able to tell you the size or products of a given business. The small business office and possibly a separate minority business division normally fall under the state department of commerce.

8) Attorney General
The state Attorney General's office is the primary consumer advocate for the state against fraudulent practices by businesses operating within the state. So, if the company you are investigating is selling consumer services or products, it would be worth the effort to check with this office. In some states the attorney generals have begun to concentrate on certain areas.

For example, the office in Denver specializes in gathering information on companies selling energy saving devices, and the one in New York investigates companies with computerized databases which provide scholarship information.

9) Food and Drug Companies
Any company which produces, manufactures or imports either food or drug products is likely to come under the jurisdiction of the state food and drug agency. This office makes routine inspections of facilities and the reports are generally accessible; however, a Freedom of Information Act request is sometimes necessary.

County and Local Sources

County and local sources can prove to be the biggest bucket of worms as far as information sources go. Unlike state government offices where there are 50 varieties to choose from, there are over 5,000 different jurisdictions at the local level. Here are some basic checkpoints that can enhance your information gathering efforts.

Local Newspapers: Business Editors

The local newspaper can provide the best leads for anything you are investigating at the local level. It is perhaps the best source mentioned in this book. A well placed telephone call to the business editor or the managing editor, if there is not a business section, can prove to be most useful. In smaller towns, and even in suburbs of larger cities where there are suburban newspapers, a local business generates a good deal of news. A local reporter often knows the company like no one else in the country. The company executives usually are more open with the local media because they like to show off about how big they are, how much the company is growing, etc. A reporter is also likely to know company employees who can corroborate or refute the executive's remarks.

Ask the local newspaper if you can get copies of all articles written about the company in question. After you review them, call the reporter to see what additional information may be stored in his or her head.

Other Checkpoints

It is worth fishing for information in a number of other places, including agencies and private organizations.

1) Chamber of Commerce
Talking to someone on the research staff or the librarian can help you identify sources within the community about a company. A friendly conversation with Chamber executives can also provide insight into a company's financial position and strategies.

2) Local Development Authority
Many local communities, counties, and regional areas have established development authorities to attract business and industry to their area. They operate pretty much the same as the state department of economic development described

above, and as a result, collect a large amount of data about the businesses in their area.

3) Local Courts

Civil and criminal court actions can provide excellent source material for company investigations. Perdue Chicken Company, a private corporation in Maryland, revealed its annual sales figures while fighting Virginia sales tax in the courts. A recent search revealed four financial-related suits filed against a large privately held political campaign fund raising firm in McLean, Virginia. If you are not in close proximity to the court, it may be worthwhile to hire a local freelance reporter or researcher. In most jurisdictions there are chronological indexes of both civil and criminal cases which are kept by the clerk of the court. These indexes record all charges or complaints made, the names of the defendants and plaintiffs in the event of civil cases, the date of the filing, the case number, and the disposition if one has been reached. Armed with the case number you can request to see the case files from the clerk.

Company Information At The Office Of Federal Regulators

The federal offices identified in the preceding section on market studies are also excellent sources for information on companies. Industry specialists within the federal government are likely to have information on companies or can refer you to other sources which may have just the information you need.

The 26 government agencies listed here are those that are involved with regulating industries and/or the companies within those industries. The information held at each federal office varies from agency to agency; however, most of the offices maintain financial or other information that most researchers would consider sensitive.

Airlines, Air Freight Carriers, and Air Taxis
Office of Community and Consumer Affairs
U.S. Department of Transportation
400 7th Street SW, Room 10405
Washington, DC 20590 (202) 366-2220/5957

Airports
Airport Section
National Flight Data Center, Room 634
Federal Aviation Administration, ATM-612
800 Independence Avenue SW
Washington, DC 20591 (202) 267-9311

Bank Holding Companies and State Members of the Federal Reserve System
Freedom of Information Act Office
Board of Governors of the Federal Reserve System
20th Street and Constitution Avenue NW
Room B1122
Washington, DC 20551 (202) 452-3684

Banks, National
Communications Division
Comptroller of the Currency
250 E St., SW
Washington, DC 20219 (202) 874-4700

Barge and Vessel Operators
Financial Analysis, Tariffs
Federal Maritime Commission

1100 L Street NW
Washington, DC 20573 (202) 523-5876

Cable Television System Operators
Cable TV Branch
Federal Communications Commission
1919 M Street NW, Room 416
Washington, DC 20554 (202) 632-7480

Colleges, Universities, Vocational Schools, and Public Schools
Office of Educational Research and Improvement
U.S. Department of Education
555 New Jersey NW, Room 600
Washington, DC 20208-5530 (202) 219-2050

Commodity Trading Advisors
National Futures Association
200 W. Madison St., Suite 1600
Chicago, IL 60606-3447 (800) 621-3570
Attn: Compliance Dept. FAX: (312) 781-1467

Consumer Products
Corrective Actions Division
U.S. Consumer Product Safety Commission
5401 Westbard Avenue
Bethesda, MD 20816 (301) 492-6608

Electric and Gas Utilities and Gas Pipeline Companies
Federal Energy Regulatory Commission
825 North Capitol Street NE
Room 9204
Washington, DC 20426 (202) 208-0200

Exporting Companies
Office of Export Trading Companies Affairs
U.S. Department of Commerce
14th and Constitution Avenue
Room 1800
Washington, DC 20230 (202) 482-5131

Federal Land Bank and Production Credit Associations
Farm Credit Administration
1501 Farm Credit Drive
McLean, VA 22102-5090 (703) 883-4000

Foreign Corporations
World Traders Data Report
U.S. Department of Commerce
Washington, DC 20230 (202) 482-4204

Government Contractors
Federal Procurement Data Center
General Services Administration
7th and D Streets, SW
Room 5652
Washington, DC 20407 (703) 401-1529

Hospitals and Nursing Homes
National Center for Health Statistics
6525 Belcrest Rd.
Hyattsville, MD 20782 (301) 436-8500

Land Developers
Office of Interstate Land Registration
U.S. Department of Housing and Urban Development
451 7th Street SW, Room 6262
Washington, DC 20410 (202) 708-0502

Mining Companies
Mine Safety and Health Administration
U.S. Department of Labor
4015 Wilson Boulevard
Arlington, VA 22203 (703) 235-1452

Information on People, Companies, and Mailing Lists

Non-Profit Institutions
U.S. Internal Revenue Service
Freedom of Information Reading Room
1111 Constitution Avenue NW, Room 1563
P.O. Box 388, Ben Franklin Station
Washington, DC 20044 (202) 566-3770

Nuclear Power Plants
Director, Office of Nuclear Reactor Regulation
U.S. Nuclear Regulatory Commission
2120 L Street NW
Washington, DC 20037 (301) 492-7000/7758

Pension Plans
Division of Inquiries and Technical Assistance
Office of Pension and Welfare Benefits Programs
U.S. Department of Labor
200 Constitution Avenue NW, Room N5658
Washington, DC 20210 (202) 219-8233

Pharmaceutical, Cosmetic and Food Companies
Associate Commissioner for Regulatory Affairs
U.S. Food and Drug Administration
5600 Fishers Lane, Room 14-90
Rockville, MD 20857 (301) 443-1594

Pesticide and Chemical Manufacturers
U.S. Environmental Protection Agency
Office of Pesticides and Toxic Substances
401 M Street SW (TS-788)
Washington, DC 20460 (202) 260-2902

Radio and Television Stations
Mass Media Bureau
Federal Communications Commission
1919 M Street NW, Room 302
Washington, DC 20554 (202) 632-6485

Railroads, Trucking Companies, Bus Lines, Freight Forwarders, Water Carriers, Oil Pipelines, Transportation Brokers, Express Agencies
U.S. Interstate Commerce Commission
12th and Constitution Avenue NW, Room 4126
Washington, DC 20423 (202) 927-7119

Savings and Loan Associations
Office of Thrift Supervision
1700 G Street NW
Washington, DC 20552 (202) 906-6000

Telephone Companies, Overseas Telegraph Companies, Microwave Companies, Public Land and Mobile Service
Common Carrier Bureau
Federal Communications Commission
1919 M Street NW, Room 500
Washington, DC 20554 (202) 632-6910

Suppliers And Other Industry Sources

If all of the above sources fail to provide information you need on a given company, your last resort is to go directly into the industry and try to extract the information by talking with insiders.

Although your telephone is an essential and perhaps the best research tool, there are two other reference sources that will help you track down industry specialists:

1) **Trade Associations** are identified in *Encyclopedia of Associations* - (Gale Research Inc., Book Tower, 835 Penobscot Building, Detroit, MI 48277, (313) 961-2242, (800) 877-4253. For prepaid order, mail check for $322 to P.O. Box 71701, Chicago, IL 60694-1701);

2) **100 Industry Analysts** at the U.S. Department of Commerce. Government Industry Analysts who cover industries such as athletic goods, dairy products or truck trailers.

Your first step is to begin casting around for someone in the industry who knows about the company in question. When hunting for an expert, it is essential that you remain determined and optimistic about eventually finding one or several individuals who will be "information jackpots."

People who know their industry will be able to give you the details you need about any company (i.e., its size, sales, profitability, market strategies). These sources probably will not be able to give you the precise figure that is on the balance sheet or profit and loss statement, but they will offer a very educated guess which is likely to be within 10 to 20% of the exact figure. And usually this estimate is good enough for anyone to work with.

The real trick is finding the right people -- the ones who know. Talk to them and get them to share their knowledge with you.

Where Else To Look For Industry Experts

Industry experts are not concentrated in Washington, DC but are located all over the world, so you need to exercise some common sense to figure out where to find them. Here are some general guidelines.

1) Industry Observers
These are specialists on staff at trade associations, think tanks, and at the U.S. Department of Commerce and other government agencies. Anyone who concentrates on an industry has familiarity with the companies that comprise that industry.

2) Trade Magazines
You will find that there is at least one magazine which reports on every industry. The editors and reporters of these trade publications are also well acquainted with individual companies.

3) Suppliers
Most industries have major suppliers which must know about the industry they service and the companies within that industry. For example, the tire manufacturers anticipate every move among auto makers well before any other outsiders. Suppliers also have to know the volume of every manufacturer to whom they sell their product because of the obvious repercussions on the supplier's business. Every company is like this, even Information USA, Inc. We are basically a publisher, and if you talk to our printers, you would get a pretty good picture of exactly what we are doing.

Company Case Studies and Databases

1) Company Case Studies For As Little As $2 Each
Case studies of major and minor companies, as well as subsidiaries of public companies, can provide valuable

Information on Any Company

competitive intelligence. Thousands of such cases are identified in an $8 publication titled *Directory of Harvard Business School Cases and Related Course Materials, 1991-92.* A supplement to the directory, covering the period between April 1987 and January 1988 is available for $5.

HBS Publications Division
Operations Department · · · (617) 495-6117/6006
Boston, MA 02163 · · · FAX: (617) 495-6985

2) Government and Commercial Databases
ABI/Inform, Disclosure, and Management Contents are just a few of the online databases which provide quick access to information about all types of companies. Additional leads for gathering intelligence about companies can be derived from diverse databases maintained by the U.S. government, many of which are identified in the *Federal Data Base Finder* (Information USA, Inc.).

Complete Financials On Franchising Companies

Franchising companies, whether public or privately held, must file detailed financial information in 14 different states. These state statutes create excellent opportunities for gathering competitive and marketing data as outlined below.

Inside Information

If the company of interest is a franchise organization, a great deal of financial information for their average franchisee is available in addition to their corporate profit and loss statements and balance sheets. A typical table of contents for a filing includes:

* biographical information on persons affiliated with the franchisor
* litigation
* bankruptcy
* franchisees' initial franchise fee or other initial payment
* other recurring or isolated fees and payments
* the franchisee's initial investment
* obligations of the franchisee to purchase or lease from designated sources
* obligations of the franchisee to purchase or lease in accordance with specifications or from approved suppliers
* financing arrangements
* obligations of the franchisor: other supervision, assistance or services
* territorial rights
* trademarks, service marks, trade names, logotypes and commercial symbols
* patents and copyrights
* obligation of the franchisee to participate in the actual operation of the franchise business
* restrictions on goods and services offered by the franchisee
* term, renewal, termination, repurchase, modification, assignment and related information
* agreements with public figures
* actual, average, projected or forecasted franchisee sales, profits and earnings
* information regarding franchises of the franchisor
* financial statements

* contracts
* standard operating statements
* list of operational franchisees
* estimate of additional franchised stores
* company-owned stores
* estimate of additional company-owned stores
* copies of contracts and agreements

Market Information and Franchising Trends

The franchise information packets often include information on the results of their market studies which establish the need for their product or service. These can provide valuable market information as well as forecasts for potential markets. Is the ice cream boom over? A quick check into Ben and Jerry's forecast for future stores will give you a clue of what the experts think.

Franchise companies are often the first to jump into current trends and fads in the U.S., for example, ice cream shops and diet centers. You can get an instant snapshot of such a trend by reviewing the marketing section of a franchise agreement.

Career Opportunities

If you ever wondered how much it would cost to open up your own bookstore, restaurant, video store, or most any other kind of venture, you can get all the facts and figures you need without paying a high-priced consultant or tipping your hand to your current employer. Just take a look at a franchise agreement from someone in a similar line of business. You can even discover the expected salary level.

New Business for Suppliers

If you are looking to sell napkins, Orange Julius or computer services to Snelling & Snelling, their franchise statements will disclose what kind of agreements they currently have with similar suppliers.

State Checkpoints for Franchising Intelligence

To obtain franchise agreements from the 14 states that require such disclosure, simply call one or more of the offices listed below and ask if a specific company has filed. Copies of the documentation are normally sent in the mail with a copying charge of $0.10 to $0.40 per page.

California
Department of Corporations, 1115 11th Street, Sacramento, 95814, (916) 445-7205. Fee is 30 cents per page. Send blank check stating $25 limit. They will call with price for orders exceeding that amount.

Hawaii
Department of Commerce and Consumer Affairs, Business Registration Department, 1010 Richards Street, Honolulu, 96813, P.O. Box 40, Honolulu, 96810, (808) 586-2730. Fee is 25 cents per page.

Illinois
Franchise Division, Office of Attorney General, 500 South Second Street, Springfield, 62704, (217) 782-1090. Charge is a $40 flat fee per company franchise.

Be patient. If any phone number is incorrect, call (area code) 555-1212 and request the new listing.

Information on People, Companies, and Mailing Lists

Indiana

Franchise Division, Secretary of State, 302 West Washington Street, Room E-111, Indianapolis, 46204, (317) 232-0735. Fee is 10 cents per page plus handling charges.

Maryland

Assistant Attorney General, Maryland Division of Securities, 200 St. Paul Place, 21st Floor, Baltimore, 21202-2020, (301) 576-6360. Maryland does not make copies. Suggests contacting Documents-To-Go, (800) 879-4949.

Minnesota

Minnesota Department of Commerce, Enforcement Division, 133 East Seventh Street, St. Paul, 55101, (612) 296-2594. Contact Ann Hagestad at (612) 296-6328. Fee is 50 cents per page.

New York

Bureau of Investor and Protection Securities, New York State Department of Law, 120 Broadway, New York, 10271, (212) 341-2200. Fee is 25 cents per page.

North Dakota

Franchise Examiner, North Dakota Securities Commission, 600 East Blvd., Fifth Floor, Bismarck, 58505, (701) 224-2910. Documents are open for the public to inspect and copy, but this office does not provide copies as a service.

Oregon

Department of Insurance and Finance, Corporate Securities Section, Division of Finance and Corporate Securities, 21 Labor and Industries Bldg., Salem, 97310, (503) 378-4387. Oregon does not keep franchise documents on file.

Rhode Island

Securities Section, Securities Division, 233 Richmond Street, Suite 232, Providence, 02903-4237, (401) 277-3048. Special request form must be used. Fee is 15 cents per page copy and $15 an hour per search time.

South Dakota

Franchise Administrator, Division of Securities, State Capitol, Pierre, 57501, (605) 773-4013. Fee is 50 cents per sheet.

Virginia

Franchise Section, Division of Securities and Retail Franchising, 1229 Bank Street, 4th Floor, Richmond, 23219, (804) 786-7751. Fee is $1 per page.

Washington

Department of Licensing, Securities Division, 405 Black Lake Blvd., SW, Olympia, 98507-9033, (206) 753-6928. No charge for orders under 30 pages, then 10 cents for each page thereafter, plus tax.

Wisconsin

Franchise Investment Division, Wisconsin Securities Commission, PO Box 1768, 111 West Wilson Street, Madison, 53701, (608) 266-3414/3364. Wisconsin does not provide copies of franchise agreements. One must come in person or hire private service.

Be patient. If any phone number is incorrect, call (area code) 555-1212 and request the new listing.

Companies In Your State

State documents on 9,000,000 public and private companies have hit the computer age. Nine states already offer online access to their files and 15 states intend to follow suit within the next year. Computerized records are such a major issue with state officials who administer corporate division offices that they have placed online access on their annual convention agenda. Furthermore, 27 states will make their complete files available on magnetic tape, and, I should say, at bargain prices. And if you are not computerized, all but a few states offer free telephone research services. Here are a dozen ways to ferret out current information on companies:

- a list of companies by SIC code within a given state or county
- names and addresses of a company's officers and directors
- a list of all new companies incorporated in a given week or month
- the location of any company with a single phone call
- a mailing list of 300,000 companies for $100
- the availability of a given company name
- a complete list of non-profit organizations
- a list of companies by city, zip, date of incorporation, or size of capital stock
- a mailing list of limited partnerships
- a listing of companies on which a given individual is an officer or board member
- a listing of trademarks for a given state
- which companies in a given state are subsidiaries of a given company

Financial Data and Other Documents on File

Although there are variations, almost all states maintain the following documents for every company doing business in their state: Certificate of Good Standing; Articles of Incorporation; Reinstated Articles of Incorporation; Articles of Amendment; Articles of Merger; Articles of Correction; Articles of Dissolution; Certificate of Incorporation; Certificate of Authority; and Annual Report (which contains list of officers and directors).

All states require corporations to file the original Articles of Incorporation, a yearly annual report and amendments to the Articles of Incorporation. Clerks can provide you with certifications of good standing stating that the corporation has complied with the regulation to file a yearly annual report. A certificate of good standing does not assure financial stability, and is only a statement that the corporation has abided by the law. You may obtain a statement of name availability if you are searching for a name for your new corporation. Most states require prepayment for copies of documents. You can mail them a blank check stipulating the amount not to exceed a certain amount. You may want to call the phone information number for details before sending in your written request.

Only a few states require financial information in their annual reports. However, every state requires companies to list the value of the capital stock in their Articles of Incorporation. Some states, such as Massachusetts used to require financial data in the past, so it may be useful to request annual reports of previous years.

Data on Six Different Types of Companies

The types of companies required to file documents with the state include: Domestic Companies (those incorporated within the state), Foreign Companies (those incorporated in another state, but doing business in the state), Partnerships, Limited Partnerships, Non-Profit Organizations, Business Names (incorporated and non-incorporated firms). It should be emphasized here that all public and private companies as well as subsidiaries of public corporations are required to reveal this information.

Company Information Available in Numerous Formats

Each state provides information about corporations in some or all of the following formats:

1) Telephone, Mail and Walk-In Services:
Telephone information lines have been established in all but one state to respond to inquiries regarding the status of a specific corporation. New Jersey and North Dakota charge for phone service. The NJ Expedite Service allows you to receive information over the phone and charge the cost of the service to your credit card. Another option for New Jersey company information is to have it sent via Western Union's electronic mail service.

Telephone operators can verify corporate names, identify the resident agent and his address, the date of incorporation, the type of corporation (foreign, domestic, etc.), and the amount of capital stock. Often these operators can either take your request for documents on file pertaining to a corporation or they can refer you to the appropriate number. Names of officers and directors are never given over the phone. This information is usually contained in a company's annual report, copies of which can be requested by phone or letter.

These state telephone lines tend to be quite busy. It is not unusual for the larger offices of a corporation to answer over 1,200 inquiries a day. Persistence and patience are essential on your part. Requests for copies of documents usually require prepayment. You can mail them a blank check stipulating the amount not to exceed a certain amount. You may want to call the phone information number for details before sending in your written request.

Information on People, Companies, and Mailing Lists

Walk-in service, with access to all documents, is an option in every state. However, if you do not want to do the research yourself, almost every state can suggest private firms which will obtain the pertinent data for you.

2) Mailing Labels:
The following six states will print mailing labels of companies on file: Arizona, Idaho, Maine, New Mexico, Mississippi, and Nebraska. However, over half the states will sell you a computer tape of their files, from which mailing labels can be generated easily by a good mailhouse or service bureau.

3) Computer Tape Files:
Currently 27 states will provide you with magnetic tapes of their corporate files. The cost is very reasonable, and in many cases the state will require the user to supply blank tapes.

4) Custom Services:
Many of the states provide custom services with outputs ranging from computer printouts and magnetic tape files to statistical tables. Such services are a valuable way to obtain specific listings of corporations such all non-profit corporations or all companies within a given SIC code. Most states that offer this option compute cost by figuring time, programming time, and printing expense.

5) New Companies:
Almost all of the states offer some type of periodic listing of newly formed companies. As a rule, these can be purchased on a daily, weekly, or monthly subscription basis.

6) Microfiche and Microfilm:
Eleven of the states will also sell you copies of their documents on microfiche or microfilm at a nominal fee.

7) Online Access:
As mentioned earlier, nine states now provide online access to their files, and 15 other states are in the active planning stages. The states currently with online systems include:

* Alaska - available through Motznik Computer Service
* Arizona - their only customer for this service is Dun and Bradstreet
* Florida - available through CompuServe
* Georgia - available through Information America
* Illinois - available through Mead Data Central
* Missouri - available through Mead Data Central
* New Mexico - available through New Mexico Technet
* Oklahoma - their only customer for this service is Dun and Bradstreet
* Texas - available through Information America

State Corporation Divisions

Alabama

Division of Corporation, Secretary of State, 4121 Carmichael Road, Montgomery, AL 36106 or P.O. Box 5616, Montgomery, AL 36103-5616, (205) 242-5324; Selected Publications: *Guide to Incorporation*. Phone Information: (205) 242-5324. Office is not completely computerized yet, but can do word search or partial name search by officer, incorporator, or serving agent. Copies of Documents on File: Available by written request for $1 per page plus $5 for certified copies. Mailing Labels: No. Magnetic Tape: No. Microfiche: No. New Corporate Listings: No. Custom Searches: Can do word search or partial name search. Online Access: Yes. Dial-up Program available. No fee for this pilot program. Contact Robina Jenkins, (205) 242-5974. This office is in the process of being computerized. When fully on computer access, fee for online service may be charged. Number of Active Corporations on File: Figures not available.

Alaska

State of Alaska, Division of Banking, Securities and Corporation, Corporation Section, P.O. Box 110808, Juneau, AK 99811-0808, (907) 465-2530. Selected Publications: *Establishing Business in Alaska* ($3), from State of Alaska, Division of Economic Development, P.O. Box 110808, Juneau, AK 99811-0808. Phone Information: (907) 465-2530. Copies of Documents on File: Complete corporate record (Articles of Incorporation, annual report, amendments, etc.). Certified copies cost $20, list of Officers and Directors cost $1, Certificate of Status cost $25. Mailing Labels: No. Magnetic Tape: IBM- compatible. Copy of complete master file, excluding Officers and Directors is priced at $100. Hard copy directory is $65. Weekly supplements are an additional $5. Requester must supply blank tape. Microfiche: Yes. Complete file for $6. New Corporate Listings: No. Custom Searches: Available directly from them soon. Online Access: Yes. Contact Mike Monagle, (907) 465-2530. Other: Printouts are available by corporation, SIC code, and zip code for $25 per list. Number of Active Corporations on File: 23,000.

Arizona

Arizona Corporations Division, Records Division, Secretary of State, 1200 W. Washington, Phoenix, AZ 85007 or P.O. Box 6019, Phoenix, AZ 85005, (602) 542-3026. Selected Publications: Sample packet with forms and statutes mailed for $4. Guideline booklets will be available soon. Phone Information: (602) 542-3026. Copies of Documents on File: Cost 50 cents per page, $5 for certified copies. Mailing Labels: No. Magnetic Tape: Master File $400, issued monthly. Requester must supply blank tape. Microfiche: All corporations statewide $75. New Corporate Listing: Monthly Listing of New Domestic Companies for $200 plus $200 for new foreign listings. Custom Searches: No. Can search by title or cross-reference by statutory agent only. Online Access: Yes. Available through Information America (1-800-235-4008), Dunn and Bradstreet and other commercial services. Number of Corporations on File: 100,000.

Arkansas

Secretary of State, Corporations Division, State Capitol Building, Room 058, Little Rock, AR 72201, (501) 682-5151. Selected Publications: *Corporate Guide*. Phone Information: (501) 682-5151. Copies of Documents on File: Call (501) 371-3431 for copies at 50 cents a page plus $5 for certified copies. Mailing Labels: No. Magnetic Tape: Master file 2 cents per name. Microfiche: No. New Corporate Listing: Statistics only. Custom Searches: Categories include foreign, domestic, profit, and non-profit corporations. Cost: 2 cents per name, 50 cents per page. Online Access: Contact Philip Hoots at (501) 682-3411. Number of Active Corporations on File: 1000,000.

California

Corporations, Supervisor of Records, Secretary of State, 1230 J Street Sacramento, CA 95814, (916) 324-1485. Selected Publications: *Corporations Checklist Booklet*. Request must be in writing and cost is $5. Phone Information: Name Availability at (916) 322-2387, Forms and Samples at (916) 445-0620. Copies of Documents on File: Cost is $1 for first page, 50 cents for each additional page plus $5 for certified copies (written requests only). You must pay in advance or send check stating limit. Mailing Labels: No. Magnetic Tape: Yes. You must supply the tapes or be charged $24 for tape. Charges for making 22 tapes is $300. Contact Kevin Tibown. Categories: Active $521; Active Stock $427; Active Non-Stock $150; Active Non-Stock by Classification $150 per tape. Microfiche: No. Custom Searches: Computer generated listing of Active Stock ($17,030), Active Non-Stock ($422), Active Non-Stock by Classification $150 per list. Contact: Patricia Gastelum, Management Services Division, Information Systems Section, 1230 J Street, Suite 242, Sacramento, CA 95814, (916) 322-0418. All orders must be submitted in writing. Basic cost of magnetic tape copy is $1.02 per 1,000 names. Basic cost of same run, for custom search, printed on paper, is $4.13 per 1,000 names. $150 minimum is applied to both. Online Access: No. Number of Corporations on File: 1,050,000.

Colorado

Corporate Division, Secretary of State, 1560 Broadway, Suite 200, Denver, CO 80202, (303) 894-2251. Selected Publications: *Corporate Guide*. Copies of

Companies In Your State

Documents on File: Cost is $1 a page, plus $5 for certification. Mailing Labels: No. Magnetic Tape: Available for $500 for complete set of five. Tapes must be purchased individually. Categories: Foreign and Domestic. Microfiche: Available at $1 a sheet (includes Summary of Master Computer File, total of 60-75 sheets - must be purchased in its entirety). New Corporate Listings: Reporting Service costs $200 a year. Weekly List of New Corporations. Written requests only. Custom Searches: Yes. Categories: Foreign and Domestic available on a cost recovery basis. The minimum fee is $50. Online Access: Available. Contact Patty Webb, (303) 894-2200, ext. 300. Fee is $300 for 3 months or $1,000 per year. Number of Corporations on File: 235,000.

Connecticut

Office of Secretary of State, Division of Corporations, 30 Trinity Street, Hartford, CT 06106, (203) 566-2448. Selected Publications: None, but to get a copy of *The Connecticut Law Book*, call (203) 458-8000 or (203) 741-3027. Phone Information: (203) 566-8570. Copies of Documents on File: Fees are $6 for plain copy, $12 for certified. Written requests only. Labels: No. Magnetic Tape: Copy of master file $110. Requester must provide tapes. Microfiche: No. New Corporate Listing: No. Custom Searches: No. Online Access: Not at this time, but Southern New England Telephone (SNET) is working on a pilot program which should be available soon. Number of Corporations on File: 325,000.

Delaware

Delaware Department of State, Division of Corporations, Secretary of State, P.O. Box 898, Dover, DE 19903, (302) 739-3073. Selected Publications: *Incorporating in Delaware*. Phone Information: (302) 739-3073. Copies of Documents on File: Available at $1 per page plus $20 for certification, $100 for long forms of good standing. Contains all documents on the corporation. Requests may be faxed to (302) 739-3812, but written requests are preferred. Requests must be paid for in advance. Call for number of pages. Documents filed prior to 1983 are not on computer and must be requested in writing. They offer Corporate Expedited Serives (same day or 24-hour service) to file or retrieve certified documents. Additional fee is $20. You can pay by MasterCard or Visa and it is sent by Federal Express. Mailing Labels: No. Magnetic Tape: No. Microfiche: No. New Corporate Listings: Monthly New Corporation Listing. Fees are $10 per month which can be paid in advance for 6 months or a year. Contact Karen Scaggs. Custom Searches: Yes. Categories include foreign and domestic which are available on cost recovery basis. For manual search of foreign corporations, the fee is $30. Online Access: Not available. Number of Active Corporations on File: 212,000.

District of Columbia

Corporations Division, Consumer and Regulatory Affairs, 614 H Street, N.W., Room 407, Washington, DC 20001, (202) 727-7278. Selected Publications: *Guideline and Instruction Sheet for Profit, Non-Profit, Foreign, or Domestic*. Phone Information: (202) 727-7283. Copies of Documents on File: Available for $5 each (all copies certified). Mailing Labels: Will be available in near future. Profit and non-profit lists updated quarterly. Magnetic Tape: No. Microfiche: No. New Corporate Listings No. Custom Searches: Computer searches on agents are available. Online Access: Possibly available in 1993. Number of Active Corporations on File: 40,000.

Florida

Division of Corporations, Secretary of State, PO Box 6327, Tallahassee, FL 32314, (904) 487-6000. Selected Publications: *Copy of the Law Chapter 607* (corporate law). Forms included. (Publications on laws of non-profit corporations and limited partnerships also available.) Phone Information: (904) 488-9000. Limit of up to 3 inquiries per call. No charge to receive hard copy of microfiche on the corporations. Copy of Documents on File: Available at $1 per page if you do it yourself. Written requests must be paid for advance: $1 for non-certified annual report; $10 for plain copy of complete file; $52.50 for any certified document including complete file. Microfiche: Yes. Contact Frank Reinhart or Ed Bagnell at Anacomp, (813) 289-1608. Categories: Officers and Directors, Registered Agents and Domestic Corporations $250; Foreign, Non-Profit $85, Limited Partnerships $50, Trademarks $75 (addresses are included). Magnetic Tape: No. New Corporate Listings: No. Custom Searches: No. Online Access: Available on CompuServe, (800) 848-8199. Address written request to Attn: Public Access, Division of Corporations, (904) 487-6866. Ask for a CompuServe Intro-Pak. Charge for connect time is $24 per hour, plus $12.50 per hour additional corporate access fee. Both are prorated by time used. CompuServe can be contacted directly at South Eastern Information Systems, P.O. Box 6867, Tallahassee, FL 32314, Attn: Keith Meyer, (904) 656-4500. As of

February, 1992, Anacomp will handle. Contact Eileen Self, (904) 487-6073 for service. Number of Active Corporations on File: 691,000.

Georgia

Division of Business Services and Regulation, Secretary of State, Suite 306, West Tower #2, Martin Luther King Drive, S.E., Atlanta, GA 30334, (404) 656-2185. Selected Publications: None, but information package sent upon request. Phone Information: (404) 656-2817. Copies of Documents on File: Available for at least a minimum of $10 and all copies certified. Bills will be sent for orders over $10. Mailing Labels: No. Magnetic Tape: Master file available for $600 a month if you supply the tape. Add $18 if they supply tape. Microfiche: No. New Corporate Listings: Quarterly Listing of New Corporations on magnetic tape. There are three lists which include Fulton County, the remainder of the state and foreign. Cost is $25 each. Send written requests to James Gullion. Custom Searches: No. Online Access: Available by subscription through Information America at (404) 892-1800. Connect fee is $50. Access time is 55 cents per minute. Monthly service charge is $25-$55 per month depending on size of the firm. Number of Active Corporations on File: 200,000

Hawaii

Business Registration Division, Department of Commerce and Consumer Affairs, 1010 Richards Street, PO Box 40, Honolulu, HI 96810, (808) 586-2727. Selected Publications: None. Phone Information: (808) 586-2727. Copies of Documents on File: Available at 25 cents per page, plus 10 cents per page for certified copies. Expedited service available for $10 fee plus 25 cents per sheet, plus $1 per page. Mailing Labels: No. Magnetic Tape: No. Microfiche: No. New Corporate Listing: Weekly printout available but only for walk-ins. Custom Searches: No. Online Access: Available through FYI for no charge. Call (808) 536-7133 (direct access number) or (808) 586-1919. Number of Active Corporations on File: 45,000.

Idaho

Corporate Division, Secretary of State, Room 203, Statehouse, Boise, ID 83720, (208) 334-2300. Selected Publications: *Idaho Corporation Law*. Phone Information: (208) 334-2300. Copies of Documents on File: Available at 25 cents per page, $2 for certified copies. Mailing Labels: Very flexible and may be combined with custom search. Fee is $10 for computer base, 25 cents for first 100 pages, 10 cents for next 500 pages, and 5 cents per page thereafter. Magnetic Tape: Available for $20 per tape if you supply the tape. They will supply diskette for additional $10. Microfiche: Available for $10, 50 cents for each additional copy of same. Custom Searches: Available on basis of serving agent, profit, non-profit, type, status, state and jurisdiction. Very flexible. Same prices and categories apply to labels, microfiche and custom search. You supply the tapes or they will at cost. Contact Everett Wholers. New Corporate Listing: No, but published weekly in *The Idaho Business Review*. Online Access: Available through Data Share Program. Fee is $150 per year plus $18 per hour plus telephone line charges. Number of Active Corporations on File: 30,000.

Illinois

Corporations Division, Centennial Building, Room 328, Springfield, IL 62756, (217) 782-6961. Selected Publications: *Guide for Organizing (Domestic, Non-profit, or Foreign)*. Phone Information: (217) 782-7880. Copies of Documents on File: Available at $5 per page up to first 10 pages; 50 cents for each page thereafter. Fee is $10 for first 10 certified copies; 50 cents for each page thereafter. Mailing Labels: No. Magnetic Tape: Yes. Categories: Domestic and Foreign cost $1,500; Not-for-Profit cost $1,500. You must supply tape. Microfiche: Only condominiums list available for $150. New Corporate Listings: Daily list of newly formed corporations costs $318 per year; Monthly List priced at $180 per year. Custom Searches: No. Other: Certified List of Domestic and Foreign Corporations (Address of Resident Agent included) costs $38 for two volume set. Online Access: Available from Mead Data Central (LEXIS), 9393 Springboro Pike, P.O. Box 933, Dayton, OH 45401, Contact: Diane Fisher at (800) 227-4908, ext. 6382. Cost is $500 per month. Number of Active Corporations on File: 240,000.

Indiana

Office of Corporation, Secretary of State, Room E018, 302 West Washington Street, Indianapolis, IN 46204, (317) 232-6582. Selected Publications: *Indiana Corporation Guide*. Phone Information: (317) 232-6576. Copies of Documents on File: Available at $1 per page and $15 to certify. May pay in advance or be billed. Mailing Labels: No. Magnetic Tape: No. Microfiche: No. New Corporate Listings: Daily Listing is published monthly for $20 a month. Custom Searches:

Information on People, Companies, and Mailing Lists

No. Online Access: Available. Tapes made into computer database by Mead Data (LEXIS) at (800) 634-9738 and by Information America (800) 235-4008. Contact Bob Gardner at (317) 232-6691. Number of Active Corporations on File: 200,000.

Iowa

Corporate Division, Secretary of State, Hoover State Office Building, Des Moines, IA 50319, (515) 281-5204. Selected Publications: *Iowa Profit Corporations*. Phone Information: (515) 281-5204. Copies of Documents on File: Available at $1 per page; certified copies cost $5. Mailing Labels: No. Magnetic Tape: Master file costs $165; detailed domestic profit $415; domestic non-profit $160 and requester must supply tape. Microfiche: No. New Corporate Listings: No. Custom Searches: Searches by Chapters of Incorporation (profit, non-profit, etc.) and or. Cost determined at time of request. Online Access: Available through Dial Up Program. Contact Allen Welsh at (515) 281-8363. Cost is $150 per year, 30 cents per minute plus telephone charges. Number of Active Corporations on File: 97,000.

Kansas

Corporate Division, Secretary of State, Capitol Building, Second Floor, Topeka, KS 66612, (913) 296-4564. Selected Publications: None. Will send out forms with instruction sheets. Phone Information: (913) 296-4564. Copies of Documents on File: Available at 50 cents per page plus $7.50 for certified copies (written requests only). Must be paid for in advance. Mailing Labels: No. Magnetic Tape: Available. Master file costs $2,000. Microfiche: No. Other: Microfilm is available for $25 a roll plus $7.50 postage for up to 50 rolls. Master File on magnetic tape will be needed to use. Contact Cathy Martin. New Corporate Listings: No. Custom Searches: No. May be available in the future. Online Access: No. May be available in near future. Number of Active Corporations on File: 66,000.

Kentucky

Corporate Division, Secretary of State, Room 154, Capitol Building, Frankfort, KY 40601, (502) 564-2848. Selected Publications: *Rules and Laws Manual* ($8). Phone Information: (502) 564-7336. Copies of Documents on File: Mail in request with payment. Call (502) 564-7330 to obtain number of copies in advance. Cost is 50 cents per page; $5 for certified copies. Mailing Label: No. Magnetic Tape: Available for $250. Tape contains all profit and non-profit corporations on file. Microfiche: No. New Corporate Listings: Available for $50 a month. Custom Searches: No. Online Access: No, but is being considered. Number of Active Corporations on File: 80,000.

Louisiana

Corporate Division, Secretary of State, 3851 Essen Lane, Baton Rouge, LA 70809, (504) 925-4704. Selected Publications: *Corporate Law Book* ($6). Phone Information: (504) 925-4704. Copies of Documents on File: Available starting at $10 for certified articles. Cost for total file is $20. Mailing Label: No. Magnetic Tape: Available in the future. Microfiche: No. New Corporate Listing: Weekly Newsletter at no charge. (Requester must supply large pre-addressed envelope). Custom Searches: No. Online Access: Dial Up Access, using a 900 number, will be available after January, 1992. Number of Active Corporations on File: 120,000.

Maine

Information and Report Section, Bureau of Corporations, Secretary of State, State House Station 101, Augusta, ME 04333, (207) 289-4195. Selected Publications: *Guide to Completing Forms of Incorporation* (Blue Guide). Phone Information: (207) 289-4195. Copies of Documents on File: Available for $1 per page, plus $5 for certified copies. Mailing Labels: No. Magnetic tape: No, but hope to have it in the near future. Contact Rebecca Wyke at (207) 289-6308. Microfiche: No. New Corporate Listings: Monthly Corporations Listing costs $8. Contact Betsy at (207) 289-4183. Custom Searches: No, but hope to have it in near future. Online Access: No. Number of Active Corporations on File: 40,000.

Maryland

Corporate Charter Division, Department of Assessments and Taxation, 301 W. Preston Street, Baltimore, Maryland 21201, (410) 225-1330. Selected Publications: *Guide to Corporations*. Phone Information: (410) 225-1330. Copies of Documents on File: Available for $1 per page, plus $6 for certified copies for walk-ins. If they make copy there is a $20 expediting fee. Mailing Labels: No. Magnetic Tape: Available for $250 weekly. Infrequent requests cost $425. Microfiche: No. New Corporate Listings: Monthly Corporate Computer Printout costs $25 a month. Custom Searches: Not at this time. Online Access: Hope to have in near future. Number of Active Corporations on File: 300,000.

Massachusetts

Corporate Division, Secretary of State, 1 Ashburton Place, Boston, MA 02108, (617) 727-2850. Selected Publications: *Organizing a Business Corporation, Organizing a Non-Profit Corporation, When You Need Information About Corporations in Massachusetts, Choose a Name for Your Business, Compendium of Corporate Law* ($15). Phone Information: (617) 727-2850. Copies of Documents on File: Available for 20 cents per page (send a minimum of 80 cents), $12 for certified copies. Mailing Labels: No. Magnetic Tape: Cost is $300 for copy of master file and record layout. Requester must supply tapes. Microfiche: No. New Corporate Listings: Semi-monthly Filings cost $15; Quarterly Filings cost $50; bi-weekly printout cost $15. Custom Searches: Available on a cost recovery basis. Online Access: Direct Access program. Cost is $149 annually. Connect time is 40 cents per minute. Number of Corporations on File: 375,000.

Michigan

Corporation Division, Corporation and Securities Bureau, Michigan Department of Commerce, PO Box 30054, 6546 Mercantile, Lansing, MI, 48909, (517) 334-6302. Selected Publications: None. Phone Information: (517) 334-6311. Copies of Documents on File: Available at a minimum of $6 for 6 pages or less, $1 for each page thereafter. Certified copies cost $10. (Request a price list.) Mailing Labels: No. Magnetic Tape: No. Microfiche: Available for $145. New Corporate Listings: Monthly Listing costs $90 per month. Custom Searches: No. Online Access: Available through Information America, (800) 235-4008 or Mead Data, (313) 259-1156. Number of Corporations on File: 251,000.

Minnesota

Corporate Division, Secretary of State, 180 State Office Building, St. Paul, MN 55155, (612) 296-2803. Selected Publications: *Guide to Starting a Business in Minnesota*. Phone Information: (612) 296-2803. Copies of Documents on File: Available for $3 per document, $8 for certified copies. Mailing Labels: Yes. Categories: Domestic, Limited Partnerships, Non-profits, Foreign, Foreign Limited, Foreign Non-profits, Trademarks, Business Trusts. Cost determined at time of request. Magnetic Tape: No. Microfiche: Available documents on file (Articles of Incorporation, annual reports, amendments) cost 21 cents sheet plus filing or retrieval fees. Paper copy of microfiche is $6 per corporation for complete file. $3 for articles of incorporation. New Corporate Listings: Daily Log costs 25 cents per page. Custom Searches: Available on a cost recovery basis. Categories same as for mailing labels. Online Access: Direct Access available for $50 annually plus transaction charge of $1 to $4. Number of Corporations on File: 194,500.

Mississippi

Office of Corporations, Secretary of State, PO Box 136, Jackson, MS 39205, (601) 359-1350 or mailing address: 202 N. Congress, Suite 601, Jackson, MS 39201. Selected Publications: None. Phone Information: (601) 359-1627. Copies of Documents on File: Available at $1 per page plus $10 for certified copies. Mailing Labels: No. Magnetic Tape: Available for $200 for set of 2. You are to supply tapes. Microfiche: No. New Corporate Listings: Monthly Listing costs $25. Custom Searches: Available to limited extent. Printout costs $2 per page. Online Access: Yes. $250 sign-up fee, plus flat monthly fee. $50 is monthly minimum for first 100 transactions. Contact Sheryl Crawford at (601) 359-1548. Number of Active Corporations on File: 80,000. This office has converted to an automated system with advanced search capabilities.

Missouri

Corporate Division, Secretary of State, 301 High Street, PO Box 77, Jefferson City, MO 65102, (314) 751-4194. Selected Publications: *Corporation Handbook*. Phone Information: (314) 751-4153. Copies of Documents on File: Available at 50 cents per page plus $5 for certified copies. Send in written requests and they will bill. Mailing Labels: No. Magnetic Tape: Cost is between $100 and $200 for copy of master file. Contact Sara Welch at (314) 751-5832. Microfiche: No. New Corporate Listings: Not usually, but can be set up on special request. Custom Searches: No. Online Access: Available through Mead Data Central (LEXIS), 9393 Springboro Pike, PO Box 933, Dayton, OH 45401, (513) 865-6800; Prentice-Hall, Dunn and Bradstreet or Information America. Direct Dial Up access is available through the State Access Center. Contact John Bluma at (314) 751-4780 or Sara Welch at (314) 751-5832. Number of Active Corporations on File: 140,000.

Be patient. If any phone number is incorrect, call (area code) 555-1212 and request the new listing.

Companies In Your State

Montana

Corporate Department, Secretary of State, Capitol Station, Helena, MT 59620, (406) 444-3665. Selected Publications: None. Phone Information: (406) 444-3665. Copies of Documents on File: Available for 50 cents per page; $2 for certification. Mailing Labels: No. Magnetic Tape: No. Microfiche: No. New Corporate Listings: No. Custom Searches: No, but can search by name of corporation only. Online Access: No. Number of Active Corporations on File: 33,000.

Nebraska

Corporate Division, Secretary of State, State Capitol, Lincoln, NE 68509, (402) 471-4079. Selected Publications: None. Phone Information: (402) 471-4079. Copies of Documents on File: Available for $1 per page, $10 for certified copies. Will bill for requests under $50. Mailing Labels: Available on a cost recovery basis. Can do for entire data base only. Contact Mr. Englert at (402) 471-2554. Magnetic Tape: Available on a cost recovery basis. Also contact Mr. Englert. Microfiche: No. New Corporate Listings: Available upon request. Will set up for number of issues customer requests. $100 per issuance. Custom Searches: No. Online Access: No. Number of Active Corporations on File: 50,000

Nevada

Office of Corporations, Secretary of State, Capitol Complex, Carson City, NV 89710, (702) 687-5203. Selected Publications: *Guidelines.* Phone Information: Corporate Status call (702) 687-5105. Copies of Documents on File: Available for $1 per page, $10 for certified copies. Written request only, prepayment required (send a blank check stating limit). Mailing Labels: No. Magnetic Tape: Copy of master file available. Corporations takes 2 tapes which requester supplies. Cost per tape is $25. Microfiche: No. New Corporate Listings: Monthly Listing of New Corporations costs $25 a month. Custom Searches: Yes. Searches may be done by location of resident agent and other ways. Cost determined at time of request. Other: A three volume listing of corporations on file, in the "Alpha Listing", is published twice a year which includes names of active and inactive corporations but not addresses. Cost for set is $25. Contact Cindy Woodgate. Online Access: Dial Up Direct Access through subscription service. Your computer needs a communication pack and you must set up trust account from which $24.50 per hour, prorated by actual minutes used, will be deducted. For ID number and password, contact Cindy Woodgate. Number of Active Corporations on File: 60,000.

New Hampshire

Corporate Division, Secretary of State, State House, Room 204, Concord, NH 03301, (603) 271-3244. Selected Publications: *How to Start a Business, New Hampshire Corporate Law.* Phone Information: (603) 271-3246. Copies of Documents on File: Available for $1 per page, plus $5 for certified copies. Mailing Labels: No. Magnetic Tape: No. Microfiche: Complete listing of all registrations. No breakdown by type of entity (updated monthly). Annual Subscription costs $200. New Corporate Listings: Monthly Subscriber List costs $15 plus postage. Custom Searches: No. Other: Booklet listing all non-profit corporations is available for $45. Online Access: No. Number of Active Corporations on File: 33,000.

New Jersey

Commercial Recording Division, Secretary of State, 820 Bear Tavern Road, West Trenton, NJ 08628, (Mailing address: CN 308), (609) 530-6400. Selected Publications: *Corporate Filing Packet.* Phone Information: General Information call (609) 530-6405; Forms call (609) 292-0013; Expedite Service call (609) 984-7107. There is a charge for standard information, $5 look-up fee for each request plus $10 expedite fee. User may use VISA or Master Charge for payment. Answers available by phone, mail or Western Union Electronic Mail. Requests and answering copies may be done through FAX at (609) 530-6433. Copies of Documents on File: Available for $10 plus $15 for certified copies. Mailing Labels: No. Magnetic Tape: No. Microfiche: No. New Corporate Listings: Monthly List of Corporations costs $100 per month. Custom Searches: Numerous search capabilities are available. Each request is reviewed on individual basis. Requester is billed for computer time. Online Access: No. Number of Active Corporations on File: 436,314.

New Mexico

State Corporation Commission, PO Drawer 1269, Santa Fe, NM 87504-1269, (505) 827-4502. Selected Publications: None. Phone Information: (505) 827-4504. Copies of Documents on File: Available for 75 cents per page, plain copy; $1 per page for certified copy. Mailing Labels: No. Magnetic Tape: No. Microfiche: No. New Corporate Listings: Yes. Monthly listings available. Requester must send manilla self-addressed envelope. Online Access: Available through New Mexico Technet, 4100 Osuna N.E., Albuquerque, NM 87109, (505) 345-6555. You may also pay the same charge as the State by purchasing it directly from the Corporation Division. They will bill you for usage monthly. Contact Mr. Salinas at (505) 827-4502. Custom Searches: Yes. Categories: Corporate Name, Domestic or Foreign, Profit or Non-profit, Date of Incorporation, Active or Inactive, Identification Number, Amount of Capital Stock, Authorized Stock, Instrument file, Principal Office Address, Officers and Directors Names (includes addresses, Social Security numbers and titles), Name of Incorporators, Registered Agent and Office, Good Standing Status, Parent/Subsidiary Information. Call or put request in writing. Only a limited number of custom searches can be performed each month. Number of Active Corporations on File: 50,000.

New York

New York State, Department of State, Division of Corporations, 162 Washington Avenue, Albany, NY 12231, (518) 474-6200. Selected Publications: *Extract of Laws for Incorporating.* Phone Information: (518) 474-6200. Copies of Documents on File: Available for $5 per document, $10 for certified copies. Mailing Labels: No. Magnetic Tape: No. Microfiche: No. New Corporate Listing: Report of Corporations is printed daily and mailed out every other day. It is available by subscription only for $125 per year, $75 for 6 months or $40 for 3 months. Online Access: Available in the near future. Number of Corporations on File: 1,200,000.

North Carolina

Division of Corporation, Secretary of State, 300 N. Salisbury Street, Raleigh, NC 27603-5909, (919) 733-4201. Selected Publications: *North Carolina Business Corporation Guidelines, North Carolina's Non-profit Corporation Handbook.* Phone Information: (919) 733-4201. Copies of Documents on File: Available for $1 per page, $5 for certified copies. Mailing Labels: No. Magnetic Tape: Available on cost recovery basis. To make a request, write Bonnie Elek. Categories: All active corporations, foreign, domestic, non-profit, and profit. Microfiche: No. New Corporate Listings: Available for $20 per month and issued in hard copy only. Custom Searches: Yes. Categories: Type of Corporation, Professional Corporations, Insurance Corporations, Banks, and Savings and Loans. Not available for the type of business a corporation conducts. This may be available in the future. Online Access: Available. Number of Active Corporations on File: 180,000.

North Dakota

Corporation Division, Secretary of State, Capitol Building, 600 East Boulevard Avenue, Bismarck, ND 58505, (701) 224-2905. Selected Publications: *North Dakota Business Corporation Act Statute,* $3. Phone Information: (701) 224-4284. Copies of Documents on File: Search of records cost $5, four pages for $1, $10 for certified copies. Written or phone requests accepted. Requester will be billed for phone orders. Mailing Labels: No. Magnetic Tape: No. Microfiche: No. New Corporate Listings: Monthly Corporation List costs $10 per month. Custom Searches: No. Online Access: No, but may be available in the future. Number of Active Corporations on File: 22,500.

Ohio

Corporation Division, Secretary of State, 30 East Broad Street, 14th Floor, Columbus, OH 43266-0418, (614) 466-3910. Selected Publications: *Corporate Checklist.* Phone Information: Corporate Status call (614) 466-3910; Name Availability call (614) 466-0590. Copies of Documents on File: Contact (614) 466-1776. Available for $1 per page, $5 for certified copies. Mailing Labels: No. Magnetic Tape: Available for $125 for 6,250 corporation names, thereafter the cost is 2 cents per corporate name with a maximum of 25,000 names. Microfiche: No. New Corporate Listing: Call (614) 466-8464. Weekly County-Wide Listing costs 25 cents per page, Weekly Statewide Listing costs 10 cents per page ($45 a month). Custom Searches: Yes. Categories: location (county), Foreign, Domestic, Profit, Non-Profit. Price structure is same as for Magnetic tape. Online Access: No. Number of Active Corporations on File: 400,000.

Oklahoma

Corporations, Secretary of State, 101 State Capitol Building, Oklahoma City, OK 73105, (405) 521-3911. Selected Publications: *Forms and Procedures to Incorporate.* Phone Information: (900) 820-2424 for record search. Charge is $3 per call. Copies of Documents on File: Available for $1 per page, $5 for certified copies. Mailing Labels: No. Magnetic Tape: $5 per tape which is supplied by

Be patient. If any phone number is incorrect, call (area code) 555-1212 and request the new listing.

Information on People, Companies, and Mailing Lists

requester. Microfiche: No. New Corporate Listings: Monthly Charter List costs $150 a month, plus Amendments $250 a month plus postage. Custom Searches: No. Online Access: Contact Beverly Curry at Information Systems, (404) 892-1800. They purchase magnetic tape of Division's master file weekly to make a database which is complete except for new names. Number of Corporations on File (Active and Inactive): 224,159.

Oregon

Corporation Division, Department of Commerce, 158 12th Street N.E., Salem, OR 97310, (503) 378-4166. Selected Publications: *Business Organizations, Assumed Trademarks, and Securities (BOATS)*. Phone Information: (503) 378-4166. Copies of Documents on File: Available for $5 for all documents in a corporation's file except annual report. Annual reports are an additional $5. Certification fee is $15. Mailing Labels: No. Magnetic Tape: Complete master file costs $190. Contact Joy Lorenz at (503) 373-7920. Requester must provide tape or charge will be an additional $20 per tape. Microfiche: No. New Corporate Listings: Statistical Report of New Corporations is available for $17 per monthly issue. Custom Searches: Yes. Numerous categories with a minimum charge of $150. Address inquiries to Attn: Joy Lorenz. Online Access: Yes. Contact Joy Lorenz, (503) 373-7920. Charges include $100 for hookup, $70 monthly fee, plus telephone charges and prorated computer time with a minimum $10 charge. Total minimum monthly cost is $80. Cost of average user is $100 per month. Mead Data, Information America and Dunn and Bradstreet also have database. Number of Active Corporations on File: 56,000.

Pennsylvania

Corporation Bureau, 308 N. Office Building, Harrisburg, PA 17120, (717) 787-1997. Selected Publications: *Corporate Guide* (currently under revision). Phone Information: (717) 787-1057. Copies of Documents on File: Available for $2 per page, $12 search fee, $28 for certified copies. Mailing Labels: No. Magnetic Tape: Copy of master file available for $900 per tape, Requester must supply 11 blank tapes. Microfiche: No. New Corporate Listings: County or area listing available for 25 cents per name. Custom Searches: Yes. Categories: Non-Profit, Domestic, Foreign, county location, Limited Partnerships, Fictitious name, Trademarks, Foreign Non-profits, Cooperatives, Professional Corporations 25 cents per name). Online Access: Available from Information America at (404) 892-1800; Prentice-Hall, Legal and Financial Services at (518) 458-8111; or Mead Data Central at (513) 865-6800. Number of Corporations on File: 616,000.

Rhode Island

Corporations Division, Secretary of State, 100 North Main Street, Providence, RI 02903, (401) 277-3040. Selected Publications: Instruction sheet, *The Rhode Island Law Book* ($10). Phone Information: (401) 277-3040. Staff will look up two corporations per call. Copies of Documents on File: Available for 50 cents per page, $5 for certified sheet. Mailing Labels: No. Magnetic Tape: Available for $250 per tape. Requester supplies tape. They will put their database on disc. You supply 5 1/4 disc, MAG high density. Printouts cost 50 cents per page. There approximately 11 names per page. Microfiche: No. New Corporate Listings: Not usually provided. New corporate listings are published weekly in *The Providence Journal*, Sunday Business Section. Send a letter requesting weekly printouts. Custom Searches: No. Online Access: No. Number of Active Corporations on File: 90,000.

South Carolina

Division of Corporations, Secretary of State, PO Box 11350, Columbia, SC 29211, (803) 734-2158. Selected Publications: None. Phone Information: (803) 734-2158. Copies of Documents on File: Available for $1 for first page, 50 cents thereafter. $2 for plain charter and $4 for certified charter. Amendments are $1 per page thereafter and it costs $2 for certification. Mailing Labels: No. Magnetic Tape: No. Microfiche: No. New Corporate Listing: Special request only; contact Amy Hoskin at (803) 734-2159. Custom Searches: No. Online Access: Yes. Available for $70 per month. Contact Bob Knight, Deputy Secretary. Number of Active Corporations on File: 250,000.

South Dakota

Corporate Division, Secretary of State, 500 East Capitol, Pierre, SD 57501, (605) 773-4845. Selected Publications: None. Phone Information: (605) 773-4845. Copies of Documents on File: Available for 50 cents per page plus $5 for certification. Mailing Labels: No. Magnetic Tape: No. Microfiche: No. New Corporate Listings: No. Custom Searches: No. Online Access: No. Number of Active Corporations on File: 30,000.

Tennessee

Office of Secretary of State, Services Division, Suite 1800, James K. Polk Building, Nashville, TN 37243-0306, (615) 741-2286. Select Publications: None. Phone Information: (615) 741-2286. Copies of Documents on File: Certified copies only are available for $10. Mailing Labels No. Magnetic Tape: Yes. Categories: All Corporations on file, Foreign, Domestic, Profit, Non-Profit, Banks, Credit Unions, Cooperative Associations. Charge of an additional $2 for each tape supplied. Cost, done on a cost recovery basis, is determined at time of request. Contact Mr. Thompson at (615) 741-0584. Microfiche: No. New Corporate Listings: Monthly New Corporation Listing on a cost recovery basis of 25 cents per page, 8 names per page. Call (615) 741-1111. Custom Searches: Yes. Categories: Same as for magnetic tape. Cost is same as for New Corporate Listing. Contact Mr. Thompson at (615) 741-0584. Online Access: No. Number of Active Corporations on File: 100,000.

Texas

Corporation Section, Statute Filing Division, Secretary of State, PO Box 13697, Austin, TX 78711, (512) 463-5586. Selected Publications: *Filing Guide to Corporations*. (Written requests only for a $15 fee.) Phone Information: (512) 463-5555. Copies of Documents on File: Available for 85 cents for first page, 15 cents for each additional page. Certification is $5 plus $1 for each additional page. Invoices are sent for order not in excess of $100. Mailing Labels: No. Magnetic Tape: No. Microfiche: Names of officers and directors available. Cost determined at time of request. New Corporate Listings: Weekly Charter Update costs $27.50 per week. Custom Searches: No. Online Access: Available through Information America (404) 892-1800. Contact Linda Gordon at (713) 751-7900. Number of Active Corporations on File: 400,000.

Utah

Corporations and UCC, Division of Business Regulations, P.O. Box 45801, 160 East 300 South Street, Second Floor, Salt Lake City, UT 84145-0801, (801) 530-6012. Selected Publications: *Going into Business*, *Doing Business in Utah*, *A Guide to Business Information*. (Send $2 to cover mailing costs.) Phone Information: (801) 530-4849. Copies of Documents on File: Available for 30 cents a page plus $10 for certified copies. Mailing Labels: No. Magnetic Tape: Yes. Categories: Profit, Non-Profit, Foreign, Domestic. Cost includes computer time and programming fee. Microfiche: No. New Corporate Listing: Weekly New Corporation List 30 cents per page, New Doing Business As (DBA) List 30 cents per page. Custom Searches: Yes. Categories: Same as for Magnetic tape. Cost includes printing charge of 30 cents per page plus computer time and programming fee. Online Access: Available for $10 per month, 10 cents per minute. Contact Ted Wiggin at (801) 530-6643 about Data Share. Number of Active Corporations on File: 40,000.

Vermont

Corporate Division, Secretary of State, 109 State Street, Montpelier, VT 05602-2710, (802) 828-2386. Selected Publications: *Doing Business in Vermont*. Phone Information: (802) 828-2386. Copies of Documents on File: Available for $1 per page, $5 for certified copies. Send the $5 certification fee in advance. They will bill you for the copies. Mailing Labels: No. Magnetic Tape: Diskettes available for $6 - $10 plus 1 cent per name. Entire date base costs $250. Microfiche: No. New Corporate Listings: Yes. Monthly New Corporations and Trade names on diskette is $6 plus 1 cent per name. Total cost is never more than $15. Out-of-State Corporations, $50 for complete list. Custom Searches: Yes. Categories: Foreign, Domestic, Non-profits, by date of registration. Cost is 1 cent per name plus $6 to run list. Online Access: Will be available mid 1992. Contact: Betty Poulin. Number of Active Corporations on File: 24,000.

Virginia

Clerk of Commission, State Corporation Commission, Secretary of State, P.O. Box 1197, Richmond, VA 23209, street address: 1220 Bank Street, Richmond, VA 23219, (804) 786-3672, FAX: (804) 371-0118. Selected Publications: *Business Registration Guide*. Phone Information: (804) 786-3733. Copies of Documents on File: Available for $1 per page, $3 for certified copies. Mailing Labels: No. Magnetic Tape: Possibly in the future. Microfiche: No. New Corporate Listings: No. Custom Searches: Yes. Categories: Foreign, Domestic, Non-profit, Professional corporation, Non-Stock, Public Service, Cooperatives. Available on cost recovery basis. Online Access: Available. Contact Betty Williams at (804) 786-6703. Free while in pilot stage, then available on cost recovery basis. Number of Active Corporations on File: 160,000.

Be patient. If any phone number is incorrect, call (area code) 555-1212 and request the new listing.

Companies In Your State

Washington

Corporate Division, Secretary of State, 2nd Floor Republic Bldg., 505 Union Ave, Mail Stop PM-21, Olympia, WA 98504, (206) 753-7120. Selected Publications: *None*. Phone Information: (206) 753-7115. Copies of Documents on File: Call (206) 586-2061 to leave recorded message for document orders. Fees are $1 for the first page and 20 cents thereafter. Certification is $10. Mailing Labels: No. Magnetic Tape: No. Microfiche: Cost is $10 a month per set. New Corporate Listings: No except for statistical sheet. Custom Searches: No. Online Access: No. Number of Active Corporations on File: 145,000. This office is not computerized.

West Virginia

Corporate Division, Secretary of State, Room 139 West, State Capitol, Charleston, WV 25305, (304) 342-8000. Selected Publications: *The Corporate Filings Requirements*. Phone Information: (304) 342-8000. Copies of Documents on File: Available for 50 cents per page, $10 for certified copies. Mailing Labels: No. Magnetic Tape: No. Microfiche: No. New Corporate Listing: Monthly Report costs $5 a month or $50 per year. Custom Searches: Yes. Cost is $1 for first hour and $5 for every hour thereafter, prorated. Online Access: No. Number of Active Corporations on File: 39,000.

Wisconsin

Corporate Division, Secretary of State, PO Box 7846, Madison, WI 53707; Street address: 30 W. Mifflin St., 9th Floor, Madison, WI 53703, (608) 266-3590. Selected Publications: *Chapter 180 Statutes Book* ($5). Phone Information: (608) 266-3590, FAX: (608) 267-6813. Copies of Documents on File: For simple copy request must be in writing. Fee is $2. Faxed copies are 50 cents per page. Requests for certified copies may be phoned in. Fee is $10. Mailing Labels: No. Magnetic Tape: Available for $175. Address inquiries to Molly O'Connell. Microfiche: Yes. Monthly New Corporations costs $11 per month. New Corporate Listing: Yes (see microfiche entry). Minimum cost is $10 per week. Custom Searches: No. Online Access: No. Number of Active Corporations on File: 176,000.

Wyoming

Corporate Division, Secretary of State, State of Wyoming, Capitol Building, Cheyenne, WY 82002, (307) 777-7311; FAX: (307) 777-5339. Selected Publications: *Wyoming Business Corporation Act* ($4). Phone Information: (307) 777-7311. Copies of Documents on File: Available for 50 cents for first 10 pages then 15 cents per page, $3 for certified copies. Mailing Labels: No. Magnetic Tape: Yes. Categories: Trademarks, New Domestic, New Foreign all available on a cost recovery basis. Other categories may be possible for $200 plus monthly fees. Information cannot be used for solicitation. Submit written request with letter of purpose. Microfiche: Available for foreign and nonprofit corporations for $15. New Corporate Listings: Yes. (See magnetic tape entry). Also, you may be put on mailing list for weekly press release that appears in local journals, Business Section. Custom Searches: Yes. Categories: Trademarks 25 cents per name and address, New Domestic $120 or $80 if in-state request, New Foreign $120 or $80 if instate request. Limited capacity for other types of searches. Information cannot be used for solicitation. Submit written request with letter of purpose. Listing of all active profit corporation can be purchased for $25. Online Access: Will soon be available. Contact Jeanie Sawyer. Number of Active Corporations on File: 25,000.

Be patient. If any phone number is incorrect, call (area code) 555-1212 and request the new listing.

State Company Directories

Market Info, Mailing Lists, Databases Available From State Company Directories

Would you like to know what kind of computing systems and software 24,000 manufacturing firms in California use? Or where to find out what materials 7,000 manufacturers in North Carolina need for their manufacturing processes? Or which of 2,700 manufacturers in Nevada have contracts with the federal government? You can get quick answers to these questions and more in the state directories of manufacturing companies.

These directories contain valuable information concerning what products are bought, sold, and distributed in each state. At the very least, each directory lists the companies' names, addresses, phone numbers, products, and SIC codes, and is cross-referenced by company name, location, and SIC code/product. So, if you want to find out which companies in Tennessee manufacture a certain type of electronic component and where they are located, all you have to do is look it up in the product index. If you want to find out what manufacturing firms are operating in a certain town or county, the geographic index will tell you. These directories can be invaluable for targeting new market areas, monitoring industry trends, developing more effective mailing lists, and much more.

The majority of these directories are put out by the individual state's Chamber of Commerce or Department of Economic Development, while private publishing firms compile and distribute the rest. The price and sophistication of these directories vary widely from state to state. While some, like Montana's, may offer only the basic information mentioned above, others, like the Illinois directory, will also include key personnel, CEO, parent company, employment figures, import/export market, computer system used, and more. Prices range from no charge for North Dakota's directory, all the way to $250 for Alabama's five volume set. Most of the prices listed below include shipping and handling, and state sales tax where applicable.

Many of these directories are also available in database formats and differ widely in cost. While there are some real bargains, such as Rhode Island's directory of 2,600 firms on diskette for $20, some, like Colorado's of 4,700 firms, will cost you $1,000. Before ordering any of these databases, make sure that the software is compatible with your own system. Mailing labels for many of the directories are also available, and many states allow you to choose the companies you want for your mailing list on a cost per label basis.

List of State Company Directories

Alabama

Alabama Development Office, Research Division, State Capitol, 135 S. Union Street, Montgomery, AL 36130; (205) 263-1171. $275/5 volumes. Listing of 6,500 companies includes name, address, phone, CEO, year established, employee figures, product lines, parent company, import/export, and SIC code. Cross-referenced by company name, location, product, parent company, international trade, and SIC code. Available on diskette or tape database format for $42 plus 3 cents per entry plus cost of software.

Alaska

Alaska Center for International Business, University of Alaska, 3211 Providence, Suite 203, Anchorage, AK 99508; (907) 786-4300. *The Alaska Trade Directory,* a listing of 150 Alaska companies and industries that import or export, includes name, address, phone, CEO, key personnel, market area, product/service, and SIC code. Cross-referenced by company name and product/SIC code. Prices available on request.

Arizona

Phoenix Chamber of Commerce, 34 West Monroe, Suite 900, Phoenix, AZ 85003; (602) 254-5521. $65. Listing of 5,000 companies includes name, address, phone, CEO, employee figures, market area, products, and SIC code. Cross-referenced by company name, location, market area, and products/SIC code.

Arkansas

Arkansas Industrial Development Foundation, P.O. Box 1784, Little Rock, AR 72203; (501) 682-1121. $50. Listing of 2,500 companies includes name, address, phone, contact person, parent company, products, and SIC code. Cross-referenced by company name, location, and product/SIC code.

California

Database Publishing Company, 523 Superior Avenue, Newport Beach, CA 92663; (800) 888-8434. $160. Listing of 24,000 companies includes name, address, phone, CEO, key personnel, sales volume, year established, parent company, products, computer brand used, import/export, employee figures, and SIC code. Cross-referenced by company name, location, products, and SIC code. Available on diskette for $975, book included.

Colorado

Business Research Division, University of Colorado, Campus Box 420, Boulder, CO 80309; (303) 492-8227. $75. Listing of 4,700 companies includes name, address, phone, employee figures, market area, CEO, products, and SIC code. Cross-referenced by company name, location, and SIC code. Available in database format for $1,250. Mailing labels: $275/set. Prices may vary.

Connecticut

Connecticut Labor Department, Employment Security Division, Attn: Business Management, 200 Folly Brook Boulevard, Weathersfield, CT 06109; (203) 566-2120. $22. The 1984 directory of 4,000 companies includes name, address, products, and SIC code. Cross-referenced by company name, location, products, and SIC codes. A quarterly updated listing is available for $7/year.

MacRae's Industrial Directories, 817 Broadway, 3rd Floor, New York, NY 10003; (800) 622-7237. $129.50. Listing of 8,200 CT and RI manufacturing firms includes name, address, phone, parent company, key personnel, employee figures, size, products, and SIC code. Cross-referenced by company name, location, and SIC code.

Delaware

Delaware State Chamber of Commerce, 1201 N. Orange Street, P.O. Box 671, Wilmington, DE 19899; (302) 655-7221. $45 for state Chamber members; $55 for non-members. The directory of commerce and industry, listing over 5,600 companies, includes name, address, phone, CEO, employee figures, products/ services, and SIC code. Cross-referenced by company name, location, and SIC code. Mailing labels: 25 cents/company.

Be patient. If any phone number is incorrect, call (area code) 555-1212 and request the new listing.

State Company Directories

Florida

Florida Chamber of Commerce, P.O. Box 11309, Tallahassee, FL 32302; (904) 425-1200. $65. Listing of over 10,000 companies includes name, address, phone, CEO, employee figures, products, import/export, and SIC code. Cross-referenced by company name, location, and SIC code. Available in database format, diskette or tape, for 12 cents/company or about $1,903.67. Mailing labels: 10 cents per company, $150 per 1,000 names, 1,000 minimum.

Georgia

Georgia Department of Industry and Trade, Directory Section, P.O. Box 56706, Atlanta, GA 30343; (404) 656-3619. $55. Listing of 8,000 companies includes name, address, market area, parent company, key personnel, employee figures, year established, products, and SIC code. Cross-referenced by company name, location and SIC code.

Hawaii

Chamber of Commerce of Hawaii, 735 Bishop Street, Honolulu, HI 96813; (808) 522-8800. $45. The current edition of over 150 companies includes name, address, phone, contact person, product, and SIC code. Cross-referenced by company name, location, and SIC code.

Idaho

Center for Business Development and Research, University of ID, Moscow, ID 83844-3227; (208) 885-6611. The new directory of over 1,300 manufacturers will include name address, phone, CEO, product/service, contact person, import/export, employee figures, and SIC code. Cross-referenced by company name, location, and SIC code. Diskette: PC compatible, $200.

Illinois

Harris Publishing Company, 2057 Aurora Road, Twinsburg, OH 44087; (800) 321-9136. $116.45. Listing of over 20,000 companies includes name, address, phone, CEO, employee figures, computer brand used, year established, sales volume, product, and SIC code. Cross-referenced by company name, location, product, and SIC code. Diskette format, containing 9,000 companies with 20 or more employees, available for $276.75.

Indiana

Harris Publishing Company, 2057 Aurora Road, Twinsburg OH 44087; (800) 321-9136. $75.65. Listing of over 8,000 companies includes name, address, phone, CEO, employee figures, year established, annual sales, computer brand used, products, and SIC code. Cross-referenced by company name, location, product, and SIC code. Diskette format, containing 6,000 companies with 10 or more employees, available for $233.75.

Iowa

Iowa Department of Economic Development, Research Section, 200 East Grand Avenue, Des Moines, IA 50309; (515) 281-3925. $55. Listing of over 5,000 companies includes name, address, phone, CEO, purchasing agent, parent company, employee figures, product, and SIC code. Cross-referenced by company name, location, product, and SIC code. Available on diskette, $125. Book and diskette, $150. Purchase address: Business Publishing Corporation, 100 4th Street, Des Moines, IA 50309; (800) 626-6000.

Kansas

Kansas Department of Commerce, 700 SW Harrison Street, Suite 1300, Topeka, KS 66603-3712; (913) 296-3481. $40. Listing of 4,000 companies includes name, address, phone, contact person, parent company, employee figures, product, and SIC code. Cross-referenced by company name, location, product, and SIC code. Diskettes will be available in 1992.

Kentucky

Department of Economic Development, Maps and Publications, 133 Holmes Street, Frankfort, KY 40601; (502) 564-4715. $30. Listing of 3,600 companies includes name, address, phone, CEO, year established, employee figures, products, and SIC code. Cross-referenced by company name, location, and SIC code.

Louisiana

Department of Economic Development, Commerce and Industry, P.O. Box 94185, Baton Rouge, LA 70804-9185; (504) 342-5361. $48. Listing of 3,000 companies includes name, address, phone, CEO, purchasing agent, marketing area, import/export, products, and SIC code. Cross-referenced by company name, location, and SIC code. Database price available on request.

Maine

Maine Manufacturing Directory, Tower Publishing Company, 34 Diamond Street, P.O. Box 7220, Portland, ME 04112; (800) 431-2665 in-state; (207) 774-9813 out-of-state. $37.50. Listing of 2,200 companies includes name, address, phone, three contact persons, employee figures, gross sales, product, and SIC code. Cross-referenced by company name, location, and SIC code. Mailing labels: $55 for first 1,000, then 5 cents each.

Maryland

Harris Publishing Company, 2057 Aurora Rd., Twinsburg, OH 44087; (800) 888-5900. $50.35. Listing of 2,500 companies includes name, address, phone, employee figures, year established, annual sales, products, key personnel, and SIC code. Divided into sections by company name, location, industry, import/export, products, and SIC code. Mailing labels: $75 per 1,000 names, minimum charge $150. Diskette available for $228.

Massachusetts

George D. Hall Publishing Company, 50 Congress Street, Boston, MA 02109; (617) 523-3745. $67.95 in-state; $56.95 out-of-state. Listing of 7,400 companies includes name, address, phone, CEO, sales volume, employee figures, products, and SIC code. Cross-referenced by company name, location, and product. Database format on diskette for any 3,000 companies available for $400. Mailing labels $225 minimum per 3,000; 6 cents per name.

Michigan

Harris Publishing Company, 2057 Aurora Road, Twinsburg, OH 44087; (800) 321-9136. $123.50. Listing of 14,000 companies includes name, address, phone, CEO, employee figures, computer brands used, year established, products, and SIC code. Cross-referenced by company name, location, product, and SIC code. Diskette format, containing 7,000 companies with 20 or more employees, available for $308.75.

Minnesota

National Information Systems, 4401 West 76th Street, Edina, MN 55435; (612) 893-8308. $83.49. Listing of 9,000 companies includes name, address, phone, contact person, employee figures, sales volume, year established, products, and SIC code. Cross-referenced by company name, location, and product/SIC code.

Mississippi

Mississippi Department of Economic and Community Development, 1400 Walter Sillers Bldg., P.O. Box 849, Jackson, MS 39205; (601) 359-3448. $50. Listing of 2,600 companies includes name, address, phone, CEO, key personnel, employee figures, parent company, products, international trade, and SIC code. Cross-referenced by company name, location, product, and SIC code. Available on diskette for $400, and $200 for yearly update.

Missouri

Harris Publishing Company, 2057 Aurora Road, Twinsburg, OH 44087; (800) 321-9136. $89.30. Listing of 8,000 companies includes name, address, phone, CEO, employee figures, computer brand used, year established, product, and SIC code. Cross-referenced by company name, location, product, and SIC code. Diskette format, containing 4,800 companies with 10 or more employees, available for $261.25.

Montana

Department of Commerce, Business Assistance Division, 1424 9th Avenue, Helena, MT 59620; (406) 444-3923. $20. Listing of 2,500 companies includes name, address, phone, owner, size classification, products, and SIC code. Cross-referenced by company name, location, product, and SIC code.

Be patient. If any phone number is incorrect, call (area code) 555-1212 and request the new listing.

Information on People, Companies, and Mailing Lists

Nebraska

Nebraska Department of Economic Development, P.O. Box 94666, Lincoln, NE 68509; (402) 471-3784. $40. Listing of 1,849 companies includes name, address, phone, CEO, parent company, employee figures, import/export, products, and SIC code. Cross-referenced by company name, location, and product/SIC code. Available on IBM compatible diskette for $150.

Nevada

Gold Hill Publishing Company, P.O. Drawer F, Virginia City, NV 89440; (702) 847-0222. $75 out-of-state; $75 plus shipping and handling in-state. Listing of 6,530 companies includes name, address, phone, parent company, CEO, key personnel, FAX #, square footage occupied, sales volume, products, import/export, federal contracts, year established, years in NV, products, and SIC code. Cross-referenced by company name, location, and product/SIC code. Available on diskette for $400.

New Hampshire

Department of Research and Economic Development, Industrial Development Office, 172 Pembroke Road, P.O. Box 856, Concord NH 03302-0856; (603) 271-2591. $34.75. Listing of 4,800 companies includes name, address, phone, CEO, ranking officers, year established, sales volume, import/export, products, and SIC code. Cross-referenced by company name, location, and product/SIC code. Available on IBM compatible diskette for $250/set of 4 + $4.74 postage and handling.

New Jersey

Commerce Register, Inc., 190 Godwin Avenue, Midland Park, NJ 07432; (800) 221-2172. $92.50. Listing of 11,000 companies includes name, address, phone, key personnel, sales volume, products, employee figures, square footage and acreage occupied, year established, SIC code, and bank, accountants, and law firms used. Cross-referenced by company name, location, and product/SIC code. Available on diskette for $153 minimum charge, depending on number of listings ordered.

New Mexico

Department of Economic Development, Joseph M. Montoya Building, 1100 St. Francis Dr., Santa Fe, NM 87503; (505) 827-0300. $25. Listing of 1,800 companies includes name, address, phone, CEO, employee figures, products/services, and SIC code. Cross-referenced by company name, location, and product/SIC code.

New York

MacRAE's Industrial Directories, 817 Broadway, 3rd Floor, New York, NY 10003; (800) 622-7237. $135. Listing of 12,000 companies includes name, address, phone, key personnel, size classification, products, location, and SIC code.

North Carolina

North Carolina Business Industry, Dept. D, P.O. Box 25249, Raleigh, NC 27611; (919) 733-4151. $52.50. The new edition of 7,000 companies includes name, address, phone, CEO, year established, employee figures, parent company, import/export, product, and purchasing and product SIC codes. Cross-referenced by company name, location, parent company, product, products purchased, and import/export capabilities. Available on IBM magnetic tape database format for $1,000.

North Dakota

North Dakota Department of Economic Development and Finance, 1833 E. Bismarck Express, Bismarck, ND 58504; (701) 224-2810. $20. Listing of over 600 companies includes name, address, phone, contact person, employee figures, products, and SIC code. Cross-referenced by company name, location, and product/SIC code.

Ohio

Harris Publishing Company, 2057 Aurora Road, Twinsburg, OH 44087; (800) 321-9136. $130.15. Listing of 18,000 companies includes name, address, phone, CEO, employee figures, year established, annual sales, computer brand used, products, and SIC code. Cross-referenced by company name, location, product, and SIC code. Diskette format, containing 8,700 companies with 20 or more employees, available for $308.75.

Oklahoma

Oklahoma Department of Commerce, P.O. Box 26980, Marketing Division, Oklahoma City, OK 73126-0980; (405) 843-9770, ext. 207. $40. Listing of 4,500 companies includes name, address, phone, owner's name, employee figures, product, and SIC code. Cross-referenced by company name, location, product, and SIC code.

Oregon

Oregon Economic Development Department, 775 Summer Street, NE, Salem, OR 97310; (503) 373-1200. $60. Listing of 7,500 companies includes name, phone, employee figures, parent company, CEO, import/export, products, and SIC code. Cross-referenced by company name, product, and SIC code. Available in database formats and mailing labels at variable cost.

Pennsylvania

Harris Publishing Company, 2057 Aurora Road, Twinsburg, OH 44087; (800) 321-9136. $130.15. Listing of 18,000 companies includes name, address, phone, CEO, employee figures, computer brand used, year established, products, and SIC code. Cross-referenced by company name, location, product, and SIC code. IBM compatible diskette format, containing 8,800 companies with 20 or more employees, available for $308.75.

Rhode Island

Department of Economic Development, Research Division, 7 Jackson Walkway, Providence, RI 02903; (401) 277-2601. $10 for RI residents; $30 for non-residents. Listing of 2,600 companies includes name, address, phone, CEO, employee figures, parent company, products, and SIC code. Cross-referenced by company name, location, and SIC code. Available on IBM or MacIntosh compatible diskette for $50. Mailing labels: 5 cents per name.

South Carolina

State Development Board, P.O. Box 927, Columbia, SC 29202; (803) 737-0400. Attn: Industrial Directory sales. $60. Listing of 3,200 companies includes name, address, phone, CEO, geographical location, purchasing agent, employee figures, product line, parent company, and SIC code. Cross-referenced by company name, location, product, and SIC code. Available on IBM compatible diskette for $500. Mailing labels: $50 set up fee, 10 cents per label.

South Dakota

Governor's Office of State Economic Development, Capitol Lake Plaza, Pierre, SD 57501; (605) 773-5032. $35. Listing of 1,000 companies includes name, address, phone number, trade name, county, FAX number, marketing area, employee figures, CEO, purchasing agent, sales manager, products, and SIC code. Cross-referenced by company name, location, and SIC code. Mailing labels: $35/set.

Tennessee

M. Lee Smith Publishers and Printers, P.O. Box 198867, Arcade Station, Nashville, TN 37219; (615) 242-7395. $68 in-state; $65 out-of-state. Listing of 5,300 companies includes name, address, phone, parent company, key personnel, employee figures, marketing area, computer brand used, products, and SIC code. Available in database format, magnetic tape or diskette: $100 conversion fee, then $250 per 1,000 chosen. Mailing labels: $90 per 1,000. Diskette is available for $395. Diskette and book available for $345.

Texas

University of Texas, Bureau of Business Research, P.O. Box 7459, Austin, TX 78713-7459; (512) 471-1616. $120. Two volume directory of 17,000 companies includes name, address, phone, key personnel, year established, sales volume, employee figures, market area, import/export, products, and SIC code. Volume 1 lists companies by name; volume 2 lists companies by product/SIC code. Available on diskette for $400 per 2,000 companies.

Utah

Utah Department of Community and Economic Development, 324 S. State St., Suite 500, Salt Lake City, UT 84111; (801) 538-8700. $26. Listing of 2,600 companies includes name, address, phone, employee figures, products, and SIC

State Company Directories

code. Cross-referenced by company name and SIC code. Available in dBase 3 database format, high or low density diskettes. Prices may vary.

Cross-referenced by company name, location, products, and SIC code. Diskette available for $495. Mailing labels, $65/1,000.

Vermont

Agency of Development and Community Affairs, Pavilion Office Building, Montpelier, VT 05609; (802) 828-3221. $12. Listing of 1,300 companies includes name, address, phone, geographical listing, plant location, CEO, parent company products trade names, products exported, employee figures, retail/mailorder/or wholesale distribution, and SIC code. Cross-referenced by company name, location, and product/SIC code. Available on diskette for $300.

Virginia

Virginia Chamber of Commerce, 9 South 5th Street, Richmond, VA 23219; (804) 644-1607. $78.38 in-state; $75 out-of-state. Listing of 4,000 companies includes name, address, phone, CEO, employee figures parent company, products, and SIC code. Cross-referenced by product, SIC code, county, and city. Available in ASCII and ABCDIC magnetic tape database formats for $225. Mailing labels vary in price.

Washington

Database Publishing Company, 523 Superior Avenue, Newport Beach, CA 92663; (800) 888-8434. $99. Listing of 4,100 companies includes name, address, phone, CEO, key personnel, sales volume, year established, parent company, products, computer brand used, employee figures, import/export, product, and SIC code.

West Virginia

Harris Publishing Company, 2057 Aurora Rd., Twinsburg, OH 44087; (800) 321-9136. $42.75. Listing of 1,200 companies includes name, address, phone, CEO, employee figures, computer brand used, year established, products, and SIC code. Cross-referenced by company name, location, product, and SIC code.

Wisconsin

WMC Service Corporation, P.O. Box 352, 501 East Washington Street, Madison, WI 53701-0352; (608) 258-3400. $89.68/member, $131.88/non-member. Listing of 9,000 companies includes name, address, phone, CEO, year established, computer brand used, employee figures, parent company, FAX #, import/export, out-of-state affiliates, products, and SIC code. Cross-referenced by company name, location, product, and SIC code. Available on IBM compatible diskette $300/member, $450/non-member.

Wyoming

Department of Commerce, Division of Economic and Community Development, Barrett Bldg. 4 North, Cheyenne, WY 82002; (307) 777-7284. No charge. Listing of 250 companies includes name, address, phone, CEO, market area, employee figures, product, and SIC code. Cross-referenced by company name, location, and SIC code.

Be patient. If any phone number is incorrect, call (area code) 555-1212 and request the new listing.

State Securities and Stockbrokers

State Securities Offices Offer Company Information, Mailing List of Brokers and More

The offices of state security regulators offer financial data on thousands of companies which are not required to file with the U.S. Securities and Exchange Commission as well as the names, addresses, financial data, and consumer information on thousands of stockbrokers and broker-dealers.

State regulation of the sale of securities in the United States began in 1911 when the Kansas legislature passed the first securities law. North Carolina enacted a law the same year; Arizona and Louisiana did so in 1912. By 1919, 32 states had followed suit. Now, all states and the federal government have laws regulating the sale of corporate securities, bonds, investment contracts and stocks.

The reason for these laws is simple enough: they protect the public, unfamiliar with the intricacies of investing, against deceitful promoters and their often worthless stocks. This is the same type of function that the U.S. Securities and Exchange Commission performs in Washington, DC. The United States covers companies trading stocks across state boundaries, and the states cover companies trading stocks within their state. The laws -- called Blue Sky laws -- prevent speculative schemes "which have no more basis than so many feet of blue sky," according to the Commerce Clearing House Blue Sky Law Reports.

The Blue Sky Law is usually administered by each state's Securities Commission or Securities Division. Securities to be sold within a state must register with this office. If the issuer is a corporation, for example, it must submit the following information:

- articles of incorporation
- purpose of proposed business
- names and addresses of officers and directors
- qualifications and business history of applicant - detailed financial data

Each state, however, has numerous exemptions. Securities issued by national banks, savings and loan associations, non-profit organizations, public utilities, and railroads are usually exempt from the Blue Sky laws, as are securities listed on the stock exchange, those issued by companies registered with the U.S. Securities and Exchange Commission, and those issued by foreign governments with which the U.S. has diplomatic relations.

Securities offices also require broker-dealer firms, the agents (or sales representatives), and investments advisers wanting to work in the state to file applications.

Agents wanting to work in one or more states now apply for registration by filing with National Association of Securities Dealers' Central Registration Depository (CRD). To keep the CRD current, agents must submit all pertinent employment and application changes. All state securities offices are hooked up to the CRD through computer terminals and use them to monitor agents registered or applying to register in their jurisdictions as well as any complaints filed against individuals.

Most states also use the system for registration of broker-dealer firms. Information kept in the repository will include registration applications, amendments to applications, complaints on file, and so forth. The purpose is to reduce the amount of paperwork for the states and to promote more uniformity.

The system is not set to accept broker-dealers' audited financial statements or annual reports so applicants will have to continue to file in the states requiring them. The broker-dealer phase of the CRD is now in operation. Several states are now trying to determine what, if any, information they will require broker-dealers to file with their securities divisions. Most of those states that have made a decision said they will continue to require annual financial reports to be filed with their offices.

Below are the names, addresses and telephone numbers for the state securities offices. Most of these offices will routinely provide information over the phone on whether specific companies, agents, or broker-dealers are registered in their states. Requests for more detailed information may have to be submitted in writing.

Securities Offices

Alabama
Securities Commission, 770 Washington Ave., Suite 570, Montgomery, AL 36130; (205) 242-2984.

Alaska
Division of Banking, Securities and Corporations, Department of Commerce and Economic Development, State Office Building #94, PO Box 110807, Juneau, AK 99811-0807; (907) 465-2521.

Arizona
Securities Division, Arizona Corporation Commission, 1200 West Washington St., Suite 201, Phoenix, AZ 85007; (602) 542-4242.

Arkansas
Securities Department, Heritage West Building, Third Floor, 201 East Markham, Little Rock, AR 72201; (501) 324-9260.

California
Securities Regulation Division, Department of Corporations, 3700 Wilshire Blvd., 6th Floor, Los Angeles, CA 90010; (213) 736-2741.

Colorado
Division of Securities, Department of Regulatory Agencies, 1580 Lincoln, Suite 420, Denver, CO 80203; (303) 894-2320.

State Securities and Stockbrokers

Connecticut
Securities and Business Investments Division, Department of Banking, Securities and Business, 44 Capitol Ave., Hartford, CT 06106; (203) 566-4560.

Delaware
Division of Securities, Department of Justice, 8th Floor, Civil Division, 820 North French St., Wilmington, DE 19801; (302) 577-2515.

District of Columbia
Division of Securities, DC Public Service Commission, 450 5th St., NW, Suite 821, Washington, DC 20001; (202) 626-5105.

Florida
Division of Securities and Investor Protection, Department of Banking and Finance, Office of Comptroller, The Capitol, LL-22, Tallahassee, FL 32399-0350; (904) 488-9805.

Georgia
Business Services and Regulations, Office of Secretary of State, Suite 315 West Tower, Two Martin Luther King Dr., Atlanta, GA 30334; (404) 656-2894.

Hawaii
Business Registration Division, Department of Commerce and Consumer Affairs, 1010 Richards St., PO Box 40, Honolulu, HI 96810; (808) 586-2737.

Idaho
Securities Bureau, Department of Finance, 700 West State St., Boise, ID 83720-2700; (208) 334-3684.

Illinois
Securities Department, Office of Secretary of State, 900 South Spring St., Springfield, IL 62704; (217) 782-2256.

Indiana
Securities Division, Office of Secretary of State, 302 W. Washington, Room E-111, Indianapolis, IN 46204; (317) 232-6681.

Iowa
Securities Bureau, Office of Commissioner of Insurance, Lucas State Office Building, 2nd Floor, Des Moines, IA 50319; (515) 281-4441.

Kansas
Office of Securities Commissioner, 618 S. Kansas, 2nd Floor, Topeka, KS 66603-3804; (913) 296-3307.

Kentucky
Division of Securities, Department of Financial Institutions, 477 Versailles Rd., Frankfort, KY 40601; (502) 564-3390.

Louisiana
Securities Commission, 1100 Poydras Street, Suite #2250, New Orleans, LA 70163; (504) 568-5515.

Maine
Securities Division, Bureau of Banking, Department of Professional and Financial Regulation, State House Station 121, Augusta, ME 04333; (207) 582-8760.

Maryland
Division of Securities, Office of Attorney General, 200 St. Paul Place, 21st Floor, Baltimore, MD 21202-2020; (410) 576-6360.

Massachusetts
Securities Division, Department of Secretary of State, 1719 John W. McCormack Building, One Ashburton Place, Boston, MA 02108; (617) 727-3548.

Michigan
Corporation and Securities Bureau, Department of Commerce, 6546 Merchantile Way, Lansing, MI 48909; (517) 334-6200.

Minnesota
Registration and Licensing Division, Department of Commerce, 133 East 7th Street, St. Paul, MN 55101; (612) 296-4026.

Mississippi
Securities Division, Office of Secretary of State, P.O. Box 136, Jackson, MS 39205; (601) 359-1350.

Missouri
Office of Secretary of State, 600 West Main, Jefferson City, MO 65101; (314) 751-4136.

Montana
Securities Department, State Auditor's Office, 126 North Sanders, Room 270, Helena, MT 59620; (406) 444-2040.

Nebraska
Bureau of Securities, Department of Banking and Finance, 1200 N Street, The Atrium #311, Lincoln, NE 68508; (402) 471-3445.

Nevada
Securities Division, Office of Secretary of State, 1771 E. Flamingo Rd., Suite 212-B, Las Vegas, NV 89158; (702) 486-4440.

New Hampshire
Department of State, Bureau of Securities Regulation, State House, Room 204, Concord, NH 03301-4989; (603) 271-1463.

New Jersey
Bureau of Securities, 153 Halsey Street, 6th Floor, Newark, NJ 07101; (201) 648-2040.

New Mexico
Securities Division, Regulation and Licensing Department, 725 St. Michaels Dr., P.O. Box 25101, Santa Fe, NM 87501; (505) 827-7140.

New York
Bureau of Investor Protection and Securities, Department of Law, 120 Broadway, 23rd Fl., New York, NY 10271; (212) 416-8200.

North Carolina
Securities Division, Department of State, 300 N Salisbury St., Suite 1000, Raleigh, NC 27603; (919) 733-3924.

North Dakota
Office of Securities Commissioner, 600 E. Boulevard, 5th Floor, Bismarck, ND 58505; (701) 224-2910.

Ohio
Division of Securities, Department of Commerce, 77 South High St, 22nd Fl., Columbus, OH 43266-0548; (614) 644-7381.

Oklahoma
Department of Securities, 2401 North Lincoln Blvd., 4th Fl., Oklahoma City, OK 73152; (405) 521-2451.

Oregon
Division of Finance and Corporate Securities, Department of Insurance and Finance, 21 Labor and Industries Bldg., Salem, OR 97310; (503) 378-4387.

Pennsylvania
Securities Commission, Division of Licensing and Compliance, 1010 North Seventh St., Second Floor, Harrisburg, PA 17102-1410; (717) 787-8061.

Rhode Island
Securities Division, Department of Business Regulation, 233 Richmond St., #232, Providence, RI 02903-4232; (401) 277-3048.

South Carolina
Securities Division, Department of State, 1205 Pendelton St., #501, Columbia, SC 29201; (803) 734-1087.

South Dakota
Division of Securities, Department of Commerce and Regulation, 118 W. Capitol, Pierre, SD 57501-2017; (605) 773-4823.

Be patient. If any phone number is incorrect, call (area code) 555-1212 and request the new listing.

Information on People, Companies, and Mailing Lists

Tennessee
Division of Securities, Department of Commerce and Insurance, Volunteer Plaza, Suite 680, 500 James Robinson Pkwy., Nashville, TN 37243; (615) 741-3187.

Texas
State Securities Board, 221 W. 6th Street, Suite 700, Austin, TX 78701; (512) 474-2233.

Utah
Securities Division, Department of Business Regulation, P.O. Box 45808, Salt Lake City, UT 84145-0808; (801) 530-6600.

Vermont
Securities Division, Department of Banking and Insurance, 89 Main Street, Drawer 20, Montpelier, VT 05620-3101; (802) 828-3420.

Virginia
Division of Securities and Retail Franchising, State Corporation Commission, PO Box 1197, Richmond, VA 23209; (804) 371-9051.

Washington
Securities Division, Department of Licensing, PO Box 9033, 405 Black Lake Blvd., SW, 2nd Floor, Olympia, WA 98507-9033; (206) 753-6928.

West Virginia
Securities Division, State Auditor's Office, Room W-118, State Capitol, Charleston, WV 25305; (304) 558-2257.

Wisconsin
Office of Commissioner of Securities, 101 East Wilson St., P.O. Box 1768, Madison, WI 53701; (608) 266-3431.

Wyoming
Securities Division, Office of the Secretary of State, State Capitol Building, Cheyenne, WY 82002; (307) 777-7370.

Be patient. If any phone number is incorrect, call (area code) 555-1212 and request the new listing.

Food and Drug Companies

If you are seeking information on sanitation or safety conditions at a particular restaurant, fast food franchise, or meat packing facility and don't want to wade through masses of information maintained by the federal government, you can always start at the state level. All state departments of health have a division that oversees the inspection and certification of food processing, storing, and serving facilities in the state.

This information might be valuable if you were interested in buying into a facility or if you have a new product that you want to market in a specific area, say sanitation shields for salad bars. Conversely, having state records can add weight to your argument if you want to close an offensive facility down, such as a slaughterhouse or noisy neighborhood bar.

Among the types of facilities most state offices regulate are:

- food processing plants
- food storage facilities
- non-alcoholic bottling plants
- public accommodations (AL)
- vending machines (CT)
- school lunch programs (NH)
- bed and breakfast facilities (NH)
- wineries (OR)

License and inspection forms are a matter of public record in most states and may be obtained by submitting a Freedom of Information Act (FOI) request. The license form will include the address of the facility, the owner's name, and the number of people employed at the facility. Inspection forms provide information on:

- structure of facility
- construction of equipment
- condition of equipment
- sanitation procedures
- how products are handled
- type of labeling
- type of packaging
- safety violations

State offices responsible for regulating the manufacture, distribution, and sale of drugs can provide computer listings of the facilities that they license and inspect.

The types of facilities most often regulated are:

- pharmacies
- drug manufacturers
- drug wholesalers
- medical device manufacturers
- research institutions using controlled substances or hazardous materials

Food And Drug Offices

Alabama

Department of Public Health, Division of Environmental Health, 515 W. Jeff Davis Ave., Montgomery, AL 36104; (205) 263-6671. This agency acts as a consultative agency and oversees the inspections of food plants and warehouses. Most of their inspections are done at the county level. The Environmental Health Division inspects and certifies all aspects of environmental health including food processing, storing and serving facilities; sanitation procedures, and safety violations. They have computerized their inspection and licensing data and will provide free printouts upon request. Licensing and inspections forms are also available through the department's legal office.

Alabama State Board of Pharmacy, 1 Perimeter Park South, Suite 425 South, Birmingham, AL 35243; (205) 967-0130. This agency licenses and inspects all state pharmacies, drug manufacturers and drug wholesalers. Application and inspection records are confidential. Some of the information has been computerized and a computer listing and mailing labels are available only if the information is to be used for continuing education purposes. A mailing list of state pharmacists is $84 and a list of pharmacies costs $25.

Alaska

Department of Environmental Conservation, Division of Environmental Health, 410 Willobough Ave., Suite 105, Juneau, AK 99801-1795; (907) 465-5280. This agency licenses and inspects restaurants, food processors, storage facilities, public accommodations, and bottling companies. Some information is stored on the computer and is available upon request. Lists of businesses are provided upon request at no charge.

Department of Commerce and Economic Development, Division of Occupational Licensing, P.O. Box D-LIC, Juneau, AK 99811. (907) 465-2534. This department licenses and inspects pharmacies, drug manufacturers and wholesalers.

Arizona

State Department of Health Services, Food Protection and Institutional Sanitation Section, 3008 N. 3rd St., Suite 207, Phoenix, AZ 85012; (602) 230-5912. Most inspections and permits are issued on the county level. This office inspects institutions contracted by the FDA and includes wholesale food manufacturers. The county is responsible for retail food and food processors. A mailing list is available for those places it inspects (around 100). Prices vary according to the nature of the request.

State Board of Pharmacy, 5060 N. 19th Ave. Suite 101, Phoenix, AZ 85015; (602) 255-5125. The State Board of Pharmacy licenses and inspects pharmacies, drug wholesalers and manufacturers. Inspection reports are available to the public. Information can be retrieved and a computer printout provided. A mailing list is available and can be sorted in any form needed.

Arkansas

Environmental Health Protection, Department of Health, Division of Sanitation Services, 4815 West Markham, Little Rock, AR 72205; (501) 661-2171. This department provides management to county agencies for inspection of retail food operations. The state is responsible for inspecting canning plants, bottling plants and manufactured milk plants. It has a contract with FDA to inspect their inventories. Individuals can receive a listing of selected facilities and inspection reports upon completion of a Freedom of Information request. Listings are $.25 per page.

Board of Pharmacy, 320 W. Capitol, Suite 802, Little Rock, AR 72201; (501) 324-9200. This agency inspects and licenses retail and hospital pharmacies, wholesale drug distributors, and medical device manufacturers. Computer listings and mailing labels are available upon written request. Application forms are public information. Computer listings of pharmacists are $75. A listing of pharmacies is $55. A complete set of pharmacy mailing labels is $75. Labels for pharmacists cost $100.

Be patient. If any phone number is incorrect, call (area code) 555-1212 and request the new listing.

Information on People, Companies, and Mailing Lists

California

State Department of Health Section, Food and Drug Branch, 601 N. 7th St., Sacramento, CA 95814; (916) 445-2263. This agency licenses and inspects food processing, packaging and storage facilities; bottled water plants, cold storage facilities, shellfish processors, frozen food lockers, water vending machines, drug and medical device manufacturers, and water haulers. Ceramic tableware manufacturers must register with the agency so that they can collect tableware samples for safety testing. Information from application forms is generally available unless the firm is under current investigation for possible violations of the law that could result in civil or criminal investigation. Licensing programs are on a database but the agency's ability to generate specific reports varies considerably depending upon the request. Computer printouts are $.25 per page. If a legal review is required before data are released, there is an extra charge. Mailing labels are available for some programs. Fees vary according to the scope of the request.

State Board of Pharmacy, 400 R St., Suite 4070, Sacramento, CA 95814; (916) 323-7018. This agency licenses and inspects pharmacies and drug wholesalers. A mailing list of the entire file is available. The list can be sorted by county, zip code. The minimum order for mailing labels or printed lists is $100.

Colorado

Colorado Department of Health, Division of Consumer Protection, 4300 Cherry Creek Drive South, Denver, CO 80222-1530; (303) 692-2000. This office inspects restaurants, retail markets, food processing plants and food warehouses, dairy farms and milk plants, schools, child care centers licensed by social services, summer camps and group homes, hotels and motels on complaint, campgrounds, and corrections facilities. It also inspects drug manufacturers, wholesalers and medical device manufacturers.

Board of Pharmacy, 1560 Broadway, Suite 1310 , Denver, CO 80202-5146; (303) 894-7750. The Board of Pharmacy licenses pharmacists and inspects and licenses state pharmacies. The office provides mailing lists and labels of both pharmacies and pharmacists. Costs range from $113 to $130. Requests must be placed in writing and be accompanied by a check.

Connecticut

State Department of Consumer Protection, Food Division, State Office Building, 165 Capitol Ave., Room 167, Hartford, CT 06106; (203) 566-3388. This department licenses non-alcoholic beverage manufacturers including bottled water; bakeries, frozen dessert manufacturers, vending machines, and apple juice ciders. It inspects all food warehouses plus those listed above. Information from application forms is public. The office provides listings of licensed establishments. Information will soon be computerized. Lists of licensed plants are free.

State Department of Consumer Protection, Division of Drug Control, State Office Building, 165 Capitol Ave., Hartford, CT 06106; (203) 566-4490. This agency licenses and inspects drug manufacturers and wholesalers. They oversee the inspection and regulation of retail pharmacies, hospitals, nursing homes, public and private clinics, and on a limited basis, dentists, physicians, nurses and veterinarians. Mailing lists are not provided but routine inspection reports can be obtained.

Professional Licensing Division, Division of Consumer Protection, Commission of Pharmacy, State Office Building, 165 Capitol Ave., Hartford, CT 06106; (203) 566-4832. This agency inspects pharmacies, pharmacists and convenience stores. Requests must be made in writing and approved by the Board. Lists can be sorted into alphabetical, numerical or zip code order. Mailing labels cost $50, printouts cost $40.

Delaware

State Department of Public Health, Office of Food and Milk Protection, P.O. Box 637, Jesse Cooper Building, Dover, DE 19903; (302) 739-3841. This agency inspects and licenses milk processors, restaurants, water distribution systems, dairy farms, and non-alcoholic bottling centers. Most inspections are done at the county level. They do not oversee wholesale food processor plants since this is regulated by the USDA. A listing of licensed facilities can be obtained at $.25 per page.

State Department of Health and Social Services, Division of Narcotics and Dangerous Drugs, Delaware Board of Pharmacy, Jesse Cooper Building, P.O Box 637, Room 205, Dover, DE 19903, (302) 739-4798. This agency regulates any facility in which drugs are prescribed, dispensed and stored and runs routine compliance inspections. They oversee the inspection and regulation of retail pharmacies, hospitals, nursing homes, public and private clinics, and on a limited basis, dentists, physicians, and veterinarians. Their data has been computerized and a mailing list of pharmacists and pharmacies is available for $25. The office also responds to consumer complaints against pharmacies and physicians that prescribe controlled drugs.

District of Columbia

Department of Consumer Regulatory Affairs, Business Regulations Administration, Food Protection Branch, 614 H Street, NW, Room 616, Washington, DC 20001; (202) 727-7250. This agency inspects and licenses approximately 1,800 District restaurants and all food processing, packaging and storage facilities. A listing of licensed restaurants is available upon request. Costs of listings vary and are based upon the amount of computer time needed to complete the request.

Board of Pharmacy, Department of Consumer and Regulatory Affairs, Pharmaceutical, Radiological and Medical Devices Control Division, Room 1016, 614 H Street, NW, Washington, DC 20001; (202) 727-7223. This office licenses all pharmacies, drug manufacturers and wholesalers in the District of Columbia and oversees the regulation of radiological and medical devices. A computer listing of regulated agencies is available upon written request. Fees for services vary according to the complexity of the request.

Florida

State Department of Agriculture and Consumer Services, Bureau of Food Grade and Standards, Lab Complex M-A, 3125 Conner Blvd., Tallahassee, FL 32399; (904) 488-3951. This bureau oversees the inspection and certification of over 22,000 food storing and serving facilities and certain food processing plants. This includes food processors, distributors, and retail stores. They do not, however, inspect meat and poultry facilities. The office provides a listing of licensed facilities at $.25 per page. Mailing labels are not available.

State Department of Health and Rehabilitative Services, Pharmacy Program Office, 2633 Mahan Dr., Tallahassee, FL 32308 ; (904) 487-1257. This department licenses and inspects retail pharmacies, prescription drug wholesalers and manufacturers; cosmetic manufacturers, device manufacturers, compressed medical gas distributors and wholesalers; and medical oxygen retail establishments. The office all inspects consumer complaints lodged against physicians, pharmacies or clinics. A listing of facilities that have obtained permits is available, free of charge. License application forms are available to the public.

Georgia

Department of Agriculture, Consumer Field Forces Division, 19 Martin Luther King Jr. Drive, Atlanta, GA 30334; (404) 656-3627. This department licenses and inspects food processors, producers, distributors and warehouses; grocery stores, wholesale seafood dealers, soft drink and bottled water manufacturers, and bedding manufacturers. This office does not routinely provide mailing lists of inspected facilities. However, the Georgia Department of Industry Trade and Tourism publishes a yearly *Georgia Manufacturing Directory* which lists information on over 9,300 manufacturing plants. For ordering information, call (404) 656-3619.

State Drugs and Narcotics Agency, Board of Pharmacy, 166 Pryor St. S.W., Atlanta, GA 30303; (404) 656-3912. This agency licenses and inspects pharmacies, drug manufacturers, and wholesalers. A mailing list of licensed facilities is available for $170. Requests should be in writing, and checks may be made out to the Board of Pharmacy. The board also provides license application information.

Hawaii

State Department of Health, Kinau Hale Building, 1250 Punchbowl St., P.O. Box 3378, Honolulu, HI 96801; (808) 586-4725. This agency is divided into a number of sections. None offer mailing lists. The Food Products Section inspects for misbranded and adulterated products and medical devices. The Consumer Products Section licenses and inspects food processors, warehouses, manufacturers and bottling plants. The Food Contamination Section oversees pesticides, frozen desserts, and monitors lead content in tableware. Inspection reports are available upon request.

Dept. of Commerce and Consumer Affairs, State Board of Pharmacy, 1010 Richards St., P.O. Box 3469, Honolulu, HI 96801; (808) 586-2698. This agency inspects and licenses pharmacies and pharmacists. A roster of pharmacies sorted alphabetically is $12.75. Requests should be made in writing and accompanied by a check made out to the Department of Commerce.

Food and Drug Administration, P.O. Box 50061, Honolulu, HI 96810; (808) 541-2661. This office licenses and inspects drug manufacturers, processors, re-

Be patient. If any phone number is incorrect, call (area code) 555-1212 and request the new listing.

Food and Drug Companies

labelers, packagers and wholesalers once a year. For information concerning a particular company, write a letter with your specific question to the Office of Legal Affairs at the address listed above.

Idaho

State Department of Health and Welfare, Food Protection Program, Bureau of Communicable Disease Prevention, Division of Health, H&W, 450 W. State St., Boise, ID 83720; (208) 334-5938. This agency consults with local health departments and monitors their performances. Inspections are done at the local level. The State Food Program Coordinator can answer general questions about an establishment or will find out specific information upon request.

Board of Pharmacy, 280 N. 8th, St., Suite 20450, Boise, ID 83720; (208) 334-2356. This agency inspects drug manufacturers, wholesalers, distributors, re-packers and non-pharmacy outlets. Mailing lists and labels are available. A listing of licensed pharmacies is $10 and pharmacists is $20. Mailing labels are provided at the same price. Lists can be sorted by zip code order or by type of facility.

Illinois

Department of Public Health, Division of Food, Drugs and Devices, 525 W. Jefferson St., Springfield, IL 62761; (217) 785-2439. There is no licensing program in Illinois. This office inspects: bottling plants, candy and cookie manufacturers, bakeries, warehouses, food processors and dairy manufacturing plants. This office also inspects drug manufacturers and medical device manufacturers. Computer listings of inspected facilities are available for $.25 per page. Inspection forms, including a description summary, are also available for $.10 per page upon written request.

State Board of Pharmacy, Office of Drug Compliance, 100 W. Randolph, Suite 9-300, Chicago, IL 60601; (312) 814-4573. This agency licenses and inspects pharmacies, drug manufacturers, wholesalers and distributors of controlled substances. Computer printouts of pharmacies and pharmacists are $58.90, each. If you provide your own mailing labels they will print the information on them for the price quoted above. Labels must be three columns across, and 4 by 1 and 7/16 inches in size.

Indiana

State Board of Health, Divisions of Retail and Manufactured Foods, 1330 West Michigan St., P.O. Box 1964, Room 136 Indianapolis, IN 46206; (317) 633-0360. This agency is divided into two divisions, retail foods and manufactured foods. The manufactured foods division licenses and inspects wholesale food processors, bottling plants, warehouses, and manufacturers. The retail foods division inspects state facilities such as the State Fair and local health departments. It also handles consumer complaints. Mailing lists are not available for commercial purposes.

State Board of Pharmacy, 402 W. Washington St, Room 041, Indianapolis, IN 46204; (317) 232-2960. In addition to inspecting pharmacies, this agency licenses pharmacists, and wholesale legend drug distributors. Under a separate division it also licenses optometrists who wish to prescribe legend drugs. The agency also contains a controlled substance advisory committee that licenses anyone who manufactures, distributes or performs research with controlled substances. Mailing lists and labels are both available. There is a base fee of $20 per listing and an additional few cents per mailing label. Individuals must first complete an application and information is released at the agency's discretion.

Iowa

State Department of Inspections and Appeals, 2nd Floor, Lucas Building, Des Moines, IA 50319; (515) 281-6538. This agency licenses and inspects all food related businesses, motels and hotels. They inspect but do not license barbers and cosmetologists. Computer listings are available for $12 per listing. Files are sorted by zip code and type of facility.

Board of Pharmacy, 1209 East Court, Des Moines, IA 50319; (515) 281-5944. This agency licenses and inspects pharmacies, drug manufacturers and distributors. Mailing lists are available. The minimum order is $20, and sorting is available by several categories. Mailing labels are also available. Requests must be made in writing. Once the agency has received your request they will forward the information to you along with an invoice.

Kansas

State Department of Health and Environment, Division of Health, Food Service, Drug and Lodging Section, 109 SW 9th St., Suite 604, Topeka, KS 66612-1271; (913) 296-1500. This agency licenses all food services, and inspects food and drug manufacturers, bakeries, bottling plants and warehouses. It also handles customer complaints. The agency no longer provides mailing lists or labels to the general public. However, the Department of Health and Environment publishes a newsletter which includes information about the Division of Health, Food Service.

Board of Pharmacy, Landon State Office Building, 900 Jackson St., Room 513, Topeka, KS 66612; (913) 296-4056. The Board of Pharmacy licenses and inspects pharmacies, distributors, retail dealers, analytical laboratories for controlled substances, and research institutions using controlled substances. Before a mailing list is released, the board must give its approval and an Open Records Act application must be completed.

Kentucky

Cabinet for Human Resources, Division of Local Health, 275 East Main St., Frankfort, KY 40621; (502) 564-3722. This agency licenses and inspects food service establishments, retail food markets, vending machines, bottling companies, frozen food lockers, shellfish re-packers, food salvage dealers, food processing plants and food warehouses. Copies of information can be obtained for $.25 per page. Computer research time requires an additional fee.

Board of Pharmacy, 1228 U.S. 127 South, Frankfort, KY 40601; (502) 564-3833. This agency licenses and inspects drug manufacturers, wholesalers, pharmacies, and grants licenses to pharmacists and pharmacy interns. Listings and self-adhering mailing labels of pharmacists and pharmacies are provided. Information is available in zip code, county or alphabetical order. A listing of licensed pharmacists is $50, a listing of pharmacies, $35. Checks may be made out to the Kentucky State Treasurer's Office and mailed to the above address. Orders may take up to two weeks to complete.

Louisiana

State Department of Health and Human Resources, Food and Drug Control Unit, 325 Loyola Avenue, P.O. Box 60630, New Orleans, 70160 (504) 568-5402. This agency licenses and inspects warehouses, manufacturers, distributors and re-packers. Computer lists are available, but are not released for commercial purposes. To receive a listing send a written request to William Swiler, Program Manager, at the address listed above. Be very specific concerning the purpose of your request. Once the office has received your letter they will inform you of costs.

Board of Pharmacy, 5615 Corporate Blvd., #8, Baton Rouge, LA 70808-2537; (504) 925-6496. This agency licenses pharmacists and licenses and inspects pharmacies and manufacturers. Approved requests for mailing labels are provided through the Louisiana Pharmacists Association. There is a base charge of $210 for the service and $.10 per label. Call (504) 767-7115 for details.

Maine

State Department of Agriculture, Division of Regulations, State House Station 28, Augusta, ME 04333; (207) 289-3841. This department licenses and inspects food processors, bakeries, bottling plants, warehouses, mobile vendors and retail stores. Computer listings are available for $1 per sheet. Sorting can only be done by type of facility.

Board of Pharmacy, State House Station 35, Augusta, ME 04333; (207) 783-9769. This agency licenses and inspects pharmacies, drug manufacturers and drug wholesalers. Mailing lists are available for $20. Mailing labels are available for $30.

Maryland

Department of Health and Mental Hygiene, Division of Food Control, 4201 Patterson Ave., Baltimore, MD 21215; (410) 764-3539. This agency acts as a consultant to counties for their inspection programs, and provides back-up support and guidance. It inspects and licenses all wholesale food facilities. This includes warehouses, food processors, and distributors. Computer listings of licensed facilities are available upon written request.

Department of Health and Mental Hygiene, Drug Control Division, 4201 Patterson Ave., Baltimore, MD 21215; (410) 764-2890. This division licenses pharmacies and drug manufacturers. It also inspects wholesale pharmacies and does field work inspection for the Board of Pharmacy. The division enforces state drug law enforcement of controlled substances, prescription and non-prescription drugs. Application information is open to the public for review. Copies and mailing labels of licensed facilities are available.

Massachusetts

Department of Public Health, Division of Food and Drugs, 305 South St., Jamaica Plain, MA 02130; (617) 522-3700. This department licenses and inspects food processors, warehouses, bottled water plants, bakeries, and distributors.

Be patient. If any phone number is incorrect, call (area code) 555-1212 and request the new listing.

Information on People, Companies, and Mailing Lists

Computer listings can be generated upon written request. There is a charge of $.20 per page plus $6 for staff computer time.

State Board of Pharmacy, State Office Building, Government Center, 100 Cambridge St., Boston, MA 02202; (617) 727-7390. This agency licenses pharmacists, pharmacies and wholesalers. A mailing list, labels or magnetic tape can be purchased, sorted by zip code or alphabetical order. A written request is required. A mailing list of pharmacies is $120. A listing of pharmacists is $320. Information on mailing labels and computer tape costs $200 for the first 1,000 names and $50 for each additional name.

Michigan

Department of Agriculture, Food Division, P.O. Box 30017, Lansing, MI 48909; (517) 373-1060. This office licenses and inspects food processors, canners, distributors, warehouses and grocery stores. Computer listings are available, the charge is based on the size of the run. The file can be sorted by county, region, zip code or alphabetical order. Requests for information should be made in writing. The office will then forward you the mailing list along with an invoice.

Office of Health Services, Board of Pharmacy, P.O. Box 30018, Lansing, MI 48909; (517) 373-0620, 335-0918. This agency licenses pharmacists, and licenses and inspects pharmacies, drug manufacturers, wholesalers, and distributors. It also deals with consumer complaints lodged against health professionals. Computer lists can be generated for $.20 per page with a $20 minimum.

Minnesota

Department of Agriculture, Food Inspection Department, 90 W. Plato Blvd., St. Paul, MN 55107; (612) 296-1592. This agency licenses and inspects food manufacturers, processors, wholesalers, warehouses, and retail stores. For mailing list information contact the Minnesota Trade Office at (612) 297-4222.

Board of Pharmacy, 2700 University Ave. West, #107, St. Paul, MN 55114-1079; (612) 642-0541. The Board of Pharmacy licenses and inspects drug manufacturers, wholesalers, and pharmacies. Mailing lists and labels are available through the State of Minnesota Mailing List Service at (612) 297-2552. Information from application forms is available to the public.

Mississippi

State Department of Health, Division of Sanitation, P.O. Box 1700, Jackson, MS 39215-1700; (601) 960-7689. This agency licenses and inspects bottling plants, warehouses and waste water installers. Permits are issued to food service establishments, recreational vehicle parks, and milk plants. Computer lists are available for a fee. Send a written request to the Office of Public Records, Health Communications, Public Relations Division at the above address.

State Board of Pharmacy, Suite D, C & F Plaza, 2310 Hwy. 80 West, Jackson, MS 39204; (601) 354-6750. This office licenses and inspects drug manufacturers, wholesalers and pharmacies for instate registrants, only. It also licenses pharmacists. A computer listing of licensed pharmacists is $125. A listing of pharmacies is $100. Information is also available on peel-off labels. A listing of pharmacies is $150, a listing of pharmacists costs $200.

Missouri

State Department of Health, Bureau of Community Sanitation, P.O. Box 570, 1730 Elm St., Jefferson City, MO 65102; (314) 751-6400. This agency licenses frozen dessert manufacturers and distributors, non-alcoholic bottlers, manufacturers and distributors, hotels and motels. It also inspects retail food establishments, food plants and warehouses. Frozen desserts and hotel and motels have been computerized. The cost is $.15 per page plus $2.50 for shipping and handling.

State Board of Pharmacy, P.O. Box 625, Jefferson City, MO 65102; (314) 751-0091. This agency licenses pharmacists in addition to licensing and inspecting drug wholesalers and distributors. Mailing lists for licensed pharmacists are $15. Mailing labels for licensed pharmacists are $45. Labels for licensed pharmacies are $25. Lists may be sorted by type or by zip code.

Montana

State Department of Health and Environmental Sciences, Food and Consumer Safety Bureau, Cogswell Building, Helena, MT 59620; (406) 444-2408. This agency licenses and inspects food warehouses, manufacturers, packagers and processors. Mailing lists are available on a limited basis. Costs vary from $5 to $20, dependent upon the size of the request.

State Board of Pharmacy, 111 N. Last Chance Gulch, Helena, MT 59620; (406) 444-3737. The Board of Pharmacy licenses pharmacists and licenses and inspects drug wholesalers and manufacturers. Mailing lists are only available for continuing education purposes. Records can, however, be inspected on site.

Nebraska

State Department of Agriculture, Dairy and Foods, 301 Centennial Mall South, PO Box 95064, Lincoln, 68509; (402) 471-2536. The food division of this agency licenses and inspects food manufacturers, processors, restaurants, retail stores and warehouses. The dairy division licenses and inspects dairy producers and plants. Files are open to the public but the only way to obtain a listing is to visit the office and hand copy the information. No information is released for commercial purposes.

Bureau of Examining Boards, State Department of Health, 301 Centennial Mall South, P.O. Box 95007, Lincoln, NE 68509; (402) 471-2115. This office licenses pharmacies and all health- related professions. Wholesalers and distributors are licensed only in-state. Listings can be sorted into hospital or community pharmacies. Fees vary according to the complexity of the request.

Nevada

State Department of Human Resources, Bureau of Health Protection Services, 505 East King St., Room 103, Carson City, NV 89710; (702) 687-4750. This agency licenses all food establishments, processors and manufacturers. All application information is available to the public. The agency is in the process of setting up computer databases. Prices will vary according to the complexity of the request. This department also licenses and inspects drug manufacturers. There are so few that a hand written list can be obtained. All financial information is confidential.

State Board of Pharmacy, 1201 Terminal Way, Suite 212, Reno, NV 89502; (702) 322-0691. The Board of Pharmacy licenses pharmacists and licenses and inspects drug wholesalers, manufacturers and pharmacies. Computer listings and mailing labels are available. Mailing lists of pharmacies and pharmacists are $10, each. Sets of mailing labels are $40, each.

New Hampshire

State Department of Health and Welfare, Division of Public and Health Services, Bureau of Food Protection, Health and Welfare Building, 6 Hazen Drive, Concord, NH 03301-6527; (603) 271-4589. New Hampshire does not inspect food processors or warehouses. It licenses restaurants, grocery stores, school lunch programs, hotels, motels, and snack bars. Individuals interested in a particular file must first place their request in writing to the director. Lists of inspected facilities are free and also available upon written request.

State Board of Pharmacy, Health and Welfare Building, 57 Regional Dr., Concord, NH 03301; (603) 271-2350. The commission oversees the licensing and inspection of retail pharmacies, wholesalers, distributors and manufacturers of prescription drugs, and health clinics. It also enforces compliance standards at hospitals, nursing homes, and public and private clinics. It also makes required visits to dentists, physicians, and veterinarians to ensure that compliance standards are maintained. Computer lists of licensed pharmacists are available for $150. Mailing labels cost $200.

New Jersey

State Health Department, Consumer Health Services, Food and Milk Program, 3635 Quaker Bridge Road, Trenton, NJ 08625; (609) 984-1370. This department licenses and inspects all food and cosmetic wholesalers, processors and distributors, plus frozen desserts and milk plants. Computer listings are available from $40 to $50, dependent upon the size of the request.

State Department of Health, Office of Drug Control, CN-367, Trenton, NJ 08625-0367; (609) 984-1308. This agency licenses and inspects drug manufacturers and packagers, and licenses all medical practitioners, except chiropractors. Directories of all manufacturers and distributors are available for $37.75, each.

Board of Pharmacy. P.O. Box 45013, 1100 Raymond Blvd., Newark, NJ 07101; (201) 504-6450. This office licenses and inspects pharmacies and licenses pharmacists. Mailing lists and labels are available. Fees vary according to the size of the request.

New Mexico

State Department of Health and Environment, Environmental Improvement Division, 4131 Montgomery Ave. N.E., Santa Fe, NM 87109; (505) 827-2850. This agency licenses dairy farms and restaurants only. A listing of licensed dairy farms is $25. A separate division inspects food processors, warehouses and bottling plants. Mailing lists are available; costs vary according to the complexity of the request.

Be patient. If any phone number is incorrect, call (area code) 555-1212 and request the new listing.

Food and Drug Companies

State Board of Pharmacy, 1650 University NE, Suite 400 B, Albuquerque, NM 87102; (505) 841-9102. This agency oversees the inspection and regulation of retail pharmacies, hospitals, nursing homes, public and private clinics, drug manufacturers and wholesalers. They also license medical professionals who deal with controlled substances such as pharmacists, physicians and veterinarians. A computer listing of pharmacists or pharmacies is available. The cost is $.10 per name or company.

New York

State Department of Agriculture and Markets, Division of Food Inspection Services, One Winners Circle, Albany, NY 12235; (518) 457-4492. This agency licenses and inspects refrigerated warehouses, salvagers, distributors, and food processing plants including over 16,000 groceries. Requests for information should be placed in writing to: Gerald Moore, Freedom of Information Officer, at the address listed above. Include the purpose of your request and be as specific as possible. There is a charge of $.25 per page for information that runs over one hundred pages.

Board of Pharmacy, Cultural Education Center, Room 3035, Albany, NY 12230; (518) 474-3848. This office licenses and registers pharmacies, manufacturers, distributors, wholesalers and re-packagers. Computer listings and magnetic tapes are available with a written request. You must include the purpose of your request in your letter. Once the office has received you request it will send you an application form and list of fees.

North Carolina

State Department of Agriculture, Food and Drug Protection Division, 4000 Reedy Creek Rd., Raleigh, NC 27607; (919) 733-7366. Under a contract with FDA, this office licenses and inspects wholesale food manufacturers, warehouses, bottling plants, bakeries, and prescription drug wholesale manufacturers. Computer listings are available and can be sorted by type of industry. There is a flat fee of $15 plus $.05 per page. Listings include: name of firm, address, city, zip and phone number. Some inspection reports are available through the Public Records Act.

Board of Pharmacy, P.O. Box 459, Carrboro, NC 27510-0459; (919) 942-4454. This office licenses and inspects pharmacies. Computer lists and mailing labels are available upon written request. The cost of all state registered pharmacies is $74.94. The cost for a listing of licensed pharmacists is $180.18. If you wish a list of those pharmacists that reside in the state, the cost is $150.86.

North Dakota

Department of Health and Consolidated Laboratories, Division of Consumer Protection, 2635 E. Main St., P.O. Box 937, Bismarck, ND 58502-0937; (701) 221-6147. This agency licenses and inspects retail food establishments, bed and breakfast facilities, vending operations, bottling plants and ice manufacturers. They are under contract with FDA to inspect food warehouses and processors. Computer listings are $.25 per page. A complete listing costs approximately $100.

State Board of Pharmacy, P.O. Box 1354, Bismarck, ND 58502; (701) 258-1535. This agency licenses pharmacists and licenses and inspects all pharmacies and wholesale drug manufacturers. Mailing labels and lists of pharmacists in charge and pharmacies are available for $20 each. Information from application forms is public.

Ohio

Department of Agriculture, Division of Foods, Dairies and Drugs, 8995 E. Main St., Reynoldsburg, OH 43068; (614) 866-6361. This department licenses and inspects food processors, cold storage warehouses, grocery stores, frozen food storage facilities, canneries, syrups and extracts, frozen desserts, bottling plants, and wholesale and home bakeries. Computer listings can be generated, sorted by county or commodity. A listing of frozen desserts and bakeries is $30, each. The remaining lists are $10, each.

State Board of Pharmacy, 77 South High St., Columbus, OH 43266-0320; (614) 466-4143. This agency licenses pharmacists and licenses and inspects retail and wholesale pharmacies, drug distributors, and industrial first aid rooms. Mailing lists and labels of pharmacies and pharmacists are available. They can be sorted by county, type of license, or zip code. Fees for printed materials are $.07 per record. Mailing labels cost $.10 per record. Requests for information should be in writing and accompanied by a check.

Oklahoma

State Department of Health, Food Protection Service, 1000 N.E. 10th St. Oklahoma City, OK 73117-1299; (405) 271-5243. This department licenses and inspects bottling plants, food processors, manufacturers and wholesalers.

Computer listings are available at $10 per listing. Requests must be made in writing. Send a letter of intent to Richard Barnes at the address listed above.

State Board of Pharmacy, 4545 Lincoln Blvd., Suite 112, Oklahoma City, OK 73105; (405) 521-3815. The Board of Pharmacy licenses and inspects pharmacies, wholesalers, manufacturers and packagers. A mailing list of pharmacies is $200. A list of pharmacists is $400. Requests must be made in writing and include a letter of intent.

Oregon

Department of Agriculture, Food and Dairy Division, 635 Capitol St., N.E., Salem, OR 97310; (503) 378-3790. This agency licenses and inspects food processors, retail stores, bakeries, food storage warehouses, bottling plants, retail meat facilities and dairies. Computer listings and mailing labels are available and can be sorted by type of facility. Fees are $.05 per name. A minimum order of $25 is required.

Board of Pharmacy, 800 N.E. Oregon St., #9, Portland, OR 97232; (503) 731-4032. The Board of Pharmacy licenses pharmacists and interns and licenses and inspects drug manufacturers, pharmacies, wholesalers, and retail outlets with over the counter drugs. Listings are $75, each. Mailing labels are $80 per set.

Pennsylvania

State Department of Agriculture, Bureau of Food Safety and Laboratory Services, 2301 N. Cameron St., Harrisburg, PA 17110-9408; (717) 787-4315. This agency licenses and inspects bakeries, bottling plants and warehouses, and issues non-alcoholic drink licenses. Mailings lists are available. Costs vary according to the size of the list.

State Department of Health, Drug Registration Section, Division of Drugs, Devices and Cosmetics, P.O. Box 90, Harrisburg, PA 17108-0090; (717) 787-2307. This agency licenses and inspects drug, cosmetic and device manufacturers. It does not normally issue computer listings.

Board of Pharmacy, P.O. Box 2649, Harrisburg, PA 17105; (717) 783-7157. This agency licenses and inspects pharmacies. Computer listings are available. There is a charge of $.005 per name plus a $71 service fee.

Rhode Island

State Department of Health, Division of Food Protection, Room 203, Canon Bldg., 3 Capitol Hill, Providence, RI 02908-5097; (401) 277-2750. Licenses and inspects food processors, wholesalers and food service establishments, dairies, vending machines and warehouses. Computer listings are available and range between $10 to $90, depending upon the complexity of the request. Interested individuals must first file a release of information request form.

State Department of Health, Division of Drug Control, 304 Cannon Bldg. 3 Capitol Hill, Providence, RI 02908. (401) 277-2837. The Division of Drug Control licenses and inspects drug manufacturers, wholesalers, retailers, pharmacies, and some devices and cosmetics. A list of pharmacies costs $42. Interested individuals must first file a release of information request form.

South Carolina

Department of Health and Environmental Control, Division of Dairy Foods and Bottling Plants, 2600 Bull St., Columbia, SC 29201; (803) 734-4970. This agency inspects soft drink bottling plants and dairy farms. Computer listings and mailing labels are available. The cost is $10 per listing plus a $3.50 set up charge for sorting the file.

Department of Agriculture, Laboratory Division, 1101 William St., P.O. Box 11280, Columbia, SC 29211; (803) 737-2070. This agency inspects non-meat manufacturers such as bakeries and warehouses. A computer listing is provided free of charge.

State Board of Pharmaceutical Examiners, 1026 Sumter St., P.O. Box 11927, Columbia, SC 29211; (803) 734-1010. This office licenses both pharmacists and pharmacies. Files are open to the public. Computer lists and mailing labels are available. Mailing lists cost $.01 per name, plus postage. Mailing labels are $.04 per name, postage, and $6 for staff computer time. Place your requests in writing to the address listed above.

South Dakota

Department of Agriculture, Division of Regulatory Services, Anderson Building, 445 East Capitol, Pierre, SD 57501; (605) 773-3724. This agency inspects milk plants, pesticide producers, fertilizer producers and nurseries. Mailing lists are available and cost between $10 and $50.

Be patient. If any phone number is incorrect, call (area code) 555-1212 and request the new listing.

Information on People, Companies, and Mailing Lists

State Board of Pharmacy, P.O. Box 518, Pierre, SD 57501; (605) 224-2338. The Board of Pharmacy licenses both pharmacists and pharmacies. A mailing list of pharmacies is $15, pharmacists cost $25. Mailing labels are also available in each category for an additional $5. Requests must be placed in writing.

Tennessee

State Department of Agriculture, Division of Quality and Standards, Ellington Agricultural Center, Melrose Station, P.O. Box 40627, Nashville, TN 37204; (615) 360-0150. The Food and Drug Administration maintains all information and inspection files on retail food stores, warehouses, processors, bottling plants, bakeries, grain elevators, and produce warehouses. Data on retail foods stores has been computerized. Requests for information must first be placed in writing to the director's office. The cost of a listing is dependent upon the information requested.

Board of Pharmacy, 500 James Robertson Parkway, 2nd Floor, Nashville, TN 37243-1149; (615) 741-2718. This office licenses and inspects drug wholesalers, distributors, manufacturers, and pharmacies. Computer listings of pharmacies and pharmacists are $100, each. Mailing labels are $50 extra. Listings can be sorted by zip code, county or alphabetical order.

Texas

Department of Health, Division of Food and Drugs, 1100 W. 49th St., Austin, TX 78756; (512) 458-7248. This agency licenses and inspects food manufacturers, bottling plants, bakeries, and retail food markets. Computer listings can be generated and information can be sorted by county or zip code order. Computer listings are $.05 per page and mailing labels, $.01 each. Faxes are $.17 per minute. Information is also available on diskette or magnetic tape. For detailed requests there is a charge of $16.50 for professional time and $8.50 for clerical support staff time. Inspection form information must be requested under the Freedom of Information Act.

State Board of Pharmacy, 8505 Cross Park Drive, Suite 110, Austin, TX 78754; (512) 832-0661. This agency licenses pharmacists and licenses and inspects pharmacies. Computer lists and labels are available. Sorting is possible, the cost varies according to the size of the request. Fees range from $10 to $40.

Utah

Department of Agriculture, Division of Food and Dairy, 350 N. Redwood Road, Salt Lake City, UT 84116; (801) 538-7124. This agency licenses and inspects food manufacturers, processors, retail stores and warehouses. Computer listings can be generated for $5 and sorted into broad categories such as zip code and type of facility. A written request is required.

Division of Occupational Licensing, Board of Pharmacy, Heber Wells Building, 160 East 300 South, Salt Lake City, UT 84145; (801) 530-6628. The Board of Pharmacy licenses pharmacists and licenses and inspects pharmacies, wholesalers, and manufacturers. Computer listings of pharmacies and pharmacists are $40, each. Mailing labels are also available. Information can be transferred onto disk, but the individual must provide the disk, himself. Information requests should be placed in writing and include disk specifications.

Vermont

Department of Health and Human Services, Environmental Health Division, P.O. Box 70, 60 Main St., Burlington, VT 05402; (802) 863-7220. This department licenses and inspects bakeries, restaurants, delis, mobil food units, and food and lodging establishments. The agency inspects the following on a complaint basis only: bottling plants, warehouses and food processors. Computer lists can be generated, there is a minimum charge of $5 with an additional cost of $.04 per page.

State Department of Agriculture, Dairy Division, 120 State Street, Montpelier, VT 05620-2901; (802) 828-2433. The Dairy Division licenses and inspects dairy farms, milk plants, dairy processors, warehouses (dairy) retail stores. Computer lists can be generated upon request. The agency does not provide a list of dairy farmers but does distribute free lists of licensed firms or establishments. A separate division licenses and inspects the plant industry. A free listing of licensed plant nurseries is available upon request.

State Board of Pharmacy, c/o Secretary of State, Office of Prof Regulation, 109 State St., Montpelier, VT 05609-1106; (802) 828-2875. This agency licenses pharmacists and inspects and licenses pharmacies and drug wholesalers. Listings of pharmacists are available at $.03 per name. Lists are also available on mailing labels at $.04 per name and on diskettes for $.01 per name. There is a $5 handling fee involved for each list. Data can be sorted alphabetically or by zip code.

Virginia

State Department of Agriculture, Bureau of Food Inspection, 1100 Bank St., P.O. Box 1163, Richmond, VA 23209; (804) 786-3520. This bureau inspects food processors, warehouses, storage plants and retail food establishments such as grocery stores. Restaurants are inspected through another agency. Information is available on a firm's inspection history. Computer listings can be generated for a processing fee.

State Board of Pharmacy, 1601 Rolling Hills Dr., Richmond, VA 23229; (804) 662-9911. This agency licenses and inspects pharmacies, drug manufacturers, wholesalers and any company handling controlled substances. For a listing, the request must be made in writing. Lists can be sorted by zip code, alphabetically or license number order. Mailing labels can also be ordered. There is a $45 minimum fee. All licensure information is confidential.

Washington

State Department of Agriculture, Food Safety and Animal Health Division, P.O. Box 42576, Olympia, WA 98504-2576; (206) 902-1876. This agency inspects and licenses in-state food processors and warehouses. It does not release listings for commercial use.

Board of Pharmacy, P.O. Box 47863, Olympia, WA 98504-7863; (206) 753-6834. The Board of Pharmacy licenses and inspects pharmacies, drug wholesalers and manufacturers and animal shelters. A computer list or mailing labels may be obtained through a written request. The cost is $.25 per page.

West Virginia

State Health Department, Environmental Health Services, Sanitation Department, 815 Quarrier St., Suite 418, Charleston, WV 25301; (304) 558-2981. This agency licenses and inspects primarily interstate commerce facilities such as food processors, bakeries, canneries, candy manufacturers and bottling plants. A mailing list of licensed facilities is provided, free of cost.

State Board of Pharmacy, 236 Capitol St., Charleston, WV 25301 (304) 558-0558. The Board of Pharmacy licenses pharmacists and licenses and inspects pharmacies, drug distributors and manufacturers. Computer printouts or labels are available. Data can be sorted alphabetically or by zip code order. Computer printouts are free. Mailing labels of pharmacies are $50. Labels for pharmacists cost $100.

Wisconsin

Department of Agriculture, Trade and Consumer Protection, Food Division, 801 West Badger Road, Madison, WI 53708; (608) 266-7240. This department licenses and inspects food processors, warehouses, bottling plants, dairy farms and bakeries. Computer lists are available for some types of establishments. There is a processing fee. Sorting is available to a limited extent. Individuals seeking mailing lists can call the open records request line at (608) 266-7210 for further information.

State Department of Regulation and Licensing, P.O. Box 8935, Madison, WI 53708; (608) 266-2112. The Board of Pharmacy licenses pharmacists and licenses and inspects pharmacies, manufacturers, and distributors. Computer listings and labels are available from the Renewal Document Processing Center (608) 266-0627. A listing of pharmacies is $21.20. A listing of pharmacists is $29. Mailing labels are available to state agencies, only.

Wyoming

Department of Agriculture, Food and Drug Section, 2219 Carey Ave. Cheyenne, WY 82002; (307) 777-6587. This agency licenses and inspects food processors, warehouses and distributors, dairy farms, and meat plants. Restaurants are licensed through another agency. Listings of licensed facilities may be obtained for $.20 per page, with a $5 minimum required.

State Board of Pharmacy, 1720 South Poplar St., #5, Casper, WY 82601; (307) 234-0294. This agency licenses pharmacists and licenses and inspects pharmacies and hospitals with retail licenses. A listing of pharmacies is available for $10 as long as it is not used for advertising purposes. Requests to the agency should be made in writing.

Be patient. If any phone number is incorrect, call (area code) 555-1212 and request the new listing.

Utility Companies

A consulting firm in New Jersey was interested in working out a deal between an electrical company that needed extra power to meet increasing consumer demands, and some private companies that had the ability to generate and sell their extra power. By determining the power needs and financial resources of the utility company, the consulting firm could then match them up with the appropriate power sources in private industry, and along the way save the public utility company millions of dollars by not having to build expensive new power plants of their own. But how did this consulting firm discover the operational and financial background of the electric company to draw up their proposals? The State Utility Regulatory Commission was their source.

If a company provides a service that its state considers a public utility, it must, at the very least, provide detailed financial statements and annual reports to the state's Utility Regulatory Commission. The URC's role is to ensure that utility companies follow the state operating guidelines and make their annual findings available to the public.

The one thing you can count on about utility regulation commissions across the U.S. is that they are all different. The utilities they regulate, the information they gather, and the way they are set up all vary from state to state. For example, Tennessee regulates the standard utilities--transportation, water and sewer, electricity, gas, and telephone--South Dakota regulates all of these along with warehouses and elevators. And while Hawaii will provide you with monthly financial and annual reports, Vermont will give you all that plus a company's tariff information, informal complaints, and special contracts, along with the state regulatory commission's proceedings reports.

Many state utility regulatory commissions have different divisions for each type of utility. Telecommunications, for example, generally include the following divisions: local and long distance telephone, radio common carriers, re-sellers, cable television, and coin operated pay telephones. Fixed utilities often include gas, electricity, water, sewer, and refuse. Many states, like Utah and Pennsylvania, also have transportation divisions that regulate trucking, railroads, taxicabs, buses, and so forth. Some states regulate utilities not regulated in other states, such as cotton gins in Oklahoma, and elevators in South Dakota.

Information in the Public Utility Commission (PUC) files is meant for and mostly used by consumers--whether individual or commercial--for the purposes of estimating and comparing costs. However, the financial information kept on file at commissions contains a wealth of information invaluable to the entrepreneur. In many states, utilities file reports on sales volume, details on revenues raised and customer base, balance sheets, and service reliability and responsiveness. All of this is important for targeting your competition, and developing

market studies, mailing lists, and much more. Most state commissions have this information on file in hard copy, but some have begun transferring it into computer formats and will do customized searches based on your specific needs.

Utility Commissions

Alabama

Wallace Tidmore, Secretary of the Commission, Public Service Commission, Box 991, Montgomery, AL 36101-0991; (205) 242-5218. Utilities regulated include: Local and long distance telephone, radio common carriers and re-sellers, coined operated telephones; some gas, electric and water (investor owned); transportation (rail, buses, taxis, trucks); gas pipeline (for safety only). Examples of Information on file include annual reports and other financial information including current operating charges and changes in rates. Format of Files and Costs: Hard copy, but efforts to automate are underway. No charge for simple requests; charges on a cost recovery basis for extensive searches. The office provides a listing of regulated companies at no cost. Publications include their free *1991 Annual Report* which includes information on the transportation, telecommunications and energy departments.

Alaska

Ray Wipperman, Public Utilities Commission, 1016 W. 6th Ave., Ste. 400, Anchorage, AK 99501; (907) 276-6222. Utilities regulated include: telephone, radio common carriers, some cable television, electricity, gas, water, sewer, steam, garbage, and refuse. Examples of information on file include: fully regulated companies file tariff and financial information. Cost for duplicating information is $.25 per page. A listing of regulated companies is available for $5. A report entitled *Notices*, published twice weekly, lists public notices on tariff filings, etc. It is available through subscription at $40 per year. Another publication, *Order List*, published weekly, lists all orders issued. It is available at $25 per year.

Arizona

Carmine Madrid, Docket Control Center, Arizona Corporation Commission, 1200 W. Washington Street, Phoenix, AZ 85007; (602) 542-4251. Utilities regulated include: water, sewer, irrigation, gas, electricity, and telephone. Examples of Information kept on file includes: annual reports; applications called Certificates of Convenience and Necessity, which cover changes in rates; current operating tariffs, and service reliability reports. The staff will make hard copies or copies of microfilm for $.50 per page. The charge is $.10 per page if the requestor comes in to the office to make copies, himself. A listing of regulated companies is available at $.50 per page. Other publications include: *Hearing Notices*, which lists dates and times and specific information about hearings and the *Hearing Calendar* which lists weekly dates and times of hearings. Both are available at $.50 per page.

Arkansas

Jan Sanders, Secretary, Public Service Commission, P.O. Box 400, Little Rock, AR 72203-0400; (501) 682-2051. This office regulates: electricity, telephone, gas, and water. Information on file includes: annual reports, complaints, rate and tariff information, and service reliability. Hard copy and older records are on microfilm. Costs are $.25 per page for duplicating. The office will also fax information to you for $3 for the first page and $2 for each additional page. Microfiche is $.25 per page. A 16-page listing of the companies regulated is also available at $.25 per page. The commission also publishes two weekly reports: the *Daily Log*, an agenda of the commission, and *Pending Rate Cases*, which lists upcoming rate hearings. Both are available for $.10 per page.

California

Office of the Director, Public Utilities Commission, Consumer Affairs Branch, 505 Van Ness Ave., San Francisco, CA 94102; (415) 557-0647. Utilities regulated include: Local and long distance telephone, telegraph, mobile telephone, cellular telephone facilities and re-sellers, gas, electricity, water, steam, gas pipeline, sewer, and transportation. Examples of information on file: Annual Reports,

Information on People, Companies, and Mailing Lists

applications, case files (orders, pleadings, correspondence, exhibits, transcripts) tariff information. The staff will make copies of requested information for $.20 per page. They will also provide listings of regulated companies. Lists are arranged by the type of company, and prices vary for from $1 to $10. For information contact the Documents Section at (415) 703-1713. Other publications available include: *Agendas for Meetings*, $75 per year; *Daily Calendar* $125 per year; *Bi-Weekly Calendar*, $50 per year; and the *Transportation Calendar*, $75 per year. The first copy of the *Annual Report*, is free. Each additional copy is $10.

Colorado

Information Center, Public Utilities Commission, Department of Regulatory Agencies, 1580 Logan St., Office Level 2, Denver, CO 80203; (303) 894-2000. Utilities regulated include: water and electricity (investor owned), gas (distribution companies only and inspection of new pipeline), telecommunications (all local and long distance only in Colorado), and transportation (taxis and hauling for hire). Examples of Information on file: annual reports, current operating tariffs, changes in rates, and all pending commission actions. Files are microfilmed as the arrive. The office provides hard copies and microfilmed copies at $.20 per printed page. Customized computer searches are available on a cost recovery basis. The office also maintains mailing lists of all active carriers, common and deregulated carriers with state depositories. The *Weekly Agenda* is available at $.20 per page through the Executive Secretary, at the above address.

Connecticut

Barney Spector, Director, Consumer Services Division, Public Utility Control, 1 Central Park Plaza, New Britain, CT 06051; (203) 827-2622. Utilities regulated include electricity, gas, water, local and cellular telephone, and cable television. Information on file includes annual reports, customer complaints, financial information, service reliability on cable companies, and changes in rates for all utilities except cable television. Hard copy files are available for $.50 per page. Listings of regulated companies are also available for $.50 per page.

Delaware

Melinda S. Carl, Public Information Officer, Public Service Commission, 1560 South Dupont Highway, P.O. Box 457, Dover, DE 19903-0457; (302) 739-4333. Utilities regulated include: Electricity, telephone and water. The commission issues franchises for cable television, and handles disputes concerning new car franchises. Information on file includes: quarterly financial reports, new service or elimination of existing service, rate changes, and issuance of stock. Information, whether on hard copy or microfilm, is $.25 per page. The office also provides a listing of regulated companies, free of charge. Other publications include the yearly *Meeting Agenda* and *Monthly Calendar*, both $18.

District of Columbia

Office of the Secretary, Service Commission, 450 5th Street, N.W., Suite 800, Washington, DC 20001; (202) 626-5100. Utilities regulated include: electricity, gas, local telephone, stock broker securities, and coin operated telephones. Examples of information on file include annual reports, other periodic accounting information, service reliability reports, changes in rates, and new tariffs or amendments. The office provides hard copy files at $.15 per sheet plus some computerized records. They also provide a listing of regulated companies, free of charge. Publications include an *Annual Report*, and the *Utility Bulletin*, their quarterly newsletter.

Florida

Steve Tribble, Director of Records and Reporting, Public Service Commission, 101 E. Gaines Street, Tallahassee, FL 32399-0850; (904) 488-7238. The commission oversees the intrastate operations of investor-owned utilities -- electric, gas, water and waste water, and telecommunications. It does not regulate publicly-owned, municipal, or cooperative utilities. Information on file includes: monthly general operating reports, earnings, current operating tariffs, rate changes, and complaints. Copies of information and a listing of regulated companies is available at $1 per page. The commission publishes *From the PSC Agenda*, a monthly consumer publication which is distributed to consumer organizations throughout the state, as well as to members of the media, legislators, and city and county government officials.

Georgia

Executive Director's Office, Public Service Commission, 244 Washington St., S.W. Atlanta, GA 30334; (404) 656-4501. Utilities regulated include: local telephone, electric, gas, radio common carriers, and transportation. Information on file includes: annual reports, changes in names, rates or management; current operating tariffs, and service reliability. Copies of information are provided at $.25 per page. The office also provides a listing of all companies by type at $.25 per page. An *Annual Report* is also available.

Hawaii

Norman Lee, Chief Engineer, Public Utilities Commission, 465 S. King St., Kekuanaoa Building, Room 103, Honolulu, HI 96813; (808) 586-2020. Utilities regulated include: local and cellular telephone, radio common carriers, electricity, gas, water, sewer, trucking, and intra-state transportation. Information on file includes: monthly financial and annual reports. The commission will make hard copies of information for individuals at $.25 per page plus postage. A listing of regulated companies is also $.25 per page.

Idaho

Commission Secretary, Public Utilities Commission, State House, Boise, Idaho 83720; (208) 334-0338. Utilities regulated include telephone, gas, electricity, water, and trucking. The office keeps information of file such as applications for rate increases, financial statements, changes in rates and current operating tariffs. Information has not been computerized. The cost of receiving hard copy of information is $.05 per page. The office can provide a list of regulated companies, free of charge. Other publications include an *Annual Report* and monthly *Summary List of Cases*. Both are free to the public.

Illinois

Chief Clerk's Office, Public Utilities Commission, 527 E. Capitol Avenue, P.O. Box 19280, Springfield, IL 62794-9280; (217) 782-7434. Utilities regulated include: local and long distance telephone, radio common carriers, customer-owned pay telephones, gas, electricity, water and sewer, gas pipeline, railroad, bus, towing and tractor-trailer haulers. This office keeps files on annual reports, service reliability, all tariff information, and general financial information. There is a $.05 per page copying charge. Publications include the *Annual Report*, which is divided into two parts: public utilities and telecommunication. Each section is available for $10. The office does publish a directory of regulated companies.

Indiana

Public Information Office, Utility Regulatory Commission, Indiana Government Center South, 302 West Washington Street, Suite E-306, Indianapolis, IN 46204; (317) 232-2715. Regulated utilities include: local telephone, WATS re-sellers, telephone cooperatives, inter-exchange carriers, radio common carriers, gas, gas transportation companies, electricity, steam, water, and sewer. Information on file includes: rates and charges, tariffs, financial reports, and changes in rates. Hard copies of information are $.15 per page. The office provides a listing of regulated companies, free of charge. The office also publishes an *Annual Report*.

Iowa

Iowa State Utilities Board, Department of Commerce, Utilities Division, Lucas State Office Building, 5th Floor, Des Moines, IA 50319; (515) 281-5979. Utilities regulated include: local and long distance telephone, telegraph, investor-owned gas and electricity. The office keeps records of annual reports, financial information, changes in rates and current operating tariffs. There is a $.50 charge for the first three pages of information. Each following page is $.15. A listing of regulated companies is provided at $.50 per page. Their *Annual Report* includes filings and description of proceedings.

Kansas

Director of Public Affairs, Corporation Commission, Utilities Division, 1500 S.W. Arrowhead Rd., Topeka, KS 66604-4027; (913) 271-3140. Utilities regulated include: local and long distance telephone, electricity, gas and water, and transportation. Examples of information on file include: annual reports, records of proceedings, current operating tariffs, and rate changes. Information is provided on hard copy. For information between 1-10 pages, the cost is $.10 per copy. Costs decrease as the number of pages increases. Microfilm copies are available at $.25 per page. There is also an additional cost for postage in both cases. The office provides a listing of regulated companies, but the caller must certify that the list will not be used for solicitation purposes.

Kentucky

Public Service Commission, 730 Schenkel Lane, Box 615, Frankfort, KY 40601; (502) 564-3940. This office regulates local and long distance telephone, WATS re-sellers, radio common carriers, cellular telephone, electricity, gas, water, sewage, and coin operated telephones. Annual reports, tariffs, and applications for changes are all kept on file. There is a charge of $.10 a page for printed copies of information and $.50 for older information on microfilm. Postage is extra. A listing of regulated companies is free. Publications include a monthly *Public Service Commission Update Listing* which lists all cases filed, hearings, and decisions. It is available for an annual fee of $63.60.

Utility Companies

Louisiana

Secretary of the Commission, Public Service Commission, One American Place, Suite 1630, Baton Rouge, LA 70825; (504) 342-4416. This office regulates: local, long distance, and cellular telephone; long distance facility-based carriers, electricity, gas, water, sewage, and transportation. Information on file includes: current operating tariffs, financial information, rate changes and service reliability reports. A listing of regulated companies is available free. Copies of information are provided at $.25 per page. Transcription hearings are $1 per page.

Maine

Mary Broad, Public Utilities Commission, 242 State Street, Station 18, Augusta, ME 04333-0018; (207) 289-3831. Regulated utilities include local exchange telephone, re-sellers, electricity, gas, and water. Annual reports, financial statements, and transfer of stock or rate changes are all kept on file. Hard copies of information are provided at $.20 per page. The office provides a listing of regulated companies, free of charge. Other publications available include: *Monthly Docket*, $10 semiannually; *Weekly Agenda*, $12 semiannually; and copies of all orders and decisions, $73 semiannually.

Maryland

Director of Consumer Assistance and Public Affairs, Public Service Commission, The American Building, 231 E. Baltimore St., Baltimore, MD 21202; (301) 333-6028. Utilities regulated include: gas, electricity, and some privately owned water and sewer companies. The office provides financial information, annual reports, rate changes and tariff information. Information is provided on hard copy. The office charges $.20 per page plus postage. A listing of regulated companies is also available at $.20 per page. The state's transportation division regulates trucking, buses and taxi cabs.

Massachusetts

Secretary of the Department of Public Utilities, Department of Public Utilities, Leverett Saltonstall Building, Government Center, 100 Cambridge St., 12th Floor, Boston, MA 02202; (617) 727-3500. Utilities regulated include: trucks, buses, and railroad; gas, water and voluntary holding companies for electricity, telecommunications, and pipeline engineering and safety. Examples of information on file include: annual reports and financial statements, service reliability reports, tariff information and rate changes. Information is provided on hard copy at $.20 per page. A listing of regulated companies is available at $.10 per page. Their last annual report was published in 1989.

Michigan

Executive Secretary, Public Service Commission of the Department of Commerce, P.O. Box 30221, Lansing, MI 48909; (517) 334-6445. Utilities regulated include: local and long distance telephone, electricity, gas and water, and transportation. This office keeps records on tariffs, annual reports, audit information, and filings to the commission. Hard copies of information and microfilm are $.05 per page. There is an additional charge for research services. A listing of regulated companies is provided, also at $.05 per page. Individuals may subscribe to listings of orders, agendas, and minutes; fees vary. Their *Annual Report* is free.

Minnesota

Department of Public Service, Public Utilities Commission, 780 American Center Building, 150 E. Kellogg Blvd., St. Paul, MN 55101; (612) 296-7124. The commission regulates: local and inter-LATA telephone, pay telephone, electricity, and gas. Information on file includes: annual financial reports, current operating tariffs, and case files. The staff will provide hard copies of information at $.25 per page. A listing of regulated companies is also available at $.25 per page. The Commission also publishes a *Biennial Report* and summary of hearings.

Mississippi

Public Service Commission, P.O. Box 1174, Jackson, MS 39215-1174; (601) 961-5400. Utilities regulated include: land-line telephone, radio common carriers, some personal paging systems, WATS re-sellers, interstate telephone, electricity, gas, water, and sewer. Annual reports, tariffs, financial information, and proceedings before the commission are all on file. Information provided on hard copy is $.50 per page. A case-tracking system was implemented in 1990 and is now being expanded. The commission provides a listing of regulated companies at $.50 per page.

Missouri

Secretary of the Commission, Public Service Commission, P.O. Box 360, Jefferson City, MO 65102; (314) 751-7494. The commission regulates: local telephone, inter-exchange facility-based carriers, inter-exchange re-sellers, pay telephones, and privately owned electricity, gas, water, and sewer companies. Information on file includes: applications, financial information, complaints, annual reports, current operating tariffs and rate changes. Information is available on hard copy and some records are computerized. The office can perform some custom searches; charges vary. Copying costs are $.30 per page and $1 for certified copies. Transcripts are $.25 per page. The office also provides a listing of regulated companies, free of charge. Other publications include: the weekly *Tariff Filing Docket*, which lists tariff matters. This is available for $24 per year. The commission also publishes a free *Weekly Docket* which lists upcoming hearings.

Montana

Public Service Commission, 1701 Prospect Ave., Helena, MT 59620-2601; (406) 444-6199. The utilities regulated by the commission include: local and long distance telephone, electricity, water and sewer, gas, and intra-state oil pipeline. Information on file includes annual reports, special reports, rules, regulations, rate increases and current operating tariffs. Information is available both on hard copy and microfilm. The charge is $.30 per page if the staff does the research, and $.15 per page if the requestor does the research. The commission also provides a listing of regulated companies, free of charge.

Nebraska

Public Service Commission, 300 the Atrium, 1200 N St., P.O. Box 94927, Lincoln, NE 68509; (402) 471-3101. Utilities regulated include: local and long-distance telephone and motor carriers, and railroads to some extent. Information on file includes: annual reports, financial information, tariffs, and proceedings of hearings. The office charges $.25 per page for copying information. Transcripts of hearings are $.50 per page. A listing of regulated companies is available, free of charge. Other publications include their free annual *Legislative Report*.

Nevada

Public Information Officer, Public Service Commission, Capitol Complex, 727 Fairview Drive, Carson City, NV 89710; (702) 687-6082. Utilities regulated include: electricity, gas, telephone, water and sewer, various motor carriers, and railroad transportation. Examples of information on file include: annual reports, insurance and operating certificates, current operating tariffs and rate changes. The commission provides copies of microfilmed and printed information for $.25 per page. It also provides a listing of regulated companies sorted alphabetically and by utility at no charge. Other free publications include a *Biennial Report and Transportation Quarterly Newsletter*.

New Hampshire

Executive Director, Public Utilities Commission, 8 Old Suncook Rd., Concord, NH 03301; (603) 271-2431. Utilities regulated include: gas, electricity, telephone, sewer, water, and steam. Examples of information on file include: service reliability, financial information, records of responsiveness and responsibility, tariff information, and changes in rates. Information printouts are $.50 per page. A listing of regulated companies is also available at $.50 per page. The office also publishes a *Biennial Report for the Legislature*.

New Jersey

Sharon Schulman, Director of Public Information, Board of Public Regulatory Commissioners, CN 350, Trenton, NJ 08625; (609) 777-3303. Utilities regulated include: electricity, gas, water, sewer, cable television, and telephone. Examples of information on file include: tariff information, annual reports on revenue, expenses, and capitalization. Information on hard copy is $1 per page. Annual reports are computerized. A listing of regulated companies is available at $1 per page. Other publications available include: *Case File Report*, published weekly. The cost is $120 per year. A bi-monthly report of the commission's agenda is also available.

New Mexico

Records Office, Public Service Commission, 224 E. Palace Ave., Santa Fe, NM 87501-2013; (505) 827-6940. Utilities regulated include: Gas, electricity, water, and sewer. Examples of information on file include: tariffs, annual reports, and hearing proceedings. Information is available on hard copy or microfilm. A listing of regulated companies is available at $.15 per page.

New York

Central Files, Public Service Commission, 3 Empire State Plaza, Albany, NY 12223; (518) 474-7080. This office regulates private and some state utilities including: water, gas, electricity, and telephone. The office keeps annual reports, financial statements, performance material, rate changes, and current operating tariffs on file. Copies of information can be obtained at $.25 per page. Requests must be of a reasonable size. Older records are on microfilm. The office

Be patient. If any phone number is incorrect, call (area code) 555-1212 and request the new listing.

Information on People, Companies, and Mailing Lists

provides a list of regulated companies, free of charge. Other publications include: *Financial Statistics of Major Utilities*, $10; *Public Service Commission Reports*, $125; and *The Weekly Bulletin*, $20.

North Carolina

Chief Clerk's Office, Utilities Commission, Box 29510, Raleigh, NC 27626-0510; (919) 733-0839. Utilities regulated include: electricity, telephone, gas, water, and sewer, transportation, and radio common carriers. The office keeps records of annual reports, applications, rates, current operating tariffs and comments from orders issued. Hard copies of information are $.20/page. Transcriptions of testimony is $1/page. The office will also provide a listing of regulated companies at $.20 per page. Other publications available include: *North Carolina Public Utilities Law Book--Rules and Regulations*, $30, and *Orders and Decisions*, $60.

North Dakota

Secretary of the Commission, Public Service Commission, 12th Floor, State Capitol, Bismark, ND 58505; (701) 224-2400. The commission regulates: electricity, gas, telephone, and transportation. Information on file includes annual reports, financial information, current operating tariffs, and rate case information. The staff will provide hard copy and microfilm information. The first ten pages copied are free, additional copies are $.10 per page. There are also additional charges if research is performed.

Ohio

Fiscal Office, Public Utilities Commission, 180 E. Broad St., Columbus, OH 43266-0573; (614) 466-3016. Utilities regulated include: heating and cooling through pipes or tubing, inter-urban railroad, water transportation through pipelines, sewage, electricity, natural gas, railroad, water works, and telephone. Annual reports, current operating tariffs, and rate changes are on file. Hard copies of information are $1 for the first page and $.10 for each subsequent page. Copies of microfilm are $.35 per page. The office does provide a listing of regulated companies, also at $.35 per page. Other publications available include: the *Commission Meeting Agenda*, *Commission Rules and Regulations and the Yearly Calendar*, all available through subscription.

Oklahoma

Office Manager, Oklahoma Corporation Commission, Public Utilities Division, Room 500, Jim Thorpe Office Building, Oklahoma City, OK 73105; (405) 521-3908. The commission regulates utilities divisions including: electricity, gas, telephone, water, and cotton gins. Information on file includes all information connected with case hearings or filing, current operating tariffs, annual reports, audit reports, and applications. Copies of information can be obtained for $.25 per page or $10 per document. The office also provides a listing of regulated companies that is available for $.25 per page. Each utility division has recodified their rules and regulations. These are available in separate reports for $10 each. An *Annual Report* is also available.

Oregon

Public Information Office, Public Utilities Commission, 550 Capitol St., NE., Salem, OR 97310-1380; (503) 378-5849. The commission regulates investor owned utilities including: gas, water, electricity and telephone; trucking, and railroad safety. Examples of information on file include: financial and operational information, current operating tariffs, rate changes and service reliability. The staff will copy information for $.25 for the first 10 pages and $.10 per each additional page. The commission also provides a free listing of regulated companies. Other free publications available include: general information pamphlets, fax sheets, and a public involvement guide.

Pennsylvania

Public Utilities Commission, P.O. Box 3265, Harrisburg, PA 17105-3265 (717) 783-1740. The commission regulates gas, electricity, water, sewer, communications, and transportation utilities. Information on file includes: annual reports, updated tariff information, rate changes, financial information and other periodic reports. The office provides hard copies of records at $.75 per page. Records are computerized and customized searches are available on a limited basis. The office will also provide you with a listing of regulated companies at $.75 per page.

Rhode Island

Commission Clerk's Office, Public Utilities Commission, 100 Orange St., Providence, RI 02903; (401) 277-3500. Utilities regulated include: gas, electricity, telephone, water, sewer, cable television, and trucking. Information on file includes: annual reports, materials from rate hearings, rate changes, current operating tariffs and complaints. Individuals can receive hard copies of information at $.25 per page.

South Carolina

Executive Director, Public Service Commission, 111 Doctor's Circle, P.O. Drawer 11649, Columbia, SC 29211; (803) 737-5135. This office regulates gas, electricity, telecommunications, water and waste water, and transportation. Records on file include: quarterly financial reports, rate-of-return, sales, cost information, rate changes, and current operating tariffs. Hard copies of information are $.25 per page. Regulated companies are listed within the commission's *Annual Report*, which is $5. The office also publishes *Rules and Regulations*, which is also $5.

South Dakota

Public Utilities Commission, 500 E. Capitol Avenue, Pierre, SD 57501; (605) 773-3201. The commission regulates telephone, electricity, and gas utilities; transportation, warehouses, and elevators. Information on file includes: current operating tariffs, rate changes and various financial information. The staff will copy requested information at $.25 per page. A listing of regulated companies is available at no charge. Other free publications include an *Annual Report*. and various consumer guide pamphlets such as *Energy Efficient Appliances*, *Rate Changes*, *Lower Phone Bills Made Easy*, and *Pulling the Plug*.

Tennessee

Public Utilities Commission, 460 James Robertson Pky., Nashville, TN 37243-0505; (615) 741-2125. Utilities regulated include: transportation, water/sewer, electricity, gas, and telephone. Information on file includes: annual reports, rate and tariff information, ad valorem tax reports, financial records, and service reliability reports. The staff will provide hard copies of information at $.25 per page. Copies of microfilm are $2.50 per page or $1.50 per page if the customer does the work, himself. Transcripts are $1.50 per page. Customized searches are available with an additional charge for computer time. The office also provides a free listing of regulated companies. Other publications include a free *Annual Report* and *Agenda of Cases*.

Texas

Public Utility Commission, 7800 Shoal Creek Blvd., Austin, TX 78757; (512) 458-0100. The commission regulates the following utilities: electricity, local telephone, and AT&T long distance telephone. Examples of information on file include: annual reports, financial information, tariff information, and transcripts of commission hearings. The office provides information on both hard copy and microfilm. The staff will copy up to 50 pages of information for free. The cost is $.85 for the following page and $.15 for each additional page. The office also provides a listing of regulated companies for $5, each. Other publications available include: news releases, new filings, and agendas. The office also provides annual reports for the electric and telephone divisions. They are sold for $10 each. *Substantive Rules* is a loose-leaf edition of all rules issued by the commission and is available for $25 per year.

Utah

Public Service Commission, 160 East 300 South, Salt Lake City, UT 84111; (801) 530-6716. Utilities regulated include: electricity, gas, water, transportation (including trucking and railroad), telephone, and steam heat companies. Annual reports, complaints, petitions, and requests for agency action are kept on file. Hard copy and microfilm for older records are available for $.50 per page. A listing of regulated companies is available at no charge. An *Annual Report* is also available, free of charge.

Vermont

Public Service Board, 120 State St., Montpelier, VT 05620-2701; (802) 828-2358. Utilities regulated include: gas, electricity, telephone, water, and cable television. The office has information on file including: proceedings, tariff information, annual reports, informal complaints, rate changes, and special contracts. Information on hard copy and microfilm are available for $.10 per page. They will also provide a listing of regulated companies, free of charge. Other publications include *Board Decisions*, which is available through a monthly subscription. Specific information can be obtained at $.10 per page.

Virginia

Division of Energy Regulation, State Corporation Commission, P.O. Box 1197, Richmond, VA 23209; (804) 786-3611. The commission regulates electricity, gas, water, and sewer. Telephone is regulated by the communications division. Examples of information on file include: financial information, transmission applications, and annual operating reports that include credit information, sales volumes and operating expenses. Individuals can receive information on hard copy for $2 for the first two pages and $.50 for each additional page. An *Annual Report* is also available. The price of the report is dependent upon production costs and varies.

Be patient. If any phone number is incorrect, call (area code) 555-1212 and request the new listing.

Utility Companies

Washington

Public Utilities and Transportation Commission, P.O. Box 47250, 1300 S. Evergreen Park Dr. SW, Olympia, WA 98504-7250; (206) 753-6423. Utilities regulated include: electricity, telephone, telecommunications, water, gas, and transportation. Balance sheets and annual reports are kept on file. Copies of information is available at $.20 per page. A free listing of regulated companies is available upon completion of a public request form. Individuals may subscribe to reports such as the *Transportation Docket,* at $43.16 per year and the *Utilities Docket* at $77.69 per year.

West Virginia

Public Service Commission, P.O. Box 812, Charleston, WV 25323; (304) 340-0300. Utilities regulated include: telecommunications, gas, water, sewer, railroad, electricity, gas pipelines, and motor carriers. Information on file includes: annual reports, financial statements, current operating tariffs, service reliability, rate changes and sales volumes. Copied and microfilmed information is available at $.20 per page.

Wisconsin

Public Service Commission, P.O. Box 7854, Madison, WI 53707-7854; (608) 267-7915. Utilities regulated include: gas, electricity, telephone, water, and sewer. The commission keeps annual reports, tariffs, rate changes and regulations on file. Copies of information and a listing of regulated companies can be obtained at $.15 per page. Each utility publishes an annual report. The same copying charges apply as listed above.

Wyoming

Public Service Commission, Herschler Building, 700 W. 21st St., Cheyenne, WY 82002; (307) 777-7427. Utilities regulated include: electricity, gas, pipelines, telephone, telegraph, radio common carriers, water, railroad, and motor carriers. Information on file includes: rates, conditions of service, contracts, and financial conditions. A directory of regulated companies is $2. A report, *Rules and Regulations,* is $5.

Be patient. If any phone number is incorrect, call (area code) 555-1212 and request the new listing.

Information on People, Companies, and Mailing Lists

Weights and Measures

Looking for a mailing list of all delicatessens in the state? This office is likely to have it for you. The same is true for any other organization which uses a scale for commercial purposes, including gas stations, pharmacies, and dairies.

Every time you buy a half pound of corned beef or gas up the car, you rely on the accuracy of the scale behind the counter or meter on the pump. These and thousands of other measuring devices are used with confidence every day by businesses and consumers, most never questioning the accuracy of the information. Who then is charged with making sure a pound is a pound and an inch an inch?

All commercial measuring devices are regularly inspected by agents of your state office of weights and measures. In addition, such offices are the official keepers of state standards of mass, length, and volume traceable to those maintained by the National Institute of Standards and Technology (formerly the National Bureau of Standards).

These offices are staffed by professionals who can answer questions as simple as a child's homework assignment or as complicated as determining the best method of sale for a particular commodity. Many types of businesses rely on the expertise of these offices: defense industries, scale companies, and store-front businesses such as fabric shops, railroads, feed stores, and so on.

In general, most agents of a state office of weights and measures conduct on-site inspections of equipment at commercial businesses and manufacturing plants, ensuring that measuring devices are being used correctly and are being maintained so as to ensure their accuracy. Investigators also inspect scales used to weigh trucks and other vehicles used for transporting goods from factory or farm to market. Among the measuring devices inspected on a regular basis are: gasoline and air pumps, gas storage tanks, dairies, truck scales, pharmacy scales, and those used by commercial businesses.

The offices also field and investigate numerous complaints, most questioning the accuracy of fuel pumps. State agents also enforce standards of the Fair Packaging and Labeling Act. This law, passed by Congress in 1966, standardized the packaging and labeling of products so that they are packaged in containers of approximate similar size and labeled so as not to mislead.

Virtually every commercial transaction involves the use of weights and measures, so the state files are extensive. Given the number of transactions, even a slight measurement error can add up to thousands of dollars. Most state offices will provide business addresses and the type and capacity of measuring devices owned by companies on their files.

The following is a listing of state offices of weights and measures.

Weights and Measures Offices

Alabama

Weights and Measures Division, Alabama Department of Agriculture and Industry, P.O. Box 3336, Montgomery, AL 36109-0336; (205) 242-2613. This agency will provide listings of licensed warehouses, free of charge. The listings are categorized by type, and include cotton gins, and cattle and grain warehouses.

Alaska

Division of Measurement Standards, 12050 Industrial Way, Huffman Business Park, Business Park Building, 99515; (907) 345-7750. No listings of inspected businesses are provided.

Arizona

Jeffrey Gonscher, Deputy Chief, Arizona Weights and Measures Division, 1951 W. North Lane, Phoenix, AZ 85021; (602) 255-5211. A computer listing of licensed businesses is $48. Requests must be in writing.

Arkansas

Acting Director, James Michael Hile, Bureau of Standards, Division of Weights and Measures, 4608 West 61st Street, Little Rock, AR 72209; (501) 562-7605. A listing of licensed scale operators is available. The division also prints an annual report. Both publications are free.

California

Darrell A. Guensler, Acting Assistant Director, Division of Measurement Standards, California Department of Food and Agriculture, 8500 Fruitridge Rd., Sacramento, CA 95826; (916) 366-5119. No listings of inspected businesses are provided.

Colorado

David Wallace, Chief, Measurement Standard Securities, Department of Agriculture, 3125 Wyandot, Denver, CO 80211; (303) 866-2845. No listings of inspected businesses are provided.

Connecticut

Department of Consumer Protection, State Office Building, Room G17, 165 Capitol Ave., Hartford, CT 06106; (203) 566-5230. This office inspects commercial and industrial scales, licenses retail gas stations and oversees motor fuel registration. They will release a listing of licensed businesses. Prices vary, according to the length of the list.

Delaware

Eugene Keeley, Supervisor, Office of Weights and Measures, Department of Agriculture, 2320 South Dupont Hwy., Dover, DE 19901; (302) 739-4811. No listings of inspected businesses are provided.

District of Columbia

Department of Consumer and Regulatory Affairs, Weights, Measures and Markets Division, 1110 U. St., SE, Washington, DC 20020; (202) 767-7923. No listings of inspected businesses are provided.

Florida

Maxwell Gray, Chief, Bureau of Weights and Measures, Department of Agriculture and Consumer Services, 3125 Conner Blvd., Lab 2, Tallahassee, FL 32399-1650; (904) 488-9140. This office will provide lists of tests reports. Costs vary according to the size of the request.

Georgia

Martin Coile, Director, Weights and Measures Laboratory, Atlanta Farmers Market, 16 Forest Parkway, Forest Park GA 30050; (404) 363-7685. Licensed scale companies are available for a nominal fee.

Be patient. If any phone number is incorrect, call (area code) 555-1212 and request the new listing.

Weights and Measures

Hawaii

George E. Mattimore, Administrator, Measurement Standards, Department of Agriculture, 725 Ilelo St., Honolulu, HI 96813; (808) 586-0886. Licensed scale companies are provided free to the public.

Idaho

Glen Jex, Chief, Bureau of Weights and Measures, Department of Agriculture, 2216 Kellogg Lane, Boise, ID 83712; (208) 334-2345. Individual test reports of specific companies can be obtained. There is no charge involved.

Illinois

Rebecca Doyle, Weights and Measures Program Manager, Bureau of Product Inspection and Standards, Department of Agriculture, P.O. Box 19281, 801 Sangamon Ave., Springfield, IL 62794-9281; (217) 782-3817. Lists of licensed or inspected businesses are released at the discretion of the agency's Freedom of Information Act officer. Put requests for information in writing, be as specific as possible, and include the purpose of your request. The agency will then respond with a decision and cost of the list.

Indiana

Sharon Rhoades, Director of Weights and Measures, State Board of Health, 1330 West Michigan St., Indianapolis, IN 46206; (317) 633-0350. No listings of inspected businesses are provided.

Iowa

Gerald Bane, Supervisor, Weights and Measures Division, Department of Agriculture and Land Stewardship, Henry A. Wallace Building, Des Moines, IA 50319; (515) 281-5794. This office will provide a listings of inspected and licensed businesses. There is a $12 set-up fee and additional charge of $.01 per line. Information provided through the basis list includes the company's license, county and location. A master list is also available with more detailed information.

Kansas

Larry Woodson, Division of Inspections, Kansas State Board of Agriculture, 7th Fl, 901 S. Kansas Ave, Topeka, KS 66612-1272; (913) 296-3511. This agency will release certain business addresses of companies that they keep on file. Individuals must place their request in writing and then complete an open records request form certifying that the information they obtain will not be used for commercial gain. Once approved, lists of information is $.35 per page.

Kentucky

Danny Willis, Director, Division of Weights and Measures, Department of Agriculture, 106 West Second St., Frankfort, KY 40601; (502) 564-4870. Copies of individual company inspection reports are filed by county and are $.10 per page. Requests must be made in writing.

Louisiana

Ronald Harold, Director, Louisiana Weights and Measures, Department of Agriculture, P.O. Box 3098, Baton Rouge, LA 70821; (504) 925-3780. No listings of inspected businesses are provided.

Maine

Clayton F. Davis, Director, Agriculture Inspections Division, Division of Regulation, Stationhouse 28, Augusta, ME 04333; (207) 289-3841. At the present time Maine is not computerized and does not release listings of licensed businesses.

Maryland

Louis Straub, Chief, Weights and Measures Section, Department of Agriculture, 50 Harry S. Truman Parkway, Annapolis, MD 21401; (410) 841-5790. No listings of inspected businesses are provided.

Massachusetts

Steven Berard, Supervising Inspector, Massachusetts Division of Standards, One Ashburton Place, Room 1115, Boston, MA 02108; (617) 727-3480. This agency provides printouts of various licensed business including: gas stations, body shops with repair licenses, indoor vendors and auctioneers. Lists are $25, each. Please make your request in writing and include a check made out to the Commonwealth of Massachusetts.

Michigan

Edward Heffron, Chief, Food Division, Department of Agriculture, 611 W. Ottawa, Box 30017, Lansing, MI 48909; (517) 373-1060. Individuals can receive printouts of licensed businesses for $.04 per page plus a base rate of $17.98 per hour. Lists are sorted by county.

Minnesota

Michael Blacik, Director, Division of Weights and Measures, State of Minnesota, Department of Public Service, 2277 Highway 36, St. Paul, MN 55113; (612) 639-4010. No listings of inspected businesses are provided.

Mississippi

William P. Eldridge, Director, Weights and Measures Division, Mississippi Department of Agriculture and Commerce, 1603 Walter Sillers Building, P.O. Box 1609, Jackson, MS 39215-1609; (601) 354-7077. No listings of inspected businesses are provided.

Missouri

Lester Barrows, Director, Weights and Measures Division, Department of Agriculture, P.O. Box 630, Jefferson City, MO 65102; (314) 751-4278. This agency provides various computer listings of businesses sorted by category. Requests should be in writing. Costs vary depending upon the type of information requested.

Montana

Jim Kimball, Division Chief, Bureau of Weights and Measures, Department of Commerce, Capitol Station, Helena, MT 59620; (406) 444-3164. No listings of inspected businesses are provided.

Nebraska

Steven A. Malone, Director, Division of Weights and Measures, Department of Agriculture, State Office Building, 301 Centennial Mall South, Lincoln, NE 68509; (402) 471-4292. No listings of inspected businesses are provided.

Nevada

William McCrea, Chief Deputy State Sealer, Bureau of Weights and Measures, Department of Agriculture, P.O. Box 11100, Reno, NV 89510-1100; (702) 688-1166. This agency will provide listings of inspected businesses on file. Costs range from $60 to $100.

New Hampshire

Mike Grenier, Director, Bureau of Weights and Measures, Department of Agriculture, P.O Box 2042, Concord, NH 03302-2042; (603) 271-3700. No business listings are provided.

New Jersey

William J. Wolfe, State Superintendent, State Office of Weights and Measures, 1261 Rts. 1 ad 9 South, Evenel, NJ 07701; (908)-815-4840. No business listings are provided.

New Mexico

Gary D. West, Chief, Standards and Consumer Services, Department of Agriculture, Department 3170, P.O. Box 30005, Las Cruces, NM 88003; (505) 646-1616. No business listings are provided.

New York

John J. Bartfai, Director, Bureau of Weights and Measures, Department of Agriculture, Building 7-A State Campus 1220 Washington Ave., Albany, NY 12235; (518) 457-3452. No business listings are provided.

North Carolina

David N. Smith, Director, Consumer Standards Division, Department of Agriculture, P.O. Box 27647, Raleigh, NC 27611; (919) 733-3313. Listings of registered scale technicians such as petroleum dispensers or gasoline station owners are available for $10, each. The agency is working on a listing of licensed businesses and will provide you with their most up-to-date copy upon request. Requests should be placed in writing and be accompanied by a check made out to the North Carolina Department of Agriculture.

North Dakota

Al Moch, Director, North Dakota Public Service Commission, Department of Weights and Measures, State Capitol, 12th Floor, Bismarck, ND 58505; (701) 224-2400. The agency does not provide listings on a regular basis,

Ohio

John J. Steinberger, Jr., Chief, Division of Weights and Measures, Ohio Department of Agriculture, 8995 East Main St., Reynoldsburg, OH 43068; (614)

Be patient. If any phone number is incorrect, call (area code) 555-1212 and request the new listing.

866-6361. This agency does provide a listing of businesses licensed through their office. The cost is $.25 per page.

Oklahoma

Charles Carter, Program Administrator, Bureau of Standards, Oklahoma Department of Agriculture, 2800 North Lincoln Blvd., Oklahoma City, OK 73105-4298; (405) 521-3864, Ext 261. Listings of licensed scale companies and standard labeling rules and regulations are provided, free of charge.

Oregon

Kendrick J. Simila, Administrator, Measures Standard Division, Dept. of Agriculture, 635 Capitol St., NE, Salem, OR 97310-0110; (503) 378-3792. The agency will provide a listing of licensed businesses. There is a $25 minimum charge.

Pennsylvania

Neil Cashman, Director, Bureau of Standard Weights and Measures, Department of Agriculture, 2301 North Cameron St., Harrisburg, PA 17110; (717) 787-6772. Listings of businesses are not provided.

Rhode Island

Lynda Agresti Maurer, Sealer of Weights and Measures, Department of Labor, Division of Professional Regulations, 220 Elmwood Ave., Providence, RI 02907; (401) 457-1863. Listings of businesses are not provided.

South Carolina

Carol Fulmer, Director, Weights and Measures, Department of Agriculture, P.O. Box 11280, Consumer Services Division, Columbia, SC 29211; (803) 734-2210. This office does maintain a listing of registered businesses. Although prices vary, lists are at least $1 per page.

South Dakota

Mike Kumm, Director, Division of Consumer Inspection, Office of Weights and Measures, 118 West Capitol Ave., Pierre, SD 57501; (605) 773-3697. Listings of businesses are not provided.

Tennessee

Bob Williams, Administrator, Director, Weights and Measures, Department of Agriculture, Box 40627, Nashville, TN 37204; (615) 360-0159. Listings of businesses are not provided.

Texas

Ed Price, Supervisor of Weights and Measures, Department of Agriculture, Box 12847, Stephen F. Austin Bldg., Austin, TX 78711; (512) 463-7530. This agency supplies listings of inspected businesses sorted by category. Requests should be placed in writing. The cost is $.05 per name for the first 1,000 and $.05 for every name thereafter.

Utah

Edison J. Stephens, Deputy Commissioner, Division of Weights and Measures, State Department of Agriculture, 350 North Redwood Road, Salt Lake City, UT 84116; (801) 538-7159. All licensed businesses must register with the state's corporation office. Information is kept on a city by city basis and listings of licensed businesses are not normally released.

Vermont

Bruce Martell, Director, Division of Weights and Measures and Retail Inspection, Department of Agriculture, Food and Markets, Consumer Assurance Section, 120 State St., Montpelier, VT 05620-2901; (802) 828-2436. This office can supply individuals with copies of retail outlets. Copies of information are $.08 per page. Requests should be placed in writing.

Virginia

Kermit Spruill, Director, Weights and Measures Section, Department of Agriculture and Consumer Services, 1100 Banks St., Room 402, Richmond, VA 23209; (804) 786-2476. Business listings are not provided.

Washington

Mike Willis, Assistant Supervisor, Department of Agriculture, Office of Weights and Measures, Consumer and Producer Protection Division, P.O. Box 42560, Olympia, WA 93504; (206) 753-5042. Business listings are not provided.

West Virginia

Stephen L. Casto, Director, Division of Weights and Measures, Department of Labor, 570 W. McCorkle Ave., St. Albans, WV 25177; (304) 727-5781. Business listings are not provided.

Wisconsin

Alan Porter, Program Manager, Bureau of Weights and Measures, Wisconsin Department of Agriculture, Trade and Consumer Protection, Box 8911, Madison, WI 53708; (608) 266-2295. Business listings are not provided.

Wyoming

Jim Bigelow, Manager, Consumer/Compliance Division, Department of Agriculture, 2219 Carey Ave., Cheyenne, WY 82002; (307) 777-6591. This office will provide a listing of licensed businesses at $.10 per page.

Be patient. If any phone number is incorrect, call (area code) 555-1212 and request the new listing.

Insurance Companies and Salesmen

An insurance company wants to compare their rates to those of their competitors. A software company with a new time saving product needs the names of all the 1,500 insurance companies in Minnesota for a mailing list. Someone shopping for auto insurance wants to see sample policies from five different insurance companies in her area before she makes a final decision. A prospective insurance buyer wants to know how many complaints have been lodged against a certain company before he signs on the dotted line. All of this information and more can be found at the State Insurance Offices.

Although the kinds of information available at each of these offices varies from state to state, all except Colorado and Hawaii have listings of the insurance companies in their state, and only nine states--Arkansas, Georgia, Hawaii, Louisiana, Maryland, Montana, New York, Texas, and Washington--do not compile comprehensive listings of the in-state insurance agents. About thirty states will provide you with these listings in the form of a computer printout and/or mailing labels. California, Indiana, and Kansas also offer these listings on computer tape or diskettes.

Most state offices also handle consumer complaints and make their findings available to the public. Illinois, for example, not only compiles a "Complaint Rating List" that will tell you the number of complaints filed against a company, they also calculate "Complaint Ratios," which show the number of complaints versus the amount of insurance a company writes. If a company writes 100 policies and has 20 complaints, chances are you shouldn't buy a policy from them. But these "Complaint Ratios" can also be used by insurance companies to find out which of their competitors' policies produce the highest number of complaints. This is invaluable information for a company that plans to sell a new type of policy and wants a market study.

When a company wants to sell certain commercial or personal lines of insurance, they must file the policy forms and endorsements at the state office. Individuals can request copies of these policies before they make a purchase to compare rates from one company to another. Some states, in fact, publish *Premium Comparison Manuals* for personal auto and homeowner's policies. For the rate charts listed in these manuals, each insurance company must take the same policy situation, such as a three bedroom house or a twenty-seven year-old driver, and prepare a rate estimate for an insurance policy.

Some state offices also require insurance companies to file their *Rate Manuals* which show their brokers how to estimate their company's insurance premiums. These are valuable sources of information for both the consumer and competitor. And if you are interested in looking into a company's history--when it was first licensed, owners and former owners--many state offices can furnish you with that information, too.

Insurance Divisions

Alabama

Insurance Department, 135 S. Union St., Montgomery, AL 36130/(205) 269-3550. Insurance Companies Documents on File: Available for $1 a page plus mailing costs from Blue Print Services, P.O. Box 1383, Montgomery, AL 36109/(205) 263-4865. Listing of Insurance Companies: *Annual Report* (List of all licensed insurance companies) is available at no charge. Number of Licensed Insurance Companies: 1,300. Licensed Agents. Listing of Agents: Published yearly and available at no cost. Listing does not contain addresses. Number of Licensed Agents: Available for a fee.

Alaska

Insurance Division, Department of Commerce and Economic Development, PO Box 110805, Juneau, AK 99811-0805/(907) 465-2515. Insurance Companies Documents on File: Cost recovery basis. Listing of Insurance Companies: Available for $25. Number of Licensed Insurance Companies: 1,058. Licensed Agents. List of Agents: Available for $25. Number of Agents: 4,800.

Arizona

Insurance Department, 3030 N. 3rd Street, Suite 1100, Phoenix, AZ 85014/(602) 255-5367. Insurance Companies Documents on File: Available for 50 cents per page. Requests must be submitted in writing. Listing of Insurance Companies: Contained in *Annual Report*, which is published yearly. Cost is $16.50. Prepayment required, (602) 255-5605. Number of Licensed Insurance Companies: 2,540. Licensed Agents. List of Agents: A computer printout is available by line of insurance. Cost is 3 cents a name. Average cost is $400. (602) 255-5605. Number of Agents: 60,000.

Arkansas

Insurance Department, 1123 S. University, STE-400, Little Rock, AR 72204/ (501) 686-2900. Insurance Companies Documents on File: Available for $1 a page. Licensed Agents. List of Agents: Not Available. Number of Agents: 31,000.

California

Insurance Department, Business, Transportation and Housing Agency, 3450 Wilshire Blvd, L.A., CA 90010/(213) 736-3582, (800) 927-4357(in state) Insurance Companies Documents on File: Annual/Quarterly Statements are available to public at a cost of 50 cents per page plus sales tax up to four pages, then an outside copy service must be brought in. There is a one dollar fee per document certification. Listing of Insurance Companies: Lists are available, either in printout format (Cheshire labels) or magnetic tape format. Cost for list of all admitted companies is $40. Other lists, including breakdowns of different classes of insurance carriers or license types are also available at prices ranging from approximately $350 to $800. Interested parties should contact the Department's Electronic Data Processing Bureau, at (916) 323-5171 to request an order form. Number of Licensed Insurance Companies: 1,344. Licensed Agents. List of Agents: Available by calling (916) 322-3555. Number of Agents: 110,000. Send written request to: Dept. of Insurance, ATTN: Lucy Chavez, 700 L. St., 3rd floor, Sacramento, CA 95140. Fee: $1,067 + postage and handling.

Colorado

Insurance Division, 1560 Broadway, Suite 850, Denver, CO 80202/(303) 894-7499. Insurance Companies Documents on File: Available to the public for 25 cents per page or $6.50 for each list sorted by line of Insurance, but a visit to the office is necessary. Listing of Insurance Companies: A current listing is not available. Number of Licensed Companies: 1,786. Licensed Agents. List of Agents: Available by calling (303) 894-7495. Lists are sorted by line of insurance and the cost is $100 a list. Number of Agents: 38,000.

Connecticut

Insurance Department, 153 Market St., Hartford, CT 06103/(203) 297-3800. Insurance Companies Documents on File: A visit to the office is necessary to copy documents. Listing of Insurance Companies: List is printed twice a year and is available for $10.75. All requests must be submitted in writing and be prepaid. Number of Licensed Companies: 1,000. Licensed Agents. List of Agents:

Be patient. If any phone number is incorrect, call (area code) 555-1212 and request the new listing.

Information on People, Companies, and Mailing Lists

Lists are available by calling (203) 297-3841. Lists are sorted by authority, company, and locality. Cost of each list is $318. Number of Agents: Not available.

Delaware

Insurance Department, 841 Silver Lake Blvd, Dover, DE 19901/(302) 739-4251. Insurance Companies Documents on File: Documents are available. Cost is 25 cents per page or $15.50 for listing. Listing of Insurance Companies: Cheshire or pressure sensitive labels are available for $75. Computer printouts are available on a cost recovery basis. Number of Insurance Companies: 1,400. Licensed Agents. List of Agents: Available by contacting (302) 739-4251. Number of Agents: 8,000.

District of Columbia

Insurance Administration, Dept. of Consumer and Regulatory Affairs Dept., P.O. Box 37200, Washington, DC 20013-7200/(202) 727-8000. Insurance Companies Documents on File: Documents may be reviewed and copied in the office. Listing of Insurance Companies: A free listing is available. Number of Insurance Companies: Not available. Licensed Agents. List of Agents: No listing available. Number of Licensed Agents: Not available. All requests must be in writing.

Florida

Dept of Insurance Agents and Agent Licensing, 200 E. Gaines, Tallahassee, FL 32399-0300/(904) 922-3100. Insurance Companies Documents on File: Copies are available for 50 cents per page and $5 for certified copies. Listing of Insurance Companies: Complimentary copy of *Year List of All Insurance Companies Licensed to Do Business in State of Florida* available upon written request. *Annual Report* also contains listing. Number of Insurance Companies; 1,800. Licensed Agents. List of Agents: List is sorted by type of insurance. They categorize 5 types of adjusters. Computer printouts are available on a cost recovery basis, as are magnetic tape formats and gummed labels. Number of Agents: 169,458.

Georgia

Insurance Commissioner, #2 Martin Luther King Dr., 7th Floor, W. Tower, Atlanta, GA 30334/(404) 656-2056. Insurance Companies Documents on File: Annual Statements are available. Listing of Insurance Companies: Computer printouts are available for $30. Number of Insurance Companies: 1,500. Licensed Agents. List of Agents: No list available, (404) 656-2100. Number of Agents: 48,000.

Hawaii

Commerce and Consumer Affairs Department, Insurance Division, 250 S. King St., Honolulu, HI 96813; (808) 586-2790. Insurance Companies Documents on File: Available for 25 cents per page. List of Insurance Companies: *Commissioner Report* available free of charge. Number of Insurance Companies: 760. Licensed Agents. List of Agents: None available. Number of Agents: 9,670. (808) 586-2788.

Idaho

Insurance Department, 500 S. 10th, Boise, ID 83720/(208) 334-2250. Insurance Companies Documents on File: Available for 50 cents per page. Listing of Insurance Companies: Company Listing available for $7.50. This order must be prepaid. Number of Insurance Companies: 1,500. Licensed Agents, (208) 334-4339. List of Agents: Computer printout available for a fee. Pressure Sensitive labels available for a fee. List and labels can be sorted by line of insurance or ZIP code. Number of Agents: 11,500.

Illinois

Insurance Department, 320 W. Washington St., 4th Floor, Springfield, IL 62767/(217) 782-4515. Insurance Companies Documents on File: Available for $1 a page. Listing of Insurance Companies: Annual Statement available quarterly. Computer Information, (217) 782-3045: Printout available for $100. Magnetic tape or diskette available for $100. Requester must supply tape or diskette. Pressure sensitive labels can be run on a cost recovery basis if requester supplies labels. Cheshire labels also available on a cost recovery basis, you supply the labels. All computer runs are in ZIP code order. Number of Insurance Companies: 1,813. Licensed Agents. List of Agents: (217) 782-3045. Computer printouts available for $100. Magnetic tape or diskette available for $600. Requester must supply tape or diskette. Cheshire labels available for $1,000. All computer runs are in ZIP code order. Number of Agents: 80,000.

Indiana

Insurance Department, 311 W. Washington St., Suite 300, Indianapolis, IN 46204/(317) 232-2405. Phone Information: (317) 232-2392. Documents on File: Available for 25 cents per page. Listing of Insurance Companies: Monthly computer run available for $25. This listing contains name of company, address, phone number, and type of insurance. Computer generated labels and listings on magnetic tape or diskette will be available in the near future. Number of Insurance Companies: 1,700, (317) 232-2410. Licensed Agents. List of Agents: Computer listing will be available in near future. Diskette available for a fee. Number of Agents: 97,000.

Iowa

Commerce Department, Insurance Division, Lucas State Office Building, Des Moines, IA 50319/ (515) 281-4033. Insurance Companies Documents on File: Documents can be reviewed in the office and may be copied for a minimal charge. Listing of Insurance Companies: Available for $5. Number of Insurance Companies: 1,487. Licensed Agents, (515) 281-4039. List of Agents: Computer printout available on a cost recovery basis. Pressure sensitive labels available on a cost recovery basis. Customized listing or labels may be sorted by type of insurance, ZIP Code, county, or company. Number of Agents: 32,170.

Kansas

Kansas Insurance Department, 420 S. West 9th St, Topeka, KS 66612/(913) 296-3071. Insurance Companies Documents on File: Documents can be copied on a cost recovery basis. Listing of Insurance Companies: Kansas Insurance Company Directory available free of charge. Listing available on magnetic tape if requester supplies the tape. (Kansas forbids use of public information for solicitation purposes.) Number of Insurance Companies: 1,200. Licensed Agents. List of Agents: Customized lists of agents by company, line of business or location are available on a cost recovery basis, (913) 296-7861. Number of Agents: 24,500.

Kentucky

Department of Insurance, PO Box 517, Frankfort, KY 40602/(502) 564-3630. Insurance Companies Documents on File: (502) 564-6081. Call and then submit written request and prepayment. Annual statements, copies 50 cents per page. Listing of Insurance Companies: Directory available for $150. Pressure sensitive labels available for $150. Number of Insurance Companies: 1,438. Licensed Agents, (502) 564-6004. List of Agents: Computer printouts are available in many formats but due to computer limitations no listing of all agents is available. The following listings are available for $5 each: ZIP Code, Company Name, and Lines of Insurance. Number of Agents: 31,340.

Louisiana

Insurance Department, PO Box 94214, Baton Rouge, LA 70804-9214/(504) 342-5900. Insurance Companies Documents on File: A written request must be submitted for all documents. All documents are available for 25 cents per page, complete list for $31.25. Listing of Insurance Companies: Report of the Commissioners of Insurance is available at no charge. It contains name, address and telephone number of all insurance companies. Number of Insurance Companies: 2,358. Licensed Agents. List of Agents: No list of agents is available. Names may be obtained by visiting the office. Number of Agents: 70,000. (504) 342-3565.

Maine

Bureau of Insurance and Financial Regulations Dept., State House #34, Augusta, ME 04333/(207) 582-8707. Insurance Companies Documents on File: Documents will be copied as staffing permits on a cost recovery basis. Listing of Insurance Companies: written request required. Computer printout available on a cost recovery basis. Printouts can be sorted by ZIP code, alphabetical, county, or type of insurance. Pressure sensitive labels available for 4 cents a name. Number of Insurance Companies: 800. Licensed Agents. List of Agents: Computer printout available on a cost recovery basis. Pressure sensitive labels available for 4 cents a name. Number of Agents: 9,000.

Maryland

Insurance Division, Licensing and Regulation Department, 501 St. Paul Pl. Baltimore, MD 21202/(301) 333-6300. Insurance Companies Documents on File: Available for $1 per page. Listing of Insurance Companies: Not Available, (301) 333-6192. Number of Insurance Companies: 1,884. Licensed Agents, (301) 333-4074. List of Agents: No listing available. Number of Agents: 75,000.

Massachusetts

Commonwealth of Massachusetts, Division of Insurance, 280 Friend St., Boston, MA 02114/(617) 727-5503. Insurance Companies Documents on File: Copies of documents may be obtained on a cost recovery basis. Listing of Insurance Companies: Computer printout available for a fee. Number of Insurance Companies: 900. Licensed Agents, (617) 727-7189 ext. 350. List of Agents: Not available. Number of Agents: 60,000.

Be patient. If any phone number is incorrect, call (area code) 555-1212 and request the new listing.

Insurance Companies and Salesmen

Michigan

Insurance Bureau, Dept. of Commerce, PO Box 30220, Lansing, MI 48909/(517) 373-9273. Insurance Companies Documents on File: Office will copy up to 14 pages free, over 15 pages documents are copies on a cost recovery basis. Listing of Insurance Companies: Computer printouts available for 20 cents per page, written request only! Number of Insurance Companies: 110. Licensed Agents. List of Agents: Written request only. Number of Agents: 60,000. (517) 373-0234.

Minnesota

Insurance Division, Minnesota Department of Commerce, 133 E. 7th St., St. Paul, MN 55101/(612) 296-6319. Insurance Companies Documents on File: Copies available for 50 cents per page. Listing of Insurance Companies: Minnesota Book Store, 117 University Avenue, St. Paul, MN 55155/(612) 297-3000. Photocopied listing available for $25 plus tax and handling cost. Mailing list office, Debbie Sabota (612) 297-2552. Number of Insurance Companies: 1,500. Licensed Agents. List of Agents: Contact Mailing List Office listed above. Number of Agents: 38,000-40,000.

Mississippi

Insurance Department, PO Box 79, Jackson, MS 39205/(601) 359-3576. Insurance Company Documents on File: Copies of documents available on a cost recovery basis if staffing permits. Listing of Insurance Companies: Company book available with written request. Pressure sensitive labels available for $360. Number of Insurance Companies: 17,000. Licensed Agents. List of Agents: Available from the Mississippi Association of Life Underwriters, P.O. Box 13649, Jackson, MS 39236/(601) 981-1522. Labels, printouts or tapes available for a fee. Number of Agents: 16,000.

Missouri

Missouri Dept. of Insurance, Regulatory Agencies, PO Box 690, 301 W. High, Room 630, Jefferson City, MO 65102/(314) 751-2562. Insurance Companies Documents on File: A Book of documents available for $10. Listing of Insurance Companies: Computer printout and pressure sensitive labels available on a cost recovery basis. Number of Insurance Companies: 1,200. Licensed Agents. List of Agents: Computer printout and pressure sensitive labels available on a cost recovery basis. Number of Agents: 64,000.

Montana

Insurance Commissioner, PO Box 4009, Helena, MT 59604-4009/(406) 444-2040. Insurance Companies Documents on File: Documents can be copied for 50 cents per pages as staffing permits. Listing of Insurance Companies: Computer printout available for $6 plus postage, (1990 latest listing). Number of Insurance Companies: 1,400. Licensed Agents. List of Agents: No listing available. Names may be viewed by visiting the office. Number of Agents: 8,310.

Nebraska

Insurance Department, Terminal Bldg, 941 O Street, Suite 1400, Lincoln, NE 68508/(402) 471-2201. Insurance Companies Documents on File: Available for 50 cents per page. Listing of Insurance Companies: Computer printouts, pressure sensitive labels, or magnetic tape can be obtained for $50. Computerized information can be sorted by ZIP code, alphabetical, or by line of insurance. Summary of Insurance Business is available annually for $20. It lists amount of premiums each company collects and the volume of business. Number of Licensed Insurance Companies: 16,500. Licensed Agents. List of Agents: Computer printouts, pressure sensitive labels or magnetic tape are available for $150. Computerized information can be sorted by ZIP code, alphabetical, or by line of insurance. Number of Agents: 22,000.

Nevada

Department of Insurance, Commerce Department, 1665 Hot Spring Rd., Suite 152, Carson City, NV 89710/(702) 687-4270. Insurance Companies Documents on File: Available for 50 cents per page or $45 for a list. Listing of Insurance Companies: Computer printouts, Cheshire and pressure sensitive labels and diskettes available on a cost recovery basis. Computerized information can be sorted by ZIP code, alphabetical, or city. Number of Insurance Companies: 2,000. Licensed Agents. List of Agents: Same as for insurance companies. Number of Agents: 18,000.

New Hampshire

Insurance Department, 169 Manchester St., Concord, NH 03301/(603) 271-2261. Insurance Companies Documents on File: Documents may be viewed by visiting the above office. List of Insurance Companies: A printout titled Licensed Companies is available on a cost recovery basis. Number of Insurance Companies: 900. Licensed Agents. List of Agents: Laser printout $50. Number of Agents: 3,500.

New Jersey

Department of Insurance, 20 W. State St, CN 325, Trenton, NJ 08625/(609) 292-5371. Insurance Company Documents on File: Free. Listing of Insurance Company: Commissioners Annual Report contains a listing of insurance companies. Number of Insurance Companies: 1,500. Licensed Agents. List of Agents: (609) 292-4390. List is available on a cost recovery basis. Number of Agents: Not available. For a list of agents, send written request to State of New Jersey, 20 W. State St., CN 327, Trenton, NJ 08625.

New Mexico

Insurance Division, Corporation Commission, 500 Old Santa Fe Trail, Santa Fe, NM 87501-1269/(505) 827-4542. Insurance Companies Documents on File: Documents will be copied on a cost recovery basis. Listing of Insurance Companies: Directory of Insurance Companies available free of charge. Number of Insurance Companies: 1,500. Licensed Agents. List of Agents: Computer printout available for $400, (505) 827-4549 (Licensing). Pressure sensitive labels available for $200. Number of Agents: 10,000.

New York

Insurance Department, Empire State Plaza, Building 1, Albany, NY 12257/(518) 474-6615. Insurance Companies Documents on File: Available for 50 cents per page. Listing of Insurance Companies: (518) 474-7159. Directory of Licensed Insurance Companies available for $1, (Out of state only). Number of Insurance Companies: 1,000. Licensed Agents. List of Agents: requests in writing only. Number of Agents: 40,000. (518) 474-6620 ext. 30.

North Carolina

Insurance Department, Box 26387, 430 N. Salisbury St., Raleigh, NC 27611/(919) 733-5633. Insurance Companies Documents on File: Available for 50 cents per page. Average cost is $10. Listing of Insurance Companies: Computer printout is available for $5. Number of Insurance Companies: 1,069. Licensed Agents, (919) 733-7487. List of Agents: Available for $175 for the first 5,000 names, for every additional 1,000 the cost is $7. Lists may be sorted by company, line of insurance, resident or nonresident, and ZIP. Number of Agents: 70,000.

North Dakota

Insurance Department, Capitol Building, 600 E. Blvd., 5th Floor, Bismarck, ND 58505/(701) 224-2440. Insurance Companies Documents on File: Available for 20 cents per page. Listing of Insurance Companies: Computer printout is available for $20 or 2 cents per name. Pressure sensitive labels are available for $100. Number of Insurance Companies: 1,300. Licensed Agents. List of Agents: Pressure sensitive labels and computer printout are available for $20 plus 2 cents a name. List may be sorted by resident or nonresident and line of insurance. Number of Agents: 10,000.

Ohio

Insurance Department, 2100 Stella Court, Columbus, OH 43266-0566/(614) 644-2658. Insurance Companies Documents on File: Available for 50 cents per page. Listing of Insurance Companies: Authorized list of Insurance Companies is available free of charge. This list contains names only. Computer printouts, pressure sensitive labels and magnetic tape are available on a cost recovery basis. Lists can be sorted by types of insurance, foreign or domestic, ZIP Code, and city. All requests must be submitted in writing. Number of licensed insurance companies: 1,665. Licensed Agents. List of Agents: Computer printout and pressure sensitive labels are available on a cost recovery basis. Number of Agents: 54,000.

Oklahoma

Insurance Department, 1901 N. Walnut, Oklahoma City, OK 73152-3408/(405) 521-3966. Insurance Companies Documents on File. Listing of Insurance Companies: Annual Report and Directory is available free with written request. Computer printouts and pressure sensitive labels available on a cost recovery basis. Magnetic tape available for $25 plus 1 cent per record. Lists may be sorted by line of insurance or ZIP code. Licensed Agents. List of Agents: Computer printouts and pressure sensitive labels available on a cost recovery basis for $200. Number of Agents: 17,000. (405) 521-3916.

Oregon

Department of Insurance and Finance, Insurance Division, 440 Labor and Industrial Bldg., Salem, OR 97310/(503) 378-4271. Insurance Companies Documents on File: Available for 50 cents per page. Listing of Insurance Companies: Directory available for $2.50. Number of Insurance Companies: 1,500. Licensed Agents. List of Agents: Computer printout is available for $25. Pressure sensitive labels are available for $50. Number of Agents: 19,000.

Be patient. If any phone number is incorrect, call (area code) 555-1212 and request the new listing.

Information on People, Companies, and Mailing Lists

Pennsylvania

Insurance Department, 1311 Strawberry Square, Harrisburg, PA 17120/(717) 787-2735. Insurance Companies Documents on File: Available for 25 cents per page. Listing of Insurance Companies: Listing is available for $20. Number of Insurance Companies: 1,500. Licensed Agents. List of Agents: (717) 787-3840, Not available. Number of Agents: 190,000.

Rhode Island

Insurance Division, Business Regulations Department, 233 Richmond St., Providence, RI 02903/(401) 277-2223. Insurance Companies Documents on File: Available for 20 cents per page. Average cost is $32. Listing of Insurance Companies: Annual Report is available for $15. It contains names and addresses of all insurance companies. Number of Insurance Companies: 900. Licensed Agents. List of Agents: Available on a cost recovery basis with written request. Number of Agents: 25,000.

South Carolina

Insurance Department, P.O. Box 100105, Columbia, SC 29202-3105/(803) 737-6120. Insurance Companies Documents on File: Available by written request for $25. Listing of Insurance Companies: Master list of all licensed companies is available for $5. Pressure sensitive labels are available on a cost recovery label. Number of Insurance Companies: 1,420. Licensed Agents, (803) 737-6095. List of Agents: Listing available for 3 cents per name. Pressure sensitive labels are available for 6 cents per label. Number of Agents: 45,000.

South Dakota

Insurance Division, Commerce and Regulations Department, 500 East Capitol, Pierre, SD 57501/(605) 773-3563. Insurance Companies Documents on File: Available for 75 cents per page. Listing of Insurance Companies: Computer printout and pressure sensitive labels are available for $25. Number of Insurance Companies: 1,464. Licensed Agents. List of Agents: Computer printouts are available for $200. Pressure sensitive labels are available for $200. Number of Agents: Not available. (605) 773-3513.

Tennessee

Commerce and Insurance Department, 500 James Robertson Pkwy, Volunteer Plaza, Nashville, TN 37243/(615) 741-1692. Insurance Companies Documents on File: All documents may be viewed in the office. Listing of Insurance Companies: Quarterly listing of companies available for free. The listing contains addresses, type of insurance, and ZIP code. Number of Insurance Companies: 1,574. Licensed Agents. List of Agents: List may be copied in the office. Number of Agents: 83,000.

Texas

Texas Dept of Insurance, 333 Guadalope, Austin, TX 78701-1998/(512) 463-6425. Insurance Companies Documents on File: Available for 50 cents per page. Listing of Insurance Companies: Computer printout available for $37.80. Send written request to Texas Dept. of Insurance Publications, PO Box 149104 #999, Austin, TX 78714. Licensed Agents. List of Agents: Available for a fee. Number of Agents: 150,000, (512) 322-4105.

Utah

Insurance Department, 3110 State Office Bldg., Salt Lake City, UT 84114/(801) 538-3800. Insurance Companies Documents on File: Available for 25 cents per page. Listing of Insurance Companies: Computer printouts are available for $1 a sheet. Average cost is $50. Pressure sensitive labels are available for $10 per page. Average cost is $140. Number of Insurance Companies: 1,500. Licensed Agents. List of Agents: Written request for pressure sensitive labels are available for $350 or $1 per page. (801) 538-3855. Number of Agents: 16,500.

Vermont

Department of Banking and Insurance, 89 Main St, Montpelier, VT 05602/(802) 828-3301. Insurance Companies Documents on File: Documents may be viewed in the office. Annual report is free. Listing of Insurance Companies: Available free of charge. Number of Insurance Companies: 1,000. Licensed Agents. List of Agents: Computer printouts, mailing labels and magnetic tape available on a cost recovery basis. Number of Agents: 7,200.

Virginia

Insurance Bureau, State Corporation Commission, 1220 Bank Street, P.O. Box 1197, Richmond, VA 23219/(804) 786-3741. Insurance Companies Documents on File: Available for $1 for first page, 50 cents each page after. Listing of Insurance Companies: Available free of charge. Number of Insurance Companies: 1,700. Licensed Agents. List of Agents: Available by company. Not available at Bureau. Number of Agents: Not available.

Washington

Insurance Commissioner, Insurance Building, PO Box 40255, Olympia, WA 98504/(206) 753-2418. Insurance Companies Documents on File: Documents available for $10. Listing of Insurance Companies: Available on a cost recovery basis. Number of Insurance Companies: 1,500. Licensed Agents. List of Agents: No list available. The state law forbids the use of names for commercial purposes. Number of Agents: Not available.

West Virginia

Insurance Department, 2100 Washington St East, Charleston, WV 25305/(304) 348-2100. Insurance Companies Documents on File: Available for 50 cents per page. Listing of Insurance Companies: Commissioners Annual Report contains names and addresses. It is available for $10. Number of Insurance Companies: 1,000. Licensed Agents, (304) 348-3386. List of Agents: Written request required. Computer printout available for $60. Pressure sensitive labels available for $60. Number of Agents: 20,000.

Wisconsin

Insurance Commission, P.O. Box 7573, Madison, WI 53707-7873/(608) 267-9456. Insurance Companies Documents on File: Available for 20 cents per page. Listing of Insurance Companies: Computer printout available for $50. Listing can be searched by ZIP code, county, line of insurance, company, and resident or nonresident. Licensed Agents, (608) 266-8699. List of Agents: Available for $50. It can be searched by ZIP code, county, line of insurance, company and resident or nonresident. Number of Agents: 50,000.

Wyoming

Insurance Department, 122 West 25th Street, Cheyenne, WY 82002- 0440/(307) 777-7401. Insurance Companies Documents on File: Available for $1 per page plus postage. Average cost $100. Listing of Insurance Companies: Computer printouts available for $50. Number of Insurance Companies: 970. Licensed Agents, (307) 777-7319. List of Agents: Computer printout is available for $50. Number of Agents: 3,100.

Be patient. If any phone number is incorrect, call (area code) 555-1212 and request the new listing.

Federal Mailing Lists

Listed below are a number of mailing lists available from the federal government. This does not represent all available mailing lists, but only the more popular ones. Remember that anywhere the government collects names and addresses, that information theoretically is available to the public. Keep this in mind as you review the other chapters in this book.

At the end of each description below is a vendor code. A listing of the complete name and address for vendor codes is at the end of the mailing list descriptions.

Abstract Newsletter Subscribers

Contains 14,000 subscribers to the National Technical Information service newsletter service which covers the most recent research findings in 26 areas of industrial, technological, and sociological interest. Format: Off-line; Price: $100/per thousand names; Vendor: NTIS.

Agexporter (formerly Foreign Agriculture)

A monthly magazine targeted at business firms selling United States farm products overseas. Provides timely information on overseas trade opportunities, including reports on marketing activities and how-to's of agricultural exporting. List ID: FA-2E; 460 paid subscribers; Vendor: GPO.

Airman's Information Manual

Subscription provides the fundamentals required in order to fly in the United States National Airspace System. It also contains items of interest to pilots concerning health and medical facts, factors affecting flight safety, a pilot/controller glossary of terms used in the Air Traffic Control System, and information on safety, accident and hazard reporting. List ID: BFAP-2D; 9,134 paid subscribers; Vendor: GPO.

Alcohol Health and Research World

Presents current research findings; prevention, treatment, and training program descriptions; and observations with opinions from those working at the base level to provide services to persons affected by alcohol-related problems. List ID: AHRW-2Q; 5,932 paid subscribers; Vendor: GPO.

Area Wage Survey

These bulletins report on earnings in 70 major metropolitan areas for occupations common to a wide variety of establishments, including office clerical, professional and technical, maintenance, custodial, and material movement occupations. List ID: AWS-2B; 327 paid subscribers; Vendor: GPO.

Business America, The Magazine of International Trade

A biweekly publication designed to help American exporters penetrate overseas markets by providing them with timely information on opportunities for trade and methods of doing business in foreign countries. List ID: CRTD-2E; 4,632 paid subscribers; Vendor: GPO.

Branch Office Deposits

The Office of Thrift Supervision contains street addresses for home offices and branch offices of 3,196 FSLIC insured institutions. Zip codes are not included. Format: Tape; Price: $150; Vendor: FHLBB.

Business Conditions Digest

Prepared in the Statistical Indicators Division of the Bureau of Economic Analysis, the Digest presents almost 500 economic indicators in a form convenient for analysis with different approaches to the study of current business conditions and prospects (e.g., the national income model, the leading indicators, and anticipations and intentions), as well as for analysts who use combinations of these approaches. List ID: BCD-2G; 4,123 paid subscribers; Vendor: GPO.

Cancergrams

Current awareness bulletins in numerous cancer-related subject areas; Vendor: GPO.

Catalog of Federal Domestic Assistance

A Government-wide summary of financial and nonfinancial Federal programs, projects, services, and activities that provide assistance or benefits to the American public administered by departments and establishments of the Federal Government. Describes the type of assistance available and the eligibility requirements for the particular assistance being sought, with guidance on how to apply. Also intended to improve coordination and communication between the Federal Government and State and local governments. List ID: COF89-1X; 4,456 paid subscribers; Vendor: GPO.

Census and You (formerly Data User News)

A monthly newsletter for users of Census Bureau statistics, which gives up-to-date information on Bureau programs, products and services and the latest news about demographic and economic data. List ID: DUN-2G; 2,941 paid subscribers; Vendor: GPO.

Census and You Mailing List (formerly Data User News)

Listing of the 394 free subscribers to the *Data User News*, which contains news highlights of current products available from the U.S. Bureau of the Census. Format: Tape; Price: $10; Vendor: CENSUS.

Children Today

Reports on Federal, State, and local services for children, child development, health and welfare laws, and other news pertinent to child welfare in the United States. List ID: CT-2S; 5,201 paid subscribers; Vendor: GPO.

Commerce Business Daily: Synopsis of United States Government Proposed Procurement, Sales, and Contract Awards

The Synopsis is of particular value to firms interested in bidding on U.S. Government purchases, surplus property offered for sale, or in seeking subcontract opportunities from prime contractors. It lists current information received daily from military and civilian procurement offices. List ID: COBD-2P; 42,106 paid subscribers; Vendor: GPO.

Commercial Info Management (CIMS)

CIMS is a decentralized database of the U.S. Dept. of Commerce that matches subscribing U.S. firms with foreign companies and governments interested in purchasing U.S. goods and services. Information connecting buyers and sellers is transmitted via telecommunications between U.S. posts in foreign counties and District Offices in the U.S. District Offices maintain data on the size, products

Be patient. If any phone number is incorrect, call (area code) 555-1212 and request the new listing.

Information on People, Companies, and Mailing Lists

and export capabilities of companies in their area. Format: Off-line; Price: $500 for entire list; Vendor: COMMERCE.

Committee on Scientific and Technical Information

List of individuals who have requested copies of the index by 22 major categories of National Technical Information Service reports that were developed and endorsed by the Committee on Scientific and Technical Information. Format: Off-line; Price: $100/per thousand; Vendor: NTIS.

Congressional Record

A verbatim report on Congressional debates and other proceedings. List ID: CR-3A; 1,698 paid subscribers. List ID: CRM-3A (Microfiche); 70 paid subscribers; Vendor: GPO.

Consumer Directory - Catalog

CERN-II is a directory of more than 2,000 organizations involved in consumer education or protection. Groups listed range from government agencies to university programs at the national, state, or local level. Retrieval information includes: address, phone number, contact person, type of organization (25 categories), staff size, funding, subject areas covered, etc. Format: Off-line; Price: Free; Vendor: GSA-CIC.

Cumulative List of Organizations

Lists contributions of organizations which are deductible under Section 170(c) of the Internal Revenue Code of 1954. List ID: CL-1L; 5,075 paid subscribers; Vendor: GPO.

Current Housing Reports

H-111. Housing Vacancies. Quarterly reports and an annual issue which give percent distributions of rental vacancies and homeowner vacancies, by facilities, number of rooms, monthly rent asked and sales price asked, etc., compared with same quarter of previous year.

H-121. Housing characteristics. Occasional reports of data for the country as a whole and for regions on selected characteristics of housing. List ID: CHR-2Q; 211 paid subscribers; Vendor: GPO.

Current Wage Development

Presents wage and benefit changes that result from collective bargaining settlements and unilateral management decisions. Also includes statistical summaries and special reports on wage trends. List ID: CWD-2M; 650 paid subscribers; Vendor: GPO.

Customs Bulletin and Decisions

Contains regulations, rulings, decisions, and notices concerning Customs and related matters of the United States Court of Appeals for the Federal Circuit and the United States Court of International Trade. List ID: CB-2E; 1,041 paid subscribers; Vendor: GPO.

Customs Regulations of the United States

Contains regulations made and published for the purpose of carrying out customs laws administered by the United States Customs Service. List ID: CRUS-1F; 3,710 paid subscribers; Vendor: GPO.

DOD FAR Supplement

This U.S. Department of Defense supplement to the Federal Acquisition Regulation contains guidelines on the provisions, clauses, and cost principles authorized for DOD contracts, as well as procedures and actions necessary for awarding and administering the contracts. List ID: DFARS-1A; 4,806 paid subscribers; Vendor: GPO.

Domestic Mail Manual

Designed to assist Postal Service customers in obtaining maximum benefits from domestic postal services. It includes applicable regulations and information about rates and postage, classes of mail, special services, wrapping and mailing requirements, and collection and delivery services.

List ID: DOM-2S; 8,631 paid subscribers; Vendor: GPO.

Economic Indicators

Gives pertinent economic information on prices, wages, production, business activity, purchasing power, credit, money and Federal finance. List ID: ECIN-2G; 4,766 paid subscribers; Vendor: GPO.

Education Statistics Mailing List

Contains over 5,000 people who requested material from the National Center for Education Statistics. Format: Tape; Price: See Vendor; Vendor: NCES.

EIA Publication New Releases (DOE-EIA-0204)

Contains 14 categories of users of U.S. Energy Department's Energy Information Administration publications with approximately 13,000 names. Format: Off-line; Price: Cost Recovery; Vendor: EIA.

Employment and Earnings

Current data on employment, hours, and earnings for the United States as a whole, for States, and for more than 200 local areas. List ID: EMEA-2M; 3,485 paid subscribers; Vendor: GPO.

Export Administration Regulations

Subscription service consists of a compilation of official regulations and policies governing the export licensing of commodities and technical data. List ID: EAR88-1A; 8,385 paid subscribers; Vendor: GPO.

FAA Aviation News

Designed to help airmen become safer pilots, this publication gives updates and major Federal Aviation Administration rule changes and proposed Changes, as well as refresher information on flight rules, maintenance airworthiness, avionics, accident analysis, and other related topics. Covers all types of aircraft, including helicopters, balloons, gliders, antique, sport and experimental. List ID: FAN-2D; 15,032 paid subscribers; Vendor: GPO.

FDA Consumer

Covers information written especially for consumers about Food and Drug Administration regulatory and scientific decisions, and about the safe use of products regulated by FDA. List ID: FDAP-2G; 23,942 paid subscribers; Vendor: GPO.

Federal Acquisition Regulations

The Federal Acquisition Regulation (FAR) is the primary regulation used by Federal Executive Branch agencies purchasing supplies and services. List ID: FEACR-1A; 13,757 paid subscribers; Vendor: GPO.

The Federal Labor-Management and Employee Relations Consultant

Presents current information in the field of labor-management and employee relations. List ID: FLMC-2G; 365 paid subscribers; Vendor: GPO.

Federal Procurement Data Center

This database contains two million records pertaining to federal procurement actions from 1979 to present. Information is on contracts totaling $25,000 or more and also includes the purchasing or contracting office, date of award, principal place of performance and dollars obligated. Format: Tape, hard copy, gummed labels, microfiche; Price: variable; Vendor: FPDC.

Federal Register

Provides a uniform system for making available to the public regulations and legal notices issued by Federal agencies. These include Presidential proclamations and Executive orders and Federal agency documents having general applicability and legal effect, documents required to be published by Act of Congress and other Federal agency documents of public interest.

Be patient. If any phone number is incorrect, call (area code) 555-1212 and request the new listing.

List ID: FR-3A; 17,085 paid subscribers; Vendor: GPO.
List ID: MFFR-3A Microfiche; 1,129 paid subscribers.

Federal Trainer

Contains news and features pertaining to programs for training Federal employees. List ID: FEDT-2Q; 164 paid subscribers; Vendor: GPO.

Fishery Bulletin

Publishes original research papers, and occasionally, reviews of topical interest, in the broad discipline of fishery science. Research fields of particular interest are ecology, oceanography, and limnology; mariculture; ocean pollution; physiology, behavior and taxonomy of marine organisms, particularly fishes; technology; gear development; and economics.
List ID: FB-2D; 214 paid subscribers; Vendor: GPO.

Foreign Economic Trends and Their Implications for the United States

Includes key economic indicators, a brief summary of the state of the economy of the subject country, the current situation and economic trends, industrial report, agricultural report, foreign trade situation, living costs, monetary situation, and conclusions and implications for the United States.
List ID: ECTR-2B; 845 paid subscribers; Vendor: GPO.

Foreign Traders Index (FTI)

A directory of manufacturers, service organizations, agent representatives, retailers, wholesalers, distributors and cooperatives in 130 countries outside the U.S. Data are maintained by the International Trade Administration at the U.S. Department of Commerce. It provides the nature of business, name of officers, size, employees and establishment date. FTI is restricted to U.S. use. It is current for 5 years and is updated quarterly. Format: Tape, hard copy, gummed labels; Price: Varies, 25 cents/per name; Vendor: ITA.

Foreign Trade Reports FT990

Highlights of United States export and import trade.
List ID: FT990-2M; 380 paid subscribers; Vendor: GPO.

FSS Agency Rehabilitation

The General Services Administration sells this mailing list which totals some 1,000 addresses. Format: Tape; Price: $50/per reel; Vendor: GSA-MLIC.

FSS Excess Property

The General Services Administration sells this mailing list which totals some 2,000 addresses. Format: Tape; Price: $50/per reel; Vendor: GSA-MLIC.

FSS Publications

The General Services Administration sells this mailing list which totals 47,000 addresses. Format: Tape; Price: $50/per reel; Vendor: GSA-MLIC.

FSS Procurement Bidders

The General Services Administration sells this mailing list which totals some 47,000 addresses. Format: Tape; Price: $50/per reel; Vendor: GSA-MLIC.

FSS Property Rehabilitation

The General Services Administration sells this mailing list which totals some 1,000 addresses. Format: Tape; Price: $50/per reel; Vendor: GSA-MLIC.

FSS Surplus Personal Property Zone (Regions 4 & 5)

Some 24,000 addresses comprise this General Services Administration mailing list. Surplus property auctioned by the federal government consists of hand and machine tools, office machines and supplies, furniture, hardware, motor vehicles, confiscated boats, airplanes and construction equipment. Format: Tape; Price: $50/per reel; Vendor: GSA-MLIC.

FSS Surplus Personal Property Zone (Regions 6 & 7)

Some 9,000 addresses comprise this General Services Administration mailing list. Surplus property auctioned by the federal government consists of hand and machine tools, office machines and supplies, furniture, hardware, motor vehicles, confiscated boats, airplanes and construction equipment.
Format: Tape; Price: $50/per reel; Vendor: GSA-MLIC.

FSS Surplus Personal Property Zone (Regions 8 - 10)

Some 38,000 addresses comprise this General Services Administration mailing list. Surplus property auctioned by the federal government consists of hand and machine tools, office machines and supplies, furniture, hardware, motor vehicles, confiscated boats, airplanes and construction equipment.
Format: Tape; Price: $50/per reel; Vendor: GSA-MLIC.

FSS Surplus Personal Property Defaulted Bidders

Some 4,000 addresses comprise this General Services Administration mailing list. Surplus property auctioned by the federal government consists of hand and machine tools, office machines and supplies, furniture, hardware, motor vehicles, confiscated boats, airplanes and construction equipment.
Format: Tape; Price: $50/per reel; Vendor: GSA-MLIC.

FSS Surplus Personal Property Zone (Regions 1, 2, 3)

Some 19,000 addresses comprise this General Services Administration mailing list. Surplus property auctioned by the federal government consists of hand and machine tools, office machines and supplies, furniture, hardware, motor vehicles, confiscated boats, airplanes and construction equipment.
Format: Tape; Price: $50/per reel; Vendor: GSA-MLIC.

Futures All Firm Directory

The National Future Association directory contains an alphabetical listing of the four categories of futures traders: Commodity Trading Advisors, Commodity Pool Operators, Futures Commission Merchants, and Introducing Brokers. Includes addresses and phone numbers. Format: Off-line; Price: $10-$25; Vendor: NFA.

Government Unit Name and Address File

Contains names, addresses, and geographic codes of local governments in the census for the years ending in 2 and 7.
Format: Tape; Price: $140/per reel; Vendor: CENSUS 2.

GPO Sales Publications Reference File

A guide to current publications offered for sale by the Superintendent of Documents arranged by GPO stock numbers; Superintendent of Documents classification numbers; and alphabetically by subjects, titles, agency series and report numbers, key words and phrases, and personal authors.
List ID: PRF-2N; 441 paid subscribers; Vendor: GPO.

GSA Rocky Mountain Bulletin

The General Services Administration sells this mailing list which totals some 3,000 addresses.
Format: Tape; Price: $50/per reel; Vendor: GSA-MLIC.

General Services Administration Training (Classes)

The GSA sells this mailing list which totals some 26,000 names and addresses.
Format: Tape; Price: $50/per reel; Vendor: GSA-MLIC.

Harmonized Tariff Schedules of the U.S. Annotated

For use in classifying imported merchandise for rate of duty and statistical purposes. List ID: TSA88-1A; 9,673 paid subscribers; Vendor: GPO.

Humanities

Published by the National Endowment for the Humanities, this publication describes the NEH program, projects, and issues in the humanities. Gives recent grants, deadlines, and useful information for applicants seeking funds.

Be patient. If any phone number is incorrect, call (area code) 555-1212 and request the new listing.

Information on People, Companies, and Mailing Lists

List ID: NR-2N; 3,671 paid subscribers; Vendor: GPO.

ICC Interstate Carrier Listing

Provides names, addresses, phone number, and motor carrier number of 51,000 active motor carriers. Types of carriers included in file are: railroads, trucking co., bus lines, freight forwarders, water carriers, property brokers, rate bureaus, and private carriers.

Format: Tape $45, Hard copy $100; Price: Cost recovery; Vendor: ICC.

ICD-9-CM International Classification of Diseases, 9th Revision, Clinical Modification, 3rd Edition:

Volumes 1 and 2; 47,684 paid subscribers; List ID: ICDP-1C.

Volume 3, Procedures Tabular List and Alphabetic Index; 108 paid subscribers; List ID: ICDH-1C.

Internal Revenue Bulletin

Announces official Internal Revenue Service rulings, Treasury Decisions, Executive Orders, legislation, and court decisions pertaining to internal revenue matters. List ID: IRB-2E; 5,027 paid subscribers; Vendor: GPO.

International Flight Information Manual

Primarily designed as a preflight and planning guide for use by United States non-scheduled operators, business and private aviators contemplating flights outside of the United States.

List ID: IFM89-1F; 1,016 paid subscribers; Vendor: GPO.

International Mail Manual

List ID: IMM-2S; 4,603 paid subscribers; Vendor: GPO.

Journal of the National Cancer Institute

An up-to-the-minute, reliable and comprehensive source of critical news and information on the latest developments in cancer research and treatment, including: prevention, clinical trials, immunology, molecular and tumor cell biology, biochemistry, carcinogenesis, epidemiology, biological response modifiers, cancer control, drug development, pharmacology, and many other fields. List ID: JNCI-2E; 2,232 paid subscribers; Vendor: GPO.

Lists of Parties Excluded from Federal Procurement or Nonprocurement Programs

List ID: CLDSC-2M; 959 paid subscribers; Vendor: GPO.

Management

Focuses attention on important developments in the Office of Personnel Management. List ID: CSJ-2Q; 1,793 paid subscribers; Vendor: GPO.

Manual on Uniform Traffic Control Devices for Streets and Highways

This manual provides detailed uniform standards for all signs, markings and devices placed on, over, or adjacent to a street or highway. Included are general specifications of sizes, shapes and colors, as well as sections on guide signs, pavement markings, traffic control signals, and islands. List ID: N-523-2A; 6,415 paid subscribers; Vendor: GPO.

Marine Fisheries Review

A review of developments and news of the fishery industries prepared in the National Marine Fisheries Service, United States Department of Commerce. List ID: MFR-2M; 177 paid subscribers; Vendor: GPO.

Master Cross Reference List

Part I, Logistics Reference No. to NSN; 379 paid subscribers; List ID: MCR01-2Q

Part II, NIIN to Logistics Reference No.; 463 paid subscribers; List ID: MCR02-2Q

Part III, FSCM and Logistics Reference to NSN; 212 paid subscribers; List ID: MCR03-2Q; Vendor: GPO

Monthly Catalog of United States Government Publications

Lists the publications printed and processed during each month. It includes the publications sold by the Superintendent of Documents, those for official use, and those sent to Depository Libraries.

List ID: MC89-1F; 1,242 paid subscribers; Vendor: GPO.

Monthly Energy Review

Illustrates current and historical statistics on United States production, storage, imports and consumption of petroleum, natural gas, and coal.

List ID: MER-2B; 1,273 paid subscribers; Vendor: GPO.

Monthly Labor Review

Includes articles on labor force, wages, prices, productivity, economic growth, and occupational injuries and illnesses. Regular features include a review of developments in industrial relations, book reviews, and current labor statistics.

List ID: MLR-2D; 6,976 paid subscribers; Vendor: GPO.

National Library of Medicine Audiovisuals Catalog

List ID: MAC89-1S; 251 paid subscribers; Vendor: GPO.

Nuclear Safety

Through this periodical the Energy Department provides concise and authoritative evaluation of scientific and technological developments relating to nuclear safety as they emerge from atomic research and development programs.

List ID: NS-2N; 535 paid subscribers; Vendor: GPO.

Occupational Outlook Quarterly

A periodical to help young people, employment planners, and guidance counselors keep abreast of current occupational and employment developments.

List ID: OOQ-2R; 22,730 paid subscribers; Vendor: GPO.

OSHA Standards and Regulations

Volume I, General Industry Standards and Interpretations; 5,056 paid subscribers; List ID: OSH01-1A

Volume II, Maritime Standards; 1,380 paid subscribers; List ID: OSH02-1A

Volume III, Construction Industry Standards and Interpretations; 4,579 paid subscribers; List ID: OSH03-1A

Volume IV, Other Regulations and Procedures; 1,631 paid subscribers; List ID: OSH04-1A

Volume V, Field Operations Manual; 1,029 paid subscribers; List ID: OSH05-1A

Volume VI, Industrial Hygiene Technical Manual; 1,102 paid subscribers; List ID: OSH06-1A; Vendor: GPO

Official Gazette of the United States Patent and Trademark Office: Patents

Contains the patents, Patent Office notices, and designs issued each week.

List ID: OG-2D; 2,313 paid subscribers; Vendor: GPO.

Official Gazette of the United States Patent and Trademark Office: Trademarks

Contains Trademarks, Trademark Notices, Marks Published for Opposition, Trademark Registrations Issued, and Index of Registrants.

List ID: OGT-2D; 1,565 paid subscribers; Vendor: GPO.

Official Summary of Security Transactions and Holdings

Contains securities holdings figures showing owners, relationships to issues, amounts of securities bought or sold by each owner, their individual holdings at the end of the reported month, and types of securities. List ID: OSST-2G; 916 paid subscribers; Vendor: GPO.

Be patient. If any phone number is incorrect, call (area code) 555-1212 and request the new listing.

Federal Mailing Lists

Postal Bulletin

Contains current orders, instructions and information relating to the United States Postal Service, and Commemorative Stamp Posters. List ID: POB-2E; 3,062 paid subscribers; Vendor: GPO.

Resources in Education

List ID: RIE-2M; 933 paid subscribers; Vendor: GPO.

Schedule B: Statistical Classification of Domestic and Foreign Commodities Exported from the United States

Contains approximately 40,007 digit commodity classifications, based on the organization framework of the Tariff Schedules of the United States, Annotated, to be used by shippers in reporting export shipments from the United States and for use in compiling official statistics on exports of merchandise from the United States. List ID: SCHB-1A; 28,436 paid subscribers; Vendor: GPO.

Schizophrenia Bulletin

Facilitates the dissemination and exchange of information about schizophrenia and provides abstracts of the recent literature on the subject. List ID: SB-2Q; 2,160 paid subscribers; Vendor: GPO.

SEC Monthly Statistical Review

Includes statistical summaries of new securities, securities sales, common stock prices, stock transactions, and other phases of securities exchange. List ID: STBU-2M; 375 paid subscribers; Vendor: GPO.

Survey of Current Business

Gives information on trends in industry, the business situation, outlook, and other points pertinent to the business world. List ID: SCUB-2D; 7,031 paid subscribers; Vendor: GPO.

Vendor List

The following is an alphabetical listing of government agencies according to their vendor symbols noted above.

CENSUS

Customer Service, Census Bureau
Data Services Division
Washington, DC 20233
(301) 763-4100

COMMERCE

U.S. Department of Commerce
World Traders Data Reports Section
14th St. and Constitution Ave., NW
Washington, DC 20230
(202) 482-4204

EIA

Energy Information Administration
Freedom of Information Office
U.S. Department of Energy
1000 Independence Ave., SW, 1G051
Washington, DC 20462
(202) 586-5955

FPDC

Federal Procurement Data Center
7th and D St., SW, Room 5652
Washington, DC 20407
(202) 401-1529

GSA-CIC

Consumer Information Center
General Services Administration
Room G142/18th and F St., NW
Washington, DC 20405
(202) 501-1794

GSA-MLIC

GSA/BSC
819 Taylor St., Room 11A05
Ft. Worth, TX 76102
(817) 334-3284

GPO

Superintendent of Documents
U.S. Government Printing Office
Washington, DC 20401
(202) 783-3238
Prices and Selections:
Cheshire labels: $85 per 1,000
minimum list user charge of $300 per order
Pressure sensitive labels: $5.30 per 1,000
Key coding (up to 5 digits): $2 per 1,000
No geographic selections available. No foreign lists available.
Shipping charges: $10 to $15.

ICC

Interstate Commerce Commission
Section of System Development
12th and Constitution, NW, #1349
Washington, DC 20423
(202) 275-7682

IRS

Internal Revenue Service Headquarters
U.S. Department of the Treasury
1111 Constitution Ave., NW
Washington, DC 20224
(202) 566-4743

ITA

International Trade Administration or
District Office
U.S. Department of Commerce
Washington, DC 20230
(202) 482-3808

MINING

Mining Information Division
Mine Safety and Health Administration
P.O. Box 2537
Denver, CO 80225
(303) 231-5475

NCES

National Center for Education Statistics/
Data Systems Branch
555 New Jersey Ave., NW, #300
Washington, DC 20208
(202) 357-6651

NFA

National Future Association
200 West Madison
Chicago, IL 60606
(312) 781-1300

Be patient. If any phone number is incorrect, call (area code) 555-1212 and request the new listing.

Information on People, Companies, and Mailing Lists

NTIS
National Technical Information Service
5285 Port Royal Road
Springfield, VA 22161
(703) 487-4812

OTS
Office of Thrift Supervision
1700 G St., NW
Washington, DC 20552
(202) 906-5900

Be patient. If any phone number is incorrect, call (area code) 555-1212 and request the new listing.

Government Auctions and Surplus Property

Looking for a bargain? Year round, the federal government offers hundreds of millions of dollars worth of property and goods -- from animals to real estate -- at remarkable prices. The Customs Service sells seized property -- jewelry, camera, rugs -- anything brought in from another country. The IRS auctions off everything imaginable -- boats, cars, businesses. The U.S. Postal Service sells unclaimed merchandise, including lots of books.

Here is one story to inspire: a New Yorker bought surplus parachutes from the Pentagon and became a supplier selling clothesline cord. If you are looking for a business, try the Small Business Administration, which sells equipment and businesses it has acquired through foreclosure. Want a good deal on a house? U.S. Department of Housing and Urban Development offers repossessed homes, sometimes for practically nothing, on government foreclosures.

Very few people know about these unique bargains because the federal government doesn't advertise them. Described below are 20 of Uncle Sam's Red Tag Specials. Contact the appropriate offices for more information. And remember, if you don't find what you want, stay at it. This is ongoing, and new merchandise and property are coming in all the time.

* Burros and Horses: Bureau of Land Management

Nevada State Office
Bureau of Land Management
U.S. Department of the Interior
850 Harvard Way (702) 785-6400
Reno, NV 89520-0006 FAX: (702) 673-6010

Or contact your local Bureau of Land Management office. The "Adopt-a-Horse" program is aimed at keeping wild herds at in the West at manageable levels, and allows individuals around the country to purchase a wild horse for $125 or a burro for $75. The animals usually have their shots. Aside from the purchase price you only need pay for shipping. If you live west of the Mississippi, call the Program Office above to find out which of the 12 adoption satellites are nearest you. If you live east of the Mississippi, call (703) 461-1365 to arrange an adoption. Representatives of the BLM travel around the country, so that you don't have to travel to Wyoming to participate. The only qualifications for adoption are that you have appropriate facilities to house the animal, that you are of legal age in your state, and that you have no record of offenses against animals. The horses and burros may not be used for any exploitative purposes such as rodeos or races, nor may they be re-sold. Upon adoption, you sign an agreement to that effect, and no title of ownership is given until one year after an adoption. Animals are usually from two to six years in age, and must be trained. The offices listed above have a brochure called *So You'd Like to Adopt a Wild Horse or Burro* on the "Adopt-a-Horse" program that gives more details.

again at a very low cost. These items are free for non-profit organizations for their own use. Permits for commercial usage may also be available. Cost depends on market value. Below are the addresses and phone numbers of Regional Bureau of Land Management Offices.

Alaska
222 W. 7th Ave. #13, Anchorage, AK 99513-5076; (907) 271-5555.

Arizona
3707 N. 7th Street, P.O. Box 16563, Phoenix, AZ 85011; (602) 640-5504.

California
2800 Cottage Way, E-2841, Sacramento, CA 95825; (916) 978-4746.

Colorado
2850 Youngfield St., Lakewood, CO 80215; (303) 239-3670.

Eastern States
7450 Ballston Blvd, Springfield, VA 22153; (703) 440-1700.

Idaho
3380 Americana Terrace, Boise, ID 83706; (208) 384-3014.

Montana
Granite Tower, 222 N. 32nd St., P.O. Box 36800, Billings, MT 59107; (406) 255-2913.

Nevada
850 Harvard Way, P.O. Box 12000, Reno, NV 89520-0006; (702) 785-6586.

New Mexico
1474 Rodeo Road, P.O. Box 27115, Santa Fe, NM 87502-0115; (505) 438-7508.

Oregon
1300 NE 44th Ave., P.O. Box 2965, Portland, OR 97208-2965; (503) 280-7287.

Utah
324 South State Street, Suite 301, Salt Lake City, UT 84111-2303; (801) 539-4019.

Wyoming
2515 Warren Ave., P.O. Box 1828, Cheyenne, WY 82003; (307) 775-6011.

* Christmas Trees, Seedling, Wooden Poles and Posts: Bureau of Land Management

U.S. Department of the Interior
Bureau of Land Management
Division of Forestry
1849 C Street, NW
Washington, DC 20240 (202) 653-8864
or U.S. Forest Service (202) 205-1389

Contact your local Bureau of Land Management (BLM), U.S. Department of Interior. In the 11 Western states, the Bureau of Land Management has a program for obtaining low-cost Christmas trees from Federal lands. By contacting your local BLM office, you may obtain a permit for a nominal fee (usually $10) to cut a tree for your own use. You will be given a map with directions as to which are permissible areas for tree-cutting. Non-profit organizations may also qualify. Non-profit may get free use permits and cut larger amounts. Trees must be for their own use and may not be resold at fundraisers.

In addition, under the Minor Forest Products program, you may collect or cut specified small trees for use as poles or posts; or, you may obtain cactus or plant seedlings from areas of natural growth where there are abundant supplies --

* Federal Depository Insurance Corporation (FDIC)

Federal Depository Insurance Corporation
550 17th St. NW
Washington, DC 20429 (202) 393-8400

Be patient. If any phone number is incorrect, call (area code) 555-1212 and request the new listing.

Government Auctions and Surplus Property

or Office of Liquidations
1776 F Street, NW
Washington, DC 20429 (202) 898-7343

The FDIC sells at auctions the furnishings and equipment of failed commercial banks. Consult the blue pages in your phone directory for the regional FDIC office nearest you. Each regional office handles their own personal property disposal. Professional auctioneers are contracted to auction off the accumulation of desks, calculators, chairs, computers and other furnishings that banks normally have. These auctions will be advertised in the auction section or classifieds of local newspapers.

The FDIC also holds open for offers costly commercial property and real estate. For a full catalog of these listings across the country, which also includes homes over $250,000 call (800) 678-3342 or (800) 445-3683. They will send *The Liquidation Book* which is the marketing list that is most current. All the property the FDIC has to sell is in this book, but if you are interested in bidding on a house under $250,000, it is wise to ask them for the phone number of the FDIC sales office in your area that is in charge of selling them, and then contact them directly. About 97 percent of the listings in it are commercial offerings such as hotels, offices, and industries. Sales of commercial real estate are advertised nationally by the FDIC in such papers as *The Wall Street Journal*.

* FHA Money May Be Waiting For You

DHUD-Distributive Shares Division
451 7th Street, SW
Washington, DC 20410
HUD Locator (202) 708-1422
DHUD-Insurance Operation Division (703) 235-8117
(800) 697-6967

If you or someone in your family has successfully paid off a mortgage on a house, there may be money waiting for you at the U.S. Department of Housing and Urban Development. HUD oversees the Federal Housing Administration (FHA) which insures mortgages that your bank lends to house buyers. Each year FHA predicts how many people will default on their loans, and based on that prediction, they calibrate how much mortgage insurance home buyers will pay during that year. If it turns out that there are fewer loan defaults than FHA predicted, those borrowers that have continued to pay their mortgages have what are called "Mutual Mortgage Dividend" checks coming to them upon completion of the loan agreement. Call (703) 235-8117 if you think you are due a one time mortgage insurance premium refund or a distributive share.

Another way you may qualify for an FHA insurance refund is to have taken out, say, a 30 year mortgage and paid the entire FHA insurance premium up front instead of in installments over the entire period of the loan. If you have completed the loan agreement in less than 30 years, you may have money coming back to you since you didn't use the insurance for the entire 30 years you've already paid for. In most cases, though, you have to carry a loan for at least 7 years to qualify for a dividend, and the longer you have a loan, the more likely it is that you will qualify for a dividend check.

In these cases where you prepay all of your mortgage insurance premium up front, your bank should let you know that you may eventually be eligible for a mutual mortgage refund upon fulfillment of the loan agreement. Also, after you have paid off your loan, your bank should notify HUD, who in turn should notify you if you have any refund coming, usually within six months. However, if HUD cannot locate you, they will add your name to a list of other individuals who cannot be located but have HUD money coming to them.

Through the Freedom of Information Act many individuals have gotten their hands on copies of this list from HUD and gone around the country tracking down the people and charging them fees to recover this HUD money. Depending on the size of the original loan, your dividend refund could be several thousand dollars, and since some of these "bounty hunters" may ask for up to 50% of the refund just for making a phone call that you could make yourself, you could be losing out on a substantial sum of money by letting them do it. In fact, all you have to do to get the same list the bounty hunters are using is to call (703) 235-8117. DHUD staff will mail to you, free of charge, an "information package" which contains the names of all the mortgagors in the state in which you reside (or request the list for), forms and basic information you would need to apply for a refund.

If you feel you may have money coming to you, or if a member of your family who took out a mortgage is now deceased and you are an heir, try to locate the original loan contract number, and then make a few calls. To apply for a refund you will need the loan number and FHA case number, which you can find on the Recorded Deed of Purchase, kept at your local county courthouse.

* Firewood: U.S. Forest Service

U.S. Forest Service
Timber Management
U.S. Department of Agriculture
14th and Independence Ave. SW
Box 96090
Washington, DC 20090-6090
Operations and Technology Information (202) 205-0855/0857

Contact your nearest National Forest Office (list below) to find out about the firewood program and to learn which national forest is near you. Also, ask these regional offices about firewood from state forestry organizations and private timber companies. Ask about availability of firewood before you make the trip. In any National Forest, you may pick up downed or dead wood for firewood for a nominal charge of $5 per cord, $10 minimum fee, after requesting a permit from the Forest of your choice. You may phone to request the permit, and must have it in your possession while collecting the wood. The Forest Service allows you to gather 2-10 cords worth of wood. Six cords are equal to 12 pick-up truck loads. Wood may not be collected for commercial purposes. All permits to cut wood are issued locally, so you must purchase permits directly from the district ranger. Regional offices do not sell permits.

Northern Region I
Federal Building, 200 East Broadway St., P.O. Box 7669, Missoula, MT 59807; (406) 329-3316. Includes Northern Idaho and Montana.

Rocky Mountain Region II
11177 West Eighth Ave., P.O. Box 25127, Lakewood, CO 80225; (303) 236-9427. Includes Colorado, Nebraska, South Dakota, Eastern Wyoming.

Southwestern Region III
Federal Building, 517 Gold Ave. SW, Albuquerque, NM 87102; (505) 842-3306. Includes New Mexico, Arizona.

Intermountain Region IV
Federal Building, 324 25th St., Ogden, UT 84401; (801) 625-5605. Includes Southern Idaho, Nevada, Utah, and Western Wyoming.

Pacific Southwest Region V
630 Sansome St., San Francisco, CA 94111; (415) 705-2870. Includes California, Hawaii, Guam, and Trust Territories of the Pacific Islands.

Pacific Northwest Region VI
333 SW First Avenue, P.O. Box 3623, Portland, OR 97208; (503) 326-3626. Includes Oregon and Washington. (Mt. Hood is the most popular national forest and may be sold out of permits. Call them in advance at (503) 666-0700. Try also the state and private timber units at (503) 326-2727 or the U.S. Forest Service at (503) 326-2877 or (503) 326-2957.)

Southern Region VIII
1720 Peachtree Rd. NW, Atlanta, GA 30367; (404) 347-4177. Includes Alabama, Arkansas, Florida, Georgia, Kentucky, Louisiana, Mississippi, North Carolina, Puerto Rico and the Virgin Islands, South Carolina, Tennessee, Texas, Virginia.

Eastern Region IX
310 West Wisconsin Ave., Room 500, Milwaukee, WI 53203; (414) 297-3600. Includes Illinois, Indiana, Ohio, Michigan, Minnesota, Missouri, New Hampshire, Maine, Pennsylvania, Vermont, West Virginia, Wisconsin and Fingerlakes section of New York.

Alaskan Region X
Federal Office Building, 709 West Ninth St., P.O. Box 21628, Juneau, AK 99802-1628; (907) 586-7840. Abundance of wood results in extensive free-use permits.

* Homes: U.S. Department of Agriculture (USDA)

USDA, FmHA
Single Family Housing Division
Loan Processing
14th and Independence Ave., SW, Room 5334
Washington, DC 20250 (202) 720-1474

Contact your local Farmers Home Administration Office. There are 1900 around the country. The Farmers Home Administration, part of the U.S. Department of Agriculture, makes low-interest loans available to qualified applicants to purchase homes or farms in rural areas (among other things). Rural settings are small towns with a population under 10,000. Check to see if the locale you are interested in qualifies. Sometimes areas of up to 25,000 in population are

Be patient. If any phone number is incorrect, call (area code) 555-1212 and request the new listing.

Government Auctions and Surplus Property

approved. Farmers Home Administration is also charged with disposing of properties that are foreclosed. First, they make any necessary repairs to the properties, then offer them for sale to people who have the same qualifications as those applying for FmHA loans (based on income, credit worthiness and other criteria). Eligible applicants also qualify to purchase the properties at special low FmHA interest rates (as low as 1%). If no eligible applicants purchase a property, it is then put up for sale to the general public at competitive prices. If the property is not sold within 10 days, it may be reduced by 10%. Sales to the general public may be through FmHA offices or through private real estate brokers. FmHA "eligible applicants" must reside on the property purchased; but if no such eligible buyers are available, other buyers may use it for investment or rental purposes. A separate program applies for farms. This program is designed to serve people of modest income and good credit who don't have enough to make a down payment on a home. Credit evaluation is done on the most recent 12 months. Bankruptcy is not looked at after 36 months. The current loan budget is one-third of what is was in the 70's. This program is being changed to eventually act as insurers to guarantee loans from professional lenders. Applicants may work in a city if their home is rural.

* Homes: U.S. Department of Housing and Urban Development

U.S. Department of Housing and Urban Development
451 7th St. SW
Washington, DC 20410-4000

HUD Locator	(202) 708-1422
Multi-Family Property Dispositions	(202) 708-1220
Single-Family Property Dispositions	(202) 708-1832

HUD homes are properties HUD owns as a result of paying the balance on foreclosed FHA insured home mortgages. Any qualified buyer can purchase a HUD home. Generally, your monthly mortgage payment should be no more than 29% of your monthly gross income. Many HUD homes require only a 3% down payment. You can move into some HUD homes with a $100 down payment. HUD will pay the real estate brokers commission up to the standard 6% of the sales price. HUD may also pay your closing costs. HUD homes are priced at fair market value. Consult your local newspapers for HUD listings; or, your regional HUD office, listed below; or, the real estate broker of your choice.

HUD's Property Disposition facilities are located within ten regional offices and various field offices around the country. Contact the nearest office for details (see listing below). Frequently, HUD will advertise upcoming auctions of foreclosed properties in a local newspaper. The properties may be apartments, condominiums, or various kinds of single-family homes. The condition of these properties varies widely, including some that are little more than shells; and that, of course, affects the price. Some may be located in less than desirable neighborhoods; but others may end up being bargains, either as investments or personal residences. Bids are placed through private real estate brokers, who then submit them to HUD. Some offers for HUD homes are made to the seller and there may be negotiations. Offers for other HUD homes are done by bids placed during an 'Offer Period.' If you bid the full asking price, it may be accepted immediately. Otherwise, all the bids are opened at the close of the 'Offer Period.' The highest bidder wins. Contact the participating broker of your choice to show you the property and submit your bid. HUD broker contracted services are free to prospective buyers. Earnest money is a flat scaled fee ranging from $500-$2000 and must accompany the bid. Bidders must furnish their own financing. HUD stresses that properties sell "as is," so HUD will not make any repairs. It is up to a potential buyer to determine the value and condition, although the listings will state major problems.

Newspaper ads list houses that will be available for the next ten days, as well as others that did not sell in previous auctions. Listings include addresses, number of bedrooms and bathrooms, and suggested prices. Remember that HUD contracts are binding and non-negotiable: once your bid has won, there's no turning back. For a step by step buying guide to purchasing HUD owned homes, call the HUD Homeline, (800) 767-4483, and request the brochure, *A Home of Your Own.* To learn about other programs at HUD that may be useful to you, call (202) 708-0685.

HUD Region I (Boston)
HUD Thomas P. O'Neill Federal Building, 10 Causeway St., Room 375, Boston, MA 02222-1092; (617) 565-5102. Field offices are located in: Bangor, ME; Burlington, VT; Hartford, CT; Manchester, NH; and Providence, RI. Ask for Property Distribution Division in these offices.

Region II (New York)
HUD New York Regional Office, 26 Federal Plaza, New York, NY 10278-0068;

(212) 264-4771. Field offices located in: Albany, NY; Buffalo, NY; Camden, NJ; Hato Rey, PR; and Newark, NJ.

Region III (Philadelphia)
HUD Philadelphia Regional Office, Liberty Square Building, 105 South Seventh St., Philadelphia, PA 19106-3392; (215) 597-2645. Field offices located in: Baltimore, MD; Charleston, WV; Pittsburgh, PA; Richmond, VA; Washington, DC; and Wilmington, DE.

Region IV (Atlanta)
HUD Atlanta Regional Office, Richard B. Russell Building, 75 Spring St., SW, Atlanta, GA 30303-3388; (404) 331-4127. Field offices located in: Birmingham, AL; Columbia, SC; Coral Gables, FL; Greensboro, NC; Jackson, MS; Jacksonville, FL; Knoxville, TN; Louisville, KY; Memphis, TN; Nashville, TN; Orlando, FL; and Tampa, FL.

Region V (Chicago)
HUD Chicago Regional Office, 626 West Jackson Blvd., Chicago, IL 60606-5601; (312) 353-6950. Field offices are located in: Cincinnati, OH; Cleveland, OH; Columbus, OH; Detroit, MI; Flint, MI; Grand Rapids, MI; Indianapolis, IN; Milwaukee, WI; Minneapolis/St. Paul, MN; and Springfield, IL.

Region VI (Fort Worth)
HUD Fort Worth Regional Office, 1600 Throckmorton, P.O. Box 2905, Fort Worth, TX 76113-2905; (817) 885-5531. Field Offices are located in: Albuquerque, NM; Dallas, TX; Houston, TX; Little Rock, AR; Lubbock, TX; New Orleans, LA; Oklahoma City, OK; San Antonio, TX; Shreveport, LA; and Tulsa, OK.

Region VII (Kansas City)
HUD Kansas City Regional Office, Professional Building, 1103 Grand Ave., Kansas City, MO 64106-2496; (816) 374-6438. Field offices are located in: Des Moines, IA; Omaha, NE; St. Louis, MO; Topeka, KS.

Region VIII (Denver)
HUD Denver Regional Office, Executive Tower Building, 1405 Curtis St., Denver, CO 80202-2349; (303) 844-4959. Field offices are located in: Casper, WY; Fargo, ND; Helena, MT; Salt Lake City, UH; and Sioux Falls, SD.

Region IX (San Francisco)
HUD San Francisco Regional Office, Phillip Burton Federal Building and U.S. Courthouse, 450 Golden Gate Ave., P.O. Box 36003, San Francisco, CA 94102-3448; (415) 556-0796. Field offices are located in: Fresno, CA; Honolulu, HI; Las Vegas, NV; Los Angeles, CA; Phoenix, AZ; Reno, NV; Sacramento, CA; San Diego, CA; Santa Ana, CA; and Tucson, AZ.

Indian Programs Office, One North First Street, 3rd Floor, P.O. Box 13468, Phoenix, AZ 85002-3468; (602) 261-4434.

Region X (Seattle)
HUD Seattle Regional Office, Arcade Plaza Building, 1321 Second Ave., Seattle, WA 98101-2054; (206) 442-4373. Field offices are located in: Anchorage, AK; Boise, ID; Portland, OR; and Spokane, WA.

Other HUD Programs
HUD offers over 100 housing programs. Some may be useful to you. To find out about all the programs offered, and what they do, call (202) 708-1420 and request *Programs of HUD.* This 119-page booklet will be sent to you free of charge. HUD offers free counseling to HUD homebuyers, homeowners and tenants. Contact your nearest HUD field office to find an approved housing counseling agency.

* Homes: H.O.P.E. 3

U.S. Department of Housing and Urban Development
Office of Community Planning and Development
Office of Affordable Housing Programs
451 7th St., SW
Washington, DC 20410-7000 (202) 708-0324

The HUD Urban Homesteading Program has been replaced by the HOPE 3 Program--with a $95 million budget--as of June 1991. It is designed to provide homeownership for low income families and individuals. The funds will be distributed to the 10 HUD regions and awarded to local governments and non-profit organizations on a competitive bidding basis. It will generally provide down payment assistance for groups to acquire or rehabilitate affordable low income housing. Call your regional HUD office to find out who has been awarded grants, and then contact them directly to see what is available.

Government Auctions and Surplus Property

You qualify for housing help through HOPE 3 under the Low Income Family Housing Act if you are a first time homebuyer and are below 80% of the median income in your area. You must also meet the affordability criteria -- which requires that the cost of principal interest, taxes and insurance for the home comes to no more than 30% of your income. Since the program is new, the quality of public dissemination of information about these programs remains to be seen. These programs are instituted to help you, so don't be afraid to be persistent in asking for information about what HOPE 3 programs are available in your area from the Community Planning and Development Office at the Field or Regional HUD office nearest you.

To find out what the programs will provide and how to apply for a grant, contact John Garrity, DHUD, Office of Urban Rehabilitation, Room 7158, 451 Seventh Street, SW, Washington, DC 20410-7000, (202) 708-0324 or look up the Monday, February 4, 1991 issue of the *Federal Register,* Part X, DHUD, 24 CFR Subtitle A called *HOPE for Homeownership for Single Family Homes Program; Notice of Program Guidelines.*

* Homes: Veterans Administration

U.S. Veterans Administration
810 Vermont Ave., NW
Washington, DC 20420 (202) 233-4000

Contact the local Veterans Administration Office in your state, or a real estate broker. Watch newspaper ads in local papers for listings of foreclosed properties. The "For Sale" signs on VA foreclosed properties are distinctive. The National Veterans Administration office in Washington, DC is not directly involved in handling the sales; for any inquiries you will be referred to a real estate broker or local VA office.

The Veterans Administration sells foreclosed properties through private real estate brokers. Properties are frequently advertised in local newspapers, giving information such as address, number of bedrooms and bathrooms, particular defects in the property, and price. Almost any real estate agent can show you the property. No broker has an exclusive listing for any of these properties. Local VA offices are the best source of information on the procedures involved in purchasing these properties. Regional offices publish lists of foreclosed properties with descriptions in multiple listing code and phone numbers to call about the property. In some cases, they will also directly send you lists of properties currently available in your area. These offices will mail out a list each time you write in a request, but unless you are a broker, they will not send the list for foreclosures to you on a monthly basis. You can, however, have the agent of your choice put on the mailing list. Others will not mail lists to you, but allow you to pick up the list from their office and/or will refer you to a broker. In either case, you must go through an agent to purchase the house, since they have the keys to the premises, and the process is very much like a regular real estate transaction. The listing has the price on it the VA wants. It will also state if the VA is willing to entertain a lower price. Except, remember, once you have put a bid on a house and won, there is no negotiating or turning back. Houses come "as is" with no guarantees, so it is important to inspect them carefully. Some are located in less than desirable neighborhoods, but there are bargains to be had as well. For the most part VA financed homes are mainstream suburban, not inner city. They are often found in neighborhoods located in economically hard hit areas -- such as the Southwest. Prices may drop on homes that are not sold in a certain period of time. VA financing is possible, but you get a 10% discount for paying cash. Also, if you plan on VA financing, in cases of a tie, the other bidder gets priority for cash offers (pre-approved financing through a commercial lender.) You must state at the time of the bid whether you intend to use VA financing or have found your own.

There are two basic avenues to arrange financing. You can be pre-qualified by lenders and then go shopping. More commonly, the real estate broker you are working with will tell you what is available in the mortgage market. The usual way it works is that you find a broker, find a house, bid on it, wind the bid and then the broker helps you to find financing.

If you should win a bid on a VA foreclosed home but be unable to procure financing, some regional offices will put the home up for bid again. Others hold backup offers and will contact the next highest bidder if the original successful bidder is unable to complete the purchase. Most listings offer to sell financing at the current rate of interest for GI loans, even if the buyer is not a GI. A purchaser who is a GI can get these rates without using his GI benefits. Call (202) 233-6388, the Central Office, if you have questions. They will direct you to the appropriate department of your regional office. If you are a GI and wish to find out about a Certificate of Eligibility, whereby you can purchase a home worth up to $184,000 without a down payment, call (202) 208-1325 or your regional office. To discusses VA loan qualifications generally, call (202) 872-1151

or your regional office.

Purchase is done through a sealed bidding process. Earnest money requirements are published in the listing, usually ranging from $500 to $1000 and are nonrefundable if the bid is accepted. This is a salvage program designed to recover what it can of the cost to the VA for purchasing the property, within a reasonable amount of time after foreclosure -- usually around 6 months.

* Miscellaneous Property: U.S. Customs Service

E.G.& G. Dynatrend
2300 Clarendon Blvd., Suite 705 (703) 351-7887
Arlington, VA 22201 (703) 351-7880

E.G.& G. Dynatrend, under contract with the U.S. Customs Service, auctions forfeited and confiscated general merchandise, including vehicles, on a nationwide basis. Items include everything from vessels--both pleasure and commercial--to aircraft, machinery, clothes (in both commercial and individual quantities), jewelry, household goods, precious stones, liquor, furniture, high technology equipment, and infrequently, real estate. Public auctions and sealed and open bid methods are all used. Items are sold only by lot and number of items in a lot vary from one to many. You must bid on the entire lot.

The U.S. Customs Public Auction Line is (703) 351-7887. Call it to subscribe to the mailing list of locations and dates of sales, to obtain general information about the custom sales program, dates of sales in your region or information about real estate sales. For $50 dollars per year you can subscribe to a mailing list of items to be auctioned nationwide; or you may subscribe to a list limited to one region of the country for $25. You will then receive fliers with descriptions of items available in upcoming auctions. Regions are divided as follows: General, Northeast sales; Southeast Sales; Northwest sales; and Southwest sales. Send your name, address, telephone number, and a money order to the above address. Allow six to eight weeks for the first flier to arrive. The fliers will then arrive three weeks prior to the viewing period and will tell you when and where the items are available for inspection and details of auction procedures. Catalogs are also available a week before the sale with additional details. For sealed bids, a deposit in cashier's check for the total bid must be submitted along with the bid. Make the cashier's check payable to U.S. Customs Service/E.G.& G. Dynatrend, Agent. Indicate sale number on cashier's check and outside on the envelope.

U.S. Customs auctions are held every nine weeks in the following eight cities: Los Angeles, CA; Laredo, TX; Nogales, AZ; Miami, FL; Edinburg, TX; Houston, TX; Chula Vista, CA (San Diego, CA area); Jersey City, NJ; El Paso, TX. Other auctions are scheduled at different times at various other cities also.

* Miscellaneous Property: U.S. Department of Defense

The Defense Reutilization Marketing Service
P.O. Box 1370 (616) 961-7331
Battle Creek, MI 49016-1370 (800) 222-DRMS

Imagine what kinds of items are used, then discarded, by a government department as big as the Defense Department: literally everything from recyclable scrap materials and weapons accessories, to airplanes, ships, trains, and motor vehicles; to wood and metalworking machinery, agricultural equipment, construction equipment, communications equipment and medical, dental and veterinary supplies. Not to forget photographic equipment, chemical products, office machines, food preparation and serving equipment, musical instruments, textiles, furs, tents, flags, and sometimes live animals such as goats and horses. No activated items with military applications are included. Neither are real estate or confiscated items such as sports cars or luxury goods.

Goods sold are either surplus or not usable by other government agencies. First priority is given to designated groups which qualify for donations. The rest is then put up for public sale. By contacting the Defense Reutilization Marketing Service at the above address or telephone, you can receive a booklet called *How to Buy Surplus Personal Property* which explains what DOD has for sale and how to bid for it. The Defense Department also lists notices of Sealed Bid property sales in the Commerce Business Daily, available from the Superintendent of Documents, Government Printing Office, Washington, DC 20402-9325; (202) 783-3238.

Sales are conducted by regional Defense Reutilization and Marketing Region (DRMR) sales offices which coordinate sales in their geographical area. Listed below are addresses and telephone numbers of the regional offices, which can direct you further as to exactly where items are physically sold. Local sales are by auction, spot bid, or on a retail basis. Auctions are held where there are

Be patient. If any phone number is incorrect, call (area code) 555-1212 and request the new listing.

Government Auctions and Surplus Property

relatively small quantities of a variety of items. Spot bids are made through forms submitted in the course of a sale--usually when the property is something with a high demand or interest. The retail sales offer small quantities at fixed, market-level prices. There are 214 retail sales offices, located on military bases.

Large quantities of goods are usually sold by sealed bid, which you submit by mail, along with a deposit, on a form you obtain in a catalog which describes the items. (You receive the catalogs once you are on the mailing list). Recyclable materials are sold through the Resource Recovery Recycling Program or through the Hazardous Property Program. Call the above listed number for further details. You can be put on a mailing list to receive advance notice of DOD sales in your region, but if you don't make any bids after two notifications it will probably be removed unless you make an additional request to remain on the list. You can also be placed on a National Bidders List for sales throughout the country. By contacting the DOD Bidders Control Office, P.O. Box 1370, Battle Creek, MI 49016-1370, (616) 961-7331, 961-7332, or (800) 222-DRMS. People under age 18 and members of the U.S. Armed Forces, including civilian employees, are not eligible to participate in these sales.

Following are the Defense Reutilization and Marketing sales offices:

DRMR: Columbus, P.O. Box 500, Blacklick, OH 43004-0500, (614) 692-2114. This region includes: MN, WI, MI, IA, NE, KS, MO, IL, IN, OH, WV, VA, DE, NJ, PA, , MD, CT, NY, RI, MA, ME, VT, NH, and District of Columbia

DRMR: Memphis, 2163 Airways Blvd., Memphis, TN 38114-0716, (901) 775-6417. This region includes: TX, OK, AR, LA, MS, AL, TN, KY, GA, FL, SC, NC.

DRMR: Ogden, P.O. Box 53, Defense Depot Ogden, Ogden, UT 84407-5001, (801) 777-6557. This region includes: ND, SD, MT, WY, ID, UT, CO, AZ, NM, WA, OR, NV, CA.

You can also take advantage of DOD sales if you live outside the United States. The DOD booklet, *How to Buy Surplus Personal Property,* lists addresses for various regions in Europe and the Pacific.

* Miscellaneous Property: U.S. Postal Service

U.S. Postal Service
475 L'Enfant Plaza, SW
Washington, DC 20260-0001 (202) 268-2000
Vehicle Management Facility (202) 268-2000

Contact the Dead Letter Branches listed below for undeliverable goods; or your local Postmaster for Vehicle Maintenance Facilities and surplus property auctions. To receive advance notice of the auctions you can write to a Dead Letter Branch and request that your name be put on the auction sales mailing list. To be on all of them, you must write to each one separately. Usually 10 days before the auction, you will be notified by postcard of the time, date and place. Viewing inspections are usually held 2 hours before the auction begins.

The Postal Service holds auctions of unclaimed merchandise which includes a wide range of property -- from electronic and household items -- to clothes, jewelry, linens, toys, all types of equipment, and lots of books. Sales are handled through five dead letter branches throughout the country listed below. However, any high value items such as art works, are sold at the New York auction. Contact your local Postmaster to ask about their auctions of surplus property and used vehicles. There are 225 post office vehicle maintenance facilities throughout the country. Their addresses and phone numbers are all listed at the back of the Zip Code Directory kept at post offices. The used vehicle sales can be good bargains, since the vehicles are somewhat fixed up, painted, and occasionally in good condition. Some jeeps, for instance, may sell for between $1200 and $1500. Recently a man bought 15 jeeps for $100 each at auction. Vehicles that do not sell off the storage lot are auctioned. Sometimes cars such as Pintos can be picked up for as little as $750. The sales conducted by the 225 Vehicle Maintenance Facilities around the country are usually fixed price sales, but 5 or 6 times per year auctions have been held at larger cities.

The dead letter items are usually sold in lots of similar goods, with the volume or quantity varying widely. Prices depend on what the goods are and the number of people bidding at a particular auction. There may be a minimum bid required, such as $20; and often cash is the only acceptable payment. Bidders are responsible for removing the items purchased.

A flier for a Postal Service auction of unclaimed and damaged merchandise in St. Paul, Minnesota advised that only those already on an established check register may pay by check; otherwise, cash is required. It also advised that potential bidders to bring their own containers -- boxes, crates, and bags -- for

packing. The Postal Service in San Francisco, California, announced that books, jewelry, sound recordings, speakers, and cabinets, as well as miscellaneous merchandise would be available.

Eastern Region
U.S. Postal Service Claims and Inquiry, Room 531 A, 2970 Market St., Philadelphia, PA 19104-9652; (215) 895-8140 (auction information and number to call to be notified by postcard of next upcoming auction). Includes Pennsylvania, Southern New Jersey, Maryland, Delaware, Ohio, Kentucky, part of Indiana, Virginia, West Virginia, North Carolina, and South Carolina.

Central Region
U.S. Postal Service Dead Letter Office, 180 E. Kellogg St., Room 932, St. Paul, MN 55101-9511; (612) 293-3083. Includes Minnesota, Michigan, Wisconsin, North Dakota, South Dakota, Wyoming, Colorado, Nebraska, Iowa, Indiana, and Illinois.

Northeast Region
U.S. Postal Service Dead Parcel Office, J.P. Farley Bldg., Room 209A, New York, NY 10099-9543; (212) 330-3859. Includes: New York, Massachusetts, Puerto Rico, Connecticut, New Hampshire, New Jersey, and Rhode Island.

Southern Region
U.S. Postal Service Undeliverable Mail Branch, 730 Great Southwest Parkway, Atlanta, GA 30304-9506; (404) 344-1625. Includes: Georgia, Florida, Louisiana, Tennessee, Arkansas, Mississippi, Oklahoma, Texas, and parts of South Carolina.

Western Region
U.S. Postal Service Claims and Inquiries, 1300 Evans Ave., Room 293, San Francisco, CA 94105-9501; (415) 543-1826. Auctions are held at 228 Harrison St., San Francisco, CA. Includes: Alaska, Oregon, Idaho, California, Washington, Nevada, Utah, Arizona, New Mexico, part of Texas, and Hawaii.

* Miscellaneous Property: General Services Administration Property

William Tesh
Chief of Sales Branch
U.S. General Services Administration
Property Management Division
Crystal Mall 4, Room 709
Washington, DC 20406 (703) 557-7785

Contact your local GSA office listed below. The GSA disposes of surplus property for most of the government agencies, and has items ranging from vehicles and scrap metals, to office furniture, office and industrial equipment, data processing equipment, boats, medical equipment, waste paper and computers; as well as aircraft, railroad equipment, agricultural equipment, textiles, food waste, photographic equipment, jewelry, watches, and clothing.

Some regional offices have no mailing list. Instead, there is a number they will give you to call that is a recorded message of all upcoming events. It will give the time, date, and location of the auction and type, such as warehouse, vehicles or office furniture. Other regions allow you to have your name placed on a mailing list to receive advance notices of auctions at no cost. Catalogs list the specific items and their condition. Sales are conducted as regular auctions, spot auctions (where bids are submitted on-the-spot in writing) and by sealed bid (written on a form and mailed in). For auctions and spot bids, you will have two days prior to the sale to view and inspect property, and one week prior for sealed bids. For sealed bid items you receive a catalog, once your are on the mailing list, describing the merchandise. If your region does not have a mailing list, you may pick up catalogs at the office or the sale. Announcements come out as property is accumulated, with March to October being the busiest period. The highest bidder wins in all cases.

Prices may range from way below wholesale for some items to close-to-market prices for others, especially automobiles and boats. Cars tend to be common American-made brands, such as Tempos, Citations, and Reliances. Prices for 4-6 year-old cars may range from around $1500 to $3000 depending on the condition. Seized cars may be newer and of a foreign make. A Mercedes-Benz was recently sold at a National Capitol Region auction. Payment may be by cash, cashier's checks, money orders, traveler's checks, government, or credit union checks; but any personal or business checks must be accompanied by an Informal Bank Letter guaranteeing payment. Full payment must be made by the following day, and bidders are responsible for removal of all property. To bid in GSA auctions, you must register at the site and obtain a bidder number. Once you are on the bidders mailing list, you must bid at least once while receiving five mailings or

Be patient. If any phone number is incorrect, call (area code) 555-1212 and request the new listing.

Government Auctions and Surplus Property

your name will be removed from the list. Then you must contact the appropriate office again to continue receiving mailings.

Some listings for a GSA sale in Bismarck, North Dakota included the following items: miscellaneous kitchen equipment, meat slicers, coffee makers, cameras, film, binoculars, screens, paper, postage meter, nuts and bolts, typewriters, lettering set, mailboxes, lamps, and a streetlight.

For information about GSA auctions in your area, contact one of the regional offices listed below:

National Capitol Region (Washington DC and vicinity)
6808 Loisdale Rd., Building A, Springfield, VA 22150; (703) 557-7785, or (703) 557-7796, for a recording.

Region I (Boston)
GSA, Surplus Sales Branch, 10 Causeway St., 9th Floor, Boston, MA, 02109; (617) 565-7326, Auction Hotline.

Region II (New York)
GSA Surplus Sales Branch, 26 Federal Plaza, Room 20-112, New York, NY, 10278; (212) 264-4824, or (212) 264-4823, for a recording.

Region III (Philadelphia)
GSA Surplus Sales Branch, 841 Chestnut, Suite 540, Philadelphia, PA 19107; (215) 597-5674 or (215) 597-SALE for a recording. (This is NCR Headquarters).

Region IV (Atlanta)
GSA Surplus Sales Branch, Attn: 4FBPS, 401 West Peachtree Street, Atlanta, GA 30365; (404) 331-0972.

Region V (Chicago)
230 S. Dearborn St., Chicago, IL 60604; (312) 353-6061, office or (312) 353-0246, hotline, for a recorded announcement.

Region VI (Kansas)
GSA Surplus Sales Branch, 4400 College Blvd., Suite 175, Overland Park, KS 66211; (913) 236-2523.

Region VII (Ft. Worth)
GSA Surplus Sales Branch, 819 Taylor St., Ft. Worth, TX 76102-6105; (817) 334-2352, office or 2351 for a recorded announcement.

Region VIII (Denver)
GSA Surplus Sales Branch, Denver Federal Center Building 41, Denver, CO 80225-0506; (303) 236-7705 or 7698.

Region IX (San Francisco)
GSA Surplus Sales PBM Section 9FBP-S, 525 Market St., 33rd Floor, San Francisco, CA 94105; (415) 744-5245, or (800) 676-SALE for catalogs and mailing lists.

Region X (Washington)
GSA Surplus Sales Branch GSA Center, Auburn, Washington 98001-6599; (509) 353-2544 or (206) 931-7566, recording.

* Miscellaneous Property: Internal Revenue Service (IRS)

IRS National Information Hotline (800) 829-1040
This office appears to be understaffed. Overloads are automatically put on busy. It is very difficult to get through. If you call before 3:30, Donica Davis may be able to help you.

The hotline can tell you which local office to call. It will tell you to consult your local newspaper, in classifieds, for a listing of IRS seized property to be sold. The listing will give phone number and details. The property sold by the IRS is seized from delinquent taxpayers rather than being used or surplus government property. Many kinds of merchandise are put up for auction, including real estate, vehicles, and office and industrial equipment. Sales are by both sealed bids and public auction. Regarding property sales, the IRS warns that land may still be redeemed by the original owner up to 180 days AFTER you, the bidder, purchase it at an auction; and therefore no deed is issued until this time period has elapsed. Buildings on land being sold by the IRS are NOT open for inspection by a potential buyer unless permission is granted by the taxpayer/owner.

Payment may be by cash, certified check, cashier's check, or money order. In some cases, full payment is required the day of the sale. Otherwise, a 20% downpayment (or $200, whichever is greater) is needed to hold the property, with the balance due at a specified time from the date of the sale, not to exceed one month.

* Miscellaneous Property: U.S. Marshals Service

U.S. Marshals Service
Seized Assets Division
U.S. Department of Justice
600 Army-Navy Drive
Arlington, VA 22202 (202) 307-9237

Contact your local Sunday newspaper for auction notices in the legal section, or the nearest U.S. Marshals Office under U.S. Department of Justice. Usually the Marshals Office is located in the Federal Building of a city. The U.S. Marshals Service or a contracted commercial sales or auction service may handle disposal of the property. Sales are always listed every other Wednesday in *USA Today* newspaper.

In 1991, the Drug Enforcement Agency managed 1.4 billion dollars worth of property from convicted drug dealers. The U.S. Marshals Service, which holds crime-related property accumulated in Federal drug-related and other confiscations, auctions much of this off to the public through 94 offices around the country. Items sold include everything from entire working businesses, to cars, houses, copiers, jewelry, rare coin and stamp collections, apartment complexes, and restaurants. The government is not giving these properties away by any means, but bargains are possible as well as opportunities to purchase some exotic goodies. Confiscated viable businesses are managed by the Service until the time of the auction in order to keep up or increase the businesses' value.

Auctions are not scheduled regularly, but occur when items accumulate. Auctions may be conducted by private auctioneers or the Marshals Service itself. No mailing list is kept to notify you individually, and there is no national listing of items, since new properties are seized daily and adjudication of drug-related cases may take years. Payment at these auctions is by cash, certified check, or special arrangements when large amounts of money are involved. One note, the Marshals Service checks out people paying for large items with cash to make sure the government is not re-selling things to drug dealers. The Marshals Service also auctions off property seized by the Drug Enforcement Agency.

* Natural Resources Sales Assistance

Small Business Administration (SBA)
409 Third Street, SW
8th Floor (800) 827-5722
Washington, DC 20416 (202) 205-6600

The federal government sells surplus property and natural resources, such as timber. SBA works with government agencies which are selling the property and resources to assure that small businesses have an opportunity to buy a fair share of them. Occasionally natural resources that the federal government is releasing on the market are made available. Small fuel companies and producers may get the option to buy their fair share of federal government coal leases. The royalty oil program enables small and independent refineries to buy oil at valuations set by the federal government - which is in excess of spot market prices. Agricultural leases may be had for land on which to graze cattle or grow crops. This SBA program is designed to ensure that small businesses get their fair share of real and personal federal property put on the market. Don't expect bargains. Write for *The U.S. Government Purchasing and Sales Directory* at the above address. This book tells you how to sell to the U.S. government, how to be put on its bidder's list, and what agencies sell property. For more information, contact Bill Berry at (202) 205-6470. To find out what SBA Natural Resources Sales Assistance programs are in your area, contact your nearest SBA office. For information on other SBA services, call (800) 827-5722 (recorded listing from which you can order brochures.)

* Real Estate: General Services Administration Property Sales

General Services Administration (GSA)
Office of Real Estate Sales (800) GSA-1313
Call this toll-free number for national listing of properties, and then contact local GSA office for the area you are interested in. You can also obtain the list by calling Asset Disposition, (202) 501-0067. The phone number of the local GSA office to contact will be provided on the list that is mailed to you free of charge upon request.

Be patient. If any phone number is incorrect, call (area code) 555-1212 and request the new listing.

Government Auctions and Surplus Property

* Real Estate: Small Business Administration (SBA)

U.S. Small Business Administration (SBA)
Portfolio Management Division
409 Third Street, SW
Washington, DC 20416 (202) 205-6660
Recording from which to order brochures (800) 827-5722

Contact your local SBA office located in 10 Regional Offices around the country, or any of the 68 District Offices. SBA does not maintain a mailing list. No district or regional SBA office is aware of what the other offices are offering. The SBA auctions off properties of people who have defaulted on home loan payments in SBA-sponsored programs. Listings of auctions are printed in local newspapers, usually in the Sunday edition in the classified section. Merchandise is identified as SBA property and sold by brokers, none of whom have the exclusive listing, or by private auctioneers. The auctioneers are chosen on a rotating basis. SBA attempts to sell to the highest bidder, but may reject a winning bid if too low. Sales are infrequent. Do not expect bargains. Items sold range from office furniture and equipment to buildings or entire bakeries, drycleaners, or other businesses. There may be parts or whole businesses available. The auctioneer may have an entire auction of SBA items, or a mixture of things from various sources. You may request to bid by sealed bid if you desire; and a deposit is required. Payment is by cash or certified check. If you are interested in certain categories of merchandise, you might want to be placed on the mailing list of one or more auctioneers who specialize in that particular type of item, such as farm equipment, for example. Since the SBA is often the guarantor of bank loans, SBA auctions are relatively infrequent and bargains are not easy to find. SBA Regional Offices follow:

Dallas: 8625 King George Dr., Dallas, TX 75235-3391; (214) 767-7633

Kansas City: 911 Walnut St., 13th Floor, Kansas City, MO 64106; (816) 426-3608

Denver: 999 18th St.,Suite 701, Denver, CO 80202; (303) 294-7186

San Francisco: 71 Stevenson St., San Francisco, CA 94105-2939; (415) 744-6402

Seattle: 2615 4th Ave.,Room 440, Seattle, WA 98121; (206) 553-5676

Boston: 155 Federal Street, 9th Floor, Boston, MA 02110; (617) 451-2023

New York: 26 Federal Plaza, Room 31-08, New York, NY 10278; (212) 264-1450

King of Prussia: 475 Allendale Rd., Suite 201, King of Prussia, PA 19406; (215) 962-3700

Atlanta: 1375 Peachtree St. N.E., 5th Floor, Atlanta, GA 30367-8102; (404) 347-2797

Chicago: 300 South Riverside Plaza, Suite 1975 South, Chicago,IL 60606-6617; (312) 353-5000

* Ships: Maritime Administration

U.S. Department of Transportation
Office of Ship Operations
Maritime Administration
400 7th St., SW, Room 7324
Washington, DC 20590 (202) 366-5111

When the government decides that a merchant ship is no longer needed or useable, it may put that ship up for sale by auction, through a sealed bid procedure. A ten percent deposit is required. It is sold to the highest bidder usually for its scrap value. Contact the above address to be put on the auction mailing list.

* Timber Sales for Small Business

Small Business Administration
409 3rd St., SW, #8800
Washington, DC 20416 (202) 205-6470

The U.S. Government regularly sells timber from the federal forests managed by the U.S. Forest Service, U.S. Department of Agriculture, and the Bureau of Land Management, U.S. Department of Interior. On occasion, timber also is sold from federally-owned forests which are under the supervision of the U.S. Department of Defense, the U.S. Department of Energy, and the Tennessee Valley Authority, and the U.S. Department of the Interior. The SBA and these agencies work together to ensure full opportunity for concerns to bid on federal timber sales. SBA and the sales agencies jointly set aside timber sales for bidding by small concerns when it appears that, under open sales, small business would not obtain a fair share at reasonable prices. Contact your local SBA office for further specific information. It is listed in the blue pages of the telephone directory. General information, if needed, is available from Bill Berry at (202) 205-6470.

Be patient. If any phone number is incorrect, call (area code) 555-1212 and request the new listing.

Government Auctions and Surplus Property

Donations To Non-Profit Organizations

* Art Exhibits

Smithsonian Institution
1100 Jefferson Dr., SW, Room 3146
Washington, DC 20560 (202) 357-3168

The Smithsonian can bring art to you, whether you live in a major metropolitan area or a rural one. The Smithsonian Institute Traveling Exhibition Service (SITES) sponsors 80 to 100 different exhibits at any given time in museums and other locations around the country. The participation fee will range from $500 to $20,000. The exhibitions range from popular culture, to fine arts, photography, historical exhibits, or topics of interest to children. The collections are from other museums and institutions, sometimes including the Smithsonian, and are most frequently sent to other museums, libraries, historic homes, or even schools and community centers. More than half the locations are in rural settings. SITES estimates that more than 11 million people view the exhibits it circulates in this program. The bigger exhibits that require special security arrangements go only to museums equipped to handle them. If interested, call the above number for the SITES *Updates* catalog.

* Books

Library of Congress
Exchange and Gift Division
1st and C Street, SE
Washington, DC 20540-4280 (202) 707-9511/9512

Government agencies, educational institutions, and other non-profit organizations may qualify to obtain free books from the U.S. Library of Congress. The books are largely technical and legal works, but from time to time contains entire collections from military installation lending libraries that have been closed. There is no way to tell what books will be available. Stock is constantly changing. Books are first offered on a competitive bidding basis. If they are not sold, they become available on a donation bidding basis. Commercial book dealers may compete in this bidding against non-profit organizations. The proceeds sustain the Book Preservation Program. Someone from the organization must choose which books are desired. He or she must have a letter from the organization or appropriate Congressional representative stating that the person it selected to choose the books acts for a non-profit organization. The Library will ship the books UPS at the organization's expense or the organization may supply the Library with pre-addressed franking labels. Congressional offices will help educational institutions such as universities and schools obtain these labels. Non-profit organizations may submit bids to purchase books. The Library will contact the organization if the bid is unacceptably low and give the bidder one chance to raise it. There is no limit on the number of books a group may order.

DHUD

HUD Library and Information Service
451 7th Street SW, Room 814
Washington, DC 20743

To find out about the over 100 programs HUD offers to assist low and moderate income housing groups and individuals, obtain *Programs of HUD* by calling (202) 708-1420.

* Food and Surplus Commodities

USDA Food Distribution Programs
or Food Distribution Division
Food and Nutrition Service
3101 Park Center Dr., Room 503
Alexandria, VA 22302 (703) 305-2680

Non-profit groups with tax-exempt status may apply for surplus commodities held by the Agriculture Department, such as grain (usually flour), oils, and sometimes milk and cheese. The large quantities of surplus cheese and milk that existed a couple of years ago are largely depleted. The items available depend somewhat on which foods are currently in surplus. Contact your state distribution agency, frequently the state Department of Agriculture, Department of Education, or Administrative Services, or the above address.

* Foreign Gifts

General Services Administration (GSA)
Crystal Mall Building #4
1941 Jefferson Davis Hwy., Room 800
Washington, DC 20406 (703) 308-0745

Non-Presidential gifts worth over $200 from foreign countries to U.S. government agencies or their representatives may be displayed by the recipient in his government office, then purchased by him at an officially assessed value. If the gift is not purchased, it may end up in a State Surplus Property office, where the general public can get a chance to buy it. Watches and jewelry are commonly available, along with books, sculptures, and various artifacts. But the souvenir from Anwar Sadat to Jimmy Carter during the Middle East peace talks goes to the U.S. Archives and possibly later to the Jimmy Carter Library.

When gifts are reported to the GSA, they first go through the federal screening cycle. Federal agencies have the first chance to purchase items at retail value price. If none exercise that option, then the recipient may purchase the item. If the item remains unsold, it enters the donation screening cycle. It may then be used for display purposes at state agencies such as libraries or museums. After that, it may be sold to the public at auction. At public auction, anyone can purchase the item. Non-profits have no special footing. Items are disposed of by GSA in basically the same way as other surplus and excess property.

Items desired by non-profit organizations should be requested through your local Surplus Property Office, which can then contact the GSA about a donation. You can find a list of foreign gifts given to government agencies published yearly in the *Federal Register*, State Department, Chief of Protocol, Washington, DC, (202) 647-4169.

* Housing For The Homeless

Judy Breitman
Chief, Real Property Branch
Division of Health Facilities Planning, ORM/OM
U.S. Department of Health and Human Services
Parklawn Building, Room 17A-10
5600 Fishers Lane (301) 443-2265
Rockville, MD 20857 FAX: (301) 443-0084

The above will send you a helpful brochure entitled *Obtaining Federal Property for the Homeless: Questions and Answers About Federal Property Programs.* If you are part of a non-profit organization ministering to the homeless, the government is currently taking applications for eligible groups to receive excess or unused federal buildings or land for homeless people. The property is leased or deeded over. To find out what properties are available call the 24 hour hotline, (800) 927-7588. Every Friday, *The Federal Register* (available from libraries or by subscription) will list which federal properties are available and where. You can also ask the National Coalition for the Homeless, (202) 265-2371, to notify you when a property becomes available. The applying organization has 60 days after notice of property availability is published to submit a written expression of interest. It will then be sent an application packet and have 90 days after that to apply for the property. Criteria is outlined in *The Federal Register.* If you think your organization may qualify, call Public Health Service, (301) 443-2265.

* Interagency Council on the Homeless

451 Seventh Street, SW
Washington, DC 20410 (202) 708-1480

This is a coordinating counsel of 16 different Federal agencies, headed by the HUD Secretary. It works with State and local governments and private organizations on homeless-related efforts. Call it for information on homeless activities. For information on financing rehabilitation or support services, contact HUD's Office of Special Needs Assistance Program at (202) 708-4300.

Title V of the McKinney Act is the "Federal Surplus Property Program." You can call (800) 927-7588 to get answers about the Title V Program and properties 24 hours per day. Under this program, federally owned surplus or unused property may be deeded, leased or made available on an interim basis at no cost

Be patient. If any phone number is incorrect, call (area code) 555-1212 and request the new listing.

Donations To Non-Profit Organizations

to homeless providers such as states, local governments and non-profit organizations. To find out about eligible properties, ask to be put on the mailing list that tells you of properties in your area as they are published by contacting your nearest field HUD office.

* Miscellaneous Property

Director, Property Management Division
Office of Transportation and Property Management
Federal Supply Service
Washington, DC 20406 (703) 308-0745

Or contact your local State Office of Surplus Property. The General Services Administration will donate items it handles to qualifying non-profit organizations which request it. Items are "as is" and range from tools, office machines, supplies and furniture, clothes, hardware, medical supplies to cars, boats, and planes. Your State Agency for Surplus Property, also called Office of Purchasing, Property Control, or General Services, makes the determination whether your group qualifies, then contacts the GSA to obtain it. There may be a charge of 2% of the value and a fee for handling and service. Groups eligible can include public agencies, and non-profit educational, public health, elderly, or homeless organizations.

* Tools for Schools

Commander, Defense General Supply Center
Attn: DGSC-OMC
8000 Jefferson Davis Hwy.
Richmond, VA 23297-5501 (804) 279-3861

This program of the Defense Logistics Agency loans used industrial equipment no longer necessary to the military or military contractors to qualifying non-profit educational institutions. The equipment must be over $5000 in value and includes such things as saws, lathes, milling equipment, drilling equipment, and grinding equipment. Loans are for five year periods, but may be renewed indefinitely.

The receiving institution must pay for the cost of transportation, packaging and handling, plus any necessary repairs. Some equipment comes "as is" and may be inoperable; other items sometimes show up almost unused. The equipment generally dates from between 1950 to 1970, but in some cases it can be of superior quality than its modern equivalent. The Defense Industrial Plant Equipment Center advises looking first hand at equipment before ordering it. Contact the above for informational brochure and application.

* Travel Aboard An Icebreaker

Ice Operations Division
U.S. Coast Guard Headquarters
2100 2nd Street, SW
Washington, DC 20593 (202) 267-1450

The Coast Guard does not evaluates scientific projects to determine if they qualify. The group that qualifies as a primary user, because it is willing to pay for fuel and part of maintenance and helicopter costs on resupply trips, may send a scientist they select to ride along with one of the two Coast Guard Icebreakers that travel to the Arctic and Antarctica. At present, for the Antarctic trip, the National Science Foundation (1800 G St. NW, Washington, DC 20550, (202) 357-9859, Information Center or (202) 357-7808, Polar Programs) is the primary user. For the Tooley, Greenland trip, the Military Sealift Command ((202) 433-6056 or (202) 443-0083) is the primary user. Other interested parties who wish to send scientists or observers, such as scientific or environmental groups must obtain the consent of the primary user for that trip. Most travelers are sponsored by government or educational organizations, but the Coast Guard is interested in any appropriate, professional project and will consider other applications as well. They can also be flexible on their itinerary to accommodate projects. Sometimes scientists on short missions may travel at no cost. In addition, special expeditions are commissioned, such as the one in 1992 by the U.S. Geological Survey. If interested, contact the primary user.

Be patient. If any phone number is incorrect, call (area code) 555-1212 and request the new listing.

Government Auctions and Surplus Property

Resolution Trust Corporation

As a result of the U.S. Savings and Loan failures, the U.S. Government has contracted the Resolution Trust Corporation (RTC) to dispose of the thousands of real property and other assets it now possesses. Inventory constantly changes, but includes single family homes, as well as commercial properties, shopping centers, loans and undeveloped land.

* The Affordable Housing Disposition Program

Stephen Allen, Director
Barry Wides, Deputy Director
Resolution Trust Corporation (RTC) (202) 416-7348
801 17th Street, NW (800) 624-HOME
Washington, DC 20434 FAX: (202) 416-2530

This program sells single and multi-family residences valued or sold at $67,500 or less. As of March 31, 1991, there were 18,816 RTC properties in the Affordable Housing Program with a total value of $1.6 billion. One to four family residences were 93% of that number and 84% of the single family properties were appraised at less than $50,000. Most of the properties are in the Southwest. More than half are in Texas. More properties in the east are becoming available. List prices are at fair market value but are negotiable. Offers are made to realtors for properties listed with clearinghouses. Such listing must be for 90 days during which only pre-qualified buyers can make offers. Generally to be eligible, your income must be less than $40,000 per year or no more than 115% of the area's median income. Contact the Housing Finance Agency in your State. You might also want to ask it about housing loans for low income persons.

The calendar gives the contact person who will show you the property and tell you the dates of the buyer's seminar you should attend to learn more about how to buy a home under the RTC Affordable Housing Program. RTC oversees the private sector auction companies who sell the homes. The auction company must set up a time for a "Buyer Awareness Seminar" to explain the process and the prerequisites of eligibility for the program and RTC financing. The auctions are usually open call; sometimes sealed bids are taken. One can bid up to the amount one has financing for. Earnest money is cash, usually $500 up front.

* Houses and Other Property From Failed Savings and Loan Companies

Resolution Trust Corporation (RTC)
801 17th Street, NW
Washington, DC 20434 (202) 416-7348

Call to have information on RTC programs mailed to you.
National Assets Specific Inquiry Program .... (800) 431-0600
RTC National Sales Center .... (800) 842-2970
Regional Assets Sales Hotline Numbers: .... (800) 348-1484
Property Listings (800) 782-3006

* Housing for the Homeless

Resolution Trust Corporation (RTC)
801 17th Street, NW
Washington, DC 20434

Contact: Diane Case or Felisa Neuringer (202) 416-7348

RTC offers real estate to public and non-profit organizations for public purposes such as day care, low and moderate income family housing and housing for the homeless. The property that is offered has been determined to not have a reasonable recovery value. When a property is deteriorated, of low value, holding costs are too high, or if there have been no offers made on it for a long time, RTC is authorized to transfer title to a designated public agency or non-profit organization which has its application for the property endorsed by a local governmental body.

RTC issues notices of properties available for public use that describes the condition, size and location of the property, gives a contact person, the public purpose for which it may be used, and date by which proposals to acquire the property must be received. The notices are sent to various agencies and to the RTC headquarters and regional offices. Upon acceptance of a proposal, the property is conveyed to the organization by quitclaim deed or deed without warranty.

* Real Estate and General Merchandise Anyone Can Buy

Call the Assets Sales Hotline number, (800) 348-1484, to receive the calendar of events of all items such as fixtures, furniture and equipment, as well as property that is being auctioned around the country. The calendar is updated twice monthly and will be mailed to you free upon request. What type of auction it is - - mixed where everyone can buy or "Affordable Housing Auctions" where only pre-qualified buyers can buy, will be stated in the calendar. It tells you what is being sold, where and who to contact. The auctioneer or contact person provides viewing locations of merchandise. Auctioneers may send you an inspection catalogue the week before the sale.

For real estate call (800) 782-3006 to receive a list of all RTC properties around the country that are not being auctioned. Transactions are conducted like any regular real estate transaction where you make an offer.

* Tenant Programs

RTC often tries to arrange for the present occupiers of an RTC held property to buy the dwelling by arranging financing for two months rent equivalent in a down payment and mortgage payments like rent.

Be patient. If any phone number is incorrect, call (area code) 555-1212 and request the new listing.

State Government Auctions

The following is a descriptive listing of state government offices which offer auctions or donations of surplus property.

Alabama

Alabama Surplus Property, P.O. Box 210487, Montgomery, AL 36121, (205) 277-5866. Alabama auctions off a variety of items about three times per year, including office equipment, heavy machinery (such as milling machines and drill presses), and vehicles, including cars, trucks, boats, and tractors. Trailers, medical equipment, tires, dossiers, and lathes are also sold. The state advertises upcoming auctions in the classified section of local newspapers. Upon written request made to the above address, you can be put on a mailing list. You will then be notified 2 or 3 weeks in advance of each upcoming auction, but you won't receive a list of items. Lists of items can be picked up at the above office 2 days before the auction. Payment can be by cash, cashier's check, or personal check with a bank letter of credit. Items are available for viewing two days prior to the auction. No bids by mail.

Alaska

Surplus Property Management Office, 2400 Viking Dr., Anchorage, AK 99501, (907) 279-0596. The Juno office is (907) 465-2172. Call it for general information and mailing list information. Alaska's Division of General Services and Supply sells surplus office equipment, including furniture and typewriters, every Tuesday from 8:30 am to 12:pm, and from 1:00 pm to 4:00 pm in a garage sale fashion with prices marked for each item. For items costing over $100, cash or cashiers checks are required. Vehicles, at various locations throughout the state, are sold during sealed bid or outcry auctions twice a year, in the spring and fall. Payment is by cashiers check after you have been notified of your winning bid.

Arizona

Office of Surplus Property, 1537 W. Jackson St., Phoenix, AZ 85007, (602) 542-5701. About four times per year, Arizona auctions off everything from vehicles to miscellaneous office equipment and computers. Items are sold by lots rather than individually; and prices, especially cars, can be below blue book price, depending upon opening bids. Vehicles range from empty frames to Jaguars. A mailing list is maintained. You can have it sent to you for no charge. Individual cities and county governments in Arizona also hold their own surplus auctions.

Arkansas

State Marketing and Redistribution Office, 6620 Young Rd., Little Rock, AR 72209, (501) 565-8645. Arkansas conducts both sealed bid and retail, fixed price sales of surplus items. On Wednesdays, between 7:30 am and 3:00 pm, buyers may view and purchase items, which include office machines, tables, and tires, valued at under $500. Larger, more valuable items, including vehicles, medical equipment, mobile homes, and machine shop and automotive supplies, are sold by sealed bid. You can have your name placed on the mailing list for various categories such as computers, autos and miscellaneous equipment. You must bid three times to keep your name on the mailing list. The state also conducts sealed bids by mail. The bid fee is $1. No personal checks are accepted for sealed bids. All items are sold "as is," with no refunds or guarantees implied or stated.

California

State of California, Office of Fleet Administration, 1416 10th St., Sacramento, CA 95814, (916) 657-2318. California sells surplus office equipment or other supplies only to schools and other non-profit or educational institutions. However, once a month on Saturdays, the General Services Department of the state holds open bid auctions at Sacramento or Los Angeles State Garages of surplus automobiles previously owned by state agencies. Vehicles can be viewed from 8:00 am to 10:00 am. The auction begins at 10:00 am. Vehicles may include sedans, cargo and passenger vans, pick-ups (mostly American-made). You can receive 2 weeks advance notice by getting on the mailing list. Auctions are occasionally advertised in the newspapers. Minimum bid prices are set for exceptionally nice cars. Only state agency vehicles are sold. Payment is by cash, cashiers check, or certified check. Personal checks are also accepted, but items may not be picked up until the check has cleared. Successful bidders have up to one week to pay for and pick up the cars (the following Friday). Out-of-state checks are frowned upon. Prices vary greatly, and some vehicles have required minimum bids.

California Highway Patrol, Used Vehicle Sales Office, 2812 Meadowview Rd., Sacramento, CA 95832, (916) 421-0285. Minimum bids are stated on a recorded telephone message. The auction is by sealed bids which are opened at 3:00 pm daily; winners may be present or notified by telephone. Payment is by cashiers check, certified check, or, money order only -- no personal checks or cash accepted. Bids may be submitted and inspection is available between 8:00 am and 3:00 pm.

Colorado

Department of Correctional Industries, State Surplus Agency, 4200 Garfield Street, Denver, CO 80216, (303) 321-2200. Several times a year, Colorado auctions off its surplus property, excepts for motor vehicles, which are not sold to the public. Auctions are pre-announced in newspaper ads, and a mailing list is also maintained. To be put on the mailing list, call the above number. The auctions of state property are held the third Thursday of every month. If you are on the mailing list, you will receive notice the weekend before the auction with a brief description of the items. Non-profit organizations have first choice of state surplus items, which can include typewriters, desks, computers, file cabinets, hospital beds, and much more. Payment may be made by cash, money order or personal checks with two IDs.

Connecticut

60 State St. Rear, Wethersfield, CT 06109, (203) 566-7018, or (203) 566-7190. Items vary from day to day. Vehicles are auctioned separately 8 or 9 times per year, with ads in the 4 largest newspapers and on 2 radio stations giving advance notice. There is no mailing list. These auctions are usually on the second Saturday of the month. Vehicles may be viewed one hour prior to the auction. Buyers may also purchase a brochure with vehicle descriptions when they pay the $3 registration fee. You may go Monday-Friday, noon to 3:45, to view and purchase smaller items in their warehouse.

Delaware

Division of Purchasing Surplus Property, P.O. Box 299, Delaware City, DE 19706, (302) 834-4550. About two, sometimes three times each year, in May and September, Delaware publicly auctions off vehicles, office furniture, and other surplus or used property. Vehicles include school buses, paddle boats, vans, pick-up trucks, heavy equipment, and sedans. Prices depend on the condition of the item and how many people are bidding for it. Vehicles may be inspected and started up prior to the auction, but may not be driven. You may get on a mailing list to be advised of upcoming auctions. A flyer with information and conditions of payment will be sent to you.

District of Columbia

District of Columbia Dept. of Public Works, 5001 Shepard Parkway, Washington, DC 20032, (202) 404-1068. DC holds vehicle auctions the 1st and 3rd Tuesday of every month. Vehicles include cars, trucks, buses, ambulances, and boats. Inspection and viewing is available at 8:00 am, one hour prior to the 9:00 am open bid auction. Prices and conditions of vehicles vary greatly. No mailing list is kept. Auctions are posted 45 days in advance in the *Washington Times*. A $50 cash entry fee must be paid to attend an auction and is refunded if no car is purchased. Cars must be paid for in full at the auction by certified or cashier's check. Twice a year confiscated bikes and property found in cars go to auction.

Be patient. If any phone number is incorrect, call (area code) 555-1212 and request the new listing.

Government Auctions and Surplus Property

District of Columbia Office of Property Control, 2250 Shannon Place, SE, Washington, DC 20032, (202) 767-7586. In the past, this office auctioned off items such as clothing, typewriters, cabinets, tools, refrigerators, and more at the DC Police Training Academy facility. Such auctions are becoming increasingly infrequent and may be discontinued altogether in the future. No mailing list is kept, but advance notices are placed in The Washington Post. Viewing of items is allowed the day of the sales. Cash only is accepted.

Florida

Department of Management Services, 813 A Lake Bradford Rd., Tallahassee, FL 32304, (904) 488-5272. DGS holds no auctions. A retail store, located at the above address, is open from 12:30 pm to 4:30 pm on weekdays for public retail-type sales of various items, excluding vehicles. Items include office supplies, computers, medical equipment, mowers, calculators, typewriters, couches, desks, chairs, tables, air conditioners, black boards, and filing cabinets.

Department of Management Services, Division of Motor Pool Bureau of Motor Vehicles, 813 B Lake Bradford Rd., Tallahassee, FL 32304, (904) 488-5178. Approximately one per month, somewhere in Florida, items are auctioned for the state by First Coast Auctions at (904) 772-0110. Descriptive information and viewing schedules are published in newspapers. Surplus items, including motorcars, heavy equipment and boats are sold. Automobile auctions take place anywhere from 7 to 15 times per year, with dates set 4 to 6 weeks in advance at various auction locations throughout the state. The auctions are advertised. Some industrial equipment is also included, along with various kinds of used and confiscated vans, trucks, and cars. Pleasure and fishing boats are also auctioned. Items may be viewed prior to the auction. (800) 766-9266 (in state).

Georgia

State of Georgia, Department of Administrative Services, Purchasing Division, Surplus Property Services, 1050 Murphy Ave, SW, Atlanta, GA 30310, (404) 756-4800. Georgia auctions vehicles, including sedans, wagons, trucks, vans, buses, and cement mixers; also shop equipment, generators, typewriters, copiers, computers, tape recorders, and other office equipment; as well as audio-visual equipment, cameras, electronic equipment, and air conditioners. They keep a mailing list and also advertise the auctions in local newspapers. Merchandise may be inspected by pre-registered bidders two days before an auction, which are held on the third Wednesday of a month -- but not necessarily every month. Auctions begin at 8:30 am if federal property is to be sold, otherwise at 9-9:30 am. Vehicles may be started up, but not driven. Sealed bids are also used, and deposits are required with these. For auctions, items are payable with cash or check with sufficient I.D. if the amount is under $501. For personal or business checks in amounts over $501, property will be held until the check clears. Items must be paid for on the day of sale. A recent Georgia auction offered 40 sedans between 3 and 15 years old, 30 pick-up trucks from 5 to 22 years old, vans dating from 1965 to 1989, tires, tractors, farm equipment, shop equipment, office equipment, and 3 lots of televisions.

Hawaii

State Government Stock Control Department, (808) 735-0348/0349. Hawaii does not conduct surplus sales at the state level. Federal public auctions are held by the Defense Reutilization Marketing Office, (808) 476-6872.

Idaho

Division of Purchasing, 9208) 327-7465. In 1991 the Idaho state legislature dissolved centralized public auctions. Each state agency now holds its own auction or has a commercial auctioneer handle its surplus. If an agency decides to auction cars through sealed bids, it must advertise in 3 newspapers for 10 days. To find out if, when, and what an agency is disposing of through auction, contact that agency directly.

Illinois

Central Management Services, Division of Property Control, 3550 Great Northern Ave., Springfield, IL 62707, (217) 793-1813. Two or three times per year this office auctions vehicles and property. Auctions are held at the Illinois state fairgrounds on Sangamon Avenue in Springfield. Auctions are always held on Saturdays. Property includes office equipment, desks, chairs, typewriters, restaurant equipment, calculators, cameras, refrigerators, and filing cabinets. Scrap metal and equipment not easily moved are sold by sealed bid. The office maintains a mailing list which costs $20/year to subscribe. Notices of auctions and bids are mailed out 3 weeks prior to the auction. The auctions are also advertised in advance in local newspapers. All the cars auctioned have a minimum mileage of 75,000 miles and were driven by state employees. Minimum bid begins at $300. Prices vary widely, but below-market prices are available. Illinois auctions off vehicles by open bid auctions. (Confiscated cars are sold at federal auctions and may present greater possibility for a bargain.)

Indiana

State Surplus Property Section, 229 W. New York St., Indianapolis, IN 46202, (317) 232-0134, warehouse; (317) 232-1365, office. Indiana holds auctions as items accumulate through open cry auctions to the highest bidder. During the summer months, the state sells surplus from the Department of Transportation and the Department of Natural Resources. There is no mailing list. Auctions are advertised the first Thursday of every month in the *Indianapolis Star*. The auction date and selected auctioneer changes every year. The switch is made during July. Call the above office in May to obtain the new schedule. Sealed bids must contain 100% deposit. Payment is by cash, certified check, cashiers check, or money order. No personal checks or letters of credit are accepted. Items vary and are all state surplus.

Iowa

Department of Natural Resources, Wallace State Office Bldg., Des Moines, IA 50319, (515) 281-5145. The Department of Natural Resources holds an auction when and if a sufficient number of items have accumulated, on the second Saturday of every May. Items disposed of include boats, fishing rods, tackle boxes, guns, and other fishing and hunting equipment, as well as office equipment. Payment is by cash or check with appropriate identification. There is no mailing list, but auctions are advertised in local newspapers.

Vehicle Dispatchers Garage, 301 E. 7th, Des Moines, IA 50319, (515) 281-5121. The Department of Transportation holds auctions, if there is sufficient accumulation, three to four times per year at 9:00 am on Saturdays. The state disposes of approximately 500 vehicles yearly through these auctions. They mostly sell patrol cars, pickups and trucks. All have at least 81,000 miles of travel on them, and prices vary widely. A deposit of $200 is required on the day of the sale, with full payment due by the following Thursday. Payment may be made by cash or check with an accompanying letter of credit guaranteeing payment by the issuing institution. Viewing is possible Friday all day and Saturday morning prior to the sale. There is a mailing list. Auctions are advertised in the local papers.

Kansas

Kansas State Surplus Property, P.O. Box 19226, Topeka, KS 66619-0226, (913) 296-2334, FAX: (913) 296-7427. The State Surplus Property office sells sedans, snow plows, and everything they have, from staples to bulldozers. Property is first offered to other state agencies at set prices for 30 days. Whatever is left over is opened to public sale at the same prices. Prices tend to be competitive. Items not sold by auction are sold by sealed bids, with a catalog available containing descriptions of items and where they are located. Confiscated vehicles are not sold to the public. They are disposed of by county courthouses, usually to county agencies. To obtain copies of catalogs describing sealed bid items, write to the above address. It will be sent to you for 3 months, after which time your name will be purged unless you re-request it.

Kentucky

Kentucky Office of Surplus Property, 514 Barrett Ave., Frankfurt, KY 40601, (502) 564-4836. Kentucky holds public auctions on Saturdays every two or three months. Items may include vehicles, desks, chairs, calculators, typewriters, file cabinets, tape recorders, electronic equipment, couches, beds, and lawnmowers, to name a few. Merchandise may be viewed the day before an auction. The office maintains a mailing list and also advertises upcoming auctions in local newspapers. Some items are auctioned by sealed bids. Property is payable by cash, certified check, or money order.

Louisiana

Division of Administration, Louisiana Property Assistance Agency, P.O. Box 94095, 1059 Brickyard Lane, Baton Rouge, LA 70804-9095, (504) 342-6849. Public auctions are held on the second Saturday of every month at 9:00 am at 1502 North 17th St. Items may be viewed at the warehouse from 8:00 am to 4:30 pm the week before. Property sold ranges from medical and office equipment, to boats, shop equipment, typewriters, file cabinets, pinball machines, bicycles, televisions, adding machines, and chairs, and vehicles. All items are sold "as is" and "where is." Payment is required in full the day of the auctions, but no

State Government Auctions

personal or company checks are accepted. In addition, all merchandise must be removed within five days after the sale. Auctions are conducted by a different auctioneer each year, depending on who wins the bid for the annual contract.

Maine

Office of Surplus Property, Station 95, Augusta, ME 04333, (207) 289-5750. Five or six times per year, Maine publicly auctions off vehicles on the grounds of the Augusta Mental Institute. You must register to be able to bid, and then you will automatically be notified of upcoming auctions. Vehicles may include police cruisers, pick-up trucks, snowmobiles, lawn mowers, and heavy equipment, such as large trucks, graders, and backhoes. Inspection is allowed between 1:00 pm and 3:00 pm on the Friday before, and 8:00 am and 10:00 am the day of the auctions, which are always held on Saturdays. The impound yard opens at 7:00 am. Vehicles may be started up but not driven. Personal checks, money orders, certified checks, and cash are all accepted. Office equipment and other non-vehicles items are sold by tag sale once per month, and prices are negotiable. Exact date, place, and time of auctions are announced in local newspapers, but there is no mailing list. Payment is due for both vehicles and other items the day of the auction or sale.

Maryland

Maryland State Department for Surplus Property, P.O. Box 122, 8037 Brock Bridge Rd., Jessup, MD 20794, (410) 799-0440. Office furniture and the like are sold or donated to non-profit organizations or state agencies, and vehicles are sold to dealers only. The state maintains a retail store for surplus property at its warehouse at the above address. After a certain length of time, items that do not go to non-profits or state agencies become available to the public at set prices at its retail store.

Massachusetts

Massachusetts State Purchasing Agency, Department of Procurement and General Services, Surplus Property, One Ashburton Place, Boston, MA 02108, (617) 727-7500. About six times per year, Massachusetts holds public auctions of surplus property. Bidders must register in the morning by filling out a card. The State Purchasing Agency places ads in The Boston Globe on the Sunday and Wednesday prior to each of the auctions, which are normally held on Saturdays. Vehicles are usually auctioned after about 60 or so accumulate. Vehicles sold include sedans, wagons, vans, and pick-ups with an average age of 7 years. The average car has over 100,000 miles. Conditions range from good to junk. Viewing is available the day before the auction from 9:00 am to 4:00 pm. Purchases are "as is". No start-ups allowed. The state does not auction other surplus property, in general, but occasionally special auctions are held for boats, parts from the Department of Public Works, and most recently, helicopters.

Michigan

State of Michigan, Department of Management and Budget, State Surplus Property, P.O. Box 30026, 3353 N. Logan, Lansing, MI 48913, (517) 335-8444. The state auctions off all kinds of office furniture, household goods, machinery, livestock, and vehicles, such as sedans, buses, trucks, and boats. Auctions are held at different locations for different categories of property. The State Surplus Property Office sends out yearly calendars with auction dates and information. Contact them at the above address to have it sent to you. Double check dates because additions or changes may occur. Auctions are also published in the local newspapers. Payment may be made by cash or check and should include the 4% state sales tax. No refunds are made. Inspections of merchandise are available either the day before from 8:00 am to 3:00 pm or the morning of an auction from 8:00 am to 9:30 am. Auctions begin at 10:00 am. Items must be paid in full on the day of sale by cash or check. Buyer has 3 working days to remove the property.

Minnesota

Minnesota Surplus Operations Office, 5420 Highway 8, New Brighton, MN 55112, (612) 639-4022; HOTLINE: (612) 296-1056. Minnesota holds about 15 auctions per year at different locations around the state. They sell vehicles such as old patrol cars, passenger cars, trucks, vans, and trucks, as well as heavy machinery, boats, snowmobiles and outboard motors. The state also auctions off furniture, office equipment, kitchen equipment, tools, and confiscated items such as vehicles, computers, jewelry, car stereos and radios, and other personal effects. Many of these items are sold under market price. You may be put on a mailing list to receive a calendar for the schedule of upcoming auctions for the year. Auctions are advertised in the locale where they occur by radio, TV, and in the Minneapolis and St. Paul newspapers. Inspection of property is held from 8:00 am to 9:30 am, an hour and a half before the auction begins; and payment is by personal check for in-state residents, cash, or money order.

Mississippi

Bureau of Surplus Property, P.O. Box 5778, Whitfield Rd., Jackson, MS 39288, (601) 939-2050. Up to three times a year, Mississippi auctions such items as machinery, textiles, ammunition boxes, and unrepairable vehicles. Contact the above office to be put on the mailing list. Auctions are advertised in state newspapers. Inspections are allowed during the two days before the auction. Payment may be made by cash, bank draft, or check with bank letter of credit.

Department of Public Safety, Support Services, P.O. Box 958, Jackson, MS 39205, (601) 987-1453. The state cars that are auctioned are mostly patrol cars, and only occasionally vans and other types of vehicles. State cars are usually wrecked or old. Most have at least 100,000 miles on them. Recent average prices have ranged from $1200 to $1500. The state is keeping cars longer, so less are being sold. These agency cars and others from the Department of Wildlife and Fisheries, military bases, Narcotics Division, and U.S. Marshal's Office -- which includes confiscated cars -- are auctioned the first Tuesday of every month by Mid South Auctions, 6655 N. State St., Jackson, MS 39213, (601) 956-2700. Call to be put on the mailing list. Many car dealers as well as the public attend these auctions, so prices are competitive. Bargains are still possible. Payment must be in cash or cashiers check -- no personal checks. The balance is due the day of the auction.

Missouri

State Of Missouri, Surplus Property Office, Materials Management Section, P.O. Drawer 1310, 117 N. Riverside Dr., Jefferson City, MO 65102, (314) 751-3415. At various times throughout the year, Missouri holds regular public auctions, as well as sealed bid auctions of merchandise located at various places in the state. The wide range of items include clothing, office equipment and vehicles. No confiscated or seized vehicles or other items are sold. You can be put on a mailing list to receive notices of upcoming auctions, plus they are advertised in local newspapers. For regular auctions, inspection is available the day before or on the day of the auction; and sealed bid items may be viewed two or three days before the deadline. Items may be sold by lot or individually. Payment may be made by cash or personal check.

Montana

Property and Supply Bureau, 930 Lyndale Ave., Helena, MT 59620-0137. (406) 444-4514. Montana holds a vehicle auction once a year, of about 300 state vehicles. Contact the above to get on the mailing list. The auctions are by open cry and sealed bid. All items are from state surplus; nothing is seized or confiscated. These auctions are advertised in local newspapers prior to the auction. In addition, the state offers other property for sale each month on the second Friday of the month. The sales include items such as office supplies, computers, chairs, tables, and vehicles including trucks, vans, sedans, highway patrol cars, and more. Payment can be by cash up to $300. Higher amounts must be paid by certified or business check, or bank check.

Nebraska

Nebraska Office of Administrative Services, Material Division, Surplus Property, P.O. Box 94901, Lincoln, NE 68509, (402) 479-4890. Three or four times a year, Nebraska auctions off office furniture, computers, couches, and more. Separate auctions are held for vehicles and heavy equipment -- also about three or four times per year. Auctions are advertised in newspapers and on radio, and a mailing list is also kept. Sealed bids for property such as scrap iron, wrecked vehicles, guard posts, and tires are taken. Items are available for viewing two days prior to the auctions, which are held on Saturdays at 5001 S. 14th St. All items are sold "as is". Payment, which can be made by cash or check, must be in full on the day of the auction.

Nevada

Nevada State Purchasing Division, Kinkead Bldg., Room 400 Capitol Complex, Carson City, NV 89710, (702) 687-4070. The sales and auction are located at the warehouse at 2250 Barnett Way, Reno, NV 89512. About once a year, Nevada holds a sale on the second Saturday in August of such items as calculators, desks, cabinets, tables and chairs. Office equipment is released for sale to the public at a set price. The sale is held to clear the warehouse, and is on a first come, first serve basis, with minimum prices to cover service and handling marked on the

Be patient. If any phone number is incorrect, call (area code) 555-1212 and request the new listing.

Government Auctions and Surplus Property

property. Very few vehicles are confiscated. Most are surplus turned in by other state agencies for resale. Vehicles and motorcycles are auctioned. Public auctions are not served by mailing lists but are advertised in the newspapers. You can be put on a mailing list to receive notice of sealed bid sales of 19 categories of merchandise, including heavy equipment, boats, and planes. Once you have requested to place your name on the mailing list, if you do not subsequently bid on two consecutive occasions, it will be removed. Payment is by cash or local check with proper I.D. No out of state checks accepted. For vehicles, you can put down a 5% deposit with 5 days to complete payment. The county, city and University of Nevada also advertise and hold public auctions.

New Hampshire

Office of Surplus Property 78 Regional Dr., Building 3, Concord, NH 03301, (603) 271-2126. New Hampshire holds two auctions per year of vehicles and other equipment, such as office furniture and machines, and refrigerators. Vehicles, which include cruisers, pickups, vans, and sometimes confiscated vehicles may be viewed the day before the auction, while other merchandise can be viewed on the same day just before the auction. A mailing list is maintained, and ads are also placed in local newspapers prior to the auctions. Acceptable payment includes cash and certified funds.

New Jersey

New Jersey Purchase and Property Distribution Center, CN-234, Trenton, NJ 08625-0234, (609) 530-3300. New Jersey auctions used state vehicles such as vans, various types of compacts, and occasionally boats, buses and heavy equipment. Frequency of auctions depends on availability which currently averages once per month. Vehicles may be inspected and started up the day before the auction from 9:00 am to 3:00 pm. Payment is by cash, money order, or certified check. No personal checks. A 10% deposit is required to hold a vehicle, and then the successful bidder has 7 calendar days to complete payment and remove the vehicle by Friday. If an item is left after that, even if paid in full, a $20 per day storage fee is charged. To be advised of auctions, put your name on the mailing list by writing the address above. Phone calls to be put on the mailing list are not accepted. A recent vehicle auction in New Jersey offered a variety of Dodge and Chevy vehicles, ages ranging from three to thirteen years, with mileages from 50,000 to 130,000. Other surplus items are not put up for public auction; rather they are offered to other state agencies.

New Mexico

New Mexico Highway and Transportation Department, SB-2, 7315 Cerrillos Road, P.O. Box 1149, Santa Fe, NM 87504-1149, (505) 827-5580. About once a year, on the last Saturday of September, New Mexico auctions off vehicles, including sedans, loaders, backhoes, snow removal equipment, pick-ups, vans, four-wheel drives, and tractors. They have some office equipment as well. The items come from state agencies. You may place your name on a mailing list to receive the exact date of the auction and descriptions of merchandise up for bidding. A public entity auction is held first. The published list of items to be publicly auctioned consists of what is left over. Everything is open auction; there are no sealed bids. Items may be inspected the day before the auction. Payment is by cash, checks with proper I.D., money orders, or cashier's checks. No credit cards.

Department of Public Safety, State Police Division, Attn: Major W.D. Morrow, P.O. Box 1628, Santa Fe, NM 87504. The above holds a public auction on the second Saturday in July at 4491 Cerrillos Road. Write to the above address to be put on the mailing list. It is also advertised in local newspapers. Items sold include everything from calculators to cars. They come from seizures and surplus from other agencies. The vehicles may be viewed and started up the Friday before the auction. Payment may be by cash, money order, cashier's check or personal check with bank letter of guarantee.

New York

State of New York Office of General Service, Bureau of Surplus Property, Building #18, W.A. Harriman State Office Building Campus, Albany, NY 12226, (518) 457-6335. The Office of General Services holds auctions continuously in locations around the state. The items are so numerous that the state finds it necessary to sell them by category. You can designate which categories you are interested in on the mailing list application. Items are sold as they become available. Sales are advertised one week in advance in local newspapers. These items include surplus and used office equipment, scrap material, agricultural items (even unborn cows). Most categories such as medical, photographic, institutional and maintenance equipment are sold through sealed bids, usually in lots of varying size. To participate in a sealed bid, you place your name on a

mailing list for items in seven different categories, then make your bid by mail. The highest bidder wins and is notified by mail. Mailings give as much information as possible about the items being auctioned; but state officials stress that merchandise is sold "as is" and "where is". They advise viewing property in person before making a bid. A ten percent deposit is required with each sealed bid. Vehicles are sold by public auction and may include cars, trucks, buses, tractors, bulldozers, mowers, compressors, plows, sanders, and other highway maintenance and construction equipment. Large items are sold individually, and smaller equipment, such as chain saws, is more likely to be sold in lots. These auctions take place about 55 times per year. It is always possible that enough surplus may not accumulate to warrant an auction. The state warns that just because an auction is scheduled is no guarantee that it will occur. Payment may be made by certified check or cash. A ten percent deposit will hold a vehicle until the end of the day.

North Carolina

State Surplus Property, P.O. Box 33900, Raleigh, NC 27636-3900, (919) 733-3889. North Carolina sells through sealed bids surplus state merchandise including vehicles and office equipment. Office equipment includes furniture, typewriters, desks, and chairs. For a fee of $15 you can be placed on a mailing list to receive weekly advisories of what is for auction, with a description of the item and its condition. Otherwise, if you visit the warehouse in person, you can pick up free samples of bid listings and look at lists of prices that items sold for in previous auctions. The warehouse is located on Highway 54 - Old Chapel Hill Road. Payment is by money order or certified check, and you have 15 days to pay for your merchandise and 15 days to pick it up. Items may be inspected two weeks before an auction from Monday to Friday between 8:00 am and 5:00 pm. On Tuesdays, the warehouse is closed between 1:00 pm and 3:00 pm when the bids are opened and the public is then invited to attend. The state may reject bids that are too low. Vehicles vary greatly in type and condition.

North Dakota

Surplus Property Office, P.O. Box 7293, Bismarck, ND 58507, (701) 224-2273. Once a year, usually in September, the Office of Surplus Property auctions through open bidding surplus office furniture and equipment, as well as vehicles and scrap materials. The auction is advertised the two days before and merchandise may be viewed the morning of the auction. The auction is held at Igo Industrial Park. Cash, cashiers checks, or money orders are acceptable forms of payment. Personal or business checks are accepted only with a bank letter of credit.

Ohio

Office of State and Federal Surplus Property, 4200 Surface Road, Columbus, OH 43228, (614) 466-5052. Ohio holds public auctions and sealed bid sales on a wide range of office machines and equipment, furniture, and vehicles. The sealed bid sales are held at various locations around the state for inoperable vehicles. These may be inspected any time after you receive your bid invitation in the mail. No mailing list is maintained. Call or write for the information. When you attend an auction, you can fill out a label that will be used to notify you of the next auction. Other vehicle auctions are held three to four times a year, depending on the amount accumulated. Inspections are available the day before. Vehicles may include sedans, trucks, vans, 4x4s, boats, mowers, tractors, and chain saws. No seized or confiscated items are sold. At the time of the auction, a 25% downpayment is required, with the balance due by the following Monday (auctions are held on Saturdays). For the sealed bid auctions, payment must be by money order or certified check.

Oklahoma

Central Purchasing, Dept. Central Services, B-4, State Capitol, Oklahoma City, OK 73105, (405) 521-3046; general information only for public auctions, (405) 521-3835; for general information and information on sealed bids, (405) 521-2110. The charge is $10 for which you will receive all the information and descriptions. Oklahoma auctions vehicles as they accumulate. The state advertises upcoming auctions in local newspapers. The state tells their condition. Vehicles often have from 80,000 to 120,000 miles on them and it is rare for a car to be rated as fair - which means it is in running condition. They are usually bought by wholesalers. State agency cars are commonly sold, but occasionally seized or confiscated cars are sold. Agencies most likely to have auctions are: Department of Human Services (occasionally vehicles and other items, but they usually take their cars to public auctions); Wildlife Department (vehicles); Department of Public Safety (vehicles); and the Department of Transportation (vehicles). The Department of Transportation has four auctions per year. The cars and trucks can have 120,000

Be patient. If any phone number is incorrect, call (area code) 555-1212 and request the new listing.

State Government Auctions

miles on them. They are usually not in good condition. The state advises that you contact each agency separately for details. Sealed bid auctions of all kinds of merchandise are also held. You may request your name to be placed on a mailing list, but if you do not bid three times, it will be removed. Otherwise, visit the office to view a catalog of listings.

Oregon

Department of General Services, Surplus Property, 1655 Salem Industrial Dr. N.E., Salem, OR 97310, (503) 378-4714 (Salem area). Oregon auctions both vehicles and other equipment, such as office furniture. Merchandise may include snow plows, horse trailers, computer equipment, desks, chairs, tires or shop equipment. Some items are in excellent condition, and bargains may be found. Items come from state agency surplus and confiscations. On rare occasions exotic items such as a Porsche and hot tub have been sold. Public sales are held every Friday at set prices. Sealed bid sales are held separately. The frequency of auctions depends on the amount of items to be disposed. The numbers of vehicles for sale is increasing. Cars are also sold every week at set prices. For info call the 24 hour information line that is always kept current, (503) 373-1392. Ads are also placed on radio and in local newspapers in the areas where the auction will be held, giving the date and location of the auction. The procedure is to register and obtain a bidder number, which you hold up when you are making a bid. The forms may be obtained at the auction site. At the same time as you register, you must show some form of identification. The conditions and terms of sale are always listed. At the public sales if you pay by Mastercard or Visa, title is immediately released. You can also pay 10% down at the auction site and pay the balance at the office with Mastercard or Visa in 3 days.

Pennsylvania

General Services Department, Bureau of Vehicle Management, 2221 Forster St., Harrisburg, PA 17105, (717) 783-3132. About 10 times per year, depending on the number of cars accumulated, the DGS auctions off all kinds of vehicles. Many have mileages under 100,000, and ages commonly range from 1979 to 1986. There are about 200 cars at each auction. They are mostly used state agency cars that have been replaced, but up to 3 seized cars are also sold each year. An inspection period begins two weeks before an auction on Monday through Friday from 9:00 am to 5:00 pm at the storage facility located at 22nd and Forster Sts. in Harrisburg. Inspection period ends 2 days before the auctions. Each car has a form detailing its condition. It will state if the car must be towed. All cars are sold "as is". Cars are started up the day of the auction, which is open cry. If you request an application, you may have your name put on a mailing list for advance advisories of auctions for a period of six months. A $100 deposit is required (cash only) if you win a bid, with full payment due within five working days by cashier's check, certified check, or postal money order. No personal or company checks accepted.

Bureau of Supplies and Surplus, Department of General Services, P.O. Box 1365, 2221 Forster St., Harrisburg, PA 17105, (717) 787-4083. The Bureau of Supplies and Surplus of the General Services Department sells such items as mainframe computers and off-loading equipment, office furniture and machines, including typewriters, desks, chairs, sectional furniture, filing cabinets, copy machines, dictaphones, and calculators. This merchandise is first offered to other state agencies, then municipalities, and is then put up for public sale after five days. There is no mailing list for notification of upcoming auctions, but ads are placed in the local newspapers in the area where an auction will be held and in the *Pennsylvania Bulletin*. You can be put on a mailing list for some specific items such as heavy equipment that is sold by sealed bid. State which categories of bidder's lists you are interested in. The notice you receive will give date, times and places to inspect and submit a bid. A $100 security deposit must accompany the bid. Property is sold at set prices. You may call to find out what items are currently for sale, or visit the warehouse which sells mostly office equipment such as computers, desks, chairs and file cabinets, between 10:00 am and 3:00 pm Monday through Friday.

Rhode Island

Department of Administration, Division of Purchase, 1 Capitol Hill, Providence, RI 02908, (401) 277-2375. Rhode Island's Division of Purchase auctions off its surplus vehicles and office equipment, as well as other items through sealed bid to a list of buyers who are usually in the business. Most of the cars sold have no plates and must be towed. They are sold primarily to wholesalers. Office equipment and supplies are primarily sold to suppliers. If the state ever does hold a public auction, it advertises two or three times in the local papers.

South Carolina

Surplus Property Office, Division of General Services, 1441 Boston Ave., West Columbia, SC 29170, (803) 822-5490. South Carolina sells items ranging from vehicles, to office and heavy equipment. Property is collected in monthly cycles and offered first to state agencies before being put up for sale to the public. No mailing list is kept for it, but you can visit the warehouse on 1441 Boston Ave. in West Columbia, which is open between 8:00 am and 4:30 pm Monday through Friday. Prices are tagged; there is no auction. Every 6 to 8 weeks, the General Services Division holds public auctions of items by lot for State, Federal, and Wildlife Department property. A mailing list is kept for advance advisories and property descriptions. There is a $15 fee, payable by check or money order, to receive the mailings annually. Items can be inspected two days prior to the sale. You are advised to make notes of the numbers of property you are interested in, then to check back to inquire if it is still available, since state agencies have first choice.

South Carolina Public Transportation Department, 1500 Shop Road, P.O. Box 191, Columbia SC 29202, (803) 737-6635, for general information; (803) 737-1488, for mailing list. About every five weeks, the South Carolina Department of Public Transportation holds auctions of its used and surplus vehicles, which include everything from patrol cars, trucks, and passenger cars, to highway equipment. To have your name put on a mailing list of upcoming auctions, call the number above. Payment is by cash, check or money order. Banking information will be requested for personal checks. Vehicles may be viewed from 9:00 am to 4:30 pm on the Monday and Tuesday before the auctions, which are always held on a Wednesdays at 10 am. You may start up the cars. It is open bidding. Usually about 100 cars are sold at each auction.

South Dakota

Bureau of Administration, State Property Management, 701 East Sioux Ave., Pierre, SD 57501-3321, (605) 773-4935. Twice a year, in the spring and fall, the Department of Transportation holds on its premises public auctions for office equipment and vehicles, including pick-ups. Most vehicles have over 85,000 miles on them and sell for well under market price. The cars usually sell for under $5000. Most are surplus or have been replaced at state agencies. A few are from seizures or confiscation. You may visually inspect the vehicles prior to the auction, but you may not enter them. However, during the auction, the vehicles are started and demonstrated. Auctions and special sales are located wherever the most property has accumulated in the state. Call or write the above office to have your name put on the mailing list. There is no charge. Terms are up to the auctioneer. Title is released only after checks clear, or immediately if accompanied by a bank letter.

Tennessee

Department of General Services Property Utilization, 6500 Centennial Blvd., Nashville, TN 37243-0543, (615) 741-1711. Tennessee auctions surplus vehicles, and machinery of various kinds -- milling machines, lathes, welders, and metal working equipment. The vehicles are of all types, including dump trucks, pick-ups, sedans, and station wagons. Auctions are held twelve times a year in Jackson, Dandridge, Nashville, and Chattanooga. A mailing list is kept, and auctions are advertised in local newspapers. Items are available for inspection the day before the auction. Keys are in the car, and start ups are allowed. Register at no charge the morning of the auction. Payment can be in cash, cashier's checks, or certified check. The state also conducts sealed bids usually 12 times a year and most commonly on office furniture.

Texas

Texas State Purchasing and General Services Commission, P.O. Box 13047, Capitol Station, Austin, TX 78711-3047, (512) 463-3445. Every two months, Texas auctions off vehicles, office furniture and machines, and highway equipment. You must apply to be put on the mailing list, which will give you a brief description of items available at the next auction (call (512) 463-3416). It will also tell you the location of the auction, which changes often. You may call the agency selling the property to arrange to inspect it; however, merchandise that is on site is available for inspection two hours before the auction. Items are mostly used state property, although some is confiscated as well. You must register to bid beforehand. Most registrations take place the day of the auction, beginning at 7:00 am. Payment on a winning bid is due at the end of the auction. Cash, cashiers check, certified check, money order, bank draft with Letter of Credit, or personal or company check with Letter of Credit are acceptable forms of payment. Items sold on site must be removed the day of the sale. For off-site items, 30 days are usually allowed for removal. Texas also holds sealed bid auctions, where you make a bid by mail. First, you indicate what category of property you are interested in, and they will send you bid forms and descriptions

Be patient. If any phone number is incorrect, call (area code) 555-1212 and request the new listing.

Government Auctions and Surplus Property

of items in that category. Sealed bid participants are notified by letter if winning bids and the exact amount due. Deposits for non-winners are returned. Also, each of the Texas state agencies hold local sales, for which each has its own mailing list and advertises in the local papers.

Utah

Utah State Surplus Office, 522 South 700 West, Salt Lake City, UT 84104, (801) 533-5885. Four or five times a year, Utah auctions of vehicles off and office furniture, as well as heavy equipment, whenever property accumulates. Most items are sold by public auction, although sealed bid auctions are sometimes held as well. Mail-in bids are accepted if you can't attend in person. A 10% deposit is required. It is refunded unless you win the bid. Most of the public auctions are held in Salt Lake City at the address above, although some are occasionally held in other parts of the state. You may request your name be put on a mailing list to receive advance notice of auctions and a description of the items. Auctions are always held on Saturdays. Property may be viewed the Friday prior to an auction. Acceptable forms of payment are cash, cashier's check, and personal checks up to $100 with two forms of I.D. No business checks are accepted. Items must be removed and payments must be made in full on the day of the auction.

Vermont

Vermont Central Surplus Property Agency, RD #2, Box 520, Montpelier, VT 05602, (802) 828-3394. Vermont sells low-priced surplus office furniture and machines on retail basis between 8:00 am and 4:00 pm daily at the Central Garage on Barre Montpelier Rd. Items include desks, chairs, file cabinets, and book shelves. Twice a year, vehicles, which may include police cruisers, dump trucks, and pick-ups, are sold by public auction, on a Saturday in late May and September. A mailing list is kept to advise you in advance of upcoming auctions. To have you name placed on it, contact the auctioneer. Local newspapers also advertise them. Vehicles may be inspected the Friday before an auction. The auctions are open bid, "as is", and "where is". There are no hold backs. The highest bid, even if it is far below market value, will take the item. A 25% deposit is due the day of the sale. The balance is due in 2 days, by the following Tuesday by 3:00 pm. Payment is up to the auctioneer, who is a private contractor. Usually, checks must be bank-certified, and a deposit is required to hold any vehicle not paid for in full the day of the auction.

Virginia

State Surplus Property, P.O. Box 1199, Richmond, VA 23231, (804) 786-3876. Virginia auctions everything but land. It sells vehicles, office equipment and furniture, computers, tractors, bulldozers, dump trucks, pick-ups, and vans. Some of the cars are in good condition. Scrap metal, tires, and batteries are sold separately. Auctions may be held on any day of the week except Sunday. Sales are by both public auction and sealed bid. Agencies have the discretion to decide which way their surplus is sold. There are sealed bid offerings every week, and as many as two auctions per week. Twice a year there are auctions for cars only. The rest are mixed. Items are occasionally seized, such as jewelry. Auction sites are at various locations around the state. You may write to place your name on a mailing list for both public auctions and sealed bid auctions; phone call requests are not honored. For sealed bid, there are usually 100 to 200 items available. Inspections are encouraged. They are allowed the day before the auction and again for a couple of hours on the day of the auction. For sealed bid items, you may call for more details on the items offered for sale or to make an appointment to inspect the items.

Washington

Office of Commodity Redistribution, 2805 C St. SW, Building 5, Door 49, Auburn, WA 98001-7401, (206) 931-3931. Every Friday the public can visit the store at the central warehouse. It is open from 12:00 noon to 2:30 pm and purchases are for cash only. Washington holds auctions of used state vehicles, conducts "silent bids" (auctions where the bids are written rather than spoken), and also sells surplus materials by sealed bid (bids are placed through the mail) via catalogs. The vehicles are auctioned about every three months and include all kinds of used state conveyances, from patrol cars, to trucks and passenger cars, most having over 100,000 miles. There are few new luxury or confiscated type vehicles. The "silent bids" are held once a month, and include large quantities of office furniture sold by the pallet, with the exception of typewriters, which are sold individually. You may visit the warehouse to inspect the items

beforehand. Payment may be made by cashiers check, money order, or cash, but no personal checks. For the sealed bids, you may request a catalog of merchandise, which includes everything from vehicles, to scrap material, office equipment, computers, clothes, cleaning fluids, tools, and pumps. For any of these sales, you may request to be put on the mailing list at the address above.

West Virginia

West Virginia State Agency Surplus Property, 2700 Charles Ave., Dunbar, WV 25064, (304) 766-2626. Contact the above to be put on the mailing list. Statewide sealed bids have a separate mailing list you must specifically request. For sealed bids, prospective buyers can inspect only by going to the site. Each month, West Virginia auctions such items as chairs, desks, telephones, computers, typewriters, office equipment and furniture, and other miscellaneous property, as well as vehicles. They are all auctioned at the same auction. The vehicles are in varying conditions. The auctions are always held on a Saturday. Inspection is available the week before the auction from 9:00 am to 6:00 pm. On auction day, the gate opens at 9:00 am. Miscellaneous property is sold until 12:00 noon. Then all the cars are sold. If time allows, any remaining miscellaneous property is auctioned. Payment may be by personal check, business check, or certified check, but no cash. Payment is due in full the same day. For sealed bids, payment is due within one week after a bid has won. Deposits, usually 20% of a bid, are returned to unsuccessful bidders, or in the case of winning bids, applied to the purchase price.

Wisconsin

Department of Transportation, P.O. Box 7396, Hill Farm Building, 4802 Sheboygan Ave., Madison, WI 53707-7396, (608) 266-3965. The Department of Transportation continuously sells a variety of merchandise from its warehouse in Madison. These items vary greatly from week to week, but may include work tables, desks, files, calculators and other office equipment and furniture, as well as vehicles. Call ahead before visiting the facility to view the property, which is sold at set prices. The few surplus items the state has are used up by other organizations or sold informally as parties express an interest. A small room stores all the items. Computers, however, and occasionally road finds accumulate. These are sold by sealed bid and you can call to get on the bid list.

Wisconsin Department of Administration, P.O. Box 7880, Madison, WI 53708, (608) 266-8024. The Department of Administration holds vehicle auctions approximately every month -- usually with around 100 vehicles, including passenger vehicles, vans, trucks, and station wagons, all of different makes and models. Most are in running condition. Cars that need towing are rare and clearly designated. The vehicles are usually at least four years old, or have at least 70,000 miles on them. The auctions begin on Saturday at 10:00 am. Cars may be inspected the Friday before from 1:00 pm to 6:00 pm. The public may also inspect and start up the cars from 8:00 am to 10:00 am on the morning of the auction. You may have your name placed on a mailing list for advance notice of auctions; however, the auctions are also advertised in local newspapers. There are no sealed bids. Payment is by cash, personal check, cashiers check, or money order. No credit cards. The full amount is due the day of the auction. Occasionally, if the auctioneer is consulted at pre-registration, a small delay for bank loan arrangements are pre-approved so that the prospective buyer can bid.

Wyoming

State Motor Pool, 723 West 19th Street, Cheyenne, WY 82002, (307) 777-7247. Although it first donates most of its surplus property to other state agencies, Wyoming does auction its remaining surplus vehicles, which may include pick-ups, vans, sedans, and jeeps, and also tires. Although most have high mileage -- from 80,000 to 100,000 miles, the majority are dependable vehicles. You can have your name placed on a mailing list to receive advance notices of auctions, which are held when items accumulate. On the average, one or two auctions are held each year. The state also advertises in local newspapers. Inspection of the vehicles is available between 3:00 pm and 6:00 pm the Friday before the auction, which is usually held on Saturdays and begins at 10:00 am. No start ups are allowed. Anything known to be wrong with the car will be on the list handed out at the auction, or sent if you are on the mailing list. Payment depends on the auctioneer who is a private contractor. Usually, cash or check with proper I.D. are acceptable. Some cars go for well below market value, but others may bid up in price, depending on the mood of the crowd.

Be patient. If any phone number is incorrect, call (area code) 555-1212 and request the new listing.

Unclaimed Money

In the United States today, experts believe that about $5 billion in unclaimed money is collecting dust in state Abandoned Property offices. Some of the monetary items that end up in a state's possessions after being declared abandoned by the holding institution include:

- forgotten bank accounts
- uncashed stock dividends
- insurance payments
- safe deposit boxes
- utility deposits
- travelers checks
- money orders

People move away, lose track of investments, or die, and the accounts or funds, after a set amount of time -- frequently five years -- are reported to the state Treasurer's Escheats, Comptroller's, or Revenue office. The state then tries to track down the owners and return the money.

If you think financial property may be held by your state, the first step is to contact the appropriate office (a state by state list follows) to find out whether your name is listed. Or, in the case of the estate of a deceased person, the listing would be under his/her name. You will then fill out a claim form which you must return together with the required identification or proof of ownership. Requirements for proving ownership may vary according to the amount of the claim and the complications involved, but frequently states will ask for such things as copies of driver's licenses, social security numbers, and bank account numbers and passbooks. Most require that the information be notarized. A few states have limitations on how long they keep abandoned property before turning it over to state coffers, but most keep it indefinitely. Some also pay interest on the money if the property was originally interest-bearing.

Honest Finders vs. Vultures

The states currently owe money from abandoned property to an estimated one in ten people in the country, according to attorney David Epstein. But many states do not have the resources to investigate every case, and do little more than advertise names of owners in local newspapers. The resulting gap is sometimes filled by professional "finders" or "heir searchers" who find the owners themselves and charge a fee or commission in exchange for returning it. They can obtain lists, legally in most cases but sometimes surreptitiously, of the names of the owners from the state offices, then conduct their own search. Some finders have charged commissions of 60% to 100%. The price of one finders fee in a past Colorado case was 30% of the dividends and all the shares of stock! Finders can, however, perform a valuable service by reuniting people with money that would have been lost to them forever. Because of cases where these finders have charged excessive fees to people for returning their own money, and because of the strain their demands have put on some already over-burdened state offices, the finders have a shady reputation in some quarters. One state office, for example, refers to them as "bounty hunters," and another calls them "vultures." Many state offices feel that the finders infringe on the owner's right to have their money returned with no charge involved, which is the goal of the state.

The National Association of Abandoned Property Administrators says that since the states never find 100% of the owners, there is a place for honest finders. For example, if a state is unable to locate the owner of a sizable property that he didn't even know about, and a finder does the job, then a service has been performed. Many states, such as Texas, limit the amount of commission a finder may charge; and others have confidentiality laws that prevent them from aiding finders in any way.

One of the biggest obstacles states face is obtaining the cooperation of the banks, insurance companies, and other institutions in reporting properties to them. Despite laws that govern how a holding institution should deal with dormant accounts, they are often low priority items in a business. A state must sometimes work hard to convince them that it is best qualified to return the money. Some states are passing laws that would penalize lax holding companies by charging them a fee.

With billions of dollars in property sitting around out there, clearly many people have an interest in what happens to it. Finders, keepers, states and businesses all have something at stake, and the losers will be those who fail to take advantage of the services that the states offer.

State Listing of Unclaimed Property Offices

Alabama

Department of Revenue and Unclaimed Property, 50 Ripley Street, Room 1116, Montgomery, AL 36104, or P.O. Box 327580, Montgomery, AL 36132-7580; (205) 242-9614. Alabama sends notices to the last known addresses of people whose unclaimed property has reverted to the Department of Revenue. The state also advertises in local newspapers four times a year - in a total of 63 different publications. In Alabama only owners, heirs or those possessing power of attorney will receive the property once it has been rightfully claimed. It usually takes at least three weeks for the claimant to receive his money once the claim has been approved. The state has no statute of limitations on how long it can hold unclaimed property.

Alaska

Alaska Department of Revenue, Income and Excise Audit Division, Unclaimed Property Section, 1111 West 8th Street, Room 106, Juneau, AK 99801; (907) 465-4653. Alaska publishes names of unclaimed property owners once a year in the three major newspapers, sends the information to state legislators, and contacts local news services in order to try to find the owners. They have a three person office, and the person in charge of refunds also makes efforts to investigate the whereabouts of owners. There is no full time locator. Alaska is currently holding an estimated 4.4 million dollars worth of unclaimed property.

Government Auctions and Surplus Property

Arizona

Arizona Department of Revenue, Unclaimed Property, 1600 West Monroe, Room 610, Phoenix, AZ 85007; (602) 542-3908. Twice a year the state runs advertisements in local newspapers with the names of people who have unclaimed property. Claimants need three pieces of I.D. to identify themselves as the rightful owners. In the case of an estate or property of a deceased person, a copy of the will and death certificate is also required. The cumulative number of people who once had, or still do have unclaimed property in Arizona is over 170,000.

Arkansas

Auditor of the State, Unclaimed Property Division, 230 State Capitol, Little Rock, AR 72201; (501) 324-9670. Arkansas publishes the names of owners yearly in local newspapers once a week for two consecutive weeks. It also sends letters to the last known address of each person. Since 1988 the state has held "The Great Arkansas Treasure Hunt " which featured TV spots in an effort to locate owners. This year out of a total of $1,666,802 in unclaimed property, the state paid out $632,428. Arkansas is one of the few states where the unclaimed property reverts to a general fund after three years in the Unclaimed Property Office. This does not mean the money escheats to the state, but once the money goes into the fund, the owner must go to the State Claims Commissioner to claim it. The state will deal only with the actual owner of the property and not with other parties, including those endowed with power of attorney unless it is court ordered. Finders are restricted to a ten per-cent commission of the total retrieved. Refunds are usually sent out within about two weeks of approval.

California

Unclaimed Property Office, P.O. Box 942850, Sacramento, CA 94250-5873; (916) 323-2827, toll free (800) 992-4647 (CA only). In California the law requires the state to advertise unclaimed properties. However, according to Tom Holland, who heads the Unclaimed Property Office, they no longer have a special locator unit, due to budget cuts. The office uses radio and television advertisements, as well as newspaper advisories to locate owners every quarter. A person inquiring about abandoned property in California can get an instant answer by phone from the Office's computer. However, they still need to fill out a claim form and show proof of identity such as birth certificate and social security card once they have determined that the property they are looking for is in the hands of the state. There are hundreds of finders in California trying to get a piece of the considerable action in a state with over 1.6 million unclaimed properties worth seven hundred million dollars. They can come to the state's office or a public library and look up information on microfiche, but are limited to a ten per cent commission. Also, the state will only make checks out amounting to 10 percent for a finder, while sending the remaining 90 percent directly to the owner.

Colorado

Colorado State Treasurer, Division of Unclaimed Property, 1560 Broadway, Suite 630, Denver, CO 80202; (303) 894-2449. Colorado has no statute of limitations on unclaimed property. Once a year in March, the state places the names of owners whose accounts they received the previous year in local newspapers. Colorado will deal only with owners. Finders may obtain a list of property owners for $130, but no research is available to them. The list has 60,000 names on it. The Unclaimed Property Office will only send checks directly to owners. Returns usually go out within four to six weeks of approval. Colorado, like other states, also stipulates that no owner is obligated to pay a finder a commission until the funds have been held by the state for 24 months or longer. The state will not go through an intermediary. Claim forms are only sent to owners. The state currently holds 200,000 names on file of unclaimed property owners.

Connecticut

Treasury Department, 55 Elm St., Hartford, CT 06106; (203) 566-5516. Accounts bearing interest are paid a 4 percent interest. Connecticut lists names of owners in local newspapers every quarter, rotating through two of the eight counties. The state has about 140 million dollars that is currently unclaimed - approximately 200,000 owners. This office is currently getting onto computer. Returns are made out to owners only. Finders are limited to a 50% commission, or 20% commission if the claim is under two years old.

Delaware

Delaware State Escheator, Abandoned Property Division, P.O. Box 8931, Wilmington, DE 19899; If you have a claim, write to Delaware State Escheator, P.O. Box 1039, Boston, MA 02103-1039; (302) 577-3349. Delaware requires

different kinds of proof of ownership, depending on the kind or amount of the claim. After approval, a return is usually mailed out in about six to eight weeks. The state publishes names of owners in local newspapers and occasionally takes the lists to state fairs. On average, Delaware receives 20,000 items per year. Delaware will send returns in joint names of finder and owner.

District of Columbia

Department of Finance and Revenue, Unclaimed Property Division, 300 Indiana Ave. N.W., Room 5008, Washington, DC 20001; (202) 727-0063. The District of Columbia requires the usual proof of ownership, plus social security numbers to identify owners. They get out the returns in about four to six weeks. DC places advertisements in newspapers in August and February, as well as sending out letters to owners. They do not have a locating unit. DC currently holds $11 million in unclaimed property. In 1991 two million dollars of unclaimed property has been returned. Finders are limited to 10% commission. Finders must wait until the District government has held an account for seven months before they can contract to recover it, and must have documentation and a contract that proves they have authority to act on behalf of the owner. The check is issued in the owner's name, but is sent to the address requested.

Florida

Office of Comptroller, Division of Finance, Abandoned Property Section, Tallahassee, FL 32399-0350; (904) 487-0510. Florida deals with owners and other parties, but finders must be licensed private investigators. Claims are advertised in newspapers. Claims may be viewed on microfiche in the office. Lists of items are sold for $30. Returns are made out only to owners or investigators. They currently have about 141 million dollars worth of unclaimed property. There is no limit to the amount of commission finders may collect.

Georgia

Georgia Department of Revenue, Unclaimed Property Office, 270 Washington St. Room 405, Atlanta, GA 30334; (404) 656-4244. Georgia is in the process of upgrading its office and soon hopes to speed up its return time on claims. Claimants may write, telephone, or come in and view lists on microfiche at the Georgia Department of Archives, (404) 656-2393 in order to determine if they have property in the office. The next step is to fill out a claim form and return it with the necessary documentation and proof of identity. Checks are then sent out within a month. The office now has 4 employees. As part of its upgrading, the Georgia office also has more resources to locate owners, through records searches and outreach programs at state public events and placing lists in state Tax Commissioners' offices. They also place advertisements in 159 county newspapers and on television. Georgia holds property in perpetuity and does not pay interest. If you call to inquire about unclaimed property you may have coming to you, the office will check its records. However, nothing has been updated since 1987 on either microfiche or computer. If you think your claim originated after 1987, you must contact the holder directly to get the needed information. The office is currently holding about 65,000 names on file - a total of $45 million dating from 1973. However, they are also holding some safe deposit box items that date back to the 1800's. Finders are not dealt with. Checks are issued only to owners. Finders must wait for 24 months until they can contract to recover claims and they may charge no more than a 10 percent commission.

Hawaii

Director of Finance, State of Hawaii, Unclaimed Property Section, P.O. Box 150, Honolulu, HI 96810; (808) 586-1590. Hawaii lists property owners names in local papers and attempts to locate people by phone. The state currently has about 200 thousand names of people who have not claimed their property. No interest is paid on accounts. The amounts range from a few cents to hundreds of thousands of dollars. Accumulation began in 1974. As of September 30, 1991, Hawaii is holding 21 million dollars of unclaimed property. Hawaii does deal with finders, in providing lists of owners names, etc, but the state will send out checks only to owners. People inquiring about unclaimed property may do so by phone, but a written request is required if there is more than one account. Records are kept on microfiche. Commission of finders is limited to 20 percent.

Idaho

Ms. Mary Weirick, State Tax Commission, Unclaimed Property Division, 700 West State St., P.O. Box 36, Boise, ID 83722-2240; (208) 334-7623. Idaho publishes a list of names once a year in local newspapers, and puts circular inserts in all state and senior citizens papers. It advertises on 2 radio stations and 3 television stations. In addition, some local radio stations announce 25 names

Be patient. If any phone number is incorrect, call (area code) 555-1212 and request the new listing.

Unclaimed Money

per day on weekdays. Also, they now have a full-time locator in the office to find potential owners. Idaho is currently holding approximately 11 million dollars in cash, 125,000 stock shares, 80,000 individual accounts, and thousands of safety deposit boxes. The state deals with finders and will sell them a list of properties worth $200 and above for $31.85. Property must be held for two years by the state before a commission may be charged. After that, checks may be mailed to finders, but they will be made out to the owner.

Illinois

Department of Financial Institutions, Unclaimed Property Division, 500 Iles Park Place, Suite 510, Springfield, IL 62718; (217) 782-8463 or (217) 782-6692. Illinois requests that inquiries to the office be in writing to facilitate their research. With sufficient detail, the search takes 3 to 4 weeks. Claim analysis takes 6 to 8 weeks. After approval, returns usually take about three months. The state advertises the names of owners twice a year in the newspapers of the county of each owner's last known address. Occasionally they advertise on radio and television. They currently have over two million names. Since 1971 over 270 million dollars have accumulated. Finders must be licensed detectives and are required to send the contract with the owners to the state office for approval. Items must be held by the state 2 years before finders make a contract on it. As of August 1990, finders are limited to a 10% commission. Checks are sent to owner and finder with power of attorney. Finders and holders are notified when claim is paid.

Indiana

Office of Attorney General Pearson, Unclaimed Property Division, 219 State House, Indianapolis, IN 46204-2794; (317) 232-6348. Indiana has a statute of limitations of 25 years before unclaimed property reverts to the Common School Building Fund. After reversion, the property can no longer be claimed. The first time this will occur is in 1993. After approval, returns take about six to eight weeks. The whole claim process takes about 3 months. The state runs newspaper advertisements as well as television spots and a cable show called *Consumer Corner* in an effort to find owners. Finders must submit the contract with the owners for approval by the state, and checks are sent directly to the owners. Also, finders are limited to 10% commission and may collect nothing on items held for less than 24 months by the state.

Iowa

Great Iowa Treasure Hunt, Treasurer's Office, Hoover Building, State Capitol Complex, Des Moines, IA 50319; (515) 281-5540/5366. You may write or call this office to see if you have unclaimed property. They will look it up on their computers. Iowa publishes owners' names in local newspapers twice a year, and has representatives at the State and County Fairs to disseminate information. Big books are brought and people can look through them. They use radio and TV advertisements for larger claims - $100 and over. Iowa currently has close to 74 thousand unclaimed properties. The office takes about two weeks to make the returns once the claim is approved. Finders must be private investigators. They may use the office's microfiche, but no lists are sold to them. Their commission is limited to 15 percent.

Kansas

State Treasurer's Office, Unclaimed Property Division, 900 Southwest Jackson, Suite 201, Topeka, KS 66612-1235; (913) 296-3171, or toll free (800) 432-0386 (KS only). Kansas will take phone or written inquiries about lost properties. They pay owners directly. Currently there are over 230,000 unclaimed properties in the state worth $22 million. The Treasurer's office makes attempts by mail and through public gatherings such as booths at state fairs to find owners. About 45 percent of properties are recovered. Finders commissions are limited to 15 percent and contracts for items held by the state for less than two years are not valid.

Kentucky

Abandoned Property Unit, Station 62, Frankfort, KY 40620; (502) 564-6823. Kentucky successfully processes 250-300 claims per year. They place advertisements in local newspapers, produce press releases, and run radio, television announcements, and at state fairs in attempts to locate owners. In addition, they try to find people by mail. Kentucky requests all inquiries to be in writing. In the past, they have even discovered people attempting fraud by using fake letterhead. One man claimed to be Thomas Edison's heir and owed $25,000. Finders need a power of attorney or other legal document. Returns are issued to owners and sent to the address requested. The office says they hope to see new legislation soon to control finders' fees.

Louisiana

Louisiana Department of Revenue and Taxation, Unclaimed Property Section, P.O. Box 91010, Baton Rouge, LA 70821-9010; (504) 925-7425. Louisiana holds unclaimed items into perpetuity. It holds about 42 million dollars worth of unclaimed items. About 1500-2000 items are successfully united with owners each year. To research records, call the office to make an appointment. You can take the whole day to view printouts. Printouts are not for sale. Claims are advertised in newspapers and letters are sent to last known address. Finders must wait two years before making contracts on items over $50. Finders commission is limited to 10 percent. Once a claim is approved, the check will be issued within 90 days.

Maine

Treasurer's Department, Abandoned Property Division, House Station 39, Augusta, ME 04333; (207) 289-2771. Maine accepts either phone or written inquiries, and will have a return in about a month from approval, although stock returns take longer. There is about a two month backlog in running computer searches. Since 1979, there has been no statute of limitation on the length of time, and the office will hold funds in perpetuity. The state currently holds about 14 million dollars worth of unclaimed property from 7000 holders and 20,000 owners. Finders cannot collect commissions on properties held less than two years and after that they are limited to 15% for items over $50. Maine uses advertising, personal letters, and booths at fairs to try to locate owners. The office has had good results in locating people. Maine pays interest that item earned at the time it was turned over to the state for up to 10 years. The office has hired a national firm to locate property.

Maryland

Comptroller of the Treasury, Unclaimed Property Section, 301 West Preston St., Baltimore, MD 21201; (410) 225-1700. Maryland has no statute of limitations governing the length of time property is held. Maryland advertises in the jurisdiction of the last known address twice a year and mails notices to the last known address. It also advertises on radio and television, and disseminates information at state fairs. The office has been in existence since 1966 and deals with both finders and owners. Claim forms must be signed by the owner if possible. Only owners may ask for claim forms. Finders cannot, even if they have a contract. Payment is made only to the claimant. As of July 1, 1991, finders need not be paid on items held by the state for less than 2 years. No limits are placed on the amount of commission finders may charge after the two years elapses.

Massachusetts

Commonwealth of Massachusetts, Treasury Department, Unclaimed Property Division, One Ashburton Place, Room 1207, Boston, MA 02108; (617) 367-3900. Massachusetts, whose office has been in existence since 1955, pays interest to owners on interest-earning property. The state holds items belonging to more than 30,000 people. They publish names in local newspapers every year to try to locate owners. Safety deposit boxes held more than 7 years are sold at auction. Once ownership has been established, the office pays returns in about four to six weeks. The state does not give returns to finders, but sells microfiche to finders for $25. There is a 30 percent cap on finders fees.

Michigan

Michigan Department of the Treasury, Escheats Division, Lansing, MI 48922; (517) 334-6550. Michigan has a statute of limitations of seven years after abandonment for amounts under $50. Michigan is a custodial state. Lists of items are advertised in each county after they go through probate. Since 1988 listings have been put on computer. Prior to 1988, unless you know the holder, it is difficult to trace a claim. Approximately 68 million dollars worth of property is being held. They get the returns out within several weeks. Finders must have a contract if they charge more than 5 percent commission. Finders need a private detective's license. The office makes out checks only to owners or heirs. Third parties are never issued checks even if they have power of attorney.

Minnesota

Minnesota Department of Commerce, Office of Unclaimed Property, 133 East 7th Street, St. Paul, MN 55101-2362; (612) 296-2568, toll free (800) 652-9747 within the state but outside Minneapolis/St.Paul area. Minnesota has about 150,000 properties currently unclaimed. Inquiries may be made by phone or in writing, and specific documentation will be required. Normally six weeks are needed to process returns. Lists are advertised in newspapers. Searchers can

Be patient. If any phone number is incorrect, call (area code) 555-1212 and request the new listing.

Government Auctions and Surplus Property

collect for owners if proper documents are presented, but there is a 10 % limit on commissions unless there is a prior agreement between the owner and the searcher. Finders may not enforce contracts for locating items that have been held by the state for less than one year.

Mississippi

Mississippi Treasurer's Office, Unclaimed Property Division, P.O. Box 138, Jackson, MS 39205; (601) 359-3600. Mississippi pays interest on accounts - 5% on interest-bearing accounts and 1% on everything else. They currently hold $5.4 million in unclaimed funds. Holding period, called dormancy, is 5 years. After that time, the holding company must turn the property over to the state. The state sets a limit of 10% commission for finders, but expects new legislation to restrict that amount further. The state is required by law to publish the names of all owners every third year with items worth $100 or more. It usually takes 30 to 60 days for returns to be processed, if all the information has been properly supplied by the claimant.

Missouri

Department of Economic Development, Unclaimed Property, Box 1272, Jefferson City, MO 65102; (314) 751-0840. Missouri pays interest on interest-bearing accounts; and finders can collect their percentages with no limitations. The office tries to locate owners through advertising twice per year in news publications, mailing postcards to last known addresses, and some searches, but they do not have investigative capability.

Montana

State Of Montana, Department of Revenue, Abandoned Property Section, Mitchell Bldg., Helena, MT 59620; (406) 444-2425. Montana's two-person office cannot conduct extensive investigations to find property owners, but are exceptionally dedicated to finding owners and have an excellent return rate. They can access state's income tax records and drivers license records for addresses. They will soon be able to access the Federal Deed Check. This office has a refund rate of 33 percent. In 1990 it took in $1.5 million and refunded one-half million dollars. Items over $100 are advertised in the county of the person's last known address. There are currently between 70 and 100 thousand accounts unclaimed. Returns are made to finders with legal contracts or power of attorney. There are no limits on finders.

Nebraska

Nebraska State Treasurer's Office, Property Capitol Building, P.O. Box 94788, Lincoln, NE 68509; (402) 471-2455. Nebraska publishes the names of property owners in local newspapers, sends out letters, and conducts research in an effort to locate the rightful owners. It does not pay interest on accounts. The office will deal with owners only and issues checks to them alone. For the first 90 days during which property is held by the state, finders may not charge more than 10 percent commission. After that there is no limit.

Nevada

State of Nevada, Unclaimed Property Division, State Mail Room, Las Vegas, NV 89158; (702) 486-4140/3000, or toll free (800) 521-0019 (NV only). Nevada currently has about 80 thousand unclaimed properties, the vast majority of which are under $500. The current unclaimed amount, which the state holds in perpetuity, is $29 million. This 9 person office is on computer. They prefer inquiries to be made in writing and will make returns in about three weeks. No interest is paid on interest bearing accounts. The state allows finders to make claims after the state has tried for two years to locate the rightful owner. Computer printouts of lists can be viewed by researchers at the office, but they are not for sale. The finders are then limited to ten percent commission, and the checks are sent only to the owner. Nevada advertises in local papers and on television and radio as part of its efforts to locate the owners.

New Hampshire

New Hampshire State Treasurer's Office, Abandoned Property Division, 25 Capitol St., State House Annex Room 121, Concord, NH 03301; (603) 271-2619. People can come to the office and look at the books. State expects to be entirely on microfiche or computer by 1993. After advertising an abandoned property for two years in a statewide newspaper and sending a letter to the last known address, New Hampshire can go to court and have the account escheated to the county involved, with 15% going to a general State Treasurer's fund. After the two year period, the owner needs a special bill in the state legislature to retrieve his money. The State advertises once again in the newspaper prior to escheatment, and they research large accounts. New Hampshire does not recognize finders; any agreement between a finder and owner is unenforceable for 24 months after a property is turned over to the state, and then the escheatment process takes over.

New Jersey

Department of Treasurer, Unclaimed Property, CN-214, Trenton, NJ 08646; (609) 292-9200. All requests must be in writing. No information on claims is given out by phone. New Jersey will not supply lists of owners' names to finders. They pay interest on interest bearing accounts as of April 14, 1989, and are a custodial state. Their efforts to find owners consist mostly of running newspaper advertisements. The state of New Jersey does not deal with finders.

New Mexico

New Mexico Taxation and Revenue Department, P.O. Box 25123, Santa Fe, NM 87504-5123; (505) 827-0767. New Mexico puts funds from unclaimed property in a special account in the General Fund, but it is still accessible to owners who make a claim. Objects such as those found in safe deposit boxes can be auctioned when they are turned over to the state, after 25 years. So far that has never happened, but it may in the future. The state currently holds 200,000 names on cards, which date back to 1959, and 70,000 names on computer, which date from March 1989 when the office was automated. The properties held total about $8 million. The state advertises owners' names statewide and sends letters to the last known addresses. Finders are subject to a gross receipts tax, but there is no limit on the commission they may charge. As of November 1, 1991, no finders may contract on items held by the state for less than two years.

New York

Administrator, Office of Unclaimed Funds, Alfred E. Smith Bldg., 9th Floor, Albany, NY 12236; (518) 474-4038, toll free (800) 221-9311 (NY only). From New York's hotline or regular phone number, owners can find out immediately if their property has been turned over to the state and if anyone has ever successfully made a claim on it. Then they will need to fill out the appropriate forms with proof of identification, which will vary for different kinds of property. New York is not a forms state. No particular application is needed, just proof that the property belongs to the claimant. Interest is paid for the first five years at the U.S. Treasury rate. There are currently seven million names of unclaimed property owners in the state, with funds amounting to two billion dollars. New York is very active in its efforts to find owners. Besides sending out letters (about three thousand per week), they have a mobile outreach program, where office personnel travel to various locations with all the computerized information, and visit senior citizens centers, malls, fairs, etc. They say this has been very successful in locating owners, whereas pilot projects to try to match names with the Department of Motor Vehicles and the Taxation and Finance Department have been less successful. The state is "not thrilled" with finders and feels that owners should be able to reclaim their property free of charge. Finders fees are limited to 15% and the office encourages people to deal directly with them.

North Carolina

Administrator, Escheat and Abandoned Property Section, Department of State Treasurer, 325 N. Salisbury St., Raleigh, NC 27603-1388; (919) 733-6876. In North Carolina, the Abandoned Property Section can return funds in less than two weeks in uncomplicated situations. By law, they must send lists of owners names to clerks of the State Supreme Court in each county and to local newspapers. They also use computer matches with the Department of Motor Vehicles and Department of Revenue, and they have a locator unit as well. Currently, North Carolina holds over 79 million dollars in abandoned monies. In 1990 they took in over ten million dollars worth. Finders must be licensed private investigators or detectives and licenses may not be transferred from state to state. Finders must state their fees in a contract with the owner. Commissions are limited to 25%.

North Dakota

North Dakota Unclaimed Property Division, 918 East Divide Ave., Suite 410, P.O. Box 5523, Bismarck, ND 58502; (701) 224-2805. North Dakota publicizes abandoned properties in local newspapers, radio, television, through mailings to last known addresses, and booths at the State Fair. They accept inquiries by phone or mail, and then require claim forms to be filled out with appropriate documents attached. Once approved, returns usually take about two weeks. The state sends checks only to owners and has a two-year waiting period before fin-

Be patient. If any phone number is incorrect, call (area code) 555-1212 and request the new listing.

Unclaimed Money

ders can contract on a property. Finders' fees are limited to 25% of the total amount. Interest earned by abandoned properties goes to a common school fund.

Ohio

Chief, Division of Unclaimed Funds, Department of Commerce, 77 South High Street, 20th Floor, Columbus, OH 43266-0545; (614) 466-4433. In Ohio, the published lists of owners' names includes a coupon in the larger newspapers that they can fill out to expedite their claim. Returns could take from eight weeks to three months, depending on the complications involved. Ohio also has an outreach program where the office sends representatives to state and county fairs, shopping malls and other public events. This includes visiting sites of the Governor's "Regional Cabinet Day" program where he picks a town to spend the day in to conduct business. The state currently has 2.8 million names on file, with funds amounting to 110 million dollars. It pays no interest on accounts and there is a 5 percent processing fee for payment of claims. Ohio is unusual in that the Unclaimed Funds Division operates on the money it is holding, at no cost to the government. The state's Department of Development also uses unclaimed funds to guarantee loans that stimulate economic development. In addition, the original holding institutions in Ohio are only required to turn 10% of the unclaimed funds over to the state, and they use the money to invest at market value. The holding company may retain the other 90 percent and invest it in secured stock in the name of the State of Ohio. The claimant still receives the full amount owed to him. The Ohio office must hold funds for two years before finders can make contracts on them, and their fees are restricted to 10%. Checks are paid to owners only unless another party has the power of attorney.

Oklahoma

Oklahoma Tax Commission, Unclaimed Property Section, 2501 Lincoln Blvd., Oklahoma City, OK 73194-0010; (405) 521-4275. Oklahoma is a custodial state and keeps unclaimed properties in perpetuity. Requests about claims must be in writing. State does not pay interest on interest-bearing accounts. The state currently holds $60 million worth of these monies. Approximately $11 million has been returned to owners. They publicize names in local newspapers twice a year and intend to have a locator service in the near future. If a finder has a power of attorney, he can submit a claim and there is a 25 percent limit on the amount of commission he can charge.

Oregon

Oregon Division of State Lands, 775 Summer Street NE, Salem, OR 97310; (503) 378-3805. Oregon will hold unclaimed property indefinitely while it is invested in the School District Fund. From the time property is reported by a holding company as unclaimed until the time it is advertised and remitted to the state, which is about 6 months duration, information about it is not public information. Inquiries during that time must be directed to the holding company. Interest earned also goes to the Fund. There is $29 million worth of unclaimed property belonging to 80,000 persons. No interest is paid on interest-bearing accounts. The state sends letters to the last known addresses of owners and advertises in local newspapers. They publish an information brochure for consumers explaining the procedures involved for claiming abandoned property. They also publish an information packet for researchers who want to find claims as a business. State emphasizes to owners that it will do the search for them. The state sends checks jointly to finders and owners and there are currently no restrictions on the amount of commission finders may charge.

Pennsylvania

Supervisor, Abandoned and Unclaimed Property Section, Pennsylvania Department of Revenue, 2850 Turnpike Industrial Park, Middletown, PA 17057; (717) 986-4641, or toll free (800) 222-2046 (PA only). Procedures and proof required to reclaim property depend on the type and size of the property, and whether the claimant is the owner, heir or estate. As of September 30, 1991, the state has collected $208 million from 500,000 accounts, of which $34 million, plus securities, has been returned. Pennsylvania checks its list of names against state tax records to help locate people and sends out notices for amounts over $100. The state also lists the names of owners in local newspapers, and passes lists on to General Assembly members. In addition, they have an outreach program that travels to public functions, such as the governor's "Capitol for the Day" program, around the state looking for owners, and they have found one in five people on their list in this manner. In Pennsylvania there are no restrictions on finders. However, before claim forms are sent to finders, they must have a notarized power of attorney.

Rhode Island

State Of Rhode Island, Unclaimed Property Division, 40 Fountain St., Providence, RI 02903; (401) 277-6505. Rhode Island takes about three to four weeks to return lost funds once the claim is made. People with more recent claims may call the state office to find out immediately from the computerized listing if they actually have money there. Older claims take a day to research. No dollar amounts are given out. They must then follow up with the proper identification. The state pays simple interest - 5% on interest-bearing accounts. They send out letters to the last known addresses of owners, and place advertisements in all the state newspapers. They also have an outreach program, where representatives of the Unclaimed Property Office travel to public functions around the state to try to locate people. The state says this program has been very effective. In March of 1988 Rhode Island advertised six thousand names of property owners and was able to locate half of them. Finders are on their own here - they receive no help from the state, nor are there restrictions on the fees they may charge. Finders' contracts are null and void if item has been in state custody for under 24 months.

South Carolina

Abandoned Property Office, South Carolina Tax Commission, P.O. Box 125, Columbia, SC 29214; (803) 737-4771. In South Carolina, a claimant looking for lost property can go to the holding institution - that is, the original business where the account or money was located - within the first sixty days after his funds have been declared abandoned. Then, he must look for them in the state office. Make an appointment. The hours are 9:00 am to 11:00 am and 2:30 pm to 4:30 pm weekdays. The information is kept on microfiche. Twice a year the office runs advertisements in county newspapers, with names of people known to have lived in each county. They also travel to the State Fair in October, as well as mail letters to the last known addresses. South Carolina currently holds $31 million in abandoned property, representing 403,000 accounts. In 1989, lists of owners' names were made available to the public for the first time, but the office will not duplicate or mail copies. Finders fees have also been limited to 15%, and the finder must be a licensed private investigator. The state now mandates it must hold a property for two years before a finder can contract to recover it.

South Dakota

Ms. Ruby Douglas, Abandoned Property, State Treasurer's Office, 500 East Capitol, Pierre, SD 57501; (605) 773-3378. Inquiries may be by phone or in writing to the office, which can do an immediate computer search to determine if a claimant's property is being held there. South Dakota has, after returns taken out, 4 million dollars of unclaimed property that has accumulated since the inception of the program. The accounts belong to about 15,000 people. Then, the claimant must submit whatever proof is required and complete the necessary paperwork. South Dakota has a successful outreach program that travels to state and county fairs with a specially-made list of names that is posted so the public may easily read it. In the past two years, they have tripled their refunds as a result of the program. In addition, the office lists names in local newspapers. Finders are limited to 25% commission and the office pays returns directly to owners only. No lists of names are made available for heir-finding purposes, although anyone who wants to see the names may come to the office by appointment only.

Tennessee

State of Tennessee, Unclaimed Property Division, Andrew Jackson State Office Bldg., 11th floor, Nashville, TN 37243-0242; (615) 741-6499. In Tennessee the Unclaimed Property Division pays only to original owner or estates in the case of money belonging to a deceased person. In all cases, they require suitable proof identification such as proof of address, social security number, etc. Returns take approximately three weeks. Interest is paid only if the original holder paid it as well. Tennessee advertises names of owners in local newspapers, sends letters to last known addresses, matches its list with other state agencies, and searches current telephone directories in an effort to locate owners. Further efforts, such as consulting credit bureaus, may be made in cases of large accounts. Since 1979, $26 million worth of abandoned property has been reported to the state office, of which $13 million has been returned. The office currently holds $30 million worth of property. Finders must make appointments with the office to view lists of names, and they are frequently booked a week in advance. The records viewed at the office are on microfiche and can be purchased for $30. Any contract made between a finder and owner must be approved by the state; and contracts are only valid after the state has held the property for one year. Finders are restricted to 10% commission or $50, whichever is greater.

Be patient. If any phone number is incorrect, call (area code) 555-1212 and request the new listing.

Government Auctions and Surplus Property

Texas

Unclaimed Money Fund, P.O. Box 12019, State Treasurer's Office, Austin, TX 78711; (512) 444-7833, or toll free (800) 321-CASH (TX only). This office has a full-time locator and aggressively pursues search for owners. Texas claimants follow procedures similar to those in most states - that is, filling out claim forms, providing notarized documentation of ownership, and submitting driver's license or social security numbers. Returns take about 90 days to process. The state advertises names in local newspapers, on radio and television, and sends notices to the last known address of the owner. The Treasurer's office has received two million accounts over the past 25 years, representing over $206 million. Of that, 25 percent has been returned to owners. Holding companies also return many items. No interest on interest-bearing accounts is paid. Finders are limited to 10% commission; and the Treasurer's office advises people who have been contacted by a finder to check with them first before paying someone a fee to return their money. Half of the money never claimed in Texas goes to a Foundation School Fund, and the other half goes to the State general revenue. However, the money is always available to the rightful owner and claimants can retrieve their funds at any time.

Utah

Utah Unclaimed Property Division, 341 South Main Street, 4th Floor, Salt Lake City, UT 84114; (801) 533-4101. Utah pays interest on accounts that were interest-bearing when they came from the bank, such as certificates of deposit; but other items such as savings accounts are closed out by the bank. The state advertises one time in the paper names they received in the past six months and publicizes on radio and television. They also run a booth at the State Fair and maintain a locator in the office. The state has over 150,000 unclaimed properties worth over $20 million at the present time. Searchers or finders can apply with a valid power of attorney and checks are issued either to owners or those with power of attorney. No agreement between owners and fee-finders is enforceable until the state has held the property for two years.

Vermont

State Treasurer's Office, Unclaimed Property Division, 133 State St., Montpelier, VT 05633-6200; (802) 533-4101. Vermont sends out letters to owners of property worth $25 or more. If the amount is over $50, the state runs advertisements in local newspapers for two consecutive weeks. They have no other investigative capability due to the very small size of the office. Books are open to the public view at the office. Vermont has collected about two million dollars worth of unclaimed property since 1965, and currently holds between 16 and 18 thousand properties. Finders can only contract with owners after the state has held a property for twelve months.

Virginia

Department of the Treasury, Division of Unclaimed Property, P.O. Box 2478, Richmond, VA 23207; (804) 225-2393, or toll free (800) 468-1088 (VA only). Virginia requires a claimant to submit proof of whatever information the state received from the holder. For example, someone claiming money in a savings account would have to produce a passbook or other proof of ownership of that account. In most cases, returns are made within two months. The state pays interest if the original holder was also paying it. There is a 5 % limit. In Virginia, unclaimed property information is classified as confidential, so the state cannot release information to finders. The public is not invited to look at the office's records. Private agreements between finders and owners are limited to a 10% commission for the finder. In addition, the property must be held for 36 months before such a contract is recognized. Approximately 600 thousand names are currently on file with the abandoned property office, and the state is holding an accumulation of some $125 million.

Washington

State of Washington Department of Revenue, Unclaimed Property Division, P.O. Box 448, Olympia, WA 98507; (206) 586-2736. Washington has an automated system that enables the office to respond immediately to inquiries about unclaimed property. Their list dates back to 1955. The office attends county and state fairs to locate owners, and will branch out soon to malls and other public locations as well. A full time locator will be added to the office who will do nothing but track down owners. A spokesperson for the office says it is anticipated this will double the amount of claims refunded. The staff searches telephone books. One found the owner of $149,000 by looking in the telephone directory. She had not even known the money was owed to her. They also place advertisements in local newspapers every six months and send out notices. Efforts to advertise through the broadcast media have been very successful. A recent television show brought 250 calls. Washington pays interest if an account was previously an interest-bearing bank and CD account, and continues to pay the same rate of interest for up to 10 years. The state currently holds about $100 million in unclaimed property, from about 600,000 owners. Last year, it paid out over five million dollars in returns, out of the fourteen million it received. Washington is one of the most restrictive states for finders, limiting them to 5% commission and subjecting them to the confidentiality law which limits what information the office can reveal about abandoned property owners. As a result, they say they have few problems with heir-finding.

West Virginia

Treasurer of the State, Unclaimed Property Division, Bldg. 1, Suite E145, State Capital, Charleston, WV 25305; (304) 343-4000. West Virginia is currently holding 6 million dollars in unclaimed funds for some 70,000 accounts. No interest is paid on interest-bearing accounts. West Virginia has a five-person office for unclaimed property, so the efforts they can make to locate owners are minimal, and returns may take some time. By law, however, the state must advertise the names in local newspapers, and send notices to the last known address within 10 days. There are no regulations on finders, but the office does not supply lists of names. Finders can view the names by visiting the office, but no information except names and addresses is released unless an owner has authorized it.

Wisconsin

Office of the State Treasurer, Unclaimed Property Division, P.O. Box 2114, Madison, WI 53701-2114; (608) 267-7977. The Wisconsin office prefers written inquiries about lost properties, including as accurate a description as possible. Once a claim is approved by the Unclaimed Property Division and the Attorney General's office, returns are made within six to eight weeks. The state pays interest if the account was interest-bearing in the first place. For properties over $50, Wisconsin runs newspaper advertisements listing the names of owners. The office is able to perform only limited research. They search current telephone directories, and try to check social security numbers with the Department of Revenue. The state holds $10 million of unclaimed property. Finders are limited to 20% commission as of May 1988. They may purchase a list of names and view the records in the office, but checks are made out only in the names of the owners.

Wyoming

Unclaimed Property Division, Wyoming State Treasury Office, State Capital, Cheyenne, WY 82002; (307) 777-7408. Wyoming's Unclaimed Property Division currently deals mainly with lost insurance policies. At present, only insurance companies are required to file unclaimed property with the state. Other holders are not required to turn over or even tell the state about unclaimed property. However, new legislation is expected soon to bring the state in line with the uniform unclaimed property law. Wyoming holds about half a million dollars worth of unclaimed funds. The claim procedures for recovering the insurance money is similar to what other states require - that is, proof of policy number, address, etc. Returns are usually made in one week. Currently Wyoming holds 4000 names on its unclaimed list. They are all on a printout list that can be purchased for $60. Wyoming has a five year statute of limitations, after which funds that are still unclaimed revert to a Common School Fund and are no longer claimable. Finders can come into the office to view the list of names and there are no restrictions on the amount of commission they may charge. However, finders have no access to property until the account has been held by the state for two years. The state deals only with owners and will remit only to claimant.

Be patient. If any phone number is incorrect, call (area code) 555-1212 and request the new listing.

Small Business and Entrepreneuring Federal Starting Places

* *See also Business and Industry Chapter*
* *See also Selling to the Government Chapter*
* *See also Information on People, Companies, and Mailing Lists Chapter*
* *See also Economics, Demographics, and Statistics Chapter*
* *See also International Trade Chapter*
* *See also Patents, Trademarks and Copyrights Chapter*

Here you will discover that the U.S. Small Business Administration is not the only federal agency that provides financial and managerial assistance to small businesses and entrepreneurs. For example, trade remedy relief is the responsibility of the U.S. International Trade Commission and the National Science Foundation offers small firms R&D opportunities. After you become more familiar with the Answer Desk, incubator programs, FTC rules, certified lenders, and other federal help, you may want to move on to the next section, State Starting Places and Money. You'll probably find a lot of help close by in the state capital and in other major metropolitan areas besides Washington, DC. State governments are increasingly responsive to small business and offer many services.

* Advocacy and Small Business

Office of Advocacy
U.S. Small Business Administration
409 3rd Street, SW
7th Floor
Washington, DC 20416 (202) 205-6533

As the watchdog for small business within the federal government, this office carries out the following: researching the effect of federal laws, programs, regulation, and taxation on small business and making recommendations to federal agencies for appropriate adjustments to meet the needs of small business; conducting economic studies and statistical research into matters affecting small business and evaluating future opportunities, problems, and needs of small business; and serving as a conduit through which small business can make suggestions and comment on policy. Available for sale from the U.S. Government Printing Office, *The State of Small Business: A Report of the President*, contains the most current information on small business performance in the economy. Also issued from this office is the *Small Business Advocate*, a monthly newsletter that reports on small business issues and actions of the Office of Advocacy. It is available through Advocacy's Office of Information by calling (202) 634-7600. For more information contact the office above.

* Answer Desk

U.S. Small Business Administration
409 3rd Street, SW
5th Floor (800) 827-5722
Washington, DC 20416 (202) 653-7561

The Small Business Answer Desk helps callers with questions on how to start and manage a business, where to get financing, and other information needed to operate and expand a business. This toll-free hotline is provided by SBA's Office of Advocacy and operates from 8:30 a.m. to 5:00 p.m. EST, Monday through Friday.

* Broadcast Entrepreneurs: Purchasing and Technical Assistance

Consumer Assistance and Small Business Division
Office of Public Affairs
Federal Communications Commission
1919 M Street, NW
Room 254
Washington, DC 20554 (202) 632-7000

The CASB Division will provide you with personal assistance in locating information concerning FCC rules, policies, procedures, and guidance concerning participation in FCC rulemaking proceedings. In addition, this office provides specialized to assistance to those interested in becoming involved in the small business telecommunications industry. They will walk you through the purchasing procedures, identify resources for financial and technical assistance, and perform license status checks for applicants. The Public Affairs office also coordinates broadcast ownership workshops, which cover these topic and more, every year across the country. Contact CASB for more information.

* Business Assistance--Directory of Federal and State

National Technical Information Service
U.S. Department of Commerce
5285 Port Royal Rd.
Springfield, VA 22161 (703) 487-4650

The *Directory of Federal and State Business Assistance* describes more than 180 Federal and 500 state programs. Each entry gives a summary of the service offered, a telephone number and address, and eligibility requirements if any. These programs are designed to help new and growing companies compete more effectively in domestic and international markets. Uses of this directory can include how to get funding for a company's research and development; where to get mail lists of potential overseas business buyers; who provides venture money; and what Federal and state contacts offer free management consulting. The *Directory* is available for $29. Contact the Sales Desk to place an order or request the free information brochure, *PR-801*.

* Business Assistance Newsletter

Public Affairs
Minority Business Development Agency
14th and Constitution Ave. NW
Room 6707
Washington, DC 20230 (202) 377-1936

Minority Business Today is a free monthly publication which highlights interesting articles, educational opportunities, loan information, and grant awards, as well as procurement and publications information, relating to minority businesses. Also included is information on international trade and Minority Business Development Centers.

* Business Loans from the SBA

Contact your local SBA office or the Small Business Answer Desk listed in this Section.

SBA offers two basic types of business loans: guaranteed loans which are made by private lenders, usually banks, and guaranteed up to 90 percent by SBA; and SBA direct loans which are available only to applicants unable to secure an SBA guaranteed loan. *Business Loans from the SBA* is a brochure available from your SBA office which gives information on these two types of loans, how to apply for a loan, terms of loans, collateral, eligibility requirements, and general size standards.

Small Business and Entrepreneuring

* Capital Formation for Small Businesses

The Office of Small Business Policy
Division of Corporation Finance
U.S. Securities and Exchange Commission (SEC)
450 5th St., NW
Washington, DC 20549 (202) 272-2644

The Securities and Exchange Commission's main responsibility under the securities laws is to protect investors and to make sure the capital markets operate fairly and orderly. However, the Commission is careful not to let its regulations impair capital formation by small businesses. Therefore, the SEC has taken a number of steps to help small businesses raise capital and to ease the burden of undue regulations under the federal securities laws. The Commission is continually examining other ways to meet these goals. For more information, contact this office.

* Coal Operator Assistance

Small Coal Operator Assistance
Land Resources
Natural Resources Management
Resource and Development
Tennessee Valley Authority (TVA)
Norris, TN 37828 (615) 632-1753

To ensure more competition and reasonable prices, TVA reserves a portion of its coal purchases for small producers. In addition, the TVA provides mining and reclamation technical assistance to small coal producers. The program is also involved in non-coal mineral abandoned mine reclamation. The percentage of contracts awarded to coal suppliers is evaluated based on the capability of the company to comply with TVA's mine reclamation programs.

* Contract Loans

Contact your local SBA office or the Small Business Answer Desk listed in this section.

The Contract Loan Program (COL) is a short term line of credit, without a revolving feature. It is available under the SBA's guaranty loan program solely to finance the estimated cost of labor and material needed to perform on a specific contract. Detailed information can be obtained from the SBA office in your area.

* Definition of a Small Business

Contact your local SBA office or the Small Business Answer Desk listed in this section.

SBA generally defines a small business as one which is independently owned and operated and is not dominant in its field. Most small, independent businesses or individuals starting a business are eligible for SBA assistance. To be eligible for SBA loans and other assistance, a business must meet a size standard set by the SBA. Specific size standard information is available through any SBA office around the country.

* Development Company Loans

Contact your local SBA office or the Small Business Answer Desk listed in this section.

Development Company Loans are made to development organizations approved by SBA for the purpose of fostering economic growth in rural and urban areas. Growth is measured primarily by job creation and retention. Loan proceeds are used by development companies to assist small business concerns with plant acquisition, construction, conversion, or expansion, including the acquisition of machinery and equipment. Contact the nearest SBA office for more information on these loans.

* Disaster Assistance

Contact your local SBA office or the Small Business Answer Desk listed in this section.

Natural disasters, such as hurricanes, floods, tornados, and earthquakes, often cause hardship to business and individuals. When the U.S. President or SBA Administrator declares a specific area to be a disaster area, two types of loans are offered by the SBA: Physical Disaster Loans and Economic Injury Disaster Loans. To obtain the pamphlets *Disaster Loans for Homes and Personal Property, Economic Injury Disaster Loans for Small Businesses,* and *Physical Disaster Business Loans,* or for more information about disaster loans, contact your local SBA office.

* Economic Database

Office of Economic Research
Office of Advocacy
U.S. Small Business Administration
409 3rd Street, SW
5th Floor
Washington, DC 20416 (202) 205-6530

The *Small Business Data Base* (SBDB) is an integrated effort for developing and organizing data on the role of small business in the U.S. Economy. It is designed to meet the needs of the research community for analyzing cause and effect relationships of small business problems and progress. *The Small Business Data Base: A User's Guide* provides an overview of Data Base files and applications, as well as methods of accessing the *Small Business Data Base.* It is designed to acquaint the first-time user with the diversity of possible uses with the SBDB. To obtain this guide or for more information, contact the office above.

* Environmental Protection Agency Small Business Ombudsman

Small Business Ombudsman
Environmental Protection Agency (EPA)
401 M Street SW
Washington, DC 20460 (703) 305-5938

The Small Business Ombudsman in the EPA Office of the Administrator provides various services to help small business comply with EPA regulations. The Ombudsman serves as information services and advocate for small business interests in the regulatory development process. It helps these small businesses with their individual problems.

* EPA-Help Hotline for Small Business

Environmental Protection Agency
401 M Street SW (800) 368-5888
Washington, DC 20460 (202) 260-2090

The Small Business Hotline is an EPA-based hotline that gives advice and information to small businesses on complying with EPA regulations. It deals with problems encountered by small-quantity generators of hazardous waste and other small businesses with environmental concerns.

* Expanding SBA Services to Business

Office of Business, Initiative, Education,
and Training (BIET)
U.S. Small Business Administration (SBA)
409 3rd St., SW, Room 6400
Washington, DC 20416 (202) 205-6665

The Private Sector Initiatives Program is a cooperative, outreach program designed to increase the effectiveness of SBA programs, particularly in providing management training and publications to the small business community. It combines the resources of trade associations, corporations, foundations, and professional societies with those of SBA in responding to the changing needs of small business. The main focus of this program is enlarging the capability of SBA to provide valuable services to small businesses through cooperative, jointly-sponsored activities with the private sector, particularly at reduced cost. Some of the ways the private sector helps SBA in delivering these services is by co-sponsoring management training programs (courses,conferences, clinics, seminars, and workshops), providing speakers, panelists, and moderators for training programs, and offering one-on-one counseling to small business persons. For additional information on this program, contact your SBA office or the office above.

* Facts About Small Businesses

Office of Business Initiative, Education, and Training (BIET)
U.S. Small Business Administration
409 3rd St., SW, Room 6400
Washington, DC 20416 (202) 205-6665

Contact this office above to obtain any the following fact sheets:

Seasonal Line of Credit Program (#4)
Contract Loan Program (#6)
Handicapped Assistance Loans (#7)
Small Business Institute Program (#11)
SCORE/ACE (#16)
Loans to Small General Contractors (#17)
Management and Technical Assistance 7(j) Program (#20)

Be patient. If any phone number is incorrect, call (area code) 555-1212 and request the new listing.

Federal Starting Places

Surety Bond Guarantee Program (#21)
Secondary Market Program - Fact Sheet for Lenders (#24)
Section 504 - Certified Development Company Program (#25)
Small Business Solar Energy and Conservation Loan Program (#29)
Interest Rate Policy (#30)
Section 8(a) Program (#36)
Facts About Certified and Preferred Lender Programs (#38)
Facts about SBA (#39)
Facts about Small Business (#40)
International Trade Assistance (#42)
Small Business Development Centers (#43)
Facts About Black-Owned Small Businesses (#44)
Facts About Women-Owned Small Businesses (#45)
Facts About Hispanic-Owned Small Businesses (#47)
Facts About Firms Owned by Asians, American Indians, and Other Minorities (#48)
Private Sector Initiatives Program (#49)
Guaranteed Loans to Employee Trusts (#50)
SBA Export-Revolving Line of Credit (#51)
Small Business Innovation Research (SBIR) Program (#52)
Loans for Vietnam-Era and Disabled Veterans (#53)

* Small Business Administration Field Offices

SBA field offices are comprised of regional offices (RO), district offices (DO), branch offices (BO), post-of-duty offices (POD), and disaster area offices (DAO). The regional offices are located in 10 major cities around the country and each directs a number of district offices within the region. Regional offices do not make individual loans or offer specific assistance to individuals or companies. District offices are the real contact point for small businesses needing information or assistance. Each district office is staffed by a team of experts in the lending, procurement, and management assistance areas who have the responsibility to consider loan applications, to offer individual management assistance, and to coordinate other small business services. Branch offices and post-of-duty offices have a smaller staff than district offices and are not quite as full-serviced. Disaster area offices are located in four cities around the country and each provides disaster assistance for their individual regions to small business owners.

Region 1

Augusta
40 Western Ave., Room 512, Augusta, ME 04330; (207) 622-8378; Fax (207) 622-8277

Boston
155 Federal St., 9th Floor, Boston, MA 02110; (617) 451-2023; Fax (617) 565-8695

Boston
10 Causeway St., Room 265, Boston, MA 02222-1093; (617) 565-5590; Fax (617) 565-5598

Concord
143 N. Main St., Room 210, Concord, NH 03302-1257; (603) 225-1400; Fax (603) 225-1409

Hartford
330 Main St., 2nd Floor, Hartford, CT 06106; (203) 240-4700; Fax (203) 240-4659

Montpelier
87 State St., Room 205, Montpelier, VT 05602; (802) 828-4422; Fax (802) 828-4485

Providence
380 Westminster Mall, 5th Floor, Providence, RI 02903; (401) 528-4561; Fax (401) 528-4539

Springfield
1550 Main St., Room 212, Springfield, MA 01103; (413) 785-0268; Fax (413) 785-0267

Region 2

Albany
445 Broadway, Room 222, Albany, NY 12207; (518) 472-6300; Fax (518) 472-7138

Buffalo
111 W. Huron St., Room 1311, Buffalo, NY 14202; (716) 846-4301; Fax (716) 846-4418

Camden
2600 Mt. Ephrain Ave., Camden, NJ 08104; (609) 757-5183; Fax (609) 757-5335

Elmira
333 E. Water St., 4th Floor, Elmira, NY 14901; (607) 734-8130; Fax (607) 733-4656

Hato Rey
Carlos Chardon Ave., Room 691, Hato Rey, PR 00918; (809) 766-5572; Fax (809) 766-5309

Melville
35 Pinelawn Rd., Room 102E, Melville, NY 11747; (516) 454-0750; Fax (516) 454-0769

New York
26 Federal Plaza, Room 31-08, New York, NY 10278; (212) 264-1450; Fax (212) 264-0900

New York
26 Federal Plaza, Room 3100, New York, NY 10278; (212) 264-2454; Fax (212) 264-4963

Newark
60 Park Place, 4th Floor, Newark, NJ 07102; (201) 645-2434; Fax (201) 645-6265

Rochester
100 State St., Room 410, Rochester, NY 14614; (716) 263-6700; Fax (716) 263-3146

St. Croix
4200 United Shopping Plaza, Room 7, St. Croix, VI 00820-4487; (809) 778-5380; Fax (809) 778-1012

St. Thomas
Veterans Drive, Room 210, St. Thomas, VI 00802; (809) 774-8530; Fax (809) 776-2312

Syracuse
100 S. Clinton St., Room 1071, Syracuse, NY 13260; (315) 423-5383; Fax (315) 423-5370

Region 3

Baltimore
10 N. Calvert St., 3rd Floor, Baltimore, MD 21202; (410) 962-4392; Fax (410) 962-1805

Charleston
550 Eagan St., Suite 309, Charleston, WV 25301; (304) 347-5220; Fax (304) 347-5350

Clarksburg
168 W. Main St., 5th Floor, Clarksburg, WV 26301; (304) 623-5631; Fax (304) 623-0023

Harrisburg
100 Chestnut St., Suite 309, Harrisburg, PA 17101; (717) 782-3840; Fax (717) 782-4839

King of Prussia
475 Allendale Rd., Suite 201, King Prussia, PA 19406; (215) 962-3700; Fax (215) 962-3743

King Prussia
475 Allendale Rd., Suite 201, King Prussia, PA 19406; (215) 962-3804; Fax (215) 962-3795

Pittsburgh
960 Penn Ave., 5th Floor, Pittsburgh, PA 15222; (412) 644-2780; Fax (412) 644-5446

Be patient. If any phone number is incorrect, call (area code) 555-1212 and request the new listing.

Small Business and Entrepreneuring

Richmond
400 N. 8th St., Room 3015, Richmond, VA 23240; (804) 771-2400; Fax (804) 771-8018

Washington
1111 18th St., 6th Floor, Washington, DC 20036; (202) 634-1500; Fax (202) 634-1803

Wilkes-Barre
20 N. Pennsylvania Ave., Room 2327, Wilkes-Barre, PA 18702; (717) 826-6497; Fax (717) 826-6287

Wilmington
920 N. King St., Suite 412, Wilmington, DE 19801; (302) 573-6295; Fax (302) 573-6060

Region 4

Atlanta
1375 Peachtree St., NE, 5th Floor, Atlanta, GA 30367-8102; (404) 347-2797; Fax (404) 347-2355

Atlanta
1720 Peachtree Rd., NW, 6th Floor, Atlanta, GA 30309; (404) 347-2749; Fax (404) 347-4745

Birmingham
2121 8th Ave., N., Suite 200, Birmingham, AL 35203-2398; (205) 731-1344; Fax (205) 731-1404

Charlotte
200 N. College, Charlotte, NC 28202; (704) 344-6563; Fax (704) 344-6769

Columbia
1835 Assembly St., Room 358, Columbia, SC 29201; (803) 765-5376; Fax (803) 765-5962

Coral Gables
1320 S. Dixie Hwy, Suite 501, Coral Gables, FL 33146-2911; (305) 536-5521; Fax (305) 536-5058

Gulfport
One Hancock Plaza, Suite 1001, Gulfport, MS 39501-7758; (601) 863-4449; Fax (601) 864-0179

Jackson
101 W. Capitol St., Suite 400, Jackson, MS 39201; (601) 965-4378; Fax (601) 965-4294

Jacksonville
7825 Baymeadows Way, Jacksonville, FL 32256-7504; (904) 443-1900; Fax (904) 443-1980

Louisville
600 Dr. Martin Luther King Place, Room 188, Louisville, KY 40202; (502) 582-5971; Fax (502) 582-5009

Nashville
50 Vantage Way, Suite 201, Nashville, TN 37228-1500; (615) 736-5881; Fax (615) 736-7232

Statesboro
52 N. Main St., Room 225, Statesboro, GA 30458, (912) 489-8719

Tampa
501 E. Polk St., Suite 104, Tampa, FL 33602; (813) 228-2594; Fax (813) 228-2111

W. Palm Beach
5601 Corporate Way S., Suite 402, W. Palm Beach, FL 33407-2044; (305) 689-3922

Region 5

Chicago
300 S. Riverside Plaza, Suite 1975, Chicago, IL 60606-6617; (312) 353-5000; Fax (312) 353-3426

Chicago
500 W. Madison St., Room 1250, Chicago, IL 60661-2511; (312) 353-4528; Fax (312) 886-5108

Cincinnati
525 Vine Street, Suite 870, Cincinnati, OH 45202; (513) 684-2814; Fax (513) 684-3251

Cleveland
1240 E. 9th St., Room 317, Cleveland, OH 44199; (216) 522-4180; Fax (216) 522-2038

Columbus
2 Nationwide Plaza, Columbus, OH 43215-2592; (614) 469-6860; Fax (614) 469-2391

Detroit
477 Michigan Ave., Room 515, Detroit, MI 48226; (313) 226-6075; Fax (313) 226-4769

Indianapolis
429 N. Pennsylvania St., Suite 100, Indianapolis, IN 46204-1873; (317) 226-7272; Fax (317) 226-7259

Madison
212 E. Washington Ave., Room 213, Madison, WI 53703; (608) 264-5261; Fax (608) 264-5541

Marquette
300 S. Front St., Marquette, MI 49885; (906) 225-1108; Fax (906) 225-1109

Minneapolis
100 N. 6th St., Suite 610, Minneapolis, MN 55403-1563; (612) 370-2324; Fax (612) 370-2303

Milwaukee
310 W. Wisconsin Ave., Suite 400, Milwaukee, WI 53203; (414) 297-3941; Fax (414) 297-4267

Springfield
511 W. Capitol St., Suite 302, Springfield, IL 62704; (217) 492-4416; Fax (217) 492-4867

Region 6

Albuquerque
625 Silver Ave., SW, Suite 320, Albuquerque, NM 87102; (505) 766-1870; Fax (505) 766-1057

Austin
300 East 8th Street, Room 520, Austin, TX 78701; (512) 482-5288; Fax (512) 482-5290

Corpus Christi
606 N. Carancahua, Corpus Christi, TX 78476; (512) 888-3331; Fax (512) 888-3418

Dallas
8625 King George Dr., Bldg. C, Dallas, TX 75235-3391; (214) 767-7633; Fax (214) 767-7870

Dallas
1100 Commerce St., Room 3C-36, Dallas, TX 75242; (214) 767-0605; Fax (214) 767-0493

El Paso
10737 Gateway W., Suite 320, El Paso, TX 79935; (915) 540-5676; Fax (915) 540-5636

Ft. Worth
819 Taylor St., Room 8A-27, Ft. Worth, TX 76102; (817) 334-3777; Fax (214) 767-0493

Harlingen
222 E. Van Buren St., Room 500, Harlingen, TX 78550; (512) 427-8533; Fax (512) 427-8537

Be patient. If any phone number is incorrect, call (area code) 555-1212 and request the new listing.

Federal Starting Places

Houston
9301 Southwest Freeway, Suite 550, Houston, TX 77074-1591; (713) 953-5900; Fax (713) 953-6279

Little Rock
2120 Riverfront Dr., Suite 100, Little Rock, AR 72202; (501) 324-5278

Lubbock
1611 Tenth St., Suite 200, Lubbock, TX 79401; (806) 743-7462; Fax (806) 743-7487

Marshall
505 East Travis, Room 103, Marshall, TX 75670; (214) 935-5257; Fax (903) 935-5258

New Orleans
1661 Canal St., Suite 2000, New Orleans, LA 70112; (504) 589-6685; Fax (504) 589-2339

Oklahoma City
200 NW 5th St., Suite 670, Oklahoma City, OK 73102; (405) 231-4301; Fax (405) 231-4876

San Antonio
7400 Blanco Rd., Suite 200, San Antonio, TX 78216; (512) 229-4535; Fax (512) 229-4556

Shreveport
500 Fannin St., Room 8A-08, Shreveport, LA 71101; (318) 226-5196; Fax (318) 226-5214

Region 7

Cedar Rapids
373 Collins Rd. NE, Room 100, Cedar Rapids, IA 52402-3147; (319) 393-8630; Fax (319) 393-7585

Des Moines
210 Walnut St., Room 749, Des Moines, IA 50309; (515) 284-4422; Fax (515) 284-4572

Kansas City
323 W. 8th St., Suite 501, Kansas City, MO 64105; (816) 374-6708; Fax (816) 374-6759

Kansas City
911 Walnut St., 13th Floor, Kansas City, MO 64106; (816) 426-3608; Fax (816) 426-5559

Omaha
11145 Mill Valley Rd., Omaha, NE 68154; (402) 221-4691; Fax (402) 221-3680

Springfield
620 S. Glenstone St., Suite 110, Springfield, MO 65802-3200; (417) 864-7670; Fax (417) 864-4108

St. Louis
815 Olive St., Room 242, St. Louis, MO 63101; (314) 539-6600; Fax (314) 539-3785

Wichita
100 E. English St., Suite 510, Wichita, KS 67202; (316) 269-6273; Fax (316) 269-6499

Region 8

Casper
100 East B St., Room 4001, Casper, WY 82602-2839; (307) 261-5761; Fax (307) 261-5499

Denver
999 18th St., Suite 701, Denver, CO 80202; (303) 294-7186; Fax (303) 294-7153

Denver
721 19th St., Room 407, Denver, CO 80201-0660; (303) 844-2607; Fax (303) 844-3984

Fargo
657 Second Ave. N, Room 218, Fargo, ND 58108-3086; (701) 239-5131; Fax (701) 239-5645

Helena
301 S. Park, Room 528, Helena, MT 59626; (406) 409-5381; Fax (406) 449-5474

Salt Lake City
125 S. State St., Room 2237, Salt Lake City, UT 84138-1195; (801) 524-5800; Fax (801) 524-4160

Sioux Falls
101 S. Main Ave, Suite 101, Sioux Falls, SD 57102-0527; (605) 330-4231; Fax (605) 330-4215

Region 9

Agana
238 Archbishop F.C. Flores St., Room 508, Agana, GM 96910; (671) 472-7277; Fax (200) 550-7365

Fresno
2719 North Air Fresno Dr., Fresno, CA 93721; (209) 487-5189; Fax (209) 487-5636

Honolulu
300 Ala Moana, Room 2213, Honolulu, HI 96850-4981; (808) 541-2990; Fax (808) 541-2976

Las Vegas
301 E. Steward St., Room 301, Las Vegas, NV 89125-2527; (702) 388-6611; Fax (702) 388-6469

Glendale
330 N. Brand, Glendale, CA 91213; (213) 894-2956; Fax (213) 894-5665

Phoenix
2828 N. Central Ave., Suite 800, Phoenix, AZ 85004-1025; (602) 640-2316; Fax (602) 640-2360

Reno
.50 S. Virginia St., Room 238, Reno, NV 895053216; (702) 784-5268

Sacramento
660 J St., Room 215, Sacramento, CA 95814-2413; (916) 551-1426; Fax (916) 551-1439

San Diego
880 Front St., Room 4-S-29, San Diego, CA 92188-0270; (619) 557-7252; Fax (619) 557-5894

San Francisco
211 Main St., 4th Floor, San Francisco, CA 94105-1988; (415) 744-6820; Fax (415) 744-6812

San Francisco
71 Stevenson St., 20th Floor, San Francisco, CA 94105-2939; (415) 744-6435; Fax (415) 744-6435

Santa Ana
901 W. Civic Ctr Dr., Room 160, Santa Ana, CA 92703-2352; (714) 836-2494; Fax (714) 836-2528

Tucson
300 W. Congress St., Room 7-H, Tucson, AZ 85701-1319; (602) 629-6715; Fax (602) 670-5047

Ventura
6477 Telephone Rd., Suite 10, Ventura, CA 93003-4459, (805) 642-1866, Fax (805) 642-9539

Region 10

Anchorage
222 W. 8th Ave., Room 67, Anchorage, AK 99513-7559; (901) 271-4022, Fax (907) 271-4545

Small Business and Entrepreneuring

Boise
1020 Main St., Suite 290, Boise, ID 83702-5745; (208) 334-1696, Fax (208) 334-9353

Portland
222 SW Columbia, Suite 500, Portland, OR 97201-6605; (503) 326-2682, Fax (503) 326-2808

Seattle
2615 4th Ave., Room 440, Seattle, WA 98121; (206) 553-5676, Fax (206) 553-4155

Seattle
915 Second Ave., Room 1792, Seattle, WA 98174-1088; (206) 553-1420, Fax (509) 353-2829

Spokane
W. 601 First Ave., 10th Floor E., Spokane, WA 99204-0317; (509) 353-2800, Fax (509) 353-2829

Disaster Area Offices

Atlanta
One Baltimore Place, Suite 300, Atlanta, GA 30308; (404) 347-3771, Fax (404) 347-3813

Niagara Falls
360 Rainbow Blvd S., 3rd Floor, Niagara Falls, NY 14303; (716) 282-4612; Fax (716) 282-1472

Ft. Worth
4400 Amon Carte Blvd., Suite 102, Ft. Worth, TX 76155; (817) 885-7600, Fax (817) 885-7616

Sacramento
1825 Bell St., Suite 208, Sacramento, CA 95825; (916) 978-4571, Fax (916) 978-4577

* Films on Small Business

National Audiovisual Center
National Archives and Records Administration
Customer Services, Section PY
8700 Edgeworth Drive
Capitol Heights, MD 20743-3701 (301) 763-1896

A number of films on small business topics are available for sale and sometimes for rental purposes. *The Media Resource Catalog* contains a list of the titles. To obtain the free catalog, contact this office.

* Financial Management and Your Business

Superintendent of Documents
U.S. Government Printing Office
Washington, DC 20402 (202) 783-3238

Financial Management: How to Make a Go of Your Business ($2.50) contains information required to familiarize the small business owner/manager with the basic concepts of financial management. Tips on financial planning, cash-flow management, forecasting and obtaining capital, and other topics are covered.

* Food and Drug Small Business Assistance

Small Business Coordinator
Food and Drug Administration (FDA)
5600 Fishers Lane
Room 1372, HFZ-220
Rockville, MD 20857 (301) 443-6597

The FDA has established the Division of Small Manufactures Assistance to help small companies learn about and comply with FDA regulations. This office can explain FDA procedures and provide assistance in dealing with the FDA. For a free copy of *A Small Business Guide to FDA* or more information contact this office.

* Franchise and Business Opportunities Rules

Federal Trade Commission (FTC)
Marketing Practices

6th and Pennsylvania Ave., NW
Washington, DC 20580 (202) 326-3128

Under the FTC's Franchise and Business Opportunities Rule, sellers of franchises and business opportunities are required to give prospective buyers a disclosure document containing specific information about the franchise and any earning claims. For more information on this regulation, contact this office or your regional FTC.

* Incubators

Business Initiative, Education and Training
U.S. Small Business Administration (SBA)
409 3rd Street, SW
6th Floor
Washington, DC 20416 (202) 205-6665

A small business incubator is a flexible method of encouraging the development of new businesses and fostering local economic development. Incubators are facilities in which a number of new and growing businesses operate under one roof with affordable rents, sharing services and equipment, and having equal access to a wide range of professional, technical, and financial programs. For more information, contact your nearest Small Business Administration office or the office listed above.

* Indian Business Development

Bureau of Indian Affairs
U.S. Department of the Interior
18th and C Sts., NW
Washington, DC 20240 (202) 208-3710

Indian tribes and small businesses may receive technical assistance and financial backing through this office. The Bureau spends more than $10 million annually to develop Indian business enterprises.

* International Visitors Program

International Visitors Liaison
U.S. Small Business Administration (SBA)
409 3rd St., SW
Washington, DC 20416 (202) 205-6720

The growing influx of foreign visitors to SBA reflects the growing world-wide interest in small business and the appreciation of small business contributions to national economies. SBA personnel are pleased to meet with government officials, embassy personnel, private sector individuals, educators, students, and other interested parties. Program policies, administration, and operational aspects can be shared through consultation, observation, and briefing sessions. If you are interested in attending a half-day, full-day, or two-day session, contact this office.

* Lenders Programs

Office of Financial Institutions
U.S. Small Business Administration
409 3rd St., SW
Washington, DC 20416 (202) 205-6510

Under the Certified Lenders Program, the lenders, acting under SBA supervision, handle much of the necessary paperwork and review client financial status - thereby speeding up loan processing and freeing SBA personnel for other assistance to small businesses. Under SBA's Preferred Lenders Program, the lenders handle all loan paperwork, processing, and servicing. For more detailed information, contact the SBA office in your area or the office above.

* Lending and Bonding for Minority Business

Minority Business Resource Center (MBRC)
Small and Disadvantaged Business Utilization (SDBU)
Director of Civil Rights
Office of the Secretary of Transportation
U.S. Department of Transportation
400 7th Street, SW, Room 9410
Washington, DC 20590 (202) 366-2852

This office offers short-term lending and bonding assistance to small businesses in the transportation industry. The Short-term Lending Program offers loans at prime interest rates, while the Bonding Assistance Program enables small firms to obtain bonding in support of transportation-related contracts. Entrepreneurs can contact MBRC for information and certification details.

Be patient. If any phone number is incorrect, call (area code) 555-1212 and request the new listing.

Federal Starting Places

* Management and Technical Assistance

Office of Minority Small Business
and Capital Ownership
U.S. Small Business Administration
409 3rd St., SW
Washington, DC 20416 (202) 205-6555

The SBA initiates, organizes, and maintains a management counseling service for small firms in the 8(a) program. Under this authority, SBA places grants, agreements, and contracts with qualified individuals, profit-making firms, state and local governments, educational institutions, and some non-profit organizations to furnish management and technical aid to SBA clients and other eligible small firms. Some of the services performed are accounting, marketing, engineering, and bookkeeping. Eligible recipients of development assistance are generally firms in SBA's 8(a) contracting program, socially or economically disadvantaged individuals, or small firms located in areas of high concentration of unemployed and low-income individuals. If you are interested in providing technical or management assistance to eligible small firms, contact the office above. If you are interested in receiving technical or management assistance, contact the SBA field office in your area.

* Medical Devices: Technical Assistance for Small Businesses

Division of Small Manufacturer's Assistance
Center for Devices and Radiological Health
Food and Drug Administration (FDA)
5600 Fishers Lane, HFZ-220
Rockville, MD 20857 (301) 443-6597

The FDA provides information to small businesses regarding device regulations and what is needed to get approval. The FDA often holds meetings and workshops to offer further assistance. The handbook, *A Small Business Guide to FDA*, explains how the FDA works and the approval process. This Center provides copies of device regulations and FDA documents, as well as guidelines and aids that simplify manufacturer requirements. The *SMA MEMO* contains articles and tips on medical device regulations and reports on Center activities.

* Minority Business Development Centers

Public Affairs
Minority Business Development Agency (MBDA)
U.S. Department of Commerce
14th St. and Constitution Ave. NW, Room 6707
Washington, DC 20230 (202) 482-1936

MBDA funds a nationwide network of 100 Minority Business Development Centers--in large minority population areas--to help minority-owned firms needing assistance in counseling, accounting, administration, business planning, inventory control, negotiations, referrals, networking, construction, and marketing. The MBDC offers entrepreneurs managerial and technical assistance for bonding, bidding, estimating, financing, procurement, international trade, franchising, acquisitions, mergers, joint ventures, and leverage buyouts. The MBDC provides vital business information from corporations, trade associations, export management companies, and federal, state, and local government agencies. The MBDC also identifies minority-owned firms for contract opportunities with state and local government agencies, and private institutions. Business referral services are provided free. The MBDCs, however, generally charge nominal fees for specific management and technical assistance services.

* Minority Business Development- State and Local Offices

Minority Business Development Agency
U.S. Department of Commerce
14th St. and Constitution Ave., NW
Washington, DC 20230 (202) 482-1936

The following is list of state and local offices which are concerned with minority business development. You may contact these offices for more information about the services and assistance they can provide.

* Minority Business Program Development

Office of Program Development
Minority Business Development Agency
U.S. Department of Commerce
14th St. and Constitution Ave., NW, Room 5096
Washington, DC 20230 (202) 482-1936

The office is responsible for designing and developing all MBDA programs, and identifying private and public sector resources in connection with the delivery of direct and indirect assistance to develop the minority business community. The Private Sector Division develops programs to encourage the creation and growth of business opportunities within the private sector by providing funding to business and trade associations, foundations, corporations, financial and education institutions, and other private sector organizations. The Public Sector Division is responsible for program development, oversight, and implementation of Federal, state, and local programs that impact on minority business enterprise.

* Minority Business Purchasing

National Minority Supplier Development Council
1412 Broadway, 11th Floor
New York, NY 10018 (212) 944-2430

The National Minority Supplier Development Council works with 47 Councils throughout the U.S. to promote the use of minority-owned firms. They assist firms in developing and marketing their capabilities, and acts as a liaison between minority companies and companies who wish to purchase their products or services. Contact the Council for more information.

* Minority Business Regional Assistance

Public Affairs
Minority Business Development Agency
U.S. Department of Commerce
14th St. and Constitution Ave. NW
Room 6707
Washington, DC 20230 (202) 482-1936

The Minority Business Development Agency conducts most of its activities through its six Regional Offices and four District Offices:

Regional Offices:

Atlanta
410 W. Peachtree St., NW, Suite 1930, Atlanta, GA 30308-3516; (404) 730-3300

Chicago
55 East Monroe St., Suite 1440, Chicago, IL 60603; (312) 353-0182

Dallas
1100 Commerce St., Room 7B23, Dallas, TX 75242; (214) 767-8001

New York
26 Federal Plaza, Room 37-20, New York, NY 10278; (212) 264-3262

San Francisco
221 Main St., Room 1280, San Francisco, CA 94105; (415) 744-3001

Washington
1255 22nd St., NW, Suite 701, Washington, DC 20036; (202) 467-0012

District Offices:

Boston
Room 418, 10 Causeway St., Boston, MA 02222; (617) 565-6850

Los Angeles
Suite 201, 977 N. Broadway, Los Angeles, CA 90012; (213) 894-7157

Miami
Room 1314, Box 25, 51 SW., 1st Ave., Miami, FL 33130; (305) 536-5054

Philadelphia
Room 10128, 600 Arch St., Philadelphia, PA 19106; (215) 597-9236

* Minority Business Week

Minority Enterprise Development Week
Minority Business Development Agency
U.S. Department of Commerce
14th St. and Constitution Ave., NW
Room 5073
Washington, DC 20230 (202) 482-1936

Minority Enterprise Development Week--MED Week--is an annual celebration to honor the contributions of minority entrepreneurs and those individuals and organizations who actively support minority business development. It is

Be patient. If any phone number is incorrect, call (area code) 555-1212 and request the new listing.

Small Business and Entrepreneuring

celebrated the first full week in October, and includes workshops, seminars, an Awards Gala, as well as a Marketplace where public and private sector buyers meet with minority vendors.

* Minority Research

Research Division
Minority Business Development Agency
U.S. Department of Commerce
14th St. and Constitution Ave., NW, Room 5701
Washington, DC 20230 (202) 482-1936

This Division conducts research on minority businesses and issues related to them. A complete listing of research studies is available for free by contacting this office.

* Minority Small Business

Contact your local SBA office or the Small Business Answer Desk listed in this section.

Members of minority groups who own or are interested in owning small businesses are eligible for all SBA programs. In addition, SBA offers special programs to assist members of minority groups who want to start small businesses or expand existing ones. Contact your SBA office for information.

* Money, Management, and Marketing

Business, Initiative, Education and Training (BIET)
U.S. Small Business Administration (SBA)
409 3rd St., SW, Room 6400
Washington, DC 20416 (202) 205-6665

Focus on the Facts is a series of information sheets issued by SBA which includes those listed below. To obtain copies, contact the office above.

How to Raise Money for a Small Business (#1)
How to Start a Small Business (#2)
Planning...The Most Important Ingredient (#3)
Knowing Your Market (#4)
Information...The Key to Success (#5)
How to Price Your Products and Services (#6)
Opportunities in Exporting (#7)
How to Start a Home-Based Business (#8)

* Patent Licensing Opportunities

U.S. Government Printing Office
Superintendent of Documents
Washington, DC 20402 (202) 783-3238

Government patents resulting from research discoveries are available for licensing to U.S. companies and citizens. Licenses are offered on a non-exclusive, exclusive, and co-exclusive basis. Non-exclusive licenses are generally granted when no large investment to market a product is expected. Exclusive and co-exclusive licenses are granted when substantial investment is required. Fees for licenses are negotiable. Lists of such patents are made available each week by the Government Printing Office in the form of the *Patent Official Gazette*. Subscriptions or single copies are available from the above address or phone number.

* Publications on Small Business

U.S. Small Business Administration (SBA)
P.O. Box 15434
Fort Worth, TX 67119

SBA has a collection of over 100 business booklets which are sold for a nominal fee (most are under $2). These publications address the most important business topics and answer the questions most asked by prospective and existing business owners. The topics include financial management and analysis, general management and planning, crime prevention, marketing, personnel management, and new products, ideas, and inventions. Some of the booklets are listed below. A free *Directory of Business Development Publications* and order forms can be received by contacting your local SBA office or by calling the Small Business Answer Desk at 1-800-368-5855. To order any of the publications below send your request to the Fort Worth, Texas address in this listing.

Financial Management and Analysis
ABC's of Borrowing: $1
Profit Costing and Pricing For Manufacturing: $1

Basic Budgets for Profit Planning: $0.50
Understanding Cash Flow: $1
A Venture Capital Primer for Small Business: $0.50
Accounting Services for Small Service Firms: $0.50
Analyze Your Records to Reduce Costs: $0.50
Budgeting in a Small Business Firm: $0.50
Sound Cash Management and Borrowing: $0.50
Recordkeeping in a Small Business: $1
Break Even Analysis: A Decision Making Tool: $1
A Pricing Checklist for Small Retailers: $0.50
Pricing Your Products and Services Profitably: $1

General Management and Planning
Effective Business Communications: $0.50
Locating or Relocating Your Business: $1
Problems in Managing a Family-Owned Business: $0.50
Business Plan for Small Manufacturers: $1
Business Plan for Small Construction Firms: $1
Planning and Goal Setting for Small Business: $0.50
Fixing Production Mistakes: $0.50
Should You Lease or Buy Equipment: $0.50
Business Plan for Retailers: $1
Choosing a Retail Location: $1
Business Plan for Small Service Firms: $0.50
Going into Business: $0.50
How to Get Started With a Small Business Computer: $1
The Business Plan For Home - based Business: $1
How to Buy or Sell a Business: $1
Purchasing for Owners of Small Plants: $0.50
Buying for Retail Stores: $1
Small Business Decision Making: $1
Business Continuation Planning: $1
Developing a Strategic Business Plan: $1
Inventory Management: $0.50
Techniques for Problem Solving: $1
Techniques for Productivity Improvement: $1
Selecting the Legal Structure for your Business: $0.50
Evaluating Franchise Opportunities: $0.50
Starting a Retail Travel Agency: $1
Small Business Risk Management Guide: $1

Crime Prevention
Reducing Shoplifting Losses: $0.50
Curtailing Crime--Inside and Out: $1
A Small Business Guide to Computer Security: $1

Marketing
Creative Selling: The Competitive Edge: $0.50
Marketing for Small Business: An Overview: $1
Is the Independent Sales Agent For You: $0.50
Marketing Checklist for Small Retailers: $1
Research Your Market: $1
Selling by Mail Order: $1
Market Overseas With U.S. Government Help: $1
Advertising: $1

Personnel Management
Checklist for Developing a Training Program: $0.50
Employees: How to Find and Pay Them: $1
Managing Employee Benefits: $1

New Products/Ideas/Inventions
Can You Make Money With Your Idea or Invention: $0.50
Introduction to Patents: $0.50

* Research and Development

Office of Small Business Innovation Research (SBIR)
National Science Foundation (NSF)
Room V 502
1800 G St., NW
Washington, DC 20550 (202) 653-5002

This office offers information and guidance on NSF programs and research opportunities for small firms involved in research and technology.

Be patient. If any phone number is incorrect, call (area code) 555-1212 and request the new listing.

Federal Starting Places

* Research and Development Funding for Small Business

National Technical Information Service
U.S. Department of Commerce
5285 Port Royal Rd.
Springfield, VA 22161 (703) 487-4650

The *Small Business Guide to Federal Research and Development Funding Opportunities* provides you with direct contacts to U.S. Government offices that contract out research and development work. It is written for smaller businesses with strong scientific and technical competence that want to do research and development work with the government. Highlighted is the Small Business Innovation Research (SBIR) Program. This program requires agencies to set aside a portion of the R&D awards for small businesses. This guide gives you steps to obtaining Federal R&D funding, an overview of Federal laboratory research efforts, criteria companies must meet, and certain laws and regulations that affect small business participation. Contact the Sales Desk to place your order or request the free information brochure, *PR-801*.

* Research Studies in Small Business

Office of Economic Research
Office of Advocacy
U.S. Small Business Administration
409 3rd St., SW, 7th Floor
Washington, DC (202) 205-6533

The Office of Advocacy conducts and coordinates applied research in a variety of areas important to small business to promote policies that strengthen the performance of American small business. *The Catalog of Completed Research Studies* is a listing of SBA contracted research studies completed between 1978 and 1986, with over 200 studies covering a broad scope of small business topics and issues, including studies on finance and credit, capital formation, taxes and regulation, government competition and procurement, job creation, innovation, and women and minority business ownership. Contact the office above to obtain this catalog.

* Seasonal Line of Credit

Contact your local SBA office or the Small Business Answer Desk listed in this section.

The Seasonal Line of Credit program is a short-term loan available under SBA's guaranty program to finance an increase in the trading assets (receivables and inventory) of eligible small businesses arising from a seasonal upswing in business. For additional information on this program, contact the nearest SBA office in your area.

* SEC Policy

The Office of Small Business Policy
Division of Corporation Finance
U.S. Securities and Exchange Commission (SEC)
450 5th St., NW
Washington, DC 20549 (202) 272-2644

This office directs the SEC's small business rulemaking goals, reviews and comments on the impact the SEC rule proposals have on small issuers, and serves as a liaison with Congressional committees, government agencies, and other groups concerned with small business. Information on security laws that pertain to small business offerings may be obtained from this office.

* Section 8(a) Program

Contact your local SBA office or the Small Business Answers Desk listed in this section.

Through the 8(a) Program, small companies owned by socially and economically disadvantaged persons can obtain federal government contracts and other assistance in developing their business. Under the 8(a) Program, SBA acts as the prime contractor and enters into all types of federal government contracts (including, but not limited to, supply, services, construction, research and development) with other government departments and agencies, and negotiates subcontracts for small companies in the 8(a) Program. Contact your SBA office for more information.

* Service Corps of Retired Executives Association (SCORE)

Service Corps of Retired Executives Association

1825 Connecticut Ave., NW, Suite 503
Washington, DC 20009 (202) 653-6279

SCORE is an independent, voluntary, non-profit association funded almost exclusively by the SBA. It is made up to over 13,000 men and women from all walks of business management, most of whom are retired, who volunteer their services to small businesses seeking managerial assistance. SCORE volunteers work in each district office and their services are free. They provide small-business community assistance in the form of one-on-one and team counseling and nominal-fee workshops. The Active Corps of Executives (ACE) is closely coordinated with SCORE. ACE volunteers are not yet retired and volunteer their services in counseling and training to supplement those offered by the retired SCORE counselors. For more information on the SCORE and ACE, contact the office above, or the SBA office in your area.

* Small Business and the SEC

Publications Section
Printing Branch, Stop C-11
U.S. Securities and Exchange Commission (SEC)
Washington, DC 20549 (202) 272-7040

The free booklet, *Q&A: Small Business and the SEC*, discusses capital formation and the federal securities laws and is designed to help you understand some of the basis, necessary requirements that apply when you wish to raise capital by selling securities. It answers such questions as:

What are the federal securities laws?
Is any special help available for a small business that wants to sell its securities?
Should my company "go public"?
How does my small business "go public"?
If my company becomes "public," what are its disclosure obligations?
Are there legal ways to sell securities without registering with the SEC?
Are there state law requirements in addition to those under the federal securities laws? and
Where can I go for more information?

* Small Business Development Centers (SBDCs)

Contact your local SBA office or the Small Business Answer Desk listed in this section.

Small Business Development Centers are located in 46 states, the District of Columbia, Puerto Rico, and the Virgin Islands. These centers provide quality assistance, counseling, and training to prospective and existing business owners. They also provide managerial and technical help, research studies, and other types of specialized assistance.

* Small Business Innovation Research (SBIR) Program

Office of Innovation, Research and Technology
U.S. Small Business Administration
1800 G. St., NW, Room V 502
Washington, DC 20416 (202) 653-5002

The Small Business Innovation Research (SBIR) Program came into existence with the enactment of the Small Business Innovation Development Act of 1982. Under SBIR, agencies of the federal government with the largest research and development budgets are mandated to set aside a legislated percentage each year for the competitive award of SBIR funding agreements to qualified high technology small business concerns. SBA was designated as the federal agency having unilateral authority and responsibility for coordinating and monitoring the government-wide activities of the SBIR program and reporting on its results annually to Congress. In line with this responsibility, SBA publishes the *SBIR Pre-Solicitation Announcement* quarterly. The *PA* contains pertinent information on the program and specific data on upcoming SBIR solicitations. To obtain the *SBIR Pre-Solicitation Announcement*, call (202) 653-6458, and for further information, contact the office above.

* Small Business Institutes (SBIs)

Contact your local SBA Office or the Small Business Answer Desk listed in this section.

SBIs are organized through the SBA on almost 500 college campuses and universities around the nation. The institutes are staffed by senior business administration students and their faculty advisors and offer free guidance and assistance to troubled small firms. Contact your local SBA district office to obtain the name and telephone number of the SBI nearest you.

Be patient. If any phone number is incorrect, call (area code) 555-1212 and request the new listing.

Small Business and Entrepreneuring

* Small Business Investment Companies (SBICs)

Finance and Investment Division
U.S. Small Business Administration
409 3rd St., SW, Room 8033
Washington, DC 20416 (202) 205-6570

SBA licenses, regulates, and provides financial assistance to privately owned and operated Small Business Investment Companies. Their major function is to make "venture" or "risk" investments by supplying equity capital and extending unsecured loans and loans not fully collateralized to small enterprises which meet their investment criteria. SBA also licenses a specialized type of SBIC solely to help small businesses owned and managed by socially or economically disadvantaged persons. This type of SBIC is a Section 301(d) SBIC, formerly referred to as a MESBIC (Minority Enterprise SBIC). For more information or to obtain the free brochure, *Small Business Investment Companies: The SBIC Program*, contact the office above.

* Solar Energy and Conservation Loans

Contact your local SBA office or the Small Business Answer Desk listed in this section.

Financial assistance is provided to small business concerns engaged in the engineering, manufacturing, distributing, marketing, installing, or servicing of energy measures designed to conserve the Nation's energy resources. Detailed information can be obtained from the SBA office in your area.

* Starting and Managing a Business From Your Home

Superintendent of Documents
U.S. Government Printing Office (GPO)
Washington, DC 20402 (202) 783-3238

The publication, *Starting and Managing a Business From Your Home*, provides descriptions of products and services to help you start your home-based business. It includes a questionnaire to help you decide if you are the typical entrepreneur, and also gives helpful information on managing your business, including tips on structure, recordkeeping, taxes, and insurance. It is available for $2 from GPO.

* Surety Bonds

Contact your local SBA office or the Small Business Answer Desk listed in this section.

Through its Surety Bond Guarantee Program, the SBA helps to make the bonding process accessible to small and emerging contractors, including minorities who find bonding unavailable to them. The SBA is authorized to guarantee to a qualified surety up to 90 percent of losses incurred under bid, payment, or performance bonds issued to contractors on contracts valued up to $1.25 million. These contracts may be for construction, supplies, manufacturing, or services provided by either a prime or subcontractor for government or non-government work. This program is administered through SBA's 10 regional offices and participating surety companies and agents throughout the nation.

* Trade Remedy Assistance for Small Businesses

The Trade Remedy Assistance Office
U.S. International Trade Commission (ITC)
500 E St., SW
Washington, DC 20436 (202) 205-2200

Small businesses are often adversely affected by U.S. trade laws, which may allow foreign products to flood the U.S. market and unfairly compete with U.S. businesses which sell similar products. The ITC, however, provides technical assistance under U.S. trade remedy laws to eligible small businesses which have experienced such effects. To qualify, businesses must have neither adequate resources nor the financial ability to obtain qualified outside assistance. ITC staff is available to meet with eligible small businesses to discuss the petition process

and to help organize and assemble relevant background material. The office has assisted eligible small businesses at the preinstitution stage in analyzing their trade-related problems and deciding which statutes may offer relief. Technical assistance may include the review of initial drafts submitted by the eligible small business and advice on additions, deletions, and possible alternative presentations, leading to the final preparation of the petition for filing with the ITC. Such assistance also includes discussion of relevant ITC precedents and publications.

* Transportation Small Business Assistance

Public Assistance Office
Interstate Commerce Commission
12th St. and Constitution Ave., NW
Washington, DC 20423 (202) 927-7597

The Commission maintains a Public Assistance Office to help the small business owner or transportation firm in such matters as how to file protests on rates, how to file new operating authority or extensions, or how to get adequate service where there is none.

* Veterans Assistance

Contact your local SBA office or the Small Business Answer Desk listed in this section.

The SBA makes special efforts to help veterans get into business or expand existing veteran-owned small firms. Acting on its own or with the help of veterans organizations, the SBA sponsors special business training workshops for veterans. The SBA also sponsors special computer-based training and long-term entrepreneurial programs for veterans. Each SBA office has a veterans affairs specialist to help give veterans special consideration with loans, training, and/or procurement. The *Veterans Handbook*, which outlines the Agency's special consideration programs for veterans, is also available from SBA district and regional offices.

* Vietnam-Era and Disabled Veterans Loans

Contact your local SBA office or the Small Business Answer Desk listed in this section.

Under a special appropriation, funds are available for direct loans to disabled and Vietnam-era veterans. These loans can be made only when financing is not available from other sources on reasonable terms. These loans may be made to establish a small firm or assist in the operation or expansion of an existing business. The administrative ceiling on these loans is $150,000. While all qualified veterans receive special consideration in connection with applications for SBA assistance, most loans are made by financial institutions and many are guaranteed by SBA. Whenever a guaranteed loan or other reasonable credit is available, the SBA cannot make a direct loan.

* Women's Business Ownership

Office of Women's Business Ownership
U.S. Small Business Administration
409 3rd St., SW
Washington, DC 20416 (202) 205-6673

This office was formed to implement a national policy to support women entrepreneurs. Its primary functions include developing and coordinating a national program to increase the number and success of women-owned businesses while making maximum use of existing government and private sector resources; researching and evaluating the special programmatic needs of current or potential women business owners, and develop and test ways of meeting them; working with federal, state, and local governments to ensure that they consider women's business ownership in their program areas.

Be patient. If any phone number is incorrect, call (area code) 555-1212 and request the new listing.

State Starting Places for Money

Who Can Use State Money?

All states require that funds be used solely by state residents. But that shouldn't limit you to exploring possibilities only in the state in which you currently reside. If you reside in Maine, but Massachusetts agrees to give you $100,000 to start your own business, it would be worth your while to consider moving to Massachusetts. Shop around for the best deal.

Types of Money And Help Available

Each state has different kinds and amounts of money and assistance programs available, but these sources of financial and counseling help are constantly being changed. What may not be available this year may very well be available next. Therefore, in the course of your exploration, you might want to check in with the people who operate the business "hotlines" to discover if anything new has been added to the states' offerings.

Described below are the major kinds of programs which are offered by most of the states.

Information

Hotlines or One-Stop Shops
Hotlines or One-Stop Shops are available in many states through a toll-free number that hooks you up with someone who will either tell you what you need to know or refer you to someone who can. These hotlines are invaluable -- offering information on everything from business permit regulations to obscure financing programs. Most states also offer some kind of booklet that tells you how to start-up a business in that state. Ask for it. It will probably be free.

Small Business Advocates
Small Business Advocates operate in all 50 states and are part of a national organization (National Association of State Small Business Advocates) devoted to helping small business people function efficiently with their state governments. They are a good source for help in cutting through bureaucratic red tape.

Funding Programs

Free Money
Free Money can come in the form of grants, and it works the same as free money from the federal government. You do not have to pay it back.

Loans
Loans from state governments work in the same way as those from the federal government -- they are given directly to entrepreneurs. Loans are usually at interest rates below the rates charged at commercial institutions and are also set aside for those companies which have trouble getting a loan elsewhere. This makes them an ideal source for riskier ventures.

Loan Guarantees
Loan Guarantees are similar to those offered by the federal government. For this program the state government will go to the bank with you and co-sign your loan. This, too, is ideal for high risk ventures which normally would not get a loan.

Interest Subsidies On Loans
Interest Subsidies On Loans is a unique concept not used by the federal government. In this case the state will subsidize the interest rate you are charged by a bank. For example, if the bank gives you a loan for $50,000 at 10% per year interest, your interest payments would be $5,000 per year. With an interest subsidy you might have to pay only $2,500 since the state would pay the other half. This is like getting the loan at 5 percent instead of 10 percent.

Industrial Revenue Bonds or General Obligation Bonds
Industrial Revenue Bonds or General Obligation Bonds are a type of financing that can be used to purchase only fixed assets, like a factory or equipment. In the case of Industrial Revenue Bonds the state will raise money from the general public to buy your equipment. Because the state acts as the middleman, the people who lend you the money do not have to pay federal taxes on the interest they charge you. As a result, you get the money cheaper because they get a tax break. If the state issues General Obligation Bonds to buy your equipment, the arrangement will be similar to that for an Industrial Revenue Bond except that the state promises to repay the loan if you cannot.

Matching Grants
Matching Grants supplement and abet federal grant programs. These kinds of grants could make an under-capitalized project go forward. Awards usually hinge on the usefulness of the project to its surrounding locality.

Loans To Agricultural Businesses
Loans to Agricultural Businesses are offered in states with large rural, farming populations. They are available solely to farmers and/or agribusiness entrepreneurs.

Loans To Exporters
Loans to Exporters are available in some states as a kind of gap financing to cover the expenses involved in fulfilling a contract.

Energy Conservation Loans
Energy Conservation Loans are made to small businesses to finance the installation of energy-saving equipment or devices.

Special Regional Loans
Special Regional Loans are ear-marked for specific areas in a state that may have been hard hit economically or suffer from

Be patient. If any phone number is incorrect, call (area code) 555-1212 and request the new listing.

Small Business and Entrepreneuring

under-development. If you live in one of these regions, you may be eligible for special funds.

High Tech Loans
High Tech Loans help fledgling companies develop or introduce new products into the marketplace.

Loans To Inventors
Loans to Inventors help the entrepreneur develop or market new products.

Local Government Loans
Local Government Loans are used for start-up and expansions of businesses within the designated locality.

Childcare Facilities Loans
Childcare Facilities Loans help businesses establish on-site day care facilities.

Loans To Women And/Or Minorities
Loans to Women and/or Minorities are available in almost every state from funds specifically reserved for economically disadvantaged groups.

Many federally funded programs are administered by state governments. Among them are the following programs:

SBA 7(A) Guaranteed and Direct Loan Program
The SBA 7(A) Guaranteed and Direct Loan Program can guarantee up to 90% of a loan made through a private lender (up to $500,000), or make direct loans of up to $150,000.

SBA 504
The SBA 504 establishes Certified Development Companies whose debentures are guaranteed by the SBA. Equity participation of the borrower must be at least 10%, private financing 60% and CDC participation at a maximum of 40%, up to $500,000.

SBIR Grants
SBIR Grants award between $20,000 to $50,000 to entrepreneurs to support six months of research on a technical innovation. They are then eligible for up to $500,000 to develop the innovation.

Small Business Investment Companies
Small Business Investment Companies (SBIC) license, regulate and provide financial assistance in the form of equity financing, long-term loans, and management services.

Community Development Block Grants
Community Development Block Grants are available to cities and counties for the commercial rehabilitation of existing buildings or structures used for business, commercial, or industrial purposes. Grants of up to $500,000 can be made. Every $15,000 of grant funds invested must create at least one full-time job, and at least 51% of the jobs created must be for low-and moderate-income families.

Urban Development Action Grants
Urban Development Action Grants, funded by the U.S. Department of Housing and Urban Development, are awarded to communities which then loan the proceeds at flexible rates to eligible businesses. Projects whose total costs are less than $100,000 are not eligible. UDAG funds should leverage at least three to four times their amount in private sector investment.

Farmers Home Administration (FmHA) Emergency Disaster Loans
Farmers Home Administration (FmHA) Emergency Disaster Loans are available in counties where natural disaster has substantially affected farming, ranching or aquaculture production.

FmHA Farm Loan Guarantees
FmHA Farm Loan Guarantees are made to family farmers and ranchers to enable them to obtain funds from private lenders. Funds must be used for farm ownership, improvements, and operating purposes.

FmHA Farm Operating Loans
FmHA Farm Operating Loans are used to meet operating expenses, finance recreational and nonagricultural enterprises, to add to family income, and to pay for mandated safety and pollution control changes that are available at variable interest rates. Limits are $200,000 for an insured farm operating loan and $400,000 for a guaranteed loan.

FmHA Farm Ownership Loans
FmHA Farm Ownership Loans can be used for a wide range of farm improvement projects. Limits are $200,000 for an insured loan and $300,000 for a guaranteed loan.

FmHA Soil And Water Loans
FmHA Soil and Water Loans must be used by individual farmers and ranchers to develop, conserve, and properly use their land and water resources and to help abate pollution. Interest rates are variable; each loan must be secured by real estate.

FmHA Youth Project Loans
Youth Project Loans enable young people to borrow for income-producing projects sponsored by a school or 4-H club.

Assistance Programs

Management Training
Management Training is offered by many states in subjects ranging from bookkeeping to energy conservation.

Business Consulting
Business Consulting is offered on almost any subject. Small Business Development Centers are the best source for this kind of assistance.

Market Studies
Market Studies to help you sell your goods or services within or outside the state are offered by many states. They all also have State Data Centers, which not only collect demographic and other information about markets within the state, but also have access to federal data which can pinpoint national markets. Many states also provide the services of graduate business students at local universities to do the legwork and analysis for you.

State Starting Places for Money

Business Site Selection

Business Site Selection is done by specialists in every state who will identify the best place to locate a business.

Licensing, Regulation, and Permits

Licensing, Regulation, and Permits information is available from most states through "one-stop shop" centers by calling a toll-free number. There you'll get help in finding your way through the confusion of registering a new business.

Employee Training Programs

Employee Training Programs offer on-site training and continuing education opportunities.

Research And Development

Research and Development assistance for entrepreneurs is a form of assistance that is rapidly increasing as more and more states try to attract high technology-related companies. Many states are even setting up clearing houses so that small businesses can have one place to turn to find expertise throughout a statewide university system.

Procurement Programs

Procurement Programs have been established in some states to help you sell products to state, federal, and local governments.

Export Assistance

Export Assistance is offered to identify overseas markets. Some states even have overseas offices to drum up business prospects for you.

Assistance In Finding Funding

Assistance in Finding Funding is offered in every state, particularly through regional Small Business Development Centers. They will not only identify funding sources in the state and federal governments but will also lead you through the complicated application process.

Special Help For Minorities And Women

Special Help for Minorities and Women is available in almost every state to help boost the participation of women and minorities in small business ventures. They offer special funding programs and, often, one-on-one counseling to assure a start-up success.

Venture Capital Networking

Venture Capital Networking is achieved through computer databases that hook up entrepreneurs and venture capitalists. This service is usually free of charge. In fact, the demand for small business investment opportunities is so great that some states require the investor to pay to be listed.

Inventors Associations

Inventors Associations have been established to encourage and assist inventors in developing and patenting their products.

Annual Governors' Conferences

Annual Governors' Conferences give small business people the chance to air their problems with representatives from state agencies and the legislature.

Small Business Development Centers

Small Business Development Centers (SBDC's), funded jointly by the federal and state governments, are usually associated with the state university system. SBDC's are a god-send to small business people. They will not only help you figure out if your business project is feasible, but also help you draw up a sensible business plan, apply for funding, and check in with you frequently once your business is up and running to make sure it stays that way.

Tourism

Tourism programs are prominent in states whose revenues are heavily dependent on the tourist trade. They are specifically aimed at businesses in the tourist industries.

Small Business Institutes

Small Business Institutes at local colleges use senior level business students as consultants to help develop business plans or plan expansions.

Technology Assistance Centers

Technology Assistance Centers help high-tech companies and entrepreneurs establish new businesses and plan business expansions.

On-Site Energy Audits

On-Site Energy Audits are offered free of charge by many states to help control energy costs and improve energy efficiency for small businesses. Some states also conduct workshops to encourage energy conservation measures.

Minority Business Development Centers

Minority Business Development Centers offer a wide range of services from initial counseling on how to start a business to more complex issues of planning and growth.

State Starting Places

Alabama

General Information

Alabama Development Office, State Capitol, 135 South Union Street, Montgomery, AL 36130, (205) 263-0048. Answers general inquiries about Alabama's programs. *Small Business is Big Business in Alabama* is a free packet with information on assistance programs, sources of financing, a licensing handbook, and tips on preparing business and financial plans.

Small Business Advocate, c/o Alabama Development Office, State Capitol, 135 South Union Street, Montgomery, AL 36130, (205) 263-0048. Assistance in cutting bureaucratic red tape. Information and expertise in dealing with state, federal and local agencies.

Small Business Development Centers

The following offices offer free and fee-based services to new and expanding businesses:

Lead Center: Alabama Small Business Development Center, University of Alabama at Birmingham, Medical Towers Building, 1717 11th Avenue South, Suite 419, Birmingham, AL 35294-7645; (205) 934-7260, FAX: (205) 934-7645

Auburn: Auburn University, Small Business Development Center, College of Business, 226 Thach Hall, Auburn, AL 36849-5243, (205) 844-4220, FAX: (205) 844-4268.

Birmingham: University of Alabama at Birmingham, Small Business Development Center, 901 South 15th Street, MCJ, Room 143, Birmingham, AL 35294-2060, (205) 934-6760, FAX: (205) 934-0534.

Small Business and Entrepreneuring

Birmingham: Alabama Small Business Procurement System, University of Alabama at Birmingham, Small Business Development Center, 1717 11th Avenue South, Suite 419, Birmingham, AL 35294-4410, (205) 934-7260.

Florence: University of North Alabama, Small Business Development Center, P.O. Box 5017, Keller Hall, Florence, AL 35632-0001, (205) 760-4629, FAX: (205) 760-4813.

Huntsville: North East Alabama Regional Small Business Development Center, P.O. Box 343, 225 Church Street, N.W., Huntsville, AL 35804-0343, (205) 535-2061, FAX: (205) 535-2050.

Jacksonville: Jacksonville State University, Small Business Development Center, 113-B Merrill Hall, Jacksonville, AL 36265, (205) 782-5271, FAX: (205) 782-5124.

Livingston: Livingston University, Small Business Development Center, Station 35, Livingston, AL 35470, (205) 652-9661, ext. 439, FAX: (205) 652-9318.

Mobile: University of South Alabama, Small Business Development Center, College of Business and Management Studies, Building 101, Mobile, AL 36688, (205) 460-6004, FAX: (205) 460-6246.

Montgomery: Alabama State University, Small Business Development Center, 915 South Jackson Street, Montgomery, AL 36195, (205) 269-1102, FAX: (205) 265-9144.

Troy: Troy State University, Small Business Development Center, Sorrell College of Business, Troy, AL 36082-0001, (205) 670-3771, FAX: (205) 670-3636.

Tuscaloosa: Alabama International Trade Center, University of Alabama, P.O. Box 870396 400-N, Martha Parham West, Tuscaloosa, AL 35487-0396, (205) 348-7621, FAX: (205) 348-6974.

Tuscaloosa: University of Alabama, Small Business Development Center, P.O. Box 870397, 400-S Martha Parham West, Tuscaloosa, AL 35487-0397, (205) 348-7011, FAX: (205) 348-9644.

Alaska

General Information

Division of Business Development, Alaska Department of Commerce and Economic Development, P.O. Box D, Juneau, AK 99811, (907) 465-2018, or 3601 C Street, Suite 722, Anchorage, AK 99503, (907) 563-2165. Answers general inquiries. A free booklet, *Establishing a Business in Alaska*, provides information on assistance programs, licensing requirements, taxation, labor laws, financial assistance programs, and state sources of information.

Small Business Advocate, Division of Business Development, Department of Commerce and Economic Development, P.O. Box D, Juneau, AK 99811, (907) 465-2018. Assistance in cutting bureaucratic red tape. Information and expertise in dealing with state, federal, and local agencies.

Small Business Development Centers

The following offices offer free and fee-based services to new and expanding businesses:

Lead Center: University of Alaska, Small Business Development Center, 430 West 7th Avenue, Suite 110, Anchorage, AK 99501; (907) 274-7232, FAX: (907) 274-9524

Anchorage: University of Alaska-Anchorage, 430 West 7th Avenue, Suite 110, Anchorage, AK 99501, (907) 274-7232; FAX: (907) 274-9524.

Fairbanks: University of Alaska-Fairbanks, Small Business Development Center, 510 Fifth Avenue, #421, Fairbanks, AK 99701, (907) 456-1701, FAX: (907) 456-1942.

Juneau: University of Alaska-Southeast, Small Business Development Center, 124 West 5th Street, Juneau, AK 99801, (907) 463-3789; FAX: (907) 463-5670.

Wasilla: University of Alaska-Anchorage/Matanuska-Susitna Borough, Small Business Development Center, 1801 Parks Highway, #C-18, Wasilla, AK 99654, (907) 373-7232; FAX: (907) 373-2560.

Arizona

General Information

Arizona Office of Economic Development, Department of Commerce, State Capitol, 1700 West Washington, Phoenix, AZ 85007, (602) 255-5374.

State Small Business Advocate, Arizona Department of Commerce, Fourth Floor, Capital Towers, 1700 West Washington, Phoenix, AZ 85007, (602) 255-5371. Assistance in cutting bureaucratic red tape. Information and expertise in dealing with state, federal, and local agencies.

Small Business Development Centers

These offices offer free and fee-based services to new and expanding businesses:

Lead Center: Arizona Small Business Development Center, 9215 N. Black Canyon Highway, Phoenix, AZ 85021; (602) 943-9818, FAX: (602) 943-3716

Coolidge: Central Arizona College, Small Business Development Center, 141 N. Main, Coolidge, AZ 85222, (602) 723-5522; FAX: (602) 426-4234.

Flagstaff: Coconino County Community College, Small Business Development Center, 3000 N. 4th Street, Suite 17, Flagstaff, AZ 86004, (602) 526-5072; FAX: (602) 526-8693; (800) 266-5072.

Holbrook: Northland Pioneer College, Small Business Development Center, P.O. Box 610, Holbrook, AZ 86025, (602) 537-2976; FAX: (602) 524-2227.

Lake Havasu City: Mojave Community College, Small Business Development Center, 1977 W. Acoma Blvd., Lake Havasu City, AZ 86403, (602) 453-1836; FAX: (602) 453-8335.

Phoenix: Rio Salado Community College, Small Business Development Center, 301 West Roosevelt, Suite D, Phoenix, AZ 85003, (602) 238-9603; FAX: (602) 340-1627.

Phoenix: Gateway Community College, Small Business Development Center, 108 N. 40th Street, Phoenix, AZ 85008, (602) 392-5220; FAX: (602) 392-5329.

Prescott: Yavapai College, Small Business Development Center, 1100 E. Sheldon Street, Prescott, AZ 86301, (602) 776-2373; FAX: (602) 776-2193.

Safford: Eastern Arizona College, Small Business Development Center, 1111 Thatcher Boulevard, Safford, AZ 85546, (602) 428-7603; FAX: (602) 428-8462.

Sierra Vista: Cochise College, Small Business Development Center, 901 N. Colombo, Room 411, Sierra Vista, AZ 85635, (602) 459-9778; FAX: (602) 459-9764; (800) 966-7943, ext. 778.

Tucson: Pima Community College, Small Business Development Center, 655 North Alvernon, #110, Tucson, AZ 85711, (602) 884-6306; FAX: (602) 884-6585.

Yuma: Arizona Western College, Small Business Development Center, 281 W. 24th Street, #128 Century Plaza, Yuma, AZ 85364, (602) 341-1650; FAX: (602) 341-0234.

Arkansas

General Information

Small Business Clearinghouse, Arkansas Industrial Development Commission, One Capitol Mall, Little Rock, AR 72201, (501) 682-7500. *Small Business Information Clearinghouse Summaries* is a spiral-bound notebook that summarizes the states' programs agency by agency.

Small Business Advocate, Coordinator, Small Business Programs, Arkansas Industrial Development Commission, One State Capitol Mall, Room 4C300, Little Rock, AR 72201, (501) 371-5273. Assistance in cutting bureaucratic red tape. Information and expertise in dealing with state, federal, and local agencies.

Small Business Development Centers

The following offices offer free and fee-based services to new and expanding businesses:

State Starting Places for Money

Lead Center: Arkansas Small Business Development Center, University of Arkansas at Little Rock, Little Rock Technology Center Building, 100 South Main, Suite 401, Little Rock, AR 72201; (501) 324-9043, FAX: (501) 324-9049

Arkadelphia: Henderson State University, Small Business Development Center, P.O. Box 7624, Arkadelphia, AR 71923, (501) 246-5511, ext. 327.

Fayetteville: University of Arkansas at Fayetteville, Small Business Development Center, College of Business - BA 117, Fayetteville, AR 72701, (501) 575-5148.

Jonesboro: Arkansas State University, Small Business Development Center, P.O. Drawer 2650, Jonesboro, AR 72467, (501) 972-3517.

California

General Information

Office of Small Business, California Department of Commerce, 1121 L Street, Suite 501, Sacramento, CA 95814, (916) 445-6545. Offers workshops, seminars, individual counseling, and publications.

Office of Local Development, California Department of Commerce, 1121 L Street, Suite 600, Sacramento, CA 95814, (916) 322-1398. Provides case studies, handbooks, slide presentations, on-site training workshops, and seminars on a wide range of topics, including: downtown revitalization, industrial development, streamlining the local permit process, and financing.

Office of Business Development, California Department of Commerce, 1121 L Street, Suite 600, Sacramento, CA 95814, (916) 322-5665. Identifies available locations for business development in California and provides site-specific information on regional economic trends, labor supply, wage rates, real estate prices, infrastructure needs, transportation costs, regulations, taxes, tax-exempt bond financing, and government-sponsored job training.

California Commission for Economic Development, Office of the Lieutenant Governor, State Capitol, Room 1028, Sacramento, CA 95814, (916) 445-8994. Publishes *Doing Business in California: A Guide for Establishing Business.* Cost: $3.

Small Business Advocate, 1120 North Street, Sacramento, CA 95814, (916) 322-6108. Provides assistance in cutting bureaucratic red tape and information and expertise in dealing with state, federal, and local agencies.

Small Business Development Centers

The following offices offer free and fee-based services to new and expanding businesses:

Lead Center: California Small Business Development Center, California Department of Commerce, Office of Small Business, 801 K Street, Suite 1700, Sacramento, CA 95814; (916) 324-5068, FAX: (916) 322-5084

Aptos: Central Coast Small Business Assistance Center, 6500 Soquel Drive, Aptos, CA 95003, (408) 479-6136; FAX: (408) 479-5743.

Auburn: Sierra College, Small Business Development Center, 560 Wall Street, Suite J, Auburn, CA 95603, (916) 885-5488; FAX: (916) 781-0455.

Bakersfield: Weill Institute, Small Business Development Center, 2101 K Street Mall, Bakersfield, CA 93301, (805) 395-4148; FAX: (805) 395-4134.

Chico: Butte College, Tri-County Small Business Development Center, 260 Cohasset Avenue, Chico, CA 95926, (916) 895-9017; FAX: (916) 895-9099.

Chula Vista: Southwestern College, Small Business Development Center and International Trade Center, 900 Otay Lakes Road, Bldg. 1600, Chula Vista, CA 91910, (619) 482-6393; FAX: (619) 482-6402.

Crescent City: North Coast Small Business Development Center, 882 H. Street, Crescent City, CA 95531, (707) 464-2168; FAX: (707) 465-3402.

Eureka: North Coast Satellite Center, 408 7th Street, Suite "E", Eureka, CA 95501, (707) 445-9720.

Fresno: Cal-State University at Fresno, Central Valley Small Business

Development Center, 2771 East Shaw Avenue, Fresno, CA 93740, (209) 278-4946; FAX: (209) 373-7740.

Gilroy: Gavilan College, Small Business Development Center, 5055 Santa Teresa Blvd., Gilroy, CA 95020, (408) 847-0373; FAX: (408) 847-0393.

La Jolla: Greater San Diego Chamber of Commerce, Small Business Development Center, 4275 Executive Square, Suite 290, La Jooa, CA 92037, (619) 453-9388; FAX: (619) 450-1997.

Lakeport: Business Development Center of Lake and Mendocino Counties, 341 North Main Street, Lakeport, CA 95453, (707) 263-6180; FAX: (707) 263-0920.

Los Angeles: Export Small Business Development Center of Southern California, 110 E. 9th, Suite A761, Los Angeles, CA 90079, (213) -892-1111; FAX: (213) - 892-8232.

Merced: Merced Satellite Center, 1632 "N" Street, Merced, CA 95340, (209) 385-7312; FAX: (209) 383-4959.

Modesto: Valley Sierra Small Business Development Center, 1012 11th Street, Suite 300, Modesto, CA 95354, (209) 521-6177; FAX: (209) 521-9373.

Napa: Napa Valley College, Small Business Development Center, 1556 First Street, Suite 103, Napa, CA 94559, (707) 253-3210; FAX: (707) 255-0972.

Oakland: East Bay Small Business Development Center, 2201 Broadway, Suite 814, Oakland, CA 94612, (510) 893-4114; FAX: (510) 893-5532.

Oxnard: Export Satellite Center, 300 Esplanade Drive, Suite 1010, Oxnard, CA 93030, (805) 981-4633.

Pomona: Eastern Los Angeles County Small Business Development Center, 363 S. Park Avenue, #105, Pomona, CA 91766, (714) 629-2247; FAX: (714) 629-8310.

Riverside: Inland Empire Small Business Development Center, 1860 Chicago Avenue, Building 1, Suite 1, Riverside, CA 92507, (714) 781-2345; FAX: (714) 781-2353.

Sacramento: Greater Sacramento Small Business Development Center, 1787 Tribute Road, Suite A, Sacramento, CA 95815, (916) 920-7949; FAX: (916) 920-7940.

San Jose: Silicon Valley - San Mateo County, Small Business Development Center, 111 N. Market Street, #150, San Jose, CA 95113, (408) 298-7694; FAX: (408) 971-0680.

San Mateo: San Mateo County Satellite Center, Bayshore Corporate Center, 1730 S. Amphlett Blvd., Suite 208, San Mateo, CA 94402, (415) 358-0271; FAX: (415) 358-9450.

Santa Ana: Rancho Santiago Small Business Development Center, 901 East Santa Ana Boulevard, Suite 108, Santa Ana, CA 92701, (714) 647-1172; FAX: (714) 835-9008.

Stockton: San Joaquin Delta College, Small Business Development Center, 814 N. Hunter, Stockton, CA 95202, (209) 474-5089; FAX: (209) 474-5605.

Suisun: Solano County Small Business Development Center, 320 Campus Lane, Suisun, CA 94585, (707) 864-3382; FAX: (707) 864-3386.

Van Nuys: Northern Los Angeles Small Business Development Center, 14540 Victory Boulevard, Suite #206, Van Nuys, CA 91411, (818) 373-7092; FAX: (818) 373-7740.

Colorado

General Information

Colorado Office of Small Business, Office of Economic Development, 1625 Broadway, Suite 1710, Denver, CO 80202, (303) 892-3840, Hotline (800) 323-7798 in Colorado. Offers information, assistance and referrals for Colorado's small business owners and operators. The Small Business Hotline provides access to the Colorado Business Clearinghouse, a computerized database that contains information on over 2,000 business resources.

Be patient. If any phone number is incorrect, call (area code) 555-1212 and request the new listing.

Small Business and Entrepreneuring

Colorado Office of Business Development, Office of Economic Development, 1625 Broadway, Suite 1710, Denver, CO 80202, (303) 892-3840. Provides information and assistance to local economic development organizations, assists in retaining and expanding existing businesses, and responds to out-of-state inquiries concerning expanding or relocating in Colorado.

State Small Business Advocate, Office of Economic Development, Suite 1710, 1625 Broadway, Denver, CO 80202, (303) 892-3840. Provides assistance in cutting bureaucratic red tape and information and expertise in dealing with state, federal, and local agencies.

Small Business Development Centers

The following offices offer free and fee-based services to new and expanding businesses:

Lead Center: Colorado Small Business Development Center, Office of Economic Development, 1625 Broadway, Suite 1710, Denver, CO 80202; (303) 892-3809, (303) 892-3840, FAX: (303) 892-3848

Alamosa: Adams State College, Small Business Development Center, Alamosa, CO 81102, (719) 589-7372, (719) 589-7199; FAX: (719) 589-7522.

Aurora: Community College of Aurora, Small Business Development Center, 16000 E. Centretech Parkway, #A201, Aurora, CO 80011-9036, (303) 360-4745; FAX: (303) 360-4761.

Canon City: Canon City (Satellite), 402 Valley Road, Canon City, CO 81212, (719) 275-5335; FAX: (719) 275-4400.

Colorado Springs: Pikes Peak Community College/Colorado Springs Chamber of Commerce, Small Business Development Center, P.O. Drawer B, Colorado Springs, CO 80901-3002, (719) 635-1551, (719) 471-4836; FAX: (719) 635-1571.

Craig: Colorado Northwestern Community College, Small Business Development Center, 50 Spruce Drive, Craig, CO 81625, (303) 824-7071; FAX: (303) 824-3527.

Delta: Delta Montrose Vocational School, Small Business Development Center, 1765 U.S. Highway 50, Delta, CO 81416, (303) 874-8772; FAX: (303) 874-8796.

Denver: Community College of Denver/Denver Chamber of Commerce, Small Business Development Center, 1445 Market Street, Denver, CO 80202, (303) 620-8076; FAX: (303) 534-3200.

Durango: Fort Lewis College, Small Business Development Center, Miller Student Center, Room 108, Durango, CO 81301, (303) 247-7188; FAX: (303) 247-7620.

Fort Collins: Fort Collins (Satellite), P.O. Box 2397, Fort Collins, CO 80522, (303) 226-2500, ext. 108; FAX: (303) 825-6819.

Fort Morgan: Morgan Community College, Small Business Development Center, 300 Main Street, Fort Morgan, CO 80701, (303) 867-3351; FAX: (303) 867-7580.

Grand Junction: Mesa State College, Small Business Development Center, 304 W. Main Street, Grand Junction, CO 81505-1606, (303) 248-7314; FAX: (303) 241-0771.

Greeley: Aims Community College/Greeley and Weld Chamber of Commerce, Small Business Development Center, 1407 8th Avenue, Greeley, CO 80631, (303) 352-3661; FAX: (303) 352-3572.

Lakewood: Red Rocks Community College, Small Business Development Center, 13300 W. 6th Avenue, Lakewood, CO 80401-5398, (303) 987-0710; FAX: (303) 969-8039.

Lamar: Lamar Community College, Small Business Development Center, 2400 South Main, Lamar, CO 81052, (719) 336-8141; FAX: (719) 336-2448.

Littleton: Arapaho Community College/South Metro Chamber of Commerce, Small Business Development Center, 7901 South Park Plaza, Suite 110, Littleton, CO 80120, (303) 795-5855; FAX: (303) 795-7520.

Pueblo: Pueblo Community College, Small Business Development Center, 900 West Orman Avenue, Pueblo, CO 81004, (719) 549-3224; FAX: (719) 546-2413.

Stratton: Stratton (Satellite), P.O. Box 28, Stratton, CO 80836, (719) 348-5596; FAX: (719) 348-5887.

Trinidad: Trinidad State Junior College, Small Business Development Center, 600 Prospect Street, Davis Building, Trinidad, CO 81082, (719) 846-5645; FAX: (719) 846-5667.

Vail: Colorado Mountain College, Small Business Development Center, 1310 Westhaven Drive, Vail, CO 81657, (303) 476-4040, (800) 621-1647; FAX: (303) 479-9212.

Westminster: Front Range Community College, Small Business Development Center, 3645 West 112th Avenue, Westminster, CO 80030, (303) 460-1032; FAX: (303) 466-1623.

Connecticut

General Information

Office of Small Business Services, Department of Economic Development, 210 Washington Street, Hartford, CT 06106, (203) 566-4051. Offers a One Stop Licensing Center for call-in or drop-in service. Publishes *Establishing a Business in Connecticut*, a free booklet for ready reference to state licensing laws.

Small Business Advocate, Department of Economic Development, 210 Washington Street, Hartford, CT 06106, (203) 566-4051. Provides assistance in cutting bureaucratic red tape, and information and expertise in dealing with state, federal, and local agencies.

Small Business Development Centers

The following offices offer free and fee-based services to new and expanding businesses:

Lead Center: Connecticut Small Business Development Center, University of Connecticut, School of Business Administration, Box U-41, Room 422, 368 Fairfield Road, Storrs, CT 06268; (203) 486-4135, FAX: (203) 486-1576

Bridgeport: Business Regional B.C., Small Business Development Center, 10 Middle Street, 14th Floor, Bridgeport, CT 06604-4229, (203) 335-3800; FAX: (203) 366-9105.

Bridgeport: University of Bridgeport, Small Business Development Center, 141 Linden Avenue, Bridgeport, CT 06601, (203) 576-4538.

Danielson: Quinebaug Valley Community College, Small Business Development Center, 742 Upper Maple Street, Danielson, CT 06239-1440, (203) 774-1133; FAX: (203) 774-7768.

Hartford: University of Connecticut/MBA, Small Business Development Center, 1800 Asylum Avenue, West Hartford, CT 06117, (203) 241-4907; FAX: (203) 241-4907.

Groton: University of Connecticut, Small Business Development Center, Administration Building, Room 313, 1084 Shennecossett Road, Groton, CT 06340-6097, (203) 449-1188; FAX: (203) 445-3415.

Middletown: Middlesex County Chamber of Commerce, Small Business Development Center, 393 Main Street, Middletown, CT 06457, (203) 344-2158; FAX: (203) 346-1043.

New Haven: Greater New Haven Chamber of Commerce, Small Business Development Center, 195 Church Street, New Haven, CT 06506, (203) 773-0782; FAX: (203) 787-6730.

Stamford: Southwestern Area Commerce and Industry Association (SACIA), Small Business Development Center, One Landmark Square, Stamford, CT 06901, (203) 359-3220; FAX: (203) 967-8294.

Waterbury: Greater Waterbury Chamber of Commerce, Small Business Development Center, 83 Bank Street, Waterbury, CT 06702, (203) 757-0701; FAX: (203) 756-3507.

Willmantic: Eastern Connecticut State University, Small Business Development Center, 83 Windham Street, Willmantic, CT 06226-2295, (203) 456-5349; FAX: (203) 456-5670.

Be patient. If any phone number is incorrect, call (area code) 555-1212 and request the new listing.

State Starting Places for Money

Delaware

General Information

Delaware Development Office, 99 Kings Highway, P.O. Box 1401, Dover, DE 19903, (302) 736-4271. Offers referrals to appropriate state agencies and other organizations. Free tabloid, *Small Business Start-Up Guide,* is available.

Small Business Advocate, Delaware Development Office, 99 Kings Highway, P.O. Box 1401, Dover, DE 19903, (302) 736-4271. Provides assistance in cutting bureaucratic red tape, and information and expertise in dealing with state, federal, and local agencies.

Small Business Development Centers

The following offices offer free and fee-based services to new and expanding businesses:

Lead Center: Delaware Small Business Development Center, University of Delaware, Purnell Hall, Suite 005, Newark, DE 19716; (302) 831-2747, FAX: (302) 831-1423

Dover: Delaware Small Business Development Center, University of Delaware, 4 The Green, Dover, DE 19901, (302) 735-8200; FAX: (302) 735-8203.

District of Columbia

General Information

Office of Business and Economic Development, District Building, 1111 E Street, N.W., Washington, DC 20004, (202) 727-6600. Offers a wide range of technical and financial assistance programs.

Small Business Development Centers

The following offices offer free and fee-based services to new and expanding businesses:

Lead Center: District of Columbia Small Business Development Center, Howard University, 6th and Fairmont Street, N.W., Room 128, Washington, DC 20059; (202) 806-1550, FAX: (202) 806-1777

Arlington: Marymount University, Small Business Development Center, Office of Continuing Education, 2807 North Glebe Road, Arlington, VA 22207-4299, (703) 522-5600.

College Park: University of Maryland (UMCP), Small Business Development Center, College of Business and Management, Tydings Hall, College Park, MD 20742, (301) 454-5072.

Landover: National Business League of Southern Maryland, Inc., Small Business Development Center, 9200 Basil Court, Suite 210, Landover, MD 20785, (301) 794-4400.

Washington: Galludet University, Small Business Development Center, Management Institute, 800 Florida Avenue, N.E., Washington, DC 20002-3625, (202) 651-5312.

Washington: George Washington University, Small Business Development Center, National Law Center, 720 20th Street, N.W., Suite SL-101B, Washington, DC 20052, (202) 994-7463.

Florida

General Information

Bureau of Business Assistance, Department of Commerce, Division of Economic Development, G-26 Collins Building, Tallahassee, FL 32399, (904) 488-9357, (800) 342-0771 in Florida. The Business Services Section operates a toll-free information and referral service for current and potential small business owners. They also sponsor workshops and business forums and an annual Small Business Development Workshop that brings together local, state, and federal agency representatives.

Small Business Advocate, Florida Department of Commerce, G-27 Collins Building, Tallahassee, FL 32399, (904) 487-4698. Assistance in cutting bureaucratic red tape. Information and expertise in dealing with state, federal, and local agencies.

Small Business Development Centers

These offices offer free and fee-based services to new and expanding businesses:

Lead Center: Florida Small Business Development Center Network, University of West Florida, 1100 University Parkway, Pensacola, FL 32514; (904) 474-3016, FAX: (904) 474-2092

AltaMonte Springs: Seminole Community College, Small Business Development Center, Seminole Chamber of Commerce, P.O. Box 150784, AltaMonte Springs, FL 32715-0784, (407) 834-4404.

Boca Raton: Florida Atlantic University, Small Business Development Center, Building T-9, P.O. Box 3091, Boca Raton, FL 33431, (407) 367-2273.

Cocoa: Brevard Community College, Small Business Development Center, 1519 Clearlake Road, Cocoa, FL 32922, (407) 951-1060, ext. 2045.

Dania: Small Business Development Center, 46 SW 1st Avenue, Dania, FL 33304, (305) 987-0100.

Deland: Stetson University, Small Business Development Center, School of business Administration, P.O. Box 8417, Deland, FL 32720, (904) 822-7326.

Fort Lauderdale: Small Business Development Center, Florida Atlantic University, Commercial Campus, 1515 West Commercial Blvd., Room 11, Fort Lauderdale, FL 33309, (305) 771-6520.

Fort Pierce: Indian River Community College, Small Business Development Center, 3209 Virginia Avenue, Room 114, Fort Pierce, FL 34981-5599, (407) 468-4756.

Fort Myers: University of South Florida, Small Business Development Center, Sabal Hall, Rooms 219 and 220, 8111 College Parkway, Fort Myers, FL 33919, (813) 489-4140.

Fort Walton Beach: University of West Florida, Fort Walton Beach Center, Small Business Development Center, 414 Mary Esther Cutoff, Fort Walton Beach, FL 32548, (904) 244-1036.

Gainesville: Small Business Development Center, 214 W. University Avenue, P.O. Box 2518, Gainesville, FL 32601, (904) 377-5621.

Gainesville: FSBDC Product Innovation Program, Florida Product Innovation Center, 2622 NW 43rd Street, Suite B-3, Gainesville, FL 32606, (904) 334-1680.

Jacksonville: University of North Florida, Small Business Development Center, College of Business, 4567 St. John's Bluff Road, South, Building 11, Room 2163, Jacksonville, FL 32216, (904) 646-2476.

Miami: Florida International University, Small Business Development Center, Trailer MO1, Tamiami Campus, Miami, FL 33199, (305) 348-2272.

Miami: Florida International University, Small Business Development Center, North Miami Campus, N.E. 151 Street and Biscayne Blvd., Academic Building #1, Room 350, Miami, FL 33181, (305) 940-5790.

Ocala: Small Business Development Center, 110 East Silver Springs Blvd., P.O. Box 1210, Ocala, FL 32670, (904) 629-8051.

Orlando: University of Central Florida, Small Business Development Center, Building CEBA II, P.O. Box 25000, Orlando, FL 32816, (407) 823-5554.

Pensacola: University of West Florida, Small Business Development Center, Building 8, 11000 University Parkway, Pensacola, FL 32514, (904) 474-2908.

St. Petersburg: University of South Florida, St. Petersburg Campus, Small Business Development Center, 830 First Street South, Room 113, St. Petersburg, FL 33701, (813) 893-9529.

Sarasota: Small Business Development Center, 5700 North Tamiami Trail, Sarasota, FL 33580, (813) 359-4292.

Be patient. If any phone number is incorrect, call (area code) 555-1212 and request the new listing.

Small Business and Entrepreneuring

Tallahassee: Florida A and M University, Small Business Development Center, 1715-B South Gadsden Street, Tallahassee, FL 32301, (904) 599-3407.

Tampa: University of South Florida, Small Business Development Center, College of Business Administration, 4202 E. Fowler Avenue, BSN 3403, Tampa, FL 33620, (813) 974-4274.

West Palm Beach: Small Business Development Center, Prospect Place, Suite 123, 3111 South Dixie Highway, West Palm Beach, FL 33405, (407) 837-5311.

Georgia

General Information

Georgia Department of Community Affairs, 1200 Equitable Building, 100 Peachtree Street, N.W., Atlanta, GA 30303, (404) 656-6200. Provides information on financing programs and other services offered by the state government.

Business Council of Georgia, 1280 South CNN Center, Atlanta, GA 30303, (404) 223-2264. The Business Council is a clearinghouse for information and makes referrals to the Georgia Department of Labor, the Georgia Department of Industry and Trade, and other agencies. The council often acts as a liaison between businesses and local chambers of commerce.

Georgia Small Business Association, 1280 South CNN Center, Atlanta, GA 30335, (404) 223-2285. GSBA is a statewide membership organization that promotes the interests of small businesses. It keeps members informed of pending legislation, changes in law/regulations, provides management assistance and advice, provides information, makes referrals, and provides a variety of other services for small businesses.

Small Business Advocate, Department of Administrative Services, West Tower, Room 1302, 200 Piedmont Avenue, Southeast, Atlanta, GA 30334, (404) 656-6315.

Small Business Development Centers

The following offices offer free and fee-based services to new and expanding businesses:

Lead Center: Georgia Small Business Development Center, University of Georgia, Chicopee Complex, 1180 East Broad Street, Athens, GA 30602; (404) 542-6785, FAX: (404) 542-6776

Albany: Small Business Development Center, Southwest Georgia District, Business and Technology Center, 230 S. Jackson Street, 3rd Floor, Suite 333, Albany, GA 31701, (912) 430-4303; FAX: (912) 430-3933.

Athens: Small Business Development Center, University of Georgia, Chicopee Complex, 1180 East Broad Street, Athens, GA 30602, (404) 542-7436; FAX: (404) 542-6825.

Atlanta: Georgia State University, Small Business Development Center, Box 874, University Plaza, Atlanta, GA 30303-3083, (404) 651-3550.

Augusta: Small Business Development Center, 1061 Katherine Street, Augusta, GA 30910, (404) 737-1790; FAX: (404) 731-7937.

Brunswick: Small Business Development Center, 1107 Fountain Lake Drive, Brunswick, GA 31520, (912) 264-7343; FAX: (912) 262-3095.

Columbus: Small Business Development Center, P.O. Box 2441, Columbus, GA 31902, (404) 649-7433; FAX: (404) 649-1928.

Decatur: DeKalb Chamber of Commerce, Small Business Development Center, 750 Commerce Drive, Decatur, GA 30030, (404) 378-8000; FAX: (404) 378-3397.

Gainesville: Small Business Development Center, 455 Jesse Jewel Parkway, Suite 302, Gainesville, GA 30501, (404) 531-5681; (404) 531-5684.

Lawrenceville: Gwinnett Technical Institute, Small Business Development Center, P.O. Box 1505, 1230 Atkinson Road, Lawrenceville, GA 30246, (404) 963-4902; FAX: (404) 962-7985.

Macon: Small Business Development Center, Baconsfield Park, 640-K North

Avenue, P.O. Box 13212, Macon, GA 31208-3212, (912) 751-3592.

Marietta: Kennesaw State College, Small Business Development Center, P.O. Box 444, Marietta, GA 30061, (404) 423-6450; FAX: (404) 423-6564.

Morrow: Clayton State College, Small Business Development Center, P.O. Box 285, Morrow, GA 30260, (404) 961-3440; FAX: (404) 961-3428.

Rome: Floyd College, Small Business Development Center, P.O. Box 1864, Rome, GA 30163, (404) 295-6326; FAX: (404) 295-6732.

Savannah: Small Business Development Center, 6555 Abercorn Street, Suite 224, Savannah, GA 31405, (912) 356-2755; FAX: (912) 353-3033.

Statesboro: Small Business Development Center, Landrum Center, Box 8156, Statesboro, GA 30460, (912) 681-5194; FAX: (912) 681-0648.

Valdosta: Small Business Development Center, Valdosta Area Office, Baytree Office Park, Suite 9, Baytree Road, Valdosta, GA 31601, (912) 245-3738; FAX: (912) 245-3741.

Warner Robins: Middle Georgia Technical Institute, Small Business Development Center, 151 Asigian Blvd., Warner Robins, GA 31088, (912) 953-9376; FAX: (912) 953-9376.

Hawaii

General Information

Small Business Information Service, Department of Business and Economic Development, P.O. Box 2359, Honolulu, HI 96804, (808) 548-7645. Assists both new and existing businesses with information on government permit and license requirements, government procurement, sources of alternative financing, marketing, preparing a business plan, and available entrepreneurship training programs.

Small Business Advocate, Department of Business Economic Development, 250 South King Street, Honolulu, HI 96813, (808) 548-4347.

Small Business Development Centers

The following offices offer free and fee-based services to new and expanding businesses:

Lead Center: Hawaii Small Business Development Center, University of Hawaii at Hilo, 523 West Lanikaula Street, Hilo, HI 96720-4091; (808) 933-3515, FAX: (808) 933-3683

Hilo: Small Business Development Center - Big Island, University of Hawaii at Hilo, 523 W. Lanikaula Street, Hilo, HI 96720-4091, (808) 933-3515.

Lihue: Small Business Development Center - Kauai, Kauai Community College, 3-1901 Kaumualii Highway, Lihue, HI 96766-9591, (808) 246-1748.

Kihei: Small Business Development Center - Maui, Maui Research and Technology Center, 590 Lipoa Parkway, Kihei, HI 96753, (808) 875-2402.

Honolulu: Small Business Development Center - Oahu, Business Action Center, 1130 N. Nimitz Highway, Suite A-254, Honolulu, HI 96817, (808) 545-7726.

Idaho

General Information

Idaho Department of Commerce, Division of Economic Development, 700 West State Street, Boise, ID 83720, (208) 334-2470.

Small Business Advocate, Department of Commerce, State House, Boise, ID 83720, (208) 334-2470.

Small Business Development Centers

The following offices offer free and fee-based services to new and expanding businesses:

Be patient. If any phone number is incorrect, call (area code) 555-1212 and request the new listing.

State Starting Places for Money

Lead Center: Idaho Small Business Development Center, Boise State University, College of Business, 1910 University Drive, Boise, ID 83725; (208) 385-1640, FAX: (208) 385-3877

Hayden: Small Business Development Center, Panhandle Area Council, 11100 Airport Drive, Hayden, ID 83835, (208) 772-0587; FAX: (208) 772-6196.

Idaho Falls: Idaho State University, Small Business Development Center, 2300 North Yellowstone, Idaho Falls, ID 83401, (208) 523-1087; FAX: (208) 523-1049.

Lewiston: Lewis-Clark State College, Small Business Development Center, 8th Avenue and 6th Street, Lewiston, ID 83501, (208) 799-2465; FAX: (208) 799-2831.

Pocatello: Idaho State University, Small Business Development Center, 1651 Alvin Ricken Drive, Pocatello, ID 83201, (208) 232-4921; FAX: (208) 233-0268; (800) 232-4921.

Sandpoint: Panhandle Area Council, Small Business Development Center, Box 724, Sandpoint, ID 83864, (208) 263-4073; FAX: (208) 263-1911.

Twin Falls: College of Southern Idaho, Small Business Development Center, Region IV, P.O. Box 1844, Twin Falls, ID 83303, (208) 733-9554, ext. 477; FAX: (208) 734-6592.

Illinois

General Information

Small Business Assistance Bureau, Illinois Department of Commerce and Community Affairs, State of Illinois Center, 100 West Randolph Street, Suite 3-400, Chicago, IL 60601, (312) 917-7179; Hotline (800) 252-2923 in Illinois. The Small Business Hotline is a "one-stop shop" for small business information. It offers quick, personalized answers to business owners' questions. Also available, *How to Start a Small Business in Illinois*, a comprehensive start- up guide.

Small Business Advocate, Small Business Assistance Bureau, Illinois Department of Commerce and Community Affairs, Suite 3-400, 100 West Randolph, Chicago, IL 60601, (312) 917-2829. Assistance in cutting bureaucratic red tape. Information and expertise in dealing with state, federal, and local agencies.

Small Business Development Centers

The following offices offer free and fee-based services to new and expanding businesses:

Lead Center: Illinois Small Business Development Center Network, Dept. of Commerce and Community Affairs, 620 East Adams Street, 6th floor, Springfield, IL 62701; (217) 524-5856, FAX: (217) 785-6328

Aurora: Waubonsee Community College/Aurora Campus, SBDC, 5 East Galena Blvd., Aurora, IL 60506, (708) 892-3334, Ext. 141.

Carbondale: Southern Illinois University/Carbondale, SBDC, Carbondale, IL 62901, (618) 536-2424; FAX: (618) 453-5040.

Centralia: Kaskaskia College (Satellite), SBDC, Shattuc Road, Centralia, IL 62801, (618) 532-2049.

Chicago: Back of the Yards Neighborhood Council (Sub-Center), SBDC, 1751 West 47th Street, Chicago, IL 60609, (312) 523-4419.

Chicago: Greater North Pulaski Economic Development Corp., SBDC, 4054 West North Avenue, Chicago, IL 60639, (312) 384-2262.

Chicago: Women's Business Development Center, SBDC, 8 South Michigan, Suite 400, Chicago, IL 60603, (312) 853-3477; FAX: (312) 853-0145.

Chicago: Olive-Harvey College, SBDC, 10001 South Woodlawn Drive, Chicago, IL 60628, (312) 660-4839.

Chicago: Industrial Council of NW Chicago, SBDC, 2023 West Carroll, Chicago, IL 60612, (312) 421-3941.

Chicago: Latin American Chamber of Commerce, SBDC, 539 North Kedzie, Suite 11, Chicago, IL 60647, (312) 252-5211; FAX: (312) 252-7065.

Chicago: Eighteenth Street Development Corp., SBDC, 1839 South Carpenter, Chicago, IL 60608, (312) 733-2287.

Chicago: Loop SBDC, DCCA, State of Illinois Center, 100 West Randolph, Suite 3-400, Chicago, IL 60601, (312) 814-2829; FAX: (312) 814-1749.

Crystal Lake: McHenry County College, SBDC, 8900 U.S. Highway 14, Crystal Lake, IL 60012-2761, (815) 455-6098; FAX: (815) 455-3999.

Danville: Danville Area Community College, SBDC, 28 West North Street, Danville, IL 61832, (217) 442-7232.

Decatur: Richland Community College, SBDC, One College Park, Decatur, IL 62521, (217) 875-7200, ext. 556.

DeKalb: Northern Illinois University, SBDC, Department of Management, 305 East Locust, DeKalb, IL 60115, (815) 753-1403.

Dixon: Sauk Valley College, SBDC, 173 Illinois Route #2, Dixon, IL 61021-9110, (815) 288-5605.

Edwardsville: Southern Illinois University/Edwardsville, SBDC, Campus Box 1107, Edwardsville, IL 62026, (618) 692-2929; FAX: (618) 692-2647.

Elgin: Elgin Community College, SBDC, 1700 Spartan Drive, Elgin, IL 60115, (708) 697-1000, ext. 7923.

Evanston: Evanston Business and Technology Center, SBDC, 1840 Oak Ave., Evanston, IL 60201, (708) 866-1841; FAX: (708) 866-1808.

Freeport: Highland Community College (Satellite), SBDC, 2998 West Pearl City, Freeport, IL 61032-9341, (815) 232-1362; FAX: (815) 235-6130.

Glen Ellyn: College of DuPage, SBDC, 22nd and Lambert Road, Glen Ellyn, IL 60137, (708) 858-2800, ext. 2771.

Grayslake: College of Lake County, SBDC, 19351 West Washington Street, Grayslake, IL 60030, (708) 223-3633.

Harrisburg: Southeastern Illinois College (Satellite), SBDC, R.R. #4, College Drive, Harrisburg, IL 62946, (618) 252-4411.

Ina: Rend Lake College, SBDC, Route #1, Ina, IL 62846, (618) 437-5321, ext. 267.

Joliet: Joliet Junior College, SBDC, Renaissance Center, Room 319, 214 North Ottawa Street, Joliet, IL 60431, (815) 727-6544, Ext. 1313.

Kankakee: Kankakee Community College, SBDC, Box 888, River Road, Kankakee, IL 60901, (815) 933-0374; FAX: (815) 933-0370.

Macomb: Western Illinois University, SBDC, 216 Seal Hall, Macomb, IL 61455, (309) 298-1128.

Mattoon: Lake Land College, SBDC, South Route #45, Mattoon, IL 61938-9366, (217) 235-3131.

East Moline: Black Hawk College, SBDC, 301 42nd Ave, East Moline, IL 61244, (309) 752-9759.

Monmouth: Maple City Business and Technology (Satellite), SBDC, 620 South Main Street, Monmouth, IL 61462, (309) 734-4664.

Oglesby: Illinois Valley Community College, SBDC, Building 11, Route 1, Oglesby, IL 61348, (815) 223-1740.

Olney: Illinois Eastern Community College, SBDC, 233 East Chestnut, Olney, IL 62450, (618) 395-3011.

Palos Hills: Moraine Valley College, SBDC, 10900 South 88th Avenue, Palos Hills, IL 60465, (708) 974-5468; FAX: (708) 974-0078.

Peoria: Bradley University, SBDC, 141 North Jobst Hall, 1st Floor, Peoria, IL 61625, (309) 677-2992; FAX: (309) 677-3386.

Rockford: Rock Valley College, SBDC, 1220 Rock Street, Rockford, IL 61102, (815) 968-4087; FAX: (815) 968-4157.

Be patient. If any phone number is incorrect, call (area code) 555-1212 and request the new listing.

Small Business and Entrepreneuring

Springfield: Lincoln Land Community College, SBDC, 200 West Washington, Springfield, IL 62701, (217) 524-3060.

East St. Louis: East St. Louis, DCCA, State Office Building, 10 Collinsville, East St. Louis, IL 62201, (618) 583-2272; FAX: (618) 588-2274.

Ullin: Shawnee College (Satellite), SBDC, Shawnee College Road, Ullin, IL 62992, (618) 634-9618.

University Park: Governor's State University, SBDC, University Park, IL 60466, (708) 534-3713.

Indiana

General Information

Small Business Advocate, Office of Business Regulatory Ombudsman, Indiana Department of Commerce, Suite 700, One North Capitol, Indianapolis, IN 46204-2243, (317) 232-5295.

Small Business Development Centers

The following offices offer free and fee-based services to new and expanding businesses:

Lead Center: Indiana Small Business Development Center, Economic Development Council, One North Capitol, Suite 420, Indianapolis, IN 46204; (317) 264-6871, FAX: (317) 264-3102

Bloomington: Greater Bloomington Chamber of Commerce, Small Business Development Center, 116 W. 3rd Street, Bloomington, IN 47404, (812) 339-8937.

Columbus: Columbus Enterprise Development Center, Inc., Small Business Development Center, 4920 North Warren Drive, Columbus, IN 47203, (812) 372-6480; FAX: (812) 372-0228.

Evansville: Evansville Chamber of Commerce, Small Business Development Center, 100 N.W. Second Street, Suite 200, Evansville, IN 47708, (812) 425-7232.

Fort Wayne: Northeast Indiana Business Assistance Corporation, Small Business Development Center, 1830 West Third Street, Fort Wayne, IN 46803, (219) 426-0040.

Jeffersonville: Hoosier Valley Economic Opportunity Corporation, Small Business Development Center, 1613 E. 8th Street, Jeffersonville, IN 47130, (812) 288-6451.

Indianapolis: Indiana University, Small Business Development Center, 1317 West Michriver, Indianapolis, IN 46202, (317) 274-8200.

Kokomo: Kokomo-Howard County Chamber of Commerce, Small Business Development Center, P.O. Box 731, Kokomo, IN 46903, (317) 457-5301.

Lafayette: Greater Lafayette Progress, Inc., Small Business Development Center, 122 N. Third, Lafayette, IN 47901, (317) 0457-5301.

Madison: Madison Area Chamber of Commerce, Small Business Development Center, 301 East Main Street, Madison, IN 47250, (812) 265-3127.

Merrillville: Northwest Indiana Forum, Inc., Small Business Development Center, 8002 Utah Street, Merrillville, IN 46410, (219) 942-3496; FAX: (219) 942-5806.

Muncie: Muncie-Delaware County Chamber, Small Business Development Center, 401 South High Street, Muncie, IN 47308, (317) 284-8144; FAX: (317) 741-5489.

Richmond: Richmond Area Chamber of Commerce, Small Business Development Center, 33 South 7th Street, Richmond, IN 47374, (317) 962-2887.

South Bend: South Bend Chamber of Commerce, Small Business Development Center, 300 North Michigan Street, South Bend, IN 46601, (219) 282-4350.

Terre Haute: Indiana State University, Small Business Development Center, School of Business, Terre Haute, IN 47809, (812) 237-3232.

Iowa

General Information

Iowa Department of Economic Development, 200 East Grand Avenue, Des Moines, IA 50309, (515) 281-3251; CALL ONE: (800) 532-1216 in Iowa only.

Small Business Advocate, Small Business Division, Iowa Department of Economic Development, 200 East Grand Avenue, Des Moines, IA 50309, (515) 281-8324.

Small Business Development Centers

The following offices offer free and fee-based services to new and expanding businesses:

Lead Center: Iowa Small Business Development Center, Iowa State University, College of Business Administration, Chamblynn Building, 137 Lynn Avenue, Ames, IA 50010; (515) 292-6351, FAX: (515) 292-0020

Ames: Iowa State University, ISU Small Business Development Center, 137 Lynn Avenue, Ames, IA 50010, (515) 292-6351; FAX: (515) 292-0020.

Ames: ISU Small Business Development Center, ISU Ames Branch, 111 Lynn Avenue, Ames, IA 50010, (515) 292-6355; FAX: (515) 292-0020.

Audubon: ISU Small Business Development Center, ISU Audubon Branch, Circle West Incubator, P.O. Box 204, Audubon, IA 50025, (712) 563-2623; FAX: (712) 563-2301.

Cedar Falls: University of Northern Iowa, Small Business Development Center, Suite 5, Business Building, Cedar Falls, IA 50614-0120, (319) 273-2696; FAX: (319) 273-6830.

Council Bluffs: Iowa Western Community College, Small Business Development Center, 2700 College Road, Box 4C, Council Bluffs, IA 51502, (712) 325-3260; FAX: (712) 325-3424.

Creston: Southwestern Community College, Small Business Development Center, 1501 West Townline, Creston, IA 50801, (515) 782-4161; FAX: (515) 782-4164.

Davenport: Eastern Iowa Community College District, Small Business Development Center, 304 West Second Street, Davenport, IA 52801, (319) 322-4499; FAX: (319) 322-3956.

Des Moines: Drake University, Small Business Development Center, Drake Business Center, Des Moines, IA 50311-4505, (515) 271-2655; FAX: (515) 271-4540.

Dubuque: Dubuque Area Chamber of Commerce, Northeast Iowa Small Business Development Center, 770 Town Clock Plaza, Dubuque, IA 52001, (319) 588-3350; FAX: (319) 557-1591.

Iowa City: University of Iowa, Oakdale Campus, Small Business Development Center, 106 Technology Innovation Center, Iowa City, IA 52242, (319) 335-4057; FAX: (319) 335-4489.

Marion: Kirkwood Community College, Small Business Development Center, 2901 Tenth Avenue, Marion, IA 53302, (319) 377-8256; FAX: (319) 377-5667.

Mason City: North Iowa Area Community College, Small Business Development Center, 500 College Drive, Mason City, IA 50401, (515) 421-4342; FAX: (515) 424-2011.

Ottumwa: Indian Hills Community College, Small Business Development Center, 525 Grandview Avenue, Ottumwa, IA 52501, (515) 683-5127; FAX: (515) 683-5263.

Sioux City: Western Iowa Tech Community College, Small Business Development Center, 5001 East Gordon Drive, Box 265, Sioux City, IA 51102, (712) 274-6302; FAX: (712) 274-6238.

Spencer: Iowa Lakes Community College, Small Business Development Center, Gateway North Shopping Center, Highway 71 North, Spencer, IA 51301, (712) 262-4213; FAX: (712) 262-4047.

Be patient. If any phone number is incorrect, call (area code) 555-1212 and request the new listing.

State Starting Places for Money

West Burlington: Southeastern Community College, Small Business Development Center, Drawer F, West Burlington, IA 52655, (319) 752-2731, ext. 103; FAX: (319) 752-4957.

Kansas

General Information

Kansas Department of Commerce, Capitol Tower Office Building, 400 West 8th Street, Suite 500, Topeka, KS 66603-3957, (913) 296-3483. Offers a "One-Stop Clearinghouse" for obtaining permits and applications necessary for establishing and operating a business.

Small Business Advocate, Director, Existing Business, Department of Commerce, 400 Southwest Eighth, Suite 500, Topeka, KS 66603-3957, (913) 296-3481.

Small Business Development Centers

The following offices offer free and fee-based services to new and expanding businesses:

Lead Center: Kansas Small Business Development Center, Wichita State University, 1845 Fairmount, Wichita, KS 67260-0148; (316) 689-3193, FAX: (316) 689-3647

Augusta: Butler County Community College, Small Business Development Center, 600 Walnut, Augusta, KS 67010, (316) 775-1124; FAX: (316) 775-1370.

Arkansas City: Cowley County Community College, Small Business Development Center, 125 S. 2nd, Strother Field Training Facility, Arkansas City, KS 67005, (316) 442-8142; FAX: (316) 442-0713.

Colby: Colby Community College, Small Business Development Center, 1255 South Range, Colby, KS 67701, (913) 462-3984, ext. 239; FAX: (913) 462-8315.

Concordia: Cloud County Community College, Small Business Development Center, 2221 Campus Drive, P.O. Box 1002, Concordia, KS 66901, (913) 243-1435; FAX: (913) 243-1459.

Dodge City: Dodge City Community College, Small Business Development Center, 2501 North 14th Avenue, Dodge City, KS 67801, (316) 225-1321, ext. 247; FAX: (316) 225-0918.

Emporia: Emporia State University, Small Business Development Center, 207 Cremer Hall, Emporia, KS 66801, (316) 343-5308; FAX: (316) 341-5418.

Garden City: Garden City Community College, Small Business Development Center, 801 Campus Drive, Garden City, KS 67846, (316) 276-9632; FAX: (316) 276-9630.

Great Bend: Barton County Community College, Small Business Development Center, 3709 N. Main, P.O. Box 136Z, Great Bend, KS 67530, (316) 792-1242; FAX: (316) 792-8035.

Hays: Fort Hays State University, Small Business Development Center, 1301 Pine, Hays, KS 67601, (913) 628-5340; FAX: (913) 628-1471.

Hutchinson: Hutchinson Community College, Small Business Development Center, 815 N. Walnut, #225, Hutchinson, KS 67501, (316) 665-4950; FAX: (316) 665-7619.

Kansas City: Kansas City Community College, Small Business Development Center, 7250 State Avenue, Kansas City, KS 66112, (913) 334-1100, ext. 228; FAX: (913) 596-9606.

Lawrence: University of Kansas, Small Business Development Center, 734 Vermont, Suite 104, Lawrence, KS 66044, (913) 843-8844; FAX: (913) 865-4400.

Liberal: Seward County Community College, Small Business Development Center, 1801 North Kansas, Liberal, KS 67901, (316) 624-1951, ext. 148; FAX: (316) 624-0637.

Manhattan: Kansas State University, Small Business Development Center, 2323 Anderson Ave., Suite 100, Manhattan, KS 66502-2947, (913) 532-5529; FAX: (913) 532-7800.

Ottawa: Ottawa University, Small Business Development Center, College Avenue, Box 70, Ottawa, KS 66067, (913) 242-5200, ext. 5457; FAX: (913) 242-7429.

Overland Park: Johnson County Community College, Small Business Development Center, CEC Building, Room 3051, Overland Park, KS 66210-1299, (913) 469-3878; FAX: (913) 469-4415.

Pittsburg: Pittsburg State University, Small Business Development Center, Shirk Hall, Pittsburg, KS 66762, (316) 231-8267; FAX: (316) 232-6440.

Pratt: Pratt Community College, Small Business Development Center, Highway 61, Pratt, KS 67124, (316) 672-5641; FAX: (316) 672-5288.

Salina: KSU-Salina College of Technology, Small Business Development Center, 2409 Scanlan Avenue, Salina, KS 67401, (913) 825-0275, ext. 445; FAX: (913) 825-8475.

Topeka: Washburn University, Small Business Development Center, 101 Henderson Learning Center, Topeka, KS 66621, (913) 231-1010, ext. 1305; FAX: (913) 231-1063.

Wichita: Wichita State University, Small Business Development Center, Brennan Hall, 2nd Floor, 1845 Fairmount, Campus Box 148, Wichita, KS 67208, (316) 689-3193; FAX: (316) 689-3647.

Kentucky

General Information

Kentucky Business Information Clearinghouse, Kentucky Commerce Cabinet, Department of Economic Development, Capital Plaza Tower, Frankfort, KY 40601, (502) 564-4252; (800) 626-2250 in Kentucky only. This office handles requests for business licensing and permit information, referrals to other state, federal and local government agencies, and problems with government red tape.

Small Business Advocate, Small Business Division, Department of Economic Development, Business Information Clearninghouse, 22nd Floor, Capital Plaza Tower, Frankfort, KY 40601, (502) 564-4252.

Small Business Development Centers

The following offices offer free and fee-based services to new and expanding businesses:

Lead Center: Kentucky Small Business Development Center, University of Kentucky, Center for Business Development, College of Business and Economics, 225 Business and Economics Building, Lexington, KY 40506-0034; (606) 257-7668, FAX: (606) 258-1907

Ashland: Ashland Small Business Development Center, Boyd-Greenup County Chamber of Commerce Building, P.O. Box 830, 207 15th Street, Ashland, KY 41105-0830, (606) 329-8011; FAX: (606) 325-4607.

Bowling Green: Western Kentucky University, Bowling Green Small Business Development Center, 245 Grise Hall, Bowling Green, KY 42101, (502) 745-2901; FAX: (502) 745-2902.

Cumberland: Southeast Community College, Small Business Development Center, Room 113, Chrisman Hall, Cumberland, KY 40823, (606) 589-4514; FAX: (606) 589-4941.

Elizabethtown: Elizabethtown Small Business Development Center, 238 West Dixie Avenue, Elizabethtown, KY 42701, (502) 765-6737; FAX: (502) 765-6737.

Highland Heights: Northern Kentucky University, North Kentucky Small Business Development Center, BEP Center, Room 463, Highland Heights, KY 41099-0506, (606) 572-6524; FAX: (606) 572-5566.

Hopkinsville: Hopkinsville Small Business Development Center, 300 Hammond Drive, Hopkinsville, KY 42240, (502) 886-8666; FAX: (502) 886-3211.

Lexington: University of Kentucky, Small Business Development Center, College of Business and Economics, 227 Business and Economics Building, Lexington, KY 40506-0034, (606) 257-7666; FAX: (606) 258-1907.

Be patient. If any phone number is incorrect, call (area code) 555-1212 and request the new listing.

Small Business and Entrepreneuring

Louisville: Bellarmine College, Small Business Development Center, School of Business, 2001 Newburg Road, Louisville, KY 40205-0671, (502) 452-8282; FAX: (502) 452-8288.

Louisville: University of Louisville, Small Business Development Center, Center for Entrepreneurship and Technology, Room 122, Burhans Hall, Louisville, KY 40292, (502) 588-7854; FAX: (502) 588-8573.

Morehead: Morehead State University, Small Business Development Center, 207 Downing Hall, Morehead, KY 40351, (606) 783-2895; FAX: (606) 783-2678.

Murray: Murray State University, West Kentucky Small Business Development Center, College of Business and Public Affairs, Murray, KY 42071, (502) 762-2856; FAX: (502) 762-3049.

Owensboro: Owensboro Small Business Development Center, 3860 U.S. Highway 60 West, Owensboro, KY 42301, (502) 926-8085; FAX: (502) 684-0714.

Pikeville: Pikeville Small Business Development Center, 222 Hatcher Court, Pikeville, KY 41501, (606) 432-5848.

Somerset: Eastern Kentucky University, Small Business Development Center, 107 West Mt. Vernon Street, Somerset, KY 42501, (606) 678-5520; FAX: (606) 678-8349.

Louisiana

General Information

Louisiana Department of Economic Development, P.O. Box 94185, Baton Rouge, LA 70804-9185, (504) 342-5359.

Small Business Advocate, Community Development Division, Louisiana Department of Commerce and Industry, Box 94185, Baton Rouge, LA 70804-9184.

Small Business Development Centers

The following offices offer free and fee-based services to new and expanding businesses:

Lead Center: Louisiana Small Business Development Center, Northeast Louisiana University, Adm. 2-57, Monroe, LA 71209; (318) 342-5506, FAX: (318) 342-5510

Alexandria: Small Business Development Center, 5212 Rue Verdun, Alexandria, LA 71306, (318) 487-5454; FAX: (318) 487-5451.

Baton Rouge: Capital Small Business Development Center, 9613 Interline Avenue, Baton Rouge, LA 70809, (504) 922-0998.

Hammond: Southeastern Louisiana University, Small Business Development Center, Box 522, SLU Station, Hammond, LA 70402, (504) 549-3831; FAX: (504) 549-2127.

Lafayette: University of Southwestern Louisiana, Arcadiana Small Business Development Center, Box 43732, Lafayette, LA 70504, (318) 262-5344; FAX: (318) 262-5296.

Lake Charles: McNeese State University, Small Business Development Center, College of Business Administration, Lake Charles, LA 70609, (318) 475-5529; FAX: (318) 475-5122.

Monroe: Northeast Louisiana University, College of Business Administration, Monroe, LA 71209, (318) 342-1224; FAX: (318) 352-5506.

Monroe: Northeast Louisiana University, Small Business Development Center, LA Electronic Assistance Program, College of Business Administration, Monroe, LA 71209, (318) 342-1215; FAX: (318) 342-1209.

Monroe: Northeast Louisiana University, Small Business Development Center, Adm. 2-57, Monroe, LA 71209, (318) 342-5506; FAX: (318) 342-5510.

Natchitoches: Northwestern State University, Small Business Development Center, College of Business Administration, Natchitoches, LA 71497, (318) 357-5611; FAX: (318) 357-6810.

New Orleans: University of New Orleans, Small Business Development Center, LA International Trade, 368 Business Administration, New Orleans, LA 70148, (504) 286-6978; FAX: (504) 286-7197.

New Orleans: Loyola University, Small Business Development Center, Box 134, New Orleans, LA 70118, (504) 865-3474; FAX: (504) 865-3347.

New Orleans: Southern University, Small Business Development Center, College of Business Administration, New Orleans, LA 70126, (504) 286-5308; FAX: (504) 286-5306 (call first).

New Orleans: University of New Orleans, Small Business Development Center, Lakefront Campus, College of Business Administration, New Orleans, LA 70148, (504) 286-6978; FAX: (504) 286-7197.

Ruston: Louisiana Tech University, Small Business Development Center, Box 10318, Tech Station, Ruston, LA 71271-0046, (318) 257-3537; FAX: (318) 257-3356.

Shreveport: Louisiana State University at Shreveport, Small Business Development Center, College of Business Administration, 1 University Place, Shreveport, LA 71115, (318) 797-5144; FAX: (318) 797-5156.

Thibodaux: Nicholls State University, Small Business Development Center, P.O. Box 2015, Thibodaux, LA 70310, (504) 448-4242; FAX: (504) 448-4922.

Maine

General Information

Business Answers, Department of Economic and Community Development, Station #59, Augusta, ME 04333; (800) 872-3838 in Maine only. Serves as a central clearinghouse of information regarding business assistance programs and services available to state businesses.

Small Business Advocate, Maine Department of Economic and Community Development, Station 59, 193 State Street, Augusta, ME 04333, (207) 289-2658; (800) 541-5872 outside Maine.

Small Business Development Centers

The following offices offer free and fee-based services to new and expanding businesses:

Lead Center: Maine Small Business Development Center, University of Southern Maine, 99 Falmouth Street, Portland, ME 04103; (207) 780-4420, FAX: (207) 780-4810

Auburn: Androscoggin Valley Council of Governments (AVCOG), Small Business Development Center, 70 Court Street, Auburn, ME 04210, (207) 783-9186.

Bangor: Eastern Maine Development Corporation, Small Business Development Center, 10 Franklin Street, Bangor, ME 04401, (207) 942-6389.

Caribou: Northern Maine Regional Planning Commission, Small Business Development Center, McElwain House, P.O. Box 779, 2 Main Street, Caribou, ME 04736, (207) 498-8736.

Machias: University of Maine at Machias, Small Business Development Center, Math and Science Building, Machias, ME 04654, (207) 255-3313.

Sanford: Southern Maine Regional Planning Commission, Small Business Development Center, Box Q, 2 School Street, Sanford, ME 04073, (207) 324-2952.

Winslow: North Kennebec Regional Planning Commission, Small Business Development Center, 7 Benton Avenue, Winslow, ME 04902, (207) 873-0711.

Wiscasset: Coastal Enterprises, Inc., Small Business Development Center, Middle Street, Box 268, Wiscasset, ME 04578, (207) 882-7552.

Be patient. If any phone number is incorrect, call (area code) 555-1212 and request the new listing.

State Starting Places for Money

Maryland

General Information

Maryland Business Assistance Center, 217 East Redwood Street, Baltimore, MD 21202, (301) 333-6975; Hotline; (800) OK-GREEN in Maryland only. A direct link to state services including public financing, facility location, state-funded employee training, government procurement assistance, help with licensing and permit processing, and information on starting a business.

Small Business Advocate, Department of Economic and Employment Development, 45 Calvert Street, Annapolis, MD 21401, (301) 974-3514. Assistance in cutting bureaucratic red tape. Information and expertise in dealing with state, federal, and local agencies.

Small Business Development Centers

The following offices offer free and fee-based services to new and expanding businesses:

Lead Center: Maryland Small Business Development Center, Department of Economic and Employment Development, 217 East Redwood Street, 10th Floor, Baltimore, MD 21202; (410) 333-6995, FAX: (410) 333-6609

Baltimore: Small Business Development Center, 1414 Key Highway, Suite 310, Baltimore, MD 21230, (301) 234-0505.

Bethesda: Montgomery College, Small Business Development Center, 7815 Woodmount Avenue, Bethesda, MD 20814, (301) 656-7482.

Cumberland: Western Region Small Business Development Center, 3 Commerce Drive, Cumberland, MD 21502, (301) 724-6716.

Elkton: Cecil Community College, Eastern Region Small Business Development Center, 107 Railroad Avenue, Elkton, MD 21921, (301) 392-3366.

Fredrick: Fredrick Community College, Small Business Development Center, 5340 Spectrum Drive, Suite K, Fredrick, MD 21701, (301) 694-4647; FAX: (301) 695-7332.

Hagerstown: Hagerstown Junior College, Small Business Development Center, Advanced Technology Center, 751 Robin Hood Drive, Hagerstown, MD 21740, (301) 790-2800, ext. 388.

Landover: Suburban Washington Small Business Development Center, 9201 Basil Court, Suite 403, Landover, MD 20785, (301) 925-5460; FAX: (301) 925-5359.

Waldorf: Charles Community College, Southern Region Small Business Development Center, 235 Smallwood Village Center, Waldorf, MD 20601, (301) 932-4155.

Massachusetts

General Information

Massachusetts Office of Business Development, 100 Cambridge Street, Boston, MA 02202, (617) 727-3221; SPIRIT: (800) 632-8181 in Massachusetts only. Operates the "SPIRIT" Business Line, a toll-free, direct hot-line service to answer business-related questions.

Small Business Development Centers

The following offices offer free and fee-based services to new and expanding businesses:

Lead Center: Massachusetts Small Business Development Center, University of Massachusetts, 205 School of Management, Amherst, MA 01003; (413) 545-6301, FAX: (413) 545-1273

Boston: University of Massachusetts at Amherst, Minority Business Assistance Center, 250 Stuart Street, 12th Floor, Boston, MA 02116, (617) 287-7016; FAX: (617) 426-7854.

Chestnut Hill: Boston College, Metropolitan Regional Small Business Development Center, 96 College Road - Rahner House, Chestnut Hill, MA 02167, (617) 552-4091; FAX: (617) 552-2730.

Chestnut Hill: Boston College, Capital Formation Service/East, Small Business Development Center, 96 College Road - Rahner House, Chestnut Hill, MA 02167, (617) 552-4091; FAX: (617) 552-2730.

Fall River: University of Massachusetts at Dartmouth, Southeastern Massachusetts Regional Small Business Development Center, 200 Pocasset Street, P.O. Box 2785, Fall River, MA 02722, (508) 673-9783; FAX: (508) 674-1929.

Salem: Salem State College, North Shore Regional Small Business Development Center, 197 Essex Street, Salem, MA 01970, (508) 741-6343; FAX: (508) 741-6345.

Springfield: University of Massachusetts, Western Massachusetts Regional Small Business Development Center, 101 State Street, Suite #424, Springfield, MA 01103, (413) 737-6712; FAX: (413) 737-2312.

Worcester: Clark University, Central Massachusetts Regional Small Business Development Center, 950 Main Street, Worcester, MA 01610, (617) 793-7615; FAX: (508) 793-8890.

Michigan

General Information

Michigan Business Ombudsman, P.O. Box 30107, Lansing, MI 48909; (517) 373-6241, (800) 232-2727 in Michigan. Acts as a mediator in resolving regulatory disputes between business and the various state departments and also provides consultation and referral services. The ombudsman also serves as a "one-stop" center for business permits.

Small Business Advocate, Michigan Department of Commerce, P.O. Box 30225, Lansing, MI 48909; (517) 335-4720. Assistance in cutting bureaucratic red tape. Information and expertise in dealing with state, federal and local agencies.

Small Business Development Centers

The following offices offer free and fee based services to new and expanding businesses.

Lead Center: Michigan Small Business Development Center, 2727 Second Avenue, Detroit, MI 48201; (313) 577-4848, FAX: (313) 577-4222

Allendale: Ottawa County Economic Development Office, Inc., Small Business Development Center, 6676 Lake Michigan Drive, Allendale, MI 49401, (616) 892-4120; FAX: (616) 895-6670.

Ann Arbor: Merra Specialty Business Development Center, Small Business Development Center, 2200 Commonwealth, Suite 230, Ann Arbor, MI 48105, (313) 930-0034; FAX: (313) 663-6622.

Bad Axe: Huron County Economic Development Corporation (Satellite), Small Business Development Center, Huron County building, Room 303, Bad Axe, MI 48413, (517) 269-6431; FAX: (517) 269-7221.

Battle Creek: Kellogg Community College, Small Business Development Center, 450 North Avenue, Battle Creek, MI 49017-3397, (616) 965-3023; (800) 955-4KCC; FAX: (616) 965-4133.

Benton Harbor: Lake Michigan College, Small Business Development Center, Corporate and Community Services, 2755 E. Napier, Benton Harbor, MI 49022-1899, (616) 927-3571, ext. 247; FAX: (616) 927-4491.

Big Rapids: Ferris State University, Small Business Development Center, Alumni 226, 901 S. State Street, Big Rapids, MI 49307, (616) 592-3553; FAX: (616) 592-3539.

Cadillac: Wexfor-Missaukee Business Development Center (Satellite), 117 W. Cass Street, Suite 1, Cadillac, MI 49601-0026, (616) 775-9776; FAX: (616) 775-1440.

Caro: Tuscola County Economic Development Corporation, Small Business Development Center, 1184 Cleaver Road, Suite 800, Caro, MI 48723, (517) 673-2849; FAX: (517) 673-2517.

Detroit: NILAC-Marygrove College, Small Business Development Center, 8425

Be patient. If any phone number is incorrect, call (area code) 555-1212 and request the new listing.

Small Business and Entrepreneuring

West McNichols, Detroit, MI 48221, (313) 945-2159; FAX: (313) 864-6670.

Detroit: Wayne State University, Small Business Development Center, School of Business Administration, 2727 Second Avenue, Detroit, MI 48201, (313) 577-4850; FAX: (313) 577-8933.

Detroit: Comerica Small Business Development Center, 8300 Van Dyke, Detroit, MI 48213, (313) 571-1040.

East Lansing: Michigan State University, International Business Development Center, 6 Kellogg Center, East Lansing, MI 48824-1022, (517) 353-4336; FAX: (517) 336-1009; (800) 852-5727.

Escanaba: 1st Step, Inc., Small Business Development Center, 2415 14th Avenue, South, Escanaba, MI 49829, (906) 786-9234; FAX: (906) 786-4442.

Flint: Genesee Economic Area Revitalization, Inc. (Satellite), Small Business Development Center, 412 S. Saginaw Street, Flint, MI 48502, (313) 238-7803; FAX: (313) 238-7866.

Grand Rapids: Grand Rapids Community College, Small Business Development Center, Applied Technology Center, 151 Fountain N.E., Grand Rapids, MI 49503, (616) 771-3600; FAX: (616) 771-3605.

Hart: Oceana Economic Development Corporation (Satellite), Small Business Development Center, P.O. Box 168, Hart, MI 49420-0168, (616) 873-7141; FAX: (616) 873-3710.

Houghton: Michigan Technological University, Small Business Development Center, Bureau of Industrial Development, 1400 Townsend Drive, Houghton, MI 49931, (906) 487-2470; FAX: (906) 487-2858.

Howell: Livingston County Business Development Center, 404 E. Grand River, Howell, MI 48843, (517) 546-4020; FAX: (517) 546-4115.

Kalamazoo: Kalamazoo College, Small Business Development Center, Stryker Center for Management Studies, 1327 Academy Street, Kalamazoo, MI 49007, (616) 383-8602; FAX: (616) 383-5663.

Lansing: Lansing Community College, Small Business Development Center, P.O. Box 40010, Lansing, MI 48901, (517) 483-1921; FAX: (517) 483-9616.

Lapeer: Lapeer Development Corporation (Satellite), 449 McCormick Drive, Lapeer, MI 48446, (313) 667-0080; FAX: (313) 667-3541.

Marlette: Thumb Area Community Growth Alliance, Small Business Development Center, 3270 Wilson Street, Marlette, MI 48453, (517) 635-3561; FAX: (517) 635-2230.

Marquette: Northern Economic Initiative Corporation, Small Business Development Center, 1009 West Ridge Street, Marquette, MI 49855, (906) 228-5571; FAX: (906) 228-5572.

Mt. Clemens: Macomb County Business Assistance Network, 115 South Groesbeck Highway, Mt. Clemens, MI 48043, (313) 469-5118; FAX: (313) 469-6787.

Mt. Pleasant: Central Michigan University, Small Business Development Center, 256 Applied Business Studies Complex, Mt. Pleasant, MI 48859, (517) 774-3270; FAX: (517) 774-2372.

Muskegon: Muskegon Economic Growth Alliance, Small Business Development Center, 349 West Webster Avenue, Suite 104, P.O. Box 1087, Muskegon, MI 49443-1087, (616) 722-3751; FAX: (616) 728-7251.

Peck: Sanilac County Economic Growth (Satellite), 175 East Aitken Road, Peck, MI 48466, (313) 648-4311; FAX: (313) 648-4617.

Port Huron: St. Claire County Community College, Small Business Development Center, 323 Erie Street, P.O. Box 5015, Port Huron, MI 48061-5015, (313) 984-3881, ext. 457; FAX: (313) 984-2852.

Saginaw: Saginaw Future, Inc., Small Business Development Center, 301 East Genesee, Fourth Floor, Saginaw, MI 48607, (517) 754-8222; FAX: (517) 754-1715.

Scottville: West Shore Community College (Satellite), Business and Industrial Development, 3000 North Stiles Road, Scottville, MI 49454-0277, (616) 845-6211;

FAX: (616) 845-0207.

Sidney: Montcalm Community College (Satellite), 2800 College Drive SW, Sidney, MI 48885, (517) 328-2111; FAX: (517) 328-2950.

Sterling Heights: Sterling Heights Area Chamber of Commerce (Satellite), 12900 Paul, Suite 110, Sterling Heights, MI 48313, (313) 731-5400.

Traverse City: Northwestern Michigan College, Center for Business and Industry, 1701 East Front Street, Traverse City, MI 49684, (616) 922-1105.

Traverse City: Travers Bay Economic Development Corporation, Traverse City Small Business Development Center, 202 E. Grandview Parkway, P.O. Box 387, Traverse City, MI 49685-0387, (616) 946-1596; FAX: (616) 946-2565.

Traverse City: Greater Northwest Regional CDC, 2200 Dendrinos Drive, Traverse City, MI 49685-0506, (616) 929-5000.

Traverse City: Traverse City Area Chamber of Commerce BDC, 202 E. Grandview Parkway, P.O. Box 387, Traverse City, MI 49685-0387, (616) 947-5075.

Troy: Walsh/O.C.C. Business Enterprise Development Center, 340 E. Big Beaver, Suite 100, Troy, MI 48083, (313) 689-4094; FAX: (313) 689-4398.

University Center: Saginaw Valley State University (Satellite), Business and Industrial Development Institute, 2250 Pierce Road, University Center, MI 48710, (517) 790-4000; FAX: (517) 790-1314.

Minnesota

General Information

Minnesota Small Business Assistance Office, 900 American Center Building, 150 East Kellogg Boulevard, St. Paul, MN 55101; (612) 296-3871; Hotline: (800) 652-9747. Small business and business licensing assistance. Provides accurate, timely and comprehensive information and assistance to businesses in all areas of start-up, operation, and expansion. Referrals to other state agencies.

Small Business Advocate, Minnesota Small Business Assistance Office, 900 American Center, 150 Kellogg Boulevard, St. Paul, MN 55101; (612) 296-3871.

Small Business Development Centers

The following offices offer free and fee-based services to new and expanding businesses:

Lead Center:, Minnesota Small Business Development Center, Department of Trade and Economic Development, 900 American Center Building, 150 East Kellogg Blvd., St. Paul, MN 55101; (612) 297-5770, FAX: (612) 296-1290

Bemidji: Customized Training Center, Small Business Development Center, Bemidji Technical College, 905 Grant Avenue, SE, Bemidji, MN 56601, (218) 751-0979.

Bloomington: Normandale Community College, Small Business Development Center, 9700 France Avenue South, Bloomington, MN 55431, (612) 832-6395.

Brainerd: Brainerd Technical College, Small Business Development Center, 300 Quince Street, Brainerd, MN 56401, (218) 828-5302.

Duluth: University of Minnesota at Duluth, Small Business Development Center, 10 University Drive, 150 SBE, Duluth, MN 55811, (218) 726-8761.

Grand Rapids: Itasca Development Corporation, Grand Rapids Small Business Development Center, 19 NE Third Street, Grand Rapids, MN 55744, (218) 327-2241; FAX: (218) 681-5519.

Hibbing: Hibbing Community College, Small Business Development Center, 1515 East 25th Street, Hibbing, MN 55746, (218) 262-6700.

Mankato: Mankato State University, Small Business Development Center, Box 145, Mankato, MN 56001, (507) 389-1648.

Marshall: Southwest State University, Small Business Development Center, ST #105, Marshall, MN 56258, (507) 537-7386.

Be patient. If any phone number is incorrect, call (area code) 555-1212 and request the new listing.

State Starting Places for Money

Minneapolis: Minnesota Project Innovation, Small Business Development Center, Suite 410, 111 Third Avenue South, Minneapolis, MN 55401, (612) 338-3280.

Moorhead: Moorhead State University, Small Business Development Center, P.O. Box 303, Moorhead, MN 56560, (218) 236-2289.

Pine City: Pine Technical College, Small Business Development Center, Pine City, MN 55063, (612) 629-7340.

Red Wing: Red Wing Technical Institute, Small Business Development Center, Highway 58 at Pioneer Road, Red Wing, MN 55066, (612) 388-4079.

Rochester: Rochester Community College, Small Business Development Center, Highway 14 East, 851 30th Avenue, S.E., Rochester, MN 55904-4999, (507) 285-7536.

Rosemount: Dakota County Technical Institute, Small Business Development Center, 1300 145th Street East, Rosemount, MN 55068, (612) 423-8262.

St. Cloud: St. Cloud State University, Small Business Development Center, Business Resource Center, 1840 E. Hwy 23, St. Cloud, MN 56301, (612) 255-4842.

St. Paul: University of St. Thomas, Small Business Development Center, 23 Empire Drive, St. Paul, MN 55103, (612) 223-8663.

Thief River Falls: Thief River Falls Technical Institute, Small Business Development Center, Highway One East, Thief River Falls, MN 56701, (218) 681-5424; FAX: (218) 681-5519.

Virginia: Mesabi Community College, Small Business Development Center, 9th Avenue and W. Chestnut Street, Virginia, MN 55792, (218) 749-7729.

Wadena: Wadena Technical College, Small Business Development Center, 222 Second Street, SE, Wadena, MN 56482, (218) 631-1502.

White Bear Lake: North/East Metro Technical College, Small Business Development Center, 3554 White Bear Avenue, White Bear Lake, MN 55110, (612) 779-5764.

Winona: Winona State University, Small Business Development Center, Winona, MN 55987, (507) 457-5088.

Willmar: Willmar Small Business Development Center, Mid-Minnesota Development Commission, 333 West 6th Street, Willmar, MN 56201, (612) 235-8504.

Mississippi

General Information

The State of Mississippi, Department of Economic Development, 3825 Ridgewood Road, Jackson, MS 39211; (601) 982-6684.

Small Business Advocate, Mississippi Department of Economics, P.O. Box 849, Jackson, MS 39205; (601) 982-6518.

Small Business Development Centers

The following offices offer free and fee-based services to new and expanding businesses:

Lead Center: Mississippi Small Business Development Center, University of Mississippi, Old Chemistry Building, Suite 216, University, MS 38677; (601) 232-5001, FAX: (601) 232-5650

Booneville: Northeast Mississippi Community College, Small Business Development Center, Cunningham Blvd., Stringer Hall, 2nd Floor, Booneville, MS 38829, (601) 728-7751, ext. 317; FAX: (601) 728-1165.

Cleveland: Delta State University, Small Business Development Center, P.O. Box 3235 DSU, Cleveland, MS 38733, (601) 846-4236; FAX: (601) 846-4443.

Greenville: Delta Community College, Small Business Development Center, P.O. Box 5607, Greenville, MS 38704-5607, (601) 378-8183; FAX: (601) 378-5349.

Hattiesburg: Pearl River Community College, Small Business Development Center, Route 9, Box 1325, 5448 U.S. Highway 49 South, Hattiesburg, MS 39401, (601) 544-0030; FAX: (601) 544-0032.

Jackson: Jackson State University, Small Business Development Center, Suite A1, Jackson Enterprise Center, 931 Highway 80 West, Jackson, MS 39204, (601) 968-2795; FAX: (601) 968-2358.

Jackson: Mississippi Department of Economic and Community Development, Small Business Development Center, P.O. Box 849, Jackson, MS 39205, (601) 359-3179; FAX: (601) 359-2832.

Long Beach: University of Southern Mississippi, Small Business Development Center, USM Gulf Park Campus, Long Beach, MS 39560, (601) 865-4578; FAX: (601) 865-4544.

Meridian: Meridian Community College, Small Business Development Center, 5500 Highway 19 North, Meridian, MS 39307, (601) 482-7445; FAX: (601) 482-5803.

Mississippi State: Mississippi State University, Small Business Development Center, P.O. Drawer 5288, Mississippi State, MS 39762, (601) 325-8684; FAX: (601) 325-8686.

Natchez: Copiah-Lincoln Community College, Small Business Development Center, Natchez Campus, Natchez, MS 39120, (601) 445-5254; FAX: (601) 446-9967.

Raymond: Hinds Community College, Small Business Development Center, International Trade Center, P.O. Box 1170, Raymond, MS 39154, (601) 857-3536; FAX: (601) 857-3535.

Tupelo: Itawamba Community College, Small Business Development Center, 653 Eason Blvd., Tupelo, MS 38801, (601) 680-8515; FAX: (601) 680-8423.

University: University of Mississippi, Small Business Development Center, Old Chemistry Building, Suite 216, University, MS 38677, (601) 234-2120; FAX: (601) 232-5650.

Missouri

General Information

Missouri Business Assistance Center, Department of Economic Development, P.O. Box 118, Jefferson City, MO 65102, First-Stop Shop: (800) 523-1434. The First-Stop Shop number for Missouri residents serves to link business owners and state government and provides information on state rules, regulations, licenses, and permits. The Business Assistance Center provides information and technical assistance to start-up and existing businesses on available state and federal programs.

Federal Information Center, Federal Building, 1520 Market Street, Kansas City, MO 64106, (800) 892-5808 in Missouri; or Federal Information Center, Federal Building, 1520 Market Street, St. Louis, MO 63103, (800) 392-7711 in Missouri. Both locations offer information regarding Missouri programs for business people.

Small Business Advocate, Department of Economic Development, P.O. Box 118, Jefferson City, MO 65102; (314) 751-4982. Assistance in cutting bureaucratic red tape. Information and expertise in dealing with state, federal, and local agencies.

Small Business Development Centers

The following offices offer free and fee-based services to new and expanding businesses:

Lead Center: Missouri Small Business Development Center, University of Missouri, Suite 300, University Place, Columbia, MO 65211; (314) 882-0344, FAX: (314) 884-4297

Cape Girardeau: Southwest Missouri State University, Small Business Development Center, 222 N. Pacific, Cape Girardeau, MO 63701, (314) 290-5965; FAX: (314) 651-5005 (call first).

Columbia: University of Missouri at Columbia, Small Business Development

Be patient. If any phone number is incorrect, call (area code) 555-1212 and request the new listing.

Small Business and Entrepreneuring

Center, 1800 University Place, Columbia, MO 65211, (314) 882-7096; FAX: (314) 882-6156.

Flat River: Mineral Area College, Small Business Development Center, P.O. Box 1000, Flat River, MO 63601, (314) 431-4593, ext. 283; FAX: (314) 431-6807.

Joplin: Missouri Southern State College, Small Business Development Center, 107 Mathews Hall, 3950 Newman Road, Joplin, MO 64801-1595, (417) 625-9313; FAX: (417) 625-3121.

Kansas City: Rockhurst College, Small Business Development Center, 1100 Rockhurst Road, Kansas City, MO 64110-2599, (816) 926-4572; FAX: (816) 926-4588.

Kirksville: Northeast Missouri State University, Small Business Development Center, 207 East Patterson, Kirksville, MO 63501, (816) 785-4307; FAX: (816) 785-4181.

Maryville: Northwest Missouri State University, Small Business Development Center, 127 South Buchanan, Maryville, MO 64468, (816) 562-1701; FAX: (816) 582-8469.

Poplar Bluff: Three Rivers Community College, Small Business Development Center, Business Incubator Building, 3019 Fair Street, Poplar Bluff, MO 63901, (314) 686-3499; FAX: (314) 686-5467 (call first).

Rolla: Center for Technology Transfer and Economic Development, University of Missouri at Rolla, Room 104, Building 1, Nagogami Terrace, Rolla, MO 65401-0249, (314) 341-4992; FAX: (314) 341-4559.

Rolla: University of Missouri at Rolla, Small Business Development Center, 223 Engineering Management Building, Rolla, MO 65401-0249, (314) 341-4561; FAX: (314) 341-2071.

St. Louis: St. Louis University, Small Business Development Center, 3642 Lindell Boulevard, St. Louis, MO 63108, (314) 534-7232; FAX: (314) 658-3897.

Springfield: Southwest Missouri State University, Small Business Development Center, Center for Business Research, 901 S. National, Box 88, Springfield, MO 65804-0089, (417) 836-5685; FAX: (417) 836-6337.

Warrensburg: Central Missouri State University, Center for Technology, Grinstead #75, Warrensburg, MO 64093-5037, (816) 543-4402; FAX: (816) 747-1653.

Warrensburg: Central Missouri State, Small Business Development Center, Grinstead #75, Warrensburg, MO 64093-5037, (816) 543-4402; FAX: (816) 747-1653.

Montana

General Information

Business Assistance Division, Department of Commerce, 1424 Ninth Avenue, Helena, MT 59620; (406) 444-3923. *A Guide to Montana's Economic Development Assistance Program*, which lists state and federal agencies and other sources of business assistance is available at no charge.

Division of Small Business Advocacy and Business Licensing, Department of Commerce, 1424 Ninth Avenue, Helena, MT 59620, (800) 221-8015 (in-state only). Offers a toll-free number for licensing and permit questions. Also acts as an advocate for small businesses.

Small Business Advocate, Business Assistance Division, Department of Commerce, 1424 Ninth Avenue, Helena, MT 59620; (406) 444-4380. Assistance in cutting bureaucratic red tape. Information and expertise in dealing with state, federal, and local agencies.

Small Business Development Centers

These offices offer free and fee-based services to new and expanding businesses:

Lead Center: Montana Small Business Development Center, Department of Commerce, 1424 Ninth Avenue, Helena, MT 59620; (406) 444-4780, FAX: (406) 444-2808

Billings: Billings Area Business Incubator, Small Business Development Center, 115 N. Broadway, 2nd Floor, Billings, MT 59101, (406) 256-6875; FAX: (406) 255-7175.

Bozeman: Bozeman Human Resources Development Council, Small Business Development Center, 321 East Main, Suite 413, Bozeman, MT 59715, (406) 587-3113; FAX: (406) 587-9565.

Butte: Butte REDI, Small Business Development Center, 305 W. Mercury Street, Suite 211, Butte, MT 59701, (406) 782-7333; FAX: (406) 782-9675.

Haver: Haver Small Business Development Center, Bear Paw Development Corporation, P.O. Box 1549, Haver, MT 59501, (406) 265-9226; FAX: (406) 265-3777.

Kalispell: Flathead Valley Community College, Small Business Development Center, 777 Grandview Drive, Kalispell, MT 59901, (406) 756-3835; FAX: (406) 786-3815.

Missoula: Missoula Incubator, Small Business Development Center, 127 N. Higgins, 3rd Floor, Missoula, MT 59802, (406) 278-9234; FAX: (406) 721-4584.

Sidney: Sidney Small Business Development Center, 123 W. Main, Sidney, MT 59270, (406) 482-5024; FAX: (406) 482-5306.

Nebraska

General Information

Department of Economic Development, Research Division, P.O. Box 94666, 301 Centennial Mall South, Lincoln, NE 69509; (402) 471-3782; (800) 426-6505 in state. One-Stop Business Assistance Program: Provides information on technical assistance, regulations licenses, and taxes as well as marketing, patents, and business counseling.

Department of Economic Development, Small Business Division, P.O. Box 94666, 301 Centennial Mall South, Lincoln, NE 69509; (402) 471-3111. Offers technical assistance to small businesses and acts as a clearinghouse for information on other state services. Activities include acting as a link between business and government contracts, promoting exports of Nebraska products to foreign markets, maintaining a job training liaison to coordinate labor training with industrial location and expansion, maintaining business finance consultants in outreach offices, and providing information on federal programs such as Community Development Block Grants, SBA loans, and FmHA Business and Industry loans.

Small Business Advocate, Small Business Division, P.O. Box 94666, 301 Centennial Mall South, Lincoln, NE 68509, (402) 471-3742. Assistance in cutting bureaucratic red tape. Information and expertise in dealing with state, federal, and local agencies.

Small Business Development Centers

These offices offer free and fee-based services to new and expanding businesses:

Lead Center: Nebraska Small Business Development Center, University of Nebraska, 60th and Dodge Street, CBA, Room 407, Omaha, NE 68182; (402) 554-2521, FAX: (402) 554-3747

Chadron: Chadron State College, Small Business Development Center, Administration Building, Chadron, NE 69337, (308) 432-6282.

Kearney: University of Nebraska at Kearney, Small Business Development Center, Welch Hall, 19th and College Drive, Kearney, NE 68849, (308) 234-8344.

Lincoln: University of Nebraska at Lincoln, Small Business Development Center, Cornhusker Bank Bldg., 11th and Cornhusker Hwy., Suite 302, Lincoln, NE 68521, (402) 472-3358.

North Platte: Mid-Plains Community College, Small Business Development Center, 416 North Jeffers, Room 26, North Platte, NE 69101, (308) 534-5115.

Omaha: University of Nebraska at Omaha, Small Business Development Center, Peter Keiwit Conference Center, 1313 Farnam, Suite 132, Omaha, NE 68182, (402) 595-2381.

Be patient. If any phone number is incorrect, call (area code) 555-1212 and request the new listing.

State Starting Places for Money

Peru: Peru State College, Small Business Development Center, T.J. Majors Building, Room 248, Peru, NE 68421, (402) 872-2274.

Scottsbluff: Small Business Development Center, Nebraska Public Power Building, 1721 Broadway, Room 408, Scottsbluff, NE 69361, (308) 635-7513.

Wayne: Wayne State College, Small Business Development Center, Connell Hall, Wayne, NE 68787, (402) 375-7575.

Nevada

General Information

State of Nevada Commission on Economic Development, Capitol Complex, Carson City, NV 89710; (702) 885-4325; (800) 336-1600 in Nevada. Publishes a pamphlet, *Backing Business in Nevada,* which lists state resources for business retention and expansion. Acts as a clearinghouse for information and technical assistance. Operates several business assistance programs and performs advertising and public relations activities on behalf of Nevada business.

Small Business Advocate, Nevada Office of Community Services, Capitol Complex, Suite 116, 1100 East William, Carson City, NV 89710; (702) 885-4602.

Small Business Development Centers

These offices offer free and fee-based services to new and expanding businesses:

Lead Center: Nevada Small Business Development Center, University of Nevada at Reno, College of Business Administration, Room 411, Reno, NV 89577-0100; (702) 784-1717, FAX: (702) 784-4305

Elko: Northern Nevada Community College, Small Business Development Center, 901 Elm Street, Elko, NV 89801, (702) 738-8493.

Las Vegas: University of Nevada at Las Vegas, Small Business Development Center, College of Business and Economics, 4505 Maryland Parkway, Las Vegas, NV 89154, (702) 739-0852.

New Hampshire

General Information

Small Business Advocate, Department of Resources and Economic Development, Division of Economics, Prescott Park, 105 Loudon Rd., Concord, NH 03301.

Small Business Development Centers

The following offices offer free and fee-based services to new and expanding businesses:

Lead Center: New Hampshire Small Business Development Center, University of New Hampshire, 108 McConnell Hall, Durham, NH 03824; (603) 862-2200, FAX: (603) 862-4468

Durham: Office of Economic Initiatives, Heidelberg Harris Building, Technology Drive, Durham, NH 03824, (603) 862-0710.

Durham: Small Business Development Center, Heidelberg Harris Building, Technology Drive, Durham, NH 03824, (603) 862-0700.

Keene: Keene State College, Small Business Development Center, Blake House, Keene, NH 03431, (603) 358-2602.

Littleton: Small Business Development Center, P.O. Box 786, Littleton, NH 03561, (603) 444-1053.

Manchester: Small Business Development Center, 1001 Elm Street, Manchester, NH 03101, (603) 624-2000.

Plymouth: Plymouth State College, Small Business Development Center, Hyde Hall, Plymouth, NH 03264, (603) 535-2523.

Nashua: Center for Economic Development, Small Business Development Center, 188 Main Street, Nashua, NH 03062, (603) 881-8333.

New Jersey

General Information

Office of Small Business Assistance, Capital Place One, 200 S. Warren Street, CN 835, Trenton, NJ 08625; (609) 984-4442. Advice on expansion and business start-ups, and marketing and procurement assistance are some of the services available to small businesses. The office also offers seminars throughout the state as part of its outreach program.

Small Business Advocate, Office of Business Advocacy, Capital Place One, 200 S. Warren Street, CN 823, Trenton, NJ 08625; (609) 292-0700. Assistance in cutting bureaucratic red tape. Information and expertise in dealing with state, federal, and local agencies.

Small Business Development Centers

The following offices offer free and fee-based services to new and expanding businesses:

Lead Center: New Jersey Small Business Development Center, Rutgers Graduate School of Management, University Heights, 180 University Avenue, Newark, NJ 07102; (201) 648-5950, FAX: (201) 648-1110

Atlantic City: Small Business Development Center, Greater Atlantic City Chamber of Commerce, 1301 Atlantic Avenue, Atlantic City, NJ 08401, (609) 345-5600; FAXL (609) 345-4524.

Camden: Rutgers - The State University Of New Jersey at Camden, Small Business Development Center, Business and Science Building, 2nd Floor, Camden, NJ 08102, (609) 757-6221; FAX: (609) 757-6231.

Lincroft: Brookdale Community College, Small Business Development Center, Newman Springs Road, Lincroft, NJ 07738, (908) 842-8685; FAX: (908) 842-0203.

Newark: Rutgers - The State University of New Jersey at Camden, Small Business Development Center, University Heights, 180 University Ave., 3rd Floor, Newark, NJ 07102, (201) 648-5950; FAX: (201) 648-1110.

Trenton: Mercer County Community College, Small Business Development Center, P.O. Box B, Trenton, NJ 08690, (609) 586-4800; FAX: (609) 890-6338.

Trenton: Mercer County Community College, Small Business Development Center, James Kerney Campus, North Broad and Academy Streets, Trenton, NJ 08608, (609) 586-4800, ext. 633.

Union: Kean College of New Jersey, Small Business Development Center, East Campus, Room 242, Union, NJ 07083, (908) 527-2946; FAX: (908) 527-2960.

Washington: Warren County Community College, Small Business Development Center, Route 57 West, Box 55A, Washington, NJ 07882-9605, (201) 689-7613; FAX: (908) 689-7488.

New Mexico

General Information

Business Development Section, Department of Economic Development and Tourism, Joseph Montoya Building, 1100 St. Francis Drive, P.O. Box 20003, Sante Fe, NM 87503; (505) 827-0300.

Small Business Advocate, Department of Economic Development and Tourism, Joseph Montoya Building, P.O. Box 20003, 1100 St. Francis Drive, Santa Fe, NM 87503; (505) 827-0300. Assistance in cutting bureaucratic red tape. Information and expertise in dealing with state, federal, and local agencies.

Small Business Development Centers

The following offices offer free and fee-based services to new and expanding businesses:

Lead Center: New Mexico Small Business Development Center, Santa Fe Community College, P.O. Box 4187, Santa Fe, NM 87502-4187; (505) 438-1362, FAX: (505) 438-1237

Be patient. If any phone number is incorrect, call (area code) 555-1212 and request the new listing.

Small Business and Entrepreneuring

Alamogordo: New Mexico State University at Alamogordo, Small Business Development Center, 1000 Madison, Alamogordo, NM 87310, (505) 434-5272.

Albuquerque: Albuquerque Technical Vocational Institute, Small Business Development Center, 525 Buena Vista SE, Albuquerque, NM 87106, (505) 224-4246.

Carlsbad: New Mexico State University at Carlsbad, Small Business Development Center, 301 South Canal, P.O. Box 1090, Carlsbad, NM 88220, (505) 887-6562.

Clovis: Clovis Community College, Small Business Development Center, 417 Schepps Blvd., Clovis, NM 88101, (505) 769-4136.

Espanola: Northern New Mexico Community College, Small Business Development Center, 1002 N. Onate Street, Espanola, NM 87532, (505) 753-7141.

Farmington: San Juan College, Small Business Development Center, 203 West Main, Suite 201, Farmington, NM 87401, (505) 326-4321.

Gallup: University of New Mexico at Gallup, Small Business Development Center, 103 W. Highway 66, P.O. Box 1395, Gallup, NM 87305, (505) 722-2220.

Grants: New Mexico State University at Grants, Small Business Development Center, 709 E. Roosevelt Ave., Grants, NM 87020, (505) 287-8821.

Hobbs: New Mexico Junior College, Small Business Development Center, 5317 Lovington Highway, Hobbs, NM 88240, (505) 392-4510.

Las Cruces: Dona Ana Branch Community College, Small Business Development Center, 3400 S. Espina Street, Box 30001, Department 3DA, Las Cruces, NM 88003-0001, (505) 527-7566.

Las Vegas: Luna Vocational Technical Institute, Small Business Development Center, Luna Camp, P.O. Drawer K. Las Vegas, NM 88701, (505) 454-2595.

Los Alamos: University of New Mexico at Los Alamos, Small Business Development Center, 901 18th Street, #18, P.O. Box 715, Los Alamos, NM 87544, (505) 662-0001.

Los Lunas: University of New Mexico at Valencia, Small Business Development Center, 280 La Entrada, Los Lunas, NM 87031, (505) 865-9596, ext. 317.

Roswell: Eastern New Mexico University at Roswell, Small Business Development Center, #57 University Ave., P.O. Box 6000, Roswell, NM 88201-6000, (505) 624-7133.

Santa Fe: Santa Fe Community College, Small Business Development Center, South Richards Avenue, P.O. Box 4187, Santa Fe, NM 87502-4187, (505) 438-1343.

Silver City: Western New Mexico University, Southwest Small Business Development Center, Glazer Hall, Continuing Education Department, P.O. Box 2672, Silver City, NM 88062, (505) 538-6320.

Tucumcari: Tucumcari Area Vocational School, Small Business Development Center, 824 W. Hines, P.O. Box 1143, Tucumcari, NM 88401, (505) 461-4413.

New York

General Information

Business Opportunity Center, New York State Department of Economic Development, Business Opportunity Center, Albany, NY 12245, (800) STATE NY. A special service that offers fast, up- to-date information on the State's business development programs and can help in making contact with appropriate agencies.

Small Business Advocate, Director of Advocacy, New York State Department of Economic Development, 1515 Broadway, 51st floor, New York, NY 10036; (212) 309-0466.

Small Business Development Centers

The following offices offer free and fee-based services to new and expanding businesses:

Lead Center: New York Small Business Development Center, State University of New York, State University Plaza, S-523, Albany, NJ 12246; (518) 443-5398, (800) 732-7232, FAX: (518) 465-4992

Albany: State University of New York at Albany (SUNY), Small Business Development Center, Draper Hall, 107, 135 Western Ave., Albany, NY 12222, (518) 442-5577; FAX: (518) 442-5582.

Binghamton: SUNY at Binghamton, Small Business Development Center, P.O. Box 6000, Vestal Parkway East, Binghamton, NY 13902-6000, (607) 777-4024; FAX: (607) 777-4029.

Brooklyn: Long Island University, Small Business Development Center, School of Business, One University Plaza, Humanities Building, 7th Floor, Brooklyn, NY 11201, (718) 852-1197; FAX: (718) 852-3447.

Buffalo: State University College at Buffalo, Small Business Development Center, 1300 Elmwood Avenue, BA 117, Buffalo, NY 14222, (716) 878-4030; FAX: (716) 878-4067.

Corning: Corning Community College, Small Business Development Center, 24-28 Denison Parkway West, Corning, NY 14830, (607) 962-9461; FAX: (607) 936-6642.

Dobbs Ferry: Rockland Community College at Suffern, Small Business Development Center, Westchester Outreach Center, Mercy College, 555 Broadway, Dobbs Ferry, NY 10522, (914) 693-4500, ext. 485; FAX: (914) 693-4996.

Farmingdale: SUNY College of Technology at Farmingdale, Small Business Development Center, Laffin Administration Building, Farmingdale, NY 11735, (516) 420-2765; FAX: (516) 293-5343.

Jamaica: York College, Small Business Development Center, Science Building, Room 107, The City University of New York, Jamaica, NY 11451, (718) 262-2880; FAX: (718) 262-2881.

Jamestown: Jamestown Community College, Small Business Development Center, P.O. Box 20, Jamestown, NY 14702-0020, (716) 665-5220, (800) 522-7232; FAX: (716) 665-6733.

New York: Pace University, Small Business Development Center, Pace Plaza, New York, NY 10038, (212) 346-1899; FAX: (212) 346-1613.

Plattsburgh: Clinton Community College, Small Business Development Center, Alpert Bldg., Route 9, Plattsburgh, NY 12901, (518) 562-4260; FAX: (518) 563-9759.

Riverdale: Manhattan College, Small Business Development Center, School of Business, Farrell Hall, Riverdale, NY 10471, (212) 884-1880; FAX: (212) 549-0089.

Rochester: Monroe Community College at Rochester, Small Business Development Center, 1000 East Henrietta Road, Rochester, NY 14623, (706) 292-2000, ext. 303D.

Sanborn: Niagara County Community College at Sanborn, Small Business Development Center, 3111 Saunders Settlement Road, Sanborn, NY 14132, (716) 693-1910; FAX: (716) 731-3595.

Stone Ridge: Ulter County Community College at Stone Ridge, Small Business Development Center, Stone Ridge, NY 12484, (914) 687-5272; FAX: (914) 687-5271.

Stony Brook: SUNY at Stony Brook, Small Business Development Center, Harriman Hall, Room 109, Stony Brook, NY 11794, (516) 632-9070; FAX: (516) 632-7176.

Suffern: Rockland Community College at Suffern, Small Business Development Center, 145 College Road, Suffern, NY 10901, (914) 356-0370; FAX: (914) 356-0381.

Syracuse: Onondaga Community College at Syracuse, Small Business Development Center, Greater Syracuse Incubator Center, 1201 East Fayette Street, Syracuse, NY 13210, (315) 475-0083; FAX: (315) 475-8460.

Utica: SUNY College of Technology at Utica/Rome, Small Business

State Starting Places for Money

Development Center, P.O. Box 3050, Utica, NY 13504-3050, (315) 792-7546; FAX: (315) 792-7554.

Watertown: Jefferson Community College at Watertown, Small Business Development Center, Watertown, NY 13601, (315) 782-9262; FAX: (315) 782-0901.

North Carolina

General Information

North Carolina Department of Commerce, Small Business Development Division, 430 N. Salisbury St., Raleigh, NC 27603; (919) 733-4151. Coordinates state small business assistance programs and financing. Includes pooled industrial revenue bonds, a certified SBA Development Company, and a long-term, fixed-rate financing program. Also provides information and referral services to small firms and prospective entrepreneurs and acts as advocate for the state's small business community.

Small Business Advocate, Small Business Development Division, North Carolina Department of Commerce, Dobbs Building Room 2019, 430 North Salisbury St., Raleigh, NC 27611; (919) 733-7980. Assistance in cutting bureaucratic red tape. Information and expertise in dealing with state, federal, and local agencies.

Small Business Development Centers

The following offices offer free and fee-based services to new and expanding businesses:

Lead Center: North Carolina Small Business Development Center, University of North Carolina, 4509 Creedmoor Road, Suite 201, Raleigh, NC 27612; (919) 571-4154, FAX: (919) 571-4161

Boone: Appalachian State University, Small Business Development Center, Northwestern Region, Walker College of Business, Boone, NC, 28608, (704) 262-2095; FAX: (704) 262-2027.

Chapel Hill: Small Business Development Center, Central Carolina Region, 608 Airport Road, Suite B, Chapel Hill, NC 27514, (919) 962-0389.

Charlotte: Small Business Development Center, Southern Piedmont Region, The Ben Craig Center, 8701 Mallard Creek Road, Charlotte, NC 28262, (704) 548-1090; FAX: (704) 548-9050.

Cullowhee: Small Business Development Center, Center for Improving Mountain Living, Western Carolina University, Cullowhee, NC 28723, (704) 227-7494; FAX: (704) 227-7422.

Elizabeth City: Elizabeth City State University, Small Business Development Center, Northeastern Region, P.O. Box 874, Elizabeth City, NC 27909, (919) 335-3247; FAX: (919) 335-3648.

Fayetteville: Fayetteville State University, Small Business Development Center, Cape Fear Region, Continuing Education Center, P.O. Box 1334, Fayetteville, NC 28302, (919) 486-1727; FAX: (919) 486-1949.

Greenville: East Carolina University, Small Business Development Center, Eastern Region, Corner of First and Reade Street, Greenville, NC, 27858-4353, (919) 757-6157; FAX: (919) 757-6992.

Wilmington: University of North Carolina at Wilmington, Small Business Development Center, Southeastern Region, Room 131, Cameron Hall, 601 South College Road, Wilmington, NC 28403, (919) 395-3744; FAX: (919) 395-3815.

Winston-Salem: Winston-Salem University, Small Business Development Center, Northern Piedmont Region, P.O. Box 13025, Winston-Salem, NC 27110, (919) 750-2030; FAX: (919) 750-2031.

North Dakota

General Information

Center for Innovation and Business Development, Box 8103, University Station, Grand Forks, ND 58202; (701) 777-3132. The "Do It Yourself" Entrepreneur Kit is a step-by-step guide, with optional software, to writing your own business and marketing plan. It is targeted to new manufacturing ventures producing new products or technology, but the guide can also be relevant to many entrepreneurs, academics, and business professionals.

Small Business Advocate, North Dakota Development Commission, Liberty Memorial Building, Bismarck, ND 58501; (701) 224-2810. Assistance in cutting bureaucratic red tape. Information and expertise in dealing with state, federal, and local agencies.

Small Business Development Centers

The following offices offer free and fee-based services to new and expanding businesses:

Lead Center: North Dakota Small Business Development Center, University of North Dakota, 118 Gamble Hall, Box 7308, Grand Forks, ND 58202; (701) 777-3700, FAX: (701) 777-5099

Bismarck: Small Business Development Center, Bismarck Regional Center, 400 East Broadway, Suite 421, Bismarck, ND 58501, (701) 223-8583; FAX: (701) 222-3843.

Dickinson: Small Business Development Center, Dickinson Regional Center, 314 3rd Avenue West, Drawer L, Dickinson, ND 58602, (701) 227-2096; FAX: (701) 225-5116.

Fargo: Small Business Development Center, Fargo Regional Center, 417 Main Avenue, Fargo, ND 58103, (701) 237-0986; FAX: (701) 235-6706.

Grand Forks: Small Business Development Center, Grand Forks Regional Center, The Hemmp Center, 1407 24th Avenue S., Suite 201, Grand Forks, ND 58201, (701) 772-8502; FAX: (701) 775-2772.

Minot: Small Business Development Center, Minot Regional Center, 1020 20th Avenue Southwest, P.O. Box 940, Minot, ND 58702, (701) 852-8861; FAX: (701) 838-2488.

Ohio

General Information

Ohio Department of Development, P.O. Box 1001, Columbus, OH 43266-0101; (614) 644-8748; (800) 248-4040, in Ohio. The Ohio One-Stop Business Permit Center provides new entrepreneurs with licensing and permit information and directs them to the proper department for specific aid.

Small Business Advocate, Small And Developing Business Division, Ohio Department of Development, 30 East Broad St., 23rd Floor, P.O. Box 100, Columbus, OH 43266-0101; (614) 466-2718. Assistance in cutting bureaucratic red tape. Information and expertise in dealing with state, federal, and local agencies.

Small Business Development Centers

The following offices offer free and fee-based services to new and expanding businesses:

Lead Center: Ohio Small Business Development Center, Department of Development, State Office Tower, P.O. Box 1001, Columbus, OH 43226-0101; (614) 466-2480, FAX: (614) 466-0829

Akron: Small Business Development Center, Akron Regional Development Board, One Cascade Plaza, 8th Floor, Akron, OH 44308, (216) 379-3170; FAX: (216) 379-3164.

Archbold: Northwest Technical College, Small Business Development Center, Star Route 34, Box 246-A, Archbold, OH 43502, (419) 267-5511; FAX: (419) 267-5233.

Athens: Ohio University, Small Business Development Center, Innovation Center, One President Drive, Suite 104, Athens, OH 45701, (614) 593-1797; FAX: (614) 593-1795.

Athens: Athens Small Business Center, Inc., 900 East State Street, Athens OH 45701, (614) 582-1188; FAX: (614) 593-7744.

Be patient. If any phone number is incorrect, call (area code) 555-1212 and request the new listing.

Small Business and Entrepreneuring

Bowling Green: Wood County Small Business Development Center, WSOS Community Action Commission, Inc., P.O. Box 48, 118 E. Oak Street, Bowling Green, OH 43402, (419) 352-7469; FAX: (419) 353-3291.

Canton: Small Business Development Center, Greater Stark Development Board, 800 Savannah Avenue, N.E., Canton, OH 44704, (216) 453-5900; FAX: (216) 453-1793.

Celina: Wright State University, Lake Campus, Small Business Development Center, 7600 State Route 703, Celina, OH 45882, (419) 586-2365; FAX: (419) 586-4048.

Chillicothe: Chillicothe-Ross Chamber of Commerce, Small Business Development Center, 165 S. Paint Street, Chillicothe, OH 45601, (614) 772-4530; FAX: (614) 772-5335.

Cincinnati: Cincinnati Small Business Development Center, IAMS Research Park, MC189, 1111 Edison Avenue, Cincinnati, OH 45216-2265, (513) 753-7141; FAX: (513) 948-2109.

Cincinnati: Clemont County Chamber of Commerce, Small Business Development Center, 4440 Glen Este-Withamsville Road, Cincinnati, OH, (513) 753-7141; FAX: (513) 753-7146.

Cleveland: Greater Cleveland Growth Association, Small Business Development Center, 200 Tower City Center, 50 Public Square, Cleveland, OH 44113-2291, (216) 621-3300; FAX: (216) 621-6013.

Columbus: Columbus Small Business Development Center, Columbus Area Chamber of Commerce, 37 North High Street, Columbus, OH 43216, (614) 221-1321; FAX: (614) 469-8250.

Coshocton: Coshocton Area Chamber of Commerce, Small Business Development Center, 124 Chestnut Street, Coshocton, OH 43812, (614) 622-5411; FAX: (614) 622-9902.

Dayton: Dayton Area Chamber of Commerce, Small Business Development Center, Chamber Plaza, 5th and Main Streets, Dayton, OH 45402-2400, (513) 226-8230; FAX: (513) 226-8294.

Fremont: North Central Small Business Development Center, Fremond Office, Terra Technical College, 1220 Cedar Street, Freemont, OH 43420, (419) 332-1002; FAX: (419) 334-2300.

Jefferson: Ashtabula County Economic Development Council, Inc., Small Business Development Center, 36 West Walnut Street, Jefferson, OH 44047, (216) 576-9134; FAX: (216) 576-5003.

Lima: Lima Technical College, Small Business Development Center, 545 West Market Street, Suite 305, Lima, OH 45801-5320, (419) 229-5320; FAX: (419) 229-5424.

Logan: Logan-Hocking Chamber of Commerce, Small Business Development Center, 11 1/2 West Main Street, Box 838, Logan, OH 43138, (614) 385-7259; FAX: (614) 385-8999.

Lorain: Lorain County Chamber of Commerce, Small Business Development Center, 6001 S. Broadway, Lorain, OH 44053, (216) 246-2833; FAX: (216) 246-4050.

Mansfield: Mid-Ohio Small Business Development Center, 193 N. Main Street, Mansfield, OH 44902, (419) 332-1002; FAX: (419) 522-4198.

Marietta: Marietta College, Small Business Development Center, Marietta, OH 45750, (614) 374-4649; FAX: (614) 374-4763.

Marion: Marion Small Business Development Center, Marion Area Chamber of Commerce, 206 S. Prospect Street, Marion, OH 43302, (614) 382-2181; FAX: (614) 387-7722.

Mentor: Lakeland Community College, Lake County Economic Development Center, Small Business Development Center, Mentor, OH 44080, (216) 951-1290; FAX: (216) 953-4413.

New Philadelphia: Tuscarawas Chamber of Commerce, Small Business Development Center, 1323 Fourth Street, NW, P.O. Box 232, New Philadelphia, OH 44663, (216) 343-4474; FAX: (216) 343-6526.

Piqua: Upper Valley Joint Vocational School, Small Business Development Center, 8811 Career Drive, North County Road 25A, Piqua, OH 45356, (513) 778-8419; FAX: (513) 778-9237.

Portsmouth: Portsmouth Area Chamber of Commerce, Small Business Development Center, P.O. Box 509, 729 Sixth Street, Portsmouth, OH 45662, (614) 353-1116; FAX: (614) 353-5824.

St. Clairsville: Department of Development of the CIC of Belmont County, Small Business Development Center, St. Clairsville Office, 100 East Main Street, St. Clairsville, OH 43950, (614) 695-9678; FAX: (614) 695-4921.

Sandusky: North Central Small Business Development Center, Sandusky Office, 407 Decatur Street, Sandusky, OH 44870, (800) 548-6507; FAX: (419) 626-9176.

Southport: Lawrence County Chamber of Commerce, Small Business Development Center, U.S. Route 52 and Solida Road, P.O. Box 488, Southport, OH 45680, (614) 894-3838; FAX: (614) 894-3836.

Steubenville: Greater Steubenville Chamber of Commerce, Small Business Development Center, 630 Market Street, P.O. Box 278, Steubenville, OH 43952, (614) 282-6226; FAX: (614) 282-6285.

Youngstown: Youngstown State University, Cushwa Center for Industrial Development, Small Business Development Center, Youngstown, OH 44555, (216) 742-3495; FAX: (216) 742-3784.

Zanesville: Zanesville Area Chamber of Commerce, Small Business Development Center, 217 North Fifth Street, Zanesville, OH 43701, (614) 452-4868; FAX: (614) 454-2963.

Oklahoma

General Information

Teamwork Oklahoma, 6601 Broadway Extension, Oklahoma City, OK 73116; (405) 843-9770; (800) 522-OKLA, in Oklahoma. Acquaints businesspersons or potential businessperson with the many financial and consulting services available in Oklahoma.

Small Business Advocate, Oklahoma Department of Commerce, Five Broadway, Executive Park, 6001 Broadway Ext. Oklahoma City, OK 73116-8214. Assistance in cutting bureaucratic red tape. Information and expertise in dealing with state, federal, and local agencies.

Small Business Development Centers

The following offices offer free and fee-based services to new and expanding businesses:

Lead Center: Oklahoma Small Business Development Center Network, Southeastern Oklahoma State University, Station A, Box 2584, Durant, OK 74701; (405) 924-0277, (800) 522-6154, FAX: (405) 924-8531

Ada: East Central State University, Small Business Development Center, 1036 East 10th, Ada, OK 74820, (405) 436-3190; FAX: (405) 521-6516.

Alva: Northwestern State University, Small Business Development Center, Alva, OK 73717, (405) 327-5883; FAX: (405) 327-1881.

Durant: Southeastern State University, Small Business Development Center, 517 University, Durant, OK 74701, (405) 924-0277; FAX: (405) 924-7071.

Edmond: University of Central Oklahoma, Small Business Development Center, 100 North University Boulevard, Edmond, OK 73034, (405) 359-1968; FAX: (405) 341-4946.

Enid: Phillips University, Enid Satellite Center, 100 South University Avenue, Enid, OK 73701, (405) 242-7989; FAX: (405) 237-1607.

Langston: Langston University, Minority Assistance Center, P.O. Box 667, Langston, OK 73050, (405) 466-3256; FAX: (405) 466-3381.

Lawton: Lawton Satellite Center, Small Business Development Center, American National Bank Building, 601 SW "D", Suite 209, Lawton, OK 73501, (405)

Be patient. If any phone number is incorrect, call (area code) 555-1212 and request the new listing.

State Starting Places for Money

248-4946; FAX: (405) 355-3560.

Midwest City: Rose State College, Procurement Specialty Center, 6420 Southeast 15th Street, Midwest City, OK 73110, (405) 733-7348; FAX: (405) 733-7495.

Oklahoma City: Oklahoma Department of Commerce, Small Business Development Center, 6601 Broadway Extension, Oklahoma City, OK 73116, (405) 841-5236; FAX: (405) 841-5199.

Poteau: Carl Albert Junior College, Poteau Satellite Center, Small Business Development Center, 1507 South McKenna, Poteau, OK 74953, (918) 647-4019; FAX: (918) 647-2980.

Tahlequah: Northeastern State University, Small Business Development Center, Tahlequah, OK 74464, (918) 458-0802; FAX: (918) 458-2193.

Tulsa: Tulsa Satellite Center, State Office Building, 440 South Houston, Suite 206, Tulsa, OK 74107, (918) 581-2502; FAX: (918) 581-2844.

Weatherford: Southwestern State University, Small Business Development Center, 100 Campus Drive, Weatherford, OK 73096, (405) 774-1040; FAX: (405) 772-5447.

Oregon

General Information

Department of Economic Development, Business Development Division, 595 Cottage St. N.E., Salem, OR 97310; (503) 373-1225. Provides information to business investors on land, buildings, financing,and other relevant issues. Provides consulting services for manufacturing and processing companies with problems. Supports local economic development organizations in expansion efforts. Manages the Oregon Enterprize Zone program which offers property tax relief incentives in 30 specified regions, and a computer-based inventory of available industrial sites and buildings in the state. The Division maintains regional offices in six locations around the state.

Office of Small Business Advocate, Department of Economic Development, 595 Cottage St. N.E., Salem, OR 97310; (503) 373-1200. Assistance in cutting bureaucratic red tape. Information and expertise in dealing with state, federal, and local agencies.

Small Business Development Centers

These offices offer free and fee-based services to new and expanding businesses:

Lead Center: Oregon Small Business Development Center, Lane Community College, 99 West 10th, Suite 216, Eugene, OR 97401; (503) 726-2250, FAX: (503) 345-6006

Albany: Linn-Benton Community College, Small Business Development Center, 6500 S.W. Pacific Boulevard, Albany, OR 97321, (503) 967-6112; FAX: (503) 967-6550.

Ashland: Southern Oregon State College, Small Business Development Center, Regional Service Institute, Ashland, OR 97520, (503) 482-5838, FAX: (503) 482-1115.

Bend: Central Oregon Community College, Small Business Development Center, 2600 N.W. College Way, Bend, OR 97701, (503) 385-5524; FAX: (503) 385-5497; (800) 422-3041, ext. 524.

Coos Bay: Southwestern Oregon Community College, Small Business Development Center, 340 Central, Coos Bay, OR 97420, (503) 267-2300; FAX: (503) 269-0323.

Eugene: Lane Community College, Small Business Development Center, 1059 Willamette Street, Eugene, OR 97401, (503) 726-2255; FAX: (503) 686-0096.

Grants Pass: Rogue Community College, Small Business Development Center, 290 N.E. "C" Street, Grants Pass, OR 97526, (503) 471-3515.

Gresham: Mount Hood Community College, Small Business Development Center, 323 NE Roberts Street, Gresham, OR 97030, (503) 667-7658, FAX: (503) 666-1140.

Klamath Falls: Oregon Institute of Technology, Small Business Development Center, 3201 Campus Drive, South 314, Klamath Falls, OR 97601, (503) 885-1760; FAX: (503) 885-1115.

Lincoln City: Oregon Coast Community College Service District, Small Business Development Center, P.O. Box 419, 4157 N.W. Highway 101, Suite 123, Lincoln City, OR 97367, (503) 994-4166; FAX: (503) 996-4958.

Medford: Small Business Development Center, 229 N. Bartlett, Medford, OR 97501, (503) 772-3478; FAX: (503) 776-2224.

Milwaukie: Clackamas Community College, Small Business Development Center, 7616 S.E. Harmony Road, Milwaukie, OR 97222, (503) 656-4447; FAX: (503) 652-0389.

Ontario: Treasure Valley Community College, Small Business Development Center, 88 S.W. Third Avenue, Ontario, OR 97914, (503) 889-2617, FAX: (503) 889-8331.

Pendleton: Blue Mountain Community College, Small Business Development Center, 37 S.E. Dorion, Pendleton, OR 97801, (503) 276-6233.

Portland: Portland Community College, Small Business Development Center, 123 N.W. 2nd Avenue, Suite 321, Portland, OR 97209, (503) 273-2828; FAX: (503) 294-0725.

Portland: Small Business International Trade Program, 121 S.W. Salmon Street, Suite 210, Portland, OR 97204, (503) 274-7482, FAX: (503) 228-6350.

Roseburg: Umpqua Community College, Small Business Development Center, 744 S.E. Rose, Roseburg, OR 97470, (503) 672-2535; FAX: (503) 672-3679.

Salem: Chemeketa Community College, Small Business Development Center, 365 Ferry Street S.E., Salem, OR 97301, (503) 399-5181; FAX: (503) 581-6017.

Seaside: Clatsop Community College, Small Business Development Center, 1240 South Holladay, Seaside, OR 97138, (503) 738-3347.

The Dalles: Columbia Gorge Community College, Small Business Development Center, 212 Washington, The Dalles, OR 97058, (503) 296-1173, FAX: (503) 296-2107.

Tillamook: Tillamook Bay Community College Service District, Small Business Development Center, 401 B Main Street, Tillamook, OR 97141, (503) 842-2551; FAX: (503) 842-2555.

Pennsylvania

General Information

Business Resource Network, Room 404, Forum Building, Harrisburg, PA 17120; (717) 783-5700. Acts as a clearinghouse to assist small business in finding resources and services available in the state.

Small Business Advocate, Office Of Enterprise Development, Business Resource Network, 404 Forum Building, Harrisburg, PA 17120; (717) 783-5700. Assistance in cutting bureaucratic red tape. Information and expertise in dealing with state, federal, and local agencies.

Small Business Development Centers

The following offices offer free and fee-based services to new and expanding businesses:

Lead Center: Pennsylvania Small Business Development Center, University of Pennsylvania, The Wharton School, 444 Vance Hall, Philadelphia, PA 19104-6374; (215) 898-1219, FAX: (215) 573-2135

Bethlehem: Lehigh University, Small Business Development Center, Rauch Business Center #37, Bethlehem, PA 18015, (215) 758-3980; FAX: (215) 758-5205.

Clarion: Clarion University of Pennsylvania, Small Business Development Center, Dana Still Building, Clarion, PA 16214, (814) 226-2060; FAX: (814) 226-2636.

Be patient. If any phone number is incorrect, call (area code) 555-1212 and request the new listing.

Small Business and Entrepreneuring

Erie: Gannon University, Small Business Development Center, 824 Peach Street, Carlisle Building, 3rd Floor, Erie, PA 16541, (814) 871-7714; FAX: (814) 871-7383.

Latrobe: St. Vincent College, Small Business Development Center, Alfred Hall, 4th Floor, Latrobe, PA 15650-2690, (412) 537-4572; FAX: (412) 537-0919.

Lewisburg: Bucknell University, Small Business Development Center, Dana Engineering Building, Lewisburg, PA 17837, (717) 524-1249; FAX: (717) 524-1768.

Loretto: Small Business Development Center, Business Resource Center, Loretto, PA 15940, (814) 472-3200; FAX: (814) 472-3202.

Middletown: Pennsylvania State University, Small Business Development Center, 777 W. Harrisburg Pike, Middletown, PA 17057-4898, (717) 948-6069; FAX: (717) 948-6031.

Philadelphia: Temple University, Small Business Development Center, Room 6, Speakman Hall, 006-00, Philadelphia, PA 19122, (215) 787-7282; FAX: (215) 787-5698.

Philadelphia: LaSalle University, Small Business Development Center, 1900 West Olney Avenue, Box 365, Philadelphia, PA 19141, (215) 951-1416; FAX: (215) 951-1547.

Philadelphia: University of Pennsylvania, Small Business Development Center, The Wharton School, 409 Vance Hall, Philadelphia, PA 19104-6357, (215) 898-4861; FAX: (215) 898-1299.

Pittsburgh: Duquesne University, Small Business Development Center, Rockwell Hall-Room 10 Concourse, 600 Forbes Avenue, Pittsburgh, PA 15282, (412) 434-6233; FAX: (412) 434-5072.

Pittsburgh: University of Pittsburgh, Small Business Development Center, Room 343 Mervis Hall, Pittsburgh, PA 15260, (412) 648-1544; FAX: (412) 648-1693.

Scranton: University of Scranton, Small Business Development Center, St. Thomas Hall, Room 588, Scranton, PA 18503, (717) 941-7588; FAX: (717) 941-4053.

Wilkes-Barre: Wilkes College, Small Business Development Center, Hollenback Hall, 192 South Franklin Street, Wilkes-Barre, PA 18766, (717) 824-4651, ext. 4340; FAX: (717) 824-2245.

Rhode Island

General Information

Rhode Island Department of Economic Development, 7 Jackson Walkway, Providence, RI 02903; (401) 277-2601. Maintains three separate divisions: Financial Services, 2) The Business Action Center, and 3) Small Business Development Division.

Small Business Advocate, Advisory Commission, Good Neighbor Alliance Corp., 1664 Cranston St., Cranston, RI 02920. Assistance in cutting bureaucratic red tape. Information and expertise in dealing with state, federal, and local agencies.

Small Business Development Centers

The following offices offer free and fee-based services to new and expanding businesses:

Lead Center: Rhode Island Small Business Development Center, Bryant College, 1150 Douglas Pike, Smithfield, RI 02917; (401) 232-6111, FAX: (401) 232-6416

Kingston: University of Rhode Island, Small Business Development Center, 24 Woodward Hall, Kingston, RI 02881, (401) 792-2451; FAX: (401) 792-4017.

Middletown: Aquidneck Island, Small Business Development Center, 28 Jacome Way, Middletown, RI 02840, (401) 849-6900; FAX: (401) 849-0815.

Providence: Bryant College, Small Business Development Center, 7 Jackson Walkway, Providence, RI 02903, (401) 831-1330; FAX: (401) 454-2819.

Providence: Community College of Rhode Island, Small Business Development Center, Providence Campus, One Hilton Street, Providence, RI 02905, (401) 455-6042; FAX: (401) 455-6047.

Smithfield: Bryant College, Export Assistance Center, 1150 Douglas Pike, Smithfield, RI 02917, (401) 232-6407; FAX: (401) 232-6416/6319.

South Carolina

General Information

Enterprise Development Department, South Carolina State Development Board, P.O. Box 927, Columbia, SC 29202; (803) 737-0400. Stimulates the formation and growth of new businesses. Step-by-step information on starting a new business in South Carolina is provided in the *Business Formation and Expansion Manual*, a free publication. Provides a network of services for development of business plans, offers assistance to small businesses on individual problems, and establishes a regional network for women-owned businesses. Technical assessments are available as well as educational and training programs and financial and marketing assistance.

Small Business Advocate, Industry-Business and Community Services, South Carolina Development Board, P.O. Box 927, Columbia, SC 29202; (803) 734-1400. Assistance in cutting bureaucratic red tape. Information and expertise in dealing with state, federal, and local agencies.

Small Business Development Centers

These offices offer free and fee-based services to new and expanding businesses:

Lead Center: South Carolina Small Business Development Center, University of South Carolina, College of Business Administration, Columbia, SC 29208; (803) 777-5118, FAX: (803) 777-4403

Beaufort: University of South Carolina at Beaufort, Small Business Development Center, 800 Carteret Street, Beaufort, SC 29902, (803) 521-4143; FAX: (803) 521-4198.

Charleston: Trident Technical College, Charleston Small Business Development Center, 66 Columbus Street, P.O. Box 20339, Charleston, SC 29413-0339, (803) 727-2020; FAX: (803) 727-2013.

Clemson: Clemson University, Small Business Development Center, 425 Sirrine Hall, Clemson, SC 29634-1392, (803) 656-3227; FAX: (803) 656-4889.

Columbia: University of South Carolina, USC Regional Small Business Development Center, College of Business Administration, Columbia, SC 29208, (803) 777-5118; FAX: (803) 777-4403.

Conway: Coastal Carolina, Small Business Development Center, School of Business Administration, Conway, SC 29526, (803) 349-2169; FAX: (803) 349-2990.

Florence: Florence Darlington Tech, Small Business Development Center, P.O. Box 100648, Florence, SC 29501-0548, (803) 661-8324; FAX: (803) 661-8041.

Greenville: Greenville Technical College, Small Business Development Center, Box 5616, Station B-GHEC, Greenville, SC 29606, (803) 271-4259; FAX: (803) 250-8514.

Greenwood: Upper Savannah Council of Governments, Small Business Development Center, SBDC Exchange Building, 222 Phoenix Street, Suite 200, P.O. Box 1366, Greenwood, SC 29648, (803) 227-6110O; FAX: (803) 229-1869.

Hilton Head Island: University of South Carolina at Hilton Head, Small Business Development Center, Suite 300, Kiawah Bldg., 10 Office Park Road, Hilton Head Island, SC 29928, (803) 785-3995; FAX: (803) 777-0333.

North Augusta: Aiken/North Augusta Small Business Development Center, Triangle Plaza, Highway 25, 215-B Edgefield Road, North Augusta, SC 29481, (803) 442-3670; FAX: (803) 641-3445.

Orangeburg: South Carolina State College, Small Business Development Center, School of Business Administration, Orangeburg, SC 29117, (803) 536-8445; FAX: (803) 536-8066.

Be patient. If any phone number is incorrect, call (area code) 555-1212 and request the new listing.

State Starting Places for Money

Rock Hill: Winthrop College, Small Business Development Center, 119 Thurmond Building, Rock Hill SC 29733, (803) 323-2283, FAX: (803) 323-3960.

Spartanburg: Spartanburg Chamber of Commerce, Small Business Development Center, P.O. Box 1636, Spartanburg, SC 29304, (803) 594-5080; FAX: (803) 594-5055.

South Dakota

General Information

Small Business Advocate, Governor's Office of Economic Development, 711 Wells Ave., Pierre, SD 57501; (605) 773-5032. Assistance in cutting bureaucratic red tape. Information and expertise in dealing with state, federal, and local agencies.

Small Business Development Centers

The following offices offer free and fee-based services to new and expanding businesses:

Lead Center: South Dakota Small Business Development Center, University of South Dakota, 414 East Clark, Vermillion, SD 57069; (605) 677-5272, FAX: (605) 677-5427

Aberdeen: Small Business Development Center, 226 Citizens Building, Aberdeen, SD 57401, (605) 225-2252.

Pierre: Small Business Development Center, 105 South Euclid, Suite C, Pierre, SD 57501, (605) 773-5941.

Rapid City: Small Business Development Center, 444 Mount Rushmore Road, #208, P.O. Box 7715, Rapid City, SD 57709, (605) 394-5311.

Sioux Falls: Small Business Development Center, 200 North Phillips, L103, Sioux Falls, SD 57102, (605) 339-3366.

Tennessee

General Information

Office of Small Business, Department of Economic and Community Development, 320 Sixth Ave. North, Nashville, TN 37219; (615) 741-1888. Serves as an advocate for the small business community. Acts as a clearinghouse on programs and projects in both the public and private sectors that assist small business.

Small Business Advocate, Department of Economic and Community Development, 7th Floor, 320 Sixth Ave. Nort, Nashville, TN 37219; (615) 741-2626. Assistance in cutting bureaucratic red tape. Information and expertise in dealing with state, federal, and local agencies.

Small Business Development Centers

The following offices offer free and fee-based services to new and expanding businesses:

Lead Center: Tennessee Small Business Development Center, Memphis State University, South Campus (Getwell Road), Building #1, Memphis, TN 38152; (901) 678-2500, FAX: (901) 678-4072

Chattanooga: Chattanooga State Technical Community College, Small Business Development Center, 4501 Amnicola Highway, Chattanooga, TN 37406-1097, (615) 697-4410; FAX: (615) 698-5653.

Chattanooga: Southeast Tennessee Development District, Small Business Development Center, 25 Cherokee Blvd., Chattanooga, TN 37405, (615) 266-5781; FAX: (615) 267-7705.

Clarksville: Austin Peay State University, Small Business Development Center, College of Business, Clarksville, TN 37044-0001, (615) 648-7764; FAX: (615) 648-7475.

Cleveland: Cleveland State Community College, Small Business Development

Center, Business and Technology, P.O. Box 3570, Cleveland, TN 37320-3570, (615) 478-6247; FAX: (615) 478-6251.

Columbia: Small Business Development Center, Memorial Building, Room 205, 308 West 7th Street, Columbia, TN 38401, (615) 388-5674.

Cookeville: Tennessee Technological University, Small Business Development Center, College of Business Administration, P.O. Box 5023, Cookeville, TN 38505-0001, (615) 372-3648; FAX: (615) 372-6112.

Dyersburg: Dyersburg Community College, Small Business Development Center, P.O. Box 648, Dyersburg, TN 38024, (901) 286-3200; FAX: (901) 286-3201.

Hartsville: Four Lakes Regional Industrial Development Authority, Small Business Development Center, P.O. Box 63, Hartsville, TN 37074-0063, (615) 374-9521; FAX: (615) 374-4608.

Jackson: Jackson State Community College, Small Business Development Center, 2046 North Parkway Street, Jackson, TN 38310-3797, (901) 424-5389; FAX: (901) 425-2647.

Johnson City: East Tennessee State University, Small Business Development Center, College of Business, P.O. Box 70, 698A, Johnson City, TN 37614-0698, (615) 929-5630; FAX: (615) 929-5274.

Knoxville: Pellissippi State Technical Community College, Small Business Development Center, P.O. Box 22990, Knoxville, TN 37933-0990, (615) 694-6660; FAX: (615) 694-6583.

Knoxville: International Trade Center, 301 E. Church Avenue, Knoxville, TN 37915, (615) 637-4283.

Memphis: Memphis State University, Small Business Development Center, 320 South Dudley Street, Memphis, TN 38104-3206, (901) 527-1041; FAX: (901) 527-1047.

Memphis: Memphis State University, Small Business Development Center, International Trade Center, Memphis, TN 38152, (901) 678-4174; FAX: (901) 678-4072.

Morristown: Walters State Community College, Small Business Development Center, Business/Industrial Services, 500 S. Davy Crockett Parkway, Morristown, TN 37813-688, (615) 587-9722; FAX: (615) 586-1918.

Murfreesboro: Middle Tennessee State University, Small Business Development Center, School of Business, P.O. Box 487, Murfreesboro, TN 37132, (615) 898-2745; FAX: (615) 898-5538.

Nashville: Tennessee State University, Small Business Development Center, School of Business, 330 10th Avenue North, Nashville, TN 37203-3401, (615) 251-1178; FAX: (615) 251-1178 (call first).

Texas

General Information

Texas Department of Commerce, Small Business Division, P.O. Box 12728, Austin, TX 78711; (512) 472-5059. Provides business counseling for both new and established firms. Helps firms locate capital, state procurement opportunities, and resources for management and technical assistance. An Office of Business Permit Assistance serves as a clearinghouse for permit-related information throughout the state and refers applicants to appropriate agencies for permit and regulatory needs.

Small Business Advocate, Texas Department of Commerce, Small Business Division, P.O. Box 12728, Austin, TX 78711; (512) 472-5059. Assistance in cutting bureaucratic red tape. Information and expertise in dealing with state, federal, and local agencies.

Small Business Development Centers

The following offices offer free and fee-based services to new and expanding businesses:

Lead Centers: North Texas Small Business Development Center, Dallas County

Small Business and Entrepreneuring

Community College, 1402 Corinth Street, Dallas, TX 75215; (214) 565-5837, FAX: (214) 565-5857

Houston Small Business Development Center, University of Houston, 601 Jefferson, Suite 2330, Houston, TX 77002; (713) 752-8444, FAX: (713) 752-8484

Northwest Texas Small Business Center, Center for Innovation, 2579 South Loop 289, Suite 114, Lubbock, TX 79423; (806) 745-3973, FAX: (806) 745-6207

South Texas Border Small Business Development Center, University of Texas at San Antonio, 801 S. Bowie, San Antonio, TX 78205; (512) 224-0791, FAX: (512) 222-9834

Abilene: Abilene Christian University, Caruth Small Business Development Center, College of Business Administration, ACU Station, Box 8307, Abilene, TX 79699, (915) 674-2776; FAX: (915) 674-2507.

Alvin: Alvin Community College, Small Business Development Center, 3110 Mustang Road, Alvin, TX 77511-4898, (713) 338-4686; FAX: (713) 388-4903.

Amarillo: West Texas State University, Panhandle Small Business Development Center, T. Boone Pickens School of Business, 1800 South Washington, Suite 110, Amarillo, TX 79102, (806) 372-5151.

Athens: Trinity Valley Small Business Development Center, 500 South Prairieville, Athens, TX 75751, (903) 675-7403; FAX: (903) 675-6316.

Austin: Austin Small Business Development Center, 221 South IH 35, Suite 103, Austin, TX 78741, (512) 326-2256; FAX: (512) 447-9825.

Baytown: Lee College, Small Business Development Center, Rundell Hall, 511 South Whiting Street, Baytown, TX 77520-4703, (713) 425-6309; FAX: (713) 425-6307.

Beaumont: John Gray Institute/Lamar University, Small Business Development Center, 855 Florida Avenue, Beaumont, TX 77705, (409) 880-2367; FAX: (409) 880-2201; (800) 722-3443.

Bonham: Bonham Small Business Development Center (Satellite), Sam Raybourn Center, Bonham, TX 75418, (903) 583-4811.

Brenham: Blinn College, Small Business Development Center, 902 College Avenue, Brenham, TX 77833, (409) 830-4137; FAX: (409) 830-4116.

Bryan: Bryan/College Station Chamber of Commerce, Small Business Development Center, 401 South Washington, Bryan, TX 77806, (409) 823-3034; FAX: (409) 822-4818.

Corpus Christi: Corpus Christi Chamber of Commerce, Small Business Development Center, 1201 North Shoreline, Corpus Christi, TX 78403, (512) 882-6161; FAX: (512) 888-5627.

Corsicana: Navarro Small Business Development Center, 120 North 12th Street, Corsicana, TX 75110, (903) 874-0658; FAX: (903) 874-4187.

Dallas: International Business Center, 2050 Stemmons Freeway, World Trade Center, Suite #150, P.O. Box 58299, Dallas, TX 75258, (214) 653-1777; FAX: (214) 748-5774.

Denison: Grayson Small Business Development Center, 6101 Grayson Drive, Denison, TX 75020, (903) 786-3551; FAX: (903) 463-5284.

Denton: Denton Small Business Development Center (Satellite), P.O. Drawer P, Denton, TX 76202, (817) 382-7151; FAX: (817) 382-0040.

DeSoto: Best Southwest Small Business Development Center, 1001 N. Beckley, Suite 606D, DeSoto, TX 75115, (214) 228-3783.

Edinburg: University of Texas/Pan American, Small Business Development Center, 1201 West University Drive, Edinburg, TX 78539-2999, (512) 381-3361; FAX: (512) 381-2322.

El Paso: El Paso Community College, Small Business Development Center, 103 Montana Avenue, Room 202, El Paso, TX 79902-3929, (915) 534-3410; FAX: (915) 534-3420.

Fort Worth: Tarrant Small Business Development Center, 1500 Houston Street, Room 163, 7917 Highway 80 West, Fort Worth, TX 76102, (817) 244-7158; FAX: (817) 877-9295.

Gainesville: Cooke Small Business Development Center, 1525 West California, Gainesville, TX 76240, (817) 665-4785; FAX: (817) 668-6049.

Galveston: Galveston College, Small Business Development Center, 4015 Avenue Q, Galveston, TX 77550, (409) 740-7380; FAX: (409) 740-7381.

Hillsboro: Hillsboro Small Business Development Center (Satellite), SOS Building, P.O. Box 619, Hillsboro, TX 76645, (817) 582-2555, ext. 282.

Houston: North Harris Community College District, Small Business Development Center, 350 N. Sam Houston Parkway, Houston, TX 77060, (713) 591-9320; FAX: (713) 591-3513; (800) 443-SBDC.

Huntsville: Sam Houston State University, Small Business Development Center, College of Business Administration, P.O. Box 2056, Huntsville, TX 77341, (409) 294-3737; FAX: (409) 294-3612.

Kingsville: Kingsville Chamber of Commerce, Small Business Development Center, 635 East King, Kingsville, TX 78363, (512) 595-5088; FAX: (512) 592-0866.

Lake Jackson: Brazosport College, Small Business Development Center, 500 College Drive, Lake Jackson, TX 77566, (409) 265-6131, ext. 380; FAX: (409) 265-7208.

Laredo: Laredo Development Foundation, Small Business Development Center, 616 Leal Street, Laredo, TX 78041, (512) 722-0563.

Longview: Kilgore College, Small Business Development Center, 300 South High, Longview, TX 75601, (903) 757-5857; FAX: (903) 753-7920.

Lubbock: Texas Tech University, Small Business Development Center, Center for Innovation, 2579 South Loop 289, Suite 114, Lubbock, TX 79423, (806) 745-1637; FAX: (806) 745-6207.

Lufkin: Angelina Community College, Small Business Development Center, P.O. Box 1768, Lufkin, TX 75902, (409) 639-1887; FAX: (409) 639-4299.

Mt. Pleasant: Northeast Texarkana Small Business Development Center, P.O. Box 1307, Mt. Pleasant, TX 75455, (214) 572-1911; FAX: (903) 572-6712.

Odessa: University of Texas/Permian Basin, Small Business Development Center, 4901 East University, Odessa, TX 79762, (915) 563-0400; FAX: (915) 561-5534.

Paris: Paris Small Business Development Center, 2400 Clarksville Street, Paris, TX 75460, (214) 784-1802; FAX: (903) 784-1801.

Plano: Collin County Small Business Development Center, Plano Market Square, 1717 East Spring Creek Parkway, #109, Plano, TX 75074, (214) 881-0506; FAX: (214) 423-3956.

San Angelo: Angelo State University, Small Business Development Center, 2610 West Avenue N, Campus Box 10910, San Angelo, .TX 76909, (915) 942-2119; FAX: (915) 942-2038.

San Antonio: UTSA, International Small Business Development Center, 801 S. Bowie, San Antonio, TX 78205, (512) 227-2997; FAX: (512) 222-9834.

Stafford: Houston Community College System, Small Business Development Center, 13600 Murphy Road, Stafford, TX 77477, (713) 499-4870; FAX: (713) 499-8194.

Stephenville: Tarleton State University, Small Business Development Center, Box T-158, Stephenville, TX 76402, (817) 968-9330; FAX: (817) 968-9329.

Texas City: College of the Mainland, Small Business Development Center, 8419 Emmett F. Lowry Expressway, Texas City, TX 77591, (409) 938-7578; FAX: (409) 935-5816.

Tyler: Tyler Small Business Development Center, 1530 South SW Loop 323, Suite 100, Tyler, TX 75701, (903) 510-2975; FAX: (903) 510-2978.

Be patient. If any phone number is incorrect, call (area code) 555-1212 and request the new listing.

State Starting Places for Money

Victoria: University of Houston-Victoria, Small Business Development Center, 700 Main Center, Suite 102, Victoria, TX 77901, (512) 575-8944; FAX: (512) 575-8852.

Waco: McLennan Small Business Development Center, 4601 North 19th Street, Waco, TX 76708, (817) 750-3600; FAX: (817) 756-0776.

Wharton: Wharton County Junior College, Small Business Development Center, Administration Building, Room 102, 911 Boling Highway, Wharton, TX 77488-0080, (409) 532-0604; FAX: (409) 532-2201.

Wichita Fall: Midwestern State University, Small Business Development Center, Division of Business, 3400 Taft Boulevard, Wichita Falls, TX 76308, (817) 696-6738; FAX: (817) 689-4374.

Utah

General Information

Small Business Advocate, Utah Small Business Development Center, University of Utah, Suite 418, 660 South 200 East, Salt Lake City, UT 84111. Assistance in cutting bureaucratic red tape. Information and expertise in dealing with state, federal, and local agencies.

Small Business Development Centers

These offices offer free and fee-based services to new and expanding businesses:

Lead Center: Utah Small Business Development Center, University of Utah, 102 West 500 South, Suite 315, Salt Lake City, UT 84101; (801) 581-7905, FAX: (801) 581-7814

Cedar City: Southern Utah University, Small Business Development Center, 351 West Center, Cedar City, UT 84720, (801) 586-5400; FAX: (801) 586-5493.

Ephraim: Snow College, Small Business Development Center, 345 West 1st North, Ephraim, UT 84627, (801) 283-4021; (801) 283-6890; FAX: (801) 283-6913.

Logan: Utah State University, Small Business Development Center, East Campus Building, Logan, UT 84322-8330, (801) 750-2277; FAX: (801) 750-3317.

Ogden: Weber State University, Small Business Development Center, College of Business and Economics, Ogden, UT 84408-3806, (801) 626-7232; FAX: (801) 626-7423.

Price: College of Eastern Utah, Small Business Development Center, 451 East 400 North, Price, UT 84501, (801) 637-1995; FAX: (801) 637-4102.

Provo: Brigham Young University, Small Business Development Center, School of Management, 790 Tanner Building, Provo, UT 84602, (801) 378-4022; FAX: (801) 378-4501.

Roosevelt: Uintah Basin Applied Technology Center, Small Business Development Center, 1100 East Lagoon, P.O. Box 124-5, Roosevelt, UT 84066, (801) 722-4523; FAX: (801) 722-5804.

St. George: Dixie College, Small Business Development Center, 225 South 700 East, St. George, UT 84770, (801) 673-4811 ext 353; FAX: (801) 673-8552.

Vermont

General Information

Vermont Economic Development Department, 109 State Street, Montpelier, VT 05602; (802) 828-3221; (800) 622-4553, in-state.

Small Business Advocate, Vermont Agency of Development and Community Affairs, Montpelier, VT 05602; (802) 828-3211. Assistance in cutting bureaucratic red tape. Information and expertise in dealing with state, federal, and local agencies.

Small Business Development Centers

These offices offer free and fee-based service to new and expanding businesses:

Lead Center: Vermont Small Business Development Center, Suite 13, One Blair Park, Williston, VT 05495-9404; (802) 878-0181, FAX: (802) 878-0245

Morrisville: UVM Extension System, Central Small Business Development Center, RFD 1 Box 2280, Morrisville, VT 05661, (802) 888-4972; FAX: (802) 888-2432.

Rutland: UVM Extension System, Southwest Small Business Development Center, Box 489, Rutland, VT 05701, (802) 773-3349; FAX: (802) 775-4840.

St. Johnsbury: UVM Extension System, Northeast Small Business Development Center, HCR 31, Box 436, Johnsbury, VT 05819, (802) 748-5512.

West Brattleboro: UVM Extension System, Southeast Small Business Development Center Resource Center, Box 2430, 411 Western Ave., West Brattleboro, VT 05301, (802) 257-7967; FAX: (802) 257-0112.

Virginia

General Information

Department of Economic Development, Office of Small Business and Financial Services, 1000 Washington Building, Richmond, VA 23219; (804) 786-3791. Helps new or expanding business by answering questions about licensing, taxes, regulations, assistance programs, etc. The office can also locate sources of information in other state agencies, and it also can identify sources of help for business planning, management, exporting, and financing.

Virginia Employment Commission Economic Information Services Division, 703 East Main St., P.O. Box 1358, Richmond, VA 23211; (804) 786-3047. Publishes the *Virginia Business Resource Directory*, a comprehensive source of information on every aspect of doing business in the state, from business planning, management and personnel issues to sources of finance, marketing assistance, and regulations and licences.

Small Business Advocate, Office of Small Business and Financial Services, Virginia Department of Economic Development, 1000 Washington Building, Richmond, VA 23219; (804) 786-3791. Assistance in cutting bureaucratic red tape. Information and expertise in dealing with state, federal, and local agencies.

Small Business Development Centers

The following offices offer free and fee-based services to new and expanding businesses:

Lead Center: Virginia Small Business Development Center, P.O. Box 798, Richmond, VA 23206-0798; (804) 371-8258, FAX: (804) 371-8185

Arlington: George Mason University/Arlington Campus, Small Business Development Center, 3401 N. Fairfax Drive, Arlington, VA 22201, (703) 993-8129; FAX: (703) 993-8130.

Big Stone Gap: Mt. Empire Community College, Southwest Small Business Development Center, Drawer 700, Route 23, Big Stone Gap, VA 24219, (703) 523-6529; FAX: (703) 523-4130.

Blacksburg: Western Virginia Small Business Development Center Consortium, VPI & SU, Economic Development Assistance Center, 404 Clay Street, Blacksburg, VA 24061-0539, (703) 231-5278; FAX: (703) 953-2307.

Charlottesville: Central Virginia Small Business Development Center, 700 Harris Street, Suite 207, Charlottesville, VA 22901-4553, (804) 295-8198, FAX: (804) 979-3749.

Fairfax: Northern Virginia Small Business Development Center, 4260 Chainbridge Road, Suite B-1, Fairfax, VA 22030, (703) 993-2131; FAX: (703) 993-2126.

Farmville: Longwood College, Small Business Development Center, Farmville, VA 23901, (804) 395-2086, FAX: (804) 395-2359.

Harrisonburg: James Madison University, Small Business Development Center, College of Business Building, Room 523, Harrisonburg, VA 22807, (703) 568-3227; FAX: (703) 568-3399.

Be patient. If any phone number is incorrect, call (area code) 555-1212 and request the new listing.

Small Business and Entrepreneuring

Lynchburg: Lynchburg Regional Small Business Development Center, 147 Mill Ridge Road, Lynchburg, VA 24502, (804) 582-6100; FAX: (804) 582-6106.

Manassas: Small Business Development Center, Dr. William E.S. Flory, 10311 Sudley Manor Drive, Manassas, VA 22110, (703) 335-2500; FAX: (703) 335-1700.

Norfolk: Hampton Roads Inc., Small Business Development Center, P.O. Box 327, 420 Bank Street, Norfolk, VA 23501, (804) 622-6414; FAX: (804) 622-5563.

Radford: New River Valley Small Business Development Center, New River Valley Planning District Commission Office, P.O. Box 3726, 1612 Wadsworth Street, Radford, VA 24143, (703) 731-9546; FAX: (703) 831-6093.

Richlands: Southwest Virginia Community College, Small Business Development Center, P.O. Box SVCC, Richlands, VA 24641, (703) 964-7345; FAX: (703) 964-9307.

Richmond: Capital Area Small Business Development Center, 403 East Grace Street, Richmond, VA 23219, (804) 648-7838; FAX: (804) 648-7849.

Roanoke: The Blue Ridge Small Business Development Center, 310 First Street, S.W. Mezzanine, Roanoke, VA 24011, (703) 983-0717; FAX: (703) 983-0723.

South Boston: South Boston Small Business Development Center, P.O. Box 1116, South Boston, VA 24596, (804) 575-0044, FAX: (804) 572-4087.

Sterling: Loudoun County Small Business Development Center, One Steeplechase at Dulles, 21736 Atlantic Boulevard, Suite 100, Sterling, VA 22170, (703) 430-7222; FAX: (703) 430-9562.

Wytheville: Wytheville Community College, Small Business Development Center, 1000 E. Main Street, Wytheville, VA 24382, (703) 228-5541, ext 314; FAX: (703) 228-2542.

Washington

Business Assistance Division, Department of Trade and Economic Development, 101 General Administration Building, AX-13, Olympia, WA 98504; (206) 586-3021

Small Business Development Centers

The following offices offer free and fee-based services to new and expanding businesses:

Lead Center: Washington Small Business Development Center, Washington State University, 245 Todd Hall, Pullman, WA 99164-4727; (509) 355-1576, FAX: (509) 335-0949

Aberdeen: Grays Harbor College, Small Business Development Center, 1602 Edward P. Smith Drive, Aberdeen, WA 98520, (206) 532-9020.

Bellevue: Bellevue Community College, Small Business Development Center, 3000 Landerholm Circle, Bellevue, WA 98009, (206) 641-2265; FAX: (206) 453-3032.

Bellingham: Western Washington University, Small Business Development Center, College of Business and Economics, 415 Park Hall, Bellingham, WA 98225, (206) 676-3899; FAX: (509) 647-4844.

Centralia: Centralia Community College, Small Business Development Center, 600 West Locust Street, Centralia, WA 98531, (206) 736-9391; FAX: (206) 753-3404.

Everett: Edmonds Community College, Small Business Development Center, 917 134th Street, S.W., Everett, WA 98204, (206) 745-0430; FAX: (206) 745-5563.

Moses Lake: Big Bend Community College, Small Business Development Center, 7662 Chanute Street, Bldg. 1500, Moses Lake, WA 98837-3299, (509) 762-6239; FAX: (509) 762-6329.

Mt. Vernon: Skagit Valley College, Small Business Development Center, 2405 College Way, Mt. Vernon, WA 98273, (206) 428-1282; FAX: (206) 428-1186.

Olympia: South Puget Sound Community College, Small Business Development Center, 2011 Mottman Road SW, Olympia, WA 98501, (206) 754-7711; FAX: (206) 586-6054.

Omak: Wenatchee Valley College, Small Business Development Center, P.O. Box 1042, Omak, WA 98841, (509) 826-5107; FAX: (509) 826-4604.

Pasco: Columbia Basin College, Small Business Development Center, 2600 North 20th, Pasco, WA 99301, (509) 547-0511; FAX: (509) 546-0401.

Seattle: South Seattle Community College, Small Business Development Center, 6000 16th Avenue, SW, Seattle, WA 98106, (206) 764-5339; FAX: (206) 764-5393.

Seattle: Washington State University at Seattle, Small Business Development Center, 2001 Sixth Avenue, Suite 2608, Seattle, WA 98121-2518, (206) 464-5450.

Seattle: North Seattle Community College, Small Business Development Center, International Trade Institute, 9600 College Way North, Seattle, WA 98103, (206) 527-3732; FAX: (206) 527-3734.

Spokane: Community College of Spokane, Small Business Development Center, West 601 First, Spokane, WA 99204, (509) 459-3741; FAX: (509) 459-3433.

Tacoma: Washington State University at Tacoma, Small Business Development Center, 950 Pacific Avenue, Suite 300, Box 1933, Tacoma, WA 98401-1933, (206) 272-7232; FAX: (206) 597-7305.

Tacoma: Pierce College, Small Business Development Center, 9401 Farwest Drive, SW, Tacoma, WA 98498, (206) 964-6776; FAX: (206) 964-6746.

Vancouver: Columbia River Economic Development Council, Small Business Development Center, 100 East Columbia Way, Vancouver, WA 98660-3156, (206) 693-2555; FAX: (206) 694-9927.

Wenatchee: Wenatchee Valley College, Small Business Development Center, 1300 Fifth Street, Wenatchee, WA 98801, (509) 662-1651; FAX: (206) 764-5393.

Yakima: Yakima Valley Community College, Small Business Development Center, P.O. Box 1647, Yakima, WA 98907, (509) 575-2284; FAX: (509) 575-2461.

West Virginia

General Information

Small Business Development Center, State Capitol Complex, Charleston, WV 24305; (304) 348-2960. Acts as a one-stop resource center for information and assistance in filing state and federal forms and coordinates assistance programs with other agencies.

Small Business Advocate, Director, Small Business Development Center, Capitol Complex, Charleston, WV 24305; (304) 348-2960. Assistance in cutting bureaucratic red tape. Information and expertise in dealing with state, federal, and local agencies.

Small Business Development Centers

The following offices offer free and fee-based services to new and expanding businesses:

Lead Center: West Virginia Small Business Development Center, West Virginia Development Office, 1115 Virginia Street, East, Capitol Complex, Charleston, WV 25310-2406; (304) 558-2960, FAX: (304) 558-0127

Athens: Concord College, Small Business Development Center, Center for Economic Action, Box D-125, Athens, WV 24712, (304) 384-5103.

Bluefield: Bluefield State College, Small Business Development Center, 219 Rock Street, Bluefield, WV 24701, (304) 327-4107; FAX: (304) 325-7747.

Fairmont: Fairmont State College, Small Business Development Center, Fairmont, WV 26554, (304) 367-4125.

Huntington: Marshall University, Small Business Development Center, 1050 Fourth Avenue, Huntington, WV 25701, (304) 696-6789.

Keyser: Potomac State College, Rural and Small Business Development Center,

State Starting Places for Money

75 Arnold Street, Keyser, WV 26726, (304) 788-3011.

Montgomery: West Virginia Institute of Technology, Small Business Development Center, Room 102, Engineering Building, Montgomery, WV 25136, (304) 442-5501.

Morgantown: West Virginia University, Small Business Development Center, P.O. Box 6025, Morgantown, WV 26506, (304) 293-5839.

Parkersburg: West Virginia University at Parkersburg, Small Business Development Center, Route 5, Box 167-A, Parkersburg, WV 26101, (304) 424-8277.

Shepherdstown: Shepherd College, Small Business Development Center, 120 North Princess Street, Shepherdstown, WV 25443, (800) 344-5231, ext 261.

Wheeling: West Virginia Northern Community College, Small Business Development Center, College Square, Wheeling, WV 26003, (304) 233-5900; ext. 206.

Wisconsin

General Information

Permit Information Center, Department of Development, P.O. Box 7970, Madison, WI 53707; (608) 266-1386. Coordinates state regulatory and business development needs by providing information on permit requirements, expedition of permit issuance, monitoring of a permit's progress in the bureaucracy, and recommending improvements in the permit process.

Small Business Advocate, Department of Development, Bureau of Advocacy, P.O. Box 7970, Madison, WI 53707; (608) 266-6747. Assistance in cutting bureaucratic red tape. Information and expertise in dealing with state, federal, and local agencies.

Small Business Development Centers

The following offices offer free and fee-based services to new and expanding businesses:

Lead Center: Wisconsin Small Business Development Center, University of Wisconsin, 432 N. Lake Street, Room 423, Madison, WI 53706; (608) 263-7794, FAX: (608) 262-3878

Eau Claire: University of Wisconsin at Eau Claire, Small Business Development Center, Schneider Hall, #113, Eau Claire, WI 54701, (715) 836-5637.

Green Bay: University of Wisconsin at Green Bay, Small Business Development Center, Library Learning Center, Room 710, Green Bay, WI 54302, (414) 465-2089.

Kenosha: University of Wisconsin at Parkside, Small Business Development Center, 234 Tallent Hall, Kenosha, WI 53141, (414) 595-2620.

La Crosse: University of Wisconsin at LaCrosse, Small Business Development Center, School of Business, La Crosse, WI 54601, (608) 785-8782.

Madison: University of Wisconsin at Madison, Small Business Development Center, 905 University Avenue, Madison, WI 53715, (608) 263-2221.

Milwaukee: University of Wisconsin at Milwaukee, Small Business Development Center, 929 North Sixth Street, Milwaukee, WI 53203, (414) 227-3241.

Oshkosh: University of Wisconsin at Oshkosh, Small Business Development Center, Clow Faculty Building, Room 157, Oshkosh, WI 54901, (414) 424-1453.

Stevens Point: University of Wisconsin at Stevens Point, Small Business Development Center, 012 Main Building, Stevens Point, WI 54481, (715) 346-2004.

Superior: University of Wisconsin at Superior, Small Business Development Center, 29 Sundquist Hall, Superior, WI 54880, (715) 394-8352.

Whitewater: University of Wisconsin at Whitewater, Small Business Development Center, 1000 Carlson, Whitewater, WI 53190, (414) 472-3217.

Wyoming

General Information

Small Business Advocate, Economic Development and Stabilization Board, Herschler Building, Cheyenne, WY 82002; (307) 777-7287. Assistance in cutting bureaucratic red tape. Information and expertise in dealing with state, federal, and local agencies.

Small Business Development Centers

The following offices offer free and fee-based services to new and expanding businesses:

Lead Center: Wyoming Small Business Development Center, 111 West 2nd Street, Suite 416, Casper, WY 82601; (307) 235-4825, FAX: (307) 473-7243

Casper: Small Business Development Center, 350 West A, Suite 200, Casper, WY 82601, (307) 235-4827.

Cheyenne: Laramie County Community College, Small Business Development Center, 1400 East College Drive, Cheyenne, WY 82007, (307) 778-1222.

Douglas: Eastern Wyoming Community College, Small Business Development Center, Douglas Branch, 203 North Sixth Street, Douglas, WY 82633, (307) 358-4090.

Gillette: Sheridan College, Small Business Development Center, 720 West 8th, Gillette, WY 82716, (307) 686-0297.

Lander: Central Wyoming College, Small Business Development Center, 360 Main Street, Lander, WY 82520, (307) 332-3394; (800) 338-1864.

Laramie: University of Wyoming, Small Business Development Center, P.O. Box 3275, University Station, Laramie, WY 82070, (307) 766-2363.

Powell: Northwest Community College, Small Business Development Center, 146 South Bent #103, Powell, WY 82435, (307) 754-3745.

Rock Springs: Western Wyoming Community College, Small Business Development Center, P.O. Box 428, Rock Springs, WY 82902, (307) 382-1830.

Small Business and Entrepreneuring

Federal Money for Business

* *See also Careers and Workplace; Research Grants in Every Field*

The following is a description of the federal funds available to small businesses, entrepreneurs, inventors, and researchers. This information is derived from the *Catalog of Federal Domestic Assistance* which is published by the U.S. Government Printing Office in Washington, DC. The number next to the title description is the official reference for this federal program. Contact the office listed below the caption for further details. The following is a description of the terms used for the types of assistance available:

Loans: money lent by a federal agency for a specific period of time and with a reasonable expectation of repayment. Loans may or may not require payment of interest.

Loan Guarantees: programs in which federal agencies agree to pay back part or all of a loan to a private lender if the borrower defaults.

Grants: money given by federal agencies for a fixed period of time and which does not have to be repaid.

Direct Payments: funds provided by federal agencies to individuals, private firms, and institutions. The use of direct payments may be "specified" to perform a particular service or for "unrestricted" use.

Insurance: coverage under specific programs to assure reimbursement for losses sustained. Insurance may be provided by federal agencies or through insurance companies and may or may not require the payment of premiums.

---

* Economic Injury Disaster Loans (EIDL) 59.002
Office of Disaster Assistance
Small Business Administration
409 3rd Street, SW
Washington, DC 20416 (202) 502-6734
To assist business concerns suffering economic injury as a result of certain Presidential, SBA, and/or U.S. Department of Agriculture disaster declarations. Types of assistance: Loans. Estimate of annual funds available in 1992: $108,000,000.

* Loans for Small Business (Business Loans 7(a)(11)) 59.003
Director, Loan Policy and Procedures Branch
Small Business Administration
409 3rd Street, SW
Washington, DC 20416 (202) 205-7511
To provide loans to small business owned by low-income persons or located in areas of high unemployment. Types of assistance: Loans, Loan Guarantee. Estimate of annual funds available in 1992: $16,800,000.

* Management and Technical Assistance for Socially and Economically Disadvantaged Businesses (7(j) Development Assistance Program) 59.007
Associate Administrator for Minority Small Business and Capital Ownership Development
409 3rd Street, SW
Washington, DC 20416 (202) 205-6423
To provide management and technical assistance through qualified individuals, public or private organizations to existing or potential businesses which are economically and socially disadvantaged or which are located in areas of high concentration of unemployment. Types of assistance: Grants. Estimate of annual funds available in 1992: $8,040,000.

* Physical Disaster Loans (7(b) Loans(DL)) 59.008
Office of Disaster Assistance
Small Business Administration
409 3rd Street, SW
Washington, DC 20416 (202) 205-6734
To provide loans to the victims of designated physical-type disasters for uninsured loans. Types of assistance: Loans, Loan Guarantee. Estimate of annual funds available in 1992: $358,300,000.

* Small Business Investment Companies (SBIC; SSBICC) 59.011
Director
Office of Investments
Small Business Administration
409 3rd Street, SW
Washington, DC 20416 (202) 205-6510
To establish privately owned and managed small business investment companies; to provide equity capital and long term loan funds and advisory services. Type of assistance: Loans, Loan Guarantees. Estimate of annual funds available in 1992: $263,539,000.

* Small Business Loans (Regular Business Loans - 7(a) Loans) 59.012
Director
Loan Policy and Procedures Branch
Small Business Administration
409 3rd Street, SW
Washington, DC 20416 (202) 205-7510
To provide guaranteed loans to small businesses which are unable to obtain financing in the private credit marketplace, but can demonstrate an ability to repay loans granted. Types of assistance: Loan Guarantees. Estimate of annual funds available in 1992: $5,133,352,000.

* Local Development Company Loans (502 Loans) 59.013
Office of Economic Development
Small Business Administration
409 3rd Street, SW, Room 720
Washington, DC 20416 (202) 205-6485

Be patient. If any phone number is incorrect, call (area code) 555-1212 and request the new listing.

Federal Money For Business

To make federal loans to local development companies to provide long-term financing to small business concerns located in their areas. Types of assistance: Loan Guarantees. Estimate of annual funds available in 1992: $34,718,000.

* Bond Guarantees for Surety Companies (Surety Bond Guarantee) 59.016

Asst. Administrator
Office of Surety Guarantees
Small Business Administration
409 3rd Street, SW
Washington, DC 20416
Dorothy Kleeschulte (202) 205-6540

To guarantee surety bonds issued by commercial surety companies for small contractors unable to obtain a bond without a guarantee. Types of assistance: Insurance. Estimate of annual funds available in 1992: $1,566,000,000.

* Handicapped Assistance Loans (HAL-1 and HAL-2) 59.021

Director, Loan Policy and Procedures Branch
Small Business Administration
409 3rd Street, SW
Washington, DC 20416 (202) 205-7510

To provide direct loans for nonprofit sheltered workshops and other similar organizations that produce goods and services. Types of assistance: Loans, Loan Guarantees. Estimate of annual funds available in 1992: $11,800,000.

* Service Corps of Retired Executives Association (SCORE) 59.026

National SCORE Office
1825 Connecticut Ave., NW
Washington, DC 20009 (202) 653-6279

To utilize the management experience of retired and active business executives to counsel and train potential and existing small businesses. Types of assistance: Grants. Estimate of annual funds available in 1992: $1,712,000.

* Veterans Loan Program (Veterans Loans) 59.038

Director, Loan Policy and Procedures Branch
Small Business Administration
409 3rd Street, SW
Washington, DC 20416 (202) 205-7510

To provide loans to small businesses owned by Vietnam-era and disabled veterans. Types of assistance: Loans. Estimate of annual funds available in 1992: $16,700,000.

* Certified Development Company Loans (504 Loans) 59.041

Office of Economic Development
Small Business Administration
409 3rd Street, SW
Washington, DC 20416 (202) 205-6485

To assist small business concerns by providing long-term financing for fixed assets through the sale of debentures to private investors. Types of assistance: Loan Guarantees. Estimate of annual funds available in 1992: $682,443,000.

* Business Loans for 8(a) Program Participants (8(a) Program Loans) 59.042

Director
Loan Policy and Procedures Branch
Small Business Administration
409 3rd Street, SW
Washington, DC 20416 (202) 205-7510

To provide direct and guaranteed loans to small business contractors receiving assistance under the subsection of 7(j) 10 and section 8(a) of the Small Business Act (15 U.S.C. 636 (a)), who are unable to obtain financing on reasonable terms in the private credit marketplace, but can demonstrate an ability to repay loans granted. Types of assistance: Loans. Estimate of annual funds available in 1992: $4,900,000.

* Women's Business Ownership Assistance 59.043

Small Business Administration
Office of Women's Business Ownership
409 3rd Street, SW
Washington, DC 20416 (202) 205-6673

To promote the legitimate interest of small business concerns owned and controlled by women and to remove, in so far as possible, the discriminatory barriers that are encountered by women in accessing the capital and other factors of production. Types of assistance: Grants. Estimate of annual funds available in 1992: $1,267,000.

* Commodity Loans and Purchases (Price Supports) 10.051

Cotton, Grain and Rice Price Support Division
Agricultural Stabilization and Conservation Service
U.S. Department of Agriculture
P.O. Box 2415
Washington, DC 20013 (202) 720-7641

To improve and stabilize farm income, to assist in bringing about balance between supply and demand of the commodities, and to assist farmers in the orderly marketing of their crops. Types of assistance: Direct Payments, Loans. Estimate of annual funds available in 1992: $7,675,721,000.

* Cotton Production Stabilization (Cotton Direct Payments) 10.052

Deputy Administrator Policy Analysis
Agricultural Stabilization and Conservation Service
U.S. Department of Agriculture
P.O. Box 2415
Washington, DC 20013 (202) 720-6734

To assure adequate production for domestic and foreign demand for fiber, to protect income for farmers, to take into account federal costs, to enhance the competitiveness of U.S. cotton for domestic mill use and export, and to conserve our natural resources. Types of assistance: Direct Payments. Estimate of annual funds available in 1992: $930,253,000.

* Dairy Indemnity Program 10.053

Emergency Operations and Livestock Program Division
Agricultural Stabilization and Conservation Service
U.S. Department of Agriculture
P.O. Box 2415
Washington, DC 20013 (202) 720-7673

To protect dairy farmers and manufacturers of dairy products who, through no fault of their own, are directed to remove their milk or dairy products from commercial markets because of contamination from pesticides which have been approved for use by the Federal government. Types of assistance: Direct Payments. Estimate of annual funds available in 1992: $200,000.

* Emergency Conservation Program (ECP) 10.054

Agricultural Stabilization and Conservation Service
U.S. Department of Agriculture
P.O. Box 2415
Washington, DC 20013 (202) 720-6221

To enable farmers to perform emergency conservation measures to control wind erosion on farmlands, or to rehabilitate farmlands damaged by wind erosion, floods, hurricanes, or other natural disasters. Types of assistance: Direct Payments. Estimate of annual funds available in 1992: $24,612,250.

* Feed Grain Production Stabilization (Feed Grain Direct Payments) 10.055

Deputy Administrator Policy Analysis
Agricultural Stabilization and Conservation Service
U.S. Department of Agriculture
P.O. Box 2415
Washington, DC 20013 (202) 720-4418

To assure adequate production for domestic and foreign demand, to protect income for farmers, to take into account federal costs, to enhance the competitiveness of United States exports. Types of assistance: Direct Payments. Estimate of annual funds available in 1992: $2,279,453,000.

Be patient. If any phone number is incorrect, call (area code) 555-1212 and request the new listing.

Small Business and Entrepreneuring

*** Wheat Production Stabilization (Wheat Direct Payments) 10.058**
Deputy Administrator Policy Analysis
Agricultural Stabilization and Conservation Service
U.S. Department of Agriculture
P.O. Box 2415
Washington, DC 20013 (202) 720-4417
To assure adequate production for domestic and foreign demand, to protect income for farmers, to take into account federal costs, to enhance the competitiveness of U.S. exports, to compact inflation, and to conserve our natural resources. Types of assistance: Direct Payments. Estimate of annual funds available in 1992: $1,712,500,000.

*** National Wool Act Payments (Wool and Mohair Support Payments) 10.059**
Deputy Administrator Policy Analysis
Agricultural Stabilization and Conservation Service
U.S. Department of Agriculture
P.O. Box 2415
Washington, DC 20013 (202) 720-6734
To encourage continued domestic production of wool at prices fair to both producers and consumers in a way which will assure a viable domestic wool industry in the future. Types of assistance: Direct Payments. Estimate of annual funds available in 1992: $179,600,000.

*** Water Bank Program 10.062**
Agricultural Stabilization and Conservation Service
U.S. Department of Agriculture
P.O. Box 2415
Washington, DC 20013 (202) 720-6221
To conserve surface waters; preserve and improve the nation's wetlands; increase migratory waterfowl habitat in nesting, breeding and feeding areas in the U.S.; and secure environmental benefits for the nation. Types of assistance: Direct Payments. Estimate of annual funds available in 1992: $21,113,713.

*** Agricultural Conservation Program (ACP) 10.063**
Agricultural Stabilization and Conservation Service
U.S. Department of Agriculture
P.O. Box 2415
Washington, DC 20013 (202) 720-6221
Control of erosion and sedimentation, encourage voluntary compliance with federal and state requirements to solve point and nonpoint source pollution, improve water quality, encourage energy conservation measures, and assure a continued supply of necessary food and fiber for a strong and healthy people and economy. Types of assistance: Direct Payments. Estimate of annual funds available in 1992: $230,147,000.

*** Forestry Incentives Program (FIP) 10.064**
Agricultural Stabilization and Conservation Service
U.S. Department of Agriculture
P.O. Box 2415
Washington, DC 20013 (202) 720-6221
To bring private non-industrial forest land under intensified management; to increase timber production; to assure adequate supplies of timber; and to enhance other forest resources through a combination of public and private investments on the most productive sites on eligible individual or consolidated ownerships of efficient size and operation. Types of assistance: Direct Payments. Estimate of annual funds available in 1992: $14,334,176.

*** Rice Production Stabilization (Rice Direct Payments) 10.065**
Deputy Administrator
Policy Analysis Division
Agricultural Stabilization and Conservation Service
U.S. Department of Agriculture
P.O. Box 2415
Washington, DC 20013 (202) 720-7923
To assure adequate production for domestic and foreign demand, to protect income for farmers, to take into account federal costs, to enhance the competitiveness of U.S. exports, and to conserve our natural resources. Types of assistance: Direct Payments. Estimate of annual funds available in 1992: $490,200,000.

*** Emergency Livestock Assistance 10.066**
Emergency Operations and Livestock Programs Division
Agricultural Stabilization and Conservation Service
U.S. Department of Agriculture
P.O. Box 2415
Washington, DC 20013 (202) 720-5621
To provide emergency feed assistance to eligible livestock owners, in a State, county, or area approved by the Executive Vice President, CCC, where because of disease, insect infestation, flood, drought, fire, hurricane, earthquake, storm, hot weather, or other natural disaster, a livestock emergency exists. Types of assistance: Direct Payments. Estimate of annual funds available in 1992: $82,000,000.

*** Grain Reserve Program (Farmer-Held and Owned Grain Reserve) 10.067**
Cotton, Grain and Rice Price Support Division
Agricultural Stabilization and Conservation Service
U.S. Department of Agriculture
P.O. Box 2415
Washington, DC 20013 (202) 720-9886
To insulate sufficient quantities of grain from the market to increase price to farmers. Types of assistance: Direct Payments. Estimate of annual funds available in 1992: $26,000,000.

*** Rural Clean Water Program (RCWP) 10.068**
Conservation and Environmental Protection Division
Agricultural Stabilization and Conservation Service
U.S. Department of Agriculture
P.O. Box 2415
Washington, DC 20013 (202) 720-6221
To achieve improved water quality in the most cost-effective manner possible in keeping with the provisions of adequate supplies of food, fiber, and a quality environment, and to help control nonpoint source agricultural pollution. Types of assistance: Direct Payments. Estimate of annual funds available in 1992: $1,235,830.

*** Conservation Reserve Program (CRP) 10.069**
Conservation and Environmental Protection Division
Agricultural Stabilization and Conservation Service
U.S. Department of Agriculture
P.O. Box 2415
Washington, DC 20013 (202) 720-6221
To protect the nation's long-term capability to produce food and fiber; to reduce soil erosion; to reduce sedimentation; to improve water quality; to create a better habitat for fish and wildlife. Types of assistance: Direct Payments. Estimate of annual funds available in 1992: $1,739,560,000.

*** Colorado River Basin Salinity Control Program (CRBSCP) 10.070**
Conservation and Environmental Protection Division
Agricultural Stabilization and Conservation Service
U.S. Department of Agriculture
P.O. Box 2415
Washington, DC 20013 (202) 720-6221
To provide financial and technical assistance to identify salt source areas; develop project plans to carry out conservation practices to reduce salt loads; install conservation practices to reduce salinity levels; and carry out research, education, and demonstration activities. Types of assistance: Direct Payments. Estimate of annual funds available in 1992: $17,366,164.

*** Small Business Innovation Research (SBIR Program) 10.212**
SBIR Coordinator
Office of Grants and Program Systems
Cooperative State Research Service
U.S. Department of Agriculture

Federal Money For Business

Room 323, Aerospace Bldg.
14th and Independence Ave., SW
Washington, DC 20250-2200 (202) 401-6852
To stimulate technological innovation in the private sector, strengthen the role of small businesses in meeting federal research and development needs, increase private sector commercialization of innovations derived from USDA supported research and development effort, and foster and encourage minority and disadvantaged participation in technological innovation. Types of assistance: Grants. Estimate of annual funds available in 1992: $5,627,503.

* Sustainable Agriculture Research and Education 10.215

Cooperative State Research Service
U.S. Department of Agriculture
Washington, DC 20520 (202) 720-4423
To promote scientific investigation and education in order to reduce pesticides, improve low-input farm management, research and take advantage of local agricultural conditions and practices. Types of assistance: Grants. Estimate of annual funds available in 1992: $6,441,709.

* Emergency Loans 10.404

Administrator
Farmers Home Administration
U.S. Department of Agriculture
Washington, DC 20250 (202) 720-1632
To assist family farmers, ranchers and aquaculture operators with loans to cover losses resulting from major and/or natural disasters. Types of assistance: Loans. Estimate of annual funds available in 1992: $72,000,000.

* Farm Labor Housing Loans and Grants (Labor Housing) 10.405

Multi-Family Housing Processing Division
Farmers Home Administration
U.S. Department of Agriculture
Washington, DC 20250 (202) 720-1604
To provide decent, safe and sanitary low-rent housing and related facilities for domestic farm laborers. Types of assistance: Loan Guarantees. Estimate of annual funds available in 1992: $11,000,000.

* Farm Operating Loans 10.406

Director, Farmer Programs Loan Making Division
Farmers Home Administration
U.S. Department of Agriculture
Washington, DC 20250 (202) 720-1632
To enable operators of not larger than family farms through the extension of credit and supervisory assistance, to make efficient use of their land, labor, and other resources. Loans also available to youths. Types of assistance: Loans, Loan Guarantees. Estimate of annual funds available in 1992: $1,600,000,000.

* Farm Ownership Loans 10.407

Administrator
Farmers Home Administration
U.S. Department of Agriculture
Washington, DC 20250 (202) 720-1632
To assist eligible farmers, ranchers, and aquaculture operators, including farming cooperatives, corporations, partnerships, and joint operations through the extension of credit to become owner-operators of not larger than family farms. Types of assistance: Loans, Loan Guarantees. Estimate of annual funds available in 1992: $555,500,000.

* Rural Rental Housing Loans 10.415

Director, Multi-Family Housing Processing Division
Farmers Home Administration
U.S. Department of Agriculture
Washington, DC 20250 (202) 720-1604
To provide economically designed and constructed rental and cooperative housing and related facilities suited for independent living for rural residents. Types of assistance: Loan Guarantees. Estimate of annual funds available in 1992: $573,900,000.

* Soil and Water Loans (SW Loans) 10.416

Administrator
Farmers Home Administration
U.S. Department of Agriculture
Washington, DC 20250 (202) 720-1632
To facilitate improvement, protection, and proper use of farmland by providing adequate financing and supervisory assistance for soil conservation, water resource development, conservation and use. Types of assistance: Loans. Estimate of annual funds available in 1992: $2,544,000.

* Indian Tribes and Tribal Corporation Loans 10.421

Director
Community Facilities Division
Farmers Home Administration
U.S. Department of Agriculture
Washington, DC 20250 (202) 720-1490
To enable tribes and tribal corporations to acquire land for the use of the tribe or its members. Types of assistance: Loan Guarantees. Estimate of annual funds available in 1992: $1,000,000.

* Business and Industrial Loans 10.422

Administrator
Farmers Home Administration
U.S. Department of Agriculture
Washington, DC 20250-0700 (202) 690-1533
To assist public, private, or cooperative organizations (profit or nonprofit), Indian tribes or individuals in rural areas to obtain quality loans for the purpose of improving, developing or financing business, industry, and employment and improving the economic and environment climate in rural communities including pollution abatement and control. Types of assistance: Loan Guarantees. Estimate of annual funds available in 1992: $101,127,500.

* Industrial Development Grants (IDG) 10.424

Director
Community Facilities Loan Division
Farmers Home Administration
U.S. Department of Agriculture
Washington, DC 20250 (202) 720-1490
To facilitate the development of small and emerging private business, industry and related employment for improving the economy in rural communities. Types of assistance: Grants. Estimate of annual funds available in 1992: $20,750,000.

* Rural Rental Assistance Payments (Rental Assistance) 10.427

Director
Multi-Housing Services and Property Management Division
Farmers Home Administration
U.S. Department of Agriculture
Washington, DC 20250 (202) 720-1599
To reduce the rents paid by low-income families occupying eligible Rural Rental Housing (RRH), Rural Cooperative Housing (RCH), and Farm Labor Housing (LH) projects financed by the Farmers Home Administration through its Sections 515, 514, and 516 loans and grants. Types of assistance: Direct Payments. Estimate of annual funds available in 1992: $319,900,000.

* Interest Rate Reduction Program 10.437

County Supervisor
Farmers Home Administrator
(in the county where the farming is located)
Or write FmHA
U.S. Department of Agriculture
Washington, DC 20250
To aid not larger than family sized farms in obtaining credit when they are temporarily unable to project a positive cash flow without a reduction in the interest rate. Types of assistance: Loan Guarantees. Estimate of annual funds available in 1992: $175,000,000.

* Intermediary Relending Program 10.439

Farmers Home Administration
Room 6321

Be patient. If any phone number is incorrect, call (area code) 555-1212 and request the new listing.

Small Business and Entrepreneuring

South Agriculture Building
Washington, DC 20250 (202) 690-4100
To finance business facilities and community development. Types of assistance: Loans. Estimate of annual funds available in 1992: $32,500,000.

★ Crop Insurance 10.450
Manager, Federal Crop Insurance Corporation
U.S. Department of Agriculture, Ste. 500
Washington, DC 20250 (202) 254-8460
To improve economic stability of agriculture through a sound system of crop insurance by providing multi-peril insurance for individual producers of commercially grown commodities against unavoidable causes of loss such as adverse weather conditions, fire, insects or other natural disasters. Types of assistance: Insurance. Estimate of annual funds available in 1992: $1,170,292,796.

★ Foreign Agricultural Market Development and Promotion 10.600
Assistant Administrator
Commodity and Marketing Programs
Foreign Agricultural Service
U.S. Department of Agriculture
Washington, DC 20250 (202) 447-4761
To create, expand, and maintain markets abroad for U.S. agricultural commodities. Types of assistance: Direct Payments. Estimate of annual funds available in 1992: $34,700,000.

★ Market Promotion Program (MPP) 10.601
Assistant Administrator
Commodity and Marketing Programs
Foreign Agricultural Service
U.S. Department of Agriculture
Washington, DC 20250 (202) 447-4761
To encourage foreign agricultural market development, and to counter or offset the adverse effect on the export of a U.S. agricultural commodity or the product thereof due to subsidy, import quota, or other unfair foreign trade practice. Types of assistance: Direct Payments. Estimate of annual funds available in 1992: $200,000,000.

★ Rural Electrification Loans and Loan Guarantees (REA) 10.850
Administrator
Rural Electrification Administration
U.S. Department of Agriculture
Washington, DC 20250-1500 (202) 720-9540
To assure that people in eligible rural areas have access to electric services comparable in reliability and quality to the rest of the nation. Types of assistance: Loan Guarantees. Estimate of annual funds available in 1992: $2,057,550,000.

★ Rural Telephone Loans and Loan Guarantees (REA) 10.851
Administrator
Rural Electrification Administration
U.S. Department of Agriculture
Washington, DC 20250 (202) 720-9540
To assure that people in eligible rural areas have access to telephone service comparable in reliability and quality to the rest of the nation. Types of assistance: Loan Guarantees. Estimate of annual funds available in 1992: $358,875,000.

★ Rural Telephone Bank Loans (Rural Telephone Bank) 10.852
Governor
Rural Telephone Bank
U.S. Department of Agriculture
Washington, DC 20250 (202) 720-9540
To provide supplemental financing to extend and improve telephone service in rural areas. Types of assistance: Loans. Estimate of annual funds available in 1992: $177,045,000.

★ Rural Economic Development Loans and Grants 10.854
Administrator
Rural Electrification Administration
U.S. Department of Agriculture
Washington, DC 20250 (202) 720-9552
To promote rural economic development and job creation projects, including funding for project feasibility studies, start-up costs, incubator projects, and other reasonable expenses for the purpose of fostering rural development. Types of assistance: Loans, Grants. Estimate of annual funds available in 1992: $8,773,000.

★ Great Plains Conservation 10.900
Deputy Chief for Programs
Soil Conservation Service
U.S. Department of Agriculture
P.O. Box 2890
Washington, DC 20013 (202) 720-1868
To conserve and develop the Great Plains soil and water resources by providing technical and financial assistance to farmers, ranchers, and others in planning and implementing conservation practices. Types of assistance: Direct Payments. Estimate of annual funds available: $16,500,109.

★ Research and Evaluation Program 11.312
David H. Geddes
Room H-7315
Economic Development Administration
U.S. Department of Commerce
Washington, DC 20230 (202) 482-4085
To assist in the determination of causes of unemployment; to promote programs that will raise income levels; to alleviate economic distress. Types of assistance: Grants. Estimate of annual funds available: $1,193,000.

★ Trade Adjustment Assistance 11.313
Daniel F. Harrington
U.S. Department of Commerce
Trade Adjustment Assistance Division
Economic Development Administration
14th and Constitution Ave. NW
Washington, DC 20230 (202) 377-3373
To provide trade adjustment assistance to firms and industries adversely affected by increased imports. Types of assistance: Grants. Estimate of annual funds available in 1992: $14,000,000.

★ Fishermen's Contingency Fund (Title IV) 11.408
Inspection Services Division
Financial Services Division
National Marine Fisheries Service
1335 East West Hwy.
Silver Spring, MD 20910 301-713-2396
To compensate U.S. commercial fishermen for damage/loss of fishing gear and 50% of resulting economic loss due to oil and gas related activities in any area of the Outer Continental Shelf. Types of assistance: Direct Payments. Estimate of annual funds available in 1992: $989,000.

★ Fishing Vessel and Gear Damage Compensation Fund (Section 10) 11.409
Chief, Financial Services Division
National Marine Fisheries Service
U.S. Department of Commerce
1335 East West Hwy.
Silver Spring, MD 20910 301-713-2396
To compensate U.S. fishermen for the loss, damage, or destruction of their vessels by foreign fishing vessels and their gear by any vessel. Types of assistance: Direct Payments. Estimate of annual funds available in 1992: $1,296,000.

★ Minority Business Development Centers (MBDC) 11.800
Assistant Director
Office of Program Operations
Room 5063, Minority Business Agency

Be patient. If any phone number is incorrect, call (area code) 555-1212 and request the new listing.

Federal Money For Business

U.S. Department of Commerce
14th and Constitution Ave., NW
Washington, DC 20230 (202) 377-8015
To provide business development services for a minimal fee to minority firms and individuals interested in entering, expanding or improving their efforts in the marketplace. Types of assistance: Grants. Estimate of annual funds available in 1992: $22,491,000.

* American Indian Program (AIP) 11.801

Assistant Director
Office of Program Development
Room 5063
Minority Business Development Agency
U.S. Department of Commerce
14th and Constitution Ave., NW
Washington, DC 20230 (202) 377-8015
To provide business development service to American Indians and individuals interested in entering, expanding or improving their efforts in the marketplace. Types of assistance: Grants. Estimate of annual funds available in 1992: $1,495,000.

* Minority Business and Industry Association-Minority Chambers of Commerce (MB and IA/C of C) 11.802

Theresa Speake, Asst. Director
Office of Program Development
Room 5096
Minority Business Development Agency
U.S. Department of Commerce
14th and Constitution Ave., NW
Washington, DC 20230 (202) 377-5770
To provide financial assistance for Minority Business and Industry Association/ Minority Chambers of Commerce (MB and IA/C of C) which act as advocates for their members and the minority community. Types of assistance: Grants. Estimate of annual funds available in 1992: $4,601,000.

* Procurement Technical Assistance for Business Firms (Procurement Technical Assistance (PTA)) 12.002

Defense Logistics Agency
Cameron Station
Office of Small and Disadvantaged Business Utilization (DLA-U)
Room 4B130
Alexandria, VA 22304-6100 (202) 274-6471
To assist eligible entities in the payment of the costs of establishing new Procurement Technical Assistance Programs and maintaining existing Procurement Technical Assistance Programs. Types of assistance: Grants. Estimate of annual funds available in 1992: $12,279,481.

* Interest Reduction Payments-Rental and Cooperative Housing for Lower Income Families (236) 14.103

Director
Office of Multifamily Housing Management
U.S. Department of Housing and Urban Development
Washington, DC 20410 (202) 708-3730
To provide good quality rental and cooperative housing for persons of low- and moderate-income by providing interest reduction payments in order to lower their housing costs. Types of assistance: Direct Payments. Estimate of annual funds available in 1992: $645,579,000.

* Mortgage Insurance-Construction or Substantial Rehabilitation of Condominium Projects (234(d) Condominiums) 14.112

Insurance Division
Office of Insured Multifamily Housing Development
U.S. Department of Housing and Urban Development
Washington, DC 20410 (202) 708-2556
To enable sponsors to develop condominium projects in which individual units will be sold to home buyers. Types of assistance: Loan Guarantees. Estimate of annual funds available in 1992: $7,679,000.

* Mortgage Insurance - Homes (203(b)) 14.117

Director, Single Family Development Division
Office of Single Family Housing
U.S. Department of Housing and Urban Development
Washington, DC 20410 (202) 708-2700
To help families undertake home ownership. Types of assistance: Loan Guarantees. Estimate of annual funds available in 1992: $44,279,662,000.

* Mortgage Insurance-Cooperative Projects (213 Cooperatives) 14.126

Policies and Procedures Division
Office of Insured Multifamily Housing Development
U.S. Department of Housing and Urban Development
Washington, DC 20410 (202) 708-2556
To make it possible for nonprofit cooperative ownership housing corporations or trusts to develop or sponsor the development of housing projects to be operated as cooperatives. Most cooperative mortgages are now obtained under 221 (d)(3). Types of assistance: Loan Guarantees. Estimate of annual funds available: Contact Office Above.

* Mortgage Insurance-Manufactured Home Parks (207(m) Manufactured Home Parks) 14.127

Policies and Procedures Division
Office of Insured Multifamily Housing Development
U.S. Department of Housing and Urban Development
Washington, DC 20410 (202) 708-2556
To make possible the financing of construction or rehabilitation of manufactured home parks. Types of assistance: Loan Guarantees. Estimate of annual funds available: Contact Office Above.

* Mortgage Insurance-Hospitals (242 Hospitals) 14.128

Hospital Program
U.S. Department of Housing and Urban Development
Washington, DC 20410 (202) 708-0599
To make possible the financing of hospitals. Types of assistance: Loan Guarantees. Estimate of annual funds available in 1992: $428,754,000.

* Mortgage Insurance-Nursing Homes, Intermediate Care Facilities and Board and Care Homes (232 Nursing Homes) 14.129

Insurance Division
Office of Insured Multifamily Housing Development
U.S. Department of Housing and Urban Development
Washington, DC 20412 (202) 708-2556
Types of assistance: Loan Guarantees. Estimate of annual funds available in 1992: $684,098,000.

* Mortgage Insurance-Purchase of Sales-Type Cooperative Housing Units 14.132

Director
Single Family Development Division
Office of Insured Family Housing
U.S. Department of Housing and Urban Development
Washington, DC 20410 (202) 708-2700
To make available good quality new housing for purchase by individual members of a housing cooperative. Now accepting applications. Types of assistance: Loan Guarantees. Estimate of annual funds available: Contact office above.

* Mortgage Insurance-Purchase of Units in Condominiums (234(c)) 14.133

Director
Single Family Development Division
Office of Insured Single Family Housing
U.S. Department of Housing and Urban Development
Washington, DC 20410 (202) 708-2700
To enable families to purchase units in condominium projects. Types of assistance: Loan Guarantees. Estimate of annual funds available in 1992: $2,904,209,000

Be patient. If any phone number is incorrect, call (area code) 555-1212 and request the new listing.

Small Business and Entrepreneuring

* **Mortgage Insurance-Rental Housing for Moderate Income Families and Elderly, Market Interest Rate (221(d)(3) and (4) Multifamily - Market Rate Housing) 14.135**

Policies and Procedures Division
Office of Insured Multifamily Housing Development
U.S. Department of Housing and Urban Development
Washington, DC 20410 (202) 708-2556

To provide good quality rental or cooperative housing for moderate income families and the elderly. Types of assistance: Loan Guarantees. Estimate of annual funds available in 1992: $666,648,000.

* **Mortgage Insurance-Rental Housing for the Elderly (231) 14.138**

Policies and Procedures Division
Office of Insured Multifamily Housing Development
U.S. Department of Housing and Urban Development
Washington, DC 20410 (202) 708-2556

To provide good quality rental housing for the elderly. Types of assistance: Loan Guarantees. Estimate of annual funds available in 1992: $2,693,000.

* **Mortgage Insurance-Rental Housing in Urban Renewal Areas 14.139**

Policies and Procedures Division
Office of Insured Multifamily Housing Development
U.S. Department of Housing and Urban Development
Washington, DC 20410 (202) 708-2566

To provide good quality rental housing in urban renewal areas, code enforcement areas, and other areas designated for overall revitalization. Types of assistance: Loan Guarantees. Estimate of annual funds available in 1992: $5,674,000.

* **Property Improvement Loan Insurance for Improving all Existing Structures and Building of New Nonresidential Structures (Title I) 14.142**

Director
Title I Insurance Division
U.S. Department of Health and Human Services (202) 708-2880
Washington DC 20410 (800) 733-4663

To facilitate the financing of improvements to homes and other existing structures and the building of new nonresidential structures. Types of assistance: Loan Guarantees. Estimate of annual funds available in 1992: $1,440,000,000.

* **Rent Supplements--Rental Housing for Lower Income Families 14.149**

Office of Multi-Family Housing Management
U.S. Department of Housing and Urban Development
Washington, DC 20410 (202) 708-3730

To make good quality rental housing available to low income families at a cost they can afford. Types of assistance: Direct Payments. Estimate of annual funds available in 1992: $50,139,000.

* **Supplemental Loan Insurance-Multifamily Rental Housing 14.151**

Policies and Procedures Division
Office of Insured Multifamily Housing Development
U.S. Department of Housing and Urban Development
Washington DC 20411 (202) 708-2556

To finance repairs, additions and improvements to multifamily projects, group practice facilities, hospitals, or nursing homes already insured by HUD or held by HUD. Types of assistance: Loan Guarantees. Estimate of annual funds available in 1992: $184,370,000.

* **Mortgage Insurance for the Purchase or Refinancing of Existing Multifamily Housing Projects (Section 223(f) Insured Under Section 207) 14.155**

Office of Insured Multifamily Housing Development

Policies and Procedures Division
U.S. Department of Housing and Urban Development
Washington, DC 20410 (202) 708-2556

To provide mortgage insurance to lenders for the purchase or refinancing of existing multifamily housing projects, whether conventionally financed or subject to federally insured mortgages. Types of assistance: Loan Guarantees. Estimate of annual funds available in 1992: $418,075,000.

* **Housing for the Elderly or Disabled (202) - 14.157**

Housing for the Elderly and Handicapped People Division
Office of Elderly and Assisted Housing
U.S. Department of Housing and Urban Development
Washington, DC 20410 (202) 708-2730

To provide for rental or cooperative housing and related facilities (such as central dining) for the elderly or disabled. Types of assistance: Loans. Estimate of annual funds available in 1992: $11,105,000.

* **Operating Assistance for Troubled Multifamily Housing Projects (Flexible Subsidy Fund) (Troubled Projects) 14.164**

Director
Management Operations Division
Office of Multifamily Housing Management
U.S. Department of Housing and Urban Development
Washington, DC 20420 (202) 708-3730

To provide assistance to restore or maintain the physical and financial soundness of certain projects assisted or approved for assistance under the National Housing Act or under the Housing and Urban Development Act of 1965. Types of assistance: Grants, Direct Payments. Estimate of annual funds available in 1992: $208,500,000.

* **Mortgage Insurance-Two Year Operating Loss Loans, Section 22 14.167**

Office of Insured Multifamily Housing Development
Policies and Procedures Division
U.S. Department of Housing and Urban Development
Washington, DC 20410 (202) 708-3730

To insure a separate loan covering operating losses incurred during the first two years following the date of completion of a multifamily project with a HUD insured first mortgage. Types of assistance: Loan Guarantees. Estimate of annual funds available in 1992: $8,155,000.

* **Mortgage Insurance--Experimental Homes (ExTech 233-Homes) 14.507**

Asst. Secretary for Policy Development and Research
Division of Innovative Technology
U.S. Department of Housing and Urban Development
451 7th Street, SW
Washington, DC 20410 (202) 708-0640

To help finance the development of homes that incorporate new or untried construction concepts designed to reduce housing costs, raise living standards, and improve neighborhood design by providing mortgage insurance. Types of assistance: Loan Guarantees. Estimate of annual funds available: Contact Office Above.

* **Mortgage Insurance--Experimental Projects Other Than Housing (ExTech 233-Projects Other Than Housing) 14.508**

Asst. Secretary for Policy Development and Research
Division of Innovative Technology
U.S. Department of Housing and Urban Development
451 7th Street, SW
Washington, DC 20410 (202) 708-0640

To provide mortgage insurance to help finance the development of group medical facilities that incorporate new or untried construction concepts intended to reduce construction costs, raise living standards and improve neighborhood design. Types of assistance: Loans. Estimate of annual funds available: Contact Office Above.

Be patient. If any phone number is incorrect, call (area code) 555-1212 and request the new listing.

Federal Money For Business

* Mortgage Insurance--Experimental Rental Housing 14.509

Asst. Secretary for Policy Development and Research
Division of Innovative Technology
U.S. Department of Housing and Urban Development
451 7th Street, SW
Washington, DC 20410 (202) 708-0640

To provide mortgage insurance to help finance the development of multifamily housing that incorporates new or untried construction concepts designed to reduce housing costs, raise living standards, and improve neighborhood design. Types of assistance: Loan Guarantees. Estimate of annual funds available: Contact Office Above.

* National Water Resource Research Program 15.806

Geological Survey
U.S. Department of the Interior
MS 424, National Center
Reston, VA 22092 703-648-6811

To support needed research into any aspect of water resource related problems deemed to be in the national interest. Types of assistance: Project Grants. Estimate of annual funds available in 1992: $1,787,000.

* Earthquake Hazards Reduction Program 15.807

Geological Survey
U.S. Department of the Interior
MS 905, National Center
Reston, VA 22092 703-648-6722

To mitigate earthquake losses that can occur in many parts of the nation by providing earth science data and assessments essential for warning of imminent damaging earthquakes, land-use planning, engineering design, and emergency preparedness decisions. Types of assistance: Project Grants. Estimate of annual funds available in 1992: $10,000,000.

* Geological Survey--Research and Data Acquisition 15.808

Geological Survey
U.S. Department of the Interior
MS 104, National Center
Reston, VA 22092 703-648-4451

To support research in any field of study that helps fulfill the Geological Survey's mission. Types of assistance: Project Grants. Estimate of annual funds available in 1992: $9,000,000.

* Protection of Ships from Foreign Seizure (Fishermen's Protection Act) 19.201

Ronald J. Bettauer
Asst. Legal Adviser for International Claims and Investment Disputes
Office of the Legal Adviser
Suite 402, 2100 K St., NW
Washington, DC 20037-7180 (202) 632-7810

To reimburse U.S. fishermen whose vessels are seized by a foreign country on the basis of claims to jurisdictions not recognized by the U.S., claims to jurisdictions recognized by the U.S. but exercised in a manner inconsistent with international law as recognized by the U.S., any general claim to exclusive fisher management with conditions and restrictions. Types of assistance: Insurance. Estimate of annual funds available in 1992: $100,000.

* Fishermen's Guaranty Fund (Section 7) 19.204

Office of Fisheries Affairs
Bureau of Oceans and International Environmental and Scientific Affairs
Room 5806
U.S. Department of State
Washington, DC 20520-7818 (202) 647-2009

To provide for reimbursement of losses incurred as a result of the seizure of a U.S. commercial fishing vessel by a foreign country on the basis of rights or claims in territorial waters or on the high seas which are not recognized by the United States. Types of assistance: Insurance. Estimate of annual funds available in 1992: $900,000.

* Airport Improvement Program (AIP) 20.106

Federal Aviation Administration
Office of Airport Planning and Programming
Grants-in-Aid Division
APP-500, 800 Independence Ave., SW
Washington, DC 20591 (202) 267-3831

To assist sponsors, owners, or operators of public-use airports in the development of a nationwide system of airports adequate to meet the needs of civil aeronautics. Types of assistance: Grants. Estimate of annual funds available in 1992: $1,900,000,000.

* Federal Ship Financing Guarantees (Title XI) 20.802

Associate Administrator for Maritime Aids
Maritime Administration
U.S. Department of Transportation
Washington, DC 20590 (202) 366-0364

To promote construction and reconstruction of ships in the foreign trade and domestic commerce of the U.S. by providing Government guarantees of obligations so as to make commercial credit more available. Types of assistance: Loan Guarantees. Estimate of annual funds available: Contact Office Above.

* Maritime War Risk Insurance (Title XII, MMA, 1936) 20.803

Edmond J. Fitzgerald, Director
Office of Trade Analysis and Insurance
Maritime Administration
U.S. Department of Transportation
Washington, DC 20590 (202) 366-2400

To provide war risk insurance whenever it appears to the Secretary of Transportation that adequate insurance for water-borne commerce cannot be obtained on reasonable terms and conditions from licensed insurance companies in the U.S.. Types of assistance: Insurance. Estimate of annual funds available in 1992: $273,000.

* Operating-Differential Subsidies (ODS) 20.804

Associate Administrator for Maritime Aids
Maritime Administration
U.S. Department of Transportation
400 7th Street, SW
Washington, DC 20590 (202) 366-0364

To promote development and maintenance of the U.S. Merchant Marine by granting financial aid to equalize cost of operating a U.S. flag ship with cost of operating a competitive foreign flag ship. Types of assistance: Direct Payments. Estimate of annual funds available in 1992: $272,210,000.

* Capital Construction Fund (CCF) 20.808

Associate Administrator for Maritime Aids
Maritime Administration
U.S. Department of Transportation
Washington, DC 20590 (202) 366-0364

To provide for replacement vessels, additional vessels or reconstructed vessels, built and documented under the laws of the U.S. for operation in the U.S. foreign, Great Lakes or noncontiguous domestic trades. Types of assistance: Direct Payments. Estimate of annual funds available in 1992: $256,000.

* Supplementary Training 20.810

Bruce J. Carlton, Director
Office of Maritime Labor and Training
Maritime Administration
U.S. Department of Transportation
Washington, DC 20590 (202) 366-5755

To train seafarers in shipboard firefighting, diesel propulsion and other such essential subjects related to safety and operations where this training is not or cannot be provided by the industry directly. Types of assistance: Other. Estimate of annual funds available in 1992: $678,000.

* Construction Reserve Fund (CRF) 20.812

Associate Administrator for Maritime Aids
Maritime Administration

Be patient. If any phone number is incorrect, call (area code) 555-1212 and request the new listing.

Small Business and Entrepreneuring

U.S. Department of Transportation
Washington, DC 20590 (202) 366-0364
To promote the construction, reconstruction, reconditioning or acquisition of merchant vessels which are necessary for national defense and to the development of U.S. commerce. Types of assistance: Direct Payments. Estimate of annual funds available in 1992: $72,000.

* Payments for Essential Air Services 20.901

Director
Office of Aviation Analysis, P-50
U.S. Department of Transportation
400 7th St. SW
Washington, DC 20590 (202) 366-1030
To provide air transportation to eligible communities by subsidizing air service. Types of assistance: Direct Payments. Estimate of annual funds available in 1992: $38,600,000.

* Promotion of the Arts--Design Arts 45.001

Director
Design Arts Program
National Endowment for the Arts
1100 Pennsylvania Ave., NW
Washington, DC 20506 (202) 682-5437
To promote excellence in architecture, landscape architecture, urban design, historic preservation, planning, interior design, graphic design, industrial design and fashion design. Types of assistance: Grants. Estimate of annual funds available in 1992: $3,777,000.

* Promotion of the Arts--Dance 45.002

Dance Program
National Endowment for the Arts
1100 Pennsylvania Ave., NW
Washington, DC 20506 (202) 682-5435
To provide support for professional choreographers, dance companies, organizations and individuals that present or serve dance. Types of assistance: Grants. Estimate of annual funds available in 1992: $8,521,000.

* Promotion of the Arts--Literature 45.004

Director
Literature Program
National Endowment for the Arts
1100 Pennsylvania Ave., NW
Washington, DC 20506 (202) 682-5451
To aid creative writers of fiction and non-fiction, poets, and translators of literary works (into English). Types of assistance: Grants. Estimate of annual funds available in 1992: $4,577,000.

* Promotion of the Arts--Media Arts: Film/Radio/Television 45.006

Cliff Whitham
Media Arts Program
National Endowment for the Arts
1100 Pennsylvania Ave., NW
Washington, DC 20506 (202) 682-5452
To provide grants in support of projects designed to advance the media arts and to encourage their practice and wider appreciation. Types of assistance: Grants. Estimate of annual funds available in 1992: $12,397,000.

* Promotion of the Arts--Theater 45.008

Director
Theater Program
National Endowment for the Arts
1100 Pennsylvania Ave., NW
Washington, DC 20506 (202) 682-5425
To provide grants to aid professional not-for-profit theater companies, individual theater artists, national theater service organizations, professional theater training institutions, and professional not-for-profit theater presenters, including festivals. Types of assistance: Grants. Estimate of annual funds available in 1992: $9,563,000.

* Promotion of the Arts--Visual Arts 45.009

Director, Visual Arts Program
National Endowment for the Arts
1100 Pennsylvania Ave., NW
Washington, DC 20506 (202) 682-5448
To provide grants to assist visual artists including: painters, sculptors, photographers, crafts artists, printmakers, artists specializing in traditional and new genres. Types of assistance: Grants. Estimate of annual funds available: $5,554,000.

* Promotion of the Arts--Museums 45.012

Director, Museum Program
National Endowment for the Arts
1100 Pennsylvania Ave., NW
Washington, DC 20506 (202) 682-5442
To provide grants in support of American museums' essential activities and the evolving needs of the museum field. Types of assistance: Grants. Estimate of annual funds available in 1992: $11,080,000.

* Promotion of the Arts--Opera-Musical Theater 45.014

Director, Opera-Musical Theater Program
National Endowment for the Arts
1100 Pennsylvania Ave., NW
Washington, DC 20506 (202) 682-5447
To support excellence in the performance and creation of professional opera and musical theater. Types of assistance: Grants. Estimate of annual funds available in 1992: $6,063,000.

* Promotion of the Arts--Folk Arts 45.015

Director
Folk Arts Program
National Endowment for the Arts
1100 Pennsylvania Ave., NW
Washington, DC 20506 (202) 682-5449
To provide grants to assist, foster, and make publicly available the diverse traditional American folk arts. Types of assistance: Grants. Estimate of annual funds available in 1992: $3,160,000.

* Arts and Artifacts Indemnity 45.201

Indemnity Administrator
Museum Program
National Endowment for the Arts
Washington, DC 20506 (202) 682-5442
To provide for indemnification against loss or damage for eligible art works, artifacts and objects. Types of assistance: Insurance. Estimate of annual funds available: Contact Office Above.

* Computer and Information Science and Engineering (CISE) 47.070

Assistant Director
Computer and Information Science and Engineering
National Science Foundation
1800 G Street, NW, Room 306
Washington, DC 20550 (202) 357-7936
To support research improving the fundamental understanding of computer and information processing, to enhance the training and education of scientists and engineers who contribute to and exploit that understanding, to enhance the personnel pool for these fields, and to provide access to very advanced computing and networking capabilities. Types of assistance: Grants. Estimate of annual funds available in 1992: $210,940,000.

* Superfund Technical Assistance Grants for Citizen Groups at Priority Sites (Superfund Technical Assistance Grants) 66.806

Office of Emergency and Remedial Response
5203-G, Environmental Protection Agency
401 M Street, SW
Washington, DC 20460
Murray Newton 703-603-8775

Federal Money For Business

To provide resources for community groups to hire technical advisors who can assist them in interpreting technical information concerning the assessment of potential hazards and the selection and design of appropriate remedies at sites eligible for cleanup under the Superfund program. Types of assistance: Grants. Estimate of annual funds available in 1992: $3,200,000.

* Superfund Innovative Technology Evaluation Program (SITE) 66.807

Richard Nalesnik, Chief
Office of Environmental Engineering Technology Demonstration
Environmental Protection Agency
401 M Street, SW, (RD-681)
Washington, DC 20460 (202) 260-2583

To promote research and development of alternative and innovative treatment technologies that can be used under the Comprehensive Environmental Response, Compensation and Liability Act (CERCLA) and to provide incentives for the development and use of such technologies. Types of assistance: Grants. Estimate of annual funds available in 1992: $12,493,000.

* Foreign Investment Guaranties 70.002

Daven Oswalt, Information Officer
Overseas Private Investment Corporation
1615 M Street, NW
Washington, DC 20527 (202) 457-7033

To guarantee loans and other investment made by eligible U.S. investors in friendly developing countries and areas. Types of assistance: Loan Guarantees. Estimate of annual funds available in 1992: $375,000,000.

* Foreign Investment Insurance (Political Risk Insurance) 70.003

Daven Oswalt, Information Officer
Overseas Private Investment Corporation
1615 M Street, NW
Washington DC 20527 (202) 457-7033

To insure investments of eligible U.S. investors in developing friendly countries and areas, against the risks of inconvertibility, expropriation, war, revolution and insurrection, certain types of civil strife, and business interruption. Types of assistance: Insurance. Estimate of annual funds available in 1992: $2,290,000,000.

* Direct Investment Loans (Dollar Loans) 70.005

Daven Oswalt, Information Officer
Overseas Private Investment Corporation
1615 M Street, NW
Washington DC 20527 (202) 457-7033

To make loans for projects in developing countries sponsored by or significantly involving U.S. small business or cooperatives. Types of assistance: Loans. Estimate of annual funds available in 1992: $25,000,000.

* Energy-Related Inventions 81.036

George Lewitt, Director
Office of Technology Evaluation and Assessment
National Institute of Standards and Technology
Gaithersburg, MD 20899 301-975-5500

To encourage innovation in developing non-nuclear energy technology by providing assistance to individual and small business companies in the development of promising energy-related inventions. Types of assistance: Grants. Estimate of annual funds available in 1992: $6,169,365.

* Basic Energy Sciences--University and Science Education (Basic Energy Sciences, High Energy and Nuclear Physics, Fusion Energy, Health and Environmental Research, Program Analysis, Field Operations Management, Superconducting Super Collider, Scientific Computing, and University & Science Education) 81.049

William Burrier
Division of Acquisition and Assistance Management
Office of Energy Research

Office of Energy, Mail Stop G-236
Washington, DC 20545 301-335-5544

To provide financial support for fundamental research, training and related activities in the basic sciences and advanced technology concepts and assessments in fields related to energy. Types of assistance: Grants. Estimate of annual funds available in 1992: $411,621,000.

* Energy Extension Service 81.050

James Demetrops, Director
State Energy Programs Division
U.S. Department of Energy, (CE-522)
Forrestal Building
1000 Independence Ave., SW
Washington, DC 20585 (202) 586-9187

To encourage individuals and small establishments to reduce energy consumption and convert to alternative energy sources. Types of assistance: Grants. Estimate of annual funds available in 1992: $4,757,000.

* Office of Minority Economic Impact Loans (OMEI Direct Loans for DOE Bid or Proposal Preparation) 81.063

Sterling Nichols
Office of Minority Economic Impact
MI-1, U.S. Department of Energy
Forrestal Building, Room 5B-110
Washington, DC 20585 (202) 586-1594

To provide direct loans to minority business enterprises (MBE) to assist them in financing bid or proposal preparation costs they would incur in pursuing DOE work. Types of assistance: Loans. Estimate of annual funds available: Contact Office Above.

* Industrial Energy Conservation 81.078

Marsha Quinn
Office of Industrial Technologies
CE-14, U.S. Department of Energy
Washington, DC 20585 (202) 586-2097

To work closely with industry to develop new technologies to improve energy efficiency and fuel flexibility in the industrial sector. To conduct programs to reduce waste generation, increase recycling, improve the use of waste as process feedstocks, and encourage adoption of new technologies. Types of assistance: Grants. Estimate of annual funds available in 1992: $3,000,000.

* Regional Biomass Programs 81.079

Mike Voorhies
Office of Natural Programs
CE-52, U.S. Department of Energy
Washington, DC 20585 (202) 586-1480

To conduct a long-term research effort to provide generic technology tailored to specific regions for feedstock, production, and conversion technologies, and municipal solid waste. Types of assistance: Grants. Estimate of annual funds available in 1992: $4,523,000.

* Conservation Research and Development (Conservation) 81.086

Barbara Twigg
Office of Management and Resources
Conservation and Renewable Energy
Washington, DC 20585 (202) 586-8174

To conduct a research effort in the areas of buildings, industry, transportation. Grants will be offered to develop and transfer to the nonfederal sector various energy conservation technologies. Types of assistance: Grants. Estimate of annual funds available in 1992: $8,258,000.

* Renewable Energy Research and Development (Renewable Energy) 81.087

Barbara Twigg
Office of Management and Resources
U.S. Department of Energy
Washington, DC 20585 (202) 586-8714

To research and develop efforts in energy technologies: solar buildings,

Be patient. If any phone number is incorrect, call (area code) 555-1212 and request the new listing.

Small Business and Entrepreneuring

photovoltaics, solar thermal, biomass, alcohol fuels, urban waste, wind, ocean, and geothermal. Grants will be offered to develop and transfer to the nonfederal sector various renewable energy technologies. Types of assistance: Grants. Estimate of annual funds available in 1992: $100,000.

* Fossil Energy Research and Development 81.089

Dwight Mottett
U.S. Department of Energy
Fossil Energy Program, FE-122
Germantown, MD 20545 (202) 903-3008

To support long-term, high risk research and development with high potential payoff to increase domestic production of oil and gas or help shift use of oil and gas to more abundant coal and oil shale resources. Types of assistance: Grants. Estimate of annual funds available in 1992: $53,777,063.

* Socioeconomic and Demographic Research, Data and Other Information 81.091

Georgia R. Johnson
U.S. Department of Energy
Forrestal Building, Room 5B-110
Washington, DC 20585 (202) 586-1593

To provide financial support for developing and enhancing socioeconomic and demographic research to determine minority energy consumption, minority income spent on energy; develop information to guide policy and assist minority education and business. Types of assistance: Grants. Estimate of annual funds available in 1992: $800,000.

* Nuclear Energy, Reactor Systems, Development, and Technology 81.095

H. Rohm, Office of Nuclear Energy (NE-40)
B-410, Germantown Building
Washington, DC 20545 301-353-6590

To provide financial support for research, design, analysis, and assessments in science and technology in fields related to nuclear energy. Types of assistance: Grants. Estimate of annual funds available in 1992: $3,500,000.

* Clean Coal Technology Program 81.096

C. Lowell Miller
U.S. Department of Energy
Fossil Energy Program
FE-22, Clean Coal Technology
Washington, DC 20585 703-235-2450

To solicit proposals to conduct cost-shared Innovative Clean Coal Technology projects to demonstrate technologies that are capable of being commercialized in the 1990's, that are more cost-effective than current technologies, and that are capable of achieving significant reduction of $SO2$ and/or NOX emissions from existing coal burning facilities, particularly those that contribute to transboundary and interstate pollution. Types of assistance: Grants. Estimate of annual funds available in 1992: $177,243,200.

* Technology Integration (TIP) 81.103

C. Sink
Office of Technology Development, EM-52
Environmental Restoration and Waste Management
Washington, DC 20545 301-903-7928

To support the mission of TIP by expediting the transfer of technologies/ information from DOE to industry and from industry to DOE. Also, to coordinate technological development for environmental restoration and waste management within DOE and between DOE and other government agencies. Types of assistance: Grants. Estimate of annual funds available: $4,000,000.

* Disabled--Innovation and Development (Research and Demonstration Projects in Education for the Disabled) 84.023

Martha Coutinho
Division of Innovation and Development
Office of Asst. Secretary of Education
400 Maryland Ave., NW
Washington, DC 20202 (202) 205-8156

To improve the education of children with disabilities through research and development projects and model programs (demonstrations). Types of assistance: Grants. Estimate of annual funds available in 1992: $21,000,000.

* Early Education for Children with Disabilities 84.024

James Hamilton
Division of Educational Services
Special Education Programs
Office of Asst. Secretary for Special Education and Rehabilitation Services
U.S. Department of Education
400 Maryland Ave., SW
Washington, DC 20202 (202) 205-9084

To support demonstration, dissemination and implementation of effective approaches to preschool and early childhood education for children with disabilities. Types of assistance: Grants. Estimate of annual funds available: $24,202,000.

* Media and Captioning for Individuals with Disabilities 84.026

Ernest Hairston
Division of Educational Services
Special Education Programs
Office of Asst. Secretary of Special Education and Rehabilitation Services
U.S. Department of Education
Washington, DC 20202 (202) 205-9172

To maintain free loan service of captioned films for the deaf and instructional media for the educational, cultural, and vocational enrichment of disabled. Provide for acquisition and distribution of media materials and equipment; provide contracts distribution of media material and equipment; provide contracts and grants for research into use of media and technology, train teachers, parents, etc. in media and technology use. Types of assistance: Grants. Estimate of annual funds available in 1992: $17,000,000.

* Educational Research and Development 84.117

U.S. Department of Education
Office of Educational Research and Improvement
555 New Jersey Ave., NW
Washington, DC 20208 (202) 219-2079

To advance knowledge about and understanding of education policy and practice, and solve, alleviate, or illuminate educational problems. Types of assistance: Grants. Estimate of annual funds available in 1992: $27,700,000.

* Technology, Educational Media and Materials for Individuals with Disabilities (Technical Development) 84.180

Ellen Schiller
Division of Innovation and Development
U.S. Department of Education
400 Maryland Ave., NW
Washington, DC 20202 (202) 205-8123

To advance the use of new technology, media, and materials in the education of disabled students and the provision of early intervention to infants and toddlers with disabilities. Types of assistance: Grants. Estimate of annual funds available: $5,593,000.

* Food and Drug Administration Research 93.103

Program and Grants Management
Grants and Assistance Agreements
Division of Contracts and Grants
Federal Drug Administration
Public Health Service
U.S. Department of Health and Human Services
HFA-520, Room 340
Parklawn Bldg., 5600 Fishers Lane
Rockville MD 20857 301-443-6170

To assist profit-making organizations, public and others, to research and disseminate information about AIDS, poison control, drug hazards, human and veterinary drugs, medical devices, diagnostic products, biologics, and radiation

Be patient. If any phone number is incorrect, call (area code) 555-1212 and request the new listing.

Federal Money For Business

emitting devices; stimulate technological innovation; use small business to meet Federal R&D needs; increase private sector commercialization of innovations derived from Federal research; foster minority and disadvantaged persons' participation in innovations. Types of assistance: Grants. Estimate of annual funds available in 1992: $10,000,000.

* Adolescent Family Life Research Grants 93.111

Ms. Eckard
Office of Adolescent Pregnancy Program
Office of Asst. Secretary for Health
Public Health Service
U.S. Department of Health and Human Services
Room 736E, Humphrey Bldg.
200 Independence Ave., SW
Washington, DC 20201 (202) 690-8181

To encourage and support research projects concerning adolescent premarital sexual practices and to resolve the negative consequences. Types of assistance: Grants. Estimate of annual funds available in 1992: $926,000.

* Biological Response to Environmental Health Hazards 93.113

Dr. Schonwalder
Scientific Programs Branch
Division of Extramural Research and Training
NIEHS, National Institutes of Health
Public Health Service
U.S. Department of Health and Human Services
P.O. Box 12233
Research Triangle Park, NC 27709 919-541-7634

To promote understanding of how chemical and physical agents cause pathological changes that manifest as diseases. Types of assistance: Grants. Estimate of annual funds available in 1992: $72,965,000.

* Applied Toxicological Research and Testing (Bioassay of Chemicals and Test Development) 93.114

Dr. Schonwalder
Scientific Programs Branch
Division of Extramural Research and Training
NIEHS, National Institutes of Health
Public Health Service
U.S. Department of Health and Human Services
P.O. Box 12233
Research Triangle Park, NC 27709 919-541-7643

To develop scientific information about potentially toxic and hazardous chemicals and develop methods for predicting human response to toxic agents. Types of assistance: Grants. Estimate of annual funds available in 1992: $6,406,000.

* Biometry and Risk Estimation--Health Risks From Environmental Exposures 93.115

Dr. Schonwalder
Scientific Programs Branch
Division of Extramural Research and Training
NIEHS, National Institutes of Health
Public Health Service
U.S. Department of Health and Human Services
Research Triangle Park, NC 27709 919-541-7643

To conduct a broad-scale effort in biometry and risk estimation of probable health risks of cancer, reproductive and neurological effects, and other adverse effects from exposures to various environmental hazards. Types of assistance: Grants. Estimate of annual funds available in 1992: $6,020,000.

* Acquired Immunodeficiency Syndrome (AIDS) Activity (AIDS) 93.118

Clara Jenkins
Grants Management Branch
Procurement and Grants Office
Centers for Disease Control
Public Health Service
U.S. Department of Health and Human Services

255 E. Paces Ferry Rd., NE
Atlanta, GA 30305 404-842-6575

To develop and implement surveillance, epidemiological research, health education, school health, and risk reduction activities of the human immunodeficiency virus, (HIV) in States and major cities. Types of assistance: Grants. Estimate of annual funds available in 1992: $232,854,000.

* Mental Health Services for Cuban Entrants 93.120

Refugee Mental Health Program
National Institute of Mental Health
Alcohol, Drug Abuse and Mental Health Administration
Public Health Service
U.S. Department of Health and Human Services
Room 18-49, Parklawn Bldg.
5600 Fishers Lane
Rockville MD 20857 301-443-2130

To support a complete range of treatment settings which are needed for mentally ill and/or developmentally disabled Cuban entrants currently in Federal custody. Entrants needing treatment cover a wide range of diagnostic categories and treatment histories. Types of assistance: Grants. Estimate of annual funds available in 1992: $3,600,000.

* Oral Diseases and Disorders Research 93.121

Ms. Ringler
Extramural Program
National Institute of Dental Research
National Institutes of Health
Public Health Service
U.S. Department of Health and Human Services
Bethesda, MD 20892 301-496-7437

To obtain improved information on the early diagnosis etiology and prevention of dental caries and improved dental care. Types of assistance: Grants. Estimate of annual funds available in 1992: $112,595,000.

* Small Business Innovation Research (SBIR Program) 93.126

Grants Management Officer
National Institute of Drug Abuse
Alcohol, Drug Abuse and Mental Health Administration
Public Health Service
U.S. Department of Health and Human Services
Room 8A-54, Parklawn Bldg.
5600 Fishers Lane
Rockville MD 20857 301-443-6710

To stimulate technological innovation; use small business to meet alcohol, drug, and mental health research and development needs; increase private sector commercialization of innovations derived from federal research and development; and encourage participation by minority and disadvantaged firms. Types of assistance: Grants. Estimate of annual funds available in 1992: $9,997,000.

* Injury Prevention and Control Research Projects 93.136

Mr. Cassell
Grants Management Officer
Procurement and Grants Office
Centers for Disease Control
Public Health Service
U.S. Department of Health and Human Services
255 E. Paces Ferry Rd., NE
Atlanta, GA 30305 404-842-6630

To support injury control research and demonstrations on priority issues. Types of assistance: Grants. Estimate of annual funds available in 1992: $14,500,000.

* Pediatric AIDS Health Care Demonstration Program 93.153

Division of Services for Children with Special Health Care Needs
Maternal and Child Health Bureau
Health Resources and Services Administration
Public Health Service

Be patient. If any phone number is incorrect, call (area code) 555-1212 and request the new listing.

Small Business and Entrepreneuring

U.S. Department of Health and Human Services
Room 18A27, Parklawn Bldg.
Rockville, MD 20857 301-443-9051
To support demonstration projects for strategies and innovative models for intervention in pediatric AIDS and coordination of services for child-bearing women and children with AIDS, or who are at-risk of contracting AIDS. Types of assistance: Grants. Estimate of annual funds available in 1992: $19,518,000.

* Rural Health Research Centers 93.155

Dr. Taylor
Office of Rural Health Policy
Office of Administration
Health Resources and Services Administration
Public Health Service
U.S. Department of Health and Human Services
Parklawn Bldg, Room 9-05
5600 Fishers Lane
Rockville, MD 20857 301-443-0835
To support the development of rural health research centers to provide an information base and policy analysis capacity on the full range of rural health issues, including reimbursement, recruitment and retention of health professionals, access to care, and alternative delivery systems. Types of assistance: Grants. Estimate of annual funds available in 1992: $2,100,000.

* Minority AIDS and Related Risk Factors Education/Preservation Grants 93.160

Mrs. Williams
Grants Management Officer
Office of Minority Health
Office of Asst. Secretary for Health
Rockwall II Bldg., Suite 1102
5515 Security Lane
Rockville, MD 20852 301-227-8758
To demonstrate that minority community-based organizations and minority institutions can effectively develop and implement human HIV infection education and prevention strategies. Types of assistance: Grants. Estimate of annual funds available in 1992: $1,300,000.

* Human Genome Research 93.172

Dr. Mark Guyer
National Center for Human Genome Research
National Institutes of Health
Public Health Service
U.S. Department of Health and Human Services
Bethesda, MD 20892 301-496-0844
To obtain genetic maps, physical maps, and determine the DNA sequences of the genomes of humans and model organisms to be used as resources in biomedical research, medicine, and biotechnology, using Small Business Innovative Research (SBIR) Program objectives. Types of assistance: Grants. Estimate of annual funds available in 1992: $91,589,000.

* Research Related to Deafness and Communication Disorders 93.173

Dr. Naunton
National Institute on Deafness and Other Communication Disorders
National Institutes of Health
Public Health Service
U.S. Department of Health and Human Services
Executive Plaza South, Room 400-B
Bethesda, MD 20892 301-496-1804
To investigate solutions to problems directly relevant to patients with deafness or disorders of human communication, such as hearing, balance, smell, taste, voice, speech, and language. Types of assistance: Grants. Estimate of annual funds available in 1992: $127,244,000.

* Mental Health Research Grants 93.242

Mr. Ringler
Grants Management Officer
National Institute of Mental Health
Alcohol, Drug Abuse and Mental Health Administration

Public Health Service
U.S. Department of Health and Human Services
Room 7C-15, Parklawn Bldg.
5600 Fishers Lane
Rockville, MD 20857 301-443-3065
To increase knowledge and improve research methods on mental and behavioral disorders. Types of assistance: Grants. Estimate of annual funds available in 1992: $368,281,000.

* Occupational Safety and Health Research Grants 93.262

Mr. Cassell
Grants Management Officer
Procurement and Grants Office
Centers for Disease Control
Public Health Service
U.S. Department of Health and Human Services
255 E. Paces Ferry Road NE, MS-E14
Atlanta, GA 30333 404-842-6630
To understand occupational safety and health problems in industry and find effective solutions in dealing with them. Types of assistance: Grants. Estimate of annual funds available in 1992: $6,747,847.

* Drug Abuse Research Programs 93.279

Ms. Denney
Grants Management Officer
National Institute of Drug Abuse
Alcohol, Drug Abuse and Mental Health Administration
Public Health Service
U.S. Department of Health and Human Services
Room 8A-54, Parklawn Bldg.
5600 Fishers Lane
Rockville, MD 20857 301-443-6710
To develop new knowledge and approaches to diagnosis, treatment and prevention of drug abuse and intravenous(IV)-related AIDS. Types of assistance: Grants. Estimate of annual funds available in 1992: $276,704,000.

* Cancer Cause and Prevention Research 93.393

Leo Buscher, Jr.
Grants Management Officer
National Cancer Institute
National Institutes of Health
Public Health Service
U.S. Department of Health and Human Services, EPS-216
Bethesda, MD 20892 301-496-7753
To identify those factors which cause cancer and develop mechanisms for preventing cancer in people. Types of assistance: Grants. Estimate of annual funds available in 1992: $324,720,000.

* Cancer Detection and Diagnosis and Research 93.394

Leo Buscher, Jr.
Grants Management Officer
National Cancer Institute
National Institutes of Health
Public Health Service
U.S. Department of Health and Human Services, EPS-216
Bethesda, MD 20892 301-496-7753
To identify cancer in patients early and precisely enough to use the latest methods of treatment. Types of assistance: Grants. Estimate of annual funds available: $74,816,000.

* Cancer Treatment Research 93.395

Leo Buscher, Jr., Grants Management Officer
National Cancer Institute
National Institutes of Health
Public Health Service
U.S. Department of Health and Human Services, EPS-216
Bethesda, MD 20892 301-496-7753
To develop the means to cure as many cancer patients as possible. Types of assistance: Grants. Estimate of annual funds available in 1992: $248,826,000.

Be patient. If any phone number is incorrect, call (area code) 555-1212 and request the new listing.

Federal Money For Business

* Cancer Biology Research 93.396

Leo Buscher, Jr.
Grants Management Officer
National Cancer Institute
National Institutes of Health
Public Health Service
U.S. Department of Health and Human Services, EPS-216
Bethesda, MD 20892 301-496-7753

To provide fundamental information on the cause and nature of cancer in humans to improve prevention, detection and diagnosis and treatment of neoplastic diseases. Types of assistance: Grants. Estimate of annual funds available in 1992: $216,223,000.

* Cancer Control 93.399

Leo Buscher
Grants Management Officer
National Cancer Institute
National Institutes of Health
Public Health Service
U.S. Department of Health and Human Services, EPS-216
Bethesda, MD 20892 301-496-7753

To reduce cancer incidence, morbidity and mortality. Types of assistance: Grants. Estimate of annual funds available in 1992: $32,159,000.

* Social Services Research and Demonstration 93.647

Division of Research and Demonstrations
Office of Policy, Planning and Legislation
Office of Human Development Service
U.S. Department of Health and Human Services
Room 684-C
370 L'Enfant Promenade, SW
Washington, DC 20201 (202) 472-3026

To promote effective social services for dependent and vulnerable populations such as the poor, the aged, children and youth, Native Americans, and the disabled. Types of assistance: Grants. Estimate of annual funds available in 1992: $10,379,000.

* Health Care Financing Research, Demonstrations and Evaluations 93.779

Joseph R. Antos, Director
Office of Research and Demonstrations (ORD)
HCFA, U.S. Department of Health and Human Services
6325 Security Blvd
Baltimore, MD 21207 301-966-6507

To support projects in efforts to resolve major health care financing issues. Types of assistance: Grants. Estimate of annual funds available in 1992: $78,380,000.

* Biophysics and Physiological Sciences 93.821

Ms. Tippery
Grants Management Officer
Office of Program Activities
National Institute of General Medical Sciences
National Institutes of Health
Public Health Service
U.S. Department of Health and Human Services
Bethesda, MD 20892 301-496-7746

To foster the application of physical and engineering principles in the study of biomedical problems. Types of assistance: Grants. Estimate of annual funds available in 1992: $164,076,000.

* Heart and Vascular Diseases Research 93.837

Thomas Turley
Grants Management Officer
Office of Program Policy and Procedures
National Heart, Lung and Blood Institute
National Institutes of Health
Public Health Service
U.S. Department of Health and Human Services
Bethesda, MD 20892 301-496-7255

To foster research and prevention, education and control of heart and vascular diseases. Types of assistance: Grants. Estimate of annual funds available in 1992: $530,543,000.

* Lung Diseases Research 93.838

Thomas Turley, Grants Management Officer
Office of Program Policy and Procedures
National Heart, Lung and Blood Institute
National Institutes of Health
Public Health Service
U.S. Department of Health and Human Services
Bethesda, MD 20892 301-496-7255

To use available knowledge and technology to solve specific diseases of the lungs and promote further studies of the lungs. Types of assistance: Grants. Estimate of annual funds available: $174,333,000.

* Blood Diseases and Resources Research 93.839

Thomas Turley
Grants Management Officer
Office of Program Policy and Procedures
National Heart, Lung and Blood Institute
National Institutes of Health
Public Health Service
U.S. Department of Health and Human Services
Bethesda, MD 20892 301-496-7255

To foster research for the prevention and improved diagnosis and treatment of blood diseases. Types of assistance: Grants. Estimate of annual funds available in 1992: $157,201,000.

* Arthritis, Musculoskeletal and Skin Diseases Research 93.846

Grants Management Officer
Division of Extramural Activities
National Institute of Arthritis, Musculoskeletal and Skin Diseases
National Institutes of Health
Public Health Service
U.S. Department of Health and Human Services
Room 732A, Westwood Bldg.
Bethesda, MD 20892 301-402-3352

To conduct research and train researchers in the above areas. Types of assistance: Grants. Estimate of annual funds available: $165,727,000.

* Diabetes, Endocrinology and Metabolism Research 93.847

John Garthune, Asst. Director
Division of Extramural Activities
National Institute of Diabetes, Digestive and Kidney Diseases
National Institutes of Health
U.S. Department of Health and Human Services
Room 637, Westwood Bldg.
Bethesda, MD 20892 301-496-7793

To support research and training for individuals interested in careers in these programs and stimulate technological innovation. Types of assistance: Grants. Estimate of annual funds available in 1992: $258,131,000.

* Digestive Diseases and Nutrition Research 93.848

John Garthune, Asst. Director
Division of Extramural Activities
National Institute of Diabetes, Digestive and Kidney Diseases
National Institutes of Health
Room 637, Westwood Bldg.
Bethesda, MD 20892 301-496-7793

To conduct research and train individuals in the above fields. Types of assistance: Grants. Estimate of annual funds available in 1992: $121,286,000.

* Kidney Diseases, Urology and Hematology Research 93.849

John Garthune, Asst. Director
Division of Extramural Activities

Be patient. If any phone number is incorrect, call (area code) 555-1212 and request the new listing.

Small Business and Entrepreneuring

National Institute of Diabetes, Digestive and Kidney Diseases
National Institutes of Health
Room 637, Westwood Bldg.
Bethesda, MD 20892 — 301-496-7793
Types of assistance: Grants. Estimate of annual funds available in 1992: $167,727,000.

* Clinical Research Related to Neurological Disorders 93.853

Ms. Whitehead
Grants Management Officer
National Institute of Neurological Disorders and Stroke
National Institutes of Health
Public Health Service
U.S. Department of Health and Human Services
Federal Bldg., Room 1004A
Bethesda, MD 20892 — 301-496-9231
To investigate solutions to neurological disorders and stroke. Types of assistance: Grants. Estimate of annual funds available in 1992: $180,983,000.

* Biological Basis Research in the Neurosciences 93.854

Ms. Whitehead
Grants Management Officer
National Institute of Neurological Disorders and Stroke
National Institutes of Health
Public Health Service
U.S. Department of Health and Human Services
Federal Bldg., Room 1004A
Bethesda, MD 20892 — 301-496-9231
To support biological basis research of the brain and nervous system and their disorders. Types of assistance: Grants. Estimate of annual funds available in 1992: $281,074,000.

* Pharmacological Sciences 93.859

Ms. Tippery
Grants Management Officer
Office of Program Activities
National Institute of General Medical Sciences
National Institutes of Health
Public Health Service
U.S. Department of Health and Human Services
Bethesda, MD 20892 — 301-496-7746
To provide an improved understanding of the biological phenomena and related chemical and molecular processes involved in the action of therapeutic drugs and their metabolites and design new ones as well as research anesthetic agents. Types of assistance: Grants. Estimate of annual funds available in 1992: $122,066,000.

* Genetics Research 93.862

Ms. Tippery
Grants Management Officer
Office of Program Activities
National Institute of General Medical Sciences
National Institutes of Health
Public Health Service
U.S. Department of Health and Human Services
Bethesda, MD 20892 — 301-496-7746
To support research aimed at prevention, therapy, and control of genetic diseases, including multifactorial illnesses with a strong hereditary component. Types of assistance: Grants. Estimate of annual funds available in 1992: $229,530,000.

* Cellular and Molecular Basis of Disease Research 93.863

Ms. Tippery
Grants Management Officer
Office of Program Activities
National Institute of General Medical Sciences
National Institutes of Health
Public Health Service

U.S. Department of Health and Human Services
Bethesda, MD 20892 — 301-496-7746
To support research that seeks greater understanding of human cells and their environment in order to prevent, treat and cure diseases resulting from disturbed or abnormal cellular activities. Types of assistance: Grants. Estimate of annual funds available in 1992: $233,476,000.

* Population Research 93.864

Mr. Clark
Office of Grants and Contracts
National Institute of Child Health and Human Development
National Institutes of Health
Public Health Service
U.S. Department of Health and Human Services
Executive Plaza North
Rockville, MD 20892 — 301-496-5001
To seek solutions to the problems of reproductive processes; to develop safer and more effective contraceptives; to understand impact of population change and structure. Types of assistance: Grants. Estimate of annual funds available in 1992: $118,517,000.

* Research for Mothers and Children 93.865

Mr. Clark
Office of Grants and Contracts
National Institute of Child Health and Human Development
National Institutes of Health
Public Health Service
U.S. Department of Health and Human Services
Executive Plaza North
Rockville, MD 20892 — 301-496-5001
To stimulate, coordinate and support fundamental and clinical, biomedical and behavioral research of fetal and childhood development. Types of assistance: Grants. Estimate of annual funds available in 1992: $235,977,000.

* Aging Research 93.866

Mr. Ellis
Grants Management Officer
Office of Extramural Affairs
National Institute on Aging
National Institutes of Health
Public Health Service
U.S. Department of Health and Human Services
Bethesda, MD 20892 — 301-496-1472
To encourage biomedical, social, and behavioral research to understand the aging process and the needs, special problems, and diseases it produces. Types of assistance: Grants. Estimate of annual funds available in 1992: $291,003,000.

* Retinal and Choroidal Diseases Research 93.867

Ms. Carolyn Grimes
Extramural Services Branch
National Eye Institute
National Institutes of Health
Public Health Service
U.S. Department of Health and Human Services
Bethesda, MD 20892 — 301-496-5884
To support research on the structure and function of the retina in health and disease. Types of assistance: Grants. Estimate of annual funds available in 1992: $96,170,000.

* Anterior Segment Diseases Research 93.868

Ms. Carolyn Grimes
Extramural Services Branch
National Eye Institute
National Institutes of Health
Public Health Service
U.S. Department of Health and Human Services
Bethesda, MD 20892 — 301-496-5884
To support research on diseases of the cornea and external ocular structures. Types of assistance: Grants. Estimate of annual funds available in 1992: $72,109,000.

Federal Money For Business

* Strabismus, Amblyopia and Visual Processing 93.871

Ms. Carolyn Grimes
Extramural Services Branch, National Eye Institute
National Institutes of Health
Public Health Service, DHHS
Bethesda, MD 20892 · 301-496-5884

To support studies of the structure and function of the central visual pathways, processing of visual information and the study of those structures in terms of their function, impairment and rehabilitation. Types of assistance: Grants. Estimate of annual funds available in 1992: $45,999,000.

* Special Loans for National Health Service Corps Members to Enter Private Practice 93.973

Director, National Health Service Corps
Health Resources and Services Administration
Public Health Service
U.S. Department of Health and Human Services
Parklawn Building, Room 7A-39
5600 Fishers Lane
Rockville, MD 20857 · 301-443-2900

To assist members of the National Health Service Corps in establishing their own private practice in a health manpower shortage area. Types of assistance: Loans. Estimate of annual funds available: Contact Office Above.

Be patient. If any phone number is incorrect, call (area code) 555-1212 and request the new listing.

Franchising: How to Select the Best Opportunity

Franchising can be the way for you to launch a new business, but it is not risk free, and needs to be entered into with a degree of caution. According to the Federal Trade Commission (FTC), there is no accurate data available to prove that franchises have a lower failure rate than new businesses, so there are a few steps you need to take in order to protect yourself. The following organizations and publications will help you find the right franchise for you.

Organizations

Federal Trade Commission
Bureau of Consumer Protection
Division of Enforcement
Pennsylvania Avenue at 6th Street, NW
Washington, DC 20580
Craig Tregillus   (202) 326-2970

Buying a franchise or a business opportunity may be appealing if you want to be your own boss, but have limited capital and business experience. However, without carefully investigating a business before you purchase, you may make a serious mistake. It is important to find out if a particular business is right for you and if it has the potential to yield the financial return you expect. A Federal Trade Commission rule requires that franchise and business opportunity sellers provide certain information to help you in your decision. Under the FTC rule, a franchise or business opportunity seller must give you a detailed disclosure document at least ten business days before you pay any money or legally commit yourself to a purchase. This document gives 20 important items of information about the business, including: the names, addresses, and telephone numbers of other purchasers; the fully-audited financial statement of the seller; the background and experience of the business's key executives; the cost required to start and maintain the business; and the responsibilities you and the seller will have to each other once you buy. The disclosure document is a valuable tool that not only helps you obtain information about a proposed business, but assists you in comparing it with other businesses. If you are not given a disclosure document, ask why you did not receive one. Some franchise or business opportunity sellers may not be required to give you a disclosure document. If any franchise or business opportunity says it is not covered by the rule, you may want to verify it with the FTC, an attorney, or a business advisor. Even if the business is not required to give the document, you still may want to ask for the data to help you make an informed investment decision.

Some Important Advice From The FTC:

1. Study the disclosure document and proposed contracts carefully.

2. Talk to current owners. Ask them how the information in the disclosure document matches their experiences with the company. Visit the franchises to be sure they really exist. One group you should interview is those who have been in business less than a year. Ask about the company's training program. Find out how long it took to break even and if the company's estimate of operating and working capital was accurate. The second group should be those in business for six years. Find out what kind of deal they got for the franchise and compare it to yours. There are strains in every franchise marriage. Find out what they are. Some franchises hire their own accountants to double check the franchises' accounting. When mistakes are made, it is often attributed to the franchise.

3. Investigate earnings claims. Earnings claims are only estimates. The FTC rule requires companies to have in writing the facts on which they base their earnings claims. Make sure you understand the basis for a seller's earnings claims.

4. Shop around: compare franchises with other available business opportunities. You may discover that other companies offer benefits not available from the first company you considered. The *Franchise Opportunities Handbook*, which is published annually by the U.S. Department of Commerce, describes more than 1,400 companies that offer franchises. Contact other companies and ask for their disclosure documents. Then you can compare offerings.

5. Listen carefully to the sales presentation. Some sales tactics should signal caution. A seller with a good offer does not have to use pressure.

6. Get the seller's promises in writing. Any important promises you get from a salesperson should be written into the contract you sign.

7. Consider getting professional advice. You may want to get a lawyer, an accountant, or a business advisor to read the disclosure document and proposed contract to counsel you and help you get the best deal.

Although the FTC cannot resolve individual disputes, information about your experiences and concerns is vital to the enforcement of the Franchise and Business Opportunities Rule. The time to protect yourself is before you buy rather than after. Only fifteen states give you private rights to sue, and there is often a limited ability to recover. A franchiser knows your financial situation, and can often outwait you. Many franchise owners have no money left to hire a lawyer to try to recoup their losses. The FTC has two phone numbers of places you can call to ask for assistance. The Franchise Complaint Line, (202) 326-3128, is staffed by a duty attorney and takes complaints about franchisers or disclosure requirements. The second number is:

Franchising

FTC Franchise Rule Information Hotline (202) 326-3220 Information on Federal Presale Disclosure Requirements for Franchise and Business Opportunity Ventures ext.2

Information on Disclosure Statements for Specific Franchise and Business Opportunity Companies . . ext.3

Information on Complaints on File for a Particular Franchise or Business Opportunity Venture ext.4

For Filing a Complaint Against a Franchise or Business Opportunity Venture ext.5

List of States with Franchise Laws and their Telephone Numbers. ext.6

List of States with Business Opportunity Laws and their Telephone Numbers. ext.7

To Speak With an Attorney ext.1

Franchise and Business Opportunities -- a four-page guide about what to consider before buying a franchise.

The Franchise Rule: Questions and Answers -- a one-page summary of the disclosure rule and penalties for infractions by the franchiser.

Franchise Rule Summary -- a seven-page, detailed technical explanation of the federal disclosure rule, which requires franchisers to furnish a document (with information on twenty topics) to the potential franchisee before a sale. This includes an explanation and description of the Uniform Franchise Offering Circular (UFOC) required in fourteen states.

State Agencies Administering Franchise Disclosure Laws

California - filing required
Franchise Division
Department of Corporations
3700 Wilshire Blvd., Suite 600
Los Angeles, CA 90010 (213) 736-2741

Hawaii - filing required
Franchise and Securities Division
State Department of Commerce
1010 Richards Street
Honolulu, HI 96813 (808) 548-2021

Illinois - filing required
Franchise Division
Office of Attorney General
500 South Second Street
Springfield, IL 62706 (217) 782-1090

Indiana - filing required
Franchise Division
Office of Secretary of State
302 W. Washington Street, #E-111
Indianapolis, IN 46204 (317) 232-6681

Maryland - filing required
Franchise Office
Division of Securities
200 St. Paul Place, 20th Floor
Baltimore, MD 21202 (301) 576-6360

Michigan - filing required
Antitrust and Franchise Unit
Office of Attorney General
670 Law Building, P.O. Box 30215
Lansing, MI 48909 (517) 373-7117

Minnesota - filing required
Franchise Division
Department of Commerce
133 East Seventh St.
St. Paul, MN 55101 (612) 296-6328

New York - filing required
Franchise and Securities Division
State Department of Law
120 Broadway
New York, NY 10271 (212) 416-8211

North Dakota - filing required
Franchise Division
Office of Securities Commission
600 East Boulevard, 5th floor
Bismarck, ND 58505 (701) 224-4712

Oregon - no filing
Corporate and Securities Division
Department of Insurance and Finance
Labor and Industries Bldg.
Salem, OR 97310 (503) 378-4387

Rhode Island - filing required
Franchise Office
Division of Securities
233 Richmond St., Suite 232
Providence, RI 02903-4232 (401) 277-3048

South Dakota - filing required
Franchise Office
Division of Securities
118 W. Capitol Ave.
Pierre, SD 57501 (605) 773-4013

Virginia - filing required
Franchise Office
State Corporation Commission
1300 E. Main St., 9th Floor
Richmond, VA 23219 (804) 371-9051

Washington - filing required
Franchise Office
Business License Services
State Securities Division
P.O. Box 9033
Olympia, WA 98507-9033 (206) 753-6928

Wisconsin - filing required
Franchise Office

Be patient. If any phone number is incorrect, call (area code) 555-1212 and request the new listing.

Small Business and Entrepreneuring

Wisconsin Securities Commission
P.O. Box 1768
Madison, WI 53701 (608) 266-8559

States With Business Opportunity Laws For Franchises

State	Phone
California	(619) 237-6553
Colorado	(203) 566-4560
Florida	(904) 488-9805
	(800) 342-2176
Georgia	(404) 651-8600
Indiana	(317) 232-6331
Iowa	(515) 281-4441
Kentucky	(502) 564-2200
Louisiana	(504) 342-7373
Maine	(207) 582-8760
Maryland	(410) 576-6360
Michigan	(517) 373-7117
Nebraska	(402) 471-2171
New Hampshire	(603) 271-3641
North Carolina	(919) 733-3924
Ohio	(614) 466-8831
	(800) 282-0515
Oklahoma	(405) 521-2451
South Carolina	(803) 734-2168
South Dakota	(605) 773-4823
Texas	(512) 475-1769
Utah	(801) 530-4849
Virginia	(804) 786-0594
	(800) 451-1525
Washington	(206) 753-6210

International Franchise Association
1350 New York Avenue, NW
Washington, DC 20005
John Reynolds, Public Relations Officer (202) 628-8000

Founded in 1960, the International Franchise Association (IFA) has more than 600 franchiser members, including thirty-five overseas. IFA members are accepted into the organization only after meeting stringent requirements regarding number of franchises, length of time in business, and financial stability. The IFA offers about twenty-five educational conferences and seminars yearly, including an annual convention and a legal symposium. There is a program on financing and venture capital designed to bring together franchisers and franchisees. Each year the association also sponsors several trade shows, open to the public, so that franchisers may attract potential franchisees. There is a library, but as yet no database, for members. Mr. Buzzy Gordon, Public Relations Officer, will answer inquiries from the public and make referrals for speakers, courses, and resources on franchising.

The International Franchise Association publishes the following publications, which you can order by phone (800-543-1038)

To Help You Buy a Franchise

Answers to the 21 Most Commonly Asked Questions - $2.25
Investigate Before Investing - $5
Is Franchising For You? - $5
Franchise Opportunities Guide - $15
Franchising: The Inside Story - $20

To Help You Franchise Your Business

Blueprint For Franchising A Business - $28
Financial Strategies For The Growing Franchisor - $25
The Franchise Advantage - $30
The Franchise Option - $26
Franchising: A Planning And Sales Compliance Guide - $48
Franchising and Licensing - $27
Franchising in the U.K. - $35
Franchising - The How-To Book - $20
How To Be A Franchisor - $8
How To Franchise Internationally - $30
How To Organize A Franchise Advisory Council - $10
McDonald's: Behind the Arches - $22
Multiple-Unit Franchising - $25
Public Relations For The Franchise - $21

Legal Information

Franchise Legal Digest - $195
Franchising: Business and the Law (VHS set) - $200
The Law of Franchising (VHS set) - $200
The IFA Compliance Kit - $225
International Franchising - $175
Legal Symposium binder - $250
Mock Trial (VHS set) - $195
Survey of Foreign Laws and Regulations Affecting International Franchising - $140

Reference Material

A Comparison of International vs. Domestic - $50
Conversion of Dealer Organizations - $395
Franchise Marketing and Sales Survey - $295
Franchising in the Economy - $25
Franchisor/Franchisee Relations Survey - $5
The Future of Franchising - $10
Glossary of Franchising Terms - $4

Audiocassettes, Videotapes, Computer Diskettes

Franchise Finder (IBM compatible) - $79
Franchise Finder (Macintosh compatible) - $79
Franchising: A World of Opportunity (VHS) - $145
Franchising: How To Be In Business For Yourself Not By Yourself (VHS) - $49.95
How to Select a Franchise (Audio) - $15
IFA: A World of Difference (VHS) - $20
Let's Talk: Bringing Your Franchise To Canada (VHS) - $95
Your Future in Franchising (VHS) - $75
Franchising World Magazine - $12

Minority Business Development Agency
U.S. Department of Commerce
14th and Constitution Ave, NW
Washington, DC 20230 (202) 377-3237

The Minority Business Development Agency (MBDA) can provide information to all business, not just minority-owned businesses, regarding franchising. They are the publishers of *Franchise Opportunities Handbook* -- a bible of franchising information, this 390 page directory includes detailed listings of 1,500 companies, facts about the franchising industry, guidance

Be patient. If any phone number is incorrect, call (area code) 555-1212 and request the new listing.

Franchising

for investing in a franchise, resource listings of helpful agencies and organizations, and a bibliography. Cost is $15; U.S. Government Printing Office, Superintendent of Documents, Washington, DC 20420; (202) 783-3238. MBDA has several other free publications to assist people who are interested in learning more about franchising. They can also answer questions regarding FTC rules, major growth areas, how does a franchise chain start, where do franchise sales come from, and other general questions.

Experts

Michael Wood
Business Development Office
U.S. Small Business Administration

1441 L Street, NW
Washington, DC 20005
(202) 205-6665

Mr. Wood is coordinator of a coalition between the International Franchising Association (IFA) and the Small Business Administration (SBA), and is available to answer questions and provide assistance to regional offices or the SBA. Mr. Wood leads training programs at various IFA exhibits and shows for people interested in buying a franchise. Your local SBA office also may run seminars on franchising. Some SBA District Offices, such as the one in Kansas City, hold large Franchise Expos, which deal with all aspects of the franchise business. The SBA has a free 4 page brochure titled, *Evaluating Franchise Opportunities*, for people considering franchises as a way to start a business. Contact your local SBA office for more information (800-827-5722 for the office nearest you).

Business and Industry General Sources

* *See also Experts Chapter*
* *See also Science and Technology Chapter*
* *See also Small Business and Entrepreneuring Chapter*
* *See also International Trade Chapter*
* *See also Law and Social Justice Chapter*
* *See also Energy Chapter*

This chapter covers big business and major industries in the U.S., such as telecommunications, mining, transportation, railroads, and shipping. Because businesses in these industries are regulated by the federal government, a significant amount of revealing information about them is often available to the public, including financial reports, safety records, business volumes, and violations of industry regulations. But you'll also find other important sources on consumer relations, hiring incentives, child care, and even help in converting your business to the metric system.

This introductory section lists general sources of information on major industries with a particular stress on sources for finding company information collected by the U.S. government.

* Airline Data

Office of Airline Statistics
Research and Special Programs Administration
U.S. Department of Transportation
400 7th Street, SW
Room 4125
Washington, DC 20590 (202) 366-9059

The Aviation Information Management (AIM) program collects information on the financial operations of air carriers. Government, industry, and the general public may access this information. Database functions are housed at the Transportation Systems Center (see entry) but this office can serve as liaison for access to air carrier reports and data requiring DOT approval for release.

* Alcohol Production Regulations

Wine and Beer Branch
Office of Compliance Operations
Bureau of Alcohol, Tobacco, and Firearms
U.S. Department of the Treasury
650 Massachusetts Ave., NW
Washington, DC 20226 (202) 927-8230

Distilled Spirit and Tobacco Branch
Office of Compliance Operations
Bureau of Alcohol, Tobacco, and Firearms
U.S. Department of the Treasury
650 Massachusetts Ave., NW
Washington, DC 20226 (202) 927-8210

These offices regulate basic permit requirements under the Federal Alcohol Administration, as well as the use, bulk sales, bottling, labeling, and advertising of wine, beer, and distilled spirits. Regulations for the sale and production of distilled spirits are also outlined in the booklet, *Laws and Regulations under the Federal Alcohol Administration Act*, available from the Bureau's Distribution Center at 7943 Angus Ct., Springfield, VA 22153.

* Alcohol, Tobacco, and Firearms Regulation Research

National Laboratory Center
Bureau of Alcohol, Tobacco, and Firearms
U.S. Department of the Treasury
1401 Research Blvd.
Rockville, MD 20850 (301) 294-0410

Laboratory services for the Bureau are conducted at the National Laboratory Center in Rockville, MD, and at regional locations in Atlanta, GA, and San Francisco, CA, in the areas of compliance and law enforcement. All alcohol-containing products sold in the United States and imported to this country are analyzed at these laboratories, and tobacco products are examined for tax classification. Specialists also investigate firearms, explosives, and arson evidence at the forensic labs. Crime lab scientists are also trained at this facility.

* Alcohol, Tobacco, and Firearms Regulations Update

Wine and Beer Branch
Bureau of Alcohol, Tobacco, and Firearms
U.S. Department of the Treasury
650 Massachusetts Ave., NW
Washington, DC 20226 (202) 927-8230

In April and October, this office publishes the *Unified Agenda* in the *Federal Register*. The *Agenda* outlines regulations that have been issued, are being proposed, or are being reviewed within a six month period by the entire Bureau to give the public ample notice of all regulatory activities. Contact this office for additional information.

* Alcohol, Tobacco, and Firearms Statistics

Public Affairs Branch
Office of Congressional and Media Affairs
Bureau of Alcohol, Tobacco, and Firearms
U.S. Department of the Treasury
650 Massachusetts Ave., NW
Washington, DC 20226 (202) 927-8500

The free booklet, *Ready Reference Statistics*, outlines the Bureau's statistical activities. Alcohol statistics include moonshine seizures; beer, wine, and distilled spirits production; the number of licensees and permittees; and federal excise tax rates. The U.S. viticulture areas (areas where wine may be produced) are also listed. The tobacco section outlines production and tax rates. The booklet also includes the number of domestic, imported, and exported manufacturers of firearms by type, as well as a listing of the number of registered weapons by state and type.

* Alcohol Trade Laws

Alcohol Import-Export Branch
Office of Industry Compliance
Bureau of Alcohol, Tobacco, and Firearms
U.S. Department of the Treasury
650 Massachusetts Ave., NW
Washington, DC 20226 (202) 927-8110

The Trade Affairs Branch informs industry of the provisions of the Federal Alcohol Administration Act, as well as issues of product compliance, permits applications, and Bureau opinions relating to the Act.

Be patient. If any phone number is incorrect, call (area code) 555-1212 and request the new listing.

General Sources

* Annual Report of Interstate Transportation Companies

Bureau of Accounts' Public Reference Room
Interstate Commerce Commission (ICC)
12th St. and Constitution Ave., NW, Room 3378
Washington, DC 20403 (202) 927-7119

Annual reports of companies regulated by the ICC contain revealing information concerning those companies, including annual income, balance sheets, expenses, types of equipment owned, and much more. These documents may be examined by the public in the Reference Room from 8:30 a.m. to 5:00 p.m. weekdays,and photocopies of these reports, at a cost of $.60 per page, with a $3 minimum charge per order, may be obtained by writing the Office of the Secretary, Room 2215, ICC, Washington, DC, 20423.

* Bureau of Alcohol, Tobacco, and Firearms Publications

Distribution Center
Bureau of Alcohol, Tobacco, and Firearms
U.S. Department of the Treasury
7943 Angus Ct.
Springfield, VA 22153 (703) 455-7801

The following is a sampling of free publications from the ATF Distribution Center:

Index of Materials Required by the Freedom of Information Act
Public Use Forms
Information to Claimants
Distilled Spirits for Fuel Use
Payment of Tax by Electronic Fund Transfer
Importation of Distilled Spirits, Wines, and Beer
Beverage Distilled Spirits Plants and Breweries Authorized to Operate
Bonded Wineries and Bonded Wine Cellars Authorized to Operate
Information for Specially Denatured Spirits Applicants
Information for Tax-Free Alcohol Applicants
Distribution and Use of Denatured Alcohol/Rum and formulas for Denatured Alcohol/Rum
Liquor Laws and Regulations for Retail Dealers
Instructions - Application for FAA Act Basic Permits: Wholesalers and Importers
Firearms Curios and Relics List
Federal Firearms Licensee Information
Importation of Arms, Ammunition, and Implements of War
Bomb Threats and Physical Security Planning

* Business Assistance Service

Office of Business Liaison
U.S. Department of Commerce
14th St. and Constitution Ave., NW
Room 5898C
Washington, DC 20230 (202) 377-3176

The Business Assistance Service provides information and guidance on programs throughout the Federal Government. The Service can answer such questions as:

How can I sell my products or services to the Federal Government?
Where do I find overseas buyers?
Where can I get Federal business loans?

The Business Assistance staff maintains a network of interagency contacts so that they can quickly provide you with current information on a wide range of subjects. People with specific questions about government programs can also find the answers by contacting the Business Assistance staff.

* Business and Transport Records

National Archives and Records Administration
Center for Electronic Records
Washington, DC 20408 (202) 501-5579

The National Archives Center for Electronic Records maintains several databases of interest to the business researcher. The standard charge for a copy of an electronic dataset on magnetic tape is $90. Photocopies of documents cost $.25 per page; microfiche costs $1.25 per fiche. Transfer of information onto CD-Rom or floppy disks is generally not available. Agencies with records available include: Civil Aeronautics Board; U.S. Department of Labor; Minerals Management Service; Bureau of Mines; National Oceans and Atmospheric Administration; President's Commission on the Coal Industry 1978-1980; U.S. Railway Association; U.S. Department of Transportation General Records; and U.S.

Department of Transportation Research and Special Programs Administration. Call for more information and for a printout of the specific records available.

* Business Briefings and Speakers

Office of Business Liaison
U.S. Department of Commerce
14th St. and Constitution Ave., NW
Room 5898C
Washington, DC 20230 (202) 377-3176

This office has an Outreach Program which organizes a series of briefings for the business community. These briefings serve a dual purpose of promoting the Department's activities to business and allowing Commerce officials to be familiar with business perspectives. The briefings are free and are held in Washington, DC. Speaking requests from business organizations are also routinely handled through this office. Sending Commerce officials across the country, promoting Departmental programs, and listening to concerns of business allows OBL to extend its outreach.

* Business Community Representation

Chamber of Commerce of the United States
1615 H St., NW
Washington, DC 20062 (202) 659-6000

The Chamber of Commerce is generally regarded as the spokesgroup for United States business. It is the world's largest business federation composed of more than 180,000 companies plus several thousand other organizations such as local and state chambers of commerce and trade and professional associations. It has an environmental department. Publications: *Nation's Business, The Business Advocate.*

* Business Radio Services

Licensing Division
Federal Communications Commission
1270 Fairfield Rd
Gettysburg, PA 17326 (717) 337-1212

The FCC authorizes and licenses all Business Radio Services used in commercial activity. Over 640,000 businesses in the U.S., from mail couriers to exterminators to plumbers, use radio services as part of their operations and must be licensed by the FCC. Updated daily, these files are available on database and can be accessed through SAFE, or at an access terminal by visiting the FCC office in person.

* Business Reference Service

Library
U.S. Department of Commerce
14th St. and Constitution Ave., NW
Washington, DC 20230 (202) 377-5511

The U.S. Department of Commerce's Library is open to the public, 1:00 p.m. to 4 p.m., Monday through Friday. Their collection is business oriented, and the staff is available to direct you to appropriate resources.

* Business Services Directory

Office of Business Liaison
U.S. Department of Commerce
14th St. and Constitution Ave., NW
Room 5898C
Washington, DC 20230 (202) 377-3176

The Business Services Directory gives you a brief description of all the programs of the U.S. Department of Commerce, including phone numbers, and is used by the business community to find sources of information within the Department. Those in business can see the activities of the various programs and how they relate to their particular business. This free directory is available from the office listed above.

* Census Information on Business

Bureau of the Census
U.S. Department of Commerce
Washington, DC 20233 (301) 763-4040

The U.S. Bureau of the Census collects a vast amount of information on business. *The Factfinder for the Nation* series summarizes reports and their availability by subject area. CFF-5 lists reference sources for Census Data and

Be patient. If any phone number is incorrect, call (area code) 555-1212 and request the new listing.

Business and Industry

is a good place to begin your research. Factfinders related to business are the following:

CFF-6 Housing Statistics - June 1991
CFF-9 Construction Statistics - September 1989
CFF-10 Retail Trade Statistics - May 1989
CFF-11 Wholesale Trade Statistics - May 1989
CFF-12 Statistics on Service Industries - July 1989
CFF-13 Transportation Statistics - September 1989
CFF-15 Statistics on Manufacturing - March 1990
CFF-16 Statistics on Mineral Industries - February 1990
CFF-20 Energy and Related Statistics - September 1991

Census Fact Finders are available for a nominal fee, usually $.25 or $.30 per copy.

* Census Statistics Business Experts

Bureau of the Census
U.S. Department of Commerce
Washington, DC 20233 (301) 763-4100

The Telephone Contact List at the Bureau of the Census can put you in touch with a census expert studying business (or other) issues. It is available free.

* Commerce Libraries

Library
U.S. Department of Commerce
14th St. and Constitution Ave., NW
Washington, DC 20230 (202) 377-5511

Many libraries within the U.S. Department of Commerce are open to the public and have collections specific to the concerns of the various Bureaus. You can contact the libraries directly regarding hours of operations, and questions on various topics:

NOAA
Library and Information Services, National Oceanic and Atmospheric Administration, 6009 Executive Blvd., Rockville, MD 20852; (301) 443-8330

NIST
Research Information Center, National Institute of Standards and Technology, Administration Bldg. 101, Room E106, Gaithersburg, MD 20899; (301) 975-3052

Patent and Trademark Office
Scientific Library, Patent and Trademark Office, 2021 Jefferson Davis Hwy., Arlington, VA 22202; (703) 557-2955

Census Bureau
Library, Bureau of the Census, Federal Office Bldg. No. 3, Room 2455, Washington DC 20233; (301) 763-5042

* Commercial and Industrial Conservation

Distributer and Marketing Services
Tennessee Valley Authority (TVA)
Power, 1101 Market St.
4S136X Missionary Ridge Pl.
Chattanooga, TN 37402 (615) 751-5103

The TVA offers businesses, industries, and other nonresidential power users free, in-depth energy conservation audits upon request, with loans available for those businesses and industries which carry out measures recommended in the audits. The program assists with water heating, space heating, and air conditioning as end uses. Contact this office for more information on energy audits and conservation.

* Communications and Information Policy

Public Information
National Telecommunications and
Information Administration
U.S. Department of Commerce
14th St. and Constitution Ave., NW, Room 4898
Washington, DC 20230 (202) 377-1551

The National Telecommunications and Information Administration's policy recommendations affect the nation's economic and technological advancement in the telecommunications industry. This includes common carrier, telephone, broadcast, and satellite communications systems. It is involved with regulatory changes that have led to increased competition in common carrier operations and the growing overlap between telecommunications and computers. In the information field, NTIA focuses attention on issues of privacy and security and the impact of U.S. and international privacy legislation on the flow of electronic data across national boundaries. Contact this office for more information.

* Communications Industry Analysis

Federal Communications Commission (FCC)
Public Reference Room
1919 M Street, NW, Room 537
Washington, DC 20554 (202) 632-0745

Documents on File: Reports required by FCC Rules and Regulations, Administrative Reports, Annual Reports to Stockholders, FCC Form 492, Rate of Return Report, Statistics of Communications Common Carriers, Quarterly Operating Data of Telephone and Telegraph Carriers, Switched Access Reports, Equal Access Implementation Reports, NECA - Pool Results, Local Exchange Rates, Monthly Bypass Request Report - AT&T, Lifeline Link-Up Reports, IAD Reports, General Reference Material from Sources. Hours of Operation: Monday through Friday, 9:00 a.m. to 1:00 p.m., 2:00 p.m. to 5:00.

* Consumer Affairs

Office of Consumer Affairs (OCA)
U.S. Department of Commerce
14th St. and Constitution Ave., NW
Room 5718
Washington, DC 20230 (202) 377-5001

The office provides advice and technical assistance to businesses on problems and issues of concern to consumers. Through cooperative projects among businesses, consumers, and local and state governments, this office works to improve companies' customer relations and the quality of goods and services. OCA also helps businesses deal with customer concerns about advertising, warranties, complaint-handling, credit, and products safety, as well as helping them establish ways to involve consumers in the development of product safety and performance standards. OCA also mediates between consumers and businesses on complaints and inquiries, helping businesses to reach equitable resolutions to such complaints.

* Consumer Information and Complaint Centers

The Interstate Commerce Commission has three regional offices which serve a variety of functions, one of which is to answer inquiries and assist the public with concerns regarding interstate bus, trucking, and railroad companies. The most frequent calls involve moving companies.

Eastern
Interstate Commerce Commission, 3535 Market St., Room 16400, Philadelphia, PA 19104; (215) 596-4040. States served: AL, CT, DE, DC, FL, GA, KY, MA, MD, ME, MS, OH, PA, NC, NH, NJ, NY, RI, SC, TN, VA, VT, WV.

Central
Interstate Commerce Commission, Xerox Center, 55 West Monroe Street, Suite 570, Chicago, IL 60603; (312) 353-6204. States served: AR, IA, IL, IN, KS, LA, MI, MO, MN, NE, ND, OK, SD, TX, WI.

Western
Interstate Commerce Commission, 211 Maine St., Suite 500, San Francisco, CA 94105; (415) 774-6520. States served: AK, AZ, CA, CO, ID, MT, NV, NM, OR, UT, WA, WY.

Questions can also be directed to the ICC office in Washington DC, at (202) 927-7597.

* Consumer Rule Guides For Businesses

Federal Trade Commission
Public Reference Branch, Room 130
6th and Pennsylvania Ave., NW
Washington, DC 20580 (202) 326-2222

The FTC publishes the following guides for businesses to help them comply with the most current consumer trade rules and regulations, on everything from offering layaways to the Federal warranty law.

Business Guide to the Federal Trade Commission's Mail Order Rule

Be patient. If any phone number is incorrect, call (area code) 555-1212 and request the new listing.

General Sources

Businessperson's Guide to Federal Warranty Law
Direct Marketer's Guide to Labeling Requirements Under the Textile and Wool Acts
Complying with the Credit Practices Rule
Guides for the Jewelry Industry
Handling Customer Complaint: In-House and Third-Party Strategies
How to Write Readable Credit Forms
Offering Layaways
Payments and Services
Rules and Regulations Under the Hobby Protection Act
Textile and Wool Acts
Writing a Care Label: How to Comply with the Amended Care Labeling Rule
Writing Readable Warranties

* Donations to the Peace Corps

Peace Corps
1990 K St., NW
Washington, DC 20526 (202) 606-3063

The Peace Corps offers corporations donate materials if a need for them materials exists. Contact this office for more information on the donation process.

* Economic Studies of Transit Industry

Industry, Economics and Finance Division (P-37)
Office of Economics
Policy and International Affairs
Office of the Secretary of Transportation
U.S. Department of Transportation
400 7th Street, SW, Room 10223
Washington, DC 20590 (202) 366-5412

Financial and economic studies of the transportation industry are prepared by this office. Air transportation is emphasized, but other modes are also evaluated. Report topics include mergers, regional marketing studies, gross receipts at airports, and intelligent vehicle highway systems. Contact this office to determine if a study has been prepared on your subject.

* Explosives: Laws and Regulations

Distribution Center
Bureau of Alcohol, Tobacco, and Firearms
U.S. Department of the Treasury
7943 Angus Ct.
Springfield, VA 22153 (703) 455-7801

ATF laws and regulations for firearms are described in the free book, *ATF: Explosives Law and Regulations.* Commerce in explosives is highlighted, describing licenses and permits, business conduct, records and reports, storage, exemptions, and unlawful acts. The impact of the regulations on the fireworks industry is also discussed.

* Federal Maritime Commission

1100 L Street NW
Washington, DC 20573 (202) 523-5725

Established in 1961, the Federal Maritime Commission (FMC) monitors relationships among carriers and also ensures that individual carriers fairly treat shippers and other members of the shipping public. The commission consists of 5 full time commissioners appointed by the President, with no more than 3 from the same political party, serving 5 year terms. The FMC has 230 full time equivalent positions and an appropriated budget of $15,452,000.

* Gifts-in-Kind Program

Office of Private Sector Development
Peace Corps
1990 K St., NW
Washington, DC 20526 (202) 606-3063

The Peace Corps allows corporations to donate materials if a need for them materials exists. Contact this office for more information on the donation process.

* Highway Contractors and Subcontractors

Office of Civil Rights (HCR-1)
Federal Highway Administration (FHWA)

U.S. Department of Transportation
400 7th St., SW
Washington, DC 20590 (202) 366-0693

This office monitors compliance with civil rights laws by requiring contractors and subcontractors of Federal highway projects to submit employment data. Equal opportunity issues are also addressed in the Disadvantaged Business Enterprise Program, which awards contracts and subcontract commitments to small and minority businesses, and in FHWA's Historically Black Colleges and Universities Programs. Data from contractor filings and a list of contractors and subcontractors, by state or county, are available from this office. You can also obtain a copy of *FHWA's Historically Black Colleges and Universities Programs,* a publication with details about those programs.

* Hiring Incentives for Employers of Veterans

Assistant Secretary for Veterans
Employment and Training
U.S. Department of Labor
200 Constitution Ave., NW, Room S1313
Washington, DC 20210 (202) 523-9116

As a hiring incentive, the Veterans Administration will pay an employer half of a Veteran's entry wages up to $10,000 for up to nine months or fifteen months for a veteran with a disability rating of 30% or more. A veteran must have served during the Korean Conflict or the Vietnam Era, and have been unemployed for 10 to 15 weeks. Employers must certify that they intend to hire the veteran upon completion of training. Adequate training facilities must be available; wages and benefits must be no less than those normally paid; and training cannot be for a position for which the Veteran already qualifies. Veterans and employers alike must apply for certification with any local job service office or VA Regional Office.

* Infrastructure Technologies

Office of Technology Assessment (OTA)
600 Pennsylvania Ave., SE
Washington, DC 20510 (202) 228-6939

Public works infrastructure, which includes roads, bridges, sewers, etc., provides essential services--moving people and goods, supplying water, and disposing of waste. And there is little disagreement about the urgency of repair, maintenance, or new construction of these vital systems. OTA is currently studying how technological, institutional, and financial alternatives could be combined to meet the challenges posed by infrastructure needs that might be required in the Federal role. Contact Edith Page, the project director, for more information.

* International Trade Administration Publications

International Trade Administration (ITA)
U.S. Department of Commerce
14th St. and Constitution Ave., NW
Washington, DC 20230 (202) 377-5487

The International Trade Administration of the U.S. Department of Commerce produces numerous publications on U.S. business, particularly related to exports and foreign domestic competition in the U.S. Publications are available from ITA, NTIS, and GPO. Contact ITA for a free publications list.

* Interstate Commerce Commission (ICC)

12th St. and Constitution Ave., NW
Washington, DC 20423 (202) 927-7597

The Interstate Commerce Commission was created as an independent regulatory agency by act of February 4, 1887 to regulate commerce. ICC's responsibilities include regulation of carriers engaged in transportation in interstate commerce and in foreign commerce to the extent that it takes place within the U.S. Surface transportation under the Commission's jurisdiction includes railroads, trucking companies, bus lines, freight forwarders, water carriers, transportation brokers, and a coal slurry pipeline. The regulatory laws vary depending on the type of transportation; however, they generally involve certification of carriers seeking to provide transportation for the public, rates, adequacy of service, purchases, and mergers. The Commission assures that the carriers it regulates will provide the public with rates and services that are fair and reasonable.

* ICC Library

Interstate Commerce Commission (ICC)
12th St. and Constitution Ave., NW, Room 3392
Washington, DC 20423 (202) 927-5642

Be patient. If any phone number is incorrect, call (area code) 555-1212 and request the new listing.

Business and Industry

The Interstate Commerce Commission's library is open to the public, and its collection focuses on transportation and transportation law. You must sign in with the building guard before going up to the library.

* Long Distance Carrier Information

Industry Analysis
Federal Communications Commission
Public Reference Room
1919 M Street, NW, Room 537
Washington, DC 20554 (202) 632-0745

The Industry Analysis division compiles information on market share for all long distance carriers whose total toll service revenue is $100 million or greater. The Downtown Copy Center has a report entitled the *Long Distance Market Share Report*, detailing this information.

* Major Developments in U.S. Shipping Trade

Federal Maritime Commission (FMC)
1100 L Street, NW
Washington, DC 20573 (202) 523-5725

The Federal Maritime Commission continually monitors developments in the major shipping markets around the world. Information on rates, capacity, and international agreements is compiled. The FMC also has information on developments with respect to the major carriers. The FMC breaks its analysis down in the following geographic manner: Transatlantic, Mediterranean, Africa, Transpacific, Latin America and the Caribbean, and the Middle East.

* Maritime Administration Activities and Statistics

MARAD - Public Affairs
U.S. Department of Transportation
400 7th Street, SW, Room 7219
Washington, DC 20590 (202) 366-5807

MARAD's annual report is an excellent place to begin your search for information on U.S. maritime activities and statistics. The report includes a profile of the U.S. Merchant Fleet, U.S. Department of Defense Cargo programs, information on maritime labor and training, and a report on maritime agreements recently concluded between the U.S. and foreign nations. Statistics include listings for worldwide ship deliveries, Federal Ship financing guarantee program, U.S. Oceangoing Merchant Marine, major world merchant fleets, U.S. Great Lakes Merchant Fleet, the National Defense Reserve Fleet, and maritime subsidy outlays. The report is available free upon request.

* Maritime Commerce Financial Analysis

Bureau of Domestic Regulation
Federal Maritime Commission
1100 L Street, NW
Washington, DC 20573 (202) 523-5796

The Bureau of Domestic Regulation provides accounting and financial expertise to help ensure the reasonableness of rates for the transportation of cargo and other services provided by common carriers in the domestic offshore waterborne commerce of the U.S. The Bureau also provides technical assistance to other activities within the Commission.

* Metals and Mining Producers

American Mining Congress (AMC)
1920 N St., NW, Suite 300
Washington, DC 20036 (202) 861-2800

The American Mining Congress is an industry association of producers of metals, coal industrial and agricultural minerals; manufacturers of mining and mineral processing machinery, equipment and supplies; and mining engineering firms. AMC publishes the *American Mining Congress Journal*, a monthly journal which focuses on mining issues and policy and is available for $30 per year. AMC can also put you in touch with members who can provide you with detailed information on most aspects of the mining industry.

* Metric Conversion Assistance

National Institute of Standards and Technology
Office of Metric Programs
U.S. Department of Commerce
Building 411, Room A146
Gaithersburg, MD, 20899 (301) 975-3689

This office coordinates Federal metric transition to promote consistency in agency plans, policies, and practices. It identifies and helps remove barriers that inhibit or block metric transition in federal, state, or local rules, standards and codes, or regulations. It also provides technical and general information about the metric system and its use to businesses, educators, the news media, and the general public. There are several free brochures and pamphlets available from the Office explaining the metric system and metric conversions.

* Mine Maps/Mine Companies Property Ownership

Division of Program Information and Analysis
Bureau of Mines
U.S. Department of the Interior
810 7th St., NW
Washington, DC 20241 (202) 501-9650

Valuable information is available from the mine maps available through the mine map repositories of the Office of Surface Mining Reclamation and Enforcement. Mine and company names, water sources, property ownership of adjoining companies and towns, latitudes and longitudes, coal outcrop seam designations, openings and emergency exits of mines, and gas and power lines are some of the topics covered. This information can be useful to local developers, engineering firms, and energy interests, as well as private citizens.

* Minerals: Data, Industries, and Technology

Publication Distribution
Bureau of Mines
U.S. Department of the Interior
Cochrans Mills Rd.
P.O. Box 18070
Pittsburgh, PA 15236 (412) 892-4338

The Bureau of Mines publishes several reports of investigations and information circulars that are free of charge to those interested in mineral research. *Mineral Industry Surveys* are published monthly, quarterly, and annually, presenting data on various minerals and metals. Reprints from *Minerals Yearbook 1987* are available and report on the mineral industry in the United States and abroad. If documents are unavailable here, they will refer you to the appropriate headquarters office.

* Multinational Corporations in Mining

Office of Mineral Commodities
Bureau of Mines
U.S. Department of the Interior
810 7th St., NW
Washington, DC 20241 (202) 501-9449

An expert in the office of mineral commodities, Mr. Balazik, can discuss the results of a major study he did for the Bureau of Mines on Multinational Corporations in the Mining industry. He examined both U.S. ownership and interest in foreign mining operations as well as foreign ownership and interest in American mining operations. The information presented in the study is based on a review of over 2200 mineral properties operated by more than 400 companies in 80 countries. The study has not yet been published, but Mr. Balazik will share the results of his study and can aid you in your research in this area.

* National Association of Manufacturers

National Association of Manufacturers (NAM)
1331 Pennsylvania Ave., NW, Suite 1500
North Lobby
Washington, DC 20004 (202) 637-3000

The National Association of Manufacturers is a voice for industry at the national level. Members are manufacturing companies from throughout the United States. Publications: *PAC Manager*, published monthly.

* National Telecommunications

National Telecommunications and Information Administration
U.S. Department of Commerce
14th St. and Constitution Ave., NW
Room 4898
Washington, DC 20230 (202) 377-1551

This Administration's broad goals include formulating policies to support the development and growth of telecommunications, information and related industries, furthering the efficient development and use of telecommunications

Be patient. If any phone number is incorrect, call (area code) 555-1212 and request the new listing.

General Sources

and information services, providing policy and management for Federal use of the electromagnetic spectrum, and providing telecommunications facilities grants to public service users. NTIA employs approximately 300 people and has an annual budget of $35,104,000.

* Ocean Commerce Statistics and Information

Bureau of Economic Analysis
Federal Maritime Commission
1100 L Street, NW
Washington, DC 20573 (202) 523-5870

The Bureau of Economic Analysis provides economic, statistical and financial analysis for the Commission. The Bureau assists in the development of long-range plans for the commission and enhances the agencies responsiveness to new developments and trends in U.S. ocean commerce and the liner shipping industry.

* On-Site Child Care

Women's Bureau
U.S. Department of Labor
200 Constitution Ave., NW, Room S3309
Washington, DC 20210 (202) 523-6652

The free publication, *Employers and Child Care: Benefiting Work and Family*, is designed for employers and employees concerned with developing programs and policies to assist in quality and cost-efficient child care programs while parents are at work. Created to help in a vast array of situations, it provides guidance to those who wish to improve employee productivity and business' ability to recruit and retain the best workers. It is designed for people who are concerned about fulfilling two essential and often conflicting responsibilities--working and caring for their families.

* Private Sector Initiatives in Mass Transit

Office of Private Sector Initiatives (UBP-30)
Office of Budget and Policy
Federal Mass Transit Administration
U.S. Department of Transportation
400 7th St., SW, Room 9300
Washington, DC 20590 (202) 366-1666

This office encourages private sector involvement in mass transit throughout the United States. Specifically, they work through the following four areas:

Competitive Contracting: Local transit authorities are encouraged to open the provisioning of services up to private sector competition.

Entrepreneurial Services: Groups in the private sector are encouraged to start self-sustaining transit services (such as taxi and bus) in cooperation with local transit authorities.

Joint Development: Federal assistance is available to help plan public/private sector joint ventures at transit facilities.

Demand Management Program: Federal funds are available to encourage local employers and merchants to develop techniques to help manage transportation and mobility problems in their areas.

* Pulp and Paper Industry

Technical Association of the Pulp and Paper Industry (TAPPI)
Box 105113 (800) 332-8636
Atlanta, GA 30348 (404) 446-1400

The Technical Association of the Pulp and Paper Industry consists of individual professionals working in pulp, paper, packaging, converting and non-wovens industries. Publications: *TAPPI Journal*.

* Rail Industry Conditions

Office of Industry, Finance and Operations (RRP-11)
Federal Railroad Administration
U.S. Department of Transportation
400 7th Street, SW, Room 8302
Washington, DC 20590 (202) 366-0386

This office serves as the principal advisory element in assessing the financial and operating condition of the railroad industry, with special emphasis on carriers in marginal or bankrupt financial condition. This office also administers programs

to improve railroad labor/management relations and monitors disputes under the Railway Labor Act.

* Railroad Industry Analysis

Office of External Affairs
Interstate Commerce Commission (ICC)
12th Street and Constitution Ave., NW
Washington, DC 20423 (202) 927-5737

The *ICC Annual Report* contains a detailed analysis of current developments in the Rail industry falling under their jurisdiction including financial conditions, reorganizations, mergers and acquisitions, labor issues, abandonments, rates, freight service, and passenger service.

* Science and Technical Business References

Science and Technology Division
Reference Section
Library of Congress
Washington, DC 20540 (202) 707-5580

Informal series of reference guides are issued free from the Science and Technology Division under the general title, *LC Science Tracer Bullet*. These guides are designed to help readers locate published material on subjects about which they have only general knowledge. New titles in the series are announced in the weekly *Library of Congress Information Bulletin* that is distributed to many libraries including:

80-3 Automotive Electronics
80-6 Lasers and Their Applications
80-19 Industrial Robots
81-9 Cable Television (Cable TV)
82-5 Jet Engines and Jet Aircraft
84-7 Biotechnology
87-9 Microcomputers
87-12 Optical Disc Technology

* Space Management Research

Office of Planning
Public Buildings Service
General Services Administration
18th and F Sts., NW
Washington, DC 20405 (202) 501-0638

Information on space management research studies which emphasize efficiency and cost productiveness can be obtained by contacting this office.

* Statistics Reports

Publications
Office of the Secretary
Interstate Commerce Commission
12th St. and Constitution Ave., NW
Washington, DC 20423 (202) 927-5930

This office compiles and publishes statistics on the various modes of transportation.

Annual

Transport Statistics in the United States. Detailed data on traffic, operations, equipment, finances, and employment for carriers subject to the Interstate Commerce Act.

A-300 Wage Statistics of Class I Freight Railroads in the United States-Calendar Year. Number of employees, service hours, and compensation by occupational group: Executive, Officials, and Staff Assistants; Professional and Administrative; Maintenance-of-Way and Structures; Maintenance of Equipment and Stores, etc.

Quarterly

Large Class I Motor Carriers of Property Selected Earnings Data. Operating revenues, net carrier operating income, net income, revenue tons hauled, operating ratio and rate of return.

Class I Freight Railroads Selected Earnings Data. Railway operating revenues, net railway operating income, income before extraordinary items, net income, revenue ton-miles of freight, and rate of return.

Large Class I Motor Carriers of Passengers Selected Earnings Data. Operating

Be patient. If any phone number is incorrect, call (area code) 555-1212 and request the new listing.

Business and Industry

revenues, net carrier operating income, net income, revenue passengers carried, operating ratio, and rate of return.

Large Class I Household Goods Carriers Selected Earnings Data. Operating revenues, net carrier operating income, net income, revenue tons hauled, operating ratio and rate of return.

Monthly

M-350 Preliminary Report of Railroad Employment, Class I Line-Haul Railroads. Number of employees at middle of month, group totals.

* Tax Credits for Employers of Targeted Groups

Employment and Training Administration
U.S. Department of Labor
200 Constitution Ave., NW, Room S2322
Washington, DC 20210 (202) 523-6871

The Targeted Jobs Tax Credit Program offers employers a credit against their tax liability for hiring individuals from nine target groups that have traditionally had difficulty obtaining and holding jobs. Groups include disadvantaged youths, the handicapped, disadvantaged veterans, ex-offenders, and recipients of state and federal assistance. An employer must request certification for the individual prior to starting work. The credit applies only to employees hired into a business or trade. For more information contact your local Employment Service offices or your local Internal Revenue Service office.

* Transport Statistics in the United States

Publications
Interstate Commerce Commission

12th St. and Constitution Ave., NW
Washington, DC 20423 (202) 927-5930

This is an annual report which contains statistics of railroads and motor carriers. It includes a complete breakdown of finances, expenses and equipment, as well as service statistics. The tables are compiled from reports filed with the Commission by railroads and motor carriers.

* Trucking Company Analysis

Office of External Affairs
Interstate Commerce Commission (ICC)
12th Street and Constitution Ave., NW
Washington, DC 20423 (202) 927-5737

The *ICC Annual Report* contains a detailed analysis of the developments in the trucking industry falling under ICC jurisdiction. The 1990 Report discusses the financial condition of the industry, mergers, rates, operating rights, safety, and insurance issues. The report is available free from the ICC.

* Updates on Industry

Industrial Reports and Studies
U.S. Department of Commerce
14th St. and Constitution Ave., NW
Washington, DC 20230 (202) 377-4356

The U.S. Department of Commerce publishes a massive yearly study on some 350 U.S. industries entitled the *U.S. Industrial Outlook*. Included in this study are analyses of the aviation, maritime, and railroad industries. It is available from the Government Printing Office, (202) 783-3238 for $38.

Be patient. If any phone number is incorrect, call (area code) 555-1212 and request the new listing.

Airlines

The Federal Aviation Administration, an arm of the U.S. Department of Transportation, is the central locus of information on aviation in the U.S. Government. Other sources of information include the Aviation Office within the Office of the Secretary of Transportation and the National Transportation Safety Board.

* Air Carrier Market Data and Statistics

Public Reference Room
Research and Special Programs Administration
U.S. Department of Transportation
400 7th Street, SW, Room 4201
Washington, DC 20590 (202) 366-4888

Start with this office for market data, financial information, and traffic statistics on air carrier passenger and cargo operations. Information is compiled by DOT from schedules that air carriers file, and some data is stored in a computerized database. For the publication, *Air Carrier Traffic Statistics*, contact the Transportation Systems Center in Cambridge. (See that entry.)

* Air Traffic Management

Office of Air Traffic Management
Federal Aviation Administration (FAA)
U.S. Department of Transportation
800 Independence Ave., SW, Room 400E
Washington, DC 20591 (202) 267-9155

This office establishes and oversees policies for civilian and military air traffic management. It also operates the FAA national and international flight information and cartographic program and coordinates U.S. policies and procedures related to international air traffic.

* Air Traffic Plans and Requirements

Air Traffic Plans and Requirements
Federal Aviation Administration (FAA)
U.S. Department of Transportation
800 Independence Ave., SW
Room 400 East
Washington, DC 20591 (202) 267-3136

The air traffic control system tracks flights automatically and tags each one with a small block of information written electronically on the radar scope used by air traffic controllers. The data block includes aircraft identity, altitude and ground speed, and transponder code. Contact this office for more information.

* Air Traffic System Errors

Quality Assurance Division
Air Traffic Services
Federal Aviation Administration (FAA)
U.S. Department of Transportation
800 Independence Ave., SW, Room 416
Washington, DC 20591 (202) 267-9205

All system errors are logged on a central file chronologically by region. The file consists of reports identifying anything wrong in the air traffic service terminal. Contact this FAA office for more information on system errors.

* Air Travel - General Information

Office of Public Affairs
Federal Aviation Administration (FAA)
U.S. Department of Transportation
800 Independence Ave., SW, Room 907B
Washington, DC 20591 (202) 267-3481

The FAA can provide you with information on many aspects of air travel. Popular publications include:

Fly Rights: A Guide to Air Travel in the U.S.
Air Travel for the Handicapped.
Child/Infant Safety Seats Recommended for Use in Aircraft.
Air Travel for Your Dog or Cat.
How Safe is Flying?

Alert: FAA Security Tips for Air Travelers.
Caution: Shipping Hazardous Materials by Air.

* Air Travelers' Rights and Complaints

Consumer Affairs Division
Intergovernmental and Consumer Affairs
Governmental Affairs
Office of the Secretary of Transportation
U.S. Department of Transportation
400 7th Street, SW
Washington, DC 20590 (202) 366-2220

If your problem cannot be resolved directly with the airline, contact this office for information on air travelers' rights and for assistance in resolving problems with airlines and charter flights. Complaints about delayed or canceled flights, reservations, lost baggage, smoking, refunds, and overbooking can also be handled here.

* Aircraft Accident Data: U.S. Air Carrier Operations

National Technical Information Services
5285 Port Royal Road
Springfield, VA 22161

The *Annual Review of Aircraft Accident Data: U.S. Air Carrier Operations* contains statistical tabulations of data compiled from reports of accidents involving revenue operations of U.S. air carriers in a particular calendar year. The report is divided into sections according to the Part of the Code of Federal Regulations under which the aircraft were flown when the accidents occurred (14 CFR Part 121 or 14 CFR Part 135). The Part 135 section is further divided into scheduled and non-scheduled operations. Information provided within each section includes a list of accidents, tabulations of injuries, types of accidents, accident causes and related factors, and accident rates. Comparisons are made of data for the given year to averages of accident data for several prior years. The publication is available for a fee from the office above. Call (703) 487-4650 for single copies and microfiche; or (703) 487-4630 for an annual subscription.

* Aircraft Accident Investigations

Biomedical and Behavioral Science Division
Office of Aviation Medicine
Federal Aviation Administration (FAA)
U.S. Department of Transportation
800 Independence Ave., SW, Room 400 East
Washington, DC 20591 (202) 366-6910

This office analyses medical data associated with victims of aviation accidents.

* Aircraft Accident Prevention

Accident Prevention Staff
General Aviation Division
Flight Standards Service
Federal Aviation Administration (FAA)
U.S. Department of Transportation
800 Independence Ave., SW, Room 2322
Washington, DC 20591 (202) 366-6321

The staff provides national guidance and policy on accident prevention in general aviation. This office supports 9 regional offices and 78 field offices. For information on available publications, tapes, slides, seminars, and speakers, contact the office at the above address or contact your local field office. General publications available from this office include the following:

The Accident Prevention Program	FAA P 8740-8
Safe Flying for Agricultural Aviation	FAA P 8740-42
Notices to Airmen	FAA P 8740-54

Be patient. If any phone number is incorrect, call (area code) 555-1212 and request the new listing.

Business and Industry

Weight and Balance: An Important Safety Consideration	FAA P 8740-5
Descent to the MDA and Beyond	FAA P 8740-9
Pilot Prerogatives	FAA P 8740-17
Dead Reckoning Navigation	FAA P 8740-22
Always Leave Yourself an Out	FAA P 8740-25
Using the System	FAA P 8740-32
The Propwatchers Guide	FAA P 8740-37
Radio Communications	FAA P 8740-47
How to Avoid a Mid-Air Collision	FAA P 8740-51

* Aircraft Accident Reports

Accident/Incident Analysis Branch
Air Traffic Service
Federal Aviation Administration (FAA)
U.S. Department of Transportation
800 Independence Ave., SW, Room 417D
Washington, DC 20591 (202) 267-9612

Accidents and incidents involving aircraft are documented in a central file maintained by this FAA branch. Contact this office for more information on the information in these files.

* Aircraft Accidents

Safety Analysis Division
Office of Aviation Safety
Federal Aviation Administration (FAA)
U.S. Department of Transportation
800 Independence Ave., SW, Room 2221A
Washington, DC 20591 (202) 366-6003

The division can provide you with information on general aviation accidents and near mid-air collisions. The Office keeps statistics on operational errors, deviations, pilot errors, accidents, and near mid air collisions.

* Aircraft Accident Statistics

Safety Data Branch
Information Management
National Field Office
Federal Aviation Administration (FAA)
U.S. Department of Transportation
P.O. Box 25082, AVN-124
Oklahoma City, OK 73125 (405) 680-6420

The FAA maintains statistics on the following: general aviation accident information; incidents (little damage or minor injury) of both air carrier and general aviation; service difficulty reports; and enforcement data and violations. Contact this office for more information.

* Aircraft Certification Service

Administrator for Regulation and Certification
Federal Aviation Administration (FAA)
800 Independence Ave SW, Room 300W
Washington DC 20591 (202) 267-7270

The certification of airworthiness goes to the heart of aviation safety. Certification occurs at three stages: the design of the aircraft; the production of the aircraft; and the operation of the aircraft. For information and a copy of a booklet on the Aircraft Certification Service, contact the above office.

* Aircraft Flight Data and Voice Recorders Investigations

Engineering Services Division
Bureau of Technology
National Transportation Safety Board (NTSB)
800 Independence Avenue, SW, Room 826
Washington, DC 20594 (202) 382-6686

For information on aircraft flight data and voice recorders examined by the NTSB, contact the office above.

* Aircraft Maintenance Data

Maintenance Analysis Center Section
AVN-140
Federal Aviation Administration (FAA)

U.S. Department of Transportation
Aeronautical Center
P.O. Box 25082
Oklahoma City, OK 73125 (405) 680-6495

Information and statistics are available regarding aircraft maintenance surveillance, mechanical interruptions, and inflight mechanical problems.

* Aircraft Noise

Noise Abatement Division
Office of Environment and Energy
Federal Aviation Administration (FAA)
U.S. Department of Transportation
800 Independence Ave., SW, Room 432
Washington, DC 20591 (202) 267-3699

This FAA division conducts research on reducing noise levels of new aircraft, and retrofitting older aircraft to reduce noise levels. Contact this office for recent noise Advisory Circulars that certify the noise levels for aircraft under Federal Aviation Regulation 36. Ask for Advisory Circulars 36-1E; 36-2C; and 36-2F.

* Aircraft Standards and Statistics Data Base

Management Standards and Statistics Division
Federal Aviation Administration (FAA)
AMS-400
U.S. Department of Transportation
800 Independence Ave., SW
Washington, DC 20591 (202) 267-8063

The FAA maintains several computerized data files on a variety of aviation-related subjects such as: aviation safety, air traffic, aviation schools, commercial and government ownership and operation of aircraft, aircraft repair stations, FAA facilities, and procurement. While the FAA does not conduct searches of these files for anyone outside the agency, they will copy any file you designate onto a blank tape that you provide for $38.

* Airline Antitrust Violations

Aviation Analysis
Federal Aviation Administration (FAA)
U.S. Department of Transportation
800 Independence Ave., SW, Room 10223
Washington, DC 20591 (202) 267-4382

The office investigates airline mergers and interlocks, unfair methods of competition among carriers, and also determines antitrust immunity. Contact this FAA office for more information on airline antitrust issues.

* Airline Data

Office of Airline Statistics
Research and Special Programs Administration
U.S. Department of Transportation (DOT)
400 7th Street, SW, Room 4125
Washington, DC 20590 (202) 366-9059

The Aviation Information Management (AIM) program collects information on the financial operations of air carriers. Government, industry, and the general public may access this information. Database functions are housed at the Transportation Systems Center (see entry) but this office can serve as liaison for access to air carrier reports and data requiring DOT approval for release.

* Airline Passenger Safety

Community and Consumer Liaison Division
Office of Public Affairs
Federal Aviation Administration (FAA)
U.S. Department of Transportation
800 Independence Ave., SW
Washington, DC 20591 (202) 267-3481

Airline passengers who have inquiries or complaints regarding airplane safety should contact this office.

* Airlines General Inquiries

Office of Public Affairs
Federal Aviation Administration (FAA)
U.S. Department of Transportation
800 Independence Ave., SW

Airlines

Washington, DC 20591 (202) 267-3481

Questions and information requests about the aviation industry can be directed to this FAA office.

* Airline Transportation Data Files

Center for Electronic Records
National Archives and Records Administration
8th St. and Pennsylvania Ave., NW, Room 20E
Washington, DC 20408 (202) 523-3267

This center has information regarding airline transportation from the U.S. Department of Transportation and the Civil Aeronautics Board. Contact the Center for a detailed listing of the data available and the fees for retrieval.

* Airmen and Aircraft Registry

Airmen and Aircraft Registry
Federal Aviation Administration (FAA)
U.S. Department of Transportation
Mike Monroney Aeronautical Center
P.O. Box 25082
Oklahoma, OK 73125 (405) 680-4331

The FAA keeps permanent records on all U.S. civil aircraft and airmen (students, private, commercial and airline transport). The Registry also issues and monitors certificates to air carrier personnel involved in international civil aviation. Contact this office for information on these records, along with the registration records of all civil aircraft.

* Airport Capacity

Office of Systems Capacity and Requirements
Airport Capacity Planning and Development
Federal Aviation Administration (FAA)
U.S. Department of Transportation
800 Independence Ave., SW, Room 723
Washington, DC 20591 (202) 267-7425

This office is involved in a variety of programs to increase the capacity of the national air system through programs of improved airport and air routes design; improved procedures that allow planes to fly in closer proximity more safely; and developing new technology in areas such as radar precision. This office's work is detailed in the Aviation System Capacity Plan, which publishes statistics and outlines FAA programs in capacity expansion.

* Airport Hubs

Office of Aviation Policy and Plans
Forecast Branch
Federal Aviation Administration (FAA)
U.S. Department of Transportation
800 Independence Ave.,SW, Room 935F
Washington, DC 20591 (202) 267-3355

The Office of Aviation Policy and Plans analyzes activity at different airport hubs around the country. There are currently 25 large hubs, encompassing 40 carrier airports, in the U.S. There are reports on all the major hubs in the U.S. Contact this office for more information. Recent reports focus on:

Washington/Baltimore Hub	October 1991
Denver Hub/Colorado Airports	October 1990
Miami/ Ft. Lauderdale (update)	December 1990
Nashville, Tn.	September 1989
Dayton, Ohio.	September 1989
Cincinnati, Ohio.	September 1989
Raleigh/Durham, N.C.	June 1989
Atlanta (update)	June 1989

* Airport Security

Airport Security Program
Civil Aviation Security Service
Federal Aviation Administration (FAA)
U.S. Department of Transportation
800 Independence Ave., SW, Room 319
Washington, DC 20591 (202) 267-9863

The FAA ensures the presence of law enforcement in U.S. airports, and approves the security programs of all airports under FAR 107. It also certifies walk-through detection devices.

* Airport Safety and Facilities

Airport Safety Data Branch
Federal Aviation Administration (FAA)
U.S. Department of Transportation
800 Independence Ave., SW
Room 616A
Washington, DC 20591 (202) 267-8730

This office collects data on airport services, schedules, runway layouts, and lighting. The data is published in the *Airport Facility Directory*. Information is available to the public, but requestors are limited to two facility inquiries per request. Those wishing to do large scale research may make an appointment and go to the Airport Safety Data Branch and use the files. The information is also available on magnetic disk. For further information, contact the Branch.

* Airport Standards

Design and Operational Criteria Division
Office of Airport Standards
Federal Aviation Administration (FAA)
U.S. Department of Transportation
800 Independence Ave., SW Room 614
Washington, DC 20591 (202) 267-3446

This office can provide you with information on standards required for constructing and operating airports. Such standards include size, length, separation between runways, snow and ice control, and crash and fire rescue equipment. Contact this office for more information.

* Airway Facilities

Associate Administrator for Airway Facilities
Planning Branch
Federal Aviation Administration (FAA)
U.S. Department of Transportation
800 Independence Ave., SW, Room 731
Washington, DC 20591 (202) 267-7304

This office is responsible for the establishment, installation and maintenance of the infrastructural facilities such as radars, communications, and navigation aids in the National Aerospace System.

* Annual Review of Aircraft Accidents

National Technical Information Services
5285 Port Royal Road
Springfield, VA 22161 (703) 557-4650

The *Annual Review of Aircraft Accident Data: U.S. General Aviation* contains statistical tabulations of data compiled from reports of accidents involving U.S. general aviation aircraft in a particular calendar year. The report is divided into sections according to the type of aircraft and also according to the purpose for which aircraft was being used at the time of an accident. Within each section, tabulations provide data describing the types, causes, and circumstances of accidents. Accident rates (total and fatal) are provided, as are comparisons of the data of the given year to averages of accident data for several prior years. This publication is available from the office above. Call (703) 487-4650 for single copies and microfiche; or (703) 487-4630 for an annual subscription.

* Aviation Accident Prevention

Flight Standards Service
Accident Prevention Program
Federal Aviation Administration (FAA)
U.S. Department of Transportation
800 Independence Ave.,SW, Room 2232
Washington, DC 20591 (202) 267-6321

The Accident Prevention Program has a variety of publications on aircraft safety. All are free and can be obtained by contacting the above office.

The Accident Prevention Program.	*FAA P 8740-8*
Safe Flying for Agricultural Aviation.	*FAA P 8740-42*
Notices to Airmen.	*FAA P 8740-54*
Weight and Balance: An Important Safety Consideration for Pilots.	*FAA P 8740-5*
Pilot Prerogatives.	*FAA P 8740-17*
Dead Reckoning Navigation.	*FAA P 8740-22*
Always Leave Yourself an Out.	*FAA P 8740-25*
Using the System.	*FAA P 8740-32*
The Propwatchers Guide.	*FAA P 8740-37*

Be patient. If any phone number is incorrect, call (area code) 555-1212 and request the new listing.

Business and Industry

Radio Communications. FAA P 8740-47
How to Avoid a Mid-Air Collision. FAA P 8740-51

* Aviation Equipment Specifications

Engineering and Specifications Division
Office of Airport Standards
Federal Aviation Administration (FAA)
U.S. Department of Transportation
800 Independence Ave., SW, Room 614
Washington, DC 20591 (202) 267-3826

This office can supply you with information on specifications for the manufacturing and installation of such aviation equipment as visual aides associated with aircraft landing and taxiing, runway lights, approach lights, beacons, and so forth.

* Aviation Forecasts

Aviation Forecasts Branch
Office of Aviation Policy
Federal Aviation Administration (FAA)
U.S. Department of Transportation
800 Independence Ave., SW, Room 935F
Washington, DC 20591 (202) 267-3103

This Branch is responsible for forecasting aviation activity for the U.S. Data collected include the number of landings, takeoffs, aircraft, enplanements, and deplanements.

The following publications are available through this office, free of charge, depending on availability; otherwise you will be referred to the Government Printing Office, where they can be purchased:

Federal Aviation Administration Aviation Forecast. This microfiche provides 12-year projections on all aspects of aviation, including total aircraft, total airborne, statute miles of U.S. air carriers, hours flown in general aviation, and fuel consumed.

Terminal Area Forecasts. This microfiche provides 10-year projections on 400 specific airports including in-plane passengers, and operations of air carriers.

North Atlantic Forecast. This report contains short, medium, and long-term forecasts of air traffic over the North Atlantic and between North America and the Caribbean area for the periods 1991-1996, 2000, 2005 and 2010. Annual forecasts are provided for total passengers and aircraft movements.

Sixteenth Annual FAA Aviation Forecast Conference Proceedings. This report discusses a variety of forecast related issues including the outlook for Hubbing, Education and Noise, and financing issues in the aviation industry.

Forecasting Civil Aviation Activity: Methods and Approaches.

FAA Flight Service Station Facility Level Forecast: Fiscal Years 1992-2002.

* Aviation History

Agency Historian
Office of Public Affairs
Federal Aviation Administration (FAA)
U.S. Department of Transportation
800 Independence Ave., SW, Room 907A
Washington, DC 20591 (202) 267-3478

This office can provide you with the facts on the history of American aviation as well as a five page brief on the history of the FAA. A list of FAA historical works is also available from this office. Books can be purchased from GPO (202) 783-3238. Additional information on aviation or FAA history can also be obtained at the FAA library, which is open to the public.

* Aviation Medicine

Biomedical and Behavioral Science Division
Office of Aviation Administration
Federal Aviation Administration (FAA)
U.S. Department of Transportation
800 Independence Ave., SW, Room 2338C
Washington, DC 20591 (202) 366-6910

The FAA conducts aeromedical research on in the following areas:

- Psychology: evaluates spatial disorientation and visual perception in the aviation environment;
- Physiology: performance and health of aircrew and air traffic controllers under diverse environmental conditions;
- Toxicology: toxic hazards such as pesticides used in aerial application, products of combustion and ionizing radiation from air shipment of radioactive cargo in the high-altitude environment;
- Protection and survival: studies of techniques for lessening or preventing crash injuries, developing concepts and evaluating survival equipment used under adverse physical conditions, establishing human physical limitations of civil aviation operations, and evaluating emergency procedures for downed aircraft.

* Aviation News

FAA General Aviation News
General Aviation and Commercial Division
Flight Standards Service, AFS-800
Federal Aviation Administration (FAA)
U.S. Department of Transportation
800 Independence Ave., SW
Room 325
Washington, DC 20591 (202) 267-8212

The bimonthly publication, *Aviation News,* is a safety magazine for general aviation pilots (for more information about content, contact the above office). It is available for $13 per year from the Government Printing Office, Superintendent of Documents, Washington, DC 20402; (202) 783-3238.

* Aviation Policy

Information Systems Branch
Policy Analysis Division, APO-130
Office of Aviation Policy and Plans
Federal Aviation Administration (FAA)
U.S. Department of Transportation
800 Independence Ave., SW
Room 937C
Washington, DC 20591 (202) 267-3350

Reports and other data are generated by approximately 18 databases to aid in aviation policy decisions on such matters as the activities of airlines, seat belt configurations, and the number of airports in the United States.

* Aviation Procedures Periodicals

Superintendent of Documents
U.S. Government Printing Office (GPO)
Washington DC 20402 (202) 783-3238

The following two periodicals from GPO contain the current internal directives of the Federal Aviation Administration:

Flight Services Handbook. Describes the procedures and terms used by personnel providing assistance and communications services ($46/subscription, #950-032-00000-6).

Data Communications Handbook. Describes teletypewriter operating procedures, applicable international teletypewriter procedures, and continuous U.S. Service weather schedules ($34/subscription, #950-004-00000-2).

* Aviation Publications

U.S Department of Transportation
M-443.2
Washington, DC 20590

Write to the above address to order free copies of the annual *Guide to Federal Aviation Administration Publications* (FAA-APA-PG-11). For approval of more that 10 copies, write to: Federal Aviation Administration, U.S. Department of Transportation, 800 Independence Ave., SW, APA-230, Washington, DC 20591. Many of the publications listed are free.

* Aviation Research and Development Efforts

System Research and Development
Federal Aviation Administration (FAA)
U.S. Department of Transportation, Room 500W
800 Independence Ave., SW
Washington, DC 20591 (202) 267-8183

Be patient. If any phone number is incorrect, call (area code) 555-1212 and request the new listing.

Airlines

This office directs, coordinates, and controls the FAA's Research, Engineering, and Development efforts aimed at bringing new into the National Aerospace System.

* Aviation Safety

Assistant Administrator for Aviation Safety
Federal Aviation Administration (FAA)
U.S. Department of Transportation
800 Independence Ave., SW, Room 1000E
Washington, DC 20591
(202) 267-9613

The Assistant Administrator is involved in all aspects of aviation safety. The Office reviews and recommends safety programs for the FAA and the aviation community. It also initiates special safety reviews and maintains reports on safety data.

* Aviation Standards

Assistant Administrator for Aviation Standards
Mike Monroney Aeronautical Center
P.O. Box 25082
Oklahoma City, OK 73125
(405) 680-3306

This office promotes flight safety, develops flight procedures, oversees the management of the airman and aircraft registry, provides for the operation and maintenance of FAA aircraft, and investigates aircraft accidents and incidents.

* Aviation Statistics--General

Information Analysis Branch
Management Standards and Statistics Division
Office of Information Technology
Federal Aviation Administration (FAA)
U.S. Department of Transportation
800 Independence Ave., SW, Room 607
Washington, DC 20591
(202) 267-8063

Historical and current aviation statistics are available on such subjects as: air traffic activities, number of aircraft, flying hours, pilots, and passengers. For a listing of available publications, contact the above office.

* Balloon Safety

Flight Standards Service
Accident Prevention Program
Federal Aviation Administration (FAA)
U.S. Department of Transportation
800 Independence Ave., SW, Room 2322
Washington, DC 20591
(202) 267-6321

The FAA publishes the following booklets on balloon safety: *Powerlines and Thunderstorms-Balloon Safety,* and *False Lift, Shears, and Rotors - Balloon Safety.* They are available free from the Accident Prevention program.

* Bird Strikes

Airport Safety Data Group
Office of Airport Standards
Federal Aviation Administration (FAA)
U.S. Department of Transportation
800 Independence Ave., SW, Room 615
Washington, DC 20591
(202) 267-8792

Birds being accidentally sucked into jet engines is a serious aviation hazard. Contact this office for information on where bird strikes occur.

* Careers in Aviation

Office of Public Affairs
Aviation Education Program
Federal Aviation Program
U.S. Department of Transportation
800 Independence Ave., SW, Room 907F
Washington, DC 20591
(202) 267-3476

Federal, state, and local government agencies are a major source of aviation jobs. The FAA publishes a booklet entitled *Aviation Careers Series* which details a variety of careers in the aviation field. It is available free.

* Commuter and Air Taxi Services

Commuter and Air Taxi Branch
Air Carrier Division
Office of Flight Operations
Federal Aviation Administration (FAA)
U.S. Department of Transportation
800 Independence Ave., SW, Room 306A
Washington, DC 20591
(202) 267-8086

Contact this office for information regarding policy, regulations, and directives for commuter and air taxi aircraft. A list is available of air taxi operators and commercial operators of small aircraft.

* Consumer Complaints

Community and Consumer Liaison Division
Office of Public Affairs
Federal Aviation Administration (FAA)
U.S. Department of Transportation
800 Independence Ave., SW
Washington, DC 20591
(202) 267-3481

Complaints involving such aviation issues as safety, noise, pesticide spraying, or broken seat belts can be directed to this office.

* Consumer Rights on Airlines

Government Printing Office (GPO)
Superintendent of Documents
Washington DC 20402
(202) 783-3238

Fly Rights is an easy-to-read booklet that explains the rights and responsibilities of air travellers. It is available at nominal cost from the GPO.

* Educational Resources in Aviation

Aviation Education Officer
Federal Aviation Administration (FAA)
U.S. Department of Transportation
800 Independence Ave., SW
Washington, DC 20591
(202) 267-3469

The FAA's Aviation Education Program offers volunteer assistance to the nation's schools through the following programs: career guidance; tours of airports, control towers, and other facilities; classroom lectures and demonstrations; aviation safety information; aviation education resource materials; computerized clearinghouse of aviation and space information; aviation science instruction programs for home/school computers; "Partnerships-in-Education" activities; and teachers' workshops. Write to the above office for more information.

* Essential Air Passenger Service

Aviation Analysis
Federal Aviation Administration (FAA)
U.S. Department of Transportation
800 Independence Ave., SW, Room 5100
Washington, DC 20591
(202) 267-5903

This office guarantees that certain cities will be served by airlines. It also represents community views. Contact this office for information on airport service.

* Essential Air Service

Office of Aviation Analysis
Policy and International Affairs
Office of the Secretary of Transportation
U.S. Department of Transportation
400 7th Street, SW, Room 6401
Washington, DC 20590
(202) 366-5903

The Departments's Essential Air Service Program ensures that certain cities will be served by air transportation. The program establishes subsidy levels, selects carriers, processes applications to change service levels, and reviews fitness of carriers. Contact the office listed for information about this program.

* Experimental Aircraft Association (EAA)

EAA Aviation Center
P.O. Box 3086
Oshkosh, WI 54903-3086
(800) 322-2412

Be patient. If any phone number is incorrect, call (area code) 555-1212 and request the new listing.

Business and Industry

The EAA brings together aircraft and aviation enthusiasts from around the country for air shows and activities. It also represents member interests in Washington DC with the FAA and promotes safety and education in aviation. It currently has 700 chapters nationwide.

* Federal Aviation Administration Academy

Federal Aviation Administration (FAA)
U.S. Department of Transportation
P.O. Box 25082, AAC-900
Oklahoma, OK 73125 (405) 680-6900

The Academy is the principal source of technical information on U.S. civil aviation. It conducts training for FAA personnel through resident or correspondence courses and occasional on-site training. Air traffic training is available for specialists who man the FAA airport traffic control towers, air route traffic control center, and flight service stations. Electronic training is also available for engineers and technicians who install and maintain navigation and traffic control communications facilities. Initial and recurrent training is also conducted for air carrier and general operations inspectors. The Academy provides air navigation facilities and flight procedures analysis to flight inspection personnel.

* Federal Aviation Administration Directives

Office of Public Affairs
Document Inspection Facility
Federal Aviation Administration (FAA)
U.S. Department of Transportation
800 Independence Ave., SW, Room 907
Washington, DC 20591 (202) 267-3883

Requests for copies of the FAA Directives list should be sent here.

* Films and Videos on Aviation

Public Inquiry Center
Federal Aviation Administration (FAA)
U.S. Department of Transportation, APA-230
Washington, DC 20591 (202) 267-3481

The FAA has a free catalog of films and videos useful both for experienced aviators as well as the general public. They describe the kinds of programs and measures that can be taken collectively to increase the safety, capacity, and efficiency of the U.S. national airspace system--in areas ranging from air traffic control to aeromedical research, meteorology, and safety. Most of the titles listed in the catalog are available in both 16mm film and 1/2" VHS videocassette. There is no charge for borrowing these FAA titles, and no admission may be charged to any audiences viewing the programs. These titles may also be purchased. For a copy of the *FAA Film/Video Catalog*, contact this office. The following is a list of some of the titles available.

Title	Number
Where Airports Begin.	*#11106*
Looking Up to Your Aviation Career.	*#10314*
Area Navigation.	*#11114*
Flight 52.	*#11127*
Aeromedical Factors.	*#19981*
Medical Facts for Pilots.	*#11138*
Dusk to Dawn.	*#11124*
Mountain Flying.	*#11140*
Overwater Flying.	*#11141*
Path to Safety.	*#11142*

* Financial Analysis of Airline Industry

Aviation Analysis
Office of the Secretary of Transportation
U.S. Department of Transportation
800 Independence Ave., SW, Room 5100
Washington, DC 20591 (202) 267-5903

Financial studies and evaluations of the air transportation industry are available on such subjects as profit margin trends, aircraft cost and performance, domestic jet trends, fuel trends, carrier lenders, passenger yield, used aircraft sales, aircraft seating trends, and airline employment.

* Flight Instruction

General Aviation Manufactures Association
1400 K. St. NW, Suite 801

Washington, DC 20005 (202) 393-1500

This association publishes a pamphlet entitled *Learning to Fly* that discusses the basics of flying and the first steps on where to go for flying lessons.

* Flight Procedures

Flight Procedures Branch
Federal Aviation Administration (FAA)
U.S. Department of Transportation
P.O. Box 25082
AVN-220900
Oklahoma, OK 73125 (405) 680-3382

The branch develops and maintains instrument flight procedures.

* Flight Standards

Flight Procedures Standards Branch
Federal Aviation Administration (FAA)
800 Independence Ave., SW, Room 305C
Washington, DC 20591 (202) 267-8277

Along with the Flight procedures branch in Oklahoma, the Flight Standards Branch plays a key role in developing flight procedures and overseeing flight inspectors.

* General Inquiries

Office of Public Affairs
Federal Aviation Administration (FAA)
U.S. Department of Transportation
800 Independence Ave., SW
Washington, DC 20591 (202) 267-3481

The stating place for any information on airlines, airports and aircraft.

* Human Factors: Aviation Research

Civil Aeromedical Institute (CAMI)
Federal Aviation Administration (FAA)
U.S. Department of Transportation
Mike Monroney Aeronautical Center
P.O. Box 25082
Oklahoma, OK 73125 (405) 680-4806

CAMI conducts research to identify human factor causes of aircraft accidents, prevent future accidents, and make accidents that do occur more survivable. Contact this Institute for more information on this research.

* International Air Transportation

Office of International Aviation
Policy and International Affairs
Office of the Secretary of Transportation
U.S. Department of Transportation
400 7th Street, SW, Room 6402
Washington, DC 20590 (202) 366-2423

This office studies and develops U.S. policy with regard to international aviation. It ensures cooperation between U.S. and foreign-flag airlines and negotiates air service agreements with other countries.

* International Aviation

Bureau of Economic and Business Affairs
U.S. Department of State
2201 C St., NW, Room 5531
Washington, DC 20520 (202) 647-7973

In handling all international aviation negotiations and agreements, this office works on expanding aviation markets overseas, aviation security, and other issues relating to international aviation, such as assisting airlines in operating overseas and monitors agreements thereof. Information is available on these topics.

* International Aviation Assistance

Office of International Aviation
International Operations Organization Division
Federal Aviation Administration (FAA)
800 Independence Ave., SW, Room 1027
Washington, DC 20591 (202) 267-3230

Be patient. If any phone number is incorrect, call (area code) 555-1212 and request the new listing.

Airlines

This office handles affairs concerning both international organizations and international assistance for foreign aviation systems. This office works with FAA technical offices on political and bureaucratic aspects of aviation policy with foreign nations. It also works with nations who request assistance for developing aviation infrastructure and training programs.

* Light Twin Engine Aircraft

Flight Standards Service
Accident Prevention Program
Federal Aviation Administration (FAA)
U.S. Department of Transportation
800 Independence Ave., SW, Room 2322
Washington, DC 20591 (202) 267-6321

The FAA publication *Flying Light Twins Safely* discusses safety with respect to light twin engine aircraft. It is available free.

* Medical Certification of Airmen

Civil Aeromedical Institute (CAMI)
Federal Aviation Administration (FAA)
U.S. Department of Transportation
Mike Monroney Aeronautical Center
P.O. Box 25082
Oklahoma, OK 73125 (405) 680-4806

CAMI operates a program for the medical certification of airmen, and educates pilots and physicians in matters related to aviation safety. It is also responsible for developing and producing brochures, slides, and training films for distribution to aviation groups and organizations. Contact CAMI for more information on certification or these education programs.

* National Aerospace System Development

Assistant Administrator for NAS Development
Federal Aviation Administration (FAA)
U.S. Department of Transportation
800 Independence Ave., SW, Room 800W
Washington, DC 20591 (202) 267-3555

This office directs FAA's requisition, engineering and management activities for NAS Planing Programs associated with the next generation of communications, navigational, surveillance, and weather systems.

* National Airport System Plan

Office of Airport Planning and Programming
National Planning Division
Federal Aviation Administration (FAA)
U.S. Department of Transportation
800 Independence Ave., SW, Room 615C
Washington, DC 20591 (202) 267-3451

Contact this office for statistical information on the National Airport System.

* National Flight Data

National Flight Data Center
Airspace--Rules and Aeronautical Information Division
Air Traffic Service
Federal Aviation Administration (FAA)
U.S. Department of Transportation
800 Independence Ave., SW, Room 634
Washington, DC 20591 (202) 267-9311

This Center can provide you with information on all civilian airports (and those military airports with joint usage), navigation aids, and procedures for the national airspace system. The Center also maintains a database which contains such items as the latitude and longitude of airports, airport runways, records of obstruction to air navigation, flight planning information, bearing and distance information, and records of hazards to air navigation.

* Pilot's Aeromedical Standards

Medical Specialties Division
Office of Aviation Medicine
Federal Aviation Administration (FAA)
U.S. Department of Transportation
800 Independence Ave., SW, Room 322
Washington, DC 20591 (202) 267-3535

Contact this FAA division for information on policy, regulations, and standards for medical certificates required for a pilot's license.

* Pilot Judgement and Accident Prevention

Flight Standards Service
Accident Prevention Program
Federal Aviation Administration (FAA)
U.S. Department of Transportation
800 Independence Ave., SW, Room 2322
Washington, DC 20591 (202) 267-6321

Most aircraft accidents occur due to human error rather than mechanical malfunction. The FAA Accident Prevention Program publishes several pamphlets on both common judgement errors and medical problems that can lead to accidents. The following are available free by contacting the above office.

Human Behavior: The No. 1 Cause of Accidents.	*FAA P 8740-38*
What's an Accident Prevention Counselor?	*FAA P 8/40-43*
Medical Facts for Pilots.	*FAA P 8740-41*
Introduction to Pilot Judgement.	*FAA P 8740-53*
Impossible Turn.	*FAA P 8740-44*
Proficiency and the Private Pilot.	*FAA P 8740-36*
Pilot Vision.	
Disorientation.	
Beyond the Medical.	
Alcohol and Flying Don't Mix!	

* Pilot Schools

U.S. Government Printing Office (GPO)
Superintendent of Documents
Washington DC 20402 (202) 783-3238

The *List of Certified Pilot Schools* provides you with an up-to-date directory of pilot training schools in the U.S. It is available for $1.75 from the GPO (#050-007-00763-9).

* Radio Frequency Systems Compatibility

Spectrum Engineering Division
Systems Research and Development Service
Federal Aviation Administration (FAA)
U.S. Department of Transportation
800 Independence Ave., SW, Room 714
Washington, DC 20591 (202) 267-9710

The FAA ensures that radio systems have frequencies on which to operate that are compatible with other frequencies. Work is also done in conjunction with international organizations on plans for future radio systems.

* Regulatory Standards for Aviation

Regulatory Standards and Compliance
Federal Aviation Administration (FAA)
U.S. Department of Transportation
800 Independence Ave, SW, Room 1040
Washington, DC 20591 (202) 267-3330

This office provides guidance relating to flight standards, aircraft certification, aircraft programs, aviation medicine, aviation security, aircraft accident investigations, airman and aircraft registry, and rulemaking.

* Relocation Assistance Near Airports

Community and Environmental Needs Division
Office of Airport Planning and Programming
Federal Aviation Administration (FAA)
U.S. Department of Transportation
800 Independence Ave., SW, Room 615B
Washington, DC 20591 (202) 267-3263

The division assists airport owners involved with airport development projects provide uniform and equitable treatment of persons displaced from their homes and businesses due to federal or federally-assisted programs. Assistance is also available on environmental impact and noise.

* Safety and Aircraft Mechanical Systems.

Flight Standards Service
Accident Prevention Program

Business and Industry

Federal Aviation Administration (FAA)
U.S. Department of Transportation
800 Independence Ave., SW, Room 2322
Washington, DC 20591 (202) 267-6321

Aircraft maintenance and performance are vital parts of aviation safety. The accident prevention program publishes a series of booklets in these areas. They are available free upon request.

Maintenance Aspects of Owning Your Own Airplane	*FAA P 8740-15A*
Meet Your Aircraft	*FAA P 8740-29*
Engine Operation for Pilots	*FAA P 8740-13*
The Silent Enemy: Pneumatic System Malfunction	*FAA P 8740-52*
All About Fuel	*FAA P 8740-35A*
Time in Your Tanks	*FAA P 8740-3*

* Security

Civil Aviation Security Service (ACS 400)
Federal Aviation Administration (FAA)
U.S. Department of Transportation
800 Independence Ave., SW, Room 320
Washington, DC 20591 (202) 267-9075

The office is a source of information and expertise on the following airport security issues: domestic and foreign aircraft hijacking; bomb threats at airports and on airplanes; compliance and enforcement of regulations; prevention of attempts; explosives and explosive devices found at airports and on airplanes; international crimes involving civil aviation; information on numbers of people screened, numbers of weapons found, and weapon detection devices.

* Small Business Procurement

Small Business Specialist Procurement Division
AAC-70A
Federal Aviation Administration (FAA)
U.S. Department of Transportation
Mike Monroney Aeronautical Center
P.O. Box 25082
Oklahoma, OK 73125 (405) 680-7702

The office provides FAA contracting and procurement support for spare parts, modifications and service contracts for the fleet of aircraft, and their air navigation and communication gear operated by the FAA.

* Standards and Statistics Data Base

Management Standards and Statistics Division
Federal Aviation Administration (FAA)
AMS-400
U.S. Department of Transportation
800 Independence Ave., SW, Room 606A
Washington, DC 20591 (202) 267-8063

The FAA maintains several computerized data files on a variety of aviation-related subjects such as: aviation safety, air traffic, aviation schools, commercial and government ownership and operation of aircraft, aircraft repair stations, FAA facilities, and procurement. While the FAA does not conduct searches of these files for anyone outside the agency, they will copy any file you designate onto a blank tape that you provide for $38.

* Takeoff and Landing Safely

Flight Standards Service
Accident Prevention Program
Federal Aviation Administration (FAA)
U.S. Department of Transportation
800 Independence Ave., SW, Room 2322
Washington, DC 20591 (202) 267-6321

Many air accidents occur during takeoff or landing. The FAA publishes a series of booklets discussing takeoff and landing safety. The following are available free from the FAA.

Planning Your Takeoff	*FAA P 8740-23*
Preventing Accidents During Aircraft Ground Operations	*FAA P 8740-20*
On Landings Parts I-III	*FAA P 8740-4-50*
Aviation Safety: The Runway Incursion Problem	

* Tariffs and Routes

Aviation Analysis
Federal Aviation Administration (FAA)
U.S. Department of Transportation
800 Independence Ave., SW, Room 10223
Washington, DC 20591 (202) 267-4382

Contact this office for information regarding carriers' passenger and cargo operations.

* Unauthorized Low Flying Aircraft

Office of Public Affairs
Federal Aviation Administration (FAA)
U.S. Department of Transportation
800 Independence Ave., SW, Room 907B
Washington, DC 20591 (202) 267-3481

Aircraft flying excessively low are not just a bother, but a threat to public safety. The FAA enforces regulations against unauthorized low flying aircraft. For information, contact the FAA and ask for the publication *How You Can Help FAA Identify Unauthorized Low Flying Aircraft.*

* Weather Factors and Flight Safety

Flight Standards Service
Accident Prevention Program
Federal Aviation Administration (FAA)
U.S. Department of Transportation
800 Independence Ave., SW, Room 2322
Washington, DC 20591 (202) 267-6321

Changes in weather patterns as well as the normal weather patterns at different points in the year pose significant hazards to pilots. The Accident Prevention Program publishes several pamphlets on flying in difficult weather. They are available free.

Density Altitude	*FAA P 8740-02*
Thunderstorms - Don't Flirt...Skirt em.	*FAA P 8740-12*
Wind Shear.	*FAA P 8740-40*
Tips on Winter Flying.	*FAA P 8740-24*
How to Obtain a Good Weather Briefing.	*FAA P 8740-30B*

Be patient. If any phone number is incorrect, call (area code) 555-1212 and request the new listing.

Communications

Given its importance to society, the Communications industry is among the most regulated of all industries by the Federal government. The two principal government entities charged with monitoring and regulating the Communications industry are the Federal Communications Commission (FCC) and the National Telecommunications and Information Administration, an arm of the U.S. Department of Commerce. You will find the FCC particularly helpful in locating information. The listings below cover a wide range of communications media including radio, television, cable television, microwave transmissions, long distance telephone service, pay per call (900) services, and political broadcasting.

* Amateur Radio Operators

National Technical Information Service (NTIS)
5285 Port Royal Road
Springfield, VA 22161 (703) 487-4808

A database of all the Federal Communications Commission's licensed amateur radio operators is available through NTIS. This magnetic tape file contains records on over 450,000 operators, including names, addresses, ages, station locations, and other licensing information. This Amateur Radio Service Master File (PB 83-220-889), available for $625 (6,250 BPI) or for $825 (BPI), is updated weekly.

* Amateur Radio Services

Consumer Assistance Branch
Federal Communications Commission (FCC)
1270 Fairfield Road
Gettysburg, PA 17326 (717) 337-1212

The FCC's Amateur Radio Services is comprised of three parts--amateur Service, amateur-satellite service, and Radio Amateur Civil Emergency Radio (RACES). During times of national crises, licensed amateur stations can assist local governments in coordinating emergency efforts. Those interested in becoming a licensed ARS operator must take a qualifying exam. Over 450,000 licensed individuals in the U.S. are ARS members.

* Applications and Publications

Services and Supply Branch
Federal Communications Commission (FCC)
1919 M Street, NW, Room B-10
Washington, DC 20554 (202) 632-7272

This office will provide you with any FCC licensing application forms, construction permits, and instructional publications on how to conform with FCC guidelines.

* Auxiliary Services Branch

Federal Communications Commission (FCC)
2025 M Street, NW, Room 7310
Washington, DC 20554 (202) 632-6485

Documents on File: FM Booster Stations, International, Intercity Relays, Remote Pickups, Translator Relays, Studio Transmitter Link, and so on. Hours of Operation: Monday through Friday, 1:00 p.m. to 5:00 p.m.

* Broadcast Ownership Reference Room

Federal Communications Commission (FCC)
1919 M Street, NW, Room 234
Washington, DC 20554 (202) 632-6993

Documents on File: Commercial and Non-Commercial Ownership Reports for Station AM, FM, and TV, Contract Files, and Network Affiliation Agreements. Information in these files includes lists of broadcast owners, directors, shares of stock sold, shareholders, media interests held by broadcasters outside their own station in areas such as newspapers. The *Ownership Report* is available from the Reference Room and details this information. Hours of Operation: Monday through Friday, 9:00am to 4:30pm.

* Broadcast Regulations

Mass Media Bureau
Federal Communications Commission (FCC)
1919 M Street, NW, Room 314
Washington, DC 20554 (202) 632-6460

The Mass Media Bureau has three major responsibilities: 1) regulating AM, FM, and television broadcast stations and related facilities; 2) administering and enforcing cable TV rules; and 3) licensing private microwave radio facilities used by cable systems. The Bureau also processes applications for licenses or other filings, analyzes complaints, and conducts investigations.

* Broadcast Violations

Field Operations Bureau
Federal Communications Commission (FCC)
1919 M Street, NW, Room 725
Washington, DC 20554 (202) 632-1940

FOB is the FCC's primary point of contact with the public. Field office personnel nationwide interact with consumers, radio communications users, and the telecommunications industry through enforcement and public service activities. The Field Operations Bureau detects violations of radio regulations, monitors transmissions, inspects stations, investigates complaints of radio interference, and issues violations notices. It also examines and licenses radio operators; processes applications for painting, lighting, and placing antenna towers; and furnishes direction-finding aids for ships and aircraft in distress. The bureau maintains over 30 field offices across the country.

* Business Radio Services

Licensing Division
Federal Communications Commission (FCC)
1270 Fairfield Rd
Gettysburg, PA 17326 (717) 337-1212

The FCC authorizes and licenses all Business Radio Services used in commercial activity. Over 640,000 businesses in the U.S., from mail couriers to exterminators to plumbers, use radio services as part of their operations and must be licensed by the FCC. Updated daily, these files are available on database and can be accessed through SAFE, or at an access terminal by visiting the FCC office in person.

* Cable Television

Federal Communications Commission (FCC)
File Room Number 2
1919 M Street, NW, Room 248
Washington, DC 20554 (202) 632-6993

Documents on File: FCC Form 325 Schedule 2, Physical System Data, Reference to files that are filed by county, state, and/or operator legal name. Hours of Operation: Monday through Friday, 9:00am to 4:30pm.

* Cable Television

Federal Communications Commission (FCC)
File Room Number 1
1919 M Street, NW, Room 244
Washington, DC 20554 (202) 632-6993

Be patient. If any phone number is incorrect, call (area code) 555-1212 and request the new listing.

Business and Industry

Documents on File: Correspondence Files, FCC Form 325 Schedule 1, Community Unit Data, 76.12 Registration (letter), 76.400 Ownership Change (Letters), Cable Antenna Relay Services (CARS), Cable Show Cause Orders, (CSC) Files, Cable Special Relief (CSR), and Cross-Ownership Files. Hours of Operation: Monday through Friday, 9:00am to 4:30pm.

* Cellular Reference Room

Federal Communications Commission (FCC)
1919 M Street, NW, Room 209
Washington DC 20554 (202) 632-6400
Documents on File: Pending Cellular Applications, Petitions. Hours of Operation: Tuesday, Thursday, and Friday, 1:00pm to 4:00pm.

* Common Carrier Bureau Reference and File Rooms

Federal Communications Commission (FCC)
Accounting and Audits Division
Public Reference Room
2000 L Street, NW, Room 812
Washington, DC 20554 (202) 634-1861
Documents on File: Accounts and Subaccounts, Continuing Property Records, Disposition Units, Pension Filings, Official Correspondence, Computer II Public Files, Depreciation Rates, Filings, Docket 86-111 Implementation Filings, Contracts between Carriers, and Affiliations Waiver Requests dealing with Accounting and Reporting. Hours of Operation: Monday through Friday, 9:00am to 4:00pm.

* Common Carrier Regulations

Common Carrier Bureau
Federal Communications Commission (FCC)
1919 M Street, NW, Room 500
Washington, DC 20554 (202) 632-6910
This office regulates wire and radio communications common carriers--paging, digital electronic message service, point-to-point microwave, multipoint distribution service, rural radio, cellular radio, offshore radio, international fixed radio, international fixed public radio, telephone, telegraph, and satellite companies. It also processes applications for licenses or other filings, analyzes related complaints, and conducts investigations into common carrier-related problems.

* Communications and Information Policy

Public Information
National Telecommunications and Information Administration
U.S. Department of Commerce
14th St. and Constitution Ave., NW, Room 4898
Washington, DC 20230 (202) 377-1551
The National Telecommunications and Information Administration's policy recommendations affect the nation's economic and technological advancement in the telecommunications industry. This includes common carrier, telephone, broadcast, and satellite communications systems. It is involved with regulatory changes that have led to increased competition in common carrier operations and the growing overlap between telecommunications and computers. In the information field, NTIA focuses attention on issues of privacy and security and the impact of U.S. and international legislation on the flow of electronic data across national boundaries. Contact this office for more information.

* Communications Networks and New Technologies

Office of Technology Assessment (OTA)
600 Pennsylvania Ave., SE
Washington, DC 20510 (202) 228-6774
Recent advances in information storage and transmission technologies, occurring in a new deregulated and intensely competitive economic climate, are rapidly changing the Nation's communication networks. OTA is studying the role of the Federal government in this area, along with how to coordinate them, resolve potential conflicts between them, and examine new communication systems abroad and their potential relationships to the U.S. systems. Contact Linda Garcia, the project director, for more information.

* Communications Treaties

Federal Communications Commission (FCC)
Treaty Library
2025 M Street, NW, Room 7112

Washington, DC 20554 (202) 632-7025
Documents available include: International Telecommunications Union Publications including International Telecommunications Convention, Radio Convention, Radio Regulations, List of Addresses of Administrations, etc., Final Acts of ITU Conferences, CCIR and CCITT Reports and Recommendations, International Frequency Assignments and specialized lists including the international frequency list, list of Coast Stations, list of Ship Stations, IFRB Weekly Circular with Annexed Special Sections, Canadian Frequency Assignment List. Hours of operation: Monday through Friday, 7:00am to 3:30pm.

* Consumer Complaints: Television, Broadcast Radio

Mass Media Division
Complaints and Investigations Branch
Federal Communications Commission (FCC)
2025 M Street, NW, Room 8210
Washington, DC 20554 (202) 632-7048
This office handles consumer complaints involving commercial, non-commercial and cable TV, and broadcast radio. These complaints generally involve transmission interference problems, complaints about indecent language, and commercial sponsorship regulations. Complaints about billing, programming, and scheduling are handled by the local governments and stations themselves.

* Database Search Service

ATA Services Inc.
2200 Mill Rd.
Alexandria, VA 22314 (703) 838-1901
The FCC has contracted ATA to provide the public with a search and retrieval service for all information contained in the FCC database files. For example, they could give you the names of all the businesses within a 70 mile radius of Washington, DC, that use mobile radios in their operations, or even equal opportunity employment statistics for TV stations in Dallas, Texas. They provide on-line access to the databases for $54 per hour, and or they will do customized searches for $55 per hour plus the cost of materials. ATA has on-line FCC information on the following areas: Private Radio Land/Mobile Licenses; Common Carrier Land/Mobile Licenses; Common Carrier Multipoint Distribution Service Licenses; Common Carrier Cellular Licenses; Pending Data on Applications for these licenses; Telephone Interconnection Data; Private Radio Bureau Administrative Tracking Information for - Aviation Ground - Marine Coast - Private Microwave. Data is available on computer tape, floppy disks, paper, and mailing labels. For a complete description of the FCC's databases and costs of searches, contact ATA.

* Domestic Facilities Division

Federal Communications Commission (FCC)
Public Reference Room
2025 M Street, NW, Room 6220
Washington, DC 20554 (202) 634-1860
Documents on File: *Point to Point Microwave, Digital Electronic Message Services, Multi-Point Distribution Services, Space Stations, Section 214,* and *Equipment Registration.* Hours of Operation: Monday through Thursday, 8:30am to 12:30pm, 1:30pm to 3:00pm.

* Domestic Telecommunication Policy Development

Office of Policy Analysis and Development (OPAD)
National Telecommunications and Information Administration
U.S. Department of Commerce
14th Street and Constitution Ave. NW, Room 4725
Washington, DC 20230 (202) 377-1880
OPAD develops policy recommendations on the introduction of competition into, and the deregulation of, the telecommunications industries, information service, radio and television broadcasting, and Cable TV. OPAD also administers NTIA's Minority Telecommunications Development Program (MTDP), which promotes minority ownership participation in the telecommunications industry.

* Electric Borrowers Operations Database

Public Information Office
Rural Electrification Administration
U.S. Department of Agriculture
Washington, DC 20250 (202) 720-9560
The Rural Electrification Administration (REA) Database contains financial and statistical information about the operations of approximately 2,160 REA electric

Be patient. If any phone number is incorrect, call (area code) 555-1212 and request the new listing.

Communications

and telephone borrowers individually and as a group. The following information can be retrieved about each borrower: outstanding loans, REA debit service repayments, balance sheet items, revenue and expense items, operating statements, and sales statistics. REA maintains a variety of files containing information, ranging from loan statistics to accounting data. Searches and printouts are available free of charge. Tapes can be purchased for a cost-recovery fee, and hard copy reports are also available.

* Electronic Equipment Authorization

Equipment Authorization Branch
Federal Communications Commission (FCC)
7435 Oakland Mills Road
Columbia, MD 21046 (410) 725-1585

All electronic equipment must be approved by the FCC before it is marketed in or imported into the U.S. The FCC's equipment authorization program also includes procedures for approving telephone equipment connected to public telephone network and for advance approval of over-the-air subscription (pay) TV systems before their authorization for use. The FCC also maintains and constantly updates a database of the equipment it authorizes. For more information on equipment application guidelines and regulations, contact EAB.

* Enforcement

Common Carrier Bureau
Federal Communications Commission (FCC)
2025 M Street, NW, Room 6202
Washington, DC 20554 (202) 632-7553

This office handles consumer complaints involving communications services provided by interstate common carriers, which include voice, record, data, video and facsimile transmissions via wire, microwave, satellite, radio marine cable, optical fiber, and other facilities. The majority of complaints generally concern a carrier's rates or practices or the accuracy of a service charge or billing practice. Contact this office for more information on lodging a complaint.

* Enforcement Reference Room

Federal Communications Commission (FCC)
2025 M Street, NW, Room 8210
Washington, DC 20554 (202) 632-6968

Documents on File: *Station Complaint Files, Congressional Correspondence, Files, and Network Correspondence Files.* Hours of Operation: Monday through Friday, 9:00am to 5:00pm.

* Equal Employment Opportunity

Federal Communications Commission (FCC)
2025 M Street, NW, Room 7218
Washington, DC 20554 (202) 632-6968

Documents on File: *FCC Form 395 Reports* (Broadcast Stations and Cable Employment Units), *Submissions that Cable Companies File in the Certification Process, Labor Force Statistics, Correspondence to and from Broadcast Stations and Cable Employment Units, and Cable Certification Process Results.* Hours of Operations: Monday through Friday, 8:00am to 4:30pm.

* Emergency Broadcast System

Federal Communications Commission (FCC)
1919 M Street, NW, Room 840
Washington, DC 20554 (202) 632-3906

The Emergency Broadcast System (EBS) was originally developed to be used by the President in times of national crisis or war. EBS may now also be used by state and local officials in all 50 states, the District of Columbia, Puerto Rico, the Virgin Islands, American Samoa, and Guam to disseminate warning and instructions to the public in situations threatening life and property. Nationally, the EBS, which can be activated only by the White House, is designed to enable the President to speak to the nation within 10 minutes of his request. This office can also provide you with documents on the history of the EBS. Contact this office for more information.

* Evolution of Broadcasting

Federal Communications Commission (FCC)
Consumer Assistance and Small Business Division
Office of Public Affairs
1919 M Street, NW, Room 254

Washington, DC 20554 (202) 632-7000

The FCC publishes several packets detailing the evolution of television, cable television, and radio broadcasting. These information packets also discuss the evolution of the rules governing mass media.

* Experimental Radio Service

Frequency Liaison Branch
Federal Communications Commission (FCC)
1919 M Street, NW, Room 7326
Washington, DC 20554 (202) 653-8141

The FCC's Experimental Radio Service permits the public to experiment with new uses of radio frequencies. Individuals or manufacturers wishing to conduct research involving radiowave propagation equipment must be licensed by the FCC. For more information on the application procedures or on the database maintained on all experimental radio licenses granted, contact this office.

* Fairness/Political Programming Branch

Federal Communications Commission (FCC)
2025 M Street, NW, Room 8202
Washington, DC 20554 (202) 632-6968

Documents on File: *Correspondence and Rulings on Fairness/Political Programming Complaints.* Hours of Operation: Monday through Friday, 8:00am to 5:30pm. In early 1992 the FCC released a new report on the Codification of the Commissions Political Programming Policies - MM Docket 91-168, detailing FCC rules and policies with respect to political programming.

* FCC Information Bulletins and Fact Sheets

Federal Communications Commission (FCC)
Consumer Assistance and Small Business Division
Office of Public Affairs
1919 M Street, NW, Room 254
Washington, DC 20554 (202) 632-7000

If you are looking for general information about communications issues or background material about the FCC, you may want to obtain copies of the following bulletins from this office. Single copies only are supplied free of charge.

Bulletins:
How to Apply for a Broadcast Station
Mass Media Services
The FCC in Brief
Radio Stations and Other Lists
Private Radio Services
Evolution of Wire and Radio Communications
Station Identification and Call Signs
Frequency Allocation
Memo to All Young People Interested in Radio
Cable Television
Field Operation Bureau

Fact Sheets:
Low Power Television (LPTV)
Multipoint Distribution Service (MDS)
Instructional Television Fixed Service (ITFS)
Direct Broadcast Service (DBS)
Cellular Radio
Satellite Program Scrambling
Indecency/Obscenity
Exparte'
Dial-a-Porn
FCC Fee Information
Specialized Mobile Radio Service (SMRS)

* FCC Library

1919 M Street NW, Room 639
Washington, DC 20554 (202) 632-7100

Documents available include the following: *Code of Federal Regulations Title 47, Telecommunications 1938-1988, FCC Annual Reports, FCC Federal Court Briefs,* selected FCC Records, FCC Reports - first and second series, *Federal Radio Commission Annual Reports, Pike and Fischer Radio Regulations* - first and second series, and the *Radio Act of 1927* and the *Communication Act of 1934* as well as other proposed and/or enacted legislation pertaining to communications, telecommunications, broadcasting, administrative procedures, and independent

Be patient. If any phone number is incorrect, call (area code) 555-1212 and request the new listing.

Business and Industry

agency regulations. Two collections that may be of particular interest to telecommunications researchers are the collection of cross indexed legislative histories which date back to the early beginnings of communication law and the wide range of scholarly periodicals (some 250) on communications.

* FCC Mass Media Bureau Reference and File Sources
Federal Communications Commission (FCC)
Mass Media, Pubic Reference Room
1919 M Street, NW, Room 239
Washington, DC 20554 (202) 632-6485
Documents on File: Station License Files, New Applications, Assignments and Transfers, Engineering Files, Construction Permits, LPTV, and ITFS. Hours of Operation: Monday through Friday, 9:00am to 5:30pm.

* FCC News Releases Recording
Federal Communications Commission (FCC)
News Media Division
Office of Public Affairs
1919 M Street, NW
Washington, DC 20554 (202) 632-0002
The Office of Public Affairs' recorded message will provide information on the latest news releases concerning the FCC and the telecommunications industry.

* FCC Open Meetings
Federal Communications Commission (FCC)
Office of Public Affairs
1919 M Street, NW, Room 856
Washington, DC 20554 (202) 632-7000
The general public is welcome to attend and observe all Commission meetings, except when the Commission finds that the public interest requires otherwise. This office can provide you with the free brochure, *A Guide To Open Meetings*, which outlines how FCC meetings work and where to obtain information on their findings.

* FCC Record of Actions
U.S. Government Printing Office
Superintendent of Documents
Washington, DC 20402 (202) 783-3238
The *FCC Record* provides a comprehensive, timely, and cost-effective source of FCC actions, including all texts released to the public daily through the FCC Office of Public Affairs. It contains a table of contents, a popular name case table, table of docket numbers, DA and FCC numbers, a list of cases by locale, and an alphabetical subject index. In addition, the *FCC Record* contains some public notices, speeches, and staff papers, and is available every two weeks through the GPO at an annual subscription rate.

* FCC Research and Copy Service
Federal Communications Commission (FCC)
1919 M Street, Room 246
Washington, DC 20037 (202) 857-3815
Any documents on file at the FCC's library or reference rooms listed below can be researched and copied for you for a fee by DCC, Inc. ITS charges $22 per hour for research, and $.08 per page for photocopying. Documents located in the Private Radio Licensing Division must be ordered from ITS, Inc., 1270 Fairfield Road, Gettysburg, PA 17325; (717) 337-1433.

* FCC Rules and Regulations
U.S. Government Printing Office
Superintendent of Documents
Washington, DC 20402 (202) 783-3238
The volumes of *FCC Rules and Regulations* must be purchased from the GPO, rather directly from the FCC. In addition to the FCC Rules, the GPO has available for purchase the following publications and documents often requested by customers:

Communications Act of 1934 (including amendments)
Volumes of FCC Reports and Decisions
FCC Annual Reports
Federal Register
Code of Federal Regulations

* FCC Rules On-line
Federal Communications Commission (FCC)
1919 M Street, NW, Room 230
Washington, DC 20554 (202) 632-4128
By visiting the FCC in person can you have the most up-to-date information on the complete FCC rules and regulations through the Automated FCC Rules Reference System. This system provides the only on-line computer access to FCC rules and regulations, and can be accessed free of charge at designated computer terminals at the FCC.

* FCC Telephone Directory
Downtown Copy Center
1114 21st Street, NW
Washington, DC 20036 (202) 452-1422
Issued on a quarterly basis, the FCC's telephone directory is available for $2.50 by mail or $1 if you pick it up in person. This directory can be a very useful research tool not only because it includes FCC telephone and room numbers of staff members, but also because it contains functional listings which identify key telephone numbers by subject areas.

* Federal Communications Commission Reference Room
Dockets Reference Room
1919 M Street, NW, Room 239
Washington, DC 20554 (202) 632-6410
The Dockets Reference Room maintains files on all rulemaking proceedings, docket files, transcripts of hearing proceedings, decisions, briefs, depositions, interrogatories, and ex parte comments. If you cannot visit the docket room in person, the FCC's copying service, ITS, Inc., will reproduce any documents you wish and send them to you for a fee.

* Federal Telecommunications Resource
Interdepartment Radio Advisory Committee (IRAC)
National Telecommunications and Information Administration
14th St. and Constitution Ave., NW, Room 1605
Washington, DC 20230 (202) 377-0319
Radio frequency spectrum management is the concern of NTIA's Office of Spectrum Management (OSM). By statute, NTIA manages the Federal government's use of the radio spectrum, while the Federal Communications Commission is responsible for non-Federal usage. OSM processes nearly 100,000 frequency assignment actions every year. It chairs and provides administrative and analytic support to the Interdepartment Radio Advisory Committee (IRAC). The IRAC is the central advisory body to NTIA regarding Federal Government radio spectrum management and use. When calling, ask for the Report of IRAC January 1, 1990 - June 30, 1990 and July 1990 - June 1991. These reports detail IRAC activities over the last few years as well as providing valuable background information.

* Foreign Press and Radio Translations
Foreign Broadcast Information Service
National Technical Information Service
U.S. Department of Commerce
5282 Port Royal Rd.
Springfield, VA 22161 (703) 487-4630
The subscription, *Foreign Press and Radio Translations*, provides a daily (paper copy) or weekly (microfiche copy) publication featuring news accounts, commentaries, and government statements from foreign broadcasts, press agency transmissions, newspapers, and periodicals published in the previous 48 to 72 hours. The selections available are the following:

People's Republic of China
Eastern Europe
Central Eurasia
East Asia
Near East and South Asia
Latin America
Western Europe
Sub Saharan Africa

The paper copy is available for $525 annually, and the microfiche copy for $230. Costs per category decline if more than one is ordered. Contact the Subscription Department to place an order or request a free information brochure *PR-376*.

Be patient. If any phone number is incorrect, call (area code) 555-1212 and request the new listing.

Communications

* Formal Complaints and Investigations

Federal Communications Commission (FCC)
2025 M Street, NW, Room 6206
Washington, DC 20554   (202) 632-4890

Documents on File: Formal Complaints and Related Pleadings, Interlocking Directorate Reports and Applications, Pole Attachment Complaints and Related Pleadings, Pole Attachment State Certifications, Enforcement Proceedings which include: mergers, acquisitions, and transfers of control files. Hours of Operation: Monday through Friday, 9:00am to 5:00pm.

* Freedom of Information Act Requests

FCC Managing Director
1919 M Street, Room 852
Washington, DC 20554   (202) 632-6390

FOIA requests for FCC materials should be submitted in writing to this office.

* Frequency Allocations History

Federal Communications Commission (FCC)
2025 M Street, NW, Room 7102
Washington, DC 20554   (202) 632-7025

This office has files of notices and orders dealing with Frequency allocations proceedings available in chronological order.

* History of FCC Rules

Publications Branch
1919 M Street, NW, Room 224
Washington, DC 20554   (202) 632-6410

Files in this Branch contain information on the history of FCC rules. It is open weekdays from 8am to 5:30pm.

* Industry Analysis

Federal Communications Commission (FCC)
Public Reference Room
1919 M Street, NW, Room 537
Washington, DC 20554   (202) 632-0745

Documents on File: Reports required by FCC Rules and Regulations, Administrative Reports, Annual Reports to Stockholders, FCC Form 492, Rate of Return Report, Statistics of Communications Common Carriers, Quarterly Operating Data of Telephone and Telegraph Carriers, Switched Access Reports, Equal Access Implementation Reports, NECA - Pool Results, Local Exchange Rates, Monthly Bypass Request Report - AT&T, Lifeline Link-Up Reports, IAD Reports, General Reference Material from Sources. Hours of Operation: Monday through Friday, 9:00am to 1:00pm, 2:00pm to 5:00pm.

* Informal Complaints and Public Inquiries Branch

Federal Communications Commission (FCC)
2025 M Street, NW, Room 6202
Washington, DC 20554   (202) 632-4890

Documents on File: Informal Written Telephone Related Complaints and Public Information. Hours of Operation: Monday through Friday, 8:00am to 5:00pm.

* Instructional Television Fixed Service (ITFS)

Federal Communications Commission (FCC)
Consumer Assistance and Small Business Division
Office of Public Affairs
1919 M Street, NW, Room 254
Washington, DC 20554   (202) 632-7000

ITFS was created over 20 years ago to provide in school instructional/cultural programming in accredited educational institutions. It can only be received using a special receiving antenna. Recent rule changes allow a licensee to air non ITFS programming using excess channel capacity or lease time to third parties on a profit making basis. A Fact Sheet on ITFS available from the FCC explains rules and procedures for applying for an ITFS station.

* Interference Complaints

FOB Public Contact Branch
Federal Communications Commission (FCC)
1919 M Street, NW, Room 725

Washington, DC 20554   (202) 634-1940

Interference happens when radio signals are picked up by consumer electronic products, most often TVs, VCRs, Hi Fi equipment, electronic organs and cordless telephones. *Something About Interference* and the *Interference Handbook* are two publications free from the FCC on interference problems. Complaints about interference and requests for free publications can be directed to the local FCC office in your area or to the FOB Public Contact Branch.

* International Broadcasting Service

Federal Communications Commission (FCC)
2025 M Street, NW, Room 8120-A
Washington, DC 20554   (202) 254-3394

The IBS sets aside a portion of the radio spectrum for stations wishing to broadcast to foreign countries. Currently, IBS regulates 18 such stations, most of which are religious-oriented. Additionally, IBS negotiates telecommunications agreements with foreign countries. Contact this office for more information.

* International Communications

Bureau of International Communications
  and Information Policy
U.S. Department of State
2201 C St., NW, Room 6317
Washington, DC 20520   (202) 647-8345

As the principal advisor to the Secretary of State on international telecommunications policy issues affecting U.S. foreign policy and national security, this bureau coordinates with other U.S. Government agencies and the private sector in formulating and implementing international policies relating to communications and information technologies. CIP provides guidance and instructions to U.S. representatives to such international organizations as the International Telecommunications Satellite Organization, the International Maritime Satellite Organization, The Information, Computers, and Communications Policy Committee of the Organization for Economic Cooperation and Development, and the International Telecommunication Union. Through bilateral negotiations and multilateral programs, CIP promotes the principles of free enterprise and the free flow of communication.

* International Communications Regulation

Federal Communications Commission (FCC)
International Facilities Division
1919 M Street, NW, Room 533
Washington, DC 20554   (202) 632-7834

Documents on File: *International Microwave Point-to-Point Files, International Fixed Radiotelephone Files, International Fixed Radiotelegraph Files, International Space Station Files, Recognized Private Operating Agency Files, Uniform Settlement Policy Files, Submarine Cable Landing License Files, International Earth Station Files, Transborder Earth Station Files, Section 214, INTELSAT, and Comsat Documents, Rulemakings, Rulings, Assignments of Licenses, Transfer of Control, and Temporary Authorities*. Hours of Operation: Monday through Friday, 8:00am to 1:00pm, 2:00pm to 5:00pm.

* International Telecommunications

Office of International Affairs (OIA)
National Telecommunications and Information Administration
14th St., NW, Room 4090
Washington, DC 20230   (202) 377-1304

This office is responsible for developing International Communications policy. OIA works to minimize unnecessary Federal and foreign government interference in the efficient functioning of international telecommunications markets. It also seeks to identify and, where feasible, lessen foreign obstacles to U.S. trade in telecommunications and information services and products. To do this, OIA assesses the communications policies of other nations and cooperates with the State Department in preparing U.S. positions before various international forums, such as the International Telecommunication Union and the Organization for Economic Cooperation and Development. Also, OIA reviews a wide rage of issues pertinent to regulatory and legislative proceedings. Contact this office for more information on international communications.

* Legislative Affairs

Office of Legislative Affairs
Federal Communications Commission (FCC)
1919 M Street, NW, Room 808

Be patient. If any phone number is incorrect, call (area code) 555-1212 and request the new listing.

Business and Industry

Washington, DC 20554 (202) 632-6405

If you have questions concerning congressional testimony, current bills, or other legislative matters related to the FCC, this office has two attorneys on staff who specialize in mass media and common carrier law to answer your questions.

* Litigation Against the FCC

Litigation Division File Room
1919 M Street, NW, Room 609-C
Washington, DC 20554 (202) 632-7112

Documents on file include all case files of actions that have been brought against the FCC; computer listings of case histories including: lists of pending cases, background histories of cases, status of cases, deadlines for submission of briefs, etc. Hours of operation: Monday through Friday, 10:00am to 12:00pm and 3:00pm to 4:00pm.

* Live TV Coverage of the FCC

The Capitol Connection
George Mason University, Kelly Drive
Fairfax, VA 22030-4444 (703) 993-3100

For residents of the Washington DC area, the Capitol Connection can provide live coverage of FCC open meetings via microwave transmissions. The service costs $795 annually. In the future, FCC meeting coverage may be available nationwide via the use of satellite transmissions. Call for more information.

* Long Distance Carrier Information

Industry Analysis
Federal Communications Commission (FCC)
Public Reference Room
1919 M Street, NW, Room 537
Washington, DC 20554 (202) 632-0745

The Industry Analysis division compiles information on market share for all long distance carriers whose total toll service revenue is $100 million or greater. The Downtown Copy Center has a report entitled the *Long Distance Market Share Report,* detailing this information.

* Low Power Television (LPTV)

Federal Communications Commission (FCC)
Consumer Assistance and Small Business Division
Office of Public Affairs
1919 M Street, NW, Room 254
Washington, DC 20554 (202) 632-7000

Established in 1982, LPTV was intended to provide opportunities for locally oriented television service in small rural communities, and in industrial communities in larger urban areas. LPTV presents a less expensive and very flexible means of delivering programming tailored to the interests of viewers in small localized areas. Today there are approximately 800 stations in 550 towns in the Continental U.S. The FCC can provide you with an information packet on LPT that includes information on starting an LPTV station.

* Marine Radio Services

Aviation and Marine Branch
Federal Communications Commission (FCC)
2025 M Street, NW, Room 5114
Washington, DC 20554 (202) 632-7175

The FCC regulates the Marine Radio Services for the safety and operational communications of non-federal maritime activities, including U.S. vessels that traverse international waters and land stations in the Maritime Mobile Radio Service. This office also regulates the Aviation Radio Services for nongovernment use of radio for aeronautical radionavigation, search and rescue, and other safety operations.

* Master Frequency File Database

Frequency Liaison Office
Federal Communications Commission (FCC)
2025 M Street, NW, Room 7326
Washington, DC 20554 (202) 653-8141

The Master Frequency File contains information on the identification, location, and technical characteristics of almost 900,000 radio and television broadcast stations, satellite stations, land mobile and microwave stations, and all other types of radio frequency transmitters. Information on each facility includes name of owner, mailing address, height of transmitting towers, power, frequency, number of mobile units, and much more. This file is available for sale from NTIS on microfiche or magnetic tape, or specialized searches can be arranged through ATA Services Inc., 2200 Mill Rd., Alexandria, VA 22314; (703) 838-1901.

* Mobile Services Division

Federal Communications Commission (FCC)
Public Reference Room
1919 M Street, NW, Room 628
Washington, DC 20554 (202) 632-6400

Documents on File: *Station Files, Maps, Diagrams, Petitions, Co-Channel Searches and Background Material Pending Files, and Cellular Granted Station Files.* Hours of Operation: Monday through Friday, 8:00am to 12:00pm.

* Multipoint Distribution Service

Federal Communications Commission (FCC)
Consumer Assistance and Small Business Division
Office of Public Affairs
1919 M Street, NW, Room 254
Washington, DC 20554 (202) 632-7000

Multipoint Distribution Service (MDS) programming is unlike conventional broadcasts in that it is designed to reach only those who subscribe to the service by obtaining a special receiving antenna capable of receiving special microwave frequencies. Operators can choose to be common or non-common carriers. While originally thought to be an effective medium for business data transmission, it has become popular for transmitting entertainment programming. Information on licensing and filing is available from the FCC.

* National Telecommunications

National Telecommunications and Information Administration
U.S. Department of Commerce
14th St. and Constitution Ave., NW, Room 4898
Washington, DC 20230 (202) 377-1551

This Administration's broad goals include formulating policies to support the development and growth of telecommunications, information and related industries, furthering the efficient development and use of telecommunications and information services, providing policy and management for Federal use of the electromagnetic spectrum, and providing telecommunications facilities grants to public service users. NTIA employs approximately 300 people and has an annual budget of $35,104,000.

* Pay Per Call (900) Services

Common Carrier Bureau
Enforcement Division
Federal Communications Commission (FCC)
2025 M Street, NW, Room 6202
Washington, DC 20554 (202) 632-7553

The FCC adopted rules governing interstate pay per call (900) services effective December 2, 1991. These rules require information providers to disclose the cost of the call and describe the service being provided, giving the caller the opportunity to hang up before charges are assessed. The rules also require local telephone companies to offer blocking of 900 services to all subscribers where technically feasible and one-time free blocking of 900 services to residential subscribers. The Enforcement Division can furnish you with complete information on FCC rules governing 900 number telephone services. The Division also logs complaints on these services.

* Policy and Program Planning

Federal Communications Commission (FCC)
1919 M Street, NW, Room 544
Washington, DC 20554 (202) 632-9342

Documents on File: *Petitions in Non-Docketed Proceedings, Comments and Replies in Non-Docketed Proceedings, Applications for Review, Petitions for Declaratory Rulings/Comments and Replies, Petitions for Waiver/Comments and Replies, CEI Plans/Comments and Replies.* Hours of Operation: Monday through Friday, 9:00am to 5:30pm.

* Political Programming Rules

Political Programming
Federal Communications Commission (FCC)

Be patient. If any phone number is incorrect, call (area code) 555-1212 and request the new listing.

Communications

2025 M Street, NW, Room 8202
Washington, DC 20554 (202) 632-7586

This office can answer questions concerning political programming rules and regulations. For example, if a station lets a legally qualified candidate for public office use its broadcast facilities, it must give "equal opportunities" to other candidates for the same office. This office can also tell you about programming costs for political candidates, who are all entitled to "lowest unit charges" for use of broadcast or cable TV facilities during 45 days preceding a primary and 60 days preceding a general election. Contact this office for more information.

* Private Radio Reference Room

Federal Communications Commission (FCC)
1270 Fairfield Road
Gettysburg, PA 17325 (717) 337-1311

Documents on File: *Land Mobile and GMRS Applications, Microwave Applications, Aviation Ground Applications, Marine Coast Applications, all Dismissals, Copies of Special Temporary Authorities (STA) or Transfers of Control.*
Hours of Operation: Monday through Friday, 8:00am to 4:30pm.

* Private Radio Licensing

Licensing Division
Federal Communications Commission (FCC)
1270 Fairfield Road
Gettysburg, PA 17325 (717) 337-1212

For information on the status of any pending applications for FCC private radio licenses, contact this office.

* Private Radio Regulations

Private Radio Bureau
Federal Communications Commission (FCC)
2025 M Street, NW, Room 5002
Washington, DC 20554 (202) 632-6940

This office regulates radio stations serving the communications needs of businesses, individuals, nonprofit organizations, and state and local governments, including the following uses: private land mobile, private operational fixed microwave, aviation, marine, personal, amateur, and disaster. It also compiles applications for licenses for processing in Gettysburg, analyzes complaints, and conducts investigations.

* Public Access Link (PAL)

Equipment Authorization Branch
Federal Communications Commission (FCC)
7435 Oakland Mill Road
Columbia, MD 21046 (410) 725-1585

The Public Access Link (PAL) provides computerized information on the status of pending applications and technical information on granted authorizations. The system remains on-line continuously, providing a twenty-hour service to the public. You can also access the FCC "Bulletin Board" of recent Commission actions which might impact on the equipment authorization program, a list of testing laboratories which have filed required information with the FCC, and grantee and manufacturer codes assigned for equipment identification. For direct, on-line hook-up with your modem, call (301) 725-1072.

* Public Service Workshops and Seminars

Federal Communications Commission (FCC)
1919 M Street, NW, Room 725
Washington, DC 20554 (202) 634-1940

The FCC conducts free seminars and workshops across the country to help the public identify and resolve telecommunications-related interference problems. For example, the FCC will train TV service technicians, telephone companies and manufacturers, and power company technicians how to eliminate interference in consumer-related products and services. Also, the FCC will conduct seminars by special request from any group which needs help addressing interference-related problems. Examples of special requests include Cable television companies, Taxi Cab Associations, and hospital paging users. These services are handled through the field offices and coordinated by the regional offices. For more information on having a seminar address your group, contact your local FCC office or contact the above office for information and the number of your local office.

* Public Service Reference

Federal Communications Commission (FCC)
1919 M Street, NW, Room 728
Washington, DC 20554 (202) 632-7240

Documents on File: *Commercial Radio Operator Application Files and Bulletins Concerning Radio Operator Matters.*

* Public Telecommunications Facilities Program (PTFP)

Office of Telecommunications Applications
National Telecommunications and Information Administration
14th Street and Constitution Ave, NW, Room 4625
Washington, DC 20230 (202) 377-1835

The PTFP expands and improves the public telecommunications services of the U.S. by providing grants for the dissemination of equipment. The major objective of the PTFP is to extend the delivery of quality public telecommunication services to unserved areas of the U.S. The PTFP concentrates mostly on TV and radio services. Recent rule changes have created a new subcategory to provide satellite downlinks at public radio and TV stations that would bring nationally distributed programming to a geographic area for the first time. Contact the above office for information on and applications for PTFP grants.

* Purchasing and Technical Assistance for Broadcast Entrepreneurs

Consumer Assistance and Small Business Division (CASB)
Office of Public Affairs
Federal Communications Commission (FCC)
1919 M St., NW, Room 254
Washington, DC 20554 (202) 632-7000

The CASB Division will provide you with personal assistance in locating information concerning FCC rules, policies, procedures, and guidance concerning participation in FCC rulemaking proceedings. In addition, this office provides specialized to assistance to those interested in becoming involved in the small business telecommunications industry. They will walk you through the purchasing procedures, identify resources for financial and technical assistance, and perform license status checks for applicants. The Public Affairs office also coordinates broadcast ownership workshops, which cover these topic and more, every year across the country. Contact CASB for more information.

* Radio-Frequency (RF) Radiation

Office of Engineering and Technology
Federal Communications Commission (FCC)
2025 M Street, NW, Room 7130
Washington, DC 20554 (202) 653-8169

Every transmitting device emits Radio Frequency (RF) radiation, and levels which exceed FCC standards can be a serious health risk. If you have questions about RF radiation in your community or workplace, contact the FCC for a free consumer information package on RF radiation, along with technical surveys and investigations of certain transmitters across the country. In particular ask for the publication *Questions and Answers about Biological Effects and Potential Hazards of Radiofrequency Radiation, OET Bulletin No. 56.* It is available free upon request.

* Rulemaking Changes at the FCC

The Secretary
Federal Communications Commission (FCC)
1919 M Street, NW, Room 222
Washington, DC 20554 (202) 632-6410

The FCC is interested in any experiences, judgments, or insights you might have that would shed light on issues and questions raised in an inquiry or rulemaking. To obtain guidelines on how to submit your ideas on any FCC rulemaking changes, contact this office.

* Spectrum Management

Office of Spectrum Management
National Telecommunications and Information Administration
U.S. Department of Commerce
14th Street and Constitution Ave, NW, Room 4099
Washington, DC 20230 (202) 377-1850

OSM is charged with developing and implementing policies and procedures regarding the use of the radio frequency spectrum. By statute, NTIA manages

Be patient. If any phone number is incorrect, call (area code) 555-1212 and request the new listing.

Business and Industry

the Federal Governments use of the spectrum, while the FCC manages all non-Federal spectrum usage. OSM also chairs the Interdepartmental Radio Advisory Committee. OSM plays an important role in the preparations for the many conferences and meetings of the International Telecommunications Union (ITU), and chairs the Frequency Management Advisory Council - which provides advice on spectrum allocation and assignment matters.

* Tariff Legal Documents

Federal Communications Commission (FCC)
1919 M Street, NW, Room 518
Washington, DC 20554 (202) 632-6387

Documents on File: *Notices of Proposed Rulemakings, Petitions against Tariffs* (including comments and replies), *Petitions for Reconsideration* (including comments and replies), *Access Tariffs, Petitions dealing with Access Tariff, Applications for Review* (comments and replies).

* Tariff Review Public Reference Room

Federal Communications Commission (FCC)
1919 M Street, NW, Room 513
Washington, DC 20554 (202) 632-6387

Documents on File: *Multipoint Distribution Service (MDS), American Telephone and Telegraph Company, Access Service Tariffs by Bell Operating Companies, National Exchange Carrier Association, and Independent Telephone Companies, Western Union Telegraph Company, International Record Carriers, and other Overseas Carriers, Specialized Common Carriers, Satellite Carriers, Microwave Carriers, Maritime Carriers, Facilities for CATV and Wide Spectrum Service, and Mobile Radiotelephone Service.* Hours of Operation: Monday through Friday, 1:30pm to 4:30pm.

* Tax Breaks For Broadcasting Entrepreneurs

Consumer Assistance and Small Business Division
Office of Public Affairs
Federal Communications Commission (FCC)
1919 M Street, NW, Room 254
Washington, DC 20554 (202) 632-7260

If an owner of a broadcast or cable facility sells that station to a minority-owned purchaser, the FCC can permit the seller to defer the payment of capital gains tax, generally for 2 to 3 years. The FCC defines minority-ownership as consisting in excess of 50 per cent of controlling interest. Also, shareholders in a minority-controlled broadcast or cable entity are eligible for tax certificates upon the sale of their shares, provided that their interest was acquired to assist in the financing of the acquisition of the facility. The FCC may also issue tax certificates in transfers to limited partnerships where the general partner is a minority individual and owns more than 20 per cent interest in the broadcast or cable facility. For more information, contact CASB.

* Telecommunications Expertise for Public Service Groups

Public Telecommunications Facilities Program
National Telecommunications and Information Administration
U.S. Department of Commerce
14th St. and Constitution Ave., NW, Room 4625
Washington, DC 20230 (202) 377-5802

By identifying public service telecommunications needs, NTIA assists schools, hospitals, libraries, policy, fire departments, and government agencies in using advanced telecommunications systems and technology to achieve their goals.

* Telecommunications Publications

Publications Information
National Telecommunications and Information Administration
U.S. Department of Commerce
14th St. and Constitution Ave., NW, Room 4625
Washington, DC 20230 (202) 377-5802

A catalog is available which lists all the reports available from NTIA. Most are technical research studies, but several deal with communications policies and standards. In 1988, NTIA issued *TELECOM 2000*, the first comprehensive review and analysis of U.S. telecommunications policy in 20 years, as well as a number

of reports regarding new computer-related communications and information services, expansion of broad-band and cable television systems, and customer options, high-definition television, and other topics.

* Telecommunications Research

Institute for Telecommunications Sciences (ITS)
National Telecommunications and Information Administration
U.S. Department of Commerce
325 Broadway
Boulder, CO 80303 (303) 497-3572

As the chief research and engineering arm of NTIA, the Institute for Telecommunication Sciences supports Administration Telecommunication objectives such as enhanced domestic competition, improved foreign trade opportunities for U.S. telecommunication firms, and more efficient and effective use of the radio frequency spectrum. ITS also serves as a principal Federal resource for assistance in solving problems of other Federal agencies, state and local governments, private corporations and associations, and international organizations. ITS conducts research in spectrum use analysis, telecommunication standards development, telecommunication systems performance, telecommunication systems planning and applied research. The *Annual Technical Progress Report* describes in more detail the research conducted, as well as listing the publications available.

* Telephone Utility Systems

Assistant Administrator--Telephone
Rural Electrification Administration
U.S. Department of Agriculture (USDA)
Room 4056 South Building
Washington, DC 20250 (202) 720-0715

The USDA lends money to approximately 1,000 rural telephone companies and maintains a staff knowledgeable in both operations and equipment. Consumer Complaints: Telephones, Faxes.

* Transcripts of FCC Hearings

Capitol Hill Reporting, Inc.
1825 K Street, NW, Suite 1122
Washington, DC 20006 (202) 466-9500

Transcripts of hearings, FCC Official Court Reporting Service, and Transcripts of Court hearings may be obtained by contacting this office.

* Unauthorized Long Distance Carrier Switch

News Media Division
Federal Communications Commission (FCC)
1919 M Street NW
Washington, DC 20554 (202) 632-5050

Long distance carriers may not switch you from one company to another without your explicit consent. The News Media Division can provide you with information on what steps long distance carriers must take in order to switch customers from one carrier to another. The Division also outlines consumer rights with respect to long distance carrier choice. *FCC Report DC-2016* outlines FCC rules and actions with regard to unauthorized switches. It is available free upon request from the above office.

* Video/Audio Tape Recordings of FCC Open Meetings

CLI Productions Inc.
4320 Hamilton Street, Suite 102
Hyattsville, MD 20871 (301) 864-6333

Video and audio tape recordings of Commission open meetings, official sessions, and FCC tutorials, are available to the public only from a this private contractor on a fee basis. Customers may buy blank tapes from this office or provide their own. Videotapes can be 3/4 inch U-Matic or 1/2 inch VHS, audio tapes C-90 (45 minutes per side) cassettes. Customers should be prepared to provide date of meetings, and, when appropriate, agenda number, unless they want this office to perform a search for a fee.

Be patient. If any phone number is incorrect, call (area code) 555-1212 and request the new listing.

Shipping and Fishing

As an island nation of continental proportions, shipping is vital to the economic well being and national security of the United States. Within the U.S. Department of Transportation, the Coast Guard and the Maritime Administration ensure set and enforce regulations for maritime safety. The Maritime Administration also monitors other aspects of shipping and marine affairs. An independent government agency, the Federal Maritime Commission, monitors private shipping, ensuring compliance by foreign and domestic shippers with U.S. shipping laws.

Fish are important both as a food source and as a part of our environment. Within the U.S. government, the Department of Commerce's, National Oceans and Atmospheric Administration monitors fish catches off the coasts of the U.S. to ensure compliance with catch limits and to monitor fish stocks off the coasts of the U.S.

* Aids to Navigation

Office of Navigation Safety and Waterways Services
U.S. Coast Guard
U.S. Department of Transportation
2100 2nd St., SW, Room 1116
Washington, DC 20593-0001 (202) 267-1965

The Coast Guard maintains aids to navigation such as lighthouses and lights, buoys, beacons, fog signals, and long-range radionavigation aids like LORAN-C and OMEGA. The aids are established to assist navigators in plotting safe courses on waters under U.S. jurisdiction and in certain international areas. The seven volumes of *Light Lists*, which detail the navigation aids in seven geographic areas, are available at varying cost from the Superintendent of Documents, Government Printing Office, Washington, DC 20402; (202) 783-3238. The *LORAN-C User Handbook*, which explains the radionavigation system and how to use it, is also available from GPO for $4.75.

* Anti-Rebate Certification Program

Bureau of Domestic Regulation
Federal Maritime Commission
1100 L Street, NW
Washington, DC 20573 (202) 523-5796

The Commission ensures that foreign commercial shippers so not receive a rebate from their countries on shipments to the U.S. Shippers not certifying their compliance with U.S. anti-rebate regulations may be assessed a civil penalty of $5,000 per day for each day the violation continues. For information on anti-rebate actions, contact the above office.

* Automated Electronic System for Ocean Pollution

Ocean Pollution Data and Information Services
Central Coordination and Referral Office
National Oceanographic Data Center
National Oceanic and Atmospheric Administration
1825 Connecticut Ave, NW
Washington, DC 20235 (202) 606-4539

The Automated Electronic System for Ocean Pollution (AESOP) is a newly developed software application created at OPDIN for making access to its ocean and Great Lakes databases quick and easy. The system contains the following: summaries of federal projects and programs - organized by department and abstracts contain project summaries; guide to marine pollution related data; handbook of federal systems and services related to marine pollution control; and marine, Great Lakes, and Arctic pollution related literature - containing several thousand citations and updated regularly.

* Boating Correspondence Course

U.S. Government Bookstore
World Savings Building
720 N. Main St.
Pueblo, CO 81003 (719) 544-3142

Designed for boaters who can't attend a boating class, *The Skipper's Course* covers basic navigation, legal requirements, anchoring, weather, emergency procedures, boat handling, and safety. A certificate of completion is awarded. Stock No: 050012002258. Price: $6.50.

* Bridges Over Navigable Waters

Bridge Administration Division
Office of Navigation Safety and Waterways Services
U.S. Coast Guard
U.S. Department of Transportation
2100 2nd St., SW, Room 1408
Washington, DC 20593-0001 (202) 267-0368

Bridges and causeways spanning navigable waterways in the U.S. are subject to Coast Guard safety regulations concerning their construction, operation, and maintenance. This office oversees bridge engineering and issues permits. For further details, contact the division listed above.

* Capital Construction Fund

Office of Maritime Aids
Maritime Administration
U.S. Department of Transportation
400 7th Street SW, Room 8126
Washington, DC 20590 (202) 366-0364

The Capital Construction Fund assists operators in accumulating capital to build, acquire, and reconstruct vessels through the deferral of Federal Income Taxes on certain deposits, as defined in Section 607 of the Merchant Marine Act of 1936. Any U.S. citizen owning or leasing an eligible vessel may enter into an agreement with the Maritime Administration to obtain tax-deferral privileges on deposits placed in the fund. Call MARAD for details.

* Cargo Preference Programs

Office of Market Development
Maritime Administration
U.S. Department of Transportation
400 7th Street, SW, Room 7209
Washington, DC 20590 (202) 366-5517

MARAD is the central authority overseeing U.S. cargo preference programs. U.S. law requires that 50% of U.S. foreign assistance deliveries and Department of Defense shipments be carried on U.S. flag vessels. For more information on this program, contact MARAD.

* Certificates of Documentation for Vessels

Vessel Documentation Branch
Merchant Vessel Inspection and Documentation Division
Office of Marine Safety, Security, and Environmental Protection
U.S. Coast Guard
U.S. Department of Transportation
2100 2nd St., SW, Room 1312
Washington, DC 20593-0001 (202) 267-1492

Be patient. If any phone number is incorrect, call (area code) 555-1212 and request the new listing.

Business and Industry

Most commercial vessels of 5 or more net tons used on U.S. waters must be documented. Commercial vessels engaged in foreign trade and recreational boats of that size, may be documented at the option of the owner. Also, undocumented vessels equipped with propulsion machinery are required to be numbered by their individual states. Lending institutions regard a documented vessel to be a more secure form of collateral, thus making bank financing easier to obtain. Considered a form of international registration, the *Certificate of Documentation* may also make customs entry and clearance easier in foreign ports. The initial documentation fee is about $100. *Certificates of Documentation* are issued by the Coast Guard at documentation offices around the U.S. The office listed above can provide you with the address of the one nearest you.

* Coast Guard Courses and Textbooks

Coast Guard Auxiliary National Board, Inc.
9949 Watson Industrial Park
St. Louis, MO 63126 (800) 336-BOAT

The following are textbooks used in Coast Guard Auxiliary public education courses. They can be ordered by writing to the above address, or you can get each textbook by taking the course of the same title through the Coast Guard. To find out where courses are offered near you, call the Courseline at (800) 336-BOAT; or (800) 245-BOAT in VA.

Boating Skills and Seamanship. Boating laws and regulations, boat handling, and navigation ($8).

Sailing and Seamanship. Same basic text as above, geared to sailboats ($8).

Advanced Coastal Piloting. How to read charts, plot courses, predict tides, and use navigation aids ($8).

* Coast Guard Regulations

Marine Safety Council, U.S. Coast Guard
U.S. Department of Transportation
2100 2nd St., SW, Room 3600
Washington, DC 20593-0001 (202) 267-1477

Rules and regulations proposed by the Coast Guard are taken under consideration and studied by this Council. Hearings are held at Coast Guard headquarters in DC and at other locations around the country. Announcements appear Monday through Friday in the *Federal Register*. For further information, contact the Council.

* Coast Guard Rescue Service

SAR Database Manager
Search and Rescue Division
Office of Navigation Safety and Waterways Services
U.S. Coast Guard
U.S. Department of Transportation
2100 2nd St., SW, Room 1422
Washington, DC 20593-0001 (202) 267-1054

The Search and Rescue (SAR) program maintains a comprehensive system of resources to save lives and prevent personal injury and property damage on the navigable waters of the U.S. This system includes rescue vessels, aircraft, and communication facilities. A cooperative international distress response system is also maintained for incidents on the high seas. For more information about the Guard's SAR program, contact the branch listed above.

* Coast Guard Reserve

Office of Readiness and Reserve
U.S. Coast Guard
U.S. Department of Transportation
2100 2nd St., SW, Room 5101 (202) 267-2350

In time of war or national emergency, the Coast Guard Reserve provides trained individuals and units for active duty. The Reserve also assists the Guard in peacetime missions during domestic emergencies and peak operations. The *Coast Guard Reservist Magazine*, available free from the office listed above, provides bimonthly news and human interest stories about Coast Guard Reservists and their activities.

* Coastal Zone Management

Office of Ocean and Coastal Resource Management
National Ocean Service
National Oceanic and Atmospheric Administration
U.S. Department of Commerce

1825 Connecticut Ave., NW, Room 724
Washington, DC 20235 (202) 606-4158

To balance the needs for preserving and developing the resources in the U.S. coastal zone, the National Ocean Service, through its Office of Ocean and Coastal Resource Management, provides the coordination and expertise at the Federal level needed for effective management of these coastal resources. NOS has begun to expand the technical assistance provided to States and territories, emphasizing special area management planning, coastal hazards mitigation, cost-effective coastal management, and the simplification of permit processes for coastal activities. Ask for Technical Bulletins 101-104, which detail activities in Coastal Zone Management and Environmental Protection.

* Commercial Fisheries Clearinghouse

Public Affairs
National Marine Fisheries Service
National Oceanic and Atmospheric Administration
U.S. Department of Commerce
1335 East-West Hwy.
Silver Spring, MD 20910 (301) 713-2370

The National Marine Fisheries Service manages the country's stocks of saltwater fish and shellfish for both commercial and recreational interests. NMFS administers and enforces the Magnuson Fishery Conservation and Management Act to assure that fishing stays within sound biological limits, and that U.S. commercial and recreational fishermen have the opportunity to harvest all the available fish within these limits. Several hundred Fisheries Service scientists conduct research relating to these management responsibilities in science and research centers in 15 states and the District of Columbia. Many of these laboratories have evolved a major field of interest, and have special knowledge of the fish in their geographical area that leads to predictions of abundance, economic forecasts, and direct assistance to sport fishermen and commercial fishing businesses. Each of the science and research centers of the National Marine Fisheries Service has their own area of expertise and knowledge of the fish in their area. Contact them directly regarding questions or publications requests.

* Commercial Vessel Inspections

Merchant Vessel Inspection and Documentation Division
Office of Marine Safety, Security, and Environmental Protection
U.S. Coast Guard
U.S. Department of Transportation
2100 2nd St., SW, Room 1400
Washington, DC 20593-0001 (202) 267-2978

The Coast Guard administers and enforces safety standards for the design, construction, equipment, and maintenance of commercial vessels and offshore structures on the Outer Continental Shelf. Foreign vessels subject to U.S. jurisdiction must also meet the required standards. Boardings are conducted to detect and prevent violations. Safety regulations cover such ship characteristics as hull structure, watertight integrity, fire safety, and navigation instrumentation. Records, mostly computerized, are kept on these inspections at district Coast Guard offices. For general information or referral to a records inspection facility near you, contact the division listed.

* Crew Certification

Licensing and Evaluation Branch
Merchant Vessel Personnel Division
Office of Marine Safety, Security, and Environmental Protection
U.S. Coast Guard, U.S. Department of Transportation
2100 2nd St., SW, Room 1210
Washington, DC 20593-0001 (202) 267-0218

To ensure that vessels are safely and sufficiently crewed with properly trained personnel, the Coast Guard develops safe manning standards for commercial vessels and administers a system for evaluation and licensing. Crew requirements on a vessel depend on factors such as route, tonnage, horsepower, and type of trade. The rules and regulations for licensing are included in the *Code of Federal Regulations*, Title 46, parts 10-14. Licensing and exams are given in applicable professional fields at regional examination centers around the country. Contact your local Coast Guard office or the branch listed above for referral to the center nearest you.

* Current Fisheries Statistics Series

Fisheries Statistics Division
National Marine Fisheries Service
National Oceans and Atmospheric Administration

Shipping and Fishing

U.S. Department of Commerce
1335 East-West Highway
Silver Spring, MD 20910 (301) 427-2328

CFS series are statistical bulletins on marine recreational fishing, commercial fishing, and on the manufacture and commerce of fishery products. For further information, or to order these bulletins, contact the above office.

* Enforcement of Shipping Law

Bureau of Hearing Counsel/Bureau of Investigation
Federal Maritime Commission
1100 L Street, NW
Washington, DC 20573 (202) 523-5783/523-5860

Under the 1984 Shipping Act, the commission has put more emphasis on enforcement activities. Through the Transpacific malpractice program, the commission seeks compliance with the 1984 Act and seeks to establish an equitable trade environment for carriers, shippers, and middlemen participating in the transpacific trades.

* Environmental Impact Statements

Office of Ship Operations
Maritime Administration
U.S. Department of Transportation
400 7th Street SW
Washington, DC 20590 (202) 366-5737

MARAD participates in international conferences on environmental issues and also develops environmental impact statements on the construction and operation of vessels, training in marine pollution abatement, and projects to producer safer more efficient vessels and operating methods.

* Federal Maritime Commission

1100 L Street, NW
Washington DC 20573 (202) 523-5725

Established in 1961, the Federal Maritime Commission (FMC) monitors relationships among carriers and also ensures that individual carriers fairly treat shippers and other members of the shipping public. The commission consists of 5 full time commissioners appointed by the President, with no more than 3 from the same political party, serving 5 year terms. The FMC has 230 full time equivalent positions and an appropriated budget of $15,452,000.

* Federal Maritime Commission (FMC) - District Offices

1100 L Street, NW
Washington, DC 20573 (202) 523-5725

FMC District Offices represent the Commission in their jurisdictions, provide liaison between the Commission and the maritime industry and the shipping public, collects and analyzes intelligence of regulatory significance, and assesses industry wide conditions for the Commission. District offices are located in the following cities:

New York . . . . (212) 264-1425
New Orleans . . . . (504) 589-6662
San Francisco . . . . (415) 744-7016
Puerto Rico . . . . (809) 766-5581
Los Angeles . . . . (213) 514-6127
Miami . . . . (305) 536-6963
Houston . . . . (713) 229-2841

* Federal Maritime Commission - Special Docket Decisions

Office of Administrative Law Judges
Federal Maritime Commission
1100 L Street, NW
Washington, DC 20573 (202) 523-5750

This office has information on a variety of special docket cases that have come before the Commission.

* Fish Exports

Office of Trade and Industry Services
National Marine Fisheries Service
National Oceanic and Atmospheric Administration

U.S. Department of Commerce
1335 East-West Hwy., Room 6212
Silver Spring, MD 20910 (301) 713-2379

This office assists seafood exporters by providing trade leads, conducting sales missions, doing market studies, and organizing "how to export" seminars. It helps industry by improving their access to markets in other countries. The Service provides inspection services for fishery commodities for export and issues official U.S. Government certificates attesting to the findings. Statistics on Fish exports can be found in the book *Fisheries of the United States* (see listing below).

* Fisheries Technical Reports

Scientific Publications Office
National Marine Fisheries Service
National Oceanic and Atmospheric Administration
U.S. Department of Commerce
7600 Sand Point Way N.E.
Seattle, WA 98115 (206) 526-6107

This office prepares the following scientific and technical publications having to do with fisheries:

Fishery Bulletin. Publishes original research reports and technical notes on investigations in fishery science, engineering, and economics. Quarterly, $24 per year.

Marine Fisheries Review. Publishes review articles, original research reports, significant progress reports, technical notes, and new articles on fisheries science, engineering, and economics, commercial and recreational fisheries, marine mammal studies, and foreign fisheries developments. Quarterly, $7 per year.

NOAA Technical Reports. Publishes scientific investigations that document long-term continuing programs of NMFS, technical papers of general interest intended to aid conservation and management, as well as many other topic areas. Indexes are available. Issued irregularly, price varies.

* Fishery Products Grading and Inspection

Utilization Research and Services
National Marine Fisheries Service
National Oceanic and Atmospheric Administration
U.S. Department of Commerce
1335 East-West Hwy., Room 6142
Silver Spring, MD 20910 (301) 713-2355

The National Marine Fisheries Service conducts a voluntary seafood inspection program on a fee-for-service bases. A wide range of inspection services are available to any interested party, including harvesters, processors, food-service distributors, and importers and exporters. These services include vessel and plant sanitation inspection, product evaluation (in-plant and warehouse lot), product specification review, label review, laboratory analyses (microbiological tests, chemical contaminant/indices of decomposition, species identification), training, and education and information. This office has a great deal of information concerning inspections, grading of products, and regulations. They also publish a document listing fishery products that have been produced in fish establishments approved by the National Marine Fisheries Service.

* Fisheries of the United States

Office of Research and Environmental Information
National Marine Fisheries Service
National Oceanic and Atmospheric Administration
U.S. Department of Commerce
1335 East-West Hwy., Room 8313
Silver Spring, MD 20910 (301) 713-2328

This publication is prepared by the Fisheries Statistics Division, and includes information on U.S. commercial fishery landings, U.S. exclusive economic zone catches, world fisheries, imports and exports, U.S. supply, and per capita fish consumption. It is an invaluable source of statistics on fishing and fishing related activities. This publication is available through Superintendent of Documents, Government Printing Office, Washington, DC 20402; (202) 783-3238, cost $6.50.

* Fisheries Publications

National Technical Information Service (NTIS)
5285 Port Royal Road (800) 553-6847
Springfield, VA 22161 (703) 487-4650

The National Marine Fisheries Service has made many of its technical reports available through NTIS. Subject areas include: Commercial fisheries, Fisheries

Be patient. If any phone number is incorrect, call (area code) 555-1212 and request the new listing.

Business and Industry

of the United States (issues published from 1939 on), State Landings, Processed Fishery Products Annual Summary (issues published from 1979 on), Marine Recreational Fishing Statistics Survey (1979 on), as well as other publications. Publications list can be obtained from the annual publications *Fisheries of the United States*, which is available from NTIS or GPO (202) 783-3238.

* Fisheries Research

Office of Research and Environmental Information
National Marine Fisheries Service (NMFS)
National Oceanic and Atmospheric Administration
U.S. Department of Commerce
1335 East-West Hwy., Room 6310
Silver Spring, MD 20910 (301) 713-2367

Contact this office for information regarding fisheries research. Topics covered include acid rain and pollution, aquaculture information, diseases of fish, ecology and fish recruitment, fishing methods, and resource abundance. Fisheries research is also undertaken at the NMFS regional offices. They can be contacted directly for information.

North East Region	(508) 281-9250
South East Region	(813) 893-3141
North West Region	(206) 526-6150
South West Region	(213) 548-2575
Alaska	(907) 586-7221

* Fisheries - Oceanography Research

Oceanic and Atmospheric Research
National Oceanic and Atmospheric Administration
U.S. Department of Commerce
1335 East-West Hwy., Room 6310
Silver Spring, MD 20910 (301) 713-2463

This research, conducted jointly with the National Marine Fisheries Service, seeks to improve understanding of the effects of atmospheric and oceanic variations on fish and shellfish.

* Fishery Statistics

Office of Research and Environmental Information
National Marine Fisheries Service
National Oceanic and Atmospheric Administration
U.S. Department of Commerce
1335 East-West Hwy., Room 8313
Silver Spring, MD 20910 (301) 713-2328

The Fisheries Statistics Division publishes statistical bulletins on marine recreational fishing and commercial fishing, and on the manufacture and commerce of fishery products. Annual publications available from this office include:

Marine Recreational Fishery Statistics
Frozen Fishery Products
Processed Fishery Products
Imports and Exports of Fishery Products
Fish Meal and Oil

* Fisheries Trade and Industry Services

Office of Trade and Industry Services
National Marine Fisheries Service
National Oceanic and Atmospheric Administration
U.S. Department of Commerce
1335 East-West Hwy.
Silver Spring, MD 20910 (301) 713-2351

This office conducts activities designed to improve the competitiveness of the U.S. fishing industry in domestic and world markets and to enhance the safety and quality of U.S. seafood products. Programs include identification of industry trade issues and problems; financial assistance in the form of loan guarantees, insurance programs, a capital construction fund, and research and development grants; administration of fishery marketing councils; administration of inspection and grading programs; and research and development of product safety, quality and use.

* Fishing Multi-Lateral Agreements

Bureau of Oceans and International Environmental and Scientific Affairs

U.S. Department of State
2201 C St., NW, Room 5806
Washington, DC 20520 (202) 647-2335

This office negotiates fishing agreements with countries who want to fish within the U.S. economic zone, along with agreements with countries within whose zone the U.S. would like to fish. They are also responsible for multi-lateral agreements dealing with fishing on the high seas, with particular attention to conservation issues. Information is available on these agreements and on fishery concerns in general.

* Fishing Vessels International Claims

Assistant Legal Advisor for International Claims
Office of the Legal Advisor
U.S. Department of State
2201 C St., NW
Washington, DC 20520 (202) 632-7810

The Fishermen's Protective Act provides for reimbursement for financial loss to owners of vessels registered in the United States for fines paid to secure the release of vessels seized for operation in waters not recognized as territorial waters by the United States. No registration or payment of premiums is required prior to the seizure in order to qualify for reimbursement.

* Foreign Fish Catches

Office of International Affairs
National Marine Fisheries Service
National Oceanic and Atmospheric Administration
U.S. Department of Commerce
1335 East-West Hwy., Room 7624
Silver Spring, MD 20910 (301) 427-2272

For information regarding foreign fishing catches (allocations) or foreign fisheries in general contact the Office of International Affairs.

* Freight Forwarders

Bureau of Domestic Regulation
Federal Maritime Commission
1100 L Street, NW
Washington, DC 20573 (202) 523-5796

Ocean freight forwarders serve export shippers by arranging for the ocean transportation of cargo by common carriers, and by handling the paperwork, legal requirements, safety requirements and other incidentals related to the shipment of cargo. The Commission is vested with the authority for the licensing and regulation for independent ocean freight forwarders. The Commission also maintains surety bonds on file for freight forwarders.

* Habitat Conservation

National Marine Fisheries Service
National Oceanic and Atmospheric Administration
U.S. Department of Commerce
1335 East-West Hwy., Room 6212
Silver Spring, MD 20910 (301) 713-2325

The Habitat Conservation Program helps minimize losses and degradation in areas where fish and shellfish grow and live by working with other federal and state agencies involved in development projects. It also helps the regional offices incorporate habitat considerations into their management plans.

* High Seas Law Enforcement

Operational Law Enforcement Division
Office of Law Enforcement and Defense Operations
U.S. Coast Guard
U.S. Department of Transportation
2100 2nd St., SW, Room 3110
Washington, DC 20593-0001 (202) 267-1890

As the primary maritime law enforcement agency for the U.S., the Coast Guard enforces Federal laws, treaties, and international agreements to which the U.S. is a party. The Coast Guard may conduct investigations when violations are suspected, such as smuggling, drug trafficking, or polluting. Empowered to board and inspect vessels routinely as well, the Guard also conducts "suspicionless" boardings to prevent violations. To report suspicious or questionable activity on boats, or to complain about an improperly conducted boarding, call the Boating Safety Hotline, (800) 368-5647; or (202) 267-0780 in DC, or contact your local Coast Guard commander. The office listed above can provide you with

Be patient. If any phone number is incorrect, call (area code) 555-1212 and request the new listing.

Shipping and Fishing

information about the Coast Guard's law enforcement role and the National Narcotics Border Interdiction System, which coordinates multi-agency and international operations with other countries to suppress narcotics trafficking.

* Impact of Human Activities on Marine Life

Office of Oceanic and Atmospheric Research
National Oceanic and Atmospheric Administration
U.S. Department of Commerce
1335 East-West Hwy., Room 6212
Silver Spring, MD 20910 (301) 713-2463

The Marine Assessment Program determines the ecological impacts of human activities, such as coastal power generation, fishing, mining, and waste disposal. Scientists conduct theoretical and laboratory experiments of chemical and dynamical processes in the deep oceans as well as in the Great Lakes estuaries.

* International Marine Environmental Efforts

Environmental Coordination Branch
Marine Environmental Response Division
Office of Marine, Safety, Security, and Environmental Protection
U.S. Coast Guard
U.S. Department of Transportation
2100 2nd St., SW, Room 1202
Washington, DC 20593-0001 (202) 267-0421

Information is available here on the Coast Guard's role in international marine environmental efforts, such as representation in the U.N. International Maritime Consultative Organization. For further information on cooperative environmental efforts, contact the branch listed.

* International Maritime Activities

Office of International Activities
Maritime Administration
U.S. Department of Transportation
400 7th Street, SW, Room 7119
Washington, DC 20590 (202) 366-5773

This office plans and coordinates MARAD participation in international activities as well as keeping track of external developments affecting U.S. shipping interests. Specific activities include information collection, analyses, contract negotiations, promotional programs and the development of contacts between U.S. and foreign governments/foreign maritime industry representatives.

* Joint Seafood Inspection Program

National Marine Fisheries Service
Industry and Consumer Liaison Branch
National Oceanic and Atmospheric Administration (NOAA)
1335 East West Highway
Silver Spring, MD 20910 (301) 713-2355

The Food and Drug Administration and NOAA are designing and pilot testing a new joint seafood inspection program based on the Hazard Analysis Critical Control Point (HACCP) concept. The final program will be a voluntary fee-for-service inspection program. The basic tenet of HACCP is the identification of critical control points, the establishment of controls for those points, and the continuous monitoring of these areas to prevent problems before they begin. For information on the progress of the pilot programs, contact Lu Cano of NOAA at the above number.

* Major Developments in U.S. Shipping Trade

Federal Maritime Commission (FMC)
1100 L Street, NW
Washington, DC 20573 (202) 523-5725

The Federal Maritime Commission continually monitors developments in the major shipping markets around the world. Information on rates, capacity, and international agreements is compiled. The FMC also has information on developments with respect to the major carriers. The FMC breaks its analysis down in the following geographic manner: Transatlantic, Mediterranean, Africa, Transpacific, Latin America and the Caribbean, and the Middle East.

* Marine Advisory Service

National Sea-Grant College Program
National Oceanic and Atmospheric Administration
U.S. Department of Commerce

1335 East-West Hwy.
Silver Spring, MD 20910 (202) 377-8090

Operated through the Sea-Grant Colleges, the marine advisory service consists of agents and specialists who are experts in areas such as seafood technology, marine economics, coastal engineering, commercial fishing, recreation, and communications. These specialists provide a link between the people who live and work in coastal areas and researchers in the universities. They sponsor workshops, conferences, and seminars on marine issues for the public and representatives of industry and government agencies. They talk to high school science classes, as well as publish bulletins, fact sheets, newsletters, technical papers, and audio-visual materials concerning marine affairs. The following is a list of Sea-Grant Colleges, and people you can contact for more information.

Sea Grant Colleges

Alabama
See Mississippi

Alaska
Alaska Sea Grant College Program
University of Alaska Fairbanks
138 Irving II
Fairbanks, AK 99775-5040 (907) 474-7086

Arizona
Environmental Research Laboratory
University of Arizona
2601 E. Airport Drive
Tucson, AZ 85706-6985 (602) 741-1990

California
California Sea Grant
University of California/San Diego
9500 Gilman Drive
La Jolla, CA 92093-0232 (619) 534-4444

Sea Grant Program
University of Southern California
University Park
Los Angeles, CA 90089-1231 (213) 740-1961

Connecticut
Connecticut Sea Grant
Marine Sciences Institute
University of Connecticut
Building 24, Avery Point
Groton, CT 06340 (203) 445-8664

Delaware
University of Delaware Sea Grant
Marine Communications Office
263 E. Main Street
Newark, DE 19716 (302) 831-8083

Florida
Florida Sea Grant
Building 803
University of Florida
Gainesville, FL 32611-0341 (904) 392-2802

Georgia
Georgia Sea Grant
Ecology Building
University of Georgia
Athens, GA 30602 (404) 542-7671

Hawaii
University of Hawaii
Sea Grant College Program
1000 Pope Road, MSB 200
Honolulu, HI 96822 (808) 956-7410

Illinois
Illinois-Indiana Sea Grant
University of Illinois
65 Mumford Hall

Be patient. If any phone number is incorrect, call (area code) 555-1212 and request the new listing.

Business and Industry

1301 W. Gregory Drive
Urbana, IL 61801 (217) 333-9448

Indiana
See Illinois

Louisiana
Louisiana Sea Grant
Center for Wetland Resources
Louisiana State University
Baton Rouge, LA 70803 (504) 388-6449

Maine
Maine Sea Grant Communications
30 Coburn Hall
University of Maine
Orono, ME 04469 (207) 581-1440

Marine Law Institute
University of Maine School of Law
246 Deering Avenue
Portland, ME 04102 (207) 780-4474

Maryland
Maryland Sea Grant
1123 Taliaferro Hall
University of Maryland
College Park, MD 20742 (301) 405-6371

National Sea Grant College Program
NOAA, SSMB-1/5206
1335 East-West Hwy.
Silver Spring, MD 20910 (301) 713-2431

Massachusetts
MIT Sea Grant
Building E-38, Room 300
Massachusetts Inst. of Technology
292 Main Street
Cambridge, MA 02139 (617) 253-7041

Sea Grant Program
Woods Hole Oceanographic Institution
Woods Hole, MA 02543 (508) 548-1400

Michigan
Michigan Sea Grant Publications
University of Michigan
2200 Bonisteel Blvd.
Ann Arbor, MI 48109-2099 (313) 764-1138

Minnesota
Minnesota Sea Grant
University of Minnesota
1518 Cleveland Ave. N, Room 302
St. Paul, MN 55108 (612) 625-9288

Mississippi
Mississippi-Alabama Sea Grant Consortium
P.O. Box 7000
Ocean Springs, MS 39564-7000 (601) 875-9341

New Hampshire
New Hampshire Sea Grant
Kingman Farm
University of New Hampshire
Durham, NH 03824 (603) 749-1565

New Jersey
Sea Grant Program
New Jersey Marine Sciences Consortium
Building No. 22
Fort Hancock, NJ 07732 (908) 872-1300

New York
New York Sea Grant Institute
Dutchess Hall Room 137

SUNY at Stony Brook
Stony Brook, NY 11794-5001 (516) 632-6905

North Carolina
North Carolina Sea Grant
North Carolina State University
Box 8605
Raleigh, NC 27695 (919) 515-2454

Ohio
Ohio Sea Grant
Ohio State University
1314 Kinnear Road
Columbus, OH 43212 (614) 292-8949

Oklahoma
Department of Chemistry
Attn. F. Schmitz
University of Oklahoma
620 Parrington Oval, Room 208
Norman, OK 73019 (405) 325-5581

Oregon
National Coastal Resources Research and
Development Inst.
528 SW Mill, Suite 222
P.O. Box 751
Portland, OR 97207 (503) 725-5725

Oregon Sea Grant
Oregon State University
AdS 402
Corvallis, OR 97331-2134 (503) 737-2716

Publications Orders
Agricultural Communications
Oregon State University
AdS 422
Corvallis, OR 97331-2119 (503) 737-2513

Puerto Rico
Puerto Rico Sea Grant Program
Communications Office
RUM-UPR P.O. Box 5000
Mayaguez, PR 00709-5000 (809) 834-4726

Rhode Island
National Sea Grant Depository
Pell Library Building
Bay Campus
University of Rhode Island
Narragansett, RI 02882 (401) 792-6114

Rhode Island Sea Grant
Publications Unit
University of Rhode Island
Bay Campus
Narragansett, RI 02882-1197 (401) 792-6842

South Carolina
South Carolina Sea Grant Consortium
287 Meeting Street
Charleston, SC 29401 (803) 727-2078

Texas
Texas Sea Grant
Texas A&M-Galveston
P.O. Box 1675
Galveston, TX 77553-1675 (409) 762-9800

Virginia
Virginia Sea Grant
Madison House
University of Virginia
170 Rugby Road
Charlottesville, VA 22903 (804) 924-5965

Be patient. If any phone number is incorrect, call (area code) 555-1212 and request the new listing.

Shipping and Fishing

Washington
Washington Sea Grant, HG-30
University of Washington
3716 Brooklyn Avenue, NE
Seattle, WA 98105 (206) 543-6600

Wisconsin
Sea Grant Institute
University of Wisconsin
1800 University Avenue
Madison, WI 53705 (608) 263-3259

* Marine Environmental Reports

Coastal Monitoring and Bioeffects Division
National Oceanic and Atmospheric Administration (NOAA)
Washington Science Center, Building 5
6010 Executive Blvd., Room 320
Rockville, MD 20852 (301) 713-2465

Under the National Status and Trends Program, NOAA produced some 63 papers and reports in 1991 dealing with a wide range of Marine environmental issues and their impact on Marine life. A list of these reports is available from NOAA at the above number. Specific questions on marine pollution research at NOAA can be directed to Dr. Andrew Robertson, Dr. Douglas Wolfe, or Dr. Thomas O'Connor.

* Marine Terminal Activities

Bureau of Domestic Regulation
Federal Maritime Commission
1100 L Street, NW
Washington, DC 20573 (202) 523-5796

The Commission is responsible for the review and processing of certain agreements and tariffs related to the Marine terminal industry under the 1984 and 1916 Acts.

* Marine Environmental Information

Pollution Response Branch
Marine Environmental Response Division
Office of Marine Safety, Security, and Environmental Protection
U.S. Coast Guard
U.S. Department of Transportation
2100 2nd St., SW, Room 2104 (202) 267-0518
Washington, DC 20593-0001 (202) 267-2611

This office responds to requests for marine environmental protection information from Congress and other federal agencies, state agencies, schools, industries, and the general public. Data is available on laws relating to the protection of the marine environment, incidents involving releases of oil or other hazardous substances, and federally funded spill response operations. Currently the Division is working on new regulations regarding dumping in the Caribbean.

* Marine Mammals Protection Enforcement

Office of Protected Resources
National Marine Fisheries Service
National Oceanic and Atmospheric Administration
U.S. Department of Commerce
1335 East-West Hwy.
Silver Spring, MD 20910 (301) 713-2322

The Marine Mammal Protection Act commits the United States to long-term management and research programs to conserve and protect these animals. Marine mammals may be taken for scientific research, public display, and incidentally to commercial fishing. The National Marine Fisheries Service grants or denies requests for exemptions, issues permits, carries out research and management programs, enforces the Act, participates in international programs, and issues rules and regulations to carry out its mission to conserve and protect marine mammals. An annual report is available for the Office of Protected Resources, which gives detailed information regarding the activities of the Office. This office can also provide you with copies of the Act, and two publications: *Handbook for the Determination of Adverse Human-Marine Mammal Interaction from Necropsies*, and *Proceedings of the Workshop to Review and Evaluate Whale Watching Programs and Management Needs*. The report *Marine Mammal Strandings in the U.S., NMFS report 98*, January 1991, is available from National Technical Information Service (703) 487-4650. Each regional office also puts out a report on stranded mammals (see Fisheries Research for their phone numbers.)

* Marine Pollutants

Office of Oceanography and Marine Assessments
National Ocean Service
National Oceanic and Atmospheric Administration
U.S. Department of Commerce
6001 Executive Blvd.
Rockville, MD 20852 (301) 443-8487

This office surveys and monitors the oceans, U.S. coastal waters and the Great Lakes to produce data and information products that are critically important for offshore oil and gas exploration, dredging operations, coastal and offshore construction, sea floor mining, waste disposal management, and for protecting the marine environment from the adverse effects of ocean and coastal pollution.

* Mariners Weather Log

National Oceanographic Data Center
National Oceanic and Atmospheric Administration
Universal Building Room 412
Washington, DC 20235 (202) 606-4561

The Mariners Weather Log is a unique source of information on marine weather and climate and their effects on operations at sea. Published quarterly by the National Oceanographic Data Center, the *Mariners Weather Log* provides comprehensive coverage of major storms of the North Atlantic and North Pacific, reports and annual summaries on tropical cyclones, information on the National Weather Service's Marine Observation Program, selected shipboard gale and wave observations, and general articles about weather and climate, hazards and safety precautions, and related marine lore. An annual subscription is available for $8 from the Superintendent of Documents, Government Printing Office, Washington, DC 20402; (202)783-3238.

* Marine Debris

National Ocean Service
Office of Ocean and Coastal Resource Management
National Oceanic and Atmospheric Administration (NOAA)
1825 Connecticut Ave., NW, Room 724
Washington, DC 20235 (202) 606-4158

There has been an explosion of plastic pollution in the world's oceans and waterways in the last 20 years. One survey stated that some 58% of fishermen had incurred costs due to damage caused by plastic debris. Ingestion and entanglement due to plastics cause the death of an estimated 100,000 marine mammals each year. The NOAA technical assistance bulletin *Marine Debris: Status Report and Bibliography* (number 104) documents the problem, discusses innovative solutions now being undertaken in several states, and contains detailed reference bibliographies on beach cleanups, entanglement, plastic article debris, and regulations on pollution. It is available free upon request.

* Marine Recreational Fishing Publications

Fisheries Statistics Division
National Marine Fisheries Service
National Oceans and Atmospheric Administration
U.S. Department of Commerce
1335 East-West Highway
Silver Spring, Md 20910 (301) 427-2328

The National Marine Fisheries Service publishes the following regional fishing reports. They are available from the above office. Marine Recreational Fishing Statistics Survey:

Atlantic and Gulf Coasts, 1987-1989, CFS #8904
Pacific Coast, 1986, CFS #8393
Atlantic and Gulf Coasts, 1986, CFS #8392
Atlantic and Gulf Coasts, 1983-1984, CFS #8326
Pacific Coast, 1983-1984, CFS #8325
Pacific Coast, 1981-1982, CFS #8323
Atlantic and Gulf Coasts, 1979 (revised) - 1980, CFS #8322
Atlantic and Gulf Coasts, 1979-1980, CFS #8321

* Marine Technology

Library, Coast Guard Research and Development Center
U.S. Coast Guard
U.S. Department of Transportation
Avery Point
Groton, CT 06340-6096 (203) 441-2648

Marine research is conducted here in areas such as ice technology, navigation

Be patient. If any phone number is incorrect, call (area code) 555-1212 and request the new listing.

Business and Industry

instrumentation technology, ocean dumping surveillance, pollution, search and rescue techniques, and marine fire and safety technology. This library is a good starting point for obtaining specific information about what research is done by the Center and for referrals to appropriate experts.

* Marine Technology Society

1828 L St NW, Suite 906
Washington, DC 20036 (202) 775-5966

This non-profit organization is dedicated to providing information about marine science and engineering. It is divided into 14 geographical sections in the U.S. and Canada, and each section holds monthly meetings, at which brief technical presentations are given. The Society has 31 professional committees that sponsor technical conferences, workshops, and short courses that are open to members and nonmembers. The staff can provide you with technical information and referrals. The Society publishes the *Journal of the Marine Technology Society*, a quarterly publication that presents technical activities of the Society, papers, conferences summaries, book reviews, and so on. It is available free of charge to members and for $5 for nonmembers.

* Maritime Administration Activities and Statistics

MARAD - Public Affairs
U.S. Department of Transportation
400 7th Street SW, Room 7219
Washington, DC 20590 (202) 366-5807

MARAD's annual report is an excellent place to begin your search for information on U.S. maritime activities and statistics. The report includes a profile of the U.S. Merchant Fleet, Department of Defense Cargo programs, information on maritime labor and training, and a report on maritime agreements recently concluded between the U.S. and foreign nations. Statistics include listings for worldwide ship deliveries, Federal Ship financing guarantee program, U.S. Oceangoing Merchant Marine, major world merchant fleets, U.S. Great Lakes Merchant Fleet, the National Defense Reserve Fleet, and maritime subsidy outlays. The report is available free upon request.

* Maritime Administration Publications

MARAD - Public Affairs
U.S. Department of Transportation
400 7th Street SW, Room 7219
Washington, DC 20590 (202) 366-5807

MARAD publishes a booklet containing a listing of all MARAD publications. Some MARAD publications are free and others are available for sale through the GPO (202) 783-3238, or NTIS (703) 487-4650. The catalogue is available free from the above address.

* Maritime Affairs

Bureau of Economic and Business Affairs
Office of Maritime and Land Transport
U.S. Department of State
2021 C St., NW, Room 5828
Washington, DC 20520 (202) 647-5840

This office is involved with all matters concerning maritime affairs, including unions, shipping regulations, the exporting and importing of cargo, and rights of passage. They also take part in the negotiations and agreements on these issues and monitor them to make sure the agreements are followed.

* Maritime Commerce Financial Analysis

Bureau of Domestic Regulation
Federal Maritime Commission
1100 L Street, NW
Washington, DC 20573 (202) 523-5796

The Bureau of Domestic Regulation provides accounting and financial expertise to help ensure the reasonableness of rates for the transportation of cargo and other services provided by common carriers in the domestic offshore waterborne commerce of the U.S. The Bureau also provides technical assistance to other activities within the Commission.

* Maritime Complaints

Office of Informal Inquiries and Complaints
Federal Maritime Commission
1100 L Street, NW

Washington, DC 20573 (202) 523-5807

This office coordinates the informal complaint handling system throughout the Commission. The Office is also responsible for the initial adjudication of reparation claims for less than $10,000 that are filed by shippers against common carriers by water engaged in the foreign and domestic offshore commerce of the U.S. The office supplies copies of procedures, dockets, and other information on complaints to the public.

* Maritime Information FOIA Requests

Office of the Secretary
Federal Maritime Commission
1100 L Street, NW
Washington, DC 20573 (202) 523-5911

Among the Secretary's responsibilities are administering Freedom of Information, Government in the Sunshine, and Privacy Acts. Requests for information under these Acts should be directed to the Secretary's office.

* Maritime and Shipping Tariffs

Bureau of Tariffs, Certification and Licensing
Federal Maritime Commission
1100 L Street, NW
Washington, DC 20573 (202) 523-5796

The 1916 and 1984 Shipping Acts require that common carriers by water file and keep open to public inspection their tariffs. The 1984 Act additionally requires that service contracts be filed and that their essential terms be made available to the public in tariff format. At the end of 1990 there were some 5757 tariffs on file. The Commission is currently working on an automatic tariff filing and information system. Information on tariffs is available to the public. Call for more information.

* Maritime Legal Cases and Petitions

Office of the General Counsel
Federal Maritime Commission
1100 L Street, NW
Washington, DC 20573 (202) 523-5740

The General Counsel provides legal counsel to the Commission. This counsel includes reviewing for legal sufficiency staff recommendations for commission action, drafting proposed rules to implement Commission policies, and preparing final decisions, orders and regulations for Commission ratification. The Office has information on a variety of recent cases and petitions brought before the Commission.

* Maritime Technology

Office of Technology Assessment
Maritime Administration
U.S. Department of Transportation
400 7th Street SW, Room 7328
Washington, DC 20590 (202) 366-1925

This office conducts technology assessment activities related to the development and use of waterborne transportation systems with application in such areas as cargo handling, fleet productivity, military sealift, port activities, trade and intermodal transportation support. It additionally serves as the focal point of maritime technological expertise within the U.S. Department of Transportation.

* Maritime Trade Statistics

Trade Analysis Division (MAR-570)
Office of Trade and Analysis and Insurance
Maritime Administration
U.S. Department of Transportation
400 7th Street, SW
Washington, DC 20590 (202) 366-2282

Records on federally subsidized shipping companies are maintained by this Division. Information includes vessel name, port dates, and crew costs. The public can visit the document inspection room or write for information.

* Market Development for U.S. Shipping

Office of Market Development
Maritime Administration
U.S. Department of Transportation
400 7th Street, SW, Room 7209

Be patient. If any phone number is incorrect, call (area code) 555-1212 and request the new listing.

Shipping and Fishing

Washington, DC 20590 (202) 366-5517

MARAD conducts programs designed to increase U.S. flag participation in the nation's overseas commerce. Contact this office for information on programs.

* Monitoring the 1984 Shipping Act

Bureau of Trade Monitoring
Federal Maritime Commission
1100 L Street, NW
Washington, DC 20573 (202) 523-5787

The Bureau of Trade Monitoring has produced a number of reports and studies relating to the 1984 Shipping Act. These include: an economic analysis of the impact of the Commissions Transatlantic Enforcement Initiative; a report on the issues surrounding the application of terminal handling charges; a profile of the North Europe trade routes; an extensive profile of the carrier services in the transpacific trade routes; the monitoring of the agreement activity in the Venezuelan trade; a report on the carryings of a controlled carrier service patterns and vessel utilization in the U.S. trades; a report on the carryings of a controlled carrier to and from U.S. Gulf ports; a report on Freight All Kinds rates and the potential abuse by controlled carriers; a report on potential trade restrictions by the Ivory Coast; and a report on trade information on carriers serving the Middle East. Contact the Trade Monitoring Bureau for information on these and other reports.

* Nautical Charts

Chart Distribution Branch
National Ocean Service
National Oceanic and Atmospheric Administration
U.S. Department of Commerce
6501 Lafayette Blvd.
Riverdale, MD 20737 (301) 436-6990

The National Ocean Service produces approximately 1,000 nautical charts for navigation in U.S. estuarine waters and navigable inland waterways, the Great Lakes, and the 2 1/2 million square miles of coastal waters of the United States and its possessions. NOAA *Chart and Map Catalogs* describe nautical charts which are listed in a series of four catalogs, one for each region of the U.S. ocean and coastal waters. NOAA bathymetric maps and special purpose charts are listed in a single catalog. A sixth catalog is a guide to NOAA nautical products and services. The catalogs contain a brief description of each nautical chart, bathymetric map, special purpose chart, and chart-related publication produced by the NOS. They also include the price of the chart of publication, other information needed to select and order nautical charting products, and a list of NOAA chart sales facilities and authorized commercial chart sales agents. Contact this office for your free catalogs.

* Ocean Commerce Statistics and Information

Bureau of Economic Analysis
Federal Maritime Commission
1100 L Street, NW
Washington, DC 20573 (202) 523-5870

The Bureau of Economic Analysis provides economic, statistical and financial analysis for the Commission. The Bureau assists in the development of long-range plans for the commission and enhances the agencies responsiveness to new developments and trends in U.S. ocean commerce and the liner shipping industry.

* Ocean Common Carrier Investigations

Bureau of Investigation
Federal Maritime Commission
1100 L Street, NW
Washington, DC 20573 (202) 523-5860

The Bureau of Investigations monitors the activities of, and conducts investigations of alleged violations by, ocean common carriers, non-vessel operating common carriers, freight forwarders, shippers, ports and terminals, and other persons to ensure compliance with the statutes and regulations issued by the commission. The Bureau maintains a staff of 48 personnel located in Washington DC, Houston, Los Angeles, Miami, New Orleans, New York, San Francisco, and Puerto Rico. District offices also provide a liaison between the Commission, industry, and the shipping public. Investigations focus on the following areas: illegal rebates by carriers; misdescriptions and misdeclarations of cargo by shippers, carriers, consignees and other persons; activities of ocean common carriers which may be in violation of the Shipping Acts; failure by carriers to charge rates in effect and on file with the Commission; and operating

as an ocean freight forwarder without a license issued by the Commission or contrary to statute or regulation.

* Oceanboard Liner Cargo

Federal Maritime Commission
1100 L Street, NW
Washington, DC 20573 (202) 523-5725

Section 10002(g)(1) of the Omnibus Trade and Competition Act of 1988 requires the Commission to include in its annual report to Congress a listing of the 20 foreign countries which generated the largest volume of bilateral oceanboard liner cargo with the U.S. for the most recent calendar year available. The Annual Report is available from the FMC at the above listed number.

* Oceanographic Data and Publications

National Oceanic and Atmospheric Administration
U.S. Department of Commerce
1825 Connecticut Ave., NW
Washington, DC 20235 (202) 606-4561

The National Oceanographic Data Center has a free publications list which includes technical reports and bulletins, as well has a variety of data reports pertaining to oceanographic research.

* Oceanographic Information

National Oceanographic Data Center
National Environmental Satellite, Data and Information Service
National Oceanic and Atmospheric Administration
U.S. Department of Commerce
1825 Connecticut Ave., NW
Washington, DC 20235 (202) 606-4561

The National Oceanographic Data Center provides global coverage of oceanographic data and services. NODC's databases cover physical and chemical properties of the world's oceans, seas, and estuaries, plus information on selected continental shelf and coastal waters. Researchers using NODC data range from industrial scientists through local, state, and national government investigators, to university or academic personnel. Information is available in various forms: publications, computer plots, computer printouts, magnetic tapes and floppy disks. NODC publishes a *Users Guide*, which describes the data and products services available. Simple questions usually can be answered without charge by telephone or mail, but more complicated ones requiring research or computer processing usually carry a fee. The fees range upward from a base of $49 per floppy disk to $110 per reel of magnetic tape. Publications available from NODC include *Newsletter on Oceanography*, the *Earth System Monitor*, published quarterly, and the *Environmental Information Bulletin*, published 4-6 times annually.

* Oceanographic Corps Jobs

Commission Personnel Division, NOAA Corps
National Oceanic and Atmospheric Administration (NOAA)
U.S. Department of Commerce
11400 Rockville Pike
Rockville, MD 20852 (301) 443-8984

The NOAA Corps is the uniformed service of the U.S. Department of Commerce responsible for operating and managing NOAA's fleet of hydrographic, oceanographic, and fisheries-research ships and for supporting NOAA scientific programs. Engineering, computer science, mathematics, and science baccalaureate or higher degree graduates are sought for positions in the Corps.

* Ocean Pollution Information Network

Ocean Pollution Data and
Information Network/CCRO
National Oceanographic Data Center
National Oceanic and Atmospheric Administration
1825 Connecticut Ave., NW
Washington, DC 20235 (202) 606-4539

The Ocean Pollution Data and Information Network facilitates user access to ocean pollution data and information generated by 11 participating Federal departments and agencies. OPDIN provides a wide range of products and services to researchers, managers, and others who need data and information about ocean pollution. OPDIN is managed by the Central Coordination and Referral Office (CCRO). The CCRO maintains a directory of Federal ocean pollution data and information systems and services, lists of ocean pollution

Be patient. If any phone number is incorrect, call (area code) 555-1212 and request the new listing.

Business and Industry

scientists and managers and their fields of expertise, and annually-updated catalogs of Federal marine pollution research, development, and monitoring projects. The CCRO also provides information and advice about ocean pollution data management and processing, as well as copies of catalogs, directories, technical reports, data inventories, and data products.

* Oil and Chemical Spills Hotline

National Response Center (NRC)
Marine Environmental Response Division
Office of Marine Safety, Security, and Environmental Protection
U.S. Coast Guard
U.S. Department of Transportation
2100 2nd St., SW, Room 2611 (800) 424-8802
Washington, DC 20593 (202) 267-2188

The NRC receives reports of oil and hazardous substance spills, investigates incidents, initiates civil penalty actions, monitors cleanups, and coordinates federally funded spill response operations. NRC's National Strike Force assists federal coordinators on the scene in responding to pollution accidents. For further details, or to report information, contact the Center toll-free.

* Panama Canal Dredging Division

Engineering and Construction Bureau
Dredging Division
c/o Panama Canal Commission
Unit 2300
APO AA 34011 011 (507) 56-6232

The Dredging Division is responsible for maintenance and construction dredging; slide removal; inspection and maintenance of the Atlantic breakwater; operation and maintenance of navigational aids; the detection, containment, recovery, and disposal of oil pollution in Canal operating areas; and the removal and control of aquatic weeds through the use of chemical and biological means. For more information on the dredging operations, contact this office.

* Panama Canal Economic and Market Research

Economic Research and Market Development Division
The Office of Executive Planning
c/o Panama Canal Commission
Unit 2300
APO AA 34011 011 (507) 52-7806

As an agency of the U.S. Government, the Panama Canal Commission has a legal obligation to operate on a break-even basis, recovering all costs of operating, maintaining, and improving the Canal through tolls revenue. The agency tries to have a high standard of service at the lowest possible cost. As a reflection of this, toll rates have gone up only four times since the Canal opened in 1914. Operating costs are very carefully controlled so that it provides an economic advantage to world trade on many routes. Even if other world trade routes may be shorter in distance, the Canal remains competitive because of its reliable, cost-effective service. For more information on operating costs, contact this office.

* Panama Canal Environmental Safeguards

Sanitation Branch
General Services Bureau
Panama Canal Commission
Unit 2300
APO AA 34011 011 (507) 52-3464

The Sanitation Branch carries out measures to control disease carrying organisms and environmental sanitation measures essential to maintaining a high standard of public health which can be enjoyed by Panama Canal Commission employees and their families. There is an effort to control insect vector and vermin by nonchemical methods. For more information, contact the above office.

* Panama Canal General Information

Office of the Secretary
Panama Canal Commission
2000 L Street, NW
Room 550
Washington, DC 20036-4996 (202) 634-6441

This office is a good place to start in acquiring general information on the Canal. It can also supply you with information related to transiting the Canal.

* Panama Canal Logistical Support

Office of Logistical Support
General Services Bureau, Panama Canal Commission
4400 Dauphine St.
New Orleans, LA 70146-6800 (504) 948-5299

The Logistical Support Division provides centralized procurement, inventory management, warehousing, distribution, contract administration, and supply and property disposal support to Canal operations. For more information, contact this office.

* Panama Canal Publications and Audiovisuals

The Office of Public Affairs
c/o Panama Canal Commission
Unit 2300
APO AA 34011 (507) 52-3165

The Office of Public Affairs has available various publications including the *Panama Canal 75th Anniversary Commemorative Album* and *The Panama Canal Spillway* as well as press releases, brochures, and other matters of related interest are distributed to the work force and the public at large. A broad range of photographic and audio-visual support services were created as well. A limited number of projection prints are available for loan to individuals and groups interested in the canal and its operation. All films are 16mm color and sound. Individuals may obtain video tapes of all subjects by submitting a blank tape in the desired format and the payment of a transfer charge. Some examples of the available films for general audiences are as follows:

The Task That Never Ends. 1984. Depicts the on going job of maintaining and improving the channel of the Panama Canal, widening, deepening and straightening the water route.

The Vital Link. 1986. Depicts the role of the Panama Canal in world commerce with a layman's introduction to the people and methods of Canal operations. Details of lockages, traffic control, and communications at the crossroads of the world.

1986 Landslide. 1987. Shows the resumption of the Cucaracha Slide in October, 1986. Measures taken to maintain Canal traffic while the obstruction was removed and remedial actions taken.

Some examples of the available films of special interest to engineers and mechanical craftsmen include the following:

Locks Overhaul - Strut Arms. 1981. A detailed description of strut arm removal prior to gate or bullwheel removal and replacement.

Locks Overhaul - Bullwheels. 1982. A detailed description of bullwheel removal and replacement.

There are also films of special interest to canal operating personnel. Films are available in both Spanish and English. For a complete listing of films produced by the Panama Canal Commission, contact the above office.

* Panama Canal Traffic Data

Economic Research and Market Development Division
The Office of Executive Planning
c/o Panama Canal Commission
Unit 2300
APO AA 34011 011 (507) 52-7961

The Panama Canal is a vital link in the world transportation chain. A large share of world trade passes through the Canal over any of the world's major trade routes. In 1988, 156.5 million long tons of cargo moved through the Canal aboard 12,318 oceangoing vessels. More than 690,962 vessels have crossed the waterway, carrying more than 4 billion long tons of the world's goods from one ocean to the other. For more information or compilations of Canal traffic data, contact this office.

* Panama Canal Transit

Canal Operations Unit
c/o Panama Canal Commission
Unit 2300
APO AA 34011 011 (507) 52-4211

This office can provide information for those considering taking a boat or ship through the canal.

Be patient. If any phone number is incorrect, call (area code) 555-1212 and request the new listing.

Shipping and Fishing

* Panama Canal Vessel Emergency Response Management

Marine Director
Marine Bureau
c/o Panama Canal Commission
Unit 2300
APO AA 34011 011 (507) 52-4500

For information on marine operations including inspections, piloting, locks, traffic management, canal services, marine safety, canal operations and maritime training, contact this Bureau. The Commission's marine risk management team is devoted to the prevention of and response to accidents involving vessels carrying hazardous cargoes. The team consists of an experienced fireman, a licensed marine engineer, a safety generalist, an experienced chemist, and lead by an experienced active duty U.S. Coast Guard officer. This team is also responsible for updating the Commission's Vessel Emergency Response Plan and in conducting vessel emergency training exercises.

* Passenger Safety Certification

Bureau of Domestic Regulation
Federal Maritime Commission
1100 L Street, NW
Washington, DC 20573 (202) 523-5796

Owners, charters, and operators of American and foreign vessels having berth or stateroom accommodations for fifty or more passengers and embarking passengers at U.S. ports must establish financial responsibility to meet any liability incurred for death or injury to passengers on voyages to or from U.S. ports and to indemnify passengers for non-performance of transportation to which they would be entitled under ticket contracts. Call this office for more information.

* Port Development

Office of Port Development
Maritime Administration
U.S. Department of Transportation
400 7th Street, SW
Washington, DC 20590 (202) 366-4357

As part of its marketing program, MARAD actively promotes the improvement of the national port facilities and advanced intermodal transportation systems. MARAD advises and assists port communities in promoting advanced, highly efficient marine terminal and intermodal operations to speed the flow of cargo. MARAD also conducts research to help ports update facilities, services, and equipment. Recent port studies include:

Report to Congress on the Status of U.S. Public Ports - 1988-89.
Water Transportation and Ports.
Changing Directions for Traditional Ports.

These are available free from MARAD.

* Port Regulations

Port Safety and Security Division
Office of Marine Safety, Security, and Environmental Protection
U.S. Coast Guard
U.S. Department of Transportation
2100 2nd St., SW, Room 1104
Washington, DC 20593-0001 (202) 267-0489

Coast Guard Captains of the Port enforce rules and regulations concerning the safety and security of ports and the anchorage and movement of vessels. This includes supervising cargo transfers and storage; conducting harbor patrols and facility inspections; establishing security zones; and surveying to prevent water pollution. The Division also administers a licensing and registration program for deepwater ports transferring oil from tankers to shore via pipelines. For information on regulations and operations, contact the division listed.

* Protection of Ships From Seizure

Assistant Legal Advisor for International Claims
Office of the Legal Advisor
U.S. Department of State
2201 C St., NW
Washington, DC 20520 (202) 632-7810

The Fishermen's Protective Act provides for reimbursement for financial loss to owners of vessels registered in the United States for fines paid to secure the release of vessels seized for operation in waters not recognized as territorial waters by the United States. No registration or payment of premiums is required prior to the seizure in order to qualify for reimbursement.

* Ready Reserve Fleet

Division of Reserve Fleet
Maritime Administration
U.S. Department of Transportation
400 7th Street SW, Room 2117
Washington, DC 20590 (202) 366-5776

MARAD maintains an inactive reserve of over 300 ships in the National Defense Reserve Fleet as a source of vessels available for the U.S. government in the event of an emergency. The Ready Reserve Force is a portion of the NDRF and can be activated in 5-20 days. MARAD activated some 78 ships during Operation Desert Shield/Storm.

* Saint Lawrence Seaway Statistics

Office of Trade and Traffic Development
Saint Lawrence Seaway Development Corporation
400 7th Street, SW, Room 5424
Washington, DC 20590 (202) 366-0091

This office keeps statistics on traffic in the Great Lakes/Seaway system. Data is recorded on the number of vessels and their size, type, cargo, and nationality. Cargo vessel statistics are published in the *Annual Traffic Report in the Saint Lawrence Seaway.*

* Saint Lawrence Seaway Publications

Public Affairs Office
Saint Lawrence Seaway Development Corporation
U.S. Department of Transportation
180 Andrews Street
Massena, NY 13662-1763 (315) 764-3232

Free publications about the Seaway are available by contacting this office. Some of the titles available include the following:

Annual Traffic Report in the Saint Lawrence Seaway. Cargo vessel statistics for traffic between Montreal and Lake Erie.

Pleasure Craft Guide: The Seaway. Information on boating in the St. Lawrence River.

The Saint Lawrence Seaway. General and historical information in French and English, including port data, schedules, and tourist information.

The Saint Lawrence Seaway Annual Report.

Seaway Regulations. Includes regulations and toll schedule, operating manual, and chart booklet.

* Sea Grant Abstracts

National Sea Grant Depository
Pell Library Building
The University of Rhode Island
Narragansett Bay Campus
Narragansett, RI 02882-1197 (401) 792-6114

Sea Grant Abstracts cites, on a quarterly basis, the majority of the literature which is received by the National Sea Grant Depository. This literature covers pure and applied science, engineering, business management, shipping and navigation, fisheries, wetlands management, law and policy, economics, and education. Each reference contains a short abstract, a bibliographic reference, and information for obtaining the document. Back issues are also available.

* Sea-Grant Colleges

Office of Oceanic Research Programs
National Oceanic and Atmospheric Administration
U.S. Department of Commerce
1335 East-West Hwy.
Silver Spring, MD 20910 (301) 713-2465

The National Sea Grant College Program is a national network of over 300 colleges, universities, research institutions, and consortia working in partnership with industry and the federal government to support Great Lakes and marine

Be patient. If any phone number is incorrect, call (area code) 555-1212 and request the new listing.

Business and Industry

research, education, and extension services. This program provides support for institutions engaged in comprehensive marine research, education, and advisory service programs, supports individual projects in marine research and development, and sponsors education of ocean scientists and engineers, marine technicians, and other specialists at selected colleges and universities.

* Sea Grant Depository

National Sea Grant Depository
Pell Library Building
University of Rhode Island
Bay Campus
Narragansett, RI 02882 (401) 792-6114

The National Sea Grant Depository is a clearinghouse for all Sea Grant publications. The scope of the collection includes a wide variety of marine topics, such as oceanography, marine education, aquaculture, fisheries, coastal zone management, recreation, and law. The collection includes journal reprints, technical and advisory reports, books, manuals, directories, annual reports, conference proceedings, and newsletters. The Depository Database includes some 22,000 citations. The Depository provides reference and online search services, and welcomes telephone, mail and inter-library loan requests. The Depository will loan documents, but does not distribute the publications (they refer you to the authors). There is a loan limit of 10 documents per request. To be sure that your request for materials is not returned, the library urges people to state clearly that you wish to borrow materials.

* Ship Construction

Office of Ship Construction (MAR-720)
Maritime Administration
U.S. Department of Transportation
400 7th Street, SW, Room 6422
Washington, DC 20590 (202) 366-1880

Contact this office for information on the cost of and market for shipbuilding. The difference between the cost of constructing ships here and abroad are also examined.

* Ship Mortgage Guarantees

Office of Ship Operations
Maritime Administration
U.S. Department of Transportation
400 7th Street, SW, Room 8122
Washington, DC 20590 (202) 366-5744

Through the Merchant Marine Act of 1936, MARAD guarantees commercially placed construction loans and ship mortgages on vessels built in the U.S. for operation on domestic or foreign trade routes. Qualified applicants can obtain long term financing on favorable terms. Contact MARAD for details.

* Shipping Analysis

Office of Domestic Shipping
Maritime Administration
U.S. Department of Transportation
400 7th Street, SW
Washington, DC 20590 (202) 366-5123

The Maritime Administration promotes U.S. domestic shipping services through analysis of the domestic fleet, its markets, the commodities it moves, and its modal competition. Information compiled or maintained by this office is available to the maritime community.

* Shipping Service Contract Regulation

Bureau of Domestic Regulation
Federal Maritime Commission
1100 L Street, NW
Washington, DC 20573 (202) 523-5796

Shippers must file service contracts with the Commission. The Commission ensures that service contracts filed with it meet the necessary statutory and regulatory requirements. The Commission does not accept service contracts which fail to contain mutually binding service and cargo commitments, or which contain meaningless liquidated damages provisions. Contact the Commission to find out shippers requirements with respect to service contracts under the 1984 Shipping Act.

* Small Passenger Vessel Safety

Marine Inspection Office
Your Local Coast Guard Office

Most small passenger vessels (less than 100 tons and carrying more than 6 people) are required to adhere to certain Coast Guard safety regulations. These include having a safety orientation procedure for passengers (announcement or placard), posting of emergency instructions, a life preserver for every person on board, and a Coast Guard safety certification. Marine Inspection Offices around the country issue the certificates. To find an Inspection Office near you, or to report a violation or complaint, call the Boating Safety Hotline (800) 368-5647; or (202) 267-0780 in DC.

* Sockeye Odyssey and Other Films

National Oceanic and Atmospheric Administration (NOAA)
U.S. Department of Commerce
14th St. and Pennsylvania Ave., NW, Room 6013
Washington, DC 20230 (202) 377-8090

A brochure is available which lists motion picture films produced by the National Oceanic and Atmospheric Administration. Most NOAA productions are available in both motion picture and video formats. Unless noted, these films are not available directly from NOAA. To borrow prints without charge, except for return postage, write to: Modern Talking Pictures, 6000 Park Street North, St., Petersburg, FL 33709. These films are heavily booked, so you must send your request as early as possible. The following is a list of their titles:

Sockeye Odyssey
The Awesome Power
The Great American Fish Story
The Great American Fish Story- The West
The Great American Fish Story- The Northeast
The Great American Fish Story- The South
The Great American Fish Story- The Lakes and Rivers
Down to the Monitor
Estuary
*FAMOUS- Boundary of Creation**
*Give Me The Tides**
Global Weather Experiment
*Longlines: An Undersea Investigation**
NOAA Corps- The Seventh Service
Trashing The Oceans

*Available directly from NOAA. Contact the office listed above for a free catalog.

* Trade Monitoring

Bureau of Trade Monitoring
Federal Maritime Commission
1100 L Street, NW
Washington, DC 20573 (202) 523-5787

The Bureau's major program activities include: administering comprehensive trade monitoring programs to identify and track relevant competitive, commercial, and economic activity in each major U.S. trade in order to keep the Commission and its staff appraised of current trade conditions, emerging trends and regulatory needs impacting on waterborne liner transportation. Other monitoring duties include: systematic surveillance of carrier activity and processing and analysis of agreements involving common carriers.

* Updates for Mariners

District Commander
Your local Coast Guard Office

The free *Local Notice to Mariners* is issued weekly by each Coast Guard District. Intended for small craft owners, it advises you of changes in the status of aids to navigation (buoys, radiobeacons, etc.); chart updates; drawbridge operations; and safety warnings for particular areas. This *Local Notice* often includes temporary changes not included in the Defense Mapping Agency's *Notice to Mariners*. To order a subscription for the *Local Notice*, send a written request to the District Commander of your local Coast Guard office. For referral to the correct address, call the Boating Safety Hotline (800) 368-5647; or (202) 267-0780 in DC.

* U.S. Living Marine Resources

National Marine Fisheries Service
Office of Predictions and Analysis

Be patient. If any phone number is incorrect, call (area code) 555-1212 and request the new listing.

Shipping and Fishing

National Oceanic and Atmospheric Administration
1335 East West Highway
Silver Spring, MD 20910 (301) 713-2363

In 1991 the NMFS published the first annual report *Our Living Oceans*, a comprehensive report on the status of U.S. living marine resources. The study contains status reports on many U.S. coastal fish stocks and regional reports detailing fisheries in the Northeast, Atlantic, Gulf of Mexico, Southeast, Pacific Coast, and Alaskan waters. The report is available in limited supply from the above office and is sold by GPO, stock number 0030200161-1, price - $6.

* U.S. Merchant Marine Academy

U.S. Merchant Marine Academy
Maritime Administration
U.S. Department of Transportation-Kings Point
Long Island, NY 11024 (516) 773-5000

Future merchant marine officers are trained here in navigation instrumentation, ship maneuvering, ship management, and communications. The Academy also administers a Federal assistance program for maritime academies in California, Maine, Massachusetts, Michigan, New York, and Texas.

* Vessel Operating Aid

Office of Maritime Aids
Maritime Administration
U.S. Department of Transportation
400 7th Street, SW
Washington, DC 20590 (202) 366-0364

The Maritime Administration pays a subsidy to U.S. Shipping companies to offset the higher cost of operating under U.S. flags. To qualify for the subsidy, a vessel operator must be a U.S. citizen who owns or leases ships to compete in foreign trade. Operators must additionally be fiscally sound and agree to make their ships available to the government in the event of a military emergency. Call or write MARAD for more information.

* War Risk Insurance for Ships

Marine Insurance Division
Office of Trade and Analysis and Insurance
Maritime Administration
U.S. Department of Transportation
400 7th Street, SW, Room 8121
Washington, DC 20590 (202) 366-4161

The War Risk Insurance Program insures operators and seamen against losses from hostile action if commercial insurance is not available to them. The program covers loss of life and materials due to war or nuclear detonation.

* Waterways Traffic Regulation

Commander G-NSP
Vessel Traffic Services Branch
Office of Navigation Safety and Waterways Services
U.S. Coast Guard
U.S. Department of Transportation
2100 2nd St., SW, Room 3202
Washington, DC 20593-0001 (202) 267-1539

To ensure the safe and orderly passage of vessels, cargo, and people, Vessel Traffic Services in major ports oversee the movement of vessels and install necessary safety equipment. Traffic is monitored closely during hazardous conditions and bad weather. To locate the Vessel Traffic Service nearest you, contact the branch listed above or your local Coast Guard office.

Be patient. If any phone number is incorrect, call (area code) 555-1212 and request the new listing.

Business and Industry

Mining

Given the central importance of minerals to the modern economy, the Federal government closely monitors the position of the U.S. with respect to key minerals. The central locus of information in the U.S. government on mine and mineral related matters is the U.S. Department of the Interior's Bureau of Mines. Another good source of information is the U.S. Geological Survey. With the creation of the U.S. Department of Energy in 1977, many policy decisions on the mining of energy producing materials such as coal and uranium and on the drilling for oil and natural gas moved largely to Energy. The Office of Surface Mining and Reclamation in the U.S. Department of the Interior can provide you with information on surface mining for coal and environmental reclamation.

* Abandoned Mine Land Reclamation

Office of Surface Mining Reclamation and Enforcement
U.S. Department of the Interior
1951 Constitution Ave., NW
Washington, DC 20240
(202) 208-5365

The surface mining law requires that operators pay a reclamation fee for each ton of coal produced. These fees are deposited with the U.S. Treasury in a fund called the Abandoned Mine Reclamation Fund and are used to reclaim sites that were mined and left unreclaimed before the surface mining law was enacted in 1977. Fifty percent of the fees collected in a state that has approved reclamation and regulatory programs is returned to that state for use in its reclamation program. The other fifty percent is the Federal share. This portion is used by the Office of Surface Mining Reclamation and Enforcement to address public health and safety emergencies caused by past mining practices, and to fund high-priority reclamation projects in non-program states. The Office of Surface Mining also publishes a booklet entitled *Abandoned Mine Reclamation: Ten Years of Progress*, which details the progress of the program. To obtain your state contact for the abandoned mine land reclamation program and for a copy of the *Abandoned Mine Reclamation* booklet, contact the office above.

* Bureau of Land Management: Mineral Publications

Bureau of Land Management (BLM)
U.S. Department of the Interior
18th and C Streets, NW
Washington, DC 20240
(202) 208-3435

The BLM has several free publications dealing with mining and minerals. The following is a partial list of publications.

Energy and Mineral Resources on Public Lands
Mining Claims and Sites on Public Domain Lands
Federal Coal Management Report
Mineral Revenues: The 1989 Report on Receipts from Federal and Indian Lands

* Bureau of Mines Educational Publications

Office of Public Affairs
Bureau of Mines
U.S. Department of the Interior
810 7th St., NW
Washington, DC 20241
(202) 501-9650

The Bureau of Mines outreach efforts are targeted at both school age children as well as adults. For elementary school children, the Bureau of Mines materials package includes a coloring book entitled *Minerals and You*. A three part package consisting of an introductory mineral information text, a coloring book, and a booklet of teacher-student activities. For adults, the Bureau of Mines publishes a 70 page book entitled *Minerals in 1991*, which profiles 34 minerals and discusses the importance of minerals to the U.S. economy.

* Bureau of Mines Field Facilities

Bureau of Mines
U.S. Department of the Interior
810 7th St., NW
Washington, DC 20241
(202) 501-9650

Alabama
Tuscaloosa Research Center, University of Alabama Campus, P.O. Box L, Tuscaloosa, AL 35486; (205) 759-9474

Alaska
Alaska Field Operations Center, 3301 C St., Suite 325, Anchorage, AK 99501; (907) 271-2454

Colorado
Intermountain Field Operations Center, P.O. Box 25086, Building 20, Denver Federal Center, Denver, CO 80225; (303) 236-0421

Minerals Availability Field Office, Building 20, Denver Federal Center, Denver, CO 80225; (303) 236-5200

Denver Research Center, P.O. Box 25086, Building 20, Denver Federal Center, Denver, CO 80225; (303) 236-0697

Minnesota
Twin Cities Research Center, 5629 Minnehaha Ave. S., Minneapolis, MN 55417; (612) 725-4610

Missouri
Rolla Research Center, P.O. Box 280, 1300 Bishop Ave., Rolla, MO 65401; (314) 364-3169

Nevada
Reno Research Center, 1605 Evans Ave., Reno, NV 89512; (702) 334-6610

Oregon
Research Center, 1450 Queen Ave., SW, Albany, OR 97321; (503) 967-5893

Pennsylvania
Pittsburgh Research Center, Cochrans Mill Rd, P.O. Box 18070, Pittsburgh, PA 15236; (412) 892-6601

Texas
Helium Field Operations, 1100 South Fillmore, Amarillo, TX 79101; (806) 376-2602

Utah
Salt Lake City Research Center, 729 Arapeen Dr., Salt Lake City, UT 84108; (801) 524-6100

Washington
Spokane Research Center, E 315 Montgomery Ave., Spokane, WA 99207; (509) 484-1610

Western Field Operations Center, E. 360 Third Ave., Spokane, WA 99202; (509) 353-2712

* Minerals Management Service Field Offices

Atlantic Region
381 Elden St., Suite 1109, Herndon, VA 22070-4817; (703) 787-1113

Be patient. If any phone number is incorrect, call (area code) 555-1212 and request the new listing.

Mining

Alaska Region
949 E. 36th Ave., Suite 604, Anchorage, AK 99508-4302; (907) 261-4070

Gulf of Mexico Region
1201 Elmwood Park Blvd., New Orleans, LA 70123-2394; (504) 736-2595

Pacific Region
1340 W. 6th St., Los Angeles, CA 90017; (213) 894-3389

Rocky Mountains
Royalty Management Program Accounting Center and Central Service Center, 6th Ave. and Kipling St., Bldg. 85, Lakewood, CO 80225; (303) 231-3162

* Bureau of Mines Programs

Office of Public Affairs
Bureau of Mines
810 7th Street, NW
Washington, DC 20241 (202) 501-9650

The Bureau of Mines publishes the booklet *The Minerals Source*, which discusses different programs os the Bureau of Mines. It is available free from the public affairs office.

* Bureau of Mines State Activities Directory

Chief, Office of State Activities
Bureau of Mines
U.S. Department of the Interior
810 7th St., NW
Washington, DC 20241 (202) 501-9650

The following offices are sources of information on state mineral activity:

Alaska
Regional Office of State Activities, Bureau of Mines, U.S. Department of the Interior, P.O. Box 20550, Juneau, AK 99802-0550; (907) 364-2111

Denver
Regional Office of State Activities, Bureau of Mines, U.S. Department of the Interior, Denver Federal Center, Bldg. #20, P.O. Box 25086, Denver, CO 80225-0086; (303) 236-0435

Pittsburgh
Regional Office of State Activities, Bureau of Mines, U.S. Department of the Interior, Cochrans Mill Rd., P.O. Box 18070, Pittsburgh, PA 15236-0070; (412) 892-6601

Reno
Regional Office of State Activities, Bureau of Mines, U.S. Department of the Interior, Reno Research Center, 1605 Evans Ave., Reno, NV 89512-2295; (702) 334-6610

Spokane
Regional Office of State Activities, Bureau of Mines, U.S. Department of the Interior, E. 360 Third Ave., Spokane, WA 99202-1413; (509) 353-2720

Tuscaloosa
Regional Office of State Activities, Bureau of Mines, U.S. Department of the Interior, University of Alabama Campus, P.O. Box L, University, AL 35486-9777; (205) 759-9465; (205) 759-9466

Tucson
Regional Office of State Activities, Bureau of Mines, U.S. Department of the Interior, 210 E. 7th St., Tucson, AZ 85705-8454; (602) 629-5111

Twin Cities
Regional Office of State Activities, Bureau of Mines, U.S. Department of the Interior, 5629 Minnehaha Ave., S., Minneapolis, MN 55417-3099; (612) 725-4534; (612) 725-4535

* Bureau of Mines Publications

Superintendent of Documents
Government Printing Office
Washington, DC 20420 (202) 783-3238

Publications of the Bureau of Mines is an annotated bibliography of new publications by the Bureau of Mines. Included in this monthly flyer are listings

of free publications, open file reports, and outside publications available concerning the mineral industry. The annual subscription price is $19, and the single copy price is $1.75 (S/N 724-004-00000-8).

* Bureau of Reclamation Regional Offices

Bureau of Mines
U.S. Department of Interior
18th and C Sts, NW
Washington, DC 20240 (202) 208-4662

Here are the regional offices which enforce strip mining and reclamation laws; also listed are the Headquarters contacts for these regions:

Lower Colorado Region
Box 61470, Boulder City, NV 89006; (702) 293-8420; DC contact (202) 208-6269

Mid-Pacific Region
2800 Cottage Way, Sacramento, CA 95825; (916) 978-4919; DC contact (202) 208-6274

Pacific Northwest Region
Box 043, 550 W. Fort St., Boise, ID 83724; (208) 334-1938; DC contact (202) 208-6271

Upper Colorado Region
Box 11568, 125 S. State St., Salt Lake City, UT 84147; (801) 524-6477; DC contact (202) 208-6751

Great Plains Region
Box 36900, 316 N. 26th St., Billings, MT 59107; (406) 657-6218; DC contact (202) 208-6267

Contact headquarters for information and addresses for international project/overseas offices in Brazil, Egypt, Guam, Pakistan, Saudi Arabia, and Saipan.

* Byproduct Metals Study

Research Division, Bureau of Mines
U.S. Department of the Interior
810 7th St., NW
Washington, DC 20241 (202) 501-9290

A new study, *Byproduct Output from Domestic Primary Copper, Lead, and Zinc Industries*, examined the collective role of byproducts with regard to the economics of mineral production, and their individual significance in terms of dollar values, end uses and strategic considerations. The study also analyzes circumstances that have affected the competitiveness and structure of the copper, lead, and zinc industries and the factors that impact byproduct availability, including production capacity at domestic smelters and refineries, process technology, changing sources and composition of ores, foreign ownership, and byproduct demand and price. Call or write for information on obtaining the study.

* Census of Minerals Industries Bibliography

Superintendent of Documents
Government Printing Office
Washington, DC 20402 (202) 783-3238

The Census of Mineral Industries, 1987, Geographic Series is featured in this bibliography, as well as the *Industry Series* subscription service.

* Claims on Federal Lands

Energy and Mineral Resources
Bureau of Land Management
U.S. Department of the Interior
18th and C Sts., NW
Washington, DC 20240 (202) 208-4201

The brochure, *Staking a Mining Claim on Federal Lands*, describes the procedure you would follow to stake a mining claim on public lands. Claims are granted to individuals for particular pieces of land, valuable for specific mineral deposits. Questions concerning the definition of a mining claim and the technicalities of recording and maintaining mining claims are also covered.

* Coal Ash Producers

American Coal Ash Association (ACAA)

Be patient. If any phone number is incorrect, call (area code) 555-1212 and request the new listing.

Business and Industry

1913 Eye St., NW, 6th Floor
Washington, DC 20006 (202) 659-2303

ACAA has been representing producers and marketers of coal combustion products (some 68 at present) as well as coal companies and suppliers of ash-related equipment and services as a "resource conservation and recovery" association since 1968. ACAA's technology development program attempts to protect and increase the use of coal ash by developing a technological base for coal ash as a commercially viable and environmentally sound alternative to virgin materials. The ACAA also collects information for members and end users of coal ash. Contact ACAA for more information.

* Coal Mining and Environmental Protection

Office of Public Affairs
Office of Surface Mining Reclamation and Enforcement
1951 Constitution Avenue, NW
Washington, DC 20240 (202) 208-2553

This office works to protect people and the environment from the side-effects of coal mining, while continuing to regulate coal mining. Lands that were affected by past coal mining operations must be repaired if left unreclaimed or abandoned. Technical assistance is provided to states so that they can perform their responsibilities under the surface mining law. State personnel are trained in the technical aspects of surface mining, such as soil compaction, revegetation, and groundwater hydrology, so that they can better enforce regulations.

* Coal Mining Research

Bureau of Mines
Research Division
U.S. Department of the Interior
810 7th St., NW
Washington, DC 20241 (202) 501-9274

The Bureau of Mines is currently researching and evaluating a system for teleoperated highwall coal mining. Teleoperations for mining is computer based, remote control of mining machinery from a protected operator compartment located distantly from the mine site, so that sensory information about the mining operation cannot be obtained directly. Video, sound, and other relevant data are gathered through sensors and transmitted electronically to the operators location. This technology offers the possibility to dramatically increase worker safety. For more information, contact the research division.

* Critical Minerals Assessment

Bureau of Mines
Research Division
U.S. Department of the Interior
810 7th St., NW
Washington, DC 20241 (202) 501-9274

The Bureau evaluates and catalogues potential mineral resources, especially those on federal land, to assist lawmakers and land use managers in making decisions. It has also been a major participant in a joint task force investigating placer resources in the U.S. Exclusive Economic Zone off the coast of Oregon.

* Deep Seabed Mining

Ocean Minerals and Energy Division
National Ocean Service
National Oceanic and Atmospheric Administration
U.S. Department of Commerce
1825 Connecticut Ave., NW
Washington, DC 20235 (202) 606-4121

Extensive information is available on deep seabed mining, which includes the annual report to Congress and an updated environmental assessment of NOAA deep seabed mining licensees' exploration plans. The Office's current focus is on exploration for Manganese nodules on the ocean floor. No mining permits for Manganese nodules on the ocean floor have been issued. This office can provide you with information regarding the research conducted concerning the environmental impact of the mining, as well as information on the regulations and licenses. The *1989* and *1991 Annual Reports to Congress* are excellent places to begin your information search. They are available free.

* Energy and Mineral Resources

Office of Energy and Marine Geology
U.S. Geological Survey
National Center, MS 915

Reston, VA 22092 (703) 648-6472

Investigations of the nature, extent, and origin of the Nation's coal, oil gas, oil shale, uranium, and geothermal resources are basic to this office's research efforts. Acquired data are placed in computerized databases, such as the National Coal Resources Data System.

* Environmental Mining Research

Environmental Technology Division
Bureau of Mines
U.S. Department of the Interior
810 7th St., NW
Washington, DC 20241 (202) 501-9271

Researchers at the Bureau of Mines are working on low-cost ways to deal with the problem of acid drainage at abandoned mines. They are developing computer programs to predict potential drainage at new mines. The Bureau's environmental research also addresses the problem of solid waste disposal and soil and water contaminated by metals. Technologies are developed that will reduce or remove the threats that these wastes pose.

* Films on the Mining Industry

Office of Technology Transfer
Bureau of Mines
U.S. Department of the Interior
810 7th Street, NW
Washington, DC 20241 (202) 501-9652

This office publishes a listing of films and videos on topics related to the mineral industry. Topics include safer coal mining equipment, mine shaft smoke and fire protection system, and a retractable diamond bit system for core drilling, among others. All of the films and videos may be purchased or can be borrowed free of charge.

* Gold Prospecting

Publications Department
Bureau of Mines
U.S. Department of the Interior
810 7th Street., NW
Washington, DC 20241 (202) 208-9650

The publications department of the Bureau of Mines distributes the free booklet, *How To Mine and Prospect for Gold.* The booklet is no longer in print, but the Bureau of Mines can send you a photocopy. It is *Information Circular 8517.*

* Indian Lands and Minerals

Office of Trust and Economic Development
Bureau of Indian Affairs
U.S. Department of the Interior
18th and C Sts., NW
Washington, DC 20240 (202) 208-5831

This office manages some 53 million acres of land held in trust by the United States for Indians. Tribes are helped in protecting their lands and in developing their forest, water, mineral, and energy resources.

* International Mineral Data

Superintendent of Documents
Government Printing Office
Washington, DC 20402 (202) 783-3238

The *Minerals Yearbook, 1985: Volume 111 (Area Reports: International)* contains the latest available mineral data from more than 150 foreign countries and discusses the importance of minerals to the economies of these nations. It reviews the international minerals industry in general and its relationship to the world economy. 1987 (S/N 024-004-02179-9, $36).

* International Minerals Research

Information and Analysis Division
Bureau of Mines
U.S. Department of the Interior
810 7th St., NW
Washington, DC 20241 (202) 501-9660

The Bureau of Mines continually assesses the world mineral situation as it impacts the United States. The U.S. Department of State regional resource officers report regularly from 10 major minerals - and mineral producing

Be patient. If any phone number is incorrect, call (area code) 555-1212 and request the new listing.

Mining

countries: Australia, Belgium, Brazil, Chile, India, Indonesia, Japan, Mexico, South Africa, and Venezuela. As part of its China studies program, the bureau in 1990 published *The Iron and Steel Industry of China.* The Bureau of Mines also closely coordinates with the United States Trade Representative on trade matters, particularly relating to Canada, Mexico, and the European Community.

* Land Management Annual Report

Bureau of Land Management (BLM)
U.S. Department of the Interior
18th and C Streets, NW
Washington, DC 20240 (202) 208-3435

The BLM *Annual Report* contains information on current BLM programs in the areas of land and mineral management. The 1989-1992 BLM report contains an excellent discussion of surface mining management initiatives. The report is available free from BLM.

* Materials Research: Wear and Corrosion

Research Division
Bureau of Mines
U.S. Department of the Interior
810 7th St., NW
Washington, DC 20241 (202) 501-9290

Advanced materials research is being conducted to eliminate wear and corrosion within the minerals industry through the use of ceramics, high-performance plastics, high-tech metals and alloys, and composites. Bureau scientists are also developing new coatings to protect equipment from the heat, corrosive chemicals, and abrasive materials found in mills, smelters, refineries, and furnaces.

* Metals and Mining Producers

American Mining Congress (AMC)
1920 N St., NW
Suite 300
Washington, DC 20036 (202) 861-2800

The American Mining Congress is an industry association of producers of metals, coal industrial and agricultural minerals; manufacturers of mining and mineral processing machinery, equipment and supplies; and mining engineering firms. AMC publishes the *American Mining Congress Journal,* a monthly journal which focuses on mining issues and policy and is available for $30 per year. AMC can also put you in touch with members who can provide you with detailed information on most aspects of the mining industry.

* Mine Map Repositories

Office of Public Affairs
Bureau of Mines
U.S. Department of the Interior
810 7th Street, NW
Washington, DC 20241 (202) 501-9650

The Mine Map Repositories were established in 1970 and are responsible for collecting and archiving mine maps both east and west of the Mississippi River and in Alaska. The brochure, *Mine Map Repositories,* provides information and statistics on the mine map repository facilities of the Office of Surface Mining Reclamation and Enforcement. The five repositories are listed with their addresses and phone numbers. They are located in Pittsburgh, PA, Wilkes-Barre, PA, Denver, CO, Spokane, WA, and Juneau, AK.

* Mine Maps/Mine Companies Property Ownership

Division of Program Information and Analysis
Bureau of Mines
U.S. Department of the Interior
810 7th St., NW
Washington, DC 20241 (202) 501-9650

Valuable information is available from the mine maps available through the mine map repositories of the Office of Surface Mining Reclamation and Enforcement. Mine and company names, water sources, property ownership of adjoining companies and towns, latitudes and longitudes, coal outcrop seam designations, openings and emergency exits of mines, and gas and power lines are some of the topics covered. This information can be useful to local developers, engineering firms, and energy interests, as well as private citizens.

* Mine Safety and Health Administration (MSHA)

Office of Public Affairs
U.S. Department of Labor
4015 Wilson Blvd., Room 601
Arlington, VA 22203 (703) 235-1452

The Labor Department's Mine Safety and Health Administration (MSHA) helps to reduce deaths, injuries and illnesses in the nations mines with a variety of activities and programs. The agency develops and enforces safety and health rules applying to all U.S. mines, helps mine operators who have special compliance problems, and makes available technical, educational and other types of assistance. MSHA's authority derives from the 1977 Federal Mine Safety and Health Act. The Office of Public Affairs can provide you with information on MSHA programs including: injury statistics; safety, health, and education training and enforcement; technical assistance; and legislation. MSHA has technical support offices in Pittsburgh and Denver.

* Mineral Commodity Summaries 1992

Minerals Information Office
Bureau of Mines/U.S. Geological Survey
U.S. Department of the Interior
18th and C Sts., MS 2647-MIB
Room 2647
Washington, DC 20240 (202) 208-5520

Mineral Commodity Summaries 1992 lists the statistics available for 82 commodities, including domestic production and uses; salient statistics - United States; recycling; import sources; tariff; depletion allowance; government stockpile; events and trends; world mine production, reserves and reserve base; world resources; and substitutes. The expert's name and phone number of each report is also listed.

* Mineral Commodity Information

Minerals Information Office
Bureau of Mines/U.S. Geological Survey
U.S. Department of the Interior
18th and C Sts., MS 2647-MIB
Room 2647
Washington, DC 20240 (202) 208-5520

The Minerals Information Office is staffed by mineral experts who distribute a wide variety of mineral-related information and publications to meet and support the needs of the public, as well as government agencies and the scientific and industrial sectors. The staff provides information on the most current as well as past published reports pertaining to minerals, mining, processing, and research, as well as updated listings of current reports.

* Mineral Deposits Database

Minerals Information Office
Bureau of Mines/U.S. Geological Survey
U.S. Department of the Interior
18th and C Sts., MS 2647-MIB
Room 2647
Washington, DC 20240 (202) 208-5520

The Bureau of Mines has three mining databases. The *Personal Computer Advanced Deposit Information Tracking System Mineral Deposit Data Base* contains information on 3,000 domestic and foreign (market economy countries) mining operations, including operation data (name, company, locations, etc.) and operation status (operation type, processing and milling methods, capacity, etc.). The database covers 34 critical and strategic commodities, representing those deposits most significant in terms of value and tonnage. The *Automated Minerals Information System (AMIS)* is an integrated system that includes information on mineral production, capacity, consumption, industrial stocks, imports, exports, reserves and recycled materials. Information on personal computer access for AMIS is available at (202) 501-9750. The *Minerals Industry Locator System (MILS)* contains nearly 200,000 records of mineral occurrences, identified and described in terms of geographic, geologic, ownership, and production information. Call for information on accessing these databases.

* Mineral Deposits Distribution

Mineral Resources
Geologic Inquiries
U.S. Geological Survey
907 National Center
Reston, VA 22092 (703) 648-4383

Be patient. If any phone number is incorrect, call (area code) 555-1212 and request the new listing.

Business and Industry

The U.S. Geological Survey assesses the distribution of the mineral resources of the United States, especially strategic and critical commodities, and studies the processes that control the occurrence of mineral deposits. New techniques and methods useful in the search for these resources are continually being developed.

* Minerals on Federal Lands

Bureau of Land Management (BLM)
U.S. Department of the Interior
18th and C Streets NW
Washington, DC 20240
(202) 208-4537

The BLM regulates and manages the exploration, development and extraction of minerals and energy sources on Federal Land and Native American lands in coordination with other Federal, State, and Local agencies. Its role is to balance the need for these resources while ensuring protection of the environment.

* Mineral Policy Analysis

Policy Analysis
Information and Analysis Division
Bureau of Mines
U.S. Department of the Interior
810 7th St., NW
Washington, DC 20241
(202) 501-9734

Bureau economists prepare special studies that analyze issues involving minerals in the United States. An ongoing assessment of the Nation's "mineral position" is conducted. Specialists examine factors that affect the competitiveness of the U.S. mineral industry and its contribution to the Nation's economy. Environmental regulations are also evaluated as to their impact on U.S. mineral production.

* Mineral Position of the United States

Bureau of Mines
U.S. Department of the Interior
810 7th St., NW
Washington, DC 20241
(202) 501-9650

The Mineral Position of the United States is an annual report published by the Department of the Interior under the Mining and Minerals Policy Act of 1970. It contains a detailed analysis and statistics for key mineral industries such as steel, copper, aluminum, and gold as well as discussing government initiatives related to mineral issues. These initiatives include new programs as well as international agreements that influence the U.S. mineral position. The final section of the report discusses research and new technologies in the mineral industry. The 1988 edition of the report is the latest available. It is free from the public affairs office.

* Mineral Processing Research

Minerals and Materials Science
Bureau of Mines
U.S. Department of the Interior
810 7th St., NW
Washington, DC 20241
(202) 501-9274

This office looks for ways to improve mineral processing operations by cutting costs and recovering more minerals contained in ores. A variety of processing methods are studied, including crushing, grinding, flotation, smelting, solvent extraction, and leaching. Their research also includes long-range efforts to apply high technology to mineral processing.

* Mineral Production and Consumption

Information and Analysis Division
Bureau of Mines
U.S. Department of the Interior
810 7th St., NW
Washington, DC 20241
(202) 501-9365

The Bureau of Mines collects information about minerals from U.S. mining companies and mineral processing plants. Mineral production and consumption is monitored throughout the world through contacts with foreign governments, U.S. embassies, international publications, and visits to mines overseas. The Bureau employs 11 state mineral specialists through cooperative data collection agreements with the states. Three regional field offices and nine research centers also gather information. The data is then made available to the public via reports, books, and computer disks.

* Mineral Resource Films

Audiovisual Library
Office of Public Affairs
Bureau of Mines
U.S. Department of the Interior
810 7th St., NW
Washington, DC 20241
(202) 501-9652

This office's brochure, *Mineral Resource Films*, lists information on borrowing and scheduling films and videocassettes, along with National distribution centers. Films available cover such topics as copper, cast iron, silver, mine fire control, the minerals challenge, wealth out of waste, tungsten, lead, boron, chromium, gold, and platinum. Recently released titles include *Out of the Rock*, *Call me Can*, and *Aluminum Recycling*.

* Mineral Resources

Mineral Resources
Geologic Inquiries
U.S. Geological Survey
907 National Center
Reston, VA 22092
(703) 648-4383

The U.S.Geological Survey assesses the distribution of the mineral resources of the United States, especially strategic and critical commodities, and studies the processes that control the occurrence of mineral deposits. New techniques and methods useful in the search for these resources are continually being developed.

* Mineral Technology Transfer

Office of Technology Transfer
Bureau of Mines
U.S. Department of the Interior
810 7th St., NW
Washington, DC 20241
(202) 501-9306

The Bureau of Mines supports an active technology and information transfer program. The objective of the program is to encourage the use by the minerals industry of valuable research and minerals data. Industry is kept informed of developments though exhibits, briefing, seminars, special workshops, patent licenses, films, and *Technology News*. Call for more information.

* Minerals and Mining Bibliography

Superintendent of Documents
Government Printing Office (GPO)
Washington, DC 20402
(202) 783-3238

Bureau of Mines publications and mineral industry publications are featured. Books describing the coal mining industry, gold availability, and the wilderness mineral potential are included. Also featured is the *Bureau of Mines List of Publications and Articles*: 1985-1989 SP-391. List number at GPO - 024-004-02218-3.

* Minerals: Data, Industries, and Technology

Publication Distribution
Bureau of Mines
U.S. Department of the Interior
Cochrans Mills Rd.
P.O. Box 18070
Pittsburgh, PA 15236
(412) 892-4338

The Bureau of Mines publishes several reports of investigations and information circulars that are free of charge to those interested in mineral research. *Mineral Industry Surveys* are published monthly, quarterly, and annually, presenting data on various minerals and metals. Reprints from *Minerals Yearbook 1987* are available and report on the mineral industry in the United States and abroad. If documents are unavailable here, they will refer you to the appropriate headquarters office.

* Minerals of Critical and Strategic Importance

Research Division
Bureau of Mines
U.S. Department of the Interior
810 7th St., NW
Washington, DC 20241
(202) 501-9290

An emphasis within the Bureau of Mines' Research Division is reducing the Nation's dependence on imports for certain minerals that have key defense and industrial applications. The Bureau is developing ways to recover strategic and

Be patient. If any phone number is incorrect, call (area code) 555-1212 and request the new listing.

Mining

critical minerals from mineral processing wastes and to recycle these minerals. Key minerals of this type include cobalt, chromium, manganese, and platinum.

* Minerals on Public Lands - Statistics

Bureau of Land Management (BLM)
U.S. Department of the Interior
18th and C Streets, NW
Washington, DC 20240   (202) 208-3435

The BLM publication *Public Land Statistics 1990*, includes statistics on oil, gas, coal and other minerals on public lands. It is available free from BLM.

* Minerals Management Service Field Offices

Bureau of Mines
U.S. Department of Interior
1951 Constitution Avenue, NW
Washington, DC 20240   (202) 208-4662

U.S. Department of Interior has the following regional offices:

Atlantic Region
381 Elden St., Suite 1109, Herndon, VA 22070-4817; (703) 787-1113

Alaska Region
949 E. 36th Ave., Suite 604, Anchorage, AK 99508-4302; (907) 261-4070

Gulf of Mexico Region
1201 Elmwood Park Blvd., New Orleans, LA 70123-2394; (504) 736-2595

Pacific Region
1340 W. 6th St., Los Angeles, CA 90017; (213) 894-3389

Rocky Mountains
Royalty Management Program Accounting Center and Central Service Center, 6th Ave. and Kipling St., Bldg. 85, Lakewood, CO 80225; (303) 231-3162

* Minerals Research

Research Division, Bureau of Mines
U.S. Department of the Interior
810 7th St., NW
Washington, DC 20241-0001   (202) 501-9290

Research is being conducted here to find cheaper, more efficient ways of mining and processing minerals. Robotics and advanced automation is also being researched for use in mining operations. Immediate problems in the industry are also studied, such as improvement of equipment and procedures.

* Minerals Today

Bureau of Mines
U.S. Department of the Interior
810 7th St., NW
Washington, DC 20241   (202) 501-9650

In 1990 the Bureau of Mines launched a new bimonthly magazine entitled *Minerals Today*. The magazine covers the latest developments, trends, and issues related to minerals and materials. The regular feature "Mineral Indicators" helps industry analysts track the flow of minerals by presenting statistics on production, supplies, and consumption. Call the public affairs office for ordering information.

* Minerals Yearbooks Bibliography

Superintendent of Documents
Government Printing Office
Washington, DC 20402   (202) 783-3238

Yearbooks on metals and minerals are listed, as well as reports on the domestic and international industry. Free.

* Mine Safety

Health, Safety, and Mining Technology
Bureau of Mines
U.S. Department of the Interior
810 7th St., NW
Washington, DC 20241   (202) 501-9321

The Bureau is studying ways to improve mine safety and to eliminate the health risks of mining. One of the areas of emphasis is finding ways to reduce a miner's exposure to respirable dust, which causes black lung and other respiratory diseases. Studies in safety precautions help companies build more stable mines with better roof support systems and more efficiently detect flammable gases and ignition sources. Research on automation and robotics to do the more hazardous jobs is also being done.

* Mines Library

Bureau of Mines
U.S. Department of the Interior
810 7th St., NW
Washington, DC 20241   (202) 501-9756

The Bureau of Mines' Library contains a wealth of technical information involving the mineral industry. Reference librarians are available to answer questions by phone or mail. Topics include state and county mineral data, mineral supply and demand analysis, congressional reports pertaining to minerals, oil and gas reports, and market studies. Free mineral publications published by the Bureau of Mines are also available. The hours of the library are 7:45 a.m. to 4:15 p.m., Monday through Friday.

* Mines Technology Transfer

Office of Technology Transfer
Bureau of Mines
U.S. Department of the Interior
810 7th St., NW
Washington, DC 20241   (202) 501-9323

The Technology Transfer Group distributes information on mining industry issues in many ways. *Technology Transfer* is a newsletter announcing the latest technology and research in mining. Free conferences are also held around the country on a variety of topics, such as advanced materials research and new technology for minerals. To be placed on the mailing list, contact the office above.

* Mining Research Update

Public Affairs
Bureau of Mines
U.S. Department of the Interior
810 7th St., NW
Washington, DC 20241   (202) 501-9323

The Bureau of Mines publication *Research 91* is an invaluable source of information on the latest Bureau of Mines research work. The publication highlights the latest developments in research, as well as updating program information. It also has a reference bibliography on all aspects of mining. It is available free from the Bureau of Mines.

* Multinational Corporations in Mining

Office of Mineral Commodities
Bureau of Mines
U.S. Department of the Interior
810 7th St., NW
Washington, DC 20241   (202) 501-9449

An expert in the office of mineral commodities, Mr. Balazik, can discuss the results of a major study he did for the Bureau of Mines on Multinational Corporations in the Mining industry. He examined both U.S. ownership and interest in foreign mining operations as well as foreign ownership and interest in American mining operations. The information presented in the study is based on a review of over 2200 mineral properties operated by more than 400 companies in 80 countries. The study has not yet been published, but Mr. Balazik will share the results of his study and can aid you in your research in this area.

* Offshore Geologic Resources

Geologic Inquiries
U.S. Geological Survey
907 National Center
Reston, VA 22092   (703) 648-4383

Using remotely sensed data, including sidescan sonar and other geophysical surveys, and direct sampling, the USGS studies the geology and assesses the potential mineral and energy resources of the continental margins and the Exclusive Economic Zone of the United States (200 miles from the coastline) and its territories. Also identified are geologic features that must be considered in the selection of sites for offshore drilling platforms and pipelines.

Be patient. If any phone number is incorrect, call (area code) 555-1212 and request the new listing.

Business and Industry

* Offshore Minerals Leasing and Management

Offshore Minerals Management
Mineral Management Service
U.S. Department of the Interior
18th and C Sts., NW
Washington, DC 20240 (202) 208-3530

The Mineral Management Service leases the rights to explore and develop oil and gas on Federal lands of the continental shelf. The "shelf" is made up of the submerged offshore areas lying seaward of the territorial sea to a depth of 200 meters (656 feet) and beyond that area to that depth which allows for mineral exploration. The brochure, *Leasing Energy Resources on the Outer Continental Shelf*, explains the leasing procedure and gives a history of the program.

* Onshore Minerals Leases

Bureau of Land Management (BLM)
U.S. Department of the Interior
18th and C Streets, NW
Washington, DC 20240 (202) 208-4636

The BLM leases and sells onshore minerals. Its responsibilities include land use planning; issuance of leases; reworking and annual filing of mines claims; review of plans for exploration and development; and inspection, enforcement and productive verification of leases and mining operators to ensure compliance with approved claims.

* Regulatory Projects Coordination

Office of Regulatory Projects Coordination
Bureau of Mines
U.S. Department of the Interior
810 7th St., NW
Washington, DC 20241 (202) 501-9732

This office serves as a focal point in the bureau, identifying, monitoring, and assessing the impact of regulations as well as evolving regulatory issues of vital concern to the minerals industry. At present, the Office's primary concern remains the regulation of mining and mineral processing solid wastes. This office is a good source for conservation and environmental information on the mining industry.

* Surface Coal Mining Reclamation

Office of Surface Mining, Public Affairs
1951 Constitution Ave, NW
Washington, DC 20420 (202) 208-2553

While surface mining for coal is less costly than underground mining, it is also more destructive to the environment. In 1977 Congress passed the Surface Mining Control and Reclamation Act (SMCRA) to coordinate the Federal and State efforts to prevent further environmental destruction from surface mining. The law mandated an environmental protection program to establish standards and procedures for approving permits and inspecting current surface coal mining and reclamation operations. It also established a reclamation program for abandoned mine lands, funded by fees that operators pay on each ton of coal mined, to reclaim land and water resources adversely affected by pre-Act coal mining. *Surface Coal Mining Reclamation: 10 Years of Programs, 1977-1987* is a report detailing progress under the SMCRA. Also available is *Abandoned Mine Reclamation: 10 Years of Progress*, which describes programs in abandoned mine reclamation under SMCRA. Both are available free.

* Steel Research

Bureau of Mines
Research Division
U.S. Department of the Interior
810 7th St., NW
Washington, DC 20241 (202) 501-9274

The Bureau of Mines is working on research in the area of powder metallurgy which offers the potential for producing steel with 2 to 4 times greater tensile strength and higher temperature resistance than conventional steel. For information on this program, contact the research division.

* Strip Mining and Reclamation

Office of Public Affairs
Office of Surface Mining Reclamation and Enforcement
U.S. Department of Interior
1951 Constitution Avenue, NW

Washington, DC 20240 (202) 208-2553

This office works to protect people and the environment from the side-effects of coal mining, while continuing to regulate coal mining. Lands that were affected by past coal mining operations must be repaired if left unreclaimed or abandoned. Technical assistance is provided to states so that they can perform their responsibilities under the surface mining law. State personnel are trained in the technical aspects of surface mining, such as soil compaction, revegetation, and groundwater hydrology, so that they can better enforce regulations.

* Strip Mining Enforcement Offices

Office of Surface Mining Reclamation and Enforcement
U.S. Department of Interior
1951 Constitution Avenue, NW
Washington, DC 20240 (202) 208-2553

Albuquerque
625 Silver Ave., SW, Suite 310, Albuquerque, NM 87102; (505) 766-1486

Appalachia
1300 New Circle Rd, Lexington, KY 40504; (606) 233-2792

Ashland
Federal Bldg., Room 120, 1430 Greenup Ave., Ashland, KY 41101; (606) 324-2828

Beckley
101 Harper Park Dr., Beckley, WV 25801; (304) 255-5265

Birmingham
135 Gemeni Circle, Suite 215, Homewood, AL 35209; (205) 290-7282

Big Stone Gap
P.O. Box 1216, Big Stone Gap, VA 24219; (703) 523-4303

Casper
Federal Bldg., 100 East B St., Room 2128, Casper, WY 82601-1918; (307) 261-5776

Columbus
2242 S. Hamilton Rd., Columbus, OH 43232; (614) 866-0578

Chattanooga
900 Georgia Ave., Room 30, Chattanooga, TN 37402; (615) 752-5175

Charleston
603 Morris St., Charleston, WV 25301; (304) 347-7158

Denver
Bldg. 20, Room B2015, P.O. Box 25065, Denver CO 80225; (303) 236-0331

Eastern
Ten Parkway Center, Pittsburgh, PA 15220; (412) 937-2828

Harrisburg
Harrisburg Transportation Ctr., Third Fl., Suite 3C, 4th and Market Sts., Harrisburg, PA 17101; (717) 782-4036

Hazard
516 Village Lane, Hazard, KY 41701; (606) 439-5843

Indianapolis
Minton-Capehart Federal Bldg., 575 N. Penn St., Room 301, Indianapolis, IN 46204; (371) 226-6700

Johnstown
Penn Traffic Bldg., Room 20, 319 Washington St., Johnstown, PA 15901; (814) 533-4223

Kansas City
934 Wynadotte St., Room 500, Kansas City, MO 64105; (816) 374-6405

Knoxville
530 Gay St., Suite 500, Knoxville, TN 37902; (615) 673-4504

Lexington
340 Legion Dr., Suite 28, Lexington, KY 40504; (606) 233-2494

Mining

London
P.O. Box 1048, London, KY 40741; (606) 878-6440

Madisonville
100 YMCA Drive, Madisonville, KY 42431; (502) 825-4500

Morgantown
P.O. Box 886, Morgantown, WVA 26505; (304) 291-4004

Norris
P.O. Box 179, Norris, TN 37828; (615) 632-1730

Olympia
Columbia Commons, 3773 C Martin Way East, Suite 104, Olympia, WA 98506; (206) 753-9538

Pikesville
Division of Audit Management, First National Bank, Room 608B, 334 Main St., Pikesville, KY 41505; (606) 432-4123

Prestonburgh
P.O. Box 306, 2664 West Mountain Parkway, West Prestonburg, KY 41668; (606) 866-1391

Springfield
509 West Capitol Avenue, 2nd Fl., Springfield IL 62701; (217) 492-4495

Tulsa
5100 East Skelley Dr., Suite 550, Tulsa, OK 74135; (918) 581-6430

Wilkes-Barre
20 N. Penn. Ave., Suite 3323, Wilkes-Barre, PA 18701; (717) 826-6333

Western
1020 15th St., 2nd Fl., Brooks Towers, Denver, CO 80202; (303) 844-2459

* Surface Mining Information and Programs

Office of Public Affairs
Office of Surface Mining Reclamation and Enforcement
U.S. Department of Interior
1951 Constitution Avenue, NW
Washington, DC 20240 (202) 208-2553

The Office of Surface Mining *Annual Report* details OSM activities under the Surface Mining Control and Reclamation Act of 1977. The report discusses Regulatory enforcement of the SMCRA and aspects of the Abandoned Mine Land Program. It is available free from the Office of Public Affairs at OSM.

* U.S. Geological Survey History

U.S. Geological Survey - Public Affairs Office
12201 Sunrise Valley Drive
Reston, VA 22092 (703) 648-4660

The *U.S. Geological Survey 1879-1989* gives an overview of the history of USGS and its role in the development of public land, Federal science and mineral resources in the U.S. It is available free.

* U.S. Geological Survey Reports

U.S. Geological Survey (USGS) - Public Affairs Office
12201 Sunrise Valley Drive
Reston, VA 22092 (703) 648-4660

The USGS publishes reports on minerals, geography and cartography, water resources, and geology. The public affairs office has an index available of current reports and their availability.

Be patient. If any phone number is incorrect, call (area code) 555-1212 and request the new listing.

Business and Industry

General Transportation

The section details general sources of information on transportation with particular emphasis on safety related issues. The key government agencies dealing with transportation safety is the National Transportation Safety Board, which investigates all major transportation accidents. Within the U.S. Department of Transportation one finds safety offices in each of the major Administrations. In addition to these programs, the DOT National Highway Traffic Safety Administration works to promote automobile and highway safety.

* Accident Briefs (Non-major Accident Reports)

Public Inquiries Section
National Transportation Safety Board (NTSB)
490 L'Enfant Plaza East, SW
Washington, DC 20594 (202) 382-6735

Reports of accidents in brief or summary format are issued for all aviation accidents and for all non-major railroad, highway, pipeline, and marine accidents investigated by or for the NTSB, for which probable cause is determined. The accident reports are issued in a publication containing up to 200 individual reports, which identify the facts, conditions, circumstances, and probable cause for each accident. The publication may include other statistical data such as tabulations by type of accident, phase of operation, casual factors, and injuries. For information on ordering these publications, which are available for a fee, contact the office above.

* Accident Investigations

Office of Aviation Safety
National Transportation Safety Board (NTSB)
490 L'Enfant Plaza, SW
Washington, DC 20594 (202) 382-6610

Office of Surface Transportation Safety
National Transportation Safety Board (NTSB)
490 L'Enfant Plaza, SW
Washington, DC 20594 (202) 382-6800

The Bureaus of Accident Investigation and Field Operations investigate or cause to be investigated all aviation and selected surface transportation accidents and incidents; develop proposed probable cause(s) of accidents; formulate recommendations to minimize their recurrence; and prepare detailed reports for use by other government agencies, the Congress, the transportation industry, and the traveling public. The Bureau of Accident Investigation manages the investigations of major transportation accidents--those accidents for which multi-disciplinary teams (go-teams) are sent to the accident site. The Bureau of Field Operations manages the investigations of the smaller-scale accidents that are usually investigated by one person from the Safety Board. For more information, contact the appropriate office listed above.

* Accident Reports (Major)

Public Inquiries Section
National Transportation Safety Board (NTSB)
490 L'Enfant Plaza East, SW
Washington, DC 20594 (202) 382-6735

Detailed narrative reports which contain the facts, conditions, circumstances, analysis, conclusions, and probable cause of major aviation, railroad, highway, pipeline, and marine accident investigations are issued for all accidents which resulted in a major investigation. Major accident reports are issued irregularly and are available for a fee from the National Technical Information Service (NTIS). For information on ordering, contact the office above.

* Alaska Pipeline

Alaska Natural Gas Pipeline Project
Office of Pipeline Safety
Research and Special Programs Administration
U.S. Department of Transportation
400 7th Street, SW
Washington, DC 20590 (202) 366-4556

Contact this office for information about the plans, programs, policies, and regulation concerning the Alaska pipeline.

* Alternative Fuels Initiative

Office of Engineering
Federal Transportation Administration (FTA)
400 7th St., SW, Room 6431
Washington, DC 20590 (202) 366-0090

Since 1988, FTA's Office of Engineering has been involved in the effort to replace today's conventional fuels with cleaner-burning alternative fuels, such as methanol, ethanol, and compressed natural gas. For more information, contact the office at the above address.

* Appealing Transportation Licensing Decisions

Office of Administrative Law Judges
National Transportation Safety Board (NTSB)
490 L'Enfant Plaza East, SW
Washington, DC 20594 (202) 382-0650

This office provides the initial forum for the review of appeals from the suspension, amendment, modification, revocation, or denial of any operation certificate or license issued by the Secretary of Transportation under the Federal Aviation Act of 1958. The primary purpose of this function is to assure fair and impartial review when appeals are taken from safety enforcement certificate actions by the Administrator of the Federal Aviation Administration against airmen or certificate holders or from denials of pilot applications for airman medical certificates. For more information on the process involved, contact the office above.

* Automobile Fuel Economy

Motor Vehicle Requirements Division
Office of Market Incentives
Rulemaking
National Highway Traffic Safety Administration (NHTSA)
U.S. Department of Transportation
400 7th Street, SW, Room 5320
Washington, DC 20590 (202) 366-0846

NHTSA issues fuel economy standards and collects information on the technological and economic capabilities of automobile manufacturers to maximize fuel efficiency. Contact this office for information and referrals.

* Auto Safety Hotline

Office of Defects Investigation (NEF-10)
National Highway Traffic Safety Administration
U.S. Department of Transportation
400 7th Street, SW, Room 5326 (800) 424-9393
Washington, DC 20590 (202) 366-0123

This toll-free hotline is accessible in all 50 states, Puerto Rico, and the Virgin Islands. Consumers may call to report automobile safety problems or to request information on recalls, defects, investigations, child safety seats, tires, drunk driving, crash test results, seat belts, air bags, odometer tampering, and other related topics. Staff will also make referrals to state and other agencies. Also ask about the New Car Assessment Program (NCAP), which provides comparable data on the frontal crashworthiness of selected new vehicles.

General Transportation

* Aviation Accident Data on Computer Tape

Analysis and Data Division
National Transportation Safety Board (NTSB)
490 L'Enfant Plaza East, SW
Washington, DC 20594 (202) 382-6672

Computerized tapes containing public data on aircraft accidents are available. Contact the office above for information on ordering the tapes.

* Aviation Accident Investigation

Office of Aviation Safety
National Transportation Safety Board (NTSB)
490 L'Enfant Plaza East, SW
Washington, DC 20594 (202) 382-6610

The Board investigates all air carrier accidents, all in flight collisions, fatal general aviation accidents, and all air taxi/commuter accidents. The Board also participates in the investigation of major airline crashes overseas involving American carriers and US manufactured airliners. The Board also takes a broader approach in investigating accidents in order to improve preventive measures. The Office produces accident reports, recommendation letters on prevention, and statistical summaries. Call for information.

* Census Statistics in Transportation

Bureau of the Census
U.S. Department of Commerce
Washington, DC 20223 (301) 763-7039

Surveys of the transportation industry are currently taken at 5 year intervals in years ending in the number "2" or "7." The 1987 Census of Transportation included a *Truck Industry and Use Survey*, which reported on the characteristics and operational use of truck resources and other than those of the Federal, State, or local governments; ambulance; buses; motor homes; and off highway vehicles. The Census also included a *Census of Selected Transportation Industries*, which covered a wide range of industries and services. *Factfinder CFF-13* lists data available on the transportation industry. It is available from customer services at the Census Bureau for $.25.

* Certificate and License Appeals

Office of Administrative Law Judges
National Transportation Safety Board (NTSB)
490 L'Enfant Plaza East, SW
Washington, DC 20594 (202) 382-0650

The Safety Board serves as the "court of appeals" for any airman or mariner whenever certificate action is taken by the Federal Aviation Administrator or the U.S. Coast Guard Commandant. The Board's administrative law judges hear, consider, and issue initial decisions on appeals from FAA certificate actions taken under Section 602(b), 609 and 501(c) of the Federal Aviation Act of 1958, as amended. Judges' decisions may be appealed to the five-member Board by the airman or FAA. The Board's review of the appeal encompasses the transcripts of the proceeding, the judge's decision, and appeal briefs submitted by the parties. For more information, contact the office above.

* Consumer Liaison

Office of Public Interest Groups
Intergovernmental and Consumer Affairs
Governmental Affairs
Office of the Secretary of Transportation
U.S. Department of Transportation
400 7th Street, SW
Washington, DC 20590 (202) 366-1524

This office acts as a liaison between Congress, state and local governments, business and industry, and public interest groups to ensure that their needs are considered when Department policy decisions are made. Public and private organizations can contact this office to communicate needs and comment on DOT programs and regulations.

* Current Department of Transportation Programs

Office of Public Affairs (A-30)
Office of the Secretary of Transportation
U.S. Department of Transportation
400 7th Street, SW, Room 10413
Washington, DC 20590 (202) 366-5580

The U.S. Department of Transportation Annual Report is an excellent place to find information on current US transportation programs. Included in the report is a summary of program initiatives as well as a breakdown by specific administrations such as Federal Highway Administration, Federal Aviation Administration, Federal Railroad Administration, and Maritime Administration. Also included are summary statistics for transportation programs. It is available free from the public affairs office.

* Economic Analysis of Transportation Policy

Office of Economics (P-30)
Policy and International Affairs
Office of the Secretary of Transportation
U.S. Department of Transportation
400 7th Street, SW, Room 10305
Washington, DC 20590 (202) 366-4416

Staff in this office analyze transportation policy issues to assess their economic and institutional implications. Studies focus on energy and environmental concerns, safety, the handicapped, user charges, and Federal assistance. Contact this office to determine what reports are available and how to obtain them.

* Economic Studies of Transit Industry

Industry, Economics and Finance Division (P-37)
Office of Economics
Policy and International Affairs
Office of the Secretary of Transportation
U.S. Department of Transportation
400 7th Street, SW, Room 10223
Washington, DC 20590 (202) 366-5412

Financial and economic studies of the transportation industry are prepared by this office. Air transportation is emphasized, but other modes are also evaluated. Report topics include mergers, regional marketing studies, gross receipts at airports, and intelligent vehicle highway systems. Contact this office to determine if a study has been prepared on your subject.

* Employment in Transportation

Central Employment Office (M18.1)
Office of Personnel
U.S. Department of Transportation
400 7th St., SW, Room 9113
Washington, DC 20590 (202) 366-9417

Employment inquiries for positions in Washington, DC, should be submitted to this office. Regional and district offices handle employment in their areas. Civil Service positions include air traffic controller; electronics maintenance technicians; civil, aeronautical, automotive, electronic, and highway engineers; and administrative, management, and clerical positions.

* Environmental Policies

Office of Transportation Regulatory Affairs (P-14)
Environmental Policy Division
U.S. Department of Transportation
400 7th Street, SW, Room 9217
Washington, DC 20590 (202) 366-4366

The National Environmental Policy Act (NEPA) requires all federal agencies to assess thoroughly the environmental consequences of any major federal action, either directly or through financial assistance, before an action decision can be taken. This office can provide you with a list of internal directives and documentation on the various Department of Transportation component Administration's procedures for considering environmental impacts. Call for information.

* Freedom of Information

Freedom of Information Act (FOIA) Division (C-12)
Office of the General Counsel
Office of the Secretary of Transportation
U.S. Department of Transportation (DOT)
400 7th Street, SW, Room 5432
Washington, DC 20590 (202) 366-4542

Inspection of some DOT documents which have proprietary information may require formal Freedom of Information Act (FOIA) requests. Each administration within DOT has a FOIA office. The central office listed here can supply you with addressees and contacts for submittal of FOIA requests.

Be patient. If any phone number is incorrect, call (area code) 555-1212 and request the new listing.

Business and Industry

* Handicapped Assistance and Mass Transit

Office of Research, Training, and Rural Transportation (UTS-30) Federal Transportation Administration (FTA) 400 7th St., SW, Room 6102 Washington, DC 20590 (202) 366-4995

FTA is involved in a Congressionally-mandated project with the National Easter Seals Committee to study accessibility problems faced by the handicapped who use mass transit. The office runs a series of demonstrations on improved arrangements to help the handicapped.

* Hazardous Material Transportation Accidents

Information Systems Division (DHM-63) Office of Hazardous Materials Transportation Research and Special Programs Administration U.S. Department of Transportation 400 7th Street, SW, Room 8108 Washington, DC 20590 (202) 366-4555

This division collects and analyzes accident data from transporters of hazardous materials by highway, rail, air, and water and from container manufacturers. Information stored in the database includes the hazardous material involved, transporter name and mode, packaging used, cause of accident, and results. Contact the above office for searches. There may be a charge.

* Highway Accident Investigation

Office of Surface Transportation Safety Highway Division National Transportation Safety Board (NTSB) 490 L'Enfant Plaza, SW Washington, DC 20594 (202) 382-6850

The Board investigates highway accidents involving issues of wide-ranging safety significance, specifically: all accidents that involve the collapse of a highway bridge structure, accidents that involve a fatality on a public transportation vehicle; and grade crossing accidents that involve collisions between trains and public transportation vehicles or hazardous materials vehicles. The Board also makes recommendations to the U.S. Department of Transportation and local agencies on highway safety issues. Statistical data is available from the National Highway Traffic Safety Administration in the U.S. Department of Transportation, (202) 366-0123.

* Lending and Bonding for Small Business

Minority Business Resource Center (MRBC) (S-44) Small and Disadvantaged Business Utilization (SDBU) Director of Civil Rights Office of the Secretary of Transportation U.S. Department of Transportation 400 7th Street, SW, Room 9410 Washington, DC 20590 (202) 366-2852

This office offers short-term lending and bonding assistance to small businesses in the transportation industry. The Short-term Lending Program offers loans at prime interest rates, while the Bonding Assistance Program enables small firms to obtain bonding in support of transportation-related contracts. Entrepreneurs can contact MBRC for information and certification details.

* Marine Accidents

Office of Surface Transportation Safety Marine Division National Transportation Safety Board (NTSB) 490 L'Enfant Plaza, SW Washington, DC 20594 (202) 382-6862

The Board investigates all major maritime accidents that occur in navigable waters of the U.S. In addition, it investigates major maritime accidents that involve US merchant vessels in international waters and accidents involving US public vessels and non-public vessels. Under the Board's criteria, a major maritime accident is one that involves the loss of six or more lives, the loss of a self propelled vessel of over 100 gross tons, property damage at more than $500,000, or an accident involving a serious threat from hazardous materials.

* Mass Transit Program Evaluation

Program Evaluation Division Federal Transportation Administration (FTA)

U.S. Department of Transportation 400 7th St., SW, Room 9306 Washington, DC 20590 (202) 366-1727

This office can provide you with information on its recent and on-going evaluations of projects and programs implemented by FTA. For information on earlier evaluations, refer to UMTRIS (see separate listing).

* NTSB Annual Report to Congress

Public Inquiries Section National Transportation Safety Board (NTSB) 490 L'Enfant Plaza East, SW Washington, DC 20594 (202) 382-6735

NTSB's Annual Report to the U.S. Congress details the major activities of the NTSB aviation, railroad, highway, pipeline, and marine safety during the previous calendar year. The biennial additions also include an appraisal, evaluation, and review, and recommendations for legislative and administrative action and change, with respect to transportation safety. It is available free from the office above.

* NTSB Directives

Public Inquiries Section National Transportation Safety Board (NTSB) 490 L'Enfant Plaza East, SW Washington, DC 20594 (202) 382-6735

NTSB Directives is a manual of orders and notices, which identify NTSB organization, policies, and procedures. The directives are updated as NTSB organization, policies, and procedures change. They are available for a fee from the office above.

* NTSB General Information

Public Inquiries Section National Transportation Safety Board (NTSB) 490 L'Enfant Plaza East, SW Washington, DC 20594 (202) 382-6735

The pamphlet, *The National Transportation Safety Board*, provides you with general information on the mission and responsibilities of the NTSB and how it accomplishes these responsibilities. The Board is the chief government investigator of transportation accidents. It is available free from the office above.

* NTSB Regional Offices

Office of Government and Public Affairs National Transportation Safety Board (NTSB) 490 L'Enfant Plaza East, SW Washington, DC 20594 (202) 382-6600

To obtain the addresses and telephone numbers of NTSB's ten regional offices located around the country, contact the office above.

* Pipeline Safety

Office of Pipeline Safety (OPS) (DPS-35) Research and Special Programs Administration U.S. Department of Transportation 400 7th Street, SW Washington, DC 20590 (202) 366-4572

OPS establishes and enforces safety standards for the transportation of gas and other hazardous materials by pipeline. A computerized reporting system is maintained to collect and analyze accident and incident data from pipeline operators. Accident reports include the operator's name, the hazardous material involved, description of the accident, and results. For database searches, contact the office listed. There may be a charge.

* Private Sector Initiatives in Mass Transit

Office of Private Sector Initiatives (UBP-30) Office of Budget and Policy Federal Transportation Administration (FTA) U.S. Department of Transportation 400 7th St., SW, Room 9300 Washington, DC 20590 (202) 366-1666

This office encourages private sector involvement in mass transit throughout the United States. Specifically, they work through the following four areas:

Be patient. If any phone number is incorrect, call (area code) 555-1212 and request the new listing.

General Transportation

Competitive Contracting: Local transit authorities are encouraged to open the provisioning of services up to private sector competition.

Entrepreneurial Services: Groups in the private sector are encouraged to start self-sustaining transit services (such as taxi and bus) in cooperation with local transit authorities.

Joint Development: Federal assistance is available to help plan public/private sector joint ventures at transit facilities.

Demand Management Program: Federal funds are available to encourage local employers and merchants to develop techniques to help manage transportation and mobility problems in their areas.

* Public Docket

Public Inquiries Section
National Transportation Safety Board (NTSB)
490 L'Enfant Plaza East, SW
Washington, DC 20594 (202) 382-6735

The Safety Board's Public Inquiries Section maintains a public docket at the Board's headquarters in Washington, DC. The docket contains the records of all Board investigations, all safety recommendations, and all safety enforcement proceedings. These records are available to the public and may be reviewed or duplicated for public use.

* Public Hearings on Accidents

Public Inquiries Section
National Transportation Safety Board (NTSB)
490 L'Enfant Plaza East, SW
Washington, DC 20594 (202) 382-6735

Following an accident, the Board may decide to hold a public hearing to collect added information and to air in a public forum the issues involved in an accident. Contact the office above for more information on obtaining accident reports from the hearings.

* Public Private Transportation Network

8737 Colesville Road
Suite 1100
Silver Spring, Maryland 20910 (800) 522-7786

The Transit Information Exchange is a free technical assistance program sponsored by the Federal Transit Administration. PPTN assists public transit agencies, private transit operators, federal state and local officials and others seeking guidance on transportation issues especially concerning identification and fostering of public/private partnerships. Assistance includes site visits by a network of industry professionals; speakers and facilitators for seminars, conferences, and workshops; and a library of technical assistance materials.

* Railroad Accidents

Office of Surface Transportation Safety
Railroad Division
National Transportation Safety Board (NTSB)
490 L'Enfant Plaza East, SW
Washington, DC 20594 (202) 382-6843

The Board places special emphasis on train accidents that involve the travelling public, such as rail rapid transit accidents. The Board's criteria for a railroad accident investigation include any accident in which damage exceeds $150,000. Safety studies in the rail mode have included such areas as the carriage of hazardous materials and track maintenance.

* Regulations of the NTSB

Public Inquiries Section
National Transportation Safety Board (NTSB)
490 L'Enfant Plaza East, SW
Washington, DC 20594 (202) 382-6735

Regulations of the NTSB are published in the *Federal Register* and codified in the *Code of Federal Regulations*, Chapter VIII, Title 49 - Transportation. These regulations are issued irregularly as procedures change. They are available free from the office above. Contact the office above for information on ordering the regulations.

* Research Abstracts

Manager, UMTRIS
Transportation Research Board
National Research Council
2101 Constitution Ave., NW
Washington, DC 20418 (202) 334-2995

Twice annually UMTRIS publishes the *Urban Transportation Abstracts* which provide all the new references added to the it transportation research database during the preceding six months. Each issue is divided into five sections: *Abstracts of Reports and Journal Articles, Summaries of New and Ongoing Research, Source Index, Author/Investigator Index,* and *Retrieval Term Index.* Summer and winter issues can be purchased individually, or through an annual subscription fee of $72.

* Research Bibliography Services

Manager, UMTRIS
Transportation Research Board
National Research Council
2101 Constitution Ave., NW
Washington, DC 20418 (202) 334-2995

Urban Mass Transit Research Information System provides computerized, online responses to transit inquiries. A computer-generated bibliography, including abstract of articles, reports, and summaries of new and ongoing research, can be created for almost any subject related to mass transportation. UMTRIS is now providing a new, low-cost extension to its online capability. The Data Base is accessible through Dialog and costs $45 per hour on line. Because transportation professionals are often interested in the same current problems, UMTRIS has made available, at a nominal fee, copies of the database literature searches that have been recently completed and may be of interest to other professionals.

* Safety Institute

Transportation Safety Institute (DTI-1)
Research and Special Programs Administration
U.S. Department of Transportation
6500 South MacArthur Blvd.
Oklahoma City, OK 73125 (405) 680-3153

The Institute supports the Department's efforts to reduce transportation accidents. It develops and conducts training programs for Federal, state, and local governments; industry; and foreign personnel. Courses are offered in aviation, highway, marine, pipeline, and railroad safety; materials analysis; transportation security; and other subjects.

* Safety Monitoring of the Trucking Industry

Motor Carrier Information and Analysis (HIA-10)
Office of Motor Carriers
Federal Highway Administration (FHWA)
U.S. Department of Transportation
400 7th St., SW, Room 3104
Washington, DC 20590 (202) 366-4023

FHWA motor carrier programs address licensing interstate and intrastate commercial truck and bus drivers and enforce uniform safety regulations for commercial motor vehicles and their cargo. Driver and vehicle tests and inspections are designed to determine safety performance on the road, and follow-up reviews are conducted when problem areas are identified. The Cargo Security Program regulates the movement of dangerous cargoes on the Nation's highways. This includes hazardous wastes, explosives, flammables, and other volatile materials. Permits are issued to regulate packaging, labeling and transporting of these materials. The transport of migrant workers is also regulated.

Carrier data by state can be obtained from the office listed above. Some information in printout form is available on a cost basis, with price varying according to the information requested. Driver and vehicle tests and inspections are conducted in the field by Motor Carrier Safety and Field Operations, Office of Motor Carriers, FHWA, USDOT, 400 7th St., SW, Room 3408, Washington, DC 20590; (202) 366-2952.

* Safety Publications

Public Inquiries Section
National Transportation Safety Board (NTSB)
490 L'Enfant Plaza East, SW
Washington, DC 20594 (202) 382-6735

Be patient. If any phone number is incorrect, call (area code) 555-1212 and request the new listing.

Business and Industry

The Safety Board makes public all of its actions and decisions in the form of accident reports, special studies, statistical reviews, safety recommendation and press releases. Details on available publications can be obtained by writing to the office above.

* Safety Recommendations

Public Inquiries Section
National Transportation Safety Board (NTSB)
490 L'Enfant Plaza East, SW
Washington, DC 20594 (202) 382-6735

Safety Recommendations are issued by the NTSB as a result of the investigation of transportation accidents and other safety problems. Recommendations usually identify a specific problem uncovered during an investigation of an accident or other safety problems and specify how to correct the situation. Such recommendations are directed to the organization best able to act on the problem, whether it is private or public. These recommendations are issued when a problem is identified, and are distributed individually and in a monthly publication. Contact the office above for information on ordering the recommendations.

* Speeches of the NTSB Members of the Board

Public Inquiries Section
National Transportation Safety Board (NTSB)
490 L'Enfant Plaza East, SW
Washington, DC 20594 (202) 382-6735

The Members of the Board are frequently asked to speak before Congressional Committees and state, local, and private organizations. Their prepared statements enunciate NTSB's positions on transportation issues. The topics of these statements vary depending on the organization before which they are speaking. Speech texts are issued irregularly. They are available free from the office above. When ordering, specify the date of the speaking engagement and the committee or organization before which the speech was made.

* Spill Maps

Public Inquiries Section
National Transportation Safety Board (NTSB)
490 L'Enfant Plaza East, SW
Washington, DC 20594 (202) 382-6735

Spill maps are developed on selected transportation accidents involving hazardous materials. The maps identify how the hazardous materials spread based on environment in the subject accident. Spill maps are issued irregularly. They are available free from the office above until limited supplies are exhausted. For information on ordering the maps, contact the office above.

* State Motor Vehicle Inspections

Records and Motor Vehicle Services Division (NTS-43)
National Highway Traffic Safety Administration (NHTSA)
U.S. Department of Transportation
400 7th Street, SW
Washington, DC 20590 (202) 366-2676

NHTSA's Motor Vehicle Inspection Program is aimed at providing car owners with preventative information on what repairs are needed to achieve greater safety, lower pollution, and better mileage. The annual *Study of the State Motor Vehicle Inspection Program* is available from this office.

* Surface Transportation Information

Office of Surface Transportation Safety
National Transportation Safety Board (NTSB)
490 L'Enfant Plaza East, SW
Washington, DC 20594 (202) 382-6800

This Office conducts accident investigations for a variety of surface transportation modes, including highway, railroad, marine, and pipeline. contact the above number for information about reports, statistics, and recent and ongoing investigations.

* Technical Transportation Information

Technology Sharing Program (DRT-1)
Office of Research and Technology
Research and Special Programs Administration (RSPA)
U.S. Department of Transportation

400 7th Street, SW
Washington, DC 20590-0001 (202) 366-4208

The RSPA develops and coordinates a comprehensive transportation information service. Contact this office for referrals and details on DOT programs, projects, contacts, available technical information on transportation-related topics. Technological areas include energy, security, emergency preparedness, and safety. Publications are available in the following areas: General Information, transit, commuter/travel demand, Highways and street maintenance, Rural Transportation, Energy, Hazardous Materials, Taxi/Personalized Transportation, Disadvantaged (Handicapped and Specialized Transportation), Water Marine, and Safety. Publications are obtained by returning an order form specifying which publications lists you would like to be on.

* Technology Exchange Programs

International Cooperative Division and Secretariat (P-25)
Office of International Transportation and Trade
Office of the Secretary of Transportation
U.S. Department of Transportation (DOT)
400 7th Street, SW
Washington, DC 20590 (202) 366-4398

DOT participates in a number of cooperative programs with other countries to exchange mutually beneficial transportation research data and state-of-the-art technical information. Areas of exchange include highway technology; ports and inland waterways; railway technology; and search and rescue operations. Contact this office for information about these programs.

* Transit Environments

Environment Division
Policy and International Affairs
Office of the Secretary of Transportation
U.S. Department of Transportation
400 7th Street, SW, Room 9217
Washington, DC 20590 (202) 366-4366

This is the DOT contact point for environmental issues. Staff can provide you with information and referrals on such subjects as highway beautification, transportation architecture, bicycle paths, historic preservation activities, wetlands laws and environmental impact statements. Office activities are governed in large part by the requirements of the National Environmental Policy Act.

* Transportation Library

Library (M-493)
Office of the Secretary of Transportation
U.S. Department of Transportation
400 7th Street, SW, Room 2200
Washington, DC 20590 (202) 366-0736

An extensive collection of literature on all aspects of transportation is housed here. Reading rooms are also available in regional offices around the country. Contact the specific administration of interest. Law Library: (202) 366-0749.

* Transportation of Hazardous Materials

Office of Hazardous Materials Transportation
Research and Special Programs Administration
U.S. Department of Transportation
400 7th Street, SW
Washington, DC 20590-0001 (202) 366-2301

This office can provide you with information on the transportation of hazardous materials by highway, rail air, and water. Data is collected directly from industry and also via compliance inspections by field staff. The quarterly *Hazardous Material Newsletter* is available free from the office above.

* Transportation Systems Center

Technical Information Center-Library
Transportation Systems Center (TSC)
Research and Special Programs Administration
U.S. Department of Transportation (DOT)
Kendall Square, 55 Broadway
Cambridge, MA 02142 (617) 494-2306

TSC is the DOT's multimodal research and analysis center to address national transportation and logistics issues. With contractual participation by industry and academia, it conducts technical, socio-economic, and human-factor studies on which the Department's transportation policy decisions are based. Areas of

Be patient. If any phone number is incorrect, call (area code) 555-1212 and request the new listing.

General Transportation

research include safety, security, transportation infrastructure, system modernization, and information technology relevant to transportation system operations. Research covers highways, rail, air, and water. The Center maintains statistics and a transportation information database which include information on aviation safety and statistical references on rail transport. The Center will provide copies of reports if they are available. New reports are listed in the acquisitions list that is published monthly. If reports are unavailable for the Center, NTIS retains copies for sale. Contact the center for more information.

* University Research on Transportation

Office of University Research (P-34)
Policy and International Affairs
Office of the Secretary of Transportation
U.S. Department of Transportation
400 7th Street, SW
Washington, DC 20590 (202) 366-0190

Grants are made to institutions of higher learning to establish and administer transportation research centers. Issues for study are determined by the Department. This office can provide you with a list of universities that receive federal money for this purpose.

* Federal Transportation Administration (FTA)

U.S. Department of Transportation
400 7th St., SW
Washington, DC 20590 (202) 366-4040

FTA assists in the development of improved mass transportation facilities, equipment, techniques, and methods; encourages the planning and establishment of area-wide urban mass transportation systems; and provides assistance to state and local governments in financing such systems.

* Federal Transportation Administration Research

Manager, UMTRIS
Transportation Research Board
National Research Council
2101 Constitution Ave., NW
Washington, DC 20418 (202) 334-2995

The Federal Transportation Administration Research Information Service is a computerized database on worldwide transportation research. Administered by the Transportation Research Board (TRB), it covers all phases of conventional, new, and automated public transportation. UMTRIS features database storage/retrieval of abstracts of technical papers, journal articles, research reports, computer program descriptions, and statistical sources, as well as state-of-the-art bibliographies. Descriptions of ongoing research, especially that sponsored by FTA, are also included. UMTRIS offers the public nearly 20,000 information references to ongoing and completed research activities, and adds 2,000 new references annually to the database. In addition to serving as the central source of technical information to the public and private sectors, UMTRIS also serves as an institutional memory for FTA projects and project reports. The database can be searched online by any computer with a modem through DIALOG Information Services File 63. UMTRIS is supported by a National Network of Transportation Libraries (18), and they serve both as repositories that house and make FTA documents available to the general public, as well as document delivery centers that provide UMTRIS users with full text copies of citations retrieved from the database.

* Vehicle Manufacturer Safety Compliance

Vehicle Manufacturer Safety Compliance (NEF-30)
Enforcement
National Highway Traffic Safety Administration
U.S. Department of Transportation
400 7th Street, SW
Washington, DC 20590 (202) 366-2832

To ensure that foreign and domestic vehicle and equipment manufacturers comply with federal motor vehicle safety standards, this office performs compliance testing, inspections, and investigations involving about 150 performance requirements and nearly 3000 equipment items.

* Vehicle Research and Testing

Vehicle Research and Test Center
Research and Development
National Highway Traffic Safety Administration (NHTSA)
U.S. Department of Transportation
P.O. BOX 37
East Liberty, OH 43319 (513) 466-4521

NHTSA evaluates the effectiveness of Federal Motor Vehicle Safety Standards. This engineering facility performs tests to obtain basic data used to establish standards for safety and fuel efficiency of motor vehicles.

Business and Industry

Highways, Waterways and Railways

The U.S. Department of Transportation's Federal Highway Administration, Federal Railroad Administration, Federal Transportation Administration, and Research and Special Programs Administration are the loci of highway and railroad expertise in the U.S. government. The Interstate Commerce Commission is an excellent source of information on road and rail transportation companies.

* **AMTRAK: National Railroad Passenger Corporation**
AMTRAK
60 Massachusetts Ave., NE
Washington, DC 20002 (202) 906-3000
AMTRAK was created in 1970 to provide a balanced national transportation system by developing, operating, and improving U.S. intercity rail passenger service.

* **AMTRAK Financial and Operating Statistics**
AMTRAK
Office of Public Affairs
60 Massachusetts Ave., NE
Washington, DC 20002 (202) 906-3860
No rail passenger system in the world makes a profit; therefore, AMTRAK does require government assistance in the form of an annual appropriation. However, AMTRAK has made significant progress in reducing its dependence on federal support while at the same time improving the quality of service. *The Annual Report* provides operating statistics and financial statements, which cover operations, cashflows, and changes in capitalization.

* **AMTRAK Passenger Services**
AMTRAK
60 Massachusetts Ave., NE
Washington, DC 20002 (202) 906-2733
The Passenger Services Department handles all of the onboard service aspects of AMTRAK, including all of its employees across the country.

* **AMTRAK Customer Relations**
AMTRAK
60 Massachusetts Ave., NE
Washington, DC 20002 (202) 906-2121
You may call or write the Customer Relations Office concerning any comments or problems with AMTRAK service. Please include your ticket receipt and dates of travel to help with the resolution of your problem.

* **AMTRAK Tickets or Travel Information**
AMTRAK
60 Massachusetts Ave., NE
Washington, DC 20002 (800) USA-RAIL
For information regarding tickets or travel on AMTRAK, call 1-800-USA-RAIL. AMTRAK also publishes a travel planner which provides travel tips and services, as well as a listing AMTRAK's vacation packages.

* **Annual Report of Interstate Transportation Companies**
Bureau of Accounts' Public Reference Room
Interstate Commerce Commission (ICC)
12th St. and Constitution Ave., NW, Room 3378
Washington, DC 20403 (202) 927-7119
Annual reports of companies regulated by the ICC contain revealing information concerning those companies, including annual income, balance sheets, expenses, types of equipment owned, and much more. These documents may be examined by the public in the Reference Room from 8:30 a.m. to 5:00 p.m. weekdays,and photocopies of these reports, at a cost of $.60 per page, with a $3 minimum

charge per order, may be obtained by writing the Office of the Secretary, Room 2215, ICC, Washington, DC, 20423.

* **Applications of Motor Carriers**
Motor and Rail Docket File
Office of the Secretary
Interstate Commerce Commission (ICC)
12th St. and Constitution Ave., NW
Room 1221
Washington, DC 20423 (202) 927-7510
As required by the Motor Carrier Act, all motor carriers must be willing to give a copy of its application package to anyone willing to pay the $10 fee. These packages include information on the type of authority requested from the ICC, the type of business run by the applicant, a history of the applicant's business, and more. Contact this office for more information on examining these applications.

* **Assistance to Foreign Highways**
International Highway Programs (HPI-10)
Associate Administrator for Policy
Federal Highway Administration (FHWA)
U.S. Department of Transportation (DOT)
400 7th St., SW
Washington, DC 20590 (202) 366-9632
FHWA administers programs which provide assistance and advice to foreign governments engaged in highway engineering and administration. Projects have included technical assistance in fabricating bridge segments, value engineering skills, development of transportation systems, materials testing, quality control, and skid testing. Through the International Visitors Program, highway specialists from over 40 countries receive training. Countries that have participated include China, Indonesia, Haiti, Kuwait, Dubai, and Saudi Arabia. Two publications available from this office are *World of Technology for Sharing* and *Highway Community on the Occasion of the 18th World Road Congress*.

* **Automobile Safety Investigation Reports**
Office of Public and Consumer Affairs (NOA-40)
National Highway Traffic Safety Administration
U.S. Department of Transportation (DOT)
400 7th Street, SW
Washington, DC 20590 (202) 366-5971
The Office of public affairs has available and posts monthly notices on ongoing defects investigations, recall notices, and the results of completed defects investigations. They are available free from the above listed office.

* **Automobile Sales Statistics**
Transportation Branch
U.S. International Trade Commission (ITC)
500 E St., SW
Washington, DC 20436 (202) 205-3392
Under Section 302 of the Tariff Act of 1930 the ITC publishes a monthly report on select economic indicators for the U.S. automobile industry. *USITC publication 2485* (February 1992) details sales and inventory figures for U.S. producers, comparing selected months in 1991 and 1990, and also lists import figures for November and December 1991. It is available free.

Be patient. If any phone number is incorrect, call (area code) 555-1212 and request the new listing.

Highways, Waterways and Railways

* Automotive Trade Statistics

Machinery and Transportation Equipment Branch
Machinery and Equipment Division
Office of Industries
U.S. International Trade Commission (ITC)
500 E St., SW, Room 500
Washington, DC 20436 (202) 205-3380

At the request of the House Ways and Means Committee, this office publishes a monthly newsletter on automobile trade and industry which includes many current statistics of interest. The *ITC Annual report* also lists ongoing investigations with respect to trade in automobiles. It is available from the ITC (202) 205-2000.

* Bridges Over Navigable Waters

Bridge Administration Division (G-NBR)
Office of Navigation Safety and Waterways Services
U.S. Coast Guard
U.S. Department of Transportation (DOT)
2100 2nd St., SW, Room 1408
Washington, DC 20593-0001 (202) 267-0368

Bridges and causeways spanning navigable waterways in the U.S. are subject to Coast Guard safety regulations concerning their construction, operation, and maintenance. This office oversees bridge engineering and issues permits. For further details, contact the division listed above.

* Bus Transportation

Office of External Affairs
Interstate Commerce Commission (ICC)
12th Street and Constitution Ave, NW
Washington, DC 20423 (202) 927-5737

Part of the *ICC Annual Report* analyzes the Bus transport industry. The report is available free from the ICC.

* Consumer Assistance

Office of Compliance and Consumer Assistance
Interstate Commerce Commission (ICC)
12th Street and Constitution Ave, NW, Room 4412
Washington, DC 20423 (202) 927-5500

This office monitors the activities of ICC regulated companies, ensuring compliance with ICC rules and assisting the public in the resolution of complaints against ICC regulated companies.

* Cargo Insurance

Office of the Secretary
Interstate Commerce Commission (ICC)
12th St. and Constitution Ave., NW, Room 2215
Washington, DC 20423 (202) 927-5480

All motor common carriers of property and freight forwarders are required to maintain cargo insurance for the protection of the shipping public. Under this protection, the insurance company is directly liable to a shipper or consignee for any cargo claim for which the motor carrier or freight forwarder may be legally liable. No limitations in the policy itself, such as deductibles, may be used as a defense by the insurance companies against claims filed under this Commission's prescribed cargo endorsements. Railroads are not required to maintain cargo insurance. The name of the insurance company may be obtained by writing the Office of the Secretary.

* Civil Emergency Preparedness - Railroads

Office of Policy (RRP-8)
Defense and Special Programs Staff
Federal Railroad Administration (FRA)
U.S. Department of Transportation (DOT)
400 7th Street, SW, Room 8307
Washington, DC 20590 (202) 366-8307

This Office directs the FRA Emergency Preparedness Program in fulfillment of FRA and DOT Federal Emergency Management Agency requirements. It also identifies and analyzes rail industry capabilities in support of national security, defense, and emergency response needs.

* Commission Reports and Orders Certification

Public Records Room
Interstate Commerce Commission (ICC)
12th Street and Constitution Ave, NW, 2115
Washington, DC 20423 (202) 927-5710

All Commission Reports and Orders are available to the public at a slight cost ($.60 per page) and can be received by contacting the Public Records Room.

* Computerized Data Base of Railroads

Office of Transportation Analysis
Interstate Commerce Commission (ICC)
12th St. and Constitution Ave., NW, Room 3219
Washington, DC 20423 (202) 927-6203

The Office of Transportation Analysis maintains a computerized data base of railroad contract summaries, which include shipper names on agricultural commodities.

* Consumer Information Brochures

Office of Public and Consumer Affairs (NOA-40)
National Highway Traffic Safety Administration (NHTSA)
U.S. Department of Transportation, Room 5232
400 7th Street, SW
Washington, DC 20590 (202) 366-5971

NHTSA issues a series of consumer fact sheets on an assortment of safety related and other questions. Fact sheets available include:

Insurance Discounts
School Bus Safety
Traffic Tips for Older Drivers
Transporting Your Child Safely
Auto Safety Defects and Recalls
Brakes
Buckle Up in the Back Seat
Motorcycle Safety Helmets
Safety Belts - Proper Use
Utility Vehicles

* Crashworthiness

Office of Crashworthiness Research (NRD-10)
Research and Development
National Highway Traffic Safety Administration
U.S. Department of Transportation (DOT)
400 7th Street, SW
Washington, DC 20590 (202) 366-4862

Research is conducted on vehicle crashworthiness and crash avoidance. To determine how drivers and passengers fare in head-on collisions, information is collected on seat belts, air bags, child safety restraints, motorcycle helmets, fuel systems, rearview mirrors, tires, door locks, seats, bumpers, and school busses. The annual publication, *Federal Motor Vehicle Safety Standards and Regulations*, is available for $82 from the Government Printing Office. Superintendent of Documents, Washington, DC 20402; (202) 783-3238. New Car Assessment Program information on selected models is available from the Auto Safety Hotline: (800) 424-9393.

* Diesel Fuel Recording

Interstate Commerce Commission (ICC)
12th St. and Constitution Ave., NW
Washington, DC 20423 (202) 927-6237

This recording states the average diesel fuel price each week after a survey is taken of fuel stations across the country.

* Driver and Pedestrian Research

Office of Driver and Pedestrian Research (NRD-40)
Research and Development
National Highway Traffic Safety Administration
U.S. Department of Transportation (DOT)
400 7th Street, SW
Washington, DC 20590 (202) 366-9591

This office studies factors affecting the safety of drivers and pedestrians. Research areas include determining the causes of unsafe driving and developing countermeasures; the effectiveness of vehicle occupant safety restraints; the effect

Be patient. If any phone number is incorrect, call (area code) 555-1212 and request the new listing.

Business and Industry

of alcohol and drugs; the safety concerns of bicycles, motorcycles, and mopeds; driver license standards; and young drivers. This office can refer you to staff researching the topic of your interest.

* Funded Traffic Safety Projects

Evaluation Staff (NTS-02.1)
Traffic Safety Programs
National Highway Traffic Safety Administration
U.S. Department of Transportation (DOT)
400 7th Street, SW
Washington, DC 20590 (202) 366-2752

Once known as the National Project Reporting System, funded project information collected by this office from each state is stored in a database. Projects are funded in areas such as occupant safety and alcohol. Findings are assembled annually in a published report providing an overview of the projects, their status, and how funding is apportioned, such as amounts to each project and within each project, amount to education, to enforcement, and to other areas. Contact the Evaluation Staff for details.

* Hazardous Material Transportation Accidents

Information Systems Division (DHM-63)
Office of Hazardous Materials Transportation
Research and Special Programs Administration
U.S. Department of Transportation (DOT)
400 7th Street, SW, Room 8112
Washington, DC 20590 (202) 366-4555

This division collects and analyzes accident data from transporters of hazardous materials by highway, rail, air, and water and from container manufacturers. Information stored in the database includes the hazardous material involved, transporter name and mode, packaging used, cause of accident, and results. Contact the above office for searches. There may be a charge.

* Highway Beautification

Environment Division
Policy and International Affairs
Office of the Secretary of Transportation
U.S. Department of Transportation (DOT)
400 7th Street, SW, Room 9217
Washington, DC 20590 (202) 366-4366

This is the DOT contact point for environmental issues. Staff can provide you with information and referrals on such subjects as highway beautification, transportation architecture, bicycle paths, historic preservation activities, and environmental impact statements.

* Highway Construction Accident Prevention

Office of Highway Safety (HHS-21)
Associate Administrator for Safety and Operations
Federal Highway Administration (FHWA)
U.S. Department of Transportation (DOT)
400 7th St., SW
Washington, DC 20590 (202) 366-2177

Highway construction safety programs are funded to remove, relocate, or shield roadside obstacles; to identify and correct hazards at railroad crossings; and to improve signing, pavement markings, and signalization. For information and referral, contact the Office of Highway Safety. The following publications are also available:

Highway Safety Improvement Programs, Annual Report
Status Report of Federal Funds Used for Highway Safety Programs.

Several other reports prepared by this office are available from National Technical Information Service, 5285 Port Royal Road, Springfield, VA 22161; (703) 487-4650. A sampling of titles follows:

Inexpensive Accident Countermeasures at Narrow Bridges
Legibility and Driver Response to Selected Lane and Road Closure Barricades
Re-Evaluation of Traffic Control at Non-Signalized Intersections
Rollover Potential of Vehicles on Embankments, Sideslopes, and Other Roadside Features; Railroad-Highway Grade Crossing Signal Visibility Improvement Program, Final Report
Studies of the Road Marking Code

Constant Warning Time Devices for Railroad-Highway Crossings: Technical Summary

* Highway Contractors and Subcontractors

Office of Civil Rights (HCR-1)
Federal Highway Administration (FHWA)
U.S. Department of Transportation (DOT)
400 7th St., SW
Washington, DC 20590 (202) 366-0693

This office monitors compliance with civil rights laws by requiring contractors and subcontractors of Federal highway projects to submit employment data. Equal opportunity issues are also addressed in the Disadvantaged Business Enterprise Program, which awards contracts and subcontract commitments to small and minority businesses, and in FHWA's Historically Black Colleges and Universities Programs. Data from contractor filings and a list of contractors and subcontractors, by state or county, are available from this office. You can also obtain a copy of *FHWA's Historically Black Colleges and Universities Programs,* a publication with details about those programs.

* Highway Environment

Environmental Operations Division (HEP-1)
Office of Environment and Planning
Federal Highway Administration (FHWA)
U.S. Department of Transportation (DOT)
400 7th St., SW
Washington, DC 20590 (202) 366-0106

FHWA assesses environmental impact so that highways are located, constructed, and designed in cooperation with environmental concerns. Water and air quality, noise abatement, vegetation management, corrosion control, and preserving wildlife are some of the factors considered. For more information on FHWA efforts in these areas, contact the office listed above.

* Highway Information

Office of Highway Information Management
40 7th Street, SW
Washington, DC 20590 (202) 366-0160

The Office of Highway Management puts out reports on many aspects of highway travel, highway accident statistics, and vehicle operating costs. Reports available include:

Highway Taxes and Fees, How They Are Collected and Distributed - 1991
Monthly Motor Fuel Reported by States
A Guide to Reporting Highway Statistics
Highway Performance Monitoring System Field Manual-1990
Toll Facilities in the United States - 1991
Fatal and Injury Accident Rates on Federal-aid and Other Highway Systems - 1990
Summary and Recommendations of the Workshop on National Urban Congestion Monitoring - September 1990
Traffic Volume Trends
Speed Monitoring Summary
Traffic Monitoring Guide
Highway Statistics
Selected Highway Statistics and Charts - 1990
Our Nation's Highways - Selected Facts and Figures - 1990
Drivers Licenses - 1990
Nationwide Personal Transportation Study - 1991
Driver License Administration Requirements and Fees - 1990
Road User and Property Taxes on Selected Vehicles - 1987
Cost of Owning and Operating Vehicles and Vans - 1992

* Highway Programs Updates

Office of Public Affairs (A-30)
U.S. Department of Transportation (DOT), Room 10413
400 7th Street, SW
Washington, DC 20590 (202) 366-5580

The U.S. Department of Transportation *Annual Report* has information on current DOT and Federal Highway Administration programs for highways. The report highlights FHWA accomplishments in the areas of safety, environment, Federal lands projects, motor carrier programs, and international highway assistance. The report also discusses FHA activities in the areas of pavement and bridge management. The report is free from the office of public affairs.

Be patient. If any phone number is incorrect, call (area code) 555-1212 and request the new listing.

Highways, Waterways and Railways

* Highway Publications

Office of Public Affairs (HPA-1)
Federal Highway Administration (FHWA)
U.S. Department of Transportation (DOT)
400 7th St., SW
Washington, DC 20590 (202) 366-0660

The *FHWA Publications Index,* free from Public Affairs, is a useful guide to current reports, manuals, and summaries generated by programs of the Federal Highway Administration. The *Index* provides contact addresses and telephone numbers for obtaining the publications from offices within FHWA or from NTIS and GPO. The titles listed below are available directly from Public Affairs:

Motor Carrier Activities of the FHWA
U.S. Highways
Commercial Motor Vehicle Safety Act of 1986
FHWA News
The Single License Requirement for Truck and Bus Drivers

* Highway R&D Programs/Publications

Federal Highway Administration (FHWA) (HRD-11)
Office of Research and Development
Turner-Fairbank Highway Research Center
6300 Georgetown Pike
McLean, VA 22101-2144 (703) 285-2144

The Office of Research, Development and Technology Annual Report details research activities at the Turner-Fairbank Highway Research Center. The report also contains a detailed list of publications. Some categories of publications include: R&D reports; Technology Sharing Reports; Implementation Packages; Rural Technical Reports; Training Materials; TFHRC Update; NCP Progress Report; Technical Summaries; and Public Roads: A Journal of Highway Research and Development.

* Highway Reports List

Federal Highway Administration (FHWA) (HRD-11)
Office of Research and Development
Turner-Fairbank Highway Research Center
6300 Georgetown Pike
McLean, VA 22101-2144 (703) 285-2144

This office can provide you with a computer runout of all reports, videos, and films produced by the FHWA. Not all items are available. Call the above number for the list or for information on specific publications.

* Highways Research Center

Technical Information Center-Library
Transportation Systems Center (TSC)
Research and Special Programs Administration
U.S. Department of Transportation (DOT)
Kendall Square, 55 Broadway
Cambridge, MA 02142 (617) 494-2306

TSC is the DOT's multimodal research and analysis center to address national transportation and logistics issues. With contractual participation by industry and academia, it conducts technical, socio-economic, and human-factor studies on which the Department's transportation policy decisions are based. Areas of research include safety, security, transportation infrastructure, system modernization, and information technology relevant to transportation system operations. Research covers highways, rail, air, and water. The Center maintains statistics and a transportation information database. There is no central point for distribution of reports, publications, data tapes, and other information available from the Center, so contact the Library above for referral to the appropriate source within the Center for the information you need.

* Highway Statistics

Office of Highway Information Management (HPM-1)
Associate Administrator for Policy
Federal Highway Administration (FHWA)
U.S. Department of Transportation (DOT)
400 7th St., SW, Room 3306
Washington, DC 20590 (202) 366-0180

This office is the centralized source for highway statistics compiled by FHWA. The *Highway Statistics Summary,* updated every ten years, summarizes historical information on the Nation's highway system, its users, and Federal, State, and local highway funding. You can also obtain statistics and information on

personal, regional, and national travel trends; fuel usage and taxes; road user and motor vehicle taxes; toll bridges, roads, tunnels, and ferries in the U.S.; traffic volume; driver licenses; and yearly statistical summaries. Contact this office to be added to the mailing list for a free subscription to *Monthly Motor Fuels Reported by State,* which indicates trends in gasoline sales.

* Highway Traffic Safety Records

Technical Reference Division (NAD-52)
Office of Administrative Operations
National Highway Traffic Safety Administration
U.S. Department of Transportation (DOT)
400 7th Street, SW
Washington, DC 20590 (202) 366-2768

NHTSA reports and records are available for public inspection at this location, and database searches can be requested for a fee. Holdings include vehicle research and test reports; investigation reports on accidents and defects; recall information; compliance reports; consumer complaints; consumer advisories; filmed records of research and tests; NHTSA *Technical Reports;* engineering specifications; and certification information. Both light and heavy highway vehicles are covered. Call ahead to ensure that the records you need will be on hand.

* Intermodal Surface Transportation Efficiency Act

Office of Public Affairs (A-30)
Federal Highway Administration (FHWA)
U.S. Department of Transportation (DOT)
400 7th St., SW
Washington, DC 20590 (202) 366-5580

On December 18, 1991 President Bush signed the Intermodal Surface Transportation Efficiency Act of 1991, providing authorizations for highways, highway safety, and mass transportation for the next six years. Total funding of about $155 billion will be available from FY 1992 - FY 1997. The Office of the Secretary of Transportation published a booklet outlining the provisions of the Act, including tables containing programmatic authorization amounts. The booklet, entitled *Intermodal Transportation Efficiency Act of 1991 - A Summary,* is free from the Office of Public Affairs.

* International Motor Vehicles Standards Harmonization

Director of International Harmonization (NOA-5)
National Highway Traffic Safety Administration
U.S. Department of Transportation (DOT)
400 7th Street, SW
Washington, DC 20590 (202) 366-2114

The Director formulates strategies for dealing with issues arising from the agencies program for harmonization of US motor vehicle safety standards and regulations with those of foreign countries. This office also contributes to policy guidance used by US negotiators at international standards conferences.

* Interstate Commerce Commission (ICC)

Interstate Commerce Commission
12th St. and Constitution Ave., NW
Washington, DC 20423 (202) 927-7597

The Interstate Commerce Commission was created as an independent regulatory agency by act of February 4, 1887 to regulate commerce. ICC's responsibilities include regulation of carriers engaged in transportation in interstate commerce and in foreign commerce to the extent that it takes place within the U.S. Surface transportation under the Commission's jurisdiction includes railroads, trucking companies, bus lines, freight forwarders, water carriers, transportation brokers, and a coal slurry pipeline. The regulatory laws vary depending on the type of transportation; however, they generally involve certification of carriers seeking to provide transportation for the public, rates, adequacy of service, purchases, and mergers. The Commission assures that the carriers it regulates will provide the public with rates and services that are fair and reasonable.

* Interstate Commerce Commission Register

Superintendent of Documents
Government Printing Office
Washington, DC 20402 (202) 783-3238

The *ICC Register* is a daily summary of motor carrier applications and of decisions and notices issued by the ICC. Subscription information is available from the Government Printing Office.

Be patient. If any phone number is incorrect, call (area code) 555-1212 and request the new listing.

Business and Industry

* Interstate Commerce Publications

Office of External Affairs
Interstate Commerce Commission (ICC)
12th St. and Constitution Ave., NW, Room 4111
Washington, DC 20423 (202) 927-5737

The *ICC Annual Report* contains a complete list of publications, including explanatory material on the operation and activities of the ICC and on special consumer-related fields, such as household goods movements and small shipments, is available. Most of the publications are available directly from the offices that publish them or from GPO.

* Interstate Commerce Rules Enforcement

Office of External Affairs
Interstate Commerce Commission (ICC)
12th Street and Constitution Ave, NW
Washington, DC 20423 (202) 927-5540

The ICC vigorously enforces rules with respect to motor carrier safety and financial responsibility under the Interstate Commerce Act. Particular commission activities have focused on ensuring that: household good transportation companies abide by applicable regulations; owner operator transportation companies do not violate regulations with respect to tariffs; and transport companies operate safely and with the proper insurance. Recent ICC enforcement activities are documented in the *Annual Report*. Complaints can be filed with the Compliance and Consumer Assistance Office.

* Interstate Commerce Speakers

Office of Government and Public Affairs
Interstate Commerce Commission (ICC)
12th St. and Constitution Ave., NW, Room 4111
Washington, DC 20423 (202) 927-5737

Speakers are available to discuss subjects relating to the Commission's organization, operations, procedures, and regulations.

* Legal Assistance

Office of the Secretary
Interstate Commerce Commission (ICC)
12th St. and Constitution Ave., NW, Room 2215
Washington, DC 20423 (202) 927-7428

To assist claimants in disputes, the Commission requires all motor carriers to designate an agent for service of legal process in each state into or through which they operate. The name of this process agent may be obtained by writing to the Office of the Secretary.

* Magnetic Levitation/High Speed Rail

Office of Railroad Development (RDV-7)
Federal Railroad Administration
U.S. Department of Transportation (DOT)
400 7th St., SW, Room 5106
Washington, DC 20590 (202) 366-6593

This office plans, develops and demonstrates technology toward the application and use of magnetic levitation (Maglev) and high speed transportation systems. This office maintains program documentation and status reports on Maglev and high speed technology programs.

* Mass Transportation Abstracts

Federal Transportation Administration (FTA)
Office of Technology Assistance and Safety
U.S. Department of Transportation (DOT), Room 6100
400 7th Street, SW
Washington, DC 20590 (202) 366-4995

The Federal Transportation Administration publishes a *Compendium of Technical Report Abstracts* that provide bibliographic information and abstracts for recently available FTAC (formerly Urban Mass Transportation Administration) - sponsored research project reports. All abstracts are logged in the transportation database (UMTRIS) and are also available online (Dialog file 63) to users of Dialog Information Services, Palo Alto, California. Research reports are available either from NTIS or FTA regional offices. Call for information and to order the Compendium.

* Maximum Speed Limit

Police Traffic Services Division (NTS-41)
Office of Enforcement and Emergency Services
Traffic Safety Programs
National Highway Traffic Safety Administration
U.S. Department of Transportation (DOT)
400 7th Street, SW, Room 5119
Washington, DC 20590 (202) 366-4295

The National Maximum Speed Limit is 65 miles per hour on certain interstate highways. This office processes annual certifications of maximum speed limit enforcement programs throughout the U.S. and assists states in developing and improving enforcement efforts.

* Minority Contracts for Rail Revitalization

Office of Civil Rights (ROA-10)
Federal Railroad Administration
U.S. Department of Transportation (DOT)
400 7th Street, SW, Room 8314
Washington, DC 20590 (202) 366-9753

The Office of Civil Rights designs, plans, and implements programs to encourage, promote, and assist minority enterprises to secure contracts and subcontracts with recipients of Federal assistance related to revitalizing the nations railroads. It also serves as the focal point/liaison with the Black Colleges Program and the Office of the Secretary of Transportation's Office of Small and Disadvantaged Business Utilization.

* Mobility Manager Technologies

Technology Sharing Program DRT-1MM
Research and Special Programs Administration
U.S. Department of Transportation (DOT)
400 7th St, SW
Washington, DC 20590 (202) 366-4208

DOT is conducting ongoing research into new technologies for local transportation organization. Electronic technologies now make possible mobility manager systems that allow people to plan trips and actually make reservations from a single point of contact. The report *Mobility Management and Market Oriented Local Transportation* (DOT-T-92-07) describes the concept and its operation in detail, explores how the service would work in practice, and sets forth criteria for continuing demonstrations. Single copies are available at no charge.

* Motor and Rail Dockets

Office of the Secretary
Motor and Rail Docket File Room
Interstate Commerce Commission (ICC)
12th St. and Constitution Ave., NW, Room 1221
Washington, DC 20423 (202) 927-5710

All the Commission's decisions and other legal documents are available for public inspection in the Office of the Secretary.

* Motor Vehicle Standards Enforcement

Office of Enforcement (NEF-01)
National Highway Traffic Safety Administration
U.S. Department of Transportation (DOT), Room 5321
400 7th Street, SW
Washington, DC 20590 (202) 366-9700

This Office ensures manufacturer compliance with Federal Laws regarding vehicle safety, fuel economy, theft prevention, damageability, consumer information and odometer fraud. Non compliance and defect recalls are also enforced by this office. It also supports an auto-safety hotline (800) 424-9323 for consumer complaints about vehicle safety related defects.

* NHTSA Congressional Liaison

Director for Intergovernmental Affairs (NOA-1)
National Highway Traffic Safety Administration (NHTSA)
U.S. Department of Transportation (DOT)
400 7th Street, SW
Washington, DC 20590 (202) 366-2105

This office provides a communications link between NHTSA and Congress, ensuring Congress understands NHTSA programs and in turn assuring that NHTSA understands Congressional concerns in the areas of highway safety and standards.

Be patient. If any phone number is incorrect, call (area code) 555-1212 and request the new listing.

Highways, Waterways and Railways

* National Driver Register

National Driver Register (NTS-24)
Traffic Safety Programs
National Highway Traffic Safety Administration
U.S. Department of Transportation (DOT)
400 7th Street, SW, Room 6124
Washington, DC 20590 (202) 366-4800

The *National Driver Register* is a central, computerized index of state records on drivers whose operator licenses have been revoked, denied, or suspended for more than 6 months. Data includes name, birthdate, height, weight, eye color, date and reason for action, and date of reinstatement. Applications for driver licenses are routinely checked against the register, and states exchange information via an electronic system.

* National Highway Traffic Safety Administration

National Highway Traffic Safety Administration (NHTSA)
U.S. Department of Transportation (DOT)
400 7th Street, SW
Washington, DC 20590 (202) 366-0123

NHTSA supports the U.S. Department of Transportation with programs to reduce automobile fuel consumption and motor vehicle crashes with resulting deaths, injuries, and economic losses, and to safeguard the public through regulation, research, information and education on motor vehicles. NHTSA concentrates on developing highway safety programs and monitoring compliance by auto manufacturers with fuel and safety standards. NHTSA has 10 regional offices. The General information number listed above can provide you with the phone number and address of the regional office for your state.

* Northeast Corridor Rail Project

Public Affairs (ROA-30)
Federal Railroad Administration
U.S. Department of Transportation (DOT)
400 7th St., SW
Room 8125
Washington, DC 20590 (202) 366-0881

Now in its final stages, the project is a major track upgrading on AMTRAK's main line from Washington, DC to Boston. The goal of the upgrading is to produce the best high-speed passenger railroad in the United States. This office can be contacted for information regarding current progress.

* Occupants Displaced by Highway Construction

Office of Right-of-Way (HRW-22)
Federal Highway Administration (FHWA)
U.S. Department of Transportation (DOT)
400 7th St., SW, Room 3219
Washington, DC 20590 (202) 366-2028

This office administers FHWA's lead role in implementing the Uniform Relocation Assistance and Real Property Acquisition Policies Act. When Federally funded highway construction projects involve displacing residents from acquired property, this Act sets policies for purchase of the land and relocating the people on it. The publication, *Your Rights and Benefits as Displaced Under the Federal Relocation Assistance Program*, is available from this office.

* Pedestrian Safety

Geometric and Roadside Design Branch (HGN-14)
Office of Engineering Program Development
Federal Highway Administration (FHWA)
U.S. Department of Transportation (DOT)
400 7th St., SW, Room 3128
Washington, DC 20590 (202) 366-1312

Highway design and roadside facilities are studied by this office to determine their impact on pedestrians and bicyclists. The publication, *Pedestrian and Bicycle Facilities*, provides you with information about the roadside designs and structures used in safety-related applications.

* Pedestrian Safety Programs

Federal Highway Administration (FHWA) (HSR-1)
Office of Safety and Traffic Operations R&D
Turner-Fairbank Highway Research Center
6300 Georgetown Pike
McLean, VA 22101-2144 (703) 285-2054

The Federal Highway Administration and the National Highway Traffic Safety Administration jointly fund the Walk Alert program, which focuses on engineering, education, and enforcement to improve pedestrian safety.

* Public Tariff File

Tariff Examining Branch
Bureau of Traffic
Interstate Commerce Commission (ICC)
12th St. and Constitution Ave., NW, Room 4360
Washington, DC 20423 (202) 927-5648

The Bureau of Traffic monitors tariff publication, filing, and interpretation, and suspends any unreasonable or unlawful tariffs before they become effective. The tariffs are available for public inspection by contacting the Tariff Examining Branch.

* Rail and Service Abandonments

Office of Transportation Analysis
Interstate Commerce Commission (ICC)
12th St. and Constitution Ave., NW, Room 3100
Washington, DC 20423 (202) 927-6203

No line of railroad may be abandoned and no rail service discontinued unless the Commission has a certificate of public convenience and necessity authorizing the abandonment or discontinuance. The Notice of Intent must be filed with the Commission at least 15 days, but not more than 30 days, prior to the filing of the abandonment application. The public may become a party to this proceeding by filing a protest, which the Commission will then investigate. For more information, contact the Office of Transportation Analysis.

* Rail Freight Carrier Assistance

Freight Assistance Division
Office of Railroad Development (RDV-11)
Federal Railroad Administration
U.S. Department of Transportation (DOT)
400 7th St., SW, Room 5411
Washington, DC 20590 (202) 366-9657

This office implements and administers Federal programs of financial and technical assistance to rail roads. It also evaluates requests for financial and technical assistance.

* Rail Industry Conditions

Office of Industry, Finance and Operations (RRP-11)
Federal Railroad Administration
U.S. Department of Transportation (DOT)
400 7th Street, SW, Room 8302
Washington, DC 20590 (202) 366-0386

This office serves as the principal advisory element in assessing the financial and operating condition of the railroad industry, with special emphasis on carriers in marginal or bankrupt financial condition. This office also administers programs to improve railroad labor/management relations and monitors disputes under the Railway Labor Act.

* Rail Transit Safety

Office of Safety (UTS-30)
Federal Transportation Administration (FTA)
400 7th St., SW, Room 6432
Washington, DC 20590 (202) 366-2896

FTA's rapid- and light-rail transit safety system is made up of the following aspects: 1) Safety Information--Reporting and Analysis System--developing a new rapid rail transit accident/incident reporting system; 2) System Safety--disseminating pertinent information to individuals working in the field of mass transit; 3) Drug and Alcohol Abuse information; and 4) Information on State Transit Programs.

* Railroad Accidents

System Support Division
Safety, RRS 22
Federal Railroad Administration
U.S. Department of Transportation (DOT) Room, 8301
400 7th St., NW
Washington, DC 20590 (202) 366-2760

Be patient. If any phone number is incorrect, call (area code) 555-1212 and request the new listing.

Business and Industry

The division maintains data accessible to the public regarding railroad accidents on a computer database, as well as in the following free publications:

Accident-Incident Bulletin (annual)
Railroad Highway Crossing Accident-Incident and Inventory Bulletin
Summary of Accidents Investigated by the Federal Railroad Administration (1987)
Railroad Employee Fatalities Investigated by the Federal Railroad Administration (quarterly)
Railroad Accident Investigation Reports (National Transportation Safety Board)

* Railroad Freight and Operations

Office of Policy Systems
Federal Railroad Administration
U.S. Department of Transportation (DOT)
400 7th Street, SW, RRP-20
Washington, DC 20590 (202) 366-2920

This office studies the use of freight cars, accounting and financial systems of railroads, coal rates, grain transportation, and mergers. Available for purchase is the yearly series *Carload Waybill Statistics (Report TD1)*, a compilation of rail freight statistics calculated annually showing traffic flows by commodity across broad geographic areas (including from Canada). You can order this report through the National Technical Information Service, or contact the above office for more information. *Freight Commodity Statistics* is available for purchase from the Association of American Railroads, and contact the above office for more information. The public use computer tape of the *Carload Waybill Sample* is available for purchase from ALK Associates, Inc., 1000 Herrontown Rd., Princeton, NJ 08540. Attn: Database Mgr.

* Railroad Industry Analysis

Office of External Affairs
Interstate Commerce Commission (ICC)
12th Street and Constitution Ave, NW
Washington, DC 20423 (202) 927-5737

The ICC Annual Report contains a detailed analysis of current developments in the Rail industry falling under their jurisdiction including financial conditions, reorganizations, mergers and acquisitions, labor issues, abandonments, rates, freight service, and passenger service.

* Railroad Information

Public Affairs (ROA-30)
Federal Railroad Administration (FRA)
U.S. Department of Transportation (DOT)
400 7th St., SW, Room 8125
Washington, DC 20590 (202) 366-0881

Contact the Public Affairs for additional information on FRA programs, publications, and activities.

* Railroad Reports

Reports Branch (RRS-22.1)
Federal Railroad Administration
U.S. Department of Transportation (DOT)
400 7th St., SW, Room 8301
Washington, DC 20590 (202) 366-2760

This office prepares Accident Investigation Reports and Employee Fatality Reports for publication and distribution. It also administers and processes Freedom of Information Act requests on matters pertaining to railroad safety.

* Railroad Research and Development

Office of Research and Development (RDV-30)
Federal Railroad Administration
U.S. Department of Transportation (DOT)
400 7th St., SW, Room 5420
Washington, DC 20590 (202) 366-0453

Call this office for information on the latest trends in railway technology and thinking. Topics include developments to improve track and track bed structures; work to reduce the effects of accidents involving tank cars carrying hazardous materials; efforts to gain a better understanding of equipment failures; development of less expensive and more effective grade crossing techniques; and research into human factors in train operation.

* Railroad Safety

Office of Safety (RRS-20)
Federal Railroad Administration
U.S. Department of Transportation (DOT)
400 7th St., SW, Room 8314
Washington, DC 20590 (202) 366-0521

This office inspects tracks, equipment, signals, and general railroad operations. It investigates accidents and complaints, and makes routine investigations. The office has jurisdiction over such areas as locomotives, signals, safety appliances, power brakes, hours of service, transportation of explosives; and human factors in rail operations. The free publication, *Safety Report*, lists federal government actions to improve railroad safety. It includes statistical compilations of accidents; incident reports, federal safety regulations, orders and standards issues by the Federal Railroad Administration; evaluation of the degree of their observance; summary of outstanding problems; analysis and evaluation of research and related activities; a list of completed or pending judicial actions for the enforcement of any safety rules, regulations, orders, or standards issued; and recommendations for additional legislation. The publication is available by contacting Public Affairs, Federal Railroad Administration, U.S. Department of Transportation, 400 7th St., SW, Room 3413, Washington, DC 20590; (202) 366-0881.

* Railway Hazardous Materials Transport

Hazardous Materials Division (RRS-12)
Federal Railroad Administration (FRA)
U.S. Department of Transportation (DOT)
400 7th Street, SW, Room 8326
Washington, DC 20590 (202) 366-0495

This office develops, reviews, analyzes, and prepares DOT exemptions to the hazardous materials regulations covering such items as package design, specifications and operating requirements for the FRA. This office coordinates its programs with the other DOT offices handling hazardous materials transport regulations.

* Railway Regulatory Analysis

Regulatory Analysis Division (RRP-31)
Federal Railroad Administration
U.S. Department of Transportation (DOT)
400 7th Street, SW, Room 8302J
Washington, DC 20590 (202) 366-0344

This office assesses the effects of proposed legislative and administrative changes to the rail regulatory system and evaluates the impact on railroads and shippers of changes implemented by Congress or the Interstate Commerce Commission.

* Rates and Charges

Bureau of Traffic
Rates and Informal Cases Section
Interstate Commerce Commission (ICC)
12th St. and Constitution Ave., NW, Room 4310
Washington, DC 20423 (202) 927-5180

A tariff is a schedule of rates and charges, and each carrier must file a copy with the ICC. If you have a complaint with a company regarding the charges, contact the Bureau of Traffic for assistance. They may be able to help resolve the matter quickly.

* Road Signs

Traffic Control Development Applications Division (HHS-32)
Traffic Control Systems
Traffic Operations Division
Office of Highway Safety
Federal Highway Administration (FHWA)
U.S. Department of Transportation (DOT)
400 7th St., SW
Washington, DC 20590 (202) 366-2187

Efforts by this division improve the effectiveness and uniformity of such traffic control devices as road signs, signal lamps, and highway markings throughout the country. Standards are developed for designing signs and using other traffic control devices. The meanings of road signs and markings are described in *Road Symbol Signs*, which can be obtained by contacting the office listed above. Two other publications on the subject, listed below, are available from the Superintendent of Documents, U.S. Government Printing Office, Washington, DC 20402; (202) 783-3238:

Highways, Waterways and Railways

Manual on Uniform Traffic Control Devices, ($22)
Standard Highway Signs Book, ($30)

* Rural Technical Assistance Program

Federal Highway Administration (FHWA) (HHI-20)
Office of Research and Development
Turner-Fairbank Highway Research Center
6300 Georgetown Pike
McLean, VA 22101-2144 (703) 285-2770

The Rural Technical Assistance Program (RTAP) is managed by the National Highway Institute, the technical training arm of the Federal Highway Administration. The RTAP provides direct technical assistance to those transportation agencies responsible for constructing or maintaining rural roads and local streets. Assistance is generated through RTAP's three supportive services: local technology transfer centers; a national clearinghouse for technical resources; and national technical projects. Contact the Turner-Fairbank center for more information.

* Special Permission Authority

Special Permission Board, Bureau of Traffic
Interstate Commerce Commission (ICC)
12th St. and Constitution Ave., NW, Room 4338
Washington, DC 20423 (202) 927-7348

Companies must give the ICC one day's notice for new or reduced rates and five to seven working days for increased rates or fares. You must contact the Special Permission Board to shorten the time period.

* Traffic Accident Data

Information Management and Analysis
Office of Highway Safety (HHS-12)
Federal Highway Administration (FHWA)
U.S. Department of Transportation (DOT)
400 7th St., SW
Washington, DC 20590 (202) 366-2159

Statistics are kept here on fatal and injury accident rates for the Nation's highways. The office accepts inquiries for specific topics of interest as well as copies of publications that contain fatality and injury data. The Office does not maintain a publications list, but will assist you in finding the information you need. The office can also transfer data onto magnetic tape. Call or write this office to request the data you need.

* Tariff Instructional Manual

Tariff Section
Bureau of Traffic
Interstate Commerce Commission (ICC)
12th St. and Constitution Ave., NW, Room 4363A
Washington, DC 20423 (202) 927-5150

The Tariff Instructional Manual is intended as a guide for carriers wishing to publish their own tariffs. It includes only the essentials and will require some adjustment to meet individual needs. This outlines the rules and regulations and offers several examples. They also include information on frequent problems and define some of the terms used in the tariff application.

* Traffic Safety Programs

Office of Traffic Safety Programs (NTS-01)
National Highway Traffic Safety Administration
U.S. Department of Transportation (DOT), Room 5125
400 7th Street, SW
Washington, DC 20590 (202) 366-1755

This office develops national goals and objectives with respect to highway safety as well as evaluating both in place and proposed state highway safety programs. It also manages national programs dealing with drunk and drugged driving, use of safety belts and child safety seats, automatic crash protection, police traffic services, emergency medical services, traffic records, pedestrian safety, and motorcycle safety.

* Transportation of Hazardous Materials

Office of Hazardous Materials Transportation (DHM-50)
Research and Special Programs Administration
U.S. Department of Transportation (DOT)

400 7th Street, SW
Washington, DC 20590-0001 (202) 366-4465

This office can provide you with information on the transportation of hazardous materials by highway, rail air, and water. Data is collected directly from industry and also via compliance inspections by field staff. The quarterly *Hazardous Material Newsletter* is available free from the office above.

* Transportation Safety Institute

Transportation Safety Institute (DTI-1)
Research and Special Programs Administration
U.S. Department of Transportation (DOT)
6500 South MacArthur Blvd.
Oklahoma City, OK 73125 (405) 680-3153

The Institute supports the Department's efforts to reduce transportation accidents. It develops and conducts training programs for Federal, state, and local governments; industry; and foreign personnel. Courses are offered in aviation, highway, marine, pipeline, and railroad safety; materials analysis; transportation security; and other subjects.

* Transport Statistics in the United States

Publications
Interstate Commerce Commission (ICC)
12th St. and Constitution Ave., NW
Washington, DC 20423 (202) 927-5930

This is an annual report which contains statistics of railroads and motor carriers. It includes a complete breakdown of finances, expenses and equipment, as well as service statistics. The tables are compiled from reports filed with the Commission by railroads and motor carriers.

* Transportation Statistics Compilation

Office of Economics
Interstate Commerce Commission (ICC)
12th Street and Constitution Ave, NW
Washington, DC 20423 (202) 927-5156

This office conducts economic and statistical analyses of the transportation industry for the ICC. It compiles and publishes transport statistics and cost studies. Contact the Office of Economic for more specific information and requests.

* Transportation Technical Reports Bibliography

Research and Special Programs Administration
John A. Volpe Transportation System Center
U.S. Department of Transportation (DOT)
Cambridge, MA 02142 (617) 494-2306

The Bibliography lists reports released by the Volpe National Transportation System Center from January 1980 to December 1990. Reports are listed by sponsoring agency and are indexed by author, title, subject, report number and performing organization. The bibliography includes reports from all of the component administrations of the U.S. Department of Transportation. It is available free from the Center.

* Trucking Company Analysis

Office of External Affairs
Interstate Commerce Commission (ICC)
12th Street and Constitution Ave, NW
Washington, DC 20423 (202) 927-5737

The *ICC Annual Report* contains a detailed analysis of the developments in the trucking industry falling under ICC jurisdiction. The 1990 Report discusses the financial condition of the industry, mergers, rates, operating rights, safety, and insurance issues. The report is available free from the ICC.

* Updates on Federal Railroad Administration Programs

Office of Public Affairs (A-30)
U.S. Department of Transportation (DOT), Room 10413
400 7th Street, SW
Washington, DC 20590 (202) 366-5580

The *U.S. Department of Transportation Annual Report* has information on current rail programs. The 1990 report highlights programs in the areas of rail safety, deregulation, labor/management disputes, services restructuring, magnetic levitation and high speed rail. The report is free from the office of public affairs.

Be patient. If any phone number is incorrect, call (area code) 555-1212 and request the new listing.

Business and Industry

* Updates on Traffic Programs

Office of Public Affairs (A-30)
U.S. Department of Transportation (DOT), Room 10413
400 7th Street, SW
Washington, DC 20590 (202) 366-5580

The U.S. Department of Transportation *Annual Report* lists the latest activities of the National Highway Traffic Safety Administration (NHTSA). Included are accident statistics, recent research on motor vehicle safety, and report summaries on highway safety. Recent litigation involving NHTSA is also outlined. The report is available free from the Office of Public Affairs.

* Vehicle Import Investigations

International Trade Commission (ITC)
500 E Street, SW
Washington, DC 20436 (202) 205-1807

The International Trade Commission investigates matters pertaining to domestic industry injury from imports and unfair trade practices. It's reports are available to the public. Reports are free from the ITC. Reports pertaining to auto imports include:

Rules of Origin Related to NAFTA and the North American Automotive Industry - USITC 2460.
All Terrain Vehicles (Japan) USITC 2071 and USITC 2163.
Automotive Glass (Mexico) USITC 2299.

The Reports Index for all *ITC Reports* is USITC 2484.

* Vehicle Performance Standards

Office of Rulemaking (NRM-1)
National Highway Traffic Safety Administration
U.S. Department of Transportation (DOT)
400 7th Street, SW
Washington, DC 20590 (202) 366-1810

This office develops and promulgates rules dealing with crash protection, crash survivability, crash avoidance, fuel economy, and theft protection of motor vehicles. It also directs programs relating to bumper standards, safety performance standards, tire standards, and other equipment standards. The Office also develops consumer information on crash protection and survivability characteristics for new and used motor vehicles and equipment.

* Waterways Traffic Regulation

Commander G-NSP
Vessel Traffic Services Branch
Office of Navigation Safety and Waterways Services
U.S. Coast Guard
U.S. Department of Transportation (DOT)
2100 2nd St., SW, Room 3202
Washington, DC 20593-0001 (202) 267-1539

To ensure the safe and orderly passage of vessels, cargo, and people, Vessel Traffic Services in major ports oversee the movement of vessels and install necessary safety equipment. Traffic is monitored closely during hazardous conditions and bad weather. To locate the Vessel Traffic Service nearest you, contact the branch listed above or your local Coast Guard office.

Selling to the Government Government Contracts

The Federal Government spends over $180 billion each year buying everything from toilet paper to bombs. They buy these goods and services from someone, and why can't that someone be you? All you need to do is learn to talk "governmentese", and get yourself into the purchasing loop. There are just a few easy steps you need to take to get you and your company into the government contracting business. Last year the government took action (either initiating or modifying) on 368,372 contracts.

Step 1

Each department within the federal government has a procurement office that buys whatever the department needs. Most of these offices have put together their own *Doing Business With the Department of _____* publication, which usually explains procurement policies, procedures, and programs. This booklet also contains a list of procurement offices, contact people, subcontracting opportunities, and a solicitation mailing list. Within each department is also an Office of Small and Disadvantaged Business Utilization, whose sole purpose is to push the interests of the small business, and to make sure these companies get their fair share of the government contracts. Another resource is your local Small Business Administration Office which should have a listing of U.S. Government Procurement Offices in your state.

Step 2

Once you have familiarized yourself with the overview, you need to find out who is buying what from whom and how much, as well as who wants what when. There are three ways to find out this information.

A. Daily Procurement News

Each weekday, the *Commerce Business Daily* (CBD) gives a complete listing of products and services (over $25,000) wanted by the U.S. government -- products and services that your business may be selling. Each listing includes the following: the product or service, along with a short description; name and address of the agency; deadline for proposals or bids; phone number to request specifications; and the solicitation number of the product or service needed. Many business concerns, including small businesses, incorporate CBD review into their government marketing activities. To obtain a $208/year subscription, contact Superintendent of Documents, U.S. Government Printing Office, Washington, DC 20402; (202) 783-3238.

B. Federal Data Systems Division (FDSD)

This Center distributes consolidated information about federal purchases, including research and development. FDSD can tell you how much the federal government spent last quarter on products and services, which agencies made those purchases, and who the contractors were. FDSD summarizes this information through two types of reports: The FDSD standard report and the FDSD special report. The standard report is a free, quarterly compilation containing statistical procurement information in "snapshot" form for over 60 federal agencies, as well as several charts, graphs, and tables which compare procurement activities by state, major product and service codes, method of procurement, and contractors. The report further includes quarterly and year-to-year breakdowns of amounts and percentages spent on small, women-owned, and minority businesses. Special reports are prepared upon request for a fee, based on computer and labor costs. They are tailored to the specific categories, which can be cross-tabulated in numerous ways. A special report can help you analyze government procurement and data trends, identify competitors and locate federal markets for individual products or services. Your Congressman may have access to the Federal Procurement Database from his/her office in Washington, which you may be able to use for free. For more information, contact Federal Data Systems Division, General Services Administration, 7th and D Street, SW, Room 5652, Washington, DC 20407; (202) 401-1529.

C. Other Contracts

For contracts under $25,000, you need to be placed on a department's list for solicitation bids on the contracts. The mailing list forms are available through the Procurement Office, the Office of Small and Disadvantaged Business Utilization, or your local Small Business Association office. Last year 18.7 billion dollars was spent on these "small" purchases, so these contracts are not to be overlooked.

Step 3: Subcontracting Opportunities

All of the federal procurement offices or Offices of Small and Disadvantaged Business Utilization (SBDU) can provide you with information regarding subcontracting. Many of the departments' prime contracts require that the prime contractor maximize small business subcontracting opportunities. Many prime contractors produce special publications which can be helpful to those interested in subcontracting. The SDBU Office can provide you with more information on the subcontracting process, along with a directory of prime contractors. Another good source for subcontract assistance is your local Small Business Administration (SBA) office, (800) 827-5722. SBA develops subcontracting opportunities for small business by maintaining close contact with large business prime contractors and referring qualified small firms to them. The SBA has developed agreements and close working relationships with hundreds of prime contractors who cooperate by offering small firms opportunities to compete for their subcontracts. In addition, to complete SBA's compliance responsibilities,

Be patient. If any phone number is incorrect, call (area code) 555-1212 and request the new listing.

Selling To The Government

commercial market representatives monitor prime contractors in order to assess their compliance with laws governing subcontracting opportunities for small businesses.

Step 4: Small Business Administration's (SBA) 8(a) Program

Are you a socially or economically disadvantaged person who has a business? This group includes, but is not limited to, Black Americans, Hispanic Americans, Native Americans, Asian Pacific Americans, and Subcontinent Asian Americans. Socially and economically disadvantaged individuals represent a significant percentage of U.S. citizens, yet account for a disproportionately small percentage of total U.S. business revenues. The 8(a) program assists firms to participate in the business sector and to become independently competitive in the marketplace. SBA may provide participating firms with procurement, marketing, financial, management or other technical assistance. A Business Opportunity Specialist will be assigned to each firm that participates, and is responsible for providing the firm with access to assistance that can help the firm fulfill its business goals. SBA undertakes an extensive effort to provide government contracting opportunities to participating businesses. SBA has the Procurement Automated Source System (PASS) which places your company's capabilities online so that they may be available to Government agencies and major corporations when they request potential bidders for contracts and subcontracts. To apply for the 8(a) program you must attend an interview session with an official in the SBA field office in your area. For more information, contact your local Small Business Administration (SBA) Office, or you can call (800) 827-5722 for the SBA office nearest you.

Step 5: Bond

A Surety bond is often a prerequisite for government and private sector contracts. This is particularly true when the contract involves construction. In order for the company to qualify for an SBA Guarantee Bond, they must make the bonding company aware of the capabilities based on past contract performance and meeting of financial obligations. SBA can assist firms to obtain surety bonding for contracts that do not exceed $1,250,000. SBA is authorized, when appropriate circumstances occur, to guarantee as much as 90 percent of losses suffered by a surety resulting from a breach of terms of a bond.

Step 6: Publications

The Government Printing Office has several publications for sale which explain the world of government contracts. For ordering information, contact Superintendent of Documents, Government Printing Office, Washington, DC 20402; (202) 783-3238.

* *U.S. Government Purchasing and Sales Directory* ($5.50): The Directory is an alphabetical listing of the products and services bought by the military departments, and a separate listing of the civilian agencies. The Directory also includes an explanation of the ways in which the SBA can help a business obtain government prime contracts and subcontracts, data on government sales of surplus property, and comprehensive

descriptions of the scope of the government market for research and development.

* *Guide to the Preparation of Offers for Selling to the Military* ($4.75)

* *Small Business Specialists* ($3.75)

* *Small Business Subcontracting Directory* ($7): designed to aid small businesses interested in subcontracting opportunities within the U.S. Department of Defense (DOD). The guide is arranged alphabetically by State and includes the name and address of each current DOD prime contractor as well as the product or service being provided to DOD.

* *Women Business Owners; Selling to the Federal Government* ($3.75)

* *Selling to the Military*, ($8)

Step 7: What is GSA?

General Services Administration (GSA) is the Government's business agent. On an annual budget of less than half a billion dollars, it directs and coordinates nearly $8 billion a year worth of purchases, sales, and services. Its source of supply is private enterprise, and its clients are all branches of the Federal Government. GSA plans and manages leasing, purchase, or construction of office buildings, laboratories, and warehouses; buys and delivers nearly $4 billion worth of goods and services; negotiates the prices and terms for an additional $2.3 billion worth of direct business between federal groups and private industry; sets and interprets the rules for federal travel and negotiates reduced fares and lodging rates for federal travelers; and manages a 92,000 vehicle fleet with a cumulative yearly mileage of over 1 billion. For a copy of *Doing Business With GSA*, *GSA's Annual Report*, or other information regarding GSA, contact Office of Publication, General Services Administration, 18th and F Streets, NW, Washington, DC 20405; (202) 501-1235. For information on GSA's architect and engineer services, such as who is eligible for GSA professional services contracts, how to find out about potential GSA projects, what types of contracts are available, and where and how to apply, contact Office of Design and Construction, GSA, 18th and F Streets, NW, Washington, DC 20405; (202) 501-1888. Information on specifications and standards of the Federal Government is contained in a booklet, *Guide to Specifications and Standards*, which is available free from Specifications Sections, General Services Administration, 470 E L'Enfant Plaza, SW, Suite 8100, Washington, DC 20407; (202) 755-0325.

Step 8: Bid and Contract Protests

The General Accounting Office (GAO) resolves disputes between agencies and bidders for government contracts, including grantee award actions. The free publication, *Bid Protests at GAO; A Descriptive Guide*, contains information on GAO's procedures for determining legal questions arising from the awarding of government contracts. Contact Information Handling and Support Facilities, General Accounting Office, Gaithersburg, MD 20877; (202) 275-6241. For Contract

Government Contracts

Appeals, the GSA Board of Contract Appeals works to resolve disputes arising out of contracts with GSA, the U.S. Departments of Treasury, Education, Commerce, and other independent government agencies. The Board also hears and decides bid protest arising out of government-wide automated data processing (ADP) procurements. A contractor may elect to use either the GSA Board or the General Accounting Office for resolution of an ADP bid protest. Contractors may elect to have their appeals processed under the Board's accelerated procedures if the claim is $50,000 or less, or under the small claims procure if the claim is $10,000 or less. Contractors may also request that a hearing be held at a location convenient to them. With the exception of small claims decisions, contractors can appeal adverse Board decisions to the U.S. Court of Appeals for the Federal Circuit. For more information, contact Board of Contract Appeals, General Services Administration, 18th and F Streets, NW, Washington, DC 20405; 202-501-0720. There are other Contract Appeals Boards for the other Departments. One of the last paragraphs in your government contract should specify which Board you are to go to if a problem arises.

Selling To The Government

Free Local Help: The Best Place To Start To Sell To The Government

Within each state there are places you can contact to receive help in getting started in the federal procurement process. As was stated previously, your local Small Business Administration (SBA) office is a good resource. In addition to their other services, the SBA can provide you with a list of Federal Procurement Offices based in your state, so you can visit them in person. Other places to turn are your local Small Business Development Center (look under Economic Development in your phone book). These offices are funded jointly by federal and state governments, and are usually associated with the state university system. They are aware of the federal procurement process, and can help you draw up a sensible business plan. Some states have established programs to assist businesses in the federal procurement process for all departments in the government. These programs are designed to help businesses learn about the bidding process, the resources available, and provide information on how the procurement system operates. They can match the product or service you are selling with the appropriate agency, and then help you market your wares. Several programs have online bid matching services, whereby if a solicitation appears in the *Commerce Business Daily* that matches what your company markets, then the program will contact you to start the bid process. They can then request the appropriate documents, and assist you to achieve your goal. These Procurement Assistance Offices (PAOs) are partially funded by the U.S. Department of Defense to assist businesses with Defense Procurement. For a current listing of PAOs contact:

Defense Logistics Agency
Office of Small and Disadvantaged Utilization
Bldg. 4, Cameron Station, Room 4B110
Alexandria, VA 22304-6100   (703) 274-6471

Let Your Congressman Help You

Are you trying to market a new product to a Department of the Federal Government? Need to know where to try to sell your wares? Is there some problem with your bid? Your Congressman can be of assistance. They want business in their state to boom, so they will make an effort to assist companies in obtaining federal contracts. Frequently, they will write a letter to accompany your bid, or if you are trying to market a new product, they will write a letter to the procurement office requesting that they review your product. Your congressman can also be your trouble-shooter. If there is some problem with your bid, your Congressman can assist you in determining and resolving the problem, and can provide you with information on the status of your bid. Look in the blue pages of your phone book for your Senators' or Representatives' phone numbers, or call them in Washington at (202) 224-3121.

Small Business Set-Asides

The Small Business Administration (SBA) encourages government purchasing agencies to set-aside suitable government purchases for exclusive small business competition. A purchase which is restricted to small business bidders is identified by a set-aside clause in the invitation for bids or request for proposals. There is no overall listing of procurements which are, or have been, set-aside for small business. A small business learns which purchases are reserved for small business by getting listed on bidders' lists. It also can help keep itself informed of set-aside opportunities by referring to the *Commerce Business Daily*. Your local SBA office can provide you with more information on set-asides, as can the Procurement Assistance Offices listed below. You can locate your nearest SBA office by calling (800) 827-5722.

Veterans Assistance

Each Small Business Administration District Office has a Veterans Affairs Officer which can assist veteran-owned businesses in obtaining government contracts. Although there is no such thing as veterans set-aside contracts, the Veterans Administration does make an effort to fill its contracts using veteran-owned businesses. Contact your local SBA office for more information.

Woman-Owned Business Assistance

There are over 3.7 million women-owned businesses in the United States, and the number is growing each year. Current government policy requires federal contracting officers to increase their purchases from women-owned businesses. Although the women-owned firms will receive more opportunities to bid, they still must be the lowest responsive and responsible bidder to win the contract. To assist these businesses, each SBA district office has a Women's Business Representative, who can provide you with information regarding government programs. Most of the offices hold a *Selling to the Federal Government* seminar, which is designed to educate the business owner on the ins and outs of government procurement. There is also a helpful publication, *Women Business Owners: Selling to the Federal Government*, which provides information on the procurement opportunities available. Contact your local SBA office or your Procurement Assistance Office for more information.

Minority and Labor Surplus Area Assistance

Are you a socially or economically disadvantaged person who has a business? This group includes, but is not limited to, Black Americans, Hispanic Americans, Native Americans, Asian Pacific Americans, and Subcontinent Asian Americans. Socially and economically disadvantaged individuals represent a significant percentage of U.S. citizens yet account for a disproportionately small percentage of total U.S. business revenues. The 8(a) program assists firms to participate in the business sector and to become independently competitive in the marketplace. SBA may provide participating firms with

Be patient. If any phone number is incorrect, call (area code) 555-1212 and request the new listing.

Free Local Help

procurement, marketing, financial, management or other technical assistance. A Business Opportunity Specialist will be assigned to each firm that participates, and is responsible for providing the firm with access to assistance that can help the firm fulfill its business goals. SBA undertakes an extensive effort to provide government contracting opportunities to participating businesses. SBA has the Procurement Automated Source System (PASS) which places your company's capabilities online so that they may be available to government agencies and major corporations when they request potential bidders for contracts and subcontracts. To apply for the 8(a) program you must attend an interview session with an official in the SBA field office in your area. Some areas of the country have been determined to be labor surplus areas, which means there is a high rate of unemployment. Your local SBA office can tell you if you live in such an area, as some contracts are set-asides for labor surplus areas. For more information contact your local Small Business Administration office, or you can call (800) 827-5722 for the SBA office nearest you.

Alabama

University of Alabama at Birmingham, School of Business, Ms. Patricia E. Thompson, UAB Station, Birmingham, AL 35294; (205) 934-7260.

Alaska

University of Alaska at Anchorage, Small Business Development Center, Ms. Jan Fredericks, 430 W. 7th Ave., Suite 110, Anchorage, AK 99501; (907) 274-7232.

Arizona

Arizona Procurement Technical Assistance Network, Arizona Department of Commerce, 3800 N. Central Ave., Bldg. D, Phoenix, AZ 85012; (602) 280-1348.

National Center for American Indians Enterprise Development, National Center Headquarters, Mr. Steve L.A. Stallings, 953 E. Juanita Ave., Mesa, AZ 85204; (602) 831-7524.

Arkansas

Southern Arkansas University (SAU), Mr. Robert E. Graham, P.O. Box 1239, Hwy. 19 North, Magnolia, AR 71753; (501) 235-4375.

California

c/o AMD, Procurement Assistance Center m/s 31, Dr. Murray P. Leavitt, 901 Thompson Place, Sunnyvale, CA 94088-3453; (408) 739-6283.

Private Industry Council of Imperial County, Inc., 1411 State Street, El Centro, CA 92243; (619) 353-5050.

Merced County Office of Economic and Strategic Development, Contract Procurement Center, Karen Prentiss, 1632 N. Street, Merced, CA 95340; (209) 752-3891.

PIC of Solano County, Business Services Division, Terrye Miller-Davis, 320 Campus Lane, Suisun, CA 94585; (707) 864-3370.

Delaware

Delaware State College, Dept. of Economics and Business, Dr. Winston Awadzi, 1200 N. Dupont Hwy., Dover, DE 19901; (302) 739-3521.

Florida

University of West Florida, Florida Procurement Technical Assistance Program, Mr. Jerry Cartwright, 11000 University Parkway, Bldg. 38, Pensacola, FL 32514; (904) 474-3016.

Georgia

Columbus College, Division of Continuing Education, Columbus, GA 31993-2399; (404) 649-1092.

Georgia Tech Research Corporation, Georgia Institute of Technology, Mr. Charles P. Catlett, O'Keefe Building, Room 246, Atlanta, GA 30332; (404) 894-6121.

Hawaii

State of Hawaii, Department of Business, Economic Development and Tourism, Mr. Larry Nelson, P.O. Box 2359, Honolulu, HI 96804; (808) 586-2598.

Idaho

Business Network, Mr. Larry Demirelli, Department of Commerce, 700 W. State St., Boise, ID 83720; (208) 334-2470.

Illinois

State of Illinois, Department of Commerce and Community Affairs, 620 East Adams, 6th Floor, Springfield, IL 62701; (217) 524-5696.

Indiana

Indiana Institute for New Business Ventures, Government Marketing Assistance Group, Mr. A. David Schaff, One North Capitol, Suite 1240, Indianapolis, IN 46204-2026; (317) 264-5600.

Iowa

State of Iowa, Iowa Department of Economic Development, Mr. Allen Williams, 200 East Grand Avenue, Des Moines, IA 50309; (319) 398-5665.

Kentucky

Kentucky Cabinet for Economic Development, Department of Existing Business and Industry, Mr. Bernard L. Williams, 500 Mero Street, Capital Plaza Tower, 23rd Floor, Frankfort, KY 40601; (800) 626-2930.

Louisiana

Jefferson Parish Economic Development Commission, The Bid Center, Ms. Phyllis McLaren, 1221 Elmwood Park Blvd., Suite 405, Harahan, LA 70123; (504) 736-6550.

Louisiana Productivity Center/USL, Procurement Technical Assistance Network, Mr. Stephen A. Killingsworth, P.O. Box 44172, 241 E. Lewis Street, Lafayette, LA 70504-4172; (318) 231-6767.

Northwest Louisiana Government Procurement Center, Greater Shreveport Economic Development, P.O. Box 20074, 400 Edwards Street, Shreveport, LA 71120-0074; (318) 677-2530.

Maine

Eastern Maine Development Corporation, Acadia Development Corporation, Mr. Richard L. Allen, One Cumberland Place, Suite 300, Bangor, ME 04402-2579; (207) 942-6389, (800) 339-6389 (ME), (800) 955-6549.

Maryland

Morgan State University, School of Business and Management, Dr. Otis Thomas, Cold Spring Lane and Hillen Road, Baltimore, MD 21239; (410) 319-3160.

Tri-County Council for Western Maryland Inc., Michael J. Wagoner, 111 South George Street, Cumberland, MD 21502; (301) 777-2158.

Michigan

Genesee County Metropolitan Planning Commission, Procurement Technical Assistance Program, 1101 Beach Street, Room 223, Flint, MI 48502; (313) 257-3010.

Be patient. If any phone number is incorrect, call (area code) 555-1212 and request the new listing.

Selling To The Government

Kalamazoo County CGA, Inc., Government Contracting Office, Ms. Sandra Ledbetter, 100 W. Michigan, Suite 294, Kalamazoo, MI 49007; (616) 342-0000.

Downriver Community Conference, Economic Development Department, 15100 Northline, Southgate, MI 48195; (313) 281-0700.

Northwest Michigan Council of Governments, Procurement Technical Assistance Center, Mr. James F. Haslinger, P.O. Box 506, Traverse City, MI 49685-0506; (616) 929-5036.

Saginaw County, Contract Procurement Office, Ms. JoAnn Crary, 301 E. Genessee, 4th Floor, Saginaw, MI 48607; (517) 754-8222.

Schoolcraft College, Ms. Judi Zima, 18600 Haggerty Road, Livonia, MI 48152-2696; (313) 462-4438.

Thumb Area Consortium/Growth Alliance, Local Procurement Office, Mr. Marvin N. Pichla, 3270 Wilson Street, Marlette, MI 48453; (517) 635-3561.

Warren, Center Line, Sterling Heights, Chamber of Commerce, Ms. Janet E. Masi, 30500 Van Dyke Ave., Suite 118, Warren, MI 48093-2178; (313) 751-3939.

West Central Michigan Employment and Training Consortium, Procurement Technical Assistance, Mr. John Calabrese, 110 Elm Street, Big Rapids, MI 49307; (616) 796-4891.

Minnesota

Minnesota Project Innovation, Procurement Assistance Center, 111 3rd Ave., S, Minneapolis, MN 55401-2554; (612) 338-3280.

Mississippi

Mississippi Contract Procurement Center, Mr. Charles W. Ryland, P.O. Box 610, Gulfport, MS 39502; (601) 864-2961.

Missouri

Curators of the University of Missouri, University Extension, Steve Wyatt, 215 University Hall, Columbia, MO 65211; (314) 882-0344.

Montana

Billings Area Business Incubator, James F. Ouldhouse, 115 No. Broadway, Suite 200, Billings, MT 59101; (406) 256-6876.

High Plains Development Authority Inc., Janet L. Seagrave, #2 Railroad Square, P.O. Box 2568, Great Falls, MT 59401; (406) 454-1934.

Procurement Technical Institute, Butte PTA Center, Greg Depuydt, 305 West Mercury, Butte, MT 59701; (406) 782-7333.

Nebraska

Nebraska Department of Economic Development, Existing Business Assistance Division, Mr. Jack Ruff, 301 Centennial Mall So., P.O. Box 94666, Lincoln, NE 68509-4666; (402) 471-3769.

Nevada

State of Nevada, Commission on Economic Development, Mr. Ray Horner, Capitol Complex, Carson City, NV 89710; (702) 687-4325.

New Hampshire

Small Business Development Center, University Center, Room 311, 400 Commercial Street, Manchester, NH 03101; (603) 743-3995, (800) 322-0390 (in NH).

New Jersey

Elizabeth Development Corporation of New Jersey, Elizabeth Procurement Assistance Center, Mr. Arthur Myers, 1045 East Jersey Street, P.O. Box 512, Elizabeth, NJ 07207-0512; (908) 289-0262.

New Jersey Institute of Technology, Defense Procurement Technical Assistance Center, Mr. John McKenna, 240 Martin Luther King Blvd., Newark, NJ 07102; (201) 596-3105.

New Mexico

State of New Mexico, Procurement Assistance Program, 1100 St. Francis Drive, Room 2006, Santa Fe, NM 87503; (505) 827-0423.

American Indian Business and Technologies Corporation, Richard A. Ailes, 2015 Wyoming Blvd. NE, Suite E, Albuquerque, NM 87112; (505) 275-7484.

New York

Cattaraugus County, Department of Economic Development and Tourism, Mr. David K. Yarnes, 303 Court Street, Little Valley, NY 14755; (716) 938-9111.

Long Island Development Corporation, Procurement Technical Assistance Program, Mr. Morris Breiman, 255 Glen Cove Road, Carle Place, NY 11514; (516) 741-5690.

New York City Office of Business Development, Procurement Outreach Program, Mr. Martin Bass, 17 John Street, New York, NY 10038; (212) 513-6356.

Rockland Economic Development Corporation, Procurement Div., Mr. Martin Penn, 1 Blue Hill Plaza, Room 812, Pearl River, NY 10965; (914) 735-7040.

South Bronx Overall Economic Development Corporation, 370 East 149th Street, Bronx, NY 10455; (212) 292-3113.

North Carolina

University of North Carolina, Small Business and Technology Development Center, Mr. Scott R. Daugherty, 4509 Creedmoor Road, Raleigh, NC 27612; (919) 571-4154.

North Dakota

State Small Business Development Center Office, Economic Development Commission, Business Development Assistance Division, Liberty Memorial Building, Bismarck, ND 58505; (701) 224-2810.

Ohio

Central State University, Developing Nations Center, Mr. James H. Sangster, Wilberforce, OH 45384; (513) 376-6514.

Columbus Area Chamber of Commerce, Central Ohio Government Marketing Assistance Program, 37 N. High Street, Columbus, OH 43215; (614) 225-6940.

Community Improvement Corporation of Lake County, Northeast Ohio Government Contract Assistance Center, 7750 Clocktower Drive, Mentor, OH 44060; (216) 951-1290.

Greater Cleveland Government Business Program, 200 Tower City Center, 50 Public Square, Cleveland, OH 44113; (216) 621-3300.

Lawrence Economic Development Corporation, Procurement Outreach Center, 101 Sand Road, P.O. Box 488, South Point, OH 45680; (614) 894-3838.

Mahoning Valley Economic Development Corporation, Mahoning Valley Technical Procurement Center, Mr. Stephen J. Danyi, 4319 Belmont Ave., Youngstown, OH 44505; (216) 759-3668.

Terra Technical College, North Central Ohio Procurement Technical Ass't Program, Ms. Ronda Gooden, 1220 Cedar St., Fremont, OH 43420; (419) 332-1002.

University of Cincinnati, CECE-Extension Unit Small Business Center, Ms. Nancy Rogers, 1111 Edison Drive, IAMS Building, Cincinnati, OH 45216; (513) 948-2082.

Oklahoma

Oklahoma Department of Vocational-Technical Education, Business Assistance and Development Division, Ms. Denise Agee, 1500 West Seventh Ave., Stillwater, OK 74074-4364; (405) 743-5574.

Be patient. If any phone number is incorrect, call (area code) 555-1212 and request the new listing.

Free Local Help

Tribal Government Institute, 111 N. Peters, Suite 200, Norman, OK 73069; (405) 329-5542.

Oregon

State of Oregon, Economic Development Department, Mr. J. Rick Evans, 775 Summer Street NE, Salme, OR 97310; (503) 888-2595.

Pennsylvania

Economic Development Council of Northeastern Pennsylvania, Local Development District, Ms. Karen D. Ostroskie, 1151 Oak Street, Pittston, PA 18640; (717) 655-5581.

Indiana University of Pennsylvania, Dr. Robert Camp, Robertshaw Building, Incubator Office, 650 South 13th Street, Suite 303, Indiana, PA 15705-1087; (412) 357-2520.

Northern Tier Regional Planning and Development Commission, Economic-Community Development, Ms. Katherine A. Shatinsky, 507 Main Street, Towanda, PA 18848; (717) 265-9103.

Northwest Pennsylvania Regional Planning and Development Commission, Mr. Richard A. Mihalic, 614 Eleventh Street, Franklin, PA 16323; (814) 437-3024.

Private Industry Council of Westmoreland/Fayette, Inc., Procurement Assistance Center, Mr. Charles R. Burtyk, 531 South Main Street, Greensburg, PA 15601; (412) 836-2600.

SEDA - Council of Governments, Mr. A. Lawrence Barletta, RD 1, Timberhaven, Lewisburg, PA 17837; (717) 524-4491.

Southern Alleghenies Planning and Development Commission, Local Development District, Mr. Daniel R. Shade, 541 58th Street, Altoona, PA 16602; (814) 949-6528.

University of Pennsylvania, PASBDC, Snider Entrepreneurial Center, Mr. Paul A. Fickes, Philadelphia, PA 19104-6374; (215) 898-1282.

Geneva College, Geneva College Government Procurement Assistance Center, Jeffrey Milroy, 3231 Fourth Ave., Beaver Falls, PA 15010; (412) 847-4022.

Johnstown Area Regional Industries, Defense Procurement Assistance Center, Robert J. Murphy, 111 Market St., Johnstown, PA 15901; (814) 539-4951.

Mon Valley Renaissance, Califoria University of Pennsylvania, Joseph E. Hopkins, California, PA 15419; (412) 938-5881.

Puerto Rico

Commonwealth of Puerto Rico (FOMENTO), Economic Development Administration, Mr. Pedro J. Acevedo, 355 Roosevelt Avenue, Hato Rey, PR 00918; (809) 752-6861.

Rhode Island

Rhode Island Department of Economic Development, Business Development Office, 7 Jackson Walkway, Providence, RI 02903; (401) 277-2601.

South Carolina

University of South Carolina, College of Business Administration, Small Business Development Center, Mr. John Lenti, Columbia, SC 29208; (803) 777-4907.

South Dakota

South Dakota Procurement Technical Assistance Center, School of Business, Mr. Stephen L. Tracy, 414 E. Clark, Vermillion, SD 57069; (605) 677-5287.

Tennessee

University of Tennessee, Center for Industrial Services, Mr. T.C. Parsons, 226 Capitol Boulevard Bldg., Suite 606, Nashville, TN 37219-1804; (615) 242-2456.

Texas

City of San Antonio Procurement Outreach Center, Department of Economic and Employment Development, Ms. Rosalie O. Manzano, P.O. Box 839966, San Antonio, TX 78283; (512) 554-7133.

Northeast Texas Community College, East Texas Procurement Technical Assistance Program, P.O. Box 1307, Mt. Pleasant, TX 75455; (903) 572-1911.

University of Houston/TIPS, Texas Information Procurement Service, 4800 Calhoun, Houston, TX 77204; (713) 752-8477.

University of Texas at Arlington, Automaton and Robotics Research Institute, P.O. Box 19125, Arlington, TX 76019; (817) 273-2105.

Angelina College, Defense PTA Center, Dr. Larry Phillips, P.O. Box 1768, Lufkin, TX 75902; (409) 639-1301.

El Paso Greater Chamber of Commerce, Wes Jury, 10 Civic Center Plaza, El Paso, TX 79901; (915) 534-0500.

Utah

Utah Department of Community and Economic Development, Utah Procurement Outreach Program, Mr. James F. Odle, 324 South State Street, Suite 235, Salt Lake City, UT 84111; (801) 538-8791.

Vermont

State of Vermont, Agency of Development and Community Affairs, Mr. William P. McGrath, 109 State Street, Montpelier, VT 05609; (802) 828-3221.

Virginia

Crater Planning District Commission, The Procurement Assistance Center, Mr. Dennis K. Morris, 1964 Wakefield Street, P.O. Box 1808, Petersburg, VA 23805; (804) 861-1667.

George Mason University, Entrepreneurship Center, Dean John O'Malley, 4400 University Drive, Fairfax, VA 22030; (703) 330-5091.

Southwest Virginia Community College, Ms. Maxine B. Rogers, P.O. Box 5VCC, Richlands, VA 24641; (703) 964-7334.

Washington

Economic Development Council of Snohomish County, Ms. C. Grace Brown, 913 134th Street SW, Everett, WA 98204; (206) 743-4567.

Spokane Area Economic Development Council, Local Business Assistance, Mr. Ken Olson, 221 N. Wall, Suite 310, Spokane, WA 99210-0203; (509) 624-9285.

Economic Development Council of Kitsap County, Earle Smith, 4841 Auto Center Way, Suite 204, Bremerton, WA 98312; (206) 377-9499.

West Virginia

Mid-Ohio Valley Regional Council, Procurement Technical Assistance Center, P.O. Box 5528, Vienna, WV 26105; (304) 295-8714.

Regional Contracting Assistance Center, Inc., Mr. Mick Walker, 1116 Smith Street, Suite 202, Charleston, WV 25301; (304) 344-2546.

Wisconsin

Aspin Procurement Institute, Inc., Mr. Mark F. Wagner, 840 Lake Avenue, Racine, WI 53403; (414) 632-6321.

Madison Area Technical College, Small Business Assistance Center, Ms. Wendy L. Lein, 211 North Carroll Street, Madison, WI 53703; (608) 258-2330.

Be patient. If any phone number is incorrect, call (area code) 555-1212 and request the new listing.

Selling To The Government

Government Buys Bright Ideas From Inventors: Small Business Innovative Research Programs (SBIR)

The SBIR stimulates technological innovation, encourages small science and technology-based firms to participate in government-funded research, and provides incentives for converting research results into commercial applications. The program is designed to stimulate technological innovation in this country by providing qualified U.S. small business concerns with competitive opportunities to propose innovative concepts to meet the research and development needs of the Federal Government. Eleven federal agencies with research and development budgets greater than $100 million are required by law to participate: The Departments of Defense, Health and Human Services, Energy, Agriculture, Commerce, Transportation, and Education; the National Aeronautics and Space Administration; the National Science Foundation; the Nuclear Regulatory Commission; and the Environmental Protection Agency.

Businesses of 500 or fewer employees that are organized for profit are eligible to compete for SBIR funding. Nonprofit organizations and foreign-owned firms are not eligible to receive awards, and the research must be carried out in the U.S. All areas of research and development solicit for proposals, and the 1992 budget for SBIR is $475 million. There are three phases of the program. Phase I determines whether the research idea, often on high-risk advanced concepts, is technically feasible, whether the firm can do high quality research, and whether sufficient progress has been made to justify a larger Phase II effort. This phase is usually funded for 6 months with awards up to $50,000. Phase II is the principal research effort, and is usually limited to a maximum of $500,000 for up to two years. The third phase, which is to pursue potential commercial applications of the research funded under the first two phases, is supported solely by non-federal funding, usually from third party, venture capital or large industrial firms. SBIR is one of the most competitive research and development programs in government. About one proposal out of ten received is funded in Phase I. Generally, about half of these receive support in Phase II. Solicitations for proposals are released once a year (in a few cases twice a year). To assist the small business community in its SBIR efforts, the U.S. Small Business Administration publishes the Pre-Solicitation Announcement (PSA) in December, March, June and September of each year. Every issue of the PSA contains pertinent information on the SBIR Program along with details on SBIR solicitations that are about to be released. This publication eliminates the need for small business concerns to track the activities of all of the federal agencies participating in the SBIR Program. In recognition of the difficulties encountered by many small firms in their efforts to locate sources of funding essential to finalization of their innovative products, SBA has developed the Commercialization Matching System. This system contains information on all SBIR awardees as well as financing sources that have indicated an interest in investing in SBIR innovations. Firms interested in obtaining more information on the SBIR Program or receiving the PSA, should contact the Office of Innovation, Research and

Technology, Small Business Association, 1441 L Street, NW, Washington, DC, (202) 205-6450.

SBIR representatives listed below can answer questions and send you materials about their agency's SBIR plans and funding.

U.S. Department of Agriculture
Office of Grants and Program Systems, U.S. Department of Agriculture, Room 323, Aerospace Center, 901 D Street, SW, Washington, DC 20250; (202) 401-4002.

U.S. Department of Defense
Small Business and Economic Utilization, Office of Secretary of Defense, Room 2A340, Pentagon, Washington, DC 20301; (800) 225-DTIC.

U.S. Department of Education
Dr. Ed Esty, The Brown Building, 1900 M Street, NW, Room 722, Washington, DC 20208; (202) 708-5366.

U.S. Department of Energy
SBIR Program, U.S. Department of Energy, ER-16, Washington, DC 20585; (301) 903-5867.

U.S. Department of Health and Human Services
Mr. Richard Clinkscales, Director, Office of Small and Disadvantaged Business Utilization, U.S. Department of Health and Human Services, 200 Independence Ave., SW, Room 513D, Washington, DC 20201; (202) 690-7300.

U.S. Department of Transportation
SBIR Program, Transportation System Center, U.S. Department of Transportation, Kendall Square, Cambridge, MA 01242; (617) 494-2051.

Environmental Protection Agency
EPA Small Business Ombudsman, 401 M Street, SW, A149-C, Washington, DC 20460; (800) 368-5888.

National Aeronautics and Space Administration
SBIR Program, National Aeronautics and Space Administration, 250 E Street, SW, Suite 380, Washington, DC 20024; (202) 488-2931.

National Science Foundation
Mr. Ritchie Coryell, Mr. Roland Tibbetts, SBIR Program Managers, National Science Foundation, 1800 G Street, NW, Washington, DC 20550; (202) 653-5002.

Nuclear Regulatory Commission
Ms. Mary Ann Riggs, SBIR Coordinator, Office of Nuclear Regulatory Research, Nuclear Regulatory Commission, Mail Stop NLS-007, Washington, DC 20555; (301) 492-3625.

Be patient. If any phone number is incorrect, call (area code) 555-1212 and request the new listing.

State Procurement Offices

The following offices are starting places for finding out who in the state government will purchase your products or services.

Alabama
Finance Department, Purchasing Division, 11 South Union, Room 200, Montgomery, AL 36130; (205) 242-7250.

Alaska
State of Alaska, Department of Administration, Division of General Services and Supply, P.O. Box 110210, Juneau, AK 99811-0210; (907) 465-2253.

Arizona
State Purchasing, Executive Tower, Suite 101, 1700 W. Washington, Phoenix, AZ 85007; (602) 542-5511.

Arkansas
Office of State Purchasing, P.O. Box 2940, Little Rock, AR 72203; (501) 324-9312.

California
Office of Procurement, Department of General Services, 1823 14th Street, Sacramento, CA 95814; (916) 445-6942.

Colorado
Division of Purchasing, 225 E. 16th Ave., Suite 900, Denver, CO 80203; (303) 866-6100.

Connecticut
State of Connecticut, Department of Administrative Services, Bureau of Purchases, 460 Silver Street, Middletown, CT 06457; (203) 638-3280.

Delaware
Purchasing Division, Purchasing Bldg., P.O. Box 299, Delaware City, DE 19706; (302) 577-3070.

District of Columbia
Department of Administrative Services, 441 4th Street NW, Room 7544, Washington, DC 20001; (202) 727-0171.

Florida
General Service Department, Division of Purchasing, Knight Bldg., 2737 Centerview Drive, 2nd Floor, Tallahassee, FL 32399-0950; (904) 488-1194.

Georgia
Administrative Services Department, 200 Piedmont Ave., Room 1308 SE, Atlanta, GA 30334; (404) 656-3240.

Hawaii
Purchasing Branch, Purchasing and Supply Division, Department of Accounting and General Services, Room 416, 1151 Punch Bowl, Honolulu, HI 96813; (808) 586-0575.

Idaho
Division of Purchasing, Administration Department, 5569 Kendall, State House Mail, Boise, ID 83720; (208) 327-7465.

Illinois
Department of Central Management Services, Procurement Services, 801 Stratton Bldg., Springfield, IL 62706; (217) 782-2301.

Indiana
Department of Administration, Procurement Division, 402 W. Washington Street, Room W-468, Indianapolis, IN 46204; (317) 232-3032.

Iowa
State of Iowa, Department of General Services, Purchasing Division, Hoover State Office Building, Des Moines, IA 50319; (515) 281-3089.

Kansas
Division of Purchasing, Room 102 North, Landon State Office Building, 900 SW Jackson Street, Topeka, KS 66612; (913) 296-2376.

Kentucky
Purchases, Department of Finance, Room 354, Capital Annex, Frankfort, KY 40601; (502) 564-4510.

Louisiana
State Purchasing Office, Division of Administration, P.O. Box 94095, Baton Rouge, LA 70804-9095; (504) 342-8010.

Maine
Bureau of Purchases, State House Station #9, Augusta, ME 04333; (207) 289-3521.

Maryland
Purchasing Bureau, 301 West Preston Street, Mezzanine, Room M2, Baltimore, MD 21201; (410) 225-4620.

Massachusetts
Purchasing Agent Division, One Ashburton Place, Room 1017, Boston, MA 02108; (617) 727-8081.

Michigan
Office of Purchasing, Mason Bldg., P.O. Box 30026, Lansing, MI 48909, or 530 West Ellegan, 48933; (517) 373-0330.

Minnesota
State of Minnesota, 112 Administration Bldg., 50 Sherburne Ave., St. Paul, MN 55155; (612) 296-6152.

Mississippi
Office of Purchasing and Travel, 1504 Sillers Bldg., Jackson, MS 39201; (601) 359-3409.

Missouri
State of Missouri, Division of Purchasing, P.O. Box 809, Jefferson City, MO 65102; (314) 751-3273.

Be patient. If any phone number is incorrect, call (area code) 555-1212 and request the new listing.

Selling To The Government

Montana
Department of Administration, Procurement Printing Division, 165 Mitchell Bldg., Helena, MT 59620-0135; (406) 444-2575.

Nebraska
State Purchasing, Material Division, 301 Centennial Mall S., P.O. Box 94847, Lincoln, NE 68509; (402) 471-2401.

Nevada
Nevada State Purchasing Division, 505 E. King Street, Room 400, Kinkead Bldg., Carson City, NV 89710; (702) 687-4070.

New Hampshire
Plant and Property Management, 25 Capitol Street, State House Annex, Room 102, Concord, NH 03301; (603) 271-2201.

New Jersey
Purchase and Property, CN-230, Trenton, NJ 08625; (609) 292-4700.

New Mexico
State Purchasing Division, 1100 St. Frances Dr., Joseph Montoya Bldg., Room 2016, Santa Fe, NM 87503; (505) 827-0472.

New York
Division of Purchasing, Corning Tower, Empire State Plaza, 38th Floor, Albany, NY 12242; (518) 474-3695.

North Carolina
Department of Administration, Division of Purchase and Contract, 116 W. Jones St., Raleigh, NC 27603-8002; (919) 733-3581.

North Dakota
Office of Management and Budget, Purchasing, 600 E Blvd., Bismarck, ND 58505-0400; (701) 224-2683.

Ohio
State Purchasing, 4200 Surface Road, Columbus, OH 43228-1395; (614) 466-5090.

Oklahoma
Office of Public Affairs, Central Purchasing Division, Room B4, State Capital Bldg., Oklahoma City, OK 73105; (405) 521-2110.

Oregon
General Services, Purchasing, 1225 Ferry Street, Salem, OR 97310; (503) 378-4643.

Pennsylvania
Procurement Department Secretary, Room 414, Harrisburg, PA 17125; (717) 787-5295.

Rhode Island
Department of Administration, Purchases Office, One Capital Hill, Providence, RI 02908-5855; (401) 277-2317.

South Carolina
Materials Management Office, General Service Budget and Control Board, 1201 Main Street, Suite 600, Columbia, SC 29201; (803) 737-0600.

South Dakota
Division of Purchasing, 523 East Capitol Ave., Pierre, SD 57501; (605) 773-3405.

Tennessee
Purchasing Division, C2-211, Central Services Bldg., Nashville, TN 37219; (615) 741-1035.

Texas
State Purchasing and General Services Commission, P.O. Box 18047, Austin, TX 78711; (512) 463-3445.

Utah
Purchasing Division, Department of Administrative Services, State Office Bldg., Room 350, Salt Lake City, UT 84114; (801) 538-3026.

Vermont
Purchasing Division, 128 State Street, Drawer 33, Montpelier, VT 05633-7501; (802) 828-2211.

Virginia
Department of General Services, Purchasing Division, P.O. Box 1199, Richmond, VA 23209; (804) 786-3172.

Washington
Office of State Procurement, 216 GA Building, P.O. Box 41017, Olympia, WA 98504-1017; (206) 753-6461.

West Virginia
Department of Administration, Purchasing Section, Room E102, Building One, 1900 Kanawha Blvd. E, Charleston, WV 25305; (304) 348-2309.

Wisconsin
Division of State Agency Services, Bureau of Procurement, 101 East Wilson, 6th Floor, P.O. Box 7867, Madison, WI 53707-7867; (608) 266-2605.

Wyoming
Department of Administration, Procurement Services, 2001 Capitol Ave., Cheyenne, WY 82002; (307) 777-7253.

Be patient. If any phone number is incorrect, call (area code) 555-1212 and request the new listing.

Selling Overseas: International Trade

There is probably more information in the United States about any country in the world than there is in the countries themselves. Expertise and assistance to exporters continue to increase at both the federal and state level.

Polypropylene In Countries That Don't Even Count People

A few years ago a Fortune 500 company asked us to identify the consumption of polypropylene resin for 15 lesser developed countries. It was a project they had been working on without success for close to a year. After telexing all over the world and contacting every domestic expert imaginable, we too came up empty-handed. The basic problem was that we were dealing with countries that did not even count people, let alone polypropylene resin.

Our savior was a woman at the U.S. Commerce Department named Maureen Ruffin, who was in charge of the World Trade Reference Room. Ms. Ruffin and her colleagues collect the official import/export statistical documents for every country in the world as soon as they are released by the originating countries. Although the data are much more current and more detailed than those published by such international organizations as the United Nations, the publications available at this federal reference room are printed in the language of origin. Because none of the 15 subject countries manufacture polypropylene resin, Ms. Ruffin showed us how to get the figures by identifying those countries which produce polypropylene and count up how much each of them exported to the countries in question. To help us even further, she also provided us with free in-house translators to help us work with the foreign documents.

Exporter's Hotline

The Trade Promotion Coordinating Committee has established this comprehensive "one-stop-shop" for information on U.S. Government programs and activities that support exporting efforts. This hotline is staffed by trade specialists who can provide information on seminars and conferences, overseas buyers and representatives, overseas events, export financing, technical assistance, and export counseling. They also have access to the National Trade Data Bank.

Trade Information Center
U.S. Department of Commerce
Washington, DC 20230
(800) USA-TRADE
FAX: (202) 377-4473
TDD: (800) 833-8723

Country Experts

If you are looking for information on a market, company or most any other aspect of commercial life in a particular country, your best point of departure is to contact the appropriate country desk officer at the U.S. Department of Commerce. These experts often have the information you need right at their fingertips or they can refer you to other country specialists.

U.S. Foreign and Commercial Services (FCS)
Export Promotion Services
U.S. Department of Commerce
Room 2810
Washington, DC 20230 (202) 377-8220

All the Department of Commerce/US & FCS field offices around the country are listed later in this chapter. (You will also find a separate roster of international trade offices maintained by the states.)

A

ASEAN	George Paine	(202) 377-3875	2308
Afghanistan	Tim Gilman	(202) 377-2954	2029B
Albania	Lynn Fabrizio	(202) 377-2645	6043
Algeria	Jeffrey Johnson	(202) 377-4652	2039
Angola	Claude Clement	(202) 377-5148	3317
Anguilla	Michelle Brooks	(202) 377-2527	3021
Antigua /Barbuda	Michelle Brooks	(202) 377-2527	3021
Argentina	Randy Mye	(202) 377-1548	3021
Aruba	Michelle Brooks	(202) 377-2527	3020
Australia	Gary Bouck	(202) 377-3646	2308
Austria	Philip Combs	(202) 377-2920	3029

B

Bahamas	Rodrigo Soto	(202) 377-2527	3021
Bahrain	Claude Clement /Jeffrey Johnson	(202) 377-5545	2039
Baltic States	Pam Green	(202) 377-4915	3413
Bangladesh	Cheryl McQueen	(202) 377-2954	2029B
Barbados	Michelle Brooks	(202) 377-2527	3021
Belgium	Simon Bensimon	(202) 377-5041	3046
Belize	Michelle Brooks	(202) 377-2527	3021
Benin	Debra Henke	(202) 377-4228	3317
Bermuda	Michelle Brooks	(202) 377-2527	3021
Bhutan	Tim Gilman	(202) 377-2954	2029B
Bolivia	Laura Zeiger	(202) 377-2521	3029
Botswana	Vacant	(202) 377-5148	3317
Brazil	Larry Farris	(202) 377-3871	3017
Brunei	Raphael Cung	(202) 377-3875	2308
Bulgaria	Lynn Fabrizio	(202) 377-2645	6043
Burkina Faso	Philip Michelini	(202) 377-4388	3317
Burma	George Paine	(202) 377-3875	2308
Burundi	Debra Henke	(202) 377-4228	3317

Be patient. If any phone number is incorrect, call (area code) 555-1212 and request the new listing.

Selling Overseas

C

Country	Contact	Phone	Ext
Cambodia	Hong-Phong B. Pho	(202) 377-3875	2308
Cameroon	Debra Henke	(202) 377-4228	3317
Canada	Jonathan Don	(202) 377-3101	3033
Cape Verde	Philip Michelini	(202) 377-4388	3317
Caymans	Michelle Brooks	(202) 377-2527	3020
Central Africa Republic	Debra Henke	(202) 377-4228	3317
Chad	Debra Henke	(202) 377-4228	3317
Chile	Roger Turner	(202) 377-1495	3017
Columbia	Laurie MacNamara	(202) 377-1659	3025
Comoros	Chandra Watkins	(202) 377-4564	3317
Congo	Debra Henke	(202) 377-4228	3317
Costa Rica	Theodore Johnson	(202) 377-2527	3021
Cuba	Rodrigo Soto	(202) 377-2527	3021
Cyprus	Ann Corro	(202) 377-3945	3044
Czechoslovakia	Mark Mowrey	(202) 377-2645	6043

D

Country	Contact	Phone	Ext
D'Jibouti	Chandra Watkins	(202) 377-4564	3317
Denmark	Maryanne Lyons	(202) 377-3254	3413
Dominica	Michelle Brooks	(202) 377-2527	3021
Dominican Republic	Rodrigo Soto	(202) 377-2527	3021

E

Country	Contact	Phone	Ext
E. Caribbean	Michelle Brooks	(202) 377-2527	3021
Ecuador	Laurie McNamara	(202) 377-1659	3025
Egypt	Thomas Sams		
	/Corey Wright	(202) 377-4441	2039
El Salvador	Theodore Johnson	(202) 377-2527	3020
Equatorial Guinea	Debra Henke	(202) 377-4228	3317
Ethiopia	Chandra Watkins	(202) 377-4564	3317
European Community	Charles Ludolph	(202) 377-5276	3036

F

Country	Contact	Phone	Ext
Finland	Maryanne Lyons	(202) 377-3254	3413
France	Elena Mikalis	(202) 377-8008	3042

G

Country	Contact	Phone	Ext
Gabon	Debra Henke	(202) 377-4228	3317
Gambia	Philip Michelin	(202) 377-4388	3317
Germany	Brenda Fisher	(202) 377-2434	3409
Germany	Joan Kloepfer	(202) 377-2841	3409
Ghana	Debra Henke	(202) 377-4228	3317
Greece	Ann Corro	(202) 377-3945	3044
Grenada	Michelle Brooks	(202) 377-2527	3021
Guadeloupe	Michelle Brooks	(202) 377-2527	3021
Guatemala	Ted Johnson	(202) 377-2527	3021
Guinea	Philip Michelini	(202) 377-4388	3317
Guinea-Bissau	Philip Michelini	(202) 377-4388	3317
Guyana	Michelle Brooks	(202) 377-2527	3021

H

Country	Contact	Phone	Ext
Haiti	Rodrigo Soto	(202) 377-2527	3021
Honduras	Theodore Johnson	(202) 377-2527	3020
Hong Kong	JeNelle Matheson	(202) 377-3583	2317
Hungary	Brian Toohey	(202) 377-2645	6043

I

Country	Contact	Phone	Ext
Iceland	Maryanne Lyons	(202) 377-3254	3037
India	John Simmons		
	/John Crown		
	/Tim Gilman	(202) 377-2954	2029B
Indonesia	Karen Goddin	(202) 377-3875	2308
Iran	Corey Wright	(202) 377-4652	2039
Iraq	Thomas Sams	(202) 377-4441	2039
Ireland	Boyce Fitzpatrick	(202) 377-2177	3039
Israel	Kate FitzGerald-Wilks		
	/Doris Nelmes	(202) 377-4652	2039
Italy	Boyce Fitzpatrick	(202) 377-2177	3045
Ivory Coast	Philip Michelini	(202) 377-4388	3317

J

Country	Contact	Phone	Ext
Jamaica	Rodrigo Soto	(202) 377-2527	3021
Japan	Ed Leslie		
	/Cantwell Walsh		
	/Eric Kennedy	(202) 377-2425	2324
Jordan	Claude Clement	(202) 377-2515	2039

K

Country	Contact	Phone	Ext
Kenya	Chandra Watkins	(202) 377-4564	3317
Korea	Jeffrey Donius		
	/Dan Duvall		
	/Renato Amador	(202) 377-4957	2327
Kuwait	Corey Wright		
	/Thomas Sams	(202) 377-2515	2039

L

Country	Contact	Phone	Ext
Laos	Hong-Phong B. Pho	(202) 377-3875	2308
Lebanon	Corey Wright		
	/Thomas Sams	(202) 377-2515	2039
Lesotho	Vacant	(202) 377-5148	3317
Liberia	Reginald Biddle	(202) 377-4388	3317
Libya	Claude Clement	(202) 377-5545	2039
Luxembourg	Simon Bensimon	(202) 377-5401	3046

M

Country	Contact	Phone	Ext
Macao	JeNelle Matheson	(202) 377-2462	2323
Madagascar	Chandra Watkins	(202) 377-4564	3317
Malawi	Vacant	(202) 337-5148	3317
Malaysia	Raphael Cung	(202) 377-3875	2308
Maldives	John Simmons	(202) 377-2954	2029B
Mali	Philip Michelini	(202) 377-4388	3317
Malta	Robert McLaughlin	(202) 377-3748	3049
Mauritana	Philip Michelini	(202) 377-4564	3317
Mauritius	Chandra Watkins	(202) 377-4564	3317
Mexico	Andrew Lowry		
	/Ingrid Mohn	(202) 377-4464	3028
Mongolia	JeNelle Matheson	(202) 377-2462	2323
Montserrat	Michelle Brooks	(202) 377-2527	3314
Morocco	Jeffrey Johnson	(202) 377-5545	2039
Mozambique	Vacant	(202) 377-5148	3317

N

Country	Contact	Phone	Ext
Namibia	Emily Solomon	(202) 377-5148	3317
Nepal	Tim Gilman	(202) 377-2954	2029B
Netherlands	Simon Bensimon	(202) 377-5401	3039
Netherlands Antilles	Michelle Brooks	(202) 377-2527	3021
New Zealand	Gary Bouck	(202) 377-3647	2308
Nicaragua	Ted Johnson	(202) 377-2527	3021
Niger	Philip Michelini	(202) 377-4388	3317

Be patient. If any phone number is incorrect, call (area code) 555-1212 and request the new listing.

International Trade

Country	Contact	Phone	Ext
Nigeria	Debra Henke	(202) 377-4228	3317
Norway	James Devlin	(202) 377-4414	3037

O

Country	Contact	Phone	Ext
Oman	Kate Fitzgerald-Wilks /Doris Nelmes	(202) 377-4652	2039

P

Country	Contact	Phone	Ext
Pacific Islands	Gary Bouck	(202) 377-3647	2308
Pakistan	Cheryl McQueen	(202) 377-2954	2029B
Panama	Theodore Johnson	(202) 377-2527	3020
Paraguay	Randy Mye	(202) 377-1548	3021
People/China	Robert Chu /Laura McCall	(202) 377-3583	2317
Peru	Laura Zeiger	(202) 377-2521	3029
Philippines	George Paine	(202) 377-3875	2308
Poland	Audrey A. Zuck	(202) 377-2645	6043
Portugal	Mary Beth Double	(202) 377-4508	3044
Puerto Rico	Rodrigo Soto	(202) 377-2527	3021

Q

Country	Contact	Phone	Ext
Qatar	Kate Fitzgerald-Wilks /Doris Nelmes	(202) 377-4652	2039

R

Country	Contact	Phone	Ext
Romania	Lynn Fabrizio	(202) 377-2645	6043
Russia CIS	Jack Brougher /Susan Lewens /Tim Smith	(202) 377-4655	3318
Rwanda	Debra Henke	(202) 377-4228	3317

S

Country	Contact	Phone	Ext
Sao Tome & Principe	Debra Henke	(202) 377-4228	3317
Saudi Arabia	Jeffrey Johnson /Claude Clement	(202) 377-4652	2039
Senegal	Philip Michelini	(202) 377-4388	3317
Seychelles	Chandra Watkins	(202) 377-4564	3317
Sierra Leone	Philip Michelini	(202) 377-4388	3317
Singapore	Raphael Cung	(202) 377-3875	2308
Somalia	Chandra Watkins	(202) 377-4564	3317
South Africa	Emily Solomon	(202) 377-5148	3317
Spain	Mary Beth Double	(202) 377-4508	3045
Sri Lanka	John Simmons	(202) 377-2954	2029B
St. Bartholomy	Michelle Brooks	(202) 377-2527	3021
St. Kitts-Nevis	Michelle Brooks	(202) 377-2527	3021
St. Lucia	Michelle Brooks	(202) 377-2527	3021
St. Martin	Michelle Brooks	(202) 377-2527	3021
St. Vincent Grenadines	Michelle Brooks	(202) 377-2527	3021
Sudan	Chandra Watkins	(202) 377-4564	3317
Suriname	Michelle Brooks	(202) 377-2527	3021
Swaziland	Vacant	(202) 377-5148	3317
Sweden	James Devlin	(202) 377-4414	3037
Switzerland	Philip Combs	(202) 377-2920	3039
Syria	Corey Wright /Thomas Sams	(202) 377-2515	2039

T

Country	Contact	Phone	Ext
Taiwan	Ian Davis /Dan Duvall		

Country	Contact	Phone	Ext
	/Paul Carroll	(202) 377-4957	2308
Tanzania	Vacant	(202) 377-5148	3317
Thailand	Jean Kelly	(202) 377-3875	2308
Togo	Debra Henke	(202) 377-4228	3021
Trinidad & Tobago	Michelle Brooks	(202) 377-2527	3021
Tunisia	Corey Wright /Thomas Sams	(202) 377-2515	2039
Turkey	Heidi Lamb	(202) 377-5373	3045
Turks & Caicos Islands	Rodrigo Soto	(202) 377-2527	3021

U

Country	Contact	Phone	Ext
Uganda	Chandra Watkins	(202) 377-4564	3317
United Arab Emirates	Claude Clement /Jeffrey Johnson	(202) 377-5545	2039
United Kingdom	Robert McLaughlin	(202) 377-3748	3045
Uruguay	Roger Turner	(202) 377-1495	3021

V

Country	Contact	Phone	Ext
Venezuela	Herbert Lindow	(202) 377-4303	3029
Vietnam	Hong-Phong B. Pho	(202) 377-3875	2308
Virgin Islands (UK)	Michelle Brooks	(202) 377-2527	3020
Virgin Islands (US)	Rodrigo Soto	(202) 377-2527	3021

Y

Country	Contact	Phone	Ext
Yemen, Rep of	Kate Fitzgerald-Wilks /Doris Nelmes	(202) 377-4652	2039
Yugoslavia	Jeremy Keller	(202) 377-2645	6043

Z

Country	Contact	Phone	Ext
Zaire	Debra Henke	(202) 377-4228	3317
Zambia	Vacant	(202) 377-5148	3317
Zimbabwe	Vacant	(202) 377-5147	3317

State Department Country Experts

If you need information that is primarily political, economic or cultural in nature, direct your questions first to the State Department Country Desk Officers.

U.S. Department of State
2201 C Street NW
Washington, DC 20520 (202) 647-6575

Foreign Specialists At Other Government Agencies

The following is a listing by subject area of other departments within the federal government which maintain country experts who are available to help the public:

1) **Mineral Resources:**
Bureau of Mines, U.S. Department of Interior, Division of International Minerals, 810 7th Street NW, Washington, DC 20241-0002, (202) 501-9666

Be patient. If any phone number is incorrect, call (area code) 555-1212 and request the new listing.

Selling Overseas

2) Foreign Agriculture:
Economic Research Service, Agriculture and Trade Analysis Division, U.S. Department of Agriculture, Room 732, 1301 New York Avenue, NW, Washington, DC 20005, (202) 219-0700

Food Safety and Inspection Service, International Programs, U.S. Department of Agriculture, Room 341-E, 14th and Independence SW, Washington, DC 20250-3700, (202) 720-3473

Animal and Plant Health Inspection Service, Import-Export, U.S. Department of Agriculture, 6505 Bellcrest Road, Hyattsville, MD 20782, (301) 436-8590

Food Transportation, International Transportation Branch, U.S. Department of Agriculture, Room 1217 South Building, Washington, DC 20250, (202) 690-1320

3) Energy Resources:
Office of Export Assistance, U.S. Department of Energy, 1000 Independence Avenue, SW, Washington, DC 20585, (202) 586-0151

Office of Fossil Energy, U.S. Department of Energy, 1000 Independence Ave., SW, Washington, DC 20585, (202) 586-7297

4) Economic Assistance to Foreign Countries:
Business Office, U.S. Agency for International Development, 320 21st Street NW, Washington, DC 20523, (703) 875-1551

5) Information Programs and Cultural Exchange:
U.S. Information Agency, 301 4th Street SW, Washington, DC 20547, (202) 619-4700

6) Seafood Certificates:
Inspection Certificates for Seafood Exports, National Oceanic and Atmospheric Administration, 1335 East-West Highway, Room 6120, Silver Spring, MD 20910, (301) 443-8910

7) Metric:
Office of Metric Programs, National Institute of Standards and Technology, Gaithersburg, MD 20899, (202) 377-0944

8) Telecommunications Information:
Bureau of International Communications and Information Policy, U.S. Dept of State, Washington, DC 20520, (202) 647-5231

9) Fisheries:
Office of Trade and Industry Services, Fisheries Promotion and Trade Matters, National Marine Fisheries Service, 1335 East-West Highway, Silver Spring, MD 20910, (301) 713-2351

Fax Directory Of Overseas Commercial Counselors

You can FAX IT, if you are looking for a market study, a client or any other piece of information in a given country. Listed below are the fax numbers of the commercial officers who work at U.S. Embassies around the world. These officers are available to assist U.S. businesses succeed in selling their products overseas.

Algeria:
Algiers 9-011-213-2-60-18-63

Argentina:
Buenos Aires 9-011-54-1775-6040

Australia:
Sydney 9-011-61-2-261-8148
Brisbane 9-011-61-7-832-6247
Melbourne 9-011-61-3-696-1820
Perth 9-011-61-9-325-3569

Austria:
Vienna 9-011-43-222-341261

Barbados:
Bridgetown 9-1-809-426-2275

Belgium:
Brussels (Emb) 9-011-32-2-512-6653
Brussels (EC) 9-011-32-2-513-1228
Antwerp 9-011-32-3-234-3698

Brazil:
Brasilia 9-011-55-61-225-3981
Belo Horizonte 9-011-55-31-224-6214
Rio de Janeiro 9-011-55-21-240-9738
Sao Paulo 9-011-55-11-853-2744

Cameroon:
Douala 9-011-237-427-790
Yaounde 9-011-237-427-790

Canada:
Ottawa 9-1-613-233-8511
Calgary 9-1-403-264-6630
Halifax 9-1-902-423-6861
Montreal 9-1-514-398-0711
Toronto 9-1-416-595-0051
Vancouver 9-1-604-685-5285

China:
Beijing 9-011-86-1-532-3297
Guangzhou 9-011-86-20-666-409
Shanghai 9-011-86-21-433-1576
Shenyang 9-011-86-24-290-074

Columbia:
Bogata 9-011-57-1-285-7945

Costa Rica:
San Jose 9-011-506-31-47-83

Cote D'Ivoire:
Abidjan 9-011-225-22-32-59
African Dev Bk 9-011-225-33-21-72

Czechoslovakia:
Prague 9-011-42-2-532-457

Denmark:
Copenhagen 9-011-45-31-42-01-75

Dominican Republic:
Santa Domingo 9-1-809-688-4838

Ecuador:
Quito 9-011-593-2-504-550
Guayaquil 9-011-593-4-324-558

Egypt:
Cairo 9-011-20-2-355-8368
Alexandria 9-011-20-3-482-9199

Finland:
Helsinki 9-011-358-0-635-332

France:
Paris (EMB) 9-011-33-1-4266-4827
Paris (ORCD) 9-011-33-1-4524-7410
Bordeaux 9-011-33-56-51-60-42

Be patient. If any phone number is incorrect, call (area code) 555-1212 and request the new listing.

International Trade

Location	Phone Number
Lyon	9-011-33-1-4266-4827
Marseille	9-011-33-1-4266-4827
Nice	9-011-33-1-4266-4827
Strasbourg	9-011-33-1-4266-4827
Germany:	
Bonn	9-011-49-228-334-649
Berlin	9-011-37-2-229-2167
Dusseldorf	9-011-49-211-594-897
Frankfurt	9-011-49-69-748-204
Hamburg	9-011-49-410-6598
Munich	9-011-49-89-285-261
Stuttgart	9-011-49-711-234-350
Greece:	
Athens	9-011-30-1-723-9705
Guatemala:	
Guatemala	9-011-502-2-317-373
Honduras:	
Teguicigalpa	9-011-504-32-0027
Hong Kong:	
Hong Kong	9-011-852-845-9800
Hungary:	
Budapest	9-011-36-1-142-2529
India:	
New Delhi	9-011-91-11-687-2391
Bombay	9-011-91-22-822-0350
Calcutta	9-011-91-33-283-823
Madras	9-011-91-44-825-0240
Indonesia:	
Jakarta	9-011-62-21-360-644
Medan	9-011-62-21-360-644
Surabaya	9-011-62-21-360-644
Iraq:	
Baghdad	9-011-964-1-718-9297
Ireland:	
Dublin	9-011-353-1-608-469
Israel:	
Tel Aviv	9-011-972-3-658-033
Italy:	
Rome	9-011-39-6-4674-2113
Florence	9-011-39-55-283-780
Genoa	9-011-39-10-207-721
Milan	9-011-39-2-481-4161
Naples	9-011-39-81-761-1869
Jamaica:	
Kingston	9-1-809-929-3637
Japan:	
Tokyo	9-011-81-3-589-4235
Tokyo (TradeCtr)	9-011-81-3-987-2447
Fukuoka	9-011-81-9-271-3922
Osaka-Kobe	9-011-81-6-361-5978
Sapporo	9-011-81-11-641-0911
Kenya:	
Nairobi	9-011-254-2-340-838
Korea:	
Seoul	9-011-82-2-739-1628
Kuwait:	
Kuwait	9-011-965-240-7368
Malaysia:	
Kuala Lumpur	9-011-60-3-242-1866
Mexico:	
Mexico City	9-011-52-5-207-8938
Mexico City (Trade Center)	9-011-52-5-566-1115
Guadalajara	9-011-52-36-26-6549
Monterrey	0-011-52-83-42-5172
Morocco:	
Casablanca	9-011-212-22-02-59
Rabat	9-011-212-7-656-61
Netherlands:	
The Hague	9-011-31-70-363-29-85
Amsterdam	9-011-64-4-781-701
Nigeria:	
Lagos	9-011-234-1-619-856
Norway:	
Oslo	9-011-47-2055-88-03
Pakistan:	
Karachi	9-011-92-21-511-381
Panama:	
Panama	9-011-507-27-1713
Peru:	
Lima	9-011-51-14-33-4687
Philippines:	
Manila	9-011-63-2-818-2684
Asian Dev Bank	9-011-63-2-834-4003
Poland:	
Warsaw	9-011-48-22-21-63-27
Portugal:	
Lisbon	9-011-351-1-726-8914
Oporto	9-011-351-2-600-2737
Romania:	
Bucharest	9-011-40-0-110-474
Saudi Arabia:	
Riyadh	9-011-966-1-488-3237
Dhahran	9-011-966-3-891-8332
Jeddah	9-011-966-2-665-8106
Singapore:	
Singapore	9-011-65-338-5010
South Africa:	
Johannesburg	9-011-27-11-331-6178
Cape Town	9-011-27-21-214-280
Spain:	
Madrid	9-011-34-1-575-8655
Barcelona	9-011-34-3-319-5621
Sweden:	
Stockholm	9-011-46-8-660-9181
Switzerland:	
Bern	9-011-41-31-43-73-36
Geneva(GATT)	9-011-41-22-799-0885
Zurich	9-011-41-4-383-9814
Taiwan:	
Taipei	9-011-886-2-757-7162
Kaohsiung	9-011-886-7-231-8237
Thailand:	
Bangkok	9-011-66-2-255-2915
Trinidad & Tobago:	
Port-of-Spain	9-1-809-622-9583
Turkey:	
Ankara	9-011-90-4-167-1366
Istanbul	9-011-90-1-152-2417
United Arab Emirates:	
Adu Dhabi	9-011-971-2-331-374
Dubai	9-011-971-4-375-121
United Kingdom:	
London	9-011-44-71-491-4022
U.S.S.R.:	
Moscow	9-011-7-095-230-2101

Be patient. If any phone number is incorrect, call (area code) 555-1212 and request the new listing.

Selling Overseas

Venezuela:

Caracas	9-011-58-2-285-0336

Yugoslavia:

Belgrade	9-011-38-11-645-096
Zagreb	9-011-38-41-440-235

(202) 336-8636 (Public Affairs)
(202) 336-8680 (Press Information)

Money For Selling Overseas

1) State Government Money Programs:
Some state government economic development programs offer special assistance for those who need financial assistance in selling overseas. See the section presented later in this chapter entitled *State Government Assistance To Exporters.*

2) Export-Import Bank Financing:
The Export-Import Bank facilitates and aids in the financing of exports of U.S. goods and services. Its programs include short-term, medium-term, and long-term credits, small business support, financial guarantees and insurance. In addition, it sponsors conferences on small business exporting, maintains credit information on thousands of foreign firms, supports feasibility studies of overseas programs, and offers export and small business finance counseling. To receive *Marketing News* Fact Sheets, or the *Eximbank Export Credit Insurance* booklet, or the Eximbank's *Program Selection Guide*, contact: Export-Import Bank, 811 Vermont Ave. NW, Washington, DC 20571, (202) 566-8860, (800) 424-5201.

3) Small Business Administration Export Loans:
This agency makes loans and loan guarantees to small business concerns as well as to small business investment companies, including those which sell overseas. It also offers technical assistance, counseling, training, management assistance, and information resources, including several excellent publications to small and minority businesses in export operations. Contact your local or regional SBA office listed in the blue pages of your telephone book under Small Business Administration, or Small Business Administration, 409 3rd St, SW, Washington, DC 20416, (202) 205-6720.

4) Overseas Private Investment Corporation (OPIC):
This agency provides marketing, insurance, and financial assistance to American companies investing in 118 countries and 16 geographic regions. Its programs include direct loans, loan guarantees and political risk insurance. OPIC also sponsors seminars for investment executives as well as conducts investment missions to developing countries. The Investor Services Division offers a computer service to assist investors in identifying investment opportunities worldwide. A modest fee is charged for this service and it is also available through the LEXIS/NEXIS computer network. Specific Info-Kits are available identifying basic economic, business and political information for each of the countries covered. In addition, it operates:

Program Information Hotline
Overseas Private Investment Corporation
1100 New York Ave., NW
Washington, DC 20527
(800) 424-OPIC (Hotline)
(202) 336-8400 (General Information)
(202) 457-7128 (Investor Services Division)

5) Agency For International Development (AID):
AID offers a variety of loan and financing guarantee programs for projects in developing countries that have a substantial developmental impact or for the exportation of manufactured goods to AID-assisted developing countries. Some investment opportunities are region specific, which include the Association of Southeast Asian National, the Philippines, and Africa. For more information contact the Office of Investment, Agency for International Development, 515 22nd Street NW, Room 301, Washington, DC 20523-0231, (202) 663-2280.

Marketing Data, Custom Studies And Company Information

Further information on any of the following services and products can be obtained by contacting a U.S. Department of Commerce/US & FCS field office listed later in this chapter, or contact the US & FCS at: United States and Foreign Commercial Services, U.S. Department of Commerce, Room 3810, HCH Building, 14th and Constitution Ave., NW, Washington, DC 20230, (202) 377-4767 or call (800) USA-TRADE.

1) International Industry Experts:
A separate Office of Trade Development at the Commerce Department handles special marketing and company problems for specific industries. Experts are available in the following international market sectors:

Aerospace:	(202) 377-2835
Automotive and Consumer Goods:	(202) 377-0823
Basic Industries:	(202) 377-0614
Capital Goods and International Construction:	(202) 377-5023
Science and Electronics and Telecommunications and Industries:	(202) 377-3548
Service:	(202) 377-5261
Textiles and Apparel:	(202) 377-3737

You can also talk to industry desk officers at the U.S. Department of Commerce. They can provide information on the competitive strengths of U.S. industries in foreign markets from abrasives to yogurt. They are listed in the "Experts" section at the end of this book and have "COMMERCE" after their name.

2) Trade Lists:
Directories of overseas customers for U.S. exports in selected industries and countries: They contain the names and product lines of foreign distributors, agents, manufacturers, wholesalers, retailers and other purchasers. They also provide the name and title of a key officials as well as telex and cable numbers, and company size data. Prices range up to $40 for a list of a category.

3) Country Trade Statistics:
Tables showing American exports of 100-150 industries to a selected country: Data are available for over 150 countries and include relative growth rates, percentage export shares and leading markets for specific U.S. products. Price is $25 per country.

Be patient. If any phone number is incorrect, call (area code) 555-1212 and request the new listing.

International Trade

4) Custom Statistical:
Export data for a particular country are presented according to customer's specifications. This service is broader in scope and more detailed in nature than the *Country Trade Statistics* service. Prices start at $50.

5) Customized Export Mailing Lists:
Selected lists of foreign companies in particular industries, countries and types of business can be requested by a client. Gummed labels are also available. Prices start at $35.

6) World Traders Data Reports:
Background reports are available on individual firms containing information about each firm's business activities, its standing in the local business community, its credit-worthiness and overall reliability and suitability as a trade contact for exporters. The price is $75 per report.

7) Agent Distributor Service:
This is a customized search for interested and qualified foreign representatives on behalf of an American client. U.S. commercial officers overseas conduct the search and prepare a report identifying up to six foreign prospects which have personally examined the U.S. firm's product literature and have expressed interest in representing the firm. The price is $90 per market.

8) New Product Information Service:
This service is designed to help American companies publicize the availability of new U.S. products in foreign markets and simultaneously test market interest in these products. Product information which meets the criteria is distributed worldwide through Commercial News USA and Voice of America broadcasts. A fee is charged for participation.

9) Customized Market Studies:
At a cost of $500 per country per product, these studies are called "Comparison Shopping Service". They are conducted by the U.S. Embassy foreign commercial attaches and can target information on quite specific marketing questions.

- Does the product have sales potential in the country?
- Who is the supplier for a comparable product locally?
- What is the going price for a comparable product in this country?
- What is the usual sales channel for getting this type of product into the market?
- What are the competitive factors that most influence purchases of these products in the market (i.e., price, credit, quality, delivery, service, promotion, brand)?
- What is the best way to get sales exposure in the market for this type of product?
- Are there any significant impediments to selling this type of product?
- Who might be interested and qualified to represent or purchase this company's products?
- If a licensing or joint venture strategy seems desirable for this market, who might be an interested and qualified partner for the U.S. company?

10) Special Opportunities in the Caribbean Basin and Latin America:
Under the Caribbean Economic Recovery Act of 1983, the government has established special incentives for American firms wishing to do business with Latin American and Caribbean Basin companies. Seminars, workshops, business development missions, business counseling as well as marketing and competitive information are available.

Latin America/Caribbean Business Development Center
U.S. Department of Commerce (202) 377-0841
Washington, DC 20230 FAX: (202) 377-2218

11) New Markets In Eastern European Countries:
The Eastern Europe Business Information Center is stocked with a wide range of publications on doing business in Eastern Europe; these include lists of potential partners, investment regulations, priority industry sectors, and notices of upcoming seminars, conferences, and trade promotion events. It also serves as a referral point for programs of voluntary assistance to the region.

Eastern Europe Business Information Center
U.S. Department of Commerce (202) 377-2645
Washington, DC 20230 FAX: (202) 377-4473

12) Opportunities for Rebuilding The Gulf:
The Gulf Reconstruction Center coordinates the U.S. Department of Commerce's reconstruction activities and counsels the U.S. business community about rebuilding opportunities in Kuwait and the Gulf region. The center serves as an information clearinghouse for business investors. It also provides American firms with materials on doing business in Kuwait. The Center is compiling a database of companies interested in business opportunities in the region, which can also be used by the Kuwaiti Government and the U.S. Army Corps of Engineers to obtain information on companies interested in Kuwait's reconstruction effort.

Counseling and Referral Services
Gulf Reconstruction Center
U.S. Department of Commerce (202) 377-5767
Washington, DC 20230 FAX: (202) 377-0878

13) Exporting to Japan: Japan Export Information Center (JEIC)
JEIC provides business counseling services and accurate information on exporting to Japan. The JEIC is the point of contact for information on business in Japan, market entry alternatives, market information and research, product standards and testing, tariffs, and non-tariff barriers. The center maintains a commercial library and participates in seminars on various aspects of Japanese business. Contact: Japan Export Information Center, (202) 377-2425; FAX: (202) 377-0469.

Trade Fairs And Missions

Trade fairs, exhibitions, trade missions, overseas trade seminars and other promotional events and services are sponsored by the Export Promotion Services Group, US & FCS, U.S. Department of Commerce, 14th and E Streets, N.W., Room 2808, Washington, DC 20230, (202) 377-8220. This office or one of its field offices which are listed later in this chapter can provide additional details on these activities.

Selling Overseas

1) Industry-Organized, Government-Approved Trade Missions:

Such missions are organized by trade associations, local Chambers of Commerce, state trade development agencies, and similar trade-oriented groups with U.S. Department of Commerce support.

2) Catalog Exhibitions:

Such exhibitions feature displays of U.S. product catalogs, sales brochures and other graphic sales materials at American embassies and consulates or in conjunction with trade shows. A Commerce Department specialist assists in the exhibition. Call (202) 377-3973; FAX: (202) 377-0178.

3) Video Catalog:

This catalog is designed to showcase American products via video tape presentation. This permits actual product demonstrations giving the foreign buyer an opportunity to view applications of American products. Federal specialists participate in these sessions. Call (202) 377-3973; FAX: (202) 377-0178.

4) U.S. Specialized Trade Missions:

These missions are distinct from those mentioned above since the U.S. Department of Commerce plans the visits and accompanies the delegation. They are designed to sell American goods and services as well as establish agents or representation abroad. The U.S. Department of Commerce provides marketing information, advanced planning, publicity and trip organization. Call (800) USA-TRADE.

5) U.S. Seminar Missions:

The objective here is to promote exports and help foreign representation for American exporters. However, unlike trade missions, these are designed to facilitate the sales of state-of-the-art products and technology. This type of mission is a 1-2 day "seminar" during which team members discuss technology subjects followed by private, sales-oriented appointments. Call (800) USA-TRADE.

6) Matchmaker Trade Delegations:

These Commerce-recruited and planned missions are designed to introduce new-to-export or new-to-market businesses to prospective agents and distributors overseas. Trade Specialists from Commerce evaluate the potential firm's products, find and screen contacts and handle logistics. This is followed by an intensive trip filled with meetings and prospective clients and in-depth briefings on the economic and business climate of the countries visited. Call Office of Export Promotion Services, (202) 377-3119; FAX: (202) 377-0178.

7) Investment Missions:

These events are held in developing countries offering excellent investment opportunities for U.S. firms. Missions introduce U.S. business executives to key business leaders, potential joint venture partners and senior foreign government officials in the host country. Call Investment Missions, (202) 457-7039; FAX: (202) 223-3514.

8) Foreign Buyer Program:

This program supports major domestic trade shows featuring products and services of U.S. industries with high export potential. Government officials world-wide recruit qualified buyers to attend the shows. Call (202) 377-8433; FAX: (202) 377-0178.

9) Trade Fairs, Solo Exhibitions, and Trade Center Shows:

The U.S. Department of Commerce organizes a wide variety of special exhibitions. These events range from solo exhibitions representing U.S. firms exclusively at trade centers overseas to U.S. pavilions in the largest international exhibitions. Call (800) USA-TRADE.

10) Agent/Distributor Service (ADS):

Looking for overseas representatives to expand your business and boost your export sales? Commerce will locate, screen, and assess agents, distributors, representatives, and other foreign partners for your business. Call (800) USA-TRADE.

11) Trade Opportunities Program (TOP):

TOP provides companies with current sales leads from international firms seeking to buy or represent their products or services. TOP leads are printed daily in leading commercial newspapers and are also distributed electronically via the U.S. Department of Commerce Economic Bulletin Board. Call (202) 377-1986; FAX: (202) 377-2164.

12) Travel and Tourism:

The U.S. Travel and Tourism Administration promotes export earnings through trade in tourism. USTTA stimulates demand for travel to the U.S., encourages and facilitates promotion in international travel markets by U.S. travel industry concerns; works to increase the number of new-to-market travel businesses participating in the export market; forms cooperative marketing opportunities for private industry and regional state, and local government; provides timely data; and helps to remove government-imposed travel barriers. Call International Congress Programs, (202) 377-4904.

13) Gold Key Service:

This customed tailored service is aimed at U.S. firms which are planning to visit a country. Offered by many overseas posts, it combines several services, such as market orientation briefings, market research, introductions to potential partners, and interpreters for meetings, assistance in developing a sound market strategy, and an effective follow-up plan. Call (800) USA-TRADE.

Special Programs For Agricultural Products

The following programs are specifically aimed at those who wish to sell agricultural products overseas. Agricultural exporters should also be sure not to limit themselves only to programs under this heading. Programs listed under other headings can also be used for agricultural products.

1) Office Space for Agricultural Exporters:

The Foreign Agriculture Service (FAS) maintains overseas agricultural trade offices to help exporters of U.S. farm and forest products in key overseas markets. The facilities vary depending on local conditions, but may include a trade library, conference rooms, office space, and kitchens for preparing product samples. Contact: Foreign Agriculture Service, U.S. Department of Agriculture, 12 Street and Jefferson Drive SW, Washington, DC 20250, (202) 720-9509; FAX: (202) 690-4374.

Be patient. If any phone number is incorrect, call (area code) 555-1212 and request the new listing.

International Trade

2) Research Services:
The Agricultural Research Service provides exporters with information, research and consultants on a wide array of topics including shipping, storage, insect control, pesticide residues, and market disorders. Contact: Agricultural Research Service, U.S. Department of Agriculture, 12th Street and Jefferson Drive SW, Washington, DC 20250, (202) 504-5605; FAX: (301) 504-5298.

3) Foreign Market Information:
A special office serves as a single contact point within the Foreign Agriculture Service for agricultural exporters seeking foreign market information. The office also counsels firms which believe they have been injured by unfair trade practices. Contact: Trade Assistance and Planning Office, U.S. Department of Agriculture, 12th Street and Jefferson Drive SW, Washington, DC 20250, (703) 305-2771; FAX: (703) 305-2788.

4) Export Connections:
The AgExport Action Kit provides information which can help put U.S. exporters in touch quickly and directly with foreign importers of food and agricultural products. The services include trade leads, a Buyer Alert newsletter, foreign buyer lists, and U.S. supplier lists. All services are free. Contact: AgExport Connections, U.S. Department of Agriculture, Washington, DC 20250, (202) 720-7103; FAX: (202) 690-4374.

5) Country Market Profiles:
Country-specific 2-4 page descriptions are available for 40 overseas markets for high value agricultural products. They provide market overview, market trends, and information on the U.S. market position, the competition, and general labeling and licensing requirements. Contact: Country Market Profiles, FAS Information Service, U.S. Department of Agriculture, Washington, DC 20250, (202) 720-7937; FAX: (202) 720-1727.

Export Regulations, Licensing, And Product Standards

Talk to ELVIS — Bureau of Export Administration (BXA)
BXA is responsible for controlling exports for reasons of national security, foreign policy, and short supply. Licenses on controlled exports are issued, and seminars on U.S. export regulations are held domestically and overseas.

Export license applications may be submitted and issued through computer via the Export License Application and Information Network (ELAIN). The System for Tracking Export License Application (STELA) provides instant status updates on license applications by the use of a touch-tone phone.

The Export Licensing Voice Information (ELVIS) is an automated attendant that offers a range of licensing information and emergency handling procedures. Callers may order forms and publications or subscribe to the *Office of Export Licensing (OEL) Insider Newsletter*, which provides regulatory updates. While using ELVIS, a caller has the option to speak to a consultant.

Office of Export Licensing	(202) 377-8536
	FAX: (202) 377-3322

ELAIN	(202) 377-4811
STELA	(202) 377-2752
ELVIS	(202) 377-4811

The National Institute of Standards and Technology provides a free service which will identify standards for selling any product to any country in the world. This federal agency will tell you what the standard is for a given product or suggest where you can obtain an official copy of the standard.

National Center for Standards and Certification
National Institute of Standards and Technology
Building 411, Room A163
Gaithersburg, MD 20899 (301) 975-4040

Cheap Office And Conference Space Overseas

If you are travelling overseas on a business trip, you may want to look into renting office space and other services through the American Embassy. Depending on the country and the space available, the embassy can provide temporary office space for as low as $25 per day, along with translation services, printing and other services. Meeting rooms, seminar or convention space along with promotion services, mailings, freight handling, and even catering may be available in many countries. Contact the U.S. Department of Commerce/US & FCS field office (listed later in this chapter) or the appropriate country desk officer at the U.S. Department of Commerce in Washington, DC.

Other Services, Resources And Databases

The following is a description of some of the additional services and information sources that can be useful to anyone investigating overseas markets:

1) World Import/Export Statistics:
For the latest information on any product imported to or exported from any foreign country, contact: Foreign and U.S. Trade Reference Room, U.S. Dept. of Commerce, Room 2233, Washington, DC 20230, (202) 377-4855.

2) Help In Selling To Developing Nations:
The U.S. Agency For International Development (AID) provides information to U.S. suppliers, particularly small, independent enterprises, regarding purchases to be financed with AID funds. U.S. small businesses can obtain special counseling and related services in order to furnish equipment, materials, and services to AID-financed projects. AID sponsors Development Technologies Exhibitions, where technical firms in the U.S. are matched up with those in lesser developed countries for the purpose of forming joint ventures or exploring licensing possibilities. AID provides loans and grants to finance consulting services that support project activities related to areas such as agriculture, rural development, health, and housing. Contact: Office of Business Relations, U.S. Agency for International Development, State Annex 14, Room 1400A, Washington, DC 20523, (703) 875-1551.

3) Foreign Demographic Profiles:
The U.S. Bureau of the Census produces detailed statistical profiles of foreign trade and demographic topics, as well as

Be patient. If any phone number is incorrect, call (area code) 555-1212 and request the new listing.

Selling Overseas

import/export statistics, and can do marketing research consultation for American exporters. The cost of the latest edition, 1989, is $7.50 (GPO: 031-024-07074-0). Contact: Superintendent of Documents, U.S. Government Printing Office, Washington, DC 20402; (202) 783-3238.

Also available from the Government Printing office is the CIA *World Factbook*. Produced annually by the CIA, this publication provides country-by-country data on demographics, economy, communications, and defense. The cost is $23 (GPO: 041-015-00169-8). Order from the above address by mail or by phone.

4) Help With Selling Commodities Abroad:
The Foreign Agricultural Service is charged with maintaining and expanding export sales of U.S. agricultural commodities and products. Staff can provide information on foreign agricultural production, trade and consumption, marketing research including areas of demand for specific commodities in foreign countries, and analyses of foreign competition in agricultural areas. Other services include financing opportunities, contributing to export promotion costs and testing market assistance. This office also handles U.S. representation to foreign governments and participates in formal trade negotiations. Contact: Foreign Agricultural Service, U.S. Department of Agriculture, 14th and Independence Avenue, S.W., Room 4647, South Bldg., Washington, DC 20250, (202) 447-6343.

5) International Prices:
Export price indexes for both detailed and aggregate product groups on a quarterly basis, as well as price trends comparisons of U.S. exports with those of Japan and Germany, are available from:

International Prices Division, Bureau of Labor Statistics, U.S. Department of Labor, 2nd Massachusetts Ave., NE, Room 3955, Washington, DC 20212, (202) 606-7100.

6) Identifying Overseas Opportunities:
The International Trade Administration (ITA) of the Commerce Department assists American exporters in locating and gaining access to foreign markets. It furnishes information on overseas markets available for U.S. products and services, requirements which must be fulfilled, economic conditions in foreign countries, foreign market and investment opportunities, etc. Operations are divided into four major areas:

- **International Economic Policy:** promotes U.S. exports geographically by helping American businesses market products in various locations abroad and by solving the trade and investment problems they encounter. This office is staffed by Country Desk Officers knowledgeable in marketing and business practices for almost every country in the world. (See details above). Contact: Office of International Economic Policy, ITA, U.S. Department of Commerce, Washington, DC 20230, (202) 377-3022. See Appendix N for country marketing experts.

- **Export Administration:** supervises the enforcement provisions of the Export Administration Act, and administers the Foreign Trade Zone Program. Personnel in its export enforcement and its administration, policy and regulations offices can offer technical advice and legal interpretations of the various export legislation which affect American businesses. Assistance in complying with export controls can be obtained directly from the Exporter Counseling Division within the Bureau of Export Administration (BXA) Office of Export Licensing in Washington, DC, (202) 377-4811.

BXA also has four field offices that specialize in counseling on export controls and regulations:

Western Regional Office	(714) 660-0144
Northern California Branch Office	(408) 748-7450
Portland Branch Office	(503) 326-5159
Eastern Regional Office	(603) 834-6300

- **Trade Development:** advises businesses on trade and investment issues, and promotes U.S. exports by industry or product classifications. Offices offer assistance and information on export counseling, statistics and trade data, licensing, trading companies, and other services. Contact: Office of Trade Development, ITA, U.S. Department of Commerce, Washington, DC 20230, (202) 377-1461; FAX: (202) 377-5697.

- **U.S. and Foreign Commercial Service:** provides information on government programs to American businesses, and uncovers trade opportunities for U.S. exporters. They also locate representatives and agents for American firms, assist U.S. executives in all phases of their exporting, and help enforce export controls and regulations. They operate through 47 district offices located in major U.S. cities and in 124 posts in 68 foreign countries. In addition, a valued asset of the US & FCS is a group of about 525 foreign nationals, usually natives of the foreign country, who are employed in the U.S. embassy or consulate and bring with them a wealth of personal understanding of local market conditions and business practices. U.S. exporters usually tap into these services by contacting the U.S. Department of Commerce/US & FCS field office in their state (listed later in this chapter), or Office of U.S. and Foreign Commercial Service, U.S. Department of Commerce, Washington, DC 20230; (202) 377-4767.

Or contact regional directors at:

Africa, Near East and South Asia	(202) 377-4836
East Asia and Pacific	(202) 377-8422
Europe	(202) 377-1599
Western Hemisphere	(202) 377-2736

FAX (Europe and Western Hemisphere) (202) 377-3159
FAX (All others) (202) 377-5179

7) Latest News On Foreign Opportunities:
In addition to technical reports on foreign research and development, National Technical Information Service sells foreign market airgrams and foreign press and radio translations. A free video is available explaining NTIS services. Contact: National Technical Information Service, U.S. Department of Commerce, 5285 Port Royal Road, Springfield, VA 22161, (703) 487-4650.

8) Planning Services for U.S. Exporters:
In its effort to promote economic development in Third World countries, the Trade and Development Program finances

Be patient. If any phone number is incorrect, call (area code) 555-1212 and request the new listing.

planning services for development projects leading to the export of U.S. goods and services. A free pamphlet is available that describes the planning services offered by the Trade and Development Program. To obtain a copy, contact: U.S. Trade and Development Program, U.S. Department of State, Room 309 SA-16, Washington, DC 20523-1602, (703) 875-4357.

9) Terrorism Abroad:

Assistance is available to companies doing business abroad to assess the security conditions and risk in certain cities and countries which may pose a threat. Contact: Private Sector Liaison Staff, Bureau of Diplomatic Security, U.S. Dept. of State, 2216 Gallows Rd., Dunn Loring, VA 22027, (703) 204-6210.

10) Trade Remedy Assistance Center:

The Center provides information on remedies available under the Trade Remedy Law. It also offers technical assistance to eligible small businesses to enable them to bring cases to the International Trade Commission. Contact: ITC Trade Remedy Assistance Center, U.S. International Trade Commission, 500 E Street SW, Washington, DC 20436, (202) 205-2200.

11) International Expertise:

Staff in the following offices will prove helpful as information sources regarding the international scope of their respective subject areas:

Economics:

International Economics, Bureau of Economic Analysis, U.S. Department of Commerce, 1401 K Street, N.W., Washington, DC 20230, (202) 523-0695

Productivity and Technology Statistics:

Bureau of Labor Statistics, U.S. Department of Labor, 2 Massachusetts Ave., NE, #2150, Washington, DC 20212, (202) 606-5600.

Investments and Other Monetary Matters:

Office of Assistant Secretary for International Affairs, U.S. Department of the Treasury, Room 3430, Washington, DC 20220, (202) 622-0060.

European Lifestyles:

European Community Information Service, 2100 M Street NW, Suite 707, Washington, DC 20037, (202) 862-9500

Population:

Barbara Boyle Torrey, Chief, Center for International Research, Bureau of Census, U.S. Department of Commerce, Room 709, Scuderi Building, Washington, DC 20233, (301) 763-4811

Population Reference Bureau, Inc., 1875 Connecticut Ave., NW, #520, Washington, DC 20009, (202) 483-1100.

Country Development:

Inter-American Development Bank, 1300 NY Ave., NW, Washington, DC 20577, (202) 623-1000

International Monetary Fund, 700 19th Street NW, Washington, DC 20431, (202) 623-7000

World Bank, 1818 H St NW, Washington, DC 20433, (202) 477-1234

12) National Trade Data Bank:

This is a "one-stop" source for export promotion and international trade data collected by 15 U.S. government agencies. Updated each month and released on CD-ROM, the Data Bank enables a user with and IBM-compatible personal computer equipped with a CD-ROM reader to access over 100,00 trade documents. It contains the latest Census data on U.S. imports and exports by commodity and country; the complete CIA World Factbook; current market research reports compiled by the U.S. and Foreign and Commercial Service; the complete Foreign Traders Index which has over 45,000 names and addresses of individuals and firms abroad interested in importing U.S. products; and many other data services. It is available for free at over 700 Federal Dispository Libraries and can be purchased for $35 per disc or $360 for a 12-month subscription. Contact: Economics and Statistics Administration, U.S. Department of Commerce, Washington, DC 20230, (202) 377-1986.

13) Global Demographics:

The Center for International Research at the U.S. Department of Commerce compiles and maintains up-to-date global demographic and social information for all countries in its International Data Base, which is accessible to U.S. companies seeking to identify potential markets overseas. The database can be purchased for $175. Contact Systems Analysis and Programming Staff, (301) 763-4811.

14) International Energy Data Base:

The Office of Fossil Energy forwards prospective energy-related leads to the Agency for International Development (AID) for inclusion in its growing trade opportunities data base in an effort to reach an extended audience seeking energy-related trade opportunities. For more information on the Fossil Energy-AID Data base contact: The Office of Fossil Energy, U.S. Department of Energy, 1000 Independence Ave SW, Washington, DC 20585, (202) 586-9680.

15) Product Info On 25 World Markets:

The Small Business Administration has an Export Information System (XIS), which are data reports providing specific product or service information on the top 25 world markets and market growth trends for the past five years. Contact: Office of International Trade, Small Business Administration, 409 Third St. SW, Washington, DC 20416, (202) 205-7264.

16) Monitoring Investments In Developing Countries:

The Agency for International Development maintains a Trade and Investment Monitoring System (TIMS) which is a user-friendly computer-based system, providing a broad array of trade and investment information to potential U.S. investors and exporters on 42 developing countries. Contact: International Business, Agency for International Development, Room 100 SA-2, Washington, DC 20253-0229, (202) 663-2660.

17) On-Line Economic Bulletin Board:

This computer-based electronic bulletin board, is an on-line sources for trade leads as well as the latest statistical releases from the Bureau of Census, the Bureau of Economic Analysis, the Federal reserve Board, and

Selling Overseas

other Federal Agencies. Subscribers pay an annual fee, plus cost per minute. Contact EBB, Office of Business Analysis, U.S. Dept. of Commerce, Washington, DC 20230, (202) 377-1986.

Now use your FAX machine to get the latest economic, financial, and trade news available from the U.S. government. Just dial (900) 786-2329 from your FAX machine's touch-tone telephone and follow the simple voice instructions. EBB/FAX™ stores the complete text of many government press releases and information files. The cost for this service is 65¢ per minute. Charges will appear on your regular phone bill and there are no registration fees. The list of files is updated every business day and the service is available 24 hours per day, 7 days per week.

18) Free Legal Assistance:
The Export Legal Assistance Network (ELAN) is a nationwide group of attorneys with experience in international trade who provide free initial consultations to small businesses on export related matters. Contact: Export Legal Assistance Network, Small Business Administration, 409 Third St. SW, Washington, DC 20416, (202) 778-3080.

19) Global Learning:
U.S. Department of Education, Business and International Education Programs. The business and international education program is designed to engage U.S. schools of business language and area programs, international study programs, public and private sector organizations, and U.S. businesses in a mutually productive relationship which will benefit the Nation's future economic interest. Approximately $2.3 million annually is available to assist U.S. institutions of higher education to promote the Nation's capacity for international understanding. Typical grantee activities include executive seminars, case studies and export skill workshops. For more information contact: Center for International Education, U.S. Department of Education, Room 3053, ROB-3, 7th and D Streets, SW, Washington, DC 20202; (202) 708-8764.

20) Export Counseling — SCORE, ACE:
The Small Business Administration can provide export counseling to small business exporters by retired and active business executives. Members of the Service Corps of Retired Executives (SCORE) and the Active Corps of Executives (ACE), with years of practical experience in international trade, assist small firms in evaluating their export potential and developing and implementing basic export marketing plans. For more information, contact your local SBA office listed in the government pages of your telephone book, or National SCORE Office, 1825 Connecticut Ave., NW, Suite 503, Washington, DC 20009; (202) 653-6279.

21) U.S. Department of Energy — Office of International Affairs and Energy Emergencies:
The U.S. Department of Energy (DOE) promotes U.S. exports of energy goods, services and technology primarily through participation in The Committee on Renewable Energy Commerce and Trade, and The Coal and Clean Technology Export Program. The following is a list of DOE's programs and the corresponding telephone numbers to call for more information.

Committee on Renewable Energy Commerce and Trade (CORECT): Through the concept of "one-stop shopping"

potential exporters can receive comprehensive advice on potential markets, financing and information on export guidelines. Call (202) 586-5517.

Coal and Technology Export Program (CTEP): CTEP serves as a reservoir for international information on U.S. coal and coal technologies, as DOE's intra-departmental coordinator, and as the USG inter-agency liaison for coal companies and technology firms. Call (202) 586-7297.

Bureau of International Affairs and Energy Emergencies' Eastern European Development Program: Eastern Europe is now threatened with severe energy shortfalls due to circumstances such as the Persian Gulf situation, the concern over environmentally hazardous nuclear reactors, and the decrease in oil supplies from the former Soviet Union. Call (202) 586-1189.

The Export Assistance Initiative: This entity in the Bureau of International Affairs has been designed to help identify overseas opportunities for U.S. companies, identify and attempt to alleviate discriminatory trade barriers, and identify possible financing alternatives for U.S. companies. Call (202) 586-0153.

Read All About It: Helpful Publications

Basic Guide to Exporting:
This publication outlines the sequence of steps necessary to determine whether to, and how to, use foreign markets as a source of profits. It describes the various problems which confront smaller firms engaged in, or seeking to enter, international trade as well as the types of assistance available. It also provides a guide to appraising the sales potential of foreign markets and to understanding the requirements of local business practices and procedures in overseas markets. The booklet is available for $8.50 from: Superintendent of Documents, U.S. Government Printing Office, Washington, DC 20402, (202) 783-3238.

Exporter's Guide to Federal Resources for Small Business:
This free booklet describes the types of assistance available for small businesses interested in international trade opportunities. It is available from any of the Small Business Administration field offices or contact: Office of International Trade, U.S. Small Business Administration, 409 3rd St., SW, 6th Floor, Washington, DC 20416, (202) 205-6720.

Markets Overseas with U.S. Government Help:
This booklet describes the various agencies of the federal government which offer programs to assist those businesses involved or contemplating international trade. It is available for 50 cents from the Small Business Administration, Box 30, Denver, CO 80201.

Commercial News USA:
This publication describes a free export promotion service that will publicize the availability of your new product to foreign markets, and test foreign market interest in your new product. There is a small fee. Contact: Marketing Programs Section, Room 2106, U.S. Department of Commerce, Washington, DC 20230, (202) 377-4918.

Be patient. If any phone number is incorrect, call (area code) 555-1212 and request the new listing.

International Trade

Export Programs: A Business Directory of U.S. Government Resources:

This guide provides an overview of U.S. government export assistance programs and contact points for further information and expertise in utilizing these programs. Contact: Trade Information Center, U.S. Department of Commerce, Washington, DC 20230, (800) 872-8723.

Business America:

The principal Commerce Department publication for presenting domestic and international business news. Each weekly issue includes a "how to" article for new exporters, discussion of U.S. trade policy, news of government actions that may affect trade, a calendar of upcoming trade show, exhibits, fairs and seminars. An annual subscription is $49. Contact: Superintendent of Documents, Government Printing Office, Washington, DC 20402, (202) 783-3238.

Key Officers of Foreign Service Posts: A Guide for Business Representatives:

Lists the names of key State and Commerce officers at U.S. embassies and consulates. Cost is $5 per copy. Contact: Superintendent of Documents, Government Printing Office, Washington, DC 20402, (202) 783-3238.

Export Trading Company (ETC) Guidebook:

This Guidebook is intended to assist those who are considering starting or expanding exporting through the various forms of an ETC. This Guidebook will also facilitate your review of the ETC Act and export trading options and serve as a planning tool for your business by showing you what it takes to export profitably and how to start doing it. Cost is $8. Contact: Superintendent of Documents, Government Printing Office, Washington, DC 20402, (202) 783-3238.

Foreign Labor Trends:

Published by the U.S. Department of Labor, theses are a series of reports, issued annually, that describe and analyze labor trends in more than 70 countries. The reports, which are prepared by the American Embassy in each country, cover labor-management relations, trade unions, employment and unemployment, wages and working conditions, labor and government, international labor activities, and other significant developments. Contact: Office of Foreign Relations, Room S 5006, 200 Constitution Ave, NW, Washington, DC 20210, (202) 523-6257.

ABC's of Exporting:

This is a special issue of Business America which goes step by step through the exporting process. It explains the federal agencies and how they can help as well as providing a directory of export sources. This publication is free and is available by contacting: Trade Information Center, U.S. Department of Commerce, Washington, DC 20230, (800) 872-8723.

Ag Exporter:

Monthly magazine published by the U.S. Department of Agriculture's Foreign Agricultural Service (FAS). The annual subscription cost is $14. Contact: Trade Assistance and Planning Office, Foreign Agricultural Service, U.S. Department of Agriculture, Washington, DC 20250; (703) 756-6001.

AID Procurement Information Bulletin:

This publication advertises notices of intended procurement of AID-financed commodities. The subscription cost is free. Contact: USAID's Office of Small and Disadvantaged Business Utilization/Minority Resource Center, Washington, DC 20523-1414; (703) 875-1551.

The Government Printing office has many more titles to choose from. For a listing, contact the GPO (listed below) by mail, or phone and ask for the Foreign Trade and Tariff Subject Bibliography (SB-123).

Government Printing Office (GPO)
Superintendent of Documents
Washington, DC 20402
(202) 783-3238

U.S. Department of Commerce/US & FCS Field Offices

Trade experts at these 64 offices advise companies on foreign markets.

Alabama

Birmingham: 2015 2nd Ave N., 35203, (205) 731-1331

Alaska

Anchorage: 222 W. 7th Ave., P.O. Box 32, 99513, (907) 271-5041

Arizona

Phoenix: 230 North 1st Avenue, Room 3412, 85025, (602) 379-3285

Arkansas

Little Rock: 320 W. Capitol Avenue, Suite 811, 72201, (501) 378-5794

California

Los Angeles: 11000 Wilshire Blvd., Room 9200, 90024, (213) 209-7104
Santa Ana: 116-A W. 4th Street, Suite 1, 92701, (714) 836-2461
San Diego: 6363 Greenwich Drive, 92122, (619) 557-5395
San Francisco: 450 Golden Gate Ave, Box 36013, 94102, (415) 556-5860

Colorado

Denver: 680 World Trade Center, 1625 Broadway, 80202, (303) 844-3246

Connecticut

Hartford: 450 Main Street, Room 610-B, 06103, (203) 240-3530

District of Columbia

Washington: 14th and Constitution Ave NW, #1068 HCHB, 20230, (202) 377-3181

Delaware

Served by Philadelphia, Pennsylvania

Florida

Miami: 51 S.W. First Avenue, Suite 224, 33130, (305) 536-5267
Clearwater: 128 North Osceola Avenue, 34615, (813) 461-0011
Jacksonville: 3100 University Blvd. South, Suite 200A, 32216, (904) 791-2796
Orlando: U.S. Dept of Commerce, c/o College of Business Administration, CEBAII, Room 346, 32802, (407) 648-1608
Tallahassee: 107 W. Gaines St., Collins Bldg., Room 401, 32304, (904) 488-6469

Georgia

Atlanta: 4360 Chamber-Dunwoody Road, 30341, (404) 452-9101
Savannah: 120 Barnard Street, A-107, 31401, (912) 944-4204

Be patient. If any phone number is incorrect, call (area code) 555-1212 and request the new listing.

Selling Overseas

Hawaii
Honolulu: 300 Ala Moana Blvd., Box 50026, 96850, (808) 541-1782

Idaho
Boise: 700 W. State Street, Boise, 83720, (208) 334-3857

Illinois
Chicago: 55 E Monroe, Room 1406, 60603, (312) 353-4450
Rockford: 515 N Court Street, 61110-0247, (815) 987-8123
Palatine: W.R. Harper College, Algonquin and Roselle Rd., 60067, (312) 397-3000, ext. 2532.

Indiana
Indianapolis: One N. Capitol, Suite 520, 46204-2227, (317) 226-6214.

Iowa
Des Moines: 210 Walnut Street, Room 817, 50309, (515) 284-4222

Kansas
Wichita: 7591 River Park Pl., Suite 580, 727 N. Waco, 67203, (316) 269-6160

Kentucky
Louisville: 601 West Broadway, Room 636B, 40202, (502) 582-5066

Louisiana
New Orleans: 2 Canal Street, Room 432, 70130, (504) 589-6546

Maine
Augusta: 77 Sewall Street, 04330, (207) 622-8249

Maryland
Baltimore: U.S. Custom House, 40 South Bay, Room 413, 21202, (301) 962-3560

Massachusetts
Boston: World Trade Center, Suite 307, 02210, (617) 565-8563

Michigan
Detroit: 477 Michigan Avenue, Room 1140, 48226, (313) 226-3650
Grand Rapids: 300 Monroe N.W., Room 409, 49503, (616) 456-2411

Minnesota
Minneapolis: 110 S. 4th Street, Room 108, 55401, (612) 348-1638

Mississippi
Jackson: 300 Woodrow Wilson Blvd., Room 328, Jackson Mall Office Center, 39213, (601) 965-4388

Missouri
St. Louis: 7911 Forsyth Blvd., Suite 610, 63105, (314) 425-3302
Kansas City: 601 East 12th Street, Room 635, 64106, (816) 426-3141

Montana
Served by Boise, Idaho

Nebraska
Omaha: 11133 O Street, 68137, (402) 221-3664

Nevada
Reno: 1755 E. Plumb Lane, #152, 89502, (702) 785-5203

New Hampshire
Served by Boston, Massachusetts

New Jersey
Trenton: 3131 Princeton Pike Bldg. 6, Suite 100, 08648, (609) 989-2100

New Mexico
Albuquerque: 625 Silver SW, 3rd Floor, 87102, (214) 767-0542
Santa Fe: Economic Development and Tourism Department, 1100 St. Francis Dr., 87503, (505) 827-0264

New York
Buffalo: 111 West Huron Street, Room 1312, Federal Building, 14202, (716) 846-4191
Rochester: 111 East Avenue, 14604, (716) 263-6480
New York: U.S. Dept. of Commerce, 26 Federal Plaza, Foley Square, 10278, (212) 264-0634

North Carolina
Greensboro: 324 West Market Street, 27402, (919) 333-5345

North Dakota
Served by Omaha, Nebraska

Ohio
Cincinnati: 550 Main Street, Room 9504, 45202, (513) 684-2944
Cleveland: 668 Euclid Avenue, Suite 600, 44114, (216) 522-4750

Oklahoma
Oklahoma City: 6601 Broadway Extension, 73116, (405) 231-5302
Tulsa: 440 S. Houston Street, Room 505, 74127, (918) 581-7650

Oregon
Portland: Suite 242, One World Trade Center, 121 SW Salmon Street, 97204, (503) 326-3001

Pennsylvania
King of Prussia: 475 Allendale Road, 19406, (215) 962-4980
Pittsburgh: 1000 Liberty Avenue, Room 2002, 15222, (412) 644-2850

Puerto Rico
San Juan: Room 659 Federal Building, 00918, (809) 766-5555

Rhode Island
Providence: 7 Jackson Walkway, 02903, (401) 528-5104, ext. 22

South Carolina
Columbia: 1835 Assembly Street, Suite 172, 29201, (803) 765-5345
Charleston: Room 128, JC Long Bldg, 9 Liberty Street, 29424, (803) 724-4361

South Dakota
Served by Omaha, Nebraska

Tennessee
Nashville: 404 James Robertson Parkway, Suite 1114, 37219, (615) 736-5161
Memphis: 22 North Front Street, Suite 200, 38103, (901) 544-4137
Knoxville: 301 E. Church Ave., 37915, (615) 549-9268

Texas
Dallas: 1100 Commerce Street, Room 7A5, 75242, (214) 767-0542
Austin: 816 Congress, First City Center Bldg., Room 1200, 78701, (512) 482-5939
Houston: 515 Rusk Street, Room 2625, 77002, (713) 229-2578

Utah
Salt Lake City: Suite 105, 324 South State Street, 84111, (801) 524-5116

Vermont
Served by Boston, Massachusetts

Virginia
Richmond: 400 North 8th Street, Room 8010, 23240, (804) 771-2246

Washington
Seattle: 3131 Elliott Avenue, Suite 290, 98121, (206) 442-5616
Spokane: West 808 Spokane Falls Blvd., Room 625, 99201, (509) 353-2922

West Virginia
Charleston: 405 Capitol St., Suite 809, 25301, (304) 347-5123

Wisconsin
Milwaukee: 517 E. Wisconsin Avenue, Room 606, 53202, (414) 291-3473

Be patient. If any phone number is incorrect, call (area code) 555-1212 and request the new listing.

Wyoming
Served by Denver, Colorado

State Government Assistance To Exporters

Last year state governments spent approximately $40,000,000 to help companies in their state sell goods and services overseas. This figure increased almost 50% over the previous two years. During the same period of time, federal monies devoted to maximizing companies' export capabilities remained virtually constant. This is another indicator of how the states are fertile sources of information and expertise for large and small businesses.

The underlying mission of these offices is to create jobs within their state. Usually their approach is to help companies develop overseas marketing strategies or to offer incentives to foreign companies to invest in their state. The major state trade development programs and services are outlined below.

1) Marketing Research and Company Intelligence:
All of the states can provide some degree of overseas marketing information. The level of detail will depend upon the resources of the state. Thirty-two states (except for Alabama, Arizona, California, Delaware, Hawaii, Idaho, Kansas, Maryland, Minnesota, Nebraska, Nevada, New Jersey, New York, South Dakota, Texas, Washington, West Virginia, and Wyoming) say they will do customized market studies for companies. Such studies are free or available for a small fee. For example, the Commonwealth of Virginia will do an in-depth market study for a company and charge $1,000. They estimate similar surveys done by the private sector cost up to $20,000. Virginia relies on MBA students and professors within the state university system who get credit for working on such projects.

Even if a state does not perform customized studies, the trade office within the department of economic development will prove to be an ideal starting place for marketing information. Some states which do not undertake comprehensive studies for prospective exporters will do a limited amount of research for free. These offices can also point to outside sources as well as the notable resources at the federal level which may be able to assist. And those states with offices overseas also can contact these foreign posts to identify sources in other countries. Moreover, many of the offices have people who travel abroad frequently for companies and also work with other exporters. Such bureaucrats can be invaluable for identifying the exact source for obtaining particular market or company intelligence.

2) Company and Industry Directories:
Many states publish directories which are helpful to both exporters and researchers. Some states publish export/import directories which show which companies in the state are exporters and what they sell as well as which are importers and what they buy. Because many of the trade offices are also interested in foreign investment within their state, many publish directories or other reference sources disclosing which companies in their state are foreign owned, and by whom. Other state publications may include export service directories which list organizations providing services to exporters such as banks, freight forwarders, translators, and world trade organizations. Some also publish agribusiness exporter directories which identify agricultural-related companies involved in exporting.

3) Free Newsletters:
All but 14 states (i.e., Alabama, Colorado, Delaware, Florida, Hawaii, Indiana, Louisiana, Minnesota, Mississippi, Michigan, Kentucky, Ohio, North Carolina, South Dakota, and Tennessee) generate international newsletters or publish a special section within a general newsletter on items of interest to those selling overseas. These newsletters are normally free and cover topics like new trade leads, new rules and regulations for exports, and details about upcoming overseas trade shows. Such newsletters can also be a source for mailing lists for those whose clients include exporters. We haven't specifically investigated the availability of such lists, but remember that all states have a law comparable to the federal Freedom of Information Act which allows public access to government data.

4) Overseas Contacts:
Finding a foreign buyer or an agent/distributor for a company is one of the primary functions of these state offices. How they do this varies from state to state. Many sponsor trade fairs and seminars overseas to attract potential buyers to products produced in their state. The more aggressive trade promotion offices may organize trade missions and escort a number of companies overseas and personally help them look for buyers or agents. Many will distribute a company's sales brochures and other literature to potential buyers around the world through their overseas offices. Some states work with the federal government and explore general trade leads and then try to match buyers with sellers. Others will cultivate potential clients in a given country and contact each directly.

5) Export Marketing Seminars:
Most all of the states conduct free or modestly priced seminars to introduce companies to selling overseas. Some of the courses are held in conjunction with the regional International Trade Administration office of the U.S. Commerce Department. The course may be general in nature, for example, *The Basics of Exporting*, or focused on specific topics such as *International Market Research Techniques*, *Letters of Credit*, *Export Financing*, or *How to do Business with Israel*.

6) State Grants and Loans for Exporters:
Many states offer financial assistance for those wishing to export. Some states even provide grants (money you do not have to pay back) to those firms which cannot afford to participate in a trade mission or trade fair. This means that they provide money to those companies which are just trying to develop a customer base overseas. More typically the state will help with financing of a sale through state-sponsored loans and loan guarantees, or assistance in identifying and applying for federal or commercial export financing.

7) Trade Leads Databases:
Because these offices provide mostly services, there are not many opportunities for them to develop databases. However, their trade leads program is one area where a number of offices have computerized. These databases consist of the names and addresses along with some background information on those overseas companies which are actively searching or might be interested in doing business with companies within the state. The number of leads in such a system could range from several

Be patient. If any phone number is incorrect, call (area code) 555-1212 and request the new listing.

Selling Overseas

hundred to five or ten thousand. None of these states seem to have made such information available on machine readable formats to those outside the office. But, in light of state Freedom of Information statutes, it may be worth making a formal inquiry if you have an interest. The states which have computerized their trade leads include: Alabama, California, Colorado, Connecticut, Florida, Georgia, Hawaii, Indiana, Iowa, Minnesota, Mississippi, Missouri, Nebraska, New Jersey, New York, North Carolina, North Dakota, Ohio, Pennsylvania, South Dakota, Tennessee, West Virginia, and Wisconsin.

State International Trade Offices

The foreign cities in parentheses after the telephone number are those locations where the state maintains a trade office.

Alabama

International Development and Trade Division, Alabama Development Office, State Capitol, Montgomery, AL 36130, (205) 263-0048; FAX: (205) 265-5078 (Hanover, Germany; Seoul, Korea; Tokyo, Japan;)

Alaska

International Trade Director, Office of International Trade, Department of Commerce and Economic Development, 3601 C Street, Suite 798, Anchorage, AK 99503, (907) 561-5585; FAX: (907) 561-4557 (Tokyo, Japan; Seoul, Korea)

Arizona

International Trade, Department of Commerce, 3800 N. Central, Phoenix, AZ 85012, (602) 280-1371

Arkansas

International Marketing, Department of Economic Development, One State Capitol Mall, Little Rock, AR 72201, (501) 682-7690 (Brussels, Belgium; Tokyo, Japan; Taipei, Taiwan)

California

California State World Trade Commission, 1121 L Street, Suite 310, Sacramento, CA 95814, (916) 324-5511; FAX: (916) 324-5791 (Tokyo, Japan; London, England; Hong Kong; Frankfort, Germany; Mexico City, Mexico)

Export Finance Office, 107 South Broadway, Room 8039, Los Angeles, CA 90012, (213) 620-2433; FAX: (213) 620-6102

Colorado

International Trade Office, Department of Commerce and Development, 1625 Broadway, Suite 680, Denver, CO 80202, (303) 892-3850

Connecticut

International Division, Department of Economic Development, 865 Brook St., Hartford, CT 06067, (203) 258-4256 (Frankfort, Germany; Tokyo, Japan)

Delaware

Delaware Development Office, Division of Economic Development, 99 Kings Highway, Box 1401, Dover, DE 19903, (302) 736-4271; FAX: (302) 736-5749

District of Columbia

DC Office of International Business, 1250 I St., Suite 1003, Washington, DC 20005, (202) 757-1576

Florida

Florida Department of Commerce, 366 Collins Building, Tallahassee, FL 32399-2000, (904) 488-6124; FAX: (904) 487-1407 (Toronto, Canada; Brussels, Belgium; Seoul, Korea; Frankfort, Germany; Tokyo, Japan; London, England)

Georgia

Department of Industry, Trade and Tourism, Suite 1100, 285 Peachtree Center Ave., Atlanta, GA 30303, (404) 656-3545; FAX: (404) 656-3567 (Brussels, Belgium; Tokyo, Japan; Toronto, Canada; Seoul, Korea)

Hawaii

International Services Branch, Department of Planning and Economic Development, P.O. Box 2359, Honolulu, HI 96804, (808) 548-7719

Idaho

Economic Development, Division of Economic and Community Affairs, 700 W. State Street, Boise, ID 83720, (208) 334-2470; FAX: (208) 334-2783

Illinois

International Business Division, Illinois Department of Commerce and Community Affairs, 100 W. Randolph Street, Suite 3-400, Chicago, IL 60601, (312) 814-7166 (Brussels, Belgium; San Paulo, Brazil; Hong Kong; Osaka and Tokyo, Japan; Warsaw, Poland; Toronto, Canada; Shenyaang, China)

Illinois Export Council, 321 N. Clark St. #550, Chicago, IL 60610, (312) 793-4995

Indiana

International Trade Division, Department of Commerce, One North Capitol, Suite 700, Indianapolis, IN 46204, (317) 232-3527 (Brussels, Belgium; Tokyo, Japan; London, England; Toronto, Canada; Tiapie, Taiwan; Beijing, China; Seoul, Korea)

Iowa

International Trade, Iowa Department of Economic Development, 200 East Grand Avenue, Des Moines, IA 50309, (515) 242-4743; FAX: (515) 242-4749 (Frankfurt, Germany; Hong Kong; Tokyo, Japan)

Kansas

Kansas Department of Commerce, 400 W. 8th, Suite 500, Topeka, KS 66603, (913) 296-4027 (Tokyo, Japan; Brussels, Belgium)

Kentucky

Office of International Marketing, Kentucky Commerce Cabinet, Capitol Plaza Tower, 24th Floor, Frankfort, KY 40601, (502) 564-2170 (Tokyo, Japan; Brussels, Belgium)

Louisiana

Office of Commerce and Industry, P.O. Box 94185, Baton Rouge, LA 70804-9185, (504) 342-9232; FAX: (504) 342-5389 (Mexico City, Mexico; Tiapie, Taiwan; Seoul, Korea)

Maine

International Trade, Maine World Trade Commission, State House, Station 59, Augusta, ME 04333, (207) 289-2656

Maryland

Maryland International Division, World Trade Center, 401 East Pratt Street, 7th Floor, Baltimore, MD 21202, (301) 333-4295 (Brussels, Belgium; Tokyo, Japan; Hong Kong)

Massachusetts

Office of International Trade, 100 Cambridge Street, Room 902, Boston, MA 02202, (617) 367-1830

Michigan

U.S./International Trade Division, Manufacturing Development Group, Michigan Department of Commerce, P.O. Box 30017, Lansing, MI 48909, (517) 373-1054; FAX: (517) 335-2521 (Toronto, Canada; Lago, Nigeria; Hong Kong; Brussels, Belgium; Tokyo, Japan)

Minnesota

Minnesota Trade Office, 1000 World Trade Center, 30 E. 7th Street, St. Paul, 55101, (612) 297-4222; FAX: (612) 296-3555 (Oslo, Norway; Stockholm, Sweden)

Mississippi

Department of Economic Development, P.O. Box 849, Jackson, MI 39205, (601) 359-3552 (Seoul, Korea; Tokyo, Japan; Hong Kong; Frankfort, Germany; Tiapie, Taiwan)

Missouri

Export Development Office, Department of Commerce and Economic Development, P.O. Box 118, Jefferson City, MO 65102, (314) 751-4855 (Tokyo, Japan; Dusseldorf, Germany; Seoul, Korea; Tiapie, Taiwan)

Be patient. If any phone number is incorrect, call (area code) 555-1212 and request the new listing.

International Trade

Montana

International Trade Office, Montana Department of Commerce, 1424 9th Avenue, Helena, MT 59620, (406) 444-3923 (Tokyo, Japan; Calgary, Canada; Tiapie, Taiwan; Kumamoto, Japan)

Nebraska

Department of Economic Development, 301 Centennial Mall South, P.O. Box 94666, Lincoln, NE 68509, (402) 471-3111

Nevada

Commission of Economic Development, Capital Complex, Carson, NV 89710, (702) 687-4325

New Hampshire

Foreign Trade and Commercial Development, Department of Resources and Economic Development, 172 Pembroke Street, P.O. Box 856, Concord, NH 03301, (603) 271-2591

New Jersey

Division of International Trade, Dept. of Commerce and Economic Development, 153 Halsey Street, Newark, NJ 07102, (201) 648-3518 (Tokyo, Japan)

New Mexico

Economic Development Division, Economic Development and Tourism Department, 1100 St. Francis Drive, Joseph Montoya Building, Santa Fe, NM 87503, (505) 827-0307; FAX: (505) 827-0263

New York

International Division, Department of Commerce, 1515 Broadway, 51st Floor, New York Department of Economic Development, New York, NY 10036, (212) 827-6100 (Tokyo, Japan; Wiesbaden, Germany; London, England; Milan, Italy; Ontario and Montreal, Canada; Hong Kong)

North Carolina

International Division, Department of Commerce, 430 North Salisbury Street, Raleigh, NC 27611, (919) 733-7193 (Dusseldorf, Germany; Hong Kong; Tokyo, Japan)

North Dakota

International Trade Consultant, Economic Development Commission, 1833 East Expressway, Bismarck, ND 58504, (701) 224-2810

Ohio

International Trade Division, Department of Development, 77 S. High Street, P.O. Box 1001, Columbus, OH 43266, (614) 466-5017 (Brussels, Belgium; Tokyo, Japan Hong Kong, Toronto, Canada)

Oklahoma

International Trade Division, Oklahoma Department of Commerce, 6601 Broadway Extension, Oklahoma City, OK 73116, (405) 841-5220

Oregon

International Trade Division, Oregon Economic Development Department, #1 World Trade Center, Suite 300, 121 Salmon Street, Portland, OR 97204, (503) 229-5625, or (800) 452-7813 (Tokyo, Japan)

Pennsylvania

International Projects Manager, Bureau of International Commerce, 433 Forum Building, Harrisburg, PA 17120, (717) 783-5107 (Frankfurt, Germany; Tokyo, Japan;)

Puerto Rico

P.R. Department of Commerce, P.O. Box 4275, San Juan, PR 00936, (809) 721-3290

Rhode Island

Business and Industry Representative, Department of Economic Development, 7 Jackson Walkway, Providence, RI 02903, (401) 277-2601 (Hong Kong)

South Carolina

International Business Development, South Carolina State Development Board, P.O. Box 927, Columbia, SC 29202, (803) 737-0400; FAX: (803) 737-0481 (Tokyo, Japan; Frankfort, Germany)

South Dakota

South Dakota International Trade Center, Capitol Lake Plaza, Pierre, SD 57501, (605) 773-5032

Tennessee

Export Promotion Office, Department of Economic and Community Development, Rachel Jackson Building, 7th Floor, Nashville, TN 37219, (615) 741-5870

Texas

International Business Development Department, Texas Dept. of Commerce, P.O. Box 12728, Austin, TX 78711, (512) 472-5059 (Mexico City, Mexico)

Utah

Export Development Committee, Economic and Industrial Development Division, 324 S. State St., Salt Lake City, UT 84111, (801) 538-3631 (Tokyo, Japan)

Vermont

International Business, Department of Economic Development, Pavilion Office Building, Montpelier, VT 05602, (802) 828-3221

Virginia

Director of International Marketing, 2 James Center, P.O. Box 798, Richmond, VA 23206, (804) 371-8100 (Tokyo, Japan; Brussels, Belgium)

Washington

Domestic and International Trade Division, Department of Trade and Economic Development, 2001 Sixth Ave, 26th Floor, Seattle, WA 98121, (206) 464-7143; FAX: (206) 464-7222 (Tokyo, Japan)

West Virginia

Governor's Office of Community and Industrial Development, State Capitol, Room 517, Charleston, WV 25305, (304) 348-2243; FAX: (304) 348-0449 (Tokyo, Japan)

Wisconsin

Bureau of International Business Development, Department of Development, 123 West Washington Avenue, Madison, WI 53702, (608) 266-1767 (Frankfurt, Germany; Hong Kong)

Wyoming

International Trade Division, Department of Commerce, Herschler Building, Cheyenne, WY 82002, (307) 777-6412; FAX: (307) 777-5840

Overseas Travel: Business Or Pleasure

The following sources and services will be helpful to anyone who is on business or vacation in any foreign country.

1) Arts America:

The U.S. Information Agency assists qualified artists and performers in arranging private tours overseas. Its aim is to present a balanced portrayal of the American scene. Past activities have included a major exhibition of American crafts shown in China, a modern dance company in the USSR, Spain, and Portugal, and a jazz ensemble in Nigeria, Senegal and Kenya. Contact: Program Manager, Office of the Associate Director for Programs, United States Information Agency, 301 4th Street SW, Room 567, Washington, DC 20547, (202) 619-4779.

2) Travel Overseas On Government Expense:

The U.S. Speakers program will pay experts, who can contribute to foreign societies' understanding of the United States, to travel abroad and participate in seminars, colloquia or symposia. Subjects treated by the program include economics, international political relations, U.S. social and political processes, arts and humanities, and science and technology. To see if you qualify contact: U.S. Speakers, Office of Program Coordination

Be patient. If any phone number is incorrect, call (area code) 555-1212 and request the new listing.

Selling Overseas

and Development, U.S. Information Agency, 301 4th Street SW, Room 550, Washington, DC 20547, (202) 619-4764.

3) Citizens Arrested Overseas:
The Arrest Unit at the State Department monitors arrests and trials to see that American citizens are not abused; acts as a liaison with family and friends in the United States; sends money or messages with written consent of arrestee; offers lists of lawyers; will forward money from the United States to detainee; tries to assure that your rights under local laws are observed. The Emergency Medical and Dietary Assistance Program includes such services as providing vitamin supplements when necessary; granting emergency transfer for emergency medical care; and short-term feeding of two or three meals a day when arrestee is detained without funds to buy his or her own meals. Contact: Arrests Unit, Citizens Emergency Center, Overseas Citizens Service, Bureau of Consular Affairs, U.S. Department of State, 2201 C Street NW, Room 4811, Washington, DC 20520, (202) 647-5225.

4) Citizens Emergency Center:
Emergency telephone assistance is available to United States citizens abroad under the following circumstances:

Arrests: (202) 647-5225 (see details above)

Deaths: (202) 647-5225; notification of interested parties in the United States of the death abroad of American citizens; assistance in the arrangements for disposition of remains.

Financial Assistance: (202) 647-5225; repatriation of destitute nationals, coordination of medical evacuation of non-official nationals from abroad; transmission of private funds in emergencies to destitute United States nationals abroad when commercial banking facilities are unavailable (all costs must be reimbursed)

Shipping and Seamen: (202) 647-5225; protection of American vessels and seamen

Welfare and Whereabouts: (202) 647-5225; search for nonofficial United States nationals who have not been heard from for an undue length of time and/or about whom there is special concern; transmission of emergency messages to United States nationals abroad. For other help contact: Overseas Citizen Services, Bureau of Consular Affairs, U.S. Department of State, 2201 C Street NW, Washington, DC 20520, (202) 647-5225

5) Country Information Studies:
For someone who wants more than what the typical travel books tell about a specific country, this series of books deals with more in depth knowledge of the country being visited. Each book describes the origins and traditions of the people and their social and national attitudes, as well as the economics, military, political and social systems. For a more complete listing of this series and price information, contact: Superintendent of Documents, U.S. Government Printing Office, Washington, DC 20402, (202) 783-3238.

6) Foreign Country Background Notes:
Background Notes on the Countries of the World is a series of

short, factual pamphlets with information on the country's land, people, history, government, political conditions, economy, foreign relations, and U.S. foreign policy. Each pamphlet also includes a factual profile, brief travel notes, a country map, and a reading list. Contact: Public Affairs Bureau, U.S. Department of State, Room 4827A, 2201 C Street NW, Washington, DC 20520, (202) 647-2518 for a free copy of *Background Notes* for the countries you plan to visit. This material is also available from the: Superintendent of Documents, U.S. Government Printing Office, Washington, DC 20402, (202) 783-3238. Single copies cost in the range of $1.50 to $56 for a set.

7) Foreign Language Materials:
The Defense Language Institute Foreign Language Center (DLIFC) has an academic library with holdings of over 100,000 books and periodicals in 50 different foreign languages. These materials are available through the national interlibrary loan program which can be arranged through your local librarian.

8) Foreign Language Training:
The Foreign Service Institute is an in-house educational institution for foreign service officers, members of their families and employees of other government agencies. It provides special training in 50 foreign languages. Its instructional materials, including books and tapes, are designed to teach modern foreign languages. Instruction books must be purchased from Superintendent of Documents, U.S. Government Printing Office, Washington, DC 20402, (202) 783-3238. Tapes must be purchased from the National Audiovisual Center, National Archive, Order Section/AV, 8700 Edgeworth Drive, Capitol Heights, MD 20743, (301) 763-1891.

9) Free Booklets for Travelers:
The following booklets and guides are available free of charge:

Travel Information: Your Trip Abroad:
Contains basic information such as how to apply for a passport, customs tips, lodging information and how American consular officers can help you in an emergency. Publications Distribution, Bureau of Public Affairs, U.S. Department of State, 2201 C Street NW, Room 5815A, Washington, DC 20520, (202) 647-9859.

Customs Information:
Provides information about custom regulations both when returning to the U.S. as well as what to expect when traveling to different parts of the world. Customs Office, P.O. Box 7118, Washington, DC 20044.

Visa Requirements of Foreign Governments:
Lists entry requirements of U.S. citizens traveling as tourists, where and how to apply for visas and tourist cards. Passport Services, Bureau of Consular Affairs, U.S. Department of State, 1425 K Street NW, Room G-62, Washington, DC 20524, (202) 647-0518.

10) Passport Information:
A recorded telephone message provides general information on what is needed when applying for a U.S. passport. Call (202) 647-0518. U.S. citizens and nationals can apply for passports at all passport agencies as well as those post offices and federal and state courts authorized to accept passport applications.

Be patient. If any phone number is incorrect, call (area code) 555-1212 and request the new listing.

Economics, Demographics and Statistics General Sources

* *See also Information on People, Companies, and Mailing Lists Chapter*
* *See also Current Events and Homework Chapter*
* *See also Expert Chapter*

During a recent hearing on Capitol Hill, a congressman asked a Bureau of the Census official why so much money needs to be spent collecting census data when all the information is contained in the popular paperback, *Information Please Almanac*. Of course, all this information comes from the Census Bureau which conducts surveys and the decennial census. This attitude is typical of those who have no idea that the U.S. Government is the largest producer of data in the world, and that anyone else selling it is probably getting it from Uncle Sam. The major publication which identifies many of the statistical sources from the federal government is the *Statistical Abstract of the U.S.* Be sure you look through the Experts Chapter where thousands of data experts are listed by name and telephone number.

* 1990 Census Block-Numbered Maps

Customer Services Branch
Data User Services Division
Bureau of the Census
Washington, DC 20233 (301) 763-4100

The 1990 census block-numbered map series includes county-wide maps prepared on the smallest possible number of map sheets at the maximum practical scale. The 1990 map series depicts each county (or county equivalent) on one or more map sheets--depending on the areal size and shape of the county, the number of blocks in the county, and the density of the block pattern--that will allow displaying all block numbers and feature identifiers, as well as show the county boundary and the MCDs/CCDs, places, and census tracts/BNAs in the county. Each county consists of one or more parent sheets at a single scale, plus insets of densely settled geographic areas as required. As a result, the maps for counties could be at different scales. Insets will be single sheets at a larger scale. In densely developed areas where an inset will not fit on one sheet, multiple-sheet insets are used. An index showing the map sheet and inset coverage are included. The standard sheet size for all maps is 36" x 42" with a maximum 32" x 32" map display area. Data users must purchase these maps from the Census Bureau; they will not be printed and sold through the Government Printing Office (GPO) as in 1980. The maps will be produced by map plotting equipment on paper by Census Bureau staff. There is a charge of $5 per map sheet.

* 1990 Tabulation and Publication Report

Customer Services Branch
Data User Services Division
Bureau of the Census
Washington, DC 20233 (301) 763-4100

The *1990 Census of Population and Housing Tabulation and Publication Program* report describes the 1990 census tabulation and publication program for the 50 States and the District of Columbia. While it is impossible to anticipate all user needs in a changing environment, the Census Bureau designed the 1990 census tabulation and publication program to meet a variety of data needs for different segments of the data user community. Highlights in the report include information on questionnaire content, sample design and disclosure avoidance, dissemination media, map products, data products, custom data products, how to obtain 1990 census data products, and a dictionary of geographic terms. For further information about the report, or to order a free copy, contact the Customer Services Branch. If you want more information about the tabulation and publication program, contact the Data Products Branch, Decennial Planning Division, Census Bureau, Washington, DC 20233; (301) 763-4908.

* X-11.2 and X-11.2Q Seasonal Adjustments

Customer Services (Diskettes)
Data User Services Division
Bureau of the Census
Washington, DC 20233 (301) 763-4100

Two improved versions of the Census-developed X-11 and 11.Q seasonal adjustment software programs are now available which adjust series that range from 3 to 30 years. They are based on the ratio-to-moving average method which provides a moving average and includes trend-cycle curves, ratios of trend-cycle estimates, and estimates of seasonal factors from those ratios. The X-11.2 program adjusts monthly series with a variety of options for adjusting special characteristics. It provides substantial practical flexibility with respect to the kinds of series that can be adjusted. Included in the package are trading and holiday routines, diagnostic plots for output, and a table of the final combined adjustment. The adjusted data can be output to a pre-specified file. The X-11.2Q program adjusts quarterly series and follows the same basic procedures as the X-11.2 program. The trading day and holiday routines are not included, and some options differ somewhat. To request a data diskette, contact Customer Services and they will mail ordering information to you for the diskette files of interest to you.

* Agriculture, Economic, and Government Areas

Data User Services Division
Customer Services
Bureau of the Census
U.S. Department of Commerce
Washington, DC 20233 (301) 763-4100

The following agriculture, economic, and government areas statistical publications are free from this office. The 1992 versions of these reports should begin to be available in 1993.

Guide to the 1987 Census of Agriculture and Related Statistics
A Review of the 1987 Census of Agriculture
Guide to the 1987 Economic Censuses and Related Statistics
An Overview of the 1987 Economic Censuses is free from the Bureau of the Census
Guide to Service Industry Statistics and Related Data

* American Housing Survey 1989 on CD-ROM

Customer Services
Data User Services Division
Bureau of the Census
Washington, DC 20233 (301) 763-4100

The *American Housing Survey* (AHS) is the largest regular national sample survey that describes people and their homes in the United States. It is sponsored by the U.S. Department of Housing and Urban Development (HUD) and conducted by the U.S. Census Bureau which uses interviews to gather information on approximately 42,000 individual housing units and the households that occupy them. The 1989 Core file is in both ASCII SDF (flat) file and SAS formats (PC SAS Version 6.03). The files are microdata files containing the results of each individual interview in the national survey. The technical documentation that comes with the disc is very detailed. It sells for $150; the technical documentation alone is $40. For a brochure containing additional ordering information, contact Customer Services.

Be patient. If any phone number is incorrect, call (area code) 555-1212 and request the new listing.

Economics, Demographics and Statistics

* Approved Recurring Reports Bulletin

Office of Records Management
Services (723)
U.S. Department of Veterans Affairs
Washington, DC 20420 (202) 233-6837

The *Approved Recurring Reports Bulletin* includes a list of reports which have been cleared by the Reporting Policy and Review Service for data collection or have been discontinued since the last printed issue. Contact the office above to obtain a copy.

* Automated Geographic Support System

Chief, Geography Division
Bureau of the Census
Washington, DC 20233 (202) 763-1580

This interagency project was created to produce geographic products for the 1990 census. The geographic component of the new generation of computer-based approaches for taking the 1990 census is called the TIGER System (Topologically Integrated Geographic Encoding and Referencing System). The TIGER File provides geographic products and services from the 1990 decennial census from a totally automated single source. This means that all mapping and geoprocessing would be in complete agreement. In conjunction with the U.S. Geological Survey, the Geography Division developed a computer-readable map file for the whole United States, providing the most complete and accurate set of maps ever prepared for the U.S.--and the first from a computer file. The TIGER System is used to produce publication quality maps on high precision computer-driven map production devices to accompany the data files for the census bureau's 1990 decennial publication programs. For detailed information on the TIGER System, ask for the *Tiger Tales Presentation* from your regional Census office or the office listed above.

* Automated Management Information System

Reporting Systems Division
Office of Information Management and Statistics
U.S. Department of Veterans Affairs
810 Vermont Ave., N.W.
Washington, DC 20420 (202) 233-6824

The Automated Management Information System (AMIS) is an agency-wide system designed to meet the U.S. Department of Veterans Affairs' statistical reporting needs. Contact the office above for further information.

* Bureau of the Census

Bureau of the Census
U.S. Department of Commerce
Washington, DC 20233 (301) 763-4040

The Bureau of the Census takes a census of the U.S. population every 10 years, and they keep the information collected from individual persons, households, or establishments strictly confidential and use it only for statistical purposes. The agency collects, tabulates, and publishes a wide variety of statistical data about the people and the economy of the U.S. These data are utilized by the Congress, the executive branch, and by the public generally in the development and evaluation of economic and social programs. Its principal functions include: 1) decennial censuses of population and housing, 2) quinquennial censuses of agriculture, state and local governments, manufacturers, mineral industries, distributive trades, construction industries, and transportation, 3) current surveys that provide information on many of the subjects covered in the censuses at monthly, quarterly, annual, or other intervals, 4) compilation of current statistics on U.S. foreign trade, including data on imports, exports, and shipping, 5) special censuses at the request and expense of states and local government units, 6) publication of estimates and projections of the population, 7) current data on population and housing characteristics; and 8) current reports on manufacturing, retail and wholesale trade, services, construction, imports and exports, state and local government finances and employment, and other subjects.

April 1, 1990, marked 200 years of census taking in America. A national census has been taken every ten years in the United States since 1790. Mandated by the U.S. Constitution, the decennial census was the basis for determining how many seats each state filled in the House of Representatives. The census provides important social and economic information about our people and our nation. Many federal, state, and local government programs, private corporations, and community agencies use census data. Each census portrays America, and over the years the census has revealed a great deal about how our country has changed as we have grown from a young agrarian nation of about 4 million people clustered along the Eastern seaboard to a complex post-industrial society

of nearly 250 million spread across the continent and beyond. Techniques for taking the census have steadily improved over the past two centuries. The 1990 Census relied heavily on computerization in field operations, processing, geography, data tabulations, and products. The 1990 Census was the most accurate census in U.S. history. Issues such as census undercount and the homeless population were important factors taken into consideration.

* Business Economics - Publications and Databases

Public Information
Bureau of Economic Analysis (BEA)
U.S. Department of Commerce
1401 K St., N.W., Room 713
Washington DC 20230 (202) 523-0777

A User's Guide to BEA Information contains program descriptions and entries for specific products and services, including publications, computer tapes, diskettes, and other information services. The first, general section of the *Guide* describes the products and services that cut across the range of BEA's work. The following sections describe the products and services related to BEA's four program areas: national economics, regional economics, international economics, and other tools for measuring, analyzing, and forecasting. Some highlights include the following:

Survey of Current Business. A monthly journal containing estimates and analyses of U.S. economic activity. Includes the *Business Situation,* a review of current economic developments and articles pertaining to the national, regional, and international economic accounts and related topics ($29 per year). This survey has incorporated information that used to be published in the *Business Conditions Digest.*

Handbook of Cyclical Indicators. Series descriptions and data for 1947-1989. It includes an explanation of how the composite indexes are constructed ($21.95).

Business Statistics. This biennial publication includes data for 1963-1991 and for series that appear in *Survey of Current Business* (20).

Evaluation of the GNP Estimates. An evaluation of the GNP estimates, covering the reliability of estimates, sources of error and types of statistical improvement, status of source data, documentation of methodology, release schedules, and security before release ($5).

Gross State Product, Annual Estimates, 1977-1989-. These estimates are the counterpart of gross domestic product and provide the most comprehensive measure of State production now available. The estimates are for the 50 States, nine BEA regions, and the United States, and for 61 industries ($100 computer tape, $60 diskettes).

* Business and Industry Data Centers

Data User Services Division
Customer Services
Bureau of the Census
U.S. Department of Commerce
Washington, DC 20233 (301) 763-4100

The Census Bureau has established four Business and Industry Data Centers as economic counterparts to the network of State Data Centers. Contact this office for a free listing.

* Consultation Over the Telephone

Data User Services Division
Customer Services
Bureau of the Census
U.S. Department of Commerce
Washington, DC 20233

Subject-matter specialists from all areas of the Census Bureau may be consulted by telephone. For detailed statistical information route calls as follows:

Government, Commerce, and Industry
Agriculture Data: (301) 763-1113
Business Data:
  Retail: (301) 763-7038
  Wholesale: (301) 763-5281
Construction Statistics: (301) 763-7163
Foreign Trade Data: (301) 763-5140
State Exports: (301) 763-2725
Government Data: (301) 763-7366

Be patient. If any phone number is incorrect, call (area code) 555-1212 and request the new listing.

General Sources

Industry Data: (301) 763-7800
Manufacturers Data: (301) 763-7666

Population, Housing, and Income
Housing Data: (301) 763-8553
International Statistics: (301) 763-4811
Population Data: (301) 763-5002
Special Demographic Studies: (301) 763-1263

* Census CD-ROM Products

Customer Services
Data User Services Division
Bureau of the Census
Washington, DC 20233 (301) 763-4100

The Census Bureau continues to produce its popular large data files in CD-ROM format. CD-ROM products include:

1990 County Business Patterns
1988 County and City Data Book
1988 Census of Agriculture
1992 Tiger/Line Extract Files
1990 Census of Population and Housing

* Census Bureau Library

Library, Bureau of the Census
U.S. Department of Commerce
Washington, DC 20233 (301) 763-5042

The Census Bureau Library collection contains general statistical information, population areas statistics, demographics, migration, foreign country censuses, and the complete collection of census publications. It is open to the public, and photocopying equipment is available.

* Census Bureau's Online Data System

Data Access and Use Staff
Data User Services Division
Bureau of the Census
Washington, DC 20233 (301) 763-2074

CENDATA is the Census Bureau's on-line service, available commercially for access from remote terminals or microcomputers, that carries selected current data, press releases, and publication lists from Bureau programs. If you need the most recent population estimates for states, counties, incorporated places, and selected towns and townships use CENDATA. CompuServe and DIALOG, information service companies, are offering CENDATA to their customers. Contact this office for more information about CENDATA content and on-line services, or call CompuServe: (800) 848-8199; or DIALOG Information Services: (800) 334-2564.

* Census Data Diskettes

Customer Services (Diskettes)
Data User Services Division
Bureau of the Census
Washington, DC 20233 (301) 763-4100

The data diskettes are available from the Bureau of the Census. These files are generated on an IBM Personal Computer and can be used with compatible microcomputers using the PC DOS 1.1 or higher operating systems. Contact this office for a complete listing of those available.

* Census Data On CD-ROM

Customer Services
Data User Services Division
Bureau of the Census
Washington, DC 20233 (301) 763-4100

The Census Bureau now makes several of its large databases available in microcomputer format. To use Compact Disc - Read Only Memory (CD-ROM) you will need a personal computer, a CD-ROM reader, and the appropriate CD-ROM software for your system. The discs are standard 4 3/4" size and are compatible with all CD-ROM readers. If you are interested in learning more about the software and hardware requirements of CD-ROM technology, request an Information Packet from this office. To demonstrate CD-ROM products, Census Bureau analysts have written various software programs for public access. The software is available to users from the following two sources:

-An electronic bulletin board accessed by modem on (301) 763-1568.
-You can obtain CD-ROM software from the University of Tennessee. This clearinghouse has information on software packages available for use with the Census Bureau's CD-ROMs and also maintains a list of private software vendors who sell software developed to access the CD-ROMs. For information from the clearinghouse, contact: Department of Marketing, Logistics, and Transportation, 309 Stokley Management Center, University of Tennessee, Attn: Center for Electronic Data Analysis, Knoxville, TN 37916; (615) 974-5311.

* Census Depository Libraries

Data User Services Division
Customer Services
Bureau of the Census
U.S. Department of Commerce
Washington, DC 20233 (301) 763-4100

There are nearly 1,500 Government and Census depository libraries; these include large public and university libraries that will have census reports in their reference collections. The holdings in the Census Bureau's library are complete. To contact the library call (301) 763-5042. A listing entitled *Government and Census Depository Libraries Holding Census Bureau Reports* is free from the Census Bureau.

* Census/Equal Employment Opportunity Special File

Customer Services Branch
Data User Services Division
Bureau of the Census
Washington, DC 20233 (301) 763-4100

This special computer tape file provides sample census data to support affirmative action planning for equal employment opportunity. The file contains tabulations showing detailed occupations and educational attainment data by age. These data are cross tabulated by sex, Hispanic origin, and race. Data are provided for all counties, MSAs, and places of 50,000 or more inhabitants. For more information on this special computer tape file, contact this office.

* Census Newsletter

Superintendent of Documents
U.S. Government Printing Office
Washington, DC 20402 (202) 783-3238

Census and You brings you the latest news about Census Bureau products and programs. This monthly newsletter cuts through the complexities of Government statistical programs and tells you where to find the statistics you need on the latest trends in various areas, what products fit your needs, how to get in touch with the experts, where to turn locally for information, and what programs the Census Bureau is planning now and how to be sure your views are heard. It is available from the Government Printing Office for $18. To FAX orders or inquiries, dial (202) 512-2250.

* Census of Agriculture Diskettes

Customer Services (Diskettes)
Data User Services Division
Bureau of the Census
Washington, DC 20233 (301) 763-4100

These diskettes include data from the *1987 Census of Agriculture Advance Reports* for each State and each county with ten or more farms. County and State data items include: farms by size, land use, value of agricultural products sold, selected expense items, operator characteristics, major livestock and poultry inventories and sales, and selected crops by State. The *1987 Census of Agriculture Preliminary Reports* for each State is available for all States. The 1992 series should begin to be available in 1993.

* Census Products and Services

Data User Services Division
Customer Services
Bureau of the Census
U.S. Department of Commerce
Washington, DC 20233 (301) 763-4100

The *Census Catalog and Guide 1992* is a one-stop guide that tells you where to look for every Census Bureau data product and service. In it you'll find information on every report, microfiche, computer tape, floppy disk, and map issued, 1980-1991; explanations of the censuses and surveys of business,

Be patient. If any phone number is incorrect, call (area code) 555-1212 and request the new listing.

Economics, Demographics and Statistics

manufacturing, and population--plus all the others; and lists of over 5,000 sources of assistance--Census Bureau specialists, other Federal statistical offices, State and local agencies, and private companies. There is also a nationwide list of Government and Census depository libraries. The book sells for $17. To fax orders or inquiries, dial (202) 512-2250. International customers should add 25% to the cost.

* Census Regional Offices

The regional offices of the Census Bureau play a vital role in the work of the Census Bureau. They offer educational, inquiry, and reference services to federal, state, and local government agencies; minority organizations; businesses; libraries; educational institutions; community service organizations; the media; and the general public. Information services specialists in the offices assist data users across the country by furnishing information about Census Bureau reports and tape files, and making presentations at workshops and conferences. The Information Services Program staff in all 12 offices can help:

Atlanta
101 Marietta St., N.E., Suite 3200, Atlanta, GA 30030; (404) 730-3833

Boston
Thomas P. O'Neill Federal Office Building, Room 553, 10 Causeway St., Boston, MA 02222-1084; (617) 565-7078

Charlotte
222 S. Church Street, Suite 505, Charlotte, NC 28202; (704) 344-6142

Chicago
175 W. Jackson Boulevard, Room 527, Chicago, IL 60604-2689; (312) 353-0980

Dallas
6303 Harry Hines Blvd., Suite 210 E, Dallas, TX 75235; (214) 767-7105

Denver
6900 W. Jefferson, P.O. Box 272020, Denver, CO 80227-9020; (303) 969-6750

Detroit
27300 W. 11 Mile Rd., Suite 200, South Field, MI 48034; (313) 354-4654.

Kansas City
Gateway Tower II, Suite 600, 400 State Ave., Kansas City, KS 66101-2410; (913) 236-3711

Los Angeles
15350 Sherman Way, Van Nuys, CA 91406; (818) 904-6339

New York
Federal Office Building, Room 37-130, 26 Federal Plaza, New York, NY 10278; (212) 264-4730

Philadelphia
105 South 7th Street, 1st Floor, Philadelphia, PA 19106; (215) 597-8313

Seattle
101 Stewart St., Suite 500, Seattle, WA 98101-1098; (206) 728-5314

* Census Reports

Data User Services Division
Customer Services
Bureau of the Census
U.S. Department of Commerce
Washington, DC 20233 (301) 763-4100

The Bureau publishes a number of guides, catalogs, indexes, Factfinders, and other user aids. Most of these materials are available for reference as well as purchase; some are free. Printed reports for the individual economic censuses usually consist of separate series for industries, geographic areas, subjects, and special reports. Some of the series are designated as preliminary and will appear several months before corresponding final reports. Preliminary reports have limited detail, however, and their figures are subject to change in the final reports. Copies of printed reports can also be obtained on microfiche.

* Census Schedules Available to the Public

National Archives and Records Service

Reference Services Branch
7th and Pennsylvania Avenue, N.W.
Washington, DC 20408 (202) 501-5400

The U.S. population census records contain a wealth of information about people. They are useful in learning about one's ancestors and about local social and economic conditions at various times in history. Microfilm copies of the original population schedules, form 1790 through 1920 are open to the public at the National Archives and its regional center and at many libraries in various parts of the United States. Most now have facilities for making paper copies from the microfilm.

* Census Statistical Areas Committees

Census statistical areas committees consist of local data users with an interest in the census statistical areas programs. These committees exist in all metropolitan statistical areas and some other counties. The committee memberships represent the data users within the community by including planners, representatives from the business community, government agencies, the media, minority organizations, and neighborhood associations. The local census statistical areas committees play an important part in defining geographic statistical areas. The committees recommend or approve the boundaries for statistical reporting units. Each local committee selects a census statistical areas key person as a liaison between the Bureau of the Census and the committee for these programs. For the key person in your area, contact the Census Bureau regional office nearest you.

* Census Telephone Contacts

Data User Services Division
Customer Services
Bureau of the Census
U.S. Department of Commerce
Washington, DC 20233 (301) 763-4100

Telephone Contacts for Data Users is free from the Census Bureau.

* Census Tract/Block Numbering Area Outline Maps

Customer Services Branch
Data User Services Division
Bureau of the Census
Washington, DC 20233 (301) 763-4100

These maps show census tract/block numbering area boundaries and numbers and the features and feature names underlying these boundaries (for example, the boundaries and names of counties, county subdivisions, and places). The scale of the maps are determined such that the number of map sheets for each area are minimal, but vary by area. For densely settled areas, where the census tract/block numbering area numbers and boundary features cannot be shown, the Census Bureau issues insets at a larger scale. These maps are available in both electrostatic plotter version and a printed version. Data users who do not wish to wait for the printed maps can purchase these maps from the Census Bureau for a fee. Data users who want printed maps can purchase the printed maps from the Superintendent of Documents.

* Census University Curriculum Support

User Training Branch
Data User Services Division
Bureau of the Census
U.S. Department of Commerce
Washington, DC 20233 (301) 763-4100

The Bureau has a Census Curriculum Support Project, designed to help university instructors teach about census concepts, methodologies, and products. The Bureau prepares such items as instructors' guides, application exercises, bibliographies, and visual aides. For further information, contact this division.

* Clearinghouse for Census Data Services

Customer Services Branch
Data User Services Division
Bureau of the Census
Washington, DC 20233 (301) 763-4100

The National Clearinghouse for Census Data Services is a referral service for users needing special assistance in obtaining and using statistical data and related products prepared by the Census Bureau. Organizations registered with the Clearinghouse offer assistance ranging from informational services, such as seminars or workshops, to technical services such as providing tape copies or performing geocoding. A list is available.

Be patient. If any phone number is incorrect, call (area code) 555-1212 and request the new listing.

General Sources

* Compensation and Working Conditions

Superintendent of Documents
Government Printing Office
Washington, DC 20402 (202) 783-3238

Each monthly issue of *Compensation and Working Conditions* includes selected wage and benefit changes, work stoppages, major agreements that expire during the next month, calendar of features, and statistics on compensation changes. The cost is $18 per year. For more information on this data, contact Office of Compensation and Working Conditions, Bureau of Labor Statistics, U.S. Department of Labor, #2 Massachusetts Ave., N.E., Room 2021, Washington, DC, 20212; (202) 606-6220.

* Consumer Expenditure and Family Budgets

Consumer Expenditure Surveys Division
Office of Prices and Living Conditions
Bureau of Labor Statistics (BLS)
U.S. Department of Labor
#2 Massachusetts Ave., N.E.
Washington, DC 20212 (202) 606-6872

The *Consumer Expenditure Studies*, a continuing annual survey of consumer expenditures and income, is the basic source of data for the revision of items and weights in the market basket of consumer purchases to be priced for the Consumer Price Index. Selected data is classified by income class, family size, and other demographic and economic characteristics of consumer units. Coverage includes the urban population of the U.S. through 1983, and the total population in 1984 and after.

* Consumer Price Index on Computer Diskette

BLS Office of Publications
U.S. Department of Labor
441 G St., N.W., Room 2831A
Washington, DC 20212 (202) 606-5888

Computer diskettes offer an easy-to-use way to manipulate data for economists, other social scientists, researchers, managers, and policy makers with an interest in measuring employment, prices, productivity, injuries and illnesses, and wages. BLS diskette users need an IBM-compatible microcomputer and Lotus 1-2-3 Version 2. Each diskette contains the named data series and a brief technical description that highlights regular revisions, if any, and typical uses for statistics. A flyer is available which describes the diskettes available and their cost.

* Consumer Price Index Within 24 hours

National Technical Information Service
U.S. Department of Commerce
5285 Port Royal Road
Springfield, VA 22161 (703) 487-4630

A Consumer Price Index (CPI) data summary is available by mailgram within 24 hours of the CPI release. It provides unadjusted and seasonally adjusted U.S. City Average data for All Urban Consumers and for Urban Wage Earners and Clerical Workers. The cost of this service is $180 per year.

* Consumer Prices

Office of Prices and Living Conditions
Bureau of Labor Statistics
U.S. Department of Labor
#2 Massachusetts Ave., N.E.
Room 3615
Washington, DC 20212-0001 (202) 606-7000

The Labor Department measures consumer price changes for a predetermined market basket of consumer goods and services for two population groups: all urban consumers, and urban wage earners and clerical workers. The fixed market basket includes items representing all goods and services purchased for everyday living by all urban residents. Monthly and bimonthly indexes are available for various geographic regions.

* Consumer Purchasing Power Index

Superintendent of Documents
Government Printing Office
Washington, DC 20402 (202) 783-3238

Each monthly issue of the *Consumer Price Index Detailed Report* provides a comprehensive summary of price movements for the month, plus statistical tables, charts, and technical notes. The report covers two indexes, the Consumer

Price Index for All Urban Consumers, and the Consumer Price Index for Wage Earners and Clerical Workers. The indexes reflect data for the U.S. city average and selected areas. An annual subscription is available for $23.

* Cost-Reimbursable Surveys from Census

Special Census Staff
Demographic Surveys Division
Bureau of the Census
U.S. Department of Commerce
Federal Bldg. 3, Room 3319
Washington, DC 20233 (301) 763-5100

Upon request the Census Bureau conducts cost-reimbursable surveys and special studies for Federal agencies on such topics as employment, health, housing, crime, and consumer expenditures. It also performs similar work for educational institutions, qualified private organizations, and takes special censuses requested by local governments needing up-to-date census figures. Contact this division for more information.

* County and City Data Book

Superintendent of Documents
Government Printing Office
Washington, DC 20402-9325 (202) 783-3238

The *County and City Data Book* is your one-stop, official source for county and city data. You can profile or compare thousands of cities and counties. It gives you quick access to comprehensive data including maps for each state highlighting metropolitan counties and cities with 25,000 or more inhabitants. It answers these questions:

What percentage of your county's population is made up of persons 65 years old and over?

Which county in your state experienced the largest increase in business establishments?

How many building permits authorized new housing in your city?

The subjects covered include agriculture, bank deposits, business, climate, crime, electric bills, employment, government finances, health care, housing, personal income, population, poverty, vital statistics, and many more. The book sells for $36 To FAX orders or inquiries, call (202) 512-2250. International customers should add 25% to the cost.

* County and City Data Books: 1983 & 1988

Customer Services (Diskettes)
Data User Services Division
Bureau of the Census
Washington, DC 20233 (301) 763-4100

The 1988 and 1983 files provide a compendia of data from the *1980 Census of Population and Housing*, the *1982 and 1977 Economic Censuses*, the *1982 and 1978 Census of Agriculture*, and other data from a variety of Federal government, private agency, and national association sources. Some data items included are vital statistics, government employment, climate, and social security.

* County Business Patterns on Diskette

Customer Services (Diskettes)
Data User Services Division
Bureau of the Census
Washington, DC 20233 (301) 763-4100

Data on diskette are available annually for every U.S. county--1983 to 1989--and show number of establishments, employment, and payroll, for industries in the Standard Industrial Classification (SIC) levels: two-digit State and county level, 2-, 3-, and 4-digit at U.S. level. Software is not provided.

* County Subdivision Maps

Customer Services Branch
Data User Services Division
Bureau of the Census
Washington, DC 20233 (301) 763-4100

These maps show the names and boundaries of all counties (or county equivalent) and subdivisions in each State, as well as all places for which the Census Bureau tabulates data for the 1990 census. They also depict American Indian reservations, including off-reservation trust lands, tribal jurisdiction statistical areas in Oklahoma, tribal designated statistical areas, Alaska Native

Be patient. If any phone number is incorrect, call (area code) 555-1212 and request the new listing.

Economics, Demographics and Statistics

Regional Corporations, and Alaska Native village statistical areas. All boundaries are as of January 1, 1990. Both electrostatically plotted (computer-generated) and printed maps are available. The plotted maps are made to order and sold separately from the data products. The electrostatic plotter paper sheet size is generally 36" x 42" with the largest size being 36" x 48" long. The number of map sheets for each area varies, depending on coverage type, size, scale and population density. The printed reports can be purchased through the Superintendent of Documents, Government Printing Office, Washington, DC 20402-9325; (202) 783-3238.

* County-to-County Migration

Customer Services Branch
Data User Services Division
Bureau of the Census
Washington, DC 20233 (301) 763-4100

Computer files are issued by state, providing summary records for all intrastate county-to-county migration streams and significant interstate county-to-county migration streams. Each record includes codes for the geographic area of origin, codes for the geographic area of destination, and selected characteristics of the persons who made up the migration stream. For more information on these special computer tape files, contact this Census office.

* Current Economic Data

Data User Services Division
Customer Services
Bureau of the Census
U.S. Department of Commerce
Washington, DC 20233 (301) 763-4100

The Census Bureau's integrated program of current surveys produced data supporting key indicators of monthly economic performance and quarterly GNP calculations covering most goods producing sectors. The Bureau has taken steps to improve and expand its economic products and services in a number of areas. The Bureau improved current merchandise trade data by re-instituting seasonal adjustments of monthly imports and exports, generating new tabulations of state-of-shipment for exports, providing monthly graphic information on trade performance, and publishing data for imports (c.i.f. basis) and imports (customs basis) simultaneously. Contact this office for more information the economic data products from Census.

* Current Employment Analyses

Office of Employment and Unemployment Statistics
Bureau of Labor Statistics
U.S. Department of Labor
#2 Massachusetts Ave., N.E.
Room 4675
Washington, DC 20212 (202) 606-6378

Labor force statistics from the *Current Population Survey* provide a comprehensive body of information on the employment and unemployment experience of the nation's population, classified by age, sex, race, and a variety of other characteristics. The data is published in a variety of sources, including the monthly news release, *The Employment Situation*, and the monthly periodical, *Employment and Earnings*. Data uses include economic indicators, measure of potential labor supply, and evaluation of wage rates and earnings trends for specific demographic groups.

* Economic Bulletin Board

Office of Business Analysis
U.S. Department of Commerce
14th St. and Constitution Ave., N.W.
Room 4887
Washington DC 20230 (202) 377-1986

The Economic Bulletin Board is a one-stop source for current economic information. It has the latest releases from the Bureau of Economic Analysis, the Bureau of the Census, the Bureau of Labor Statistics and other Federal agencies. The Bulletin Board includes summaries of economic news from the U.S. Department of Commerce, economic indicators, GNP, Consumer Price Index, and special economic studies and reports, as well as listings of new publications and databases. The Bulletin Board is available 24 hours a day. Contact the office listed above for more information regarding the Bulletin Board and subscription fees.

* Economic Data

Center for Electronic Records
National Archives and Records Administration
8th St. and Pennsylvania Ave., N.W., Room 18E
Washington, DC 20408 (202) 501-5579

The Center has a vast amount of economic data from various government agencies, such as the Bureau of Economic Analysis, Agencies for Economic Opportunity and Legal Services, Economic Stabilization Programs, Economics, Statistics, and Cooperative Service, and the Bureau of the Census. Contact this office for a complete listing of information available from each agency.

* Economic Indicators

Public Information (BE-53)
Bureau of Economic Analysis (BEA)
U.S. Department of Commerce
Washington DC 20230 (202) 523-0777

The Bureau of Economic Analysis can provide you with basic information on such key issues as economic growth, inflation, regional development, and the Nation's role in the world economy. BEA's current national, regional, and international estimates usually appear first in news releases. The information is available to the general public in three forms: on recorded telephone messages, online through the Economic Bulletin Board, and in *BEA Reports*. The recorded messages are available 24 hours a day for several days following release. The usual time of release (eastern standard time) and the telephone numbers to call are as follows:

Composite Index Indicators: The message is updated weekly, usually on Monday, to include recently available component data. Release time: 8:30 a.m. Call (202) 898-2450.

Gross National Product. Release time: 8:30 a.m. Call (202) 898-2451.

Personal Income and Outlays. Release time: 10:00 a.m. Call (202) 898-2452.

Merchandise Trade, Balance of Payments Basis or U.S. International Transactions. Release time: 10:00 a.m. Call (202) 898-2453.

News releases are available on the Economic Bulletin Board shortly after their release. Selected estimates and articles are also available. The Bulletin Board is available by subscription from the U.S. Department of Commerce, Office of Business, Room 4885, Washington DC 20230; (202) 482-1986. The *BEA Reports* present information contained in BEA news releases and are mailed the day after estimates are released. An annual subscription can be ordered from the Bureau. Contact the Public Information Office listed above for more information and a list of release dates for BEA estimates.

* Economic Census in the U.S.

Data User Services Division
Customer Services
Bureau of the Census
U.S. Department of Commerce
Washington, DC 20233 (301) 763-4100

Taken every 5 years, the economic censuses include the manufacturing, service, construction, and mineral industries; retail and wholesale trade; transportation; agriculture; and governments. For more information on the censuses of the U.S. economy, contact this office.

* Economic Monitoring

The Office of Economic Analysis
U.S. Securities and Exchange Commission (SEC)
450 5th St., N.W., Room 9000
Washington, DC 20549 (202) 272-7104

The SEC's Office of Economic Analysis deals with the economic and practical issues that affect the Commission's regulatory activities. To accomplish this, it builds and maintains different computer databases, designs programs to access data, and develops and tests research methods. The staff looks at how market regulations affect issuers, broker-dealers, investors, and the economy in general. The office also closely watches the national market structure and regulation changes that affect the ability of small businesses to raise capital. Significant developments in the marketplace are analyzed, as are new trends in the securities market and new types of securities. Results of the studies are occasionally published with the Commission's approval. For more information on current and past studies, contact this office.

Be patient. If any phone number is incorrect, call (area code) 555-1212 and request the new listing.

General Sources

* Economic Policy Development

U.S. Department of Commerce
14th St. and Constitution Ave., NW
Room 4855
Washington DC 20230 (202) 377-2235

Economic Affairs analyzes economic developments, develops economic policy options and oversees the collection and distribution of a major share of federal government economic and business developments; promotes efforts to improve productivity; and analyzes supply and demand for strategic materials.

* Economic Reports

What follows is a list of the Federal Reserve Banks across the U.S., along with their free consumer publications available:

Board of Governors of the Federal Reserve System
Publications Services, MS-138
20th St. and C Streets, NW
Washington, DC 20551 (202) 452-3244

Consumer Handbook on Adjustable Rate Mortgages. Explains adjustable rate mortgages and some of the risks and advantages.

Consumer Handbook to Credit Protection Laws. Tells how consumer credit laws can help in shopping for and applying for credit and in keeping a good credit record.

Consumer's Guide to Mortgage Settlement Costs. Explains the mortgage closing process.

Consumer's Guide to Mortgage Lock-Ins. Describes various aspects of mortgage lock-ins.

Consumer's Guide to Mortgage Refinancing. Discusses the process and some of the risks and advantages to mortgage refinancing.

Federal Reserve Glossary. Defines many of the terms used in monetary policy and in bank supervision.

Guide to Business Credit for Women, Minorities and Small Businesses. Advises consumers of their rights under the Act when applying for a business loans and helps consumers prepare effective loan presentations.

How to File a Consumer Credit Complaint. Tells how to file a complaint against a bank.

Federal Reserve Bank of Atlanta
Public Information Department
104 Marietta St. NW
Atlanta, GA 30303-2713 (404) 521-8500

Economic Review. A bimonthly publication presenting new research and articles on the economy of the Southeast.

Federal Reserve Bank of Boston
Bank and Public Services Department
Office of Public and Community Affairs
600 Atlantic Ave., P.O. Box 2076
Boston, MA 02106-2076 (617) 973-3459

Checkpoints. Explains how to write, deposit, and cash checks; also available in Spanish and Portuguese.

Consumer Education Catalog. Lists consumer education materials published by the System.

New England Economic Indicators. Quarterly report of statistical data for the nation and New England states.

New England Economic Review. Publishes articles of broad economic interest six times a year.

Federal Reserve Bank of Chicago
Public Information Center
230 S. LaSalle St.
Chicago, IL 60690 (312) 322-5111

Economic Perspectives. Bimonthly publication on banking, business, and agriculture.

Agriculture Letter. Monthly publication on agricultural conditions for the five states of the 7th Federal Reserve District.

Fedwire. Monthly publication on current Federal Reserve automated services such as electronic payment and automated clearinghouses.

Federal Reserve Bank of Cleveland
Public Information Department
P.O. Box 6387
Cleveland, OH 44101 (216) 579-2047

Economic Review. Quarterly publication featuring monetary, economic, and banking topics of district and national interest.

Economic Trends (Chartbook). Tracks latest economic statistics and briefly discusses the current economy.

Economic Commentary. Bimonthly newsletter that highlights a current banking or economic issue.

Federal Reserve Bank of Dallas
Public Affairs Department
Station K
Dallas, TX 75223 (214) 922-5270

Crossroads. Discusses regional agricultural, economic and financial developments.

Economic Review. Bimonthly publication of articles on economic and financial topics.

Energy Highlights. Summarizes developments in the energy industry.

Federal Reserve Bank of Kansas City
Public Affairs Department
925 Grand Ave.
Kansas City, MO 64198 (816) 881-2402

Economic Review. Discusses a variety of economic and financial topics; 4 issues per year.

Federal Reserve Bank of Minneapolis
Public Affairs
P.O. Box 291
250 Marquette Ave.
Minneapolis, MN 55480-291 (612) 340-2446.

Agricultural Credit Conditions. Quarterly survey of district farm economy.

Consumer Credit Protection: Do You Know Your Rights? Easy-to-understand summary of consumers' credit protection rights.

Fedgazette: This quarterly newspaper includes articles, editorials and statistics on the district economy.

Quarterly Review. Includes feature articles on the district economy.

Federal Reserve Bank of New York
Public Information Department
33 Liberty Street
New York, NY 10045 (212) 720-6134

Consumer Credit Regulators (Fedpoints 17). Reviews the responsibilities of the 12 Federal organizations charged with administering consumer regulations.

Quarterly Review. Reports on business activities and the money and bond markets.

Federal Reserve Bank of Philadelphia
Public Information Department
10 Independence Mall
Philadelphia, PA 19106 (215) 574-6115

Business Outlook Survey. Reports on manufacturing in the district and provides forecasts for the next six months; monthly.

Business Review. Bimonthly articles for readers with a general interest in economics.

Buying Treasury Securities. Provides basic information on investing in Treasury bills, notes, and bonds.

Electronic Banking for Today's Consumer. Explains electronic services such as ATMs, direct deposit, bill-paying services, and point-of-sale terminals, as well as consumer projections of Regulation E.

Fair Debt Collection Practices Act. Summarizes the main provisions of the Act.

Give Yourself Credit. Guides consumers through various credit protection laws.

How the New Equal Credit Opportunity Act Affects You. Outlines the Act's main provisions for consumers.

Plastic Fraud: Getting a Handle on Debit and Credit Cards. Discusses consumer awareness concerning credit and debit card fraud and the regulations protecting consumers.

Quarterly Regional Economic Report. Analyzes the economy of the district.

Your Credit Rating. Describes the importance of credit histories and consumers' rights when using credit, including ways to correct records.

How to Establish and Use Credit. Guidelines on obtaining credit and using it wisely.

Frauds and Scams. Tips on how to avoid telephone and mail fraud.

Federal Reserve Bank of Richmond
Public Services Department
P.O. Box 27622
Richmond, VA 23261 (804) 697-8000

Black Banks. Profiles operating revenue and distribution by profit/loss size of black banks.

Community Affairs Officers at Federal Reserve Banks. Outlines the Community Affairs Officer's role, duties, and responsibilities, particularly those related to the

Be patient. If any phone number is incorrect, call (area code) 555-1212 and request the new listing.

Economics, Demographics and Statistics

Community Reinvestment Act.
Cross Sections. Quarterly reviews of business and economic developments.

Federal Reserve Bank of St. Louis
Public Information Office
P.O. Box 442
St. Louis, MO 63166 (314) 444-8444
Regional Economist. Quarterly summary of national and district businesses and agricultural developments.
Annual U.S. Economic Data. Provides selected economic statistics.
Review. Examines national and international economic developments; analyzes various sectors of the district; ten issues per year.

Federal Reserve Bank of San Francisco
Public Information Department
P.O. Box 7702
San Francisco, CA 94120 (415) 974-2163
Give Yourself Credit. Guides the consumer through various credit protection laws.
Review. Discusses selected economic, banking, and financial topics; quarterly.

* Economic Studies

The Office of Economic Analysis
U.S. Securities and Exchange Commission
450 5th St., NW
Washington, DC 20549 (202) 272-7104
The following are just a few of the many economic studies that are available from the SEC. Contact this office to obtain one of the following or a complete listing of all the reports available:

Spillover Effects of Shelf Registration
Transcript of Proceedings in the Matter of: Economic Forum on Tender Offers
Institutional Ownership, Tender Offers, and Long-Term Investments
The Economics of Any-or-All, Partial, and Two-Tier Tender Offers
Shark Repellents and Stock Prices: The Effects of Anti-takeover Amendments Since 1980
Eurodollar Bonds: Alternative Financing for United States Companies
Do Bad Bidders Become Good Targets?

* Economists: Regional, National, International

Public Information
Bureau of Economic Analysis
U.S. Department of Commerce
1401 K St., NW
Washington DC 20230 (202) 523-0777
The Bureau can provide you with an extensive list of telephone numbers of economists who can be contacted for information pertaining to their area of expertise. The list includes a wide rage of economic issues within national, regional, and international economics.

* Education-Related Surveys

Data User Services Division
Customer Services
Bureau of the Census
U.S. Department of Commerce
Washington, DC 20233 (301) 763-4100
In the educational field, a set of surveys provide information about principals and teachers, teacher supply and demand, staffing patterns, working conditions in the schools, policies of schools and school districts, and other data. Contact this office for more information on educational surveys.

* Elderly Statistics

Data User Services Division
Customer Services
Bureau of the Census
U.S. Department of Commerce
Washington, DC 20233 (301) 763-4100
The Census Bureau, playing a major role in collecting, publishing, and distributing statistics on the older population, is cosponsor of the Federal Interagency Forum on Aging-Related Statistics, as are the National Institute on Aging and the National Center for Health Statistics. Contact this office for more information on available statistics.

* Employment Projections

Office of Employment Projections
Bureau of Labor Statistics
U.S. Department of Labor
#2 Massachusetts Ave., N.E.
Washington, DC 20212 (202) 606-5700
Projections of U.S. economic growth and industry employment provides a framework for studying the factors affecting long-range economic growth. Data available include projections of total gross national product (GNP), demand and income composition of GNP, and aggregate components of demand specified by 160 industry groups under alternative assumptions for basic economic variables and government economic policies. Reference period for projections is for approximately 10 years ahead.

* Employment and Unemployment: Monthly Data and Estimates

Office of Employment and Unemployment Statistics
Bureau of Labor Statistics
#2 Massachusetts Ave., N.E.
Washington, DC 20212 (202) 606-6347
This office collects, analyzes, and publishes detailed industry data on employment, wages, hours, and earnings of workers on payrolls of non-agricultural business establishments. It also publishes monthly estimates of state and local area unemployment for use by federal agencies in allocating funds as required by various federal laws. In addition, the office provides current data on occupational employment for most industries for economic analysis and for vocational guidance and education planning.

* Exhibits and Conventions at Census

User Training
Bureau of the Census
U.S. Department of Commerce
Washington, DC 20233 (301) 763-2370
For information on exhibits and conventions, contact this office.

* Factfinder for the Nation

Customer Services Branch
Data User Services Division
Bureau of the Census
Washington, DC 20233 (301) 763-4100
The *U.S. Bureau of the Census Factfinder for the Nation* describes, in a series of reports, the range of Census Bureau materials available on a given subject and suggests some of their uses. *Factfinders* are published on an irregular basis as topical brochures that may be used individually, in groupings of related topics, or as a complete series:

No. 1. *Statistics on Race and Ethnicity*. 4 pp. 1981. 6 pp. 1991. .40.
No. 2. *Availability of Census Records About Individuals*. 4 pp. 1991. .25.
No. 3. *Agricultural Statistics*. 4 pp. 1989. 4 pp. .25
No. 4. *History and Organization*. 12 pp. 1988 .40.
No. 5. *Reference Sources*. 12 pp. 1988. .40.
No. 6. *Housing Statistics*. 4 pp. 1991 .40.
No. 7. *Population Statistics*. 4 pp. 1991. .40.
No. 8. *Census Geography--Concepts and Products*. 8 pp. 1991. .40.
No. 9. *Construction Statistics*. 4 pp. 1989. .25.
No. 10. *Retail Trade Statistics*. 4 pp. 1989. .25.
No. 11. *Wholesale Trade Statistics*. 4 pp.. 1989. .25.
No. 12. *Statistics on Service Industries*. 4 pp. 1989. .25.
No. 13. *Transportation Statistics*. 4 pp. 1989. .25.
No. 14. *Foreign Trade Statistics*. 4 pp. 1990. 4 pp. .25.
No. 15. *Statistics on Manufacturers*. 8 pp. 1990. .30.
No. 16. *Statistics on Mineral Industries*. 4 pp. 1990. .25.
No. 17. *Statistics on Governments*. 4 pp. 1990. .25.
No. 18. *Census Bureau Programs and Products*. 24 pp. 1990. $1.
No. 19. *Enterprise Statistics*. 4 pp. 1991. .25.
No. 20. *Energy and Related Statistics*. 4 pp. 1991. 4 pp. .25.
No. 21. *International Programs*. 4 pp. 1991. .25.
No. 22. *Data for Communities*. 12 pp. 1991. .75.

These *Factfinders* are available from Customer Services. A 25% discount is available on orders of 100 copies or more sent to a single address.

Be patient. If any phone number is incorrect, call (area code) 555-1212 and request the new listing.

General Sources

* Federal Budget: Economic Impact

Publications Office
Congressional Budget Office (CBO)
House Office Building Annex #2
Second and D Streets, SW
Washington, DC 20515 (202) 226-2809

All information published by CBO is available to the public in print form only. Most analysis results in publications, but there are also working papers and memoranda available. Among the major on-going publications at CBO are the following:

Economic Forecasts. This biannual forecast of the American economy focuses on such issues as unemployment, interest and inflation rates, the gross national product, and the overall short- and long-term outlook for the entire economy.

Baseline Budget Projections. These biannual baseline projections start with the most recently completed budgetary decisions made by Congress and show the effect on the budget if no new policy decisions were made during the next five years. These baselines act as a benchmark when considering spending and taxing policies.

Bill Cost Estimates. CBO prepares cost estimates for nearly every public bill reported by Congressional committees and shows how these legislative proposals would affect spending or revenues over the next five years.

Analysis of the President's Budget. CBO publishes an analysis of the President's annual budget that examines the scope and impact of the Administration's revenue and spending proposals.

Scorekeeping. CBO provides Congress with up-to-date tabulations of Congressional action on revenue and spending bills in order to measure the status of Congressional actions against targets or limits set in the budget.

Annual Report on Budget Options. This annual report includes a discussion of national budget priorities. It examines alternative ways to reduce the deficit and provides specific spending and revenue options for Congress to consider.

The Sequestration Report. This biannual advisory report provides CBO's economic assumptions of real economic growth, estimates budget base levels according to current spending and taxing law and the effects on deficit targets, and calculates the amount of money to be sequestered to eliminate any excess.

Washington, DC 20515 (202) 226-2809
CBO has published thousands of papers since its inception in 1974, and all are available to the general public. These reports are written to provide Congress with budget-related information and with analyses of alternative fiscal, budgetary, and programmatic policies. A listing of all CBO publications is available from the CBO Publications Office. All publications are available from that office, and many are available from GPO. CBO studies fall into categories including U.S. economy and fiscal policy; federal budget; commerce, industry, and trade; social programs; national security; and government operations. Congressional Office Division, U.S. Government Printing Office, Washington, DC 20402; (202) 512-2471.

* Federal Economic Policy

Office of the Assistant Secretary
of the Treasury for Economic Policy
U.S. Department of the Treasury
1500 Pennsylvania Ave., NW
Washington, DC 20220 (202) 622-2200

Under the Secretary of the Treasury, this office recommends economic policy and formulates policies that have general significance for the nation's economy.

* Finding and Using the Data

Census Office of Public Affairs
U.S. Department of Commerce
Public Affairs Office, (2705-3)
Washington, DC 20233 (301) 763-4040

Census Bureau products are available in a variety of places. Libraries across the country have printed reports, and an increasing number have microfiche. Current publications are kept for reference and order at the 12 Bureau of the Census regional offices and the 47 U.S. Department of Commerce district offices. Summary-tape, public-use microdata, and geographic reference files, and flexible diskettes, as well as those microfiche (including recent out-of-print reports), maps, and publications not sold by the GPO can be ordered from the Census Bureau. Help is also available through the Bureau's national headquarters. Copies of products and materials generally can be purchased from the Census office above or from the Superintendent of Documents, U.S. Government Printing Office, Washington, DC 20402; (202) 783-3238.

* Fiscal and Federal Budget Alternatives

Publications Office
Congressional Budget Office (CBO)
House Office Building Annex #2
Second and D Streets, SW

* Financial Statistics

Division of Research and Statistics
Federal Reserve System, Room B3048
20th St. and Constitution Ave., NW
Washington, DC 20551 (202) 452-3301

Economic and financial information is available on such topics as government finances, business conditions, wages, prices, and productivity. A variety of reports and studies are published regularly. Contact this office or any Federal Reserve Bank for more information on available financial statistics.

* Foreign Investment Statistics

International Investment Division
Bureau of Economic Analysis (BEA)
U.S. Department of Commerce
1401 K St., NW, (BE-150)
Washington DC 20230 (202) 523-0659

BEA's international economics program encompasses international transactions accounts (balance of payments) and the direct investment estimates. The international transactions accounts, which measure U.S. transactions with foreign countries, include merchandise trade, trade in services, the current-account balance, and capital transactions. The direct investment estimates cover estimates of U.S. direct investment abroad and foreign direct investment in the United States, income and other flows associated with these investments, and other aspects of the operations of multinational enterprises. Contact this office for further information on direct investment and international services.

* Foreign Money Markets

Foreign Exchange and Gold Operations
U.S. Department of the Treasury
1500 Pennsylvania Ave., NW, Room 2409
Washington, DC 20220 (202) 622-2650

This office monitors the foreign money markets for the U.S. Department of the Treasury. Contact them for more information.

* Foreign Portfolio Investment

Office of Foreign Portfolio Investment Survey
Office of the Assistant Secretary
of the Treasury for International Affairs
U.S. Department of the Treasury
1500 Pennsylvania, Ave., NW
Washington, DC 20220 (202) 622-2240

Once every five years, this office conducts a survey of foreign portfolio investment within the United States. The last survey was conducted in 1989.

* General Accounting Office

General Accounting Office (GAO)
441 G St., NW
Washington, DC 20548 (202) 275-5067

GAO assists the Congress, its committees, and its members in carrying out their legislative and oversight responsibilities; carries out legal, accounting, auditing, and claims settlement functions of federal government programs and operations; and makes recommendations designed to provide for more efficient and effective government operations.

* General Accounting Office Annual Report

Information Handling and Support Facilities
General Accounting Office
P.O. Box 6015

Be patient. If any phone number is incorrect, call (area code) 555-1212 and request the new listing.

Economics, Demographics and Statistics

Gaithersburg, MD 20877 (202) 275-6241

The GAO's *Annual Report to Congress* highlights its efforts for the present fiscal year. It contains budget information, a list of recommendations to Congress, and a catalog of Audit Reports issued during the fiscal year. As with most GAO publications, the annual report is available free of charge for the first copy ordered (thereafter, $2 per copy).

* General Accounting Office Reports

Information Handling and Support Facilities
General Accounting Office
P.O. Box 6015
Gaithersburg, MD 20877 (202) 275-6241

Each month the Comptroller General sends a list of GAO reports and testimony issued or released during the previous month to Congress, its committees, and its members. Up to one copy of each GAO report is provided free of charge, and $2 is charged for each additional copy.

* Geography of the Census

Data User Services Division
Customer Services
Bureau of the Census
U.S. Department of Commerce
Washington, DC 20233 (301) 763-4100

The Bureau collects and publishes data for two kinds of geographical areas:

Governmental

-the United States, Puerto Rico, and outlying areas under U.S. sovereignty or jurisdiction
-States, counties, and county equivalents
-incorporated places (e.g., cities, villages) and minor civil divisions (MC's) of counties (such as townships)
-congressional districts and election precincts
-American Indian reservations and Alaska Native villages

Statistical

-four census regions (Northeast, South, Midwest, and West) and nine census divisions, all of which are groupings of States
-Metropolitan areas
-census country divisions in States where minor civil division boundaries are not satisfactory for statistical purposes
-census designated places
-urbanized areas
-census tracts and block numbering areas averaging about 4,000 people
-census blocks--generally equivalent to city blocks
-enumeration districts--census administrative areas, averaging around 700 inhabitants, where block statistics are not available
-block groups--counterparts to enumeration districts, averaging 900 population, in areas with census blocks
-Neighborhoods--subareas locally defined by participants in the Bureau's Neighborhood Statistics Program
-ZIP Codes--Postal Service administrative areas independent of either governmental or other statistical areas.

In the census of retail trade, the Bureau publishes data for central business districts (CAD's) and major retail centers outside CAD's; in the census of governments, for school districts and other special districts; and in foreign trade and international research, for countries and world areas. Generally, survey data are published only for the larger areas, such as the U.S., its regions, and some States, while census data are made available for smaller areas as well. Contact this office for more information on Census geography.

* Government Auditing Standards

Superintendent of Documents
Government Printing Office
Washington, DC 20548 (202) 275-9359

Revised and updated in 1988, the *Yellow Book--Government Auditing Standards* (#02000000243-3) carries standards for audits of government organizations, programs, activities and functions; and of government money received by contractors, non-profit organizations, and other non-government organizations. The standards are to be followed by auditors and audit organizations where regulated by law, regulation agreement, or policy. The statements pertain to the auditors' professional quality, quality of audit effort, and the character of professional and meaningful audit reports. $3.50.

* Government Income and Expenses: Monthly

Superintendent of Documents
Government Printing Office
Washington, DC 20402 (202) 783-3238

For monthly information on the U.S. Government's monthly income and expenses, subscribe to the publication, *Monthly Treasury Statement of Receipts and Outlays of the United States Government*. The annual price is $27 (S/N 748-009-00000-1).

* Government Transactions

Government Division
Bureau of Economic Analysis
U.S. Department of Commerce
1401 K St., NW, Room 506
Washington DC 20230 (202) 523-0715

BEA's national economics program encompasses the government transactions on a national income and product accounting basis, which include estimates of government receipts, expenditures, and surplus of deficit. The estimates are prepared separately for Federal and for State and local governments. Contact the office listed above for further information.

* Guide to the 1992 Economic Censuses and Related Statistics

Customer Services Branch
Data User Services Division
Bureau of the Census
Washington, DC 20233 (301) 763-4100

The *Guide to the 1992 Economic Censuses and Related Statistics* describes the scope, coverage, classification system, data items, and publications for each of the economic censuses and the related surveys that provide monthly and annual data. It also reviews other Census Bureau data series that provide information of value to economic statistics users. Single copies are free from this office. A revised version will be available in 1993.

* Detailed Census Information

For detailed information about the contents of specific censuses, programs, or publications, contact the following offices:

General Trade

Retail Trade: (301) 763-7038
Wholesale Trade: (301) 763-5281
Service Industries: (301) 763-7039
Transportation: (301) 763-2662
Establishment Data: (301) 763-5281
Truck, commodity surveys: (301) 763-2662

Manufacturers

Durable Goods: (301) 763-7304
Nondurable Goods: (301) 763-2510
Mineral Industries: (301) 763-5938
Construction Industries: (301) 763-5435

Minority- and Women-Owned

Businesses: (301) 763-5517
Enterprise Statistics: (301) 763-5470
Puerto Rico and other U.S. possessions: (301) 763-5134

* Homeless Statistics

Population Division
U.S. Bureau of the Census
U.S. Department of Commerce
Room 2332-3
Washington, DC 20233 (301) 763-7883

As part of the 1990 Census the Census Bureau made special efforts to include homeless persons in census counts and to meet public demand for information about homeless persons. The Census Bureau used two operations designed to count the homeless. A "shelter and street night" count took place that counted people in hotels and motels identified beforehand as shelters for the homeless, or that cost $12 or less per night. It also included "emergency" shelters and open locations in the streets, parks, and other areas not intended for habitation. Contact this office for a fact sheet of their study.

Be patient. If any phone number is incorrect, call (area code) 555-1212 and request the new listing.

General Sources

* Hours and Earnings Monthly Survey

Office of Employment and Unemployment Statistics
Bureau of Labor Statistics
U.S. Department of Labor
#2 Massachusetts Ave., N.E.
Washington, DC 20212 (202) 606-6555

A monthly survey provides hours and earnings data collected from payroll records of business establishments. The data available includes gross hours and earnings of production or non-supervisory workers in a variety of industries, and overtime hours in manufacturing industries. The data are published in a variety of sources, and are used as economic indicators, wage negotiations, and economic research and planning.

* Income and Program Participation Survey

Data User Services Division
Customer Services, Bureau of the Census
U.S. Department of Commerce
Washington, DC 20233 (301) 763-4100

New information on important aspects of household economic activity has continued to emerge from the *Survey of Income and Program Participation* (SIPP), including more detailed observations on income flows and frequency of participation in government assistance programs. Special reports issued from SIPP were *Who's Helping Out--Support Networks Among American Families*, and *Pensions: Worker Coverage and Retirement Income*. For information on these special reports, or questions about the *Survey of Income and Program Participation*, contact this office.

* Industry and Employment Projections

Office of Economic Growth and Employment Projections
Bureau of Labor Statistics
U.S. Department of Labor
#2 Massachusetts Ave., N.E.
Room 2135
Washington, DC 20212 (202) 606-5720

State and area employment data classified by industry division, and gross weekly hours and earnings for production and related workers in manufacturing is available, as is other data, including demographic employment/unemployment, monthly labor force and unemployment, occupational employment, and area wage surveys.

* Industry-Occupation Employment Matrix

Office of Economic Growth and Employment Projections
Bureau of Labor Statistics
U.S. Department of Labor
#2 Massachusetts Ave., N.E.
Washington, DC 20212 (202) 606-5730

The National Industry-Occupation Employment Matrix provides detailed information on the distribution of occupational employment by industry. Coverage is for over 400 detailed occupations--wage and salary, self-employed, and unpaid family workers, and wage and salary workers only for over 300 detailed industries.

* Industry Productivity Measurements

Industry Productivity and Technology Studies
Office of Productivity and Technology
U.S. Department of Labor
#2 Massachusetts Ave., N.E.
Room 2150
Washington, DC 20210 (202) 606-5600

The Industry Productivity Measurement Program develops annual indexes of productivity for individual industries. Available data include annual indexes of output per employee hour, output per employee, output, employment, and employee hours, as well as annual indexes of industry multifactor productivity (labor and capital combined). Data are published in a variety of sources, including the annual bulletin, *Productivity Measures for Selected Industries*.

* Information Resources

Office of Information Resources, Policies and Oversights (72)
U.S. Department of Veterans Affairs
810 Vermont Ave., NW
Washington, DC 20420 (202) 233-2423

This office is the information management and statistical research branch of the VA. It provides statistical data and analyses to VA management of budgeting, program management, and policy formulation, and coordinates the Agency's internal, interagency, and public use reporting needs. This office is also responsible for VA-wide information resources management policy, paperwork management, records management, forms and correspondence management policy, and mail and travel policy. Contact the office above for more information. Contact this office for information on obtaining the following publications:

Summary of Medical Programs. Presents facility specific program data. *Trend Data*. An annual publication which presents up to 25 years of data related to VA activities.

* Industry Wage Statistics

Office of Compensation and Working Conditions
Bureau of Labor Statistics
U.S. Department of Labor
#2 Massachusetts Ave., N.E.
Washington, DC 20212 (202) 606-6300

Data available from industry surveys include averages and distributions of straight-time earnings for representative occupations--nationwide, regions, selected areas--by size of establishment and other characteristics, depending on industry and how they were studied. Published in summaries and in *Industry Wage Surveys*, the data are useful for wage and salary administration, union contract negotiation, arbitration, and government policy considerations.

* Information Services Specialists

Data User Services Division
Customer Services
Bureau of the Census
U.S. Department of Commerce
Washington, DC 20233 (301) 763-4100

Customer Services staff and subject specialists at Bureau headquarters, as well as information services specialists in its regional offices, are equipped to answer questions about census and survey data and provide personalized attention to your needs. To receive a telephone contact list, contact the office above.

* Interindustry Economics

Interindustry Economics Division (BE-51)
Bureau of Economic Analysis
U.S. Department of Commerce
1401 K St., NW, Room 608
Washington DC 20230 (202) 523-0857

Input-output accounts for the United States show how industries interact--providing input to, and taking output from, each other--to produce the GNP. *Benchmark tables, based largely on the economic census, are prepared every 5 years. Annual tables are prepared using basically the same procedures as used for the benchmark tables, but with less comprehensive and less reliable source data. For more information contact the office listed above.

* Internal Auditing

Information Handling and Support Facilities
General Accounting Office
P.O. Box 6015
Gaithersburg, MD 20877 (202) 275-6241

The free book, *Accounting Principles and Standards for Federal Agencies* (#123095), provides guidance for internal auditing in federal agencies.

* International Comparisons of Productivity, Labor Costs, Economic Indicators, and Unemployment

International Training Division
Office of Productivity and Technology
Bureau of Labor Statistics
U.S. Department of Labor
#2 Massachusetts Ave., N.E.
Room 2150
Washington, DC 20210 (202) 523-5632

This office develops comparisons of productivity and labor costs to assess U.S. economic performance relative to other countries. Data available include indexes

Be patient. If any phone number is incorrect, call (area code) 555-1212 and request the new listing.

Economics, Demographics and Statistics

of output per employee hour, hourly compensation, and unit labor costs in manufacturing. The coverage includes 11 industrial countries plus regional groupings. Also available are data concerning labor force, employment, and unemployment for foreign countries, by selected characteristics, approximating U.S. concepts. This office also makes comparisons of prices, compensation costs, and other major economic indicators in industrial countries.

* International Energy Economic Research

Office of Middle East and Energy Policy
Room 5132
U.S. Department of the Treasury
1500 Pennsylvania Ave., NW
Washington, DC 20220 (202) 622-4140

This office under the Secretary of the Treasury studies international energy resources and technology and their impact on the United States' economy.

* International Finance

Division of International Finance
Federal Reserve System
Room B1252B
20th St. and Constitution Ave., NW
Washington, DC 20551 (202) 452-3614

For information relating to foreign financial markets, international banking, U.S./international transactions, international development, world payments, and economic activity, contact this office.

* International Price Indexes: Export and Import

Office of Prices and Living Conditions
Bureau of Labor Statistics
U.S. Department of Labor
#2 Massachusetts Ave., N.E.
Room 3955
Washington, DC 20212 (202) 272-5025

This office measures change in the prices of commodities exported from and imported into the United States. Quarterly price indexes are available for all exported and imported items and major subgroups, such as food, beverages and tobacco, crude materials except fuels, animal and vegetable oils, fats and waxes, chemicals, manufactured goods, machinery and transport equipment, and miscellaneous manufactured articles.

* International Statistics

Data User Services Division
Customer Services
Bureau of the Census
U.S. Department of Commerce
Washington, DC 20233 (301) 763-4100

The Bureau published demographic statistics for the world's countries in cooperation with the Agency for International Development and also developed international data bases on AIDS, youth, and aging for developing countries. Also, the Census Bureau is assisting 25 countries in planning, conducting, or analyzing population censuses.

* International Visitors Program

International Visitors Program
Bureau of the Census
International Statistical Program Center
U.S. Department of Commerce
Washington, DC 20233 (301) 763-2839

The International Visitors Program provides an opportunity for consultation with experts at the Census Bureau. Consultation sessions can last for a day to a week. Workstudy tours are also available, generally lasting two to six weeks. Statistical consultations are offered on surveys, data processing, and technical and analytical aspects of census and survey taking.

* Labor Statistics Availability

Division of Information Services
Bureau of Labor Statistics (BLS)
U.S. Department of Labor
#2 Massachusetts Ave., N.E.
Washington, DC 20212 (202) 606-7828

The Bureau of Labor Statistics can provide you with a tentative release schedule for BLS major economic indicators. The schedule lists the information available (i.e., employment situation, consumer price index, productivity and costs, etc.), as well as the date and time of the information release. The *BLS Update* also contains the release dates for the quarter.

* Local Area Employment and Unemployment

Office of Employment and Unemployment Statistics
Bureau of Labor Statistics
U.S. Department of Labor
#2 Massachusetts Ave., N.E., Room 4675
Washington, DC 20212 (202) 606-6390

This office provides labor force, employment, and unemployment data estimated by state employment security agencies. These data are used primarily to allocate federal funds to local jurisdiction. The coverage includes annual average data with demographic detail for 50 states, the District of Columbia, 30 large metropolitan areas, and 11 of their central cities, and monthly data to include 50 states, 330 areas, 3,100 counties, and 500 cities of 50,000 or more. The data are published in a variety of sources, including the annual bulletin, *Geographic Profile of Employment and Unemployment,* and the monthly periodical, *Employment and Earnings.*

* Longitudinal Employment Surveys

Office of Economic Research
Bureau of Labor Statistics
U.S. Department of Labor
#2 Massachusetts Ave., N.E.
Washington, DC 20212 (202) 606-7386

Every couple of years, this office updates *The National Longitudinal Surveys,* which study employment profiles of certain age groups. The groups include: young women who were 14-24 in 1968; mature women who were 30-44 in 1967; and youth who were 14-21 in 1979. Information available includes labor market activities, characteristics of jobs, earnings, unemployment, social and demographic characteristics, education, and training.

* Mapping Algorithms

Customer Services Branch
Data User Services Division
Bureau of the Census
Washington, DC 20233 (301) 763-4100

The Census Bureau is making the FORTRAN source code routines available that it used to produce TIGER maps on its Unisys 1100 Series mainframe computers, so that experienced FORTRAN systems analysts can learn how Census mapping algorithms work. However, the routines do not run on any computer system without extensive additional programming, and the Bureau will not support the routines, nor answer questions about them. If you would still like to obtain these algorithms to assist you in your own programming efforts, you can order them on computer tape together with documentation on the TIGER data structure for $600 from the office above.

* Map Products from Census

Customer Services Branch
Data User Services Division
Bureau of the Census
Washington, DC 20233 (301) 763-4100

Superintendent of Documents
Government Printing Office
Washington, DC 20402-9325 (202) 783-3238

Each of the following map types are available for purchase separately. Listed are descriptions of the map products offered through the 1990 census program. This listing includes only those maps that are sold separately; it does not include maps that are prepared and included in the printed reports.

1) Count Block Map (1990): This is the most detailed of the series. It is county-based and contains block numbers and physical features, and the boundaries, names and codes for legal and statistical entities in the county. The scale varies by county and may include inset sheets.
2) P.L. 94-171 County Block Map: This is the same as the County Block Map described above and includes codes and boundaries of voting districts where these were delineated by states for the 1990 census.
3) Entity-Based County Block Map: The three series included in this category

Be patient. If any phone number is incorrect, call (area code) 555-1212 and request the new listing.

General Sources

are: American Indian Area Block Map (1990); Alaska Native Area Block Map (1990); and Place Block Map (1990) -- for places in more than one county. The content is the same as the County Block Map. Scales are adjusted to focus on the subject entity.

4) Census Tract/Block Numbering Area Outline Map: This county-based map shows the boundaries and codes of census tracts or block numbering areas, the features and feature names underlying the boundaries, and the names and boundaries of counties, county subdivisions, places, and American Indian and Alaska Native areas. The scale varies by county and may include inset sheets.

5) Voting District Outline Map: This county-based map shows voting district boundaries, names, and codes; the features and feature names underlying the boundaries; and the names of counties, county subdivisions, places, and American Indian and Alaska Native areas. The scale varies by county and may include inset sheets.

6) County Subdivision Outline Map: This state-based map shows the boundaries and names of all counties and statistically equivalent areas, county subdivisions, places, and American and Alaska Native areas. The scale varies by state and may include inset sheets.

7) Urbanized Area Boundary Map: The urbanized area-based map shows 1990 urbanized area boundaries, the underlying features,and their names. It also shows the boundaries and names of states, American Indian and Alaska Native areas, counties, county subdivisions and places. The scale varies by urbanized area.

* Market News Reports

Information Staff
Agricultural Marketing Service
U.S. Department of Agriculture
Room 3510, South Building
P.O. Box 96456
Washington, DC 20090-6456 (202) 720-5115

Skilled market reporters gather and document marketing information that is distributed quickly throughout the U.S. via telephone recorders, newspapers, radio, television, and in printed reports. The reports are available for seven commodities: dairy, tobacco, cotton, fruits and vegetables, livestock, grain, and poultry, and they contain information on supply and demand and shipping point reports that cover prices paid by types of sale. Much of the information is gathered and distributed by local field offices via satellite.

* Monetary Affairs

Bureau of Economic and Business Affairs
U.S. Department of State
21st and C Streets, NW, Room 6820
Washington, DC 20520 (202) 647-3105

This office evaluates foreign policy aspects of the functioning of the International Monetary System and examines international banking and taxation issues. A member of the Joint IMF-IBID, this office also conducts multilateral negotiations of rescheduling of foreign debts to the United States.

* National Income and Wealth Economics

National Income and Wealth Division
Bureau of Economic Analysis
U.S. Department of Commerce
1401 K St., NW, Room 800
Washington DC 20230 (202) 523-0669

The national income and product accounts show the value and composition of the Nation's output and the distribution of incomes generated in its production. The accounts include estimates of gross national product (GNP), GNP price measures, the goods and services that make up GNP in current and constant dollars, national income, personal income, and corporate profits. Contact the office listed above for more information.

* New Census Materials

Data User Services Division
Customer Services
Bureau of the Census
U.S. Department of Commerce
Washington, DC 20233 (301) 763-4100

The *Monthly Product Announcement* is a free listing of every new report, computer tape, microfiche, and so forth, from the Census Bureau complete with price and ordering information, as it is issued. It is available from Customer Services office above.

* Online Economic Indicators

BLS Electronic News Releases Service
Bureau of Labor Statistics
U.S. Department of Labor
INC-Room 2860
#2 Massachusetts Ave., N.E.
Washington, DC 20212 (202) 523-1913

Economic indicators from the Bureau of Labor Statistics are available electronically at the time of their release. There is no charge for the data. Users pay only for the actual computer time used. More than 100 releases a year are available online, including monthly releases on consumer and producer prices, earnings, employment and unemployment, as well as quarterly releases on productivity, employment costs, collective bargaining, and import and export price indexes.

* Policy and Procedures Manual

Information Handling and Support Facilities
General Accounting Office (GAO)
P.O. Box 6015
Gaithersburg, MD 20877 (202) 275-6241

The GAO publishes the *Policy and Procedures Manual for Guidance of Federal Agencies*, the official medium through which the Comptroller announces principles, standards, and related requirements for accounting to be observed by the federal departments and agencies. Formation report forms designed by these agencies for the collection of information from the public are required to be cleared by GAO before they may be issued. The review and clearance functions are to ensure that information is obtained with minimum burden on those businesses required to provide the information, to eliminate duplicate data collection efforts, and to ensure that collected information is tabulated so as to maximize its usefulness.

* Population and Housing 1990

Superintendent of Documents
U.S. Government Printing Office
Washington, DC 20402 (202) 783-3238.

The Census Bureau provides the results of the 1990 census in various printed reports in different subject title series. The 1990 subject titles are *Census of Population and Housing* (1990 CPH), *Census of Population* (1990 CP) and *Census of Housing* (1990 CH). Most report series contain one report for each state, the District of Columbia and a United States Summary. They are available from the GPO.

* Population and Housing Statistics

Data User Services Division
Customer Services
Bureau of the Census
U.S. Department of Commerce
Washington, DC 20233 (301) 763-4100

The following population and housing publications are available free from Census: *Neighborhood Statistics From the 1990 Census*; and *Subject Index to Current Population Reports*.

* Population Survey

Data User Services Division
Customer Services
Bureau of the Census
U.S. Department of Commerce
Washington, DC 20233 (301) 763-4100

The *Current Population Survey* continues to generate the Nation's official measures of employment, unemployment, income, and poverty. Plans are in the works to redesign the survey early in the 1990s. The Bureau continues working with agencies sponsoring other recurring surveys on such topics as consumer expenditures, housing, crime, job training, and health, including the development of data on Acquired Immune Deficiency Syndrome (AIDS). For more information about the current population survey, contact this Census office.

* Prices and Living Conditions

Office of Prices and Living Conditions
Bureau of Labor Statistics
U.S. Department of Labor
#2 Massachusetts Ave., N.E.

Be patient. If any phone number is incorrect, call (area code) 555-1212 and request the new listing.

Economics, Demographics and Statistics

Washington, DC 20212 (202) 606-7000
This office develops a wide variety of information on prices in retail and primary markets and conducts research to improve the measurement of price change. The program also includes Consumer Price Indexes, Producer Price Indexes, and export and import price indexes for U.S. foreign trade. The Bureau can also provide you with information on its studies of consumer expenditures, income assets, and liabilities of all U.S. families.

* Private Sector Productivity

Productivity Research Division
Office of Productivity and Technology
Bureau of Labor Statistics
U.S. Department of Labor
#2 Massachusetts Ave., N.E.
Washington, DC 20212 (202) 606-5606

This office develops measures for the business, non-farm business, and manufacturing sectors of the economy, as well as for nonfinancial corporations. Available information includes quarterly and annual levels, indexes, and percent changes for output per hour for all persons and related measures, such as unit labor cost, real and current dollar compensation per hour, and unit labor payments. Monthly employment and employee hour data are available.

* Producer Prices and Price Indexes

Office of Prices and Living Conditions
U.S. Department of Labor
#2 Massachusetts Ave., N.E.
Washington, DC 20212 (202) 606-7000

This office provides measures of changes in prices received by producers at the level of the first commercial transaction for many commodities and a few services. Price indexes are available for virtually all industries in the mining and manufacturing sectors. *Producer Price Indexes* is a monthly periodical, which includes a comprehensive report on price movements for the month, plus regular tables and technical notes. A subscription is available for $23 per year from: Superintendent of Documents, Government Printing Office, Washington, DC 20402; (202) 783-3238.

* Productivity and Technology Statistics

Office of Productivity and
Technology Studies
Bureau of Labor Statistics
U.S. Department of Labor
#2 Massachusetts Ave., N.E.
Washington, DC 20210 (202) 606-5606

This office is responsible for three major research programs. The productivity program compiles and analyzes productivity and related statistics on the U.S. business economy and its major sectors, and on individual industries and government. The technological studies program investigates trends in technology and their impact on employment and productivity. And the international labor statistics program compiles and analyzes data on productivity and related factors in foreign countries for comparison with the U.S. experience. A publication, *Productivity: A Selected Annotated Bibliography*, is available through the Government Printing Office, Washington, DC 20402; (202) 783-3238.

* Productivity and Technology Trends

Office of Productivity and Technology
Bureau of Labor Statistics
U.S. Department of Labor
#2 Massachusetts Ave., N.E.
Washington, DC 20210 (202) 523-9394

To better understand the factors underlying productivity change, this office measures productivity trends in the economy, major sectors, industrial industries, and government. The staff also investigates and can provide you with information on the nature and effect of technological change within industries and across industry lines.

* Program Evaluation

Program Evaluation and Methodology Division
General Accounting Office
Room 5868
441 G St. NW
Washington, DC 20548 (202) 275-1854

This office evaluates the effectiveness of virtually any government program. These evaluations focus on both improving government, and introducing innovations in the evaluation of such programs. The Division encourages and maintains contacts with evaluation professionals in other federal agencies, universities, professional societies, and state and local governments, and fosters improved communication within the evaluation community. It makes available a series of papers introducing such topics as how to design program evaluations, and how to conduct survey questionnaires.

* Public Debt of the United States: Monthly

Superintendent of Documents
Government Printing Office
Washington, DC 20402 (202) 783-3238

For a monthly description of the public debt of the United States Government, subscribe to *Monthly Statement of the Public Debt of the United States*. The price is $28 (S/N 748-008-00000-4).

* Public-Use Microdata Sample for the Older Population

Customer Services Branch
Data User Services Division
Bureau of the Census
Washington, DC 20233 (301) 763-4100

The Census Bureau produces this product to meet the increasing demand for data on the older population. This file could be used to generate sufficient data, especially for the oldest age groups, to construct detailed cross tabulations by age, sex, race, and other characteristics. Contact this office for more information.

* Regional Economic Forecast

Regional Economic Analysis Division
Bureau of Economic Analysis (BEA)
U.S. Department of Commerce
1401 K St., NW, Room 308
Washington DC 20230 (202) 523-0946

BEA's regional economics program provides estimates, analyses, and projections by region, State, metropolitan statistical area, and county. Estimates of total and per capita personal income are used by the Federal government in formulas to distribute funds to States and local areas, by State and local governments for revenue projections, and by businesses in marketing and plant location studies. BEA also maintains econometric models to forecast annual changes in economic activity and to analyze the impacts of projects and programs. In conjunction with the projections work, BEA has developed estimates of gross state product. Contact this office for more information.

* Report Guidelines for GAO

Superintendent of Documents
General Accounting Office (GAO)
DHIS, P.O. Box 6015
Gaithersburg, MD 20877 (202) 275-6241

The *Checklist for Report Writers and Reviewers* (#091096) standardizes the report format and shows how it should be organized. It breaks a GAO report down to its components--cover, transmittal letter, digest--and poses questions to use in judging how well each was written. The booklet includes reminders of GAO reporting policies, principles taught in Producing Organized Writing and Effective Reviewing (POWER), recurring reporting problems, and technical reporting requirements. Another publication, *From Auditing to Editing* (#095119), is a guide for teaching report writing. Each book is on microfiche and one copy per individual is available upon request.

* Resources, Community, and Economic Development

Resources, Community, and Economic Development Division
General Accounting Office (GAO)
441 G St. NW, Room 1842
Washington, DC 20548 (202) 275-3567

As with most sections of GAO, this section does most of its work in the form of reports requested specifically by the Congress. However, the division does share its reports, testimony and studies with interested groups outside the government. This division coordinates GAO's work in the areas of food, domestic housing and community development, environmental protection, land use planning arrangement and control, transportation systems and policies, and water and water-related programs. The division also provides GAO audit coverage at the U.S. Departments of Agriculture, Commerce, Energy, Housing and Urban

Be patient. If any phone number is incorrect, call (area code) 555-1212 and request the new listing.

General Sources

Development, Interior, and Transportation; the Army Corps of Engineers (civil function); the Environmental Protection Agency; the Small Business Administration; the Interstate Commerce, Federal Maritime and Federal Communications Commissions; the National Railroad Passenger Corporation (Amtrak); the Washington Metropolitan Area Transit Authority; the U.S. Railway Association; the Civil Aeronautics Board; the Federal Emergency Management Agency; and a variety of boards, commissions, and quasi-governmental entities.

* Revenue from Public Lands

Management Services, Bureau of Land Management
U.S. Department of the Interior
18th and C Sts., NW
Washington, DC 20240 (202) 343-4864

This office collects and disburses revenues and receipts generated from public lands. The Bureau of Land Management is a primary generator of revenues in the Federal government, with more than $235 million collected annually from a variety of sources, including timber sales, sale of public lands, grazing leases, right-of-way leases, permits, and mineral receipts.

* Seminars at the Census Bureau

User Training Branch
Data User Services Division
Bureau of the Census
U.S. Department of Commerce
Washington, DC 20233 (301) 763-1510

Seminars are available for librarians, government personnel, and for the general public to help you identify the types of statistical data available from Census and other Federal agencies as well as how to use these data. Seminars last from one-half day to four days, and there is a nominal fee. Current courses include:

Understanding Federal Statistics
Census Bureau Data on CD-ROM
In the Eye of the Tiger: Understanding and Using the TIGER System

From time to time the Bureau also trains people in preparing population projections and estimates, and on special topics. Contact the office above for information on fees and scheduling.

* Special Computer Tape Files

Customer Services Branch
Data User Services Division
Bureau of the Census
Washington, DC 20233 (301) 763-4100

The Census Bureau will produce and release several special computer tape files in 1993 to meet unique data needs. Others may be produced based on user demand and availability of resources. Contact this office for a list of these upcoming files.

* Special Services of the Census

The Director
Bureau of the Census
Washington, DC 20233

The Bureau of the Census can provide you with special services on a cost-reimbursable basis, such as designing and carrying out sample surveys (including collecting data by mail or field enumeration), providing population estimates and projections, making special tabulations of data collected in censuses and surveys, and giving other technical assistance. The Bureau of the Census may act as consultant to or agent for groups on special statistical problems. Inquiries concerning special services should be addressed to the office above.

* Special Tabulations Program

William Downs
Housing and Household Economic Statistics Division
Bureau of the Census
U.S. Department of Commerce
Washington, DC 20233 (301) 763-8553

This division handles specialized needs of the data user that are not met through the 1990 standard data products or the User-Defined Areas Program. Such needs include specialized cross tabulations, product formats, or geographic areas which require splitting blocks. The computer process for this program generally involves retabulating data from the confidential internal record files. The Census Bureau prepares these special tabulations on a user-fee basis. The Census Bureau provides free estimates of the cost and time required to produce a special tabulation. To obtain these estimates, the user must provide specific information on the proposed data content as well as the geographic areas. Contact this office for more information on available special services.

* State and Metropolitan Area Data Book

Superintendent of Documents
Government Printing Office
Washington, DC 20402-9325 (202) 783-3238

The *State and Metropolitan Area Data Book* contains statistics for states, metropolitan statistical areas, 738 component counties, and 510 central cities. You can use this edition to find the areas that are growing the fastest, with the highest median family income, or the most college graduates, to determine where your metro area ranks in amount of Federal contracts, retail sales, or service receipts, or to track past employment trends by industry between areas or patterns within an area. The book also contains explanatory notes, and source citations for finding additional information. The 1991 version sells for $26. To FAX orders or inquiries, call (202) 552-1250. International customers should add 25% to the cost.

* State and Metropolitan Area Data Book 1991 on Diskettes

Customer Services (Diskettes)
Data User Services Division
Bureau of the Census
Washington, DC 20233 (301) 763-4100

These diskettes present selected data from the book. There are over 1,800 variables for states, about 300 for metropolitan areas and component counties, and over 80 for central cities. A wide variety of subject areas are included. Sources include the Bureau of the Census and several other national agencies both public and private. Note that free sampler diskettes previewing this product are available from Customer Services. To request a data diskette, contact Customer Services and they will mail ordering information to you for the diskette files of interest to you.

* State Data Centers

Data User Services Division
Customer Services
Bureau of the Census
U.S. Department of Commerce
Washington, DC 20233 (301) 763-4100

The Census Bureau began the State Data Center program to make statistical information more readily available to the public. There are State Data Centers (in almost all States, the District of Columbia, the Virgin Islands, and Puerto Rico) and private and public organizations registered with the Bureau's National Clearinghouse for Census Data Services located throughout the country. The Bureau furnishes data products, training in data access and use, technical assistance, and consultation to States. For more information on the State Data Center Program, call (301) 763-1580. Listings of the centers are available upon request from the Census division listed above.

* Statistical Abstract of the United States

Superintendent of Documents
Government Printing Office
Washington, DC 20402-9325 (202) 783-3238

The official *Statistical Abstract of the United States* is the one reference book to have in your home, office, school, or library. It is an extensive collection of statistics on social, economic and political subjects from over 200 sources. It includes source notes for each table and a guide to statistical publications for more information, a list of telephone contacts for key Federal statistical agencies, a special section on State rankings, a comprehensive index, many graphs and tables depicting analytical percents and rankings, and the latest available official data--quoted and used by experts in every field. The 1992 paper edition is $29. To FAX orders or inquiries, call (202) 512-2250. International customers should add 25% to the cost.

* Statistical Briefs

Data User Services Division
Customer Services

Be patient. If any phone number is incorrect, call (area code) 555-1212 and request the new listing.

Economics, Demographics and Statistics

Bureau of the Census
U.S. Department of Commerce
Washington, DC 20233 (301) 763-4100

The Bureau produces the *Statistical Brief Series*--short, nontechnical presentations on such policy-related topics as child care, pension coverage, computer usage, consumer markets in China, and housing in selected metropolitan areas. Briefs are distributed to audiences ranging from Congress and government officials to the general public. Contact this office for more information.

* Statistical Methodology

Data User Services Division
Customer Services
Bureau of the Census
U.S. Department of Commerce
Washington, DC 20233 (301) 763-4100

Internationally recognized researchers have worked with Census Bureau specialists on a variety of statistical challenges. Studies included economic development in ghettos, undercount adjustment, value of fringe benefits, effect of income fluctuations on poverty rates, improving state-to-state migration estimates, and recalibration of earlier occupation and industrial classification to make them more compatible with 1990 census data. Contact this office for more information on these statistical studies.

* Statistics Services

Data User Services Division
Customer Services
Bureau of the Census
U.S. Department of Commerce
Washington, DC 20233 (301) 763-4100

Population, housing, business, agriculture, government finances, foreign trade--the Bureau of the Census gathers data on these and many other subjects. Do you need statistics like the following?

Which areas have the fastest growing populations?
What is the average value of houses in my neighborhood?
How do shoe sales in my area compare with sales in other parts of the country?
How many acres of wheat did farmers grow in my county?
How much money did my county government spend on road maintenance last year, and how did that compare with the neighboring counties?
How well do imports and exports balance in U.S. trade with the Mideast?

For more information on these and other statistics, contact this service division.

* Supplementary Reports

Customer Services Branch
Data User Services Division
Bureau of the Census
Washington, DC 20233 (301) 763-4100

Supplementary reports present special compilations of census data dealing with specific population and housing subjects as well as for sub-groups of the population. The types of reports vary from census to census. Some examples of supplementary reports include *Advance Estimates of Social, Economic, and Housing Characteristics; Social, Economic, and Housing Characteristics for Redefined Metropolitan Statistical Areas;* graphic chartbooks; thematic maps portraying 1990 census data; and an atlas of census maps that contain the printed publication maps. Contact this office for more information.

* Teaching Materials From Census

User Training Branch
Data User Services Division
Bureau of the Census
U.S. Department of Commerce
Washington, DC 20233 (301) 763-1510

CCSP Update keeps college instructors informed about new resources, teaching materials, and projects for students. It is available for no cost from the Census Bureau.

* Thematic Statistical Maps

Customer Services Branch
Data User Services Division

Bureau of the Census
Washington, DC 20233 (301) 763-4100

The maps, which the Census Bureau issues as part of the GE-50 map series, usually depict a wide variety of statistical topics. In the past, the Census Bureau issued these maps as a single sheet wall map. Similar maps also appeared in selected printed report series as page-size maps. For more information on statistical maps, contact this office.

* TIGER Data Base

U.S. Dept. of Commerce
Geography Division
Bureau of the Census
Washington, DC 20233

The TIGER database contains digital data for all 1990 census map features (such as roads, railroads, and rivers) and the associated collection geography (such as census tracts and blocks), political areas (such as cities and townships), feature names and classification codes, alternate feature names, 1980 and 1990 census geographic area codes, Federal Information Processing Standard codes, and within metropolitan areas, address ranges and ZIP Codes for streets. Contact this office for more information on the TIGER database.

* TIGER/Line Comments

State and Regional Programs Staff
Data User Services Division
Bureau of the Census
Washington, DC 20233

The Bureau of the Census would like to find out how you are using TIGER/Line data, especially your specific applications. Please send your comments to this address.

* TIGER/Line Files

Customer Services Branch
Data User Services Division
Bureau of the Census
Washington, DC 20233 (301) 763-4100

The TIGER database is not available to the public; however, TIGER/Line Files are. The TIGER/Line File is an extract of selected geographic and cartographic information from the TIGER database. The normal geographic coverage for a TIGER/Line File is a county. Each file contains appropriate census geographic area codes, latitude/longitude coordinates, the name and type of the feature, the relevant census feature class code identifying the feature segment by category and, for portions of metropolitan and highly populated areas, the address ranges and associated Zip Codes for each side of a street segment. The files can be combined to cover the whole nation. The TIGER/Line Files are available to data users as follows:

1) The 1990 Census version of the TIGER/Line files includes final 1990 census tabulation geographic areas and their codes. These files also include census designated places and final voting districts as well as map feature corrections reported by local officials during the post-census local review operation. It also provides some address range enhancements resulting from the Census Bureau's address list development work in urban areas. In addition, the Bureau has added permanent record numbers, as well as Federal Information Processing Standards Codes for minor civil divisions/census county divisions and places, and American Indian Reservations and have made some minor modifications to the record format. The version replaces the Initial Voting District Codes (VTD) version.

The public can use a TIGER/Line file to combine the geographic and cartographic data of a TIGER/Line file with other statistical information--such as population, housing, income, or any other type of data--using either mainframe or personal computers and appropriate software for various applications. Some examples of its uses are mapping/thematic mapping, geocoding of spatially-referenced data for marketing research, routing, address matching, redistricting, and applications into geographic information systems.

The 1990 Census TIGER/Line files are available on 9 track, 1600 bi or 6250 bi computer tape, ASCII or EBCDIC, labeled, or tape cartridges (IBM 3480 compatible). The price of the computer tapes and cartridges is $200 for the first county ordered in each state, plus $25 for each additional county in that state ordered at the same time. The data set for the entire United States is $87,450, with Puerto Rico and Other Outlying Areas it is $90,150. Documentation for the files is provided with each order but can also be obtained separately for $10. The 1990 Census TIGER/Line files are also available on CD-ROM (Compact Disc -

Be patient. If any phone number is incorrect, call (area code) 555-1212 and request the new listing.

General Sources

Read Only Memory) that can record 650 megabytes of data. The discs are standard size and are compatible with all CD-ROM readers in your personal computers. The price of the CD-ROMs is $250 each. To order the TIGER/Line files write to the Customer Services Branch, or to charge your order to your VISA or Master Card, or to establish a deposit account, call the number listed above. For tape orders, specify either 1600 or 6250 bpi, 9 track tape or tape cartridge, ASCII or EBCDIC.

* TIGER System Information Assistance

Data Developments
Data User Services Division
Bureau of the Census
Washington, DC 20233 (301) 763-4100

Additional information about TIGER/Line and its various extracts, as well as training and technical assistance, are available from the Census Bureau, its regional offices or agencies participating in the State Data Center Program.

* Trade Product Classification

Data User Services Division
Customer Services
Bureau of the Census
U.S. Department of Commerce
Washington, DC 20233 (301) 763-4100

The Census Bureau has prepared for implementation of the complex new Harmonized System of trade product classification. Meetings were held to inform exporters of the changes, and domestic product classifications were produced to support better analyses of production and trade flows. Researchers are studying the statutory request for constant-dollar information on U.S. merchandise trade. Contact this office for more information.

* Treasury Bulletin

Superintendent of Documents
Government Printing Office
Washington, DC 20402 (202) 783-3238

Treasury Bulletin is a quarterly synopsis of Treasury activities, covering financial operations, budget receipts and expenditures, debt operations, cash income and outgo, internal revenue collections, capital movements, yields of long-term bonds, ownership of Federal securities, and other Treasury activities. The annual subscription price is $29 (S/N 748-007-00000-8).

* Types of Data Files

Customer Services Branch
Data User Services Division
Bureau of the Census
Washington, DC 20233 (301) 763-4100

The Bureau of the Census gathers data on many subjects, but only a fraction of this information is published. To help meet needs not met by these regular publication sources, the Census Bureau maintains an extensive holding of data in computerized form. Almost 1,500 separate data files are available, the majority of which are products of the Bureau's regular data collection and tabulation programs. The types of files include:

Summary Data. Resemble information in published reports; however, data files are often more detailed and cover more geographic areas.

Public-Use Microdata Samples. Include records for unidentifiable individual observations--persons, households, and housing units in a form that protects the confidentiality of the responses, but allows users to design their own tabulations. The Census Bureau does limit the sample size and geographic identification on microdata files.

Geographic Reference Files. List geographic codes associated with specific areas; present computerized representations of maps; and relate various geographic concepts to Census Bureau geography.

Special Tabulations. Statistical information specially prepared by the Census Bureau at the request and expense of the user. These data are furnished on computer tape, printouts, or microfiche, and cannot be sold by the Census Bureau as a standard product for approximately 6 months after completion.

For a brief description of selected tape files and a list of files issued within the past five years showing the number of tape reels, price of technical documentation and references to the Data Development containing a more detailed file description, contact the office listed above.

* User-Defined Areas

Adrienne Quasney
Decennial Management Division/DPD
Bureau of the Census
Attention: UDAP
U.S. Department of Commerce
Washington, DC 20233 (301) 763-4282

This program gives the Census Bureau a generalized capability to produce data based on locally specified geographic areas not available in census tabulations and publications. Through this program, participants are provided population and housing data for their specified area on a user-fee basis. The primary objective of the program is to process requests for data for specialized geography efficiently to ensure timely delivery of the program products for reasonable user fees. If you are interested in obtaining further information about the User-Defined Areas Program, contact the office above.

* Voting District Outline Maps

Customer Services Branch
Data User Services Division
Bureau of the Census
Washington, DC 20233 (301) 763-4100

The maps in this series show voting district numbers and boundaries as well as the underlying features such as roads, railroads, and rivers. They also show the boundaries and names of counties, county subdivisions, and places. The mapping unit is a county with a variable scale. The maps are created on demand are expensive to produce. These maps are produced using map plotting equipment on paper by Census Bureau staff. Contact this office for more information.

* Wage and Price Indexes on Computer Tape

Bureau of Labor Statistics (BLS)
U.S. Department of Labor
#2 Massachusetts Ave., N.E.
Washington, DC 20212 (202) 606-5888

BLS major data series are available on magnetic tape. The standard format is 9-track, 6250 BPI. In addition to the data files listed, BLS makes some microdata tapes and also prepares customized data files on a cost-for-service basis. Available data files include consumer expenditures, consumer price index, export-import price indexes, and labor force, as well as many others. A brochure is available which describes the tapes, ordering information, and the cost of each tape.

* Wage Surveys: Area, Industry and White Collar Earnings

Office of Compensation and Working Conditions
Bureau of Labor Statistics
U.S. Department of Labor
#2 Massachusetts Ave., N.E.
Washington, DC 20210 (202) 606-6220

This office conducts three different types of wage surveys. The area and industry surveys provide annual data on averages and distributions of earnings for selected occupations in major industry groups in metropolitan areas. *The Professional, Administrative, Technical and Clerical Survey* has been revised. *The White Collar Pay Survey,* as it is now known, will resume annual publication in 1993. The survey is used in the federal pay-setting process and provides data on salaries in white-collar occupations from a national sample of establishments.

* Women Worker Data

Office of Publications
Bureau of Labor Statistics
#2 Massachusetts Ave., N.E.
Room 2860
Washington, DC 20212 (202) 606-7828

This office publishes a wide array of information about women in the labor force. This information is presented to the public through a variety of publications, including news releases, periodicals, bulletins, reports, tapes, and diskettes. The pamphlet, *Where to Find BLS Statistics on Women,* identifies the particular publications in which specific data services may be found, along with information on how to obtain BLS publications. The data includes information

Be patient. If any phone number is incorrect, call (area code) 555-1212 and request the new listing.

Economics, Demographics and Statistics

labor force status, employment, and unemployment, earnings and hours of work, education, occupational injuries and illness, and unpublished data.

* Workshops on Census Data

Data User Services Division
Customer Services
Bureau of the Census
U.S. Department of Commerce
Washington, DC 20233 (301) 763-4100

The Bureau conducts workshops for data users. For more information, contact the office above or the Data User Training Program at (301) 763-1510.

* World Population Data Base

International Demographic Data Center
Scuderi Building, Room 614
Camp Springs, MD 20748 (202) 763-4811

The World Population database contains population data for the overall world, its regions (i.e. Latin America, Asia, etc.) and 205 individual countries. Population statistics include total population, estimated projections, growth rate, migratory rate, and crude (number per 1,000) birth and death rates. Data is collected from a survey conducted every two years. The latest statistics were added in 1991, and the time span covered is 1950 through 2050 (projections). Contact this office for free searches and print-outs or to purchase tapes.

State Crime Statistics

* *See also Law and Social Justice Chapter*

You wouldn't put your kid in a day care center near an outdoor drug market or buy a fast-food franchise in an area where the crime rate is ten times the national average, but how can you stay away from such areas if the crime statistics aren't common knowledge? Among the largest databases maintained by states are those pertaining to crime and to law enforcement. These statistics provide a fairly accurate profile of how an area is affected by crime and how the police and the criminal justice system react.

The data are valuable for students and researchers, political aspirants, real estate companies, urban planners, journalists, private rehabilitation facilities, burglar alarm and security services firms, and, in particular, any business seeking a fairly safe place from which to operate.

Before drawing conclusions from state crime data, a number of factors should be considered, including:

* Strength of local police departments
* Economic profile
* Density and size of the area and surrounding communities
* Cultural factors such as education, recreation, ethnic makeup and religion
* attitudes of residents toward police, crime
* Policies and characteristics of other components in the law enforcement system
* Organization and cooperation of adjoining and overlapping police departments
* Membership and attitudes toward special police organizations
* Climate
* Standards of appointments to local police force
* Crime reporting practices
* Age makeup

Crime statistics are available from 47 states. Only Louisiana, Nevada and Tennessee do not provide statistics on crime. For those states, the U.S. Department of Justice can provide you with some data. Call (800) 732-3277 for Justice Statistics and (800) 638-8736 for Juvenile Statistics.

Examples of the type of data available from your state office include:

* number of juveniles arrested in your state for possession of illegal drugs
* number of shoplifting convictions in your county
* incidents of white-collar crime in major metropolitan areas
* number of armed robberies that have occurred in the last three years

Most states have publications that report crime data. Forty-six states publish Annual Reports or pamphlets which summarize annual statistics. Connecticut and South Dakota each publish a

Quarterly Report. The following states publish reports containing information on crime: California, Connecticut, Delaware, District of Columbia, Illinois, Massachusetts, and Wyoming. Most reports are in the form of statistical tables with an introduction explaining how to use the information and a summary. Tables are presented on such categories as crime, arrests, process, personnel, expenditures, and correctional actions. Other categories may include adult felony arrest offenses, adult misdemeanor offenses, adult probation, juvenile probation. They are published on a yearly basis and most are available at no cost.

Each state's annual crime and delinquency report summarizes data pertaining to its own criminal justice system. Information is available on a state-wide or county-wide basis. In addition, some states will retrieve data not available in published sources if requested in writing. Usually there is a fee for such services.

Computer printouts available from California and Delaware require a fee for this service. To obtain a printout in District of Columbia you must submit a Freedom of Information Request. Oregon has only standard output reports available, whereas most other states will do some individualized searching for data. The following states will produce data only upon special request: Kentucky, Maryland and North Carolina.

Data are available on magnetic tape from California, Georgia, Idaho, Indiana, Kansas, Michigan, North Carolina, South Carolina, North Dakota, South Dakota and Wisconsin.

Although West Virginia's files are not computerized, they will search manually for data. Nevada is in the process of computerizing its files.

List of State Crime Statistics Offices

Alabama

Criminal Justice Information Center, 770 Washington Ave., Suite 350, Montgomery, AL 36830; (205) 242-4900. This division publishes the *Crime in Alabama Annual Report*. Computer printouts of selected data are provided if the information is readily available. Special statistical analysis of data not found in the annual report is also provided. There is no cost for these services.

Alaska

Department of Public Safety, Information Systems, Uniform Crime Reporting Section, 5700 E. Tudor Rd., Anchorage, AK 99507; (907) 269-5659. The *Crime in Alaska Annual Report* is free. Computer printouts are not provided at this time.

Arizona

Department of Public Safety, Uniform Crime Reporting Section, P.O. Box 6638, Phoenix, AZ 85005; (602) 223-2222. The department publishes the *Arizona Uniform Crime Annual Report*. Computer printouts of selected data are provided at no charge.

Arkansas

Crime Information Center, Uniform Crime Reporting Section, 1 Capitol Mall, Room 4D 200, Little Rock, AR 72201; (501) 682-2222. The Crime Information

Be patient. If any phone number is incorrect, call (area code) 555-1212 and request the new listing.

Economics, Demographics and Statistics

Center publishes an annual report entitled *A Public Opinion Report* from the Arkansas Crime Poll. Computer printouts of selected data are provided at no charge. Requests should be placed in writing and may be faxed to: (501) 682-7444.

California

Department of Justice, Bureau of Criminal Statistics and Special Services, P.O. Box 903427, Sacramento, CA 94270; (916) 739-5598. Publications include the *Crime and Delinquency in California Report* and *Annual Criminal Justice Profile*, which are free upon request. Computer printouts are provided at $.30 per page. Requests for computer reports cost $150 per hour. Information is also available on diskette or magnetic tape. There is no additional charge for the software involved. Fees are based only on programming services.

Colorado

Department of Public Safety, Division of Criminal Justice, 700 Kipling St., Suite 1000 Denver, CO 80215; (303) 239-4442. Publications include *Community Corrections Annual Report*. The office does not provide crime statistics printouts upon request.

Connecticut

Department of Public Safety, Department of State Police, Uniform Crime Reporting Program, Crimes Analysis Division, 294 Colony St., Meriden, CT 06450; (203) 238-6575. Publications include the *Annual Uniform Crime Report* and *Crime in Connecticut Quarterly Report*. Computer printouts of selected data are not available.

Delaware

Delaware State Police, State Bureau of Identification, P.O. Box 430, Dover, DE 19903; (302) 739-5871. Publications and Services: This bureau publishes the *Crime in Delaware Annual Report* plus monthly computer printout reports of various statistics on the state and county level. Selected data runs are also available. Fees vary according to the complexity of the request.

District of Columbia

Metropolitan Police Department, Crime Research and Analysis Section (CRAS), Room 3125, 300 Indiana Ave., NW, Washington, DC 20001; (202) 727-4100. Publications include the *Statistical Report of Crime Index Offenses and Arrests* which is published monthly and annually. Computer printouts of selected data are provided with a Freedom of Information request. There is a charge of $10 per request. Information that is simply copied is $.10 per page.

Florida

Department of Law Enforcement, Uniform Crime Reporting Section, P.O. Box 1489, Tallahassee, FL 32302; (904) 488-5221. This department publishes a four-page summary pamphlet of Florida crime statistics which is available at no cost. Computer printouts of selected data are available at no charge. Information that was included in previous annual reports is also available upon request.

Georgia

Georgia Bureau of Investigation, Georgia Crime Information Center, P.O. Box 370748, Decatur, GA 30037; (404) 244-2748. The Crime Information Center publishes an annual *Georgia Criminal Justice Data Report*. Computer printouts of selected data are also provided upon request, generally at no cost. On a case by case basis information can be transferred to magnetic tape and diskette.

Hawaii

Criminal Justice Data Center, 465 S. King St., Room 101, Honolulu, HI 96813; (808) 587-3100. A *Crime in Hawaii Annual Report* is published. Computer printouts of selected data are available depending upon the complexity of the request.

Idaho

Criminal Identification Bureau, 6064 Corporal Lane, Boise, ID 83704; (208) 327-7130. The Crime Identification Bureau publishes an annual *Uniform Crime Reporting Program Report*. Computer printouts of selected data are provided free upon request. Some information is available on diskette or magnetic tape if you supply your own software.

Illinois

Department of State Police, Division of Forensic Services and Identification, Bureau of Identification, 100 Armory Bldg., P.O. Box 19461, Springfield, IL 62794-9461; (217) 782-7583. Publications include the *Crime in Illinois Annual Report*. The office will re-run monthly special reports for individuals upon request. There is no charge for this service.

Indiana

Indiana State Police, Data Division, 100 Indiana Government Center North, 100 N. Senate, Indianapolis, IN 46204-2259; (317) 232-8289. Although this office doesn't publish an annual report, it will provide individuals with computer printouts or copies of crime statistics. There is no charge involved in these instances. Data is also available on diskette or magnetic tape. Charges vary according to the complexity of the request. Detailed requests should be placed in writing.

Iowa

Department of Public Safety, Plans, Training and Research Bureau, Wallace State Office Building, Des Moines, IA 50319; (515) 281-5524. This department publishes the *Iowa Uniform Crime Annual Report*. Computer printouts are not available at this time although they are planning to expand their services in 1993.

Kansas

Statistical Analysis Center, Kansas Bureau of Investigation, 1620 Tyler, Topeka, KS 66612; (913) 232-6000. The Statistical Analysis Center publishes the *Crime in Kansas Annual Report*. Computer printouts of selected data is free upon request if the data is available. If you provide your own magnetic tapes or diskettes the staff will transfer the data onto them at no extra cost.

Kentucky

State Police, Information Section. 1250 Louisville Road, Frankfort, KY 40601; (502) 227-8717. Publications include the *Crime in Kentucky Annual Report* and *Traffic Accident Facts Report*. Computer printouts of selected data are available in special circumstances, depending upon the request. Most printouts are free. Some accident data requires an additional charge.

Louisiana

State Police, Office of Public Affairs, Box 66614, Baton Rouge, LA 70896; (504) 925-6202. The Office of Public Affairs publishes a brochure on highway safety. It does not provide statistics on crime to the general public.

Maine

Dept. of Public Safety, Uniform Crime Reporting Division, 36 Hospital St., Station # 42, Augusta, ME 04333; (207) 289-2025. Publications include the *Crime in Maine Annual Report*. Computer printouts of selected data is available on a limited basis, usually at no charge.

Maryland

Maryland State Police, Uniform Crime Reporting Unit, 1711 Belmont Ave., Baltimore, MD 21244, Attn. UCR; (301) 298-3444. Publications include the annual *Crime in Maryland Report*. Computer printouts are not generally provided, but can be done upon special request.

Massachusetts

Commissioner of Public Safety, 1010 Commonwealth Ave., Boston, MA 02215; (617) 566-4500. Publications include a *Hate Crime Statistics Report* and yearly crime comparison reports. Computer services are available on a very limited basis.

Michigan

Department of State Police, 714 S. Harrison Rd., Uniform Crime Reporting, E. Lansing, MI 48823. (517) 322-1150. The Uniform Crime Reporting Division publishes an annual *Michigan Crime Report*, which is free upon request. Computer printouts of selected data are also free. If you supply your own diskettes or magnetic tapes the division will transfer information on to them at no additional cost.

Minnesota

Department of Public Safety, Office of Information Systems, 395 John Ireland Blvd., St. Paul, MN 55155; (612) 296-7589. Publications include an *Annual Report*. Computer printouts of selected data are provided at no charge if the information is readily available. Complex requests may involve a $25 per hour fee.

Mississippi

Department of Public Safety, City of Jackson Police Department, Box 16, Crime Analysis Unit, Jackson, MS 39205; (601) 987-1212. Publications include an annual report. Mississippi does not have a central agency for collecting crime statistics. Each county or city has a department of safety that keeps individual records of criminal data. Computer printouts are not available.

Be patient. If any phone number is incorrect, call (area code) 555-1212 and request the new listing.

State Crime Statistics

Missouri

State Highway Patrol, Criminal Records Division, P.O. Box 568, Jefferson City, MO 65102; (314) 751-3313. The Criminal Records Division publishes an annual Missouri Crime Index Report. Their data is not computerized, so no printouts are available.

Montana

Montana Board of Crime Control, 303 North Roberts, Helena, MT 59620; (406) 444-3604. Publications available include the *Crimes of Montana Annual Report* which is $4. Computer printouts of selected data are provided upon written request.

Nebraska

Commission on Law Enforcement and Criminal Justice, 301 Centennial Mall South, P.O. Box 94946, Lincoln, NE 68509; (402) 471-2194. The Commission publishes a *Crime In Nebraska Annual Report* which is free upon request. Individual computer printouts are not provided.

Nevada

Department of Public Safety, Criminal Repository Division, 555 Wrightway, Carson City, NV 89711; (702) 687-5713. Nevada does not have a central agency for collecting crime statistics. Each county or city has a department of safety that keeps individual records of criminal data. At present, computer printouts are not available. The state is in the process of compiling statistics and plans to have a computerized database in 1993. Each county has a sheriffs department that keeps records of criminal data. The state's main county department is: Nevada Highway Patrol, 555 Wrightway, Carson City, NV 89711; (702) 687-5300.

New Hampshire

Department of State Police, Uniform Crime Reports, 10 Hazen Drive, Concord, NH 03301; (603) 271-2509. Publications include the *Crime Statistics In New Hampshire Annual Report*. Computer printouts of selected data are provided at no charge upon written request.

New Jersey

Department of Law and Public Safety, Division of State Police, Uniform Crime Reporting Unit, Box 7068, West Trenton, NJ 08628-0068; (609) 882-2000. The *Crime In New Jersey Report* is published annually. The office does not supply computer printouts of selected data.

New Mexico

Department of Corrections, Data Processing, P.O. Box 27116, Santa Fe, NM 87502-0116; (505) 827-8606. Publications include an *Annual Report*. Computer printouts of selected data are available upon written request. There is a nominal fee for most requests unless significant computer programming time is involved.

New York

Division of Criminal Justice Services, Executive Park Tower, Stuyvesant Plaza, Albany, NY 12203; (518) 457-8393. This division publishes the *Crime and Justice Annual Report* which is free upon request. Computer printouts are available at no cost.

North Carolina

Division of Criminal Information, 407 N. Blount St., Raleigh, NC 27601; (919) 733-3171. The *Crime in North Carolina Annual Statistics Report* is available for $15. Printouts of statistics already collected in their annual report are provided at no cost, if requests are reasonable. Individualized computer runs can also be performed but may become expensive. Costs vary according to the complexity of the request.

North Dakota

State Crime Bureau, Bureau of Criminal Investigation, P.O. Box 1054, Bismarck, ND 58502; (701) 221-6180. Publications include an *Annual Report* which is free upon request. Computerized printouts of crime data are available. In most cases the cost is minimal. Detailed requests should be placed in writing. Information can also be transferred to computer diskette or magnetic tape if you supply the software, yourself.

Ohio

Governor's Office of Criminal Justice Services, Capitol Square, 400 E. Town St., Suite 120, Columbus, OH 43215-4242; (614) 466-5126. This office publishes a report entitled *Crime and Arrest Data by County* which is free upon request. The office does not provide computer printouts of selected data.

Oklahoma

Oklahoma State Bureau of Investigation, Northeast 36th At Eastern, P.O. Box 11497, Oklahoma City, OK 73136; (405) 848-6724. The statistics unit publishes the *Crime in Oklahoma Annual Report*. Computer printouts of selected data are provided at no cost.

Oregon

State Executive, Law Enforcement Data System, 155 Cottage Street, NE, Salem, OR 97310; (503) 378-3057. Publications and Services: This division publishes the *Criminal Offenses and Arrests Annual Report* which is available for $10. Computer services are not available, but standard output reports can be obtained upon request.

Pennsylvania

Pennsylvania State Police, Commission on Crime and Delinquency, P.O. Box 1167, Federal Square Station, Harrisburg, PA 17108-1167; (717) 787-5152. The *Commission on Crime and Delinquency Annual Report* is free upon request. Computer printouts of annual data are also provided at no charge.

Rhode Island

Governor's Justice Commission, 222 Quaker Lane, West Warwick, RI 02886; (401) 277-2620. The commission publishes the *Serious Crime in Rhode Island Annual Report* for $7. Computerized data is not available.

South Carolina

South Carolina Law Enforcement Division, Uniform Crime Reporting, 4400 Broad River Road Columbia, SC 29210; (803) 737-9000. This division publishes the *Crime in South Carolina Annual Report* which is $3. Computer printouts of selected data are provided. The cost varies and is based on the complexity of the request. Requests should be made in writing and as specific as possible. Direct inquiries to: Lt. Jerry Hamby, c/o SLED, UCR Dept., P.O. Box 21398, Columbia, SC 29221-1398. Certain data may be available on diskette or magnetic tape on a case by case basis.

South Dakota

Division of Criminal Investigation, Statistical Analysis Center, 500 E. Capitol St., Pierre, SD 57501; (605) 773-6312. Publications include a newsletter and annual and quarterly reports which are free upon request. Computerized printouts of selected crime data are available at no cost. Detailed requests should be placed in writing. Information can also be transferred to computer diskette or magnetic tape if you supply the software yourself.

Tennessee

Crime Information Center, 545 Marriott Drive, Suite 850, Nashville, TN 37210; (615) 871-0013. Tennessee does not have a central agency for collecting crime statistics. Each county or city has a department of safety that keeps individual records of criminal data. Computer printouts are not available. The Crime Information Center provides statistics to state departments of safety.

Texas

Department of Public Safety, Statistical Services, Uniform Crime Reporting, Crime Records, Box 4143, Austin, TX 78765; (512) 465-2000. Publications include the *Crime In Texas Annual Report*. Computer printouts of selected data are provided free, upon request.

Utah

Department of Public Safety, Bureau of Criminal Identification, 4501 South, 2700 West, Salt Lake City, UT 84119; (801) 965-4566. Publications include the *Crime in Utah Annual Report* which is free upon request. Computer printouts of selected data are available, usually at no cost.

Vermont

Department of Public Safety, Vermont Criminal Information Center, P.O. Box 189, Waterbury VT 05676 (802) 244-8763. The Criminal Information Center publishes the *Vermont Annual Crime Report* which is free upon request. Computer printouts of selected data are not available.

Virginia

Department of State Police, Uniform Crime Reporting Section, P.O. Box 27472, Richmond, VA 23261; (804) 674-2000. The *Crime in Virginia Annual Report* is available for $5. Computer printouts of selected data are provided on a cost recovery basis.

Be patient. If any phone number is incorrect, call (area code) 555-1212 and request the new listing.

Economics, Demographics and Statistics

Washington

Washington Association of Sheriffs and Police Chiefs, P.O. Box 826, Olympia, WA 98507; (206) 586-3221. This organization produces the *Crime in Washington State Annual Report*, which is free upon request. Information that is not included in the annual report but readily accessible in their data banks is available to the public upon request.

West Virginia

Department of Public Safety, Uniform Crime Reporting Division, 725 Jefferson Road, South Charleston, WV 25309; (304) 746-2192. The UCR Division publishes a *Crime in West Virginia Annual Report*. No computer services are available, but data can be retrieved manually and the staff will fill requests as needed.

Wisconsin

Office of Justice Assistance, Wisconsin Statistical Analysis Center, 222 State St., 2nd Floor, Madison, WI 53702; (608) 266-3323. The Statistical Analysis Center publishes a free *Crime and Arrests Annual Report* which is available upon request. Computer printouts of selected data provided at no charge.

Wyoming

Criminal Justice Information Section, 316 W. 22nd St., Cheyenne, WY 82002; (307) 777-7523. Publications include the *Uniform Crime Annual Report*. Computer printouts of selected data are provided at no charge. The office will supply furnish special reports if the data requested is of the type they usually collect. These reports are usually in table or letter form. Services are free unless there is significant computer programming involved. Complex requests should be placed in writing.

Be patient. If any phone number is incorrect, call (area code) 555-1212 and request the new listing.

State Labor Offices

* *See also Careers and Workplace Chapter*

Labor market information departments are an overlooked resource within state governments. These little-known offices can provide current, customized data such as:

- which cities have the highest concentration of restaurants or credit agencies;
- how many Hispanic males were living in Bridgeport, Connecticut in 1987;
- which zip codes have the fastest growing population of working women in managerial positions;
- the name, address and size of each new business or business expansion in a given state;
- which U.S. counties offer the highest entry level salaries for market research analysts.

Two reasons for tapping state government labor offices for market and demographic data are that in most cases the information is free and less than one year old.

Sources of Data

The primary function of each state labor information office is to collect data in conjunction with the federal government in order to produce employment, unemployment, occupational and wage information. The most interesting data sources are state unemployment contribution forms filled out by every employer in the state. This form is filed quarterly revealing total wages and number of employees for companies by SIC code in each city and county.

In addition, each state compiles data showing future manpower needs within the state. By studying labor trends, economic conditions and school enrollments, these agencies project the future supply and demand for up to 1,000 different occupations. Many offices also supplement their information with data from the U.S. Bureau of Census as well as other state data collection agencies to provide additional studies and forecasts.

More Current Than Federal Data

If you are a user of the Census Bureau's *County Business Patterns*, you are aware that the latest information available is nearly two years old. But, are you aware that right now you can obtain basically the same information from most states that was collected only six months ago? This information is 18 months more current than Census data? If you are looking for personal income figures by state, county or city, the latest available data from the federal government dates back two years. Moreover, the majority of personal income is made up of wage data which is available from most states much more recently.

Also remember that all data, such as state unemployment information, are passed on to the federal government for publication, but are available from state governments several weeks before being released from Washington.

State Data More Detailed, Cheaper and More Accessible Than Federal Data

Unemployment rate data are released by the U.S. Bureau of Labor Statistics for approximately 150 major cities. However, the state of Connecticut alone can provide unemployment data for 169 cities. If you are looking for salary by type of occupation, the Bureau of the Census covers about 400 occupations in their data. But state governments will cover up to one thousand occupations based on data which can be up to three years more current.

Federal policies combined with the public's increased reliance on traditional federal data sources have caused many of major federal statistical agencies to increase prices and to decrease services. In contrast, using state labor information centers is like walking into virgin data territory. Almost everything is still free from these offices, and state employees are eager to do a lot of free research for those who call. In a conversation I had with the labor information office in Ohio, the director recounted how a local bank requested demographic data for a few dozen zip codes in a three state area. Not only did the state office assemble this information but also gave it to the bank on diskettes...all for free.

Multiple Uses of Labor Market Data

State labor data provide an endless array of uses, but here are some of the primary applications.

1) Marketing:
The marketing information available from the states is overwhelming. The data cover both the consumer and industrial markets. It can be used for determining your current market size as well as identifying new or emerging marketing opportunities. For example, you can find:

- monthly employment and average wages by SIC code, by county;
- annual employment for up to 1,000 occupations, by county, by SIC code;
- which counties have the highest concentration of hairdressers making over $20,000 per year;
- how many bartenders are working in a given city;
- how many hotels with fewer than 100 employees operate in a given city;
- what are the fastest growing jobs or industries in any county or city;
- one year projections (1987) of demographic data for each city and county; or

Be patient. If any phone number is incorrect, call (area code) 555-1212 and request the new listing.

Economics, Demographics and Statistics

- five to ten year projections of industries and occupations by city and county.

Many labor market information centers also offer special market studies to cover specific industries which may be important within the state. You can get free studies covering the hospital industry, ski industry, finance industry and many high-tech related industries.

2) Company Information:
These offices can tell you how many companies in a given SIC code are located in any county or city. States also can provide the median salary and average starting salary for up to 1,000 different jobs, and can even tell you how many people are employed in all these companies by type of job. Many states keep information on any company which is a newcomer to the state or undertaking major business expansion. And, almost every state can give you the number of employees for any manufacturer in the state.

3) Business Location:
Whether you are establishing a new plant, a real estate business, or fast food franchise, these offices can help you locate the best location with regard to labor availability, customer availability and competition. The state labor experts can furnish specifics on how many college graduates, typists or computer programmers with three years of experience are looking for work in any given area. Or, how many are unemployed and looking for work, or how many are working for other companies in the area and their salaries. You can discover what wages are being paid by your competitors in the area for these jobs. Some states volunteer to provide information on union activity in any area. Some states can give you an indication of the work ethic of potential employees. Work ethic can be quantified by showing the number of days off taken by specific employees in certain industries. And if your customers are going to be consumers or businesses in the area, these labor market specialists can share estimates on your potential clientele.

4) Employee Development:
If you are worried about the availability of skilled employees for the future growth of your business, these offices can forecast for you the exact number of people who will be available from school training programs and other employers. This can help you determine if your business will have to move to another location or begin an in-house training program to ensure a plentiful supply of trained labor.

5) Labor Negotiations:
You can find out what the average entry wage for a typist is in your area or what the average fringe benefit package looks like for businesses in your industry. What is the maximum amount of days off allowed for sick leave in your industry? How many companies in your industry offer paid dental care? Answers to these, and other employee benefit questions, can be useful leverage in negotiating employee benefit packages.

6) Affirmative Action, EEOC and Government Contracts:
Organizations which have to comply with EEOC and affirmative action criteria can get all the data necessary from these offices. Labor force data for any area can pinpoint how many women, Hispanics, etc., are in the labor force for various

occupations. Such data can be compared with a company's current employee demographics. This information can be useful when seeking government contracts. Also, remember that many government contracts are set aside for those companies in high unemployment areas. This data, too, can be obtained from these offices to see if you qualify.

7) Economic Analysis:
If you are interested in any local area economic forecasting or economic monitoring, this is an ideal place to start. All of these offices have monthly and quarterly newsletters which plot economic health down to the city and county level. If your business is dependent on the economic conditions of a specific region, state, city or county, this approach is an easy way to keep your finger on the pulse of what is happening.

8) Careers and Job Search:
An important function of each of these offices is to provide career and job counseling information. If you are looking for a job, each office has access to a state database which identifies available job openings throughout the state. They project which jobs will be in demand in the next 10 to 20 years. And more importantly, the future supply is projected for these positions so that you can more easily spot important opportunities. Moreover, you can obtain the starting salaries and median wages for approximately 1,000 occupations in hundreds of industries. Many states give out free books designed for job seekers, as well as information on how to participate in training programs and vocational education opportunities.

9) Computer Formats and Special Services:
You must remember that no two states operate in the same manner or generate identical data. Although many offer the same reports, some may break down the data into 2-digit SIC codes and others into 4-digit SIC codes. What you must never forget is that although one state may NOT provide the data in the format you need, this does not rule out the possibility when dealing with other states. A few states now have their data online and more are beginning to offer diskettes and computer tapes. But if a state labor office says it does not provide computer readable formats, you may be able to convince them to let you be the first. These offices all seem to be very flexible and not heavily encumbered in bureaucracy.

Be sure to investigate any special services which may be offered by the state. Some offer free sources on how to interpret and use labor data and others provide customized affirmative action reports.

State Labor Offices

Alabama
Department of Industrial Relations, Research and Statistics Division, 649 Monroe St., Montgomery, AL 36131, (205) 242-8855; Selected Publications: *Monthly Labor Market, Annual Average Labor Force, Area Trends in Employment and Unemployment;* Computer Readable Formats: No; Custom Research: Limited amount available free.

Alaska
Department of Labor, Research and Analysis, P.O. Box 25501, Juneau, AK 99802-5501, (907) 465-4500; Selected Publications: *Economic Trends, Akcens Quarterly Newsletter, Career Guide, Industry-Occupation Outlook to 1994, Micro-Computer Occupational Information System (Micro-OIS), Wage Rates,*

Be patient. If any phone number is incorrect, call (area code) 555-1212 and request the new listing.

State Labor Offices

Occupational Supply and Demand Information, Occupational Injury and Illness Information, Population Overview, Special Demographic Reports, Directory of Licensed Occupations, Residency Analysis of Alaska's Workers by Firm, Employment Insurance, Actuarial Study and Financial Handbook, State Salary Survey; Computer Readable Formats: Limited availability; Custom Research: Limited amount available free.

Arizona

Department of Economic Security West, Research Administration, 1789 West Jefferson, Site Code 733A, Phoenix, AZ 85007, (602) 542-3871; Selected Publications: *Arizona Economic Trends, First Job, Staying in School, Job Searchers Guide, Job Leads; Where to Look, Metro, Non-Metro Affirmative Action Planning Information, Annual Planning Information, Applying for Government Jobs, Arizona Labor Market Newsletter, Arizona Licensed Occupation Requirements, Arizona Occupational Employment Forecasts, Arizona Occupational Profiles, Employer Wage Survey, Employment Interview Guide, Helpful Hints for Job Seekers, Map of Major Employers, The Resume, Summer Jobs For Students;* Computer Readable Formats: Forthcoming; Custom Research: Charge for special projects; all shelf publications are free.

Arkansas

Employment Security Department, Labor Market Information Section, P.O. Box 2981, Little Rock, AR 72203, (501) 682-3197; Selected Publications: *Annual Planning Information, Annual Report, Annual Report of the Employment Security Division, Arkansas Labor Force Statistics, Covered Employment and Earnings, Interface Supply and Demand, Statistical Review, Current Employment Developments, Monthly Employment Trends, Monthly County Labor Market Information, Directory of Licensed Occupations, Job Hunters Guide to AR, Occupational Trends, Staffing Patterns;* Computer Readable Formats: Occupational trends on disk; Custom Research: A limited amount is available free.

California

Employment Development Department, Labor Market Information Division, 7000 Franklin Blvd., #1100, Sacramento, CA 95823, (916) 262-2162; Selected Publications: *Annual Planning Information, California Labor Market Bulletin, Labor Market Information for Affirmative Action Programs, Labor Market Conditions in California, California Occupational Guides, California Employment and Payrolls, Projections of Employment By Industry and Occupation;* Computer Readable Formats: Limited; Custom Research: Most everything is free.

Colorado

Department of Labor and Employment, Labor Market Information Section, 393 S. Harland Street, Lakewood, CO 80226; (303) 937-4935; Selected Publications: *Affirmative Action Packets, Annual Planning Information Report, Colorado Springs Labor Force, Employment and Wages Quarterly, Occupational Employment Outlook Projection, Job Bank Wage Listing, Occupational Employment in Selected Industries, Quarterly Occupational Supply/Demand Outlook, Pueblo Labor Force, Occupational Supply and Demand, Denver, Boulder, Front Range, Western Slope, Occupational Employment Survey Publishing, Employment Projections;* Computer Readable Formats: No; Custom Research: Free on a limited basis.

Connecticut

Department of Labor, Office of Research and Information, 200 Folly Brook Blvd, Wethersfield, CT 06109-1114, (203) 566-3472; Selected Publications: *Annual Report of the Commission of the Labor in Economy Work Force and Training Needs in Connecticut, Planning for the Future Publishing, Work Place 2000, Labor Situation, Labor Force Data, Annual Planning Information, The Occupational Outlook, New Manufacturing Firms* ($7 per year fee), *Occupations in Demand, Labor Market Review, Occupational Projections and Training Data;* Computer Readable Formats; No: Custom Research: Free.

Delaware

Labor Department, Occupational and Labor Market Information Office, University Office Plaza, Newark, DE 19714, (302) 368-6962; Selected Publications: *Delaware Annual Brief, Delaware Monthly Digest, Delaware Jobs to 2005* $7.50, *Delaware Career Compass, Career Guidance-High School Information on Job Growth, ES202 Series, Occupational Wage Data-Government and Educational Services* (three year cycle), *Delaware Labor Supply and Demand:*

Occupational and Industrial Projections; Computer Readable Formats: Inquire requested; Custom Research: Limited amount available free.

District of Columbia

Employment Services Department, Labor Market Information, Room 201, 500 C St., NW, Washington, DC 20001, (202) 639-1175; Selected Publications: *Area Labor Summary, Labor Market Information for Affirmative Action Programs, Directory of 200 Major Employers, Occupational Employment in Selected Industries, Annual Population Estimates By Census Tract;* Computer Readable Formats: No; All shelf publications are free.

Florida

Department of Labor and Employment Security, Bureau of Labor Market Information, Suite 200, Hartman Building, 2012 Capital Circle, S.E., Tallahassee, FL 32399-2151, (904) 488-1048; Selected Publications: *Affirmative Action Statistical Packets, Florida Employment Statistics, Florida Industry and Occupational Employment 1995, Florida Occupational Employment in Hospitals, Labor Force Summary, Labor Market Trends, Occupational Employment in Federal Government, Occupations Employment in the Finance, Insurance and Real Estate Industry, Occupational Employment in the Services Industry, Occupational Wage Surveys;* Computer Readable Formats: Bulletin board system for direct downloading.

Georgia

Department of Labor, Labor Information Systems, 148 International, Atlanta, GA 30303, (404) 656-3177; Selected Publications: *Area Labor Profiles, Civilian Labor Force Estimates, GA Employment and Earnings, GA Employment and Wages, GA Labor Market Trends, GA Occupational Employment, Civilian Labor Force Estimates, Data on Occupational Supply and Demand, Earnings by Industry and Area;* Computer Readable Formats: No; Custom Research: Charge for Large projects, all others free.

Hawaii

Labor Market and Employment Services Branch, Labor and Industrial Relations Dept., 830 Punchbowl St., Room 302, Honolulu, HI 96813, (808) 586-8711; Selected Publications: *Labor Shortages in Agriculture, Demand Occupations, Occupations in Communication Industry, Job Hunters's Guide, Selected Wage Information, Unemployment Insurance Fact Book, Licensed Occupations, Occupational Employment Statistics, Occupational Illness and Injuries, Wage Rate, Workers Compensation, Characteristics of the Insured Unemployed, Employment and Payrolls, Permanent Mass Layoffs and Plant Closings 1988, Labor Area News, Labor Force Information for Affirmative Action Programs;* Computer Readable Formats: No; Custom Research: Free.

Idaho

Department of Employment, Research and Analysis Bureau, 317 Main St., Boise, ID 83735, (208) 334-6469; Selected Publications: *Economic Projects of Idaho Cities and Counties, LMI Directory, Idaho Monthly employment Newsletter, Labor Forces in idaho, Basic Economic Data, Annual Demographics Report, Affirmative Action Statistics, Area Employment Newsletter, Employment and Wages by Industry in Idaho;* Computer Readable Formats: Forthcoming; Custom Research: Most everything is free, Fee for larger projects.

Illinois

Employment Security Bureau, Research and Analysis, 401 South State St., Chicago, IL 60605, (312) 793-2316; Selected Publications: *Country Labor Force Summary-2000, Labor Market Review, Illinois at Work, Affirmative Action Information, Occupational Employment Statistics, Occupational Projections, Wage Survey, Where Workers Work, Illinois Employment Industrial Summary;* Computer Readable Formats: No; Custom Research: Nominal fee.

Indiana

Employment Security Division, Labor Market Information, 10 N. Senate Ave., Indianapolis, IN 46204, (317) 232-7701; Selected Publications: *Annual County Employment Patterns, Indiana Employment Review, Labor Force Estimates, Quarterly Covered Employment and Payrolls, Regional Economic Profiles, Occupational Employment Projections, Occupational Wage Surveys, Occupations In Demand, Hours and Earnings of Production Workers;* Computer Readable Formats: No; All shelf publications are free.

Be patient. If any phone number is incorrect, call (area code) 555-1212 and request the new listing.

Economics, Demographics and Statistics

Iowa

Department of Employment Services, Labor Market Information Unit, 1000 E. Grand Ave., Des Moines, IA 50319, (515) 281-8182; Selected Publications: *Condition of Employment Report/Analysis of the Iowa Market, Labor Force Employment and Unemployment Information, Labor Market Information for Service Delivery Areas, State-Wide Wage Surveys, Labor Market Information for Affirmative Action Programs, Industry/Occupational Projections, Job Insurance Benefits, Iowa Occupational Planning Guide, Licensed Occupations, Labor Market Information Directory, Wages and Employment Covered by Employment Security, Affirmative Action Data for Iowa, Condition of Employment;* Computer Readable Formats: Electronic bulletin board; Custom Research: Free, nominal fee for larger projects.

Kansas

Department of Human Resources, Division of Employment and Training, Research and Analysis Section, 401 S.W. Blvd., Topeka, KS 66603, (913) 296-5058; Selected Publications: *Occupational Staffing Patterns, Kansas Unemployment Insurance Claims, Monthly Labor Market Summary, Kansas Wage Survey, Affirmative Action Packet, Labor Market Review, Report on Employment-Hours and Earnings, Labor Force Estimates, Employment by Area and Industry;* Computer Readable Formats: Limited; Custom Research: Charge for large projects, all others free.

Kentucky

Department for Employment Services, Research and Statistics, CHR Bldg 2C, Frankfort, KY 40621, (502) 564-7976; Selected Publications: *Non-Agricultural Wage and Salary Employment, Kentucky Labor Market Newsletter, Estimate of Production Workers and Average Hours and Earnings, Labor Force Estimates, Occupational Outlook, Occupational Career Brief, Occupational Profiles, Labor Area Summary, Labor Area Profile, Annual Planning Information, Affirmative Action, Labor Supply Estimates, Characteristics of Insured Unemployed, Average Covered Monthly Workers in Manufacturing by Industry Division and County, Total Wages by Industrial Division and County, Average Weekly Wages by Industrial Division and County;* Computer Readable Formats: No; Custom Research: Limited.

Louisiana

Department of Employment Security, Research and Statistics Unit, P.O. 94094, Baton Rouge, LA 70804-9094, (504) 342-3141; Selected Publications: *Occupational Projections-1999-2000, Quarterly Employment and Wages, Annual Employment and Wages, Monthly Labor Market Information, Manpower for Affirmative Action, Annual Planning Report, Occupational Employment Statistics, Average Weekly Wage, LA Occupational Injuries and Illnesses;* Computer Readable Formats: Limited; Custom Research: Limited amount available free.

Maine

Bureau of Employment Security, Division of Economic Analysis and Research, 20 Union St., Augusta, ME 04330-6826, (207) 289-2271; Selected Publications: *Labor Market Digest Monthly, Maine Occupational Staffing Patterns in Hospitals-Government-Manufacturing/Nonmanufacturing-Trade, Careers In Maine Woods;* Computer Readable Formats: Yes; Custom Research: Charge for larger projects, all others free.

Maryland

Department of Human Resources, Research and Analysis, Employment and Training, 1100 N. Eutaw St., Baltimore, MD 21201, (410) 333-5007; .PA Selected Publications: *Affirmative Action Data, Maryland Occupational Industrial Outlook, Civilian Labor Force Employment and Unemployment by Place of Residence, Claims Processed for Unemployment Insurance Benefits, Occupations in Maryland, Current Employment Statistics, Labor Market Dimensions, Employment and Payrolls Covered by the Unemployment Insurance Law of Maryland, Zoned Employment and Unemployment Statistics, Industries in Maryland, Highlights of Maryland's Population Projections, Maryland Rural Manpower Report, Occupational Wage Information, Year in Review, Population and Labor Force in Maryland, A Profile: Services Industry in Maryland 1980-Present;* Computer Readable Formats: No. Customer Research: Limited amount available free.

Massachusetts

Division of Employment Security, Massachusetts Employment and Training Center, 19 Saniford Street, Charles F. Hurley Building, Boston, MA 02114, (617) 727-6531; Selected Publications: *Planning Data: Massachusetts, Employment and Wages, Massachusetts Employment Review* (monthly), *Careers and Training in Allied Health, Occupational Profiles of Manufacturing Industries, Career Choices in a Changing Economy, New England Economic Indicators;* Computer Readable Formats: No; Publications free when available.

Michigan

Employment Security Commission, Bureau of Research and Statistics, 7310 Woodward Ave., Detroit, MI 48202, (313) 876-5439; Selected Publications: *Affirmative Action Information Report, Annual Planning Information, Claims Counter, Covered Employment Statistics, Monthly Labor Market Review, Occupational Employment Statistics Survey Publications, Occupations in Education, Occupational Wage Information, Michigan Regulated and Trade Industries, Occupational Projections and Training Data, Michigan Occupation/Industry Outlook 2000, Michigan Metropolitan Areas Occupation/Industry Outlook 2000, Michigan Non-metropolitan Areas Occupation/Industry Outlook 2000, Michigan Occupational Supply/Demand Report, Occupational Projections and Training Information for Michigan-OPTIM, Civilian Labor Force, Employment and Unemployment Estimates, Employment Hours and Earnings Estimates, Unemployment Insurance Program Statistics, Employment Trends, Hours and Earnings Trends, Women Employment Trends 1982 to Present, Production Worker Employee Trends 1982 to Present;* Computer Readable Formats: Limited, electronic bulletin board forthcoming; Custom Research: Limited amount available free.

Minnesota

Department of Jobs and Training, Research Office, 390 North Robert St., St. Paul MN 55101, (612) 296-8716; Selected Publications: *Consumer Price Index, Career Bulletin, Minnesota Projections and Monthly Reports* (available on diskette), *Employment Outlook by Region, Minnesota Wage Data by Industry and Area, Minnesota Employment Outlook to 1996, Important MN Occupations by Industry by Area, Minnesota Careers, MN Wage Data By Industry and Size of Firm, Employment and Wage Data By County, Minnesota Labor Market Review;* Computer Readable Format: Some data available via electronic bulletin board; Custom Research: Charge for large projects, all others free.

Mississippi

Employment Security Commission, Labor Market Information Department, P.O. Box 1699, Jackson, MS 39215-1699, (601) 961-7424; Selected .PA Publications: *Guide to Labor Market Information, LMI Catalogue, Annual Labor Force Averages, Annual Report, Employment and Job Openings 2005, Farm Income and Expenditures, Affirmative Action Programs, Monthly Labor Market Data, Labor Market Trends for Jackson Metro Area, Mississippi's Business Population, Occupational Employment and Job Openings by Unit of Analysis, by Major Sources, Quarterly Labor Market Summary, Transfer Payments by Major Sources;* Computer Readable Formats: Yes, some publications available on diskettes; Customer Research: Limited amount available free.

Missouri

Division of Employment Security, Research and Analysis, P.O. Box 59, Jefferson City, MO 65104, (314) 751-3602; Selected Publications: *Monthly Labor Area Trends, Labor Market Information for Affirmative Action Programs, Wages Paid in Selected Occupations, Employment Outlook;* Computer Readable Formats: Electronic bulletin board; Custom Research: Limited research available.

Montana

Department of Labor and Industry, Research and Analysis Bureau, P.O. Box 1728, Helena, MT 59624, (406) 444-2430; Selected Publications: *Wage Surveys of the Private Sector, Wage Surveys of the Public Sector, Wage Surveys of Public Education, Quarterly Employment and Labor Force, Monthly Statistics in Brief, Annual Planning Information, Montana Supply and Demand Report, Montana Apprenticeable Occupations;* Computer Readable Formats: Forthcoming; Custom Research: Limited Amount available free.

Nebraska

Department of Labor, Labor Market Information, 550 South 16th St., Lincoln, NE 68509, (402) 471-2600; Selected Publications: *Prairie/Farm and Ranch Profile, NE Labor Market Information, Supply and Demand/Selected Occupations, Careers*

Be patient. If any phone number is incorrect, call (area code) 555-1212 and request the new listing.

State Labor Offices

and Education in Nebraska, *Monthly Labor Area Summary, Occupational Employment Statistics by Industry, Monthly Labor Force, Affirmative Action, Survey of Average Hourly Wage Rates, Occupational Newsletter, Nebraska Job Prospects;* Computer Readable Formats: No; Custom Research: Limited amount available for free.

Nevada

Employment Security Department, Employment Security Research Section, 500 E Third St., Carson City, NV 89713, (702) 687-4550; Selected Publications: *Area Labor Review, Directory of Labor Market Information, Quarterly and Monthly Economic Update, Nevada Wage Survey, Occupational Projections, Job Finding Techniques;* Computer Readable Formats: Limited; Custom Research: Limited amount available free.

New Jersey

Labor Department, Labor Market Information Office, John Fitch Plaza CN056, Trenton, NJ 08625, (609) 292-7376; Selected Publications: *Regional Labor Market Reviews, Regional Labor Market Newsletters, PA Compendium of New Jersey Wage Surveys, Employment and Economy Newsletter, Employment Trends, Economic Indicators Monthly;* Computer Readable Formats: Limited electronic bulletin board usage; Custom Research: Limited amount available free.

New Hampshire

Employment Security Department, Economic Analysis and Reports and Labor Market Information Bureau, 32 South Main St., Concord, NH 03301, (603) 224-3311; Selected Publications: *Wage Survey, Vital Signs, Staffing Patterns in NH, Annual Report, Annual Planning Information, Annual Planning Information MSA's, Community Patterns NH, Economic Conditions, Employment and Wages by County, Employment and Wages MSA's, Employment and Wages by Planning Region, Fact Book: Cities and Towns, Firms By Size, Local Area Unemployment Statistics, NH Affirmative Action Data, NH Occupational Outlook 2005, Users Guide to Labor Market Information;* Computer Readable Formats: Call for availability and cost; Custom Research: Free.

New Mexico

Department of Employment Security, Economic Research and Analysis, P.O. Box 1928, Albuquerque, NM 87103, (505) 841-8645; Selected Publications: *Covered Employment and Wages, Basic Concepts, Monthly Labor Market Review, Nonagricultural Wage and Salary Employment, Facts and Figures about New Mexico, Hours and Earnings Estimates, Albuquerque Small Employer Wage Survey, Jobs to 2000, Area Job Market Flyers, Large Employers in New Mexico by County;* Computer Readable Formats: Limited; Customer Research: Limited amount available for free.

New York

Department of Labor, Division of Research and Statistics, State Office Bldg. Campus #12, Albany, NY 12240, (518) 457-3800; Selected Publications: *Statistics on Operations, Characteristics of Job Openings, Civilian Labor Force by Occupation, Selected Demographic Groups, Regular and Extended Benefits, State Unemployment Insurance, Collective Bargaining Settlements, Directory of Labor Unions and Employee Organizations in New York State Employment Review, Current Population Survey Data, A Guide to Career Opportunities in New York State Government, Earnings and Hours in Selected Industries, The Job Seeker, Labor Area Summary Monthly Statistical Report, Labor Area Summary Quarterly Analytical Report, Labor Market Assessment: Occupational Supply and Demand, Occupational Brief, Occupational Projections, Occupational Employment Statistics, Occupational Guide, Occupational Needs, Occupation Licensed or Certified by New York State, Operations, Resident Employment Status of the Civilian Labor Force, Careers Exploration and Job Seeking, Total and Civilian Labor Force Summary, Selected Demographic Groups - NYS, Counties and SMSA's, Selected Labor Research Reports, Apprentice Training Hours and Earnings, Insured Employment and Payrolls, Local Area Unemployment Statistics, Non-Agricultural Wage and Salary Employment, Unemployment Insurance Operating Statistics;* Computer Readable Formats: Forthcoming; Custom Research: Charge for large projects, all others free.

North Carolina

Employment Security Commission, Labor Market Information Division, P.O. Box 25903, Raleigh, NC 27611, (919) 733-2936; Selected Publications:

Employment and Wages in NC Quarterly, Market Areas Newsletter, Past High School Intentions of NC Graduates by County, Equal Employment Data Series, Occupational Trends: Year 2000: NC, NC Metro State Planning Regions A-F; G-L; M-R, Announced New and Expanding Manufacturing Firms, NC Preliminary Civilian Labor Force Estimates, Active Job Applicants by County, Registered Applicants and Job Openings, Follow-Up Survey of NC High School Graduates by County, Wage Rates in Selected Occupations; Computer Readable Formats: Forthcoming; Custom Research: Free, charge for larger projects.

North Dakota

Job Service, Research and Statistics, P.O. Box 1537, Bismarck, ND 58502, (701) 224-3048; Selected Publications: *Occupational Supply/Demand Report, Employment and Wages, Monthly Labor Market Advisor, Occupations Wage Surveys and Benefits for Major Cities, Occupational Projections to 2000, Employment Surveys by Major City, Annual Planning Report;* Computer Readable Formats: No; Custom Research: Charge for large amounts, all others free.

Ohio

Bureau of Employment Services, Labor Market Information Division, 145 South Front St., Columbus, OH 43216, (614) 466-4636; Selected Publications: *Employment and Unemployment Estimates, Covered Employment and Payroll, Trend Tables, Monthly Labor Market Review, County Labor Force Reports, Labor Force Estimates, Metropolitan Profile, Occupational Projections, Composition of Job Placements, Summary of Ohio Worker Training Program Activities;* Computer Readable Formats: Yes; Custom Research: Charge for large projects, all others free.

Oklahoma

Oklahoma Employment Security Commission, Economic Analysis, 2401 N. Lincoln Blvd., Oklahoma City, OK 73105, (405) 557-7104; Selected Publications: *Labor Market Information, Handicap Labor Force Data for Selected Areas, Manpower Information for Affirmative Action, Annual Report to the Governor, Handbook of Employment Statistics, County Employment and Wage Data, Occupational Wage Surveys, OK Monthly Economic Newsletter;* Computer Readable Formats: Yes; Custom Research: Charge for large projects, all other free.

Oregon

Employment Division, Research and Statistics, 875 Union NE, Salem, OR 97311, (503) 378-8656; Selected Publications: *Oregon Work Force at Risk, Dislocated Workers, Oregon Works, Affirmative Action Programs, Agricultural Employment, Average Weekly Earnings-Hours, Business and Employment Outlook, Monthly Local Labor Trends, Occupational Program Planning System, Oregon Wage Information;* Computer Readable Formats: No; Custom Research: Charge for large projects, all others free.

Pennsylvania

Department of Labor and Industry, Research and Statistics Division, 7th and Forster Sts., Harrisburg, PA 17121, (717) 787-2114; Selected Publications: *Work Force 2000, Civilian Work Force Data by Labor Market Area of Residence, Annual Average Labor Force Data, Civilian Labor Force Series by Labor Market Area, PA Labor Market Areas Ranked on Basis of Rate of Unemployment, PA Unemployment Fact Sheet, Directory of Occupational Wage Information, Occupational Trends and Outlook for Total Civilian Employment, Industry Trends and Outlook 2000, Employment and Wages of Workers Covered by the PA Unemployment Compensation Law, Occupations Employment in Hospital Occupational Staffing Patterns for Selected Non-Manufacturing Industries, Annual Planning Information, Affirmative Action Report, Labor Market Job Guides, Directory of Licensed Occupational Information Systems, Labor Demand-Supply Relationships, Career Guide, Labor Market Letters, PA Employment and Earnings, PA's Microcomputer Occupational Information System, Hours and Earnings, Current Trends in Employment and Wages in PA Industries, PA Labor Force, Annual Planning Information Report, Hours and Earnings in Manufacturing and Selected Non-manufacturing Industries, Industry Trends and Outlook Projected 1995;* Computer Readable Formats: Yes; Custom Research: Charge for large projects, all others free.

Rhode Island

Department of Employment Security, Research and Statistics, 101 Friendship St.,

Be patient. If any phone number is incorrect, call (area code) 555-1212 and request the new listing.

Economics, Demographics and Statistics

Providence, RI 02903, (401) 277-3706; Selected Publications: *Occupational Projections 2000, Monthly Labor Force Statistics, Characteristics of Insured Unemployed, RI Employment Newsletter, Quarterly Labor Supply and Demand Report, Employment and Wages by City and Industry, Annual Planning Information, Manpower Information for Affirmative Action Programs, Employment In RI Hospitals;* Computer Readable Format: No; Custom Research: Free.

South Carolina

Employment Security Commission, Labor Market Information Division, P.O. Box 995, Columbia, SC 29202, (803) 737-2660; Selected Publications: *Industrial Monographs, Wage Survey, SC Job Search Assistance Guide, Labor Market Review, Employment Trends, Occupational Projections 2000, Labor Force in Industry, Employment and Wages in SC;* Computer Readable Formats: Limited; Custom Research: Charge for large projects, all others free.

South Dakota

Department of Labor, Labor Market Information Center, P.O. Box 4730, Aberdeen, SD 57402-4730, (605) 622-2314; Selected Publications: *Labor Availability Studies, Labor Bulletin, Occupational Wage Information, Occupational Outlook Handbook, Employment and Earnings, Affirmative Action Package, Statewide Job Listings;* Computer Readable Formats: Yes; Custom Research: Limited amount available free.

Tennessee

Department of Employment Security, Research and Statistics Division, 11th Floor, James Robertson Parkway, Nashville, TN 37245-1040, (615) 741-3639; Selected Publications: *Occupational Wage and Benefit Information, Minorities in Tennessee, Occupations in Demand, Licensed Occupations in Tennessee, Monthly Available Labor, Monthly Labor Force Summary, Commuting Patterns, Tennessee Employment Projections 2000, Tennessee Youth Report, Veterans in Tennessee, Women in the Labor Force, Tennessee High School Graduates;* Computer Readable Formats: Limited; Custom Research: Limited amount available free.

Texas

Texas Employment Commission, Economic Research and Analysis Dept., Room 208-T, TEC Building, Austin, TX 78778, (512) 463-2616; Selected Publications: *Labor Force Estimates, Current Population Survey, Nonagricultural Wage and Salary Employment Estimates, Average Hours and Earnings Data, Employment and Wages by Industry and County, Affirmative Action Packets, Characteristics of the Insured Unemployed, Regional Reports, Labor Demand Projects by 2000, Occupational Employment Statistics;* Computer Readable Formats: Limited; Custom Research: Charge for large projects, all others free.

Utah

Utah Department of Employment Security, Labor Market Information Services, P.O. Box 11249, Salt Lake City, UT 84147, (801) 536-7800; Selected Publications: *Annual Labor Market Research, Licensed Occupations in Utah, Monthly Utah Labor Market Report, Utah Directory of Business and Industry;* Computer Readable Formats: On a limited basis. Custom Research: Free.

Vermont

Department of Employment and Training, Labor Market Information, P.O. Box 488, Montpelier, VT 05601, (802) 229-0311; Selected Publications: *Occupation, Wage and Employment Survey, Job Openings, Affirmative Action Planning Data, Annual Planning Information, Combined Annual Report of DET and JTPA, Directory of Labor Market Information Employment and Earnings, Labor Market Area Bulletins, Profile of Active Applicants, Vermont Labor Market, Employment and Wages Covered by Unemployment Insurance, Licensed Occupations in Vermont Mining and Quarrying, Construction, Unemployment Compensation Statistical Table, Vermont Economic and Demographic Profile Series, Vermont*

Industrial Projections to 2000, Vermont Occupational Projections to 2000; Computer Readable Formats: Forthcoming; Custom Research: Upon request, limited time available.

Virginia

Virginia Employment Commission, Labor Market and Demographics Analysis Section, P.O. Box 1358, Richmond, VA 23211, (804) 786-8222; Selected Publications: *Guide to Establishing a Business, LMI Directory, Business Registration Guide, Work Force 2000, Labor Force by Sex and Minority Status, Commuting Patterns, Data on Public Schools, Economic Assumptions for the U.S. and VA, Economically Disadvantaged Data, Employment and Training Indicators, Employment and Wages in Establishments, Employment and Wages in VA, Monthly Labor Market Review, Wage Survey Selected Manufacturers Occupation, Licensed Occupations in VA, List of Employers By Size, State and County Veteran Population, Trends in Employment-Hours and Earnings, Quarterly Virginia Economic Indicators, Virginia Business Resource Directory.* Computer Readable Formats: ALICE (Virginia based only); Custom Research: Limited for nominal fee.

Washington

Employment Security Group, Labor Market and Economic Analysis Branch, 605 Woodland Square Loop S.E., Lacey, WA 98503, mailing address P.O. Box 9046, Olympia, WA 98507-9046, (206) 438-4804; Selected Publications: *Labor Area Summaries, Washington Labor Market, LMI Review, Affirmative Action Information, Annual Demographic Information, Area Wage Survey, Employment and Payrolls in Washington, Occupational Profiles and Projections, Labor Market Monthly;* Computer Readable Formats: Some; Custom Research: Large projects are charged on a contract basis.

West Virginia

Employment Security Department, Labor and Economic Research, 112 California Ave., Charleston, WV 25305, (304) 558-2630; Selected Publications: *Affirmative Action, West Virginia Women in the Labor Force, Annual Planning Information, Metropolitan Statistical Areas Annual Planning Information, Job Training Partnership Act, West Virginia County Profiles, WV Economic Summary, Employment and Earnings Trends, Insured Workers Summary, Occupational Projections, Veterans Report, Wage Survey, Youth Report, Directory of Publications, Licensed Occupations in West Virginia;* Computer Readable Formats: Forthcoming; Custom Research: Limited amount available free.

Wisconsin

Department of Industry, Labor and Human Relations, Employment and Training Library, P.O. Box 7944, Madison, WI 53707, (608) 267-9613; Selected Publications: *LMI: A Reference Guide of WI Publications, Labor Market Planning Information, Employment, Wages, Taxes Due Covered by Wisconsin U.C. Law, Wisconsin Projections 1988-2000, Affirmative Action Data, Career Connection, Monthly Wisconsin Economic Indicators, Civilian Labor Force Estimates, Consumer Price Index, Current Population Survey, Employment and Wages, Wage Survey, Covered Employment By Size of Industry and County, Wisconsin Employment Picture, Wisconsin Works, Inform Bi-Monthly;* Computer Readable Formats: Some; Custom Research: Charge for large projects.

Wyoming

Employment Security Commission, Research and Analysis, P.O. Box 2760, Casper, WY 82602, (307) 235-3200; Selected Publications: *Occupational Employment Statistics: Manufacturing and Hospitals, Occupational Employment Statistics, Wyoming's Annual Planning Report, Wyoming's Covered Employment and Wage Data, Labor Force Trends, Applicants and Job Openings in Wyoming, Affirmative Action Package;* Computer Readable Format: No; Custom Research: Limited amount available.

Be patient. If any phone number is incorrect, call (area code) 555-1212 and request the new listing.

State Health Statistics

* *See also Health and Medicine Chapter*

Vital And Infectious Disease Statistics

The last few years have witnessed explosive growth in products and services aimed at the health-conscious baby-boomers and their aging parents. In order to market products and services, many businesses use state health statistics and records. State health data are used to great success by insurance companies, individual medical providers and doctor groups, private health care clinics and rehabilitative service centers, diet and natural food producers, pharmaceutical and cosmetic companies, and even publishers.

A state's health care registration system is often the best place to start researching specific health data for an entire state's population. In addition, each state makes available its annual health report in a number of formats.

Some insurance companies use this information to steer away from areas where cancer rates are too high or to zero in on areas where rates are lower than the national norm. Along this same line, a new doctor might search for an area where there is a greater demand for his or her specific medical expertise.

Exercise equipment manufacturers can use the data to target upscale, "yuppie" markets for their sales campaigns -- or identify clusters of older hospitals with on-site physical therapy facilities that might need new equipment. Other examples include:

- how many people have cancer, diabetes, or high blood pressure by zip code
- hospitals with CAT scans and other sophisticated medical equipment
- vaccination records to find which homes have babies, preschoolers, grade schoolers, etc.
- names, addresses and neighborhoods with the most senior citizens
- names and addresses of ambulatory care facilities and state-funded birth control/venereal disease counseling clinics
- neighborhoods not immediately serviced by existing drug stores

Data are collected and used to assess the current status of health and health care in a state and to help state officials better anticipate future health care needs and resources. In addition, the information provides baseline data for medical research, charts population shifts, and identifies specific groups, communities, neighborhoods, etc. for special state and federal health programs.

Annual reports, available from state vital statistics departments, contain information on births, deaths, marriages and divorces, with narrative and graphic highlights of emerging demographic and health issue trends.

Annual reports from a state's office of epidemiology contain specific data on the incidence of notifiable communicable diseases and related information reported by area physicians, hospitals and health clinics.

Computer printouts of selected data provide the most current health and health care information in detail, much of which does not make it into a state's annual reports. Data can be sorted and printed to assist individuals and businesses with statistical research projects. Most states are staffed with experts to help with individual research requests. Most offices prefer that information requests be placed in writing. State offices release aggregate data that includes no names or personal identifiers.

All states will provide computer printouts of selected data, at least on limited basis. In most instances, there is no charge for printouts. When requesting specific data not found in a state's annual report, place your information request in writing, be as specific as possible in what you are asking, and specify your computer system's requirements.

The following states provide information on magnetic tape or diskette. Fees vary from state to state depending upon the complexity of the request.

Magnetic tape: Arizona, California, Delaware, Florida, Georgia, Idaho, Illinois, Indiana, Kentucky, Maine, Maryland, Mississippi, Missouri, Montana, New Hampshire, New York, North Carolina, Oklahoma, South Carolina, South Dakota, Tennessee, Texas, Utah, Virginia, West Virginia, Washington, Wyoming

Diskette: Alaska, Arizona, California, Delaware, Florida, Georgia, Idaho, Illinois, Kentucky, Maine, Maryland, Minnesota, Mississippi, Missouri, Montana, Nebraska, New Hampshire, New Mexico, New York, North Carolina, Oklahoma, Oregon, South Carolina, South Dakota, Tennessee, Texas, Utah, Virginia, West Virginia, Wyoming

Offices For Vital And Infectious Disease Statistics

Alabama

Department of Public Health, Center for Health Statistics, P.O. Box 5625, Montgomery, AL 36130; (205) 242-5033. This office will provide computer printouts of selected data. There is a charge of $15 per printout. At present, data is not available on diskette or magnetic tape. Their publications include an *Annual Report; Teenage Birth Statistics,* and *Detailed Mortality Statistics.*

Bureau of Preventive Health Services, Epidemiology Division, Department of Health, 434 Monroe St., Room 900, Montgomery, AL 36130-1701; (205) 242-5131. Publications include their 1990 annual report, *Notifiable Diseases in Alabama.* The office can supply limited computer printouts of selected aggregate data on communicable diseases.

Be patient. If any phone number is incorrect, call (area code) 555-1212 and request the new listing.

Economics, Demographics and Statistics

Alaska

State Department of Health, Division of Public Health, P.O. Box 110610, Juneau AK 99811-0610; (907) 465-3090. Publications include the *Vital Statistics Annual Report.* Information is available on computer printouts and on diskette on a limited basis. Fees vary according to the complexity of the request.

State Department of Health, Office of Epidemiology, P.O. Box 240249, Anchorage, AK 99524-0249; (907) 561-4406. Publications include the *Epidemiology Bulletin.* Information is available on computer printouts, usually free of charge.

Arizona

Department of Health Services, Office of Policy and Planning, 1740 West Adams St., Phoenix, AZ 85007; (602) 542-1216. Publications include *Abortion Surveillance Report, Accidental Deaths in Arizona,* and *Health Status and Vital Statistics.* The office provides aggregate data on computer printouts, free of charge. Special requests for selected data are handled on a limited basis. There is a minimum charge of $25 for computer programming time.

Department of Health Services, Office of Infectious Diseases, Epidemiology, 3008 N. 3rd St., Phoenix, AZ 85012; (602) 230-5927. Publications include *Communicable Diseases in Arizona.* This office provides computer printouts of selected data. If you send them a blank diskette they will transfer the information requested on to it, free of charge.

Arkansas

Department of Health, Office of Vital Records, State Health Building, 4815 W. Markham, Little Rock, AR 72205; (501) 661-2371. This office publishes an *Annual Report.* Computer printouts are available for certain items for a processing fee. If you provide a diskette, the office will process it for you.

Department of Health, Epidemiology Program, Division of Health Maintenance, 4815 W. Markham, Little Rock, AR 72205; (501) 661-2264. Publications include an *Annual Report, Annual Morbidity Report,* and *Physician's Bulletin* which contains 1991 data. The office provides computer printouts of selected data, free of charge.

California

California Department of Health Data and Services, 714 P. St., Sacramento, CA 95814; (916) 657-3057. Publications include: *Vital Statistics of California, General Fertility Rates and Age-Specific Live Births by Age of Mother, Suicides in California, Multiples Causes of Death,* and *California's Non-licensed Marriages -- A first Look at Their Characteristics.* Publication prices vary and a complete catalogue of titles can be obtained from this office. Specific computer searches are available. Information is provided on computer printout, diskette and magnetic tape. Fees vary according to the complexity of the request.

Colorado

Department of Health, Health Statistics Section, 4210 East 11th Ave., Denver, CO 80220; (303) 331-4895. Publications include the 400-page *Colorado Vital Statistics Report.* The office does provide specialized computer runs of extracted data at a minimum cost of $40. Computer printouts are provided, but no information is distributed on diskette or magnetic tape.

Department of Health, Division of Disease Control and Environmental Epidemiology, 4210 East 11th Ave., Denver, CO 80220; (303) 331-8330. Publications include the bi-monthly *Colorado Disease Bulletin* which contains yearly totals of infectious diseases.

Connecticut

Department of Health Services, Division of Health Surveillance and Planning, 150 Washington St., Hartford, CT 06106; (203) 566-7886. Publications include an *Annual Report.* Computer printouts and machine readable forms are offered through this office for a fee.

Department of Health Services, Epidemiology Program, 150 Washington St., Hartford, CT 06106; (203) 566-5058. Although this office provides information on infectious diseases such as hepatitis, separate statistics on AIDS, cancer and tuberculosis are handled through individual offices. There is no charge for computer printouts of statistical reports.

Delaware

Delaware Health Statistics Center, Bureau of Health Planning, Resource Management, P.O. Box 637, Dover, DE 19903; (302) 739-4776. Publications include an *Annual Report.* Computer printouts and information on diskette and magnetic tape are generally provided free of charge.

Bureau of Disease Prevention, Division of Public Health, P.O. 637, Dover, DE 19903; (302) 739-5617. This office's publications include a *Monthly Surveillance Report.* Computer printouts of data are generated, usually at no cost.

District of Columbia

Department of Human Services, Research and Statistics Division, 425 I St. N.W., Room 3007, Washington, DC 20001; (202) 727-0681.--Publications include the *1990 Annual Report of Vital Statistics.* Statistical data tables are available on computer printout form.

Florida

Department of Health and Rehabilitative Services, Public Health Statistics, P.O. Box 210, Jacksonville, FL 32231-0042; (904) 359-6963. Publications include the: *Florida Vital Statistics, Vital News and Quarterly Vital Statistics Report.* This office can provide a computer printout of data records, at $.12 per record. Programming is $50.65 per hour. They will send two to three pages of data at no charge. Anything above that contains a handling charge of $18 per hour. Information is also provided on computer diskette. The fees are the same as those for computer printouts.

Department of Health and Rehabilitative Services, 1317 Winewood Blvd. Tallahassee, FL 32399-0700; (904) 487-2542. Publications include a *Monthly Report,* and *Florida Morbidity Statistics.* Computer printouts of selected data are provided on a limited basis.

Georgia

Department of Human Resources, Vital Records, 47 Trinity Ave., SW, Room 217-H, Atlanta, GA 30334; (404) 894-6482. Publications include an *Annual Report.* Information requests must be made in writing. There is a $25 minimum charge for computer printouts of selected data. Information is available on diskette and on magnetic tape. Fees vary depending upon the scope of the project.

Department of Human Resources, Epidemiology Section, 878 Peachtree St. N.E., Room 210, Atlanta, GA 30309; (404) 894-6531. Publications include a *Communicable Disease Morbidity Annual Report* and *Annual Report.* Computer printouts on certain selected statistics are available.

Hawaii

Vital Records Section, State Dept of Health, P.O. Box 3378, Honolulu, HI, 96801-9984; (808) 586-4602. Publications include the *1990 Statistical Report,* which is free. Computer printouts of information are available on a limited basis. Detailed information requests should be in writing. The office can retrieve some information from databases on tape but it depends on the time frame involved and the resources available. At present, there is no charge for computer printouts.

Department of Health, Epidemiology Branch, Kinau Hale Building, 1250 Punchbowl St., Room 107, Honolulu, HI 96813; (808) 586-4586. Publications include *Communicable Disease Report* which is published bi-monthly.

Idaho

Department of Health and Welfare, Bureau of Vital Statistics, Statehouse, Boise, ID 83720; (208) 334-5980. Publications include an *Annual Report.* The office provides reports, free of charge, of existing data tables. Tables can also be placed on diskette for a fee of $25 to $50. There is a charge of $15 if computer programming runs over an hour. Records are legally confidential, so the use of magnetic tapes is possible only as long as data is not potentially identifying.

Department of Health and Welfare, Communicable Disease Prevention, Statehouse, Boise, ID 83720; (208) 334-5930. This office publishes a *Biweekly Disease Surveillance Report.* Computer printouts of information are available.

Be patient. If any phone number is incorrect, call (area code) 555-1212 and request the new listing.

State Health Statistics

Illinois

Department of Public Health, Division of Vital Records, Division of Data Processing, 605 W. Jefferson, Springfield, IL 62702-5097; (217) 785-1064. Publications include the *Vital Statistics Annual Report*. Computer printouts of selected data are copied at $.25 per page. Magnetic tapes of birth/death data are available for a fee. If you supply the office with a blank diskette they will transfer the information on to it for a fee.

Department of Public Health, Division of Infectious Diseases, 525 W. Jefferson, Springfield, IL 62761; (217) 785-7165. Computer printouts are available through individual departments. You must fill out a data request form before information is released.

Indiana

State Board of Health, Division of Public Health Statistics, 1330 West Michigan St., P.O. Box 1964, Indianapolis, IN 46206-1964; (317) 232-0307 Publications include *Indiana Abortion Report*, and *1990 Indiana County Population Estimates*. Computer printouts and tapes are available on a limited basis. Programming fees vary depending upon the complexity of the request. The office also publishes an annotated list of publications.

State Board of Health, Disease Intervention, 1330 West Michigan St., P.O. Box 1964, Indianapolis, IN 46206; (317) 633-8414. Publications include an *Annual Report* Computer printouts are provided, if data exists.

Iowa

Department of Public Health, Statistic Services, 321 E. 12th St., Lucas State Office Building, Des Moines, IA 50319-0075; (515) 281-4945. Publications include a *Vital Statistics Annual Report*. This office provides yearly data tables. Information is available on computer printouts and fees vary according to the complexity of the request.

Department of Public Health, Epidemiology Section, Lucas State Office Building, Des Moines, IA 50319; (515) 281-5424. Weekly health updates are available through this office.

Kansas

Department of Health and Environment, Research and Analysis, Office of Communication Services, Forbes Field, Bldg. 740, Topeka, KS 66620; (913) 296-0632. Publications include an *Annual Report*. This office will provide printouts of selected data. There is a fee for reports over 25 pages. Information is available on computer diskette and there is a fee which is dependent upon the amount of programming time involved.

Department of Health and Environment, Bureau of Disease Control, Suite 605, Mills Building, 109 S.W. 9th St., Topeka, KS 66612; (913) 296-5586. Publications include their *Annual Report*. Computer printouts are available, free of charge.

Kentucky

Cabinet for Human Resources, Health Data Branch, 275 East Main St., Frankfort, KY 40621; (502) 564-2757. Publications include a monthly report and year-end summary table. Computer printouts of selected data are available for $10 per printout. Diskettes and magnetic tapes are available. The cost depends upon the scope of the request.

Cabinet for Human Resources, Division of Epidemiology, 275 East Main St., Frankfort, KY 40621; (502) 564-3418. Publications include monthly and year- end summary reports of specific diseases plus their *Monthly Epidemiologic Notes and Reports*. The office does provide computer printouts of selected data but information on diskette or magnetic tape is not available.

Louisiana

Department of Health and Human Resources, Public Health Statistics, P.O. Box 60630, New Orleans, LA 70160; (504) 568-5458. This office publishes an *Annual Report*. Computer printouts are available, if the data is complete. There is no charge.

Department of Health and Human Resources, Office of Epidemiology, P.O. Box 60630, New Orleans, LA 70160; (504) 568-5005. This office publishes an *Annual Report*. Computer printouts of 1991 data are provided free of charge.

Maine

Department of Human Services, Department of Vital Records, 221 State St., Augusta, ME 04333; (207) 624-5445. Publications include the *1991 Annual Report of Vital Statistics* which is available at $10.50. This office will provide raw data via printouts, diskettes and magnetic tapes. There is a base fee of $27.50 per diskette and $52 per magnetic tape. All request should be in writing, and be as specific as possible regarding the data that you request and the requirements of your computer system. The office encourages callers to provide their own disk or magnetic tape when possible.

Bureau of Health, Division of Disease Control, State House Station 11, Augusta, ME 04333; (207) 289-3591. Publications include the *Epigram* which is published every two months on topics of health concern to Maine residents. A limited amount of raw data can be provided to callers on computer printouts. All requests for detailed information should be in writing.

Maryland

Department of Health and Mental Hygiene, Division of Health Statistics, 201 West Preston St., Baltimore, MD 21201; (410) 225-5950. Publications include the *1989 Vital Statistics Preliminary Report*. Computer printouts of tables of selected data are provided. Requests for information should be in writing. Information is available on magnetic tape and diskette. Fees vary according to the amount of information requested.

Department of Health and Mental Hygiene, Communicable Diseases Surveillance, 201 West Preston St., 3rd Floor Baltimore, MD 21201; (410) 225-6712. This office publishes *Annual Report* that is free of charge.

Massachusetts

Department of Public Health, Division of Health Statistics and Research, 153 Tremont, 5th Floor, Jamaica Plains, MA 02111; (617) 239-4257. Publications include an *Annual Report*. Computer printouts of selected data are provided, free of charge.

Department of Public Health, Epidemiology Program, 305 South St., Jamaica Plains, MA 02130; (617) 522-3700. Publications include fact sheets on various communicable diseases.

Michigan

Department of Public Health, Office of State Registrar, Center for Health Statistics, Statistical Services Section, P.O. Box 300195, Lansing, MI 48909; (517) 335-8656. Publications include: *Health Statistics Pocket Guide, Abortions in Michigan, Cancer Incidence and Mortality, Michigan Perinatal Effectiveness Index, Infant and Maternal Health Statistics*, most of which are free. Requests for computer printouts should be placed in writing. There is a fee for services.

Department of Public Health, Division of Disease Surveillance, P.O. Box 30035, Lansing, MI 48909; (517) 335-8050. Publications include weekly surveillance reports of communicable diseases. These are available for researchers.

Minnesota

State Health Department, Center for Health Statistics, 717 Delaware St., S.E., P.O. Box 9441, Minneapolis, MN 55410-9441; (612) 623-5353. Publications include the *Annual Report of Health Statistics*. This office will provide you with selected tables from their annual report at no cost. The fees for information transferred to computer diskette would depend upon the complexity of the request.

State Health Department, Acute Epidemiology Department, 717 Delaware St., S.E., Minneapolis, MN 55414; (612) 623-5414. Publications include various statistical reports on all reportable diseases. Computer printouts of summary data can be obtained from the Center for Health Statistics, described above.

Mississippi

Department of Health, Vital Records Division, Statistical Services, P.O. Box 1700, 2423 N. State St., Jackson, MS 39205; (601) 960-7635. Publications include the *1990 Annual Report*. Computer printouts of specific information require a written request. The office will provide photocopies of tables at no charge. If you furnish your own magnetic tape or computer diskette they will transfer information on to it for you.

Be patient. If any phone number is incorrect, call (area code) 555-1212 and request the new listing.

Economics, Demographics and Statistics

Department of Health, Office of Epidemiology, P.O. Box 1700, Jackson, MS 39215; (601) 960-7725. Publications include the *Mississippi Morbidity Report* which includes annual case tabulation. Aggregate data is available via computer printouts and diskettes.

Missouri

Department of Health, Vital Records Department, P.O. Box 570, Jefferson City, MO 65102; (314) 751-6400. Publications include the *Annual Report of Vital Statistics*. Requests for information should be in writing. Printouts of data, such as tables already printed in the annual report, are free of charge. A special computer run of a selected year of data is $43.50, including programming time and shipping and handling. Each additional year of data requested is $21. Information transferred to floppy disk costs $100. Information transferred to magnetic tape costs $250.

Department of Health, Bureau of Communicable Disease Control, 1730 E. Elm St., P.O. Box 570, Jefferson City, MO 65102; (314) 751-6128. Publications include the *1991 Annual Report* and the bi-monthly *Missouri Epidemiologist*. The office will distribute data information included in their Annual Report, free of charge.

Montana

Department of Health, Bureau of Records and Vital Statistics, Helena, MT 59620; (406) 444-2614. Publications include the *Annual Report of Vital Statistics*. Specific data can be provided on computer printout, diskette and magnetic tape. Fees vary according to the complexity of the request and the amount of programming time involved.

Department of Health and Environmental Sciences, Communicable Disease Section of Preventive Health Services Bureau, Cogswell Building, Helena, MT 59620; (406) 444-2737. Computer printouts of aggregate data are available on a limited basis.

Nebraska

Department of Health, Bureau of Vital Statistics, P.O. Box 95007, Lincoln, NE 68509-5007; (402) 471-2871. Publications include the *1990 Annual Report of Vital Statistics*. The Health Data and Statistical Research Department will help with statistical information on the phone as well as provide information on computer printout and diskette. The cost of computer time is $20 per hour. Requests for selected data should be made in writing. Be as specific as possible, including your computer system's requirements as well as diskette size and density.

Department of Health, Division of Disease Control, 301 Centennial Mall South, P.O. Box 95007, Lincoln, NE 68509-5007; (402) 471-2937. Publications include the *Nebraska Morbidity Report*. Computer printouts of data are available on a limited basis.

Nevada

Department of Human Resources, Division of Health, Section of Vital Statistics, 505 East King St., Carson City, NV 89710; (702) 687-4481. Publications include the *1990 Vital Statistics Report*. Computer printouts on selected data are available free of charge.

Department of Human Resources, Office of Disease Control, 505 East King St., Room 304 Carson City, NV 89710; (702) 687-4800. This office provides numerous publications on a variety of communicable diseases. They are not staffed to do selected computer runs.

New Hampshire

Department of Health and Welfare, Bureau of Vital Records and Health Statistics, Health and Human Services Building, 8 Hazen Drive, Concord, NH 03301; (603) 271-4651. Publications include an *Annual Report*. Requests are for specific information are handled on a case by case basis. Fees vary according to the amount of computer programming involved. Computer printouts, diskettes and magnetic tapes are available.

Department of Health and Welfare, Bureau of Communicable Disease Control, Health and Human Services Building, 6 Hazen Dr., Concord, NH 03301-6527; (603) 271-4477. Publications include several bimonthly bulletins. Computer printouts are available of selected data.

New Jersey

Department of Health, Bureau of Vital Statistics, CN 370, Trenton, NJ 08625; (609) 292-4087. Publications include an *Annual Report*. Computer printouts are available for a fee.

Department of Health, Division of Epidemiology and Disease Control, University Office Plaza, CN 369, Trenton, NJ 08625; (609) 588-7500. This office will answer specific questions over the phone, but does not provide computer printouts.

New Mexico

Department of Health and Environment, Office of Vital and Health Statistics, Public Health Division, P.O. Box 26110, Santa Fe, NM 87503-6110; (505) 827-2539. Publications include the *1990 Annual Report*. Detailed requests for information not found in their annual report should be placed in writing. Information can be provided on diskette. Fees vary according to the complexity of the request.

Department of Health, Division of Epidemiology, P.O. Box 26110, Santa Fe, NM 87502; (505) 827-0006. Publications include their monthly *Epidemiology Report*. Requests for information not found in their monthly report should be placed in writing. If you provide them with a blank diskette they will download data on to it for you and omit any identifiers.

New York

Department of Health, Bureau of Biometrics, Empire State Plaza, Concourse Room C144, Albany, NY 12237-0044; (518) 474-3189. Publications include the *1989 Annual Report of Vital Statistics*. Requests for information should be placed in writing. Information that is readily available, such as tables printed in the 1989 Annual Report, are distributed at no cost. A specific data run of information is $191. Some information is available on diskette and magnetic tape. Fees vary, according to the complexity of the request.

Department of Health, Bureau of Communicable Disease Control, Tower Bldg., Room 651, Empire State Plaza, Albany, NY 12237; (518) 474-3187. Publications include the *1998-1989 Annual Report*. The office will run computer searches of aggregate data, depending upon the purpose of the request.

North Carolina

North Carolina Center for Health and Environmental Statistics, P.O. Box 29538, Raleigh, NC 27626-0538; (919) 733-4728. Publications include an *Annual Report* and *1990 Vital Statistics Report*, among others. Information requests should be in writing. If requesting a magnetic tape, be sure to include your system requirements. Computer printouts, diskettes, and magnetic tapes are provided on a limited basis. The charge for magnetic tapes is the cost of the tape and the computer time involved.

North Dakota

Department of Health, Administrative Services Section, 600 E. Blvd., Second Floor, Judicial Wing, State Capitol, Bismarck, ND 58505-0200; (701) 224-2392. Publications include the *1990 Vital Statistics Annual Report*. Computer searches and printouts are provided free of charge.

Department of Health, Division of Disease Control, 600 E. Blvd., State Capitol, Bismarck, ND 58505-0200; (701) 224-2378. This office publishes a variety of publications on communicable diseases. Computer searches and printouts are not provided.

Ohio

Statistical Analysis Unit, Health Policy Data Center, Ohio Department of Health, P.O. Box 118, Columbus, OH 43266-0118, (614) 644-7800. Publications include the *1990 Annual Report of Vital Statistics* which is $9. The office also publishes a *Vital Statistics Summary Fact Sheet*, which is free. Special computer runs are $25 per data year. Extensive programming is extra, and the amount depends upon the complexity of the request. Information is provided via computer printouts.

Oklahoma

Department of Health, Division of Data Management, 1000 N.E. 10th St., P.O. Box 53551, Oklahoma City, OK 73117; (405) 271-4542. Publications include the

Be patient. If any phone number is incorrect, call (area code) 555-1212 and request the new listing.

State Health Statistics

1990 Annual Report of Vital Statistics. Computer searches and printouts are provided, usually free of charge. If you supply your own magnetic tape or diskette, they will transfer information to it for you. Fees vary according to the complexity of the request. All information for specific data runs should be in writing. Be sure to include information describing your computer system's requirements.

Department of Health, Office of General Communicable Diseases-0305, 1000 N.E. 10th St., Oklahoma City, OK 73117-1299; (405) 271-4060. Publications include a monthly *Epidemiological Bulletin* and *Epidemiologic Annual Summary of Communicable Diseases*. Computer searches and printouts are provided free. All requests for information should be submitted in writing at least two weeks before the data is needed. Fees vary according to the complexity of the request.

Oregon

State Health Department, Division of Vital Statistics, P.O. Box 14050, Portland, OR 97214; (503) 731-4108. Publications include: *1990 Oregon Vital Statistics, Oregon Deaths Due to Drugs and Alcohol*, and their newsletter, *Oregon Health Trends*. Information is available on computer printout and diskette. Fees vary according to the complexity of the request.

State Health Department, Division of Epidemiology Control, P.O. Box 116, Portland, OR 97202; (503) 731-4025. Publications include the *Current Disease Summary*, which is published every other week. This office is not equipped to provide printouts of selected data that do not already exist in published form.

Pennsylvania

Department of Health, Health Statistics and Research, State Health Data Center, P.O. Box 90, Harrisburg, PA 17108; (717) 783-2543. Publications include the *County Profile*. Computer searches and printout requests must be made in writing. Costs are $150 for one year of data, $75 for each additional year.

Department of Health, Division of Epidemiology, Health and Welfare Building, 7th and Forster Sts., P.O. Box 90, Harrisburg, PA 17120; (717) 787-3350. Publications include an *Annual Report*. Computer searches and printouts are available, free of charge.

Rhode Island

Department of Health, Vital Records, Room 101, 75 Davis St., Providence, RI 02908; (401) 277-2812. Publications include the *1988 Annual Report of Vital Statistics*. Printouts of information are available depending upon whether or not the data is available on computer. Requests for individualized reports must be made in writing. Fees vary and are based upon the amount of computer programming needed to fulfill a request.

Department of Health, Office of AIDS-Sexually Transmitted Diseases, 3 Cannon Building, Providence, RI 02908; (401) 277-2577. Publications include the bimonthly *Disease Bulletin*. This office does not provide selected data printouts.

South Carolina

Department of Health and Environmental Control, Office of Vital Records and Public Health Statistics, 2600 Bull St., Columbia, SC 29201; (803) 734-4810. Publications include the *South Carolina Vital and Morbidity Report*. Computer searches, printouts, and information on diskette and magnetic tape are provided. Information requests should be in writing, be sure to specify your computer system requirements. Each request is evaluated individually. Although in-house printouts are free, individual requests for selected data require a fee based on the complexity of the request and computer time involved.

Department of Health and Environmental Control, Communicable Disease Control Section, Robert Mills Complex, Box 101106, Columbia, SC 29211; (803) 737-4165. Publications include the *1991 South Carolina Reportable Diseases Report*. Computer searches and printouts of information are provided. Requests for information should be in writing. Information on diskette is provided on a limited basis. Since patient data is confidential, aggregate data is releases without any personal identifiers.

South Dakota

State Health Department, Center for Health Policy and Statistics, 445 E. Capitol St., Pierre, SD 57501-3185; (605) 773-3693. Publications include the *1990 Vital Statistics Annual Report* for $10.50. Once the office receives a written request for

information they will respond with an estimate of computer charges. Information is available on diskette and magnetic tape on a limited basis.

State Health Department, Division of Public Health, 523 E. Capitol Bldg., Pierre, SD 57501; (605) 773-3361. Publications include a monthly newsletter and *1991 South Dakota Vital Statistics and Health Status* report. Computer reports of selected data are provided free of charge. Diskettes and magnetic tapes can be provided on a limited basis. All information requests should be in writing.

Tennessee

Department of Health and Environment, Center for Health Statistics, 419 Cordell Hull Building, Nashville, TN 37247-0360; (615) 741-1954. Publications include an *Annual Report of Vital Statistics*. There is also a series of four publications, *Tennessee's Health*, which gives a detailed health profile based on 1990 statistics. The series can be ordered in its entirety for $30. You can purchase the volumes separately, also. *Picture of the Present* is $5, *Picture of the Present, Part II*, $15, *Guidelines for Growth*, $5, and *Focus on the Future*, is also $5. Printouts are provided free of charge. The office will also download limited data to a magnetic tape or diskette at no charge, but you must supply them with the materials needed. All requests for information should be in writing, and be sure to include you computer system's specifications in your letter.

Texas

Department of Health, Bureau of Vital Statistics, Statistical Services Division, 1100 West 49th St., Austin, TX 78756; (512) 458-7111. Publications include *1990 Texas Vital Statistics*. The office will provide information on computer printouts, diskettes and magnetic tapes. Printouts are available at $150 per hour, diskettes at approximately $25 per tape. Programming charges are $30 per hour. Department of Health, Bureau of Disease Control and Epidemiology, 1100 West 49th St., Austin, TX 78756; (512) 458-7455. Publications include their annual summary, *Reported Morbidity and Mortality in Texas*. Computer searches and printouts are provided at no cost.

Utah

Department of Health, Division of Vital Records, P.O. Box 16700, Salt Lake City, UT 84116; (801) 538-6186. Publications include the *1990 Vital Statistics Report*. Information is provided via computer printouts, diskettes and magnetic tapes. The office does charge for the use of the computer and the statistician's time. Fees vary according to the complexity of the request. If detailed information is required, requests should be made in writing. Be sue to include the specifications needed for diskettes or magnetic tapes.

Department of Health, Bureau of Epidemiology, P.O. Box 16660, Salt Lake City, UT 84116-0660; (801) 538-6191. Publications include the monthly *Epidemiology Newsletter*. The Department of Health is the process of creating a centralized statistics center. This should be in full operation as of Fall, 1992.

Vermont

Department of Health and Human Services, Vital Records Statistics, P.O. Box 70, Burlington, VT 05402; (802) 863-7275. Publications include the *1990 Vital Statistics Report*. Computer searches and printouts are available through this office.

Department of Health and Human Services, Division of Epidemiology and Disease Prevention, P.O. Box 70, Burlington, VT 05402; (802) 863-7240. Publications include the *Vermont Disease Control Bulletin* which is published bi-monthly. Reportable disease totals for the previous year are listed through this publication. The office releases county specific information.

Virginia

Department of Health, Center for Health Statistics, 109 Governors St., 307 Madison Bldg., P.O. Box 1000, Richmond, VA 23208-1000; (804) 786-6206. Publications include the *1990 Annual Report* for $10. Computer searches are available and information is provided via printouts, diskettes and magnetic tapes. The minimum charge for a selected data search is $25. All information requests should be in writing.

Department of Health, Office of Epidemiology, James Madison Building, P.O. Box 2448, 109 Governor St., Richmond, VA 23218; (804) 786-6261. Publications include the monthly *Virginia Epidemiology Bulletin*. The office provides county specific information. No diskettes or magnetic tapes are available.

Be patient. If any phone number is incorrect, call (area code) 555-1212 and request the new listing.

Economics, Demographics and Statistics

Washington

Department of Health, Center for Health Statistics, Office Building #2, Olympia, WA 98504; (206) 753-5936. Publications include the *Annual Summary Report of Statistics for 1990, Selected Pregnancy Reports of Statistics for 1990, Age Adjusted Death Rates for 1986-1989,* and *Minority Health in Washington.* The office provides computer searches for selected data and computer printouts. Information is not provided on diskette. One year of aggregate data on magnetic tape costs $600.

West Virginia

State Health Department, Epidemiology and Health Promotion, Surveillance and Disease Control, State Capitol Complex, Charleston, WV 25305; (304) 558-9100. Publications include the *Annual Report of Vital Statistics* and the *1989 County Health Profile* which is being updated for publication in 1992. The office provides computer printouts of selected data, free of charge. Magnetic tapes and diskettes can be obtained on a limited basis for a fee.

Wisconsin

Department of Health and Social Services, Vital Statistics Department, 1 West Wilson St., Madison, WI 53701; (608) 266-1939. Publications include the *Annual Report of Vital Statistics.* Information requests should be in writing. Computer printouts of selected data are provided at no cost.

Department of Health and Social Services, Community Communicable Disease Section , P.O. Box 309, Madison, WI 53701; (608) 267-9003. Publications include the quarterly *Wisconsin Epidemiologic Bulletin.* Requests for information should be made in writing. Information is available on computer printout, free of cost.

Wyoming

Department of Health and Social Services, Division of Health and Medical Services, Vital Records Services, Hathaway Building, Cheyenne, WY 82002; (307) 777-7591. Publications include the *1990 Vital Statistics Report.* The office does provide computer searches and information is available on printouts, diskettes and magnetic tapes. There is a flat fee of $25 for computer searches. Diskettes and magnetic tapes require additional fees that vary with the complexity of the request.

Department of Health and Social Services, Division of Health and Medical Services, Preventive Medicine, Hathaway Building, Cheyenne, WY 82002; (307) 777-6004. Publications include the *Epidemiologic Bulletin.* Basic information is provided on computer printouts and diskette at no charge. Detailed requests should be in writing.

Be patient. If any phone number is incorrect, call (area code) 555-1212 and request the new listing.

Highway Accident Statistics

* *See also Your Community Chapter*
* *See also Business and Industry Chapter*

A car runs a red light and slams into your brand new Jeep Cherokee, doing $1,500 worth of damage. You shout, they shout, a police officer comes and files an accident report. Guess what? You've just become part of your state's traffic accident database. Not just your name, mind you, but every little detail about the accident will be entered into a computer file and stored for posterity -- or until someone asks the state for the information.

A state accident database is a file made up of reports completed by all law enforcement agencies which investigate accidents. While it might seem that this data should be confidential, it is freely available to engineers, lobbyists, courts, safety organizations, and such citizen-action groups as Mothers Against Drunk Drivers (MADD).

In most instances, the computerized system can be searched and printouts provided by a number of variables.

* The Human Element: driver sex, age, equipment used by age, charged driver violations, pedestrian age.

* Environmental Elements: accident type vs. highway conditions, traffic control vs. accident site, accident type vs. weather, and accident type vs. light conditions.

* Accident Characteristics: county, month of year, time of day, rural/urban road system, hit and run severity, holiday accidents, fatal accidents, alcohol involved, property damage, type of car, accidents caused by animals in the highway.

Our research indicates that state highway accident database searches can be tailored to individual requests within reason. In some states, state employees will perform computer searches and provide printouts--all free of charge. Other states charge up to $150 per hour or require a Freedom of Information Act request.

States that do not provide data searches and printouts are: Arkansas, Colorado, District of Columbia, Georgia, Minnesota, Mississippi, Ohio, West Virginia, Wisconsin.

A statewide accident summary and a breakdown of accident problems by specific areas can be obtained by contacting the state offices listed below.

Highway Department Offices

Alabama
Alabama Highway Department, Accident Identification and Surveillance Section, Traffic Engineering, 1409 Coliseum Blvd., Montgomery, AL 36130; (205) 242-6128. A report, *Alabama Traffic Accident Facts*, is available to individuals at no cost. The accident database can be searched, sorted and a printout produced.

This service is free unless it is to be used for legal purposes. In those instances there is a $100 fee per computer run.

Alaska
Department of Transportation and Public Facilities, 3132 Channel Drive, Juneau, AK 99801-7908; (907) 465-2777. Publications include a free annual report. Accident database printouts are provided. If you supply your own computer disks the department will transfer data on to them at no additional charge.

Arizona
Arizona Department of Transportation, Traffic Records Unit, 1739 W. Jackson Ave., Phoenix, AZ 85007; (602) 255-7724. Publications include the *Arizona Traffic Accident Summary*. The accident database can be searched, sorted and a printout provided at no charge.

Arkansas
Arkansas State Highway and Transportation Division, P.O. Box 2261, Little Rock, AR 72203; (501) 569-2564. Publications include an annual *State Accident Data Report*. Information from accident databases is not released on a routine basis.

California
Department of Transportation, Caltrans, 1120 N. St., P.O. Box 1499, Room 4123, Sacramento, CA 95807; (916) 654-2852. Publications include the annual *Accident Data on California Highways Report*. The accident database can be searched, sorted and a printout provided on a cost recovery basis.

Colorado
Department of Highways, Staff Traffic Division, 4201 E. Arkansas Ave., Room 172, Denver, CO 80222; (303) 757-9271. This department's publications include: *Accidents by County*, and *Accidents by City*. Both are free. A report entitled, *Accidents by Rates*, is $5. The Department of Revenue issues standard summaries of motor vehicle reports for a nominal fee. Information from accident databases is not released as a general policy.

Connecticut
Department of Transportation, Planning Inventory and Data, Bureau of Planning, 2175 Berlin Turnpike, Newington, CT 06111; (203) 665-0072. The accident database can be searched, sorted, and a printout provided at no cost to state and non-profit agencies. Others are charged a fee of $.50 per page. Requests should be in writing. Publications include a *Statewide Accident Summary* and *1989 Connecticut Accidents Facts Booklet* which are $5.30 each. Traffic accident surveillance reports are available on microfiche. There is a $.50 per page copying fee.

Delaware
State Police Headquarters, Delaware State Traffic Section, P.O. 321, Dover, DE 19901; (302) 739-4865. Publications include monthly and annual reports. The database can be searched, sorted, and a printout provided at no cost.

District of Columbia
Traffic Analysis, Traffic Enforcement Branch, 501 New York Ave., NW, Washington, DC 20001; (202) 727-6533. No listings are provided on a regular basis. General questions are answered over the telephone.

Florida
Department of Highway Safety and Motor Vehicles, Office of Management and Planning, Statistics Division, 2900 Appalachia Parkway, Room A-430, Tallahassee, FL 32399; (904) 488-3666. Publications include the *Florida Traffic Accident Facts Report* which is free upon request. The accident database can be searched, sorted, and a printout provided, usually free of charge. If the department must perform a mainframe computer search there is an additional charge.

Be patient. If any phone number is incorrect, call (area code) 555-1212 and request the new listing.

Economics, Demographics and Statistics

Georgia

Department of Public Safety, Accident Reporting Section, P.O. Box 1456, Atlanta, GA 30371; (404) 624-7660. Standard accident summaries and an annual report is free upon request. Copies of individual accident reports are also provided. The agency does not routinely provide computer printouts of accident data.

Hawaii

Department of Transportation, Traffic Branch, 869 Punchbowl Street, Room 120, Honolulu, HI 96813; (808) 587-2171. Publications include *Major Traffic Accidents in Hawaii* which is available for $30. The accident database has information up to 1990. Printouts are available. Charges vary according to the complexity of the request.

Idaho

Office of Highway Safety, Idaho Transportation Department, P.O. Box 7129, Boise, ID 83707-1129; (208) 334-8100. Publications include the *Idaho Traffic Accident Analysis*, which is free upon request. The accident database can be searched, sorted and a printout provided. A broad search of the data base is usually under $10, but fees vary depending upon the complexity of the request. A specific accident report is $4 plus tax and shipping.

Illinois

Department of Transportation, Division on Traffic Safety, 3215 Executive Park Dr., Springfield, IL 62764; (217) 782-2575. Publications include an *Accident Facts Report*. The accident database can be searched, sorted and a printout provided at no cost.

Indiana

State Police Data Section, Indianapolis Government Center North, 100 N. Senate Ave., Indianapolis, IN 46204; (317) 232-8289. Publications include monthly and annual summaries of motor vehicle traffic accidents. The accident database can be searched, sorted and a printout provided on a cost recovery basis. A written request is required.

Iowa

Iowa Department of Transportation, Driver Services, Lucas State Office Building, Des Moines, IA 50319; (515) 237-3054. Publications include the *Accident Facts Report*. The accident database can be searched, sorted and a printout provided for a cost recovery fee.

Kansas

Department of Transportation, Office of Traffic Safety, 217 S.E. 4th St., 2nd Floor, Thatcher Building, Topeka, KS 66603-3504; (913) 296-3756. Publications include the *Annual Summary of Accident Statistics*, *Kansas Traffic Accident Facts*, and an *Age, Alcohol and Traffic Accidents Report*. The accident database can be searched, sorted and a printout provided at no cost.

Kentucky

State Police, Records Center, 1250 Louisville Road, Frankfort, KY 40601; (502) 227-8717. Publications include an *Accident Facts Book*. The accident database can be searched for records dating back to 1985, sorted, and a printout provided. A written request is required and there is a charge of $2 for the first 10 pages and $.10 for every following page.

Louisiana

Department of Public Safety and Corrections, Highway Safety Commission, P.O. Box 66336, 265 S. Foster Dr., Baton Rouge, LA 70896; (504) 925-6991. This department publishes an annual *Louisiana Traffic Accident Report* which is free upon request. The accident database can be searched, sorted and a printout provided upon written request. Information not found in their annual report may require an additional charge.

Maine

Department of Highway Safety, 36 Hospital St., Augusta, ME 04333; (207) 624-8756. The accident database can be searched, sorted and a printout provided at no cost upon request.

Maryland

Ron Lips, State Highway Administration, Traffic Safety, 7491 Connelly Dr., Hannover, MD 21076; (410) 787-5849. The staff will supply data tailored to individual needs within reasonable requests. There is normally no charge, but fees are based on the amount of data requested and staff time involved.

Massachusetts

Registry of Motor Vehicles, Accident Records, 100 Nashua St., Boston, MA 02114; (617) 727-3730. The accident database can be searched, sorted, and a printout provided in most cases. There is a fee for the data retrieval service. Requests should be in writing. Requests for an entire year's worth of data can be very expensive. A magnetic tape of 1991 accident report data costs $7,640.

Michigan

Michigan State Police, Office of Highway Safety Planning, 300 S. Washington Square, Suite 300, Lansing, MI 48913; (517) 334-5198. Publications include the annual *Traffic Accident Facts Book*. The department does provide computer printouts of selected data. Requests should be made in writing. Easily accessible information is provided at no cost. Detailed searches may require an additional fee.

Minnesota

Department of Public Safety, Office of Traffic Safety, Room 207, Transportation Bldg., St. Paul, MN 55155; (612) 296-6953. Publications include the *1991 Crash Facts Report*. This department does not provide accident database searches.

Mississippi

Department of Public Safety, Statistical Bureau, P.O. Box 958, Jackson, MS 39205; (601) 987-1212. This department does not provide accident database searches. General questions are handled over the phone.

Missouri

State Highway Patrol, Traffic Division, P.O. Box 568, Jefferson City, MO 65102; (314) 751-3313. Publications include the annual *Missouri Traffic Crashes Report*. The accident database can be searched, sorted and a printout provided upon special request. Fees vary and are based on a cost recovery basis.

Montana

Montana Highway Patrol, Records Bureau, 303 N. Roberts, Helena, MT 59601; (406) 444-3278. Publications include their free *Annual Statistical Report*. The accident database can be searched, sorted and a printout provided at no cost.

Nebraska

Department of Roads, Highway Safety Bureau, Accident Records, P.O. Box 94669, Lincoln, NE 68509; (402) 479-4645. Publications include the annual *Traffic Accident Facts Report*. The accident database can be searched, sorted and a printout provided, usually at no cost.

Nevada

Department of Transportation, Safety Engineering, 1263 S. Stewart St., Carson City, NV 89712; (702) 687-3468. Publications include the annual *Nevada Traffic Accidents Report*. The accident database can be searched, sorted and a printout provided. There is a fee of $35 per hour for staff computer time unless the requestor is a non-profit or government agency.

New Hampshire

Department of Safety, Data Processing Division, 10 Hazen Drive, Concord, NH 03305; (603) 271-2554. A *Fatal Accident Summary* is free to the public. The accident database can be searched, sorted and a printout provided for a fee of $.50 per page. Thirty-five accidents are listed per page.

New Jersey

Department of Law and Public Safety, Division of Highway Traffic Safety, Quackerbridge Drive, Building 5, 3rd Floor, CN 048, Trenton, NJ 08625; (609) 588-3750. Publications include a *Fatal Statistics Report* and *Annual Report*. Both are free to the public. The accident database can be searched, sorted and a printout provided. Requests should be made in writing. There may be a fee depending upon the amount of computer programming time involved.

New Mexico

Highway and Transportation Department, Traffic Safety Bureau, P.O. Box 1149, Santa Fe, NM 87502; (505) 827-0427. Publications include the annual *New Mexico Traffic and Crash Data Report*. The accident database can be searched, sorted and a printout provided at no cost. Requests for data not found in the annual report should be placed in writing.

New York

State Department of Motor Vehicles, Accident Safety Division, Empire State Plaza, Albany, NY 12228; (518) 474-0679. Publications include an annual *Summary of Motor Vehicle Accidents Report*. The accident database can be

Be patient. If any phone number is incorrect, call (area code) 555-1212 and request the new listing.

Highway Accident Statistics

searched, sorted and a printout provided. Fees vary according to the complexity of the request.

North Carolina

Division of Motor Vehicles, Collision Reports, 1100 New Bern Ave., Raleigh, NC 27697; (919) 733-7250. Publications include a free report entitled *Traffic Accident Facts*. The accident database can be searched, sorted and a printout provided for a fee from: Highway Safety Research Center, 13040 1/2 E. Franklin St., CB 3430, UNC Campus, Chapel Hill, NC 27599; (919) 962-2202.

North Dakota

State Highway Department, Drivers License and Traffic Safety Division, Accident Records Section, 608 East Boulevard Ave., Bismarck, ND 58505; (701) 224-4352. Publications include the *Annual Accident Report*. The accident database can be searched, sorted and a printout provided. There is a $7 minimum charge.

Ohio

Department of Highway Safety, Public Information Office, 240 Parsons Ave. Columbus, OH 43266; (614) 466-2550. The accident database can be searched, sorted and a printout provided to other government agencies. At the present time, individual requests are not handled on a regular basis. A 70-page publication entitled *Crash Facts Book* is available that is updated annually.

Oklahoma

Department of Public Safety, Accident Records Division, Box 11415, Oklahoma City, OK 73136; (405) 425-2192. Publications include the annual *Oklahoma Traffic Accident Facts Report*, which is free. Computer printouts are available upon written request. Fees vary according to the complexity of the data search.

Oregon

Department of Transportation, Accident Data Division, 2001 Front St., N.E. Salem St. (503) 378-2309. Publications include an *Oregon Accident Rate Table* which is $20. The accident database can be searched, sorted and a printout provided at no cost.

Pennsylvania

Department of Transportation, Center for Highway Safety, Safety Management, Room 203, Transportation and Safety Building, Harrisburg, PA 17120; (717) 787-3393. This office publishes a free report entitled *Traffic Accident Facts and Statistics*. The accident database can be searched, sorted and a printout provided. Fees vary according to the scope of the request. All requests should be made in writing.

Rhode Island

Department of Transportation, Planning Section, Two Capitol Hill, Room 372, Providence, RI 02903; (401) 277-2694. Standard tables of accident reports are published yearly and are available upon request. The accident database can be searched, sorted and a printout provided upon special, written request. Individuals must first complete an open records request. Costs vary according to the actual research and computer time involved.

South Carolina

Department of Highways, Safety Office, P.O. Box 191, Columbia, SC 29202; (803) 737-1162. Publications include the *South Carolina Traffic Accidents Report* which is $3. The accident database can be searched, sorted and a printout provided. The minimum charge is $43.75.

South Dakota

Department of Transportation, Accident Records, 118 W. Capitol, Pierre, SD 57501; (605) 773-3868. Publications include an annual *South Dakota Accident Facts Book*. Individuals can receive copies of individual accident reports for $4, each. Individual computer runs of selected data are provided generally at no cost.

Tennessee

Department of Safety, 1150 Foster Ave., Nashville, TN 37249-1000; (615) 251-5220. Publications include a *1987 Accident Facts Book* and *1991 Annual Report*. The accident database can be searched, sorted and a printout provided. There is a minimum charge of $500.

Texas

Department of Public Safety, Statistical Services, Box 15999, Austin, TX 78761-1599; (512) 465-2000. Publications include the *Motor Vehicle Traffic Accidents Report*, and a report entitled *A Look at DWI... Accidents, Victims, Arrests*. The accident database can be searched, sorted and a printout provided for a cost recovery fee.

Utah

Department of Transportation, Division of Traffic Safety, 4501 South, 2700 West, Salt Lake City, UT 84119; (801) 965-4284. Publications include *Utah Annual Safety Report*. The accident database can be searched and printouts provided. Requests should be in writing and individuals must first complete a request form. Fees for computer printouts vary. Individuals may receive data within the last five years at a cost of $10 per year. Printouts of older data cost $15 per year.

Vermont

Agency for Transportation, Planning Division, 133 State St., Montpelier, VT 05633. (802) 828-3440. Publications include an annual report. The accident database can be searched, sorted and printouts provided. Costs for individual searches vary depending upon the scope of the request. Requests should be made in writing to the attention of Jeff Squires.

Virginia

Department of Transportation, Traffic Engineering, 1401 E. Broad St., Richmond, VA 23219; (804) 786-2969. Publications include an *Accident Summary Book*. The accident database can be searched, sorted and printouts provided upon special, written request. There may be a charge depending upon the complexity of the information requested.

Washington

Department of Transportation, Public Transportation Plan, Accident Data, 310 Maple Park Ave., S.E., Olympia, WA 98504-7300; (206) 753-6182. Publications include the *Washington State Department of Transportation Highway Traffic Report*. The accident database can be searched, sorted and a printout provided. Normally, there is a charge of $20 to $25 per hour. Most requests usually require only one hour of staff time.

West Virginia

Department of Highways, Traffic Engineering Division, 1700 Kanawah Blvd., Capitol Complex, Building 5, Room A550, Charleston, WV 25305; (304) 558-3063. Publications include the *West Virginia Accident Data Report* which is free. The accident database is not available to the general public.

Wisconsin

Department of Transportation, Bureau of Traffic Accidents, P.O. Box 7917, Madison, WI 53707; (608) 266-8753. Publications include a report entitled *Wisconsin Traffic Crash Facts* which is free to the public. Computer printouts not normally available.

Wyoming

Highway Safety Branch, Wyoming Highway Department, P.O. Box 1708, Cheyenne, WY 82002; (307) 777-7296. Publications include the *Wyoming Comprehensive Report on Traffic Accidents*. The accident database can be searched and printouts provided at no cost.

Be patient. If any phone number is incorrect, call (area code) 555-1212 and request the new listing.

Economics, Demographics and Statistics

State Data Centers

Approximately 1,300 organizations nationwide receive data from the U.S. Bureau of the Census and in turn disseminate the information to the public free of charge or on a cost recovery basis. These organizations are called state data centers and serve as ideal information sources for both local and national markets. The centers listed in this report are the major offices for each state. If you are looking for national markets, start with a center in your state. If you are searching for local market data, contact the center located in the relevant area.

Demographics and Target Market Identification

State data center offices are most frequently used for obtaining information on target markets. For instance, the Army and Navy used such services to identify which areas are populated with large numbers of teenagers in order to open recruiting offices and focus their advertising campaign. Avon door-to-door sales reps used state data center generated demographic maps to identify homes with highest potential. L.L. Bean relied on a center to determine large Hispanic populations for a special promotion of outdoor recreational products. These offices could provide current data including:

- The age distribution within a given county;
- Moving patterns for particular geographical areas;
- The number of wells and mobile homes in 85 counties;
- How many gravel pits in the state of Montana;
- Counties with the highest rate of illegitimate children;
- Analysis of why certain stores in an auto parts chain are doing better than others;
- Demographic profile of a person in need of child care;
- The top 25 markets by zip code;
- The number of male secretaries in a dozen contiguous counties.

Forecasting Future Markets

The biggest opportunities often lie in knowing the future of a market. Many of the state data centers have developed specific software for analyzing Census and other data to project growth of specific markets. Here is a sampling of what some centers can do:

- Population projections for every three years to the year 2020 (done by California center);
- State population changes by the year 2000;
- What year the white population will not be in the majority;
- The number of teenagers by the next century;
- Series of economic indicators for plotting future economic health in state (Oklahoma center provides such data).

Site Location

Another major area of interest is in providing information to companies considering relocating into a state. Because most states are aggressively trying to attract business, numerous customized services receive a high priority. Local centers can provide information such as the number of fast food restaurants in the area and the best location for another one. And some states, like Arkansas, have special site evaluation software which can manipulate Census data to show the demographic characteristics for market radiuses which are 2, 5 or 10 miles from a given site. Oklahoma and other states have free data sheets covering every community in their state which are loaded with specifics for choosing a location. Their reports contain data on:

- Distance from major cities
- Population: past and future
- Climate
- Municipal services
- Utilities
- Labor market analysis
- List of major manufacturers
- List of major employers
- Transportation
- Commercial services
- Major freight lines and truck terminals
- Educational facilities
- Financial institutions
- Tax structure
- Housing and churches
- Medical facilities
- Retail business in city
- Industrial financial assistance
- Water analysis report
- Recreational facilities
- Wholesale business in city
- Items deserving special consideration

Professional and Personal Relocation

The same services that are intended to help businesses relocate also can be useful to individuals and professionals. For example, if you are looking for a place to start an orthodontics practice, a local data center could determine which counties and cities have the most affluent families with young people -- a prime market for braces. Also, if you get an offer for a new job in another city, obtaining a data sheet on the local community like the one described above provides insight into the types of housing, schools, churches, and recreational facilities available.

Business Proposals Plus Loan and Grant Applications

If you are looking for money for either a grant, a loan or even

Be patient. If any phone number is incorrect, call (area code) 555-1212 and request the new listing.

venture money, data centers can provide the information needed for proposal writing. Grantors must have information such as what percent of people live below poverty line, and banks want to know current business patterns for a new enterprise when seeking a loan. These sorts of data can be obtained easily from these centers.

Level of Detail

Because the data centers use information from other sources in addition to the Bureau of Census, the level of detail will vary according to subject area as well as the state and office contacted. Much of the Census data can be provided at the state, county, city, census tract and block group level (which is normally even smaller than a zip code). Data according to zip code are also available for many categories of information. All states also have the public use micro data sample, which do not contain aggregate data, but actual questionnaire information filled out by respondents. They can be manipulated into any kind of special detail required.

Custom Work, Workshops and Other Services

A lot of work performed by the data centers is customized in nature. The organizations collect data from other federal and state sources to enhance their Census information. Many have arrangements with other state data centers to send any computer file needed to do special analysis. This is how local centers can provide national information or inter-market comparisons. Some centers will even perform custom census projects for clients, which means raw data collection for market research.

Free and low cost workshops about services and information opportunities are sponsored in some areas for potential users. These workshops are important at the local level because in the past they were readily available from the Bureau of Census, but recent budget cuts have reduced their frequency and increased their price. Because of the centers' familiarity of census data, these offices are excellent starting places for almost any information search.

Formats

Data centers offer some of the most sophisticated formats you are likely to find from public organizations. They all provide computer tapes, off-the-shelf reports, custom reports from computer analysis, and quick answers over the telephone. Most are also set up to provide custom analysis and/or raw data on computer diskettes, and some -- like Ohio -- have developed a PC database from which they can generate standard reports and download onto diskettes. Colorado and other states are beginning to make data accessible online.

Prices

Although the U.S. government provides most of the data to these centers, the feds do not interfere with fee schedules. Most offices try to give out information free, but some charge on a

cost recovery basis. Some states do not charge for the first so many pages of a report but charge a nominal fee for additional pages. Some say they have a minimum fee of $20 for customized computer runs. It is interesting that these centers sell you computerized data cheaper than the U.S. Bureau of the Census in Washington. In contrast to the Bureau's fee of $140, Illinois and Georgia only charge $50 for a data tape file, and in Florida, the cost is $15 for a file.

In the dozens of interviews we conducted with these centers about the complicated market research reports they have provided to clients, the highest figure we found they ever charged was $2,000. That amount of money would buy virtually nothing from most marketing consultants.

State Data Centers

Below is a roster of data centers in all 50 states as well as the District of Columbia, Puerto Rico and Virgin Islands. Some of these Census Bureau information providers are based in state departments and agencies, universities, business colleges, and libraries. Each center listed below includes the name and phone number of the data expert.

Alabama

Center for Business and Economic Research, University of Alabama, P.O. Box 870221, Tuscaloosa, AL 34587-0221, Ms. Annette Walters, (205) 348-2953.

Alabama Department of Economic and Community Affairs, Office of State Planning, P.O. Box 250347, 3465 Norman Bridge Road, Montgomery, AL 36125-0347, Mr. Parker Collins, (205) 284-8630.

Alabama Public Library Service, 6030 Monticello Drive, Montgomery, AL 36130, Ms. Hilda Dent, (205) 277-7330.

Alaska

Alaska State Data Center, Research and Analysis, Department of Labor, P.O. Box 25504, Juneau, AK 99802-5504, Ms. Kathryn Lizik, (907) 465-4500.

Office of Management and Budget, Division of Policy, Pouch AD, Juneau, AK 99811, Mr. Jack Kreinheder, (907) 465-3568.

Department of Education, Division of Libraries and Museums, Alaska State Library, Pouch G, Juneau, AK 99811, Ms. Catherine Gruenberg, (907) 465-2927.

Department of Community and Regional Affairs, Division of Municipal and Regional Assistance, P.O. Box BH, Juneau, AK 99811, Ms. Laura Walters, (907) 465-4756.

Institute for Social and Economic Research, University of Alaska, 3211 Providence Drive, Anchorage, AK 99508, Mr. Jim Kerr, (907) 786-7710.

Arizona

Arizona Department of Economic Security, Mail Code 045Z, 1789 West Jefferson Street, Phoenix, AZ 85007, Ms. Betty Jeffries, (602) 255-5984.

Center for Business Research, College of Business Administration, Arizona State University, Tempe, AZ 85287, Mr. Tom Rex, (602) 965-3961.

College of Business Administration, Northern Arizona University, Box 15066, Flagstaff, AZ 86011, Dr. Joseph Walka, (602) 523-3657.

Federal Documents Section, Department of Library, Archives, and Public Records, 1700 West Washington, 2nd Floor, Phoenix, AZ 85007, Ms. Janet Fisher, (602) 621-4121.

Division of Economic and Business Research, College of Business and Public Administration, University of Arizona, Tucson, AZ 85721, Ms. Holly Penix, (602) 621-2155.

Be patient. If any phone number is incorrect, call (area code) 555-1212 and request the new listing.

Economics, Demographics and Statistics

Arkansas

State Data Center, University of Arkansas-Little Rock, 2801 South University, Little Rock, AR 72204, Ms. Sarah Breshears, (501) 569-8530.

Arkansas State Library, 1 Capitol Mall, Little Rock, AR 72201, Ms. Mary Honeycutt, (501) 682-2864.

Research and Analysis Section, Arkansas Employment Security Division, P.O. Box 2981, Little Rock, AR 72203, Mr. Coy Cozart, (501) 682-3159.

California

State Census Data Center, Department of Finance, 915 L Street, Sacramento, CA 95814, Ms. Linda Gage, Director, (916) 322-4651, Mr. Richard Lovelady, (916) 323-2201.

Sacramento Area COG, 106 K Street, Suite 200, Sacramento, CA 95814, Mr. Bob Faseler, (916) 441-5930.

Association of Bay Area Governments, Metro Center, 8th and Oak Streets, P.O. Box 2050, Oakland, CA 94604-2050, Ms. Patricia Perry, (415) 464-7937.

Southern California Association of Governments, 818 West 7th Street, 12th Floor, Los Angeles, CA 90017, Mr. Javier Minjares, (213) 236-1800.

San Diego Association of Governments, First Federal Plaza, 401 B Street, Suite 800, San Diego, CA 92101, Ms. Karen Lamphere, (619) 236-5353.

State Data Center Program, University of California-Berkeley, 2538 Channing Way, Berkeley, CA 94720, Ms. Ilona Einowski/Fred Gey, (415) 642-6571.

Association of Monterey Bay Area Governments, 977B Pacific Street, P.O. Box 190, Monterey, CA 93942, Mr. Steve Williams, (408) 373-6116.

Colorado

Division of Local Government, Colorado Department of Local Affairs, 1313 Sherman Street, Room 521, Denver, CO 80203, Mr. Reid Reynolds/Ms. Rebecca Picasso, (303) 866-2156.

Business Research Division, Graduate School of Business Administration, University of Colorado-Boulder, Boulder, CO 80309, Mr. Richard Wobbekind, (303) 492-8227.

Natural Resources and Economics, Department of Agriculture, Colorado State University, Fort Collins, CO 80523, Ms. Sue Anderson, (303) 491-5706.

Documents Department, The Libraries, Colorado State University, Fort Collins, CO 80523, Ms. Suzanne Taylor, (303) 491-1880.

Connecticut

Comprehensive Planning Division, Connecticut Office of Policy and Management, 80 Washington Street, Hartford, CT 06106-4459, Mr. Theron Schnure, (203) 566-8285.

Government Documents, Connecticut State Library, 231 Capitol Avenue, Hartford, CT 06106, Mr. Albert Palko, (203) 566-4971.

Connecticut Department of Economic Development, 865 Brook Street, Rocky Hill, CT 06067-3405, Mr. Jeff Blodgett, (203) 258-4239.

Employment Security Division, Connecticut Department of Labor, 200 Folly Brook Boulevard, Wethersfield, CT 06109, Mr. Richard Vannuccini, (203) 566-2120.

Delaware

Delaware Development Office, 99 Kings Highway, P.O. Box 1401, Dover, DE 19903, Ms. Judy McKinney-Cherry, (302) 739-4271.

College of Urban Affairs and Public Policy, University of Delaware, Graham Hall, Room 286, Academy Street, Newark, DE 19716, Mr. Ed Ratledge, (302) 451-8406.

District of Columbia

Data Services Division, Mayor's Office of Planning, Room 570, Presidential Bldg., 415 12th Street, N.W., Washington, DC 20004, Mr. Gan Ahuja, (202) 727-6533.

Metropolitan Washington Council of Governments, 777 North Capitol Street, Suite 300, Washington, DC 20006, Mr. Robert Griffith/Ms. Jenean Johanningmeier, (202) 962-3200.

Florida

Florida State Data Center, Executive Office of the Governor, Office of Planning and Budgeting, The Capitol, Tallahassee, FL 32399-0001, Mr. Steve Kimble, (904) 487-2814.

Center for the Study of Population, Institute for Social Research, 654 Bellemy Building, Florida State University, Tallahassee, FL 32306-4063, Dr. Ike Eberstein, (904) 644-1762.

State Library of Florida, R.A. Gray Building, Tallahassee, FL 32399-0250, Ms. Linda Close, (904) 487-2651.

Bureau of Economic Analysis, Florida Department of Commerce, 107 East Gaines Street, 315 Collins Building, Tallahassee, FL 32399-2000, Ms. Sally Ramsey, (904) 487-2568.

Georgia

Division of Demographic and Statistical Services, Georgia Office of Planning and Budget, 254 Washington Street, S.W., Room 640, Atlanta, GA 30334, Ms. Marty Sik, (404) 656-0911.

Documents Librarian, Georgia State University, University Plaza, Atlanta, GA 30303, Ms. Gayle Christian, (404) 651-2185.

Robert W. Woodruff Library for Advanced Studies, Emory University, Atlanta, GA 30322, Ms. Elizabeth McBride, (404) 727-6880.

Main Library, University of Georgia, Athens, GA 30602, Ms. Susan C. Field, (404) 542-0664.

Georgia Department of Community Affairs, Office of Coordinated Planning, 100 Peachtree Street, N.E. #1200, Atlanta, GA 30303, Mr. Phil Thiel, (404) 656-5526.

Documents Librarian, State Data Center Program, Albany State College, 504 College Drive, Albany, GA 31705, Ms. Juanita Miller, (912) 430-4799.

Documents Librarian, State Data Center Program, Georgia Southern College, Statesboro, GA 30460, Ms. Lynn Walshak, (912) 681-5117.

State Data Center Program, Mercer University Law Library, Mercer University, Macon, GA 31207, Mr. Ismael Gullon, (912) 752-2668.

Data Services, University of Georgia Libraries, 6th Floor, Athens, GA 30602, Ms. Hortense Bates, (404) 542-0727.

Price Gilbert Memorial Library, Georgia Institute of Technology, Atlanta, GA 30332, Mr. Richard Leacy, (404) 894-4519.

Guam

Guam Department of Commerce, 590 South Marine Drive, Suite 601, 6th Floor GITC Building, Tamuning, Guam 96911, Mr. Peter R. Barcinas, (671) 646-5841.

Hawaii

Hawaii State Data Center, Department of Business and Economic Development, Kamamalau Building, Room 602A, 220 S. King Street, Suite 400, Honolulu, HI 96813, Mailing Address: P.O. Box 2359, Honolulu, HI 96804, Mr. Robert Schmitt, State Statistician/Ms. Emogene Estores, (808) 586-2482.

Information and Communication Services Division, State Department of Budget and Finance, Kalanimoku Building, 1151 Punchbowl Street, Honolulu, HI 96813, Ms. Joy Toyama, (808) 548-6180.

Idaho

Idaho Department of Commerce, 700 West State Street, Boise, ID 83720, Mr. Alan Porter, (208) 334-2470.

Institutional Research, Room 319, Business Building, Boise State University, Boise, ID 83725, Mr. Don Canning, (208) 385-1613.

The Idaho State Library, 325 West State Street, Boise, ID 83702, Ms. Stephanie Nichols, (208) 334-2150.

Be patient. If any phone number is incorrect, call (area code) 555-1212 and request the new listing.

State Data Centers

Center for Business Research and Services, Campus Box 8450, Idaho State University, Pocatello, ID 83209, Dr. Paul Zelus, (208) 236-2304.

Illinois

Division of Planning and Financial Analysis, Illinois Bureau of the Budget, William Stratton Building, Room 605, Springfield, IL 62706, Ms. Suzanne Ebetsch, (217) 782-1381.

Census and Data Users Services, Department of Sociology, Anthropology and Social Work, Illinois State University, 604 South Main Street, Normal, IL 61761-6901, Dr. Roy Treadway, (309) 438-5946.

Center for Governmental Studies, Northern Illinois University, Social Science Research Bldg., DeKalb, IL 60115, Ms. Ruth Anne Tobias, (815) 753-1901, ext 221.

Regional Research and Development Service, Southern Illinois University at Edwardsville, Box 1456, Edwardsville, IL 62026-1456, Mr. Charles Kofron, (618) 692-3500.

Chicago Area Geographic Information Study, Room 2102, Building BSB, P.O. Box 4348, University of Illinois at Chicago, Chicago, IL 60680, Mr. Jim Bash, (312) 996-6367.

Northeastern Illinois Planning Commission, 400 West Madison Street, Chicago, IL 60606-2642, Max Dieber/Mary Cele Smith, (312) 454-0400.

Indiana

Indiana State Library, Indiana Data Center, 140 North Senat Avenue, Indianapolis, IN 46204, Mr. Ray Ewick, Director/Ms. Roberta Eads, (317) 232-3733.

Indiana Business Research Center, Indiana University, 10th and Fee Lane, Bloomington, IN 47405, Dr. Morton Marcus, (812) 335-5507.

Indiana Business Research Center, P.O. Box 647, 801 West Michigan, B.S. 4013, Indianapolis, IN 46202-5151, Ms. Carol Rogers, (317) 274-2205.

Research Division, Indiana Department of Commerce, 1 North Capitol, Suite 700, Indianapolis, IN 46204, Mr. Robert Lain, (317) 232-8959.

Iowa

Research Section, Iowa Department of Economic Development, 200 E. Grand Avenue, Des Moines, IA 50309, (515) 281-3005.

State Library of Iowa, East 12th and Grand, Des Moines, IA 50319, Ms. Beth Henning, (515) 281-4350.

Center for Social and Behavioral Research, University of Northern Iowa, Cedar Falls, IA 50614, Dr. Robert Kramer, (319) 273-2105.

Census Services, Iowa State University, 320 East Hall, Ames, IA 50011, Dr. Willis Goudy, (515) 294-8337.

Iowa Social Science Institute, University of Iowa, 345 Shaeffer Hall, Iowa City, IA 52242, Mr. Brian Dalziel, (319) 335-2371.

Census Data Center, Department of Education, Grimes State Office Building, Des Moines, IA 50319, Mr. Steve Boal, (515) 281-4730.

Kansas

State Library, Room 343-N, State Capitol Building, Topeka, KS 66612, Mr. Marc Galbraith, (913) 296-3296.

Division of the Budget, Room 152-E, State Capitol Building, Topeka, KS 66612, Ms. Teresa Floerchinger, (913) 296-2436.

Institute for Public Policy and Business Research, 607 Blake Hall, The University of Kansas, Lawrence, KS 66045-2960, Ms. Thelma Helyar, (913) 864-3123.

Center for Economic Development and Business Research, Box 48, Wichita State University, Wichita, KS 67208, Ms. Janet Nickel, (316) 689-3225.

Population and Resources Laboratory, Department of Sociology, Kansas State University, Manhattan, KS 66506, Dr. Jan L. Flora, (913) 532-5984.

Kentucky

Urban Studies Center, College of Urban and Public Affairs, University of Louisville, Louisville, KY 40292, Mr. Ron Crouchs, (502) 588-7990.

Office of Policy and Management, State of Kentucky, Capitol Annex, Frankfort, KY 40601, Mr. Steve Rowland, (502) 564-7300.

State Library Division, Department for Libraries and Archives, 300 Coffeetree Road, P.O. Box 537, Frankfort, KY 40601, Ms. Brenda Fuller, (502) 875-7000.

Louisiana

Office of Planning and Budget, Division of Administration, P.O. Box 94095, Baton Rouge, LA 70804, Ms. Karen Paterson, (504) 342-7410.

Division of Business and Economic Research, University of New Orleans, Lake Front, New Orleans, LA 70122, Mr. Vincent Maruggi, (504) 286-6248.

Division of Business Research, Louisiana Tech University, P.O. Box 10318, Ruston, LA 71272, Dr. Edward O'Boyle, (318) 257-3701.

Reference Department, Louisiana State Library, P.O. Box 131, Baton Rouge, LA 70821, Mrs. Blanche Cretini, (504) 342-4918.

Center for Life Cycle and Population Studies, Department of Sociology, Room 126, Stubbs Hall, Louisiana State University, Baton Rouge, LA 70803, Mr. Pete McCool, Director, (504) 388-5359.

Center for Business and Economic Research, Northeast Louisiana University, Monroe, LA 71209, Dr. Jerry Wall, (318) 342-1215.

Maine

Division of Economic Analysis and Research, Maine Department of Labor, 20 Union Street, Augusta, ME 04330, Mr. Raynold Fongemie, Director, Ms. Jean Martin, (207) 289-2271.

Maine State Library, State House Station 64, Augusta, ME 04333, Mr. Gary Nichols, (207) 289-5600.

Maryland

Maryland Department of State Planning, 301 West Preston Street, Baltimore, MD 21201, Mr. Michel Lettre/Mr. Robert Dadd, (301) 225-4450.

Computer Science Center, University of Maryland, College Park, MD 20742, Mr. John McNary, (301) 405-3037.

Government Reference Service, Pratt Library, 400 Cathedral Street, Baltimore, MD 21201, Mr. Wesley Wilson, (301) 396-5468.

Small Business Development Center, 217 E. Redwood Street, 9th Floor, Baltimore, MD 21202, Mr. Eliot Rittenhouse, (301) 333-6995.

Massachusetts

Massachusetts Institute for Social and Economic Research, 128 Thompson Hall, University of Massachusetts, Amherst, MA 01003, Dr. Steve Coelen, Director, (413) 545-3460, Ms. Nora Groves, (413) 545-0176.

Massachusetts Institute for Social and Economic Research, Box 219, The State House, Room 50, Boston, MA 02133, Mr. William Murray, (617) 727-4537.

Michigan

Michigan Information Center, Department of Management and Budget, Office of Revenue and Tax Analysis, P.O. Box 30026, Lansing, MI 48909, Mr. Eric Swanson, (517) 373-7910.

MIMIC/Center for Urban Studies, Wayne State University, Faculty/ Administration Bldg., 656 W. Kirby, Detroit, MI 48202, Dr. Mark Neithercut/ Kurt Metzger, (313) 577-8350.

The Library of Michigan, Government Documents Service, P.O. Box 30007, Lansing, MI 48909, Ms. F. Anne Diamond, (517) 373-1307.

Minnesota

State Demographer's Office, Minnesota State Planning Agency, 300 Centennial Office Building, 658 Cedar Street, St. Paul, MN 55155, Mr. David Birkholz, (612) 297-2360, Mr. David Rademacher, (612) 297-3255.

Be patient. If any phone number is incorrect, call (area code) 555-1212 and request the new listing.

Economics, Demographics and Statistics

Interagency Resource and Information Center, Department of Education, 501 Capitol Square Building, St. Paul, MN 55101, Ms. Patricia Tupper, (612) 296-6684.

Mississippi

Center for Population Studies, The University of Mississippi, Bondurant Bldg., Room 3W, University, MS 38677, Dr. Max Williams, Director/Ms. Pattie Byrd, Manager, (601) 232-7288.

Governor's Office of Federal-State Programs, Department of Community Development, 301 West Pearl Street, Jackson, MS 39203-3096, Mr. Jim Catt, (601) 949-2219.

Division of Research and Information Systems, Department of Economic and Community Development, 1200 Walter Sillas Building, P.O. Box 849, Jackson, MS 39205, Ms. Linda Penton, (601) 359-3739.

Missouri

Missouri State Library, 2002 Missouri Boulevard, P.O. Box 387, Jefferson City, MO 65102, Ms. Marlys Davis, (314) 751-3615.

Office of Administration, 124 Capitol Building, P.O. Box 809, Jefferson City, MO 65102, Mr. Ryan Burson, (314) 751-2345.

Urban Information Center, University of Missouri-St. Louis, 8001 Natural Bridge Road, St. Louis, MO 63121, Dr. John Blodgett, (314) 553-6014.

Office of Social and Economic Data Analysis, University Missouri-Columbia, 224 Lewis Hall, Columbia, MO 65211, Ms. Evelyn J. Cleveland, (314) 882-7396.

Geographic Resources Center, University of Missouri-Columbia, 4 Stewart Hall, Columbia, MO 65211, Dr. Christopher Salter.

Montana

Census and Economic Information Center, Montana Department of Commerce, 1424 9th Avenue, Capitol Station, Helena, MT 59620-0401, Ms. Patricia Roberts, (406) 444-4393.

Montana State Library, 1515 East 6th Avenue, Capitol Station, Helena, MT 59620, Ms. Kathy Brown, (406) 444-3004.

Bureau of Business and Economic Research, University of Montana, Missoula, MT 59812, Mr. Jim Sylvester, (406) 243-5113.

Survey Research Center, Wilson Hall, Room 1-108, Montana State University, Bozeman, MT 59717, Ms. Lee Faulkner, (406) 994-4481.

Research and Analysis Bureau, Employment Policy Division, Montana Department of Labor and Industry, P.O. Box 1728, Helena, MT 59624, Ms. Cathy Shenkle, (406) 444-2430.

Nebraska

Center for Applied Urban Research, The University of Nebraska-Omaha, Peter Kiewit Conference Center, 1313 Farnam-on-the-Mall, Omaha, NE 68182, Mr. Jerome Deichert/Mr. Tim Himberger, (402) 595-2311.

Policy Research Office, P.O. Box 94601, State Capitol, Room 1319, Lincoln, NE 68509-4601, Ms. Prem L. Bansal, (402) 471-2414.

Federal Documentation Librarian, Nebraska Library Commission, 1420 P Street, Lincoln, NE 68508-1683, (402) 471-2045.

The Central Data Processing Division, Department of Administration Services, 1312 State Capitol, Lincoln, NE 68509-5045, Mr. Skip Miller, (402) 471-4862.

Nebraska Department of Labor, 550 South 16th Street, P.O. Box 94600, Lincoln, NE 68509-4600, Mr. Robert H. Shanahan, (402) 471-2518.

Natural Resources Commission, 301 Centennial Mall South, P.O. Box 94876, Lincoln, NE 68509-4876, Mr. Mahendra Bansal, (402) 471-2081.

Nevada

Nevada State Library, Capitol Complex, 401 North Carson, Carson City, NV 89710, Ms. Joan Kerschner/Ms. Betty McNeal, (702) 687-5160.

New Hampshire

Office of State Planning, 2-1/2 Beacon Street, Concord, NH 03301, Mr. Tom Duffy, (603) 271-2155.

New Hampshire State Library, 20 Park Street, Concord, NH 03301-6303, Mr. John McCormick, (603) 271-2239.

Office of Biometrics, University of New Hampshire, James Hall, 2nd Floor, Durham, NH 03824, Mr. Owen Durgin, (603) 862-1700.

New Jersey

New Jersey Department of Labor, Division of Labor Market and Demographic Research, CN 388-John Fitch Plaza, Trenton, NJ 08625-0388, Ms. Connie O. Hughes, Asst. Director, (609) 984-2593.

New Jersey State Library, 185 West State Street, CN 520, Trenton, NJ 08625-0520, Ms. Beverly Railsback, (609) 292-6220.

CIT - Information Services, Princeton University, 87 Prospect Avenue, Princeton, NJ 08544, Ms. Judith S. Rowe, (609) 258-6052.

Center for Computer and Information Services, Rutgers University, CCIS-Hill Center, Busch Campus, PO Box 879, Piscataway, NJ 08854, Ms. Mary Jane Face Cedar, (908) 932-2889.

Rutgers University - The State University, Kilmer Campus, Lucy Stone Hall, B Wing, New Brunswick, NJ 08903, Dr. James Hughes, Chair and Graduate Director, (908) 932-3822.

New Mexico

Economic Development and Tourism Department, 1100 St. Francis Drive, Santa Fe, NM 87503, Mr. John Beasley, (505) 827-0272.

New Mexico State Library, 325 Don Gaspar Avenue, P.O. Box 1629, Santa Fe, NM 87503, Ms. Laura Chaney, (505) 827-3826.

Bureau of Business and Economic Research, University of New Mexico, 1920 Lomas NE, Albuquerque, NM 87131, Mr. Kevin Kargacin, (505) 277-6626, Ms. Julian Boyle, (505) 277-2216.

Department of Economics, New Mexico State University, Box 30001, Las Cruces, NM 88003, Dr. Kathleen Brook, (505) 646-4905.

New York

Division of Policy and Research, Department of Economic Development, 1 Commerce Plaza, Room 905, 99 Washington Avenue, Albany, NY 12245, Mr. Robert Scardamalia, (518) 474-6005.

CISER Data Archive, Cornell University, 262 Caldwell Hall, Ithaca, NY 14853, Ms. Ann Gray, (607) 255-4801.

Nelson A. Rockefeller Institute of Government, 411 State Street, Albany, NY 12203, (518) 255-1300.

New York State Library, Cultural Education Center, Empire State Plaza, Albany, NY 12230, Ms. Mary Redmond, (518) 474-3940.

Division of Equalization and Assessment, 16 Sheridan Avenue, Albany, NY 12210, Mr. Wilfred B. Pauquette, (518) 474-6742.

North Carolina

North Carolina Office of State Budget and Management, 116 West Jones Street, Raleigh, NC 27603-8005, Ms. Francine Stephenson, Director of State Data Center, (919) 733-7061.

State Library, North Carolina Department of Cultural Resources, 109 East Jones Street, Raleigh, NC 27611, Mr. Joel Sigmon, (919) 733-3683.

Institute for Research in Social Science, University of North Carolina, Manning Hall CB 3355, Chapel Hill, NC 27599-3355, Mr. Glenn Deane, (919) 966-3346.

Division of Land Resources, P.O. Box 27687, Raleigh, NC 27611, Ms. Karen Siderelis/Tim Johnson, (919) 733-2090.

Be patient. If any phone number is incorrect, call (area code) 555-1212 and request the new listing.

State Data Centers

North Dakota

Department of Agricultural Economics, North Dakota State University, Morrill Hall, Room 224, P.O. Box 5636, Fargo, ND 58105, Dr. Richard Rathge, (701) 237-8621.

Office of Intergovernment Assistance, State Capitol, 14th Floor, Bismarck, ND 58505, Mr. Jim Boyd, (701) 224-2094.

Department of Geography, University of North Dakota, Grand Forks, ND 58202, Mohammad Hemmasi, (701) 777-4246.

North Dakota State Library, Liberty Memorial Building, Capitol Grounds, Bismarck, ND 58505, Ms. Susan Pahlmeyer, (701) 224-2490.

Ohio

Ohio Data Users Center, Ohio Department of Development, P.O. Box 1001, Columbus, OH 43266-0101, Mr. Barry Bennett, (614) 466-2115.

State Library of Ohio, 65 South Front Street, Columbus, OH 43215, Mr. Clyde Hordusky, (614) 644-7051.

Cleveland State University, Northern Ohio Data and Information Service, Euclid Avenue and East 24th Street, Cleveland, OH 44115, Mr. Mark Salling, (216) 687-2209.

Ohio State University Library/ Census Data Center, 126 Main Library, 1858 Neil Avenue Mall, Columbus, OH 43210, Ms. Marge Murfin, (614) 292-6175.

Southwest Ohio Regional Data Center, Institute for Policy Research, Mail Loc. 132, Cincinnati, OH 45221, (513) 556-5082.

Oklahoma

Oklahoma State Data Center, Oklahoma Department of Commerce, 6601 Broadway Extension, (Mailing address) P.O. Box 26980, Oklahoma City, OK 73126-0980, Ms. Karen Selland, (405) 841-5184.

Oklahoma Department of Libraries, 200 N.E. 18th Street, Oklahoma City, OK 73105, Mr. Steve Beleu, (405) 521-2502.

Oregon

Oregon State Library, State Library Building, Salem, OR 97310, Mr. Craig Smith, (503) 378-4276.

Bureau of Governmental Research and Service, University of Oregon, Hendricks Hall, Room 340, P.O. Box 3177, Eugene, OR 97403, Ms. Karen Seidel, (503) 346-5232.

Center for Population Research and Census, Portland State University, P.O. Box 751, Portland, OR 97207-0751, Mr. Ed Shafer/Ms. Maria Wilson-Figueroa, (503) 725-3922.

Oregon State Housing Agency, 1600 State Street, Suite 100, Salem, OR 97310-0161, Mr. Mike Murphy, (503) 373-1611.

Pennsylvania

Pennsylvania State Data Center, Institute of State and Regional Affairs, Pennsylvania State University at Harrisburg, Middletown, PA 17057-4898, Mr. Michael Behney, (717) 948-6336.

Pennsylvania State Library, Forum Building, Harrisburg, PA 17120, Mr. John Gerswindt, (717) 787-2327.

Penn State at Harrisburg, Acquisitions, Heindel Library, Middletown, PA 17057-4898, Ms. Grace M. Finn, (717) 948-6074.

Puerto Rico

Puerto Rico Planning Board, Minillas Government Center, North Bldg., Avenida De Diego, P.O. Box 41119, San Juan, PR 00940-9985, Sra. Lillian Torres Aguirre, (809) 728-4430.

Recinto Universitario de Mayaguez, Edificio Anexo Pineiro, Carretera Num 2, Mayaguez, PR 00708, Prfa. Grace Quinones Seda, (809) 834-4040.

Biblioteca Carnegie, Ave. Ponce de Leon, Parada 1, San Juan, PR 00901, Sra. Carmen Martinez, (809) 724-1046.

Rhode Island

United Way of Rhode Island, 229 Waterman Street, Providence, RI 02908, Ms. Jane Nugent, (401) 521-9000.

Rhode Island Department of State Library Services, 300 Richmond Street, Providence, RI 02903, Mr. Frank Iacona, (401) 277-2726.

Social Science Data Center, Brown University, P.O. Box 1916, Providence, RI 02912, Dr. Alden Speare, (401) 863-2550.

Department of Administration, Office of Municipal Affairs, 1 Capitol Hill, Providence, RI 02908-5873, Mr. Paul Egan, (401) 277-6493.

Office of Health Statistics, Rhode Island Department of Health, 3 Capitol Hill, Providence, RI 02908, Dr. Jay Buechner, (401) 277-2550.

Rhode Island Department of Economic Development, 7 Jackson Walkway, Providence, RI 02903, Mr. Vincent Harrington, (401) 277-2601.

South Carolina

Division of Research and Statistical Services, South Carolina Budget and Control Board, Rembert Dennis Bldg. Room 425, Columbia, SC 29201, Mr. Bobby Bowers/Mr. Mike Macfarlane, (803) 734-3780.

South Carolina State Library, P.O. Box 11469, Columbia, SC 29211, Ms. Mary Bostick, (803) 734-8666.

South Dakota

Business Research Bureau, School of Business, University of South Dakota, 414 East Clark, Vermillion, SD 57069, Ms. DeVee Dykstra, (605) 677-5287.

Documents Department, South Dakota State Library, Department of Education and Cultural Affairs, 800 Governors Drive, Pierre, SD 57501-2294, Ms. Margaret Bezpaletz, (605) 773-3131.

Labor Market Information Center, South Dakota Department of Labor, 420 S. Roosevelt, Box 4730, Aberdeen, SD 57402-4730, Ms. Mary Susan Vickers, (605) 622-2314.

Center for Health Policy and Statistics, South Dakota Department of Health, Foss Building, 523 E. Capitol, Pierre, SD 57501, Mr. Brian Williams, (605) 773-3693.

Rural Sociology Department, South Dakota State University, Scobey Hall 226, Box 504, Brookings, SD 57007, Mr. Jim Satterlee, (605) 688-4132.

Tennessee

Tennessee State Planning Office, John Sevier State Office Bldg., 500 Charlotte Ave., Suite 307, Nashville, TN 37243-0001, Mr. Charles Brown, (615) 741-1676.

Center for Business and Economic Research, College of Business Administration, University of Tennessee, Room 100, Glocker Hall, Knoxville, TN 37996-4170, Ms. Betty Vickers, (615) 974-5441.

Texas

State Data Center, Texas Department of Commerce, 9th and Congress Streets, (Mailing address) P.O. Box 12728, Capitol Station, Austin, TX 78711, Ms. Susan Tully, (512) 472-9667.

Department of Rural Sociology, Texas A & M University System, Special Services Building, College Station, TX 77843-2125, Dr. Steve Murdock, (409) 845-5115 or 5332.

Texas Natural Resources Information System (TNRIS), P.O. Box 13231, Austin, TX 78711, Mr. Charles Palmer, (512) 463-8399.

Texas State Library and Archive Commission, P.O. Box 12927, Capitol Station, Austin, TX 78711, Ms. Diana Houston, (512) 463-5455.

Utah

Office of Planning and Budget, State Capitol, Room.116, Salt Lake City, UT 84114, Mr. Brad Barber, Director/Ms. Linda Smith, (801) 538-1036.

Bureau of Economic and Business Research, 401 Garff Building, University of Utah, Salt Lake City, UT 84112, Mr. Frank Hachman, (801) 581-6333.

Be patient. If any phone number is incorrect, call (area code) 555-1212 and request the new listing.

Economics, Demographics and Statistics

Population Research Laboratory, Utah State University, UMC 07, Logan, UT 84322, Mr. Yun Kim, (801) 750-1231.

Department of Employment Security, 174 Social Hall Avenue, P.O. Box 11249, Salt Lake City, UT 84147, Mr. Ken Jensen, (801) 533-2372.

Vermont

Office of Policy Research and Coordination, Pavilion Office Building, 109 State Street, Montpelier, VT 05602, Mr. Bernie Johnson, (802) 828-3326.

Center for Rural Studies, University of Vermont, 207 Morrill Hall, Burlington, VT 05405-0106, Ms. Cathleen Gent, (802) 656-3021.

Vermont Department of Libraries, 111 State Street, Montpelier, VT 05602, Ms. Patricia Klinck, State Librarian, (802) 828-3265.

Vermont Agency of Development and Community Affairs, Pavilion Office Building, 109 State Street, Montpelier, VT 05602, Mr. Jed Guertin, (802) 828-3211.

Virginia

Virginia Employment Commission, 703 East Main Street, Richmond, VA 23219, Mr. Dan Jones, (804) 786-8308.

Center for Public Service, University of Virginia, Dynamics Bldg., 4th Floor, 2015 Ivy Road, Charlottesville, VA 22903-1795, Dr. Michael Spar, (804) 924-7451.

Virginia State Library, Documents Section, 11th Street at Capitol Square, Richmond, VA 23219-3491, Mr. Robert Keeton, (804) 786-2175.

Virgin Islands

University of the Virgin Islands, Caribbean Research Institute, Charlotte Amalie, St. Thomas, VI 00802, Dr. Frank Mills, (809) 776-9200.

Virgin Islands Department of Economic Development, P.O. Box 6400, Charlotte Amalie, St. Thomas, VI 00801, Mr. Richard Moore, (809) 774-8784.

Washington

Estimation and Forecasting Unit, Office of Financial Management, 450 Insurance Bldg., MS: AQ-44, Olympia, WA 98504-0202, Ms. Sharon Estee, (206) 586-2504.

Documents Section, Washington State Library, AJ-11, Olympia, WA 98504, Ms. Ann Bregent, (206) 753-4027.

Puget Sound Council of Govts., 215 1st Avenue South, Seattle, WA 98104, Ms. Elaine Murakami, (206) 464-5355.

Social Research Center, Department of Rural Sociology, Washington State University, Pullman, WA 99164-4006, Dr. Annabel Kirschner Cook, (509) 335-4519.

Department of Sociology, Demographic Research Laboratory, Western Washington University, Bellingham, WA 98225, Mr. Lucky Tedrow, Director, (206) 676-3167.

Applied Social Data Center, Department of Sociology, Central Washington University, Ellensburg, WA 98926, Dr. David Kaufman, (509) 963-1305.

West Virginia

Community Development Division, Governor's Office of Community and Industrial Development, Capitol Complex, Building 6, Room 553, Charleston, WV 25305, Ms. Mary C. Harless, (304) 348-4010.

Reference Library, West Virginia State Library Commission, Science and Cultural Center, Capitol Complex, Charleston, WV 25305, Ms. Karen Goff, (304) 348-2045.

Office of Health Services Research, Health Science Center South, West Virginia University, Morgantown, WV 26506, Ms. Stephanie Pratt, (304) 293-2601.

The Center for Economic Research, West Virginia University, 323 Business and Economic Building, Morgantown, WV 26506-6025, Dr. Tom Witt, Director/Ms. Linda Culp, (304) 293-5837.

Wisconsin

Demographic Services Center, Department of Administration, 101 S. Webster St., 6th Floor, P.O. Box 7868, Madison, WI 53707-7868, Ms. Nadene Roenspies/Mr. Robert Naylor, (608) 266-1927.

Applied Population Laboratory, Department of Rural Sociology, University of Wisconsin, 1450 Linden Drive, Room 316, Madison, WI 53706, Mr. Michael Knight, (608) 262-3097.

Wyoming

Survey Research Center, University of Wyoming, P.O. Box 3925, Laramie, WY 82071, Mr. G. Fred Doll, (307) 766-2931.

Department of Administration and Fiscal Control, Emerson Building 327E, Cheyenne, WY 82002-0060, Ms. Mary Byrnes, Director/Kreg McCollums, (307) 777-7504.

Campbell County Library, 2101 Four J Road, Gillette, WY 82716, (307) 682-3223.

Be patient. If any phone number is incorrect, call (area code) 555-1212 and request the new listing.

State Statistical Abstracts

For years researchers have been aware of the importance of keeping around the latest edition of the *Statistical Abstract of the United States* (available for $25 from Superintendent of Documents, U.S. GPO, Washington, DC 20402, (202) 783-3238). Now if you are interested in local or regional opportunities, trends or markets, almost every state government offers their own *State Statistical Abstract* or something comparable. Most of the states produce their abstract on an annual basis. There are only eleven states which do not publish abstracts: Alabama, Arkansas, Delaware, Kansas, Massachusetts, Michigan, New Hampshire, New Mexico, Texas, Virginia, and Wisconsin.

Tables and graphs are used to illustrate the performance of the economy. Where comparisons can be made, state, regional, and national data can be compared. Market analysts, businesses and researchers will find the following kinds of information in a statistical abstract:

- how many of Fortune magazine's top 500 companies have manufacturing plants in the state;
- the number of jobs directly or indirectly related to exports;
- largest sources of personal income;
- number of people employed in agricultural/non-agricultural jobs;
- how a state ranks in population and land size;
- number of acres of forest land;
- number of airports, number privately owned;
- number of registered aircraft;
- changes in population-age distribution;
- percentage of 17- and 18-year-olds graduating from high school;
- number of state universities, vocational schools;
- motor vehicle registrations;
- crime rates; and
- traffic fatalities.

Similar to the *Statistical Abstract of the U.S.* in providing important data in charts and tables, these state abstracts offer important leads to more detailed sources of information. Although the specific charts and tables may not offer the exact detail of data you require on a particular topic, they will identify the offices which generate this type of information. By contacting the specific office you are likely to get the precise data you require. They can't publish everything they have in a single statistical abstract, but they can dig it out of their files for you.

Statistical Abstract Offices

Alaska

Alaska Department of Labor, Research and Analysis, P.O. Box 25501, Juneau, AK 99802; (907) 465-4500. Publication: *Employment and Earnings Report, Statistical Quarterly* (free).

Arizona

Arizona Department of Economic Security Research Administration, P.O. Box 6123, Phoenix, AZ 85005; (602) 542-3871. Publication: *Labor Market Information-Annual Planning Information* (free).

California

Department of Finance, 915 L Street, 8th Floor, Sacramento, CA 95814; (916) 322-2263. Publication: *California Statistical Abstract* (free).

Colorado

State Planning and Budget, Room 1111, State Capitol Building, Denver, CO 80203; (303) 866-3386. Publication: *Economic Perspective* (free).

Connecticut

Office of Policy and Management, Budget and Financial Management Division, 80 Washington St., Hartford, CT 06106; (203) 566-8342. Publication: *Economic Report of the Governor* (free).

District of Columbia

Office of Policy and Program Evaluation, Room 208, District Building, 1350 Pennsylvania Ave. NW, Washington, DC 20004; (202) 727-6979. Publication: *Indices* ($21).

Florida

University Presses of Florida, 15 N.W. 15th St., Gainesville, FL 32603; (904) 392-1351. Publication: *Florida Statistical Abstract* ($22.95).

Georgia

Georgia Office of Budget and Planning, 254 Washington St. SW, Suite 614, Atlanta, GA 30334-8500; (404) 656-0911. Publications: *Georgia Descriptions and Data - A Statistical Abstract* ($10).

Hawaii

State of Hawaii, Business and Economic Development, P.O. Box 2359, Honolulu, HI 96804, Attention: Information Office; (808) 586-2466. Publication: *State of Hawaii Statistical Abstract* ($8).

Idaho

Secretary of State, Room 203, State House, Boise, ID 83720; (208) 334-2300. Publication: *Idaho Blue Book* ($5).

Illinois

University of Illinois, Bureau of Economic and Business Research, 1206 S. 6th St., 428 Commerce West, Champaign, IL 61820; (217) 333-2330. Publication: *Illinois Statistical Abstract* ($40).

Indiana

Indiana Department of Commerce, Division of Economic Analysis, One North Capitol, Suite 200, Indianapolis, IN 46204; (317) 264-3110. Publication: *Indiana: Its Economy, Its People* ($2).

Iowa

Iowa Development Commission, 200 East Grand Ave., Des Moines, IA 50309; (515) 243-4871. Publication: *Statistical Profile of Iowa* (free).

Kentucky

Cabinet for Economic Development, 133 Holmes St., Frankfort, KY 40601; (502) 564-4715. Publication: *Kentucky Economic Statistics* ($10).

Maine

Business Development Office, State House Station #59, Augusta, ME 04333; (207) 289-3195. Publication: *Maine Statistical Summary* (free).

Be patient. If any phone number is incorrect, call (area code) 555-1212 and request the new listing.

Economics, Demographics and Statistics

Maryland

Dept. of Economic and Employment Development, 217 East Redwood, 11th Floor, Baltimore, MD 21202, (410) 333-6953. Publication: *Statistical Abstract* ($39).

Minnesota

Department of Trade and Economic Development, Business Development Analysis Division, 900 American Center Building, 150 East Kellogg, St. Paul, MN 55101; (612) 297-2335 or 297-2872. Publication: *Compare Minnesota* (free). They do not have an abstract.

Mississippi

Mississippi State University, Division of Business Research, College of Business and Industry, Drawer 5288, Mississippi State, MS 39762; (601) 325-3817. Publications: *Mississippi Statistical Abstract* ($35).

Missouri

University of Missouri, B & PA Research Center, 10 Professional Building, Columbia, MO 65211; (314) 882-4805. Publications: *Statistical Abstract* ($25).

Montana

Department of Commerce, Census and Economic Information Center, 1424 9th Ave. Helena, MT 59620; (406) 444-4393. Publication: *Montana Statistical Abstract* (from 1984, free). *State Summary Volume*, from the Montana County Profile Series.

Nebraska

Dept. of Economic Development, Research Division, P.O. Box 94666, Lincoln, NE 68509; (402) 471-3111. Publication: *Nebraska Statistical Handbook* ($10).

Nevada

Vital Statistics, 505 East King Street, Room 102, Carson City, NV 89710; (702) 687-4480. Publication: *Statistical Abstract* (free).

New Jersey

Office of Economic Policy, New Jersey Department of Commerce, 20 W. State St., Trenton, NJ; (609) 292-3860.

New York

Rockefeller Institute of Government, 411 State St., Albany, NY 12203; (518) 443-5522. Publication: *New York Statistical Yearbook* ($50 + $4 s/h).

North Carolina

State Planning Office, Office of the State Budget, 116 W. Jones St., Raleigh, NC 27603; (919) 733-4131. Publication: *North Carolina State Statistical Abstract* ($25 + tax).

North Dakota

The Bureau of Business and Economic Research, College of Business and Public Administration, Box 8255, University of North Dakota, Grand Forks, ND 58202; (701) 777-3365. Publication: *North Dakota Statistical Abstract* ($20).

Ohio

Ohio Data Users, P.O. Box 1001, Columbus, OH 43266; (614) 466-2115. Publication: *County Profiles* ($50).

Oklahoma

University of Oklahoma, Center for Economic and Management Research (CEMR), College of Business Administration, 307 W. Brooks St., Room 4, Norman, OK 73019; (405) 325-2931. Publication: *Statistical Abstract* ($22).

Oregon

Economic Development Department, 775 Summer Street, Salem, OR 97310, Attn: Publications; (503) 373-1290. Publication: *Oregon Economic Profile* ($3.50).

Pennsylvania

State Data Center, State University at Harrisburg, Capitol College, Middletown, PA 17057; (717) 948-6336. Publication: *Statistical Abstract* ($35).

Rhode Island

Department of Economic Development, 7 Jackson Walkway, Providence, RI 02903; (401) 277-2601. Publication: *Annual Economic Trend Series* (free).

South Carolina

Division of Research and Statistical Services, 1000 Assembly St., Rembert C. Dennis Building, Suite 425, Columbia, SC 29201; (803) 734-3793. Publication: *South Carolina Statistical Abstract* ($20).

South Dakota

Businesses Research Bureau, School of Business, The University of South Dakota, 414 East Clark St., Vermillion, SD 57069-2390; (605) 677-5287. Publication: *South Dakota Community Abstract* ($20).

Tennessee

University of Tennessee, Center for Business and Economic Research, S. 100 Glocker Hall, College of Business Administration, Knoxville, TN 37996; (615) 974-5441. Publication: *Tennessee State Statistical Abstract* ($36 + $3 shipping and handling).

Texas

Department of Commerce, Research and Planning Division, State Data Center, P.O. Box 12728, Austin, TX 78711; (512) 463-1166.

Utah

Office of Planning and Budget, Room 116, State Capitol Building, Salt Lake City, UT 84115; (801) 538-1027. Publication: *Economic Report to the Governor* ($12).

Vermont

Agency of Development and Community Affairs, Montpelier, VT 05602; (802) 828-3211. Publication: *Vermont Selected Statistics* (free).

Washington

Office of Forecast Council, Evergreen Plaza, Room 300, Mailstop FJ33, Olympia, WA 98504; (206) 586-6785. Publication: *Economic and Revenue Forecast for Washington State* ($4.50 per issue in state, $9 per issue out of state; $18 per year in state subscription, $36 per year out of state subscription).

West Virginia

Chamber of Commerce, Research and Strategic Planning, P.O. Box 2789, Charleston, WV 25330; (304) 342-1115.

Wyoming

Division of Economic Analysis, Room 327E, Emerson Building, Cheyenne, WY 82002-0060; (307) 777-7504. Publication: *The Wyoming Data Handbook* (Free).

Be patient. If any phone number is incorrect, call (area code) 555-1212 and request the new listing.

State Forecasting Centers

State planning offices can provide vast quantities of local market information, demographic data, and company intelligence -- more than you would believe possible. Every state has a bureau equivalent to a planning office to assist the Governor in charting future economic change. Of course, the quantity of information varies from one state to the next as does the sophistication level of methods used to gather and analyze data. However, most information is generated to support decision-making for policies and legislative initiatives which will affect the current and future status of the state economy. These blueprints for the future usually include plans for attracting new businesses and industries as well as improving the quality of housing, education and transportation.

It should be noted that there is a wide disparity in the research and strategic focus of these state planning offices. The position of this function within the state bureaucratic structure often provides clues about the scope of its mission. In most states this forecasting operation is housed in the Department of Economic Development or a separate policy office under the Governor's office. However, in our survey of all 50 states, we discovered this crucial function in unexpected places. In South Carolina, for example, there is a special Commission on the Future within the Lieutenant Governor's office, and in Texas, a comparable office falls under the jurisdiction of the state comptroller.

The types of information available from these offices are outlined below.

Business Expansion and Economic Outlook

If you currently do business in a state or intend to establish a business there, it would be wise to learn about the Governor's long-term strategy. Keep in mind that no one is more concerned about the state's future than this elected official. If your company sells to farmers, inquire at the planning office about the Governor's agricultural policies. If your firm relies on high-tech complementary businesses, see whether there is a plan to attract high-tech companies. Or, if you are interested in consumer markets, be aware of demographic projections conducted by the planning agency for the state as well as for specific regions and counties. Many states appear to be charting future population patterns on a regular basis, as is evident with the sampling of publications noted here.

Indiana: *Some Aspects of Demographic Change in Indiana from 1980 to 2000*
California: *California's Economic Future -- Building New Foundations for a Competitive Society*
Michigan: *Population Projections for Michigan to the Year 2010*
Utah: *Utah 2000*
Nebraska: *Nebraska Industry -- A Survey of Concerns, Needs and Future Plans*
New Jersey: *Annual Economic Forecast*

Demographics and Market Studies

Most of these offices are aware of the current demographic situation within their state. They also continually monitor the major industries in the state as well as emerging industries. Their data are usually derived from a combination of federal, state and locally generated information. Sometimes these offices are part of the state data center program run by the U.S. Bureau of the Census. Demographic studies as well as state statistical abstracts are readily available.

Arizona: *Community Profiles*
Montana: *County Profiles*
Washington DC: *Housing Monographs by Ward*
Nevada: *Community Profiles -- Demographic Facts*
New Hampshire: *Changes in Households and Households Size for Towns and Cities*
Iowa: *A Statistical Profile of Iowa*
Maryland: *State Statistical Abstract*

These state planning offices often produce in-depth market studies on diverse topics:

Arizona: *Aerospace in Arizona -- An Assessment of Market Opportunities*
Delaware: *Food Processors, Banking, and Automotive Just-In-Time Suppliers*
Maryland: *Impact of Professional Sports on the Maryland Economy*
Michigan: *Machine Tool Industry Update*
Missouri: *Home Health Care and the Homemaker*
Nebraska: *Profit Opportunities in Nebraska for Manufacturers of Pet Food*
New York: *Statistical Profile of the Printing and Publishing Industry*
Florida: *Monthly Tourist Surveys*
Virginia: *High Technology Communications in Virginia*

Company Information and Industry Directories

Many of these offices are responsible for maintaining information on the companies which are located within their state. It is not unusual for the state to collect the following data on every manufacturer and corporation:

- Name of company;
- Address and telephone number;
- Names of principal officers;
- Types of products or services produced;
- Number of employees; and
- Sales estimate.

You stand to learn more about a company, especially its finan-cial picture, if the business in question received some type of

Economics, Demographics and Statistics

economic assistance from the state. After all, once a company takes taxpayer money, the public has a right to know. There is a growing number of companies that fall into this category. Recently we received a list of over 100 firms which obtained financial assistance from Pennsylvania just during the past year.

Other handy resources available from many state planning offices are company directories, many of which concentrate on one industry sector.

Kansas: *Directory of Kansas Warehouse and Distribution Centers*
Michigan: *Michigan Private 100*
Montana: *Consumer Products Buyer's Directory*
Oregon: *Directory of Oregon Electronic Products*

Databases and Special Services

Because these planning agencies share their forecasts and statistical data with other offices within the state government, often the data are readily available to the public, usually for free or on a cost recovery basis. Many have already established customized databases, some of which permit direct online access. Examples include:

- Idaho's database linking entrepreneurs with investors;
- Colorado's community profiles database covering 63 counties and 260 municipalities;
- Florida's nine public access databases; and
- Nevada's computerized databank on land availability, labor resources and economic statistics.

Difficulties Tracking Down Forecasting Data

Since numerous offices within a state are engaged in forecasting, expect to run into some obstacles. Don't be discouraged if, when you contact one office for specific market data, you are told there is "no way" they would keep such information. The odds are that some other state bureaucrat has the information, so always patiently ask for other offices you could call. For example, practically every state publishes a directory of manufacturers, but it may not be produced by the planning office but by some other agency across town. This holds true when hunting for statistical information, market studies, and databases.

State Planning Offices

The address and telephone numbers are included for the primary planning offices in each state as well as the District of Columbia. The publications listed with the office do not represent the entire universe of hardcopy data available. These titles are included only when the office is capable of providing us with a current listing. There are states which have publications, but do not have any sort of catalog. For those states you must request data under specific topic headings.

Alabama

Alabama Department of Economic and Community Affairs, P.O. Box 25037, Montgomery, AL 36125-0347; (205) 284-8910. Publications: *Annual Report.*

Alaska

State Planning Office, Division of Policy, Commerce and Economic Development, Office of Management and Budget, P.O. AM, Juneau, AK 99811; (907) 465-3568.

Arizona

Arizona Department of Commerce, 3800 N. Central, Phoenix, AZ 85012; (602) 280-1300. Publications: *Annual Report, Arizona Annual Economic Profile, Arizona Developments Quarterly Newsletter, Directory of High Technology Companies, Guide to Establishing a Business in Arizona, Arizona Agribusiness Profiles, Arizona Community Profiles* ($18), *Arizona Indian Profiles, Arizona Industrial Profiles* ($15), *Arizona Main Street Newsletter, Common Questions About Planning Newsletter, Planning and Zoning Handbook* ($20), *Rural Economic Development Resource Directory* ($5), *Financial Resources for Business Development, Request for Proposal Handbook, Bi-Weekly Report of Federal and State Proposals Under Review, Clearinghouse Manual, Federal Assistance Award Data System Report, Arizona Energy Data Report, Community Energy Profile Handbook, So-Easy Energy Saving Packet, Energy Checklist, Ease the Squeeze Driving Hints, Apartment Energy Conservation Guide, Home Energy Conservation Guide, Mobile Home Energy Conservation Guide, Energy Fact Sheets, Arizona Exporters Directory, Arizona World Trade Review Quarterly Newsletter, Directory of International Services, Twenty Questions about the Community Development Block Grants, Energy News, Local State Funding Report.*

Arkansas

Office of Industrial Development, State of Arkansas, #1 Capitol Mall, Little Rock, AR 72201; (501) 682-1121. Publications: *Breaking Down Old Walls-Laying a New Foundation, Annual Report.*

California

Commission on Economic Development, State of California, State Capitol, Room 1028, Sacramento, CA 95814; (916) 445-1025. Publications: *Annual Report* ($2.50), *Doing Business in California-A Guide for Establishing a Business* (old version $3, new version $1.67 postage), *An International Trade Policy for California* ($2, photocopy charged for postage), *Poisoning Prosperity-The Impact of Toxics in California's Economy* ($5, follow-up version $3), *Assessment of Reduced Revenue on California Local Law Enforcement* ($2, postage charged).

Colorado

State of Colorado, Division of Commerce and Development, Department of Local Affairs, 1313 Sherman St., Room 523, Denver, CO 80203; (303) 866-2205. Publications: *Directory of Services* (free to state employees only), *Stateline* (state newsletter, only for state employees). Other Services: Community Profiles Database, covering 63 counties and 260 municipalities. More information on demographics can be obtained from State of Colorado, Division of Local Government, Department of Local Affairs, Room 521, Denver, CO 80203; (303) 866-2156.

Connecticut

Connecticut Department of Economic Development, Marketing Department, 865 Brook Street, Rocky Hill, CT 06067; (203) 258-4288. Publications: *Annual Report.*

Delaware

Delaware Development Office, State of Delaware, Executive Department, 99 Kings Highway, P.O. Box 1401, Dover, DE 19903, (302) 739-4271. Publications: *Three-Year Capital Budget Plan, Delaware Data Book* ($25), *Comparison of Estimated State and Local Family Tax Burdens, Small Business Start-Up Guide,* and *Procurement Guide.* Other Services: Business Research Section maintains an extensive library of data resources and responds to requests for economic, demographic and travel information. Selective online access available to a computerized real estate file. A computerized hotel reservation system is also available.

District of Columbia

Office of Planning, Deputy Mayor for Economic Development, Government of the District of Columbia, Washington, DC 20004; (202) 727-6492. Publications: *Census Tract Map* ($2), *Citizen's Guide to Zoning, Comprehensive Plan and Land Use Map, Development Process in the District of Columbia* ($50), *District of Columbia Zoning Map* ($3), *Market Assessment for Downtown Washington, Housing Monograph by Ward, Population Monograph by Ward, Land Use Monograph by Ward, 1982 Housing Unit Estimates Washington, DC, Planning for the Future/The Ward Planning Process, Proposal to Establish Development Zones East of the Anacostia River, Population Estimates Washington, DC, Connecticut Avenue Corridor Study, Anacostia Metro Station Action Plan, Benning Road Action Plan, Fort Totten Metro Station Action Plan, Fourteenth Street and Potomac*

State Forecasting Centers

Avenue Metro State Area Action Plan, Howard Gateway Action Plan, New York Avenue Industrial Corridor Action Plan, Rhode Island Avenue Metro Station Action Plan, Taylor and Upshur Street Action Plan, Street Address Directory ($4), *The State of the Wards Report.*

Florida

Bureau of Economic Analysis, Florida Department of Commerce, Division of Economic Development, Tallahassee, FL 32301; (904) 487-2971. Publications: *Monthly Tourist Surveys, County Comparisons, Florida and the Other Forty-Nine, Agency Functional Plan, A Guide to Florida Environmental Permitting.* Special Services: Five public access databases, and customized research requests; (909) 488-4255.

Georgia

Office of Planning and Budget, 254 Washington Street, S.W., Atlanta, GA 30334-8500; (404) 656-3820. Publications: *Governor's Policy Statement, Memos from Growth Issues Resources Council.*

Hawaii

Department of Business, Economic Development and Tourism, 11th floor, 220 S. King Street, Honolulu, HI 96813; (808) 586-2406.

Idaho

Department of Commerce, Room 108, State Capitol, Boise, ID 83720; (208) 334-3417. Publications: *Economic Development Agenda.*

Illinois

Illinois Department of Commerce and Community Affairs, 620 East Adams Street, Springfield, IL 62701; (217) 782-3233. Publications: *Annual Report* (free).

Indiana

Indiana Economic Development Council, One North Capitol, Suite 425, Indianapolis, IN 46204; (317) 631-0871. Publications: *The Futures of Indiana-Trends Affecting Economic Change 1986-2000, Indiana's Infrastructure Strategy-An Outline for Action, 1986 Indiana Economic Development Congress, Defining Vocational Education, Vocational Education: Who Are The Students, Vocational Education in Indiana, Vocational Education and Economic Development in Indiana, A Future of Learning and Work, The Investment Effects of Indiana's Preliminary Tax Abatement Programs, An Evaluation of Property Tax Abatement in Indiana, Looking Back-The Update of Indiana's Strategic Economic Development Plan.*

Iowa

Iowa Department of Economic Development, 200 East Grand Avenue. Des Moines, IA 50309; (515) 281-3251. Publications: *Statistical Profile of Iowa, Economic Developments.*

Kansas

Department of Economic Development Research, 400 W 8th St. 5th Floor, Topeka, KS 66603; (913) 296-3564. Department of Commerce; (913) 296-3481. Publications: *Annual Report, Directory of Kansas Manufacturers and Products* ($10.53), *Directory of Kansas Warehouse and Distribution Centers, Directory of Kansas Job Shops, Fortune 500 Facilities in Kansas* (hasn't been revised since 1987), *Kansas Manufacturing Firms in Exports, Kansas Association Directory, Firms Headquartered In Kansas, Kansas New and Expanding Manufacturers, Kansas Economic Development Statutes* (being revised, may not be available to the public).

Kentucky

Center for Business and Economic Development, 302 Matthews Building, College of Business and Economics, University of Kentucky, Lexington, KY 40506; (606) 257-7675. Publications: *Annual Economic Report.*

Louisiana

State Planning Office, Division of Administration, 1051 North Riverside Mall, Baton Rouge, LA 70804; (504) 342-7410.

Maine

Economic and Community Development Office, State House Station 59, Augusta, ME 04333; (207) 289-2656. Also, Data Census Manager, 20 Union Street, Augusta, ME 04330-6827; (207) 289-2271.

Maryland

Division of Research, Department of Economic and Community Development, 45 Calvert St., Annapolis, MD 21401; (301) 974-3629. Publications: *The Impact of Professional Sports on the Maryland Economy, An Econometric Analysis of Variations in Workers' Compensation Rates, The Fiscal Impact of Professional Sports, The Economic Impact of the Preakness on the Maryland Economy, Workers' Compensation Insurance, Competitive Rating in Workers' Compensation Insurance, The Economic Impact of the University of Maryland's Football Program, Report of the Special Advisory Committee on Professional Sports and the Economy, Maryland Statistical Abstract, Workers' Compensation in Maryland, Technical Notes on 27 Issues in Workers' Compensation, Workers' Compensation in Maryland, Workers' Compensation Summary of Major Studies, Prompt Payment of Temporary Total Disability Benefits, Maryland Workers' Compensation Claims Experience, Workers' Compensation Medical Claims and Benefits Written Opinions, A Comparative Analysis of Accident Patterns by Industry and by State, Report of the Governor's Commission to Study the Workers' Compensation System, Addendum to the Report of the Governor's Commission to Study the Workers' Compensation System, A Preliminary Feasibility Study of Ferry Service on the Chesapeake Bay, A Guide to the Calculation of Workers' Tax Payments, The Impact of the Commercial Fishing Industry on the Maryland Economy, Telecommunications Taxation, Selected Economic Indications-Monthly.*

Massachusetts

Executive Office of Economic Affairs, One Ashburton Place, Room 2101, Boston, MA 02108; (617) 727-1130.

Michigan

Business Research Office, Department of Commerce, State of Michigan, P.O. Box 30225, Lansing, MI 48909; (517) 373-7401. Publications: *Business Guide to Understanding Michigan Sales and Use Tax, Comparison with Illinois, Comparison with Indiana, Comparison with Kentucky, Comparison with Ohio, Comparison with Tennessee, Comparison with Wisconsin, County Business Climate Overview and Highlights for each of 83 Counties, Food Processing Overview, Michigan as a Place to do Business - A Review of Recent Studies, Michigan's Labor Force Characteristics, Michigan's Market Potential, Michigan Property Tax System - Overview of the, Ontario - Brief Look at Augusta, Ontario vs. Michigan - A Comparison, Review of Michigan Taxes, Crain's Detroit Business List of Top Privately Held Companies, Crain's Detroit Business List of Top Publicly Held Companies, Fortune 500 Companies Headquartered in Michigan, Michigan Private 100, The Michigan 100, Employment Size Study, Industrial Construction Trends by County, Industrial Real Estate Market Survey, Michigan Economic Update, Michigan Economy-Overview, New Business Incorporations, New Capital Expenditures in Michigan, Population Projections for Michigan to the Year 2010, Questions and Answers About Small Business, REMI Employment Multipliers, U.S. Dept. of Commerce, Bureau of Economic Analysis Projections, Metal Fabricating Industry Study, Michigan Chemical Industry-An Overview, Michigan Machine Tool Industry Update, Michigan Machinery Industry Overview, Michigan Service Industry Overview, Michigan-State of the Future, Plastics Industry, Basic Business Sources-SMU Business Library, Business Reference Sources-Library of Michigan, Business Taxes in Michigan, The Case for Michigan, Commercial Redevelopment Act, Community Growth Alliances, Export Assistance, Food Processing Opportunities in Michigan, Forest Products Opportunities in Michigan, Governor's Commission on Jobs and Economic Development Adopts Labor Training, Labor Training, Leader in Automated Systems Manufacturing, Michigan-The Leader in Metalworking, Michigan's Expanding Plastics Industry, Michigan's Improving Business Future, Michigan Main Street-Downtown Revitalization Assistance, Property Tax Incentives, Small Business Centers, State Financial Assistance.*

Minnesota

State Planning Agency, Administration, 300 Centennial Bldg., 658 Cedar St., St. Paul, MN 55155; (612) 296-3985. Publications: *Minnesota State Hospital Facilities and Alternative Use, Minnesota State Hospital Use and Cost, A Profile of Minnesota State Hospital Employees, The Economic Impact of Minnesota State Hospitals, Public Opinions About State Hospitals, Residents/Patients in Minnesota State Hospitals, Opinions and Recommendations for the Minnesota State Hospital System, Minnesota State Hospitals-Executive Summary, Mental Health Commission Report, Studies of the Academies for the Deaf and the Blind, Disabilities and Technology, Real Homes Real Education Real Job: A New Way of Thinking.*

Department of Trade and Economic Development, 900 American Center Building, 150 East Kellogg, St. Paul, MN 55701; (612) 296-8341. Publications: *Compare Minnesota* (free).

Mississippi

Mississippi Research and Development Center, 3825 Ridgewood Rd., Jackson, MS 39211; (601) 325-3817. Publications: *Bibliography of Publications, Budget Facts: Facts on Financing Mississippi State Government, Catalog of Audiovisual Materials Available on Loan, Checklist for New Manufacturers in Mississippi, A*

Economics, Demographics and Statistics

Comparison of the 1980 Census Count in Mississippi with the Mississippi Research and Development Center's 1980 County Population Projections, Directory of Master Parent Companies of Mississippi Manufacturers, Electrical Peak Demand Control System, Factors Affecting the Location of Technology Intensive Industries, Facts and Figures, Handbook of Selected Data for Mississippi, Highlights of Mississippi's Changing Economy, How to Develop a Business Plan, Industrial Incentives, Major Government Regulations Affecting Small Retail Business in Mississippi, Mississippi County Data Bank, Mississippi Industrial Services Communicator, Mississippi Manufacturers Directory ($35), Mississippi Manufacturing Atlas, Mississippi's Public Junior College Vocational-Technical Courses of Interest to Industry, R & D Economic Brief, R & D Annual Report, Services for Mississippi Businesses.

Missouri

Missouri Office of Administration, Division of Budget and Planning, P.O. Box 809, Jefferson City, MO 65102; (314) 751-2345. Publications: *Missouri Demographic and Economic Profile, An Analysis of the Missouri Agribusiness Sector, Missouri's Statewide Economic Development Planning Program, A Directory of Missouri Data Sources ($23), An Economic Analysis of Energy Supply and Demand in Missouri, Export Trade of the State of Missouri, Home Health Care and The Homemaker, Housing Program Utilization in Missouri, Missouri Housing Situation, Missouri Transportation System: Condition, Capacity and Impediments to Efficiency, Transportation Trends, Potential Industrial Opportunities for Missouri's Resource Base, A User's Guide to Missouri Maps.*

Montana

Business Assistance Division, Department of Commerce, State of Montana, 1424 9th Ave., Helena, MT 59620; (406) 444-3923. Publications: *County Profiles, Montana Statistical Abstract, 1984, Montana Manufacturers and Products Directory, Business and Industrial Location Guide, Consumer Products Buyers' Directory.*

Nebraska

Nebraska Department of Economic Development, P.O. Box 94666-State Office Bldg., 301 Centennial Mall South, Lincoln, NE 98509; (402) 471-3111, (800) 426-6505. Publications: *The Ethanol Distilling Industry-An Industrial Opportunity in Nebraska, Pharmaceuticals and Related Industries: Opportunities in Nebraska, Threshold Estimates and Other Tools for Retail Analysis, Frozen Potato and Onion Processing Opportunities in Nebraska, Investment of Nebraska Public Pension Funds, Nebraska as a World Class Center for Communications Industry, Equity Capital for Nebraska Small Business, Nebraska Visitors Survey, Nebraska Industry: A Survey of Their Concerns, Needs and Future Plans, Characteristics of Nebraska Immigrants and Outmigrants, 1984 Nebraska Air Service Study, The Nebraska Economic Indicators Survey, Hazardous Waste in Nebraska, Profit Opportunities in Nebraska for Manufacturers of Pet Food, Opportunities for Nebraska Businesses in India, Nebraska Profit Opportunities for Manufacturers of Scientific, Measuring and Controlling Instruments, Vegetable Production, Processing and Marketing in Nebraska, Service as a Leading Sector in Economic Development, Nebraska's Economic Performance, Building Prosperity: Nebraska Economic Development Strategy, Nebraska Statistical Handbook ($8), Nebraska Facts and Figures, Nebraska Directory of Manufacturers and their Products ($20), Nebraska Community Profiles.*

Nevada

Commission on Economic Development, State of Nevada, Capitol Complex, Carson City, NV; (702) 885-4325. Publications: *State Plan for Economic Diversification and Development, Nevada Industrial Directory, Community Profiles-Demographic Facts, Quarterly Newsletter, State Economic Development Brochure, The Nevada Development Handbook.* Other: Development of a statewide database to provide access to information about land availability, labor sources and economic statistics.

New Hampshire

Office of State Planning, State of New Hampshire, Executive Department, 2 1/2 Beacon St., Concord, NH 03301; (603) 271-2155. Publications: *Current Year Population for New Hampshire Communities, Selected Economic Characteristics for New Hampshire Municipalities, Current Estimates and Trends in New Hampshire's Housing Supply Update-Annual, New Hampshire Population Projections for Counties and Municipalities, Current Estimates and Trends in New Hampshire's Housing Supply-1970-1981, New Hampshire Population Trends, Changes in Households and Household Size for Towns and Cities in New Hampshire, Taxable Valuation Per Person in New Hampshire Communities.*

New Jersey

Office of Economic Analysis, State of New Jersey, 1 West State St. Trenton, NJ 08625; (609) 292-3860. Publications: *Economic Report of the Governor-Annual, Economic Forecast-Annual.*

New Mexico

Economic Development Department, 1100 St. Francis Drive, Santa Fe, NM 87503; (505) 827-0302. Publications: *Annual Report, New Mexico USA (Economic Development), The New Mexico Rio Grande Research Corridor, New Mexico Magazine, The New Mexico Manufacturing Directory, The New Mexico Fact Book, Community Surveys, Brochure on International Trade, Brochure on Writing a Business Plan, Financial Resources in New Mexico.*

New York

Bureau of Business Research, NYS Department of Economic Development, Room 910, One Commerce Plaza, Albany, NY 12245; (518) 443-5522. Publications: *The Alpine Ski Industry in New York State, The Apparel Industry in New York State-A Statistical Profile, Business Trends in New York State-Monthly, Economic Trends in Selected Metropolitan Areas of New York State, Financial Services Industries in New York State, Industrial Development Bond report, New York State Business Fact Book Supplement-Annual, New York State Tax Structure-State Taxes-Local Taxes outside NYC, Local Taxes New York City, Personal Income in Areas and Counties of New York State-Annual, Profile of People, Jobs and Housing for New York State-New York City-Each County, A Statistical Profile of the Printing and Publishing Industry in New York State, A Statistical Report on High Technology Industries in New York State, Summaries of Selected Business and Business Climate Surveys, Summary of Business Statistics-Quarterly and Annual, Tax Incentives and Financing for Industrial Location, Tax Incentives-New York State, Tax Incentives-New York City.*

North Carolina

Office of Policy and Planning, NC Department of Administration, 116 Jones St., Raleigh, NC 27603-8003; (919) 733-4131.

North Dakota

North Dakota Scanning Network, State of North Dakota, Office of the Governor, Bismarck, ND 58505; (701) 224-2810. Publications: *Prairie Scans,* a newsletter identifying important issues and problems the state may face in the future. North Dakota Economic Development Commission, Liberty Memorial Building, Bismarck, ND 58505, (701) 224-2810. Publications: *Annual Planning Report, North Dakota Economic Indicators, New Wealth Creating in North Dakota, North Dakota Growth Indicators, North Dakota Taxes, Available Buildings in North Dakota, North Dakota Economic Development Commission Work Plan, Financial and North Dakota, Resources and North Dakota, Manufacturers and North Dakota, Network Newsletter.*

Ohio

State of Ohio, Department of Development, P.O. Box 1001, Columbus, OH 43216; (614) 466-2609. Publications: *Annual Report.*

Oklahoma

Oklahoma Futures Commission, Department of Commerce, 6601 Broadway Extension, P.O. Box 26980, Oklahoma City, OK 73126-0980; (405) 843-9770. Publications: *Five Year Plan.*

Oregon

Oregon Economic Development Department, 775 Summer Street NE, Salem, OR 97310; (503) 373-1200. Publications: *Starting a Business in Oregon, A Summary of Oregon Taxes, Financial Incentives for Business Expansion: Building the Long-Term Financing Gap for Small Business, Directory of Manufacturing Plants, Oregon County Economic Indicators ($3.50), Oregon Economic Development Revenue Bonds, Directory of Oregon Manufacturers ($60), Oregon Industrial and Commercial Announced Investments, Oregon Economic Trends Project ($50), Oregon International Trade Directory ($30), Exporter's Handbook ($25), Helping Export Firms, Personalized Export Panel, Asia Representatives Office, Directory of Oregon Electronic Products, Directory of Oregon Industrial Equipment and Supplies, Directory of Forest Products Equipment and Services.*

Pennsylvania

Pennsylvania Department of Commerce, 446 Forum Bldg., Harrisburg, PA 17120; (717) 783-1132. Publications: *Annual Report.*

Rhode Island

Rhode Island Statewide Planning Program, 265 Melrose St., Providence, RI 02907; (401) 277-2601. Publications: *State Guide Plan and Strategic Plan, The Housing Report of the Governor's Human Services Advisory Council, Interim Ground Transportation Plan-Year 2010, Access Update-Telecommunications Device for the Deaf in State Government, Forensic Services Security Issues, Quonset State Airport Master Plan, Jerusalem Master Plan, Hazard Mitigation Plan, Ocean State Outdoors-Recreation and Conservation Strategies for Rhode Island, Highway*

State Forecasting Centers

Jurisdiction in Rhode Island, *Methods for Calculating Vehicle Miles of Travel in Rhode Island, Transportation and Land Use, Rhode Island Coastal Resources Management Program, Water Resources Issues in Land Use Policy, Reevaluation of Statewide Travel Demand Model, Federally Assisted Rental Housing, Quonset State Airport Master Plan, Unified Work Program for Transportation Planning, Work Program 1987-1988, Policy Statement-Proposals for New or Restructured Public Transit Facilities or Service, Port of Galilee-A Case Study of Port Redevelopment, The Feasibility of Closing Ladd Center, Unified Work Program for Transportation Planning, Siting High-Level Nuclear Waste Repositories, Ocean State Outdoors-Recreation and Conservation Strategies for Rhode Island.*

South Carolina

Commission on the Future of South Carolina, Office of Lieutenant Governor, Post Office Box 142, Columbia, SC 29202; (803) 734-2080.

South Dakota

Governor's Office of Economic Development, Capitol Lake Plaza, 711 Wells Ave., Pierre, SD 57501-3369; (605) 773-5032. Publications: *Economic Development Programs, Directory of Manufacturers and Processors* ($35).

Tennessee

Department of Economic and Community Development, 320 Sixth Ave., North, Nashville, TN 37219; (615) 741-1888. Publications: *Economic Growth in Tennessee, Tennessee Economic Statistics, Tennessee Population.*

Texas

Comptroller of Public Accounts, LBJ State Office Building, Austin, TX 78774; (512) 463-1778. Publications: *Annual Financial Report, 1988-1989 Biennial Revenue Estimate, Taxes and Texas: A National Survey on Alternatives and Comparisons, Texas Fees-Putting a Price on State Services, Quarterly Survey of Business Expectations in Texas, Sales and Franchise Tax Exemptions, Time of Change-Time of Choice, State Government's Use of Outside Services, Decontrolling Natural Gas-The Impact on Texas Prices and Tax Revenue, The High Finance of Higher Education, The Petroleum Industry and the Texas Sales Tax, The Geography of State Spending, Productivity Ideas and Cost Cutting Alternative to Control of State Budget Growth, Hazardous Waste in Texas, The Geography of Texas Taxes.*

Utah

State Data Center, Office of State Planning and Budget, State of Utah, 116 Capitol Bldg, Salt Lake City, UT 84114; (801) 533-6082. Publications: *1987 Baseline Projections, Economic Report to the Governor, State of Utah Revenue Forecast* (quarterly), *Utah Data Guide* (quarterly), *Budget in Brief* (annual), *Capital Budget* (annual), *Historic and Projected Long Term Revenues and Expenditures, Historic Analysis of Preliminary Taxes, The Impact of the Gramm-Rudman-Hollings Deficit Reduction Act, The Import of the Tourism-Travel and Recreation Industry in Utah, The Importance of the Agricultural Industry in Utah, Retail Sales and Service Analysis, Flooding and Landslides in Utah-An Economic Impact Analysis, The Economic and Demographic Impacts of the Intermountain Power Project, Final Socio-economics Technical Report-Utah Basin Synfuels Development, Utah-2000, Energy-2000, Socioeconomic Impacts of the Boulder to Bullfrog Road Improvement, The Economic Issues Surrounding the Vitro Remedial Action Alternatives, Utah Facts, Utah Directory of Business and Industry, Utah Export Directory, Utah Economic Development Plan, Utah Economic and Business Review, Construction Report* (quarterly), *Statistical Abstract of Utah.*

Vermont

Office of Policy Research and Coordination, Pavillion Office Building, 109 State St., Montpelier, VT 05602; (802) 828-3326. Services and Responsibilities: Monitor Trends and Anticipate the Impact of Evolving Technologies such as Telecommunications, Provide Staff for the Governor's Council of Economic Advisors, Data on Vermont's Economy.

Virginia

Governor's Office, Department of Economic Development, 1000 Washington Building, Richmond, VA 23219; (804) 786-3791. Publications: *Virginia Facts and Figures 1987, Economic Developments-A Statistical Summary, Quarterly Economic Development Report, High Technology Communications in Virginia, Corporate Headquarters in Virginia, Metalworking Industries-Advantages of a Virginia Location, High Technology-Biomedical and Related Industries-Advantages of a Virginia Location, Printing Industry-Cost Savings in Virginia, Virginia Small Business Financing Authority, High Technology Applied Here, Virginia-Local Taxes on Manufacturers, Virginia-Export Management/Trading Companies, International Business Services Directory, Mountains of Hardwood-Virginia's Southern Mountain Region, Virginia-A Guide to Establishing a Business, Are You Ready? A Guide to Community Preparedness for Industrial Development in Virginia, Manufacturing in Virginia, Allegheny County-Clifton Forge-Covington-Virginia-A New Thrust for Industry, The Virginia Economy, Foreign Investment in Virginia.*

Washington

Washington State, Department of Trade and Economic Development, 101 General Administration Bldg., Olympia, WA 98504; (206) 753-5630. Publications: *Foreign Exports and the Washington Economy, The Aquaculture Industry in Washington State-An Economic Overview, Washington State Department of Trade and Economic Development-The First Two Years.*

West Virginia

Research and Strategic Planning, Department of Industrial and Community Development, 1900 Washington St., East Bldg. 6, Room 504, Charleston, WV 25305; (304) 348-3810.

Wisconsin

Bureau of Research, Department of Development, 123 West Washington Ave., P.O. Box 7970, Madison, WI 53707; (608) 267-9214. Publications: *Profiles in Success-Wisconsin Business Developments, New Industries and Plant Expansions Reported in Wisconsin, Models of State Entrepreneurial Development Programs, Youth Unemployment in Wisconsin, Entrepreneurial Culture in Wisconsin, Out-of-State Certified Minority Businesses, Industrial Revenue Bond Financing in Wisconsin, Analysis of State Investment Board Investments to Enhance the Wisconsin Economy, Biennial Report on Tax Incremental Financing, Industrial Revenue Bond Financing, Economic Development Lending Activities of the Wisconsin Housing Development Authority, Wisconsin Long-range Economic Forecast 1985-1995, An Economic Analysis of Wisconsin Regions, Advertising Conversion Results 1983 and 1986, Ozone Air Quality Management and Economic Development in Southeastern Wisconsin, The Relationship of State and Local Government Spending and Taxing to Economic Performance-An Econometric Analysis of States from 1972 to 1984, Labor Management Cooperation in Wisconsin, The Wisconsin Tourism Industry-Analysis of Market Share and Trends, The Economic Development Potential of the Service Sector Industries in Wisconsin, A Statistical Profile of Minority Population, Employment and Business Ownership in Wisconsin, Development Preparedness Task Force, Task Force Tourism Funding, The Flow of Federal Funds to Wisconsin, Exchange Rate and Interest Rates Effects on Wisconsin Employment, Management Assistance and Business Growth in Wisconsin, A Comparative Study of U.S. and Wisconsin Productivity-Analysis of Manufacturing Industries 1963-1982, Employment Potential of Wisconsin Industry Groups- An Analysis and Industry Classification, Local Economic Development in Wisconsin.*

Wyoming

Economic Development and Stabilization Board, Herschler Building, 2nd Floor West, Cheyenne, WY 82002; (307) 777-7284. Publications: *Wyoming, Directory of Manufacturing and Mining, Business Development Kit, Mineral Yearbook.*

Be patient. If any phone number is incorrect, call (area code) 555-1212 and request the new listing.

International Relations and Defense Foreign Policy

* *See also Economics, Demographics and Statistics*
* *See also Experts*
* *See also Current Events Reports and Homework*
* *See also Drug and Chemical Dependence; Law Enforcement*
* *See also International Trade*
* *See also Law and Social Justice; Immigration*
* *See also Tracking Federal Legislation*
* *See also Vacations and Business Travel*

The U.S. Department of State, the Agency for International Development (AID), and nearly half a dozen other government agencies study the changing political, social, and economic situations in every region of the world. All this intelligence is spun off into studies and reports as well as informative and readable material such as the State Department's Dispatch. If you are considering travel abroad, information about a country's history and culture is readily available. Anyone doing research on any region of the world can benefit from using the historical resources available as well as the country desk officers who track daily developments abroad. International treaties, peace and conflict resolution, and international organizations such as the World Bank also erase boundaries for obtaining information about our increasingly inter-dependent world. International agreements from Law of the Sea to the Nuclear Test Ban Treaty are spelled out in materials that the average person can understand. You'll also find plenty of public information on weapons systems and other aspects of the U.S. military.

* Advisory Commission on Public Diplomacy

United States Advisory Commission on Public Diplomacy
United States Information Agency (USIA)
301 Fourth St., SW, Room 600
Washington, DC 20547 (202) 619-4700

The seven Presidentially-appointed Commissioners oversee the operations of USIA and make a yearly report of findings and recommendations to the President, Congress, the Secretary of State, the Director of USIA, and the American people. The free report is available from this office.

* African Countries and US Foreign Policy

Bureau for African Affairs
U.S. Department of State
2201 C St., NW, Room 3509
Washington, DC 20520 (202) 647-7371

This Bureau develops implementation of U.S. policy in 46 Sub-Sahara African countries. The Office advises the Secretary of State on foreign policy issues, especially those focusing on democracy, economics, and human rights. Information is available on each of the countries, including *Background Notes*, foreign economic trend reports, and GIST summaries.

* Agency for International Development Library

Development Information Center, Room 105 SA-18
Agency for International Development (AID)
Washington, DC 20523-1801 (703) 875-4818

The library collections include: reference collection of current and retrospective runs of the major AID program documents and financial reports, such as *Congressional Presentations, Country Development Strategy Statements, Action Plans, Policy Papers, Current Technical Service Contracts and Grants*, and *U.S. Overseas Loans and Grants*, also the current *AID Handbook*; microfiche collection; historical off-site collection; Women in Development collection; current book collection of commercial publication, directories, yearbooks, and reports from other bilateral and international development agencies, private voluntary organizations, and research institutions which deal with current development issues. Access is through an online catalog. Although the library contains some information on development in general, most materials relate to AID-supported research and projects. The library holdings focus on those countries in which AID has or has had project or program activities, and on those subjects related to the Agency's work. If you are flexible about the countries and topics you are willing to investigate, you will have a much better chance of finding relevant information. A list of countries with AID missions is available in AID's *Project History List*, by Country Name in a black binder located on the right as you enter the library.

* Agriculture Assistance

Office of Agriculture
Bureau for Research and Development, Room 409, SA-18
Agency for International Development (AID)
Washington, DC 20523-1809 (703) 875-4300

This office provides technical leadership in the broad range of activities related to international agriculture development. The focus of the AID's agriculture, rural development, and nutrition program is to increase the incomes of the poor and expand the availability and consumption of food while maintaining the country's natural resource base. To obtain a copy of *A Program Guide to the Office of Agriculture, Bureau for Science and Technology*, contact this office.

* Agriculture Information

Office of Public Affairs
U.S. Department of Agriculture
Washington, DC 20250 (202) 720-7507

The USDA *Annual Report* and the annual *Fact Book of Agriculture* discuss important Agricultural foreign trade and policy developments. They are available free along with the *List of Available Publications*, which details USDA publications for sale. Publications include:

AIB 516 *Trade Liberalization in World Farm Markets*, 1987 p.ERS
PB 87-190559-AS PC AO3 MF AO1.

FAER 227 *Exporting U.S. Food to Sweden, Norway, and Finland*, 1987 57 p.ERS
PB 87-204582 PC AO5 MF AO1.

* Agricultural Policy

Economic Research Service
U.S. Department of Agriculture
1301 New York Ave., Room 208
Washington, DC 20005 (202) 219-0515

While Agriculture makes up a very small part of the economies of the industrialized world, it has become a very large and contentious foreign policy issue for industrialized nations, stalling trade negotiations and creating animosity.

Foreign Policy

The Economic Research Service publishes a wealth of information for those interested in agricultural issues and foreign policy. Publications can be ordered toll free in the U.S. and Canada by calling 1-800-999-6779, elsewhere call 301-725-7937, and include:

Agricultural Outlook - the premier USDA agriculture magazine it presents long term analyses of such issues as U.S. agricultural policy, trade forecasts and export-market development, food safety, and the environment. 11 issues Order # AGO, cost - 1 yr, $26; 2 yrs, $51; 3 yrs, $75.

World Agriculture - deals with worldwide developments in agricultural markets and trade. It is based on research ongoing in ERS. quarterly, Order # WAS. 1 yr,$21; 2 yrs, $41; 3 yrs, $60.

Foreign Agricultural Trade of the United States - updates the quantity and value of U.S. farm exports and imports, plus price trends. It also tracks U.S. in relation to the world market. 4 issues plus 2 supplements. Order # FAT. 1 yr, $25; 2 yrs, $49; 3 yrs, $72.

* A.I.D. Information

Development Information Center
Research and Reference Services
Room 105 SA-18
Agency for International Development (AID)
Washington, DC 20523-1801 (703) 875-4818

Information about the structure and administration of the AID is available from the series of *AID Handbooks* from the above reference section of the library. General information about AID's plans in a particular country can be found in the *Country Development Strategy Statements* (CDSS's) in the serials room. Also in the serials room are *Congressional Presentations* (CPs) and *Annual Budget Submissions* (ABSs), which contain financial information on AID projects. Information on all phases on AID projects is available in project documents (PD's).

* A.I.D. Magazine and Newsletter

Office of Publications
Agency for International Development (AID)
320 21st St., NW
Washington, DC 20523 (202) 647-4330

The Agency for International Development (AID) publishes a free quarterly newsletter, *AID Highlights*, which describes a different AID program in each issue. This publication is designed for those in the general public interested in Agency activities. *Frontlines* is a monthly newspaper, available to Agency staff and retirees that also highlights the current activities of the AID.

* A.I.D. Reference Services

Development Information Center
Room 105 SA-18
Agency for International Development (AID)
Washington, DC 20523-1801 (703) 875-4818

The library's holding of AID documents catalogued since 1974 are available on microfiche and can be read on microfiche readers in the library. Hard copies or microfiche copies of documents can be ordered from AID's Document Information Services Clearinghouse in Arlington, Va. The library's historical (pre-1974) documents are stored off-site, but may be retrieved upon request at the reference desk (be sure to have a full citation and complete call number). For more information, contact the office above.

* A.I.D. Speakers Bureau

Office of Public Liaison
Bureau for External Affairs
Agency for International Development (AID)
320 21st St., NW, Room 4889
Washington, DC 20523 (202) 647-4213

Speakers within the AID organization are available to address meetings and conferences. A wide variety of topics can be discussed, including women's issues, health, economic policy, agriculture, world hunger, and disaster relief. A letter must be sent to the office above outlining the format of the meeting, the number of people attending, the location of the meeting, and the subject of the presentation. A minimum of two weeks is needed to secure a speaker.

* Alien Registration Information

Central Office
Immigration and Naturalization Service
425 I Street, NW
Washington, DC 20536 (202) 307-1501

Publications and tape recorded messages about immigration are available from this central office. However, field offices operate in most states and these local phone numbers appear in the Law and Social Justice Chapter and, of course, are easy to obtain from the directory assistance operators. When calling the tape recorded telephone number listed above, enter one of the number codes below which corresponds to the information about immigration and naturalization that you need:

401 Permanent alien residency card
402 Applying for a replacement alien residency card (I-90)
403 If you never received your alien residency card (I-90)

* American and Foreign Teachers Exchange Program

Office of Academic Programs
United States Information Agency (USIA)
301 Fourth St., SW, Room 353
Washington, DC 20547 (202) 619-4555

The Advising, Teaching, and Specialized Programs Division serves overseas education advising centers, foreign exchange students in the U.S., and administers the International Student Exchange Program for one-to-one exchange of university students. Its Teacher Exchange Branch arranges one and two way exchanges of U.S. and foreign teachers, and summer seminars for U.S. teachers to study abroad. Free brochures and applications are available.

* American Books Overseas Distribution

Book Programs Division
Office of Cultural Centers and Resources
Bureau of Educational and Cultural Affairs
United States Information Agency (USIA)
301 Fourth St., SW, Room 320
Washington, DC 20547 (202) 619-4896

USIA helps in the translation, publication, and promotion of American books overseas. The Promotion Branch organizes traveling book exhibits and supports an American presence at international book fairs. The Field Operations Branch supports the translation and publication of a broad range of titles, mostly in the social sciences and humanities.

* American Business and A.I.D. Coordination

Office of Trade and Investment
Agency for International Development (AID)
320 21st St., NW, Room 3253
Washington, DC 20523 (202) 647-9100

This office assists, coordinates, and advises on the involvement of the U.S. business community with AID to achieve Agency objectives. Cooperative projects between AID and the U.S. business community within AID's guidelines are encouraged. Contact this office for more information. For regional information one can also contact the Development Center at the U.S. Department of Commerce at (202) 377-0841.

* American Enterprise Institute

1150 17th St., NW
Washington, DC 20036 (202) 862-5800

AEI is an independent, non-partisan organization dedicated to the "maintenance of a free and prosperous economic order, a resolute national defense, and tradition-proven cultural and political values." AEI conducts research in three general areas: domestic and international economic policy; foreign and defense policy; and social and political studies. A free catalogue of AEI books and publications is available.

* American Experts Overseas Lecture Tour

Office of Program Coordination and Development
United States Information Agency (USIA)
301 Fourth St., SW, Room 550
Washington, DC 20547 (202) 619-4720

AmParts are experts in a field--usually economics, international affairs, literature, the arts, U.S. political and social processes, sports, science, or technology--sent

Be patient. If any phone number is incorrect, call (area code) 555-1212 and request the new listing.

International Relations and Defense

abroad by USIA to meet with groups or individual professional counterparts. Recruited on the basis of requests of USIA staff in other countries, AmParts often engage in informal lecture/discussions with small groups, grant media interviews, or speak before larger audiences. Those interested in the American Participant program are invited to submit a brief letter indicating times of availability, along with a curriculum vitae and at least two lecture topics with brief talking points. A free brochure on the program is available from this office.

★ American Foreign Policy Information Clearinghouse

Bureau of Public Affairs
U.S. Department of State
2201 C St., NW, Room 5819
Washington, DC 20520 (202) 647-6575 or 6576

The State Department in Washington, DC receives thousands of reports daily, and produces hundreds of publications, speeches, and conferences are produced each year. The Bureau of Public Affairs informs the American people on foreign policy and advises the Secretary of State on public opinion. To request information or express an opinion, contact the above office. If unable to answer an inquiry directly, staff will direct you to the appropriate source. This bureau issues various publications covering U.S. foreign relations, some of which are free. In 1991 the State Department phased out many of its publications including *Gist Series, Current Policy Series, Special Report Series, Selected Documents Series, Regional Briefs,* and the *Historical Issues Series.* The information in these documents can now be found in the new U.S. Department of State *Dispatch.* Contact the above office for further information.

★ American Publications Translated and Distributed Worldwide

Superintendent of Documents
Government Printing Office (GPO)
Washington, DC 20402 (202) 783-3238

The United States Information Agency publishes many teaching materials, including books, maps, complete teaching modules, and 14 magazines in 20 languages. By law most USIA publications may be distributed only in foreign countries. However, by congressional action, two magazines are available in the United States. *English Teaching Forum,* a quarterly for English teachers worldwide, is published by USIA's English Language Programs Division. *Problems of Communism* is a bi-monthly forum for American and foreign scholars discussing communist and socialist affairs. It is published in English and Spanish. Both these magazines are available through the GPO.

★ American Schools and Hospitals Abroad

Bureau for Food and Humanitarian Assistance
Agency for International Development (AID), SA-8
Washington, DC 20523 (703) 351-0232

Each year this Bureau gives grants on a competitive basis to private, non-profit schools, hospitals, and libraries known for their excellence in demonstrating U.S. ideas and practices of education and medicine to citizens of other countries. Grant recipients must by U.S.-based, tax-exempt, private citizens' organizations which have founded and/or sponsor overseas institutions on a continuing basis. Eligible schools must be for secondary or higher level educations, while hospitals must conduct medical education and research. Grants are made to the U.S. sponsors for the exclusive benefit of the overseas institutions and customarily carry matching or cost-sharing provisions. Contact the office above for more information.

★ American Studies for Foreigners

Division of Study of the U.S.
United States Information Agency (USIA)
301 Fourth St., SW, Room 256
Washington, DC 20547 (202) 619-4557

The Division for the Study of the U.S. promotes foreign education through conferences, seminars, exchange programs for foreign educators, grants, and development of school resource materials. The Academic Specialist Branch provides grants for American teachers to instruct their peers at foreign educational institutions. Contact this office for more information.

★ Aquaculture and Fishing in Third World

Fisheries Specialist
Office of Programming and Training Support
Peace Corps, 1990 K St., NW

Washington, DC 20526 (202) 606-3402

In helping people help themselves, fishery specialists provide information and techniques to farmers and fishermen on stocking, managing, feeding, and harvesting fish.

★ Arab-Israeli Conflict Study

United States Institute of Peace
1550 M St., NW, Suite 700
Washington, DC 20005-1708 (202) 457-1700

In July 1991 the Institute of Peace convened a study group to examine diplomatic techniques that might be useful in reaching a peaceful settlement of the Arab-Israeli conflict. *Making Peace Among Arabs and Israelis* documents the results of this study and is available free from the Institute.

★ Arctic and Antarctic International Policy

Office of Oceans
Bureau of Oceans and International Environmental and Scientific Affairs
U.S. Department of State
2201 C St., NW, Room 5801
Washington, DC 20520 (202) 647-3262

This office is concerned with all issues concerning the Arctic and Antarctic, including the environment and marine life, such as whales and seals. They are also closely involved with the many science stations located on the Antarctic.

★ Artistic Ambassador Program

United States Information Agency (USIA)
301 4th St., SW, Room 216
Washington, DC 20547 (202) 619-5338

Begun in 1983, the Artistic Ambassador Program is designed to utilize the wealth of often undiscovered American musical talent to enhance the USIA mission of cross-cultural understanding. Musicians are sent on tours ranging from 4-6 weeks. Since the programs inception, 41 musical ambassadors have visited 79 nations. For information, contact the above office.

★ Assistance to Foreign Highways

International Highway Programs (HPI-10)
Associate Administrator for Policy
Federal Highway Administration (FHWA)
U.S. Department of Transportation
400 7th St., SW
Washington, DC 20590 (202) 366-0111

FHWA administers programs which provide assistance and advice to foreign governments engaged in highway engineering and administration. Projects have included technical assistance in fabricating bridge segments, value engineering skills, development of transportation systems, materials testing, quality control, and skid testing. Through the International Visitors Program, highway specialists from over 40 countries receive training. Countries that have participated include China, Indonesia, Haiti, Kuwait, Dubai, and Saudi Arabia. Two publications available from this office are *World of Technology for Sharing* and *Highway Community on the Occasion of the 18th World Road Congress.*

★ Atomic Energy

International Atomic Energy Agency (IAEA)
Wagramerstrasse 5
P.O. Box 100
A-1400 Vienna, Austria

The IAEA twin goals are to promote the peaceful use of Atomic energy and to supervise civilian installations to prevent the military use of nuclear fuel. The IAEA supports the safeguards regime set out by the Nuclear Non-Proliferation Treaty of 1968, through periodic inspections of facilities arranged by the host nations.

★ Balance of Payments Support

International Monetary Fund (IMF)
700 19th St., NW
Washington, DC 20431 (202) 623-7000

The IMF's primary purpose is to provide short term balance of payments assistance to members experiencing temporary difficulties. The Fund also operates a Compensatory Financing Facility to support members, particularly

Be patient. If any phone number is incorrect, call (area code) 555-1212 and request the new listing.

Foreign Policy

those producing primary products which suffer from fluctuations in export receipts. The Fund issues a broad range of studies, reports, and publications on its activities and related economic subjects.

* Bilateral and Multilateral International Aid Donors

International Donor Programs
Policy Office
Agency for International Development (AID)
320 21st St., NW, Room 3637
Washington, DC 20523 (202) 647-0600

This Bureau coordinates AID policies and programs with other bilateral assistance donors, United Nations development organizations, and multilateral development banks. In close collaboration with State, Treasury, and other interested government agencies, the Bureau reviews programs, budgets, and staffing of the international development organizations. Recommendations are made on the U.S. Government's position regarding these matters, and guidance is provided to U.S. representatives to these organizations.

* Binational Libraries and Cultural Centers Worldwide

Library Programs Division
Bureau of Educational and Cultural Affairs
United States Information Agency (USIA)
301 Fourth St., SW, Room 314
Washington, DC 20547 (202) 619-4915

USIA maintains or supports libraries and reading rooms in 160 cities in 89 countries, as well as library programs at 111 binational centers in 17 countries. Collections focus on fostering foreign understanding of U.S. people, history, and culture. A bi-weekly bibliography, listing 80-100 titles on international relations and developments in the U.S., is one of many library services provided for the overseas posts, including reference and research assistance. More information on the program can be obtained in the Bowker Annual Library and Book Trade Information Manual, which can be found in many libraries.

* Black Medical Schools and International Development

Agency Center for University Cooperation and Development
Bureau for Research and Development, Room 900, SA-38
Agency for International Development (AID)
Washington, DC 20523-3801 (703) 816-0295

AID has initiated a program to increase participation by historically black medical schools in AID-supported international activities. The program links each of four participating medical schools with a major U.S. School of Public Health that already has extensive overseas experience. Through a set of Joint Memoranda of Understanding (JMOU), program support grants have been awarded to the eight participating institutions to increase their capacity to provide technical assistance to AID field missions in implementing health, population, and nutrition policies and strategies. Contact this office for more information.

* Brookings Institution

1775 Massachusetts Ave., NW
Washington, DC 20036 (202) 797-6105

Brookings can be considered the "dean" of public policy/foreign policy think tanks in Washington. With 50 full time scholars and 200 staff assistants, the Institution pursues research in the areas of Economic Studies, Foreign Policy Studies, Governmental Studies, and Public Policy Education. Each research area is headed by a nationally renowned scholar. Contact Brookings for information on current research projects and for the latest catalogue of books.

* Business Development Teaching Overseas

Peace Corps
1990 K St., NW
Washington, DC 20526 (202) 606-3412

Volunteers teach new ways of conducting business and trade by introducing basic accounting skills, administration, and marketing to farmers, fisherman, and village women.

* Caribbean and Latin America Field Project Histories

Inter-American Foundation
1515 Wilson Blvd.
Rosslyn, VA 22209 (703) 841-3830

IAF is compiling 267 project file-based histories and 13 field- based project histories which outline the background, results, and lessons learned of each of IAF's funded projects in Latin America and the Caribbean. These histories are valuable research tools for those interested in development efforts in these regions.

* Caribbean Basin Employment and Trade

Office of International Economic Affairs
Bureau of International Economic Affairs
U.S. Department of Labor
200 Constitution Ave., NW, Room S5355
Washington, DC 20210 (202) 523-7597

The annual report, *Trade and Employment Effects of the Caribbean Basin Economic Recovery Act*, describes the provisions included in the CBERA, along with the benefits they provide to beneficiary countries. It also analyzes changes in U.S. trade with CBERA countries, and looks at trends in U.S. employment in those industries which have undergone the most significant changes in trade flows. Contact this office for more information on the report.

* Carnegie Endowment for International Peace

11 Dupont Circle NW, Suite 900
Washington, DC 20036 (202) 862-7900

Established in 1910 through a gift from Andrew Carnegie, the Endowment conducts programs of research, discussion, publication, and education in international affairs and American foreign policy. Special projects include the Middle East Arms Control Project; Immigration Policy Project; and the U.S.-Soviet Relations Study Group. For a list of current research projects and internship opportunities, contact the Endowment.

* Center for the Study of Foreign Affairs

Foreign Service Institute
1400 Key Blvd., Room 304
Arlington, VA 22209 (703) 875-5183

The Center for the Study of Foreign Affairs aims to enrich traditional Foreign Service training by keeping government officials in many agencies abreast of emerging foreign policy concepts. Its program of conferences, research, and publications combines new perspectives developed by private scholarship with the practical experience of foreign affairs personnel. The Center publishes full-length studies of various foreign policy issues in its *Study of Foreign Affairs series*, many of which are based on conferences and workshops held at the Center.

* Central and Eastern Europe Assistance Programs

Peace Corps
Eastern European Desk
1990 K St., NW
Washington, DC 20526 (202) 606-3547

The revolutions of 1989 that swept the communists from power in Eastern Europe also swept in the Peace Corps for the first time since their creation in 1961. Peace Corps volunteers now serve in Poland, Czechoslovakia, Bulgaria, Romania, Yugoslavia, Albania, and in the former USSR. Initially, most volunteers taught english at the secondary school and university level. Plans are being developed for programs in Agriculture, Child Survival, Environmental Protection, and Small Business Development. Currently there are 461 volunteers in Eastern Europe. For background information on the current programs, contact the above office.

* Central Intelligence Agency Information

Public Affairs
Central Intelligence Agency (703) 351-2053
Washington, DC 20505 (703) 482-7676

The Public Affairs office can provide declassified information and respond to inquiries.

* Central Intelligence Agency Reports Published Before 1980

Photoduplication Service
Library of Congress
Washington, DC 20540 (202) 707-1636

The Library of Congress distributes CIA reports that have been released to the

Be patient. If any phone number is incorrect, call (area code) 555-1212 and request the new listing.

International Relations and Defense

public. These reports detail foreign government structures, trade news, economic conditions, and industrial development. Orders must be prepaid or charged to a standing account at the Library of Congress. For $13 the projects unit for the CIA in the Photoduplication Service can also provide you with a list of CIA reports available. Reports can be purchased on microfilm for $.50 per exposure or $30 per reel.

* Childhood Communicable Disease Control

Health Programmer
Office of Programming and Training Coordination
Peace Corps
1990 K St., NW
Washington, DC 20526 (202) 254-8400

The Peace Corps has developed child survival programs that train parents as well as children with curricula designed to teach better nursing skills, with an emphasis on vaccination.

* Child Survival in the Third World

Document Information Services Clearinghouse
1500 Wilson Blvd., Suite 1010
Arlington, VA 22209-2404 (703) 351-4006

The child health publications listed below can be viewed in the Library on microfiche, and paper copies may be obtained from the address above. Note that document identification call numbers follow the identification number. Their telefax number is (301) 951-9624.

The A.I.D. Diarrheal Disease Control Strategy (Oral Rehydration Therapy and Related Interventions). Washington, DC; U.S. Agency for International Development, 1986. (616.3427.A288) (PN-AAX-052).

Birth Spacing and Child Survival. Maine, Deborah and Regina McNamara. Sponsored by the U.S. Agency for International Development, Bureau for Science and Technology, Office of Population, New York: Columbia University, Center for Population and Family Health, 1985. (613.94.M225) (PN-AAV-575).

Child Survival: A Third Report to Congress. Washington, DC: U.S. Agency for International Development, 1987. (613.0432.C536 1987) (PN-AAZ-401).

Child Survival: Risks and the Road to Health. Galway, Katrina, Brent Wolff and Richard Sturgis. Sponsored by the U.S. Agency for International Development, Bureau for Science and Technology, Office of Population. Columbia, MD: Westinghouse Company, Institute for Resource Development, Inc. 1987. (362.19892.G183) (PN-AAX-157).

Child Survival Strategy, 1987-1990: Bureau for Africa, U.S. Agency for International Development. Washington, DC: U.S. Agency for International Development, Bureau for Africa, Office of Technical Resources, 1987. (613.0432.C536) (PD-AAU-969).

Health and Family Planning in Community-Based Distribution Programs. Mawer, Maria, Sandra Huffman, Deborah Cebula and Richard Osbor, eds. Sponsored by the U.S. Agency for International Development, Bureau for Science and Technology, Office of Population, Boulder, CO: Westview Press, 1985. (362.1.W356) (PN-AAT-004).

Immunizations. Primary Health Care Issues Series. Sabin, Edward and Wayne Stinson. Washington, D.C: American Public Health Association, 1981. (614.47.I33) (PN-AAJ-782).

Notes From the Field: A.I.D.-Supported Oral Rehydration Therapy Activities. Sanghvi, Tina and Patricia E. Scully. Proceedings from the International Conference on Oral Rehydration Therapy, 2nd, Washington, DC, December 10-13, 1985. Washington, DC: Creative Associates, Inc. for the U.S. Agency for International Development, 1985. (616.3427.S225) (PN-AAU-137).

* Child Survival Action Program

Office of Health
Bureau for Research and Development, Room 709, SA-18
Agency for International Development (AID)
Washington, DC 20523 (703) 875-4600

Each year, fourteen to fifteen million children in developing countries die of disease and malnutrition before they reach the age of five. In February 1985, A.I.D. demonstrated its commitment to helping these children by establishing the Child Survival Action Program (CSAP) to deliver simple, inexpensive, and proven technologies to save the lives of these children and to improve their prospects for a healthy future. A.I.D.'s child survival strategy includes four basis interventions: oral rehydration therapy (ORT), immunization, birth spacing, and better infant and child nutrition. For information on CSAP, contact the office above.

* CIA Catalog of Maps and Publications

Public Affairs
Central Intelligence Agency (CIA)
Washington, DC 20505 (703) 351-2053

The CIA declassifies many of its maps which are available from the National Technical Information Service, 5285 Port Royal Road, Springfield, VA 22161 (703) 487-4650. The catalog, titled *CIA Maps and Publications Released to the Public*, is available free from the CIA. Some of the titles include *The Impact of Gorbachev's Policies on Soviet Economic Statistics* (NTIS SOV 88-10049); *Chiefs of State and Cabinet Members of Foreign Governments* (NTIS LDA-CS 88-001); *The World Factbook* (NTIS PB 88-928009) and *OECD Trade with the Middle East* (PB-91-928012).

* Citizenship and Naturalization

Central Office
Immigration and Naturalization Service
425 I Street, NW
Washington, DC 20536 (202) 307-1501

Publications and tape recorded messages about immigration and naturalization are available from this central office. However, field offices operate in most states and these local phone numbers appear in the Law and Social Justice Chapter and, of course, are easy to obtain from the directory assistance operators. When calling the tape recorded telephone number listed above, enter one of the number codes below which corresponds to the information about immigration and naturalization that you need:

801 Citizenship and Naturalization requirements (N-400)
805 Residency requirements for naturalization
804 Derivative citizenship for children of U.S. citizens
802 Citizenship for children born outside the United States (N-600)
803 Naturalization based upon military service
807 Replacement of certificate of citizenship or naturalization (N-565)
806 How to file for naturalization on behalf of a child
808 To renounce or forfeit United States citizenship

* Commercial Library Program Publications List

Foreign Affairs Information Management Center
2201 C St., NW, Room 3239
U.S. Department of State
Washington, DC 20520 (202) 647-1062

This list provides a wide-ranging selection of publications useful to commercial reference facilities. It contains annotated bibliographies of directories, buyers' guides, yearbooks, atlases, etc., in general and in special product areas. State manufacturing and industrial directories are included, as are telex directories.

* Commerce and Foreign Affairs

International Trade Administration
U.S. Department of Commerce
14th St. between E St. and Constitution Ave NW.
Washington, DC 20230 (202) 377-2000

In the post-Cold War international environment, trade and economic issues will take on increased foreign policy importance for the United States. The International Trade Administration is a good source of information on the political aspects of trade negotiations such as the Uruguay Round of multilateral trade negotiations. For further information, contact ITA at the number above and ask to speak to the officer for the country or region you are interested in.

* Conflict Resolution

United States Institute of Peace
1550 M St., N.W.
Washington, DC 20005 (202) 457-1700

The Jeanette Rankin library program supports the expansion of the Institute's and the nation's information resources on issues in the fields of peace and international conflict management. The Institute also conducts the annual National Peace Essay Contests for high school students, and has many television and other media projects on such subjects as the history of U.S.--USSR summitry and issues and ideas in peacemaking. Publications of the Institute include the biennial report; the bimonthly Journal which provides information on the Institute's programs and achievements and increases public knowledge of important projects and points of view; and *In Brief*, a new series highlighting results from Institute projects, as well as books and papers.

Be patient. If any phone number is incorrect, call (area code) 555-1212 and request the new listing.

Foreign Policy

Institute reports available include the following:

Biennial Report of the United States Institute of Peace, 1989.
Contributions to the Study of Peacemaking: A Summary of Completed Grant Projects (12/90)
The Gulf Crisis: Finding A Peaceful Solution (1990).
Guide to Specialists (Institute fellow and staff areas of expertise, 1991-92).
Making Peace Among Arabs and Israelis: Lessons from Fifty Years of Negotiating Experience (1991).
Prospects for Conflict or Peace in Central and Eastern Europe (1990).

* Congress-Bundestag Youth Exchange Program

Youth Programs Division
United States Information Agency (USIA)
301 4th St., SW, Room 357
Washington, DC 20547 (202) 619-6299

Jointly funded by the United States Congress and the German Bundestag, this program is designed to strengthen ties between the two countries. The program provides full scholarships or a year of study, homestay, and work internships. The program serves approximately 800 American and German students each year, most of whom are in high school.

* Congressional Research Service (CRS)

Foreign Affairs and National Defense Division
Room 315, Library of Congress
Washington, DC 20540 (202) 707-5700

The Congressional Research Service is an excellent source for foreign affairs information. The foreign affairs division has some 60 full time analysts writing and updating reports as well as answering special requests for Congress. Individual analysts are superb sources for information as they often follow issues for years. CRS reports are not normally available to the public, but can be obtained through your Congressman's or Senator's office. If you contact CRS directly, see if the report you are interested in has been inserted into the Congressional Record and/or a House or Senate report. A complete list of CRS reports has been reprinted in the Current Events and Homework section.

* Cooperatives and Credit Unions

Office of Private and Voluntary Cooperation
Bureau for Food and Humanitarian Assistance, Room 712, SA-8
Agency for International Development (AID)
Washington, DC 20523 (703) 351-0211

U.S. cooperatives provide business services and outreach in cooperative development to underdeveloped countries for their U.S. membership. These organizations support the participation of rural and urban poor people in their countries' development. These organizations are not charitable or fund-raising groups and rely almost exclusively on AID funding for their international programs.

* Country and Territory Info Pamphlets

Superintendent of Documents
Government Printing Office
Washington, DC 20402 (202) 783-3238

Background Notes, a series of short, factual pamphlets about various countries and territories of the world, plus selected international organizations, contain up-to-date information on each country's people, culture, geography, history, government, political conditions, economy, defense, and foreign relations with other countries, including the United States. A reading list provides additional sources of information about the country, and travel notes, maps, and occasional photographs are often included. A complete set can be purchased from the Government Printing Office for $63.

* Country "Desks"

Country Desk Officers
U.S. Department of State
2201 C St., NW
Washington, DC 20520 (202) 647-4000

The State Department's Country Desk Officers are responsible for following all activities in their assigned countries, from the political, economic, and social perspectives. These officers are in contact with the embassies; deliver and receive documents from the embassies; and write reports on the current activities in the country. The officers can provide the most current information available about

their country. Call the number above and ask for the country you wish to find information about. Also see the Expert Chapter for a complete roster giving the name and phone number of the country specialists.

* Country Intelligence and Research Coordination

U.S. Department of State
Bureau of Intelligence and Research
2201 C St., NW, Room 8732
Washington, DC 20520 (202) 647-2025

This bureau coordinates programs of intelligence, research, and analysis for the State Department and for other Federal agencies, and produces intelligence studies and current intelligence analyses essential to foreign policy determination and execution. The Office of Research maintains a liaison with cultural and educational institutions on a wide range of matters relating to Government contractual and private foreign affairs research.

* Cultural and Educational International Exchange

Office of Public Liaison
United States Information Agency (USIA)
301 Fourth St., SW, Room 602
Washington, DC 20547 (202) 619-2355

The USIA distributes the free *Directory of Resources for Cultural and Educational Exchanges and U.S. Information,* a treasure trove of information on cultural and educational exchange programs in the U.S. The directory provides contacts and background information of government agencies and non-profit and private organizations which sponsor exchange programs.

* Development Aid Policy and Budget

Directorate of Finance Administration
Policy Office
Agency for International Development (AID)
320 21st St., NW, Room 3756
Washington, DC 20523 (202) 647-9110

AID's program and budget is formulated and revised as needed by the Bureau for Program and Policy Coordination. This Bureau presents the Agency's program to Congress, and reviews country program strategies and project proposals. The Bureau develops economic assistance policies, provides guidance on long-range program planning, economic analysis, sector assistance strategies, and project analysis and design.

* Development Assistance

World Bank
1818 H. Street, NW
Washington, DC 20433 (202) 477-1234

The World Bank is made up of three separate institutions - the International Bank for Reconstruction and Development (IBRD), The International Development Association (IDA), and the International Finance Corporation (IFC) - which share the common goal of helping to raise standards of living of the people in the developing countries by channelling financial resources from developed countries to the developing world. World Bank institutions support programs of technical assistance and research in support of its development goals.

* Development Fund for Africa

Bureau of African Affairs
Office of Development Policy
New State, Room 2495
Agency for International Development (AID)
Washington, DC 20523 (202) 647-3362

In 1987 Congress consolidated many of the aid programs to Sub-Saharan Africa into the Development Fund for Africa. The implementation of the DFA since its inception has been focused on helping African governments and people to achieve the goal of sustainable broad-based, market-oriented economic growth. Contact this office for the following reports: *The Development Fund for Africa* report, 1991; and *U.S. Assistance for Africa - The Development Fund for Africa (DFA): An Action Plan,* May 1989.

* Development Information System

Center for Development Information and Evaluation
Policy Coordination Office

Be patient. If any phone number is incorrect, call (area code) 555-1212 and request the new listing.

International Relations and Defense

Agency for International Development (AID)
Washington, DC 20523-1801 (703) 875-4818
This Center operates and maintains the A.I.D. Development Information System (DIS), which provides online access to development assistance experience from almost 9,000 A.I.D.-funded projects and over 70,000 A.I.D.-generated technical, evaluation, and research reports. The *A.I.D. Technical Reports* is a monthly acquisitions list which presents citations recently added to the DIS of technical reports from Agency sponsored projects and activities. The *A.I.D. Project Descriptions* is a quarterly acquisitions list which presents abstracts of grant agreements, project design documents, and project identification documents recently added to the DIS. Citations are organized by sector and within sector by title. Contact the office above for further information.

Patrons outside the Washington metropolitan area may request searches of DIS by writing to A.I.D., Development Information Center, Room 105, SA-18, Washington, DC 20523-1801. Include your return address and in 4-6 weeks you will receive a computer print-out listing projects, with descriptions, and document bibliographies. This search service is free. Patrons outside the Washington metropolitan area may request searches of DIS by writing to A.I.D., Development Information Center, Room 105 SA-18, Washington, DC 20523-1801. Include your return address and in 4 to 6 weeks you will receive a computer print out listing projects, with descriptions, and document bibliographies. This search service is free.

* Diplomatic Archives in Foreign Countries

Office of the Historian
Bureau of Public Affairs
S A-1, Room 3100
U.S. Department of State
Washington, DC 20522 (202) 663-1122
The monograph, *Public Availability of Diplomatic Archives in Foreign Countries*, lists each country and its archival rules, requirements, and documents made available by contacting GPO, Superintendent of Documents, Washington, DC, 20402-6518, (202) 783-3238. A list of important published works on archival sources is also available.

* Drug War

Bureau of International Narcotics Matters
U.S. Department of State
2201 C St., NW, Room 7331
Washington, DC 20520 (202) 647-6936
To coordinate the worldwide effort to halt the production and flow of illegal drugs to the United States, this bureau works closely with foreign governments and international organizations. Under bilateral agreements and international treaties, it provides technical and material assistance to foreign governments for such programs as eradication of narcotics crops, destruction of illicit laboratories, and training of antinarcotics interdiction personnel. This office also produces the *International Narcotics Control Strategy Report*, which is available for purchase at the GPO (202) 783-3238.

* East Asia and Pacific Region Clearinghouse

Bureau of East Asia and Pacific Affairs
U.S. Department of State
Public Affairs, Room 5209
2201 C St., NW
Washington, DC 20520 (202) 647-2538
This Bureau is responsible for U.S. relations with the countries in East Asia and the Pacific, which include Australia, New Zealand, China, Indonesia, Malaysia, Brunei, Singapore, Japan, North and South Korea, Philippines, the Pacific Islands, Taiwan, Thailand, Burma, Vietnam, Laos, and Cambodia. This office advises the Secretary on foreign policy issues, especially those focusing on democracy, economics, and human rights.

* Economic and Social Conditions Worldwide

Center for Development Information and Evaluation
Agency for International Development (AID)
PPC/CDIE, SA-18
Washington, DC 20523-1802 (703) 875-4818
The Economic and Social Data System (ESDS) contains statistical information gathered from government agencies and organizations from around the world. Countries worldwide are characterized according to the Country's economy, financial situation, demographics, poverty indicators, labor force, social factors,

and the levels of education, nutrition, health, and food. This database is for use by AID employees and contractors only.

* Economic Development in the Third World

Office of Economic and Institutional Development
Bureau for Research and Development, Room 608, SA-18
Agency for International Development (AID)
Washington, DC 20523 (703) 875-4710
This office's goal is to create broadly based and sustainable economic growth and the active economic participation of the poor in underdeveloped countries. The staff of economists, anthropologists, and social and management scientists work on policy and institutional change and technology transfer in three key areas: employment and enterprise development; decentralization and public management; and natural resources and regional economic systems analysis and management. Contact this office for more information.

* Economic Development Projects Involving Women

Women in Development
Office of Training and Program Support
Peace Corps, 1990 K St., NW
Washington, DC 20526 (202) 606-2366/4472
This office ensures that Peace Corps programs are designed to fully integrate women into the economic development process of their countries and communities. This office provides programming, training, and evaluation to the field workers. *The Exchange*, a quarterly newsletter, is published and distributed to 6,000 volunteers and staff in the field, with a focus on projects involving women.

* Economic Policy

Bureau of International Organization Affairs
U.S. Department of State
2201 C St., NW, Room 5328
Washington, DC 20520 (202) 647-8270
This office, as coordinator of U.S. economic policy within the United Nations, is responsible for the analysis and handling of international economic issues as they arise in international organizations, especially those in force in the U.N. system.

* Economic Support Fund

Office of Finance Administration and Budgeting
Bureau of Finance Administration
Agency for International Development (AID)
320 21st St., NW, Room 3847
Washington, DC 20523 (202) 647-6671
The Economic Support Fund supports U.S. economic, political, and security interests and advances U.S. foreign policy objectives. The resources that ESF provides curb the spread of economic and political disruption and help friends and allies to deal with threats on their security and independence. ESF is flexible economic assistance provided on a grant or loan basis. It may be used to sustain economic activity to address basic development needs, or to improve the basic framework of the existing system. Additional information is available in the *AID Congressional Presentation Document*, which is available from the Office of Legislative Affairs, (202) 647-8441.

* Education Development in Developing Countries

Office of Education
Bureau for Research and Development, SA-18 Room 609
Agency for International Development (AID)
Washington, DC 20523-1815 (703) 875-4700
This office helps developing countries more efficiently allocate and use of their education resources, especially at the primary school level. To improve the quality of education, the office also develops appropriate and effective teaching technologies. And by developing educational communications and social marketing systems, researchers help improve AID's health and agriculture extension services. Contact the office above for a portfolio directory of projects and for further information.

* Energy Assessments

Energy Assessments Division
Forrestal Bldg., Room 7G-076
U.S. Department of Energy

Be patient. If any phone number is incorrect, call (area code) 555-1212 and request the new listing.

Foreign Policy

Washington, DC 20585 (202) 586-6140
This office develops strategic assessments on critical international energy issues including: world oil market conditions, petroleum stocks, natural gas security, electricity policy, and energy environmental concerns.

* Energy Emergencies

Office of Energy Emergencies Operations
Forrestal Bldg., Room 8F-073
U.S. Department of Energy
Washington, DC 20585 (202) 586-3271
This office is responsible for improving the Federal Government's ability to meet U.S. and allied energy requirements during catastrophic disasters.

* Energy Policy

Office for International Affairs and Energy Emergencies
Room 7C-016, Forrestal Building
U.S. Department of Energy
Washington, DC 20585 (202) 586-5800
The office of the Assistance Secretary for International Affairs and Energy Emergencies is responsible for developing and directing international energy policy, including the international component of overall energy policy, and for coordinating the Department's energy emergency preparedness planning, and the encouragement of free trade in energy resources, services, equipment, and technology.

* Energy Development in Developing Countries

Office of Energy and Infrastructure
Bureau for Research and Development
Agency for International Development (AID)
SA-18, Room 508
Washington, DC 20523 (703) 875-4203
With the AID's Missions and Regional Bureaus, this office helps assisted countries develop appropriate energy services. Program goals with respect to programs in Less Developed Countries include: increased consideration of environmental criteria in projects; increased technical efficiency and financial performance of energy systems; greater private enterprise involvement in energy development and management; and expanded use of sustainable indigenous energy resources. Office projects include: Energy Planning and Policy Development Project; Energy and Environmental Policy Planning Project; and Biomass Energy Systems and Technology Project (BEST). The *Program Plan*, available from the office above, explains the programs of this office in pursuit of that goal and how the Office is organized to implement those programs.

* Energy Organizations

Office of International Energy Organizations and Policy Development
Forrestal Bldg., Room 7G-046
U.S. Department of Energy
Washington, DC 20585 (202) 586-6140
This office develops objectives, generic policy positions, specific policies with respect to individual foreign countries, and prepares briefing papers for all U.S. Government energy-related bilateral and multilateral Ministerial meetings.

* Energy Publications

AID Document Information Services Clearinghouse
1500 Wilson Blvd, Suite 1010
Arlington, VA 22209-2404 (703) 351-4006 ext. 9624
The following reports of the Office of Energy and Infrastructure, Bureau for Research and Development, can be obtained from the office above (the Document no. follows the Office of Energy Report no.):

New Direction for A.I.D., Renewable Energy Activities. February 1988 (88-01; PN-ABB-532).
Assessment of Integrated Coal Gasification Combined Cycle Technology for India. May 1988 (88-06; PN-AAZ-893).
The A.I.D. Experience with Independent Power Generation. August 1988 (88-14; PN-ABB-535).
Options to Increase Private Participation in Electric Power Development in A.I.D.-Assisted Countries. December 1987 (88-15; PN-ABB-536).
Private Sector Participation in the Energy/Power Sector of Jamaica, Sept. 1990 (PN-ABH-191)
Poland: An Energy and Environmental Overview, Oct. 1990 (PN-ABH-045).

* European and Canadian Affairs

U.S. Department of State
2201 C St., NW, Room 5229
Washington, DC 20520 (202) 647-6925
This office studies and guides government to government foreign relations with the Soviet Union, Canada, and Eastern and Western Europe. Their work involves economic affairs, OECD, and NATO. The Office of Regional Political and Economic Affairs follows developments within the European Community affecting American political, business, and security interests. This office can provide information with regard to the above.

* Farmer-to-Farmer Program

Agriculture Sector Specialist
Office of Training and Program Support
Peace Corps, 1990 K St., NW
Washington, DC 20526 (202) 606-3402
Working in collaboration with the Agency for International Development (AID) and Volunteers in Overseas Cooperative Assistance (VOCA), the Peace Corps has added this program to its Agriculture Sector. This office provides specific short-term (30 to 120 days) technical assistance to countries whose requests are approved in such areas as dairy production, vegetable production, and vegetable handling.

* Federal Aviation Administration (FAA)

U.S. Department of Transportation
Washington, DC 20590 (202) 267-3883
The problems of aircraft hijacking and sabotage remain pressing concerns of the FAA. The agencies response has included tightened airport security and the planned deployment of advanced explosive-detection systems around the world in coming years.

* Fishing Multi-Lateral Agreements

Bureau of Oceans and International Environmental and Scientific Affairs
U.S. Department of State
2201 C St., NW, Room 5806
Washington, DC 20520 (202) 647-2335
This office negotiates fishing agreements with countries who want to fish within the U.S. economic zone, along with agreements with countries within whose zone the U.S. would like to fish. They are also responsible for multi-lateral agreements dealing with fishing on the high seas, with particular attention to conservation issues. Information is available on these agreements and on fishery concerns in general.

* Fishing Vessels International Claims

Assistant Legal Advisor for International Claims
Office of the Legal Advisor
U.S. Department of State
2201 C St., NW
Washington, DC 20520 (202) 632-7810
The Fishermen's Protective Act provides for reimbursement for financial loss to owners of vessels registered in the United States for fines paid to secure the release of vessels seized for operation in waters not recognized as territorial waters by the United States. No registration or payment of premiums is required prior to the seizure in order to qualify for reimbursement.

* Food and Agricultural Production

Food and Agricultural Organization (FAO)
Viale delle Terme di Caracalla
00100 Rome, Italy
The FAO gives direct, practical help in the developing world through technical assistance projects in all areas of food and agriculture.

* Food For Peace Program

Bureau for Food and Humanitarian Assistance
Office of Food for Peace
Room 300, SA-8
Agency for International Development (AID)
Washington, DC 20523 (703) 351-0107

Be patient. If any phone number is incorrect, call (area code) 555-1212 and request the new listing.

International Relations and Defense

To obtain information on the Food for Peace Program, contact the office above. To receive a copy of the *Food for Peace 1988 Annual Report,* contact the Operations office (703) 351-0112, or the U.S. Department of Agriculture.

* Foreign Affairs Education

Foreign Service Institute
1400 Key Boulevard SA-3
Arlington, VA 22209 (703) 235-8727

The Foreign Service Institute provides foreign affairs and language training for employees of the State Department and other government agencies involved with foreign affairs.

* Foreign Attitudes of USA

Office of Research
United States Information Agency (USIA)
301 Fourth St., SW, Room 352
Washington, DC 20547 (202) 619-4965

Assessing foreign attitudes is one of USIA's prime responsibilities. A daily summary of worldwide media reaction to events of concern to the United States is used throughout the official diplomatic community. The research staff also amasses information for use by the White House, the U.S. Department of State, government agencies and USIA staff in assessing issues. Interested persons can obtain USIA research reports from depository libraries throughout the country. A list of these libraries is available.

* Foreign Aid Development Reports

AID Document Information Services Clearinghouse
1500 Wilson Blvd, Suite 1010
Arlington, VA 22209-2404 (703) 351-4006 ext. 9624

AID's Center for Development Information and Evaluation (CDIE) produces an evaluation publications series includes a broad range of subjects of interest to those working in international development. The series comprises project impact evaluations, program evaluations, special studies, program design and evaluation methodology reports, and discussion papers. The *CDIE Evaluation Publications List* is arranged by general subject category and by type of report within each category or subcategory. Each document has an identification number and is available in hard copy or on microfiche. A partial list of the documents follows:

A.I.D.'s Experience in Latin America and The Caribbean. May 1990, N. 69 (PN-AAX-232).

A.I.D. Assistance to Local Government: Experience and Issues. November 1983, No. 17 (PN-AAL-026).

Agricultural Policy Analysis and Planning: A Summary of Two Recent Analyses of A.I.D.-Supported Projects Worldwide. August 1988, No. 55 (PN-AAX-205).

Agricultural Research in Northeastern Thailand. May 1982, No. 34 (PN-AAJ-615).

An Evaluation of the African Emergency Food Assistance Program in Chad. 1984-1985, June 1987, No. 48 (PN-AAL-091).

Child Survival Programs in Egypt. Feb. 1990, No. 73 (PN-AAX-235).

Conducting Mini Surveys in Developing Countries. Dec. 1990, No. 15 (PN-AAX-249).

Development Assistance and Health Programs: Issues of Sustainability. October 1987, No. 23 (PN-AAL-097).

Natural Resource Management: A.I.D.'s Experience in Nepal. Oct. 1990, No. 41 (PN-AAX-247).

Private Sector: Ideas and Opportunities -- A review of Basic Concepts and Selected Experience. June 1982, No. 14 (PN-AAJ-618).

Private Volunteer Organizations and the Promotion of Small-Scale Enterprise. July 1985, No. 27 (PN-AAL-055).

Promoting Trade and Investment in Constrained Environments: A.I.D. Experience in Latin America and the Caribbean. May 1990. No. 69 (PN-AAX-237).

Small Farmer Attitudes and Aspirations. May 1989, No. 26 (PN-AAX-217).

Terms of Endowment: A New A.I.D. Approach to Institutional Development. Dec. 1990, No. 3 (PN-ABG-001).

The Impact of Irrigation on Development: Issues for Comprehensive Evaluation Study. October 1980, No. 9 (PN-AAJ-208).

Reaching the Rural Poor: Indigenous Health Practitioners Are There Already. March 1979, No. 1 (PN-AAG-685).

Rural Development: Lessons From Experience -- Highlights of the Seminar Proceedings. January 1989, No. 25 (PN-AAX-214).

Strengthening the Agriculture Research Capacity of the Less Developed Countries: Lessons From A.I.D. Experience. September 1983, No. 10 (PN-AAL-020).

Study of Family Planning Program Effectiveness. April 1979, No. 5 (PN-AAG-672).

Universities for Development: Report of the Joint Indo-U.S. Impact Evaluation of

the Indian Agricultural Universities. September 1988, No. 68 (PN-AAX-206).

Women in Development: A.I.D.'s Experience, 1973-1985. Vol. I, Synthesis Paper, March 1987, No. 18 (PN-AAL-087).

For more information on ordering documents or to obtain the CDIE Evaluation Publications List, contact the clearinghouse listed above.

* Foreign Aid Effectiveness and Assessment

National Security and International Affairs Division
General Accounting Office
441 G St. NW, Room 5055
Washington, DC 20548 (202) 275-5518

This office serves as GAO's lead division for the international affairs issues. This division provides GAO audit coverage for the U.S. Department of State, the Agency for International Development, the International Development Cooperation Agency, the Central Intelligence Agency, the Export-Import Bank of the United States, the U.S. Information Agency, and the Panama Canal Commission, as well as for the international activities of numerous other federal entities. International Division personnel staff GAO's overseas offices.

* Foreign Aid Projects Database

Development Information Center
Room 105 SA-18
Agency for International Development (AID)
Washington, DC 20523-1801 (703) 875-4818

The Development Information System (DIS) contains information on A.I.D. projects, programs, policies, and research, as well as associated project, research, and technical documents. Anyone can search DIS databases through the easy-to-use Menu DOS system on the library's public computer terminal. Records can be located by subject, author, title, project number, date, project status, or bibliographic type (e.g. project paper, evaluation, research report). All of these fields can be combined during one search. The MenuDIS quick reference guide to the right of the terminal can help you with your search. For more information on A.I.D.'s three main databases, "Document," "Project," and "Library Catalog," contact the office above.

* Foreign Assistance Funding

House Committee on Appropriations
Subcommittee on Foreign Operations
U.S. House of Representatives
H-218 Capitol Building
Washington, DC 20515 (202) 225-2041

In recent years, the House Appropriations Subcommittee on Foreign Operations has played a very important role in the allocation of American foreign assistance. Subcommittee hearings, reports, and markup bills provide a rich source of information on foreign assistance policy. For more information, contact the subcommittee. To order bills and reports, contact the House Documents room at (202) 225-3456 and have the House Resolution or Public Law number ready. Prints are free if in stock.

* Foreign Disaster Assistance

Office of U.S. Foreign Disaster Assistance (OFDA)
Agency for International Development (AID)
320 21st St., NW, Room 1262A
Washington, DC 20523 (202) 647-8924

The office administers AID's overseas disaster assistance program. The office involves other U.S. Government agencies, voluntary and international organizations, and the U.S. private sector to meet the demands of disaster relief, rehabilitation, preparedness, early warning, and mitigation in countries stricken or threatened by natural or man-made disasters, including earthquakes, floods, cyclones, volcanoes, accidents, and civil strife. OFDA provides technical assistance and training for the development of government disaster assistance programs, technology transfer for improved prediction and warning systems, and material and personnel resources for emergency relief and rehabilitation. An *Annual Report* detailing this office's activities is available by calling the above number.

* Foreign Economic Aid Projects

AID Document Information Services Clearinghouse
1500 Wilson Blvd, Suite 1010
Arlington, VA 22209-2404 (703) 351-4006 ext. 9624

Foreign Policy

Reports containing information on AID's projects may be obtained from the above facility for a minimal fee. One may also wish to subscribe to *Research and Development Abstracts* for a listing of available material for $10 per year.

* Foreign Economic Impact on U.S. Employment

Office of International Economic Affairs
Bureau of International Labor Affairs
200 Constitution Ave., NW, Room S5325
Washington, DC 20210 (202) 523-7610

The Labor Department's foreign economic research program evaluates the effects of foreign economic developments on the earnings and employment of U.S. workers. This includes quantitative analysis of the impact of policies on international trade, investment, and technology transfer. Often undertaken in response to congressionally-mandated studies or to requests from other executive branch agencies, research is conducted by staff economists and supplemented by outside research contractors. Studies undertaken during FY 1991 include: the effects of the Proposed North American Free Trade Area on U.S. workers; the implications for U.S. workers and the lessons on economic integration of EC 1992; and seventh annual report on the Caribbean Basin Economic Recovery Act. Studies are also released through the Labor Department's *Economic Discussion Paper* series. A complete list of the research is available by contacting this office.

* Foreign Language Training

Defense Language Institute
Foreign Language Center
Non-Resident Division
Presidio of Monterey, CA 93944 (408) 647-5516

The Defense Language Institute is one of the world's largest language training centers. The holdings of its library--over 100,000 books in 50 languages--are available through a national inter-library loan program. The non-resident division offers foreign language courses for sale. A catalog of the languages available may be obtained for $5.25. Write or call for brochures on the Institute and information regarding inter-library loans.

* Foreign Policy and Energy

Office of International Affairs
Forrestal Bldg., Room 7C-034
U.S. Department of Energy
Washington, DC 20585 (202) 586-5918

This office is responsible for the development and conduct of international energy policy consistent with U.S. foreign policy objectives. It also promotes international energy research and development collaboration policy and the strengthening of the international nuclear non-proliferation regime.

* Foreign Policy Briefings and Speakers

Office of Public Liaison
Bureau of Public Affairs
2201 C St NW, Room 5831
U.S. Department of State
Washington, DC 20520 (202) 647-1710

Foreign policy briefings are arranged on request for interested groups to the extent that resources permit. These briefings can be on a variety of topics, such as foreign economic environment or human rights.

* Foreign Policy Public Forums

Office of Public Programs
Bureau of Public Affairs
U.S. Department of State
2201 C St., NW, Room 5831
Washington, DC 20520 (202) 647-2234

The State Department encourages public dialogue on foreign policy topics through nationwide public appearances by Department officials. The following is a list of public programs available:

Conferences - National foreign policy conferences are scheduled throughout the year for leaders from business, labor, government, and other organizations. Regional foreign policy conferences are held several times a year in major cities. These day-long meetings involve senior department officials, a variety of local co-sponsoring organizations, and flexible formats to encourage the free exchange of information and opinions.

Seminars - Foreign policy seminars attract 30 to 40 specialists from the private sector together with Department officials for informal discussions. The Bureau offers 1 or 2 day seminars for business executives and media representatives, emphasizing international economic and other foreign policy issues.

Liaison with Nongovernmental Organizations - NGO liaison is initiated and maintained with national organizations interested in foreign policy issues. Briefings on these issues are organized for NGO leaders and staffers and other special interest groups.

* Foreign Press Centers

Washington Foreign Press Center
529 Fourteenth St., NW, Suite 898
Washington, DC 20045 (202) 724-1640

New York Foreign Press Center
110 E. 59th St.
New York, NY 10022 (212) 826-4722

Los Angeles Foreign Media Liaison Office
11000 Wilshire Blvd.
Los Angeles, CA 90024 (310) 575-7693

Press offices in Washington, DC, New York, and Los Angeles assist foreign journalists, resident and visiting, in acquiring press credentials and gaining access to newsmakers. Facilities at the Press Centers include Wire New Services, television monitors, copying machines, TV and Radio studios, and a conference facilities.

* Foreign Service Career Counseling

Personnel Office
Special Services Branch
United States Information Agency (USIA)
301 Fourth St., SW, Room 525
Washington, DC 20547 (202) 619-4695

Information on career opportunities for serving Foreign Service Officers is available from this office.

* Foreign Service Careers

Personnel Office
Special Recruitment Office
United States Information Agency (USIA)
301 Fourth St., SW, Room 518
Washington, DC 20547 (202) 619-4659

Information is available for those interested in taking the Foreign Service Exam. Call or write in August or September for a registration and sample Foreign Service exam test booklet.

* Foreign Studies of America and English

Division for the Study of the U.S.
Office of Academic Programs
Bureau of Educational and Cultural Affairs
United States Information Agency (USIA)
301 Fourth Street, SW
Room 256
Washington, DC 20547 (202) 619-4557

USIA supports academic programs for the study of America, as well as the study of the English language. It acts as liaison between American and foreign universities, academic associations, and scholars, and supports 200 cultural centers and binational centers in 100 countries for the study of the English language. It publishes teaching materials in many languages and numerous publications, including "English Teaching Forum," a professional quarterly for English teachers worldwide. It also sponsors many seminars, institutes, study tours, exchange programs and curriculum support geared to the study of America in foreign countries.

* Forest Management and Education Worldwide

Natural Resources Sector
Office of Training and Programming Support
Peace Corps
1990 K St., NW
Washington, DC 20526 (202) 606-3100

Be patient. If any phone number is incorrect, call (area code) 555-1212 and request the new listing.

International Relations and Defense

Working in 38 countries, forestry specialists design and execute forest management plans designed to help combat the overcutting, droughts, and deserts that are beginning to threaten many tropical forests around the world. They also help establish nurseries, curricula in environmental education, and skills in tropical fruit cultivation.

* Forestry, Environment, and Natural Resources

Office of Environment and Natural Resources
Bureau for Research and Development, Room 509 SA-18
Agency for International Development (AID)
Washington, DC 20523-1812 (703) 875-4106

To maximize the amount of development that is sustainable, the Agency is working toward networking of worldwide development planning. This office's strategy includes providing technical assistance to government and non-government agencies working toward the development of national environmental policy and programs which will contribute to sustainable economic development; and to provide assistance in research and the transfer of appropriate technologies. For more information or to obtain the *User's Guide to the Office of Environment and Natural Resources*, contact the office above.

* Fulbright Foreign Policy Scholarships

Office of Academic Programs
The Bureau of Educational and Cultural Affairs
United States Information Agency (USIA)
301 Fourth St., SW, Room 234
Washington, DC 20547 (202) 619-4556

This office develops and runs all academic programs of USIA, including the best-known educational exchange, the Fulbright Scholarship program. About 5,000 Fulbright grants are awarded each year to American students, teachers, and scholars to work abroad and to foreign citizens to teach, study, and conduct research in the U.S. In addition to the Fulbright program, the Academic Exchange Programs Division of this office administers grants to private agencies conducting complementary programs to the Fulbright academic exchanges, and has responsibilities for foreign research centers, Fulbright commissions, and seminars for foreign Fulbright students. Contact this office for more information and application forms for the Fulbright program.

* Fulbright Teacher Exchange Program

Office of Academic Programs
United States Information Agency (USIA)
301 Fourth St., SW, Room 353
Washington, DC 20547 (202) 619-4555

Opportunities are available for elementary and secondary school teachers and administrators, and college faculty to attend seminary or teach in schools abroad. Grants in most cases include round trip transportation. Applications must be submitted by October 15 for the following summer or academic years' program. Contact the Office of Academic Programs for information/applications.

* General Accounting Office International Affairs Reports

U.S. General Accounting Office
Post Office Box 6015
Gaithersburg, MD 20877 (202) 275-6241

GAO publishes dozens of reports each year on different American programs overseas. These reports, as well as reports published in previous years, are available free by request from GAO, up to five copies. Collectively, these reports are a treasure trove of information on U.S. policy. In addition, this office can put you on the mailing list for the monthly index of reports. Reports published in 1991 include:

Foreign Assistance:
International Resource Flows and Development Assistance to Developing Countries. GAO/NSIAD 91-25FS

Eastern Europe:
Donor Assistance and Reform Efforts. GAO/NSIAD 91-21

Cambodia:
Multilateral Relief Efforts in Border Camps. GAO/NSIAD 91-99FS

Agricultural Trade Negotiations:
Stalemate in the Uruguay Round. GAO/NSIAD 91-129.

Promoting Democracy:
National Endowment for Democracy's Management of Grants Needs Improvement. GAO/NSIAD 91-162.

U.S.-Mexico Trade:
Information on Environmental Regulations and Enforcement. GAO/NSIAD 91-227.

* Geographic Boundaries and Disputes

Office of the Geographer
Bureau of Intelligence and Research
U.S. Department of State
2201 C St., NW, Room 8742
Washington, DC 20520 (202) 647-1205

This office distributes several publications which contain a variety of geographical information. Some of them include:

Geographic Notes. Contains brief analyses of current issues relevant to United States foreign policy. These analyses provide a geographical perspective on such foreign policy-related topics such as boundary, sovereignty, and territorial disputes. Subscriptions cost $8 per year and can be ordered from the above office or from GPO (202) 783-3238.

International Boundary Studies. This is a series of specific boundary papers. Recent studies analyze developments in the borders between Iraq-Saudi Arabia, Iraq-Kuwait, and Argentina-Chile.

Cartoanalytic Briefs. These are occasionally published large thematic maps depicting developments in such regions as the former U.S.S.R. or Yugoslavia. They are available from the National Information Technical Service (703) 487-4630.

* Geographic Bureaus

Agency for International Development (AID)
320 21st St., NW
Washington, DC 20523

These Bureaus are the principal AID line offices with responsibility for the planning, formulation, and management of United States economic development and/or supporting assistance programs in their respective areas overseas. An annual budget of proposed Bureau activities is submitted for approval, and a program and budget is presented to Congress through the Policy Coordination Office. The Bureaus also represent the agency before the press and public as required.

Bureau for Africa: (202) 647-9232
Bureau for Latin America and the Caribbean: (202) 647-8246
Bureau for Asia: (202) 647-7302
Bureau for Europe and the Near East: (202) 647-9119
Bureau for the Near East: (202) 647-0462

* Grants for International Research Development

Agency Center for University Cooperation and Development
Bureau of Research and Development, SA-38, Room 900
Agency for International Development (AID)
Washington, DC 20523-3801 (703) 816-0295

AID links the land grant universities with the historically black colleges and universities both in the United States and abroad in an effort of cooperation. Research grants, usually in the amount of $100,000, are given in the areas of health, agriculture, rural development and nutrition to historically black colleges and universities in 30 countries. The presidentially appointed Board for International Food and Agricultural Development formulates policy and projects to foster the working relationship of agricultural universities in AID programs. Research projects are listed in the *Commerce Business Daily* for which colleges and universities can compete. Unsolicited research proposals by individuals are also considered, but only a limited number are accepted. For information on the guidelines for these proposals, contact the above office.

* Grassroots Assistance to Africa

African Development Foundation
1400 I St., NW, 10th Floor
Washington, DC 20005 (202) 673-3916

This is a non-profit, government corporation formed to support self-help development activities in economically depressed communities in Africa and to promote friendship between Africa and the U.S. The Foundation makes grants,

Be patient. If any phone number is incorrect, call (area code) 555-1212 and request the new listing.

Foreign Policy

loans, and loan guarantees to Africans engaged in peaceful development efforts. Call the number listed to request a free African Development information packet and for further information about the Foundation.

* Health Assistance

World Health Organization (WHO)
20 Avenue Appia
1211 Geneva 27, Switzerland

The WHO helps countries strengthen their health systems by building up services for the individual, family, and community; health institutions, referral systems; and the provision of essential drugs, other supplies and equipment. The organization promotes research on appropriate health technologies, and social and behavioral approaches that could lead to healthier lives in both the industrialized and developing societies. WHO has major programs to combat global diarrhoeal disease, smallpox, and river blindness. In addition, it has expanded the immunization program in recent years and hopes to protect all the worlds children in 1990 from diphtheria, pertussis, tetanus, measles, polio, and tuberculosis.

* Health Development

Office of Health
Bureau for Research and Development
Room 1200, SA-18
Agency for International Development (AID)
Washington, DC 20523 (703) 875-4600

This office serves as AID's principal source of technical expertise and assistance on international health issues and projects. Contact this office for more information, or to obtain a copy of the *Directory of the Office of Health, Bureau for Research and Development.*

* High Seas Law Enforcement

Operational Law Enforcement Division
Office of Law Enforcement and Defense Operations
U.S. Coast Guard
U.S. Department of Transportation
2100 2nd St., SW, Room 3110
Washington, DC 20593-0001 (202) 267-1890

As the primary maritime law enforcement agency for the U.S., the Coast Guard enforces Federal laws, treaties, and international agreements to which the U.S. is a party. The Coast Guard may conduct investigations when violations are suspected, such as smuggling, drug trafficking, or polluting. Empowered to board and inspect vessels routinely as well, the Guard also conducts :"suspicionless" boardings to prevent violations. To report suspicious or questionable activity on boats, or to complain about an improperly conducted boarding, call the Boating Safety Hotline, (800) 368-5647; or (202) 267-0780 in DC, or contact your local Coast Guard commander. The office listed above can provide you with information about the Coast Guard's law enforcement role and the National Narcotics Border Interdiction System, which coordinates multi-agency and international operations with other countries to suppress narcotics trafficking.

* Historian of the State Department

Bureau of Public Affairs
Columbia Plaza Office Building
2401 E St., NW, Room 3100
U.S. Department of State
Washington, DC 20522 (202) 663-1122

The office of the Historian has twin missions: to compile and publish the official diplomatic record of the United States in the series *Foreign Relations of the United States;* and to prepare policy-related historical research studies for the key officers of the U.S. Department of State. *Foreign Relations of the United States* is a multi-volume series in which the Historian's staff seeks, arranges, and edits principal papers which comprise the record of American foreign policy. Although principally based on State Department records, the series also is derived from White House files, the archives of other agencies, and, where relevant, papers and recollections of former officials. Resources and the pace at which the documents are declassified determine the rate at which the series is published. The office also publishes the *AMERICAN FOREIGN POLICY* series which contains texts of official messages, addresses, statements, reports, and communications which best convey the objectives of U.S. foreign policy. Microfiche supplements of documents are also available. These publications are available from GPO.

* Historically Black Colleges and International Development Research

Agency Center for University Cooperation and Development
Bureau for Research and Development, Room 900, SA-38
Agency for International Development (AID)
Washington, DC 20523-3801 (703) 816-0295

AID's Historically Black Colleges and Universities (HBCUs) Research Program seeks to take advantage of the strong interest of HBCUs in development assistance activities. Through this program, AID hopes to involve researchers from HBCUs in the problems of developing countries. Inclusion in the research program is determined through an AID formal review process. Contact this office for more information.

* House Committee on Foreign Affairs

U.S. House of Representatives
2170 Rayburn House Office Building
Washington, DC 20515 (202) 225-5021

The House Foreign Affairs Committee is a rich source of information on most all aspects of American foreign policy. Committee hearings include testimony from Government experts, academics, think tanks, and interested private individuals. For committee hearings and reports, contact the above number or call the House Documents room at (202) 225-3456. When calling the House Documents room, have the bill or Public Law number ready. Further information is available from the geographic subcommittees.

Subcommittees:
Africa: (202) 226-7807
Arms Control, International Security: (202) 225-8926
Asian and Pacific Affairs: (202) 226-7801
Europe and the Middle East: (202) 225-3345
Human Rights and International Organizations: (202) 226-7825
International Economic Policy: (202) 225-7820
International Operations: (202) 225-3324
Western Hemisphere: (202) 226-7812

* Housing in Developing Countries

Office of Housing and Urban Programs
Bureau for Private Enterprise
Agency for International Development (AID)
320 21st St., NW, Room 401, SA-2
Washington, DC 20523-0214 (202) 663-2530

This program facilitates private financing for shelter for lower income families in developing countries by guaranteeing repayment to U.S. lenders for projects requested by these countries. Innovative programs are financed, such as upgrading the provisions of sewerage, potable water, electricity, and home improvements. Basic urbanized lots are financed for the construction of family dwellings, and low-cost, expandable core housing units are made available. An Annual Report detailing office activities is available.

* Human Rights Violations Worldwide U.S. Department of State

Bureau of Human Rights and Humanitarian Affairs
2201 C St., NW, Room 7802
Washington, DC 20520 (202) 647-1383

Country Reports on Human Rights in 1991 covers the human rights practices of all nations that receive U.S. foreign assistance, those nations that do not receive it but are members of the United Nations, and those few nations that are not members of the U.N. Each country's section begins with a brief description of the country, including information on political parties and security forces. It then is broken down into several area. The first deals with respect for human rights and includes information on political killings, disappearances, torture, and denial of public trial. Other sections include information on respect for civil liberties, such as freedom of speech, press and religion, respect for political rights and worker rights, as well as information on discrimination. This annual report can be purchased from the Government Printing Office, Superintendent of Documents, Washington, DC 20402; (202) 783-3238.

* Immigrant Visas and Immigrant Status

Central Office
Immigration and Naturalization Service
425 I Street, NW

Be patient. If any phone number is incorrect, call (area code) 555-1212 and request the new listing.

International Relations and Defense

Washington, DC 20536 (202) 307-1501

Publications and tape recorded messages about immigration are available from this central office. However, field offices operate in most states and these local phone numbers appear in the Law and Social Justice Chapter and, of course, are easy to obtain from the directory assistance operators. When calling the tape recorded telephone number, (202) 307-1501, enter one of the number codes below which corresponds to the information about immigration and naturalization that you need:

301 Filing petitions to obtain immediate relative status (I-130)
302 Filing petitions to sponsor prospective immigrant employee (I-140)
303 How an alien in the United States may request a change of status to permanent resident status (I-485)
304 When a United States citizen marries a foreign national outside the USA
506 Fiance/fiancee visa (I-129F)
305 How to file joint petitions for spouse to remove conditional basis of their permanent resident status (I-751)
307 Orphan petitions (I-600)
306 Immigration benefits for adoption before 16th birthday (I-130)
308 Application for asylum in the USA (I-589)
309 Permanent residence for beneficiaries of approved asylum applications

* Immigration Act of 1990

Central Office
Immigration and Naturalization Service
425 I Street, NW
Washington, DC 20536
(800) 755-0777
(202) 307-1501

On November 29, 1990 President Bush signed into law the Immigration Act of 1990. This resulted in major changes in immigration which affect immigrants and non-immigrants, Philippine WWII veterans desiring American citizenship, El Salvadorean nationals, and many others with immigration related concerns. One major provision offers Temporary Protective Status (TPS) to nationals of El Salvador. Call the toll-free number listed above to obtain up-to-the-minute information on Immigration Act regulations and procedures as they become finalized. To hear recorded messages detailing established INS regulations, contact the "Ask Immigration" system at (202) 307-1501.

* Impact of Human Rights Activities on Foreign Policy

U.S. Department of State
Bureau of Human Rights and Humanitarian Affairs
2201 C St., NW, Room 7802
Washington, DC 20520 (202) 647-1383

This bureau ensures that consideration of human rights is a regular part of U.S. foreign policy decision-making, as expressed through direct contacts between the U.S. and individual countries, quiet diplomacy, and continuous public activity. In the 1970's, Congress passed a series of laws linking human rights conditions in specific countries to actions by the U.S. government, such as most-favored-nation tariff status, U.S. government credits guaranties, and economic and military assistance. Congress has mandated that this bureau submit an annual report reviewing human rights practices country by country.

* Industry Productivity Trends

Industry Productivity Studies Division
Office of Productivity and Technology
U.S. Department of Labor
200 Constitution Ave., NW, Room S4315
Washington, DC 20210 (202) 523-9267

This office looks at a variety of technological trends. One study analyzes major impending changes in products, materials, and production methods in selected industries; their present and future applications; and their effect on output, productivity, employment, skill levels, training, and occupational requirements. Another study analyzes technological changes that have major effects on more than one industry. Coverage includes selected innovations such as computers and numerical control of machine tools, with an emphasis on innovations that will be important in the next five to 10 years. For a list of reports call (202) 523-9267.

* Intelligence: The Acme of Skill

Public Affairs
Central Intelligence Agency
Washington, DC 20505 (703) 351-2053

Two free CIA brochures are available to the public include *Intelligence: The Acme of Skill*, and *The Factbook on Intelligence*. The Factbook contains

background information on the CIA as well as information on how to order CIA publications available to the public.

* Inter-American Affairs

Public Affairs
Bureau of Inter-American Affairs
U.S. Department of State
2201 C St., NW, Room 5913
Washington, DC 20520 (202) 647-472

This bureau prepared foreign policy documents relating to U.S. relations with all countries of the Western Hemisphere except Canada. The documents focus on issues revolving around democracy, human rights, economic policy, narcotics, and promotion of U.S. security and commercial interests.

* Inter-American Foundation Publications

Inter-American Foundation (IAF)
Publications Office
1515 Wilson Blvd.
Rosslyn, VA 22209 (703) 841-3821

Established in 1969 by Congress as an independent agency, the Foundation makes grants to agricultural cooperatives, community associations, and small urban enterprises in Central and Latin America. The IAF also grants fellowships to University students from the Western Hemisphere. The following is a sampling of the free titles published in English, Spanish, and Portuguese.

The Inter-American Foundation and the Small- and Micro-Enterprise Sector
What to Think About Cooperatives: A Guide From Bolivia
In Support of Women: Ten Years of Funding by the Inter-American Foundation
A Review of the Inter-American Foundation's Support for Health Activities
Bottom-up Development in Haiti
The Inter-American Foundation in the Making
In Partnership with People: An Alternative Development Strategy
Grassroots Development
Inter-American Foundation Annual Report.
Direct to the Poor: An Anthology of articles from Grassroots Development.

* Inter-American Grassroots Development Video Series

West Glen Communications, Inc.
1430 West Broadway
New York, NY 10018 (212) 921-2800

The following videos, which are part of the Inter-American Foundation's "Grassroots Development Video Series," are available for sale or on loan. Each video is $22.95 from West Glen Communications at the above address, or on loan from Modern Talking Picture Service, 500 Park Street North, St. Petersburg, FL 33709. For a complete list of videos call the IAF at (703) 841-3869.

A Cooperative Without Borders: The First Step (21 minutes). Depicts the struggle of a group of Mexican migrant workers and their hope for the future to improve economic conditions as an alternative to migration (1987). Teacher's guide available.

The Women's Construction Collection (13 minutes). The story of 25 unemployed women selected from the poorer neighborhoods of Kingston, Jamaica, and trained in construction trades (1986).

Alpacas: An Andean Gamble (28 minutes). The peasant community of Aquia, Peru, bets on its future by repopulating its communal highlands with alpacas. Teachers' guide available.

* International Aid Public Information

Office of Public Inquiry
Bureau for External Affairs
Agency for International Development (AID)
320 21st St., NW
Washington, DC 20523 (202) 647-1850

For further information on the programs and projects within the Agency, contact the office above.

* International Aid Report to Congress

Office of Public Inquiry
Bureau for External Affairs
Agency for International Development (AID)
320 21st St., NW

Be patient. If any phone number is incorrect, call (area code) 555-1212 and request the new listing.

Washington, DC 20523 (202) 647-1850

Congressional Presentation is a seven volume document that describes the AID program of each developing country. Statistical information is included for present and prior years. Copies are available in limited supply from the above office and are also available for use at the Center for Development Information and Evaluation, 1601 N. Kent St., Room 105, Arlington, VA; (703) 875-4818.

* International Air Transportation

Office of International Aviation Policy and International Affairs Office of the Secretary of Transportation U.S. Department of Transportation 400 7th Street, SW, Room 6402 Washington, DC 20590 (202) 366-2423

This office studies and develops U.S. policy with regard to international aviation. It ensures cooperation between U.S. and foreign-flag airlines and negotiates air service agreements with other countries.

* International Conferences Coordination

Bureau of International Organization Affairs U.S. Department of State 2201 C St., NW, Room 1517 Washington, DC 20520 (202) 647-6875

This office organizes over 700 intergovernmental conferences each year. They accredit all participating delegations and decide who represents the U.S. and what information is allowed to be shared.

* International Development Resource Materials

Development Information Center Room 105 SA-18 Agency for International Development (AID) Washington, DC 20535-1801 (703) 875-4818

The AID Library also has a collection of non-AID materials. You can identify materials acquired after April 1984 using the on-line catalog in the Development Information System, and earlier acquisitions will be found in the card catalog.

* International Energy Analysis

Office of International Energy Analysis Forrestal Bldg., Room 7G-090 U.S. Department of Energy (DOE) Washington, DC 20585 (202) 586-5893

This office is responsible for monitoring and analyzing world energy market developments and the international political, economic and strategic factors that influence these developments; providing policy recommendations on international energy issues; and managing U.S./DOE participation in international energy related organizations.

* International Law Library

Law Library Library of Congress Washington, DC 20540 (202) 707-5073

As the world's largest and most comprehensive library of foreign, international, and comparative law, the Law Library provides information for all known legal systems including common law, civil law, Roman law, canon law, Chinese law, Jewish and Islamic law, and ancient and medieval law. Specialists with knowledge of more than fifty languages provide reference and research service in all known legal systems. U.S. legislative documents housed here include the *Congressional Record* (and its predecessors), the serial set, a nearly complete set of bills and resolutions, current documents, committee prints, reports, hearings, etc. plus a complete set of U.S. Supreme Court records and briefs and collections of U.S. Court of Appeals records and briefs. The law library has five major divisions:

American-British Law

United States, Australia, Canada, Great Britain, India, New Zealand, Pakistan, certain other countries of the British Commonwealth and their dependent territories, and Eire: (202) 707-5077.

European Law

Nations of Europe and their possessions, except Spain and Portugal: (202) 707-5088.

Hispanic Law

Spain and Portugal, Latin America, Puerto Rico, the Philippines, and Spanish- and Portuguese-language states of Africa: (202) 707-5070.

Far Eastern Law

Nations of East and Southeast Asia including China, Indonesia, Japan, Korea, Thailand, and former British and French possessions in the area: (202) 707-5085.

Near Eastern and African Law

Middle Eastern countries, including the Arab states, Turkey, Iran, and Afghanistan, and all African countries, except Spanish- and Portuguese-language states and possessions: (202) 707-5073.

* International Visitors Program

Bureau of Educational and Cultural Affairs United States Information Agency (USIA) 301 Fourth St., SW, Room 255 Washington, DC 20547 (202) 619-5217

Some 2,600 foreign leaders from many fields are invited each year by USIA to meet with their counterparts in the United States, either joining group projects or an individually tailored program to learn about our society. Arrangements for visitors' programs are made by USIA, often with the cooperation of several private non profit organizations with support from the Agency. In addition to these visits, partially or wholly funded by USIA, another 2,000 Voluntary Visitors participate in similar programs, traveling at their own or their governments' expense.

* International Youth Exchange

The Bureau of Educational and Cultural Affairs United States Information Agency (USIA) 301 Fourth St., SW, Room 357 Washington, DC 20547 (202) 619-6299

This office administers grants to non-profit organizations for international educational and cultural exchanges for youths 15 to 30 years of age. The principal objective of youth exchange programming is the promotion of better understanding of U.S. society among foreign youth. The program has stimulated over 22,000 exchanges since its inception in 1982. Organizations wishing to become sponsors, or individuals wishing to be put in contact with sponsoring organizations, can receive free information from this office.

* Japan-United States Friendship Commission

1200 Pennsylvania Avenue, NW, Suite 3416 Washington, DC 20004 (202) 275-7712

The Commission was established in 1975 as an independent government agency to promote friendship and cultural understanding between the United States and Japan. The endowment fund contained some $14 million in 1990. The Commission funds five categories of projects: Japanese Study in American Education; American Studies in Japanese Education; Policy-oriented Research; Public Affairs/Education; and The Arts. To this end, it provided some $1.8 million and 240 million Yen in grants in FY 1990. Grant information and applications can be obtained from the above address.

* Junior Foreign Service Officer Trainee Program

Personnel Office Special Recruitment Branch United States Information Agency (USIA) 301 Fourth St., SW, Room 525 Washington, DC 20547 (202) 619-4667

Each December the Foreign Service Officer Examination is held at many locations in this country and overseas to screen candidates for the Junior Officer Trainee Program. Date, locations, and other information is available from this office.

* Labor Standards

International Labour Organization 4 route des Morillons 1211 Geneva 22, Switzerland

The ILO brings together government, labor, and management to recommend international minimum standards and to draft international labor conventions on such subjects as human rights, freedom of association, wages, hours of work, minimum ages for employment, conditions of work for various classes of

Be patient. If any phone number is incorrect, call (area code) 555-1212 and request the new listing.

International Relations and Defense

workers, workmen's compensation, social insurance, vacation with pay, employment services and labor inspection. The organization also has opportunities for advanced study and training in Geneva, Switzerland at the International Institute for Labor Studies.

* Latin American/Caribbean Foreign Assistance

Inter-American Foundation
Program Office
1515 Wilson Blvd.
Rosslyn, VA 22209 (703) 841-3855

The Inter-American Foundation database monitors projects that receive IAF funding, and can be search by the following areas: type of project, urban/rural area, type of beneficiary, whether it generates income, and more. Contact this office for more information on the database or searching the files.

* Law of the Sea Treaty

Office of Oceans Law and Policy
Bureau of Oceans and International Environmental and Scientific Affairs
U.S. Department of State
2201 C St., NW, Room 5805A
Washington, DC 20520 (202) 647-9098

In working out policy regarding use of the world's oceans, this office monitors countries to see if they conform to the Law of the Sea Treaty, and negotiate U.S. policy regarding the Treaty. This is a large treaty with over 300 articles, dealing with such issues as uses of the outer continental shelf, pollution, fishing, use of Straits and territorial zones. As of early 1992 51 nations had ratified the treaty. The treaty comes into force when ratified by 60 countries. The United States has not signed the treaty due to concerns about the seabed mining article, but observes the provisions of the treaty as customary law.

* Law Enforcement Overseas

Federal Bureau of Investigation (FBI)
10th and Pennsylvania Ave, NW
Washington, DC 20535 (202) 324-3000

While primarily a domestic law enforcement agency, the FBI does engage in some law enforcement activities overseas. The Bureau posts legal attaches in some American embassies overseas as well as maintaining liaison functions with foreign police forces. In certain areas, the United States maintains extraterritorial jurisdiction. For further information contact your local FBI office or the above number.

* Limited Resource Farming Projects

Agriculture Sector Specialist
Office of Training and Program Support
Peace Corps, 1990 K St., NW
Washington, DC 20526 (202) 606-3402

The Peace Corps' agricultural specialists provide personnel and services to 46 countries, and have recently become especially proficient in bee-keeping projects. They help teach and establish crop production techniques, basic production research, small animal husbandry, and are currently developing a project for iguana production in Honduras. This project, though, is only in the early planning stages and would not be implemented until the 1990s; it is being designed as a food resource and forest preservation program. They also work closely with volunteers in the U.S. and abroad to share culturally related information regarding such topics such as limited resource farming practices here and abroad.

* Marine Environmental Efforts

Environmental Coordination Branch
Marine Environmental Response Division
Office of Marine, Safety, Security, and Environmental Protection
U.S. Coast Guard
U.S. Department of Transportation
2100 2nd St., SW, Room 2100
Washington, DC 20593-0001 (202) 267-0421

Information is available here on the Coast Guard's role in international marine environmental efforts, such as representation in the U.N. International Maritime Consultative Organization. For further information on cooperative environmental efforts, contact the branch listed.

* Marine Science and International Policy

Office of Oceans and Fisheries Affairs
2201 C St., NW, Room 5801
U.S. Department of State
Washington, DC 20520 (202) 647-3262

This office handles international marine environment concerns, from the protection of whales to cleaning up oil spills, by negotiating bilateral and multilateral agreements.

* Maritime Boundaries

Office of Ocean Law and Policy
Bureau of Oceans and International Environmental and Scientific Affairs.
2201 C St., NW, Room 5805A
U.S. Department of State,
Washington, DC 20520 (202) 647-5123

This office tracks and analyzed national claims to maritime jurisdictions. It publishes *Limits in the Seas*, which details maritime boundaries. Contact the above office for more information.

* Maritime Organization

International Maritime Organization (IMO)
4 Albert Embankment
London SE1 7SR, England

The IMO's main objective is to facilitate co-operation among Governments on technical matters affecting international shipping and to ensure the highest standards of maritime safety, navigational efficiency, and prevention of maritime pollution of the sea. To these ends it prepares international conventions, recommendations, codes and other material on the technical aspects of shipping and related maritime matters.

* Maritime Trade Statistics

Trade Analysis Division (MAR-570)
Office of Trade and Analysis and Insurance
Maritime Administration
U.S. Department of Transportation
400 7th Street, SW
Washington, DC 20590 (202) 366-2282

Records on federally subsidized shipping companies are maintained by this Division. Information includes vessel name, port dates, and crew costs. The public can visit the document inspection room or write for information.

* Narcotics Cultivation Worldwide

Policy Coordination Office
Narcotics Coordinator
Agency for International Development (AID)
320 21st Street, NW
Washington, DC 20523 (202) 647-8383

AID in conjunction with other international agencies collects data about narcotics growing areas of the world and attempts channel economic development for narcotics producing areas into alternative crops and rural development. AID missions are involved in research for developing and testing alternative crops. Other agencies are responsible for the monitoring of enforcement and eradication of illegal narcotics cultivation.

* Natural Resources and the Environment

Document Information Services Clearinghouse
Agency for International Development (AID)
1500 Wilson Blvd., Suite 1010
Arlington, VA 22209-2404 (703) 351-4006

The following documents may be viewed in the Library on microfiche. Hard copies may be obtained from the address above. Note document identification numbers are included. Also, AID publishes a collection of *Country Environmental Profiles* which may assist persons doing research on the environmental issues of a specific country. A listing of these *Country Environmental Profiles* is available at the reference desk of the Library.

Arid and Semiarid Rangelands: Guidelines for Development. Handbook/Manual/Guide, 1987. PN-AAY-730.
Ecological Development in the Humid Topics: Guidelines for Planners. AID Supported Study by the Winrock International Institute of Agricultural

Be patient. If any phone number is incorrect, call (area code) 555-1212 and request the new listing.

Foreign Policy

Development, 1987. PN-ABB-421.

Economics and Biological Diversity: Developing and Using Economic Incentives to Conserve Biological Resources. AID Supported Study, Nov. 1988. PN-ABA-988 (Not available on microfiche).

Environment and Natural Resources. A.I.D. Policy Paper. Apr. 1988. PN-AAV-464.

Forest for the Trees: Government Policies and the Misuse of Forest Resources. AID Supported Study, May 1988. PN-ABB-973 (Not available on microfiche).

Progress in Conserving Tropical Forests and Biological Diversity in Developing Countries: The 1987 Annual Report to Congress on the Implementation of Sections 118 and 119 of the Foreign Assistance Act, as amended. AID Program Document, 27 June 1988. PN-AAY-764.

Thailand Natural Resources Profile: Is the Resource Base for Thailand's Development Sustainable? AID Environmental Assessment, Jan. 1987. PD-AAY-099.

* Near Eastern and South Asian Countries Update

Bureau of Near Eastern and South Asian Affairs
U.S. Department of State
2201 C St., NW, Room 6243
Washington, DC 20520 (202) 647-5151

This office develops United States foreign policy for the countries in North Africa, north of the Sahara, the Middle East, the Persian Gulf and West Asia. They follow political, social, and economic developments and prepare policy papers. Specialized offices and functions include the Special Envoy to the Afghan Resistance and the Office for Regional and Multilateral Force Observers Affairs. *Background Notes* and GIST summaries are available on the various countries, as well as foreign policy papers and speeches.

* Newspapers and Periodicals Worldwide

Library of Congress
Washington, DC 20540 (202) 707-5650

Hundreds of different newspapers and periodicals from all fifty states and countries around the world are available on microfilm for $30 for domestic and $35 for foreign publications. Subscriptions are available or single issues can be ordered. Orders must be prepaid or charged to a standing account at the Library of Congress.

* Nonimmigrant Visas and Nonimmigrant Status

Central Office, Immigration and Naturalization Service
425 I Street, NW
Washington, DC 20536 (202) 307-1501

Publications and tape recorded messages about immigration are available from this central office. However, field offices operate in most states and these local phone numbers appear in the Law and Social Justice Chapter and are easy to obtain from the directory assistance operators. When calling the tape recorded telephone number above, enter one of the number codes below which corresponds to the information about immigration and naturalization that you need:

501 Nonimmigrant or temporary visas
505 Temporary visitor's visa
502 How to request an extension of temporary stay (I-539)
504 Applying for a replacement arrival-departure document I-94 (I-102)
503 Change of status from one nonimmigrant classification to another nonimmigrant classification for purpose of work (I-506)
510 Requirements for classification as nonimmigrant treaty trader E-1 or treaty investor E-2.
508 Requirements for classification as nonimmigrant exchange alien J-1
507 Requirements for classification as nonimmigrant temporary workers H-1, H-2, and H-3, (I-129B)
509 Intracompany transfers L-1 (I-129L, I-129S)

* Non-Violent Conflict Resolution Grants

United States Institute of Peace
1550 M St., NW
Washington, DC 20005 (202) 429-3844

The Grants Program provides financial support to nonprofit organizations, official public institutions, and individuals to fund projects on various themes and topics of interest. Past projects have included the role of third-party negotiators in the resolution of regional conflicts, religious and ethical questions in war and peace, and the use of non-violent sanctions in confronting political violence. Call or write for more information regarding grant application procedures.

* Nuclear Non-Proliferation

Office of Nuclear Nonproliferation Policy
Forrestal Building, Room 7G-050
U.S. Department of Energy
Washington, DC 20585 (202) 586-6175

Implements U.S. Department of Energy non-proliferation programs and activities.

* Nutrition and Health Education in Developing Countries

Health Programmer
Office of Training and Programming Support
Peace Corps
1990 K St., NW
Washington, DC 20526 (202) 606-3100

Volunteers work to teach modern health-care techniques through programs on vaccination and hygiene and nursing. They design health curricula as well as teaching basic elements of nutrition.

* Nutrition and Food Science

Office of Nutrition
Bureau for Research and Development, Suite 411, SA-18
Agency for International Development (AID)
Washington, DC 20523-1808 (703) 875-4003

This office's resources are invested at the "cutting edge" of nutrition science, food science, and technology and in creating mechanisms for adapting food and nutrition content to specific conditions and needs of host countries. As a result of these efforts, the Office has created programs in three major categories: child survival, household food security, and nutribusiness. The *1989 Interim Directory: Sustained Enhanced Nutritional Status for Everyone* (SENSE) will help you better understand this Bureau's nutrition programs. For more information on the Office of Nutrition, or to obtain a copy of the *Directory*, contact the office above.

* Opportunities for Women in Developing Countries

International Women's Program
Bureau of International Organization Affairs
U.S. Department of State
2201 C St., NW, Room 4334A
Washington, DC 20520 (202) 647-1155

Working through the United Nations Commission, this office strives to improve the lives of women in developing countries. Toward this end, this office develops and introduces resolutions to the U.N., and focuses on such issues as increasing literacy, equality in the law, and the availability of credit information.

* Organization of American States (OAS)

Documents Officer
Permanent Mission of the U.S.A. to the
Organization of American States
U.S. Department of State
2201 C St., NW, Room 6489
Washington, DC 20520 (202) 647-8650

The Documents Officer can provide you with all reference documents and other general information concerning the Organization of American States.

* Organization of the U.S. State Department

Bureau of Public Affairs
U.S. Department of State
2201 C St., NW, Room 5819
Washington, DC 20520 (202) 647-6575

Department of State Today is a free publication which outlines the general organization of the State Department, including descriptions of the various Bureaus and their responsibilities. A list of public services is available, along with a section of charts, maps, and tables.

* Panama Canal Crisis Hotline

Office of the Ombudsman
Panama Canal Commission
Unit 2300
APO AA 34011 011 (507) 52-3305

Be patient. If any phone number is incorrect, call (area code) 555-1212 and request the new listing.

International Relations and Defense

The Office of the Ombudsman handles administrative problems, inefficiencies, and policy conflicts existing within the Panama Canal Commission and other US Government agencies on the Isthmus of Panama resulting from the Treaty. The office does its best to improve employee morale and their quality of life. Due to the recent political unrest in Panama, a "hotline" was established to help employees, dependents, area residents and others previously employed with U.S. Federal agencies on the Isthmus, work through their concerns and hardships. For more information, contact this office.

* Panama Canal Dredging Division

Engineering and Construction Bureau
Dredging Division
c/o Panama Canal Commission
Unit 2300
APO AA 34011   011 (507) 56-6232

The Dredging Division is responsible for maintenance and construction dredging; slide removal; inspection and maintenance of the Atlantic breakwater; operation and maintenance of navigational aids; the detection, containment, recovery, and disposal of oil pollution in Canal operating areas; and the removal and control of aquatic weeds through the use of chemical and biological means. For more information on the dredging operations, contact this office.

* Panama Canal Economic and Market Research

Economic Research and Market Development Division
The Office of Executive Planning
c/o Panama Canal Commission
Unit 2300
APO AA 34011   011 (507) 52-7806

As an agency of the U.S. Government, the Panama Canal Commission has a legal obligation to operate on a break-even basis, recovering all costs of operating, maintaining, and improving the Canal through tolls revenue. The agency tries to have a high standard of service at the lowest possible cost. As a reflection of this, toll rates have gone up only four times since the Canal opened in 1914. Operating costs are very carefully controlled so that it provides an economic advantage to world trade on many routes. Even if other world trade routes may be shorter in distance, the Canal remains competitive because of its reliable, cost-effective service. For more information on operating costs, contact this office.

* Panama Canal Environmental Safeguards

Sanitation Branch, General Services Bureau
Panama Canal Commission
Unit 2300
APO AA 34011   011 (507) 52-3464

The Sanitation Branch carries out measures to control disease carrying organisms and environmental sanitation measures essential to maintaining a high standard of public health which can be enjoyed by Panama Canal Commission employees and their families. There is an effort to control insect vector and vermin by nonchemical methods. For more information, contact the above office.

* Panama Canal Logistical Support

Office of Logistical Support
General Services Bureau
Panama Canal Commission
4400 Dauphine St.
New Orleans, LA 70146-6800   (504) 948-5299

The Logistical Support Division provides centralized procurement, inventory management, warehousing, distribution, contract administration, and supply and property disposal support to Canal operations. For more information, contact this office.

* Panama Canal Publications and Audiovisuals

The Office of Public Affairs
c/o Panama Canal Commission
Unit 2300
APO AA 34011   (507) 52-3165

The Office of Public Affairs has available various publications including the *Panama Canal 75th Anniversary Commemorative Album* and *The Panama Canal Spillway* as well as press releases, brochures, and other matters of related interest are distributed to the work force and the public at large. A broad range of photographic and audio-visual support services were created as well. A limited number of projection prints are available for loan to individuals and groups interested in the canal and its operation. All films are 16mm color and sound. Individuals may obtain video tapes of all subjects by submitting a blank tape in the desired format and the payment of a transfer charge. Some examples of the available films for general audiences are as follows:

The Task That Never Ends. 1984. Depicts the on going job of maintaining and improving the channel of the Panama Canal, widening, deepening and straightening the water route.

The Vital Link. 1986. Depicts the role of the Panama Canal in world commerce with a layman's introduction to the people and methods of Canal operations. Details of lockages, traffic control, and communications at the crossroads of the world.

1986 Landslide. 1987. Shows the resumption of the Cucaracha Slide in October, 1986. Measures taken to maintain Canal traffic while the obstruction was removed and remedial actions taken.

Some examples of the available films of special interest to engineers and mechanical craftsmen include the following:

Locks Overhaul - Strut Arms. 1981. A detailed description of strut arm removal prior to gate or bullwheel removal and replacement.

Locks Overhaul - Bullwheels. 1982. A detailed description of bullwheel removal and replacement.

There are also films of special interest to canal operating personnel. Films are available in both Spanish and English. For a complete listing of films produced by the Panama Canal Commission, contact the above office.

* Panama Canal Traffic Data

Economic Research and Market Development Division
The Office of Executive Planning
c/o Panama Canal Commission
Unit 2300
APO AA 34011   011 (507) 52-7961

The Panama Canal is a vital link in the world transportation chain. A large share of world trade passes through the Canal over any of the world's major trade routes. In 1988, 156.5 million long tons of cargo moved through the Canal aboard 12,318 oceangoing vessels. More than 690,962 vessels have crossed the waterway, carrying more than 4 billion long tons of the world's goods from one ocean to the other. For more information or compilations of Canal traffic data, contact this office.

* Panama Canal Transit

Canal Operations Unit
c/o Panama Canal Commission
Unit 2300
APO AA 34011   011 (507) 52-4211

This office can provide information for those considering taking a boat or ship through the canal.

* Panama Canal Treaty Implementation

Office of the Secretary
Panama Canal Commission
2000 L St., NW, Room 550
Washington, DC 20036-4996   (202) 634-6441

On September 7, 1977, the United States and the Republic of Panama signed the Panama Canal Treaty of 1977. The Treaty provided for the establishment of the Panama Canal Commission on October 1, 1979, to assume certain operational responsibilities for the Canal until December 31, 1999. When the Treaty terminates on December 31, 1999, the Republic of Panama shall assume total responsibility for the management, operation, and maintenance of the Panama Canal, which shall be turned over in operating condition and free of liens and debts, except as the two parties may otherwise agree. Of the permanent current work force, 84 percent are Panamanians. This office can also supply annual reports and a packet of general information on the Canal. For more information, contact this office.

* Panama Canal Vessel Emergency Response Management

Marine Director
Marine Bureau

Be patient. If any phone number is incorrect, call (area code) 555-1212 and request the new listing.

Foreign Policy

c/o Panama Canal Commission
Unit 2300
APO AA 34011 011 (507) 52-4500
For information on marine operations including inspections, piloting, locks, traffic management, canal services, marine safety, canal operations and maritime training, contact this Bureau. The Commission's marine risk management team is devoted to the prevention of and response to accidents involving vessels carrying hazardous cargoes. The team consists of an experienced fireman, a licensed marine engineer, a safety generalist, an experienced chemist, and lead by an experienced active duty U.S. Coast Guard officer. This team is also responsible for updating the Commission's Vessel Emergency Response Plan and in conducting vessel emergency training exercises.

* Peace and International Conflict Resolution Clearinghouse

Education and Public Information Program
United States Institute of Peace
1550 M St., NW
Washington, DC 20005 (202) 429-3844
The Jeanette Rankin library program supports the expansion of the Institute's and the nation's information resources on issues in the fields of peace and international conflict management. The Institute also conducts the annual *National Peace Essay Contests* for high school students, and has many television and other media projects on such subjects as the history of U.S.--USSR summitry and issues and ideas in peacemaking. Publications of the Institute include the biennial report; the bimonthly *Journal* which provides information on the Institute's programs and achievements and increases public knowledge of important projects and points of view; and *In Brief,* a new series highlighting results from Institute projects, as well as books and papers.

* Peace Corps Environment Education Curricula

Natural Resources Sector
Office of Training and Program Support
Peace Corps
1990 K St., NW
Washington, DC 20526 (202) 606-3100
In charge of the forestry sector, natural resources encompasses wildlife management, national parks management, soil conservation, and environmental education curricula.

* Peace Corps Reference Manuals

Information Collection and Exchange (ICE)
Office of Training and Program Support
Peace Corps
1990 K St., NW
Washington, DC 20526 (202) 606-3087
The Peace Corps publishes a number of handbooks and materials written by their experienced Peace Corps volunteers which are designed to assist new volunteers abroad:

Community Health Education in Developing Countries
Cooperatives
Disaster Procedures
Freshwater Fish Pond Culture and Management
A Glossary of Agricultural Terms
Health and Sanitation Lessons--Africa
Pesticide Safety
The Photonovel--A Tool for Development
Programming and Training for Small Farm Grain Storage
Self-Help Construction of One-Story Buildings
Water Purification, Distribution, and Sewage Disposal

* Peace Corps Regional Bureaus

Peace Corps
1900 K St., NW
Washington, DC 20526 (202) 606-3886
The Peace Corps has regional bureaus for Asia, Africa, Interamerican Affairs, and Eastern Europe. These offices can answer questions about specific projects and countries. For further information call:
Africa Bureau: 202-606-3181
Inter-American Bureau: 202-606-3714
Eastern Europe: 202-606-3606

* Political Asylum

Office of Asylum Affairs
Bureau of Human Rights and Humanitarian Affairs
U.S. Department of State
SA-17, Room 520
Washington, DC 20520 (202) 326-6110
This office handles the U.S. Department of State's responsibilities regarding political asylum by providing advisory opinions on the cases to the Immigration and Naturalization Service.

* Population Planning

Office of Population
Bureau for Research and Development, Room 811, SA-18
Agency for International Development (AID)
Washington, DC 20523-1819 (703) 875-4402
Here population projects are designed to strengthen USAID assistance to country family planning programs worldwide. The projects fall into two broad categories: those which support current family planning service delivery, and research to enhance future efforts in the population field. Contact the office above for more information.

* President's Eastern European Initiative

U.S. Information Agency (USIA)
301 4th St., Room 753
Washington, DC 20547 (202) 619-5066
Begun in 1989, the Presidents EEI is designed to strengthen democratic values in the newly democratic Eastern European nations. The program is organized into four pillars: *The John Marshall Pillar:* emphasizing legislative and judicial reform; *The Noah Webster Pillar:* emphasizing English teaching; *The Alexander Hamilton Pillar:* emphasizing free enterprise; and *The Samuel Gompers Pillar:* emphasizing free trade unionism.

* Private Voluntary Organizations

Office of Private and Voluntary Cooperation
Bureau for Food and Humanitarian Assistance
Room 260, SA-8
U.S Agency for International Development (AID)
Washington, DC 20523 (703) 351-0201
AID has long recognized the important contribution made by private voluntary organizations (PVOs) to development efforts in the Third World. According to AID, PVOs are tax-exempt non-profit organizations which receive some portion of their annual revenue from the private sector (demonstrating their private nature) and receive voluntary contributions of money, staff time, or in-kind support from the general public (a demonstration of their voluntary nature). For information on AID available to PVOs, grants reserved for registered PVOs, and for general information including program descriptions and a breakdown of program funding, contact the office above. Also ask for a copy of *The AID-PVO Partnership: Sharing Goals and Resources in the Work of Development* and the *Voluntary Agencies Registered with AID (Volag) Report.*

* Problems of Communism and Socialism

Superintendent of Documents
Government Printing Office (GPO)
Washington, DC 20402 (202) 783-3238
The United States Information Agency publishes many teaching materials, including books, maps, complete teaching modules, and 14 magazines in 20 languages. By law most USIA publications may be distributed only in foreign countries. However, by congressional action, two magazines are available in the United States. *English Teaching Forum,* a quarterly for English teachers worldwide, is published by USIA's English Language Programs Division. *Problems of Communism* is a bi-monthly forum for American and foreign scholars discussing communist and socialist affairs. It is published in English and Spanish. Both these magazines are available through the GPO.

* Radio Free Europe/Radio Liberty

Board for International Broadcasting
1201 Connecticut Avenue, NW, Suite 400
Washington, DC 20036 (202) 457-6900
The Board for International Broadcasting's annual reports, available free of charge to the public, cover Radio Free Europe's and Radio Liberty's research, audience, technical facilities, future plans, and more. RFE's Research and Analysis

Be patient. If any phone number is incorrect, call (area code) 555-1212 and request the new listing.

International Relations and Defense

Department is the largest center in the West for research on Eastern Europe. RAD's analytical staff produce papers in English on a broad range of subjects, including the internal situations in the countries to which RFE broadcasts. Also available are situation and background reports, along with special publications covering timely topics in those countries. RL publications covering activities in the Soviet Union are also available, including research reports and bulletins, and press surveys and monitoring reports. Specific reports include the *Soviet/East European Report*, and the *RFE/RL Daily Report*. Contact this office for more information on how to order these research publications.

* Radio Free Europe/Radio Liberty Library

Reference Library
1775 Broadway
New York, NY 10019 (212) 397-5343

This library contains over 17,000 volumes, 3,000 reels of microfilm, 355 subscriptions to periodicals and newspapers in English, Russian, and other languages, and RFE/RL Archival Material.

* Radio Free Europe/Radio Liberty Research Report

1775 Broadway
New York, NY 10019 (212) 397-5300

This report was introduced in January 1992 and replaces the *Report on the USSR* and the *Report on Eastern Europe*, and will be the size of these two publications combined. In North America the annual subscription cost will be $150, $75 for students. Contact the above office for information.

* RAND

1700 Main St.
PO Box 2138
Santa Monica, CA 90406-2138 (213) 393-0411

RAND began as a research project sponsored by the United States Air Force with the Douglas Aircraft Corporation in 1946. While RAND is a private, non-profit institution, most of its research contracts were security oriented and sponsored by the Air Force and other government agencies. RAND operates three Federally Funded Research and Development Centers: Project AIR FORCE; the Arroyo Center; and the National Defense Research Institute. Today, while Defense and Foreign policy work still predominates, RAND does do some nondefense related research and has developed significant non-government support. For further information, a publications list, and a sample of the *RAND Research Review*, contact the above address.

* Refugees, Permanent Residents, Students, and Aliens Travel

Central Office
Immigration and Naturalization Service
425 I Street, NW
Washington, DC 20536 (202) 307-1501

Publications and tape recorded messages about immigration are available from this central office. However, field offices operate in most states and these local phone numbers appear in the Law and Social Justice Chapter and, of course, are easy to obtain from the directory assistance operators. When calling the tape recorded telephone number, above, enter one of the number codes below which corresponds to the information about immigration and naturalization that you need:

701 Departure from the USA by permanent residents: reentry permits (I-131)
703 Travel authorization for refugees: Refugee travel documents (I-570)
705 Travel by an alien whose application for permanent resident status is still pending
704 Emergency travel requests
702 Student travel outside the USA

* Refugee Resettlement and Asylum

Bureau of Refugee Programs
U.S. Department of State
2201 C St., NW, Room 5824
Washington, DC 20520 (202) 647-5767

At the center of a cooperative effort between the State Department, other Government agencies, private voluntary organizations, and international agencies, this bureau provides assistance to refugees in countries of first asylum, and to implement the admission policies to the United States for refugee resettlement.

Some of the programs for which this bureau is responsible include relief and repatriation of refugees, and the selection, processing, and training of refugees to be admitted to the United States.

* Resolution of Human Rights Violations

Bureau of International Organization Affairs
U.S. Department of State
2201 C St., NW, Room 4334A
Washington, DC 20520 (202) 647-2708

This office focuses on human rights issues within the United Nations, with the hope of improving the state of human rights in foreign countries. They also oversee U.N. human rights organizations and write U.S. government replies to accusations of U.S. human rights violations.

* Sahel Development Program

Office of West Africa and the Sahel
Bureau for Africa, Room 3491
Agency for International Development (AID)
Washington, DC 20523 (202) 647-5993

AID participates in a long-term program for the development of the Sahelian region of West Africa as part of the Development Fund for Africa. The objectives of the Sahel Development Program are to promote regional food self-reliance and self-sustaining economic growth. The program is coordinated, planned, and designed by the Club du Sahel, comprised of nine Sahel states: Mali, Chad, Niger, Burkina Faso, Senegal, Mauritania, Cape Verde, the Gambia, and Guinea-Bissau; the United States; and over 20 participating governments and international organizations.

* Samantha Smith Memorial Exchange Program

Youth Programs Division
United States Information Agency (USIA)
301 4th St., SW, Room 357
Washington, DC 20547 (202) 619-6299

Private Organizations and schools are invited to submit proposals for grants in support of exchanges of young people under the age of 21 between the U.S. and the countries of Eastern Europe and the former Soviet Union.

* Science and Technology Development

Bureau for Research and Development, Room 4942
Agency for International Development (AID)
Washington, DC 20523-0057 (202) 647-1827

Multi-disciplinary science expertise from this office work closely with regional and field staffs, offering needed technical assistance, and serve as a link to U.S. and international development specialists. A major responsibility is to identify and support research having interregional or worldwide implications and research on the "cutting edge" of technology generation, such as biotechnology and the use of genetic engineering techniques. Contact this office for more information.

* Science Capacity-Building in Third World

Office of the Research Advisor
Agency for International Development (AID)
Room 320, SA-18
Washington, DC 20523-1818 (703) 875-4444

This office coordinates the more innovative and collaborative approaches to the problems and processes of development research, technology transfer, and related capacity-building programs and activities in the development of Third World countries. Scientific and technological needs and opportunities in developing countries are identified, and resources are found to meet those needs from the United States and foreign public and private sources. Effective communication is ensured between the United States scientific and technological capacities and the development programs in which the United States participates.

* Seabed Mining, Outer Continental Shelf and Other Ocean Policies

Office of Oceans Law and Policy
Bureau of Oceans and International Environmental and Scientific Affairs
U.S. Department of State

Foreign Policy

2201 C St., NW, Room 5805A
Washington, DC 20520 (202) 647-5123
This series of studies deals with a variety of topics concerning the seas, such as sea boundaries, straight baselines, and national maritime claims. Call or write for copies of specific studies and more information.

* Senate Foreign Relations Committee

Suite SD-419 Dirksen Senate Office Building
Washington, DC 20510 (202) 224-4651
The Senate Foreign Relations Committee reviews all aspects of American foreign relations. In particular, the SFRC is a good source for information on treaties, as it reviews them before they go to the full Senate for ratification.

* Small Business Contracts with A.I.D.

Office of Small and Disadvantaged Business Utilization
Agency for International Development (AID), SA-14
Washington, DC 20523-1414 (703) 875-1551
Information and other handout materials are provided for AID procurement for small and disadvantaged businesses. A weekly bulletin is published that lists the current need of the agency. For a packet of information on the requirements for securing business with AID, write to the office above.

* State Department Speakers

Office of Public Programs
Bureau of Public Affairs
U.S. Department of State
2201 C St, NW, Room 5831
Washington, DC 20520 (202) 647-2234
Speaking engagements are arranged with organizations throughout the country. To make the best use of the speakers' time, the bureau normally tries to schedule other events during trips, such as media interviews, informal discussion with community leaders, and visits to academic institutions.

* State of World Peace Survey

United States Institute of Peace
1550 M St., NW
Washington, DC 20005 (202) 429-3838
The Institute has decided to undertake a task of presenting critical information on the state of peace worldwide to the American public and to the international community. A number of valuable studies are available in areas such as human rights and global ecology. The Institute's report will be a periodically updated survey seeking to identify trends, causes, and consequences of armed international conflict on a region-by-region basis. In addition, efforts will be made to standardize methods of statistical reporting on the state of world peace.

* Student Visa Information

Central Office
Immigration and Naturalization Service
425 I Street, NW
Washington, DC 20536 (202) 307-1501
Publications and tape recorded messages about immigration are available from this central office. However, field offices operate in most states and these local phone numbers appear in the Law and Social Justice Chapter and are easy to obtain from the directory assistance operators. When calling the tape recorded telephone number above, enter one of the number codes below which corresponds to the information about immigration and naturalization that you need:

601 Permission to go to school (I-20, I-134)
606 How to maintain your student status
604 Visas for spouse and dependent children of student
602 Student visa extension (I-538)
603 Permission to work (I-538)
605 F-1 Transfer to another school (I-538) and M-1 Transfer to another school (I-538)

* Teaching in the Third World

Education Sector
Office of Programming and Training Support
Peace Corps
1990 K St., NW

Washington, DC 20526 (202) 606-2366
Volunteers are trained to teach people of other cultures by experienced educators. Programs are planned here to fit the basic needs of the countries being served.

* Technology Assessment Reports

Office of Technology Assessment (OTA)
Publications Order
U.S. Congress
Washington, DC 20510-8025 (202) 224-8996
The Office of Technology Assessment explores issues relating to science and technology for Congress. These OTA publications are available through the office above, the Government Printing Office, and the National Technical Information Service. To find out correct ordering information and prices, along with brief summaries of the following studies, contact the OTA office above and request their current publications catalog.

Africa Tomorrow: Issues in Technology, Agriculture, and U.S. Foreign Aid (TM-F-31)
Continuing the Commitment: Agricultural Development in the Sahel (F-308)
Enhancing the Quality of U.S. Grain for International Trade (F-399)
Grain Quality in International Trade: A Comparison of Major U.S. Competitors (F-402)
A Review of U.S. Competitiveness in Agriculture Trade (TM-TET-29)
Sustaining Tropical Forest Resources: Reforestation of Degraded Lands (BP-F-18)
Sustaining Tropical Forest Resources: U.S. and International Institutions (BP-F-19)

* Technology Transfer in the Third World

Office of the Science Advisor
Agency for International Development (AID)
Room 320, SA-18
Washington, DC 20523-1818 (703) 875-4444
This office responds to the interest of Congress in supporting innovative, collaborative approaches in Third World development research and technology transfer. A small, highly competitive research grant program funds the more experimental and less widely known technologies that might later be incorporated into AID's mainstream programs. This grant program is designed to encourage the involvement of scientists in the developing countries and seeks to support research that will lead to solutions to serious developing-country problems. Research Modules include: Biotechnology/Immunology; Chemistry for World Food Needs; Plant Biotechnology; and Global Climate Change. The office also helps support a National Academy of Sciences program to establish research networks among institutions in the developing countries that can identify underexploited resources of potential economic value. Contact the office above for more information.

* Trade Agreements

Developed Countries Trade Division
Bureau of Economic and Business Affairs
U.S. Department of State
2201 C St., NW, Room 3822
Washington, DC 20520 (202) 647-1162
In handling the U.S. relationship with developed countries regarding bilateral and multilateral trade agreements, this offices examine all aspects of trade, such as restrictions on exports, customs, and licensing requirements. Information is available on these agreements and other issues concerning trade with these developed countries.

* Trade-Related Employment Issues

U.S. Department of Labor
200 Constitution Ave., NW, Room S2235
Washington, DC 20210 (202) 523-6043
The Bureau of International Labor Affairs represents the U.S. Department of Labor in the development of international economic and trade policies that affect the welfare of U.S. workers. This role includes conducting research on trade-related employment issues, coordinating advice received from Labor Advisory Committees on Trade authorized by the Trade Agreements Act of 1979, and acting as a liaison between other federal departments, agencies, and organized labor. The Bureau is also a member of various interagency committees charged with trade policy functions, and continues to participate in the formulation of U.S. immigration policy. Contact this office for information on studies in progress.

Be patient. If any phone number is incorrect, call (area code) 555-1212 and request the new listing.

International Relations and Defense

* Training Engineers Overseas

Office of Programming and Training Support
Peace Corps, 1990 K St., NW
Washington, DC 20526
(202) 606-3398

Civil, mechanical, mining, environmental, and metallurgical engineers help train people to develop water, sanitation, and transportation systems, as well as building bridges and roads.

* Transportation Technology Exchange

International Cooperative Division and Secretariat (P-25)
Office of International Transportation and Trade
Office of the Secretary of Transportation
U.S. Department of Transportation (DOT)
400 7th Street, SW
Washington, DC 20590
(202) 366-4368

DOT participates in a number of cooperative programs with other countries to exchange mutually beneficial transportation research data and state-of-the-art technical information. Areas of exchange include highway technology; ports and inland waterways; railway technology; and search and rescue operations. China and the Soviet Union are among the countries participating. Contact this office for information about these programs.

* Travel Advisories and Alerts for Unstable Countries

Overseas Citizens Services
U.S. Department of State
2201 C St., NW, Room 4800
Washington, DC 20520
(202) 647-5225

This office can provide you with visa requirements for U.S. citizens wishing to travel to foreign countries. They stress that this information is subject to change and that definitive information regarding visas can come only from the foreign embassies. This taped message lists all the countries, their current visa requirements, travel advisories for the countries, and the embassies' phone numbers.

* Treaties and International Agreements

Office of Legal Advisor
U.S. Department of State
2201 C St., NW, Room 5420
Washington, DC 20520
(202) 647-2044

Information on treaties and international agreements to which the U.S. is a party is prepared by the Office of Legal Advisor. The following publications can be purchased from the Superintendent of Documents, Government Printing Office, Washington, DC 20402; (202) 783-3238:

United States Treaties and Other International Agreements. This multivolume series presents the texts of all treaties and other international agreements of the U.S. entered into force since January 1, 1950. It contains the official, legal texts of agreements in their original languages, with English translations when necessary.

Treaties and Other International Agreements of the United States of America, 1776 - 1949. This contains the texts of bilateral, multilateral, and other international agreements entered into by the United States.

Treaties in Force. Lists the treaties and other international agreements in effect for the United States on record in the U.S. Department of State at the beginning of each year ($16).

Treaties and Other International Acts Series (TIAS). TIAS provides in pamphlet form the texts of treaties and international agreements to which the U.S. is a party. Purchase is by subscription or single copy ($89 per year).

* United Nations Documents and Reference

Bureau of International Organization Affairs
U.S. Department of State
2201 C St., NW, Room 3428
Washington, DC 20520
(202) 647-6878

This office performs general reference on United Nations matters for the State Department. There is limited availability for U.N. documents.

* United Nations Educational Scientific and Cultural Organizations (UNESCO)

UNESCO Affairs
Bureau of International Organization Affairs
U.S. Department of State
2201 C St., NW, Room 5331
Washington, DC 20520
(202) 647-6882

Although the United States withdrew from UNESCO in 1984, it still maintains a foreign service officer observes UNESCO and reports their activities to the State Department. This office can provide you with general information regarding UNESCO.

* United Nations Information

United Nations Association of the United States of America
1010 Vermont Ave., NW, Suite 904
Washington, DC 20005
(202) 347-5004

The Association provides information and educational services on the work of the U.N. and on other global issues for students, scholars, Congress, and the media. UNA-USA also supports the model U.N. program in which some 60,000 high school and college students assume the role of diplomats and debate issues from the U.N. agenda. UNA-USA also publishes studies on the U.N., the environment, international economics, and the role of the U.S. in the United Nations. A list of publications with prices is available from the above office.

* United Nations Special Agencies

Office of Technical Specialized Agencies
Bureau of International Organization Affairs
U.S. Department of State
2201 C St., NW, Room 5331
Washington, DC 20520
(202) 647-2330

In overseeing U.S. relationships with United Nations technical and specialized organizations, this office is responsible for planning, coordinating, and implementing U.S. policy toward these organizations and other programs within the United Nations. They work closely with other offices, governmental agencies, and organizations.

* United States Coast Guard

U.S. Department of Transportation
Washington, DC 20590
(202) 267-1587

In the last several years, the Coast Guard has played a central role in the war against illicit drugs. The Coast Guard patrols the American shores, intercoastal waterways, rivers, and the Great Lakes.

* University Expertise in International Development

Agency Center for University Cooperation and Development
Bureau for Research and Development, Room 900, SA-38
Agency for International Development (AID)
Washington, DC 20523-3801
(703) 816-0295

U.S. universities are the primary centers which generate knowledge and the development of skills essential to the U.S. role in development assistance. The overseas missions of AID in particular need to be able to draw upon the scientific community in order to apply the most current technical expertise and judgment to mission plans and programs. In response to this need, AID has established a Joint Career Corps (JCC) to encourage certain exchanges of work assignments between university faculty and Agency staff. Candidates proposed by their universities must be tenured faculty, at least at the Associate Professor level, with established scientific reputations, leadership qualities, and the ability to provide both technical and policy related advice to missions and high-level host country officials. Contact this office for more information.

* Urban Development in Third World

Office of Housing and Urban Programs
Bureau for Private Enterprise
Agency for International Development (AID)
320 21st St., NW
Washington, DC 20523
(202) 663-2530

This office supports a program of research and technical assistance in urban development. New tools are developed and applied to the analysis of urban issues and urban investment strategies to strengthen their effectiveness.

* U.S. Exports to Developing Countries

Commercial, Legislative and Business Affairs
Bureau of Economic and Business Affairs
U.S. Department of State

Be patient. If any phone number is incorrect, call (area code) 555-1212 and request the new listing.

Foreign Policy

2201 C St., NW, Room 6822
Washington, DC 20520 (202) 647-1942

This office acts as a clearinghouse within the State Department for general questions concerning international business exporting and U.S. Government programs to support U.S. business and exports. It also works with the U.S. Department of Commerce to support U.S. commercial assistants working in 140 U.S. embassies overseas.

* U.S. Foreign Policy Press Materials

Press and Publications Service
Bureau of Programs
United States Information Agency (USIA)
301 Fourth St., SW, Room 406
Washington, DC 20547 (202) 619-4265

USIA prints materials to project an accurate image of the United States and its foreign policy abroad. The Wireless File, a radioteletype network which now can also be accessed computer-to-computer, sends five regional transmissions of policy statements and interpretation each weekday. Each contains 20,000 to 30,000 words in English, but also includes Spanish, French, and Arabic portions, and is sent to U.S. personnel abroad for background information and to distribute to foreign opinion leaders and news media. The Express File transmits material from the Wireless directly into the news rooms of foreign media. This division also distributes articles, photographs, and Dateline America news-feature service. USIA also prints 14 magazines and commercial bulletins in 20 languages, mostly at foreign locations. Generally, they contain reprints from American periodicals for distribution abroad. Publications printed in Washington, DC, are *America Illustrated*, a monthly printed in Russian; *Topic*, published six times a year for sub-Saharan Africa, in English and French; *Dialogue*, a quarterly devoted to American culture and ideas, printed in English, French, and Spanish, as well as other translations put out by field posts; *Economic Impact*, an English and Spanish quarterly; *English Teaching Forum*, a quarterly for English teachers around the world; and *Problems of Communism*. The latter two are available in the United States through the Government Printing Office. Other magazines printed overseas are *al-Majal*, an Arabic monthly; *Span*, an English monthly published in India; and *Trends*, a Japanese bi-monthly. USIA also distributes pamphlets and leaflets in more than 100 countries.

* U.S. Information Agency Library

United States Information Agency (USIA)
301 Fourth St., SW, Room 135
Washington, DC 20547 (202) 619-5947

The Washington library of USIA houses a varied collection, including a Russian language section. Access is restricted: permission to use the library can be obtained through the Office of Congressional and Public Liaison, address above, Room 602, (202) 619-4355.

* U.S. Representation at International Organizations

Bureau of International Organization Affairs
U.S. Department of State
2201 C St., NW, Room 6334
Washington, DC 20520 (202) 647-9490

This bureau explains the United States' foreign policy positions to other nations and does the day-in and day-out work of representing the U.S. and presenting U.S. policies at the United Nations. They work with many international organizations, such as the International Labor Organization, and take part in over 700 international conferences each year. Concerns include UN peace keeping operations in the Middle East, nuclear facility safeguards and refugee assistance.

* U.S. Role in United Nations

United States Mission to the United Nations
799 United Nations Plaza
New York, NY 10017 (212) 415-4404

This office can provide information regarding the activities and positions of U.S. representatives as well as the delegations of other countries at the United Nations. Specific areas reviewed include UN Peacekeeping Operations in the Middle East, nuclear facility safeguards, and refugee assistance. Specialized sections within the Mission include: the Economic and Social Affairs Section; the Legal Section; the Resources and Management Section; the Military Staff; and the Press/Publications Office.

* U.S.-Soviet Exchange Initiative

President's U.S.-Soviet Exchange Initiative
United States Information Agency (USIA)
301 Fourth St., SW, Room 751
Washington, DC 20547 (202) 619-4548

This office is implementing the General Exchanges Agreement signed by the U.S. and the Soviet Union in 1985 to resume academic, cultural, and performing artists exchanges, officially suspended since 1979. It is also charged with facilitating a new, extensive initiative to foster direct contact between their citizens, endorsed by the leaders of both countries. Presidents Bush and Gorbachev upgraded the program in June 1990, expanding exchanges of U.S. and Soviet undergraduates by 1000 in each direction. Guidance is provided to private-sector groups interested in establishing exchanges in the areas of performing arts, exhibitions, education, health, sports, television, film, youth, citizen and professional counterparts.

* Videos and Transcripts on the Persian Gulf Crisis

Center for Defense Information (CDI)
1500 Massachusetts Ave., NW
Washington, DC 20005 (202) 862-0700

CDI, an independent military affairs research organization, produces a weekly TV show, AMERICA'S DEFENSE MONITOR, which aired a series of three episodes dealing with the Persian Gulf Crisis. Copies of VHS tapes can be purchased from the above address for $65 plus $2 postage and handling. Or order transcripts of the episodes for $5 each, plus $2 postage and handling.

* Visa Information for Aliens

Visa Services, U.S. Department of State
Bureau of Consular Affairs
Columbia Plaza Office Building
2401 E St., NW, Room 1353
Washington, DC 20520 (202) 647-0510

This office provides visa information for citizens of foreign countries who wish to come to the United States for a temporary stay, such as for studies, tourism, or medical treatment. To obtain a visa you must contact the nearest American embassy or consulate. This office can direct you to the closest place, as well as inform you of documents necessary for the application process.

* Voice of America International Broadcasting

Office of External Affairs
Voice of America (VOA)
United States Information Agency (USIA)
330 Independence Ave., SW, Room 3323
Washington, DC 20547 (202) 619-2538

On the air since 1942, VOA has built an audience of more than 127 million adults, listening to some 1200 hours of broadcasting a week in 43 languages. With 34 studios at headquarters in Washington, DC, three more in New York, one in Los Angeles, and one in Miami, VOA beams programs worldwide through a satellite network. VOA maintains news bureaus in 26 cities, and uses part-time correspondents in many countries to supplement its own staff. Radio Marti broadcasts seven days a week to Cuba, and a test of TV Marti has been funded. Information on the VOA and its program schedules is available. Forty-five-minute tours of VOA facilities are given weekdays, except holidays. Call for reservations.

* Voice of America Facilities

Office of Engineering and Technical Operations
Voice of America (VOA)
United States Information Agency (USIA)
330 Independence Ave., SW, Room 3348
Washington, DC 20547 (202) 619-1060

The Voice of America has a Master Control and Network Control Center in Washington, DC, facilities in New York City, Chicago, Los Angeles, and Miami, 107 transmitters worldwide, and 15 satellite circuits to use in reaching audiences all over the globe. A Satellite Interconnect System (SIS) is in the beginning phases of operation and will eventually improve reception of VOA broadcasts in many remote areas. The public can receive free of charge information on the technical operations of VOA, including a descriptive leaflet on SIS, a table of VOA relay stations, showing the locations, transmitters, power range, and area reached, and a frequency schedule.

Be patient. If any phone number is incorrect, call (area code) 555-1212 and request the new listing.

International Relations and Defense

* Voluntary Relief Organizations Reports

Bureau for Food and Humanitarian Assistance
Room 260, SA-8
Agency for International Development (AID)
Washington, DC 20523 (703) 351-0201

Voluntary Foreign Aid Programs: Report of American Voluntary Agencies Engaged in Overseas Relief and Development Registered with the Agency for International Development describes the general nature of the work being carried out by the Private and Voluntary Organizations (PVOs) which are registered with AID. Included is such information as a PVO's geographic focus and sectorial concentration, as well as summaries of support, revenue, and expenditures. Contact the office above to obtain a copy.

* War Risk Insurance for Ships

Marine Insurance Division
Office of Trade and Analysis and Insurance
Maritime Administration
U.S. Department of Transportation
400 7th Street, SW, Room 8121
Washington, DC 20590 (202) 366-4161

The War Risk Insurance Program insures operators and seamen against losses from hostile action if commercial insurance is not available to them. The program covers loss of life and materials due to war or nuclear detonation.

* Water and Sanitation Assistance and Training

Office of Training and Program Support
Peace Corps
1990 K St., NW
Washington, DC 20526 (202) 606-2174

This office works at encouraging and implementing better methods of sanitation and water purification.

* Weekly Updates on Foreign Policy

U.S. Department of State Dispatch
Office of Public Communication
Bureau of Public Affairs
Washington, DC 20520-6810 (202) 647-6317

The U.S. Department of State Dispatch chronicles U.S. foreign policy on a weekly basis. Containing original source material and indexed every six months (index is included in the subscription), *DISPATCH* incudes speeches and Congressional testimony; fact sheets on critical international issues and organizations; analyses of foreign policy; photographs; maps and profiles of countries in the news; updates on U.S. initiatives abroad; treaty actions and other foreign policy topics. Several subscription options are available: $75 per year 3rd Class Mail; $142, First Class; $93.75 foreign mail. Order from Superintendent of Documents, Government Printing Office, Washington, DC 20402-9371, (202) 783-3278. Overnight delivery is available for $430 from National Technical Information Service, U.S. Department of Commerce, 5285 Port Royal Road, Springfield, VA 22161-2171, (703) 487-4630 (Pub. No. : PB90-923500ACT). For Electronic Subscriptions, contact the State Department's Computer Information Delivery Service (CIDS) at (703) 802-5700.

* Who's Who in the Diplomatic Community

Bureau of Public Affairs
U.S. Department of State
2201 C St., NW, Room 5815A
Washington, DC 20520 (202) 647-6575

The Bureau of Public Affairs publishes a sales catalog, which lists their publications, as well as ordering information. The following publications are also available from the Superintendent of Documents Government Printing Office, Washington, DC 20402; (202) 783-3238. Documents can also often be obtained at a local GPO bookstore. Check for one in your area.

Diplomatic List ($4.50 per issue). Prepared quarterly, the Diplomatic List includes the names of the members of the diplomatic staffs of all missions and their spouses, as well as the addresses and phone numbers of the foreign missions.

Employees of Diplomatic Missions ($2.50 per issue). This quarterly publication lists all the members of the technical, administrative, and service staffs of more than 130 foreign missions. It gives the employee's name, function, and home address.

Key Officers of Foreign Service Posts ($1.75 per issue). Produced three times a

year, this publication lists all key officers at Foreign Service posts whom business representatives would most likely need to contact. Addresses and phone numbers are included.

State Department Organizational Directory ($11). It includes detailed organizational listings of State, AID, ACDA, and the U.S. Information Agency, with titles, names, and phone numbers. There is a directory of services listing available services within the Department of State.

Update From State (free). A new bimonthly publication dedicated to informing the public about the policies, operations, and diplomatic efforts of the U.S. Department of State and the Foreign Service.

* Women in Development Program

Development Information Center
Room 105, SA-18
Agency for International Development (AID)
Washington, DC 20523-1801 (703) 875-4818

Contact this Center for information on AID's Women in Development subject collection of papers and documents assembled and organized by the AID Women in Development Office. Access is through a handlist.

* Women Empowerment in Third World

Bureau of Research and Development
Agency for International Development (AID)
Room 714, SA-18
Washington, DC 20523 (703) 875-4474

Women in developing countries play a significant role in economic production, family support, and the overall development process of the national economies. Bilateral aid is therefore administered to give particular attention to the programs, projects, and activities that tend to integrate women and improve their status in these countries. Materials on experiences within this program are available through the Center for Development Information and Evaluation, 1601 N. Kent St., Room 105, Arlington, VA (703) 875-4818.

* Work Permits for Foreigners

Labor Certification Division
Employment Service
Employment and Training Administration
U.S. Department of Labor
200 Constitution Ave., NW, Room N4456
Washington, DC 20210 (202) 535-0163

If an employer wishes to hire foreign workers, he must first obtain a foreign labor certificate, which is a statement from the U.S. Department of Labor stating that there is no U.S. citizen available to fill the job. The Department investigates to make sure that the wages and working conditions of the foreign workers will not seriously affect the wages and working conditions of U.S. workers. An employer applies for a foreign labor certificate through the local state employment service office, which then conducts a job hunt before sending the application form to the area regional office for approval or disapproval.

* WORLDNET Radio and Television Satellite Network

Public Liaison
Television and Film Service
United States Information Agency (USIA)
601 D St., NW
Washington, DC 20547 (202) 501-7806

The first live global satellite television network, WORLDNET now reaches every continent, transmitting five days a week. Designed to link overseas posts and embassies with Washington and to provide news and feature programming for foreign broadcast media, WORLDNET allows the U.S. to explain our foreign policy with new immediacy and to act quickly in response to global events. "Dialogues" are an innovative way to demonstrate American press freedom by linking American newsmakers electronically with foreign journalists in unrehearsed, live "telepress conferences." The network utilizes Intelsat and regional satellites. Nearly 200 U.S. embassies, consulates, and cultural centers around the world are equipped with antennae to receive WORLDNET programming and distribute it to local broadcasters. Topics covered on WORLDNET include Arts and Literature, Business and Economics, Current Events, Entertainment, Sports, Environment, Language Instruction, Science, and American Society. A free brochure on WORLDNET is available. On August 22, 1988, RIAS-TV joined RIAS (Radio in the American Sector), a 40-year-old U.S.-German cooperative effort.

Be patient. If any phone number is incorrect, call (area code) 555-1212 and request the new listing.

Arms Control and World Peace

In the United States, the Arms Control and Disarmament Agency (ACDA) coordinates the ongoing negotiations between the United States, Russia, and other nuclear powers to reduce their arsenals. This federal agency also takes the lead in other efforts to reduce the risk of war by, for example, verifying other countries' compliance with the Nuclear Non-Proliferation Treaty and other international agreements. Information about these developments as well as technical materials are identified here. Weapons sales to foreign governments, technology transfer, and treaties are also important elements of arms control. As Congressional approval is necessary for these actions, the foreign affairs and armed services committees as well as other congressional panels serve as additional information sources, often providing a different approach to the objectives of the President and the ACDA.

* Arms Control and Disarmament Agreements

Arms Control and Disarmament Agency (ACDA)
320 21st St., NW
Washington, DC 20451 (202) 647-4800

The 1990 edition of *Arms Control and Disarmament Agreements* contains all the texts and histories of all major arms control agreements to which the U.S. was a participant up through May 1988. The publication is for sale at the GPO (202) 783-3238, stock number 002000-00096-2. Cost is $15.

* Current and Future Negotiations

Bureau of Strategic and Nuclear Affairs
Arms Control and Disarmament Agency (ACDA)
320 21st St., NW
Washington, DC 20451 (202) 647-6566

This office coordinates with other agencies on research and policy studies to support the development of a comprehensive and effective arms control program. The Bureau also conducts external research on the technical and political implications of current and proposed negotiating options. This research supports implementation of existing agreements, ongoing negotiations, and planning for future negotiations.

* Defense Facts and Analyses

Center for Defense Information (CDI)
1500 Massachusetts Ave., NW
Washington, DC 20005 (202) 862-0700

In pursuit of its goal to lessen the possibility of nuclear war, CDI analyzes military issues and collects information, facts, and statistics. The staff includes many former military officers and civilians trained in military analysis. CDI regularly presents information to the Pentagon, State Department, and Congress. This information is also made available to the public and the media through a variety of services and publications. Members of CDI's Military Advisory Council (MAC) are available to speak to civic, school and business groups. Contact the Center at the telephone number listed above.

* Defense Systems Impact on Arms Control

Defense Programs and Analysis
Bureau of Nuclear Non-Proliferation Policy
Arms Control and Disarmament Agency (ACDA)
320 21st St., NW
Washington, DC 20451 (202) 647-1300

Arms Control Impact Statement, an annual report to Congress, contains details on certain weapons systems and analyses on the impact that such systems have on arms control agreements, treaties, and negotiations. Those weapon systems include nuclear weapon-related programs, defense programs which exceed specified cost ceilings, and other technology and weapons systems which the Executive Branch certifies as having significant effects on arms control. Impact statements are intended to be of value to the executive branch, to the Congress, and to the general public in evaluating the arms control implications of the development of major U.S. nuclear and non-nuclear weapons systems. Impact statements are intended to enhance the likelihood that arms control considerations become and remain integral to the decision making process on major U.S. defense programs, and that ACDA be instrumental in the process. This office can provide further information in this regard. Contact the public affairs office (202-647-4800) to obtain a copy of this annual publication.

* Diplomatic Coordination

Office of Public Affairs
Arms Control and Disarmament Agency (ACDA)
320 21st St., NW, Room 5843
Washington, DC 20451 (202) 647-8677

As part of an interagency public diplomacy group, this office prepares, coordinates, and publishes materials to support the Administration's conduct of public diplomacy activities. ACDA also provides guidance on arms control matters to press spokesmen of other Federal agencies, assists in preparation of information for use abroad, conducts special programs and conferences for nongovernmental organizations and the news media, and conducts briefings for media representatives, visiting students, and scholars.

* Disarmament Activities and Documents

Superintendent of Documents
Government Printing Office
Washington, DC 20402 (202) 783-3238

Each volume of ACDA's historical series, *Documents on Disarmament*, contains complete details on significant arms control and disarmament activities by printing the textual materials of treaties, agreements, laws, reports, statements, resolutions, communiques, proposals, declarations, and speeches of both U.S. and foreign origin.

* Economic Analysis of Arms Control Programs

Defense Programs and Analysis Division
Bureau of Nuclear Non-Proliferation Policy
Arms Control and Disarmament Agency (ACDA)
320 21st St., NW
Washington, DC 20451 (202) 647-1300

This division is responsible for the Agency's economic analysis of defense and arms control programs, and the analysis of weapons technology. Contact them for more information on these issues.

* Economic Impact of Arms Reduction Treaties

Office of Public Affairs
Arms Control and Disarmament Agency (ACDA)
320 21st St., NW, Room 5843
Washington, DC 20451 (202) 647-8677

Research relevant indirectly to negotiation support and directly to assessing the economic impact of treaties and agreements is an important part of ACDA's activities. They analyze the economics of defense strategies, and are currently building data banks on worldwide defense and economic information. One of the objectives of arms control is the reduction of global military expenditures, and research in support of this objective includes analyses of the economic impact

Be patient. If any phone number is incorrect, call (area code) 555-1212 and request the new listing.

International Relations and Defense

of the INF Treaty, defense spending and national budgets, and military procurement. ACDA economists review Russian and Eastern European countries' national accounts, and prepare an annual submission on U.S. defense spending for the U.N. military expenditures reporting program. For questions regarding economics research, contact this office.

* Europe

Theater Affairs Division
Bureau of Strategic and Nuclear Affairs
Arms Control and Disarmament Agency (ACDA)
320 21st St. NW
Washington, DC 20451 (202) 647-8253

Europe is the most heavily militarized continent on the planet. Even in the post Cold-War era, the danger of conflict remains. The task of arms control in Europe is to reduce the danger of war. Contact this bureau for more information on European arms control programs.

* Foreign Military Sales

Defense Security Assistance Agency
Operations Directorate
The Pentagon, Room 4B740
Washington, DC 20301-2800 (703) 697-8108

This office administers the Foreign Military Sales (FMS) Program, which deals with U.S. government sales of defense articles and services to foreign governments. A free booklet containing information on the Program and the U.S. Defense Security Assistance Agency is available upon request.

* Foreign Weapon Sales Statistics

FMS Reports and Controls Division
Defense Security Assistance Agency
The Pentagon, Room 4B659
Washington, DC 20301-2800 (703) 693-1057

This office publishes a free annual publication, *Foreign Military Sales, Foreign Military Construction Sales, and Military Assistance Facts*, which contains information and detailed statistics on all grant programs, sales, and Federal financing of security assistance to foreign countries. Write or call for a copy.

* INF Treaty Q & A

Office of Public Affairs
Arms Control and Disarmament Agency (ACDA)
320 21st St., NW, Room 5834
Washington, DC 20451 (202) 647-4800

Understanding the INF Treaty reviews the post-World War II history leading up to the treaty, its negotiation, ratification, and implementation. This 36-page booklet provides the historical context to NATO's 1979 two-track decision, a history of the negotiations themselves, the ratification process that took place in both countries, an overview of the inspection and elimination procedures that are now being implemented, and an addendum that addresses may questions frequently asked about the INF Treaty.

* Legal Advice on Arms Control Treaties

The Office of the General Counsel
Arms Control and Disarmament Agency (ACDA)
320 21st St., NW
Washington, DC 20451 (202) 647-3582

This office is responsible for all matters of domestic and international law relevant to ACDA's work. It provides advice and assistance in drafting and negotiating arms control treaties and agreements, and on questions regarding their approval by Congress, and their implementation, interpretation, ratification, and revision. Attorneys from the office also serve as legal advisers on U.S. arms control negotiating delegations. The office also handles the legal aspects of Agency policies and operations in the areas of personnel, ethics, security, patents, contracts, procurement, and fiscal and administrative matters.

* Military Equipment Export Licenses

Office of Defense Trade Controls
Bureau of Politico-Military Affairs
U.S. Department of State, SA-6
Washington, DC 20520 (703) 875-6650

Being responsible for the licensing and regulation of commercial exports of military equipment and services, this office develops policy guidance on munitions exports, and registers all U.S. exports of arms, ammunition, and implements of war.

* Multilateral Arms Control Negotiations

Bureau of Multilateral Affairs
Arms Control and Disarmament Agency (ACDA)
320 21st St. NW
Washington, DC 20451 (202) 647-5999

This office develops arms control policy, strategy, and tactics for ongoing multilateral arms control negotiations, and provides organizational support, delegation staffing, and Washington backstopping for multilateral negotiations, such as multilateral and bilateral chemical weapons negotiations and the First Committee of the United Nations General Assembly. Contact this bureau for more information relevant to multilateral affairs.

* Newsletter

Office of Public Affairs
Arms Control and Disarmament Agency (ACDA)
320 21st St., NW, Room 5832
Washington, DC 20451 (202) 647-4800

Arms Control Update, an eight-page, serially-published ACDA newsletter, reviews recent developments in arms control and contains excerpts from administration statements on U.S. arms control policy. Recent issues contain broad overviews of U.S. arms control activities and information about other, more in-depth, publications. Contact this office to receive a free subscription.

* Non-Proliferation Evaluation

International Nuclear Affairs Division
Bureau of Nuclear and Weapons Control
Arms Control and Disarmament Agency (ACDA)
320 21st St. NW
Washington, DC 20451 (202) 647-3466

This division provides advice, assessments, and policy recommendations on the international relations aspects of nonproliferation. It also assesses each proposed agreement for peaceful cooperation and provides ACDA views on U.S. nuclear export control issues.

* Non-Proliferation Policy

Office of Nuclear Non-Proliferation Policy
U.S. Department of Energy
Room 7G-050 Forrestal Bldg.
Washington, DC 20585 (202) 586-6175

This office implements U.S. Department of Energy programs and activities derived from formal international non-proliferation agreements.

* Non-Proliferation Treaty Compliance

Office of Non-Proliferation and Export Policy
Bureau of Oceans and International Environmental and Scientific Affairs
U.S. Department of State
2201 C St., NW, Room 7828
Washington, DC 20520 (202) 647-4812

Concerned with non-proliferation policy, this office makes sure that materials having nuclear weapons potential are not exported without careful consideration of the Nuclear Non-Proliferation Treaty.

* Nuclear Risk Reduction Center

Nuclear Risk Reduction Center
U.S. Department of State
2201 C St., NW, Room 7532
Washington, DC 20520 (202) 647-0025

The United States Nuclear Risk Reduction Center and its Soviet counterpart have been established to reduce the risk of conflict that might result from accident, misinterpretation, or miscalculation. The increasing complexity of arms control agreements associated with the end of the Cold War has led to the expansion of the centers.

Be patient. If any phone number is incorrect, call (area code) 555-1212 and request the new listing.

Arms Control and World Peace

* Nuclear Technologies

Nuclear Safeguards and Technology Division
Bureau of Nuclear Non-Proliferation Policy
Arms Control and Disarmament Agency (ACDA)
320 21st St. NW
Washington, DC 20451 (202) 647-1140

This division provides advice and policy recommendations on safeguard systems, nuclear fuel cycles, and the technology aspects of nonproliferation. It also assesses the safeguards and nonproliferation implications of emerging technologies. Contact this division for more information.

* Peace and International Conflict Grants

Jennings Randolph Program for International Peace
United States Institute of Peace
1550 M St., NW
Washington, DC 20005 (202) 457-1700

This Program provides fellowships to scholars and leaders in peace to undertake research and other appropriate forms of communication on issues of international peace and the management of international conflict. The Fellowship Program has three levels: Jennings Randolph Distinguished Fellows are individuals whose careers show extraordinary accomplishment concerning questions of international peace; United States Institute of Peace Fellows are individuals also of accomplishment, but of somewhat less eminence; and United States Institute of Peace Scholars are individuals working on doctoral dissertations in the field.

* Policy Coordination

Bureau of Strategic and Nuclear Affairs
Arms Control and Disarmament Agency (ACDA)
320 21st St. NW
Washington, DC 20451 (202) 647-6566

This office is responsible for U.S.-Soviet nuclear arms control. In coordination with other U.S. agencies, it develops U.S. nuclear arms control policies for Presidential approval, supports negotiations on nuclear arms control, and provides analytical support for these efforts. Its responsibilities also include consultation and coordination with allied and other foreign governments on U.S./Soviet arms control negotiations. This bureau maintains the official record of all relevant documents, speeches, significant comments, and general material related to bilateral arms control and negotiations.

* Politico-Military Considerations

Bureau of Politico-Military Affairs
U.S. Department of State
2201 C St., NW, Room 7321
Washington, DC 20520 (202) 647-1256

The bureau advises the Secretary of State on the military aspects of various foreign policy matters, such as arms control negotiations, regional security arrangements, security assistance, arms sales programs, and technology transfers. It has primary responsibility for coordinating U.S. arms sales, military assistance, and Economic Support Fund programs to other nations. With a role in ongoing arms control negotiations, the bureau prepares talks with the Russians and other powers on reduction of strategic nuclear weapons, defense and space issues, and nuclear testing. It also is involved in multilateral negotiations to ban chemical weapons and reduce conventional forces in Europe.

* Press Releases

Office of Public Affairs
Arms Control and Disarmament Agency (ACDA)
320 21st St., NW, Room 5843
Washington, DC 20451 (202) 647-4800

This office publishes and distributes a daily compilation of press clippings; dispatches a daily cable containing selected press releases on arms control to U.S. Diplomatic posts overseas; and supplies numerous updates of arms control topics in its *Issues Brief* series. Contact this office for more information on these news releases.

* Proposals in U.S. Congress

Office of Congressional Affairs
Arms Control and Disarmament Agency (ACDA)
320 21st St. NW
Washington, DC 20451 (202) 647-3612

This office responds to congressional interest in arms control and negotiations by arranging briefings and consultations between ACDA officials and Members of Congress and staff; arranging arms control seminars for Congressional staff with ACDA officials and officials from other agencies; working with Congressional committee staffs in arranging hearings at which ACDA officials appear as witnesses; and distributing informational material on arms control issues to Members of Congress and their staffs. In response to requests from Senators and staff, this office provides information and coordinated briefings, seminars, and speakers.

* Proposed Arms and Technology Transfers

Arms Transfer Division
Bureau of Nuclear Non-Proliferation Policy
Arms Control and Disarmament Agency (ACDA)
320 21st St. NW
Washington, DC 20451 (202) 647-3466

This office assesses the arms control implications of proposed arms transfers and technology transfers, represents the Agency in the preparation of the Administration's annual security assistance programs, and participates in the implementation of the Missile Technology Control Regime. Contact this office for more information concerning arms transfer.

* Proposed Weapons Sales Analysis

Office of Security Assistance and Sales (OSAS)
Bureau of Politico-Military Affairs
U.S. Department of State
2201 C St., NW, Room 7424
Washington, DC 20520 (202) 647-9792

OSAS sets policy regarding transfer or sales of arms to foreign countries with respect to geographic regions and the technology allowed in the regions. They also deal with the transfer of arms regarding their purpose for use, as well as third country transfers, where a country who bought arms from the U.S. wants to sell these arms to another country. This office handles munitions control which concerns the licensing of items with military applications. Working closely with the U.S. Department of Defense on many of these areas, OSAS also helps in formulating the budget for military needs.

* Public Information on Arms Control Policies

Office of Public Affairs
Arms Control and Disarmament Agency (ACDA)
320 21st St., NW, Room 5834
Washington, DC 20451 (202) 647-4800

This office distributes and coordinates public information on arms control and disarmament. The staff works to ensure accurate and complete media coverage of U.S. arms control policies, and makes the public aware of arms control activities through speaking engagements and publications. This office also responds to information requests, and provides Agency leaders with advice on public perceptions of U.S. arms control policies.

* Safeguards and Arms Control Research

Office of Public Affairs
Arms Control and Disarmament Agency (ACDA)
320 21st St., NW, Room 5834
Washington, DC 20451 (202) 647-8677

ACDA's sponsored external research covers a wide range of arms control issues, such as verification, nuclear safeguards, nuclear test ban monitoring, and crisis stability issues. Specific examples of projects include Retrieval of Public Statements on Verification, and a Computer Model for Simulating Conventional Warfare. Conferences and seminars on related issues are also arranged. Contact this office for more information on these projects and other on-going external research.

* Science, Technology, and Arms Control

Office of the Science Advisor
Arms Control and Disarmament Agency (ACDA)
320 21st St. NW
Washington, DC 20451 (202) 647-5477

This office, created by Congress as part of the 1990 ACDA authorization, will serve as the focal point within ACDA and the US government for matters of science and technology in arms control and for coordination of arms control verification research and development. The Chief Science advisor also serves as

Be patient. If any phone number is incorrect, call (area code) 555-1212 and request the new listing.

International Relations and Defense

the chair of the ACDA Research Review Board, which recommends the research budget requirements and allocates ACDA external research funds. Contact this office for more information.

* Soviet Compliance with Arms Control Agreements

Office of Public Affairs
Arms Control and Disarmament Agency (ACDA)
320 21st St., NW, Room 5834
Washington, DC 20451   (202) 647-4800

The President's annual *Report on Soviet Noncompliance* to Congress presents in detail an evaluation of Soviet actions with respect to arms control obligations. Annually, ACDA also prepares for the President to submit to the Congress the report, *Adherence to and Compliance with Agreements*. This report contains details of the process by which the U.S. Government ensures U.S. compliance with its arms control obligations, detailed responses to Soviet charges of U.S. noncompliance, and an evaluation of other nations' compliance with international arms control agreements.

* Speakers on Arms Control

Office of Public Affairs
Arms Control and Disarmament Agency (ACDA)
320 21st St., NW, Room 5834
Washington, DC 20451   (202) 647-8677

Officers of the U.S. Arms Control and Disarmament Agency will address audiences in all parts of the country if speaking engagements can be worked into their schedules.

* Status of Current Arms Control Activities

Office of Public Affairs
Arms Control and Disarmament Agency (ACDA)
320 21st St., NW, Room 5834
Washington, DC 20451   (202) 647-4800

Each year the President is required to send to the Congress an annual report on the activities of ACDA and the nation's arms control agenda. The report includes a complete review of arms control and disarmament goals, research, and activities, as well as appraisals of the status and prospects of arms control negotiations and of arms control measures in effect. Contact this office of more information on this report.

* Treaty Verification Operations

Division of Verification
Bureau of Verification and Implementation
Arms Control and Disarmament Agency (ACDA)
320 21st St., NW
Washington, DC 20451   (202) 647-8091

The ACDA VAX computer helps evaluate and improve treaty verification procedures, assess treaty compliance, and verify provisions of proposed treaties, along with other facets of negotiation support. One of the VAX programs, for example, keeps track of all arms control-related external research conducted throughout the U.S. Government. All agencies are informed of on-going research to ensure that no duplication of work occurs. Contact this office for more information on computer aided research and arms control.

* Verification of Soviet Compliance

Bureau of Verification and Implementation
Arms Control and Disarmament Agency (ACDA)
320 21st St. NW
Washington, DC 20451   (202) 647-8091

This bureau provides a focal point within ACDA and the U.S. Government for formulating U.S. arms control verification policy and for assessing Soviet compliance with arms control agreements.

* Weapons Reduction Research and Arms Control Options

Office of Public Affairs
Arms Control and Disarmament Agency (ACDA)
320 21st St., NW, Room 5834
Washington, DC 20451   (202) 647-8677

Research, both short-run and long-run, on all aspects of arms control and disarmament, is one of the Arms Control and Disarmament Agency's principal functions. While most research projects support the immediate requirements of ongoing negotiations, others have been directed toward the goal of a world free from war and the dangers of armaments. Over the years, ACDA has accumulated a wealth of information on every conceivable aspect of arms control and disarmament. ACDA also coordinates research and studies by or for other government agencies, and analyzes selected defense programs for their arms control implications. Contact this office for information on specific research topics.

* World Peace Assessment

United States Institute of Peace
1550 M St., NW
Washington, DC 20005   (202) 457-1700

The Institute has decided to undertake a task of presenting critical information on the state of peace worldwide to the American public and to the international community. A number of valuable studies are available in areas such as human rights and global ecology. The Institute's report will be a periodically updated survey seeking to identify trends, causes, and consequences of armed international conflict on a region-by-region basis. In addition, efforts will be made to standardize methods of statistical reporting on the state of world peace.

* Worldwide Military Expenditures and Arms Transfers

Superintendent of Documents
Government Printing Office
Washington, DC 20402   (202) 783-3238

This annual publication provides a compilation of annual military and other relevant statistics for each of 145 countries over a decade, as well as essays on pertinent topics and special analyses. Military data include military spending, numbers of armed forces, and arms exports and imports in value and quantity terms. Comparative economic data include gross national product, central government expenditures, population, and total exports and imports. This publication also provides worldwide military and other relevant statistics for the period 1979-1986, as well as arms transfer data through 1987.

Be patient. If any phone number is incorrect, call (area code) 555-1212 and request the new listing.

Military and National Security

* *See also Information from Lawmakers Chapter*
* *See also Selling to the Government Chapter*
* *See also Science and Technology Chapter*
* *See also Foreign Policy section at the beginning of this chapter*

The military-industrial complex is vast. Many of the research and development centers and laboratories identified below are useful information sources. Defense procurement and contracts are included here as well as in the *Selling to the Government* Chapter. Military installations, personnel, spending, and other dimensions to the armed forces are contained in this chapter. There are 108 House and Senate committees and subcommittees that not only oversee the Pentagon but also have the last word on the defense budget. Listings for them can be found here as well as in the *Information from Lawmakers* Chapter. Policy concerning weapons sales and technology transfer to foreign governments are also addressed in the preceding section on arms control and disarmament.

Main phone numbers and public affairs offices are good places to get started when seeking information. Military and National Security affairs are the preserve of the State and Defense Departments. The State Departments main switchboard number is (202) 647-4000. The Defense Departments main switchboard number is (703) 545-6700. In the State Department, the Bureau of Politico-Military Affairs is the main action bureau in military affairs. The Arms Control and Disarmament Agency also has good information resources. The Regional desks have information on their individual areas. The size of the Defense Department inevitably makes it more complicated. Good places to start hunting are the Office of the Secretary of Defense's public affairs office, and the individual services public affairs offices. When calling, explain what you need as clearly as possible. Given the overlapping jurisdictions in this area, expect to get mis-routed at least once. Hang in there and you'll get to where you need to go. Keep in mind that often times bureaucrats in these areas (and others as well) think in terms of people as often as issues, meaning that when you request information on some topic their first thought is "who do I know that handles that type of thing?" Calling is probably more effective than writing because you are more likely to get into the right network and therefore find the right person to answer your question.

* Aeromedical Research
Strughold Aeromedical Library
U.S. Department of the Air Force
School of Aerospace Medicine
Brooks Air Force Base, TX 78235 (512) 536-3321
This library will provide inter-library loans, and can help you identify reports and refer you to the appropriate source. Strughold is linked to the OCLC and Doc Line systems (symbol TBM) and is located in the Amigos region of these systems.

* Aerospace Research Library
Information Management Division
National Air and Space Museum, Room 3100
Smithsonian Institute
Washington, DC 20560 (202) 357-3133
The Museum has a research library devoted to books and journals on aviation history, space exploration history, and science and technology in the fields of astronomy, astrophysics, engineering, geology, and space medicine. Appointments are strongly recommended as there is a limit of 5 researchers a day permitted due to limited staff resources. The library is open weekdays, 10am to 5pm.

* Aeronautical Systems Clearinghouse
Aeronautical Systems Division
Office of Public Affairs
U.S. Department of the Air Force
Wright-Patterson Air Force Base, OH 45433 (513) 255-3334
This office develops and acquires aeronautical systems, their components, and related aerospace equipment, including aircraft engines, airborne communications systems, special reconnaissance projects, and interpretation facilities. Fact sheets are available for each of the 200 programs administered by the agency. Write or call the above office for a free brochure describing the Division's mission.

* Aerospace Structures
Aerospace Structures Information
and Analysis Center
U.S. Department of the Air Force
WRDC/FIBR
Wright-Patterson AFB, OH 45433 (513) 255-6688
This Center is a central point for the collection and distribution of aerospace structures information. It maintains a library of reports done by various government agencies, and can refer you to other libraries and sources. Requests for specific information are served for researchers or contractors with a "need to know" status. Write or call for *How to Get It: A Guide to Defense-related Information Sources* and a free brochure describing the Center, its services, and user eligibility.

* Aeronautics Research: Air Force
U.S. Department of the Air Force
Arnold Engineering Development Center
Air Force Systems Command
Arnold Air Force Base, TN 37389 (615) 454-5586
This center has test laboratories in which atmospheric conditions, orbital, space flight, and ballistic conditions can be simulated. A brochure on the base, its programs, and mission, along with fact sheets on technical subjects, including wind tunnels, aeropropulsion systems, and rocket test facilities can be obtained by writing or calling the above office.

* Aircraft Armament Research
U.S. Air Force Systems Command
Eglin Air Force Base, FL 32542 (904) 882-3931
This Command conducts research, development, testing, and evaluation of guns and other aircraft weapons, explosives, chemical-biological weapons, and missile systems. Other units based at or associated with Eglin include the Air Force Tactical Air Warfare Center, 33rd Tactical Fighter Wing, 919th Special Operations Group, 20th Surveillance Squadron, the 6th Ranger Training

Be patient. If any phone number is incorrect, call (area code) 555-1212 and request the new listing.

International Relations and Defense

Battalion, and the Naval School, Explosive Ordnance Disposal. The office will respond to requests for information on specific technical topics.

* Aircraft Test Flights

Air Force Flight Test Center
Public Affairs Office
Edwards Air Force Base, CA 93523-5000 (805) 277-3510

This office can supply you with fact sheets on all aircraft tested on its facilities, the history of the Test Center, significant historical events, biographies of famous people associated with the base, and tour information.

* Air Force Aeronautical Systems

U.S. Department of the Air Force
Aeronautical Systems Division
Public Affairs Office
Wright-Patterson Air Force Base, OH 45433-6503 (513) 255-2725

The Public Affairs Office's brochure, *What's Happening at ASD*, lists the major programs in all the Aeronautical Systems Division offices, the contractors involved, and the program status. Also available is a brochure describing the five laboratories which make up the Wright Research and Development Center: aeropropulsion and power, flight dynamics, materials, avionics, and electronic technology.

* Air Force Armament Museum

Eglin Air Force Base, FL 32542 (904) 882-3931

The Armament museum at Eglin AFB is the only facility in the U.S. dedicated to the display of Air Force armament. The main attractions are the 18 aircraft on display including an SR-71 Blackbird, a B-17 Flying Fortress, and an F-4 Phantom. The indoor museum features many World War II and Korean War aircraft including a P-51 Mustang and a F-80 Shooting Star. The museum is open seven days a week, 9:30-4:30.

* Air Force Aviation History

U.S. Department of the Air Force
1352 AVSDOLD - Media Center
Air Force Central Visual Information Library
Norton Air Force Base, CA 92409-5996 (714) 382-2493

This library will loan copies from their collection, which includes visual productions of documentaries, training materials, the history of aviation, and W.W.II and Korean War produced by the Air Force. Written requests for information are preferred.

* Air Force Casualty Reporting

U.S. Department of the Air Force
Casualty Matters
Headquarters, AFMPA/DPMC
Randolph Air Force Base, TX 78150-6001 (512) 652-2710

To obtain information on Air Force personnel who are injured, deceased, missing in action, or taken prisoner, call the above number 24 hours a day, 7 days a week.

* Air Force Directives, R & D, Goals

U.S. Department of the Air Force
Air Force Information for Industry Office
5001 Eisenhower Ave.
Alexandria, VA 22333 (202) 247-5838

The Air Force Information for Industry Office offers information, assistance, and resources to aid potential contractors in doing business with the Air Force. You may write or call their office. The following are among the free publications available: *Air Force Logistics Needs, Mission Element Need Statements (MENS), Program Element Descriptive Summaries, Program Management Directive, R & D Planning Summaries, Technical Objective Documents, Technology Needs Documents,* and *Selling to the United States Air Force.*

* Air Force Historical Records

Air Force Historical Research Agency
HQUSAFHRC/HD
Maxwell Air Force BASE, AL 36112-6678 (205) 953-5342

This is the principal repository for Air Force historical records. It holds the most extensive collection of documentary source material on the history of U.S. military action, and has its own historical studies and oral histories collection. The Center is open to researchers, scholars, as well as the general public. The library operates on a non-circulating, research basis, ie. reference librarians take written requests for information and pull information for patrons. Inter-library loan is available for items it has duplicates of within its collection. Microfilm copies of records are available for $20 per roli; each roll contains 2000 frames. Hours of operation are Monday-Saturday, 8am-4:45pm.

* Air Force Historical Research Library

Secretary of the U.S. Air Force
Public Resource Library
The Pentagon, Room 5C945
Washington, DC 20330-1000 (703) 697-4100

The Resource Library is able to answer a broad range of Air Force related questions and has printed material available such as biographies of prominent Air Force generals, fact sheets on Air Force related topics (such as aircraft, weapons systems, missions), and "Speech Inserts" from key speeches by Air Force leadership. Contact this office for a catalogue of fact sheets.

* Air Force Housekeeping Programs

U.S. Air Force Engineering Agency
Morale, Welfare and Recreation
Public Affairs Office
Tyndall Air Force Base, FL 32403-6001 (904) 283-6476

This Center conducts research and forms Air Force policy for the managing of food services, laundry services, and billeting on Air Force bases worldwide. They can provide fact sheets on their programs and engineering activities.

* Air Force Information Fact Sheets

Secretary of the Air Force
Office of Public Affairs
Washington, DC 20330-1000 (703) 697-3329

The Air Force has fact sheets available on virtually all of its systems, bases, commands, services, and programs. Call or write for the master list. Fact sheets are available electronically via modem by dialing commercial (512) 925-8608 and downloading from the AFNEWS T-COMM Bulletin Board.

* Air Force Military History

Office of Air Force History
Building 5681, Room 200
Bolling AFB, Washington, DC 20332-6098 (202) 767-0412

This office has a small library and archives on Air Force military history going back to the Civil War era, and is available to researchers and scholars. It has holdings on microfilm of the Air Force Historical Research Center in Alabama. Research is by appointment. Copies cost 7 cents, but the first 20 are free. It offers a brochure on Air Force research programs with opportunities for research fellowships. Also ask for a publications list, which contains titles on the air-force role in World Wars I and II, as well as Korea and Vietnam. The list contains prices and ordering information.

* Air Force Patents

The Judge Advocate General
Patents Division, AF/JACP
1900 Half St., SW
Washington, DC 20324-1000 (202) 475-1386

This office grants licenses for commercial use of government-owned patents. For information on the patents available, contact the above office.

* Air Force Procurement

U.S. Air Force
Air Force Information for Industry Office (AFIFIO)
5001 Eisenhower Ave.
Alexandria, VA 22333 (202) 274-9305

This office maintains a research and development, technical reading room open to DOD contractors, and will provide research and development planning and requirement documents to qualified users. A security clearance and, in the case of private firms, a government contract, is necessary to enter the reading room as most material is classified. The office can also give information on the Air

Be patient. If any phone number is incorrect, call (area code) 555-1212 and request the new listing.

Military and National Security

Force Potential Contractors Program, which was instituted to facilitate technology transfer between the military and industry. Write or call for the free brochure explaining eligibility requirements and how to access the reading room, as well as how to enroll in the Potential Contractors Program and gain access to the Defense Technology Information Center.

* Air Force Research Grants

Office of Scientific Research
U.S. Air Force
Bolling Air Force Base
Washington, DC 20332 (202) 767-4910

This office accepts proposals for scientific research and requests for grants. Current research interests lie in the areas of Aerospace Sciences, Chemical and Materials Sciences, Physics and Electronics, Life and Environmental Sciences, and Mathematical and Computer Sciences. Write or call for copies of the *Research Interest* pamphlet, *Proposer's Guide*, *Grant Brochure* (which lists types of grants available), and technical brochures on Air Force research programs.

* Air Force Space and Missile Museum

U.S. Air Force
P.O Box 893
Cape Canaveral, FL 32920-0893 (407) 853-3245

The Museum documents America's race to the Space Age. Exhibits include *Thor*, *Minuteman 1*, *Polaris A-3*, and many other missiles presently or formerly in America's active arsenal. Within the Museum, the Center for Aerospace Technology contains documents and records which will enable scholars to analyze ballistic missile warfare ideas and technology. Call or write for more information.

* Air Force Special Missions

Headquarters, U.S. Air Force Reserve
Public Affairs Office
Robins Air Force Base, GA 31098 (404) 926-1113

Write for photographic reproductions of Air Force aircraft, including the one and only C130 spray mission airplane used for drug enforcement and control. The office also has fact sheets available containing little known but interesting data on other special missions of the Air Force Reserve, including the Central American support flights.

* Aircraft Carriers

U.S. Department of the Navy
OP-553
Washington, DC 20350-2000 (703) 697-9360

The aircraft carrier is the centerpiece of the American Navy, capable of deploying airpower anywhere in the world. Carrier aircraft played an important role in the air war against Iraq in January-February 1991. For vital statistics on the carrier fleet, contact the above office.

* Airport Security: Hijacking, Bomb Threats

Civil Aviation Security Service (ACS 400)
Federal Aviation Administration (FAA)
U.S. Department of Transportation
800 Independence Ave., SW, Room 319
Washington, DC 20591 (202) 267-9075

The FAA ensures the presence of law enforcement in U.S. airports, and approves the security programs of all airports under FAR 107. It also certifies walk-through detection devices. The office is a source of information and expertise on the following airport security issues: domestic and foreign aircraft hijacking; bomb threats at airports and on airplanes; compliance and enforcement of regulations; prevention of attempts; explosives and explosive devices found at airports and on airplanes; international crimes involving civil aviation; information on numbers of people screened, numbers of weapons found, and weapon detection devices.

* Air Warfare and Missile Systems Research

U.S. Navy
Crane Division
Naval Surface Warfare Center
Public Affairs Office
Crane, IN 47522 (812) 854-1394

This Center conducts research and development, testing, and evaluation on air warfare and missile systems. Write or call for their free brochure containing vital statistics on the Center, its mission, and personnel, and which lists major contractors in the local area. Copies of technical reports may be ordered from the Center, a list of reports is also available.

* American Military History 15th Century On

Army Military History Institute
Carlisle Barracks, PA 17013-5008 (717) 245-3611

The Institute collects original source material on American military history dating as far back as the 15th Century, and holds over one million catalogued items. The Institute provides research and reference assistance to researchers on site and by written and telephone request. The library does lend its materials through inter-library loan programs. No appointment is necessary for research. Photocopies are limited to 100 per year, with a cost of $3.50 for the first 6 copies (including service fee) and 10 cents per page thereafter. The library is open weekdays 8am to 4:30pm.

* Ammunition, Combat, Weapons Testing

U.S. Army
Public Affairs Office (AMSTE-PA)
Aberdeen Proving Ground, MD 21005 (301) 278-3840

This facility conducts research, development, and testing of weapons, systems, ammunition, and combat and support vehicles. Their pamphlet entitled *This is TECOM* explains the Command, its mission, organization, structure, history, and methods of testing. The booklet *Facts and Figures* provides statistics on property values, energy consumption, number of employees, and population figures. Both are free upon request.

* Army Active Personnel Locator

U.S. Department of the Army
Worldwide Locator, EREC
Ft. Benjamin Harrison, IN 46249-5301 (317) 542-4211

To locate a missing relative in the active army, contact the above office. There is a small fee for the search.

* Army Aircraft Worldwide

U.S. Department of the Army
Aviation Systems Command
Federal Center, 4300 Goodfellow Blvd.
St. Louis, MO 63120-1798 (314) 263-1164

This Command maintains all Army aircraft. It publishes a booklet entitled *AVSCOM - Worldwide*, containing facts and figures on troops, world locations, resources, and assets of the Command. To obtain a free copy, write or call the above office.

* Army and Air Force Base Exchanges Procurement

Army and Air Force Exchange Service
P.O. Box 222305
Dallas, TX 75222 (214) 312-2011

This office handles procurement of resale merchandise for Army and Air Force base exchanges in the continental United States. Write or call for free fact sheets on the Service and a *Vendor's Fact Book* explaining how to sell to the exchanges.

* Army and Navy Historic Photographs

Still Picture Branch
7th and Pennsylvania Ave., NW
National Archives and Records Administration
Washington, DC 20408 (202) 501-5455

This office holds photographs from all Federal agencies, including the historical Matthew Brady Civil War collection, and Army and Navy photographs from World War II. Copies may be obtained at cost.

* Army Budget and Forces

Community Relations Division
U.S. Army Public Affairs
The Pentagon, Room 2E631
Washington, DC 20310 (703) 695-5732

Be patient. If any phone number is incorrect, call (area code) 555-1212 and request the new listing.

International Relations and Defense

The Posture of the Army and the *Department of the Army Budget Estimates* is published each fiscal year and contains information on the status and direction of Army forces and the budget overview. The Fiscal Year 92/93 Posture Statement contains information on the Army's restructuring for the post Cold-War international security environment. Write or call to obtain a copy of the statement.

* Army Computer Procurement

Public Affairs Office
U.S. Army Information Systems Selection
and Acquisition Agency
2461 Eisenhower Ave.
Alexandria, VA 22331 (703) 325-9762

This office is responsible for the procurement of all Army computer systems. Write for its fact sheet which describes the agency's mission, philosophy, and procurement process.

* Army Corps of Engineers Historical References

U.S. Army Corps of Engineers
Attn: Office of History
Humphreys Engineering Center
Ft. Belvoir, VA 22060-5577 (703) 355-3554

This office will respond to reference inquiries regarding the history of the Army Corps of Engineers. Permission is granted to serious researchers for the use of its archival library, which maintains historical documents dating from the beginning of the Corps. Historical studies analyze the role of the Corps in, among other things, the construction of Washington DC, Yellowstone park, the St. Lawrence Seaway, and the Mississippi River Basin. Recent information is available on the Corps' involvement in the 1989 Alaskan oil spill, the California earthquake, and Hurricane Hugo. The office publishes numerous books and reports and a free list of publications is available on request. The Center extends an open invitation for visitors to drop in.

* Army Discharged Personnel Locator Service

National Personnel Records Center
9700 Page Blvd.
St. Louis, MO 63132-5200 (314) 538-4261

To locate a relative or friend who is has been discharged from the Army, or who is deceased, contact the above office. The locator service's records go back to 1912; you may be able to find out what your great-great grandfather did in the Army. The above number leads to a recording with detailed information. All requests must be in writing. There is a small fee for the search.

* Army Engineers' Environmental Publications

U.S. Army Corps of Engineers
Public Affairs
20 Massachusetts Ave., NW
Washington, DC 20314 (202) 272-0011

The Corps offers free brochures on a wide variety of subjects, including archaeology, camping, environment, erosion control, flood control, flood plain management, history, safety, waste-water treatment and water supply. For a publications list, call or write the above office or call the publications office directly at (301) 436-2065.

* Army Exploration Maps

Cartographic and Architectural Branch
National Archives and Records Administration
Washington, DC 20408 (703) 756-6700

This office provides reference service on maps and architectural drawings in its holdings, which include survey maps, early Army exploration maps of the Old West dating from 1860. This office has over 2 million maps and drawings. Call or write for assistance and specify area and time period you are interested in. For in person visits, the center is located at 841 S. Pickett St., Alexandria, Va. The Center is open daily from 8am to 4 pm. Do not send written requests to this address; use the above National Archives address.

* Army Historical Publications

U.S. Army Center for Military History
Federal Center SE./Navy Yard, Bldg 159
Washington, DC 20374-5088 (202) 475-2587

The Army Center for Military History publishes books, monographs and series on Army military related history. A small sampling of the selections include *The Military and the Media, The Final Years,* a series on the Korean War, the Vietnam era, and a series on World War II. Write or call to order their 50-page brochure listing over 200 publications. The center is open 7:30 am to 4 pm weekdays. Appointments are requested. Researchers may peruse the stacks themselves. Microfilm copies of documents are not for sale.

* Army Historical Research

U.S. Army Center of Military History
Historical Resources Branch
Federal Center SE./ Navy Yard, Bldg. 159
Washington, DC 20374-5088 (202) 475-2580

The Army Center of Military History maintains a library and archives which may be used by serious researchers. For information about use of the library and its holdings, write or call the above office.

* Army Information Technology Laboratory

U.S. Army Corps of Engineers
Waterways Experiment Station
Public Affairs Office
3909 Halls Ferry Road
Vicksburg, MS 39180-6199 (601) 634-2504

ITL operates one of the Army's largest computers and is also responsible for developing, managing and coordinating research and development projects in computer-aided interdisciplinary engineering areas; computer science; automation; visual information; etc. For more information, contact the Laboratory.

* Army Medical Library

Stimson Library
U.S. Department of the Army
Academy of Health Science
Building 2840, Room 106
Ft. Sam Houston, TX 78234-6100 (512) 221-6900

This library will provide inter-library loans, answer information requests, or give referrals to serious researchers. The collection is particularly good on physical therapy, health care administration, and materials on Army medical history.

* Army Medical Research

U.S. Department of the Army
Army Medical Research and Development Command
Attn: SGRD-PA
Fort Detrick
Frederick, MD 21702 (301) 663-2732

This Command conducts research and development in medical sciences, supplies, and equipment. Write or call for free copies of the brochure describing the Command, a quarterly newsletter, and the *Broad Agency Announcement* describing the research areas for which they solicit and instructions for submitting proposals.

* Army Patents

Intellectual Property Law Division
Patents, Copyrights and Trademarks Division
U.S. Army Legal Services Agency
5611 Columbia Pike, Room 332A
Falls Church, VA 22041-5013 (703) 756-2617

This office grants licenses for commercial use of government-owned patents. For information on the patents available and the cooperative research and development agreements with Army regional laboratories, contact the above office.

* Army Personnel Locator

U.S. Army Worldwide Locator
ELREC
Fort Benjamin Harrison, IN 46249 (317) 542-4211

To locate a long lost relative who is still on active duty in the Army, contact this office by letter. There is a small fee for their services ($3.50 in early 1992). The telephone recording will give you information on the procedure and the data they need from you to initiate their search.

Be patient. If any phone number is incorrect, call (area code) 555-1212 and request the new listing.

Military and National Security

* Army Procurement

U.S. Army
Technical Industrial Liaison Office (TILO)
5001 Eisenhower Ave.
Alexandria, VA 22333
(202) 274-8948

This office maintains a research and development, technical reading room open to DOD contractors, and will provide research and development planning and requirement documents to qualified users. Security clearance is required to enter the reading room. The office can also give information on the Army Potential Contractors Program, which was instituted to facilitate technology transfer between the military and industry. Write or call for the free brochure explaining eligibility requirements and how to access the reading room, as well as how to enroll in the Potential Contractors Program and gain access to the Defense Technology Information Center.

* Army Recruitment Audiovisuals

Army Recruiting Support Command
Cameron Station, Building 6
Alexandria, VA 22304
(703) 274-6670

Civic groups may request the Army's recruiting films for community fairs and youth events. The Army has a traveling slide projection show with short subject presentations on American history, the Federal government, development of the English language, Army basic training, and the Army nursing program. If interested in this service, contact your local Army recruiter for information and to request the Audiovisuals.

* Army Research Grants

U.S. Army Research Office
P.O. Box 12211
Research Triangle Park, NC 27709-2211
(919) 549-0641

This office considers requests for support of basic scientific research from educational institutions and nonprofit organizations. Army special research areas include the following: Young Investigator Program, Short Term Innovative Research Program, and the Research Instrumentation Program. The Army also has a strong interest in research conducted at Historically Black Colleges or Minority Institutions. Write or call for a free pamphlet entitled *Broad Agency Announcement*, which describes the type of research being solicited by the Army, how to fashion a proposal and how to apply for a grant.

* Army Research Labs, Speakers on Technology

U.S. Department of the Army
Army Research Laboratory
AMSLC-PA
2800 Powder Mill Rd.
Adelphi, MD 20783-1145
(301) 394-3590

This Command oversees the work of the seven major U.S. Army research laboratories. Laboratory work is done in the areas of advanced computing and electronics; battlefield environmental effects; materials and structures; power sources; signal processing; and survivability enhancement. A brochure on the laboratories' missions and programs is available, and the Command can provide public speakers for civic groups in the field of technology development. Write or call for information.

* Army Reserve and Retiree Locator

Army Reserve Personnel Center
U.S. Department of the Army
9700 Page Blvd.
St. Louis, MO 63132-5200
(314) 263-3901

To locate a missing relative in the Army reserve (who is not assigned to a unit), or to locate a living Army retiree, contact this office. Requests for information must be made in writing.

* Army Speakers Bureau

Community Relations Division
U.S. Army Public Affairs
The Pentagon, Room 2E631
Washington, DC 20310
(703) 697-2707

The Army supplies speakers on a wide range of subjects to civic groups across the country, including chaplains, doctors, and nutritionists. They have experts in their Wildlife and Environment Conservation Program and Drug and Alcohol Abuse Program who will speak to you about how to start and run your own community programs. Contact your nearest Army installation, or the above office, for a referral.

* Army Technology Transfer and Commercialization

U.S. Department of the Army
Army Research Office
P.O. Box 12211
Triangle Park, NC 27709-2211
(919) 549-0641

The Army Research Office sponsors programs to further technology development and technology transfer in the United States. Its Technology Transfer Program allows private industry to enter into patent agreements with the Army, making possible the commercialization of Army technological findings. Write or call for free brochures and information describing these programs.

* Army Weapons Systems and Prime Contractors

U.S. Government Printing Office
Superintendent of Documents
Washington, DC 20402-6518
(202) 783-3238

The U.S. Department of the Army publishes the *Army Weapons Systems Handbook*, which contains photographs and descriptions of the major weapons systems in the Army, their program status, and a list of the prime contractors involved. It also gives information on Soviet counterparts. A copy can be ordered through the Government Printing Office for a moderate charge.

* Astronomy: Naval Observatory

Naval Observatory
34th and Massachusetts Ave.
Washington, DC 20392-5100
(202) 653-1541

Monday night tours are conducted at the Observatory; call for reservations. A tour brochure and fact sheets on topics such as telescopes, planetariums, and astronomy may be obtained by writing or calling the above office. (Note: The Observatory does not have a planetarium.)

* Atlantic Fleet

U.S. Department of the Navy
Pubic Affairs Office
Commander in Chief
U.S. Atlantic Fleet
Code NO2P
Norfolk, VA 23511-5100
(804) 444-6294

The Atlantic Fleet provides the forces for the United States Second Fleet in the Atlantic, the Sixth Fleet in the Mediterranean and the Middle East Force in the Persian Gulf-Indian Ocean area.

* Atomic Era Veterans Hotline

Defense Nuclear Agency
Public Affairs Office
6801 Telegraph Rd.
Alexandria, VA 22310-3398
(800) 462-3683

This toll free number is for "atomic" era veterans and their families to call for information on whether he or she was exposed to dangerous radiation in the course of their military duty. Call or write for more information.

* Atmospheric Nuclear Test Era

Defense Nuclear Agency
Public Affairs Office
6801 Telegraph Rd.
Alexandria, VA 22310-3398
(703) 325-7095

The Agency maintains a public reading room holding information and historical documents pertaining to the atmospheric nuclear testing era. Appointments are required. This specific reading room is administered by the Nuclear Test Personnel Review Program of the U.S. Department of Defense.

* Aviation History

Information Management Division
National Air and Space Museum, Room 3100
Smithsonian Institute
Washington, DC 20560
(202) 357-3133

Be patient. If any phone number is incorrect, call (area code) 555-1212 and request the new listing.

International Relations and Defense

The Museum archives have photographs, manuscripts, and personal papers related to major figures in aviation history from the turn of the century to the present. Holdings include NASA "moon shots," and the official collection of Air Force photographs dating back from 1955 to the earliest days of aviation, including both World Wars and the Korean War. Write for their information brochure.

* Aviation Services

U.S. Army Aviation Systems Command
4300 Goodfellow Blvd.
Attn: AMSAV-Z
St. Louis, MO 63120-1798 (314) 263-1164

This Command is responsible for depot activities and services, serving all four branches of the military. The Command has a Speakers Bureau which responds to requests from civic organizations, of any age group, to speak on scientific and technological topics, as well as the varied personal hobbies of its members. Write or call for free brochures describing the Command's mission, programs, and functions.

* Ballistic Missiles Procurement

U.S. Department of the Army
Strategic Defense Command
Public Affairs Office
P.O. Box 1500
Huntsville, AL 35807-3801 (205) 955-3887

This Command conducts advanced research and development in the fields of radar, interceptors, optics, and other technical aspects of ballistic missile defense. It publishes fact sheets on the various research programs of the Command, and booklets entitled *Doing Business with the U.S. Army Strategic Defense Command* and *U.S. Army--First in Space and Strategic Defense.*

* Ballistic Research and Engineering

Ballistic Research Laboratories
314 Ryan Building
Aberdeen Proving Ground, MD 21005-5066 (301) 278-6954

This is an advanced technology laboratory conducting basic and applied research in mathematics, physics, chemistry, biophysics, and engineering related to defense ballistics. Write or call for more information.

* Ballistic Missile Submarines

U.S. Department of the Navy
OP-02P
Washington, DC 20350 (703) 697-8704

Ballistic missile submarines form the backbone of the United States nuclear deterrent. The Navy currently has some 35 strategic submarines in its force, armed with Trident I and II missiles. For information on submarine classes and armament, contact the above office.

* Base Closures and Economic Impact

Office of Economic Adjustment
U.S. Department of Defense
400 Army Navy Drive, Suite 200
Arlington, VA 22202-1155 (703) 695-1800

With cutbacks in defense, the President and Congress established the Defense Base Closure and Realignment Commission to gather recommendations for streamlining the domestic military base structure. The Office of Economic Adjustment assists local communities, areas or states affected by U.S. Department of Defense actions, such as base closures, establishment of new installations, and cutbacks or expansion of activities. It publishes a number of free publications on these issues, including *Communities in Transition, Planning Civilian Reuse of Former Military Bases, Civilian Reuse of Former Military Bases.* The office also puts out additional information for Communities concerned about base closings. Write or call for more information.

* Bases Overseas

Foreign Military Rights Affairs
International Security Affairs
U.S. Department of Defense
The Pentagon, Room 4D830
Washington, DC 20301 (703) 695-6386

This office can supply you with information on the status of negotiations for U.S. bases in foreign countries. As much of this information is classified, you may also want to call the public affairs offices at the State and Defense departments.

* Biological Defense Research

U.S. Department of the Army
Dugway Proving Ground
Public Affairs Office STEDP-PA
Dugway, UT 84022-5000 (801) 831-2116

This facility conducts biological defense research and field and lab tests to evaluate chemical and radiological weapons and defense systems. This center also conducts Smoke Program training exercises in operating under conditions of battlefield obscurement. Dugway is aligned under the Army's Test and Evaluation Command at Aberdeen Proving Ground, MD. Its technical library can be made accessible to approved researchers; requests for technical reports are handled on a case by case basis. Write or call for a brochure describing the installation.

* Biological Research in Medical Defense

U.S. Army Medical Research Institute
for Infectious Diseases
Public Affairs Office
Fort Detrick, MD 21701 (301) 663-2285

This Institute conducts research on biological agents of military significance and development of vaccines, anti-toxins, toxoids and drugs for medical defense. Write or call for a free brochure on the Institute; copies of technical reports are also available.

* Burial of Veterans

Superintendent
Arlington National Cemetery
Arlington, VA 22211 (703) 695-3250

Many veterans are eligible to be buried or inurned at Arlington. As burial space is limited mainly to holders of the nations highest military decorations or 20 year or more veterans. Arlington constructed a Columbarium which opened in 1980. Any honorably discharged veteran and their spouse and dependent children can be inurned there. Write or call this office for information on eligibility requirements and procedures.

* Casualty Reporting: Army

Casualty Services Division
U.S. Department of the Army
Hoffman Building, Room 920
Alexandria, VA 22331 (703) 325-7990

The Casualty Services Division is responsible for the Army's casualty reporting and notification system worldwide, and provides a survivor and next-of-kin assistance program. The office is available for calls 24 hours a day, seven days a week. Army policy is that next of kin can be notified on injuries over the phone. Next of kin are notified of deaths in person. A free brochure is available explaining their procedures.

* Central Command

Public Affairs Office
McDill AFB, FL 33608 (813) 830-6393

The Central Command's responsibilities include, countries in Europe, Asia, and Africa. Included within its Area of Responsibility (AOR) is the volatile Persian Gulf region, which contains over 70% of the world's oil reserves. Senior command at CENTCOM rotates between an Army and Marine senior officer. American and allied forces during the Gulf War came under the CENTCOM command and its senior commander, U.S. Army General Schwarzkopf. This office is a good place to start searching for information on the Gulf War. Requests for Gulf War information should be made in writing.

* Ceramics and Metals Research

U.S. Department of the Army
Army Materials Technology Lab
Watertown, MA 02172-0001 (617) 923-5278

This Center specializes in research regarding metals and ceramics. Major programs currently include: the battle against *Corrosion; Advanced Armor; Structural Ceramics; Elastomers;* and *Composite Materials Hull.* The Lab's work

Be patient. If any phone number is incorrect, call (area code) 555-1212 and request the new listing.

Military and National Security

has done much to improve the armors of American mechanized forces. It maintains a library open to approved researchers, and copies of technical reports are available upon request. Write or call for free brochures describing the Center, its mission, and programs.

* Chemical and Biological Weapons

U.S. Department of the Army
Public Affairs Office STEDP-PA
Dugway Proving Ground, UT 84022-5000 (801) 831-2116

This facility conducts biological defense research, and field and lab tests to evaluate chemical and radiological weapons and defense systems. A post guide, economic impact statement, and fact sheets on the history of the post, and its mission are available. Write or call for free copies.

* Chemical Defense, Bald Eagles and Peregrine Falcons

U.S. Department of the Army
Chemical Research Development
and Engineering Center
Aberdeen Proving Ground, MD 21010-5423 (301) 671-4345

While the Center's primary mission is concerned with research on chemical defensive material, the Center has become very involved in wildlife conservation programs because of its location on the Chesapeake Bay. The Center is especially experienced in a Bald Eagle program and a Peregrine Falcon program. Fact sheets on these and other wildlife issues may be obtained by writing or calling the above office.

* Chemical Defense Technologies

U.S. Army Medical Research Institute of Chemical Defense
Attn: SGRD-UV-R
Aberdeen Proving Ground, MD 21010-5425 (301) 671-3653

This Institute conducts research, development, testing, and evaluation of medical/chemical defense technologies. Write or call for a free brochure describing the work of the Institute and a list of technical reports.

* Chemical Propulsion Resource Center

The Johns Hopkins University
Applied Physics Laboratory
Chemical Propulsion Information Agency (CPIA)
10630 Little Patuxent Parkway
Columbia, MD 21044-3200 (410) 992-7307

CPIA provides products, specialized reference service, database searches, and copies of technical reports on all areas of chemical propulsion. Publications include *The Chemical Propulsion Abstracts, The CPIA/M1 Rocket Motor Manual, the CPIA/M2 Solid Propellant Manual, the CPIA/M6 Airbreathing Propulsion Manual, The JANNAF Propulsion Meeting*, and *Selected Papers*. CPIA also puts out a monthly bulletin updating subscribers on its activities. Write or call for a free pamphlet explaining their services and how to become a subscriber. Note, however, that this service is primarily for DOD contractors.

* Civil Air Patrol (CAP)

HQ Civil Air Patrol
U.S. Department of the Air Force
Office of Public Affairs
Maxwell AFB, AL 3611-5572 (205) 953-5463

The Civil Air Patrol has three main missions: 1) emergency services; 2) aerospace education; and 3) a cadet program for high school students. CAP has offices in all 50 states and in the District of Columbia. CAP flies most of the search and rescue hours requested by the Air Force. Write or call for a leaflet explaining the programs, the benefits of membership, and a list of CAP posts in your area.

* Civil Engineering and Construction Research

Naval Civil Engineering Laboratory
Naval Construction Battalion Center
U.S. Department of the Navy
Port Hueneme, CA 93043 (805) 982-4493

This Center is the principal research, development, test, and evaluation center for shore and sea-floor facilities and for support of Navy and Marine Corps construction forces. The Public Affairs Office of the Center has a brochure on the Laboratory's mission, programs, and personnel entitled *Tech Activities*. There

are also two procurement offices located at the Center. Write or call the above office for further information.

* Civil War Photographs

Still Picture Branch
7th and Pennsylvania Ave. NW
National Archives and Records Administration
Washington, DC 20408 (202) 501-5455

The American Civil War was the first large scale conflict in history to be captured on film. The Still Picture Branch has the famous Brady collection of photos. The Collection includes photos of Army life, Generals in the field, Navies, battlefields, and famous figures from both the Blue and the Gray. Call or write for a list of the photos available.

* Coast Guard Reserve

Office of Readiness and Reserve
U.S. Coast Guard
U.S. Department of Transportation
2100 2nd St., SW, Room 5101
Washington, DC 20593-0001 (202) 267-2350

In time of war or national emergency, the Coast Guard Reserve provides trained individuals and units for active duty. The Reserve also assists the Guard in peacetime missions during domestic emergencies and peak operations. The *Coast Guard Reservist Magazine*, available free from the office listed above, provides bimonthly news and human interest stories about Coast Guard Reservists and their activities.

* Coastal Engineering Research Center (CERC)

U.S. Army Corp of Engineers
Waterways Experiment Station
Public Affairs Office
3909 Halls Ferry Road
Vicksburg, MS 39180-6199 (601) 634-2504

CERC is the nations foremost research and development for coastal engineering. Research focuses on problems relating to shore and beach erosion control; flooding and storm protection; coastal dredging; and design, construction, and maintenance of coastal navigation. Contact WES for more information.

* Cold Environments Research

U.S. Army Corps of Engineers
Army Cold Regions Research and Engineering Laboratory
72 Lyme Rd.
Hanover, NH 03755-1290 (603) 646-4100

This Laboratory conducts research on living, working, traveling, building and military operations in cold environments. A Speakers Bureau will provide experts to speak before civic groups. The Laboratory also has an extensive library on cold regions research. The Library of Congress prepares the *Bibliography on Cold Regions Science and Technology*. Write or call for brochures explaining the mission and programs, accessing information from the library, and how to do business with the Laboratory.

* Communications and Electronic Government Contracts

U.S. Army Communications-Electronics Command
Ft. Monmouth, NJ 07703 (908) 532-1258

This Command is concerned with research, development and acquisition of communications tactical data, command and control systems, and the components and materials of electronic communications. Its Technical/Industrial Liaison and Special Projects Office will supply information and literature on Advance Planning Briefings for Industry and how to do business with CECOM.

* Conscientious Objectors and Reclassification

U.S. Department of Defense
Force Management and Personnel
The Pentagon, Room 3E764
Washington, DC 20301-4000 (703) 695-7402

For information on conscientious objectors and POW's, including reclassification and discharge data, contact the above office.

Be patient. If any phone number is incorrect, call (area code) 555-1212 and request the new listing.

International Relations and Defense

* Contracting with the Defense Logistic Agency

Public Affairs (DLA-B)
Defense Logistics Agency
Cameron Station
Alexandria, VA 22304-6100 (703) 274-6135

This office has information on all Defense Logistics Agency business and activities, and a pamphlet on it mission, *The ABC's of DLA*. It also offers a *DLA Index to Publications*, a *DLA Index to Forms*, and the brochure, *An Identification of Commodities Purchased by the Defense Logistics Agency*.

* Contracting Research and Development with the Defense Department

Defense Technical Information Center (DTIC)
DTIC, Attn: FDRB
Cameron Station
Alexandria, VA 22304-6145 (703) 274-7633

DTIC is the clearinghouse for the U.S. Department of Defense's collection of scientific and technological research and development information. The booklet entitled *Registration and Certification for Scientific and Technical Services* will explain who is eligible to use the Center's services and how to register as a user. The manual also contains a list of contractors, their offices and phone numbers, and information on the potential contractor program. The *Handbook for Users* and the *Green and White* brochure (DTIC-BC-1) explain the two major databases available to contractors and potential contractors: one for completed research and technological reports and one for ongoing research and development information.

* Construction Productivity Partnership

U.S. Army Corps of Engineers
Public Affairs Office
20 Massachusetts Ave., NW
Washington, DC 20314-1000 (202) 272-0010

The Army Corps of Engineers sponsors the Construction Productivity Advancement Research Program (CPAR), in which the Corps joins in partnership with city government, public utilities, or private industry to fund research which will benefit the U.S. construction industry as a whole. Write or call for their booklet describing the program and participation guidelines.

* Contractors and Government Procurement

Defense Logistics Agency
Defense Contract Administration Service (DCAS)
Cameron Station
Alexandria, VA 22304-6100 (703) 274-6135

The nine regional offices of this Service provide post-award contract administration. Booklets are available which explain the services of the agency and the procedure for obtaining a government contract, and the staff will answer questions on current contractors and contracts. Contact your regional office or the above office to locate the office nearest you.

* Correcting Errors in Air Force Records

Air Force Board for the
Correction of Military Records
U.S. Department of the Air Force
The Pentagon, Room AFBCMR
Washington, DC 20330-1430 (703) 692-4726

This Board handles appeals for correction of Air Force military records containing errors or unjust information. Write or call for the appropriate application forms.

* Correcting Errors in Army Records

Army Board for Correction of
Military Records
U.S. Department of the Army
1914 Jefferson Davis Hwy.
CM4, 2nd Floor, Room 220
Arlington, VA 22202-4508 (703) 607-1601

This Board handles appeals for correction of Army military records containing errors or unjust information. Write or call for the appropriate application forms.

* Correcting Errors in Navy Records

Board for the Correction
of Naval Records
U.S. Department of the Navy
Arlington Navy Annex, Room 2432
Washington, DC 20370-5100 (703) 614-1765

This Board handles appeals for correction of Navy military records containing errors or unjust information. Write or call for the appropriate application forms.

* Cost Comparison of U.S. and former Soviet Defense Activities

Public Affairs
Central Intelligence Agency (CIA)
Washington, DC 20505 (703) 351-2053

The CIA declassifies many of its publications including *A Dollar Cost Comparison of Soviet and U.S. Defense Activities, 1968-1978* which is available from the Library of Congress Photoduplication Service, Washington, DC 20540 (202) 707-5650. More recent studies such as 1988 *USSR Defense Industries* (SOV88-10043) are sold through the National Technical Information Service, 5285 Port Royal Road, Springfield, VA 22161 (703) 487-4650; or the Government Printing Office, Washington, DC 20402 (202)783-3238. A publications catalog titled *CIA Maps and Publications Released to the Public* is available free.

* Critical and Strategic Mineral Commodities

Minerals Information Office
Bureau of Mines/U.S. Geological Survey
U.S. Department of the Interior
18th and C Sts., MS 2647-MIB
Room 2647
Washington, DC 20240 (202) 208-5512

The *Personal Computer Advanced Deposit Information Tracking System Mineral Deposit Data Base* contains information on 3,000 domestic and foreign (market economy countries) mining operations, including operation data (name, company, locations, etc.) and operation status (operation type, processing and milling methods, capacity, etc.). The database covers 34 critical and strategic commodities, representing those deposits most significant in terms of value and tonnage. This information is not printed, but visitors can look at it on the Minerals Information Office computer system or can request the information on disk from the Minerals Availability Branch.

* Defense Analysis

Center for Defense Information
1500 Massachusetts Ave NW
Washington, DC 20005 (202) 862-0700

The Defense Monitor, published about 10 times per year, provides analyses, statistics, facts, quotes and information about military programs and spotlights military issues of national importance. Issues are available for $1 each (half price for 10 or more) from the above address. Some titles included are as follows:

The Stealth Bomber
U.S. Invasion of Iraq: Appraising the Option
Space Warfare: A New Cold War Battleground
Nuclear Bomb Factories: The Danger Within
What Should We Defend?
Defending the Environment? The Record of the U.S. Military

* Defense Budget and Military Spending Reports

National Technical Information Service
5285 Port Royal Rd.
Springfield, VA 22161 (703) 487-4650

The Service has both paper copy and microfiche copy of U.S. Department of Defense budget reports, including *Program Acquisition Costs by Weapons System; Construction Programs; Research, Development, Test and Evaluation Program;* and *Procurement Programs*. For price and ordering information, write or call the above office. The office is open weekdays 8:30 to 5:30.

* Defense Contractor Fraud Hotline

The Pentagon (703) 693-5080
Washington, DC 20301-1900 (800) 424-9098

Call this number to report fraud or corruption by anyone working for a U.S.

Be patient. If any phone number is incorrect, call (area code) 555-1212 and request the new listing.

Military and National Security

Department of Defense contractor. The Hotline people are eager to supply your office with posters, brochures, and wallet size cards displaying their number.

* Defense Data Worldwide Network

Ada Information Clearinghouse
c/o IIT Research Institute
4600 Forbes Blvd.
Lanham, MD 20706 (703) 685-1477

This organization supplies comprehensive services and information to Ada database users worldwide. It offers a free quarterly newsletter, a calendar of events, a list of resources for reusing the Ada code, information on how to access the *Defense Data Network*, a list of Ada compilers, a list of Ada serial publications, a list of classes and seminars, a free monthly handout on new products and tools for Ada, a catalog of college courses, and two bulletin boards with comprehensive Ada information. Call or write for an information packet explaining their services and resources.

* Defense Department General Information

Directorate for Public Communication
U.S. Department of Defense
The Pentagon, Room 2E777
Washington, DC 20301-1400 (703) 697-5737

This office answers general questions concerning the work of the U.S. Department of Defense, including defense spending and defense policy. Upon request, the office can supply copies of major speeches delivered by officials in the Office of the Secretary of Defense, reports issued by the Office, and fact sheets on defense issues. Speeches are referenced by date delivered. Write or call for more information.

* Defense Department Manpower Statistics

Washington Headquarter Services
Directorate for Information Operations
and Reports
1215 Jefferson Davis Hwy., Suite 1204
Arlington, VA 22202-4302 (703) 746-0786

A free catalog is available which lists this office's publications covering DOD manpower statistics, including financial management data, logistic data, health care statistics, and prime contract award data. Write or call to order a copy.

* Defense Department Organization and Functions

Directorate for Organizational
and Management Planning
U.S. Department of Defense
The Pentagon, Room 3A326
Washington, DC 20301-1100 (703) 697-1142

This office publishes the *Defense Organizational and Functions Guidebook*, which outlines the functions of the major components of the U.S. Department of Defense. It contains a functional statement citing the pertinent charter and detailed information on the authority and responsibilities of each organization, including an organizational chart. To request a free copy, write or call the above office.

* Defense Department Publications List

Directorate for Public Communication
U.S. Department of Defense
The Pentagon, Room 2E777
Washington, DC 20301-1400 (703) 697-5737

The Directorate for Public Communication puts out a list of Defense Department publications available from DOD, NTIS, or GPO. Call or write for the list. Publications include:

Allied Contributions to the Common Defense
Armed Forces Insignia Poster
Defense Industrial Base: Report to Congress
Defense Issues (speech texts)
Joint Military Net Assessment
National Security Strategy
Security Assistance Programs: Congressional Presentation Document
Military Forces in Transition (formerly Soviet Military Power)
Strategic Defense Initiative Annual Report

* Defense Energy Consumption

Defense Energy Policy Directorate
Office of the Assistant Secretary of Defense
DEF/P&L/L(EP), The Pentagon, Room 1D760
Washington, DC 20301-3000 (703) 697-2500

This office can provide you with wholesale petroleum data and facility energy consumption data. Inquiries will be answered on a cost recovery basis and should be made in writing.

* Defense Maps and Charts Toll-free Number

Defense Mapping Agency
Combat Support Center
Attn: Customer Assistance Office (800) 826-0342
Washington, DC 20315-0010 (301) 227-2495

The Defense Mapping Agency makes available at cost a broad range of maps and charts. There are four categories available: aeronautical, topographic, hydrographic, and digital (lists those products available on magnetic tape). Each map costs $2.75 each.

* Defense Monthly Magazine

American Forces Information Service
1735 N. Lynn St.
Arlington, VA 22209 (703) 274-4847

The Information Service publishes *Defense 92*, a bi-monthly magazine devoted to defense issues and policy. You can order it through the Government Printing Office, Superintendent of Documents, Washington, DC 20402; (202) 783-3238.

* Defense Technical Information and Referral Center

Defense Technical Information Center (DTIC)
Cameron Station
Alexandria, VA 22304-6145 (703) 617-7931

DTIC maintains a *Referral Data Bank Directory* of major resource and holding centers in the U.S. Department of Defense. Write or call the above office for more information.

* Defense Videos

Center for Defense Information (CDI)
1500 Massachusetts Ave NW
Washington, DC 20005 (202) 862-0700

CDI's weekly TV show, "America's Defense Monitor", covers military and international affairs and is available on VHS for $25 per episode plus $2 shipping and handling. Transcripts are $5 each plus $2 postage and handling. Contact the above listing for more information. Some of the titles available are as follows:

The Spread of Nuclear Weapons
Testing Nuclear Arms
The Face of the "Enemy"
The Stealth Bomber

* Desert Shield/Desert Storm - Air Force Role

Office of the Secretary of the Air Force
Public Affairs Office
Washington, DC 20330-1000 (703) 695-9664

The Air Force published several items documenting its role in the Gulf War. The August 1991 commemorative issue of *Airman*, the Magazine of the Air Force, has personal stories from airmen who took part in the conflict, including interviews with men who were taken prisoner in Iraq. Also ask for the Air Force White Paper and Backgrounder on the Gulf War, both of which provide analysis of the air campaign against Iraq and the performance of the many aircraft and air delivered munitions used in the conflict. All of these publications are free but availability may be limited.

* Desert Shield/Desert Storm - Army Role

Association of the United States Army
Institute for Land Warfare (ILW)
2425 Wilson Blvd.
Arlington, VA 22201-3385 (703) 841-4300

The ILW publishes numerous fact sheets and special reports on all aspects of land warfare. Reports on the Persian Gulf War include:

Be patient. If any phone number is incorrect, call (area code) 555-1212 and request the new listing.

International Relations and Defense

AUSA Background Brief, No. 30, Summary of Authorities Available to the President in Emergencies Short of Declared War - January 1991

AUSA Background Brief , No. 34, Army equipment performance in Operation Desert Storm - April 1991

Landpower Essay Series, No. 91-1, The Impact of Desert Storm and the Growing Soviet Military Dissatisfaction with Defense Doctrine, by MG Edward b. Atkeson, USA Retired, March 1991

Special Report - The U.S. Army in Operation Desert Storm - An Overview, June 1991

Landpower Essay Series, No.91-2, Desert Storm Fire Support - Classic Airland Battle Operations, by BG Paul F. Pearson, USA Retired, and General Glenn K. Otis, USA Retired, June 1991

Special Report - Operations Desert Shield and Desert Storm: The Logistics Perspective, September 1991

Defense Report 91-1, Victory in the Persian Gulf War -- Only America Could Do It, March 1991

Defense Report 91-2, How We Did It -- Smart Weapons Operated by Smart People, March 1991

* Desert Shield/Desert Storm - Navy Role

U.S. Department of the Navy
Office of Information
Washington, DC 20350-1200 (703) 697-2904

The Navy has published several items highlighting Navy and Marine roles in the U.S. victory in the Gulf War. The Special Issue of the U.S. Navy official magazine *All Hands,* includes articles on Sealift, Marine combat engagements, and Navy Medicine in the Gulf. The Office of the Chief of Naval Operations has also published a book entitled *The United States Navy in Desert Shield/Desert Storm.* This book details the Navy and Marine role in the conflict and outlines lessons learned for the future. Both publications are available free to the public but supplies may be limited.

* Desert Shield/Desert Storm - GAO Analyses

General Accounting Office
National Security and International Affairs Division
Post Office Box 6015
Gaithersburg, MD 20877 (202) 275-6241

In the afterglow of the Persian Gulf War, the General Accounting Office has been studying logistical and equipment problems in order to improve military performance in future conflicts. Reports on the War include:

Operation Desert Storm: The Services Efforts to Provide Logistics Support for Selected Weapon Systems. GAO/NSIAD 91-321, Sept 26, 1991.

Operation Desert Storm: Army's Use of Water Purification Equipment. GAO/NSIAD 91-325, Sept. 26 1991.

Operation Desert Storm: Problems Encountered by Activated Reservists. GAO/NSIAD 91-290, Sept 27, 1991.

Call for a complete list of reports.

* Desert Shield/Desert Storm - Logistics

Military Traffic Management Command (MTMC)
5611 Columbia Pike
Falls Church, VA 22041-5050 (703) 756-1242

The MTMC has facts and figures on the astonishing logistical movements that made Desert Shield/Storm such a monumental and successful operation. Ask for the MTMC facts, which details the number of ships used and vehicles moved in the operation. It is available free upon request.

* Dictionary of Military Terms

U.S. Government Printing Office
Superintendent of Documents
Washington, DC 20402-6518 (202) 783-3238

The Joint Staff has published a comprehensive *Dictionary of Military and Associated Terms,* available for approximately $15. Contact the Government Printing Office for current price and ordering information.

* Doing Business with the Military

Director, Office of Small and
Disadvantaged Business Utilization
Undersecretary of Defense for Acquisition

The Pentagon, Room 2A340
Washington, DC 20301 (703) 614-1151

This office has an information package on how to sell to the U.S. Department of Defense. It contains a booklet of rules and regulations in selling to the military, a booklet listing all the procurement offices worldwide, and a subcontracting directory.

* Electronic Warfare

U.S. Navy
Crane Division
Naval Surface Warfare Center
Public Affairs Office
Crane, IN 47522 (812) 854-1394

As the Gulf War vividly demonstrated, electronic warfare has become an indispensable part of modern combat. The Naval Surface Warfare Center engages in research in Microelectronic Technology, Microwave components, electronic warfare, and electronic module test and repair. Contact the above office for further information.

* Electromagnetic Technology

Directorate for Public Communication
U.S. Department of Defense
The Pentagon, Room 2E777
Washington, DC 20301-1400 (703) 697-5737

This office can provide you with general information about electromagnetic technology, including annual reports, newsletters and fact sheets, and will make referrals for you if you need more detailed information.

* Excavation and Dredging Regulation Regulatory Branch

U.S. Army Corps of Engineers
20 Massachusetts Ave., NW, Room 6235
Washington, DC 20314 (202) 272-0397

You must obtain a Corps permit if you plan to locate a structure, excavate, or discharge dredged or fill material in waters of the United States, including wetlands, or if you plan to transport dredged material for the purpose of dumping it into ocean waters. Contact the appropriate District Engineer office for current information and to apply for a permit. You may contact the above office for addresses and telephone numbers of the District offices.

* Federal Helium Stockpile

Helium Operations
Bureau of Mines
U.S. Department of the Interior
810 7th St, NW
Washington, DC 20241 (202) 501-9244

The Bureau of Mines' Federal Helium Program provides helium for the current and foreseeable needs of essential government activities and assists individual enterprises with the production and distribution of helium. Approximately 300 million cubic feet of helium is withdrawn annually from the Bureau's Cliffside Helium Storage Reservoir near Amarillo, Texas. After purification, this helium is distributed to federal agencies, the private helium industry, and to university and college research facilities.

* Federal Technological Resources Directory

National Technical Information Service
Springfield, VA 22161 (703) 487-4650

The *Directory of Federal Technological Resources* listing all federal resources for services, expertise, and facilities of interest to engineers, scientists, and technology-oriented businesses may be ordered from this service for a moderate charge.

* Film Footage

U.S. Department of Defense
Motion Media Records Center
Building 248
Norton Air Force Base, CA 92409-0218 (714) 382-2307

This Center holds Army, Navy, and Marine Corps stock footage from 1964 to the present. Contact the National Archives for footage from prior years. They will

Be patient. If any phone number is incorrect, call (area code) 555-1212 and request the new listing.

Military and National Security

assist researchers, educators, or commercial enterprises in locating specific scenes for a moderate fee. Write for their free brochure describing the holdings and how to access the Center.

* Flight Testing and Aerial Support Systems

Air Force Flight Test Center
Air Force Systems Command
U.S. Department of the Air Force
Edwards Air Force Base, CA 93523 (805) 277-3510

This Test Center conducts advanced development programs in flight testing and evaluation of new aircraft, rocket propulsion systems, aerial support systems (parachutes, delivery and recovery systems), and the training of research pilots. Its technical library may be made available for approved researchers. Fact sheets on the history, mission, aircraft, and space shuttle, as well as photographs of the base and aircraft are available at no charge upon request.

* Foreign Language Training

Defense Language Institute
Foreign Language Center
Non-Resident Division
Presidio of Monterey, CA 93944 (408) 647-5104

The Defense Language Institute is one of the world's largest language training centers. The holdings of its library--over 100,000 books in 50 languages--are available through a national inter-library loan program. The non-resident division offers foreign language courses for sale. A catalog of the languages available may be obtained for $5.25. Write or call for brochures on the Institute and information regarding inter-library loans.

* Foreign Military Sales

Defense Security Assistance Agency
The Pentagon, Room 4D720
Washington, DC 20301-2800 (703) 697-8108

This office administers the Foreign Military Financing Program (FMFP) Program, which deals with U.S. government sales of defense articles and services to foreign governments. A free booklet containing information on the Program and the U.S. Defense Security Assistance Agency is available upon request.

* Foreign Weapon Sales Statistics

FMS Reports and Controls Division
Defense Security Assistance Agency
The Pentagon, Room 4B659
Washington, DC 20301-2800 (703) 693-1057

This office publishes a free annual publication, *Foreign Military Sales, Foreign Military Construction Sales, and Military Assistance Facts*, which contains information and detailed statistics on all grant programs, sales, and Federal financing of security assistance to foreign countries. Write or call for a copy.

* Freedom of Information Access

Defense Intelligence Agency
Attn: RTS-1B
Washington, DC 20340-3299 (202) 373-8361

For access to information held by the Defense Intelligence Agency and subject to the provisions of the Freedom of Information Act, contact this office. A brochure, *Brief History of DIA*, which gives information on the various functions and the mission of the agency is available upon request.

* Fuel Suppliers and Consumption in the Military

Public Affairs Office
Defense Fuel Supply Center
Defense Logistics Agency
Cameron Station
Alexandria, VA 22304-6160 (703) 274-6489

This office will supply information on almost anything you will want to know concerning fuel supply in the military. The staff will explain how to contract for the Strategic Petroleum Reserve, and how to request information under the Freedom of Information Act, such as statistics on fuel consumption patterns in the military and copies of current contracts with major suppliers. You may request a free copy of their *Fact Book*, which tells how much was spent on fuel throughout the U.S. Department of Defense, the sources of supply, and how the fuel was allocated. It includes line graphs and pie charts, with a national

geographic distribution breakdown. This office also publishes the magazine *Fuel Line*, available by subscription.

* Genealogy Searches Military Service

General Reference Branch
National Archives and Records Administration
Washington, DC 20408 (202) 501-5402

This office holds military service and pension records of people who served prior to 1900. The office accepts written requests only. Ask for *Form NATF 80*.

* Geotechnical Research

U.S. Army Corps of Engineers
Waterways Experiment Station
3909 Halls Ferry Rd.
Vicksburg, MS 39180-6199 (601) 634-2504

A component of the Geotechnical Lab, the Pavements and Soil Trafficability Information Analysis Center (PSTIAC) provides products and specialized reference services to the public. The staff can be tasked to provide evaluative engineering and/or analytical service on pavements, trafficability, vehicle mobility, and terrain, primarily relevant to military needs. Database searches are performed on a cost recovery basis, and requests are approved on a case by case basis. The Station's library participates in the national inter-library loan system, and copies of technical reports are distributed on a first come, first served basis. (Reports are thereafter available from DTIC.) The Public Affairs Office can provide a summary of publications, fact sheets on the Center's programs, brochures on subject areas, and a comprehensive book entitled *Summary of Capabilities* describing the Center's work. Time on the Center's super computer is available for sale to academic researchers.

* Government Films, Videos, and Slides

National Audio-Visual Center
8700 Edgeworth Dr.
Capital Heights, MD 20743 (301) 763-1891

This is the sole source from which to purchase all U.S. government produced films, video tapes and slide sets. Write or call their office for a list of the specialty catalogs available; the catalogs are free, the products are for sale.

* Guided Missiles and Rocket Launching

Naval Ordnance Missile Test Facility
White Sands Missile Range, NM 88002 (505) 678-1134

This facility is used for the testing and evaluation of guided missiles, and endo- and exo-atmospheric research in rocket launching. Testing is conducted by the armed services, NASA, and private corporations. The Range also has a thriving wildlife reserve. Write or call for a free brochure detailing the type of research conducted on the facility and its range capabilities.

* High Seas Law Enforcement

Operational Law Enforcement Division
Office of Law Enforcement and Defense Operations
U.S. Coast Guard
U.S. Department of Transportation
2100 2nd St., SW, Room 3110
Washington, DC 20593-0001 (202) 267-1890

As the primary maritime law enforcement agency for the U.S., the Coast Guard enforces Federal laws, treaties, and international agreements to which the U.S. is a party. The Coast Guard may conduct investigations when violations are suspected, such as smuggling, drug trafficking, or polluting. Empowered to board and inspect vessels routinely as well, the Guard also conducts "suspicionless" boardings to prevent violations. To report suspicious or questionable activity on boats, or to complain about an improperly conducted boarding, call the Boating Safety Hotline, (800) 368-5647; or (202) 267-0780 in DC, or contact your local Coast Guard commander. The office listed above can provide you with information about the Coast Guard's law enforcement role and the National Narcotics Border Interdiction System, which coordinates multi-agency and international operations with other countries to suppress narcotics trafficking.

* History Museums in U.S. and Germany

U.S. Army Center of Military History
Attn: DAMH-HSM
Federal Center SE/Navy Yard, Bldg. 159

Be patient. If any phone number is incorrect, call (area code) 555-1212 and request the new listing.

International Relations and Defense

Washington, DC 20374-5088 (202) 475-2580
The Army Center of Military History administers 73 public museums throughout the U.S. and West Germany. Write or call the above office for a list of museum locations and collections.

* House of Representatives Hearings and Research

House Armed Services Committee
Suite 2120, Rayburn House Office Building
Washington, DC 20515 (202) 225-4151
The House Armed Services Committee concerns itself with defense, military personnel and installations, procurement, nuclear systems, research and development, seapower, and strategic and critical materials such as petroleum and Chromium. To be placed on the mailing list for hearing dates, call the above telephone number. Transcripts of committee hearings may be obtained directly from the committee or you may ask your representative for help. Copies of House bills and committee reports can also be obtained free of charge from the House Documents room (202) 225-3456. Your Congressman can also obtain Congressional Research Reports on national defense issues for you. A list of reports is located in the back of this book.

* Installations Public Works Construction

U.S. Department of the Army
Public Affairs Office
Construction Engineering Research Laboratory
P.O. Box 4005
Champaign, IL 61824-4005 (217) 373-7216
This office has copies of technical reports on research related to the construction, operation, maintenance, and repair of public works facilities at military installations. For a free brochure detailing your nearest Construction Engineering Research Laboratory and where to obtain reports, contact this office.

* Joint Chiefs of Staff

Historical Division
Joint Chiefs of Staff
U.S. Department of Defense
The Pentagon, Room 1A-714
Washington, DC 20318-0400 (703) 697-3088
This office publishes a number of military history series and volumes, including *Joint Chiefs of Staff and National Policy (1945-1954)* and *The Chairmen of the Joint Chiefs of Staff*, discussing the evolution of the office and profiles of its chiefs and *The Organizational Development of the Joint Chiefs of Staff: 1942-1989*. Write or call the above office for the availability of the publications. Publications are free but quantities are limited.

* Land and Aeronautical Target Survivability

Survivability/Vulnerability Information Analysis Center
WL/FIVS/SURVIAC
Wright-Patterson AFB, OH 45433 (513) 255-4840
SURVIAC maintains and operates a database of non-nuclear survivability/ vulnerability data, information, methodologies, models, and analyses relating to U.S. and foreign land and aeronautical targets. The Center is a source for products, database searches, and technical reports offered on a cost recovery basis. Specialized reference services are available for questions that exceed the limits of resources available for an inquiry response. Requests must be relevant to SURVIAC's primary areas of interest and funded by the requestor. Contact SURVIAC to order services or obtain general information.

* Land Warfare

Association of the United States Army
Institute for Land Warfare
2425 Wilson Blvd.
Arlington, VA 22201-3385 (703) 841-4300
The Institute's mission is to inform national leaders and the American public about the nature of land warfare and the importance of the U.S. Army. The ILW publishes Defense Reports, Special Reports, Fact Sheets, and Background Briefs. For a list of publications, contact the above number.

* Largest Defense Contractors

Directorate for Information Operations and Reports
Washington Headquarters Services

1215 Jefferson Davis Hwy., Suite 1204
Arlington, VA 22202 (703) 746-0786
This office publishes such reports as *100 Companies Receiving the Largest Dollar Volume of Prime Contract Awards* and the *Atlas/Data Abstract for the United States and Selected Areas*, which contains a map showing all the military installations and a compendium of U.S. Department of Defense statistics for each state. Write or call for their free catalog list all their publications available through the Government Printing Office.

* Laser Research

High Energy Laser Systems Test Facility
White Sands Missile Range
Public Affairs Office
New Mexico, NM 88802 (505) 678-1134
This Facility tests and evaluates high energy laser systems, subsystems and components. For information on tests and facilities, contact the above office.

* Lawrence Livermore Computer Facility

Visitors Center
Lawrence Livermore National Laboratory
Greenville Road
Livermore, CA 94550 (510) 422-9797
The National Laboratory conducts public tours of its computing center. You must, however, be 18 years of age or older. For information, contact the Visitors Center.

* Lawrence Livermore National Laboratory

Laboratory Communications and
Public Information
Lawrence Livermore National Laboratory
7000 East Ave. (Mail Stop L-404)
Livermore, CA 94550 (510) 422-4599
The Laboratory maintains a library accessible to researchers able to demonstrate a "need to know." The collection includes reports, texts, and journals on biomedicine, physics, energy, and military weapons design. Their *Rainbow* brochure outlines the programs, functions, and mission of the laboratory, and *Science and Engineering on the Grand Scale* gives an overview of each laboratory department. Free booklets on a broad range of subjects are available, including physics, the national magnetic fusion energy computing center, biomedical cancer research, solar energy research, and history of the National Laboratory and its role in weapons research.

* Logistics Research

U.S. Army
Ordnance Center and School Library
(AMATSL-SE-LI)
Aberdeen Proving Ground, MD 21004 (301) 278-5615
The Center's school has several technical libraries devoted to military logistics, supply and maintenance, which are open to approved researchers. Part of the collection is closed. Materials are available through inter-library loan. For additional information on their holdings and accessibility, contact the above office.

* Marine Corps Historical Research and Internships

U.S. Marine Corps Historical Center
Building 58, Navy Yard
9th and M Sts., SE
Washington, DC 20374-0580 (202) 433-3840
The Historical Center encompasses a museum, library, archives, reference section, a world historical section, and a publishing department. The library is open to serious researchers. The Center sponsors an internship program whereby students may earn college credit for performing research work at the Center. Write or call for brochures describing both the museum and the library. A free publications catalog is also available.

* Marine Corps Information Clearinghouse

Marine Corps-Public Affairs
Headquarters, U.S. Marine Corps
Washington, DC 20380-0001 (703) 614-1492
This office publishes material describing Marine Corps programs, personnel, and

Military and National Security

budget. Publication indexes and checklists are also available for a small fee. Write for information.

* Medical History Research

National Museum of Health and Medicine
Building 54, South Wing
Walter Reed Army Medical Center
Washington, DC 20606-6000 (202) 576-2348

The museum maintains an archives and a behind-the-scenes collection available for serious researchers. Write or call for brochures and information on the collection and for information on the tax-exempt, non-profit foundation headed by Surgeon General Dr. Koop for a new national health museum.

* Medical Scholarships through the Air Force

U.S. Department of the Air Force
Headquarters, USAFRS/RSH (512) 652-4334
Randolph Air Force Base, TX 78150-5421 (800) 531-5980

The Air Force offers Health Professions Scholarships in return for military service obligation. These scholarships are for those entering medical school. At the completion of medical school scholarship recipients can begin their obligation or file for a deferment in order to seek specialized training. Educational costs determine the length of service to the Air Force required. Contact the above office or call toll-free number for further information. Local Air Force recruiters also have information on this program.

* Microcomputers and Semiconductors

Reliability Analysis Center (RAC)
P.O. Box 4700
Rome, NY 13440-8200 (315) 337-9933

Evaluation engineering, analytical services, products, and specialized reference services are provided by RAC in the areas of microcircuits, semiconductors, nonelectric devices, and electronic modules. Reliability and maintainability data on planned and operational systems and equipment is stored in a database. A user's catalog, searches, and technical reports can be obtained on a cost recover basis. Searches cost $50 for two or more records found; there is generally no charge if less than two records are recovered. The Center does not release documents, but documents can be ordered from the Defense Technical Information Service in Alexandria, Va. (703) 274-7633.

* Military Academies

Training and Education
Manpower, Installation and Logistics
U.S. Department of Defense
The Pentagon, Room 3B930
Washington, DC 20301 (202) 607-0512

To meet a portion of the long-range requirement for career military officers the U.S. Military Academy, U.S. Naval Academy, and the U.S. Air Force Academy were established. These schools offer curricula specifically designed to train students as professional officers. For more information on these academies, contact them at the following addresses:

U.S. Military Academy, West Point, NY 10996; (914) 938-4011
U.S. Naval Academy, Annapolis, MD 21402; (301) 267-4361
U.S. Air Force Academy, USAFA, CO 80840; (719) 472-4050

* Military and Civilian Employment Records

National Personnel Center
9700 Page Blvd.
St. Louis, MO 63232 (314) 538-4261

This Center holds both military and civilian Federal personnel records dating from 1900 to the present. The Center prefers written requests for reference assistance.

* Military Archives

U.S. Department of Defense
Still Media Records Center, Code SSRC-PSa
Building 168 Naval Imaging Command
Anacostia Naval Station
Washington, DC 20374-1681 (202) 433-2166

This photographic archives/library maintains 100,000 photographs and a ready access slide file for all four branches of the military. Its holdings date from 1982 to the present (photographs prior to this have been transferred to the National Archives), and include pictures of ships, tanks, missiles, rockets, the Grenada invasion, and military exercises in Honduras. Research assistants are available to help patrons, and the Center will do research for fee of $5 for the first 15 minutes and $20 per hour after that. The Center is open 9am to 3 pm daily but access is by appointment only.

* Military Commands

Directorate for Public Communication
U.S. Department of Defense
The Pentagon, Room 2E777
Washington DC 20301-1400 (703) 697-5737

The United States military is organized into Specified and Unified Commands that combine forces from different services. Unified commands are organized on a regional basis. For information about the commands, contact the above number or contact the commands directly:

Atlantic Command (804) 444-6294
Pacific Command (808) 471-9779
Space Command (719) 554-6889
Central Command (813) 830-6393
European Command 011 49 711 680 8486 (Germany)
Southern Command (507) 82-4278 (Panama)
Special Operations Command (813) 830-4600
Strategic Air Command (402) 294-4130
Forces Command (404) 669-7301

* Military Photographs Prior to 1982

National Archives and Records Administration
Still Picture Branch
Washington, DC 20408

Contains photographic records for the armed services prior to 1982. Air Force records predating 1954 can be ordered from the National Air and Space Museum, Information Management Division, Smithsonian Institution, Washington, DC 20560.

* Military Records 19th Century On

Suitland Reference Branch
National Archives and Records Administration
Washington, DC 20409 (703) 763-7410

This office holds historical material, including Land Office records, State Department personnel overseas post records since 1935, the Japanese war relocation records, records of the U.S. military government of Germany and Japan, as well as records of all military actions from World War II through the Vietnam War. The office provides reference assistance in locating historical material, and will accept reference questions both in writing and by phone. The Library is open Monday through Saturday 8am to 4:15 pm. If requesting materials over the phone, the Library charges $6 minimum fee and 25 cents a page for any requests costing more than $6.

* Military Systems Reports and Audits

General Accounting Office (GAO)
Post Office Box 6015
Gaithersburg, MD 20877 (202) 275-6241

The National Security and International Affairs Division of the General Accounting office authored some 125 reports on defense and security matters in 1991. As GAO is the auditing agency of Congress, the reports are generally critical in nature, calling for reforms to improve program efficiency. Past year reports are also available. The first five copies of GAO reports are free. The following is a small sample of what's available.

Naval Aviation: The V-22 Osprey - Progress and Problems. GAO/NSIAD 91-45 October 12, 1991

Defense Reorganization: DOD's Efforts to Streamline the Special Operations Command. GAO/NSIAD 91-24BR November 23, 1991

Army Budget: Potential Reductions in Helicopter Programs. GAO/NSIAD 91-55BR December 5, 1991

Weapons Production: Impacts of Production Rate Changes on Aircraft Unit Costs. GAO/NSIAD 91-12 December 18, 1991

Antisubmarine Warfare: Tactical Surveillance Sonobuoy and Related Software Need to be Tested Together. GAO/NSIAD 91-41 January 9, 1991

Be patient. If any phone number is incorrect, call (area code) 555-1212 and request the new listing.

International Relations and Defense

Enlisted Force Management: Past Practices and Future Challenges. GAO/NSIAD 91-48 January 22, 1991

Battleships: Issues Arising from the Explosion Aboard the USS Iowa. GAO/NSIAD 91-4 January 4, 1991

Chemical Weapons: DOD's Successful Effort to Remove US Chemical Weapons from Germany. GAO/NSIAD 91-105 February 13, 1991

* Military Traffic Management

Military Traffic Management Command
U.S. Department of Army
5611 Columbia Pike
Falls Church, VA 22041-5050 (703) 756-1242

This Command manages all DOD freight and passenger movement in the United States, and all Army transport activities worldwide; however, the Command's expertise and responsibilities are considerably more complex and far-ranging. Upon request, this office will supply you with a 25-page brochure entitled *Ensuring Combat Power Gets to Its Place of Business,* an information brief on specific traffic management topics and projects, a copy of their *Traffic Management Progress Report* (published quarterly), a pamphlet on how to do business with the Command, and MTMC Facts, which outlines the structure of the command as well as providing statistics on the monumental logistics involved with Operations Desert Shield and Desert Storm. All are free of charge.

* Minerals of Critical and Strategic Importance

Research Division, Bureau of Mines
U.S. Department of the Interior
810 7th St., NW
Washington, DC 20241-0002 (202) 501-9649

An emphasis within the Bureau of Mines' Research Division is reducing the Nation's dependence on imports for certain minerals that have key defense and industrial applications. The Bureau is developing ways to recover strategic and critical minerals from mineral processing wastes and to recycle these minerals. Key minerals of this type include cobalt, chromium, manganese, and platinum.

* Mine Sweeping and Other Naval Coastal Activities

Coastal Systems Station - Dahlgrin Division
Naval Surface Warfare Center
Panama City, FL 32407-5000 (904) 234-4083

The Center is involved in research and development in support of naval missions and operations in the coastal (Continental Shelf) regions, including mine sweeping, diving and salvage, and amphibious operations. Experts may be obtained from their Speakers Bureau to talk on naval research and development issues, and their office will make every effort to answer specific questions from serious researchers. Write or call for a brochure describing their work and programs, and for information on their Tour Program for civic groups.

* Mine Warfare

U.S. Department of the Navy
OP-744
Washington, DC 20350 (703) 694-7334

Both mine warfare and mine countermeasures are vital for controlling essential sea areas. In 1987 the U.S. commissioned the USS Avenger, the first new mine countermeasures ship to be built since the 1950s. The Navy is also currently working on the MHC-51 (Osprey) class mine hunter. For information on mine warfare, contact the above office.

* Missile and Space Launchers

HQ 20th USAF
Office of Public Affairs
Vandenberg Air Force Base, CA 93437-5000 (805) 866-3016

This center conducts developmental and operational testing of missile and space launchers. It is the only test launch facility in the U.S. for ICBMs, and the only facility to have launched test orbiters into polar orbit. The public is invited to its annual open house, held usually in the spring. Fact sheets on the base, its mission, programs, and history can be obtained by writing or calling the above office.

* Missile and Weapons Testing

Naval Air Weapons Station
Office of Public Affairs

Code 6033
Point Mugu, CA 93042-5011 (805) 989-8094

This Center tests and evaluates Naval weapons systems and devices and provides logistics and training support. Included are guided missiles, rockets, free-fall weapons, fire control and radar systems, drones and target drones, electronic devices, countermeasures equipment, test planning, simulations, and data collection. Reports are available only through Freedom of Information Act requests. For further details, contact Public Affairs.

* Missile Research

U.S. Army Missile Command
Redstone Arsenal, AL 35898 (205) 842-0560

This Command conducts research and development on rockets, guided missiles, air defense weapons systems, meteorology, missile launching, and associated equipment. Write or call for a free brochure on the Command and its history, which contains pictures and descriptions of virtually every missile the U.S. Army has ever used. Also ask for a pamphlet on how to do business with the Command. Copies of technical reports are also available upon request.

* Missile Testing Center

U.S. Department of the Army
Public Affairs Office
Building 122
White Sands Missile Range, NM 88002-5047 (505) 678-2101

This research and missile testing center invites the public to an open house twice a year, which includes a visit to the "Trinity Site" where the first atomic detonation took place. The center publishes a brochure and fact sheets on its history, mission, and wide range of programs. Facilities at White Sands are shared by the U.S. Naval Ordinance Missile Test Station, Atmospheric Sciences Laboratory, National Aeronautics and Space Administration, and the U.S. Army's Training and Doctrine Command's Analysis Command. The test range also functions as a wildlife preserve. Write or call for their free publications and information on open house days.

* Museum of Health and Medicine

National Museum of Health and Medicine
Building 54, South Wing
Walter Reed Army Medical Center
Washington, DC 20606-6000 (202) 576-2348

The museum is open to the public every day of the week, and features exhibits illustrating health and disease in their social and historical contexts. You may see organ specimens dating from the Civil War, the bullet that killed President Lincoln, a famous collection of microscopes dating from their invention, and currently an "interactive" exhibit on AIDS and another on "Headache Art"-- migraine sufferers' depiction on paper on what a migraine headache is like. Notable exhibits are "Living In a World With AIDS," and "The Patient is Abraham Lincoln" and "Substance Abuse Prevention." Call or write for more information. Write or call for a free brochure on the museum and its hours.

* National Air and Space Archives

Paul E. Garber Preservation
Restoration and Storage Facility
Building 12
3904 Old Silver Hill Road
Suitland, MD 20746 (301) 238-3480

The NASM library houses more than 35,000 books, 7000 bound journals as well as collections of microforms and other technical documents.The collection encompasses the history of aviation and space, flight technology, the aerospace industry, rocketry, earth and planetary sciences, and astronomy. The libraries hours are 8:30-4:30 weekdays. Appointments are necessary. Inquiries may be made by phone, fax, or mail. The staff will photocopy up to 25 documents while you wait, larger orders are sent out to external vendors and then forwarded to researchers. Loans are not made to individuals.

* National Guard Bands

National Guard Bureau
Attn: NGB-PAC
4501 Ford Ave.
Alexandria, VA 22301-1457 (703) 695-0421

Local National Guard units provide bands, color guards, and flight demonstrations for community events upon request of civic groups. The Guard

Be patient. If any phone number is incorrect, call (area code) 555-1212 and request the new listing.

Military and National Security

also sponsors annual open houses and conducts tours of the local bases. A Speakers Bureau will provide experts to speak on defense and local issues, and the Guard sponsors orientation trips for civic leaders. Call or write for more information on the Guard's varied community assistance programs, including the loan of equipment to civic groups.

* National Guard Statistical Information

National Guard Bureau
NSB-PA, Room 23261
The Pentagon
Washington, DC 20310-2500 (703) 695-0421

The Guard publishes a brochure entitled *National Guard Updates* which discusses the Federal and State mission, force structure, overseas deployments, and personnel statistics, and an *Annual Review* of its work and accomplishments. Write or call for a free copy.

* National Guard Posters and History

National Guard Bureau
Attn: PAH
The Pentagon
Washington, DC 20310-2500 (703) 695-0421

Posters and lithographs of historical events involving the Guard, which date from 1636 to the present, are available free of charge. This office will provide advice and help in obtaining information on specific Guard Units.

* National Security Research

The Rand Corporation
1700 Main Street
P.O. Box 2138
Santa Monica, CA 90407-2138 (213) 393-0411

The National Defense Research Institute conducts research in several areas of national security affairs. Contact RAND for a list of available publications.

* National Strategy

Directorate for Public Communications
Office of Assistant Secretary of Defense
for Public Affairs
The Pentagon, Room 2E777
Washington, DC 20301 (703) 697-6462

This Public Affairs office will answer your general questions regarding American National Security Strategy. It can also provide you with the document *National Security Strategy of the United States*. This document, published annually, provides good insight into Administration thinking on security issues. Call or write for a copy.

* Naval Air Procurement

Naval Air Warfare Center
Aircraft Division
Public Affairs Division
Lakehurst, NJ 08733-5041 (908) 323-2620

This Center conducts research, development, testing, and evaluation of aircraft launching and landing equipment and airborne weapons systems. Write or call the Center for copies of a mission statement, historical background sheet, and information on contracting.

* Naval Avionics Development Center

U.S. Department of the Navy
Naval Air Warfare Center
Code 094, Small Business Office
Warminster, PA 18974 (215) 441-2456

This laboratory researches, develops, tests, and evaluates naval avionic systems. Write or call for their free pamphlet, *Doing Business with the Naval Air Development Center*.

* Naval Avionics Procurement

Naval Air Warfare Center
Aircraft Division
Public Affairs Office

6000 E. 21st St.
Indianapolis, IN 46219 (317) 353-4009

This Center conducts research and development on avionics and related equipment. Call or write for free brochures describing the Center, its programs, statistics on its employees, and a booklet on *How to Do Business with NAC*.

* Naval Construction Battalion Center

Commander Port Hueneme Division
Naval Surface Warfare Center
Port Hueneme, CA 93043 (805) 982-4493

This is the training center for the Navy's Construction Battalion (the "Seabees"). The Center has a base guide, a profile sheet giving statistical information on the base, and a brochure on the history of the Center, which was founded during W.W. II. They will accept written or phone requests for information.

* Naval Guided Weapons Systems

U.S. Department of the Navy
Public Affairs Office
Naval Surface Warfare Center
Port Hueneme, CA 93043-5007 (805) 982-7972

This Station conducts research and development, testing, and evaluation on ships' guided weapons systems. To obtain information about the station, its programs, and activities, write or call for the booklets, *PHDNSWC*, *Your Navy in Ventura County*, and a copy of their 25th anniversary magazine containing articles about the various departments.

* Naval Historical Research

Naval Historical Center
Washington Navy Yard
Washington, DC 20374 (202) 433-2210

The Navy Historical Center's research library and operational archives is open to private researchers. Its holdings include a still photographic collection of over 225,000 views and an art collection of over 8,000 pieces. Write or call for their free catalog of books in print, which includes an 8-volume series *Dictionary of American Naval Fighting Ships* and a 9-volume series *Naval Documents of the American Revolution*. Of current interest are *Origins of the Maritime Strategy* and *Power and Change: The Administrative History of the Chief of Naval Operations*, 1946-1989. Books may be ordered through GPO. Center hours are 8:30 to 4:30 daily and no appointment is necessary. Parts of the library are classified.

* Naval Observatory Library

34th and Massachusetts Ave.
Washington, DC 20392-5100 (202) 653-1541

The Naval Observatory's research library is open to the public by appointment. Its holdings (over 75,000 volumes) include many rare books on astronomy as well as the current literature. A list of publications is available at no charge, which includes the *Astronomical Almanac*, the *Nautical Almanac*, the *Air Almanac*, the *Almanac for Computers*, *Astronomical Phenomena*, various periodicals, and reference materials. For publications call (202) 653-1547.

* Naval Ordinance

Naval Ordinance Missile Test Station
Public Affairs Office
White Sands Missile Range
New Mexico, NM 88002 (505) 678-1134

The NOTMS tests land based weapons and directed energy weapons as well as engaging in rocket launch support research. The Station is the only test station capable of firing all versions of the Standard Missile. For more information, contact the above office.

* Naval Patents

Deputy Counsel
Office of the Chief of Naval Research
(Intellectual Property)
800 N. Quincy St.
Arlington, VA 22217-5000 (703) 696-4000

This office grants licenses for commercial use of government-owned patents. For information on the patents available for licensing, contact the above office.

Be patient. If any phone number is incorrect, call (area code) 555-1212 and request the new listing.

International Relations and Defense

* Naval Reservists

Naval Reserve Recruiting Office
Naval Reserve Center
2600 Powder Mill Road
Adelphi, MD 20783-1198 (301) 394-2510

Naval Reservists are prepared for mobilization with equipment and training programs that parallel those of the regular Navy, including participation in fleet exercises. The Recruiting Office can provide information and brochures about the Reserve.

* Navy Band

U.S. Navy Band
Public Affairs Office
Washington Navy Yard
Washington, DC 20374-1052 (202) 433-2394

The U.S. Navy Concert Band and its specialty units--including the Commander's Trio, Windjammers, Tuba-Euphonium Quartet, Sea Chanters, Country Current, and the Commodores--are available to perform at community events nationwide. Units of the band perform a wide range of musical styles, from jazz, folk, and blue grass to classical chamber and cocktail music. Band bookings are done through the operations office, at (202) 433-3676. Write or call for information on how to request the Band.

* Navy Budget and Forces Summary

Comptroller of the Navy, NCB33
Crystal City Mall, No. 2, Room 606
Statistical and Report Branch
Washington, DC 20350-1100 (703) 607-0875

This office publishes a *Budget and Forces Summary* covering the overall Navy budget for current and prior years, and a projection for the coming year. It contains a complete breakdown of Nay appropriations and is published annually, usually in mid April of each year. Write or call for a free copy.

* Navy Exchanges Procurement

Navy Resale and Services Support Office
Naval Station New York
Staten Island, NY 10305-5097 (718) 390-3700

This office handles procurement of resale merchandise for Navy exchanges and commissary stores. Write or call for the free *Guide for Doing Business with the Navy Resale System.*

* Navy Information Clearinghouse

U.S. Navy, Office of Information
The Pentagon
Washington, DC 20350-1200 (703) 695-6915

This office answers a broad range of general questions pertaining to Navy affairs. It can also supply a copy of the *Navy Fact File* containing general information on ships, aircraft and weapons systems, ship programs, and other statistics.

* Navy Medical Research

Navy Medical Research and Development Command
Attn: Code 40C
Bethesda, MD 20814 (301) 295-0325

This Command conducts research, development, testing, and evaluation in diving medicine, submarine medicine, aviation medicine, fleet health care, infectious diseases, and dental health. A list of their technical reports is available upon request.

* Navy Procurement

Navy Acquisition, Research and
Development Information Center (NARDIC)
5001 Eisenhower Ave.
Alexandria, VA 22333 (703) 274-9315

This Center maintains a research and development, technical reading room open to DOD contractors, and will provide research and development planning and requirement documents to qualified users. The Center can also give information on the Navy Potential Contractors Program, which was instituted to facilitate technology transfer between the military and industry. Write or call for the free brochure explaining eligibility requirements and how to access the reading room,

as well as how to enroll in the Potential Contractors Program and gain access to the Defense Technology Information Center.

* Navy Ship Historic Plans

Cartographic and Architectural Branch
National Archives and Records Administration
Washington, DC 20408 (703) 756-6700

This office compiles the plans of all U.S. Navy ships since the Navy was founded to 1939. If you make your request in writing, provide ship name and designation. The office will accept no more than three requests at a time. Cost for the service is $1.80 per print foot. The average request costs $5.40 - $7.20. Call or write for assistance.

* Navy Ship Historic Photographs and Drawings

Still Picture Branch
7th and Pennsylvania Ave., NW
National Archives and Records Administration
Washington, DC 20408 (202) 501-5455

The Still Picture Branch has drawings and photos of many Navy ships commissioned from the founding of the republic to the eve of World War II. The Collection includes: Thomas Birche's famous drawing of the battle between the USS Constitution (Old Ironsides) and the British Warship Guerriere in the War of 1812; a photo of the battleship Maine shortly before she mysteriously exploded in Havana harbor touching off the Spanish-American War; and the aircraft carrier Yorktown. 8x10 reproductions cost $6.25. Call or write for details.

* Night Vision Research

Office of Public Affairs
Night Vision and Electro-Optics Laboratories (NVEOL)
Fort Belvoir, VA 22060-5677 (703) 664-5066

NVEOL conducts research and development into electro-optical low-energy lasers, all-weather systems, infrared, radiation, visionics, and image intensification. The laboratories provide the Army with equipment to enable it to carry out nocturnal operations efficiently. This office can offer information and referral on laboratory programs.

* North Atlantic Treaty Organization

Bureau of Public Affairs
Office of Public Communication
U.S. Department of State, Room 5815A
Washington, DC 20520-6816 (202) 647-6317

This office publishes the bimonthly magazine *NATO Review*, which contains timely articles on European defense issues as well as copies of recent unclassified Alliance documents. The magazine is free and can be ordered by contacting the above office.

* Nuclear Armaments Research

U.S. Army Armament Research and Development Command
U.S. Department of the Army - ARDEC
Picatinny Arsenal, NJ 07806-5000 (201) 724-6364

This Command conducts research, development, life-cycle engineering, and initial acquisition of various nuclear and non-nuclear weapons and ammunition. The Command accepts requests for information on specific technical topics on a case-by-case basis. Write or call for their information pamphlet and brochures on the research center and current programs.

* Nuclear Attack Submarines

U.S. Department of the Navy
OP-02PA
Washington, DC 20350-2000 (703) 697-8704

Nuclear attack submarines play a vital role in the Navy's strategy. As of May 1989, the United States deployed some 96 nuclear attack submarines, of which 41 were Los Angeles Class. Navy plans currently foresee the deployment of one ultra modern SSN-21 Seawolf class attack submarine.

* Nuclear Weapons Effects Testing

Field Command Defense Nuclear Agency
Defense Nuclear Agency

Be patient. If any phone number is incorrect, call (area code) 555-1212 and request the new listing.

Military and National Security

6801 Telegraph Road
Alexandria, VA 22310-3398 (703) 325-7095

This Command carries out much of the operational work done by the DNA and maintains a liaison with the military services and is located in Kirtland Air Force Base, New Mexico. The Command is also responsible for operations and maintenance on Johnson Atoll. The mission of the DNA personnel on Johnston Atoll is to maintain facilities to resume nuclear tests in treaty prohibited environments, should this be required. This mission is specified in the legislation passed by Congress in ratifying the Limited Test Ban Treaty of 1963. For more information on the Field Command or Johnston Atoll, contact the DNA.

* Overseas Navy Exchanges

Navy Exchange Service Command
Naval Station New York
Staten Island, NY 10305-5097 (718) 390-3700

Overseas Navy exchanges in Guam, Hawaii, Italy, Japan, Spain, and the United Kingdom have independent purchasing authority for themselves and one or more branch exchanges. Those interested in selling to these exchanges can contact the Exchange Service Command for the addresses of the overseas exchanges, which may then be contacted directly.

* Pacific Fleet

United States Navy
Commander in Chief
U.S. Pacific Fleet
Public Affairs Office
Pearl Harbor, HI 96860-7000 (808) 471-9779

Based in Pearl Harbor, the Commander in Chief, U.S. Pacific Fleet command encompasses 102 million square miles of ocean, just over half of the earths ocean area. Operational commands include the Seventh fleet, Third Fleet, Task Force Fourteen, Task Force Twelve, Maritime Defense Zone, and Submarine Force Pacific.

* Patents Owned by Uncle Sam

National Technical Information Service
U.S. Department of Commerce
5285 Port Royal Rd.
Springfield, VA 22161 (703) 487-4650

This Service has a list of government patents available for licensing, as well as copies of all patents issued by the U.S. Patent Office. Call or write for ordering information.

* Pension Genealogy Searches

General Reference Branch
National Archives and Records Administration
Washington, DC 20408 (202) 501-5402

This office holds military service and pension records of people who served prior to 1900. The office accepts written requests only. Ask for *Form NATF 80*.

* Pentagon Budget Statistics

Office of Assistant Secretary of Defense
Public Affairs
The Pentagon, Room 2E777
Washington, DC 20301-1400 (703) 697-5737

This office can furnish you with copies of the book *Construction Programs (C-1)*, *DOD Budget for Fiscal Year 1992*, the *Annual Report to Congress*, and the *Defense '92 Almanac*, which gives statistics on manpower, organization charts, force charts, DOD budget, and international relations data. Write or call for free copies.

* Pentagon Products and Services

National Technical Information Service
Springfield, VA 22161 (703) 487-4650

This agency collects and publishes the results all government-sponsored research carried out by corporations, universities, and government agencies. The *Products and Services Catalog* gives an overview of the agency's services, and describes by subject the reports, subscription newsletters, database and microfiche services available. The catalog is free; publications and services may be purchased at cost. Write or telephone the above office for more information.

* Persian Gulf Crisis - Videos and Transcripts

Center for Defense Information (CDI)
1500 Massachusetts Ave. NW
Washington, DC 20005 (202) 862-0700

CDI, an independent military affairs research organization, produces a weekly TV show, "America's Defense Monitor", which aired a three part series on the Persian Gulf Crisis. Copies on VHS tapes can be purchased from the above address for $65 plus $2 postage and handling. Or order transcripts of the episodes for $5 each, plus $2 postage and handling.

* Persian Gulf Minesweeping

U.S. Department of the Navy
Office of Information
Washington, DC 20350-1200 (703) 697-2904

Three years before Operations Desert Shield/Storm the U.S. Navy undertook Operation Earnest Will. This operation protected reflagged Kuwaiti oil tankers from mines in the Persian Gulf and was the largest mine sweeping operation since the Korean War. The Office of Information can provide you with free information on Earnest Will and mine sweeping in general.

* Photographic Archives

Still Picture Branch (NNSP)
National Archives Records Administration
Seventh and Pennsylvania Ave., NW
Room 18N
Washington, DC 20408 (202) 523-3236

The archives holds the official photographic collection for the Army, Navy, and Marine Corps dating 1955 back to the founding of the country. Patrons can order photographic reproductions and posters for a small fee. Write or call for a price sheet, a "Select List" of period topics--including The Civil War, World War II, the Old West, the American Revolution, Indians, Navy Ships, and American Cities--and a catalog entitled *War and Conflict*.

* Photographic Archives of U.S. Military

U.S. Department of Defense
Still Media Records Center
Anacostia Naval Station
Building 168
Washington, DC 20374-1681 (202) 433-2168

This Center holds over one million negatives from all four military services, dating from the mid-1950s to present. Its archives are open to the public (appointments are preferred), and copies of negatives may be purchased. The Center maintains a research file by subject, and the staff will do research on a fee basis.

* Plastics and Adhesives Research

Plastics Technical Evaluation Center
U.S. Army Armament Research, Development
and Engineering Center (ARDEC)
Building 355-N
Picatinny Arsenal, NJ 07806-5000 (201) 724-4222

Technical information related to plastics, adhesives, and organic matrix composites is generated, evaluated, stored, and distributed at this Center, with an emphasis on performance and properties. Computerized databases are maintained on the compatibility of polymers with propellants and explosives and on materials deterioration. The Center provides services on a fee basis, including consulting, state-of-the-art studies, handbooks, analysis, evaluation, and bibliographic and literature searches. To arrange for services or to get information, contact PLASTEC at the number listed above.

* Plastics: Adhesives and Sealants Expert

Arthur Landrock
PLASTEC
U.S. Army/ARDEC
Building 355-N
Picatinny Arsenal, NJ 07806-5000 (201) 724-4222

Mr. Landrock, a materials engineer at PLASTEC, is an expert frequently consulted nationwide in the fields of adhesives and sealants. He has authored two books, including *Adhesives Technology Handbook* from Noyse Publications.

Be patient. If any phone number is incorrect, call (area code) 555-1212 and request the new listing.

International Relations and Defense

* Potential Military Contracts

Defense Advanced Projects Research Agency
3701 N. Fairfax Dr. Room 905
Arlington, VA 22203-1714 (703) 696-2402

This office will answer your general questions regarding the Defense Advanced Research Projects Agency (DARPA), which supports high-risk, high-payoff programs for research and technology development. Brochures available include the *Defense Advanced Research Projects Agency* updated annually, *Information, Science and Technology Office Research Programs* which lists current research programs, and the report, *Strategic Computing: Seventh Annual Report November 1991*. Technical program offices include the areas of Aerospace technology; Defense Sciences; Directed Energy; and Information Science and Technology. DARPA works closely with the Small Business Administration. All publications are free on request, as well as press releases on major events sponsored by DARPA. Write or call also for their *User's Guide for Potential Contractors*.

* President's National Security Council

National Security Council (NSC)
Old Executive Office Building
17th St. and Pennsylvania Ave., NW
Washington, DC 20506 (202) 395-4974

The NSC is responsible to assess and appraise the objectives, commitments, and risks of the United States in relation to our actual and potential military, economic, and political power, in the interest of national security, and to consider policies on matters of common interest to the department and agencies of the Government, and to make such recommendations and reports to the President as it deems appropriate or as the President may require. Council members are the President, the Vice President, the Secretary of State, and the Secretary of Defense, as prescribed by statute. The Chairman, Joint Chiefs of Staff, and the Director of Central Intelligence are statutory advisors. The Council's staff is headed by the Executive Secretary and provides day-to-day support for the President and his Assistant for National Security Affairs.

* Prisoners of War and Reclassification

U.S. Department of Defense
Force Management and Personnel
The Pentagon, Room 3E767
Washington, DC 20301-4000 (703) 695-7402

For information on conscientious objectors and POW's, including reclassification and discharge data, contact the above office.

* Radiobiology Research

Armed Forces Radiobiology Research Institute (AFRRI)
Defense Nuclear Agency
National Naval Medical Center, Building 42
Bethesda, MD 20814 (301) 295-2017

The Institute conducts tours of the facility, and makes its library available to approved researchers. AFRRI scientists conduct research on the biological effects of radiation and their relationship to national defense, space exploration, and medical progress. Its *Annual Report* summarizes the current work being performed in radiobiological research, and a brochure explains the Institute and its various programs. To request literature, contact the AFRRI's parent institution, the Defense Nuclear Agency at (703) 325-7306. Literature is free upon request.

* Relocation Assistance

Realty Services Division
Corps of Engineers Real Estate
U.S. Army Corps of Engineers
Attn: CERE-R
Washington, DC 20314-1000 (202) 272-0517

This office administers the Uniform Relocation Assistance Act for the U.S. Department of the Army. The Act provides benefits to landowners, tenants, businesses, and farmers who must move or must move property as a result of government acquisition of real property for Federal projects. Benefits include reimbursement for moving, costs, replacement housing, and direct losses. For further information, contact the Realty Services Division.

* Research and Development for Small Business

U.S. Army Laboratory Command
2800 Powder Mill Road

Attn: AMSLC-SP
Adelphi, MD 20783-1145 (301) 394-3590

The Command has a collection of hand-outs relating to Army research and development programs. These free pamphlets intended for small businesses include the *Laboratory Command Small Business Guide*, *Unsolicited Proposal Guide*, and *Technical/Industrial Liaison Guide*.

* Research and Development Standards or Military Contractors

Tri-Service Industry Information Center
5001 Eisenhower Ave.
Alexandria, VA 22333 (703) 274-8948

This office provides information on research and development, planning, and requirements information to suppliers of military equipment for the Army, Navy, and Air Force. To enter the research center, you must have a DOD contract and a personal security clearance. Write or call to obtain brochures on how to use the center and for its publications, including *Air Force Logistics Needs*, *Mission Element Need Statements (MENS)*, *Program Element Descriptive Summaries*, *Program Management Directive*, *R&D Planning Summaries*, *Technical Objective Documents Technology Needs Documents*, and *Selling to the United States Air Force*.

* Retirement Home

Public Relations
U.S. Soldiers' and Airmen's Home
3700 North Capitol St., NW
Washington, DC 20317 (202) 722-3386

The Home was established for retired or discharged enlisted and warrant officer personnel, men and woman, who have served 20 years or more in the Army or Air Force; or who have a service-connected disability preventing them from earning a living; or who have served during periods of war and have a nonservice connected disability preventing their earning a livelihood. For general information and brochures, contact the office listed above. For admissions, call (202) 722-3336. For information about the U.S. Soldiers' and Airmen's Home National Cemetery, contact the following address: 21 Harewood Road, NW, Washington, DC 20011; (202) 695-3190.

* Revolutionary War Paintings and Drawings

Still Picture Branch
7th and Pennsylvania Ave. NW
National Archives and Records Administration
Washington, DC 20408 (202) 501-5455

The Still Picture Branch has reproduced hundreds of famous scenes from the Revolutionary War. Pictures include the battles of Lexington, Concord, and Bunker Hill; the signing of the Declaration of Independence; and the surrender of Cornwallis at Yorktown. Call or write for the list of pictures available and prices.

* ROTC: Reserve Officers Training Corps

Training and Education
Manpower, Installation and Logistics
U.S. Department of Defense
The Pentagon, Room 3B930
Washington, DC 20301 (703) 695-2618

The Reserve Officers Training Corps (ROTC) program is conducted at over 500 U.S. colleges and universities and is the single largest source of officers for the Armed Forces, both career and non-career. For further details about ROTC, contact the office listed above or contact the programs directly at the individual colleges and universities.

* Science and Engineering Army Apprenticeships

U.S. Department of the Army
Chemical Research Development
and Engineering Center
Aberdeen Proving Ground, MD 21010-5423 (301) 671-4345

This Center sponsors a science and engineering apprenticeship program for high school students, summer "associateships" for high school faculty, and a faculty research and engineering program for university level scientists. The Center further welcomes requests from high schools for assistance with "Science Fairs" not only locally, but at the national and regional level.

Military and National Security

* Science Fairs and Research Grants

U.S. Department of the Army
Army Research Office
P.O. Box 12211
Triangle Park, NC 27709-2211 (919) 549-0641

This office administers the nation-wide Science Fair program, which sponsors science competition at the high school level, and the Defense Research Initiative, which is a competitive grant program for government funding of university research. Write or call for free brochures and information describing these programs.

* Security Assistance/ Foreign Assistance Funding

Agency for International Development
Bureau for External Affairs
Office of Publications
320 21 St., NW
Washington DC 20523 (202) 647-4330

This office can provide you with statistics on American foreign assistance, which includes security assistance, broken down both by country and program. Copies of the statistical tables are free.

* Security Assistance Journal

Defense Institute for Security Assistance Management
DISAM Journal
Wright-Patterson AFB, OH 45433-5000 (513) 255-2994

The Institute publishes the *DISAM Journal,* a must for those interested in security assistance policy. The Journal analyzes management issues and programs as well as annual security assistance legislation in Congress. The Journal also reprints the testimony of key Executive branch officials on security assistance. The Journal is published quarterly. Subscriptions cost $12 per year and can be ordered from the above office. The Institute also has a library specializing in security assistance matters.

* Security Assistance Policy

Defense Security Assistance Agency (DSSA)
The Pentagon 4B659
Washington DC 20301-2800 (703) 693-1057

Each February the State Department and the Defense Department jointly release the *Congressional Presentation Document for Security Assistance Programs.* This document, mandated by law, contains a complete list of security assistance programs descriptions as well as country by country breakdowns with discussion of current American security assistance programs in each country. The document also contains funding requests for the next fiscal year as well as final aid figures for the prior two fiscal years. The Document costs $25 and can be ordered from the DSAA at the above number.

* Selective Service Fact Sheets: Deferments, Exemptions, Etc.

Public Affairs
Selective Service System
1023 31st St., NW
Washington, DC 20435 (202) 724-0790

The Selective Service System provides free to the public fact sheets which contain information on certain aspects of the Selective Service System.

Address Verification Program
Aliens and Dual Nationals
Federal Student Aid, Job Training Benefits and Federal Employment
Postponements, Deferments, Exemptions
Selective Service and the Immigration Reform and Control Act of 1986
Alternative Service for Conscientious Objectors
Appeals Boards
Draft Cards

* Selective Service Regulations

Public Affairs, Selective Service System
1023 31st St., NW
Washington, DC 20435 (202) 724-0790

The documents listed below are usually available in the government documents section of major libraries:

Military Selective Service Act of June 24, 1948. This is the law under which the Selective Service System operates.
Code of Federal Regulations. Selective Service Regulations are contained within.

* Selective Service Registration: Induction, Claims, and Appeals

Public Affairs
Selective Service System
1023 31st St., NW
Washington, DC 20435 (202) 724-0790

The booklet, *Information for Registrants,* furnishes information about Selective Service responsibilities, and registrant rights and obligations. It also explains the induction, claims, and appeals process. To obtain a copy, contact this office.

* Selective Service Registration Status

Registration Information Office
P.O. Box 4638
North Suburban, IL 60197-4638 (708) 688-6888

If you have any questions regarding an individual's status and the requirement to register, call or write this office.

* Selective Services Semiannual Update

Public Affairs
Selective Service System
1023 31st St., NW
Washington, DC 20435 (202) 724-0790

Every six months, the Selective Service System publishes a summary of its program. Copies of the report can be obtained from this office.

* Selling to the Army: Commodity Commands

U.S. Army Materiel Command
Public Affairs
5001 Eisenhower Ave.
Alexandria, VA 22333 (703) 274-8010

The U.S. Army Materiel Command encompasses seven commodity commands which contract for both products and research and development. The Materiel Command buys everything the soldier uses, both personally and professionally. The commodity commands include the Armament, Munitions and Chemical Command; the Aviation Systems Command; the Communications-Electronics Command; the Laboratory Command (which contracts for research); the Missile Command; the Tank-Automotive Command; and the Troop Support Command (includes portable sanitary equipment, food, and uniforms). Call or write for a free brochure explaining what the Material Command encompasses.

* Selling to the Army: Small Business

U.S. Army Material Command
Small and Disadvantaged Business
Utilization Office
5001 Eisenhower Ave.
Alexandria, VA 22333 (703) 274-8185

A series of brochures is available for small and women-owned businesses on how to sell their products and services to the Army. *How to Do Business with AMC* lists the commodity commands and each Small Business Office at each command. *Selling to the Military, Small Business Specialists,* and *Small Business Subcontracting* all cover information on the application process through the U.S. Department of Defense. Also available are other free brochures explaining finance regulations for small businesses and how to prepare offers.

* Selling to the Military

Defense Logistics Agency
DFSC-DU
Cameron Station
Alexandria, VA 22304-6160 (703) 274-6135

DOD contracts literally hundreds of billions of dollars worth of goods and services annually. Call and request the book *Selling to the Military,* and *Guide to the Preparation of Offers For Selling to the Military,* both musts for getting started in this area. The publications are free upon request.

Be patient. If any phone number is incorrect, call (area code) 555-1212 and request the new listing.

International Relations and Defense

* Selling to the Marine Corps

Commandant of the Marine Corps
Morale Welfare Recreation Support Center
3044 Catlin Ave
Quantico, VA 22134-5099 (703) 640-3800

This office supplies fact sheets listing Marine Corps installations worldwide and explaining how to sell to the military exchanges on those installations. Requests for information must be made in writing.

* Selling to Navy Exchanges

Navy Exchange Services Command
Naval Station - NY
Staten Island, NY 10305-5097 (718) 390-3841

This office supplies the brochure, *The Navy Resale System*, which explains how to sell to the Navy military exchanges. Call or write for a free copy.

* Service Classification: Aliens, Conscientious Objectors, Ministers

Selective Service System
1023 31st. St., NW
Washington, DC 20435 (202) 724-0820

Classification is the process of determining who is available for military service and who is deferred or exempted from such service. Classification categories include conscientious objectors, ministers, veterans, and alien and dual nationals. For more information, contact this office.

* Small Business Pentagon Procurement Assistance

Small Business Office
Defense Fuel Supply Center
5010 Duke St.
Cameron Station, Building 8
Alexandria, VA 22304-6160 (703) 274-7428

This Small Business Office will refer potential contractors to the major buying centers within the Defense Logistics Agency for the commodity or service they wish to market. They have two standard brochures, *Selling to the Military* and *Guide to Preparation*. Write or call for free copies.

* Small Business and Disadvantaged Procurement

Small Business Office
U.S. Department of Defense (DOD)
The Pentagon 2A340
OUSD(A)SADBU
Washington, DC 20301-3061 (703) 697-9383

This office will supply information and guidance to small and disadvantaged businesses. Free copies are available of a list of the 700 DOD procurement offices and a book listing the major prime DOD contractors and the products and services they provide. Write or call their office to get on the solicitors' mailing list.

* Software Development and Technology

Data and Analysis Center for Software (DACS)
P.O. Box 120
Utica, NY 13503 (315) 336-0937

DACS provides products and specialized reference services on software development and maintenance programs. Subsets of its database can be obtained on hard copy or magnetic tape. Database searches and copies of technical reports are furnished on a cost recovery basis. Write or call for a free products and services brochure containing ordering and price information.

* Solid State Laser Research

Documents Office
Naval Research Laboratory (NRL)
Code 4827, 4555 Overlook Ave., SW
Washington, DC 20375-5000 (202) 767-2949

The Laboratory conducts research on low- and medium-power solid state lasers and infrared detectors. Technical reports can be obtained on the research from National Technical Information Service, 5285 Port Royal Road, Springfield, VA 22161; (703) 487-4650. A few are available from NRL directly. Contact the Documents Office for details.

* Space Command

HQ NORAD
Director Public Affairs
Peterson AFB, CO 80914 (719) 554-6889

This Command is in charge of America's early warning systems for detecting attacks launched against North America.

* Space and Missile Product Engineering

Office of Public Affairs
Western Space and Missile Center
U.S. Department of the Air Force
U.S. Department of Defense
Vandenberg AFB, CA 93437-6021 (805) 866-3016

Research, development, and product engineering in support of U.S. space and missile programs are conducted at this Center. Work focuses on radar, telemetry, electro-optics, communications range and mission control, weather timing, aircraft impact location, and data handling. Contact the Office of Public Affairs for information and referral.

* Space and Missile Test Range Research

45th Space Wing/ PA
Patrick Air Force Base, FL 32925 (407) 494-5933

This center conducts research and development activities in test range instrumentation and provides support for the Defense Department's missile and space programs. This involves radar, trajectory computers, tracking and target analysis, communications, timing and firing systems, telemetry, and data storage. For more information, contact research and development staff at the address listed above.

* Space Technology Research

U.S. Air Force Space Technology Center
Kirtland Air Force Base, NM 87117-6008 (505) 846-1911

This Center overseas the work of the three major Air Force research laboratories: the Weapons Laboratory at Kirtland; the Astronautics Laboratory at Edwards Air Force Base, California; and the Geophysics Laboratory at Hanscom Air Force Base, Massachusetts. Free fact sheets on all three labs and their programs are available from this Center, including fact sheets on the SDI program, the relay mirror experiment, the Alpha chemical laser experiment, "Brilliant Pebbles" research, optics research, microwaves, plasma physics, and nuclear weapons effects research. The Center offers a Speakers Bureau of experts and intern programs for outside researchers.

* Speakers Bureau: Chemical Weapons

U.S. Department of the Army
Chemical Research Development and Engineering Center
Aberdeen Proving Ground, MD 21010-5423 (301) 671-4345

While the Center's mission is to conduct research on chemical defense materials, it also provides a variety of programs involving the Center in the civic and scientific communities. Through its Speakers Bureau the Center will provide experts on scientific and technological topics. Write or call for a brochure explaining the laboratory, the Center's programs, and statistics on the post. Interested persons from the business and scientific community may call or write to be added to their mailing list for Advance Planning Briefings to Industry and notices of conferences and seminars.

* Special Forces

Special Operations Command (SOC)
Public Affairs Office
McDill AFB, FL 33608-6001 (813) 830-4600

SOC was formed in 1987 as a result of the Cohen-Nunn amendment to the National Defense Authorization Act of 1987. It currently has approximately 42,000 active, reserve, and national guard forces. Special forces throughout the military, including the Army Rangers, Navy SEALs, and the Air Force Special Tactic Units, come under this command.

* Specifications and Standards

Naval Publications and Printing Service
Standardization Documents Order Desk
700 Robins Ave. Bldg. 4D

Be patient. If any phone number is incorrect, call (area code) 555-1212 and request the new listing.

Military and National Security

Philadelphia, PA 19111-5094 (215) 697-2179

This Center is the DOD's distribution point for unclassified specifications and standards used to determine requirements for military procurement. Military personnel can obtain the *Index of Specifications and Standards* from this Center. The general public can obtain it from the Government Printing Office, Superintendent of Documents, Washington, DC 20402; (202) 783-3238. Contact the Center for the following types of information:

Military specifications and standards
Federal specifications and standards
Qualified product lists
Military handbooks
Air Force-Navy aeronautical specifications and standards
Air Force specifications
Air Force specifications bulletins
Air Force-Navy aeronautical bulletins

* Star Wars and Advanced Defense Technology

Strategic Defense Initiative Organization (SDI)
The Pentagon
Washington, DC 20301-7100 (703) 695-8743

SDI is responsible for overseeing development of the defensive system popularly known as Star Wars - a defensive system against enemy ballistic missiles. Under the authority and direction of the Secretary of Defense, SDI manages and directs research in advanced technology that will provide the technological basis for national defense decisions relating to nuclear ballistic missiles and defensive system. The agency utilizes the services of the military, the U.S. Department of Energy, private industry, and educational and research institutions. Some publications are available to the public from the above listed office, including *SDI's Annual Report to Congress* and various booklets about SDI activities. For further information, contact the above office.

* Star Wars and Other Defense Research Information

Office of Assistant Secretary of Defense
Public Affairs, Directorate for Defense Information
Pentagon 2E765
Washington, DC 20301-1400 (703) 695-3886

This office can supply you with fact sheets, press releases, and reports on defense programs such as Star Wars, the DOD Laser and Space Program, and the Defense Advanced Research Projects Agency (DARPA) activities, and related Congressional activity. Staff can also direct you in making FOIA requests for Defense contract information.

* Strategic Bomber Forces

Strategic Air Command, HQ/SAC/PA
901 SAC Blvd. Suite 1A1
Offutt AFB, NE 68113-5150 (402) 294-4130

This Command is headquarters for America's B-52, B-1 and B-2 strategic bomber forces, as well as America's arsenal of intercontinental missiles. SAC also has bases at Beale AFB, California; Barksdale AFB, Louisiana; March AFB, California; and Vandenberg AFB; California. For more information on SAC, its forces and its mission, contact SAC at the above address.

* Strategic Defense Research

U.S. Army Strategic Defense Command
Public Affairs Office
P.O. Box 1500
Huntsville, AL 35807-3801 (205) 955-3887

The U.S. Army Strategic Defense Command conducts programs designed to defeat ballistic missile attacks at each phase of their trajectory. The program has recently been expanded to include Theater missile defense. Army programs work on developing technologies for Systems Analysis/ Battle Management as well as various types of energy weapons. In conjunction with the Strategic Defense Initiative, the Army is conducting programs on ground based interceptors and tracking. For information and fact sheets on individual programs, call or write to the Command.

* Surplus Property from Defense Department

Defense Reutilization and Marketing Service
Public Affairs Office
P.O. Box 1370

Battle Creek, MI 49016-1370 (616) 961-7331

This office manages and disposes of surplus property from all U.S. Department of Defense agencies. Many items are for sale by public auction. Write or call for free pamphlets on how to buy DOD surplus property and applications for the national bidders mailing list. For local sales, contact the nearest DRMS office or the above office for a referral.

* Tactical Weapons: Database Searches for Contractors

GACIAC/IIT Research Institute
10 W. 35th St.
Chicago, IL 60616 (312) 567-4345

This organization offers user guides, a bi-monthly bulletin, and complex database searches on tactical weapons guidance and control, information, and analysis. Write or call for further information; requesters must be registered DOD contractors.

* Tanks and Armor Research

U.S. Army Tank Automotive Command
ATTN. AMSTA-CB
Warren, MI 48397-5000 (313) 574-5388

This Command conducts research into combat tactical and special purpose vehicles. Component programs involve engines, transmissions, suspensions, electrical and miscellaneous vehicular components. Call or write for more information.

* Technical Assistance to Foreign Countries

U.S. Army Corps of Engineers
Attn: CEMP-MG
20 Massachusetts Ave., NW
Washington, DC 20314-1000 (202) 272-0641

Through its Foreign Military Sales Program, the Army Corps of Engineers can provide a full range of services to foreign governments, including construction management, research and development, procurement, training, and engineering design. For information, contact the above office.

* Technical Exchange Between Government and Industry

Government Industry Data Exchange Program
GIDEP Operations Center
Corona, CA 91720-5000 (714) 736-4677

GIDEP is a data exchange program between government and industry. Members have access to five databases, grouped by subject: Failure Experience; Engineering; Reliability, Maintainability and Quality; Metrology; and Value Engineering. In addition, GIDEP has a newsletter and an *Urgent Data Request System*. For a free information package on program services, membership, and application forms, write or call the above office.

* Technical Expertise at Federal Labs

Defense Technical Information Center
Cameron Station, DTIC-BC
Alexandria, VA 22304-6145 (703) 274-6434

The Defense Technical Information Center maintains a Domestic Technology Referral Data Base, supplying a broad referral to federal laboratories and their areas of expertise. The service is available to all legitimate requesters; the requester need not be a "registered user." Call or write for information.

* Technology Research Army Libraries

U.S. Army Materiel Command
Information Systems Command
Public Affairs Office
Timberlake, AZ (602) 538-8609

Each Army Materiel Command installation has a technological library. It is usually possible to gain access to the library if you obtain prior approval. Contact your local AMC for information, or the above office for a referral to your closest installation.

* Technology Transfer and Systems Engineering

Director of Publications, DRI-P
Defense Systems Management College

Be patient. If any phone number is incorrect, call (area code) 555-1212 and request the new listing.

International Relations and Defense

Ft. Belvoir, VA 22060-5426 (703) 664-5082

This College publishes 28 books and a bi-monthly magazine entitled *Program Manager* (subscription, $7.50 per year). Titles include *Systems Engineering Management Guide* (a Government Printing Office all-time best-seller), *Cost Estimating, Subcontract Management Guide, Skill in Communications,* and *Program Office Guide to Technology Transfer.* All apply to acquisition and program management. Write for a free publications list explaining where to purchase them, stock numbers, and prices. Non-government employees must order publications through GPO at (202) 783-3238. The editor will also supply a sample copy of the *Program Manager* upon written request.

* Technology Transfer Competitiveness

Administrator
Federal Laboratory Consortium (FLC)
P.O. Box 545
Sequim, WA 98382 (206) 683-1005

The mission of the Consortium is to facilitate technology transfer among government, business, and academic entities in order to foster American economic and technological competitiveness. It sponsors conferences and seminars and publishes a free monthly newsletter (currently no charge). For very specific questions from bona fide researchers who find themselves at an impasse, the Consortium will conduct a database search to refer the inquirer to an appropriate lab. Write or call for a free general information packet explaining the organization, how to access its services, facilities available for testing, and examples of technology transfers. Also ask for the Consortium's newsletter *News Link,* which regularly provides updates on FLC activities. The FLC also has regional contacts:

Far West Region . . . . (619) 553-2101
Midwest Region . . . . (513) 255-2006
Northeast Region . . . . (609) 484-6689
Mid-Atlantic Region . . . . (202) 653-1442
Washington DC Rep . . . . (202) 331-4220
Southeast Region . . . . (601) 688-2042
Mid-Continental Region . . . . (501) 541-4516

* Test Flight History

Air Force Flight Test Center
Air Force Systems Command
U.S. Department of the Air Force
Edwards Air Force Base, CA 93523 (805) 277-3510

The History Office on Edwards Air Force Base has an archival library of history documents about the base. Videotapes of historical events are also available for viewing on site. Call or write the above office for information on its holdings.

* Time: Naval Observatory's Atomic Clock

Atomic Clock
National Observatory
34th and Massachusetts Ave.
Washington, DC 20392-5100 (202) 653-1541

The Observatory's Master Clock is the source for all standard time in the United States. For the correct time, call the number above, or dial 1-900-410-TIME if you are outside of the DC area.

* Training Methods Speakers Bureau

U.S. Army Research Institute for
Behavioral and Social Sciences
5001 Eisenhower Ave., Room 6E06
Alexandria, VA 22333 (703) 274-8683

The Institute conducts research for the military on educational and training methods and organizational effectiveness. Requests may be made to its Speakers Bureau for experts in the field. Copies of its published reports may be obtained through the Defense Technology Information Center.

* Training Military Doctors

Uniformed Services University of Health Sciences
U.S. Department of Defense
4301 Jones Bridge Road, Room A1045
Bethesda, MD 20814 (301) 295-3101

Physicians for the military services and for the Public Health Service are educated at this institution. In addition to a school of medicine and graduate and continuing education programs, the university incorporates the Military Medical Education Institute which provides combat training for health care professionals in the military service. You can obtain information and brochures from the above address.

* Trinity Test Site

Public Affairs Office
White Sands Missile Range
New Mexico, NM 88002 (505) 678-1700

This was the site of the first Atomic test explosion, July 16, 1945. While the site still has trace radiation from the test, a short visit exposes one to no more radiation than many other activities undertaken in a typical year. Call the Range for more information on visiting Trinity.

* Underwater Defense Systems Research

Office of Public Affairs
Naval Underwater Systems Center
U.S. Department of the Navy
Newport Laboratory
Newport, RI 02840 (401) 841-2182

Underwater warfare systems and components, undersea surveillance systems, navigation systems, and related technologies are developed, tested, and analyzed at the Center. The Office of Public Affairs sometimes has publications on hand or can refer you to appropriate information sources within the Center.

* U.S. Military Installations Atlas

Directorate for Information Operations and Reports
Washington Headquarters Services
1215 Jefferson Davis Hwy., Suite 1204
Arlington, VA 22202 (703) 746-0786

The *Atlas/Data Abstract for the United States and Selected Areas* contains a map showing all the military installations and a compendium of U.S. Department of Defense statistics for each state. Write or call for their free catalog list all their publications available through the Government Printing Office.

* Vendor Sales to Military Exchanges

Headquarters
Army and Air Force Exchange Service
Attn: PA-I
P.O. Box 660202
Dallas, TX 75266-0202 (214) 312-2011

This office supplies the brochure, *Suppliers Handbook,* which explains how to sell to the Army and Air Force military exchanges. Call or write for free copies.

* Vietnam Casualty Computer Printout

Center for Electronic Records
National Archives and Records Administration
Washington, DC 20408 (202) 501-5402

This office holds all Federal records on computer disk, which include all recent DOD records and the casualty lists from the Vietnam War. Copies may be purchased.

* Voluntary Draft and Selective Service Compliance

Selective Service System
1023 31st St., NW
Washington, DC 20435 (202) 724-0820

Applicants for Title IV federal student aid, Job Training Partnership Ace benefits, and those young men seeking employment with the federal government who are required to register must be in compliance with the registration requirement in order to be eligible for those programs. For more information, contact this office.

* Waterways and Wetlands R & D

Research and Development Division
U.S. Army Corps of Engineers
CERD-ZA
20 Massachusetts Ave NW
Washington, DC 20314-1000 (202) 272-0254

Be patient. If any phone number is incorrect, call (area code) 555-1212 and request the new listing.

Contact this office for information and referral on Corps of Engineers research and development into reservoir water quality; coastal ecology; aquatic plant control; environmental impact of development projects; designing dams, locks, and other hydraulic structures for earthquakes; river ice and winter navigation; battlefield environment; Army installations; and combat engineering.

* Weapons Lab Super Computer Center

U.S. Air Force Super Computer Center
Kirtland Air Force Base, NM 87117-6008 (505) 646-5354

The Super Computer Center is administered by the Weapons Laboratory. Academic researchers sponsored by the U.S. Department of Defense may have access to the Cray 1 and Cray 2 super computer services and a bi-monthly

newsletter. Write or call for their brochure on how to subscribe for time on the computer, eligibility for use, and prices.

* Weapons Museum

U.S. Army Ordnance Museum
Aberdeen Proving Ground
Aberdeen, MD 23005 (301) 278-3602

This museum holds the free world's largest collection of military weapons and paraphernalia, including captured W.W. II German V-2 rockets, the one and only atomic cannon, and handguns with curved barrels to shoot around corners. It's open to the public Tuesday through Sunday, and admission is free. You can also write for their pamphlet, *Welcome to the U.S. Army Ordnance Museum.*

Be patient. If any phone number is incorrect, call (area code) 555-1212 and request the new listing.

Science and Technology General Sources

* *See also Experts*
* *See also Current Events and Homework*
* *See also Economics, Demographics, and Statistics*
* *See also Patents, Trademarks and Copyrights*
* *See also National Security and International Affairs*

Part of the reason we are suffering from an information explosion can be attributed to technology. About 90 percent of all scientific knowledge has been generated since 1950. And, according to the U.S. Department of Commerce, this knowledge is expected to double again in the next ten to fifteen years. Technology, once again, has recaptured the interest and investment of both American business and the public. In 1982, *Time* magazine selected the computer as its "Man of the Year." Continuing this trend, April 22-28, 1992 was designated National Science and Technology Week. In 1992 President Bush also launched his National Technology Initiative to increase U.S. strength in new technology. In line with this initiative, the National Institute of Standards and Technology held a special series of conferences on new technology throughout 1992.

This section will introduce you to the major sources of information about technology throughout the government, including those located at the National Technical Information Service (NTIS), the Science and Technology Reading Room at the Library of Congress, the Office of Technology Assessment, and the U.S. Department of Defense. Through these sources you'll find sources of information on everything from Alzheimer's disease and genetic fingerprinting to supercomputers and commercial biotechnology.

* 3 Million Science and Technical Books

Science and Technology Division
Library of Congress
Washington, DC 20540
(202) 707-5639

The Science and Technology collection contains more than 3 million scientific and technical books and pamphlets and 3 million technical reports, including those issued by the U.S. Department of Energy, NASA, the U.S. Department of Defense, and other government agencies. The collections, which are particularly strong in aeronautical materials, contain first editions of Copernicus and Newton and the personal papers of the Wright Brothers and Alexander Graham Bell. Computer terminals provide principal access to the collections. Special scientific finding aids, such as abstracting and indexing journals, are part of the division's reference collection. This Division also prepares an informal series of reference guides called *Tracer Bullets*, which are available free upon request. More extensive bibliographies are published from time to time.

* Adolescent Health

Office of Technology Assessment (OTA)
600 Pennsylvania Ave., SE
Washington, DC 20510
(202) 228-6590

OTA is working on a project to assess the health status of adolescents 10 to 18 years old and identify factors that put adolescents at risk for health problems, including racial and ethnic backgrounds, socioeconomic status, gender, and developmental stage. Particular attention will be paid to the availability, effectiveness, and accessibility of health services for adolescents. Contact Denise Dougherty, the project director, for more information.

* Aging Nuclear Power Plants

Office of Technology Assessment (OTA)
600 Pennsylvania Ave, SE
Washington, DC 20510
(202) 228-6285

Existing nuclear power plants supply 20% of the nations electricity. Some plants are nearing the end of their initial 40 year license. Preliminary analyses indicate that it may be safe and cost effective to extend these licenses another 20 years. The OTA is currently working on a study to examine the economic, technical, institutional, and safety factors determining the useful lives of existing nuclear power plants. It will examine both the prospects for life extension of nuclear plants and the cost and performance of those plants in attaining their currently licensed operating lives. Decommissioning technology will also be examined. Contact project director Robin Roy for more information.

* Agrichemical Contaminations of Groundwater

Office of Technology Assessment (OTA)
600 Pennsylvania Ave., SE
Washington, DC 20510
(202) 228-6516

To assess agricultural technology that may reduce groundwater contamination, OTA is reviewing data and literature on extent, types, and sources of agrichemical contamination, and on hydrogeological, crop type, and cropping system relationships. The study will also assess likely impacts of these new technologies, especially on the environment farm economics, rural communities, and the structure of agriculture. Contact Alison Hess, the project director, for more information.

* Agriculture Research Service (ARS) Programs

Information Staff
Beltsville Agricultural Research Center, Room 307A
10301 Baltimore Blvd
Beltsville, MD 20705
(301) 504-6264

The ARS of the USDA conducts research in several areas designed to increase the quality of American crops, livestock, and nutrition. ARS also conducts research designed to improve the competitiveness of U.S. agriculture on the world market. For more information on specific ARS programs, contact the information office listed above.

* Air Force Research Grants

Office of Scientific Research
U.S. Air Force, Bolling Air Force Base
Washington, DC 20332
(202) 767-4910

This office accepts proposals for scientific research and requests for grants. Current research interests lie in the areas of Aerospace Sciences, Chemical and Materials Sciences, Physics and Electronics, Life and Environmental Sciences, and Mathematical and Computer Sciences. Write or call for copies of the *Research Interest* pamphlet, the *Proposer's Guide*, the *Grant Brochure* (which lists the types of grants available), and technical brochures on Air Force research programs.

Be patient. If any phone number is incorrect, call (area code) 555-1212 and request the new listing.

General Sources

* American Association for the Advancement of Science

1333 H Street, NW
Washington, DC 20005 (202) 326-6400

The largest scientific organization in the country with membership exceeding 136,000, this association was formed to promote increased public understanding of science and technology. Its activities are divided regionally and by field of interest, and it also sponsors international events such as its annual meeting which brings together scientists from all over the world. The Association can provide information about major scientific and technological issues, and staff will help you locate both specialists and printed materials. It publishes *Science Magazine* as well books about topics of immediate scientific interest, as well as directories and other materials of interest to its members.

* Association for Computing Machinery

1515 Broadway
New York, NY 10036 (212) 869-7440

This large educational and scientific society is concerned with all aspects of computer science and its applications. The Association's 32 Special Interest Groups (SIGs) and numerous local chapters throughout the US provide members with a variety of forums and continuing education programs. The SIGs focus on subjects ranging from Automata and Computability Theory (ACT) to Software Engineering (SIGSOFT). Each group holds an annual conference, the proceedings of which are published by the Association, and publishes 11 journals covering different aspects of R&D and application in the computer field. A free publications catalog is available.

* Association of Science-Technology Centers (ASTC)

1025 Vermont Ave, NW, Suite 500
Washington, DC 20005-3516 (202) 783-7200

With over 400 members, this association of science museums and science/ technology centers promotes public understanding of science and technology. It publishes a quarterly calendar of museum exhibits. ASTC sponsors conferences which are open to the public. It sells surveys about computers, along with a bimonthly newsletter. Call for more information and for a publications list.

* Biological Research on Addiction

Office of Technology Assessment (OTA)
600 Pennsylvania Ave, SE
Washington, DC 20510 (202) 228-6692

Substance abuse costs the U.S. billions of dollars each year in crime, health costs, and lost productivity/human potential. OTA is currently evaluating the state of the art of biological research on addiction to various substances as well as other studies on addition and treatment. Contact project director Kevin O'Connor for more information.

* Ballistic Research and Engineering

Ballistic Research Laboratories
314 Ryan Building
Aberdeen Proving Ground, MD 21005-5066 (301) 278-6954

This is an advanced technology laboratory conducting basic and applied research in mathematics, physics, chemistry, biophysics, and engineering related to defense ballistics. Write or call for more information.

* Basic Energy Sciences Research

Office of Basic Energy Sciences
Office of Energy Research
U.S. Department of Energy
19901 Germantown Rd.
Germantown, MD 20585 (301) 903-3081

The Basic Energy Sciences office supports some 1,400 research projects and is organized to manage research in five areas: Materials Science, Chemical Sciences, Engineering and Geosciences, Advanced Energy Projects, and Energy Biosciences.

Materials Research

This research seeks to mitigate unforseen materials problems in advanced energy systems. The current emphasis of the program is on high temperature superconductivity, use of supercomputers in calculations and modeling of materials phenomena, polymer research, surfaces and interface research, and materials synthesis and processing science. [Contact at DOE: (301) 903-3427.]

Chemical Sciences Research

This Chemical Sciences subprogram includes research that impacts such fields as photovoltaics, production of fuels and chemicals from coal, catalysis, nuclear waste separation, conversion of biomass into liquid fuels, separation of metals from low-grade mineral resources, combustion, and detection and measurement of harmful by products of energy processes. [Contact at DOE: (301) 903-5804.]

Engineering and Geosciences

The objective of the engineering research program is to provide experimental tests of theories and models of processes needed for energy production facilities and for increased energy efficiency. The geosciences research is aimed at developing a quantitative, predictive understanding of the energy-related aspects of geological, geophysical and geochemical processes both in the earth and at the solar-terrestrial interface. [Contact at DOE: (301) 903-5822.]

Applied Mathematical Sciences

This program supports research in mathematics and computer science required by DOE researchers.

Advanced Energy Projects

This program supports research that explores the feasibility of novel energy-related concepts evolving from basic research. Projects are supported typically for about three years, at which time it is expected that they will transferred to a technology program or private industry. [Contact at DOE: (301) 903-5995.]

Energy Biosciences

This subprogram focuses on understanding the limits of productivity in green plants how plants adapt to suboptimal conditions of growth and the mechanisms of microbial conversion of various biomass forms. An integral part of the subprogram is the development of genetic information that may ultimately be used to produce new or improved microorganisms and plants to facilitate the production of fuels or petroleum-saving chemicals or to yield biotechnologies capable of conserving energy. [Contact at DOE: (301) 903-2873.]

* Biotechnology and a Global Economy

Office of Technology Assessment (OTA)
600 Pennsylvania Ave., SE
Washington, DC 20510 (202) 228-6692

OTA is currently working on a study to identify current U.S. capabilities in various applications of biotechnology and compare these capabilities with efforts underway internationally. They will also address trade, export, and international intellectual property issues relevant to the safe and timely commercialization of products derived from biotechnology. Contact Kevin O'Connor, the project director, for more information.

* Ceramics and Metals Research

U.S. Department of the Army
Army Materials Technology Lab
Watertown, MA 02172-0001 (617) 923-5278

This Center specializes in research regarding metals and ceramics. Major programs currently include: the battle against Corrosion; Advanced Armor; Structural Ceramics; Elastomers; and Composite Materials Hull. The Lab's work has done much to improve the armors of American mechanized forces. It maintains a library open to approved researchers, and copies of technical reports are available upon request. Write or call for free brochures describing the Center, its mission, and programs.

* Cold Environments Research

U.S. Army Corps of Engineers
Army Cold Regions Research and Engineering Laboratory
72 Lyme Rd.
Hanover, NH 03755-1290 (603) 646-4100

This Laboratory conducts research on living, working, traveling, building and military operations in cold environments. A Speakers Bureau will provide experts to speak before civic groups. The Laboratory also has an extensive library on cold regions research. The Library of Congress prepares the *Bibliography on Cold Regions Science and Technology*. Write or call for brochures explaining the mission and programs, accessing information from the library, and how to do business with the Laboratory.

* Commercial Low-Level Radioactive Waste

Office of Technology Assessment (OTA)

Be patient. If any phone number is incorrect, call (area code) 555-1212 and request the new listing.

Science and Technology

600 Pennsylvania Ave., SE
Washington, DC 20510 (202) 228-6852
OTA is working on a project to analyze the Federal effort and State progress in implementing the Low-Level Radioactive Waste Policy Amendments Act, which identifies Federal activities needed to help States meet milestones for developing disposal facilities. Contact Gretchen Hund McCabe, the project director, for more information.

* Communications Networks and New Technologies

Office of Technology Assessment (OTA)
600 Pennsylvania Ave., SE
Washington, DC 20510 (202) 228-6774
Recent advances in information storage and transmission technologies, occurring in a new deregulated and intensely competitive economic climate, are rapidly changing the Nation's communication networks. OTA is studying the role of the Federal government in this area, along with how to coordinate them, resolve potential conflicts between them, and examine new communication systems abroad and their potential relationships to the U.S. systems. Contact Linda Garcia, the project director, for more information.

* Computer Information/Research

National Technical Information Service (NTIS)
U.S. Department of Commerce
5285 Port Royal Rd.
Springfield, VA 22161 (703) 487-4650
NTIS puts out the following reports related to computers and information systems:

American National Dictionary for Information Systems. Offers precise definitions of terms relating to information systems and services as the official source for US Government contract terminology in this area. Price - $50.

Computer Viruses and Related Threats. Addresses the current problem of computer viruses, analyzing where they attack and why they are on the rise. Price - $17.

Federal Information Processing Standards Program. These standards serve as the official source within the Federal Government for information on the approval, implementation and maintenance of FIPS resulting from the provisions of Public Law 89-306. Call for prices.

POSIX Conformance Test Suite (PCTS). This program tests the conformance of computer operating system environments to the FIPS release 151, which defines the standard for functional interface between an operating environment and applications to promote applications portability. Price - $2,500.

* Computerized Data File Directory

Directory of Computerized Datafiles
National Technical Information Service
U.S. Department of Commerce
5285 Port Royal Rd.
Springfield, VA 22161 (703) 487-4650
The annual, *Computerized Data File Directory* contains more than 1,300 source files for unique Federal numeric and text data. This publication offers its readers a single, convenient reference to important datafiles prepared by a variety of Federal agencies. The cost is $55. Call the Sales Desk to place an order or ask for a free information brochure *PR-629*.

* Computer Software Directory

Directory of Computer Software
National Technical Information Service
U.S. Department of Commerce
5285 Port Royal Rd.
Springfield, VA 22161 (703) 487-4650
This directory contains detailed descriptions of software applications and tools. Information has been compiled in cooperation with hundreds of U.S. Government agencies. More than 1,700 programs are arranged under 21 subject headings. Full indexes by subject, hardware, language, and sponsoring agency are included. Agencies providing programs include the National Library of Medicine, Environmental Protection Agency, U.S. Department of Defense, the U.S. Department of Energy, plus many others. The cost is $55. Contact the Sales Desk of place an order or ask for a free information brochure *PR-261*.

* Congressional Fellowships

Personnel Office
Office of Technology Assessment (OTA)
Congress of the United States
Washington, DC 20510 (202) 224-9241
OTA awards up to six fellowships each year, providing an opportunity for individuals of demonstrated outstanding ability to gain a better understanding of science and technology issues facing Congress, along with the ways in which Congress establishes national policy related to these issues. Applications must be received by January 31. Stipends range from $28,000 to $55,000, depending upon background and experience. For further information, write this office.

* Critical Technologies

National Technical Information Service
U.S. Department of Commerce
5285 Port Royal Rd.
Springfield, VA 22161 (703) 487-4650
The President's Council on Competitiveness has examined America's declining position in the area of critical technologies and makes recommendations as to what the country must do to regain its position as world leader in this area. The cost of this report is $20. Order number is PB91-180281CAU.

* Current Technology Assessment Activities

Publishing Office
Office of Technology Assessment (OTA)
600 Pennsylvania Ave.
SE, Washington, DC 20510 (202) 224-8996
Free upon request, this booklet provides Members of Congress with brief summaries of OTA's current work projects and their anticipated completion dates.

* Cystic Fibrosis Research

Office of Technology Assessment (OTA)
600 Pennsylvania Ave, SE
Washington, DC 20510 (202) 228-6690
Cystic fibrosis is the most common lethal genetic disease in the U.S. Pressure is building or widespread carrier screening for the disorder. This OTA assessment will: gather technical information on cystic fibrosis diagnosis and treatment; examine prospects for additional DNA tests to detect additional cystic fibrosis mutations; analyze legal, economic, and ethical issues in population screening for the disorder. Contact project director Robyn Nishimi for more information.

* Defense Technical Information and Referral Center

Defense Technical Information Center (DTIC)
Cameron Station
Alexandria, VA 22304-6145 (703) 617-7931
DTIC maintains a *Referral Data Bank Directory* of major resource and holding centers in the U.S. Department of Defense. Write or call the above office for more information.

* Digital Spatial Data and Mapping Software

U.S. Geological Survey
Reston-ESIC
507 National Center
Reston, VA 22092 (703) 648-6045
The U.S. Geological Survey's Earth Science Information Center (ESIC) now offers inventories of digital spatial data sets and cartographic applications software in two bound listings. These inventories provide up-to-date bibliographic descriptions of data sets and software available from federal, state, and local government agencies and the private sector.

Sources for Digital Spatial Data. Describes more than 500 data sets containing spatially referenced base or thematic categories of data. The data sets are indexed by geographic area of coverage and cross-indexed by type of data.

Sources for Software for Computer Mapping and Related Disciplines. Describes more than 700 subroutines, programs, and systems that can be used in geographic information systems, map and chart plotting and construction, image processing and analysis, surveying, photogrammetry, data modeling and analysis, coordinate conversion, and other applications. Each publication is $22.

Be patient. If any phone number is incorrect, call (area code) 555-1212 and request the new listing.

General Sources

* Defense Nuclear Waste and Contamination Cleanup

Office of Technology Assessment (OTA)
600 Pennsylvania Ave., SE
Washington, DC 20510 (202) 228-6862

Today there is a large backlog of high-level, transuranic, low-level, hazardous, and mixed nuclear waste at the 15 facilities in the U.S. Department of Energy's nuclear weapons complex. OTA is currently studying how best to clean up this nuclear waste problem using technologies for waste management and minimizations. Contact Peter Johnson, the project director, for more information.

* Digital Spatial Data Applications Cooperation

U.S. Geological Survey
Reston-ESIC, 507 National Center
Reston, VA 22092 (703) 648-6899

If your organization is involved in digital spatial data applications, the Earth Science Information Center invites you to contribute information about your holdings. Your data and software may be valuable to other users.

* Drug Labeling in Developing and Newly-Industrialized Countries

Office of Technology Assessment (OTA)
600 Pennsylvania Ave., SE
Washington, DC 20510 (202) 228-6590

The U.S. pharmaceutical industry is a major supplier of pharmaceuticals to developing countries, but the industry has been criticized for mislabeling certain drugs sold in those countries. OTA is currently studying whether inappropriate labeling is occurring today to allow health workers in those developing countries to use drugs safely and effectively. Contact Bob McDonough, the project director, for more information.

* Earth System Data Directory

National Oceanographic Data Center
NOAA/NESDIS E/OCx7
Washington, DC 20235 (202) 673-5548

The NOAA Earth System Data Directory provides users with an on-line catalogue and index to data files and data sets held by elements of the National Oceanographic and Atmospheric Administration. Most entries at this time describe data held by NOAA's three national data centers, but the directory will become increasingly comprehensive as other NOAA offices add descriptions of their data holdings. The directory may be searched by scientific discipline, measured parameters, time period, geographic location, project, and other criteria. The directory was developed by NASA. For more information, contact NOAA at the above listing.

* Education Technologies

Office of Technology Assessment (OTA)
600 Pennsylvania Ave., SE
Washington, DC 20510 (202) 228-6936

New curriculum requirements, shortages of qualified teachers in some subjects, sparse student enrollment in some regions, and rising costs for educational services contribute to an increasing need for effective methods for providing instruction. OTA is currently studying these problems and the various technological options, their costs, effectiveness, and tradeoffs, in the K-12 school setting. Contact Linda Roberts, the project director, for more information.

* Electromagnetic Technology

Directorate for Public Communication
U.S. Department of Defense
The Pentagon, Room 2E777
Washington, DC 20301-1400 (703) 697-5737

This office can provide you with general information about electromagnetic technology, including annual reports, newsletters and fact sheets, and will make referrals for you if you need more detailed information.

* Emerging Agricultural Technology

Office of Technology Assessment (OTA)
600 Pennsylvania Ave., SE
Washington, DC 20510 (202) 228-6521

OTA is studying the emerging agricultural technologies for the 1990s and the structure of the research system that gives rise to these technologies, which include biotechnology, information technology, and low input technology for the food and agricultural sector. Contact Mike Phillips, the project director, for more information.

* Emerging Technologies

National Technical Information Service
U.S. Department of Commerce
5285 Port Royal Rd.
Springfield, VA 22161 (703) 487-4650

This report identifies twelve technologies in four commercial areas that will create markets for an estimated $1 trillion in sales by the year 2000. The four commercial areas covered are: advanced materials; electronics and information systems, manufacturing systems, and life sciences applications. The cost of this document is $19, order number PB90-216557CAU.

* Energy and Environmental Technology Transfer to Eastern Europe

Office of Technology Assessment (OTA)
600 Pennsylvania Ave, SE
Washington, DC 20510 (202) 228-6427

Aiding the formerly communist nations of Eastern Europe and the Soviet Union through the transfer of energy and environmental technology can benefit the West by reducing their demand for energy supplies and by controlling pollution. This OTA study will review the energy technology needs in Eastern Europe and the former Soviet Union with an eye towards increasing the efficiency of energy use and production. The study will also determine which technologies the U.S. can supply and outline options to Congress for U.S. policy in this area. For more information, contact project director Alan Crane.

* Energy Bioscience Research

Office of Energy Research
Energy Biosciences Division
U.S. Department of Energy
19901 Germantown Rd., Room G-34
Germantown, MD 20585 (301) 903-2873

This office funds fundamental research in the plant and microbial sciences that will underpin new biotechnologies related to energy matters.

* Energy Pollutants Health Research

Health Effects and Life Sciences Research Division
Office of Health and Environmental Research
U.S. Department of Energy
19901 Germantown Rd.
Germantown, MD 20585 (301) 903-5468

This Division conducts studies to characterize and develop a basis for understanding biological phenomena used in predicting human health effects from exposure to energy pollutants. It conducts fundamental research into structural, molecular, and cellular biology, and develops technologies and resources needed to characterize the molecular nature of the human genome.

* Energy Related Chemical Research

Office of Energy Research
Chemical Sciences Division
19901 Germantown Rd., Room G-34
Germantown, MD 20585 (301) 903-5804

This office funds and administers programs in energy-related chemical sciences research such as photochemistry, radiation chemistry, hot atom chemistry, chemical dynamics, theoretical chemistry, spectroscopy, and the physics of ions, atoms, and molecules. It also supports research in the area of chemical thermodynamics related to energy resources such as coal. Contact this office for more information on facilities available for researchers.

* Energy Science and Technology Database

National Technical Information Service
U.S. Department of Commerce
5285 Port Royal Rd.
Springfield, VA 22161 (703) 487-4929

Be patient. If any phone number is incorrect, call (area code) 555-1212 and request the new listing.

Science and Technology

The ESTD is a multidisciplinary file containing two and a half million references to the world's scientific and energy related literature. In addition to nuclear science and technology and basic scientific studies in biology, chemistry, engineering, geology, physics, nuclear medicine, computers, and environment and pollution, it contains more than a million entries in areas not considered strictly energy fields, e.g. nuclear medicine computers, and mathematical models. Contact NTIS for more information.

* Energy Services in Developing Nations

Office of Technology Assessment (OTA)
600 Pennsylvania Ave SE
Washington, DC 20510 (202) 228-6267

Energy is an essential ingredient for development. Increased energy demand must be carefully managed so as to ensure resources are not wasted and do not cause environmental damage. This study will examine how technology can contribute to the goal of sound and productive energy development in the world's poorer nations, and the role of U.S. policy and the relevant international organizations in encouraging the rapid adoption of improved technologies. Contact Joy Dunkerly for more information.

* Energy Systems Vulnerability

Office of Technology Assessment (OTA)
600 Pennsylvania Ave., SE
Washington, DC 20510 (202) 228-6427

A study is underway at OTA to assess the vulnerability of certain energy producing and delivery systems--electricity, natural gas, and refined oil products--to disruption by either terrorist actions or massive natural disasters. Contact Alan Crane, the project director, for more information.

* Environmental Research Technology Transfer

Center for Environmental Research Information
Environmental Protection Agency (EPA)
26 West Martin Luther King Dr.
Cincinnati, OH 45263 (513) 569-7391

The Office of Research and Development of the EPA has centralized most of its information distribution and technology transfer activities in the Center for Environmental Research Information listed above. CERI also serves as a central point of distribution for ORD research results and reports.

* European Technology and U.S. Trade

Office of Technology Assessment (OTA)
600 Pennsylvania Ave., SE
Washington, DC 20510 (202) 228-6354

The OTA is currently studying how the European Commission's Single Market Act and the technology projects of Europe affect U.S. manufacturers and trade, particularly in high-technology sectors like microelectronics, computers, and telecommunications equipment. The study is comparing how technology development in chosen industrial sectors has worked in both Europe and East Asia, and assessing the conditions under which governmental participation and collaboration between firms, universities, and government has succeeded or failed. Contact Julie Gorte, the project director, for more information.

* European Technology in Computers, Telecommunications and Electronics

National Technical Information Service
U.S. Department of Commerce
5285 Port Royal Rd.
Springfield, VA 22161 (703) 487-4650

This report, prepared by the Department of the Navy, provides material important for those doing business in the areas of computers, telecommunications, and electronics. The report looks at the impact of microcomputers, distributed systems, supercomputers, and minicomputers are having on the European computer market. It also describes the European programs in the area of Integrated Services Digital Network. Cost is $19; order number PB90-215773CAU.

* Federal Laboratory Consortium (FLC)

U.S. Department of Agriculture
Extension Service
14th and Independence Ave., S.W.

Room 3865, South Building
Washington, DC 20250-0900 (202) 720-7185

FLC is a national network of 300 individuals from federal laboratories and centers across the country. Members are responsible for assessing the technologies developed at their facility and then passing that knowledge onto industry, government, and the general public. Through the FLC the public can gain access to all unclassified research conducted by the federal government. The FLC director can refer you to an FLC member in your specialty or geographical area. Its *Federal Laboratory Directory 1985* provides data on 388 federal laboratories with ten or more full-time professionals engaged in R&D. Information is provided about staff size, mission, and major scientific or testing equipment. The Directory can be obtained for free from the NTIS, 5285 Port Royal Rd., Springfield, VA 22161, (703) 487-4600.

* Federal Research in Progress Database

National Technical Information Service
U.S. Department of Commerce
5285 Port Royal Rd.
Springfield, VA 22161 (703) 487-4650

FEDRIP summarizes 120,000 US Government funded research projects currently in progress. These summaries make it possible to determine progress in specific areas before technical reports or journal literature become available. The database content focuses on health, physical sciences, agriculture, engineering, and life sciences. Each listing describes a research project, its project, its objectives, and when available, preliminary findings. For a free brochure describing this service, contact NTIS and ask for PR847/827.

* Fermi National Accelerator Laboratory

Public Information Office
PO Box 500
Batavia, IL 60510 (312) 840-3351

This laboratory was established in 1967 to explore the field of elementary particle physics so that the understanding of the basic structure of matter may be broadened. A related mission is the improvement of accelerator design that has resulted in numerous technological spinoffs: the development of various applications other than magnets for superconductivity; fast electronics and particle detector technology; and special computers and computer programs.

* Forensic Uses of DNA Tests

Office of Technology Assessment (OTA)
600 Pennsylvania Ave., SE
Washington, DC 20510 (202) 228-6690

OTA is working on a project to gather technical information on the reliability of the various genetic techniques, assess costs and procedural uses raised by the rapid adoption of forensic genetic testing, and outline issues that will emerge as the genetic tests are more widely used. Contact Robyn Nishimi, the project director, for more information.

* Fusion Energy Research

Office of Fusion Energy
Office of Energy Research
U.S. Department of Energy
19901 Germantown Rd.
Germantown, MD 20585 (301) 903-4941

Magnetic fusion is a long term energy option that could become a principal energy source in the next century. The role of the Federal government in magnetic fusion is to establish the scientific and technological base required for an assessment of the feasibility of magnetic fusion as an energy source. Four issues are currently at the forefront of magnetic fusion research: improving magnetic confinement systems; determining the properties of burning plasmas; developing economic and environmentally suitable materials fusion systems; and developing nuclear technologies that can be successfully integrated into advanced fusion systems. Contact this office for more information on the current status of magnetic fusion research.

* Geotechnical Research

U.S. Army Corps of Engineers
Waterways Experiment Station
3909 Halls Ferry Rd.
Vicksburg, MS 39180-6199 (601) 634-2504

A component of the Geotechnical Lab, the Pavements and Soil Trafficability

General Sources

Information Analysis Center (PSTIAC) provides products and specialized reference services to the public. The staff can be tasked to provide evaluative engineering and/or analytical service on pavements, trafficability, vehicle mobility, and terrain, primarily relevant to military needs. Database searches are performed on a cost recovery basis, and requests are approved on a case by case basis. The Station's library participates in the national inter-library loan system, and copies of technical reports are distributed on a first come, first served basis. (Reports are thereafter available from DTIC.) The Public Affairs Office can provide a summary of publications, fact sheets on the Center's programs, brochures on subject areas, and a comprehensive book entitled *Summary of Capabilities* describing the Center's work. Time on the Center's super computer is available for sale to academic researchers.

* Health and Environmental Research

Office of Health and Environmental Research
Office of Energy Research
U.S. Department of Energy
19901 Germantown Rd.
Germantown, MD 20585 (301) 903-3251

The Office of Health and Environmental Research seeks to understand the long term health effects and environmental consequences of energy use and development. To this end, its program focus is on research in atmospheric, marine and terrestrial processes; molecular and subcellular mechanisms underlying human somatic and genetic processes and their responses to energy related environmental toxicants; nuclear medicine and epidemiology; and structural biology.

* Health Services Research

Health Services Research (152)
U.S. Department of Veterans Affairs
810 Vermont Ave., NW
Washington, DC 20420 (202) 233-5478

The goal of this research is to improve the effectiveness and efficiency of the U.S. Department of Veterans Affairs health care delivery system. Health services researchers develop and distribute information designed to help clinicians, investigators, and administrators select medical interventions and administrative actions that are most appropriate to the Agency's mission: the provision of quality medical care services to the veteran patient.

* High Energy Physics Advisory Panel

U.S. Department of Energy
19901 Germantown Rd., Room F-336
Germantown, MD 20585 (301) 903-4140

This Advisory Panel provides guidance to the Secretary of Energy on high energy physics research program which encompasses the Superconducting Super Collider (SSC) activities. The panel, among other things, recommends changes in the program based on scientific and technological advances.

* High Energy and Nuclear Physics Program

Office of Energy Research
U.S. Department of Energy
19901 Germantown Rd.
Germantown, MD 20585 (301) 903-3713

The High Energy and Nuclear Physics Programs seek a deeper understanding of the nature of matter and energy and the basic forces that exist between the fundamental constituents of matter. The program focuses on obtaining an understanding of the ultimate structure of all matter and energy through the study of properties of elementary particles. This program is supported by three major research laboratories:

Fermi National Accelerator Laboratory - Batavia, Illinois.
The Tevatron, currently the worlds only superonducting proton synchrotron, is capable of accelerating particles to the highest energies available anywhere in the world.

Stanford Linear Accelerator Center - Menlo Park, CA.
The Stanford Linear Accelerator Center carries out experimental and theoretical research in high energy physics, and also developmental work in new techniques for particle acceleration and for experimental instrumentation. The Stanford Linear Collider project recently began and promises to be a major step toward reducing the cost of future high energy electron-positron colliders. It also gives U.S. physicists early access to the physics resulting from production of "Z" particles.

Brookhaven National Laboratory - Upton, NY.
The Alternating Gradient Synchrontron provides a facility for research using beams of protons, polarized protons, and various secondary particles, at energies up to 33 GeV. The main focus of the present research program using the proton primary beam are on studies of very rare decays of the K meson.

* Ice Navigational Technology

Planning Branch
Research and Development Staff
Office of Engineering and Development
U.S. Coast Guard
U.S. Department of Transportation
2100 2nd St., SW, Room 6208
Washington, DC 20593-0001 (202) 267-1030

Information can be obtained here about research conducted by the Coast Guard in support of its operations and responsibilities. Areas of study include ice operations, ocean dumping, law enforcement, environmental protection, port safety and security, navigation aids, search and rescue procedures, recreational boating, energy, and advanced marine vehicles. For referral to specific personnel working in these areas, contact the Planning Branch.

* Information Technology and Research

Office of Technology Assessment (OTA)
600 Pennsylvania Ave., SE
Washington, DC 20510 (202) 228-6787

Advanced information technology is having a major impact on the conduct of science and engineering research in nearly all disciplines--supercomputers, high resolution color displays, artificial intelligence software, and more. OTA is assessing the impact of advanced information technology on research, with particular emphasis on Federal programs to provide access to supercomputers and the Federal role in developing a national scientific network. Contact James Curlin, the project director, for more information.

* Infrastructure Technologies

Office of Technology Assessment (OTA)
600 Pennsylvania Ave., SE
Washington, DC 20510 (202) 228-6939

Public works infrastructure, which includes roads, bridges, sewers, etc., provides essential services--moving people and goods, supplying water, and disposing of waste. And there is little disagreement about the urgency of repair, maintenance, or new construction of these vital systems. OTA is currently studying how technological, institutional, and financial alternatives could be combined to meet the challenges posed by infrastructure needs that might be required in the Federal role. Contact Edith Page, the project director, for more information.

* Institute of Electrical and Electronics Engineers

IEEE Headquarters
345 East 47th Street
New York, NY 10017 (212) 705-7867

This large engineering society focuses on advancing the theory and practice of electrical engineering, electronics, computer engineering and computer science. IEEE consists of 30 technical societies corresponding to essentially every recognized discipline or interest area. There are, for example, societies for biomedical engineering, control systems, communications, and power engineering. The largest is the IEEE Computer Society. Staff at IEEE can respond to questions and refer you to members in regional chapters around the US. One of the organization's main functions is publishing technical literature, and presently it is credited with publishing 15% of the world's technical papers in the electrical and electronic fields. Each Society publishes one or more technical periodicals, usually called *Transactions* or *Journals*, which cover such fields as aerospace and electronic systems, electron devices, lightwave technology, microwave theory and techniques, and quantum electronics. The primary periodical is *IEEE Spectrum* which contains state-of-the-art news, reviews, and application articles of interest to many engineers and scientists. Call (212) 705-7890 for information on technical activities; and (201) 981-1393 for publications from the Piscataway, NJ, Service Center.

* Japanese Technology Evaluation Center

National Technical Information Service
U.S. Department of Commerce
5285 Port Royal Rd.

Be patient. If any phone number is incorrect, call (area code) 555-1212 and request the new listing.

Science and Technology

Springfield, VA 22161 (703) 487-4650
The Japanese Technology Evaluation Center issues a series of reports written by panels of U.S. industrial, government, and academic experts. These reports are definitive assessments of emerging Japanese efforts in selected high-technology areas. The JTEC evaluations provide technical input for those who make technology forecasts and competitive assessments and establish a direction for U.S. research and trade policies. The Center has numerous reports available. Call for a list of reports.

* Japanese Technical Resources

Directory of Japanese Technical Resources
National Technical Information Service
U.S. Department of Commerce
5285 Port Royal Rd.
Springfield, VA 22161 (703) 487-4650

The directory, *Japanese Technical Resources*, allows government, industry, and the academic community to find U.S. sources of Japanese high-technology information. It is divided into four parts: 1) an alphabetical list of commercial organizations that collect, abstract, translate, or distribute Japanese technical information; 2) a list of government agencies with programs and services involving Japanese technical information; 3) a list of libraries that have extensive holdings of Japanese technical information; and 4) a list of Japanese technical reports translated by the U.S. Government and available to the public. It is available for $36.

* Laser Research

High Energy Laser Systems Test Facility
White Sands Missile Range
Public Affairs Office
New Mexico, 88802 (505) 678-1134

This Facility tests and evaluates high energy laser systems, subsystems and components. For information on tests and facilities, contact the above office.

* Lawrence Berkeley Laboratory

1 Cyclotron Road
Berkeley, CA 94720 (510) 486-5771

The Lawrence Berkeley Laboratory is managed by the University of California for the U.S. Department of Energy. The laboratory has more than 3,000 employees and an operating budget of more than $235 million. The laboratory conducts research in the following areas: acceleration and fusion research, energy and environment, cell and molecular biology, chemical biodynamics, earth sciences, chemical sciences, materials sciences, nuclear science, physics, research medicine and radiation biophysics, engineering, information and computing sciences, and environment, safety and health. The *LBL Research Review*, a quarterly publication, is a good way to keep up with current research activities at the laboratory. For more information on programs or to get a sample copy of the *LBL Research Review*, contact the above office.

* Materials Research: Wear and Corrosion

Research Division
Bureau of Mines
U.S. Department of the Interior
810 7th St., NW
Washington, DC 20241-0001 (202) 501-9274

Advanced materials research is being conducted to eliminate wear and corrosion within the minerals industry through the use of ceramics, high-performance plastics, high-tech metals and alloys, and composites. Bureau scientists are also developing new coatings to protect equipment from the heat, corrosive chemicals, and abrasive materials found in mills, smelters, refineries, and furnaces.

* Medical Research

Medical Research Service
Veterans Health Services and Research Administration
U.S. Department of Veterans Affairs
810 Vermont Ave., NW
Washington, DC 20420 (202) 233-5041

VA efforts in this area fall into two broad categories: research on medical, dental, and psychiatric problems that are specific to the veteran population (spinal cord injury, Agent Orange, etc); and research on general health problems that are particularly prevalent among veterans (e.g., alcoholism, aging, and schizophrenia). Most of the investigators are VA clinicians and the close links between research and patient care functions give the research program a clinical orientation that is directly related to its goal of providing quality medical care to the veteran patient. For more information, contact the office above.

* Medicare's Prescription Drug Benefit

Office of Technology Assessment (OTA)
600 Pennsylvania Ave., SE
Washington, DC 20510 (202) 228-6590

OTA will study the experience of public and private payers of prescription drugs, including how they set payment rates, promote appropriate use, and control total expenditures. The study will apply this experience to develop methods the Medicare program might use to pay for multiple- and single-source drugs, and pharmaceutical services. Contact Jane Sisk, project director, for more information.

* Microcomputers and Semiconductors

Reliability Analysis Center (RAC)
P.O. Box 4700
Rome, NY 13440-8200 (315) 337-9933

Evaluation engineering, analytical services, products, and specialized reference services are provided by RAC in the areas of microcircuits, semiconductors, nonelectric devices, and electronic modules. Reliability and maintainability data on planned and operational systems and equipment is stored in a database. A user's catalog, searches, and technical reports can be obtained on a cost recover basis. Searches cost $50 for two or more records found; there is generally no charge if less than two records are recovered. The Center does not release documents, but documents can be ordered from the Defense Technical Information Service in Alexandria, VA; (703) 274-7633.

* Mines Technology Transfer

Office of Technology Transfer, Bureau of Mines
U.S. Department of the Interior
810 7th St., NW, MS 6201
Washington, DC 20241-0001 (202) 501-9323

The Technology Transfer Group distributes information on mining industry issues in many ways. *Technology Transfer* is a newsletter announcing the latest technology and research in mining. Free conferences are also held around the country on a variety of topics, such as advanced materials research and new technology for minerals. These conferences are announced through the newsletter *Technology Transfer Announcement*. To be placed on the mailing list, contact the office above.

* Multinationals and the U.S. Technology Base

Office of Technology Assessment (OTA)
600 Pennsylvania Ave, SE
Washington, DC 20510 (202) 228-6434

OTA is currently undertaking a project to determine how MNCs influence the U.S. economy and why MNCs decide to conduct or not to conduct state of the art manufacturing in the U.S. The study will examine the incentive structures for high technology manufacturing in the U.S., the European Community, and Japan. Contact project manager William Keller for more information.

* National Critical Technologies Panel Report

National Technical Information Service
U.S. Department of Commerce
5285 Port Royal Rd.
Springfield, VA 22161 (703) 487-4650

This report describes 22 technologies identified as critical to the economic prosperity and national defense of the United States. How the technologies were identified is described in the appendix. Some of the broad areas selected include materials, manufacturing, information and communications, biotechnology and life sciences, and energy and environment. Each of these areas is further broken down into specific technologies. The report costs $16. The order number is PB91-156869CAU.

* Neuroscience Studies

Office of Technology Assessment (OTA)
600 Pennsylvania Ave, SE
Washington, DC 20510 (202) 228-6676

Neurological disorders affect 50 million Americans each year. Costs of care,

Be patient. If any phone number is incorrect, call (area code) 555-1212 and request the new listing.

General Sources

treatment and loss of productivity range as high as $300 billion. OTA has undertaken the following series of neuroscience studies to be released between 1990 and 1992.

Neurotoxicity: Identifying and Controlling the Poisons of the Nervous System
Neural Grafting: Repairing the Brain and Spinal Cord
Biological Rhythms: Implications for the Worker
The Biological Basis of Mental Illness

* New Energy Technologies and Developing Countries

Office of Technology Assessment (OTA)
600 Pennsylvania Ave., SE
Washington, DC 20510 (202) 228-6267

OTA is currently working on a study to examine how technology can contribute to the goal of sound and productive energy development in the world's poorer countries, and the role of U.S. policy and the relevant international organizations in encouraging the rapid adoption of improved technologies. Contact Joy Dunkerley, the project director, at OTA for more information.

* Night Vision Research

Office of Public Affairs
Night Vision and Electro-Optics
Laboratories (NVEOL)
Fort Belvoir, VA 22060-5677 (703) 664-5066

NVEOL conducts research and development into electro-optical low-energy lasers, all-weather systems, infrared, radiation, visionics, and image intensification. The laboratories provide the Army with equipment to enable it to carry out nocturnal operations efficiently. This office can offer information and referral on laboratory programs.

* Non-indigenous Species Introduction

Office of Technology Assessment (OTA)
600 Pennsylvania Ave, SE
Washington, DC 20510 (202) 228-6533

Through the growth of knowledge, transportation, and communications, non-indigenous species are increasingly being introduced to new areas. Intentional introductions, such as potatoes and wheat, have become important crops. Unintended introductions such as fire ants and zebra mussels cause billions in damage. OTA will review the process of introducing non-indigenous species into new areas, and look at methods to control or eliminate unwanted species. Contact Phyllis Windle, project director, for more details.

* NTIS Alert on Computers

National Technical Information Service
U.S. Department of Commerce
5285 Port Royal Rd.
Springfield, VA 22161 (703) 487-4630

This bulletin describes new software and datafiles received by the Federal Computer Products Center. It also includes abstracts of Government research in computers and information technology, such as computer hardware; control systems and theory; information processing standards; information theory; and pattern recognition and image processing.

* NTIS Data Base Searches

Selected Research in Microfiche (SRIM)
National Technical Information Service
5285 Port Royal Rd.
Springfield, VA 22161 (703) 487-4929

Selected Research in Microfiche (SRIM) automatically provides selected technical reports as they are issued. Using SRIM, customers design (or select) their own subscription parameters, choosing from more than 350 subject topics. They then receive all reports that fall within their selections. Customers pay only $1.25 for each report they receive. Call SRIM Product Manager to start your subscription or request the free information brochure, *PR-271.*

* NTIS Foreign Technology Alert

National Technical Information Service
U.S. Department of Commerce
5285 Port Royal Rd.
Springfield, VA 22161 (703) 487-4630

This newsletter covers significant breakthroughs in foreign research and industrial technology. Coverage includes the areas of advanced microelectronics structural ceramics, superconductivity, and biotechnology. Subscription price for the *Alert* is $165 per year. A free brochure is available *(PR-842/827)* that describes the service.

* NTIS Index

National Technical Information Service (NTIS)
U.S. Department of Commerce
5285 Port Royal Rd.
Springfield, VA 22161 (703) 487-4650

NTIS Title Index is a microfiche list that provides an economical means of locating reports for sale from NTIS. It cites titles, order numbers, and prices of reports input into NTIS for a two-year period. A key-word-out-of-context title listing index is provided along with a personal author index and an order/report number index. The price for a two-year subscription is $400. Call the Sales Desk to place an order or request the free information brochure, *PR-567.*

* NTIS Products

National Technical Information Service
U.S. Department of Commerce
5285 Port Royal Rd.
Springfield, VA 22161 (703) 487-4630

The NTIS information products and services presented in this section give you ready access to the results of both U.S. and foreign government-sponsored research. The U.S. Government alone invests billions of dollars in research and development and engineering programs. Much of the resulting knowledge and technology is available through NTIS. And in the case of applied technology, this information can be of great value because it is not proprietary and may be used freely. The following newsletters are available through NTIS:

NTIS Alerts. These weekly bulletins present summaries of the most recent U.S. and foreign government research and development and engineering results. Prices range from $125- $175 depending upon subject area. For more information, request the free brochure, *PR-797.*

Computers, Control and Information Theory Abstract Newsletter. This bulletin provides early notice of new software and datafiles as they are received by the Federal Computer Products Center. It also includes abstracts of Government research in computers and information theory. A subscription is available for $150 per year. For more information, request the free brochure, *PR-797.*

Tech Notes. This is a monthly service providing access to the Federal laboratory activities and resources. An NTIS Tech Notes subscription provides selected *Fact Sheets* on the latest U.S. government-developed technologies and know-how. This low-cost service provides concise, illustrated one page announcements describing new processes, instruments, materials, equipment, software, services, and techniques. Each month more than 100 fact sheets are arranged under twelve subject headings. A subscription is available for $157 per year. For more information request the free brochure, *PR-365.*

Government Reports Announcements and Index Journal. This journal is issued twice monthly for those who want to see all of the research and development and engineering results announced annually by NTIS. Its comprehensive coverage provides 2,500 results within each issue. Entries are arranged under 38 major subject headings and then further sorted within more than 350 subheadings. A subscription is available for $495 per year. For more information, request the free information brochure, *PR-195.*

* NTIS Product Services Catalog

National Technical Information Service
U.S. Department of Commerce
5285 Port Royal Rd.
Springfield, VA 22161 (703) 487-4650

NTIS Product Services Catalog describes the bulletins, journals, catalogs, and directories produced by NTIS and available for sale. It also includes descriptions of more than eighty subscription items produced by other government agencies and made available from NTIS. Call for your free copy.

* Nuclear Physics/High Energy Research

Office of High Energy and Nuclear Physics
Office of Energy Research

Be patient. If any phone number is incorrect, call (area code) 555-1212 and request the new listing.

Science and Technology

19901 Germantown Rd.
Germantown, MD 20585 (301) 903-3713
This office establishes basic research policies for nuclear physics and high energy research and funds meritorious research programs at Federal laboratories, universities, and industrial institutions. It also provides scientific and technical knowledge for development of technology options and technology transfer of those projects which show promise of becoming important as energy technologies.

* Ocean Science Information Exchange

National Oceanographic Data Center
User Services Branch
NOAA/NESDIS E/OC21
Washington, DC 20235 (202) 673-5549
This is an experimental prototype system developed to provide frequent NODC users with on-line access to information about its data sets and services. In addition to containing most of the information contained in the *NODC Users Guide,* it also contains modules that provide searchable inventories of some of NODCs major data files, as well as other useful features. Contact NODC for more information on this database.

* Office of Technology Assessment (OTA) Publications and Reports

Office of Technology Assessment
Publications Order, U.S. Congress
Washington, DC 20510-8025 (202) 224-8996
These OTA publications are available through the office above, the Government Printing Office, and the National Technical Information Service. To find out correct ordering information and prices, contact the OTA office above and request their current publications catalog. Free executive summaries of each of these reports are available from this office.

Agriculture and Forestry

Acid Rain and Transported Air Pollutants: Implications for Public Policy (0-204)
Accommodating Uses Producing Outputs, and Sustaining Ecosystems (F-505)
Africa Tomorrow: Issues in Technology, Agriculture, and U.S. Foreign Aid (TM-F-31)
Agricultural Commodities as Industrial Raw Materials (F-476)
Agricultural Postharvest Technology and Marketing Economics Research (TM-F-21)
Agricultural Research and Technology Transfer Policies for the 1990s (F-448)
Assessing Biological Diversity in the United States: Data Considerations (BP-F-39)
An Assessment of the U.S. Food and Agricultural Research System (F-155)
Commercial Biotechnology: An International Analysis (BA-218)
Continuing the Commitment: Agricultural Development in the Sahel (F-308)
Drugs in Livestock Feed (F-91)
Emerging Food Marketing Technologies (F-79)
Energy From Biological Processes (E-124)
Enhancing Agriculture in Africa: A Role for Development Assistance (F-356)
Enhancing the Quality of U.S. Grain for International Trade (F-399)
Environmental Contaminants in Food (F-103)
Food Information Systems (F-35)
Grain Quality in International Trade: A Comparison of Major U.S. Competitors (F-402)
Grassroots Conservation of Biological Diversity in the United States (BP-F-38)
Grassroots Development: The African Development Foundation (F-378)
Impacts of Applied Genetics: Micro-Organisms, Plants, and Animals (HR-132)
Impacts of Technology on U.S. Cropland and Rangeland Productivity (F-166)
Innovative Biological Technologies for Lesser Developed Countries (BP-F-29)
Integrated Renewable Resource Management for U.S. Insular Area (F-325)
Nutrition Research Alternatives (F-74)
Open Shelf-Life Dating of Food (F-94)
Organizing and Financing Basic Research To Increase Food Production (F-49)
Perspectives on Federal Retail Food Grading (F-47)
Pest Management Strategies in Crop Protection (F-98)
Pesticide Residues in Food (F-398)
Plants: The Potential for Extracting Protein, Medicines, and Other Useful Chemicals (BP-F-23)
A Review of U.S. Competitiveness in Agriculture Trade (TM-TET-29)
Setting Strategic Direction Under RPA (F-441)
Sustaining Tropical Forest Resources: Reforestation of Degraded Lands (BP-F-18)
Sustaining Tropical Forest Resources: U.S. and International Institutions (BP-F-19)
Technologies To Benefit Agriculture and Wildlife (BP-F-34)
Technologies To Maintain Biological Diversity (F-330)

Technologies To Sustain Tropical Forest Resources (F-214)
Technology and the American Economic Transition (TET-283)
Technology, Public Policy, and the Changing Structure of American Agriculture (F-285)
Technology, Public Policy, and the Changing Structure of American Agriculture: A Special Report for the 1985 Farm Bill (F-272)
Technology, Renewable Resources, and American Crafts (BP-F-27)
Water-Related Technologies for Sustainable Agriculture in U.S. Arid/Semiarid Lands (F-212)
Water-Related Technologies for Sustainable Agriculture in U.S. Arid/Semiarid Lands: Selected Foreign Experience (BP-F-20)
Wetlands: Their Use and Regulation (0-206)
Wood Use: U.S. Competitiveness and Technology (ITE-210)

Biological Applications

Alternatives to Animal Use In Research, Testing, and Education (BA-273)
Artificial Insemination: Practice in the United States (BP-BA-48)
Assessment of Technologies for Determining Cancer Risk From the Environment (H-138)
Biological Rhythms: Implications for the Worker (BA-463)
Biotechnology in a Global Economy (BA-494)
Commercial Development of Tests for Human Genetic Disorders (Staff Paper)
Commercial Biotechnology: An International Analysis (BA-218)
Federal Policies and the Medical Devices Industry (H-229)
Federal Regulation and Animal Patents (Staff Paper)
Genetic Monitoring and Screening in the Workplace (BA-455)
Hearing Impairment and Elderly People (BP-BA-30)
Humane Gene Therapy (BP-BA-32)
Identifying and Controlling Immunotoxic Substances (BP-BA-75)
Impacts of Applied Genetics: Micro-Organisms, Plants, and Animals (HR-132)
Impacts of Neuroscience (BP-BA-24)
Infertility: Medical and Social Choices (BA-358)
Innovative Biological Technologies for Lesser Developed Countries (BP-F-29)
Institutional Protocols for Decisions About Life-Sustaining Treatments (BA-389)
Life-Sustaining Technologies and the Elderly (BA-306)
Loosing a Million Minds: Confronting the Tragedy of Alzheimer's Disease and Other Dementias (BA-323)
Mapping Our Genes: Genome Projects - How Big, How Fast? (BA-373)
Medical Monitoring and Screening in the Workplace: Results of a Survey (BP-BA-67)
Methods for Locating and Arranging Health and Long-Term Care for Persons With Dementia (BA-403)
Neural Grafting: Repairing the Brain and Spinal Cord (BA-462)
Neurotoxicity: Identifying and Controlling the Poisons of the Nervous System (BA-436)
New Developments in Biotechnology: Field-Testing Engineered Organisms: Genetic and Ecological Issues (BA-350)
New Developments in Biotechnology: Ownership of Human Tissue and Cells (BA-337)
New Developments in Biotechnology: Patenting Life (BA-370)
New Developments in Biotechnology: Public Perceptions in Biotechnology (BP-BA-45)
New Developments in Biotechnology: U.S. Investment in Biotechnology (BA-360)
Preventing Illness and Injury in the Workplace (H-256)
Reproductive Health Hazards in the Workplace (BA-266)
The Role of Genetic Testing in the Prevention of Occupational Disease (BA-194)
Status of Biomedical Research and Related Technology for Tropical Diseases (H-258)
Technologies for Detecting Heritable Mutations in Human Beings (H-298)
Technologies for Managing Urinary Incontinence (HCS-33)
Technology and Aging in America (BA-264)
Transgenic Animals (Staff Paper)
US Dairy Industry at a Crossroad: Biotechnology and Policy Choices (F-470)
World Population and Fertility Planning Technologies: The Next 20 Years (HR-157)

Defense

Adjusting to a New Security Environment: The Defense Technology and Industrial Base Challenge (BP-ISC-79)
Arming Our Allies: Cooperation and Competition in Defense Technology (ISC-449)
Advanced Space Transportation
Alternative Cargo Policies (BP-O-36)
American Military Power: Future Needs and Future Choices (BP-ISC-80)
Anti-Satellite Weapons, Countermeasures, and Arms Control (ISC-281)
Arms Control in Space (BP-ISC-28)
An Assessment of Alternative Economic Stockpiling Policies (M-36)
Ballistic Missile Defense Technology (ISC-254)

General Sources

Big Dumb Boosters: A Low Cost Transportation Option (Background Paper)
The Border War On Drugs (0-336)
Containment of Underground Nuclear Explosions (ISC-414)
Cooperative Aerial Surveillance in International Agreements (ISC-480)
Commercial Newsgathering From Space (TM-ISC-40)
Defending Secrets, Sharing Data: New Locks and Keys for Electronic Information (CIT-310)
The Defense Technology Base: Introduction and Overview (ISC-374)
Directed Energy Missile Defense in Space (BP-ISC-26)
The Effects of Nuclear War (NS-89)
Energy Technology Transfer to China (TM-ISC-30)
Global Arms Trade: Commerce in Advanced Military Technology and Weapons (ISC-460)
Holding the Edge: Maintaining the Defense Technology Base - 2 vols. (ISC 420 and 432)
International Cooperation and Competition in Civilian Space Activities (ISC-239)
Launch Options for the Future: A Buyer's Guide (ISC-383)
Managing Research and Development for Cooperative Arms Control Monitoring Measures (ISC-488)
Monitoring and Preventing Accidental Radiation Release at the Nevada Test Site MX Missile Basing (ISC-140)
New Structural Materials Technologies: Opportunities for the Use of Advanced Ceramics and Composites (TM-E-32)
New Technologies for NATO: Implementing Follow-On Forces Attack (ISC-309)
Nuclear Proliferation and Safeguards (E-48)
Piloted Space Transportation Technologies
Redesigning Defense: Planning the Transition to the Future U.S. Defense Industrial Base (ISC-500)
Reducing Launch Operations Costs: New Technologies and Practices (TM-ISC-28)
Remote Sensing and the Private Sector: Issues for Discussion (TM-ISC-20)
Review of the FAA 1982 National Airspace System Plan (STI-176)
Scientific Validity of Polygraph Testing: A Research Review and Evaluation (TM-H-15)
SDI: Technology, Survivability, and Software (ISC-353)
Seismic Verification of Nuclear Testing Treaties (ISC-361)
Space Stations and the Law: Selected Legal Issues (BP-ISC-41)
Strategic Materials: Technologies To Reduce U.S. Import Vulnerability (ITE-248)
Taggants in Explosives (ISC-116)
Technology Against Terrorism: The Federal Effort (ISC-481)
Technologies for NATO's Follow-On Forces Attack Concept (ISC-312)
Technology and East West Trade (ISC-101)
Technology and East West Trade: An Update (ISC-209)
Technology Transfer to China (ISC-340)
Technology Transfer to the Middle East (ISC-173)
UNISPACE '82: A Context for International Cooperation and Competition (TM-ISC-26)
U.S.-Soviet Cooperation in Space (TM-STI-27)

Trade Adjustment Assistance: New Ideas for an Old Problem (ITE-346)
Transportation of Hazardous Materials (SET-304)
Transportation of Hazardous Materials: State and local Activities (SET-301)
The Use of Integrity Tests for Pre-Employment Screening (SET-442)
Worker Training: Competing in the New International Economy (ITE-457)

Energy and Mineral Resources

Advanced Material by Design: New Structural Materials Technologies (E-351)
Analysis of Laws Governing Access Across Federal Lands: Options for Access in Alaska (M-82)
Application of Solar Technology to Today's Energy Needs (E-66)
An Assessment of Alternative Economic Stockpiling Policies (M-36)
An Assessment of Development and Production Potential of Federal Coal Leases (M-150)
An Assessment of Information System Capabilities Required to Support U.S. Materials Policy Decision (M-40)
An Assessment of Oil Shale Technologies (M-118)
Benefits of Increased Use of Continuous Casting by the U.S. Steel Industry (TM-ISC-2)
Changing Energy Structure of U.S. Industry
Coal Exports and Port Development (TM-0-8)
Coastal Effects of Offshore Energy Systems (0-37)
Commercialization High-Temperature Superconductivity (ITE-388)
Conservation and Solar Energy Programs of the Department of Energy: A Critique (E-120)
Copper: Technology and Competitiveness (E-367)
The Direct Use of Coal: Prospects and Problems of Production and Combustion (E-86)
Electric Power-Wheeling and Dealing: Technological Considerations for Increasing Competition (E-409)
Energy and Efficiency of Building in Cities (E-168)
Energy Efficiency in the Federal Government: Government by Good Example? (E-492)
Energy From Biological Processes (E-124)
Energy in Developing Countries (E-486)
Energy Technology Choices: Shaping our Future (E-493)
Energy Technology Transfer to China (TM-ICS-30)
Energy Use and the U.S. Economy (BP-E-57)
Engineering Implications to Chronic Materials Scarcity (M-44)
Enhanced Oil Recovery Potential in the United States (E-59)
Environmental Protection in the Federal Coal Leasing Program (E-237)
The Future of Liquefied Natural Gas Imports (E-110)
Gas Potential From Devonian Shales of the Appalachian Basin (E-57)
Gasohol (TM-E-1)
High Temperature Superconductivity in Perspective (E-440)
A History and Analysis of the Federal Prototype Oil Shale Leasing Program (M-119)
Increased Automobile Fuel Efficiency and Synthetic Fuels: Alternatives for Reducing Oil Imports (E-185)
Improving Automobile Fuel Economy: New Standards, New Approaches (E-504)
Industrial and Commercial Cogeneration (E-192)
Industrial Energy Use (E-198)
Management of Fuel and Nonfuel Minerals in Federal Lands (M-88)
Marine Applications for Fuel Cell Technology (TM-O-37)
Marine Minerals: Exploring Our New Ocean Frontier (O-342)
Materials and Energy From Municipal Waste (M-93)
New Electric Power Technologies: Problems and Prospects for the 1990's (E-246)
New Structural Materials: Opportunities for the Use of Advanced Ceramics and Composites (TM-E-32)
Nonferrous Metals: Industrial Structure (BP-E-62)
Nuclear Power in an Age of Uncertainty (E-216)
Nuclear Powerplant Standardization: Light Water Reactors (E-134)
Nuclear Proliferation and Safeguards (E-48)
Ocean Thermal Energy Conversion (O-62)
Oil and Gas Technologies for the Arctic and Deepwater (O-270)
Oil Production in the Arctic National Wildlife Refuge: The Technology and the Alaskan Oil Context (E-394)
Oil Transportation by Tankers: An Analysis of Marine Pollution and Safety Measures (O-9)
Patterns and Trends in Federal Coal Lease Ownership, 1950-80 (TM-M-7)
Physical Vulnerability of Electrical Systems to Natural Disasters and Sabotage (E-453)
Polar Prospects: a Minerals Treaty for Antarctica (O-428)
Potential Effects of Section 3 of the Federal Coal Leasing Amendments Act of 1976 (E-300)
Power Frequency and Electromagnetic Fields: Exposure, Effects, Research and Regulation (BP-E-53)

Education and Training

Alternatives to Animal Use in Research, Testing, and Education (BA-273)
Automation and the Workplace: Selected Labor, Education, and Training Issues (TM-CIT-25)
Automation of America's Offices (CIT-287)
Computer Technology in Medical Education and Assessment (BP-H-1)
Computerized Manufacturing Automation: Employment, Education, and the Workplace (CIT-235)
Demographic Trends and the Scientific and Engineering Work Force (TM-SET-35)
Displaced Homemakers: Programs and Policy (ITE-292)
Educating Scientist and Engineers: Grade School to Grad School (SET-377)
Elementary and Secondary Education for Science and Engineering (TM-SET-41)
Higher Education for Science and Engineering (BP-SET-62)
Higher Education for Science and Engineering (BP-SET-52)
Informational Technology and Its Impact on American Engineers (CIT-187)
Life-Sustaining Technologies and the Elderly (BA-306)
Linking for Learning: A New Course for Education (SET-430)
Plant Closing: Advance Notice and Rapid Response (ITE-321)
Performance Standards for Secondary School Vocational Education (April 1989)
Potential Office Hazards and Controls (Contractor Report)
Power On! New Tools for Teaching and Learning (SET-379)
Preventing Illness and Injury in the Workplace (H-256)
Reproductive Health Hazards in the Workplace (BA-266)
Research Funding As An Investment: Can We Measure the Returns? (TM-SET-36)
Role of Technology in the Education, Training, and Retraining of Adult Workers (Contractor Document)
Technology and Handicapped People (H-179)
Technology and Structural Unemployment: Reemploying Displaced Adults (ITE-250)

Science and Technology

Recent Developments in Ocean Thermal Energy (TM-O-3)
Replacing Gasoline: Alternative Fuels for Light Duty Vehicles (E-364)
Residential Energy Conservation (E-92)
Royalty Management Program's Auditing and Financial System: Technical Issues (July 1990)
Solar Power Satellite Systems (E-144)
Starpower: The U.S. and the International Quest for Fusion Energy (E-338)
Strategic Materials: Technologies to Reduce U.S. Import Vulnerability (ITE-248)
Technical Options for Conservation of Metals (M-97)
Technologies for Improving Minerals Royalty Management
Technologies for Prehistoric and Historic Preservation (E-319)
Technologies for Underwater Archaeology and Maritime Preservation (BP-E-37)
Technology for Soviet Energy Availability (ISC-153)
A Technology Assessment of Coal Slurry Pipelines (E-60)
Technology Transfer to the Middle East (ISC-173)
Transportation of Liquefied Natural Gas (TM-E-12)
U.S. Natural Gas Availability: Conventional Gas Supply Through the Year 2000 (TM-E-12)
U.S. Natural Gas Availability: Gas Supply Through the Year 2000 (E-245)
U.S. Oil Import Vulnerability: The Technical Replacement Capability (E-503)
U.S. Oil Production: The Effect of Low Oil Prices (E-348)
U.S. Vulnerability to an Oil Import Curtailment: The Oil Replacement Capability (E-243)
Western Surface Mine Permitting and Reclamation (E-279)
World Petroleum Availability: 1980-2000 (TM-E-5)

Environment and Pollution

Acid Rain and Transported Air Pollutants: Implications for Public Policy (O-204)
Are We Cleaning Up? 10 Superfund Case Studies (ITE-362)
Assessing Contractor Use In Superfund (BP-ITE-51)
Assessment of Technologies for Determining Cancer Risks From the Environment (H-138)
Beneath the Bottom Line: Agricultural Approaches to Reduce Agrichemical Contaminants of Groundwater (F-418)
Catching Our Breath: Next Steps for Reducing Urban Ozone (O-412)
Changing By Degrees: Steps to Reduce Greenhouse Gases (O-482)
Complex Cleanup: The Environmental Legacy of Nuclear Weapons Production (O-484)
The Direct Use of Coal: Prospects and Problems of Production and Combustion (E-86)
Environmental Containments in Food (F-103)
Environmental Protection in the Federal Coal Leasing Program (E-237)
An Evaluation of Options for Managing Greater-Than-Class-C Low-Level Radioactive Waste (BP-0-40)
Facing America's Trash: What Next for Municipal Solid Waste? (O-424)
Finding The Rx for Managing Medical Wastes (O-459)
From Pollution to Prevention: A Progress Report on Waste Reduction (ITE-347)
Habitability of the Love Canal Area: An Analysis of the Technical Basis for the Decision on the Habitability of the Emergency Declaration Area (TM-M-13)
Impacts of Applied Genetics: Micro-Organisms, Plants, and Animals (HR-132)
Issues in Medical Waste Management (BP-O-49)
Long Lived Legacy: Managing High Level and Transuranic Waste at the DOE Nuclear Weapons Complex (BP-O-83)
Managing the Nation's Commercial High-Level Radioactive Waste (O-171)
Marine Applications for Fuel Cell Technology (TM-O-37)
Monitoring and Preventing Accidental Radiation Release at the Nevada Test Site
Municipal Solid Waste Management
New Clean Air Act Issues (O-412)
Nonnuclear Industrial Waste: Classifying for Hazards Management (TM-M-9)
Ocean Incineration: Its Role in Managing Hazardous Waste (O-313)
Oil and Gas Technologies for the Arctic and Deepwater (O-270)
Oil Transportation by Tankers: An Analysis of Marine Pollution and Safety Measures (O-9)
Partnerships Under Pressure: Managing Commercial Low-Level Radioactive Waste (O-426)
Passive Smoking in the Workplace: Selected Issues (Staff Paper)
Protecting the Nation's Groundwater From Contamination (O-233)
Serious Reduction of Hazardous Waste (ITE-317)
Superfund Implementation:
- *Coming Clean: Superfund problems can be solved...*(ITE-433)
- *Assessing contractor use in Superfund* (BP-ITE-51)
- *Are we cleaning up: 10 Superfund case studies* (ITE-362)

Superfund Strategy (ITE-252)
Technologies and Management Strategies for Hazardous Waste Control (M-196)
Technologies for Prehistoric and Historic Preservation (E-319)
Technologies for the Preservation of Prehistoric and Historic Landscapes (BP-E-44)

Technologies for Reducing Dioxin in the Manufacture of Bleached Wood Pulp (BP-O-54)
Technologies for Reducing Dioxin in the Manufacture of Pulp and Paper
Technologies for Underwater Archaeology and Maritime Preservation (BP-E-37)
Technology and Oceanography: An Assessment of Federal Technologies for Oceanographic Research and Monitoring (O-141)
Trade Adjustment Assistance: New Ideas for an Old Program (ITE-346)
Transportation of Hazardous Materials (SET-304)
Transportation of Hazardous Materials: State and Local Activities (SET-301)
Urban Ozone and the Clean Air Act: Problems and Proposals for Change (Staff paper)
Wastes in Marine Environments (O-334)
Western Surface Mine Permitting and Reclamation (E-279)
Wetlands: Their Use and Regulation (O-206)

Health

Abstracts of Case Studies in the Health Technology Case Study Series (P-225)
Acid Rain and Transported Air Pollutants: Implications for Public Policy (O-204)
Adolescent Health-Volume I: Summary and Policy Options (H-468)
Adolescent Health-Volume II: Background and the Effectiveness of Selected Prevention and Treatment Services (H-466)
Adolescent Health-Volume III: Crosscutting Issues in the Delivery of Health and Related Services (H-467)
Adolescent Health Insurance Status: Analyses of Trends in Coverage and Preliminary Estimates of the Effects of an Employer Mandate and Medicaid Expansion on the Uninsured (BP-H-56)
AIDS and Health Insurance: An OTA Survey (Staff Paper)
Artificial Insemination: Practice in the United States (BP-BA-48)
Assessing the Efficacy and Safety of Medical Technologies (H-75)
Assessment of Four Common X-Ray Procedures (BP-H-14)
Assessment of Technologies for Determining Cancer Risks From the Environment (H-138)
Assistive Devices for Severe Speech Impairments (HCS-26)
Biology, Medicine, and Bill of Rights (CIT-371)
Blood Policy and Technology (H-260)
Boston Elbow (HCS-29)
Cancer Testing Technology and Saccharin (H-55)
Children's Dental Services under the Medicaid Program (BP-H-78)
Confused Minds, Burdened Families: Finding Help for People with Alzheimer's and Other Dementias (BA-403)
Costs and Effectiveness of Screening for Cervical Cancer in the Elderly (Contractor Paper)
Children's Mental Health: Problems and Services (BP-H-33)
Costs and Effectiveness of Screening for Cholesterol in the Elderly (Contractor Paper)
Colorectal Cancer Screening in the Elderly (Staff Paper)
Commercial Biotechnology: An International Analysis (BA-218)
Compensation for Vaccine-Related Injuries (TM-H-6)
Computer Technology in Medical Education and Assessment (BP-H-1)
Contact Lenses (HCS-31)
Cost-Effectiveness Analysis of Influenza Vaccine (H-152)
The Cost-Effectiveness of Digital Subtraction Angiography in the Diagnosis of Cerebrovascular Disease (HCS-34)
Cost of AIDS and Other HIV Infections: Review of the Estimates (Staff Paper)
Defining Rural Areas: Impact on Health Care Policy and Research (July 1989)
Development of Medical Technology: Opportunities for Assessment (H-34)
Diagnostic Related Groups (DRGs) and the Medicare Program: Implications for Medical Technology (TM-H-17)
Diagnosis Related Groups (DRGs) and the Medicare Program: Using Diagnosis Related Groups in Hospital Payment-The New Jersey Experience
The Direct Use of Coal: Prospects and Problems of Production and Combustion (E-86)
Do Insects Transmit AIDS? (Staff Paper)
Drug Labeling in Developing Countries
The Effectiveness of Costs of Alcoholism Treatment (HCS-22)
Effects of Federal Policies on Extracorporeal Shock Wave Lithotripsy (HCS-36)
The Effects of Nuclear War (NS-89)
The Efficacy and Cost Effectiveness of Psychotherapy (BP-H-6)
Efficacy, Safety, and the Cost-Effectiveness of Continuous Ambulatory Peritoneal Dialysis (HCS-35)
Environmental Contaminants in Food (F-103)
Federal Policies and the Medical Devices Industry (H-229)
Federal Response to AIDS
Forecasts of Physician Supply and Requirements (H-113)
Healthy Children: Investing in the Future (H-344)
Health Care in Rural America (H-434)
Hearing Impairment and Elderly People (BP-BA-30)

General Sources

Hemodialysis Equipment (HCS-32)
How Effective is AIDS Education?
Human Gene Therapy (BP-BA-32)
Identifying and Regulating Carcinogens (BP-H-42)
Impact of AIDS on the Northern California Region of Kaiser Permenente (Staff Paper)
The Impact of Randomized Clinical Trials on Health Policy and Medical Practice (BP-H-22)
The Impacts of Neuroscience (BP-BA-24)
The Implications of Cost-Effectiveness Analysis of Medical Technology (H-126)
Indian Health Care (H-290)
Indian Adolescent Mental Health (H-446)
Infertility: Medical and Social Choices (BA-358)
The Information Context of Premanufacture Notices (BP-H-17)
Institutional Protocols for Decisions About Life-Sustaining Treatments (BA-389)
Intensive Care Units (ICU's) Clinical Outcomes, Costs, and Decisionmaking (HCS-28)
Issues in Medical Waste Management (BP-O-49)
Life-Sustaining Technologies and the Elderly (BA-306)
Losing a Million Minds: Confronting the Tragedy of Alzheimer's Disease and Other Dementias (BA-323)
The Management of Health Care Technology in Ten Countries (BP-H-7)
Mandatory Passive Restraint Systems in Automobiles: Issues and Evidence (BP-H-15)
The Market of Wheelchairs: Innovation and Federal Policy (HCS-30)
Medical Technology and the Costs of the Medicare Program (H-227)
Medical Technology Under Proposals To Increase Competition in Health Care (H-190)
Medical Testing and Health Insurance (H-384)
Medicare's Prospective Payment System: Strategies for Evaluating Cost, Quality, and Medical Technology (H-262)
MEDLARS and Health Information Policy (TM-H-11)
Methodological Issues and Literature Review (BP-H-5)
Methods for Locating and Arranging Health and Long-Term Care for Persons With Dementia (BA-403)
Monitoring and Preventing Accidental Radiation Release at the Nevada Test Site
Municipal Solid Waste Management
Neonatal Intensive Care for Low Birthweight Infants: Costs and Effectiveness (HCS-38)
New Clean Air Act Issues (O-412)
Nuclear Magnetic Resonance Imaging Technology: A Clinical, Industrial, and Policy Analysis (HCS-27)
Nurse Practitioners, Physician Assistants, and Certified Nurse-Midwives: A Policy Analysis (HCS-37)
Nutrition Research Alternatives (F-74)
Ocean Incineration: Its Role in Managing Hazardous Waste (O-313)
Outpatient Immunosuppressive Drugs under Medicare (H-452)
Passive Smoking in the Workplace: Selected Issues (Staff Paper)
Payment for Physician Services: Strategies for Medicare (H-294)
Plants: The Potentials for Extracting Protein, Medicine, and Other Useful Chemicals (BP-F-23)
Policy Implications of Medical Information Systems (H-56)
Policy Implications of the Computed Tomography (CT) Scanner (H-72)
Policy Implications of the Computed Tomography (CT) Scanner: An Update (BP-H-8)
Postmarketing Surveillance of Prescription Drugs (H-189)
Potential Office Hazards and Controls (Contractor Report)
Preventive Health Services for Medicare Beneficiaries: Policy and Research Issues (H-416)
Preventing Illness and Injury in the Workplace (H-256)
Procurement and Evaluation of Medical Devices by the Veterans Administration (TM-H-16)
Protecting the Nation's Groundwater From Contamination (O-233)
The Quality of Medical Care: Information for Consumers (H-386)
Quality Relevance of Research and Related Activities at the Gorgas Memorial Laboratory (TM-H-18)
Reproductive Health Hazards in the Workplace (BA-266)
A Review of Selected Federal Vaccine and Immunization Policies Based on Case Studies of Pneumococcal Vaccine (H-96)
Recombinant Erythropoietin: Payment Options for Medicare (H-451)
Review of the Public Health Service's Response to AIDS (TM-H-24)
The Role of Genetic Testing in the Prevention of Occupational Disease (BA-194)
Rural Emergency Medical Services (H-445)
The Safety, Efficacy, and Cost Effectiveness of Therapeutic Apheresis (HCS-23)
Screening for Open-Angle Glaucoma in the Elderly (Staff Paper)
Selected Telecommunication Devices for Hearing-Impaired Persons (BP-H-16)
Selected Topics in Federal Health Statistics (H-90)

Status of Biomedical Research and Related Technology for Tropical Diseases (H-258)
Strategies for Medical Technology Assessment (H-181)
Superfund Strategy (ITE-252)
Technologies for Detecting Heritable Mutations in Human Beings (H-298)
Technologies for Managing Urinary Incontinence (HCS-33)
Technology and Aging in America (BA-264)
Technology and Handicapped People (H-179)
Technology and Learning Disabilities (HCS-25)
Technology Dependent Children: Hospital v. Home Care (TM-H-38)
Technology Transfer at the National Institutes of Health (TM-H-10)
Technology Transfer to the Middle East (ISC-173)
The Use of Preventive Services by the Elderly (Staff Meeting)
Update of Federal Activities Regarding the Use of Pneumococcal Vaccine (TM-H-23)
Urban Ozone and the Clean Air Act: Problems and Proposals for Change (Staff Paper)
Unconventional Cancer Treatments (H-405)
Variations in Hospital Length of Stay: Their Relationship to Health Outcomes (HCS-24)
World Population and Fertility Planning Technologies: The Next 20 Years (HR-157)

Industry

AIDS and Health Insurance: An OTA Survey (Staff Paper)
Alternative Cargo Policies (BP-O-36)
An Assessment of Maritime Trade and Technology (O-220)
An Assessment of Technology for Local Development (B-129)
Automation and the Workplace: Selected Labor, Education, and Training Issues (TM-CIT-25)
Automation of America's Offices (CIT-287)
Benefits of Increased Use of Continuous Casting by the U.S. Steel Industry (TM-ISC-2)
Boston Elbow (HCS-29)
Census of State Government Initiatives for High-Technology Industrial Development (BP-STI-21)
Changing Energy Structure of the U.S. Industry
Commercial Biotechnology: An International Analysis (BA-218)
Commercial Development of Tests for Human Genetic Disorders (Staff Paper)
Commercializing High-Temperature Superconductivity (ITE-388)
Communications Systems for an Information Age (CIT-407)
Competing economies: America, Europe, and the Pacific Rim (ITE-498)
Computer-Based National Information Systems: Information and Public Policy (CIT-146)
Computerized Manufacturing Automation: Employment, Education, and the Workplace (HCS-31)
Contact Lenses (HCS-31)
Copyright and Home Copying
Displaced Homemakers: Programs and Policy (ITE-292)
Drug Labeling in Developing Countries
The Effectiveness and Costs of Alcoholism Treatment (HCS-22)
The Effects of Information Technology on Financial Services Systems (CIT-202)
The Efficacy and Cost Effectiveness of Psychotherapy (BP-H-6)
Electric Power - Wheeling and Dealing: Technological Considerations for Increasing Competition (E-409)
Encouraging High-Technology Development (BP-STI-25)
Federal Policies and the Medical Devices Industry (H-229)
Federal Regulation and Animal Patents (Staff Paper)
Gearing Up for Safety: Motor Carrier Safety in a Competitive Environment (SET-382)
Hemodialysis Equipment (HCS-32)
The Impact of Randomized Clinical Trials on Health Policy and Medical Practice (BP-H-22)
Impacts of Applied Genetics: Micro-Organisms, Plants, and Animals (HR-132)
Industrial and Commercial Cogeneration (E-192)
Industrial Energy Use (E-198)
Information Technology R&D: Critical Trends and Issues (CIT-268)
Informational Technology and Its Impact on American Education (CIT-187)
Informing the Nation: Federal Information Dissemination in an Electronic Age (CIT-396)
Intellectual Property Rights in an Age of Electronics and Information (CIT-302)
International Competition in Services: Banking, Building, Software, Know-How (ITE-328)
International Competitiveness in Electronics (ISC-200)
Making Things Better: Competing in Manufacturing (ITE-443)
Marine Applications for Fuel Cell Technology (TM-O-37)
The Market for Wheelchairs: Innovation and Federal Policy (HCS-30)

Be patient. If any phone number is incorrect, call (area code) 555-1212 and request the new listing.

Science and Technology

Medical Testing and Health Insurance (H-384)
Microelectronics R&D (BP-CIT-40)
New Developments in Biotechnology: U.S. Investment in Biotechnology (BA-360)
Nuclear Magnetic Resonance (NMR) Imaging Technology: A Clinical, Industrial, and Policy Analysis (O-270)
Oil and Gas Technologies for the Arctic and Deepwater (O-270)
Paying the Bill: Manufacturing and America's Trade Deficit (ITE-390)
Plant Closing: Advance Notice and Rapid Response (ITE-321)
Policy Implications of the Computed Tomography (CT) Scanner (H-72)
Policy Implications of the Computed Tomography (CT) Scanner: An Update (BP-H-8)
Power Frequency and Electromagnetic Fields: Exposure, Effects, Research, and Regulation (BP-E-53)
Preventing Illness and Injury in the Workplace (H-256)
R&D in the Maritime Industry (BP-O-35)
Reproductive Health Hazards in the Workplace (BA-266)
Role of Technology in the Education, Training, and Retraining of Adult Workers (Contractor Document)
Safe Skies for Tomorrow: Aviation Safety in a Competitive Environment (SET-381)
Safer Skies With TCAS: Traffic Alert and Collision Avoidance System (SET-431)
Scientific Use of Supercomputers (BP-CIT-31)
Services in the U.S. Balance of Payments 1982-84: Documentation of OTA Estimates (Working Paper)
Strategies for Medical Technology Assessment (H-181)
Technology and Steel Industry Competitiveness (M-122)
Technology and Structural Unemployment: Reemploying Displaced Adults (ITE-250)
Technology and the American Economic Transition (TET-283)
Technology and the Future of the U.S. Construction Industry
Technology, Innovation, and Regional Economic Development (STI-238)
Technology, Innovation, and U.S. Trade
Technology, Trade, and the U.S. Residential Construction Industry (TET-315)
Transgenic Animals (Staff Paper)
Transportation of Hazardous Materials: State and Local Activities (SET-301)
U.S. Industrial Competitiveness: A Comparison of Steel, Electronics, and Automobiles (ISC-135)
The U.S. Textile and Apparel Industry: A Revolution in Progress (TET-332)
Wood Use: U.S. Competitiveness and Technology (ITE-210)

Information Technology and Services
An Assessment of Alternatives for a National Computerized Criminal History System (CIT-161)
An Assessment of Information System Capabilities Required To Support U.S. Materials Policy Decision (M-40)
Automation and the Workplace: Selected Labor, Education, and Training Issues (TM-CIT-25)
Automation of America's Offices (CIT-287)
Big Picture: HDTV and High Resolution Systems (BP-CIT-64)
Biology, Medicine, and the Bill of Rights (CIT-371)
Book Preservation Technologies (O-375)
Computer Software and Intellectual Property (BP-CIT-61)
Costs and Effectiveness of Screening for Cervical Cancer in the Elderly (Contractor Paper)
Children's Mental Health: Problems and Services (BP-H-33)
Costs and Effectiveness of Screening for Cholesterol in the Elderly (Contractor Paper)
Colorectal Cancer Screening in the Elderly (Staff Paper)
Communications Systems for an Information Age (CIT-407)
Computer-Based National Information Systems: Technology and Public Policy Issues (CIT-146)
Computerized Manufacturing Automation: Employment, Education, and the Workplace (CIT-235)
Copyright and Home Copying
Costs of AIDS and Other HIV Infections: Review of the Estimates (Staff Paper)
Criminal Justice, New Technologies, and the Constitution (CIT-366)
Critical Connections: Communication for the Future (CIT-407)
Defending Secrets, Sharing Data: New Locks and Keys for Electronic Information (CIT-310)
Democratic Governance Through Information and Communications Technologies (BP-CIT-59)
Do Insects Transmit AIDS? (Staff Paper)
Educating Scientists and Engineers: Grade School to Grad School (SET-377)
Effects of Information Technology on Financial Services Systems (CIT-202)
Efficacy and Cost Effectiveness of Psychotherapy (BP-H-6)
Electronic Delivery of Public Assistance Benefits: Technology Options and Policy Issues (BP-CIT-47)

Electronic Bulls and Bears: U.S. Securities Markets and Information Technology (CIT-469)
The Electronic Supervisor: New Technology, New Tensions (CIT-333)
Elementary and Secondary Education for Science and Engineering (TM-SET-41)
Energy Technology Transfer to China (TM-ISC-30)
Federal Government Information Technology: Electronic Record Systems and Individual Privacy (CIT-296)
Federal Government Information Technology: Electronic Surveillance and Civil Liberties (CIT-293)
Federal Government Information Technology: Management, Security, and Congressional Oversight (CIT-297)
Federal Government Information Technology: The Social Security Administration and Information Technology (CIT-311)
Federal Response to AIDS
Helping America Compete: the Role of Federal Scientific and Technical Information (CIT-454)
Higher Education for Science and Engineering (BP-SET-52)
High Performance Computing and Networking for Science (BP-CIT-59)
Impact of Randomized Clinical Trials on Health Policy and Medical Practice (BP-H-22)
Implications of Electronic Mail and Message Systems for the U.S. Postal Service (CIT-183)
The Information Context of Premanufacture Notices (BP-H-17)
Information Technology R&D: Critical Trends and Issues (CIT-268)
Informational Technology and Its Impact on American Education (CIT-187)
Informing the Nation: Federal Information Dissemination in an Electronic Age (CIT-396)
Intellectual Property Rights in an Age of Electronics and Information (CIT-302)
International Cooperation and Competition in Civilian Space Activities (ISC-239)
Medical Testing and Health Insurance (H-384)
MEDLARS and Health Information Policy (TM-H-11)
Patent-Term Extension and the Pharmaceutical Industry (CIT-143)
Payment for Physician Services: Strategies for Medicare (H-294)
Plant Closing: Advance Notice and Rapid Response (ITE-321)
Policy Implications of Medical Information Systems (H-56)
Power On! New Tools for Teaching and Learning (SET-379)
A Preliminary Assessments of the National Crime Information Center and the Computerized Criminal History System (I-80)
The Quality of Medical Care: Information for Consumers (H-386)
Radiofrequency Use and Management: Impacts From the World Administrative Radio Conference of 1979 (CIT-163)
Review of Postal Automation Strategy: A Technical and Decision Analysis (TM-CIT-22)
Role of Technology in the Education, Training, and Retraining of Adult Workers (Contractor Document)
Rural America at the Crossroads: Networking for the Future (TCT-471)
Science, Technology, and the Constitution (BP-CIT-43)
Science, Technology, and the First Amendment (CIT-369)
Scientific Validity of Polygraph Testing: A Research Review and Evaluation (TM-H-15)
Screening for Open-Angle Glaucoma in the Elderly (Staff Paper)
Seeking Solutions: High Performance Computing for Science (BP-TCT-77)
Selected Electronic Funds Transfer Issues: Privacy, Security and Equity (BP-CIT-12)
Strategies for Medical Technology Assessment (H-181)
Technology and Structural Unemployment: Reemploying Displaced Adults (ITE-250)
Trading Around the Clock: Global Securities Markets and Information Technology (BP-CIT-66)
The Use of Preventative Services by the Elderly (Staff Paper)

International Trade, Competition, and Cooperation
Arms Control in Space (BP-ISC-28)
Civilian Space Policy and Applications (STI-177)
Civilian Space Stations and U.S. Future in Space (STI-241)
Commercial Biotechnology: An International Analysis (BA-218)
Copper: Technology and Competitiveness (E-367)
Energy Technology Transfer to China (TM-ISC-30)
Enhancing Agriculture in Africa: A Role for Development Assistance (F-356)
Enhancing the Quality of U.S. Grain for International Trade (F-399)
Grain Quality in International Trade: A Comparison of Major U.S. Competitors (F-402)
International Competition in Services: Banking, Building, Software, Know-How (ITE-328)
International Competitiveness in Electronics (ISC-200)
International Cooperation and Competition in Civilian Space Activities (ISC-239)
Paying the Bill: Manufacturing and America's Trade Deficit (ITE-390)

Be patient. If any phone number is incorrect, call (area code) 555-1212 and request the new listing.

General Sources

A Review of U.S. Competitiveness in Agricultural Trade (TM-TET-29)
Salyut: Soviet Steps Toward Permanent Human Presence in Space (TM-STI-14)
Services in the U.S. Balance of Payments 1982-84: Documentation of OTA Estimates (Working Paper)
Starpower: The U.S. and the International Quest for Fusion Energy (E-338)
Technology and East-West Trade (ISC-101)
Technology and East-West Trade: An Update (ISC-209)
Technology and Soviet Energy Availability (ISC-153)
Technology and Structural Unemployment: Reemploying Displaced Adults (ITE-250)
Technology, Innovation, and U.S. Trade
Technology, Trade, and the U.S. Residential Construction Industry (TET-315)
Technology Transfer to China (ISC-340)
Technology Transfer to the Middle East (ISC-173)
Technology Transfer to the United States: The MIT-Japan Science and Technology Program (April 1989)
Trade in Services: Exports and Foreign Revenues (ITE-316)
UNISPACE '82: A Context for International Cooperation and Competition (TM-ISC-26)
U.S. - Soviet Cooperation in Space (TM-STI-27)
U.S. Universities and Development Assistance (BP-F-71)

Oceans and Water Resources
Alternative Cargo Policies (BP-O-36)
An Assessment of Maritime Trade and Technology (O-220)
Bioremediation for Marine Oil Spills (BP-O-70)
The Border War on Drugs (TM-O-8)
Coal Exports and Port Development (TM-O-8)
Competition in Coastal Areas: An Evaluation of Foreign Maritime Activities in the 200 Mile EEZ (BP-O-55)
Coping With an Oiled Sea (P-O-63)
Costal Effects of Offshore Energy Systems (O-37)
Establishing a 200-Mile Fisheries Zone (O-46)
An Evaluation of Options for Managing Greater-Than-Class-C Low-Level Radioactive Waste (BP-O-40)
Extending Cabotage Policy to All Commercial Maritime Activities in the EEZ
Integrated Renewable Resource Management for U.S. Insular Areas (F-325)
Issues in Medical Waste Management (BP-O-49)
Marine Applications for Fuel Cell Technology (TM-O-37)
Marine Minerals: Exploring Our New Ocean Frontier (O-342)
Municipal Solid Waste Management
Ocean Incineration: Its Role in Managing Hazardous Waste (O-313)
Ocean Margin Drilling (TM-O-4)
Ocean Thermal Energy Conversion (O-62)
Oil and Gas Technologies in the Arctic and Deepwater (O-270)
Oil Transportation by Tankers: An Analysis of Marine Pollution and Safety Measures (O-9)
Protecting the Nation's Groundwater From Contamination (O-233)
R&D in the Maritime Industry (BP-O-35)
Recent Developments in Ocean Thermal Energy (TM-O-3)
Technologies for Underwater Archaeology and Maritime Preservation (BP-E-37)
Technology and Oceanography: An Assessment of Federal Technologies for Oceanographic Research and Monitoring (O-141)
Transportation of Liquefied Natural Gas (O-53)
Use of Models for Water Resources Management, Planning, and Policy (O-159)
Using Desalination Technologies for Water Treatment (BP-O-46)
Wastes in Marine Environments (O-334)
Wetlands: Their Use and Regulation (O-206)

Science and Technology, Research and Development
Advanced Materials by Design: New Structural Materials Technologies (E-351)
Alternatives to Animal Use in Research, Testing, and Education (BA-273)
Anti-Satellite Weapons, Countermeasures, and Arms Control (ISC-281)
Assessment of Technologies for Determining Cancer Risks From the Environment (H-138)
An Assessment of the United States Food and Agriculture Research System (F-155)
Ballistic Missile Defense Technology (ISC-254)
Biology, Medicine, and the Bill of Rights (CIT-371)
Blood Policy and Technology (H-260)
Book Preservation Technologies (O-375)
Cancer Testing Technology and Saccharin (H-55)
Civilian Space Policy and Applications (STI-177)
Civilian Space Stations and U.S. Future in Space (STI-241)
Commercial Biotechnology: An International Analysis (BA-218)
Commercial Development of Tests for Human Genetic Disorders (Staff Paper)
Commercializing High-Temperature Superconductivity (ITE-388)

Criminal Justice, New Technologies, and the Constitution (CIT-366)
Demographic Trends and the Scientific and Engineering Work Force (TM-SET-35)
Education Scientists and Engineers: Grade School to Grad School (SET-377)
Elementary and Secondary Education for Science and Engineering (TM-SET-41)
Energy Technology Transfer to China (TM-ISC-30)
Federally Funded Research: Decisions for a Decade (SET-490)
Federal Regulations and Animal Patents (Staff Paper)
Global Models, World Futures, and Public Policy (R-165)
Human Gene Therapy (BP-BA-32)
Identifying and Regulating Carcinogens (BP-H-42)
Impacts of Applied Genetics: Micro-Organisms, Plants, and Animals (HR-132)
Impacts of Neuroscience (BP-BA-24)
Information Technology R&D: Critical Trends and Issues (CIT-268)
Microelectronics R&D (BP-CIT-40)
New Developments in Biotechnology: Field Testing Engineered Organisms: Genetic and Ecological Issues (BA-350)
New Developments in Biotechnology: Ownership of Human Tissues and Cells (BA-337)
New Developments in Biotechnology: Patenting Life (BA-370)
New Developments in Biotechnology: Public Perceptions of Biotechnology (BP-BA-45)
New Developments in Biotechnology: U.S. Investment in Biotechnology (BA-360)
New Structural Material Technologies: Opportunities for the Use of Advanced Ceramics and Composites (TM-E-32)
Patent-Term Extension and the Pharmaceutical Industry (CIT-143)
Power On! New Tools for Teaching and Learning (SET-379)
R&D in the Maritime Industry (BP-O-35)
The Regulatory Environment for Science (TM-SET-34)
Research Funding As An Investment: Can We Measure the Returns? (TM-SET-36)
The Role of Genetic Testing in the Prevention of Occupational Disease (BA-194)
Salyut: Soviet Steps Toward Permanent Human Presence in Space (TM-STI-14)
Science, Technology, and the Constitution (BP-CIT-43)
Science, Technology, and the First Amendment (CIT-369)
Scientific Use of Supercomputers (BP-CIT-31)
Scientific Validity of Polygraph Testing: A Research Review and Evaluation (TM-H-15)
SDI: Technology, Survivability, and Software (ISC-353)
Seismic Verification of Nuclear Test Ban Treaties (ISC-361)
Space Science Research in the United States (TM-STI-19)
Status of Biomedical Research and Related Technology for Tropical Diseases (H-258)
Technologies for Detecting Heritable Mutations in Human Beings (H-298)
Technology Transfer at the National Institutes of Health (TM-H-10)
Technology Transfer to China (ISC-340)
Transgenic Animals (Staff Paper)

Space
Access to Space: the Future of U.S. Space Transportation Systems (ISC-415)
Advanced Space Transportation Technologies
Affordable Spacecraft Design and Launch Alternatives (BP-ISC-60)
Anti-Satellite Weapons, Countermeasures, and Arms Control (ISC-281)
Arms Control in Space (BP-STI-28)
Ballistic Missile Defense Technology (ISC-254)
Big Dumb Boosters: A Low Cost Transportation Option (Background Paper)
Civilian Space Policy and Applications (STI-177)
Civilian Space Stations and U.S. Future in Space (STI-241)
Commercial Newsgathering From Space (TM-ISC-40)
Directed Energy Missile Defense in Space (BP-ISC-26)
Exploring the Moon and Mars (ISC-502)
International Cooperation and Competition in Civilian Space Activities (ISC-239)
Launch Options for the Future: A Buyer's Guide (ISC-383)
Orbital Debris: A Space Environmental Problem (BP-ISC-72)
Piloted Space Transportation Technologies
Reducing Launch Operations Costs: New Technologies and Practices (TM-ISC-28)
Remote Sensing in the Private Sector: Issues for Discussion (TM-ISC-20)
Round Trip to Orbit: Human Spaceflight Alternatives (ISC-419)
Salyut: Soviet Steps Toward Permanent Human Presence in Space (TM-STI-14)
SDI: Technology, Survivability, and Software (ISC-353)
Seismic Verification of Nuclear Test Ban Treaties (ISC-361)
Solar Power Satellite Systems (E-144)
Space Science Research in the United States (TM-STI-19)
Space Stations and the Law: Selected Legal Issues (BP-ISC-41)
UNISPACE '82: A Context for International Cooperation and Competition (TM-ISC-26)
U.S. - Soviet Cooperation in Space (TM-STI-27)

Science and Technology

Transportation

Advanced Space Transportation Technologies
Airport and Air Traffic Control Systems (STI-175)
Airport System Development (STI-231)
Automated Guideway Transit: An Assessment of Personal Rapid Transit and Other New Systems (T-8)
Big Dumb Boosters: A Low Cost Transportation Option (Background Paper)
The Border War On Drugs (O-336)
Changes in the Future Use and Characteristics of the Automobile Transportation System (T-83)
Civilian Space Policy and Applications (STI-177)
Delivering the Goods: Public Works Technologies, Management, and Financing (SET-477)
The Direct Use of Coal: Prospects and Problems of Production and Combustion (E-86)
Energy From Biological Processes (E-124)
An Evaluation of Railroad Safety (T-61)
Gasohol (TM-E-1)
Gearing Up for Safety: Motor Carrier Safety in a Competitive Environment (SET-382)
Safer Skies With TCAS: Traffic Alert and Collision Avoidance System (SET-431)
Impact of Advanced Air Transport Technology: Pt.1-Advanced High-Speed Aircraft (T-112)
Impact of Advanced Air Transport Technology: Pt.2-Air Cargo (BP-T-10)
Impact of Advanced Air Transport Technology: Pt.3-Air Services to Small Communities (T-170)
Impact of Advanced Air Transport Technology: Pt.4-Financing and Program Alternatives for Advanced High-Speed Aircraft (BP-T-14)
Impact of Advanced Group Rapid Transit Technology (T-106)
Increased Automobile Fuel Efficiency and Synthetic Fuels: Alternatives for Reducing Oil Imports (E-185)
Launch Options for the Future: A Buyer's Guide (ISC-383)
Managing the Nation's Commercial High-Level Radioactive Waste (O-171)
Mandatory Passive Restraints in Automobiles: Issues and Evidence (BP-H-15)
Moving Ahead: 1991 Surface Transportation Legislation (SET-496)
New Ways: Tiltrotor Aircraft and Magnetically Levitated Vehicles (SET-507)
Oil Transportation by Tankers: An Analysis of Marine Pollution and Safety Measures (O-9)
Piloted Space Transportation Technologies
Rebuilding the Foundations: State and Local Public Works Financing and Management (SET-447)
Reducing Launch Operations Costs: New Technologies and Practices (TM-ISC-28)
Review of the FAA 1982 National Airspace System Plan (STI-176)
Safe Skies for Tomorrow: Aviation Safety in a Competitive Environment (SET-381)
Safer skies with TCAS (Traffic Alert and Collision Avoidance System) (SET-432)
Strategic Materials: Technologies to Reduce U.S. Import Vulnerability (ITE-248)
A Technology Assessment of Coal Slurry Pipelines (E-60)
Transportation of Hazardous Materials (SET-304)
Transportation of Hazardous Materials: State and Local Activities (SET-301)
U.S. Passenger Rail Technologies (STI-222)
Wastes in Marine Environments (O-334)

* Pharmaceutical Research and Development

Office of Technology Assessment (OTA)
600 Pennsylvania Ave., SE
Washington, DC 20510 (202) 228-6590

OTA is working on a project to examine trends in the structure, process, and products of pharmaceutical R&D in the U.S., with the goal of developing and implementing a system for estimating and tracking R&D costs over time. The study will also describe the organization of the pharmaceutical R&D enterprise, identifying how costs differ by therapeutic class or biological research area. Contact Judith Wagner, the project director, for more information.

* Plastics and Adhesives Research

Plastics Technical Evaluation Center
U.S. Army Armament Research, Development
and Engineering Center (ARDEC)
Building 355-N
Picatinny Arsenal, NJ 07806-5000 (201) 724-4222

Technical information related to plastics, adhesives, and organic matrix composites is generated, evaluated, stored, and distributed at this Center, with an emphasis on performance and properties. Computerized databases are maintained on the compatibility of polymers with propellants and explosives and on materials deterioration. The Center provides services on a fee basis, including

consulting, state-of-the-art studies, handbooks, analysis, evaluation, and bibliographic and literature searches. To arrange for services or to get information, contact PLASTEC at the number listed above.

* Science Information Tracer Bullets

Science and Technology Division
Reference Section
Library of Congress
Washington, DC 20540 (202) 707-5580

Informal series of reference guides are issued free from the Science and Technology Division under the general title, *LC Science Tracer Bullet*. These guides are designed to help readers locate published material on subjects about which they have only general knowledge by providing detailed bibliographies and search strategies for topics of interest. New titles in the series are announced in the weekly Library of Congress *Information Bulletin* that is distributed to many libraries. The following is a list of *Tracer Bullets* currently available:

TB No.	Title
80-1	*Green Revolution*
80-3	*Automotive Electronics*
80-4	*Aging*
80-5	*Low-Level Ionizing Radiation: Health Effects*
80-6	*Lasers and Their Applications*
80-7	*Solar Energy*
80-8	*Electric and Hybrid Vehicles*
80-9	*Terminal Care*
80-10	*Infrared Applications*
80-11	*Drug Research on Human Subjects*
80-12	*Ocean Thermal Energy*
80-14	*Automotive Maintenance and Repair*
80-15	*The History of Psychology II*
80-16	*Synthetic Fuels*
80-18	*Health Foods*
80-19	*Industrial Robots*
81-2	*Medicinal Plants*
81-3	*Alcoholism*
81-5	*Wind Power*
81-6	*Pets and Pet Care*
81-9	*Cable Television (Cable TV)*
81-10	*Manned Space Flight*
81-11	*Mariculture*
81-13	*Wood As Fuel*
81-14	*Volcanoes*
81-15	*History of American Agriculture*
81-17	*Epilepsy*
82-1	*Food Additives*
82-2	*Gardening*
82-3	*Earth Sheltered Buildings*
82-4	*Extraterrestrial Life*
82-5	*Jet Engines and Jet Aircraft*
82-6	*Biological Control of Insects*
82-8	*Chemical and Biological Warfare (CBW)*
82-9	*Sickle Cell Anemia*
83-1	*Biofeedback*
83-2	*Power Metallurgy*
83-3	*Hazardous Wastes (Non-nuclear)*
83-4	*Science Policy*
83-5	*Plant Exploration and Introduction*
83-6	*Mental Retardation*
83-7	*Quarks*
83-8	*Women in the Sciences*
83-9	*Geothermal Energy*
83-10	*High Technology*
84-1	*Aquaculture*
84-2	*Edible Wild Plants*
84-3	*Japanese Science and Technology*
84-4	*Sharks*
84-5	*Scientific and Technical Libraries: Administration and Management*
84-7	*Biotechnology*
85-1	*Herbs and Herb Gardening*
85-2	*Landscape Gardening*
85-3	*Endangered Species (Animals)*
85-4	*Computer Security*
85-5	*Black Scientists*

Be patient. If any phone number is incorrect, call (area code) 555-1212 and request the new listing.

General Sources

Number	Topic
85-6	*Acupuncture*
85-7	*CAD/CAM (Computer Aided Design/ Computer Aided Manufacture)*
85-8	*Anorexia Nervosa/Bulimia*
85-10	*Rose Culture*
85-11	*Acquired Immune Deficiency Syndrome (AIDS)*
86-1	*Artificial Intelligence*
86-2	*Mars (Planet)*
86-3	*Jojoba and Other Oilseed Plants*
86-4	*Composite Materials*
86-5	*Electromagnetic Fields--Physiological and Health Effects*
86-6	*Diabetes Mellitus*
86-8	*Indoor Air Pollution*
86-10	*Career Opportunities in Science and Technology*
86-11	*Acid Rain*
87-1	*Asbestos*
87-2	*Alzheimer's Disease*
87-3	*Cellular Radio*
87-4	*The History of Technology*
87-5	*Science and Technology in China*
87-6	*Stress: Physiological and Psychological Aspects*
87-7	*Osteoporosis*
87-8	*The Future: Science and Technology Enter the 21st Century*
87-9	*Microcomputers*
87-10	*Tribology*
87-11	*Inventions and Inventors*
87-12	*Optical Disc Technology*
88-1	*Algae*
88-2	*Fiber Optics*
88-3	*Biographical Sources in the Sciences*
88-4	*Science Fair Projects*
88-5	*Soil Erosion*
88-6	*Noise Pollution*
89-1	*Science Policy--Foreign and International*
89-2	*Japanese Technology*
89-3	*Space Science Projects*
89-4	*Municipal Solid Waste Management*
89-5	*Human Diet and Nutrition*
89-6	*Endangered Species (Plants)*
89-7	*Allergy and Asthma*
89-8	*Earthquakes and Earthquake Engineering*
89-9	*Blacks in Science and Related Disciplines*
89-10	*Halocarbons and the Stratospheric Ozone Layer*
90-1	*Soviet Union and Eastern Europe: State of the Environment*
90-2	*Environmental Science Projects*
90-3	*High Speed Rail Transportation*
90-4	*Poisonous Plants*
90-5	*The Crisis in Science Education*
90-6	*Women in the Sciences*
90-7	*Freshwater Ecology*
90-8	*Astronomy and Astrophysics*
90-9	*Chemical And Biological Warfare*
90-10	*The Brain: an Overview*
91-1	*Unidentified Flying Objects*
91-2	*Civil Engineering: Public Works/Infrastructure*
91-3	*Dyslexia*
91-4	*Bioethics*
91-5	*Desalination*
91-6	*Career Opportunities in the Sciences*
91-7	*Breast Cancer*
91-8	*Medicinal Plants*
91-9	*Acquired Immunodeficiency Syndrome (AIDS)*
91-10	*Dolphins*
91-11	*Chemical Exposure: Toxicology, Safety, and Risk Assessment*
91-12	*Science Fair Projects*

* Ozone Depletion and Greenhouse Effect

Office of Technology Assessment (OTA)
600 Pennsylvania Ave., SE
Washington, DC 20510 (202) 228-6845

OTA is currently studying the major contributors to climate change, ozone depletion, and the greenhouse effect for both the developed and developing world. OTA will identify areas where gains in efficiency, product substitution, conservation, or other options can slow climate change. Contact Rosine Bierbaum, the project director, for more information.

* Patent, Trademark, and Copyright Monitoring

Intellectual Property Owners, Inc.
1255 23rd St., NW, #850, Washington, DC 20037; (202) 466-2396. IPO is a non-profit trade association representing people who own patents, trademarks, and copyrights. It gathers and disseminates information on legislative and regulatory matters, and monitors international events and intellectual property developments. It publishes the *IPO News* which keeps members up-to-date on developments in the field.

Patent Office Society
Commissioner of Patents and Trademarks, 2021 Jefferson Davis Highway, Crystal City, VA 22202; (703) 415-0350. This professional society for patent examiners promotes the patent system to the general public. It publishes the *Journal of the Patent Office Society* and the *Official Gazette*. The *Official Gazette* is printed every Tuesday for those trying to secure patents. It can be purchased from the Government Printing Office.

Commissioner of Patents and Trademarks
Public Service Center, Office of Patents and Trademarks, 2021 Jefferson Davis Highway, Crystal City, VA 20231; (703) 308-HELP or (703) 557-4636. The Center publishes a newsletter that includes a listing of publications and brochures put out by the Patent and Trademark Office. The staff tries to answer all questions such as finding the right office or locating publications. Patent specifications and drawings, as well as trademarks, are $3 each. You must have the patent or trademark number.

Search Room--Patents
2021 Jefferson Davis Highway, Crystal City, VA 22202; (703) 308-0595, (703) 557-4636 for general information; (703) 308-0808 for the Scientific Library. This service will search for any patent, and give the vendor's name, the issue date, and the title. You can also go in and search all patents in any field. The Scientific Library contains all US and foreign patents and is open to the public.

Search Room--Trademarks
2021 Jefferson Davis Highway, Crystal City, VA 22202; (703) 308-9800. To search a trademark, you must either go to this office or call the Trademark Library, which is open to the public.

Trademark Information Office
2021 Jefferson Davis Highway, Crystal City, VA 22202; (703) 308-9000. This office will answer questions on different aspects of trademarks, and has a booklet describing trademarks and what the Patents and Trademarks Office does.

Copyright Office
Reference and Bibliographic Section, Library of Congress, Washington, DC 20559; (202) 707-6850. This office will research the copyright you need and send you the information by mail. Requests must be in writing and you must specify exactly what it is you need to know.

United States Trademark Association
6 East 45th Street, New York, NY 10017; (212) 986-5880. The USTA keeps abreast of all aspects of the trademark field. Forums, educational meetings and an annual meeting are held. It maintains a comprehensive library that offers access to source material on all aspects of trademarks. Publications include *The Trademark Reporter, The Executive Newsletter*, and over 50 bulletins which are published each year, reporting on general news, publications, and events related to trademark law, advertising, marketing, and design.

American Intellectual Property Law Association
2001 Jefferson Davis Highway, Suite 203, Arlington, VA 22202; (703) 415-0780. AIPLA tries to promote better understanding of the patent, trademark, and copyright systems. Its law library is open to the public which makes available a wide range of material on patents. Publications include *AIPLA Bulletin* ($40/year), *AIPLA Quarterly Journal* ($45/year), and *An Overview of Intellectual Property* ($.25/pamphlet).

* Publications Prepared by the Science and Technology Division

Science and Technology Division
Library of Congress

Be patient. If any phone number is incorrect, call (area code) 555-1212 and request the new listing.

Science and Technology

Washington, DC 20540 (202) 707-5655

The Library of Congress' Science and Technology Division recently released a report entitled *Fifty Years of Science*, which lists hundreds of publications produced by the Division over the past fifty years with abstracts. Contact the Division to obtain a copy of the list.

* Renewable Energy Technology

Office of Technology Assessment (OTA)
600 Pennsylvania Ave, SE
Washington, DC 20510 (202) 228-6274

New concerns over energy security, economic growth, and environmental quality are once again focusing interest on renewable energy technologies. This study will evaluate a wide variety of renewable technologies and resources on the basis of their security, economic, and environmental costs and benefits in the near, middle, and long term. Systems to be considered include solar, wind, hydro, biomass, geothermal, and ocean resources. For more information, contact project director Sam Baldwin.

* Scientific and Technical Information

National Technical Information Service
U.S. Department of Commerce
5285 Port Royal Rd.
Springfield, VA 22161 (703) 487-4650

The U.S. government publishes a directory that provides an overview of Federal agencies' responsibilities in disseminating scientific and technical information originating with Federal research and development programs. It lists that major agencies involved and is a guide to comprehending the scope and relationships of Federal STI programs. It includes a table that shows the policy and operational roles of Federal agencies and their R&D budgets. Directory cost - $30. Order number PB91-180216CAU.

* Science and Technology Resources in U.S. Industry

National Technical Information Service
U.S. Department of Commerce
5285 Port Royal Rd.
Springfield, VA 22161 (703) 487-4650

The National Science Foundation has prepared a report that explores American industrial science and technological resources in terms of R&D activities, employment and use of scientists, engineers, and technicians. It examines how a country's competitive position is largely determined y its investment in human and capital resources dedicated to science and technology. Cost is $26; order number PB90-107194CAU.

* Science Fairs and Research Grants

U.S. Department of the Army
Army Research Office
P.O. Box 12211
Triangle Park, NC 27709-2211 (919) 549-0641

This office administers the nation-wide Science Fair program, which sponsors science competition at the high school level, and the Defense Research Initiative, which is a competitive grant program for government funding of university research. Write or call for free brochures and information describing these programs.

* Science Resources Center

National Science Resources Center
Smithsonian Institution
Arts and Industries Building
Room 1201
Washington, DC 20560 (202) 357-2555

The National Science Resources Center was established to improve the teaching of science and mathematics in the nation's schools. The NSRS has established a science and mathematics curriculum resource collection and database, developed and disseminates resources materials for science and mathematics teachers, and offers a program of outreach and leadership-development activities. One resource guide, *Science for Children: Resources for Teachers*, is a guide designed to help teachers and science educators identify teaching materials and resources that can be used to improve science teaching in elementary schools. Contact the Resource Center for more information.

* Solid State Laser Research

Documents Office
Naval Research Laboratory (NRL)
Code 4827
4555 Overlook Ave., SW
Washington, DC 20375-5000 (202) 767-2949

The Laboratory conducts research on low- and medium-power solid state lasers and infrared detectors. Technical reports can be obtained on the research from National Technical Information Service, 5285 Port Royal Road, Springfield, VA 22161; (703) 487-4650. A few are available from NRL directly. Contact the Documents Office for details.

* Standards for Industrial Engineering

Technical Reports Section
Science and Technology Division
Library of Congress
Washington, DC 20540 (202) 707-5655

The Standards Collection of the Science and Technology Division contains almost 500,000 items. In addition to the hundreds of organizations who have contributed to the collection, the *Technical Reports Section* holds a complete set of standards issued and sponsored by the American National Standards Institute (ANSI) as well as a complete set of U.S. Federal/Military and DOD adopted standards and specifications. The collection also includes a complete hardbound set of standards for the former Soviet Union, the Peoples Republic of China, and the Republic of South Africa. They are the only complete set of standards available to the public located in the U.S. For a list of the organizations whose standards are held by the Library of Congress, contact the Technical Reports Section at the above number.

* Superconducting Super Collider

Office of the Superconducting Super Collider
Office of Energy Research
U.S. Department of Energy
1000 Independence Ave., SW
Room 6E-034
Washington, DC 20585 (202) 586-7170

The SSC will be the worlds largest particle accelerator, with two rings of superconducting magnets in a 53-mile circumference race-track shaped tunnel. Continued progress in high-energy physics research in the late-1990s will require the study of collisions at energy levels that cannot be achieved with any accelerator now in operation. The total budget for the project is currently projected at $5.9 billion, with an expected completion around the year 1998. The site chosen for the Collider is located about 25 miles south of Dallas and 35 miles south-east of Fort Worth. For more information on the Collider, contact the above office.

* Superfund Technology

Center for Environmental Research Information
Environmental Protection Agency
26 West Martin Luther King Dr.
Cincinatti, OH 45263 (513) 569-7391

The Center for Environmental Research Information can provide you with the publication entitled *Compendium of Superfund Program Publications*, which details, among other things, the technologies used for the superfund cleanup programs of hazardous waste sites around the country.

* Technical Agriculture Resources

National Agricultural Library (NAL)
10301 Baltimore Blvd.
Beltsville, MD 20705 (301) 504-3755

NAL provides comprehensive information services for the food and agricultural sciences through a variety of sources, which include bibliographies, personal reference services, loans, photocopies, and online data files. Services are provided to agricultural colleges, research institutions, government agencies, agricultural associations, industry, individual scientists, and the general public. NAL cooperates with the Library of Congress and the National Library of Medicine to provide access to publications worldwide in the agricultural, chemical, and biological sciences. NAL houses one of the largest collections in the free world on agricultural subjects--2.3 million volumes and 26,000 periodicals--including biology, chemistry, nutrition, forestry, soil sciences, and much more.

Be patient. If any phone number is incorrect, call (area code) 555-1212 and request the new listing.

General Sources

* Technical Bibliographies

Published Searches
National Technical Information Service (NTIS)
U.S. Department of Commerce
5285 Port Royal Rd.
Springfield, VA 22161 (703) 487-4650

Published Searches contains bibliographies available on more than 3,000 topics from NTIS and 23 international information sources. These specialized bibliographies are created not only from material announced by NTIS, but also from published scientific journal articles gathered from 23 other international information sources. Each bibliography is chosen for its current interest to a particular audience. Most titles are updated annually. For a copy of the *NTIS Published Search Master Catalog* listing more the 3,000 titles, contact NTIS and ask for *PR-186.*

* Technical Memoranda

Publishing Office
Office of Technology Assessment (OTA)
600 Pennsylvania Ave., SE
Washington, DC 20510 (202) 224-8996

Issued at the request of Members of Congress, OTA *Technical Memoranda* are issued on specific subjects analyzed in recent OTA reports or in projects currently in process at OTA.

* Technology Research Army Libraries

U.S. Army Materiel Command
Information Systems Command
Public Affairs Office
Timberlake, AZ (602) 538-8609

Each Army Materiel Command installation has a technological library. It is usually possible to gain access to the library if you obtain prior approval. Contact your local AMC for information, or the above office for a referral to your closest installation.

* Technological Opportunities for Defense Conversion

Office of Technology Assessment (OTA)
600 Pennsylvania Ave, SE
Washington, DC 20510 (202) 228-6353

This OTA study will compliment a February 1992 study on projected defense needs. This study will look at the potential for converting facilities and technologies from defense to commercial activities and also explore possibilities for continued support of research and technology development relevant to the civilian economy that now depends on defense funding. It will examine innovative policies for R&D and the application of new technology to commercial production for technology transfers and diffusion, and for economic incentives for investment. Contact project director Katherine Gillman for more information.

* Technology Assessment Background Papers

Publishing Office
Office of Technology Assessment (OTA)
600 Pennsylvania Ave., SE
Washington, DC 20510 (202) 224-8996

Useful to a variety of different parties, the information in the *Background Papers* supports formal OTA assessments or is an outcome of internal exploratory planning and evaluation. The papers are free of charge, and can be requested through this office.

* Technology Assessment with Patents

Office of Documentation Information
Patent and Trademark Office
U.S. Department of Commerce
1921 Jefferson Davis Hwy., Room 304
Arlington, VA 22202 (703) 308-4357

The Technology Assessment and Forecast (TAF) Program's mission is to stimulate the use and enhance the usability of the more than 27 million documents which make the categorized U.S. patent file. The PTO has assembled the TAF database which covers all U.S. patents. The PTO extracts meaningful information about the U.S. patent file from the TAF database, analyzes the information, and makes it available in a variety of formats. Users of TAF information include patent attorneys, researchers, PTO employees and other government agencies. Patent information from the TAF database is distributed to users through publications, such as *Patent Profiles* and *Technology Assessment and Forecast Reports,* as well as through custom patent reports and statistical reports. Contact this office for more information on the TAF database, and ordering information for TAF publications.

* Technology Catalogs

National Technical Information Service
U.S. Department of Commerce
5285 Port Royal Rd.
Springfield, VA 22161 (703) 487-4650

Each of the *Federal Technology Catalogs: Guides to New and Practical Technologies* contains more than 1,000 summaries of selected processes, instruments, materials, equipment, software, services, and techniques. In conjunction with Federal agencies and their laboratories, key practical and applied results are screened for interest to U.S. engineers, research and development managers, and business planners. Most entries give a telephone contact for further detailed information or for specific technical discussion. Each catalog is subdivided into 23 subject headings making it easy to scan for exact references. Each entry includes full bibliographic information, full summaries, and how to obtain additional information. Catalogs are available for each year going back to 1981, and range in price from $27 to $36. Contact the Sales Desk to place an order or request the free information brochure, *PR-801.*

* Technology Commercialization

Office of Commercial Affairs (OCA)
Technology Administration
U.S. Department of Commerce
14th St. and Constitution Ave., NW
Room 4203
Washington, DC 20230 (202) 377-4743

This office works with industry to develop a consensus regarding technology opportunities and foreign competitive challenges. OCA facilitates cooperative joint ventures with U.S. industry in areas of research and technology development, and aims to improve the ability of U.S. industry to access federally-funded technology. This office also provides specific assistance in targeting and coordinating information activities in areas such as Japanese science and technology and metric conversion. Key activities include facilitating the adoption of flexible computer-integrated manufacturing by small- and medium-sized businesses by encouraging the establishment of private sector-funded joint centers and by working with other federal agencies and industry to remove barriers and create incentives. Contact this office for more information.

* Technology Exchange Programs

International Cooperative Division and Secretariat (P-25)
Office of International Transportation and Trade
Office of the Secretary of Transportation
U.S. Department of Transportation (DOT)
400 7th Street, SW
Washington, DC 20590 (202) 366-4368

DOT participates in a number of cooperative programs with other countries to exchange mutually beneficial transportation research data and state-of-the-art technical information. Areas of exchange include highway technology; ports and inland waterways; railway technology; and search and rescue operations. China and the Soviet Union are among the countries participating. Contact this office for information about these programs.

* Technology, Innovation, and U.S. Trade

Office of Technology Assessment (OTA)
600 Pennsylvania Ave., SE
Washington, DC 20510 (202) 228-6354

The international diffusion of technology has resulted in increased competition from a growing number of countries, in a widening array of products, and cut into the market share of U.S. manufacturers. OTA is currently examining how changes in the competitiveness of U.S. manufacturing industries affect the ability of the U.S. economy to create new jobs in various sectors. The study will also assess how technology, coupled with strategic responses by U.S. firms, could reverse the erosion of U.S. market shares. Contact Julie Gorte, the project director, for more information.

Be patient. If any phone number is incorrect, call (area code) 555-1212 and request the new listing.

Science and Technology

* Technology Policy

Office of Technology Policy (OTP)
Technology Administration
U.S. Department of Commerce
14th St. and Constitution Ave., NW
Room 4818
Washington, DC 20230 (202) 377-1581

This office analyzes and advocates the removal of technical and non-technical barriers to the commercialization of technology, including such macroeconomic policies as antitrust, trade, product liability, tax, regulatory, and intellectual property laws. The OTP staff also evaluate civilian technology trends and commercial potential in the U.S., and assesses options for greater cooperation among industry, government, and academia. This office assists state, local, and regional organizations in their support of technology-oriented companies and institutions through a clearinghouse with information on the initiatives and experiences of these organizations to date. Contact this office for more information on technology policy.

* Technology, Productivity, and Innovation

Technology Administration
U.S. Department of Commerce
14th St. and Constitution Ave., NW
Room 4824
Washington, DC 20230 (202) 377-1984

This administration identifies opportunities or barriers affecting U.S. commercial innovation, quality, productivity, and manufacturing, and advocates Federal policies and programs to eliminate government-wide statutory, regulatory, or other barriers to the rapid commercialization of U.S. science and technology. The Technology Administration represents U.S. commercial interests in international science and technology agreements and forums, and promotes joint efforts involving business, industry, educational institutions, and state and local organizations to encourage technology commercialization.

* Technological Risks and Opportunities for Future U.S. Energy Supply and Demand

Office of Technology Assessment (OTA)
600 Pennsylvania Ave., SE
Washington, DC 20510 (202) 228-6275

The OTA is currently studying the current views of the U.S. future energy outlook to identify key technical uncertainties and risks that affect the validity of these views, and to evaluate energy policy options for dealing with these uncertainties and risks. Contact Steven Plotkin, the project director, for more information.

* Technology Resources Directory

National Technical Information Service
U.S. Department of Commerce
5285 Port Royal Rd.
Springfield, VA 22161 (703) 487-4650

The *Directory of Federal Laboratory and Technology Resources* guides readers to hundreds of Federal agencies, laboratories, and engineering centers willing to share their expertise, equipment--and sometimes even their facilities--to aid in U.S. research efforts. The current edition contains detailed summaries of more than 1,000 unique resources, including descriptions of some 90 technical information centers. The name, address, and telephone number of a personal contact is listed for each entry, along with a detailed descriptive summary. The directory is available for $36. Contact the Sales Desk to place an order or to request the free information brochures, *PR-746* and *PR-801*.

* Technology Transfer in Agriculture

National Agriculture Library, room 1402
10301 Baltimore Blvd.
Beltsville, MD 20705-2351 (301) 504-7098

The TTIC works to convert agriculture related technology and innovations into practical commercial products. Increasing emphasis has been placed on technology transfer in recent years. A 1989 report *Technology Transfer: A Profile of Agency Activities in USDA*, details technology transfer activities in U.S. Department of Agriculture. Several projects are currently underway with respect to wood products. For more information, contact the TTIC.

* Technology Transfer Competitiveness

Technology Transfer Competitiveness
Administrator, Federal Laboratory Consortium
P.O. Box 545
Sequim, WA 98382 (206) 683-1828

The mission of the Consortium is to facilitate technology transfer among government, business, and academic entities in order to foster American economic and technological competitiveness. It sponsors conferences and seminars and publishes a free monthly newsletter (currently no charge). For very specific questions from bona fide researchers who find themselves at an impasse, the Consortium will conduct a database search to refer the inquirer to an appropriate lab. Write or call for a free general information packet explaining the organization, how to access its services, facilities available for testing, and examples of technology transfers.

* Technology Transfer and Systems Engineering

Director of Publications, DRI-P
Defense Systems Management College
Ft. Belvoir, VA 22060-5426 (703) 664-5082

This College publishes 28 books and a bi-monthly magazine entitled *Program Manager* (subscription, $7.50 per year). Titles include *Systems Engineering Management Guide* (a Government Printing Office all-time best-seller), *Cost Estimating*, *Subcontract Management Guide*, *Skill in Communications*, and *Program Office Guide to Technology Transfer*. All apply to acquisition and program management. Write for a free publications list explaining where to purchase them, stock numbers, and prices. Non-government employees must order publications through GPO at (202) 783-3238. The editor will also supply a sample copy of the *Program Manager* upon written request.

* U.S. Government Datafiles for Computers

National Technical Information Service
U.S. Department of Commerce
5285 Port Royal Rd.
Springfield, VA 22161 (703) 487-4650

The Directory of U.S. Government Datafiles for Mainframe and Minicomputers describes 1600 datafiles for unique Federal numeric and textual data. It offers a convenient reference to datafiles prepared by Federal agencies.

* U.S. Government Software

National Technical Information Service
U.S. Department of Commerce
5285 Port Royal Rd.
Springfield, VA 22161 (703) 487-4650

The U.S. Government publishes a directory of software for mainframes and microcomputers. It describes software applications and tools available from NTIS for more than 2000 programs arranged under 21 subject headings. For a free brochure on the directory, ask for *PR-261/827*. Directory cost is $59; order number is PB92-100106CAU.

* U.S.-Mexico Trade, Technology, and Investment

Office of Technology Assessment (OTA)
600 Pennsylvania Ave, SE
Washington, DC 20510 (202) 228-6345

OTA will examine investment in Mexico by the U.S. and Japan with an eye toward explaining the factors that induce investment. In particular OTA will look at the quality of Mexican labor, its receptiveness to training and Mexico's infrastructural ability to support technologically sophisticated manufacturing. OTA will assess the impact of the Free Trade Agreement on U.S. industries and exports. Contact John Alic, project manager, for more information.

* Waste Disposal and Product Design

Office of Technology Assessment (OTA)
600 Pennsylvania Ave, SE
Washington, DC 20510 (202) 228-6270

One innovative way to attack the waste disposal problem is by designing products that are more environmentally friendly when disposed of. This study will explore how technologies of "post consumption" wastes could be coupled more fully into the initial design processes. Incentives for producers to do this will be explored. Contact project manager Gregory Eyring for more information.

Be patient. If any phone number is incorrect, call (area code) 555-1212 and request the new listing.

Aerospace Technology / Space Research

* Aeronautical Engineering

National Technical Information Service (NTIS)
U.S. Department of Commerce
5285 Port Royal Rd.
Springfield, VA 22161   (703) 487-4630

This publication is prepared monthly for joint use by NASA, the FAA, and the scientific and technical community concerned with the field of aeronautical engineering. Each entry consists of a standard bibliographic citation and an abstract. This information includes a subject, personal author, and contract number.

* Aeronautical Systems Clearinghouse

Aeronautical Systems Division
Office of Public Affairs
U.S. Department of the Air Force
Wright-Patterson Air Force Base, OH 45433   (513) 255-3334

This office develops and acquires aeronautical systems, their components, and related aerospace equipment, including aircraft engines, airborne communications systems, special reconnaissance projects, and interpretation facilities. Fact sheets are available for each of the 200 programs administered by the agency. Write or call the above office for a free brochure describing the Division's mission.

* Aeronautics Research: Air Force

U.S. Department of the Air Force
Arnold Engineering Development Center
Air Force Systems Command
Arnold Air Force Base, TN 37389   (615) 454-5586

This center has test laboratories in which atmospheric conditions, orbital, space flight, and ballistic conditions can be simulated. A brochure on the base, its programs, and mission, along with fact sheets on technical subjects, including wind tunnels, aeropropulsion systems, and rocket test facilities can be obtained by writing or calling the above office.

* Aerospace Commercial Assistance

Boeing/Peat Marwick
Commercial Space Group
2001 M St., NW
Washington, DC 20024   (202) 467-3083

In 1986, NASA contracted with the Boeing Company and Peat Marwick to provide professional support to companies interested in exploring the potential benefits of space by providing the following services at no charge: current space activity briefings; concept formulation; technical planning and feasibility studies; experiment design assistance; market research; economic feasibility and business planning; financial alternatives and tax analysis; and links with other expertise in academia, industry, or NASA. If you are interested in pursuing a specific project or need assistance in space-related commercial areas, contact this office.

* Aerospace Commercialization Agreements

National Aeronautical and Space Administration (NASA)
Office of Commercial Programs
Code C/PAO
Washington, DC 20546   (703) 557-5609

NASA uses a number of innovative and functional agreements which provide private industry with assistance, services, and facilities to help reduce the risks associated with their commercial space ventures. This family of agreements include:

Joint Endeavor Agreements: Involving no exchange of funds between NASA and the private company, JEAs are designed to encourage early space ventures and demonstrate the use of space technology to meet marketplace needs. Private industry funds the experiments and NASA provides transportation and other services.

Space Systems Development Agreements: SSDAs provide industry with a deferred payment schedule for Shuttle launch services. This allows the entrepreneur to have a more favorable cash flow during a time when capital investment costs are typically the greatest.

Technical Exchange Agreements: TEAs are designed for companies interested in applying microgravity or other technologies to their commercial operations, but who are not yet ready to commit to a specific space flight experiment or venture. Under the agreement, NASA and a company agree to exchange technical information and cooperate in the conduct and analysis of ground-based research programs. The company funds its own participation, while at the same time gaining direct access to and results from NASA facilities and research.

* Aerospace Commercialization Publications

Office of Commercial Programs
National Aeronautics and Space Administration (NASA)
Code C/PAO
Washington, DC 20546   (703) 557-5609

The following publications on the commercial applications of space are available from this office:

Spinoff: An illustrated summary of NASA's major aeronautical and space programs, their goals and directions, their contributions to American scientific and technological growth, and their potential for practical benefits in new products and processes.

Aerospace Spinoffs: Twenty-Five Years of Technology Transfer.

Commercial Use of Space: A New Economic Strength for America.

NASA Commercial Programs: A Progress Report 1990. The Progress reports detail the years activities and include such information as discussion of the latest commercial program development, discussions of technology transfer activities, and Small Business Innovation Research Awards.

* Aerospace Commercial Users Catalog

Commercial Development Division (Code CC)
Office of Commercial Programs
National Aeronautics and Space Administration (NASA)
Washington, DC 20546   (703) 557-9528

This catalog, *Accessing Space: A Catalog of Process Equipment, and Resources for Commercial Users*, provides a broad range of information for the commercial developer of space seeking to understand and experience the areas of microgravity research and remote sensing. This publication provides an inventory along with information about the equipment and facilities that are being used and developed for commercial space applications.

* Aerospace Research Library

Information Management Division
National Air and Space Museum, Room 3100
Smithsonian Institute
Washington, DC 20560   (202) 357-3133

The Museum has a research library devoted to books and journals on aviation history, space exploration history, and science and technology in the fields of astronomy, astrophysics, engineering, geology, and space medicine. Appointments are strongly recommended as there is a limit of 5 researchers a day permitted due to limited staff resources. The library is open weekdays, 10am to 5pm.

* Aerospace Structures

Aerospace Structures Information
  and Analysis Center
U.S. Department of the Air Force
WRDC/FIBR

Be patient. If any phone number is incorrect, call (area code) 555-1212 and request the new listing.

Science and Technology

Wright-Patterson AFB, OH 45433 (513) 255-6688

This Center is a central point for the collection and distribution of aerospace structures information. It maintains a library of reports done by various government agencies, and can refer you to other libraries and sources. Requests for specific information are served for researchers or contractors with a "need to know" status. Write or call for *How to Get It: A Guide to Defense-related Information Sources* and a free brochure describing the Center, its services, and user eligibility.

* Aerospace Technology Briefs

Office of Commercial Programs National Aeronautical and Space Administration (NASA) Code C/PAO Washington, DC 20546 (703) 557-5609

Each issue of NASA's *Tech Briefs* contains concise descriptions of newly developed products and processes arising from NASA research and development efforts, and identifies and highlights information on new aerospace technologies which appear to have potential non-aerospace uses. Once you've identified a specific technology you are interested in, you can request a *Technology Support Package*, which provides more detailed information. Contact this office to be put on the *Tech Briefs* mailing list.

* Air Force Aeronautical Systems

U.S. Department of the Air Force Aeronautical Systems Division Public Affairs Office Wright-Patterson Air Force Base, OH 45433-6503 (513) 255-2725

The Public Affairs Office's brochure, *What's Happening at ASD*, lists the major programs in all the Aeronautical Systems Division offices, the contractors involved, and the program status. Also available is a brochure describing the five laboratories which make up the Wright Research and Development Center: aeropropulsion and power, flight dynamics, materials, avionics, and electronic technology.

* Ames Research Center

National Aeronautics and Space Administration (NASA) Moffett, CA 94035 (415) 604-4044

Located in the heart of "Silicon Valley" at the southern end of San Francisco Bay, Ames specializes in scientific research, exploration, and applications aimed toward creating new technology for the Nation. The center's major program responsibilities are concentrated in computer science and applications, computational and experimental aerodynamics, flight simulation, flight research, hypersonic aircraft, rotorcraft and powered-lift technology, aeronautical and space human factors, life sciences, space sciences, solar system exploration, airborne science and applications, and infrared astronomy. The center also supports military programs, the Space Shuttle, and various civil aviation projects such as the National Aerospace Plane. The center's laboratories are equipped to study solar and geophysical phenomena, life evolution and life environmental factors, and to detect life on other planets.

* Army Information Technology Laboratory

U.S. Army Corps of Engineers Waterways Experiment Station Public Affairs Office 3909 Halls Ferry Road Vicksburg, MS 39180-6199 (601) 634-2504

ITL operates one of the Army's largest computers and is also responsible for developing, managing and coordinating research and development projects in computer-aided interdisciplinary engineering areas; computer science; automation; visual information; etc. For more information, contact the Laboratory.

* Army Medical Research

U.S. Department of the Army Army Medical Research and Development Command Attn: SGRD-PA Fort Detrick Frederick, MD 21702 (301) 663-2732

This Command conducts research and development in medical sciences, supplies, and equipment. Write or call for free copies of the brochure describing the Command, a quarterly newsletter, and the *Broad Agency Announcement*

describing the research areas for which they solicit and instructions for submitting proposals.

* Army Research Labs, Speakers on Technology

U.S. Department of the Army Army Research Laboratory AMSLC-PA 2800 Powder Mill Rd. Adelphi, MD 20783-1145 (301) 394-3590

This Command oversees the work of the seven major U.S. Army research laboratories. Laboratory work is done in the areas of advanced computing and electronics; battlefield environmental effects; materials and structures; power sources; signal processing; and survivability enhancement. A brochure on the laboratories' missions and programs is available, and the Command can provide public speakers for civic groups in the field of technology development. Write or call for information.

* Army Technology Transfer and Commercialization

U.S. Department of the Army Army Research Office P.O. Box 12211 Triangle Park, NC 27709-2211 (919) 549-0641

The Army Research Office sponsors programs to further technology development and technology transfer in the United States. Its Technology Transfer Program allows private industry to enter into patent agreements with the Army, making possible the commercialization of Army technological findings. Write or call for free brochures and information describing these programs.

* Astronaut Candidates

Astronaut Selection Office, Mail Code AHX National Aeronautics and Space Administration (NASA) Johnson Space Center Houston, TX 77058

NASA accepts applications on a continuous basis and selects astronaut candidates as needed. Civilians and military personnel are considered for the one-year training program. Current regulations require that preference be given to U.S. citizens when they are available. Contact this office for more information on pilot astronaut or mission specialist opportunities.

* Automated Space Flight

Office of Space Science and Applications National Aeronautics and Space Administration (NASA) 400 Maryland Avenue, SW Washington, DC 20546 (202) 453-1547

The NASA automated space flight program is directed toward scientific investigations of the solar system using ground-based, airborne, and space techniques, including rockets, Earth satellites, and deep space probes. This office oversees research and development activities leading to programs that demonstrate the application of space systems, space environment, and space-related or derived technology for the benefit of the world. These activities involve such disciplines as weather and climate, pollution monitoring, Earth resources survey, and Earth and ocean physics.

* Big Bang Theory

Goddard Space Flight Center Greenbelt, MD 20771 (301) 286-6255

The Cosmic Background Explorer (COBE), a spacecraft built at Goddard, has been deployed to test the "Big Bang" theory about the origins of our universe, and gain answers to such questions as, What started the formation of galaxies? What caused galaxies to be arranged in giant clusters? The results from the COBE have begun to come in. Contact Goddard for more information concerning the project and its results.

* Bioserve ITA Materials Experiment

National Aeronautics and Space Administration (NASA) Office of Commercial Programs Code C/Room 1223 CG4 Washington, DC 20546 (703) 557-5609

Shuttle flights are increasingly used for scientific experimental research programs carried out by private companies in conjunction with NASA. In July 1991,

Be patient. If any phone number is incorrect, call (area code) 555-1212 and request the new listing.

Aerospace Technology

Instrumentation Technology Associates of Pennsylvania and BioServe Space Technologies of Colorado carried out a series of space experiments using a Materials Dispersion Apparatus developed by the companies. The objective of the experiments was to further obtain scientific and technical knowledge regarding the commercial potential of biomedical manufacturing processes and fluid science processing in the microgravity environment of space. In an experiment using the MDA, Urokinase crystals that take from 6 months to 3 years to grow on earth were grown in less than 7 days. Research on Urokinese may lead to significant progress in fighting cancer spreading and metastasis. The success in growing the crystals so quickly holds promise for future research in this area.

* Black Holes, Quasars, and Exploding Galaxies

Goddard Space Flight Center
Greenbelt, MD 20771 (301) 286-6255

The Gamma Ray Observatory (GRO) will try to study the processes that propel the energy-emitting objects of deep space: exploding galaxies, black holes, and quasars. One of the instruments used in this study is the Energetic Gamma-Ray Experiment Telescope. Contact Goddard for more information.

* Balloon Projects at NASA

Goddard Space Flight Center
Wallops Flight Facility
Wallops Island, VA 23337 (804) 824-1579

Wallops manages and coordinates NASA's Scientific Balloon Projects using thin film, helium-filled balloons to provide approximately 45 scientific missions each year. When fully inflated, the balloons can expand to nearly 600 feet in diameter with a volume of more than 50 million cubic feet. Contact Wallops for more information.

* Business in Space

Office of Commercial Programs
National Aeronautics and Space Administration (NASA)
400 Maryland Avenue, SW, Code C
Washington, DC 202546 (703) 557-5609

This office provides the focus within NASA for an agency-wide program to expand U.S. private sector investment and involvement in civil space activities. The office is responsible for programs actively supporting new, high technology commercial space ventures, the commercial application of existing aeronautics and space technology, and expanding commercial access to available NASA capabilities and services.

* Centers for the Commercial Development of Space

Office of Commercial Programs
Commercial Development Division
National Aeronautics and Space Administration (NASA)
Washington, DC 20546 (703) 557-9528

NASA's 17 Centers for the Commercial Development of Space are non-profit consortia of industry, universities, and government which conduct space-based, high-technology research and development in specific areas ranging from materials processing to remote sensing. These CCDS serve as incubators for future commercial space ventures, enabling their industrial affiliates to explore the economic value of space in a program where financial and technical risks are shared. For more information on becoming an industrial affiliate, contact one of the following centers:

Space Automation and Robotics Center, P.O. Box 134001, Ann Arbor MI 48105; (313) 994-1200, x2381.

The SPARC has three major focuses: 1. To develop Key Space Industrialization Enabling Technologies: Machine Vision and Sensing Systems, Robotics and Automated Manufacturing Concepts and Systems. 2. To develop commercial and technical plans as well as key components for space servicing applications: Design of Space Systems for Robotic Servicing, Space Services Technology, Tooling, and Systems. 3. To provide support for terrestrial Robotics and Automation applications: Servicing industrial systems, Robotics systems for operations in hazardous environments.

Wisconsin Center for Space Automation and Robotics (WCSAR), University of Wisconsin, Madison, 1357 University Avenue, Madison, WI 53715-1020; (608) 262-5524.

The WCSAR was established in 1989 to conceive, demonstrate and stimulate commercialization of space and terrestrial technology in the areas of ASTROBOTICS, to enhance the ability of humans to perform functional tasks required to travel, explore, and live in space; ASTROCULTURE, to develop technologies fora bioregenerative life support system required for long duration space missions ad for the establishment of permanently manned space settlements; and ASTROFUEL, to demonstrate that the thermonuclear fuel, Helium-3 (He3), uniquely present on the moon, can be of critical importance to the economies and future energy supplies of the Earth and for development of technologies to recover minerals from the lunar regolith.

Center for Mapping, The Ohio State University, 1216 Kinnear Rd., Columbus, OH 43212; (614) 292-6642.

This Center has four key objectives: timely collection of data that allows accurate location of surface features in terms of their geographical coordinates; merging these data; converting the data in useful information through the use of application and process models; and providing the information to those who need it.

ITD Space Remote Sensing Center, Building 1103, Suite 118, John Stennis Space Center, MS 39529; (601) 688-2509.

The Space Remote Sensing Center (SRSC)is providing commercial space applications development of satellite remote sensing, image processing, and geographic information systems.

Bioserve Space Technologies, University of Colorado-Boulder, Department of Aerospace Engineering Sciences, Campus Box 429, Boulder, CO 80309; (303) 492-7613.

There are approximately 30 projects now underway in the different Bioserve locations. Projects fall under one of the following four general headings: Biomedical Isomorphism - the study of earthly disease disorders that may have space-borne counterparts that could facilitate study in both Space and on Earth; Controlled Ecological Life Support Systems (CELSS) - a system is being set up at the University of Colorado; Bioprocessing and Bioproduct Research - Biological self assembly processes are under active study; and Related Hardware Development Tasks - Bioserve is engaged in a range of projects to develop hardware for its research.

Center for Cell Research, Pennsylvania State University, 204 South Frear Laboratory, University Park, PA 16802; (814) 865-2407.

The CCR focuses on commercial, product and process-oriented, biomedical/biotechnology projects in three main areas: physiological testing - using test animals and tissues in space research; bioseparations - this program offers American industry access to continuous flow electrophoresis and aqueous two phase partitioning in space; and illumination - this program seeks to develop photometric equipment for biological experiments.

Center for Macromolecular Crystallography, University of Alabama at Birmingham, Box 7, THT, UAB Station, Birmingham, AL 35294-0005; (205) 934-5329.

This center specializes in space-grown crystals of biological materials which are identified by participating firms in pharmaceutical, biotechnology and chemical industries. Its goal is to develop the technology and applications for the space-based material processing of biological crystals.

Advanced Materials Center, Battelle, 505 King Ave, Columbus, OH 43201-2693; (614) 424-6376.

The Advanced Materials CCDS conducts ground based research and microgravity flight experiments on advanced materials and processes, including polymers, industrial catalysts, electronic materials, metals, ceramics and superconductors.

Center for Commercial Crystal Growth in Space, Clarkson University, NASA Center for Crystal Growth, Clarkson University, 103 CAMP Building, Potsdam, NY 13699-5665; (315) 268-6446.

This center focuses on the following: developing commercial crystal growth in space by developing larger, more perfect unique crystals in the space environment; and a broad spectrum of crystal growth techniques, theoretical modelling, complementary thermophysical property measurement, and structural and electronic characterization.

Consortium for Materials Development in Space, University of Alabama at Huntsville, Research Institute Building, 4701 University Drive, Huntsville, AL 35899; (205) 895-6620.

This center focuses on commercial materials development projects that benefit from the unique attributes of space. Principal activities include physical vapor transport growth of highly non-linear optical inorganic and organic crystals and thin films, surface coatings and surface particle inclusions by electrodeposition, material preparations and longevity in hyperthermal atomic oxygen, physical

Science and Technology

properties of immiscible polymers and unique polymer production, and powdered metal sintering.

Space Vacuum Epitaxy Center, University of Houston, Science and Research Building, 4800 Calhoun Road, Houston, TX 77204-5507; (713) 749-3701. This center focuses its primary research efforts on exploring R&D and commercial possibilities of thin film growth and materials purification in space. Major research efforts are in the areas of definition and development of epitaxially-grown compound semiconductor materials for enhancement under space ultra-vacuum conditions and the definition/development of superconduction epitaxially grown thin films with low earth orbit space enhanced characteristics.

Center for Space Power, Texas A&M University, 223 Wisenbaker Engineering Research Center, The Texas A&M University System, College Station, TX 77843-3118; (409) 845-8768. CSP conducts research relevant to space power, and develops and demonstrates technology associated with the commercial use of space. Its goal is to demonstrate that providing power in space is an attractive commercial venture. The center supports a series of projects related to the production, storage and transmission of power.

CCDS Power and Advanced Electronics, Auburn University, Space Power Institute, Auburn, AL 36849-5320; (205) 844-5894. The overall objective of the center's efforts in space power is to identify critical technological impediments to the economic deployment of power systems in space, advance these technologies, and develop new products to meet power generation, storage, conditioning, and distribution needs.

Center for Space Transportation and Applied Research, University of Tennessee Space Institute, UT-Calspan Center for Aerospace Research, PO Box 850, Tullahoma, TN 37388; (615) 454-9294. The mission of CSTAR is to develop and commercialize aerospace technologies and thereby enhance the competitive position of US industry. The primary emphasis areas are: Space Propulsion, Aerospace Transportation and Infrastructure.

Center for Materials and Space Structures, Case Western Reserve University, White Bldg, Room 219, 10900 Euclid Ave, Cleveland, OH 44106; (216) 368-4203. This center focuses on providing materials for space structures that are capable of being processes in space and capable of withstanding the space environment. Research projects will focus on the following six areas: Polymeric composites; Metallic composites; Ceramic composites; Organic coatings; and Metallic coatings.

Center for Satellite and Hybrid Communication Networks, University of Maryland Systems Research Center, A.V. Williams Bldg, College Park, MD 20742; (301) 405-6606. The focus of this center is space-based communications, especially in the context of hybrid networks which integrate terrestrial and extra-terrestrial communication technologies.

Center for Space Communications Technology, Florida Atlantic University Research Corporation, Space Communications Technology Center, Florida Atlantic University, Boca Raton, FL 33431; (407) 367-3411. The mission of this center is to develop the commercial use of digital transmission techniques for transmitting video, audio and data to the earth by satellite.

* Regional Technology Transfer Centers

Mid-Atlantic RTTC NASA Industrial Applications Center,823 William Pitt Union, Pittsburgh, PA 15260; (412) 648-7000.

Far-West RTTC NASA Industrial Applications Center, Research Annex, Room 200, University of Southern California, 3716 South Hope Street, Los Angeles, CA 90007; (213) 743-7477.

Northeast RTTC Center for Technology Commercialization, Massachusetts Technology Park, 100 North Drive, Westborough, MA 01581; (508) 870-0042.

Technology Applications Team Research Triangle Institute, P.O. Box 12194, Research Triangle Park, NC 27709; (919) 541-7202.

Southeast RTTC Southern Technology Applications Center, University of Florida, College of Engineering, One Progress Boulevard, Box 24, Alachua, FL 32615; (904) 462-3913, or (800) 225-0308.

Mid-West RTTC Battelle Memorial Institute, Great Lakes Industrial Technology Center, 25000 Great Northern Corporate Center, Suite 450, Cleveland, OH 44070; (216) 734-0094.

Mid-Continent RTTC Commercial Technology Services, Texas Engineering Experiment Station, The Texas A&M University System, 237 Wisenbaker Engineering Research Center, College Station, TX 77843-3401.

National Technology Transfer Center Wheeling Jesuit College, 316 Washington Ave., Wheeling, WV 26003; (304) 243-2455.

Technology Applications Center University of New Mexico, 2808 Central SE, Albuquerque, NM 87131; (505) 277-3622.

Center for Aerospace Information PO Box 8757, Baltimore, MD 21240; (410) 859-5300, x241.

Computer Software Management and Information Center University of Georgia, 382 East Broad St., Athens, GA 30602; (404) 542-3265.

* Challenger Center for Space Science Education

1055 North Fairfax St.
Suite 100 (800) 969-5747
Alexandria, VA 22314 (703) 683-9740

The Challenger Center, founded as a living memorial to the Challenger crew, plans to construct a series of simulated space environment centers linked to museums, science centers, and school districts throughout the world through a comprehensive, international endowment program. The first center, the Challenger Center Space-Life Station, will be build in the Washington, DC, area, and will serve as headquarters for the network. The Marsville project is the first project in the Center's Adventures in Exploration program. In it, students will be asked to create a new human world, a multi-national settlement on Mars. The program is currently being piloted at thirty sites nationally. An educator membership is available that includes a journal, newsletter, updates, and conference information. There will be 30 Challenger Learning Center Sites open by the end of 1992. Contact the center for information on sites in your area.

* Chemical Propulsion Resource Center

The Johns Hopkins University
Applied Physics Laboratory
Chemical Propulsion Information Agency (CPIA)
10630 Little Patuxent Parkway
Columbia, MD 21044-3200 (410) 992-7307

CPIA provides products, specialized reference service, database searches, and copies of technical reports on all areas of chemical propulsion. Publications include *The Chemical Propulsion Abstracts, The CPIA/M1 Rocket Motor Manual, the CPIA/M2 Solid Propellant Manual, the CPIA/M6 Airbreathing Propulsion Manual, The JANNAF Propulsion Meeting,* and *Selected Papers.* CPIA also puts out a monthly bulletin updating subscribers on its activities. Write or call for a free pamphlet explaining their services and how to become a subscriber. Note, however, that this service is primarily for DOD contractors.

* Commercial Flight Program

Office of Commercial Programs
National Aeronautics and Space Administration (NASA)
Code C/PAO
Washington, DC 20546 (703) 557-5609

Under this program, businesses can gain access to NASA space capabilities and use the unique environment of space to conduct investigations that may lead to new, high-value products and technological advances. Certain portions of the Space Shuttle, Spacelab, and the Space Station Freedom payloads, for example, are being set aside for commercial uses.

Be patient. If any phone number is incorrect, call (area code) 555-1212 and request the new listing.

Aerospace Technology

* Commercial Payloads Video

Office of Commercial Programs
Commercial Development Division
National Aeronautics and Space Administration (NASA)
Washington, DC 20546 (703) 557-5609

NASA's Commercial Development Division is producing a videotape which shows how commercial payloads on spacecraft are developed, managed, and processed. The film is designed to provide viewers with a perspective on the basic flow of payload processing from concept, through ground processing, to post-mission analysis. It will be available through NASA's Headquarters, Centers for the Commercial Development of Space, and Field Centers.

* Commercial Programs Advisory Committee

National Aeronautics and Space Administration (NASA)
Office of Commercial Programs
Washington, DC 20546 (703) 557-5609

As a subcommittee of the NASA Advisory Council, the CPAC assists NASA by reviewing policies and programs, and recommending strategies to implement the national space policy goals to promote greater investment and participation by the U.S. private sector in America's civil space program. The Committee holds meetings that are open to the public. A free brochure, *Charting the Course: U.S. Space Enterprise and Space Industrial Competitiveness*, which includes highlights of the Committee's findings, is available.

* Commercial Programs Newsletter

Office of Commercial Programs
National Aeronautics and Space Administration (NASA)
Code C/PAO
Washington, DC 20546 (703) 557-5609

The free bimonthly publication, *Office of Commercial Programs Newsletter*, covers the latest news related to the NASA's commercial programs, including new publications, projects, committee meetings, grants, congressional actions, and technology transfer. For more information on obtaining copies, contact this office.

* Commercial Space Developments

FUTRON Corporation
490 M. St. SW, W305
Washington, DC 20024 (202) 479-0025

Under contract from NASA, the FUTRON Corporation produces a bimonthly newsletter updating recent developments in the area of commercial activities in space. Newsletters include information on developments in the Office of Commercial Programs and the Centers for the Commercial Development of Space, news on payloads recently launched, policy changes in the White House and Congress, and news about key players in the field. Contact FUTRON for more information and to order *Commercial Space Developments*.

* Competitive Contract Space Launches

National Aeronautics and Space Administration (NASA)
Office of Commercial Programs
Code C/Room 1223, CG4
Washington, DC 20546 (703) 557-5609

The Office of Commercial Programs (OCP) is sponsoring two sounding rocket series through a unique program developed with the consortium for Materials Development in Space (CDMS) based at the University of Alabama at Huntsville. The Sounding Rocket Program, initiated in 1988, acquires commercial suborbital launch services through competitive procurements and provides a range of early flight opportunities for various commercial payloads. The key element of the program is that the UAH CDMS seeks commercial launch services, specifying the requirements needed for the flight. The contractors then bid on the flights. The first series, named Consort, has had three successful flights in four attempts. The experiments vary according to flight.

* Computer Software Management/Information Center

University of Georgia
382 E. Board Street
Athens, GA 30602 (404) 542-3265

NASA and other government agencies develop many types of computer programs that frequently can be adapted--with little or no modification--to secondary uses, often remote from their original purpose. In the interests of national productivity, COSMIC offers adaptable programs to business and

industry at a fraction of their original cost. An additional benefit of the program is that COSMIC provides the source codes for the programs, allowing users to modify or adapt the programs and then sell them commercially. COSMIC publishes, in four different formats, a catalog of the some 1,400 programs available for purchase: on microfiche ($10); printed copies ($25); on IBM PC-compatible diskettes ($30); and on computer magnetic tape ($50).

* Crystal Growth in Space

National Aeronautics and Space Administration (NASA)
Office of Commercial Programs
Code C/Room 1223, CG4
Washington, DC 20546 (703) 557-5609

Protein crystal growth experiments have been conducted aboard 11 Shuttle flights over the past six years. The first four flights used hand held prototype equipment to test vapor diffusion technology. On the next four flights several protein crystals were produced by the vapor diffusion process within Refrigerator/Incubator Modules. Results from these experiments were encouraging and have led to two more flights in which crystals were grown using a new hardware configuration known as the Protein Crystallization Facility. The purpose of these experiments is to grow crystals that are larger and more pure than those which are produced on earth.

* Deep Space Network

Jet Propulsion Laboratory
4800 Oak Grove Drive
Pasadena, CA 91109 (818) 354-4862

JPL operates the worldwide deep space tracking and data acquisition network (DSN). As part of its DSN facilities, JPL oversees the use of the world's largest satellite receiving dishes located near Death Valley, California, measuring over 90 meters in diameter each.

* Dryden Flight Research Facility

Ames Research Center
Hugh L. Dryden Flight Research Facility
P.O. Box 273
Edwards, CA 93523 (805) 258-3441

Located at in the Mojave Desert about 80 miles north of Los Angeles, California, Ames-Dryden has developed a unique and highly specialized capability for conducting flight research programs. The facility was actively involved in the Approach and Landing Tests of the Space Shuttle Orbiter Enterprise and continues to support Shuttle landings from space. Currently, Ames-Dryden is conducting research on the X-29 program in a variety of advanced aero technologies, including forward swept wings, aeroelastic tailoring, and thin supercritical wings.

* Dual Use Technology

Office of Commercial Programs
National Aeronautics and Space Administration (NASA)
Code C/PAO
Washington, DC 20546 (703) 557-5609

Through the Small Business Innovation Research Program, established by Congress in 1982, NASA has worked with hundreds of small businesses on developing technologies useful for both the space program and commercial uses. Spinoffs from technologies originally developed primarily for the space program have benefitted the following areas: food safety, structural analysis of items such as oil drilling platforms, X-ray imaging, ultrasonic maintenance, aircraft collision avoidance, fire protection, flight simulation, performance testing, lightning protection, transportation safety, automotive design, and health monitoring. This information is detailed in the NASA publication *Spinoffs 1991*, which is available free from the Office of Commercial Programs.

* Earth Observing System (EOS)

Goddard Space Flight Center
Greenbelt, MD 20771 (301) 286-8955

Eos, the Earth Observing System, is a planned NASA program for observing the Earth from space using unmanned platforms in conjunction with the Space Station. Its goal is to understand the Earth as an integrated system. The platform will be equipped with remote sensing instruments, and launched into polar orbit so that all parts of the globe can be viewed. Contact Goddard for more information.

Be patient. If any phone number is incorrect, call (area code) 555-1212 and request the new listing.

Science and Technology

* Electronic Still Camera Experiment

National Aeronautics and Space Administration (NASA)
Office of Commercial Programs
Code C/Room 1223, CG4
Washington, DC 20546 (703) 557-5609

NASA, in conjunction with Autometric Inc. of Alexandria, VA are evaluating and analyzing the commercial potential of a high-resolution Electronic Still Camera developed by the Johnson Space Center. Electronic still photography is a developing technology providing the means by which a hand-held camera electronically captures and produces a digital image with resolution approaching film quality. The image can be computer enhanced and/or downlink transmitted. This technology will greatly aid Space Shuttle and Space station capabilities in Earth observations and on-board photo documentation. During STS-42 mission, the Shuttle crew will operate the ESC. NASA will evaluate the results of this test after the mission.

* Fluid Experiment Apparatus

National Aeronautics and Space Administration (NASA)
Office of Commercial Programs
Code C/Room 1223, CG4
Washington, DC 20546 (703) 557-5609

The Fluid Experiment Apparatus is a modular microgravity chemistry and physics laboratory used on the Space Shuttle for materials processing research. The FEA is used for the float-zone crystal growth process, which results in the production of pure crystals from samples. The project is being carried out in conjunction with Rockwell International.

* Goddard Space Flight Center

Greenbelt, MD 20771 (301) 286-6255

Located 10 miles northeast of Washington, DC, Goddard's research is centered in six space and Earth Science laboratories and in the management, development, and operation of several near-Earth space systems: The Hubble Space Telescope is an important astronomical telescope in space, studying the stars, planets, and interstellar space. The Upper Atmosphere Research Satellite will be launched to look back at Earth's atmosphere to help understand its composition and dynamics. As part of the Space Station program, Goddard will develop the detailed design, construction, and test and evaluation of the automated free-flying polar platform and provisions for instruments and payloads to be attached externally to the Space Station.

* HL-20 Space Launch System

Langley Research Center
MS 146
Hampton, VA 23665-5225 (804) 864-3293

For the past several years NASA has been studying an enhanced lifting body candidate for manned orbital missions. The concept, designated HL-20, has been designed for low operations cost, improved flight safety, and conventional runway landings. The orbiter is designed to take crews but not bulky cargo into space and return. Notably, unlike the Space Shuttle, the HL-20 would not have a payload bay nor main engines. Its size, only 20% of the Shuttle, would reduce maintenance time on the ground, reducing cost. Contact Langley for information on the continuing research on the HL-20.

* Hubble Space Telescope

Goddard Space Flight Center
Greenbelt, MD 20771 (301) 286-6255

The Hubble Space Telescope is an important astronomical telescope in space. Its deployment in space allows Hubble to see things more clearly than its counterparts on earth, which have to look through the atmosphere into space. Its movements are controlled from Goddard's Space Telescope Operations Control Center, as the observatory's five scientific instruments study the stars, planets, and interstellar space. The Space Telescope Science Institute in Baltimore, Maryland, is analyzing much of the data generated from the Hubble Space Telescope.

* Jet Propulsion Laboratory

4800 Oak Grove Drive
Pasadena, CA 91109 (818) 354-4862

Located 20 miles northeast of Los Angeles, California, JPL is engaged in activities associated with deep space automated scientific missions--engineering subsystem and instrument development, and data reduction and analysis required in deep space flight. Current NASA flight projects under JPL include Voyager, Galileo, Magellan, and the Mars Observer. JPL also designs and tests flight systems, including complete spacecraft, and provides technical direction to contractor organizations. JPL also operates the worldwide deep space tracking and data acquisition network (DSN) and maintains a substantial technology program to support present and future NASA flight projects.

* Langley Research Center

Hampton, VA 23665-5225 (804) 864-6123

Located about 100 miles south of Washington, DC, Langley's primary mission is the research and development of advanced concepts and technology for future aircraft and spacecraft systems, with particular emphasis on environmental effects, performance, range, safety, and economy. Examples of this research are projects involving flight simulation, composite structural materials, and automatic flight control systems. Work is continuing in the development of technology for avionic systems for reliable operations in terminal areas of the future. Efforts continue to improve supersonic flight capabilities for both transport and military aircraft. The center also works with the general aviation industry to help solve problems concerning aircraft design and load requirements and to improve flight operations. Overall about 60% of the work done at Langley is related to Aeronautics, while 40% relates to the Space program. Langley's newest major project is developing technology for the National Aero-Space Plane.

* Manned Space Flight Research

Lyndon B. Johnson Space Center
Houston, TX 77058 (713) 483-3671

Located 20 miles southeast of downtown Houston, Texas, the Johnson Center is NASA's primary center for design, development, and testing of spacecraft and related systems for manned flight; selection and training of astronauts; planning and conducting manned missions; and extensive participation in the medical, engineering, and scientific experiments carried aboard space flights. Johnson has program management responsibility for the Space Shuttle program and the Space Station, along with the interfaces between the two. The Johnson Center also directs the operations of the White Sands Test Facility in Las Cruces, New Mexico, which supports the Space Shuttle propulsion system, power system, and materials testing.

* Marshall Space Flight Center

Huntsville, AL 35812 (216) 433-6043

Located in Huntsville, Alabama, the Marshall Center, along with being NASA's launch vehicle development center, manages projects involving scientific investigation and application of space technology to the solution of problems on Earth. The Center provides the Shuttle orbiter's engines, the external tank that carries liquid hydrogen and liquid oxygen for those engines, and the solid rocket boosters that assist in lifting the Shuttle orbiter from the launch pad. Marshall's Orbital Maneuvering Vehicle will be carried into orbit also by the Shuttle to perform a number of activities, including moving satellites from one orbit to another. Marshall will also design the living and working, laboratory, and life support modules for the Space Station, along with an environmental control system.

* Michoud Assembly Facility

NASA SA-39
P.O. Box 29300
New Orleans, LA 70189 (504) 257-2601

Located about 15 miles east of downtown New Orleans, Louisiana, Michoud's primary mission is the systems engineering, engineering design, manufacture, fabrication, and assembly for the Space Shuttle external tank.

* NASA Activities Newsletter

Superintendent of Documents
Government Printing Office
Washington, DC 20402 (202) 783-3238

NASA Activities covers current agency highlights, including new programs and projects, personnel activities, field center news, relevant legislation, community activities, and more. It is available by subscription from GPO for $8 per year.

* NASA Formal Series Reports

National Technical Information Service
Springfield, VA 22161 (703) 487-4630

Be patient. If any phone number is incorrect, call (area code) 555-1212 and request the new listing.

Aerospace Technology

Through NTIS you can obtain full copies of scientific and technical reports produced by NASA. Original copies of these reports are sent to you as they are printed, even before they are announced to the general public by NASA. You can order reports under one of the ten following categories: Aeronautics, Astronautics, Chemistry and Materials, Engineering, Geosciences, Life Sciences, Mathematical and Computer Sciences, Physics, Social Sciences, and Space Sciences. Price per copy is $18.

* NASA Headquarters

400 Maryland Avenue, SW
Washington, DC 20546 (202) 453-1000

NASA Headquarters manages the space flight centers, research centers, and other installations that make up the National Aeronautics and Space Administration. The staff at Headquarters determine the programs and projects; establish management policies, procedures, and performance criteria; evaluate progress; review and analyzes all phases of the aerospace program.

* NASA Magazine

Internal Communications
Code P-2
NASA Headquarters
Washington, DC 20546 (202) 453-8332

Founded in 1991, the *NASA Magazine* is a quarterly news and information publication detailing the latest goings on at NASA as well as containing interesting articles on topics related to Space research.

* NASA Monetary Awards for Inventions

Staff Director
Inventions and Contributions Board
National Aeronautics and Space Administration (NASA)
Washington, DC 20546 (202) 453-2890

NASA makes monetary awards to individuals or organizations for scientific or technical contributions which have been used and have proven to be of verifiable value to NASA. Many qualified contributions have been produced during the performance of contracts for NASA. Contact this office for information concerning the criteria for eligibility and the procedure for submitting an application for an award.

* NASA Patent Bibliography

National Technical Information Service
5285 Port Royal Road
Springfield, VA 22101 (703) 487-4600

The *NASA Patent Abstracts Bibliography*, a semiannual updated compendium of over 4,000 NASA patented inventions, is published as a service to companies, firms, and individuals seeking new licensable products for the commercial market. For convenience, each issue has a separately bound *Abstract Section* ($13.75 per issue) and *Index Section* ($29 per copy). The *Abstract Section* covers only the indicated 6 month period, while the *Index Section* is cumulative, covering all NASA-owned inventions announced since May 1969.

* NASA Procurement Report

National Aeronautics and Space Administration (NASA)
Office of Procurement
Central Promenade
425 L'Enfant Plaza SW
Washington, DC 20546 (202) 453-2130

The *NASA Semiannual Procurement Report* presents summary data on all NASA procurement actions and detailed information on contracts, grants, agreements, and other procurements over $25,000 awarded by NASA during a six month period. Contact this office for your free copy.

* NASA STAR Journal

National Technical Information Service
Springfield, VA 22161 (703) 487-4630

The *NASA STAR Journal* is a microfiche copy of NASA's biweekly *STAR* journal, which indexes and abstracts all of NASA's research and development results, as well as other research and engineering related to aerodynamics and space. The price is $70 per year for 24 issues.

* National Aerospace Plane

Aerospace Plane Research and Development
Wright-Patterson Air Force Base
Dayton, OH 45433-6503 (513) 255-2725

The National Aerospace Plane, the X-30, capable of achieving low orbit but taking off and landing like a plane, could be one of the most significant technologies of the early 21st century. The NASA program isn't geared to developing the Orient Express high speed airliner that President Reagan referred to in his 1986 State of the Union address. To achieve orbit, the plane must be able to accelerate to Mach 25, or 17,500 miles per hour. At the same time, it has to both be able to carry enough fuel to get to orbit but in a small enough container so the plane isn't too large. Currently there are several labs working on the project, with Wright-Patterson coordinating the research effort. Contact the above office for more information on the project.

* National Space Technology Laboratories

Building 1100
Education and Productivity Office
Stennis Space Center
NSTL, MS 39529-6000 (601) 688-2739

Located near Bay St. Louis, Mississippi, NSTL's main mission is the support of Space Shuttle main engine and main orbiter propulsion system testing. NSTL is also a center of excellence in the area of remote sensing and is involved in Earth sciences programs of national and international significance, which are conducted at its Earth Resources Laboratory. NSTL also conducts data systems and commercial utilization studies in support of the Space Station.

* NASA Technology Transfer Network

NASA Field Centers
Office of Commercial Programs
Technology Transfer Division, Code CU
Washington, DC 20546 (703) 557-8160

The following NASA field centers can provide you with information on technology transfer activities and sources of information on NASA technical activities.

Ames Research Center
Office of Commercial and Community Programs, Mail Stop 223-3, Moffett Field CA 94035-1000; (415) 604-4044.

Goddard Space Flight Center
Office of Commercial Programs, Technology Utilization Office, Mail Code 702, Greenbelt, MD 20771; (301) 286-6242.

Jet Propulsion Laboratory
NASA Resident Office, Mail Stop 180-801, 4800 Oak Grove Dr., Pasadena, CA 91109; (818) 354-4862.

Johnson Space Center
Technology Utilization Office, Mail Code IC4, Houston, TX 77058; (713) 483-3809.

Kennedy Space Center
Technology Utilization Office, Mail Stop PT-PAT-A, Kennedy Space Center, FL 32899; (407) 867-3017.

Langley Research Center
Technology Utilization and Applications Office, Mail Stop 200, Hampton, VA 23665-5225; (804) 864-2484.

Lewis Research Center
Technology Utilization Office, Mail Stop 7/3, 21000 Brookpark Rd., Cleveland, OH 44135; (216) 433-5568.

Marshall Space Flight Center
Technology Utilization Office, Mail Code AT01, MSFC, AL 35812; (205) 544-2223.

Stennis Space Center
Technology Utilization Office, Mail Code HA30, SSC, MS 39529-6000; (601) 688-2042.

Be patient. If any phone number is incorrect, call (area code) 555-1212 and request the new listing.

Science and Technology

* National Space Council

Executive Office of the President
Washington, DC 20500
(202) 395-6175

Established by Executive Order 12675 in March 1989 under the Office of the Vice President, the National Space Council oversees the United States National Space Strategy. The five elements of this strategy are: transport - to develop U.S. space transport infrastructure and ability; exploration - to establish a permanent space station and study the possibility of a permanent Moon presence and a mission to Mars; solutions - to use Space technologies to solve problems here on Earth; opportunity - to foster economic well being on Earth; and freedom - so that space will be free for exploration and development. Contact the Space Council for more information on its activities and in particular for an annual report detailing its activities.

* Naval Avionics Development Center

U.S. Department of the Navy
Naval Air Warfare Center
Code 094, Small Business Office
Warminster, PA 18974
(215) 441-2456

This laboratory researches, develops, tests, and evaluates naval avionic systems. Write or call for their free pamphlet, *Doing Business with the Naval Air Development Center.*

* Oceans and Space

Goddard Space Flight Center
Greenbelt, MD 20771
(301) 286-8955

NASA's Laboratory for Oceans at Goddard works to expand the applications of space technology in oceanographic research by demonstrating new research uses of satellite data and initiating new flight instrument concepts for satellite flight missions.

* Ozone and Chlorofluorocarbons

Goddard Space Flight Center
Greenbelt, MD 20771
(301) 286-8955

Using such tools as Goddard's Total Ozone Mapping Spectrometer (TOMS) aboard the Nimbus-7 Spacecraft, NASA conducts research missions over Antarctica and Arctic regions to measure ozone, aerosol profiles, and other constituents of the atmosphere. Recent studies look at the relationship between fluorocarbons and ozone holes in the atmosphere. Contact Goddard for more information.

* Polymer Membrane Processing Experiments

National Aeronautics and Space Administration (NASA)
Office of Commercial Programs
Code C/Room 1223, CG4
Washington, DC 20546
(703) 557-5609

This experiment was sponsored by the Battelle Advanced Materials Center, a NASA Center for the Commercial Development of Space (CCDS), based in Columbus, Ohio. The objective of this payload was to investigate the physical and chemical processes that occur during the formation of polymer membranes in microgravity so that the improved technology base can be applied to commercial membrane processing techniques. Preliminary results from previous experiments indicate that membranes with significantly different porous qualities can be obtained in microgravity environments. Polymer membranes have been used by the separations industry for many years in such areas as water desalinization and kidney dialysis.

* Polymer Morphology Tests in Space

National Aeronautics and Space Administration (NASA)
Office of Commercial Programs
Code C/Room 1223, CG4
Washington, DC 20546
(703) 557-5609

As part of a joint endeavor agreement between NASA and 3M, a shuttle mission in November 1989 conducted the first real time study of microgravity on polymers as they change from solids to liquids and back to solids, using a Fourier Transform Infrared (FTIR) spectrometor to gather data samples as the polymers underwent the melt processing.

* Private Investment in Space

U.S. Government Printing Office

Washington, DC 20402

A recent Congressional Budget Office report entitled *Encouraging Private Investment in Space,* examines the current status of private ivestment in space activities in three areas: the provision of space launch services by large-capacity launch vehicles; the production of information based on data gathered by satellites through remote sensing; and the processing of materials in space, along with the provision of necessary orbital facilities.

* Propulsion Systems Research

NASA Lewis Research Center
21000 Brookpart Road
Cleveland, OH 44135
(216) 433-2899

Located about 20 miles southwest of Cleveland, Ohio, Lewis is NASA's leading center for research, technology, and development in aircraft propulsion, space propulsion, space power, and satellite communication. Lewis has the responsibility for developing the largest space power system ever designed to provide the electrical power necessary to accommodate the life support systems and research experiments to be conducted aboard the Space Station. In addition, Lewis will support the Station in other major areas, such as auxiliary propulsion systems and communications. This center is also working on materials and propulsion development for the National Aerospace Plane. Other facilities here include a zero-gravity drop tower, wind tunnels, space environment tanks, chemical rocket thrust stands, and chambers for testing jet engine efficiency and noise.

* Remote Sensing Systems Research

KPMG Marwick
Commercial Space Group
2001 M St., NW
Washington, DC 20036
(202) 467-3098

Currently there are two systems non-military systems that provide remote sensing data: the French SPOT system and the American Landsat. KPMG has produced a report that examines how a small satellite system could be commercially operated based on demand estimates for world-wide consumption of satellite data. Computer based maps have created an explosive demand for geographic information systems that can provide a full range of data and geographic analysis. Upgrades in satellite capability would be needed to fill this demand. The KPMG report looks at the scenario for a small specialized MAPSAT remote sensing system.

* Robot Space Retrieving Equipment

Goddard Space Flight Center
Greenbelt, MD 20771
(301) 286-8955

NASA is developing an autonomous free flying robot for retrieving equipment or a spacewalking astronaut drifting in separated flight near the Space Station. Recent test flights have been flown from the Space Shuttle's cargo bay. Contact Goddard for more information.

* Satellite-Aided Search and Rescue

Goddard Space Flight Center
Greenbelt, MD 20771
(301) 286-8955

In a cooperative project sponsored by the U.S., Canada, France, and the Soviet Union, NASA is working on a satellite system, SARSAT, that greatly reduces the time required to rescue air, sea, and other distress victims and to find victims which otherwise might not be found. Contact Goddard for more information.

* Satellite Repair In Space

Goddard Space Flight Center
Greenbelt, MD 20771
(301) 286-8955

The Satellite Servicing Project is working on ways to expand the operational life of satellites to be launched in the future. Not only does this project repair satellites, it also allow for planned routine maintenance calls in space which will maximize the longevity of the satellites and save money. Contact Goddard for more information.

* Spacecraft and Launch Vehicles

Office of Space Operations
National Aeronautics and Space Administration (NASA)
400 Maryland Avenue, SW, Code T
Washington, DC 20546
(202) 453-2019

Be patient. If any phone number is incorrect, call (area code) 555-1212 and request the new listing.

Aerospace Technology

This office tracks activities involving aeronautical research aircraft, space launch vehicles, and spacecraft. It also acquires and distributes technical and scientific data from these spacecraft. Contact this office for more information on this subject.

* Space Exploration

Office of Exploration
National Aeronautics and Space Administration (NASA)
400 Maryland Avenue, SW, Code Z
Washington, DC 20546
(202) 453-8394

The office develops long range plans for exploration and expansion of human presence beyond Earth into the solar system, along with a roadmap which provides opportunities and options leading to the commitment to national space exploration initiatives by 1992.

* Space Exploration Initiative

National Space Council
Executive Office of the President
Washington, DC 20500
(202) 395-6175

The National Space Council is involved with the planning for the Space Exploration Initiative. The goal of this initiative is to establish a permanent presence on the Moon and then use this base for robust exploration actities on Mars using both robotic and human missions.

* Space Launches

John F. Kennedy Space Center
Kennedy Space Center, FL 32899
(407) 867-7110

Located on the east coast of Florida, 150 miles south of Jacksonville, the Kennedy Space Center serves as the primary center within NASA for the test, checkout, and launch of space vehicles, which presently includes the launch of manned and unmanned vehicles at Kennedy, Cape Canaveral, and Vandenberg Air Force base in California. The Center is also responsible for the assembly, checkout, and launch of Space Shuttle vehicles and their payloads, landing operations, and the turn-around of Space shuttle orbiters between missions.

* Space Research and Technology

Office of Aeronautics and Space Technology (OAST)
National Aeronautics and Space Administration (NASA)
400 Maryland Avenue, SW, Code R
Washington, DC 20546
(202) 453-2754

This office plans, directs, executes, evaluates, documents, and distributes the results of NASA research and technology development programs. These programs are conducted primarily to demonstrate the feasibility of a concept, structure, or component system which may have general application to the nation's aeronautical and space objectives. For information on specific research programs, contact this NASA office.

* Space Shuttle and Spacelab

Office of Space Flight
National Aeronautics and Space Administration (NASA)
400 Maryland Avenue, SW, Code M
Washington, DC 20546
(202) 453-4164

To permit humans to explore space and perform missions which will lead to increased knowledge and the quality of life on Earth, this office directs the development of space transportation and the required supporting systems for humans to perform missions in space. One of the major program now underway is the Space Shuttle, and this office is responsible for scheduling Space Shuttle flights, including the Spacelab. This office also develops financial plans and pricing structures for these flights; provides services to users; manages expendable launch services and upper stages; and manages of NASA's advanced program activities.

* Space Shuttle Program Book

Superintendent of Documents
Government Printing Office (GPO)
Washington, DC 20402
(202) 783-3238

The NASA publication *Space Shuttle: The Renewed Promise*, discusses the changes made in the Shuttle program in the wake of the Challenger accident and the achievements of the program to date. Contact the GPO for price and availability.

* Space Flight History

Office of Space Flight
National Aeronautics and Space Administration (NASA)
400 Maryland Avenue, SW, Code M
Washington, DC 20546
(202) 453-4164

The publication *Space Flight: The First 30 Years*, details the history of the space program and includes information on the Mercury, Gemeni, Apollo, Skylab and Space Shuttle missions. It is available free from this office.

* Space Station

Office of Space Station
National Aeronautics and Space Administration (NASA)
600 Independence Avenue, SW, Code S
Washington, DC 20546
(202) 453-4164

This office manages and directs all aspects of NASA's Space Station program whose goal is to develop a permanently manned Space Station by the mid 1990s; to encourage other nations to participate in the Space Station program; and to promote private sector investment in space through enhanced space-based operational capabilities.

* Space-Type Freeze-Dehydrated Foods

GEWA Visitor Center Gift Shop
Goddard Space Flight Center
Greenbelt, MD 20771
(301) 286-6476

The Gift Shop at Goddard sells samples of foods that astronauts eat during space flights. The food, however, is for sale only in the Gift Shop--no mail orders. Other companies that can provide you with information on space-type, freeze dried foods include the following: Spaceland Enterprises, Inc., 1970 Carroll Ave., San Francisco, CA 94124; and Sky-Lab Foods, Inc., 177 Lake Street, White Plains, NY 10604.

* Space Telescope Science Institute (STSI)

Johns Hopkins Homewood Campus
Baltimore, MD 21218
(301) 338-4514

Located in Baltimore, Maryland, STSI plans and conducts science operations for the Edwin P. Hubble Space Telescope, a cooperative venture between NASA and the European Space Agency (ESA). Scheduled for launch aboard the Space shuttle, the telescope spacecraft will orbit the Earth at approximately 350 miles sending data and receiving commands through NASA's Tracking and Data Relay Satellite System.

* Space Technology Research

U.S. Air Force Space Technology Center
Kirtland Air Force Base, NM 87117-6008
(505) 846-1911

This Center overseas the work of the three major Air Force research laboratories: the Weapons Laboratory at Kirtland; the Astronautics Laboratory at Edwards Air Force Base, California; and the Geophysics Laboratory at Hanscom Air Force Base, Massachusetts. Free fact sheets on all three labs and their programs are available from this Center, including fact sheets on the SDI program, the relay mirror experiment, the Alpha chemical laser experiment, "Brilliant Pebbles" research, optics research, microwaves, plasma physics, and nuclear weapons effects research. The Center offers a Speakers Bureau of experts and intern programs for outside researchers.

* Stars in the Sky

R. Woods, Consumer Information Center-2A
P.O. Box 100
Pueblo, CO 81002

The Consumer Information Catalogue has two inexpensive publications available dealing with stars. *A Look at the Planets* contains full-color photos and descriptions of the planets ($1), and *Stars in Your Eyes: A Guide to the Northern Skies* provides helpful hints on how to find the seven best know constellations ($1.50).

* Star Wars and Other Defense Research Information

Office of Assistant Secretary of Defense
Public Affairs
Directorate for Defense Information
Pentagon 2E765
Washington, DC 20301-1400
(703) 695-3886

Be patient. If any phone number is incorrect, call (area code) 555-1212 and request the new listing.

Science and Technology

This office can supply you with fact sheets, press releases, and reports on defense programs such as Star Wars, the DOD Laser and Space Program, and the Defense Advanced Research Projects Agency (DARPA) activities, and related Congressional activity. Staff can also direct you in making FOIA requests for Defense contract information.

* Super-Maneuverable Jet Fighter

Ames Research Center
Hugh L. Dryden Flight Research Facility
P.O. Box 273
Edwards, CA 93523 (805) 258-8381

Ames-Dryden is testing a specially instrumented F-18 fighter jet to investigate high alpha or high angle of attack flight which may result in airplanes capable of "supermaneuvers." Contact Ames for more information.

* Technology Transfer Statistics

Office of Commercial Programs
National Aeronautical and Space Administration (NASA)
Washington, DC 20546 (202) 453-1123

NASA is currently studying the economic impact of their technology transfer programs in both the aerospace industry and the nation at large. When completed, the study will be available through this office. For more information on the study, contact this office.

* Technology Utilization Officers

Technology Utilization Division
NASA Scientific and Technical Information Facility
P.O. Box 8757
Baltimore, MD 21240

Within the NASA technology transfer network, Technology Utilization Officers (TUOs) are placed at each of NASA's field centers. They work with industry, providing information on new technologies developed at the center and matching and cross-correlating NASA technologies with industrial needs. They also provide a link to NASA's engineers and scientists, who can help clients locate, adapt, and implement NASA technology. The following is a list of the NASA field centers and their technology utilization officers.

Ames Research Center, Mail Code 223-3, Moffett Field, CA 94035/Larry Milov/(415) 694-6471.

Goddard Space Flight Center, Mail Code 702, Greenbelt, MD 20771/Donald Friedman/(301) 286-6242.

Lyndon B. Johnson Space Center, Mail Code EA4, NASA Road One, Houston, TX 77058/Dean Glenn/(713) 483-3809

Langley Research Center, Mail Stop 139A, Hampton, VA 23665/John Samos/(804) 865-3281.

Marshall Space Flight Center, Code AT01, MSFC, AL 35812/Ismail Akbay/(205) 544-2223.

Lewis Research Center, Mail Stop 7-3, 21000 Brookpark Road, Cleveland, OH 44135/Daniel Soltis/(216) 433-5567.

Jet Propulsion Laboratory, Mail Stop 156-211, 4800 Oak Grove Drive, Pasadena, CA 91109/Norman Chalfin/(818) 354-2240.

National Space Technology Laboratories, Code GA-00, NSTL Station, MS 39529/Robert Barlow/(601) 688-1929.

John F. Kennedy Space Center, Mail Stop PT-TPO-A, Kennedy Space Center, FL 32899/Thomas Hammond/(305) 867-3017.

NASA Resident Office-JPL, Mail Stop 180-801, 4800 Oak Grove Drive, Pasadena, CA 91109/Gordon Chapman/(818) 354-4849.

* Tethered Satellite System

Marshall Space Flight Center
Huntsville, AL 35812 (216) 433-6043

Marshall manages the Tethered Satellite System, expected to be in orbit by 1990, which will be carried by the Space Shuttle into space and suspended from the orbiter's cargo bay on a tether to study electrodynamic phenomena and the Earth's upper atmosphere for magnetospheric, atmospheric, and gravitational data.

* Tracking and Data Relay Satellite System

Goddard Space Flight Center
Greenbelt, MD 20771 (301) 286-6255

Voice and data transmissions between Earth and orbital regions are multiplying rapidly, and to accommodate this communications growth NASA is building a new Earth-to-orbit and orbit-to-Earth communications link called the Tracking and Data Relay Satellite System. When completed, TDRSS, along with two other communications satellites, will comprise NASA's Space Network, and will be one of the biggest advances in space communications technology to date. For more information, contact Goddard.

* Transonic Wind Tunnels

Langley Research Center
Hampton, VA 23665-5225 (804) 864-6123

Included in Langley's research labs are a variety of wind tunnels covering the entire Mach-number speed range. The National Transonic Facility is a new cryogenic wind tunnel providing a unique opportunity for conducting high Reynolds number research at subsonic and transonic speeds.

* Upper Atmosphere Research Satellite (UARS)

Goddard Space Flight Center
Greenbelt, MD 20771 (301) 286-8955

To investigate current upper atmospheric changes, UARS will provide for the first time the global data required in probing the chemistry, dynamics, and radiative inputs of the stratosphere and mesosphere. Contact Goddard for more information.

* Wallops Flight Facility

Goddard Space Flight Center
Wallops Island, VA 23337 (804) 824-1579

A part of Goddard Space Flight Center, Wallops manages and implements NASA's sounding rocket projects which use suborbital rocket vehicles to accommodate approximately 50 scientific missions each year. Approximately 100-150 rocket launches are conducted each year from the Wallops Island site. In cooperative and commercial projects, Wallops provides support which includes launching, tracking, aircraft flights, and data reduction, to various segments of the U.S. Department of Defense and commercial and educational ventures. Wallops also conducts Earth and ocean physics, ocean biological and atmospheric science field experiments; satellite correlative measurements; and developmental projects for new remote sensor systems.

* X-Ray Astrophysics

Goddard Space Flight Center
Greenbelt, MD 20771 (301) 286-8955

When completed, NASA's X-ray Astrophysics Facility (AXAF) will permit astronomers to extend their observations of the cosmos beyond the normal visible band to the X-ray region of the spectrum, providing valuable new information on phenomena spanning our Milky Way galaxy and stretching to the farthest reaches of the known universe. Contact Goddard for more information.

Be patient. If any phone number is incorrect, call (area code) 555-1212 and request the new listing.

Geology and Earth Science

* Do You Love GOLD?

USGS Book and Report Sales
P.O. Box 25425
Denver, CO 80225

The U.S. Geological Survey has several free publications dealing with Gold.

Gold - discusses the nature of gold, its origins, and the geologic environments in which it is found.

Prospecting for Gold in the United States - describes various kinds of gold deposits and their locations.

Suggestions for Prospecting - compares modern prospecting techniques with those of earlier years.

* Drilling Core Library

Core Library
U.S. Geological Survey (USGS)
MS 975, Building 810
Box 25046, Federal Center
Denver, CO 80225 (303) 236-1931

The USGS Core Library collects, stores, and makes available to the public valuable core material from boreholes drilled for oil and gas. The cores are collected from a variety of public and private sources, most of them being from the Rocky Mountain and the Great Plains regions. The cores are processed into core slabs, a more usable and easily archived form. You can examine the processed cores at the facility.

* Earth Science Bibliography

Superintendent of Documents
Government Printing Office
Washington, DC 20402 (202) 783-3238

Earthquake and volcano publications are listed in this bibliography. *Earthquakes and Volcanoes*, a bimonthly subscription service is featured at an annual cost of $6.50. The *Preliminary Determination of Epicenters* subscription service is listed at a yearly cost of $14. Space and satellite publications are also included. Free.

* Earth Science Data Directory

National Technical Information Service
5285 Port Royal Road
Springfield, VA 22161 (703) 487-4929

The *ESDD* is a comprehensive listing of available databases in earth sciences and natural resources. References include databases on global change the *Arctic Environment Data Directory*, and geographic and socioeconomic databases. Contributors include governmental agencies, academic institutions, and the private sector. For more information on the database itself, contact USGS at (703) 648-7112.

* Earth Science Information Centers

Reston-ESIC
U.S. Geological Survey (USGS)
507 National Center
Reston, VA 22092 (800) 872-6277 (703) 648-6045

The Earth Science Information Office operates a nationwide information and sales service for the results of earth science research, maps, and related products and publications. A network of Earth Science Information Centers provides information about geologic, hydrologic, topographic, and land-use maps; books and reports; aerial, satellite, and radar images and related products; earth science and map data in digital form and related applications software; and geodetic data. ESIC offices can take orders for such customized products as aerial photographs and orthophotoquads, digital cartographic data, and geographic names gazetteers. These centers also function as over-the-counter dealers for USGS books and maps.

Anchorage
ESIC, U.S. Geological Survey, 4230 University Dr., Room 101, Anchorage, AK 99508-4664; (907) 786-7011.

Anchorage
ESIC, U.S. Geological Survey, U.S. Courthouse, Room 113, 222 W. 7th Ave., #53, Anchorage, AK 99513-7546; (907) 271-2754

Denver
ESIC, U.S. Geological Survey, 169 Federal Building, 1961 Stout St., Denver, CO 80294; (303) 844-4169

Lakewood
ESIC, U.S. Geological Survey, Box 25046, Federal Center, MS 504, Denver, CO 80225-0046; (303) 236-5829

Menlo Park
ESIC, U.S. Geological Survey, Building 3, MS 532, 345 Middlefield Rd., Menlo Park, CA 94025; (415) 329-4309

Reston
ESIC, U.S. Geological Survey, 507 National Center, Reston, VA 22092; (703) 648-6045

Rolla
ESIC, U.S. Geological Survey, 1400 Independence Rd., MS 231, Rolla, MO 65401; (314) 341-0851

Salt Lake City
ESIC, U.S. Geological Survey, 8105 Federal Building, 125 S. State St., Salt Lake City, UT 84138; (801) 524-5652

San Francisco
ESIC, U.S. Geological Survey, 504 Custom House, 555 Battery St., San Francisco, CA 94111; (415) 705-1010.

Sioux Falls
ESIC U.S. Geological Survey, EROS Data Center, Sioux Falls, SD 57198; (605) 594-6151.

Spokane
ESIC, U.S. Geological Survey, 678 U.S. Courthouse, W. 920 Riverside Ave., Spokane, WA 99201; (509) 353-2524

Stennis Space Center
ESIC, U.S. Geological Survey, Bldg. 3101, Stennis Space Center, MS 39529; (601) 688-3544

Washington, DC
ESIC, U.S. Geological Survey, Department of the Interior Building, 18th and C Sts. NW, Room 2650, Washington, DC 20240; (202) 208-4047

* Earth Science Information Just A Phone Call Away

ESDD Project Manager
U.S. Geological Survey (USGS)
801 National Center
Reston, VA 22092 (703) 648-7112

The *Earth Science Data Directory* (ESDD) is a directory of earth-science data bases that is administered by the USGS. Between 400-600 references to data bases are being added annually. The referenced data bases involve a wide range of earth science fields including geology, hydrology, cartography, and biology. Contact this office for more information.

* Earth Science Teaching Materials

Geologic Inquiries Group

Be patient. If any phone number is incorrect, call (area code) 555-1212 and request the new listing.

Science and Technology

U.S. Geological Survey (USGS)
907 National Center
Reston, VA 22092 (703) 648-4383

Packets of geological teaching aids for different grade levels and geographic location are available from the Geologic Inquiries Group and from the Earth Science Information Centers listed elsewhere in this book. These packets include lists of reference materials, various maps and map indexes, and a selection of general interest publications. Requests for teachers packets should be sent on school letterhead, indicating the grade level and subject of interest.

* Earthquake Information

National Earthquake Information Center
U.S. Geological Survey (USGS)
Mail Stop 967
Box 25046, Federal Center
Denver, CO 80225 (303) 236-1500

The National Earthquake Information Center compiles, computes, and distributes digital and analog data on earthquakes that have occurred around the world. Using the Global Digital Seismic Network and other sources the Center compiles digital data on earthquakes measuring 5.5 or higher onto Event Tapes. For more information, contact the Center.

* Earthquake Safety

S. James, Consumer Information Center- 2A
P.O. Box 100
Pueblo, CO 81002

Safety and Survival in an Earthquake explains actions you take before, during and after an earthquake which may save you and your family's lives. Learn what to do at home and in your community (146Y, $2).

* Energy Engineering and Geoscience Research

Office of Basic Energy Sciences
Engineering and Geosciences Division
U.S. Department of Energy
19901 Germantown Rd.
Germantown, MD 20585 (301) 903-5822

This Division supports the U.S. Department of Energy's central fundamental research activities in the engineering and geoscience disciplines conducted by universities, Federal Laboratories, and industrial firms throughout the U.S. Emphasis in geoscience research is given to the geophysics and geochemistry of rock/fluid systems.

* Energy Science Research

Accelerator and Fusion Research Division
Lawrence Berkeley Laboratory
1 Cyclotron Road
Mail Stop 50A/5104
Berkeley, CA 94720 (510) 486-5771

The Lawrence Berkeley Laboratory undertakes a wide ranging research program in Energy Sciences, which includes geology, chemistry, materials sciences, physics and engineering. LBL pursues basic research and seeks ways of practical application of the basic results. The work of this division of the Laboratory is designed to reflect Energy Department priorities in finding ways to explore and recover energy resources, as well as protecting people and the environment from possible hazards. Contact the above office for further information.

* Environmental Geology

Geologic Division
U.S. Geological Survey (USGS)
National Center, MS 911
Reston, VA 22092 (703) 648-6600

The U.S. Geological Survey (USGS) conducts geologic mapping and gathers other basic information about the Nation's geologic framework and the processes that have shaped it. Scientists also determine the age and distribution of different types of rocks, climatic changes and their effect on land and water resources, and variations in the Earth's gravity and magnetic field.

* EROS Data Center

U.S. Geological Survey (USGS)
EROS Data Center

Sioux Falls, SD 57198 (605) 594-6151

The EROS data center receives, processes, and distributes earth-image data acquired by satellite and aircraft and investigates new uses for such data. The Center also develops computerized land information systems and studies new ways of handling data and information. The EDC also sells high and low altitude photographs as well as photographs from NASA's manned spacecraft. In cooperation with NOAA, the Center also distributes LANDSAT data. Contact the center for more information.

* Field Record Collections

U.S. Geological Survey (USGS)
Mail Stop 914, Building 20
Box 25046, Federal Center
Denver, CO 80225 (303) 236-1005

The Field Records collection is the depository for the original materials produced by the USGS geologists during their field investigations. The collection consists primarily of materials on the U.S. and holdings consist of 15,600 notebooks, 2000 folders, 2400 map groups, and 60,000 aerial photographs. Contact the Denver office to inquire about specific records and the possibility of having them sent to a more convenient library for examination.

* Free Information on Earthquakes and Volcanoes

USGS Book and Report Sales
P.O. Box 25425
Denver, CO 80225

The U.S. Geological Survey has the following free publications dealing with earthquakes and volcanoes:

Earthquakes - explains the nature and causes of earthquakes.

Safety and Survival in an Earthquake - describes the hazards posed by earthquakes and offers instructions for individual action before, during, and after a tremor.

The San Andreas Fault - describes the nature, behavior, and earthquake history of this major fault system.

Volcanoes - describes the principal types of volcanoes, different types of eruptions, associated volcanic phenomena, their geologic settings, and how volcanoes are monitored.

Volcanic Hazards of Mount Shasta, California - describes the kinds of volcanic activity that have occurred in the past, shows areas that could be affected in the future, and suggests ways of reducing the risks.

* Geodetic Information

National Geodetic Data Center
National Ocean Service
National Oceanic and Atmospheric Administration
U.S. Department of Commerce
11400 Rockville Pike
Rockville, MD 20852 (301) 443-8631

The National Geodetic Data Center collects, maintains, publishes, and distributes a complete range of information pertaining to the National Geodetic Reference System, including data on vertical and horizontal geodetic survey stations, geodetic control diagrams for the conterminous United States, Alaska, and Hawaii, gravity values for over 1 million points, calibration base line data, astronomic and Doppler satellite data, computer programs for geodetic applications, and geodetic publications and historical records. NGDC has catalogs available describing a variety of maps, slide sets, and educational tools which are appropriate for both technical and non-technical audiences. Data is broken down into ten categories: solid earth geophysics, earthquake seismology, geomagnetic survey data, marine geological data, marine geophysical data, solar-terrestrial data, solar activity data, geomagnetic variations data, ionospheric data and glaciology. Databases, bulletins, and reports are available within each category. A *Directory of Data Services* lists researchers who can be contacted for technical information about data and products.

* Geologic Names Committee

U.S. Geological Survey (USGS)
National Center, MS 902
Reston, VA 22092 (703) 648-4311

Be patient. If any phone number is incorrect, call (area code) 555-1212 and request the new listing.

Geology and Earth Science

The Geologic Names Committee defines and recommends policy and rules governing stratigraphic nomenclature and classification for the USGS. *Stratigraphic Notes* is published to announce changes in official geologic names usage. Lexicons are compiled that show domestic geologic names usage, and a file is maintained of geologic names reserved future use.

* Geologic Inquiries

U.S. Geological Survey (USGS)
National Center, MS 907
Reston, VA 22092 (301) 648-4383

To obtain technical information on such geologic topics as earthquakes and volcanoes, energy and mineral resources, the geology of specific areas, and geologic maps, contact this office.

* Geologic Science

Office of Scientific Publications
Geologic Division
U.S. Geological Survey (USGS)
National Center, MS 904
Reston, VA 22092 (703) 648-6077

This office reviews all scientific publications in the geologic field for scientific accuracy. Both internal and outside publications are analyzed. All must comply with the Geological Survey's standards.

* Geology Films

Visual Services
U.S. Geological Survey (USGS)
790 National Center
Reston, VA 22092 (703) 648-4379

The geology motion picture films are available on a free short-term loan to educational and scientific communities, professional and technical societies, civic and industrial groups, and other established organizations. Those marked by an asterisk should be borrowed from: Modern Talking Picture Service, 5000 Park St. North, St. Petersburg, FL 33709.

In The Beginning * - Upper Elementary, Junior High
When The Earth Moves * - College, State Agencies
1955 Eruption of Kilauea Volcano, Hawaiian Islands - Elementary
Inside Hawaiian Volcanoes * - Elementary
The Alaskan Earthquake, 1964 * - Elementary
John Wesley Powell: Canyon Geologist * - Junior High
Geology of the Berlize Barrier Reef - High School, College
The 1923 Surveying Expedition of the Colorado River in Arizona - Junior High
The Subject is Water * - High School
Flow in Alluvial Channels - College
The Sea River - High School
The Little Plover (River) Project, A Study in Sand Plains Hydrology - High School
The Water Below - Elementary
To Fill The Gap - Elementary
National Petroleum Reserve in Alaska - Junior High
Yakutat - High School

* Geology Information Centers

Public Inquiries Offices are a network of earth-science information offices that are especially convenient for walk-in customers but also answer inquiries made by mail or telephone. In addition to assisting the public in the selection and ordering of all USGS products, the PIO's provide counter service for USGS topographic, geologic and water-resources maps and reports. The offices furnish information about the USGS and its programs and are a link to information held by State and other federal offices. PIO's distribute catalogs, circulars, indexes, and leaflets and provide bibliographic and geographic reference searches. Most PIO's (those not located near regional USGS centers) maintain libraries of USGS book reports and are regional depositories for Open-File Reports. Below are PIO locations, regions of specialization, addresses, and phone numbers:

Public Inquiries Office
U.S. Geological Survey (USGS)
Room 101
4230 University Dr.
Anchorage, AK 99508-4664 (907) 271-4320
(Alaska)

Public Inquiries Office
Earth Science Information and Sales
U.S. Geological Survey (USGS)
E-146 Federal Building, Box 53
701 C Street
Anchorage, AK 99513 (907) 271-4307

Public Inquiries Office
U.S. Geological Survey (USGS)
169 Federal Building
1961 Stout St.
Denver, CO 80294 (303) 844-4169
(AK, AZ, CO, KS, MT, NE, ND, SD, UT, WY)

Public Inquiries Office
U.S. Geological Survey (USGS)
7638 Federal Building
300 North Los Angeles St.
Los Angeles, CA 90012 (213) 894-2850
(AK, AZ, CA, HI, NV, OR, WA)

Public Inquiries Office
U.S. Geological Survey (USGS)
Building 3, Room 3128
Mail Stop 533
345 Middlefield Rd.
Menlo Park, CA 94025 (415) 329-4390
(AK, AZ, CA, HI, ID, NV, OR, UT, WA)

Public Inquiries Office
U.S. Geological Survey (USGS)
503 National Center
Room 1-C-402
12201 Sunrise Valley Dr.
Reston, VA 22092 (703) 648-6892
(all States)

Public Inquiries Office
U.S. Geological Survey (USGS)
8105 Federal Building
125 South State St.
Salt Lake City, UT 84138 (801) 524-5652
(AZ, CO, ID, NV, NM, UT, WY)

* Geology Publications

U.S. Geological Survey (USGS)
Distribution Support Section
582 National Center
12201 Sunrise Valley Dr.
Reston, VA 22092

Write to the address listed above to get on the free mailing list for the monthly list of new publication of the U.S. Geological Survey. *Guide to Obtaining USGS Information* is a free publication which describes sources of USGS information and lists in tabular form USGS products and their sources. To receive your copy write: Books and Open File Reports Section, USGS, Federal Center, Box 25425, Denver, CO 80225.

* Geology Teacher Packets

Geologic Inquiries Group
U.S. Geological Survey (USGS)
907 National Center
Reston, VA 22092 (703) 648-4383

National Cartographic Information Center (NCIC)
U.S. Geological Survey (USGS)
507 National Center, Room 1-C-107
12201 Sunrise Valley Dr.
Reston, VA 22092 (703) 648-5963

Contact for NCIC Office nearest you.

Packets of teaching aids, which differ according to subject, grade level, and geographic location, are available through the Geologic Inquiries Group (GIG) and the National Cartographic Information Center (NCIC). These packets include lists of reference materials, various maps and map indexes, and a

Be patient. If any phone number is incorrect, call (area code) 555-1212 and request the new listing.

Science and Technology

selection of general interest publications. Requests for teachers packets should be sent on school letterhead to GIG or NCIC, as appropriate, and should indicate the grade level and subject of interest. GIG compiles two packets; 1) "Selected Packet of Geologic Teaching Aids," for elementary- and secondary-school teachers of general science courses, and 2) "Teachers Packet of Geologic Materials," for Secondary-school and college teachers of earth-science courses. NCIC compiles specialized packets emphasizing mapping. Requests for packets should include specific details about the needs and/or interest of a particular class.

* Geophysical and Solar-Terrestrial Information

National Geophysical Data Center (NGDC)
National Oceanic and Atmospheric Administration
U.S. Department of Commerce
325 Broadway
Boulder, CO 80303 (303) 497-6215

The National Geophysical Data Center combines in a single center all data activities in the fields of solid earth geophysics, marine geology and geophysics, and solar-terrestrial physics. NGDC produces numerous publications which catalog and document data. In addition, NGDC has available a variety of maps, slide sets, and educational tools which are appropriate for both technical and non-technical audiences.

Marine Data . . . . (303) 497-6338
Land Data . . . . (303) 497-6123
Seismological Data . . . . (303) 497-6472

* Geoscience Research: Department of Energy

Office of Fossil Energy
Office of Geoscience Research
U.S. Department of Energy
1000 Independence Ave, SW, Room 3E-028
Washington, DC 20585 (202) 586-5600

This office is the chief coordinator for geoscience programs of the U.S. Department of Energy. It also manages and directs the Hydrocarbon Geoscience Research Coordinating Committee activities, which includes as ex-officio members from the National Science Foundation, the U.S. Department of Interior's Geological Survey and Minerals Management Service.

* Geoscience Research - Grand Junction

Grand Junction Projects Office
PO Box 2567
Grand Junction, CO 81502 (303) 248-6000

The primary mission of the Grand Junctions projects office is to apply its project management, engineering, and geoscience capabilities to support national programs in environmental restoration, geoscience, and energy. Activities include: the Grand Junction Uranium Mill Tailings Remedial Action (UMTRA) vicinity properties project; the Monticello, Utah, mill site and vicinity properties project; the remediation of DOE's Grand Junction Projects Office; and the DOE-Wide Long Term Surveillance and Maintenance Program.

* Geology and Earth Science Libraries

The USGS library system is one of the largest earth science library systems in the world. Holdings include 1.1 million monographs and serials 385,000 maps; 355,000 pamphlets; and 340,000 reports and dissertations in microform. The libraries are open to the public and some materials may be available on inter-library loan.

Reston, VA
USGS Library, 950 National Center, Room 4-A-100, 12201 Sunrise Valley Dr., Reston, VA 22092; (703) 648-4302.

Menlo Park, CA
USGS Library, Mail Stop 955, 345 Middlefield Road, Menlo Park, CA 94025; (415) 329-5090.

Denver, CO
USGS Library, Mail Stop 914, Building 20, Box 25046, Federal Center, Denver, CO 80225; (303) 236-1000.

Flagstaff, AZ
USGS Library, 2255 North Gemini Dr., Flagstaff, AZ 86001; (602) 527-7009.

* International Geology

Geologic Division
U.S. Geological Survey (USGS)
National Center, MS 917
Reston, VA 22092 (703) 648-6047

Through scientific cooperation and exchange programs, this office coordinates geologic activities and research with other countries, including developing nations.

* Landslide Information

Landslide Information Center
U.S. Geological Survey (USGS)
Box 25046, MS 966, Federal Center
Denver, CO 80225 (303) 236-1599

This center responds to inquiries on landslide research and maintains files of landslide documents, newspaper clippings, and photographs that may be examined or photocopied at the Center.

* Earthquakes and Other U.S. Geological Survey Publications

U.S. Geological Survey (USGS)
Book and Report Sales
Box 25425
Denver, CO 80225 (303) 236-7476

This is a listing of some of the general interest publications available through the U.S. Geological Survey. They are free unless otherwise indicated. Also ask about getting of the mailing list for new publications.

The Antarctic and its Geology
Earthquakes
Eruptions of Hawaiian Volcanoes: Past, Present and Future ($4)
Eruptions of Mount St. Helens: Past, Present, and Future ($2.75)
Geologic History of Cape Cod, Massachusetts
Geology of Caves
The Great Ice Age
The Interior of the Earth
Landforms of the United States
Marine Geology: Research Beneath the Sea
Our Changing Continent
Permafrost
Safety and Survival in an Earthquake
The San Andreas Fault
Volcanoes
Geysers
Natural Steam for Power
Elevations and Distances in the United States
Geologic Maps: Portraits of the Earth
Steps to the Moon
Tree Rings: Timekeepers of the Past

* Global Seismology

Branch of Global Seismology and Geomagnetism
U.S. Geological Survey (USGS)
Mail Stop 967, Box 25046, Federal Center
Denver, CO 80225 (303) 236-1369

Current and historical magnetic-declination information can be obtained from this Branch. Contact this office for further information.

* Mineral Information

Minerals Information Office
U.S. Department of the Interior
1849 C. St., NW, Room 2647
Washington, DC 20240 (202) 208-5512

The U.S. Department of the Interior can answer questions and provide you with information on minerals and mineral science. The Minerals information office can provide you with publications and data base searches also.

* Rock Collecting

USGS Book and Report Sales
P.O. Box 25425

Be patient. If any phone number is incorrect, call (area code) 555-1212 and request the new listing.

Geology and Earth Science

Denver, CO 80225

Collecting Rocks is a free publication, which describes the origin of major rock types and how rocks can provide clues to the Earth's history. It includes suggestions for starting a rock collection, identifying specimens, and housing such a collection.

* State Geoscience Agencies

Many State geoscience agencies sell U.S. Geological Survey (USGS) products (book reports, maps, etc.) that pertain to their regions or States. Some State geoscience agencies are also affiliated with the National Cartographic Information Center. The USGS cooperates with State geoscience agencies in a variety of projects; publications resulting from these projects are commonly available from both organizations. In addition to selling USGS products, many State geoscience agencies allow the public to consult, but not borrow, these materials. Certain State geoscience agencies are also designated as depositories of specific USGS Open-File Reports.

Alabama
Geological Survey of Alabama, PO Box O, University Station, Tuscaloosa, AL 35486; (205) 349-2852.

Alaska
Department of Geological and Geophysical Surveys, 794 University Ave., Fairbanks, AK 99709; (907) 474-7147.

Arizona
Bureau of Geology and Mineral Technology, 845 North Park Avenue, Tucson, AZ 85719; (602) 882-4795.

Arkansas
Arkansas Geological Commission, 3815 West Roosevelt Road, Little Rock, AR 72204; (501) 371-1488.

California
California Division of Mines and Geology, 1416 Ninth Street, Room 1341, Sacramento, CA 95814; (916) 445-1923.

Colorado
Colorado Geological Survey, 1313 Sherman Street, Room 715, Denver, CO 80203; (303) 866-2611.

Connecticut
Department of Environmental Protection, Natural Resource Center, 165 Capitol Avenue, Room 553, Hartford, CT 06106; (203) 566-3540.

Delaware
Delaware Geological Survey, University of Delaware, 101 Penny Hall, Newark, DE 19716; (302) 451-2833.

Florida
Florida Geological Survey, 903 West Tennessee Street, Tallahassee, FL 32304-7795; (904) 488-9380.

Georgia
Georgia Geologic Survey, Room 400, 19 Martin Luther King Jr Drive, SW, Atlanta, GA 30334; (404) 656-3214.

Hawaii
Department of Land and Natural Resources, Division of Water and Land Development, PO Box 373, Honolulu, HI 36809; (808) 548-7533.

Idaho
Idaho Geological Survey, University of Idaho Campus, Morris Hall, Room 332, Moscow, ID 83843; (208) 885-7991.

Illinois
Illinois State Geological Survey, 615 East Peabody Dr., Room 121, Champaign, IL 61820; (217) 333-5111.

Indiana
Indiana Geological Survey, Department of Natural Resources, 611 North Walnut Grove, Bloomington, IN 47405; (812) 335-2862.

Iowa
Iowa Geological Survey, 123 North Capitol Street, Iowa City, IA 52242; (319) 338-1575.

Kansas
Kansas Geological Survey, 1930 Constant Avenue, Campus West, The University of Kansas, Lawrence, KS 66046; (913) 864-3965.

Kentucky
Kentucky Geological Survey, University of Kentucky, 228 Mining and Mineral Resources, Lexington, KY 40506; (606) 257-5500.

Louisiana
Louisiana Geological Survey, Department of Natural Resources, Box G, University Station, Baton Rouge, LA 70893; (504) 388-5320.

Maine
Maine Geological Survey, Department of Conservation, State House, Station 22, Augusta, ME 04333; (207) 299-2801.

Maryland
Maryland Geological Survey, 2300 St. Paul St., Baltimore, MD 21218; (301) 554-5500.

Massachusetts
Department of Environmental Quality Engineering, Coastal Zone Management, 100 Cambridge St., 20th Floor, Boston, MA 02202; (617) 292-5690.

Michigan
Geological Survey Division, Michigan Department of Natural Resources, Steven T. Mason Building, PO Box 30028, Lansing, MI 48909; (517) 334-6923.

Minnesota
Minnesota Geological Survey, 2642 University Ave., St. Paul, MN 55114-1057; (612) 627-4780.

Mississippi
Department of Natural Resources, Bureau of Geology, PO Box 5348, Jackson, MS 39216; (601) 354-6228.

Missouri
Department of Natural Resources, Division of Geology and Land Survey, 111 Fairgrounds Road, PO Box 250, Rolla, MO 65401; (314) 364-1752.

Montana
Montana Bureau of Mines and Geology, Montana College of Mineral Science and Technology, Butte, MT 59701; (406) 496-4180.

Nebraska
Conservation and Survey Division, 113 Nebraska Hall, The University of Nebraska, Lincoln, NE 68588-0517; (402) 472-3471.

Nevada
Nevada Bureau of Mines and Geology, University of Nevada, Reno, NV 89557-0088; (702) 784-6691.

New Hampshire
Department of Resources and Economic Development, 117 James Hall, University of New Hampshire, Durham, NH 03824; (603) 862-3160.

New Jersey
New Jersey Geological Survey, CN-029, Trenton, NJ 08638; (609) 292-1185.

New Mexico
New Mexico Bureau of Mines and Mineral Resources, Campus Station, Socorro, NM 87801; (505) 835-5420.

New York
New York State Geological Survey Room 3136, Cultural Education Center, Albany, NY 12230; (518) 474-5816.

North Carolina
North Carolina Geological Survey Section, PO Box 27687, Raleigh, NC 27611; (919) 733-3833.

North Dakota
North Dakota Geological Survey, University Station, Box 8156-58202, Grand Forks, ND 58202; (701) 777-2231.

Ohio
Division of Geological Survey, Fountain Square, Building B, Columbus, OH

Be patient. If any phone number is incorrect, call (area code) 555-1212 and request the new listing.

Science and Technology

43224; (614) 265-6605.

Oklahoma
Oklahoma Geological Survey, The University of Oklahoma, 830 Van Fleet Oval, Room 163, Norman, OK 73019; (405) 325-3031.

Oregon
Department of Geology and Mineral Industries, 910 State Office Building, Portland, OR 97201-5528; (503) 229-5580.

Pennsylvania
Bureau of Topographic and Geologic Survey, PO Box 2357, Harrisburg, PA 17120; (717) 787-2169.

Rhode Island
Department of Geology, Green Hall, The University of Rhode Island, Kingston, RI 02881; (401) 792-2265.

South Carolina
South Carolina Geological and Geodetic Survey, Harbison Forest Road, Columbia, SC 29210; (803) 737-9440.

South Dakota
South Dakota Geological Survey Science Center, University of South Dakota, Vermillion, SD 57069; (605) 677-5227.

Tennessee
Department of Conservation, Division of Geology, 701 Broadway, Nashville, TN 37219-5237; (615) 742-6691.

Texas
Bureau of Economic Geology, The University of Texas at Austin, University Station, Box X, Austin, TX 78713-7508; (512) 471-1534.

Utah
Utah Geological and Mineral Survey, 606 Black Hawk Way, Salt Lake City, UT 84108-1280; (801) 581-6831.

Vermont
Vermont Geological Survey, 103 South Main St., Center Building, Waterbury, VT 05676; (802) 224-5164.

Virginia
Virginia Division of Mineral Resources, PO Box 3667, Charlottesville, VA 22903; (804) 293-5121.

Washington
Division of Geology and Earth Resources, Department of Natural Resources, Olympia, WA 98504; (206) 459-6372.

West Virginia
West Virginia Geological Survey, PO Box 879, Morgantown, WV 26507; (304) 594-2331.

Wisconsin
Wisconsin Geological and Natural History Survey, University of Wisconsin Extension, 3817 Mineral Point Rd., Madison, WI 53705; (608) 262-1705.

Wyoming
Geological Survey of Wyoming, PO Box 3008, University Station, Laramie, WY 82071; (307) 742-2054.

Puerto Rico
Servicio Geologico de Puerto Rico, Department de Recursos Naturales, Apartado 5887, Puerta de Tierra, San Juan, PR 00906; (809) 723-2716.

* U.S. Geological Survey Regional Information Offices

For information, you can contact the office in your geographic area or contact the Reston, VA office or Washington, DC office, which handle all states.

Anchorage
Public Inquiries Office, U.S. Geological Survey, Room 101, 4230 University Dr., Anchorage, AK 99508-4664; (907) 271-4320

Anchorage
Public Inquiries Office, U.S. Geological Survey, Federal Building, Room E-146, Box 53, 701 C St., Anchorage, AK 99513; (907) 271-4307

Denver
Public Inquiries Office, U.S. Geological Survey, Federal Building, Room 169, 1961 Stout St., Denver, CO 80294; (303) 844-4169

Los Angeles
Public Inquiries Office, U.S. Geological Survey, Federal Building, Room 7638, 300 N. Los Angeles St., Los Angeles, CA 90012; (213) 894-2850

Menlo Park
Public Inquiries Office, U.S. Geological Survey, Building 3 (Stop 533), Room 3128, 345 Middlefield Rd., Menlo Park, CA 94025; (415) 329-4390

Reston
Public Inquiries Office, U.S. Geological Survey, 503 National Center, Room 1C402, 12201 Sunrise Valley Dr., Reston, VA 22092; (703) 648-6892

Salt Lake City
Public Inquiries Office, U.S. Geological Survey, Federal Building, Room 8105, 125 South State St., Salt Lake City, UT 84138; (801) 524-5652

San Francisco
Public Inquiries Office, U.S. Geological Survey, Customhouse, Room 504, 555 Battery St., San Francisco, CA 94111; (415) 556-5627

Spokane
Public Inquiries Office, U.S. Geological Survey, U.S. Courthouse, Room 678, West 920 Riverside Ave., Spokane, WA 99201; (509) 456-2524

Washington, DC
Public Inquiries Office, U.S. Geological Survey, Main Interior Building, 2600 Corridor, 18th and C Sts., NW, Washington, DC 20240; (202) 343-8073

* Volcanoes and Earthquakes

Science and Technology Division
Reference Section
Library of Congress
Washington, DC 20540 (202) 707-5580

Informal series of reference guides are issued free from the Science and Technology Division under the general title, *LC Science Tracer Bullet*. These guides are designed to help readers locate published material on subjects about which they have only general knowledge. New titles in the series are announced in the weekly Library of Congress *Information Bulletin* that is distributed to many libraries. Two relevant *Tracer Bullets* currently available are: *TB 81-14 Volcanoes*, and *TB 89-8 Earthquakes and Earthquake Engineering*.

* Want To Learn About Earthquakes?

U.S. Geological Survey (USGS)
Mail Stop 967
Box 25046, Federal Center
Denver, CO 80225 (303) 236-1500

The National Earthquake Information Center compiles, computes, and distributes digital and analog data on earthquakes that have occurred around the world. NEIC routinely publishes earthquake data. The NEIC publications are the principal sources of current earthquake information for thousands of seismologists around the world for use in fundamental research and in the evaluation of earthquake hazards. Other publications include an annual *United States Earthquakes*, and state seismicity maps which are available to the public from the Geological Survey.

Be patient. If any phone number is incorrect, call (area code) 555-1212 and request the new listing.

National Institute of Standards and Technology

A good idea often isn't good enough anymore. As U.S. firms have discovered in international markets, innovation by itself does not ensure commercial success. Unless a new technology is quickly translated into an efficiently manufactured, high-quality product, a faster-acting competitor is likely to capitalize on the advance and reap most of the market returns. The National Institute of Standards and Technology (NIST), formerly the National Bureau of Standards, as a world-class center for science and engineering research, is uniquely positioned to help U.S. firms strengthen their competitive performance.

NIST has been a valuable behind-the-scenes partner of industry and academia, providing the standards and measurement techniques that foster technological advance, domestic and international commerce, and, ultimately, economic progress. NIST is also responsible for speeding innovation and accelerating the adoption of new technologies and new ideas by U.S. companies. That's why about half of the organization's scientists and engineers focus their work on the fastest-moving and, perhaps, most commercially attractive areas of science: advanced materials, electronics, superconductivity, automation, computing, biotechnology, and thin-layer technology.

The National Institute of Standards and Technology provides advisory and consulting services to assist government and industry in the development of standards. As the national reference for physical measurement, NIST produces measurement standards data necessary to create, make, and sell U.S. products and services at home and abroad. Staff work with industry and consumers at every level. Generally, a staffer can lead you to major companies, research centers, experts, and literature. Listed below are the NIST laboratories and centers which can provide you with scientific and technological services as well as measurement, instrumentation and standards information.

* Advanced Measurement Techniques

Office of Physical Measurement Services
National Measurement Laboratory
National Institute of Standards and Technology (NIST)
B362 Physics Bldg
Gaithersburg, MD 20899 (301) 975-2005

The National Measurement Laboratory develops advanced measurement techniques for complex physical and chemical systems for use in areas such as chemical manufacturing, waste disposal, biotechnology, and environmental studies. Contact this office for more information.

* Alloys: New and Improved

Metallurgy Division
Institute for Materials Science and Engineering
National Institute of Standards and Technology (NIST)
B261 Materials Bldg
Gaithersburg, MD 20899 (301) 975-5963

The Institute for Materials Science and Engineering explores and quantifies processing technologies to produce new and improved alloys. For more information, contact this division.

* Analytical Mass Spectrometry

Chemical Science and
Technology Laboratory
A21 Physics Bldg.
National Institute of Standards and Technology (NIST)
Gaithersburg, MD 20899 (301) 975-4109

Analytical mass spectrometry has played a key role in industries, such as the semiconductor industry, that require accurate measurements of trace elements in raw materials, products, and product containers. The NIST inorganic mass spectrometry program is concerned with developing analytical capabilities for making highly accurate determinations of trace inorganics using stable isotope compositions, as well as highly accurate measurements of absolute isotopic compositions to redetermine atomic weights. Areas of research include instrumentation in thermal source, inductively coupled plasma source, and ionization and chemical separations at the trace level using chromatography and other techniques.

* Applications Portability Profile

Systems and Software Technology Division
National Computer Systems Laboratory
National Institute of Standards and Technology (NIST)
B266, Bldg. 225
Gaithersburg, MD 20899 (301) 975-3290

The ability to move or port an application from one operating system environment to another is important for cost effective computing. The National Computer Systems Laboratory is working with users and industry to define and implement the Applications Portability Profile (APP), a group of standard elements, including database management, data interchange, network services, user interfaces, and programming services. Workshops for vendors and users are sponsored to explore common requirements for software portability, and to reach agreements on common ways to implement the standards that are being developed. Contact this office for more information on portability and workshops.

* Applied Mathematics

Computing and Applied Mathematics
B112 Technology Building
National Institute of Standards and Technology (NIST)
Gaithersburg, MD 20899 (301) 975-2732

The Center for Applied Mathematics conducts research and supports NIST activities and other Federal agencies in selected fields of the mathematical and computer sciences. The Center also develops such mathematical tools as scientific software, statistical models and computational methods, mathematical handbooks, and manuals. Contact this office for more information.

* Atomic Mapping

Chemical Science and Technology
National Institute of Standards and Technology (NIST)
A309 Chemistry Bldg.
Gaithersburg, MD 20899 (301) 975-3143

The National Measurement Laboratory has developed a tool for "atomic mapping" of the magnetic characteristics of material surfaces. A boon to the $40 billion magnetic recording industry, the instrument will be produced commercially by a U.S. firm. Contact this Center for more information on atomic mapping.

Be patient. If any phone number is incorrect, call (area code) 555-1212 and request the new listing.

Science and Technology

* Atomic Scale Measuring Machine

Manufacturing Engineering Laboratory
A117 Metrology
National Institute of Standards and Technology (NIST)
Gaithersburg, MD 20899 (301) 975-3490

By the year 2001, uncertainty requirements for dimensional metrology of step heights, surface roughness, linewidth, and line spacing for the integrated circuit and optics industries will be 0.1nm to 1nm. Furthermore these uncertainties must be held over areas ranging from several square millimeters to fractions of a square meter. To address these needs, NIST is building the molecular measuring machine (M^3) It will be capable of positioning and measuring atomic-scale accuracies over an area of 25 square centimeters. The machine represents a combined effort of NIST and several universities, Watson Research Center, AT&T Bell Laboratories, and Zygo Corporation.

* Automated Manufacturing Data Handling

Automated Manufacturing Research Facility
Manufacturing Technology Centers Program
National Institute of Standards and Technology (NIST)
B326 Metrology
Gaithersburg, MD 20899 (301) 975-3400

In a very real sense, the cornerstone of the "factory of the future" will be information. The hardware of the facility--robots, machine tools and sensors--is very visible, but the ability to generate, store, retrieve, and transfer information accurately and on time will be just as important as any hardware. Special features of this unseen part of the Automated Manufacturing Research Facility include the use of distributed databases and a data communications system. Contact this facility for more information on the on-going data handling projects.

* Automated Manufacturing Data Preparation

Automated Manufacturing Research Facility
Manufacturing Technology Centers Program
National Institute of Standards and Technology (NIST)
B326 Metrology Bldg.
Gaithersburg, MD 20899 (301) 975-3400

At the Automated Manufacturing Research Facility, research is underway to determine exactly what sorts of data are required by a factory's manufacturing and inspection systems, and how these data can be generated automatically by the various data preparation systems in use in the facility. Contact this facility for more information on this research.

* Bioanalytical Sensors

Chemical Science and Technology Laboratory
B158 Chemistry
National Institute of Standards and Technology (NIST)
Gaithersburg, MD 20899 (301) 975-4109

Biosensors are a new generation of analytical devices with the potential for widespread use in biomedical and industrial monitoring applications. Biosensors will incorporate the latest advances in biotechnology to provide high specificity and sensitivity. NIST is conducting research using a variety of optical techniques for detection and amplification of changes detected.

* Biotechnology Research

Chemical Science and Technology Laboratory
A353 Chemistry Bldg.
National Institute of Standards and Technology (NIST)
Gaithersburg, MD 20899 (301) 975-3128

Working in several areas of DNA chemistry, NIST scientists are actively manipulating DNA to produce proteins, developing methods for measuring DNA damage on the molecular level, and developing methods for characterizing DNA, including profiling. NIST scientists are working on new methods for DNA profiling, ranging from developing well-characterized DNA fragment standards for restriction fragment length polymorphisms to performing research for rapid determination of DNA profiles y polymerase chain reaction amplification ad automated detection of fragments.

* Building Environment

Building Environment Division
B304 Building and Fire Research Lab.
National Institute of Standards and Technology (NIST)
Gaithersburg, MD 20899 (301) 975-5851

The Building Environment Division develops fundamental data, measurement techniques, test methods, and models for the design, construction, and operation of the building envelope and building mechanical and electrical systems. The division also develops software performance criteria, interface standards, and test methods needed to make effective use of modern computer-aided design hardware and software and database management systems within the disaggregated construction industry. Sample outputs for the division include testing and rating procedures and computer models for the performance of heating and air conditioning systems, predictive models for estimating peak heating/cooling requirements and annual building energy use, and indoor air quality, criteria for improving thermal performance of insulating materials, and criteria for measuring and improving the lighting in buildings. The division also has computer aids to assist in formulating building standards and expert systems. Contact this office for more information.

* Building Materials Research

Building Materials Division
B348 Building and Fire Research Lab
National Institute of Standards and Technology (NIST)
Gaithersburg, MD 20899 (301) 975-6707

The Building Materials Division conducts laboratory, field and analytical research and develops methods for evaluating the performance and durability of building materials and components. The division also develops chemical, physical, microstructural, and mechanical characterization procedures and mathematical methods for describing microstructures for building materials. Also, the division conducts voluntary laboratory inspection and proficiency sample programs to aid maintenance of quality in execution of standard tests on materials used in building and highway construction. Researchers at NIST are working to gain a better understanding of the lifespan of inorganic materials such as cement and concrete used in building. Artificial intelligence systems are being developed for optimizing the selection of materials and for diagnosing the causes of material degradation. Researchers are also looking into the lifespans of organic building materials such as protective coatings for steel, roofing materials, and asphalt. Contact this office for guidelines for selecting building materials, or for more information on the on-going research in building materials.

* Building Technology

Building and Fire Research Lab
National Institute of Standards and Technology (NIST)
Gaithersburg, MD 20899 (301) 975-5900

The Center for Building Technology is the national building research laboratory. It works cooperatively with other organizations, private and public, to improve building practices. It conducts laboratory, field, and analytical research. It develops technologies to predict, measure, and test the performance of building materials, components, systems, and practices. This knowledge is required for responsible and cost effective decisions in the building process and cannot be obtained through proprietary research and development. The Center provides technologies needed by the building community to achieve the benefits of advanced computation and automation. It does not distribute building standards or regulations, but its technologies are widely used in the building industry and adopted by governmental and private organizations which have standards and codes responsibilities. Contact this Center for more information.

* Building Technology Presentations and Symposia

B222 Building and
Fire Research Lab
National Institute of Standards and Technology (NIST)
Gaithersburg, MD 20899 (301) 975-5900

Staff at the Center for Building Technology make a number of presentations at professional societies and at technical meetings of building community organizations. Also, the center presents a monthly series of Building Technology Symposia, in cooperation with other organizations concerned with building research and practice. Contact this Center for further information.

* Calibration Services

Manufacturing Engineering Laboratory
B326 Metrology
National Institute of Standards and Technology (NIST)
Gaithersburg, MD 20899 (301) 975-3400

The Center for Manufacturing Engineering maintains the national standards for the length, force, and a number of subsidiary standards. It offers primary calibration services for these standards. Under unique circumstances, the Center

Be patient. If any phone number is incorrect, call (area code) 555-1212 and request the new listing.

National Institute of Standards and Technology

accepts especially complex or sensitive measurement assignments of national significance. Contact this Center for more information.

* Center for Advanced Biotechnology Research

9600 Gudelsky Dr.
Rockville, MD 20850 (301) 251-2244

At this center, jointly established by the University of Maryland, Montgomery County, MD, and NIST, researchers study protein structure/function relationships. They are focusing on the measurement of protein structure by X-ray crystallography and nuclear magnetic resonance spectroscopy, and the manipulation of structure by molecular biological techniques including site-directed mutagenesis. Protein modeling and molecular dynamics and computational chemistry are used to understand protein structure to predict the effects of specific structural modifications on the properties of proteins and enzymes.

* Center for Analytical Chemistry Services

Chemical Science and Technology Laboratory
National Institute of Standards and Technology (NIST)
A309 Chemistry Bldg.
Gaithersburg, MD (301) 975-3145

The availability of Center for Analytical Chemistry analytical expertise to other institutions is an important service function. In addition to service analyses, the Center is frequently called upon to consult or advise, to provide various metrological calibrations of a chemical nature on a wide variety of industrial and research materials, and to provide analytical services of a unique nature such as compositional mapping, depth profiling, or ultra-trace analysis. These services are available to private industry when the uniqueness of the Center capability has been demonstrated, and similar services are not available in the private sector. Contact this office for more information.

* Center for Analytical Chemistry Technical Activities

Center for Analytical Chemistry
National Institute of Standards and Technology (NIST)
A309 Chemistry Bldg.
Gaithersburg, MD 20899 (301) 975-3145

Center for Analytical Chemistry Technical Activities annual report summarizes the technical activities in the Inorganic Analytical Research Division, the Organic Analytical Research Division, and the Gas and Particulate Science Division. It also describes certain special activities in the Center, including quality assurance and voluntary standardization coordination. Contact this office for a free copy.

* Center for Manufacturing Engineering

Manufacturing Engineering Laboratory
B326 Metrology
National Institute of Standards and Technology (NIST)
Gaithersburg, MD 20899 (301) 975-3400

The Center for Manufacturing Engineering provides competence and develops technical data, findings, and standards in manufacturing engineering, mechanical metrology, automation, robotics, control technology, and precision mechanical engineering to support the discrete parts manufacturing industries. Contact this office for more information on the research and developments at the Center.

* Ceramic and Metal Powder Production

Office of Nondestructive Evaluation
Materials Science and Engineering Laboratory
National Institute of Standards and Technology (NIST)
B344 Materials Bldg.
Gaithersburg, MD 20899 (301) 975-5727

The *Nondestructive Evaluation Technical Activities 1989* annual report reviews the technical activities and developments at NIST, including ceramic and metal powder production and consolidation, formability of metals, composites processing and interfaces, and standards and methods. Also included are listings of the various seminars and invited talks which were presented in 1989. A listing of the Office's publications are also available.

* Ceramics Program

Ceramics Division
Institute for Materials Science and Engineering
National Institute of Standards and Technology (NIST)
A256 Materials Bldg.

Gaithersburg, MD 20899 (301) 975-6119

The Institute for Materials Science and Engineering conducts a high-tech ceramics program geared to help U.S. industry stay competitive in the worldwide race to expand production and application of these materials. Direct your inquiries to the above office.

* Chemical Engineering Center

Center for Chemical Engineering
National Institute of Standards and Technology (NIST)
325 Broadway
Boulder, CO 80303 (303) 497-5366

The Center for Chemical Engineering performs research in process metrology, thermophysical properties of fluids and solids, and unit operations and processes; provides measurement practices and standards, fundamental engineering data, calibration and measurement services, and engineering science for the chemical and related industries, academe, and Government.

* Chemical Engineering Separations

Chemical Science and Technology Laboratory
Division 832
National Institute of Standards and Technology (NIST)
Boulder, CO 80303 (303) 497-3416

Separation and purification are critical steps in the manufacture of chemical products using existing and emerging process technologies, such as energy production or environmental protection. Separation processes affect both the economies of production and the fundamental ability to produce a product of desired form or purity. NIST is creating an engineering science based on separations.

* Chemical Process Research

Chemical Process Metrology Division
Center for Chemical Engineering
B304 Physics Bldg.
National Institute of Standards and Technology (NIST)
Gaithersburg, MD 20899 (301) 975-2601

Research is on-going in the Chemical Process Metrology Division to develop measurement standards and provide measurement services for flow (volume and mass rates), liquid density, liquid volume, and humidity. Experimental and theoretical research is conducted to characterize fluid behavior.

* Chemical Reference Laboratory

Chemical Science and Technology Laboratory
National Institute of Standards and Technology (NIST)
A309 Chemistry Bldg.
Gaithersburg, MD 20899 (301) 975-3143

The National Measurement Laboratory serves as the nation's reference laboratory for the more than 250 million chemical composition measurements made each day in the United States for industrial process control, environmental protection, toxic substances control, and health services. Working with a U.S. firm, the National Measurement Laboratory designed a new instrument for more efficient and more accurate separation and analysis of chemical elements in a sample. Contact this Lab for more information.

* Chemical Research

Chemical Science and Technology Laboratory
A309 Chemistry Bldg.
National Institute of Standards and Technology (NIST)
Gaithersburg, MD 20899 (301) 975-3145

Current programs at the Center for Analytical Chemistry include the following: Clinical Standards, Environmental Standards, Metal Standards, Gas Standards, Biomaterial Standards, Acid Rain, Environmental Analysis, Particle Analysis, Specimen Banking, and Nutrient Analysis. Research interests include atom reservoirs, bioanalytical sensors, bioanalytical techniques, compositional mapping, electrochemical techniques, high resolution chromatography, laboratory automation, laser enhanced ionization in flames, and multicomponent analysis. Contact the Center for more information about research interests or its current programs.

* Commercialization of Advanced Technology

Manufacturing Technology Centers Program
Manufacturing Engineering Laboratory

Be patient. If any phone number is incorrect, call (area code) 555-1212 and request the new listing.

Science and Technology

B326 Metrology Bldg
National Institute of Standards and Technology (NIST)
Gaithersburg, MD 20899 (301) 975-3400

Through the Advanced Technology Program, NIST is directed to speed the commercialization of new technology and the development of new, generic manufacturing techniques. NIST may support or participate in research consortia to develop and test new equipment or production processes, provided that they are "generic" to a particular industry or group of industries. The program will be aimed at small- to mid-sized, high technology firms or consortia. The idea is to "leverage" the relatively small financial resources of NIST by using the Institute's support to encourage private investment in each project. For more information, contact this office.

* Computer and Telecommunications Standards Assistance

Information Systems Engineering Division
Computer Systems Laboratory
National Institute of Standards and Technology (NIST)
A259 Technology Bldg
Gaithersburg, MD 20899 (301) 975-3262

The National Computer Systems Laboratory helps computer manufacturers, communications companies, and domestic and international standards-writing groups to produce and test standards for off-the-shelf compatibility of computer and related telecommunications systems. Contact this NIST division for more information.

* Computer Assistance for Organizations

Computer Systems Laboratory
National Institute of Standards and Technology (NIST)
B154 Technology Bldg
Gaithersburg, MD 20899 (301) 975-2822

The National Computer Systems Laboratory works on techniques and tools to help organizations make effective use of computers and information technology, reduce training costs, and improve productivity. Contact this Lab for more information.

* Computer Information Technology

Computer Systems Laboratory
National Institute of Standards and Technology (NIST)
B154 Technology Bldg
Gaithersburg, MD 20899 (301) 975-2822

Computers are indispensable tools of the Information Age. Current uses, however, tap neither the full potential of rapidly improving hardware and software, nor the growing opportunities arising from new telecommunications technology that can simultaneously transmit data, image, and voice signals. The National Computer Systems Laboratory is helping to ensure that the manufacturers and users of information technology will reap the anticipated benefits--better products, the growth of markets, and production applications of information technology. Beyond providing technical assistance, NCSL serves government and industry by developing standards, test methods, and computer security measures. It consists of the following divisions:

Information Systems Engineering Division, A266 Technology Bldg.; (301) 975-3262

Systems and Software Technology Division, B266 Technology Bldg.; (301) 975-3290

Computer Security Division, A216 Technology Bldg.; (301) 975-2934

Systems and Network Architecture Division, B217 Technology Bldg.; (301) 975-3618

Advanced Systems Division, A224 Technology Bldg.; (301) 975-2904

* Computer Security Consulting

Computer Security Division, Computer Systems Laboratory
National Institute of Standards and Technology (NIST)
A216, Technology Bldg
Gaithersburg, MD 20899 (301) 975-2929

The National Computer Systems Laboratory (NCSL) provides federal agencies with advice and assistance in computer security planning, training, and related activities. With the National Security Agency, NCSL reviews and comments on agency security plans for sensitive, unclassified systems. Regular workshops, meetings, and a national computer security conference comprise the ongoing program to facilitate the interchange of ideas, needs, guidance, and standards.

* Computer Systems Consulting

Computer Systems Laboratory
National Institute of Standards and Technology (NIST)
B154 Technology Bldg
Gaithersburg, MD 20899 (301) 975-2822

The National Computer Systems Laboratory (NCSL) consults with federal agencies to solve technical problems. Carried out on a cost-reimbursable basis, projects are selected for their broad applicability to federal agency information processing and their contributions to NCSL programs. The professional staff is uniquely qualified to address technical problems in computer security, software engineering, advanced computer systems, database management and graphics systems, and distributed processing. For specific information on how NCSL's products, services, and expertise can help your organization, contact this laboratory.

* Cooperative Data Programs

Reference Center
Standard Reference Data
National Institute of Standards and Technology (NIST)
A323 Physics Building
Gaithersburg, MD 20899 (301) 975-2208

The need for high quality data far exceeds the resources of the Standard Reference Data Program. as a result, NIST participates in numerous cooperative data projects which have been set up to meet the needs. In a typical project, the NIST technical centers work together with an outside group, such as a technical society, industry group, or government agency to develop databases. Contact this Center for more information.

* Cooperative Research With NIST Experts

Cooperative Research Program
National Institute of Standards and Technology (NIST)
A363 Physics Bldg
Gaithersburg, MD 20899 (301) 975-4505

Researchers from industry and universities regularly work in NIST laboratories with Institute experts on projects of mutual interest. For example, engineers, machinists, and computer specialists from private companies, other government agencies, and universities have joined NIST researchers to develop the quality control techniques and the computer software interface standards needed for the automated factory of the future. For information on conducting cooperative research at the Institute write or call David Edgerly, or call the individual division listed previously that applies to your interests directly.

* Data Evaluation Centers

An important part of the National Standard Reference Data System is the data evaluation centers active in major areas of physics, chemistry, and materials science. These centers represent a long-term commitment to assessing and improving the quality of data in each area. Each of the centers maintains a close working relationship with other government agencies, private-sector organizations, and international groups active in its area. The centers welcome inquiries and opportunities for cooperative projects. The data centers are, unless otherwise indicated, located at the National Institute of Standards and Technology, Gaithersburg, MD 20899.

Chemistry

Aqueous Electrolyte Data Center, A164 Chemistry Building
Chemical Kinetics Information Center, A147 Chemistry Building
Chemical Thermodynamics Data Center, A158 Chemistry Building
Fluids Mixtures Data Center, Mail Code 774.00, National Institute of Standards and Technology, Boulder, CO 80303
Ion Kinetics and Energetics Data Center, A147 Chemistry Building
Molten Salts Data Center, Rensselaer Polytechnic Institute, Department of Chemistry, Troy, NY 12181
Radiation Chemistry Data Center, University of Notre Dame, Radiation Laboratory, Notre Dame, IN 46556
Thermodynamics Research Center, Texas A&M University, College Station, TX 77843-3111

Materials Science

Alloy Phase Diagram Data Center, B150 Materials Building
Center for Information and Numerical Analysis and Synthesis, Purdue University, 2595 Yeager Road, West Lafayette, IN 47906
Corrosion Data Center, B259 Materials Building
Crystal Data Center, A207 Materials Building

National Institute of Standards and Technology

Phase Diagrams for Ceramists Data Center, A229 Materials Building
Tribology Information Center, A247 Materials Building

Physics
Atomic Collision Cross Section Data Center, Joint Institute for Laboratory Astrophysics, University of Colorado, Boulder, CO 80309
Atomic Energy Levels Data Center, A167 Physics Building
Atomic Transition Probabilities Data Center, A267 Physics Building
Fundamental Constants Data Center, B258 Metrology Building
Molecular Spectra Data Center, B268 Physics Building
Photon and Charged-Particle Data Center, C311 Radiation Physics Building

* Dielectric Properties of Materials

Electronics and Electrical Engineering Laboratory
National Institute of Standards and Technology (NIST)
Boulder, CO 80303 (303) 497-3339

Inadequate knowledge of the electromagnetic properties of materials inhibits development of new technologies, drives up the cost of systems and components, and may prevent achievement of optimal performance levels. A relatively new NIST program in materials is aimed at developing primary standards for measuring the dielectric materials of properties of materials used in electromagnetic applications.

* Dynamic Pressure and Temperature Research

Chemical Science and Technology Laboratory
B312 Physics
National Institute of Standards and Technology (NIST)
Gaithersburg, MD 20899 (301) 975-4813

U.S. industry increasingly relies on real-time monitoring of process parameters, particularly temperature and pressure, to produce efficiently a desired endproduct, to warrant safe operation and to assure equity in commerce. NIST has a research program and is developing a test facility to provide a reliable basis for the evolution and calibration of transducer dynamical response functions. This research seeks to develop a primary standard for dynamic temperature and pressure based on the fundamental properties of the molecular constituents of the dynamic system. Contact NIST for more information.

* Earthquake Safety

Building and Fire Research Laboratory
National Institute of Standards and Technology (NIST)
B250 Building Research Bldg
Gaithersburg, MD 20899 (301) 975-5900

The National Engineering Laboratory uses a specially designed computerized facility to test how full-scale bridge and building components would perform in earthquakes. Contact this Center for more information.

* Electromagnetic Interference and Compatibility

Electronics and Electrical Engineering Laboratory
Div. 813.03
National Institute of Standards and Technology (NIST)
Boulder, CO 80303 (303) 497-5320

NIST researchers are engaged in a wide range of projects aimed at quantifying electromagnetic interference and electromagnetic compatibility. One thrust of NIST work is to develop measurement techniques and methodologies for measuring the emission of unintentional radiation from electronic devices. Another aspect under active investigation is the susceptibility of electronic equipment to such radiation. Success of this research should lead to the development of new standards which can be adopted both in the U.S. and internationally.

* Electromagnetic Technology/Magnetics

Electronics and Electrical Engineering Laboratory
Div. 814.05
National Institute of Standards and Technology (NIST)
325 Broadway
Boulder, CO 80303 (303) 497-3785

NIST researchers characterize magnetic materials, such as ferromagnetic and magnetoresistive films, recording tapes and disks, ferromagnetic steels, very weakly magnetic alloys, amorphous ribbons, spin glasses, ferrites, and permanent magnets as a function of magnetic field and temperature. Attention in this work is given to calibration accuracy measurement precision and instrument

development. The research done in this lab has applications in basic physics and in applied engineering.

* Electronic Publishing

Systems and Software Technology Division
Computer Systems Laboratory
National Institute of Standards and Technology (NIST)
B218, Technology Bldg.
Gaithersburg, MD 20899 (301) 975-3290

The National Computer Systems Laboratories' Electronic Publishing Laboratory assists federal agencies in the selection and use of publishing systems by demonstrating the capabilities and limitations of different publishing technologies. Laboratory demonstrations focus on electronic publishing and the role of standards in electronic document processing and interchange. To visit the laboratory, contact the office above.

* Electrical Metrology with Optical Sensors

Electronics and Electrical Engineering Laboratory
Room B344, Metrology Bldg
National Institute of Standards and Technology (NIST)
Gaithersburg, MD 20899 (301) 975-2403

Researchers at NIST are developing electro-optical methods to measure electrical quantities and phenomena as part of a program to develop theory, methods, and physical standards for measuring electrical quantities in advanced high-voltage/high power systems.

* Electronics and Electrical Engineering

Electronics and Electrical Engineering Laboratory
B352 Metrology
National Institute of Standards and Technology (NIST)
Gaithersburg, MD 20899 (301) 975-2220

This Center conducts research and development in the field of electronic and electrical materials, devices, instruments, and systems. The Center develops engineering data, measurement methods, theory, physical standards, and associated technology, and provides technical services, national reference standards, and engineering measurement traceability for the benefit of government, industry, and the scientific community. Contact this office for more information.

* Emerging Technologies in Manufacturing Engineering

Manufacturing Engineering Laboratory
National Institute of Standards and Technology (NIST)
B326 Metrology Bldg.
Gaithersburg, MD 20899 (301) 975-3400

Emerging Technologies in Manufacturing Engineering is an internal report produced by the managers and staff of the Center for Manufacturing Engineering for planning purposes only. It represents their current best thinking about emerging technologies in manufacturing engineering, the impact these technologies will have on their programs, and the directions their programs will go if sufficient resources are available. The emerging technologies discussed are those that they believe will require increased support and leadership from CME in coming years. Contact this office for a free copy.

* Energy Efficient Chemical Separation

Chemical Engineering Science Division
Chemical Science and Technology Laboratory
National Institute of Standards and Technology (NIST)
325 Broadway
Boulder, CO 80303 (303) 497-5366

The Chemical Engineering Science Division creates mass transfer models and heat transfer codes for new, energy efficient separation concepts.

* Energy-Related Inventions Program

Office of Technology Evaluation and Assessment
Energy-Related Inventions
National Institute of Standards and Technology (NIST)
Gaithersburg, MD 20899 (301) 975-5500

The National Institute of Standards and Technology evaluates all promising non-nuclear energy-related inventions, particularly those submitted by independent inventors and small companies for the purpose of obtaining direct grants for

Be patient. If any phone number is incorrect, call (area code) 555-1212 and request the new listing.

Science and Technology

their development from the U.S. Department of Energy. The Energy-Related Inventions Program provides an opportunity for inventors to obtain Federal assistance in developing and commercializing their inventions. For a leaflet answering questions about qualifying, the evaluation process, types of assistance, patent policy, and other frequently asked questions about the program; and to request an Evaluation Request Form, contact the office above.

* European Community Approach to Standards Development

Office of Standards Code and Information
A629 Administration Bldg
Gaithersburg, MD 20899 (301) 975-4029

The Commission of the European Communities (EC) is acting swiftly to turn the 12-member countries into a single integrated market of 320 million people by the end of 1992. EC legislation dealing with standardization is likely to have a profound effect on U.S. exports. *A Summary of the New European Community Approach to Standards Development* contains a list of EC and U.S. government contacts for information on various aspects of EC activities related to standardization. For a copy, send a self-addressed mailing label to Patrick Cooke at the address above.

* Fire Center Research Grants

Fire Science and Engineering
Building Fire and Research Laboratory
National Institute of Standards and Technology (NIST)
B218 Building Research Bldg
Gaithersburg, MD 20899 (301) 975-6850

The Center for Fire Research (CFR) awards, mostly to universities, about 25 research grants annually that are integrated with the in-house program by CFR technical monitors who have related project responsibilities. Contact this Center for more information on the research grants. FIREDOC is the automated database of the Fire Research Information Services bibliographic collection. The collection contains national and international fire research reports, books, journal articles and conference proceedings. FIREDOC contains the references and, if possible, abstract and keywords. The full text of the document is not included in the database. FIREDOC is available 23 hours per day, Monday through Friday. It is not available between 8:30 a.m. and 9:30 a.m. eastern time. On Saturdays and Sundays, it is available 24 hours per day. For detailed instructions on how to access the database and how to perform bibliographic searches, you can get the *FIREDOC User's Manual* for $11.95 from National Technical Information Service (NTIS), 5285 Port Royal Rd., Springfield, VA 22161; (703) 487-4650. For additional information, call Nora Jason at the NIST office above.

* Fire Hazard Analysis

Building and Fire Research Laboratory
A249 Polymer
National Institute of Standards and Technology (NIST)
Gaithersburg, MD 20899 (301) 975-6879

The U.S. has one of the worst fire records in the industrialized world. NIST researchers are helping to reduce the losses and cost of fire protection by providing scientific and engineering bases needed by manufacturers and the fire protection community. The project relies on numerical and hand calculation methods as well as computer graphics and design techniques.

* Fire Measurement and Research Developments

Fire Science and Engineering
Building and Fire Research Laboratory
National Institute of Standards and Technology (NIST)
Gaithersburg, MD 20899 (301) 975-6866

Contact this division for information on studies which identify and measure potentially harmful combustion products and their effects on living organisms, and studies to develop less flammable furnishings.

* Fire Research and Consulting

Building and Fire Research Laboratory
National Institute of Standards and Technology (NIST)
B218, Building Research Bldg
Gaithersburg, MD 20899 (301) 975-6850

The Center for Fire Research (CFR) provides technical support to voluntary standards and codes groups, the engineering and design community, the building industry, fire services, and fire protection organizations. It also provides scientifically-based recommendations to other government agencies on fire-related issues. CFR also conducts fire research for private industry when CFR facilities or expertise are unique and when the requested research complements the on-going CFR program. Contact this Center for more information.

* Fire Research Center

Building and Fire Research Laboratory
National Institute of Standards and Technology (NIST)
Gaithersburg, MD 20899 (301) 975-6850

This Center performs and supports research to provide the scientific and technical basis for reducing fire losses and the cost of fire protection. The Center's technical promotes the development and widespread use of scientifically-based fire protection engineering practices, promote the continued advance in knowledge of the physics and chemistry behind actual fires, and maintain the technical capability for timely response to current fire problems. The Center maintains a definitive fire research information center for its use and as a resource for the fire community. The Center also manages a grants program for basic and applied fire research to complement in-house research. For more information, contact this Center.

* Fire Research Computer Bulletin Board

Building and Fire Research Laboratory
National Institute of Standards and Technology (NIST)
B218, Building Research Bldg
Gaithersburg, MD 20899 (301) 975-6850

The Center for Fire Research Computer Bulletin Board is a public access computer bulletin board featuring computer programs developed by the Center for Fire Research. The bulletin Board also contains information on FIREDOC and Center for Fire Research activities. You will find fire simulation programs developed at the Center, information on upcoming activities at the Center, including conferences, workshops and seminars, a listing of recent reports from the Center, and more. Contact this Center for more information on accessing the bulletin board.

* Fire Research Publications, 1987

National Technical Information Service
5825 Port Royal Rd
Springfield, VA 22161 (703) 487-4650

Interested in the combustion toxicity of various plastics? cigarette fire-safety? sprinklers? smoke control? soot formation? The NIST Center for Fire Research issued publications and articles on these topics and many others, all of which are compiled in the bibliography, *Fire Research Publications, 1987.* NIST conducts research on how fires start and spread and how they can be detected and suppressed. This research leads to realistic material test methods, cost-effective fire safety design concepts, and new methods of fire control and extinguishment. Copies are $14.95 prepaid through the office above.

* Fire Safety

Building and Fire Research Laboratory
National Institute of Standards and Technology (NIST)
A218 Building Research Bldg
Gaithersburg, MD 20899 (301) 975-6850

The National Engineering Laboratory develops computer-based models and engineering tools that predict fire and its effects for use by the fire protection and building communities in designing safer buildings. Contact this Center for more information.

* Fire Safety in Transportation Vehicles

Fire Science and Engineering
Building and Fire Research Laboratory
National Institute of Standards and Technology (NIST)
Gaithersburg, MD 20899 (301) 975-6864

This division makes recommendations for upgrading fire safety of mass transportation vehicles such as subway cars and trains.

* Fire Science and Engineering

Fire Science and Engineering Division
Building and Fire Research Laboratory
National Institute of Standards and Technology (NIST)

Be patient. If any phone number is incorrect, call (area code) 555-1212 and request the new listing.

National Institute of Standards and Technology

Gaithersburg, MD 20899 (301) 975-6863

This Division develops new methods for determining fire hazard and risk and extends them into engineering practice. The division provides information and analytical methods for advancing the science of fire protection, develops comprehensive and user-friendly computer models of fire and its effects within complex structures, performs experiments and analysis on the growth and spread of fire on materials and within structures, and develops measurement techniques and analyses to study the dynamics of water in putting out fires. Sample outputs include a fire hazard assessment method that addresses smoke transport and the behavior and effects on people, a handbook of smoke control, an improved room fire growth computer model, and a salt water analog technique for determining the motion of smoke in complex structures. Contact this division for more information on fire science and engineering developments.

* Fire Sensing Research

Building and Fire Research Laboratory
A250 Polymer
National Institute of Standards and Technology (NIST)
Gaithersburg, MD 20899 (301) 975-6866

NIST researchers are working on a new generation of fire detectors that will detect fires earlier and avoid the high current rate of false alarms generated by current sensing technologies.

* Fracture and Deformation Research

Materials Reliability Division
Institute for Materials Science and Engineering
National Institute of Standards and Technology (NIST)
Division 430
Boulder, CO 80303 (303) 497-3268

Understanding how and why structural materials fail--the aim of the Materials Reliability Division--can yield enormous benefits. When used in the design and fabrication of structure, detailed, quantitative knowledge of the mechanics of fracture and deformation can improve safety and reliability, increase productivity, and even avert disaster, such as bridge collapses and railroad derailments that stem from stresses and flows in materials. The division's staff studies nonlinear fracture mechanics, arc physics, acoustoelasticity, the mechanics of composite materials, and the relationship between the structure, properties, and mechanical behavior of materials. Materials are examined over a wide range of temperatures. The division conducts studies for other government agencies and provides technical services to industry and public and private research institutions. For more information, contact this NIST division.

* Frequency, Time, and Phase Noise Measurement

Physics Laboratory, Division 847
National Institute of Standards and Technology (NIST)
Boulder, CO 80303 (303) 497-3772

Advancements in communication and navigation systems require atomic oscillators with increased performance. NIST has several programs aimed at providing advanced frequency standards with the potential for benefitting commercial atomic standards. NIST has also begun a program to develop methods for measuring phase noise over a broad frequency range.

* Fuel Consumption Maximization

Chemical Science and Technology Laboratory
B308 Physics Bldg
National Institute of Standards and Technology (NIST)
Gaithersburg, MD 20899 (301) 975-2609

NIST is working on research to help U.S. industry obtain maximum energy output from fuel consumption. The researchers are studying the dynamics of spray flames to investigate droplet vaporization, pyrolysis, combustion, and particulate formation processes and to delineate the effect of chemical and physical properties of fuels on the above processes. The research will lay the necessary groundwork for developing and validating spray combustion models.

* GATT Standards Code Activities of the National Bureau of Standards 1987

Office of Standards Code and Information
A629 Administration Bldg
Gaithersburg, MD 20899 (301) 975-4029

GATT Standards Code Activities of the National Bureau of Standards 1987 is an annual report that describes NIST's role over the past year as the official U.S. GATT (General Agreement on Tariffs and Trade) inquiry point for information on standards and certification activities that might significantly affect U.S. trade. The NIST effort included coordinating comments on proposed foreign regulations, translating of foreign texts, and operating the GATT "hotline" (301) 975-4041, not toll free) that provides the latest information on foreign notifications from the GATT Secretariat in Geneva, Switzerland. The 1987, highlights were participation in the GATT Standards Code meeting on information exchange and the ISONET (International Organization for Standardization Information Network) workshop on international trade; publication of an introduction to standardization, certification, and laboratory accreditation; and background research for the Canadian Free Trade Agreement. Contact the office above to obtain a copy.

* Guest Researcher Opportunities in Building Technology

Building and Fire Research Laboratory
B222, Building Research Bldg
National Institute of Standards and Technology (NIST)
Gaithersburg, MD 20899 (301) 975-5900

The Center for Building Technology performs cooperative research with other organizations, private and public. There are many opportunities for engineers, scientists, and students from private and public organizations to participate in CBT research:

- Research Associates (from industry and academia),
- Guest Researchers (from U.S. and international organizations),
- Postdoctoral Research Associates (selected by National Academies),
- Engineers and Scientists from State and local governments,
- Visiting Scholars from universities, and
- Cooperative and Summer Students

Contact this office for more information on guest researcher opportunities.

* HAZARD I

National Fire Protection Association
One Stop Data Shop
Batterymarch Park
Quincy, MA 02269

National Technical Information Service
Springfield, VA 22161

Center for Firesafety Studies
Worcester Polytechnic Institute
Worcester, MA 01609

Building and Fire Research Laboratory
Room A-247, Building 224
Gaithersburg, MD 20899

HAZARD I is a method for predicting the hazards to the occupants of a building from a fire therein. Within prescribed limits, *HAZARD I* allows you to predict the outcome of a fire in a building populated by a representative set of occupants in terms of which persons successfully escape and which are killed, including the time, location, and likely cause of death for each. Specific applications vary, but some include material/product performance evaluation, fire reconstruction and litigation, evaluation of code changes or variances, fire department pre-planning, and extrapolation of fire test data to additional physical configurations. *HAZARD I* consists of a three volume report and a set of computer disks and costs $225 per copy from the National Fire Protection Association or the National Technical Information Service. Training programs are planned for a variety of target groups at the Center for Firesafety Studies. For more information, contact the Center for Fire Research.

* Hydrocarbon Engineering Properties

Office of Standard Reference Data
National Institute of Standards and Technology (NIST)
A323 Physics Building
Gaithersburg, MD 20899 (301) 975-2208

A new database for calculating viscosity, density, and other important engineering property data of hydrocarbons--natural gas, petroleum, and organic materials, including mixtures of fluids--has been developed by NIST. The "DDMIX" database was developed as part of a research project sponsored by an industry consortium of petroleum, chemical, and gas processing firms. Available on a floppy disk for personal computers, it provides rapid access to important information on the storage and transportation of fluids, and for the design of new chemical processes. Among other things, the program allows users to

Be patient. If any phone number is incorrect, call (area code) 555-1212 and request the new listing.

Science and Technology

calculate quickly various thermodynamic and transport properties of fluid mixtures. To order the *DDMIX--Mixture Property Program (1988), NIST Standards Reference Database 14*, a floppy disk for personal computers for $400, contact the office above.

* Image Recognition

Computer Systems Laboratory
A216 Technology
National Institute of Standards and Technology (NIST)
Gaithersburg, MD 20899 (301) 975-2080

Image-recognition research at NIST focuses on developing methods for evaluating image quality, compression efficiency, and image systems used in optical character recognition. The methods being developed are used for automated fingerprint recognition, automation of data entry from images of forms, and measurement of recognition systems on realistic applications.

* Industry Pollution Reduction

Chemical Science and Technology Laboratory
B112 Physics Bldg
National Institute of Standards and Technology (NIST)
Gaithersburg, MD 20899 (301) 975-2610

The chemical and associated industries produce enormous amounts of byproducts. To avoid wasting industrial resources and polluting the environment, the impact of these byproducts must be minimized. The solution of the problem lies in the following: minimizing waste at the source by modifying industrial processes; recovering energy and chemicals for reuse; and converting pollutants to acceptable species. NIST is pursuing research in the area of thermal treatments, which seems to be the most promising approach to the problem. Contact NIST for information on facilities and current research.

* Industrial Quality Control

Office of Standard Reference Materials
National Measurement Laboratory
National Institute of Standards and Technology (NIST)
B311 Chemistry Bldg
Gaithersburg, MD 20899 (301) 975-2016

The National Measurement Laboratory contributes to improved industrial quality control by developing Standard Reference Materials and calibrating equipment and devices. Contact this office for more information.

* Information Resource Dictionary System

Information Systems Engineering Division
Computer Systems Laboratory
National Institute of Standards and Technology (NIST)
A259, Technology Bldg
Gaithersburg, MD 20899 (301) 975-3262

The Information Systems Engineering Laboratory research initiative resulted in the Information Resource Dictionary System (IRDS) standard and an IRDS prototype, a software system that records, stores, and processes information about an organization's data and data processing resources. The IRDS enables federal government users to improve productivity by identifying information resources that can be shared within an organization and between organizations. Contact this office for more information on IRDS and its uses.

* Information Services

Technology Services
Room A128, Administration Bldg
National Institute of Standards and Technology (NIST)
Gaithersburg, MD 20899 (301) 975-3058

The Office of Information Services maintains a comprehensive international collection of information in scientific disciplines such as metrology, mathematics, computer science, and materials science. The NIST staff participate in national and international publications and technical information networks and consortia, as well as a document exchange program to ensure that NIST publications are available to interested parties. An inquires service assists the public in obtaining information about past and present NIST programs, projects, and publications.

* Information Systems Engineering Assistance

Information Systems Engineering Division
Computer Systems Laboratory

National Institute of Standards and Technology (NIST)
A259, Technology Bldg
Gaithersburg, MD 20899 (301) 975-3262

The Information Systems Engineering Division supports standards development and provides technical assistance to government and industry in data administration; data management; computer graphics; geographic information systems; standards validation; and programming language technologies. Contact this division for more information on available assistance.

* Information Technology Research

Information Systems Engineering Division
Computer Systems Laboratory
National Institute of Standards and Technology (NIST)
A266 Technology Bldg
Gaithersburg, MD 20899 (301) 975-3262

The National Computer Systems Laboratory conducts research on parallel processing performance, speech recognition, and other rapidly evolving applications of information technology to provide a basis for standards development.

* Information Technology Standards

Information Systems Engineering Division
Computer Systems Laboratory
National Institute of Standards and Technology (NIST)
A266 Technology Bldg
Gaithersburg, MD 20899 (301) 975-3262

The National Computer Systems Laboratory helps the information technology industry and users develop cost-effective national and international standards for open systems that erase incompatibility barriers and allow exchange of information between the systems of different manufacturers. Contact this division for more information.

* Integrated Services Digital Networks

Advanced Systems Division
Computer Systems Laboratory
National Institute of Standards and Technology (NIST)
A231, Technology Bldg
Gaithersburg, MD 20899 (301) 975-2904

The National Computer Systems Laboratory investigates standards and develops conformance test methods for Integrated Services Digital Networks (ISDN), a new telecommunications technology that makes it possible to send and receive voice, data, and image signals simultaneously over digital telephone networks. Researchers in this area focus on the measurement capabilities and testbed facilities required to develop conformance tests and performance metrics for engineering ISDN standards. NCSL established the North American ISDN User's Forum to create a strong user voice in the implementation of ISDN. Contact this office for more information.

* Integrated-Circuit Test Structure Metrology

Electronics and Electrical Engineering Laboratory
Room B360 Technology Bldg
National Institute of Standards and Technology (NIST)
Gaithersburg, MD 20899 (301) 975-2052

Integrated -circuit (IC) test structures and test methods developed by NIST are used widely by the semiconductor industry and other government agencies. These devices can be used to evaluate manufacturing processes and equipment used to manufacture semiconductors and to test the reliability of the finished product. NIST engineers are investigating pattern recognition techniques for the rapid diagnosis of IC manufacturing processes and for establishing methods to determine the reliability of thin films used in state-of-the-art microcircuits.

* Intelligent Processing of Materials

Materials Science and Engineering Laboratory
B344 Materials
National Institute of Standards and Technology (NIST)
Gaithersburg, MD 20899 (301) 975-5727

Advanced materials are capable of providing outstanding properties, but they generally require unusual processing operations and tend to be expensive. Intelligent processing offers the potential to design and produce materials with improved quality, reduced lead time, and increased production flexibility. Research sponsored by the Office of Intelligent Processing of Materials is directed to process models, sensors, and intelligent control systems.

Be patient. If any phone number is incorrect, call (area code) 555-1212 and request the new listing.

National Institute of Standards and Technology

* Laboratory Automation for Organic Analysis

Chemical Science and Technology Laboratory
A343 Chemistry Bldg
National Institute of Standards and Technology (NIST)
Gaithersburg, MD 20899 (301) 975-4132

NIST has joined with industry and other government agencies in a cooperative project to develop automated analytical devices for organic analysis based on new chemistries and apparatus, as well as on laboratory robotic systems.

* Law Enforcement Standards Laboratory

Law Enforcement Standards Laboratory
National Institute of Standards and Technology (NIST)
Gaithersburg, MD 20899 (301) 975-2757

The Law Enforcement Standards Laboratory conducts research and provides technical services to the U.S. Department of Justice and State and local governments in support of law enforcement agencies. The division develops standards for police bullet-resistant equipment, handguns, shotguns, communications equipment, physical security equipment, tear gas devices, speed measuring devices, and evidential breath testers. The division also provides guides for selecting and applying commercial intrusion systems, facsimile equipment, and protective equipment. Technical reports on various related subjects such as handgun ammunition, blood/breath alcohol analysis, and arson investigation, are available. Contact this laboratory for more information.

* Low-Alloy Steel Calibration Standards

Office of Standard Reference Materials
National Institute of Standards and Technology (NIST)
B311 Chemistry Bldg
Gaithersburg, MD 20899 (301) 975-6776

NIST has developed a new graded series of seven low-alloy steel standards for calibrating optical emission and x-ray fluorescence spectrometers. Great care has been used in preparing these materials to obtain a high level of homogeneity to meet the demands of new, highly precise instruments used in the quality control of alloy materials. *Standard Reference Materials* (SRM's) 1761-1767, prepared in consultation with ASTM and industry, are available for $135 each in the form of disks approximately 34 mm in diameter and 19 mm thick. To obtain information on the certified values of each disk, or to order the new graded series of calibration standards, contact the office above.

* Low-Temperature Electronics

Electronics and Electrical Engineering Laboratory
Division 814.03
National Institute of Standards and Technology (NIST)
Boulder, CO 80303 (303) 497-5341

Cyrogenic, and especially superconducting electronics, provide remarkably high speed and sensitivity, coupled with exceptionally low power dissipation. NIST has a complete facility for fabricating superconducting integrated circuits from conventional low-temperature superconductors and is developing a similar capability for high-temperature ceramic superconductors. NIST's work in this area has established numerous world performance records over the years with such devices as analogue-to-digital converters, samplers, electrometers, microwave and infrared detectors, lithographed antennas, and magnetic flux detectors using SQUIDs. NIST works closely with private industry in this area.

* Malcolm Baldrige National Quality Awards

National Institute of Standards and Technology (NIST)
Inquiries Unit
E128 Administration Bldg
Gaithersburg, MD 20899 (301) 975-2758

A goal of the National Institute of Standards and Technology is to aid firms in building a competitive advantage. NIST manages the annual Malcolm Baldrige National Quality Awards to work towards this goal. Winning firms achieve continuous improvement in their manufacturing processes and final products. They, like formidable foreign competitors, have succeeded in meshing efficiency, flexibility, quality, and innovation in a single operation. Contact this office for more information on the awards.

* Manufacturing Engineering Publications

Manufacturing Engineering Laboratory
National Institute of Standards and Technology (NIST)
B119 Technology Bldg

Gaithersburg, MD 20899 (301) 975-3400

The current edition of the *Publications of the Center for Manufacturing Engineering* covers the period January, 1978 through December, 1988. This listing reflects the diversity of scientific and technical problems which have been attacked over the past ten years in fulfillment of the Center's mission. Publications, indexed by subject area, cover research done by the Center in the areas of high precision dimensional measurement and precision engineering; robotics and intelligent machines; manufacturing data description, data administration, and information processing; and sensors for manufacturing processes. Contact this Center for a free copy.

* Manufacturing Engineering Research

Manufacturing Engineering Laboratory
B326 Metrology Bldg
National Institute of Standards and Technology (NIST)
Gaithersburg, MD 20899 (301) 975-3400

NIST is recognized as the Nation's finest general purpose scientific and engineering laboratory. The mission of the Center for Manufacturing Engineering is to bring the resources of this laboratory to bear on the standards and measurements problems associated with America's discrete parts manufacturing. In fulfillment of its mission, the Center conducts active programs of research in the areas of high precision dimensional measurement; sensing and measurement of force, sound, vibration, and surface finish characteristics; and application of advanced control and sensing techniques to automated machines, manufacturing systems, and robot manipulators. Contact this Center for more information on current research.

* Manufacturing Systems Integration

Manufacturing Engineering Laboratory
A127 Metrology Bldg
National Institute of Standards and Technology (NIST)
Gaithersburg, MD 20899 (301) 975-2802

Despite years of product development, truly modular, flexible, integrated manufacturing systems are still not prevalent in the U.S. Information sharing across engineering product management and control systems is still not possible. NIST has begun a manufacturing systems integration project to develop a prototype environment for conducting integration experiments. NIST is working on this project with several major universities, auto companies, aerospace companies, and vendors. In a related project, NIST is researching the "process of design," with the hopes of creating a more integrated process rather than one-shot design programs.

* Manufacturing Technology Centers Program

Manufacturing Technology Centers Program
B112 Metrology Bldg
National Institute of Standards and Technology (NIST)
Gaithersburg, MD 20899 (301) 975-3414

To bring automated manufacturing technology to small- and mid-sized manufacturing firms, NIST has begun a manufacturing technology centers program. The program is designed to establish regional centers that will help these companies improve their technical capabilities and competitiveness. Their central activity is working hands-on with small and mid-size firms to 1) determine their particular technology needs; 2) develop a technology up-grade plan; 3) assist with business and financial planning to make the up-grade possible; and 4) help in the implementation of the new technology. The program will help to move new technology into the marketplace and will accelerate adoption of well-established "off-the-shelf" technologies to improve competitiveness of U.S.-based firms. The Centers invite inquiries from small and mid-sized manufacturers who want to find out more about their services. For more information about the program, or for phone numbers contact the above office.

* Materials Science

Materials Science and Engineering Laboratory
National Institute of Standards and Technology (NIST)
B309 Materials Bldg
Gaithersburg, MD 20899 (301) 975-5658

Without new and better materials, technological progress would come to a halt. Increasingly, advances in fields ranging from electronics to construction depend on the mastery of an almost infinitesimally small domain, the arrangements of atoms and molecules that determine material properties. MSEL's research staff investigate all classes of advanced materials: ceramics, polymers, composites, and metallic alloys. The results are data, measurement tools, and services for

Be patient. If any phone number is incorrect, call (area code) 555-1212 and request the new listing.

Science and Technology

understanding, improving, predicting, and controlling the processing and performance of materials. From autos to aerospace, improved materials are changing our lives. Car bodies and airplane parts are being made from polymer composites. Unconventional processing or synthesizing techniques are giving metal, ceramic, and polymer alloys increased strength or unusual properties. The laboratory consists of the following divisions:

Office of Intelligent Processing of Materials, B344 Materials Bldg; (301) 975-5727
Ceramics Division, A256 Materials Bldg.; (301) 975-6119
Fracture and Deformation Division, 430.0 NIST, Boulder, CO 80303; (303) 497-3251
Polymers Division, A305 Polymer Bldg.; (301) 975-6762
Metallurgy Division, B261 Materials Bldg.; (301) 975-5963
Reactor Radiation Division, A106 Reactor Bldg.; (301) 975-6210

* Materials Science and Engineering Laboratory Annual Report

Director, Materials Science and Engineering Laboratory
National Institute of Standards and Technology (NIST)
B309 Materials Bldg
Gaithersburg, MD 20899 (301) 975-5658

The *Materials Science and Engineering Laboratory Annual Report* describes in detail the technical activities of each of the Laboratory's major units and is available on request from the Lab above.

* Mathematical Analysis

Mathematical Analysis Division
Computing and Applied Mathematics Laboratory
National Institute of Standards and Technology (NIST)
Gaithersburg, MD 20899 (301) 975-2732

The Mathematical Analysis Division provides consulting services in applied economics. The Division also performs research and collaborates in the application of mathematical analysis, mathematical modeling, and requisite computer-based methods to science and engineering. Contact this division for more information on the services offered, or the research conducted.

* Mathematical Software

Scientific Computing Division
Center for Applied Mathematics
National Engineering Laboratory
National Institute of Standards and Technology (NIST)
Gaithersburg, MD 20899 (301) 975-3816

The Center for Applied Mathematics puts out the *Guide to Available Mathematical Software*. Contact this office to obtain a copy.

* Measurement Technology

Office of Measurement Services
National Institute of Standards and Technology (NIST)
A309 Chemistry Bldg
Gaithersburg, MD 20899 (301) 975-3143

The National Measurement Laboratory's researchers subscribe to the maxim: If a process cannot be measured or a product characterized, then it is not completely understood. Their work takes them to the frontiers of the physical and chemical sciences, the birthplace of many new technologies. And it takes them to the manufacturing floor, where their technical understanding is translated into sensors, analytical methods, and other tools required for efficient production of high-technology materials and products. NML also coordinates the U.S. measurement system with those of other nations, facilitating international trade. It consists of the following centers:

Center for Basic Standards, B160 Physics Bldg.; (301) 975-4203
Center for Radiation Research, C229 Radiation Physics Bldg.; (301) 975-6090
Center for Chemical Physics, A363 Physics Bldg.; (301) 975-4500
Center for Analytical Chemistry, A309 Chemistry Bldg.; (301) 975-3143
Office of Standard Reference Data, A323 Physics Bldg.; (301) 975-2200
Office of Standard Reference Materials, B311 Chemistry Bldg.; (301) 975-2012
Office of Physical Measurement Services, B362 Physics Bldg.; (301) 975-2005

* Metals Quality and Cost

Metallurgy Division
Materials Science and Engineering Laboratory

National Institute of Standards and Technology (NIST)
B261 Materials Bldg
Gaithersburg, MD 20899 (301) 975-5963

The Institute for Materials Science and Engineering works with the U.S. metals industry and other federal laboratories to develop and exploit technologies that will improve the quality and reduce the cost of domestic steel, aluminum, and other metals. For more information, contact this division.

* Metallurgy Process Control

Materials Science and Engineering Laboratory
B144 Materials
National Institute of Standards and Technology (NIST)
Gaithersburg, MD 20899 (301) 975-6168

Special facilities at NIST enable researchers to develop advanced measurement methods and standards for application in process modeling and control for intelligent processing of materials. Measurement methods available include ultrasound, eddy currents, and acoustic emission. Coupled with state-of-the-art materials processing equipment and expertise these facilities offer a unique opportunity to ascertain feasibility and develop prototype specifications for a wide spectrum of sensor needs.

* Microwave/Millimeter-Wave Metrology

Electronics and Electrical Engineering Laboratory
National Institute of Standards and Technology (NIST)
Boulder, CO 80303 (303) 497-3148

Rapidly developing and expanding microwave technology requires research in advanced microwave measurements and standards. NIST researchers have developed highly accurate six-port techniques for automated measures of microwave power, attenuation, impedance, scattering parameters, and noise. They currently are developing greatly improved power and impedance standards and extending measurement services to cover millimeter waves and subminiature coaxial connectors.

* National Computer Systems Laboratory Newsletter

Computer Systems Laboratory
National Institute of Standards and Technology (NIST)
B154 Technology Bldg
Gaithersburg, MD 20899 (301) 975-2832

Published every six weeks, the *National Computer Systems Laboratory Newsletter* includes information on conferences, Federal Information Processing Standards, and NCSL special publications. Contact this office for more information on the *NCSL Newsletter*.

* National Engineering Laboratory

National Engineering Laboratory
National Institute of Standards and Technology (NIST)
B119 Technology Bldg
Gaithersburg, MD 20899 (301) 975-2300

Scores of studies have emphasized the importance of manufacturing to the competitive position of U.S. industry. The National Engineering Laboratory researchers are making accelerated efforts to provide the measurements and technology U.S. firms need to compete in burgeoning markets for ever faster semiconductors and optical communications equipment. On NEL's agenda are safety, public health, and the environment, as reflected in studies of fire prevention, evaluations of alternatives to ozone-depleting chlorofluorocarbons, and research supporting development of effective building regulations. It consists of the following centers:

Center for Computing and Applied Mathematics, A438 Administration Bldg.; (301) 975-2728
Center for Electronics and Electrical Engineering, B358 Metrology Bldg.; (301) 975-2220
Center for Manufacturing Engineering, B322 Metrology Bldg.; (301) 975-3400
Center for Building Technology, B250 Building Research Bldg.; (301) 975-5900
Center for Fire Research, A247 Polymer Bldg.; (301) 975-6850
Center for Chemical Engineering, 770.0, NIST, Boulder, CO 80303; (303) 497-5108

* National Innovation Workshops

Office of Energy-Related Inventions
National Institute of Standards and Technology (NIST)

Be patient. If any phone number is incorrect, call (area code) 555-1212 and request the new listing.

National Institute of Standards and Technology

Gaithersburg, MD 20899 (301) 975-5500

The Office of Energy-Related Inventions conducts a series of National Innovation Workshops for inventors and small businesses. Contact this office for more information.

* National Measurement Standards

Center for Basic Standards, B160 Physics Bldg
National Institute of Standards and Technology (NIST)
Gaithersburg, MD 20899 (301) 975-4023

The National Measurement Laboratory maintains and improves national standards for mass, length, time, temperature, and electric current. Inquiries should be directed to this Center.

* National Technical Information Service

National Technical Information Service
5825 Port Royal Rd.
Springfield, VA 22161 (703) 487-4650

The National Institute of Standards and Technology publications are sold by the National Technical Information Service. They can supply microfiche, or paper copy from microfiche, at any time. *Federal Information Processing Standards, NIST Interagency Reports* (a special series of interim or final reports on work performed by NIST for outside sponsors), and *Grant/Contract Reports* are available only from NTIS. Place orders on (800) 336-4700. For more information call the office above.

* Network Management

Computer Systems Laboratory
B217 Technology Bldg
National Institute of Standards and Technology (NIST)
Gaithersburg, MD 20899 (301) 975-3618

NIST researchers are working with industry to establish a set of standards for exchanging network management information between heterogeneous management systems. Their goal is to establish a standard enabling integrated, interoperable, automated management of multivendor computer systems, routers, bridges, switches, multiplexors, modems, and provider services.

* Neutron-Scattering Experiments

Reactor Radiation Division
Institute for Materials Science and Engineering
National Institute of Standards and Technology (NIST)
A106, Reactor
Gaithersburg, MD 20899 (301) 975-6242

Neutron-scattering methods of research permit studies of bulk samples, often yielding information on submicroscopic materials behavior and structure that is unsurpassed in detail and accuracy. Division scientists are engaged in a broad research program aimed at understanding and measuring the structure and properties of virtually all classes of materials used by industry, including high-temperature superconductors, advanced ceramics, catalysts, artificially structured materials, hydrogen in metals, and others that hold promise for high-technology applications. They are also furthering the uses of neutron diffraction and radiography for nondestructive evaluation. Other activities include efforts to develop new instrumentation and to strengthen the theoretical foundation of neutron-scattering research. Contact the office above for information on free services, including descriptive literature, telephone or on-site descriptions of the facilities, and discussion of problems.

* NIST List of Publications by Subject Category

National Institute of Standards and Technology (NIST)
U.S. Department of Commerce
Publications and Program Inquiries
E128 Administration Bldg
Gaithersburg, MD 20899 (301) 975-3058

A complimentary abridged journal of research, the *NIST List of Publications by Subject Category* compiles the NIST publications that are available, along with ordering information. It also contains a listing of depository libraries and a listing of Dept. of Commerce District Offices, two other sources of NIST publications.

* NIST Nonperiodical Technical Publications

Superintendent of Documents
Government Printing Office

Washington, DC 20402 (202) 783-3283

The nonperiodical publications from the National Institute of Standards and Technology include:

Monographs. Major contributions to the technical literature on various subjects related to the Institute's scientific and technical activities.

Handbooks. Recommended codes of engineering and industrial practice (including safety codes) developed in cooperation with interested industries, professional organizations, and regulatory bodies.

Special Publications. Includes proceedings of conferences sponsored by NIST, NIST annual reports, and other special publications appropriate to this grouping such as wall charts, pocket cards, and bibliographies.

Applied Mathematics Series. Mathematical tables, manuals, and studies of special interest to physicists, engineers, chemists, biologists, mathematicians, computer programmers, and others engaged in scientific and technical work.

National Standard Reference Data Series. Provides quantitative data on the physical and chemical properties of materials, compiled from the world's literature and critically evaluated.

Building Science Series. Disseminates technical information developed at the Institute on building materials, components, systems, and whole structures. The series presents research results, test methods, and performance criteria related to the structural and environmental functions and the durability and safety characteristics of building elements and systems.

Technical Notes. Studies or reports which are complete in themselves but restrictive in their treatment of a subject. Analogous to monographs but not so comprehensive in scope or definitive in treatment of the subject area. Often serve as a vehicle for final reports of work performed at NIST under the sponsorship of other government agencies.

Voluntary Product Standards. Developed under procedures published by the U.S. Department of Commerce, these standards establish nationally recognized requirements for products, and provide all concerned interests with a basis for common understanding of the characteristics of the products. NIST administers this program as a supplement to the activities of the private sector standardizing organizations.

Consumer Information Series. Practical information, based on NIST research and experience, covering areas of interest to the consumer. Easily understandable language and illustrations provide useful background knowledge for shopping in today's technological marketplace.

Order the above NIST publications from the Government Printing Office (see the address listed above).

* NIST Research Reports

Public Information Division
National Institute of Standards and Technology (NIST)
A903 Administration Bldg
Gaithersburg, MD 20899 (301) 975-2758

NIST Research Reports is a special publication which includes a research update, a listing of new NIST publications, and a conference calendar. It also includes specific NIST research reports of general public interest. Contact this office to obtain a copy.

* Nondestructive Evaluation Research

Office of Intelligent Processing of Materials
Materials Science and Engineering Laboratory
National Institute of Standards and Technology (NIST)
B344, Materials Bldg
Gaithersburg, MD 20899 (301) 975-5727

Nondestructive evaluation (NDE) is concerned with inspecting structures and products such as nuclear reactors, aircraft, and pipelines--an essential component of safety programs. Researchers are also concerned with monitoring important properties and characteristics of materials while they are being processed. In this capacity, NDE provides the information necessary for guiding or controlling production processes, assuring uniform high-quality products, and reducing waste. Contact the office above for more information.

Be patient. If any phone number is incorrect, call (area code) 555-1212 and request the new listing.

Science and Technology

* Non-Energy Invention Assistance

Office of Non-Energy Inventions
National Engineering Laboratory
National Institute of Standards and Technology (NIST)
Gaithersburg, MD 20899   (301) 975-5504

The National Institute of Standards and Technology is developing a new program to reach out to individuals. Any inventor will be able to submit an invention to NIST for evaluation, so long as it is non-nuclear. Drawing on a national network of science and engineering consultants, NIST--for *free*--will evaluate the technical feasibility and marketability of the invention: Will it work? Will anyone buy it? Recommendations for support will go elsewhere for marketing assistance or development grants. This program is not yet operational as it is awaiting congressional approval, but if you wish to submit a non-energy invention to the program, you may put your name on a waiting list. For more information, contact the office above.

* Oil Spill Cleanup

National Institute of Standards and Technology (NIST)
Gaithersburg, MD 20899   (301) 975-6668

In the wake of the Exxon Valdez accident and the Persian Gulf War, researchers have been searching for better ways to cleanup oil spills. One possible solution would be to burn the oil. NIST researchers have developed methods for more accurately determining the airborne concentration of smoke particles billowing off major oil fires. Using this information, local authorities may decide that less environmental damage would be caused by burning the oil than by other cleanup options.

* Open Systems Interconnection Technology

Systems and Network Architecture Division
National Computer Systems Laboratory
National Institute of Standards and Technology (NIST)
B217, Bldg 225
Gaithersburg, MD 20899   (301) 975-3618

The National Computer Systems Laboratory supports private industry and government through testing and standards implementation activities. For example, the Laboratory established OSINET, a cooperative government/ industry research network which tests commercial Open Systems Interconnection (OSI) technology products to see how well they operate together. Contact this division for more information about the program to advance the standards necessary for effective integrated network management.

* Optical Disk Media

Advanced Systems Division
National Computer Systems Laboratory
National Institute of Standards and Technology (NIST)
A224, Bldg 225
Gaithersburg, MD 20899   (301) 975-2904

The National Computer Systems Laboratory is developing a testing methodology that predicts life expectancy of optical disk media. This research will assist government managers in planning how long information may safely be stored on these media. Contact this office for more information.

* Optical Electronics Research

Electronics and Electrical Engineering Laboratory
Div. 814.02
National Institute of Standards and Technology (NIST)
Boulder, CO 80303   (303) 497-5341

NIST researchers are studying optical fiber measurements, optical communication device metrology, laser measurements, and optical fiber sensors. This research results in publication of new technology and measurement procedures and calibration services to support the laser and optical communications industries.

* Origins of Historical Artifacts

Materials Science and Engineering Laboratory
National Institute of Science and Technology
B309 Materials Bldg
Gaithersburg, MD 20899   (301) 975-5658

In a remote Asian village, an archaeologist unearths a bronze art object. Though the object appears similar to many discovered in other excavations, a basic question must be answered before it can be catalogued or displayed in a museum: Where did it originate? More specifically, where did the raw materials come from that make up the object? One of the most useful techniques of tracing an ancient artifact or verifying the authenticity of a piece is lead isotope ratio analysis. Scientists at the National Institute of Standards and Technology are using the technique in collaboration with museum researchers who seek to pinpoint just where precious art pieces come from. For more information, contact this laboratory.

* Phase Diagram Databases

Institute for Materials Science and Engineering
National Institute of Standards and Technology (NIST)
B309 Materials Bldg
Gaithersburg, MD 20899   (301) 975-5658

The Institute for Materials Science and Engineering works with professional societies to develop phase diagram databases that will help improve processing control and use of metals, ceramics, and polymers. For more information, contact this Institute.

* Photoduplicated Copies of NBS Publications

Photoduplication Service
Library of Congress
Washington, DC 20540   (202) 287-5640

Photoduplicated copies of many old National Bureau of Standards publications can be purchased from this Library of Congress service.

* Polymer Composites

Materials Science and Engineering Laboratory
National Institute of Standards and Technology (NIST)
A209 Polymer Building
Gaithersburg, MD 20899   (301) 975-6837

Researchers in industry, universities, and government are invited to participate in an NIST research program that addresses the most critical barriers in high-performance polymer composite processing which producers must overcome to meet increasing international competition. The U.S. market for high technology plastic products is expected to grow. The United States now has the technological lead in the use of high performance polymer composites in defense and aerospace applications. In high-volume mass markets, however, U.S. industries face intense competition. For more information, contact Donald L. Hunston at the above office.

* Polymer Science

Polymers Division
Materials Science and Engineering Laboratory
National Institute of Standards and Technology (NIST)
A305 Polymer Bldg
Gaithersburg, MD 20899   (301) 975-6762

The uses of polymers and polymer-based composites are virtually unlimited, and the materials are even displacing metals in many structural and high-performance applications, including automobiles and commercial and military aircraft. Advances in polymer science have paced important technological developments. The Polymers Division supports U.S. industries that produce, process, or use synthetic polymers. Its basic research programs are devoted to strengthening the scientific foundation that sustains continued advances in this important class of materials. These programs are designed according to the perceived needs of industry. The division is developing novel sensors for monitoring viscosity, flow, molecular orientation, and mixing. For more information on polymers research, contact this NIST division.

* Product Development Exchange Research

Manufacturing Engineering Laboratory
A127 Metrology
National Institute of Standards and Technology (NIST)
Gaithersburg, MD 20899   (301) 975-3511

Product data is an integral part of the information shared across computer applications and organizations forming a critical part of any integration scheme. Currently no commercial products exist that allow systems to share information in a standard way so as to be integrated. The Standard for the Exchange of Product Model Data (STEP) will help to alleviate the integration problem. NIST is also working on testing STEP, evaluating proposed standards with respect to applications.

Be patient. If any phone number is incorrect, call (area code) 555-1212 and request the new listing.

National Institute of Standards and Technology

* Protecting Computerized Information

Computer Security Division
Computer Systems Laboratory
National Institute of Standards and Technology (NIST)
A216 Technology Bldg
Gaithersburg, MD 20899 (301) 975-2934

The National Computer Systems Laboratory develops standards and guidelines for protecting computerized information from threats of all kinds--operator error, power losses, natural disasters, and unauthorized users. Contact this division for more information.

* Quality Assurance

Building and Fire Research Laboratory
National Institute of Standards and Technology (NIST)
B226, Building Research Laboratory
Gaithersburg, MD 20899 (301) 975-5900

The Center for Building Technology provides a quality assurance program for over 1000 public and private construction materials testing laboratories nationwide that is relied upon by owners, designers, builders, and State and local governments responsible for buildings and transportation facilities. Contact this Center for more information on the Quality Assurance Program.

* Quality in Automation Program

Manufacturing Engineering Laboratory
B106 Sound
National Institute of Standards and Technology (NIST)
Gaithersburg, MD 20899 (301) 975-6618

This program is an effort to achieve higher part accuracy from existing discrete parts manufacturing equipment. A four layer closed loop control architecture has been proposed, and three layers are presently being implemented. The Real Time and Process Intermittent loops use algorithms to predict systematic errors and compensate for them in real time. The Post Process loop verifies the cutting process and is also a check for errors that evade the first two loops. NIST is also working on research in machine tool performance, based on the premise that errors in manufacturing are repeatable, and thus predictable and correctable. Working closely with academia and industry, this research should result in improved manufacturing quality in the future.

* Radiation Measurements

Center for Radiation Research
National Measurement Laboratory
National Institute of Standards and Technology (NIST)
C229 Radiation Physics Bldg
Gaithersburg, MD 20899 (301) 975-6090

The National Measurement Laboratory designs dosimeters used to assure accurate measurement of radiation for diagnostic and therapeutic uses, personnel monitoring, and the production of materials. Contact this Center for more information on radiation measurement.

* Radiation Research

Center for Radiation Research
National Institute of Science and Technology
C229 Radiation Physics Bldg
Gaithersburg, MD 20899 (301) 975-6090

The Center for Radiation Research develops and maintains the scientific competencies and experimental facilities necessary to provide the Nation with a central basis for uniform physical measurements, measurement methodology, and measurement services in the areas of near infra-red radiation, optical radiation, ultraviolet radiation, and ionizing radiation; provides government, industry, and the academic community with essential calibrations for field radiation measurements needed in such applied areas as nuclear power, lighting, solar radiation processing, advanced laser development, and radiation protection for public safety; and carries out research in order to develop improved radiation standards, new radiation measurement technology, and improved understanding of atomic, molecular, and ionizing radiation processes, and to elucidate the interaction of radiation and particles with inanimate and biological materials. Contact this Center for a copy of the annual report summarizing the activities that were carried out in 1989, and listing publications, talks, and professional interactions.

* Research and Testing Facilities

National Institute of Standards and Technology (NIST)
U.S. Department of Commerce
E128 Administration Bldg
Gaithersburg, MD 20899 (301) 975-2758

The NTIS has some of the premier research and testing facilities in the United States, several of which are unequaled anywhere in the world. To aid firms in building a competitive advantage, NIST makes available for cooperative and proprietary work its varied research and testing facilities at its headquarters in Gaithersburg, Maryland, and its site in Boulder, Colorado. To contact a facility, see the previous listing of centers and laboratories. The following is a listing of some of the special facilities that are available to conduct research at various centers and laboratories:

Chemical Science and Technology Laboratory

Research Reactor
NIST has a 20-megawatt research reactor used in materials research, molecular structure determination, and neutron activation analysis. This analysis is applicable to a wide variety of biomedical problems such as nutrition, the role of trace elements in human development, bioaccumulation, the role of trace elements in disease processes, investigations of metal-containing drugs, and utilization of cold neutrons.

Microprobe Facilities
The Center's microanalysis facilities are among the most advanced and complete in the world. Instruments include an analytical electron microscope, ion microprobe, secondary ion mass spectrometer, time of flight secondary ion mass spectrometer, laser microprobe mass analyzer, and a Raman microprobe. The latter two instruments provide molecular information from micro-regions and offer great potential in biomedical applications.

Trace Element Facilities
The Center for Analytical Chemistry has a wide variety of instruments used for the determination of trace element concentrations in virtually any matrix. These instruments include the following: atomic absorption spectrometer, spark atomic emission spectrometer, inductively coupled plasma spectrometer, dc plasma spectrometer, laser enhanced ionization spectrometer, spark source mass spectrometer, thermal ionization mass spectrometer, electrochemical analyzers, neutron activation analysis

Trace Organic Analysis
The Center performs basic and applied research in many areas of organic analysis. They have a variety of research instruments for this research.

Specimen Bank Research Facility
This facility contains separate clean areas for organic and inorganic sample preparation, biohazard hoods, cryogenic homogenization apparatus, and low temperature storage facilities. The specimen bank project is part of a multi-agency program in environmental monitoring and health research.

Ultrapure Reagents Facility
Modern trace analysis requires the use of high-purity reagents to minimize contamination problems commonly associated with measurements at parts-per-million and lower levels. A new reagents facility has been completed for the preparation of key trace analytical reagents.

Fluid Metering Research Facility
This facility combines primary calibration techniques with the capability to conduct detailed surveys of fluid velocity profiles in temperature controlled water flows using laser Doppler velocimetry (LDV). An industry - government consortium currently supports a research program on flowmeter installation effects, and the US Navy is sponsoring a series of tests to assess the performance of selected flow transfer standards in a range of non-ideal conditions. It is also used to generate critical databases to update the national standards on generic fluid metering topics.

Nitrogen Flow Measurement Facility
The facility is a mass-based reference system capable of both liquid and gas flow measurement. Well instrumented for temperature and pressure, the facility is adaptable and capable of a variety of piping arrangements. The Flow Facility can be used for testing a variety of flow measurement instrumentation, including flow meters, temperature sensors, pressure sensors, and densimeters.

Be patient. If any phone number is incorrect, call (area code) 555-1212 and request the new listing.

Science and Technology

Neutron Depth Profiling Facility
This facility uses a neutron beam for non-destructive evaluation of elemental depth distribution materials. Working with the Institute's 20MW nuclear reactor, researchers use the technique to provide concentration profiles for characterizing the near-surface regime of semiconductors, metals, glasses, and polymers to depths of several micrometers. With the neutron beam provided by the reactor, depth profiling can be carried out with sensitivities approaching 10^{13} atoms/cm^2.

Manufacturing Engineering Laboratory

Automated Manufacturing Research Facility
This facility is the major national laboratory for research in automated manufacturing. The facility provides a "test-bed" where researchers from NIST, industrial firms, universities, and other government agencies can work together on projects of mutual interest. Their research concentrates on the standards and measurement techniques required for successful automated manufacturing. The supporting technology for future computer integrated manufacturing systems are developed.

Computing and Applied Mathematics Laboratory

Consolidated Scientific Computing System
This major computation facility provides services through telecommunications links.

Evans and Sutherland PS-300 Dynamical Graphics System
This facility provides local display at video rates and includes 3-D perspective and orthographics projections, zoom, rotation and scaling on three axes, and variable-depth contrast. Transformed data may be transmitted back to the host computer after graphical treatment is completed. The system offers a "window" capability for difficult mathematical operations, such as the problem of visualizing a large data set at some intermediate stage of a large scale computation.

Perkin-Elmer 3230 Minicomputer
This facility is best suited to moderate-size scientific software development and limited production computing. A major feature of the 3230 is its wide I/O bandwidth which supports large local memory graphics terminals.

Raster Technologies ONE/380 Graphics System
This facility provides high resolution color raster images of three-dimensional objects or 24-bit color imaging data. The objects may be point clouds, wire frames, or solid objects with hidden surface removal, and lighting models for solid rendering. Local object manipulations include perspective or orthographic projections, translation, rotation, and scaling in three axes. All local operational parameters can be recovered by the host computer. High level graphics software available for major host computers at NIST supports this terminal. Applications include CAD/CAM rendering, four-dimensional data using color as the fourth dimension, and interaction with mathematical models through surface rendering.

Electronics and Electrical Engineering Laboratory

Data Converter Testing Facility
This facility offers regular calibration service for static parameters of high-accuracy A/D and D/A converters, particularly for linearity and differential linearity measurements. The facility also includes testing of data converters under certain dynamic conditions, e.g., settling time measurements and noise measurements.

High Voltage Measurement Facility
This facility provides tests at high voltages requiring accurate measurements and sensitive diagnostics. The equipment includes high-speed photographic equipment for electrical breakdown diagnostics, Kerr effect electro-optical equipment for space charge diagnostics, equipment for partial discharge measurements, and equipment for dielectric loss measurements. Additionally, precision dividers provide for high voltage measurements under steady-state and transient conditions.

Semiconductor Processing Facility
This facility occupies about 4,000 sq. ft. of space, half of it clean room space, and has the capability of state-of-the-art semiconductor processing for research applications. It produces specialized test specimens, experimental samples, customized device prototypes, and carefully prepared materials under extremely well-controlled and flexible conditions.

Antenna Scanning Facility
The planar, near-field antenna scanning range in Boulder, Colorado, represents the state-of-the-art in measurement accuracy for such facilities, utilizing a highly accurate verified technique. It can be used to characterize antennas of various types indoors, at lower cost, at high accuracies, and with more resultant information than that yielded by conventional outdoor antenna range techniques. It can also be used for measurements not possible inn other types of facilities. Using theory, new measurement techniques, and computer software, a laser interferometer controlled probe precisely scans the antenna under test to determine near-field antenna parameters which are then converted to the desired far-field characteristics.

Near Field Scanning Facility for Antenna Measurements
The automated facility is designed to measure the near-zone phase and amplitude distributions of the fields radiated from an antenna under test. Mathematical transformations are used to calculate the desired antenna characteristics. The facility has several applications. Its primary use is for determining the gain, pattern and polarization of antennas. Near-field data can also be used to compute near-field interactions of antennas and radiated field distributions in the near zone. Near-field scanning is also a valuable tool for identifying problems and for achieving optimal performance of various types of antenna systems.

Mode-Stirred Chambers
NIST researchers have designed and constructed mode-stirred (reverberating) chambers to measure radiated electromagnetic emissions and the susceptibility of electronic equipment and shielding effectiveness of materials and cable/connector materials. It can be used to perform radiated emission or susceptibility measurements of electronic equipment. It can additionally measure the effectiveness of different composites, gaskets and other materials frequently used in shielding radio frequencies.

Transverse Electromagnetic Cells
NIST has designed several traverse electromagnetic cells that are available for use. These cells are used to perform electromagnetic emission and susceptibility measurements of electronic equipment. The TEMs can be used for electromagnetic compatibility/interference testing, the calibration of antennas and the structure of biological effects of radio-frequency radiation.

Electromagnetic Anechoic Chamber
The electromagnetic anechoic chamber is a facility for generating standard (known) electronic fields which are fundamental to the research, development, and evaluation of antennas field probes, and EM material properties.

Manufacturing Engineering Laboratory

Automated Manufacturing Research Facility
This facility is a research laboratory for study of the measurement and standards problems of the "factory of the future." An extensive network of computers makes up the real-time control, distributed data administration, and manufacturing engineering elements of the facility. Research is currently supported on sensors, real-time control, deterministic metrology, production management and scheduling, data administration, communications, and preparation of manufacturing data.

Acoustical Anechoic Chamber
This facility provides a free-field environment for research and calibrations on measurement of the directivity of sound sources and the directional response of microphones and sensor arrays.

Building and Fire Research Laboratory

Large Scale Structural Test Facility
This facility, with a 45 foot reaction wall and its 12-million pound capacity universal testing machine, is capable of testing large-scale structural components 60-feet in length. Specimens can also be subjected to lateral loading up to 1 million pounds. It is the largest facility of its kind in the free world.

Tri-Directional Structural Testing Facility
This facility is a unique computer-controlled apparatus capable of applying forces or displacements in three directions simultaneously to large-scale structural components and systems. This facility currently supports NIST's research role in developing seismic design and construction standards for reducing the hazards of earthquakes.

National Institute of Standards and Technology

Environmental Chambers

These facilities support development of thermal performance modeling techniques required for predicting human comfort, energy efficiency, and fire safety in buildings. The chambers can automatically control temperatures with automatic humidity control.

Calibrated Hot-Box Facility

This facility provides precise measurements of heat, air, and moisture transfer through full-scale building wall and roof sections including door and window openings. The facility can simulate worldwide climatic conditions through the use of temperature, humidity, and air control. The measurements provide the basis for standard measurement methods used in private laboratories.

Five Story Plumbing Research Facility

This facility, with its high-speed preprogrammed computerized data acquisition systems, is used to study the performance of and develop measurement methods for plumbing fixtures, water supply, and waste drainage systems. The technology developed is used in building codes and standards.

Reverberation Chamber

This facility is used to develop sound pressure coefficients and to calibrate test equipment in other laboratories. The chamber supports research to define the acoustical parameters for building materials and spaces and to develop models and test methods for evaluating acoustical performance.

Construction Materials Reference Laboratories

In conjunction with other laboratories, this facility serves over 1,000 public and private laboratories nationwide by providing proficiency samples, inspections, and field test methods for cost effective quality assurance in materials.

Outdoor Energy Conservation Test Site

This facility includes a passive solar test house containing over 400 sensors and transducers for measuring the thermal performance of such solar features as clerestory windows, mass storage wall, and direct-gain cell. Six single-room test houses provide data on heat exchange. Other facilities study solar heat pumps and domestic hot water systems.

Image Analysis Laboratory

This facility has two special-purpose image analysis computers and cameras for obtaining images and converting them into digital form. The facility is used extensively in studies of materials degradation involving images from the scanning electron microscope or photographs of surfaces of full-scale structures.

Fire Test Building

This facility is designed for large scale fire experiments. Smoke abatement equipment permits large fires to be conducted safely without pollution of the environment. Some of the experimental capabilities are single room fire experiments; room-corridor fire experiments; rate of heat release (small to large scale including material samples, single items of furniture, full size rooms); fire endurance furnace with unique high rate of temperature increase capability; room-corridor smoke travel experiments; and two-story smoke travel experiments.

NIST Annex

This facility serves as a field station for experiments not readily accommodated in the main laboratories. Some of the experimental capabilities include multiroom single story structure for smoke movement studies; two story, four bay, steel frame structure for studies of steel framing movement and deflection and floor/ceiling performance with significant fire exposures; compartment fire facility for studying vent flows; sprinkler facility for droplet distribution studies; small scale gas-well simulation blow-out experiment; small scale aircraft cabin fire experiment.

Center for Fire Research Laboratory Facilities

The Center for Fire Research Laboratories' facilities include Lateral Ignition and Flame Spread Test for wall materials; vertical flame heat transfer rig; salt water smoke movement analog facilities; Fire Simulation Laboratory with dedicated mini-computer and high resolution graphics capability; apparatus for combustion product toxicity studies; Fire Research Information Service--a library of over 30,000 fire research documents; droplet imaging system for size and velocity distribution measurements in sprays.

Line Heat Source Guarded Hot Plate

The 1-m guarded hot plate apparatus measures thermal conductivity of building insulation. NIST researchers use the hot plate to provide calibration specimens for guarded hot plates in other laboratories. The hot plate also is used to investigate edge heat loss from thick thermal insulation materials.

National Measurement Laboratory

Free-Electron Laser User Facility

This laboratory is constructing a national free-electron laser user facility for research in physics, chemistry, biophysics, materials science, and medical sciences.

Materials Science and Engineering Laboratory

The specialized facilities include an array of metals and ceramics laboratories for controlled materials synthesis and process; a 12-million-pound test rig for evaluating large-scale mechanical material properties; experimental stations for studying arc-welding processes; specialized small-angle and texture x-ray diffractometers particularly suited for polymer characterization; and a 20-megawatt reactor for neutron scattering experiments.

Metals Processing Laboratory

This NIST laboratory contains special facilities for the production of rapidly solidified alloys, including equipment for gas atomization and electrohydrodynamic atomization to produce rapidly solidified alloy powders, melt spinning to produce rapidly solidified alloy ribbons, and electron beam surface melting to produce rapidly solidified surface layers. These facilities are designed to produce alloy research samples that otherwise are difficult for users to obtain. Typically, industrial companies or universities send workers to NIST to participate in preparing alloys of special industrial and scientific interest for further analyses in their home laboratories and to collaborate NIST scientists in investigations of generic relationships between processing conditions and resulting alloy microstructures and their properties.

Polymer Composite Fabrication Facility

This facility permits the preparation of well-controlled polymer composite samples for scientific studies and the evaluation of results from NIST's processing science program in a realistic fabrication environment. This lab can be used for a variety of fiber related studies.

Powder Characterization and Processing Laboratory

This facility offers specialized instrumentation for measuring physical properties, phase composition, and surface chemical properties of powders. Facilities also exist for processing and synthesizing ultrapure powders. Some of this labs capabilities include: physical properties, surface, and interface chemistry measurements; phase composition research; solid state imaging, for the identification of impurities, chemical state, and composition; powder synthesis and colloidal suspensions.

Mechanical Behavior Laboratories

Mechanical property measurement facilities at NIST permit characterization of all mechanical properties over a wide range of force levels and temperatures. Facilities are available for outside sponsors and tests can be conducted at temperatures ranging from 4 degrees Kelvin to 2800 degrees Kelvin.

Small-Angle X-Ray Scattering Facility

Small angle x-ray scattering is a technique used to probe the structures of materials on the scale size of 0.1nm to 100nm. Materials exhibiting structure in this size range include polymers, biological macromolecules, ceramics, metals, and alloys. This technique is used to study molecular conformation, microphase domain structures, crystallization phenomena, network formation, craze initiation, void distribution, and other phenomena resulting from fluctuation in the electron density within a material.

Cold Neutron Research Facility

This facility is the nation's first for "cold Neutron" studies, filling a serious void in the nation's materials science and engineering research. The facility provides beams of deeply penetrating low-energy neutrons, essential for important experiments that are impractical or even impossible with conventional neutron sources. The facility is available to all U.S. users for the study of materials research, molecular structure determination, and neutron activation analysis.

Center for Chemical Engineering

Gas Flow Measurement Facility/Boulder

This facility measures the flow rate of gas on a mass basis. Gas flows through the meter to be tested and then is condensed by passing the gas through a cryogenic system and into a weigh tank. The time integrated mass flow rate passing through the test meter is the same as the mass accumulated in the weigh tank. This facility provides high accuracy and the only mass-based continuous gas flow measurement in the world.

Be patient. If any phone number is incorrect, call (area code) 555-1212 and request the new listing.

Science and Technology

Water Flow Facilities
These facilities employ weighing and timing techniques as the means to make primary determination of the quantity of water flowing through the device or system under test.

Computer Systems Laboratory

CD-ROM Technology Evaluation Laboratory
The Compact Disk-Read Only Memory technology evaluation laboratory provides a site where Federal users can evaluate CD-ROM hardware and retrieval systems. More than 25 CD-ROM disks and 6 CD-ROM players have been installed; the National Computer Systems Laboratory solicited disk and equipment donations for the laboratory from the private sector. Other available CD-ROM databases include library catalogs, journal indexes, zip code directories, dictionaries, and product catalogs. CD-ROM drives and interfaces include systems manufactured by Phillips, Toshiba, Hitachi, and Sony.

Information Systems Engineering Facility
This facility consists of labs with computer hardware and software needed for research and development of standards, guidance to federal agencies, and validation tests. The following areas are included: graphics; programming languages; database management systems; distributed database management systems; object database management; data dictionary systems; data administration, especially database design; data interchange; knowledge-based and expert systems; and geographic information systems.

Computer and Network Security Facility.
The NIST computer and network security facility is used to improve the current security posture of federal computer and telecommunication systems ad to provide security for these systems as they migrate toward open system environments. Research done in the facility is aimed at applying methods to protect the secrecy and integrity of information in computer systems and data networks; evaluating personal identification and authentication techniques to control access to information resources; and developing computer and network security architectures to determine proper implementation of controls for integrity and confidentiality of information and authentication of users.

ISDN and Distributed Systems Facility
The NIST Integrated Services Digital Network (ISDN) and distributed systems facility provides laboratories for research and development, standards, and conformance testing in distributed computer systems and advanced computer communications, including ISDN and the fiber distributed data interface (FDDI). Significant research and development programs include open distributed systems, transaction processing, distributed multimedia, ISDN applications, ISDN conformance testing and broadband ISDN.

Physics Laboratory

Synchrotron Ultraviolet Radiation Facility-II
The SURF-II is a 300 MeV electron storage ring that radiates synchrotron radiation which is highly collimated, nearly linearly polarized, and of calculable intensity. It is well suited for studies in radiometry, atomic, molecular, bimolecular, and solid-state physics, surface and materials science, electro-optics, and surface chemistry and radiation effects on matter.

Low Background Infrared Radiation Facility
In this facility, radiant background noise levels less than a few nanowatts are attained in a large vacuum chamber by cooling internal cryoshields to temperatures less than 20K using a closed cycle helium refrigerator system. This unique facility can be used to measure total radiant power from sources such as cryogenic blackbodies. Ongoing improvements will allow measurement of spectral distribution of radiation from sources and characterization of infrared detectors and optical components.

Electronic Paramagnetic Resonance Facility
NIST is leading a national and international effort in electron paramagnetic resonance dosimetry for measuring ionizing radiation. In the EPR experiment, irradiated materials are placed in a magnetic field and electron spin transitions are induced by an electromagnetic field of the appropriate frequency. This process is used as a non-destructive probe of the structure and concentration of paramagnetic centers. Industrial applications include radiation protection/accident dosimetry, for retrospective dose assessment of clothing or biological tissue; clinical radiology, ionizing radiation doses administered in cancer therapy can be measured for enteral beam therapy using dosimeters of

crystalline alanine or validated for internally bone seeking radiopharmaceuticals using bone biopsies; industrial radiation processing, monitoring of radiation process meats, shellfish, and fruits using bone, shell, or seed.

Radiopharmaceutical Standardization Laboratory
Radioactivity measurements for diagnostic and therapeutic nuclear medicine in the U.S. are based on measurements at NIST. Recent development work has focused on therapeutic nuclides for nuclear medicine, radioimmunotherapy, and bone palliation. The lab provides calibration for gamma ray emitting radionuclides equipment for users requiring higher standards than can be attained using commercial equipment.

Magnetic Microstructure Measurement Facility
The magnetic microstructure of materials can be measured with very high spatial resolution by a technique called scanning electron microscopy with polarization analysis. This unique measurement facility can be used for research in magnetic thin films, high-coercivity magnetic materials, high density magnetic storage media, and other advanced magnetic materials.

* Research Associate Program

Office of Research and Technology Applications
National Institute of Standards and Technology (NIST)
Room A537, Administration Bldg
Gaithersburg, MD 20899 (301) 975-3087

The National Institute of Standards and Technology's Research Associate Program is an effective means for the transfer of technology, and in particular, measurement technology. The Program offers the opportunity to work under the supervision of and consult with NIST professionals of recognized stature in their fields, makes available the extensive laboratory and related facilities at NIST, and is an effective means of communicating industrial views and needs directly to NIST. Contact this office for more detailed information.

* Research of the National Institute of Standards and Technology (NIST)

Superintendent of Documents
Government Printing Office
Washington, DC 20402-9371 (202) 783-3238

For $13 a year, you can't afford not to know what's going on at the Nation's Measurement Science Laboratory. The *Journal of Research of the National Institute of Standards and Technology* brings you up-to-date scientific articles and information on NIST research and development in physics, chemistry, engineering, mathematics, and computer sciences. Papers cover a broad range of subjects, with major emphasis on measurement methodology and the basic technology underlying standardization. Also included from time to time are survey articles on topics closely related to the Institute's technical and scientific programs, cooperative research opportunities and grants, conference reports, and more. The journal is issued six times a year. Contact GPO to subscribe.

* Robotics Demonstrations

Manufacturing Engineering Laboratory
B126 Metrology Bldg
National Institute of Standards and Technology (NIST)
Gaithersburg, MD 20899 (301) 975-3414

Demonstrations of robot-tended machining workstations, and inspection machines, as well as demonstrations of optical measurement of surface finish are presented for the public. To schedule a tour, contact this Center.

* Robot Systems Division

The Robot Systems Division
Manufacturing Engineering Laboratory
B126 Metrology Bldg
National Institute of Standards and Technology (NIST)
Gaithersburg, MD 20899 (301) 975-3418

The Robot Systems Division develops and maintains competence in robotics, real-time sensory interactive control technology, robot programming languages and standards, and interface standards for computer-integrated manufacturing systems and advanced robotic systems. The division conducts research into new techniques of sensing and control, sensory data processing, and uses databases, communications, world models, robot programming languages and techniques, interactive graphics for programming and intelligent, real-time control for industrial military, space, and construction applications. Work is on-going to develop experimental hardware and software, and measures of system

Be patient. If any phone number is incorrect, call (area code) 555-1212 and request the new listing.

National Institute of Standards and Technology

performance for a wide variety of robot applications. Research in robot safety, robot assembly of parts, tools, and fixtures, and applications of intelligent control to military and industrial systems is performed. Contact this division for more information.

* Scientific Computer Users Newsletter

Computer Planning and Analysis Center for Applied Mathematics National Institute of Standards and Technology (NIST) Gaithersburg, MD 20899 (301) 975-3801

The Office of Computer Planning and Analysis puts out a bi-monthly newsletter for scientific computer users. Contact this office for information on subscriptions.

* Scientific Computing Services

Scientific Computing Division Computing and Applied Mathematics Laboratory National Institute of Standards and Technology (NIST) Gaithersburg, MD 20899 (301) 975-3816

The Scientific Computing Division provides consulting services; performs research, and collaborates in the application of computer science and technology to computation problems in physical science and engineering at NIST.

* Seismic Safety of Structures

Building and Fire Research Laboratory B168 Building Research National Institute of Standards and Technology (NIST) Gaithersburg, MD 20899 (301) 975-6707

Under the National Earthquake Hazards Reduction Program, NIST does research and development work that is used in standards for seismic safety of structures. Research is underway to develop knowledge for design and construction standards for new and existing buildings as well as lifeline structures.

* Semiconductor Electronics

Electronics and Electrical Engineering Laboratory Room A305, Technology Bldg National Institute of Standards and Technology (NIST) Gaithersburg, MD 20899 (301) 975-2060

NIST conducts research in semi-conductor materials, processes, devices and integrated circuits to provide the necessary basis for understanding measurement-related requirements in semiconductor technology. As part of this program, NIST scientists are using electrical, optical, and X-ray methods to study the resistivity, dopant distribution, and concentration of electrically inactive impurities, such as carbon and oxygen in silicon. Other studies are looking at compound semiconductors for devices that need structures unable to be fabricated from silicon.

* Semiconductor Industry

Manufacturing Engineering Laboratory National Institute of Standards and Technology (NIST) B322 Metrology Bldg Gaithersburg, MD 20899 (301) 975-3400

The National Engineering Laboratory (NEL) helps the semiconductor industry improve the quality, cost, and reliability of U.S. manufactured semiconductor devices through new measurement methods and calibration services. NEL is developing, with a major electronics firm, a computerized "expert" system to help process engineers pinpoint probable causes of errors in semiconductor manufacturing.

* Small Business Specialist

Small Business Specialist National Institute of Standards and Technology (NIST) U.S. Department of Commerce Gaithersburg, MD 20899 (301) 975-6343

NIST's small business specialist is the contact for small businesses who wish to use the services of the National Institute of Standards and Technology.

* Small-Scale Advanced Manufacturing

Center for Manufacturing Engineering

National Engineering Laboratory National Institute of Standards and Technology (NIST) B119 Technology Bldg Gaithersburg, MD 20899 (301) 975-2300

Small job shops--operations with fewer than 50 employees--make up about 85 percent of U.S. metal fabrication facilities and account for about 75 percent of all U.S. metal fabrication. They are running substantially behind their overseas competitors in the use of modern technology. The National Institute of Standards and Technology is working to answer questions such as What modern technologies are commercially available, affordable, and useful to the small job shop? and What return on investment might be expected? To help answer these questions, NIST is using its own job shop to conduct an experiment in the practical implementation of computer-integrated manufacturing. Contact this Center for more information.

* Speech Recognition Research

National Computer Systems Laboratory National Institute of Standards and Technology (NIST) B154 Technology Bldg Gaithersburg, MD 20899 (301) 975-2822

Computers that understand spoken language and can carry on conversations with humans are a science fiction staple. But in reality, comprehending and responding to spoken language is a difficult process for most computers. Interactions between people and machines still are limited mostly to communicating through mechanical means such as a keyboard. NIST researchers are developing improved algorithms and software for phonetically-based recognition of speech and ways to measure the performance of automatic speech recognizes. Basic research as well as measurement methods are needed to advance the technology. For more information on speech recognition research, contact this laboratory.

* Speech Recognition Shared Databases

Computer Systems Laboratory A216 Technology Bldg National Institute of Standards and Technology (NIST) Gaithersburg, MD 20899 (301) 975-2935

Speech recognition databases are typically too large and costly for any one organization to develop. To improve the technology, the research community in this area relies heavily on shared uses of databases and standard test methodologies. Using CD-ROM technology, NIST in cooperation with the Defense Advanced Research Projects Agency, has distributed material to over 100 research organizations.

* Standards Certification Activities in the United States

Office of Standards Code and Information A629 Administration Bldg Gaithersburg, MD 20899 (301) 975-4029

Certification programs, considered a vital link between product standards and actual products, have significant impact on the marketplace. *The ABC's of Certification Activities in the United States* describes the different types of programs or schemes used to produce written assurance that a product or service conforms to a standard or specification. A sequel to *The ABC's of Standards-Related Activities in the United States* (1987), the new report provides a further introduction to certification for those not familiar with this important standards-related activity. Included are descriptions of product quality; self certification; third-party certification; federal, state, international, and regional programs; choice of standards; certification methodology; and certification marks. The report also addresses some of the potential problems with certification programs. To obtain a copy send a self-addressed mailing label to Maureen A. Breitenberg at the above address.

* Standards for Federal Government Certification Programs

Superintendent of Documents Government Printing Office Washington, DC 20402-9371 (202) 783-3238

Federal Government Certification Programs is a guide for manufacturers, distributors, state and local government officials, importers, consumers, and others concerned with standards and procedures used in federal certification programs. It contains information on manufactured products, agricultural commodities, medical services--devices and drugs, defense procurement items, transportation, and the voluntary inspection and uniform grading of such food

Be patient. If any phone number is incorrect, call (area code) 555-1212 and request the new listing.

Science and Technology

items as dairy products, meats, and produce. Each entry describes the scope and nature of the program, lists the testing and inspection practices, standards used, methods of identification and enforcement, reciprocal recognition or acceptance of certification, and a contact point in the federal agency. The updated directory is a joint effort by NIST and the U.S. Department of Agriculture. The directory costs $12 prepaid through GPO.

* Standard Reference Data

Reference Center
Standard Reference Data
National Institute of Standards and Technology (NIST)
A323 Physics Building
Gaithersburg, MD 20899 (301) 975-2208

The Standard Reference Data Program aims to provide reliable, well-documented data to scientists and engineers for use in technical decision making, research and development. Experts in the physical, chemical, and materials sciences critically evaluate data that result from experimental measurements, calculations, and theory. The evaluations are carried out through a network of data centers, projects, and cooperative programs that comprise the National Standard Reference Data System. Experienced researchers in each area assess the accuracy of the data reported in the literature, prepare compilations, and recommend best values. The outputs are widely distributed as publications and computer-readable databases. Some of the databases are also accessible via on-line data systems. For a free complete catalog of publications and databases, contact the office above.

* Standard Reference Data Grants

Reference Center
Standard Reference Data
National Institute of Standards and Technology (NIST)
A323 Physics Building
Gaithersburg, MD 20899 (301) 975-2200

Each year, the Standard Reference Data Program, in cooperation with other government funding agencies, administers a grant program aimed at involving experts in universities, industry, and government in data evaluation projects. This competitive program focuses on high priority short-term projects within the overall chemistry, physics, and materials scope of the program. Contact this office for more information and application procedures.

* Standard Reference Materials Catalog

Office of Standard Reference Materials
National Institute of Science and Technology
B311 Chemistry Bldg
Gaithersburg, MD 20899 (301) 975-6776

Nearly 1,000 Standard Reference Materials available from NIST are listed in the *NBS Standard Reference Materials Catalog 1988-89*. The materials, certified for specific *chemical and physical properties, include cements, ores, metals, glass, plastics, food, and environmental and clinical items. The expanded list of nutrition and health standards includes materials to calibrate instruments to detect marijuana in a human urine sample and to improve the precision of tests for elevated levels of the enzyme aspartate aminotransferase (AST) to detect heart attacks. Two new micro-length standards also are listed. The first commercial space-made product, 10-Micrometer Polystyrene Spheres, is available on a glass slide to calibrate microscopes. The second commercial space-made product, 30 Micrometer Polystyrene Spheres, is a new measurement standard for powder manufacturers. Also available is a series of seven individual low-alloy steels widely used in industry. Contact the office above to obtain the catalog.

* Standard Technical Data

Office of Standard Reference Data
National Institute of Standards and Technology (NIST)
A323 Physics Bldg
Gaithersburg, MD 20899 (301) 975-2200

The National Measurement Laboratory provides reliable technical data required by industry, government, and academia to increase the effectiveness of U.S. science and technology. For information on this data, contact this office.

* State Technology Programs Clearinghouse

Director
National Institute of Standards and Technology (NIST)
Manufacturing Technology Centers Program

Bldg. 220, Room B111
Gaithersburg, MD 20899 (301) 975-3414

This clearinghouse gathers and analyzes information on the many State and local technology development programs across the nation. The idea is to develop a central base of information on what programs are available, what has been tried, and what the results have been. The clearinghouse will be a resource for state and local governments when deciding on new technology policies. The information will be shared through workshops and other mechanisms. For more information, contact this office.

* Statistical Engineering Services

Statistical Engineering Division
Computing and Applied Mathematics Laboratory
A335 Administration Bldg
National Institute of Standards and Technology (NIST)
Gaithersburg, MD 20899 (301) 975-2839

The Statistical Engineering Division provides consulting services in the application of mathematical statistics to physical science experiments and engineering tests. The division conducts studies of computational methods and prepares reports, manuals, handbooks, and tools for statistical computing. The outputs include the Handbook for Development and Implementation of Measurement Assurance Programs, and DATAPLOT computer software for data analysis and model building. Contact this division for more information.

* Structures Research

Structures Division
Building and Fire Research Laboratory
B170 Building Research Bldg
National Institute of Standards and Technology (NIST)
Gaithersburg, MD 20899 (301) 975-6061

The Structures Division conducts laboratory, field, and analytical research in structural and earthquake engineering, investigates structural failures, characterizes normal and extreme loads on buildings occurring during construction and in service, develops design criteria for reduction of damage caused by natural hazards, and develops advanced computation methods for evaluating static and dynamic response of structures. Work is on-going to enhance building safety. Sample outputs include technical data and design criteria for loads on buildings and technical data for building performance in earthquakes. Contact this division for more information.

* Superconductor Measurements

Electronics and Electrical Engineering Laboratory
Division 814.05
National Institute of Standards and Technology (NIST)
Boulder, CO 80303 (303) 497-3785

Recent advances in superconductivity have resulted in a critical need for measurement technology to characterize the different types of superconductors, which now range from very fine filament alloy conductors to high-temperature ceramic superconductors. Active research programs at NIST involve measurement techniques for critical current, critical magnetic field, ac losses, magnetic hysterisis, and electron tunneling. Recent breakthroughs in conductivity between normal metals and high- temperature superconductors has been made, and a new reference manual for large currents is being prepared.

* Technology at a Glance

Public Affairs Division
A903 Administration Bldg
National Institute of Standards and Technology (NIST)
Gaithersburg, MD 20899 (301) 975-3392

Technology at a Glance is a monthly publication published by NIST containing updates on current research activities and upcoming events sponsored by or coordinated by NIST. Contact NIST for copies of the latest issue and for subscription information.

* Technology Development and Small Business Innovation

Technology Services
Room A343 Physics Bldg
National Institute of Standards and Technology (NIST)
Gaithersburg, MD 20899 (301) 975-3084

One of NIST's most important jobs is to aid in the transfer of technology to

Be patient. If any phone number is incorrect, call (area code) 555-1212 and request the new listing.

National Institute of Standards and Technology

American businesses. Staff members help members of the private sector to locate experts in NIST that can be of assistance to them. In a separate program, NIST evaluates proposals sent to the U.S. Department of Commerce for small business grants. Phase I awards receive $35,000 to support studies of technological feasibility. In Phase II, applicants may receive up to $200,000 to support development of promising technologies. Contact this office for more information on this program.

* Technology Extension Programs

Director
National Institute of Standards and Technology (NIST)
Manufacturing Technology Centers Program
Bldg. 220, Room B111
Gaithersburg, MD 20899 (301) 975-3414

The NIST is making efforts to forge new ties to the many State and local technology extension services that have been created throughout the country. NIST can establish cooperative agreements with state or local programs to develop programs that transfer federally developed technology to business within their area. State and local extension services typically emphasize business advice rather than dealing with sophisticated technology. Ties with NIST will help to coordinate the state and local extension services with federal technology transfer programs. Through workshops, seminars, and other mechanisms, NIST plans to help technology extension agents make the best use of federal resources.

* Technology Services

Technology Services
National Institute of Standards and Technology (NIST)
A363 Physics Bldg
Gaithersburg, MD 20899 (301) 975-4500

For many U.S. businesses, the tools for building a competitive advantage already exist--in other firms, in university or federal laboratories, or even in off-the-shelf technology available from suppliers. The National Institute of Technology and Standard's industrial technology services, a still evolving array of outreach programs, aim to get the productivity-enhancing equipment and methods to the companies that need them. Technology Services provides technical support, and in some cases financial assistance, to U.S. industry, especially small and medium-sized businesses, to facilitate the commercialization of products based on new scientific discoveries. Among the services are

- Providing technical support and financial assistance to regional centers for transferring manufacturing technology to small and medium-sized firms.
- Developing Standard Reference Materials and Standard Reference Data and calibrating equipment and devices to aid in improving industrial quality control.
- Promoting technology innovation by technically evaluating innovations, inventions, and new technologies.
- Providing technical assistance to private, local, national, and international standards-writing organizations to ensure equity in the marketplace.

Contact the office above for more information on the available services.

* The Journal of Research of the National Bureau of Standards

Superintendent of Documents
Government Printing Office
Washington, DC 20402-9371 (202) 783-3238

The proceedings of a 1987 symposium, *Accuracy in Trace Analysis--Accomplishments, Goals, Challenges*, have been reprinted in this special edition of the journal. The 4-day event at NIST covered such topics as the history of trace analysis, robotics in the chemistry lab, measuring vitamins in foods, and the use of microwaves to dissolve samples. The proceedings consist of nearly 140 technical reports. This special edition is $3 prepaid through GPO.

* Thermal Radiometry

Physics Laboratory
A221 Physics
National Institute of Standards and Technology (NIST)
Gaithersburg, MD 20899 (301) 975-2355

NIST researchers are investigating the use of thermal imaging cameras as a temperature-measuring tool. These devices may prove to be very useful in determining the quality of products and in investigating changes in different processes.

* Thermochemical Tables Available Online

Office of Standard Reference Data
National Institute of Standards and Technology (NIST)
A323 Physics Bldg
Gaithersburg, MD 20899 (301) 975-2200

The third edition of the (Joint-Army-Navy-Air Force) *JANAF Thermochemical Tables*, published by NIST, has been computerized to provide scientists and engineers with rapid access to information on the performance of materials at high temperatures. The database is available to subscribers on STN International (Scientific and Technical Network), an on-line private sector retrieval service offered worldwide. The numerical data can be used to make quick performance calculations for chemical reactors such as rocket engines, air pollution control equipment, internal combustion engines, coal gasifiers, and furnaces. The database is designed to list in one table all of the values for a given property of a chemical compound when the values for that compound appear in more than one tabulation. Information can be obtained by chemical name, the formula, or by the *Chemical Abstracts Registry Number*. For information on the new JANAF file through STN, contact the office above.

* Thermomechanical Processing for Metals/Manufactures

Materials Science and Engineering Laboratory
Division 853
National Institute of Standards and Technology (NIST)
Boulder, CO 80303 (303) 497-5545

NIST researchers have designed and built a computerized, laboratory scale, hot-deformation apparatus that can simulate the manufacturing processes, such as forging and plate rolling and measure important properties incurred during processing. This approach offers more economy and versatility than the use of pilot scale or production facilities for the development of new alloys or manufacturing schedules.

* Thermophysical Computer Programs

Thermophysics Division
Center for Chemical Engineering
A103 Physics
National Institute of Standards and Technology (NIST)
Gaithersburg, MD 20899 (301) 975-2483

The Thermophysics Division creates computer programs for the calculation of thermodynamic and transport properties of industrial chemicals and fuels (for improved commercial exchange of fluids and process design).

* Tours of the Facilities

Public Affairs
National Institute of Standards and Technology (NIST)
Gaithersburg, MD 20899 (301) 975-2758

Free tours of the various facilities at NIST are given on Thursdays at 9:30 a.m. They generally last for two hours, and the public is welcome, but should schedule reservations in advance through Jan Hauber at the office above.

* Trace Gas Measurement Research

Chemical Science and Technology Laboratory
B158 Chemistry
National Institute of Standards and Technology (NIST)
Gaithersburg, MD 20899 (301) 975-3916

Accurate measurement of gaseous species is of great importance to many industries for applications ranging from quantification of pollutant and toxic gas emissions to the quality control of products. Current NIST research is focusing on new detection systems.

* UV Optics Testbed

Physics Laboratory
A253 Physics
National Institute of Standards and Technology (NIST)
Gaithersburg, MD 20899 (301) 975-6892

Be patient. If any phone number is incorrect, call (area code) 555-1212 and request the new listing.

Science and Technology

The emerging field of high reflectance, normal incidence, soft X-ray/extreme ultraviolet (xuv) optics has a wide range of applications. The ability to produce high-quality images at wavelengths below 40nm has allowed construction of xuv solar telescopes with unprecedented resolution; xuv microscopes able to study living biological samples with sub-micron resolution; and xuv photolithographic systems that will produce the next generation of integrated circuits. NIST is construction a new test facility that will allow for increased resolution and accuracy and will extend measurement capabilities to shorter wavelengths.

* Video Processing

Electronics and Electrical Engineering Laboratory
Room B344
Metrology Bldg
National Institute of Standards and Technology (NIST)
Gaithersburg, MD 20899 (301) 975-4230

Data compression, motion encoding, scan-rate conversion, scientific visualization, image analysis, and other video processing research topics are being explored at NIST using a massively parallel supercomputer, The Princeton Engine, capable of 14 giga instruction per second image processing and simulating video rate signals. Research using this system has focused on advancing the state of the art in high-definition systems.

* Voluntary Laboratory Accreditation

Technology Services
Room A146 TRF
National Institute of Standards and Technology (NIST)
Gaithersburg, MD 20899 (301) 975-4016

Staff of the NIST National Voluntary Laboratory Accreditation Program evaluate the competencies and technical qualifications of public and private laboratories for conducting specific tests or types of tests in key areas of commerce, health, and safety. Testing provides both as an internal quality check for those certified and as an external identification as a quality laboratory. Contact the staff at NIST to inquire about the types of laboratories certified and certification procedures.

* Weights and Measures Certification

Technology Services
Room A617 Administration Bldg
National Institute of Standards and Technology (NIST)
Gaithersburg, MD 20899 (301) 975-4004

One of NIST's longest running and most well known programs is assisting the states and local governments in the ensurance of the equity of weights and measures in the market place. The NIST staff produce numerous publications and also maintain an electronic bulletin board to keep people informed of changing developments. Contact this office for more information.

Be patient. If any phone number is incorrect, call (area code) 555-1212 and request the new listing.

Patents, Trademarks and Copyrights

Protecting your invention, copyrighting your work, and obtaining a patent or trademark are often necessary parts of doing business. Described below are the major sources you can consult when you need information about these procedures. For additional information on monitoring patents and copyrights, refer to the Section on Technology.

Patent and Trademark Office

United States patent and trademark laws are administered by the Patent and Trademark Office (PTO). States also have trade secret statutes, which generally state that if you guard your trade secret with a reasonable amount of care, you will have rights. The PTO examines patent and trademark applications, grants protection for qualified inventions, and registers trademarks. (It also collects, assembles, and disseminates the technological information patent grants). The PTO maintains a collection of more than 5 million United States patents issued to date, several million foreign patents, and 1.2 million trademarks, together with supporting documentation. Here's how to find what you need.

What a Great Idea

To help you get started with patenting your invention, the Patent and Trademark Offices will send you a free booklet upon request called *Summary of How the Patent Process Works.* (Address and phone number for the PTO are given below). There are three legal elements in the process of invention: the conception of the idea, diligence in working it out, and reducing it to practice -- i.e., getting a finished product that actually works. If you have a great idea you think might work, but you need time to develop it further before it is ready to be patented, what should you do?

Protect Your Idea for $6

You can file a Disclosure Statement with the Patent and Trademark Office. They will keep it in confidence as evidence of the date of conception.

Disclosure Statement
Commissioner of Patents and Trademarks
Patent and Trademark Office
Washington, DC 20231

Recorded Message	(703) 557-3158
Disclosure Office	(703) 308-HELP
Legal Counsel	(703) 308-HELP

Send an 8 1/2 x 13" drawing, a copy, signed disclosure, SASE, and a check or money order for $6 to file. Upon request, the above office will also send you a free brochure on Disclosure Statements.

This is a way to keep the idea you are working on completely secret and yet document the date you conceived the idea. You can file the Disclosure Statement at any time after the idea is conceived, but the value of it will depend on how much you put into it -- so put as much detail into it as you can.

Another way to document the date of conception is to have someone vouch for you. Explain your idea to another person who is able to understand it and have them acknowledge what you have said to them in a signed, dated, notarized affidavit. Keep the voucher statement in a safe place in case you should ever need to produce it as proof of conception.

Either of the above two methods produces documentation you can use as evidence if someone else later claims to have thought of your idea first and patents it before you do. The drawback to the voucher method is that it does not preserve absolute secrecy as does filing a disclosure statement. The person you told may tell someone else.

Telling the World

Another way to document the date of conception is to publish it in a journal. Suppose that while in your basement to see why your old furnace is not working, you trip over your stationary exercise bicycle, which you never use, and hit your head. You also hit upon a way to heat your home by hooking up the furnace to one of the bike wheels and pedalling for 15 minutes. You're not sure if this method will work with any other furnace except your own, but it might. If you publish the idea in a journal, your idea is protected for a year.

Publication acts as collateral evidence of the date of conception. If you are the first to conceive of an idea, and no one else has previously filed a Disclosure Statement on it or taken a Voucher Affidavit or published it, then for a year no one can patent your idea. Note that during the year you have to patent your invention you may not know whether someone else has documented an earlier conception date. The other catch to this method is that you have only a year to act. The heat is on because after a year you are barred from patenting your own invention! This is because the government wants you to use a reasonable amount of diligence in putting the idea to work.

The Purpose of Documenting the Date of Conception

If someone else should try to patent your idea, filing a Disclosure Statement shows that you thought of it first. Filing a Disclosure Statement does not legally protect your invention. Only being granted a patent does that. Documentation of the conception date gives you time to patent your invention, and is

Be patient. If any phone number is incorrect, call (area code) 555-1212 and request the new listing.

Patents, Trademarks and Copyrights

invaluable if you need to prove when you thought of your idea if a dispute should arise. (Note that filing a Disclosure Statement gives you limited defensive legal protection only if you follow it up with a patent in two years. Unlike a patent, it cannot be used offensively, to stop someone else from patenting the same idea.) When you go to file for a patent, if you and a competitor get into a dispute as to who was the first to invent it, the PTO will hold an Interference Proceeding. If you thought of the idea first, your Disclosure Statement or Voucher Affidavit will go a long way towards establishing that you were the first inventor and should get the patent. (If you published your idea before anyone else documented a prior date of conception, no one but you will be granted a patent to the idea for a year.)

Research Resources That Can Help You Turn Your Idea Into Reality

While diligently working out the details of your invention you can use the very extensive resources of over 150,000 scientific and technical journals, articles and books at the Scientific Document Library at the PTO in Crystal City, VA.

Facilitating public access to the more than 25 million cross-referenced United States patents is the job of PTO's Office of Technology Assessment and Forecast (OTAF), (703) 557-5652. It has a master database which covers all United States patents, and searches are available for a fee which depends on the size of the project. The minimum search fee is $150. No fee is charged if the information you need is already in a report they have on hand. This office can run a search for you based on classification, sub-class, country or company name, but not by work or topic. An OTAF search will not result in an in-depth patent search. (More on that, and how to find classifications in the *Conducting Your Own Patent Search* section below.) OTAF extracts information from its database and makes it available in a variety of formats, including publications, custom patent reports, and statistical reports. The purpose of most of the reports generated by an OTAF search is to reveal patent trends.

Copies of the specifications and drawings of all patents are available from PTO. Design patents and trademark copies are $1.50 each. Plant patents not in color are $10 each. Plant patents in color are $20 each. To request, you must have the patent number. For copies, contact:

Commissioner of Patent and Trademarks
U.S. Department of Commerce
U.S. Patent and Trademark Office
P.O. Box 9
Washington, DC 20231
Public Information Line (703) 308-HELP

Patenting Your Invention

To patent your invention, order the Patent Booklet called *General Information Concerning Patents*, and Application Form.

Superintendent of Documents
U.S. Government Printing Office
Washington, DC 20402 (202) 783-3238

The cost is $2 and may be charged to Mastercard, VISA or Choice Card. The booklet must be ordered by stock number 003-004-00641-2.

The application will ask you for a written description, oath and drawing where possible. The cost to file for a patent to individuals or small businesses of under 15 employees (defined by SBA standards) is $315. It generally takes 18 months to two years for the PTO to grant a patent. Rights start the date the patent is granted. If you use your invention prior to being granted a patent, you can put "patent pending" on your product. This warns competitors that you have taken the necessary steps, but otherwise affords you no legal protection. Before embarking on the patenting process, you will want to conduct a patent search to make sure no one else has preceded you.

Conducting Your Own Patent Search

Before investing too much time and money on patenting your idea, you will want to see if anyone has already patented it. The PTO will only conduct searches on a specific inventors' name that you request. The fee is $10 and covers a 10-year time span. Call (703) 308-0595. If you wish to hire a professional to do your patent search, consult the yellow pages or obtain a copy of *Patent Attorneys and Agents Registered to Practice Before the U.S. Patent and Trademark Office*. View this publication at the PTO Search Room, or obtain it from the U.S. Government Printing Office. Even if your search is not as in-depth as that of a patent attorney or a patent agent, you may still find out what you need to know. You may conduct your patent search at the Patent and Trademark Office Search Room located at:

Patent and Trademark Office
Washington, DC 20231 (703) 308-0595

You may also conduct your patent search at any one of the 72 Patent Depository Libraries (PDLs) throughout the country. For information about the Patent Depository Library Program and the location of a library near you, call the toll-free number listed below.

Office of Patent Depository Library Programs
U.S. Patent and Trademark Office
1921 Jefferson Davis Highway
Crystal Mall 2, Room 306 (800) 435-7735
Arlington, VA 22202 (703) 557-9685

The mailing address is:

Office of Patent Depository Libraries Office
U.S. Patent and Trademark Office
Crystal Mall 2, Room 306
Washington, DC 20231

This office distributes the information to the 72 PDL's. The information is kept on CD-Rom discs, which are constantly updated. You or the library personnel can use them to do a patent search. CD-Rom discs have been combined to incorporate CASSIS (Classification and Search Support Information System). CD-Rom discs do not give you online access to the PTO database. Online access will be available through APS (Automated Patent Systems) within two years. APS is presently

Be patient. If any phone number is incorrect, call (area code) 555-1212 and request the new listing.

Patents, Trademarks and Copyrights

available only to patent examiners, public users of the PTO Search Room and to 14 of the 72 Patent Depository Libraries on a pilot program basis. Each PDL with the online APS has its own rules regarding its use. To use the online APS at the PTO Search Room, you must first sign up and take a class at the Search Room. Online access costs $40 for connect hour, and the charge for paper used for printouts is additional.

If you do not live near a PDL, the three CD-Rom discs are available through subscription. You may purchase the Classification disc, which dates back to 1790, for $210; the Bibliography disc, which dates back to 1969, for $210; and the ASIST disc, which contains a roster of patent attorneys, assignees, and other information for $151. You can also conduct your patent search and get a copy of it through commercial database services such as:

Mead Data Central, NEXIS Express, LEXPAT; (800) 543-6862, FAX: (513) 865-7418. Searches are done free of charge on patent topics. The charge for information found is $30 for a list of abstracts, plus print charges. Copies of patents (which you may decide to order after viewing the listing, or order directly if you already know which patent you want) cost $20. Copies include full text and detailed description of drawing, but no actual drawing because it is pulled from the electronic database.

If complete secrecy or doing your own search is your object, you may also subscribe to LEXPAT through the full library service. Cost is $28 per hour access charge plus 65 cents per minute connect time. To subscribe call (800) 843-6476.

Derwent, 1313 Dolly Madison Blvd., Suite 401, McLean, VA 22101; (800) 451-3451, (703) 790-0400, FAX: (703) 790-1426. Patent searches are $360 per hour plus 80 cents per record and $40 per hour for technical time. Copies of patents are $13-16 for the first 25 pages and 67 cents for each additional page thereafter.

Rapid Patent, 1921 Jefferson Davis Highway, Suite 1821D, Arlington, VA 22202; (800) 336-5010, (703) 920-5050, FAX: (703) 685-3987. Minimum costs for patent searches are: $240 for Mechanical, $290 for Electrical or Chemical. They are done manually. Delivery time is 4 weeks. Copies of patents cost $3.25 for each 25 pages.

CompuServe, (800) 848-8199. There is a $39.95 one-time fee. Search time is $12.50 per hour or 21 cents per minute. Searches are available for abstracts ($4), full listing ($4), or classification ($4).

If you are going to do your own patent search at your local Patent Depository Library, begin with the *Manual and Index to U.S. Patent Classifications* to identify the subject area where the patent is placed. Then use the CD-Rom discs to locate the patent. CD-Rom discs enable you to do a complete search of all registered patents but do not enable you to view the full patent, with all its specific details. Lastly, view the patent, which will be kept on microfilm, cartridge or paper. What is there to view varies by library, depending on what they have been able to purchase. If the library you are using does not have the patent you want, you may be able to obtain it through inter-library loan.

Copies of patents can be ordered from the PTO, (703) 308-1200, or more quickly, but for a price, from commercial services such as Derwent or Rapid Patent. Depending on which each individual PDL has available, copies of patents can be obtained for no fee.

To obtain a certified copy of a patent, call (703) 308-1200 (Patent Search Library at the PTO). The fee is $5 and you must have the patent number. For a certified copy of an abstract of titles, the fee is $15. For a certified copy of patent assignments, with a record of ownership from the beginning until present, call (703) 308-9700. The cost is $15 and to request you must have the reel and frame number.

Trademarks

Registering a trademark for your product or service is the way to protect the recognition quality of the name you are building. The PTO keeps records on more than 1.2 million trademarks and records. The over 500,000 active trademarks are kept on the floor of the library. "Dead" trademarks are kept on microfilm. Books contain every registered trademark ever issued, starting in 1870. You can visit the Patent and Trademark Office to research a trademark. There you can conduct your search manually for no charge or use their Trademark Search System (T-Search) for $40 per hour, plus ten cents per page and $25 per hour for office staff assistance time.

Trademark Search Library
2900 Crystal Drive
Second Floor, Room 2B30
Arlington, VA 22202 (703) 308-9800/9805

If that's not possible, you can hire someone to do the search for you. For an agent consult the yellow pages under "Trademark Agents/Consultants" or "Trademark Attorneys". You can also locate an agent by calling your local bar association for a list of recommendations.

To conduct your own search at a Patent Depository Library (POL) use the CD-Rom disc on trademarks. It is not presently available for purchase. The CD-Rom disc contains trademarks but not images. Images are in the *Official Gazette*, which contains most current and pending trademarks. Subscriptions to the *Gazette* for trademarks cost $312 per year. The *Gazette* for patents costs $583 per year. Both are issued every two weeks and can be ordered from the U.S. Government Printing Office. You can also purchase an image file which contains pending and registered trademarks and corresponding serial or registration numbers through Thomson and Thomson, (800) 692-8833. It dates back to April 1, 1987 and is updated by approximately 500 images weekly. However, the PDL you use is likely to have an image of the trademark on microfilm or cartridge, and also have copies of the *Official Gazette*. If not, and you have the registration number, you may obtain a copy of the trademark you want for $1.50 from the PTO. Contact:

The Patent and Trademark Office
U.S. Department of Commerce
P.O. Box 9
Washington, DC 20231
Public Information Line (703) 557-4357

Be patient. If any phone number is incorrect, call (area code) 555-1212 and request the new listing.

Patents, Trademarks and Copyrights

There are also commercial services you can use to do trademark searches.

CompuServe, (800) 848-8199. Fees are: $39.95 one time charge, plus $12.80 per hour or 21 cents per minute online time plus $4 per search and $4 for full entry call-up.

Trademark Scan (produced by Thomson and Thomson - can be purchased, (800) 692-8833), or accessed directly via Dialog. Trademark Scan is updated three times per week, includes state and federal trademarks, foreign and domestic. To access Trademark Scan you must already have Dialog. Cost is $130 per hour. Call (703) 524-8004 or (800) 334-2564. FAX for Trademark Producer Scan (People who actually own the database): (617) 786-8273.

Derwent, (800) 451-3451, is a commercial service that will conduct the search for you. They will access the Trademark Scan database via Dialog. Cost is $60 per mark plus $1 per record. If required, 24 hour turnaround time is available.

Visual image of trademarks are not available on any of the electronic services above.

Online services and database discs for both patents and trademarks are constantly being expanded. For information on an extensive range of existing and projected products, call the PTO Office of Electronic Information at (703) 557-5652 and ask for the U.S. Department of Commerce, PTO Office of Information Systems' *Electronic Products Brochure*. For example, there is a Weekly Text File, containing text data of pending and registered trademarks. Information can be called up by almost any term. It can be purchased from IMSMARQ, (215) 834-5089, the Trademark Register through Bell Atlantic Gateway, (800) 638-6363 Operator 2606, and Thomson and Thomson, (800) 692-8833.

How to Register a Trademark

Get a copy of the booklet, *Basic Facts about Trademarks* from the U.S. Government Printing Office. It is free upon request from the Trademark Search Library. Call (703) 308-9800/9805. The mark you intend to use needs to be in use before you apply. The fee to register your trademark is $175. The time to process it can take up to 14 months.

The Right Way to Get a Copyright

Copyrights are filed on intellectual property. A copyright protects your right to control the sale, use of distribution and royalties from a creation in thought, music, films, art or books. For information, contact:

Library of Congress
Copyright Office, Room 401
101 Independence Ave., SE

Washington, DC 20540
Public Information Office
(202) 479-0700
(202) 707-2100

If you know which copyright application you require, you can call the Forms Hotline, open 7 days per week, 24 hours per day at (202) 707-9100. The fee is $20 for each registration.

The Library of Congress provides information on copyright registration procedures and copyright card catalogs which cover 28 million works that have been registered since 1870. The Copyright Office will research the copyright you need and send you the information by mail. Requests must be in writing and you must specify exactly what it is you need to know. Contact the Copyright Office, Reference and Bibliography, Library of Congress, 101 Independence Ave., SE, Washington, DC 20559; (202) 707-6850, public information 479-0700. The fee for the search is $30 per hour. You can get a certificate stating the search was conducted by qualified researchers. There is no fee if you conduct the search yourself. Staff at the Library of Congress will show you how. You may then, if you wish, request a certificate. The Copyright Office will conduct its own search, but your work will probably reduce the time of the search and save you money.

Subscriptions to the following parts of the Library of Congress *Catalogue of Copyright Entries* are available from the Superintendent of Documents, U.S. Government Printing Office, Washington, DC 20402-9325. Each lists material registered since the last issue was published. Order by stock number using Mastercard, VISA, check or money order. To order, call the Government Printing Office Order Desk at (202) 783-3238. FAX for delays in receiving orders: (202) 275-7810. For help or complaints call the Superintendent of Documents Office at (202) 275-3050.

Part 1: Nondramatic Literary Works - this quarterly costs $16 per year. Stock number 730-001-0000-2.

Part 2: Serials and Periodicals - this semiannual costs $5 per year. Stock number 730-002-0000-9.

Part 3: Performing Arts - this quarterly costs $16 per year. Stock number 730-003-0000-5.

Part 4: Motion Pictures and Filmstrips - this semiannual costs $5 per year. Stock number 730-004-0000-1.

Part 5: Visual Arts - this semiannual does not include maps and costs $5 per year. Stock number 730-005-00000-8.

Part 6: Maps - this semiannual costs $4 per year. Stock number 730-006-0000-4.

Part 7: Sound Recordings - this semiannual costs $7.50 per year. Stock number 730-007-0000-1.

Part 8: Renewal - this semiannual costs $5 per year. Stock number 730-008-0000-7.

Be patient. If any phone number is incorrect, call (area code) 555-1212 and request the new listing.

Agriculture and Farming Management and Productivity

* *See also Experts Chapter*
* *See also International Trade*
* *See also Information from Lawmakers Chapter*
* *See also Environment and Nature Chapter*
* *See also Careers and Workplace; Research Grants in Every Field Chapter*

Most farmers, ranchers, and growers are aware of only a fraction of the resources available from the federal government but consumers, chefs, gardeners, and ordinary folks know even les. about the help and information readily accessible from the U.S. Department of Agriculture (USDA). A local telephone call to your USDA extension service will bring instantaneous advice on how to get rid of a wasp's nest or termites. Extension services in local communities offer classes on a wide variety of other topics that range from career opportunities to hydroponic farming. The National Agricultural Library is another mammoth information center with its numerous databases and publications. Youngsters between the ages of 10 to 20 years are eligible for start-up USDA loans to launch businesses ranging from lawn-mowing services to roadside produce stands. Incentives for agriculture cooperatives and new alternative approaches to farming also can be exploited. The government, along with many land grant colleges and universities, can share the latest research findings about soil and water conservation, farmland preservation, crop yields, or genetic engineering. In addition to farming, aquaculture, and forestry information there are answers to questions concerning the quality of meat, poultry, dairy, produce and other food information that reaches the supermarket.

Family farmers, agricultural cooperatives, medium size growers, and corporate agribusiness all can benefit from the technical expertise, resources, loan and loan guarantee programs, and other incentives offered by numerous government offices. Efforts to modernize farming in developing countries, notably by the Peace Corps, are included in the International Relations and Defense Chapter.

* AGRICOLA Database

National Agricultural Library (NAL)
Reference Branch, Room 111
10301 Baltimore Blvd.
Beltsville, MD 20782 (301) 501-5479

The bibliographic database consists of records for literature citation of journal articles, monographs, theses, patents, software, audiovisual materials, and technical reports relating to all aspects of agriculture. It also includes materials not in the NAL collection. Access to AGRICOLA is available on-site, on a cost-recovery basis and online through DIALOG and BRS, and on CD-ROM from several vendors. For more information contact NAL at the above address.

* African Aquaculture Documents

Aquaculture Information Center
U.S. Department of Agriculture
10301 Baltimore Blvd.
Beltsville, MD 20705 (301) 504-5558

The Food and Agriculture Organization of the United Nations and the National Agricultural Library recently launched a cooperative international project, code named REGIS, to promote better access to information on aquaculture in Africa. The REGIS system contains the entire text of the *Aquaculture Regional Section Survey for the African Region* compiled by the Aquaculture Development and Coordination Program. Subscriptions are required for both on-line and CD-Rom access to REGIS. Contact Deborah Hanfman or Eileen M. McVey at NAL Aquaculture Information Center for more information on REGIS.

* Agricultural Cooperative Service Publications

Agricultural Cooperative Service (ACS)
U.S. Department of Agriculture
PO Box 96576
Washington, DC 20090-6576 (202) 720-2556

The Agricultural Cooperative Service devotes its efforts to preserving and improving the family farm. Family farmers use cooperatives as an extension of their farm businesses to jointly purchase production supplies, process and market products, and perform related services. ACS publications series include:

Agricultural Cooperative Service; Directories; History and Statistics;

Organization: Members, Organizing a Cooperative, Principles and Practices, Structure and Scope;

Operations: Communications, Education and Training, Finance, Legal and Legislative;

Marketing: Crops - cotton, Food and feed grains, fruits and vegetables, specialty, foreign trade; Livestock - dairy, other; Other marketing;

Purchasing: Animal health, Agrichemicals, Feed, Petroleum, Seed, Other;

Rural Development.

Also inquire about the magazine *Farmers Cooperatives*, which covers all aspects of cooperatives. Annual subscriptions are available through Government Printing Office, (202) 783-3238 for $14 annually, domestic.

* Agricultural Diseases Database

Emergency Programs Information Center Data Bank
Veterinary Services
Animal and Plant Health Inspection Service (APHIS)
U.S. Department of Agriculture
6505 Belcrest Rd.
Hyattsville, MD 20782 (301) 436-8687

The Emergency Program Information Center (EPIC) maintains a computerized database with bibliographic information for all literature stored on microfilm by the center. The EPIC Data Bank consists of worldwide literature covering diseases of livestock and poultry exotic to the U.S. Complete services, including bibliographic printouts and copies of cited articles, are primarily for personnel working in Federal and cooperating State animal disease-control and eradication programs. Users outside APHIS are generally only provided citations; however, requests are handled on an individual basis. The center has prepared standard bibliographies on 17 different topics, which are available to the general public. The *PIC Brucellosis file* is included in the AGRICOLA system.

Be patient. If any phone number is incorrect, call (area code) 555-1212 and request the new listing.

Agriculture and Farming

* Agricultural Stabilization and Conservation Service

Agricultural Stabilization and Conservation Service (ASCS)
Information Division
P.O. Box 2415
Washington, DC 20013   (202) 720-7962

The Agricultural Stabilization and Conservation Service, an agency of the United States Department of Agriculture, administers farm commodity, conservation, environmental protection, and emergency programs. These programs provide for commodity loans and price support payments to farmers; commodity purchases from farmers and processors; acreage reduction; cropland set-aside and other means of production adjustment; conservation cost-sharing; and emergency adjustment. The ASCS has offices in most every state in the country. It also provides an extensive amount of information on commodity support programs available from the USDA and the Commodity Credit Corporation. The most common methods of farm support are price supports, income supports, and supply controls. The following is a list of free fact sheets available from the ASCS on commodity support programs.

Flue-Cured Tobacco, Other Tobaccos,Burley Tobacco, Peanuts, Mohair, Wool, Upland Cotton Program, Extra Long Staple Cotton, Soybeans and Minor Oilseeds, Sugar Beets and Sugarcane, Rye, Rice, Honey, Wheat, Dairy Refund Payment Program, Conservation Reserve Program, Feed Grain Program, Dairy Indemnity Payment Program, Dairy Price Support Program, Wheat Program.

* Agriculture and Food Marketing Revolution

Yearbook Editor, Publications
U.S. Department of Agriculture (USDA)
Room 535-A
Washington, DC 20250   (202) 720-9434

Each year, the USDA publishes a yearbook which explores one theme in depth. The 1988 yearbook, *Marketing U.S. Agriculture*, written by experts from farms, industry, universities, and government, describes the revolution in the food marketing system caused by new technology, social changes, and increased competition for world markets.

* Agricultural Chemicals

National Agricultural Chemicals Association (NACA)
1155 15th St., NW
Madison Building, Suite 900
Washington, DC 20005   (202) 296-1585

The National Agricultural Chemicals Association consists of companies producing chemical controls for fungi, rodents, pests and weeds. In addition to representing member interests in Washington, DC, NACA also pursues environmental programs. The NACA Alliance for a Clean Rural Environment (ACRE) provides information on the best management practices to help farmers and other users of agricultural chemicals to protect water quality. The ACRE program publishes *Dealer Environment* for agrichemical dealers. The NACA also publishes a pamphlet entitled *Protecting Our Groundwater: A Growers Guide*. Finally, a good source on the NACA is its quarterly newsletter called *Growing Possibilities*. The NACA puts out several other publications, some of which are free. Contact them for a publications list.

* Agriculture Electronic Bulletin Board

National Agricultural Library (NAL)
Public Services Division
Beltsville, MD 20705   (301) 504-6778

The Agricultural Library Forum, or ALF, is an electronic bulletin board operated by the NAL. ALF provides a convenient, economical medium for the electronic communication of information about NAL and its products. The ALF also provides a forum for the exchange of agricultural information between individuals. It is free of charge, save the cost of the call into the system, and accessible 24 hours a day, 7 days a week. It can be accessed by dialing (301) 504-5496; (301) 504-5111; (301) 504-5497; or (301) 504-6510 from your computer modem. Contact the above office for more information on the ALF system.

* Agricultural Environmental Engineering

American Society of Agricultural Engineers (ASAE)
2950 Niles Rd.
St. Joseph, MI 49085   (616) 429-0300

The American Society of Agricultural Engineers is the national association for engineers working on problems of importance to agricultural interests including irrigation and other large scale projects with environmental significance. In addition to technical papers and general interest material, the society publishes books in the following substantive areas: power and machinery, forest engineering, energy, Agriculture equipment design, electronics, soil and water, irrigation, wastewater treatment, plant environment, animal housing, food and process engineering, and tractor history. Call or write for a publications list and order form.

* Agricultural Libraries Information Notes

National Agricultural Library (NAL), Room 203
10301 Baltimore Blvd.
Beltsville, MD 20705-2351   (301) 504-6778

The Agricultural Libraries Information Notes (ALIN) contains information, features and updates on many NAL programs. It also contains a schedule of upcoming activities for those interested in agriculture research. Contact the ALIN editor about getting on the mailing list.

* Agricultural Pests and Insects

Public Awareness, LPAS
Animal and Plant Health Inspection Service (APHIS)
U.S. Department of Agriculture
Federal Building, Room 700
6505 Belcrest Road
Hyattsville, MD 20782   (301) 436-8536

The following is a sampling of fact sheets intended for consumers, farmers, scientists, journalists, and others. All publications are free; however, if ordering multiple quantities, an explanation is requested.

Mediterranean Fruit Fly (August 1985). For farmers and the general public, it describes the appearance and life cycle of the fly, and explains how eradication is accomplished by survey, regulatory actions, and control.

International Programs in APHIS (January 1983). For the general public, it describes protective measures taken worldwide to prevent spread of agricultural pests and diseases through imports and exports. Lists APHIS overseas offices and their activities.

* Agricultural Productivity

Eastern Regional Research Center (ERRC)
600 E. Mermaid Lane
Philadelphia, PA 19118   (215) 233-6400

Through basic, applied, and developmental research, scientists at nine research centers at ERRC are involved with projects to improve productivity of animals and crop plants and reduce losses; develop new and improved products and processing technology; upgrade nutritional value; open new and expand existing domestic and foreign markets; reduce marketing costs; eliminate health-related problems; and minimize energy consumption.

* Agricultural Publications

Office of Public Affairs
Publishing and Visual Communication
U.S. Department of Agriculture (USDA)
Room 542A
Washington, DC 20250   (202) 720-6623

The USDA has literally hundreds of publications available on all aspects of agriculture. Some documents can be purchased through GPO or NTIS, while others can be obtained directly from USDA. Publication topics include: agricultural economics, agricultural engineering, conservation, entomology, foresting, home economics, marketing, plant science, rural development, cooperatives, and statistics. Call or write for a free copy of the *List of Available Publications*.

* Agricultural Research Magazine

Superintendent of Documents
P.O. Box 371954
Pittsburgh, PA 15250-7954   (202) 783-3238

The Agricultural Research Service of the USDA publishes a monthly magazine entitled *Agriculture Research*. It contains articles about ongoing research and agricultural programs around the U.S. Subscriptions are available for $28 per year. It can be ordered from the above address. Information and sample copies can be obtained from ARS at (301) 504-8296.

Be patient. If any phone number is incorrect, call (area code) 555-1212 and request the new listing.

Management and Productivity

* Agriculture Document Delivery Service

National Agriculture Library, USDA
Document Delivery Services Branch, 6th floor
10301 Baltimore Blvd.
Beltsville, MD 20705-2351 (301) 504-5755

The National Agricultural Library (NAL) supplies agriculture materials not found elsewhere to other libraries. Requests for materials should first be submitted to your local state libraries or university library. Libraries can borrow materials through an inter-library loan system. NAL will photocopy articles for individuals for a fee. Contact the NAL for a fee schedule and for information request requirements.

* Agriculture Research Service Programs (ARS)

Information Staff
Beltsville Agricultural Research Center, Room 307A
10301 Baltimore Blvd.
Beltsville, MD 20705 (301) 504-6264

The ARS of the USDA conducts research in several areas designed to increase the quality of American crops, livestock, and nutrition. ARS also conducts research designed to improve the competitiveness of U.S. agriculture on the world market. For more information on specific ARS programs, contact the information office listed above.

* Agriculture Yearbooks

Yearbook Editor, Publications
U.S. Department of Agriculture (USDA)
Room 542-A
Washington, DC 20250 (202) 720-9434

Each year the USDA publishes a yearbook that explores one agriculture related topic in depth. Yearbooks have been published since 1894. Between 1894 and 1935 they were simply called *Yearbook of Agriculture*. Since 1935 each book has had an individual theme. A complete list of book titles is available from the Yearbook office. Books published since 1983 are in print and are available from the Superintendent of Documents. Available books (with prices) are as follows:

1983 Using Our Natural Resources ($7)
1984 Animal Health - Livestock and Pets ($10)
1985 U.S. Agriculture in a Global Economy ($10)
1986 Research for Tomorrow ($9.50)
1987 Our American Land ($9.50)
1988 Marketing American Agriculture ($9.50)
1989 Farm Management ($10)
1990 Americans in Agriculture, Portraits in Diversity ($10)
1991 Agriculture and the Environment ($12)

* Alternative Agricultural Opportunities

Executive Officer
Local Extension Service
U.S. Department of Agriculture (USDA)
Room 340A Administration Building
Washington, DC 20250 (202) 720-6283

The USDA operates an extension program in 3,165 counties located in all of the 50 states and the U.S. territories. Federal, state, and local governments share in financing and conducting cooperative extension educational programs to help farmers, processors, handlers, farm families, communities, and consumers apply the results of food and agricultural research including Alternative Agricultural Opportunities, which helps farmers use a distinctive approach to alternative crop and livestock enterprises to integrate marketing, management, and production factors into a total business plan.

* Alternative Farming Systems

Alternative Farming Information Center (AFIC)
U.S. Department of Agriculture
10301 Baltimore Blvd., Room 304
Beltsville, MD 20705 (301) 504-6559

This center covers organized farming or gardening that includes low-input, sustainable, or regenerative agriculture. Conservation tillage and other cultivation practices, such as intercropping, crop rotation, and use of green manures, are also covered. The AFIC has quick bibliographies and other information available free. Information products available include:

QB 92-24 Air Pollution Effects on Crops and Forests

QB 92-09 Alternative Farming Systems - Economic Aspects
QB 92-04 Compost and Composting of Organic Wastes
QB 91-122 Double Cropping and Inter-planting
QB 92-11 Green Manures and Cover Crops
QB 90-02 Legumes in Crop Rotations
QB 91-84 Solar Energy Alternatives for Agriculture
QB 91-37 Wind Energy in Agriculture

* American Agriculture News Service

News Features (202) 488-8358

This recorded message gives you daily news announcements on a variety of agriculture-related topics.

* Animal Disease Control

Animal Disease Management Information Center
Animal-Plant Health Inspection Service
Room 741, Federal Building
6505 Belcrest Road.
Hyattsville, MD 20782 (301) 436-8687

Veterinary Services (VS) is responsible for protecting the health of U.S. livestock and poultry. VS continually monitors diseases in the U.S. and abroad and investigates suspected incursions of foreign diseases into the U.S. The Information Center has approximately 68,000 articles accessible through the AGRICOLA system. Call for more information and for a list of *Emerpro files* on animal diseases.

* Animal Welfare

Animal Welfare Information Center (AWIC)
U.S. Department of Agriculture
10301 Baltimore Blvd.
Beltsville, MD 20705 (301) 504-6212

This center handles matters of animal care and handling, as well as housing and caging, training guides and manuals for animal care personnel, ethical issues involving animals, legislation, and regulation, and testing alternatives for drug toxicology studies. The Center publishes a list containing the titles and order forms for AWIC bibliographies, reference briefs and fact sheets. Call or write for a publications list. All publications are free. Publications include:

QB 90-48 Ethical and Moral Issues Relating to Animals
QB 91-06 Stress in Horses
QB 91-07 Training Materials for Animal Facility Personnel
SRB 90-02 Animal Euthanasia
- Animal Information Center User Tips

* Aquaculture and Fish Farming

Aquaculture Information Center
U.S. Department of Agriculture
10301 Baltimore Blvd.
Beltsville, MD 20705 (301) 504-5558

This center covers culture of aquatic plants and animals in freshwater, brackish water, and marine environments. Examples include catfish farming, oyster culture, freshwater prawn culture, and trout farming. Staff can also answer questions about animal parasitology. Patrons can use AquaRef, a system containing aquaculture information on computer. Call or write for a publications list. All publications are free. Publications and bibliographies include:

QB 91-85 Aquaculture: Economics and Marketing
QB 91-29 Aquaculture: Integrated Farming System
QB 91-88 Catfish Farming
QB 90-85 Shellfish Diseases and Control.
QB 91-47 Trout Culture

Short Bibliographies and Topic Series include:
Aquaculture - July 1991
Aquaculture and Hydroponics - June 1991
Salmon Culture - March 1992

* Aquaculture Loans

Farmers Home Administration
U.S. Department of Agriculture
South Agriculture Building 5420

Be patient. If any phone number is incorrect, call (area code) 555-1212 and request the new listing.

Agriculture and Farming

Washington, DC 20250 (202) 720-1632

The Farmers Home Administration extends credit to aquaculture operators, farmers, ranchers, rural residents, and communities. Loans for aquaculture purposes may generally be used for the husbandry of aquatic organisms under a controlled or selected environment.

* Bees and Beekeeping

Honeybee Breeding Genetics
and Physiology Research Lab
U.S. Department of Agriculture
ARS, 1157 Ben Hur Rd.
Baton Rouge, LA 70820 (504) 766-6064

This Lab does most of its research on protecting bees against pests and disease. Scientists are currently at work trying to protect the beekeeping industry and the public from the advent of the Africanized bees that are due to arrive in mid 1990. Research projects include use of a toxic substance that will attract bees and kill them, a repellent that will keep these aggressive bees from stinging, and ways of protecting commercial queen bee farms from invasion of Africanized bees. The Lab has also recently imported bees from Europe to test them for resistance to certain diseases. The Lab works with the private bee industry and the Agriculture Extension Service to disseminate the results of its work to industry.

* Biotechnology and Genetic Engineering

Biotechnology Information Center
U.S. Department of Agriculture
10301 Baltimore Blvd.
Beltsville, MD 20705 (301) 504-5340

Subject areas covered by this center include genetic engineering, plant and animal tissue culture, single cell protein, immobilized enzymes, legislation and regulations, transgenic animals, and detoxification using microbes. The Center's staff will also perform brief, complimentary searches of the AGRICOLA data base on specific topics of your choice, or more exhaustive searches on a cost-recovery basis. Call for a list of free bibliographies and publications. Available free Quick Bibliographies include the following:

QB 91-113 Biotechnology: Forestry and Forest Products
QB 91-114 Biotechnology: Genetic Linkage Studies in Plant Systems, 1989-91.
QB 91-81 Biotechnology: Plant Protection from Viruses, 1988-91.
- List of Directories Related to Biotechnology.

* Biotechnology Information On-Line

Biotechnology Information Center
U.S. Department of Agriculture
10301 Baltimore Blvd.
Beltsville, MD 20705 (301) 504-5340

The National Biological Impact Assessment Program (NBIAP) is designed to facilitate and assess the safe application of new techniques for genetically modifying plants, animals and microorganisms to benefit agriculture and the environment. This Information System combines a monthly News Report with direct access to an extensive series of databases. Access to the system is free up to 30 minutes a day. For access dial (703) 231-3858 on your computer modem, enter the registration information and choose a password. From then on you can enter the system using a toll free number [800-624-2723]. Contact the Biotechnology Information Center for more information on this service.

* Business Start-Up Loans for 10-20 Year Olds

Production Loan Division
U.S. Department of Agriculture (USDA)
Farmers Home Administration
Washington, DC 20250 (202) 720-1452

The USDA lends up to $5,000 to youths from 10 to 20 years of age. The loans can be used to support both farm and non-farm ventures, such as small crop farming, livestock farming, roadside stands, and custom work. They are normally made in conjunction with youth groups and require parental consent.

* Chemical and Fertilizer Hotline

Chemical Referral Center (800) CMA-8200
(202) 887-1315 (DC and collect calls from AK)

This toll-free service provides non-emergency referrals to companies that manufacture chemicals and to state and federal agencies for health and safety information and information regarding chemical regulations. It operates 9 a.m. to 6 p.m. eastern time.

* Commodities Market News

Information Staff
Agricultural Marketing Service
U.S. Department of Agriculture
Room 3510, South Building
P.O. Box 96456
Washington, DC 20090-6456 (202) 720-8998

Skilled market reporters gather and document marketing information that is distributed quickly throughout the U.S. via telephone recorders, newspapers, radio, television, and in printed reports. The reports are available for seven commodities: dairy, tobacco, cotton, fruits and vegetables, livestock, grain, and poultry, and they contain information on supply and demand and shipping point reports that cover prices paid by types of sale. Much of the information is gathered and distributed by local field offices via satellite.

* Communicable Diseases Affecting Cattle and Poultry

Animal and Plant Health Inspection Service
U.S. Department of Agriculture
Room 729
Washington, DC 20250 (202) 436-8711

A staff of specialists studies communicable diseases and pests affecting livestock and poultry.

* Compost and Improved Soil

Soil Microbial Systems
U.S. Department of Agriculture
Building 318, Room 108 BARC-E
Beltsville, MD 20705 (301) 344-3163

This office provides technical assistance on the production and use of compost, soil, and microbes.

* Cooperative Agricultural Research Projects

NFEIA
NFERC/Tennessee Valley Authority (TVA)
Muscle Shoals, AL 35660-1010 (205) 386-3095

The Agricultural Research Department has several cooperative research projects under way around the U.S. to compliment their in house research activities and to promote information transfer. Projects are generally 2-3 years in duration. Current project areas include: evaluation of winter crops for reducing nitrate leaching; soil nitrate test development; enhanced ammonium nutrition research; phosphorous research; fertilizer, soil and crop management research; agrichemical research; and water utilization research. Contact Bert R. Bock at the TVA for information on specific projects and their progress.

* Crop and Soil Agronomy

American Society of Agronomy (ASA)
677 South Segoe Rd.
Madison, WI 53711 (608) 273-8080

The American Society of Agronomy promotes the acquisition and diffusion of knowledge concerning the nature and interrelationship of plants, soils and the environment. Publications: Agronomy Journal, Crops and Soils, Journal of Environmental Quality, Journal of Natural Resources and Life Science Education, Agronomy News, Crop Science, Soil Science Society of America Journal, Journal of Production Agriculture, Soil Survey Horizons, Agronomy Abstracts. The Society also publishes numerous books, monographs, and special publications. Call or write for a list of publications as well as the price list for the journals.

* Crop Acreage Certification

Agricultural Stabilization and Conservation Service (ASCS)
Information Division
P.O. Box 2415
Washington, DC 20013 (202) 720-7962

Farmers certify their crop acreages when they report program crop data, acreage conservation reserve (ACR) and other crop acres. Farmers who are growing barley, corn, grain sorghum, rice, upland cotton, or wheat who wish to be eligible for price support and other program benefits must report crop acreages. Farmers

Be patient. If any phone number is incorrect, call (area code) 555-1212 and request the new listing.

growing crops but not participating in current programs should report acreages to insure the opportunity to fully participate in future programs. For more information on what to certify and procedures for doing so, contact the ASCS.

* Crop Insurance Coverage

Manager, Federal Crop Insurance Corporation
U.S. Department of Agriculture (USDA)
Washington, DC 20250 (202) 254-8224
OR: Your local crop insurance agent

The USDA runs a crop insurance program to improve the economic stability of agriculture through a sound system of crop insurance that provides multiple-peril insurance for individual farmers to ensure a basic income against droughts, freezes, insects, and other natural causes of disastrous crop losses. Any owner or operator of farmland who has an insurable interest in a crop in a county where insurance is offered on that crop is eligible unless the land is not classified for insurance purposes.

* Crop Production Losses

Agricultural Stabilization and Conservation Service (ASCS)
Information Division
P.O. Box 2415
Washington, DC 20013 (202) 720-7962

The ASCS administers disaster assistance programs to provide payments to producers sustaining crop production losses in either 1990 or 1991. To be eligible, producers must have less than $2 million gross annual revenue and be in compliance with highly erodible land and wetland conservation provisions of the law. Disaster payments may be made for losses of commercially-grown crops under the categories of participating program crops, nonparticipating program crops, sugar, tobacco, peanuts, soybeans, sunflowers, nonprogram crops and ornamental crops. Contact the ASCS for more information on eligibility and payments.

* Current Awareness Literature Service

Information Systems Division
National Agricultural Library (NAL)
10301 Baltimore Blvd.
Beltsville, MD 20705 (301) 504-5755

The Current Awareness Literature Service is a computer based literature search system designed to keep researchers up to date with current information in their fields. It is available free to USDA personnel. Call for information on developing a profile or for a users guide to the system.

* Dairy Indemnity Payment Program

Agricultural Stabilization and Conservation Service (ASCS)
U.S. Department of Agriculture
Room 3702, South Building
Washington, DC 20250 (202) 720-5237

The Dairy Indemnity Payment Program provides indemnity payments to dairy farmers whose milk has been removed from the commercial market because it contained residues of chemicals or toxic substances, including nuclear radiation fallout.

* Educational Programs: Farmers and their Families

Executive Officer
U.S. Department of Agriculture (USDA)
Room 340A, Administration Building
Washington, DC 20250 (202) 720-4111

The USDA operates an extension program in 3,165 counties located in all of the 50 states and the U.S. territories. Federal, state, and local governments share in financing and conducting cooperative extension educational programs to help farmers, processors, handlers, farm families, communities, and consumers apply the results of food and agricultural research. The Extension Service has targeted 9 national initiatives to provide a new focus for educational efforts.

Alternative Agricultural Opportunities: Helps farmers use a distinctive approach to alternative crop and livestock enterprises to integrate marketing, management, and production factors into a total business plan.

Building Human Capital: Helps people develop marketable job skills, make informed career decisions, and expand available opportunities.

Competitiveness and Profitability of American Agriculture: To enhance farmers' competitiveness and profitability, Extension helps farmers improve production, finance, and management skills; develop new technology; adjust profitability to global market changes; and strengthen business and support systems.

Conservation and Management of Natural Resources: Helps people benefit from natural ecosystems without destroying them, sustain a productive natural resource base, market natural resource goods and services, and formulate and implement sound public policies.

Family and Economic Well-Being: Helps families manage finances and make sound financial decisions; confront and deal with such problems as alcohol and drug abuse, teenage pregnancy, and unemployment; and develop strategies for retirement.

Improving Nutrition, Diet, and Health: Extension offers up-to-date information about the relationship of dietary practices to lifestyle factors; the safety, quality, and composition of foods; and consumers' needs and perceptions about the food industry.

Revitalizing Rural America: In cooperation with local governments, Extension programs emphasize how to increase competitiveness and efficiency of rural programs, explore methods to diversify local economies and attract new business, adjust to impact of change, develop ways to finance and deliver services, and train leaders to make sound policy decisions for rural communities.

Water Quality: Work with consumers, producers and local government to learn more about the importance of high-quality ground water and the conservation of water resources. Emphasis is also put on the effects of agricultural chemicals and contaminants on water quality.

Youth at Risk: Extension is helping expand youth outreach resources to meet the needs of youth, develop programs for the most susceptible youth populations, provide leadership and job skills, and increase training of professionals and volunteers to work in communities to prevent and treat problems.

* Emergency Programs

Agricultural Stabilization and Conservation Service (ASCS)
Information Division
P.O. Box 2415
Washington, DC 20013 (202) 720-7962

The ASCS provides assistance to agricultural producers in emergencies caused by natural disasters through: haying and grazing privileges on cropland placed in the Acreage Conservation Reserve and in Conservation Use; the Livestock Feed Program; and the Emergency Conservation Program. Contact the ASCS regarding specific eligibility requirements.

* Emerging Agricultural Technology

Office of Technology Assessment (OTA)
600 Pennsylvania Ave., SE
Washington, DC 20510 (202) 228-6521

OTA is studying the emerging agricultural technologies for the 1990s and the structure of the research system that gives rise to these technologies, which include biotechnology, information technology, and low input technology for the food and agricultural sector. Contact Mike Phillips, the project director, for more information.

* Erosion Control

Information Division
U.S. Department of Agriculture
Agricultural State Conservation Service (ASCS)
P.O. Box 205
Kansas City, MO 64141 (202) 720-5237

The Agricultural State Conservation Service (ASCS) directs a number of conservation programs to preserve and improve American farmland: Conservation Reserve Program (CRP): Targets the most fragile farmland by encouraging farmers to stop growing crops on land designated by conservationists as "highly erodible" and plant grass or trees on it instead. The farmer receives rent on the land for a term of ten years. Cost-share programs are also available for permanent planting of grass and trees in these areas.

Be patient. If any phone number is incorrect, call (area code) 555-1212 and request the new listing.

Agriculture and Farming

* Farm Labor Housing Loans

Farmers Home Administration
U.S. Department of Agriculture
South Agriculture Building 5013
Washington, DC 20250 (202) 720-5177

The Farmers Home Administration makes loans and grants to finance low-rent housing for domestic farm laborers. Funds may be used to build, buy, improve, or repair farm labor housing and to provide related facilities. Loan funds can also be used to finance some amenities, but cannot be used to refinance debts.

* Farm Operating Loans

Farmers Home Administration
U.S. Department of Agriculture
South Agriculture Building 5420
Washington, DC 20250 (202) 720-1632

Operating loans may be used to pay for items needed for farm operations, including livestock, farm and home equipment, feed, seed, fertilizer, fuel, chemicals, and hail and other crop insurance; family living expenses, minor building improvements, purchase of stock in certain cooperative associations, creditor payments; purchase of milk base; and refinancing of debts. Family farmers and ranchers are eligible.

* Farm Ownership Loans

Farmers Home Administration
U.S. Department of Agriculture
South Agriculture Building 5420
Washington, DC 20250 (202) 720-1632

Farm Ownership Loans may be used to buy, improve or enlarge farms. Uses may include construction, improvement, or repair of farm homes and service buildings; improvement in on-farm water supplies; installation of pollution control or energy conservation measures; refinancing debts; clearing or improving forests; and establishing non-agricultural enterprises to help farmers supplement their income.

* Farm Ownership Loans for Socially Disadvantaged Persons

Farmers Home Administration
U.S. Department of Agriculture
South Agriculture Building 5420
Washington, DC 20250 (202) 720-1632

The Federal Home Administration is authorized by the Agricultural Credit Act of 1987 (P.L. 100-233) to set aside funds for farm ownership loans to eligible members of socially disadvantaged groups who will operate family-size farms. Eligible groups are blacks, American Indians or Alaskan Natives, Hispanics,, and Asians or Pacific Islanders.

* Farm Credit Administration Freedom of Information Act Requests

Freedom of Information Act Officer
Farm Credit Administration
1510 Farm Credit Drive
McLean, VA 22102 (703) 883-4056

Contact the office above for Freedom of Information Act requests.

* Farm Credit Administration Library

Library
Farm Credit Administration
1501 Farm Credit Drive
McLean, VA 22102 (703) 883-4296

For information on obtaining reference material through inter-library loan, contact the office above.

* Farm Facility Loan Program

Agricultural Stabilization and Conservation Service (ASCS)
U.S. Department of Agriculture
Room 3608, South Building
Washington, DC 20250 (202) 720-6778

The Farm Facility Loan Program helps qualifying farmers obtain on-site storage for their crops. Applications for these loans are accepted by county ASCS offices only during periods announced by the Secretary of Agriculture. Contact the above listed office for more details.

* Farm Money and Credit Reports

Office of Congressional and Public Affairs
Farm Credit Administration
1501 Farm Credit Drive
McLean, VA 22102 (703) 883-4056

Information on obtaining publications and documents can be obtained from the office above. Some of the documents it has which are available include news releases issued since January 1, 1972, biographies of Farm Credit Administration (FCA) officials, and speeches by FCA officials. Other publications include:

FCA Handbook - Statutes and Regulations (fee charged)
FCA Examination Manual (Set fee Charged)
FCA Bulletin (Published 10 days after each meeting of the FCA Board)
FCA Report (Published on an as-needed basis)
FCA Orders
FCA Money and Credit Market Report
FCA Organization Chart
FCA Board Policies
FCA Annual Report

* Farming Cooperatives

Agricultural Cooperative Service
U.S. Department of Agriculture (USDA)
Washington, DC 20250 (202) 653-6976

The USDA will assist any group interested in starting or developing agricultural cooperatives, and will also work with them to solve organizational, operational, or management problems. They will also help a cooperative expand export markets.

* Farming Profitability and Competitiveness

Executive Officer
Local Extension Service
U.S. Department of Agriculture (USDA)
Room 340A Administration Building
Washington, DC 20250 (202) 720-4111

The USDA operates an extension program in 3,165 counties located in all of the 50 states and the U.S. territories. Federal, state, and local governments share in financing and conducting cooperative extension educational programs to help farmers, processors, handlers, farm families, communities, and consumers apply the results of food and agricultural research including Competitiveness and Profitability of American Agriculture: To enhance farmers' competitiveness and profitability, Extension helps farmers improve production, finance, and management skills; develop new technology; adjust profitability to global market changes; and strengthen business and support systems.

* Farmer-Owned Lending Institutions

Office of Congressional and Public Affairs
Farm Credit Administration
1501 Farm Credit Drive
McLean, VA 22102 (703) 883-4056

The Farm Credit System is a network of farmer-owned lending institutions and specialized service organizations. More than 70 years ago Congress created the System to provide American agriculture with a dependable source of credit at competitive rates. Today the System provides about one-third of the total credit used by America's farmers, ranchers, and their cooperatives. The *Farm Credit System 1989 Information Guide*, which provides information on the Farm Credit System, including a list of the System's banks, is available free from the office above.

* Farmland Conservation Efforts

Information Division
U.S. Department of Agriculture
14th and Independence Ave, SW, SAG
Washington, DC 20250 (202) 720-5237

The Agricultural Stabilization Conservation Service (ASCS) directs a number of conservation programs to preserve and improve American farmland: Conservation Reserve Program (CRP): Targets the most fragile farmland by encouraging farmers to stop growing crops on land designated by

Be patient. If any phone number is incorrect, call (area code) 555-1212 and request the new listing.

conservationists as "highly erodible" and plant grass or trees on it instead. The farmer receives rent on the land for a term of ten years. Cost-share programs are also available for permanent planting of grass and trees in these areas. Agricultural Conservation Program (ACP): This program is designed to solve soil, water, and related resource problems through costsharing. ACP assistance is available to install soil-saving practices, including terraces, grass, sod waterways, and other measures to control erosion. It also helps reduce sediment, chemicals, and livestock waste that contaminate streams and lakes.

* Farmland Natural Disaster Relief

Office of Government and Public Affairs
U.S. Department of Agriculture (USDA)
Washington, DC 20250 (202) 720-2791

This free publication provides an overview of USDA's disaster assistance programs. It describes types of assistance available and where to apply for assistance. Local extension agents in each county can approve disaster applications for the following: conservation structures (when located on eligible lands); rehabilitation of farm lands destroyed by disaster; crop payment subsidies for disruption caused by disaster to regular crop schedules; sale of animal feed at below market price in emergency situations; animal grazing on reserve or conservation lands in emergency situations; donation of animal feed to Indian reservations when needed; and donation of grain to migratory wildfowl domains. The federal government will also remove debris from a major disaster from publicly- or privately-owned lands or waters.

* Farm Management and Improvements

The National Fertilizer and Environmental Center
Tennessee Valley Authority (TVA)
Muscle Shoals Reservation
Muscle Shoals, AL 35660 (205) 386-2598

The TVA is involved in a broad range of agricultural services. Thousands of demonstration farms have been created to test agricultural improvements. Current research focuses on farm management and record-keeping, planning and specialization, new crops, weed and pest control, and marketing, as well as continued improvements in fertilizer use and production practices. Current agricultural programs include developing alternative fuels from hardwood trees and farm crops, along with recycling nutrients found in farm and municipal waste.

* Farm Products Cash Value

National Center for Agricultural Utilization Research
U.S. Department of Agriculture
ARS, 1815 N. University St.
Peoria, IL 61604 (309) 685-4011

The research goal of this center is to increase the cash value of farm products in domestic and foreign markets through improved quality and safety of food and feed, enhanced use of plant materials as renewable resources, and increased efficiency of crop production.

* Fertilizer and Chemical Development

The National Fertilizer and Environmental Center
Tennessee Valley Authority
Muscle Shoals Reservation
P.O. Box 1010
Muscle Shoals, AL 35660 (205) 386-2593

The National Fertilizer Development Center plans and manages research and development programs for new and improved fertilizers and processes for their manufacture; for testing and demonstrating methods of chemical and organic fertilizer use as an aid to soil and water conservation and to the improved use of agricultural and related resources; and for operating and maintaining facilities to serve as a national laboratory for research and development in chemistry and chemical engineering related to fertilizers essential to national defense. The center conducts research to develop improved technology for converting cellulosic materials, including trees, to ethanol and other chemicals. Currently, there is an emphasis to demonstrate ways to minimize pollution problems during the handling and use of fertilizers in order to protect the environment.

* Financial Assistance For Rural Residents and Communities

Farmers Home Administration (FmHA)
U.S. Department of Agriculture

Washington, DC 20250 (202) 720-4323

FmHA provides financial assistance to rural people and communities that cannot obtain commercial credit at affordable terms. Applicants must be unable to obtain credit from usual commercial sources. Examples of the types of loans available are Emergency Loans, Youth Project Loans, Housing Repair Loans and Grants, and Business and Industry Loan Guarantees.

* Forest Insect and Disease Management

Contact: your State Forester or the state office of the U.S. Forest Service, usually located in the state capitol.

To reduce loss and damage to forests and lands by forest insects and diseases, the USDA provides technical and financial assistance in prevention, detection, evaluation, and suppression of forest insect and disease outbreaks on state and private lands.

* Forestry Incentives Program

Agricultural Stabilization and Conservation Service (ASCS)
Information Division
P.O. Box 2415
Washington, DC 20013 (202) 720-7962

The Forestry Incentive Program, the Federal Government shares the cost of planting trees and improving timber stands with private landowners. Contact the ASCS to inquire if your land is eligible and for more information on the program.

* Grain Reserve Program

Agricultural Stabilization and Conservation Service (ASCS)
U.S. Department of Agriculture
Room 3702, South Building
Washington, DC 20250 (202) 720-5237

The Grain Reserve Program is authorized for farmer owned wheat, corn, grain, sorghum, oats, and barley. When entry into the Reserve is authorized by the Secretary of Agriculture, producers may enter into a contract extending their 9 month loan an additional 27 months and receive quarterly storage payments. Loans may be repaid at any time. Contact ASCS for more details.

* Great Plains Conservation Work

Soil Conservation Service
U.S. Department of Agriculture
Washington, DC 20250 (202) 690-0547

Land users living in the Great Plains states can seek assistance from the Soil Conservation Service (SCS), which offers technical assistance and cost-sharing funds to farmers, ranchers, and other land users in the Great Plains. Cost-share rates can range up to 80 percent for urgently needed conservation work. Contact SCS or your local Soil Conservation Office.

* Gypsy Moth Control

Printing and Distribution Management Branch, APHIS
U.S. Department of Agriculture
Federal Building, Room G-100
6505 Belcrest Rd.
Hyattsville, MD 20782 (301) 436-7176

The following publication is available free of charge from APHIS: *Don't Move the Gypsy Moth* (July 1985). This tells how to make sure outdoor household articles don't spread gypsy moths.

* Horticulture Clearinghouse

U.S. Department of Agriculture
10301 Baltimore Blvd.
Beltsville, MD 20705 (301) 501-5340

This center covers technical horticultural or botanical question, economic botany, wild plants of possible use, herbs, bonsai, and floriculture.

* Hydroponic Farming

Environmental Research Laboratory
2601 East Airport Dr.
Tucson, AZ 85706 (602) 741-1990

Be patient. If any phone number is incorrect, call (area code) 555-1212 and request the new listing.

Agriculture and Farming

This lab can provide you with information and expertise on hydroponics, the process of growing crops without soil.

* Insects Identification and Control

Contact your local USDA Extension Service agent

Technical assistance is available to help you identify and eliminate any problems you may have caused by insects and bugs. You are encouraged to catch one of the insects which are causing the problem and send it in for analysis. Contact your local Extension Service for more information.

* Limited Resource Farm Loans

Farmers Home Administration
U.S. Department of Agriculture
South Agriculture Building 5420
Washington, DC 20250
(202) 720-1632

The Farmers Home Administration makes loans to help low income farmers and ranchers who live on not larger than family farms including small family farms, improve their farming and earn a better living. These loans are made on better terms than ordinary farm loans, and those who cannot pay the regular rate of interest because of low income.

* Livestock and Veterinary Services

Livestock and Poultry Sciences
Room 217, Bldg. 200
Beltsville Agricultural Research Center
Beltsville, MD 20705
(301) 504-8431

Specialists study many topics, including domestic animal diseases, beef production, dairy production, foreign animal diseases, poultry production and diseases, production of sheep and fur-bearing animals, swine production, and livestock facilities.

* Livestock Rangeland

Rangeland Resources
Bureau of Land Management (BLM)
U.S. Department of the Interior
1620 L St., NW
Washington, DC 20006
(202) 653-9193

The Bureau of Land Management has administration of 170 million acres of public lands where livestock graze. About 18,800 ranchers and farmers graze livestock on BLM-managed lands. A majority of these permittees have small (less than 100 head) or medium (100 to 500 head) livestock operations.

* Multiple Uses of Crops

Alternative Farming Center
U.S. Department of Agriculture
10301 Baltimore Blvd.
Beltsville, MD 20705
(301) 504-5724

This center covers new crops or new uses for old crops, including forest products and especially crops from which "natural rubber" can be produced.

* National Agriculture Clearinghouse

National Agricultural Library (NAL)
U.S. Department of Agriculture
10301 Baltimore Blvd.
Beltsville, MD 20705
(301) 504-3755

The National Agricultural Library (NAL) has established 12 specialized information centers to provide enhanced services to its current clientele, as well as to develop new service relationships with the public and private sectors. Aside from agricultural researchers, centers also serve educators, consumers, and the private sector. Each center has a coordinator responsible for planning the center's activities, including reference services, collection development, developing information products, coordinating outreach activities, and establishing distribution networks.

* National Agriculture Library Services

National Agricultural Library (NAL)
10301 Baltimore Blvd.

Beltsville, MD 20705
(301) 504-3755

NAL provides comprehensive information services for the food and agricultural sciences through a variety of sources, which include bibliographies, personal reference services, loans, photocopies, and online data files. Services are provided to agricultural colleges, research institutions, government agencies, agricultural associations, industry, individual scientists, and the general public. NAL cooperates with the Library of Congress and the National Library of Medicine to provide access to publications worldwide in the agricultural, chemical, and biological sciences. NAL houses one of the largest collections in the free world on agricultural subjects--2.3 million volumes and 26,000 periodicals--including biology, chemistry, nutrition, forestry, soil sciences, and much more.

* National Agriculture Statistics

Agricultural Statistics Board
U.S. Department of Agriculture
South Agriculture Building, Room 5809
Washington, DC 20250
(202) 720-7017

The National Agricultural Statistics Service, through its Washington DC headquarters and 45 field offices serving all 50 states, annually publishes hundreds of reports detailing production and prospects for crops, livestock, dairy, and poultry. Other releases outline stocks, prices, labor, weather and similar items concerning farmers, ranchers and those associated with agriculture. Information is gathered from agricultural producers and available to the public. The information is also available electronically through the Departments Computerized Information Delivery (CID) System. When calling, ask for a copy of the *Agricultural Statistics Board Catalogue*, which contains contact names as well as a complete list of reports broken down by topic area. It is available free.

* Non-Farm Enterprise Loans

Farmers Home Administration
U.S. Department of Agriculture
South Agriculture Building 6321
Washington, DC 20250
(202) 690-4100

The Farmers Home Administration makes loans to family farmers and ranchers and gives technical and management assistance for development and operation of non-farm enterprises to supplement farm income. Enterprises for which loans can be made include: repair and service shops, restaurants and grocery stores, camping sites, and riding stables.

* Orchard and Forest Tree Losses

Agricultural Stabilization and Conservation Service (ASCS)
Information Division
P.O. Box 2415
Washington, DC 20013
(202) 720-7962

The ASCS administers disaster assistance programs to provide payments to producers sustaining orchard and forest tree losses in either 1990 or 1991. To be eligible, producers must have less than $2 million gross annual revenue and be in compliance with highly erodible land and wetland conservation provisions of the law. To qualify, owners must own at least one acre of orchard or forest trees, but not more than 500 acres of orchard trees (not more than 1,000 acres in the case of forest trees) and must have owned the trees at the time of the disaster.

* Patent Licensing Opportunities

National Patent Program
Room 401, Building 005
BARC-West
Beltsville, MD 20705
(301) 504-2518

Government patents resulting from agricultural research discoveries are available for licensing to U.S. companies and citizens. Licenses are offered on a non-exclusive, exclusive, and co-exclusive basis. Non-exclusive licenses are generally granted when no large investment to market a product is expected. Exclusive and co-exclusive licenses are granted when substantial investment is required. Fees for licenses are negotiable. An annual catalog listing all patents available for license plus technical abstracts is available. The necessary regulations and forms are included.

* Patents on Seeds

Plant Variety Protection Office
Commodities Scientific Support Division
AMS, NAL, Room 500
Beltsville, MD 20705
(301) 504-2518

Be patient. If any phone number is incorrect, call (area code) 555-1212 and request the new listing.

Management and Productivity

Unique seeds, with few exceptions, that are sexually reproduced can be protected by patents, The protection, which extends for 18 years, provides owners with exclusive rights to sell, reproduce, export, and produce the seed.

* Pesticide and Quarantine Programs

Animal and Plant Health Inspection Service (APHIS)
Plant Protection and Quarantine
6505 Belcrest Rd.
Hyattsville, MD 20782 (301) 436-7799

The USDA helps states and growers control or eradicate pests and diseases that cause plant loss. APHIS cooperates with state agencies to establish quarantines, pesticide spray programs, or release of sterile insects to reduce pest populations.

* Pesticides Database

National Pesticides Information Retrieval System (NPIRS)
CERIS/NPIRS
1231 Cumberland Ave., Suite A
West Lafayette, IN 47906-1317 (317) 494-6614

NPIRS databases provide on-line dial-up access available to the public of more than 80,000 pesticide products which are now or have been registered with the Environmental Protection Agency (EPA). NPIRS also contains registration information from 36 of the 54 U.S. States and Territories. Product information includes: product name and status; registrant name and address; EPA registration number; formulation (chemical, dust); signal word (ie.danger, warning, caution); type of pesticide; active ingredients; active ingredients and percentages; sites on which products are used; pests against which products are used; use classification; registration action dates/updates.

* Pesticide Dissipation in Soil

The National Fertilizer and Environmental Center (NFERC)
Tennessee Valley Authority
Muscle Shoals Reservation
P.O. Box 1010
Muscle Shoals, AL 35660 (205) 386-2593

NFERC researchers are currently evaluating the influence on management practices, such as the use of cover crops and variations in nitrogen application rates, on the adsorption and degradation of pesticides in soil. Relative emphasis is placed on the effects on the potential movement of pesticides to groundwater. Laboratory studies have been initiated to examine the effect of cover crop residuals, such as wheat and canola, on adsorption, degradation and movement. For more information, contact principal investigator Sidney S. Harper.

* Pesticides Documents Management System

National Pesticides Information Retrieval System
CERIS/NPIRS
1231 Cumberland Ave., Suite A
West Lafayette, IN 47906-1317 (317) 494-6614

PDMS is an automated index containing over 220,000 citations of studies or documents, most of which have been submitted to the EPA in support of pesticides registrations. This database had been found useful to pesticides registrants, consultants, state and federal regulatory officials and others seeking information related to health and safety.

* Pesticide Information Hotline (PIN)

National Pesticide Telecommunications Network (800) 858-7378

This service of the U.S. Environmental Protection Agency and Texas Tech University is open 24 hours, 7 days a week. It responds to non-emergency questions about the effects of pesticides, toxicology and symptoms, environmental effects, disposal and cleanup, and safe use of pesticides.

* Pesticides Information Network

Office of Pesticide Programs
Environmental Protection Agency (H7507C)
401 M St., SW
Washington, DC 20460 (703) 305-7499

The Pesticide Information Network is a collection of files each containing up to date pesticide information. The PIN is located on a personal computer and is accessible by data-phone similar to a PC to PC bulletin board. Files available in PIN are: Pesticides Monitoring Inventory; Restricted Use Products File; and The Chemical Index. Access to the network is free. Call for more information.

* Pesticide Products Inventory

Office of Pesticide Programs
Environmental Protection Agency (EPA)
401 M St., SW
Washington DC 20460 (202) 557-7090

EPA administers two Congressionally mandated statutes to control the more than 45,000 pesticide products registered for use in the United States. The EPA monitors the distribution and use of these pesticides, issuing civil or criminal penalties for violations. EPA also sets tolerances or maximum legal limits for pesticide residues on food commodities and feed grains to prevent consumer exposure to unsafe pesticide levels.

* Pesticides Rules and Regulations

Environmental Protection Agency
H7506C
401 M Street, SW
Washington, DC 20460 (703) 305-5805

The Pesticides Docket provides public access to documentation for each Registration Standard under development when the Agency begins review of data for the Registration Standard or upon publication of a notice setting out the list and sequence of Registration Standards. The docket contains documentation of pre-special and special reviews of pesticides, memoranda, all comments, correspondence, documents, proposals, or other materials concerning a pending pesticide regulatory decision provided to the Agency by a person or party outside of government (other than confidential business information).

* Plant and Entomological Services

Information Staff
Beltsville Agricultural Research Service
U.S. Department of Agriculture
Room 307, Bldg. 307
BARC West
Beltsville, MD 20705 (301) 504-6875

Specialists study and can provide you with information on biological control of pests, corn and sorghum production, crop mechanization and pest control equipment, crop pollination, bees and honey, insect control, forage crop production, range management, plant genetics and breeding, pesticide use and impacts, plant pathology, weed control, small grains production, sugar crop production, and plant physiology.

* Plant Breeders Protection

Plant Variety Protection Office
U.S. Department of Agriculture
National Agricultural Library (NAL) Building
Agricultural Marketing Service (AMS)
Room 500
10301 Baltimore Blvd.
Beltsville, MD 20705 (301) 504-5518

Federal legislation protects the ownership rights of breeders of plants that reproduce through seeds. The Agricultural Marketing Service will certify whether or not a new variety is entitled to patent protection.

* Plant Genome Data and Information Center

National Agricultural Library (NAL)
10301 Baltimore Blvd.
Beltsville, MD 20705 (301) 504-6875

The Plant Genome Data and Information Center provides a variety of information services and publications on all aspects of plant and animal genome mapping including: nucleotide and protein sequencing; physical and cytogenetic maps; plant breeding efforts based on or using mapping efforts. The Center can furnish you with quick bibliographies or special reference briefs on genome mapping. The information center is also associated with several databases on genetic research. Also ask about *Probe*, the newsletter of the USDA Plant Genome Research Program. Some of the quick bibliographies include:

QB 91-107 Biotechnology: Genetic Engineering for Crop Plant Improvement
QB 89-73 Biotechnology: Gene Mapping in Insect and Animal Systems
QB 89-06 Biotechnology: Plant Protection
QB 90-17 Biotechnology: Plant Germplasm Maintenance and Storage
SRB 90-02 Catalogue of Agricultural, Scientific, and Research related software available at the NAL.

Be patient. If any phone number is incorrect, call (area code) 555-1212 and request the new listing.

Agriculture and Farming

* Post-Harvest Processing

Southern Regional Research Center
U.S. Department of Agriculture
1100 Robert E. Lee Blvd.
ARS, Box 19687
New Orleans, LA 70179 (504) 286-4200

Research at this center relates primarily to post-harvest processing, product enhancement, and the safety and use of agricultural commodities produced in the southern U.S.

* Production, Coops, and Marketing Groups

Your local Extension Agent or
Office for the Assistant Secretary
Science and Education Department
U.S. Department of Agriculture (USDA)
Washington, DC 20250 (202) 720-5923

The USDA will provide educational and technical assistance to any agricultural production or marketing association, group, or cooperative. They provide the latest USDA land grant university research findings, discuss new technology, and share the results of feasibility studies, market analysis reports, and the development of new products and markets.

* Quarterly Report to Congress

Current Information Branch
Agricultural Research Service
U.S. Department of Agriculture, Building 005
Beltsville, MD 20705 (301) 504-8296

The free *Quarterly Report To Congress* summarizes research findings of projects conducted by USDA. Reports cover livestock, poultry, crops, insect pest control, soil and water resources, human nutrition, post-harvest technology, and commercial uses for commodities.

* Quick Bibliography Series

National Agricultural Library (NAL)
10301 Baltimore Blvd.
Beltsville, MD 20705 (202) 504-5755

An invaluable resource for the researcher, the *Quick Bibliography* series can provide you with article, book, and conference paper citations and abstracts. Cites are taken from the AGRICOLA system. Contact the NAL information centers to inquire about the availability of *Quick Bibliographies* in your area of interest. They are available free.

* Seed Quality and Inspection Labs

Federal Seed Lab
U.S. Department of Agriculture
Beltsville, MD 20705 (301) 504-8089

The federal government can test seeds to determine their quality and whether they are free from contamination. They will also prosecute any agent that transfers contaminated or mislabeled seed from state to state. Seeds are examined by or at a state agent's request, and there may be some fee involved.

* Soil and Farmland Protection Programs

Soil Conservation Service (SCS)
U.S. Department of Agriculture
P.O. Box 2890
Washington, DC 20013 (202) 720-9149

Soil surveys are used not only for conservation purposes but also to identify suitable lands for a wide variety of uses, from maintaining crops to urban uses. Information about soil helps prevent major construction mistakes and misuse of land that can be productively put to use. Soil maps identify flood-prone areas and sources of water pollutants. The SCS has a tremendous amount of material available on all aspects of soil conservation. The following is a list of some of the publications available from the SCS.

Assistance Available from the SCS - Program Aid 1352
Clean Water: Our Conservation Commitment - Program Aid 1475
The Field Office Technical Guide to Conservation - Program Aid 1471
Conservation Assistance Around the World - Program Aid 1431
The Earth Needs You: Volunteers for Soil and Water Conservation - Program Aid 1451.
Going Wild with Soil and Water Conservation - Program Aid 1363

Tillage Options for Conservation Farmers - Program Aid 1416
Save Soil Systematically - Program Aid 1366
National Plant Materials Program - Program Aid 1473
Snow Surveys and Water Supply Forecasting - Agriculture Information Bulletin 536
Soil Erosion by Wind - Agriculture Information Bulletin 555
Soil Erosion by Water - Agriculture Information Bulletin 513

* Soil and Water Loans

Farmers Home Administration
U.S. Department of Agriculture
South Agriculture Building 5420
Washington, DC 20250 (202) 720-1632

The Farmers Home Administration makes soil and water loans and provides technical management assistance to owners or operators of farms and ranches for developing, conserving, and making proper use of their land and water resources. Activities eligible for these loans include irrigation, farmstead water, drainage, soil and water conservation, forestry, fish farming, land development, certain pollution abatement or control activities.

* Soil Conservation Service (SCS) Magazine

Superintendent of Documents
P.O. Box 371954
Pittsburgh, PA 15250-7954 (202) 783-3238

The SCS publication *SOIL and Water Conservation News* is a bimonthly magazine containing articles on a variety of conservation related issues. It costs $6 per year. Sample copies may be obtained from the SCS information office by calling (202) 720-9149.

* Soil Conservation Technical Expertise

Soil Conservation Service (SCS)
U.S. Department of Agriculture
P.O. Box 2890
Washington, DC 20013 (202) 720-1845

Technical expertise is available in such areas as irrigation, drainage, landscape architecture, construction, sanitary and water quality, and hydrology.

* Soil Conservation Volunteers

The Earth Team
7515 N.E. Ankeny Road
Ankeny, IA 50021 (800) THE SOIL

Earth Team volunteers work to improve the soil where they live and represent the local volunteer arms of the SCS. Call for a free information packet and information on the Earth Team.

* Soil, Water, and Air Sciences

ARS Information Staff
U.S. Department of Agriculture
Room 307-A, Building 005
Beltsville, MD 20705 (301) 504-6264

Specialists study such topics as environmental quality, erosion and sedimentation, soil fertility and plant nutrition, organic wastes, pesticide degradation, water use efficiency and tillage practices, and weed control. Contact the ARS staff for answers to questions on these and other conservation-related topics.

* State-based Farming Research

Cooperative State Research Service
Aerospace Bldg.
901 D. St., SW
Washington, DC 20224 (202) 401-4268

More than half of the publicly funded agricultural research in the U.S. is conducted at State Agricultural Experiment Stations (SAES), located on land-grant universities in each state and territory in the U.S. The SAES serve as an early warning system for problems and opportunities. Such advancements as iodized salt, fluoride toothpaste, and mineral and vitamin additives for food came from these laboratories. Scientists are involved with experiments to reduce food costs for the consumer, reforest our landscape with genetically improved trees free from insects and diseases, produce leaner meat, control pests, prevent acid rain, and fight insect pests. Since the SAES are located at the land-grant universities, the Cooperative Extension Service readily transfers research to the classroom and to citizens.

Be patient. If any phone number is incorrect, call (area code) 555-1212 and request the new listing.

Management and Productivity

* Technology Assessment Reports

Office of Technology Assessment (OTA)
Publications Order
U.S. Congress
Washington, DC 20510-8025 (202) 224-8996

These OTA publications are available through the office above, the Government Printing Office, and the National Technical Information Service. To find out correct ordering information and prices, along with brief summaries of the following studies, contact the OTA office above and request their current publications catalog.

Agriculture and Forestry

Africa Tomorrow: Issues in Technology, Agriculture, and U.S. Foreign Aid (TM-F-31)
Agricultural Postharvest Technology and Marketing Economics Research (TM-F-21)
Assessing Biological Diversity in the United States: Data Considerations (BP-F-39)
An Assessment of the U.S. Food and Agricultural Research System (F-155)
Commercial Biotechnology: An International Analysis (BA-218)
Continuing the Commitment: Agricultural Development in the Sahel (F-308)
Drugs in Livestock Feed (F-91)
Emerging Food Marketing Technologies (F-79)
Energy From Biological Processes (E-124)
Enhancing Agriculture in Africa: A Role for Development Assistance (F-356)
Enhancing the Quality of U.S. Grain for International Trade (F-399)
Grain Quality in International Trade: A Comparison of Major U.S. Competitors (F-402)
Grassroots Conservation of Biological Diversity in the United States (BP-F-38)
Grassroots Development: The African Development Foundation (F-378)
Impacts of Applied Genetics: Micro-Organisms, Plants, and Animals (HR-132)
Impacts of Technology on U.S. Cropland and Rangeland Productivity (F-166)
Innovative Biological Technologies for Lesser Developed Countries (BP-F-29)
Pest Management Strategies in Crop Protection (F-98)
Pesticide Residues in Food (F-398)
Plants: The Potential for Extracting Protein, Medicines, and Other Useful Chemicals (BP-F-23)
A Review of U.S. Competitiveness in Agriculture Trade (TM-TET-29)
Sustaining Tropical Forest Resources: Reforestation of Degraded Lands (BP-F-18)
Sustaining Tropical Forest Resources: U.S. and International Institutions (BP-F-19)
Technologies To Benefit Agriculture and Wildlife (BP-F-34)
Technologies To Maintain Biological Diversity (F-330)
Technologies To Sustain Tropical Forest Resources (F-214)
Technology and the American Economic Transition (TET-283)
Technology, Public Policy, and the Changing Structure of American Agriculture (F-285)
Technology, Public Policy, and the Changing Structure of American Agriculture: A Special Report for the 1985 Farm Bill (F-272)
Technology, Renewable Resources, and American Crafts (BP-F-27)
Water-Related Technologies for Sustainable Agriculture in U.S. Arid/Semiarid Lands (F-212)
Water-Related Technologies for Sustainable Agriculture in U.S. Arid/Semiarid Lands: Selected Foreign Experience (BP-F-20)
Wetlands: Their Use and Regulation (0-206)
Wood Use: U.S. Competitiveness and Technology (ITE-210)

* Technology Transfer Information Center (TTIC)

National Agriculture Library
Room 1402
10301 Baltimore Blvd.
Beltsville, MS 20705-2351 (301) 504-7098

The TTIC works to convert agriculture related technology and innovations into practical commercial products. Increasing emphasis has been placed on technology transfer in recent years. A 1989 report *Technology Transfer: A Profile of Agency Activities in USDA,* details technology transfer activities in USDA. Several projects are currently underway with respect to wood products. For more information, contact the TTIC.

* Tobacco Inspection

Tobacco Division
U.S. Department of Agriculture
AMS, P.O. Box 96456
Washington, DC 20090-6456 (202) 205-0567

Tobacco sold at auction in designated U.S. markets, along with imported tobacco (except cigar and oriental varieties), are inspected.

* Transportation Services for Agricultural Products

Office of Transportation
U.S. Department of Agriculture
P.O. Box 96575
Washington, DC 20090-6575 (202) 690-1303

This office recognizes that transportation facilities are an integral part of the agribusiness system. Farmers, shippers, farm organizations and local or state agencies who wish to bring about changes in freight service or rates for food products can seek assistance through this office.

* TVA Fertilizer R & D

National Fertilizer and Environmental Development Center
Resource Development
Tennessee Valley Authority (TVA)
Muscle Shoals Reservation
Muscle Shoals, AL 35660 (205) 386-2593

At its National Fertilizer Development Center, TVA operates the world's leading facility for developing new fertilizer technology. Major objectives of this program have been to reduce energy requirements for fertilizer production and increase the efficiency of fertilizer use. Also, emphasis is on an environmental initiative aimed at avoiding an adverse environmental impact from fertilizer production, distribution, and use. Various activities with agricultural colleges and fertilizer industries take place, including model plant compliance demonstrations and educational audiovisuals.

* U.S. Agriculture Department Resources

Information Office
U.S. Department of Agriculture (USDA)
Office of Public Affairs, Room 402-A
Washington, DC 20250 (202) 720-2791

The information staff can help you get the facts you need. USDA also publishes a variety of publications. Some of the general, more helpful ones are:

Fact Book of Agriculture. Published annually, this monograph details the mission of the many USDA agencies, and provides a plethora of information about agriculture in the U.S.

How to Get Information from USDA: Lists sources of information in the USDA agencies.

Your United States Department of Agriculture: Provides some history of the USDA and describes how this huge agency serves farms, local communities, as well as the world agricultural communities.

Report of the Secretary of Agriculture: Published annually, this report gives a summary of progress and initiatives for the policy making agencies in USDA--a great source of "what's new" at the USDA.

* U.S. Department of Agriculture Economic Agencies Reports

Economic Management Staff
U.S. Department of Agriculture (USDA)
1301 New York Avenue, NW (800) 999-6779
Washington, DC 20005 (202) 219-0494

The USDA agricultural economics agencies publish a quarterly catalogue entitled *Reports.* It contains a list of available reports form the Economic Research Service, the National Agricultural Statistics Service, and the World Agricultural Outlook Board. It is available free.

* Water Quality and Natural Resources Education

Executive Officer
Local Extension Service
U.S. Department of Agriculture (USDA)
Room 340A Administration Building
Washington, DC 20250 (202) 720-7947

The USDA operates an extension program in 3,165 counties located in all of the 50 states and the U.S. territories. Federal, state, and local governments share in financing and conducting cooperative extension educational programs to help farmers, processors, handlers, farm families, communities, and consumers apply the results of food and agricultural research, including Conservation and Management of Natural Resources, which helps people benefit from natural ecosystems without destroying them, sustain a productive natural resource base,

Be patient. If any phone number is incorrect, call (area code) 555-1212 and request the new listing.

Agriculture and Farming

market natural resource goods and services, and formulate and implement sound public policies. In the Water Quality program officials work with consumers, producers and local government to teach them more about the importance of high-quality ground water and the conservation of water resources. Emphasis is also put on the effects of agricultural chemicals and contaminants on water quality.

* Water Quality and Preservation

U.S. Department of Agriculture (USDA)
Deputy for Programs, SCS
Box 2890
Washington, DC 20013 (202) 720-4527

The USDA manages a variety of water resource programs to aid landowners and agricultural operators use existing water resources wisely. These programs also promote reclamation and preservation of water sources that have been contaminated or allowed to fall into disrepair. USDA will provide technical and financial assistance for approved projects that meet its criteria.

* Water Quality/Environmental Monitoring

The National Fertilizer and Environmental Center (NFERC)
Agricultural Research Projects
Tennessee Valley Authority
Muscle Shoals Reservation
P.O. Box 1010
Muscle Shoals, AL 35660 (205) 386-2593

The NFERC is currently working to increase awareness of its expertise in environmentally related activities among Congressional staff, administrators of other Federal agencies, such as the EPA, NOAA, and USGS and many other policy makers. NFERC researchers monitor and comment on legislative proposals and reports.

* Water Quality Information Center (WQIC)

National Agricultural Library (NAL), Room 1402
10301 Baltimore Blvd.
Beltsville, MD 20705-2351 (301) 504-6077

The WQIC was established in 1990 as part of the USDA's coordinated plan responding to the President's initiative on water quality. The primary focus of the

Center is on the quality of water resources as they affect or are affected by agricultural production practices. Information from the WQIC is available on the ALF electronic network. Call or write for a publications list. Some of the free bibliographies include:

QB 91-145 Water Quality Implications of Conservation Tillage
QB 91-125 Animal Wastes: Environmental Aspects
QB 91-101 Climate, Fertilizers, and Soil Fertility
QB 91-53 Water Quality and Forestry
QB 91-30 Water Quality in Aquaculture
QB 90-62 Groundwater Contamination

* Wood Pests

Your local Forest Service or
Extension Office, or
Forest Insect and Disease Research
U.S. Department of Agriculture (USDA)
Auditors Building
201 14th Street, SW
Washington, DC 20250 (202) 205-1532

The USDA provides technical assistance for insect and diseases to wood, whether it is in use, stored, wood products, or urban trees. All insect and disease suppression projects must meet specific criteria for federal participation.

* Young, Beginning, and Small Farmers

Farm Credit Administration (FCA)
1501 Farm Credit Drive
McLean, VA 22102 (703) 883-4056

Each Federal Land Bank Association, Production Credit Association, Federal Land Credit Association, and Agricultural Credit Association is required by law, under policies established by each Farm Credit district board, to prepare a program for furnishing sound and constructive credit and related services to young beginning, and small farmers. Specific efforts generally focus on educational efforts and assistance in the extension of credit. Education programs emphasize the need for sound recordkeeping and management practices. Credit program assistance usually involves efforts to coordinate regular loan programs with special assistance from the Federal, State, and local agencies. For information on specific programs, contact the FCA.

Food Quality and Distribution

* *See also Health and Medicine; Food Facts, Nutrition and Diets Chapter*
* *See also Consumer Chapter*

* Beef and Meat Grading and Certification

Meat Grading and Certification Branch
U.S. Department of Agriculture
AMIS, Room 2628-SAG
Washington, DC 20250 (202) 720-1113

All meat is federally inspected on a mandatory basis. All other product grading is voluntary. Grading of meat, poultry, eggs, and dairy products and fresh and processed fruits and vegetables is provided on request for a fee. For further information, contact the appropriate office.

* Child and Adult Care Food Program (CACFP)

Food and Nutrition Service
U.S. Department of Agriculture (USDA)
3101 Park Center Drive
Alexandria, VA 22302 (703) 305-2286

The Child and Adult Care Food Program provides Federal funds and USDA donated foods to nonresidential child care and adult day care facilities to serve nutritious meals and snacks to participants. Federal funds come in the form of reimbursements to participating institutions for meals served under the program. CACFP generally operates in child care centers, outside-school-hours care centers, family day care homes, and certain adult day-care centers. The program spent nearly $1 billion in 1991.

* Cotton, Dairy, Produce, Meat Regulations

Agricultural Marketing Service
U.S. Department of Agriculture
Information Staff, AMS
P.O. Box 96456
Washington, DC 20090-6456 (202) 720-8998

This office regulates the following segments of the agricultural industry: cotton, dairy products, fruits and vegetables, some livestock, poultry, grains, seeds, and also tobacco.

* Crop Yields and Food Research

Beltsville Agricultural Research Center (BARC)
Room 227, Building 003
BARC-W
U.S. Department of Agriculture
Beltsville, MD 20705 (301) 504-6078

BARC is among the largest and most diversified agricultural complexes in the world. About 900 scientists and technicians who specialize in a wide variety of research projects, have a long list of accomplishments to their credit. Animal researchers study livestock diseases, animal nutritional needs, and animal genetics and physiology. Plant specialists seek greater crop yields by breeding plants that use light and nutrients more efficiently. Broad research topics include animals, insects, plants, soil, air water, human nutrition, and family resources.

* Dairy Products Grading and Inspection

Dairy Grading Branch
Dairy Division, Room 2750-SAG
U.S. Department of Agriculture
Washington, DC 20250 (202) 720-3171

All eggs (liquid or frozen) are federally inspected on a mandatory basis. All other product grading is voluntary. Grading of meat, poultry, eggs, and dairy products and fresh and processed fruits and vegetables is provided on request for a fee. For further information, contact the appropriate office.

* Egg Products Inspection

Agricultural Marketing Service (AMS)
Food Safety and Inspection Service

U.S. Department of Agriculture
Room 1160, South Agriculture
Washington, DC 20250 (202) 720-9113

Under the Egg Products Inspection Act, the AMS provides continuous mandatory inspection in all plants processing liquid, dried, or frozen egg products. In 1989, the AMS inspected some 1.6 billion pounds of liquid, frozen, and dried egg products in 83 processing plants.

* Emergency Relief and Excess Food

Commodity Operations Division
U.S. Department of Agriculture
ASCS, Room 5755
South Building
Washington, DC 20250 (202) 720-5074

The Commodity Credit Corporation buys, stores, and distributes such commodities as dry milk, wheat, rice, and corn, which are acquired through price support programs. The commodities are sent overseas as donations, distributed to domestic food programs, or given to relief agencies in times of emergencies.

* Emergency Food Assistance Program

Food and Nutrition Service
U.S. Department of Agriculture (USDA)
3101 Park Center Drive
Alexandria, VA 22302 (703) 305-2286

This program gives needy Americans, including low income and unemployed persons, USDA donated foods for household use. The program has donated millions of pounds of food bought under USDA programs designed to support agriculture prices.

* Food and Nutrition Information Center

Food and Nutrition Service
U.S. Department of Agriculture
10301 Baltimore Blvd.
Beltsville, MD 20705 (301) 504-5719

This center acquires books, journal articles, and audiovisual materials pertaining to human nutrition, food service management, and food science. Items in the FNIC collection are listed in AGRICOLA, NAL's computerized bibliographic database, which can be accessed through Dialog (800-3-DIALOG) or BRS (800-345-4BRS). FNIC also has a unique demonstration center for food and nutrition microcomputer software. The extensive collection of dietary analysis, nutrition education, and food service programs is available for on-site review by appointment only. The FNIC produces a series of pamphlets and bibliographies called Nutritopics. Most publications are free. Quick Bibliographies include:

QB 90-59 *Childhood Obesity and Cardiovascular Disease*
QB 91-100 *Infant Nutrition*
QB 91-34 *Nutrient Composition of Selected Grains as Food*
SRB 91-07 *Nutrition and AIDS*

Contact the FNIC for a full list of publications. Any four can be ordered free at one time.

* Food Distribution Process Studies

Commodities Scientific Support Division
AMS, Box 96456
U.S. Department of Agriculture
Washington, DC 20090-6456 (202) 720-5231

Studies are available on a wide variety of markets covering all aspects of the distribution process: wholesaling, packaging, transportation, and more. For a listing of studies available, contact the above office.

Be patient. If any phone number is incorrect, call (area code) 555-1212 and request the new listing.

Agriculture and Farming

* Food Inspection and Official Standards

Food Safety and Inspection Service (FSIS)
U.S. Department of Agriculture
Information Division, Room 1160 SAG
Washington, DC 20250 (202) 720-9113

This office inspects all meats, poultry, and egg products shipped interstate and abroad, and ensures that labels on these products are truthful. Food inspection is mandatory for the following animals and birds used for human food: cattle, calves, swine, goats, sheep and lambs, horses, chickens, turkeys, ducks, geese and guineas. FSIS tests product samples for microbial or chemical contaminants. They also develop official grade standards for meat, poultry, eggs, dairy products, and fresh and processed fruits and vegetables.

* Food Irradiation Safety

Food Irradiation
U.S. Department of Agriculture
10301 Baltimore Blvd.
Beltsville, MD 20705 (301) 504-5719

This center covers the use of ionizing radiation to process foods. Print and audio-visual aids are available in food science, nutrition, safety and wholesomeness, labeling, economics, and other subjects.

* Food Nutrition Service Programs

U.S. Department of Agriculture (USDA)
Food and Nutrition Service
3101 Park Center Drive, Room 502
Alexandria, VA 22302 (703) 305-2680

The USDA Food and Nutrition Service coordinates a variety of programs to get food to those in need. Special Nutrition Programs aim at improving children's nutrition through school breakfast and lunch programs. The Special Supplemental Food Program for Women, Infants, and Children provides specified nutritious food supplements to and nutrition education for pregnant women, nursing women up to 12 months postpartum, non-nursing women up to 6 months postpartum, and children up to 5 years old.

* Food Poisoning or Improper Packaging

Food Safety and Inspection Service
U.S. Department of Agriculture
Washington, DC 20250 (800) 535-4555

This service takes calls from consumers on cases of meat or poultry food poisoning or complaints about meat or poultry spoilage due to improper packaging or processing. They can also provide you with health-oriented information on safe handling and storage of meats and poultry.

* Food Safety and Supply

Western Regional Research Center
U.S. Department of Agriculture
ARS, 800 Buchanan St.
Albany, CA 94710 (510) 559-6082

Research here is generally focused on food problems. Scientists try to increase agricultural productivity through preventing loss and ensuring safety of the food supply and improving market quality of agricultural products. They also have a program to find new means to convert agricultural materials to value-added food and nonfood products.

* Food Safety Research

Eastern Regional Research Center (ERRC)
600 East Mermaid Lane
Philadelphia, PA 19118 (215) 233-6400

The ERRC conducts research to enhance food safety. Their research objectives are: to investigate the chemical and physical parameters that influence the formation of potentially carcinogenic components in foods, particularly cured meats and to develop means for their reduction or elimination; develop methodologies capable of identifying meats and poultry that have been subjected to low dose ionizing radiation; and to investigate the efficacy and safety of ionizing radiation treatments of fresh and processed meats and poultry to improve microbiological safety and shelflife of products while preserving vitamin content. Another ERRC unit carries out microbiological research on eliminating harmful food bacteria.

* Foreign Food Assistance - PL 480

Commodity Credit Corporation
U.S. Department of Agriculture
PO Box 2415
Washington, DC 20013 (202) 720-5237

Under the Agriculture Trade Development and Assistance Act of 1954, PL 480, as amended, the Commodity Credit Corporation (CCC) carries out assigned foreign assistance activities, such as the guaranteeing of U.S. agricultural commodities abroad. Major emphasis is also being directed toward meeting the needs of developing nations. The Corporation also encourages U.S. financial institutions to provide financing to developing nations under the Export Credit Guarantee Programs.

* Free Food For Non-Profit Institutions

Food Distribution Program
Food and Nutrition Service
U.S. Department of Agriculture (USDA)
3101 Park Center Dr., Room 502
Alexandria, VA 22302 (703) 305-2680

Charitable and rehabilitation institutions are usually eligible to receive surplus commodities stored by USDA. The commodities available are dairy products, grain oil, and peanuts.

* Grading and Inspecting Poultry

Poultry Grading Branch
AMS Poultry Division
U.S. Department of Agriculture
Room 3938, South Building
Washington, DC 20250 (202) 720-3272

All poultry are federally inspected on a mandatory basis. Tobacco sold at auction in designated U.S. markets, along with imported tobacco (except cigar and oriental varieties), are also inspected. All other product grading is voluntary. Grading of meat, poultry, eggs, and dairy products and fresh and processed fruits and vegetables is provided on request for a fee. For further information, contact the appropriate office.

* Grading Food Products

Agricultural Marketing Service
U.S. Department of Agriculture (USDA)
Room 3510, South Building
Washington, DC 20250 (202) 720-8998

USDA provides producers, packers, processors, shippers, wholesalers, and consumers with official certification of the quality of food and farm products to aid in establishing a market value for the product. For most commodities a fee is charged to cover the cost of the service, and the service may be conducted during packing or processing or at supply depots. The official grading or inspection certificate is accepted as prima facie evidence in court.

* Grain Inspection

Administrator, Federal Grain Inspection Service
U.S. Department of Agriculture
Room 1094 South Building
Washington, DC 20250 (202) 720-0219

This office establishes federal standards for grain and performs inspections to ensure compliance. They also regulate the weighing of all grain for export.

* Indian Reservation Food Distribution

Food and Nutrition Service (FNS)
U.S. Department of Agriculture
3101 Park Center Drive
Alexandria, VA 22302 (703) 305-2286

This program provides monthly food packages to Indians living on or near a reservation. While the program is administered Federally by the FNS, state agencies are responsible for all aspects of the programs operation.

* Livestock Health and Safety

Packers and Stockyards Administration
U.S. Department of Agriculture
Room 3408 South Building

Food Quality and Distribution

Washington, DC 20250 (202) 720-3128

This office regulates trade practices of businesses involved in marketing livestock, meat, and poultry.

* Meat and Poultry Hotline

Food Safety and Inspection Service
U.S. Department of Agriculture
Washington, DC 20250 (800) 535-4555

This service takes calls from consumers on cases of meat or poultry food poisoning or complaints about meat or poultry spoilage due to improper packaging or processing. They can also provide you with health-oriented information on safe handling and storage of meats and poultry.

* Milk Order Marketing Program

Market Information Branch
Dairy Division
Agricultural Marketing Service (AMS)
PO Box 96456
Washington, DC 20090-6456 (202) 720-7461

Federal milk orders define the terms under which handlers of milk in a specified market purchase milk from dairy farmers. They are legal instruments designed to promote orderly market conditions. Orders assist farmers in developing steady, dependable markets and help correct conditions of price instability and needless fluctuations in price. More information is available from the AMS, which can also provide you with the publications: The Federal Milk Marketing Order Program; The Market News; Federal Milk Order Statistics; Questions and Answers On Federal Milk Marketing Orders; and Daily Market News ($30 per year). Recorded phone messages on the program are available as follows:

Chicago (708) 858-8188
Madison, WI (608) 266-0706
Minneapolis (612) 725-3641
New York (212) 687-8078
Seattle (206) 282-3974

* Milk Research

Eastern Regional Research Center
600 East Mermaid Lane
Philadelphia, PA 19118 (215) 233-6400

Biochemical, microbial, and chemical technology research is conducted in critical areas of milk processing and utilization. Results of basic and applied studies are used to develop the science, technology and knowledge needed to improve food quality, processing, and storage.

* Nutritional Labeling

Meat and Poultry Standards and Labeling Division
Federal Safety and Inspection Service (FSIS)
U.S. Department of Agriculture (USDA)
Room 1165, South Building
Washington, DC 20250 (202) 205-0042

A number of labeling regulations apply across-the-board to all meat and poultry products. These include: appropriate product name; ingredients listed from most to least; net quantity of package contents; name and address of the manufacturer; USDA mark of inspection. The FSIS can provide you with a brochure entitled *Meat and Poultry Products: A Consumer Guide to Content and Labeling Requirements* which details requirements for meat and poultry products labels.

* Packers and Stockyards Program

Packers and Stockyards Administration
U.S. Department of Agriculture (USDA)
Room 3039, South Agriculture
Washington, DC 20250 (202) 720-7051

The USDA's packers and stockyards specialists work with private producers and trade organizations to investigate complaints and file any complaint on violations of fair and open competition in the marketing of livestock.

* Perishable Agricultural Commodities

PACA Branch
Agricultural Marketing Service
U.S. Department of Agriculture

Room 2095, South Agriculture
Washington, DC 20250 (202) 720-2272

The USDA's Agricultural Marketing Service (AMS) prohibits unfair trading practices among buyers and sellers of perishable items. The AMS will provide advice on your rights and responsibilities and try to bring disputing parties together for informal settlements.

* Pick Your Own Fruits and Vegetables

Contact your local U.S. Department of Agriculture
Extension Service agent

Many farmers allow consumers to pick produce directly from their fields at substantial savings.

* Processed Fruits and Vegetables Inspection

Processed Products Branch
Fruit and Vegetable Division, AMS
U.S. Department of Agriculture
Box 96456
Washington, DC 20090-6456 (202) 720-4693

Grading of meat, poultry, eggs, and dairy products and fresh and processed fruits and vegetables is provided on request for a fee. For further information, contact this office.

* Protection From Animal Pests and Diseases

Animal and Plant Health Inspection Service
Veterinary Services
U.S. Department of Agriculture
6505 Belcrest Rd.
Hyattsville, MD 20782 (202) 436-8093

For control or eradication of livestock/poultry pest or disease, a state government or industry can receive cooperation from the federal government to establish quarantines, vaccination procedures, and destruction of diseased or exposed animals.

* Quality Control Regulations

Marketing Order Administration Branch
U.S. Department of Agriculture
Room 2525, South Agriculture
Washington, DC 20250 (202) 720-2491

This office administers programs that give growers the authority to work together to develop dependable markets for their products. Methods used include establishing minimum quality standards to keep inferior products from depressing markets for an entire crop, research and promotion projects to improve production, and volume controls to stabilize the short-term rate of commodity shipments.

* Residue Testing in Meat and Poultry

Food Safety and Inspection Service (FSIS)
U.S. Department of Agriculture
Room 4436, South Building
Washington, DC 20250 (202) 720-3311

The FSIS runs a National Residue Program designed to detect illegal or potentially harmful levels of residues on meat and poultry. Each year the FSIS collects about 1.5 million test results on 450,000 meat and poultry samples from U.S. plants. Call or write for more information on the program.

* Salmonella and Food Safety

Food Safety and Inspection Service
U.S. Department of Agriculture
Room 1160 South Building
Washington, DC 20250 (202) 720-9113

After 20 years of research, it is still impossible to economically produce "salmonella free" raw meat and poultry. Routine food safety practices can destroy salmonella and other bacteria. The FSIS produces a background information sheet on safe handling of meat and poultry to prevent food borne illness.

* Seed Quality and Inspection Labs

Federal Seed Lab

Be patient. If any phone number is incorrect, call (area code) 555-1212 and request the new listing.

Agriculture and Farming

U.S. Department of Agriculture
Beltsville, MD 20705 (301) 504-8089

The federal government can test seeds to determine their quality and whether they are free from contamination. They will also prosecute any agent that transfers contaminated or mislabeled seed from state to state. Seeds are examined by or at a state agent's request, and there may be some fee involved.

* Summer Food Service Program

Food and Nutrition Service
U.S. Department of Agriculture
3101 Park Center Drive
Alexandria, VA 22302 (703) 305-2286

The Summer Food Service Program funds meals and snacks for children in needy areas when school is not in session. In local areas, the program is operated by local sponsors, which receive reimbursement from USDA. Sponsorship is limited to public or private nonprofit school food authorities; state, local, or municipal county governments; public or private non-profit colleges and universities that are operating the National Youth Sports Program; public or private non-profit residential summer camps; and private non-profit organizations that operate special summer or school vacation programs.

* Technology Assessment Reports

Office of Technology Assessment (OTA)
Publications Order
U.S. Congress
Washington, DC 20510-8025 (202) 224-8996

These OTA publications are available through the office above, the Government Printing Office, and the National Technical Information Service. To find out correct ordering information and prices, along with brief summaries of the following studies, contact the OTA office above and request their current publications catalog.

Food Information Systems (F-35)
Nutrition Research Alternatives (F-74)
Open Shelf-Life Dating of Food (F-94)
Organizing and Financing Basic Research To Increase Food Production (F-49)
Perspectives on Federal Retail Food Grading (F-47)
Pesticide Residues in Food (F-398)

* Transportation Food Containers

Office of Transportation
Director, International Division
U.S. Department of Agriculture
P.O. Box 96575
Washington, DC 20090-6575 (202) 653-6275

This office regulates the standards for manufacture of container equipment used to move agricultural products between the U.S. and foreign countries.

* Transportation and Marketing Division

U.S. Department of Agriculture
Agricultural Marketing Service (AMS)
PO Box 96456
Washington, DC 20090-6456 (202) 690-1300

On January 1, 1991 USDA's office of Transportation was incorporated into the AMS to improve coordination of transportation and marketing policies. TMD conducts economic and analyses of domestic and international transportation systems and represents agriculture and rural transportation interests in policy and regulatory forums. TMD also conducts research in cooperation with industry on packaging and refrigeration transport for perishables.

* Volume Food Buyers

Agricultural Marketing Service
U.S. Department of Agriculture (USDA)

Room 3943
South Agriculture
Washington, DC 20250 Poultry Division: (202) 720-7693

USDA specialists work with volume food buyers in developing specifications for food commodities using specifications, grades, and standards that have been developed by USDA for this purpose. Graders examine food and certify the food buyers' purchases prior to delivery. Any processor, wholesaler, retailer, hospital, restaurant, governmental agency, educational institution, airline, or other public or private group buying food in large quantities may ask USDA for their inspection services by contacting this office. Fruit/Vegetable division (202) 720-6391; Livestock (202) 720-2650; general program information (202) 720-8998.

* Wholesale Food Distribution

Marketing Facilities Branch
U.S. Department of Agriculture
AMS, Room 2649-S
Box 96456
Washington, DC 20090-6456 (202) 720-8317

This office performs general research aimed at getting food on the table more cheaply by working with wholesale food distribution facilities and farmers markets to reduce the price spread between what the farmer gets for his products and what the consumer pays.

* Wholesalers and Volume Food Buyers

Special Inspection Services
Agricultural Marketing Service
U.S. Department of Agriculture (USDA)
Washington, DC 20250 Dairy Products: (202) 720-3171

USDA specialists work with volume food buyers in developing specifications for food commodities using specifications, grades, and standards that have been developed by USDA for this purpose. Graders examine food and certify the food buyers' purchases prior to delivery. Any processor, wholesaler, retailer, hospital, restaurant, governmental agency, educational institution, airline, or other public or private group buying food in large quantities may ask USDA for their inspection services by contacting this office.

Fruits and Vegetables Fresh: . . . . (202) 720-5870
Fruits and Vegetables Processed: . . . . (202) 720-4693
Meat: . . . . (202) 720-1116
Poultry Division: . . . . (202) 720-7693

* Women, Infants and Children Food Program (WIC)

Food and Nutrition Service
U.S. Department of Agriculture
3101 Park Center Drive
Alexandria, VA 22302 (703) 305-2286

The WIC program provides supplemental foods, plus health care referrals and nutrition education at no cost to low-income pregnant breastfeeding and nonbreastfeeding postpartum women, infants, and young children up to 5 years of age who are found to be at nutritional risk. To be eligible, persons must: meet a state residency requirement; meet an income standard or participate in Aid to Families with Dependent Children Program, the Food Stamp Program, or Medicaid; and be individually determined to be at risk by a health professional.

* World Food Donations

Agency for International Development
Bureau of Food and Humanitarian Assistance
State Annex #8
Washington, DC 20523 (202) 875-4901

By working with groups like CARE and the World Food Program, the Food For Peace program helps needy people abroad by sending food and other agricultural commodities.

Be patient. If any phone number is incorrect, call (area code) 555-1212 and request the new listing.

Trade and Marketing

* *See also the International Trade Chapter*
* *See also the Experts Chapter*

* Agricultural Analyses and Forecasts

Economic Research Service and
National Agricultural Statistical Service
U.S. Department of Agriculture
Box 1608
Rockville, MD 20850

(800) 999-6779
(202) 720-7017

Several publications are available which provide information about the world trade situation. *Situation and Outlook Reports* provide analyses and forecasts of all major agricultural commodities and such related topics as finance, farm inputs, land values, and world regional developments (each year and are available in one-year ($10), two-year $19 or three-year $27 subscriptions); *Agricultural Statistics Reports* estimate production, stocks, inventories, disposition, utilization, and prices of about 40 agricultural commodities and other items such as labor and farm numbers; *The Journal of Agricultural Economics Research* his journal covers technical research in agricultural economics, including econometric models and statistics focusing on methods employed and results of U.S. Department of Agriculture economic research ($7/year; two years: $13, and three years: $18).

* Agricultural/Food Trade Policy

Bureau of Economic and Business Affairs
U.S. Department of State
2201 C St., NW, Room 3526
Washington, DC 20520
(202) 647-3090

This office handles agricultural trade issues and agreements, including the General Agreement on Tariffs and Trade (GATT) negotiations. Besides monitoring such food commodities as coffee, cocoa and jute, this office also is responsible for foreign policy aspects of food aid and shipment, and acts as liaison with the U.S. Department of Agriculture.

* Agricultural Import Quotas

Foreign Agricultural Service
Import Policies and Trade Analysis
U.S. Department of Agriculture
Room 5533 South Building
Washington, DC 20250
(202) 720-2916

This office regulates the imports of beef, dairy products, and other commodities by administering quotas imposed by the President.

* Agricultural Industry Investigations

Office of Investigations
U.S. International Trade Commission (ITC)
500 E St., SW, Room 615
Washington, DC 20436
(202) 205-3160

This office coordinates the ITC's investigations involving antidumping, reviews, escape-clause and market disruptions, and determinations of whether imports of agricultural products are interfering with programs of the U.S. Department of Agriculture. For more information regarding these investigations, contact this office.

* Agricultural Marketing Service (AMS)

U.S. Department of Agriculture (USDA)
P.O. Box 96456
Washington, DC 20090-6456
(202) 720-1238

The Agricultural Marketing Service is the focal point for a variety of marketing programs operated by the USDA. The free publication *This is the AMS* provides a good overview of AMS programs.

* Agricultural Trade and Marketing

Agricultural Trade and Marketing
U.S. Department of Agriculture
10301 Baltimore Blvd.
Beltsville, MD 20705
(301) 504-5704

This center covers agricultural trade and marketing, trade policies, barriers, trade agreements and negotiations, agricultural domestic policy and international trade, and many other trade-related matters. Staff can also answer questions relating to the economics of urbanization and urban policies in developing countries.

* Agriculture Exports Clearinghouse

Information Division
Foreign Agricultural Service
U.S. Department of Agriculture
5074 South Building
Washington, DC 20250
(202) 720-9330

For supply and demand information of agricultural products in other countries, contact the above office.

* Animal and Pet Import and Export Restrictions

Import--Export Staff Veterinary Services
APHIS/U.S. Department of Agriculture (USDA)
6505 Belcrest Rd., Room 765
Hyattsville, MD 20782
(301) 436-5785

The USDA will provide certification to exporters or importers of animals and animal products, or pet birds to prevent the introduction of agricultural pests and diseases from foreign countries into the U.S. and to aid exporters meeting foreign importers standards.

* Attache Educational Program (AEP)

Trade Assistance and Planning Office
Foreign Agricultural Service
U.S. Department of Agriculture (USDA)
3001 Park Center Drive, Room 1103
Alexandria, VA 22302
(703) 305-2771

The AEP enables U.S. agricultural producers and exporters to benefit from the experience of USDA agricultural counselors and trade officers who have recently returned from overseas posting. These officers are available to make presentations, participate in panel discussions and provide one-on-one export counseling. Groups eligible to participate in the AEP include international trade development centers; land grant and historically black colleges and universities; state wide, regional, and national farm organizations; and State departments of agriculture.

* Commodities Programs

Agricultural Stabilization and Conservation Service (ASCS)
U.S. Department of Agriculture
Room 3608, South Agriculture
Washington, DC 20250
(202) 720-6778

The ASCS administers the Commodity Credit Corporation's (CCC) commodity stabilization programs for wheat, corn, cotton, seed cotton, soybeans, peanuts, rice, tobacco, milk, wool, mohair, barley, oats, sugarbeets, sugarcane, grain sorghum, rye and honey. For most commodities, loans are made directly to producers on the unprocessed commodity through the ASCS's county offices. If market prices rise above loan levels, producers or their agents can pay off their loans and market their commodities. If market prices fail to rise above loan levels, producers or their agents ca forfeit or deliver the commodity to the CCC, thereby discharging their obligations in full.

Be patient. If any phone number is incorrect, call (area code) 555-1212 and request the new listing.

Agriculture and Farming

* Commodity Reports

Reports Officer - Foreign Agricultural Service (FAS)
U.S. Department of Agriculture (USDA)
Room 6078, South Building
Washington, DC 20250-1000 (202) 720-8924

Commodities reports by USDA officers posted overseas are available to the public at cost. The current subscription program is done by commodity only. Major commodities have weekly reports while other commodities are less frequent. Call FAS for a list of commodity reports, prices, and frequency of publication.

* Dairy Export Incentive Program

Commodity Credit Corporation
Operations Division
U.S. Department of Agriculture (USDA)
Room 4503, South Building
Washington, DC 20250-1000 (202) 720-9150

The Dairy Export Incentive Program (DEIP) enables U.S. exporters to meet prevailing world prices for targeted dairy products and destinations. Under the program, the USDA pays cash to exporters as bonuses, allowing them to sell certain dairy products in targeting countries at prices below the exporters cost of acquiring them. The program is designed to help U.S. farmers meet subsidized competition and also to demonstrate the quality of U.S. products. Milk powder, butterfat, and Cheddar Cheese are currently eligible for inclusion in DEIP. Contact the FAS for information on qualifications for participating in the program.

* Electronic Export Data Available

Special Programs Division
U.S. Department of Agriculture (USDA)
Office of Information
Room 536-A
Washington, DC 20250 (202) 720-5505

Daily, weekly, and monthly reports showing foreign trade opportunities, exports to major markets, highlights of trade and production, import/export prices, and policy developments are available electronically through USDA's Electronic Dissemination of Information (EDI) systems.

* Expert Export Assistance

FAS Coordinator
U.S. Department of Agriculture (USDA)
Room 4951 South Building
Washington, DC 20050 (202) 720-7103

The USDA's Foreign Agricultural Service offers private companies and cooperatives assistance in marketing their products overseas. The Agricultural Information and Marketing Service (AIMS), for example, provides foreign trade opportunities and contacts to U.S. food and agricultural businesses by collecting and publicizing information on foreign buyers and advertising U.S. export availability. The export marketing services offered include Trade Leads, Buyer Alert, Foreign Buyer Lists, and U.S. Supplier Lists. This material is available in print or through various computer information suppliers, for a charge, depending on the information you request.

* Export Assistance Programs

Foreign Agricultural Service
U.S. Department of Agriculture (USDA)
Room 4503, South Agriculture
Washington, DC 20250 (202) 720-5540

Several export assistance programs are designed to counter or offset the adverse effects from competitors unfair trade practices on U.S. agriculture. These programs include the Export Enhancement Program (EEP), the Dairy Export Incentive Program (DEIP), the Sunflowerseed Oil Assistance Program (SOAP), and the Cottonseed Oil Assistance Program (COAP). Contact the USDA for information on these programs. Also ask for a copy of the *Agricultural Export Assistance Quarterly Report*, which describes all the current U.S. export assistance programs.

* Export Credit Guarantees

Commodity Credit Corporation
Operations Division
U.S. Department of Agriculture (USDA)

Washington, DC 20250-1000 (202) 720-6211

This program encourages the development or expansion of overseas markets for U.S. agricultural commodities by providing guarantees on private financing of U.S. exports to foreign buyers purchasing on credit terms. The guarantees ensure that the exporter or banks will be repaid in the event the foreign purchaser breaks their promise to pay for the goods. The USDA programs differ in their length of the credit periods they cover. The Export Credit Guarantee Program (GSM 102) covers loans with credit terms of six months to three years. This program issued some $4 billion in guarantees in 1990. The Intermediate Export Credit Guarantee Program (GSM 103) promotes exports on a longer term basis. The CCC considers coverage on sales of any U.S. agricultural commodity that has the potential of expanding U.S. export markets. A U.S. exporter, foreign buyer, or foreign government may submit requests that may result in authorized guarantee coverage.

* Export Publications and Manuals

FAS Information Services
Room 5922
U.S. Department of Agriculture (USDA)
Washington, DC 20250 (202) 720-7937

The Foreign Agricultural Service (FAS) issues various reports and publications each year based on information from agricultural attaches and counselors stationed around the world.

AgExporter: This monthly magazine features articles which analyze conditions affecting trade and highlighting market development and export promotion. $14 U.S., $17 foreign.

World Agricultural Production Report: Monthly report of USDA production estimates for grain, cotton, and oilseeds in major countries and selected regions of the world. $29 domestic.

Agricultural Trade Offices: One-Stop Service Overseas. Directory of U.S. agricultural trade offices and what they do to assist exporters of U.S. food and agricultural products. Free.

U.S. Farmer's Export Arm: Describes the services of the FAS. Free.

Partners in Trade Promotion: Directory and description of the FAS market development cooperator program. Free.

Agriculture's Emissaries Overseas: Directory and description of agricultural counselor/attache offices overseas. Free.

Food and Agricultural Export Directory: Listing of export services and key contacts in the export business. Free.

U. S. Export Sales: Weekly report that summarizes sales and exports of selected U.S. agricultural commodities by country bases on reports from private exporters. Free. For more information call (202) 720-9212.

Free brochures also are available on such topics as FAS agricultural trade offices and attaches abroad, export financing, Public Law 480, technical requirements for export products, and the FAS market development program.

* Farm Export Information Round-the-Clock

Information Division
U.S. Department of Agriculture (USDA)
Room 5074, FAS
Washington, DC 20250 (202) 720-3448

News reports announcing agreements and allocations for farm exports are available by facsimile. Also, 24-hour information is available on export credit guarantee activities and on Export Enhancement Program (EEP) news. The Weekly Roundup of World Production and Trade offers current news items and trade statistics on various commodities, along with a summary of recent developments in world production and trade.

* Export Opportunities For Small and Minority Businesses

Minority and Small Business Program
U.S. Department of Agriculture (USDA)
Park Office Center
3101 Park Center Drive

Trade and Marketing

Alexandria, VA 22302 (703) 305-2771

This program provides small and minority companies with a broad range of support services and assistance in selling their products overseas.

* Farm Imports and Exports

ERS/NASS
U.S. Department of Agriculture (USDA)
Box 1608 (800) 999-6779
Rockville, MD 20850 (202) 720-7017

Foreign Agricultural Trade of the United States updates the quantity and value of U.S. farm exports and imports, plus price trends. Subscriptions for one year cost $20, two years $39, and three years $57.

* Federal Milk Order Programs

U.S. Department of Agriculture (USDA)
Agricultural Marketing Service
Dairy Division
Room 2753, South Agriculture
Washington, DC 20250 (202) 720-7461

The Federal Milk Order Program sets the prices that producers of milk receive when selling to milk processors. This division collects monthly statistics on prices, numbers of producers, quantities of milk sold, and its final end use. The division also oversees the national dairy promotion and research program, dairy inspection programs, and standards programs with respect to the content of butter and cheese.

* Import Interference With Agricultural Programs

The Office of Investigations
U.S. International Trade Commission (ITC)
500 E St., SW, Room 615
Washington, DC 20436 (202) 205-3160

At the direction of the U.S. President, the ITC conducts investigations to determine whether any articles are being or are about to be imported into the U.S. under such conditions and in such quantities as to have a negative effect on the U.S. Department of Agriculture's programs for agricultural commodities or products. If investigation find that import interference exists, the U.S. President may decide to restrict the imports in question by imposing either import fees or quotas.

* International Trade Shows

High Value Products Division, FAS
U.S. Department of Agriculture (USDA)
Room 4951-S
Washington, DC 20250-1000 (202) 720-7103

The USDA offers a cost-effective service for U.S. firms to explore foreign markets. FAS organizes national pavilions in major international food shows throughout the world. Participation includes individual booths, lounge, advance public relations work, product shipment, and customs clearance for the show. Copies of the current trade show calendar are available.

* Livestock, Meat and Wool Market Reports

Agricultural Marketing Service (AMS)
Livestock and Grain Market News
U.S. Department of Agriculture (USDA)
Room 2623, South Building
PO Box 96456
Washington, DC 20090-6456 (202) 720-6231

The AMS produces a variety of commodity reports, covering the latest prices and other important information from regional markets around the country. The following reports are available for a fee:

National Carlot Meat Trade Report - Daily
Livestock, Meat and Wool - Weekly
Georgia Livestock - Weekly
California Livestock - Weekly
National Wool Market Review - 33 issues
Grain, Feed and Market News - Weekly
Pacific Northwest Grain Market News - Weekly
Pacific Northwest Feed Market News - Weekly
Hay Market News - Weekly
Rice Market News - Weekly

Bean Market News - Weekly and Annual National
Molasses Market News - Weekly and Annual National
Hops Market News - Monthly
Grain Stocks Report - Weekly
Durum Wheat Reports - Quarterly

Call for current prices. Also request a free copy of *The Market News Services*, which lists numbers in each state for dairy updates and livestock information and grain market information.

* Mandated Dairy Sales Program

Commodity Credit Corporation (CCC)
Operations Division
U.S. Department of Agriculture (USDA)
Room 4503, South Building
Washington, DC 20250-1000 (202) 720-9150

This program requires that in each of the fiscal years 1990 through 1995 the Commodity Credit Corporation export not less than 150,000 metric tons of CCC owned dairy products. These sales cannot disrupt domestic US markets or world prices and patterns of commercial trade.

* Market News

Agricultural Marketing Service (AMS)
U.S. Department of Agriculture (USDA)
Room 3510, South Agriculture
Washington, DC 20250 (202) 720-8998

The Federal-State Market News Service, carried out by USDA's AMS in cooperation with 41 state agencies, US AID, and Agriculture Canada, reports up to the minute information on prices, supply, and demand for most agricultural commodities. The reports cover buying and selling of these commodity groupings: cotton and cottonseed; domestic fruits and vegetables, including truck rates; floral products and specialty crops; livestock, meat, poultry, eggs, grain, hay, feeds and wool; dairy products and tobacco.

* Market Promotion Program (MPP)

Foreign Agricultural Service
Marketing Operations Staff
U.S. Department of Agriculture (USDA)
Washington, DC 20250 (202) 720-4327

The Market Promotion Program is designed to increase US exports of farm commodities and value added agricultural commodities. Under the MPP, funds from the Commodity Credit Corporation (some $200 million annually) are used to partially reimburse program participants conducting specific foreign market development projects for eligible products in specified countries. Contact the program for information on products and participants in the program.

* Market Prospects Overseas

Information Division
FAS, U.S. Department of Agriculture (USDA)
Room 5922-S
Washington, DC 20250-1000 (202) 720-7937

A series of background publications describing market prospects for U.S. food and farm products in many countries is available from this office.

* Marketing Regulations

Agricultural Marketing Service (AMS)
U.S. Department of Agriculture (USDA)
Room 3529, South Agriculture
Washington, DC 20250 (202) 720-6766

The AMS administers and enforces regulatory laws with respect to marketing. Farmers can file complaints under the Agricultural Fair Practices Act if processors refuse to deal with them because they are members of a producer's bargaining or marketing association.

* Plant Import and Export Restrictions

Plant Protection Quarantine Unit
Room 632, APHIS
U.S. Department of Agriculture (USDA)
6505 Belcrest Rd.
Hyattsville, MD 20782 (301) 436-8295

Be patient. If any phone number is incorrect, call (area code) 555-1212 and request the new listing.

Agriculture and Farming

The USDA will provide certification to exporters or importers of plants and plant products as well as animals and animal products, or pet birds to prevent the introduction of agricultural pests and diseases from foreign countries into the U.S. and to aid exporters meeting foreign importers standards.

* Sunflower and Cottonseed Oil Assistance Programs

Commodity Credit Corporation
Operations Division
U.S. Department of Agriculture (USDA)
Room 45255, South Building
Washington, DC 20250-1000 (202) 720-5540

The Sunflowerseed Oil Assistance Program (SOAP) and the Cottonseed Oil Assistance Program (COAP) are designed to help US exporters meet prevailing world prices for sunflowerseed oil and cottonseed oil in targeted markets. Under the programs, the USDA pays cash to US exporters as bonuses, making up the difference between the higher US cost and lower world market price. Contact the FAS for information on eligibility for participating in the program.

* Tobacco Markets

Agricultural Marketing Service (AMS)
Tobacco Division
Room 502 - Annex Building
PO Box 96456
Washington, DC 20090-6456 (202) 205-0489

The Agricultural Marketing Service Tobacco division issues annual reports on tobacco stocks, and the tobacco market for different grades of tobacco produced. A publications list is also available.

* Trade Assistance

Trade Assistance and Planning Office (TAPO)
Foreign Agricultural Service
U.S. Department of Agriculture (USDA)
3101 Park Center Dr., Suite 1103
Alexandria, VA 22302 (703) 756-6001

The Trade Assistance and Planning Office of the FAS was established by the Omnibus Trade and Competitiveness Act of 1988. It provides a single point of contact within the FAS for agriculture exporters who need information and export assistance as well as those who believe they have been injured by unfair trade practices. The following products can be ordered from TAPO:

- *Agricultural Trade Assistance Folder*
- *Agexport Action Kit*
- *Trade Policies and Market Opportunities for U.S. Farm Products*
- *U.S. Agricultural Trade Goals and Strategies.*
- *U.S. legislation Counters Unfair Foreign Trade Practices*
- *Section 301: Protecting U.S. Trade Rights*
- *The GATT and What It Means for U.S. Agriculture*
- *Working Toward a North American Free Trade Area*
- *Status of Assistance to the Former Soviet Union*
-- Also available are marketing prospecti for some 16 countries.

* Trade Development Centers for Agriculture

Cooperative State Research Service
U.S. Department of Agriculture (USDA)
Suite 329, Aerospace Center
Washington, DC 20250-2200 (202) 401-4555

The Federation of International Trade Development Centers assists firms and individuals in expanding exports of U.S. produced agricultural, aquacultural, and forest products. The centers are affiliated with universities located in 12 states. Outreach activities available consist of training and assistance on the mechanics of exporting, trade statistics, trade lead information, and the characteristics of export markets. Promotional advice and services are available from several centers. Centers are located in the following states: Washington, North Dakota, Kentucky, Kansas, Iowa, West Virginia, Oklahoma, Oregon, Idaho, and Maryland.

* Trade Leads

Foreign Agricultural Service
U.S. Department of Agriculture (USDA)
Room 4647, South Building
Washington, DC 20250-1000 (202) 720-7103

The USDA issues a weekly publication entitled *Trade Leads*, which lists agricultural products sought by foreign buyers, as well as contact names and phone numbers. Leads are also available by FAX. New trade leads are placed on the machines each Wednesday at 12:00 noon, Eastern time. The same set of leads will be available 24 hours per day. To receive the Trade Leads on your machine, simply dial one of the numbers listed below on your fax machine and then press start. The leads come through like a regular transmission. FAX numbers and the leads they cover are listed below.

Machine 1 - (202) 60-2088
Condiments, Candy, Beverages, and Other Specialty Foods.

Machine 2 - (202) 690-1753
Grains, Pulses, Grain Products, and Animal Feeds.

Machine 3 - (202) 720-5165
Fruits, Vegetables, Nuts (Fresh, Processed, Packaged, or Juices) Meats, Poultry, Seafood, and Dairy Products.

Machine 4 - (202) 720-8980
Oils, Oilseeds, and Oilseed products; Live Animals and animal byproducts; Tobacco, Cotton, Seeds for Planting, Nursery Stock, and Cut Flowers; Lumber and Forest Products.

Machine 5 - (202) 205-2963
All of the four machines listed above, plus information on up coming Trade Shows, Notice of Foreign Proposals Concerning Standards in Agriculture, and more.

* U.S. Agricultural Trade Information

Information Division
Foreign Agricultural Service (FAS)
U.S. Department of Agriculture (USDA)
Room 4644, South Building
Washington, DC 20250-1000 (202) 720-7937

The Foreign Agricultural Service issues hundreds of reports every year, based on information from agricultural counselors, attaches, and trade officers stationed around the world. Contact the above office for a copy of the brochure *How to Get Information on U.S. Agricultural Trade*, which lists all the publications available. Publications include:

FAS Circulares - reports which present the U.S. and world production and trade statistics for a variety of commodities.

Foreign Agriculture - presents agricultural profiles on more than 70 countries, focusing on production, marketing, and trade.

Brochures - FAS brochures cover a variety of export related topics, aiding exports in tapping overseas markets.

Fact Sheets - FAS fact sheets provide concise up to date information o FAS export program operations and key issues in agricultural trade.

Market Profiles - focus on specific countries and prospects for U.S. agricultural exports. Entire set of 50 is available. For information call (202) 720-7937.

Electronic Reports - Daily, weekly, and monthly reports showing foreign trade opportunities, exports to major markets, import/export prices, and policy developments are available electronically through USDA's Computerized Information Delivery System. For Information call (202) 720-5505.

* Wholesale Market Development Program

Wholesale Market Branch
Transportation and Marketing Division
Agricultural Marketing Service (AMS)
U.S. Department of Agriculture (USDA)
PO Box 96456
Washington, DC 20090-6456 (202) 720-8317

The Wholesale Market Development Program conducts research to find new ways to improve the efficiency of American food marketing. An important element of the program is research to develop new wholesale food marketing centers and farmers' markets. Over the years some 75 extensive studies have been conducted in cities throughout the U.S.; about half of these studies have led to the construction of new wholesale food distribution centers and specialized

Be patient. If any phone number is incorrect, call (area code) 555-1212 and request the new listing.

industrial parks for food firms. For more information on this program, contact the AMS. The Branch also has an extensive publications list covering both the Market Development Program as well as commodities and livestock research.

* World Agricultural Databases

Economic Research Service Databases
U.S. Department of Agriculture (USDA)
ERS/NASS
P.O. Box 1608
Rockville, MD 20850 (800) 999-6779

The Economic Research Service has developed more than 60 databases dealing in a wide variety of U.S. and world agricultural economics topics. Data products are shipped on DOS-compatible discs or on unlabeled, 9-track 6250 b.p.i. magnetic tapes as appropriate. A complete listing of ERS electronic products and ordering information is available by contacting the above center.

* World Agricultural Trade Database

Chief, Trade and Marketing Branch
Foreign Agricultural Service
U.S. Department of Agriculture (USDA)
Washington, DC 20250 (202) 720-1294

The Foreign Agricultural Service (FAS) maintains a database of selected foreign agricultural trade information for the U.S. and 100 nations that conduct agricultural trade. The database contains information from a variety of sources, including United Nations trade tapes from the Food and Agriculture Organization and data from the Bureau of the Census. Examples of retrievable information include long-term U.S. exports by destination; foreign country import and export data; foreign production, supply, and distribution of agricultural products; and other export marketing information. Searches and print-outs are provided on a cost-recovery basis. Staff prefers request by phone so that they can discuss your needs and thereby supply you with appropriate information.

* World Competition

Yearbook Editor, Publications
U.S. Department of Agriculture (USDA)
Room 535-A
Washington, DC 20250 (202) 720-9434

Each year, the USDA publishes a yearbook which explores one theme in depth. The 1988 yearbook, *Marketing U.S. Agriculture*, written by experts from farms, industry, universities, and government, describes the revolution in the food marketing system caused by new technology, social changes, and increased competition for world markets.

Agriculture and Farming

State Agriculture Information

In most states, agriculture is the leading industry. Farming has become highly specialized, and modern farmers and agribusinesses must stay abreast of a wide range of current data: crop prices, price and production projections, field statistics, test results, and more. The U.S. Department of Agriculture (USDA) publishes the greatest number of reports and surveys in such areas, routinely publishing data on crop conditions, long-term and short-term weather forecasts, research developments, and current and projected market conditions for specific crops at home and abroad. Decisions involving billions of dollars are made each year based on this information.

USDA reports are most often used to track crop and livestock production and prices and to maximize production by ensuring that the best equipment and storage techniques are used for each crop. But the federal government does not hold a monopoly on agricultural information. States also collect and disseminate a great deal of farm data, and obtaining information from a state agency is generally less time-consuming and expensive than going through the USDA offices in Washington, DC.

Market News and Surveys

Individual states contribute to the Market News Service. Major wire services, newspapers, and radio stations use this service to track developments in agriculture. The service is used by virtually all persons involved in the sale or purchase of grain, livestock, poultry, or poultry products, as well as by insurance and investment companies and government agencies.

State agencies often make available employment and income surveys -- publications providing information of farms and the families who operate them, the quality of services provided, income generated from all sources, and analysis of this data. Special state agricultural directories are also a good source of information, providing the name, address, and telephone number of every agricultural producer in a state by commodity. They also include data on production levels, acreage, and farm dollar values for each commodity.

Information on Agribusiness and Growers

In terms of collecting information on agricultural companies, most states maintain a computerized licensing and product registration system and will provide mailing lists for a minimum fee. Included in the databases are names and addresses of agricultural processors, distributors, and manufacturers, as well as all registered products. States maintain records on the number of products and licenses held by each company, and inspection reports for retailers, wholesalers, and packagers are usually available for a fee. In addition, some states require that you file a Freedom of Information Act request to obtain this information.

Marketing or Agricultural Development Programs

State agriculture offices may offer their biggest help in promoting products grown within a state. Each state has a marketing and development program to protect, conserve, and develop state agriculture and natural resources. The objectives of such programs are to develop new and existing markets (including foreign) for state agricultural products and to ensure that state farms and ranches are using the best production techniques available. These offices also:

* improve agricultural profitability by encouraging the development of value-added products and new, high-value crops.

* encourage and support research issues which have an impact upon agricultural growth within the state.

* serve as clearinghouses for trade leads and provide various support services for state farmers and agribusinesses, including grading, inspection, promotion, and market intelligence.

* assist the agricultural producer, processor, shipper and exporter to expand trade volume and to broaden marketing areas, to reduce distribution and transportation costs, and to gain freer access to foreign markets.

To obtain overseas contracts, companies have their name and product(s) registered in the state export directory free of charge. Foreign investors and importers look to state directories for new ideas and areas in which to expand their business interests.

State departments of agriculture also rent booths at agricultural trade shows both at home and overseas. For example, if you have a small seafood company or are in the pasta and noodle business, renting a booth through the state at the Japan Food Show will go a long way to promote your product and may net you a tax-free trip to the Orient as well.

States also help promote your product overseas and may prove valuable in helping your small businesses expand through foreign franchises. Another example: a popular soft yogurt company was able to franchise in several overseas markets with the help of the Maryland State Agricultural Department.

Statistical Reporting Service (SRS)

The purpose of SRS is to collect and disseminate current statistics on the nation's agriculture. SRS maintains a network of 44 field offices which service all 50 states through cooperative agreements with state departments of agriculture or state universities. These State Statistical Offices (SSOs)

State Agriculture Information

regularly survey thousands of farmers, ranchers, and agri-businesses that voluntarily provide data on a confidential basis.

Statisticians consolidate these reports with field observations, objective yield measurements, and other data to produce state farm and ranch estimates. These data are then forwarded to SRS headquarters in Washington, DC, where they are combined and released as a national profile. In addition, SRS issues about 300 national and 9,000 state farm reports each year. The reports provide broad coverage of agriculture, including 120 crops and 45 livestock items.

Many statistical publications are also available directly from the USDA/NASS Agricultural Statistics Board Publications, Room 5829 South Building, Washington, DC 20250-2000.

Agricultural Stabilization and Conservation Service

The Agricultural Stabilization and Conservation Service (ASCS) administers a variety of farm commodity, conservation, environmental, and emergency/disaster programs. Its commodity programs are designed to stabilize agricultural prices so as to avoid unnecessary or violent price swings. ASCS administers commodity stabilization programs for wheat, corn, grain sorghum, barley, oats, rye, soybeans, rice, tobacco, peanuts, milk, cotton, wool, mohair, sugar, and honey.

The ASCS also makes loans to eligible farmers. The ASCS is also involved in a variety of conservation programs designed to reduce soil erosion. ASCS offices are located in 49 of the 50 states, usually in the state capital. County offices are listed in the telephone directory under "U.S. Department of Agriculture."

State Agricultural Offices

The following is a list of state agricultural departments and the products and services they can provide:

Alabama

Agricultural Statistics Service, M.L. Dantzler, Box 1071, Montgomery, AL 36192; (205) 223-7263. Publications: *Alabama Farm Facts* (issued twice monthly): *Agricultural Prices; Crop Production or Forecasts, Intended and Actual Plantings, and Grain Stocks; Fruits, Nuts and Vegetables; Livestock Numbers, Production, Slaughter and Milk; Poultry and Eggs; Broiler Report* (issued each Wednesday); *Crop Weather* (issued each Monday, March-December); *County Data: Cattle, Hogs, Poultry, Corn, Cotton, Hay, Oats, Peanuts, Sorghum Grain, Soybeans, Wheat; Alabama Agricultural Statistics, Fact Sheet on Alabama Agriculture, Alabama Agriculture Perspective.*

Department of Agriculture and Industries, P. O. Box 3336, Montgomery, AL 36193; (205) 242-5872. Publications: *Fruit and Vegetable Direct Marketing Directory, Alabama Farmers' Bulletin, Ag Talk, The Alabama Food and Agricultural Export Directory.*

Agricultural Stabilization and Conservation Service Office, PO Box 891, Montgomery, AL 36192-4101; (205) 223-7230.

Alaska

State Statistical Service, D.A. Brown, Box 799, Palmer, AK 99645; (907) 745-4272. Publications: *Alaska Agricultural Statistics; Alaska Farm Reporter* (monthly); *Crop Weather* (weekly). Combined fee for all three publications is $15 per year.

Department of Natural Resources, Division of Agriculture, P.O. Box 949, Palmer, AK 99645; (907) 745-7200. Programs: *Agricultural Revolving Loan Fund, Alaska Grown Program, Alaska Grown Logo Program, Plant Materials Center for Alaskan Grown Plants.* Publications: *Alaska Agricultural Statistics; Alaska Food and Farm Directory.*

Agricultural Stabilization and Conservation Service Office, 624 South Valley Suite 102, Palmer Business Plaza, Palmer AK 99645; (907) 745-7982.

Arizona

Agricultural Statistics Service, B. L. Boyd, 201 East Indianola, Suite 250, Phoenix, AZ 85012; (602) 640-2573. Publications: *Arizona Agricultural Statistics, Crop Release, Livestock Release, Crop and Weather Report, Annual Bulletin.*

Arizona Department of Agriculture, 1688 West Adams, Phoenix, AZ 85007; (602) 542-0951. *Annual Report, Agriculture 91, 1990 Arizona Agricultural Statistics.*

Arkansas

Agricultural Statistics Service, D. H. Von Steen, Box 3197, Little Rock, AR 72203; (501) 324-5145. Publications: *Arkansas Farm Report* (issued twice a month); *Weather and Crop Bulletin; Weekly Broiler* (weekly); *County Estimates; Agricultural Statistics for Arkansas.*

Cooperative Extension Service, University of Arkansas, P.O. Box 391, Little Rock, AR 72203; (501) 671-2117. Publication: *Annual Report of Accomplishments.* Publication topics are the following: Agricultural Chemicals, Agricultural Engineering, Agronomy - general, Agronomy - Cotton, Agronomy - Feed Grains, Agronomy - Pastures and Forages, Agronomy - Rice, Agronomy - Soybeans, Clothing and Textiles, Entomology, Farm Management, Fisheries, Food Marketing, Food and Nutrition, Forestry, Horticulture, Livestock and Livestock Products, Marketing, and Plant Pathology.

Agricultural Stabilization and Conservation Office. P.O. Box 2781, Little Rock, AR 72203; (501) 378-5220.

California

Agricultural Statistics Service, H. J. Tippett, Box 1258, Sacramento, CA 95806; (916) 551-1533. Publications: *California Agriculture; Exports of California Agricultural Products; California Agricultural Export Directory; Summary of County Agricultural Commissioners' Reports; Field Crop Statistics; Prices Received by California Producers for Farm Commodities; Fruit and Nut Acreage, Fruit and Nut Statistics, Grape Crush Report; Grape Acreage Bulletin; Grapes, Raisins, and Wine; Walnuts, Raisins, and Prunes, Vegetable Crops; Livestock Statistics; Eggs, Chickens, and Turkeys; Dairy Industry Statistics; Complete Set of County Agricultural Commissioner Report Data, Commodity by County.*

State of California, Food and Agriculture, 1220 N. St., Sacramento, CA 94271; (916) 654-0466. Programs: *Agricultural Export Program (AEP)*: first of its kind by a state, AEP provides assistance, service, and support in developing sales in foreign markets. It is a five year matching funds partnership in which the costs of foreign market development are equally shared between the California Department of Food and Agriculture and program cooperators. The program is open to all private companies, marketing boards, and commissions or associations who are producers, processors, or marketers of California agricultural products. The AEP program is developing its own "California specific" trade lead network which will electronically provide information on buyer leads, best market prospects, trade barriers, and export assistance. Publications: *California Department of Food and Agriculture and What it Does for You; California Agriculture: 1990 Statistics; Taste California: 1992 Food and Wine Festivals; Straight From the Farm to You: Farmer to Consumer Direct Marketing; Taste the Californias: California Fresh Produce Guide.*

Agricultural Stabilization and Conservation Service Office, 1303 J Street, Suite 300, Sacramento, CA 95814-2916; (916) 551-1801.

Colorado

Agricultural Statistics Service, C. A. Hudson, Box 150969, Lakewood, CO 80215; (303) 236-2300. The Colorado Legislature has eliminated funding for agricultural statistics. Publications: *Agricultural Update* (bi-monthly); *Crop-Weather Report* (weekly, March-November); *Colorado Agricultural Statistics Bulletin* (Annual).

Colorado Department of Agriculture, 700 Kipling St., Suite 4000, Lakewood, CO 80215; (303) 239-4100. Programs: 1) The Department administers the Colorado Agricultural Development Authority which makes low interest loans to producers. 2) Project ARC (Agricultural Resources in Colorado): rebate funds are offered to assist farmers with the identification and promotion of innovative agricultural practices.

Agriculture and Farming

Agricultural Stabilization and Conservation Service Office, 655 Parfet Street, Suite E301, Lakewood, CO 80215; (303) 236-2866.

Connecticut

For Connecticut agricultural statistics, contact the Marketing Division at the Connecticut Department of Agriculture below.

Connecticut Department of Agriculture, State Office Building, Room 243, 165 Capitol Ave., Hartford, CT 06106; (203) 566-4276. Program: Joint Venture Program: $50,000 in matching funds is available to agricultural commodity groups and organizations for promotion of "Connecticut Grown" products. Publications: *Connecticut Grown, Annual Report, Farm Fresh Directory, Connecticut Sugarhouses, Connecticut Wineries, Pick Your Own: Orchards, Vegetables, Christmas Trees, Berries; Connecticut Farmers Markets, Fair List, Connecticut Agricultural Directory, Connecticut Agricultural Statistics.*

Agricultural Stabilization and Conservation Service Office, 88 Day Hill Road, Windsor, CT 06095; (203) 285-8483.

Delaware

Agricultural Statistics Service, 2320 S. Dupont Highway, Dover, DE 19901; (302) 739-4811. Publications: *Annual Delaware Agricultural Statistics Report, Delaware Agri-Facts, Delaware Weekly Crop and Weather Report, Delmarva Broiler Chicks.*

Delaware Department of Agriculture, 2320 S. Dupont Highway, Dover, DE 19901; (302) 739-4811. Publications: *Delaware Agricultural Statistics, Delaware AGenda, Century Farms, Delaware Land Survey, Report of State Farmland Evaluation Advisory Council, Agricultural Bulletin, Delaware's State Forests, Delaware Agriculture - An Overview, Delaware Farmers Markets Directory, Delaware Food/Agriculture Export Directory, Delaware Produce Buyers Guide, Pesticide Briefs.*

Agricultural Stabilization and Conservation Service Office, 179 West Chestnut Hill Rd. S.7, Newark DE 19713; (302) 573-6536.

Florida

Agricultural Statistics Services, R. L. Freie, 1222 Woodward St., Orlando, FL 32803; (407) 648-6013. Publication: *Florida Agricultural Statistics, Field Crops, Citrus and Tropical Fruits, Vegetables, Celery, Tomatoes, Livestock - Dairy and Poultry, Broilers, Weather and Crop News, Numbers of Workers and Wage Rates, Prices and Cash Receipts, Citrus Acreage and Tree Numbers, Citrus Historic Maturity and Yield, Annual Summaries* for the following crops: Citrus, Vegetables, Livestock, Poultry, Dairy, Field Crops.

Department of Agriculture, 3125 Conner Blvd, Conner Building, Tallahassee, FL 32399-1650; (904) 488-7000. Publications: *Annual Report; Agricultural Groups Directory; Dollars and $ense; Flowers, Trees, and Shrubs: Native and Exotic; Native Trees of Florida; Vegetable Gardening; Touring Florida Agriculture; Lemon Log.* Information is also available from the Agricultural Institute of Florida - (904) 236-3488.

Agricultural Stabilization and Conservation Service Office, PO Drawer 670, Gainesville, FL 32602-0670; (904) 372-8549.

Georgia

Agricultural Statistics Service, L. E. Snipes, Stephens Federal Building, Suite 320, Athens, GA 30613; (404) 546-2236. Publications: *Georgia Farm Report* includes the following reports: *Crop production, Grain stocks, Vegetable production, Fruit production, Prices received and paid by farmers, Hog inventory, Pig crop, Egg production, Hatchery data, Milk production, Livestock slaughter, Cash receipts, Farm Labor, Weather and Crops; Weekly Hatchery; Georgia Agricultural Facts, Georgia Poultry Facts.*

Department of Agriculture, Capitol Square, 19 Martin Luther King Jr. Drive, Atlanta, GA 30334; (404) 656-3645, (800) 282-5852. Publications: *Farmers and Consumers Market Bulletin; Annual Report; Agricultural Fact Book.*

Agricultural Stabilization and Conservation Service Office, PO Box 1907, Athens GA 30613-4299; (404) 546-2266.

Hawaii

Agricultural Statistics Service, A. R. Davis, State Department of Agriculture Building, 1428 S. King St., Honolulu, HI 96822; (808) 973-9588. Publication: *Hawaii Agricultural Statistics; Avocados; Bananas; Coffee; Fruits; Ginger Root; Guavas; Herbs; Macadamia Nuts; Papayas; Pineapples; Sugarcane; Taro; Vegetables; Anthurimes; Floriculture and Nursery Products; Poinsettias; Cattle; Chickens and Eggs; Hogs; Honey; Milk; Crop-Weather Report; Farm Labor; and Prices Paid-Feed.*

Department of Agriculture, P.O. Box 22159, Honolulu, HI 96823-2159; (808) 973-9599. Programs: 1) Agricultural Loan Program: credit is available to qualified farmers, partnerships, corporations, and agricultural cooperatives to promote agricultural development in Hawaii. 2) New Farmer Program: provides initial start-up loans to new farmers. 3) Orchard Development Program: allows tax relief to qualified orchardists during the developmental period of certain fruit and nut crops. 4) Aquaculture Loan Program: provides loans for the development of aquacultural enterprises (independent). 5) Sugar Grower Loan Program: provides supplementary direct loans to independent sugar growers to cover deficits during current period of insufficient national protection against foreign sugar imports. 6) Agricultural and New Farmer Loan Program: loans to encourage the development of agricultural enterprises in the State. Publications: *Annual Report, Hawaii Agricultural and Food Products Export Directory.*

Agricultural Stabilization and Conservation Service Office, 300 Ala Moana Blvd. PO Box 50008, Honolulu, HI 96850; (808) 541-2644.

Idaho

Agricultural Statistics Service, R. C. Max, Box 1699, Boise, ID 83701; (208) 334-1507. Publication: *Annual Report, Agriculture in Idaho, Potato Reports, Weekly Crop Weather Reports.*

Idaho Department of Agriculture, Marketing and Development, P.O. Box 790, Boise, ID 83701; (208) 334-2718. Program: Rural Rehabilitation Loans: this lending program helps stabilize rural Idaho by providing funds to small family farmers and to youths who want to continue in agricultural pursuits. Publication: *Department of Agriculture Annual Report.*

Agricultural Stabilization and Conservation Service Office, 3220 Elder Street, Boise, ID 83705; (208) 334-1486.

Illinois

Agricultural Statistics Service, J. Clampett, Box 19283, Springfield, IL 62794; (217) 492-4295. Publications: *Illinois Farm Report, Illinois Weather and Crop Reports, Annual Summary - Illinois Agricultural Statistics - 1992.*

Department of Agriculture, Division of Administrative Services, State Fairgrounds, P.O. Box 4906, Springfield, IL 62708; (217) 785-9272. Programs: Illinois Grain Insurance Corporation (IGIC): provides full protection to Illinois farmers who store their grain in country elevators; "T by 2000". This program is a nationwide model aimed at controlling soil erosion of fragile lands by the turn of the century. Publication: *Illinois Agricultural Statistics Annual Summary.*

Agricultural Stabilization and Conservation Service Office, PO Box 19273, Springfield, IL 62794-9723; (217) 492-4180.

Indiana

Agricultural Statistics Service, R. W. Gann, 1148 Agricultural Administration Building, Purdue University, Room 223, West Lafayette, IN 47907; (317) 494-8371. Publications: *Indiana Agricultural Statistics, Indiana Weekly Crop and Weather Report, Indiana Agriculture Report.*

Indiana Department of Agriculture, Office of the Commissioner of Agriculture, 150 West Market Street, Suite 414, Indianapolis, IN 46204; (317) 232-8770. Programs: 1) Hoosier Homestead and Hoosier Business Award Programs: farms and businesses that have been a working factor in the same family for at least 100 years receive an award. 2) Treasurer's Farm Program (TFP) provides low interest loans to farmers facing cash flow difficulties. 3) Value Added Grant Program: This program is designed to increase the value of Indiana produced agricultural commodities, thereby increasing the net worth of the state's agriculture. 4) Domestic and International Marketing Program: Works to identify markets within the U.S. and abroad for Indiana Agriculture. Publications: *Indiana Food Processors Directory, Grown in Indiana: You Pick Directory, Agricultural Exports Directory, Indiana Agriculture Book, Indiana Agriculture: A Strategic Plan, Indiana Agricultural Statistics.*

Agricultural Stabilization and Conservation Service Office, 5981 Lakeside Blvd. Indianapolis, IN 46278-1996; (317) 290-3030.

Iowa

Agricultural Statistics Service, D. M. Skow, 210 Walnut St., Room 833, Des Moines, IA 50309; (515) 284-4340. Publications: *Iowa Crop Report, Iowa Crops and Weather, Iowa Livestock Report, Agri News.*

Be patient. If any phone number is incorrect, call (area code) 555-1212 and request the new listing.

State Agriculture Information

Department of Agriculture, Information Bureau, Wallace Building, Des Moines, IA 50319; (515) 281-5681. Programs: Agricultural Diversification Program: assists farms with an alternative crop and livestock program. Agricultural Development Authority: assists beginning farmers in acquiring agricultural land, property, and agricultural improvements by offering loans at low interest rates. Publications: *Beginning Farmer Loan Program, Iowa Department of Agriculture and Land Stewardship, Recycling: The Right Thing to Do, History of Agriculture in Iowa, Iowa's Apple Orchards, Honey Producers of Iowa, Biennial Report, Agricultural Commodity and Farm Organization List for 1991-92.*

Agricultural Stabilization and Conservation Service Office, Federal Building, Room 937, 210 Walnut St. Des Moines, IA 50309; (515) 284-4210.

Kansas

Agricultural Statistics Service, T.J. Byram, P.O. Box 3534, Topeka, KS 66601-3534; (913) 233-2230. Publications: *Weekly Crop Weather; Crops; Prices; Livestock; Hogs and Pigs; Bluestem Pasture; Grain Marketing and Transportation; Custom Rates; Farm Facts; Wheat Quality; Wheat Varieties; Farm Bankruptcies; Agricultural Land Values.*

State Board of Agriculture, 109 SW 9th Street, Topeka, KS 66612; (913) 296-3556.

Agricultural Stabilization and Conservation Service Office, 2601 Anderson Ave. Manhattan, KS 66502-2898; (913) 539-3531.

Kentucky

Agricultural Statistics Service, D. D. Williamson, Box 1120, Louisville, KY 40601; (502) 582-5293. Publications: *AGRI-NEWS, Crop Weather Reports, Livestock Reports, Dairy Reports, Poultry Reports, Price Reports, Miscellaneous Reports, Crop Weather, County Estimates.*

Department of Agriculture, 7th Floor, 500 Nero St., Frankfort, KY 40601; (502) 564-4696, (800) 372-7602 (consumer line). Program: FARMLOT (800-327-6568): free marketing service to persons across the state who are interested in buying and/or selling farm commodities as well as receiving regional up-to-date farm market prices. Publication: *Kentucky Agricultural Statistics, Preview of the Tobacco Market, Report and Market Review, Kentucky Agricultural News, Kentucky Agricultural Facts, Kentucky Agricultural Almanac, Export Directory, Farmers Markets, Christmas Tree Directory, Kentucky Local Agricultural Fairs, Kentucky Livestock, Kentucky Hay Testing Program.*

Agricultural Stabilization and Conservation Service Office, 333 Waller Ave. Lexington, KY 40504; (606) 233-2726.

Louisiana

Agricultural Statistics Service, A.D. Frank, Box 5524, Alexandria, LA 71307; (318) 841-5140. Publication: *Statistical Report, Louisiana Farm Reporter, Annual Crop Summary, Weekly Crop-Weather Report, All County Estimates for Cotton, Rice, Soybeans, Wheat, Corn, Sugarcane, Sorghum, and Livestock.*

Department of Agriculture and Forestry, P.O. Box 65038, Baton Rouge, LA 70896; (504) 922-1234. Program: Farm Youth Loan Program: provides loan and loan guarantees to youths who are involved in an organized school program in agriculture. Publication: *Market Bulletin.*

Agricultural Stabilization and Conservation Service Office, 3737 Government St. Alexandria, LA 71302; (318) 473-7721.

Maine

For specific statistical information on Maine's agricultural products contact the Commissioner's Office of the Department of Agriculture, Food and Rural Resources, (207) 287-3871.

Department of Agriculture, Food and Rural Resources, Commissioner's Office, State House Station 28, Augusta, ME 04333; (207) 287-3871. Publications: *Maine Agricultural Report, Maine Agricultural Buyers Guide, Producer to Consumer, Peat Task Force Report, How to Organize Agricultural Marketing Cooperatives, Annual Report on the Main Agricultural Fairs, Saving Energy in Rural Maine or Who is Doing What on the Farm, Useable Waste Products for the Farm.*

Agricultural Stabilization and Conservation Service Office, 444 Stillwater Ave. Suite 1, PO Box 406, Bangor, ME 04401-3521; (207) 942-0342.

Maryland

Agricultural Statistics Service, M. B. West, 50 Harry S. Truman Parkway, Suite

202, Annapolis, MD 21401; (410) 841-5740. Publications: *Maryland Agri-Facts* - which includes the following types of information - crop production, grain stocks, vegetable production, fruit production, prices received and paid by farmers, livestock production and inventories, poultry and egg production, hatchery data, milk production, livestock slaughter, farm income and finance, farm labor, miscellaneous reports; *Maryland Crop Weather; Delmarva Broiler Chicks; Maryland Agricultural Summary.*

Maryland Department of Agriculture, 50 Harry S. Truman Parkway, Annapolis, MD 21401; (410) 841-5700. Publication: *The Maryland Department of Agriculture Yesterday, Today and Tomorrow; Agricultural Maryland.*

Agricultural Stabilization and Conservation Service Office, Rivers Center 10270 B Old Columbia Rd., Columbia, MD 21406; (410) 381-4550.

Massachusetts

For specific agricultural statistics, contact the Department of Food and Agriculture listed below.

Massachusetts Department of Food and Agriculture, 100 Cambridge, Boston, MA 02202; (617) 727-3018. Programs: Municipal Farmland Identification Program: information on available farmland will be mapped and on record. It provides the communities and farmers with an inventory on the possible crop production of an area and assists in planning decisions. Agricultural Preservation Restriction Program: protects diminishing farmland resources through the purchase of Agricultural Preservation Restrictions, commonly known as development rights.

The Department is currently initiating its own, complimentary data-collection program which will be transformed into a reliable computerized data base. Publications: *Massachusetts Agriculture Annual Report. The Fresh Connection* - newsletter to help local growers find new markets, and to help improve communications between local producers and restaurant chefs, *Farm and Market Report.*

Agricultural Stabilization and Conservation Service Office, 451 West Street, Amherst, MA 01002-2953; (413) 256-0232.

Michigan

Agricultural Statistics Service, D. J. Fedewa, Box 20008, Lansing, MI 48901; (517) 377-1831. Publications: *Michigan Agricultural Statistics, Agriculture Across Michigan, Crop Weather, Fruit Survey, Equine Survey.*

Department of Agriculture, P.O. Box 30017, Lansing, MI 48909; (517) 373-1104. Program: Agricultural Assistance Network: provides assistance to Michigan farmers and related agribusinesses facing financial hardship as a result of economic crisis. A toll free hotline (1-800-346-FARM) is available to anyone with problems related to loans, human service needs, legal referrals, and financial farm management. Publications: *You Pick Fruit and Vegetable Markets; County Agricultural Economy Directory; Agriculture Business Directory for Exports.*

Agricultural Stabilization and Conservation Service Office, Room 116, 1405 S. Harrison Road East Lansing, MI 48823-5202; (517) 337-6659.

Minnesota

Agricultural Statistics Service, C. C. Rock, Box 7068, St. Paul, MN 55107; (612) 296-2230. Publications: *Agri-View, Minnesota Weekly Crop-Weather Report, Potato Stocks, Monthly Turkey Report, Minnesota Agricultural Statistics Book.*

Department of Agriculture, 90 West Plato Blvd. Saint Paul, MN 55107; (612) 297-1551. Publication: *Minnesota Agriculture.*

Agricultural Stabilization and Conservation Service Office, 400 Farm Credit Services Bldg. 375 Jackson Street, St. Paul, MN 55101-1852; (612) 290-3651.

Mississippi

Agricultural Statistics Service, G. R. Knight, Box 980, Jackson, MS 39205; (601) 965-4575. Publication: *Mississippi Agricultural Statistics, Crop Weather Report, Weekly Broiler Report.*

Mississippi Department of Agriculture and Commerce, P.O. Box 1609, Jackson, MS 39215; (601) 354-6734. Publication: *Annual Report.*

Agricultural Stabilization and Conservation Service Office, PO Box 14995 Jackson, MS 39236-4995; (601) 965-4300.

Be patient. If any phone number is incorrect, call (area code) 555-1212 and request the new listing.

Agriculture and Farming

Missouri

Agricultural Statistics Service, P.A. Walsh, P.O. Box 1, Columbia, MO 65205; (314) 876-0950. Publications: *Farm Facts; Crop and Weather Report; Crop and Livestock Report.*

Missouri Department of Agriculture, P.O. Box 630, Jefferson City, MO 65102; (314) 751-2672. Publication: *Missouri Farm Facts.*

Agricultural Stabilization and Conservation Service Office, 555 Vandiver Dr. Columbia, MO 65202; (314) 875-5201.

Montana

Agricultural Statistics Service, J. Sands, Box 4369, Helena, MT 59604; (406) 449-5303. Publication: *Agricultural Statistics Bulletin, Crop Weather Report, Reporter.*

Department of Agriculture, Agriculture/Livestock Building, Capitol Station, Helena, MT 59620; (406) 444-3144. Programs: Agricultural Assistance Program: provides confidential one-on-one assistance to financially distressed farmers and ranchers (800) 722-FARM; Agricultural Development: makes grants and low interest rate loans available to rural youth organizations and other qualified farmers and ranchers. Publications: *Legal Aspects of Difficult Choices, Farm and Ranch Debt, Junior Agricultural Loan Program, Rural Assistance Loan Program, Growth Through Agriculture Loan Program, Agricultural Assistance Program, and Farm/Ranch Hotline.*

Agricultural Stabilization and Conservation Service Office, PO Box 670 Bozeman, MT 59771-0670; (406) 587-6872.

Nebraska

Agricultural Statistics Service, J. L. Aschwege, Box 81069, Lincoln, NE 68501; (402) 437-5541. Publications: *Nebraska Agricultural Statistics, Crop-Weather, Agri-Facts, Crops and Weather Summary.*

Department of Agriculture, Nebraska Agricultural Development, P.O. Box 94947, Lincoln, NE 68509; (402) 471-4876, (800) 422-6692. Programs: The Nebraska Department of Agriculture has identified four key areas for development. Livestock - further develop markets for this most important industry; Bulk Commodities - generate trade leads for grain; Value Added - assist companies for international marketing of Nebraska value added food products; Nontraditional Agriculture - development of new crops for Nebraska agriculture. Publication: *Nebraska Agriculture, Nebraska Agricultural Products Trade Directory, Ag Report, Facts About Nebraska Agriculture, Nebraska Beef.*

Agricultural Stabilization and Conservation Service Office, PO Box 57975 Lincoln, NE 68505-7975; (402) 437-5581.

Nevada

Agricultural Statistics Service, C. R. Lies, Box 8880, Reno, NV 89507; (702) 784-5584. Publication: *Nevada Agricultural Statistics, Prospective Plantings; Crop Production; Annual Crop Production Summary; Weather, Crops, and Livestock; Farm Income; Livestock Inventory.*

Nevada State Department of Agriculture, Box 11100, Reno, NV 89510; (702) 789-0180. Publication: *Nevada and Its Agriculture.*

Agricultural Stabilization and Conservation Service Office, 1755 East Plumb Lane, Suite 202, Reno, NV 89502; (702) 784-5411.

New England

Agricultural Statistics, Maine, New Hampshire, Vermont, Connecticut, Rhode Island, Massachusetts, A.R. Davis Jr., 22 Bridge St., P.O. Box 1444, Concord, NH 03302-1444; (603) 224-9639. Publications: *Ag Review Monthly, Cranberries, Maple, Potato Grade and Size Report, Wild Blueberries, and Crop Weather.*

New Hampshire

New Hampshire Department of Agriculture, Caller Box 2042, Concord, NH 03302; (603) 271-3688. Publication: *Weekly Market Bulletin.*

Agricultural Stabilization and Conservation Service Office, PO Box 1398 Concord, NH 03302-1298; (603) 224-7941.

New Jersey

Agricultural Statistics Service, R. J. Battaglia, CN-330 New Warren St., Trenton, NJ 08625; (609) 292-6385. Publications: *Farm Facts, Weekly Weather Crop,*

Annual Vegetable Summary, Fertilizer Report.

Department of Agriculture, Health and Agriculture Building, CN-330, Trenton, NJ 08625; (609) 292-8896. Programs: administers nine commodity councils dedicated to research, education and agricultural promotion. Agricultural Development Program: through a variety of tours and educational activities, this program informs the non-farming public about New Jersey's agriculture. Publication: *New Jersey Agriculture, Pick Your Own Guide, NJ Certified and Plant Dealers, Roadside Stand Directory, NJ Farm Market Directory.*

Agricultural Stabilization and Conservation Service Office, Mastoris Professional Plaza, 163 Rte. 130 Building 1, Suite E, Bordentown, NJ 08505; (609) 298-3446.

New Mexico

Agricultural Statistics Service, D. G. Gerhardt, Box 1809, Las Cruces, NM 88004; (505) 523-8168. Publications: *Weekly Crop Weather, New Mexico Agri-Info:* includes information on Crop Acreages and Production, Livestock Inventory and Production; other publications - *Chile Summary, New Mexico Agricultural Statistics.*

New Mexico Department of Agriculture, NMSU Campus, Box 3189, Las Cruces, NM 88003; (505) 646-2804. Programs: Rangeland Protection Program: implements brush control programs on lands within the state. ADC Program: assists agricultural producers with the control of prairie dogs and kangaroo rats on rangeland, planted pastures, and field crops. Publications: *Biennial Report, New Mexico Agricultural Export Directory.*

Agricultural Stabilization and Conservation Service Office, PO Box 1458, Albuquerque, NM 87103-1458; (505) 766-2472.

New York

Agricultural Statistics Service, R.E. Schooley, 1 Winners Circle, Albany, NY 12235; (518) 457-5570. Publication: *New York Agricultural Statistics, New York Crop and Livestock Report, Weather and Crops, Fruit, Vegetables, Potatoes, Maple Production, Cash Receipts and Farm Income, Apples in Storage, Cold Storage, Corn, Wheat, Oats, and Hay Acreage and Production by County, Cattle Inventory by County, Milk Production by County, New York Equine Survey.*

New York Department of Agriculture and Markets, 1 Winners Circle, Albany, NY 12235; (518) 457-5981. Program: Institutional Procurement Assistance Program (1-800-NY-CROPS) assists state institutional facilities in purchasing foods grown, produced,and processed in the state. The program utilizes a computerized database of farmers, institutional buyers, and food wholesalers to provide buyers and sellers with detailed information on sources and marketing opportunities for New York State fresh fruits and vegetables. Publications: *New York Agriculture 2000, Frontiers for Agriculture: An Action Agenda for New York State, Annual Report, New York Wine Guide, Apple Country, Make a Splash with New York Grape Juice, New York Agriculture in the Classroom, Uncork New York, Export Directory, Local Laws and Agricultural Districts, Maple Syrup Recipe Book, NYS Community Farmers Market Directory, NYS Guide to Fresh Farm Food, NYS Guide to Fresh Meat, Bulletin 424: list of Milk Plants and Dealers in NYS, Agricultural Fairs List, Annual Report, Governor's Conference o the Kosher Food Industry, Safeguarding Your Food, New York is an Agricultural State.*

Agricultural Stabilization and Conservation Service Office, 811 Federal Building, 100 South Clinton St. Syracuse, NY 13260; (315) 423-5176.

North Carolina

Agricultural Statistics Service, B.M Murphy, Box 27767, Raleigh, NC 27611; (919) 856-4394. Publication: *North Carolina Farm Report* - which includes the following reports: Crop Production, Grain Stocks, Vegetable Production, Prices received and paid by farmers, Hog inventory and pig crop, Egg Production, Hatchery data, Milk production, Livestock slaughter, Cash receipts, Farm labor; *Weather and Crops; Broiler Reports, North Carolina Agricultural Statistics; North Carolina Farm Income;* County Estimates of these crops: Corn, Soybeans and Wheat, Tobacco, Peanuts, and Cotton, Sweet potatoes, Cattle and Hogs, Chickens.

North Carolina Department of Agriculture, P.O. Box 27647, Raleigh, NC 27611; (919) 733-4216. Program: Public Affairs Department features reports on agricultural business violations; Market NewsLine: a new electronic version of market news that transmits instant reports on farm market prices, supply and demand information,and weather. Publications: *Market Summary, Livestock Report, Agricultural Review, Agriculture Information Sourcebook.*

Agricultural Stabilization and Conservation Service Office, PO Box 27327 Raleigh, NC 27611-7327; (919) 790-2958.

Be patient. If any phone number is incorrect, call (area code) 555-1212 and request the new listing.

State Agriculture Information

North Dakota

Agricultural Statistics Service, R. F. Carver, Box 3166, Fargo, ND 58102; (701) 237-5771. *Agricultural Statistics.*

Department of Agriculture, State Capitol, Bismarck, ND 58505; (701) 224-2231. Programs: Northern Crops Institute: established to foster cooperation of farm commodity and agri-business organizations. Centennial Farm Award Program: awards given to families who have retained ownership of their farm for 100 years or more. Publication: *North Dakota Biennial Report.*

Agricultural Stabilization and Conservation Service Office, PO Box 3046, Fargo, ND 58108; (701) 239-5224.

Ohio

Agricultural Statistics Service, J.E. Ramsey, 200 N. High St., Room 608, Columbus, OH 43215; (614) 469-5590. Publication: *Ohio Agricultural Statistics, Ohio Farm Report, Crop-Weather Report, Ohio Farm Income, Timber Prices, Farm Real Estate.*

Ohio Department of Agriculture, 65 South Front St., Columbus, OH 43215; (614) 466-2732. Programs: Ohio Farm Financial Management Program: offers seminars on Farm Financial Management In Time of Stress; a $500,000 grant is being used to help farmers with new financing techniques using a computer generated program. International Trade Program: designed to foster international trade relationships between foreign buyers and Ohio agribusiness firms via a trade-leads match-making service. The focus of this program is toward small businesses. Publication: *Ohio Food Products Directory.*

Agricultural Stabilization and Conservation Service Office, 200 North High Street, 540 Federal Building, Columbus, OH 43215-2495; (614) 469-6735.

Oklahoma

Agricultural Statistics Section, R. P. Bellinghausen, 2800 N. Lincoln Blvd. Oklahoma City, OK 73105; (405) 525-9226. Publication: *Oklahoma Agricultural Statistics; Crop Weather Summary; Farm Statistics.*

State Department of Agriculture, 2800 North Lincoln Blvd., Oklahoma City, OK 73105; (405) 521-3864. Publication: *The Oklahoma Department of Agriculture and You, Poultry Newsletter, Urban Forestry Grant Information; Branch Out in Oklahoma; Certified Greenhouse and Nursery Directory; Hybrid Sorghum; Licensed Commercial and Non Commercial Pesticide Applicators; Firewood Facts; Planting Trees and Shrubs to Improve Wildlife Habitat in Oklahoma.*

Agricultural Stabilization and Conservation Service Office, Agricultural Center Building, McFarland and Farm Road, Stillwater, OK 74074; (405) 624-4110.

Oregon

Agricultural Statistics Service, P.M. Williamson, 1220 S.W. 3rd Avenue, Portland, OR 97204; (503) 526-2131. Publication: *Oregon Agriculture and Fisheries Statistics, Crop Weather Report, Agrifacts.*

Department of Agricultural and Resource Economics, Oregon State University, Administrative Services A422, Corvallis, OR 97331; (503) 737-2713. Publications: *Farming and Ranching in Oregon, Oregon County and State Agricultural Estimates, Commodity Data Sheets* for: grains, hay, field crops, tree fruits and nuts, small fruits and berries, vegetables and truck crops, specialty products, livestock and poultry; the Extension service also publishes a booklet listing an extensive number of publications available.

Also contact Department of Agriculture, Marketing, 121 South West Salmon St., Portland, OR, 97204; (503) 229-6734 and the Information Office in Salem; (503) 378-3713. Publications: *Department of Agriculture Mission Statement, Export Service Center, Biennial Report, Oregon Agriculture and Fisheries Statistics 1990-91.*

Agricultural Stabilization and Conservation Service Office, 1220 SW Third Avenue, Room 1524, Portland, OR 97204; (503) 326-2741.

Pennsylvania

Agricultural Statistics Service, W. C. Evans, 2301 N. Cameron St., Room G-19, Harrisburg, PA 17110; (717) 787-3904. Publications: *Crop and Livestock Annual Summary, Keystone Digest, Special Dairy Report, Broilers, Annual Manufactured Dairy, Machinery Custom Rates, Weekly Crop and Weather Round-Up.*

Department of Agriculture, 2301 North Cameron St., Harrisburg, PA 17110; (717) 787-4694. Publication: *Annual Report.*

Agricultural Stabilization and Conservation Service Office, One Credit Union Place, Suite 320, Harrisburg, PA 17110; (717) 782-4547.

Rhode Island

For specific agricultural statistics in Rhode Island contact the office listed below.

Rhode Island Department of Environmental Management, Division of Agriculture and Marketing, Roger Williams Building, 22 Hayes St., Providence, RI 02908; (401) 277-2781. Programs: Purchase of Development Rights: designed to retain agricultural land by purchasing right to develop the land for purposes other than agriculture. Farm, Forest and Open Space: encourages the maintenance of Rhode Island's productive agriculture and forestland. The use value assessment is based on the current use of land rather than the potential development value. Publications: *Weekly Wholesale Reports, Seasonal Crop Reports, Pick-Your-Own* brochures and information, *Farmers Market* brochures and information, *Crop Brochures* featuring Nutritional, Storage, Buying and Cooking information on Rhode Island grown crops. *Rhode Island Agricultural Statistics, Export Directory, Agriculture Facts Book.*

Agricultural Stabilization and Conservation Service Office, West Bay Office Park, 40 Quaker Lane West Warwick, RI 02893; (401) 828-8232.

South Carolina

Agricultural Statistics Service, H. J. Power, Box 1911, Columbia, SC 29202; (803) 765-5333. Publications: *Weekly Crop Weather; Farm Facts for Field Crops, Fruits and Vegetables; Farm Facts for Livestock and Poultry; Farm Facts for Agriculture Prices; Annual Cash Receipts Bulletin; Vegetable Statistics Bulletin; Fruit Tree Survey Bulletin; Annual Agricultural Statistics Bulletin.*

Department of Agriculture, P.O. Box 11280, Columbia, SC 29211; (803) 734-2210. Publications: *Annual Report,* individual reports: *Tobacco, Soybean, Cattle, Beef, Pork, Peach, Watermelon, Egg, Peanut and Tomato, Commodity Promotions and Consumer Information, Poultry Grading, Fruit and Vegetables, Ag Study Tours, Small Farms, Fruit and Vegetable Market News, International Trade, Livestock Market News, Consumer Services.*

Agricultural Stabilization and Conservation Service Office, Strom Thurmond Federal Building, 1835 Assembly Street, Room 909, Columbia, SC 29201-2488; (803) 765-5186.

South Dakota

Agricultural Statistics Service, J.C. Ranek, Box 5068, Sioux Falls, SD 57117; (605) 330-4235. Publications: *Crop and Livestock Reporter, Crop-Weather Summary, South Dakota Agriculture, South Dakota's Rank in Agriculture.*

Department of Agriculture, Anderson Building, 445 E. Capitol Ave., Pierre, SD 57501; (605) 773-3375. Program: Adult Farm and Ranch Business Management Program: assists farmers and ranchers in developing a farm accounting system. Publications: *Statewide Annual Report, South Dakota Agriculture, South Dakota Exporters Directory, South Dakota Agricultural Statistics, Horizons, Pesticide Program, Guide to Animal Waste Management and Assistance for Livestock Producers, South Dakota Conservation Districts, Gypsy Moth Trapping and Detection Program, Agricultural Marketing Program, Agricultural Enterprise Program, Rural Development Loan Participation, Livestock Loan Programs, Farm Loan Mediation Program, Nursery Inspection Program, Coordinated Soil and Water Conservation Program, Egg Inspection Program, Grassroots Restoration, Register of Big Trees, Protect Your Forest Home From Wildlife, Project Learning Tree, Tree Farming, Chemical Weed Control in Trees, The Capitol Grounds Arboretum Trail, Arbor Day, South Dakota's Forests, Windbreaks.*

Agricultural Stabilization and Conservation Service Office, 200 Fourth Street SW, Room 208 Huron, SD 57350; (605) 353-1092.

Tennessee

Agricultural Statistics Service, C. R. Brantner, Box 41505, Nashville, TN 37204; (615) 781-5300. Publications: *Tennessee Weather and Crops, Tennessee Farm Facts, Agricultural Statistics.*

Department of Agriculture, Ellington Agricultural Center, P.O. Box 40627, Nashville, TN 37204; (615) 360-0160. Program: Overseas Market Program: new-to-export companies receive counseling via state-sponsored educational seminars and individual meetings with marketing personnel. Advice is also available on international financing. Publications: *Producer to Consumer Directory, Tennessee Hay Directory,* and *Tennessee Agriculture: A Century Farms Perspective.*

Be patient. If any phone number is incorrect, call (area code) 555-1212 and request the new listing.

Agriculture and Farming

Agricultural Stabilization and Conservation Service Office, 579 U.S. Courthouse, 801 Broadway, Nashville, TN 37203; (615) 736-5555.

Texas

Agricultural Statistics Service, D. S. Findley, Box 70, Austin, TX 78767; (512) 482-5581. Publications: *Texas Agricultural Facts, Texas Historic Livestock Statistics, Texas Historic Crops Statistics, Texas County Statistics, Texas Custom Rates Statistics, Texas Citrus Tree Inventory Survey, Weekly Crop-Weather, Monthly Citrus, Monthly Onions, Quarterly Vegetable Acreage, Monthly Cattle on Feed, Weekly Broilers.*

Department of Agriculture, P.O. Box 12847, Austin, TX 78711; (512) 463-7624. Program: International Marketing Program: this network ties into the USDA's computerized trade lead system that spans the world to gather buyer inquiries on a daily basis. Publications: *Texas Agriculture Facts, Gazette, Taste of Texas.*

Agricultural Stabilization and Conservation Service Office, PO Box 2900, College Station, TX 77841-2900; (409) 260-9207.

Utah

Agricultural Statistics Service, D. J. Gneiting, Box 25007, Salt Lake City, UT 84125; (801) 524-5003. Publications: *Annual Bulletin, Utah Agriculture, Weekly Crop-Weather.*

Department of Agriculture, 350 North Redwood Road, Salt Lake City, UT 84116; (801) 533-5421. Programs: Computerized Branding: Utah is the first state to have a computerized brand renewal system which processed 24,000 brands in one year. Agricultural Resource Development Loan (ARDL): low interest loans to establish conservation practices. Resource Inventory and Monitoring Systems (RIMS): loans to implement soil and water conservation. Publications: *Market News, Biennial Report.*

Agricultural Stabilization and Conservation Service Office, PO Box 11547, Salt Lake City, UT 84147; (801) 524-5013.

Vermont

Vermont Department of Agriculture, State Office Building, 120 State St., Montpelier, VT 05620-2901; (802) 828-2416. Contact: Office of Information for various free directories and brochures including: *Hay Directory and Specialty Foods Directory,* and the following Vermont titles: *Beef, Wool, Game, Cheese, Sugarhouses, Pork, Turkey, Milk, Lamb, Christmas Trees, Maple by Mail.*

Agricultural Statistics: Vermont is included in the New England State Statistical Office. Contact: New England State Statistical Office, P.O. Box 1444, Concord, NH 03302; (603) 224-9639.

Agricultural Stabilization and Conservation Service Office, 346 Shelburne Street, Burlington, VT 05401; (802) 951-6715.

Virginia

Agricultural Statistics Service, R. Bass, Box 1659, Richmond, VA 23213; (804) 786-3500. Publications: *Crops and Livestock, Poultry, Milk and Dairy, Prices and Income, Virginia Agricultural Statistics, Tobacco Sales.*

Department of Agriculture and Commerce, Post Office Box 1163, Richmond, VA 23209-1163; (804) 786-2373. Program: Rural Virginia Development Foundation: researches and evaluates potential venture investment opportunities, established a computerized information exchange system statewide- tel-o-auction, to promote livestock sales. Publications: *Bulletin, Year in Review, Commodity Newsletter.*

Agricultural Stabilization and Conservation Service Office, 400 North Eighth Street, Richmond, VA 23240; (804) 771-2581.

Washington

Agricultural Statistics Service, D. A. Hasslen, Box 609, Olympia, WA 98507; (206) 586-8919. Publication: *Washington Statistical Bulletin.*

Department of Agriculture, PO Box 42560, Olympia, WA 98504-2560; (206) 586-6108. Publications: *Washington State Food and Agricultural Suppliers Directory, Biennial Report, Washington Agricultural Exports Statistical Bulletin, Washington Agricultural Statistics, Washington State Livestock Brand Book, AG-2000 Economic Strategies for Washington Agriculture, The Regulation Handbook for Direct Farm Marketers, Processed Food Marketing in Japan, Business Opportunities Report, Agri-Facts, Crop-Weather Report, Livestock Market News, Fruit and Vegetable Market News, Agriculture Trade Facts, WSDA Pesticide Notes.*

Agricultural Stabilization and Conservation Service Office, US Courthouse, Room 391, West 920 Riverside, Spokane, WA 99201; (509) 353-2307. Publications: *Agri-Facts* which includes the following crop information - *Crop production, Grain Stocks, Vegetables, Fruit, Agricultural Prices, Hogs, Eggs, Milk, Cattle, Cattle on Feed, Farm Labor, Potatoes and Cold Storage; Potato Stocks and Processing; Crop-Weather.* Publications can also be ordered from Agricultural Statistics Board Publications, U.S. Department of Agriculture, NASS, Room 5829, South Building, Washington, DC 20250-2000.

West Virginia

Agricultural Statistics Service, D. Loos, c/o State Department of Agriculture, 1990 N. Kanawha Blvd East, Charleston, WV 25305; (304) 348-2217. Publications: *West Virginia Mountain State Reporter* [includes statistics on major crops and livestock in the state], *West Virginia Crop Weather Bulletin, West Virginia Agricultural Statistics.*

Department of Agriculture, State Capitol, Charleston, WV 25303; (304) 348-3708. Publications: *The Market Bulletin;* The following publications are divided by subject - Cattle: *External Parasite Control, Beef Cattle for Beginners, Herd Health, Identification in West Virginia, Summer Management, Winter Cow Management, Recognizing and Handling Calving Problems, Leptospirosis, an infectious disease of livestock and pets, Abortion in Cattle in West Virginia, Roundworms in Cattle, Breeding Season Management, Dehorning, What You Should Know About Blackleg;* Sheep: *Quality Lamb Production, Winter Ewe Management, Early Weaning of Lambs;* Horses: *Housing Recommendations, Broodmare Management, Internal Parasites in Horses, Equine Foot Care, Horses in West Virginia;* Goats: *Goat Management Guide;* Gardening: *Growing Strawberries in West Virginia, Gardening for Beginners, Home Vegetable Garden Pest Control, Beginning a Backyard Orchard, West Virginia Home Orchard Spray Schedule, Home Gardening is Fun, Beginning with Grapes - No. 1, Grape Pest Control - No. 2;* Bees and Beekeeping: *Beekeeping in West Virginia, Transferring Bees from Box Hives into Modern Equipment, The Diagnosis and Treatment of American Foulbrood, Controlling the Wax Moth in Honey Comb, Swarming of Honey Bees;* Consumer Guides and Recipes: *West Virginia Apples - Consumer Guide and Recipes, A Peach Potpourri, West Virginia Strawberry Recipes, Beef - A Consumer Guide and Recipes, Pork - A Consumer Guide and Recipes, Cooking with Cornmeal, EGG-ceptional Recipes Using Eggs, Egg Facts You Should Know, Turkey Recipes, A Pickle Potpourri, A Roundup of Relishes, 1987 Prizewinning Recipes.*

Agricultural Stabilization and Conservation Service Office, PO Box 1049, Morgantown, WV 26507; (304) 291-4351.

Wisconsin

Agricultural Statistics Service, L. Pratt, Box 9160, Madison, WI 53715; (608) 264-5317. Publication: *Agricultural Statistics; Dairy Facts; Agricultural Land Sales and Rental Rates; Annual Dairy Summary; Custom Rates; Cash Receipts; Farm Costs and Returns; Mink Production; Trout Production.* Several publications are available directly from the USDA/NASS Agricultural Statistics Board Publications, Room 5829 South Building, Washington DC 20250-2000. These include: *Wisconsin Farm Reporter; Crop and Weather; Snow and Frost; Vegetables; Manufacturing Grand Milk Prices; Livestock Review; and Poultry.*

Department of Agriculture, 801 W. Badger Rd., P.O. Box 8911, Madison, WI 53708; (608) 266-2939. Publications: *Direct Marketing Guide, Take Home Guide.*

Agricultural Stabilization and Conservation Service Office, 6515 Watts Road, Suite 100, Madison, WI 53791-2726; (608) 264-5301.

Wyoming

Agricultural Statistics Service, R.W. Coulter, Box 1148, Cheyenne, WY 82003; (307) 772-2181. Publications: *Biweekly Ag Statistics, Winter Wheat Variety, Winter Wheat County Estimates, Barley County Estimates, Hay County Estimates, Sheep and Lamb Loss, Crop Weather Report, Wyoming Agricultural Statistics.*

Department of Agriculture, 2219 Carey Avenue, Cheyenne, WY 82002; (307) 777-6792. Publications: *Your Agriculture Business Plan, Annual Statistical Report, Agricultural Trade Directory, Working With Agricultural Lenders: Understanding the Loan Approval Process, Annual Report, Food Handlers Guide, Wyoming State Fair Preview, Wyoming Agriculture Strategic Plan: 1990-2000, Wyoming Coordinated Resource Management Workbook, Agricultural Loan Volume and Market Shares by Lender, Wyoming Farm and Ranch Finance Survey, Credit for Wyoming Agricultural and Commercial Sectors, Wyoming Farm and Ranch Land Market, Costs of Producing Crops, Prices Received by Wyoming Farmers and Ranchers.*

Agricultural Stabilization and Conservation Service Office, PO Box 920, Casper WY 82602; (307) 261-5231.

Energy General Sources

* *See also Experts Chapter*
* *See also Current Events and Homework Chapter*
* *See also Careers and Workplace; Research Grants in Every Field Chapter*
* *See also Economics, Demographics and Statistics Chapter*
* *See also Environment and Nature Chapter*
* *See also Housing and Real Estate Chapter*
* *See also Weather and Maps Chapter*
* *See also Science and Technology Chapter*
* *See also Housing and Real Estate Chapter*

As the Persian Gulf War made vividly clear, finding new and more efficient sources and uses of energy is one of the most pressing issues facing the world today. Here you'll find information leads on everything from international energy agreements to how you can better insulate your home to lower your heating bills. Not only can you find out about the newest energy-related legislation or the newest developments in geothermal power, but you'll also find sources on such volatile issues as nuclear reactor safety and offshore oil exploration. Whether you're a business that needs an energy audit or a student doing a report on solar energy, these up-to-date resources will provide you with the answers.

* Agricultural Use of Energy

Input Supply and Demand Section
Production System Branch
Economic Research Service
U.S. Department of Agriculture
1301 New York Ave., Room 424
Washington, DC 20005-4788 (202) 219-0459

The Economic Research Service can provide you with current and historical statistics on energy use, prices, and expenditure in agriculture by fuel source such as gasoline, diesel, liquified petroleum gas, fuel oil, etc. The office can also provide you with information on grain based fuels such as alcohol.

* Albuquerque Operations Office

Public Information Office
U.S. Department of Energy (DOE)
PO Box 5400
Albuquerque, NM 87115 (505) 845-5596

This facility provides field level planning for nuclear weapons research and development. It also provides direction for non weapons projects in the areas of nuclear, solar, wind, and geothermal energy projects as well as waste management and transportation research.

* Alcohol Fuel Plant Permits

Distribution Center
Bureau of Alcohol, Tobacco, and Firearms
U.S. Department of the Treasury
7943 Angus Ct.
Springfield, VA 22153 (703) 455-7801

The free booklet, *Alcohol Fuel Plants*, outlines the general provisions of the alcohol fuel plant permit system. Questions and answers are included to clarify certain points in reference to alcohol fuel plant application and operations. If you need further information, contact the Bureau's Regional Office located in your state.

* Alcohol Fuel Production Loans

Office of Alcohol Fuels
Conservation and Renewable Energy
U.S. Department of Energy (DOE)
1000 Independence Ave., SW, Room 5F-086
Washington, DC 20585 (202) 586-2340

Contact this office for information on the Energy Security Act's loan guarantee program (Title II Renewable Energy), designed in part to encourage the private sector to construct alcohol fuel production facilities. The office also monitors the remaining cooperative agreements and feasibility studies under this program.

* American Public Power Association

2301 M. St. NW
Washington, DC 20037 (202) 775-8300

This Association represents municipally owned electric utilities, public utility districts, State and county owned electrical systems and rural cooperatives. It also maintains a 6000 volume library on the electrical power industry as well as compiling statistics and conducting research programs.

* Appliance Labeling

Building Equipment Division
Conservation and Renewable Energy, CE-80
U.S. Department of Energy (DOE)
1000 Independence Ave., SW, Room 6C-016
Washington, DC 20585 (202) 586-9123

Energy guide labels, required by law to be on the back of all major appliances, provide information as to energy efficiency and cost of operation of the particular equipment. Contact this office for information on the Appliance Standards Program.

* Appliance Testing and Evaluation

Building Equipment Division
Building and Community Systems
Conservation and Renewable Energy
U.S. Department of Energy (DOE)
1000 Independence Ave., SW, Room 5H-048
Washington, DC 20585 (202) 586-9123

DOE's Building Equipment Division develops or modifies test procedures for measuring energy saving design procedures in major household appliances. The office also develops minimum energy efficiency standards for these appliances. Contact the office for further information.

* Appropriate Technology Assistance Service

U.S. Department of Energy (DOE)
P.O. Box 2525 (800) 428-2525
Butte, MT 59702-2525 (800) 428-1718 (MT)

National Appropriate Technology Assistance Service (NATAS) provides tailored

Be patient. If any phone number is incorrect, call (area code) 555-1212 and request the new listing.

Energy

information and technical and commercialization assistance by toll-free telephone or mail. NATAS provides two types of assistance services: technical engineering assistance, which can include help with system design, component comparisons, system problem solving, economic analysis, and sources of local help; and commercialization assistance, which includes industry overviews, microeconomic analyses and tailored help to identify and evaluate market trends and locate potential funding sources. In addition to responding to written or phone requests, NATAS also responds via computer bulletin boards and electronic networks such as Dialcom, Login, and Econet.

* Architecture and Engineering

Buildings Systems Division
Buildings and Community Systems
Conservation and Renewable Energy
U.S. Department of Energy (DOE)
1000 Independence Ave., SW, Room 5E-098
Washington, DC 20585 (202) 586-9445

The Buildings Systems Division distributes information and runs outreach programs on energy efficient buildings. The work of this Division focuses on how systems, subsystems, and components of buildings function independently and how they interact. This Division also develops and promotes research on construction and operation methods and standards for application to new or existing structures. Contact this office for detailed program information and information on available publications, or contact the National Energy Information Center and the National Technical Information Service for information.

* Atmospheric Fluid Dynamics

Battel Northwest
Richland Operations Office, DOE
P.O. Box 999
Richland, WA 99352 (509) 375-2121

This office collects and manages research on atmospheric fluid dynamics as they apply to design, performance, and operation of wind turbines. Recent work includes wind turbine wake research, microscale turbulence analyses for dynamic stress load studies, flow characterization, and micrositing in complex terrain. This laboratory has performed wind energy resource assessments for the U.S. and has also developed an international wind energy resource assessment. Contact this office for more detailed information on its projects.

* Audit and Accounting Files

Division of Public Affairs
Federal Energy Regulatory Commission
825 North Capitol Street, NE
Washington, DC 20426 (202) 208-1088

Contact this office for information on examining the accounting files and FERC audits of gas, electric, and oil companies.

* Automobile Fuel Economy

Motor Vehicle Requirements Division
Office of Market Incentives, Rulemaking
National Highway Traffic Safety Administration (NHTSA)
U.S. Department of Transportation
400 7th Street, SW, Room 5320
Washington, DC 20590 (202) 366-0846

NHTSA issues fuel economy standards and collects information on the technological and economic capabilities of automobile manufacturers to maximize fuel efficiency. Contact this office for information and referrals.

* Basic Energy Sciences Advisory Committee

U.S. Department of Energy (DOE)
19901 Germantown Rd.
Germantown, MD 20585 (301) 903-5565

This Committee was established in 1986 to provide the Secretary of Energy with advice on elements of the Department's Basic Energy Sciences Program.

* Biofuels

Biofuels and Municipal Waste Technology Division
Conservation and Renewable Energy
U.S. Department of Energy (DOE)
1000 Independence Ave., SW, Room 5H-072

Washington, DC 20585 (202) 586-5350

DOE researchers provide the technology base for the production of cost-competitive liquid and gaseous fuels from biomass resources. During the early stages of biofuels development, DOE provides leadership and sponsors long-term, high-risk research and development (R&D). As technology is developed, industry's level of cooperation and cost sharing increases. Finally, when the technology is sufficiently advanced and the economics are sufficiently defined, industry assumes responsibility for commercialization of the developed technology. Contact this office for the program summary and other information.

* Biomass Feedstock Fuels

Biofuels and Municipal Waste Technology Division
U.S. Department of Energy (DOE)
1000 Independence Ave., SW, Room 5H-086
Washington, DC 20585 (202) 586-5350

This office directs long-term research and development into increasing supplies of biomass feedstocks. Researchers also develop conversion technologies for producing heat, gas, and liquid fuels from a variety of biomass and municipal waste feedstocks. They also investigate aquatic, herbal, and wood crops with potential for increased biomass yields, as well as related systems. Regional programs focus on technology transfer and matching local feedstocks to conversion technologies.

* Biomass Energy Directory - 1992

Independent Energy Inc.
620 Central Avenue North
Milaca, MN 56353-1788 (612) 983-6892

This directory contains listings for hundreds of companies involved in the area of biomass energy. Listings include company name, address, and a description of their activities in the biomass field. The directory sells for $27.

* Bulletins: Ocean Thermal to Wind Power

Science and Technology Division
Reference Section, Library of Congress
Washington, DC 20540 (202) 707-5580

Informal series of reference guides are issued free from the Science and Technology Division under the general title, *LC Science Tracer Bullet*. These guides are designed to help readers locate published material on subjects about which they have only general knowledge. New titles in the series are announced in the weekly Library of Congress *Information Bulletin* that is distributed to many libraries. The following is a list of *Tracer Bullets* currently available:

80-7	*Solar Energy*
80-8	*Electric and Hybrid Vehicles*
80-12	*Ocean Thermal Energy*
80-16	*Synthetic Fuels*
81-5	*Wind Power*
81-13	*Wood As Fuel*
83-9	*Geothermal Energy*

* Computer Control of Power Systems

Computer Systems Section
Power System Control Center
Tennessee Valley Authority (TVA)
2N 10A Power Control Center
Chattanooga, TN 37401 (615) 751-8678

The Computer Systems Section develops and maintains the software systems that control such functions as economic dispatch, automatic generation control, and logging. Telemetered information from TVA's plants, substations, and from interconnection points with utilities is analyzed and processed to help the load coordinators determine the most economical and reliable method to run the power system. Personnel also are responsible for program development and maintenance of the software for the five area dispatch control centers and a microwave alarm logger.

* Conservation Technology Transfer

State Energy Programs Division, CE-54
Office of Technical Assistance Programs
U.S. Department of Energy (DOE)
1000 Independence Ave., SW
Washington, DC 20585 (202) 586-5517

Be patient. If any phone number is incorrect, call (area code) 555-1212 and request the new listing.

General Sources

The Energy Extension Service helps market and transfer energy conservation technology and information to businesses. Contact this office to find more out about the information and technology available. For publications, contact the CAREIRS center at (800) 523-2929.

* Consumer Countries

Office of Global Energy
Bureau of Economics and Business Affairs
U.S. Department of State
2201 C St., NW, Room 3336
Washington, DC 20520 (202) 647-4017

This office deals with energy-consuming countries--countries that use more energy than they produce. The primary portfolio is dealing with the International Energy Agency in Paris, which was begun in response to the oil crisis. This office, which coordinates policy regarding energy and energy crises, is broken down into the various energy sources (oil, natural gas, coal, nuclear, solar, wind and electricity) with each looking at the stock and emergency preparedness. They also each follow a handful of countries and track international organizations. Along with the Departments of Energy and Commerce, they try to sell energy when they can.

* Consumers and Energy Issues

Congressional, Intergovernmental and Public Affairs
U.S. Department of Energy (DOE)
1000 Independence Ave., SW, Room 8G-026
Washington, DC 20585 (202) 586-5373

This office analyzes how U.S. Department of Energy policies affect the public energy consumer. It is a source of referral for specific program information to other offices in the U.S. Department of Energy.

* Consumption Statistics

Energy End-Use Division
Energy Markets and End Use
Energy Information Administration
U.S. Department of Energy (DOE)
1000 Independence Ave., SW, Room 2F-065
Washington, DC 20585 (202) 586-1112

This office compiles statistics on energy consumption in U.S. residential, commercial, industrial, and transportation sectors by sector and by fuel type. Contact this office for more information and available publications.

* Deep Seabed Mining

Ocean Minerals and Energy Division
National Ocean Service
National Oceanic and Atmospheric Administration (NOAA)
U.S. Department of Commerce
1825 Connecticut Ave., NW
Washington, DC 20235 (202) 606-4121

Extensive information is available on deep seabed mining, which includes the annual report to Congress and an updated environmental assessment of NOAA deep seabed mining licensees' exploration plans. This office can provide you with information regarding the research conducted concerning the environmental impact of the mining, as well as information on the regulations and licenses. The 1989 and 1991 annual reports are particularly good for information.

* Defense Energy Emergencies

Energy Emergency Operations
International Affairs and Energy Emergencies
U.S. Department of Energy (DOE)
1000 Independence Ave., SW, Room 8F0973
Washington, DC 20585 (202) 586-3271

This office conducts programs to ensure that the U.S. can meet its defense energy needs and that government and industry can continue their essential functions in a catastrophic emergency. It works to reduce U.S. vulnerability to such emergencies and to help improve energy emergency decision making. Contact this office for more detailed information.

* Department of Energy Annual Report

Office of Public Affairs
U.S. Department of Energy (DOE)

1000 Independence Ave., SW, Room 8H-068
Washington, DC 20585 (202) 586-5575

The Division of Budget and Administration prepares the U.S. Department of Energy's annual budget and *Annual Report*. For copies of these and other Department of Energy Publications, contact the office of Public Affairs, a good starting point for any quest for information from the Department of Energy.

* Diesel Fuel Recording

Interstate Commerce Commission
12th St. and Constitution Ave., NW
Washington, DC 20423 (202) 927-6237

This recording states the average diesel fuel price each week after a survey is taken of fuel stations across the country.

* Department of Energy Budget

Office of the Controller
Office of Management and Administration
U.S. Department of Energy (DOE)
1000 Independence Ave., SW, Room 4A-139
Washington, DC 20585 (202) 586-4171

The free publication, *Budget Highlights*, summarizes, in statistics and narrative description, the current budget and programs of the U.S. Department of Energy.

* DOE Energy Education Programs

Office of Energy Research
Office of University and Science Education Programs
U.S. Department of Energy (DOE)
1000 Independence Ave., SW, Room 3F-061
Washington, DC 20585 (301) 586-8949

Education has been an important part of the U.S. Department of Energy's mission since its creation in 1977. While the Department has traditionally concentrated its efforts on education at the University level through graduate fellowships and research appointments, the Department has expanded its approach and now also funds significant programs for precollege education and science literacy. The Office of University and Science Education Programs was formed within the Office of Energy Research in 1990 to coordinate education programs within the Department. The *Education Programs Catalog* details Dept. of Energy programs at the pre-college, under-graduate, graduate, and general public level. It also contains a list of the National Laboratories run by or affiliated with the Dept. of Energy and the education programs they sponsor.

* DOE Energy Research

Office of Energy Research
U.S. Department of Energy (DOE)
1000 Independence Ave., SW, Room 7B-058
Washington, DC 20585 (301) 586-5430

The Office of Energy Research gives advice on U.S. Department of Energy research programs, university-based education and training activities, as well as grants and other forms of energy assistance. Office programs support both energy research and technologies that have non-energy related spinoffs. Contact this office for available program information, including the publication, *Programs of the Office of Energy Research*, which provides a summary of office research and education programs.

* DOE Public Reading Rooms

U.S. Department of Energy (DOE)
Public Reading Room
1000 Independence Ave., SW, Room 1E-90
Washington, DC 20585 (800) 638-8081

A variety of program documents are available at DOE Public Reading Rooms and Information Offices listed below. Nuclear Regulatory Commission materials are available at the listed NRC Local Public Document rooms. For further information about the Local Public Document Room Program, call the above office.

Albuquerque
Operations Office, National Atomic Museum, P.O. Box 5400, Kirtland Air Force Base, E, Albuquerque, NM 87115; (505) 844-8443

Bartlesville
Institute for Petroleum and Energy Research Library, U.S. Dept. of Energy, 220 N. Virginia Ave.,PO Box 2128, Bartlesville, OK 74003; (918) 337-4371.

Be patient. If any phone number is incorrect, call (area code) 555-1212 and request the new listing.

Energy

Boston
Support Office, U.S. Department of Energy, 10 Causeway Street, Room 1197, Boston, MA 02222-1035; (617) 565-7700

Chicago
Operations Office, Building 201, 9800 South Cass Ave., Argonne, IL 60439; (312) 972-2010

Idaho
Operations Office, Public Reading Room, 1776 Science Drive, Idaho Falls, ID 83402; (208) 526-1144

Morgantown
Energy Technology Center Library, 3610 Collins Ferry Road, PO Box 880, Morgantown, WV 26507-0880; (304) 291-4183.

Nevada
Operations Office, Public Reading Room, U.S. Department of Energy, P.O. Box 98518, Las Vegas, NV 89193-8518; (702) 295-1128

Oak Ridge
Operations Office, Federal Building, 200 Administration Road, PO Box 2001, Oak Ridge, TN 37830; (615) 576-1216

Pittsburgh
Energy Technology Center, U.S. Department of Energy, Cochran Mill Road, Building 95, PO Box 10940, Pittsburgh, PA 15236-0940; (412) 892-4751.

Richland
Operations Office, U.S. Department of Energy, 825 Jadwin Avenue, PO Box 1970, A1-65, Richland, WA 99352; (509) 376-8583

Rocky Flats Office. Front Range Community College, 3645 West 112 Avenue, Westminster, CO 80030; (303) 469-4435.

San Francisco
Operations Office, Wells Fargo Bank Building, 1333 Broadway, Oakland, CA 94612; (415) 273-4428

Savannah River
Operations Office, DOE Public Documents Reading Room, Gregg-Graniteville Library, Second Floor, University of South Carolina-Aiken, 171 University Parkway, Aiken, SC 29801; (803) 725-2889.

Southeastern Power Administration
U.S. Department of Energy, Legal Library, Samuel Elbert Building, Public Square, Elberton, GA 30635; (404) 283-9911.

* Donation of Energy-Related Laboratory Equipment

University and Industry Programs
Office of Field Operations Management, ER-80
U.S. Department of Energy (DOE)
1000 Independence Ave., SW
Washington, DC 20585 (202) 586-8949

Used energy equipment is donated to nonprofit educational institutions of higher learning for use in appropriate programs. Lists of eligible equipment can be found in the *Energy-Related Laboratory Equipment Guide* and on the Eligible Equipment Grants Access Data System. Contact the office for further information and details.

* Economics and Statistics

Economics and Statistics Division
Office of Energy Markets and End Use
Energy Information Administration
U.S. Department of Energy (DOE)
1000 Independence Ave., SW, Room 2G-089
Washington, DC 20585 (202) 586-1441

This office compiles economic and financial energy statistics, including domestic and international trends.

* Electric Power Data

Electric Power Division
Coal, Nuclear, Electric and Alternate Fuels

Energy Information Administration
U.S. Department of Energy (DOE)
1707 H Street, NW
Washington, DC 20585 (202) 254-5419

This office collects analytical data on electric power supply, including capacity, generation, distribution, fuel use, finances, and rates. It also prepares projections of capacity, generation, fuel use, costs, rates, financial requirements, and distribution of electric power. The effects of policy and regulatory actions on the electric utilities' rates, costs, capacity, generation, distribution, finance, and consumption of input fuels are also studied. Contact this office for more information.

* Electric Power Supply and Rates

Transmission and Consumer Service
Distributer and Marketing Services, MR5S
Tennessee Valley Authority (TVA)
Chattanooga, TN 37402-2801 (615) 751-6886

TVA has a goal to operate a more competitive power system by not increasing its power rates for its consumers for three years. Rate stability in 1988 avoided a 6 percent rate increase and resulted in $300 million in savings for consumers. For information on electric power supply and rates, or to receive brochures with coal and electricity statistics, including breakdowns of monthly residential and industrial electric bills, and the use of TVA revenue dollars, contact this office.

* Electric Utility Systems

Administrator, Rural Electrification Administration
U.S. Department of Agriculture (USDA), Room 4051
Washington, DC 20250 (202) 720-9542

USDA lends money to about 1,000 rural electric companies and maintains a staff that is knowledgeable on both operations and equipment.

* Electricity - Generation and Transmission

Office of Energy Management
Utility Systems Division
U.S. Department of Energy (DOE)
1000 Independence Ave, SW, Room 5F-064
Washington, DC 20585 (202) 586-2828

This division plans and manages research and development programs that will result in new technologies to improve the generation and transmission of electricity, the reliability of electric networks, and impacts resulting from generating and transmission activities. It also researches new methods and techniques for addressing energy demand and supply options that will enable more efficient delivery and use of energy in community shared systems.

* Emergencies

Energy Emergency Plans and Integration
International Affairs and Energy Emergencies
U.S. Department of Energy (DOE)
1000 Independence Ave., SW, Room GH-060
Washington, DC 20585 (202) 586-4000

This office develops energy emergency plans and responses to energy emergencies, and manages international cooperation in response to energy emergencies. Contact this office for more detailed information.

* Emergency Policy

Energy Policy and Evaluation
International Affairs and Energy Emergencies
U.S. Department of Energy (DOE)
1000 Independence Ave., SW, Room GE-262
Washington, DC 20585 (202) 586-2442

This office defines, analyzes, and coordinates energy emergency policy issues, focusing on resolving problems that may hinder effective U.S. responses to energy emergencies. This office also assesses the impact of proposed responses on all levels of government, private industry, and individuals. Contact the office for further information.

* Energy Analysis

Energy Information Administration
Energy Analysis and Systems Division
U.S. Department of Energy (DOE)
1707 H St. NW

Be patient. If any phone number is incorrect, call (area code) 555-1212 and request the new listing.

General Sources

Washington, DC 20585 (202) 254-5392

This Division develops and maintains statistical information and short term forecasting systems related to coal, nuclear, electric, and alternative fuels. It assesses existing and potential resources and reserves, analyzes historical trends, produces forecasts for the short term, performs quality control, and improves and maintains systems for data collection and analysis.

* Energy and Mineral Resources

Office of Energy and Marine Geology
U.S. Geological Survey
National Center, MS 915
Reston, VA 22092 (703) 648-6470

Investigations of the nature, extent, and origin of the Nation's coal, oil and gas, oil shale, uranium, and geothermal resources are basic to this office's research efforts. Acquired data are placed in computerized databases, such as the National Coal Resources Data System.

* Energy Conservation and Solar Power

Office of Energy Conservation and Energy Management
Tennessee Valley Authority (TVA)
703 Power Building
Chattanooga, TN 37401 (615) 632-4100

The Tennessee Valley Authority publishes a number of brochures and information bulletins on energy conservation and on the use of solar energy in your home. The following publications are available free from TVA.

Introduction to Solar Energy
Solar Energy in New Homes
Read Your Electric Meter
Save on Your Electric Bills
Insulate Your Attic
Insulate Your Water Heater
Water Source Heat Pump: How to get home heating and cooling from your own backyard.
The New Variable Speed Heat Pump
Let the Sun Get You in Hot Water
Build-It-Yourself Solar Water Heater
Shading Devices
Seasonal Sun and Home Orientation
Natural Cooling

* Energy Extension Services

Energy Management and Extension Branch, CE-522
Office of State and Local Assistance Programs
U.S. Department of Energy (DOE)
1000 Independence Ave., SW
Washington, DC 20585 (202) 586-9645

The Energy Extension Service (EES) provides small-scale energy users, such as individuals, small businesses, and local governments, with personalized information and on-site technical assistance for practical energy conservation, including the uses of renewable energy resources. EES supplies block grants for approved programs. All states, as well as U.S. territories and the District of Columbia, offer this conservation assistance. Contact the State and Territorial Energy offices, listed at the end of this section, for information on particular programs.

* Energy Information Administration

U.S. Department of Energy (DOE)
1000 Independence Ave., SW, Room 2F-095
Washington, DC 20585 (202) 586-1094

The Energy Information Administration's *Annual Report* provides a good summary of the Administrations' structure and key informational contacts within the offices.

* Energy Information Directory

National Energy Information Center
Energy Information Administration
U.S. Department of Energy (DOE)
1000 Independence Ave., SW, Room E1-231
Washington, DC 20585 (202) 586-8800

The National Energy Information Center is the central distribution point for most U.S. Department of Energy publications, including the free *Energy Information Administration Publications Directory: A Users Guide*. *The Directory* includes current program information sources; an index of DOE, State, and Federal Agency contacts; a directory of DOE technical information with descriptions of computerized databases and other resources; Congressional Committees and Subcommittees that have jurisdiction over various components of the Civilian Radioactive Waste Management Program; and DOE Public Reading Rooms and Information Offices, and NRC local public document rooms; and listings of selected publications. Also ask for the latest edition of the *Energy Information Directory*, a comprehensive guide to energy information in the Federal government. The NEIC should be an early contact in any energy research project.

* Energy Inventions and Innovation

Office of National Programs
Inventions and Innovations Division
U.S. Department of Energy (DOE)
1000 Independence Ave, SW, Room 5E-052
Washington, DC 20585 (202) 586-1479

Two principal programs of this division, the Energy Related Inventions Program (ERIP) and the Innovative Concepts Program (ICP) help non-Federal entities to identify, evaluate, and provide financial and technical support for inventions and innovations that may have a significant impact on energy production or utilization. ERIP provides assistance the commercialization of recommended technologies. ICP provides assistance for the development of technologies beyond the concept stage. Contact this office for more information.

* Energy Markets Development/Analysis

Office of Policy, Planning, and Analysis
Office of Electricity, Coal, Nuclear,
and Renewable Policy
U.S. Department of Energy (DOE)
1000 Independence Ave., SW, Room 7H-075
Washington, DC 20585 (202) 586-5727

This office analyzes factors that influence energy demand such as economic, technical, environmental, regulatory, and institutional developments. Major areas of concentration include analysis of electrical power, coal, and nuclear resource markets, incentives designed to stimulate production and availability for more efficient use of resources and enhance U.S. energy security.

* Energy Publications Directory, 1977-1989

Energy Information Administration
National Energy Information Center
U.S. Department of Energy (DOE)
1000 Independence Ave.,SW
Washington, DC 20585 (202) 586-8800

The Energy Information Administration has compiled a massive directory that lists some 895 Energy publications written between 1977 and 1989. The report is indexed by subject, title, and report number. Contact the National Energy Information Center for a copy of the Directory.

* Energy Research Grants

Office of Energy Research
U.S. Department of Energy (DOE)
1000 Independence Ave., SW, Room 7B-058
Washington, DC 20585 (301) 586-5430

The Office of Energy Research sponsors research, training, and related activities in the following program areas: Basic Energy Sciences, Field Operations Management, Fusion Energy, Health and Environmental Research, High Energy and Nuclear Physics, Scientific Computing Staff, Superconduction Super Collider, University and Science Education Programs, Program Analysis, and other program areas that are announced in the Federal Register. The Office of Energy Research *Grant Application and Guide* lists different research division projects with contact numbers for the programs. It is available free.

* Energy-Saving Equipment in Buildings

Building Equipment Division
Conservation and Renewable Energy
U.S. Department of Energy (DOE)
1000 Independence Ave., SW, Room 5H-048
Washington, DC 20585 (202) 586-9123

Be patient. If any phone number is incorrect, call (area code) 555-1212 and request the new listing.

Energy

This Division supplies the private sector with the technological base on which to develop and test high efficiency energy equipment used in operating residential and commercial buildings. This office is also responsible for administration of the Appliance Standards Program. Contact this office for more information.

* Energy Science Research

Accelerator and Fusion Research Division
Lawrence Berkeley Laboratory (LBL)
1 Cyclotron Road
Mail Stop 50A/5104
Berkeley, CA 94720 (510) 486-5771

The Lawrence Berkeley Laboratory undertakes a wide ranging research program in Energy Sciences. Research is carried out by four divisions: material sciences, chemical sciences, energy and environment, and earth sciences. LBL pursues basic research and seeks ways of practical application of the basic results. The work of this division of the Laboratory is designed to reflect Energy Department priorities in finding ways to explore and recover energy resources, as well as protecting people and the environment from possible hazards. Contact the above office for further information.

* Environmental Impact Statements

Office of National Environmental Policy Act (NEPA)
Project Assistance
Environment, Safety, and Health
U.S. Department of Energy (DOE)
1000 Independence Ave., SW, Room 3E-080
Washington, DC 20585 (202) 586-4610

NEPA documents prepared for DOE activities are reviewed and approved through this office to determine whether DOE programs require Environmental Impact Statements. This office also reviews energy-related Environmental Impact Statements from other agencies. Contact this office for more detailed information.

* Environmental Issues and Energy Development

Office of Environmental Analysis, PE-63
Assistant Secretary for Environment, Safety and Health
U.S. Department of Energy (DOE)
1000 Independence Ave., SW, Room 4G-036
Washington, DC 20585 (202) 586-2061

This office analyzes proposed environmental policies, laws, and regulations to determine their effects on energy development and use. The office also assesses the potential impact on the environment of energy technologies being developed by the Department of Energy, along with the potential impact of national energy strategies at both the national and regional level. Contact the office for more detailed information.

* Environmental Guidance

Office of Environment, Safety and Health
Office of Environmental Guidance
U.S. Department of Energy (DOE)
1000 Independence Ave., SW, Room GA-098
Washington, DC 20585 (202) 586-8505

This office is responsible for developing written compliance policies, standards, guidance documents, and internal DOE orders which cover the full range of environmental statutes and regulations. The division monitors regulatory and legislative developments, keeps DOE personnel abreast of emerging and changing environmental requirements, coordinates the development of Departmental positions, and serves as the advocate for DOE's position with regard to other agencies rulemaking efforts.

* Environmental Protection, International

Bureau of Oceans and International Environmental and Scientific Affairs
U.S. Department of State
2201 C St., NW, Room 4325
Washington, DC 20520 (202) 647-9266

This office looks at international environmental issues and concerns, such as pollution, acid rain, global climate changes, the ozone, and toxic waste. They monitor bilateral and multilateral agreements, and work with other agencies in trying to develop ways to handle these environmental concerns.

* Federal Energy Management

Federal Energy Management Program (FEMP), CE-44
Office of Conservation and Renewable Energy
U.S. Department of Energy (DOE)
1000 Independence Ave., SW
Room 5E-080
Washington, DC 20585 (202) 586-1211

This office coordinates the Federal government's energy management efforts. The *FEMP Update*, published quarterly by the FEMP, provides information that will assist Federal managers in their energy management responsibilities. On August 17, 1991 President Bush signed an Executive Order (12759) which directs all Federal Agencies to improve the energy efficiency of their buildings by 20% from 1985-2000. A subgoal of the President's strategy is to reduce motor vehicle petroleum use by 10% by 1995 over 1991 levels. Contact this office above for further information, or to obtain a copy of FEMP's *Annual Report to Congress for Fiscal Year 1990*.

* Federal Energy Policy

Commerce Clearing House, Inc.
4025 West Peterson Ave.
Chicago, IL 60646 (312) 583-8500

The *Federal Energy Guidelines* is a set of loose-leaf publications dealing primarily with DOE programs, certain other Federal energy activities, and general data regarding energy policy are produced from an automated data base. Nongovernment offices can obtain a subscription by contacting the office above.

* Federal Energy Regulatory Commission

Federal Energy Regulatory Commission (FERC)
Division of Public Affairs
825 North Capitol Street, NE
Room 2214
Washington, DC 20426 (202) 208-1088

This office can supply you with information on the work of the Federal Energy Regulatory Commission (FERC). This office can also assist you in obtaining copies of FERC official documents.

* Federal Energy Regulatory Commission Publications

Reference and Information Services Branch
Federal Energy Regulatory Commission (FERC)
825 North Capitol Street, NE
Room 1000
Washington, DC 20426 (202) 208-1371

The *Federal Energy Regulatory Commission Publications Directory* provides descriptions, sources, stock numbers, and prices, when applicable, of the latest editions of publications and staff reports issued by the Federal Energy Regulatory Commission or the former Federal Power Commission. Many reports and data files are available on diskette. Contact the office above to obtain a free copy. Orders from FERC for publications must be sent in writing.

* Films on Energy Issues

Civilian Radioactive Waste Group
901 D St. Suite 201B
Washington, DC 20024 (202) 586-2835

This group has two video tapes for loan to the public. The first tape looks at the issue of monitored retrievable storage facilities for nuclear waste. The second examines worldwide nuclear waste management. In addition, this group will make you a compilation tape that examines several issues in the area of nuclear waste management. This service is free, all you have to do is supply a blank VHS tape.

* Financial Statistics and Projections

Economics and Statistics Division
Energy Markets and End Use
Energy Information Administration
U.S. Department of Energy (DOE)
1000 Independence Ave., SW, Room 2G-089
Washington, DC 20585 (202) 586-1441

This office compiles economic and financial energy statistics and projections, and periodic assessments of the U.S. energy situation are made. Additionally, it evaluates and interprets current trends and events in the U.S. and international energy situations. For available information and publications, contact this office.

Be patient. If any phone number is incorrect, call (area code) 555-1212 and request the new listing.

General Sources

* Fuel Economy and State Motor Vehicle Inspections

Records and Motor Vehicle Services Division (NTS-43)
National Highway Traffic Safety Administration (NHTSA)
U.S. Department of Transportation
400 7th Street, SW
Washington, DC 20590 (202) 366-2676

NHTSA's Motor Vehicle Inspection Program is aimed at providing car owners with preventative information on what repairs are needed to achieve greater safety, lower pollution, and better mileage. The annual *Study of the State Motor Vehicle Inspection Program* is available from this office.

* Fuel Efficiency and Vehicle Research and Testing

Vehicle Research and Test Center
Research and Development
National Highway Traffic Safety Administration (NHTSA)
U.S. Department of Transportation
P.O. Box 37
East Liberty, OH 43319 (513) 666-4511

NHTSA evaluates the effectiveness of Federal Motor Vehicle Safety Standards. This engineering facility performs tests to obtain basic data used to establish standards for safety and fuel efficiency of motor vehicles.

* General Accounting Office Studies

Energy Issue Area Resources
U.S. General Accounting Office (GAO)
441 G. St. NW
Washington, DC 20548 (202) 275-1441

The GAO's Energy Issue Area conducts in-depth studies of the production, regulation, and consumption of all forms of energy. Aspects of the GAO's work include evaluating the effectiveness of energy security policies and programs, the management of energy research and development programs and nuclear waste disposal programs, the safety of defense and commercial nuclear facilities, and the procedures and controls governing energy programs. Recent reports of interest includes *Bibliography of GAO Documents* January 1986 - December 1989 (GAO/RCED 90-179). To get on the GAO's mailing list or to order this free report, call (202) 275-6241.

* Genetic Research

Life Sciences Program
Lawrence Berkeley Laboratory
One Cyclotron Rd.
Mail Stop 50A/5104
Berkeley, CA 94720 (510) 486-5771

The Life Sciences Program at the Lawrence Berkeley Laboratory undertakes research into genes and related aspects of genetic structure. It also researches radiobiology, nuclear medicine, biotechnology, and cellular and molecular damage caused by energy-related environmental hazards. Contact this office for more detailed information on its programs.

* Geothermal Energy

Geothermal Technology Division
Conservation and Renewable Energy
U.S. Department of Energy (DOE)
1000 Independence Ave., SW, Room 5H-065
Washington, DC 20585 (202) 586-5340

Geothermal energy technology improvements are needed before the more difficult resources--moderate-temperature hydrothermal fluids, geopressured brines, hot dry rock, and magma--can compete economically with conventional power generation technologies. Until these technologies become available for industry use, this resource cannot meet its full potential in the Nation's energy supply mix. This division supports geothermal technology development and transfer through government/industry cooperation. Research that promises future economic expansion of geothermal development and use is given priority. Contact this office for more information and the program summary.

* Grand Coulee and Other Dams

Commissioner's Office, Bureau of Reclamation
U.S. Department of the Interior
18th and C Sts., NW
Washington, DC 20240 (202) 208-4662

Across the West, the Bureau of Reclamation annually supplies over 210,000 billion gallons of water to more than 23 million people for municipal, industrial, and agricultural use. The best known Reclamation projects are the Grand Coulee Dam on the Columbia River and the Hoover Dam on the Colorado River. Project water is delivered to almost 10 million acres of farmland to produce crops valued at $7.5 billion annually. The Bureau's non-polluting hydroelectric powerplants supply electricity to 17 million persons. Reclamation reservoirs also provide millions of visitors with facilities for fishing, swimming, picnicking, and sightseeing.

* Heat Pump Program

Residential Energy Services Program
Tennessee Valley Authority (TVA)
3N45B Signal Place
1101 Market St.
Chattanooga, TN 37402-2801 (615) 751-5261

TVA and participating local power distributors offer a heat pump program to encourage the installation of energy-efficient heat pumps in existing residential dwellings. The plan includes an on-site inspection to ensure the heat pump is correctly installed. In addition, distributors may offer such incentives as cash payments, electric bill credits, or low-interest loans. Loans may be used for approved weatherization improvements, such as attic and floor insulation and storm windows, installed along with a heat pump. No down payment is required, and customers may take up to 10 years to repay the loans.

* Home Energy Audits

Office of Technical Assistance Programs
U.S. Department of Energy (DOE)
1000 Independence Ave, SW
Washington, DC 20585 (202) 586-5517

Through the Residential Conservation Service, eligible gas and electric customers can request that their large utility companies give them home energy audits and related services to help them use energy more efficiently. Owners and renters of single-family residences and multifamily residences in buildings with up to four units are being targeted for this service. Given a free energy audit of their premises and cost information on recommended energy-saving measures, residents would take energy-saving actions. Contact this office for more information.

* Household Energy Consumption and Expenditures, 1987

Office of Energy Markets and End Use
Energy End Use Division
Energy Information Administration
U.S. Department of Energy (DOE)
1000 Independence Ave., SW, Room 2F-065
Washington, DC 20585 (202) 586-1122

Household Energy Consumption and Expenditures, 1987 is the second report based on 1987 RECS data. The 1987 RECS, the seventh in a series of national surveys of households and their energy suppliers, provides baseline information on how households in the United States use energy. A randomly selected set of housing units that includes single-family detached homes, townhouses, apartment buildings, condominiums, and mobile homes were selected for the survey. Data from the RECS and a companion survey, the *Residential Transportation Energy Consumption Survey*, are available to the public in published reports such as this one and on public use tapes.

* Housing Energy Characteristics 1987

Office of Energy Markets and End Use
Energy End Use Division
Energy Information Administration
U.S. Department of Energy (DOE)
1000 Independence Ave., SW, Room 2F-065
Washington, DC 20585 (202) 586-1122

Housing Characteristics 1987 is the first of a series of reports based on data from the 1987 RECS, the seventh in the series of national surveys of households and their energy suppliers. These surveys provide baseline information on how households in the U.S. use energy. Contact this office for more information.

* Hydroelectric Power

Resource Management
Bureau of Reclamation
U.S. Department of the Interior

Be patient. If any phone number is incorrect, call (area code) 555-1212 and request the new listing.

Energy

P.O. Box 25007
Denver CO 80225 (303) 236-3289

The Bureau of Reclamation is currently operating 49 powerplants at different sites throughout the West. For further information on the impact of hydroelectric power and the Bureau's efforts, contact this office.

* Hydroelectric Power Films

U.S. Army Corps of Engineers
Directorate of Information Management
Visual Information Branch
20 Massachusetts Ave., NW
Washington, DC 20314 (202) 272-0017

This office maintains a still photographic library and offers a free film loan and video distribution program. The Corps has educational and public relations films on their recreational facilities, navigation, flood control, hydro-electric power, and environmental systems. Write for information on the how to participate in the program.

* Industrial Energy Bibliography

Office of Scientific and Technical Information
U.S. Department of Energy (DOE)
P.O. Box 62
Oak Ridge, TN 37831 (615) 576-1196

The *Technical Reports Bibliography* is the first annotated publication containing information on all scientific and technical reports sponsored by the DOE Industrial Energy Conservation Program during the years 1974-1987. Contact this office for information on ordering.

* Industrial Energy Conservation

National Technical Information Service
5285 Port Royal Road (800) 553-6847
Springfield, VA 22161 (703) 557-4660

The monthly publication, *Industrial Energy Conservation*, announces the current worldwide information on all aspects of energy conservation in industry, including alternative energy sources; improved materials, equipment, and processes; waste heat recovery; and industrial waste management. This publication contains the abstracts of DOE reports, journal articles, conference papers, patents, theses, and monographs added to the Energy Data Base (EDB) during the past month. Also included is information obtained through acquisition programs or interagency agreements and through the International Energy Agency's Energy Technology Data Exchange or government-to-government agreements. The digests in *IEC* and other citations on energy conservation in industry technologies back to 1974 are available for on-line searching and retrieval on EDB. Current information, added daily to EDB, is available to DOE and its contractors through the DOE Integrated Technical Information System. Customized profiles can be developed to provide current information to meet each user's needs. The entire Energy Data Base is available on commercial on-line retrieval systems. (Order #PB89-93390011).

* Industrial Energy Technologies

Office of Industrial Programs
Deputy Assistant Secretary for Conservation
U.S. Department of Energy (DOE)
1000 Independence Ave., SW, Room 6B-052
Washington, DC 20585 (202) 586-2098

Here researchers develop new energy technologies for improved energy efficiency in the industrial process and greater fuel flexibility. This office can supply you with several basic reports describing what programs are being undertaken. Reports on the results of their studies are available from the National Technical Information Service.

* Industrial Programs: Research in Progress

National Technical Information Service
U.S. Department of Commerce
5285 Port Royal Rd.
Springfield, VA 22161 (703) 557-4660

The report, *Office of Industrial Programs: Research in Progress* contains summaries for currently active projects supported by the Office of Industrial Programs. The report was prepared from the DOE Research-in-Progress database maintained by the Office of Scientific and Technical Information. Write to the office above to obtain a copy of this report.

* Institutional Energy Conservation Grants

Conservation and Renewable Energy Programs, CE-531
Institutional Conservation Program Division
U.S. Department of Energy (DOE)
1000 Independence Ave., SW, Room 5G-063
Washington, DC 20585 (202) 586-8034

Public and private nonprofit schools and hospitals can get matching, cost-shared grants to make detailed energy analyses and energy-saving capital improvements. The government will contribute 50 percent of the cost of these conservation projects, and in certain hardship cases, they may provide more. Contact this office for more information.

* Integrated Technical Information System

U.S. Department of Energy (DOE)
Office of Scientific and Technical Information (OSTI)
P.O. Box 62
Oak Ridge, TN 37831 (615) 576-1222

The Integrated Technical Information System (ITIS), developed by the DOE, provides access to DOE databases in the Energy Data Information System; information merging for customized information products; and electronic mail, a communications link among OSTI, DOE, and contractor offices. Library specialists, information managers, and researchers can work from remote terminals to search various databases on ITIS. The following databases are part of the ITIS system.

Energy Science and Technology Database. This database contains citations in associated sciences, medicine ecology and other fields outside the conventional energy areas. The database is updated nightly.

Management Information File (MIF). MIF contains selected data elements from all records entered into the Energy Science and Database since 1974, as well as Controlled Access File records. MIF records contain enough information for report ordering.

Reports Holding File (RHF). This is a directory of DOE and non-DOE reports processed and held at the Office of Scientific and Technical Information from 1947 to the present.

Research in Progress (RIP). This database contains administrative and technical information on all current and recently completed unclassified research projects performed or funded by the U.S. Department of Energy. Citations are maintained in the database for five years after project completion.

Controlled Access File (CAF). This database contains records of DOE documents and other materials that are not classified but which legal reasons, such as patent or copyright questions, restrict distribution.

Minority Economic Impact (MEI). Found here are bibliographic references to selected books, reports, and journal articles concerned with the impact of energy on minorities.

Nevada Nuclear Waste (NNW). Found here are references to research and site characterization studies for the proposed high-level radioactive waste repository at Yucca Mountain, Nevada. NNW is a subset of the Energy Science and Technology Database.

Energy Science and Technology Software (ESTS). This database contains citations to available software developed in all subject areas relative to programs of the U.S. Department of Energy and the Nuclear Regulatory Commission.

Numeric Database Directory (NDB). This is a directory of machine-readable numeric and factual databases currently available in the field of scientific and technical information. NDB includes descriptions for both federal and private sector data-bases.

Foreign Research in Progress (FRP). Records of current energy-related research abroad are found here. Information about ongoing foreign research is acquired through exchange agreements with such organizations as the International Energy Agency, International Nuclear Energy Agency, and Energy Technology Data Exchange.

New Technology from DOE (NTD). This database contains brief descriptions of DOE research results having potential for commercialization by U.S. industry. NTD incorporates older materials known as Applications Assessments Records and current Technology Assessment Records submitted by each Office of

Be patient. If any phone number is incorrect, call (area code) 555-1212 and request the new listing.

General Sources

Research and Technology Applications, as required by the Stevenson-Wydler Technology Innovation Act of 1980.

Contact the office above for more information about on-line access to these databases. The Access fee for this service is $30 per hour plus $.25 per record for downloading/printing.

* International Annual Energy Outlook

National Energy Information Center
Energy Information Center
U.S. Department of Energy (DOE)
1000 Independence Ave., SW, Room 1F-048
Washington, DC 20585 (202) 586-8800

The *Annual Energy Outlook* is a survey of the U.S. and world energy situation. It includes projections of production and prices in the U.S. and overseas. Contact NEIC for information on obtaining a copy of the report.

* International Energy Affairs

International Research and Development Policy
International Affairs and Energy Emergencies
U.S. Department of Energy (DOE)
1000 Independence Ave., SW, Room 1E-218
Washington, DC 20585 (202) 586-6777

This office coordinates and assists the development of energy research and development cooperation involving the United States and other nations. Contact the office for more detailed information.

* International Energy Data

International and Contingency Information Division
Energy Markets and End Use
Energy Information Administration
U.S. Department of Energy (DOE)
1000 Independence Ave., SW, Room 2G-060
Washington, DC 20585 (202) 586-1130

This Branch compiles international energy information, including current international energy market assessments, international energy projections, contingency planning studies, prices, distribution, and other quick response or special purpose analyses. In addition, the Branch reports U.S. energy data to international organizations. Contact office for information on its research reports and publications.

* International Energy Analysis

Bureau of International Affairs and Energy Analysis
Office of International Energy Analysis
U.S. Department of Energy (DOE)
1000 Independence Ave., SW, Room 7G-090
Washington, DC 20585 (202) 586-5893

This office manages and analyzes world energy market developments and the international political, economic, and strategic factors that influence these developments. It also manages U.S. participation in international energy organizations.

* International Energy Supply

Office of Energy Markets and End Use
Energy Information Administration
U.S. Department of Energy (DOE)
1000 Independence Ave., SW, Room 2G-060
Washington, DC 20585 (202) 586-1130

This office forecasts international energy supply and demand under various assumptions of international institutional arrangements and other international factors. Contact this office for more detailed program information.

* Lawrence Berkeley Laboratory

Lawrence Berkeley Laboratory
One Cyclotron Rd., Bldg. 50C
Berkeley, CA 94720 (510) 486-5771

Lawrence Berkeley Laboratory is a multi-program national laboratory run by the University of California under contract to the U.S. Department of Energy. It undertakes a wide range of unclassified research activities, including Accelerator and Fusion Research, Applied Science, Life Science, Earth Science, Energy

Sciences, Engineering, General Sciences, Information and Computing Sciences, Materials and Chemical Sciences, Nuclear Science and Physics. The Laboratory describes its function as being four-fold: research, education, developing and operating national experimental facilities, and fostering productive relations between LBL research programs and private industry. Contact the Public Affairs office for copies of their annual report and catalog of programs. Also ask for a couple sample copies of the *LBL Research Review*, which contains articles on research projects ongoing at the Laboratory.

* Legislation

Division of Public Affairs
Federal Energy Regulatory Commission
825 North Capitol Street, NE
Washington, DC 20426 (202) 208-0055

You can get information on energy-related legislative matters under consideration by Congress, after release by the Committee or Member of Congress involved. For more information current or past legislation, contact this office.

* Legislation on Energy Issues

Congressional and Intergovernmental Affairs
U.S. Department of Energy (DOE)
1000 Independence Ave., SW, Room 8E-070
Washington, DC 20585 (202) 586-5450

Daily actions by Congress on energy legislation, are tracked through this office, and the staff can provide you with current status of the legislation. The office prepares briefing books and issues papers for U.S. Department of Energy witnesses, and compiles membership lists of Congressional committees concerned with DOE programs. The office also prepares and distributes reports of all daily energy related Congressional activity. Contact this office for more information on current energy legislation. For information on legislation in the House call (202) 586-2764; for information on Senate legislation, call (202) 586-5468.

* Libraries, Energy

The Energy Library
U.S. Department of Energy (DOE)
1000 Independence Ave., SW, Room GA-138
Washington, DC 20585 (202) 586-9534

This library compiles material on administrative and regulatory matters, non-nuclear research and development and alternative energy sources. The following are the major libraries of the U.S. Department of Energy:

Federal Energy Regulatory Commission Library, 825 N. Capitol Street, NW, Room 8502, Washington, DC 20426; (202) 208-2179. Focuses on regulatory matters.

Germantown Branch, U.S. Department of Energy, Germantown Branch, Room 6034, Washington, DC 20585; (301) 903-4301. This library focuses on material on nuclear energy and fossil fuels, energy research, and environmental protection, safety and emergency preparedness.

* Liquid Biomass Fuels in Vehicles

Office of Alcohol Fuels
U.S. Department of Energy (DOE)
1000 Independence Ave., SW, Room 5G-086
Washington, DC 20585 (202) 586-9220

Contact this office for information on the use of liquid biomass fuels in vehicles. The office handles market analysis, market testing, research and development, and commercialization programs involving these fuels. It consolidates information about federal alcohol fuel efforts and education activities designed to increase public awareness and use of alcohol fuels. For further information on available publications, contact this office.

* Load Management

Marketing Services
3N45B Signal Pl.
Tennessee Valley Authority (TVA)
1101 Market St.
Chattanooga, TN 37402-2801 (615) 751-7611

The TVA, in cooperation with power distributors, is trying out a number of ways to flatten out the peaks in consumer power demand, which requires the use of more expensive generating facilities. One of these load management demonstrations involves remote controlled "cycling" of hot water heaters and

Be patient. If any phone number is incorrect, call (area code) 555-1212 and request the new listing.

Energy

space-conditioning units in homes. About 120,000 remote switches have been installed for power distributors to investigate larger capacity storage small element water heaters.

* Load Research

Load Research Efforts
Tennessee Valley Authority (TVA)
Power, 1100 Market St.
2N-48A Signal Place
Chattanooga, TN 37402-2801 (615) 751-6741

Researchers are currently sampling TVA power customers to determine when and how much electricity they consume. Homes and businesses are monitored to determine hourly load information, which will be gathered for studies of cost of service, rate design, and planning and marketing. Contact this office for more information on power usage statistics in the TVA regions.

* Maps from TVA

Maps and Surveys Department
Maps Information and Records Unit
100 Haney Building
Chattanooga, TN 37401 (615) 751-3248

The Tennessee Valley Authority can provide you with a variety of maps and land surveys for areas under their jurisdiction. Contact them for a free catalog.

* Marketing Federally Generated Power

Power Marketing Coordination
Office of the Assistant Secretary
Conservation and Renewable Energy
U.S. Department of Energy (DOE)
1000 Independence Ave., SW, Room 8G-061
Washington, DC 20585 (202) 586-2008

Contact the above office for information on the marketing of power generated at Federal facilities. The Judicial Administrations are listed below:

Alaska Power Administration, Robert J. Cross, Administrator, 2770 Sherwood Avenue, Juneau, AK 99801; (907) 586-7405

Bonneville Power Administration, Randall Hardy, Administrator, P.O. Box 3621, Portland, OR 97208; (503) 230-5101

The Bonneville Power Administration serves the Pacific Northwest area including Washington, Oregon, Idaho, and western Montana. It also provides power to California in the summer. In addition to managing a series of hydroelectric and nuclear stations, the Power Administration is also involved in many conservation activities related to Salmon.

Washington, DC Office, Lee Johnson, Assistant Administrator, FORSTL, Room 8G033; (202) 586-5640

Southeastern Power Administration, Johnny McAllister, Administrator, Samuel Elbert Building, Elberton, GA 30635; (708) 283-9911

Headquartered in Elberton, GA, this administration markets surplus power generated at reservoir projects operated in the states of West Virginia, Virginia, North Carolina, South Carolina, Georgia, Florida, Alabama, Mississippi, Tennessee, and Kentucky.

Southwestern Power Administration, JM Shafer, Administrator, P.O. Box 1619, Tulsa, OK 74101; (918) 581-7474

This Administration provides power from hydroelectric dams to citizens in Oklahoma, Missouri, Arkansas, Louisiana, Kansas, and Eastern Texas.

Western Area Power Administration, William Clagett, Administrator, P.O. Box 3402, 1627 Cole Boulevard, Golden, CO 80401; (303) 231-1511

* Markets and End Use

Office of Energy Markets and End Use
Energy End Use Division
Energy Information Administration
U.S. Department of Energy (DOE)
1000 Independence Ave., SW, Room 2F-065
Washington, DC 20585 (202) 586-1122

Here research produces models for short-and medium-term energy demand in end use sectors: residential, industrial, commercial, and transportation. The

research includes regional and demographic breakdowns, analyses of market penetration, the impact of conservation, and new technologies. The office can provide you with reports detailing its programs, as well as some subject reports.

* Minorities and Energy Programs

National Minority Energy Information Clearinghouse
U.S. Department of Energy (DOE)
1000 Independence Ave., SW, Room 5R-110
Washington, DC 20585 (202) 586-5876

This Clearinghouse is a centralized repository for information about energy programs and the economic impact of those programs on minorities, minority businesses, and minority educational institutions. The following services are available from the Clearinghouse: research, referrals, information transfer, selective distribution of information, and searches of minority energy information retrieval systems as well as commercial and other Federal databases. The Department of Energy is also forging ahead with programs to encourage more minority participation in the sciences through initiatives such as The Minorities Honors Training and Industrial Assistance Program, the Minority Educational institution Assistance Program, the Minority Undergraduate Training for Energy-Related Careers Program, and the Minority Math/Science Leadership Development Program and Recognition Program, and the Cooperative Developmental Energy Program. The Office also coordinates Departmental activities with respect to the Historically Black Colleges and Universities Initiative.

* National Association of Energy Service Companies

1440 New York Ave, NW
Washington, DC 20005 (202) 371-7000

Members of this association include individuals and firms providing energy efficiency services or electrical or thermal energy as an unregulated business activity using a range of performance based contacting and financing mechanisms. Its purpose is to provide industry representation at all regulatory levels in the government as well as to inform the public regarding performance contracting and financing of alternative energy and energy conservation programs. Information on activities is available through its bimonthly newsletter *NAESCO NEWS.*

* National Center for Appropriate Technology (NCAT)

3040 Continental Drive
PO Box 3838
Butte, MT 59702 (406) 494-4572

The National Center for Appropriate Technology is a non-profit organization whose purpose is to develop and promote practical solutions in the areas of energy, housing, agriculture, and the environment. Through NATAS, NCAT helps people choose and implement energy conservation and energy saving renewable technologies. It also works with public utilities and provides information to low-income energy assistance program managers via a national clearinghouse funded by the U.S. Department of Health and Human Services. The NCAT annual report is a good resource of basic information on NCAT. The following is a list of NCAT publications available for a fee.

Conservation in Buildings: A Northwest Perspective, 1985
Window Insulation: How to Sort Through the Options, 1984
Moisture and Home Energy Conservation, 1983
Introducing Supplemental Combustion Air to Gas-Fired Home Appliances, 1983
Using the Earth to Heat and Cool Homes, 1983
NCAT Energy Conservation and Renewable Energy Bibliography, 1992
Directory of State Energy Programs, 1992
Conservation for Window Air Conditioners, 1978
Heat Recovery Ventilation for Housing: Air-to-Air Heat Exchanges, 1984
Energy Efficient Home Construction: Basic Superinsulation Techniques, 1984
Mobile Home Weatherization: A Status Report, 1985
Mobile Home Weatherization: A Guidebook for Installers, 1986
The NCAT/Penelec Mobile Home Weatherization Series, 1990
Community Energy Management: An Introduction to Saving Energy Dollars, 1981
Appropriate Technology Management Information System (ATMIS), 1984
Appropriate Technology at Work, 1983
NCAT's Best: Outstanding Projects Funded by NCAT from 1977 to 1980, 1981
NCAT Technical Publications Catalog, 1992
Solar Greenhouse and Sunspaces: Lessons Learned, 1984
Low-Cost Passive Solar Greenhouses, 1981
Solar Greenhouses: Suggested Reading Lists, 1992
Solar Water Heating: Suggested Reading List 1992

Be patient. If any phone number is incorrect, call (area code) 555-1212 and request the new listing.

Cold Frame Construction: A Beginners Guide, 1981
The Caterpillar Cold Frame, 1980
Breadbox Solar Water Heaters, 1981
Vertical Solar Air Heaters, 1981
Solar Energy: Suggested Readings, 1992
Drying Wood With the Sun: How to Build a Solar Heated Firewood Dryer, 1983
Homemade Electricity: An Introduction to Small-Scale Wind, Hydro, and Photovoltaic Systems, 1984
Photovoltaics: Suggested Readings, 1984
Microhydroelectric Energy: Suggested Readings, 1992
Independent Power Systems: Suggested Readings, 1990
Fuel Alcohol: Answers to Common Questions, 1981
Fuel Alcohol Production: A Selective Survey of Operating Systems, 1981
Making More Fuel Alcohol: An Operator's Guide to Improve Starch Conversion and Fermentation, 1981
Alcohol Fuels: Suggested Readings, 1992

* National Energy Extension Service Advisory Board

U.S. Department of Energy (DOE)
1000 Independence Ave., SW, Room 6A-055
Washington, DC 20585 (202) 586-1893

Established in 1980, this advisory board provides a continuing review of the comprehensive Energy Extension Service Program (EES) and approved plans of the Governors of each state for implementing EES activities.

* National Energy Information Center

Energy Information Administration (EIA)
U.S. Department of Energy (DOE)
1000 Independence Ave., SW, Room 1F-048
Washington, DC 20585 (202) 586-8800

The National Energy Information Center can provide you with statistical and analytical data, information, and referral assistance on virtually an energy-related issue. The Center operates the EIA microfilm control center, providing access to data collection surveys and historical documents available to the public. National Energy Information Center (NEIC) Energy Information Administration's data and projections on energy productions, consumption, prices, and supplies, are available by mail or telephone. The NEIC has subject specialists to handle the following areas: Coal, Electrical and Nuclear Power, Natural Gas, Petroleum, Renewable Energy Resources/Conservation, and Data Survey forms.

* National Energy Software Center

U.S. Department of Energy (DOE)
Earth Science and Technology Software Center
PO Box 1020
Oak Ridge, TN 37831 (615) 576-2606

Operated under contract for DOE's Office of Scientific and Technical Information, this center is DOE's centralized software management center. Software exchange and information center activities for the U.S. Nuclear Regulatory Commission (NRC) are carried with support from the NRC's Office of Resource Management. NESC provides a central computer software information and resource facility in support of DOE and NRC research and development programs. It also serves as a focal point for intra-agency sharing of software and for the transfer and exchange of computer technology to other U.S. and foreign agencies, as well as to the U.S. private sector. Contact the office above for more information.

* New Energy Technologies and Developing Countries

Office of Technology Assessment
600 Pennsylvania Ave., SE
Washington, DC 20510 (202) 228-6267

The Office of Technology Assessment (OTA) is currently working on a study to examine how technology can contribute to the goal of sound and productive energy development in the world's poorer countries, and the role of U.S. policy and the relevant international organizations in encouraging the rapid adoption of improved technologies. Contact Joy Dunkerley, the project director, at OTA for more information.

* News Releases

National Energy Information Center, EI-231
Energy Information Administration (EIA)

Room 1F-048, Forestall Building
Washington, DC 20585 (202) 586-8800

EIA New Releases is published six times per year and contains information on issues of special interest, periodicals, machine-readable files, and how to order EIA publications. This is a valuable publication for keeping up with the latest publications and developments in EIA.

* Ocean Energy

Wind and Oceans Technologies Division
Conservation and Renewable Energy, 5H-047
U.S. Department of Energy (DOE)
1000 Independence Ave., SW
Washington, DC 20585 (202) 586-8086

Here researchers develop technologies to harness ocean energy in a cost-effective and environmentally safe manner. Researchers look to develop ocean energy technology to the point where businesses accurately assess whether applications of the technology are viable energy conversion alternatives, or supplements, to systems currently in use. Contact this office for more program information.

* Petroleum Overcharge Refunds

Office of Hearings and Appeals
U.S. Department of Energy (DOE)
1000 Independence Ave., SW, Room 6G-087
Washington, DC 20585 (202) 586-2094

Cash refunds are available to any people, business firms, and governments that purchased refined petroleum products in the U.S. between August 1973 and January 1981. This office distributes millions of dollars in oil overcharges collected through the DOE enforcement program between those years. This office can give you further details.

* Petroleum Price Regulation

Economic Regulatory Administration (ERA)
Press Office, U.S. Department of Energy (DOE)
1000 Independence Ave., SW, Room 8G-087
Washington, DC 20585 (202) 586-5810

This office serves as the first public contact point for information on petroleum enforcement actions for crude oil price and allocation regulations prior to January 28, 1981. ERA also regulates natural gas imports and exports; administers programs for the conversion of oil- and gas-fired utilities to alternate fuels; and licenses both exports of electricity from the United State and transmission lines crossing U.S. borders. Contact this office for more information.

* Photovoltaic Materials and Devices

Solar Energy Technologies
Deputy Assistant Secretary for Renewable Energy
Conservation and Renewable Energy
U.S. Department of Energy (DOE)
1000 Independence Ave., SW, Room 5H-088
Washington, DC 20585 (202) 586-1721

This office conducts research and development leading toward potentially low-cost, advanced photovoltaic materials and devices which are environmentally sound. Contact this office for more program information.

* Photovoltaics

Photovoltaics Technology Division
Conservation and Renewable Energy
U.S. Department of Energy (DOE)
1000 Independence Ave., SW, Room 5H-088
Washington, DC 20585 (202) 586-1720

Researchers are currently developing photovoltaic technology--which converts sunlight directly into electricity--for the large-scale generation of economically competitive electric power in the U.S. Eventually photovoltaic energy products will significantly contribute to the mix of renewable energy sources on which the U.S. will depend. Contact this office for its program summary.

* Power Control Centers

Power Control Center
Tennessee Valley Authority (TVA)
2N 10A Power Control Center

Be patient. If any phone number is incorrect, call (area code) 555-1212 and request the new listing.

Energy

Chattanooga, TN 37401 (615) 751-8678

TVA's five area dispatch control centers (ADCCs) monitor the 15,000 miles of transmission lines across which power is carried to the distributors of TVA power and large industries in the Valley. The dispatchers at the ADCCs and the load coordinators at the Power System Control Center work together to coordinate the maintenance of the transmission network to ensure the safety of the men working on the lines, and to make sure there are no transmission lines scheduled to be out of service that would cause an interruption in power service.

* Power Information Center

Interagency Advanced Power Group (IAPG)
c/o Horizon Data Corporation
10700 Parkridge Blvd., Suite 250
Reston, VA 22091 (703) 758-0531

The Interagency Advanced Power Group (IAPG) promotes the exchange of information in advanced power fields by 1) maintaining a database of projects sponsored by its member agencies (Army, Navy, Air Force, NASA, and DOE); and 2) arranging semiannual meetings in the following areas of interest: chemical, electrical, magnetohydrodynamics, mechanical, nuclear, solar, and systems R&D. Members of industry and academia who are frequently invited to serve as presenters or participants at these meetings can receive IAPG publications by subscribing to NTIS. Membership and associated benefits are free to employees of the IAPG member agencies.

* Power System Control

Power System Control Center
Tennessee Valley Authority (TVA)
2N 10A
Chattanooga, TN 37401

TVA provides a reliable supply of power at the lowest possible cost to the consumers. This center manages the resources needed to meet the daily load of the TVA power system, the largest in the U.S. Through control of generation, interchange transactions with other utilities, and load management, the staff at the Center ensures that the residents and industrial customers have ample power on hand to meet their needs.

* Press Services

Press Secretary to the Secretary
U.S. Department of Energy (DOE)
Office of Communications
FORSTL, CP-60, Room 8G087
Washington, DC 20585 (202) 586-8325

DOE's Press Service produces news releases and answers inquiries from the media of a general nature in all program areas, including nuclear energy and national defense programs within DOE. The office also arranges press conferences and media interviews for the Secretary of Energy and other DOE officials.

* Princeton Plasma Physics Laboratory

Information and Administrative Services
PO Box 451
Princeton, NJ 08543 (609) 243-2755

This lab performs research aimed at the development of magnetic fusion energy as an inexhaustible, safe, and environmentally acceptable means of generating electricity. The laboratory operates two major magnetic fusion devices: the Tokamak Fusion Test Reactor and the Princeton Beta Experiment - Modified. A third device, called Compact Ignition Tokamak is currently under construction. Research at the Princeton lab is also being applied to research in other areas such as X-ray technology and the plasma etchings of electronic circuitry on semiconductor chips.

* Producing Countries

Office of Energy Producer - Country Affairs
Bureau of Economics and Business Affairs
U.S. Department of State
2201 C St., NW, Room 3329
Washington, DC 20520 (202) 647-1476

This office handles all foreign affairs concerning energy producing countries. Subjects studies include OPEC, natural gas, uranium, as well as the importing and exporting of oil and gas.

* Propulsion Technology

Office of Propulsion Systems
Advanced Propulsion Division
U.S. Department of Energy (DOE)
1000 Independence Ave, SW, Room 5G-046
Washington, DC 20585 (202) 586-8012

This office manages the development of a national advanced transportation, propulsion, and demonstration program of advanced engine and vehicular systems development. It emphasized high-risk technology research for advanced propulsion systems such as ceramic gas turbines, adiabatic diesels, and magnetic levitation.

* Publications

Public Affairs
Division of Public Affairs
U.S. Department of Energy (DOE)
1000 Independence Ave., SW, Room 8H-068
Washington, DC 20585 (202) 586-6827

This office writes and publishes the DOE's newspaper, *DOE This Month* and produces written material describing DOE programs and policies in a variety of formats, including speech texts, talking points, letters to editors, magazine/journal articles, and fact sheets. *DOE This Month* contains articles on recent developments in energy policy as well as new programs and a calendar of upcoming events. Contact this office for more information on the publications available from DOE.

* Publications--Free

Publications Branch
Technical Information Center (TIC)
U.S. Department of Energy (DOE)
P.O. Box 62
Oak Ridge, TN 37831 (615) 576-1301

Contact TIC office for a complete listing of their free publications.

* Regional Biomass Energy Programs

Office of National Programs
U.S. Department of Energy (DOE)
1000 Independence Ave., SW
Washington, DC 20585 (202) 586-9104

The Regional Program's goal is to transfer current and reliable information about biomass fuel to energy users with the long term goal of increasing the use of biomass fuels. The United States has been divided into seven regions by the program. Each of them can be contacted for information.

NORTHEAST. CONEG Policy Research Center Inc., Suite 382, 400 North Capitol St., NW, Washington, DC 20001; (202) 624-8454.

OAK RIDGE OPERATIONS. U.S. Department of Energy, 200 Administration Road, PO Box 2008, Oak Ridge, TN 37831-8600; (615) 576-1763.

WESTERN. Western Area Power Administration, 1627 Cole Blvd., PO Box 3402, Golden, CO 80401; (303) 231-1615.

GREAT LAKES. Council of Great Lakes Governors, 35 East Wacker Drive, Suite 1850, Chicago, IL 60601; (312) 407-0177.

NORTHWEST. Bonneville Power Administration, 905 NE 11th Avenue, Portland, OR 97232; (503) 230-3449.

SOUTHEAST. Tennessee Valley Authority, 435 Chemical Engineering Building, Muscle Shoals, AL 35660; (205) 386-3086.

The Southeast Power Administration can provide you with the following information on their biomass program: a list of publications, a Six-Year Report 1983-89, *Wood Energy Guide for Agricultural and Small Commercial Applications, Watts Bar Conversion to Whole Tree Energy - Vol. I and II., Residential Fuelwood Consumption in the Southeastern United States.*

* Regulation

Federal Energy Regulatory Commission (FERC)
Office of External Affairs
825 North Capitol Street, NE
Washington, DC 20426 (202) 208-1371

Be patient. If any phone number is incorrect, call (area code) 555-1212 and request the new listing.

General Sources

The free *Annual Report of the Federal Energy Regulatory Commission* details last year's energy regulatory activities of the FERC, as well as giving a summary of the structure and functions of each office within FERC.

* Regulation Hotline

Office of Congressional Affairs
Energy Regulatory Commission
U.S. Department of Energy (DOE)
1000 Independence Ave., SW
Washington, DC 20585 (202) 208-0870

Call this office for information on energy regulation matters.

* Regulatory Files

Division of Public Affairs
Federal Energy Regulatory Commission (FERC)
825 North Capitol Street, NE
Washington, DC 20426 (202) 208-0870

Records and files of the Federal Energy Regulatory Commission are available for public inspection or copying at FERC's North Capitol Street office. Contact the office of Public Affairs for more detailed information on consulting records. The following is a summary of the available information:

- All filings submitted to the Commission which comprise formal records. This includes applications, petitions and other pleadings requesting FERC action; responses, protests, motions, contracts, briefs, rate schedules, tariffs and related filings; and FERC staff correspondence relating to any proceedings.
- Transcripts of hearings, hearing exhibits, proposed testimony and exhibits filed with the Commission but not yet offered or received in evidence.
- Administrative law judges' actions, orders, and correspondence in connection with FERC proceedings.
- Commission orders, notices, opinions, decisions, letter orders, and approved Commission minutes.
- Agendas and lists of actions taken at Commission meetings, which are open to the public.
- Environmental impact statements prepared by FERC staff pursuant to the National Environmental Policy Act of 1969.
- Agendas, minutes, and draft papers relating to the National Power Survey, Natural Gas Policy Council and other FERC advisory committee meetings, all open to the public.
- Filings and recordings in court proceedings to which the Commission is a party and FERC correspondence with the courts.
- News releases and announcements issued by FERC.
- Subject index of Commission actions.

* Renewable Energy Information Hotline

P.O. Box 8900
Silver Spring, MD 20907 (800) 523-2929

Conservation and Renewable Energy Inquiry and Referral Service (CAREIRS) answers questions for the general public by toll-free telephone or mail. This center can answer questions on such topics as active/passive solar, solar thermal, photovoltaics, wind, biomass, alcohol fuels, hydroelectric, geothermal, and ocean thermal energy. This service is the successor to the National Solar Heating and Cooling Information Center. Call (800) 462-4983 in Pennsylvania, or (800) 233-3071 in Alaska and Hawaii.

* Renewable Energy Publications

National Renewable Energy Laboratory
Technical Inquiry Service
1617 Cole Boulevard
Golden, CO 80401-3393 (303) 231-1000

You can get any of the following series of documents on the renewable energy programs sponsored by the U.S. Department of Energy at no charge by writing the office above. A list of publications is available from the National Technical Information Service (NTIS); (703) 487-4650. Publications may also be ordered from NTIS.

Solar Building Program Summaries
Wind Energy
Energy Storage and Distribution
Solar Thermal Energy
Biofuels

Geothermal Energy
Photovoltaic Energy
Ocean Energy
Technical and Financial Assistance (for energy conservation)
Energy for Today: Renewable Energy
CORRECT: Committee on Renewable Energy Commerce and Trade

* Renewable Energy Publications

Conservation and Renewable Energy Inquiry
and Referral Service (CAREIRS)
Renewable Energy Information
Box 8900
Silver Spring, MD 20907 (800) 523-2929

The following are some of the free energy information publications available through the above CAREIRS service. Bulk copies are not available. The service asks that each request be limited to 8 publications.

Fact Sheets:

FS 104 Conserving Energy and Heating Your Swimming Pool with Solar Energy.
FS 105 Alternative Heat Sources for Heat Pumps
FS 109 Planning for a Homeowner Installation
FS 110 Converting a Home to Solar Heat
FS 113 Solar Energy Systems Consumer Tips
FS 115 Solar Heat Storage
FS 118 Solar Energy and You (for middle grades)
FS 120 Earth-Sheltered Houses
FS 124 Sunspaces and Solar Greenhouses
FS 135 Wind Energy Systems
FS 141 Energy Efficient Lighting
FS 142 Insulation
FS 150 Municipal Resource Recovery
FS 176 Solar Energy and Your Home: Questions and Answers
FS 178 Low-Cost Passive and Hybrid Solar Retrofits
FS 183 Facts About Ethanol
FS 188 Geothermal Energy
FS 185 Residential Indoor Air Pollution
FS 190 Movable Insulation
FS 203 Caulking and Weatherstripping
FS 204 Hot Water Energy Conservation
FS 207 Buying an Energy Efficient House
FS 208 Moisture Control in Your Home
FS 214 Biofuels as a Source of Energy
FS 216 Improving the Energy Efficiency of Windows
FS 217 Small-Scale Hydropower Systems
FS 218 Learning About Energy Conservation (for elementary grades)
FS 220 Landscaping for Energy-Efficient Homes
FS 222 Energy Efficient Factory Built Homes
FS 224 Home Energy Audits
FS 228 Fans and Ventilation
FS 230 Options for Saving Energy and Reducing Costs with Electric Heating
FS 234 Electric Vehicles

Books and Brochures:

SD 107 Tips for Energy Savers
SD 109 Regional Guidelines for Building Passive and Energy Conserving Homes
SD 115 Protecting Solar Access for Residential Development
SD 133 Site Planning for Solar Access
SD 234 Improving the Efficiency of Your Oil Heating System
SD 243 Energy Conservation Information for Vehicle Owners
SD 247 Attic Radiant Barrier Fact Sheet
SD 256 Improving the Efficiency of Your Gas Heating System

Bibliographies:

DC 150 Renewable Energy Reading List for Young Adults
DC 169 Passive Solar Construction - Design and Performance
DC 175 Wind Energy
DC 189 Photovoltaics Stand Alone Applications Reading List

* Renewable Energy Technologies

Conservation and Renewable Energy Inquiry
and Referral Service (CAREIRS)
P.O. Box 8900 (800) 523-2929
Silver Spring, MD 20907 (800) 233-3071 (AK and HI)

CAREIRS provides information on the full spectrum of renewable energy

Be patient. If any phone number is incorrect, call (area code) 555-1212 and request the new listing.

Energy

technologies and energy conservation, including active/passive solar, solar thermal, photovoltaics, wind, biomass, alcohol fuels, hydroelectric, geothermal, and ocean thermal energy. In addition, the Service maintains contact with a nationwide network of public and private organizations that specialize in highly technical or regionally specific information. Information on two other programs can also be obtained from CAREIRS. The first is the Center for Analysis of Demonstrated Energy Technology, or CADET program which consists of 14 member nations and is based in Holland. The second is the Committee on Renewable Energy Commerce and Trade, or CORRECT. Contact CAREIRS for information on these programs. Telephone service is available 9am to 5pm Eastern Standard Time.

* Renewable Energy Technologies

Deputy Assistant Secretary for Renewable Energy
Conservation and Renewable Energy
U.S. Department of Energy (DOE)
1000 Independence Ave., SW, Room 5H-095
Washington, DC 20585 (202) 586-8089

This office conducts research and development of biomass energy technology, energy from municipal waste, and geothermal/small hydropower energy technology. They emphasize the development of renewable technology with potential to increase significantly the Nation's supply of fuel, heat, and electricity. Contact the office for program information.

* Research and Technology Development

Program Integration Analysis Division
Office of Energy Research
U.S. Department of Energy (DOE)
19901 Germantown Road
Germantown, MD 20585 (301) 903-5544

The Office of Energy Research undertakes advanced and fundamental research to support the Energy Department's long-term energy technology development. *Programs of the Office of Energy Research* describes the Office's research activities in sufficient detail to enable researchers to understand current Energy Department research programs. A copy is available free through the office.

* Research Facilities

Office of Energy Research
Office of Field Operations Management
U.S. Department of Energy (DOE)
1000 Independence Ave., SW, Room 7B-040
Washington, DC 20585 (202) 586-5447

The *Capsule Review of DOE Research and Development and Field Facilities* surveys DOE research facilities, with brief descriptions of the work of the various offices.

* Residential Energy Conservation Database

Office of Energy Markets and End Use
Energy End Use Division
Energy Information Administration
U.S. Department of Energy (DOE)
1000 Independence Ave., SW, Room 2F-065
Washington, DC 20585 (202) 586-1122

The database, *Technical Documentation, 1984 Residential Energy Consumption Survey and 1985 Residential Transportation Energy Consumption Survey*, contains data concerning energy consumption in the U.S. residential sector. The *RECS* data file contains basic data concerning housing unit characteristics, including weather and weighing variables. The file contains 5,611 sample households from the contiguous U.S. representing 85.8 million weighted households. The 1985 *RTECS* data provide information on how energy is used in households for personal transportation based on the number and type of vehicles per household and, for each vehicle, annual miles traveled, gallons of fuel consumed, type of fuel used, price paid for fuel, and vehicle miles-per-gallon. Contact this office for more information on these databases.

* Safety Inspections - Non-Nuclear

Office of Safety and Quality Assurance
Office of Safety Appeals
U.S. Department of Energy (DOE)
19901 Germantown Road
Germantown, MD 20585 (301) 903-3548

This office conducts independent technical safety appraisals of DOE-owned, contractor-operated non-nuclear facilities to assure they meet DOE safety requirements. The office also performs technical reviews necessary for the independent recommendations regarding construction, startup, and restart of selected non-nuclear facilities.

* Short-Term and Long-Term Energy Statistics

Energy Analysis and Forecasting Division
Energy Markets and End Use
Energy Information Administration
U.S. Department of Energy (DOE)
1000 Independence Ave., SW, Room BG-057
Washington, DC 20585 (202) 586-6160

This division compiles statistics on both short-term (up to 18 months) and the long-term (primarily within the next 15 years) energy supply and demand. Contact this office for more information.

* Small Business Assistance - Energy

Office of Small and Disadvantaged Business Utilization
U.S. Department of Energy (DOE)
1707 H. St NW, Room 905
Washington, DC 20585 (202) 254-5583

This office is responsible for policy, plans, implementation, and oversight of functions related to programs for small businesses, small disadvantaged businesses, minority and women owned businesses.

* SocioEconomic Research and Analysis Program

National Minority Energy Information Clearinghouse
U.S. Department of Energy (DOE)
1000 Independence Ave., SW, Room 5R-110
Washington, DC 20585 (202) 586-5876

The Office of Minority programs has begun a major research program to collect information on the energy consumption and expenditure patterns of minorities as compared to other segments of the population. The long range hope is to use the information both to improve DOE's program sensitivity to minority needs and to expand opportunities for minority owned businesses/entrepreneurs and minority communities. Another goal is to improve the capabilities of the policy sensitive Minority Energy Assessment Model "MEAM" by improving the level of minority representation in the data bank. For more information on this ongoing program, contact the Office of Minority Economic Impact listed above.

* Solar Building Technology

Office of Building Energy Research
Conservation and Renewable Energy, CE-421
U.S. Department of Energy (DOE)
1000 Independence Ave., SW
Washington, DC 20585 (202) 586-8163

Research from this office provides the solar and buildings industries with the technology needed to develop reliable solar systems that can contribute significantly to a building's space heating, hot water, cooling, and lighting requirements at competitive costs. Major research activities are aimed at improving the overall effectiveness of solar water and space heating systems, increasing solar cooling system performance, increasing daylighting system contributions, and increasing overall building energy contributions from individual solar heating, cooling, and daylighting technologies through systems integration. These activities are planned and executed in close cooperation with the solar and building industries to ensure that the results can readily be adopted by the private sector. Contact this office for further information.

* Solar Energy and Wind Information

National Climatic Data Center
National Oceanic and Atmospheric Administration
U.S. Department of Commerce
Federal Building
Asheville, NC 28801 (704) 259-0682

The National Climatic Data Center has a great deal of information regarding solar energy and wind data. Information includes solar radiation averages, measurements, and sunshine averages, as well as wind statistics. Reference manuals and indexes are also available. Prices vary depending upon the information requested. The Center can provide you with more detailed information regarding the data available.

Be patient. If any phone number is incorrect, call (area code) 555-1212 and request the new listing.

General Sources

* Solar Energy Research

National Renewable Energy Laboratory
1617 Cole Boulevard
Golden, CO 80401 (303) 231-7303

Solar Energy Research Institute (SERI) is the lead organization for advanced solar research and development in the U.S. Its Technical Inquiry Service responds to questions related to SERI's research and the solar research conducted in other laboratories and universities from the scientific, industrial, and business communities. Central inquiry and referral services are provided to the general public through the Conservation and Renewable Energy Inquiry and Referral Service, (CAREIRS). The Document Distribution Service, (303) 231-1243, responds to requests for single copies, prior to NTIS announcements, of selected SERI-produced technical reports and publications in hard copy format for a fee. Contact the above office for more information.

* Solar Technical Information Service

National Renewable Energy Laboratory
1617 Cole Boulevard
Golden, CO 80401 (303) 231-7303

Solar Energy Research Institute Technical Inquiry Service (SERI/TIS) solar technical information requested by scientific and industrial professional by telephone or mail.

* Solar Thermal Technology

Solar Thermal Technology Division
Conservation and Renewable Energy
U.S. Department of Energy (DOE)
1000 Independence Ave., SW, Room 5H-072
Washington, DC 20585 (202) 586-8121

Here researchers are looking to improve the overall performance of solar thermal systems and provide cost-effective energy options that are strategically secure and environmentally sound. Major research activities include energy collection technology, energy conversion technology, and systems and applications technology for both CR and DR systems. This research is being conducted through research laboratories in close coordination with the solar thermal industry, utility companies, and universities. This research program is also pursuing the development of critical components and subsystems for improved energy collection and conversion devices.

This development follows two basic paths: 1) For CR systems, critical components include stretched membrane heliostats, direct absorption receivers (DARs), and transport subsystems for molten salt heat transfer fluids. These components offer the potential for a significant reduction in system costs; and 2) For DR systems, critical components include stretched membrane dishes, reflux receivers, and Stirling engines. These components will significantly increase system reliability and efficiency, which will reduce costs.

The major thrust of the program is to provide electric power; however, there is an increasing interest in the use of concentrated solar energy for such applications as detoxifying hazardous wastes and developing high-value transportable fuels. These potential uses of highly concentrated solar energy still require additional experiments to prove concept feasibility. The research's goal of economically competitive energy production from solar thermal systems is being cooperatively addressed by both industry and government. Contact this office or the Solar Energy Research Institute for more information and a copy of the program summary.

* State Energy Conservation

Energy Management and Extension Branch, CE-522
State Energy Programs
U.S. Department of Energy (DOE)
1000 Independence Ave., SW
Washington, DC 20585 (202) 586-9645

To reduce the growth rate of energy demand, States voluntarily participate in a cooperative effort with the U.S. Department of Energy (DOE), which provides technical and cost-shared financial assistance, while the states develop and implement comprehensive plans for achieving specific energy goals. At present, all states, as well as the District of Columbia and U.S. territories, participate in this conservation program. Recent regulatory and legislative changes have given States flexibility to engage in a much broader range of program measures to promote energy efficiency and conservation, thereby enabling them to take advantage of available petroleum violation escrow funds. For more information on this, contact your State office. (Listing are found at the end of this section.)

* Statistics

National Energy Information Center
Energy Information Administration
U.S. Department of Energy (DOE)
1000 Independence Ave., SW, Room E1-231
Washington, DC 20585 (202) 586-8800

This Center can provide you with National energy statistics and general data services. Contact them for more information on the types available.

* Statistics on Production/Sales

Energy and Chemicals Division
International Trade Commission (ITC)
500 E. St. SW
Washington, DC 20406 (202) 205-3343

The ITC monitors U.S. production, sales and international trade flows of petroleum, natural gas, and other chemical agents. Contact them for information on acquiring statistics.

* Systems Vulnerability

Office of Technology Assessment (OTA)
600 Pennsylvania Ave., SE
Washington, DC 20510 (202) 228-6427

A study is underway at OTA to assess the vulnerability of certain energy producing and delivery systems--electricity, natural gas, and refined oil products--to disruption by either terrorist actions or massive natural disasters. Contact Alan Crane, the project director, for more information.

* Technical Information

Office of Scientific and Technical Information
U.S. Department of Energy (DOE)
P.O. Box 62
Oak Ridge, TN 37831 (615) 576-1192

Both DOE-originated information and worldwide literature regarding advances in subjects of interest to DOE researchers are collected, processed, and distributed through this office. The major databases in this system are available within the United States through commercial on-line systems such as DIALOG and to those outside the United States through formal governmental exchange agreements. This service is mainly for DOE and its contractors but the information is available through the National Technical Information Service in Springfield, VA, at (703) 467-4650.

* Technical Energy Information

Office of Scientific and Technical Information
U.S. Department of Energy (DOE)
P.O. Box 62
Oak Ridge, TN 37831 (615) 576-8401

Office of Scientific and Technical Information, Technical Information Center (OSTI/TIC) access to bibliographic databases for the government, contractors, libraries, and research institutions, and supplies reports to the National Technical Information Service for sale to the public. OSTI also serves as the central processing and distribution point and repository for DOE scientific and technical reports; develops data sets to provide access to energy literature, DOE research in progress and DOE developed software. This office also maintains a registry of energy publications produced by the department for the public. For information on technical reports, call (615) 576-8401; for information on data bases, call (615) 576-1175.

* Technical Information Center

U.S. Department of Energy (DOE)
P. O. Box 62
Oak Ridge, TN 37831 (615) 576-8401

The Technical Information Center distributes energy information resulting from DOE-funded research and development, as well as relevant technical literature produced worldwide for use by the DOE community. The Center also maintains the DOE Energy Data Base (EDB) with over 1.8 million citations to technical energy literature, and the central DOE Research-in-Progress (RIP) database. It also publishes abstract journals and bibliographies and provides on-line retrieval through DOE-RECON. Contact this office for more information on the Center's information services.

Be patient. If any phone number is incorrect, call (area code) 555-1212 and request the new listing.

Energy

* Technological Risks and Opportunities for Future U.S. Energy Supply and Demand

Office of Technology Assessment (OTA)
600 Pennsylvania Ave., SE
Washington, DC 20510
(202) 228-6275

The OTA is currently studying the current views of the U.S. future energy outlook to identify key technical uncertainties and risks that affect the validity of these views, and to evaluate energy policy options for dealing with these uncertainties and risks. Contact Steven Plotkin, the project director, for more information.

* Technology Hotline

National Appropriate Technology
Assistance Service (NATAS)
U.S. Department of Energy (DOE)
P.O. Box 2525
(800) 428-2525
Butte, MT 59702-2525
(800) 428-1718 (MT)

Both businesses and consumers can call this toll-free hotline for information on implementing energy-saving technologies. NATAS provides more detailed technical assistance than other programs and helps entrepreneurs develop appropriate technology.

* Tennessee Valley Authority (TVA)

Power Control Center
Tennessee Valley Authority
2N 10 A Power Center
Chattanooga, TN 37401
(615) 751-8678

The TVA serves an area in the southeast U.S. consisting of 91,000 square miles and over seven million residents in parts of seven states. TVA has a total generating capacity in excess of 32,000 megawatts, made up of 11 operating coal-fired power plants, two licensed nuclear plants, 29 hydro plants, four combustion turbine installations, and the Raccoon Mountain Pumped-Storage Plant. The TVA works toward achieving competitive power rates, a reliable transmission system, research on clean-coal technology, industrial development in the region, improved quality and costs, and excellent fossil and hydro facilities performance.

* TVA Energy Publications

Office of Communications
Governmental and Public Affairs
Tennessee Valley Authority (TVA)
1101 Market St., SP3N
Chattanooga, TN 37402-2801
(615) 632-4402

TVA provides publications on energy for research studies and the general public. They contain general information on the TVA and also specific information on such subjects as dams and steam plants, nuclear power, energy alternatives, and energy conservation, including buying guides for appliances. Though solar energy projects are no longer being carried out at TVA, you can still obtain information on past research. The following is a partial list of publications:

Annual Report
Answers to the Most Frequently Asked Questions About TVA
Financial Statement (of TVA)
History of TVA
Power Quarterly Report
TVA Act (1933 TVA Constitution)
A Student History
Electricity
TVA and Electric Power
TVA and Regional Development

* Unleaded Gas and Fuels Hotline

Environmental Protection Agency
Region I, JFK Federal Bldg.
Boston, MA 02203
(800) 821-1237
(800) 631-2700 (MA)

The Unleaded Fuel Tank Hotline is an enforcement-related line that takes calls about tampering with vehicles, pumps, and other problems related to unleaded fuels. It provides this service for Region I states: Connecticut, Massachusetts, New Hampshire, Rhode Island, Vermont. The 800 listed above is only good in New England. For information in your region, check the Environment chapter of this book for your local number or call the Environmental Protection Agencies main number at (202) 260-2090.

* United States Alternative Fuels Council

U.S. Department of Energy (DOE)
1000 Independence Ave., SW, Room 7H-021
Washington, DC 20585
(202) 586-3891

This Council was established in 1990 to provide advice to the Interagency Commission on Alternative Fuels to help in the Commissions efforts to ensure commercial development for alcohol, natural gas, and other potential alternative motor fuels.

* U.S. Council for Energy Awareness

1776 Eye Street, NW, Suite 400
Washington, DC 20006
(202) 293-0770

This organization consists of representatives from electrical utilities, manufacturers, industrial firms, research and service organizations, educational institutions, labor groups and government agencies engaged in development and utilization of nuclear energy especially nuclear produced electricity, and other energy matters. It maintains a speakers bureau, compiles statistics and public attitude data. It's library consists of books, articles, periodicals, government documents, and audiovisual material on energy related topics.

* U.S. House of Representatives: Energy Information

Committee on Energy and Commerce
Majority Staff
2125 Rayburn House Office Building
Washington, DC 20515
(202) 225-2927

This committee can provide you with a variety of information on energy policy as well as information on legislation currently being considered by the House of Representatives that relates to energy.

* United States Senate: Energy Information

Committee on Energy and Natural Resources
Majority Staff
364 Senate Dirksen Office Building
Washington, DC 20510-6150
(202) 224-4971

This committee can provide you with a variety of information on energy exploration and policy as well as information on current legislation being considered by the Senate relating to energy.

* Waste Operations

Office of Environmental Restoration and Waste Management
Office of Waste Operations
U.S. Department of Energy (DOE)
1000 Independence Ave., SW, Room 6B-170
Washington, DC 20585
(202) 586-0370

This office is responsible for all DOE facilities, operations, or sites that are used for the storage, treatment, or disposal of radioactive, hazardous waste materials that have been packaged or labelled or used exclusively for long term storage of DOE waste material. Sites and operations managed by the Office of Civilian Radioactive Waste Management are excepted.

* Water Heater Program

Residential Energy Services Program
Tennessee Valley Authority (TVA)
1101 Market St.
3N 45B Signal Place
Chattanooga, TN 37402-2801
(615) 751-5161

The TVA's water heater program is designed to encourage homeowners in the region to install electric water heaters in new and existing homes. The program, available through local power distributors, offers participation incentives, which include cash payments, credits on electric bills, or financing. Water heater distributors may also offer free or reduced-cost water heaters, or make special offers for maintenance or installation. Loans may be used for a heat pump and related items such as electronic air cleaners, programmable thermostats, and extended warranties. No down payment, and the loan may be repaid over a period of up to 10 years.

* Weatherization Assistance

Weatherization Assistance Programs Branch, CE-532
U.S. Department of Energy (DOE)

Be patient. If any phone number is incorrect, call (area code) 555-1212 and request the new listing.

General Sources

1000 Independence Ave., SW, Room 5G-023
Washington, DC 20585 (202) 586-2204
To reduce high fuel costs for heating and air conditioning, low-income families, the elderly, and the handicapped can receive assistance to weatherize their homes and apartments. Those in need can have caulking and weatherstripping, storm windows, attic insulation, and heating system improvements installed at little or no charge. Contact this office or your state energy office for more detailed information on this assistance.

* Weapons Materials and Planning

Office of Weapons and Materials Planning
Weapons Planning Division
U.S. Department of Energy (DOE)
19901 Germantown Road
Germantown, MD 20585 (301) 903-6699
This office is responsible for strategic planning, liaison, and management direction related to the nuclear weapons stockpile, and strategic planning related to nuclear materials. It also manages nuclear weapons planning, acquisition, and retirement. The office also prepares the DOE portion of the annual surety report to the President.

* Wind Energy Information Contacts

With existing technological resources, a recent study concluded that wind energy could supply 20% of this country's electricity, with advanced technology currently under development, wind energy, in theory, could supply more than the current consumption of electricity of the U.S. Research has been steadily reducing the per kilowatt hour cost of wind generated electricity, making it increasingly economical. The following is a list of contact points for acquiring more information on wind energy development.

U.S. Department of Energy, Washington, DC 20585.
Office of Utility Technologies CE-10; (202) 586-9275.
Office of Renewable Energy Conservation, CE-12; (202) 586-8084.
Wind/Hydro/Ocean Division, CE-121; (202) 586-5630.
National Renewable Energy Laboratory, 1617 Cole Boulevard, Golden, CO 80401-3393; (303) 231-7650.
Pacific Northwest Laboratory, PO Box 999, Richland, WA 99352; (509) 376-6653.
Sandia National Laboratories, PO Box 5800, Alburquerque, NM 87185-5800; (505) 844-5253.

* Wind Energy Test Center

National Renewable Energy Laboratory
1617 Cole Boulevard
Golden, CO 80401 (303) 231-7111
SERI's Wind Energy Test Center is the focal point for wind technology research activities in the U.S. The objective is to establish a technology base in a support industry in confirming the viability of wind energy as an alternative energy source. Basic research in wind turbine dynamics is conducted to understand the random nature of the wind, characterize its complex interaction with the wind turbine, and determine the effects of this interactions on performance, structural loads reliability and lifetime. Research is also scheduled to establish the feasibility of such technological advances as high performance airfoils, variable speed generators, and controls. Cooperative research and test programs with the wind industry will also take place over the next 5 years. SERI can provide you with information on its current activities and publications.

* Wind/Hydro/Ocean Division

Office of Conservation and Renewable Energy
U.S. Department of Energy (DOE)
1000 Independence Ave, SW, Room 5H-095
Washington, DC 20585 (202) 586-8086
This division is responsible for managing the development, implementation, and evaluation of a national program of technology and development of hydroelectric, wind, and ocean energy.

* State and Territorial Energy Offices

Alabama
Science, Technology, and Energy Division, 3465 Norman Bridge Road, Montgomery, AL 36105-0939; (205) 284-8936.

Alaska
Rural Development Division Energy Programs, 949 East 36th Ave., Suite 403, Anchorage, AK 99508; (907) 563-1955.

American Samoa
Territorial Energy Office, Office of the Governor, Pago Pago, American Samoa 96799; 011 (684) 699-1325.

Arizona
Dept. of Commerce, 3800 North Central Avenue, Suite 1400, Phoenix, AZ 85012; (602) 280-1402.

Arkansas
Energy Office, One State Capitol Mall, Little Rock, AR 72201; (501) 682-7315.

California
Energy Commission, 1516 Ninth Street, Sacramento, CA 95814; (916) 324-3000.

Colorado
Office of Energy Conservation, 112 East 14th Ave., Denver, CO 80203; (303) 894-2144.

Connecticut
Office of Policy and Management, Energy Division, 80 Washington St., Hartford, CT 06106; (203) 566-2800.

Delaware
Energy Office, P.O. Box 1401, Dover, DE 19901; (302) 739-5644.

District of Columbia
Energy Office, 613 G Street, NW, 5th Floor, Washington, DC 20001; (202) 727-9700.

Florida
Governor's Energy Office, 214 South Bronough St., Tallahassee, FL 32399-0001; (904) 488-6764.

Georgia
Office of Energy Resources, 270 Washington, SW, Room 615, Atlanta, GA 30334; (404) 656-5176.

Guam
Energy Office, P.O. Box 2950, Agana, Guam 96910; (671) 472-8711.

Hawaii
State Energy Division, Dept. of Planning and Economic Development, 335 Merchant Street, Room 109, Honolulu, HI 96813; (808) 548-2306.

Idaho
Dept. of Water Resources, Division of Energy Resources, 1301 North Orchard, Boise, ID 83706; (208) 327-7900.

Illinois
Dept. of Energy and Natural Resources, 325 West Adams, Room 300, Springfield, IL 62706; (217) 785-2800.

Indiana
Dept. of Commerce, Division of Energy Policy, One North Capitol, Suite 700, Indianapolis, IN 46204-2288; (317) 232-2701.

Iowa
Dept. of Natural Resources, Energy and Geological Division, Wallace State Office Building, Des Moines, IA 50319; (515) 281-6682.

Kansas
Research and Energy Analysis Division, Kansas Corporation Commission, 1500 S.W. Arrowhead Road, Topeka, KS 66604; (913) 271-3260.

Kentucky
Governors Office of Coal and Energy Policy, P.O. Box 11888, Lexington, KY 40578; (606) 252-5535.

Louisiana
Dept. of Natural Resources, P.O. Box 94396, Baton Rouge, LA 70804-9396; (504) 342-4534.

Be patient. If any phone number is incorrect, call (area code) 555-1212 and request the new listing.

Energy

Maine
Department of Economics and Community Development, State House Station No. 53, Augusta, ME 04333; (207) 289-6000.

Maryland
Energy Office, 45 Calvert St., Annapolis, MD 21401; (301) 974-3755.

Massachusetts
Executive Office of Energy Resources, 100 Cambridge Street, Room 1500, Boston, MA 02202; (617) 727-4732.

Michigan
Office of Energy Programs, P.O. Box 30221, 6545 Mercantile Way, Lansing, MI 48909; (517) 334-6272.

Minnesota
Energy Information Center, Department of Public Service, Energy Division, 900 American Center Building, 150 East Kellogg Boulevard, St. Paul, MN 55101; (612) 296-5175.

Mississippi
Dept. of Energy and Transportation, 510 George Street, Dickson Building, Suite 100, Jackson, MS 39202-3096; (601) 359-6600.

Missouri
Dept. of Natural Resources, Division of Energy, P.O. Box 176, Jefferson City, MO 65102; (314) 751-4000.

Montana
Dept. of Natural Resources and Conservation, Energy Division, 1520 East Sixth Avenue, Helena, MT 59620-2301; (406) 444-6697.

Nebraska
Energy Office, P.O. Box 95085, State Capitol Building, 9th Floor, Lincoln, NE 68509; (402) 471-2867.

Nevada
State Office of Community Services, Capitol Complex, Carson City, NV 89710; (702) 687-4990.

New Hampshire
Governor's Energy Office, 2 1/2 Beacon St., Concord, NH 03301; (603) 271-2711.

New Jersey
Division of Energy Planning and Conservation, 101 Commerce St., Newark, NJ 07102; (201) 648-6289.

New Mexico
Dept. of Minerals and Natural Resources, Energy Management and Conservation Division, 2400 South Pacheco, Santa Fe, NM 87505; (505) 827-5900.

New York
State Energy Office, Two Rockefeller Plaza, Albany, NY 12223; (518) 473-4375.

North Carolina
Dept. of Economic and Community Development, Energy Division, P.O. Box 25249, Raleigh, NC 27611; (919) 733-2230.

North Dakota
Office of Intergovernmental Assistance, State Capitol Building, Bismarck, ND 58505; (701) 224-2094.

Ohio
Office of Energy Conservation, Ohio Dept. of Development, 77 South High Street, 24th Floor, Columbus, OH 43266-0413; (614) 466-6797.

Oklahoma
Dept. of Commerce, Division of Community Affairs and Development, 6601 Broadway Extension, Suite 200, Oklahoma City, OK 73116; (405) 841-9326.

Oregon
Dept. of Energy, 625 Marion Street, NE, Salem, OR 97310-0831; (503) 378-4040.

Pennsylvania
Energy Office, 116 Pine Street, Harrisburg, PA 17101; (717) 783-9981.

Puerto Rico
Office of Energy, PO Box 4109-Minillas Station; (809) 726-4740.

Rhode Island
Office of Energy Assistance, 275 Westminster Mall, Providence, RI 02903; (401) 277-3370.

South Carolina
Governor's Division of Energy, Agriculture, and Natural Resources, 1205 Pendleton Street, 3rd Floor, Columbia, SC 29201; (803) 758-3208.

South Dakota
Governors Office of Energy Policy, 217 1/2 West Missouri, Pierre, SD 57501; (605) 773-3603.

Tennessee
Energy Division, Department of Economic and Community Development, 320 Sixth Ave., North, 8th Floor, Nashville, TN 37219; (615) 741-2372.

Texas
Energy Management Center, Governor's Office of Budget and Planning, P.O. Box 12428, Capitol Station, Austin, TX 78711; (512) 463-1962.

Utah
Energy Office, 355 West North Temple, Three Triad Center, Suite 450, Salt Lake City, UT 84180-1204; (801) 538-5428.

Vermont
Energy Efficiency Division, Department of Public Services, State Office Building, 120 State Street, Montpelier, VT 05602; (802) 828-2393.

Virginia
Department of Mines, Minerals, and Energy, 2201 West Broad Street, Richmond, VA 23220; (804) 367-6851.

Virgin Islands
Energy Office, Old Customs House, Frederickston, St. Croix, VI 00840; (809) 772-2616.

Washington
State Energy Office, 809 Legion Way SE, Mail Stop FA-11, Olympia, WA 98504; (206) 956-2000.

West Virginia
Governor's Office of Community and Industrial Development, Building 6, Capital Complex, Charleston, WV 25305; (304) 348-4010.

Wisconsin
Division of Energy and Intergovernmental Relations, 101 South Webster Street, 6th Floor, Madison, WI 53707-7868; (608) 266-8234.

Wyoming
Economic Development and Stabilization Board, Herschler Building, West Wing, 2nd Floor, Cheyenne, WY 82002; (307) 777-7284.

Mariana Islands
Office of Energy and Environment, P.O. Box 340, Saipan, Mariana Islands 96950

Puerto Rico
Office of Energy, P.O. Box 41089, Minillas Station, Santurce, Puerto Rico 00940

Virgin Islands
Energy Office, Room 233, Building 3, Lagoon Complex, Fredericksted, St. Croix, U.S. Virgin Islands 0084

Be patient. If any phone number is incorrect, call (area code) 555-1212 and request the new listing.

Fossil Fuels: Oil, Coal, and Natural Gas

* Alaska Natural Gas Pipeline

Alaska Natural Gas Pipeline Project
Office of Pipeline Safety, DPS-12
Research and Special Programs Administration, Room 8417
U.S. Department of Transportation
400 7th Street, SW
Washington, DC 20590 (202) 366-4556

Contact this office for information about the plans, programs, policies, and regulation concerning the Alaska pipeline.

* Atmospheric Fluidized Bed Combustion

Fluidized Bed Combustion Projects
Tennessee Valley Authority
Power, P.O. Box 1010
CEB-2W201A
Muscle Shoals, AL 35660 (615) 751-7438

This office can provide you with up-to-date information on atmospheric fluidized bed combustion, a new technology which burns pulverized coal at a lower temperature than conventional pulverized coal technology in a bed of limestone particles, resulting in lower nitrogen oxide emissions. The by-product is more easily disposed of, and therefore, it is more environmentally desirable. A 160 megawatt atmospheric fluidized bed demonstration plant was recently completed in Paducha, Kentucky, at the Shaunyee Plant. The U.S. Department of Energy's Office of Fossil Fuels also has a contact for this program at (301) 903-3991.

* Clean Coal Technology

Clean Coal Technology
Demonstration Project
U.S. Department of Energy
1000 Independence Ave., NW, FE-22
Washington, DC 20585 (202) 586-7165

Through DOE's Clean Coal Technology (CCT) Demonstration Program, the most promising of the advanced coal-based technologies are being moved into the marketplace through demonstration. The demonstration effort is at a large enough scale to generate all data needed by the public sector to judge the commercial potential of the processes being developed. These technologies will reduce or eliminate the economic and environmental impediments that limit the full use of coal, and will work toward resolving the conflict between the increasing use of coal and the growing concern about the environmental impact of such use. Contact the above office for further information, including a copy of their report *Clean Power From Clean Coal*.

* Coal Combustion and Control Systems

Fossil Energy
U.S. Department of Energy
19901 Germantown, Rd.
Germantown, MD 20585 (301) 908-4348

This office oversees research in atmospheric and pressurized fluidized bed combustion, coal-water mixtures, coal preparation and advanced combustion techniques. The office also develops advanced environmental control technology, including management of solid wastes produced by advanced fossil energy technologies. Contact the office for further program information.

* Coal Education Information

American Coal Foundation
1130 17th St. NW, Suite 220
Washington, DC 20036 (202) 466-8630

This association provides publications for grades K-12, some of which are available in classroom sets; a film guide, activities and science fair ideas. Also available free of charge is a coal sample kit that contains samples of peat, lignite, bitomous coal and anthracite, along with a brief description of the formation of different types of coal. Also available for purchase or free loan (grades 7-12 and adult groups) is a slide presentation "Understanding the Greenhouse Effect and Global Climate Change." The complete kit numbers 53 slides, a script, teachers guide, brochure, and a one page summary.

* Coal Energy Research

Research and Development
Power and Business Operations
Missionary Ridge Place, 3N41A
1101 Market St.
Chattanooga, TN 37402-2801 (615) 751-7438

This office can provide you with information on TVA's two most promising technologies for better use of coal: fluidized bed combustion, and advanced sulfur dioxide control technology to capture sulfur in conventional coal-fired boilers.

* Coal Liquefaction

Pittsburgh Energy Technology Center
P.O. Box 10940
Pittsburgh, PA 15236 (412) 892-6128

This laboratory conducts research and development in coal liquefaction, alternative fuels, coal slurries, advanced combustion, magnetohydrodynamics, coal preparation, flue gas cleanup, and university coal research. Contact this office for available information on its research.

* Coal Supply and Demand

Coal Division
Coal, Nuclear, Electric and Alternate Fuels
Energy Information Administration
U.S. Department of Energy
1707 H. St. NW
Washington, DC 20585 (202) 254-5392

This office monitors all supply and demand aspects of coal, including production, prices, and distribution. It identifies and analyses coal reserves; examines new technologies for deriving energy from coal; and, studies existing and proposed legislation and regulations affecting coal supply and demand. Contact this office for more program information.

* Coal Use Technology Database

Pittsburgh Energy Technology Center
P.O. Box 10940
Pittsburgh, PA 15236 (412) 892-8029

This Center does research on all aspects of coal. Contact this office for information on its database on emerging coal use technologies.

* Defense Energy Consumption

Defense Energy Policy Directorate
Office of the Assistant Secretary of Defense
DEF/P&L/L(EP)
The Pentagon, Room 1D760
Washington, DC 20301-3000 (703) 697-2500

This office can provide you with wholesale petroleum data and facility energy consumption data. Inquiries will be answered on a cost recovery basis.

* Defense Energy Consumption

Defense Energy Policy Directorate
Office of the Assistant Secretary of Defense
DEF/P&L/L(EP)
The Pentagon, Room 1D760
Washington, DC 20301-3000 (202) 697-2500

This office can provide you with wholesale petroleum data and facility energy consumption data. Inquiries will be answered on a cost recovery basis.

Be patient. If any phone number is incorrect, call (area code) 555-1212 and request the new listing.

Energy

* Eastern Region Coalbed Methane Information Center

The University of Alabama
Box 870211
205 Tom Bevill Building
Tuscaloosa, AL 35487 (205) 348-2839

This Center can provide you with information and research assistance on all aspects of coalbed methane research, development and field activities. The Center focuses primarily on the Black Warrior and San Juan basins, but also provides materials covering less known basins including the Pineance, Powder River Arkoma, Illinois, Wind River, Green River, and all of the Appalachian areas. While the library at the Center is non-circulating, photocopies may be obtained for a nominal fee.

* Energy and Mineral Resources

Office of Energy and Marine Geology
U.S. Geological Survey
National Center, MS 915
Reston, VA 22092 (703) 648-6470

Investigations of the nature, extent, and origin of the Nation's coal, oil and gas, oil shale, uranium, and geothermal resources are basic to this office's research efforts. Acquired data are placed in computerized databases, such as the National Coal Resources Data System.

* Energy Price Patterns

Energy Markets and Information Division
Energy Information Administration (EIA)
U.S. Department of Energy
1000 Independence Ave., SW, Room 2G-089
Washington, DC 20585 (202) 586-1441

This office performs analyses and short-term forecasting of world oil markets and energy demand patterns and prices. It assesses the factors that influence world energy prices. This office also acts as the center for the collection and analysis of enterprise level data within EIA.

* Export Assistance for Coal and Coal Technologies Industry

National Technical Information Service
U.S. Department of Commerce
Springfield, VA 22161 (703) 487-4650

The *Guide to Federal Export Assistance Activities Applicable to the U.S. Coal and Coal Technologies Industry* provides coal and coal technology firms with a single reference source for identifying U.S. government agencies, programs, and contacts that might aid in exporting. The *Guide* contains an in-depth discussion of the eight major agencies offering export assistance and identifies pertinent activities performed by other federal agencies that might assist coal and coal technologies exporters. Write to the office above to obtain a copy.

* Fossil Energy Developments

Communications Staff
Fossil Energy, 4G-085
U.S. Department of Energy
Washington, DC 20585 (202) 586-6503

Fossil Energy Review provides an update of key events in the Department of Energy's Fossil Energy program. It is published as part of the Office of Fossil Energy's technology transfer efforts conducted in response to the Stevenson-Wydler Technology Innovation Act of 1980 and the Technology Transfer act of 1986. Contact this office or the Government Printing Office for subscription availability.

* Fossil Energy Research

Western Research Institute (WRI)
P.O. Box 3395, University Station
Laramie, WY 82071 (307) 721-2211

This fossil energy research center specializes in environmental assessment, extraction process development, and fuels upgrading. Research efforts focus on conversion of oil shale, tar sands, coal, and waste products to useful hydrocarbon products and environmentally acceptable wastes. Contact this Institute for more information on fossil energy.

* Fossil Fuel Research Solicitations

National Institute for Petroleum
and Energy Research (NIPER)
P.O. Box 2128
Bartlesville, OK 74005 (918) 337-4375

NIPER solicit fossil fuel technology research not only from government agencies, but from the private sector as well. Contact this office for more information.

* Fossil Fuel Technology

National Institute for Petroleum
and Energy Research (NIPER)
P.O. Box 2128
Bartlesville, OK 74005 (918) 337-4375

This office conducts research and development covering all phases of liquid fossil fuel technology. This program includes research on petroleum extraction using enhanced oil recovery methods and improved drilling technology; the extraction of natural gas from Western tight sands; processing and thermodynamic properties of conventional oils, as well as liquid products made from coal, oil shale, and tar sands; recycling of waste lubricating oil; and improving automotive engine emissions. Databases on crude oil analyses, alternative fuels, enhanced oil recovery are maintained, and the public has free access to them. Contact this office for more information on fossil fuel technology and accessing information on the Institute's databases.

* Fuel Suppliers and Consumption in the Military

Public Affairs Office
Defense Fuel Supply Center (DFSC)
Defense Logistics Agency
Cameron Station
Alexandria, VA 22304-6160 (703) 274-6489

This office will supply information on almost anything you will want to know concerning fuel supply in the military. The staff will explain how to contract for the Strategic Petroleum Reserve, and how to request information under the Freedom of Information Act, such as statistics on fuel consumption patterns in the military and copies of current contracts with major suppliers. You may request a free copy of their *Fact Book*, which tells how much was spent on fuel throughout the U.S. Department of Defense, the sources of supply, and how the fuel was allocated. It includes line graphs and pie charts, with a national geographic distribution breakdown. Also ask for a copy of the DFSC's magazine *Fuel Line*.

* Gas Research Institute (GRI)

8600 West Bryn Mawr Avenue
Chicago, IL 60631 (312) 399-8100

This institute is a non-profit membership organization of the natural gas industry. GRI plans, manages, and develops financing for a research and development program designed to advance natural gas supply, transport, storage, and end-use technologies and to conduct related basic research. new products processes, and information resulting from GRI's results oriented program provide cost savings and other benefits for the natural gas industry and gas consumers nationwide.

* Morgantown Energy Technology Center

U.S. Department of Energy
Public Affairs Manager
PO Box 880
Morgantown, WV 27507-0880 (304) 291-4308

The main goal of this center is to work with industry and research organizations to commercialize new ways to find and utilize domestic supplies of coal, oil and natural gas. Research is conducted on site and at many locations throughout the United States.

* Natural Gas Information

American Gas Association
1515 Wilson Blvd.
Arlington, VA 22209 (703) 841-8400

This association provides information on sales, finance utilization, research, management, safety, accounting, and all phases of gas transmission and distribution. It also sponsors competitions among primary and secondary students as well as public service and informational advertising. It also compiles a wide range of national and regional statistical, economic, marketing and

Be patient. If any phone number is incorrect, call (area code) 555-1212 and request the new listing.

Fossil Fuels: Oil, Coal, and Natural Gas

financial studies as well as developing operating practices and gas rate schedules for virtually all gas companies.

* Naval Petroleum Reserves

Office of Naval Petroleum and Oil Shale Reserves
Fossil Energy
U.S. Department of Energy
1000 Independence Ave., SW, Room 3H-076
Washington, DC 20585 (202) 586-4685

This office oversees the operations of the Naval Petroleum and Oil Shale Reserves, including the protection, conservation, maintenance, and production of Reserves. A Naval petroleum reserve program has existed since before the Second World War. Contact the above office for information or references to further information on the program.

* Office of Natural Gas

Office of Natural Gas
Fossil Energy
U.S. Department of Energy
1000 Independence Ave., SW, Room 3H-087
Washington, DC 20585 (202) 586-9482

Working in conjunction with the State department and other federal agencies, this office performs policy analysis related to the importation and exportation of natural gas. It also works on the major issues involving pipeline systems for natural gas across state and international boundaries.

* Offshore Geologic Resources

Geologic Inquiries
U.S. Geological Survey (USGS)
907 National Center
Reston, VA 22092 (703) 648-4383

Using remotely sensed data, including sidescan sonar and other geophysical surveys, and direct sampling, the USGS studies the geology and assesses the potential mineral and energy resources of the continental margins and the Exclusive Economic Zone of the United States (200 miles from the coastline) and its territories. Also identified are geologic features that must be considered in the selection of sites for offshore drilling platforms and pipelines.

* Offshore Oil and Gas Leasing

Offshore Minerals Management
Mineral Management Service
U.S. Department of the Interior
18th and C Sts., NW
Washington, DC 20240 (202) 208-3530

The Mineral Management Service leases the rights to explore and develop oil and gas on Federal lands of the continental shelf. The "shelf" is made up of the submerged offshore areas lying seaward of the territorial sea to a depth of 200 meters (656 feet) and beyond that area to that depth which allows for mineral exploration. The brochure, *Leasing Energy Resources on the Outer Continental Shelf*, explains the leasing procedure and gives a history of the program.

* Offshore Oil Lease Revenues

Land Resources Division
National Park Service
U.S. Department of the Interior
1100 L St., NW
Washington, DC 20005 (202) 523-5252

The National Park System is able to purchase land for its use with the revenues received from off-shore oil leases. Revenues from these leases also are credited to the Land and Water Conservation Fund and the Historic Preservation Fund for efforts in these areas.

* Oil and Gas Data

Office of Oil and Gas
Energy Information Administration
U.S. Department of Energy
1000 Independence Ave., SW, 2H-058
Washington, DC 20585 (202) 586-6401

This office designs, develops and maintains oil and gas statistical data and current short-term forecasting information systems.

* Oil and Gas: Economic Issues

Office of Policy, Planning, and Analysis
U.S. Department of Energy
1000 Independence Ave., SW, 7H-063
Washington, DC 20585 (202) 586-5667

This office analyzes the international oil and gas markets. Major areas of concentration include economic analyses of the Organization of Petroleum Exporting Countries (OPEC), market responses to changing oil prices, incentives designed to stimulate increased oil production and conservation, and Government policies designed to deregulate oil and gas markets and enhance U.S. energy security.

* Oil and Gas Leasing on Public Lands

Energy and Mineral Resources Division
Bureau of Land Management
U.S. Department of the Interior
18th and C Sts., NW
Washington, DC 20240 (202) 208-4201

Public lands are available for oil and gas leasing only after they have been evaluated through the Bureau of Land Management. In areas where development of oil and gas resources would conflict with the protection or management of other resources or public land uses, mitigating measures are identified and may appear on leases as either stipulations to uses or as restrictions on surface occupancy. Two types of leases are issued: competitive and noncompetitive.

* Oil and Gas Reserves

Reserves and Natural Gas Division
Energy Information Administration
U.S. Department of Energy
1000 Independence Ave., SW, Room BE-054
Washington, DC 20585 (202) 586-6090

Energy reserves and production are vital to America's energy security for the future. This office maintains statistical and short-term forecasting information systems for domestic oil and gas reserves and production and on the natural gas industry.

* Oil and Gas Royalties

Royalty Management
Mineral Management Service
U.S. Department of the Interior
Kipling at Sixth Ave., Bldg. 85
Box 25165
Denver, CO 80225 (303) 231-3058

The Royalty Management Program collects and accounts for bonuses, rentals, and royalties due on the Outer Continental Shelf, federal and Indian mineral leases. It then distributes the money to States, Indians, or other Federal agencies. Owners of federal and Indian leases are required, by regulation and lease terms, to pay an annual lease rental fee and/or monthly royalties on the value of minerals removed or sold from a lease. Mineral revenues from Federal and Indian lands were nearly $4.6 billion in 1990. The publication *Mineral Revenues 1990* details royalties on a state by state basis and also has some interesting figures on oil, gas, and coal production.

* Oil and Natural Gas: Production, Marketing, Legislation

Office of Economic Analysis
Policy, Planning and Analysis
U.S. Department of Energy
1000 Independence Ave., SW, Room 7H-063
Washington, DC 20585 (202) 586-5667

This office prepares analyses and advises the Secretary of Energy on government policies affecting the discovery, production, refining, marketing, and consumption of oil and natural gas. This promotes free market policies and regulatory reform, thereby increasing the economic efficiency of oil and natural gas markets, increasing domestic consumer welfare, and reducing the Nation's vulnerability to energy supply disruptions. To accomplish this objective, the staff currently prepares analyses of natural gas legislation, restrictions on Alaskan oil exports, acquisition/drawdown policies for the Strategic Petroleum Reserve, domestic refinery policy, tax reform policy, and the Crude Oil Windfall Profits Tax. Contact this office for information on the availability of these and other reports and program information.

Be patient. If any phone number is incorrect, call (area code) 555-1212 and request the new listing.

Energy

* Oil, Gas, and Shale Technology

Oil, Gas, and Shale
Fossil Energy
U.S. Department of Energy
19901 Germantown Road
Germantown, MD 20585
(301) 903-2877

This office is responsible for Federal technology programs for recovery of natural gas from hydrocarbon reserves, Eastern gas shales, and Western tight gas sands; for the recovery of methane from coal; and for recovery of other unconventional gas resources. The office is also responsible for the advancement of the science and engineering database for gas extraction technologies. Contact this office for program information.

* Oil Potential in the U.S.

Oil, Gas, Shale and Special Technologies
Office of Fossil Energy
U.S. Department of Energy
19901 Germantown Road
Germantown, MD 20585
(301) 903-2877

The document, *Federal Oil Research: A Strategy for Maximizing the Producibility of Known U.S. Oil*, summarizes the current American oil situation. It traces Federal programs designed to maximize U.S. oil potential, and describes the program's present status. Contact the above office for further information.

* Oil Recyclers

National Oil Recyclers Association (NORA)
2266 Bellfield Avenue
Cleveland, OH 44106
(216) 791-7316

The National Oil Recyclers Association is comprised of primary producers of recycled used oil fuel. Its purpose is to represent the interests of used oil recyclers to the Environmental Protection Agency to ensure regulations on used oil are carried out and to encourage recycling. NORA will send you a free information package upon request.

* Oil Shale Conversion

Oil, Gas, and Shale Technology
Fossil Energy
U.S. Department of Energy
19901 Germantown Road
Germantown, MD 20585
(301) 903-3514

This office is involved with oil shale conversion to liquid fuels, including the development of a sound technology base for surface and in-situ processes and the investigation of improved environmental mitigation strategies and systems. Call or write the above office for more information.

* Outer Continental Shelf Oil and Gas

Operations Management
Offshore Minerals Management
Mineral Management Service
U.S. Department of the Interior
18th and C Sts., NW
Washington, DC 20240
(202) 208-3530

Management of the oil and gas operations following leasing agreements with the Mineral Management Service is outlined in the publication, *Managing Oil and Gas Operations on the Outer Continental Shelf*. This booklet describes activities through the drilling and production process to lease relinquishment.

* Petroleum Industry Interest Group

American Petroleum Institute (API)
1220 L St., NW
Washington, DC 20005
(202) 682-8375

The American Petroleum Institute is the petroleum industry trade association representing major oil companies, independent oil producers and fuel distributors, and service-station owners. It publishes extensive statistics about the industry. Publications: *Petroleum Today, Washington Report.*

* Petroleum Information Systems

Petroleum Marketing Division
Oil and Gas

Energy Information Administration
U.S. Department of Energy
1000 Independence Ave., SW, Room EI-431
Washington, DC 20585
(202) 586-5986

This office compiles information on crude oil and refined petroleum product prices and the industry market. The office can provide you with regular statistical reports on heating oil, gasoline, and other refined product prices and on sales of fuel oil and kerosene. Contact this office for available information and publications.

* Petroleum Marketing Information

Petroleum Marketing Division
Energy Marketing Division
Energy Information Administration
U.S. Department of Energy
1000 Independence Ave., SW, Room 2G-051
Washington, DC 20585
(202) 586-5214

Since 1973 the price of oil has been one of the most important factors influencing economic growth in this country. This office designs, develops, and maintains crude oil and refined petroleum product price and marketing statistical information.

* Petroleum Overcharge Refunds

Office of Hearings and Appeals
U.S. Department of Energy
1000 Independence Ave., SW, Room 6G-087
Washington, DC 20585
(202) 586-2094

Cash refunds are available to any people, business firms, and governments that purchased refined petroleum products in the U.S. between August 1973 and January 1981. This office distributes millions of dollars in oil overcharges collected through the DOE enforcement program between those years. This office can give you further details.

* Petroleum Research

Bartlesville Project Office
U.S. Department of Energy
P.O. Box 1398
Bartlesville, OK 74001
(918) 337-4293

This Center is involved with research and engineering in petroleum and natural gas, including the improvement and demonstration of technologies in exploration, producing, refining, and use. A database on crude oil production and marketed fuel properties is also maintained. Research into automobile fuels is also undertaken. Contact this office for information on the database.

* Petroleum Statistics

Petroleum Supply Division
Oil and Gas
Energy Information Administration
U.S. Department of Energy
1000 Independence Ave., SW, Room 2G-020
Washington, DC 20585
(202) 586-6860

This office compiles statistics and projections for crude oil and refined petroleum products, including their availability, production, imports, processing, transportation, stocks, and distribution. For available information and publications, contact this office.

* Pipeline Safety

Office of Pipeline Safety (OPS), DPS-35
Research and Special Programs Administration
U.S. Department of Transportation
400 7th St., SW
Washington, DC 20590
(202) 366-4572

OPS establishes and enforces safety standards for the transportation of gas and other hazardous materials by pipeline. A computerized reporting system is maintained to collect and analyze accident and incident data from pipeline operators. Accident reports include the operator's name, the hazardous material involved, description of the accident, and results. For database searches, contact the office listed. There may be a charge.

* Public Lands Oil and Gas Leasing

Energy and Mineral Resources Division
Bureau of Land Management

Be patient. If any phone number is incorrect, call (area code) 555-1212 and request the new listing.

Fossil Fuels: Oil, Coal, and Natural Gas

U.S. Department of the Interior
18th and C Sts., NW
Washington, DC 20240 (202) 208-4201

Public lands are available for oil and gas leasing only after they have been evaluated through the Bureau of Land Management. In areas where development of oil and gas resources would conflict with the protection or management of other resources or public land uses, mitigating measures are identified and may appear on leases as either stipulations to uses or as restrictions on surface occupancy. Two types of leases are issued: competitive and noncompetitive.

* Small Coal Operator Assistance

Small Coal Operator Assistance
Land Resources
Natural Resources Management
Resource and Development
Tennessee Valley Authority (TVA)
Norris, TN 37828 (615) 632-1753

To ensure more competition and reasonable prices, TVA reserves a portion of its coal purchases for small producers. In addition, the TVA provides mining and reclamation technical assistance to small coal producers. The program is also involved in non-coal mineral abandoned mine reclamation. The percentage of contracts awarded to coal suppliers is evaluated based on the capability of the company to comply with TVA's mine reclamation programs.

* Strategic Petroleum Reserve

New Orleans Project Management Office
Oak Ridge Operations Office
U.S. Department of Energy
900 Commerce Rd. East
New Orleans, LA 71023 (504) 734-4201

Petroleum Reserves
Fossil Energy
U.S. Department of Energy
1000 Independence Ave., SW, Room 3G-072
Washington, DC 20585 (202) 586-4415

The Strategic Petroleum Reserve was established to provide a stock of petroleum products to serve as at least a partial cushion in case of another cut off of oil products from overseas. Reports on the reserve and its progress are available

from the above offices. The New Orleans office can answer specific questions on project implementation, site locations, construction, technical problems, and related matters, and the Washington office can provide you with information on the project's overall direction.

* Strategic Petroleum Reserve: Quarterly Report

Office of Petroleum Reserves
Assistant Secretary for Fossil Energy
U.S. Department of Energy
1000 Independence Ave., SW, Room 3G-024
Washington, DC 20585 (202) 586-4410

Strategic Petroleum Reserve: Quarterly Report details the current status of the Strategic Petroleum Reserve project, designed to have a stock on hand of petroleum in case of future supply disruptions. Contact the office of the National Energy Information Center for information on availability.

* Underground Storage Tank Regulations

Environmental Protection Agency
2800 Crystal Dr., North Towers
Arlington, VA 22022 (703) 308-8850

The Underground Storage Tank (UST) Docket provides public access to regulatory information supporting the Agency's regulatory action on USTs. As of April 1, 1987, there are seven dockets: (1) UST Notification Form; (2) Technical Standards for USTs Containing Petroleum; (3) Financial Responsibility Requirements for USTs Containing Petroleum; (4) State Program Approval; (5) Report to Congress on Exempt Tanks; (6) Consolidated Rules of Practice Governing the Administrative Assessment of Civil Penalties and Revocation or Suspension of Permits; and (7) Financial Responsibility Requirements for USTs Containing Hazardous Substances.

* World Petroleum Prices

Energy Plastics Branch
Energy and Chemicals Division
U.S. International Trade Commission
500 E St., SW, Room 513
Washington, DC 20436 (202) 205-3348

This office can provide you with the study, *Possible Effects of Changing World Crude Petroleum Prices.*

Be patient. If any phone number is incorrect, call (area code) 555-1212 and request the new listing.

Energy

Nuclear Energy and Waste

* Abnormal Occurrences at Nuclear Facilities

Superintendent of Documents
Government Printing Office (GPO)
Washington, DC 20402 (202) 783-3238

The Nuclear Regulatory Commission (NRC) prepares a quarterly *Report to Congress on Abnormal Occurrences* which also serves to communicate significant event information to licensees, other government agencies, and the public. This publication reports abnormal occurrences, which are unscheduled incidents or events which the NRL determined significant from the standpoint of public health and safety, involving facilities and activities regulated by the NRL and those regulated by the agreement states. For more information on the content of the reports, contact the Office of Analysis and Evaluation of Operational Data, Nuclear Regulatory Commission, Washington, DC 20555; (301) 492-9809. Contact GPO for ordering information.

* Accidents and Incidents

Division of Operational Events Assessment
Office of Nuclear Reactor Regulation
Nuclear Regulatory Commission (NRC), Room 11 E1
Washington, DC 20055 (301) 504-1163

This division implements programs and procedures to systematically assess and screen daily reactor events; to provide daily reports; to recommend immediate corrective plant-specific and generic actions; and to coordinate the follow-up to events by assigning and tracking follow-up actions. This Division maintains and administers "on-call officer" roster to assure notification of management for events requiring prompt actions. They also respond to emergencies, and serve as the Incident Assessment Team contact.

* Antitrust Review of Nuclear Industry

Office of the General Counsel
Nuclear Regulatory Commission (NRC), Room 15D19
Washington, DC 20555 (301) 504-1532

During the licensing process, the NRC and the Attorney General conduct antitrust reviews of license applications, and an antitrust hearing may be required. Contact this office for more information on past or current antitrust reviews.

* Atomic Safety and Licensing Appeal Panel

Nuclear Regulatory Commission (NRC)
4530 East-West Highway, Room 534A
Bethesda, MD 20814 (301) 492-7662

Three-member appeal boards are selected from this panel to review individual licensing board decisions. These include proceedings for the licensing of nuclear power plants and other nuclear facilities. The Appeal Board decision is subject only to judicial review in a Federal court of appeals.

* Atomic Safety and Licensing Board Panel

Nuclear Regulatory Commission (NRC)
4530 East-West Highway, Room 422
Bethesda, MD 20814 (301) 492-7814

Three-member licensing boards are drawn from this panel. They are made up of lawyers and others with expertise in various technical and environmental fields to conduct public hearings on applications to build and operate nuclear power plants and other matters related to the possession and use of nuclear facilities and materials.

* Atomic Vapor Laser Isotope Separation

Advanced Technology Projects
and Technology Transfer
Uranium Enrichment
Nuclear Energy
U.S. Department of Energy

19901 Germantown Rd.
Germantown, MD 20585 (301) 903-4781

This office researches and develops techniques to process atomic vapor laser isotope separation (AVLIS). More detailed information is available from the above office.

* Audiovisuals, Nuclear Waste

Information Services Division
Office of Civilian Radioactive Waste Management (OCRWM)
U.S. Department of Energy
1000 Independence Ave., SW
Washington, DC 20585 (202) 586-2835

The *OCRWM Audiovisual Directory* lists abstracts of videotapes, audiocassettes, slides and films on the subject of waste management. These products are available for loan to Federal, State, and local governments; Indian Tribes; the media; professionals; and the general public. The directory contains both current and historical footage and features citation listings numerically and alphabetically by titles. The directory also indexes products by subject keywords. In addition to a printed directory, the information is available online through the *OCRWM Product Record System*.

* Citizen's Guide to U.S. Nuclear Regulatory Commission

Public Affairs
Nuclear Regulatory Commission (NRC)
Washington, DC 20555 (301) 634-3273

The *Citizen's Guide to U.S. Nuclear Regulatory Commission Information* is designed to acquaint the public with the availability of information pertaining to the licensing and regulation of nuclear energy, and of all commercial high-level and low-level radioactive waste and uranium recovery activities in the United States.

* Civilian Reactor Development

Nuclear Energy
Office of Civilian Reactor Development
U.S. Department of Energy
19901 Germantown Rd.
Germantown, MD 20585 (301) 903-5330

This office is responsible for supporting the national energy supply policy by developing and implementing programs to ensure that nuclear energy remains a safe, economically competitive and environmentally acceptable energy option.

* Construction Permits for Nuclear Facilities

Office of Nuclear Reactor Regulation
Nuclear Regulatory Commission (NRC)
Room 12 D1
Washington, DC 20555 (301) 504-1270

Obtaining an NRC construction permit is the first objective of a utility or other company seeking to operate a nuclear power reactor or other nuclear facility under NRC licensing authority. The process begins with the filing and acceptance of an application, generally comprising many volumes of data, covering both safety and environmental considerations, in accord with NRC requirements and guidance. Contact this office for more information concerning the construction permit process.

* Criminal Incidents

Emergency Programs Center
U.S. Department of Justice
10th St. and Constitution Ave., NW
Room 6101
Washington, DC 20530 (202) 514-2000

If you would like to know the facts of any case of criminal activity involving nuclear incidents, the files of the Emergency Programs Center is for you. This

Be patient. If any phone number is incorrect, call (area code) 555-1212 and request the new listing.

Nuclear Energy and Waste

office of the U.S. Department of Justice coordinates the government's activity in any such case. For instance, if you want the facts on the real-life case of nuclear extortion seen in the movie, *The Falcon and the Snowman*, this is the place to go. Maybe you are interested in writing your own thriller on nuclear espionage; contact the Emergency Programs Center and read accounts of actual incidents to give your writing that tinge of reality. Whatever your interest may be, here's where you'll get the facts.

* Daily Nuclear Documents

Public Document Room (PDR)
Nuclear Regulatory Commission (NRC)
2120 L. Street, NW
Washington, DC 20037 (202) 634-3273

The *PDR Daily Accession List* describes agency documents that are made publicly available each weekday. There is ordinarily at least a two-to-three-week delay in the public availability of new documents. The PDR collection includes all publicly available forms of communication generated by NRC or sent to NRC by the companies and institutions it regulates. The Accession Lists are organized by NRC topics, and all documents appropriate to a topic and their file location are listed in one place. A free publication, *How to Use The Public Document Room's Daily Accession List*, is available from the office above, and explains the *Daily Accession List*, the PDR request policy, as well as the classification scheme.

* Decommissioning Nuclear Facilities

Remedial Action Program Information Center (RAPIC)
Martin Marietta Energy Systems Inc.
P.O. Box 2003, Building K-1210, MS-7256
Oak Ridge, TN 37831-7256 (615) 576-0568

The *Nuclear Facility Decommissioning and Site Remedial Action* database serves as a comprehensive source of technical information relevant to the DOE Remedial Action Program, under which nuclear facilities are decommissioned and cleaned up. The RAPIC data center scans both foreign and domestic reports, journals, books and theses and currently contains some 8,500 references. Computerized literature searches of RAPIC databases are available upon request at no charge.

* Environmental Review of Proposed Nuclear Facilities

Office of Nuclear Reactor Regulation
Nuclear Regulatory Commission (NRC)
Room 12 D1
Washington, DC 20555 (301) 504-1270

An environmental review begins with an analysis of the consequences to the environment of the construction and operation of the proposed nuclear facility at the proposed site. Upon completion of the analysis, a draft Environmental Statement is published and distributed to all interested parties. Comments are then taken into account in the preparation of a final Environmental Statement. During this same period, the NRC is conducting analysis and preparing a report on the site suitability aspects of the proposed licensing action. Contact this office more information on the review process and reports.

* Exhibits, Nuclear Waste

U.S. Department of Energy
Office of Civilian Radioactive Waste Management (OCRWM)
ERAP/ISD (RW-43) (Exhibits)
Washington, DC 20585 (202) 586-2835

OCRWM has one full-size (9' X 20') exhibit and several tabletop (3' X 8') exhibits which describe the radioactive waste management program. These exhibits are used at public meetings and events around the country.

* Export and Import Controls

Nuclear Energy and Energy Technology Affairs
Bureau of Oceans and International Environmental
and Scientific Affairs
U.S. Department of State
2201 C St., NW, Room 7820
Washington, DC 20520 (202) 647-4101

This office works closely with the Nuclear Regulatory Commission with regard to the licensing requests for nuclear imports and exports. They also study the development and transfer of nuclear technology in foreign countries. This office monitors the Nuclear Non-Proliferation Treaty, making sure that the countries which signed the treaty are following its regulations. They also oversee the export

and import of items which are not nuclear, but which could be used for nuclear purposes, such as super computers. The export of these items must follow the guidelines set in the Nuclear Non-Proliferation Treaty.

* Export-Import Licensing

International Programs
Nuclear Regulatory Commission (NRC)
Room 3H1
Washington, DC 20555 (301) 504-2344

This NRC office formulates and recommends policies concerning nuclear exports and imports, international safeguards, international physical security, nonproliferation matters, and international cooperation and assistance in nuclear safety and radiation protection. NRC is responsible for licensing the import or export of nuclear-related materials and equipment. This export authority extends to production and utilization facilities, to special nuclear and source material, to byproduct materials, and to certain nuclear-related components and other material.

* Freedom of Information Act Requests

Office of Administration
Nuclear Regulatory Commission (NRC)
7920 Norfolk Ave., Room 378C
Bethesda, MD 20814 (301) 492-8133

All Freedom of Information Act Requests should be addressed to the Office listed above.

* Fuel Cycle Plants and Material Safety

Industrial and Medical Nuclear Safety Division
Office of Nuclear Material Safety and Safeguards
Nuclear Regulatory Commission (NRC)
Room 6H1
Washington, DC 20555 (301) 504-3426

This office analyzes health physics, radiation and nuclear safety, quality, licensing, and follow-up review of all fuel cycle plants. Contact this office for more information on its studies.

* Fuel Cycle Programs

Office of Facilities and Fuel Cycle Programs
Fuel Cycle Programs Division
U.S. Department of Energy
19901 Germantown Rd.
Germantown, MD 20585 (301) 903-2915

This division manages fuel development and fabrication activities necessary to assure adequate fuel supply for uninterrupted operations by key nuclear test facilities. It also performs equipment development and verification testing to support various fuel cycle options, improve operational efficiency, and reduce future fuel cycle costs.

* Fusion Energy and Basic Science Research

General Sciences
Lawrence Berkeley Laboratory
One Cyclotron Rd.
Mail Stop 50A/5104
Berkeley, CA 94720 (510) 486-5771

The General Sciences section of the Lawrence Berkeley Laboratory researches the basic nature of matter to provide basic understanding of the elements of the universe, making progress possible in many fields of science. Of particular interest in the work of this division is investigation of the potential development of nuclear fusion energy sources. Contact this office for more information.

* Fusion Technology

Office of Fusion Energy
Energy Research
U.S. Department of Energy
19901 Germantown Rd.
Germantown, MD 20585 (301) 903-3347

The office works to develop sound physical and engineering technological foundations needed for the design, construction, and operation of complex nuclear fusion experiments and facilities. Contact the office for more detailed program information.

Be patient. If any phone number is incorrect, call (area code) 555-1212 and request the new listing.

Energy

* Gas Centrifuge and Isotope Separation Research

Uranium Enrichment Advanced Technology Project
U.S. Department of Energy
19901 Germantown Rd.
Germantown, MD 20585 (301) 903-4781

This project conducts research and development of gas centrifuge technology and advanced isotope separation techniques. It publishes an annual report which covers statistical information pertaining to uranium research and development. Contact the office for further information.

* High-Level Nuclear Waste

High-Level Waste Management Division
Office of Nuclear Material Safety and Safeguards
Nuclear Regulatory Commission (NRC)
Room 4H1
Washington, DC 20555 (301) 504-3404

This Division develops and manages the Agency's program for the licensing, inspection, and regulation of the U.S. Department of Energy's high-level waste repository program. They also provide the lead for all Agency activities under the Nuclear Waste Policy Act.

* Inspection of Nuclear Reactors

Nuclear Reactor Regulation
Nuclear Regulatory Commission (NRC)
Room 12E23
Washington, DC 20402 (301) 504-1274

A basic element in NRC reactor regulation is the inspection of licensed reactor facilities to determine the state of reactor safety, to confirm that the operations are in compliance with the provisions of the license, and to ascertain whether other conditions exist which have safety implications serious enough to warrant corrective action. The NRC conducts a program to deal with unsafe or potentially unsafe events or conditions which occur at individual plant sites or other facilities involving licensed operation ("reactive" inspections).

* Interim Waste Storage

Superintendent of Documents
U.S. Government Printing Office
Washington, DC 20402 (202) 783-3238

The Monitored Retrievable Storage Review Commission's report, *Nuclear Waste: Is There A Need For Federal Interim Storage?*, reflects the Commission's extensive technical work and public policy deliberations. It is available for sale from the office above.

* International Reactor Development

Office of Technology Support Program
U.S. Department of Energy
19901 Germantown Rd. Room H407
Germantown, MD 20585 (301) 903-3609

Under the Civilian Reactor Technology Support Program, this office coordinates and cooperates with other Federal agencies in developing and executing international programs for power reactor development. Contact this office for more information.

* International Nuclear and Energy Association

645 North Michigan Ave. Suite 860
Chicago, IL 60611 (312) 642-9502

This association seeks to unify and develop new sources of energy. To this end it conducts workshops, seminars, research, and other technical studies as well as compiling statistics.

* Justifying Nuclear Energy

Office of Program Support, Nuclear Energy
U.S. Department of Energy (DOE)
19901 Germantown Rd. Room 5A-157
Germantown, MD 20585 (301) 903-5462

This office is responsible for justifying and defending DOE's Nuclear Energy programs before internal agency, Office of Management and Budget (OMB), and Congressional reviews. More detailed information is available from the above office.

* Licensee Event Reports

Superintendent of Documents
Government Printing Office
Washington, DC 20402 (202) 783-3238

Licensee Event Report Compilation is a monthly publication which contains summaries of reported operational information submitted to the Nuclear Regulatory Commission (NRC) by nuclear powerplant licensees in accordance with Federal regulations. The summaries are arranged alphabetically by facility name and chronologically by event data for each facility, with components, system, and keyword indexes following the summaries. The complete documents are available for review at the Public Document Room, Nuclear Regulatory Commission, 2120 L Street, NW, Washington, DC 20037; (202) 634-3273.

* Licensing Nuclear-Related Operations

Office of Nuclear Reactor Regulation
Nuclear Regulatory Commission (NRC), Room 12 D1
Washington, DC 20402 (301) 504-1270

The Nuclear Regulatory Commission grants licenses for nuclear power operations and other possession and use of nuclear materials, including the transportation and disposal of nuclear materials and wastes. Contact this office for more information on the licensing process.

* Limited Work Authorization

Office of Nuclear Reactor Regulation
Nuclear Regulatory Commission (NRC)
Room 12 D1
Washington, DC 20555 (301) 504-1270

The NRC may decide to grant a Limited Work Authorization to an applicant in advance of a final decision on the construction permit, in order to allow certain work to begin at the site. Such a step could save seven months' construction time.

* Liquid Metal Fast Breeder Reactor

Office of Technology Support Program
U.S. Department of Energy
19901 Germantown Rd. Room H407
Germantown, MD 20585 (301) 903-3609

This office is the principal point of contact for information on the National Liquid Metal Fast Breeder Reactor (LMFBR). Program details are available from the above office.

* Local Public Document Rooms

Nuclear Regulatory Commission (NRC) (800) 38-8081
Washington, DC 20555 (301) 492-4344

The Local Public Documents Room (LPDR) in your area can provide you with information on nuclear plants and low level waste disposal facilities in your area. Many of the LPDRs have documents on microfiche for all publicly available documents issued since January 1981.

The following list, organized by state, contains the addresses of LPDR libraries. Under each library is a list of the nuclear facilities whose records are available there. An asterisk along side the listing indicates that the library has a microfiche file containing all NRC publicly available records issued since January 1981.

Alabama

* Athens Public Library, 405 E. South Street, Athens, AL 35611; (205) 232-1233.
Browns Ferry Nuclear Power Station; Browns Ferry Low-Level Rad Waste Facility.

* Houston-Love Memorial Library, 212 W. Burdeshaw Street, PO Box 1369, Dothan, AL 36302; (205) 793-9767.
Joseph M. Farley Nuclear Plant.

* Scottsboro Public Library, 1002 South Broad Street, Scottsboro, AL 35768; (205) 574-4335.
Bellefonte Nuclear Plant.

Arizona

* Phoenix Public Library, 12 East McDowell Road, Phoenix, AZ 85004; (602) 262-4636.
Palo Verde Nuclear Station.

Be patient. If any phone number is incorrect, call (area code) 555-1212 and request the new listing.

Nuclear Energy and Waste

Arkansas

* Tomlinson Library, Arkansas Tech University, Russellville, AR 72801; (501) 968-0366.
Arkansas Nuclear One.

California

* Humbolt County Library, 421 I Street, Eureka, CA 95501; (707) 445-7284.
Humbolt Bay Power Plant.

* University of California - Irvine, Main Library, PO box 19557, Irvine, CA 92713; (714) 856-7234.
San Onofre Nuclear Station.

* West Los Angeles Regional Library, 11360 Santa Monica Boulevard, Los Angeles, CA 90025; (213) 312-8323.
UCLA Training Reactor.

* Martin Luther King Regional Library, 7340 24th Street Bypass, Sacramento, CA 95822; (916) 421-3151.
Rancho Seco Nuclear Generating Station.

* California Polytechnic State University, Government Documents and Maps Dept, Robert E. Kennedy Library, San Luis Obispo, CA 93407; (805) 756-1364.
Diablo Canyon Power Plant.

Colorado

* Weld Library District, Lincoln Park Branch, 919 7th Street, Greely, CO 80631; (303) 350-9210.
Fort St. Vrain Nuclear Generating Station.

Connecticut

* Russell Library, 123 Broad Street, Middletown, CT 06457; (203) 347-2520.
Haddam Neck Plant.

* Learning Resources Center, Thames Valley State Technical College, 574 New London Turnpike, Norwich, CT 06360; (203) 886-0177.
Millstone Nuclear Power Station.

Florida

* Technical Services, Coastal Region Library, 8619 W. Crystal Street, Crystal River, FL 32629; (904) 795-3716.
Crystal River Nuclear Plant.

* Charles S. Miles Learning Resources Center, Indian River Community College, 3209 Virginia Avenue, Ft. Pierce, FL 34954-9003; (407) 468-4700.
St. Lucie Plant.

* Urban and Regional Documents Collection Library, Florida International University, University Park, Miami, FL 33199; (305) 348-3138.
Turkey Point Plant.

Georgia

* Appling County Public Library, 301 City Hall Drive, Baxley, GA 31513; (912) 367-8103.
Edwin I. Hatch Nuclear Plant.

* Burke County Library, 412 4th Street, Waynesboro, GA 30830; (404) 554-3277.
Alvin W. Vogtle Nuclear Plant.

Illinois

* Byron Public Library District, 109 N. Franklin, PO Box 434, Byron, IL 61010; (815) 234-5107.
Byron Station.

* Vespasian Warner Public Library, 120 West Johnson Street, Clinton, IL 61727; (217) 935-5174.
Clinton Power Station.

* Dixon Public Library, 221 Hennepin Avenue, Dixon, IL 61021; (815) 284-7621.
Quad Cities Station; Sheffield Low-Level Radioactive Waste Disposal Facility.

* Morris Area Public Library District, 604 Liberty Street, Morris, IL 60450; (815) 942-6880.
Dresden Nuclear Power Station; Morris Operations, General Electric.

* Jacobs Memorial Library, Illinois Valley Community College, Oglesby, IL 61348; (815) 224-2720. Lasalle County Station.

* Waukegan Public Library, 128 N. County Street, Waukegan, IL 60085; (708) 623-2041.
Zion Nuclear Power Station.

* West Chicago Public Library, 332 E. Washington Street, West Chicago, IL 60185; (708) 231-1552.
Kerr-Mcgee, West Chicago.

* Wilmington Public Library, 201 South Kankakee Street, Wilmington, IL 60481; (815) 476-2834.
Braidwood Station.

Iowa

* Cedar Rapids Public Library, 501 1st Street SE, Cedar Rapids, IA 52401; (319) 398-5123.
Duane Arnold Energy Center.

Kansas

* William Allen White Library, Emporia State University, 1200 Commercial Street, Emporia, KS 66801; (316) 343-1200 x5049.
Wolf Creek Generating Station.

* Washburn University School of Law, Topeka, KS 66621; (913) 231-1688.
Wolf Creek Generating Station.

Louisiana

* Troy H. Middleton Library, Government Documents Department, Louisiana State University, Baton Rouge, LA 70803; (504) 388-2570.
River Bend Station.

* Clairborne Parish Library, 901 Edgewood Drive, Homer, LA 71040; (318) 927-3845.
Clairborne Enrichment Center.

* Earl K. Long Library, University of New Orleans, Lakefront Drive, New Orleans, LA 70148; (504) 286-7275.
Waterford Generating Station.

Maine

* Wiscasset Public Library, High Street, PO Box 367, Wiscasset, ME 04578; (207) 882-7161.
Maine Yankee Atomic Power Plant.

Maryland

* Calvert County Public Library, 30 Duke Street, PO Box 405, Prince Frederick, MD 20678; (301) 535-0291.
Calvert Cliffs Nuclear Power Plant.

Massachusetts

* Greenfield Community College, Library Learning Resource Center, One College Drive, Greenfield, MA 01301; (413) 774-3131.
Yankee Rowe Nuclear Power Station.

* Plymouth Public Library, 132 South Street, Plymouth, MA 02360; (508) 830-4250.
Pilgrim Nuclear Station.

Michigan

* Hope College, Van Wylen Library, Holland, MI 49423; (616) 394-7790.
Palisades Nuclear Plant.

* Ellis Reference and Information Center, Monroe County Library System, 3700 S. Custer Road, Monroe, MI 48161; (313) 241-5277.
Enrico Fermi Atomic Power Plant.

* North Central Michigan College, 1515 Howard Street, Petoskey, MI 49770; (616) 348-6615.
Donald C. Cook Nuclear Power Plant.

* Maude Preston Palenske Memorial Library, 500 Market Street, St. Joseph, MI 49085; (616) 983-7167.
Donald C. Cook Nuclear Power Plant.

Minnesota

* Minneapolis Public Library, Technology and Science Department, 300 Nicollet Mall, Minneapolis, MN 55401; (612) 372-6642.
Monticello Nuclear Generating Plant; Prairie Island Nuclear Station.

Be patient. If any phone number is incorrect, call (area code) 555-1212 and request the new listing.

Energy

Mississippi
* Judge George W. Armstrong Library, S. Commerce at Washington Streets, Natchz, MS 39120; (601) 445-8862.
Grand Gulf Nuclear Station.

Missouri
* Callaway County Public Library, 710 Court Street, Fulton, MO 65251; (314) 642-7261.
Callaway Plant.

Nebraska
* Auburn Public Library, 1118 15th Street, PO Box 324, Auburn, NE 68305; (402) 274-4023.
Cooper Nuclear Station.

* W Dale Clark Library, Business, Science and Technology Department, 215 s. 15th Street, Omaha, NE 68102; (402) 444-4817.
Fort Calhoun Station.

Nevada
* James R. Dickinson Library, University of Nevada at Las Vegas, 4505 Maryland Parkway, Las Vegas, NV 89154; (702) 739-3252.
Nevada Nuclear Waste Storage Investigations.

* University of Nevada at Reno, University Library, Government Publications Department, Reno, NV 89557-0044; (702) 784-6579.
Nevada Nuclear Waste Storage Investigations.

New Hampshire
* Exeter Public Library, Founders Park, Exeter, NH 03833; (603) 772-3101.
Seabrook Nuclear Station.

New Jersey
* Pennsville Public Library, 190 S. Broadway, Pennsville, NJ 08070; (609) 678-5473.
Hope Creek Nuclear Station.

* Salem Free Public Library, 112 West Broadway, Salem, NJ 08079; (609) 935-0526.
Salem Nuclear Generating Station.

* Ocean County Public Library, 101 Washington Street, Toms River, NJ 08753; (908) 349-6200.
Oyster Creek Nuclear Power Plant.

New York
* Buffalo and Erie County Public Library, Science and Technology Department, Lafayette Square, Buffalo, NY 14203; (716) 858-7098.

* Penfield Library, Reference and Documents Department, State University of New York at Oswego, Oswego, NY 13126; (315) 341-3539.
James A. Fitzpatrick Nuclear Power Station; Nine Mile Point Nuclear Station.

* Rochester Public Library, Business, Economics and Law Division, 115 South Avenue, Rochester, NY 14604; (716) 428-7328.
Robert Emmet Ginna Nuclear Plant.

* Shoreham-Wading River Public Library, Route 25A, Shoreham, NY 11786; (516) 929-4488.
Shoreham Nuclear Power Station.

* White Plains Public Library, 100 Martine Avenue, White Plains, NY 10601; (914) 422-1477.
Indian Point Station.

North Carolina
* University of North Carolina at Charlotte, J. Murrey Atkins Library, UNCC Station, Charlotte, NC 28223; (704) 547-2243.
William B. Mcguire Nuclear Station.

* Cameron Village Regional Library, 1930 Clark Avenue, Raleigh, NC 27605; (919) 856-6710.
Shearon Harris Nuclear Power Plant.

* University of North Carolina at Wilmington, William Madison Randall Library, 601 S. College Road, Wilmington, NC 28403; (919) 395-3760 (reference desk), (919) 395-3277 (documents desk). Brunswick Steam Electric Plant.

Ohio
* Cuyahoga County Public Library, Garfield Heights Branch, 5409 Turney Road, Garfield Heights, OH 44125; (216) 475-8178.
Chemerton Corporation.

* Perry Public Library, 3753 Main Street, Perry OH 44081; (216) 259-3300.
Perry Nuclear Power Plant.

* University of Toledo, Government Documents Collection, William Carlson Library, 2801 West Bancroft Avenue, Toledo, OH 43606; (419) 537-2171.
Davis-Besse Nuclear Power Station.

Oklahoma
* Stanley Tubbs Memorial Library, 101 E. Cherokee, Sallisaw, OK 74955; (918) 775-4481.
Sequoyah Fuels.

Oregon
* Branford Price Millar Library, Portland State University, 934 SW Harrison, PO Box 1151, Portland, OR 97207; (503) 725-4735.
Trojan Nuclear Plant.

Pennsylvania
* BF Jones Memorial Library, 663 Franklin Avenue, Aliquippa, PA 15001; (412) 375-7174.
Beaver Valley Power Station.

* Apollo Memorial Library, 219 N. Pennsylvania Avenue, Apollo, PA 15613; (412) 478-4214.
B&W Apollo Site; B&W Parks Township Site.

* State Library of Pennsylvania, Law/Government Documents Section, Walnut Street and Commonwealth Avenue, Box 1601, Harrisburg, PA 17105; (717) 783-5973.
Three Mile Island Nuclear Station, Peach Bottom Atomic Power Station.

* Pottstown Public Library, 500 High Street, Pottstown, PA 19464; (215) 970-6551.
Limerick Generating Station.

* Saxton Community Library, 911 Church Street, Saxton, PA 16678; (814) 635-3533.
Saxton Nuclear Experimental Facility.

* Osterhout Free Library, 71 South Franklin Street, Wilkes-Barre, PA 18701; (717) 823-0156.
Susquehanna Steam Electric Station, Susquehanna Low-Level Radioactive Waste Facility.

Rhode Island
* Cross Mills Public Library, PO Box 1680, 4417 Post Road, Charlestown, RI 02813; (401) 364-6211.
United Nuclear Wood River Junction Site.

South Carolina
* Barnwell County Public Library, Hagood Avenue, Barnwell, SC 29812; (803) 259-3612.
Barnwell Reprocessing Plant, Barnwell Low-Level Radioactive Waste Disposal Facility.

* Hartsville Memorial Library, Nuclear Information Depository, 220 N. Fifth Street, Hartsville, SC 29550; (803) 332-5115.
H.B. Robinson Plant, Robinson Independent Spent Fuel Storage Installation.

* York County Library, 138 East Black Street, PO Box 10032, Rock Hill, SC 29731; (803) 324-3055.
Catawba Nuclear Station.

* Oconee County Library, 501 W. South Broad Street, Walhalla, SC 29691; (803) 638-4133.
Oconee Nuclear Station.

* Fairfield County Library, 300 Washington Street, Winnsboro, SC 29180; (803) 635-4971.
Virgil C. Summer Nuclear Station.

Be patient. If any phone number is incorrect, call (area code) 555-1212 and request the new listing.

Nuclear Energy and Waste

Tennessee

* Chattanooga-Hamilton County Library, Business, Science and Technology Department, 1001 Broad Street, Chattanooga, TN 37402; (615) 757-5114. Sequoyah Nuclear Plant, Watts Bar Nuclear Plant, Sequoyah Low-Level Radioactive Waste Facility.

Texas

* University of Texas at Arlington, Library-Government Publications/Maps, 701 South Cooper, PO Box 19497, Arlington, TX 76019; (817) 273-3391. Commanche Peak Steam Electric Station.

* J.M. Hodges Learning Center, Wharton County Junior College, 911 Boling Highway, Wharton, TX 77488; (409) 532-4560. South Texas Project.

Vermont

* Brooks Memorial Library, 224 Main Street, Brattleboro, VT 05301; (802) 254-5290. Vermont Yankee Nuclear Power Station.

Virginia

* University of Virginia, Alderman Library, Special Collections Department, Charlottesville, VA 22903-2498. (804) 924-3025. North Anna Power Station.

* Swem Library, College of William and Mary, Documents Department, Williamsburg, VA 23185; (804) 221-3064. Surry Power Station, Surry Independent Spent Fuel Storage Installation.

Washington

* W.H. Abel Memorial Library, 125 Main Street South, Montesano, WA 98563; (206) 249-4211. WPPSS Nuclear Project.

* Richland Public Library, 955 Northgate, Richland, WA 99352; (509) 943-7446. WPPSS Nuclear Project, Richland Low-Level Waste Disposal Facility.

Wisconsin

* University of Wisconsin, Cofrin Library, 2420 Nicolet Drive, Green Bay, WI 54311-7001; (414) 465-2547. Kewaunee Nuclear Power Plant.

* LaCrosse Public Library, 800 Main Street, LaCrosse, WI 54601; (608) 789-7122. Lacross Boiling Water Reactor.

* Joseph Mann Library, 1516 16th Street, Two Rivers, WI 54241; (414) 793-5585. Point Beach Nuclear Plant.

* Low-Level Nuclear Waste

Division of Low-Level Waste Management and Decommissioning
Office of Nuclear Material Safety and Safeguards
Nuclear Regulatory Commission (NRC)
Room 5E1
Washington, DC 20555 (301) 504-3342

This division directs the NCR's program for the licensing, inspection, and regulation to assure safety and quality associated with the management, treatment, and commercial disposal of low-level nuclear waste.

* Marketing Support for Nuclear Programs

Office of Marketing Technology Deployment and Strategic Planning
Uranium Enrichment, Nuclear Energy
U.S. Department of Energy
1000 Independence Ave., SW, Room A170
Washington, DC 20585 (301) 353-4610

This office is oversees marketing activities which support uranium enrichment programs. It is also responsible for the preliminary design and construction planning for a potential Atomic Vapor Laser Isotope Separation (AVLIS) production plant. More detailed information is available from the above office.

* Material Review and Licensing

Medical, Academic, and Commercial Use Safety Branch
Division of Industrial and Medical Nuclear Safety
Office of Nuclear Material Safety and Safeguards

Nuclear Regulatory Commission (NRC), Room 6 H24
Washington, DC 20555 (301) 504-3418

This Branch conducts health physics, radiation safety, and other appropriate analyses, licensing, and follow-up review of byproduct, medical, academic, industrial, and other source and special nuclear materials, including the preparation of environmental assessments and impact statements, determination of quality evaluations of sealed sources and devices, and licensing of exempt distribution of consumer products.

* NRC Docket Breakdown

Public Document Room
Nuclear Regulatory Commission (NRC)
2120 L Street, NW
Washington, DC 20555 (202) 634-3273

Each organization engaged in a nuclear activity licensed and regulated by NRC is assigned a docket (case) number. Documents exchanged between NRC and the license applicant or licensee are filed together under that number. The docket files are open to the public in the Public Documents Room.

* NRC Information Digest

Division of Budget and Analysis
Office of the Controller
Nuclear Regulatory Commission (NRC)
Washington, DC 20555 (301) 492-7988

The *Information Digest* is a great starting source about both the NRC and nuclear power in the U.S. The *Digest* discusses the role of the NRC as a regulatory agency as well as discussing the worldwide commercial nuclear energy sector. Nuclear material safety and waste disposal planning is also discussed. Appendices list a variety of statistics related to nuclear power. Call for your free copy.

* NRC News Releases and Speeches

Public Affairs Office
Nuclear Regulatory Commission (NRC)
Washington, DC 20555 (301) 504-2240

The NRC Public Affairs Office provides copies of NRC news releases and speeches in response to requests from news media. Members of the media may also be placed on a mailing list to receive copies of all NRC news releases and speeches. The Public Documents Room maintains a complete microform file of NRC and Atomic Energy Commission news releases and speeches. Contact the public affairs office for further information.

* Nuclear Regulatory Commission (NRC) Reports

Superintendent of Documents
Government Printing Office
Washington, DC 20402 (202) 783-3238

The NRC has several categories of reports available to the public, broken down by specific report code. General Reports, those not case specific, are prepared on a variety of areas related to nuclear power/regulation. Reference reports serve as sources for further information on NRC actions/proceedings. The following reports are available.

Annual Report (NUREG-1145)
Handbook of Acronyms and Initialisms (NUREG-0544)
NRC Organizational Charts (NUREG-0325)
Regulatory and Technical Reports (NUREG-0090)
Report to Congress on Abnormal Occurrences (NUREG-0386)
The List of Documents Made Publicly Available (NUREG-0540)

* NRC Rules and Regulations

Division of Information Support Services
Nuclear Regulatory Commission (NRC)
Washington, DC 20555 (301) 492-4534

The NRC issues a loose-leaf publication entitled *U.S. NRC Rules and Regulations*. This four volume set contains all Rules and Regulations, Policy Statements, Memoranda of Understanding, a listing of Regulatory Guides, and brief summaries of selected General Notices issued by the NRC and other agencies that are published in the *Federal Register*. This publication is also available on a subscription basis.

Be patient. If any phone number is incorrect, call (area code) 555-1212 and request the new listing.

Energy

* Nuclear Documents System

Division of Information Support Systems
Nuclear Regulatory Commission (NRC)
Washington, DC 20555 (301) 492-9863

The Nuclear Documents System (NUDOCS) information system stores bibliographic data for more than one million reports, correspondence and other issuances related to the NRC's regulatory, licensing, safety, research, and enforcement programs, including such items as NUREG reports, Regulatory Guides, NRC Regulations, Generic Letters, Inspection Reports, NRC Bulletins, Environmental Reports, and Licensee Events Reports. This service is accessible from anywhere in the United States. Contact the Information Support Systems division for information on access.

* Nuclear Materials Compliance Division

Office of Environment Safety and Health
U.S. Department of Energy
1000 Independence Ave., SW
Room 3G-089
Washington, DC 20585 (202) 586-7882

This division ensures that facilities managed by the operations in Chicago, Idaho, Richland, and the Savannah River Site as well as the special programs which report directly to DOE headquarters are operated in compliance with applicable environmental requirements. These facilities and programs are primarily responsible for nuclear materials production, energy research, and certain remedial actions.

* Nuclear Power Plant Performance

Nuclear Energy
Office of Nuclear Plant Performance
U.S. Department of Energy
19901 Germantown Rd.
Germantown, MD 20585 (301) 903-3773

This office performs economic analyses to compare the costs of various forms of electrical power generation to nuclear generation, as well as comparing the costs of different nuclear technologies. It also coordinates with the nuclear power industry in developing strategies to address the various impediments to the further development of the nuclear power option. The office maintains a current data base on status, performance, and related information on all U.S. nuclear power plants as well as monitoring critical nuclear plant events including emergency situations on a real time basis for the Department of Energy.

* Nuclear Power Publications

U.S. Council for Energy Awareness
1776 Eye St. NW
Suite 400
Washington, DC 20006-2495 (202) 293-0770

The Council on Energy Awareness can provide you with a number of publications and videos on nuclear energy. The following publications are available and cost up to $3.

Nuclear Energy: Benefits for All Americans
Safety in Motion: Transportation of Radioactive Materials
How Nuclear Energy Plants Work
Radiation in Perspective
Nuclear Energy Plant Safety
Low-Level Nuclear Waste: A Safe, Permanent Solution
High-Level Nuclear Waste: A Safe, Permanent Solution
Nuclear Energy: A Renewable Resource
Look Who's Talking: What People Think About Nuclear Energy
Nuclear Energy: Foundations of Excellence
Monitored Retrievable Storage: Questions and Answers
Advanced Design Nuclear Energy Plants: Competitive, Economical Electricity
The Map Book: Electricity from Nuclear Energy (1991-92 ed.)
A Citizens Guide to Monitored Retrievable Storage of Used Nuclear Power Plant Fuel
Journalists Guide to Nuclear Energy
Guide to Nuclear Energy Experts
Communicating with the Public about Radiation
Another Environmentalist for Nuclear Energy
Source Book on Soviet-designed Nuclear Power Plants [cost $200]
Nuclear Energy and the Environment
Good News for the Environment and Energy Independence
Decommissioning Nuclear Power Plants: Completing the Task

Transporting Low-Level Radioactive Waste: Questions and Answers

Contact the Council for information on price and availability. Members receive discounts on publications.

* Nuclear Regulatory Commission (NRC)

Office of Public Affairs
Nuclear Regulatory Commission
Washington, DC 20555 (301) 492-2240

This office serves as a public inquiry point for information on the following:

- Licensing (including decommissioning) of commercial nuclear power plants and other nuclear facilities and the possession and use of nuclear materials for medical, industrial, educational, and research purposes.
- Inspections and investigations designed to assure that licensed activities are conducted in compliance with the agency's regulations and other requirements and enforcement of compliance.
- Search in the areas of safety, safeguards, and environmental assessment and the establishment of regulations, standards, and guidelines governing the use of nuclear facilities and materials.
- Safeguarding nuclear facilities and materials from diversion or sabotage.
- Implementation of agency responsibilities under the Nuclear Waste Policy Act of 1982 (high-level radioactive wastes), the Low-Level Radioactive Waste Policy Act of 1980, and the Uranium Mill Tailings Radiation Control Act of 1978.
- Packaging of radioactive materials for transport.

* Nuclear Safety Policy

Office of Nuclear Safety Policy and Standards
Nuclear Safety Policy Division
U.S. Department of Energy
19901 Germantown Rd.
Germantown, MD 20585 (301) 903-3465

This division manages the development, review, issuance interpretation, and maintenance of the Department's nuclear safety policies. It interfaces with Federal and international agencies professional societies, and advisory committees on nuclear-safety related issues.

* Nuclear Waste Policy Act

Education and Information Division
Office of Civilian Radioactive Waste Management (OCRWM)
U.S. Department of Energy
1000 Independence Ave., SW, Room 5A-051
Washington, DC 20585 (202) 586-2835

This legislation established a national policy for safely storing, transporting, and disposing of spent nuclear fuel and high level radioactive waste. This act also established the Office of Civilian Radioactive Waste Management within the U.S. Department of Energy to develop and manage the waste management system. Under this act the U.S. may establish a permanent repository for nuclear waste at Yucca Mountain in Nevada. The act also provides for the construction of a Monitored Retrievable Storage Site (MRS) as a temporary storage place for spent fuel before being transported to permanent sites. The OCRWM can provide you with a background information package on the NWPA and other aspects of nuclear waste transport and storage.

* Open and Closed Meetings of the NRC

Office of the Secretary
Nuclear Regulatory Commission (NRC), 16H1
Washington, DC 20555 (301) 492-1969

The public is welcome to observe all Commission meetings, unless a meeting is closed because it involves one or more of the "exempted" subjects described in NRC Regulations. "Exempted" subjects usually involve classified information, investigations, enforcement actions, internal rules and practices, or personnel matters. Advance notices of Commission meetings are published in the *Federal Register*, posted in the Public Document Room, and mailed to those on a regular list. Contact the Office of the Secretary to be added to the list. Current information on scheduled Commission meetings may be obtained by calling the recorded message number: (301) 492-0292. Transcripts are made of Commission meetings. These are available in the Public Document Room for inspection or duplication.

Nuclear Energy and Waste

* **Operating Statistics on Nuclear Plants**
Licensed Operating Reactors
Superintendent of Documents
Government Printing Office
Washington, DC 20402 (202) 783-3238
Also referred to as the "Gray Book," *Monthly Operating Units Status Reports* provides data on the operation of nuclear units as timely and accurately as possible. It contains three sections: highlights and statistics for commercial operating units, detailed information on each unit, and an appendix for miscellaneous information such as spent fuel storage capabilities.

* **Operations Analysis**
Nuclear Operations Analysis Center (NOAC)
Nuclear Regulatory Commission (NRC)
P.O. Box Y
Oak Ridge National Laboratory
Oak Ridge, TN 37831 (615) 574-0393
The Nuclear Operations Analysis Center performs analysis tasks, as well as information-gathering activities, for the Nuclear Regulatory Commission. It conducts a number of tasks related to the analysis of nuclear power experience, including an annual operation summary for U.S. power reactors, generic case studies, plant operating assessments, and risk assessments. NOAC also publishes staff studies and bibliographies, disseminates monthly nuclear power plant operating event reports, and cooperates in the preparation of Nuclear Safety.

* **Peaceful Uses of Nuclear Technology**
Office of Nuclear Technology and Safeguards
Bureau of Oceans and International Environmental and Scientific Affairs
U.S. Department of State
2201 C St., NW, Room 7828
Washington, DC 20520 (202) 647-3310
Concerned with peaceful uses of nuclear power, such as nuclear energy, this office negotiates cooperative agreements with other countries for the safe functioning of nuclear reactors, and also becomes involved where nuclear reactor accidents occur.

* **Power Plant Emissions**
Radioactive Emissions Standards
Office of Radiation Programs
Environmental Protection Agency (EPA)
401 M St., SW, Room NE108
Washington DC 20460 (202) 233-9320
The EPA, with a number of other federal agencies, protects the public from unnecessary exposure to ionizing radiation. EPA's major responsibilities are to set radioactive emissions standards and exposure limits, assess new technology, and monitor radiation in the environment in four areas: radiation from nuclear accidents, radon emissions, land disposal of radioactive waste, and radiation in groundwater and drinking water. The EPA fulfills these responsibilities by setting emissions standards for nuclear power plants, and for radionuclides in drinking water and in the air. EPA also prescribes work practices to reduce emissions of radon from underground uranium mines, develops radioactive waste disposal standards, and issues guidance to limit occupational exposure.

* **Public Participation in Nuclear Licensing**
Atomic Safety and Licensing Board Panel
Nuclear Regulatory Commission (NRC)
Room 422, 4350 East-West Highway
Bethesda, MD 20814 (301) 492-7814
As part of the licensing process, a mandatory public hearing is carried out by a three-member Atomic Safety and Licensing Board, which then makes an initial decision as to whether a construction permit should be granted. A notice of a public hearing is published in the Federal Register and in local newspapers, giving 30 days for members of the public to petition to intervene in the proceeding.

* **Radiation in Vicinity of Reactors**
NRC TLD Direct Radiation Monitoring Network
Government Printing Office
Superintendent of Documents
Washington, DC 20402 (202) 783-3238

This quarterly publication provides the status and results of the NRC thermoluminescent dosimeter (TLD) direct radiation monitoring. It presents the radiation levels measured in the vicinity of NRC licensed facility sites throughout the country.

* **Radioactive Waste Management**
U.S. Department of Energy
Office of Civilian Radioactive Waste Management (OCRWM)
Office of External Relations and Policy
Information Services Division
1000 Independence Ave., SW, Mail Stop RW-43
Washington, DC 20585 (202) 586-2835
Radioactive Waste Management is a monthly publication that provides digests of current information available on the topics of spent fuel transport and storage, radioactive effluents from nuclear facilities, techniques of processing radioactive waste, remedial actions and environmental aspects of radioactive waste management. Those wishing to receive this publication should call (703) 487-4630 and request document number PB88-902900.

* **Radioactive Waste Management Bulletin**
U.S. Department of Energy
Office of Civilian Radioactive Waste Management (OCRWM)
Office of External Relations and Policy
Information Services Division
1000 Independence Ave., SW, Mail Stop RW-43
Washington, DC 20585 (202) 586-2835
The *OCRWM Bulletin,* a monthly publication, provides information about OCRWM program activities, milestones, events, publications, and documents to assist interested individuals in keeping abreast of the radioactive waste management program. In addition, the text of the *Bulletin* is available on *INFOLINK.*

* **Reactor Construction Surveillance**
Division Of License Performance and Quality Evaluation
Office of Nuclear Reactor Regulation
Nuclear Regulatory Commission (NRC)
Room 10H1
Washington, DC 20555 (301) 504-1004
This Division develops and implements a program for assuring quality and reliability of reactor license facilities design, fabrication, construction, testing, and operation.

* **Reactor Inventory in the U.S.**
Office of Scientific and Technical Information
Nuclear Energy
U.S. Department of Energy
1000 Independence Ave., SW, Room 5A-157
Washington, DC 20585 (202) 586-6684
Nuclear Reactors Built, Being Built or Planned is a survey of American nuclear reactors in operation, under construction or planned. Contact this office for a copy. This publication is handy reference for information on reactors currently in operation.

* **Reactor Programs**
Nuclear Energy
Office of Reactor Programs
U.S. Department of Energy
19901 Germantown Rd.
Germantown, MD 20585 (301) 903-3218
This office is responsible for the technical direction and management of the advanced liquid metal reactor division and the modular high temperature gas reactor (HTGR) R&D programs. Also included in the responsibilities of this office is the R&D initiative on waste management improvements through actinide recycle, coordination with the New Production Reactor for common HTGR development tasks, licensing interactions with industry and technology transfer.

* **Reactor Safeguards Advisory Committee**
Advisory Committee on Reactor Safeguards (ACRS)
Nuclear Regulatory Commission (NRC), Room 440
Washington, DC 20555 (301) 492-4516

Be patient. If any phone number is incorrect, call (area code) 555-1212 and request the new listing.

Energy

This statutory body of 15 scientists and engineers reviews and makes recommendations to the Commission on all applications to build or operate nuclear power reactors and on related nuclear safety matters. The ACRS provides advice to the Commission on potential hazards of proposed safety standards. The ACRS reviews requests for pre-application site and standard plant approvals, for each application for a construction permit or an operating license for power reactors, and for applications for licenses to construct or operate test reactors.

* Reactor Safety Research

Division of Systems Research
Office of Nuclear Regulatory Research
Nuclear Regulatory Commission (NRC), Room 369
Washington, DC 20555 (301) 492-3500

This Division plans, develops, and directs comprehensive safety research programs for predicting nuclear reactor and plant systems behavior under normal, accident, and severe accident conditions. Responsibilities include evaluating challenges to containments, development of accident source terms, performance and review of probable risk assessments, and accident sequence analysis. Contact this office for more information on the research.

* Reactors and National Security

Office of New Production Reactors
U.S. Department of Energy
1000 Independence Ave., SW, Room 7A-175
Washington, DC 20585 (202) 586-5750

To meet national security requirements, this office acquires and constructs new production reactors, along with developing a strategy to consider their safety, quality, environmental, and performance. Contact this office for further information.

* Reactor Training Center

NRC Technical Training Center
Nuclear Regulatory Commission (NRC)
Osborne Office Center
Chattanooga, TN 37411 (615) 855-6500

The NRC Technical Training Center (TTC) was established to develop and implement policy and programs for technical training of NCR staff. The TTC provides technical training in broad areas of reactor technology and specialized technical training.

* Regulation Dockets

Superintendent of Documents
Government Printing Office
Washington, DC 20402 (202) 783-3238

Title List of Documents Made Publicly Available contains descriptions of the information received and generated by the Nuclear Regulatory Commission. The information includes docketed material associated with civilian nuclear power plants and material received and generated by the Commission pertinent to its role as a regulatory agency. "Docketed" refers to the system by which the Commission maintains its regulatory records. A monthly subscription price is available for $108 per year.

* Regulation Hotline

(800) 368-223
(202) 479-0487 (in DC)

DOE's toll-free hotline announces upcoming technical meetings of DOE and the Nuclear Regulatory Commission (NRC). The public is invited to attend these meetings, and may call the 800 telephone number to determine the date, time and location of the meetings. A telephone recording service has also been established to announce upcoming meetings related to the waste management program of the NRC. The number is (800) 368-5642, ext. 20436. Washington, DC, area residents should call (301) 492-0436.

* Regulation Public Documents

Nuclear Regulatory Commission (NRC)
2120 L. Street, NW
Washington, DC 20037 (202) 634-3273

The Public Document Room maintains over 1.5 million agency documents in hard copy and microfiche. The majority of these documents relate to the licensing and inspection of nuclear facilities and to the use, transport and disposal of nuclear materials. There is generally about a two week processing delay before documents are available in the PDR. The PDR files are open for public use, and reference librarians assist on-site patrons in their use. The reference staff also respond to telephone and letter requests. The PDR on-line catalog contains citations to public documents received after October 1978, and the computer searches are free of charge. In addition, the Commission has approximately 100 local Public Document Rooms around the country. Call the office above for information on the locations.

* Regulatory and Technical Reports

Government Printing Office (GPO)
Superintendent of Documents
Washington, DC 20402 (202) 783-3238

Regulatory and Technical Reports is a quarterly compilation, cumulated annually with the fourth quarter, of regulatory and technical reports and conference proceedings issued by the NRC staff and contractors. Contact GPO for ordering information.

* Regulatory Bulletins

Division of Information Support Services
Nuclear Regulatory Commission (NRC)
Washington, DC 20555 (202) 634-3273

Generic Letters, Bulletins, and *Information Notices* are written NRC notifications sent to groups of licensees that identify specific problems, developments, or other matters of interest of which licensees should be aware or for which the NRC is calling for or recommending specific steps be taken by the licensees. These technical documents are placed in the Public Document Room, and can be automatically sent to interested groups or organizations who are on the mailing list.

* Regulatory Enforcement

Office of Enforcement, 7H1
Nuclear Regulatory Commission (NRC)
Washington, DC 20402 (301) 492-0741

This office develops policies and programs for enforcement of NRC requirements. It manages major enforcement actions and assesses the effectiveness and uniformity of enforcement actions taken by the regional offices. Enforcement powers include notices of violation, fines, and orders for license modification, suspension, or revocation.

* Regulatory Guides

Superintendent of Documents
Government Printing Office
Washington, DC 20402 (202) 783-3238

Nuclear Regulatory Commission (NRC) regulatory guides describe methods acceptable to the NRC staff of implementing specific parts of the Commission's regulations and, in some cases, describe techniques used by the staff in evaluating specific problems or postulated accidents. Guides also may advise applicants regarding information the NRC staff needs in reviewing applications for permits and licenses. Comments on the guides are encouraged. The following guides are currently issued. *Division 1: Power Reactor Guides; Division 2: Research and Test Reactor Guides; Division 3: Fuels and Materials Facilities Guides; Division 4: Environmental and Siting Guides; Division 5: Materials and Plant Protection Guides; Division 6: Product Guides; Division 7: Transportation Guides; Division 8: Occupational Health Guides; Division 9: Antitrust and Financial Review Guides; Division 10: General Guides.*

* Regulatory Library

Nuclear Regulatory Commission (NRC)
7920 Norfolk Avenue
Room 190
Bethesda, MD 20814 (301) 492-8501

The Nuclear Regulatory Commission's library is open to the public, and its focus is on nuclear energy. The library does not make loans or allow photocopying of documents, but the public is free to come in and use the facilities on site. It is open M-F from 8:00 to 4:00. Reference staff are available to assist you.

* Regulatory Publications

Superintendent of Documents
Government Printing Office

Be patient. If any phone number is incorrect, call (area code) 555-1212 and request the new listing.

Nuclear Energy and Waste

Washington, DC 20402 (202) 783-3238
Nuclear Regulatory Commission Issuances is a monthly publication containing opinions, decisions, denials, memorandum, and orders of the Commission, the Atomic Safety and Licensing Appeal Board, the Atomic Safety and Licensing Board, and the Administrative Law Judge. A subscription is available for $102 per year ($5.50 per copy). Semiannual and Quarterly indexes are also available.

* Regulatory Research

Office of Nuclear Regulatory Research
Nuclear Regulatory Commission (NRC)
Room 254
Washington, DC 20555 (301) 504-3700

The Nuclear Regulatory Commission (NRC) is mandated by law to conduct an extensive conformatory research program in the areas of safety, safeguards, and environmental assessment. In addition, the agency establishes regulations, standards, and guidelines governing the various licensed uses of nuclear facilities and materials.

* Repository for Nuclear Waste

Yucca Mountain Information Office
P.O. Box 69
Beatty, NV 89003 (702) 295-1312

The Nuclear Waste Policy Amendments Act of 1987 named Yucca Mountain, Nevada as the only candidate site to be characterized for a repository. Contact this DOE office for further information and for a copy of *DOE's Yucca Mountain Studies*, which explains basic nuclear waste disposal policy in layman's terms and also describes current research being done on the Yucca Mountain site.

* Safeguards

Division of Safeguards and Transportation
Office of Nuclear Safety and Safeguards
Nuclear Regulatory Commission (NRC)
Room 4E1
Washington, DC 20555 (301) 504-3365

This Division develops overall agency safeguards policy and conducts safeguards licensing, inspection, and regulatory functions applicable to nuclear materials, nonreactor facilities, transportation of nuclear materials, and nonreactor inspection activities.

* Safeguards Inspection

Division of Reactor Inspection and Safeguards
Office of Nuclear Reactor Regulation
Nuclear Regulatory Commission (NRC)
Room 9EI
Washington, DC 20555 (301) 504-2093

This Division performs special reactor inspection, vendor inspections, reactor safeguards licensing, and regulatory effectiveness reviews, and quality assurance reviews for reactors. This Division also performs inspections in response to allegations and reports of defective and substandard components and equipment in nuclear service or being offered for nuclear service.

* Safety Review for Nuclear Plants

Office of Nuclear Reactor Regulations
Nuclear Regulatory Commission (NRC)
Room 8EI
Washington, DC 20555 (301) 492-0884

An applicant for a nuclear plant construction permit lays out the proposed nuclear plant design in *Preliminary Safety Analysis Report* (PSAR). The NRC staff examines the applicant's PSAR to determine whether the plant design is safe and consistent with NRC rules and regulations; whether valid methods of calculation were employed and accurately performed; and whether the applicant has conducted its analysis and evaluation in sufficient depth and breadth to support staff approval as to assured adequate levels of safety.

* Savannah River Operations Office

Office of External Affairs
U.S. Department of Energy
PO Box A
Aiken, SC 29802 (803) 725-2889

As an element of the DOE nuclear weapons complex, the Savannah River Operations Office carries out the following activities: production of special nuclear materials, management of nuclear waste production of naval fuel materials, and the protection and management of environmental resources.

* Speakers, Nuclear Waste

Yucca Mountain Project Office
U.S. Department of Energy
P.O. Box 98518
Las Vegas, NV 89193-8518 (702) 794-7920

Members of the OCRWM program staff are available to speak to various groups interested in the radioactive waste management program. Qualified speakers can discuss the OCRWM program in general or address specific topics of special interest to a particular organization. To request a speaker from the Speakers' Bureau in the Nevada Project Office, contact the office above.

* Spent Fuel Options

U.S. Council on Energy Awareness
1776 Eye St., NW, Suite 400
Washington, DC 20006-02495 (202) 293-0770

The Council on Energy Awareness can provide you with information on the disposal of spent nuclear fuel as well as facts on other aspects of the nuclear power industry. The Energy Products Research Institute, or EPRI (415-855-2788), a utility operated research institute, may also be able to provide you with technical information concerning ongoing research in this area.

* Standards for Nuclear Safety

Division of Engineering
Office of Nuclear Regulatory Research
Nuclear Regulatory Commission (NRC)
Room 254
Washington, DC 20555 (301) 504-3800

This Division plans, develops, and directs comprehensive research programs and standards development for nuclear safety in the design, qualification, construction, inspection, testing, operation, and decommissioning of nuclear power plants. This office maintains liaison and provides technical input to other Federal agencies, the American National Standards Institute, professional societies, and international organizations.

* State Nuclear Programs

State, Local and Indian Tribe Programs
Office of Governmental and Public Affairs
Nuclear Regulatory Commission (NRC)
Room 3D21
Washington, DC 20555 (301) 492-0321

This office plans and directs NRC's program of cooperation and liaison with States, local governments, interstate and Indian Tribe organizations. They also develop and direct administrative and contractual programs for coordinating and integrating Federal and State regulatory activities.

* Supply and Demand: Nuclear and Alternative Fuel

Nuclear and Alternate Fuels Division
Coal, Nuclear, Electric and Alternate Fuels
Energy Information Administration
U.S. Department of Energy
1707 H St. NW
Washington, DC 20585 (202) 254-5570

The office prepares, analyzes, and projects the availability, production, cost, processing, transportation, and distribution of nuclear and alternate energy sources, including solar, wind, and wood. Contact this office for more information and publications.

* Three Mile Island

Three Mile Island Program
Nuclear Energy
U.S. Department of Energy (DOE)
1000 Independence Ave., SW, Room E461
Washington, DC 20585 (301) 903-3456

This office manages DOE's Three Mile Island Research and Development Programs. Contact the office for further information.

Be patient. If any phone number is incorrect, call (area code) 555-1212 and request the new listing.

Energy

* TVA Nuclear Power Plants

Nuclear Power
Tennessee Valley Authority (TVA)
1101 Market St.
Chattanooga, TN 37402-2801 (615) 751-8689

TVA has two licensed nuclear plants with a total of five reactors in operation. Two additional plants, with a total of four reactors, are under construction. The division's responsibilities include demonstrating safe and reliable performance, making sure that operating plants to meet or exceed industry standards of excellence, increasing productivity and reliability of nuclear units to meet or exceed the industry average, and maintaining a competitive human resources program.

* Uranium Enrichment

Nuclear Energy
Office of Uranium Enrichment
U.S. Department of Energy
19901 Germantown Rd.
Germantown, MD 20585 (301) 903-4321

This office ensures that requirements for uranium enrichment services meet domestic, foreign and U.S. government needs in the most economical, reliable, safe, secure and environmentally acceptable manner.

* Uranium Mine Clean Up

Uranium Mill Tailings Remedial Action Project Office
Albuquerque Operations Office
U.S. Department of Energy
P.O. Box 5400
Albuquerque, NM 87115 (505) 353-2585

This office performs clean-up activities at 24 inactive uranium mill tailings sites and associated vicinity properties in 11 States and the Navajo Indian Reservation. After clean-up is completed, the sites will be owned by DOE and licensed by the Nuclear Regulatory Commission. You can get further information on U.S. Dept. of Energy nuclear waste management programs from the above office.

* Uranium Mining and the Environment

Grand Junction Projects Office (GJPO)
Idaho Operations Office
U.S. Department of Energy
P.O. Box 2567
Grand Junction, CO 81502 (303) 242-8621

This office assesses the environmental effects of uranium mining and milling operations, and manages uranium leases on lands under DOE control. This office also provides geoscientific support in characterizing sites under consideration as repositories under DOE's Civilian Radioactive Waste Management Program. It also participates in international technical exchanges under several programs administered by the Organization for Economic Cooperation and Development's Nuclear Energy Agency and the International Atomic Energy Agency. Contact this office for further information on DOE nuclear waste management programs.

* Waste Advisory Committee

Advisory Committee on Nuclear Waste
Nuclear Regulatory Commission (NRC), Room 2G1
Washington, DC 20555 (301) 492-4516

The Advisory Committee on Nuclear Waste is an independent committee established by the Commission to provide it with advice and recommendations concerning all aspects of nuclear waste management for which the NRC has responsibility. Its primary focus is on waste disposal, but its work also includes other aspects of waste management, such as the handling, processing, transportation, storage, and safeguarding of nuclear wastes, including spent fuel, nuclear wastes mixed with other hazardous substances, and uranium mill tailings.

* Waste Background Information

U.S. Department of Energy
Office of Civilian Radioactive Waste Management (OCRWM)
Office of External Relations and Policy
Information Services Division
Mail Stop RW-5.1
1000 Independence Ave., SW
Washington, DC 20585 (202) 586-5722

The *OCRWM Backgrounders* provide current background information on program facts, issues and initiatives. *Backgrounders* are published periodically by the Office of External Relations and Policy and are distributed to individuals and organizations on the *OCRWM Bulletin* mailing list and by individual requests.

* Waste Clean Up

Office of Remedial Action and Waste Technology
Nuclear Energy
1000 Independence Ave., SW, Room E435
Washington, DC 20585 (301) 903-5006

This office provides plans, develops, and executes DOE programs for civilian nuclear waste treatment and low-level waste management. It also works to clean up and decommission both contaminated DOE and legislatively-authorized non-Government facilities and sites. Beneficial uses of nuclear waste byproducts are also studied. Further information on U.S. Department of Energy nuclear waste management programs can be obtained from the above office.

* Waste Management

Information Services Division
Office of Civilian Radioactive Waste Management (OCRWM)
U.S. Department of Energy
1000 Independence Ave., SW, Room 5A-051 (800) 225-NWPA
Washington, DC 20585 (202) 488-5513

The *Publications Catalog, Office of Civilian Radioactive Waste Management*, is a detailed summary of office reports and studies on nuclear waste management. This catalog provides citations of selected technical and public information on nuclear waste management. The free brochure, *Managing the Nation's Nuclear Waste*, is also available from this office.

* Waste Management Factsheets

U.S. Department of Energy
Office of Civilian Radioactive Waste Management (OCRWM)
Office of External Relations and Policy
Information Services Division
Mail Stop RW-5.1
1000 Independence Ave., SW
Washington, DC 20585 (202) 586-5722

OCRWM has published factsheets that describe the overall OCRWM program, the repository program, the monitored retrievable storage (MRS) system and the transportation program. Call or write for a package.

* Waste Management Publications

U.S. Department of Energy
Office of Civilian Radioactive Waste Management (OCRWM)
Office of External Relations and Policy
Information Services Division
Mail Stop RW-5.1
1000 Independence Ave., SW
Washington, DC 20585 (202) 586-5722

The OCRWM publications catalog contains abstracts of printed documents on the topic of high-level radioactive waste management that are of interest to Federal, State and local government officials and staff; affected Indian Tribes; advisory groups; special interest groups; the media; information science professionals; and students and the general public. The catalog features citation listings alphabetically by titles, an index by keywords and an index by corporate authors. In addition to a printed catalog, the information is available online through the *OCRWM Product Record System*.

Be patient. If any phone number is incorrect, call (area code) 555-1212 and request the new listing.

Weather and Maps Climate and Forecasts

* *See also Science and Technology; Geology and Earth Science*
* *See also Current Events and Homework*

The National Weather Service is a well-known federal institution but the general public probably is unaware of the Landslide Information Center and other government offices which track and analyze climate changes. General information and technical materials on other "Acts of God" such as volcano eruptions and earthquakes are identified in the Science and Technology Chapter. Many agencies are using the most sophisticated methods for cartography from the National Archives to the National Air and Space Administration. By and large the primary distributor of all sorts of maps is the U.S. Geological Survey.

* Acid Rain, Aerosols, and Climate Impact

Environmental Research Laboratory
National Oceanic and Atmospheric Administration
U.S. Department of Commerce
8060 13th St.
Silver Spring, MD 20910 (301) 427-7684

The Air Resources Laboratory (ARL) performs weather research to understand and predict human influences on the environment, especially those involving atmospheric transport and dispersion of pollutants such as acid rain and ozone. The ARL also monitors and interprets trends in natural and man-made substances, such as $CO_2$5, halocarbons, aerosols, and ozone which can potentially modify the climate. In addition, ARL studies solar radiation for its role in climate change. An annual report is available, which describes in more detail the current research being undertaken at ARL.

* Aeronomy Research

Earth's Atmosphere Research
Environmental Research Laboratories
National Oceanic and Atmospheric Administration
U.S. Department of Commerce
325 Broadway
Boulder, CO 80303 (303) 497-6286

The Aeronomy Laboratory studies the physical and chemical processes of the Earth's atmosphere to advance our capability for monitoring, predicting, and controlling these processes. Recent emphasis is on the greenhouse effect, stratospheric and tropospheric ozone.

* Air Quality and Atmospheric Research

Environmental Sciences Group
Environmental Research Laboratories
National Oceanic and Atmospheric Administration
U.S. Department of Commerce
325 Broadway
Boulder, CO 80303 (303) 497-6286

The Environmental Sciences Group includes the Climate Research Program (studies of short- and long-term climate change), the Weather Research Program (research to improve short-range weather predictions and warning, especially regarding storm systems and flash floods), the Weather Modification Program (evaluations of data from various states' weather modification programs), and the Program for Regional Observing and Forecasting Services (transfer of technology such as interactive computer workstations to operational agencies like the National Weather Service). Contact the Public Affairs Office for information.

* Atmospheric Sciences Central Library

Central Library
National Oceanic and Atmospheric Administration
U.S. Department of Commerce
6009 Executive Blvd.
Rockville, MD 20852 (301) 443-8330

The library maintains a collection of books, journals, technical reports, microfiche, and compact discs to support research in the atmospheric sciences, oceanography, geophysics, and related disciplines. The library uses a wide array of products and services to meet its clientele's needs. Computers provide for information retrieval and bibliographic control of materials. Online services include access to hundreds of databases, which are available through systems such as Dialog, BRS, NEXIS, and LEXIS. The library's facilities and collection are available for the general public to use on-site during normal business hours.

* Beaches and Resort Weather Forecasts

Location	Phone
Cape Cod, MA	(617) 771-0500
Key West, FL	(305) 296-2011
Miami, FL	(305) 661-5065
Myrtle Beach, SC	(803) 744-3207
Nags Head, NC	(919) 995-5610
Ocean City, MD	(301) 289-3223
Orlando, FL	(305) 851-7510
Rehoboth, DE	(302) 856-7633
St Augustine/Daytona, FL	(904) 252-5575
St Petersburg/Tampa, FL	(813) 645-2506
Virginia Beach, VA	(804) 853-3013

* Climate Change

Global Change Division
Environmental Protection Agency (EPA)
401 M St., SW
Washington, DC 20460 (202) 260-8825

This office can provide you with information regarding the effects of global climate change on the U.S. A report to Congress and various articles on the greenhouse effect are available, as well as information on EPA's Sea Level Rise project and the relationship between the changing climate and the coast.

* Climatic Information

National Climatic Data Center (NCDC)
National Environmental Satellite, Data and Information Service
U.S. Department of Commerce
Federal Building
Asheville, NC 28801 (704) 259-0682

The National Climatic Data Center compiles and distributes global historical climate information. It is the collection center for all United States weather records and the world's largest climate data center. Many millions of weather facts are stored in NCDC's computer banks, available for quick response. Nearly one-third of the inquiries received are from attorneys seeking to establish circumstances surrounding legal events. Simple questions can be answered on the phone; however, those requests which need detailed digging may carry a research charge. Much data is available free or by fee in printed form.

* Cumulative Climatic Data Summaries

National Climatic Data Center
National Environmental Satellite, Data and Information Service

Be patient. If any phone number is incorrect, call (area code) 555-1212 and request the new listing.

Weather and Maps

National Oceanic and Atmospheric Administration
U.S. Department of Commerce
Federal Building
Asheville, NC 28801 (704) 259-0682

Local Climatological Data is a monthly and annual publication for each of approximately 290 National Weather Service stations. Each issue includes daily and monthly temperatures, dew point temperatures, heating and cooling degree days, weather, precipitation, snowfall, pressure, wind, sunshine, and sky cover. Three-hourly weather observations and hourly precipitation data are also presented for most stations. *Climatological Data* is a monthly and annual publication issued for each state containing much the same information. Contact this office for current prices.

* Cyclones and Other Oceanographic Forecasts

National Oceanographic Data Center
National Oceanic and Atmospheric Administration
Universal Building Room 412
Washington, DC 20235 (202) 673-5549

The Mariners Weather Log is a unique source of information on marine weather and climate and their effects on operations at sea. Published quarterly by the National Oceanographic Data Center, the *Mariners Weather Log* provides comprehensive coverage of major storms of the North Atlantic and North Pacific, reports and annual summaries on tropical cyclones, information on the National Weather Service's Marine Observation Program, selected shipboard gale and wave observations, and general articles about weather and climate, hazards and safety precautions, and related marine lore. An annual subscription is available for $6 from the Superintendent of Documents, Government Printing Office, Washington, DC 20402; (202)783-3238.

* Environmental Satellite Systems

National Environmental Satellite,
Data And Information Service (NESDIS)
National Oceanic and Atmospheric Administration
U.S. Department of Commerce
Federal Office Bldg. 4
Washington, DC 20233 (202) 763-4690

The National Environmental Satellite, Data and Information Service manages the nation's civil earth observing satellite systems for meteorology and oceanography. NESDIS operates low-altitude polar-orbiting satellites and high-altitude geostationary satellites which together monitor weather and surface conditions over the entire globe each day, providing advance warning of hurricanes, flash floods, and other severe weather conditions. Its satellites play an increasingly important role in monitoring global climate changes and such related phenomena as changes in ozone distribution over the Earth, plus changes in the marine environment. Contact this office for more information regarding satellite and data topics.

* Environmental Research Publications

Environmental Research Laboratories
National Oceanic and Atmospheric Administration (NOAA)
U.S. Department of Commerce
325 Broadway
Boulder, CO 80303 (303) 497-6286

As the research arm of NOAA, the Environmental Research Laboratories support the present responsibilities and the development of future services of NOAA. Programs include investigation of ocean processes and their interactions with the atmosphere; studies of the ocean environment as it is affected by waste disposal and development of energy and food resources; atmosphere and ocean research on weather and climate change; and much, much more. *Environmental Research Laboratories Publication Abstracts* lists all scientific and technical papers and reports available in a given year, as well as ordering information. The *Abstracts* are arranged alphabetically by Laboratory, and an author index is included.

* Federal Emergency Management

Federal Emergency Management Agency (FEMA)
P.O. Box 70274
Washington DC 20024 (202) 646-3484

The Motion Picture Catalog (FEMA-2) contains a current list of motion pictures of the Federal Emergency Management Agency. These films are in 16mm color or black and white. Topics covered include tornadoes, earthquakes, hurricanes, and public safety. Contact FEMA for your free catalog.

* Floods

S. James
Consumer Information Center 2A
P.O. Box 100
Pueblo, CO 81002

In The Event of a Flood explains what to do in a flood, and how to minimize loss of life and property (590Y, $1).

* Floods: Audiovisuals

Public Affairs, National Weather Service
U.S. Department of Commerce
8060 13th. St., Room 1326
Silver Spring, MD 29010 (301) 427-8090

The National Weather Service has films, videotapes, slide programs, and informational pamphlets dealing with floods. Contact the Public Affairs Office for more information.

* Greenhouse Effect, Ozone and Related Research

Environmental Research Laboratories
National Oceanic and Atmospheric Administration
U.S. Department of Commerce
325 Broadway
Boulder, CO 80303 (303) 497-6286

The Environmental Research Laboratories conducts an integrated program of fundamental research, related technology development, and services to improve understanding and prediction of the geophysical environment comprising the oceans and inland waters, the lower and upper atmosphere, the space environment, and the Earth. Activities at its laboratories address such major areas as stratospheric and tropospheric ozone, the greenhouse effect and atmospheric chemistry, acid rain sources, transport and deposition, ocean role in climate, meteorological phenomena, solar disturbances, and computer modeling of oceanic conditions. Contact this office for more information about the Laboratories.

* Hurricanes and Tropical Weather Research

Environmental Research Laboratories
Atlantic Oceanographic and Meteorological Laboratory (AOML)
National Oceanic and Atmospheric Administration
U.S. Department of Commerce
34301 Rickenbacher Causeway
Miami, FL 33149 (305) 361-4300

The Atlantic Oceanographic and Meteorological Laboratory performs tropical weather research to improve the description, understanding, and prediction of hurricanes, and to explore methods for modifying them. AOML's oceanographic studies focus on exchanges of energy and matter through the air-sea interface, and hydrothermal processes of mineralization at seafloor spreading centers. An annual report is available which describes the research conducted at AOML, including a listing of the technical reports published by AOML researchers.

* Mariners Weather Log

National Oceanographic Data Center
National Oceanic and Atmospheric Administration
Universal Building Room 412
Washington, DC 20235 (202) 673-5549

The Mariners Weather Log is a unique source of information on marine weather and climate and their effects on operations at sea. Published quarterly by the National Oceanographic Data Center, the *Mariners Weather Log* provides comprehensive coverage of major storms of the North Atlantic and North Pacific, reports and annual summaries on tropical cyclones, information on the National Weather Service's Marine Observation Program, selected shipboard gale and wave observations, and general articles about weather and climate, hazards and safety precautions, and related marine lore. An annual subscription is available for $6 from the Superintendent of Documents, Government Printing Office, Washington, DC 20402; (202)783-3238.

* Meteorological National Center

National Meteorological Center
National Weather Service
National Oceanic and Atmospheric Administration
U.S. Department of Commerce
5400 Auth Rd., Room 101,

Be patient. If any phone number is incorrect, call (area code) 555-1212 and request the new listing.

Climate and Forecasts

Camp Springs, MD 20033 (301) 763-8016

At the National Meteorological Center (NMC) in Maryland, more than 100,000 weather observations are incorporated daily into models of the atmosphere to produce weather forecasts from 48 hours to as far as 10 days ahead. Monthly and seasonal predictions of temperature and precipitation over North America also are produced. NMC guidance goes to National Weather Service facilities in every part of the nation where it helps meteorologists and hydrologists prepare local warnings and forecasts.

* Meteorologists Society

American Meteorological Society (AMS)
45 Beacon St.
Boston, MA 02108 (617) 227-2425

The American Meteorological Society certifies consulting meteorologists and grants a Seal of Approval to television and radio meteorologists. Publications: *Journal of Climate and Applied Meteorology, Journal of Atmospheric Sciences, Journal of Physical Oceanography, Meteorological and Geoastrophysical.*

* Meteorology and Climate Analysis

ASRL-Meteorology
Environmental Protection Agency
Research Triangle Park, NC 27711

This library's major field of interest is the meteorological aspects of air pollution, including model development and application, climatic analysis, and geophysical studies. The library holds a collection of climatic data material consisting of approximately 4,000 climatic data material reports on microfiche, over 400 rolls of film of synoptic data, surface and vorticity charts, and a large body of topographic maps.

* National Environmental Data Clearinghouse

NEDRES Office
National Oceanic And Atmospheric Administration
U.S. Department of Commerce
1825 Connecticut Ave., NW, Room 412
Washington, DC 20235 (202) 673-5548

The National Environmental Data Referral Service (NEDRES) is designed to provide convenient, economical, and efficient access to widely scattered environmental data. NEDRES is a publicly available service which identifies the existence, location, characteristics, and availability conditions of environmental data sets. NEDRES database contains only descriptions, not the actual data. It is a national network of federal, state, and private organizations cooperating to improve access to environmental data. Major subject categories include climatology and meteorology, oceanography, geophysics and geology, geography, hydrology and limnology, terrestrial resources, toxic and regulated substances, and satellite remotely sensed data. NEDRES also produces the following printed catalogs with references to available environmental data on selected topics and regions:

Finding the Environmental Data You Need (free)
NEDRES Memorandum of Agreement (free)
NEDRES Database User Agreement (free)
NEDRES Data Base User Guide ($7.50)
Guideline for the Description of Environmental Data Files for the Nedres Database ($10)
North American Climatic Data Catalog: Part 1 ($10)
North American Climatic Data Catalog: Part 2 ($10)
Satellite Remote Sensing of the Marine Environment: Literature and Data Sources ($10)
Coastal and Estuarine Waters of California, Oregon, and Washington ($10)
Chesapeake Bay and Adjacent Wetlands
Chesapeake Bay Environmental Data Directory (free to federal and state agencies)
Environmental Data Review (free)

For more information on the NEDRES database and the user charges, contact the office listed above.

* Ocean and Weather Films

Modern Talking Picture Service
5000 Park Street North
St. Petersburg, FL 33709 (800) 243-MTPS

The National Oceanic and Atmospheric Administration (NOAA) has produced several films on weather, oceans, and ocean life, which are available for free loan through the Modern Talking Picture Service. These films are most often requested by teachers from elementary schools through universities, as well as members of the general public who are interested in learning about the weather. Some requests have even come from video and commercial film production companies who need shots of lightning and thunder or flash floods for their videos. The titles include:

Down to the Monitor
Estuary
*FAMOUS- Boundary of Creation**
Flood
*Give Me The Tides**
Global Weather Experiment
Hurricane
*Longlines: An Undersea Investigation**
NOAA Corps- The Seventh Service
Sentinels In Space
Sockeye Odyssey
Terrible Tuesday (Tornado Safety)
The Awesome Fish Story
The Great American Fish Story
The Great American Fish Story- The West
The Great American Fish Story- The Northeast
The Great American Fish Story- The South
The Great American Fish Story- The Lakes and Rivers
Trashing the Oceans

For a free descriptive brochure contact: NOAA Public Affairs, U.S. Department of Commerce, Room 6913, Washington DC 20230; (202) 377-8090. Films followed by an asterisk are available directly from NOAA.

* Oceanographic Data and Publications

National Oceanic and Atmospheric Administration
U.S. Department of Commerce
1825 Connecticut Ave., NW
Washington, DC 20235 (202) 673-5549

The National Oceanographic Data Center has a free publications list which includes technical reports and bulletins, as well has a variety of data reports pertaining to oceanographic research.

* Oceanographic Information

National Oceanographic Data Center (NODC)
National Environmental Satellite, Data
and Information Service
National Oceanic and Atmospheric Administration
U.S. Department of Commerce
1825 Connecticut Ave., NW
Washington, DC 20235 (202) 673-5549

The National Oceanographic Data Center provides global coverage of oceanographic data and services. NODC's databases cover physical and chemical properties of the world's oceans, seas, and estuaries, plus information on selected continental shelf and coastal waters. Researchers using NODC data range from industrial scientists through local, state, and national government investigators, to university or academic personnel. Information is available in various forms: publications computer plots, computer printouts, magnetic tapes and floppy disks. Simple questions usually can be answered without charge by telephone or mail, but more complicated ones requiring research or computer processing usually carry a fee.

* Permafrost, Ice Age and Other Publications

Book and Report Sales
Box 25425
Denver, CO 80225 (303) 236-7476

This is a listing of some of the general interest publications available through the U.S. Geological Survey. They are free unless otherwise indicated.

The Great Ice Age
The Interior of the Earth
Landforms of the United States
Marine Geology: Research Beneath the Sea
Our Changing Continent
Permafrost
Geysers
Glaciers: A Water Resource

Weather and Maps

* Satellites and Other Instruments for Atmosphere, Geodesy, Navigational Study

Office of Legislative Affairs
National Oceanic and Atmospheric Administration
U.S. Department of Commerce
14th St. and Constitution Ave., NW, Room 6228 (800) 648-6209
Washington, DC 20230 (202) 842-7460 (DC area)

The National Oceanic and Atmospheric Administration (NOAA) has a free *Product Information Catalog* (PIC) which lists over 600 products related to the atmosphere, oceans, navigation, fisheries, mammals, geodesy, satellites, and other environmental concerns. These products span the range from simple pamphlets to technical reports. Each listing includes price and ordering information. NOAA has designed a system, the NOAA Information Service (NIS) to provide high-speed, automated retrieval of the PIC via an electronic database management system. A NOAA Information Specialist will answer inquiries about NOAA products and services and make in-house referrals to technical representatives. Call (206) 526-9403 in Washington State.

* Satellite Data

National Climate Center
National Environmental Satellite, Data, and Information Service
National Oceanic and Atmospheric Administration (NOAA)
U.S. Department of Commerce
World Weather Building, Room 100
Washington, DC 20233 (301) 763-8111

The Satellite Data Services Division (SDSD) of the National Climatic Data Center manages a database of environmental satellite data and information and provides products from this database to requesters. A unique source of data and information, the environmental database contains film imagery and digital data collected by a number of environmental satellites from 1960 to the present. It includes data from NOAA's operational environmental satellites and selected data from NASA and the U.S. Department of Defense. While much of the data is nominally meteorological, its oceanographic applications have been very extensive, and the data and information has been of interest to agronomists, hydrologists, and geologists. Contact the office listed above for more information on the data and services available.

* Space Environment Research

Space Environment Laboratory
Environmental Research Laboratories
National Oceanic and Atmospheric Administration
U.S. Department of Commerce
325 Broadway
Boulder, CO 80303 (303) 497-3313

The Space Environment Laboratory provides real-time space environment monitoring and forecasting services, develops techniques for improving forecasts of solar disturbances and their effect on the near-Earth space environment, and conducts research in solar-terrestrial physics. An annual report is available which goes into more detail about the Laboratory, the research conducted, and lists the technical reports published.

* Severe Storms Forecast Center

National Severe Storms Forecast Center (NSSFC)
National Weather Service
National Oceanic and Atmospheric Administration
U.S. Department of Commerce
601 E. 12th St.
Kansas City, MO 64106 (816) 426-5922

The National Severe Storms Forecast Center is the office responsible for forecasting tornadoes and severe thunderstorms throughout the contiguous United States. In addition to this, NSSFC prepares aviation forecasts and advisories to aircraft in-flight, weather analyses based on interpretation of satellite data, and national weather summaries. The national weather summaries are issued twice daily and are distributed nationally for use by radio, television, newspapers, and other media interests. They are written in narrative form and contain information on significant weather that has occurred in the Nation. An extensive list of technical reports is available from NSSFC, most of which deal with tornado and severe thunderstorm forecasting.

* Solar Energy and Wind Information

National Climatic Data Center
National Oceanic and Atmospheric Administration

U.S. Department of Commerce
Federal Building
Asheville, NC 28801 (704) 259-0682

The National Climatic Data Center has a great deal of information regarding solar energy and wind data. Information includes solar radiation averages, measurements, and sunshine averages, as well as wind statistics. Reference manuals and indexes are also available. Prices vary depending upon the information requested. The Center can provide you with more detailed information regarding the data available.

* Storms and Natural Disaster Detection

National Ocean Service
National Oceanic and Atmospheric Administration
U.S. Department of Commerce
6001 Executive Blvd.
Rockville, MD 20852 (301) 443-8487

The Office of Oceanography and Marine Assessments surveys and monitors the oceans, U.S. coastal waters, estuarine waterways, and the Great Lakes to produce data and information products that describe the physical properties of these waters for a wide range of engineering and navigational applications. This office also conducts studies to assess the environmental impact of human activities in U.S. coastal waters. Many of these marine data and information products are essential for protecting life and property from storms and other destructive natural forces. Other marine products, such as predictions of the times and heights of tides and descriptions of tidal currents, are vital for safe navigation.

* Stratospheric Ozone

Global Change Division
Environmental Protection Agency
401 M St., SW, W739
Washington, DC 20460 (202) 260-7497

This Office can provide you with all the information you need to know regarding the Ozone, including information on ozone-depleting chemicals and ideas for reducing these chemicals. Publications include a *Handbook for Reducing and Eliminating Chlorofluorocarbons In Flexible Polyurethane Foams* and the *Executive Summary of the Ozone Trends Panel.*

* Tornados, Hurricanes and Floods- Free Weather Films

National Weather Service
National Oceanic and Atmospheric Administration
8060 13th St., Room 1326
Silver Spring, MD 20910 (301) 713-0622

The National Weather service has several films, videos, and slides available for free loan on such topics as tornados, floods, hurricanes, and winter storms. These films are often used to teach civil defense personnel and storm spotters, and are suitable from grade four through college students. Contact this office for more information and for your free brochure.

* Undersea Research

National Undersea Research Program (NURP)
National Oceanic and Atmospheric Administration (NOAA)
U.S. Department of Commerce
6010 Executive Blvd.
Rockville, MD 20852 (301) 443-8391

The National Undersea Research Program develops programs and provides support to scientists and engineers for the study of biological, chemical, geological, and physical processes in the world's oceans and lakes. NURP assist researchers in conducting what are considered by NOAA and the marine community to be crucial research programs. In order to execute these programs, NURP provides investigators with a suite of the modern undersea facilities including submersibles, habitats, air and mixed gas SCUBA, and remotely operated vehicles. A major part of the research program is carried out by a network of National Undersea Research Centers. Contact this office for more information on the research conducted or the research centers.

* Weather Data Archive and Analyses

Selective Guide to Climatic Data Sources
National Climatic Data Center
National Oceanic and Atmospheric Administration
U.S. Department of Commerce
Federal Building

Be patient. If any phone number is incorrect, call (area code) 555-1212 and request the new listing.

Climate and Forecasts

Asheville, NC 28801 (704) 259-0682

The *Selective Guide to Climatic Data Sources* is designed to assist potential users of climatological information by acquainting them with the various forms in which these data are archived and the products or publications that are prepared from these data. Each listing contains the file name, format, contents, and an abstract. The Data Center also has the ability to prepare other statistical tabulations, climatological analyses, and special studies other than those listed in the *Guide*. Further information on the cost for preparing such specialized products, or the cost for items listed in the *Guide*, may be obtained from the Data Center. A meteorologist is available to assist you in locating appropriate data or answering your questions.

* Weather Films and Publications

National Weather Service
National Oceanic and Atmospheric Administration
U.S. Department of Commerce
8060 13th St., Room 1326
Silver Spring, MD 20910 (301) 427-8090

A list of films, videotapes, and slides, as well as brochures is available from the National Weather Service. These publications deal with tornados, thunderstorms, floods, and hurricanes. Contact this office for your free list.

* Weather Forecasts

National Weather Service
National Oceanic and Atmospheric Administration
U.S. Department of Commerce
8060 13th St., Room 1326
Silver Spring, MD 20910 (301) 427-8090

A listing is available of the weather information phone numbers for major cities throughout the U.S., as well as several resort towns. Recordings are available at most National Weather Service offices. For a listing of these phone numbers, see the city's telephone directory under "United States Government, Department of Commerce, National Weather Service" or "Weather." Large capacity weather information recordings are operated by telephone companies at some locations with forecasts supplied by the National Weather Service. For these listings, turn back to the first page of this chapter.

* Weather Maps

Public Affairs
National Oceanic and Atmospheric Administration
U.S. Department of Commerce
14th St. and Constitution Ave., NW
Room 6013
Washington, DC 20230 (202) 377-8090

This office has free copies of the weekly series of daily weather maps. The maps include the highest and lowest temperatures chart, and the precipitation areas and amounts chart. Annual subscriptions are available for $60 per year. Contact the Public Affairs Office for more information.

* Weather Forecasts for U.S. Cities

City	Phone
Albany, NY	(518) 476-1122
Albuquerque, NM	(505) 243-1371
Atlanta, GA	(404) 936-1111
Birmingham, AL	(205) 942-8430
Bismarck, ND	(701) 223-3700
Boise, ID	(208) 342-8303
Boston, MA	(617) 567-4670
Buffalo, NY	(716) 634-1615
Caribou, ME	(207) 496-8931
Charleston, WV	(304) 344-9811
Cheyenne, WY	(307) 635-9901
Chicago, IL	(312) 298-1413
Cincinnati, OH	(513) 241-1010
Cleveland, OH	(216) 931-1212
Columbia, SC	(803) 796-8710
Denver, CO	(303) 639-1212
Des Moines, IA	(515) 288-1047
Detroit, MI	(313) 941-7192
Elko, NV	(702) 738-3018
El Paso, TX	(915) 778-9343
Eugene, OR	(503) 484-1200
Fort Worth, TX	(817) 336-4416
Great Falls, MT	(406) 453-5469
Indianapolis, IN	(317) 222-2362
International Falls, MN	(218) 283-4615
Jackson, MS	(601) 936-2121
Jacksonville, FL	(904) 757-3311
Little Rock, AR	(501) 834-0316
Los Angeles, CA	(213) 554-1212
Louisville, KY	(502) 363-9655
Lubbock, TX	(806) 762-0141
Memphis, TN	(901) 757-6400
Miami, FL	(305) 661-5065
Milwaukee, WI	(414) 744-8000
Minneapolis, MN	(612) 452-2323
New Orleans, LA	(504) 465-9212
New York City, NY	(212) 315-2705
Oklahoma City, OK	(405) 360-8106
Omaha, NE	(402) 571-8111
Philadelphia, PA	(215) 627-5578
Phoenix, AZ	(602) 957-8700
Pittsburgh, PA	(412) 644-2881
Portland, ME	(207) 775-7781
Portland, OR	(503) 236-7575
Raleigh, NC	(919) 860-1234
Redding, CA	(916) 221-5613
Reno, NV	(702) 793-1300
Salt Lake City, UT	(801) 575-7669
San Antonio, TX	(512) 828-3384
San Francisco, CA	(415) 936-1212
Savannah, GA	(912) 964-1700
Seattle, WA	(206) 526-6087
Sheridan, WY	(307) 672-2345
Shreveport, LA	(318) 635-7575
Sioux Falls, SD	(314) 928-1198
St. Louis, MO	(314) 928-1198
Topeka, KS	(913) 234-2592
Washington, DC	(202) 936-1212
Wichita, KS	(316) 942-3102

* World Climate Data

National Climatic Data Center
National Oceanic And Atmospheric Administration
U.S. Department of Commerce
Federal Building
Asheville, NC 28801 (704) 259-0682

The National Climatic Data Center has a wide variety of world climate data sources, some of which include *Climates of the World*, *World Weather Records*, *Monthly Climatic Data for the World*, *Defense Department Foreign Data*, and *Foreign Data Publications Collection*. They also have several guides and catalogs on world weather. Contact the Center for more information on these and other publications and their current price list.

Be patient. If any phone number is incorrect, call (area code) 555-1212 and request the new listing.

Weather and Maps

Maps and Geography

* Aeronautical Charts

Chart Distribution Branch
National Ocean Service
National Oceanic and Atmospheric Administration (NOAA)
U.S. Department of Commerce
Riverdale, MD 20737 (301) 436-6990

The National Ocean Service Distribution Branch provides NOAA aeronautical charts and chart-related publication for the U.S. Air Space System. NOAA aeronautical charts depict navigation data and flight regulation information critically important for flight planning, flight navigation, landings and take-offs, and air traffic control. The *Catalog of Aeronautical Charts and Related Publications* contains a brief description of each aeronautical chart and chart-related publication produced by the NOS, as well as aeronautical charts produced by the U.S. Defense Mapping Agency for civilian use. It also includes the price of the chart or publication, other information needed to select and order aeronautical chart products, and a list of NOAA chart sales facilities and authorized commercial chart sales agents.

* Airborne-Geophysical Information

Branch of Geophysics
U.S. Geological Survey (USGS)
MS 964, Box 25046
Denver Federal Center
Denver, CO 80225 (303) 236-1343

State index maps and information about available aeromagnetic and aerodiometric maps and profiles can be obtained from this office.

* Antarctic Maps

Distribution Branch
U.S. Geological Survey (USGS), Building 810
Denver Federal Center, Box 25286
Denver, CO 80225 (800) USA-MAPS

Antarctic maps are available that show contour intervals of 200 meters and bathymetric information for coastal areas. The 1:250,000 -scale topographic maps are the primary map source for the planning, logistic support, and multidisciplinary investigations of the U.S. Antarctic Research Program. In the 1:500,000 series, the satellite imagery was recorded by NASA's Landsat, including the coastal areas of Wilkes Land and Enderby Land.

* Atlas of Military Installations in U.S.

Directorate for Information Operations and Reports
Washington Headquarters Services
1215 Jefferson Davis Hwy., Suite 1204
Arlington, VA 22202 (202) 746-0786

The *Atlas/Data Abstract for the United States and Selected Areas* contains a map showing all the military installations and a compendium of U.S. Department of Defense statistics for each state. Write or call for their free catalog list all their publications available through the Government Printing Office.

* Automatic Mapping Program

National Technical Information Service
U.S. Department of Commerce
5285 Port Royal Road
Springfield, VA 22151 (703) 487-4650

The Cartographic Automatic Mapping Program performs many cartographic functions and can be used in conjunction with the World Data Bank II noted below. CAM software, microfiche, and documents are available from NTIS.

* Cadastral Survey Publications

Branch of Cadastral Survey Development, SC 678
Bureau of Land Management Service Center

U.S. Department of the Interior
Denver Federal Center, Bldg. 50
P.O. Box 25047
Denver, CO 80225-0047

The following publications on surveying are available from this office:

Surveying Our Public Lands. Informative account of survey history, the growth of the public domain, the rectangular survey system, and the role of the federal cadastral surveyor (Free, #P-25).

Surveys and Surveyors of the Public Domain. To be used in training cadastral surveyors in the application of surveying principles, survey laws and their formation, and a study of the people who performed the surveys ($8, #P-140).

Preparation of Special Instructions. A required quasi-legal document authorizing a cadastral survey or resurvey. The book contains important guidelines for the proper and adequate preparation of this and other related documents ($1.85, #P-171).

Durability of Bearing Trees. Prepared as a guide for cadastral surveyors and others involved in the search for old bearing trees as well as identifying and evaluating various species of trees for marking new bearing trees ($1.40).

Manual of Surveying Instructions, 1973. Describes in detail all aspects of how cadastral surveys are made in conformance to statutory law and its judicial interpretation ($16, Superintendent of Documents, Government Printing Office, S/N 024-011-00052-6).

Selected Computations of Astronomical Computations. Discusses the following topics: Motion of the Earth, Solar Time, Sidereal Time, 24-Hour Clock, Time Signals, Azimuth Determination, Polaris, Selected Examples for Azimuth Determination - Sun, Polaris Observation for Azimuth, Equatorial Star Identification Equatorial Star/Hour Angle Observation (Free, #T/N 318).

* Cartographic Archives

Cartographic and Architectural Branch
Special Archives Division
National Archives and Records Administration
8th St. and Pennsylvania Ave., NW
Washington, DC 20408 (703) 756-6700

The Cartographic and Architectural Branch has over 11 million maps, charts, aerial photographs, architectural drawings, patents, and ship plans, which constitute one of the world's largest accumulations of such documents. The Branch holds architectural and engineering drawings created by civilian and military agencies. All the holdings can be examined in the research room at 841 South Pickett St., Alexandria, VA, from 8:00am to 4:30pm, Monday through Friday. Reproductions can be furnished for a fee.

* Cartographic Research and Experimental Maps

Geographic and Cartographic Research
National Mapping Division
U.S. Geological Survey (USGS)
National Center, MS 521
Reston, VA 22092 (703) 648-4505

The U.S. Geological Survey acquires, stores, and uses geographic data in studies that combine geographic analyses with new cartographic concepts and techniques. New types of cartographic data and experimental maps result and are used to solve environmental problems and to aid in resource management.

* Central Cartographer: Defense Mapping Agency

Defense Mapping Agency
Combat Support Center
Attn: Customer Assistance Office (800) 826-0342
Washington, DC 20315-0010 (301) 227-2495

Be patient. If any phone number is incorrect, call (area code) 555-1212 and request the new listing.

Maps and Geography

The Defense Mapping Agency makes available at cost a broad range of maps and charts. There are four categories available: aeronautical, topographic, hydrographic, and digital (lists those products available on magnetic tape). Each map costs $2.75 each. Write or call to order copies.

* China Map

Public Affairs Office
Central Intelligence Agency
Washington, DC 20505 (703) 351-2053

The Central Intelligence Agency Cartographic Automated Mapping Program and World Data Bank have generated a one-page multi-colored map which incorporates the new Pinyin (phonetic alphabet) spelling of names that became effective in 1979. The gazetteer on the reverse side of the map includes both the Pinyin and Wade-Giles rendition of geographic names. This Pinyin Edition (S/N 041-015-00106-0) can be purchased from the Government Printing Office, Washington, DC 20402; (202) 783-3238.

* CIA Catalog of Declassified Maps

Public Affairs
Central Intelligence Agency (CIA)
Washington, DC 20505 (703) 351-2053

The CIA declassifies many of its maps which are available from the National Technical Information Service, 5285 Port Royal Road, Springfield, VA 22161 (703) 487-4650. The catalog, titled *CIA Maps and Publications Released to the Public*, is available free from the CIA.

* CIA World and Country Maps

Public Affairs
Central Intelligence Agency
Washington, DC 20505 (703) 351-2053

Hundreds of maps generated by the Central Intelligence Agency are sold through NTIS. There are country maps as well as maps of continents are available. smaller geographical areas and city maps such as Moscow and Vicinity; Middle East Area Oilfields and Facilities; Israeli Settlement in the Gaza Strip; South Africa: Industrial Activity and Production; Africa Ethnolinguistic Groups.

* Comet Haley Atlas

Superintendent of Documents
Government Printing Office
Washington, DC 20402 (202) 783-3238

Census statistics publications are listed in this bibliography. One may send for the Railroad Maps of North America, featuring 5,000 maps and surveys. Weather and political atlases are listed, as well as an atlas to the Comet Haley. Free.

* Digital Cartography

Earth Science Information Center
U.S. Geological Survey (USGS)
507 National Center
Reston, VA 22092 (703) 648-6045

U.S. Geodata is the effort of the U.S. Geological Survey to expand its mapping program with digital cartography, involving the collection, storage, processing, analysis, and display of map data with the aid of computers. This includes a collection of planimetric, elevation, and geographic names information. This data may be combined with other data for cartographic applications. Users are able to plot their own maps with appropriate software. Calculations can be performed related to spatial analysis.

* Digital Spatial Data and Mapping Software

U.S. Geological Survey (USGS)
Reston-ESIC, 507 National Center
Reston, VA 22092 (703) 648-6045

The U.S. Geological Survey's Earth Science Information Center (ESIC) now offers inventories of digital spatial data sets and cartographic applications software in two bound listings. These inventories provide up-to-date bibliographic descriptions of data sets and software available from federal, state, and local government agencies and the private sector.

Sources for Digital Spatial Data. Describes more than 500 data sets containing spatially referenced base or thematic categories of data. The data sets are indexed by geographic area of coverage and cross-indexed by type of data.

Sources for Software for Computer Mapping and Related Disciplines. Describes more than 700 subroutines, programs, and systems that can be used in geographic information systems, map and chart plotting and construction, image processing and analysis, surveying, photogrammetry, data modeling and analysis, coordinate conversion, and other applications. Each publication is $22.

* Digital Spatial Data Applications Cooperation

U.S. Geological Survey (USGS)
Reston-ESIC
507 National Center
Reston, VA 22092 (703) 648-6899

If your organization is involved in digital spatial data applications, the Earth Science Information Center invites you to contribute information about your holdings. Your data and software may be valuable to other users.

* Earth Observation System

Customer User Services
Earth Resources Observation System Data Center (EROS)
U.S. Geological Survey (USGS)
Sioux Falls, SD 57198 (605) 594-6511

Aerial photographs are available from this center for most geographical regions of the country. Prices range from $6 to $65, depending on whether they are black and white or color photographs. Contact this office for ordering information.

* Earth-Science Films

Visual Information Services Group
U.S. Geological Survey (USGS)
790 National Center
Reston, VA 22092 (703) 648-4376

The Visual Information Services Group provides earth-science movies on a free-loan, short-term (2 or 3 day) basis to educational institutions and professional and scientific societies.

* Geographic Boundaries and International Disputes

Office of the Geographer
Bureau of Intelligence and Research
U.S. Department of State
2201 C St., NW, Room 8742
Washington, DC 20520 (202) 647-2022

This office distributes several publications which contain a variety of geographical information. Some of them include:

Geographic Notes. Contains brief analyses of current issues relevant to United States foreign policy. These analyses provide a geographical perspective on such foreign policy-related topics such as boundary, sovereignty, and territorial disputes.

International Boundary Studies. This is a series of specific boundary papers.

* Geographic Data and Research

Geographic and Cartographic Research
National Mapping Division
U.S. Geological Survey (USGS)
National Center, MS 521
Reston, VA 22092 (703) 648-4505

The U.S. Geological Survey acquires, stores, and uses geographic data in studies that combine geographic analyses with new cartographic concepts and techniques. New types of cartographic data and experimental maps result and are used to solve environmental problems and to aid in resource management.

* Geographic Names Information

Branch of Geographic Names
U.S. Geological Survey (USGS)
National Center, MS 523
Reston, VA 22092 (703) 648-4547

The USGS Branch of Geographic Names maintains a national research, coordinating, and information center to which all problems and inquiries concerning domestic geographic names can be directed. This office compiles name information, manages a names data repository, maintains information files, and publishes materials on domestic geographic names. The USGS, in

Be patient. If any phone number is incorrect, call (area code) 555-1212 and request the new listing.

cooperation with the Board on Geographic Names, maintains the *National Geographic Names Data Base* and compiles *The National Gazetteer of the United States of America* on a state-by-state basis.

* Geological Cartography Exhibits
Exhibits Committee
U.S. Geological Survey (USGS)
790 National Center
Reston, VA 22092 (703) 648-4357
Exhibits illustrating recent work in cartography, geography, geology, water resources, and other aspects of the USGS research are available to scientific associations for professional meetings and conferences. Contact this office for availability and scheduling information.

* Geological Survey Field Records Collection
Field Records
U.S. Geological Survey (USGS)
MS 914, Building 20
Box 25046, Federal Center
Denver, CO 80225 (303) 236-1005
The Field Records collection consists of the original materials produced by the USGS during its field investigations. Holdings include 15,600 notebooks, 2,000 folders, 2,400 map groups, and 60,000 aerial photographs. Upon gaining approval, you may examine these records at the Denver Library or make arrangements for the materials to be sent to a more convenient USGS library.

* Geologic Maps Hotline
Distribution Branch
U.S. Geological Survey (USGS)
Building 810
Denver Federal Center, Box 25286
Denver, CO 80225 (800) USA-MAPS
Geologic maps are made by USGS as part of a continuing program of examining geological structure, mineral resources, and products. These maps range in scale from 1:20,000 to 1:2,500,000, depending on the type of information shown.

Geologic Quadrangle Maps. Show the bedrock, surficial, or engineering geology of selected quadrangles in the United States.
Black-and-White or Multicolor Miscellaneous Field Studies Maps. Are preliminary reports on geologic aspects of mineral and environmental studies.
Mineral Investigations Resource Maps. Feature mineral distribution of metallic and nonmetallic minerals.
Geophysical Investigations Maps. Show the results of surveys to measure geomagnetism, gravity, and radioactivity in selected areas of the country.
State Geologic Maps. Show rock types and named geologic units exposed at the surface, geologic faults, anticlines, and synclines.
Antarctic Geologic Maps. Define rock type and named units of exposed and inferred rocks in ice-free areas.
Oil, Gas, and Coal Investigations Maps.

* Geologic Names Committee
U.S. Geological Survey (USGS)
National Center, MS 902
Reston, VA 22092 (703) 648-4311
The Geologic Names Committee defines and recommends policy and rules governing stratigraphic nomenclature and classification for the USGS. *Stratigraphic Notes* is published to announce changes in official geologic names usage. Lexicons are compiled that show domestic geologic names usage, and a file is maintained of geologic names reserved future use.

* Ground Water, Floods and Other Hydrologic Investigative Maps
Distribution Branch
U.S. Geological Survey (USGS)
Building 810
Denver Federal Center, Box 25286
Denver, CO 80225 (800) USA-MAPS
Hydrologic investigations atlases are either black and white or multicolor maps showing a wide range of water-resources information, such as depth to ground water, floods, irrigated acreage, producing aquifers, availability of water on

Indian lands, surface-water discharge to the oceans, chemical or mineral content of water, surface impoundments, and water temperature.

* Is There A Wetland Near You?
National Wetlands Inventory
Fish and Wildlife Service
U.S. Department of Interior
1849 C St., NW
Washington, DC 20240 (703) 358-2201
The National Wetlands Inventory identifies, plots, and maps all the wetlands in the U.S. These maps are available for sale through the U.S. Geologic Service by calling 800-USA-MAPS.

* Land Use and Land Cover Maps
Distribution Branch
U.S. Geological Survey (USGS), Building 810
Denver Federal Center, Box 25286
Denver, CO 80225 (800) USA-MAPS
Land use maps and land cover maps are available for most of the United States. Land use maps refer to human uses of the land (housing and industry) and land cover maps describe the vegetation, water, natural surface, and construction on the land surface. The scale used ranges from 1:100,000 for a few maps in the Western states to 1:250,000 for most other maps.

* Library of Congress Geography and Map Resources
Geography and Map Division
Library of Congress
Washington, DC 20540 (202) 707-6277
The Library's cartographic collections, which include 4 million maps, nearly 51,000 atlases, 500 globes, and some 8,000 reference books, are the largest and most comprehensive in the world. The collections include atlases published over the last five centuries covering individual continents, countries, states, counties, and cities as well as the world. Official topographic, geologic, soil, mineral, and resource maps and nautical and aeronautical charts are also available for most countries. There are also complete LANDSAT microimage data sets of images produced by several satellites revolving around the Earth. Subscription information on the microfiche data sets is available from EOSAT, 4300 Forbes Blvd., Lanham, MD 20706; (800) 344-9933.

* Mapping Research Reference Collection
National Mapping Division Research Reference Collection
U.S. Geological Survey (USGS)
521 National Center
Reston, VA 22092 (703) 648-4562
The National Mapping Division Office of Research maintains a collection of over 3,000 technical reference works in the fields of cartography and geography. The collection also includes the National Mapping Historical Archives, containing over 150,000 sheets. Functioning primarily to support research of the National Mapping Division, it is also open for use by other USGS personnel and the public. Items may be borrowed by the public through inter-library loans at local libraries.

* Maps
State affiliate National Cartographic Information Center offices distribute free pamphlets, poster-leaflets, and topographic map indexes. Many State affiliates sell maps of their respective States. The State affiliates also provide ordering assistance for custom cartographic products (including aerial photographic and satellite imagery).

Alabama
Geological Survey of Alabama
P.O. Box O, University Station
Tuscaloosa, AL 35486 (205) 349-2852

Alaska
Geophysical Institute
University of Alaska- Fairbanks
Fairbanks, AK 99775-0880 (907) 474-7487

Arizona
Arizona State Land Department

Be patient. If any phone number is incorrect, call (area code) 555-1212 and request the new listing.

Maps and Geography

Resource Analysis Division
1616 West Adams
Phoenix, AZ 85007 (602) 542-4061

Arkansas
Arkansas Geological Commission
3815 West Roosevelt Road
Little Rock, AR 72204 (501) 371-1488

California
Map and Imagery Laboratory Library
University of California
Santa Barbara, CA 93106 (805) 961-2779

Connecticut
Natural Resource Center
Department of Environmental Protection
State Office Building, Room 553
165 Capitol Ave.
Hartford, CT 06106 (203) 566-3540

Delaware
Delaware Geological Survey
University of Delaware
101 Penny Hall
Newark, DE 19716 (302) 451-8262

Florida
Florida Resources and Environmental Analysis Center
361 Bellamy Building
Florida State University
Tallahassee, FL 32306 (904) 644-2883

Georgia
Office of Research and Information
Department of Community Affairs
100 Peachtree St., Room 1200
Atlanta, GA 30303 (404) 656-5526

Hawaii
Department of Planning and Economic Development
Kamamalu Building
250 South King St.
Honolulu, HI 96813 (808) 548-3047

Idaho
Idaho State Historical Library
610 N. Julia Davis Dr.
Boise, ID 83702 (208) 334-3356

Illinois
University of Illinois at Urbana-Champaign
Map and Geography Library
1408 West Gregory Dr.
Urbana, IL 61801 (217) 333-0827

Indiana
Agricultural Data Network
214 Entomology Hall
Purdue University
West Lafayette, IN 47907 (317) 494-6305

Iowa
Iowa Geological Survey
123 N. Capitol St.
Iowa City, IA 52242 (319) 335-1575

Kansas
Kansas Geological Survey
1930 Constant Avenue
Campus West
The University of Kansas
Lawrence, KS 66046 (913) 864-3965

Kentucky
Kentucky Geological Survey
228 Mining and Min. Res.

University of Kentucky
Lexington, KY 40506 (606) 257-5500

Louisiana
Office of Public Works
Department of Transportation and Development
P.O. Box 94245 Capitol Station
Baton Rouge, LA 70804-9245 (504) 379-1473

Maine
Maine Geological Survey
State House Station #22
Augusta, ME 04333 (207) 289-2801

Maryland
Maryland Geological Survey
2300 St. Paul St.
Baltimore, MD 21218 (301) 554-5500

Massachusetts
University of Massachusetts
Cartographic Information Research Services
Hasbrouck Hall, Room 102D
Amherst, MA 01003 (413) 545-0359

Michigan
Division of Land Resource Programs
Michigan Department of Natural Resources
Steven T. Mason Building, Box 30028
Lansing, MI 48909 (517) 373-9123

Minnesota
Minnesota State Planning Agency
Land Management Information Center
300 Centennial Office Building
658 Cedar St.
Saint Paul, MN 55155 (612) 296-1201

Mississippi
Geographic Information Systems Division
Mississippi Research and Development Center
3825 Ridgewood Road
Jackson, MS 39211 (601) 982-6606

Missouri
Missouri Department of Natural Resources
Division of Geology and Land Survey
P.O. Box 250
Rolla, MO 65401 (314) 364-1752

Montana
Montana Bureau of Mines and Geology
Montana Tech
Main Hall, Room 200
Butte, Mt 59701 (406) 496-4167

Nebraska
Conservation and Survey Division
University of Nebraska
901 North 17th St.
Lincoln, NE 68508 (402) 472-2567

Nevada
Nevada Bureau of Mines and Geology
University of Nevada, Reno
Reno, NV 89557-0088 (702) 784-6691

New Hampshire
Documents Department
Dimond Library
University of New Hampshire
Durham, NH 03824 (603) 862-1777

New Jersey
Department of Environmental Protection
New Jersey Geological Survey, CN-029
Trenton, NJ 08625 (609) 292-2576

Be patient. If any phone number is incorrect, call (area code) 555-1212 and request the new listing.

Weather and Maps

New Mexico
University of New Mexico
Technology Applications Center
2808 Central Ave., SE
Albuquerque, NM 87131 (505) 277-3622

New York
Map Information Unit
New York Department of Transportation
Albany, NY 12232 (518) 457-3555

North Carolina
Geological Survey Section
Division of Land Resources, DNRCD
P.O. Box 27687
Raleigh, NC 27611 (919) 733-2423

North Dakota
North Dakota State Water Commission
State Office Building
900 East Blvd.
Bismarck, ND 58505 (701) 224-2750

Ohio
Ohio Division of Soil and Water Conservation
Remote Sensing Section- NCIC
Fountain Square, Building E
Columbus, OH 43224 (614) 265-6770

Oklahoma
Oklahoma Geological Survey
830 Van Vlett Oval
University of Oklahoma
Norman, Ok 73019 (405) 325-3031

Oregon
Oregon State Library
Public Service
Salem, OR 97310 (503) 378-4368

Pennsylvania
Department of Environmental Resources
Bureau of Topographic and Geologic Survey
P.O. Box 2357
Harrisburg, PA 17120 (717) 787-2169

Rhode Island
Rhode Island Cartographic Information Center
Pell Library
University of Rhode Island
Narragansett, RI 02882 (401) 792-6539

South Carolina
South Carolina Land Resources Conservation Commission
2221 Devine St., Suite 222
Columbia, SC 29205 (803) 758-2823

South Dakota
South Dakota Geological Survey
Science Center
University of South Dakota
Vermillion, SD 57069 (605) 677-5895

Texas
Texas Natural Resources Information System
P.O. Box 13231
Austin, TX 78711 (512) 463-8337

Utah
Utah Geological and Mineral Survey
606 Black Hawk Way
Research Park
Salt Lake City, UT 84108-1280 (801) 581-6831

Vermont
University of Vermont
Documents/Map Department

Bailey/Howe Library
Burlington, VT 05405 (802) 656-2503

Virginia
Department of Conservation and Economic Development
Division of Mineral Resources
Mineral Resources Building, Box 3667
Charlottesville, VA 22903 (804) 293-5121

Washington
Washington State Library
Information Services Division
Olympia, WA 98504 (206) 753-4027

West Virginia
West Virginia Geological and Economic Survey
West Virginia Cartographic Center
P.O. Box 879
Morgantown, WV 26507 (304) 594-2331

Wisconsin
State Cartographer's Office
155 Science Hall
550 North Park St.
Madison, WI 53706 (608) 262-6850

Wyoming
State Engineer
Herschler Building
Cheyenne, WY 82002 (307) 777-7354

* Maps and Atlases: United States and Foreign

Superintendent of Documents
Government Printing Office
Washington, DC 20402 (202) 783-3238

Census statistics publications are listed in this bibliography. One may send for the Railroad Maps of North America, featuring 5,000 maps and surveys. Weather and political atlases are listed, as well as an atlas to the Comet Haley. Free.

* Maps of Moon and Planets

Distribution Branch
U.S. Geological Survey (USGS), Building 810
Denver Federal Center, Box 25286
Denver, CO 80225 (800) USA-MAPS

The USGS established an astrogeology program on behalf of NASA to support lunar and planetary exploration. Many maps of the Moon, Mars, Venus, and Mercury are available.

* Maps: Technical Information

Geologic Inquiries
U.S. Geological Survey (USGS)
National Center, MS 907
Reston, VA 22092 (301) 648-4383

To obtain technical information on such geologic topics as earthquakes and volcanoes, energy and mineral resources, the geology of specific areas, and geologic maps, contact this office.

* Meteorological Topographic Maps

ASRL-Meteorology
Environmental Protection Agency
Research Triangle Park, NC 27711

This library's major field of interest is the meteorological aspects of air pollution, including model development and application, climatic analysis, and geophysical studies. The library holds a collection of climatic data material consisting of approximately 4,000 climatic data material reports on microfiche, over 400 rolls of film of synoptic data, surface and vorticity charts, and a large body of topographic maps.

* Mine Companies and Property Ownership Maps

Division of Program Information and Analysis
Surface Mining Reclamation and Enforcement

Be patient. If any phone number is incorrect, call (area code) 555-1212 and request the new listing.

Maps and Geography

U.S. Department of the Interior
1951 Constitution Ave., NW
Washington, DC 20240 (202) 343-5907

Valuable information is available from the mine maps available through the mine map repositories of the Office of Surface Mining Reclamation and Enforcement. Mine and company names, water sources, property ownership of adjoining companies and towns, latitudes and longitudes, coal outcrop seam designations, openings and emergency exits of mines, and gas and power lines are some of the topics covered. This information can be useful to local developers, engineering firms, and energy interests, as well as private citizens.

* Mine Map Repositories

Office of Public Affairs
Surface Mining Reclamation and Enforcement
U.S. Department of the Interior
1951 Constitution Ave., NW
Washington, DC 20240 (202) 343-4953

The Mine Map Repositories were established in 1970 and are responsible for collecting and archiving mine maps both east and west of the Mississippi River and in Alaska. The brochure, *Mine Map Repositories*, provides information and statistics on the mine map repository facilities of the Office of Surface Mining Reclamation and Enforcement. The five repositories are listed with their addresses and phone numbers. They are located in Pittsburgh, PA, Wilkes-Barre, PA, Denver, CO, Spokane, WA, and Juneau, AK.

* National Atlas Updates

Distribution Branch
U.S. Geological Survey (USGS), Building 810
Denver Federal Center, Box 25286
Denver, CO 80225 (800) USA-MAPS

The *National Atlas of the United States* (1970) contains 765 maps and charts on 335 pages. Out of print and no longer for sale, it can still be found in most libraries. However, separate sheets of selected reference maps and thematic maps from the *Atlas* are available from the USGS. Some of the sheets have been updated. Some updated thematic maps include potential natural vegetation (1985), monthly average temperature (1986) monthly minimum temperature (1986), monthly maximum temperature (1986), networks of ecological research (1983), and territorial growth (1986).

* National Gazetteer of the United States of America

Books and Open File Reports
U.S. Geological Survey (USGS)
Box 25425, Federal Center
Denver, CO 80225 (303) 236-7476

The National Gazetteer of the United States of America is a geographic dictionary of place and feature names, published on a state-by-state basis. It includes a glossary of terms and abbreviations, a map of counties in a state, and an alphabetical listing of USGS topographic quadrangle maps of the state, as well as the information contained in the *National Geographic Names Data Base*. Also listed are names of features from other historical sources. Variant names are listed and cross-referenced to their official names. A variant name is any other known name or spelling applied to a feature other than the official name.

* National Mapping Activities

National Mapping Division
U.S. Geological Survey (USGS)
National Center, MS 516
Reston, VA 22092 (703) 648-5748

The National Mapping Program of the U.S. Geological Survey compiles, updates, and prints topographic maps as well as thematic maps that combine topographic data with other spatial data, such as geology, hydrology, rainfall, land use, and population. Four regional Mapping Centers, located in Reston, VA, Rolla, MO, Denver, CO, and Menlo Park, CA, are responsible for map production and for coordinating joint mapping activities with other Federal and State agencies. Maps are sold through the Earth Science Information Centers and private dealers.

* National Mapping System

Distribution Branch
U.S. Geological Survey (USGS)
Building 810
Denver Federal Center, Box 25286

Denver, CO 80225 (800) USA-MAPS

The USGS National Mapping System is a rich source of numerous types of maps. The brochure, *Catalog of Maps*, describes in detail the different maps available. Contact either the above office for a price list or one of the Earth-Science Information Centers for more information on the maps available.

* National Park Maps

Technical Information Center
National Park Service
Denver Service Center
12795 W. Alameda Parkway
P.O. Box 25287
Denver, CO 80225-0287 (303) 969-2130

The Technical Information Center has been designated by the National Park Service as the central repository for all National Park Service-generated planning, design, and construction maps, drawings, and reports as well as related cultural, environmental, and other technical documents. Bibliographic data on aerial photography is also maintained. The Center reproduces and delivers copies of the available materials for the Service, other agencies, and the public, both here and abroad. Today, the system has a holding of 100,000 data records, which represent about 500,000 microfilm aperture cards of maps, plans, and drawings; 1,000 records of resource and site aerial photography; and 25,000 planning, design, environmental, cultural resource, and natural resource documents.

* Nautical Charts

Chart Distribution Branch
National Ocean Service
National Oceanic and Atmospheric Administration (NOAA)
U.S. Department of Commerce
Riverdale, MD 20737 (301) 436-6990

The National Ocean Service produces approximately 1,000 nautical charts for navigation in U.S. estuarine waters and navigable inland waterways, the Great Lakes, and the 2 1/2 million square miles of coastal waters of the United States and its possessions. NOAA *Chart and Map Catalogs* describe nautical charts which are listed in a series of four catalogs, one for each region of the U.S. ocean and coastal waters. NOAA bathymetric maps and special purpose charts are listed in a single catalog. A sixth catalog is a guide to NOAA nautical products and services. The catalogs contain a brief description of each nautical chart, bathymetric map, special purpose chart, and chart-related publication produced by the NOS. They also include the price of the chart of publication, other information needed to select and order nautical charting products, and a list of NOAA chart sales facilities and authorized commercial chart sales agents. Contact this office for your free catalogs.

* Photoimage Maps

Distribution Branch
U.S. Geological Survey (USGS)
Building 810
Denver Federal Center, Box 25286
Denver, CO 80225 (800) USA-MAPS

Photoimage maps are published in three types: orthophotomaps, orthoquads, and border maps of US./Mexico and U.S/Canada. Satellite (Landsat) image maps are multi-color photograph-like maps made from data collected by Earth resources satellites. They are available for selected areas in about half of the states, along with such areas as Antarctica, the Bahamas, and Iceland.

* Portraits of the Earth

U.S. Geological Survey (USGS)
Book and Report Sales
Box 25425
Denver, CO 80225 (303) 236-7476

Geologic Maps: Portraits of the Earth is one of many maps available from the U.S. Geological Survey.

* Railroad Maps of North America

Superintendent of Documents
Government Printing Office
Washington, DC 20402 (202) 783-3238

Census statistics publications are listed in this bibliography. One may send for the Railroad Maps of North America, featuring 5,000 maps and surveys. Weather and political atlases are listed, as well as an atlas to the Comet Haley. Free.

Be patient. If any phone number is incorrect, call (area code) 555-1212 and request the new listing.

Weather and Maps

* Scholarly Sources on Cartography

Smithsonian Institution Press
Dept. 900
Blue Ridge Summit, PA 17214 (717) 794-2148

Produced by the Woodrow Wilson International Center for Scholars, the *Guides to Scholarly Sources* are designed to be descriptive, evaluative surveys of source materials. The Guide titled *Cartography and Remote Sensing* is divided into two parts. Part I examines area collections - libraries; archives and manuscript depositories; art, film, music, and map collections; and data banks. Part II focuses on pertinent activities of Washington-based organizations, public and private. Given for each are its related functions, materials and products.

* Slides Of The Earth

National Geophysical Data Center
NOAA E/GC3 Dept. 874
325 Broadway
Boulder, CO 80303-3328 (303) 497-6338

Relief Globe Slides is a set of 20 slides containing 14 global view of the Earth in full color shaded relief, showing land and undersea topography. The planet is seen from vantage points over the poles and each major ocean and land mass. Also included are a rectangular Mercator projection view of the whole Earth, as well as displays of crustal plates and their relation to world seismic activity. Other views may be generated on request, either as slides or computer files. The cost is $40.

* Space Photographs

Customer Services
Earth Resources Observation System Data Center (EROS)
U.S. Geological Survey (USGS)
Sioux Falls, SD 57198 (605) 594-6511

The EROS Data Center maintains photographs from many of the space missions, including those of the space shuttle, Apollo, and Gemini. Contact the center directly for information concerning specific topics.

* State Topographic Maps

Earth Science Information Center
U.S. Geological Survey (USGS)
507 National Center
Reston, VA 22092 (703) 648-6045

Two types of directories are now available listing topographic maps for each state. *An Index to Topographic and Other Map Coverage* and its companion, *Catalog of Topographic and Other Published Maps*, contain information on the types of state maps that are available. The *Index* shows you how to locate your general area of interest and then the specific location and name of the area for which you want a map in each state. The *Catalog* lists cities and geographic areas for which maps are available.

* Topographic and Topographic-Bathymetric Maps

Distribution Branch
U.S. Geological Survey (USGS)
Building 810
Denver Federal Center, Box 25286
Denver, CO 80225 (800) USA-MAPS

Topographic maps of the USGS use brown contours to show the shape and elevation of the terrain. The maps show and name prominent natural and man-made features. The best known USGS maps are those of the 7.5-minute, 1:24,000-scale quadrangle series. Fifteen-minute maps are also available, particularly for the Hawaiian Islands, but some detail is omitted or generalized.

Other topographic maps include the U.S. 1:100,000 scale series, county map series, U.S. 1:250,000-scale series, state map series, National Park series, and shaded-relief maps.

On the topographic-bathymetric maps, contour lines show elevations of the land areas above sea level, and isobaths (depth contours) show the form of the land below the water. Some bathymetric maps also show magnetic and gravity data. The combined map serves the needs of oceanographers, marine geologists, land use planners, physical scientists, conservationists, and others having an interest in management of the coastal zone, the wetlands, and the offshore environment.

* U.S. Geological Survey Photographs

Photographic Library, MS 914
U.S. Geological Survey (USGS)
Box 25046, Federal Center
Denver, CO 80225 (303) 236-1010

The Photographic Library of the U.S. Geological Survey contains a special collection of approximately 250,000 photographs. The Library may be used by the public as well as by personnel of other government agencies. Persons who wish to obtain prints, copy negatives, and duplicate transparencies from the collection are encouraged to visit the library. If this is not possible, the staff will prepare lists of specific photographs in response to requests. Many photographs are selected by searching U.S. Geological Survey publications and are identified by title and number of the publication as well as the number of the page and plate of the figure found. To obtain information on purchasing prints, negatives, or transparencies, contact the library directly.

* U.S. Geological Survey: New Publications

Branch of Data Systems
U.S. Geological Survey (USGS)
National Center, MS 582
Reston, VA 22092 (703) 648-6045

New Publications of the U.S. Geological Survey is a free monthly catalog of new publications released by the U.S. Geological Survey. To be placed on the mailing list, contact the office above.

* Weather Maps

Public Affairs
National Oceanic and Atmospheric Administration
U.S. Department of Commerce
14th St. and Constitution Ave., NW
Room 6013
Washington, DC 20230 (202) 377-8090

This office has free copies of the weekly series of daily weather maps. The maps include the highest and lowest temperatures chart, and the precipitation areas and amounts chart. Annual subscriptions are available for $60 per year. Contact the Public Affairs Office for more information.

* World Data Bank II

National Technical Information Service
U.S. Department of Commerce
5285 Port Royal Road
Springfield, VA 22151 (703) 487-4650

The CIA produced a cartographic data base which represents natural and man-made features of the world in a digital format. Approximately six million points are contained on five separate geographic area files. All four volumes (PB 87-184-768) on magnetic tape can be purchased from NTIS.

Be patient. If any phone number is incorrect, call (area code) 555-1212 and request the new listing.

Environment and Nature General Sources

* *See also Careers and Workplace; Research Grants in Every Field Chapter*
* *See also Current Events and Homework Chapter*
* *See also Energy Chapter*
* *See also Health and Medicine Chapter*
* *See also Vacations and Business Travel Chapter*

Ozone depletion, dioxins, chemical dumps, medical waste, and the disappearance of tropical rain forests are just a few of the environmental issues making news headlines daily. These and other topics, including the tug-of-war between conservation and development, are covered in this chapter. Besides the hundreds of Environmental Protection Agency sources, you'll also find several interest and lobby groups which are useful sources on practically any environmental issue, from details about proposed Clean Air Act amendments to municipal garbage incinerators and indoor air quality. Bird watchers and naturalists will find a complete state-by-state listing of the National Wildlife Refuges here, but should also browse through the Vacations and Business Travel Chapter for information on National Parks and other points of interest.

* Aircraft Noise

Noise Abatement Division
Office of Environment and Energy
Federal Aviation Administration (FAA)
U.S. Department of Transportation
800 Independence Ave., SW, Room 432
Washington, DC 20591 (202) 267-3553

This FAA division conducts research on reducing noise levels of new aircraft, and retrofitting older aircraft to reduce noise levels.

* Alternative Energy Sources

Solar Energy Research Institute (SERI)
Technical Inquiry Service
1617 Cole Blvd.
Golden, CO 80401 (303) 231-7303

SERI produces and disseminates technical communication publications, technical articles, awareness publications, videos, and exhibits on energy efficiency and renewable energy with include: solar, photovoltaic, biofuels, wind energy, ocean energy, and energy storage. SERI provides specific technical responses to limited audiences through the Technical Inquiry Service. Contact SERI for more information.

* Arctic and Antarctic Science Stations

Office of Polar Affairs
Bureau of Oceans and International Environmental and Scientific Affairs
U.S. Department of State
2201 C St., NW, Room 5801
Washington, DC 20520 (202) 647-3262

This office is concerned with all issues concerning the Arctic and Antarctic, including the environment and marine life, such as whales and seals. They are also closely involved with the many science stations located on the Antarctic.

* Army Corps of Engineers Publications

U.S. Army Corps of Engineers
Public Affairs
20 Massachusetts Ave., NW
Washington, DC 20314 (202) 272-0011

The Corps offers free brochures on a wide variety of subjects, including archaeology, camping, environment, erosion control, flood control, flood plain management, history, safety, waste-water treatment and water supply. For a publications list, call or write the above office.

* Asbestos Ombudsman Clearinghouse

Environmental Protection Agency (EPA)
401 M St., SW (800) 368-5888
Washington DC 20460 (703) 557-1938 (in VA)

The assigned mission of the Asbestos Ombudsman Clearinghouse is to provide to the public sector, including individual citizens and community services, information on handling and abatement of asbestos in schools, the workplace, and the home. In addition, interpretation of the asbestos-in-school requirements, and publications are provided to explain recent legislation. More specifically, the EPA Asbestos Ombudsman receives complaints and requests for information and provides assistance with regard to them.

* Asbestos Regulations

Toxic Substances Control Act Information
Environmental Protection Agency (EPA)
401 M St., SW
Washington DC 20460 (202) 554-1404

This service can provide you with technical information on asbestos, as well information on regulations and publications. They have publications which interpret the regulations, as well as guidance documents on abatement, sampling, respiratory protection, and waste remove.

* Automated Laboratory Library

Central Regional Laboratory (CRL) Library
839 Bestgate Rd.
Annapolis, MD 21401 (301) 266-9180

This library was established in support of the Regional Laboratory which started in Annapolis in 1964. The subjects in the collection focus on biology, chemistry, ecology, engineering, hazardous waste hydrology, and oceanography. To serve the highly diversified expertise of the laboratory scientists and engineers, material is provided in aquatic biology, analytical chemistry, automated laboratory techniques, industrial wastewater monitoring, toxic and hazardous substances, and mathematical modelling. A special collections covers the Chesapeake Bay.

* Basic Sciences Clearinghouse

Library Services Office
Research Triangle Park, NC 27711 (919) 541-2777

The Research Triangle Park (RTP) library's collection concentrates on chemical toxicity, all aspects of air pollution as well as the basic sciences, with some coverage of business and economics. Databases maintained here include BRS, CAS On-line, DIALOG, Hazardline, Hazardous Waste Database, and NLM.

Be patient. If any phone number is incorrect, call (area code) 555-1212 and request the new listing.

Environment and Nature

* Coastal Zone Management

Office of Ocean and Coastal Resource Management
National Ocean Service
National Oceanic and Atmospheric Administration
U.S. Department of Commerce
1825 Connecticut Ave., NW, Room 706
Washington, DC 20235 (202) 673-5111

To balance the needs for preserving and developing the resources in the U.S. coastal zone, the National Ocean Service, through its Office of Ocean and Coastal Resource Management, provides the coordination and expertise at the Federal level needed for effective management of these coastal resources. NOS has begun to expand the technical assistance provided to States and territories, emphasizing special area management planning, coastal hazards mitigation, cost-effective coastal management, and the simplification of permit processes for coastal activities.

* Coast Guard Environmental Protection

Planning Branch
Research and Development Staff
Office of Engineering and Development
U.S. Coast Guard
U.S. Department of Transportation
2100 2nd St., SW, Room 6208
Washington, DC 20593-0001 (202) 267-1030

Information can be obtained here about research conducted by the Coast Guard in support of its operations and responsibilities. Areas of study include ice operations, ocean dumping, law enforcement, environmental protection, port safety and security, navigation aids, search and rescue procedures, recreational boating, energy, and advanced marine vehicles. For referral to specific personnel working in these areas, contact the Planning Branch.

* Community-College Environmental Curricula Grants

National Workforce Development Staff
Office of Research and Development
Environmental Protection Agency (EPA)
401 M St., SW, Room NE312
Washington DC 20460 (202) 260-2573

The National Workforce Development Staff awards money to community colleges to support the development of environment-related curriculum, allowing these colleges to then train State employees. The office also awards fellowships to State employees to continue their education concerning the environment. The fellowship applications are given out through the individual States. Contact this office for more information.

* Consumer Publications

Public Information Center
Environmental Protection Agency (EPA)
401 M St., SW, PM-211 B
Washington DC 20460 (202) 260-7751

The EPA's Public Information Center maintains a wide selection of publications on major environmental topics. The materials distributed by the Center are nontechnical and have been prepared as sources of general environmental information for the public. Technical documents are available through the EPA Library, the National Technical Information Service, or the publishing office within EPA. The *Public Information Center Publications List* is updated monthly and is free.

* Drinking Water Programs

Office of Drinking Water
Environmental Protection Agency (EPA)
401 M St., SW, Room E1011
Washington, DC 20460 (202) 260-5543

This EPA office develops national programs, technical policies, and regulations for water pollution control and water supply. It also administers part of the Safe Drinking Water Act.

* Ecology Research

National Ecology Center
U.S. Fish and Wildlife Service
4512 McMurray Ave.
Fort Collins, CO 80525 (303) 226-9100

The center conducts research, develops new tools, and transfers information so that scientists can better understand and manage fish and wildlife resources, habitats, and ecosystems. All endangered marine mammal research is performed here. Workshops are held in refuge management and habitat model development for those within the Interior Department and scientists in Federal and State agencies and foreign countries. Studies are reported in the Center's *Biological Report* series and through extension education brochures.

* Educational Materials and Programs

Environmental/Energy Education
Land Resources Division
Resource Development
Tennessee Valley Authority (TVA)
Norris, TN 37828 (615) 632-1640

Much of TVA's environmental education effort is accomplished through university-based environmental education centers. The TVA has worked with several universities and colleges across the Valley and seven states to develop environmental education teaching aids and programs for schools, along with workshops for teachers. At the national level, the TVA has been involved in coordinating programs with the Environmental Protection Agency. In addition, TVA offers teacher workshops and interpretive programs for groups at Land Between the Lakes, an experimental area for schools and the public to study total resource management. Contact this office of more information on the TVA's environmental education programs.

* Education Materials from the EPA

Public Information Center
Environmental Protection Agency (EPA)
401 M St., SW, PM-211 B
Washington DC 20460 (202) 260-7751

Environmental Education Materials For Teachers and Young People is a free annotated list of educational materials on environmental issues. Entries include diverse materials ranging from workbooks and lesson plans to newsletters, films, and computer software intended for young people. Educational materials available from sources other than EPA are listed alphabetically following the name of their sponsoring organization or group. A separate listing of selected EPA publications and other material available from EPA's Public Information Center is included in this pamphlet, as well as a short descriptive list of environmental education resource facilities. Contact this office to order your free copy.

* Energy Conservation- Help Is Just A Phone Call Away

Conservation and Renewable Energy Inquiry and
Referral Service (CAREIRS)
U.S. Department of Energy
P.O. Box 8900
Silver Spring, MD 20907 (800) 523-2929

CAREIRS provides fact sheets and bibliographies on the full spectrum of energy efficiency and renewable energy technologies. CAREIRS also maintains a referral network of hundreds of public and private organizations to respond to requests that are regionally or State specific, or highly technical in nature. CAREIRS provides general information on energy efficiency and renewable energy technologies such as: caulking and weatherstripping, efficient windows and lighting systems, recycling, photovoltaics, wind energy, and solar energy.

* Energy Efficiency For You

Public Affairs
U.S. Department of Energy
Washington, DC 20585 (202) 586-5575

The U.S. Department of Energy has a wide variety of information available regarding energy efficiency. They have information sheets on automatic and programmable thermostats, solar energy, appliance labeling, fans and ventilation, heat pumps, hot water conservation, insulation, as well as many more. Two booklets that provide a wealth of information as well as some helpful suggestions include: *Tips For Saving Energy In Small Business*, and *Tips For An Energy Efficient Apartment*. All are free.

* Energy Information Clearinghouse

Office of Scientific and Technical Information (OSTI)
U.S. Department of Energy
P.O. Box 62
Oak Ridge, TN 37831 (615) 576-8401

Be patient. If any phone number is incorrect, call (area code) 555-1212 and request the new listing.

General Sources

OSTI is the program office responsible for managing DOE's scientific and technical information. OSTI primarily serves the information needs of DOE and its contractors. Information collected and managed by OSTI is also made available through specific databases on superconductivity and new technology and abstract periodicals in specific subject areas such as *Buildings Energy Technology* and *Synthesis Gas Conversion Technology Update.* OSTI also distributes handbooks, brochures, flyers, posters and other information products to the public at no charge.

* Enforcement and Investigations

National Enforcement Investigations Center Library (NEIC)
Building 53, Box 25277
Denver Federal Center
Denver, CO 80225 (303) 236-5122

This library's collection comprises case files, technical reports, data compilations, and background information used to develop the basis for field studies and enforcement actions; research and development reports on municipal, industrial, and agricultural pollution abatement practices; enforcement conference documents and environmental law materials; technical reference materials covering chemistry, pesticides, toxic substances, air technology, and hazardous wastes. Databases maintained here include BRS, CDS, CIS, Consent Decree System, DIALOG, FINDS, Ground Water On-line, HWDMS, ISI, LEXIS/NEXIS, NLM, PCS, SFFAS, STORET, VV-Text, and Westlaw.

* Enforcement of Environmental Laws

Civil Enforcement
Enforcement and Compliance Monitoring
Environmental Protection Agency (EPA)
401 M St., SW, Room W1035
Washington DC 20460 (202) 260-4137

When regulated entities fail to comply voluntarily with EPA requirements, the EPA, in partnership with State agencies, can take a number of enforcement actions. These alternatives include compliance promotion; administrative money penalties; negotiated compliance schedules; and ultimately, judicial enforcement involving criminal proceedings in federal court. Contact this office for more information regarding enforcement of environmental laws.

* Environmental Impact Statements

Special Programs and Analysis Division
Office of Federal Activities
Environmental Protection Agency (EPA)
401 M St., SW, Room 2119
Washington DC 20460 (202) 260-8799

This office reviews and completes a compliance check on *Environmental Impact Statements* (EISs) to ensure that they meet the criteria required of an EIS. They comment on the impact statement and then publish it in the *Federal Register.* These *Statements* are documents required of Federal agencies by the National Environmental Policy Act for major projects or legislative proposals significantly affecting the environment. A tool for decision making, they describe the positive and negative effects of the undertaking and lists alternative actions. This office can also refer you to a Federal agency responsible for an *Environmental Impact Statement* on a specific topic.

* Environmental Engineering and Technology

Office of Environmental Engineering and Technology
Office of Research and Development
Environmental Protection Agency (EPA)
401 M St., SW, Room W635E
Washington, DC 20460 (202) 260-2600

Research in environmental engineering and technology studies pollution from industrial and municipal sources, and analyzes alternative control technologies. Examples of research includes exploring innovative techniques for removing and disposing of pollutants, and developing cost-effective methods of providing safe drinking water.

* Environment Library As Close As Your Phone

EPA's National Computer Center
EPA Research Triangle Park Library
Research Triangle Park, NC 27711 (919) 541-2777

EPA Online Library System puts a wealth of environmental information at your disposal. Anyone with access to a terminal with a modem can use OLSD. The holdings of EPA's Network Libraries are accessible using this system. The system can be searched using titles, authors, and keywords. For a User Guide and password information, contact the office listed above.

* Environmental Regulations

Superintendent of Documents
Government Printing Office
Washington DC 20402 (202) 783-3238

Single copies of *Federal Registers* with environmental regulations can be obtained from this office.

* EPA Bibliography

National Technical Information Service (NTIS)
5825 Port Royal Rd.
Springfield, VA 22161 (703) 487-4650

EPA Publications Bibliography, Quarterly Abstract Bulletin is a quarterly update listing and indexing EPA technical reports and journal articles added to the NTIS collection during the preceding quarter. The fourth issue of each year contains bibliographic citations with abstracts for the preceding quarter and cumulative indexes for the calendar year. Single copies are $25, and a yearly subscription is $90.

* EPA Freedom of Information Requests

Freedom of Information Officer
Environmental Protection Agency (EPA)
401 M St., SW, Room W227
Washington DC 20460 (202) 260-4048

All Freedom of Information requests should be addressed to the Officer listed above.

* EPA Libraries

EPA Headquarters Library
401 M St., SW
Room 2904 WSM
Washington, DC 20460 (202) 260-5921

The EPA Headquarters Library provides information services covering a wide range of environmental and related subjects of interest to EPA staff and the general public. Major areas include air and radiation, chemistry, hazardous waste, management, noise abatement, pesticides, resource recovery, solid waste, toxicology, wastewater treatment, water quality, and water supply. Databases maintained here include CAS On-line, CIS, DIALOG, Ground Water On-line, Hazardous Waste Database, ISI, LEXIS/NEXIS, NLM, and Newsnet. The library's special collection covers hazardous waste.

There are 28 EPA network libraries located in Headquarters, and all regional offices and laboratories to support the EPA offices. The libraries and other information services contain a combined collection of over 128,900 books, 5,088 journals subscriptions, 357,146 hard copy reports, 3,166,500 documents on microfilm and microfiche, 9,000 journal article reprints, and 2,000 maps. A free publication, *Guide to EPA Libraries And Information Services,* lists each of the libraries, as well as their location, collection emphasis, loan policy, and the services they offer. What follows is a list of the EPA's regional libraries:

Region 1 Library
JFK Federal Bldg., Boston, MA 02203; (617) 565-3300. The EPA Region 1 Library's collection still reflects some older New England river basin reports, but has been extensively developed in the areas of air pollution and control, pesticides and toxic substances, groundwater, solid and hazardous waste, health effects, water pollution and control. Databases maintained here include BRS, CAS On-line, CIS, DIALOG, Ground Water On-line, Hazardous Waste Database, and LEXIS/NEXIS. Special collections include the Hazardous Waste collection, Envirofiche since 1980, New England materials: Connecticut, Maine, Massachusetts, New Hampshire, Rhode Island, and Vermont.

Region 2 Library
26 Federal Plaza, New York, NY 10278; (212) 264-2881. This library embraces all aspects of EPA's environmental mission. Databases maintained here include DIALOG, Hazardous Waste Database, and ISI. Its general collection covers human resources management.

Region 2 Field Office Library
2890 Woodbridge Ave., Edison, NJ 08837; (201) 321-6762. This library includes

Be patient. If any phone number is incorrect, call (area code) 555-1212 and request the new listing.

Environment and Nature

materials on all EPA programs: air, solid waste, hazardous waste, toxic substances, pesticides, water, and radiation.

Region 3 Library
841 Chestnut St., Philadelphia, PA 19107; (215) 597-0580. This Center (IRC) provides information support for a wide range of environmental programs and activities conducted by the Regional office. It also serves as an information resource for the general public. Subject areas include air pollution, pesticides, employee development, radiation, environmental law, toxic substances, hazardous waste, toxicology, management, water pollution, and wetlands. Databases maintained here include CIS, DIALOG, Ground Water On-line, Hazardline, Hazardous Waste Database, and LEXIS/NEXIS. There are also special collections on wetland ecology and hazardous waste and law. In addition, a special effort is made to acquire published information on environmental conditions and trends within the five states and the District of Columbia which comprise Region 3.

Region 4 Library
345 Courtland St., NE, Atlanta, GA 30365-2401; (404) 347-4216. The Region 4 Library provides a full range of library and information services, covering subjects from air and water pollution to toxics and hazardous waste with a variety of technical reports, reference books, journals, and online computer services. Databases maintained here include CAS On-line, CIS, DIALOG, Dun & Bradstreet, Hazardous Waste Database, ISI, LEXIS/NEXIS, NLM, NPIRS, and OHS.

Region 5 Library
230 South Dearborn St., Room 1670, Chicago, IL 60604; (312) 353-2022. The subject areas of this library's collection cover air pollution, air quality, groundwater, hazardous waste, noise, pesticides, recycling and resource recovery, solid waste management, toxic substances, water pollution, water quality, and water supply (drinking water). The emphasis is on the Great Lakes and the six states in the Region: Illinois, Indiana, Michigan, Minnesota, Ohio, and Wisconsin. Databases maintained here include BRS, CIS, DIALOG, Ground Water On-line, Hazardous Waste Database, ISI, LEXIS/NEXIS, NLM, and ORBIT.

Region 6 Library
1445 Ross Ave., Allied Bank Tower, Dallas, TX 75202-2733; (214) 655-6444. The EPA Region 6 Library includes materials on all EPA programs: air pollution, radiation, hazardous waste, solid waste, noise, toxic substances, pesticides, and water pollution.

Region 7 Library
726 Minnesota Ave., Kansas City, KS 66101; (913) 551-7241. The Region 7 Library provides information on a wide range of environmental subjects of interest to the Regional staff and the general public. Subject areas include agricultural pollution, air pollution, environmental law, hazardous waste, pesticides, radiation, solid waste management, water pollution, water quality, and water supply. Databases maintained here include CIS, Hazardous Waste Database, LEXIS/NEXIS, NLM, and Watstore.

Region 8 Library
999 18th St., Suite 1300, Denver, CO 80202-22413; (303) 293-1444. The Region 8 Library includes materials on all EPA programs: air, water, hazardous and solid waste, pesticides, toxic substances, noise and radiation, particularly as they relate to the states within the Region. In addition, because the Rocky Mountain area is rich in energy resources, the library collects material relating to energy resource development and its relationship to the environment. And finally, to support other Agency programs, the collection incorporates publications relating to economics, planning, transportation, management and employee development. Databases maintained here include CARL, CIS, DIALOG, Ground Water On-line, and Hazardous Waste Database.

Region 9 Library
215 Fremont St., 6th Floor, San Francisco, CA 94105. The Region 9 Library's major subject areas include air pollution and control, pesticides, environmental health and safety, radiation, hazardous waste, research and development, law, solid waste. Databases maintained include CIS, DIALOG, Hazardline, and Hazardous Waste Database. Special collections here include Environmental Impact Statements, hazardous waste, and speeches given by EPA Senior Staff.

Region 10 Library
1200 Sixth Ave., Seattle, WA 98101; (206) 442-1289. The Region 10 Library's holdings include monographs, serials, a basic environmental law collection, EPA reports (both hard copy and microfiche), and local and state government reports. The collection was originally heavily oriented toward water pollution, but has

since been developed to encompass all other areas of environmental quality. Databases maintained here include CIS, DIALOG, Ground Water On-line, Hazardous Waste Database, LEXIS/NEXIS, and NLM. Special collections include Environmental Impact Statements and hazardous waste.

* EPA Newsletter

Superintendent of Documents
Government Printing Office
Washington DC 20402 (202) 783-3238

Published six times a year, the *EPA Journal* presents articles concerning the environment, State and local actions, and EPA activities. A subscription is available for $8 per year. For more information concerning the EPA Journal contact: Editor, *EPA Journal*, 401 M St, SW, A-107, Washington DC 20460; (202) 382-4393.

* Exposure to Toxic Substances

Health and Environment Review Division
Office of Toxic Substances
Environmental Protection Agency (EPA)
401 M St., SW, Room E315B
Washington, DC 20460 (202) 260-4241

This EPA division studies human and environmental exposure to chemical substances in support of OTS risk assessment activities. EED provides standards, guidance, and rule development. It reviews available information relevant to chemical exposure to humans and develops guidelines for epidemiological data.

* Free Environment Information

Consumer Information Center
Pueblo, CO 81009

Consumer Information Catalog lists 200 free or low cost publications from a variety of federal agencies. The publications cover environment, health, federal benefits, money management, housing, childcare, employment, small business, education, food and nutrition, consumer protection, and more. The catalog is published quarterly and is free. Write for your free copy.

* Free Technology Newsletter

Center for Environmental Research Information (CERI)
ORD Publications Unit
Environmental Protection Agency (EPA)
Cincinnati, OH 45268 (513) 569-7369

This free newsletter lists titles and description of printed publications that available from CERI, including seminar publications, manuals, handbooks, and guides. Also included is a listing of technology transfer seminars and meetings.

* Grants For Your Environmental Research

Research Grants Program
Center for Environmental Research Information
ORD Publications Unit
Environmental Protection Agency (EPA)
26 W. Martin Luther King Jr. Dr.
Cincinnati, OH 45268 (513) 569-7562

The EPA Research Program Guide provides descriptions of the research programs organized first by media such as air, water, hazardous waste, etc. These categories are further broken down into research foci such as scientific assessment, monitoring and quality assurance, health effects, environmental processes, and engineering technology. Each description is a every broad summary of research being done, where it is occurring, who to contact for more information about the program, and both the approximate total funding for that area and the percentage of total funding which is reserved by EPA for in-house research.

* Greenhouse Effect

Office of Technology Assessment (OTA)
600 Pennsylvania Ave., SE
Washington, DC 20510 (202) 224-8996

OTA has studied the major contributors to climate change, ozone depletion, and the greenhouse effect for both the developed and developing world. OTA identifies areas where gains in efficiency, product substitution, conservation, or other options can slow climate change. *Ozone Depletion and the Greenhouse Effect* is the resulting publication.

Be patient. If any phone number is incorrect, call (area code) 555-1212 and request the new listing.

General Sources

* Guide to the Environmental Protection Agency

Public Information Center
Environmental Protection Agency (EPA)
401 M St., SW, PM-211B
Washington, DC 20460 (202) 260-7551

Your Guide to the United States Environmental Protection Agency describes how the EPA is addressing the major environmental problems that confront the U.S. It looks at the organization, and the laws for which the EPA is responsible, as well as providing a listing of regional offices and research facilities. Contact this office for your free copy.

* Gulf Breeze Environmental Center

Environmental Research Laboratory (ERL) Library
Sabine Island
Gulf Breeze, FL 32561 (904) 932-9218

The Gulf Breeze Environmental Research Laboratory (GBERL) library provides information services to GBERL employees and the general public. The library's subject areas include aquatic toxicology, microbiology, genetic engineering, pathobiology, marine ecology, and pesticide science. Databases maintained here include DIALOG and Ground Water On-line.

* Health Effects of Chemicals

Health and Environmental Review Division
Office of Toxic Substances
Environmental Protection Agency (EPA)
401 M St., SW, Room E617
Washington, DC 20460 (202) 260-4241

The Health and Environmental Review Division studies the hazards posed by new chemicals to human health and the environment, and for integrating these studies with exposure information from other EPA divisions.

* Health Risks and the Environment

Office of Health Research
Research and Development
Environmental Protection Agency (EPA)
401 M St., SW, Room 3100
Washington DC 20460 (202) 260-5900

This office conducts health assessment research which provides an integrated, scientific basis for evaluating environmental risks and effects stemming from exposure to various substances, and provides data needed to estimate human mortality and illness caused by pollutants.

* Help With Risk Assessment

Office of Toxic Substances
Chemical Library, TS-793
Environmental Protection Agency (EPA)
401 M St., SW
Washington, DC 20460 (202) 260-3944

Risk Assessment, Management, and Communication: A Guide to Selected Sources is a series of risk management bibliographies. References are gathered from the environmental, medical and scientific literature. Also available is *Communicating Environmental Risks: A Guide to Practical Evaluations* (EPA230-01-91-001), which was designed to help staff evaluate the effectiveness of their risk communication activities.

* Hotlines: EPA State and Local Site-Specific

Region II (800) 732-1223
This is a local hotline that provides site-specific regulatory information on Resource Conservation and Recovery Act only in the Region II areas of New York, New Jersey, Puerto Rico, and the Virgin Islands.

Region III (800) 438-2474
The EPA Region III Hotline provides general information on Agency programs to the public and makes referrals as needed. It provides this information for all Region III states: Washington, DC, Delaware, Maryland, Pennsylvania, Virginia, and West Virginia.

Region IV (800) 241-1754
The EPA Region IV Hotline provides general information on Agency programs to the public and makes referrals as needed. It provides this information for all Region IV states: Alabama, Florida, Georgia, Kentucky, Mississippi, North Carolina, South Carolina, and Tennessee.

Region V (800) 621-8431; (800) 572-2515 (IL)
The EPA Region V Hotline provides general information on Agency programs to the public and makes referrals as needed. It provides this information for all Region V states: Indiana, Michigan, Illinois, Minnesota, Ohio, and Wisconsin.

Region VII
The Region VII Hotline provides general information on Agency programs to the public and makes referrals a needed. It provides this information for all Region VII states: Iowa, Kansas, Missouri, and Nebraska. Kansas: (800) 221-7749; Nebraska, Iowa, and Missouri: (800) 223-0425.

Region VII (800) 223-0424
The Resource Conservation and Recovery Act Hotline in Region VII provides information on implementation of RCRA in Iowa.

Region VIII (800) 525-3022
The Region VIII Hotline provides general information on Agency programs to the public and makes referrals as needed. It provides this information for all Region VIII states: Colorado, Montana, North Dakota, South Dakota, Utah, and Wyoming.

Region IX (800) 231-3075
This is a local hotline that provides site-specific regulatory information on Resource Conservation and Recovery Act only in the Region IX areas of Arizona, California, Hawaii, Nevada, Guam, and Samoa.

* How Does The EPA Decide What's Good Or Bad For The Environment?

Environmental Impact
Office of Federal Activities
401 M St., SW
Washington, DC 20460 (202) 260-5075

An Environmental Impact Statement (EIS) is a document required of federal agencies for major projects or legislative proposals significantly affecting the environment. A tool for decision making, it describes the positive and negative effects of the undertaking and lists alternative actions. EPA reports all filed environmental impact statements in the Federal Register weekly. In addition, EPA's comments on the EOS are also published in the weekly *Federal Register*. For each EIS listed in the Register, a public contact is listed, along with the filing agency name and phone number. Contact the office listed above for referral information on EIS and copies of EPA comments only.

* Indian Affairs Field Offices

Bureau of Indian Affairs
U.S. Department of the Interior
Code 130, Room 4627N
Washington, DC 20240 (202) 208-3711

For information on American Indian lands, address your correspondence to: Area Director, Bureau of Indian Affairs, followed by the address listed below.

Alaska
P.O. Box 3-8000, Juneau, AK 99802; (907) 586-7177. Serving: Alaska

Arizona
P.O. Box M, Window Rock, AZ 86515; (602) 871-5151, ext. 5106. Serving: Navajo Reservations only, Arizona, Utah, and New Mexico
P.O. Box 10, Phoenix, AZ 85001; (602) 379-6600. Serving: Arizona, Nevada, Utah, and Idaho

California
Federal Office Building, 2800 Cottage Way, Sacramento, CA 95825; (916) 484-4682. Serving: California

Minnesota
Chamber of Commerce Building, 15 South Fifth St., 10th Floor, Minneapolis, MN 55402; (612) 349-3631. Serving: Minnesota, Iowa, Michigan and Wisconsin

Montana
316 North 26th St., Billings, MT 59101; (406) 657-6315. Serving: Montana and Wyoming

Environment and Nature

New Mexico
P.O. Box 26567, Albuquerque, NM 87125-6567; (505) 766-3170. Serving: Colorado and New Mexico

North Dakota
115 4th Ave., SE, Aberdeen, SD 57401; (605) 226-7261. Serving: Nebraska, North Dakota, and South Dakota

Oklahoma
WCD-Office Complex, P.O. Box 368, Anadarko, OK 73005; (405) 247-6673. Serving: Kansas and West Oklahoma
Old Federal Building, 5th and Okmulgee St., Muskogee, Oklahoma 74401; (918) 687-2296. Serving: East Oklahoma

Oregon
Federal Building, 1002 N.E. Holladay St., Portland, OR 97232-4182; (503) 231-6702. Serving: Oregon, Washington, and Idaho

Virginia
1000 N. Glebe Road, Arlington, VA 22201; (703) 235-3006. Serving: New York, Maine, Louisiana, Florida, North Carolina, Mississippi, Connecticut, and Rhode Island

Eastern Area
1951 Constitution Ave. NW, MS260, Washington, DC 20245; (703) 235-2571.

* Innovative/Alternative Environmental Clearinghouse

Innovative/Alternative Projects (304) 293-4191
This Clearinghouse provides information on innovative and alternative projects to enable communities and grant applicants to identify and contact other sources with experience in technologies.

* Inspector General's Whistle Blower Hotline

Environmental Protection Agency (EPA)
401 M St., SW
Washington DC 20460 (800) 424-4000
The Inspector General's Whistle Blower Hotline receives reports of EPA-related waste, fraud, abuse, or mismanagement from public and from EPA and other government employees. All calls are kept confidential. The Hotline operates Monday through Friday, 10:00 a.m. to 3:00 p.m.(EST).

* Insular Islands Assistance

Territorial and International Affairs
U.S. Department of the Interior
18th and C Sts., NW
Washington, DC 20240 (202) 208-4754
Technical assistance in the areas of social, political, and economic development is given to the Insular Islands by this office. The office is no longer involved in the government of the islands.

* Interior Department Freedom of Information

Freedom of Information Appeals Officer
U.S. Department of the Interior
18th and C Sts., NW, Room 2248
Washington, DC 20240 (202) 208-5339
Each bureau under the U.S. Department of the Interior has a separate office that handles concerns under the Freedom of Information Act. If you wish to obtain the officer's name within a particular bureau or wish to file with the central office, contact the officer above.

* International Environmental Conservation

Office of Ecology, Health and Conservation
Bureau of Oceans and International
Environmental and Scientific Affairs
U.S. Department of State
2201 C St., NW, Room 4325
Washington, DC 20520 (202) 647-2418
This office handles matters in two basic areas: 1) the conservation of nature and natural resources, such as wildlife, plant issues, and tropical deforestation; 2) international health issues, particularly AIDS. This office also works with other agencies in developing an international approach for the United States in dealing with these problems. Recently, they have been looking at debt leverage in third world countries to set aside land for new parks or to protect habitats.

* International Environment Policy

Bureau of Oceans and International Environmental
  and Scientific Affairs
U.S. Department of State
2201 C St., NW, Room 7831
Washington, DC 20520 (202) 647-1561
International political and economic relationships are increasingly affected by science and technology and by environmental issues. This bureau deals with U.S. foreign policy such specialized fields as nuclear physics, marine science, biotechnology, global climate, acid rain, and wildlife conservation. The bureau also manages bilateral science and technology agreements with ten countries and guides the development and implementation of several hundred other science and technology arrangements.

* International Marine Environmental Efforts

Environmental Coordination Branch
Marine Environmental Response Division
Office of Marine, Safety, Security, and Environmental Protection
U.S. Coast Guard
U.S. Department of Transportation
2100 2nd St., SW, Room 1202
Washington, DC 20593-0001 (202) 267-0421
Information is available here on the Coast Guard's role in international marine environmental efforts, such as representation in the U.N. International Maritime Consultative Organization. For further information on cooperative environmental efforts, contact the branch listed.

This office also handles all antarctic issues, law of the seas, maritime boundaries, and coordinates international marine science programs. Experts are available to answer questions and provide information.

* International Marine Science and Policy

Office of Marine Science and Polar Affairs
2201 C St., NW, Room 5801
U.S. Department of State
Washington, DC 20520 (202) 647-3262
This office handles international marine environment concerns, from the protection of whales to cleaning up oil spills, by negotiating bilateral and multilateral agreements.

* Land Use Engineering

Division of Engineering
Bureau of Land Management
U.S. Department of the Interior
1725 I St., NW
Washington, DC 20006 (202) 653-8811
For technical information concerning environmental engineering of roads, buildings, and recreational structures, contact the above office.

* Law Library

EPA Law Library
401 M St., SW
Room 2902
Washington, DC 20460 (202) 260-5919
The EPA Law Library provides information services to the Agency's legal and enforcement personnel, and to the ten Regional Counsels. The collection contains approximately 9,000 volumes of legal and law-related material concentrating on Federal law, with special emphasis on administrative and environmental law. Included are statutes, codes, regulations, case reports, digests, citators, and legal reference sources, as well as looseleaf services, newspapers, and 70 current law reviews and periodicals.

* Legislation

Environmental Legislative Library
832 West Tower, 401 M St., SW
Washington, DC 20460 (202) 260-5425
The Legislative Library primarily supports the Office of Legislative Analysis, but

Be patient. If any phone number is incorrect, call (area code) 555-1212 and request the new listing.

General Sources

also provides information for other EPA staff on request. The collection consists primarily of federal environmental legislation and related federal information. The library is mainly geared to the current Congress, but there are many older documents in the collection. The library responds to reference requests from EPA staff; supplies copies of Congressional documents when possible; tracks status of current environmental legislation; and compiles current status of pending environmental legislation organized by subject area. Databases maintained include Legi-Slate and the Congressional Quarterly Data Base (CQ).

* Minnesota-Based Environmental Lab

Environmental Research Laboratory Library
6201 Congdon Boulevard
Duluth, MN 55804 (218) 720-5538

This library's major fields of interest are analytical chemistry, fisheries biology, and water pollution. Its general collections cover analytical chemistry and fisheries biology.

* Minority and Disadvantaged Small Business Hotline

Office of Small and Disadvantaged Business Utilization
Environmental Protection Agency (EPA)
401 M St., SW (800) 368-5888
Washington DC 20460 (202) 557-7015 (DC area)

The Small Business Hotline is an EPA-based hotline that gives advice and information to small businesses on complying with EPA regulations. It deals with problems encountered by small-quantity generators of hazardous waste and other small businesses with environmental concerns.

* Monitoring Pollution

Office of Modeling, Monitoring Systems and Quality Assurance
Research and Development
Environmental Protection Agency (EPA)
401 M St., SW, Room 3702
Washington DC 20460 (202) 260-5776

This office provides data on monitoring systems and quality assurance research which develops standardized methods to measure and monitor pollutants in various media (water, air, soil).

* National Environmental Data Network

National Environmental Data Referral Service
NEDRES Office
National Oceanic And Atmospheric Administration
U.S. Department of Commerce
1825 Connecticut Ave., NW, Room 412
Washington, DC 20235 (202) 606-4548

The National Environmental Data Referral Service (NEDRES) is designed to provide convenient, economical, and efficient access to widely scattered environmental data. NEDRES is a publicly available service which identifies the existence, location, characteristics, and availability conditions of environmental data sets. NEDRES database contains only descriptions, not the actual data. It is a national network of federal, state, and private organizations cooperating to improve access to environmental data. Major subject categories include climatology and meteorology, oceanography, geophysics and geology, geography, hydrology and limnology, terrestrial resources, toxic and regulated substances, and satellite remotely sensed data. For more information on the NEDRES database and the user charges, contact the office listed above. NEDRES also produces the following printed catalogs with references to available environmental data on selected topics and regions:

Finding the Environmental Data You Need (free)
NEDRES Memorandum of Agreement (free)
NEDRES Database User Agreement (free)
NEDRES Data Base User Guide ($7.50)
Guideline for the Description of Environmental Data Files for the Nedres Database ($10)
North American Climatic Data Catalog: Part 1 ($10)
North American Climatic Data Catalog: Part 2 ($10)
Satellite Remote Sensing of the Marine Environment: Literature and Data Sources ($10)
Coastal and Estuarine Waters of California, Oregon, and Washington ($10)
Chesapeake Bay and Adjacent Wetlands
Chesapeake Bay Environmental Data Directory (free to federal and state agencies)
Environmental Data Review (free)

* Natural Landmarks Registry

National Registry of Natural Landmarks
National Registry Branch
National Park Service
U.S. Department of the Interior
1100 L St., NW
Washington, DC 20005 (202) 343-9536

The Park Service conducts natural region studies to identify areas that are of potential national significance. These areas are then studied in the field by scientists. Natural areas considered of national significance are cited by the Secretary of the Interior as eligible for recognition as Registered Natural Landmarks. The owner may apply for a certificate and bronze plaque designating the site.

* Natural Resources Library

Natural Resources Library
U.S. Department of the Interior
18th and C Sts., NW
Washington, DC 20240 (202) 208-5815

Information is provided to the general public on such topics as Native American Indians, mining and minerals issues, land reclamation and management, fish and wildlife, water resources, parks and outdoor recreation, and the preservation of scenic and historic sites. The library is open from 7:45 a.m. to 5:00 p.m., Monday through Friday. Computer searches can also be performed by their reference librarians.

* Need Help Finding The Right Expert?

Technical Assistance Directory
Center for Environmental Research Information
ORD Publications Unit
Environmental Protection Agency (EPA)
Cincinnati, OH 45268 (513) 569-7369

The *Technical Assistance Directory* is a free publication which lists programs, areas of expertise, and primary contacts in each of the major research and development areas within the EPA. This information is provided to improve communication and technology transfer, and would be useful for the environmental community, other federal agencies, and individuals who need to locate specific programs within ORD.

* One-Stop Shopping For Environmental Data

Gerald Barton
NOAA/NODC
1825 Connecticut Ave., NW
Washington, DC 20235 (202) 606-4548

The *NOAA Earth System Data Directory* helps pull together all the NOAA data files that are scattered throughout the U.S. This is an on-line computer guide to environmental data. This office can also provide you with a free monthly newsletter, *Earth System Monitor,* which is a guide to NOAA's Data and Information Services.

* Oregon-Based Environmental Lab

Environmental Research Laboratory Library
200 SW 35th St.
Corvallis, OR 97333 (503) 757-4731

The Corvallis Environmental Research Laboratory (CERL) Library was established in 1966with an emphasis on marine, estuarine, and fresh water quality, air and terrestrial research. At present the laboratory has three branches: Toxics and Pesticides, Hazardous Materials, and Water, and the Air. Research concerns acid precipitation and its effects on the ecosystem, wildlife toxicology, genetic engineering, wetlands, and hazardous waste. Databases maintained here include CIS, DIALOG, and NLM. General collections of the library include acid rain, air pollution-ecology, biology, estuarine research, genetic engineering, wetlands, wildlife toxicology. The library's special collection covers acid rain.

* Outer Continental Shelf Management

Offshore Minerals Management
Mineral Management Service
U.S. Department of the Interior
18th and C Sts., NW
Washington, DC 20240 (202) 208-3530

Management of the oil and gas operations following leasing agreements with the

Be patient. If any phone number is incorrect, call (area code) 555-1212 and request the new listing.

Environment and Nature

Mineral Management Service is outlined in the publication, *Managing Oil and Gas Operations on the Outer Continental Shelf.* This booklet describes activities through the drilling and production process to lease relinquishment.

* Outside Help For The EPA

Science Advisory Board (SAB), A-101
Environmental Protection Agency (EPA)
401 M St., SW, Room 1145 West Tower
Washington, DC 20460 (202) 260-4126

The SAB was established by Congress to provide independent scientific and engineering advice to the Administrator of the EPA on the technical basis for EPA regulations. The SAB deals with risk assessment (hazard identification, dose-response assessment, exposure assessment, and risk characterization) and only that portion of risk management that deals strictly with the technical issues associated with various control options. The SAB produces approximately 25 scientific reports a year in addition to a monthly newsletter called *Happenings,* and the *Annual Report of the Staff Director.*

* Park Service Technical Information

Technical Information Center
National Park Service
Denver Service Center
12795 W. Alameda Parkway
P.O. Box 25287
Denver, CO 80225-0287 (303) 969-2130

The Technical Information Center has been designated by the National Park Service as the central repository for all National Park Service-generated planning, design, and construction maps, drawings, and reports as well as related cultural, environmental, and other technical documents. Bibliographic data on aerial photography is also maintained. The Center reproduces and delivers copies of the available materials for the Service, other agencies, and the public, both here and abroad. Today, the system has a holding of 100,000 data records, which represent about 500,000 microfilm aperture cards of maps, plans, and drawings; 1,000 records of resource and site aerial photography; and 25,000 planning, design, environmental, cultural resource, and natural resource documents.

* Pipeline Safety

Office of Pipeline Safety (OPS)
Research and Special Programs Administration
U.S. Department of Transportation
400 7th Street, SW
Washington, DC 20590 (202) 366-4572

OPS establishes and enforces safety standards for the transportation of gas and other hazardous materials by pipeline. A computerized reporting system is maintained to collect and analyze accident and incident data from pipeline operators. Accident reports include the operator's name, the hazardous material involved, description of the accident, and results. For database searches, contact the office listed. There may be a charge.

* President's Council on Environmental Quality

Council on Environmental Quality
722 Jackson Place, NW
Washington, DC 20503 (202) 395-5750

This office was established by the National Environmental Policy Act of 1969 to formulate and recommend national policies to promote the improvement of the quality of the environment. There are three members on the Council appointed by the President by and with the consent of the Senate. The Council's major responsibilities are to provide opinion and policy advice to the President on environmental matters, to act with White House advisors and other agencies to develop international environmental policy, to interact as a liaison with representatives of foreign governments and international organizations about global environmental issues, to assist in coordinating federal environmental programs that involve more than one agency, to act in the review process for proposed legislation on environmental quality, and to prepare the annual *Environmental Quality Report* on environmental activities of all levels of government and of private entities.

* Prevent Pollution Near You

Pollution Prevention Clearinghouse
Pollution Prevention Office
Environmental Protection Agency (EPA)

401 M St., SW
Washington, DC 20460 (703) 821-4800

Through the Pollution Prevention Information Clearinghouse (PPIC) EPA's Pollution Prevention Office provides information on government and industry pollution prevention programs, grant and project funding opportunities, upcoming events, conferences, and seminars and contains the Electronic Information Exchange System (EIES). The EIES is a computerized information network that anyone can access, either through a PC with appropriate communication software or through the RCRA/Superfund Hotline (800-424-9346). The EIES lists documents available, provides a directory of experts and calendar of events, and enables you to leave your question on the bulletin board and the appropriate person will respond. The hotline provides a telephone service to answer or refer any pollution prevention questions, access information in the PPIC, provide instruction on accessing the EIES databases, and assist in document searches and ordering.

* Public Access to EPA Actions

Environmental Protection Agency (EPA)
401 M St., SW
Washington DC 20460 (202) 260-5926

The Public Information Reference Unit provides public access to regulatory information supporting the EPA's actions administered under the Clean Air Act and the Clean Water Act. Records are submitted to this office by the programs within EPA or the regions for public inspection and photocopying. This office also has information supporting other EPA regulations issued under the following statutes: Resource Conservation and Recovery Act, Safe Drinking Water Act, Noise Control Act, and the Marine Protection, Research and Sanctuaries Act.

* Quality Assurance

Office of Modeling, Monitoring Systems
and Quality Assurance
Research and Development
Environmental Protection Agency (EPA)
401 M St., SW, Room 3702
Washington DC 20460 (202) 260-5767

This office provides data on monitoring systems and quality assurance research which develops standardized methods to measure and monitor pollutants.

* Radon and Radiation Control

Office of Radiation Programs
Environmental Protection Agency (EPA)
401 M St., SW, Room NE108
Washington DC 20460 (202) 260-9600

The EPA, with a number of other federal agencies, protects the public from unnecessary exposure to ionizing radiation. EPA's major responsibilities are to set radioactive emissions standards and exposure limits, assess new technology, and monitor radiation in the environment in four areas: radiation from nuclear accidents, radon emissions, land disposal of radioactive waste, and radiation in groundwater and drinking water. The EPA fulfills these responsibilities by setting emissions standards for nuclear power plants, and for radionuclides in drinking water and in the air. EPA also prescribes work practices to reduce emissions of radon from underground uranium mines, develops radioactive waste disposal standards, and issues guidance to limit occupational exposure.

* Radon: Citizen's Guide

Public Information Center
Environmental Protection Agency (EPA)
401 M St., SW, PM-211 B
Washington DC 20460 (202) 260-7751

A Citizen's Guide to Radon helps readers understand the radon problem and decide if they need to take action to reduce radon levels in their homes. It explains what radon is, how it is detected, and what the results mean. Contact this office for your free copy.

* Radon Indoors

Radon Division
Office of Radiation Programs
Environmental Protection Agency (EPA)
401 M St., SW, Room NE200
Washington DC 20460 (202) 260-9622

Be patient. If any phone number is incorrect, call (area code) 555-1212 and request the new listing.

General Sources

The EPA's indoor radon program assists States in identifying areas with high indoor radon levels, researches, demonstrates, and evaluates techniques to reduce radon levels, and establishes standard methods for measuring radon levels. Contact this office for more information on radon standards.

* Reclamation Bibliography

Superintendent of Documents
Government Printing Office
Washington, DC 20402
(202) 783-3238

Publications on priorities within the Bureau are listed, including the safety of dams and a water measurement manual used in irrigation and municipal water facilities.

* Regulatory Information References

Environmental Protection Agency (EPA)
401 M St., SW
Washington DC 20460
(202) 260-5926

PIRU provides public access to regulatory information supporting the Agency's actions administered under (1) the Clean Air Act (primarily the State Implementation Plans), and (2) the Clean Water Act (primarily the Effluent Limitation Guidelines). Records are submitted to PIRU (indexed) by the programs within EPA or the Regions for public inspection and photocopying. PIRU also has information supporting other EPA regulations issued under the following statutes: Resource Conservation and Recovery Act (RCRA), Safe Drinking Water Act, Noise Control Act, and The Marine Protection, Research and Sanctuaries Act.

* Research Center

Andrew W. Briedenbach Environmental
Research Center Library
26 W. Martin Luther King
Cincinnati, OH 45268
(513) 569-7703

The major subjects in this library's collection are bacteriology, biology, biotechnology, chemistry, engineering, hazardous wastes, hydrobiology, microbiology, solid waste management, toxicology, water pollution, and water quality. Databases maintained here include BRS, CAS On-line, CIS, DIALOG, Dun & Bradstreet, Hazardous Waste Database, LEXIS/NEXIS, NLM, Toxline, and Toxnet. General collections include bacteriology, biology, biotechnology, microbiology, physics, solid waste management. This library's special collections cover the environment, Canada, legal issues, hazardous waste, and solid waste.

* Research Labs

Environmental Research Laboratories
National Oceanic and Atmospheric Administration
U.S. Department of Commerce
325 Broadway
Boulder, CO 80303
(303) 497-6286

The Environmental Research Laboratories conducts an integrated program of fundamental research, related technology development, and services to improve understanding and prediction of the geophysical environment comprising the oceans and inland waters, the lower and upper atmosphere, the space environment, and the Earth. Activities at its laboratories address such major areas as stratospheric and tropospheric ozone, the greenhouse effect and atmospheric chemistry, acid rain sources, transport and deposition, ocean role in climate, meteorological phenomena, solar disturbances, and computer modeling of oceanic conditions. . *Environmental Research Laboratories Programs and Plans* is a free publication which contains highlights of Laboratory accomplishments and abbreviated summaries of immediate objectives. More comprehensive and detailed descriptions of activities, results, and plans may be found in the laboratories' annual reports.

* Research and Technology Transfer

Center for Environmental Research Information (CERI)
Environmental Protection Agency (EPA)
401 M St., SW
Washington DC 20460
(513) 569-7562

The Office of Research and Development has centralized most of its information distribution and technology transfer activities in the Center for Environmental Research Information listed above. CERI also serves as a central point of distribution for ORD research results and reports.

* Resident Environmental Education

Environmental/Energy Education
Land Between The Lakes
Resource and Development
Tennessee Valley Authority
Golden Pond, KY 42231
(502) 924-1309

The Youth Station and Brandon Spring at Land Between The Lakes operates the residential education program to promote better environmental understanding, aesthetic appreciation, and man's place in nature. These dorm-style activity areas are open year-round and accommodate kindergarten through college-level groups. Groups are welcome to carry out their own programs, or the staff can help in developing them. Activities include canoeing, pond studies, and nature walks. With Murray (Kentucky) State University Center for Environmental Education, the staff provides additional workshops for area teachers and in-service students.

* Resource Conservation and Recovery Act Docket

Environmental Protection Agency (EPA)
401 M Street SW
Washington, DC 20460
(202) 260-9327

This Docket provides public access to regulatory information supporting the Agency's actions under RCRA. Records support Federal Register notices, Delisting Petitions, and other Office of Solid Waste (OSW) publications. RCRA Docket publishes a semiannual catalog of frequently requested documents. The RCRA Docket staff performs two primary functions: maintaining the docket and responding to information requests. The activities which are required for each function include maintaining the RCRA Docket, tracking regulations, organizing and storing information, and distributing and ordering documents.

* Resource Conservation and Recovery Hotline

CERCLA/RCRA Hotline
Environmental Protection Agency (EPA)
401 M St., SW
Washington DC 20460
(800) 424-9346
(703) 920-9810

This hotline answers questions concerning the Resource Conservation and Recovery Act, Superfund, and hazardous waste regulations. Requests for certain documents from the *Federal Register* and public laws are also handled in addition to referral to appropriate contacts. See also RCRA/CERCLA Hotline and Superfund Hotline.

* Right to Know Information Center (PIC)

Environmental Protection Agency (EPA)
401 M St., SW
Washington DC 20460
(202) 260-2080

The Public Information Center answers inquiries from the public about EPA, its programs, and activities and offers a variety of general, non-technical information materials.

* Safe Drinking Water Hotline

Environmental Protection Agency (EPA)
401 M St., SW
Washington DC 20460
(800) 426-4791

The Safe Drinking Water Hotline responds to questions concerning the Safe Drinking Water Act, Water Standards, Regulations, and the Underground Injection Program. It will also provide selected publications relevant to these issues. It operates Monday through Friday, 8:30 a.m. to 4:30 p.m. (EST).

* Sea-Grant Colleges

Office of Oceanic Research Programs
National Oceanic and Atmospheric Administration
U.S. Department of Commerce
1335 East-West Hwy.
Silver Spring, MD 20910
(301) 427-2448

The National Sea Grant College Program is a national network of over 300 colleges, universities, research institutions, and consortia working in partnership with industry and the federal government to support Great Lakes and marine research, education, and extension services. This program provides support for institutions engaged in comprehensive marine research, education, and advisory service programs, supports individual projects in marine research and development, and sponsors education of ocean scientists and engineers, marine technicians, and other specialists at selected colleges and universities.

Be patient. If any phone number is incorrect, call (area code) 555-1212 and request the new listing.

Environment and Nature

* Small Business EPA-Help Hotline

Environmental Protection Agency (EPA)
401 M Street SW (800) 368-5888
Washington, DC 20460 (202) 557-1938

The Small Business Hotline is an EPA-based hotline that gives advice and information to small businesses on complying with EPA regulations. It deals with problems encountered by small-quantity generators of hazardous waste and other small businesses with environmental concerns.

* Space Environment and Solar-Terrestrial Physics

Space Environment Laboratory
Environmental Research Laboratories
National Oceanic and Atmospheric Administration
U.S. Department of Commerce
325 Broadway
Boulder, CO 80303 (303) 497-3313

The Space Environment Laboratory provides real-time space environment monitoring and forecasting services, develops techniques for improving forecasts of solar disturbances and their effect on the near-Earth space environment, and conducts research in solar-terrestrial physics. An annual report is available which goes into more detail about the Laboratory, the research conducted, and lists the technical reports published.

* State Environmental Libraries

The following is a list of State Environmental Libraries which is part of an EPA initiative to support information sharing between EPA and the States. The collections vary from State to State, each having their own area of emphasis. These libraries are good local starting places.

Alabama
Alabama Public Library Service
6030 Monticello Dr.
Montgomery, AL 37130 (205) 277-7330

Alaska
Alaska Department of Environmental
Conservation Library
P.O. Box O
3032 Vintage Park Blvd.
Juneau, AK 99811-1800 (907) 465-2692

Arizona
Attorney General
Civil Division Research Room
1275 W. Washington
Phoenix, AZ 85007 (602) 542-1410

Arizona Department of Environmental Quality Library
2005 N. Central Ave.
Phoenix, AZ 85004 (602) 257-6959

Arizona Department of Water Resources Library
15 South 15th Ave.
Phoenix, AZ 85007 (602) 542-1550

Arkansas
Arkansas Department of Pollution Control and Ecology
Records Section
8001 National Dr.
Little Rock, AR 72219 (501) 562-7444

California
State Water Resources Control Board Law Library
901 P St.
Sacramento, CA 95801 (916) 323-0220

California Air Resources Board Library
1800 115th St.
Sacramento, CA 95812 (916) 323-8376

Department of Health Services
Toxic Substances Control Division
Technical Reference Library
714/744 P St.

P.O. Box 942732
Sacramento, CA 94234 (916) 324-5898

California State Resources Agency Library
1416 Ninth St., Room 117
Sacramento, CA 95814 (916) 445-7752

Delaware
Superfund Branch Library
Department of Natural Resources and Environmental Control, Superfund Branch
715 Grantham Lane
New Castle, DE 19720 (302) 323-4540

Florida
Environmental Library of Sarasota County
7112 Curtiss Ave.
Sarasota, FL 34231 (813) 924-9677

Florida Department of Environmental Regulation Information Center
2600 Blair Stone Rd.
Tallahassee, FL 32301 (904) 488-0890

State of Florida
Department of Natural Resources
903 W. Tennessee St.
Tallahassee, FL 32304-7795 (904) 488-9380

Georgia
Fernbank Science Center Library
156 Heaton Park Dr., NE
Atlanta, GA 30307 (404) 378-4311

Hawaii
Hawaii State Library
634 Pensacola St.
Honolulu, HI 96813 (808) 586-3500

Illinois
Illinois Hazardous Waste Research and Information Center Library
One East Hazelwood Dr.
Champaign, IL 61820 (217) 333-8957

Illinois Environmental Protection Agency Library
2200 Churchill Rd.
Springfield, IL 62794 (217) 782-9691

Indiana
Indiana Department of Environmental Management Law Library
105 South Meridian St., Fifth Floor
Indianapolis, IN 46206 (317) 232-8591

Iowa
Technical Library
Iowa Department of Natural Resources
Henry A. Wallace Building
Des Moines, IA 50319 (515) 281-8897

Kansas
Kansas Department of Health and Environment Library
Landon State Office Building
10th Floor
900 Jackson
Topeka, KS 66612 (913) 296-7901

Kentucky
Environmental Protection Information Center
18 Reilly Rd.
Frankfort, KY 40601 (502) 564-2150

Louisiana
Air Quality Information Resources Center
Air Quality Division
Department of Environmental Protection
625 North Fourth St., 8th Floor
Baton Rouge, LA 70804 (504) 342-1241

Be patient. If any phone number is incorrect, call (area code) 555-1212 and request the new listing.

General Sources

Ground Water Protection Library
Ground Water Protection Division
Department of Environmental Protection
P.O. Box 44274
Baton Rouge, LA 70804 (504) 342-8950

Waste Minimization Library
P.O. Box 44066
Baton Rouge, LA 70804 (504) 342-4656

Water Resources Library
Water Resources Division
Department of Environmental Protection
P.O. Box 44274
Baton Rouge, LA 70804 (504) 342-6363

Maine
Department of Environmental Protection and
 Department of Conservation Library
State House, Station #17
Augusta, ME 04333 (207) 289-7843

Maryland
Maryland State Department of the Environment
Toxics Information Center
2500 Broening Highway
Baltimore, MD 21224 (301) 631-3818

Massachusetts
Massachusetts Water Resources Authority Library
100 First Ave.
Boston, MA 02129 (617) 242-6000

State Library of Massachusetts
State House
Room 341
Boston, MA 02133 (617) 727-2590

Michigan
Michigan Department of Natural Resources
Surface Water Quality Division
P.O. Box 30028
Lansing, MI 48909 (517) 373-6794

Minnesota
Minnesota Department of Natural Resources
DNR Library
500 Lafayette Rd., Box 21
St. Paul, MN 55155 (612) 296-1305

Minnesota Pollution Control Agency
520 Lafayette Rd. North
St. Paul, MN 55155 (612) 296-7719

Montana
Department of Natural Resources and Conservation
 Research Center
1520 East Sixth Ave.
Helena, MT 59620 (406) 444-6700

New Hampshire
New Hampshire Department of Environmental Services
6 Hazen Dr.
Concord, NH 03301 (603) 271-2975

New Jersey
New Jersey Department of Environmental Protection
Information Resource Center
432 East State St, CN409
Trenton, NJ 08625 (609) 984-2249

North Carolina
Environmental Resources Library
North Carolina Department of Environment, Health, and Natural Resources
P.O. Box 27687
512 N. Salisbury St.
Raleigh, NC 27611 (919) 733-4984

North Dakota
North Dakota State Department of Health and Consolidated Laboratories
P.O. Box 5520
Bismarck, ND 58502 (701) 224-2374

Ohio
Ohio Environmental Protection Agency Library
1800 Watermark Dr.
Columbus, OH 43266 (614) 644-3024

Oklahoma
Oklahoma Department of Libraries
U.S. Documents Division
200 Northeast 18th St.
Oklahoma City, OK 73105 (405) 521-2502

Puerto Rico
Centro de Informacion
Environmental Quality Board
Biblioteca
Apartado 11488
Santurce, Puerto Rico 00910 (809) 767-7712

South Carolina
South Carolina Department of Health and Environmental
Control Library
Mill Building
2600 Bull St.
Columbia, SC 29201 (803) 737-3945

Texas
Texas Air Control Board Library
6330 Highway 290 East
Austin, TX 78723 (512) 451-5711

Texas Water Commission Library
1700 North Congress
P.O. Box 13087
Austin, TX 78711 (512) 463-7834

Virginia
Bureau of Toxic Substances Library
Virginia Department of Health
109 Governor St., Room 918
Richmond, VA 23219 (804) 786-1763

Virginia State Water Control Board Library
2111 North Hamilton St.
P.O. Box 11143
Richmond, VA 23230 (804) 367-6340

Washington
Department of Ecology Library
State of Washington Mailstop PV11
Olympia, WA 98504 (206) 459-6150

Wisconsin
Department of Natural Resources
P.O. Box 7921
Madison, WI 53707 (608) 266-8933

Alternate State Environmental Contacts
The following states do not have an environmental library, but are willing to provide environmental information upon request at the address and phone number listed below their state name.

Colorado
Colorado Department of Health
4210 East 11th Ave.
Denver, CO 80220 (303) 331-4510

Colorado Joint Review Process
Department of Natural Resources
1313 Sherman St., Room 719
Denver, CO 80203 (303) 866-3311

Be patient. If any phone number is incorrect, call (area code) 555-1212 and request the new listing.

Environment and Nature

Connecticut
Department of Environmental Protection
122 Washington St.
Hartford, CT 06106 (203) 566-3672

Idaho
Idaho Department of Health and Welfare
Division of Environment
450 West State St, Fifth Floor
Boise, ID 83720 (208) 334-5839

Mississippi
Mississippi Department of Natural Resources
Southport Center
2380 Highway 880 West
P.O. Box 20305
Jackson, MS 39209 (601) 961-5000

Missouri
Missouri Department of Natural Resources
Jefferson State Office Building
Jefferson City, MO 65102 (314) 751-3443

Nebraska
Nebraska Department of Environmental Quality
301 Centennial Mall South, Fourth Floor
P.O. Box 94877
Lincoln, NE 68509 (402) 471-4223

Nevada
Nevada Department of Conservation and Natural Resources
201 South Fall St.
Carson City, NV 89710 (702) 687-4670

New York
New York Department of Environmental Conservation
50 Wolf Rd.
Albany, NY 12233 (518) 457-5400

Rhode Island
Rhode Island Department of Environmental Management
9 Hayes St.
Providence, RI 02903 (401) 277-2771

North Dakota
Department of Water and Natural Resources
523 East Capitol St.
Pierre, SD 57501 (605) 773-3151

Tennessee
Bureau of Environment
Tennessee Department of Health and Environment
150 9th Ave.
Nashville, TN 32247 (615) 741-3657

Utah
Division of Environmental Health
Utah Department of Health
288 North 1460 West
Salt Lake City, UT 84116 (801) 538-6121

Vermont
Vermont Environmental Board
103 South Main St.
Waterbury, VT 05676 (802) 828-3309

West Virginia
State of West Virginia
Department of Natural Resources
Charleston, WV 26305 (304) 348-2754

Wyoming
Department of Environmental Quality
122 West 25th St.
Cheyenne, WY 82002 (307) 777-7938

* Tennessee Valley Authority Environmental Policy

Environmental Quality Staff
Tennessee Valley Authority (TVA)
Summer Place Building
Knoxville, TN 37902-6604 (615) 632-6578

Environmental protection and enhancement are a natural part of all TVA programs that affect the water, air, and land. This office provides centralized environmental guidance and direction to the entire agency, and is TVA's point of contact with Federal and State environmental regulators. To ensure meaningful citizen involvement in TVA's environmental activities and decisions, this office conducts periodic meetings with members of the environmental community to discuss matters of mutual interest. The public is also kept informed through advertised public meetings and the news media.

* Terminology and Acronyms

Public Information Center
Environmental Protection Agency (EPA)
401 M St., SW, PM-211 B
Washington DC 20460 (202) 260-7751

The free *Glossary of Environmental Terms and Acronym List* is designed to provide you with an explanation of the more commonly used environmental terms appearing in the EPA publications, news releases, and other Agency documents. The terms and definitions in this publication were selected to give the user a general sense of what a term or phrase means in relatively non-technical language. Contact this office for your free copy.

* Territorial and International Affairs

Territorial and International Affairs
U.S. Department of the Interior
18th and C Sts., NW
Washington, DC 20240 (202) 208-4822

International affairs within the U.S. Department of the Interior are handled by this office. If more than one Bureau is involved in an international effort, this office acts as the coordinator and liaison between the Department and the foreign constituent. The Department of the Interior has administrative responsibility for coordinating Federal policy in the territories of American Samoa, Guam, the Virgin Islands and the Trust Territory of the Pacific Islands, as well as oversight of all federal programs and funds in the freely associated states of the Republic of the Marshall Islands and the Federated States of Micronesia.

* Testing At The EPA

EPA Test Methods
Region 1 Library
Environmental Protection Agency (EPA)
JFK Federal Building
Boston, MA 02203 (617) 565-3298

Test methods are approved procedures for measuring the presence and concentration of physical and chemical pollutants, evaluating properties, such as toxic properties, of chemical substances, or measuring the effects of substances under various conditions. *Index to EPA Test Methods* consists of the following three sections: Numeric List by method number, Alphabetical List by chemical substance or method name, and Source List by document number. This is an attempt to coordinate, in one publication, an index to sources of EPA test methods and sampling procedures for laboratory analysis.

* Training Clearinghouse

EPA Institute
Environmental Protection Agency (EPA)
401 M St., SW
Washington DC 20460 (202) 260-6678

The national clearinghouse for all Agency training activities, from environmental science to enforcement to personal and professional development. The Institute focuses on in-house training, but serves as the Agency's training "broker" with other Federal agencies, State, and local governments, associations, and environmental organizations. Contact this Institute for more information on specific training programs.

* Transit Environments

Environment Division
Policy and International Affairs
Office of the Secretary of Transportation

Be patient. If any phone number is incorrect, call (area code) 555-1212 and request the new listing.

General Sources

U.S. Department of Transportation
400 7th Street, SW, Room 9217
Washington, DC 20590 (202) 366-4366

This is the DOT contact point for environmental issues. Staff can provide you with information and referrals on such subjects as highway beautification, transportation architecture, bicycle paths, historic preservation activities, environmental impact statements, and disabled access.

* TVA Natural Resources Protection

Resource Development
Tennessee Valley Authority (TVA)
400 W. Summit Hill Dr.
Knoxville, TN 37921 (615) 632-6367

The TVA's work with natural resources involves the whole range of environmental concerns. Today, with 20 million acres of forests in the Valley, TVA is working to adapt computer-age management to this valuable resource. TVA lakes and their 11,000 miles of shoreline provide an extensive resource for waterfowl protection, game management, and fisheries research. Industrial development and increased population intensify the necessity of protecting the natural environment. Research and testing continue to seek better ways to protect air and water; to dispose of and make use of wastes; to plan for the wise use and management of land; and to protect and preserve water tables and mineral resources, along with free-flowing streams, plants, and animal life.

* Undersea Research

National Undersea Research Program (NURP)
National Oceanic and Atmospheric Administration (NOAA)
U.S. Department of Commerce
6010 Executive Blvd.
Rockville, MD 20852 (301) 427-2427

The National Undersea Research Program develops programs and provides support to scientists and engineers for the study of biological, chemical, geological, and physical processes in the world's oceans and lakes. NURP assist researchers in conducting what are considered by NOAA and the marine community to be crucial research programs. In order to execute these programs, NURP provides investigators with a suite of the modern undersea facilities including submersibles, habitats, air and mixed gas SCUBA, and remotely operated vehicles. A major part of the research program is carried out by a network of National Undersea Research Centers. Contact this office for more information on the research conducted or the research centers.

* Up-To-The-Minute Research

Center for Environmental Research Information
Environmental Protection Agency (EPA)
ORD Publications Unit
Cincinnati, OH 45268 (513) 569-7369

The *ORD Publication Announcement* lists titles of printed publications from ORD. These lists provide interested parties with access to the broad range of currently available documents produced by ORD. Contact this office for your free copy.

* Want To Commercialize The Latest Technology?

Office of Technology Transfer and Regulatory Support
Larry Fradkin
Office of Research and Development
Environmental Protection Agency (EPA)
26 W. Martin Luther King Dr.
Cincinnati, OH 45268 (513) 569-7960

The Federal Technology Transfer Act makes possible cooperative research and development agreements (CRDAs) between federal laboratories, industry, and academic institutions. CRDAs set forth the terms of government/industry collaboration to develop and commercialize new technologies. Information about the FTTA and the associated CRDAs can be obtained from this office. They also have a one-page flier on the opportunities for Cooperative R&D with the EPA: The Federal Technology Transfer Act.

* Water Quality Criteria

Standards and Applied Science Division
Office of Water Regulations and Standards
Environmental Protection Agency (EPA)
401 M St., SW, Room E829
Washington, DC 20460 (202) 260-7301

The Clean Water Act requires each state to set water quality standards for every significian body of surface water within its borders. To set these standards, states specify the uses of each body of water (such as drinking water, recreation, commercial fishing), and restrict pollution to levels that permit those uses. The EPA assists the states in setting these standards and monitors them to make sure they meet the minimum required.

* What's The Latest At The EPA

EPA Publications
Information Management and Services Division, PM-211D
Environmental Protection Agency (EPA)
401 M St., SW
Washington, DC 20460 (202) 475-8710

The *EPA Publications Bibliography* contains bibliographic citations with abstracts for reports generated by EPA. It lists and indexes EPA technical reports and journal articles submitted to NTIS. This Bibliography is available for sale: National Technical Information Service (NTIS), Springfield, VA 22161; (703) 487-4650, (800) 553-NTIS.

* Woodsy Owl and Children's Materials

U.S. Department of Agriculture
Forest Service, P.O. Box 96090
Washington, DC 20090-6090 (202) 205-1785

To increase children's awareness of our delicate environment, the Forest Service's Woodsy Owl campaign has a variety of free materials available, including coloring sheets, detective sheets, song sheets, patches, *Woodsy Owl on Camping* (brochure), and stickers.

Be patient. If any phone number is incorrect, call (area code) 555-1212 and request the new listing.

Environment and Nature

Water and Air Quality

* Acid Rain and Aquatic Species Chart
Superintendent of Documents
Government Printing Office
Washington, DC 20402 (202) 783-3238
The wall chart, *Acid Rain: The Effect on Aquatic Species*, illustrates the survival of selected aquatic species in an acidic environment. Information is given on acid rain, its causes, and the effect on aquatic life. Measures 17 by 22 inches (S/N 024-010-00675-7, $3.25).

* Acid Rain Headquarters
National Acid Precipitation Assessment Program (NAPAP)
1100 Vermont Ave., NW
Washington, DC 20503 (202) 296-1002
NAPAP was established because of concern that acid rain might contribute to adverse effects on aquatic systems, forests, agricultural crops, construction materials and cultural resources, atmospheric visibility, and human health. NAPAP coordinates federally funded research and assessment activities concerning acid rain, and investigates the causes and effects of acid rain, as well as analyzing alternative strategies to control or mitigate those effects. NAPAP compiled the most comprehensive and quality-assured data base ever assembled for an environmental issue. Major activities of NAPAP will include interagency research, monitoring and assessment to determine whether acid rain impacts are reduced as a result of the mandated emissions reductions, and to assess the value of the improvements. A free quarterly newsletter is available which contains articles and information concerning acid rain, as well as listing recent NAPAP publications. Several important publications are available from: Superintendent of Documents, Government Printing Office, Washington, DC 20402; (202) 783-3238.

* *National Acid Precipitation Program 1990: Integrated Assessment Report*

* *1989 Annual Report of the National Acid Precipitation Assessment Program to the President and Congress, June 1990* (available from NAPA)

* *Background on Acidic Deposition and the National Acid Precipitation Assessment Program, September 5, 1990* (available from NAPA)

* *Acidic Deposition: State of Science and Technology* (6,200 pages long; a separate 250-page Summary Document is also available)

VOLUME 1 Emissions, Atmospheric Processes and Deposition
Report 1 Emissions Involved in Acidic Deposition Processes
Report 2 Atmospheric Processes Research and Process Model Development
Report 3 Regional Acid Deposition Modeling
Report 4 The Regional Acid Deposition Model and Engineering Model
Report 5 Evaluation of Regional Acidic Deposition Models
Report 6 Deposition Monitoring: Methods and Results
Report 7 Air Quality Measurements and Characterizations for Terrestrial Effects Research
Report 8 Relationships Between Atmospheric Emissions and Deposition/Air Quality

VOLUME 2 Aquatic Processes and Effects
Report 9 Current Status of Surface Water Acid-Base Chemistry
Report 10 Watershed and Lake Processes Affecting Surface Water Acid-Base Chemistry
Report 11 Historical Changes in Surface Water Acid-Base Chemistry in Response to Acidic Deposition
Report 12 Episodic Acidification of Surface Waters Due to Acidic Deposition
Report 13 Biological Effects of Changes in Surface Water Acid-Base Chemistry
Report 14 Methods for Projecting Future Changes in Surface Water Acid-Base Chemistry
Report 15 Liming Acidic Surface Waters

VOLUME 3 Terrestrial, Materials, Health and Visibility Effects

Report 16 Changes in Forest Health and Productivity in the United States and Canada
Report 17 Development and Use of Tree and Forest Response Models
Report 18 Response of Vegetation to Atmospheric Deposition and Air Pollution
Report 19 Effects of Acidic Deposition on Materials
Report 20 Processes of Deposition t Structures
Report 21 Distribution of Materials Potentially at Risk from Acidic Deposition
Report 22 Direct Health Effects of Air Pollutants Associated with Acidic Precursor Emissions
Report 23 Indirect Health Effects Associated with Acidic Deposition
Report 24 Visibility: Existing and Historical Conditions- Causes and Effects

VOLUME IV Control Technologies, Future Emissions, and Effects Valuation
Report 25 Technologies and Other Measures for Controlling Emissions: Performance, Costs and Applicability
Report 26 Methods for Modeling Future Emissions and Control Costs
Report 27 Methods for Valuing Acidic Deposition and Air Pollution Effects

* Acid Rain Program
Atmospheric Deposition Analysis
Water Resources Division
U.S. Geological Survey
National Center, MS 416
Reston, VA 22092 (703) 648-6875
The Geological Survey, in cooperation with other Federal agencies and many State agencies, is participating in a coordinated nationwide program to monitor the chemical composition of precipitation and selected streams and lakes that are now or may be affected by acid rain. Selected watersheds are also being studied to gain a better understanding of the hydrologic and geochemical processes that determine whether or not acid rain will ultimately affect the quality of water coming from the watershed.

* Air and the TVA
Atmospheric Science Department
Tennessee Valley Authority (TVA)
400 W. Summit Hill Dr.
Knoxville, TN 37902 (205) 386-2555
The Department assess trends in regional air quality, identifies air quality problems in the Valley, and provides technical assistance to air regulatory agencies and industry in correcting air quality problems. Information documents are produced to inform the public of regional air quality (both indoor and outdoor) problems and issues.

* Air Pollution and State Motor Vehicle Inspections
Records and Motor Vehicle Services Division (NTS-43)
National Highway Traffic Safety Administration (NHTSA)
U.S. Department of Transportation
400 7th Street, SW
Washington, DC 20590 (202) 366-2676
NHTSA's Motor Vehicle Inspection Program is aimed at providing car owners with preventative information on what repairs are needed to achieve greater safety, lower pollution, and better mileage. The annual *Study of the State Motor Vehicle Inspection Program* is available from this office.

* Air Pollutants, Asbestos and Consumer Safety Hotline
Consumer Product Safety Commission (CPSC) Hotline
5401 Westbard Avenue
Bethesda, MD 20207 (800) 638-2772
The CPSC hotline provides information on consumer safety and guidelines on exposure to formaldehyde, asbestos, and air pollutants. They offer copies of studies and other related documents.

Be patient. If any phone number is incorrect, call (area code) 555-1212 and request the new listing.

Water and Air Quality

* Air Pollution Emissions Hotline

Control Technology Center Hotline (919) 541-0800

The Control Technology Center Hotline is the component of EPA's Air Toxics Strategy. The Hotline provides information to State and local pollution control agencies on sources of emissions of air toxics. It operates Monday through Friday, 8:00 a.m. to 4:30 p.m. (EST). It also offers a wide range of engineering assistance and technical guidance. A quarterly newsletter containing relevant articles and a list of CTC publications is available.

* Air Quality and Climate Change

Atmospheric Sciences Department
Tennessee Valley Authority (TVA)
Resource Development
Chemical Engineering Bldg.
Muscle Shoals, AL 35660 (205) 386-2556

The TVA is working on a large scale air pollution control program. A current report, *How Clean Is Our Air?*, evaluates the levels of traditional air pollutants, as well as discussing emerging air quality issues, which include regional oxident pollution, acidic deposition, indoor air quality, toxic air pollutants, and climate change. A full-scale report will focus on various specific regional programs that address these issues. One example, the Middle Tennessee Ozone Study, is investigating the levels and sources of ozone in the greater Nashville metropolitan area as a cooperative effort between the TVA and the Tennessee Division of Air Pollution Control. Contact this office for more information on the study and the regional air quality control programs.

* Air Quality Planning and Standards

Office of Air Quality Planning and Standards
Environmental Protection Agency
Research Triangle Park, NC 27711 (919) 541-5618

This office develops national standards for air quality, emission standards for new stationary and mobile sources, and emission standards for hazardous pollutants. Contact this office for information on specific standards.

* Air Quality Standards Library

Office of Air Quality Planning
and Standards (OAQPS) Library
826 Mutual Plaza, MD-16
Research Triangle Park, NC 27711 (919) 541-5618

This library focuses on air pollution and control technology, including material on costs, chemical technology, minerals, and statistics. The reference collection emphasizes chemistry and engineering.

* Air Resources Laboratory (ARL)

Environmental Research Laboratory
National Oceanic and Atmospheric Administration
U.S. Department of Commerce
8060 13th St.
Silver Spring, MD 20910 (301) 427-7684

The Air Resources Laboratory performs weather research to understand and predict human influences on the environment, especially those involving atmospheric transport and dispersion of pollutants such as acid rain and ozone to distances up to thousands of kilometers. The ARL also monitors and interprets trends in natural and man-made substances, such as $CO_4$25, halocarbons, aerosols, and ozone which can potentially modify the climate. In addition, ARL studies solar radiation for its role in climate change. An annual report is available, which describes in more detail the current research being undertaken at ARL.

* Air Risk Hotline

Pollutant Assessment Branch, MD-13
Environmental Protection Agency
Research Triangle Park, NC 27711 (919) 541-0888

The primary purpose of the Air Risk Hotline is to provide an initial quick response based upon available health and exposure data and the expertise of EPA and its contractors. They can answer any question from companies, industry, or other EPA offices regarding indoor or outdoor air and can direct your call to the appropriate expert. The Clearinghouse collects, classifies, and disseminates air Toxics information submitted by State and local air agencies. The database contains two categories of information: air pollution control agency data and citations/abstracts.

* Air Toxics Information Clearinghouse

National Air Toxics Information Clearinghouse
MD-13
Environmental Protection Agency
Research Triangle Park, NC 27711 (919) 541-0850

The National Air Toxics Information Clearinghouse (NATICH) assists states in developing air toxics programs and setting emission levels. The Clearinghouse has a bimonthly newsletter, special reports, and a computerized database.

* Aquaculture Information

Aquaculture Information Center
National Agricultural Library Building
Beltsville, MD 20705 (301) 504-5704

This Information Center can answer questions regarding the culture of aquatic plants and animals in freshwater, brackish, and marine environments. They can also handle requests on eel culture, alligator farming, Spirulina farming, and aqatic snail culture (no fisheries industry information). They have access to a database, bibliographic information, and other publications.

* Aquatic Plants

Aquatic Biology Department
Resource Development
River Basin Operations
Water Resources
Tennessee Valley Authority (TVA)
Muscle Shoals, AL 35660 (205) 386-2278

TVA's two major weapons for controlling the spread of pesky aquatic plants, such as Eurasian watermilfoil, spiny-leaf naiad, and hydrilla in its reservoirs, is the winter and summer draw downs and the selective spraying of herbicides. Reservoir levels may be lowered several feet in the late summer to dry out and kill the roots of these plants embedded in shallow areas of the reservoirs; while at other times, lake levels may be held higher than normal to prevent sunshine from penetrating to the bottom and thus prevent germination and growth of new colonies. Selective use of approved herbicides in high priority use areas, such as swimming beaches, developed shoreline, and marinas, is another effective control method. Several experimental control strategies also are being tested on TVA lakes. One of the most promising is a cooperative effort between TVA and the U.S. Army Corps of Engineers. TVA proposes to conduct large scale demonstrations on Guntersville reservoir on the use of Grass Carp, hydrilla fly, a fungus to control watermilfoil, and other methods being currently tested on a smaller scale by the Corps Waterways Experiment Station.

* Aquatic Toxicology and Water Quality Research

Environmental Research Laboratory Library
College Station Rd.
Athens, GA 30613 (404) 546-3302

The Athens Environmental Research Laboratory (ERL) Library provides information services covering a wide range of environmental and management subjects. Subject areas include aquatic toxicology, microbiology, biology, pesticides, chemistry, water pollution, engineering, and water quality. Databases maintained here include CIS, DIALOG, and Ground Water On-line.

* Bibliography: Water Pollution and Resources

Superintendent of Documents
Government Printing Office
Washington, DC 20402 (202) 783-3238

Water conservation and management books are featured. The *National Water Summary* books on hydrologic events and the subscription service, *Soil and Water Conservation News*, are among the selections. Free.

* Boulder Canyon and Other Water Projects

Office of Public Affairs
Bureau of Reclamation
U.S. Department of the Interior
P.O. Box 25007
Denver Federal Center
Denver, CO 80225 (303) 236-7000

Contact the office above for their recent publications listing. Topics available include the following: annual reports and project data from the Bureau, Boulder Canyon Project reports, design standards, engineering manuals, research reports, technical records, and design and construction records, and other reports on

Be patient. If any phone number is incorrect, call (area code) 555-1212 and request the new listing.

Environment and Nature

subjects such as canals, dams, economic planning, environment, geology and rock mechanics, hydrology, and safety.

* Chesapeake Bay Regional Library

Central Regional Laboratory (CRL) Library
839 Bestgate Rd.
Annapolis, MD 21401 (301) 266-9180

This library was established in support of the Regional Laboratory which started in Annapolis in 1964. The subjects in the collection focus on biology, chemistry, ecology, engineering, hazardous waste hydrology, and oceanography. To serve the highly diversified expertise of the laboratory scientists and engineers, material is provided in aquatic biology, analytical chemistry, automated laboratory techniques, industrial wastewater monitoring, toxic and hazardous substances, and mathematical modelling. A special collections covers the Chesapeake Bay.

* Clean Air Act

Air Docket
Environmental Protection Agency
401 M St., SW, Room M 1500
Washington DC 20460 (202) 260-7548

The Air Docket provides public access to regulatory information which supports the Agency's actions administered under the Clean Air Act. The docket consists of files containing a series of file folders for each category of documents. Most of the records are on microfilm. Contact this office for more information.

* Clean Lakes Clearinghouse

Environmental Protection Agency
401 M St., SW
Washington, DC 20460 (800) 726-5253

The main purpose of the Clean Lakes clearinghouse is to collect, organize, and disseminate information on lake restoration, protection, and management to researchers, EPA personnel, lake managers, and state and local governments. A computerized database provides abstracts and citations to journal articles, technical reports, and conference papers. The Clearinghouse also responds to inquiries and provides printed bibliographies on lake topics. There is a Clean Lakes Clearinghouse Information Packet available free of charge. The Clearinghouse operated by the Terrene Institute for the EPA offers several EPA publications on lake topics including posters, fact sheets, Nonpoint Source publications, and the following:

Handbooks
Handle with Care: Your Guide to Preventing Water Pollution ($9.95)
Organizing Lake Users: A Practical Guide ($10)
Urban Runoff and Stormwater Management Handbook ($4.50)
Your ABC Guide to the Environment ($12.95)
Lake Maintenance Handbook (TBA)
Decisionmaker's Stormwater Handbook (TBA)
Pesticide Publications (TBA)

The regional Offices of the Clean Lakes program are as follows:

Region 1
Water Management Division
U.S. EPA-Region 1
JFK Federal Building
Boston, MA 02203 (617) 565-3515
(CT, ME, MA, NH, RI, VT)

Region II
U.S. EPA-Region II
Room 805
26 Federal Plaza
New York, NY 10278 (212) 264-8708
(NJ, NY, PR, VI)

Region III
U.S. EPA-Region III
841 Chestnut St.
Philadelphia, PA 19107 (214) 597-3429
(DE, DC, MD, PA, VA, WV)

Region IV
U.S EPA-Region IV

345 Courtland St., NE
Atlanta, GA 30365 (404) 347-2126
(AL, FL, GA, KY, MS, NC, SC, TN)

Region V
U. S. EPA-Region V
230 S. Dearborn St.
Chicago, IL 60604 (312) 886-0209
(IL, IN, MN, OH, WI)

Region VI
U.S. EPA-Region VI
1445 Ross Ave.
Dallas, TX 75202 (214) 655-7140
(AR, LA, NM, OK, TX)

Region VII
U.S. EPA-Region VII
Water Management Div.
726 Minnesota Ave.
Kansas City, KS 66101 (913) 551-7500
(IA, KS, MO, NE)

Region VIII
U.S. EPA-Region VIII
Suite 5000, 999 18th St.
Denver, CO 80202 (303) 293-1574
(CO, MT, ND, SD, UT, WY)

Region IX
U.S. EPA-Region IX
75 Hawthorn St.
San Francisco, CA 94105 (415) 744-2018
(AS, AZ, CA, GU, HI, MP, NV, TT)

Region X
U.S. EPA-Region X
1200 Sixth Ave.
Seattle, WA 98101] (206) 553-6911
(AK, ID, OR, WA)

* Dams and Steam Plants

Governmental and Public Affairs
Community Relations
Tennessee Valley Authority (TVA)
400 W. Summit Hill Dr.
Knoxville, TN 37902 (615) 632-2101

Washington Representative
Tennessee Valley Authority (TVA)
412 1st St, Room 300
Washington, DC 20444 (202) 479-4412

The TVA has constructed a system of dams and reservoirs to promote navigation on the Tennessee River and its tributaries, and to control destructive flood waters in the Tennessee and Mississippi drainage basins, and to also produce electric power. Citizens are welcome to tour and visit the dams and steam plants.

* Dam Safety

Engineering and Research
Bureau of Reclamation
U.S. Department of the Interior
P.O. Box 25007
Denver, CO 80225 (303) 236-6988

Safety of dams will continue to be a Bureau of Reclamation priority. The Department revises safety ratings annually, based on the latest technical information available for each dam operated by the Bureau.

* Deep Seabed Mining

Ocean Minerals and Energy Division
National Ocean Service
National Oceanic and Atmospheric Administration
U.S. Department of Commerce
1825 Connecticut Ave., NW

Water and Air Quality

Washington, DC 20235 (202) 673-5121
Extensive information is available on deep seabed mining, which includes the annual report to Congress and an updated environmental assessment of NOAA deep seabed mining licensees' exploration plans. This office can provide you with information regarding the research conducted concerning the environmental impact of the mining, as well as information on the regulations and licenses.

* Drinking Water Rules and Regulations

Environmental Protection Agency
401 M Street SW
Washington, DC 20460 (202) 260-3027
The Drinking Water Docket currently contains information on the following regulatory phases: (1) Volatile Organic Chemical (VOC) (Phase I); (2) Fluoride (Phase IIA); (3) Synthetic Organic Chemicals (SOC) (Phase II); (4) Surface Water Treatment Rule (SWTR); and (5) Radionuclides (Phase III). Others will be developed as new Maximum Contaminant Level Goals (MCLG) and Maximum Contaminant Levels (MCL) are proposed. These materials include appropriate *Federal Register* notices, letters, public hearing transcripts, National Drinking Water Advisory Council materials, public comments, technical support documents, and other materials.

* Drought Information

Tom Ross
Hydrologic Information Unit
Water Resources Division
U.S. Geologic Survey
419 National Center
Reston, VA 22092 (703) 648-6814
The Hydrologic Information Unit has up-to-date information on the drought conditions. They have over 500 collection sites from which they draw their data. They also have some limited historical information on droughts.

* Effluent Guidelines

Office of Water Regulations and Standards
Environmental Protection Agency
401 M St., SW
Washington DC 20460 (202) 260-7120
The Clean Water Act was designed to control the discharge of pollution into U.S. waters. Any industry that pumps waste water into U.S. waters must have a permit. The EPA develops effluent guidelines which set pollution limits for specific industries.

* Emissions Clearinghouse

Emission Factor Clearinghouse, MD-14
Environmental Protection Agency
Research Triangle Park, NC 27711 (919) 541-5477
The Clearinghouse is a means of exchanging information on air pollution control matters. It addresses the criteria pollutants and toxic substances from stationary and area sources, as well as mobile sources. Emission Factor Clearinghouse Newsletter is issued quarterly, and contains information on recent publications, inquiries about EPA emission inventory policy, newly developed emission factors, and requests for assistance in dealing with general or specific air pollution emissions. The Clearinghouse does have a database.

* Emissions Hotline

Control Technology Center Hotline (919) 541-0800
The Control Technology Center Hotline is the component of EPA's Air Toxics Strategy. The Hotline provides information to State and local pollution control agencies on sources of emissions of air toxics. It operates Monday through Friday, 8:00 a.m. to 4:30 p.m. (EST).

* English and Spanish Publications

Book and Report Sales
Box 25425
Denver, CO 80225 (303) 236-7476
This is a listing of some of the general interest publications available through the U.S. Geological Survey. They are free unless otherwise indicated.

Glaciers: A Water Resource
Ground Water

Ground Water and the Rural Homeowner
Rain: A Water Resource (Also available in Spanish)
River Basins of the United States
Save Water....Save Money
Water in the Urban Environment: Erosion and Sediment
The Water of the World
Water Use in the United States
What Is Water? (Also available in Spanish)
Why Is the Ocean Salty? (Also available in Spanish)

* Global Change

Environmental Protection Agency
401 M St., SW, W739
Washington, DC 20460 (202) 260-7750
This office works on curbing the use of greenhouse gases, such as Carbon dioxide and methane gas. They also work to protect the ozone layer through writing the national regulations for the Clean Air Act. They can provide you with information regarding global change.

* Great Lakes Research

Great Lakes Environmental Research Laboratory
Environmental Research Laboratories
National Oceanic and Atmospheric Administration (NOAA)
2205 Commonwealth Blvd.
Ann Arbor, MI 48105 (313) 668-2235
The Great Lakes Environmental Research Laboratory (GLERL) conducts research in support of resource management and environmental services in coastal and estuarine water, with special emphasis on the Great Lakes. The scientific programs are organized into six coordinated research programs considered critical to the NOAA mission and Great Lakes problems, and include: non-indigenous species, coordinated ecosystem research, climate variability and global change, pollutant research, climate effects, marine hazards and water management, and Green Bay coordinated research. Contact this office for more information.

* Greenhouse Effects and the Ozone

Climate Monitoring and Diagnostics Laboratory
Environmental Research Laboratories
National Oceanic and Atmospheric Administration
Boulder, CO 80303-3328 (303) 497-6966
Much of the Laboratory's advanced research focuses on three contemporary issues: greenhouse gas climate warming, stratospheric ozone depletion, and El Nino-Southern Oscillation effects on larger space-scale weather and climate. Levels are increasing for the gases that cause changes in the atmosphere, such as choloroflourocarbons. New, less damaging, but not damage free species are being introduced (ex. hydroflourocarbons), and this lab is responsible for long-term monitoring of these species.

* Greenhouse Effect- What Is It And What Are We Doing About It?

Committee on Earth and Environmental Sciences
C/O U.S. Geological Survey
104 National Center
Reston, VA 22092 (703) 648-4450
The Global Change Research Program was developed by a U.S. Federal interagency group, the Working Group on Global Change of the Committee on Earth and Environmental Sciences (CEES). An unprecedented partnership has evolved not only among the agencies of the U.S. government with global and regional environmental science responsibilities, but also with the scientific community. The agencies involved included the U.S. Departments of Interior, Energy, Commerce, and Agriculture, as well as the EPA, NASA, and NSF. The CEES formulated a comprehensive plan for the U.S. Global Change Research Program in Our Changing Planet: The FY 1990 Research Plan. This Plan reviewed the Earth system changes that have occurred in the past, the forces that are at work today, and the strengths and weaknesses in current environmental monitoring, understanding of fundamental processes, and predictive capabilities. Our Changing Planet: The FY 1991 Research Plan focused on establishing the research required to provide the scientific information needed as input to current environmental policy issues, e.g., stratospheric ozone depletion and climate change, including greenhouse warming. This publication outlines the research proposed, policy issues, current knowledge, the problems being faced, and possible solutions. The agency research projects that make up the Program are

Be patient. If any phone number is incorrect, call (area code) 555-1212 and request the new listing. 1111

Environment and Nature

summarized in the Appendix. The FY 1992 Report continues this theme outlining the research being conducted by each agency. This Office can assist you in locating the researcher responsible for conducting a specific experiment for further information.

* Groundwater and Contaminants

Robert S. Kerr Environmental Research
Laboratory Library
P.O. Box 1198
Ada, OK 74820 (405) 332-8800

The Robert S. Kerr Environmental Research Laboratory (RSKERL) is the Agency's center of expertise for investigation of the soil and subsurface environment. Important areas of research at RSKERL include the study of the chemical and microbial contamination of groundwater and the mathematical and computer modeling of both the movement of groundwater and the influence of various contaminants in this area of the environment. Sources of pollution, as well as migration and degradation of pollutants, are all topics of concern at RSKERL. Databases maintained here include Ground Water On-line.

* Groundwater Management

Resource Management, Bureau of Reclamation
U.S. Department of the Interior
P.O. Box 25007
Denver CO 80225 (303) 236-8367

A priority of the Bureau of Reclamation is groundwater management. The Bureau continues to work with state, regional, and local entities in support of the theory that the responsibility for groundwater management, allocation, and protection rests with the states. Several programs are focused on coordinating the use of surface water and groundwater, desalinization and improvement of water quality, control of high water tables through drainage, and technical assistance to other governmental agencies.

* Help Close To Home For Your Indoor Air Issues

Indoor Air Division (ANR-445-W)
Office of Air and Radiation
Environmental Protection Agency
401 M St., SW
Washington, DC 20460 (703) 308-8470

The *Directory of State Indoor Air Contacts* is a guide to locating individuals who can provide information and assistance on indoor air quality problems. It brings together information on more than 17 issues, from asbestos to wood preservatives, for the range of agencies involved in addressing those issues, from health agencies to energy departments. In most states, as well as at the federal level, indoor air quality issues are dealt with by a variety of agencies with the authority or expertise to focus on a particular problem or set of problems. This free directory is intended to make it easier to find the right contact.

* Home Water Treatment

R. Woods
Consumer Information Center-2A
P.O. Box 100
Pueblo, CO 81002

Buying a Home Water Treatment Unit is a pamphlet which discusses various units on the market and how to protect yourself from deceptive sales practices (429Y, $1.50).

* How Much Water Do We Have?

WATSTORE Program
Water Resources Division
U.S. Geological Survey
National Center
Reston, VA 22092 (703) 648-5686

Water-data stations at selected locations throughout the U.S. are used by the Geological Survey to obtain records on stream discharge (flow) and stage (height), reservoir and lake stage and storage, ground water levels, well and spring discharge, and the quality of surface and ground water. These data provide a continuing record of the quantity and quality of the Nation's surface- and ground-water resources. All data collected are stored in WATSTORE (National Water Data Storage and Retrieval System), and can be retrieved in machine-readable form or as computer printed tables or graphs, statistical analyses, and digital plots.

* How Much Water Do You Use?

National Water-Use Information Program
Branch of Water-Use Information
U.S. Geological Survey
Reston, VA 22092 (703) 648-5670

This program provides for the comprehensive and systematic collection of data on water use throughout the U.S. Cooperating states collect the water-use data and aggregate these data by county and hydrologic unit. The point data are stored in a state level data base; the aggregated data are compiled by the Geological Survey for incorporation into the computerized National Water-use Data System.

* Hydroelectric Power

Resource Management
Bureau of Reclamation
U.S. Department of the Interior
P.O. Box 25007
Denver CO 80225 (303) 236-1058

The Bureau of Reclamation is currently operating 49 powerplants at different sites throughout the West. This office has design and technical and other publications on hydroelectric power. They can answer questions and refer you to other experts in the field. For further information on the impact of hydroelectric power and the Bureau's efforts, contact this office.

* Hydrographic Research

Commission Personnel Division, NOAA Corps
National Oceanic and Atmospheric Administration (NOAA)
U.S. Department of Commerce
11400 Rockville Pike
Rockville, MD 20852 (301) 443-8648

The NOAA Corps is the uniformed service of the U.S. Department of Commerce responsible for operating and managing NOAA's fleet of hydrographic, oceanographic, and fisheries-research ships and for supporting NOAA scientific programs. Engineering, computer science, mathematics, and science baccalaureate or higher degree graduates are sought for positions in the Corps.

* Is Your Drinking Water Safe?

Public Information Center (PIC)
Environmental Protection Agency
401 M St., SW, PM-211B
Washington, DC 20460 (202) 260-7751

PIC can provide you with free general publications on the safety of your drinking water, including: *Is Your Drinking Water Safe?*- This brochure explains the Safe Drinking Water Act, drinking water standards, what the numbers mean, and your state resources.

* Lake Protection and Restoration

Clean Lakes Program
Office of Water Regulations and Standards
Environmental Protection Agency
401 M St., SW
Washington DC 20460 (202) 260-7105

The EPA's Clean Lakes Program provides technical and financial assistance to States for programs dealing with lake restoration and protection.

* Lead and Your Drinking Water

Public Information Center
Environmental Protection Agency
401 M St., SW, PM-211 B
Washington DC 20460 (202) 260-7751

The free brochure, *Lead and Your Drinking Water*, explains the dangers of lead in your drinking water, how it gets there, and steps you can take to remove the lead.

* Local Air Pollution Control Hotline

Best Available Control Technology
Lowest Achievable Emission Rate Clearinghouse
Environmental Protection Agency

Be patient. If any phone number is incorrect, call (area code) 555-1212 and request the new listing.

Water and Air Quality

Research Triangle Park, NC 27711 (919) 541-2736 This Clearinghouse was established to enable State and local air pollution control agencies to exchange information on Reasonably Available Control Technology, BACT/LAER determinations for new or modified sources, and to facilitate more consistent emission levels.

* Marine, Coastal, Estuarine Water Quality

Environmental Research Laboratory Library South Ferry Rd. Narragansett, RI 02882 (401) 782-3025

The Environmental Research Laboratory Narragansett (ERLN), with its field station in Newport, Oregon, is the EPA's center for marine, coastal, and estuarine water quality research. General collections cover aquatic toxicology, biological oceanography, biomedical science, coastal research, fisheries biology, marine biology, marine ecology, marine organisms. The special collections cover: o Estuarine and marine disposal and discharge of complex wastes, dredged materials, and other wastes; o Water use designation and quality criteria for estuarine and marine water and sediment; o Environmental assessment of ocean discharge.

* Marine Environment and Ocean Dumping

Wetlands, Oceans, and Watersheds Environmental Protection Agency 401 M St., SW Washington DC 20460 (202) 260-7102

This office carries out the duties covered under the Marine Protection, Research and Sanctuaries Act, which is designed to protect the marine environment from the harmful effects of ocean dumping. The Act establishes a permit program to ensure that ocean dumping does not cause degradation of the marine environment. Contact this office for more information on ocean dumping regulation.

* Mosquito Control

Aquatic Biology Department River Basin Operations Water Resources 1220SA Tennessee Valley Authority (TVA) Muscle Shoals, AL 35660 (205) 386-3430

This office investigates complaints regarding the mosquito population around the TVA waters and lands. They will use an adulticide and a larvacide if needed. This office has done research regarding the killing of mosquitoes. They also run an inspection program May through October. If you have a mosquito problem outside the TVA jurisdiction, contact your local health department. You may be part of a mosquito control abatement district. The health department may also have information regarding mosquitoes.

* Motor Vehicle Emissions

Motor Vehicle Emissions Laboratory Library 2565 Plymouth Rd. Ann Arbor, MI 48105 (313) 668-4311

This library provides information services concentrated on automotive engineering to EPA staff and the general public. Subject areas include air pollution from mobile sources, alternative alcohol fuels, and motor vehicle retrofit devices.

* Motor Vehicle Emissions

Motor Vehicle Anti-Tampering Program Office of Mobile Sources EN-397F 401 M St., SW Washington, DC 20460 (202) 260-2640

The Motor Vehicle Anti-Tampering Program is administered by the Office of Mobile Sources. The program provides the public (especially gas station and garage owners, and the oil and gas industry) with information pertaining to enforcement of tampering regulations in the form of pamphlets and public documents as well as information over the phone. They inspect gas stations and garages regarding compliance with tampering regulations and coordinate state and local inspection programs. Staff can answer questions concerning regulation, gasoline additives and emissions standards. They also can respond to catalytic converter warranty inquiries.

* Municipal, Recreation, Industrial Water Supply

U.S. Department of Agriculture (USDA) Deputy for Programs, SCS Box 2890 Washington, DC 20013 (202) 720-4527

The USDA manages a variety of water resource programs to aid landowners and agricultural operators use existing water resources wisely. These programs also promote reclamation and preservation of water sources that have been contaminated or allowed to fall into disrepair and to monitor recreation, municipal, and industrial water supply.

* National Ocean Service

National Oceanic and Atmospheric Administration U.S. Department of Commerce 6001 Executive Blvd. Rockville, MD 20852 (301) 443-8487

The Office of Ocean Resources, Conservation and Assessments surveys and monitors the oceans, U.S. coastal waters, estuarine waterways, and the Great Lakes to produce data and information products that describe the physical properties of these waters for a wide range of engineering and navigational applications. This office also conducts studies to assess the environmental impact of human activities in U.S. coastal waters. Many of these marine data and information products are essential for protecting life and property from storms and other destructive natural forces. Other marine products, such as predictions of the times and heights of tides and descriptions of tidal currents, are vital for safe navigation.

* National Water Conditions Monthly Update

Hydrologic Information Unit Water Resources Division U.S. Geological Survey 419 National Center Reston, VA 22092 (703) 648-6817

National Water Conditions is a monthly summary of hydrologic conditions in the United States and southern Canada. Subscriptions are free upon application.

* Ocean and Coastal Pollution

Office of Ocean Resources, Conservation and Assessments National Ocean Service National Oceanic and Atmospheric Administration U.S. Department of Commerce 6001 Executive Blvd. Rockville, MD 20852 (301) 443-8487

This office surveys and monitors the oceans, U.S. coastal waters and the Great Lakes to produce data and information products that are critically important for offshore oil and gas exploration, dredging operations, coastal and offshore construction, seafloor mining, waste disposal management, and for protecting the marine environment from the adverse effects of ocean and coastal pollution.

* Ocean Dumping Surveillance and Marine Technology Library

Coast Guard Research and Development Center U.S. Coast Guard U.S. Department of Transportation Avery Point Groton, CT 06340-6096 (203) 441-2648

Marine research is conducted here in areas such as ice technology, navigation instrumentation technology, ocean dumping surveillance, pollution, search and rescue techniques, and marine fire and safety technology. This library is a good starting point for obtaining specific information about what research is done by the Center and for referrals to appropriate experts.

* Oceanographic Corps Jobs

Commission Personnel Division NOAA Corps National Oceanic and Atmospheric Administration (NOAA) U.S. Department of Commerce 11400 Rockville Pike Rockville, MD 20852 (301) 443-8648

The NOAA Corps is the uniformed service of the U.S. Department of

Be patient. If any phone number is incorrect, call (area code) 555-1212 and request the new listing.

Environment and Nature

Commerce responsible for operating and managing NOAA's fleet of hydrographic, oceanographic, and fisheries-research ships and for supporting NOAA scientific programs. Engineering, computer science, mathematics, and science baccalaureate or higher degree graduates are sought for positions in the Corps.

* Ocean Pollution Information Network

Ocean Pollution Data and
Information Network/CCRO
National Oceanographic Data Center
National Oceanic and Atmospheric Administration
1825 Connecticut Ave., NW
Washington, DC 20235 (202) 606-4539

The Ocean Pollution Data and Information Network (OPDIN) facilitates user access to ocean pollution data and information generated by 11 participating Federal departments and agencies. OPDIN provides a wide range of products and services to researchers, managers, and others who need data and information about ocean pollution. OPDIN is managed by the Central Coordination and Referral Office (CCRO). The CCRO maintains a directory of Federal ocean pollution data and information systems and services, lists of ocean pollution scientists and managers and their fields of expertise, and annually-updated catalogs of Federal marine pollution research, development, and monitoring projects. The CCRO also provides information and advice about ocean pollution data management and processing, as well as copies of catalogs, directories, technical reports, data inventories, and data products.

* Oil and Chemical Spills Hotline

National Response Center (NRC)
Marine Environmental Response Division
Office of Marine Safety, Security, and Environmental Protection
U.S. Coast Guard
U.S. Department of Transportation
2100 2nd St., SW, Room 2611 (800) 424-8802
Washington, DC 20593 (202) 267-2188

The NRC receives reports of oil and hazardous substance spills, investigates incidents, initiates civil penalty actions, monitors cleanups, and coordinates federally funded spill response operations. NRC's National Strike Force assists federal coordinators on the scene in responding to pollution accidents. For further details, or to report information, contact the Center toll-free.

* Ozone Database

Office of Air and Radiation
Environmental Protection Agency
401 M St., SW
Washington, DC 20460 (202) 260-9403

OZONET is an electronic database that supplies information regarding substitutes and alternative processes to ozone-depleting solvents. In addition, it includes contacts, regulatory information, relevant articles, an electronic bulletin board, and other services.

* Ozone Production

Aeronomy Laboratory
Environmental Research Laboratory
National Oceanic and Atmospheric Administration
Boulder, CO 80303 (303) 497-5785

Extensive research is being conducted concerning regional and global ozone production, as well as studying the ozone in the Antarctic. Research is also being conducted on hydrocloroflourocarbons which are becoming the substitutes for the ozone-destroying CFCs. This laboratory can direct you to the appropriate researcher for your area of interest, and can provide you with relevant articles and reports.

* Pacific Research

Pacific Marine Environmental Laboratory
Environmental Research Laboratories
National Oceanic and Atmospheric Administration
7600 Sand Point Way NE
Bin No. C15700
Seattle, WA 98115 (206) 526-6810

The Pacific Marine Environmental Laboratory carries out interdisciplinary scientific investigations in oceanography, marine meteorology, and related

subjects. Current programs focus on climate, marine observation and prediction, marine resources, and marine environmental assessment. Contact this office for further information.

* Pollution Response Operations

Pollution Response Branch
Marine Environmental Response Division
Office of Marine Safety, Security,
and Environmental Protection
U.S. Coast Guard
U.S. Department of Transportation
2100 2nd St., SW, Room 2104 (202) 267-0518
Washington, DC 20593-0001 (202) 267-2611

This office responds to requests for marine environmental protection information from Congress and other federal agencies, state agencies, schools, industries, and the general public. Data is available on laws relating to the protection of the marine environment, incidents involving releases of oil or other hazardous substances, and federally funded spill response operations.

* Project Skywater: Cloud Seeding

Cloud Seeding - Project Skywater
Water Augmentation Group, Code D-3720
Research and Laboratory Services Division
Bureau of Reclamation
U.S. Department of the Interior
P.O. Box 25007
Denver, CO 80225-0007 (303) 236-4346

Project Skywater is a weather modification project which attempts to change natural phenomena such as clouds, rain, snow, hail, lightning, thunderstorms, tornadoes, fog, and hurricanes so they are more beneficial or less destructive. Foreign assistance programs are also underway with Morocco, and Thailand.

* Radon Hotline

National Radon Hotline
Box 16622
Alexandria, VA 22302 (800) 767-7236

This is a 24 hour toll free hotline where a message records your name and address and a brochure on radon is sent via first class mail. The brochure gives some basic information concerning radon, as well as information on a radon detection kit available from the National Safety Council.

* Radon Removal

Public Information Center PM211-B
Environmental Protection Agency
401 M St., SW
Washington, DC 20460 (202) 260-7751

The EPA has published the following free publications regarding Radon and its removal;

A Citizen's Guide to Radon: What It Is And What To Do About It- designed to help readers understand the radon problem and decide if they need to take action to reduce radon levels in their homes.

Removal Of Radon From Household Water- the EPA is studying ways to reduce radon in houses; including methods to remove the gas from water to prevent its release in houses when the water is used. While the work has not yet answered all the questions about household water treatment systems, they are publishing what information they have that may be of immediate use to homeowners.

Radon Reduction in New Construction- This is designed to provide radon information for those involved in new construction and to introduce methods that can be used during construction to minimizer radon entry and facilitate its removal after construction is complete.

Radon Reduction Methods: A Homeowner's Guide- This is designed for homeowners who have already tested their houses for radon and decided that they need to take some action, as well as those who are still uncertain. The information provided should be helpful for homeowners who have the skills and equipment needed for "do-it-yourself" radon reduction work, as well as for homeowners who decide to hire contractors to perform the needed work.

Be patient. If any phone number is incorrect, call (area code) 555-1212 and request the new listing.

Water and Air Quality

* Regional Hydrologists

Water Resources Division
U.S. Geological Survey
409 National Center
Reston, VA 22092 (703) 648-5215

The U.S. Geological Survey has the following hydrologist field offices:

Northeastern Region
Regional Hydrologist, U.S. Geological Survey, 433 National Center, Reston, VA 22092; (703) 648-5817. Serving: CT, DE, IL, IN, ME, MD, MA, MI, MN, NH, NJ, NY, OH, PA, RI, VT, VA, DC, WV, WI

Southeastern Region
Regional Hydrologist, U.S. Geological Survey, Spalding Woods Office Park, Suite 160, 3850 Holcomb Bridge Rd., Norcross, GA 30092; (404) 409-7700. Serving: AL, AR, FL, GA, KY, LA, MS, NC, PR, SC, TN, Virgin Islands

Central Region
Regional Hydrologist, U.S. Geological Survey, Mail Stop 406, Box 25046, Denver Federal Center, Lakewood, CO 80225; (303) 236-5920. Serving: CO, IA, KS, MO, MT, NE, NM, ND, OK, SD, TX, UT, WY

Western Region
Regional Hydrologist, U.S. Geological Survey, 345 Middlefield Rd., Mail Stop 470, Menlo Park, CA 94025. Serving: AK, AR, CA, Guam, HI, ID, NV, OR, WA

* Rural Non-Source Water Pollution

U.S. Department of Agriculture (USDA)
Deputy for Programs, SCS
Box 2890
Washington, DC 20013 (202) 720-4527

The USDA manages a variety of water resource programs to aid landowners and agricultural operators use existing water resources wisely. The Rural Clean Water Program to reduce non-source water pollution is one of its programs, which aims to prevent or reduce the amount of sediment, chemicals, livestock wastes, and other agricultural pollutants from entering streams and lakes.

* Safe Drinking Water Hotline

Environmental Protection Agency
401 M Street SW
Washington, DC 20460 (800) 426-4791

The Safe Drinking Water Hotline responds to questions concerning the Safe Drinking Water Act, Water Standards, Regulations, and the Underground Injection Program. It will also provide selected publications relevant to these issues. It operates Monday through Friday, 8:30 a.m. to 4:30 p.m. (EST).

* Sea-Grant Colleges

Office of Oceanic Research Programs
National Oceanic and Atmospheric Administration
U.S. Department of Commerce
1335 East-West Hwy.
Silver Spring, MD 20910 (301) 427-2448

The National Sea Grant College Program is a national network of over 300 colleges, universities, research institutions, and consortia working in partnership with industry and the federal government to support Great Lakes and marine research, education, and extension services. This program provides support for institutions engaged in comprehensive marine research, education, and advisory service programs, supports individual projects in marine research and development, and sponsors education of ocean scientists and engineers, marine technicians, and other specialists at selected colleges and universities.

* State Drinking Water Programs

State Programs Division
Office of Drinking Water
Environmental Protection Agency
401 M St., SW, Room E1101
Washington DC 20460 (202) 260-5526

This office oversees the drinking water regulations that are part of the Clean Water Act at the regional and State level. They make sure a State's standards meet at least the minimum requirements of the law, and they are also responsible for their enforcement.

* State Radon Contacts

Your State Radon Office can answer all your questions regarding radon, including providing informational brochures and referrals for testing and removal of radon gas.

Alabama
Radiological Health Branch
Alabama Department of Public Health
State Office Building
Montgomery, AL 36130 (205) 261-5313

Alaska
Alaska Department of Health and Social Services
P.O. Box H-06F
Juneau, AK 99811 (907) 465-3019

Arizona
Arizona Radiation Regulatory Agency
4814 South 40th St.
Phoenix, AZ 85040 (602) 255-4845

Arkansas
Division of Radiation Control and Emergency Management
Arkansas Department of Health
4815 W. Markham St.
Little Rock, AR 72205 (501) 661-2301

California
Indoor Quality Program
California Department of Health Services
2151 Berkeley Way
Berkeley, CA 94704 (415) 540-2134

Colorado
Radiation Control Division
Colorado Department of Health
4210 E. 11th Ave.
Denver, CO 80220 (303) 331-4812

Connecticut
Connecticut Department of Health Services
Toxic Hazards Section
150 Washington St.
Hartford, CT 06106 (203) 566-8167

Delaware
Division of Public Health
Delaware Bureau of Environmental Health
P.O. Box 637
Dover, DE 19903 (302) 736-4731

District of Columbia
DC Department of Consumer and Regulatory Affairs
614 H St., NW, Room 1014
Washington, DC 20001 (202) 727-7728

Florida
Florida Office of Radiation Control
Building 18, Sunland Center
P.O. Box 15490
Orlando, FL 32858 (305) 297-2095

Georgia
Georgia Department of Natural Resources
Environmental Protection Division
205 Butler St., SE
Floyd Towers East, Suite 1166
Atlanta, GA 30334 (404) 656-6905

Hawaii
Environmental Protection and Health Services Division
Hawaii Department of Health
591 Ala Moana Blvd.
Honolulu, HI 96813 (808) 548-4383

Idaho
Radiation Control Section

Be patient. If any phone number is incorrect, call (area code) 555-1212 and request the new listing.

Environment and Nature

Idaho Department of Health and Welfare
Statehouse Mall
Boise, ID 83720 (208) 334-5879

Illinois
Illinois Department of Nuclear Safety
Office of Environmental Safety
1035 Outer Park Dr. (217) 546-8100
Springfield, IL 62704 (800) 225-1245 (in State)

Indiana
Division of Industrial Hygiene and Radiological Health
Indiana State Board of Health
1330 W. Michigan St.
P.O. Box 1964
Indianapolis, IN 46206 (317) 633-0153

Iowa
Bureau of Environmental Health
Iowa Department of Public Health
Lucas State Office Building
Des Moines, IA 50319 (515) 281-7781

Kansas
Kansas Department of Health and Environment
Forbes Field, Building 321
Topeka, KS 66620 (913) 862-9360 ext. 288

Kentucky
Radiation Control Branch
Cabinet of Human Resources
275 East Main St.
Frankfort, KY 40621 (502) 564-3700

Louisiana
Louisiana Nuclear Energy Division
P.O. Box 14690
Baton Rouge, LA 70898 (504) 925-4518

Maine
Division of Health Engineering
Maine Department of Human Services
State House Station 10
Augusta, ME 04333 (207) 289-3826

Maryland
Radiation Control
Department of the Environment
7th Floor Mailroom
201 W. Preston St. (301) 333-3130
Baltimore, MD 21201 (800) 872-3666

Massachusetts
Radiation Control Program
Massachusetts Department of Public Health
23 Service Center (413) 586-7525
North Hampton, MA 01060 (617) 727-6214 (Boston)

Michigan
Michigan Department of Public Health
Division of Radiological Health
3500 North Logan
P.O. Box 30035
Lansing, MI 48909 (517) 335-8190

Minnesota
Section of Radiation Control
P.O. Box 9441
717 SE Delaware St.
Minnesota Department of Health (612) 623-5350
Minneapolis, MN 55440 (800) 652-9747

Mississippi
Division of Radiological Health
Mississippi Department of Health
P.O. Box 1700
Jackson, MS 39215 (601) 354-6657

Missouri
Bureau of Radiological Health
Missouri Department of Health
1730 E. Elm, P.O. Box 570
Jefferson City, MO 65102 (314) 751-6083

Montana
Occupational Health Bureau
Montana Department of Health and
Environmental Sciences
Cogswell Building A 113
Helena, MT 59620 (406) 444-3671

Nebraska
Division of Radiological Health
Nebraska Department of Health
301 Centennial Mall South
P.O. Box 95007
Lincoln, NE 68509 (402) 471-2166

Nevada
Radiological Health Section
Health Division
Nevada Department of Human Resources
505 King St. Room 202
Carson City, NV 89710 9702) 885-5394

New Hampshire
New Hampshire Radiological Health Program
Health and Welfare Building
6 Hazen Dr.
Concord, NH 03301 (603) 271-4588

New Jersey
New Jersey Department of Environmental Protection
380 Scotch Rd. CN-411 (609) 530-4000
Trenton, NJ 08625 (800) 648-0394

New Mexico
Surveillance Monitoring Section
New Mexico Radiation Protection Bureau
P.O. Box 968
Santa Fe, NM 87504 (505) 827-2957

New York
Bureau of Environmental Radiation Protection
New York State Health Department
Empire State Plaza, Corning Tower (518) 473-3613
Albany, NY 12237 (800) 458-1158

North Carolina
Radiation Protection Section
North Carolina Department of Human Resources
701 Barbour Dr.
Raleigh, NC 27603 (919) 733-4283

North Dakota
Division of Environmental Engineering
North Dakota State Department of Health and Consolidated Laboratories
Missouri Office Building
1200 Missouri Ave., Room 304
Bismarck, ND 58502 (701) 224-2348

Ohio
Radiological Health Program
Ohio Department of Health
1224 Kinnear Rd. (614) 481-5800
Columbus, OH 43212 (800) 523-4439

Oklahoma
Radiation and Special Hazards Service
Oklahoma State Department of Health
P.O. Box 53551
Oklahoma City, OK 73152 (405) 271-5221

Oregon
Oregon State Health Department

Be patient. If any phone number is incorrect, call (area code) 555-1212 and request the new listing.

Water and Air Quality

1400 SW 5th Ave.
Portland, OR 97201 (503) 229-5797

Pennsylvania
Bureau of Radiation Protection
Pennsylvania Department of Environmental Resources
P.O. Box 2063
Harrisburg, PA 17120 (717) 787-2480

Puerto Rico
Puerto Rico Radiological Health Division
GPO Call Box 70184
Rio Piedras, PR 00936 (809) 767-3563

Rhode Island
Division of Occupational Health and Radiological Control
Rhode Island Department of Health
206 Cannon Bldg.
75 Davis St.
Providence, RI 02908 (401) 277-2438

South Carolina
Bureau of Radiological Health
South Carolina Department of Health and Environmental Control
2600 Bull St.
Columbia, SC 29201 (803) 734-4700

South Dakota
Office of Air Quality and Solid Waste
South Dakota Department of Water and Natural Resources
Joe Foss Building
Room 217
523 E. Capital
Pierre, SD 57501 (605) 773-3153

Tennessee
Division of Air Pollution Control
Custom House
701 Broadway
Nashville, TN 37219 (615) 741-4634

Texas
Bureau of Radiation Control
Texas Department of Health
1100 West 49th St.
Austin, TX 78756 (512) 835-7000

Utah
Bureau of Radiation Control
Utah State Department of Health
State Health Department Building
P.O. Box 16690
Salt Lake City, UT 84116 (801) 538-6734

Vermont
Division of Occupation and Radiological Health
Vermont Department of Health
Administration Building
10 Baldwin St.
Montpelier, VT 05602 (802) 828-2886

Virginia
Bureau of Radiological Health
Department of Health
109 Governor St.
Richmond, VA 23219 (804) 786-5932
(800) 468-0138

Washington
Environmental Protection Section
Washington Office of Radiation Protection
Thurston AirDustrial Center
Building 5, LE-13
Olympia, WA 98504 (206) 753-5962

West Virginia
Industrial Hygiene Division
West Virginia Department of Health

151 11th Ave.
South Charleston, WV 25303 (304) 348-3526

Wisconsin
Division of Health
Section of Radiation Protection
Wisconsin Department of Health and Social Services
5708 Odana Rd.
Madison, WI 53719 (608) 273-5180

Wyoming
Radiological Health Services
Wyoming Department of Health and Social Services
Hathway Building
4th Floor
Cheyenne, WY 82002 (307) 777-7956

* Toxic Substances in Water

Toxic Substances Hydrology Program (TSHP)
Water Resources Division
U.S. Geological Survey
National Center
Reston, VA 22092 (703) 648-6862

The TSHP is an interdisciplinary program designed to provide the hydrologic information necessary both to improve waste-disposal practices and also to help mitigate existing and future surface and ground-water contamination problems. This program focuses on the occurrence, movement, and fate of toxic substances in the hydrologic system by 1) studying major types of contaminants of ground and surface waters, and 2) developing new methods and protocols to assess the extent of contamination.

* Unleaded Gas and Fuels Hotline

Environmental Protection Agency
Region I
JFK Federal Bldg. (800) 821-1237
Boston, MA 02203 (800) 631-2700 (MA)

The Unleaded Fuel Tank Hotline is an enforcement-related line that takes calls about tampering with vehicles, pumps, and other problems related to unleaded fuels. It provides this service for Region I states: Connecticut, Massachusetts, New Hampshire, Rhode Island, Vermont.

* Want To Know More About Acid Rain?

Acid Rain Division
Environmental Protection Agency
401 M St., SW
Washington, DC 20460 (202) 260-9400

Acid rain affects both the health of humans and our environment and is an issue with which the EPA is actively involved. EPA can provide information on research, regulation, and other issues associated with acid rain. EPA publishes *Acid Rain: A Student's First Sourcebook* designed for grades 4-8 and their teachers, which describes the effects of acid rain, solutions, experiments, and activities. This office also has EPA Journal articles on acid rain, background information, and updates on EPA's activities. The EPA is part of the National Acid Precipitation Assessment Program, and is conducting the National Surface Water Survey designed to provide information on the status of lakes and streams believed to be susceptible to change as a result of acid rain. Contact this office for more information.

* Wastewater Information

Wastewater Treatment and Information Exchange
Bulletin Board System
P.O. Box 6064
Morgantown, WV 26506 (304) 293-4191

This Bulletin Board allows for the exchange of information on wastewater related material through its main board and its specialized conferences. They also publish a *User's Guide*.

* Wastewater Treatment Clearinghouse

Small Flows Clearinghouse
613 N. Spruce St.
Morgantown, WV 26505 (800) 624-8301

Be patient. If any phone number is incorrect, call (area code) 555-1212 and request the new listing.

Environment and Nature

The National Small Flows Clearinghouse provides information on wastewater treatment technologies for small communities, and participates in a national training effort to assist states in implementing small flows technology at the community level. Two free newsletters are produced by the Clearinghouse. *Small Flows* provides technical information and is geared toward the engineering and regulatory communities, and *Pipeline* presents information about various wastewater topics for community officials. The Clearinghouse has a computer bulletin board, databases, provides telephone consultation and referral service, maintains a large inventory of instructional products (books, brochures, and videotapes) and instructional materials. Workshops, seminars, and presentations are also sponsored. This clearinghouse was mandated by the Clean Water Act Amendments of 1977.

* Water Clearinghouse

Water Resources Scientific Information Center (WRSIC)
Water Resources Division
U.S. Geological Survey
National Center
Reston, VA 22092 (703) 648-6821

WRSIC was established to increase the availability and knowledge of water-related scientific and technical information. WRSIC abstracts water-resource publications from throughout the world and makes this information available to the water-resources community and the public through publications and computerized bibliographic information services.

* Water Conservation

U.S. Department of Agriculture (USDA)
Deputy for Programs, SCS
Box 2890
Washington, DC 20013 (202) 720-4527

The USDA manages a variety of water resource programs to aid landowners and agricultural operators use existing water resources including Resource Conservation and Development which encourages state and local governments and non-profit organizations to develop programs to accelerate water conservation and development.

* Water Contamination by Metals

Environmental Technology Division
Bureau of Mines
U.S. Department of the Interior
2401 E St., NW
Washington, DC 20241 (202) 634-1263

Researchers at the Bureau of Mines are working on low-cost ways to deal with the problem of acid drainage at abandoned mines. They are developing computer programs to predict potential drainage at new mines and to develop ways to treat the water after it's been contaminated. The Bureau's environmental research also addresses the problem of solid waste disposal and soil and water contaminated by metals. Technologies are developed that will reduce or remove the threats that these wastes pose.

* Water Data Exchange (NAWDEX)

National Water Data Exchange
Water Resources Division
U.S. Geological Survey
National Center, MS 421
Reston, VA 22092 (703) 648-5677

The National Water Data Exchange is a confederation of Federal and non-Federal water-oriented organizations working together to improve access to available water data. Information on sites for which water data is available, the types of data available, and the organizations that store the data is available from NAWDEX.

* Water Online and Other Databases

Environmental Research Laboratory Library
College Station Rd.
Athens, GA 30613 (404) 546-3302

The Athens Environmental Research Laboratory (ERL) Library provides information services covering a wide range of environmental and management subjects. Subject areas include aquatic toxicology, microbiology, biology, pesticides, chemistry, water pollution, engineering, and water quality. Databases maintained here include CIS, DIALOG, and Ground Water On-line.

* Water Pollution

Nonpoint Source Information Exchange
Office of Water Assessment and Watershed Protection Division
401 M St., SW
Environmental Protection Agency
Washington, DC 20460 (202) 260-7085

The Exchange provides response to inquiries regarding the management of nonpoint sources of water pollution and the EPA's control program under Section 319 of the Clean Water Act. Publications include *Nonpoint Sources NEWS-NOTES* and a *Technical Bulletin*.

* Water Pollution and Hydrobiology Clearinghouse

Andrew W. Briedenbach Environmental
Research Center Library
26 W. Martin Luther King
Cincinnati, OH 45268 (513) 569-7703

The major subjects in this library's collection are bacteriology, biology, biotechnology, chemistry, engineering, hazardous wastes, hydrobiology, microbiology, solid waste management, toxicology, water pollution, and water quality. Databases maintained here include BRS, CAS On-line, CIS, DIALOG, Dun & Bradstreet, Hazardous Waste Database, LEXIS/NEXIS, NLM, Toxline, and Toxnet. General collections include bacteriology, biology, biotechnology, microbiology, physics, solid waste management. This library's special collections cover the environment, Canada, legal issues, hazardous waste, and solid waste.

* Water Quality Assessment

Office of Water Quality
Water Resources Division
U.S. Geological Survey
National Center, MS 412
Reston, VA 22092 (703) 648-6884

The National Water Quality Assessment Program is designed to address a wide range of water-quality issues that include chemical contamination, acidification, eutrophication, salinity, sedimentation, and sanitary quality. The program strives to provide nationally consistent descriptions of current water-quality conditions and to define long-term trends in water quality.

* Water Quality Information Center

National Agriculture Library Building
Beltsville, MD 20705 (301) 504-6875

This Information Center can answer questions regarding the quality of freshwater and coastal water resources, point and nonpoint source pollution of both surface and ground water, the quality of drinking water, wetlands issues, and much more,. They have access to a database, bibliographies, and other publications. Contact the Center for more information.

* Water Quality Networks

Office of Water Quality
Water Resources Division
U.S. Geological Survey
National Center, MS 412
Reston, VA 22092 (703) 648-6884

The National Water-Quality Networks Program describes and appraises the Nation's water resources. The largest of these networks is the National Stream Quality Accounting Network (NASQAN), which consists of more than 400 sampling sites used to measure a comprehensive list of physical and chemical characteristics on a quarterly or bimonthly schedule to fulfill information needs of national and regional water resources planners and managers. Other networks within the program include the Radiochemical Surveillance Network, the Tritium Network, and the Hydrologic Bench-Mark Network. This last network monitors the natural streamflow and water quality of small river basins that are known to be relatively little affected by man's activities.

* Water Research Grants

Office of External Research
Water Resources Division
U.S. Geological Survey
National Center, MS 409
Reston, VA 22092 (703) 648-6807

The Water Research Grants Program is a national program of grants to support technology development and research in major water resource problem areas.

Be patient. If any phone number is incorrect, call (area code) 555-1212 and request the new listing.

Water and Air Quality

State Water Resources Research and Technology Institutes, qualified educational institutions, private foundations, private firms, individuals, and agencies of local or state governments are eligible to receive grants on a dollar-for-dollar matching basis for research concerning any aspect of a water-resource related problem deemed to be in the national interest.

* Water Resources Activities

Hydrologic Information Unit
Water Resources Division
U.S. Geological Survey
419 National Center
Reston, VA 22092 (703) 648-6817

The current hydrology program in each state is outlined in pamphlets entitled *Water-Resources Activities of the Geological Survey in (State)*. Pamphlets are available through the regional hydrologists offices listed elsewhere in this book.

* Water Resources Clearinghouse

Water Resources Scientific Information Center (WRSIC)
U.S. Geological Survey
425 National Center
Reston, VA 22092 (703) 648-6821

WRSIC was established as a national center to increase the availability and knowledge of water-related scientific and technical information. To accomplish this purpose, WRSIC abstracts water resources publications from throughout the world and makes this bibliographic information available to the water resources community and the public through publications and computerized bibliographic information services.

* Water Resources Division District Offices

The Water Resources Division District Offices are NAWDEX Assistance Centers that provide the public with information on WATSTORE and answer questions on the water resources of their specific regions. Each State publishes an Annual Report on Water Resources Data, and can provide you with information on surface-water resources, water supply and use, ground water quality, and ground-water resources. They also publish current water-resources activities in your State, which includes a publication list and other hydrologic information.

Alabama
Water Resources Division District Office
U.S. Geological Survey
520 19th Ave.
Tuscaloosa, AL 35401 (205) 752-8104

Alaska
Water Resources Division District Office
U.S. Geological Survey
4230 University Dr., Suite 201
Anchorage, AK 99508-4664 (907) 271-4138

Arizona
Water Resources Division District Office
U.S. Geological Survey
Federal Building, FB 44
300 West Congress St.
Tucson, AZ 85701 (602) 629-6671

Arkansas
Water Resources Division District Office
U.S. Geological Survey
2301 Federal Office Building
700 West Capitol Ave.
Little Rock, AR 72201 (501) 378-6391

California
Water Resources Division District Office
U.S. Geological Survey
Federal Building, Room W-2235
2800 Cottage Way
Sacramento, CA 95825 (916) 978-4633

Colorado
Water Resources Division District Office
U.S. Geological Survey

Box 25046, Federal Center
Mail Stop 415
Denver, CO 80225 (303) 236-4882

Connecticut
Connecticut Office Water Resources Division
U.S. Geological Survey
525 Ribicoff Federal Building
450 Main St.
Hartford, CT 06103 (203) 240-3060

Delaware
Delaware Office
Water Resources Division
U.S. Geological Survey
1201 Federal Building
300 South New Street
Dover, DE 19901 (302) 734-2506

Florida
Water Resources Division District Office
U.S. Geological Survey
227 North Bronough St., Suite 3015
Tallahassee, FL 32301 (904) 681-7620

Georgia
Water Resources Division District Office
U.S. Geological Survey, Suite B
6481 Peachtree Industrial Blvd.
Doraville, GA 30360 (404) 986-6860

Hawaii
Water Resources Division District Office
U.S. Geological Survey
P.O. Box 50166
300 Ala Moana Blvd., Room 6110
Honolulu, HI 96850 (808) 541-2653

Idaho
Water Resources Division District Office
U.S. Geological Survey
230 Collins Rd..
Boise, ID 83702 (208) 334-1750

Illinois
Water Resources Division District Office
U.S. Geological Survey
Champaign County Bank Plaza
102 East Main, Fourth Floor
Urbana, IL 61801 (217) 398-5353

Indiana
Water Resources Division District Office
U.s. Geological Survey
5957 Lakeside Blvd.
Indianapolis, IN 46278 (317) 290-3333

Iowa
Water Resources Division District Office
U.s. Geological Survey
P.O. Box 1230
269 Federal Building
400 South Clinton St.
Iowa City, IA 52244 (319) 337-4191

Kansas
Water Resources Division District Office
U.S. Geological Survey
1950 Constant Ave.- Campus West
University of Kansas
Lawrence, KS 66046 (913) 864-4321

Kentucky
Water Resources Division District Office
U.S. Geological Survey
2301 Bradley Ave.
Louisville, KY 40217 (502) 582-5241

Be patient. If any phone number is incorrect, call (area code) 555-1212 and request the new listing.

Environment and Nature

Louisiana
Water Resources Division District Office
U.s. Geological Survey
P.O. Box 66492
6554 Florida Blvd.
Baton Rouge, LA 70896 (504) 389-0281

Maine
Maine Office
Water Resources Division
U.S. Geological Survey
26 Ganneston Dr.
Augusta, ME 04330 (207) 622-8201

Maryland
Water Resources Division District Office
U.S. Geological Survey
208 Carroll Building
8600 LaSalle Rd.
Towson, MD 21204 (301) 828-1535

Massachusetts
Water Resources Division District office
U.S. Geological Survey
150 Causeway St., Suite 1309
Boston, MA 02114 (617) 565-6860

Michigan
Water Resources Division District Office
U.S. Geological Survey
6520 Mercantile Way, Suite 5
Lansing, MI 48910 (517) 377-1608

Minnesota
Water Resources Division district office
U.S. Geological Survey
702 Post Office Building
St. Paul, MN 55101 (612) 229-2600

Mississippi
Water Resources Division District Office
U.S. Geological Survey
Federal Building, Suite 710
100 West Capitol Street
Jackson, MS 39269 (601) 965-4600

Missouri
Water Resources Division District Office
U.S. Geological Survey
Mail Stop 200
1400 Independence Rd.
Rolla, MO 65401 (314) 341-0824

Montana
Water Resources Division District Office
U.S. Geological Survey
301 South Park Ave.
428 Federal Building
Drawer 10076
Helena, MT 59626 (406) 449-5363

Nebraska
Water Resources Division District Office
U.S. Geological Survey
406 Federal Building 100 Centennial Mall, North
Lincoln, NE 68508 (402) 437-5082

Nevada
Nevada Office Water Resources Division
U.S. Geological Survey
224 Federal Building
705 North Plaza St.
Carson City, NV 89701 (702) 882-1388

New Hampshire
New Hampshire Office
Water Resources Division

U.S. Geological Survey
525 Clinton St., RFD 2
Bow, NH 03301 (603) 225-4681

New Jersey
Water Resources Division District Office
U.S. Geological Survey
Mountain View Office Park, Suite 206
810 Bear Tavern Rd.
West Trenton, NJ 08628 (609) 771-3900

New Mexico
Water Resources Division District Office
U.S. Geological Survey
720 Western Bank Building
505 Marquette, Northwest
Albuquerque, NM 87102 (505) 262-6630

New York
Water Resources Division District Office
U.S. Geological Survey
P.O. Box 1669
343 U.S. Post Office and Courthouse Building
Albany, NY 12201 (518) 472-3107

North Carolina
Water Resources Division District Office
U.S. Geological Survey
P.O. Box 2857
300 Fayetteville Street Mall
436 Century Postal Station
Raleigh, NC 27602 (919) 856-4510

North Dakota
Water Resources Division District Office
U.S. Geological Survey
821 East Interstate Ave.
Bismarck, ND 58501 (701) 250-4611

Ohio
Water Resources Division District Office
U.S. Geological Survey
975 West Third Ave.
Columbus, OH 43212 (614) 469-5553

Oklahoma
Water Resources Division District Office
U.S. Geological Survey
Room 621
215 Dean A. McGee Ave.
Oklahoma City, OK 73102 (405) 231-4256

Oregon
Water Resources Division District Office
U.S. Geological Survey
847 NE. 19th Ave., Suite 300
Portland, OR 97232 (503) 231-2009

Pennsylvania
Water Resources Division District Office
U.S. Geological Survey
P.O. Box 1107
Federal Building, Fourth Floor
228 Walnut St.
Harrisburg, PA 17108 (717) 782-4514

Puerto Rico
Water Resources Division District Office
U.S. Geological Survey
GPO Box 4424
GSA Center, Building 652
Highway 28, Pueblo Viejo
San Juan, PR 00936 (809) 783-4660

Rhode Island
Rhode Island Office
Water Resources Division

Be patient. If any phone number is incorrect, call (area code) 555-1212 and request the new listing.

Water and Air Quality

U.S. Geological Survey
Pastore Federal Building and U.S. Post Office
Room 237
Providence, RI 02903 (401) 528-5135

South Carolina
Water Resource Division District Office
U.S. Geological Survey
Suite 658
1835 Assembly St.
Columbia, SC 29201 (803) 765-5966

South Dakota
Water Resources Division District Office
U.S. Geological Survey
317 Federal Building
200 Fourth St., SW
Huron, SD 57350 (605) 353-7176

Tennessee
Water Resources Division District Office
U.S. Geological Survey
A-413 Federal Building and U.S. Courthouse
Nashville, TN 37203 (615) 736-5424

Texas
Water Resources Division District Office
U.S. Geological Survey
649 Federal Building
300 East Eighth St.
Austin, TX 78701 (512) 832-5791

Utah
Water Resources Division District Office
U.s. Geological Survey
Room 1016
Administration Building
1745 West 1700 South
Salt Lake City, UT 84104 (801) 524-5663

Vermont
See listing for Massachusetts

Virginia
Virginia Office
Water Resources Division
U.W. Geological Survey
3600 West Broad St., Room 606
Richmond, VA 23230 (804) 771-2427

Washington
Water Resources Division District Office
U.S. Geological Survey
1201 Pacific Ave., Suite 600
Tacoma, WA 98402 (206) 593-6510

West Virginia
Water Resources Division District Office
U.S. Geological Survey
603 Morris St.
Charleston, WV 25301 (304) 347-5130

Wisconsin
Water Resources Division District Office
U.S. Geological Survey
6417 Normandy Lane
Madison, WI 53719 (608) 274-3535

Wyoming
Water Resources Division District Office
U. S. Geological Survey
P.O. Box 1125
4004 J.C. O'Mahoney Federal Center
2120 Capitol Ave.
Cheyenne, WY 82003 (307) 772-2153

---

* Water Resources: National Survey

National Water Summary Branch
Water Resources Division
U.S. Geological Survey
National Center, MS 407
Reston, VA 22092 (703) 648-6851

The National Water Summary Program brings together information about the availability, quantity, quality, and use of water resources and organizes it in ways to show the Nation's water resources condition to national, state, and local officials and to the general public. *National Water Summary Reports* are published annually.

* Water Resources Information

Hydrologic Information Unit (HIU)
Water Resources Division
U.S. Geological Survey
National Center, MS 419
Reston, VA 22092 (703) 648-6817

Contact this office for requests for general information on water resources of an area or the Nation and on activities of the Water Resources Division. The Hydrologic Information Unit answers general questions on hydrology, water resources, hydrologic mapping, publications, activities, projects, and services of the Water Resources Division, making referrals to appropriate field and Headquarters offices when necessary. HIU also maintains limited stocks of Geological Survey general-interest publications. This publication series consists of short presentations in the form of leaflets, booklets, essay reprints, brochures, and water fact sheets.

* Water Resources Library

Departmental Library
Bureau of Reclamation
U.S. Department of the Interior
P.O. Box 25007, D79231
Denver Federal Center
Denver, CO 80225-0007 (303) 236-6963

This library within the Bureau of Reclamation holds a wealth of information on the Bureau's water conservation activities. Library materials may be used only at the library or may be checked out through the inter-library loan system at your local library. Key topics include hydrology engineering, groundwater management, dam safety, soil mechanics, and business related issues.

* Watershed Protection

U.S. Department of Agriculture (USDA)
Deputy for Programs, SCS
Box 2890
Washington, DC 20013 (202) 720-4527

The USDA manages a variety of water resource programs to aid landowners and agricultural operators use existing water resources wisely including Watershed Protection Projects which provides flood management prevention; watershed protection; agricultural water management.

* Water Supply, Flood Plain Management

U.S. Army Corps of Engineers
Public Affairs
20 Massachusetts Ave., NW
Washington, DC 20314 (202) 272-0011

The Corps offers free brochures on a wide variety of subjects, including archaeology, camping, environment, erosion control, flood control, flood plain management, history, safety, waste-water treatment and water supply. For a publications list, call or write the above office.

* Water Supply Situation

Resource Management
Bureau of Reclamation
U.S. Department of the Interior
P.O. Box 25007
Denver Federal Center
Denver, CO 80225 (303) 236-3289

The Bureau assists water users and development agencies in reviewing state and federal water laws in an ongoing effort to conserve the Nation's water supply.

Be patient. If any phone number is incorrect, call (area code) 555-1212 and request the new listing.

Environment and Nature

* Western Reservoirs and Water Projects Photographs and Videos

Visual Communication Services
Bureau of Reclamation
U.S. Department of the Interior
P.O. Box 25007, Denver Federal Center
Denver, CO 80225 (303) 236-7000

Photographs depicting Bureau of Reclamation activities may be borrowed from this office. Videocassettes, slide shows, black and white photos, and color slides are available, showing water and power activities, such as recreation, irrigation, agriculture, research, and reservoirs, within the Western region. The following videos are available for free loan:

A Bursting Bubble - Cavitation
A New Horizon
Adventure in Glen Canyon
Build-up On The Bighorn
California Flooding
Central Arizona Project-Lifeline to the Future
Central Utah Project
Challenge at Glen Canyon
Coachella Canal Relining
The Colorado
The Columbia A Fountain of Life
Design and Construction of Safe Dams
From Snowfall to Sandstone
Giant on the Bighorn
Great Web of Water
Hoover Dam
Hoover Dam Construction
Hoover Dam 50th Anniversary
How Water Won the West
Hydropower
Hydropower - a Twentieth Century Force
Lake Powell - Jewel of the Colorado
Living Waters of the Colorado
Miracle of Water
Mountain Skywater
New Technologies and New Solutions
Operation Glen Canyon
Powering One Corner of the World
Rio Grande-Ribbon of Life
Take Pride in America
Take Pride in America - A Legacy of Caring
Taming of Black Canyon
Teton - Decision and Disaster
To Build A Dream - The Story of Hoover Dam
Water In The West - Tomorrow's Challenge

* Western Water Quality and Supply

Engineering and Research
Bureau of Reclamation

U.S. Department of the Interior
P.O. Box 25007
Denver, CO 80225 (303) 236-6988

The Bureau of Reclamation provides programs and leadership to improve water quality, to eliminate environmental pollution and protect Western water supplies from other threats of pollution. Other related programs include fish and wildlife enhancement, reduction of salinity and other pollutants in streams and reservoirs, agricultural drainage control, and protection against contamination of underground and surface water sources.

* Wetlands Protection

Office of Wetlands Protection
Environmental Protection Agency (EPA)
401 M St., SW
Washington DC 20460 (202) 260-7791

This office implements EPA statutory responsibilities in the Clean Water Act as they relate to the filling of wetlands and other aquatic resources. Designed to raise the importance of wetlands, this office works with other governmental bodies to encourage wetlands protection.

* Wild and Scenic Rivers

Land and Renewable Resources
Bureau of Land Management (BLM)
U.S. Department of the Interior
18th and C Sts., NW
Washington, DC 20240 (202) 208-4896

The Bureau of Land Management manages about 2,200 miles of the Wild and Scenic River System, primarily in the western United States. These areas are located in the directory, *Recreation Guide to BLM Public Lands*, available from the Office of Public Affairs, Bureau of Land Management, U.S. Department of the Interior, Washington, DC 20240.

* Undersea Research

National Undersea Research Program (NURP)
National Oceanic and Atmospheric Administration (NOAA)
U.S. Department of Commerce
6010 Executive Blvd.
Rockville, MD 20852 (301) 427-2427

The National Undersea Research Program develops programs and provides support to scientists and engineers for the study of biological, chemical, geological, and physical processes in the world's oceans and lakes. NURP assist researchers in conducting what are considered by NOAA and the marine community to be crucial research programs. In order to execute these programs, NURP provides investigators with a suite of the modern undersea facilities including submersibles, habitats, air and mixed gas SCUBA, and remotely operated vehicles. A major part of the research program is carried out by a network of National Undersea Research Centers. Contact this office for more information on the research conducted or the research centers.

Be patient. If any phone number is incorrect, call (area code) 555-1212 and request the new listing.

Forests and Land Conservation

* *See also Business and Industry Chapter*
* *See also Vacations and Business Travel Chapter*

* Abandoned Mine Land Reclamation

Office of Surface Mining Reclamation and Enforcement
U.S. Department of the Interior
1951 Constitution Ave., NW
Washington, DC 20240 (202) 208-5365

The surface mining law requires that operators pay a reclamation fee for each ton of coal produced. These fees are deposited with the U.S. Treasury in a fund called the Abandoned Mine Reclamation Fund and are used to reclaim sites that were mined and left unreclaimed before the surface mining law was enacted in 1977. Fifty percent of the fees collected in a state that has approved reclamation and regulatory programs is returned to that state for use in its reclamation program. The other fifty percent is the Federal share. This portion is used by the Office of Surface Mining Reclamation and Enforcement to address public health and safety emergencies caused by past mining practices, and to fund high-priority reclamation projects in non-program states. To obtain your state contact for the abandoned mine land reclamation program, contact the office above.

* A Forest In Your Community?

Urban and Community Forestry
Forest Service, U.S. Department of Agriculture
14th and Independence Ave., SW
Washington, DC 20250 (202) 205-1694

The Urban and Community Forestry program promotes and improves the economic, environmental, and social well-being of communities through the planting and management of trees, shrubs, and other vegetation. These efforts enhance the city environment, make important contributions to soil, water, and air quality, and help conserve energy and reduce atmospheric carbon dioxide. Contact this office for more information.

* Agents and Rangers for Public Lands

Office of Public Information
Bureau of Land Management (BLM)
U.S. Department of the Interior
18th and C Sts., NW
Washington, DC 20240-0001 (202) 208-3435

As a caretaker of more than 300 million acres, the BLM manages and protects these lands and the resources associated with them. BLM has highly trained Special Agents and uniformed rangers to enforce applicable Federal laws on public lands. Special agents are responsible for conducting criminal investigations and making arrests. Rangers primarily patrol the public lands where they prevent law violations and assist stranded visitors. Contact the office above for the pamphlet *Protecting Public Land Resources* for a listing of Field Offices to contact for employment.

* Bureau of Land Management State Offices

Bureau of Land Management (BLM)
U.S. Department of the Interior
Washington, DC 20240 (202) 208-5717

Specific information about opportunities to enjoy the benefits of the public lands and resources can best be obtained from the state office responsible for the areas of interest:

Alaska
Bureau of Land Management, 701 C St., P.O.Box 13, Anchorage, AK 99513; (907) 271-5555

Arizona
Bureau of Land Management, 3707 N 7th St., Phoenix, AZ 85014; (602) 241-5504

California
Bureau of Land Management, Federal Building, Room E-2841, 2800 Cottage Way, Sacramento, CA 95825; (916) 978-4746

Colorado
Bureau of Land Management, 2850 Youngfield St., Lakewood, CO 80215; (303) 236-1700. Also serves Kansas

Eastern States
Bureau of Land Management, 350 South Pickett St., Alexandria, VA 22304; (703) 461-1369. Serves states bordering and east of the Mississippi River.

Idaho
Bureau of Land Management, 3380 Americana Terr., Boise, ID 83706; (208) 334-1771.

Montana
Bureau of Land Management, 222 N 32nd Street, P.O. Box 36800, Billings, MT 59107; (406) 255-2913. Also serves North Dakota and South Dakota.

Nevada
Bureau of Land Management, 300 Booth St., P.O. Box 12000, Reno, NV 89520; (702) 328-6386.

New Mexico
Bureau of Land Management, South Federal Pl., P.O. Box 1449, Santa Fe, NM 87501; (505) 988-6316. Also serves Oklahoma and Texas.

Oregon
Bureau of Land Management, 825 NE Multnomah St., P.O. Box 2965, Portland, OR 97208; (503) 231-6274. Also serves Washington.

Utah
Bureau of Land Management, 324 South State Street, Suite 301, Salt Lake City, UT 84111-3146; (801) 539-4021.

Wyoming
Bureau of Land Management, 2515 Warren Ave., P.O. Box 1828, Cheyenne, WY 82001; (307) 772-2111. Also serves Nebraska.

* Bureau of Reclamation Regional Offices

Bureau of Mines
U.S. Department of Interior
1951 Constitution Avenue, NW
Washington, DC 20240 (202) 501-9649

Here are the regional offices which enforce strip mining and reclamation laws:

Lower Colorado Region
Box 427, Nevada Hwy. and Park St., Boulder City, NV 89005; (702) 293-8420

Mid-Pacific Region
2800 Cottage Way, Sacramento, CA 95825; (916) 978-4919

Pacific Northwest Region
Box 043, 550 W. Fort St., Boise, ID 83724; (208) 334-1938

Upper Colorado Region
Box 11568, 125 S. State St., Salt Lake City, UT 84147; (801) 524-5403

Great Plains Region
Box 36900, 316 N. 26th St., Billings, MT 59107; (406) 657-6218

* Cadastral Survey

Branch of Cadastral Survey Development
Bureau of Land Management (BLM)
U.S. Department of the Interior
1725 I St., NW
Washington, DC 20240 (202) 653-8798

Be patient. If any phone number is incorrect, call (area code) 555-1212 and request the new listing.

Environment and Nature

The Office of Cadastral Surveys is responsible for the creation, restoration, marking, and defining of the boundaries of public lands. Under the cadastral system, the public domain is plotted into a grid of squares, each approximately 6 miles to the side, called "townships." In recent years, modern technology has replaced the traditional "chain" measuring tape with electronic instruments. Microwave, light wave, laser beam, photogrammetry, and gyroscopic orientations are among the scientific mediums integrated in the cadastral surveyor's array of working tools.

* Christmas Trees - Free

Division of Forestry, Bureau of Land Management (BLM)
U.S. Department of the Interior
Washington, DC 20240 (202) 653-8864

The BLM officials issue permits to cut Christmas trees for a nominal fee on Bureau of Land Management-administered lands in the 11 Western states and Alaska. Free-use permits are available from the Bureau to non-profit organizations for timber and trees to be used exclusively by that organization. This excludes the resale of any free timber or trees by those organizations.

* Cooperative Forest Fire Control

Fire Protection Staff
U.S. Department of Agriculture
Forest Service, P.O. Box 96090
Washington, DC 20090-6090 (202) 205-1508

State and Federal governments cooperate to protect non-federal timberland, potential timberland, certain non-forested watershed lands, and other rural lands from serious fire damage. For information, contact a regional forester or area Forest Service director or the above office.

* Cooperative Forest Insect and Disease Management

Contact: your State Forester or the state office of the U.S. Forest Service, usually located in the state capitol.

To reduce loss and damage to forests and lands by forest insects and diseases, the USDA provides technical and financial assistance in prevention, detection, evaluation, and suppression of forest insect and disease outbreaks on state and private lands.

* Erosion Control

Information Division
U.S. Department of Agriculture
ASCS, P.O. Box 205
Kansas City, MO 64141 (202) 720-5237

The Agricultural State Conservation Service (ASCS) directs a number of conservation programs to preserve and improve American farmland:

Conservation Reserve Program (CRP): Targets the most fragile farmland by encouraging farmers to stop growing crops on land designated by conservationists as "highly erodible" and plant grass or trees on it instead. The farmer receives rent on the land for a term of ten years. Cost-share programs are also available for permanent planting of grass and trees in these areas.

* Federal Lands Energy Leasing

Offshore Minerals Management
Mineral Management Service
U.S. Department of the Interior
18th and C Sts., NW
Washington, DC 20240 (202) 208-6906

The Mineral Management Service leases the rights to explore and develop oil and gas on Federal lands of the continental shelf. The "shelf" is made up of the submerged offshore areas lying seaward of the territorial sea to a depth of 200 meters (656 feet) and beyond that area to that depth which allows for mineral exploration. The brochure, *Leasing Energy Resources on the Outer Continental Shelf,* explains the leasing procedure and gives a history of the program.

* Fire and Land Management

Fire and Aviation Management
Bureau of Land Management (BLM)
U.S. Department of the Interior
1620 L Street NW, Room 407
Washington, DC 20036 (202) 653-8800

BLM's fire management program is divided into two areas: wildfire suppression and prescribed fire. Wildfire suppression includes all aspects of preparing for, detecting, and fighting wildland fire, and for rehabilitation of severely burned areas. Fire is also used under prescribed conditions to help achieve land management objectives. An average of 700 prescribed (intentionally set and controlled) fires are conducted each year by BLM to make room for new forage for livestock and wildlife. They are also used to prepare a site for seeding or the planting of seedlings.

* Fire Safety Bibliography

Superintendent of Documents
Government Printing Office
Washington, DC 20402 (202) 783-3238

Fire safety publications are listed, including improving the fire safety of cigarettes and the effect of cigarettes on the ignition of furnishings. Free.

* Forest and Park Films

Office of Public Affairs
National Park Service
U.S. Department of the Interior
P.O. Box 37127
Washington DC 20013 (202) 208-7394

The National Park Service has an extensive list of films available for rent or sale. The films cover a variety of topics including parks, history, great Americans, and travel. Often they are used for all grade levels, as well as various civic organizations and clubs, such as Civil War Round Tables. Contact the Park Service for a listing of their films and ordering information. The Harpers Ferry Historical Association serves as a distributing agency for the Park Service and can be reached at: Harpers Ferry Historical Association Inc., P.O. Box 197, High St., Harpers Ferry, WV 25425; 304-535-6881.

* Forest Fire Reports

Aviation and Fire Management
U.S. Department of Agriculture
Current Forest Fire Situation
Washington, DC 20013 (202) 205-1486

This office can provide you with information on forest fires anywhere in the U.S. They maintain all statistics for forest fires. During the fire season (June-Sept.), a special fire hotline is established to answer questions on current fires. For that number, contact Public Affairs, (202) 205-0957.

* Forest Management and Education Worldwide

Natural Resources Sector
Office of Training and Programming Support
Peace Corps
1990 K St., NW
Washington, DC 20526 (202) 606-3100

Working in 38 countries, forestry specialists design and execute forest management plans designed to help combat the overcutting, droughts, and deserts that are beginning to threaten many tropical forests around the world. They also help establish nurseries, curricula in environmental education, and skills in tropical fruit cultivation.

* Forest Products Utilization

Cooperative Forestry
Forest Service
U.S. Department of Agriculture
Room 125-A CW P.O. Box 2417
Washington, DC 20013 (202) 205-1383

Technical assistance is available to wood processors and harvesters of wood products in cooperation with private consultants and state agencies. Assistance can range from improving efficiency to marketing assistance.

* Forest Ranger Recruitment

Forest Service
U.S. Department of Agriculture
Recruitment
P.O. Box 2417
Washington, DC 20013 (703) 235-2730

Contact this office for information on a career as a forest ranger.

Be patient. If any phone number is incorrect, call (area code) 555-1212 and request the new listing.

Forests and Land Conservation

* Forest Research and Technical Expertise

Deputy for Research
Forest Service
U.S. Department of Agriculture
Box 96690
Washington, DC 20090-6090 (202) 205-1507

Basic research is conducted by a large staff on such topics as forest insects and diseases, forest fire and atmosphere sciences, forest resource economics, biodiversity, global climate change, watershed and aquatic habitat, range and wildlife ecology, wood chemistry and fiber products, and structural and forest system engineering.

* Forests and Land Management

Forestry Division
Bureau of Land Management (BLM)
U.S. Department of the Interior
1725 I St., NW
Washington, DC 20006 (202) 653-8864

The Bureau of Land Management administers 90 million acres of forested lands, most of which are in Alaska. In the lower 48 states, some 26 million acres are managed, including 21 million acres of woodlands and 5 million acres of commercial forest lands.

* Forest Service Films

Office of Public Affairs
Forest Service
U.S. Department of Agriculture
P.O. Box 96090
Washington DC 20090 (202) 205-1438

The Forest Service maintains regional film libraries across the country. The films cover a wide range of topics, such as acid rain and management of national forests, and many of the newer one cover region-specific issues. The films are appropriate for elementary school children through college, as well as foresters. Most of the films from the Forest Service are available for free loan. Contact the film library nearest you for a free catalog and ordering information.

Region I
Film Library
U.S.D.A. Forest Service
University of Montana
Missoula, Montana 59812 (406) 243-5976

Region II
J&A Film Service
P.O. Box 20034
Denver CO 80220 (303) 321-3030

Region III
Public Service Audience Planners
5107 Douglas Fir Rd.
Calabasas, CA 91302 (818) 884-3100
Southwest Region

Region IV
Utah State Library
USU
Audiovisual Service, UMC-31
Logan, UT 84322 (801) 750-2658

Region V
California- same as Region III

Region X
Alaska Department of Education
Attn: State Libraries
P.O. Box G
Juneau, AK 99811 (907) 465-2910

* Forest Service Regional Offices

Public Affairs
14th and Independence Ave., SW
Washington, DC 20250 (202) 205-1760

The Forest Service has an annual report which outlines the activities of each of its programs. Contact the office listed above for your free copy. The following is a list of Forest Service Regional Offices:

Forest Service, USDA
Northern Region (R-1)
Federal Building
P.O. Box 7669
Missoula, MT 59807 (406) 329-3511

Forest Service, USDA
Rocky Mountain Region (R-2)
11177 West 8th Ave.
P.O. Box 25127
Lakewood, CO 80225 (303) 236-9431

Forest Service, USDA
Southwestern Region (R-3)
Federal Building
517 Gold Ave., SW
Albuquerque, NM 87102 (505) 842-3293

Forest Service, USDA
Intermountain Region (R-4)
Federal Building
324 25th St.
Ogden, UT 84401 (801) 625-5352

Forest Service, USDA
Pacific Southwest Region (R-5)
630 Sansome St.
San Francisco, CA 94111 (415) 705-2870

Forest Service, USDA
Pacific Northwest Region (R-6)
319 S.W. Pine St.
P.O. Box 3623
Portland, OR 97208 (503) 326-2971

Forest Service, USDA
Southern Region (R-8)
1720 Peachtree Rd., NW
Atlanta, GA 30367 (404) 347-2384

Forest Service, USDA
Western Region (R-9)
310 West Wisconsin Ave., Room 500
Milwaukee, WI 53203 (414) 297-3693

Forest Service, USDA
Alaska Region (R-10)
P.O. Box 21628
Juneau, AK 99802 8-907-586-8863

* Forests Near TVA Reservoirs

River Basin Operations
Land Resources
Natural Resources Management
Forest Resource Development
Tennessee Valley Authority (TVA)
Norris, TN 37828 (615) 632-1631

The Forest Resource Development staff maintains forests around TVA's reservoirs to prevent development and thereby protect the water from siltation. The forests are kept in good health to allow for hunting--within the bounds of state regulations--and recreational parks. The Service also creates jobs and encourages economic development by assisting industry in utilizing forest resources. The staff also works with state agencies in reforestation efforts and fire control programs.

* Free Books and Posters on Forests

Forest Service Publications
Forest Service
U.S. Department of Agriculture
Washington, DC 20090 (202) 205-1760

The Forest Service publishes the following fact sheets, booklets and posters,

Be patient. If any phone number is incorrect, call (area code) 555-1212 and request the new listing.

Environment and Nature

which they offer free to the public. Contact the Office listed above for a current publications list. Titles include:

Making Paper from Trees
How a Tree Grows (poster)
Why Leaves Change (Color)
What the Forest Service Does
How a Tree Grows (Booklet)
Forestry Fact Sheet
How Fire Ruins Timber
Conservation Fact Sheet
Suggestions for Intergrating Forestry in the Modern Curriculum
Wilderness Sanitation
What we get from Trees (poster, Color and B&W)
Career Profiles
Investigating Your Community Environment
You Can Be a Forest Service Volunteer
Investigating Your Environment (Packet)
State Trees and Arbor Day
Is the Water Safe
Plant A Tree for a Special Occasion
The National Resource and Environmental Education Program of the Forest Service
Room to Roam
Timeless Heritage
A Guide to Your National Forests (map)
Managing the Range

* Free Land Films and Videos

Division of Public Affairs
Bureau of Land Management (BLM)
U.S. Department of the Interior
Washington DC 20240 (202) 208-6468

The Bureau of Land Management has produced three films, three videos, and a slide show dealing with areas covered by BLM. Titles include:

Promise of the Land (film)- explains multiple use management on public lands.

Dapples, Bays, Pintos and Grays (film)- presents wild horse and burro adopt a horse program.

Antiquities (film)- details issue of looting and vandalism of our cultural resources.

Measuring America: The Cadastral Story (slide show)- explains cadastral surveying.

BLM Backcountry Byways (video)- looks at recreational opportunities provided by BLM's backcountry byways program.

Fish and Wildlife 2000 (video)- explains managing wildlife and fisheries habitat on public lands.

Automating the Past (video)- details effort at automating old land records.

These films are often requested by educational institutions (elementary and junior high), as well as civic organizations interested in the outdoors or finding out how their tax dollars are being spent. Even the Boy Scouts have borrowed films for evening entertainment. Contact this office for more information on the films and videos available for free loan.

* Gold Prospecting

Publications Department
Bureau of Mines
U.S. Department of the Interior
18th and C Sts., NW, Room 2647
Washington, DC 20240 (202) 501-9649

The publications department of the Bureau of Mines distributes the free booklet, *How To Mine and Prospect for Gold.*

* Great Plains Conservation Work

Soil Conservation Service
U.S. Department of Agriculture
Washington, DC 20250 (202) 720-4525

Land users living in the Great Plains states can seek assistance from the Soil Conservation Service (SCS), which offers technical assistance and cost-sharing funds to farmers, ranchers, and other land users in the Great Plains. Cost-share rates can range up to 80 percent for urgently needed conservation work. Contact SCS or your local Soil Conservation Office.

* Help With Forest Pests

Forest Pest Management
Forest Service
U.S. Department of Agriculture
14th and Independence Ave., SW
Washington, DC 20250 (202) 205-1600

Forest Pest Management provides protection from insects and diseases on all Federal and non-Federal lands. Pest management projects also helped protect recreation areas, wildlife habitats, and watersheds. The Forest Service aerial and ground surveys detected and evaluated vegetation damage or pest populations on 134 million acres of National Forest System lands and 44 million acres of other Federal lands. For information on pest outbreak prevention and suppression contact the office listed above.

* Indian Land Trust

Office of Trust and Economic Development
Bureau of Indian Affairs
U.S. Department of the Interior
18th and C Sts., NW
Washington, DC 20240 (202) 208-5831

This office manages some 53 million acres of land held in trust by the United States for Indians. Tribes are helped in protecting their lands and in developing their forest, water, mineral, and energy resources.

* Land Management Library

Bureau of Land Management (BLM) Library, SC 324A
U.S. Department of the Interior
Denver Federal Center
P.O. Box 25007
Denver, CO 80225 (303) 236-6649

A vast collection of information on issues concerning land management is available to the public through this library. The reference staff and an automated card catalog system aid researchers in exploring the following topics: cadastral engineering; forest resources management; land reserve studies; legislation and public land laws; range management; watershed management; mineral, oil, and gas leasing; oil shale; and conservation and use of public lands.

* Land Use and Land Cover Maps

Distribution Branch
U.S. Geological Survey
Building 810
Denver Federal Center, Box 25286
Denver, CO 80225 (800) USA-MAPS

Land use maps and land cover maps are available for most of the United States. Land use maps refer to human uses of the land (housing and industry) and land cover maps describe the vegetation, water, natural surface, and construction on the land surface. The scale used ranges from 1:100,000 for a few maps in the Western states to 1:250,000 for most other maps.

* Livestock Rangeland

Rangeland Resources
Bureau of Land Management (BLM)
U.S. Department of the Interior
1725 I St., NW
Washington, DC 20006 (202) 653-9193

The Bureau of Land Management has administration of 170 million acres of public lands where livestock graze. About 18,800 ranchers and farmers graze livestock on BLM-managed lands. A majority of these permittees have small (less than 100 head) or medium (100 to 500 head) livestock operations.

* Minerals Management Service Field Offices

Bureau of Mines
U.S. Department of Interior
1951 Constitution Avenue, NW

Be patient. If any phone number is incorrect, call (area code) 555-1212 and request the new listing.

Forests and Land Conservation

Washington, DC 20240 (202) 208-3983

U.S. Department of Interior has the following regional offices:

Atlantic Region
381 Elden St., Suite 1109, Herndon, VA 22070-4817; (703) 787-1113

Alaska
949 E. 36th Ave., Suite 604, Anchorage, AK 99508-4302; (907) 261-4010

Gulf of Mexico
1201 Elmwood Park Blvd., New Orleans, LA 70123-2394; (504) 736-0557

Pacific Region
1340 W. 6th St., Los Angeles, CA 90017; (213) 894-2050

Central Region
6th Ave. and Kipling St., Bldg. 85, Lakewood, CO 80225; (303) 231-3058

* Mining Claims on Federal Lands

Energy and Mineral Resources
Bureau of Land Management (BLM)
U.S. Department of the Interior
18th and C Sts., NW
Washington, DC 20240 (202) 208-4201

The brochure, *Staking a Mining Claim on Federal Lands*, describes the procedure you would follow to stake a mining claim on public lands. Claims are granted to individuals for particular pieces of land, valuable for specific mineral deposits. Questions concerning the definition of a mining claim and the technicalities of recording and maintaining mining claims are also covered.

* National Firefighting Coordination

Fire and Aviation Management
Bureau of Land Management (BLM)
U.S. Department of the Interior
1725 I St., NW
Washington, DC 20006 (202) 653-8800

The goal of the Boise Interagency Fire Center is to provide the nationwide coordination of fire support activities among Federal and state firefighting agencies. The Fire Center is also called upon to help during many types of natural disasters when local, state, and regional resources are exhausted.

* National Park Off-Shore Oil Leases Revenues

Land Resources Division
National Park Service
U.S. Department of the Interior
1100 L St., NW
Washington, DC 20005 (202) 343-4828

The National Park System is able to purchase land for its use with the revenues received from off-shore oil leases. Revenues from these leases also are credited to the Land and Water Conservation Fund and the Historic Preservation Fund for efforts in these areas.

* National Park Service Regional Offices

National Park Service
U.S. Department of the Interior
1100 L St., NW
Washington, DC 20005 (202) 208-7394

Here are the contact points for the field offices of the National Park Service.

Alaska
2525 Gambell St., Room 107, Anchorage, AK 99503; (907) 271-4196

Mid-Atlantic
143 South Third St., Philadelphia, PA 19106; (215) 597-3679. Serving: PA, VA, WV, DE, MD

Midwest
1709 Jackson St., Omaha, NE 68102; (402) 221-3448. Serving: NE, MO, KS, IA, IL, IN, WI, MI, MN, OH

National Capital
1100 Ohio Dr., SW, Washington, DC 20242; (202) 426-6700

North-Atlantic
15 State St., Boston, MA 02109-3572; (617) 223-3793. Serving: NY, NJ, CT, RI, MA, NH, VT, ME

Pacific Northwest
2001 6th Avenue, Seattle, WA 98104; (206) 442-4830. Serving: WA, OR, ID

Rocky Mountains
12795 W. Alameda Pkwy, P.O. Box 25287, Denver, CO 80225; (303) 234-3095. Serving: MT, ND, SD, WY, UT, CO

Southeast
75 Spring St., Atlanta, GA 30303; (404) 221-4998. Serving: MS, TN, AL, GA, FL, SC, NC, KY, Virgin Is., PR

Southwest
P.O. Box 728, Santa FE, NM 87504-0728; (505) 988-6375. Serving: NM, TX, LA, OK, AR

Western
450 Golden Gate Ave., P.O. Box 36063, San Francisco, CA 94102; (415) 556-5186. Serving: CA, AZ, NV, HI, Guam, Northern Marianas Is., Am Samoa, Micronesia, Marshall Is., Palau.

* Native American Indians Land Rights

Office of Public Affairs
Bureau of Indian Affairs
U.S. Department of the Interior
18th and C Sts., NW
Washington, DC 20240 (202) 208-7315

The free booklet, *American Indians Today: Answers to Your Questions, 1988*, contains useful information on the Native American Indians and their relationship to the Bureau of Indian Affairs. Programs within the Bureau, including education, health services, and housing are briefly outlined and contain recent statistics. Many questions are answered within the booklet, including the rights of the Indians to own land and have their own governments. A map locates the Indian lands and communities, showing Federal and State Indian Reservations and other Indian groups. An excellent bibliography, prepared by the Smithsonian Institution, is included.

* Need Some Help Managing Your Forest?

Forest Resource Management
Forest Service
U.S. Department of Agriculture
14th and Independence Ave., SW
Washington, DC 20250 (202) 205-1374

The Forest Resource Management program cooperates with State forestry agencies to provide technical assistance to non-industrial private landowners for managing their forest lands. During 1990, this program helped landowners manage 3.5 million acres by assistance through multi-resource management plans.

* Offshore Information

Office of Offshore Information and Publication
Minerals Management Service
381 Elden St., MS 642
Herndon, VA 22070 (703) 787-1037

The Minerals Management Service manages more than a billion offshore acres and collects billions of dollars in mineral revenues annually. One of its two primary missions is to run the federal government's program for managing mineral resources on the Outer Continental Shelf (OCS). The Offshore Information Office can provide you with any information regarding the OCS, including publications on leasing and managing energy resources, brochures on oil-spill prevention, as well as scientific and technical publications of the Offshore Minerals Management Program.

* Outdoor Recreation

Land Between The Lakes (LBL)
Tennessee Valley Authority (TVA)
100 Van Morgan Dr.
Golden Pond, KY 42211 (502) 924-1243

LBL is a 40-mile long, wooded peninsula bordered on three sides by the water

Be patient. If any phone number is incorrect, call (area code) 555-1212 and request the new listing.

Environment and Nature

of Kentucky Lake and Lake Barkley. LBL is a national outdoor recreation and environmental education area managed by the TVA. In LBL you can enjoy camping, hiking, fishing, bicycling, sightseeing, and other traditional outdoor activities. Four State resort parks are nearby which have lodging and restaurant facilities. For more information including maps, an LBL calendar of events, and other information, contact the address listed above.

* Pacific Yew - Anticancer Drug

Jim Sanders
Forest Service
U.S. Department of Agriculture
14th and Independence Ave., SW
Washington, DC 20250 (202) 205-1772

Taxol, a chemical extracted from the Pacific Yes, is an extremely effective anticancer drug. Patients with ovarian cancer have shown a 40 percent response rate to taxol treatment even when they had previously shown no response to other drugs. Breast cancer patients are predicted to show a 50-percent response. Taxol is expected to become a major cancer-treating chemical. This will require a large and steady supply of the raw material- Pacific yew bark. Attempts to produce taxol synthetically have not been successful. The National Cancer Institute and the Forest Service are working together on short and long-range approaches to the taxol supply from Pacific yew bark. To provide long-term bark supply, the Institute and the Forest Service are collecting bark and branchlet samples to send to the Institute for taxol-content determination and to the National Forest Genetic Tectrophoresis Laboratory for test of genetic variation. Mr. Sanders has a wealth of information on taxol, including the range, amount, collect, and current research. He can also refer you to the proper researchers for more technical information.

* Parks Pass

National Park Service
U.S. Department of the Interior
P.O. Box 37127
Washington, DC 20013 (202) 208-7394

Some federal parks, refuges and facilities can be entered and used free of charge. Other areas and facilities require payment of entrance fees, user fees, special recreation permit fees, or some combination. There are five Congressionally authorized entrance passes. The annual Golden Eagle passport and the two lifetime passes, the Golden Age Passport and Golden Access Passport, can be used at all federally operated outdoor recreation areas which charge entrance fees. The Federal Duck Stamp serves as an annual entrance fee permit to national wildlife refuges, and Park Pass is an annual entrance permit to a specific park. Contact the office listed above for more information.

* Publications On National Parks

Office of Public Affairs
National Park Service
U.S. Department of the Interior
Washington, DC 20240 (202) 208-4747

The Office of Public Affairs can provide you with a list of publications available from the National Park Service. They publish the *National Park Handbooks*, which are compact introductions to the great natural and historic places administered by the Park Service. They are published to promote understanding and enjoyment of the parks. Each is intended to be informative reading and a useful guide before, during, and after a park visit. They also publish the following general publications:

The National Parks: Camping Guide 1991
The National Parks: Index 1989
The National Parks: Lesser-Know Areas
The National Parks: Shaping the System
The National Park System Map and Guide, 1990 edition
Welcome to Washington, 1990 edition
The White House

* Public Lands National Parks

Division of Interpretation
National Park Service
U.S. Department of the Interior
1100 L St., NW, Room 2101
Washington, DC 20240 (202) 523-5270

The National Park Service assists its facilities in planning and carrying out their exhibits and visitor programs. Their future plans include more involvement in environmental education programs to be offered at the Park Service sites.

* Public Lands Oil and Gas Leasing

Energy and Mineral Resources Division
Bureau of Land Management (BLM)
U.S. Department of the Interior
18th and C Sts., NW
Washington, DC 20240 (202) 208-4201

Public lands are available for oil and gas leasing only after they have been evaluated through the Bureau of Land Management. In areas where development of oil and gas resources would conflict with the protection or management of other resources or public land uses, mitigating measures are identified and may appear on leases as either stipulations to uses or as restrictions on surface occupancy. Two types of leases are issued: competitive and noncompetitive.

* Public Lands Photos

Forestry, Range, Realty
Office of Public Affairs
Bureau of Land Management (BLM)
U.S. Department of the Interior
18th and C Sts., NW
Washington, DC 20240 (202) 208-5717

Thousands of black and white photographs and color slides are available, including forestry, realty, minerals, and range subjects.

* Public Lands Recreation

Office of Public Affairs
Bureau of Land Management (BLM)
U.S. Department of the Interior
18th and C Sts., NW
Washington, DC 20240 (202) 208-5717

In recognition of the importance of outdoor recreation to Americans, *Recreation 2000 Executive Summary* sets forth the commitment of the Bureau of Land Management to the management of outdoor recreation resources in public lands. The plan highlights the areas in which the Bureau intends to concentrate future efforts, such as visitor information, resource protection, land ownerships, partnerships, volunteers, tourism programs, facilities, and permits, fees, and concessions.

* Public Land Renewable Resources Management

Land and Renewable Resources
Bureau of Land Management (BLM)
U.S. Department of the Interior
18th and C Sts., NW
Washington, DC 20240 (202) 208-4896

The Bureau of Land Management issues leases, rights-of-way, and use permits for a wide variety of public lands including parks; power transmission and distribution lines; petroleum products collection and transmission systems.

* Public Lands Revenue: Grazing, Timber Sales, Mining

Management Services, Bureau of Land Management (BLM)
U.S. Department of the Interior
18th and C Sts., NW
Washington, DC 20240 (202) 208-4864

This office collects and disburses revenues and receipts generated from public lands. The Bureau of Land Management is a primary generator of revenues in the Federal government, with more than $800 million collected annually from a variety of sources, including timber sales, sale of public lands, grazing leases, right-of-way leases, permits, and mineral receipts.

* Public Land Statistics

Superintendent of Documents
Government Printing Office
Washington, DC 20402 (202) 783-3238

The publication, *Public Land Statistics*, contains valuable information regarding the land administered by the Bureau of Land Management. Tables include the following topics: land disposition and use, range management, resource conservation and development, forest management, wildlife habitat management, wild horse and burro management, cultural resource management, outdoor

Be patient. If any phone number is incorrect, call (area code) 555-1212 and request the new listing.

Forests and Land Conservation

recreation, areas of critical environmental concern, energy and mineral resources, public land surveys, fire protection, and finance.

* Rural Community Fire Protection

Fire and Aviation Management Staff
Forest Service, U.S. Department of Agriculture
14th and Independence Ave., SW
Washington, DC 20250 (202) 205-1483

The Farmers Home Administration funds Rural Community Fire Protection, and the Forest Service administers the program in cooperation with State foresters. The program contributes matching funds to strengthen volunteer fire departments in communities of less than 10,000 people. The funds provide for organizing, training, and equipping rural fire departments.

* Smokey Bear and Fire Prevention

Smokey Bear Headquarters
U.S. Forest Service
14th and Independence Ave., NW
Washington, DC 20250 (202) 205-1483

To make children aware of the campaign to fight forest fires, the Forest Service makes a variety of materials available to children, including posters, signs, patches, bookmarks, bumper stickers, and comic books.

* Soil and Farmland Protection Programs

Soil Conservation Service (SCS)
U.S. Department of Agriculture
P.O. Box 2890
Washington, DC 20013 (202) 720-4543

Soil surveys are used not only for conservation purposes but also to identify suitable lands for a wide variety of uses, from maintaining crops to urban uses. Information about soil helps prevent major construction mistakes and misuse of land that can be productively put to use. Soil maps identify flood-prone areas and sources of water pollutants.

* Soil Conservation Technical Expertise

Soil Conservation Service (SCS)
U.S. Department of Agriculture
P.O. Box 2890
Washington, DC 20013 (202) 720-4543

Technical expertise is available in such areas as irrigation, drainage, landscape architecture, construction, sanitary and water quality, and hydrology.

* State Soil-Saving Conservation

Information Division
U.S. Department of Agriculture
ASCS, P.O. Box 205
Kansas City, MO 64141 (816) 926-6502

The Agricultural State Conservation Service (ASCS) directs a number of conservation programs to preserve and improve American farmland: Agricultural Conservation Program (ACP): This program is designed to solve soil, water, and related resource problems through costsharing. ACP assistance is available to install soil-saving practices, including terraces, grass, sod waterways, and other measures to control erosion. It also helps reduce sediment, chemicals, and livestock waste that contaminate streams and lakes.

* Soil, Water, and Air Sciences

ARS Information Staff
U.S. Department of Agriculture
Room 307-A, Building 005
Beltsville, MD 20705 (301) 344-2264

Specialists study such topics as environmental quality, erosion and sedimentation, soil fertility and plant nutrition, organic wastes, pesticide degradation, water use efficiency and tillage practices, and weed control. Contact the ARS staff for answers to questions on these and other conservation-related topics.

* Strip Mining and Reclamation

Office of Public Affairs
Office of Surface Mining Reclamation and Enforcement

U.S. Department of Interior
1951 Constitution Avenue, NW
Washington, DC 20240 (202) 208-2553

This office works to protect people and the environment from the side-effects of coal mining, while continuing to regulate coal mining. Lands that were affected by past coal mining operations must be repaired if left unreclaimed or abandoned. Technical assistance is provided to states so that they can perform their responsibilities under the surface mining law. State personnel are trained in the technical aspects of surface mining, such as soil compaction, revegetation, and groundwater hydrology, so that they can better enforce regulations. An *Annual Report* is available.

* Strip Mining Enforcement Offices Nationwide

Office of Surface Mining Reclamation and Enforcement
U.S. Department of Interior (DOI)
1951 Constitution Avenue, NW
Washington, DC 20240 (202) 208-2553

The following are field offices of DOI's Surface Mining and Reclamation Office:

Albuquerque
625 Silver Ave., SW, Suite 310, Albuquerque, NM 87102; (505) 766-1486

Appalachia
350 Elaine Dr., Suite 2300, Lexington, KY 40504; (606) 233-2792

Ashland
Federal Bldg., Room 120, 1430 Greenup Ave., Ashland, KY 41101; (606) 325-4735

Beckley
101 Harper Park Dr., Beckley, WV 25801; (304) 255-5265

Birmingham
280 W. Valley, Room 302, Homewood, AL 35209; (205) 731-0890

Big Stone Gap
P.O. Box 626, Big Stone Gap, VA 24219; (703) 523-4303

Casper
Federal Bldg., 100 East B St., Room 2128, Casper, WY 82601-1918; (307) 261-5776

Columbus
2242 S. Hamilton Rd., Columbus, OH 43232; (614) 866-0578

Chattanooga
900 Georgia Ave., Room 30, Chattanooga, TN 37402; (615) 752-5175

Charleston
603 Morris St., Charleston, WV 25301; (304) 347-7158

Denver
Bldg. 20, Room B2015, P.O. Box 25065, Denver CO 80225; (303) 236-0331

Eastern
Ten Parkway Center, Pittsburgh, PA 15220; (412) 937-2828

Harrisburg
Harrisburg Transportation Ctr., Third Fl., Suite 3C, 4th and Market Sts., Harrisburg, PA 17101; (717) 782-4036

Hazard
516 Village Lane, Hazard, KY 41701; (606) 439-5843

Indianapolis
Minton-Capehart Federal Bldg., 575 N. Penn St., Room 301, Indianapolis, IN 46204; (371) 226-6700

Johnstown
Penn Traffic Bldg., Room 20, 319 Washington St., Johnston, PA 15901; (814) 533-4223

Kansas City
1103 Grand Ave., Room 502, Kansas City, MO 64106; (816) 374-6405

Be patient. If any phone number is incorrect, call (area code) 555-1212 and request the new listing.

Environment and Nature

Knoxville
530 Gay St., Suite 500, Knoxville, TN 37902; (615) 673-4504

Lexington
340 Legion Dr., Suite 28, Lexington, KY 40504; (606) 233-7327

London
P.O. Box 1048, London, KY 40741; (606) 878-6440

Lebanon
Two Acre Task Force: P.O. Box 487, Lebanon, VA 24266; (703) 889-4032

Madisonville
Segebarth Bldg., Box F, 2100 N. Main St., Madisonville, KY 42431; (502) 825-4500

Morgantown
P.O. Box 886, Morgantown, WV 26507; (304) 291-4004

Norris
P.O. Box 295, Norris, TN 37828; (615) 632-1699

Olympia
Columbia Commons, 3773 C Martini Way East, Suite 104, Olympia, WA 98506; (206) 753-9538

Pikesville
Division of Audit Management, First National Bank, Room 608B, 334 Main St., Pikesville, KY 41505; (606) 432-4123

Prestonburgh
P.O. Box 306, 2664 West Mountain Parkway, West Prestonburg, KY 41618; (606) 886-1391

Springfield
600 East Monroe St., Room 20, Springfield IL 62701; (217) 492-4495

Tulsa
5100 East Skelley Dr., Suite 550, Tulsa, OK 74135; (918) 581-6430

Wilkes-Barre
20 N. Penn. Ave., Suite 3323, Wilkes-Barre, PA 18701; (717) 826-6333

Western Region
1050 15th St., 2nd Fl., Brooks Towers, Denver, CO 80202; (303) 844-2459

* Timber and Woodland Analysis

River Basin Operations
Natural Resources Management
Land Resources, Forestry Resource Development
Tennessee Valley Authority
Norris, TN 37828 (615) 632-1631

This Land Resources group has developed a number of user-friendly, reliable, PC software programs, which allow the public, the timber industry, and consultants to analyze timber supply, inventory, and finances by providing growth and yield information. Inventory processing helps foresters to determine maximum financial returns by calculating, for example, the optimal time to schedule harvesting. To stay abreast of all new technologies, this resource group also conducts safety seminars, field days, and hardware demonstrations, and to stay abreast of all new technology.

* Tree Growing and Lumber Bibliography

Superintendent of Documents
Government Printing Office
Washington, DC 20402 (202) 783-3238

Tree publications are listed, including those of interest to tree growers and the lumber industry. Also featured is a guide to Christmas Tree diseases and books listing the tropical timbers of the world. Free.

* Utilize Your Forest Wisely

Forest Products Utilization
Forest Service
U.S. Department of Agriculture

14th and Independence Ave., SW
Washington, DC 20250 (202) 205-1394

Utilization, marketing, and technology transfer activities are important aspects of the outreach delivery provided by Cooperative Forestry staff. Key accomplishments include the monthly technology transfer newsletter *Utilization and Marketing Review* which provides current information on research and technology transfer to assist scientists and nonindustrial private landowners. Also available includes the *Technology Opportunities* packet, which contains concepts, emerging technologies, recent developments, and state-of-the-art knowledge from the Forest Products Laboratory and experiment stations. The Integrated Mill Production and Recovery Options for Value and Efficiency (IMPROVE) System package will increase sawmill, veneer mill, or plywood plant output by improving manufacturing efficiency. Other technology transfer activities include central tire inflation, wood protection using diffusible preservatives, and hardwood use for structural application.

* Wetlands and Land Conservation

Information Division
U.S. Department of Agriculture
ASCS, P.O. Box 205
Kansas City, MO 64141 (202) 720-5237

The Agricultural State Conservation Service (ASCS) directs a number of conservation programs: plant trees, improve timberstands, prevent loss of wetlands for migratory waterfowl, and control water pollution.

* Wildland Fire Database

FIREBASE Operations
U.S. Department of Agriculture Forest Service
Boise Interagency Fire Center
3905 Vista Ave.
Boise, ID 83705 (208) 389-2604

FIREBASE is a collection of bibliographic citations and abstracts of wildland fire-related information. The database is international in scope and topic include wildland fire detection; prevention and suppression; fire management analysis; planning and training; and fire statistics, indexes, and hazards.

* Youth Conservation Corps Regional Offices

Washington Office
Youth Program Officer
National Park Service
U.S. Department of the Interior
Room 4415, P.O. Box 37127
1100 L St., NW
Washington, DC 20013-7127 (202) 343-5514

Youngsters interested to gain experience in environmental protection can contact the nearest field office of the National Park Service listed below to inquire about summer job opportunities:

Alaska
2525 Gambell St., Room 107, Anchorage, AK 99503; (907) 261-2690

Mid-Atlantic
Second and Chestnut Sts., Philadelphia, PA 19106; (215) 597-2284. Serving: PA, VA, WV, DE, MD

Midwest
1709 Jackson St., Omaha, NE 68102; (402) 221-3431. Serving: NE, MO, KS, IA, IL, IN, WI, MI, MN, OH

National Capital
1100 Ohio Dr., SW, Washington, DC 20242; (202) 485-9813

North-Atlantic
15 State St., Boston, MA 02109-3572; (617) 565-8841. Serving: NY, NJ, CT, RI, MA, NH, VT, ME

Pacific Northwest
83 South King St., Suite 212, Seattle, WA 98104; (206) 442-5565. Serving: WA, OR, ID

Rocky Mountains
12795 W. Alameda Pkwy, P.O. Box 25287, Denver, CO 80225; (303) 969-2875. Serving: MT, ND, SD, WY, UT, CO

Be patient. If any phone number is incorrect, call (area code) 555-1212 and request the new listing.

Forests and Land Conservation

Southeast
75 Spring St., Atlanta, GA 30303; (404) 331-5185. Serving: MS, TN, AL, GA, FL, SC, NC, KY, Virgin Is., PR

Southwest
P.O. Box 728, Santa FE, NM 87504-0728; (505) 988-6388. Serving: NM, TX, LA, OK, AR

Western
450 Golden Gate Ave., P.O. Box 36063, San Francisco, CA 94102; (415) 556-4196. Serving: CA, AZ, NV, HI, Guam, Northern Marianas Is., Am Samoa, Micronesia, Marshall Is., Palau.

Environment and Nature

Fish and Wildlife

* *See also Vacations and Business Travel Chapter*

* Acid Rain and Aquatic Species Chart

Superintendent of Documents
Government Printing Office
Washington, DC 20402 (202) 783-3238

The wall chart, *Acid Rain: The Effect on Aquatic Species*, illustrates the survival of selected aquatic species in an acidic environment. Information is given on acid rain, its causes, and the effect on aquatic life. Measures 17 by 22 inches (S/N 024-010-00675-7, $3.25).

* Alaska Fish and Wildlife Research

Alaska Fish and Wildlife Research Center
U.S. Fish and Wildlife Service
1011 E. Tudor Rd.
Anchorage, AK 99503 (907) 786-3512

The Alaska Fish and Wildlife Research Center in Anchorage, in association with its field stations in Kodiak and Fairbanks, is responsible for planning and conducting research on fish, wildlife, and their habitats in Alaska. Areas of research include: the status and trends of marine mammal populations; the distribution, abundance, and population trends of coastal and marine birds; waterfowl population dynamics; productivity and stock of anadromous fish; advanced technology and its use in studying arctic and subarctic fish and wildlife; and identifying and resolving conflicts between wildlife and the utilization of Alaska's natural resources.

* Arctic and Antarctic Science Stations

Office of Polar Affairs
Bureau of Oceans and International Environmental and Scientific Affairs
U.S. Department of State
2201 C St., NW, Room 5801
Washington, DC 20520 (202) 647-3262

This office is concerned with all issues concerning the Arctic and Antarctic, including the environment and marine life, such as whales and seals. They are also closely involved with the many science stations located on the Antarctic.

* Bald Eagles and Peregrine Falcons

U.S. Department of the Army
Chemical Research Development and Engineering Center
Aberdeen Proving Ground, MD 21010-5423 (301) 671-4912

While the Center's primary mission is concerned with research on chemical defensive material, the Center has become very involved in wildlife conservation programs because of its location on the Chesapeake Bay. The Center is especially experienced in a Bald Eagle program and a Peregrine Falcon program. Fact sheets on these and other wildlife issues may be obtained by writing or calling the above office.

* Banded Waterfowl Recovery

Office of Migratory Bird Research
Patuxent Wildlife Research Center
U.S. Fish and Wildlife Service
Laurel, MD 20708 (301) 498-0300

If you happen to capture, find, or shoot a banded bird is obtained, you should remove the band, flatten and tape it securely to a piece of heavy paper or cardboard, and mail it to the address above. Include the following information: 1) Names and address of person sending the band: 2) All numbers and letters on the band (in case the band is lost from the envelope); 3) Date the band was obtained; 4) Place where band was found (mileage and direction from the nearest town, including County and State); 5) How the band was obtained (on a bird shot, found dead, etc.). Mark the envelope *Hand Cancel*.

* Birds Bibliography

Superintendent of Documents
Government Printing Office
Washington, DC 20402 (202) 783-3238

This listing includes booklets on the Atlantic Barrier Islands and their plant and animals life, the Chesapeake Bay's bird population, and field guide to fifty birds to observe in your own town. The Duck Stamp Collection subscription service is also outlined. Free.

* Bird Strikes

Airport Safety Data Group
Office of Airport Standards
Federal Aviation Administration
U.S. Department of Transportation
800 Independence Ave., SW, Room 615
Washington, DC 20591 (202) 267-8792

Birds being accidentally sucked into jet engines is a serious aviation hazard. Contact this office for information on where bird strikes occur.

* Birds, Buffalo, and Other Publications

U.S. Fish and Wildlife Service
4401 N. Fairfax Dr.
Arlington, VA 22203 (703) 358-1711

For a free listing of general interest publications from the Fish and Wildlife Service, contact the office above. General interest publications are available free of charge, but when ordering more than five publications, the need must be justified. Titles include the following:

American Bald Eagle
America's Sea Turtles
Attracting and Feeding Birds
Chesapeake Bay
Conservation Notes on American Buffalo
Ducks at a Distance
Duck Stamp Story
Endangered Species
Facts about Federal Wildlife Laws
Lead Poisoning in Waterfowl
People and Wildlife-Public Involvement in Fish and Wildlife Administration
Waterfowl Regulations

Also available is a *Wildlife Biologue Series* of various species of wildlife, including endangered species. The series includes a one page life history of the species. They are free of charge when ordering under five copies. Contact the above office for a listing.

* Buffalo and Cattle Refuges

Division of Refuges
U.S. Fish and Wildlife Service
4401 N. Fairfax Dr.
Arlington, VA 22203 (703) 358-1744

Buffalo and Texas longhorn cattle, as well as deer and elk, can be enjoyed at wildlife refuges maintained by the U.S. Department of the Interior. Wichita Mountains in Oklahoma and Fort Niobrara in Nebraska preserve these animals in their natural habitat. The government periodically auctions these animals to the public at these locations. For more information, contact the refuge managers directly: Fort Niobrara National Wildlife Refuge, Hidden Timber Route, HC 14, Box 67, Valentine, NE 69201; (402) 376-3789. Wichita Mountains Wildlife Refuge, Rt. 1, Box 448, Indiahoma, OK 73552; (405) 429-3222. You can see Buffalo also at the National Bison Range in Moiese, Montana. For more information on this refuge, contact National Bison Range, Moiese, MT 59824; (406) 644-2211.

Be patient. If any phone number is incorrect, call (area code) 555-1212 and request the new listing.

Fish and Wildlife

* Captive Breeding of Endangered Species

Patuxent Wildlife Research Center
U.S. Fish and Wildlife Service
Laurel, MD 20708
(301) 498-0300

The Endangered Species Branch at Patuxent conducts research on several endangered species in their native habitats throughout the United States and its territories. Current studies focus on such species as the Puerto Rican parrot, California condor, Hawaiian forest birds, Kirtland's warbler, and eastern timber wolf. Along with studying the endangered species, the scientists breed them in captivity for release to bolster wild populations. Key endangered species, as well as closely related surrogate species, are maintained for captive propagation research. The physiological, behavioral, and veterinary characteristics of these species are evaluated to gain a better understanding of possible biological problems as well as to assist with management of the species in the wild.

* Conservation Law Enforcement Training

Law Enforcement Division
U.S. Fish and Wildlife Service
4401 N. Fairfax Dr.
Arlington, VA 22203
(703) 358-1949

Through this division, state conservation officers are trained in the area of criminal law as it applies to the enforcement of wildlife protection.

* Duck and Geese Population

North American Waterfowl Management Plan
U.S. Fish and Wildlife Service
Federal Building
Fort Snelling
Twin Cities, MN 55111
(612) 290-3131

The United States and Canada have joined forces to reverse the decline in certain populations of ducks and geese. This plan has inspired cooperation between Federal, Provincial, and State governments, as well as private conservation agencies in the two countries. Joint ventures, formed among public and private corporations, are developing economic incentives to change land use practices, striking agreements with private landowners, and improving water management.

* Duck Stamps

Federal Duck Stamp Office
U.S. Fish and Wildlife Service
1849 C Street, NW
Suite 2058
Washington, DC 20240
(202) 208-4355

The Federal Duck Stamp program has become one of the most successful conservation programs ever initiated. To date, over 350 million duck stamp dollars have gone to preserve over 4 million acres of wetland refuges for North American waterfowl. A sheet of duck stamps from 1987-1988, Redheads, can be purchased for $10, as well as the 1988-1989 Snow Goose stamps. The 1989-1990 Lesser Scaup stamps are available for $12.50, and the 1990-1992 Black-bellied Whispering Ducks for $12.50. To order your Duck Stamps, contact U.S. Postal Service, Philatelics Sales Division, Washington, DC 20265-9997.

Subscriptions to the Duck Stamp Collection are available at $12 each from the Superintendent of Documents. The collection includes a data sheet on each duck stamp issued since the first one in 1934. Each sheet includes a photograph of the stamp and original art, short biography of the artist, names of the designers and engravers, inscription, first date of sale, and number of stamps sold. The subscription service provides the entire collection to date plus one update per year for an indeterminate period of time.

* Duck Stamp Design Competition

Federal Duck Stamp Office
U.S. Fish and Wildlife Service
4401 N. Fairfax Drive
Arlington, VA 22203
(703) 358-2020

Each year, a Duck Stamp Design Competition is held, with the winning design chosen by a panel of waterfowl and art experts. Any artist can enter the contest by submitting a 7 X 10 inch waterfowl design and paying an entry fee. The winner receives a pane of stamps bearing his or her design. Winning artists also sell prints of their prize entries which are eagerly sought by collectors.

* Ecosystems and Wildlife Habitat Models

National Ecology Center
U.S. Fish and Wildlife Service
2627 Redwing Rd.
Fort Collins, CO 80526-2899
(303) 226-9100

The center conducts research, develops new tools, and transfers information so that scientists can better understand and manage fish and wildlife resources, habitats, and ecosystems. All endangered marine mammal research is performed here. Workshops are held in refuge management and habitat model development for those within the Interior Department and scientists in Federal and State agencies and foreign countries. Studies are reported in the Center's *Biological Report* series and through extension education brochures.

* Endangered Species

S. James
Consumer Information Center 2A
P. O. Box 100
Pueblo, CO 81002

Endangered Species is a publication which explains government efforts to protect and restore species in danger of extinction and what you can do to help (587Y, $1).

* Endangered Wildlife and Plants

Office of Endangered Species
U.S. Fish and Wildlife Service
4401 N. Fairfax Dr.
Arlington, VA 22203
(703) 358-2171

The Fish and Wildlife Service follows a formal procedure in determining which species should be placed on the *U.S. List of Endangered and Threatened Wildlife and Plants*. The proposed ruling is published in the *Federal Register*, and after a suitable period for public comment and possible revision, it is published as a final rule. To obtain a listing of the endangered and threatened wildlife and plants and other information on this topic, contact the office above.

* Exotic and Warm Water Fish Husbandry

National Fisheries Research Center
U.S. Fish and Wildlife Service
7920 NW 71 St.
Gainesville, FL 32606
(904) 378-8181

Exotic and warm water fish of the southeastern United States and the Gulf Coast are studied at the National Fisheries Research Center in Gainesville, Florida, and at its field station in Marion, Alabama. Research of fish husbandry of southeastern fishes is also conducted. Aquatic weed control as it relates to the survival of these fishes is also a priority.

* Fish and Marine Life Bibliography

Superintendent of Documents
Government Printing Office
Washington, DC 20402
(202) 783-3238

Fisheries and fish research publications are featured in this bibliography, along with marine fish posters of the California, Great Lakes, and Gulf and South Atlantic waters. Free.

* Fish and Wildlife Films and Videos

Office of Public Affairs
Fish and Wildlife Service (FWS)
U.S. Department of Interior
Washington DC 20240
(202) 208-5611

The Fish and Wildlife Service has many films and videos available for free loan and are distributed through their regional offices. Some of the topic areas covered include current research and environmental issues, as well as fish and wildlife. The Offices also distribute some non-FWS videos which cover similar topics. Some of the titles available include:

America's Wetland
Wildlife, Wetlands and You- The Duck Stamp Story
Chain of Life- The Aleutian Islands
So Little Time
Where The Fish Will Be
Patuxent Wildlife Research Center
The Role of Research

Be patient. If any phone number is incorrect, call (area code) 555-1212 and request the new listing.

Environment and Nature

A Great White Bird
Birds of the Indian Monsoon
In Celebration of America's Wildlife

These films are used in elementary schools through college, and are often part of environmental group meetings. Contact your regional office for a free catalog, or you may contact the Office of Public Affairs for information regarding the Office nearest you.

* Fish and Wildlife Technical Publications

Office of Information Transfer
U.S. Fish and Wildlife Service
1025 Pennock Pl., Suite 212
Fort Collins, CO 80524 (303) 493-8401

Many technical publications are produced by the U.S. Fish and Wildlife Service. Copies of publications are available to selected individuals or organizations concerned with environmental issues.

Resource Publication
Fish and Wildlife Leaflet
Investigations in Fish Control
Fish Disease Leaflet
North American Fauna
Fish and Wildlife Research
Fish and Wildlife Technical Report
Biological Report

Fisheries Review and *Wildlife Review* are also available on a subscription basis from the Superintendent of Documents, Government Printing Office. *Fisheries Review* is $16/year and *Wildlife Review* is $22/year.

* Fish and Wildlife Year 2000

Office of Public Affairs
Bureau of Land Management
U.S. Department of the Interior
18th and C Sts., NW
Washington, DC 20240 (202) 208-5717

The full-color brochure, *Fish and Wildlife 2000: A Plan for the Future*, describes the future management plan of the public lands and their resources. These resources include recreation, range, forest, minerals, watershed, fish and wildlife, wilderness and natural, scenic, scientific, educational, and cultural values. A strategic plan is outlined, including the management of wildlife habitats, fisheries habitats, threatened and endangered species, and human resources.

* Fish and Wildlife Cooperative Research

Cooperative Fish and Wildlife
Research Units Center
U.S. Fish and Wildlife Service
4401 N. Fairfax Dr.
Arlington, VA 22203 (703) 358-1709

Cooperative fish and wildlife research field stations are located at various universities throughout the country. Research finds answers to a broad spectrum of fish and wildlife management questions, from habitat requirements of individual species to the effects of development projects on populations of fish and wildlife. Graduate education is provided to resource managers at the M.S. and Ph.D. levels and in-service training and continuing education is given to employees of conservation agencies. Technical assistance is made available to fish and wildlife resource managers and to the public. For a complete listing of field stations, contact the office above.

* Fish and Wildlife Photographs

Audio Visuals
U.S. Fish and Wildlife Service
18th and C Sts., NW
Washington, DC 20240 (202) 208-5611

The Audio Visual Department of the U.S. Fish and Wildlife Service has an extensive collection of both black and white pictures and color slides of fish and wildlife. There is no charge for their lending service, which extends 30 or 90 days. If the photographs or slides are used in publications, the photographer and the U.S. Fish and Wildlife Service must be given credit.

* Fish Disease and Chemical Cures

National Fisheries Research Center
U.S. Fish and Wildlife Service
P.O. Box 818
LaCrosse, WI 54602-0818 (608) 783-6451

The National Fisheries Research Center at LaCrosse, Wisconsin, has been designated by the Fish and Wildlife Service to negotiate registration for fishery chemicals with regulatory agencies. Pesticides are registered with the U.S. Environmental Protection Agency, and therapeutants for controlling fish diseases are registered with the U.S. Food and Drug Administration. Once a fishery chemical is registered by the Federal government, states will generally allow the use of that chemical for fish culture and management.

* Fisheries Contaminant Research

National Fisheries Contaminant Research Center
U.S. Fish and Wildlife Service
Rt. 2, 4200 New Haven Rd.
Columbia, MO 65201 (314) 875-5399

All fisheries contaminant research under the U.S. Fish and Wildlife Service, except for the Great Lakes area, is conducted at the National Fisheries Contaminant Research Center and its eight field stations. The Center is actively studying the effects of pesticides and other contaminants on aquatic ecosystems. Research equipment is designed to study the long-term effects of contaminants on growth, life stages, and biochemistry of fishes and other aquatic forms under realistic pollution conditions. The Center has capabilities to conduct special studies of national concern with striped bass, Atlantic and Pacific salmon, grayling, and Arctic char. Scientists and special groups are welcome at the Center, and special arrangements can be made for visiting scientists to conduct cooperative research with laboratory investigators.

* Fish Hatcheries Scientific Advice

Office of Information Transfer
U.S. Fish and Wildlife Service
1025 Pennock Pl., Suite 212
Fort Collins, CO 80524 (303) 493-8401

This office distributes technical information to scientists, refuge managers, and fish hatchery managers within and outside of the U.S. Fish and Wildlife Service. At office meetings scientists present research findings and provide technical advice to others. In turn, they have a rare opportunity to meet the users of their findings face to face. Information is also transferred through synthesis documents, which bring together information from a variety of sources on a particular topic of interest. Each package is then distributed to a specific audience, such as refuge managers or fish hatchery managers. Contact the office above to be placed on the mailing list for periodic announcements of new publications.

* Fish Health Research

National Fisheries Center
U.S. Fish and Wildlife Service
Box 700
Kearneysville, WV 25430 (304) 725-8461 x5333

The National Fisheries Center and its five field stations are world-renowned as a focal point for fish health research and fisheries development. Studies include nutrition, genetics, diseases, management technology, and technical services. The facility contains a training academy of fish husbandry.

* For The Latest Ecology Research. . . .

National Ecology Research Center
4512 McMurry Ave.
Fort Collins, CO 80525 (303) 226-9100

There is a continuing need for information that can help resolve the myriad of natural resource issues facing endangered species, nongame and declining species, and on a larger scale, terrestrial, riverine, and wetlands systems. The National Ecology Research Center strives to fill these needs. The Centers develop new technologies, conduct research on threatened and endangered animals, and give attention to nongame and declining species. The following is a list of field research stations, including some of the research which they conduct.

San Simeon, CA- movements, reproductive biology, and foraging ecology of sea otters; distribution and and seasonal abundance of birds and reptiles in riparian areas near Piedras Blancas.

Be patient. If any phone number is incorrect, call (area code) 555-1212 and request the new listing.

Fish and Wildlife

Santa Cruz, CA- interaction of sea otters with their nearshore food resources.

Gainesville, FL- long-term life history and population studies of manatees, reptiles, and amphibians.

Albuquerque, NM- ecology, distribution, and status of reptiles and amphibians in the arid southwest.

Washington, DC- curation of the North American collection of amphibians, eptiles, birds, and mammals at the U.S. National Museum of Natural History; status of amphibians in the eastern United States.

Auburn, AL- aquatic research and instream flow assessments for fishes, mussels, and insects.

* Grain Surpluses for Wildlife

Commodities Operations
U.S. Department of Agriculture
ASCS, Room 2415
Washington, DC 20013 (202) 720-3217

Upon request of the U.S. Department of the Interior, bulk grain is available in emergency situations to feed wildlife and birds as long as grain surpluses exist.

* Great Lakes Fish Spawning and Survival

National Fisheries Research Center
U.S. Fish and Wildlife Service
1451 Green Rd.
Ann Arbor, MI 48105 (313) 994-3331

The primary objective of the National Fisheries Research Center in Ann Arbor and its eight biological stations and research vessels is to develop the knowledge and technical basis for assessing, protecting, enhancing, and rehabilitating the valuable resources and habitats of the Great Lakes. Laboratory experiments provide information on how natural and man-induced changes in the lakes may affect important fish populations. Particular emphasis is placed upon the spawning requirements, survival of early life stages, and forage requirements of important species such as lake trout.

* Marine Environmental Pollution Response

Pollution Response Branch
Marine Environmental Response Division
Office of Marine Safety, Security and Environmental Protection
U.S. Coast Guard
U.S. Department of Transportation
2100 2nd St., SW, Room 2104
Washington, DC 20593-0001 (202) 267-2611

This office responds to requests for marine environmental protection information from Congress and other federal agencies, state agencies, schools, industries, and the general public. Data is available on laws relating to the protection of the marine environment, incidents involving releases of oil or other hazardous substances, and federally funded spill response operations.

* Marine Life Posters

Superintendent of Documents
Government Printing Office
Washington, DC 20402 (202) 783-3238

The following is a list of Marine Life Posters available from the National Marine Fisheries Service through the Government Printing Office. The posters are printed on washable non-glare plasticized paper, and cost $5.50 each.

Marine Fishes of the California Current and Adjacent Waters
Marine Fishes of the Gulf and South Atlantic
Fishes of the Great Lakes
Mollusks and Crustaceans of the Coastal U.S.

* Marine Mammals Rescue and Protection

Office of Protected Resources
National Marine Fisheries Service
National Oceanic and Atmospheric Administration
U.S. Department of Commerce
1335 East-West Hwy.
Silver Spring, MD 20910 (301) 713-2322

The Marine Mammal Protection Act commits the United States to long-term management and research programs to conserve and protect these animals. Marine mammals may be taken for scientific research, public display, and incidentally to commercial fishing. The National Marine Fisheries Service grants or denies requests for exemptions, issues permits, carries out research and management programs, enforces the Act, participates in international programs, and issues rules and regulations to carry out its mission to conserve and protect marine mammals. An annual report is available for the Office of Protected Resources, which gives detailed information regarding the activities of the Office. This office can also provide you with copies of the Act, and the publication *Proceedings of the Workshop to Review and Evaluate Whale Watching Programs and Management Needs.*

* Migratory Bird Research

Migratory Birds Research Branch
Patuxent Wildlife Research Center
U.S. Fish and Wildlife Service
Laurel, MD 20708 (301) 498-0300

Research at Patuxent on migratory game birds includes methods of assessing the status of various species, discovering reasons for declines in particular bird populations, and investigating relationships between bird populations and environmental variables to determine ecologically sound resource management techniques. Non-game migratory bird research at Patuxent studies particular habitat requirements for breeding, migration, and wintering.

* National Fisheries Library

U.S. Fish and Wildlife Service
P.O. Box 818
LaCrosse, WI 54602-0818 (608) 783-6451

The Center's library has the world's most complete collection of publications on fishery chemicals, their use, and their effects on the environment. Computer hook-ups provide access to over 200 databases.

* National Wildlife Refuges Visitor's Guide

Office of Public Affairs
U.S. Fish and Wildlife Service
18th and C Sts., NW
Washington, DC 20240 (703) 358-1711

National Wildlife Refuges: A Visitor's Guide is a listing of all of the National Wildlife Refuges that provide visitor opportunities; not all of the refuges in the system are included. A map locating each of these refuges is featured, along with public facilities, including visitor's centers, foot trails, auto tours, bicycling, boating, environmental study areas, hunting, fishing, camping, picnicking, swimming, and food and lodging. For a state-by-state listing of these refuges, see the listing below under "Wildlife Refuges National System."

* Nuisance Fish Control

National Fisheries Research Center
U.S. Fish and Wildlife Service
P.O. Box 818
LaCrosse, WI 54602-0818 (608) 783-6451

The National Fisheries Research Center at La Crosse, along with its field station at Hammond Bay, Michigan, have played an important role in the development and registration of toxicants that are useful for controlling populations of the dreaded sea lamprey, a predator of Great Lakes fishes. Intensive research and control efforts have greatly reduced the sea lamprey population through the use of larval lampricides. The Center is also responsible for all research under the U.S. Fish and Wildlife Service to control nuisance fish.

* Ocean and Coastal Pollution

Ocean Resources, Conservation, and Assessments
National Ocean Service
National Oceanic and Atmospheric Administration
U.S. Department of Commerce
6001 Executive Blvd.
Rockville, MD 20852 (301) 443-8487

This office surveys and monitors the oceans, U.S. coastal waters and the Great Lakes to produce data and information products that are critically important for offshore oil and gas exploration, dredging operations, coastal and offshore construction, seafloor mining, waste disposal management, and for protecting the marine environment from the adverse effects of ocean and coastal pollution.

Be patient. If any phone number is incorrect, call (area code) 555-1212 and request the new listing.

Environment and Nature

* Parrots, Gray Whale and 2,700 Videos and Films

National Audiovisual Center
8700 Edgeworth Dr.
Capitol Heights, MD 20743-3701 (800) 788-6282

The National Audiovisual Center contains more than 2,700 titles of videocassettes, films and slide/sound programs. Among them are some wonderful presentations produced by the National Park Service and the U.S. Fish and Wildlife Service. Materials may be rented or purchased. Contact the Audiovisual Center for specific information.
Some titles include:

Everglades: Seeking a Balance
Gulf Island Beaches, Bays, Sands, and Bayous
California Gray Whale
Environmental Awareness
Giant Sequoia
One Man's Alaska
Sanctuary: The Great Smoky Mountains
Crater Lake
Yellowstone
Washington, DC: Fancy Free
Glacier Bay
Bighorn Canyon Experience
Cape Cod
What is a Mountain?
Living Waters of the Big Cypress
National Parks: Our Treasured Lands
Mt. McKinley
America's Wetlands
Parrots of Luquillo
Where the Fish Will Be
Patuxent Wildlife Research Center
Minnesota Valley National Wildlife Refuge

To Build A Dream- The Story of Hoover Dam
Take Pride in America
Hoover Dam 50th Anniversary
Guam, USA
Commonwealth of the Northern Mariana Islands
Managing the Floods of '86- California's Ordeal
A Page In Time
The Colorado
Central Utah Project
Challenge At Glen Canyon Dam
Colorado River Operations
From Snowfall to Sandstone
Hydropower
Hydropower "A 20th Century Force"
Horizons
Waterpower 87 Wrap Up
For Want of Water
Taming of Black Canyon
The Spillways of Glen Canyon Dam
1983 The Record Water Year
Yuma Desalting Plant

These films are most often requested by elementary and junior high school teachers, or by people who have visited the dams while on vacation and would like to learn more about them. Contact the Bureau for more information regarding these videos.

* Patuxent Wildlife Center Film

National Audiovisual Center
8700 Edgeworth Dr.
Capitol Heights, MD 20743-3701 (800) 788-6282

This film informs the viewers about the wildlife research activities at the Patuxent Wildlife Research Center in Laurel, Maryland. It describes the wildlife research on endangered species, environmental contaminants, migratory waterfowl, and urban wildlife carried on at the center and at field stations around the world. This 20 minute film is available on 16mm film, and on Beta and VHS videocassettes. The film can be rented for $40 or purchased for $210. The videocassettes can be purchased for $95 each.

* Restoring America's Wildlife

Superintendent of Documents
Government Printing Office
Washington, DC 20402 (202) 783-3238

Illustrated with photographs and paintings by nationally known artists, *Restoring America's Wildlife 1937-1987* describes the impact of modern wildlife management on nearly a score of popular species and describes the many economic and recreational opportunities created by the Pittman-Robertson Federal Aid in Wildlife Restoration Act. 1986 (S/N 024-010-00671-4, $20).

* River and Water Films

Visual Communication Services
Bureau of Reclamation
P.O. Box 25007
D-1500
Denver, CO 80225 (303) 236-6973

The Bureau of Reclamation provides water for farms, towns, and industries, and is responsible for the generation of hydroelectric power, river regulation and flood control, outdoor recreation opportunities, and the enhancement and protection of fish and wildlife habitats. There are films available for free loan on a variety of the Bureau's projects. The titles include:

Central Arizona Project- Lifeline to the Future
California Flooding
Cofferdam Failure
How Water Won the West
Rio Grande- Ribbon of Life

* Salmon and Other Pacific Fish

National Fisheries Research Center
U.S. Fish and Wildlife Service
Building 204, Naval Station Puget Sound
Seattle, WA 98115-5007 (206) 526-6282

Fishery research problems of the Pacific Coast, except for those of Alaska, are solved at the National Fisheries Research Center in Seattle, Washington, and at its field stations in Cook, Washington, Nordland, Washington, and Reno, Nevada. Projects involving the study of Pacific salmon, trout, and steelhead provide valuable information to the economy of the Pacific Northwest and to the recreational fishing of this area. The Center has two main research groups: fish health and environment, and fish ecology. Willard Field Station near Cook, Washington, studies fish living in the Columbia River Basin and the effects of many hydropower projects in the area. The Marrowstone Field Station in Nordland, Washington, is the U.S. Fish and Wildlife Service's only marine laboratory where salmon and steelhead are studied as they leave their native streams and enter the oceans. The third field station in Reno, Nevada, works with threatened and endangered species native to the area.

* Saltwater Fish and Shellfish Stocks

Public Affairs
National Marine Fisheries Service
National Oceanic and Atmospheric Administration
U.S. Department of Commerce
1335 East-West Hwy.
Silver Spring, MD 20910 (301) 713-2370

The National Marine Fisheries Service manages the country's stocks of saltwater fish and shellfish for both commercial and recreational interests. NMFS administers and enforces the Magnuson Fishery Conservation and Management Act to assure that fishing stays within sound biological limits, and that U.S. commercial and recreational fishermen have the opportunity to harvest all the available fish within these limits. Several hundred Fisheries Service scientists conduct research relating to these management responsibilities in science and research centers in 15 states and the District of Columbia. Many of these laboratories have evolved a major field of interest, and have special knowledge of the fish in their geographical area that leads to predictions of abundance, economic forecasts, and direct assistance to sport fishermen and commercial fishing businesses.

* Toxic Chemicals in Fish

Office of Ocean Resources Conservation and Assessment (ORCA)
National Ocean Service
National Oceanic and Atmospheric Administration
6001 Executive Blvd.
Rockville, MD 20852 (301) 443-8487

ORCA monitors the concentrations of toxic chemicals and trace elements in

Be patient. If any phone number is incorrect, call (area code) 555-1212 and request the new listing.

Fish and Wildlife

bottom-feeding fish, shellfish, and sediments at almost 300 coastal and estuarine locations in the US. The program's objective is to determine the status and long-term trends of toxic contamination. Samples are analyzed to determine levels of DDTs, PCBs, PAHs, and toxic trace elements (e.g. mercury and lead).

* U.S. Fish and Wildlife Regional Offices

U.S. Fish and Wildlife Service
Washington, DC 20240 (202) 208-5634

Here are the field offices of the Interior Department's Fish and Wildlife Service.

Region 1
1002 NE Holladay Street, Portland, OR 97232; (503) 231-6118

Region 2
Box 1306, Albuquerque, NM 87103; (505) 766-2321

Region 3
Federal Building, Fort Snelling, Twin Cities, MN 55111; (612) 725-3563

Region 4
Richard B. Russell Federal Building, 75 Spring St., SW, Atlanta, GA 30303; (404) 331-3588

Region 5
One Gateway Center, Suite 700, Newton Corner, MA 02158; (617) 965-5100

Region 6
Box 25486, Denver Federal Center, Denver, CO 80225; (303) 236-7920

Region 7
1101 E. Tudor Rd., Anchorage, AK 99503; (907) 786-3542

Region 8
Matomic Building, Mail Stop 527, Washington, DC 20240; (202) 208-6394

* Vertebrate Research

Biological Survey/National Ecology Center
U.S. Fish and Wildlife Service
U.S. Department of the Interior
Museum of Natural History Building
10th and Constitution Ave., NW
Washington, DC 20560 (202) 357-1930

This laboratory performs systematic and ecological studies of vertebrates and their communities, particularly in their relationship to land use practices. Studies also include work with endangered species. Qualified researchers may inquire about possible study through the laboratory.

* Volunteers: Fish and Wildlife Service

U.S. Fish and Wildlife Service
Washington, DCC 20240 (202) 208-5634

Would you like to spend some time banding birds at a national wildlife refuge, feeding fish at a national fish hatchery, or doing research in a laboratory? Then consider volunteering with the U.S. Fish and Wildlife Service. There are no age requirements; however, anyone under 18 must have written parental approval. Young people under 16 years of age are encouraged to volunteer as part of a supervised group, such as a Boy Scout troop, Girl Scout troop, or 4H Club. Contact one of the U.S. Fish and Wildlife regional offices for possible volunteer programs in your area.

* Waterfowl and Migratory Birds

Northern Prairie Wildlife Research Center
U.S. Fish and Wildlife Service
P.O. Box 2096
Jamestown, ND 58402 (701) 252-5363

This research center gathers information to improve the management of migratory birds, particularly waterfowl west of the Mississippi River. Results of their studies are applied to National Wildlife Refuges and other Federal, State, and private lands. Field and experimental studies are conducted from the headquarters near Jamestown, North Dakota, and through field stations at Woodworth, North Dakota; Davis, California; and La Crosse, Wisconsin. Studies are also conducted on the ecology of the prairie pothole and upper Mississippi River areas.

* Waterfowl Hunting Regulations

Office of Migratory Bird Management
U.S. Fish and Wildlife Service
4401 N. Fairfax Dr.
Arlington, VA 22203 (703) 358-1714

Aerial surveys of waterfowl breeding populations and habitats, post-hunting surveys, and the banding program provide useful biological data for developing annual waterfowl hunting regulations. Before the rules are set, the current waterfowl picture is presented to the public through news releases, publication of proposed regulations in the *Federal Register*, and a series of late July and early August public meetings where survey data and Fall flight forecasts are reviewed. The decisions of each state are then published in the *Federal Register*.

* Wetlands and Wintering Waterfowl

National Wetlands Research Center
U.S. Fish and Wildlife Service
1010 Gause Blvd.
Slidell, LA 70458 (504) 646-7564

This center focuses on research and development studies of issues related to the protection, restoration, and management of wetlands, with an emphasis on wintering waterfowl. The Center gathers data on plant and animal ecology in both managed and natural wetland systems. Most current information is published in the *Biological Report* series. Field stations are located in Baton Rouge, LA, Corpus Christi, TX, and Vicksburg, MS.

* Wetlands Information

Public Information Center
PM-211B
Environmental Protection Agency (EPA)
401 M St., SW
Washington, DC 20460 (202) 260-7751

The U.S. is losing one of its most valuable and perhaps irreplaceable resources-the wetlands. Today less than half of the U.S.'s original wetlands remain. The EPA has an Environmental Backgrounder which provides information on the wetlands, as well as laws, sanctions, and EPA and State actions. Further information is available.

* Wetlands Protection

Office of Wetlands Protection
Environmental Protection Agency (EPA)
401 M St., SW
Washington DC 20460 (202) 260-7791

This office implements EPA statutory responsibilities in the Clean Water Act as they relate to the filling of wetlands and other aquatic resources. Designed to raise the importance of wetlands, this office works with other governmental bodies to encourage wetlands protection.

* Wetlands Protection Hotline

Geo/Resource Consultants, Inc.
1555 Wilson Blvd. Suite 500
Arlington, VA 22209 (800) 832-7828

The Environmental Protection Agency's Wetlands Protection Hotline is responsive to public interest, questions and requests for information about the values and functions of wetlands, and options for their protection. The Hotline acts as the central point of contact for the Wetlands Protection Division of the Office of Wetlands, Oceans, and Watersheds to provide a wide range of oral and written information on wetlands protection efforts involving EPA and other public and private programs. Wetlands Protection: A Local Government Handbook is available which reviews federal and state laws and programs that promote wetlands preservation. In addition, the Hotline uses an extensive contact list to provide referrals to callers when necessary. The Hotline also provides information on the availability of wetlands related documents and accepts requests for certain wetlands publications.

* Wetlands Video

National Association of Conservation Districts
P.O. Box 855
League City, TX 77574 (800) 825-5547

The U.S. Department of Agriculture and Interior, as well as private corporations cooperatively produces a 23-minute videotape which includes interviews with five farmers who believe there is a place for wetlands on their farms. Also included

Be patient. If any phone number is incorrect, call (area code) 555-1212 and request the new listing.

Environment and Nature

are brief overviews of wetlands losses, restoration methods, and sources of help in wetlands conservation and restoration. The video is available for $10.

* Whale Watching

Office of Protected Resources
National Marine Fisheries Service
National Oceanic and Atmospheric Administration
U.S. Department of Commerce
1335 East-West Hwy.
Silver Spring, MD 20910 (301) 713-2322

The Marine Mammal Protection Act commits the United States to long-term management and research programs to conserve and protect these animals. The National Marine Fisheries Service grants or denies requests for exemptions, issues permits, carries out research and management programs, enforces the Act, participates in international programs, and issues rules and regulations to carry out its mission to conserve and protect marine mammals. An annual report is available for the Office of Protected Resources, which gives detailed information regarding the activities of the Office. This office can also provide you with copies of the Act, and two publications: *First Aid For Stranded Marine Mammals*, and *Proceedings of the Workshop to Review and Evaluate Whale Watching Programs and Management Needs*.

* Wild Burros and Horses for Adoption

Office of Public Information
Bureau of Land Management (BLM)
U.S. Department of the Interior
18th and C Sts., NW
Washington, DC 20240-0001 (202) 208-5717

Wild burros and horses that roam on public lands are put up for adoption after a short time to decrease their numbers. If you are interested in adopting one of these animals, you should contact a local BLM adoption center, and there is a fee of $125 per horse and $75 per burro. You must also transport the animals home and provide for their future upkeep. The booklet, *So You'd Like to Adopt A Wild Horse Or Burro?*, answers many of the questions you might have when handling this responsibility. Contact the office above for the adoption centers near you.

* Wildlife Contaminant Research

Environmental Contaminants Research Branch
Patuxent Wildlife Research Center
U.S. Fish and Wildlife Service
Laurel, MD 20708 (301) 498-0300

Research on environmental contaminants is one of the major efforts at the Patuxent Wildlife Research Center. Field research is conducted at contaminated sites and demonstrates the relation between the presence of contaminants in the environment or tissues of a wildlife species and the degree of risk to the species. Controlled laboratory studies measure effects of mixtures of chemical contaminants on growth, survival, reproduction, metabolism, behavior, and well-being.

* Wildlife Disease Control

National Wildlife Health Research Center
U.S. Fish and Wildlife Service
6006 Schroeder Rd.
Madison, WI 53711 (608) 271-4640

This center offers services and conducts activities to prevent and control wildlife diseases. Workshops and seminars are sponsored at the Center and other locations throughout the country. The information produced through research findings and field observations is issued in the form of original articles in scientific journals, *Service Research Information Bulletins*, brochures, and special communications projects. A video presentation on lead poisoning in migratory birds was recently produced that is now widely used by the conservation community.

* Wildlife Habitats on Public Lands

Wildlife and Fisheries Division
Bureau of Land Management (BLM)
U.S. Department of the Interior
1725 I St., NW
Washington, DC 20006 (202) 653-9202

Wildlife habitats for more than 3,000 species are managed on public lands by the Bureau of Land Management. Included in this count are 140 threatened or endangered plant and animal species. The Bureau also protects and manages the key riparian areas along 85,000 miles of streams. BLM manages habitats for one out of every five big game animals in the United States, including caribou, brown and grizzly bears, desert bighorn sheep, moose, mule deer, and antelope.

* Wildlife Import Restrictions

Publications Unit
U.S. Fish and Wildlife Service
4401 N Fairfax Dr.
Arlington, VA 22203 (703) 358-1711

Before travelling overseas, learn what items cannot be imported. Write for a copy of *Facts About Federal Wildlife Laws* and a list of protected species at the above address.

* Wildlife Refuge National System

Refuges and Wildlife
U.S. Fish and Wildlife Service
18th and C Sts., NW
Washington, DC 20240 (202) 358-1744

The National Wildlife Refuge System is a network of United States lands and waters managed specifically for the enhancement of wildlife. Refuges are vitally important for they provide food, water, shelter, and space for approximately 60 endangered species and hundreds of species of birds, mammals, reptiles, amphibians, fish, and plants. Over 440 refuges, encompassing over 90 million acres in 49 states and five trust territories, now comprise the system. An estimated 30 million people visit these lands annually.

Alabama

Bon Secour, P.O. Box 1650, Gulf Shores, AL 36542; (205) 968-8623. Choctaw, Box 808, 2704 Westside College Ave., Jackson, AL 36545; (205) 246-3583. Eufaula, Rte. 2, Box 97-B, Eufaula, AL 36027; (205) 687-4065. Wheeler (Blowing Wind Cave, Fern Cave, Watercress Darter), Rte. 4, Box 250, Decatur, AL 35603; (205) 353-7243.

Alaska

Alaska Maritime (Alaska Peninsula Unit, Bering Sea Unit, Chukchi Sea Unit, Gulf of Alaska Unit), 202 West Pioneer Ave., Homer, AK 99603; (907) 235-6546. Aleutian Islands Unit, Box 5251, Naval Air Station Adak, FBO Seattle, WA 98791; (907) 592-2406. Alaska Peninsula (Becharof), P.O. Box 277, King Salmon, AK 99613; (907) 246-3339. Arctic, Box 20, 101-12th Ave., Fairbanks, AK 99701; (907) 456-0250. Innoko, Box 69, McGrath, AK 99627; (907) 524-3251. Izembek, Box 127, Cold Bay, AK 99571; (907) 532-2445. Kanuti, Box 11, 101-12th Ave., Fairbanks, AK 99701; (907) 456-0329. Kenai, 2139 Ski Hill Road, Soldotna, AK 99669-2139; (907) 262-7021. Kodiak, 1390 Buskin River Rd., Kodiak, AK 99615; (907) 487-2600. Koyukuk, P.O. Box 287, Galena, AK 99741; (907) 656-1231. Nowitna, P.O. Box 287, Galena, AK 99741; (907) 656-1231. Selawik, P.O. Box 270, Kotzebue, AK 99572; (907) 442-3799. Tetlin, P.O. Box 155, Tok, AK 99780; (907) 883-5312. Togiak, P.O. Box 270, Dillingham, AK 99576; (907) 842-1063. Yukon Delta, P.O. Box 346, Bethel, AK 99559; (907) 543-3151. Yukon Flats, Box 14, 101-12th Ave., Fairbanks, AK 99701; (907) 456-0440.

Arizona

Buenos Aires, P.O. Box 109, Sasabe, AZ 85633; (602) 823-4251. Cabeza Prieta, 1611 N. Second Ave., Ajo, AZ 85321; (602) 387-6483. Cibola, P.O. Box AP, Blythe, CA 92226; (602) 857-3253. Havasu, P.O. Box 3009, Needles, CA 92363; (619) 326-3853. Imperial, P.O. Box 72217, Martinez Lake, AZ 85365; (602) 783-3371. Kofa, P.O. Box 6290, 356 W. 1st, Yuma, AZ 85366-6290; (602) 783-7861. San Bernardino, Rural Rte. 1. Box 228R, Douglas, AZ 85607; (602) 364-2104.

Arkansas

Felsenthal (Overflow), P.O. Box 1157, Crossett, AR 71635; (501) 364-3167. Holla Bend (Logan Caves), Box 1043, 115 S. Denver St., Russellville, AR 72801; (501) 968-2800. N.E. Arkansas Refuges, P.O. Box 279, Turrell, AR 72384; (501) 343-2595. Big Lake, P.O. Box 67, Manila, AR 72442; (501) 564-2429. Cache River, P.O. Box 279, Turrell, AR 72384; (501) 343-2595. Wapanocca, P.O. Box 279, Turrell, AR 72384; (501) 343-2595. White River, Box 308, 321 W. 7th St., De Witt, AR 72042; (501) 946-1468.

California

Cibola, P.O. Box AP, Blythe, CA 92226; (602) 857-3253. Havasu, P.O. Box 3009, Needles, CA 92363; (619) 326-3853. Imperial, P.O. Box 72217, Martinez Lake, AZ 85365; (602) 783-3371. Kern (Bitter Creek, Blue Ridge, Hopper Mountain, Pixley, Seal Beach), P.O. Box 670, Delano, CA 93216-0219; (805) 725-2767, (805)

Be patient. If any phone number is incorrect, call (area code) 555-1212 and request the new listing.

Fish and Wildlife

725-5284. Klamath Basin Refuges (Bear Valley (OR), Clear Lake, Klamath Forest (OR), Lower Klamath (OR & CA), Tule Lake, Upper Klamath (OR)), Rte. 1, Box 74, Tule Lake, CA 96134; (916) 667-2231. Modoc, P.O. Box 1610, Alturas, CA 96101; (916) 233-3572. Sacramento (Butte Sink WMA, Delevan, Willow Creek-Lurline WMA), Rte. 1, Box 311, Willows, CA 95988; (916) 934-2801. Salton Sea, P.O. Box 120, Calipatria, CA 92233; (619) 348-5278, (619) 348-5310. Tijuana Slough (Coachella Valley, Sweetwater Marsh), P.O. Box 335, Imperial Beach, CA 92032; (619) 575-1290. San Francisco Bay (Antioch Dunes, Castle Rock, Ellicott Slough, Farallon, Humboldt Bay, Salinas Lagoon, San Pablo Bay), P.O. Box 524, Newark, CA 94560; (415) 792-0222. San Luis (East Grasslands WMA, Grasslands WMA, Kesterson, Merced, San Joaquin River), P.O. Box 2176, Los Banos, CA 93635; (209) 826-3508.

Colorado

Alamosa/Monte Vista, P.O. Box 1148, Alamosa, CO 81101; (303) 589-4021. Arapaho (Bamforth (WY), Hutton Lake (WY), Pathfinder (WY)), P.O. Box 457, Walden, CO 80480; (303) 723-8202. Browns Park, 1318 Hwy. 318, Maybell, CO 81640; (303) 365-3613.

Connecticut

Salt Meadow, P.O. Box 307, Charlestown, RI 02813; (401) 364-9124. Stewart B. McKinney, U.S. Federal Bldg., Room 210, 915 Lafayette Blvd., Bridgeport, CT 06604; (203) 579-5617.

Delaware

Bombay Hook, Rte. 1, Box 147, Smyrna, DE 19977; (302) 653-9345. Prime Hook, Rte. 3, Box 195, Milton, DE 19968; (302) 684-8419.

Florida

Arthur R. Marshall Loxahatchee (Hobe Sound), Rte. 1, Box 78, Boynton Beach, FL 33437; (407) 732-3684. Chassahowitzka (Crystal River, Egmont Key, Passage Key, Pinellas), 7798 S. Suncoast Blvd., Homosassa, FL 32646; (904) 382-2201. Florida Panther (Ten Thousand Lakes), 2629 S. Horseshoe Dr., Naples, FL 33942; (813) 643-2636. J.N. "Ding" Darling (Caloosahatchee, Island Bay, Matlacha Pass, Pine Island), One Wildlife Dr., Sanibel, FL 33957; (813) 472-1100. Lake Woodruff, P.O. Box 488, DeLeon Springs, FL 32028; (904) 985-4673. Lower Suwannee (Cedar Keys), P.O. Box 1193 C, Chiefland, FL 32626; (904) 493-0238. Merritt Island (Pelican Island, St. Johns), P.O. Box 6504, Titusville, FL 32780; (305) 867-0667. National Key Deer (Crocodile Lake, Great White Heron, Key West), P.O. Box 510, Big Pine Key, FL 33043; (305) 872-2239. St. Marks, P.O. Box 68, St. Marks, FL 32355; (904) 925-6121. St. Vincent, P.O. Box 447, Apalachicola, FL 32320; (904) 653-8808.

Georgia

Eufaula, Rte. 2, Box 97-B, Eufaula, AL 36027; (205) 687-4065. Okefenokee (Banks Lake), Rte. 2, Box 338, Folkston, GA 31537; (912) 496-7366. Piedmont, Rte. 1, Box 670, Round Oak, GA 31038; (912) 986-5441. Savannah Coastal Refuges (Blackbeard Island, Harris Neck, Pinckney Island (SC), Savannah, Tybee, Wassaw, Wolf Island), P.O. Box 8487, Savannah, GA 31412; (912) 944-4415.

Hawaii

Hawaiian and Pacific Islands Complex, P.O. Box 50167, 300 Ala Moana Blvd., Honolulu, HI 96850; (808) 541-1201. Hakalau Forest, 154 Waianuenue Ave., Federal Bldg., Room 219, Hilo, HI 96720; (808) 969-9909. Kilauea Point, P.O. Box 87, Kilauea, Kauai, HI 96754; (808) 828-1413. Remote Island Refuges (Baker Island, Hawaiian Islands, Howland Island, Jarvis Island, Johnston Atoll, Rose Atoll), P.O. Box 50167, 300 Ala Moana Blvd., Honolulu, HI 96850; (808) 541-1201. Wetlands Refuges (Hanalei, Huleia, James C. Campbell, Kakahaia, Pearl Harbor), P.O. Box 50167, 300 Ala Moana Blvd., Honolulu, HI 96850; (808) 541-1201.

Idaho

Deer Flat, P.O. Box 448, Nampa, ID 83653; (208) 467-9278. Kootenai, HCR 60, Box 283, Bonners Ferry, ID 83805; (208) 267-3888. Southeast Idaho Refuge Complex (Oxford Slough WPA), 1246 Yellowstone Ave., A-4, Pocatello, ID 83201-4372; (208) 237-6615. Bear Lake, 370 Webster, Box 9, Montpelier, ID 83254; (208) 847-1757. Camas, 2150 E. 2350 N., Hamer, ID 83245; (208) 662-5423. Grays Lake, 74 Grays Lake Rd., Wayan, ID 83285; (208) 574-2755. Minidoka, Rte. 4, P.O. Box 290, Rupert, ID 83350; (208) 436-3589.

Illinois

Chautauqua (Meredosia), Rte. 2, Havana, IL 62644; (309) 535-2290. Crab Orchard, P.O. Box J, Carterville, IL 62918; (618) 997-3344. Mark Twain, 311 North 5th St., Suite 100, Great River Plaza, Quincy, IL 62301; (217) 224-8580. Annada District, P.O. Box 88, Annada, MO 63330; (314) 847-2333. Brussels District, P.O. Box 142, Brussels, IL 62013; (618) 883-2524. Wapello District, Rte. 1, Wapello, IA 52653; (319) 523-6982. Upper Mississippi River National Wildlife and Fish Refuge, 51 East 4th St., Winona, MN 55987; (507) 452-4232. Savanna District, Post Office Bldg., Savanna, IL 61074; (815) 273-2732. Cypress Creek, Route 1, Box 53D, Ullin, IL 62492; (618) 634-2231.

Indiana

Muscatatuck, Rte. 7, Box 189A, Seymour, IN 47274; (812) 522-4352. Patoka, P.O. Box 510, Winslow, IN 47598; (812) 789-2102.

Iowa

DeSoto, Rte. 1, Box 114, Missouri Valley, IA 51555; (712) 642-4121. Union Slough, Rte. 1, Box 52, Titonka, IA 50480; (515) 928-2523. Upper Mississippi River National Wildlife and Fish Refuge, 51 East 4th St., Winona, MN 55987; (507) 452-4232. McGregor District, P.O. Box 460, McGregor, IA 52157; (319) 873-3423. Walnut Creek, P.O. Box 399, Prairie City, IA 50228; (515) 994-2415.

Kansas

Flint Hills, P.O. Box 128, Hartford, KS 66854; (316) 392-5553. Kirwin, Rte. 1, Box 103, Kirwin, KS 67644; (913) 543-6673. Quivira, Rte. 3, Box 48A, Stafford, KS 67578; (316) 486-2393.

Louisiana

Bogue Chitto (Breton, Delta), 1010 Gause Blvd., Bldg. 936, Slidell, LA 70458; (504) 646-7555. Cameron Prairie, Rte. 1, Box 643, Bell City, LA 70630; (318) 598-2216. Catahoula, P.O. Drawer Z, Rhinehart, LA 71363-0201; (318) 992-5261. D'Arbonne (Upper Ouachita), P.O. Box 3065, Monroe, LA 71201; (318) 325-1735. Lacassine (Shells Keys), Rte. 1, Box 186, Lake Arthur, LA 70549; (318) 774-5923. Lake Ophelia, P.O. Box 256, Marksville, LA 71351; (318) 253-4238. Sabine, Hwy. 27, 3000 Main St., Hackberry, LA 70645; (318) 762-3816. Tensas River, Rte. 2, Box 295, Tallulah, LA 71282; (318) 574-2664. Louisiana WMD, P.O. Box 1601, Monroe, LA 71210; (318) 325-1735.

Maine

Moosehorn (Cross Island, Carlton Pond WPA, Franklin Island, Seal Island, Sunkhaze Meadows), P.O. Box 1077, Calais, ME 04619; (207) 454-3521. Petit Manan, P.O. Box 279, Milbridge, ME 04658; (207) 546-2124. Pond Island, Northern Blvd., Plum Island, Newburyport, MA 01950; (508) 465-5753. Rachel Carson, Rte. 2, Box 751, Wells, ME 04090; (207) 646-9226. Sunkhaze Meadows, USDA Bldg., Room221, Orono, ME 04469; (207) 581-3670.

Maryland

Blackwater (Martin, Susquehanna), Rte. 1, Box 121, Cambridge, MD 21613; (301) 228-2692. Chincoteague, Box 62, Chincoteague, VA 23336; (804) 336-6122. Eastern Neck, Rte. 2, Box 225, Rock Hall, MD 21661; (301) 639-7056. Patuxent, Rte. 197, Laurel, MD 20708; (301) 498-0300.

Massachusetts

Great Meadows (John Hay (NH), Massasoit, Monomoy, Nantucket, Oxbow, Wapack (NH)), Weir Hill Rd., Sudbury, MA 01776; (508) 443-4661. Parker River (Pond Island (ME), Thacher Island), Northern Blvd., Plum Island, Newburyport, MA 01950; (508) 465-5753. Rachel Carson, Rte. 2, Box 751, Wells, ME 04090; (207) 646-9226.

Michigan

Seney (Harbor Island, Huron), Seney, MI 49883; (906) 586-9851. Shiawassee (Michigan Islands, Wyandotte), 6975 Mower Rd., Rte. 1, Saginaw, MI 48601; (517) 777-5930.

Minnesota

Agassiz, Middle River, MN 56737; (218) 449-4115. Big Stone, 25 NW 2nd St., Ortonville, MN 56278; (612) 839-3700. Minnesotoa Valley, 4101 E. 80th St., Bloomington, MN 55420; (612) 854-5900. Minnesota Wetlands Complex, Rte. 1, Box 76, Fergus Falls, MN 56537; (218) 739-2291. Morris WMD, Rte. 1, Box 208, Mill Dam Rd., Morris, MN 56267; (612) 589-1001. Detroit Lakes WMD, Rte. 3, Box 47D, Detroit Lakes, MN 56501; (218) 847-4431. Fergus Falls WMD, Rte. 1, Box 76, Fergus Falls, MN 56537; (218) 739-2291. Litchfield WMD, 305 North Sibley, Litchfield, MN 55355; (612) 693-2849. Rice Lake (Mille Lacs, Sandstone), Rte. 2, Box 67, McGregor, MN 55760; (218) 768-2402. Sherburne, Rte. 2, Zimmerman, MN 55398; (612) 389-3323. Tamarac, Rural Rte., Rochert, MN 56578; (218) 847-2641. Upper Mississippi River Complex, P.O. Bldg., Box 2484, La Crosse, WI 54602; (608) 784-5540. Upper Mississippi River National Wildlife and Fish Refuge (IA, IL, MN, WI), 51 East 4th St., Winona, MN 55987; (507) 452-4232. Winona District, 51 East 4th St., Winona, MN 55987; (507) 452-4232.

Mississippi

Mississippi Sandhill Crane, 7200 Coane Ln., Gautier, MS 39553; (601) 497-6322. Noxubee, Rte. 1, Box 142, Brooksville, MS 39739; (601) 323-5548. Yazoo

Be patient. If any phone number is incorrect, call (area code) 555-1212 and request the new listing.

Environment and Nature

(Hillside, Mathews Brake, Morgan Brake, Panther Swamp), Rte. 1, Box 286, Hillandale, MS 38748; (601) 839-2638. Mississippi WMD, P.O. Box 1070, Grenada, MS 38901; (601) 226-8286. St. Catherine Creek, P.O. Box 13639, Natchez, MS 39122; (601) 442-6696.

Missouri

Mingo, Rte. 1, Box 103, Puxico, MO 63960; (314) 222-3589. Squaw Creek, P.O. Box 101, Mound City, MO 64470; (816) 442-3187. Swan Lake, P.O. Box 68, Sumner, MO 64681; (816) 856-3323.

Montana

Benton Lake, P.O. Box 450, Black Eagle, MT 59414; (406) 727-7400. Bowdoin (Black Coulee, Creedman Coulee, Hewitt Lake, Lake Thibadeau), P.O. Box J, Malta, MT 59538; (406) 654-2863. Charles M. Russell (Hailstone, Halfbreed Lake, Lake Mason, Nichols Coulee, UL Bend, War Horse), P.O. Box 110, Lewistown, MT 59457; (406) 538-8706. Fort Peck Wildlife Station, P.O. Box 166, Fort Peck, MT 59223; (406) 526-3464. Jordan Wildlife Station, P.O. Box 63, Jordan, MT 59337; (406) 557-6145. Sand Creek Wildlife Station, P.O. Box 89, Roy, MT 59471; (406) 464-5181. Lee Metcalf, P.O. Box 257, Stevensville, MT 59870; (406) 777-5552. Medicine Lake (Lamesteer), HC 51, Box 2, Medicine Lake, MT 59247; (406) 789-2305. National Bison Range (Nine-Pipe, Pablo), Moiese, MT 59824; (406) 644-2211. Northwest Montana WMD (Swan River), 780 Creston Hatchery Rd., Kalispell, MT 59901; (406) 755-7870, (406) 755-9311. Red Rock Lakes, Monida Star Rte., Box 15, Lima, MT 59739; (406) 276-3347.

Nebraska

Crescent Lake (North Platte), HC 68, Box 21, Ellsworth, NE 69340; (308) 762-4893. DeSoto, Rte. 1, Box 114, Missouri Valley, IA 51555; (712) 642-4121. Fort Niobrara/Valentine, Hidden Timber Route, HC 14, Box 67, Valentine, NE 69201; (402) 376-3789. Valentine, Hidden Timber Route, HC 14, Box 67, Valentine, NE 69201; (402) 376-3789. Rainwater Basin WMD, P.O. Box 1686, Kearney, NE 68847; (308) 236-5015.

Nevada

Desert National Wildlife Range (Amargosa Pupfish Station), 1500 North Decatur Blvd., Las Vegas, NV 89108; (702) 646-3401. Ash Meadows, P.O. Box 2660, Pahrump, NV 89041; (702) 372-5435. Pahranagat, Box 510, Alamo, NV 89001; (702) 725-3417. Ruby Lake, Ruby Valley, NV 89833; (702) 779-2237. Sheldon, P.O. Box 111, Room 308, U.S. Post Office Bldg., Lakeview, OR 97630; (503) 947-3315. Stillwater (Anaho Island, Fallon), P.O. Box 1236, Fallon, NV 89406-1236; (702) 423-5128.

New Hampshire

John Hay, Weir Hill Rd., Sudbury, MA 01776; (508) 443-4661. Wapack, Weir Hill Rd., Sudbury, MA 01776; (508) 443-4661.

New Jersey

Edwin B. Forsythe (Brigantine Division), Great Creek Rd., Box 72, Oceanville, NJ 08231; (609) 652-1665. Barnegat Division, 70 Collinstown Rd., Barnegat, NJ 08005; (609) 698-1387. Great Swamp, Pleasant Plains Rd., RD 1, Box 152, Basking Ridge, NJ 07920; (201) 647-1222. Killcohook, Suite 104, Scott Plaza 2, Philadelphia, PA 19113; (215) 521-0662. Supawna Meadows, RD 3, Box 540, Salem, NJ 08079; (609) 935-1487.

New Mexico

Bitter Lake, P.O. Box 7, Roswell, NM 88201; (505) 622-6755. Bosque del Apache, P.O. Box 1246, Socorro, NM 87801; (505) 835-1828. San Andres, P.O. Box 756, Las Cruces, NM 88001; (505) 382-5047. Sevilleta, General Delivery, San Acacia, NM 87831; (505) 864-4021. Grulla, P.O. Box 228, Umbarger, TX 79091; (806) 499-3382. Las Vegas, Rte. 1, Box 399, Las Vegas, NM 87701; (505) 425-3581. Maxwell, P.O. Box 276, Maxwell, NM 87728; (505) 375-2331.

New York

Iroquois, P.O. Box 517, Casey Rd., Alabama, NY 14003; (716) 948-9154. Montezuma, 3395 Rte. 5/20 East, Seneca Falls, NY 13148; (315) 568-5987. Wertheim (Amagansett, Conscience Point, Elizabeth A. Morton, Lido Beach, Oyster Bay, Seatuck, Target Rock), P.O. Box 21, Shirley, NY 11967; (516) 286-0485. Seatuck, P.O. Box 21, Shirley, NY 11967; (516) 581-1538.

North Carolina

Alligator River (Currituck), P.O. Box 1969, Manteo, NC 27954; (919) 473-1131. Pea Island, (919) 987-2394. Great Dismal Swamp, 3100 Desert Rd., P.O. Box 349, Suffolk, VA 23434; (804) 986-3705. Mackay Island, P.O. Box 31, Knotts Island, NC 27950; (919) 429-3100. Mattamuskett (Cedar Island, Pungo, Swanquarter), Rte. 1, Box N-2, Swanquarter, NC 27885; (919) 926-4021. Roanoke River, 102 Dundee St., Box 430, Windsor, NC 27983; (919) 794-5326.

North Dakota

Arrowwood (Chase Lake, Slade), Rural Rte. 1, Pingree, ND 58476; (701) 285-3341. Long Lake, Rural Rte. 1, Box 23, Moffit, ND 58560; (701) 387-4397. Valley City WMD, Rural Rte. 1, Valley City, ND 58072; (701) 845-3466. Audubon, Rural Rte. 1, Coleharbor, ND 58531; (701) 442-5474. Lake Ilo, Dunn Center, ND 58626; (701) 548-4407. Des Lacs (Lake Zahl), P.O. Box 578, Kenmare, ND 58746; (701) 385-4046. Crosby WMD, P.O. Box 148, Crosby, ND 58730; (701) 965-6488. Lostwood, Rural Rte. 2, Box 98, Kenmare, ND 58746; (701) 848-2722. Devils Lake WMD (Lake Alice, Sullys Hill National Game Preserve), P.O. Box 908, Devils Lake, ND 58301; (701) 662-8611. J. Clark Salyer, Box 66, Upham, ND 58789; (701) 768-2548. Kulm WMD, P.O. Box E, Kulm, ND 58456; (701) 647-2866. Tewaukon, Rural Rte. 1, Cayuga, ND 58013; (701) 724-3598. Upper Souris, Rural Rte. 1, Foxholm, ND 58738; (701) 468-5467.

Ohio

Ottawa (Cedar Point, West Sister Island), 14000 W. State Rte. 2, Oak Harbor, OH 43449; (419) 898-0014.

Oklahoma

Little River (Little Sandy), P.O. Box 340, Broken Bow, OK 74728; (405) 584-6211. Salt Plains, Rte. 1, Box 76, Jet, OK 73749; (405) 626-4794. Sequoyah (Oklahoma Bat Caves), Rte. 1, Box 18A, Vian, OK 74962; (918) 773-5251. Tishomingo, Rte. 1, Box 151, Tishomingo, OK 73460; (405) 371-2402. Washita (Optima), Rte. 1, Box 68, Butler, OK 73625; (405) 664-2205. Wichita Mountains Wildlife Refuge, Rte. 1, Box 448, Indiahoma, OK 73552; (405) 429-3221.

Oregon

Klamath Forest and Upper Klamath, Rte. 1, Box 74, Tule Lake, CA 96134; (916) 667-2231. Lewis and Clark, HC 01, Box 910, Ilwaco, WA 98624-9707; (206) 484-3482. Malheur, HC 72, Box 245, Princeton, OR 97721; (503) 493-2612. Sheldon/Hart Mountain Complex, P.O. Box 111, Room 308, U.S. Post Office Bldg., Lakeview, OR 97630; (503) 947-3315. Sheldon, P.O. Box 111, Room 308, U.S. Post Office Bldg., Lakeview, OR 97630; (503) 947-3315. Hart Mountain, P.O. Box 111, Room 308, U.S. Post Office Bldg., Lakeview, OR 97630; (503) 947-3315. Umatilla (Cold Springs, McKay Creek), P.O. Box 239, Umatilla, OR 97882; (503) 922-3232. McNary, P.O. Box 308, Burbank, WA 99323; (509) 547-4942. Toppenish, Rte. 1, Box 1300, Toppenish, WA 98948; (509) 865-2405. Western Oregon Refuge Complex, 26208 Finley Refuge Rd., Corvallis, OR 97333; (503) 757-7236. Ankeny, 2301 Wintel Rd., Jefferson, OR 97352; (503) 327-2444. Baskett Slough, 10995 Hwy. 22, Dallas, OR 97338; (503) 623-2749. William L. Finley (Bandon Marsh, Cape Meares, Oregon Islands, Three Arch Rocks), 26208 Finley Refuge Rd., Corvallis, OR 97333; (503) 757-7236.

Pennsylvania

Erie, RD 1, Wood Duck Ln., Guys Mills, PA 16327; (814) 789-3585. Tinicum National Environmental Center (Killcohook (NJ)), Suite 104, Scott Plaza 2, Philadelphia, PA 19113; (215) 521-0662. Supawna Meadows (NJ), RD 3, Box 540, Salem, NJ 08079; (609) 935-1487.

Puerto Rico

Caribbean Islands (Buck Island (Virgin Islands), Cabo Rojo, Culebra, Desecheo, Green Cay (Virgin Islands), Sandy Point (Virgin Islands)), Box 510, Carr. 301, KM 5.1, Boqueron, PR 00622; (809) 851-7258.

Rhode Island

Ninigret (Block Island, Pettaquamscutt Cove, Sachuest Point, Salt Meadow (CT), Trustom Pond), P.O. Box 307, Charlestown, RI 02813; (401) 364-9124. Stewart B. McKinney, U.S. Federal Bldg., Room 210, 915 Lafayette Blvd., Bridgeport, CT 06604; (203) 579-5617.

South Carolina

Cape Romain, 390 Bulls Island Rd., Awendaw, SC 29429; (803) 928-3368. Carolina Sandhills, Rte. 2, Box 330, McBee, SC 29101; (803) 335-8401. Pee Dee, P.O. Box 780, Wadesboro, NC 28170; (704) 694-4424. Pinckney Island, P.O. Box 8487, Savannah, GA 31412; (912) 944-4415. Santee, Rte. 2, Box 66, Summerton, SC 29148; (803) 478-2217.Ace Basin, P.O. Box 1785, Mt. Pleasant, SC 29465; (803) 762-1200.

South Dakota

Lacreek, HWC 3, Box 14, Martin, SD 57551; (605) 685-6508. Lake Andes (Karl E. Mundt), Rural Rte. 1, Box 77, Lake Andes, SD 57356; (605) 487-7603. Madison WMD, P.O. Box 48, Madison, SD 57042; (605) 256-2974. Sand Lake (Pocasse), Rural Rte. 1, Box 25, Columbia, SD 57433; (605) 885-6320. Waubay, Rural Rte. 1, Box 79, Waubay, SD 57273; (605) 947-4521.

Tennessee

Cross Creeks, Rte. 1, Box 556, Dover, TN 37058; (615) 232-7477. Hatchie

Be patient. If any phone number is incorrect, call (area code) 555-1212 and request the new listing.

Fish and Wildlife

(Chickasaw, Lower Hatchie), P.O. Box 187, Brownsville, TN 38012; (901) 772-0501. Reelfoot (Lake Isom), Rte. 2, Hwy. 157, Union City, TN 38261; (901) 538-2481. Tennessee, P.O. Box 849, Paris, TN 38242; (901) 642-2091.

Texas

Anahuac (Moody), P.O. Box 278, Anahuac, TX 77514; (409) 267-3337. McFaddin/Texas Point, P.O. Box 609, Sabine Pass, TX 77655; (409) 971-2909. Aransas (Matagorda), P.O. Box 100, Austwell, TX 77950; (512) 286-3559. Attwater Prairie Chicken, P.O. Box 518, Eagle Lake, TX 77434; (409) 234-5940. Brazoria (Big Boggy), P.O. Box 1088, Angleton, TX 77516-1088; (409) 849-6062. San Bernard, P.O. Box 1088, Angleton, TX 77516-1088; (409) 849-6062. Buffalo Lake (Grulla (NM)), P.O. Box 228, Umbarger, TX 79091; (806) 499-3382. Muleshoe, P.O. Box 549, Muleshoe, TX 79347; (806) 946-3341. Hagerman, Rte. 3, Box 123, Sherman, TX 75090-9564; (214) 786-2826. Laguna Atascosa, P.O. Box 450, Rio Hondo, TX 78583; (512) 748-3607. Lower Rio Grande Valley/Santa Ana Complex, 320 N. Main, Room A-103, McAllen, TX 78501; (512) 630-4636.

Utah

Fish Springs, P.O. Box 568, Dugway, UT 84022; (801) 522-5353. Ouray (Bear River Migratory Bird Refuge), 1680 W. Hwy. 40, Room 1220, Vernal, UT 84078; (801) 789-0351.

Vermont

Missisquoi, P.O. Box 163, Swanton, VT 05488; (802) 868-4781.

Virginia

Back Bay (Plum Tree Island), 4005 Sandpiper Rd., P.O. Box 6286, Virginia Beach, VA 23456; (804) 721-2412. Chincoteague (Wallops Island), Box 62, Chincoteague, VA 23336; (804) 336-6122. Eastern Shore of Virginia (Cedar Island, Fisherman Island), RFD 1, Box 122B, Cape Charles, VA 23310; (804) 331-2760. Great Dismal Swamp (Nansemond), 3100 Desert Rd., P.O. Box 349, Suffolk, VA 23434; (804) 986-3705. Mason Neck (Featherstone, Marumsco), 14416 Jefferson Davis Hwy., Suite 20A, Woodbridge, VA 22191; (703) 690-1297. Presquile, P.O. Box 620, Hopewell, VA 23860; (804) 458-7541.

Washington

Columbia (Saddle Mountain), 735 E. Main St., P.O. Drawer F, Othello, WA 99344; (509) 488-2668. McNary, P.O. Box 308, Burbank, WA 99323; (509) 547-4942. Nisqually (San Juan Islands), 100 Brown Farm Rd., Olympia, WA 98506; (206) 753-9467. Coastal Refuges Office (Dungeness, Protection Island, Washington Islands), P.O. Box 698, Sequim, WA 98382; (206) 457-8792. Ridgefield (Pierce Ranch, Steigerwald Lake), 301 N. Third St., P.O. Box 457, Ridgefield, WA 98642; (206) 887-4106. Toppenish, Rte. 1, Box 1300, Toppenish, WA 98948; (509) 865-2405. Turnbull, S. 26010 Smith Rd., Cheney, WA 99004; (509) 235-4723. Umatilla, P.O. Box 239, Umatilla, OR 97882; (503) 922-3232. Willapa (Lewis and Clark (OR)), HC 01, Box 910, Ilwaco, WA 98624-9707; (206) 484-3482. Julia Butler Hansen (Formerly Columbian White-tailed Deer), P.O. Box 566, Cathlamet, WA 98612; (206) 795-3915. Conboy Lake, P.O. Box 5, Glenwood, WA 98619; (509) 364-3410.

Wisconsin

Horicon (Fox River, Gravel Island, Green Bay), W. 4279 Headquarters Rd., Mayville, WI 53050; (414) 387-2658; Necedah, Star Rte. West, Box 386, Necedah, WI 54646; (608) 565-2551. Upper Mississippi River Complex, P.O. Bldg., Box 2484, La Crosse, WI 54602; (608) 784-5540. Trempealeau, Rte. 1, Trempealeau, WI 54661; (608) 539-2311. Upper Mississippi River National Wildlife and Fish Refuge, 51 East 4th St., Winona, MN 55987; (507) 452-4232. La Crosse District, P.O. Bldg., Box 415, La Crosse, WI 54601-0415; (608) 784-3910.

Wyoming

Bamforth, P.O. Box 457, Walden, CO 80480; (303) 723-8202. Hutton Lake, P.O. Box 457, Walden, CO 80480; (303) 723-8202. National Elk Refuge, P.O. Box C, Jackson, WY 83001; (307) 733-9212. Pathfinder, P.O. Box 457, Walden, CO 80480; (303) 723-8202. Seedskadee, P.O. Box 67, Green River, WY 82935; (307) 875-2187.

* Wildlife Refuge Regional Offices

Region 1

911 NE 11th Ave., Portland, OR 97232; (503) 231-6118, (503) 231-6214.

Region 2

P.O. Box 1306, Albuquerque, NM 87103; (505) 766-2321, (505) 766-1829.

Region 3

Federal Bldg., Fort Snelling, Twin Cities, MN 55111; (612) 725-3563, (612) 725-3507.

Region 4

Richard B. Russell Federal Bldg., 75 Spring St., SW, Atlanta, GA 30303; (404) 331-3588, (404) 331-0833.

Region 5

One Gateway Center, Suite 700, Newton Corner, MA 02158; (617) 965-5100, (617) 965-9222.

Region 6

Box 25486, Denver Federal Center, Denver, CO 80225; (303) 236-7920, (303) 236-8145.

Region 7

1011 E. Tudor Rd., Anchorage, AK 99503; (907) 786-3542, (907) 786-3545.

* Youth Conservation Corps

United States Youth Conservation Corps
U.S. Fish and Wildlife Service
National Park Service
Washington, DC 20240 (202) 343-5514

The Youth Conservation Corps is a summer employment program for young men and women, ages 15 through 18, who work, learn, and earn wages accomplishing needed conservation work on public lands. The program is also administered by the Forest Service of the U.S. Department of Agriculture. Projects include constructing trails, building campground facilities, planting trees, collecting litter, clearing streams, improving wildlife habitats, and office work. Limited positions are available.

Be patient. If any phone number is incorrect, call (area code) 555-1212 and request the new listing.

Environment and Nature

Hazardous and Solid Waste

* *See also Health and Medicine; Chemicals, Toxics, and Other Health Hazards Chapter*

* 45,000 Pesticide Products Inventory
Office of Pesticide Programs
Environmental Protection Agency (EPA)
401 M St., SW
Washington DC 20460 (703) 305-7090
EPA administers two Congressionally mandated statutes to control the more than 45,000 pesticide products registered for use in the United States. The EPA monitors the distribution and use of these pesticides, issuing civil or criminal penalties for violations. EPA also sets tolerances or maximum legal limits for pesticide residues on food commodities and feed grains to prevent consumer exposure to unsafe pesticide levels.

* Abandoned Mines Acid Drainage Disposal
Environmental Technology Division
Bureau of Mines
U.S. Department of the Interior
2401 E St., NW
Washington, DC 20241 (202) 634-1263
Researchers at the Bureau of Mines are working on low-cost ways to deal with the problem of acid drainage at abandoned mines. They are developing computer programs to predict potential drainage at new mines. The Bureau's environmental research also addresses the problem of solid waste disposal and soil and water contaminated by metals. Technologies are developed that will reduce or remove the threats that these wastes pose.

* Animal Poison Control Hotline
National Animal Poison Control Center (217) 333-3611
The National Animal Poison Control Center, at The University of Illinois, provides 24-hour consultation in diagnosis and treatment of suspected or actual animal poisonings or chemical contaminations. Its emergency response team will rapidly investigate such incidents in North America, and perform laboratory analysis of feeds, animal specimens, and environmental materials for toxicants and chemical contaminants.

* Arctic Environmental Assessment
Office of Ocean Resources Conservation and Assessment (ORCA)
National Ocean Service
National Oceanic and Atmospheric Administration
6001 Executive Blvd.
Rockville, MD 20852 (301) 443-8487
ORCA manages a large scientific program of environmental assessments on the effects of oil and gas development on Alaska's outer continental shelf. General areas of investigation include description of Alaskan coastal and marine environments and ecosystems, development of pollutant transport models, and evaluation of the potential effects of petroleum development on coastal and marine resources.

* Asbestos in Your Home
R. Woods, Consumer Information Center-2A
P.O. Box 100
Pueblo, CO 81002
Asbestos in the Home discusses what asbestos is and the dangers it presents; how to tell if it's in your home and what to do about it (124Y, $1.50).

* Chemical Hazards Guide
Publications Dissemination
National Institute for Occupational Safety and Health
4676 Columbia Parkway
Cincinnati, Ohio 45226 (513) 533-8287
A Pocket Guide To Chemical Hazards is intended as a source of general industrial hygiene information for workers, employers, and occupational health professionals. It presents key information and data in abbreviated tabular for 398 chemicals or substance groupings that are found in the work environment and that have existing Occupational Safety and Health Administration regulations. The information includes chemical structures or formulas, identification codes, synonyms, exposure limits, chemical and physical properties, incompatibilities and reactivities, measurement methods, respirator selections, signs and symptoms of exposure, and procedures for emergency treatment. This Guide is free.

* Chemical Hazards Management Bibliography
Superintendent of Documents
Government Printing Office
Washington, DC 20402 (202) 783-3238
Hazardous and toxic waste management are topics within this bibliography. A pocket guide to chemical hazards and a septic systems and ground-water protection guide are featured. Free.

* Chemical Health and Safety Hotline
Chemical Referral Center (800) CMA-8200
(202) 887-1315 (in DC)
This toll-free service provides non-emergency referrals to companies that manufacture chemicals and to state and federal agencies for health and safety information and information regarding chemical regulations. It operates 9 a.m. to 6 p.m. eastern time. Residents in Arkansas can call (202) 887-1315 collect.

* Chemical Risk Management
Chemical Control Division
Office of Toxic Substances
Environmental Protection Agency (EPA)
401 M St., SW, Room E513
Washington DC 20460 (202) 260-3749
This office performs the risk management functions for the Office of Toxic Substances. They manage the new chemical and biotechnology programs.

* Chemicals' Impact on Eagles and Falcons
U.S. Department of the Army
Chemical Research Development and Engineering Center
Aberdeen Proving Ground, MD 21010-5423 (301) 671-4345
While the Center's primary mission is concerned with research on chemical defensive material, the Center has become very involved in wildlife conservation programs because of its location on the Chesapeake Bay. The Center is especially experienced in a Bald Eagle program and a Peregrine Falcon program. Fact sheets on these and other wildlife issues may be obtained by writing or calling the above office.

* Chemicals in Your Community
Public Information Center PM-211B
Environmental Protection Agency (EPA)
401 M St., SW
Washington, DC 20460 (202) 260-7751
Congress passes a law designed to help America's communities deal safely wand effectively with the many hazardous substances that are used throughout our society. The law is called the Emergency Planning and Community Right-to-Know Act; and this booklet has been written to help you understand and take advantage of your rights and opportunities under this far-reaching law. The first part of the guide describes how the law works; what its provisions were intended to accomplish; and how all members of the community can play an active part in making sure the law is carried out. The second part discusses specific groups and organizations affected by the law; describes what they can do or are required to do to make it work; and tells how they can benefit from it.

Be patient. If any phone number is incorrect, call (area code) 555-1212 and request the new listing.

Hazardous and Solid Waste

* Commercial Low-Level Radioactive Waste

Office of Technology Assessment
600 Pennsylvania Ave., SE
Washington, DC 20510 (202) 224-8996

OTA has worked on a project to analyze the Federal effort and State progress in implementing the Low-Level Radioactive Waste Policy Amendments Act, which identifies Federal activities needed to help States meet milestones for developing disposal facilities. *Partnerships Under Pressure: Managing Commercial Low-Level Radioactive Waste* is the resulting publication.

* Concerned About Pesticides?

Public Information Center, PM-211B
Environmental Protection Agency (EPA)
401 M St., SW
Washington, DC 20460 (202) 260-7751

The EPA has several publications which provide the consumer with information concerning pesticides. Some of the publications include:

Citizen's Guide to Pesticides- An informative brochure describing how to choose and use pesticides, how to pick a pest control company, and what to do in the event of a problem.

Regulating Pesticides- This brochure explains EPA's registration process and how they classify pesticides.

* Damage Assessment

Office of Ocean Resources Conservation and Assessment (ORCA)
National Ocean Service
National Oceanic and Atmospheric Administration
6001 Executive Blvd.
Rockville, MD 20852 (301) 443-8487

ORCA conducts comprehensive assessments of damages to NOAA trust resources from discharges of oil or releases of hazardous substances. ORCA works with EPA to address natural resource concerns at these sites through its cleanup efforts. ORCA conducts damage assessments to enable NOAA to file claims against the potentially responsible parties. ORCA is currently working to assess damages resulting from the Exxon Valdez oil spill in Alaska.

* Defense Nuclear Waste and Contamination Cleanup

Office of Technology Assessment (OTA)
600 Pennsylvania Ave., SE
Washington, DC 20510 (202) 224-8996

Today there is a large backlog of high-level, transuranic, low-level, hazardous, and mixed nuclear waste at the 15 facilities in the U.S. Department of Energy's nuclear weapons complex. OTA has studied how best to clean up this nuclear waste problem using technologies for waste management and minimizations. *Cleaning Up the Nation's Defense Nuclear Waste and Contamination* is the resulting publication.

* Dioxin Hotlines

The following hotlines provide callers with information on dioxin and related concerns for contaminated areas in New York, New Jersey, and Missouri:

New Jersey . . . . (800) 346-5009
New York . . . . (800) 722-1223
Missouri . . . . (800) 892-5009

* Do You Want To Learn More About Hazardous Substances?

Public Information Center PM211 B
Environmental Protection Agency (EPA)
401 M St., SW
Washington, DC 20460 (202) 260-2080

Hazardous Substances In Our Environment: A Citizen's Guide to Understanding Health Risks and Reducing Exposure is a guidebook which can help answer questions you may have about health risks from hazardous substances after reading statements in newspapers, book and government reports. The term hazardous substances can apply to any man-made or naturally occurring chemical or mineral substance found in air, water, soil, or food that can cause any type of human illness. Part 1 describes different hazardous substances and how they get into your environment, and Part 2 describes government actions, community activities and personal actions you can take. Also included is a list of publications and resources for further information.

* Emergency Plans for Acutely Toxic Chemicals

Emergency Planning and Community Right to Know (800) 535-0202
(703) 920-9877

This EPA hotline provides communities with help in preparing for accidental releases of toxic chemicals by providing documents and other publications necessary. Communities can call to obtain interim guidelines regarding *Acutely Toxic Chemicals*. These guidelines cover organizing a community, developing a chemical contingency plan, and gathering site-specific information. The hotline also provides a list of more than 400 acutely toxic chemicals. They can also direct you to sources for obtaining information about chemicals stored in your community.

* Environmental Hazards in Your Home

R. Woods
Consumer Information Center-2A
P.O. Box 100
Pueblo, CO 81002

Homebuyer's Guide to Environmental Hazards explains the dangers of radon, asbestos, lead, hazardous waste, contaminated ground water, and formaldehydes. This publication explains the risks, what to do, and where to get help (432Y, $1.50).

* Fishery Chemicals Research

National Fisheries Research Center
U.S. Fish and Wildlife Service
P.O. Box 818
LaCrosse, WI 54602-0818 (608) 783-6451

The National Fisheries Research Center at LaCrosse, Wisconsin, has been designated by the Fish and Wildlife Service to negotiate registration for fishery chemicals with regulatory agencies. Pesticides are registered with the U.S. Environmental Protection Agency, and therapeutants for controlling fish diseases are registered with the U.S. Food and Drug Administration. Once a fishery chemical is registered by the Federal government, states will generally allow the use of that chemical for fish culture and management.

* Geologic Hazards and Hazardous Waste

Geologic Inquiries
U.S. Geological Survey
911 National Center
Reston, VA 22092 (703) 648-4380

This division evaluates environmental hazards which are associated with earthquakes, volcanoes, floods, droughts, toxic materials, landslides, subsidence, and other ground failures. Methods of hazards prediction are developed through the study of the Earth's internal structure. Engineering problems are identified and solved, including problems in the selection of sites for power stations, highways, bridges, dams, and hazardous waste disposal.

* Guide to Hazardous Waste Publications

Headquarters Library, PM-211A
Environmental Protection Agency (EPA)
401 M St., SW
Washington, DC 20460 (202) 260-5934

The Hazardous Waste Superfund Collection is housed in 17 libraries in the EPA Library Network. This publication explains the various document types comprising the Hazardous Waste Superfund collection, including sources of documents, contacts, public access, and information pertaining to the availability of documents. This is published annually.

* Hazardous Materials Technical Hotline

Hazardous Materials Technical Center (800) 638-8958
(301) 468-8858

This center provides various services related to hazardous materials, including a clearinghouse technical inquiry line, a newsletter for the U.S. Department of Defense about hazardous materials, maintenance of a collection of publications on hazardous management, and abstracting and publishing of literature related to hazardous materials. The services provided are free only to the U.S. Department of Defense; others must pay a fee to use them.

Be patient. If any phone number is incorrect, call (area code) 555-1212 and request the new listing.

Environment and Nature

* Hazardous Material Transportation Accidents

Information Systems Division (DHM-63)
Office of Hazardous Materials Transportation
Research and Special Programs Administration
U.S. Department of Transportation
400 7th Street, SW, Room 8112
Washington, DC 20590 (202) 366-4555

This division collects and analyzes accident data from transporters of hazardous materials by highway, rail, air, and water and from container manufacturers. Information stored in the database includes the hazardous material involved, transporter name and mode, packaging used, cause of accident, and results. Contact the above office for searches. There may be a charge.

* Hazardous Materials Transportation Hotline

U.S. Department of Transportation Department Hotline
400 7th Street, SW, Room 8112
Washington, DC 20590 (202) 366-2301

This U.S. Department of Transportation Hotline provides informational assistance pertaining to federal regulations for transportation of hazardous materials. This includes those regulations contained in CFR-49.

* Hazardous Waste Bibliography and Technology Transfer

Office of Solid Waste and Emergency Response
Environmental Protection Agency (EPA)
401 M St., SW
Washington DC 20460 (202) 260-6940

This bibliography, prepared by the Technology Transfer Task Force, lists and abstracts the most important technical materials that should be readily available to all Federal and State hazardous waste staffs and their contractors. It assigns each document a level of importance as primary reference documents for Federal and State headquarters, regional, and field staffs. Contact this office to obtain a copy.

* Hazardous Waste Hotline

RCRA/Superfund Hotline
Environmental Protection Agency (EPA)
401 M St., SW (800) 424-9346
Washington DC 20460 (703) 920-9810

Under the Resource Recovery and Conservation Act, the EPA is responsible for identifying general and specific categories of hazardous wastes, developing standards, and enforcing compliance with those standards. Hazardous wastes regulated under RCRA include toxic substances, caustics, pesticides, and other flammable, corrosive, or explosive materials. EPA establishes criteria for classifying land disposal facilities according to their environmental acceptability and publishes a national inventory of unacceptable facilities. Contact this hotline for more information on hazardous wastes and the regulations associated with them. A free catalog is available.

* Hazardous Waste Ombudsman Hotline

Hazardous Waste Ombudsman Program
Environmental Protection Agency (EPA)
401 M St., SW
Washington DC 20460 (202) 260-9361

EPA has established this office to handle complaints from the public and regulated community, and to assist them in resolving problems concerning any program or requirement under the hazardous waste law. The Hazardous Waste Ombudsman Program assists citizens and the regulated community who have had problems voicing a complaint or getting a problem resolved about hazardous waste issues. It serves as a last resort to the RCRA/CERCLA Hotline.

Region 1 . . . . (617) 573-5758
Region 2 . . . . (212) 264-2980
Region 3 . . . . (215) 597-9636
Region 4 . . . . (404) 347-7109
Region 5 . . . . (312) 886-0981
Region 6 . . . . (214) 655-6760
Region 7 . . . . (913) 551-7680
Region 8 . . . . (303) 293-1603
Region 9 . . . . (415) 744-2074
Region 10 . . . . (206) 553-4280

* Help With Chemical Assessment Problems

Office of Toxic Substances
Environmental Protection Agency (EPA)
401 M St., SW
Washington, DC 20460 (202) 260-3442

The Chemical Assessment Desk is an outreach service to other EPA Offices. The Desk offers technical consultation and information on chemical risk-related issues under the OTS Existing Chemicals Program. The Desk also provides estimates of chemical toxicity and environmental fate based on structure-activity relationships in the absence of experimental data, assists in identifying related risk assessment activities, and provides comments on technical aspects of OTS evaluations and risk assessments. For State and local agencies, the Chemical Assessment Desk operates through Regional coordinators as follows:

Region 1
Boston 617-565-3704

Region 2
New York 201-321-6893

Region 3
Philadelphia 215-597-7904

Region 4
Atlanta 404-347-4216

Region 5
Chicago 312-886-6006

Region 6
Dallas 214-655-7244

Region 7
Kansas City 913-236-2970

Region 8
Denver 303-293-1730

Region 9
San Francisco 415-974-7280

Region 10
Seattle 206-442-1072

* Help With Solid Waste Issues

RCRA Information Center
Environmental Protection Agency (EPA)
401 M St., SW
Washington, DC 20460 (800) 424-9346

Is your community facing or edging toward a solid waste crisis? Do you understand all the available solid waste management options and how to integrate them to your community's advantage? To help local solid waste managers address these questions, EPA has compiled and published the *Decision-Maker's Guide to Solid Waste Management*. This free publication will help you devise and implement a solid waste management system that benefits your community economically and environmentally.

* Lead-Based Paint

R. Woods
Consumer Information Center
P.O. Box 100
Pueblo, CO 81002

What You Should Know About Lead-Based Paint in Your Home explains how lead poisoning is hazardous to you and your family's health. Learn how to detect lead in paint, what to do to reduce exposure, and safety guidelines for removing lead-based paint (435Y, $1.50).

* Medical Waste and Recycling

Office of Technology Assessment (OTA)
600 Pennsylvania Ave., SE
Washington, DC 20510 (202) 228-6854

OTA is currently studying medical waste handling and disposal as comparisons of incineration and alternative management technologies and their associated

Hazardous and Solid Waste

risks, along with waste reduction and recycling options for medical waste management. Contact Kathryn Wagner, the project director, for more information.

* National Response Center Hotline

Coast Guard Hotline (800) 424-8802

(202) 426-2675

This U.S. Department of Transportation National Response Center can be used to report spills of oil and other hazardous materials where required. It can also be used to report incidents in transportation where hazardous materials are responsible for death, serious injury, property damage in excess of $50,000 or continuing danger to life and property.

* New Pesticide Registration

Registration Division
Office of Pesticide Programs
Pesticides and Toxic Substances
Environmental Protection Agency (EPA)
401 M St., SW
Washington DC 20460 (703) 305-5447

The EPA registers (licenses) thousands of pesticide products for use in and around homes. No pesticide may legally be sold in the U.S. unless its label bears an EPA registration number. The Federal Insecticide, Fungicide and Rodenticide Act (FIFRA), which governs the registration of pesticides, prohibits the use of any pesticide products in a manner that is inconsistent with product labeling. Contact this office for more information.

* Northeast Industrial Waste Clearinghouse

Northeast Industrial Waste Exchange (315) 422-6572

The Northeast Industrial Waste Exchange provides information on waste exchange in the Northeast but with access to other areas. This exchange joins those who generate waste with those who desire waste.

* Nuclear Waste Hydrology

Nuclear Waste Program
Water Resources Division
U.S. Geological Survey
National Center, MS 410
Reston, VA 22092 (703) 648-5719

Hydrologic and geologic research and field studies are conducted to develop better understanding of radionuclide transport in ground-water systems. The program also supports Interior's role in the national high-level nuclear waste repository program, providing information on the management of low-level nuclear waste.

* Ocean Dumping

Office of Marine and Estuarine Protection
Environmental Protection Agency (EPA)
401 M St., SW
Washington DC 20460 (202) 260-1952

This office carries out the duties covered under the Marine Protection, Research and Sanctuaries Act, which is designed to protect the marine environment from the harmful effects of ocean dumping. The Act establishes a permit program to ensure that ocean dumping does not cause degradation of the marine environment. Contact this office for more information on ocean dumping regulation.

* Oil and Chemical Spills Hotline

National Response Center (NRC)
Marine Environmental Response Division
Office of Marine Safety, Security, and Environmental Protection
U.S. Coast Guard
U.S. Department of Transportation
2100 2nd St., SW, Room 2611 (800) 424-8802
Washington, DC 20593 (202) 267-2188

The NRC receives reports of oil and hazardous substance spills, investigates incidents, initiates civil penalty actions, monitors cleanups, and coordinates federally funded spill response operations. NRC's National Strike Force assists federal coordinators on the scene in responding to pollution accidents. For further details, or to report information, contact the Center toll-free.

* Oil Spills and Hazardous Waste Response Hotline

Coast Guard Hotline, U.S. Coast Guard
U.S. Department of Transportation
2100 2nd St., SW, Room 2611 (800) 424-8802
Washington, DC 20593 (202) 426-2675

This U.S. Department of Transportation National Response Center can be used to report spills of oil and other hazardous materials where required. It can also be used to report incidents in transportation where hazardous materials are responsible for death, serious injury, property damage in excess of $50,000 or continuing danger to life and property.

* PCBs and Asbestos Hotline

Toxic Substances Control Act Hotline
Environmental Protection Agency (EPA)
401 M St., SW
Washington DC 20460 (202) 554-1404

The Toxic Assistance Office at EPA will answer questions and offer general and technical assistance on the Toxic Substances Control Act. Staff will help to obtain guidance on TSCA regulations, including guidance on PCBs and asbestos issues. Publications are also available through the hotline.

* Pesticides and Toxic Substances Library

Office of Toxic Substances Library
401 M St., SW
Washington, DC 20460 (202) 260-3944

Part of the Office of Pesticides and Toxic Substances, the OTS Library houses collections relevant to toxic substances. The library also maintains some pesticides publications. Hours of operation are Monday through Friday, 8:00 a.m. to 4:30 p.m. Databases maintained here include DIALOG, NLM, STN, and CIS.

* Pesticide Information Hotline

National Pesticide Telecommunications Network (800) 858-7378

(806) 743-3091 (TX)

This service of the U.S. Environmental Protection Agency and Texas Tech University is open 24 hours, 7 days a week. It responds to non-emergency questions about the effects of pesticides, toxicology and symptoms, environmental effects, disposal and cleanup, and safe use of pesticides.

* Pesticide Problems

Frank Davido
Pesticide Incident Response Officer
Field Operations Division (H-7506C)
Office of Pesticide Programs
Environmental Protection Agency (EPA)
401 M St., SW
Washington, DC 20460 (703) 305-0576

The EPA is interested in receiving information on any adverse effects associated with pesticide exposure. You should provide as complete information as possible, including any official investigation report of the incident and medical records concerning adverse health effects. Medial records will be held in confidence.

* Pesticides Database

Pesticides Information Retrieval System
CERIS
1231 Cumberland Avenue, Suite A
N. Lafayette, IN 47906 (317) 494-7309

This computer database provides public access to current information on over 36,000 pesticide products. The system development has been jointly funded by USDA and EPA and is managed by Purdue University.

* Pesticides Rules and Regulations

Environmental Protection Agency (EPA)
401 M Street SW
Washington, DC 20460 (703) 305-5805

The Pesticides Docket provides public access to documentation for each Registration Standard under development when the Agency begins review of data for the Registration Standard or upon publication of a notice setting out the list and sequence of Registration Standards. The docket contains documentation of pre-special and special reviews of pesticides, memoranda, all comments,

Be patient. If any phone number is incorrect, call (area code) 555-1212 and request the new listing.

Environment and Nature

correspondence, documents, proposals, or other materials concerning a pending pesticide regulatory decision provided to the Agency by a person or party outside of government (other than confidential business information).

* Pipeline Safety

Office of Pipeline Safety (OPS)
Research and Special Programs Administration
U.S. Department of Transportation
400 7th Street, SW
Washington, DC 20590   (202) 366-4572

OPS establishes and enforces safety standards for the transportation of gas and other hazardous materials by pipeline. A computerized reporting system is maintained to collect and analyze accident and incident data from pipeline operators. Accident reports include the operator's name, the hazardous material involved, description of the accident, and results. For database searches, contact the office listed. There may be a charge.

* Poison Control Centers

24 hours a day, 7 days a week

These centers answer specific questions about situations involving poisons. While most calls received involve questions regarding children, a significant number of calls involve adults exposed to some form of toxic substance. These Centers provide medical treatment guidance and can answer general questions about air toxics, including paint fumes and pesticides. Regional poison control centers service many areas throughout the United States.

Alabama Poison Center
(205) 345-0600
(800) 462-0800 (AL only)

Arizona Poison Control System
(602) 626-7899
(602) 626-6016 (Tucson)
(602) 253-3334 (Phoenix)
(800) 362-0101 (AZ only)

Central Ohio Poison Center
(614) 461-2012
(614) 228-1323
(800) 682-7625

Blodgett Regional Poison Center
(616) 774-7854
(800) 442-4571 (616 area code only)

Cardinal Glennon Children's Hospital Regional Poison Center
(314) 772-8300
(314) 772-5200
(800) 392-9111 (MO only)

Maryland Poison Center
(301) 528-7606
(301) 528-7701
(800) 492-2414 (MD only)

Duke University Poison Control Center
(919) 684-4438
(919) 684-8111
(800) 672-1697 (NC only)

Georgia Poison Control Center
(404) 589-4400
(800) 282-5846 (GA only)
(404) 525-3323 (TTY)

Hennepin Regional Poison Center (Minnesota)
(612) 347-3144
(612) 347-3141
(612) 347-6219 (TTY)

Intermountain Regional Poison Control Center
(801) 581-7504
(801) 581-2151
(800) 662-0062 (UT only)

Kentucky Regional Poison Center of Kosair Children's Hospital
(502) 562-7263
(502) 589-8222
(800)722-5725 (KY only) (TDD)

Long Island Regional Poison Control Center
(516) 542-3707
(516) 542-2323

Los Angeles County Medical Association Regional Poison Control Center
(213) 664-1212
(213) 484-5151

Louisiana Regional Poison Control Center
(318) 674-6364
(318) 425-1524
(800) 535-0525 (LA only)

Massachusetts Poison Control System
(617) 735-6607
(617) 232-2120
(800) 492-2414 (MD only)

Michigan Poison Control Center
(313) 745-5329
(313) 745-5711
(800) 462-6642 (313 area code only)
(800) 572-1655 (remainder of MI)

Mid-Plains Poison Center
(402) 390-5434
(402) 390-5400
(800) 642-999 (NE only)
(800) 228-9515 (surrounding states)

New Jersey Poison Information and Education System
(201) 926-7443
(201) 923-0764
(800) 432-6866 (NJ only)

New Mexico Poison and Drug Information Center
(505) 277-4261
(505) 843-2551
(800) 432-6866 (NM only)

New York City Poison Control Center
(212) 340-4497
(212) 340-4494

North Central Texas Poison Center
(214) 920-2586
(214) 920-2400
(800) 441-0040 (TX only)

Oregon Poison Control and Drug Information Center
(503) 225-7799
(503) 225-8968 (Portland, OR)
(800) 452-7165

Pittsburgh Poison Center
(412) 647-5600
(412) 681-6669

Rocky Mountain Poison Center
(303) 893-7774
(303) 629-1123
(800) 332-3073 (CO only)
(800) 525-5042 (MT only)
(800) 442-2702 (WY only)

San Diego Regional Poison Center
(619) 294-3666
(619) 294-6000

San Francisco Gay Area Regional Poison Control Center
(415) 821-8324
(415) 476-6600

Be patient. If any phone number is incorrect, call (area code) 555-1212 and request the new listing.

Hazardous and Solid Waste

Southwest Ohio Regional Poison Control System
(513) 872-5111
(800) 872-5111

Tampa Bay Regional Control System
(813) 251-6911
(813) 253-444
(800) 282-3171

Texas State Poison Center
(409) 761-3332
(409) 765-1701 (Houston)
(713) 654-1701 (Austin)
(800) 392-8548 (TX only)

UCDMC Regional Poison Control Center
(916) 453-3414
(916) 453-3692

West Virginia Poison Center
(304) 347-1212
(304) 348-4211
(800) 642-3625 (WV only)

Washington DC
(202) 625-3333

* Pollution Prevention and the Environment

Public Information Center, PM-211B
Environmental Protection Agency (EPA)
401 M St., SW
Washington, DC 20460 (202) 260-7751

The EPA's Public Information Center supplies non-technical publications about the environment and related issues, including information on household hazards, family recycling tips, and book suggestions for all ages. All of these are free and provide a wealth of helpful information.

Books for Young People on Environmental Issues
Earth Trek...Explore Your Environment
The President's Environmental Youth Awards
1991 Gas Mileage Guide: EPA Fuel Economy Estimates
Be An Environmentally Alert Consumer
Citizen's Guide to Pesticides
Citizen's Guide to Radon: What It Is and What To Do About It
Environmental Enforcement: A Citizen's Guide
A Family Guide to Pollution Prevention
Glossary of Environmental Terms and Acronym List
The Inside Story: A Guide to Indoor Air Quality
Meeting the Environmental Challenge
Protecting Our Ground Water
Superfund: Looking Back, Looking Ahead
Termiticides: Consumer Information

* Radioactive and Radon Exposure

Office of Radiation Programs
Environmental Protection Agency (EPA)
401 M St., SW, Room NE108
Washington DC 20460 (202) 260-9600

The EPA, with a number of other federal agencies, protects the public from unnecessary exposure to ionizing radiation. EPA's major responsibilities are to set radioactive emissions standards and exposure limits, assess new technology, and monitor radiation in the environment in four areas: radiation from nuclear accidents, radon emissions, land disposal of radioactive waste, and radiation in groundwater and drinking water. The EPA fulfills these responsibilities by setting emissions standards for nuclear power plants, and for radionuclides in drinking water and in the air. EPA also prescribes work practices to reduce emissions of radon from underground uranium mines, develops radioactive waste disposal standards, and issues guidance to limit occupational exposure.

* Recycling Help For Teachers

RCRA Docket Information Center
Office of Solid Waste
Environmental Protection Agency (EPA)

401 M St., SW (800) 424-9346
Washington, DC 20460 (703) 920-9810

Let's Reduce and Recycle: Curriculum for Solid Waste Awareness provides lesson plans for grades K-12, and is a curriculum guide that emerged as part of a public education campaign to promote recycling awareness. Activities, skits, bibliographies, and other resources are included. This is a free publication.

* Recycling Information

Public Information Center
Environmental Protection Agency (EPA)
401 M St., SW, PM-211 B
Washington DC 20460 (202) 260-7751

Recycling Works! is a free booklet that provides information about successful recycling programs initiated by state and local agencies. It also describes private recycling efforts and joint recycling ventures of government and businesses.

* Resource Conservation and Recovery Act (RCRA)

Environmental Protection Agency (EPA)
401 M St., SW
Washington, DC 20460 (202) 260-9327

The Resource Conservation and Recovery Act (RCRA) Docket provides public access to regulatory information supporting the EPA's actions under RCRA. Records support *Federal Register* notices, *Delisting Petitions*, and other Office of Solid Waste publications. RCRA Docket publishes a semiannual catalog of frequently requested documents titled, *A Catalog of Hazardous and Solid Waste Publications*. Contact this office for more information on these and other RCRA documents.

* Resource Recovery Emergency Response Hotline

RCRA On-Scene Coordinators Hotline (214) 767-2666

The Resource Conservation and Recovery Act On-Scene Coordinators Hotline in Region VI responds 24 hours a day to questions and to reports of chemical spills and other emergencies for all Region VI states: Arkansas, Louisiana, New Mexico, Oklahoma, and Texas.

* Restricted Pesticides

Office of Pesticides and Toxic Substances
Environmental Protection Agency (EPA)
Washington, DC 20460 (703) 305-5805

This office has a publication titled *Suspended, Cancelled and Restricted Pesticides* which is a summary and clarification of actions taken by EPA for pesticides that the Agency has suspended, cancelled, or otherwise restricted because of concern for potentially adverse effects. This listing identifies the current status and references the legal history of each pesticide, as well as the criteria of concern for which the chemical was reviewed by the Agency (EPA/EN-342).

* Save the Whales

Office of Ocean Affairs
U.S. Department of State
Room 5801
Washington, DC 20520 (202) 647-3262

This office can provide you with up to the minute information on the protection of whales. They put together the U.S. whaling policy, attend meetings of the international whaling commission, and follow the mandates of the Marine Mammal Protection Act. This office can direct you to other organizations and associations concerned with the protection of whales.

* Solid Waste Information Clearinghouse and Hotline (SWICH)

Solid Waste Information Clearinghouse
P.O. Box 7219
8750 Georgia Ave., Suite 140
Silver Spring, MD 20910 (800) 67-SWICH

SWICH was developed to help increase the availability of information in the field of solid waste management, and is comprised of a library system and an electronic bulletin board (EBB). The library includes journals, reports, studies, proceedings, periodicals, case studies, curricula, films and videotapes all focusing on solid waste issues. Topic covered include source reduction, recycling, composting, planning, education and training, public participation, legislation and

Be patient. If any phone number is incorrect, call (area code) 555-1212 and request the new listing.

Environment and Nature

regulation, waste combustion, collection, transfer, disposal, landfill gas, and special wastes. The EBB provides updated information on solid waste issues including: meeting and conference information, message inquiries, case studies, new technologies, new publications, expert contact information, and much more. A quarterly newsletter is also published.

* Solid Waste Management Clearinghouse

Andrew W. Briedenbach Environmental Research Center Library 26 W. St. Clair St. Cincinnati, OH 45268 (513) 569-7703

The major subjects in this library's collection are bacteriology, biology, biotechnology, chemistry, engineering, hazardous wastes, hydrobiology, microbiology, solid waste management, toxicology, water pollution, and water quality. Databases maintained here include BRS, CAS On-line, CIS, DIALOG, Dun & Bradstreet, Hazardous Waste Database, LEXIS/NEXIS, NLM, Toxline, and Toxnet. General collections include bacteriology, biology, biotechnology, microbiology, physics, solid waste management. This library's special collections cover the environment, Canada, legal issues, hazardous waste, and solid waste.

* State Pesticide Agencies

State Pesticide Agencies regulate the use of pesticides and license people who purchase restricted use permits and for people who use it for their business, such as farmers. Typically, people must pass a test, carry a certain amount of insurance, and attend recertification classes in order to get a license. This office can answer question regarding pesticide use, and can explain the label on your pesticide container. If you hired someone to treat your home or yard, and you had damage as a result of that treatment, you should contact this office. They are charged with seeing that pesticides are used properly, and will investigate your complaint.

REGION 1

Connecticut Director Department of Environmental Protection Hazardous Materials Management Unit State Office Building 165 Capitol Ave. Hartford, CT 06115 (203) 566-5148

Maine Director Board of Pesticide Control Dept. of Agriculture State House- Station 28 Augusta, ME 04333 (207) 289-2731

Massachusetts Chief Pesticides Bureau Dept. of Food and Agriculture 100 Cambridge St., 21st Floor Boston, MA 02202 (617) 727-2863

New Hampshire Director Division of Pesticides Control Department of Agriculture Caller Box 2042 Concord, NH 03301 (603) 271-3550

Rhode Island Chief Division of Agriculture and Marketing Dept. of Environmental Management 22 Hayes St. Providence, RI 02908 (401) 277-2781

Vermont Director Plant Industry Laboratory of Standards Division Dept. of Agriculture 116 State St. State Office Bldg. Montpelier, VT 05602 (802) 828-2431

REGION 2

New Jersey Chief, Bureau of Pesticide Control NJ Dept. of Environmental Protection 380 South Rd. Est Trenton, NJ 08624 (609) 530-4123

New York Director Bureau of Pesticides Department of Environmental Conservation Room 404, 50 Wolf Rd. Albany, NY 12233-0001 (518) 457-7482

Puerto Rico Director Analysis and Registration of Agricultural Materials Division of Laboratory Puerto Rico Dept. of Agriculture P.O. Box 10163 Santurce, PR 00908 (809) 796-1715

Virgin Islands Director Pesticide Programs Division of Natural Resources Management Dept. of Conservation and Cultural Affairs 14 F Bldg. 111 Watergut Homes Christiansted, St. Croix U.S. Virgin Islands 00820 (809) 773-0565

REGION 3

Delaware Delaware Dept. of Agriculture 2320 S. DuPont Highway Dover, DE 199901 (302) 736-4815

District of Columbia Pesticide Section Dept. of Consumer and Regulatory Affairs District of Columbia 611 H St., NW Washington, DC 20013 (202) 783-3190

Maryland Chief Pesticide Applicators Law Section Maryland Dept. Of Agriculture 50 Harry S. Truman Parkway Annapolis, MD 21401 (301) 841-5710

Pennsylvania Chief Agronomic Services Bureau of Plant Industry PA Dept. Of Agriculture 32301 N. Cameron St. Harrisburg, PA 17110 (717) 787-4843

Virginia Supervisor Office of Pesticide Management VA Dept. of Agriculture and Consumer Service P.O. Box 1163 Richmond, VA 23209 (804) 786-3798

West Virginia Plant Pest Control Division W VA Dept. of Agriculture State Capitol Bldg. Charleston, WV 25305 (304) 348-2212

Be patient. If any phone number is incorrect, call (area code) 555-1212 and request the new listing.

Hazardous and Solid Waste

REGION 4

Alabama
Director
Agricultural Chemistry/Plant Industry Division
Alabama Dept. of Agriculture and Industries
P.O. Box 336
Montgomery, AL 36193 (205) 242-2656

Florida
Pesticide Registration Section
Bureau of Pesticides
Division of Inspection
Dept. of Agriculture and consumer Services
Mayo Bldg., Room 213
Tallahassee, FL 32301 (904) 487-2130

Georgia
Agricultural Manager
Entomology and Pesticides Division
Dept. of Agriculture
19 Martin Luther King Jr. Drive, SW
Atlanta, GA 30334 (404) 656-4958

Kentucky
Director
Division of Pesticides
Kentucky Dept. of Agriculture
Capitol Plaza Tower
Frankfort, KY 40601 (502) 564-7274

Mississippi
Division of Plant Industry
Dept. of Agriculture and Commerce
P.O. Box 5207
Mississippi State, MS 30762 (601) 325-3390

North Carolina
Administrator
Pesticides
Food and Drug Pesticide Section
Dept. of Agriculture
State Agriculture Bldg.
Raleigh, NC 27611 (919) 733-3556

South Carolina
Head
Pesticide
Dept. of Fertilizer/Pest Control
256 Poole Agriculture Center
Clemson University
Clemson, SC 29634 (803) 656-3171

Tennessee
Director
Plant Industries Division
Dept. of Agriculture
P.O. Box 40627, Melrose Station
Nashville, TN 37204 (615) 360-0130

REGION 5

Illinois
Chief
Bureau of Plant and Apiary Protection
Dept. of Agriculture
State Fair Ground
P.O. Box 19281
Springfield, IL 62794 (217) 785-2427

Indiana
Administrator
Pesticide
Office of the State Chemist
Dept. of Biochemistry
Purdue University
West Lafayette, IN 47907 (317) 494-1492

Michigan
Pesticide and Plant Pest Management Division
Dept. of Agriculture
Ottawa Building
N. Tower, 4th Floor
611 W. Ottawa St.
P.O. Box 30017
Lansing, MI 48909 (517) 373-1087

Minnesota
Director
Division of Agronomy Services
Dept. of Agriculture
90 West Plato Blvd.
St. Paul, MN 55107 (612) 296-1161

Ohio
Specialist in Charge of Pesticide Regulation
Division of Plant Industry
Dept. of Agriculture
8995 East Main St.
Reynoldsburg, OH 43068 (614) 866-6361

Wisconsin
Director
Groundwater and Regulatory Service Section
Dept. of Agriculture
Trade and Consumer Protection
801 West Badger Rd.
P.O. Box 8911
Madison, WI 53708 (608) 266-9459

REGION 6

Arkansas
Director
Division of Feed, Fertilizer and Pesticides
Arkansas State Plant Board
#1 Natural Resources Dr.
Little Rock, AR 72205 (501) 225-1598

Louisiana
Office of Agricultural and Environmental Sciences
Louisiana Dept. of Agriculture
P.O. Box 3596
Baton Rouge, LA 760821 (504) 925-3763

New Mexico
Director
Division of Agricultural and Environmental Services
N.M. State Dept. of Agriculture
p.O. Box 3005-3AQ1
N.M. State University
Las Cruces, NM 88003 (505) 545-2133

Oklahoma
Chief
Pest Management Section
Plant Industry Division
Oklahoma State Dept. of Agriculture
2800 N. Lincoln Blvd.
Oklahoma City, OK 73105 (405) 521-3864

Texas
Director
Division of Agricultural and Environmental Sciences
Texas Dept. of Agriculture
P.O. Box 12847
Austin, TX 78711 (512) 463-7534

REGION 7

Iowa
Supervisor
Pesticide Control Bureau Section
Iowa Dept. of Agriculture
Henry A. Wallace Building

Be patient. If any phone number is incorrect, call (area code) 555-1212 and request the new listing.

Environment and Nature

E. 9th St. and Grand Ave.
Des Moines, IA 50319 (515) 281-8591

Kansas
Director, Plant Health Division
Kansas State Board of Agriculture
109 SW 9th St.
Topeka, KS 66612 (913) 296-2263

Missouri
Supervisor
Bureau of Pesticide Control
Dept. of Agriculture
P.O. Box 630
Jefferson City, MO 65102 (314) 751-2462

Nebraska
Director
Bureau of Plant Industry
Nebraska Dept. of Agriculture
301 Centennial Mall South
Lincoln, NE 68509 (402) 471-2341

REGION 8
Colorado
Supervisor
Pesticide Section
Division of Plant Industry
Colorado Dept of Agriculture
1525 Sherman St., 4th Floor
Denver, CO 80203 (303) 866-2838

Montana
Administrator
Environmental Management Division
Montana Dept. of Agriculture
Agriculture-Livestock Building
Room 317 Capitol Station
6th and Roberts
Helena, MT 59620 (406) 444-2944

North Dakota
Director
Pesticide/Noxious Weed Division
N.D. Dept. of Agriculture
600 East Boulevard, 6th Floor
Bismarck, ND 58505 (701) 224-4756

South Dakota
Director
Division of Regulatory Services
S.D. Dept. of Agriculture
Anderson Bldg.
445 East Capitol
Pierre, SC 57501 (605) 773-3724

Utah
Director
Division of Plant Industries
Utah Dept. of Agriculture
350 North Redwood Rd.
Salt Lake City, UT 84116 (801) 538-7123

Wyoming
Manager
Pesticide Division
Wyoming Dept. of Agriculture
2219 Carey Ave.
Cheyenne, WY 82002 (307) 777-6590

REGION 9
Arizona
Director
Agricultural Chemical and Environmental Services Division
AZ Commission of Agriculture and Horticulture

1688 West Adams, Suite 103
Phoenix, AZ 85007 (602) 542-4373

California
Associate Deputy
Director
Division of Pest Management
Environmental Protection and Worker Safety
California Dept. of Food and Agriculture
1220 N. St.
Sacramento, CA 95814 (916) 322-6315

Hawaii
Director
Division of Plant Industry
Hawaii Dept. of Agriculture
P.O. Box 22159
Honolulu, HI 96822 (808) 548-7110

Nevada
Director
Division of Plant Industry
Nevada Dept. of Agriculture
350 Capitol Hill Ave.
P.O. Box 11100
Reno, NV 89510 (702) 789-0181

Guam
Director
Air and Land Program Division
Guam Environmental Protection Agency
P.O. Box 2999
Agana, GU 96910

American Samoa
Director
Dept. of Agriculture
P.O. Box 366
Pago Pago, American Samoa 96799

Trust Territory of the Pacific Islands
Executive Officer
Trust Territory
Environmental Protection Board
Office of the High Commissioner
Trust Territory of the Pacific Islands
Saipan, Mariana Islands 96950

Commonwealth of the Northern Mariana Islands
Environmental Engineer
Division of Environmental Quality
Commonwealth of the Northern Mariana Island
Dr. Torres Hospital
Saipan Mariana Island 96950

REGION 10
Idaho
Chief
Bureau of Pesticides
Idaho Dept. of Agriculture
P.O. Box 790
Boise, ID 83701 (208) 334-3243

Oregon
Assistant Chief
Plant Division
Oregon Dept. of Agriculture
635 Capitol St., NE
Salem, OR 97301

Washington
Chief
Chemicals Branch
Washington Dept. of Agriculture
406 General Administration Bldg.
Olympia, WA 98504 (206) 753-5064

Be patient. If any phone number is incorrect, call (area code) 555-1212 and request the new listing.

Hazardous and Solid Waste

Alaska
Director Division of Environmental Health
Alaska Dept. of Environmental Conservation
P.O. Box 'O'
Juneau, AK 99811 (907) 465-2609

* Superfund Cleanup Bulletin Board

Clean-Up Information Bulletin Board System (CLU-IN)
OSWER Electronic Bulletin Board, OS-110W
Environmental Protection Agency (EPA)
401 M St., SW
Washington, DC 20460 (301) 589-8366

The CLU-IN Bulletin Board offers a number of services including online messages and bulletins; computer files, programs, and databases, and Special Interest Group conference areas. The system targets those involved in hazardous waste remediation and corrective action activities, and is intended to provide an efficient mechanism for the exchange of technological information. CLU-IN is open to the public although access to several Special Interest Group areas are restricted to use by select EPA employees.

* Superfund Compensation and Liability Regulations

Environmental Protection Agency (EPA)
401 M Street SW
Washington, DC 20460 (202) 260-3046

The Superfund Docket provides public access to information supporting all regulatory decisions issued under the Comprehensive Environmental Response, Compensation, Liability Act of 1980 (CERCLA) as amended. This includes records of proceeding under the Emergency Planning and Community Right to Know Act of 1986, Title III of the Superfund Amendments and Reauthorization Act (SARA) of 1986. The Docket also includes CERCLA guidance documents and information supporting rulemaking under authority of Section 3012 of the Resource Conservation and Recovery Act.

* Superfund Hotline

Environmental Protection Agency (EPA)
401 M St., SW (800) 424-9346
Washington DC 20460 (703) 920-9810 (DC area)

This hotline answers questions concerning the Resource Conservation and Recovery Act, Superfund, and hazardous waste regulations. Requests for certain documents from the *Federal Register* and public laws are also handled in addition to referral to appropriate contacts. The hotline operates 8:30 a.m. to 7:30 p.m. (EST). A free catalogue of publications is available.

* Superfund National Priorities List Regional Docket Contacts

Nancy Smith, HSS-CAN-7
US EPA, Region 1
J.F. Kennedy Federal Bldg.
Boston, MA 02203 (617) 573-9697

Ben Conetta
US EPA, Region 2
26 Federal Plaza, Room 13-1000
New York, NY 10278 (212) 264-6696

Kurt Schenk, 3HW13
US EPA, Region 3
841 Chestnut St.
Philadelphia, PA 19107 (215) 597-6633

Deborah Vaugn-Wright
US EPA, Region 4
345 Courtland St., NE
Atlanta, GA 30365 (404) 347-5065

Jeanne Griffin, 5HSM-TUB7
US EPA, Region 5
230 South Dearborn St.
Chicago, IL 60604 (312) 886-3007

Bill Taylor, 6H-MA
US EPA, Region 6

1445 Ross Ave.
Dallas, TX 75202 (214) 655-6740

Karla Ashberry
US EPA, Region 7-Library
726 Minnesota Ave.
Kansas City, KS 66101 (913) 551-7595

Gregory Oberley, 8HWM-SM
US EPA, Region 8
999 18th St., Suite 500
Denver, CO 80202 (303) 294-7598

Lisa Nelson
US EPA, Region 9
1235 Mission St.
San Francisco, CA 94103 (415) 744-2347

David Bennett, HW-093
US EPA, Region 10
1200 Sixth Ave.
Seattle, WA 98101 (206) 553-2103

* Toxicology Databases and Clearinghouse

Andrew W. Briedenbach Environmental
Research Center Library
26 W. St. Clair St.
Cincinnati, OH 45268 (513) 569-7703

The major subjects in this library's collection are bacteriology, biology, biotechnology, chemistry, engineering, hazardous wastes, hydrobiology, microbiology, solid waste management, toxicology, water pollution, and water quality. Databases maintained here include BRS, CAS On-line, CIS, DIALOG, Dun & Bradstreet, Hazardous Waste Database, LEXIS/NEXIS, NLM, Toxline, and Toxnet. General collections include bacteriology, biology, biotechnology, microbiology, physics, solid waste management. This library's special collections cover the environment, Canada, legal issues, hazardous waste, and solid waste.

* Toxic Substances Control Act Hotline

Environmental Protection Agency (EPA)
401 M Street SW
Washington, DC 20460 (202) 554-1404

The Toxic Assistance Office at EPA will answer questions and offer general and technical assistance on the Toxic Substances Control Act. Staff will help you obtain guidance on TSCA regulations including guidance on PCBs and asbestos issues.

* Toxic Substances Non-Confidential Information

Office of Toxic Substances
Non-Confidential Information Center
401 M St., SW (EPA7565)
Northeast Mall, Room B002
Washington, DC 20460 (202) 260-3944

This office's library covers chemical literature in areas of biotechnology, health, chemical industry and process technology, international chemical control, ecology, and pesticides.

* Toxic Substances Rules and Regulations

Office of Toxic Substances
Environmental Protection Agency (EPA)
401 M Street SW
Washington, DC 20460 (202) 260-3587

The Office of Toxic Substances (OTS) Public Information Office houses the official copies of all OTS administrative records supporting regulatory decisions promulgated under the Toxic Substances Control Act (TSCA). The Public Information Office also maintains original materials submitted by industry in compliance with TSCA regulations. The contents of the dockets vary according to the proposed regulation and the particular Section of the Act which is being promulgated. However, generally all dockets contain the following types of supporting documentation: *Federal Register* notices; various health, environmental, and exposure assessment documents; published references; communications; and test data.

Environment and Nature

* Transportation of Hazardous Materials

Office of Hazardous Materials Transportation
Research and Special Programs Administration
U.S. Department of Transportation
400 7th Street, SW
Washington, DC 20590-0001 (202) 366-2301

This office can provide you with information on the transportation of hazardous materials by highway, rail air, and water. Data is collected directly from industry and also via compliance inspections by field staff. The quarterly *Hazardous Material Newsletter* is available free from the office above.

* Underground Storage Tanks

Office of Underground Storage Tanks
Solid Waste and Emergency Response
Environmental Protection Agency (EPA)
401 M St., SW, Room 2107
Washington DC 20460 (202) 308-8850

Storage tanks for volatile liquids have been buried underground to reduce the risk of fire and explosion, but leaking tanks are a major source of groundwater contamination and a great risk to human health and the environment. The EPA has issued regulations addressing leak detection, corrective action requirements, standards for new tanks, and other tank management practices. This Office can provide you with details concerning leaking tanks, as well as information regarding the cleanup required.

* Underground Storage Tank Docket

Environmental Protection Agency (EPA)
401 M Street SW
Washington, DC 20460 (202) 260-9720

The Underground Storage Tank (UST) Docket provides public access to regulatory information supporting the Agency's regulatory action on USTs. As of April 1, 1987, there are seven dockets: (1) UST Notification Form; (2) Technical Standards for USTs Containing Petroleum; (3) Financial Responsibility Requirements for USTs Containing Petroleum; (4) State Program Approval; (5) Report to Congress on Exempt Tanks; (6) Consolidated Rules of Practice Governing the Administrative Assessment of Civil Penalties and Revocation or Suspension of Permits; and (7) Financial Responsibility Requirements for USTs Containing Hazardous Substances.

* Waste Reduction and Minimization Hotline

Waste Minimization Hotline, Region III
Environmental Protection Agency (EPA)
841 Chestnut St. (800) 826-5320
Philadelphia, PA 19107 (800) 334-2467 (PA)

The Waste Minimization Hotline provides technical assistance and education on waste minimization. It provides this information for all Region III states: Washington, DC, Delaware, Maryland, Pennsylvania, Virginia, and West Virginia.

* What Can Be Done with Hazardous Waste?

Alternative Treatment Technology Information
Center (ATTIC)
TRI, 3202 Tower Oaks Blvd., Suite 200
Rockville, MD 208552 (301) 231-5250

ATTIC has three components: The RCRA/CERCLA Hotline, Clean-Up Information Bulletin Board, and a reference library that consists of the EPA's Hazardous Waste Superfund Collection. These services are available to groups involved in Superfund cleanup activities.

* What Helps With Oil Spills And Other Problems?

Office of Ocean Resources Conservation
and Assessment (ORCA)
National Ocean Service
National Oceanic and Atmospheric Administration
6001 Executive Blvd.
Rockville, MD 20852 (301) 443-8487

As the Scientific Support Coordinator to the Coast Guard, ORCA provides critical information on spill trajectory projections, chemical hazard analyses, and assessment of marine and estuarine sensitivity to spills. ORCA's Hazardous Materials (HAZMAT) Response Program responds to about 100 oil spills a year. The program provides similar support to the EPA;s Superfund Program during emergency responses at, and for the cleanup of, abandoned hazardous waste sites in coastal areas. The program has implemented the CAMEO (Computer-Aided Management of Emergency Operations) program designed to help emergency planners and first responders safely handle chemical accidents. CAMEO currently is being used by over 3,000 fire departments.

Be patient. If any phone number is incorrect, call (area code) 555-1212 and request the new listing.

Freedom of Information Act (FOIA) Government Records and Privacy

A Citizen's Guide on Using the Freedom of Information Act and the Privacy Act of 1974 to Request Government Records

Introduction

A popular Government without popular information or the means of acquiring it, is but a Prologue to a Farce or a Tragedy or perhaps both. Knowledge will forever govern ignorance, and a people who mean to be their Governors, must arm themselves with the power knowledge gives. -- James Madison

The Freedom of Information Act (FOIA) established a presumption that records in the possession of agencies and departments of the Executive Branch of the United States government are accessible to the people. This was not always the approach to federal information disclosure policy. Before enactment of the Freedom of Information Act in 1966, the burden was on the individual to establish a right to examine these government records. There were no statutory guidelines or procedures to help a person seeking information. There were judicial remedies for those denied access.

With the passage of the FOIA, the burden of proof shifted from the individual to the government. Those seeking information are no longer required to show a need for information. Instead, the "need to know" standard has been replaced by a "right to know" doctrine. The government now has to justify the need for secrecy.

The FOIA sets standards for determining which records must be made available for public inspection and which records can be withheld from disclosure. The law also provides administrative and judicial remedies for those denied access to records. Above all, the statute requires federal agencies to provide the fullest possible disclosure of information to the public.

The Privacy Act of 1974 is a companion to the FOIA. The Privacy Act regulates federal government agency record keeping and disclosure practices. The Act allows most individuals to seek access to federal agency records about themselves. The Act requires that personal information in agency files be accurate, complete, relevant, and timely. The Act allows the subject of a record to challenge the accuracy of the information. The Act requires that agencies obtain information directly from the subject of the record and that information gathered for one purpose not be used for another purpose. As with the FOIA, the Privacy Act provides civil remedies for individuals whose rights have been violated.

Another important feature of the Privacy Act is the requirement that each federal agency publish a description of each system of records maintained by the agency that contains personal information. This prevents agencies from keeping secret records.

The Privacy Act also restricts the disclosure of personally identifiable information by federal agencies. Together with the FOIA, the Privacy Act permits disclosure of most personal files to the individual who is the subject of the files. The two laws restrict disclosure of personal information to others when disclosure would violate privacy interests.

While both the FOIA and the Privacy Act encourage the disclosure of agency records, both laws also recognize the legitimate need to restrict disclosure of some information. For example, agencies may withhold information classified in the interest of national defense or foreign policy, trade secrets, and criminal investigatory files. Other specifically defined categories of confidential information may also be withheld.

The essential feature of both laws is that they make federal agencies accountable for information disclosure policies and practices. While neither law grants an absolute right to examine government documents, both laws provide a right to request records and to receive a response to the request. If a requested record cannot be released, the requester is entitled to a reason for the denial. The requester has a right to appeal the denial and, if necessary, to challenge it in court.

These procedural rights granted by the FOIA and the Privacy Act make the laws valuable and workable. The disclosure of government information cannot be controlled by arbitrary or unreviewable actions.

Which Act To Use

The access provisions of the FOIA and the Privacy Act overlap in part. The two laws have different procedures and different exemptions. As a result, sometimes information exempt under one law will be disclosable under the other.

In order to take maximum advantage of the laws, an individual seeking information about himself or herself should normally cite both laws. Requests by an individual for information that does not relate solely to himself or herself should be made under the FOIA.

Congress intended that the two laws be considered together in the processing of requests for information. Many government agencies will automatically handle requests from individuals in a way that will maximize the amount of information that is disclosable. However, a requester should still make a request in a manner that is most advantageous and that fully protects all available legal rights. A requester who has any doubts about which law to use should always cite both the FOIA and the

Freedom of Information Act (FOIA)

Privacy Act when seeking documents from the federal government.

The Scope of the Freedom of Information Act

The federal Freedom of Information Act applies to documents held by agencies in the executive branch of the federal Government. The executive branch includes cabinet departments, military departments, government corporations, government controlled corporations, independent regulatory agencies, and other establishments of the executive branch.

The FOIA does not apply to elected officials of the federal government, including the President, Vice President, Senators, and Congressmen, or the federal judiciary. The FOIA also does not apply to private companies; persons who received federal contracts or grants; tax-exempt organizations; or state or local governments.

All States and some localities have passed laws like the FOIA that allow people to request access to records. In addition, there are other federal and state laws that may permit access to documents held by organizations not covered by the FOIA.

What Records Can Be Requested Under FOIA?

The FOIA requires agencies to publish or make available some types of information. This includes: (1) Description of agency organization and office addresses; (2) statements of the general course and method of agency operation; (3) rules of procedure and descriptions of forms; (4) substantive rules of general applicability and general policy statements; (5) final opinions made in the adjudication of cases; and (6) administrative staff manuals that affect the public. This information must either be published or made available for inspection and copying without the formality of an FOIA request.

All other "agency records" may be requested under the FOIA. However, the FOIA does not define "agency record." Material that is in the possession, custody, or control of an agency is usually considered to be an agency record under the FOIA. Personal notes of agency employees may not be agency records. A record that is not an "agency record" will not be available under the FOIA.

The form in which a record is maintained by an agency does not affect its availability. A request may seek a printed or typed document, tape recording, map, computer printout, computer tape, or a similar item.

Of course, not all records that can be requested must be disclosed. Information that is exempt from disclosure is described below in the section entitled "Reasons Access May Be Denied Under the FOIA."

The FOIA carefully provides that a requester may ask for records rather than information. This means that an agency is only required to look for an existing record or document in response to an FOIA request. An agency is not obliged to create a new record to comply with a request. An agency is not required to collect information it does not have. Nor must an

agency do research or analyze data for a requester.

Requesters may ask for existing records. Requests may have to be carefully written in order to obtain the information that is desired. Sometimes, agencies will help a requester identify the specific document that contains the information being sought. Other times, a requester may need to be creative when writing an FOIA request in order to identify an existing document or set of documents containing the desired information.

There is a second general limitation on FOIA request. The law requires that each request must reasonably describe the records being sought. This means that a request must be specific enough to permit a professional employee of the agency who is familiar with the subject matter to locate the record in a reasonable period of time.

Because different agencies organize and index records in different ways, one agency may consider a request to be reasonably descriptive while another agency may reject a similar request as too vague. For example, the Federal Bureau of Investigation has a centrex index for its primary record system. As a result, the FBI is able to search for records about a specific person. However, agencies that do not maintain a central name index may be unable to conduct the same type of search. These agencies may reject a similar request because the request does not describe records that can be identified.

Requesters should make their requests as specific as possible. If a particular document is required, it should be identified as precisely as possible, preferably by date and title. However, a request does not have to be that specific. A requester who cannot identify a specific record should clearly explain his or her needs. A requester should make sure, however, that the request is broad enough to cover the information that is needed.

For example, assume that a requester wants to obtain a list of toxic sites near his home. A request to the Environmental Protection Agency for all records on toxic waste would cover many more records than are needed. The fees for such a request might be very high, and it is possible that the request might be rejected as too vague.

A request for all toxic waste sites within three miles of a particular address is very specific. But it is unlikely that EPA would have an existing record containing data organized in that fashion. As a result, the request might be denied because there is no existing record containing the information.

The requester might do better to ask for a list of toxic waste sites in his city, county, or state. It is more likely that existing records might contain this information. The requester might also want to tell the agency in the request letter exactly what information is desired. The additional explanation will help the agency to find a record that meets the request.

Many people include their telephone number in their requests. Sometimes questions about the scope of a request can be resolved quickly when the agency employee and the requester talk. This is an efficient way to resolve questions that arise during the processing of FOIA requests.

Be patient. If any phone number is incorrect, call (area code) 555-1212 and request the new listing.

Government Records and Privacy

It is to everyone's advantage if requests are as precise and as narrow as possible. The requester benefits because the request can be processed faster and cheaper. The agency benefits because it can do a better job of responding to the request. The agency will also be able to use its scarce resources to respond to more requests. The FOIA works best when both the requester and the agency act cooperatively.

Making an FOIA Request

The first step in making a request under the FOIA is to identify the agency that has the records. An FOIA request must be addressed to a specific agency. There is no central government records office that services FOIA requests.

Often, a requester knows beforehand which agency has the desired records. If not, a requester can consult a government directory such as the *United States Government Manual*. This manual has a complete list of all the federal agencies, a description of agency functions, and the address of each agency. A requester who is uncertain about which agency has the records that are needed can make FOIA requests at more than one agency.

All agencies normally require that FOIA requests be in writing. Letters requesting records under the FOIA can be short and simple. No one needs a lawyer to make an FOIA request. Appendix 1 of this Guide contains a sample request letter.

The request letter should be addressed to an agency's FOIA officer or to the head of the agency. The envelope containing the written request should be marked "Freedom of Information Act Request" in the bottom left-hand corner.

There are three basic elements to an FOIA request letter. First, the letter should state that the request is being made under the Freedom of Information Act. Second, the request should identify the records being sought as specifically as possible. Third, the name and address of the requester must be included.

In addition, under the 1986 amendments to the FOIA, the fees chargeable vary with the status or purpose of the requester. As a result, requesters may have to provide additional information to permit the agency to determine the appropriate fees. Different fees can be charged to commercial users, representatives of the news media, educational and noncommercial scientific institutions, and individuals. The next section explains the new fee structure in more detail.

There are several optional items that are often included in an FOIA request. The first is the telephone number of the requester. This permits an agency employee processing a request to talk to the requester if necessary.

A second optional item is a limitation on the fees that the requester is willing to pay. It is common for requesters to ask to be contacted if the charges will exceed a fixed amount. This allows a requester to modify or withdraw a request if the cost is too high.

A third optional item sometimes included in an FOIA request is a request for waiver or reduction of fees. The 1986 amendments waived or reduced the rules for fee waivers. Fees must be waived or reduced if disclosure of the information is in the public interest because it is likely to contribute significantly to public understanding of the operations or activities of the government and is not primarily in the commercial interest of the request. Decisions about granting fee waives are separate from and different from decisions about the amount of fees that can be charged to requesters.

Requesters should keep a copy of their request letter and related correspondence until the request has been fully resolved.

Fees and Fee Waivers

FOIA requesters may have to pay fees covering some or all of the costs of processing their request. As amended in 1986, the law establishes three types of charges that may be imposed on requesters. The 1986 law makes the process of determining the applicable fees more complicated. However, the new rules reduce or eliminate entirely the cost for small, noncommercial requests.

First, fees can be imposed to recover the costs of copying documents. All agencies have a fixed price for making copies using copying machines. Requesters are usually charged the actual cost of copying computer tapes, photographs, or other nonstandard documents.

Second, fees can also be imposed to recover the costs of searching for documents. This includes the time spent looking for material responsive to a request. Requesters can minimize search charges by making clear, narrow requests for identifiable documents whenever possible.

Third, fees can be charged to recover review costs. Review is the process of examining documents to determine whether any portion is exempt from disclosure. Before the effective date of the 1986 amendments, no review charges were imposed on any requester. Effective April 25, 1987, review charges may be imposed on commercial requesters only. Review charges only include costs incurred during the initial examination of a document. An agency may not charge for any costs incurred in resolving issues of law or policy that may arise while processing a request.

Different fees apply to different categories of requesters. There are three basic groups of FOIA requesters. The first includes representatives of the news media, and educational or noncommercial scientific institutions whose purpose is scholarly or scientific research. Requesters in this category who are not seeking records for commercial use can only be billed for reasonable standard document duplication charges. A request for information from a representative of the news media is not considered to be for commercial use if the request is in support of a news gathering or dissemination function.

The second group includes FOIA requesters seeking records for commercial use. Commercial use is not defined in the law, but generally includes profit making activities. Commercial users pay reasonable standard charges for document duplication, search, and review.

Freedom of Information Act (FOIA)

The third group of FOIA requesters includes everyone not included in either of the first two groups. People seeking information for their own use, public interest groups, and non-profit organizations are examples of requesters who fall into the third group. Charges for these requests are limited to reasonable standard charges for document duplication and search. No review charges may be imposed. The 1986 amendments did not change the fees charged to these requesters.

Small requests are free to requesters in the first and third groups.

This includes all requesters except commercial users. There is no charge for the first two hours of search time and the first 100 pages of documents. Noncommercial requesters who limit their requests to a small number of easily found records will not pay any fees at all.

In addition, the law also prevents agencies from charging fees if the cost of collecting the fee would exceed the amount collected. This limitation applies to all requests, including those seeking documents for commercial use. Thus, if the allowable charges for any FOIA request are small, no fees are imposed.

Each agency sets charges for duplication, search, and review based on its own costs. The amount of these charges is included in the agency FOIA regulations. Each agency also sets its own threshold for minimum charges.

The 1986 FOIA amendments changed the law on fee waivers. The new rules require that fees must be waived or reduced if disclosure of the information is in the public interest because it is likely to contribute significantly to public understanding of the operations or activities of the government and is not primarily in the commercial interest of the requester.

The new rules for fees and fee waivers have created some confusion. Determinations about fees are separate and apart from determinations about eligibility for fee waivers. For example, a news reporter may only be charged duplication fees and may ask that the duplication fees be waived. There is no need for a reporter to ask for a waiver of search and review costs because search and review costs are not charged to reporters.

Only after a requester has been categorized to determine applicable fees does the issue of a fee waiver arise. A requester who seeks a fee waiver should include a separate request in the original request letter. The requester should describe how disclosure will contribute to the public understanding of the operations or activities of the government. The sample request letter in the appendix includes optional language asking for a fee waiver.

Any requester may ask for a fee waiver. Some will find it easier to qualify than others. A news reporter who is charged only duplication costs may still ask that the charges be waived because of the public benefits that will result from disclosure. Representatives of the news media and public interest groups are very likely to qualify for a waiver of fees. Commercial users will find it more difficult to qualify.

The eligibility of other requesters will vary. A key element in qualifying for a fee waiver is the relationship of the information to public understanding of the operations or activities of government. Another important factor is the ability of the requester to convey that information to other interested members of the public. A requester is not eligible for a fee waiver solely because of indigence.

Requirements for Agency Responses

Each agency is required to determine within ten days (excluding Saturdays, Sundays, and legal holidays) after the receipt of a request whether to comply with the request. The actual disclosure of documents is required to follow promptly once the determination has been made. If a request for records is denied in whole or in part, the agency must tell the requester the reasons for the denial. The agency must also tell the requester that they have a right to appeal any adverse determination to the head of the agency.

The FOIA permits agencies to extend the time limits up to ten days in unusual circumstances. These circumstances include the need to collect records from remote locations, review large numbers of records, and consult with other agencies. Agencies are supposed to notify the requester whenever an extension is invoked.

The statutory time limits for responses are not always met. Agencies sometimes receive an unexpectedly large number of FOIA requests at one time and are unable to meet the deadlines. Some agencies assign inadequate resources to FOIA offices. The Congress does not condone the failure of any agency to meet the law's limits. However, as a practical matter, there is little that a requester can do about it. The courts have been reluctant to provide relief solely because the FOIA's time limits have not been met.

The best advice to requesters is to be patient. The law allows a requester to consider a request to be denied if it has not been decided within the time limits. This permits the requester to file an administrative appeal. However, this is not always the best course of action. The filing of an administrative or judicial appeal does not normally result in any faster processing of the request.

Agencies generally process requests in the order in which they were received. Some agencies will expedite the processing of urgent requests. Anyone with a pressing need for records should consult with the agency FOIA officer about how to ask for expedited treatment of requests.

Reasons Access May Be Denied Under the FOIA

An agency may refuse to disclose an agency record that falls within any of the FOIA's nine statutory exemptions. The exemptions protect against the disclosure of information that would harm national defense or foreign policy, privacy of individuals, proprietary interests of business, functioning of government, and other important interests.

A record that does not qualify as an "agency record" may be denied because only agency records are available under the FOIA. Personal notes of agency employees may be denied on this basis.

An agency may withhold exempt information, but it is not always required to do so. For example, an agency may disclose an exempt internal memorandum because no harm would result from its disclosure. However, an agency is not likely to agree to disclose an exempt document that is classified or that contains a trade secret.

When a record contains some information that qualifies as exempt, the entire record is not necessarily exempt. Instead, the FOIA specifically provides that any reasonably segregable portions of a record must be provided to a requester after the deletion of the portions that are exempt. This is a very important requirement because it prevents an agency from withholding an entire document simply because one line or one page is exempt.

Exemption 1: Classified Documents

The first FOIA exemption permits the withholding of properly classified documents. Information may be classified to protect it in the interest of national defense or foreign policy. Information that has been classified as "Confidential," "Secret," or "Top Secret" under the procedures of the Executive Order on Security Classification can qualify under the first exemption.

The rules for classification are established by the President and not the FOIA or other law. The FOIA provides that, if a document has been properly classified under the President's rules, the document can be withheld from disclosure.

Classified documents may be requested under the FOIA. An agency can review the document to determine if it still requires protection. In addition, the Executive Order on Security Classification establishes a special procedure for requesting the declassification of documents. If a requested document is declassified, it can be released in response to an FOIA request. However, a document that was formerly classified may still be exempt under other FOIA exemptions.

Exemption 2: Internal Personnel Rules and Practices

The second FOIA exemption covers matters that are related solely to an agency's internal personnel rules and practices. As interpreted by the courts, there are two separate classes of documents that are generally held to fall within exemption two.

First, information relating to personnel rules or internal agency practices is exempt if it is a trivial administrative matter of no genuine public interest. A rule governing lunch hours for agency employees is an example.

Second, internal administrative manuals can be exempt if disclosure would risk circumvention of law or agency regulations. In order to fall into this category, the material will normally have to regulate internal agency conduct rather than public behavior.

Exemption 3: Information Exempt Under Other Laws

The third exemption incorporates into the FOIA other laws that restrict the availability of information. To qualify under exemption three, a statute must require that matters be withheld from the public in such a manner as to leave no discretion to the agency. Alternatively, the statute must establish particular criteria for withholding or refer to particular types of matters to be withheld.

One example of a qualifying statute is the provision of the Tax Code prohibiting the public disclosure of tax returns and tax law designating identifiable census data as confidential. Whether a particular statute qualifies under Exemption 3 can be a difficult legal determination.

Exemption 4: Confidential Business Information

The fourth exemption protects from public disclosure two types of information: trade secrets and confidential business information. A trade secret is a commercially valuable plan, formula, process, or device. This is a narrow category of information. An example of a trade secret is the recipe for a commercial food product.

The second type of protected data is commercial or financial information obtained from a person which is privileged or confidential. The courts have held that data qualifies for withholding if disclosure by the government would be likely to harm the competitive position of the person who submitted the information. Detailed information on a company's marketing plans, profits, or costs can qualify as confidential business information. Information may also be withheld if disclosure would be likely to impair the government's ability to obtain similar information in the future.

Only information obtained from a person other than a government agency qualifies under the fourth exemption. A person is an individual, a partnership, or a corporation. Information that an agency created on its own cannot normally be withheld under exemption four.

Although there is no formal requirement under the FOIA, many agencies will notify a submitter of business information that disclosure of the information is being considered. The submitted can file suit to block disclosure under the FOIA. Such lawsuits are generally referred to as "reverse" FOIA lawsuits because the FOIA is being used in an attempt to prevent rather than to require disclosure of information. A reverse FOIA lawsuit may be filed when a submitter of documents and the government disagree whether the information is confidential.

Exemption 5: Internal Government Communications

The FOIA's fifth exemption applies to internal government documents. One example is a letter from one government department to another about a joint decision that has not yet been made. Another example is a memorandum from an agency employee to his supervisor describing options for conducting the agency's business.

The purpose of the exemption is to safeguard the deliberative

Freedom of Information Act (FOIA)

policymaking processes of government. The exemption encourages frank discussions of policy matters between agency officials by allowing supporting documents to be withheld from public disclosure. The exemption also protects against premature disclosure of policies before final adoption.

While the policy behind the fifth exemption is well-accepted, the application of the exemption is complicated. The fifth exemption may be the most difficult FOIA exemption to understand and apply. For example, the exemption protects the policymaking process, but it does not protect purely factual information related to the policy process. Factual information must be disclosed unless it is inextricably intertwined with protected information about an agency decision.

Protection for the decision making process is appropriate only for the period while decisions are being made. Thus, the fifth exemption has been held to distinguish between documents that are predecisional and therefore may be protected, and those which are post-decisional and therefore not subject to protection. Once a policy is adopted, the public has a greater interests in knowing the basis for the decision.

The exemption also incorporates some of the privileges that apply in litigation involving the government. For example, papers prepared by the government's lawyers are exempt in the same way that papers prepared by private lawyers for clients are not available through discovery in civil litigation.

Exemption 6: Personal Privacy

The sixth exemption covers personnel, medical, and similar files the disclosure of which would constitute a clearly unwarranted invasion of personal privacy. This exemption protects the privacy interests of individuals by allowing an agency to withhold from disclosure intimate personal data kept in government files. Only individuals have privacy interests. Corporations and other legal persons have no privacy rights under the sixth exemption.

The exemption requires agencies to strike a balance between an individual's privacy interests and the public's right to know. However, since only a clearly unwarranted invasion of privacy is a basis for withholding, there is a perceptible tilt in favor of disclosure in the exemption. Nevertheless, the sixth exemption makes it hard to obtain information about another individual without the consent of the individual.

The Privacy Act of 1974 also regulates the disclosure of personal information about individuals. The FOIA and the Privacy Act overlap in part, but there is no inconsistency. Individuals seeking records about themselves should cite both laws when making a request. This ensures that the maximum amount of disclosable information will be released. Records that can be denied to an individual under the Privacy Act are not necessarily exempt under the FOIA.

Exemption 7: Law Enforcement

The seventh exemption allows agencies to withhold law enforcement records in order to protect the law enforcement process from interference. The exemption was amended slightly in 1986, but it still retains six specific subexemptions.

Exemption (7)(A) allows the withholding of law enforcement records that could reasonably be expected to interfere with enforcement proceedings. This exemption protects active investigations from interference through premature disclosure.

Exemption (7)(B) allows the withholding of information that would deprive a person of a right to a fair trial or an impartial adjudication. This exemption is rarely used.

Exemption (7)(C) recognizes that individuals have a privacy interest in information maintained in law enforcement files. If the disclosure of information could reasonably be expected to constitute an unwarranted invasion of personal privacy, the information is exempt from disclosure. The standards for privacy protection in Exemption 6 and Exemption (7)(C) differ slightly. Exemption (7)(C) refers only to unwarranted invasions of personal privacy rather than to clearly unwarranted invasions.

Exemption (7)(D) protects the identity of confidential sources. Information that could reasonably be expected to reveal the identity of a confidential source is exempt. A confidential source can include a state, local, or foreign agency or authority, or a private institution that furnished information on a confidential basis. In addition, the exemption protects information furnished by a confidential source if the data was compiled by a criminal law enforcement authority during a criminal investigation or by an agency conducting a lawful national security intelligence investigation.

Exemption (7)(E) protects from disclosure information that would reveal techniques and procedures for law enforcement investigations or prosecutions or that would disclose guidelines for law enforcement investigations or prosecutions if disclosure of the information could reasonably be expected to risk circumvention of the law.

Exemption (7)(F) protects law enforcement information that could reasonably be expected to endanger the life or physical safety of any individual.

Exemption 8: Financial Institutions

The eighth exemption protects information that is contained in or related to examination, operating, or condition reports prepared by or for a bank supervisory agency such as the Federal Deposit Insurance Corporation, or the Federal Reserve, or similar agencies,.

9. Exemption 9: Geological Information

The ninth FOIA exemption covers geological and geophysical information, data, and maps about wells. This exemption is rarely used.

FOIA Exclusions

The 1986 amendments to the FOIA gave limited authority to agencies to respond to a request without confirming the existence of the requested records. Ordinarily, any proper request must receive an answer stating whether there is any responsive information, even if the requested information is exempt from disclosure.

Government Records and Privacy

In some narrow circumstances, acknowledgement of the existence of a record can produce consequences similar to those resulting from disclosure of the record itself. In order to avoid this type of problem, the 1986 amendments established three "record exclusions." However, these exclusions do not broaden the ability of agencies to withhold documents.

The exclusions allow agencies to treat certain exempt records as if the records were not subject to the FOIA. Agencies are not required to confirm the existence of three specific categories of records. If those records are requested, agencies may state that there are no disclosable records responsive to the request. However, these exclusions give agencies no authority to withhold additional categories of information from the public.

The first exclusion is triggered when a request seeks information that is exempt because disclosure could reasonably be expected to interfere with a current law enforcement investigation. There are specific prerequisites for the application of this exclusion. First, the investigation in question must involve a possible violation of criminal law. Second, there must be a reason to believe that the subject of the investigation is not already aware that the investigation is underway. Third, disclosure of the existence of the records -- as distinguished from contents of the records -- could reasonably be expected to interfere with enforcement proceedings.

When all three of these conditions are present, an agency may respond to an FOIA request for investigatory records as if the records are not subject to the requirements of the FOIA. In other words, the agency's response does not have to reveal that it is conducting an investigation.

The second exclusion applies to informant records maintained by a criminal law enforcement agency under the informant's name or personal identifier. The agency is not required to confirm the existence of these records unless the informant's status has been officially confirmed. This exclusion helps agencies to protect the identity of confidential informants. Information that might identify informants has always been exempt under the FOIA.

The third exclusion applies only to records maintained by the Federal Bureau of Investigation which pertain to foreign intelligence, counterintelligence, or international terrorism. When the existence of those type of records is classified, the FBI may treat the records as not subject to the requirements of FOIA.

This exclusion does not apply to all classified records on the specific subjects. It only applies when the records are classified and when the existence the records is also classified. Since the underlying records must be classified before the exclusion is relevant, agencies have no new substantive withholding authority.

In enacting these exclusions, congressional sponsors stated that it was their intent that agencies must inform FOIA requesters that these exclusions are available for agency use. Requesters who believe that records were improperly withheld because of the exclusions can seek judicial review.

Administrative Appeal Procedures

Whenever an FOIA request is denied, the agency must inform the requester of the reasons for the denial and the requester's right to appeal the denial to the head of the agency. A requester may appeal the denial of a request for a document or for fee waiver. A requester may contest the type or amount of fees that were charged. A requester may appeal any other adverse determination including a rejection of a request for failure to describe adequately the documents being requested. A requester can also appeal because the agency failed to conduct an adequate search for the documents that were requested.

A person whose request was granted in part an denied in part may appeal the partial denial. If an agency has agreed to disclose some but not all of the requested documents, the filing of an appeal does not affect the release of the documents that are disclosable. There is no risk to the requester in filing an appeal.

The appeal to the head of an agency is a simple administrative appeal. A lawyer can be helpful, but no one needs a lawyer to file an appeal. Anyone who can write a letter can file an appeal. Appeals to the head of the agency often result in the disclosure of some records that have been withheld. A requester who is not convinced that the agency's initial decision is correct should appeal. There is no charge for filing an appeal.

An appeal is filed by sending a letter to the head of the agency. The letter must identify the FOIA request that is being appealed. The envelope containing the letter of appeal should be marked in the lower left hand corner with the words "Freedom of Information Act Appeal."

Many agencies assign a number to all FOIA requests that are received. The number should be included in the appeal letter, along with the name and address of the requester. It is a common practice to include a copy of the agency's initial decision letter as part of the appeal, but this it not required. It can also be helpful for the requester to include a telephone number in the appeal letter.

An appeal will normally include the requester's arguments supporting disclosure of the documents. A requester may include any facts or any arguments supporting the case for reversing the initial decision. However, an appeal letter does not have to contain any arguments at all. It is sufficient to state that the agency's initial decision is being appealed. Appendix 1 includes a sample appeal letter.

The FOIA does not set a time limit for filing an administrative appeal of an FOIA denial. However, it is good practice to file an appeal promptly. Some agency regulations establish a time limit for filing an administrative appeal. A requester whose appeal is rejected by an agency because it is too late may refile the original FOIA request and start the process again.

A requester who delays filing an appeal runs the risk that the documents could be destroyed. However, as long as an agency is considering a request or an appeal, the agency must preserve the documents.

Freedom of Information Act (FOIA)

An agency is required to make a decision on an appeal within twenty days (excluding Saturdays, Sundays, and federal holidays). It is possible for an agency to extend the time limits by an additional ten days. Once the time period has elapsed, a requester may consider a that the appeal has been denied and may proceed with a judicial appeal. However, unless there is an urgent need for records, this is not always the best course of action. The courts are not sympathetic to appeals based solely on an agency's failure to comply with the FOIA's time limits.

Filing a Judicial Appeal

When an administrative appeal is denied, a requester has the right to appeal the denial in court. An FOIA appeal can be filed in the United States District Court in the district where the requester lives. The requester can also file suit in the district where the documents are located or in the District of Columbia. When a requester goes to court, the burden of justifying the withholding of documents is on the government. This is a distinct advantage for the requester.

Requesters are sometimes successful when they go to court, but the results vary considerably. Some requesters who file judicial appeals find that an agency will disclose some documents previously withheld rather than fight about disclosure in court. This does not always happen, and there is no guarantee that the filing of a judicial appeal will result in any additional disclosure.

Most requesters require the assistance of an attorney to file a judicial appeal. A person who files a lawsuit and substantially prevails may be awarded reasonable attorney fees and litigation costs reasonably incurred. Some requesters may be able to handle their own appeal without an attorney. Since this is not a litigation guide, details of the judicial appeal process have been not included. Anyone considering filing an appeal can begin by reviewing the provisions of the FOIA on judicial review.

The Privacy Act of 1974

The Privacy Act of 1974 provides safeguards against an invasion of privacy through the misuse of records by federal agencies. In general, the Act allows citizens to learn how records are collected, maintained, used, and disseminated by the federal government. The Act also permits individuals to gain access to most personal information maintained by federal agencies and to seek amendment of any incorrect or incomplete information.

The Privacy Act applies to personal information maintained by agencies in the executive branch of the federal government. The executive branch includes cabinet departments, military departments, government corporations, government controlled corporations, independent regulatory agencies, and other establishments in the executive branch. Agencies subject to the Freedom of Information Act (FOIA) are also subject to the Privacy Act. The Privacy Act does not generally apply to records maintained by state and local governments or private companies or organizations.

The Privacy Act grants rights only to United States citizens and to aliens lawfully admitted for permanent residence. As a result, foreign nationals cannot use the Act's provisions. However, foreigners may use the FOIA to request records about themselves.

The only records subject to the Privacy Act are records about individuals that are maintained in a system of records. The idea of a "system of records" is unique to the Privacy Act and requires explanation.

The Act defines a "record" to include most personal information maintained by an agency about an individual. A record contains information about education, financial transactions, medical history, criminal history, or employment history. A system of records is a group of records from which information is actually retrieved by name, social security number, or other identifying symbol assigned to an individual.

Some personal information is not kept in a system of records. This information is not subject to the provisions of the Privacy Act, although access may be requested under the FOIA. Most personal information in government files is subject to the Privacy Act.

The Privacy Act also establishes general records management requirements for federal agencies. In summary, there are five basic requirements that are more relevant to individuals.

First, agencies must establish procedures allowing individuals to see and copy records about themselves. An individual may also seek to amend any information that is not accurate, relevant, timely, or complete. The rights to inspect and to correct records are the most important provisions of the Privacy Act. This Guide explains in more detail how an individual can exercise these rights.

Second, agencies must publish notices describing all systems of records. The notices include a complete description of personal-data record keeping policies, practices, and systems. This requirement prevents the maintenance of secret record systems.

Third, agencies must make reasonable efforts to maintain accurate, relevant, timely, and complete records about individuals. Agencies are prohibited from maintaining information about how individuals exercise rights guaranteed by the First Amendment to the U.S. Constitution unless maintenance of the information is specifically authorized by statute or relates to authorized law enforcement activity.

Fourth, the Act establishes rules governing the use and disclosure of personal information. The Act specifies that information collected for one purpose may not be used for another purpose without notice to or the consent of the subject of the record. The Act also requires that agencies keep a record of some disclosures of personal information.

Fifth, the Act provides legal remedies that permit individuals to seek enforcement of rights under the Act. In addition, there are criminal penalties that apply to federal employees who fail to comply with the Act's provisions.

Locating Records

There is no central index of federal government records. An

Be patient. If any phone number is incorrect, call (area code) 555-1212 and request the new listing.

Government Records and Privacy

individual who wants to inspect records about himself or herself must first identify which agency has the records. Often, this will not be difficult. For example, an individual who was employed by the federal government knows that the employing agency or the Office of Personnel Management maintains personnel files.

Similarly, an individual who receives veterans' benefits will normally find the related records at the Veterans Administration or at the Defense Department. Tax records are maintained by the Internal Revenue Service, social security records by the Social Security Administration, passport records by the State Department, etc.

For those who are uncertain about which agency has the records that are needed, there are several sources of information. First, an individual can ask an agency that might maintain the records. If that agency does not have the records, it may be able to identify the proper agency.

Second, a government directory such as the *United States Government Manual* contains a complete list of all federal agencies, a description of agency functions, and the address of the agency and its field offices. An agency responsible for operating a program normally maintains the records related to that program.

Third, a Federal Information Center can help to identify government agencies, their functions, and their records. These Centers, which are operated by the General Services Administration, serve as clearinghouses for information about the federal government. There are several dozen Federal Information Centers throughout the country.

Fourth, the Office of Federal Register publishes an annual compilation of system of records notices for all agencies. These notices contain a complete description of each record system maintained by each agency. The compilation -- which is published in five large volumes -- is the most complete reference for information about federal agency personal information practices. The information that appears in the compilation is also published occasionally in the *Federal Register.*

The compilation -- formally called Privacy Act Issuance -- maybe difficult to find. Copies will be available in some federal depository libraries and possibly in other libraries as well. Although the compilation is the best single source of detailed information about personal records maintained by the federal agencies, it is not necessary to consult the compilation before making a Privacy Act request.

A requester is not required to identify the specific system of records that contains the information being sought. It is sufficient to identify the agency that has the records. Using information provided by the requester, the agency will determine which system of records has the files that have been requested.

Those who request records under the Privacy Act can help the agency by identifying the type of records being sought. Large agencies maintain dozens or even hundreds of different record systems. A request is processed faster if the requester tells the agency that he or she was employed by the agency, was the recipient of benefits under an agency program, or had other specific contacts with the agency.

Making a Privacy Act Request for Access

The fastest way to make a Privacy Act request is to identify the specific system of records. The request can be addressed to the system manager. Few people do this. Instead, most people address their requests to the head of the agency that has the records or the agency's Privacy Act Officer. The envelope containing the written request should be marked "Privacy Act Request" in the bottom left-hand corner.

There are three basic elements to a request for records under the Privacy Act. First, the letter should state that the request is being made under the Privacy Act. Second, the letter should include the name, address, and signature of the requester. Third, the request should describe as specifically as possible the records that are wanted. Appendix 1 includes a sample Privacy Act request letter. It is a common practice for an individual seeking records about himself or herself to make the request both under the Privacy Act of 1974 and the Freedom of Information Act. See the discussion in the front of this Guide about which act to use.

A requester can describe the records by identifying a specific system of records by describing his or her contacts with an agency, or by simply asking for all records about himself or herself. The broader and less specific a request is, the longer it may take for an agency to respond.

It is a good practice for a requester to describe the type of records that he or she expects to find. For example, an individual seeking a copy of his service record in the Army should state he was in the Army and include the approximate dates of service. This will help the Defense Department narrow its search to record systems that are likely to contain the information being sought. An individual seeking records from the Federal Bureau of Investigation may ask that files in specific field offices be searched in addition to the FBI's central office files. The FBI dose not routinely search field office records without a specific request.

Agencies generally require requesters to provide some proof of identity before records will be disclosed. Agencies may have different requirements. Some agencies will accept a signature; others may require a notarized signature. If an individual goes to the agency to inspect records, standard personal identification may be acceptable. More stringent requirements may apply if the records being sought are especially sensitive.

Agencies will inform requesters of a special identification requirements. Requesters who need records quickly should first consult regulations or talk to the agency's Privacy Act Officer to find out how to provide adequate identification.

An individual who visits an agency office to inspect a Privacy Act record may wish to bring along a friend or relative to review the record. When a requester brings another person, the agency may ask the requester to sign a written statement authorizing discussion of the record in the presence of that person.

Freedom of Information Act (FOIA)

It is a crime to knowingly and willfully request or obtain records under the Privacy Act under false pretenses. A request for access under the Privacy Act can be made only by the subject of the record. An individual cannot make a request under the Privacy Act for a record about another person. The only exception is for a parent or legal guardian who can request records for a minor or a person who has been declared incompetent.

Fees

Under the Privacy Act, fees can be charged only for the cost of conveying records. No fees may be charged for the time it takes to search for the records or the time it takes to review the records to determine if any exemptions apply. This is a major difference from the FOIA. Under the FOIA, fees can sometimes be charged to recover search costs and review costs. The different fee structure in the two laws is one reason many requesters seeking records about themselves cite both laws. This minimizes allowable fees.

Many agencies will not charge fees for making copies of files under the Privacy Act, especially when the files are small. If paying the copying charges is a problem, the requester should explain in the request letter. An agency can waive fees under the Privacy Act.

Requirements for Agency Responses

Unlike FOIA, there is no fixed time when an agency must respond to a request for access to records under the Privacy Act. It is good practice for an agency to acknowledge receipt of a Privacy Act request within ten days and to provide the requested records within thirty days.

At many agencies, FOIA and Privacy Act requests are processed by the same personnel. When then is a backlog of requests, it takes longer to receive a response. As a practical matter, there is little that a requester can do when an agency response is delayed. Requesters can be patient.

Agencies generally process requests in the order in which they were received. Some agencies will expedite the processing of urgent requests. Anyone with a pressing need for records should consult the agency Privacy Act Officer about how to ask for expedited treatment of requests.

Reasons Access May Be Denied Under the Privacy Act

Not all records about an individual must be disclosed under the Privacy Act. Some records may be withheld to protect important government interests such as national security or law enforcement.

The Privacy Act exemptions are different from the exemptions of the FOIA. Under the FOIA, any record may be withheld from disclosure if it contains exempt information when a request is received. The decision to apply an FOIA exemption is made only after a request has been made. In contrast, Privacy Act exemptions apply not only to records but to systems of records. Before an agency can apply a Privacy Act exemption, the agency must first issue a regulation stating that there may be exempt records in that system of records. Thus, there is a procedural prerequisite for the application of the Privacy Act exemptions.

Without reviewing agency regulations, it is hard to tell whether particular Privacy Act records are exempt from disclosure. However, it is a safe assumption that any system of records that qualifies for an exemption has been exempted by the agency.

Since most record systems are not exempt, the exemptions are not relevant to most requests. Also, agencies do not automatically rely upon the privacy Act exemptions unless there is a specific reason to do so. Thus, some records that are exempt may be disclosed upon request.

Because Privacy Act exemptions are complex and used infrequently, most requesters need not worry about them. The exemptions are discussed here for those interested in the law's details and for reference when an agency withholds records. Anyone interested in more information about the Privacy Act's exemptions can begin by reading the relevant sections of the Act. The complete text of the Act is reprinted in the Appendix to this Guide.

The Privacy Act's exemptions differ from those of the FOIA in another important way. The FOIA is mostly a disclosure law. Information exempt under the FOIA is exempt from disclosure only. That is not true under the Privacy Act. It imposes many separate requirements on personal records. No system of records is exempt from all Privacy Act requirements.

For example, no system of records is ever exempt from the requirement that a description of the system be published. No system of records can be exempted from the limitations on disclosure of the records outside the agency. No system is exempt from the requirement to maintain an accounting for disclosures. No system is exempt from the restriction against the maintenance of unauthorized information on the exercise of First Amendment rights. All systems are subject to the requirement that reasonable efforts be taken to assure that records disclosed outside the agency be accurate, complete, timely, and relevant. Agencies must maintain proper administrative controls and security for all systems. Finally, The Privacy Act's criminal penalties remain fully applicable to each system of records.

1. General Exemptions

There are two general exemptions under the Privacy Act. The first applies to all records maintained by the Central Intelligence Agency. The second general exemption applies to selected records maintained by an agency or component whose principal function is any activity pertaining to criminal law enforcement. Records of these criminal law enforcement agencies can be exempt under the Privacy Act if the records consists of (A) information compiled to identify individual criminal offenders and which consist only of identifying that and notations of arrests, the nature and disposition of criminal charges, sentencing, confinement, release, and parole or probation status: (B) criminal investigatory records associated particular individual compiled at any stage from arrest through release from supervision.

Systems of records subject to these general exemptions may be exempted from many of the Privacy Act's requirements. Exemption from the Act's access and correction provisions is the most important. Individuals have no right under the Privacy Act to ask for a copy of records that are generally exempt or to seek correction of erroneous records.

In practice, these exemptions are not as expansive as they sound. Most agencies that have exempt records will accept and process Privacy Act requests. The records will be reviewed on a case-by-case basis. Agencies will often disclose any information that does not require protection. Agencies also tend to follow a similar policy for requests for correction.

Individuals interested in obtaining records from the Central Intelligence Agency or from law enforcement agencies should not be discouraged from making requests for access. Even if the Privacy Act access exemption is applied, portions of the records may still be disclosable under the FOIA. This is a primary reason individuals should cite both the Privacy Act and the FOIA when requesting records.

The general exemption from access does not prevent requesters from filing a lawsuit under the Privacy Act when access is denied. The right to sue under the FOIA is not changed because of a Privacy Act exemption.

2. Specific Exemptions

There are seven specific Privacy Act exemptions that can be applied to many systems of records. Records subject to these exemptions are not exempt from as many of the Act's requirements as are the are the records subject to the general exemptions. However, records exempt under the specific exemptions are exempt from the Privacy Act's access and correction provisions. Nevertheless, since the access and correction exemptions are not always applied when available, those seeking records should not be discouraged from making a request. Also, the FOIA can be used to seek access to records exempt under the Privacy Act.

The first specific exemption covers record systems containing information that is properly classified. Classified information is also exempt from disclosure under the FOIA. Information that has been classified in the interest of national defense or foreign policy will normally be unavailable under either the FOIA or the Privacy Act.

The second specific exemption applies to systems of records containing investigatory material compiled for law enforcement purposes other than material covered by the general law enforcement exemption. The specific law enforcement exemption is limited when -- as a result of the maintenance of the records -- an individual is denied any right, privilege, or benefit to which he or she would be entitled by federal law or for which he or she would otherwise be entitled. In such a case, disclosure is required except where disclosure would reveal the identity of a confidential source who furnished information to the government under an express promise that the identity of the source would be held in confidence. If the information was

collected from a confidential source before the effective date of the Privacy Act (September 27, 1975), an implied promise of confidentiality is sufficient to permit withholding of the identity of the source.

The third specific exemption applies to systems of records maintained in connection with providing protective services to the President of the United States or other individuals who receive protection from the Secret Service.

The fourth specific exemption applies to systems of records required by statute to be maintained and used solely as statistical records.

The fifth specific exemption covers investigatory material compiled solely to determine suitability, eligibility, or qualifications for federal civilian employment, military service, federal contracts, or access to classified information. However, this exemption applies only to the extent that disclosure of information would reveal the identity of a confidential source who provided the information under a promise of confidentiality.

The sixth specific exemption applies to systems of records that contain testing or examination of material used solely to determine individual qualifications for appointment or promotion in federal service, but only when disclosure would compromise the objectivity or fairness of the testing or examination process. Effectively, this exemption permits withholding of questions used in employment tests.

The seventh specific exemption covers evaluation material used to determine potential for promotion in the armed services. The material is only exempt to the extent that disclosure would reveal the identity of a confidential source who provided the information under a promise of confidentiality.

3. Medical Records

Medical records maintained by federal agencies -- for example, records at Veterans Administration hospitals -- are not formally exempt from the Privacy Act's access provisions. However, the Privacy Act authorizes a special procedure for medical records that operates, at least in part, like an exemption.

Agencies may deny individuals direct access to medical records, including psychological records, if the agency deems it necessary. An agency normally reviews medical records requested by an individual. If the agency determines that direct disclosure is unwise, it can arrange for disclosure to a physician selected by the individual or possibly to another person chosen by the individual.

4. Litigation Records

The Privacy Act's access provisions include a general limitation on access to litigation records. The Act does not require an agency to disclose to an individual any information compiled in reasonable anticipation of a civil action or proceeding. This limitation operates like an exemption, although there is no requirement that the exemption be applied to a system of records before it can be used.

Freedom of Information Act (FOIA)

Administrative Appeal Procedures for Denial of Access

Unlike the FOIA, the Privacy Act does not provide for an administrative appeal of the denial of access. However, many agencies have established procedures that will allow Privacy Act requesters to appeal a denial of access without going to court. An administrative appeal is often allowed under the Privacy Act, even though it is not required, because many individuals cite both the FOIA and Privacy At when making a request. The FOIA provides specifically for an administrative appeal, and agencies are required to consider an appeal under the FOIA.

When a privacy Act request for access is denied, agencies usually inform the requester of any appeal rights that are available. If no information on appeal rights is included in the denial letter, the requester should ask the Privacy Act Officer. Unless an agency has established an alternative procedure, it is possible that an appeal filed directly with the head of the agency will be considered by the agency.

When a request for access is denied under the Privacy Act, the agency explains the reason for the denial. The explanation must name the system of records and explain which exemption is applicable to the system. An appeal may be made on the basis that the record is not exempt, that the system of records has not been properly exempted, or that the record is exempt but no harm to an important interest will result if the record is disclosed.

There are three basic elements to a Privacy Act appeal letter. First, the letter should state that the appeal is being made under the Privacy Act of 1974. If the FOIA was cited when the request for access was made, the letter should state that the appeal is also being made under the FOIA. This is important because the FOIA grants requesters statutory appeal rights.

Second, a Privacy Act appeal letter should identify the denial that is being appealed and the records that were withheld. The appeal letter should also explain why the denial of access is improper or unnecessary.

Third, the appeal should include the requester's name and address. It is good practice for a requester to also include a telephone number when making an appeal. Appendix 1 includes a sample letter of appeal.

Amending Records Under the Privacy Act

The Privacy Act grants an important right in addition to the ability to inspect records. The Act permits an individual to request a correction of a record that is not accurate, relevant, timely, or complete. This remedy allows an individual to correct errors and to prevent those errors from being disseminated by the agency or used unfairly against the individual.

The right to seek a correction extends only to records subject to the Privacy Act. Also, an individual can only correct errors contained in a record that pertains to himself or herself. Records disclosed under the FOIA cannot be amended through the Privacy Act unless the records are also subject to the Privacy Act. Records about unrelated events or about other people cannot be amended unless the records are in a Privacy Act file maintained under the name of the individual who is seeking to make the correction.

A request to amend a record should be in writing. Agency regulations explain procedures in greater detail, but the process is not complicated. A letter requesting an amendment of a record will normally be addressed to the Privacy Act Officer of the agency or to the agency official responsible for the maintenance of the record system containing the erroneous information. The envelope containing the request should be marked "Privacy Act Amendment Request" on the lower left corner.

There are five basic elements to a request for amending a Privacy Act record.

First, the letter should state that it is a request to amend a record under the Privacy Act of 1974.

Second, the request should identify the specific record and the specific information in the record for which an amendment is being sought.

Third, the request should state why the information is not accurate, relevant, timely, or complete. Supporting evidence may be included with the request.

Fourth, the request should state what new or additional information, if any, should be included in place of the erroneous information. Evidence of the validity of the new or additional information should be included. If the information in the file is wrong and needs to be removed rather than supplemented or corrected, the request should make this clear.

Fifth, the request should include the name and address of the requester. It is a good idea for the requester to include a telephone number. Appendix 1 includes a sample letter requesting amendment of a Privacy act record.

Appeals and Requirements for Agency Responses

An agency that receives a request for amendment under the Privacy Act must acknowledge receipt of the request within ten days (not including Saturdays, Sundays, and legal holidays). The agency must promptly rule on the request.

The agency may make the amendment requested. If so, the agency must notify any person or agency to which the record had previously been disclosed of the correction.

If the agency refuses to make the change requested, the agency must inform the requester of: (1) the agency's refusal to amend the record; (2) the reason for refusing to amend the request; and (3) the procedures for requesting a review of the denial. The agency must provide the name and business address of the official responsible for conducting the review.

An agency must decide an appeal of a denial of a request for amendment within thirty days (excluding Saturdays, Sundays, and legal holidays), unless the time period is extended by the agency for good cause. If the appeal is granted, the record will be corrected.

Be patient. If any phone number is incorrect, call (area code) 555-1212 and request the new listing.

Government Records and Privacy

If the appeal is denied, the agency must inform the requester of the right to judicial review. In addition, a requester whose appeal has been denied also has the right to place in the agency file a concise statement of disagreement with the information that was the subject of the request for amendment.

When a statement of disagreement has been filed and an agency is disclosing the disputed information, the agency must mark the information and provide copies of the statement of disagreement. The agency may also include a concise statement of its reasons for not making the requested amendments. The agency must also give a copy of the statement of disagreement to any person or agency to whom the record had previously been disclosed.

Finding a Judicial Appeal

The Privacy Act provides a civil remedy whenever an agency denies access to a record or refuses to amend a record. An individual may sue an agency if the agency fails to maintain records with accuracy, relevance, timeliness, and completeness as is necessary to assure fairness in any agency determination and the agency makes a determination that is adverse to the individual. An individual may also sue an agency if the agency fails to comply with any other Privacy Act provision in a manner that has an adverse effect on the individual.

The Privacy Act protects a wide range of rights about personal records maintained by federal agencies. The most important are the right to inspect records and the right to seek correction of records. Other rights have also been mentioned here, and still others can be found in the text of the Act. Most of these rights can become the subject of litigation.

An individual may file a lawsuit against an agency in the federal district court in which the individual lives, in which the records are situated, or in the District of Columbia. A lawsuit must be filed within two years from which the basis for the lawsuit arose.

Most individuals require the assistance of an attorney to file a judicial appeal. An individual who files a lawsuit and substantially prevails may be awarded reasonable attorney fees and litigation costs reasonably incurred. Some requesters may be able to handle their own appeal without an attorney. Since this is not a litigation guide, details about the judicial appeal process have not been included. Anyone considering filing an appeal can begin by reviewing the provisions of the Privacy Act on civil remedies.

Appendices

Appendix 1: Sample Request and Appeal Letter

A. Freedom of Information Act Request Letter

Agency Head [or Freedom of Information Act Officer]
Name of Agency
Address of Agency
City, State, Zip Code
Re: Freedom of Information Act Request.

Dear :

This is a request under the Freedom of Information Act.

I request that a copy of the following documents [or documents containing the following information] be provided to me: [identify the documents or information as specifically as possible].

In order to help determine my status to assess fees, you should know that I am (insert a suitable description of the requester and the purpose of the request).

[Sample requester descriptions:

a representative of the news media affiliated with the newspaper (magazine, television station, etc.) and this request is made as part of new gathering and not for a commercial use.

affiliated with an educational or noncommercial scientific institution and this request is made for a scholarly or scientific purpose.

an individual seeking information for personal use and not for a commercial use.

affiliated with a private corporation and am seeking information for use in the company business.]

[Optional] I am willing to pay fees for this request up to a maximum of $. If you estimate that the fees will exceed this limit, please inform me first.

[Optional] I request a waiver of all fees of this request. Disclosure of the requested information to me is in the public interest because it is likely to contribute significantly to public understanding of the operations or activities of the government and is not primarily in my commercial interest. [Include a specific explanation.]

Thank you for your consideration of this request.

Sincerely,

Name
Address
City, State, Zip Code
Telephone number [Optional]

B. Freedom of Information Act Appeal Letter

Agency Head or Appeal Officer
Name of Agency
Address of Agency
City, State, Zip Code
Re: Freedom of Information Act Appeal

Dear :

This is an appeal under the Freedom of Information Act.

On (date), I requested documents under the Freedom of Information Act. My request was assigned the following identification number: . On (date), I received a response to my request in a letter signed by (name of official). I appeal the denial of my request.

[Optional] The documents that were withheld must be disclosed under the FOIA because * * *.

[Optional] I appeal the decision to deny my request for a waiver of fees. I believe that I am entitled to a waiver of fees. Disclosure of the documents I requested is in the public interest because the information is likely to contribute significantly to public understanding of the operations or activities of government and is not primarily in my commercial interests. (Provide details)

[Optional] I appeal the decision to require me to pay review costs for this request. I am not seeking the documents for a commercial use. (Provide details)

[Optional] I appeal the decision to require me to pay search charges for this request. I am a reporter seeking information as part of news gathering and not for commercial use.

Thank you for your consideration of this appeal.

Sincerely,

Name
Address
City, State, Zip Code
Telephone number [Optional]

C. Privacy Act Request for Access Letter

Privacy at Officer [or System of Records Manager]
Name of Agency
City, State, Zip Code
Re: Privacy Act Request for Access.

Dear :

This is a request under the Privacy Act of 1974.

Be patient. If any phone number is incorrect, call (area code) 555-1212 and request the new listing.

Freedom of Information Act (FOIA)

I request a copy of any records [or specifically named records] about me maintained at your agency.

[Optional] To help you to locate my records, I have had the following contacts with your agency: [mention job applications, periods of employment, loans or agency programs applied for, etc.).

[Optional] Please consider that this request is also made under the Freedom of Information Act. Please provide any additional information that may be available under the FOIA.

[Optional] I am willing to pay fees for this request up to a maximum of $. If you estimate that the fees will exceed this limit, please inform me first.

[Optional] Enclosed is [a notarized signature or other identifying document] that will verify my identity.

Thank you for your consideration of this request.

Sincerely,

Name
Address
City, State, Zip Code
Telephone number [Optional]

D. Privacy Act Denial of Access Letter

Agency Head or Appeal Officer
Name of Agency
City, State, Zip Code
Re: Appeal of Denial of Privacy Act Access Request.

Dear :

This is an appeal under the Privacy Act of the denial of my request for access to records.

On (date), I requested access to records under the Privacy Act of 1974. My request was assigned the following identification number: . On (date), I received a response to my request in a letter signed by (name of official). I appeal the denial of my request.

[Optional] The records that were withheld should be disclosed to me because * * *.

[Optional] Please consider that this appeal is also made under the Freedom of Information Act. Please provide any additional information that may be available under the FOIA.

Thank you for your consideration of this appeal.

Sincerely,

Name
Address
City, State, Zip Code
Telephone number [Optional]

E. Privacy Act Request to Amend Records

Privacy Act Officer [or System of Records Manager]
Name of Agency
City, State, Zip Code
Re: Privacy Act Request to Amend Records

Dear :

This is a request under the Privacy Act to amend records about myself maintained by your agency.

I believe that the following information is not correct: [Describe the incorrect information as specifically as possible].

The information is not (accurate) (relevant) (timely) (complete) because * * *.

[Optional] Enclosed are copies of documents that show that the information is incorrect.

I request that the information be [deleted] [changed to read:]

Thank you for your consideration of this request.

Sincerely,

Name
Address
City, State, Zip Code
Telephone number [Optional]

F. Privacy Act Appeal of Refusal to Amend Records

Agency Head or Appeal Officer
Name of Agency
City, State, Zip Code
Re: Privacy Act Request to Amend Records

Dear :

This is an appeal made under the Privacy Act of the refusal of your agency to amend records as I requested.

On (date), I was informed by (name of official) that my request was rejected. I appeal the rejection of my request.

The rejection of my request for amendment was wrong because * * *.

[Optional] I enclose additional evidence that shows that the records are incorrect and that the amendment I requested is appropriate.

Thank you for your consideration of this appeal.

Sincerely,

Name
Address
City, State, Zip Code
Telephone number [Optional]

Be patient. If any phone number is incorrect, call (area code) 555-1212 and request the new listing.

Federal FOIA Offices

The Office of Information and Privacy (OIP) is the principal contact point within the executive branch for advice and policy guidance on matters pertaining to the administration of the Freedom on Information Act (FOIA). Through OIP's FOIA Counselor Service, experienced FOIA attorneys are available to respond to FOIA-related inquiries at the U.S. Department of Justice, Office of Information and Privacy, 10th and Constitution Ave., NW, Room 7238, Washington, DC 20530, (202) 514-4251.

The following list contains the principal FOIA legal and administrative contacts at all federal agencies that deal regularly with FOIA matters. In some instances (e.g., the U.S. Department of Defense), all major agency components are listed individually under the agency. In other instances (e.g., the Food and Drug Administration), major agency components are listed separately. In still other instances (e.g., the U.S. Department of Labor), no components are listed, as it is the agency's preference that all FOIA contacts be made through its main FOIA office.

All telephone numbers are FTS numbers unless a local area code is shown. Where both the legal and the administrative contacts (marked "L" and "A," respectively) are at the same address, the common address follows the name of the administrative contact. OIP should be notified whenever there is a change in a legal or administrative contact or any change in title, telephone number, or address.

ACTION

Steward A. Davis (202-606-4833) (L)
Deputy General Counsel
Ulysses G. Parnell (202-606-5242) (A)
Management Analysis Division
806 Connecticut Ave., NW
Washington, DC 20525

Administrative Conference of the United States

Gary J. Edles (202-254-7020 (L)
General Counsel
2120 L St., NW, Suite 500
Washington, DC 20037

Agriculture Department

Kenneth E. Cohen (202-720-5565) (L)
Assistant General Counsel
Room 2321, South Bldg.
Washington, DC 20250-1400

Milton E. Sloane (202-720-8164) (A)
FOIA/PA Coordinator
Room 536A, Administration Bldg.
Washington, DC 20250

American Battle Monuments Commission

Col. William E. Ryan (202-272-0536) (A)
Director of Operations and Finance
20 Massachusetts Ave., NW, Room 5127
Washington, DC 20314-0300

Appalachian Regional Commission

Joseph E. Napolitano (202-673-7822) (A)
Special Assistant to the Co-Chairman
1666 Connecticut Ave., NW
Washington, DC 20235

Arms Control and Disarmament Agency

Frederick Smith, Jr. (202-647-0932) (L)
Information/Privacy Officer
320 21st St., NW, Room 5731
Washington, DC 20451

Board for International Broadcasting

John A. Lindburg (202-254-8040) (L)
General Counsel
1201 Connecticut Ave., NW
Washington, DC 20036

Central Intelligence Agency

W. George Jameson (703-874-3118) (L)
Associate General Counsel
Office of General Counsel
John H. Wright (703-351-2770) (A)
Information and Privacy Coordinator
Office of Information Services
Washington, DC 20505

Commerce Department

Gordon Fields (202-377-5384) (L)
Chief, General Law Division
Geraldine LeBoo (202-377-4115) (A)
Chief, Mgt. Support Division
Washington, DC 20230

Commission on Civil Rights

Emma Monroig (202-376-8375) (L)
Solicitor
1121 Vermont Ave., NW, Room 606
Washington, DC 20425

Commodity Futures Trading Commission

Glynn L. Mays (202-254-9880) (L)
Senior Assistant General Counsel
Edward W. Colbert (202-254-3382) (A)
Assistant Sec'y to the Commission
2033 K St., NW
Washington, DC 20581

Comptroller of the Currency

Peter Lieberman (202-874-5330) (L)
Assistant Director
Legan Advisory Services Division
Frank Vance, Jr. (202-874-4700) (A)
Disclosure Officer
Washington, DC 20219

Be patient. If any phone number is incorrect, call (area code) 555-1212 and request the new listing.

Freedom of Information Act (FOIA)

Consumer Product Safety Commission

Alan C. Shakin (301-504-0980) (L)
Assistant General Counsel
Todd A. Stevenson (301-504-0785) (A)
FOI Officer
5401 Westbard Ave.
Washington, DC 20207

Council on Environmental Quality

Elizabeth Blaug (202-395-5754) (A)
Staff Attorney
Office of the General Counsel
722 Jackson Pl, NW
Washington, DC 20503

Customs Service

Kathryn C. Peterson (202-566-8681) (L)
Chief, Disclosure Law Branch
Gerald Crowley (202-566-8681) (A)
Paralegal Specialist
1301 Constitution Ave., NW
Washington, DC 20229

Defense Department

Maurice E. White (703-695-6804) (L)
Senior Attorney
OGC/LC, Room 3E988
Charlie Y. Talbott (703-697-1180) (A)
Chief, FOI Division
OASD (PA), Room 2C757
The Pentagon
Washington, DC 20301

Air Force

Carole Cheatham (703-614-4075) (L)
HQ USAF/JACL
Washington, DC 20324-1000

Roger T. McNamara (703-695-6552) (L)
Office of General Counsel, Room 4c941
Anne Turner (703-697-3491) (A)
SAF/AADADF, Room 4A1088C
The Pentagon
Washington, DC 20330

Army

Terry Schriefer (703-697-8029) (L)
Office of General Counsel, Room 2E725
The Pentagon
Washington, DC 20310-0104

A. Graham Shirley (703-614-4316) (L)
Administrative Law Division
The Pentagon, Room 2E433
Washington, DC 20310-2200

Edith M. Miley (703-692-2022) (A)
FOIA/PA Division
USAISC-P (ASQNS-OP-F)
Crystal Center 2, Suite 201
Arlington, VA 22201

Marine Corps

Kevin H. Winters (703-614-2510) (L)
Judge Advocate Division
HQMC (JAR), Room 1102
B.L. Thompson (703-614-3685) (A)
Management Information Systems Div.
HQMC (Code MI-10), Room 4327, Navy Annex
Washington, DC 20380

Navy

Geoffrey P.Lyon (703-614-1781) (L)
Office of the Judge Advocate General
200 Stovall St.
Alexandria, VA 22332

Theodore Fredman (703-602-2725) (L)
Office of General Counsel, Room 480
Crystal Plaza 5
Washington, DC 20360-5110

Gwen R. Aitken (703-697-1459) (A)
CNO (OP-09B30)
The Pentagon, Room 5E521
Washington, DC 20350-2000

Defense Contract Audit Agency

Dave Hanshall (703-274-4400) (A)
Information and Privacy Advisor
Information Resources Management Br.
Cameron Station (CMR)
Alexandria, VA 22304-6178

Defense Intelligence Agency

Terry Bathen (703-697-3945) (L)
Assistant General Counsel
The Pentagon, Room 2E238
Robert Richardson (202-373-8361) (A)
Chief, FOIA/PA Staff, RTS-1B
Washington, DC 20340

Defense Logistics Agency

Susan Salus (703-617-7583) (A)
Administrative Management Branch
DLA-XAM, Cameron Station
Alexandria, VA 22304-6100

Education Department

Robert Wexler (202-401-3690) (L)
Office of the General Counsel, Room 4122
Alexia J. Roberts (202-708-9263) (A)
Office of Public Affairs, Room 2089
FOB 6, 400 Maryland Ave., SW
Washington, DC 20202

Energy Department

Ralph D. Goldenberg (202-586-8665) (L)
Assistant General Counsel
P.J. Paradis (202-586-5955) (A)
1000 Independence Ave., SW
Washington, DC 20585

Environmental Protection Agency

Marlyne Lipfert (202-260-5460) (L)
Office of General Counsel (LE-132G)
Jeralene G. Green (202-260-4048) (A)
FOIA Officer (A-101)
401 M St., SW
Washington, DC 20460

Equal Employment Opportunity Commission

Nicholas M. Inzeo (202-663-4640 (L)
Assistant Legal Counsel
1801 L St., NW, Room 6006
Washington, DC 20507

Executive Office of the President, Office of Administration

Bruce Overton (202-395-2273) (L)
General Counsel
468 Old Executive Office Bldg.
Washington, DC 20500

Stacia Cropper (202-395-6963) (A)
Executive Secretary
480 Old Executive Office Bldg.
Washington, DC 20503

Export-Import Bank

Stephen G. Glazer (202-566-8864) (L)
Associate General Counsel

Be patient. If any phone number is incorrect, call (area code) 555-1212 and request the new listing.

Federal FOIA Offices

811 Vermont Ave., NW, Room 957
Washington, DC 20571

Farm Credit Administration

Ronald H. Erickson (703-883-4113) (A)
FOI Officer
Office of Cong. and Public Affairs
1501 Farm Credit Dr.
McLean, VA 22102-5090

Federal Aviation Administration

John M. Walsh (202-376-6406) (L)
Chief, General Law Branch, AGC-110
Gladys Stewart (202-267-3490) (A)
Office of Public Affairs, APA-220
800 Independence Ave., SW
Washington, DC 20591

Federal Communications Commission

Lawrence S. Schaffner (202-632-6990) (L)
Assistant General Counsel
1919 M St., NW, Room 622
Washington, DC 20554

Federal Deposit Insurance Corporation

Thomas A. Schulz (202-736-0520) (L)
Assistant General Counsel
John Adams (202-898-3819) (A)
Senior Attorney, Room F-405
550 17th St., NW
Washington, DC 20429
Resolution Trust Corp.
Linda L. Robinson (703-908-6131) (A)
FOIA/PA Unit
1735 North Lynn St.
Rosslyn, VA 22209

Federal Election Commission

Vincent J. Convery, Jr. (202-219-3690) (L)
Office of General Counsel
Fred S. Eiland (202-219-4155) (A)
FOI Officer
999 E St., NW
Washington, DC 20463

Federal Emergency Management Agency

Patricia Gemley (202-646-4105) (L)
General Counsel, Room 840
Sandra Jackson (202-646-3840) (A)
FOI/PA Specialist, Room 840
500 C St., SW
Washington, DC 20472

Federal Energy Regulatory Commission

Denise O'Brien (202-208-0457) (L)
Office of General Counsel, Room 8002
Sanford McAllister (202-208-1088) (A)
Director, Public Affairs, Room 9200
825 N. Capitol St., NE
Washington, DC 20426

Federal Home Loan Mortgage Corporation

Maud Mater (703-903-2801) (L)
Assistant General Counsel
8200 Jones Branch Dr.
McLean, VA 22102

Federal Labor Relations Authority

William E. Persina (202-382-0781) (L)
Solicitor, Room 222
David L. Feder (202-382-0834) (A)
Assistant General Counsel, Suite 326
500 C St., SW
Washington, DC 20424

Federal Maritime Commission

Joseph C. Polking (202-523-5725) (A)
Secretary
1100 L St., NW, Room 11101
Washington, DC 20573

Federal Mediation and Conciliation Service

Eileen Hoffman (202-653-5305) (L)
General Counsel
2100 K St., NW
Washington, DC 20427

Federal Mine Safety and Health Review Commission

Richard Baker (202-653-5625) (L)
Executive Director
1730 K St., NW, Room 614
Washington, DC 20006

Federal Reserve Board

Elaine M. Boutilier (202-452-2418) (L)
Legal Division
20th and C Sts., NW, Room B1051B
Washington, DC 20551

Federal Trade Commission

William Golden (202-326-2494) (L)
Office of the General Counsel
Sandra Bolden (202-326-2406) (A)
Sixth St. and Pennsylvania Ave., NW
Washington, DC 20580

Food and Drug Administration

Gerald H. Deighton (202-443-1812) (A)
5600 Fishers Lane, (HFI-30)
Rockville, MD 20857

Foreign Claims Settlement Commission

Judith H. Lock (202-208-7727) (A)
Administrative Officer
601 D St., NW, Suite 10,000
Washington, DC 20579

General Accounting Office

Douglas Faulkner (202-275-6404) (L)
Assistant General Council
441 G St., NW, Room 6800
Washington, DC 20548

General Services Administration

Helen C. Maus (202-501-1460) (L)
Attorney-Advisor
Mary Cunningham (202-501-2691) (A)
18th and F Sts., NW
Washington, DC 20405

Health and Human Services Department

Richard Friedman (202-619-0162) (L)
Office of the General Counsel
Room 5362, Cohen Bldg.
330 Independence Ave., SW
Carl Coleman (202-472-7453) (A)
Director, FOIA/Privacy Division
Room 645F, HHH Bldg.
200 Independence Ave., SW
Washington, DC 20201

Health Care Finance Administration

Rosario Cirrincione (410-966-5352) (A)
Director, FOI Division
6660 Security Blvd., Room 100
Baltimore, MD 21207

Housing and Urban Development Department

Jeffrey Rock (202-708-0553) (L)

Be patient. If any phone number is incorrect, call (area code) 555-1212 and request the new listing.

Freedom of Information Act (FOIA)

Attorney Advisor, Room 10250
Yvette Magruder (202-708-3054)
Departmental FOIA Officer, Room 10139
451 7th St., SW
Washington, DC 20410

United States Information Agency

Lorie J. Nierenberg (202-619-6975) (L)
Assistant General Counsel
Lola L. Secora (202-619-5499) (A)
FOIA/PA Officer
301 4th St., SW
Washington, DC 20547

Inter-American Foundation

Charles M. Berk (703-841-3812) (L)
General Counsel
Melvin Asterken (703-841-3869) (A)
FOI Officer
1515 Wilson Blvd.
Rosslyn, VA 22209

Interior Department

Robert Moll (202-208-5216) (L)
Acting Assistant Solicitor
Alexandra Mallus (202-208-5342)
Departmental FOIA Officer
18 and E Sts., NW
Washington, DC 20240

Internal Revenue Service

Peter V. Filpi (202-566-4109) (L)
Assistant Chief Counsel
Randy Hartman (202-566-3359) (A)
Chief, FOIA/PA Branch
1111 Constitution Ave., NW
Washington, DC 20224

International Development Cooperation Agency

Jan Miller (202-647-8218) (L)
Assistant General Counsel for Employee
and Public Affairs, Room 6892
James L. Harper (202-647-1850) (A)
Office of Public Inquiries, Room 5756
320 21st St., NW
Washington, DC 20523

International Trade Commission

W.W. Gearhart (202-205-3091) (L)
Assistant General Counsel
Kenneth R. Mason (202-205-2000) (A)
Secretary to the Commission
500 E St., SW
Washington, DC 20436

Interstate Commerce Commission

Robert S. Burk (202-927-7312) (L)
General Counsel, Room 5211
S. Arnold Smith (202-927-6317) (A)
FOIA/PA Officer, Room 3132
12th and Constitution Ave., NW
Washington, DC 20423

Justice Department

Richard L. Huff (202-514-FOIA) (L)
Daniel J. Metcalfe
Co-Directors, Room 7238
Office of Information and Privacy
Washington, DC 20530

Patricia Harris (202-514-1938) (A)
FOIA/PA Section, Room B-327
Justice Management Division
Washington, DC 20530

Antitrust Division
Leo D. Neshkes (202-514-2692) (A)
FOIA/PA Officer, Room 3232
Washington, DC 20530

Bureau of Prisons
Yvonne Hinkson (202-633-5641) (A)
FOIA/PA Officer, Room 401 NALC
Washington, DC 20534

Civil Division
Elizabeth A. Pugh (202-514-3178) (L)
Federal Programs Branch, Room 1062
Leonard Schaitman (202-514-3441) (L)
Appellate Staff, Room 3614
James M. Kovakas (202-514-2319) (A)
FOIA/PA Office, Room 808
Washington, DC 20530

Civil Rights Division
Nelson D. Hermilla (202-514-4209) (A)
Chief, FOI/PA Branch, Room 7339
Washington, DC 20530

Criminal Division
Frank Newett (202-606-4910) (A)
Chief, FOI/PA Unit, Room 1003 UBS
Washington, DC 20530

Drug Enforcement Administration
John Phillips (202-307-7596) (A)
Chief, FOI Section, Room W.6060 LP-2
Washington, DC 20537

Executive Office for U.S. Attorneys
Bonnie L. Gray (202-501-7826) (A)
Attorney-in-Charge, Room 6410 PAT
Washington, DC 20530

Federal Bureau of Investigation
J. Kevin O'Brien (202-324-5520) (A)
Chief, FOI/PA Section, Room 6296 JEH
Washington, DC 20535

Immigration and Naturalization Service
Russell A. Powell (202-514-1554) (A)
FOIA/PA Section, Room 5056 CAB
Washington, DC 20536

Environment and Natural Resources Division

Christine Kurek (202-514-4362) (A)
Paralegal Specialist, Room 2129
Washington, DC 20530

Marshals Service

Florastine P. Graham (202-307-9054) (A)
FOI/PA Officer
600 Army Navy Drive
Arlington, VA 22202-4210

Parole Commission

Pamela Posch (202-492-5959) (A)
5550 Friendship Blvd., Room 420
Chevy Chase, MD 20815

Tax Division

J. Brian Ferrel (202-307-6423) (L)
Assistant Chief, CTS, Central Region
Room 6124 JCB
Pamela Jones (202-307-0462) (A)
FOIA Unit, Room 6823 JCB
Washington, DC 20530

Labor Department

Miriam McD. Miller (202-523-8188) (L)
Office of the Solicitor, Room N-2428

Be patient. If any phone number is incorrect, call (area code) 555-1212 and request the new listing.

Federal FOIA Offices

200 Constitution Ave., NW
Washington, DC 20210

Legal Services Corporation

Joanne Gretch (202-863-1823) (L)
FOIA Officer
400 Virginia Ave., SW
Washington, DC 20024-2751

Library of Congress

Dorothy M. Schrader (202-707-8380) (L)
General Counsel
William C. Froelich (202-707-8394) (A)
Copyright Office, Dept. 17
1st St. and Independence Ave., SE
Washington, DC 20540

Merit Systems Protection Board

Michael K. Martin (202-653-7171) (L)
Office of the General Counsel
Michael H. Hoxie (202-653-7200) (A)
Director, Information Services Div.
1120 Vermont Ave., NW
Washington, DC 20419

National Aeronautics and Space Administration

George E. Reese (202-453-2465) (L)
Associate General Counsel (Code GG)
Patricia M. Riep (202-453-2939) (A)
FOIA Officer (Code PS)
400 Maryland Ave., SW
Washington, DC 20546

National Archives and Records Administration

Gary L. Brooks (202-501-5535) (L)
General Counsel
John A. Constance (202-501-5110) (A)
7th and Pennsylvania Ave., NW
Washington, DC 20408

National Credit Union Administration

Hattie M. Ulan (202-682-9630) (L)
Office of the General Counsel
1776 G St., NW
Washington, DC 20456

National Endowment for the Arts

Marlene Cleavland (202-682-5418) (L)
FOIA Officer
1100 Pennsylvania Ave., NW
Washington, DC 20506

National Endowment for the Humanities

David C. Fisher (202-786-0322) (L)
General Counsel
1100 Pennsylvania Ave., NW
Washington, DC 20506

National Labor Relations Board

John W. Hornbeck (202-254-9350) (L)
Office of the General Counsel, Room 1107
John J. Toner (202-254-9430) (A)
Associate Executive Secretary, Room 701
1717 Pennsylvania Ave., NW
Washington, DC 20570

National Mediation Board

Ronald M. Etters (202-523-5944) (L)
General Counsel
1425 K St., NW, Suite 910
Washington, DC 20572

National Railroad Passenger Corporation (AMTRAK)

William F. Erkelenz (202-906-3975) (L)

General Solicitor
Medaris W. Oliveri (202-906-2728) (A)
FOIA Officer
60 Massachusetts Ave., NE
Washington, DC 20002

National Science Foundation

D. Matthew Powell (202-357-9435) (L)
Assistant General Counsel, Room 501
Maryellen Schoolmaster (202-357-9494) (A)
FOIA Officer, Room 527
1800 G St., NW
Washington, DC 20550

National Security Agency

Vito T. Potenza (301-688-6054) (L)
Assistant General Counsel/Litigation
Michael Conn (301-688-6527) (A)
Chief, Information Policy Division
Ft. George C. Meade, MD 20755-6000

National Security Council

Nicholas Rostow (202-456-6538) (L)
Legal Adviser
368 Old Executive Office Bldg.
Steven Tilley (202-395-3103) (A)
Director for Information Discolsure
392 Old Executive Office Bldg.
Washington, DC 20506

National Transportation Safety Board

Ronald S. Battocchi (202-382-6546) (L)
Office of General Counsel, Room 818
B. Michael Levins (202-382-6700) (A)
Bureau of Administration, Room 802
800 Independence Ave., SW
Washington, DC 20594

Nuclear Regulatory Commission

Mary Pat Siemien (301-504-1565) (L)
Attorney, Office of General Counsel
Robert Hardzog (202-492-8133) (A)
Chief, FOI/LPDR
Washington, DC 20555

Occupational Safety and Health Review Commission

Earl R. Ohman, Jr. (202-634-4015) (L)
General Counsel
Linda A. Whitsett (202-634-7943) (A)
1825 K St., NW
Washington, DC 20006

Office of Government Ethics

William Gressman (202-523-5757) (L)
Attorney Advisor
Office of the General Counsel
1201 New York Ave., NW
Washington, DC 20005

Office of Management and Budget

Mac Reed (202-395-5600) (L)*
Assistant General Counsel
464 Old Executive Office Bldg.
Darrell A. Johnson (202-395-7250) (A)
Assistant Director for Administration
9026 New Executive Office Bldg.
Washington, DC 20503

* For policy guidance on the Privacy Act and on FOIA fee matters, contact OMB's Robert N. Veeder, at 202-395-4814

Office of Personnel Management

Stephanie Peters (202-606-1920) (L)
Office of the General Counsel

Be patient. If any phone number is incorrect, call (area code) 555-1212 and request the new listing.

Freedom of Information Act (FOIA)

C. Ronald Trueworthy (703-908-8550) (A)
Information Policy Branch
Washington, DC 20415

Office of Science and Technology Policy
Barbara Ferguson (202-395-7347) (A)
Administrative Officer
431 Old Executive Office Bldg.
Washington, DC 20500

Office of the Special Counsel
Robert Lane (202-653-8982) (L)
General Attorney, Suite 1100
1120 Vermont Ave., NW
Washington, DC 20005

Office of Thrift Supervision
Kathy Semone (202-906-5900) (A)
Director, Information Services
1700 G St., NW
Washington, DC 20552

Office of U.S. Trade Representative
Dorothy S. Balaben (202-395-3432) (A)
FOIA Officer
600 17th St., NW
Washington, DC 20506

Office of the Vice President
John Howard (202-456-2816) (L)
Counselor to the Vice President
271 Old Executive Office Bldg.
Washington, DC 20501

Overseas Private Investment Corporation
Richard Horanburg (202-336-8417) (L)
Office of the General Counsel
1100 New York Ave., NW
Washington, DC 20527

Panama Canal Commission
Barbara A. Fuller (202-634-6441) (A)
Assistant to the Secretary for Commission Affairs
2000 L St., NW, Suite 550
Washington, DC 20036-4996

Peace Corps
Robert L. Martin (202-606-3114) (L)
Associate General Counsel
Ronald Kendall (202-606-3420) (A)
1990 K St., NW
Washington, DC 20526

Pension Benefit Guaranty Corporation
Philip R. Hertz (202-778-8820) (L)
Office of the General Counsel, Room 7204
E. William Fitzgerald (202-778-8839) (A)
Disclosure Officer, Room 7106
2020 K St., NW
Washington, DC 20006

Pennsylvania Avenue Development Corporation
Staff (202-724-9091)
1331 Pennsylvania Ave., NW
Suite 1220 North
Washington, DC 20004

Postal Service
Charles D. Hawley (202-268-2971) (L)
Assistant General Counsel
Philip J.G. Skelly (202-268-2924) (A)
Records Officer
475 L'Enfant Plaza West, SW
Washington, DC 20260

Railroad Retirement Board
Karl T. Blank (312-751-4941) (L)
Bureau of Law
LeRoy F. Blommaert (312-751-4548) (A)
FOIA Officer
844 Rush St.
Chicago, IL 60611

United States Secret Service
Melvin Laska (202-435-5838) (A)
FOIA/PA Officer
Liason Division, Room 720
1800 G St., NW
Washington, DC 20223

Securities and Exchange Commission
Richard M. Humes (202-272-2454) (L)
Assistant General Counsel
Gayla Sessons (202-272-7443) (A)
FOIA Officer
450 5th St., NW
Washington, DC 20549

Selective Service System
Henry N. Williams (202-724-1167) (L)
General Counsel
1023 31st St., NW
Washington, DC 20435

Small Business Administration
Mona K. Mitnick (202-205-6645) (L)
Office of General Counsel
Beverly K. Linden (202-653-6460) (A)
Chief, Office of FOI/PA
409 3rd St., SW
Washington, DC 20416

Social Security Administration
Ellen Reichenbach (410-925-3154) (L)
Office of General Counsel
Room 622, Altmeyer Bldg.
Harris Factor (410-965-4011) (A)
FOIA Officer, Room 4100 Annex
6401 Security Blvd.
Baltimore, MD 21235

State Department
Kathryn Skipper (202-647-5154) (L)
Attorney-Adviser, Room 4427A
Frank M. Machak (202-647-7740) (A)
FOIA Coordinator, Room 1239
2201 C St., NW
Washington, DC 20520

Tennessee Valley Authority
Maureen H. Dunn (615-632-4131) (L)
Assistant General Counsel
Michael Patterson (615-632-8063) (A)
Information Services
400 West Summit Hill Dr.
Knoxville, TN 37902

Transportation Department
Robert I. Ross (202-366-9154) (L)
Office of General Counsel (C-10)
Rebecca H. Lima (202-366-4542) (A)
Chief, FOIA Division (A-32)
400 7th St., SW
Washington, DC 20590

Treasury Department
Nicole Jenkins (202-566-2327) (L)
Office of General Counsel, Room 1410
Alana Johnson (202-566-2789) (A)
Disclosure Officer, Room 1054

Be patient. If any phone number is incorrect, call (area code) 555-1212 and request the new listing.

1500 Pennsylvania Ave., NW
Washington, DC 20220

810 Vermont Ave., NW
Washington, DC 20420

Veterans Affairs Department

Mark McDonough (202-633-7222) (L)
Office of General Counsel (024K)
B. Michael Berger (202-233-3616) (A)
Director, PMRS (73)

The White House

C. Boyden Gray (202-456-2632) (L)
Counsel to the President
1600 Pennsylvania Ave., NW
Washington, DC 20500

Be patient. If any phone number is incorrect, call (area code) 555-1212 and request the new listing.

Freedom of Information Act (FOIA)

State FOIA Offices

How To Use State Open Records Laws: Freedom of Information

Just as the Freedom of Information Act, enacted by Congress in 1966, gave individuals the right to request and receive information held by the federal government, all states have laws giving the public access to their government records. Many of these laws, often called the Open Record laws, are modeled after the federal act.

The state statutes have some similarities. What is covered under the act, for example, invariably includes all books, maps, photographs and other documents made or received by any government agency in transaction with public business. And just as the federal act has exemptions to the rules, so do the state laws. While most of them exempt personnel, medical and other personal files, as well as criminal intelligence information and "trade secrets," there are less common ones. For example, in South Dakota, commercial fertilizer reports are exempt. In Florida, information provided to an agency for the purpose of ride-sharing arrangements is exempt, and in New Hampshire, meat inspection records are closed.

Companies can get a wide range of information from the state's Open Records laws. Here are a few examples of how these laws have been successfully used at the state level:

Bookstore Gets School Reading List
In Maryland, a bookstore used the state Open Records Law to obtain the required reading list for various courses at the state university in order to stock those books for the coming school year.

Plumber Opens Up Contracting Info
A plumbing company in New York that was the unsuccessful bidder for a project was granted access through the Open Records Law to the successful bid proposal as well as the agency's findings.

Environmental Group Obtains Damaging Drinking Water Study
In New York, an environmental group was able to get reports, analyses, and records concerning soil borings regarding a drinking water treatment plant prepared by a consulting firm for the City of Niagara Falls.

Hospital Gets Billing Practices of Competitors
In Illinois, a hospital in the same market as another hospital was able to get information on its competitive billing practices concerning ambulance service.

Advertiser Gets State's Mailing List
Through the Open Records Law in Mississippi, a company wishing to expand its advertising list was able to get a list of all the state residents who had a driver's license.

The way laws are administered varies. Some states have time limits for agencies to respond to requests -- usually between three and ten working days; others do not. Some states have administrative review processes available to individuals who have been denied their request. In other states a person's only recourse is to go to court. Some laws state whether or not the motive of the requester is relevant in allowing access to records; some provide sanctions for violations of the statutes, others do not.

In addition, several states publish pamphlets explaining their law and how to file a request for records. New York, for example, has a Committee on Open Government composed of members from the government and the public. It furnishes advice to agencies, the public and the news media and annually reports its recommendations and observations to the governor and the legislature. Unlike the federal act, which has been amended only a few times, state acts are often changed on a frequent basis.

Information on a state's FOIA can usually be obtained from the office of attorney general. Listed below are their addresses, telephone numbers, and some information about the laws and their exemptions. The common exemptions -- personal records, criminal investigation files, library and academic files -- are not listed for each state. Some of the exemptions that are listed are exempted by other state laws.

States may charge fees to cover the cost of searches and/or the cost of copying records.

State Freedom of Information Offices

Alabama
Office of Attorney General, Alabama State House, 11 South Union Street, Montgomery, AL 36130; (205) 242-7300. Exemptions include income tax returns, records of child care facilities, certain conservation and natural resource information.

Alaska
Office of Attorney General, Department of Law, P.O. Box K - State Capitol, Juneau, AK 99811; (907) 465-3600. Exemptions because of other state laws include: geological and other information submitted for persons applying to lease or buy land, reports, logs and surveys held by the Department of Natural Resources relating to oil wells for which a permit to drill was issued by the department, information contained in audit reports or tax returns. There is no time limit for responding to requests.

Arizona
Office of Attorney General, 1275 W. Washington, Phoenix, AZ 85997; (602) 542-4266. Exemptions include consumer fraud reports, racketeering investigations, minutes of executive sessions of public bodies.

Arkansas
Office of Attorney General, 323 Center, Suite 200, Little Rock, AR 72201; (501) 682-2007. Exemptions include state income tax records, grand jury minutes. Records specifically declared open include motor vehicle citations and blood alcohol tests, payroll records of covered bodies and juvenile court records.

Be patient. If any phone number is incorrect, call (area code) 555-1212 and request the new listing.

State FOIA Offices

Records must be made available within three working days at the time of the request.

California

Office of Attorney General, Department of Justice, 1515 K St., Sacramento, CA 95814; (916) 324-5437. Exemptions include requests for bilingual election materials, records of regulation of financial institutions, records of utility systems development or market or crop reports, real estate appraisals, statements of finances required by licensing agency. Agencies have 10 working days to comply with request. If denied access, an individual may request a review with the Information Practices Coordinator.

Colorado

Office of Attorney General, 1525 Sherman Street, Third Floor, Denver, CO 80203; (303) 866-3611. Access may be denied for information pertaining to licensing, specific details of state research projects, real estate appraisals by the state before any purchase. Records must be turned over within three working days after a request is made.

Connecticut

Freedom of Information Commission, 97 Elm Street, Rear, Hartford, CT 06106; (203) 566-5682. Exemptions include real estate appraisals, collective bargaining, anti-trust investigations, states sales and use tax. Any person denied the records requested may appeal to the Freedom of Information Commission.

Delaware

Office of the Attorney General, 820 North French Street, Eighth Floor, Wilmington, DE, 19801; (302) 577-3047. Exemptions include labor negotiations, anonymous contributors to charity, and records of permits for concealed weapons.

District of Columbia

Office of Corporate Counsel, District Building, 1350 Pennsylvania Ave., NW, Washington, DC 20004; (202) 727-6248. Exemptions include information related to civil anti-trust investigations, fire loss information furnished by insurer to fire marshal. Records declared open include names, salaries, title and dates of employment of all employees or officers of the mayor and an agency.

Florida

Office of Attorney General, The Capitol, Tallahassee, FL 32399-1050; (904) 487-1963. Exemptions include home addresses, phone numbers and photos of law enforcement personnel. Records held legally open include autopsy reports, inspection records of nursing homes compiled by the Department of Health, appraisal reports of land acquisitions made by a city, vote sheets, final orders and other documents of the Public Service Commission.

Georgia

Office of Attorney General, Department of Law, 132 State Judicial Building, Atlanta, GA, (404) 656-3300. Exemptions include tax returns, medical peer review group records. Records declared to be confidential by court decision or attorney general's opinions include: salary information of county employees contained only in personnel files and not included as part of another public record.

Hawaii

Department of Attorney General, Hawaii State Capitol, Room 405, Honolulu, HI 96813; (808) 586-1500. Exemptions through other state laws include applications for licenses to manufacture or sell motor vehicles, fire investigation records of county fire chiefs may be withheld. There is no time limit for responding to requests.

Idaho

Office of Attorney General, Boise, ID 83722; (208) 334-2400. Exemptions include papers filed with the judicial council or masters appointed by the supreme court concerning removal, discipline or retirement of judges or justices.

Illinois

Office of Attorney General, State of Illinois, Springfield, IL 62706; (217) 782-1090. Exemptions include taxpayer information, research data, proposals and bids for contracts, grants and agreements, architects' and engineers' plans.

Indiana

Office of Attorney General, 219 State House, Indianapolis, IN 46204; (317) 232-6201. Exemptions include information concerning research conducted under the auspices of institutions of higher learning. Information that may be withheld includes negotiations in progress with industrial, research, or commercial prospects.

Iowa

Office of Attorney General, Department of Justice, Hoover Building, Des Moines, IA, 50319; (515) 281-5164. Exemptions include: appraisal information for possible public land purchase, Iowa Development Commission information on industrial prospects in negotiations, and financial statements submitted to the state Commerce Commission. Records that have been legally open include the Book of Accounts required to be kept by county auditors, and jury lists.

Kansas

Office of Attorney General, Kansas Judicial Center - Second floor, Topeka, KS 66612-1597; (913) 296-2215. Exemptions include appraisals of property, software programs, well samples, logs and surveys, census and research records, and records of utility customers.

Kentucky

Office of Attorney General, Capitol Building, Frankfort, KY 40601; (502) 564-7600. Exemptions include details of possible real estate acquisitions, prospective locations of unannounced business. Records legally open include coroner's reports, tax records in the custody of the property valuation administrator, records of disciplinary actions of the state board of medical licensure. A public body must respond in three working days to a request.

Louisiana

Office of Attorney General, Department of Justice, 234 Loyola Building --Seventh floor, New Orleans, LA 70112-2096; (504) 342-7013. Exemptions include tax return information, financial institution records, confidential mineral reports, records in control of supervisor of public funds. Records held open under the law includes: budget requests of a city parish, records of associations of public officials. An agency has three days to respond to a request.

Maine

Office of Attorney General, State House Station - Six, Augusta, ME 04333; (207) 289-3661. Exemptions include materials prepared exclusively for labor negotiations, information on hazardous waste. Records legally opened include private appraisal reports obtained by the Bureau of Parks and Recreation in connection with proposed land acquisitions. A public official has 10 days to respond to a request.

Maryland

Office of Attorney General, Munsey Building, Calvert and Fayette Streets, Baltimore, MD 21202-1909; (301) 576-6300. Records that may be withheld include details of state research projects, real estate appraisals made for state. Records that must be withheld include confidential financial, geological, data, professional licensing records of individuals. Response to a request must not exceed 30 days.

Massachusetts

Office of Attorney General, One Ashburton Place, Boston, MA 02108; (617) 727-2200. Exemptions include real estate appraisals, name and address of any person contained in an application to carry firearms.

Michigan

Department of Attorney General, 525 W. Ottawa St., Lansing, MI 48913; (517) 373-1110. Exemptions include public bids, real estate appraisals, archaeological site information, records of any campaign committee. A public body has five working days to respond to a request.

Minnesota

Office of Attorney General, 102 Capitol Building, St. Paul, MN 55155; (612) 296-6196. Exemptions include property complaint data, real estate appraisals, social recreation data, energy and financial data, public safety data.

Mississippi

Office of Attorney General, P.O. Box 220, Jackson, MS 39205; (601) 359-3680. Exemptions include individual tax records, certain appraisal records, archaeological records, commercial and financial records.

Missouri

Office of Attorney General, Supreme Court Building, Jefferson City, MO 65102; (314) 751-3321. Exemptions include records of state militia, records of national guard, records of labor negotiations.

Be patient. If any phone number is incorrect, call (area code) 555-1212 and request the new listing.

Freedom of Information Act (FOIA)

Montana

Office of Attorney General, Justice Building, 215 N. Sanders, Helena, MT 59620; (406) 444-2026. Exemptions include unfair trade practices investigations, artificial insemination information, certain vehicle accident reports, reports of financial institutions to the Department of Commerce, and tax records. There is no time limit for responding to a request.

Nebraska

Office of Attorney General, 2115 State Capitol Building, Lincoln, NE 68509; (402) 471-2682. Exemptions include appraisal and negotiation records concerning purchase or sale of property, sales and use tax records, and income tax records.

Nevada

Office of Attorney General, Heroes Memorial Building, Carson City, NV 89710; (702) 687-4170. Exemptions include certain vital statistics, certain divorce records, certain prison commission records.

New Hampshire

Office of Attorney General, State Capitol Annex, 25 Capitol St., Concord, NH 03301-6397; (603) 271-3658. Exemptions include certain bank records, Cancer Commission records, certain records of Human Rights Commission, records of malpractice claims, certain tax information. Records legally open include city real estate records, salary information of school boards.

New Jersey

Office of Attorney General, Richard Hughes Complex Center, CN-080, Trenton, NJ 08625; (609) 984-1548. Exemptions include cancer incidence reports, certain records of Casino Control Commission, Health Department Research Studies, audits of life insurance companies.

New Mexico

Office of Attorney General, P.O. Box 1508, Santa Fe, NM 87504; (505) 827-6000. Exemptions include certain historical or educational materials, certain vital statistics.

New York

Department of State, Committee On Open Government, 162 Washington Ave., Albany NY 12231; (518) 474-2518. Exemptions include records that if disclosed would impair contract awards and collective bargaining. An agency must respond to a request within five business days of receipt of request.

North Carolina

Department of Justice, P.O. Box 629, Raleigh, NC 27602-0629; (919) 733-3377. Exemptions include certain bank records, commercial feed information, communicable disease records, national guard records, and tax records.

North Dakota

Office of the Attorney General, State Capitol, Bismarck, ND 58505; (701) 224-2210. Exemptions include air pollution records, health department studies, medical review records, legislative investigation records, veterans' records. Records legally open include medical coroner's records, school district records, State Highway Department records, Water Conservation Commission records, state engineer records, and records of charitable records on file with the secretary of state.

Ohio

Office of Attorney General, State Office Tower, 30 E. Broad St., Columbus, OH 43266-0410; (614) 466-4320. Exemptions include victim impact statements, tax information, statistics concerning veterans' exposure to caustic agents. Records legally open include city jail logs, employee address and payroll records of township trustees, complaints filed with the Division of Real Estate.

Oklahoma

Office of Attorney General, State of Oklahoma, Room 112 State Capitol, Oklahoma City, OK 73105; (405) 521-3921. Exemptions include income tax returns filed with the Oklahoma Tax Commission, certain bank records, income tax records, motor vehicle accident reports.

Oregon

Department of Justice, Justice Building, Salem, OR 97310; (503) 378-4400. Exemptions include records received or compiled by the superintendent of banks, mortality studies, motor vehicle accident reports, bank examinations, corporate tax information, personal property tax returns.

Pennsylvania

Office of Attorney General, Strawberry Square, 16th Floor, Harrisburg, PA 17120; (717) 787-3391. Exemptions include records of the state ethics commission, records of the Judicial Inquiry and Review Board, records of the PA Crime Commission. Records legally open include salaries and employment addresses of Commonwealth employees.

Rhode Island

Department of Attorney General, 72 Pine St., Providence, RI 02903; (401) 274-4400. Exemptions include charitable contributions requesting anonymity, collective bargaining, all tax returns, real estate appraisals and engineering feasibility estimates.

South Carolina

Office of Attorney General, Rembert C. Dennis Building, P.O. Box 11549, Columbus, SC 29211; (803) 734-3970. Exemptions include income tax returns, certain records of the Board of Financial Institutions, Board of Denistry records, contagious disease records, certain information given to the Securities Commission, State Development Board records. Each public body has 15 days to respond to a written request.

South Dakota

Office of Attorney General, 500 E. Capitol, State Capitol Building, Pierre, SD 57501; (605) 773-3215. Exemptions include commercial fertilizer reports, taxpayer information, hospital inspection information, savings and loan association records.

Tennessee

Office of Attorney General, 450 James Robertson Pkwy, Nashville, TN 37219-5025; (615) 741-6474. Exemptions include appraisal of real and personal property, bank examinations, records of the Medical Review Committee, tax records.

Texas

Office of Attorney General, Supreme Court Building, Austin, TX 78711-2548; (512) 463-2100. Exemptions include real and personal property appraisals and purchase price, agency reports concerning the supervision of financial institutions, geological information concerning wells, personal property tax records, sales use tax records.

Utah

Office of Attorney General, 236 State Capitol, Salt Lake City, UT 84114; (801) 538-1015. Exemptions include income tax returns, certain Insurance Commission records, certain Liquor Control Commission records, motor vehicle accident reports, sales tax returns, savings and loan association records.

Vermont

Office of Attorney General, 109 State Street, Montpelier, VT 05602; (802) 828-3171. Exemptions include tax return records, real estate appraisals, contract negotiation records. A right to appeal a request denial to the agency head exists.

Virginia

Office of Attorney General, 101 N. 8th St., Richmond, VA 23219; (804) 786-2071.

Washington

Public Disclosure Commission, 403 Evergreen Plaza, Mail Stop F-42, Olympia, WA 98505-3342; (206) 753-6200. Exemptions include taxpayer information, real estate appraisals, research data, information identifying archaeological sites, bank exams, salary and fringe information survey.

West Virginia

Office of Attorney General, Charleston, WV 25305; (303) 348-2021. Exemptions include motor vehicle accident reports, labor dispute records, tax returns, bar disciplinary records.

Wisconsin

Department of Justice, 123 W. Washington Ave., P.O. Box 7857, Madison, WI 53707-7857; (608) 266-1221. Exemptions include air pollution control records, savings bank exams, public utility accident reports.

Wyoming

Office of Attorney General, 123 Capitol Building, Cheyenne, WY 82002; (307) 777-7841. Exemptions may include details of research projects, real estate appraisals. Other statutory exemptions include motor vehicle accident reports, hospital inspection records, use tax records.

Be patient. If any phone number is incorrect, call (area code) 555-1212 and request the new listing.

Information From Lawmakers Tracking Federal Legislation

The U.S. Congress is accustomed to answering questions and sharing information with the public. Here is how you can quickly learn about any bill or resolution pending before the House of Representatives or Senate:

Free Legislation Database

This Bill Status Office can tell you the latest action on any federal legislation within seconds. Every bill and resolution for the current session as well as all House and Senate legislation dating back to 1975 are contained in LEGIS, a computerized database. When you call, it is best to give a key word or phrase (i.e., product liability, hazardous waste) which will help the congressional aides search LEGIS. This office can provide such detailed information as:

Have any bills been introduced covering a given topic?
Who is the sponsor of the bill?
How many co-sponsors are there?
When was it introduced?
Which committees have the bills been referred to?
Have any hearings been held?
Has there been any floor action?
Has a similar bill been introduced in the other chamber?
Has there been any action on the other side of the Hill?
Have the House and Senate agreed to a compromise bill?
Has the bill been sent to the White House?
Has the President signed or vetoed the bill?
What is the PL (public law) number?

Telephone assistance is free, and printouts from LEGIS are available for $.20 per page but must be picked up at the Bill Status Office. However, by making arrangements with your Representative's or Senator's office, you can avoid this nominal charge and also have the printout mailed to your home or office. Contact: LEGIS, Office of Legislative Information, House Office Building Annex 2, 3rd and D Streets, SW, Room 696, Washington, DC 20515; (202) 225-1772.

Bill Sponsor's Legislative Assistant

The aide to the Senator or Representative who is the sponsor of a particular bill is the best person to contact next. The Bill Status Office can tell you the sponsor, and the Capitol Hill Switchboard at (202) 224-3121 can transfer you to the appropriate office; then ask to speak to the person in charge of the particular bill. Usually, this congressional aide will offer to send you a copy of the bill, a press announcement, and other background information. Don't lose this opportunity to get your first of many predictions about the likelihood of the bill becoming law.

Committee Staff

Committees and subcommittees are the real work centers of the Congress. After you touch base with the Bill Status Office (LEGIS), it is wise to double-check that information with the House or Senate committees which have jurisdiction over the legislation you are tracking. The Capitol Hill Switchboard at (202) 224-3121 can connect you with any committee. Once you reach the committee staffer who handles the bill in question, you are now in a position of obtaining the following information:

Are hearings expected to be held?
Has the subcommittee or committee chair promised a vote on the measure?
What is the timetable for committee "markup" and consideration of amendments?
What is the Administration's position on the legislation?
Has the committee filed its report on the bill?
Is there any action on a similar proposal on the other side of the Hill?

You can get free copies of House bills, resolutions, and House committee reports by sending a self-addressed mailing label to the House Document Room, 2nd and D Sts., SW, Room B18, Washington, DC 20515; (202) 225-3456. Similarly, you can direct your requests for Senate documents to the Senate Document Room, Senate Hart Bldg., Room B-04, Washington, DC 20510; (202) 224-7860. Public laws, often called slip laws, can be obtained from either the House or Senate Document Rooms, but call the Bill Status Office to get the public law number. You can get printed copies of hearings by contacting the committee which conducted the inquiry, but expect several months lag time before it becomes available.

If the legislation you are concerned about is scheduled for action on the floor of the House or Senate, you can monitor its activity by the hour by listening to the following recorded messages:

House of Representatives Cloakroom
Democrat (202) 225-7400
Republican (202) 225-7430

Senate Cloakroom
Democrat (202) 224-8541
Republican (202) 224-8601

Be patient. If any phone number is incorrect, call (area code) 555-1212 and request the new listing.

Information from Lawmakers

Play Constituent

Your Representative's or Senator's office also can help with your questions about specific bills, particularly when you have difficulty getting through to committee or subcommittee staffers. Remember that Members of Congress are eager to serve their constituents, especially for simple requests such as sending you copies of bills or new public laws. The Capitol Hill Switchboard Operator at (202) 224-3121 can connect you with the Washington office of your Representative and Senators.

Additional Tools for Monitoring Federal Legislation

There are sophisticated variations of the free LEGIS database described above. One reason for the growth of commercial databases is that direct online access to LEGIS is limited to Members of Congress and their staff. The following databanks cover every bill or resolution pending before the current session:

• Electronic Legislative Search System
This online system tracks all current federal legislation (as well as all 50 states) and also provides introductory bill summaries and legislative histories. Contact: Commerce Clearinghouse, 4025 W. Peterson Avenue, Chicago, IL 60646, (312) 583-8500.

• Legi-Slate
This computerized system provides information based primarily on the *Congressional Record*, the official edited transcript of the House and Senate floor proceedings. This database also contains committee schedules, all recorded votes and analyses voting patterns. Contact: Legi-Slate, 777 N.Capitol St., NE, Suite 900, Washington, DC 20002; (202) 898-2300.

• Washington Alert Service
This database covers all bills introduced in the U.S. Congress and includes information on committee schedules, release of committee reports and other documents, all recorded votes as well as full text of the publication, *CQ Weekly Report*. Contact: Congressional Quarterly, 1414 22nd Street, NW, Washington, DC 20037; (202) 887-8500.

There are plenty of specialized trade publications designed to help lobbyists stay apprised of developments on the Hill. Online access is available to some of these newsletters, for instance, the Bureau of National Affairs' *Daily Tax Advance* and *Daily Congressional and Presidential Calendar* (BNA OnLine, 1227 25th St., NW, Room 3-268, Washington, DC 20037; (800) 862-4636 or (202) 452-4453). Another example is Budgetrack, a database produced by the editors of *Aviation Week and Space Technology*, which monitors the budget for the U.S. Defense Department and NASA from presidential submission to final congressional action (Budgetrack is available online from Data Resources, Inc., 1750 K St., NW, Washington DC 20006).

The American Enterprise Institute, the Brookings Institution, and other Washington-based think tanks generate position papers on specific legislative initiatives and often will share their information with the public. Other useful outside sources which can shed light on activities on the Hill are both small,

specialized trade associations and large ones, for example, the National Paint and Coating Association and the U.S. Chamber of Commerce. How successful you are at getting these organizations to help you depends in large measure on how good you are on the telephone.

Congressional Experts

An estimated 4,000 legislative assistants and committee aides fall into the category of "professional staff." Because these congressional aides often draft bills and amendments and play a critical role in the negotiations with special interest groups, they are valuable sources of information, but some are much more open and candid than others. When dealing with these experts, remember they are at the beck and call of an elected official. It doesn't hurt to appeal to their egos and offer to call them when they aren't quite so busy.

Investigations and Special Reports

There are approximately 50 congressional committees and subcommittees which do not have legislative authority but serve as watchdogs with responsibility for reviewing existing laws. Some examples include the Senate Permanent Subcommittee on Investigations, House Select Committee on Aging, the Joint Economic Committee, and the House Science and Technology Subcommittee on Investigations and Oversight. These congressional panels conduct full-scale hearings on a wide range of subjects. A complete listing of these committees appears in the U.S. Congress Committees section. Some hearings conducted by the House Energy and Commerce Subcommittee on Oversight and Investigations during the 100th Congress include the following examples:

"Biotechnology: Vaccine Development"
"EPA's Asbestos Regulations"
"Sulfites"
"Ground Water Monitoring"
"Unfair Foreign Trade Practices"
"SEC and Corporate Audits"
"SEC: Oversight of the Edgar System"

Many of these committees will put you on their mailing lists to receive notices of upcoming hearings as well as their *Committee Calendar*, which lists all of the hearings held during the previous year.

Congressional Caucuses

Approximately 100 non-legislative caucuses formed by Members of Congress serve as in-house think tanks. Some of these coalitions, such as the Congressional Clearinghouse on the Future, provide information to the public. The House Steel Caucus, the Senate Coal Caucus, the Congressional Port Caucus, and others work to get their particular legislative initiatives through the Congress. The staff directors of these organizations can be good sources because these congressional aides have access to all government studies and also have close contact with industry and special interests that the caucus is going to bat for.

Tracking Federal Legislation

Many of these "informal groups" dissolve after work on its legislative priorities is completed, so you should expect that these organizations come and go. A list of these organizations appear next in U.S. Congress Committees section. Note that the Capitol Hill Switchboard at (202) 224-3121 or your Member of Congress can help you find out if a particular special interest caucus exists. A list of the current caucuses appears in the U.S. Congress Committee section.

Federal Agencies Legislative Affairs Offices

Every federal department and agency has an office which makes the Administration's case for the President's proposed budget or legislation. These offices within the executive branch usually are termed the "Offices of Legislative Affairs," which concentrate on particular bills. This is in contrast to an agency's own Office of Congressional Relations, which tends to respond to requests made by lawmakers or their staff. The office of legislative affairs also makes available written testimony by agency officials who appeared as witnesses at congressional hearings.

Arms of Congress

In addition to the 47 House and Senate committees, the following four organizations produce volumes of information and reports to aid lawmakers. These studies and recommendations by these arms of Congress are available to the public.

* **Congressional Budget Office**
House Office Building Annex 2
2nd and D Streets SW
Washington, DC 20515 (202) 226-2800
Scorekeeping reports, special studies and other economic assessments are all available free to the public.

* **Congressional Research Service**
Library of Congress
See also the Current Events and Homework Chapter for a comprehensive listing of all CRS studies which cover practically every current event topic. You must arrange to get copies of any CRS publications through your Member of Congress.)

* **General Accounting Office**
Office of Public Affairs Room 7049
441 G Street NW
Washington, DC 20548 (202) 275-2812
Reports and audit information about every government program.

* **Office of Technology Assessment**
U.S. Congress
Information Center
Washington, DC 20510 (202) 228-6150
Studies and executive summaries are available on a whole range of subjects.

Be patient. If any phone number is incorrect, call (area code) 555-1212 and request the new listing.

Information from Lawmakers

U.S. Congress Committees

There is virtually *no* subject that is ignored by some office of the legislative branch of the federal government. Why? The voters back home raise all sorts of concerns with their elected officials. Every special interest group lobbies for this or that. And, each year the President proposes a federal budget which affects every taxpayer. Since Congress controls the government's purse strings, lawmakers ultimately decide the fate of practically every issue facing the country.

Every subject, from aquaculture to zinc, is monitored by some congressional employee. Many committees have authority over all these subjects. Over 100 House and Senate committees and subcommittees oversee the defense; the U.S. Department of Housing and Urban Development is subject to the jurisdiction of over 84 committees; and 54 House panels and 21 Senate panels have responsibility for some aspect of the "War on Drugs." Using the seven phone call rule, you will find someone who can be a useful information source. It may be an aide who works directly for a Senator or Congressman, a subcommittee staffer who serves either the Democratic or Republican Members of that subcommittee, an employee at one of the special interest congressional organizations such as the Senate Wine Caucus, or a specialist at the Congressional Research Service or another think tanks of the legislative branch.

The staff at the committees, subcommittees, special interest caucuses, and other congressional organizations listed here can all share their expertise over the phone, refer you to other specialists, and send publications to you free of charge. Congress tends to be particularly responsive to information requests because almost every legislator wants your vote.

Telephone Connection with Lawmakers and Staff

Although there is no central office for the U.S. Congress, the central switchboard operators at (202) 224-3121 can connect you with every Washington office of every Senator, every member of the House of Representatives, every committee, and most of the in-house congressional caucuses. To contact members of the Senate staff call or write the Senate Locator, U.S. Senate, Washington, DC 20510; (202) 224-3207, or the House Finance office, U.S. Capitol, Washington, DC 20515; (202) 225-6514. You needn't bother with room numbers and office buildings when writing to various offices. Simply address correspondence to any Senator or Senate office, followed by U.S. Capitol, Washington, DC 20510; and for any Member of the House or House committee, write the U.S. Capitol, Washington, DC 20515.

Senate Legislative Committees

The work of drafting and considering legislation is done largely by 16 "standing" or permanent committees. They evaluate proposed federal laws authored by individual Senators, the executive branch, and outside organizations and experts. Each bill and resolution is usually referred to the appropriate committee or committees, which may report a bill out in its original form, favorably or unfavorably recommend amendments, or allow the proposed legislation to die in committee without action. Committees are divided into subcommittees which conduct hearings, consider and amend legislation, and may either approve or reject the bills. On behalf of the Senate, these committees, with rare exception, determine what reaches the floor. In the process they modify--sometimes extensively--proposals referred to them.

In addition, committees serve as congressional watchdogs of the executive branch. They oversee the organization and operations of the executive branch agencies and are responsible for knowing how efficiently and effectively the agencies perform their duties and whether and how they are carrying out the intent of the laws enacted by Congress. Under the Senate's "advise and consent" responsibility, these committees decide whether or not to confirm the President's nominees to the executive and judicial branches.

These legislative committees produce reams of studies, committee reports, published hearings, and the committee staff are specialists in the areas which fall within the committee's jurisdiction. Both the majority committee staff, currently the Democrats who control the Senate, and the minority staff, the Republican committee staff, operate independently of one another and both can provide different viewpoints on issues, predictions about the fate of particular bills, and suggest people to contact both in the executive branch and organizations lobbying for or against pending legislation.

* Senate Committee on Agriculture, Nutrition and Forestry
Suite SR-328A Russell Senate Office Building
Washington, DC 20510 (202) 224-2035
Topics covered: agriculture; forestry and forest reserves; farm credit; school nutrition; and food stamp programs.

Be patient. If any phone number is incorrect, call (area code) 555-1212 and request the new listing.

U.S. Congress Committees

Subcommittees:
Agricultural Credit
Agricultural Production and Stabilization of Prices
Agricultural Research, and General Legislation
Conservation and Forestry
Domestic and Foreign Marketing and Product Promotion
Nutrition and Investigations
Rural Development and Rural Electrification

* Senate Committee on Appropriations

Suite S-128 Capitol
Washington, DC 20510 (202) 224-7282
Topics covered: appropriations of revenues for executive agencies and Federal programs.

Subcommittees:
Agriculture and Related Agencies . . . . (202) 224-7240
Commerce, Justice, State, and Judiciary . . . . (202) 224-7277
Defense . . . . (202) 224-7255
District of Columbia . . . . (202) 224-2731
Energy and Water Development . . . . (202) 224-7260
Foreign Operations . . . . (202) 224-7284
HUD-Independent Agencies . . . . (202) 224-7231
Interior and Related Agencies . . . . (202) 224-7214
Labor, Health and Human Services, Education, and
Related Agencies . . . . (202) 224-7288
Legislative Branch . . . . (202) 224-7338
Military Construction . . . . (202) 224-7276
Transportation and Related Agencies . . . . (202) 224-0330
Treasury, Postal Service, and General Government . . . . . . (202) 224-6280
VA, HUD and Independent Agencies . . . . (202) 224-7231

* Senate Committee on the Armed Services

Suite SR-228 Russell Senate Office Building
Washington, DC 20510 (202) 224-3871
Topics covered: military and defense matters.

Subcommittees:
Strategic Forces and Nuclear Deterrence
Conventional Forces and Alliance Defense
Projection Forces and Regional Defense
Defense Industry and Technology
Readiness, Sustainability, and Support
Manpower and Personnel

* Senate Committee on Banking, Housing, and Urban Affairs

Suite SD-534 Dirksen Senate Office Building
Washington, DC 20510 (202) 224-7391
Topics covered: banks and other financial institutions; public and private housing; Federal monetary policy; urban development; mass transit; and certain foreign trade matters.

Subcommittees:
Housing and Urban Affairs . . . . (202) 224-6348
International Finance and Monetary Policy
Securities
Consumer and Regulatory Affairs
[The rest of the subcommittees can be reached at (202) 224-7391.]

* Senate Committee on the Budget

SD-621 Dirksen Senate Office Building
Washington, DC 20510 (202) 224-0642
Topics covered: coordination of appropriations and revenues in Federal budget.
This committee has no subcommittees.

* Senate Committee on Commerce, Science, and Transportation

Suite SD-508 Dirksen Senate Office Building
Washington, DC 20510 (202) 224-5115

Topics covered: regulation of interstate transportation, including railroads, buses, trucks, ships, pipelines, and civil aviation; Coast Guard; Merchant Marine; science and technology research policy; communications; non-military aeronautical and space sciences; coastal zone management; and oceans policy.

Subcommittees:
Aviation
Communications
Consumer
Foreign Commerce and Tourism
Merchant Marine
Science, Technology, and Space
Surface Transportation
National Ocean Policy Study

* Senate Committee on Energy and Natural Resources

Suite SD-304 Dirksen Senate Office Building
Washington, DC 20510 (202) 224-4971
Topics covered: regulation, conservation, and research and development of all forms of energy; mining; national parks; wilderness areas and historical sites; and territorial possessions of the U.S.

Subcommittees:
Energy Regulation and Conservation
Energy Research and Development
Mineral Resources Development and Production
Public Lands, National Parks and Forests
Water and Power

* Senate Committee on Environment and Public Works

Suite SD-458 Dirksen Senate Office Building
Washington, DC 20510 (202) 224-6176
Topics covered: environmental protection; water resources and flood control; public works and buildings; highways; and noise pollution.

Subcommittees:
Environmental Protection
Nuclear Regulation
Superfund, Ocean and Water Protection
Toxic Substances, Environmental Oversight, Research and Development
Water Resources, Transportation and Infrastructure

* Senate Committee on Finance

Suite SD-205 Dirksen Senate Office Building
Washington, DC 20510 (202) 224-4515
Topics covered: taxes; tariffs; import quotas; old-age and survivors insurance; Medicare; unemployment insurance; general revenue sharing.

Subcommittees:
Defecit, Debt Management and International Debt
Energy and Agricultural Taxation
Health for Families and the Uninsured
International Debt
International Trade
Medicare and Long Term Care
Private Retirement Plans and Oversight of the Internal Revenue Service
Social Security and Family Policy
Taxation and Debt Management

* Senate Committee on Foreign Relations

Suite SD-419 Dirksen Senate Office Building
Washington, DC 20510 (202) 224-4651
Topics covered: foreign policy; treaties; diplomatic affairs; United Nations.

Subcommittees:
African Affairs
East Asian and Pacific Affairs
European Affairs
International Economic Policy, Trade, Oceans and Environment
Near Eastern and South Asian Affairs
Terrorism, Narcotics, and International Communications
Western Hemisphere and Peace Corps Affairs

Be patient. If any phone number is incorrect, call (area code) 555-1212 and request the new listing.

Information from Lawmakers

* Senate Committee on Governmental Affairs

Suite SD-340 Dirksen Senate Office Building
Washington, DC 20510 (202) 224-4751
Topics covered: budget and accounting matters; organization and reorganization of executive branch; intergovernmental relations; municipal affairs of the District of Columbia; civil service; postal service; and the census.

Subcommittees:

Federal Services, Post Office, and Civil Service .... (202) 224-2254
General Services, Federalism, and the District of Columbia .. (202) 224-4718
Government Information and Regulation .... (202) 224-9000
Oversight of Government Management .... (202) 224-3682
Permanent Subcommittee on Investigations .... (202) 224-3721

* Senate Committee on the Judiciary

Suite SD-224
Dirksen Senate Office Building
Washington, DC 20510 (202) 224-5225
Topics covered: Federal courts and judges; civil rights and civil liberties; constitutional amendments; interstate compacts; legislative apportionment; antitrust and monopoly; and immigration and naturalization.

Subcommittees:

Antitrust, Monopolies and Business Rights .... (202) 224-5701
Constitution .... (202) 224-5573
Courts and Administrative Practice .... (202) 224-4022
Immigration and Refugee Affairs .... (202) 224-6098
Patents, Copyrights, and Trademarks .... (202) 224-7704
Technology and the Law .... (202) 224-8254

* Senate Committee on Labor and Human Resources

Suite SD-428 Dirksen Senate Office Building
Washington, DC 20510 (202) 224-5375
Topics covered: education, labor, health, and public welfare.

Subcommittees:

Aging .... (202) 224-3239
Children, Family, Drugs and Alcoholism .... (202) 224-5630
Education, Arts, and Humanities .... (202) 224-7666
Employment and Productivity .... (202) 224-5575
Disabilities Policies .... (202) 224-6265
Labor .... (202) 224-5546

* Senate Committee on Rules and Administration

Suite SR-305 Russell Senate Office Building
Washington, DC 20510 (202) 224-6352
Topics covered: rules of the Senate; Senate employees; management of the Senate; Federal elections; Presidential succession; the Smithsonian Institution; the Library of Congress. The Committee has no subcommittees.

* Senate Committee on Small Business

Suite SR-428A Russell Senate Office Building
Washington, DC 20510 (202) 224-5175
FAX: 224-5619
Topics covered: measures relating to small businesses generally, and to the Small Business Administration.

Subcommittees:

Competitive and Economic Opportunities
Export Expansion
Government Contracting and Paperwork Reduction
Innovation, Technology, and Productivity
Rural Economy and Family Farming
Urban and Minority-Owned Business Development

* Senate Committee on Veterans' Affairs

Suite SR-414 Russell Senate Office Building
Washington, DC 20510 (202) 224-9126
Topics covered: veterans' affairs, including pensions, medical care, life insurance, education, and rehabilitation. This Committee has no subcommittees.

Senate Think Tanks and Committees

Congressional studies and policy options are byproducts of these Senate committees. Usually established for a limited period of time, these committees ordinarily deal with more specific issues and problems than do the legislative committees. The political party organizations are permanent committees, but others are usually established for a specific period of time or until the project for which they have been created has been completed. Most select committees may investigate, study, and make recommendations, but they have no authority to make legislation. The Select and Special Committees of the Senate are as follows:

Special Committee on Aging
Room SD G-31 Dirksen Senate Office Building; Washington, DC 20510; (202) 224-5364.

Select Committee on Ethics
Room SH-220 Hart Senate Office Building; Washington, DC 20510; (202) 224-2981.

Select Committee on Indian Affairs
Room SH-838 Hart Senate Office Building; Washington, DC 20510; (202) 224-2251; FAX: 224-2309.

Select Committee on Intelligence
Room SH-211 Hart Senate Office Building; Washington, DC 20510; (202) 224-1700.

Democratic Policy Committee
Rooms S-118 and S-318 The Capitol; Washington, DC 20510; (202) 224-5551.

Democratic Senatorial Campaign Committee
430 South Capitol St., SE; Washington, DC 20003; (202) 224-2447; FAX: 485-3120.

National Republican Senatorial Committee
425 Second St., NE; Washington, DC 20002; (202) 675-6000; FAX: 675-6058.

Conference of the Minority
Room SH-405 Hart Senate Office Building; Washington, DC 20510; (202) 224-2764.

Republican Policy Committee
Room SR-347 Russell Senate Office Building; Washington, DC 20510; (202) 224-2946.

Senate Division POW-MIA Committee
Hart Senate Office Bldg.; Suite 705; Washington, DC 20510-6500; (202) 224-2306.

House of Representatives Legislative Committees

The work of drafting and considering legislation is done largely by 22 committees. The jurisdictions of the House committees are similar to the 16 Senate committees; however, the House subcommittees usually play a much more important role than their Senate counterparts. The committees and subcommittees, with rare exception, determine what legislation will be considered by the entire House. In the process they modify--sometimes extensively--proposals referred to them. The committees, like the Senate committees, serve as congressional watchdogs of the executive branch. They oversee the organization and operations of the executive branch agencies--for knowing how efficiently and effectively the agencies perform their duties, and for knowing whether and how they are carrying out the intent of the laws enacted by Congress. These

Be patient. If any phone number is incorrect, call (area code) 555-1212 and request the new listing.

U.S. Congress Committees

legislative committees are tremendous generators of information on all the issues over which they have jurisdiction, and both the committee and subcommittee staff are accessible and useful contacts.

* House Committee on Agriculture

1301 Longworth House Office Building
Washington, DC 20515 · (202) 225-2171
Topics covered: agriculture and forestry measures, including farm credit, crop insurance, soil conservation, rural electrification, domestic marketing, and nutrition.

Subcommittees:
Conservation, Credit, and Rural Development
Cotton, Rice, and Sugar
Department Operations, Research and Foreign Agriculture
Domestic Marketing, Consumer Relations, and Nutrition
Forests, Family Farms, and Energy
Livestock, Dairy, and Poultry
Tobacco and Peanuts
Wheat, Soybeans, and Feed Grains

* House Committee on Appropriations

H-218 Capitol Building
Washington, DC 20515 · (202) 225-2771
Topics covered: appropriation of revenue for executive agencies and Federal programs and activities.

Subcommittees:
Commerce, Justice, State, The Judiciary, and
 Related Agencies · (202) 225-3351
Defense · (202) 225-2847
District of Columbia · (202) 225-5338
Energy and Water Development · (202) 225-3421
Foreign Operations, Export Financing, and Related Programs · (202) 225-2041
Interior · (202) 225-3081
Labor, Health and Human Services, Education, and
 Related Agencies · (202) 225-3508
Legislative · (202) 225-5338
Military Construction · (202) 225-3047
Rural Development, Agriculture, and Related Agencies · (202) 225-2638
Transportation · (202) 225-2141
Treasury, Postal Service, and General Government · (202) 225-5834
VA, HUD, and Independent Agencies · (202) 225-3241

* House Committee on Armed Services

2120 Rayburn House Office Building
Washington, DC 20515 · (202) 225-4151
Topics covered: defense matters, including procurement practices, weapons systems, manpower, military intelligence, naval petroleum reserves, and military applications of nuclear energy.

Subcommittees:
Investigations
Military Installations and Facilities
Military Personnel and Compensation
Procurement and Military Nuclear Systems
Readiness
Research and Development
Seapower and Strategic and Critical Materials

* House Committee on Banking, Finance, and Urban Affairs

2129 Rayburn House Office Building
Washington, DC 20515 · (202) 225-4247
Topics covered: banking and currency legislation; international financial organizations; public and private housing.

Subcommittees:
Consumer Affairs and Coinage

Domestic Monetary Policy
Economic Stabilization
Financial Institutions Supervision, Regulation, and Insurance
General Oversight and Investigations
Housing and Community Development
International Development, Finance, Trade, and Monetary Policy
Policy Research and Insurance

* House Committee on the Budget

214 House Office Building
Annex I
Washington, DC 20515 · (202) 226-7200
Topics covered: coordination of spending and revenues in Federal budget.

Task Forces:
Budget Process, Reconciliation, and Enforcement
Community Development and Natural Resources
Defense, Foreign Policy and Space
Urgent Fiscal Issues
Human Resources
Economic Policy, Projections, and Revenues

* House Committee on the District of Columbia

1310 Longworth House Office Building
Washington, DC 20515 · (202) 225-4457
Topics covered: Municipal affairs and administration of the District of Columbia.

Subcommittees:
Fiscal Affairs and Health
Government Operations and Metropolitan Affairs
Judiciary and Education

* House Committee on Education and Labor

2181 Rayburn House Office Building
Washington, DC 20515 · (202) 225-4527
Topics covered: education and labor legislation, including vocational rehabilitation, minimum wage legislation, and school lunch programs.

Subcommittees:
Elementary, Secondary, and Vocational Education
Employment Opportunities
Health and Safety
Human Resources
Labor-Management Relations
Labor Standards
Postsecondary Education
Select Education

* House Energy and Commerce Committee

2125 Rayburn House Office Building
Washington, DC 20515 · (202) 225-2927
Topics covered: National energy policy generally, including energy pricing, transmission, and conservation; interstate commerce; communications; securities and exchanges; health care; biomedical research; railroads and railroad labor; and consumer affairs and protection.

Subcommittees:
Commerce, Consumer Protection, and Competitiveness · (202) 226-3160
Energy and Power · (202) 226-2500
Health and the Environment · (202) 225-4952
Oversight and Investigations · (202) 225-4441
Telecommunications and Finance · (202) 226-2424
Transportation and Hazardous Materials · (202) 225-9304
Minority Staff · (202) 225-3641

* House Committee on Foreign Affairs

2170 Rayburn House Office Building
Washington, DC 20515 · (202) 225-5021
Topics covered: foreign relations; international trade and economic policy; Food For Peace; international commodity agreements.

Be patient. If any phone number is incorrect, call (area code) 555-1212 and request the new listing.

Information from Lawmakers

Subcommittees:

Africa . . . . (202) 226-7807
Arms Control, International Security, and Science . . . . (202) 225-8926
Asian and Pacific Affairs . . . . (202) 226-7801
Europe and the Middle East . . . . (202) 225-3345
Human Rights and International Organizations . . . . (202) 226-7825
International Economic Policy and Trade . . . . (202) 226-7820
International Operations . . . . (202) 225-3424
Western Hemisphere Affairs . . . . (202) 226-7812

* House Committee on Government Operations

2157 Rayburn House Office Building
Washington, DC 20515 (202) 225-5051

Topics covered: Executive branch reorganization, intergovernmental relations, and revenue sharing.

Subcommittees:

Commerce, Consumer, and Monetary Affairs . . . . (202) 225-4407
Employment and Housing . . . . (202) 225-6751
Environment, Energy, and Natural Resources . . . . (202) 225-6427
Government Activities and Transportation . . . . (202) 225-7920
Government Information, Justice, and Agriculture . . . . (202) 225-3741
Human Resources and Intergovernmental Relations . . . . (202) 225-2548
Legislation and National Security . . . . (202) 225-5147

* House Committee on House Administration

H-326 Capitol Building
Washington, DC 20515 (202) 225-2061

Topics covered: House administration and management; Federal election legislation; Library of Congress; and the Smithsonian Institution.

Subcommittees:

Accounts . . . . (202) 226-7540
Elections . . . . (202) 226-7616
Libraries and Memorials . . . . (202) 226-2307
Office Systems . . . . (202) 225-1608
Personnel and Police . . . . (202) 226-7641
Procurement and Printing . . . . (202) 225-4568
Task Force on Legislative Service Organizations . . . . (202) 225-2061

* House Committee on Interior and Insular Affairs

1324 Longworth House Office Building
Washington, DC 20515 (202) 225-2761

Topics covered: public lands; national parks and military cemeteries; irrigation; reclamation; U.S. territories and possessions; Indian affair; and regulation of domestic nuclear energy industry.

Subcommittees:

Energy and the Environment . . . . (202) 226-4085
General Oversight and Investigations . . . . (202) 225-8331
Insular and International Affairs . . . . (202) 225-9297
Mining and Natural Resources . . . . (202) 226-7761
National Parks and Public Lands . . . . (202) 226-7736
Water, Power, and Offshore Energy Resources . . . . (202) 225-6042
Indian Affairs Office . . . . (202) 226-7393

* House Committee on the Judiciary

2137 Rayburn House Office Building
Washington, DC 20515 (202) 225-3951

Topics covered: Federal courts; constitutional amendments; immigration and naturalization; Presidential succession; antitrust and monopolies; impeachment resolutions; and patents, trademarks, and copyrights.

Subcommittees:

Administrative Law and Governmental Relations . . . . (202) 225-5741
Civil and Constitutional Rights . . . . (202) 226-7680
Courts, Intellectual Property, and the Administration
 of Justice . . . . (202) 225-3926
Crime and Criminal Justice . . . . (202) 226-2406
Economic and Commercial Law . . . . (202) 225-2825
Immigration, Refugees, and International Law . . . . (202) 225-5727

* House Committee on the Merchant Marine and Fisheries

1334 Longworth House Office Building
Washington, DC 20515 (202) 225-4047

Topics covered: regulation and protection of fisheries and wildlife; Coast Guard; merchant marine; and the Panama Canal.

Subcommittees:

Coast Guard and Navigation . . . . (202) 226-3587
Fisheries and Wildlife Conservation and the Environment . . . (202) 226-3533
Merchant Marine . . . . (202) 225-6785
Oceanography, Great Lakes and Outer Continental Shelf . . . . (202) 226-3504
Oversight and Investigations . . . . (202) 226-3508

* House Committee on the Post Office and Civil Service

309 Cannon House Office Building
Washington, DC 20515 (202) 225-4054

Topics covered: Postal Service; civil service; and Federal statistics.

Subcommittees:

Census and Population . . . . (202) 226-7523
Civil Service . . . . (202) 225-4025
Compensation and Employee Benefits . . . . (202) 226-7546
Human Resources . . . . (202) 225-2821
Investigations . . . . (202) 225-6295
Postal Operations and Services . . . . (202) 225-9124
Postal Personnel and Modernization . . . . (202) 226-7520

* House Committee on Public Works and Transportation

2165 Rayburn House Office Building
Washington, DC 20515 (202) 225-4472

Topics covered: public buildings and roads; bridges and dams; flood control; rivers and harbors; watershed development; mass transit; surface transportation excluding railroads; and civil aviation.

Subcommittees:

Aviation . . . . (202) 225-9161
Economic Development . . . . (202) 225-6151
Investigations and Oversight . . . . (202) 225-3274
Public Buildings and Grounds . . . . (202) 225-9961
Surface Transportation . . . . (202) 225-9989
Water Resources . . . . (202) 225-0060

* House Committee on Rules

H-312 Capitol Building
Washington, DC 20515 (202) 225-9486

Topics covered: resolutions governing the disposition of business on the House floor; rules of the House (except for the House Code of Official Conduct); and waivers relating to legislative deadlines imposed by the Congressional Budget Act.

Subcommittees:

Rules of the House . . . . (202) 225-9588
The Legislative Process . . . . (202) 225-1037

* House Committee on Science, Space, and Technology

2320 Rayburn House Office Building (202) 225-6371
Washington, DC 20515 FAX 225-8280

Topics covered: astronautical research and development; energy research and development; space; and scientific research and development.

Subcommittees:

Energy Research and Development . . . . (202) 225-8056
Investigations and Oversight . . . . (202) 225-4494
International Scientific Cooperation . . . . (202) 226-3636
Science, Research, and Technology . . . . (202) 225-9622
Space Science and Applications . . . . (202) 225-8844
Transportation, Aviation, and Materials . . . . (202) 225-8105

Be patient. If any phone number is incorrect, call (area code) 555-1212 and request the new listing.

U.S. Congress Committees

* House Committee on Small Business

2361 Rayburn House Office Building
Washington, DC 20515 (202) 225-5821

Topics covered: measures related to small business generally, and to the Small Business Administration.

Subcommittees:

Antitrust, Impact of Deregulation and Privatization .... (202) 225-6026
Environment and Labor .... (202) 225-7673
Exports, Tax Policy, and Special Problems .... (202) 225-8944
Procurement, Tourism, and Rural Development .... (202) 225-9368
Regulation, Business Opportunity, and Energy .... (202) 225-7797
SBA, The General Economy, and Minority
Enterprise Development .... (202) 225-5821

* House Committee on Standards of Official Conduct

HT-2, Capitol Building
Washington, DC 20515 (202) 225-7103

Topics covered: enforcement of Code of Official Conduct. The Committee has no subcommittees.

* House Committee on Veterans' Affairs

335 Cannon House Office Building
Washington, DC 20515 (202) 225-3527

Topics covered: veterans' affairs, including pensions, medical care, life insurance, education, and rehabilitation.

Subcommittees:

Hospitals and Health Care .... (202) 225-9154
Compensation, Pension, and Insurance .... (202) 225-3569
Oversight and Investigations .... (202) 225-3541
Education, Training and Employment .... (202) 225-9166
Housing and Memorial Affairs .... (202) 225-9164

* House Committee on Ways and Means

1102 Longworth House Office Building
Washington, DC 20515 (202) 225-3625

Topics covered: taxation, social security, tariffs, and health care programs financed through payroll taxes.

Subcommittees:

Health .... (202) 225-7785
Human Resources .... (202) 225-1025
Oversight .... (202) 225-5522
Select Revenue Measures .... (202) 225-9710
Social Security .... (202) 225-9263
Trade .... (202) 225-3943

House Investigative Committees and Think Tanks

Many of these House committees conduct hearings and issue reports and recommendations. The Committee on Intelligence, which oversees the Central Intelligence Agency (CIA) and other national security operations, has both investigative and legislative authority. Several of these select committees, such as the Committee on Aging and the Committee on Children, Youth, and Family, will most likely continue their work well into the 1990s. The various political party organizations, such as the Democratic Study Group, issue numerous policy papers on such broad issues as health care, education, and defense. Don't overlook these committees; the staff experts are very knowledgeable.

Permanent Select Committee on Intelligence
Room H-405, The Capitol Building, Washington, DC 20515; (202) 225-4121.
Subcommittees: Legislation .... (202) 225-7311;
Oversight and Evaluation .... (202) 225-5658;
Program and Budget Authorization .... (202) 225-7690

Select Committee on Aging
Room H1-712, House Office Building Annex I, 300 New Jersey Ave., SE, Washington, DC 20515; (202) 226-3375.

Select Committee on Narcotics and Abuse and Control
Room H2-234, House Office Building Annex 2, Second and D Streets, SW, Washington, DC 20515; (202) 226-3040.

Select Committee on Children, Youth, and Families
H2-385 House Office Building Annex 2, Washington, DC 20515; (202) 226-7660.

Select Committee on Hunger
Room H2-505 House Office Building Annex 2, Second and D Sts., SW, Washington, DC 20515; (202) 226-5470.

Federal Government Service Task Force
Room H2-301, House Office Building Annex 2, Washington, DC 20515; (202) 226-2494.

Democratic Congressional Campaign Committee
430 South Capitol St., SE, Washington, DC 20003; (202) 863-1500.

Democratic Steering and Policy Committee
Room H-226, The Capitol Building, Washington, DC 20515; (202) 225-8550.

Democratic Study Group
Room 1422, Longworth House Office Building, Washington, DC 20515; (202) 225-5858.

National Republican Congressional Committee
320 First St., SE, Washington, DC 20003; (202) 479-7000.

Republican Policy Committee
Room 1616 Longworth House Office Building, Washington, DC 20515; (202) 225-6168.

Minority WHIP Committee
Room 1620 Longworth House Office Building, Washington, DC 20515; (202) 225-0197.

Joint Committees of the U.S. Congress

Congress uses joint committees for study and administrative purposes. Usually joint committees study broad and complex areas of interest to the entire Congress. They are usually permanent bodies composed of an equal number of House and Senate members. Members of these committees are appointed under the provisions of the measure establishing them.

Joint Committee on the Library of Congress
Room H1-103, House Annex I, Washington, DC 20510; (202) 226-7633.

Joint Committee on Printing
Room SH-818, U.S. Hart Senate Office Building, Washington, DC 20510-6650; (202) 224-5241; FAX: 224-1176. Arm of the Committee: Congressional Record Index Office; U.S. Government Printing Office, Room C-738, North Capitol and H Sts., Washington, DC 20401; (202) 512-0275.

Joint Committee on Taxation
Room 1015 Longworth House Office Building, Washington, DC 20515-6453; (202) 225-3621.

Joint Economic Committee
Room SD-G01 Dirksen Senate Office Building, Washington, DC 20510; (202) 224-5171.
Subcommittees: International Economic Policy Technology and National Security Economics; Economic Growth, Trade, and Taxes; Fiscal and Monetary Policy; Economic Goals and Intergovernmental Policy; Economic Resources and Competitiveness; and Investment, Jobs, and Prices; Education and Health.

Congressional Budget Office
2nd and D Streets, SW, Washington, DC 20515; (202) 226-2621. This nonpartisan think tank works closely with the House and Senate Budget Committees and helps lawmakers analyze both the fiscal and budgetary consequences of

Information from Lawmakers

legislation and the interaction between the federal budget and the nation's economy. CBO maintains current tabs of spending actions, prepares cost estimates for bills, provides funding alternatives for bills, reports annual projections for new budget activities, and issues advisory reports that estimate whether the projected deficit exceeds that allowed by law.

Special Interest Congressional Organizations

Congressional Member Organizations (CMOs)–commonly known as informal groups, caucuses, coalitions, or ad hoc task forces–are voluntary associations of Members of Congress created to play a role in the policy process. Unlike the formal leadership and party organizations, these groups operate without direct recognition in the chamber rules or line item appropriations. At least 114 congressional Member organizations are currently operating. Listed below are some of the groups which Senators and Congressmen have formed to exercise a stronger voice about certain regional, ethnic, industrial, or other concerns related to their state or congressional district. Some caucuses have a primary mission to disseminate information, while others serve as an informal in-house lobby on various policies. Listed are groups which may be of particular interest to the public as all caucuses produce reports, monitor legislation, and can serve as useful resources.

Adoption, Congressional Coalition on
332 Dirksen Senate Office Bldg., Washington, DC 20510; (202) 224-2841

Afghanistan, Congressional Task Force on
SH-531 Hart Bldg., Washington, DC 20510; (202) 224-2841

Agricultural Caucus
Northeast-1127 Longworth Bldg., Washington, DC 20515; (202) 225-3665

Agricultural Forum
Congressional-1226 Longworth Bldg., Washington, DC 20510; (202) 225-6605

Air and Space Caucus
Senate-SH-313 Hart Bldg., Washington, DC 20510; (202) 224-5744

Alcohol Fuels Caucus
Congressional-SH-317 Hart Bldg., Washington, DC 20510; (202) 224-2321

Anti-Terrorism Caucus
Senate-SH-520 Hart Bldg., Washington, DC 20510; (202) 224-6542

Arms Control and Foreign Policy Caucus
H2-501 House Office Bldg., Annex 2, Washington, DC 20515.

Arts Caucus
Congressional-H2-345 House Office Bldg. Annex 2, Washington, DC 20515; (202) 226-2456

Arts, Concerned Senators for the
SR-140 Senate Russell Bldg., Washington, DC 20510; (202) 224-2315

Automotive Caucus
Congressional-2366 Rayburn Bldg., Washington, DC 20515; (202) 225-2806

Aviation Forum
2311 Rayburn Bldg., Washington, DC 20515; (202) 225-6216

Balanced Budget, Congressional Leaders United For a
1034 Longworth Bldg., Washington, DC 20515.

Baltic States and Ukraine, Ad Hoc Congressional Committee on the
2442 Rayburn Bldg., Washington, DC 20515; (202) 225-6276. Will change in January.

Bearing Caucus
Congressional-119 Cannon Bldg., Washington, DC 20515.

Beef Caucus
House-118 Cannon Bldg., Washington, DC 20515; (202) 225-6730

Black Caucus
Congressional-H2-344 House Office Bldg. Annex 2, Washington, DC 20515; (202) 226-7790

Border Caucus
Congressional-440 Cannon Bldg., Washington, DC 20515; (202) 225-4831

California Democratic Congressional Delegation
503 House Office Bldg. Annex 1, Washington, DC 20515.

Children's Caucus
Senate-SR-444 Russell Bldg., Washington, DC 20510; (202) 224-5630

China Trade Caucus
U.S. Senate-SR-421 Russell Bldg., Washington, DC 20510.

Coal Caucus
Senate-SR-173A Russell Bldg., Washington, DC 20510; (202) 224-1160

Corn Caucus, Congressional-SH-331 Hart Bldg., Washington, DC 20510; (202) 224-2854

Crime Caucus
Congressional-SH-303 Hart Bldg., Washington, DC 20510; (202) 224-4254

International Narcotics Control
Senate-SH-328 Hart Bldg., Washington, DC 20510; (202) 224-5042

Education Study Group, House;Senate International
SR-444 Russell Bldg., Washington, DC 20510; (202) 224-2823

Environmental and Energy Study Conference
H2-515 House Office Bldg. Annex 2, Washington, DC 20515; (202) 226-3300

Ethiopian Jewry, Congressional Caucus for
1536 Longworth Bldg., Washington, DC 20515; (202) 225-2361

Family, Senate Caucus on the
SH-328 Hart Bldg., Washington, DC 20510; (202) 224-4521

Fire Services Caucus
1233 Longworth Bldg., Washington, DC 20515; (202) 225-2011

Footwear Caucus
House-221 Cannon Bldg., Washington, DC 20515; (202) 225-8273

Forestry 2000 Task Force
431 Cannon Bldg., Washington, DC 20515; (202) 225-5831

Future, Clearinghouse on the, Congressional
H2-555 House Office Bldg., Annex 2, Washington, DC 20515; (202) 226-3434

Hispanic Caucus, Congressional
H2-557 House Office Bldg. Annex 2, Washington, DC 20510; (202) 226-3430

Human Rights Caucus, Congressional
H2-552 House Office Bldg., Annex 2, Washington, DC 20515

Human Rights Monitors, Congressional Friends of
2448 Rayburn Bldg., Washington, DC 20515; (202) 225-6465

Insurance Caucus, House
120 Cannon Bldg., Washington, DC 20515; (202) 225-2276

Ireland, Friends of
2229 Rayburn Bldg., Washington, DC 20515; (202) 225-3215

Maritime Caucus
Congressional-H2-531 House Office Bldg. Annex 2, Washington, DC 20515.

Mining Caucus, Congressional
438 Cannon Bldg., Washington, DC 20515; (202) 225-4665

Be patient. If any phone number is incorrect, call (area code) 555-1212 and request the new listing.

U.S. Congress Committees

New York State Congressional Delegation
2108 Rayburn Bldg., Washington, DC 20515; (202) 225-4916

Northeast-Midwest Congressional Coalition
H2-530 House Office Bldg. Annex 2, Washington, DC 20515; (202) 226-3920

Olympic Caucus

Pennsylvania Congressional Delegation
2186 Rayburn Bldg., Washington, DC 20515

Population and Development, Congressional Coalition
1019 Longworth Bldg., Washington, DC 20515; (202) 225-3411

Populist Caucus, Congressional
328 Cannon Bldg., Washington, DC 20515; (202) 225-5905

Pro-Life Caucus
2440 Rayburn Bldg., Washington, DC 20515; (202) 225-7669

Rail Caucus, Senate
SR-154 Russell Bldg., Washington, 20510; (202) 224-3244

Rural Caucus, Congressional
2134 Rayburn Bldg., Washington, DC 20515; (202) 225-2876

Rural Health Caucus, Senate
SH-511 Hart Bldg., Washington, DC 20510; (202) 224-2551

Science and Technology, Congressional Caucus for
1717 Longworth Bldg., Washington, DC 20515; (202) 225-5425

Social Security Caucus, Congressional
2407 Rayburn Bldg., Washington, DC 20515; (202) 225-5961

Southern Africa, Congressional Ad Hoc Monitoring Group on
2232 Rayburn Bldg., Washington, DC 20515; (202) 225-3335

Soybean Caucus, Congressional
SH-506 Hart Bldg., Washington, DC 20510; (202) 224-5641

Soviet Jews, Congressional Coalition of
2365 Rayburn Bldg., Washington, DC 20515; (202) 225-7023

Space, Coalition for Peaceful Uses of
2188 Rayburn Bldg., Washington, DC 20515; (202) 225-6161

Space Caucus, Congressional
2188 Rayburn Bldg., Washington, DC 20515; (202) 225-6161

Steel Caucus, Congressional
H2-556 House Office Bldg. Annex 2, Washington, DC 20515; (202) 225-8792

Sunbelt Caucus, Congressional
H2-561 House Office Bldg. Annex 2, Washington, DC 20515; (202) 226-2374

Tennessee Valley Congressional Caucus
125 Cannon Bldg., Washington, DC 20515; (202) 225-6831

Territorial Caucus, Congressional
1130 Longworth Bldg., Washington, DC 20515; (202) 225-1188

Textile Caucus, Congressional
H2-368 House Office Bldg. Annex 2, Washington, DC 20515; (202) 226-3070

Third World Debt Caucus
330 Cannon Bldg., Washington, DC 20515; (202) 225-3661

Travel and Tourism Caucus, Congressional
H2-246 House Office Bldg. Annex 2, Washington, DC 20515; (202) 225-3935

Trucking Caucus, Senate
SD-105 Dirksen Bldg., Washington, DC 20510; (202) 224-4822

Vietnam Era Veterans in Congress
328 Cannon Bldg., Washington, DC 20515; (202) 225-5903

Western State Coalition, Senate
SR-328 Hart Bldg., Washington, DC 20510; (202) 224-4521

Wine Caucus, Senate
SH-720 Hart Bldg., Washington, DC 20510; (202) 224-3841

Women's Issues, Congressional Caucus for
2471 Rayburn Bldg., Washington, DC 20515; (202) 225-6740

For the latest information about the formation of new congressional caucuses or your Member of Congress by calling the Capitol Hill Switchboard Operator at (202) 224-3121.

Information from Lawmakers

Legislative Branch Sources

In addition to the powerful information sources of congressional committees and think tanks, the offices of your U.S. Senators and Representatives can be very helpful. In this section you'll also find out where to find financial information on federal campaign finance, television coverage of Congress, congressional salaries, and even how to get a flag that was raised over the U.S. Capitol.

* Bicentennial Celebration and Free Publications

The Office of the Historian
House of Representatives
138 Cannon Building
Washington, DC 20515-6701 (202) 225-1153

The Office of the Historian acts as a clearinghouse for historical information on the House of Representatives, for the Members, the public, and the press. Books and other reference information. The following publications are available free of charge from the Office:

A Guide to Research Collections of Former Members of the U.S. House of Representatives 1789-1987
Women in Congress
Origins of the U.S. House of Representatives: A Documentary Record

* Bills and Laws: Document Rooms

House Document Room
U.S. House of Representatives
2nd and D Sts.,SW, B-18
Washington, DC 20515-6622 (202) 225-3456

Senate Document Room
Senate Hart Office Bldg., Room B-04
Washington, DC 20510 (202) 224-7860

Free copies of all bills introduced in the House and Senate are available. Legislation approved by committees and also passed by the full House and/or Senate along with committee reports are available free of charge. To request a bill, you must send a self-addressed mailing label and include the bill number or report number. No more than six requests may be presented at a time. Requests for Senate documents may be made to either of your Senators, and your Representative can get copies of House bills and reports. The Document Rooms maintain current files of legislation including public laws (slip laws). Periodically public laws on a variety of subject areas are compiled and are available for $157 per session from the Government Printing Office.

* Biographical Directory of the U.S. Congress 1774-1989

Superintendent of Documents
Government Printing Office
Washington, DC 20402 (202) 783-3238

The Biographical Directory of the U.S. Congress 1774-1989, contains authoritative biographies of the more than 11,000 men and women who have served in the U.S. Congress from 1789 to 1989, and in the Continental Congress between 1774 and 1789. Many features include a listing of all chairmen of standing committees, all major formal leadership positions, bibliographic citations, and major revisions of political party affiliations reflecting the latest scholarship. You'll also find complete rosters of State congressional delegations for the First through 100th Congresses. This bicentennial edition is the most comprehensive *Biographical Directory of the United States Congress* ever issued. The latest edition published at the beginning of the 101st Congress is available through the Government Printing Office for $82.

* Calendar of the House of Representatives and History of Legislation

Superintendent of Documents
Government Printing Office
Washington, DC 20402 (202) 783-3238

House Document Room
U.S. House of Representatives
2nd and D Sts., SW, B-18
Washington, DC 20515-6622 (202) 225-3456

This calendar contains a list of bills in conference, a list of bills through conference, the *Union Calendar*, the *House Calendar*, a history of actions on each bill of the current session, a subject index of active legislation, and more. It is a weekly (when Congress is in session) publication available on subscription for $159 a year. Free copies can be picked up at the House Document Room.

* Campaign Finance Information

Press Office
Federal Election Commission (FEC)
999 E Street, NW
Washington, DC 20463 (202) 219-4155

Staff of the Press Office are the FEC's official media spokespersons. In addition to publicizing FEC actions and releasing statistics on campaign finance, they respond to all questions from representatives of the print and broadcast media.

* Campaign Finance Records

Public Records Office
Federal Election Commission (FEC)
999 E Street, NW
Washington, DC 20463 (202) 219-4140

Commission disclosure of campaign finance activity is based on the reports submitted by political committees. These reports, available from the Public Records Office within 48 hours of receipt as required by law, focus on the flow of money in and out of campaigns and the sources of campaign support.

* Compilation of All Legislation

Congressional Research Service
Bill Digest Section
Library of Congress
Washington, DC 20540 (202) 707-6996

The *Digest Public General Bills and Resolutions* provides summaries of public bills and resolutions and their current status in order of introduction in Congress. The *Digest* includes subject, author, and title. Subscription service consists of cumulative issues for each session of each Congress (two sessions per Congress). Prices per issue vary but average around $40. Subscription information is available from the Superintendent of Documents, Government Printing Office, Washington, DC 20402; (202) 783-3238.

* Congress and the Nation

Clerk of the House
House of Representatives
The Capitol
Washington, DC 20515 (202) 225-7000

Congress and the Nation is a summary of material in the *Congressional Quarterly Almanac*. *Volume I* covers the years 1945-1964; thereafter, it is published every four years.

* Congressional Directory

Superintendent of Documents
Government Printing Office

Be patient. If any phone number is incorrect, call (area code) 555-1212 and request the new listing.

Legislative Branch Sources

Washington, DC 20402 (202) 783-3238

The *Congressional Directory* has been the official handbook for the Congress since 1821 and is also widely used by Federal agency officials and the general public. Its contents include lists of addresses, rooms, and phone numbers of Members, biographical sketches of Members, Capitol officers and officials, committees, departments, and information on diplomatic offices and statistics. It also includes lists of members of the press admitted to the House and Senate galleries. The *1989-1990 Official Congressional Directory of the 101st Congress* is available for $15 in paperback, $20 in hardback, and $25 for a hardback copy with a thumb index.

* Congressional Documents, Reports, and Hearings

Law Library
Library of Congress (202) 707-5079
Washington, DC 20540 (202) 707-5065

All Senate and House documents, reports, hearings since 1970, and all bills back to the First Congress are available. Material can be obtained on microfilm.

* Congressional Leaders and Presiding Officers

Ceremonial Office of the Vice President
Old Executive Office Bldg, Room 272
Washington, DC 20501 (202) 456-6605

Speaker's Office
Room H-204, The Capitol
Washington, DC 20510 (202) 225-5604

Senate Majority Leader
Room S-221, The Capitol
Washington, DC 20510 (202) 224-5556

The Vice President of the United States is the Presiding Officer of the Senate, and in his absence the duties are taken over by a President pro tempore, elected by that body, or someone designated by him. The Presiding Officer of the House of Representatives, the Speaker, is elected by the House; he may designate any Member of the House to act in his absence. The Senate Majority Leader is elected at the beginning of each new Congress by a majority vote of the Senators in the political party which controls the Senate. In cooperation with their party organizations, leaders are responsible for the design and achievement of a legislative program involving legislation, expediting noncontroversial measures, and keeping Members informed regarding proposed action on pending business. The Majority Leader serves as an ex officio member of this party's policy making and organizational bodies and is aided by an assistant floor leader (whip) and a party secretary.

* Congressional Record: House and Senate Floor Debate

The Superintendent of Documents
Government Printing Office
Washington, DC 20402 (202) 783-3238

Proceedings of Congress are published in the *Congressional Record*, which is issued when Congress is in session. Publication of the *Record* began in March of 1873; it was the first record of debate officially reported, printed, and published directly by the Federal Government. The *Daily Digest of the Congressional Record*, printed in the back of each issue of the *Record*, summarizes the proceedings of that day in each House, and before each of their committees and subcommittees, respectively. The *Digest* also presents the legislative program for each day and, at the end of the week, gives the program for the following week. The subscription price is $225 per year. For information on the Senate portion of the *Congressional Record*, call (202) 224-2658; for the House portion, call (202) 224-5848; for information on committee activities, call Senate (202) 224-2120; House (202) 225-4470.

* Congressional Record Index

House Documents Room
U.S. House of Representatives
2nd and D Sts. SW, B-18
Washington, DC 20515-6622 (202) 225-3456

About once every two weeks, the *Congressional Record Index* is distributed listing *Congressional Record* matters by subject, member, bill number, bill title and every other sort of cross-reference combination. For instance, you can look up a member's name and find everything he or she introduced, made remarks on, submitted, reported, and gave a speech about. You can also look up a subject

and find all related articles, editorials, bills, letters, tables, and press releases included during the previous two weeks in the *Congressional Record*.

* Congressional Telephone Directories

The Superintendent of Documents
Government Printing Office
Washington, DC 20402 (202) 783-3238

Telephone directories for the U.S. Senate and the House of Representatives are available for sale. Abbreviated pamphlets providing Members and committees telephone numbers and addresses are available from the Secretary of the Senate and the Clerk of the House.

* Daily Congressional Schedule

Published weekdays in the *Washington Post* newspaper, the *Today in Congress* column gives a daily rundown on times and subjects of all House and Senate committee hearings and meetings and indicates which are open to the public.

* Election Assistance

Federal Election Commission (FEC)
Information Services
999 E Street, NW
Washington, DC 20463 (202) 219-3420

In an effort to promote voluntary compliance with the law, this office provides technical assistance to candidates and committees and others involved in elections. Staff will research and answer questions on the Federal Election Campaign Act and FEC regulations, procedures, and advisory opinions; direct workshops on the law; and publish a wide range of materials.

* Federal Election Commission Publications

Federal Election Commission (FEC)
Information Services
999 E Street, NW (800) 219-3420
Washington, DC 20463 (202) 376-3120

The following publications are available free of charge from the FEC:

Federal Election Campaign Laws. A complete compilation of Federal election campaign laws.

FEC Regulations. FEC regulations appear in Title 11 of the Code of Federal Regulations, including subject indexes.

FEC Record. This monthly newsletter is the primary source of information on FEC activity, covering reporting, advisory opinions, litigation, legislation, statistics, regulations compliance, and more.

FEC Annual Report.

Supporting Federal Candidates: A Guide for Citizens. For the general public, this booklet discusses how citizens can support Federal candidates through contributions, volunteer work, and independent expenditures.

The First 10 Years. Graphs and text describe the FEC's work during its first decade, including a brief history of campaign finance legislation and an overview of FEC operations.

Campaign Guides. Four separate guides explain how the law affects candidates, parties, corporations/unions, and nonconnected PACs. Election law requirements are explained and illustrated with examples of completed FEC forms.

The FEC and the Federal Campaign Finance Law. Gives a brief overview of the major provisions of the Federal Election Campaign Act and the FEC's role in administering it.

Public Funding of Presidential Elections. For the general public, this brochure gives a brief history of Presidential public funding and describes how the process works.

Using FEC Campaign Finance Information. Explains how to gather information about the financial activity of Federal political committees. It describes FEC's computer indexes and ways to use them.

* Federal Campaign Finance Law Complaints

Federal Election Commission (FEC)
999 E Street, NW
Washington, DC 20463 (202) 219-3690

If you believe a violation of the Federal campaign finance law has taken place, you may file a complaint with the Federal Election Commission. Send the Commission a letter explaining why you believe the law may have been violated, describe the specific facts and circumstances, and name the individuals or

Be patient. If any phone number is incorrect, call (area code) 555-1212 and request the new listing. 1189

Information from Lawmakers

organizations responsible. The letter must be sworn to, signed, and notarized. Complaints of alleged violations receive case numbers and are called MURs, Matters Under Review.

* Federal Elections Clearinghouse

Federal Election Commission (FEC)
999 E Street, NW
Washington, DC 20463 (202) 219-3670

The Election Clearinghouse assists election officials and the general public by responding to inquiries concerning the electoral process, publishing research, and conducting workshops on all matters related to Federal election administration.

* Federal Elections Library

Federal Election Commission (FEC) Library
999 E Street, NW, Room 801
Washington, DC 20463 (202) 219-3312

The FEC Library's collection includes basic legal research tools and materials dealing with political campaign finance, corporate and labor political activity, and campaign finance reform. The Library staff prepares indexes to Advisory Opinions and Matters Under Review (MURs), as well as a *Campaign Finance and Federal Election Law Bibliography*, which are available for purchase from the FEC's Public Records Office.

* Financial Disclosure Database on Federal Candidates

Federal Election Commission (FEC)
Data Systems Development Division
999 E Street, NW
Washington, DC 20463 (202) 219-3730

The FEC maintains a computer database of information from all reports filed by political committees, individuals, and other entities since 1972. The data is sorted into indexes which permit a detailed analysis of campaign finance activity and, additionally, provide a tool for monitoring contribution limitations. The data can be searched by specific candidate or contributor. By contacting this office, individuals can have searches done on twenty names or less free of charge. For searches of more than 20 names, cost varies depending on computer time needed.

* GAO Congressional Staff Assignments

Congressional Relations
General Accounting Office (GAO)
441 G St., NW, Room 7025
Washington, DC 20548 (202) 275-5456

Each year GAO assigns between 75 to 125 staff members directly to Congressional committees to help carry out their responsibilities or to assist them in using the results of GAO studies. In addition, GAO provides staff assistance to committees having jurisdiction over revenues, appropriations, and expenditures, and often to other committees as well. The agency does not, however, assign staff to individual members of Congress.

* General Accounting Office Bibliographic Database

GAO/IHSF
P.O. Box 6015
Gaithersburg, MD 20877 (202) 275-5456

The GAO maintains a database which provides bibliographic information on GAO documents and reports. The studies cover a vast array of subjects, as the agency must produce a report on any topic Congress assigns. Reports have ranged from financial audits of government agencies to policy studies of health-related programs. Searches are generally conducted by subject area and specific time period. Searches and printouts are available free of charge by calling (202) 275-5388. GAO will also mail you up to five copies of any report listed, without charge. Each copy requested beyond that is $2. Contact the office above for information regarding the contents of the reports.

* History of the Senate

Senate Historical Office
Secretary of the Senate
The Capitol, Room SH 201
Washington, DC 20510 (202) 224-6900

The Senate Historical Office collects and disseminates information on Senate history and Senate members, including photographs, unpublished documents, and oral history. A free newsletter, *Senate History*, is available, as well as a series of addresses to the Senate on subjects related to its history and traditions, including a list of citations with dates, subjects, and page numbers.

* House Committees Roster

Clerk of the House
House of Representatives
The Capitol
Washington, DC 20515 (202) 225-7000

This listing contains all official and unofficial House committees. The members of each committee are included.

* House Leadership and Ceremonial Posts

Office of the House Majority Leader
Room H-114, The Capitol
Washington, DC 20515 (202) 225-0100

Office of the House Republican Leader
Room H-232, The Capitol
Washington, DC 20515 (202) 225-0600

The leadership of the House of Representatives is elected at the beginning of each Congress. Under the tradition of the two party system in the United States, the leader of the party with the largest number of Members becomes the Majority Leader. The Minority Leader is invariably the Member nominated by the minority party for the Senate.

Sergeant at Arms of the House
Room H-124, The Capitol
Washington, DC 20515 (202) 225-2456

This office enforces the rules of the house and maintains decorum during sessions of the House. The Sergeant at Arms also is in charge of the Mace, the symbol of legislative power and authority. Maintaining the general security of the House buildings and the Capitol is his major responsibility. Another major responsibility is management of the House bank which disburses Members' salaries and travel expenses.

Clerk of the House
Room H-105, The Capitol
Washington, DC 20515 (202) 225-7000

The Clerk is the chief legislative, administrative, and budgetary officer of the U.S. House of Representatives. The Clerk is responsible for directing legislative activities of the House, such as keeping the Journal, taking all votes, certifying passage of bills, and processing all legislation. The Clerk also prepares the budget for the House, disburses funds, serves as the contracting officer of the House, and issues a report available to the public on salaries and expenses. In addition, the Clerk is the purchaser and provider of all furnishings, office equipment, and office supplies.

Doorkeeper of the House
Room H-154, The Capitol
Washington, DC 20515 (202) 225-3505

The Doorkeeper is responsible for physical arrangements for joint sessions and joint meetings of the Congress, announcements of messages from the President and the Senate, announcement of the arrival of the President when he addresses Congress in person, and escorting dignitaries visiting the Capitol.

Chaplain of the House
Room HB-25, The Capitol
Washington, DC 20515 (202) 225-2509

The Chaplain is responsible for the opening prayer at each session of the House, and occasionally invites other clergy to serve as guest chaplains. The Chaplain's Office also coordinates use of the Prayer Room and makes arrangements for pastoral services for Members and staff.

* House of Representatives Research and Library

U.S. House of Representatives and Committees Library
Cannon House Office Bldg., Room B 18
Washington, DC 20515 (202) 225-0462

This library is the official depository of House documents, reports, bills, and more. Its primary function is to serve House members and their staffs. It is open to the public, but no photocopying is permitted.

Be patient. If any phone number is incorrect, call (area code) 555-1212 and request the new listing.

Legislative Branch Sources

* House Telephone Directory

The Committee on House Administration
The Capitol, Room H-326
Washington, DC 20515 (202) 225-2061

The *House Telephone Directory* is produced yearly by the Committee on House Administration. It provides a listing for representatives, a listing for House committees, an alphabetical staff listing, a listing of staffs by representatives, a listing of staffs by committee, listings for senators and Senate committees, a listing for executive branch leaders, a listing for government agencies, and more. It is available for $17 from the House Committee (202) 512-2471.

* How Our Laws Are Made

Superintendent of Documents
Government Printing Office
Washington, DC 20402 (202) 783-3238

The booklet, *How Our Laws Are Made,* is prepared by the House of Representatives and provides a plain language explanation of how a legislative idea travels the complex passageways of the federal lawmaking process to become a statute. It is available for $2.50 from the Superintendent of Documents.

* Legislative Archives

National Archives and Records Administration
8th St. and Pennsylvania Ave., NW, Room 8E
Washington, DC 20408 (202) 501-5350

The Legislative Archives Center is responsible for the appraisal, preservation, arrangement, description, reference service, and outreach activities associated with all records of the U.S. Senate, House of Representatives, congressional committees, and agencies. The Center includes the Legislative Reference Branch, which provides reference services to Congress and the public pertaining to congressional records, and the Legislative Projects Branch, which has just completed writing two guides to the congressional records.

* Legislative Branch Audit Site

Legislative Branch Audit Site
Accounting and Financial Management Division
General Accounting Office
2nd and D Sts., SW
Washington, DC 20515 (202) 226-2480

This office assists Congress by doing 15 regular annual financial audits of such units as the House Recording Studio and the Senate Restaurant. On a less formal basis, the staff also offers advice and assistance on administrative matters. For free copies (up to five) of Audit Site reports, contact: Information Handling and Support Facilities, General Accounting Office, P.O. Box 6015, Gaithersburg, MD 20877; (202) 275-6241.

* Legislative Histories and Research

Law Library
Library of Congress, LM240
Washington, DC 20540 (202) 707-5065

The Law Library compiles legislative histories which include versions of new public statutes from the time of introduction, through congressional hearings, House and Senate floor debate, vote tallies, and votes.

* Live TV Coverage of House and Senate Chambers

Cable Satellite Public Affairs Network (C-SPAN)
400 North Capitol St., NW, Suite 650
Washington, DC 20001 (202) 737-3220

C-SPAN is a basic cable service specializing for more than a decade in the coverage of Congress. It shows lawmaking in the raw on Capitol Hill. Created to provide live gavel-to-gavel coverage of the U.S. House of Representatives C-SPAN II began in 1986 to cablecast the live sessions off the U.S. Senate, in their entirety. In addition, C-SPAN offers a front row seat to other public events from the nation's capitol and across the country. Events are aired without commentary or analysis. Each morning at 8 and each evening at 6:30, the network presents "Viewer Call-in" where viewer's questions about major news events are discussed. To receive C-SPAN call your local cable company.

* Monthly Checklist of State Publications

Exchange and Gift Division

State Documents Section
Library of Congress
Washington, DC 20540 (202) 707-9468

The *Monthly Checklist of State Publications* lists documents and publications received in the Library of Congress that are issued by the administrative, judicial, and legislative branches and state university systems of the states and territories. The subscription price is $32 per year and can be purchased from the Superintendent of Documents, Government Printing Office, Washington, DC 20402; (202) 783-3238.

* New Federal Laws

Office of the Federal Register
National Archives and Records Administration
800 N. Capitol St. NW, Room 700
Washington, DC 20408 (202) 523-5230

This office receives all laws enacted by Congress for publication in the *Federal Register* and can provide information regarding these laws. They also publish *United States at Large,* a compilation of laws enacted during a particular year.

* New Laws: Free Copies of these Statutes

House Documents Room
U.S. House of Representatives
2nd and D Sts. SW, B-18
Washington, DC 20515-6622 (202) 219-4155

The 101st Congress has passed only 149 laws to date. For a complete listing of the new laws passed by the 101th Congress, contact the House Documents Room and ask for a House Calendar which will list the new laws and their bill numbers.

* Online Access to FEC Financial Database

Federal Election Commission (FEC)
Press Office
999 E Street, NW (800) 424-9530
Washington, DC 20463 (202) 376-3155

The FEC offers an online computer information system designed for owners of personal computers. The system furnishes campaign finance information in formatted computer indexes and in raw data form. For a specific candidate or committee, the system provides the following information for election cycles beginning in 1985: total receipts and expenditures; total cash on hand; and total debts owed. Contact this office for more information on accessing this information.

* Photographs of Every Member of Congress

The Superintendent of Documents
Government Printing Office
Washington, DC 20402 (202) 783-3238

The *Congressional Pictorial Directory* contains photographs of the President, Vice President, members of the Senate and House, Officers of the Senate and House, Officials of the Capitol, and a list of the Senate delegations and an alphabetical list of senators and representatives. The paperback edition is $5, and the hardback copy is $15.

* Presidential Political Appointments: The "Plum" Book

Senate Government Affairs Committee
Dirksen Office Building, Room SD 353
Washington, DC 20510 (202) 783-3238

Superintendent of Documents
Government Printing Office
Washington, DC 20402 (202) 275-3030

U.S. Policy and Supporting Positions, more commonly known as the *Plum Book,* lists some 3,000 political appointment jobs and describes the type of appointment, tenure, grade, and salary. It is available for sale at the Superintendent of Documents for $13 per copy.

* Public Laws Tape Recording

Office of the Federal Register
National Archives and Records Administration
800 N. Capitol St. NW, Room 700
Washington, DC 20408 (202) 523-6641

Be patient. If any phone number is incorrect, call (area code) 555-1212 and request the new listing.

Information from Lawmakers

This recording lists the most recent laws which have come to the office for publication in the *Federal Register*.

* Published Congressional Hearings

Documents Clerk
Relevant House Committee (202) 225-3456
Relevant Senate Committee (202) 224-7860

Superintendent of Documents
Government Printing Office
Washington, DC 20402 (202) 783-3238

House and Senate committees and subcommittees conduct hundreds of informational and investigative hearings practically every week of the year. All of these congressional hearings are published and often available free of charge from the documents clerk of the committee or subcommittee which held the hearings. Many of the hearings also are sold by the Superintendent of Documents.

* Radio Coverage of Committee Hearings and International Events

C-SPAN Audio Networks
400 North Capitol St., NW, Suite 650
Washington, DC 20001 (202) 737-3220

The C-SPAN Audio Networks were created to provide audio coverage of congressional committee hearings and other public affairs events. They are intended to supplement the round-the-clock floor coverage of the House and Senate provided by the C-SPAN and C-SPAN II cable television networks. In addition, the Audio Networks air international public affairs events through retransmissions of foreign English-language shortwave radio programming. C-SPAN Audio I combines the Washington, DC, and international programming. Future audio programming will provide historical perspective through programming of public events from the past, drawn from the National Archives and other Sources. C-SPAN Audio 2 provides 24-hour retransmissions of the BBC World Service.

* Raise a Flag Over the Capitol

c/o The Capitol
Washington, DC 20515 (202) 224-3121

You can arrange to purchase flags that have been flown over the Capitol by getting in touch with your U.S. Senator or Representative. A certificate signed by the Architect of the Capitol accompanies each flag. Flags are available for purchase in sizes of 3'x5' or 5'x8' in fabrics of cotton and nylon.

* Salaries and Expenses of House of Representatives

Members and Employees
House Document Room
U.S. House of Representatives
2nd and D Sts. SW, B-18
Washington, DC 20515-6622 (202) 225-3456

The *Report of the Clerk of the House* includes the salaries of House members' staffs, committee staffs, and House officers and employees. This quarterly report includes a listing of House expenditures.

* Salaries and Expenses of U.S. Senators and Their Staff

Senate Document Room
B-04 Senate Hart Office Building
Washington, DC 20510 (202) 224-7860

The biannual *Report of the Secretary of the Senate* lists expenditures and details the salaries of senators' staff, members, committee staff members, and officers and employees of the Senate.

* Senate Committees Roster

Office of the Secretary of the Senate
The Capitol, Room S-208
Washington, DC 20510 (202) 224-2115

A listing is available of official Senate committees. These include the members of each committee. Also available is the *Unofficial List of Senators*, which gives the names of all Senators, their states, their party affiliations, and the year they are up for reelection.

* Senate Leadership or Ceremonial Posts

Senate Minority Leader
Room S-230, The Capitol
Washington, DC 20510 (202) 224-3135

The Minority Leader is elected at the beginning of each new Congress by the Senators in the political party which does not have a working majority in the Senate. This leader works closely with its party organizations and currently with the White House in terms of getting the President's legislative program enacted.

Secretary of the Senate
Room S-208, The Capitol
Washington, DC 20510 (202) 224-2115

The Secretary is the custodian of the seal of the Senate, and handles the payroll for the Senators, officers, committee staff, and employees, and issues a report disclosing such salaries and expenses. The Secretary's executive duties include certification of extracts from the Journal of the Senate; the attestation of bills and joint, concurrent, and Senate resolutions; in impeachment trials, issuance, under the authority of the Presiding Officer, of all orders, mandates, writs, and precepts, authorized by the Senate; and certification of the President of the United States of the advice and consent of the Senate to ratification of treaties and the names of persons confirmed or rejected upon the nomination of the President.

Sergeant at Arms of the Senate
Room S-321, The Capitol (202) 224-2341
Washington, DC 20510 FAX: 224-7690

The Senate elects the Sergeant at Arms who serves as its Executive Officer. As law enforcement officer, the Sergeant of Arms has statutory power to make arrests; to locate absentee Senators for a quorum; and to enforce Senate rules and regulations. As Protocol Officer, he is responsible for many aspects of ceremonial functions, including the Presidential inauguration; funeral arrangements of Senators who die in office; escorting the President when he addresses a Joint Session of Congress or attends any function in the Senate; and escorting heads of state when they visit the Senate.

Chaplain of the Senate
Room SH-204A, Hart Senate Office Bldg.
Washington, DC 20510 (202) 224-2510

The Chaplain of the Senate serves as pastor to the Senators and their families. He opens the sessions of the Senate each day with a prayer. His office is a resource center for information concerning the Bible, various religious denominations, and the subject of religion in general.

* Senate Research and Library

Senate Library
The Capitol, Suite S-332
Washington, DC 20510 (202) 224-7106

The Senate Library is the official depository of senate documents. Its primary function is service to Senate members and their staffs. To use the library a researcher must have a letter of introduction from a Senator.

* State Access to Financial Disclosure Database

Federal Election Commission (FEC)
Public Records Office
999 E Street, NW
Washington, DC 20463 (202) 219-4140

Under the State Access Program, individuals and organizations in 15 states now have immediate online access to several standard FEC computer indexes which provide descriptive information on all registered political committees, the total receipts and disbursements of committees, and a listing of all PAC contributions to federal candidates. Participating states with operational terminals within their State Election Offices include: Arizona, Colorado, Connecticut, Georgia, Illinois, Iowa, Massachusetts, Michigan, New Jersey, New Mexico, Ohio, Tennessee, Vermont, Washington, and Wisconsin.

* State Election Finance Records

Federal Election Commission (FEC)
Public Records Office
999 E Street, NW (800) 424-9530
Washington, DC 20463 (202) 219-4140

Researchers can obtain campaign finance reports from the records office in each state. Contact this FEC office to order a list of the names, addresses, and phone numbers of national and state disclosure offices.

Be patient. If any phone number is incorrect, call (area code) 555-1212 and request the new listing.

Legislative Branch Sources

* Treaties and Nominations

Senate Document Room
Hart Building, Room B-04
Washington, DC 20510 (202) 224-7860

For information on and copies of treaties submitted to the Senate for ratification, contact the Senate Document Room or your Senators.

* U.S. Senate Manual

Superintendent of Documents
Government Printing Office
Washington, DC 20402 (202) 783-3238

Senate Committee on Rules and Administration
Russell Senate Office Building, Room 305
Washington, DC 20510 (202) 224-6352

The biennial *Senate Manual* includes *Jefferson's Manual*, standing rules, orders, and laws and resolutions affecting the business of the U.S. Senate. A list of senators and members of the Executive Branch is also provided. It is published every two years with each new Congress, and sells for $24 from the Superintendent of Documents.

* World's Largest Law Library

Law Library
Library of Congress
Washington, DC 20540 (202) 707-5065

As the world's largest and most comprehensive library of foreign, international, and comparative law, the Law Library provides information for all known legal systems including common law, civil law, Roman law, canon law, Chinese law, Jewish and Islamic law, and ancient and medieval law. Specialists with knowledge of more than fifty languages provide reference and research service in all known legal systems. U.S. legislative documents housed here include the *Congressional Record* (and its predecessors), the serial set, a nearly complete set of bills and resolutions, current documents, committee prints, reports, hearings, etc. and a complete set of U.S. Supreme Court records and briefs and collections of U.S. Court of Appeals records and briefs. The law library has five major divisions:

American-British Law
United States, Australia, Canada, Great Britain, India, New Zealand, Pakistan, certain other countries of the British Commonwealth and their dependent territories, and Eire: (202) 707-5077.

European Law
Nations of Europe and their possessions, except Spain and Portugal: (202) 707-5088.

Hispanic Law
Spain and Portugal, Latin America, Puerto Rico, the Philippines, and Spanish- and Portuguese-language states of Africa: (202) 707-5070.

Far Eastern Law
Nations of East and Southeast Asia including China, Indonesia, Japan, Korea, Thailand, and former British and French possessions in the area: (202) 707-5085.

Near Eastern and African Law
Middle Eastern countries, including the Arab states, Turkey, Iran, and Afghanistan, and all African countries, except Spanish- and Portuguese-language states and possessions: (202) 707-5073.

Be patient. If any phone number is incorrect, call (area code) 555-1212 and request the new listing.

Tracking State Legislation

* *See also Information Starting Places; State Information Starting Places Chapter*
* *See also Current Events and Homework Chapter*

Bill Status Information

Most state legislatures maintain an office responsible for providing bill status information to the public. In Ohio, for example, a bank of telephone reference experts answer questions about current or past legislation on any given subject. The researchers rely on their own files and also have access to a computerized database updated by the Senate Clerk's office. Usually these offices can search their databases or indexes in several ways, by keyword or phrase, by specific subject, or by state senator or representative.

About half of the legislatures can send you this information in the form of a computer printout free of charge. In those states which do not operate a central bill status office, it is necessary to contact the Clerk of the House for information on bills pending before the House and similarly a call to the Secretary or Clerk of the Senate for updates on legislation pending before that body. Many legislatures have toll-free numbers which can be accessed only if you are calling from inside the state. Most of the State House hotlines operate just during the regular session of the legislature and, as you might expect, some of the "800" numbers change from one session to the next.

Your initial call to the bill status office will lead you to the appropriate committees, and if no action has been taken on a particular bill, this legislative information office can provide you with the sponsor of the legislation whom you can call directly for more details.

Copies of Bills and Other Legislative Documents

In most states, the legislative information office can send you copies of bills. Indiana is the only state that charges $.10 per page if the bill is more than 10 pages long. All states print the bills at the time of introduction. Over half reprint the amended legislation after committee action, and about two-thirds of all chambers print the legislation after the floor vote. Unlike the U.S. Congress, legislative documentation is skimpy when it comes to committee hearings as well as floor debate. Only about a third of all legislative bodies tape all committee sessions. You can make arrangements with the Clerk's office to listen to the tapes, and some states, like the Minnesota House, sell audio tapes of committee meetings and floor debates for $12.50 per copy.

Advanced Strategy for Monitoring One or All 50 State Legislatures

Coverage of a state legislature can be substantially enhanced in many ways; some are inexpensive and others can be costly:

• Clipping Service:

Newspapers, especially those published in the state capital, can prove to be a cost effective way of staying informed provided the issues of concern are controversial or significant enough to capture the attention of the local media.

• Local Chamber of Commerce:

This organization may offer information about certain issues it is following on behalf of the business community.

• Stringers:

Often expensive, but there may be no substitute for hiring someone who is in frequent contact with legislators and is a familiar face in the document rooms and statehouse corridors.

• Governor's Legislative Liaison Office:

On major legislative initiatives and politically "hot" issues, try telephoning this office.

• National Conference of State Legislators (NCSL):

Although this organization serves legislators, the staff will respond to requests from the public. The Conference maintains a list of reports and studies by investigative committees in all 50 states. Access to its in-house database may be possible in the future. This national organization of state legislators and legislative staff aims to improve the quality and effectiveness of state legislators, to ensure states a strong, cohesive voice in the federal decision-making process and to foster interstate communication and cooperation. Contact either of the two offices at 1560 Broadway, Suite 700, Denver, CO 80202; (303) 830-2200; or 444 North Capitol St., NW, Suite 515, Washington, DC 20001; (202) 624-5400.

• Council of State Governments/State Information Center:

This arm of the Council of State Governments publishes several useful directories, including *The Book of States, State Administration Officials Classified By Function,* and *State Legislative Leadership Committees and Staff.* Its database may soon be available to the public. Contact: State Information Center, Council of State Governments, P.O. Box 11910, Iron Works Pike, Lexington, KY 40578; (606) 231-1939.

• Commerce Clearing House (CCH):

CCH offers the "State Legislative Reporting Service" as well as the Electronic Legislative Search System. The Reporting Service allows you to select only those legislatures you are interested in, whereas the online search system tracks all current legislation in all 50 states. Contact: CCH, 4025 West Peterson Avenue, Chicago, IL 60646; (312) 583-8500.

• Information for Public Affairs:

This private firm offers online access to its database containing the status of legislation pending before the current session of

Tracking State Legislation

all 50 state legislatures. Contact: PAI, 1900 14th St., Sacramento, CA 95814; (916) 444-0840.

* **Other Private Legislative Reporting Services:**
Legi-Tech Corporation and other firms specialize in tracking one or two statehouses. About half of the legislatures are covered by such information brokers.

Reports And Resources Available From State Legislatures

A trend among state legislatures is the creation of special investigative committees which have responsibility for oversight and often the power to subpoena. These watchdogs usually have permanent full-time staff and produce reports throughout the year. Frequent contact with these committees is necessary to stay informed about their activities.

Here is a sampling of reports issued by the Virginia Joint Legislative Audits and Review Committee:

Outpatient Care in Virginia
Medical Assistance Programs in Virginia: An Overview
Homes for Adults in Virginia
Social Services (including day care) in Virginia
Vehicle Cost Responsibility in Virginia
Highway Construction, Maintenance, and Transit Needs
The Occupational and Professional Regulatory System
Consolidation of Office Space in Northern Virginia
Special Report: Use of State-Owned Aircraft
Towns in Virginia
Virginia's Correctional System: Population Forecasting

Even those legislatures that compress their work into 60 or 90 day sessions are active year-round. Information about hearings, meetings, and reports produced throughout the Interim can be provided by each state house legislative information office.

State Legislatures: Bill Status Information Offices

You will find more than 50 information offices listed here because some state houses do not have one centralized legislature reference office.

Alabama

Senate Bill Status, 11 S.Union, Room 709, New State House, Montgomery, AL 36130; (205) 242-7826. This office can respond to questions about all Senate bills and refer you to the appropriate committee, document room, etc.

House Bill Status, 11 S.Union, Room 512, New State House, Montgomery, AL 36130; (205) 242-7630. This office can provide information on all bills pending before the House of Representatives and can refer you to the appropriate committees, document rooms, etc.

Alaska

Legislative Information, 130 Seward St., Suite 313, Juneau, AK 99801-2197; (907) 465-4648. This office can provide information on the status of House and Senate bills. It can do subject searches by accessing a database but at this time Legislative Information cannot provide computer printouts. Copies of bills will be sent out by this office.

Arizona

Information Desk, House of Representatives, State House, 1700 West Washington Street, Phoenix, AZ 85007; (602) 542-4221. This Information Desk is the best starting point to learn the status of all bills pending before the House of Representatives. This office will refer you to the appropriate committees, document room, etc.

Senate Information Desk, State House, 1700 West Washington Street, Phoenix, AZ 85007; (602) 542-3559. This Information Desk maintains current information on all bills pending before the Arizona Senate. This office will refer you to the appropriate committees, document rooms, etc.

Arkansas

Office of Legislative Counsel, State Capitol Building, Room 315, Little Rock, AR 72201; (501) 682-1937. This office can provide status information on all legislation pending before the House of Representatives and the Senate. It also has scheduling information and can refer you to the appropriate committees, document rooms, etc.

California

Office of the Chief Clerk, State Assembly, State Capitol, Room 3196, Sacramento, CA 95814; (916) 445-3614. This office can respond to questions regarding legislation pending before the State Assembly and Assembly committees. This office can refer you to the appropriate offices in the State Capitol such as the document rooms.

Secretary of the Senate, State Capitol, Room 3044, Sacramento, CA 95814; (916) 445-4251. This office can provide information about bills pending before the Senate and the Senate committees. The Secretary of the Senate also will refer you to appropriate offices in the State Capitol such as where to obtain copies of Senate bills.

Colorado

Legislative Information Center, State Capitol Building, Room 0101, 200 E. Colfax Ave., Denver, CO 80203; (303) 866-3055. This office can provide information on the status of both House and Senate bills. The Legislative Information Center also can send you copies of bills as well as mail out status sheets which target on bills pertaining to a specific subject.

Connecticut

Bill Information Room, Law and Legislative Reference Dept., State Library, 231 Capitol Avenue, Hartford, CT 06106; (203) 566-5736. This office can provide information about both House and Senate bills and send you copies of bills. Besides doing a key word or subject search, this office can mail you a printout of all legislation pertaining to one topic.

Delaware

Division of Research, Legislative Counsel, Legislative Hall, Dover, DE 19901; (302) 739-4114; (800) 282-8545. This office can provide status information on both House and Senate bills and send you copies of bills. It can access a legislative computerized database and do searches for free. The toll-free number operates year-round.

Florida

Legislative Information Division, 11 W. Madison St., Room 704, Tallahassee, FL 32399-1400; (904) 488-4371; (800) 342-1827. This office can provide status information on all House and Senate bills. It can send you single copies of up to 10 bills and mail out printouts of all House and Senate bills pertaining to a specific subject.

Georgia

Clerk of the House, 309 State Capitol, Atlanta, GA 30334; (404) 656-5015. This office can provide up-to-date information on all House bills and send you copies of House bills. The Clerk of the House also will search its database to tell you all legislation that has been introduced on a specific topic.

Secretary of the Senate, State Capitol, Room 353, Atlanta, GA 30334; (404) 656-5040; (800) 282-5803. This office can respond to questions about all bills

Information from Lawmakers

pending before the Georgia Senate. The Secretary of the Senate can send you copies of Senate bills and search its database for legislation pertaining to a specific subject.

Hawaii

Clerk of the House, State Capitol of Hawaii, Honolulu, HI 96813; (808) 586-6400. This office can respond to questions about bills pending before the House and refer you to the appropriate offices in the State Capitol such as the document room.

Clerk of the Senate, State Capitol of Hawaii, Honolulu, HI 96813; (808) 586-6720. This office can provide status information on all legislation pending before the Hawaii Senate. It can refer you to the appropriate offices in the State Capitol such as the document room.

Idaho

Legislative Information Center, State House Room 301, Boise, ID 83720; (208) 334-2411. This office can give you information on the status of all House and Senate bills. It also can send you copies of bills as well as a printout of all legislation pertaining to a specific topic.

Illinois

Clerk of the House, State Capitol Building, Room 424, Springfield, IL 62706; (217) 782-6010; (800) 252-6300. This office can respond to questions about both House and Senate bills, and provide you with copies of bills. The Clerk's office can send you printouts, for example, a list of all bills sponsored by one legislator.

Indiana

Legislative Information, Legislative Services Agency, 302 State House, Indianapolis, IN 46204; (317) 232-9856. The agency can give you bill status information and do searches by key word, subject or legislator. Legislative Information can send you copies of bills but charge $.15 per page.

Iowa

Legislative Public Information Office, State Capitol, Room 16, Des Moines, IA 50319; (515) 281-5129. This office can provide information on all House and Senate bills and send you copies of bills. It can access a computerized database and mail you a printout of all legislation pertaining to a specific subject.

Kansas

Legislative Reference, State Library, State Capitol Third Floor, Topeka, KS 66612; (913) 296-2149; (800) 432-3924. This office can tell you the status of all current House and Senate legislation as well as provide bill histories. Legislative Reference can send you copies of bills and voting records.

Kentucky

Bill Status, State Capitol, Room 80, Frankfort, KY 40601; (502) 564-8100; (800) 633-4171. This office can provide information on House and Senate bills pending before the legislature. It can also send you copies of bills.

Louisiana

Legislative Research Library, House of Representatives, P.O. Box 94012, Baton Rouge, LA 70804-9012; (504) 342-2431; (800) 272-8186. During the session call toll-free PULS Line (if out-of-state, (504) 342-2425) for bill status information and send you copies of House and Senate bills. When the legislature is not in session contact the Legislative Research Library.

Maine

Legislative Information Office, State House, Room 314, Station 115, Augusta, ME 04333; (207) 289-1692. This office can respond to questions about House and Senate bills and do key word or subject searches of its database.

Maryland

Legislative Information Desk, Dept. of Legislative Reference, 90 State Circle, Annapolis, MD 21401; (410) 841-3886; (800) 492-7122. This office can provide

status information on all House and Senate bills and send you copies of bills. It also can provide you with a printout of all bills which pertain to a specific subject area.

Massachusetts

Citizen Information Service, 1 Ashburton Place, 16th Floor, Boston, MA 02108; (617) 727-7030. This office can provide bill status information and supply copies of bills but you must know the bill number. To obtain bill numbers and other information contact the Clerk of the House which is listed below.

Clerk of the House, House of Representatives, State House, Boston, MA 02133; (617) 722-2356. This office can respond to questions about House and Senate bills and will refer you to the document room and other appropriate offices within the State House.

Michigan

Clerk of the House, State Capitol, Lansing, MI 48909; (517) 373-0135. This office can provide information on the status of House bills and can do searches of its database to identify legislation which pertains to a specific subject. It will refer you to the House document room for copies of bills.

Secretary of the Senate, P.O. Box 30036, Lansing, MI 48933; (517) 373-2400. This office can provide Senate bill status information and also can send you copies of bills.

Minnesota

House Index Office, State Capitol Building, Room 211, St Paul, MN 55155; (612) 296-6646. This office can tell you the status of all House bills but will refer you to the Chief Clerk's office for copies of all House bills. It can search its database to identify all bills that pertain to a specific subject.

Senate Index Office, State Capitol Building, Room 231, St Paul, MN 55155, 612-296-2887-- This office can provide bill status information on all Senate legislation and will refer you to the Secretary of the Senate if you want to obtain copies of bills. It can search its database and identify all bills pertaining to a specific subject.

Mississippi

House Docket Room, PO Box 1018, New Capitol Room 305, Jackson, MS 39215; (601) 359-3358. This office can tell you the status of all House bills and send you copies of proposed laws pending before the House.

Senate Docket Room, PO Box 1018, New Capitol Room 308, Jackson, MS 39215; (601) 359-3229. This office can respond to questions about bills pending before the Mississippi Senate and send you copies of Senate bills.

Missouri

House Information Bill Status, State Capitol, Room 307B, Jefferson City, MO 65101; (314) 751-3659. This office can provide information on bills pending before the House and will refer you to the appropriate offices within the State Capitol such as the document room.

Senate Research, State Capitol Room B-9, Jefferson City, MO 65101; (314) 751-4666. This office can respond to questions about bills pending before the Senate and will refer you to the appropriate offices such as the document room.

Montana

Legislative Counsel, State Capitol, Room 138, Helena, MT 59620; (406) 444-3064, (800) 333-3408. The in-state toll-free number may change in subsequent sessions of the Montana legislature. The Legislative Counsel office can respond to inquiries year-round and send you copies of bills.

Nebraska

Hotline, Office of the Clerk, State Capitol, Room 2018, Lincoln, NE 68509; (402) 471-2709; (800) 742-7456. This office operates an in-state hotline during the session that can provide information on all bills pending before this unicameral legislature. The Clerk can respond to questions year-round.

Be patient. If any phone number is incorrect, call (area code) 555-1212 and request the new listing.

Tracking State Legislation

Nevada

Chief Clerk of the Assembly, Legislative Building, Room 124, 401 S. Carson St., Carson City, NV 89710; (702) 885-5739. This office can provide information about the status of bills pending before the Assembly. The Chief Clerk will refer you to the appropriate offices in the State Capitol such as the documents room or the Clerk of the Senate.

New Hampshire

State Library Government, Information Bureau, 20 Park Street, Concord, NH 03301; (603) 271-2239. This office can respond to questions about House and Senate bills pending before the legislature. It can send you copies of bills and search its database for bills pertaining to specific subject areas.

New Jersey

Office of Legislative, Services - Bill Room, Executive Statehouse, Room #6, Statehouse CN 068, Trenton, NJ 08625; (609) 292-6395; (800) 792-8630. This office can provide information about House and Senate legislation and send you copies of bills. It will refer you to other offices within the State House if necessary.

New Mexico

Legislative Counsel, State Capitol, Room 334, Sante Fe, NM 87503; (505) 986-4600. This office can provide bill status information on House and Senate legislation. It will refer you to the appropriate offices within the State Capitol such as the document room.

New York

Public Information Office, Room 202 LOB 2nd Floor Empire State Plaza, Albany, NY 12248; (518) 455-4218; (800) 342-9860. This office can provide information on the status of House and Senate bills and send you copies of bills. It may refer you to your local library if you want a search done to identify all bills which pertain to a specific subject.

North Carolina

Clerk of the House, State Legislative Building, Room 2320, Raleigh, NC 27601; (919) 733-7760. This office can provide information about House and Senate bills and will refer you to the appropriate offices within the State Capitol such as where to obtain copies of bills.

North Dakota

Legislative Counsel Library, State Capitol, Bismarck, ND 58505; (701) 224-2916. This office can provide information about House and Senate bills year-round and will refer you to appropriate offices in the State Capitol. The legislature maintains an in-state toll-free number during the biannual session.

Ohio

Legislative Information, State House, Columbus, OH 43266-0604; (614) 466-8842; (800) 282-0253. This office can provide information on the status of House and Senate legislation and do subject searches. This telephone bank of researchers will route your requests (i.e., copies of bills). In-state toll-free access is available throughout the year.

Oklahoma

Chief Clerk, House of Representatives, State Capitol Bldg., Oklahoma City, OK 73105; (405) 521-2711, (800) 522-8502. This office can respond to questions about bills pending before the House and Senate. It will refer you to the appropriate offices within the State Capitol.

Oregon

Legislative Library, State Capitol S-347, Salem, OR 97310; (503) 378-8871, (800) 332-2313. This office can provide information on House and Senate bills year-round. During the biannual session the legislature offers an in-state toll-free number for bill information.

Pennsylvania

Legislative Reference Bureau, History Room, Main Capitol Building, Room 648, Harrisburg, PA 17120-0033; (717) 787-2342. This office can provide information on House and Senate bills be consulting its card index and computerized database. It will refer you to the appropriate offices, for example, where to obtain copies of bills.

Rhode Island

State Library, State House Room 208, Providence, RI 02903; (401) 277-2473. This office can provide you with information on the status of House and Senate bills and send you copies of bills. It will refer you to the appropriate legislators or committees.

South Carolina

Legislative Information Systems, Room 112, Blatt Building, 1105 Pendleton St., Columbia, SC 29201; (803) 734-2923, (800) 922-1539. This office can respond to inquiries about House and Senate bills and will refer you to the appropriate offices such as where to obtain copies of bills. It can do subject searches but is unable to send out a printout.

South Dakota

Public Information Clerk, Legislative Research Counsel, State Capitol Building, 500 East Capitol, Pierre, SD 57501; (605) 773-4498, (605) 773-4296. Clare Cholik can provide information on the status of House and Senate bills. She can access a computerized database and do a search to identify legislation which pertains to a specific subject.

Tennessee

Office of Legislative Services, Room G-20, War Memorial Bldg, Nashville, TN 37243; (615) 741-3511. This office can provide information on House and Senate bills and will send you copies of bills. It can identify all legislation pending on specific subjects.

Texas

Legislative Reference Library, PO Box 12488, Capitol Station, Austin, TX 78711; 512) 463-1252. This office can provide information on the status of all House and Senate bills. It can search its database to identify all legislation which pertains to a specific subject. It will refer you to the appropriate offices such as the document room.

Utah

Legislative Research and General Counsel, 436 State Capitol, Salt Lake City, UT 84114; (801) 538-1032. This office can respond to questions about House and Senate bills. It will refer you to the appropriate offices within the State Capitol.

Vermont

Clerk of the House, Attn: Cathleen Cameron, State House, Montpelier, VT 05633-5501; (802) 828-2247. Ms. Cameron can provide you with information on legislation pending before the House and do subject searches by accessing a computerized database. She will refer you to the appropriate offices in the State House.

Clerk of the Senate, State House, Montpelier, VT 05633-5501; (802) 828-2241. This office can respond to questions about legislation pending before the Senate and will refer you to the appropriate legislators, committees, document rooms, etc.

Virginia

Legislative Information, House of Delegates, P.O. Box 406, Richmond, VA 23203; (804) 786-6530. This office can provide information on House and Senate bills and can send you copies of bills. It can consult a printed index which is updated daily to identify bills which pertain to a specific subject.

Washington

House Workroom, Legislative Building, Third Floor Capitol Campus, Olympia, WA 98504; (206) 786-7780; (800) 562-6000. This office can provide information

Be patient. If any phone number is incorrect, call (area code) 555-1212 and request the new listing.

Information from Lawmakers

on the status of bills pending before the House. It can also provide copies of bills. The toll-free number (out of state should call 206-786-7763) is in operation only during the session.

Senate Workroom, Legislative Building AS32, Third Floor Capitol Campus, Olympia, WA 98504; (206) 786-7592; (800) 562-6000. This office can provide information on bills pending before the Senate and can supply you with copies of bills. An in-state toll-free number (out of state call 206-786-7763) provides both House and Senate bill information but only during the session.

West Virginia

Clerk of the House, House of Delegates, 1900 Kanawha Blvd. E, Bldg.1, Room M212, Charleston, WV 25305-0470; (304) 340-3200. This office can respond to questions about legislation pending before the House of Delegates and House committees. It will refer you to the appropriate offices in the State Capitol such as where to obtain legislative documents.

Clerk of the Senate, 1900 Kanawha Blvd. E, Bldg., Room M-215, Charleston, WV 25305-0470; (304) 357-7800. This office can provide information on the status of bills pending before the Senate. It will refer you to the appropriate offices in the State Capitol.

Wisconsin

Legislative Reference Bureau, 100 N. Hamilton St., POB 2037, Madison, WI 53701-2037; (608) 266-0341; (800) 362-9472. The legislature operates a Legislative Hotline during the session (if calling from inside Madison, dial 608-266-9960). The Legislative Reference Bureau can respond to questions year-round will refer you to the document room, etc.

Wyoming

Legislative Service Office, State Capitol Building, Room 213, Cheyenne, WY 82002; (307) 777-7881, (800) 342-9570 within Wyoming. When the Wyoming legislature is not in session it is necessary to contact this office. During the session, bill status questions are best directed to the two offices noted below.

Senate Information Clerk, State Capitol Building, Cheyenne, WY 82002; (307) 777-6185; (307) 777-7711. This office can respond to questions about the status of bill pendings before the Senate. It will refer you to the Bill Room to obtain copies of bills.

House Information Clerk, State Capitol Building, Cheyenne, WY 82002; (307) 777-7765; (307) 777-7852. This office can provide current information on legislation pending before the House. It will refer you to the proper offices in the State Capitol, for instance, the Bill Room.

Be patient. If any phone number is incorrect, call (area code) 555-1212 and request the new listing.

Books and Libraries Library of Congress

The Library of Congress is the world's largest library, but there are more than dusty old books stored here. The more than 20 million books in 470 languages that it holds represent less than a fourth of the holdings of the Library. There are 3,000,000 books in the science and technology field. There are also massive collections of manuscripts, maps, music, prints and photographs, and film. In 1800 the Library was founded simply to help Congress make the laws. But now the Library is much more. For instance, more than a million handicapped readers borrow materials in braille and recorded forms each year. And the Library also registers copyright for books, music, films, computer programs, and other works. In celebration of the arts, the Library holds concerts by the Juilliard String Quartet, poetry readings, folk music and dance performances, and showings of classic films. More than 900 specialists provide extensive research and analysis for Congress, much of which is available to you through your Congressman's office. The Library is a major world center for scholarly research with specialists in its 22 reading rooms and in other areas ready to provide information on just about any subject you can name. And much of this information is available to you from exhaustive databases both in printed form and on magnetic tape.

* Books Published Since 1454

Enhanced Catalog Division
LA 2004, Library of Congress
Washington, DC 20540 (202) 707-5965

The *National Union Catalog* lists the world's books published since 1454 and held in approximately 1,100 North American libraries and other union catalogs that record the location of books in Slavic, Hebraic, Japanese, and Chinese languages (if Romanized). The catalog is produced on microfiche, and is in many libraries.

* Center for the Book: Reading Project

Center for the Book
Library of Congress
Washington, DC 20540 (202) 707-5221

A partnership between the federal government and private industry, the Center for the Book works closely with other organizations to explore important issues dealing with books and educational communities. The Center encourages reading and research about books and reading and serves as a catalyst by bringing together authors, publishers, librarians, booksellers, educators, scholars, and readers to discuss common concerns. Four primary concerns are: television and the printed word, reading development, international role of the book, and publishing. The center is funded by tax-deductible contributions.

* Central Intelligence Agency Declassified Reports

Photoduplication Service
Library of Congress
Washington, DC 20540 (202) 707-5650

The Library of Congress distributes CIA reports that have been released to the public. These reports detail foreign government structures, trade news, economic conditions, and industrial development. Orders must be prepaid or charged to a standing account at the Library of Congress. For $13, the Photoduplication Service can also provide you with a list of CIA reports available. Reports can be purchased on microfilm for $24 per reel if you write to: CIA, Office of Public and Agency Information, Washington, DC, 20205; the list of CIA Reports is free.

* Children's Literature Center

Children's Literature Center
National Programs
Library of Congress
Washington, DC 20540 (202) 707-5535

The Center prepares lists and scholarly bibliographies and provides other reference services for individuals who serve children, including scholars, writers, teachers, librarians, and illustrators. The center also has many publishers' catalogs that list titles to be published in the upcoming year, a wide range of periodicals about children's literature, and lists from rare and used book sellers. *Books for Children*, a guide to reference sources for children's literature

published annually for $1 per issue, is available from the Superintendent of Documents, Government Printing Office, Washington, DC 20402; (202) 783-3238. Guides available:

#6-1989-S/N 030-00100-133-4
#7-1990- S/N 030-001-00135-1
#8-1991- S/N 030-001-00138-5

* Computer-Generated Bibliographies

Customer Services Section
Cataloging Distribution Service
Library of Congress
Washington, DC 20541 (202) 707-6100

Readers who cannot do their own research in the Library of Congress can request a search of its catalog databases on a fee basis. Through this service, a bibliographic listing referred to as Select Marc; Restrspective Conversion Service, can provide you with their complete manual on readable magnetic tape. For more information contact Barbara Jones (202) 707-1313.

* Congressional Documents, Reports, and Hearings

Law Library
Library of Congress
Washington, DC 20540 (202) 707-5079

All Senate and House documents, reports, hearings since 1970, and all bills back to the First Congress are available. Material can be obtained on microfilm.

* Congressional Research Service (CRS) Reports

Contact your Member of Congress (202) 224-3121
Refer to Current Events Reports and Homework Chapter for complete listing of these reports and issue briefs.

The Congressional Research Service at the Library of Congress prepares hundreds of non-partisan background *Reports* each year on current issues, large and small, domestic and foreign, social and political. CRS also publishes hundreds of major *Issue Briefs* each year designed to keep members of Congress informed on timely issues. Written in simple and direct language, these briefs provide background information and are updated daily. Free printed copies can be obtained from your Congressman's office. *Audio Briefs* are audio cassette programs produced on topics of Congressional interest, including specially produced programs on issues before Congress featuring CRS experts and nationally recognized experts. CRS products are listed in the *Guide to CRS Products*, published quarterly, and in monthly cumulative supplements entitled *Update to the Guide to CRS Products*. Copies are available from your Congressman.

* Copernicus to Star Wars

Science and Technology Division

Be patient. If any phone number is incorrect, call (area code) 555-1212 and request the new listing.

Books and Libraries

Library of Congress
Washington, DC 20540 (202) 707-5639

The Science and Technology collection contains more than 3 million scientific and technical books and pamphlets and 3 million technical reports, including those issued by the U.S. Department of Energy, NASA, the U.S. Department of Defense, and other government agencies. The collections, which are particularly strong in aeronautical materials, contain first editions of Copernicus and Newton and the personal papers of the Wright Brothers and Alexander Graham Bell. Computer terminals provide principal access to the collections. Special scientific finding aids, such as abstracting and indexing journals, are part of the division's reference collection. This Division also prepares an informal series of reference guides called *Tracer Bullets*, which are available free upon request. More extensive bibliographies are published from time to time.

* Copyright Entries Catalogs

Superintendent of Documents
Government Printing Office
Washington, DC 20402 (202) 783-3238

The following copyright catalogs, which list materials registered only during the period covered by each issue, are available on microfiche only and are sold as individual subscriptions:

Part 1: Nondramatic Literary Works (quarterly) $14 per year.
Part 2: Serials and Periodicals (semi-annually) $5 per year.
Part 3: Performing Arts (quarterly) $13 per year.
Part 4: Motion Pictures and Filmstrips (semi-annually) $5 per year.
Part 5: Visual Arts (excluding maps) (semi-annually) $5 per year.
Part 6: Maps (semi-annually) $5 per year.
Part 7: Sound Recordings (semi-annually) $7.50 per year.
Part 8: Renewals (semi-annually) $5 per year.

Information on copyrights from 1978 to the present is available online through terminals located in the Copyright Office, and records on all copyrights back to the 1800s are kept in the Copyright Card Catalog Office, Room 459; (202) 707-5063.

* Copyright Examining Practices

Copyright Office
Certifications and Documents
Library of Congress
Washington, DC 20559 (202) 707-6800

The *Compendium II of Copyright Office Practices* is intended as a general guide for those with special interest in copyright examining practices which concern the registration of applications for copyright under the 1976 Copyright Act. It is available for $51 from the Government Printing Office, Washington, DC 20402; (202) 783-3238.

* Copyright Office

Copyright Office
Library of Congress
Washington, DC 20559 (202) 707-3000

The Library of Congress Copyright Office grants exclusive rights to reproduce or prepare derivative works on the copyrighted work in copies or on phonorecords and to distribute them to the public by sale, rental, lease, or loan. Copyrightable works include books, periodicals, and other literary works; musical compositions, song lyrics, dramas, and dramatico-musical compositions; pantomimes and choreographic works; pictoral, graphic, and sculptural works; motion pictures and other audiovisual works; and sound recordings. The Library provides information on copyright registration procedures and copyright card catalogs covering more than 16 million works that have been registered since 1870.

* Copyright Research Service

Copyright Office
Reference and Bibliographic Section
Library of Congress
Washington, DC 20559 (202) 707-6850

For a fee of $20 per hour or part thereof, the Copyright Office will research the copyright you need and send you the information by mail. Requests must be in writing, and you must specify exact details you require.

* Domestic and Foreign Periodicals Division

Serial and Government Publication Division
Library of Congress, LM 133
Washington, DC 20540 (202) 707-5647

The Library of Congress has an extensive collection of both domestic and foreign periodicals, government serials, microfilms, and newspapers.

* Folklife Center

American Folklife Center
Library of Congress
Washington, DC 20540-8100 (202) 707-6590

This Center collects and maintains archives, conducts scholarly research, and coordinates the development of field projects, performances, exhibitions, festivals, workshops, publications, and audiovisual programs on American folklife. *Folk Life Center News* is a free quarterly newsletter on folklife activities and programs. The Center maintains and administers an extensive collection of folk music, folk culture, ethnomusicology, and grass-roots oral history--both American and international--in published and unpublished forms. The Archive houses more than 30,000 hours of folk-related recordings, manuscripts, and raw materials. The Archive Reading Room contains more than 4,000 books and periodicals, plus unpublished theses, and dissertations, field notes, and many textual and some musical transcriptions and recordings. A free listing of the Archive's publications is available.

* Free LOC Catalog Cards

Cataloging Distribution Service
Library of Congress
Washington, DC 20541 (202) 707-6100

Individuals or organizations wishing to establish libraries may receive Library of Congress catalog cards free by establishing an account with the above office.

* Geography and Maps Division

Geography and Map Division
Library of Congress
Washington, DC 20540 (202) 707-6277

The Library's cartographic collections, which include 4 million maps, nearly 51,000 atlases, 500 globes, and some 8,000 reference books, are the largest and most comprehensive in the world. The collections include atlases published over the last five centuries covering individual continents, countries, states, counties, and cities as well as the world. Official topographic, geologic, soil, mineral, and resource maps and nautical and aeronautical charts are also available for most countries. There are also complete LANDSAT microimage data sets of images produced by several satellites revolving around the Earth. Subscription information on the microfiche data sets is available from EOSAT, 4300 Forbes Blvd., Lanham, MD 20706; (800) 344-9933.

* High School and Intercollegiate Debate Topics

Your Member of Congress (202) 224-3121

A series of free reports are prepared by the Congressional Research Service of the Library of Congress that contain pertinent excerpts, bibliographic references, and other materials related to debate topics for that year. For high school debate teams, the topics are selected by the National University Extension Service Association, and for college, the topics are selected by the American Speech Association.

* Historical Sound Recordings Division

Motion Picture, Broadcasting,
and Recorded Sound Division
Room 338
Library of Congress
Washington, DC 20540 (202) 707-5840

The sound recording collection reflects the entire spectrum of history of sound from wax cylinders to quadraphonic discs and includes such diverse media as wire recordings, aluminum discs, zinc discs, acetate-covered glass discs, rubber compound discs, and translucent plastic discs. The division has also recently made all of its materials recorded prior to 1909 available on 8-inch compressed audio discs for individual users in the Recorded Sound Reading Room using a micro computer. Included are the Berliner collection, from the company which invented and introduced disc recording, radio news commentaries from 1944 to 1946, eyewitness descriptions of marine combat and House of Representatives debates. For purchase by researchers, the Division's laboratory is prepared to

Be patient. If any phone number is incorrect, call (area code) 555-1212 and request the new listing.

Library of Congress

make taped copies of recordings in good physical condition, when not restricted by copyright, performance rights, or provisions of gift or transfer. The requester is responsible for any necessary search--by mail or in person--of Copyright Office records to determine the copyright status of specific recordings. The Division also offers copies of some of its holdings for sale in disc form. These include a number of LP records of folk music, poetry, and other literature.

* Humanities Library

National Endowment for the Humanities (NEH)
1100 Pennsylvania Ave., NW, Room 217
Washington, DC 20506 (202) 606-8244

This library focuses on the needs and interests of NEH and has materials on a variety of humanities-related subjects. Individuals may use this library by appointment only.

* Information On Demand

National Reference Service
Library of Congress, LJ 144
Washington, DC 20540 (202) 707-5522

If you need information that is contained in the material in the Library of Congress collections, the reference staff will find it for you and relay it over the phone. If the information you require is too extensive, however, the reference staff will refer you to private researchers who work on a fee basis.

* Last Resort Interlibrary Loan

Loan Division
Library of Congress
Washington, DC 20540 (202) 707-5444

The Loan Division will loan materials to other libraries when they have exhausted other means of locating the material. If you are having trouble finding material, first contact your local library.

* Law Library on All Legal Systems

Law Library
Library of Congress
Washington, DC 20540 (202) 707-5080

As the world's largest and most comprehensive library of foreign, international, and comparative law, the Law Library provides information for all known legal systems including common law, civil law, Roman law, canon law, Chinese law, Jewish and Islamic law, and ancient and medieval law. Specialists with knowledge of more than fifty languages provide reference and research service in all known legal systems. U.S. legislative documents housed here include the *Congressional Record* (and its predecessors), the serial set, a nearly complete set of bills and resolutions, current documents, committee prints, reports, hearings, etc. plus a complete set of U.S. Supreme Court records and briefs and collections of U.S. Court of Appeals records and briefs. The law library has five major divisions:

American-British Law: United States, Australia, Canada, Great Britain, India, New Zealand, Pakistan, certain other countries of the British Commonwealth and their dependent territories, and Eire: (202) 707-5077.

European Law: Nations of Europe and their possessions, except Spain and Portugal: (202) 707-5088.

Hispanic Law: Spain and Portugal, Latin America, Puerto Rico, the Philippines, and Spanish- and Portuguese-language states of Africa: (202) 707-5070.

Far Eastern Law: Nations of East and Southeast Asia including China, Indonesia, Japan, Korea, Thailand, and former British and French possessions in the area: (202) 707-5085.

Near Eastern and African Law: Middle Eastern countries, including the Arab states, Turkey, Iran, and Afghanistan, and all African countries, except Spanish- and Portuguese-language states and possessions: (202) 707-5073.

* Legislative Histories and Research

Law Library
Library of Congress, LM240
Washington, DC 20540 (202) 707-5065

The Law Library compiles legislative histories which include versions of new

public statutes from the time of introduction, through congressional hearings, House and Senate floor debate, vote tallies, and votes.

* Library of Congress Color Slides

Photoduplication Service
Library of Congress
Washington, DC 20540 (202) 707-5640

Color slides of the Library's buildings and items from its collections are available at $10 per slide. Slides can also be made from a bound volume for $20. Minimum order charge is $25.

* Library of Congress Free Catalog

Office Systems Services
Library of Congress (LC)
Washington, DC 20540 (202) 707-5590

The free annual catalog, *Publications in Print*, offers a comprehensive listing of the materials published by or in cooperation with the Library of Congress. Publications may be in print, recorded, or video formats. As new LC publications are issued, they are announced in the weekly *Library of Congress Information Bulletin*, and in the *Monthly Catalog of United States Government Publications* available from the Superintendent of Documents, Government Printing Office, Washington, DC 20402; (202) 783-3238.

* Library of Congress Guide

Sales Office
Library of Congress
Washington, DC 20540 (202) 707-0204

Written for both the researcher and the casual visitor, this colorful guide explores the Library's history, architecture, exhibits, holdings, and services. It is available for $5.95 at the Library's Information Counter, or by mail for $5.95 plus $3.50 shipping and handling from the above address. Out of print; if funds are available will be ready in 1994.

* Library of Congress Tours

Visitor Services Office
Library of Congress
Washington, DC 20540 (202) 707-5458

The Visitor Services Office shows a film tour, (Monday to Saturday starting at 9 a.m. and 1 p.m. to 5 p.m. on Sunday) of the Library every half hour. Actual tours of the Library are conducted at 10:00 a.m., 1:00 p.m., and 3:00 p.m., weekdays. The tours highlight the art and architecture of the Thomas Jefferson Building, and provide an overview of the Library activities. Tour reservations for groups over 10 must be made in advance.

* Library Services for Blind and Physically

Handicapped Readers Reference Section
National Library Service for the Blind and
Physically Handicapped
Library of Congress
Washington, DC 20542 (202) 707-9275
OR: Your local library

The National Library Service (NLS) maintains a large collection of books, magazines, journals, and music materials in braille, large type, and recorded formats for individuals who cannot read or use standard printed materials because of temporary or permanent visual loss or physical limitations. Reading materials and necessary playback equipment for books on record and cassette are distributed through a national network of cooperating libraries. Books in the collection are selected on the basis of their appeal to a wide range of interests. Bestsellers, biographies, fiction, and how-to books are in great demand.

* Main Reading Room

Main Reading Room
National Reference Service
Library of Congress, Room LJ 100
Washington, DC 20540 (202) 707-5522

Located on the first floor of the Thomas Jefferson Building, the main reading room contains material on American history, economics, fiction, language and literature, political science, government documents, and sociology. A reference collection for these materials is also housed there. These reading rooms are not equipped to answer reference questions over the telephone, but will provide

Be patient. If any phone number is incorrect, call (area code) 555-1212 and request the new listing.

Books and Libraries

information on their collections, hours of operation, and the like.

Social Science . . . . (202) 707-5522
Microform . . . . (202) 707-5471
Local History and Genealogy . . . . (202) 707-5537
Newspapers and Current Periodicals . . . . (202) 707-5690
Science . . . . (202) 707-5639
Law Library . . . . (202) 707-5079
Performing Arts Library at the Kennedy
Center . . . . (202) 707-6245
Motion Picture, Broadcasting, and Recorded Sound . . . . . . (202) 707-5840
Archive of Folk Culture . . . . (202) 707-5510
Prints and Photographs . . . . (202) 707-6394
Manuscripts . . . . (202) 707-5387
Music . . . . (202) 707-5507
Rare Book and Special Collections . . . . (202) 707-5434
Geography and Map . . . . (202) 707-6277
Hispanic . . . . (202) 707-5400
European . . . . (202) 707-5858
Asian . . . . (202) 707-5428
African and Middle Eastern Division . . . . (202) 707-5528

* Manuscripts Division

Manuscript Division
Special Collections, LM 101
Library of Congress
Washington, DC 20540 (202) 707-5387

More than 40 million pieces of manuscript material are housed in the Manuscript Division, including the letters, diaries, speech drafts (including the copy of the Gettysburg Address), scrapbooks, telegrams, and so forth of influential people. For instance, the Library owns the papers of 23 of the presidents from George Washington to Calvin Coolidge, as well as materials of Clara Barton, Sigmund Freud, and Benjamin Franklin. The Manuscript is open to persons engaged in serious research who present proper identification. Hours of operation are 8:30 a.m. to 5:00 p.m., Monday through Friday (except national holidays).

* Motion Picture and Broadcasting Division

Motion Picture, Broadcasting, and Recorded
Sound Division, LM 336
Library of Congress
Washington, DC 20540 (202) 287-5840

The Library's film and television collections contain more than 100,000 titles, and more than 1,000 titles are added each month through copyright deposit, purchase, gift, or exchange. Items selected from copyright deposits include feature films and short works of all sorts, fiction and documentary, exemplifying the range of current film and video production. The collections also include some 90,000 stills. The film and television collections are maintained for research purposes. Limited viewing and listening facilities for individual users are provided in the reading rooms.

* Music Arts Reading Room

Music Arts Reading Room
Room LM113
Library of Congress
Washington, DC 20540 (202) 707-5507

The Performing Arts Reading Room houses the Library of Congress's non-book collections in the performing arts area: music, dance, sound recordings, motion pictures, and television. The collection includes more than 4,000,000 pieces of music and manuscripts, some 300,000 books and pamphlets, and about 350,000 sound recordings reflecting the development of music in Western civilization from earliest times to the present. Reference services are available. Adjacent to the reading room is the Recorded Sound Reference Center, Room LM 115, (202) 707-7833, for users primarily interested in sound recordings and radio materials. Listening facilities are available in the reading room, but their use is limited of those doing research of a specific nature leading to publication or production. Musicians who wish to play music drawn from the Library's collection may use the piano available in an adjacent sound proof room.

* Newspapers and Periodicals From Around the World

Library of Congress
Washington, DC 20540 (202) 707-5640

Hundreds of different newspapers and periodicals from all fifty states and countries around the world are available on microfilm for $30 for domestic and $35 for foreign publications. Subscriptions are available or single issues can be ordered. Orders must be prepaid or charged to a standing account at the Library of Congress.

* Performing Arts

Performing Arts
John F. Kennedy Center for Performing Arts
2700 F St., NW Library (202) 416-8780
Washington, DC 20566 Exec ofc (202) 416-8000

The Performing Arts Library is a joint project of the Library of Congress and the Kennedy Center, and offers information and reference assistance on dance, theater, opera, music, film and broadcasting.

* Preservation: Newspapers to Motion Pictures

National Preservation Program Office
Library of Congress, LMG 21
Washington, DC 20540 (202) 707-1840

The Preservation Office is involved in a constant race against time to preserve its millions of items from disintegration. Newspapers are immediately microfilmed, motion pictures are rushed to refrigerated vaults, manuscripts are put in fumigating vaults, and maps are encased in polyester envelopes. But the main problem for preservationists is acid and its affect on paper. Recently the Library's chemists developed a technique whereby wood pulp books are placed in huge vacuum tanks which are flooded with diethyl zinc gas, thus deacidifying them for another hundred years. Research continues on longstanding preservation problems. A series of leaflets on various preservation and conservation topics is available from the office.

* Prints and Photographs Division

Prints and Photographs Division
Library of Congress, LM 337
Washington, DC 20540-4840 (202) 707-6394

More than 10 million items in the Library of Congress chronicle American life and society from its earliest days to the present through its prints and photographs. Items include architectural plans, posters, cartoons, drawings, and advertising labels. Reference librarians will assist those doing their own research, and they can furnish names of freelance picture researchers for individuals who cannot get to the Library.

* Private Library Space for Researchers

Research Facilities Section
General Reading Rooms
Library of Congress
Washington, DC 20540 (202) 707-5211

For increased convenience, full-time scholars and researchers may apply for study desks in semi-private areas within the Library of Congress.

* Public Bills, Resolutions and Laws

Congressional Research Service
Bill Digest Section
Library of Congress
Washington, DC 20540 (202) 707-6996

The *Digest Public General Bills and Resolutions* provides summaries of public bills and resolutions and their current status in order of introduction in Congress. The *Digest* includes subject, author, and title. Subscription service consists of cumulative issues for each session of each Congress (two sessions per Congress). Prices per issue vary but average around $40. Subscription information is available from the Superintendent of Documents, Government Printing Office, Washington, DC 20402; (202) 783-3238.

* Publishers' ISBN Catalog Numbers

Cataloging-in-Publication
Library of Congress
Washington, DC 20540 (202) 707-6372

Through a program in cooperation with American publishers to print cataloging information in current books, Library of Congress card catalog numbers are assigned by the Cataloging-in-Publication Office prior to publication.

Library of Congress

* Rare Books Division

Rare Book and Special Collections Division
Library of Congress
LJ 256
Washington, DC 20540   (202) 707-5434

The Rare Books Division contains about 300,000 volumes and 200,000 pamphlets, broadsides, theater playbills, title pages, manuscripts, posters, and photographs. The collection includes documents of the first fourteen congresses of the United States, the personal libraries of Thomas Jefferson and Harry Houdini, incunabula; miniature books and dime novels, and the Russian Imperial collection. The division has its own central card catalog plus special card files that describe individual collections or special aspects of books from many collections.

* Reproduce Library of Congress Materials

Photoduplication Service
Library of Congress, G1011
Washington, DC 20540   (202) 707-5640

Photostats, microfilms, and other photocopies of manuscripts, prints, photographs, maps, and book materials not subject to copyright and other restrictions are available for a fee. In general, there is, however, a four-to-six-week turnaround time for this service. Order forms for photo reproduction and price schedules for this and other copying services are available.

* Science and Technology Resources

National Reference Services
Library of Congress
Washington, DC 20540   (202) 707-5522

The *Science, Technology, and Social Science Database* is a computerized directory of more than 14,000 organizations or individuals who will provide information to the general public on topics primarily in science, technology, and the social sciences. Citations generally contain the name of the organization or person, mailing address, telephone number, areas of interest, special collections, publications, and special services.

* Science Information Tracer Bullets

Science and Technology Division
National Reference Services
Library of Congress (LC)
Washington, DC 20540   (202) 707-5522

The *LC Science Tracer Bullet* is an informal series of literature guides designed to help a reader begin to locate published materials on a subject about which he or she has only a general knowledge. Among its major features are a weighted list of subject headings to be used in searching a card, book, or computer catalog; lists of basic texts, bibliographies, state-of-the-art reports, conference proceedings, or government publications; a list of abstracting and indexing services useful in finding journal articles and technical reports; and the names and addresses of organizations to contact for additional information. Because these compilations are intended to put a reader "on target," they are called *Tracer Bullets*. New titles in the series are announced in the *Library of Congress Information Bulletin* that is distributed to many libraries. Each Bullet is available, without charge, from the Science Reference Section of the Science and Technology Division at the address given above.

TB No.Title

- 81-3 *Alcoholism*
- 81-5 *Wind Power*
- 81-6 *Pets and Pet Care*
- 81-9 *Cable Television (Cable TV)*
- 81-10 *Manned Space Flight*
- 81-11 *Mariculture*
- 81-13 *Wood As Fuel*
- 81-14 *Volcanoes*
- 81-15 *History of American Agriculture*
- 81-17 *Epilepsy*
- 82-1 *Food Additives*
- 82-2 *Gardening*
- 82-3 *Earth Sheltered Buildings*
- 82-4 *Extraterrestrial Life*
- 82-5 *Jet Engines and Jet Aircraft*
- 82-6 *Biological Control of Insects*
- 82-9 *Sickle Cell Anemia*
- 83-1 *Biofeedback*
- 83-2 *Powder Metallurgy*
- 83-3 *Hazardous Wastes (Non-nuclear)*
- 83-4 *Science Policy*
- 83-5 *Plant Exploration and Introduction*
- 83-6 *Mental Retardation*
- 83-7 *Quarks*
- 83-9 *Geothermal Energy*
- 83-10 *High Technology*
- 84-1 *Aquaculture*
- 84-2 *Edible Wild Plants*
- 84-3 *Japanese Science and Technology*
- 84-4 *Sharks*
- 84-5 *Scientific and Technical Libraries: Administration and Management*
- 84-7 *Biotechnology*
- 85-1 *Herbs and Herb Gardening*
- 85-2 *Landscape Gardening*
- 85-3 *Endangered Species (Animals)*
- 85-4 *Computer Security*
- 85-6 *Acupuncture*
- 85-7 *CAD/CAM (Computer Aided Design/Computer Aided Manufacture)*
- 85-8 *Anorexia Nervosa/Bulimia*
- 85-10 *Rose Culture*
- 86-1 *Artificial Intelligence*
- 86-2 *Mars (Planet)*
- 86-3 *Jojoba and Other Oilseed Plants*
- 86-4 *Composite Materials*
- 86-5 *Electromagnetic Fields--Physiological and Health Effects*
- 86-6 *Diabetes Mellitus*
- 86-8 *Indoor Air Pollution*
- 86-11 *Acid Rain*
- 87-1 *Asbestos*
- 87-2 *Alzheimer's Disease*
- 87-3 *Cellular Radio*
- 87-4 *The History of Technology*
- 87-5 *Science and Technology in China*
- 87-6 *Stress: Physiological and Psychological Aspects*
- 87-7 *Osteoporosis*
- 87-8 *The Future: Science and Technology Enter the 21st Century*
- 87-9 *Microcomputers*
- 87-10 *Tribology*
- 87-11 *Inventions and Inventors*
- 87-12 *Optical Disc Technology*
- 88-1 *Algae*
- 88-2 *Fiber Optics*
- 88-3 *Biographical Sources in the Sciences*
- 88-5 *Soil Erosion*
- 88-6 *Noise Pollution*
- 89-1 *Science Policy--Foreign and International*
- 89-2 *Japanese Technology*
- 89-3 *Space Science Projects*
- 89-4 *Municipal Solid Waste Management*
- 89-5 *Human Diet and Nutrition*
- 89-6 *Endangered Species (Plants)*
- 89-7 *Allergy and Asthma*
- 89-8 *Earthquakes and Earthquake Engineering*
- 89-9 *Blacks in Science and Related Disciplines*
- 89-10 *Halocarbons and the Stratospheric Ozone Layer*
- 90-1 *Soviet Union and Eastern Europe: State of the Environment*
- 90-2 *Environmental Science Projects*
- 90-3 *High Speed Rail Transportation*
- 90-4 *Poisonous Plants*
- 90-5 *The Crisis in Science Education*
- 90-6 *Women in the Sciences*
- 90-7 *Freshwater Ecology*
- 90-8 *Astronomy and Astrophysics*
- 90-9 *Chemical and Biological Warfare*
- 90-10 *The Brain: An Overview*
- 91-1 *Unidentified Flying Objects*
- 91-2 *Civil Engineering: Public Works/Infrastructure*
- 91-3 *Dyslexia*
- 91-4 *Bioethics*
- 91-5 *Desalination*
- 91-6 *Career Opportunities in the Sciences*
- 91-7 *Breast Cancer*
- 91-8 *Medicinal Plants*
- 91-9 *Acquired Immunodeficiency Syndrome (AIDS)*
- 91-10 *Dolphins*

Books and Libraries

91-11 Chemical Exposure: Toxicology, Safety, and Risk Assessment
91-12 Science Fair Projects

* Selling to the Library of Congress

Procurement and Supply Division
Library of Congress
1701 Brightseat Rd.
Landover, MD 20785 (202) 707-0419

Those interested in doing business with the Library of Congress must request the pamphlet, *How and What We Purchase* from the above office in writing.

* Social Science Resource Center

National Reference Services
Library of Congress
Washington, DC 20540 (202) 707-5522

The *Science, Technology, and Social Science Database* is a computerized directory of more than 14,000 organizations or individuals who will provide information to the general public on topics primarily in science, technology, and the social sciences. Citations generally contain the name of the organization or person, mailing address, telephone number, areas of interest, special collections, publications, and special services.

* Sound Recordings of Poetry and Other Literature

Motion Picture, Broadcasting,
and Recorded Sound Division
Library of Congress
Washington, DC 20540 (202) 707-5840

The Library of Congress offers copies of some of its poetry and literature holdings for sale in disc form. Contact this office for information on what's available, along with prices.

* State Government and University Publications List

Exchange and Gift Division
State Documents Section
Library of Congress
Washington, DC 20540 (202) 707-9468

The *Monthly Checklist of State Publications* lists documents and publications received in the Library of Congress that are issued by the administrative, judicial, and legislative branches and state university systems of the states and territories. The subscription price is $32 per year and can be purchased from the Superintendent of Documents, Government Printing Office, Washington, DC 20402, (202) 783-3238.

* Surplus Books Giveaway

Exchange and Gift Division
Library of Congress
Washington, DC 20540 (202) 707-9511

Tens of thousands of surplus books in a wide variety of subjects are available to government agencies, private citizens, and non-profit organizations. The books come from a wide variety of sources including extras from the Copyright Division, books that are not acquired by not selected for the Library's collections, and from private gifts. Government agencies can select from the books available first at no charge. The general public (referred to as book dealers by the Library) can select from books next. They must bid on books by the lot, and the minimum bid is $25. Everything left over is available to non-profit organizations free of charge.

* Telephone Reference Service

Library of Congress
Washington, DC 20540 (202) 707-5522

This service provides information to callers about the collections within the Library of Congress and how they can be used. In planning your research, remember that the Library of Congress is the library of last resort--all other inter-library loan avenues must be exhausted before you may borrow a book from the Library of Congress. Always begin your research with your local library.

Be patient. If any phone number is incorrect, call (area code) 555-1212 and request the new listing.

Federal Libraries

* African Art

Smithsonian Institution
950 Independence Ave., SW
Washington, DC 20560 (202) 357-4875
The Library maintains a collection of 15,000 books and 280 periodical titles on traditional and contemporary arts of Africa, including sculptural and decorative arts, ethnography, anthropology, craft, architecture, archeology, history, oral tradition and folklore, and African retentions in the New World. The Library is open to the public by appointment.

* Agriculture, U.S. Department of

National Agricultural Library (NAL)
10301 Baltimore Blvd.
Beltsville, MD 20705 (301) 504-5755
NAL provides comprehensive information services for the food and agricultural sciences through a variety of sources, which include bibliographies, personal reference services, loans, photocopies, and online data files. Services are provided to agricultural colleges, research institutions, government agencies, agricultural associations, industry, individual scientists, and the general public. NAL cooperates with the Library of Congress and the National Library of Medicine to provide access to publications worldwide in the agricultural, chemical, and biological sciences. NAL houses one of the largest collections in the free world on agricultural subjects--1.6 million volumes--including biology, chemistry, nutrition, forestry, soil sciences, and much more.

* Air Force, U.S. Department of the

Resource Library
SAF/PAR
Washington, DC 20330-1000 (703) 697-4100
Not open to the public but they do accept mail requests. They have general information about the air force, as well as biographies. Mail requests to:

* Air Force, U.S. Department of the

History Library
USAF/CHO, Building 5681
Bolling Air Force Base
Washington, DC 20330 (202) 767-0412
Library is open to the public 8:00am to 4:30pm. Collection includes history of Air Force, history of aircraft, and biographies dating back to WWI. Call for appointment.

* Air Force, U.S. Department of the

Historical Resource Center
USAFHRC/RF
Maxwell A.F.B., AL 36112-6678 (205) 953-5342
Open 8:00am to 4:30pm. This is a repository of all Air Force historical documents. It contains 550,000 documents and 60 million pages of information.

* American History Branch

National Museum of American History
Smithsonian Institute
Room 5016
14th and Constitution Ave., NW
Washington, DC 20560 (202) 357-2414
The Library houses a collection of 165,000 volumes of book and bound journals on engineering, transportation, military history, science, applied science, decorative arts, and domestic and community life in addition to American history and the history of science and technology. They have special collections of trade literature and materials about world fairs. The Library is open to the public by appointment, 10am to 5:15pm, Monday-Friday.

* Architect of the Capitol

U.S. Capitol Bldg.
Curators Office
House Terrace Level, #3
Washington, DC 20515 (202) 225-1222
This small reference library is open by appointment only. It is open 9am - 4:30pm, Monday through Friday, and one must secure a visitor's pass to enter.

* Arms Control and Disarmament Agency (ACDA), U.S.

320 21st St., NW, Room 5840
Washington, DC 20451 (202) 647-5969
As a complement to the much larger State Department Library, the ACDA Library maintains a current collection of books, periodicals, documents, and reference materials relevant to arms control and disarmament issues. The library also includes an information retrieval system and inter-library loan services. Individuals wishing to use the library must call and make an appointment.

* Arts and Museum Management Library

National Endowment for the Arts (NEA)
1100 Pennsylvania Ave., NW
Washington, DC 20506 (202) 682-5485
This library focuses on the needs and interests of NEA and has materials on the arts and arts management. Individuals may use this library by appointment only.

* Binational Libraries and Cultural Centers Worldwide

Library Programs Division
Bureau of Educational and Cultural Affairs
United States Information Agency (USIA)
301 Fourth St., SW, Room 314
Washington, DC 20547 (202) 619-4915
USIA maintains or supports 156 libraries and reading rooms in 95 countries, as well as library programs at 111 binational centers in 24 countries. Collections focus on fostering foreign understanding of U.S. people, history, and culture. A bi-weekly bibliography, listing 80-100 titles on international relations and developments in the U.S., is one of many library services provided for the overseas posts, including reference and research assistance.

* Commerce, U.S. Department of

1400 and Constitution Ave. NW, Room 7046
Washington, DC 20230 (202) 482-5511
This collection includes business directories, periodicals, and newspapers.

* Comptroller of Currency, Office of the

U.S. Department of the Treasury
250 E. St., SW
Washington, DC 20219 (202) 874-5000

* Congressional Budget Office

2nd and D Sts., SW
Room 472
Washington, DC 20515 (202) 226-2635
Open 9am to 5:30pm, Monday through Friday, this library contains information on economics and studies on the budget process. Appointment preferred.

* Consumer Product Safety Commission (CPSC)

5401 Westbard Ave., NW, Room 546
Washington, DC 20207 (301) 504-0044
The CPSC library's collection includes reference materials on engineering, economics, and health sciences, which CPSC staff and other researchers may use

Be patient. If any phone number is incorrect, call (area code) 555-1212 and request the new listing.

Books and Libraries

for background on product safety issues. The library does not include CPSC documents and publications. Open to the public 8:30am to 5:00pm, Monday to Friday.

* Council on Environmental Quality Library

Executive Office of the President
722 Jackson Pl., NW
Washington, DC 20503 (202) 395-5750
This small library contains environmental publications for researchers. Call ahead for an appointment.

* Court of Appeals for the Federal Circuit and U.S. Claims Court, U.S.

Library, 717 Madison Place, NW
Washington, DC 20439 (202) 633-5871
This joint library is accessible only to members of the Bar and those involved in cases within the courts.

* Customs Services, U.S.

U.S. Department of Treasury
1301 Constitution Ave., NW
Washington, DC 20229 (202) 927-1350

* Defense, U.S. Department of

Pentagon Library
Room 1A518, Pentagon
Washington, DC 20310 (703) 697-4301
This library is not open to the public 9am to 4pm, Monday-Friday, inquiries will be directed to another appropriate library.

* Doris and Henry Dreyfuss Study Center

Cooper-Hewitt Museum
Smithsonian Institution's National Museum of Design
2 East 91st St.
New York, NY 10128 (212) 860-6887
The Study Center and Library serve as a resource for scholars, researchers, designers, and students for the study of design. This library contains fifty thousand volumes, with specialized holdings in decorative arts, textiles, and needlework, wallcoverings, architecture, pattern and ornament, landscape design, industrial design, interior design, theater design, and graphic design. Researchers are asked to call or write in advance. Photographs may be ordered through the museum's Photographic Services Department.

* Education, U.S. Department of Reference Facility

555 New Jersey Ave., NW, MS-1139
Washington, DC 20208 (202) 219-1884
Collection focuses on education and related social sciences information.

* Energy, U.S. Department of

1000 Independence Ave., SW, Room GA138
Washington, DC 20585 (202) 586-9534
This energy library is available to U.S. Department of Energy employees, government employees from other agencies, members of the armed forces if in uniform, and for those escorted by a U.S. Department of Energy employee.

* Environmental Protection Agency

401 M St., SW, Room 2904 Reference Desk (202) 260-5921
Washington, DC 20460 Main Desk (202) 260-5922
The library's collection focuses on environmental issues.

* Federal Aviation Administration

800 Independence Ave., SW
Washington, DC 20591 (202) 267-3115
Open to the public 9am to 4pm. Collection focuses on commercial and general

aviation. Historical aviation information is located at Smithsonian's Air and Space Museum.

* Federal Communications Commission (FCC)

1919 M St., NW, Suite 639
Washington, DC 20554 (202) 632-7100
The FCC Library is a collection of various types of legal and technical information. The legal collection includes federal and statutory case histories, indexes, reference works, treatises, and looseleaf services. The technical collection covers telecommunications and related subjects. The library also includes a special collection of cross-indexed legislative histories dating back to the early beginnings of communications law, along with a special collection of trade journals, and law and literature reviews. Open to the public 1pm to 4pm Monday-Friday.

* Federal Deposit Insurance Corporation (FDIC)

550 17th St., NW, Room 4060
Washington, DC 20429 (202) 898-3631
The FDIC library collection focuses on banking law, with emphasis on bank regulation and supervision, state codes, deposit insurance, international banking, bankruptcy, and consumer affairs. The library is open to the public Tuesdays through Thursdays, 8:30am to 5:15pm. Call at least one day in advance to make an appointment to visit.

* Federal Emergency Management Agency

500 C St., SW, Room 123
Washington, DC 20472 (202) 646-3768/3769
The library's collection focuses on emergency management topics. Open to the public 8am to 4:30pm.

* Federal Energy Regulatory Commission

Reference Room and Information Center
U.S. Department of Energy
941 N. Capitol St.
Washington, DC 20426 (202) 208-3171
This reference center maintains the file of the applications for the Commission. The public is invited to use the facility from 8:30am - 5:00pm, Monday through Friday.

* Federal Reserve Board Research

Room BC241
20th St. and Constitution Ave., NW
Washington, DC 20551 (202) 452-3333
The Federal Reserve System research library contains material on banking, finance, economics, and other areas related to the Federal Reserve System. Open to the public on Thursday 9-5. Appointment required. Call one day in advance.

* Federal Reserve System Banking Law

Room B1066
20th St. and Constitution Ave., NW
Washington, DC 20551 (202) 452-3284
For information on specific banking laws, contact the Federal Reserve System Banking Law Library. Open 9am to 5pm, Monday-Friday by appointment only.

* Federal Trade Commission (FTC)

6th and Pennsylvania Ave., NW
Room 630
Washington, DC 20580 (202) 326-2395
Contact the FTC's library to use the 120,000 volumes on legal, economic, and business subjects, 1,500 periodicals, interlibrary loans, and photocopy facilities. Open to the public 8am - 5pm, Monday-Friday. Picture I.D. required.

* General Accounting Office

441 G St., NW, Room 7016
Washington, DC 20548 (202) 275-5180
This library provides information of GAO interest and has access to databases,

Be patient. If any phone number is incorrect, call (area code) 555-1212 and request the new listing.

Federal Libraries

government documents, dissertations, research in progress, and organizations. *Library Focus*, published monthly, lists the latest books acquired. Open to the public 8am to 4:45pm, Monday-Friday, picture I.D. required.

language section. Access is restricted: permission to use the library can be obtained through the Office of Congressional and Public Liaison, address above, Room 602, Congressional (202) 619-6828, Public (202) 619-4355.

* General Accounting Office Law Library

441 G St., NW, Room 7056
Washington, DC 20548 (202) 275-2585

This library's references include the Legislative History Collection, which documents the creation of public documents and bills. The collection can be read in the library on weekdays between 8am and 4:45pm. A picture ID is required.

* General Services Administration

18th and F Sts., NW, Room 1033
Washington, DC 20405 (202) 501-2789

Collection includes the Federal Acquisition Institute library. Open to the public 8am to 4:30pm, Monday-Friday for research only, book check out not available.

* Health and Human Services, U.S. Department of

Information Center
P.O. Box 1133 (301) 565-4167 in MD
Washington, DC 20013 (800) 336-4797

This center should be the initial phone call because it can direct you to more specialized clearinghouses as well as health organizations and foundations. The Information Center, through its resource files and database (DIRLINE), responds to questions regarding health concerns and can send publications, bibliographies, and other material. A library focusing on health topics is open to the public, 9am-5pm, Monday-Friday, advance notice is preferred. The National Health Information Center Library is located at 1010 Wayne Dr., Silver Springs, MD 20091. The Center also produces many different directories, and resource guides, which are available for a minimal cost. A publications catalog is free of charge.

* House of Representatives Research and Library

Cannon House Office Bldg., Room B-18
Washington, DC 20515 (202) 225-0462

This library is the official depository of House documents, reports, bills, and more. Its primary function is to serve House members and their staffs. It is open to the public, but no photocopying is permitted. The hours are 9am to 5:30pm Monday through Friday.

* Housing and Urban Development (HUD), U.S. Department of

Library
451 7th St., SW, Room 8141
Washington, DC 20410 (202) 708-2370

This library contains a wealth of information on financing, home building, mortgages, and other HUD related topics. Also included are archival documents of old housing agencies. Hours are 8:45am - 5:15pm, Monday through Friday. The Program Information Center at the Library is a source of information on HUD programs. The number is (202) 755-6420.

* Information Agency (USIA), U.S.

Programs Division
Bureau of Educational and Cultural Affairs
301 Fourth St., SW, Room 314
Washington, DC 20547 (202) 619-4545

USIA maintains or supports 156 libraries and reading rooms in 95 countries, as well as library programs at 111 binational centers in 24 countries. Collections focus on fostering foreign understanding of U.S. people, history, and culture. A bi-weekly bibliography, listing 80-100 titles on international relations and developments in the U.S., is one of many library services provided for the overseas posts, including reference and research assistance.

* Information Agency, U.S.

301 Fourth St., SW, Room 135
Washington, DC 20547 (202) 619-5947

The Washington library of USIA houses a varied collection, including a Russian

* Interior, U.S. Department of the

Natural Resources Library
18th and C Sts., NW
Washington, DC 20240 (202) 343-5815

Information is provided on such topics as Native American Indians, mining and minerals, land reclamation and management, fish and wildlife, water resources, parks and outdoor recreation, and the preservation of scenic and historic sites. The library is open from 7:45am - 5:00pm, Monday through Friday.

* Interior, U.S. Department of the

U.S. Geological Survey Library
National Center, MS 950
4th Floor
Reston, VA 22092 (703) 648-4302

This library contains valuable publications on subjects related to the Geological Survey; however geology, including ground water and water resources, is the primary topic. The hours are 7:30am -4:15pm, Monday through Friday.

* International Development Cooperation Agency, U.S.

1601 North Kent Street
Room 105
Rosslyn, VA

Agency for International Development (AID)
Development Information Center (Mailing Address)
Room 105 SA18
Washington, DC 20523-1801 (703) 875-4818

The reference desk is open between 10:00am and 4:00pm, Monday-Friday. They maintain a database listing all of AID materials. It includes 150 journals of country development, strategy statements.

* International Trade Commission (ITC), U.S.

International Trade Library
Office of Data Systems
500 E St., SW, Room 300
Washington, DC 20436 (202) 205-2626

As one of the most extensive libraries on international trade in the United States, the ITC's main library maintains a 100,000-volumes and subscribes to about 2,400 periodicals. Publications on international trade and U.S. tariff commercial policy are housed along with many business and technical journals. An audiovisual room enables visitors to listen to audio tapes and to view video tapes relating to international trade. A rare-book room is also maintained, and the library staff has begun to establish special collection areas for use with ongoing ITC projects. The library is open to the public from 8am to 5:15pm.

* International Trade Commission (ITC) Law Library

500 E St., SW, Room 614
Washington, DC 20436 (202) 205-3287

The Law Library, a resource of the ITC's Office of the General Counsel, contains more than 10,000 volumes, participates in an exchange program with other libraries, and maintains a comprehensive file on documents on legislation affecting U.S. trade. It is open to the public for research.

* Interstate Commerce Commission

12th St. and Constitution Ave., NW, Room 3392
Washington, DC 20423 (202) 927-7328

The Interstate Commerce Commission's library is open to the public, and its collection focuses on transportation and transportation law. You must sign in with the building guard before going up to the library.

* John F. Kennedy Center for the Performing Arts

Performing Arts Library
2700 F St., NW
Washington, DC 20566 (202) 416-8000

Be patient. If any phone number is incorrect, call (area code) 555-1212 and request the new listing.

Books and Libraries

The Performing Arts Library is a joint project of the Library of Congress and the Kennedy Center, and offers information and reference assistance on dance, theater, opera, music, film, and broadcasting.

* Justice, U.S. Department of

U.S. Parole Commission
Public Reading Room
U.S. Department of Justice
5550 Friendship Blvd.
1 N. Park Bldg.
Chevy Chase, MD 20015 (301) 492-5990

Federal Bureau of Investigation
Public Reading Room
U.S. Department of Justice
9th St. and Pennsylvania Ave., NW
Washington, DC 20535 (202) 324-3477
Open by appointment only.

* Labor, U.S. Department of

200 Constitution Ave., NW, Room N2439
Washington, DC 20210 (202) 523-6992
Collection includes information on trade unions, labor movements, women issues, and legal and regulatory topics related to labor.

* Land Management Library, Bureau of

U.S. Department of the Interior
SC 653
Denver Federal Center
6th Ave. and Kippling
P.O. Box 25047
Denver, CO 80225 (303) 236-6649
A vast collection of information on issues concerning land management is available to the public through this library. The following topics are included: cadastral engineering; forest resources management; land reserve studies; legislation and public land laws; range management; watershed management; mineral, oil and gas leasing; oil shale; and conservation and use of public lands. Open 8am - 4:30pm.

* Library of Congress

Washington, DC 20540 (202) 707-5000 General information
(202) 707-6372 catalog number

The Library of Congress is the world's largest library, but there are more than dusty old books stored here. The more than 20 million books in 470 languages that it holds represent less than a fourth of the holdings of the Library. There are also massive collections of manuscripts, maps, music, prints and photographs, and film. In 1800 the Library was founded simply to help Congress make the laws. But now the Library is much more. For instance, more than a million handicapped readers borrow materials in braille and recorded forms each year. And the Library also registers copyright for books, music, films, computer programs, and other works. In celebration of the arts, the Library holds concerts by the Juilliard String Quartet, poetry readings, folk music and dance performances, and showings of classic films. More than 900 specialists provide extensive research and analysis for Congress, much of which is available to you through your Congressman's office. The Library is a major world center for scholarly research with specialists in its 22 reading rooms and in other areas ready to provide information on just about any subject you can name. And much of this information is available to you from exhaustive databases both in printed form and on magnetic tape.

* Library of Congress International Law Library

Washington, DC 20540 (202) 707-5080
As the world's largest and most comprehensive library of foreign, international, and comparative law, the Law Library provides information for all known legal systems including common law, civil law, Roman law, canon law, Chinese law, Jewish and Islamic law, and ancient and medieval law. Specialists with knowledge of more than fifty languages provide reference and research service in all known legal systems. U.S. legislative documents housed here include the *Congressional Record* (and its predecessors), the serial set, a nearly complete set of bills and resolutions, current documents, committee prints, reports, hearings,

etc. plus a complete set of U.S. Supreme Court records and briefs and collections of U.S. Court of Appeals records and briefs. The law library has five major divisions:

American-British Law
United States, Australia, Canada, Great Britain, India, New Zealand, Pakistan, certain other countries of the British Commonwealth and their dependent territories, and Eire: (202) 707-5077.

European Law
Nations of Europe and their possessions, except Spain and Portugal: (202) 707-5088.

Hispanic Law
Spain and Portugal, Latin America, Puerto Rico, the Philippines, and Spanish- and Portuguese-language states of Africa: (202) 707-5070.

Far Eastern Law
Nations of East and Southeast Asia (including China, Indonesia, Japan, Korea, Thailand, and former British and French possessions in the area: 9202) 707-5085.

Near Eastern and African Law
Middle Eastern countries, including the Arab states, Turkey, Iran, and Afghanistan, and all African countries, except Spanish- and Portuguese-language states and possessions: (202) 707-5073.

* Library of Congress: Services for Readers with Vision Impairment and Handicaps

Library Services for Blind and Physically Handicapped
Readers Reference Section
National Library Service for the Blind and
Physically Handicapped
Washington, DC 20540 (202) 707-9287
or: Your local library

The National Library Service (NLS) maintains a large collection of books, magazines, journals, and music materials in braille, large type, and recorded formats for individuals who cannot read or use standard printed materials because of temporary or permanent visual loss or physical limitations. Reading materials and necessary playback equipment for books on record and cassette are distributed through a national network of cooperating libraries. Books in the collection are selected on the basis of their appeal to a wide range of interests. Bestsellers, biographies, fiction, and how-to books are in great demand.

* Library of Congress Law Library

Legislative Histories and Research
LM 240
Washington, DC 20540 (202) 707-5080
This section of the library provides information on legislative history.

* Merit Systems Protection

1120 Vermont Ave., NW, Room 828
Washington, DC 20419 (202) 653-7133
The Library's collection specializes in legal aspects of personnel issues. A reference librarian on staff can direct you to appropriate resources. The library is open to the public, but you should call for an appointment.

* Minerals Management Service

Resource Center
Congressional Liaison Office
U.S. Department of the Interior
18th and C Sts., NW
Room 4241
Washington, DC 20240 (202) 208-3502
This small reference center contains documents including offshore minerals management statistics from the Service. Hours are 8am - 4pm, Monday through Friday. Please call ahead for an appointment.

* Mines, Bureau of

U.S. Department of the Interior
2401 E St., NW, Room 127
Washington, DC 20241 (202) 501-9755

Be patient. If any phone number is incorrect, call (area code) 555-1212 and request the new listing.

Federal Libraries

Topics relating to the minerals industry are contained in this library, such as state and county mineral data, mineral supply and demand analyses, congressional reports pertaining to minerals, oil and gas reports, and market studies. The hours are 7:45am - 4:15pm, Monday through Friday.

* National Aeronautics and Space Administration

300 E. St., SW
600 Independence Ave., SW
Washington, DC 20546 (202) 358-0168
The library focuses on aeronautics and space information.

* National Air and Space Museum Branch

National Air and Space Museum
7th and Independence Ave., SW
Room 3100
Washington, DC 20590 (202) 357-3133
This library houses more than 30,000 books, 4,700 periodical titles, 6,000,000 technical reports, and is enriched by a documentary archival collection which includes 900,000 photographs, drawings, and other documents. The scope of the collection covers history of aviation and space, flight technology, aerospace industry, biography, lighter-than-air technology and history, rocketry, earth and planetary sciences, and astronomy. The Library is open to the public by appointment, 10am to 5pm, Monday-Friday.

* National Credit Union Administration (NCUA)

1776 G St., NW
Washington, DC 20456 (202) 682-9630
The NCUA Law Library is open to the public. A part-time librarian is on duty to offer assistance. You must call for an appointment.

* National Endowment for the Arts (NEA)

1100 Pennsylvania Ave., NW
Washington, DC 20506 (202) 682-5485
This library focuses on the needs and interests of NEA and has materials on the arts and arts management. Individuals may use this library by appointment only.

* National Endowment for the Humanities (NEH)

1100 Pennsylvania Ave., NW
Room 216
Washington, DC 20506 (202) 606-8244
This library focuses on the needs and interests of NEH and has materials on a variety of humanities--related subjects. Individuals may use this library by appointment only, 8am - 5pm, Monday-Friday.

* National Energy Information Center

Public Reading Room
U.S. Department of Energy
1000 Independence Ave., SW, Room 1F048
Washington, DC 20585 (202) 586-8800
This reading room contains research materials pertaining to the energy industry. Hours are 8am - 5pm, Monday through Friday. A picture ID is required.

* National Gallery of Art

Constitution and 6th St., NW
Washington, DC 20565 (202) 842-6511
The Gallery's library has over 150,000 volumes with a specialty in Renaissance and Baroque art. The collection covers the period from Post-Byzantine to the present, focusing on the history and criticism of art. The stacks themselves are closed; however, the library is open to the public, but you should call for the hours to make an appointment.

* National Labor Relations Board

1717 Pennsylvania Ave., NW
Room 900
Washington, DC 20570 (202) 254-9055
The Board's library collection focuses on labor law and labor relations. The library is open to the public and no appointment is necessary.

* National Mediation Board Reading Room

1425 K Street, NW
Washington, DC 20570 (202) 523-5996
Mediation files are available for inspection by appointment.

* National Science Foundation

1800 G Street, NW, Room 245
Washington, DC 20550 (202) 357-7811
The library is open to the public between 7:30am to 5:00pm, Monday-Friday. Specialty is science policy, technological innovation, research and development management, science and engineering education.

* National Technical Institute for the Deaf (NTID)

NTIC Resource Center
One Lomb Memorial Dr.
Rochester, NY 14623 (716) 475-6823

* National Zoological Park Branch

Education/Administration Building
3000 Connecticut Ave., NW
Washington, DC 20008 (202) 673-4771
This library houses a collection of 3,500 books and 350 periodical titles on animal behavior, animal nutrition, capture and care of animals in captivity, conservation and endangered species, horticulture, pathology, veterinary medicine, and zoology. The library is open to the public by appointment.

* Natural History Branch Library

Smithsonian Institute
10th and Constitution Ave., NW, Room 51
Washington, DC 20560 (202) 357-4696
This library houses 330,000 books and bound journals and receives 1,963 journal subscriptions. The library consists of a main location and several subject-based locations. Topics covered include biology, geology, paleontology, ecology, anthropology, botany, entomology, and mineral sciences. Call to make an appointment or for information on the location of the subject-based libraries.

* Navy, U.S. Department of the Navy Library

9th and M Sts.
Building 44
Washington Navy Yard
Washington, DC 20374-5060 (202) 433-4131
Open 8:30am to 4:30pm, Monday-Friday. The library contains historical information dating back to the 18th century. They have historical documents and abstracts. They loan books through the interlibrary loan system.

* Nuclear Regulatory Commission

Norfolk Ave. (301) 492-7748 reference library
Bethesda, MD 20555 (301) 492-8501
The library is open to the public between 8:00am to 4:00pm.

* Office of Technology Assessment

600 Pennsylvania Ave., SE
Third Fl., Room 304
Washington, DC 20510-8025 (202) 228-6150
This library contains periodicals, books, and archives of the Office of Technology Assessment. One must call ahead for an appointment. Hours are 8:30am - 5:30pm, Monday through Friday.

* Occupational Safety and Health Review Commission

1825 K Street, NW, Room 400
Washington, DC 20006 (202) 634-7933
The collection focuses on federal laws. Open to the public 8:30am to 4:45pm.

* Office of Personnel Management

1900 E Street, NW, Room 4516
Washington, DC 20415 (202) 606-1381

Be patient. If any phone number is incorrect, call (area code) 555-1212 and request the new listing.

Books and Libraries

The library is open to the public between 8:30am to 4:30pm by appointment only. The specialty of the library is personnel management

* Peace Corps

1900 K Street, NW
Room 5353
Washington, DC 20526 (202) 606-3307

The library is open to the public between 8:30am to 4:30pm. The specialty of the library is the countries the Peace Corps serves and Peace Corps services, volunteerism, and languages.

* Pennsylvania Avenue Development Corporation

1331 Pennsylvania Ave, NW
Suite 1220 N
Washington, DC 20005 (202) 724-9091

Their central files contain records of the Corporation and are open to the public by appointment.

* Postal Service, U.S.

475 L'Enfant Plaza, SW
Room 11800
Washington, DC 20260-1641 (202) 268-2904

Along with a working collection of materials in law, the social sciences, and technology, the Postal Library contains a unique collection of postal materials, legislative files from the 71st Congress to date, reports, pamphlets, clippings, photographs, general postal histories, periodicals of the national postal employee organizations, Universal Postal Union studies, and Postal laws and regulations handbooks and manuals. The library is open to the public weekdays from 9am to 4pm. Reading Rooms are located on the 11th Floor North.

* Presidential Libraries

National Archives and Records Administration
8th St. and Pennsylvania Ave., NW
Room 104
Washington, DC 20408 (202) 501-5700

Through the Presidential Libraries, which are located on sites selected by the presidents and built with private funds, the National Archives preserves and makes available for use the Presidential records and personal papers that document the actions of a particular president's administration. In addition to providing reference services on Presidential documents, each library prepares documentary and descriptive publications and operates a museum to exhibit documents, historic objects, and other memorabilia of interest to the public. Each library provides research grants to scholars and graduate students for the encouragement of research in Presidential libraries' holdings and of publication or works based on such research. Public programs of the libraries include conferences, lectures, films, tours, commemorative events, and seminars. For further information, contact the President library of your choice.

Herbert Hoover Library, West Branch, IA 52358; (319) 643-5301
Franklin D. Roosevelt Library, Hyde Park, NY 12358; (914) 229-8114
Harry S. Truman Library, Independence, MO 64050; (816) 833-1400
Dwight D. Eisenhower Library, Abilene, KS, 67410; (913) 263-4751
John F. Kennedy Library, Boston, MA 02125; (617) 929-4577
Lyndon B. Johnson Library, Austin, TX 78705; (512) 482-5137
Gerald R. Ford Library, Ann Arbor, MI 48109; (313) 668-2218
Gerald R. Ford Museum, Grand Rapids, MI 49504; (161) 456-2675
Nixon Presidential Materials Staff, Washington, DC 20408; (703) 756-6498
Jimmy Carter Library, Atlanta, GA 30307; (404) 331-3942
Ronald Reagan Library, Simi Valley, CA, 93065; (805) 522-8511

* Reclamation, Bureau of

Water Resources Library
U.S. Department of the Interior
P.O. Box 25007, D79231
Denver Federal Center
6th and Kippling
Denver, CO 80225-000 (303) 236-6963

The key topics covered at this library include hydrology engineering, groundwater management, dam safety, soil mechanics, and business related issues. Materials can be checked out only through the inter-library loan system.

* Securities and Exchange Commission (SEC)

450 5th St., NW
Washington, DC 20549 (202) 272-2618

The SEC Library contains resource material on Federal Securities Laws, accounting, economics, and other general financial information. It also houses all SEC published materials. The library is open to the public from 9:00am to 5:30pm, Monday through Friday.

* Senate Research and Library

The Capitol, Suite S-332
Washington, DC 20510 (202) 224-7106

The Senate Library is the official depository of senate documents. Its primary function is service to Senate members and their staffs. To use the library a researcher must have a letter of introduction from a Senator.

* Small Business Administration

409 3rd St., SW (202) 205-7033 Main Library
Washington, DC 20416 (202) 205-6847 Law Library

To review reference material pertaining to small business, contact the SBA's library. The library is open to the public for reference use only.

* Smithsonian Astrophysical Observatory (SAO)

Smithsonian Institute
Perkin Building
Center for Astrophysics
60 Garden St.
Cambridge, MA 02138 (617) 495-7289

The collection of 50,000 books and 600 current journal titles are owned jointly by SAO and Harvard College Observatory. Subjects covered include all aspects of astronomy and astrophysics, related fields of physics, mathematics, engineering, and computer science. The library is open to the public by appointment.

* Smithsonian Museum Support Center

Smithsonian Institution
42210 Silver Hill Rd. (301) 238-3666
Suitland, MD 20746 FAX: (301) 238-3667

This library provides information about conservational of materials and museum objects, conservation science, which includes archaeometry, the study of museum environments, and the analysis of materials by such means as x-ray, diffraction, and gas chromatography. This library is open to the public by appointment.

* Smithsonian Institution Libraries

10th St. and Constitution Ave., NW
Washington, DC 20560 (202) 357-2139

The libraries of the Smithsonian Institution include approximately 950,000 volumes, with strengths in natural history, museology, history of science, and the humanities. Inquiries on special subjects or special collections should be addressed to the appropriate branch library or to the Central Reference and Loan.

* State, U.S. Department of

2201 C St., NW, Room 3239
Washington, DC 20520 (202) 647-1099
Mailing address:
U.S. Dept. of State
A/OIS/LR, Room 3239
Washington, DC 20520-2442

The library, whose collection specializes in the area of foreign affairs, is open to the public only if the information you are looking for cannot be found elsewhere in the Washington area. You must, however, call for an appointment.

* Supreme Court of the United States

Library
1 First St., NE
Washington, DC 20543 (202) 479-3037

Supreme Court records and briefs are available to the public for reproduction. However, only government attorneys and members of the Bar are permitted to use the general collection.

Be patient. If any phone number is incorrect, call (area code) 555-1212 and request the new listing.

Federal Libraries

* Tennessee Valley Authority (TVA)
TVA Corporate Library
400 W. Summit Hill Dr., WT 2F
Knoxville, TN 37902 (615) 632-3464
The TVA library facilities are open to the public, 8am to 4:45pm, Monday-Friday, while its specialty libraries cater to various organizations within TVA. Cataloged books, current technical journals, and reports relating to ongoing research in each division are available.

* Transportation, U.S. Department of
400 7th St., SW
M49133, Room 2200
Washington, DC 20590 (202) 366-0746
Collection covers all modes of transportation except aviation. The library is open 8:30am to 5:30pm with limited staff.

* Treasury, U.S. Department of
1500 Pennsylvania Ave., NW, Room 5310
Washington, DC 20220 (202) 622-0045

By appointment only. The collection includes law, economics, and finance information.

* U.S. Trade Representative, Office of the
Public Documents Room
Executive Office of the President
600 17th St., NW, Room 101
Washington, DC 20506 (202) 395-6186
You must schedule an appointment to visit this documents area, open 10 to 12am and 1 to 4 p.m, Monday through Friday.

* Veterans Affairs, U.S. Department of
Central Office Library
810 Vermont Ave., NW, Room 976 (202) 233-3085
Washington, DC 20420 Circulation desk (202) 233-3085
Library resources include circulation collections of books, journals, and audiovisuals. Open to the public, 9am to 5pm, Monday-Friday.

Be patient. If any phone number is incorrect, call (area code) 555-1212 and request the new listing.

Books and Libraries

Government Printing Office

The U.S. Government Printing Office (GPO) along with the National Technical Information Service (NTIS) are Uncle Sam's primary publishers. The Superintendent of Documents at GPO is the official sales agent for many government publications. Approximately 21,000 titles are for sale in a wide variety of subject areas, including business and industry, children and families, careers, and energy. There are how-to guides, government manuals, and in-depth studies on nearly every subject imaginable. GPO publishes many different types of listings of their publications, from the popular *U.S. Government Books*, which lists selected popular recent releases, to the exhaustive *Publications Reference File*, which lists *all* GPO titles. GPO also provides access to their publications through a nationwide system of 1400 libraries and through 24 bookstores located across the country. Online connection through DIALOG is also possible.

* 320 Subject Bibliographies

Subject Bibliography Index
Superintendent of Documents
Government Printing Office (GPO)
Washington, DC 20402 (202) 783-3238

More than 320 subject bibliographies listing books, periodicals, and subscriptions published by government agencies are available free from GPO. Topics range from accidents to zoning, and touch on most facets of human life. A complete listing of these subject bibliographies, called the *Subject Bibliography Index*, is available free upon request.

* Bestsellers from Uncle Sam

U.S. Government Books
Free Catalog
P.O. Box 37000
Washington, DC 20013-7000

The Government Printing Office has a catalog of new and popular books sold by the government about agriculture, energy, children, space, health, history, business, vacations, and much more. Find out what government books are all about by ordering this free catalog.

* Bookstores Around the Country

Superintendent of Documents
U.S. Government Printing Office (GPO)
Office of Marketing
Stop: SM
Washington, DC 20402 (202) 512-2420

GPO operates 24 bookstores that display and sell the most popular of the more than 21,000 titles for sale by the government. If the bookstore does not stock the book you are looking for, they will order it and have it sent to you. Bookstores accept VISA, MasterCard, and Superintendent of Documents deposit account orders. All stores are open Monday through Friday, except Kansas City which is open 7 days a week. The following is a listing of the bookstores:

Alabama
O'Neill Building, 2021 Third Ave., North, Birmingham, AL 35203; (205) 731-1056

California
ARCO Plaza, C-Level, 505 South Flower St., Los Angeles, CA 90071; (213) 239-9844
Room 1023, Federal Building, 450 Golden Gate Ave., San Francisco, CA 94102; (415) 252-5334

Colorado
Room 117, Federal Building, 1961 Stout St., Denver, CO 80294; (303) 844-3964
Norwest Bank Building, 201 West 8th St., Pueblo, CO 81003; (719) 544-3142

District of Columbia
U.S. Government Printing Office, 710 N. Capitol St., NW, Washington, DC 20401 (202) 512-0132
1510 H St. NW, Washington, DC 20005; (202) 653-5075

Florida
100 West Bay St., Suite 100, Jacksonville, FL 32202; (904) 353-0569

Georgia
First Union Plaza, 999 Peachtree St. NE, Suite 120, Atlanta, GA 30309-3964; (404) 347-1900

Illinois
One Congress Center, 401 South State St., Suite 124, Chicago, IL 60605; (312) 353-5133

Maryland
U.S. Government Printing Office, Warehouse Sales Outlet, 8660 Cherry Lane, Laurel, MD 20707; (301) 953-7974; 792-0262

Massachusetts
Thomas P. O'Neill Building, 10 Causeway St., Room 179, Boston, MA 02222; (617) 720-4180

Michigan
Suite 160, Federal Building, 477 Michigan Ave., Detroit, MI 48226; (313) 226-7816

Missouri
120 Bannister Mall, 5600 E. Bannister Rd., Kansas City, MO 64137; (816) 765-2256

New York
Room 110, 26 Federal Plaza, New York, NY 10278; (212) 264-3825

Ohio
Room 1653, Federal Building, 1240 E. 9th St., Cleveland, OH 44199; (216) 522-4922
Room 207, Federal Building, 200 N. High St., Columbus, OH 43215; (614) 469-6956

Oregon
1305 S.W. First Ave., Portland, OR 97201-5801; (503) 221-6217

Pennsylvania
Robert Morris Building, 100 N. 17th St., Philadelphia, PA 19103; (215) 597-0677
Room 118, Federal Building, 1000 Liberty Ave., Pittsburgh, PA 15222; (412) 644-2721

Texas
Room 1C50, Federal Building, 1100 Commerce St., Dallas, TX 75242; (214) 767-0076
Texas Crude Building, 801 Travis St., Suite 120, Houston, TX 77002; (713) 228-1187

Washington
Room 194, Federal Building, 915 Second Ave., Seattle, WA 98174; (206) 553-4270

Be patient. If any phone number is incorrect, call (area code) 555-1212 and request the new listing.

Government Printing Office

Wisconsin
Room 190, Federal Building, 517 E. Wisconsin Ave., Milwaukee, WI 53202; (414) 297-1304

* Catalog of Federal Domestic Assistance

Superintendent of Documents
U.S. Government Printing Office (GPO)
Washington, DC 20402 (202) 783-3238

The *Catalog of Federal Domestic Assistance* is government-wide summary of financial and non-financial Federal programs, projects, services, and activities that provide assistance or benefits to the American public administered by departments and establishments of the Federal government. It describes the type of assistance available and the eligibility requirements for the particular assistance being sought, with guidance on how to apply. Also intended to improve coordination and communication between the federal government and state and local governments. Annual subscriptions, which consist of a basic manual and supplementary material for an indeterminate period, are $46.

* Congressional Record and Calendars

Superintendent of Documents
Congressional Information Specialist, Stop: SSOI
U.S. Government Printing Office (GPO)
Washington, DC 20402 (202) 783-3238

GPO publishes major Congressional publications, including the *Congressional Record*, House and Senate *Calendars*, all bills and laws, and related information. All of this information is available by subscription.

* Data Tapes of Government Publications

Superintendent of Documents
U.S. Government Printing Office (GPO)
941 N. Capitol St.
Washington, DC 20402 (202) 512-2406

Government publications produced in electronic format are now available in magnetic tape form. Tapes may be purchased on an individual tape basis or by subscription. Individual publications on tape include the *Budget of the United States*, the *Congressional Directory*, and the *Government Manual*. Some of the subscriptions available are the *Congressional Record*, *Federal Register*, and *Daily Bills*.

* Deposit Accounts for Government Publications

U.S. Government Printing Office (GPO)
Receipts and Processing Branch
Stop: SSOR
Washington, DC 20402 (202) 512-0822

Deposit accounts are a convenient way to order materials from GPO. A minimum of $50 is required to open the account, and monthly statements are issued. Telephone orders are accepted for any account containing sufficient funds, and order forms are provided for mail orders.

* Discounts on Government Books

Superintendent of Documents
Director, Documents Sales Service
U.S. Government Printing Office (GPO)
Washington, DC 20402 (202) 783-3238

Designated bookdealers and educational institution bookstores receive a 25 percent discount on publications and subscriptions whether single copies or in bulk. Any customers ordering 100 or more copies of a publication to be delivered to the same address may also receive the discount.

* Federal Depository Libraries

Superintendent of Documents
Library Marketer
Stop: SM
Washington, DC 20402 (202) 512-2420

A national system of nearly 1400 public, academic, and law libraries maintains collections of most government publications. The libraries are located in nearly every state. Their staffs will help you with research questions and can provide information on price and order numbers if you wish to purchase copies. If your library does not have the publication you need, they will borrow it for you. To determine which library serves you, contact your public library or the above.

* Federal Register

Superintendent of Documents
U.S. Government Printing Office (GPO)
Washington, DC 20402 (202) 783-3238

The *Federal Register*, with daily issues Monday through Friday, except on a legal holidays, announces to the public regulations and legal notices issued by Federal agencies. These include Presidential proclamations and Executive orders and Federal agency documents having general applicability and legal effect, documents required to be published by Act of Congress and other Federal agency documents of public interest. Subscribers to this service will automatically receive copies of the *Federal Register Index* and the *Code of Federal Regulations*, and *LSA List of CFR Sections Affected*, at no additional cost. Subscriptions are $415 per year; or $207.50 for six months; or $4.50 for single copies.

* Government Periodicals and Subscription Services

Superintendent of Documents
U.S. Government Printing Office (GPO)
Washington, DC 20402 (202) 783-3238

Better known as PL 36, *Government Periodicals and Subscription Services* lists all materials available on a subscription basis complete with ordering information and order forms. Single copies of this publication are available.

* Government Publications: Complete Listing

Superintendent of Documents
U.S. Government Printing Office (GPO)
Washington, DC 20402 (202) 783-3238

A complete master file of GPO publications, entitled *Sales Publications Reference File* (PRF), is available by subscription on microfiche $120, and magnetic tape $850, from GPO. It is also available to subscribers of the DIALOG Information Retrieval System. Users of the system can perform on-line searches of GPO's sales inventory to determine if the publication is for sale, if the item is in stock, and its stock number and current price. DIALOG users can order documents via DIALORDER, a feature of DIALOG, Information Service, Inc., 3460 Hillview Ave., Palo Alto, CA 94304.

* Government Publications Ordering Information

Superintendent of Documents
U. S. Government Printing Office (GPO)
Washington, DC 20402 (202) 783-3238

Orders for government books, pamphlets, posters, and periodicals can be placed by calling the above telephone number between 7:30 a.m. and 4:00 p.m., eastern time. This number may also be used to obtain catalogs of publications plus information on prices, stock numbers, and availability of sales publications. Orders may be charged to MasterCard, VISA, or prepaid Superintendent of Documents deposit accounts.

* How to Do Business With the Government Printing Office

U.S. Government Printing Office (GPO)
General Procurement Division, Stop: MMG
Washington, DC 20401 (202) 512-0916

If you are interested in doing business with the GPO, contact the above office to be put on a bidder list and to receive the 129 Commodities Newsletter and brochure, *How to do Business With the GPO*.

* Information on GPO Publications

Superintendent of Documents
Research and Analysis Section, Stop: SSOP
Washington, DC 20402 (202) 783-3238

Call or write at the above address for general information on materials available from GPO or for bibliographies, catalogs, or current brochures. For more extensive information on government published information, contact the nearest Federal Depository Library, which maintains copies of all GPO-published materials. To find the library nearest you, contact your local library.

* International Orders

Superintendent of Documents
U. S. Government Printing Office (GPO)
Washington, DC 20402 (202) 783-3238

Be patient. If any phone number is incorrect, call (area code) 555-1212 and request the new listing.

Books and Libraries

Orders for delivery outside the U.S. are subject to a 25% surcharge to provide for the special handling required by international mailing regulations. Orders are mailed surface mail unless airmail is requested (at an additional cost). Payment must accompany every order in U.S. dollars and be in the form of a check drawn on a bank located in the U.S. or Canada, a UNESCO coupon, or an International Postal Money Order made payable to the Superintendent of Documents.

* Mailing Lists

Superintendent of Documents
U.S. Government Printing Office (GPO)
Mail List User Program, Stop: SM
Washington, DC 20402 (202) 512-2427

Individuals interested in direct mail promotions to subscribers of government periodicals can obtain paid subscriber lists for approximately 70 different government periodicals from GPO. The lists are available on a one-time use basis only.

* Maps, Posters, Charts, Pictures, and Decals

Superintendent of Documents
Research and Analysis Section
Stop: SSOP
Washington, DC 20402 (202) 783-3238

A wide variety of posters, maps, and decals are sold by GPO, including facsimiles of the *Declaration of Independence*, the *Constitution*, NASA posters, and a wide variety of depictions of nature. For a complete price listing, contact the above address.

* New Government Titles

Superintendent of Documents
U.S. Government Printing Office (GPO)
Washington, DC 20402-9325 (202) 783-3238

The *New Books* catalog is a sampling of new releases from GPO. It is organized by subject area such as agriculture, education, computers, and transportation. These bimonthly listings are available free on a subscription basis. Contact the above address or your nearest U.S. Government bookstore.

* Printing Contracts from GPO

U.S. Government Printing Office (GPO)
Bid Section
Stop: PPSB
Washington, DC 20401 (202) 512-0526

GPO awards approximately 46,000 printing contracts to commercial printers each year. To get in on the action, ask for the GPO bidders's information packet, which contains everything necessary to get started.

* Priority Publication Announcements

U.S. Government Printing Office (GPO)
Office of Marketing, Stop: SM
Washington, DC 20401 (202) 512-2427

If you are interested in staying up to date in a certain subject, you can request that notification be sent to you when the government publishes something new in your area of interest. GPO maintains lists of materials--called *Priority Announcements*--for nearly 100 subject areas, free from GPO.

* Selling Ink to GPO

U.S. Government Printing Office (GPO)
Ralph Miller
Stop: QC
Washington, DC 20401 (202) 512-0785

If you are a commercial contractor interested in selling ink to GPO, write or call for the brochure, *How to Sell Ink to GPO*, which is designed to provide the necessary information.

* Selling Paper to GPO

U.S. Government Printing Office (GPO)
Paper Procurement Section
Stop, MMPP
Washington, DC 20401 (202) 512-2022

Information is available on procedures for selling paper to GPO.

* Standing Orders: Government Publications

Standing Order Specialist
Publication Order Branch
Stop SSOP
U.S. Government Printing Office (GPO)
Washington, DC 20402-9322 (202) 512-2315

For your convenience, GPO has instituted a standing order service for many recurring publications. This allows you to place an order once and automatically receive all subsequent editions or issuances in the same series. For complete information and the necessary authorization form, contact the above office.

* Tours of Government Printing Office

U. S. Government Printing Office (GPO)
Office of Public Affairs
Stop: PA
Washington, DC 20401 (202) 512-1995

For a tour of the world's largest printing plant, contact the above office. Tours given by appointment only on Tuesday, Wednesday, Thursday, beginning at 9:00 AM. Maximum of 20 per tour group, more than one group may be taken at a time.

Be patient. If any phone number is incorrect, call (area code) 555-1212 and request the new listing.

Government Databases and Bulletin Boards Federal Government Databases

Much of the data found in the thousands of federal databases are not available anywhere else, which makes them unique and invaluable sources of information for research on almost any topic. And because the government agencies do not make an effort to solicit public access, in many instances the existence of government databases is known to only a few specialists. In those cases where commercial vendors are selling government data, you will discover that you can get the data directly from the federal or state agency for much less money. Searches and printouts of many of these databases can be arranged, and often a tape or diskette of a file can be purchased. There are literally tens of thousands of databases generated by federal agencies. Here is just a sampling of what is available. If you are looking for databases other than those listed below, refer to the Information Starting Places Chapter or review Information USA's reference books, the *Federal Data Base Finder* and the *State Data and Database Finder*.

For a listing of those databases which can be accessed exclusively on-line see the next section titled Electronic Bulletin Boards.

* Abandoned Land Mines

George Stone, Branch Chief
National Inventory Update Committee
U.S. Department of the Interior
Office of Surface Mining
1951 Constitution Ave., Room 120-SIB
Washington, DC 20240 (202) 208-2999

This system provides an inventory of all abandoned mined lands in the United States so that land reclamation may be complete and systematic. For each abandoned mine problem area the following information is provided: location, general features, cost of reclamation and financing to date. The database can be searched by individual states or problem areas. Searches are available upon request and there is no charge.

* Adopt-A-Horse Data System

Dick Stark, Bureau of Land Management
Denver Federal Center, Building 50
U.S. Department of the Interior
PO Box 25047
Denver, CO 80225-0047 (303) 236-0157

This database supports the Wild Horse and Burro Program. It maintains a listing of several thousand individuals who have applied to adopt wild horses or burros. The listing includes names, addresses, and telephone numbers of each applicant; the species, number and sex of the animals. It also maintains a listing of adopters, their adopters, their addresses, and telephone numbers, and the individual identification numbers for animals obtained and the agency offices approving the adoptions. The data are updated when adopted animals die or are reassigned to other adopters and when titles of ownership are transferred to the adopters. Searches are provided upon request for a fee. Hard copy reports are produced showing applicants or adopters, mailing addresses and related information as requested.

* Adverse Drug Reaction Reporting System

Gerald Deighton
FOI Staff HFI-35
U.S. Food and Drug Administration
5600 Fishers Lane
Rockville, MD 20857 (301) 443-6310

This office maintains data files from 1969 to present consisting of adverse reactions to marketed drugs and biologics as reported by manufacturers, hospitals, physicians, and contracted collection efforts for the Division of Epidemiology and Surveillance (DES). For more information contact James Moore at (301) 443-4580.

* AGRICultural OnLine Access (AGRICOLA)

Technical Services Division
National Agricultural Library
U.S. Department of Agriculture
Beltsville, MD 20705 (301) 504-5755

AGRICOLA is a bibliographic database consisting of records for literature citations of journal articles, monographs, these, patents, software, audiovisual materials and technical reports relating to all aspects of agriculture. It is one of the largest collections of agricultural literature in the world with over 1.8 million volumes. AGRICOLA has been available in magnetic tape form since 1970. It currently has over 2.5 million records. AGRICOLA has many access points, searching approaches include: personal and corporate authors, subject category codes, date of journal issues, journal titles or journal title abbreviations, languages of text, source codes, subject heading, indexing terms. Online access is offered by the following commercial vendors: DIALOG, BRS Information Technologies. Magnetic tapes for both the current and retrospective files may be purchased from NTIS.

* Agriculture Research Results Database

Jim Hall, Agricultural Research Service, USDA
Room 404, Building 005
Beltsville, MD 20705 (301) 504-5345

This database contains over 1500 one-page narratives of recent research discoveries that are ready for distribution to farms, ranches, and rural communities. The subject matter covers animal and plant production, protection, and agricultural economics. Database reports are available 9 to 18 months before information becomes available through literature publications. The research work included is supported by U.S. Department of Economic Research Service. Free searches and printouts are available through most state extension services, U.S. Department of Agriculture and through Land Grant Universities on a limited basis. Online searching can also be done on the ITT Dailcom system.

* Aircraft Registration Master File

Federal Aviation Administration (FAA)
Data Services Division, AC-340
U.S. Department of Transportation
P.O. Box 25082
Oklahoma City, OK 73125

The file contains a listing of all civil aircraft registered in the United States. Information given includes data on the aircraft, the engine, the registrant, the base airport, the airworthiness, operation, use, and avionics equipment capability of the aircraft. Printouts are available at 25 cents per page from FAA, Flight Standards Technical Division, Aircraft Registration Branch, P.O. Box 25082, Oklahoma City, Oklahoma 73125 (Attn. AAC 250). To obtain copy on magnetic tape, send a written request to the Data Services Division, listed above.

Be patient. If any phone number is incorrect, call (area code) 555-1212 and request the new listing.

Government Databases and Bulletin Boards

* Air Industry Data Base System

Office of the Secretary, TAD-25
U.S. Department of Transportation
400 7th St., SW
Washington, DC 20590 (202) 366-4000

The data, available in machine readable form, provide a record for each month for each flight segment of every commercially scheduled airline flight. They describe the originating and destination terminals, detail the aircraft configuration, and report upon utilization of the aircraft. Machine readable reports on activities between city pairs by frequency of flight, load factors, and number of people traveling are generated. Airborne and ground delay time reports are also produced. Contact the office listed above.

* Annual Petroleum Supply Reporting System

National Energy Information Center
U.S. Department of Energy
Room 1F-048
Washington, DC 20585 (202) 586-8800

This system assembles statistical data on an annual basis on liquid hydrocarbon products. It provides data measuring current and sustainable capacity of the significant facilities at all refineries located in the United States, and U.S. Territories. Data are collected on type of plant, storage capacity by product, type of refining facility and capacity. Historical data are available from 1970 to present in automated form.

* Annual Survey of Occupational Injuries and Illnesses

Information Services
U.S. Department of Labor
Bureau of Labor Statistics
2 Massachusetts Ave., NE
Washington, DC 20212 (202) 606-6170

This system provides information about the incidence of job-related fatalities and job-related non-fatal injuries and illnesses among employees in the private and public sector. The system provides the Occupational Safety and Health Administration and similar state agencies information to effectively set standards, guide enforcement and consulting activities, and establish educational and training programs. Data are tabulated at the 4-digit Standard Industrial Classification (SIC) level in manufacturing, and 3-digit level in construction, and other non-manufacturing industries. Data are from about 280,000 establishments representing 5 million workplaces. Customized data files, tapes, diskettes or printouts are available on a cost recovery basis.

* Area Resource File System (ARFS) Health Services County Comparison

Inga Franklin
Office of Health Professions Analysis and Research (OHPAR)
U.S. Department of Health and Human Services
Public Health Service
5600 Fishers Lane
Parklawn Room 847
Rockville, MD 20857 (301) 443-6920

This system includes 104 separate state reports. Each report contains health resources, trends and socio-demographic information for each state and its counties. Each state report contains two volumes: Selected Geographic Resources and Geographic Trends in Resources. The first volume includes summary material on key measures related to health care resources and delivery for the state and its counties and contains a ranking profile of how each state and county compare on over 30 measures. The trends volume contains time-series tables for health professions supply, population, vital statistics and health facilities. Also included is a detailed profile of physicians by specialty. All 104 separate state reports, diskettes and tapes are for sale from NTIS.

* Bilingual Education Management Information System (BEMIS)

Office of Bilingual Education and Minority Languages Affairs
U.S. Department of Education
330 C St., SW
Washington, DC 20202 (202) 205-5463

The system contains information about English education programs for students who do not speak fluent English. Retrievable information includes the name and addresses of the grantees, the period of the grant, the amount of the grant, the native languages of the students served, the number of students in the program, the grade levels of the students, and the school and districts that participate in the program. Searches can be done in a variety of ways. Tapes are not available, but printouts can be ordered. Simple requests are free of charge but the office will charge on a cost recovery basis for more extensive searches.

* BIOETHICSLINE

Center for Bioethics Library
Kennedy Institute of Ethics
Georgetown University
Washington, DC 20057 (202) 687-3885

BIOETHICSLINE contains bibliographic citations and abstracts of literature related to moral or ethical public policies issues in medicine, medical research and health care. Journal articles, court cases, laws,, government documents and books addressing the legal, medical, philosophical and social- science aspect of bioethics are cited. Topics include professional/patient relationships, allocation of health-care resources, contraception, abortion, reproductive technologies, genetics, human experimentation, animal laboratory research, death and dying, and the prolongation of life. The database can be searched for keyword, author, title and time period. The system was started in 1973 and currently contains 26,000 records. It is updated bimonthly. Searches and printouts are available free of charge from the Bioethics Library. BIOETHICSLINE is accessible free of charge or the National Library of Medicine's MEDLARS System for which there is a nominal fee.

* Bird Banding Database

John Tautin
Bird Banding Laboratory
U.S. Fish and Wildlife Service
Laurel, MD 20708-4037 (301) 498-0423

This database contains information about game and non-game birds banded and/or recovered since the Banding Program began in 1921. Records exist on all birds banded in North America as well as their recovery from all over the world. The database is international in scope, as birds have been recovered by participants in countries such as Russia, Brazil and India. The database is used to produce quarterly reports to the person who bands the bird and certificates of appreciation to band reporters. It is also used for extensive data analysis of migratory bird populations. The database contains 2.6 million banding records. Searches and printouts are available. Depending upon the nature of your request, you may or may not be charged a fee. There is no determined fee schedule.

* Boating Accident Report (BAR)

Policy Planning and Evaluation Staff (G-BP)
U.S. Department of Transportation
2100 Second St., SW
Washington, DC 20593 (202) 267-2229

The system, updated monthly, provides annual statistical summaries on motorboat accidents. The principal data elements are case number, date, state, county, cause, facilities, injuries, operator age, vessel types, time, and environmental conditions. Thirty-two annual reports are generated by this system. One of them is the *Coast Guard Boating Statistics*, which is available upon request. Other data for internal use only.

* Bureau of Labor Statistics Electronic News Releases Service

Kathryn Hoyle
Office of Publications
Bureau of Labor Statistics
441 G St., NW
Washington, DC 20212 (202) 606-5902

BLS Electronic News Service provides direct dial-in access to subscribers of Boeing Computer Services, interested in the Bureau's economic indicators. The BLS releases, available online as soon as the data are officially released to the public include: producer price indexes; employment situation; state and metropolitan area employment and unemployment; consumer price index; real earnings; productivity and costs; and the employment cost index. The service is updated continually. Cost of the Electronic News Releases, which can be transmitted over telephone lines to computer terminals and other remote-access devices, varies. For contract information call Ronald S. Mizerak at Boeing.

Be patient. If any phone number is incorrect, call (area code) 555-1212 and request the new listing.

Federal Government Databases

* Cardiac Pacemaker Registry (CPR)

Gerald Deighton
FOI Staff HFI-35
U.S. Food and Drug Administration
5600 Fishers Lane
Rockville, MD 20857 (301) 443-6310

Contains data on all pacemakers and leads paid for under Medicare since April of 1985. Some information cannot be released. For more information contact Stuart Crumpler at (301) 427-1134.

* Catalog of Information on Water Data

Mary Bell Peters
National Water Data Exchange (NAWDEX)
U.S. Geological Survey
U.S. Department of Interior
12201 Sunrise Valley Dr.
421 National Center
Reston, VA 22090 (703) 648-5684

This computer file contains over 400,000 entries on streams, lakes, reservoirs, estuaries, and ground water. It contains sources, measurement locations, parameter types, frequency of measurement, and periods of record for data-acquisition programs of Federal/non-Federal agencies and organizations. It also contains water-data collection techniques for surface water, ground water, sediment, biological sediment, soil water, drainage basin characteristics, snow and ice and hydrometeorologic hydrometeorological observations. Computer printouts, maps, catalogs, referrals and publications are available.

* Census Bureau Transportation Statistics

Bureau of the Census
Data Users Services Division
Customer Services
Washington, DC 20233 (301) 763-4100

The following two data files are available representing survey results taken at 5 year intervals by the Census of Transportation: The Trucking Inventory and Use Survey; and the Commodity Transportation Survey. These surveys present benchmark data on the physical and operational characteristics of our national trucking resources and aggregate statistics on commodity movements by various modes. A machines readable tape is available for each survey. Printed reports and microfiche reports are also generated.

* Climate Assessment Database (CADB)

NOAA, National Meteorological Center W353
WWB, Room 800
Washington, DC 20233 (301) 763-8071

Designed for easy public access, this system provides users with information about short-term climate conditions in the United States and throughout the world. Anyone with a compatible terminal (most home computers are) and telephone linkup can obtain a password and dial directly into the system. Users can then select from a menu of 50 data files summarizing meteorological data on a weekly, monthly and seasonal basis. Examples of data include: temperature, precipitation, weather indexes, heating and cooling days, energy conditions, and assessment of climate on crops. The system contains global surface data collected from 6,000 stations worldwide. Data are contributed from 8,000 stations worldwide. The system is updated continually. For the price of a phone call, anyone with compatible equipment can use the system. Contact Director, Mr. McPherson's office at NOAA, (301) 763-8016, to find out if your terminal and telephone linkup are compatible. His office will give you an eight-letter password and the telephone number you can use to enter the system. The users fee ranges from $48-$600.

* Coal Consumption-Manufacturing Plants

Bruce Quade, Survey Manager
Coal Division - Data Systems Branch
Energy Information Administration
Washington, DC 20585 (202) 254-5461

This information system provides a quarterly census of coal consumption by U.S. manufacturing plants. The data are derived from coal receipts, consumption and stocks. Contact NTIS to purchase tapes or diskettes.

* Coal Distribution

Bruce Quade, Survey Manager
Coal Division - Data Systems Branch

Energy Information Administration
Washington, DC 20585 (202) 254-5461

The information system covers 99.5 percent of the U.S. coal production and distribution. Data are collected on coal production and purchases, stocks and distribution, including district or origin, method of transportation, and destination by: consumer category and census region and state. Data are collected quarterly, and the system contains over 20,000 records. Contact NTIS to purchase tapes or diskettes.

* Codes for Named Populated Places, Primary Country Divisions and Other Locations Entities of the U.S.

U.S. Department of Commerce
National Technical Information Service (NTIS)
5285 Port Royal Rd.
Springfield, VA 22161 (703) 487-4807

This ninth update of the Federal Information Processing Standard (FIPS) 55 data file provides a two-character State code and five-character numeric place code to uniquely identify each listed entity. Areas of the United States covered are the fifty states, the District of Columbia, and all outlying territories with significant self-administration. An exhaustive list is carried of incorporated places, census designated places (CDP's), primary county divisions (such as townships, New England towns, and census county divisions), recognized Indian reservations and Alaska Native villages, and counties. The listing also includes unincorporated places, military bases, National parks, airports, and ground transportation points. A two-character class code distinguishes over seventy entity types. Each entity is identified by the county or counties in which it is located. Zip codes are provided for all Post Offices. Available in: 9 track 1600 or 6250 BPI, order number PB87-1424326/HAL at a cost of $525. Bookstore and Information Center (703) 487-4604.

* Commuter Air Carrier Statistics: Online O & D and Flight and Traffic Statistics

Richard S. Strite
U.S. Department of Transportation
Research and Special Programs Administration
Washington, DC 20590 (202) 366-9058

Online O&D (origination and destination) contains the number of passengers and amount of mail and cargo transported by commuter air carriers between city pairs in scheduled services. Flight and Traffic Statistics provide data on the number of aircraft hours, miles, departures, revenue passenger-miles, available seat-miles, revenue ton-miles and available ton-miles transported by commuter air carriers in scheduled service. The disclosure of data on the file is restricted for a period of 12 months after the close of the year to which the data relate from 1971 to the present. Customized reports are available from these files upon written request. Data tapes are available for a fee.

* Continuing Survey of Food Intakes by Individuals (CSFII)

Gerald Deighton
FOI Staff HFI-35
U.S. Food and Drug Administration
5600 Fishers Lane
Rockville, MD 20857 (301) 443-6310

Annual nationwide food consumption survey of men and women 19-50 and children 1-5 conducted by U.S.D.A. Survey began in 1985. Provides data on food and nutrient intakes (up to six non-consecutive days) and vitamin/mineral supplement use. Contains companion food composition data. For more information contact Youngmee K. Park at (202) 205-5489.

* Contractor Accident Injury/Employment System

Richard Smith, Chief
Manager Safety and Health Technology Center
U.S. Department of Labor
Division of Mining Information Systems
PO Box 25367, DFC, Federal Building
Denver, CO 80025-0367 (303) 231-5449

This system collects, edits, updates, stores and reports information pertaining to contractor identification, employment, accidents, injuries and fatalities chargeable to mine, coal metal/non-metal contractors. The information published from this system, including incidence rates and other statistical data, i.e., coal production

Be patient. If any phone number is incorrect, call (area code) 555-1212 and request the new listing.

Government Databases and Bulletin Boards

in tons, is used by many mine industry related organizations, as well as by government personnel. The system is used to store and report contractor identification, address, accident, injury and illness information and statistics computed from these data. Individualized search requests are accepted. Searches are free as long as the information can be extracted easily and is reasonable quantity. Current data is kept for two years. Large projects are accepted and charged a fee under Freedom of Information Act. Data files are also available to purchase for complex projects.

* Countries, Dependencies, and Areas of Special Sovereignty

U.S. Department of Commerce
National Technical Information Service
Springfield, VA 22161 (703) 487-4807

The file contains data from Table 1 of Federal Information Processing Standard Publication (FIPS PUB) 10-3 *Countries, Dependencies, Areas of Special Sovereignty, and Their Principal Administrative Divisions,* including its change notices 1 and 2. The file includes the names and alphabetic two-character codes of each basic entity. In addition, it includes the name and four-character code of each principal division for those basic entities whose divisions are included in FIPS-PUB 10- 3. Records are sequenced in alphabetic order by basic entity. A typical entry consists of the country (basic entity) code and name and, if the basic entity is subdivided, the principal division codes and names. It is available in 9 track 1600 or 6250 BPI, order number PB85-222859/HAL, at a cost of $210.

* Defense Technical Information Center Collection (DTIC Online, DROLS)

National Technical Information Service (NTIS)
5285 Port Royal Rd.
Springfield, VA 22161 (703) 487-4600

DTIC maintains data banks with information about planned, ongoing, and completed DOD-related research and development activities. The collection is multi-disciplinary in scope and spans all fields of science and technology, covering topics such as: aeronautics, missile technology, navigation, space and technology, nuclear science, biology, chemistry, environmental science, oceanography, computer science, and human factors engineering. The four principle data banks are: the Technical Reports (TR) Program which contains bibliographic information on classified/unclassified reports generated by federally sponsored research; the Research and Technology Work Unit Information System (WUIS) containing information about current research being performed; the Research and Development Planning (R&DPP) database, consisting of information about proposed projects; and the Independent Research & Development (IR&D) data bank with information contractors have supplied DOD regarding their independent research efforts. The DTIC collection currently contains two million records and is updated continually. Universities, U.S. government agencies and associated contractors, subcontractors, and grantees are eligible for most DTIC services. In addition, research and development organization without current contracts may become eligible for service by obtaining a military service authorization under the defense potential contractors programs. If you are registered user for DTIC services, you can obtain direct online access to the DTIC system, have searches and printouts done free of charge, and purchase DTIC documents for a minimal fee - generally $1.50 to $3. If you are not DTIC-eligible, you can contact the National Technical Information Service (NTIS) to obtain a limited search of DTIC's Technical Reports Program database. NTIS charges for its services.

* Dental Research Projects

Deane Hill
Grants: Ron Ruben or Carla Flora
National Institute of Dental Research (NIDR)
Research Data and Management Information Section
5333 Westbard Ave., Room 707
Bethesda, MD 20814 (301) 496-7843

NIDR maintains a data bank of information about nationwide research activities in all areas of dental health. The data set is called Dental Proj. The research projects range from very basic to very applied, and most of the listings are NIDR-supported grants, contracts, or in-house projects. Retrievable data include: project title and number; name and address of the principle investigator; grant or contract specialists; project funding plus dates of commencement and completion; and a brief description of the project. Limited information is also available on worldwide dental research activities. Records go back to 1972. The contracts file, which is updated monthly, currently contains 100 active reports. The grants file presently holds 3,600 records and is updated daily. Searches and

printouts are available free of charge and only from NIDR. Data will be available online through the National Library of Medicine in the future.

* Dictionary of Occupational Titles, 4th Edition, and 1986 DOT Supplement

U.S. Department of Commerce
National Technical Information Service
Springfield, VA 22161 (703) 487-4807

This is the master file for the fourth edition of the Dictionary of Occupational Titles. it is comprehensive compilation of 12,099 coded (9-digits) job definitions classified in nine defined major categories, 82 defined 2 digit divisions, and 559 defined 3 digit groups. More than 28,800 job titles are in the file. Also included are master titles and definitions, term titles and definitions, glossary terms and 220 industry designation definitions. Available in: 9 track, 1600 or 6250 BPI, order number PB87-194528/HAL, at a cost of $210.

* Diet and Health Surveys

Gerald Deighton
FOI Staff HFI-35
U.S. Food and Drug Administration
5600 Fishers Lane
Rockville, MD 20857 (301) 443-6310

Analysis of national consumer attitudes towards diet and health, updated every two years since 1982. For more information contact Alan S. Levy at (202) 205-5657.

* Driver License Administration Requirements and Fees

Highway Statistics Division
Federal Highway Administration
U.S. Department of Transportation
400 7th St., SW
Washington, DC 20590 (202) 366-0180

Data cover the administrative requirements and qualifications necessary to obtain drivers' licenses in the 50 states and DC and Canada. Contains narrative summary and 10 detailed tables showing data by state, including requirements for regular licenses and classified licenses; training; examination and renewal; license reciprocity; fees; and suspension, revocation, and reinstatement provisions. Data is updated biennially. Contact the office listed above.

* Drug Quality Reporting System (DQRS)

Gerald Deighton
FOI Staff HFI-35
U.S. Food and Drug Administration
5600 Fishers Lane
Rockville, MD 20857 (301) 443-6310

Nation's pharmacists reporting on the quality of drugs, both RX and OTC, in the U.S. marketplace. (Replaced the former Drug Product Problem Reporting System.) Years covered are 1971 to present. For more information contact George R. Bolger at (301) 443-6044.

* Duck Breeding Ground Survey Database

Thomas J. Dwyer, Acting Chief
Office of Migratory Bird Management
U.S. Department of the Interior
Fish and Wildlife Service
Washington, DC 20240 (703) 358-1714

This survey provides data tables for use in estimating the size of waterfowl populations. It uses a master file of aerial survey data collected each year in July. It provides an index to the number of broods produced and the number of adult birds that are still on nesting territories. Data on age class and number of young per brood are recorded to determine progress and success of the nesting season. Information from this survey is most reliable for the most abundant and widely distributed species such as the mallard; it is less so for species of low abundance or for those species whose nesting is partly outside the survey area. Information is public and questions will be answered for members of the general public. Search requests are accepted through state agencies and University Land Grant Programs.

Be patient. If any phone number is incorrect, call (area code) 555-1212 and request the new listing.

Federal Government Databases

* Earth Science Data Director (ESDD)

C. R. Baskin
ESDD Project Manager
U.S. Geological Survey
12201 Sunrise Valley Dr.
801 National Center
Reston, VA 22092 (703) 648-7112

ESDD is designed to identify earth science and natural resource databases maintained by government agencies, academic institutions, and private sector entities. Users can locate indices, systems, files, documents, maps and other data sets. Databases referenced include those storing information on geologic, hydrologic, cartographic, biologic and conservation sciences. A computer terminal equipped with a modem can access ESDD with no on-line access charge. Menus, cross-referencing, and powerful search features make using the database easy. It is available on CD from OCLC (614-764-6000) in combination with GEOINDEX and USGS LIBRARY. Contact Mr. Baskin to arrange on-line use.

* Earth Science Information Center

Earth Science Information Center (ESIC)
U.S. Geological Survey
507 National Center, Room 1-C-402 (800) USA-MAPS
Reston, VA 22092 (703) 648-6045
or
Contact the ESIC nearest you. There are approximately 58 state affiliates. Consult your telephone book under U.S. Govt., Department of the Interior, USGS

The Earth Science Information Office operates a nationwide information and sales service for earth science research, maps, products and publications from both governmental and private sources. This network of ESICs (formerly known as National Cartographic Information Centers) provide information about geologic, hydrologic, topographic and land-use maps and publications; aerial, satellite and radar images and related products; cartographic data in digital form (see GeoData entry); and geodetic data. Some of the information dates back to 1700, and the Center has access to EROS Center databases of aerial/space imagery. ESIC staff will search these vast computerized records of cartographic data at your request. Several of the individual USGS databases are described in this section. Most of ESIC's research services are free, and many materials are available for order through ESIC. For others, you will be referred to the proper source.

* Economic and Industry Employment Projections

Howard Fullerton
Office of Economic Growth Projections
U.S. Department of Labor Statistics
2 Massachusetts Ave., NE
Washington, DC 20212 (202) 606-5711

The purpose of this system is to provide current and projected information in labor market trends. Information is divided by geographic location, industry and occupation and is intended for use in career guidance, educational planning and training programs. This system contains data on national employment, and projections on about 700 occupations in industries. Data are available for 1982 and projected to 1995. Bureau of Labor Statistics provides a number of services upon request for users of statistical data. These include release of certain categories of unpublished data; development of special surveys and tabulations; duplication of machine-readable data files on either diskettes or magnetic tapes; and sales of statistical software programs. Customized data files are available on a cost recovery basis.

* Economic and Social Data System (ESDS)

Maury Brown
Center for Development Information and Evaluation
U.S. Agency for International Development (AID)
Room 209, SA-1B
Washington, DC 20523 (703) 875-4902

ESDS is a statistical database consisting of development-related information about each country. The data are in a time series format, and collected from government agencies and organization conditions, demography, poverty indicators, labor force, social characteristics; and the population's education, nutrition, health, and food. The general public can obtain standardized reports, prepared from ESDS database searches, for a minimal fee from AID-Document Information and Handling Faculty (DIHF). Contact DIHF to obtain a free listing of available reports. Free specialized searches for AID contractors and federal, state, local and foreign government agencies. Non-AID users should contact the AID library to arrange a search.

* Economic Development Administration Socioeconomic Data System

U.S. Department of Commerce
Economic Development Administration
Herbert C. Hoover Bldg, Room 7116
Washington, DC 20230 (202) 482-3621

This system identifies socioeconomic characteristics of areas in which the Economic Development Administration (EDA) has approved projects. It includes data for all counties in the U.S. as well as for cities with population over 25,000. Data files are formatted to permit custom retrieval of specified data elements. Data files available through the system include Census Data Files, County Merge, County Business Patterns Files, Income Files, Bureau of Labor Statistics data and population and income figures. Arrangements can be made for individualized searches by EDA.

* Economic Impact Forecast System (EIFS)

Department of Urban and Regional Planning
ETIS Support Center
1003 West Nevada St.
Urbana, IL 61801 (217) 333-1369

EIFS is an information source and analytical tool that allows planners to predict the impact of proposed changes in an activity on the economy of affected areas. The system, which has statistics for every county in the U.S., can gather this information into any size multi-county region to analyze potential impacts. The database contains selected U.S. Department of Commerce statistics of social and economic characteristics in all U.S. counties and a variety of other types of information, including the Census of Population, Housing, and Manufacturers, the Bureau of Economic Analysis estimates, and County Business Patterns reports. EIFS contains records on all 3,200 counties in the country. Direct access via a remote terminal is available to ETIS subscribers for a $200 one time fee plus $90 per hour of computer connect time. Anyone can become an ETIS subscriber and thereby also obtain direct access to other databases maintained by ETIS. ETIS will conduct searches for nonsubscribers. A cost recovery fee, based on $90 per hour computer time, plus $25 staff time is charged. The average search generally takes 10 minutes.

* Electronic Catalog System

Satellite Data Services Division
Princeton Executive Center
5627 Allentown Rd., Suite 100
Camp Springs, MD 20746 (301) 763-8399

The Electronic Catalog System is a computerized locator system for digital data transmitted by polar orbit satellite and archived by NOAA. Data can be retrieved by time period, type of satellite, a particular sensor in a satellite, type of coverage, and geographical area. The system, formerly called the Spinner Program, was started in 1979, and currently contains 103,000 records. Nearly 800 records are added weekly. Searches and printouts (listing of digital data) are provided for a fee. Actual digital tapes must be purchased from NOAA.

* Electronic Dissemination Information System (EDI)

Russell Forte
National Agriculture Statistical Service
U.S. Department of Agriculture
Administration Building, Room 441W
Washington, DC 20250 (301) 720-5505

Information includes situation and outlook summaries and reports from ER's as well as market reports, crop and livestock statistics, foreign agricultural trade loads, export sales reports and other timely information from AMS, NASS, FAS and other USDA agencies.

* Employment Cost Index System

Albert Schwenk
Information Services
U.S. Department of Labor
Bureau of Labor Statistics

Be patient. If any phone number is incorrect, call (area code) 555-1212 and request the new listing.

Government Databases and Bulletin Boards

2 Massachusetts Ave., NE
Washington, DC 20212 (202) 606-6203

The purpose of this system is to produce indexes and rates of change in wage rates and total employee compensation by major industry and occupation groups. The system converts wage and benefit data to a cents-per-hour worked basis and inputs for non-response before generating the indexes and percent changes. Data are collected quarterly from approximately 2,000 occupational employment composition of the private non-farm economy. The major exclusions are self-employed, unpaid family workers and private household employees. The Bureau of Labor Statistics provides a number of services upon request for users of statistical data. These include release of certain categories of unpublished data; development of special surveys and tabulations; duplication of machine-readable data files on either diskettes or magnetic tapes; and sale of statistical software programs. Customized data files are available on a cost recovery basis.

* Employment Hours and Earnings

Albert Schwenk
Information Services
U.S. Department of Labor
2 Massachusetts Ave., NE
Washington, DC 20212 (202) 606-6203

This program provides current employment, hours, and earnings by industry for the nonagricultural sector of the economy. Data provided are fundamental inputs into the economic decision process at all levels of government, private enterprise and organized labor. It includes a sample of 210,000 nonagricultural establishments, monthly information on employment, wages received and the number of paid hours. Bureau of Labor Statistics provides a number of services upon request for users of statistical data. These include release of certain categories of unpublished data; development of special surveys and tabulations; duplication of machine-readable data files on either diskettes or magnetic tapes; and sales of statistical software programs. Customized data files are available on a cost-of-service basis.

* Establishment Registration (RGN)

Gerald Deighton
FOI Staff HFI-35
U.S. Food and Drug Administration
5600 Fishers Lane
Rockville, MD 20857 (301) 443-6310

Information gathered on these firms includes firm name, address, type of activity, owner/operator name and address, official correspondent name and address, and phone number and other business trading names. Years covered are 1977 to present, and updates are daily. For more information contact Ann C. Tornese at (301) 427-1152.

* Export Grain Information System (EGIS)

USDA, EGIS
Resources Management Division
Room 1642-South
PO Box 96454
Washington, DC 20090-96454 (202) 720-8732

The Export Grain Information System (EGIS) documents U.S. grain exports which were inspected and/or weighed under provisions of the U.S. Grain Standards Act. The database includes information about the quantity and quality of exported grain lots. The system documents information for wheat, corn, soybeans, sorghum, barley, rye, oats, flaxseed, sunflower seeds, and triticale. The database contains information from January 1983, to present, and is updated weekly.

* Fatal Accident Reporting System (FARS)

National Center for Statistics and Analysis
U.S. Department of Transportation
Fatal Accident Reporting System
NRD-32
Washington, DC 20590 (202) 366-4820

FARS is a census of data on all fatal traffic accidents within the 50 states, the District of Columbia and Puerto Rico. To be included in the system the accident must involve a motor vehicle traveling on a traffic way customarily open to the public and result in the death of a person (occupant of a vehicle or non-motorist) within 30 days of the accident. The FARS file contains descriptions, in a standard format, or each fatal accident reported. Each accident

has upwards of 90 different coded data elements that characterize the accident, the vehicles and the people involved. Specific data elements may be modified slightly each year to conform to changing user needs, vehicle characteristics and highway safety emphasis areas. Printouts are available at no charge and response time is normally within two weeks. Data are also available on computer tape.

* FDA Import Alert Retrieval System (FIARS)

Gerald Deighton
FOI Staff HFI-35
U.S. Food and Drug Administration
5600 Fishers Lane
Rockville, MD 20857 (301) 443-6310

Contains current information on import alerts and import bulletins (approximately 220) accessible through "keyword" or "text" search. For more information contact John Browne at (301) 443-6553.

* Federal Bureau of Investigation (FBI)

Director of the FBI
Freedom of Information Act Request
10th and Pennsylvania Ave., NW
Washington, DC 20535 (202) 324-5520

The FBI will search their central records system if you write a Freedom of Information Act (FDIA) Request letter describing in as much detail as possible the information you are seeking. Even before the FDIA was enacted the Research Unit, Office of Public and Congressional Affairs provided information in response to requests from the public. They would find the information requested, analyze it, and paraphrase the information. The office has published a 33 page booklet titled *Conducting Research in FBI Records*, which explains what type of information is available and how to use it. The booklet is available from the Research Unit, FBI Office of Congressional and Public Affairs, 10th and Pennsylvania Ave., NW, Room 7350, Washington, DC 20535; (202)324-5611.

* Federal Legal Information Through Electronics (FLITE)

Judge Advocate General's Department
United States Air Force
HQ USAF/JAS
Denver, CO 80279-5000 (303) 676-7531

FLITE is an automated legal research system. In addition to its own search system, FLITE has online access to other systems including: JURIS, LEXIS, WESTLAW, DIALOG, LEGI-SLATE and REG-ULATE. These combined resources include federal, State, and military court decisions, administrative agency decisions, statutes, pending regulations, law review articles and many related but non-legal databases of interest to attorneys. FLITE does not render legal opinions. It is available free to U.S. Department of Defense and selected federal agencies. Other federal agencies are charged $50 per database searched. FLITE is available only for problems related to government business. It is not restricted to attorneys. Your Member of Congress may be able to get FLITE search done for you.

* Federal Procurement Data Center (FPDC)

Liz Smith or Deborah Thompson
Federal Procurement Data Center
General Services Administration
4040 North Fairfax Dr., Suite 900
Arlington, VA 22203

FPDC stores information about federal procurement actions, from 1979 to present, that totaled $25,000 or more. The system will eventually contain 45 data elements, including: purchasing or contracting office; date of award; principal place of performance; dollars obligated; principal product or service; business and labor requirements; type of procurement action; methods of contracting; socioeconomic data; name and address of contractor; and foreign trade data. Examples of federal buying range from research and development to supplies and equipment and services. The database was started in 1979 and contains two million records. Approximately 400,000 contract actions are added yearly. Searches and printouts are available on a cost recovery basis. Requests should be made in writing. If a search on a contractor is requested, the DUNS number will be helpful.

Be patient. If any phone number is incorrect, call (area code) 555-1212 and request the new listing.

Federal Government Databases

* Financial Disclosure Database on Federal Candidates

Kent Cooper, Public Records Office
Federal Election Commission
999 E St., NW
Washington, DC 20463
(202) 219-3420
(800) 424-9530

The Financial Disclosure database has both financial and reference information on every candidate for federal office since 1977 and on contributing Political Action Committees and political parties. The system can be searched by specific candidate or contributor, and retrievable data include exact dollar amounts and contact information. The database was started in 1977 and contains nearly 3 1/2 million records. It is updated daily. Searches and printouts amounting to 20 records or less are available free of charge. A nominal fee is charged for each record.

* Financial Markets

Patrick Decker
Financial Markets
International Section
Federal Reserve System
Washington DC 20551
(202) 452-3314

This computer tape contains data on foreign exchange rates and foreign time deposit rates. Data only available on computer tape. Floppy diskettes and printouts not available.

* FIPS State/County Code Tape

U.S. Department of Commerce
National Technical Information Service
Springfield, VA 22161
(703) 487-4807

This tape contains two files: FIPS PUB 5-1 (incl. change notices 1-4) Standard Abbreviations and Codes for States and Outlying Areas of the U.S. and FIPS PUB 6-3 (incl. change notices 1-4), Counties and County Equivalents of the States of the United States and the District of Columbia. Records in File 1 are sequenced in alphabetic order of the states (incl. DC), followed by the major outlying areas. Records in File 2 are sequenced in alphabetic order of county name, within each state and outlying area. Progression of the numeric county code is consistent with alphabetic order of the counties within each state. Available in: 9 track 1600 or 6250 BPI, order number PB85-152288/HAL, at a cost of $210.

* Firm Profile File (MPQA)

Gerald Deighton
FOI Staff HFI-35
U.S. Food and Drug Administration
5600 Fishers Lane
Rockville, MD 20857
(301) 443-6310

Current compliance status for all drug and medical device manufacturers and repackers for each profile class (manufacturing process) and date of last GMP inspection of each process. For more information contact Anna M. Colandreo at (301) 443-3590.

* Fish and Wildlife Reference Service (FWRS) Database

U.S. Department of the Interior
Fish and Wildlife Service
Washington, DC 20240
(800) 582-3421

FWRS operates a bibliographic database containing indexed fish and wildlife-related documents from the following sources: the Federal Aid in Fish and Wildlife Restoration Program; the Adronomous Fish Conservation Program; the Endangered Species Grants program; work done at the Cooperative Fishery and Wildlife Agencies. Documents are selected for their research value to biologists in more than one state. Indexed materials include reports, published papers, technical publications, theses, and special materials such as endangered species recovery plans. Subject coverage includes birds, botany, fish management, hunting and fishing, water resources, pesticides, land use, habitat management and many other topics. The database has over 15,000 records, some dating back to 1945, and is updated continually. Bibliographic searches and documents can be obtained from FWRS. Individuals working on projects funded by FWRS contributors and full-time employees of state fish and wildlife agencies are eligible for "cooperator" status. Free literature searches are performed for "cooperators" and they are not charged for photocopying and microfiche services unless the cost exceeds $10. All others termed "clients" are charged a flat fee of $30 for a new literature search.

* Foreign Buyer

Foreign Agricultural Service
U.S. Department of Agriculture
Agricultural Information and Marketing
Services (AIMS)
Room 4951 - South
Washington, DC 20250-1000
(202) 720-4327

AIMS maintains a database of approximately 13,000 foreign firms from over 70 countries. American firms can obtain lists and match their products with prospective buyers. Foreign buyer lists provide company name, contact, address, telephone, telex, cable, and/or facsimile number. The lists can be formatted to provide foreign buyers by product for the entire world; or foreign buyers by country for all products.

* Foreign Geographic Names

Chief
Geographic Names Branch (GNB)
Defense Mapping Agency
Hydro-Graphic Topal-Graphic Center
Washington, DC 20315

This database manages information about all standardized foreign geographic names approved by GNB. The system is searchable by foreign country and its subdivisions such as listing of a particular country's rivers, populated places, or valleys. Retrievable data include proper name and spelling, longitude/latitude, and type of feature (i.e., city, mountain, administrative area, etc). In the near future, records will exist on all foreign countries. Searches and printouts are expected to be available on a cost recovery basis.

* Foreign Importer Listings Database

Foreign Agricultural Service
U.S. Department of Agriculture
Agricultural Information Marketing Service
4951-South Bldg
Washington, DC 20250
(202) 720-4327

The system includes names, addresses, and telex numbers of firms currently dealing in food and agricultural products in specific countries and of companies which have requested U.S. products in specific countries and of companies who have requested U.S. products during the past three years. Listings are available for all foreign countries for a single product or all importers of all agricultural products in a single country. There is a fee for each listing.

* Foreign Products Estimates

Ed Cissel
U.S. Department of Agriculture
Foreign Agriculture Service
Foreign Production Estimates Division
6503 South Building
Washington, DC 20250
(202) 720-0888

Various commodity databases are available that contain total production figures on foreign raw commodities. Commodities included in these files are grains, rice, dairy, poultry, livestock, oilseeds, cotton, coffee, sugar and tobacco. The Foreign Production Estimates Division can search the database by country or commodity. Each commodity has an expert available to assist with searches. There is no charge for such searches.

* Foreign Trade Statistics

Dick Preuss
U.S. Department of Commerce
Bureau of the Census
Foreign Trade Division
Washington, DC 20233
(301) 763-7754

This statistics system involves the compilation and distribution of a large body of data relating to the imports and exports of the U.S. It is designed to meet the needs of a variety of users. Non-government users in industry, finance, research institutions, transportation and other fields use the data as a statistical base to appraise the general trade situation and outlook, market analysis and market penetration studies; product and market development and for measuring the impact of competition. Special searches and tabulations are furnished at a cost which is determined on the basis of the quantity of data requested, complexity of data specification and costs for personnel and equipment.

Be patient. If any phone number is incorrect, call (area code) 555-1212 and request the new listing.

Government Databases and Bulletin Boards

* Foreign Traders Index (FTI)

Your U.S. District Office of the
International Trade Administration
or
Information Management Division
U.S. Department of Commerce
IRA/U.S. & FCS/EPS
Room 1322
Washington, DC 20230 (202) 482-0727

The Foreign Traders Index is a list-filing file describing foreign firms, their long-term interests and the types of activities they engage in. The database can be searched according to agents, sellers, distributors, users, companies, geographic location, date and number of employees. As of March 1989, the system contains 56,000 records, the majority added within the last few years. Charges include a set-up and per name fee.

* General Accounting Office Bibliographic Database (GAO)

GAO/IHSF
PO Box 6015
Gaithersburg, MD 20877 (202) 275-6241

GAO Bibliographic Database contains citations for every GAO document produced since 1976, and references for some GAO reports produced in the preceding four years. GAO studies cover a vast array of subjects, as the agency must produce a report on any topic Congress assigns. Reports have ranged from financial audits of government agencies to policy studies of health-related programs. Other topics have included environmental issues, social security, foreign relations, commerce, quotas for imported tuna and organized crime. Searches are generally conducted by subject area and specific time period. The system currently holds citations for 40,000 documents, some dating back to 1972. It is updated daily. Searches and printouts are available free of charge. GAO will also mail you up to five copies of any report listed; this service is also free.

* Geographic Information Retrieval and Analysis System (GIRAS)

U.S. Geological Survey
Earth Science Information Center (ESIC)
507 National Center, Room 1-C-402 (703) 648-6045
Reston, VA 22092 (800) USA-MAPS

The U.S. Geological Survey produces land use and land cover maps and associated overlays for the United States. These maps have been digitized, edited and incorporated into a digital database. The data is available to the public in both graphic and digital form and statistics derived from the data are published. Users are able to search for either locations or attributes. To obtain information from this database, contact ESIC.

* Geographic Names Information System (GNIS)

Roger Payne
Manager, GNIS
U.S. Geological Survey
12201 Sunrise Valley Dr.
523 National Center
Reston, VA 22092 (703) 648-4544

GNIS is an automated data system developed by USGS to standardize and disseminate information on geographic names. Primary information is provided for all know places, features, and areas in the U.S. identified by a proper name. The system is composed of 3 data bases: National Geographic Names Data Base (NGN), USGS Topographic Map Names Data Base, and Generic Data Base. The Generic Data Base defines the terms used by USGS for 63 broad categories of feature types found in the NGN Data Base (i.e., "stream" is used for rivers, creeks, brooks, etc.). It also contains annotated bibliographic listings of sources used to create the NGN Data Base. NGN and USGS Topographic Map Names Data Base are described in separate entries in this section. Printouts and searches from GNIS are available on a cost recovery basis.

* GEOINDEX

Geologic Division
U.S. Geological Survey
12201 Sunrise Valley Dr.
907 National Center
Reston, VA 22092 (703) 648-4383

GEOINDEX consists of bibliographic and location data for all published geologic maps of the U.S. and its territories. Indexed are individual maps; maps in books, journals and guidebooks; USGS Open-File Reports; and maps published by states, universities, societies, and commercial publishers. Maps now out of print are included. Fields include author, date, title, publisher, series, scale, county or region, latitude and longitude extremes and centers, area, and notes. GEOINDEX is available commercially on CD-ROM from OCLC, Inc.

* Geologic Names of the United States (GEONAMES)

Geologic Division
U.S. Geologic Survey
12201 Sunrise Valley Dr.
907 National Center
Reston, VA 22092 (703) 648-4383

GEONAMES is an annotated index of the formal geologic nomenclature of the United States and its territories. Data reflects distribution, geologic age, USGS usage, lithology, thickness, type locality, and a reference to the naming paper. Printouts are not available. Diskettes containing data for 2 or more adjacent states are available from USGS Open-File and Publications, Box 25425 Federal Center, Denver, Colorado 80225 (303) 236-7476. Magnetic tapes can be obtained from NTIS.

* Guaranteed Student Loan Information System

Pat Bridges
Guaranteed Student Loan Branch
Office of Post Secondary Education
U.S. Department of Education
7th and D Sts., SW
Washington, DC 20202 (202) 708-8242

This database contains information on the amount of money the U.S. government paid to private guarantee agencies for defaulted student loans. Statistical records are kept on the number of loans made under this program, the number of loans each guarantee agency has guaranteed, the banks participating in the program and the number of defaulted student loans each year. Information on individuals is not available to the public. However, inquiries by borrowers about their loans will be honored. Printouts are free for simple requests. Customized computer tapes are available for about $140.

* Hazardous Material Shipper Census/Identification

Linda Giles, Task Manager
Bureau of Motor Carrier Safety, HMC-10
Federal Highway Administration
U.S. Department of Transportation
400 7th St., SW
Washington, DC 20590 (202) 366-2971

This on-line system, updated daily, contains data, such as name, address, and types of hazardous materials shipped on approximately 21,000 shippers of hazardous materials. Data is for internal use and will be made available to the public as authorized by the Administration.

* Hazardous Materials Incident Reporting System

U.S. Department of Transportation
Research and Special Programs Administration
Information Systems Branch
DHM-63, Room 8112
400 7th St., SW
Washington, DC 20590 (202) 366-4433

This database provides a statistical compilation of all accidents and incidents involving hazardous materials. The system contains information on each reported incident and consists of data elements such as: the date of the accident, location, shipper, carrier, commodity involved and other detailed information concerning the packaging and nature of the incident. Customized searches are available upon request. There is a $30 minimum charge.

* Highway Statistics System

Federal Highway Administration
Highway Statistics Division
U.S. Department of Transportation
400 7th St., SW
Washington, DC 20590 (202) 366-0180

Be patient. If any phone number is incorrect, call (area code) 555-1212 and request the new listing.

Federal Government Databases

State data includes numbers and characteristics of registered vehicles, drivers' licenses, motor fuel consumed, tax and other highway related revenue, highway bonding, toll financing, roadway extent and characteristics, expenditures by type of governmental highway activity and highway travel. National summary includes highway statistics, national truck characteristics report, drivers' licenses, highway taxes and fees, road user and property fees, and special hard copy reports as required. Data are primarily byproducts of state and local planning, accounting, and administrative data files and are updated on an ongoing basis. Contact the Highway Statistics Division, listed above.

* Industrial Chemical Residues

Gerald Deighton
FOI Staff HFI-35
U.S. Food and Drug Administration
5600 Fishers Lane
Rockville, MD 20857 (301) 443-6310

Analytical properties of industrial chemical residues, updated annually. For more information, contact Marion O. Clower, Jr., at (202) 205-4036.

* Industrial Directory

Lynda DiNenna
Bureau of the Census, FB-3, Room 2585
U.S. Department of Commerce
Washington, DC 20233 (301) 763-7078

This system is a collection of business firms and the addresses of their offices and plants. It is compiled, maintained and used by the Bureau of the Census on a continuous basis. It contains basic economic information on five and a half million businesses. The following information is maintained for each company: primary name, secondary name, mailing address, actual address, standard industrial classification code, enterprise code, legal form of organization, employer identification number and directory identification number. Reimbursable projects are performed by the Bureau for requesting agencies or organizations.

* Information on Nuclear Sites

Argonne National Laboratory
Environmental Impact Studies Division
9700 S. Cass Ave.
Argonne, IL 60493

System to support efforts of the Nuclear Regulatory Commission (NRC) to develop site evaluation guidelines, to establish a general base of information for use by the NRC in other regulatory activities.

* INFOTERRA

U.S. National Focal Point for INFOTERRA
PM 211-A
U.S. Environmental Protection Agency
Washington, DC 20460 (202) 260-2080

INFOTERRA is an information referral service for sources of environmental information. The database contains government agencies, public and private organizations, universities, individuals, etc. from the U.S. and 134 countries worldwide. All those listed have agreed to answer questions and supply information regarding their particular area(s) of expertise. Sources are provided for 26 categories ranging from air to waste. The database can be searched by more than 1,000 different subject terms and retrievable information includes: description of source, contact information, source's output and the availability of materials, the regional area served, and the organization's sponsorship, activities and working language. INFOTERRA contains 10,000 records of which 1,400 refer to United States resources. It is updated every two years. Searches and printouts are available free of charge.

* Inlife

Gerald Deighton
FOI Staff HFI-35
U.S. Food and Drug Administration
5600 Fishers Lane
Rockville, MD 20857 (301) 443-6310

Data captured on an experimental animal during its lifetime, including weight, raw data for food or water consumption calculations, observations and animal removal data. The database covers 1986 to present and is updated daily. For more information contact (703) 790-4257.

* Integrated Technical Information System (ITIS)

Office of Science and Technical Information
U.S. Department of Energy (DOE)
PO Box 62
Oak Ridge, TN 37831 (615) 576-1272

The Integrated Technical Information System (ITIS), an online system developed by the DOE Office of Scientific and Technical Information, provides access to DOE databases and electronic mail service among DOE and contractor offices. Databases available on ITIS include the most recent 12 months of the Energy Data Base, reports Holding File, DOE Research in Progress, National Energy Software, etc. ITIS, which was established when DOE/RECON was discontinued in 1986, is available only to DOE and contractor employees.

* International Demographic Database (IDB)

Peter Johnson
Center for International Research
Scuderi Building, Room 614
U.S. Bureau of Census
Washington, DC 20233 (301) 763-4811

The International Demographic Center is developing its International Database which will contain demographic, social, and economic data about every country in the world. Presently, IDB focuses on developing nations, but data on other countries are being added continually. For each country logged, IDB contains 93 different subject tables. Variable stores include the following: an urban/rural breakdown, population by age and sex, birth and death rates, marital status, household size, labor force information, education data, and growth rates. Eventually, IDB will contain the World Population Database. Selected World Bank Data, United Nations material, and a bibliographic file may be added. Online access to the file is available to federal agencies and others may purchase magnetic tapes. Individual searches are available on a limited basis.

* International Marketing Profiles

Foreign Agricultural Service
U.S. Department of Agriculture
Agricultural Information and Marketing Service
Room 4951, South Building
14th Street and Independence Ave., SW
Washington, DC 20250 (202) 720-4327

This database presents statistical information on agricultural trade activity using two profiles: Product Marketing Profiles which examine market performance of specific agricultural products and Country Marketing Profiles which examine the agricultural trade activity in particular countries. Each profile includes an export brief, a list of exporter services, foreign importer mailing list information and a fact sheet summarizing Foreign Agricultural Service responsibility and key contact. There is a $15 fee for each profile.

* International Prices Program

Information Services
U.S. Department of Labor
Bureau of Labor Statistics
2 Massachusetts Ave., NE
Washington, DC 20212 (202) 606-7100

The purpose of this system is to provide measures of price changes for U.S. exports and imports and to analyze these price trends in world markets. The fundamental data in the system are price indexes for over 5,000 detailed commodities sold in the primary markets in the U.S. Price data are collected monthly from producers for more than 50,000 items covering more than 5,000 commodities. Data tapes and diskettes are available for all published producer price indexes.

* International Trade

U.S. Department of Commerce
International Trade Administration
Office of Trade and Investment Analysis System
14th and Pennsylvania Ave., NW, Room 2202
Washington, DC 20230 (202) 482-2568

This system contains comprehensive information on direct foreign investment transactions in the United States from 1974 to present. The information is for completed transactions only, and it covers manufacturing and all other sectors including real estate. There are data on U.S. enterprises, foreign investors and the terms of the transactions. This information is available on magnetic tape. The typical cost is less than $50.

Be patient. If any phone number is incorrect, call (area code) 555-1212 and request the new listing.

Government Databases and Bulletin Boards

* Inter-University Consortium for Political and Social Research (ICPSR)

ICPSR
PO Box 1248
Ann Arbor, MI 48106 (313) 764-2570

This membership-based organization comprised of over 300 colleges and universities receives, processes and distributes machine readable data on social phenomena occurring in over 130 countries. Surveys of mass and elite attitudes, census records, election returns, international interactions, and legislative records are maintained and easily searched. The contents of the archive extends across economic, sociological, historical, organizational, psychological and political concerns. The largest data collections are U.S. election data (including county and state level variables from 1790 through 1986). Direct access to ICPSR resources are available through CDNet for member schools.

* Jail Contracting Management System

U.S. Marshals Service
600 Army Navy Drive
Arlington, VA 22202 (202) 307-9320

This system monitors performance of approximately 800 contracts with local jails, as well as the financial aspects of these contracts. It contains such information as costs and obligation, population trends and jail inspection data. It produces hard copy reports on an as-required basis on jail and cost information on as well as allowing interactive file/record query.

* Labor Statistics (LABSTAT)

Connie DiCesare, Chief
Division of Information Services
U.S. Department of Labor
Bureau of Labor Statistics
2 Massachusetts Ave., NE
Washington, DC 20212 (202) 606-5886

LABSTAT is the overall system for storing, retrieving and manipulating BLS data. The database contains historic time series data which are generally aggregated at the macro level. The system is the repository for data collected from 20 different broad surveys providing data on the labor force, Consumer Price Index, Producer Price Index, Occupational Safety and Health, productivity data for industry and government, international labor comparisons, unemployment data, and more. Information is retrievable by numerous categories. LABSTAT contains 140,000 historical time series records and two million variable records with time series data. The system is updated 20 times a month. Each BLS division is responsible for data retrieval in its subject area, so contact the appropriate office for the data you need. Some offices may not be familiar with the term LABSTAT; therefore, it's best to simply request the information you need. The office will then try to assist you by consulting its data files, which are actually part of LABSTAT. Depending on the office and your request, you may or may not be charged a fee. To order data tapes, contact the Division of Planning and Financial Management, Room 1077, Bureau of Labor Statistics, U.S. Department of Labor, 441 G Street, NW, Washington, DC 20212.

* Low Acid Canned Foods (LACF)

Gerald Deighton
FOI Staff HFI-35
U.S. Food and Drug Administration
5600 Fishers Lane
Rockville, MD 20857 (301) 443-6310

The file, updated monthly, contains all low acid canned products and processes registered for use in the U.S. by domestic and foreign firms. Process data is not available to the public. For more information contact Sharon Schoen at (202) 205-4420.

* Mental Health Research Grants Application System

National Institute of Mental Health
National Institute of Health
Parklawn Building, Room 15-81
5600 Fishers La.
Rockville, MD 20857 (301) 443-3104

This management information system provides data for use in research grant analysis, planning, and administration. It covers all National Institute of Mental Health (NIMH) research grant applications. The file consists of all administrative

facts about applications including title, investigator, budget, project dates, sponsoring institution, location, review actions, and funding. A yearly sourcebook is produced. Searches and printouts for specific grant information can be arranged.

* Merchant Vessels of the United States

Information and Analysis Staff (G-MA)
U.S. Department of Transportation
2100 Second Street, SW
Washington, DC 20593 (202) 267-2229

This database is an annual listing of all American merchant vessels and yachts registered, including vessels lost, abandoned, transferred to aliens, or removed from registration. The file contains foreword, glossary, listings, and indexes. For registered vessels, listing shows official number, call letters, rig, name, tonnage, dimensions, hull type, when and where built, horsepower, service, owner, and home port. For vessels removed or subject to removal, listings show official number, rig, name of vessel, gross tons, and disposition. A monthly supplement (published 1867-present) presenting data on new registrations and changes is also issued. Contact the office listed above for data on microform or paper.

* Metals and Ceramics Information Center (MCIC)

CINDS
Perdue University
2595 Yeager Rd.
West Lafayette, IN 47906 (317) 494-9393

MCIC, a DOD-sponsored Information Center, maintains a bibliographic database for worldwide literature pertaining to metals and ceramics technologies. Major emphasis is placed on structural alloys, and retrievable information includes citations, abstracts, and analyses of technical documents from government reports and worldwide open literature. The scope includes selected metals, ceramics, and composite materials of interest to DOD and its contracts and material suppliers. Information cited on all three types of materials covers coatings, environmental effects, physical properties, materials applications, test methods, sources/suppliers, specifications, design characteristics, and various strength steels, and superalloys. Ceramics covered include borides, carbides, carbon/graphite, nitrides, oxides, sulfides, silicides, selected glass, and glass ceramics. MCIC maintains both a computerized and manual database. The computerized portion was started in 1975 and has access to more than 130,000 records. It is updated daily. MCIS will do searches for all sectors of government and industry. Simple searches are done free of charge, while more complex requests are assessed at a cost recovery fee. DOD agencies and contractors can get direct access to the database through the Defense Technical Information Center's DTIC online system (DROLS) which is described earlier in this section.

* Mineral Resources Data Systems

Donald F. Huber
U.S. Department of the Interior
Branch of Resource Analysis
345 Middlefield Rd., Mail Stop 984
Menlo Park, CA 94025 (415) 329-5358

This system serves as a storage and retrieval facility for mineral commodity data, data resulting from the two degree sheet studies, data contributed by other organizations under various types of contracts, and other sources. This system makes it possible on a short notice to search out and synthesize great quantities of diverse data on mineral resources and on individual deposits. Data are available in five versions to public users. Where interest is in less than 10 or less data items, tables or listing can be provided for the desired geographical areas or commodities. Printouts of full or practical versions are available. Computer generated maps can also be made. For large data set requests, the data are provided in tape and diskette form.

* Monthly Motor Gasoline Reported by States

Federal Highway Administration
U.S. Department of Transportation
400 7th St., SW
Washington, DC 20590 (202) 366-0180

This database stores monthly data from taxation reports on gasoline (including gasohol) consumption by state. Data are current to 2-4 months preceding issue date, as state reports become available. Contents include daily average consumption, monthly gasoline consumption for last 4 months and cumulative for the calendar year, monthly and cumulative gasohol consumption, and

Be patient. If any phone number is incorrect, call (area code) 555-1212 and request the new listing.

Federal Government Databases

12-month moving total of gasoline sales. Contact the office listed above for data available on magnetic tape.

* Monthly Petroleum Supply Reporting System

National Energy Information Center
U.S. Department of Energy
Room 1F, O48
Washington, DC 20585 (202) 586-8800

This system assembles statistical data collected monthly on liquid hydrocarbon products. Information includes production, stock, imports, exports, shipping movements and refinery input. The system provides a comprehensive collection of data on supply and disposition of crude oil and refined products in the United States and its territories. Tapes may be purchased from the National Technical Information Service (NTIS).

* Motor Carrier Census Identification

Linda Giles, Task Manager
Federal Highway Administration
Bureau of Motor Carrier Safety (BMCS), HMC-12
U.S. Department of Transportation
400 7th St., SW
Washington, DC 20590 (202) 366-2971

This on-line system, updated daily, contains data, such as name, address, type and area of operation, commodities (including hazardous materials transported), compliance ratings, numbers of vehicles and drivers used, mileage operated, and audit dates for approximately 190,000 interstate motor carriers subject to BMCS jurisdiction. Contact the office listed above concerning availability of data.

* Mourning Dove Reports

David Dolton
Office of Migratory Bird Management
U.S. Department of Interior
Fish and Wildlife Service
Patuxent Wildlife Research Center
Laurel, MD 20708 (301) 498-0306

Records from the results of the Annual Call-Count Survey, are collected according to various ecological strata. The records are used to produce a meaningful index of the size of the mourning dove breeding population and to set annual mourning dove hunting regulations. It is updated annually. Searches and printouts are available. Depending upon the nature of your request, you may or may not be charged a fee. Some information in the database is restricted under the Privacy Act. A States report is produced each year.

* MSA: Metropolitan Statistical Areas Data Tape

U.S. Department of Commerce
National Technical Information Service
Springfield, VA 22161 (703) 487-4807

A total of 257 MSAs are recognized. In addition, there are 23 CMSAs, consisting of 78 PMSAs. This tape contains computer files documenting titles, components and Federal Information Processing Standards (FIPS) codes for Metropolitan Statistical Areas and related statistical areas. It includes two computer files to convert titles, components, and FIPS codes from SMSA to MSA definitions. Available in 9 track 1600 or 6250 BPI, order number PB85-161115/HAL at a cost of $210.

* Munitions Control Database System

James DePalma
Office of Munitions Control
Bureau of Politico-Military Affairs
U.S. Department of State
Washington, DC 20520 (703) 875-7391

The system is designed to record licenses issued authorizing the export of U.S. munitions, list equipment to foreign countries and international organizations, and record the exports against said licenses. Information in the system pertaining to equipment authorized for export includes applicant/licensee, license number, date issued/shipped, quantity, and commodity value. Requests for information contained in the database must be made through the Freedom of Information Act Office. The cost of obtaining the information is charged according to a fee schedule of: professional time at $12 per hour, clerical time at $7 and a cost for reproduction of documents.

* NASA Center for Aerospace Information (NASA NASA/RECON)

NASA STI Facility
Attn: Registration Services
P.O. Box 8757
BWI Airport
Baltimore, MD 21240 (401) 859-5300

NASA STI Database provides bibliographic information for worldwide literature in aeronautics, space, and the vast array of topics of interest to NASA via NASA/RECON. The broad-based system contains more than 100 different categories ranging from aerodynamics to urban technology. Many of the reports, journals, books and conference papers cited are highly technical. NASA's wide interests in science include the environment and properties of the earth, moon, and planets; the sun and its relationship to the earth and the rest of the solar system; the space environment; the physical nature of the universe; and the search for extraterrestrial life. In technology, NASA's interests include spacecraft and launch vehicles; aircraft; propulsion; auxiliary power; human factors; electronics; and structures and materials. In applications, NASA's interests include astronomical, geophysical, meteorological and communications systems, as well as emphasis on earth resources, air and water pollution, and urban transportation. The system was started in 1968 and currently has approximately 2.7 million records. NASA offers different levels of service depending on your needs.

* National Accident Sampling System

Grace Hazzard
National Center for Statistics and Analysis (NRD-32)
National Highway Traffic Safety Administration (NHTSA)
400 Seventh St., SW
Washington, DC 20590 (202) 366-4820

This system provides detailed information on all police-reported traffic accidents since 1979. It contains data on more than 10,000 accidents per year in communities ranging from the most rural to the most urban in the nation. Data include: victim's age, sex, height, weight, admission and discharge dates, specific injuries and cause of death of fatally injured victims. This information is coded to provide general statistics while protecting the identity and privacy of the individuals involved. Data are available in report form or magnetic tape.

* National Agricultural Pest Information Services (NAPIS)

Dave Talpas
PPQ/APIS
U.S. Department of Agriculture
Federal Building, Room 640
Hyattsville, MD 20782 (301) 436-8247

This database contains information about insects, weeds, plant diseases and nematodes. Each state collects data and transmits it to the U.S. Department of Agriculture's National Plant Pest Quarantine Office (PPQ) in Maryland. Data from each state include observation date, State, county, crop, crop growth stage, pest, pest life stage, abundance or incidence, damage or severity and detection method. Searches and printouts are generally available for free.

* National Asset Seizure and Forfeiture System

Office of Legal Counsel
U.S. Marshal Service
600 Army Navy Drive
Suite 1090
Arlington, VA 22202-4210 (202) 307-9221

The system maintains a complete inventory of property seized by the government and placed in the custody of the U.S. Marshals Service. The system will also maintain a complete record of all funds expended to maintain and dispose of the property. Output includes inventory listings, summary reports on inventory items by category and financial reports. To obtain a printout, send a written Freedom of Information request to the above office.

* National Crime Information Center (NCIC)

Criminal Justice Services Division
Technical Services Division
Federal Bureau of Investigation
10th and Pennsylvania Ave., NW
Washington, DC 20535 (202) 324-2606

Government Databases and Bulletin Boards

NCIC provides information on-line to criminal justice agencies concerning wanted persons, missing persons, stolen property, and computerized criminal histories. Input and retrieval are performed via federal, state and local computer/terminal interface with a central FBI computer. Retrievable data includes information on criminal careers and permits authorities to track criminals through the criminal justice system. The system contains more than nine million records and updates are performed on a 24-hour day online basis. Searches and printouts are free and restricted to criminal justice agencies.

* National Diabetes Information Clearinghouse (NDIC)

National Diabetes Information Clearinghouse
Box NDIC
9000 Rockville Pike
Bethesda, MD 20892 (301) 468-2162

This online database contains citations and abstracts of diabetic patient education materials including books, audiovisuals, teaching manuals and journal articles. Basic information about diabetes, its complications, and information about programs designed for diabetics and health professionals is also stored. The database is patient oriented and does not include highly technical, clinical or research materials. The system, which is updated monthly, became operational in 1985 and contains 6,000 records. NDIC will do searches and provide a bibliographic printout (with abstracts and acquisition source free of charge). It is also available commercially through CHID (Combined Health Database).

* National Financial Summary

Linda Farmer
U.S. Department of Agriculture
Economic Research Service
1301 New York Ave., NW
Washington, DC 20005-4788 (202) 219-0804

This database includes farm income, cash receipts by components, production expenses, capital expenditures, off-farm income, non-money and farm-related income components. It also includes U.S. balance sheet data, 1944-87, and related data on assets and debt. Data disk is available in Lotus for $45. For ordering information, call (800) 999-6779. Stock number 88010.

* National Referral Center Library of Congress

Resources Analysis Section
General Reading Rooms Division
Library of Congress
Washington, DC 20540 (202) 707-5522

The database of Library of Congress's defunct National Referral Center still exists. This data bank consists of a directory listing more than 12,000 organizations or individuals qualified and willing to provide information on topics primarily in science, technology, and social sciences to the general public. A typical citation contains the name of the resource, mailing address, telephone number, areas of interest, special collections, databases, publications, and special services. Organizations can be located by name or subject. To obtain a listing of sources for your area of interest or a particular industry contact the General Reading Room and if you have difficulties contact your U.S. Representative or Senator.

* National Resources Inventory (NRI)

U.S. Department of Agriculture
Resources Inventory Division
Soil Conservation Service
PO Box 2890
Washington, DC 20013 (202) 720-4530

This database contains basic information on the U.S. natural resources, such as land use, soil, water and wind erosion, land cover, conservation practices, and treatment needs. These data are collected on sample sites on private lands that were selected using a systematic randomized sampling procedure. The data are site specific, but the data are considered reliable aggregated to the state and national level. The file is updated on a periodic basis and contains approximately 350,000 megabytes. Magnetic tapes are available that can be searched by: kind of soil, by state, by land use, etc. Tapes normally cost less than $100. Hard copy is also available upon request.

* National Standard Reference Data System (NSRDS)

Joan Sauerwein
A 320 Physics Building
National Institute of Standards and Technology
Gaithersburg, MD 20899 (301) 975-2208

Each NSRDS Data Center maintains databases of evaluated physical and chemical properties of substances. The system supports NBS' responsibility to promote numerical data in the physical sciences. The evaluations are carried out through a national network of 22 NSRDS Centers and special projects conducted by universities, government laboratories and industry. Each center is responsible for a well-defined technical scope and for compiling a comprehensive indexed bibliographic file with analyses of the world literature within its scope. The Centers assess the accuracy of the data reported in the literature, prepare compilations, and recommend best values. The resulting bibliographic and numeric physical, chemical, and property databases are then made available through publications, magnetic tapes, and online systems. The Center's activities are aggregated into three application-oriented program areas: 1) Energy and Environmental Data, which includes data from fields such as chemical kinetics, spectroscopy, and radiation physics and chemistry which have application to energy-related R&D and environmental modeling; 2) Industrial Process Data, which covers primarily thermodynamic and transport properties of substances important to the chemical and related industries; and 3) Materials Properties Data, which includes structural, electrical, optical, and mechanical properties of solid materials of broad interest.

* National Victim Resource Center (NVAC)

Stephanie L. Greenhouse
Office of Justice Assistance, Research and Statistics
U.S. Department of Justice
Box 6000 AIQ (301) 251-5525
Rockville, MD 20850 (301) 251-5519

This system is a computerized national program database containing description of all types of victim assistance programs throughout the country. A legislative database has been developed to track pending and enacted legislation on victim assistance and compensation programs. It also collects and makes literature available (i.e., books, articles, reports and audiovisual materials). This system has access to more than 7,000 victim related books and articles. Information specialists can help you with the federally sponsored victim related research studies, national victimization statistics and information on State victims compensation programs.

* Nationwide Examination of X-Ray Trends (NEXT)

Fred Rueter
Radiological Health
DIGP HF2
5600 Fishers Lane
Rockville, MD 20857 (301) 443-2436

NEXT contains statistical data and exposure/dose information about diagnostic medical and dental x-rays taken nationwide. Tabulations can be done according to hospitals, private facilities, geographical areas, x-ray techniques, and body organs. Started in 1973, NEXT currently holds 60,000 records. It is updated continuously. Searches and printouts are available free of charge.

* New NEXT (NX2)

Gerald Deighton
FOI Staff HFI-35
U.S. Food and Drug Administration
5600 Fishers Lane
Rockville, MD 20857 (301) 443-6310

The new NEXT (Nationwide Experience in X-ray Trends) system is designed to collect data gathered in states on the performance of X-ray equipment used in radiographic exams measuring exposure values in real life situations. The database is updated annually and covers the years 1984 to present. For more information contact Fred Rueter at (301) 443-2436.

* NHTSA Auto-Safety Hotline

National Highway Traffic Safety Administration (NHTSA)
Auto-Safety Hotline
U.S. Department of Transportation

Be patient. If any phone number is incorrect, call (area code) 555-1212 and request the new listing.

Federal Government Databases

400 Seventh St., SW (202) 366-0123
Washington, DC 20590 (800) 424-9393

NHTSA maintains a database of safety information about automobiles manufactured in the past 10 years. The system can be searched by car make, model, year, or equipment. Retrievable information includes: crash test results; repairability and damage statistics; safety recall information; insurance and accident costs; consumer complaints filed about a car; used-car information; and tire treadwear and skid resistance. The database was started in 1972 and is updated daily. Searches and printouts are available free of charge. Unless your request is complex, you can get the data you need quickly by calling the Hotline. An operator will conduct a search while you are still on the phone and a printout will be mailed within 24 hours. NHTSA encourages individuals to call the Hotline whenever they want to register a safety complaint about the automobile. Often NHTSA will investigate the complaint and if necessary contact the manufacturer on the owner's behalf.

* NIOSHTIC

Bill Bennett
Information Acquisition Data Systems
National Institute of Occupational Safety and Health
4676 Columbia Pkwy.
Cincinnati, OH 45226 (513) 533-8317

NIOSHTIC contains bibliographic citations and abstracts of occupational safety and health materials. Input is gathered from U.S. and foreign literature, the personnel files of several distinguished researchers in the field. The system currently contains more than 150,000 records and is increasing by 500 a month. This database dates back to 1860. Currently searches and printouts are available free of charge. This database is available commercially from Dialog, Pergamon and Orbit.

* National Rehabilitation Information Center

National Rehabilitation Information Center
National Institute on Disabled and Rehabilitation Research
Macro Systems, Inc.
8455 Colesville Rd., Suite 935
Silver Spring, MD 20910 (800) 34-NARIC

Updated continually, this bibliographic database contains abstracts of materials on all aspects of disability and rehabilitation. Appropriate research and proceedings reports, books, journals and audiovisual materials are referenced. Examples of subject areas covered include accessibility, behavior modification, deinstitutionalization, funding, statistics, and workers' compensation. The database contains more than 21,000 items, some dating back to the 1950s. The Center will search its own database and several other commercially available databases. The basic charge is $10 for the first 100 citations, and $5 for the next 100. No one will be denied access to these resources because of inability to pay. This database is available commercially on BRS.

* Commercial Building Energy Consumption Surveys

Marty Johnson
Office of Energy Markets and End Use
End Use Division
U.S. Department of Energy
1000 Independence Ave., SW
Washington, DC 20585 (202) 586-1135

This system is used to determine the energy consuming characteristics of a national scientific sample of non-residential buildings. The information is used for such projects as assessing the possibilities for financial incentives for the installation of energy conservation measures. Data include square footage, type of business, and maintained temperature. Energy consumption and expenditure figures are gathered from fuel suppliers of the sampled buildings. Contact Ms. Oliver or the National Energy Information Center (202) 586-8800 to have specific information retrieved from the database. To purchase the complete tape, contact NTIS, (703) 487-4650.

* Official Establishment Inventory

Gerald Deighton
FOI Staff HFI-35
U.S. Food and Drug Administration
5600 Fishers Lane
Rockville, MD 20857 (301) 443-6310

Current inventory, updated monthly, of establishments or individuals whose activities fall under jurisdiction of Food and Drug Administration. Includes

name, address, establishment types, industries' date of last inspection, classification, date of last violative inspection, and so on. For more information, contact Norma Hanna at (301) 443-3330.

* Operator Sailing Schedules

James E. Saari
FOI Officer
Office of Information Resources Management
Maritime Administration
U.S. Department of Transportation
400 7th St., SW
Washington, DC 20590 (202) 366-5746/4181

This system collects advertised sailing schedules of time service operator's vessels. Requests for access to this database, developed for use by the Maritime Administration, may be subject to Privacy Act regulations.

* The Opportunity Bank

Overseas Private Investment Corporation
Opportunities Bank
1100 New York Ave., NW (800) 424-OPIC
Washington, DC 20527 (202) 336-8799

This database contains information on U.S. companies with interest in possible joint venture investment opportunities in developing countries as well as information about foreign companies and individuals interested in locating American joint venture projects. There is no fee to be included into the database. Access to the system costs $50 for information on 10 or fewer leads that meet your requirements. Currently, the Opportunity Bank contains more than 1000 investment project profiles on a broad cross-section of potential joint venture enterprises in more than 75 countries in the developing world. The company file contains more than 4000 potential investors.

* Personal Census Records Service System

Census History Staff
U.S. Bureau of the Census
Washington, DC 20233 (301) 763-7936

A personal search of census records is available upon proof of authorized representation--parent, spouse, sibling (a named individual or authorized representative heir with proof of death). A staff of employees provide personal data from census records for those individuals who lack documents of birth or citizenship. Extracts of these records are accepted as evidence of age, place of birth, social security benefits, passports and other purposes. The data files contain complete historical census reports since 1920. Personal search requests cost $15.

* Petroleum Marketing Monthly

National Energy Information Center
U.S. Department of Energy
1000 Independence Ave., SW
Room 1-F 048
Washington, DC 20585 (202) 586-8800

This system, corresponding to the hard-copy publication with the same title, is a collection of information on petroleum products, including the following: propane, gasoline, kerosene, distillates, aviation fuels, and residual fuel oils. Summaries have been developed to provide petroleum product information, such as distribution, sales volume, and selling prices per state. Some summaries contain the anticipated supply for individual states for the following month. Computer tapes are available from NTIS.

* Physicians Data Query Cancer Information System (PDQ)

International Cancer Information Center
National Cancer Institute
U.S. Department of Health and Human Services
International Cancer Research Program
R.A. Bloch Building
9030 Old Georgetown Rd.
Bethesda, MD 20892 (301) 496-5583

Files are hierarchial and must be obtained together. Files are menu driven. A version of PDQ has been developed which uses a MUMPS-based retrieval system which can run on either mini or micro computers. Data on 87 treatments, 12,000 physicians, 1,500 organizations, 1,000 protocols are included in these files.

Be patient. If any phone number is incorrect, call (area code) 555-1212 and request the new listing.

Government Databases and Bulletin Boards

Each file updated monthly. Data are updated monthly. However, addition of chemotherapeutic agents, dose modification and AIDS treatment information limits comparability of current and historical data.

* PIERS

James E. Saari, FOI Officer
Office of Information Resources Management
Maritime Administration
U.S. Department of Transportation
400 7th St., SW
Washington, DC 20590 (202) 366-5746/4181

This database stores, sorts and, retrieves statistical data on U.S. imports and exports. Requests for access to this database, developed for use by the Maritime Administration, may be subject to Privacy Act regulations.

* PLASTEC Automated Bibliographic Services

Suseela Chandresekar
Plastics Technical Evaluation Center (PLASTEC)
U.S. Army Armament Research Development Center
Dover, NJ 07801 (201) 724-2778

PLASTEC, a DOD-sponsored information and analysis center, maintains a bibliographic database with abstracts for worldwide technical literature related to plastics, adhesives, and organic matrix composites. References cover all plastic-related technology from applied research through fabrication, with emphasis on properties and performance. Subject areas include structural, electrical, electronic, and packaging applications. Databases containing millions of citations, abstracts, or research summaries can be searched. It is updated every two months, and approximately 3,000 new citations are added yearly. In addition to its own bibliographic database, online access to PLASTEC is available only to government agencies, contractors, and the defense community through OTIC, NASA STI, Dialog and SOC. The center maintains a staff of materials specialists who provide a wide range of services.

* Procurement Automated Source System (PASS)

Your local SBA Office
or
Glen Harwood
Procurement Automated Source System
U.S. Small Business Administration
1441 L St., NW, Room 627
Washington, DC 20416 (800) 827-5722

PASS is a centralized inventory and referral system of small businesses interested in being prime contractors for federal agencies or subcontractor for companies. More than 26,000 minority owned, 27,000 female owned and over 40,000 veteran owned businesses nationwide are listed in the fields of research and development, manufacturing, construction, and services. PASS uses a keyword system which identifies the capabilities of the company. The system can be searched for firms by geographic location, type of ownership, labor surplus area, zip code, minority type, and over 3,000 keywords. PASS, started in October 1978, currently holds reports about 130,000 firms and increases by 200 firms monthly. There are 300 direct access users. Anyone seeking to purchase a product or service from a small business can contact SBA to have a search run. Searches and printouts are provided free of charge. Firms wanting to be listed (no charge) should contact the SBA regional PASS specialist. Federal agencies and prime contractors have online direct access to PASS.

* Profile: National Automated Minority Business Source List Service

James L. Thomas
Information Clearinghouse
Minority Business Development Agency, Room 6708
U.S. Department of Commerce
Washington, DC 20230 (202) 482-2414

This system serves as a minority business locator system established for government purchasing agents. The database contains information about more than 27,000 minority-owned businesses nationwide. It can be searched by specific minority ownership (i.e., black, veteran, etc.), type of firm, size, geographic location and product or service supplied. Retrievable data include contact information and a short profile of the firm describing its capabilities, services, gross sales, and more. It is updated continually. Access is limited.

* Project Share

Ms. Joseph, Project Manager
Project Share
P.O. Box 2309 (301) 231-9539
Rockville, MD 20852 (800) 537-3784

This database has bibliographic citations and abstracts of literature about improving the delivery and management of human services. Topics include long-term care, substance abuse, transportation, cost effectiveness, vocational rehabilitation, juvenile delinquency, health insurance, grants, fundings and group homes. Cited materials are geared toward managers, supervisors and policy-makers. The database contains 15,000 records on current literature and is updated frequently. Most searches, with printouts, cost $45. Several standard searches are available for $10 each.

* Railroad Accident/Incident Reporting System (RAIRS)

Bruce George
Office of Safety RRS-21
Federal Railroad Administration
U.S. Department of Transportation
400 Seventh St., SW
Washington, DC 20590 (202) 366-0533

RAIRS presents historical data on rail-highway crossing accidents/incidents for 1979 through 1988. It combines information from the rail-highway crossing accident/incident file with data in the National Rail-Highway Crossing Inventory and highlights relationships between certain grade-crossing characteristics and accident frequencies. It also gives the physical and operational statistics for all public, at-grade rail-highway crossings, described in the National Inventory of May 1985. The principal data elements includes railroad codes, casualty information, damage costs, location of the accident, train speed, weather, and other grade crossing information. Reports containing detailed tables are available. These statistics are published in various reports by the Federal Railroad Administration and can be obtained by contacting the above office or any of the public information offices located in the FRA regional and division offices around the country.

* Rare-Earth Information Center (RIC)

Joel Calhoun
Rare-Earth Information Center
Energy and Minerals Resources Institute
Iowa State University
Ames, IA 50011 (515) 294-2272

RIC is a bibliographic database of worldwide literature concerning the physical and application aspects of rare-earth. RIC's main emphasis is the physical metallurgy and solid state physics of rare-earth metals and their alloys. Citations of journal articles on ceramics, technology, geochemistry, and toxicity of the elements and their compounds are also provided. RIC can be searched by author, title, time period and subject. The system currently stores 40,000 references, some dating back to 1966. RIC is updated by 3,000 references annually. Searches and printouts are available for a minimum fee of $50 which entitles you to up to 25 citations. Twenty-five dollars is assessed for each additional increment of 25 citations, and $2 per citation over 25. Fees are waived under special circumstances.

* Recall Monitoring (REC)

Gerald Deighton
FOI Staff HFI-35
U.S. Food and Drug Administration
5600 Fishers Lane
Rockville, MD 20857 (301) 443-6310

This system tracks product recalls from their initial classification as potential recalls through the completion of any necessary product recall and verification by Food and Drug Administration field personnel. Years covered are 1972-1988. For more information, contact James Merritt at (301) 427-1122.

* Red Meats and Poultry Supply and Use

Richard Stillman
Mark Weimar
U.S. Department of Agriculture
Economic Research Service
1301 New York Ave., NW
Washington, DC 20005-4788 (202) 219-0713

Be patient. If any phone number is incorrect, call (area code) 555-1212 and request the new listing.

Federal Government Databases

Contains supply and use data for beef, pork, veal, lamb, and all red meats, broilers, other chicken, turkey, all poultry, and all red meats and poultry. Quarterly and annual data are included for 1960-87. A data disk in Lotus is available for $25. For ordering information, call (800) 999-6779. Stock number 89008.

* Registry of Toxic Effects of Chemical Substances (RTECS)

Doris Sweet
Information Retrieval and Analyses Section
National Institute for Occupational Safety and Health (NIOSH)
4676 Columbia Pkwy.
Cincinnati, OH 45226 (513) 533-8317

RTECS stores data about 98,000 individual chemicals that have been studied for toxicity. The following information can be retrieved for each chemical: main name, 8+9 collective index name, synonym, molecular weight, and toxicity data. NIOSH will run one or two chemicals and provide printouts at no charge. For more detailed searches for which there is a fee, contact the National Library of Medicine or EPA Chemical Information System.

* Regulated Persons Index Master List

Joseph C. Polking
Secretary
Federal Maritime Commission (FMC)
U.S. Department of Transportation
Washington, DC 20573 (202) 523-5773

This is an alphabetized listing of entities subject to FMC regulation, including vessel operating common carriers, non-vessel operating common carriers, marine terminal operators and licensed freight forwarders. This database is available at a modest charge in either hard copy or floppy format. Other files available from this office include Regulated Persons Index--a listing of vessel operating common carriers; and Regulated Persons Index--a listing of non vessel operating common carriers and a Listing of Licensed Freight Forwarders.

* Reliability Analysis Center (RAC)

Gina Nash
Reliability Analysis Center
PO 4700
Rome, NY 13440-8200 (315) 330-4151

RAC maintains six databases with bibliographic and technical information pertaining to the reliability characteristics of components and systems. The databases are the following: VLSI, on very large scale circuits; IC, on integrated circuits; Hybrid Circuits; Non-Electronic Devices; and Failures Related to Static Electricity (FRSC). Non-operating reliability database equipment is not operational. The scope includes reliability and failure mode/mechanism information that is generated during all phases of component fabrication, testing, equipment assembly, and operation. Information and data on research and development studies, process control, quality analysis practices, screening and burn-in, qualification and environmental testing, failure analysis, reliability protection methods, reliability demonstrations, and field testing and mission deployment are incorporated in the databases. The IC database covers 10,000 devices and has records on 50,000 test results; VLSI covers 300 devices; Hybrid 1,000 devices; FRSE 5,000 devices; and Non- Electric 2,000. Searches and printouts are available on a cost recovery basis. Generally, a bibliographic search runs about $125 to $150.

* Residential Energy Consumption Survey

Wendel Thompson, Survey Manager
Energy Information Administration
U.S. Department of Energy
1000 Independence Ave., SW
Washington, DC 20585 (202) 586-1119

This survey provides information on household energy consumption patterns for use in developing effective conservation plans. It aids in monitoring conservation goals, and serves as input for modeling efforts designed to measure the economic impact of proposed energy policies. Households provide such information as energy consumed, house income data, type of heating equipment, area heated, and house characteristics. Tapes are available through National Technical Information Service (NTIS) for $140. The hard copy of the 1987 edition of the survey costs approximately $10

* Resource Allocation and Mine Costing Model

National Energy Information Center
U.S. Department of Energy
1000 Independence Ave., SW, Room 1F-048
Washington, DC 20585 (202) 252-8800

The model is designed to develop coal supply curves. Thirty coal type categories, defined by BTU and sulfur content ranges, are considered. The potential annual production and minimum acceptance price of each mine category are calculated, and the production is ordered by price to produce the supply curve. Prices are based on the cost of five surface mine types and four underground mine types, and adjusted for regional factors. The model data originate back to 1974 and the file program is currently being updated. Searches and printouts are available from NTIS.

* Rural Electrification Administration Database (REA)

Glen Sperle
Statistics and Data Processing Division
Rural Electrification Administration
U.S. Department of Agriculture
14th St. and Independence Ave., SW
Washington, DC 20250 (202) 720-0943

REA contains financial and statistical information about the operations of approximately 2,150 REA electric borrowers individually and as a group. The borrowers are commercial companies and cooperatives providing electric and telephone service in rural areas throughout the U.S. The following information can be retrieved about each borrower: outstanding loans; REA debit service repayments; balance sheet items; revenue and expense items; operations statements, and sales statistics. REA maintains a variety of files containing information, ranging from loan statistics to accounting data. The REA database stores records on about 2,160 borrowers, 43,000 rural revolving accounts and 603,000 bank accounts. Searches, printouts and tapes are available on a cost recovery basis. Hard copy reports are also available. To arrange for searches or tapes contact the Public Information Office, REA, U.S. Department of Agriculture, Washington, DC 20250; (202) 382-1255.

* Safety Recommendation Information System (SRIS)

J. Richard Vanwoerkom
National Transportation Safety Board (NTSB)
Office of Safety Recommendations
490 L'Enfant Plaza E., SW
Washington, DC 20594 (202) 382-6817

This interactive online database contains information about all federal safety recommendations issued by NTSB regarding transportation. The system consists of 10-20 categories for each of the following modes of transportation: aircraft, marine, pipeline, highway and railroad. Special studies and evaluations of federal transportation measures and practices are also stored. SRIS can be searched by such keywords as type of operation, vehicle or accident; human and casual factors; and type of recommendation. The system was started in 1976 with information back to 1967 and contains 7800 safety recommendations. It is updated monthly or more often. Searches and printouts are available free of charge.

* Small Business Administration (SBA): 8.9 Million Company Database

Bruce Phillips
Director of Database Branch
Office of Advocacy
U.S. Small Business Administration
1441 L St., NW
Washington, DC 20146 (800) 827-5722

The SBA is under a congressional directive to maintain information on all businesses in the country. The result is a database that is the largest government source of company information outside the IRS. The data are derived from the Dun and Bradstreet Corporation, the Yellow Pages, and other sources. It contains names, addresses, and some financial information on all of these companies, as well as statistical data compiled over the years which can identify business growth areas and opportunities. Off-the-shelf reports, customized printouts, and data tapes are all available from SSSI (Scientific Social Systems, Inc.).

Be patient. If any phone number is incorrect, call (area code) 555-1212 and request the new listing.

Government Databases and Bulletin Boards

* Snow Survey Centralized Forecasting System (CFS)

Gale Teselle
Director, Resources Inventory Division
Soil Conservation Service
P.O. Box 2890
Washington, DC 20013 (202) 720-4530

CFS is an automated information system related to water supply forecasting such as streamflow, precipitation, snow depth and snow water equivalent, and reservoir data. These data are available for the current water year (September 30 through October 1) and for historical water years. Numerous routines and interactive programs for manipulating water supply data are included in utility programs within CFS. CFS also provides access to hydrologic data and interpretative products for a wide variety of governmental agencies and the general public. The system can be accessed by most computers, and it is menu driven for ease of use. These data reside in an automated database consisting of monthly data for 1,700 snow courses, 600 stream gauges, 300 reservoirs, and 1,200 precipitation stations, as well as daily data from 550 SNOTEL sites and 2,000 climatological stations.

* Soils Information Retrieval System

U.S. Army Corps of Engineers
ETIS Support Center
1003 West Nevada St.
Urbana, IL 61801 (217) 333-1369

SOILS provides interaction data retrieval of soils series data. The data is compiled from the U.S. Department of Agriculture's Soil Conservation Services (SCS) reports on the characteristics and interpretive properties of all soils in the United States. Examples of soil information include use restrictions, potential habitat, description of soil, and much more. Information is organized only by soil series. The database and be accessed directly by remote terminal, and SIRS currently contains 16,000 soil series and over 175,000 soil mapping units in the U.S.. Approximately 4,000 charges are made monthly to the data. Direct access is available to ETIS subscribers for $200 one time charge, plus $90 per hour of connect time. Anyone can become an ETIS subscriber and, thereby, also gain access to three other databases maintained by ETIS. ETIS will conduct searches for non-subscribers. A cost recovery fee, based on $90 and staff time, is charged. The average search generally takes 10 minutes. ETIS and SOILS subscriptions and assistance are available from ETIS of the University of Illinois, Department of Urban and Regional Planning. SOILS is a cooperative venture between ETIS, the Department of Urban and Regional Planning at the University of Illinois in Urbana-Champaign, the U.S. Army Construction Engineering Laboratory (U.S.A-CERL) and the U.S. Department of Agriculture, Soil Conservation Services (U.S.DA-SCS). U.S.A-CERL obtains updated data tapes from the Statistical Laboratory at Iowa State University in Ames, IA.

* Standard Industrial Classification (SIC)

U.S. Department of Commerce
National Technical Information Service
Springfield, VA 22161 (703) 487-4807

The Standard Industrial Classification (SIC) is the statistical classification standard underlying all establishment-based Federal economic statistics classified by industry. The SIC is used to promote the comparability of establishment data describing various facets of the U.S. economy. The classification covers the entire field of economic activities and defines industries in accordance with the composition and structure of the economy. Available in: 9 track 1600 or 6250 BPI, order number PB87-100020/HAL, at a cost of $210.

* Standard Industrial Classification (SIC) Manual (for Microcomputers)

U.S. Department of Commerce
National Technical Information Service
Springfield, VA 22161 (703) 487-4807

The Standard Industrial Classification (SIC) is the statistical classification standard underlying all establishment- based Federal economic statistics classified by industry. The SIC is used to promote the comparability of establishment data describing various facets of the U.S. economy. The classification covers the entire field of economic activities and defines industries in accordance with the composition and structure of the economy. It is available in 5 1/4 inch diskette, IBM-PC compatible, order number PB87-199568/HAL at a cost of $275; 5 1/4 inch diskette, AT-compatible (1.2 Mb), order number PB87- 199576/HAL, at a cost of $175; 3 1/2 inch diskette, Apple MacIntosh, order number PB87-199584/HAL, at a cost of $425.

* Standard Occupational Classification (SOC)

U.S. Department of Commerce
National Technical Information Service
Springfield, VA 22161 (703) 487-4807

The SOC provides a statistical classification system for occupations that should make statistics compiled by different agencies much more comparable, as the Standard Industrial Classification does for industries. The system includes all occupations in which work is performed for pay or profit including family members in family-operated businesses. Available in: 9 track 1600 or 6250 BPI, order number PB81-162513/HAL, at a cost of $210.

* State Alcoholism and Drug Abuse Profile (SADAP)

David S. Sanchez, Computer Systems Analyst
Division of Biometry and Epidemiology
NIAAA, Public Health Service
U.S. Department of Health and Human Services
Room 14C-26, Parklawn Building
5600 Fishers Lane
Rockville, MD 20857 (301) 443-4897

A numeric (aggregate) file containing data voluntarily submitted by the 50 states, Puerto Rico, and the Virgin Islands during state fiscal year 1985 on their alcoholism and drug abuse treatment, research, and prevention programs. There are 100 variables for 52 observations. Coverage of the file is nationwide, and individual states are identified. Data pertain to fiscal year 1985. This file may be purchased from the Alcohol Epidemiologic Data System, CSR, Inc., Suite 600, 1400 Eye St., NW, Washington, DC 20005; (202) 847-7600 or National Institute on Alcohol Abuse and Alcoholism at a price to be determined.

* State and Area CPS and Research Database

Local Area Unemployment Statistics
U.S. Department of Labor
Bureau of Labor Statistics (BLS)
2 Massachusetts Ave., NE
Washington, DC 20212 (202) 606-6392

This system is designed to provide current population survey (CPS) benchmarked for local area unemployment statistics (LAUS) estimates and to support publication of detailed labor force data by state and area, and also to support research in methods for estimating state and area unemployment. The system provides information on state and area employment and unemployment, including CPS data by demographic, social, economic characteristics, and unemployment insurance (UI) based data for research analysis. BLS provides a number of services including: the release of certain categories of unpublished data, development of special surveys and tabulations; customized data files are available on a cost recovery basis. Diskettes or magnetic tapes, as well as statistical software programs, can be purchased from the Division of Planning and Financial Management, Room 1077 BLS, U.S. Department of Labor, 441 G Street, NW, Washington, DC 20212.

* State Data on Pesticide Residues in Foods (FOODC ONTAM)

Gerald Deighton
FOI Staff HFI-35
U.S. Food and Drug Administration
5600 Fishers Lane
Rockville, MD 20857 (301) 443-6310

A national system to compile and summarize existing data on state analysis of food samples for pesticide and industrial chemical residues. Currently includes about 15,000 sample results from the states of California, Florida, Massachusetts, New York, Virginia, and Wisconsin. Years covered are 1986-1988. For more information, contact Heinz G. Wilms at (301) 443-3360.

* State Financial Summary

Linda Farmer
U.S. Department of Agriculture
Economic Research Service
1301 New York Ave., NW
Washington, DC 20005-4788 (202) 219-0804

This summary includes state-level farm income and balance sheet accounts for 1982-87. It also includes cash receipts by commodity, government payments, and related data. Data disk available in Lotus for $85. For ordering information, call (800) 999-6779. Stock number 88012.

Be patient. If any phone number is incorrect, call (area code) 555-1212 and request the new listing.

Federal Government Databases

* Tanker Database

James E. Saari
FOI Officer
Office of Information Resources Management
Maritime Administration
U.S. Department of Transportation
400 7th St., SW
Washington, DC 20590 (202) 366-5746/4181

Information is provided on physical, financial, and employment characteristics of privately-owned U.S. flag tanker fleet. Requests for access to this database, developed for use by the Maritime Administration, may be subject to Privacy Act regulations.

* Tax Exempt and Non-Profit Organizations

Exempt Organizations Support and Services
Internal Revenue Service
U.S. Department of Treasury
Washington, DC 20224 (202) 566-2000

This IRS file contains the names, addresses, and other pertinent information on over 900,000 U.S. tax exempt organizations. Organizations can be selected by asset size, income, type of organization, and more. Printouts are available for a cost of $100 plus 1.2 cents per name. This database corresponds to the annual publication (#78) available from GPO for $150.

* Tides: Hourly Heights

Tidal Datums Section (N/OMA123)
National Ocean Service
U.S. Department of Commerce
6001 Executive Blvd.
Room 609, WSC-1
Rockville, MD 20852 (301) 443-8467

Tidal hourly heights are the records of the height of the water level (in feet) for each hour of each day at tide observation stations. All heights are referenced to a datum. All tide data are processed in monthly increments and added to the station data file. Users of this data include federal, state, and local agencies, waterborne commerce, port authorities, marinas, coastal industries, engineering, surveying, construction firms, law firms, academia and foreign governments. The records for stations in the National Tide Observation Network (NTON) are available on hard copy and on tape with costs determined by format and amount of information ordered.

* Trade Lead Service

Foreign Agricultural Service
Agricultural Information Marketing Service
U.S. Department of Agriculture
South Building, Room 4951
Washington, DC 20250 (202) 720-9461

This file provides timely sales leads from overseas firms seeking to purchase or represent U.S. agricultural products. Trade leads can be received several ways. Commercial electronic dissemination whereby trade leads are produced daily and available the same day to American exporters through a number of commercial vendors. *Export briefs* is a weekly bulletin which includes all processed trade leads. There is a charge for the commercial electronic dissemination process. To subscribe to the direct mail or export briefs, call the number above. The information is published three times a year in the *Journal of Commerce.*

* Trade Opportunities Program (TOP)

U.S. Department of Commerce
The Economic Bulletin Board
Office of Business Analysis
Washington, DC 20230 (202) 482-3870
or
Information Management Division
U.S. Department of Commerce
ITA/U.S. & FCS/EPS
Room 1322
Washington, DC 20230 (202) 482-0727

TOP provides subscribers with up-to-date information about short-term and immediate trade opportunities with foreign agents (government and companies). The system can be searched by country of interest, type of opportunity, notice of listing, and agent or distributor. Collected information is immediately passed to subscribers. Approximately 50 to 100 reports are added daily and rolled over.

Data are archived. Only TOP subscribers are eligible for services which cost $25 (one-time fee) to establish an account, and then $37.50 for the first 50 leads you receive. Bulletin and computer tapes can also be purchased.

* Urban Mass Transportation Research Information System (UMTRIS)

Suzanne D. Crowther
UMTRIS
U.S. Department of Transportation
Transportation Research Board
490 L'Enfant Plaza E., SW
Washington, DC 20594 (202) 334-2933/3251

This system provides transportation administrators, researchers, planners, designers, engineers, economists, operators, and government agencies rapid access to information about ongoing and completed transit and transit-related activities. Approximately 19,000 citations are available and 2,500 more are added to the file annually. UMTRIS is one of the active subfiles of the Transportation Research Information Services database which coordinates more than 200,000 citations on modes such as highways, railroads, maritime, and aviation. Fee for literature searches is done on case by case basis. UMTRIS also is available commercially through Dialog. An electronic bulletin board is being considered.

* U.S. Department of Education Investigative Case Tracking System

John Hendrickson
Office of the Inspector General
U.S. Department of Education
330 C St., SW
Washington, DC 20202-1510 (202) 205-8772

The system contains data on criminal cases and criminal allegations involving all federal education programs. Many of the investigations pertain to possible abuses in the government's student loan and college aid programs. Records are kept of allegations, criminal cases, and their outcomes. Statistics on the number of ongoing investigations, the number of indictments and other relevant information are maintained. The information dates back to 1980 and is updated daily. Semi-annual reports containing statistical information are available free of charge. Staff will share other statistical data but will not release information about specific cases.

* U.S. Foreign Trade Forecast

James E. Saari
FOI Officer
Office of Information Resources Management
Maritime Administration
U.S. Department of Transportation
400 7th St., SW
Washington, DC 20590 (202) 366-5746/4181

Forecasting data is included on foreign and domestic trade for general cargo, dry bulk, and tanker fleet. Requests for access to this database, developed for use by the Maritime Administration, may be subject to Privacy Act regulations.

* World Agricultural Supply and Demand Estimates (WASDE)

Roger Smith and Raymond Bridge
World Agricultural Outlook Board (WAOB)
U.S. Department of Agriculture (202) 720-9807 (Smith) or
Washington, DC 20250 (202) 720-5447 (Bridge)

The WASDE report is reported into USDA's Electronic Dissemination of Information System during the second week of each month (see EDI separate entry). It reports global supply/demand short-term commodity forecasts and two years of historical data covering the United States and abroad. At 12:00 noon, the second work day of each week, WAOB inputs the International Weather and Crop (IWC) Summary into EDI. The IWC report is a joint report of the National Oceanic and Atmospheric Administration (NOAA) and the USDA which assesses the impact of recent meteorological events on domestic and foreign agriculture.

* World Data Bank II

Central Intelligence Agency
Washington, DC 20505

Be patient. If any phone number is incorrect, call (area code) 555-1212 and request the new listing.

Government Databases and Bulletin Boards

Available from:
National Technical Information Service
5285 Port Royal Rd.
Springfield, VA 22161 (703) 487-4807

This machine readable data file includes the following: a file set of geographic reference files, each file containing digital representation of a portion of the world. Five geographic areas of coverage include N. America, S. America, Europe, Africa, and Asia. Three files exist for each portion of the world represented containing data for coastlines, islands, and lakes; rivers and international boundaries. Order number PB-271869.

* World Population

Peter Johnson
Center for International Research, Room 407
U.S. Census Bureau
Washington, DC 20233 (301) 763-4811

The system contains population data for the overall world, its regions (i.e., Latin America, Asia) and 200 individual countries. Population statistics include the following: total population, estimated projections, growth rate, migratory rate, and crude (number per 1,000) birth and death rates. Data are collected from a survey conducted every two years. The latest statistics were added in March 1983, and the time span covered is 1950 to 1990 (projections). Tapes can be purchased for $175. Online access is intended only for federal employees.

Be patient. If any phone number is incorrect, call (area code) 555-1212 and request the new listing.

Electronic Bulletin Boards

If you need quick information on microcomputers, highway construction, or even national weather trends, electronic bulletin boards may have the answers. Electronic bulletin boards can offer you low-cost, online access to unique information and resources not normally available through commercial database vendors. And what is more important, the information on electronic bulletin boards is often updated daily, providing you with the newest information not yet available in larger, conventional databases. Another advantage to electronic bulletin boards is their relative easy access. Where accessing conventional online databases may require special knowledge of computer languages, bulletin boards are frequently driven by simple, user-friendly menus.

One of the nicer features of these bulletin boards which most online databases lack is that they often allow dialogue to take place between the user and the system operator (sysop), and even between different users. The Air Force's Small Computer Technical Center, for example, allows you to leave a message on the bulletin board outlining, say, a computer software problem you are having, and if the system operator or one of the other users can help, they can leave you a message, sometimes on the same day. While some bulletin boards require a subscription fee, many do not, which means you pay only for any long distance telephone charges.

Listed below are a sampling of the principal bulletin boards available. Additional online systems are identified in the preceding section on federal government databases.

* Agricultural Library Forum (ALF)

National Agricultural Library (NAL)
U.S. Department of Agriculture
10301 Baltimore Blvd.
Beltsville, MD 20705

Voice: (301) 504-5113
Data: (301) 504-6510
Data: (301) 504-5111
Data: (301) 504-5496
Data: (301) 504-5497
Fax: (301) 504-5472

ALF provides a convenient, low-cost tool for electronically accessing information about NAL programs, projects, products and services, and for the exchange of agricultural information resources among libraries, information centers, and other interested users.

ALF supports four types of communications: messaging, bulletins, file transfers, and conferencing. The messages system allows participants to electronically exchange comments or ideas. Bulletins (Bullets) are brief announcements about library policies, BBS system features, programs, services, contacts, recent publications, upcoming events, training workshops, job vacancies, and more. Transfer files are available for hundreds of items including some full-text bibliographic documents, technical notes, newsletters and information lists developed by NAL. The conferences system allows callers to participate in special interest groups discussions. There are 14 public conferences including a roundtable for ("AGRICOL") NAL's AGRICOLA database users, and forums on subjects such as animal welfare ("AWF"), biotechnology ("BT"), rural development or rural health ("RIC"), or water quality ("WIN"). Updates occur as necessary. Availability: 24 hours/day; 7 days/week. Cost: telephone call. Sysop: Karl Schneider.

* Bureau of the Census Personnel Division Bulletin Board System

Bureau of the Census
U.S. Department of Commerce
Personnel Division
Washington, DC 20233

Voice: (301) 763-5780
Data: (301) 763-4574

This service exists solely for job placement. The purpose of this board is to display Census Bureau vacancies from entry level to senior management. The Census Bureau offers a unique opportunity to be at the leading edge of statistical research and computer science technology in an historically state-of-the-art Federal Agency. All features (i.e., downloading, uploading, electronic mail) have been "disabled." You may leave messages (please leave your name, phone number, and position you are interested in) so a Personnel Specialist may return your call. Two other options are available. They are a listing of pay grades and position summaries.

* Bureau of the Public Debt

Office of Automated Information Systems
Bureau of the Public Debt
200 Third Street
Parkersburg, WV 26101

Voice: (304) 480-6025
Data: (304) 480-6083

This bulletin board contains computer security information and the latest version of F-PROT.

* BXR Information Center

Internal Revenue Service
U.S. Department of the Treasury
Systems Services Branch
Washington, DC 20224

Voice: (703) 756-6280
Data: (703) 756-6109

The main message base for this bulletin board concerns technical computer-related topics such as hardware, software, graphics, word-processing and computer security. There are 11 areas for users to discuss ways to enhance productivity. 24 hours/day, 7 days/week. Sysop: Marianne Crockford.

* Center for Exposure Assessment Modeling Electronic Bulletin Board System

U.S. Environmental Protection Agency (EPA)
960 College Station Road
Athens, GA 30605

Voice: (706) 546-3549
Data: (706) 546-3402

This bulletin board contains exposure assessment models.

* Computerized Information Delivery Service (CIDS)

Office of Public Affairs
U.S. Department of Agriculture
Room 536-A
Washington, DC 20250

Voice: (202) 720-5505
Data: Must subscribe first

Contains government information about developments and statistics dealing with the agriculture industry.

* Detroit Service Center Bulletin Board Service

Office of Personnel Management
477 Michigan Avenue
Detroit, MI 48226

Voice: (313) 226-7520/2095
Data: (313) 226-4423

This bulletin board contains job information for 14 states in the Chicago region.

Be patient. If any phone number is incorrect, call (area code) 555-1212 and request the new listing.

Government Databases and Bulletin Boards

* DOC Office Automation Bulletin Board

Bureau of the Census
Personnel Office
Room 3110 FB3
Washington, DC 20233 Data: (301) 763-4574

This electronic bulletin board includes census personnel bureau facts and vacancies available at the census bureau.

* Economic Bulletin Board of the U.S. Department of Commerce

DOC Office of Business Analysis
Economics and Statistics Administration
U.S. Department of Commerce Voice: (202) 482-1986
Washington, DC 20230 Data: (202) 482-3870

Users may tap in to the latest releases from the Bureau of Economic Analysis, Bureau of the Census, Bureau of Labor Statistics and other federal agencies. Some of the information available includes: wholesale trade sales and inventories, the employment situation, Federal Reserve positions and factors affecting reserves, weekly money supply report, historical money supply report, producer price index, consumer installment credit. Nonsubscribers: please use GUEST as your user ID. GUEST users may access the bulletin system and read and download informational bulletins and registration information. As a GUEST user, you are not permitted to access the EBB file area. The bulletins provide general EBB information, a list of all files available on the EBB, several sample EBB files, and notices about other sources of economic information. To subscribe, call the Office of Business Analysis, (202) 482-1986. Subscribers, use your account number as your User ID. Cost for a subscription is $35 including a credit for $12 connect time. Rates are based on Eastern Standard Time:

8:00 a.m. to 12:00 noon - .20 per minute
12:00 noon to 6:00 p.m. - .15 per minute
6:00 p.m. to 8:00 a.m. - .05 per minute

Plus telephone charges. Updates occur on a daily basis.

* Electronic Publishing System (EPUB)

National Energy Information Center E1 231
Energy Information Administration (EIA)
Forrestal Building, Room 1 F-048 Voice: (202) 586-8800
Washington, DC 20585 Data: (202)586-1181

The Energy Information Administration maintains the Electronic Publishing System (EPUB) to allow the general public to electronically access many of EIA's statistical reports. The EPUB system is a menu-driven, bulletin board type system with extensive online help capabilities that can be accessed free of charge 24 hours a day by using a terminal or PC with an asynchronous modem. One can access EPUB to list data reports to their terminal screen, download reports to their printer, or download reports to their PC or a diskette.

* EPA Region 10 Bulletin Board System

U.S. Environmental Protection Agency (EPA)
1200 Sixth Avenue Voice: (206) 553-1026
Mail Stop MD103 Voice: (206) 553-2910
Seattle, WA 98101 Data: (206) 553-2241

This bulletin board contains facilities communications on environmental concerns among EPA, state, and local governments, and the public.

* Eximbank Bulletin Board Service

Export-Import Bank of the United States
811 Vermont Ave., NW Voice: (202) 566-4490
Washington, DC 20571 Data: (202) 566-4699

The bulletin board offers descriptions of some of the bank's lending programs and the Foreign Credit Insurance Association policies. It includes application forms, press releases, seminar schedules, a referral list of banks in the EIB programs and an EIB staff directory. More specialized material is also available including Organization for Economic and Cooperation and Development (OECD) country categories. Eximbank lending rates, commercial interest reference rates and special buyer facilities. Updates occur on an as needed basis. Cost: telephone call.

* Fannie Mae Information Service

Federal National Mortgage Association (Fannie Mae)
3900 Wisconsin Ave., NW

Washington, DC 20016-2899 (800) 752-6440 (fee-based)

The quasi-government agency Fannie Mae utilizes MORNET electronic bulletin boards to broadcast information and provide a message exchange network to meet the needs of the mortgage industry. Topics include pricing, regional office contact lists, news, analysis, legislative reports, debt information and updates to Fannie Mae guides. Availability: 7 days/week; 24 hours/day.

* FCC Public Access Link (PAL Online)

Federal Communications Commission (FCC)
7435 Oakland Mills Road Voice: (301) 725-1585, ext. 216
Columbia, MD 21046 Data: (301) 725-1072

Limited public access to this BBS is available. It is intended as a means to provide communications equipment manufacturers and importers with the status of their applications for approval of their equipment. However, there is some information on activities and other procedures of the Commission, i.e., general information on part 68 registration, FCC's distribution procedures, how to obtain copies of records.

Please be advised that with the exception of general information pertaining to Part 68 Registration requirements as they relate to radiofrequency devices, no information relative to Form 730 and status of part 68 telephone equipment is available in PAL. Parties interested in Part 68 registration information may direct inquiries to: Federal Communications Commission, Common Carrier Bureau, Domestic Facilities Division, Room 6101, 2025 M Street, NW, Washington, DC 20554; (202) 634-1833. Pending and granted application data is accessible only by the proposed to validated FCC ID. The applicant/grantee may or may not be the manufacturer. In applying for a grant of equipment authorization, and accepting a grant, the applicant/grantee assumes responsibility for the equipment identified on the grant pursuant to Section 2.931 of the Rules. Therefore, no data is collected, or is available, for manufacturers.

Information under PAL main menus: Access equipment authorization data base; definitions; applying for an equipment authorization; other commission activities and procedures; FCC laboratory operational information; public notices; rulemakings; help; information hotline. Sysop: Robert Weber.

* Federal Deposit Insurance Corporation Electronic Bulletin Board

Federal Energy Regulatory Commission Issuance Posting Service (CIPS)
Federal Energy Regulatory Commission
Information Resource Management Voice: (202) 208-2474
941 Capitol Street, NE, Room 3100 Data: (202) 208-1781 for 9600 bps
Washington, DC 20429 Data: (202) 208-1397 for 300, 1200 and 2400 bps

CIPS provides the full text of the FERC daily issuances, press releases, the Commission agenda, daily listing of all filings, and formal document issue list made to the Commission. Availability: 23 hours/day. (down 8 a.m.-9 a.m.) Monday-Friday. Updates occur twice a day at 10 a.m. and 3 p.m. Users are permitted up to 60 minutes connect time for each call, and an unlimited number of calls. Cost: telephone call. Sysop: Judy Martin.

* Federal Highway Administration Electronic Bulletin Board System (FEBBS)

Federal Highway Administration
U.S. Department of Transportation Voice: (202) 366-9022
400 7th St., SW Data: (202) 366-3764
Washington, DC 20590 Fax: (202) 366-9037

Sysops: Carl Shea, Donna Avallone

FEBBS is intended for informal communications among Federal Highway Administration staff and interested members of the public about the Federal highway and motor carrier programs and the information technology that supports those programs. Information here includes such things as the text of the Intermodal Surface Transportation Efficiency Act of 1991, and the revised U.S. Code, a Conference for FHWA employees only with Questions and Answers on ISTEA, and an Open Forum for discussion of non-technical topics. Technical discussions on computers and software can be found in the <T>echTalk message section. Information includes: Policies of FEBBS - all new users must read this!; FEBBS Documentation available; Wanted - Articles for FHWA ADP Newsbrief; FEBBS Conference List; FEBBS Message Board List; New Files: (added last 7 days) updated daily; Key to New Files List; current FEBBS User List. Updates occur continually as new information becomes available. Cost: telephone call. Sysop: Donna Avalon.

Be patient. If any phone number is incorrect, call (area code) 555-1212 and request the new listing.

Electronic Bulletin Boards

* Federal Job Opportunities Bulletin Board System

Staffing Service Center
Office of Personnel Management Voice: (912) 545-3100
Macon, GA Data: (912) 471-3771

This bulletin board contains Federal job opportunities for this region.

* Federal Jobs Bulletin Board

Philadelphia Service Center
Office of Personnel Management
William J. Green Federal Bldg.
600 Arch Street Voice: (215) 597-7440
Philadelphia, PA 19106 Data: (215) 580-2216

This bulletin board contains Federal jobs and related information.

* Federal Reserve Economic Data (FRED)

Tom Pollmann
Federal Reserve Bank of St. Louis
P.O. Box 442 Voice: (314) 444-8562
St. Louis, MO 63166 Data: (314) 621-1824

This bulletin board contains information on banking, interest rates and the economy.

* Fed Flash Bulletin Board

Linda Rueffer
Federal Reserve Bank of Dallas
2200 North Pearl Street Voice: (214) 922-5173
Dallas, TX 75201 Data: (214) 922-5199

This bulletin board contains regional economic and banking information and national economic information.

* FE TELENEWS

Office of Fossil Energy Voice: (202) 586-6503
U.S. Department of Energy Data: (202) 586-6496
Washington, DC 20585 Fax: (202) 586-5146

FE TELENEWS is a free online service for coal, oil, gas and petroleum reserves information, including news announcements, congressional testimony, fact sheets, speeches, federal research and development programs facts. A free user guide is available from TELENEWS Staff, FE-10, Room 4G-085 at the above address. Availability: 24 hours/day, 7 days/week. Updates occur as necessary on a daily/weekly basis. Cost: telephone call.

Additional services:

1) Fuels Program Bulletin Board
2) Automated Fax Service: Fossil Energy Tech Line *Fax On Demand* Voice: (202) 586-4300 (recording of most recent items added to the information system and order directory. Hard copy is faxed to callers fax machine. Cost: telephone call.

* FJOB - Federal Job Opportunity BBS

U.S. Office of Personnel Management
Staffing Service Center Voice: (912) 757-3100
Macon, GA Data: (912) 471-3771

The purpose of this board is to provide information about jobs that are available in the Federal government. They cannot take applications. If you see a job you want to apply for, please contact the agency that posted the job for more information.

Regional Bulletin Boards
Washington, DC area (202) 606-1113
Southeastern States (404) 730-2370
Northeastern States (215) 580-2216
North Central States (313) 226-4423
Mountain and Southwestern States (214) 767-0316
Western States (818) 575-6521

* Hay Locator Bulletin Board

Keith D. Johnson
Hay Locator project
Purdue University

Agronomy Department Voice: (317) 494-8494
Lilly Hall (800) 872-1920
West Lafayette, IN 47907 Data: (317) 494-6643

This up-to-date, computerized listing of hay and straw for buyers and sellers across the nation can be searched by hay types, location, sellers, and buyers. Available free with 500, 1200, or 2400 baud connection. The system operates on a single user dial-up computer that provides access to the information and some of the programs available in the Indiana FACTS network. Extension newsletters, news stories from Purdue's Agricultural Communications Service and other sources are put on the system daily in preassigned groupings called "topics." Users can search for items of interest and then globally or selectively display items on their terminal screen or to a printing terminal. Subject areas include agricultural, agribusiness and home management. Intended users are any private citizens normally served by the extension. Cost: telephone call.

* Hazardous Materials Information Exchange Bulletin Board System

Cathy Gerard
Argonne National Laboratory
9700 South Cass Avenue
Building 900 Voice: (800) 752-6367
Argon, IL 60439 Data: (708) 972-3275

This bulletin board contains government and private-sector information on hazardous materials emergency management, training, resources, technical assistance and regulations. Lots of technical bulletins and files, and video resources are also listed.

* Internal Revenue Service Information Reporting Program Bulletin Board

Martinsburg Computer Center Information Reporting Project
Internal Revenue Service
P.O. Box 359 Voice: (304) 263-8700
Martinsburg, WV 25401 Data: (304) 263-2749

This bulletin board contains the information reporting program and listings of publications available. Electronic filing features are limited to approved filers of information returns.

* Kimberley Bulletin Board System

Public Affairs
Federal Reserve Bank of Minneapolis
250 Marquette Avenue Voice: (612) 340-2443
Minneapolis, MN 55401 Data: (612) 340-2489

This bulletin board contains regional economic and banking information and national economic information.

* MOAA MASC Library Bulletin Board

National Oceanographic and Atmospheric Administration (NOAA)
U.S. Department of Commerce
325 Broadway Voice: (303) 497-3271
Boulder, CO 80303 Data: (303) 497-5848

Online access to PCSIG CD-ROM.

* National Aeronautics and Space Administration (NASA) Johnson Space Center Bulletin Board

Johnson Space Center
2101 NASA Rd. 1
AP4 Voice: (713) 483-8674
Houston, TX 77058 Data: (713) 483-2419

This bulletin board is a read-only system providing shuttle mission schedules and TV transmission/transponder information.

* National Aeronautics and Space Administration (NASA) Spacelink

NASA Educational Affairs Division
Marshall Space Flight Center
Huntsville, AL Data: (205) 895-0028

The NASA Spacelink system was made public in February, 1988. Information on NASA scientific projects and educational programs is provided to NASA Spacelink by education specialists at NASA Headquarters and the NASA field

Be patient. If any phone number is incorrect, call (area code) 555-1212 and request the new listing.

Government Databases and Bulletin Boards

centers. While NASA understands that people from a wide variety of backgrounds will use NASA Spacelink, the system is specifically designed for teachers. Unlike bulletin board systems, NASA Spacelink does not provide interaction between callers. However, it allows teachers and other callers to leave questions and comments for NASA. Information is available on: NASA News, Aeronautics, Space Exploration: Before the Shuttle, Space Educational Services, Classroom Materials, Space Program Spinoffs/Technology Transfer.

* National Ecology Research Center (NERC) Bulletin Board

National Ecology Research Center
4512 McMurry Avenue Voice: (303) 226-9335
Ft. Collins, CO 80549 Data: (303) 226-9365

This bulletin board contains information from NERC Habitat Model Reference Library; messages and discussions; conferences include statistics, habitat models, negotiating strategies, habitat simulation, and temperature models.

* National Education Bulletin Board System

U.S. Department of Education Voice: (202) 219-1526
Office of Educational Research and Improvement Data: (800) 222-4922
Washington, DC 20208 Data: (202) 219-1511
Fax: (202) 219-1859

Full access to the OERI bulletin board system is available to persons employed in the field of education; the general public has limited access. Full status to qualified new users will be granted within one working day. Information available includes: Library Computer-Based Training Using Hypercard; Library Programs Applications for New Awards; New Information from OERI; Application Request for National Reading Center; Effective Education Performance Tests; Files Available for Reading Research into the Year 2000. Updates occur weekly. Cost: telephone call. Sysop: Joyce Benton.

* National Institute of Standards and Technology Computer Systems Laboratory

Computer Security Bulletin Board System Voice: (301) 975-3359
National Institute of Standards and Technology Data: (301) 948-5717
A216 Technology Building Data: (301) 948-5140
Gaithersburg, MD 20899 Fax: (301) 948-0279
Sysop: Larry Keys

The NIST Computer Security Bulletin Board makes available for use by Federal agencies and the general public a wide variety of computer security information and encourages the sharing of information which can help users and managers protect their data and systems. Information available includes an events calendar, software reviews, publications, bibliographies, lists of organizations and other government bulletin board numbers. Updates occur daily. Cost: telephone call. Note: This bulletin board is connected to the NTIS Gateway.

* National Pesticide Information Retrieval System

U.S. Environmental Protection Agency (EPA)
1231 Cumberland Avenue
Suite A Voice: (317) 494-6614
West Lafayette, IN 47906 Data: Call for subscription

Provides information to subscribers only on pesticide products registered by EPA. Registration support documents, commodity/tolerance data, materials handling documents, and state product registration data are provided.

* Navinfonet

Navigation Division
NAVINFONET Staff-STD44
Hydrographic/Topographic Center
Defense Mapping Agency Voice: (301) 227-3296
4600 Sangamore Road Data: (301) 227-4424 (9600)
Bethesda, MD 20816-5003 Data: (301) 227-4360 (2400)

This bulletin board contains public information for mariners; marine advisories; global positioning; chart corrections and light list corrections.

* Navy Regional Data Automation Center Remote Bulletin Board System (NARDAC)

U.S. Department of the Navy
Commanding Officer

Naval Computer Telecommunications Voice: (804) 444-8487
Area Master Station LANT Voice: AUTOVON 564-8487
Norfolk, VA 23511-5355 Data: (804) 445-1121

NARDAC has been replaced by OASIS, "Online Automated System," a new online service which has government-related information and software. The system is free and available only to military and civil service personnel. OASYS can provide a forum which can be customized to fit users command or agency and can include: bulletins, message bases, file areas and news. A fee is charged to sponsor a forum. Availability: 24 hours/day access.

* NERC Habitat Model Reference Library

National Ecology Research Center (NERC)
4512 McMurry Avenue Voice: (303) 226-9293
Ft. Collins, CO 80549 Data: (303) 226-9365

This bulletin board contains habitat model information (species, author, geographic applications.

* New England Electronic Economic Data Center

Department of Economics
University of Maine
Orono, ME 04469 Voice: (207) 581-1850
Data: (207) 581-1867

Sponsored by the University of Maine, The Federal Reserve Bank of Boston, the Bureau of Economic Analysis, and the National Trade Data Bank, this service provides economic data for New England including data sets on states, counties and metropolitan areas. Bureau of Economic Analysis Gross State Product data from 1977 to the present, number of unemployed, U.S. Bureau of Labor Statistics Unemployment rate, U.S. Labor Statistics. Contact: Dr. Buse.

* NIDDKUH Electronic Bulletin Board

Division of Kidney Urologic, and
Hematologic (KUH) Diseases
National Institute of Diabetes and Digestive
and Kidney Diseases
Building 31
Bethesda, MD 20892 Data: (301) 492-2221

This bulletin board is offered for researchers and others interested in KUH meetings and programs. The service, called NIDDKKUH, gives researchers quick, easy access to information about upcoming meetings and current research opportunities related to kidney, urologic, and hematologic diseases. NIDDKKUH's main components are news flashes and files containing information about meetings, conferences, and research solicitations. The DATES file (MEETINGS directory) provides topics, dates, and names of contact persons for upcoming meetings. The RFAs file (RFAs directory) lists Requests for Applications, Program Announcements, and Requests for Contracts issued by the KUH.

* NTIS FedWorld

Technology Administration
National Technical Information Service
U.S. Department of Commerce Voice: (703) 487-4608
Springfield, VA 22161 Data: (703) 321-8020

NTIS FedWorld^{TM} is a pilot project set up by the National Technical Information Service (NTIS) that connects users electronically to many Federal departments and agencies with over 100 computer bulletin board systems. These systems contain hundreds of datafiles, programs, databases and information. Files can be downloaded from both FedWorld and Gateway systems.

To connect to FedWorld, use your communications software package to dial FedWorld at (703) 321-8020. Set your parity to NONE, Data Bits to 8, and Stop Bit to 1 (N,8,1). Set your terminal emulation to ANSI or VT-100.

If you have technical problems or questions, please call (703) 487-4608 weekdays, 10:00 am to 4:00 pm. You can also leave questions in the form of E-mail on FedWorld to SYSOP.

These U.S. Government Computer Systems can be accessed by calling FedWorld:

###:Usage:Name	Comment
1: 1734:ADA ALS (US Navy)	ADA Language System/Navy BB
2: 3807:ALF (Dept of Agri)	National Agricultural Library BBS
3:12181:ALIX (Lib of Congress)	Automated Library Information Exchange

Be patient. If any phone number is incorrect, call (area code) 555-1212 and request the new listing.

Electronic Bulletin Boards

4: 1078:BOM-BBN (Dept of Int) Bureau of Mines-Bulletin Board Network
5: 1133:ISM-SIS (IRS) ISM Support Info System
6: 8066:CIC-BBS (GSA) Consumer Information Center
7: 3840:CLU-IN (EPA) Superfund Data and Information
8: 1116:CPO-BBS (Census) Lists open jobs at Census Dept.
9: 1611:CRS-BBS (Dept/Justice) Amer. With Disabilities Act Info
10: 4415:Computer Security (NIST) Computer Sys Lab Computer Sec BBS
11: 2457:DCBBS (DC Govt) DC Government Info
12: 1151:DMIE (NIST/CSL) NIST/CSL Data Mgmt Info
13: 6275:EBB (Dept/Commerce) Economic data and info
14: 638:ELISA System (DOD) DOD Export License Tracking System
15: 1970:EOUSA-BBS (Dep/Justice) BBS for U.S. Attorneys
16: 2134:EPUB (Dept of Energy) Energy information and data
17: 1141:FDA's BBS (FDA) FDA info and policies
18: 766:FDA/DMMS (FDA) PMA, IDE, 510K, guidance documents
19: 595:FERC-CIPS BBS (DOE) Fed Energy Regulatory Commission
20: 978:FEBBS (Fed Hwy Adm) FHWA information and data
21: 280:FRBBS (NIST) FRBBS-Info on fire research
22: 2816:FEDERAL BBS (GPO) GPO and Govt Data (Fee Based)
23: 2047:OSS-BBS (GSA) GSA online schedules system
24: 1863:ImExbank BBS Import/Export Bank data and info
25: 763:JAG-NET (US Navy) Navy Judge Advocate General
26: 4838:Labor News (Dep/Labor) Dept of Labor info and files
27: 2863:Megawatt 1 (DOE) Information on energy and DOE
28: 235:NADAP (US Navy) Navy Drug and Alcohol Abuse Prevention
29: 341:NAVTASC (US Navy) NAVCOMTELSTA Washington, DC
30: 584:NCTS BBS (US Navy) Nav Computer and Telecom System
31: 983:NDB-BBS (Dep of Agric) Human Nutrition Information Service
32: 740:NSSDC/NASA/Goddard The NASA NODIS Locator system
35: 369:OIS (Bureau of Prisons) U.S. Bureau of Prison employees
36: 96:OPBO-BBS (Dep/Comm) Internal communicat for DOC employees
37: 1061:WTIE-BBS (EPA) Wastewater Treatment info exchange
38: 542:QED-BBS (USGS) Quick epicenter determ and EQ data
39: 1777:SALEMDUG-BBS (FEMA) State and local FEMA user groups
40: 3297:SBA online (SBA) SBA information and data (9600 bps)
41: 5199:SBA online (SBA) SBA information and data (2400 bps)
42: 468:SBAI-BBS (SBA) SBA internal BBS
43: 627:Sample weather data (NWS) Sample data from fee based system
44: 3944:OPM Mainstreet OPM-Job info, personnel guidance
45: 684:TELENEWS (DOE) Data and info on fossil fuels
46: 2106:USA-GPCS BBS (Army) US Army info system software
47: 1505:USCS-BBS (Customs) Customs and Exchange rate data and info
48: 3843:USGS-BBS (USGS) Geological Survey BBS/CD-ROM info
49: 1065:USNO ADS (US Navy) GPS data, sunrise/set/surveying data
50: 1474:FMS-BBS (US Treas) Inventory mgmt data and programs
51: 2592:OASH-BBS (HHS) Health and AIDS info and reports
52: 1959:FEDIX Links fed data to higher education
53: 5230:DASC-ZD (Def Log Agcy) PC information and files
54: 1134:GPSIC (Coast Guard) GPS, Loran and Omega info/status
55: 1521:SESD-EBB (US Army) PC software and contract info
56: 1843:PPIC-BBS (EPA) Pollu. preven, clean product, ozone
57: 430:Gulfline (EPA/NOAA) Gulf Coast pollution info
58: 317:FAA Safety Exchange (FAA) Small plane safety reports/info
60: 5499:LC News Service (LOC) Library of Congress news service
61: 7680:STIS (NSF) Science and technology info system
62: 394:MI-BBS (DOE) DOE minority impact bulletin board
64: 3054:Census-BEA (Census) Census BEA electronic forum
65: 146:IHS-BBS (HHS) Indian Health Service BBS
66: 2541:NOAA-ESDD (NOAA) NOAA Earth system data directory
67: 556:Offshore-BBS (Interior) Offshore oil and gas data
68: 4708:TQM-BBS (T.Glenn) Total quality management
69: 105:NIDR online (NIH) Nat. Institute of Dental Research
70: 365:NIHGL (NIH) Nat. Inst. of Health grant line BBS
71: 955:PayPerNet #1 (OPM) Fed pay and performance mgmt BBS
72: 401:PayPerNet #2 (OPM) Fed pay and performance mgmt
73: 729:CASUCOM (GSA) Interagency shared services/resources
74: 556:ATTIC (EPA) Alternative treatment tech info center
75: 1519:NCJRS-BBS (Justice) National Criminal Justice reference sys
76: 293:DRIPSS (EPA) Drinking water info processing support
77: 394:PIM BBS (EPA) Pesticide information network
78: 126:SWICH BBS (EPA/SWANA) Solid waste mgmt
79: 651:NPS-BBS (EPA) Nonpoint source program BBS
80: 1198:OEA BBS (Interior) Interior's Ofc. of Environment. Affairs
81: 1083:Metro-Net (US Army) Army morale, welfare, recreation
82: 3520:CABB (Dept of State) Passport info/travel alerts
83: 1383:BUPERS access (Navy) Navy personnel information
84: 2303:FCC-State link (FCC) FCC daily digest and carrier stats/report
85: 1393:HUD-N&E BB (HUD) HUD news and events BB/press releases
86: 1670:NGWS BBS (US Navy) Naval Gun Weapon System BBS
87: 3562:FREND #1 (Natl Archives) Fed Register electronic news delivery
88: 1498:FREND #2 (Natl Archives) Fed Register electronic news delivery
89: 149:HSOL-BBS (HHS/UMd) Head Start online BBS (region III)
90: 258:WSCA-BBS (Dept of Labor) Board of wage & service contract appeal
91: 637:TEBBS (OGE) Office of government ethics BBS
92: 332:HSETC MD (US Navy) Naval health sci edu and training comnd
93: 2606:PPCUG/RDAMIS (DOD) Pentagon users group BBS
94: 1001:ORDBBS (EPA) EPA Office of Research & Develop BBS
95: 1010:CBEE (Coast Guard) Coast Guard online magazine and news
96: 290:ATD BBS (FAA) Air transport division BBS
97: 610:ATOS-BBS (FAA) Air traffic operations service BBS
98: 8:AEE BBS (FAA) FAA Office of Environment and Energy
99: 187:NAVAIRES (US Navy) NAVAIRES Alameda
100: 6:TeamNet (US Navy) To be 100th gateway
101: 499:Airports BBS #1 (FAA) Airport operators and designers
102: 2770:PR-online Some cong. committee press releases
103: 2433:FAA HQ BBS (FAA) FAA headquarters BBS
104: 1761:IRS-SOI (IRS) Public taxpayer statistical info
105: 35:ARA-BBS (FAA) Aviation rulemaking advisory BBS
106: 943:IIAC BBS (US Army) Integration and analysis center BBS
107: 104:Digital Express
108: 947:ACT-BBS (HHS) Admin. for children and families
109: 957:NTIA-BBS (Commerce) Radio freq mgmt issues
110: 157:OMEI-BBS (DOE) Minority energy info clearinghse
111: 2129:BHPr-BBS (HHS) Medical and health services info
113: 998:Marine Data BBS (NOAA) Marine databases and files
114: 342:Call-ERS BBS (USDA) Agriculture economic research info
115: 132:Call ERS (USDA) Economic research line service line 2
116: 329:ABLE INFORM (Dof Ed) Disability and rehab data and info
117: 111:Ada 9X BBS (DOD) Ada clearinghouse info center
118: 1467:PerManNet (State) US Agency for Internat'l Development

* OAQPS Technology Transfer Network

SRAB
U.S. Environmental Protection Agency
Building 4201, Mail Drop 14 Voice: (919) 541-5384
Research Triangle Park, NC 27711 Data: (919) 541-5742

This is a network of 10 independent bulletin boards with technical information, documents, files, and messages on air pollution control (Clean Air Act Amendments).

* Office of Fuels Programs Management Information System (MIS)

Lavine Moore
U.S. Department of Energy (DOE)
Office of Fuel Programs
Office of Fossil Energy
1000 Independence Avenue, SW Voice: (202-586-9478
Washington, DC 20580 Data: (202-586)9478

DOE's Office of Fossil Energy has expanded its electronic information services to include a publicly accessible computer bulletin board with information on natural gas import and export authorizations and permits for transboundary electric transmission lines. The bulletin board can be accessed by dialing the above number. Among the information available are Presidential Permits, connection, operation, and maintenance of electric transmission lines which cross the U.S. international border; DOE Orders authorizing electricity exports; DOE Opinions and Orders authorizing natural gas imports and exports; and the departments Quarterly Report on Natural Gas Imports and Exports. It will also make available historical regulatory actions of the Office of Fuels Programs in the near future.

* Office of Program Planning and Evaluation Bulletin Board

Office of Budget, Planning and Organization
U.S. Department of Commerce Voice: (202) 482-2949
Washington, DC 20230 Data: (202) 482-1423

This electronic bulletin board is primarily an internal communications mechanism for planning, budget and management organizations of the U.S. Department of Commerce. Most of the information and files located on this board pertain to these functions, and will be of limited or no interest to external organizations. Information available includes: About this board (general info for

Be patient. If any phone number is incorrect, call (area code) 555-1212 and request the new listing.

Government Databases and Bulletin Boards

users), Commerce planning activities and upcoming events, MBO planning meeting schedule, Decision Analysis Center schedule, major Department of Commerce goals (list of strategic policy goals), Departmental program priorities (under revision), recent studies and reports (Synopsis of materials of interest to DOC Planning and Budget community), DOC library resources for total quality management, OPPE organization and personnel. Contact: Pat Spencer.

* Office of Research and Development Electronic Bulletin Board

Office of Technology Transfer and Regulatory Support
Center for Environmental Research Information
U.S. Environmental Protection Agency (EPA)
EPA-CR1-G75 Voice: (513) 569-7272
266 W. Martin Luther King Drive Data: (800) 258-9605
Cincinnati, OH 45268 Data: (513) 569-7610

This bulletin board contains information on water, biotechnology, and other research; several conferences, biotechnology, regional EPA operations, water regulations, methods standardization; and ORD research paper bibliographic database.

* Online Library System (OLS)

Library Services (MD-35) Voice: (919) 541-2777
U.S. Environmental Protection Agency (EPA)Data: (919) 549-0700 (2400)
Research Triangle Park, NC 27711 Data: (919) 549-0720 (9600)

This system contains several databases: the EPA national catalog Hazardous Waste collection, and a list of departments and services called ACCESS 92.

* OPM Atlanta Region Bulletin Boards System

Atlanta Regional Office
Office of Personnel Management (OPM)
75 Sprint St., SW Voice: (404) 331-3459
Atlanta, GA 30303 Data: (404) 730-2370

This bulletin board contains job listings and agency directives.

* Pilot Examiner Bulletin Board

Federal Aviation Administration (FAA)
U.S. Department of Transportation (DOT)
FAA, AFS-634
P.O. Box 25082 Voice: (405) 954-4753
Oklahoma City, OK 73125 Data: (405) 954-4530

This bulletin board is sponsored by the Federal Aviation Administration's Pilot Examiner Section, AFS-634 Serving Pilot Examiners and Written Test Examiners. Designed for themselves and AFS-634. Aviation safety inspectors, certified flight instructors, or anyone seeking information concerning aviation safety are encouraged to use this system.

* Portland MMEL Bulletin Board

Federal Aviation Administration (FAA)
U.S. Department of Transportation
Ed Johnson Flight Standards
District Office - OS
Portland International Jet Port
2 AL McKay Avenue Voice: (207) 780-3263
Portland, ME 04102 Data: (207) 780-3297

This bulletin board is operated by the Federal Aviation Administration's Flight standards District Office in Portland, Maine. It makes available selected FAA information publications, documents, and allows submission to the FAA requests and applications for various authorizations, and to submit certain reports. It is open to all with a legitimate interest in aviation and aviation safety.

* Space Environment Lab Bulletin Board

National Oceanographic and Atmospheric Administration (NOAA)
U.S. Department of Commerce
325 Broadway Voice: (303) 497-3188

Boulder, CO 80303 Data: (303) 497-4006

This NOAA bulletin board contains highlights and forecasts of geomagnetic and solar activity.

* Technology Transfer Bulletin Board

John Harkens
Municipal Facilities Branch
Water Management Division
U.S. Environmental Protection Agency (EPA)
42M-MF
345 Cortland Street, NE Voice: (404) 347-3633
Atlanta, GA 30365 Data: (404) 347-1767

Wastewater, small communities, innovative and alternative technology, waste supply, water quality, stormwater research information is available on this bulletin board. EPA Region 4 activities are also listed.

* United States Courts

These bulletin boards contain online opinions and related information from US Circuit Courts.

1st U.S. Circuit Court Data: (215) 597-5315

3rd U.S. Circuit Court Data: (215) 597-5315

4th U.S. Circuit Court Data: (804) 771-8084

5th U.S. Circuit Court Data: (504) 589-6850

6th U.S. Circuit Court Voice: (513) 684-2953
Data: (513) 684-2842

7th U.S. Circuit Court Voice: (312) 435-5584
Data: (312) 435-5560

8th U.S. Circuit Court Voice: (314) 539-3600
Data: (314) 539-3576

* WashNet

Washington Area Service Network Bulletin Board
U.S. Office of Personnel Management (OPM) Voice: (202) 606-1848
Washington Area Service Center Data: (202) 606-1848
Fax: (202) 606-0848

This bulletin board contains primarily job information, including files on job information in each OPM region, and job fair listings. Plan to add training course listings. Limited access to schools, universities, Congressional Offices, Government agencies, libraries, organizations and special interest groups. There are more than 1,000 registered participants and eight telephone lines. You must call the sysops at the voice telephone number to get permission and password before you can access this BBS.

* Whistleblower Bulletin Board System

Washington, DC Data: (202) 225-5527

Attention all taxpayers and federal employees!! There is a new computer bulletin board that permits you to report on fraud, waste, and abuse in the federal government. The Whistleblower Bulletin Board System is operated by an investigative subcommittee of the House of Representatives. If you have any information on fraud, waste, or abuse in federal agencies, programs, grants, or contracts, call. Pseudonyms are encouraged. Your identity will be protected. Messages are not made public. Updated weekdays daily for each region of the United States and overseas. Cost: telephone call. Sysop: Bill Robinson.

IMPORTANT: Please note that there are no public messages or files to download on this BBS.

Be patient. If any phone number is incorrect, call (area code) 555-1212 and request the new listing.

More Info-Power Hits

Every chapter is filled with all sorts of free publications, posters, and gift ideas. Some special souvenirs and freebies are grouped here along with an assortment of other odds and ends ranging from pet advice to beekeeping.

* 50th Wedding Anniversary Card Signed By the President

Presidential Correspondence
Old Executive Office Building, Room 94
Washington, DC 20500 (202) 456-1111

50th wedding anniversary cards and 80th birthday cards signed by the President are available to the public. The requests must be written and should be received at least one month before the event. Photographs are also available through a written request. Contact the office above, 9 a.m.-5 p.m.

* 80th Birthday Card Signed by the President

Presidential Correspondence
Old Executive Office Building, Room 94
Washington, DC 20500 (202) 456-1111

Birthday cards signed by the President are available to the public. The requests must be written and should be received at least one month before the event. Photographs are also available through a written request. Contact the office above, 9 a.m.-5 p.m.

* Aerial Photographs

Customer User Services
Earth Resources Observation System Data Center (EROS)
U.S. Geological Survey
Sioux Falls, SD 57198 (605) 594-6511

Aerial photographs are available from this center for most geographical regions of the country. Prices range from $6 to $65, depending on whether they are black and white or color photographs. Contact this office for ordering information.

* American Flags

c/o The Capitol
Washington, DC 20515 (202) 224-3121

You can arrange to purchase flags that have been flown over the Capitol by getting in touch with your U.S. Senator or Representative. A certificate signed by the Architect of the Capitol accompanies each flag. Flags are available for purchase in sizes of 3 x 5 or 5 x 8 in fabrics of cotton and nylon.

* Animal Poison Control Hotline

National Animal Poison Control Center
(900) 680-0000 $2.95 per minute or
(800) 548-2423 $30 per case, charge on a major credit card

The National Animal Poison Control Center, at The University of Illinois, provides 24-hour consultation in diagnosis and treatment of suspected or actual animal poisonings or chemical contaminations. Its emergency response team will rapidly investigate such incidents in North America, and perform laboratory analysis of feeds, animal specimens, and environmental materials for toxicants and chemical contaminants.

* Bees and Beekeeping

Honeybee Breeding Genetics
and Physiology Research Lab
U.S. Department of Agriculture
ARS, 1157 Ben Hur Rd.
Baton Rouge, LA 70820 (504) 766-6064

Scientists are currently at work trying to protect the beekeeping industry and the public from the advent of the Africanized bees that are due to arrive in mid 1990. Research projects include use of a toxic substance that will attract bees and kill them, a repellent that will keep these aggressive bees from stinging, and ways of protecting commercial queen bee farms from invasion of Africanized bees.

* Bugs and Other Household Pests

Executive Officer
U.S. Department of Agriculture
SEA, Room 33A
Administration Building
Washington, DC 20250 (202) 720-3377
OR local County Cooperative Extension Service

Free technical advice is available to aid in controlling cockroaches and other critters. To identify an insect, the local county cooperative extension service often will ask you to send a representative sample in order to suggest the best way to rid your home of this menace.

* Cheese Making

Dairy Laboratory
U.S. Department of Agriculture, AR-NER
Eastern Regional Center
600 East Mermaid Lane
Philadelphia, PA 19118 (215) 233-6400

The Dairy Lab has accumulated information on the process of making cheese at home and can share their expertise with you.

* Christmas Trees

Division of Forestry
Bureau of Land Management (BLM)
U.S. Department of the Interior
Washington, DC 20240 (202) 653-8864

The BLM officials issue permits to cut Christmas trees for a nominal fee on Bureau of Land Management-administered lands in the 11 Western states and Alaska. Free-use permits are available from the Bureau to non-profit organizations for timber and trees to be used exclusively by that organization. This excludes the resale of any free timber or trees by those organizations.

* Comet Haley Atlas

Superintendent of Documents
Government Printing Office
Washington, DC 20402 (202) 783-3238

Census statistics publications are listed in this bibliography. One may send for the Railroad Maps of North America, featuring 5,000 maps and surveys. Weather and political atlases are listed, as well as an atlas to the Comet Haley. Free.

* Dial the Exact Time: The Master Clock

Atomic Clock
Naval Observatory
3450 Massachusetts Ave.
Washington, DC 20392-5100 (202) 653-1800

The Observatory's Master Clock is the source for all standard time in the United States. For the correct time, call the number above, or dial 1-900-410-TIME if you are outside of the DC area.

* Family Counseling

Family Economics Research Group
U.S. Department of Agriculture
6505 Belcrest Rd., Room 439A

Be patient. If any phone number is incorrect, call (area code) 555-1212 and request the new listing.

More Info-Power Hits

Hyattsville, MD 20782 (301) 436-8461

This center answers questions about families throughout the lifecycle, from marital relationships and childbearing families to empty nest families and retirement, and deals with matters concerning social environment and family economics education.

* First Lady's Daily Schedule

Office of the First Lady
The White House
Attention: Scheduling Office
Washington, DC 20500 (202) 456-7910

For more information write or call to the office above.

* Free County Educational Programs

Executive Officer
County Cooperative Extension Service
U.S. Department of Agriculture (USDA)
Room 340A, Administration Building
Washington, DC 20250 (202) 720-3377

The USDA operates an extension program in 3,165 counties located in all of the 50 states and the U.S. territories. Federal, state, and local governments share in financing and conducting cooperative extension educational programs to help farmers, processors, handlers, farm families, communities, and consumers apply the results of food and agricultural research. The Extension Service helps people develop marketable job skills, make informed career decisions, and expand available opportunities. It offers guidance to families such as ways to manage finances and make sound financial decisions; confront and deal with such problems as alcohol and drug abuse, teenage pregnancy, and unemployment; and develop strategies for retirement. The extension offers up-to-date information about the relationship of dietary practices to lifestyle factors. Another major area is revitalizing rural America: programs emphasize how to increase competitiveness and efficiency of rural programs, explore methods to diversify local economies and attract new business, adjust to impact of change, develop ways to finance and deliver services, and train leaders to make sound policy decisions for rural communities. It works with consumers, producers and local government to learn more about the importance of high-quality ground water and the conservation of water resources. Emphasis is also put on the effects of agricultural chemicals and contaminants on water quality. The extension is helping expand youth outreach resources to meet the needs of youth, develop programs for the most susceptible youth populations, provide leadership and job skills, and increase training of professionals and volunteers to work in communities to prevent and treat problems.

* Free Firewood

Contact your nearest forest ranger

Where supply exceeds demand, free firewood is available from public lands. Just contact your nearest forest ranger.

* Free Manure

College Park Holsteins
University of Maryland Dairy Barns
College Park, MD 20742 (301) 405-1298

Many Extension Service offices offer free manure for gardeners. In the Washington, DC, area, manure is available by the barrel or truckload at the above address.

* Genealogy: Plant a Family Tree

Communications Office
U.S. Postal Service
475 L'Enfant Plaza, SW, Room 5300
Washington, DC 20260-3121 (202) 268-2143

The Postal Service launched a "Plant a Family Tree" program to encourage the nation's children to discover their family's genealogy by writing to their grandparents and by filing in a "family tree" made available through post offices.

* Geologic Publications: Caves to Volcanoes

U.S. Geological Survey
Branch of Publications
Box 25286
Denver, CO 80225 (303) 236-7477

This is a listing of some of the general interest publications available through the U.S. Geological Survey. They are free unless otherwise indicated.

The Antarctic and its Geology
Eruptions of Hawaiian Volcanoes: Past, Present and Future ($4)
Eruptions of Mount St. Helens: Past, Present, and Future ($2.75)
Geologic History of Cape Cod, Massachusetts
Geology of Caves
The Great Ice Age
The Interior of the Earth
Landforms of the United States
Marine Geology: Research Beneath the Sea
Our Changing Continent
Permafrost
The San Andreas Fault
Volcanoes
Geysers
Gold
Natural Steam for Power
Glaciers: A Water Resource
Elevations and Distances in the United States
Geologic Maps: Portraits of the Earth
Building Stones of Our Nation's Capital
Steps to the Moon
Tree Rings: Timekeepers of the Past
The Naming (and Misnaming) of America

* Gold Prospecting

Publications Department
Bureau of Mines
U.S. Department of the Interior
810 7th Street West
Room 303
Washington, DC 20241 (202) 501-9757

The publications department of the Bureau of Mines distributes the free booklet, *How To Mine and Prospect for Gold.*

* Greeting Cards and Gift Items

Jefferson Gift Shop
Library of Congress
Washington, DC 20540 (202) 707-0204

Many gift items, including greeting cards, notepaper, bookplates, posters, recordings, T-shirts, are available from the gift shop, which is open 9 a.m. to 5 p.m., Monday through Saturday.

* Medals of the United States Mint

Customer Service Center
U.S. Mint
U.S. Department of the Treasury
10001 Aerospace Dr.
Lanham, MD 20706 (301) 436-7400

You can purchase many different types of medals that honor famous people from the U.S. Mint. Medals of all of the U.S. Presidents are available in 3" and 1 5/16" sizes. The Secretaries of the Treasury are featured in a 3" medal series, as well as the Directors of the Mint. Various medals has been issued that commemorate veterans, and famous army and navy heroes. Others include aviation heroes, leaders and statesmen, those who contributed to the arts and culture, doctors, and Chief Justices of the Supreme Court. Checks or Visa and MasterCard payments are accepted.

* Moon and Planets Maps

Distribution Branch
U.S. Geological Survey (USGS)
Building 810
Denver Federal Center
Box 25286
Denver, CO 80225 (800) USA-MAPS

The USGS established an astrogeology program on behalf of NASA to support lunar and planetary exploration. Many maps of the Moon, Mars, Venus, and Mercury are available.

Be patient. If any phone number is incorrect, call (area code) 555-1212 and request the new listing.

More Info-Power Hits

* National Atlas Updates

Distribution Branch
U.S. Geological Survey (USGS)
Building 810
Denver Federal Center, Box 25286
Denver, CO 80225 (800) USA-MAPS

The *National Atlas of the United States* (1970) contains 765 maps and charts on 335 pages. Out of print and no longer for sale, it can still be found in most libraries. However, separate sheets of selected reference maps and thematic maps from the *Atlas* are available from the USGS. Some of the sheets have been updated. Some updated thematic maps include potential natural vegetation (1985), monthly average temperature (1986) monthly minimum temperature (1986), monthly maximum temperature (1986), networks of ecological research (1983), and territorial growth (1986).

* Nation's Capitol: History, Books, Tapes

U.S. Capitol Historical Society
200 Maryland Ave., NE
Washington, DC 20002 (202) 543-8919

A non-profit educational organization chartered by Congress, this historical society puts out many publications, including *We the People* and *Washington Past and Present*. The society also sells VHS video cassette tapes, such as *City Out of Wilderness*, which tells the story of Washington, DC, and the Capitol. It sells for $35, which including postage, or $30 in the Capitol. *Place of Resounding Deeds*, a thirty minute video tour of the Capitol, sells for $29.95 with postage, or $25 in the Capitol. The society has a sales desk in the rotunda with miscellaneous items such as postcards and various books for the public. Symposiums are held annually and are published for the public. Speakers from the Society are available provided advance notice is given.

* Pet Food and Medications

Center for Veterinary Medicine
Division of Animal Feeds
Food and Drug Administration (FDA)
7500 Standish Place, Room 432, HFV 220
Rockville, MD 20855 (301) 295-8728

The Food and Drug Administration is responsible for ensuring that animal drugs, devices, and medicated feeds are safe and effective and that food from treated animals is safe to eat. They also make sure the animal and pet foods are safe and properly labeled. Flyers and memos are available for the general public and professionals regarding veterinary medicine. The *FDA Veterinarian*, a bimonthly publication, outlines the latest developments in the field of veterinary medicine, and is available for $5 per year from Superintendent of Documents, Government Printing Office, Washington, DC 20402, (202) 783-3238.

* Pet Problems and Sickness

Executive Officer
U.S. Department of Agriculture
SEA, Room 33A Administration Building
Washington, DC 20250 (202) 720-3377
OR local County Cooperative Extension Service

Free technical advice is available to aid in diagnosing sick pets. Your local county cooperative extension service often will analyze your pet's stool and offer guidance over the telephone.

* Pets and Animal Health

Public Information, LPAS
Animal and Plant Health Inspection Service (APHIS)
U.S. Department of Agriculture
Federal Building, Room 613
6505 Belcrest Road
Hyattsville, MD 20782 (301) 436-7799

Pets--They Need Proper Care to Travel by Air is one of the publications available free. Many other fact sheets are published by APHIS such as housing and caging, training guides and manuals for animal care personnel.

* Presidential Homes and Washington Buildings

Bureau of Engraving and Printing
U.S. Department of the Treasury
14th and C Sts., SW, Room 602-11A
Washington, DC 20228 (202) 874-3714/3715

Vignettes of famous Washington buildings and presidential homes are available in the 6" x 8" size for $4. The Great Seal of the U.S. and the Department of Treasury Seal, lithographed in color, are also available.

* Presidential Portraits

Bureau of Engraving and Printing
U.S. Department of the Treasury
14th and C Sts., SW, Room 602-11A
Washington, DC 20228 (202) 874-3714/3715

Small presidential portraits (6" x 8") and larger presidential portraits (9" x 12") are available from the Bureau of Engraving and Printing for $4 and $4.50, respectively. Prices are slightly less at the facility store. There are also 6" x 8" portraits of the Chief Justices of the Supreme Court, available for $4.

* President's Schedule

Office of Presidential Scheduling
The White House
1600 Pennsylvania Ave., NW
Washington, DC 20500 (202) 456-7560

Contact this office for information on the President's daily schedule, or call (202) 456-2343 to hear a recorded message.

* Public Debt Donations

Office of the Commissioner
Bureau of the Public Debt
U.S. Department of the Treasury
999 E St., NW
Washington, DC 20239 (202) 219-3300

Since the U.S. Government maintains a public debt of more than $1.9 trillion dollars, and is currently paying $176 billion in interest to pay off this debt, they are asking for donations from the general public to pay off the debt. The Treasury has an account into which money received as gifts is deposited. The money is used to pay at maturity, or to redeem or buy before maturity, an obligation of the Government included in the public debt. Donations can be sent to: Bureau of the Public Debt, Department G, Washington, DC 20239-0601.

* Rock Collecting

U.S. Geological Survey
Branch of Publications, Box 25286
Denver, CO 80225 (303) 236-7477

Collecting Rocks is a free booklet available from the USGS for those youngsters and adults interested in pursuing this hobby and learning more about geology.

* Sick Plants

Executive Officer
U.S. Department of Agriculture
SEA, Room 33A Administration Building
Washington, DC 20250 (202) 720-3377
OR local County Cooperative Extension Service

Free technical advice is available to aid in diagnosing and curing diseases of indoor and outdoor plants by contacting your local county cooperative extension service.

* Space Photographs

Customer Services
Earth Resources Observation System Data Center (EROS)
U.S. Geological Survey
Sioux Falls, SD 57198 (605) 594-6511

The EROS Data Center maintains photographs from many of the space missions, including those of the space shuttle, Apollo, and Gemini. Contact the center directly for information concerning specific topics.

* Stamp Collecting

Philatelic Sales Division
P.O. Box 449995
Kansas City, MO 64144-9995 (816) 455-0970

Anyone interested in philately, the collecting and study of stamps, can receive a free booklet called *Introduction to Stamp Collecting*.

Be patient. If any phone number is incorrect, call (area code) 555-1212 and request the new listing.

More Info-Power Hits

* Tell the President!

The President of the United States
White House
1600 Pennsylvania Avenue, NW
Washington, DC 20500 (202) 456-7639

White House operators will take messages for the president. You can also write to the Commander-in-Chief and share your views about current issues.

* Wild Burros and Horses for Adoption

Office of Public Information
Bureau of Land Management
U.S. Department of the Interior
18th and C Sts., NW
Washington, DC 20240-0001 (202) 208-5717

Wild burros and horses that roam on public lands are put up for adoption after a short time to decrease their numbers. If you are interested in adopting one of these animals, you should contact a local BLM adoption center, and there is a fee of $125 per horse and $75 per burro. You must also transport the animals home and provide for their future upkeep. The booklet, *So You'd Like to Adopt*

A Wild Horse Or Burro?, answers many of the questions you might have when handling this responsibility. Contact the office above for the adoption centers near you.

* Wine: Home Production

National Agriculture Library
U.S. Department of Agriculture
Beltsville, MD 20705 (301) 504-5248

The U.S. Department of Agriculture has accumulated documentation and can share information to assist you in making wine at home.

* Woodsy Owl: Toys for Tots

U.S. Department of Agriculture
Forest Service, P.O. Box 96090
Washington, DC 20090-6090 (202) 205-1785

To increase children's awareness of our delicate environment, the Forest Service's Woodsy Owl campaign has a variety of materials available, including coloring sheets, detective sheets, song sheets, patches, and stickers.

Be patient. If any phone number is incorrect, call (area code) 555-1212 and request the new listing.

The Government Works for Kids, Too

The government offers a bonanza of information and services specifically designed for kids, and those who love kids. When we first started to do research into what was offered, it was a bit like opening Pandora's box. We discovered an unexpected bounty of material. To our surprise, there are publications, programs, slides, games, and even computer software available for personal and classroom use. So, whether you are a student, parent, teacher or scout leader, why not take advantage of the wealth. Here are a few ideas to get you started.

Term Papers With Pizazz

When I was in school, the first mention of a term paper caused me to nod off in my seat. I knew that, like it or not, I would be spending the next month copying out-of-date facts from a dusty encyclopedia. Fortunately, this no longer has to be the case. Kids today can take advantage of publications that are available from the government with up-to-the-minute facts and figures.

Say your elementary age child wants to do a term paper on a particular animal, bird or reptile that interests him. The U.S. Fish and Wildlife Service has dozens of easy-to-read brochures and publications on anything from armadillos to weasels. There are also publications devoted just to endangered species such as the Brown Pelican or Spotted Owl.

If a history paper is assigned, why have your child read second-hand accounts when first-hand reports are available? The National Archives puts out a publication, *A More Perfect Union: The Creation of the U.S. Constitution* that contains facsimiles of the featured documents and transcriptions of what the founding fathers wrote. If he is more interested in recent events, the U.S. Government Printing Office has a transcript of the Apollo 11 post-flight press conference with the astronauts' actual descriptions of what it was like to travel into space.

Decorating In a Flash

Why not decorate your child's bedroom with a colorful poster or map? The Smithsonian offers portraits of such historical figures as Frederick Douglass or Sitting Bull for a nominal fee. Or, start teaching your child about geology at home. The U.S. Geological Survey has a number of geologic maps available for purchase.

If your classroom needs a little sprucing up, the California Energy Extension Service offers the Classroom Energy Poster Puzzle, a bulletin board-size poster for children in grades K-4. It is a great teaching aid to focus on energy use and abuse in the classroom. Are your kids space happy? The National Aeronautics and Space Administration produces posters for educators, students, and the general public through the U.S. Government Printing Office. Posters range from a near life-sized picture of an astronaut to a poster detailing the size and make-up of the planets.

Teacher Opportunities

Teachers who are interested in attending workshops have a wide selection of government sponsored programs from which to choose. For example, the NASA Education Workshop for Elementary School Teachers (NEWEST) gives outstanding elementary teachers a chance to personally experience the U.S. aerospace program. Or, if your interests lie closer to home, the National Museum of Natural History offers workshops for elementary and middle school teachers on topics ranging from dinosaurs to ocean reefs.

The earth sciences is just one topic that is covered in teacher workshops held each summer by Aerospace Education Services Program (AESP) specialists at NASA field centers, elementary and secondary schools, and on college campuses. Workshops cover astronomy, life in space, principles of rocketry and remote sensing and include hands-on activities to help teachers incorporate what they learn into classroom programs and activities.

Classroom Tools for the 90's

NASA also offers a large selection of computer software education materials that are available for the classroom. The Hubble Space Telescope, Space Shuttle Commander and Astronomy diskettes are available for use on Apple Computers. The U.S. Public Information Agency also puts out a guide, *Environmental Education Materials for Teachers and Young People (Grades K-12)* which includes computer software designed to teach students how to keep our environment clean.

Teachers can use films to teach schoolchildren about the importance of aeronautics through a program sponsored through the National Air and Space Museum. Or, introduce them to the visual arts. The National Gallery of Art now loans films free of charge to educational institutions, community groups and individuals.

The examples above are just a sampling of what is available. The following chapter includes a long list of classroom resources plus enough information, products and services to keep kids busy from kindergarten through graduation.

4-H

California Energy Extension Service
1400 Tenth St., Room 209
Sacramento, CA 95814   (916) 323-4388

The *4-H Home Conservation Guide* is a collection of 12 hands-on projects which teach home energy conservation skills for a 4-H group.

Be patient. If any phone number is incorrect, call (area code) 555-1212 and request the new listing.

The Government Works for Kids, Too

ACID RAIN

Public Information Center
U.S. Environmental Protection Agency
401 M Street, SW, PM-211B
Washington, DC 20460 (202) 260-2080

The EPA frequently receives requests for information on acid rain from school systems, teachers, and individuals. In response to these requests, EPA has developed the study guide *Acid Rain: The Student's First Sourcebook.* The purpose of the guide, which is for students in grades 4-8, is to help students better understand the science, citizen actions, and research issues that are part of the acid rain problem. *EPA's Acid Rain Program: Charting a New Course in Environmental Protection* and the *Environmental Backgrounder: Acid Rain* are two additional publications which provide information on the acid rain issue.

Office of Environmental Education
Pennsylvania Department of Education
333 Market St.
Harrisburg, PA 17126 (717) 783-6994

Acid rain is one of the many topics covered in Paul E. Beals' activity book *The Newspaper: A Tool for Teaching Environmental Awareness.* It also covers topics such as forest preservation, waste disposal, and recycling. This activity book contains newspaper articles and uses them to teach about environmental awareness.

AFRICAN-AMERICAN ART

Office of Educational Program
National Museum of American Art
Smithsonian Institution
Washington, DC 20560 (202) 357-3095

African-American Art: 20th Century Selections is a brochure appropriate for teachers of grades 5-12 which discusses various African-American artists.

Division of Education, Room B1026
National Museum of American History
Smithsonian Institution
Washington, DC 20560

Field to Factory: Afro-American Migration, 1915-1940 is an educational kit which teaches about the migration of Afro-American from 1915-1940. It is appropriate for grades upper-elementary and up and is available at a cost.

Education Office
Federal Aviation Administration
U.S. Department of Transportation (DOT)
DOT Building
Room PL100
400 7th Street, SW
800 Independence Ave., SW
Washington, DC 20590 (202) 366-7018

The *August Martin Activities Book* is a great tool to help teach your child about the world's first black airline pilot.

AGRICULTURE

Ag in the Classroom
Room 317-A Administration Building
U.S. Department of Agriculture
Washington, DC 20350

The mission of the U.S. Department of Agriculture's Ag in the Classroom program is to help students in grades K-12 acquire the knowledge needed to become agriculturally literate. The objective of Ag in the Classroom is to encourage educators to teach more about our food and fiber system and the role of agriculture in our economy and society. The program is primarily carried out in each state by a group composed of educators, government officials, and representatives from agricultural organizations and agribusinesses. Materials available for the program include the following appropriate for elementary-school educators:

Resource Guide to Educational Materials About Agriculture: A Project of Ag in the Classroom. This guide provides a listing of materials relating to agriculture that are available from private and public sources. The listings are divided into four sections: Printed Materials; Audio-Visuals and Audio-Visual Kits; Resource Guides or Catalogs; and miscellaneous items such as posters, wall charts, and computer software. Materials included are primarily about agriculture and related issues. Those concerned with nutrition, food preparation (recipes), promotional information, or buying advice on food and fiber are not included.

Library Guide to Books About Agriculture describes books with factual information about agriculture as well as fiction with an agricultural theme.

Ag in the Classroom Folders are attractive pocket folders which can be used for conferences, teacher training workshops, etc.

Ag in the Classroom Brochures are red, white, and blue and are eye-catching and informative. Distribute them at fairs, teacher conferences, or other outreach activities.

Glossary of Farm Terms, a "mini-dictionary" of farm terms, was originally prepared by Bank of America NT&SA in 1983 and has been revised and reprinted by USDA with permission of Bank of America.

Ag in the Classroom Notes is a bimonthly newsletter about Ag in the Classroom activities around the country.

Ag in the Classroom Fact Sheet is a one-page summary of Ag in the Classroom: its purpose, the basic concepts, how it works, and the role of the U.S. Department of Agriculture.

State Updates tell about Ag in the Classroom organizations and activities in each state and lists the State Contacts.

Model State Action Plan helps states organize task forces to implement Ag in the Classroom programs.

Ag in the Classroom Exhibit in red, white, and blue -- table-top or free-standing -- can be borrowed for fairs, conferences, and conventions.

Video Tapes that can be borrowed and copied.

1986 Ag in the Classroom shows how Ag in the Classroom works and offers a glimpse of enthusiastic teachers and students involved in Ag in the Classroom around the country. (16 minutes.)

America's Most Crucial Industry helps viewers of all ages understand agriculture's vital role in the American economy. This tape can also be purchased for $12 from: Video Transfer, 4709-B Arundel Avenue, Rockville, MD 20852. (14 minutes.)

AIDS

S. James
Consumer Information Center - Y
P.O. Box 100
Pueblo, CO 81002

AIDS and the Education of Our Children: A Guide for Parents and Teachers addresses issues and questions you may face when talking with children about AIDS. It also lists sources for more information. 34 pp. (1988 ed.) 550X.

AIR POLLUTION

Department of Air Pollution Control
Commonwealth of Virginia
P.O. Box 10089
Richmond, VA 23240 (804) 225-2722

Teach your children about air pollution through the coloring book *Airy Canary Learns to Fly.* It is about a bird who is having difficulty learning to fly because of the presence of Nasty Nitrogen Dioxide, Otto Ozone the Air Pollutant, and Sully Sulfur Dioxide. Children in the lower elementary grades will enjoy coloring this 16-page book, while learning about pollutants and the need for clean air.

Resource Center
Public Education and Risk Communication Division
Environmental and Occupational Health Sciences Institute
45 Knightsbridge Road
Piscataway, NJ 08854 (908) 932-0110

Children in grades 4-6 can also learn about air pollution through the following two videos. *Keeping the Lid on Air Pollution* is a 20 min. video about Terry who has a homework assignment which is to write about two pollution controls. He ends up inside the school library computer and learns about different types of air pollutants (focusing on ozone) and air pollution controls. *The Inside Story on Air Pollution* is a 19 min. video about Danny, Terry's friend, and his sister who go into the computer to investigate the sources and health effects of indoor air pollution in the home. They also learn how to reduce and prevent indoor air pollution problems. Contact the office above for cost and ordering information:

Be patient. If any phone number is incorrect, call (area code) 555-1212 and request the new listing.

Resource Center
Public Education and Risk Communication Division
Environmental and Occupational Health Sciences Institute
45 Knightsbridge Road
Piscataway, NJ 08854 (908) 932-0110
Fifth grade educators can use the lesson plan *Exploring Air Pollution* to teach their students about air pollution. This lesson plan helps students learn about major sources of air pollutants (including indoor air pollution) and their major health impacts. The concepts of occupational safety and health are introduced. They also learn about methods for reducing air pollution and about the role of government agencies and regulations in protecting worker and community health.

ALCOHOL AND DRUG ABUSE PREVENTION

National Clearinghouse for Alcohol and Drug Information
P.O. Box 2345
Rockville, MD 20852 (301) 468-2600
Elementary School Children and Alcohol Education includes audiovisuals, programs descriptions, professional and organizational resources to assist educators and parents of young childcare. It is available free from the office above. (# MS315)

Drug Video Program
Office of Public Affairs
U.S. Department of Education
400 Maryland Ave., SW
Washington, DC 20202
Drug prevention videos are available from the U.S. Department of Education for parents and educators. Originally designed for schools these video programs are now available for home use. Each program is closed captioned and comes with its own Parent's or Teacher's Guide to help you discuss each program's message and the serious problem of drug abuse with your child. Programs for elementary children include:

The Drug Avenger. ($35, 73 minutes, 16-page Parent's Guide, 1988, VHS Order No. DGA17535). Three children from the future travel back to the 20th Century to take on the life-threatening problem of drug abuse in 10 animated programs.

Fast Forward Future. ($30, 61 minutes, 23-page Teacher's Guide, 1988., VHS Order No. DGA 17532). Actor Richard Kiley as "Mentor" shows three elementary students the future with the Fast Forward machine. The students see the effects of using drugs and staying drug free.

Straight Up. ($40, 90 minutes, 2-page Teacher's Guide, 1988, VHS Order No. DGA17529). Academy award winning actor Lou Gosset, Jr., as Cosmo takes a boy named Ben, played by Chad Allen of NBC's "Our House", on a journey in the "fate" elevator. Ben's travels teach him valuable lessons about why drugs are harmful and how to refuse them.

Demand Reduction Section
Drug Enforcement Administration
U.S. Department of Justice
Washington, DC 20537 (202) 307-7936
Healthy Bodies Don't Need Drugs! Learning and Activity Book is a fifteen-page publication designed to educate children about the need to take care of their bodies and to say "No!" to drugs.

National Crime Prevention Council
1700 K Street, NW, 2nd Floor
Washington, DC 20006 (202) 466-6272
Help teach your children to say "No!" through the use of the following McGruff materials. They are available from the National Crime Prevention Council. Materials include:

Elementary School Materials Package. This package contains materials that can be photocopied for students and parents. It was sent to 51,000 elementary schools, and limited quantities are still available from the National Crime Prevention Council. Free.

If You Want to Fit In, Be Drug Free: Welcome to McGruff's Drug-Free Park. This colored poster shows McGruff with children playing basketball, baseball, riding bicycles, and reading - all alcohol- and other drug-free activities. $2.50.

Licensed Products Package. The National Crime Prevention Council has many specialty items available to teach elementary youth about prevention. This package includes information on a talking robot, a puppet package, stickers, calendars, and many other items. Free.

McGruff's Drug Abuse Prevention Kit. This kit includes different games, puzzles, a video, and recorded songs for children. Two items are for parents, and they give tips for teaching children how to say no. Materials come as reproducible masters. $30.

McGruff's Drug Abuse Prevention Kit: The No Show. The video is part of McGruff's Drug Abuse Prevention Kit. All parts of the Kit including the video, are reproducible for nonprofit educational purposes. Animation is used throughout 25 percent of the video. The video kids create a rock video about refusing drugs. $12.

To Be What You Want To Be: Be Drug Free. This poster has people from many professions with the slogan "To be what you want to be, be drug free". It has room for the child to draw himself into the picture. $2.50.

National Clearinghouse for Alcohol and Drug Information
P.O. Box 2345
Rockville, MD 20852 (800) 729-6686 (301) 468-2600
The National Clearinghouse for Alcohol and Drug Information (NCADI) is an excellent source of information for alcohol and drug abuse prevention. In 1987 it was established as the central point within the Federal Government for current print and audiovisual materials about alcohol and other drugs. NCADI answers more than 18,000 telephone and mail inquiries each month and distributes some 18 million printed items a year, which include the following posters and publications appropriate for elementary school children:

Ayundando a sus alumnos a decirle que no (Helping Your Students Say 'No') Teacher's Guide (1990). In English and Spanish, explains the effects of alcohol on the body, why children start to drink, how teachers can help their students say "No" to alcohol and deal with the first signs of drinking, and where teachers can go for more information. 13 pp. PH284.

Buzzy's Rebound: Fat Albert and the Cosby Kids (1990). In comic book format, depicts the story of Buzzy, a young basketball player and friend of the Cosby Kids, who gets into trouble with alcohol and is helped by his coach, and a school counselor. 18 pp. PH232.

The Fact Is ... You Can Prevent Alcohol and Other Drug Problems Among Elementary School Children (1988). Includes videotapes, program descriptions, and professional and organizational resources to assist educators and parents of young children. 17 pp. MS349.

Growing Up Drug Free: A Parent's Guide to Prevention (1989). This handbook outlines what children at four key stages of development should know about drugs and suggests family activities to reinforce children's motivation to avoid alcohol and other drugs. 52 pp. PHD533.

The Herschel Walker Poster (1989). Herschel Walker, football star, salutes the drug-free youth of America in a 22 in. by 27 in. color poster. Reference is made to NCADI as a source for more information. AVD45.

Learning to Live Drug Free: A Curriculum Model for Prevention (1990). Provides a flexible framework for classroom-based prevention efforts for kindergarten through grade 12. Presents the states of child development as they relate to drug prevention, facts about drugs, suggested lesson plans, tips on working with parents and the community, and a resource section for further information. Teachers can learn how to integrate prevention messages into their classroom presentations. BKD51.

Little League Drug Education Program (1991). This video has two parts: Part 1, Friend to Friend, Featuring Orel Hershiser, is directed toward today's Little Leaguer. The film tells the story of a Little League player who is tempted by drugs. Part 2, Big League Advice: Helping Your Little Leaguers Say No, is for parents and coaches of Little League players. The film depicts a discussion among Little League parents and baseball Hall-of-Famers 'Hank' Aaron and Jim Palmer. These great ball players offer frank and important advice to parents on how to talk to young people about drugs and alcohol. 30 minutes. VHS29.

Live the Dream, Say No to Alcohol and Drug Abuse (1989). Poster features Dr. Martin Luther King, Jr. Appropriate for all ages, 15 1/2 in. by 22 in. AV165.

McGruff's Surprise Party (1989). A comic book that helps children understand the importance of saying "No" to alcohol and other drugs, as told by McGruff, the crime dog. Also teaches children techniques for resisting peer pressure. For ages 8 to 10. 14 pp. PH271.

McGruff: Say 'No' to Crack and Other Drugs (1989). Bright red and white poster

Be patient. If any phone number is incorrect, call (area code) 555-1212 and request the new listing.

The Government Works for Kids, Too

featuring McGruff, the Crime Dog. McGruff tells kids that crack is poison and a very dangerous drug. Tells them to say a big "no" and walk away. Also provides the NIDA hotline number (800-662-HELP) and a cocaine hotline number (800-COCAINE). 64 in. by 88 in. AVD14.

Parent Training is Prevention (1991). Contains information to help communities identify and carry out programs on parenting. Details roles parents play in rearing children who are free of alcohol and other drug problems, highlights ethnic and cultural considerations, and gives characteristics of effective prevention programs. 184 pp. BK 184.

Pointers for Parents Card (1989). Provides easy steps parents can take to help prevent their child from using alcohol or other drugs. Excellent handout for special events such as fairs, workshop, or conferences. 3 1/2 in. by 8 1/2 in. card. PH260.

Prevention Resource Guide: Elementary Youth (1991). This Resource Guide includes materials specifically developed for youth that may be used in an elementary school setting, as well as relevant information on parenting. It is designed for teachers, administrators, and program leaders who come in contact with elementary youth. 23 pp. MS421.

Quick List: 10 Steps to Help Your Child Say "No" (1990). Also available in Spanish. Identifies ten things that parents can do to help their children stay away from alcohol and other drugs, from talking with your child to being a good role model. Three-panel fold out mini-poster. PH230.

Snappy Answers Card for Kids (1989). Suggests responses young people can use to say "No" if offered alcohol or other drugs. Excellent handout for special events such as fairs, workshops, or school events. 3 1/2" by 8 1/2" card. PH 261.

Public Affairs Section
Drug Enforcement Administration
U.S. Department of Justice
Washington, DC 20537 (202) 307-7977

The *Soozie and Katy Workbook* was created to acquaint children with the purpose of medicine, its appropriate use, the legal distribution of drugs, and the dangers which can accompany misuse. Appropriate for home and classroom discussion, it begins with the idea that each child is responsible for the care of his body and should protect it. Teaching the child the doctor-pharmacist-parent sequence of drug distribution will help the child accept the administration of medicine without fear, and it will also begin to explore the idea that there are illegal channels of drug distribution.

National Clearinghouse for Alcohol and Drug Information
P.O. Box 2345
Rockville, MD 20852 (800) 729-6686

Use the *Be Smart Game* board game to help teach your children to say "No!" to drugs. It is printed on a heavy sheet of paper, allows two-four players, and requires dice and a coin for each player. Going around the board, players have opportunities to say "No!" to drugs and to discover alternate activities.

ALLIGATORS

U.S. Fish and Wildlife Service
U.S. Department of the Interior
4401 N. Fairfax Drive
Mail Stop 130
Arlington, VA 22203 (703) 358-1711

Use the publication, *American Alligator*, to help teach your children about one type of endangered species. Contact the office above to receive a publication on this and other endangered species.

AMERICAN INDIANS

Attn: Public Inquiries Office
Bureau of Indian Affairs
Mail Stop 2620 (MIB)
U.S. Department of Interior
Washington, DC 20240 (202) 208-3711

The U.S. Department of Interior's Bureau of Indian Affairs is a wonderful source of information for those who want to teach their children about American Indians. Use the booklet *American Indians Today: Answers to Your Questions* to help answer some of the common questions your children may have about Indians. Teach your children about famous Indians through the use of *Famous Indians: A Collection of Short Biographies*. From Pocahontas to Sitting Bull, this

publication describes the history and lives of twenty famous American Indians. Help your children locate the Indian reservation nearest them through *Indian Land Areas*. This map of the United States displays federal Indian reservations, along with state reservations.

Office of Education, Room 212
Mail Stop 158
National Museum of Natural History
Washington, DC 20560 (202) 357-2747

Use the slide set *Native Peoples of North America* to enhance curricula for school children. It is available for a three-week loan free of charge from The National Museum of Natural History.

Office of Public Information
Department of Anthropology
National Museum of Natural History
Smithsonian Institution
Washington, DC 20560 (202) 357-1592

The Department of Anthropology of the National Museum of Natural History has a wonderful selection of bibliographies and leaflets on American Indians, including *Native American Resources*, a bibliography of reading material for elementary school children. Use this and the following publications to enlighten your children about the American Indian culture:

American Indian Basketry. Bibliography
American Indian Food. Bibliography
American Indian Languages. Leaflet.
Arts and Crafts of the American Indians of the Southwest. Bibliography.
Arts and Crafts of the Northwest Coast Indians and Eskimos. Bibliography.
Arts and Crafts of the Plains Indians. Bibliography.
Genealogical Research. Leaflet.
Native American Games, Dances, and Crafts. Bibliography.
Native American Resources. Bibliography.
Native Americans. Bibliography.
North American Indian Art. Bibliography.
North American Indian Healing and Medicine. Bibliography.
North American Indian Mythology. Bibliography.
North American Indian Ritual and Religion. Bibliography.
North American Indian Silverwork. Bibliography.
North American Indian Women. Bibliography.
North American Symbolism and Design. Bibliography.
Origin of the American Indians. Leaflet.
Southwest Indian Pottery. Bibliography.
Southwest Indian Textiles and Weaving. Bibliography.

Office of Public Information
Department of Anthropology
National Museum of Natural History
Smithsonian Institution
Washington, DC 20560 (202) 357-1592

Educators can use the *North American Indians* teacher's resource packet to find out how to obtain different teaching materials. Available at no charge.

Photographic Services
American History Building
Room CB-054
Smithsonian Institution
Washington, DC 20560 (202) 357-1933

The *Sitting Bull* poster provides an excellent visual tool for those who want to educate their children about American Indians. Cost is $3.

Office of Education, Room 212
Mail Stop 158
National Museum of Natural History
Washington, DC 20560 (202) 357-2747

The National Museum of Natural History has several different programs and activities held throughout the school year for visiting preschool and elementary school children. For Indian enthusiasts there is the *Indian Walkaround*, a teacher-directed walk-through of the Indian and Eskimo halls. Volunteers staff small display stations throughout the exhibit, offer objects to touch, and tell about the people who made them. There also is *Indians and Eskimos*. Sitting in front of museum exhibits and using Indian children's toys, students learn what grandparents of Indian children did in the past, what parents do today, and what Indian children might do when they grow up. Lesson includes Eskimo, Woodland, Plains, Northwest Coast, and Southwest peoples. For grades 1 and up there also are museum lesson tours. With *Indians and Eskimos* students discover the wide diversity of the indigenous cultures past and present in North

Be patient. If any phone number is incorrect, call (area code) 555-1212 and request the new listing.

The Government Works For Kids, Too

America. On the tour they explore the relationships between environment and culture by focusing on the basic human need for food, shelter, clothing, and tools. Teachers are urged to request pre-visit materials that will help them before and during the visit. Call the office above to obtain the dates of these programs and activities.

ANCIENT CULTURES

Office of Education, Room 212
Mail Stop 158
National Museum of Natural History
Washington, DC 20560 (202) 357-2747

A slide set on *Ancient Cultures: 10,000 B.C. - 600 A.D.* is available for a three-week loan free of charge from the National Museum of Natural History.

ANIMALS

Office of Public Affairs
National Institute of Mental Health
5600 Fishers Lane, Room 7C02
Rockville, MD 20857 (301) 443-4513

Let's Visit a Research Laboratory: Introduction and Lesson Plans (for schoolchildren in grades 2-5) helps answer the many questions children may have about research laboratories. The supplemental poster that is included provides teachers with helpful illustrations for classroom discussion and activities.

Office of Education, Room 212
Mail Stop 158
National Museum of Natural History
Washington, DC 20560 (202) 357-2747

The National Museum of Natural History is an excellent place to teach your students about different types of animals. Several programs and activities on animals are held throughout the school year for visiting preschool and elementary school children. Activities for preschool and kindergarten children include:

Animals - students see real examples of the different kinds of animals that make up the Animal Kingdom - birds, mammals, fish, amphibians, and reptiles - and learn to tell them apart by using external characteristics.

Discover Dinosaurs - students receive a short introduction to "what is a fossil?" by means of a puppet show, investigate dinosaur skeletons and dioramas in the Dinosaur Hall, and participate in hands-on activities relating to dinosaur exhibits.

Museum lesson tours for grades 1 and up include *Animals, Endangered Species and Extinction,* and *Prehistoric Life.* Teachers are urged to request pre-visit materials that will help them before and during the visit.

Office of Education, Room 212
Mail Stop 158
National Museum of Natural History
Washington, DC 20560 (202) 357-2747

The National Museum of Natural History offers two workshops for teachers (of elementary and middle school students) interested in preparing a visit for their classes to the museum. *Dinosaurs* is a walk through the Dinosaur Hall to help teachers and aides design a visit for their classes, followed by an informal lecture on major dinosaur groups represented in the exhibit hall. *Climate and Endangered Species* is a workshop designed to help teachers and aides design a visit or prepare for a guided tour. The identification of all endangered and extinct modern animals on exhibit is followed by an informal talk about why certain groups of animals are more vulnerable than others. For specific dates and more information contact the office above.

U.S. Fish and Wildlife Service
U.S. Department of the Interior
4401 N. Fairfax Drive
Mail Stop 130
Arlington, VA 22203 (703) 358-1711

Would you or your child like to learn more about America's sea turtles, diving ducks, or the golden eagle? Or what about endangered species such as the grizzly bear, spotted owl or gray wolf? Why not decorate your classroom or child's bedroom with some of the 30 portraits of fish they have available? The U.S. Fish and Wildlife Service has dozens of easy-reading brochures and publications which can provide information for school reports, 4-H club assignments, or Boy Scout projects. Some of the publications include the following:

American Bald Eagle
America's Sea Turtles
Conservation Note 1- Birds
Conservation Note 4 - America's Upland Game Birds
Conservation Note 5 - Bird Banding: The Hows and Whys
Conservation Note 6 - Snakes (In Press)
Conservation Note 8 - Migration of Birds (In Press)
Conservation Note 11 - Pronghorn Antelope
Diving Ducks
Ducks Get Sick, Too
Endangered Species
Endangered and Threatened Wildlife and Plants
Estuaries: Cradles of Life
In Celebration of America's Wildlife - Teacher's Guide to Learning
Know Before You Go
National Wildlife Refuge System
National Wildlife Refuges - A Visitor's Guide
Pesticide Use and Endangered Species
Take Pride in America with Mark Trail - A Coloring Book
Waterfowl for the Future

Available also are publications on endangered species:

General Information
American Alligator
Red Wolf
Gray Wolf
California Condor
Black-Footed Ferret
Grizzly Bear
Whooping Crane
Bald Eagle
Polar Bear
Spotted Owl

Other publications include those on:

Beaver
Giant Panda
Dolphins
Key Deer
Pronghorn Antelope
Sandhill Crane
Coyote
Bobcat
Rocky Mountain Goat
Muskrat
Black Bear
Cougar
Opossum
Armadillo
Trumpeter Swan
American Elk
Pacific Salmon
Caribou
Trout
Racoon
Prairie Dog
Great Horned Owl
Snowy Owl
Ring-necked Pheasant
Life in a Fox Den
American Buffalo

Posters available include:

Raptors - Hunters On the Wing!
Steel Shot - Are You Using the Right Load?
The Difference Between Endangered and Extinct is Forever
Wetlands - We need 'em..- Wildlife needs 'em too.

Natural Heritage Division
Illinois Department of Conservation
524 S. 2nd St.
Springfield, IL 62706

Nature Discovery II: Wild Mammals of Illinois is a publication for students and teachers and is available to teachers in Illinois. It includes various activities on different mammals and even has a "Guide to Mammal Signs". The publication is written for children in grades 4-8.

Be patient. If any phone number is incorrect, call (area code) 555-1212 and request the new listing.

The Government Works for Kids, Too

Public Information Center
U.S. Environmental Protection Agency
401 M Street, SW, PM-211B
Washington, DC 20460 (202) 260-2080
Use the coloring book *Save Our Species: Endangered Species Coloring Book* to introduce your children to 21 endangered and threatened plants and animals found in the United States. As they color the pages, they will journey to oceans, swamps, deserts, and islands and bring to life a variety of plants and animals.

Center for Veterinary Medicine
Food and Drug Administration
Public Health Service
U.S. Department of Health and Human Services
5600 Fishers Lane
Rockville, MD 20857 (301) 295-8755
Prepare your child how to care for a pet before it arrives. The Center for Veterinary Medicine has several fact sheets which parents can use to teach their children how to care for pets properly.

ANTELOPES

U.S. Fish and Wildlife Service
U.S. Department of the Interior
4401 N. Fairfax Drive
Mail Stop 130
Arlington, VA 22203 (703) 358-1711
The U.S. Fish and Wildlife Service has publications on various kinds of animals including the Pronghorn Antelope.

ARCHAEOLOGY

Office of Education, Room 212
Mail Stop 158
National Museum of Natural History
Washington, DC 20560 (202) 357-2747
Use the slide set *An Introduction to Archaeology* to learn more about archaeology. It is available for a three-week loan free of charge from the National Museum of Natural History.

ARCHITECTURE

Architect of the Capitol
Washington, DC 20515 (202) 225-1200
The United States Capitol contains a wealth of architectural history. Publications are provided from the office above which can be used to teach schoolchildren about the history of the U.S. Capitol so that they may attain a greater appreciation of U.S. history and architecture. The publications include the following:

Architects of the Capitol
Flags Over the East and West Central Fronts of the United States Capitol
Cornstalk or Corncob Columns and Capitals
History of the Old Subway Transportation System Connecting the Capitol and the Russell Office Building
Minton Title in the U.S. Capitol
Statuary Hall: Old Hall of the House
Statue of Freedom
The Architecture of the Unites States Capitol
The Canopy in the Rotunda of the U.S. Capitol
The United States Capitol
The United States Capitol: A Brief Architectural History
Those Who Have Lain in State in the Rotunda

National Graphic Center
205 West Jefferson Street
Falls Church, VA 22046 (703) 533-8700
Learn about the U.S. Capitol's architecture through photographs and slides from the Collection of the Architect of the Capitol.

ARMADILLOS

U.S. Fish and Wildlife Service
U.S. Department of the Interior
4401 N. Fairfax Drive
Mail Stop 130
Arlington, VA 22203 (703) 358-1711

Teachers and parents can use the publication *Armadillos* to teach their children about this unusual animal.

ART

Office of Educational Program
National Museum of American Art
Smithsonian Institution
Washington, DC 20560 (202) 357-3095
Afro-American Art: 20th Century Selections is a brochure appropriate for grades 5-12 which discusses various African-American artists.

Office of Elementary and Secondary Education
Arts and Industries Building
Room 1163
Smithsonian Institution
Washington, DC 20560 (202) 357-3049
The Smithsonian Institution's Office of Elementary and Secondary Education has an excellent guide to educational materials from the Smithsonian Institution, the National Gallery of Art, and the John F. Kennedy Center for the Performing Arts. The *Resource Guide For Teachers* is available for $10 from the office above.

National Gallery of Art
Publications Mail Order Department
2000B South Club Drive
Landover, MD 20785 (301) 322-5900
Enlighten your students or children with reproductions from the National Gallery of Art. The *National Gallery of Art Color Reproductions Catalogue* lists hundreds of different portraits and paintings available in postcards, plaques, double mats, 11x14" format, or large unframed reproductions. Included also is information on ordering slides.

Department of Extension Programs
National Gallery of Art
Washington, DC 20565
The National Gallery of Art is continually exploring ways to develop awareness in the visual arts and make its collections accessible to everyone, no matter how far away from the Gallery they may live. They now have an Extension Program which loans slide programs, films, and videocassettes free of charge to educational institutions, community groups, and to individuals throughout the U.S. Write to the office above for more information on how you may bring the National Gallery of Art to your students.

Office of Educational Program
National Museum of American Art
Smithsonian Institution
Washington, DC 20560 (202) 357-3095
Use the brochure *Hispanic-American Art/El Arte Hispanoamericano* to teach children in grades 5-12 about Hispanic American art.

Office of Elementary and Secondary Education
Smithsonian Institution
Washington, DC 20560 (202) 357-2404
Art to Zoo is a publication dedicated to promoting the use of community resources among students and teachers nationally. It brings news from the Smithsonian Institution to teachers of grades three through eight. Its purpose is to help teachers use museums, parks, libraries, zoos, and many other resources within their community to open up learning opportunities for their students. Contact the above address if you want your school to be placed, free of charge, on the *Art to Zoo* mailing list.

AUSTRALIA

Education Department
Kennedy Center
Washington, DC 20566 (202) 416-8800
Teach your students about Australia's performing arts (music, drama, dance) through the use of the booklet *An Australian Experience*. For students in grades 1-8. $1 copy; $2 shipping and handling.

AVIATION

Education Office
Federal Aviation Administration
U.S. Department of Transportation
400 7th Street, SW

Be patient. If any phone number is incorrect, call (area code) 555-1212 and request the new listing.

The Government Works For Kids, Too

Washington, DC 20590 (202) 366-7500

Help teach your children about the history of aviation and the role it plays in today's society through the publications available from the Federal Aviation Administration's Education Office. These publications are designed to provide instructional materials consisting of accurate, timely information to enrich and enhance general study programs with concepts relating to aviation. The following publications are distributed free of charge:

Aviation and Space Curriculum Guide K-3. The purpose of this guide is to provide an array of aviation and space activities which may be used by teachers to enrich locally-designed programs.

Aviation Science Activities for Elementary Grades. Pamphlet containing science demonstrations pertaining to physical properties of air. Experiments use simple equipment.

Demonstration Aids for Aviation Education. Set of science teaching strategies for independent or classroom work.

How We Made the First Flight. In Orville Wright's own words, a description of his and Wilbur's first flights.

Nuestro Primer Vuelo. Spanish version of How We Made the First Flight.

Teacher's Guide for Aviation Education for Grades 2-6. Study unit lessons of science, health, social studies, communications arts, and career education.

August Martin Activities Book. Learning activities based on a biography of the world's first black airline pilot.

A Trip to the Airport. Contains English-Spanish bilingual materials. Bilingual text plus supplemental teaching materials.

A Flying Start. Tells the basic story of flying and getting a private pilot license.

AWARDS PROGRAMS

EPA Region 1
(Connecticut, Massachusetts, Maine, New Hampshire, Rhode Island, Vermont)
JFK Federal Building
Boston, MA 02203 (617) 565-3424

EPA Region 2
(New Jersey, New York, Puerto Rico, Virgin Islands)
26 Federal Plaza
New York, NY 10278 (212) 264-2515

EPA Region 3:
(Delaware, Maryland, Pennsylvania, Virginia, West Virginia, District of Columbia)
841 Chestnut Street
Philadelphia, PA 19107 (215) 597-9370

EPA Region 4:
(Alabama, Florida, Georgia, Kentucky, Mississippi, North Carolina, South Carolina, Tennessee)
345 Courtland Street NE
Atlanta, GA 30365 (404) 347-3004

EPA Region 5:
(Illinois, Indiana, Michigan, Minnesota, Ohio, Wisconsin)
230 South Dearborn Street
Chicago, IL 60604 (312) 353-2072

EPA Region 6:
(Arkansas, Louisiana, New Mexico, Oklahoma, Texas)
1445 Ross Avenue
Dallas, TX 75202-2733 (214) 655-2200

EPA Region 7:
(Iowa, Kansas, Missouri, Nebraska)
726 Minnesota Avenue
Kansas City, KS 66101 (913) 551-7003

EPA Region 8:
(Colorado, Montana, North Dakota, South Dakota, Utah, Wyoming)

One Denver Place
999 18th Street
Denver, CO 80202-2405 (303) 293-1692

EPA Region 9:
(Arizona, California, Hawaii, Nevada, American Samoa, Guam, Trust Territories of the Pacific)
75 Hawthorne Street
San Francisco, CA 94105 (415) 744-1020

EPA Region 10:
(Alaska, Idaho, Oregon, Washington)
1200 Sixth Avenue (800) 424-4EPA
Seattle, WA 98101 (206) 744-1020

Help get some recognition for your child's interest in saving the environment by sponsoring him or her in the President's Environmental Youth Awards Program. The program encourages individuals, school classes, schools, summer camps, public interest groups, and youth organizations to promote local environmental awareness and to channel this awareness into positive community involvement. To be eligible, a young person, or group of young persons, must have completed an environmental project while in grades kindergarten through twelve, and the project must be sponsored by at least one adult representative of their school, camp, youth group, or public interest group. For additional information, contact your regional office listed below:

Martin Luther King Jr. Federal Holiday Commission
451 7th St., SW, Suite 5182
Washington, DC 20410

The Martin Luther King Jr. Federal Holiday Commission has an awards program for those individuals and organizations that are in keeping with Dr. King's standards of service to others. For more information obtain the *National and International Martin Luther King Jr. Heritage Action Project Guidelines* publication from the office above.

President's Council on Physical Fitness and Sports
450 5th St., NW
Washington, DC 20001 (202) 272-3421

American youth have participated in the Presidential Physical Fitness Award Program or the 'President's Challenge" since 1966. The program includes all young people from ages six through 17, including those students with special needs. In addition, two awards have been added to go with the prestigious Presidential Physical Fitness Award for outstanding achievement. The National Physical Fitness Award was introduced in 1987 and is for those who reach a basic yet challenging level of fitness. A new award called the Participant Physical Fitness Award, introduced in the Fall of 1991, is for those who attempt the President's Challenge but don't qualify for a Presidential or National Award. The booklet *Get Fit! A Handbook for Youth Ages 6-17* will help children become as physically fit as they can be.

Take Pride in America
P.O. Box 1339
Jessup, MD 20794

A national awards program exists with the Take Pride in America campaign. Take Pride in America is a public awareness campaign specifically designed to restore respect for the Nation's public lands and to promote voluntary stewardship of America's vast and valuable resources.

BADGERS

U.S. Fish and Wildlife Service
U.S. Department of the Interior
4401 N. Fairfax Drive
Mail Stop 130
Arlington, VA 22203 (703) 358-1711

Upper elementary school children can use the publication *Badger* to learn more about this interesting animal.

BATS

U.S. Fish and Wildlife Service
U.S. Department of the Interior
4401 N. Fairfax Drive
Mail Stop 130
Arlington, VA 22203 (703) 358-1711

Bats and Their Conservation can serve as a supplement when teaching about this unusual animal.

The Government Works for Kids, Too

Department of Vertebrate Zoology
Room 369, National Museum of Natural History
Smithsonian Institution
Washington, DC 20560

The Smithsonian Institution has available the pamphlet *Bats* which can help answer questions children may have on bats. For students in grades 1-9. Free.

BEARS

U.S. Fish and Wildlife Service
U.S. Department of the Interior
4401 N. Fairfax Drive
Mail Stop 130
Arlington, VA 22203 (703) 358-1711

Would you like to teach your child about bears? You can do so through the publication *Grizzly Bear*, available from the office above.

BEAVERS

U.S. Fish and Wildlife Service
U.S. Department of the Interior
4401 N. Fairfax Drive
Mail Stop 130
Arlington, VA 22203 (703) 358-1711

Learn about beavers through the U.S. Fish and Wildlife Service's publication *Beaver*.

BILINGUALISM

Center for Applied Linguistics
118 22nd Street NW
Washington, DC 20037-0037 (202) 429-9551

The Educational Resources Information Center (ERIC) is a nationwide information network designed to provide users with ready access to education literature. The ERIC System, managed by the U.S. Department of Education, Office of Educational Research and Improvement, consists of 16 Clearinghouses, four Adjunct Clearinghouses, and 4 support components. One of the Clearinghouses, *Languages and Linguistics*, specializes in languages and language sciences; all aspects of second language instruction and learning in all commonly and uncommonly taught languages, including English as a second language; bilingualism and bilingual education; cultural education in the context of second language learning; intercultural communication; study abroad and international education exchange; all areas of linguistics, including theoretical and applied linguistics, sociolinguistics, and psychololinguistics.

BILL OF RIGHTS

Education Branch (NEEE)
National Archives and Records Administration
Washington, DC 20408 (202) 724-0454

Teach upper elementary and secondary students about the Bill of Rights through the use of the National Archives teaching aid, *Bill of Rights*. Published by the National Archives and SIRS, Inc., it contains about 50 reproductions of documents - charts, photographs, letters, drawings, and posters - and a detailed teacher's guide. The materials deal with certain key issues of the period, with governmental and political responses to these issues, and with public attitudes. Cost is $40 each. To order, send a purchase order to: SIRS, Inc., P.O. Box 2348, Boca Raton, FL 33427-2348; or call toll free: (800) 232-SIRS (except AK and FL call collect 407-994-0079). To find out what grade level it is appropriate for and for information on other teaching aids contact the office above.

BIRDFEEDERS

U.S. Fish and Wildlife Service
U.S. Department of the Interior
4401 N. Fairfax Drive
Mail Stop 130
Arlington, VA 22203 (703) 358-1711

Would you like to build your child a birdfeeder? Use the U.S. Fish and Wildlife Service's publication, *Build a Birdfeeder for About a Buck*, to learn how to do so.

BIRDS

U.S. Fish and Wildlife Service
U.S. Department of the Interior
4401 N. Fairfax Drive

Mail Stop 130
Arlington, VA 22203 (703) 358-1711

The U.S. Fish and Wildlife Service is a wonderful resource of information on different kinds of birds, from ducks to pelicans. Listed below are some of the publications they have available:

Conservation Note 1- Birds
Conservation Note 4 - America's Upland Game Birds
Conservation Note 8 - Migration of Birds (In Press)
Diving Ducks
Ducks Get Sick, Too
California Condor
Whooping Crane
Bald Eagle
Spotted Owl
Trumpeter Swan
Great Horned Owl
Snowy Owl
Ring-necked Pheasant

BOARD GAMES

National Clearinghouse for Alcohol and Drug Information
P.O. Box 2345
Rockville, MD 20852 (800) 729-6686

Have fun saying "No!" to drugs when playing the *Be Smart Game*, a board game printed on a heavy sheet of paper. It requires dice and a coin for each player and allows two-four players. Going around the board, players have opportunities to say "No!" to drugs and to discover alternate activities.

Energy Center
Sonoma State University
1801 East Cotati Ave.
Rohnert Park, CA 94928 (707) 664-2577

Learn about California history and geography from an energy perspective with the board game *California Challenge: An Educational Tour of California* (appropriate for children in grades 4-5.) The cost is $20 for a full game which includes instructions, map, cards, 4 game pieces and 1 die.

BOBCATS

U.S. Fish and Wildlife Service
U.S. Department of the Interior
4401 N. Fairfax Drive
Mail Stop 130
Arlington, VA 22203 (703) 358-1711

Teach your children about bobcats after reading the publication *Bobcat*.

BUFFALO

U.S. Fish and Wildlife Service
U.S. Department of the Interior
4401 N. Fairfax Drive
Mail Stop 130
Arlington, VA 22203 (703) 358-1711

Use the publication *American Buffalo* to enlighten your children about this interesting animal.

CALIFORNIA

Energy Center
Sonoma State University
1801 East Cotati Ave.
Rohnert Park, CA 94928 (707) 664-2577

Learn about California history and geography from an energy perspective with the board game *California Challenge: An Educational Tour of California* (appropriate for children in grades 4-5.) The cost is $20 for a full game which includes instructions, map, cards, 4 game pieces and 1 die.

California Air Resources Board
Public Information Office
P.O. Box 2815
Sacramento, CA 95812 (916) 322-2990

The California Air Resources Board has materials available for Californians. Single copies are available free to non-Californians as well.

Be patient. If any phone number is incorrect, call (area code) 555-1212 and request the new listing.

The Government Works For Kids, Too

CAPITOL, U.S.

Architect of the Capitol
Washington, DC 20515 (202) 225-1200

Help your children learn about the history of the U.S. Capitol through fact sheets available from the office of the Architect of the Capitol. These fact sheets can be used to teach schoolchildren about the history of the U.S. Capitol so that they may attain a greater appreciation of U.S. history and architecture. The book, *The United States Capitol: A Brief Architectural History*, is available for $3.

Architect of the Capitol
Washington, DC 20515 (202) 225-1200

Use photos and slides of the U.S. Capitol when teaching your students about it. They are available from the Collection of the Architect of the Capitol. For ordering information contact the National Graphic Center, 205 West Jefferson Street, Falls Church, VA 22046 (703-533-8700). For information on the collection contact the office above.

CARBON MONOXIDE

Public Information Center
U.S. Environmental Protection Agency
401 M Street, SW, PM-211B
Washington, DC 20460 (202) 260-2080

Use the publication *Environmental Backgrounder: Ozone and Carbon Monoxide* to supplement science curricula when teaching about the pollutants carbon monoxide and ozone.

CARIBBEAN FESTIVALS

Office of Education, Room 212
Mail Stop 158
National Museum of Natural History
Washington, DC 20560 (202) 357-2747

Use the instructional kit *Caribbean Festival Arts* to teach your school children about the festivals of the Caribbean (based on the 1989 exhibition Caribbean Festival Arts).

CARIBOU

U.S. Fish and Wildlife Service
U.S. Department of the Interior
4401 N. Fairfax Drive
Mail Stop 130
Arlington, VA 22203 (703) 358-1711

Would you like to teach your kids about caribou? The U.S. Fish and Wildlife Service can help you by sending you the publication *Caribou*.

CD-ROMS

Education Services Department
MRC 305
National Air and Space Museum
Mail Response Room
Washington, DC 20560 (202) 786-2109

If you are an educator and are interested in teaching your kids aerospace-related information through the use of CD-roms, you may want to visit the Education Resource Center (ERC) of the National Air and Space Museum (NASM). Additional information on the ERC and other NASM educational programs may be obtained by writing to the address above.

CHESAPEAKE BAY

U.S. Fish and Wildlife Service
U.S. Department of the Interior
4401 N. Fairfax Drive
Mail Stop 130
Arlington, VA 22203 (703) 358-1711

For Chesapeake Bay enthusiasts who would like to enlighten their children about this area of water, let the U.S. Fish and Wildlife Service send you the publications *Chesapeake Bay - Its Beauty and Bounty* and *Chesapeake Bay Restoration*.

Smithsonian Environmental Research Center
P.O. Box 28
Edgewater, MD 21037 (301) 798-4424

Are you planning on taking your students on a field trip to the Chesapeake Bay?

Then get the loose-leaf manual *Estuarine Dock Activities Guidebook*. Includes information on crabs, oyster bars, weather and tides. For students in grades 4-6. $9.50.

Public Information Center
U.S. Environmental Protection Agency
401 M Street, SW, PM-211B
Washington, DC 20460 (202) 260-2080

Use the coloring book *Chessie: A Chesapeake Bay Story*, to help teach kids the importance of keeping the Chesapeake Bay clean. Learn about Chessie, popularized cousin of Nessie (Scotland's Loch Ness monster), a sea monster who people have reported seeing for at least half a century. Through hearing the tale of Chessie children will learn how and why we all need to keep the Chesapeake Bay clean.

CHICAGO RIVER

Public Information Office
Metropolitan Water Reclamation District of Greater Chicago
100 East Erie
Chicago, IL 60611 (312) 751-6633

Learn how the city of Chicago helps keep the Chicago River and Lake Michigan clean. *Color It Blue* is a coloring book which offers children a creative way of learning about sewage treatment.

CHILD CARE

California Energy Extension Service
1400 Tenth St., Room 209
Sacramento, CA 95814 (916) 323-4388

Need some ideas for your child care program? Why not teach them about energy? *Let's Get Energized* is a collection of 36 energy education and awareness activities designed for after-school enrichment and child care programs. Call the office above to obtain a copy.

CIVIL WAR

Education Branch (NEEE)
National Archives and Records Administration
Washington, DC 20408 (202) 724-0454

Teach your upper elementary and secondary students about the Civil War through the use of the teaching unit, *The Civil War: Soldiers and Civilians*. Published by the National Archives and SIRS, Inc., the unit contains about 50 reproductions of documents - charts, photographs, letters, drawings, and posters - and a detailed teacher's guide. The materials deal with certain key issues of the period, with governmental and political responses to these issues, and with public attitudes. The cost is $40. To order, send a purchase order to: SIRS, Inc., P.O. Box 2348, Boca Raton, FL 33427-2348: or call toll free: (800) 3327-0513 (except AK and FL call collect 407-994-0079). To find out for what grade level it is appropriate, and for information on other teaching aids, contact the office above.

CLOUDS

Superintendent of Documents
Dept. 33
Washington, DC 20402 (202) 783-3238

Use the *Cloud Code Chart* to help teach children about cloud formations. This chart illustrates and describes the 36 cloud formations according to the international system of classification. 1972. Rep. 1988. 31 x 19 ins. Shipped folded. (S/N 003-018-00050-4, $2.25).

COAL

Office of Fossil Energy Communications
1000 Independence Ave., SW
Room 4G-085
Washington, DC 20585 (202) 586-6503

Teach kids where coal comes from and the importance of it. *Dinosaurs and Power Plants* is a 16-page brochure designed for students that relates the story of mining and drilling for coal, gas, and oil, the environmental concerns involved, and modes of transportation. *Clean Coal Technology* is also available.

Office of Fossil Energy, Room 4G 085
U.S. Department of Energy
1000 Independence Ave., SW
Washington, DC 20585 (202) 586-6503

Be patient. If any phone number is incorrect, call (area code) 555-1212 and request the new listing.

The Government Works for Kids, Too

Call the office above to receive *The Clean Coal Path* poster. It traces the route of several new advances in the clean use of coal, America's most abundant fossil energy resource. During the 1990's, many of these improvements will be used for the first time in power plants to generate new supplies of electricity without polluting the nation's air.

COAST GUARD, U.S.

Public Affairs
U.S. Coast Guard
U.S. Department of Transportation
2100 Second Street, SW
Washington, DC 20593-0001 (202) 267-1587

Our Day with the Coast Guard provides a fun way for children to learn about the U.S. Coast Guard. By providing information in a coloring book format, kids can learn what it's like to be in the Coast Guard. The coloring book includes activities such as a maze and connect-the-dots.

COLLEGES

Higher Education Clearinghouse
The George Washington University
One Dupont Circle, NW, Suite 630
Washington, DC 20036-1183 (202) 296-2597

The Educational Resources Information Center (ERIC) is a nationwide information network designed to provide users with ready access to education literature. The ERIC System, managed by the U.S. Department of Education, Office of Educational Research and Improvement, consists of 16 Clearinghouses, four Adjunct Clearinghouses, and 4 support components. One of the Clearinghouses, *Higher Education* contains information on topics relating to college and university conditions, problems, programs, and students; curricular and instructional programs; and institutional research at the college or university level.

COLORADO

U.S. Geological Survey
P.O. Box 25425
Denver, CO 80225

Mountains and Plains: Denver's Geologic Setting is an excellent source of information about the nature and structure of the rocks that underlie Denver, Colorado, and part of the adjacent Front Range. Provides a road log to explain the natural features of the area. Students can use this publication to supplement special reports and science projects.

COLORING BOOKS

Department of Air Pollution Control
Commonwealth of Virginia
P.O. Box 10089
Richmond, VA 23240 (804) 225-2722

Get your kids interested in the need for clean air through the coloring book *Airy Canary Learns to Fly*. It is about a bird who is having difficulty learning to fly because of the presence of Nasty Nitrogen Dioxide, Otto Ozone the Air Pollutant, and Sully Sulfur Dioxide. Children in the lower elementary grades will enjoy coloring this 16-page book, while learning about pollutants and the need for healthy air.

Beth Lester
P.O. Box 10089
Richmond, VA 23240 (804) 786-7913

Available from the office above are the coloring books *Color Your Environment* and *Air Bear*. Single copies are free; check for prices on quantity orders.

Public Information Center
U.S. Environmental Protection Agency
401 M Street, SW, PM-211B
Washington, DC 20460 (202) 260-2080

For at least half a century people have reported seeing a "sea monster" in the Chesapeake Bay. Affectionately known as "Chessie," popularized cousin of Nessie (Scotland's Loch Ness monster), the creature is reported to be gentle and good natured. In the coloring book *Chessie: A Chesapeake Bay Story*, Chessie discusses how and why we need to keep the Chesapeake Bay clean.

Public Information Office
Metropolitan Water Reclamation District of Greater Chicago

100 East Erie
Chicago, IL 60611 (312) 751-6633

Learn how the city of Chicago helps keep the Chicago River and Lake Michigan clean. *Color It Blue* is a coloring book which offers children a creative way of learning about sewage treatment.

Public Information Center
U.S. Environmental Protection Agency
401 M Street, SW, PM-211B
Washington, DC 20460 (202) 260-2080

Save Our Species: Endangered Species Coloring Book will introduce children to 21 endangered and threatened plants and animals found in the United States. As they color the pages, they will journey to oceans, swamps, deserts, and islands and bring to life a variety of plants and animals.

Public Information Center
U.S. Environmental Protection Agency
401 M Street, SW, PM-211B
Washington, DC 20460 (202) 260-2080

Children will enjoy learning about the need for recycling while reading and coloring the publication, *There Lived a Wicked Dragon*. Written by Martha Finan for the federal solid waste management programs, it provides a creative way to learn about an important issue.

Office of Public Affairs
U.S. Environmental Protection Agency
77 West Jackson
Chicago, IL 60604 (312) 886-7935

Teach your kids how to take care of the earth through the coloring book *The Happy Earth Day Coloring and Activities Book*.

Bureau of Mines
U.S. Department of the Interior
Cochrans Mill Road
P.O. Box 18070
Pittsburgh, PA 15236 (412) 892-4338

Contact the office above to receive a copy of the coloring book *Take Pride in America with Mark Trail*. Children will enjoy coloring in the pictures while learning the importance of keeping the environment clean.

Public Affairs
U.S. Coast Guard
U.S. Department of Transportation
2100 Second Street, SW
Washington, DC 20593-0001 (202) 267-1587

Our Day with the Coast Guard provides a fun way for children to learn about the U.S. Coast Guard. By providing information in a coloring book format, kids can learn what it's like to be in the Coast Guard. The coloring book includes activities such as a maze and connect-the-dots.

COMET, HALLEY'S

NASA CORE
Lorain County Joint Vocational School
15181 Route 58 South
Oberlin, OH 44074 (216) 774-1051

NASA CORE makes available to educators an educational aid on Halley's Comet. Appropriate for grades 4 -12 are the slides *The Return of Halley's Comet* which examine an event heralded by man since the beginning of time.

COMIC BOOKS

Smithsonian Institution Traveling Exhibition Service
1100 Jefferson Dr., SW
Room 3146
Washington, DC 20560

As a teacher did you ever want to use comics in the classroom? M. Thomas Inge's publication *Comics in the Classroom* can help you to do so. It is a teacher's guide and contains suggestions for both the elementary and secondary levels. $1.

National Clearinghouse for Alcohol and Drug Information
P.O. Box 2345 (800) 729-6686
Rockville, MD 20852 (301) 468-2600

In 1987, the National Clearinghouse for Alcohol and Drug Information was established as the central point within the Federal Government for materials

Be patient. If any phone number is incorrect, call (area code) 555-1212 and request the new listing.

The Government Works For Kids, Too

about alcohol and other drugs. A few of the publications available are in comic book format, so kids can enjoy reading them while learning about important issues. The following two comic books are appropriate for elementary kids:

McGruff's Surprise Party (1989). A comic book that helps children understand the importance of saying "No" to alcohol and other drugs, as told by McGruff, the crime dog. Also teaches children techniques for resisting peer pressure. For ages 8 to 10. 14 pp. PH271.

Buzzy's Rebound: Fat Albert and the Cosby Kids is a comic book which depicts the story of Buzzy, a young basketball player and friend of the Cosby Kids, who gets into trouble with alcohol and is helped by his coach, and a school counselor. 18 pp. PH232.

Forest Service
U.S. Department of Agriculture
14th and Independence, SW
P.O. Box 96090
Washington, DC 20090-6090 (202) 205-0957

Fire prevention can also be taught through the use of comic books. The comic book *The True Story of Smokey Bear* is one of many fire prevention materials available from the office above.

Food and Drug Administration
Consumer Communications HFE-88
Rockville, MD 20857

Dennis the Menace Takes a Poke at Poison is a comic book that teaches children to "always ask first" before they taste. Write to the office above for a free copy.

Donna Darling
Director
Office of Public Information
Texas Water Development Board
P.O. Box 13231
Austin, TX 78711-3231 (512) 463-8422

Comic books appropriate for environmental education programs may be found in the *Environmental Education Books*, which lists water and environmental education programs and/or materials suitable for use in public schools. In addition to comic books, materials listed include classroom curriculum, pamphlets, dramas, speakers bureaus, workshops, seminars, and field trip opportunities.

COMMUNITY RESOURCES

Office of Elementary and Secondary Education
Smithsonian Institution
Washington, DC 20560 (202) 357-2404

Art to Zoo is a publication dedicated to promoting the use of community resources among students and teachers nationally. It brings news from the Smithsonian Institution to teachers of grades three through eight. Its purpose is to help teachers use museums, parks, libraries, zoos, and many other resources within their community to open up learning opportunities for their students. Write to the address above if you want your school to be placed, free of charge, on the *Art to Zoo* mailing list.

COMPUTER GRAPHICS

Education Division
NASA Headquarters
Washington, DC 20546

NASA Spacelink is a collection of NASA information and educational materials stored on a computer at the Marshall Space Flight Center in Huntsville, Alabama. The system may be accessed over regular telephone lines. Classroom materials include computer graphics in addition to a variety of information useful in the classroom.

COMPUTER SOFTWARE

NASA CORE
Lorain County Joint Vocational School
15181 Route 58 South
Oberlin, OH 44074 (216) 774-1051

The NASA Central Operation of Resources for Educators (CORE) serves as the national distribution center for NASA produced education materials. Computer Software (on 5 1/4" diskettes for use on Apple Computers) includes the following:

Astronomy. Programs provide a variety of calculation functions including rising and setting times, planet locations, eclipse dates, calendar conversions and astrophotography data. Educational programs include the "Griffith Observatory Museum Disk" which contains an astronomy term hangman game, a space exploration and astronomy quiz, and a program about the user's birth dates on the planets. Produced by public domain sources. Grade 4 - 6.

Hubble Space Telescope Educational Software Project. Four Apple II disks with reproducible information sheets and reference materials: *Windows to the Universe* chronicles the history of astronomical observations from the unaided eye through the Hubble Space Telescope; *Telescopes* explains the science of optics and the design and characteristics of telescopes; *Introduction to the Hubble Space Telescope* explains the design and operation of the Hubble Space Telescope; *Images From Space* describes the process through which light is captured by the Hubble space Telescope and converted into images on Earth; *Activities Disk* contains a collection of classroom activities and illustrations relating to telescopes; *Glossary* contains an Appleworks data base of more than 300 astronomy terms. Also includes two Macintosh Applications Software (requires Pagemaker program 3.02 version or higher): *Hubble Space Telescope Model* contains the pattern and instructions for making a detailed model of NASA's Hubble Space Telescope: *Telescope Primer* outline of the basic principles behind the design and operation of telescopes. Includes many diagrams that can be enlarged and used for making transparencies. Grade 5 - 8.

Space Shuttle Mission Facts Data Base. A data base that provides information on the first 30 space shuttle missions including: mission number, orbiter, date, commander and pilot. To use this data base you must have the Apple works program. Produced by Oklahoma State University. Grade K - Adult.

Space Shuttle Commander. Side A introduces students to Newton's laws of motion by asking them to imagine that they are the commander of the space shuttle. Takes a nonmathematical approach to this topic and concentrates on concept formation. Side B contains four question banks to use for practice or evaluation. Copyrighted by and reproduced with permission from Lloyd P. Reiber. Grade 4 - 8.

Education Division, MRC 305
National Air and Space Museum
Washington, DC 20560 (202) 786-2109

The Education Resource Center (ERC) of the National Air and Space Museum (NASM) is open to teachers of all levels and disciplines and offers teachers access to educational materials pertaining to aviation, space, and the Museum's collections. Aerospace-related public domain computer software is available for use with Apple II series and IBM PC computers and is available for duplication when you visit the ERC, as well as through the mail. In both cases, teachers must provide blank diskettes. (Contact the ERC for a current catalog and mail-in procedures.) A growing collection of IBM PC and Apple II series commercial software on aerospace topics is also available on a preview-only basis for visiting teachers.

Ag in the Classroom
Room 317-A Administration Building
U.S. Department of Agriculture
Washington, DC 20350

Ag in the Classroom is a U.S. Department of Agriculture program designed to help students in grades K-12 acquire the knowledge needed to become agriculturally literate. The program is primarily carried out in each state by a group composed of educators, government officials, and representatives from agricultural organizations and agribusinesses. Computer software and other educational materials are available. Contact the office above for a copy of the *Resource Guide to Educational Materials About Agriculture: A Project of Ag in the Classroom* which lists where to obtain these materials.

Public Information Center
U.S. Environmental Protection Agency
401 M Street, SW, PM-211B
Washington, DC 20460 (202) 260-2080

Environmental Education Materials for Teachers and Young People (Grades K-12) is an excellent source of resources for educators interested in teaching their students how to keep our environment clean. Computer software is just one of the many types of materials available. Contact the office above to obtain a copy.

CONDORS

U.S. Fish and Wildlife Service
U.S. Department of the Interior
4401 N. Fairfax Drive

Be patient. If any phone number is incorrect, call (area code) 555-1212 and request the new listing.

The Government Works for Kids, Too

Mail Stop 130
Arlington, VA 22203 (703) 358-1711

Learn about the intriguing bird, the condor, so you can teach your children about it. Call the U.S. Fish and Wildlife Service for the following two publications, *The California Condor - Needs Our Help!* and the *California Condor.*

CONSTELLATIONS

R. Woods
Consumer Information Center - Y
P.O. Box 100
Pueblo, CO 81002

Stars in Your Eyes: A Guide to the Northern Skies contains helpful hints on how to find the seven best known constellations and an explanation on how they were named. 23 pp. (1988. DOD) 155X. $1.50. Write to the office above to receive a copy.

CONSTITUTION, U.S.

Education Branch (NEEE)
National Archives and Records Administration
Washington, DC 20408 (202) 724-0454

Interested in teaching your upper elementary students about the U.S. Constitution? Contact the Education Branch of the National Archives for the publication *A More Perfect Union: The Creation of the U.S. Constitution* (#200105, ISBN 0-922333-24-X). This particular booklet includes a historical introduction, transcriptions, and facsimiles of the featured documents, and can be ordered from the address above. (8 1/2 x 11, approx. 25 pages each, illustrations, 1986. Softcover only, $2.50 each.) Also available is the teaching unit *The Constitution: Evolution of a Government.* Published by the National Archives and SIRS, Inc., this unit contains about 50 reproductions of documents - charts, photographs, letters, drawings, and posters - and a detailed teacher's guide. The materials deal with certain key issues of the period, with governmental and political responses to these issues, and with public attitudes. The unit's cost is $40. To order, send a purchase order to: SIRS, Inc., P.O. Box 2348, Boca Raton, FL 33427-2348: or call toll free: (800) 3327-0513 (except AK and FL call collect 407-994-0079). For information on other educational materials available contact the address above.

COUGARS

U.S. Fish and Wildlife Service
U.S. Department of the Interior
4401 N. Fairfax Drive
Mail Stop 130
Arlington, VA 22203 (703) 358-1711

Call the U.S. Fish and Wildlife Service to obtain their publication *Cougar* so you can learn more about this fascinating animal.

COUNSELING

Counseling and Personnel Services Clearinghouse
University of Michigan
School of Education, Room 2108
610 East University Street
Ann Arbor, MI 48109-1259 (313) 764-9492

The Counseling and Personnel Services Clearinghouse of the Educational Resources Information Center (ERIC) prepares and supervises counselors at all educational levels. It is a resource for counselors seeking information on the theoretical development of counseling and guidance; personnel procedures such as testing and interviewing and the analysis and dissemination of the resultant information; group and case work; nature of pupil, student, and adult characteristics; personnel workers and their relation to career planning; family consultations; and student orientation activities.

COYOTES

U.S. Fish and Wildlife Service
U.S. Department of the Interior
4401 N. Fairfax Drive
Mail Stop 130
Arlington, VA 22203 (703) 358-1711

For all you coyote enthusiasts, the U.S. Fish and Wildlife Service has a publication called *Coyote.* Read about this interesting animal so you can teach you children about it.

CRANE, WHOOPING

U.S. Fish and Wildlife Service
U.S. Department of the Interior
4401 N. Fairfax Drive
Mail Stop 130
Arlington, VA 22203 (703) 358-1711

Would you like to learn more about the Whooping Crane? Call the U.S. Fish and Wildlife Service for its publication *Whooping Crane.*

CRATERS

Venus Names
Magellan Project Office
Mail Stop 230-201
Jet Propulsion Laboratory
4800 Oak Grove Drive
Pasadena, CA 91109 (818) 354-4321

Get your students interested in the craters on Venus by having them help choose an official name for them! Scientists of the Magellan Project, in association with the U.S. Geological Survey, are inviting the public to propose names of notable women for the many impact craters and large volcanic vents being discovered on Venus by the Magellan spacecraft's imaging radar. Names sent to the Magellan Project offices at NASA's Jet Propulsion Laboratory will be compiled for the Working Group of Planetary Systems Nomenclature, a committee of the International Astronomical Union (IAU). The IAU gives final approval to names for bodies in the solar system. Because the IAU meets only every 3 years and its last meeting was in July, 1991, names newly proposed for Venusian features will not be considered until the following meeting in 1994. But names proposed this year, if accepted as provisional by the nomenclature committee, may be used on published maps and in articles, pending final approval by the IAU. For more information, including the criteria for the names submitted, write to the office above.

CREATIVE THINKING

Project XL
U.S. Patent and Trademark Office
Washington, DC 20231 (703) 557-1610

PROJECT XL has been initiated by the U.S. Patent and Trademark Office as a national partnership designed to encourage proliferation of such programs and to develop new programs and materials which will promote critical and creative thinking and problem-solving skills for all children in our nation's schools. Through critical and creative thinking and problem-solving, ideas become reality as children create inventive solutions, illustrate their ideas, and make models of their inventions. The *Inventive Thinking Curriculum Project* provides children with opportunities to develop and practice higher order thinking skills. Call the office above to obtain a copy of this teacher's guide and *The Inventive Thinking Resource Directory,* a directory designed to assist the classroom teacher or school administrator who is interested in helping students become better thinkers, problem-solvers, and decision makers. Also available is *Black Innovators in Technology: Inspiring a New Generation.*

CUBA

Education Branch (NEEE)
National Archives and Records Administration
Washington, DC 20408 (202) 724-0454

Available for educators of upper elementary through secondary schools is *The Cuban Missile Crisis: Kennedy's Address to the Nation* (#200113, ISBN 0-911333-59-2, $2.50.), a teaching aid available from the National Archives. It contains a historical introduction and transcriptions and facsimiles of the featured documents.

CULTURE

Office of Education, Room 212
Mail Stop 158
National Museum of Natural History
Washington, DC 20560 (202) 357-2747

The National Museum of Natural History has a workshop for elementary and middle school teachers on understanding culture. *Understanding Culture: Introducing Culture Into Your Classroom and/or Curricula.* The workshop provides an understanding of culture and how it works, a perspective on world cultures and the concepts of multiculturalism and Eurocentrism. Included are suggestions for resources, learning activities, and strategies for integrating an understanding of culture into social studies, geography, history, biology, language

Be patient. If any phone number is incorrect, call (area code) 555-1212 and request the new listing.

The Government Works For Kids, Too

arts, art, sociology, and anthropology. Workshop involves using museum exhibits for teaching.

CURRICULUM, ELEMENTARY SCHOOLS

Superintendent of Documents
Dept. 33
Washington, DC 20402 (202) 783-3238

James Madison Elementary School: A Curriculum for American Students presents a model elementary school curriculum for kindergarten through the eighth grade. It includes suggestions for teaching English, social studies (history, geography, and civic), mathematics, science, foreign languages, fine arts, physical education, and health. It also includes profiles of seven actual schools which have demonstrated curricular excellence. 1988. 61 pp. (S/N 065-000-00350-3, $2.50).

DATA BASES

NASA CORE
Lorain County Joint Vocational School
15181 Route 58 South
Oberlin, OH 44074 (216) 774-1051

Teach your students interesting facts about the Space Shuttle missions. Use the *Space Shuttle Mission Facts Data Base* to obtain information on the first 30 space shuttle missions including mission number, orbiter, date, commander and pilot. To use this data base you must have the Apple works program. Appropriate for kids in grades K-12. Produced by Oklahoma State University.

Educational Resources Information Center (ERIC)
Office of Educational Research and Improvement (OERI)
U.S. Department of Education
555 New Jersey Ave., NW
Washington, DC 20208-5720 (202) 219-2289

The Educational Resources Information Center (ERIC) is a nationwide information network designed to provide users with ready access to education literature. Established in 1966 to make educational research and practice available from a single source, ERIC collects, analyzes, and distributes information from local, state, federal, and international agencies, as well as private sources. At the heart of ERIC is the largest education database in the world - containing more than 735,000 bibliographic records of documents and journal articles; approximately 2,600 records are added monthly. Papers, conference proceedings, literature reviews, and curricula materials, along with articles from nearly 800 education-related journals, are indexed and abstracted for entry into the ERIC database.

DEER

U.S. Fish and Wildlife Service
U.S. Department of the Interior
4401 N. Fairfax Drive
Mail Stop 130
Arlington, VA 22203 (703) 358-1711

Call the U.S. Fish and Wildlife Service to obtain its publication called *Key Deer*.

DEERE, JOHN

Department of Public Programs
Room BB53, National Museum of American History
Smithsonian Institution
Washington, DC 20560 (202) 357-4187

Would your students or children like a poster of a 1924 John Deere Model D farm tractor? Cost is $8.

DINOSAURS

Office of Education, Room 212
Mail Stop 158
National Museum of Natural History
Washington, DC 20560 (202) 357-2747

The National Museum of Natural History periodically conducts workshops for elementary and middle school teachers. One of the workshops is *Dinosaurs* which includes a walk through the Dinosaur Hall to help teachers and aides design a visit for their classes, followed by an informal lecture on major dinosaur groups represented in the exhibit hall.

Office of Education, Room 212
Mail Stop 158

National Museum of Natural History
Washington, DC 20560 (202) 357-2747

Available from the National Museum of Natural History is the slide set *Dinosaurs and Other Giants*. It is available for a three-week loan free of charge. Use it to enhance curricula for school children.

Office of Education, Room 212
Mail Stop 158
National Museum of Natural History
Washington, DC 20560 (202) 357-2747

Discover Dinosaurs is a program for preschool and kindergarten children offered by the National Museum of Natural History. In this program students receive a short introduction to "What is a fossil?" by means of a puppet show, investigate dinosaur skeletons and dioramas in the Dinosaur Hall, and participate in hands-on activities relating to dinosaur exhibits.

DOGS

Center for Veterinary Medicine
Food and Drug Administration
Public Health Service
U.S. Department of Health and Human Services
5600 Fishers Lane
Rockville, MD 20857 (301) 295-8755

Dogs are one of the many pets children like to have. There are many factors, however, involved in the care and feeding of a household pet. The office above has several fact sheets which parents can use to teach their children how to care for pets properly.

Office of Public Affairs
Alcohol, Drug Abuse, and Mental Health Administration
Public Health Service
U.S. Department of Health and Human Services
5600 Fishers Lane, Room 13C05
Rockville, MD 20857 (301) 443-8956

Dogs are also one of the many types of animals used for medical research. By learning how scientists perform medical research in laboratories, children can better understand how and why doctors are able to help people to get well. *Let's Visit a Research Laboratory: Introduction and Lesson Plans* (for schoolchildren in grades 2-5) helps answers the many questions children may have about research laboratories. The supplemental poster that is included provides teachers with helpful illustrations for classroom discussion and activities.

U.S. Fish and Wildlife Service
U.S. Department of the Interior
4401 N. Fairfax Drive
Mail Stop 130
Arlington, VA 22203 (703) 358-1711

Learn about the prairie dog through the publication *Prairie Dog*.

DOLPHINS

U.S. Fish and Wildlife Service
U.S. Department of the Interior
4401 N. Fairfax Drive
Mail Stop 130
Arlington, VA 22203 (703) 358-1711

Would you like to learn more about the gentle and intriguing mammal, the dolphin? Contact the U.S. Fish and Wildlife Service for the publication *Dolphins*.

Marine Mammal Commission
1825 Connecticut Ave., NW, #512
Washington, DC 20009 (202) 606-5504

Children of all ages (and even adults!) will enjoy learning how to draw whales, seals and dolphins. *How to Draw Whales and Seals* shows you how to draw these mammals in four or five easy steps.

DOUGLASS, FREDERICK

Smithsonian Institution Traveling Exhibition Service
1100 Jefferson Drive, SW
Room 3146
Washington, DC 20560

Help teach your children about Frederick Douglass through the poster *The Frederick Douglass Years: 1817-1895*. It includes biographies of abolitionists and black leaders, and a bibliography. Cost is $1.

Be patient. If any phone number is incorrect, call (area code) 555-1212 and request the new listing.

The Government Works for Kids, Too

DRAMA

Education Department
Kennedy Center
Washington, DC 20566 (202) 416-8800

Introduce theater to children in grades K-6 with help from the booklet *Imaginations at Work: Kids Invent Theatre.* $2.50 copy; $2 shipping and handling.

DRUG AND ALCOHOL ABUSE PREVENTION

Drug Video Program
Office of Public Affairs
U.S. Department of Education
400 Maryland Ave., SW
Washington, DC 20202

Drug prevention videos are available from the U.S. Department of Education for parents and educators. Originally designed for schools these video programs are now available for home use. Each program is closed captioned and comes with its own Parent's or Teacher's Guide to help you discuss each program's message and the serious problem of drug abuse with your child. Programs for elementary children include:

The Drug Avenger. ($35, 73 minutes, 16-page Parent's Guide, 1988, VHS Order No. DGA17535). Three children from the future travel back to the 20th Century to take on the life-threatening problem of drug abuse in 10 animated programs.

Fast Forward Future. ($30, 61 minutes, 23-page Teacher's Guide, 1988., VHS Order No. DGA 17532). Actor Richard Kiley as "Mentor" shows three elementary students the future with the Fast Forward machine. The students see the effects of using drugs and staying drug free.

Straight Up. ($40, 90 minutes, 2-page Teacher's Guide, 1988, VHS Order No. DGA17529). Academy award winning actor Lou Gosset, Jr., as Cosmo takes a boy named Ben, played by Chad Allen of NBC's "Our House", on a journey in the "fate" elevator. Ben's travels teach him valuable lessons about why drugs are harmful and how to refuse them.

Demand Reduction Section
Drug Enforcement Administration
U.S. Department of Justice
Washington, DC 20537 (202) 307-7936

Healthy Bodies Don't Need Drugs! Learning and Activity Book is a fifteen-page publication designed to educate children about the need to take care of their bodies and to say "No!" to drugs.

National Crime Prevention Council
1700 K Street, NW, 2nd Floor
Washington, DC 20006 (202) 466-6272

Help teach your children to say "No!" through the use of the following McGruff materials. They are available from the National Crime Prevention Council. Materials include:

Elementary School Materials Package. This package contains materials that can be photocopied for students and parents. It was sent to 51,000 elementary schools, and limited quantities are still available from the National Crime Prevention Council. Free.

If You Want to Fit In, Be Drug Free: Welcome to McGruff's Drug-Free Park. This colored poster shows McGruff with children playing basketball, baseball, riding bicycles, and reading - all alcohol- and other drug-free activities. $2.50.

Licensed Products Package. The National Crime Prevention Council has many specialty items available to teach elementary youth about prevention. This package includes information on a talking robot, a puppet package, stickers, calendars, and many other items. Free.

McGruff's Drug Abuse Prevention Kit. This kit includes different games, puzzles, a video, and recorded songs for children. Two items are for parents, and they give tips for teaching children how to say no. Materials come as reproducible masters. $30.

McGruff's Drug Abuse Prevention Kit: The No Show. The video is part of McGruff's Drug Abuse Prevention Kit. All parts of the Kit including the video, are reproducible for nonprofit educational purposes. Animation is used throughout 25 percent of the video. The video kids create a rock video about refusing drugs. $12.

To Be What You Want To Be: Be Drug Free. This poster has people from many professions with the slogan to be what you want to be, be drug free. It has room for the child to draw himself into the picture. $2.50.

National Clearinghouse for Alcohol and
Drug Information
P.O. Box 2345 (800) 729-6686
Rockville, MD 20852 (301) 468-2600

The National Clearinghouse for Alcohol and Drug Information is an excellent source of information for alcohol and drug abuse prevention. In 1987 it was established as the central point within the Federal Government for current print and audiovisual materials about alcohol and other drugs. NCADI answers more than 18,000 telephone and mail inquiries each month and distributes some 18 million printed items a year, which include the following posters and publications appropriate for elementary school children:

Ayundando a sus alumnos a decirle que no (Helping Your Students Say "No") Teacher's Guide (1990). In English and Spanish, explains the effects of alcohol on the body, why children start to drink, how teachers can help their students say "No" to alcohol and deal with the first signs of drinking, and where teachers can go for more information. 13 pp. PH284.

Buzzy's Rebound: Fat Albert and the Cosby Kids (1990). In comic book format, depicts the story of Buzzy, a young basketball player and friend of the Cosby Kids, who gets into trouble with alcohol and is helped by his coach, and a school counselor. 18 pp. PH232.

Elementary School Children and Alcohol Education includes audiovisuals, programs descriptions, professional and organizational resources to assist educators and parents of young childcare. It is available free from the office below. MS315.

The Fact Is ... You Can Prevent Alcohol and Other Drug Problems Among Elementary School Children (1988). Includes videotapes, program descriptions, and professional and organizational resources to assist educators and parents of young children. 17 pp. MS349.

Growing Up Drug Free: A Parent's Guide to Prevention (1989). This handbook outlines what children at four key stages of development should know about drugs and suggests family activities to reinforce children's motivation to avoid alcohol and other drugs. 52 pp. PHD533.

The Herschel Walker Poster (1989). Herschel Walker, football star, salutes the drug-free youth of America in a 22 in. by 27 in. color poster. Reference is made to NCADI as a source for more information. AVD45.

Learning to Live Drug Free: A Curriculum Model for Prevention (1990). Provides a flexible framework for classroom-based prevention efforts for kindergarten through grade 12. Presents the states of child development as they relate to drug prevention, facts about drugs, suggested lesson plans, tips on working with parents and the community, and a resource section for further information. Teachers can learn how to integrate prevention messages into their classroom presentations. BKD51.

Little League Drug Education Program (1991). This video has two parts: Part 1, Friend to Friend, Featuring Orel Hershiser, is directed toward today's Little Leaguer. The film tells the story of a Little League player who is tempted by drugs. Part 2, Big League Advice: Helping Your Little Leaguers Say No, is for parents and coaches of Little League players. The film depicts a discussion among Little League parents and baseball Hall-of-Famers 'Hank' Aaron and Jim Palmer. These great ball players offer frank and important advice to parents on how to talk to young people about drugs and alcohol. 30 minutes. VHS29.

Live the Dream, Say No to Alcohol and Drug Abuse (1989). Poster features Dr. Martin Luther King, Jr. Appropriate for all ages, 15 1/2 in. by 22 in. AV165.

McGruff's Surprise Party (1989). A comic book that helps children understand the importance of saying "No" to alcohol and other drugs, as told by McGruff, the crime dog. Also teaches children techniques for resisting peer pressure. For ages 8 to 10. 14 pp. PH271.

McGruff: Say 'No' to Crack and Other Drugs (1989). Bright red and white poster featuring McGruff, the Crime Dog. McGruff tells kids that crack is poison and a very dangerous drug. Tells them to say a big "no" and walk away. Also provides the NIDA hotline number (800-662-HELP) and a cocaine hotline number (800-COCAINE). 64 in. by 88 in. AVD14.

The Government Works For Kids, Too

Parent Training is Prevention (1991). Contains information to help communities identify and carry out programs on parenting. Details roles parents play in rearing children who are free of alcohol and other drug problems, highlights ethnic and cultural considerations, and gives characteristics of effective prevention programs. 184 pp. BK 184.

Pointers for Parents Card (1989). Provides easy steps parents can take to help prevent their child from using alcohol or other drugs. Excellent handout for special events such as fairs, workshop, or conferences. 3 1/2 in. by 8 1/2 in. card. PH260.

Prevention Resource Guide: Elementary Youth (1991). This Resource Guide includes materials specifically developed for youth that may be used in an elementary school setting, as well as relevant information on parenting. It is designed for teachers, administrators, and program leaders who come in contact with elementary youth. 23 pp. MS421.

Quick List: 10 Steps to Help Your Child Say "No" (1990). Also available in Spanish. Identifies ten things that parents can do to help their children stay away from alcohol and other drugs, from talking with your child to being a good role model. Three-panel fold out mini-poster. PH230.

Snappy Answers Card for Kids (1989). Suggests responses that young people can use to say "No" if offered alcohol or other drugs. Excellent handout for special events such as fairs, workshops, or school events. 3 1/2 in. by 8 1/2 in. card. PH 261.

Drug Enforcement Administration
U.S. Department of Justice
Washington, DC 20537 (202) 307-7977

The *Soozie and Katy* workbook was created to acquaint children with the purpose of medicine, its appropriate use, the legal distribution of drugs, and the dangers which can accompany misuse. Appropriate for home and classroom discussion, it begins with the idea that each child is responsible for the care of his body and should protect it. Teaching the child the doctor-pharmacist-parent sequence of drug distribution will help the child accept the administration of medicine without fear, and it will also begin to explore the idea that there are illegal channels of drug distribution.

National Clearinghouse for Alcohol and Drug Information
P.O. Box 2345
Rockville, MD 20852 (800) 729-6686

Use the *Be Smart Game* board game to help teach your children to say "No!" to drugs. It is printed on a heavy sheet of paper, allows two-four players, and requires dice and a coin for each player. Going around the board, players have opportunities to say "No!" to drugs and to discover alternate activities.

R. Woods
Consumer Information Center
Pueblo, CO 81008

Growing Up Drug Free (#551X) is an educational booklet intended for parents, available at no charge. To order, send a written request (including the stock number) to the above address.

DUCKS

U.S. Fish and Wildlife Service
U.S. Department of the Interior
4401 N. Fairfax Drive
Mail Stop 130
Arlington, VA 22203 (703) 358-1711

The U.S. Fish and Wildlife Service has several publications available on ducks including *Diving Ducks*, and *Ducks Get Sick, Too*. Teach your students about these adorable birds!

EAGLES

U.S. Fish and Wildlife Service
U.S. Department of the Interior
4401 N. Fairfax Drive
Mail Stop 130
Arlington, VA 22203 (703) 358-1711

Use the U.S. Fish and Wildlife Service's publications to teach your students about our national symbol, the bald eagle. Call to receive *Bald Eagle*.

EARTH

U.S. Geological Survey
P.O. Box 25425
Denver, CO 80225

The Interior of the Earth explains the structure and nature of the Earth's crust, mantle, and core. Describes procedures used to obtain this information through studies of seismic wave patterns. To obtain a copy, write to the office above.

Teaching Resource Center
Jet Propulsion Laboratory
4800 Oak Grove Dr.
Mail Stop CS-530
Pasadena, CA 91109 (818) 354-6916

Earth: Views from Moon and Space Shuttle can be an excellent educational aid for classroom use. It is available as a slide set and consists of twenty 35 mm slides held in a plastic vue-file sleeve which will fit into a three ring binder. Many sets have a fact sheet included which lists the title of the slides and may have a brief description or topic. Cost is $6.

EARTH SCIENCES

Elementary and Secondary Programs Branch
Educational Affairs Division
Mail Code XEE
NASA Headquarters
Washington, DC 20546

The earth sciences is just one topic that is covered in teacher workshops held each summer by Aerospace Education Services Program (AESP) specialists at NASA field centers, elementary and secondary schools, and on college campuses. Workshops also cover astronomy, aeronautics, life in space, principles of rocketry, and remote sensing. A typical workshop includes how-to and hands-on activities to help teachers incorporate what they learn into classroom activities and programs to supplement existing curricula.

Missouri Department of Natural Resources
Division of Geology and Land Survey
P.O. Box 250
Rolla, MO 65401

Earthquakes in Missouri contains information not only about earthquakes in Missouri but also general information on understanding earthquakes, measuring earthquakes, and the hazards of earthquakes. This publication can serve as an educational aid for upper-elementary school children learning about earthquakes.

Geologic Inquiries Group
U.S. Geological Survey
907 National Center
Reston, VA 22092 (703) 648-4383

The office above answers questions on topics such as the geology of specific areas, geologic maps and mapping, earthquakes, and energy and mineral resources. Educators and students can contact the office if they have any questions relating to these topics.

Geologic Inquiries Group
U.S. Geological Survey
907 National Center
Reston, VA 22092 (703) 648-4383

The *Selected Packet of Geologic Teaching Aids* is prepared for elementary school teachers (and high school teachers) of general science, geography, social studies, environmental education and other earth science-related subjects. It contains leaflets, booklets, reference lists, and an activity sheet ("Make Your Own Paper Model of a Volcano"). To receive a packet, send a request on school letterhead indicating the subject that is taught and the grade level to the office listed above.

Earth Science Information Center
U.S. Department of the Interior
1849 C Street, NW, Room 2650
Washington, DC 20240 (202) 208-4047

Contact the office above for information on the U.S. Geological Survey's map products and earth science publications. They may help answer questions you have.

U.S. Geological Survey
P.O. Box 25425
Denver, CO 80225

The following publications are an excellent source of information for both upper elementary students and educators. Students can use them to supplement special

Be patient. If any phone number is incorrect, call (area code) 555-1212 and request the new listing.

The Government Works for Kids, Too

reports and science projects and teachers can use them to enhance their curricula. To obtain single copies write to the office above.

"The Big Five" - Some Facts and Figures on our Nation's Largest Rivers. Presents statistics for maximum, minimum, and mean flows for the Nation's largest rivers - - the Mississippi, St. Lawrence, Columbia, Ohio, and the Missouri.

A Brief History of the U.S. Geological Survey. Describes the bureau's growth, activities, and achievements from its founding in 1879 to its centennial in 1979.

Collecting Rocks. Describes the origin of major rock types and how rocks can provide clues to the Earth's history. Includes suggestions for starting a rock collection, identifying specimens, and housing such a collection.

Earthquakes. Explains the nature and causes of earthquakes. Describes the techniques used to detect, record, measure, and predict seismic disturbances. Provides historical data on several world-famous earthquakes that have occurred since 1755.

The Exclusive Economic Zone: An Exciting New Frontier. Describes the geologic processes that form the ocean floors. Discusses the importance of the mineral potential of the Exclusive Economic Zone, which provides the Nation with nearly 3 billion acres of new frontier for study and exploration.

Geologic Maps: Portraits of the Earth. Explains the nature of geologic maps, how they are made, and the ways they may be used to determine relationships of rocks on and beneath the Earth's Surface. Shows examples of maps.

Geologic Time. Explains relative and radiometric time scales and how geologists measure the age of the Earth. Illustrates the scientific processes that are used to interpret the Earth's geologic history.

Gold. Discusses the nature of gold, its origins, and the geologic environments in which it is commonly found. Provides information about the uses of gold and a brief historical account of production in the U.S.

Glaciers: A Water Resource. Discusses the relationship between glacial ice and the amount of water on land surfaces. Describes the types of glaciers, their origins, and the natural processes that regulate the melting of ice.

Ground Water: An Undervalued Resource. Describes the need for using ground water, the role of ground water in the economy, and an analysis of regional aquifer systems. Discusses the ways in which ground water and surface water interact.

Ground Water and the Rural Homeowner. Presents a short description of ground water, some of the problems associated with ground water, and some suggestions for help with problems.

Ground Water Contamination--No "Quick Fix" in Sight. Explains how ground water is contaminated by septic tanks or cesspools, municipal lagoons, sewers, landfills, or tailings piles, and the need for further research in contamination prevention.

How Much Water in a 12-ounce Can? A Perspective on Water-Use Information. Provides information on how water was a free resource but now is considered an expensive commodity. Demonstrates how the ever-increasing use of water by industry and in the home is depleting existing supplies.

The Hydrologic Cycle. Explains the natural process by which water is circulated from the seas to the atmosphere, to the land, and back to the seas in a continuous cycle.

The Interior of the Earth. Explains the structure and nature of the Earth's crust, mantle, and core. Describes the procedures used to obtain this information through studies of seismic wave patterns.

John Wesley Powell's Exploration of the Colorado River. Describes Powell's daring voyage in 1869 through the canyons of the Colorado River, starting at Green River Station, Wyoming, and ending at the junction of the Colorado and Virgin Rivers in Arizona.

Landforms of the United States. Discusses the sculpturing of landforms and the effects of wind, water, and chemical processes. Lists major physiographic divisions of the U.S. and describes their characteristic features.

Mountains and Plains: Denver's Geologic Setting. Describes the nature and

structure of the rocks that underlie Denver, Colorado, and part of the adjacent Front Range. Provides a road log to explain the natural features of the area.

The Naming (and Misnaming) of America. Describes how some localities came to be names, the derivation of these geographic names, and why the U.S. Board on Geographic Names was established.

Natural Steam for Power. Describes the investigation of geothermal steam as a potential source of energy for power needs worldwide. Discusses the nature and behavior of steam formed underground.

Our Changing Continent. Discusses the evidence and techniques scientists use to reconstruct the history of the changing land surface of the North American continent.

Permafrost. Defines permafrost and summarizes its geographic distribution. Explains how construction activities alter local permafrost conditions and discusses how best to counteract unfavorable changes.

Prospecting for Gold in the United States. Describes various kinds of gold deposits and their locations. Offers a brief review of the problems faced by present-day prospectors and lists available maps and services.

Rain: A Water Resource. Provides information on the annual precipitation in areas of the United States, with specific data on several major cities. Explains how to express rainfall as quantities of water. Also available in Spanish.

River Basins of the United States: A Series. Lists basic facts including historical notes, flow characteristics, and physical statistics on selected river basins.

Safety and Survival in an Earthquake. Describes the hazards posed by earthquakes and offers instructions for individual action before, during, and after a tremor to minimize loss of life and damage to property. Also available in Spanish.

The San Andreas Fault. Describes the nature, behavior, and earthquake history of this major fault system that extends from northern California to the Gulf of California.

Tree Rings: Timekeepers of the Past. Explains how past environmental conditions have been recorded in tree rings and how scientists interpret this information.

Volcanic Hazards at Mount Shasta, California. Describes the kinds of volcanic activity that have occurred in the past, shows areas that could be affected in the future, and suggests ways of reducing the risks.

Volcanoes. Describes the principal types of volcanoes, different types of eruptions, associated volcanic phenomena, their geologic settings, and how volcanoes are monitored. Explains how volcanic activity endangers and helps mankind.

Water Dowsing. Provides a brief history of water dowsing. Explains how hydrologists of the USGS and other agencies use scientific methods to locate ground water.

Water in the Urban Environment: Erosion and Sediment. Explores the dual role that water plays as both a resource and a hazard. Discusses possible actions that minimize erosion and sedimentation.

The Water of the World. Discusses the amount of water contained in the world's atmosphere, on the surface, and underground. Describes the world's water balance.

Water Use in the United States, 1980. Summarizes the use of the Nation's water supply for domestic, industrial, rural, and irrigation purposes.

What is Water?. Describes the basic chemical properties of water and its diverse physical characteristics. Briefly explains the formation of water on Earth. Also available in Spanish.

Why is the Ocean Salty? Discusses the origin of the oceans and the sources of their salinity. Also available in Spanish.

EARTHQUAKES

Geologic Inquiries Group
U.S. Geological Survey
907 National Center

Be patient. If any phone number is incorrect, call (area code) 555-1212 and request the new listing.

The Government Works For Kids, Too

Reston, VA 22092 (703) 648-4383

Would you like to teach your students or children about earthquakes, but you have some questions about them yourself? Call the Geologic Inquiries Group of the U.S. Geological Survey. This office answers questions not only on topics such as earthquakes, but also questions on energy and mineral resources, the geology of specific areas, and geologic maps and mapping.

Missouri Department of Natural Resources
Division of Geology and Land Survey
P.O. Box 250
Rolla, MO 65401

Earthquakes in Missouri contains information not only about earthquakes in Missouri but also general information on understanding earthquakes, measuring earthquakes, and the hazards of earthquakes. This publication can serve as an educational aid for upper-elementary school children learning about earthquakes.

U.S. Geological Survey
P.O. Box 25425
Denver, CO 80225

The following publications are an excellent source of information on earthquakes for both upper elementary students and educators. Students can use them to supplement special reports and science projects and teachers can use them to enhance their curricula. To obtain single copies write to the office above.

Earthquakes. Explains the nature and causes of earthquakes. Describes the techniques used to detect, record, measure, and predict seismic disturbances. Provides historical data on several world-famous earthquakes that have occurred since 1755.

Safety and Survival in an Earthquake. Describes the hazards posed by earthquakes and offers instructions for individual action before, during, and after a tremor to minimize loss of life and damage to property. Also available in Spanish.

The San Andreas Fault. Describes the nature, behavior, and earthquake history of this major fault system that extends from northern California to the Gulf of California.

ECOLOGY

U.S. Fish and Wildlife Service
U.S. Department of the Interior
4401 N. Fairfax Drive
Mail Stop 130
Arlington, VA 22203 (703) 358-1711

Learn more about ecology through the U.S. Fish and Wildlife Service's publication *Ecology.*

ECONOMICS

California Energy Extension Service
1400 Tenth St., Room 209
Sacramento, CA 95814 (916) 323-4388

Energy awareness does not have to be taught only in science classes. *100 Ways to Celebrate NEED* is a guide which promotes energy awareness and links lessons to not only science, but also to social studies, history, economics, fine arts and language arts. This guide contains 100 activities for children in grades K-12, along with a glossary and teacher background information.

EISENHOWER, DWIGHT D.

Education Branch (NEEE)
National Archives and Records Administration
Washington, DC 20408 (202) 724-0454

Atoms for Peace: Dwight D. Eisenhower's Address to the United Nations (#200016, ISBN 0-911333-76-2) is booklet offered to teachers of upper elementary through secondary school students. It includes a historical introduction and transcriptions and facsimiles of the featured documents. Cost is $2.50.

ELECTRICITY

National Energy Information Center (NEIC)
Energy Information Administration, EI-231
1000 Independence Ave., SW
Room 1F-048
Washington, DC 20585 (202) 586-8800

Do you have a question about electricity? Contact the National Energy Information Center which is the information dissemination service for DOE's Energy Information Administration (EIA). It is responsible for the collection, analysis, and distribution of energy statistics and provides 20 information sheets free. In addition to electricity, these one-page capsules cover such energy topics as petroleum, natural gas, coal, and renewable energy. Also available is *Energy Facts,* a pocket-size statistical reference providing brief facts on a variety of domestic and international energy data.

ELKS

U.S. Fish and Wildlife Service
U.S. Department of the Interior
4401 N. Fairfax Drive
Mail Stop 130
Arlington, VA 22203 (703) 358-1711

The publication *American Elk* may provide new information on this intriguing animal.

ELLINGTON, DUKE

Department of Public Programs
Room BB53
National Museum of American History
Smithsonian Institution
Washington, DC 20560 (202) 357-4187

Use the poster *Duke Ellington* to educate your students about this extraordinary person.

EMANCIPATION PROCLAMATION

Education Branch (NEEE)
National Archives and Records Administration
Washington, DC 20408 (202) 724-0454

The Education Branch of the National Archives offers teachers of upper elementary through secondary school students publications and teaching units to aid in the teaching of historical documents and eras. *The Emancipation Proclamation* (#200103, ISBN 0-911333-40-1) is one of these teaching aids. This booklet includes a historical introduction and transcriptions and facsimiles of the featured documents. Cost is $2.50.

ENDANGERED SPECIES

U.S. Fish and Wildlife Service
U.S. Department of the Interior
4401 N. Fairfax Drive
Mail Stop 130
Arlington, VA 22203 (703) 358-1711

Would you like to teach your students about endangered species? The Fish and Wildlife has some excellent publications to help you. Call them to receive *Endangered Species,* and *Pesticide Use and Endangered Species.*

Office of Education, Room 212
Mail Stop 158
National Museum of Natural History
Washington, DC 20560 (202) 357-2747

The National Museum of Natural History conducts a visiting program, include one on endangered species. The museum has on display over 100 mounted specimens of animals that are endangered. With *Endangered Species and Extinction* students learn about changes on our planet and discover how those changes affect life on Earth. Choose either a "Modern" (living endangered species and immediate reasons for their problems - recommended for K-3) or "Fossil and Modern" (global climate changes as documented in fossil and modern scientific record - recommended for Grade 3 and up) focus.

Office of Education, Room 212
Mail Stop 158
National Museum of Natural History
Washington, DC 20560 (202) 357-2747

The National Museum of Natural History also conducts workshops for teachers, including *Climate and Endangered Species.* This workshop is designed to help teachers and aides design a visit or prepare for a guided tour. The identification of all endangered and extinct modern animals on exhibit is followed by an informal talk about why certain groups of animals are more vulnerable than others.

Be patient. If any phone number is incorrect, call (area code) 555-1212 and request the new listing.

The Government Works for Kids, Too

ENERGY EDUCATION (CONSERVATION AND AWARENESS)

California Energy Extension Service
1400 Tenth St., Room 209
Sacramento, CA 95814 (916) 323-4388

The *4-H Home Conservation Guide* is a collection of 12 hands-on projects which teach home energy conservation skills for a 4-H group. Contact the office above to obtain a copy.

California Energy Extension Service
1400 Tenth St., Room 209
Sacramento, CA 95814 (916) 323-4388

The *Animated Bibliography* is a sampler of energy education materials. The descriptions of curriculum materials include complete ordering information as well as a sample activity.

Energy Center
Sonoma State University
1801 East Cotati Ave.
Rohnert Park, CA 94928 (707) 664-2577

The teaching activity/game *California Challenge: An Educational Tour of California* highlights California history and geography from an energy perspective, and is appropriate for children in grades 4-5. The cost is $20 for a full game which includes instructions, map, cards, 4 game pieces and 1 die.

Conservation and Renewable Energy
Inquiry and Referral Service (CAREIRS)
P.O. Box 8900
Silver Spring, MD 20907 (800) 523-2929

The office above has information sheets that educators can use to supplement their curricula. They include the following:

Biofuels as a Source of Energy
Geothermal Energy
Hot Water Energy Conservation
Learning About Energy Conservation
Learning About Renewable Energy
Ocean Energy
Recycling Waste to Save Energy
Renewable Energy: An Overview
Renewable Energy Reading List for Young Adults
Solar Energy and You
Sunspaces
Wood Fuel

California Energy Extension Service
1400 Tenth St., Room 209
Sacramento, CA 95814 (916) 323-4388

Let's Get Energized is a collection of 36 energy education and awareness activities designed for after-school enrichment and child care programs. Call the office above to obtain a copy.

Office of Fossil Energy, Room 4G 085
U.S. Department of Energy
1000 Independence Ave., SW
Washington, DC 20585 (202) 586-6503

Call the office above to receive *The Clean Coal Path* poster. It traces the route of several new advances in the clean use of coal, America's most abundant fossil energy resource. During the 1990's, many of these improvements will be used for the first time in power plants to generate new supplies of electricity without polluting the nation's air.

Bureau of Mines
U.S. Department of the Interior
Cochrans Mill Road
P.O. Box 18070
Pittsburgh, PA 15236 (412) 892-4338

Children in the upper elementary grades will enjoy the *Coal Products Tree* illustration and learning all the products that are available from coal. While all the common products are listed, some surprisingly uncommon ones are listed as well, including baking powder, perfumes, and food preservatives.

Conservation and Renewable Energy
Inquiry and Referral Service (CAREIRS)
P.O. Box 8900
Silver Spring, MD 20907 (800) 523-2929

Conservation Activities for the Classroom lists activities that other teachers have used to promote awareness of energy conservation and renewable energy in the classroom.

Office of Fossil Energy Communications
1000 Independence Ave., SW
Room 4G-085
Washington, DC 20585 (202) 586-6503

Teach kids where coal comes from and the importance of it. *Dinosaurs and Power Plants* is a 16-page brochure designed for students that relates the story of mining and drilling for coal, gas, and oil, the environmental concerns involved, and modes of transportation. *Clean Coal Technology* is also available.

California Energy Extension Service
1400 Tenth St., Room 209
Sacramento, CA 95814 (916) 323-4388

Energy Math is a set of materials which will assist in integrating the primary math and physical science curricula with respect to the energy theme. Teacher-led activities, learning center activities, and self-correcting worksheets for individual completion are all included.

Energy Center
Sonoma State University
1801 East Cotati Ave.
Rohnert Park, CA 94928 (707) 664-2577

Conserve and Renew: Energy Activities is a collection in interdisciplinary energy activities for children in grades 4-6 to be used either as a unit on energy, or as individual activities to complement existing curricula. While the main focus is on conservation and renewables, recycling and ethics are also included. Cost is $10.

California Energy Extension Service
1400 Tenth St., Room 209
Sacramento, CA 95814 (916) 323-4388

Energy awareness does not have to be taught only in science classes. *100 Ways to Celebrate NEED* is a guide which promotes energy awareness and links lessons to not only science, but also to social studies, history, economics, fine arts and language arts. This guide contains 100 activities for children in grades K-12, along with a glossary and teacher background information.

California Energy Extension Service
1400 Tenth St., Room 209
Sacramento, CA 95814 (916) 323-4388

The publication *Energy Activities for the Primary Classroom* is a compilation of ten different activities educators can use to help students become more energy conscious. Any child in grades K-6 can benefit from these activities.

Conservation and Renewable Energy
Inquiry and Referral Service (CAREIRS)
P.O. Box 8900
Silver Spring, MD 20907 (800) 523-2929

Educators can use the publication *Learning About Energy Conservation* to teach their students the meaning of renewable and nonrenewable energy and ways in which one can conserve energy. Call the office above for a copy of this ten page publication.

California Energy Extension Service
1400 Tenth St., Room 209
Sacramento, CA 95814 (916) 323-4388

The *Classroom Energy Poster Puzzle* is a bulletin board-size poster for children in grades K-4. It serves as a great teaching aid to focus on energy use and abuse in the classroom. Also available is a step-by-step guide called *Energy Patrol* which actively involves students in the upper elementary grades in reducing their school's energy consumption. (A video of this is also available - send a blank VHS tape).

National Energy Information Center
Energy Information Administration
Room 1F-048
Forrestal Building
1000 Independence Ave., SW
Washington, DC 20585 (202) 586-8800

Energy Education Resources is the result of a study undertaken by the National Energy Information Center (NEIC), a service of the Energy Information Administration (EIA), to provide its customers with a list of generally available free or low-cost energy-related educational materials for primary and secondary students and educators. The list is updated once a year.

Be patient. If any phone number is incorrect, call (area code) 555-1212 and request the new listing.

The Government Works For Kids, Too

California Energy Extension Service
1400 Tenth St., Room 209
Sacramento, CA 95814 (916) 323-4388
Energy Facts for Classroom Teachers is a publication anyone can use to obtain interesting facts on recycling, oil and natural gas, and other energy conservation-related topics.

Conservation and Renewable Energy
Inquiry and Referral Service (CAREIRS)
P.O. Box 8900
Silver Spring, MD 20907 (800) 523-2929
What is Your Energy I.Q.? is a two page publication students can use to test their energy I.Q. Questions asked include: What is energy from the sun called? Why do we need to conserve our nonrenewable forms of energy? and What changes sunlight into electricity?

National Energy Information Center, EI-231
Energy Information Administration
Forrestal Building
Washington, DC 20585 (202) 586-8800
Contact the office above for a copy of *Energy Information Sheets*, available free of charge. Information ranging from crude oil production to coal consumption to nuclear power generation is provided. The information can be used by teachers and upper elementary students to supplement curricula and reports.

California Energy Extension Service
1400 Tenth St., Room 209
Sacramento, CA 95814 (916) 323-4388
The Energy Tech-Knowledgy Program promotes energy awareness to children in grades kindergarten through junior high. Grade-level specific materials are available to teachers and are designed to make it easy for them to include energy conservation education as part of their regular classroom instruction. Contact the office above for more information.

Office of Plans and Evaluations
Office of Nuclear Energy
U.S. Department of Energy
1000 Independence Ave., SW
Washington, DC 20585 (202) 586-9720
Would you like to teach your students about nuclear energy? The office above has several publications available, some of which are listed below, to more fully understand this valuable source of energy and the role it plays. Teachers can supplement their science curricula with the use of these publications:

Answers to Questions
Approaches to Nuclear Safety
Atoms to Electricity
The First Reactor
High-Level Nuclear Waste: A Safe, Permanent Solution
The History of Nuclear Energy
How Nuclear Energy Plants Work
Light Water Breeder Reactor
Low-Level Nuclear Waste: Safe, Permanent Disposal
Nuclear Energy: Benefit for All Americans
Nuclear Energy Economics
Nuclear Energy Plant Safety
The Nuclear Fuel Cycle
Nuclear Power in Space
Nuclear Powerplant Safety: Design and Planning
Nuclear Powerplant Safety: Operations
Nuclear Powerplant Safety: Source Terms
Radiation in Perspective
Radioisotopes: Today's Applications
Understanding Radiation

Bureau of Mines
U.S. Department of the Interior
Cochrans Mill Road
P.O. Box 18070
Pittsburgh, PA 15236 (412) 892-4338
The Petroleum Tree illustration shows all the dozens of products that are obtainable from crude oil. This illustration serves as an excellent learning tool for students in the upper elementary grades.

Conservation and Renewable Energy
Inquiry and Referral Service (CAREIRS)
P.O. Box 8900

Silver Spring, MD 20907 (800) 523-2929
People are trying to find new ways to heat their homes, factories, offices, and schools without using so much expensive oil and gas. *Solar Energy and You* helps teach children about solar energy and solar heat. Call the office above for this four page publication.

California Energy Extension Service
1400 Tenth St., Room 209
Sacramento, CA 95814 (916) 323-4388
Teaching Energy Education Activities is a 126-page publication of activities especially prepared for elementary substitute teachers as an alternative to social studies and science lesson plans. There are dozens of activities from which to choose to keep young minds thinking. Call the office above to receive a copy.

U.S. Geological Survey
P.O. Box 25425
Denver, CO 80225
Natural Steam for Power describes the investigation of geothermal steam as a potential source of energy for power needs worldwide. Discusses the nature and behavior of steam formed underground.

Governor's Office of Planning and Research
1400 Tenth St., Room 209
Sacramento, CA 95814 (916) 323-4388
This Service is a U.S. Department of Energy funded program which provides information and training on renewable energy and energy efficiency to schools, small businesses and Indian tribes. It provides materials for the teacher, including lesson plans and class activities for grades kindergarten through twelve. An available publication, *Animated Bibliography, A Sample of Energy Education Curriculum Materials: K-12*, lists available materials and where to obtain them. All are free of charge.

Governor's Energy Office
The Capitol
Tallahassee, FL 32399-0001 (904) 488-2475
This office focuses on solar energy and conservation. *Solar and Energy Conservation Projects for Students* was produced by the Florida Solar Energy Center and is available from the office above to elementary school teachers. Another publication, *Energy Research Projects Guide*, will assist students in their selection of an energy topic for science fair projects. Also available is the *Florida Middle School Energy Education Project*. All are free of charge.

State Capitol
9th Floor
P.O. Box 95085
Lincoln, NE 68509 (402) 471-2867
The office above provides energy-related curriculum materials, including instructional materials (films), video tapes, curriculum guides, slides, and resource books and materials, and are available to Nebraska educators only.

ENVIRONMENTAL AWARENESS

Public Information Center
U.S. Environmental Protection Agency (EPA)
401 M Street, SW, PM-211B
Washington, DC 20460 (202) 260-2080
Acid rain affects both the health of humans and our environment and is an issue with which the EPA is actively involved. EPA frequently receives requests for information on acid rain from school systems, teachers, and individuals. In response to these requests, EPA has developed the study guide *Acid Rain: The Student's First Sourcebook*. The purpose of the guide, which is for students in grades 4-8, is to help students better understand the science, citizen actions, and research issues that are part of the acid rain problem. *EPA's Acid Rain Program: Charting a New Course in Environmental Protection* and the *Environmental Backgrounder: Acid Rain* are two additional publications which provide information on the acid rain issue.

Department of Air Pollution Control
Commonwealth of Virginia
P.O. Box 10089
Richmond, VA 23240 (804) 225-2722
Airy Canary Learns to Fly is a coloring book about Airy Canary, a bird who is having difficulty learning to fly because of the presence of Nasty Nitrogen Dioxide, Otto Ozone the Air Pollutant, and Sully Sulfur Dioxide. Children in the lower elementary grades will enjoy coloring this 16-page book, while learning about pollutants and the need for clean air.

Be patient. If any phone number is incorrect, call (area code) 555-1212 and request the new listing.

The Government Works for Kids, Too

Office of Environmental Education
Pennsylvania Department of Education
333 Market St.
Harrisburg, PA 17126 (717) 783-6994

The Baily Twins' Outdoor Adventures is an illustrated publication with stories, games, and activities, designed to teach upper elementary schoolchildren about the environment.

Illinois Environmental Protection Agency
Office of Public Information
2200 Churchill Road
P.O. Box 19276
Springfield, Illinois 62794-9276 (217) 782-5562

Books for Young People on Environmental Issues is a selection of books from 1970 to present prepared by Gretl Cox of EPA's Headquarters Library. It is arranged in two sections. The first section is for children from kindergarten through the sixth grade with books grouped by grade level. The second section is for students in grades seven through twelve; books are listed by subject area.

Bureau of Mines
U.S. Department of the Interior
Cochrans Mill Road
P.O. Box 18070
Pittsburgh, PA 15236 (412) 892-4338

Children in grades K-5 will enjoy watching the video *Call Me Can* (18:20 mins.). Can is a lively aluminum beverage can who calls out one day in a grocery store to a young boy named Dan. Can has new and exciting stories to tell Dan about recycling, and sings a song about how wonderful it is to be made of aluminum, because he can be recycled over and over. There is no charge for borrowing this video. It is available in 3/4" U-Matic and 1/2" VHS formats only.

Public Information Center
U.S. Environmental Protection Agency
401 M Street, SW, PM-211B
Washington, DC 20460 (202) 260-2080

For at least half a century people have reported seeing a "sea monster" in the Chesapeake Bay. Affectionately known as "Chessie," popularized cousin of Nessie (Scotland's Loch Ness monster), the creature is reported to be gentle and good natured. In the coloring book *Chessie: A Chesapeake Bay Story*, Chessie discusses how and why we need to keep the Chesapeake Bay clean.

Public Information Office
Metropolitan Water Reclamation District of Greater Chicago
100 East Erie
Chicago, IL 60611 (312) 751-6633

Learn how the city of Chicago helps keep the Chicago River and Lake Michigan clean. *Color It Blue* is a coloring book which offers children a creative way of learning about sewage treatment.

Texas Water Development Board
Office of Public Information
P.O. Box 13231
Austin, TX 78711-3231 (512) 463-8028

Do You Know How to Keep Our Water Clean? is a publication written for children which addresses the need for a clean environment. It discusses the "story on water" and recycling. It is a twenty page publication which ends with a crossword puzzle.

Office of Coastal Zone Management
National Oceanic and Atmospheric Administration
3300 Whitehaven St., NW
Washington, DC 20235

Coastal Awareness: A Resource Guide for Teachers in Elementary Science was developed for elementary school teachers who would like to instill in children and young adults an appreciation of the ecologic value of the coast. (Resource Guides for junior high and high school teachers are also available). The purpose of this guide is not to present a definitive work on coastal ecology, but to entice teachers to explore ecological aspects of coastal awareness. A more complete understanding of the coast requires study of the interactions of ecology with economics, humanities, and government. An understanding of coastal ecological processes will aid students as they participate in future decision making.

Motion Picture Service
National Oceanic and Atmospheric Administration
U.S. Department of Commerce
12231 Wilkins Ave.
Rockville, MD 20852 (301) 443-8411

The need to protect our nation's coasts is becoming increasingly important. Use the following films (which are appropriate for elementary-age children) to educate your students about coastal awareness. They may be obtained without charge by writing to the office above.

The Biologist and the Boy. 14 minutes. An encounter between a biologist and a boy on the Gulf of Mexico. Discusses conservation and awareness.

Estuarine Heritage. 28 minutes. Shows threats to estuarine resources and stresses the importance of estuaries.

Estuary. 28 minutes. Stresses the value of the estuary and its uses for food resources and recreation.

The Great American Fish Story. 28 minutes. A series of five films (each is 28 minutes long) which tells the story of the American fishing industry. The first film is an overview and the other four each concentrate on one area of the country -- The West, The Northeast, The South, The Lakes and Rivers. Every aspect of the fishing industry is covered from catching to cooking.

Hurricane Decision. 14 minutes. A hurricane awareness and preparedness film. Points out the dangers of storm surge, wind and inland flooding caused by hurricanes.

It's Your Coast. 28 minutes. Discusses coastal zone problems with people from Florida, Maine, Illinois and Washington. Land development, oil pollution, and beach erosions are discussed. Stresses the importance of the coast.

Watermen of Chesapeake. 28 minutes. A film about the impact of Chesapeake Bay on a large segment of America.

Public Information Center
U.S. Environmental Protection Agency
401 M Street, SW, PM-211B
Washington, DC 20460 (202) 260-2080

Environmental Education Materials for Teachers and Young People (Grades K-12) is an excellent source of resources for educators. Entries are diverse with materials described ranging from workbooks to curriculum plans, to posters and pamphlets, to newsletters, films, and computer software. The publication's citations have been organized into two major sections according to the private and public sector organizations that have developed and produced environmental education materials for teachers, other educators, and students. A third section describes opportunities for educators to participate in workshops and to use other resources that can enable them to better cover environmental topics in their work with young people.

Public Information Center
U.S. Environmental Protection Agency
401 M Street, St., PM-211B
Washington, DC 20460 (202) 260-2080

Children will enjoy learning about the need for recycling while reading and coloring the publication, *There Lived a Wicked Dragon*. Written by Martha Finan for the federal solid waste management programs, it provides a creative way to learn about an important issue.

Public Information Center
U.S. Environmental Protection Agency
401 M Street, SW, PM-211B
Washington, DC 20460 (202) 260-2080

The *Glossary of Environmental Terms and Acronyms List* can help educators and students clarify the meaning of environmental terms. It is designed to give the user an explanation of the more commonly used environmental terms appearing in EPA publications, news releases, and other Agency documents available to the general public.

Public Information Office
Metropolitan Water Reclamation District of Greater Chicago
100 East Erie
Chicago, IL 60611 (312) 751-6633

Earth Trek....Explore Your Environment is an activity book designed to educate elementary schoolchildren about our need to protect our water, air, and land. The booklet's layout allows its pages to be duplicated so that each student can have a copy for use in class.

Public Information Center
U.S. Environmental Protection Agency
401 M Street, SW, PM-211B

Be patient. If any phone number is incorrect, call (area code) 555-1212 and request the new listing.

The Government Works For Kids, Too

Washington, DC 20460 (202) 260-2080

General Motors has produced a video entitled *I Need the Earth and the Earth Needs Me.* Initially distributed by the Environmental Protection Agency to 4th graders, it is available from the Public Information Center to children of all ages. Children will enjoy watching this video while learning the importance of keeping our air, water, and soil clean.

Public Information Center
U.S. Environmental Protection Agency (EPA)
401 M Street, SW, PM-211B
Washington, DC 20460 (202) 260-2080

Earthnotes is published in February, May, August and November by the U.S. EPA. It is the intent of EPA to provide an open forum for the exchange of teaching aids, comments, and brief essays concerning environmental education in the elementary grades.

Education Specialist: SSI
Ohio Department of Natural Resources
Division of Litter Prevention and Recycling
1889 Fountain Square Ct. - F-2
Columbus, OH 43224 (614) 265-6333

Super Saver Investigators is an interdisciplinary environmental studies activity guide book about solid waste, recycling, and natural resources for grades kindergarten through 8th and was developed by the Ohio Department of Natural Resources in cooperation with the Ohio Department of Education and Ohio teachers actively involved in environmental studies education. *Super Saver Investigators* contains over 65 hands-on learning activities for grades K-8. The activities are related to science and social studies lessons normally taught by elementary teachers. The activities include skill-building handouts in language arts, math, reading comprehension, creative writing, art and design. It is made available to schools and teachers in Ohio at no cost, through workshops or inservice training. For out-of-state requests there is a charge. Call or write for availability and price information.

EPA Region 1:
(Connecticut, Massachusetts, Maine, New Hampshire, Rhode Island, Vermont)
JFK Federal Building
Boston, MA 02203 (617) 565-3424

EPA Region 2:
(New Jersey, New York, Puerto Rico, Virgin Islands)
26 Federal Plaza
New York, NY 10278 (212) 264-2515

EPA Region 3:
(Delaware, Maryland, Pennsylvania, Virginia, West Virginia, District of Columbia)
841 Chestnut Street
Philadelphia, PA 19107 (215) 597-9370

EPA Region 4:
(Alabama, Florida, Georgia, Kentucky, Mississippi, North Carolina, South Carolina, Tennessee)
345 Courtland Street NE
Atlanta, GA 30365 (404) 347-3004

EPA Region 5:
(Illinois, Indiana, Michigan, Minnesota, Ohio, Wisconsin)
230 South Dearborn Street
Chicago, IL 60604 (312) 353-2072

EPA Region 6:
(Arkansas, Louisiana, New Mexico, Oklahoma, Texas)
1445 Ross Avenue
Dallas, TX 75202-2733 (214) 655-2200

EPA Region 7:
(Iowa, Kansas, Missouri, Nebraska)
726 Minnesota Avenue
Kansas City, KS 66101 (913) 551-7003

EPA Region 8:
(Colorado, Montana, North Dakota, South Dakota, Utah, Wyoming)
One Denver Place
999 18th Street
Denver, CO 80202-2405 (303) 293-1692

EPA Region 9:
(Arizona, California, Hawaii, Nevada, American Samoa, Guam, Trust Territories of the Pacific)
75 Hawthorne Street
San Francisco, CA 94105 (415) 744-1020

EPA Region 10:
(Alaska, Idaho, Oregon, Washington)
1200 Sixth Avenue (800) 424-4EPA
Seattle, WA 98101 (206) 744-1020

Young people in all fifty states are invited to participate in the President's Environmental Youth Awards program, which offers them, individually and collectively, an opportunity to become an environmental force within their community. The program encourages individuals, school classes, schools, summer camps, public interest groups, and youth organizations to promote local environmental awareness and to channel this awareness into positive community involvement. To be eligible, a young person, or group of young persons, must have completed an environmental project while in grades kindergarten through twelve, and the project must be sponsored by at least one adult representative of their school, camp, youth group, or public interest group. For additional information on this awards program, contact your regional office (see listings above).

Office of Public Affairs
U.S. Environmental Protection Agency
77 West Jackson Blvd., PI-19S
Chicago, IL 60604 (312) 886-7935

Children of all ages will enjoy coloring *The Happy Earth Day Coloring and Activities Book* while learning how to take care of the earth. For a free copy, contact the office above.

Resource Center
Public Education and Risk Communication Division
Environmental and Occupational Health Sciences Institute
45 Knightsbridge Road
Piscataway, NJ 08854 (908) 932-0110

"Healthy Environment - Healthy Me" is a interdisciplinary, supplementary environmental and occupational health curriculum. As an "environmental health promotion" curriculum, it is designed to provide young people with the knowledge and understanding for creating a safe and healthful environment at home, in their future workplaces and in their communities. The primary audience is schoolchildren in kindergarten through sixth grade. Lesson plans and videos are available.

Videos

(VHS 1/2" $85 each, 3/4" $99 each, previews $25 - previews are available for 2 weeks, the fee may be applied to the purchase price).

Alexandria's Clean-Up Fix-Up Parade (15 min., grades K-2)
Alexandria decides to get the community involved in a litter pick-up campaign after seeing the harm that litter caused a swan family in the park.

Alu-Man the Can (15 min., grades K-3)
This video teaches children about recycling through the adventures of Alu-Man the Can, Nettie Newspaper, Benjamin J. Bottle III, and Mr. "G" the garbage can.

Safety Sense (14 min., grades K-3)
Jason and Alice are safety detectives as they explore the possible health hazards of using and storing hazardous products incorrectly.

Sam's Safety Star Award (15 min., grades 1-3)
Sam, the TV camera, learns that risks are part of everyday activities like crossing the road, driving a bicycle, swimming and riding in a car. He learns to look and think before he acts.

Down the Drain (22 min., grades 3-5)
As Chris begins to pour some Polish-All down the drain, the sink comes alive. The animated sink explains why certain products can pollute the water supply. Chris learns the proper way to dispose of hazardous waste.

Keeping the Lid on Air Pollution (20 min., grades 4-6)
Terry has a homework assignment to write about two pollution controls. He ends up inside the school library computer and learns about different types of air pollutants (focusing on ozone) and air pollution controls.

The Inside Story on Air Pollution (19 min., grades 4-6)
Danny, Terry's friend, and his sister go into the computer to investigate the

Be patient. If any phone number is incorrect, call (area code) 555-1212 and request the new listing.

The Government Works for Kids, Too

sources and health effects of indoor air pollution in the home. They also learn how to reduce and prevent indoor air pollution problems.

What to Do With All Our Garbage? (20 min., grades 4-6)
Kate, Jenny, and Greg explore the garbage crisis and possible solutions. Source reduction, recycling, sanitary landfills and incineration are discussed. The focus is on what consumers can do to reduce the amount of garbage we generate.

Lessons
($29 each)

My Environment and Me (Kindergarten)
Children learn why clean water, air and soil are important for people to stay healthy. They also learn about taking responsibility for keeping the environment clean by doing an "environmental clean-up."

Recycling: A Community Pollution Solution (First Grade)
Children explore the health consequences of living in a polluted environment and specifically the problems of garbage disposal and solid waste management. Children learn about recycling aluminum, glass and newspaper - one positive community solution to the garbage problem.

Using My Safety Sense (Second Grade)
Children learn to identify and safely handle hazardous household products by recognizing warning words on labels, demonstrating proper storage of products, and practicing handling emergencies with confidence.

Creating a Safer Environment (Third Grade)
As "Safety Detectives" children search out safe situations and hazardous situations in their school and at home. Using problem solving skills they identify a safety problem involving a threat to their health, suggest positive solutions, carry out one solution, and analyze the results. They also learn to discriminate between risks caused by individual behavior and risks caused by the actions or non-actions of those responsible for maintaining a safe environment.

Exploring Water Pollution Issues (Fourth grade)
Students discuss water pollution and the steps individuals and groups can take to protect water quality. The hydrologic cycle, water conservation, waste-water treatment and correct disposal methods of hazardous household wastes are covered. Children research water pollution issues and develop a newspaper to communicate the information they have learned.

Exploring Air Pollution Issues (Fifth Grade)
Students learn about major sources of air pollutants (including indoor air pollution) and their major health impacts. The concepts of occupational safety and health are introduced. They also learn about methods for reducing air pollution and about the role of government agencies and regulations in protecting worker and community health.

Garbage, Garbage, Garbage (Sixth Grade)
Students examine technical topics in solid waste management, specifically: source reduction, recycling, sanitary landfills, incineration, hazardous waste, and household hazardous waste.

Water Watch
Division of Water
Department for Environmental Protection
Frankfort Office Park
18 Reilly Road
Frankfort, KY 40601 (502) 564-3410
Contact the office above to obtain a copy of *A Field Guide to Kentucky Lakes and Wetlands*. This booklet offers an illustrated guide and discussion for field observation along and within Kentucky's lakes and wetlands. It can be used by educators and upper elementary schoolchildren.

Water Watch
Division of Water
Department for Environmental Protection
Frankfort Office Park
18 Reilly Road
Frankfort, KY 40601 (502) 564-3410
A Field Guide to Kentucky Rivers and Streams was developed for Water Watch, a public participation program that encourages citizens to adopt a stream, lake or wetland, and then gain hands on experience in protecting and enhancing their adopted water resource. To learn about Kentucky's rivers and streams, contact the office above.

Water Watch
Division of Water
Department for Environmental Protection
Frankfort Office Park
18 Reilly Road
Frankfort, KY 40601 (502) 564-3410
For information on wild rivers in Kentucky, contact the office above to obtain the brochure, *Kentucky Wild Rivers*. Learn about the Kentucky wild river system and the uses of the rivers.

Office of Environmental Education
Pennsylvania Department of Education
333 Market St.
Harrisburg, PA 17126 (717) 783-6994
Land and Soil is a publication comprised of several activities for schoolchildren, and is designed to promote environmental awareness.

Office of Environmental Education
Pennsylvania Department of Education
333 Market St.
Harrisburg, PA 17126 (717) 783-6994
Paul E. Beals' publication *The Newspaper: A Tool for Teaching Environmental Awareness* is an activity book for children in grades K-12. It covers such topics as acid rain, forest preservation, waste disposal, and recycling. This activity book contains newspaper articles and uses them to teach about environmental awareness.

Forest Service
U.S. Department of Agriculture
14th and Independence, SW
P.O. Box 96090
Washington, DC 20090-6090 (202) 205-0957
Suggestions for Incorporating Forestry into the School Curriculum (FS-62) is a brochure intended to provide a variety of suggestions for incorporating the study of forestry and other environmental topics within existing school curricula. By incorporating environmental studies into existing programs, the teacher is able not only to add a new dimension to the material but also to further the understanding of the environment as an integral part of all other studies.

Forest Service
U.S. Department of Agriculture
14th and Independence, SW
P.O. Box 96090
Washington, DC 20090-6090 (202) 205-0957
The publication *Why Leaves Change Color* (FS-12) can be used by adults and upper elementary schoolchildren to learn why leaves change their color. It also contains instructions on how to copy leaves with crayons and how to make leaf prints with a stamp pad.

Bureau of Mines
U.S. Department of the Interior
Cochrans Mill Road
P.O. Box 18070
Pittsburgh, PA 15236 (412) 892-4338
Contact the office above to receive a copy of the coloring book *Take Pride in America with Mark Trail*. Children will enjoy coloring in the pictures while learning the importance of keeping the environment clean.

Public Information Center
U.S. Environmental Protection Agency
401 M Street, SW, PM-211B
Washington, DC 20460 (202) 260-2080
Learn about the pollutants ozone and carbon monoxide in the *Environmental Backgrounder: Ozone and Carbon Monoxide*. This six-page publication provides important information on these two major public health concerns and can be used by educators to supplement science curricula.

Office of Environmental Education
Pennsylvania Department of Education
333 Market St.
Harrisburg, PA 17126 (717) 783-6994
Available from the office above is *The Friendly Forest Fun Book*, an activity book designed to help elementary teachers enhance students' awareness and knowledge about Pennsylvania's forest lands, the resources the forest provides to both wildlife and the consumer, and the enjoyment that can be obtained from the proper use of our forests.

Be patient. If any phone number is incorrect, call (area code) 555-1212 and request the new listing.

The Government Works For Kids, Too

Office of Environmental Education
Pennsylvania Department of Education
333 Market St.
Harrisburg, PA 17126 (717) 783-6994

I'm a Blue Ribbon Recycler! is an activity book that teaches children in grades K-6 about the various aspects of recycling. This includes teaching about trash, environmental shopping, and composting. The activity book concludes by awarding the user a blue ribbon. Its fun activities, which include coloring and connecting-the-dots, encourage children to learn about recycling in a creative manner.

Forest Service
U.S. Department of Agriculture
14th and Independence, SW
P.O. Box 96090
Washington, DC 20090-6090 (202) 205-0957

To learn more about recycling and the Forest Service's involvement in it, contact the office above for a copy of *Expanding Recycling Horizons*.

Public Information Center
U.S. Environmental Protection Agency
401 M Street, SW, PM-211B
Washington, DC 20460 (202) 260-2080
or
Resource Conservation and Recovery Act
Hotline (800) 424-9346

The following materials are available from either office above.

Recycle Today! Educational Materials for Grades K-12 (EPA/530-SW-90-025). Presents the goals and objectives of EPA's School Recycling Program, and describes this handbook as well as the following materials.

Let's Reduce and Recycle: Curriculum for Solid Waste Awareness (EPA/530-SW-90-005). Presents lessons and activities to teach students in grades K-12 about solid waste generation and management. Each unit presents a series of related lessons with vocabulary words, discussion questions, and projects. Practical teaching aids, such as handouts, worksheets, clip art, and a short skit are also included, along with a bibliography of additional sources of information.

Adventures of the Garbage Gremlin: Recycle and Combat a Life of Grime (EPA/530-SW-90-024). Introduces students in grades 4-7 to the benefits of book approach. Students are lead on an adventure in which their peers foil the "Garbage Gremlin" and learn about recycling.

Ride the Wave of the Future: Recycle Today! (EPA/530-SW-90-010). Promotes recycling through a colorful poster designed to appeal to all grade levels. Can be displayed in conjunction with recycling activities or used to help foster recycling.

School Recycling Programs: A Handbook for Educators (EPA/530-SW-90-023). Describes a number of school recycling program options, along with step-by-step instructions on how to set one up. It focuses on implementing actual recycling projects as a way of teaching the importance and benefits of recycling.

Conservation and Renewable Energy
Inquiry and Referral Service (CAREIRS)
P.O. Box 8900
Silver Spring, MD 20907 (800) 523-2929

Available from this office is *Recycling: What You Can Do*. This two page publication discusses the reasons to recycle and what materials can be recycled.

Office of Environmental Education
Pennsylvania Department of Education
333 Market St.
Harrisburg, PA 17126 (717) 783-6994

Regeneration: You and Your Environment contains activities for kids in grades K-12. A poster is included with the activity book.

Public Information Center
U.S. Environmental Protection Agency
401 M Street, SW, PM-211B
Washington, DC 20460 (202) 260-2080

The poster *Beneficial Use of Sewer Sludge: Land Application* discusses the various uses of sewer sludge. It shows how sewer sludge is a valuable resource that can be used to improve plant growth and soil quality.

Soil Conservation Service
U.S. Department of Agriculture

P.O. Box 2890
Washington, DC 20013 (202) 720-5157

Publications are available from the office above to help teach elementary school children about soil conservation. One educational publication includes the program aid, *Teaching Soil and Water Conservation: A Classroom and Field Guide*.

Forest Service
U.S. Department of Agriculture
14th and Independence, SW
P.O. Box 96090
Washington, DC 20090-6090 (202) 205-0957

Trees offer many benefits to the environment and play a vital role in reducing water and wind erosion, keeping rivers and streams clean, and counteracting the greenhouse effect. To learn more about trees and how they help the environment, contact the office above to receive a copy of *Trees are the Answer....to America's Growing Environmental Concerns*. Also available is *What We Get From Trees* which lists the various products, ranging from chewing gum to mop handles, which come from trees.

Forest Service
U.S. Department of Agriculture
14th and Independence, SW
P.O. Box 96090
Washington, DC 20090-6090 (202) 205-0957

The poster *How a Tree Grows* (FS-8) teaches about photosynthesis, enzymes, and the various parts of a tree. Its colorful illustrations make it a useful teaching aid. The eight-page publication *How a Tree Grows* supplements the poster and provides more information on how a tree grows.

Texas Water Development Board
Office of Public Information
P.O. Box 13231
Austin, TX 78711-3231 (512) 463-8028

Land Use and the Water Cycle is a black and white poster which illustrates the water cycle and different uses of land. It can be used by educators as a teaching aid or by students as a component to a report.

Texas Water Development Board
Office of Public Information
P.O. Box 13231
Austin, TX 78711-3231 (512) 463-8028

The Texas Water Education Network Directory is a collection of water education materials suitable for use in public schools.

Texas Water Development Board
Office of Public Information
P.O. Box 13231
Austin, TX 78711-3231 (512) 463-8028

Water Education Teams, or WETs, are groups of young people who work together to understand and preserve the water resources in their local environment. The WET Project in intended as a supplemental or extracurricular activity for schoolchildren, or a special project for youth organizations. WETs select and survey a local surface water body, which may be a creek, lake, stream, reservoir or river. Then, through water testing, local observation and problem solving, WETs work to identify existing or potential sources of pollution. The students conclude by preparing community awareness projects to share what they have learned. Contact the office above to receive a copy of the *WET Project Instruction Handbook* which contains WET student activities, teacher resources and references, and sections on the basics of water quality. There also is a section of indoor/outdoor activities for areas without access to a body of water.

Texas Water Development Board
Office of Public Information
P.O. Box 13231
Austin, TX 78711-3231 (512) 463-8028

Invasion of the Water Hogs is a four page publication on water conservation written for children and describes the various ways in which water conservation can be achieved.

Public Information Center (PM-211B)
U.S. Environmental Protection Agency
401 M Street, SW, PM-211B
Washington, DC 20460

America's Wetlands: Our Vital Link Between Land and Water provides information on the types of wetlands, wetland values, status and trends of wetlands, and wetlands protection. Both educators and students can benefit from the information provided.

Be patient. If any phone number is incorrect, call (area code) 555-1212 and request the new listing.

The Government Works for Kids, Too

Forest Service
U.S. Department of Agriculture
14th and Independence, SW
P.O. Box 96090
Washington, DC 20090-6090 (202) 205-0957
Give a hoot! Don't pollute! *Woodsy Owl's 1991-92 Campaign Catalog* is filled with dozens of items children can use (such as bike stickers, bookmarks, name tags, balloons, pens, pencils, lunch bags) that have the Woodsy Owl logo on them. Contact the office above for a catalog or the National Association of State Foresters/Woodsy Owl Campaign at (803) 737-8800.

Public Information Office
California Air Resources Board
P.O. Box 2815
Sacramento, CA 95812 (916) 322-2990
Contact the office above to receive materials aimed to Californians. Single copies available free to non-Californians as well.

Legislation and Public Affairs
California Integrated Waste Management Board
1020 9th Street, Suite 300
Sacramento, CA 95814 (916) 255-2473
Contact the office above for information on the Solid Waste Environmental Education Program (SWEEP). It includes two lesson plans, *The Wizards of Waste* (grades 2-4) and *The Trash Monster* (grades 5-7). Each 10-lesson plan includes a teacher's guide, a filmstrip and cassette tape, pre- and post-lesson tests, picture cards, home information leaflets, and pupil booklets. Also includes self-contained, interdisciplinary units designed to teach students resource conservation skills they can apply in their daily lives. Free list including price information is available upon request.

Public Information
Florida Department of Environmental Regulation
2600 Blair Stone Road
Tallahassee, FL 32399-2400 (904) 488-9334
Call the office above for information on receiving *Your Environment (Grades 3-8)*, a 21-page booklet about Florida's environment for students. It includes puzzles, games, how you can help the environment, and contacts for further information.

Division of Natural Heritage
Illinois Department of Conservation
Lincoln Town Plaza
524 South Second Street
Springfield, IL 62706 (217) 785-8774
This office makes available to Illinois teachers the curriculum guide *Nature Discovery 2 - Wild Mammals of Illinois* (grades K-8).

Environmental Education Consultant
Iowa State Department of Education
Grimes State Office Building
Des Moines, Iowa 50319 (515) 281-3146
Available is a bibliography of books relating to children's literature that presents a listing of selected publications and describes a learning cycle approach to using literature. The story makes students aware of an environmental concept and provides an application phase, whereby students can apply their knowledge through hands on experiences. Also available is the *Iowa Developed Energy Activity Sampler K-12 (IDEAS)*, a 1989 edition of energy education materials. The packets (K-2 and3-5 and 6-12) offer multidisciplinary teaching and learning possibilities. Each activity is presented within a learning cycle consisting of a framework of an awareness stage, conceptual development stage and application stage. Materials are provided free to Iowa educators. Educators outside Iowa can request more information including cost from the address above.

Department for Environmental Protection
Kentucky Natural Resources and
Environmental Protection Cabinet
Frankfort Office Park
18 Reilly Road
Frankfort, KY 40601 (502) 564-3410
Free pamphlets available include *Kentucky Wild Rivers* and *10 Ways You Can Help Keep Kentucky Water Resources Clean*. *A Field Guide to Kentucky Rivers and Streams* and *A Field Guide to Kentucky Lakes and Wetlands* are available to teachers. Also available is information on the *Water Watch Program*, a program conducted by the Division of Water with services designed to encourage and support citizen participation in the wise management of community water resources, including streams, lakes, wetlands and groundwater. Any individual,

group, family, organization, school or business can become an official "Kentucky Water Watcher".

Donna Spreitzer
California Local Government Commission
909 12th St., #205
Sacramento, CA 95814 (916) 448-1198
Available from this office is *Toxic is My Home? You Bet!*, for grades K-3, 4-6, 7-8, and 9-12 (available in Spanish only). Developed by Golden Empire Health Planning Center as a one-week course of instruction, this school curriculum identifies: toxics in the home environment; methods for reducing exposure to household toxics; unsafe circumstances involving toxic products; and safer alternatives to using such products. Step by step teaching instructions, masters for worksheets, teacher answer guides, and evaluation methods are all included.

Director
Bureau of Environmental Education
New York State Department of Environmental Conservation
50 Wolf Road, Room 504
Albany, NY 12233-4500
Pamphlets describing various materials are available to New York State teachers.

David Landis
Division of Litter and Prevention Recycling
Ohio Department of Natural Resources
Fountain Square, Bldg. F-2
Columbus, OH 43224 (614) 265-6444
Available from the office above is *Super Saver Investigators* (grades K-8), an interdisciplinary environmental studies activity guidebook about solid waste, recycling, and natural resources. It contains over 65 hands-on learning experiences related to science and social studies lessons normally taught by elementary teachers. Includes skill-building handouts in language arts, math, reading comprehension, creative writing, art and design. Illustrations enhance student interest. Test is secured in a 3-ring binder. For cost and ordering information write to above addressee.

Amy Pearlmutter
San Francisco Recycling Program
City Hall, Room 271
San Francisco, CA 94102 (415) 554-6194
Available from this office is *Fourth R* (grades K-5), a curriculum on recycling, reuse, and waste reduction. Send $10 payable to City and County of San Francisco. Resource fact sheets and general recycling information are available free upon request.

Renee Carlson
Office of Public Information
Texas Water Development Board
P.O. Box 13231
Capitol Station
Austin, TX 78711-3231 (512) 463-8028
The W.E.T. (Water Education Team) Program (grades 4-6) is intended to supplement the regular elementary curriculum or for use as a special project by youth organizations. However, many of the activities are appropriate for K-12 classes. Water Education Teams work together to understand and preserve the water resources in their local environment. Through water quality activities, student teams study pollution problems, understand the importance of water and realize the need to preserve water supplies. Adopt-a-Creek activities enable students to survey a local body of water, test its waters and help resolve its problems. Indoor/outdoor activities provide hands on experiments for students in areas where no surface water is available.

Donna Darling
Director
Office of Public Information
Texas Water Development Board
P.O. Box 13231
Austin, TX 78711-3321 (512) 463-8422
The annual publication, *Texas Water Education Network Directory*, lists water and environmental education programs and/or materials suitable for use in public schools. A contact is provided for each resource listed. The materials listed include classroom curriculum, comic books, pamphlets, dramas, speakers bureaus, workshops, seminars, and field trip opportunities.

University of California Extension Media Center
2176 Shattuck Ave.
Berkeley, CA 94704 (415) 642-0460

Be patient. If any phone number is incorrect, call (area code) 555-1212 and request the new listing.

The Government Works For Kids, Too

A free catalog listing environmental films and videos for young people is available upon request.

Jan Lingenfelter
Washington State Department of Ecology
4350 150th Ave., NE
Redmond, WA 98052-5301 (206) 867-7043

Available from the office above is *A-Way With Waste*, 3rd Edition, 1990 (grades K-12), a waste management and recycling curriculum and school program. The goal of the program is to reduce waste and increase recycling at home, at school and in the community. It includes a 602 page interdisciplinary guide of 117 activities. Three sections cover concepts in Solid Waste Management, Hazardous Waste, and Waste and Water. Articles, research reports, glossary, bibliography, fact sheets and resources are also included. This book is free to Washington State teachers who take a workshop. Write or call for prices to purchase curriculum.

U.S. Environmental Protection Agency
Public Information Center (PM-211B)
401 M St., SW
Washington, DC 20460

All materials listed below are free. Note: materials listed are available as of Winter 1991. Selection of materials changes periodically.

I Need the Earth and the Earth Needs Me (grade 4). A curriculum for fourth graders. Package includes a videocassette and companion teacher's guide. General Motors provided the packages to all fourth grade teachers in spring 1990. Suggest checking school's library before requesting a package. Request must be on school letterhead.

Earth Trek...Explore Your Environment (grades 3,4,5). Illustrated booklet describes measures to protect water, air, and land, safe uses of toxic substances and pesticides, and federal environmental laws. Booklet's layout allows its contents, including student activities, to be duplicated.

Books for Young People on Environmental Issues (grades K-12). A selected bibliography of published books on environmental issues, which are generally available at local public libraries.

President's Environmental Youth Awards (grades K-12). Information on carrying out environmental projects that may earn regional and national awards for students. Brochure includes application.

Educators Earth Day Sourcebook (grades K-6 and 7-12). Booklets on how to incorporate Earth Day into the classroom every day.

Don't Bug Me (grades K-3). A pamphlet illustrating the safe use of pesticides. Includes pictures and captions.

Acid Rain: A Student's First Source Book (Teachers and students grades 4-8). Content explains what acid rain is, its impact on people, on natural and man-made materials, and resources. Tell what can and is being done to combat it. Book suggests classroom and individual activities and describes experiments students can perform. Glossary and bibliography complete the content.

Once There Lived a Wicked Dragon (grades K-4). A story/coloring book about the need to protect the environment, and what the world would be like if we didn't.

Limited quantities of the following are available for residents in the six-state Region 5 area (Illinois, Indiana, Michigan, Minnesota, Ohio, Wisconsin).

The Happy Earth Day (grades K-3). Coloring and activities book that informs children on simple ways to preserve and conserve.

Film Brochure. Lists films available to educational and organized group audiences free of charge.

50 Ways to Make Your World a Better Place (grades K-12). Poster lists common sense ideas to help protect and improve your home and community environment.

Welcome to the Wetlands (grades K-12). Coloring poster explains how wetlands help us and what is a threat to wetlands. Included is information on animals, birds, fish and plants that thrive in wetlands.

U.S. EPA Region 5
Office of Public Affairs

77 West Jackson Blvd., PI-195
Chicago, IL 60604 (312) 353-2000

The following materials are available to New York and Pennsylvania residents in addition to Region 5 residents.

The Great Lakes in My World (grades K-8). Environmental Education curriculum that focuses on the Great Lakes.

Great Minds, Great Lakes Curriculum Sampler (grades K-12). This is a companion piece to both *The Great Lakes in My World* and *The Great Lakes Environmental Atlas.*

Information Services
Great Lakes Regional Office
International Joint Commission
P.O. Box 32869
Detroit, MI 48232-2869 (313) 226-2170

More than 600 educators were surveyed to produce the publication *Directory of Great Lakes Education Materials*, a free-for-the-requesting directory that contains information on pamphlets, technical reports, booklets, videotapes, curriculum based and classroom-based materials for classes concentrating on Great Lakes studies.

ESKIMOS

Education Department
Kennedy Center
Washington, DC 20566 (202) 416-8800

Appropriate for grades K-6 is the booklet *An Eskimo Experience: Inuit Arts and Environment.* It serves as an excellent way to introduce the culture of the Eskimo people to school children. The publication includes a bibliography and classroom activities. Cost is $1.

Office of Education
Room 212
Mail Stop 158
National Museum of Natural History
Washington, DC 20560 (202) 357-2747

Indians and Eskimos is one of the several programs and activities held throughout the school year for visiting preschool and elementary school children by the National Museum of Natural History.. With this particular program students (sitting in front of museum exhibits and using Indian children's toys) learn what grandparents of Indian children did in the past, what parents do today, and what Indian children might do when they grow up. Lesson includes Eskimo, Woodland, Plains, Northwest Coast, and Southwest peoples. Teachers are urged to request pre-visit materials that will help them before and during the visit.

Indian Arts and Crafts Board
Mail Stop 4004 (MIB)
U.S. Department of Interior
Washington, DC 20240 (202) 208-3773

Would you like to give your child some crafts made by Eskimos? An easy way to do this is to obtain the publication *Indian, Eskimo, Aleut Owned and Operated Arts and Crafts Businesses: Source Directory.* It serves as an essential resource for students, parents, and teachers who wish to obtain authentic Indian arts and crafts.

ESTUARIES

U.S. Fish and Wildlife Service
U.S. Department of the Interior
4401 N. Fairfax Drive
Mail Stop 130
Arlington, VA 22203 (703) 358-1711

Estuaries: Cradles of Life provides information on estuaries so you can teach your students about them.

Smithsonian Environmental Research Center
P.O. Box 28
Edgewater, MD 21037 (301) 798-4424

Are you planning on taking your students on a field trip to the Chesapeake Bay? Then get the loose-leaf manual *Estuarine Dock Activities Guidebook.* Includes information on crabs, oyster bars, weather and tides. For students in grades 4-6. $9.50.

Be patient. If any phone number is incorrect, call (area code) 555-1212 and request the new listing.

The Government Works for Kids, Too

Motion Picture Service
National Oceanic and Atmospheric Administration
U.S. Department of Commerce
12231 Wilkins Ave.
Rockville, MD 20852 (301) 443-8411

Estuarine Heritage is a 28-minute film which shows the threats to estuarine resources and stresses the importance of estuaries. It is appropriate for elementary-age children and may be obtained without charge by writing to the office above.

FERRETS

U.S. Fish and Wildlife Service
U.S. Department of the Interior
4401 N. Fairfax Drive
Mail Stop 130
Arlington, VA 22203 (703) 358-1711

The U.S. Fish and Wildlife Service's publication *Black-Footed Ferret* will introduce you and your upper-elementary child to this interesting and unusual animal.

FILMS

Education Division, MRC 305
Education Resource Center
National Air and Space Museum
Washington, DC 20560 (202) 786-2109

Use films to teach your schoolchildren about the importance of aeronautics. The Education Resource Center (ERC) of the National Air and Space Museum (NASM) has a large collection of filmstrips available for preview. The Center offers teachers access to educational materials pertaining to aviation, space, and the Museum's collections, and is open to teachers of all levels and disciplines. NASM-produced filmstrips may be obtained from the National Audiovisual Center, 8700 Edgewood Drive, Capitol Heights, MD 20743, (301) 763-1896. For information on other material available from the Center, contact the office above.

Department of Extension Programs
National Gallery of Art
Washington, DC 20565

The National Gallery of Art is continually exploring ways to develop awareness in the visual arts and make its collections accessible to everyone, no matter how far away from the Gallery they may live. Films are now available for loan free of charge to educational institutions, community groups, and to individuals throughout the U.S. Write to the office above for more information on how you may bring the National Gallery of Art to your students.

Motion Picture Service
National Oceanic and Atmospheric Administration
U.S. Department of Commerce
12231 Wilkins Ave.
Rockville, MD 20852 (301) 443-8411

The National Oceanic and Atmospheric Administration makes available films appropriate for elementary-age children. They may be obtained without charge by writing to the office above.

The Biologist and the Boy. 14 minutes. An encounter between a biologist and a boy on the Gulf of Mexico. Discusses conservation and awareness.

Estuarine Heritage. 28 minutes. Shows threats to estuarine resources and stresses the importance of estuaries.

Estuary. 28 minutes. Stresses the value of the estuary and its uses for food resources and recreation.

The Great American Fish Story. 28 minutes. A series of five films (each is 28 minutes long) which tells the story of the American fishing industry. The first film is an overview and the other four each concentrate on one area of the country -- The West, The Northeast, The South, The Lakes and Rivers. Every aspect of the fishing industry is covered from catching to cooking.

Hurricane Decision. 14 minutes. A hurricane awareness and preparedness film. Points out the dangers of storm surge, wind and inland flooding caused by hurricanes.

It's Your Coast. 28 minutes. Discusses coastal zone problems with people from

Florida, Maine, Illinois and Washington. Land development, oil pollution, and beach erosions are discussed. Stresses the importance of the coast.

Watermen of Chesapeake. 28 minutes. A film about the impact of Chesapeake Bay on a large segment of America.

Institute of Agriculture and Natural
Resources Nebraska
Cooperative Extension Service
University of Nebraska - Lincoln
Department of Entomology
210 Plant Industry Bldg.
Lincoln, NE 68583-0816 (402) 472-2125

Environmental films concerning the use of nonchemical control of pests and low uses of pesticides are available from the office above. A pamphlet which describes videotapes and a field scout manual can also be purchased.

University of California Extension Media Center
2176 Shattuck Ave.
Berkeley, CA 94704 (415) 642-0460

Environmental films for young people can also be obtained from the address above. For a free catalog, contact this office.

U.S. EPA Region 5
Office of Public Affairs
77 West Jackson Blvd., PI-19S
Chicago, IL 60604 (312) 353-2000

Available from the U.S. Vironmental Protection Agency (for residents in the six-state Region 5 area -- Illinois, Indiana, Michigan, Minnesota, Ohio, Wisconsin) is the publication *Film Brochure*, which lists films available to educational and organized group audiences free of charge.

Warning and Forecast Branch, W/OM11
National Weather Service
National Oceanic and Atmospheric Administration
SSMCII
1325 East West Highway, Room 14370
Silver Spring, MD 20910

Weather warning and forecast films can be used by educators to teach school children about safety during natural disasters. The following 16 mm films are available:

Minneapolis Tornado of July 1986 (Copyrighted)
Terrible Tuesday
Day of the Killer Tornadoes
Tornado at Pleasant Hill
Tornado: A Spotter's Guide (Copyrighted)
Tornado: On the Spot Training (silent and with soundtrack)
Neosho
The Awesome Power
Flash Flood
Flood
A Lady Named Camille
Hurricane Decision
Hurricane
Survival in the Cold
An Ill Wind
Rising Waters
Watch Along the Watershed
Earthwatch
NOAA, A Global View
Galaxy
Before It Hits Home
Hurricane: Before the Storm
Hurricane Aetna: Date with Disaster
Cities Don't Die
Winter Storm

NASA CORE
Lorain County Joint Vocational School
15181 Route 58 South
Oberlin, OH 44074 (216) 774-1051

Propulsion: Space Shuttle is one film available from NASA's Central Operation of Resources for Educators (CORE). This particular film, appropriate for children in grades 4-12, highlights the NASA Space Transportation System, its functions, and possible uses for the future.

Be patient. If any phone number is incorrect, call (area code) 555-1212 and request the new listing.

The Government Works For Kids, Too

FINE ARTS

California Energy Extension Service
1400 Tenth St., Room 209
Sacramento, CA 95814 (916) 323-4388

Learning about the fine arts should be an essential part of a child's education, as should learning about energy awareness. Classroom activities integrating the two can be found in the publication *100 Ways to Celebrate NEED*. This guide promotes energy awareness and links lessons to not only the fine arts, but also to science, social studies, history, economics, and the language arts. It contains 100 activities for children in grades K-12, along with a glossary and teacher background information.

FIRE PREVENTION

United States Fire Administration
National Academy
Federal Emergency Management Agency
16825 S. Seton Avenue
Emmitsburg, MD 21727 (301) 447-1122

The U.S. Fire Administration has developed a public education program called "Curious Kids Set Fires" to help reduce fire deaths by education and counseling the child setter. Contact the office above to receive a kit, which includes: handouts for the school classroom, lesson plans and poster for teachers, camera-ready print public service announcements, a press release announcing your local program, a sample letter for the local paper, a resource guide with additional materials you may want to get, and descriptions of pre-adolescent fire prevention and counseling programs from other communities.

Attn: Sesame Street Fire Safety
Federal Emergency Management Agency
P.O. Box 70274
Washington, DC 20024

The Sesame Street Fire Safety Project was developed by the Community Education Services division of the Children's Television Workshop (CTW). The first edition of the *Sesame Street Fire Safety Resource Book* is still available in English and Spanish versions. The second edition of the *Sesame Street Fire Safety Book* contains the original Muppet skits and activities that inspired thousands to teach young children fire safety. Each book is accompanied by an audio cassette that contains five songs. Also included is a five page color brochure highlighting the Sesame Street research study on mass media fire education for young children. To order your free copy, write to the office above.

Forest Service
U.S. Department of Agriculture
14th and Independence, SW
P.O. Box 96090
Washington, DC 20090-6090 (202) 205-0957

Contact the office above to receive Smokey Bear fire prevention materials, including *The True Story of Smokey Bear* comic book.

FEMA Warehouse
P.O. Box 70274
Washington, DC 20024 (202) 646-3484

Contact the office above for the following publications:

Arson Resource Directory
Public Fire Education Resource Directory
Public Fire Education Today: Fire Service Programs From Across America
Juvenile Firesetter Handbook: Dealing with Children Ages 7-14
Interviewing and Counseling Juvenile Firesetters: The Child Under Seven Years of Age
Adolescent Firesetter Handbook: Ages 14-18

Bureau of Fire Prevention
Chicago Fire Department
333 North Dearborn St.
Chicago, IL 60610 (312) 744-6691

Contact the office above for information on "Mike, Tom, and Matches", a fire prevention slide presentation on burn prevention and the dangers on match play suitable for children in grades three to six. Cost: $12 (slides with script), $15 (slides, script and tape).

Program Coordinator
Juvenile Firesetters Program
300 N. 4th St.
Columbus, OH 43215 (614) 222-7641

This fire prevention program includes a psychological assessment through interviews based on USFA/FEMA guidelines as well as an extensive fire education program. The coordinator follows up on the firesetter periodically for two years. The Consumer Product Safety Division's "Little Birdie Told Me" is used with younger children. Many National Fire Protection Association programs are used to educate older children. A 13-unit training manual is currently being produced which discusses past programs as well as existing programs, the difference between juvenile firesetting and juvenile arson, arson laws, and fire safety education. The Columbus Fire Department has also formed the Strategic Action for Fire Education Committee (SAFE) in cooperation with the city council. SAFE has developed a preschool fire safety education curriculum based on Sesame Street characters.

Executive Director
Fall River Firefighters' Museum Program
1181 N. Main St.
Box 2888
Fall River, MA 02720 (508) 674-1810

This program is a good example of networking in the community to provide the services necessary for a comprehensive program. By working with state mental health agencies and the court system the Museum is able to offer services such as psychological counseling that the organization couldn't afford to contract with privately. All materials used are original. These include slide presentations, video presentations and flannel board activities. Letters to parents incorporating preschool safety lessons in Cambodian and Portuguese have also been developed. The program works with firesetters of all ages.

Fire Investigator
Juvenile Firesetter Program
Mesa Fire Department
13 W. 1st St.
Mesa, AZ 85201 (602) 644-2622

The Mesa fire prevention program emphasizes working with the family. For example, after the first meeting the family is asked to plan a home drill together. Children who graduate from the program are named "Junior Fire Marshals representing Mesa" and are given fire marshal badges to underscore the importance of fire safe behavior. Educational materials used include pamphlets on E.D.I.T.H. (Exit Drills in the Home), and a slide show developed by the Mesa Fire Department. They have developed a slide show on responsible and irresponsible uses of fire; one directed to juvenile boys, and one directed to juvenile girls.

Fire Commissioner
Juvenile Firesetters Intervention Program
Bureau of Investigation
250 Livingston Street
Brooklyn, NY 11201 (718) 403-1508

The fire investigators in this program have police powers to ensure that children and their families attend education and/or counseling sessions. The program provides a good example of networking as well as data collection and storage. E.D.I.T.H. pamphlets are used as well as "Stop, Drop, and Roll" educational materials. Materials include: a picture book illustrating safe/unsafe uses of fire; a comprehensive annual report; a school survey which indicates that many more children play with fires than most people suspect; and some literature developed in Spanish.

Juvenile Firesetter Program Coordinator
55 Southwest Ash
Portland, OR 97204 (503) 823-3806

In this program the entire family is involved in counseling and fire safety education. Educational techniques used include the following film/TV spots: "Donald Duck's Fire Survival Plan" (Walt Disney Educational Media Company), "Matches" (Coronet MTI Film and Video), and "Smush the Fire Out" (Coronet MTI Film and Video). Literature produced includes "Beyond Burned Fingers" - a one-half hour video on firesetting and Portland's program, TV PSA on their Juvenile Firesetter program which urges parents to call in with questions, and the Oregon Juvenile Firesetter Resource Directory - a statewide resource manual.

Fire Related Youth (FRY) Coordinator
150 Plymouth Avenue South
Public Safety Building, Room 300
Rochester, NY 14614 (716) 428-7036

This fire prevention program is a very well known program in which the fire investigators have police powers to ensure participation. FRY also works closely with the University of Rochester which offers a variety of excellent resources including psychological counseling and data analysis. Materials include: a study revealing that play is extremely widespread among school-age children; a

Be patient. If any phone number is incorrect, call (area code) 555-1212 and request the new listing.

The Government Works for Kids, Too

curriculum for primary schools which incorporates fire safety education into general education; and two annual reports which include valuable information on the setting problem and setting up and maintaining a program.

Public Educator
Fireplay Intervention Program
110 E. 11th St.
St. Paul, MN 55101 (612) 228-6203

This program teaches curiosity setters about the dangers of fire. Educational materials used include *Matches, Lighters, Crackers are not Toys* by Dorothy Schad (part of the *Safety Town* series) for preschoolers to seven-year olds. For children ages 7 to 10 they offer *If You Could See Me Now* with pictures of burn victims, available from the Tulsa, Oklahoma, Fire Department. They had printed flyers describing the program put into grocery bags. St. Paul is currently developing a pamphlet describing the program. They have also developed a computer program designed to store information on all setters.

Fire Chief
San Francisco Fire Department
260 Golden Gate Ave.
San Francisco, CA 94102 (415) 861-8000

The San Francisco program has evolved over many years. From 1971-1979 it was a counseling program. From 1979-1986 it used the "Firehawks" fighter buddy system which provided adult companions for child firesetters. Since 1987, the USFA/FEMA intervention and education guidelines have been followed. Educational techniques used include the National Fire Protection Association's "Learn Not to Burn" materials. The program's philosophy is positive - scare tactics such as pictures of burn victims are not used.

Juvenile Firesetters Prevention
Task Force
3600 Tremont Road
Upper Arlington, OH 43221 (614) 457-5080

The task force provides a variety of services including: a general public awareness campaign; family interview/screening sessions to determine the cause of firesetting; family intervention sessions to assist families with local mental health referrals when necessary; and maintaining communications with local juvenile justice and protective services. Educational techniques used include Project Burn Prevention education materials. Daniel Strohl's program has developed a puppet show for younger children. For the older child, demonstrations on such topics as flammable vapors have been created. A manual describing Upper Arlington's program and interviewing techniques has also been developed.

FLOODS

Warning and Forecast Branch, W/OM11
National Weather Service
National Oceanic and Atmospheric Administration
SSMCII
1325 East West Highway, Room 14370
Silver Spring, MD 20910

Educators can use the following audiovisuals to teach school children about safety during flash floods.

16 mm Films:
The Awesome Power
Flash Flood
Flood

Videotape:
The Awesome Power

Slides:
Flash Floods: Myths or Realities
Flash Flood Preparedness

FLORIDA

Communications Office
Department of Environmental Protection
3900 Commonwealth Blvd.
Mail Station 30
Tallahassee, FL 32399 (904) 488-9334

Call the office above for information on receiving *Your Environment (Grades 3-8)*, a 21-page booklet about Florida's environment for students. It includes puzzles, games, how you can help the environment, and contacts for further information.

FORESTS

Office of Environmental Education
Pennsylvania Department of Education
333 Market St.
Harrisburg, PA 17126 (717) 783-6994

Available from the office above is *The Friendly Forest Fun Book*, an activity book designed to help elementary teachers enhance students' awareness and knowledge about Pennsylvania's forest lands, the resources the forest provides to both wildlife and the consumer, and the enjoyment that can be obtained from the proper use of our forests.

Forest Service
U.S. Department of Agriculture
14th and Independence, SW
P.O. Box 96090
Washington, DC 20090-6090 (202) 205-0957

Suggestions for Incorporating Forestry into the School Curriculum (FS-62) is a brochure intended to provide a variety of suggestions for incorporating the study of forestry and other environmental topics within existing school curricula. By incorporating environmental studies into existing programs, the teacher is able not only to add a new dimension to the material but also to further the understanding of the environment as an integral part of all other studies.

Office of Education, Room 212
Mail Stop 158
National Museum of Natural History
Washington, DC 20560 (202) 357-2747

Old-Growth Forests: Moist, Massive, and Magnificent is an instructional kit available from the National Museum of Natural History. Slides, videos, teacher's guides to classroom activities and discussions, and a wall poster provide teachers and group leaders with a range of tools for investigating the ecology of old-growth forests, their benefits, and the controversy over our use of them. It is designed for grades 6-8 but easily adapted for younger and older students. Material may be used effectively without a museum visit. Kit may be borrowed for one week. The Museum also offers a visiting program and a teacher workshop on this topic; call the office above to receive more information.

FOXES

U.S. Fish and Wildlife Service
U.S. Department of the Interior
4401 N. Fairfax Drive
Mail Stop 130
Arlington, VA 22203 (703) 358-1711

Reading *Life in a Fox Den* is one way to learn about how foxes live. Use this publication to educate your children about the lives of foxes.

GAS, NATURAL

National Energy Information Center (NEIC)
Energy Information Administration, EI-231
U.S. Department of Energy
1000 Independence Ave., SW, Room 1F-048
Washington, DC 20585 (202) 586-8800

Would you like to learn more about natural gas? Information on natural gas can be obtained from The National Energy Information Center (NEIC) of the U.S. Department of Energy. The NEIC provides one-page information sheets not only on natural gas but also on petroleum, coal, electricity, and renewable energy.

California Energy Extension Service
1400 Tenth St., Room 209
Sacramento, CA 95814 (916) 323-4388

Learn interesting facts on natural gas and other energy conservation-related topics (including recycling) in the publication *Energy Facts for Classroom Teachers*.

Office of Fossil Energy Communications
1000 Independence Ave., SW
Room 4G-085
Washington, DC 20585 (202) 586-6503

Public education-related information on natural gas and other sources of energy are available from the office above. *Dinosaurs and Power Plants*, a 16-page

Be patient. If any phone number is incorrect, call (area code) 555-1212 and request the new listing.

The Government Works For Kids, Too

brochure designed for students that relates the story of mining and drilling for coal, gas, and oil, is available free.

GEMINI MISSIONS

NASA CORE
Lorain County Joint Vocational School
15181 Route 58 South
Oberlin, OH 44074 (216) 774-1051

Gemini Science is a video, appropriate for students in grades 4 and up, in which scientists explain life science experiments developed for the Gemini missions. It includes a brief synopsis of the missions.

GEOGRAPHY

R. Woods, Consumer Information Center
Pueblo, CO 81008

Get your child interested in an important, but often neglected, aspect of education - geography. *Helping Your Child Learn Geography* ($.50, #454X) provides tips to both parents and educators.

U.S. Geological Survey
P.O. Box 25425
Denver, CO 80225

A great way to get your students interested in geography is to teach them how localities got their names. Use the publication *The Naming (and Misnaming) of America* to learn how some localities came to be named, the derivation of these geographic names, and why the U.S. Board on Geographic Names was established.

GEOLOGY

Geologic Inquiries Group
U.S. Geological Survey
907 National Center
Reston, VA 22092 (703) 648-4383

This office answers questions on topics such as earthquakes, energy and mineral resources, the geology of specific areas, and geologic maps and mapping. Educators and students can contact the office if they have any questions relating to the topics above.

Geologic Inquiries Group
U.S. Geological Survey
907 National Center
Reston, VA 22092 (703) 648-4383

The *Selected Packet of Geologic Teaching Aids* is prepared for elementary school teachers (and high school teachers) of general science, geography, social studies, environmental education and other earth science-related subjects. It contains leaflets, booklets, reference lists, and an activity sheet ("Make Your Own Paper Model of a Volcano"). To receive a packet, send a request on school letterhead indicating the subject that is taught and the grade level to the office listed above.

GLACIERS

U.S. Geological Survey
P.O. Box 25425
Denver, CO 80225

Glaciers: A Water Resource discusses the relationship between glacial ice and the amount of water on land surfaces. Describes the types of glaciers, their origins, and the natural processes that regulate the melting of ice. Upper elementary teachers can use it to help teach their students about glaciers.

GOATS

U.S. Fish and Wildlife Service
U.S. Department of the Interior
4401 N. Fairfax Drive
Mail Stop 130
Arlington, VA 22203 (703) 358-1711

Rocky Mountain Goat will introduce your students to this interesting animal.

GOLD

U.S. Geological Survey
P.O. Box 25425
Denver, CO 80225

The U.S. Geological Survey has two publications on gold. *Gold* discusses the nature of gold, its origins, and the geologic environments in which it is commonly found. It also provides information about the uses of gold and a brief historical account of production in the U.S. *Prospecting for Gold in the United States* describes various kinds of gold deposits and their locations. It offers a brief review of the problems faced by present-day prospectors and lists available maps and services. Students can use these publications to supplement special reports and science projects, and teachers can use them to enhance their curricula.

GREAT DEPRESSION

Education Branch (NEEE)
National Archives and Records Administration
Washington, DC 20408 (202) 724-0454

The Great Depression and The New Deal is a teaching unit published by the National Archives and SIRS, Inc. It is designed to help students in upper elemtary and secondary classes of U.S. history, government, and economics to understand the process by which history is written and to develop analytical skills. It contains about 50 reproductions of documents - charts, photographs, letters, drawings, and posters - and a detailed teacher's guide. The materials deal with certain key issues of the period, with governmental and political responses to these issues, and with public attitudes. Cost is $40. To order, send a purchase order to: SIRS, Inc., P.O. Box 2348, Boca Raton, FL 33427-2348, or call toll free, (800) 3327-0513 (except AK and FL call collect 407-994-0079). For more information on this and other teaching units, contact the office above.

GREAT LAKES

U.S. EPA Region 5
Office of Public Affairs
77 West Jackson Blvd, PI-195
Chicago, IL 60604 (312) 353-2000

If you live in Illinois, Indiana, Michigan, Minnesota, Ohio or Wisconsin, you can obtain the publication *The Great Lakes in My World* (grades K-8), an environmental education curriculum that focuses on the Great Lakes. *Great Minds, Great Lakes Curriculum Sampler* (grades K-12), a companion piece to both *The Great Lakes in My World* and *The Great Lakes Environmental Atlas*, is also available to residents from the states noted above, in addition to New York and Pennsylvania.

GROUND WATER

U.S. Geological Survey
P.O. Box 25425
Denver, CO 80225

Do you want your students to do a report on ground water? Have them obtain the following publications for information:

Ground Water: An Undervalued Resource. Describes the need for using ground water, the role of ground water in the economy, and an analysis of regional aquifer systems. Discusses the ways in which ground water and surface water interact.

Ground Water and the Rural Homeowner. Presents a short description of ground water, some of the problems associated with ground water, and some suggestions for help with problems.

Ground Water Contamination--No "Quick Fix" in Sight. Explains how ground water is contaminated by septic tanks or cesspools, municipal lagoons, sewers, landfills, or tailings piles, and the need for further research in contamination prevention.

GUTHRIE, WOODY

Smithsonian/Folkways Recordings
416 Hungerford Dr., Suite 320
Rockville, MD. 20850

Introduce your child to Woody Guthrie's children's songs, available for purchase from Smithsonian/Folkways Recordings. Administered by the Smithsonian Institution's Office of Folklife Programs, Folkways Records is one of the ways the Office supports cultural conservation and continuity, integrity, and equity for traditional artists and cultures. Children's recordings are one of the many categories of recordings available. Children's songs by Pete Seeger and Ella Jenkins can also be purchased, along with dozens of recordings by lesser-known yet still very talented artists.

Be patient. If any phone number is incorrect, call (area code) 555-1212 and request the new listing.

The Government Works for Kids, Too

HALLEY'S COMET

NASA CORE
Lorain County Joint Vocational School
15181 Route 58 South
Oberlin, OH 44074 (216) 774-1051

The Return of Halley's Comet examines an event heralded by man since the beginning of time, Halley's Comet and its place in the Universe. Available as slides for grades 4-12.

Teaching Resource Center
Jet Propulsion Laboratory
4800 Oak Grove Dr.
Mail Stop CS-530
Pasadena, CA 91109 (818) 354-6916

Halley's Comet is a slide set available to teachers for $6. It consists of twenty 35 mm slides held in a plastic vue-file sleeve which will fit into a three ring binder. It can be an excellent educational aid for classroom use.

HANDICAPPED CHILDREN

Council for Exceptional Children
1920 Association Drive
Reston, VA 22091-1589 (703) 620-3660

Education literature on handicapped children is available from the Education Resources Information Center (ERIC), a nationwide information network designed to provide users with ready access to education literature. Information on all aspects of the education and development of disabled and gifted children, including identification, assessment, intervention, and enrichment, both in special settings and within the mainstream, is available.

HEAT, SOLAR

Conservation and Renewable Energy
Inquiry and Referral Service (CAREIRS)
P.O. Box 3048
Merrifield, VA 22116 (800) 523-2929

People are trying to find new ways to heat their homes, factories, offices, and schools without using so much expensive oil and gas. *Solar Energy and You* helps teach children about solar energy and solar heat.

HISTORY AND ENERGY AWARENESS

California Energy Extension Service
1400 Tenth St., Room 209
Sacramento, CA 95814 (916) 323-4388

Energy awareness does not have to be taught only in science classes. *100 Ways to Celebrate NEED* is a guide which promotes energy awareness and links lessons to not only science, but also to social studies, history, economics, fine arts and language arts. This guide contains 100 activities for children in grades K-12, along with a glossary and teacher background information.

HUBBLE SPACE TELESCOPE

NASA CORE
Lorain County Joint Vocational School
15181 Route 58 South
Oberlin, OH 44074 (216) 774-1051

Are you looking for some computer software that can help teach your kids about the Hubble Space Telescope? *Hubble Space Telescope Educational Software Project* includes four Apple II disks with reproducible information sheets and reference materials. *Windows to the Universe* chronicles the history of astronomical observations from the unaided eye through the Hubble Space Telescope. *Telescopes* explains the science of optics and the design and characteristics of telescopes. *Introduction to the Hubble Space Telescope* explains the design and operation of the Hubble Space Telescope. *Images From Space* describes the process through which light is captured by the Hubble space Telescope and converted into images on Earth. *Activities Disk* contains a collection of classroom activities and illustrations relating to telescopes. *Glossary* contains an Appleworks data base of more than 300 astronomy terms. Also includes two Macintosh Applications Software (requires Pagemaker program 3.02 version or higher); *Hubble Space Telescope Model* contains the pattern and instructions for making a detailed model of NASA's Hubble Space Telescope; and *Telescope Primer* which is an outline of the basic principles behind the design and operation of telescopes. Includes many diagrams that can be enlarged and used for making transparencies. For children in grades 5-8.

HURRICANES

Warning and Forecast Branch, W/OM11
National Weather Service
National Oceanic and Atmospheric Administration
SSMCII
1325 East West Highway, Room 14370
Silver Spring, MD 20910

The office above has the following audiovisuals available which can be used by educators to teach school children about safety during natural disasters.

16 mm Films:
A Lady Named Camille
Hurricane Decision
Hurricane

Videotapes:
Hurricane
Before the Hurricane Strikes
Everyday Weather Project: Hurricanes

Slides:
Hurricane Hugo
Hurricane Eloise
Hurricane Preparedness
Hurricane Alicia
Hurricane Frederick

ILLINOIS

Natural Heritage Division
Illinois Department of Conservation
524 S. 2nd St.
Springfield, IL 62706

Nature Discovery II: Wild Mammals of Illinois is a publication for students and teachers and is available to teachers in Illinois. It includes various activities on different mammals and even has a "Guide to Mammal Signs". The publication is written for children in grades 4-8.

INDIA

Office of Education, Room 212
Mail Stop 158
National Museum of Natural History
Washington, DC 20560 (202) 357-2747

The Living Arts of India is an instructional kit available on loan for a three-week period. Based on the Aditi exhibition (1985), this truly comprehensive kit is contained in a large, brass-bound Indian dowry box. Designed for elementary and secondary students, the kit includes a library of books, pamphlets and catalogs, two dozen objects, a 45-minute videotape, four audio tapes, a two-volume teacher's manual plus four supplemental manuals on children's games, theater activities, Indian fairs and festivals, and Mughul art and history.

INDIANS, AMERICAN

Attn: Public Inquiries Office
Bureau of Indian Affairs
Mail Stop 2620 (MIB)
U.S. Department of Interior
Washington, DC 20240 (202) 208-3711

The U.S. Department of Interior's Bureau of Indian Affairs often receives inquiries from students who have questions about American Indians. Publications are available to help answer questions. They serve as a wonderful source of information for students and teachers. The publications available include:

American Indians Today: Answers to Your Questions. This booklet is an attempt to answer briefly the most commonly asked questions, to list some other resources for information about Indians and, finally, to provide a good, up-to-date bibliography to help inquirers do their own research through local library systems.

Famous Indians: A Collection of Short Biographies. From Pocahontas to Sitting Bull, this publication describes the history and lives of twenty famous American Indians. All were leaders in a great struggle to preserve treasured lands and lifeways. With their tribesmen, they are inseparably linked to our country's history from its earliest beginnings through generations of growth.

Be patient. If any phone number is incorrect, call (area code) 555-1212 and request the new listing.

The Government Works For Kids, Too

Indian Land Areas. This map of the United States displays federal Indian reservations, along with state reservations. It serves as an essential teaching aid for schoolchildren who are learning about Indian reservations.

Office of Education, Room 212
Mail Stop 158
National Museum of Natural History
Washington, DC 20560 (202) 357-2747

The National Museum of Natural History has programs and activities held throughout the school year for visiting preschool and elementary school children. Programs on American Indians include:

Indian Walkaround: (For preschool and kindergarten children.) The Indian Walkaround is a teacher-directed walk-through of the Indian and Eskimo halls. Volunteers staff small display stations throughout the exhibit, offer objects to touch, and tell about the people who made them. Students find out about different kinds of Indians and Eskimos, examine authentic Native American artifacts, and participate in hands-on activities.

Indians and Eskimos: (For preschool and kindergarten children.) Sitting in front of museum exhibits and using Indian children's toys, students learn what grandparents of Indian children did in the past, what parents do today, and what Indian children might do when they grow up. Lesson includes Eskimo, Woodland, Plains, Northwest Coast, and Southwest peoples.

Indians and Eskimos: (For grades 1 and up.) Students discover the wide diversity of the indigenous cultures past and present in North America. On the tour they explore the relationships between environment and culture by focusing on the basic human need for food, shelter, clothing, and tools. Students also examine authentic Indian and Eskimo artifacts, both contemporary and old, to complete the learning experience.

JENKINS, ELLA

Smithsonian/Folkways Recordings
416 Hungerford Dr., Suite 320
Rockville, MD. 20850

Administered by the Smithsonian Institution's Office of Folklife Programs, Folkways Records is one of the ways the Office supports cultural conservation and continuity, integrity, and equity for traditional artists and cultures. Ella Jenkins is one of those artists whose recordings are available for purchase. Children's songs by Pete Seeger and Woody Guthrie can also be purchased, along with dozens of recordings by lesser-known yet still very talented artists.

JUPITER

Superintendent of Documents
U.S. Government Printing Office
Washington, DC 20402 (202) 783-3238

Teach your kids about the planet Jupiter with the help of *The Voyager Flights to Jupiter and Saturn,* an illustrated nontechnical guide that describes the Voyager flights from the Jupiter and Saturn flybys. For sale by the Superintendent of Documents, U.S. Government Printing Office. $5.50. Stock No. 033-000-00854-6.

Teaching Resource Center
Jet Propulsion Laboratory
4800 Oak Grove Dr.
Mail Stop CS-530
Pasadena, CA 91109 (818) 354-6916

The Teacher Resource Center of the Jet Propulsion Laboratory makes available educational aids for classroom use, including the slide/cassette program *Jupiter: Voyagers 1 & 2* ($11) and the video *Jupiter, Saturn, Uranus and Neptune* ($25).

KENNEDY CENTER FOR THE PERFORMING ARTS

Office of Elementary and Secondary Education
Arts and Industries Building
Room 1163, MRC-402
Smithsonian Institution
Washington, DC 20560 (202) 357-3049

The John F. Kennedy Center for the Performing Arts is one of several resources which provides educational materials for teachers. The *Resource Guide for Teachers* contains educational materials available from the Kennedy Center, in addition to the National Gallery of Art and the Smithsonian Institution. The materials include bibliographies, posters, slide sets, films teacher's manuals, videocassettes, and curriculum units.

KENNEDY SPACE CENTER

Teaching Resource Center
Jet Propulsion Laboratory
4800 Oak Grove Dr.
Mail Stop CS-530
Pasadena, CA 91109 (818) 354-6916

Kennedy Space Center Tour is a video which will delight curious minds. Cost is $25.

KENNEDY, JOHN F.

Education Branch (NEEE)
National Archives and Records Administration
Washington, DC 20408 (202) 724-0454

Use two documents available from the Education Branch of the National Archives and Records Administration to help teach your students about John F. Kennedy's presidential speeches. *Kennedy's Inaugural Address of 1961* (#200110, ISBN 0-911333- 53-3) and *The Cuban Missile Crisis: Kennedy's Address to the Nation* (#200113, ISBN 0-911333-59-2) are part of a series of booklets which focus on some of the great documents that have shaped the course of U.S. history. Each booklet includes a historical introduction, transcriptions and facsimiles of the featured documents. 8 1/2 x 11, approx. 25 pages each, illustrations, 1986. Softcover only, $2.50 each.

KENTUCKY

Department for Environmental Protection
Frankfort Office Park
14 Reilly Road
Frankfort, KY 40601 (502) 564-3410

Free pamphlets available include *Kentucky Wild Rivers* and *10 Ways You Can Help Keep Kentucky Water Resources Clean. A Field Guide to Kentucky Rivers and Streams* and *A Field Guide to Kentucky Lakes and Wetlands* are available to teachers. Also available is information on the *Water Watch Program,* a program conducted by the Division of Water with services designed to encourage and support citizen participation in the wise management of community water resources, including streams, lakes, wetlands and groundwater. Any individual, group, family, organization, school or business can become an official "Kentucky Water Watcher".

KING, JR.; MARTIN LUTHER

Martin Luther King Jr. Federal Holiday Commission
451 7th St., SW, Suite 5182
Washington, DC 20410

Are you looking for educational materials to help teach your students about Martin Luther King, Jr.? Look no further than the Martin Luther King, Jr., Federal Holiday Commission. Available items include pledge cards, posters, teaching materials, and selected speeches. Use this resource to heighten your students knowledge of Dr. King.

National Clearinghouse for Alcohol and Drug Information
P.O. Box 2345 (800) 729-6686
Rockville, MD 20852 (301) 468-2600

Use the poster *Live the Dream, Say No to Alcohol and Drug Abuse* (1989) to help teach your kids about Martin Luther King, Jr., and the need to say no to alcohol and drugs. Appropriate for all ages, 15 1/2 in. by 22 in. AV165.

LANGUAGE ARTS

California Energy Extension Service
1400 Tenth St., Room 209
Sacramento, CA 95814 (916) 323-4388

Use the language arts to promote energy awareness among school children. *100 Ways to Celebrate NEED* is a guide which promotes energy awareness and links lessons to not only the language arts, but also to social studies, history, economics, and the fine arts. This guide contains 100 activities for children in grades K-12, along with a glossary and teacher background information.

LANGUAGES

Center for Applied Linguistics
118 22nd Street NW
Washington, DC 20037-0037 (202) 429-9551

The Educational Resources Information Center (ERIC) is a nationwide

The Government Works for Kids, Too

information network designed to provide users with ready access to education literature. The ERIC System, managed by the U.S. Department of Education, Office of Educational Research and Improvement, consists of 16 clearinghouses, four adjunct clearinghouses, and four support components. One of those clearinghouses contains information on languages and language sciences. It includes information on all aspects of second language instruction and learning in all commonly and uncommonly taught languages, including English as a second language; bilingualism and bilingual education; cultural education in the context of second language learning; intercultural communication; study abroad and international education exchange; all areas of linguistics, including theoretical and applied linguistics, sociolinguistics, and psycholinguistics.

LEAVES

Forest Service, U.S. Department of Agriculture
14th and Independence, SW
P.O. Box 96090
Washington, DC 20090-6090 (202) 205-0957

The publication *Why Leaves Change Color* (#FS-12) can be used by adults and upper elementary schoolchildren to learn about this natural process. It also contains instructions on how to copy leaves with crayons and how to make leaf prints with a stamp pad.

LITTLE LEAGUE

National Clearinghouse for Alcohol and Drug Information
P.O. Box 2345 (800) 729-6686
Rockville, MD 20852 (301) 468-2600

The video *Little League Drug Education Program* (1991) combines a child's interest in Little League with a parent's desire to teach him how to say no to drugs and alcohol. This video has two parts: Part 1, "Friend to Friend", featuring Orel Hershiser, is directed toward today's Little Leaguer. The film tells the story of a Little League player who is tempted by drugs. Part 2, "Big League Advice: Helping Your Little Leaguers Say No", is for parents and coaches of Little League players. The film depicts a discussion among Little League parents and baseball Hall-of Famers 'Hank' Aaron and Jim Palmer. These great ball players offer frank and important advice to parents on how to talk to young people about drugs and alcohol. 30 minutes. VHS29.

LOUISIANA PURCHASE

Education Branch (NEEE)
National Archives and Records Administration
Washington, DC 20408 (202) 724-0454

The Louisiana Purchase (ISBN 0-911333-54-1) is part of the Milestone Document series available from the National Archives and Records Administration. This ongoing series of booklets focuses on some of the great documents that have shaped the course of U.S. history. The booklet includes a historical introduction and transcriptions and facsimiles of the featured documents. 8 1/2 x 11, approx. 25 pages, illustrations, 1986. Softcover only, $2.50 each.

MAMMALS

Marine Mammal Commission
1825 Connecticut Ave., NW, #512
Washington, DC 20009 (202) 606-5504

Children of all ages (and even adults!) will enjoy learning how to draw whales, seals and dolphins. *How to Draw Whales and Seals* shows you how to draw these mammals in four or five easy steps.

Division of Natural Heritage
Lincoln Town Plaza
524 South Second Street
Springfield, IL 62701 (217) 785-8774

This office makes available to Illinois teachers the curriculum guide *Nature Discovery 2 - Wild Mammals of Illinois* (grades K-8).

MAPS

Geologic Inquiries Group
U.S. Geological Survey
907 National Center
Reston, VA 22092 (703) 648-4383

The geology of specific areas can be taught through the use of maps. The Geologic Inquiries Group has various kinds of geologic maps available for you to purchase.

MARS

Teaching Resource Center
Jet Propulsion Laboratory
4800 Oak Grove Dr.
Mail Stop CS-530
Pasadena, CA 91109 (818) 354-6916

The Teaching Resource Center of the Jet Propulsion Laboratory has selected video programs and color slide packages on space and planetary subjects available, including a few about the planet Mars. They are the 40 color slides/cassette program *Viking Lands on Mars* ($11), the 20-slide set program *Vikings Missions to Mars* ($6), and the video *Mars and Mercury* ($25).

NASA CORE
Lorain County Joint Vocational School
15181 Route 58 South
Oberlin, OH 44074 (216) 774-1051

Mars, The Next Step is a video that depicts a mission to Mars involving three vehicles launched from Earth, six months of interplanetary travel, and the establishment of a base on the martian soil. For students in grades 4-8.

MARTIN, AUGUST

Education Office
Federal Aviation Administration
U.S. Department of Transportation
400 7th Street, SW
Washington, DC 20590 (202) 366-7500

The *August Martin Activities Book* is a great tool to help teach your child about the world's first black airline pilot.

MATH

California Energy Extension Service
1400 Tenth St., Room 209
Sacramento, CA 95814 (916) 323-4388

Energy Math is a set of materials which will assist in integrating the primary math and physical science curricula with respect to the energy theme. Teacher-led activities, learning center activities, and self-correcting worksheets for individual completion are all included.

The Ohio State University
1200 Chanbers Road, Room 310
Columbus, OH 43212-1792 (614) 292-6717

Science, Mathematics, and Environmental Education (SE) is one of the many clearinghouses that are a part of the Educational Resources Information Center (ERIC), a nationwide information network designed to provide users with ready access to education literature. This particular clearinghouse provides information on science, mathematics, and environmental education at all levels, and within these three broad subject areas, the following topics; development of curriculum and instructional materials; teachers and teacher education; learning theory/outcomes (including the impact of parameters such as interest level, intelligence, values, and concept development upon learning in these fields); educational programs; engineering; research and evaluative studies; medical applications; and computer applications.

R. Woods
Consumer Information Center
Pueblo, CO 81008

Help Your Child Learn Math ($0.50, #452X) is one of the many publications for parents available from the Consumer Information Center. Make check or money order payable for Superintendent of Documents. For a copy, send your check or money order to the address above.

MEDICAL RESEARCH

Office of Public Affairs
National Institute of Mental Health
U.S. Department of Health and Human Services
5600 Fishers Lane, Room 7C02
Rockville, MD 20857 (301) 443-8956

By learning how scientists perform medical research in laboratories, children can better understand how and why doctors are able to help people to get well. *Let's Visit a Research Laboratory: Introduction and Lesson Plans* (for schoolchildren in grades 2-5) helps answer the many questions children may have about research laboratories. The supplemental poster that is included provides teachers with helpful illustrations for classroom discussion and activities.

Be patient. If any phone number is incorrect, call (area code) 555-1212 and request the new listing.

The Government Works For Kids, Too

MERCURY FLIGHTS

NASA CORE
Lorain County Joint Vocational School
15181 Route 58 South
Oberlin, OH 44074 (216) 774-1051

Project Mercury: An Early Step is a video appropriate for students in grades four and up that summarizes the project Mercury flights of the 60's. It shows the designing and building of the spacecraft, the training of the seven original astronauts, the MR-2 launch with the chimp HAM, and highlights of Alan Shepard's first flight, as well as the flights of other Mercury astronauts.

Teaching Resource Center
Jet Propulsion Laboratory
4800 Oak Grove Dr.
Mail Stop CS-530
Pasadena, CA 91109 (818) 354-6916

Mercury and Gemini Spacecraft Missions is a video available from the Teaching Resource Center at the Jet Propulsion Laboratory. It serves as an excellent educational aid for classroom use. Cost is $25.

MERCURY (PLANET)

Teaching Resource Center
Jet Propulsion Laboratory
4800 Oak Grove Dr.
Mail Stop CS-530
Pasadena, CA 91109 (818) 354-6916

Show your students the video *Mars and Mercury* and watch their interest grow as they learn about these planets. Cost is $25.

METRIC SYSTEM

Superintendent of Documents
U.S. Government Printing Office
Washington, DC 20402 (202) 783-3238

The National Institute of Standards and Technology (formerly the National Bureau of Standards) of the U.S. Department of Commerce has produced a 29"x45" poster called *The Modernized Metric System.* Available from the Superintendent of Documents (special publication 304), it is an excellent visual tool educators can use to teach their students about the metric system.

MIGRATION

Division of Education, RoomB1026
National Museum of American History
Smithsonian Institution
Washington, DC 20560 (202) 357-4187

Appropriate for upper elementary through twelfth grade students is the educational outreach kit, *Field to Factory: Afro-American Migration, 1915-1940.* It includes a teacher's manual, slides, and poster, in addition to other educational tools.

MINERALS

Bureau of Mines
U.S. Department of the Interior
Cochrans Mill Road
P.O. Box 18070
Pittsburgh, PA 15236 (412) 892-4338

Minerals in 1991 contains information on 34 minerals identified as highly important to the economy or defense of the United States. Students in the upper elementary grades can use this brochure to learn about various minerals, including copper, gold, silver, and tin.

Bureau of Mines
U.S. Department of the Interior
Cochrans Mill Road
P.O. Box 18070
Pittsburgh, PA 15236 (412) 892-4338

To learn about your state's mineral activities, contact the office above for a copy of *Minerals in the 50 States.* This publication contains historical information and is an excellent resource for schoolchildren who need to write reports on the history of their state.

Geologic Inquiries Group
U.S. Geological Survey

907 National Center
Reston, VA 22092 (703) 648-4383

Do you have a question on mineral resources? Contact the Geologic Inquiries Group. This office answers questions not only on mineral resources, but also questions on earthquakes, energy resources, the geology of specific areas, and geologic maps and mapping.

Office of Education, Room 212
Mail Stop 158
National Museum of Natural History
Washington, DC 20560 (202) 357-2747

The National Museum of Natural History has a visiting program for grades one and up called *Rocks and Minerals.* In it students are introduced to rocks and the major rock-forming minerals by examining exhibited specimens in the Earth and Mineral exhibition halls and by participating in a hands-on classroom activity. Students distinguish between rocks and minerals; identify seven common minerals using the physical properties of luster, color, hardness, and streak; classify seven rock specimens according to their origin (igneous, sedimentary, or metamorphic); and explore the relationship between texture and mineral composition of rocks and the processes that form them.

Office of Education, Room 212
Mail Stop 158
National Museum of Natural History
Washington, DC 20560 (202) 357-2747

The National Museum of Natural History also has workshops for teachers, including one called *Rocks and Minerals.* Here teachers can work with a geologist in developing ways to introduce students to rocks and minerals. Time is spent in the Earth and Mineral exhibition halls, as well as in a classroom. Activities are designed to provide experience in distinguishing between a rock and a mineral, describing minerals by their physical properties, and using rock texture to classify rocks according to their origin.

MISSOURI

Missouri Department of Natural Resources
Division of Geology and Land Survey
P.O. Box 250
Rolla, MO 65401

Students who wish to learn interesting facts about Missouri should obtain the publication *Earthquakes in Missouri.* It contains information not only about earthquakes in Missouri but also general information on understanding earthquakes, measuring earthquakes, and the hazards of earthquakes. This publication can serve as an educational aid for upper-elementary school children.

MONEY

Bureau of Engraving and Printing
U.S. Department of the Treasury
14th and C St., SW
Washington, DC 20228 (202) 874-2778

Did you know that 95% of the notes printed each year are used to replace notes already in circulation? That 48% of the notes printed are $1 notes? These facts and others can be obtained from the Bureau of Engraving and Printing. Parents and teachers can use the information to provide a greater appreciation of U.S. currency. Children can use it to supplement school reports. Some of the information sheets available include:

Bibliography of Numismatic Books and Periodicals
Changes in $1 From July 1929
Difference Between United States Notes and Federal Reserve Notes
Engravers and Engraving
Expanded Use of the Motto "In God We Trust" in United States Currency
Fun Facts About Dollars
The Great Seal of the United States
Use of the National Motto "In God We Trust" on United States Currency
The Story of Money

Bureau of Engraving and Printing
U.S. Department of the Treasury
14th and C St., SW
Washington, DC 20228 (202) 874-2778

The Bureau of Engraving and Printing is pleased to offer uncut currency for sale to the general public. Imagine a child's surprise and curiosity when they see uncut currency! Contact the office above for more information. Prices are:

Be patient. If any phone number is incorrect, call (area code) 555-1212 and request the new listing.

The Government Works for Kids, Too

One ($1) Notes	Visitors Center	Mail Order
4-subject	$ 7.50	$10.25
16-subject	$21.50	$28.00
32-subject	$40.50	$47.00

Two ($2) Notes	Visitors Center	Mail Order
4-subject	$12.00	$14.75
16-subject	$38.50	$45.00

MOON

Superintendent of Documents
U.S. Government Printing Office
Washington, DC 20402 (202) 783-3238

First Lunar Landing as Told by the Astronauts (20th anniversary issue) is a transcript of the Apollo 11 post-flight press conference, a first-hand narration of mankind's historic first trip to another celestial body by the men who made the journey. (24 pages, stock no. 033-00-01054-1, $2.50).

NASA CORE
Lorain County Joint Vocational School
15181 Route 58 South
Oberlin, OH 44074 (216) 774-1051

NASA CORE makes available to educators educational slides and videos, including the following three educational aids. *Moon Landing - Apollo 11* is a set of slides that tells the story of the most famous spaceflight in history, man's first moon landing. Appropriate for students in grades 4-12. *Return To The Moon Videoconference Kit* is a video of the taping of an interactive teleconference on January 26, 1990. Students joined Apollo astronaut Michael Collins and NASA guest educator Dr. Lynn Bondurant on a "Return to the Moon", participating in a series of unique problem-solving and hands on activities. Accompanying curriculum material includes an activity booklet, slides and a moon map (for grades 5-8). *The Time of Apollo* is a video tribute to the historical accomplishments of the Apollo missions (for grades 4-adult).

Teaching Resource Center
Jet Propulsion Laboratory
4800 Oak Grove Dr.
Mail Stop CS-530
Pasadena, CA 91109 (818) 354-6916

Both the *Apollo 11: The First Moon Landing* ($11) set of 40 color slides with cassette narration and the video *Apollo Moon Landings* ($25) are available from the Teacher Resource Center of the Jet Propulsion Laboratory.

MOTOR RACING

Photographic Services
American History Building
Room CB-054, Smithsonian Institution
Washington, DC 20560 (202) 357-1933

American Motor Racing: Richard Petty Car is a wonderful color poster available for all car enthusiasts. $10.

MOTORCYCLES

Department of Public Programs
Room CC53, National Museum of American History
Smithsonian Institution
Washington, DC 20560 (202) 357-4187

Get your child the color poster *American Motorcycles, 1900-1940.* $8.

MT. ST. HELENS

Teaching Resource Center
Jet Propulsion Laboratory
4800 Oak Grove Dr.
Mail Stop CS-530
Pasadena, CA 91109 (818) 354-6916

Teach your students about the eruption of Mt. St. Helens with the help of the following two programs. *Mt. St. Helens Erupts* is a set of 40 color slides with cassette narration ($11) and *Eruption of Mt. St. Helens* is a 30-minute video ($25).

MUSIC

Smithsonian/Folkways Recordings
416 Hungerford Dr., Suite 320

Rockville, MD. 20850

Administered by the Smithsonian Institution's Office of Folklife Programs, Folkways Records is one of the ways the Office supports cultural conservation and continuity, integrity, and equity for traditional artists and cultures. Children's recordings are one of the many categories of recordings available. Children's songs by Pete Seeger, Ella Jenkins, and Woody Guthrie can be purchased, along with dozens of recordings by lesser-known yet still very talented artists. They include *Latin American Folk Songs Sung in Spanish by Chago Rodrigo, Singing Streets: The Childhood Memories of Ireland and Scotland, Children's Songs from Spain,* and *French Folk Songs for Children.* Write to the office above to obtain *The Whole Folkways Catalogue* which contains these and other recordings.

MUSKRATS

U.S. Fish and Wildlife Service
U.S. Department of the Interior
4401 N. Fairfax Drive
Mail Stop 130
Arlington, VA 22203 (703) 358-1711

Interested in learning more about the muskrat? Obtain the publication *Muskrat* from the U.S. Fish and Wildlife Service.

NATIONAL AERONAUTICS AND SPACE ADMINISTRATION

Superintendent of Documents
U.S. Government Printing Office
Washington, DC 20402 (202) 783-3238

The National Aeronautics and Space Administration produces educational publications for educators, students, and the general public. All are offered for sale by the Superintendent of Documents, U.S. GPO. Prices may change.

NASA CORE
Lorain County Joint Vocational School
15181 Route 58 South
Oberlin, OH 44074 (216) 774-1051

The NASA Central Operation of Resources for Educators (CORE), established in cooperation with Lorain County Joint Vocational School, serves as the national distribution center for NASA produced education materials. For a minimal charge the NASA CORE will provide a valuable service to educators unable to visit one of the NASA Teacher Resource Centers (TRC), by making NASA educational audiovisual materials available through its mail order service. Also available are different memorabilia items which can be used by teachers as awards for students. They include a NASA logo patch, pencils, hats, T-shirts, mugs, and astronaut ice cream.

Elementary and Secondary Programs Branch
Educational Affairs Division
Mail Code XEE
NASA Headquarters
Washington, DC 20546

The Aerospace Education Services Program (AESP), previously known as Spacemobile, is the Educational Affairs Division's premier outreach program. AESP specialists, all former teachers themselves, reach millions of students each year. They cross the country from September to June each year, assisting schools so students and teachers can see first-hand what NASA is all about. Visits are scheduled by field center, and because each field center performs a specific service for NASA, each center's program is a little different from the others. All emphasize current NASA programs, such as the Space Shuttle and the Freedom Space Station. Because of this program's popularity, a visit should be requested well in advance. Although field centers make every effort to accommodate the date a school requests, there is currently about a 2-year waiting list.

Education Division
NASA Headquarters
Washington, DC 20546

NASA Spacelink is a collection of NASA information and educational materials stored on a computer at the Marshall Space Flight Center in Huntsville, Alabama. The system may be accessed over regular telephone lines. It is designed to communicate with a wide variety of computers and modems, especially those most commonly found in classrooms and home. NASA Spacelink is free, but you'll owe your phone company for long distance calls. It includes a listing of all the major NASA educational programs. Subjects include the Aerospace Education Services Project, Urban Community Enrichment Program, Summer High School Apprenticeship Research Program, Space Science Student Involvement Project, Teacher Workshops, Educators Mailing

Be patient. If any phone number is incorrect, call (area code) 555-1212 and request the new listing.

The Government Works For Kids, Too

List, Telelectures, Teacher Resource Centers, and Science Fair support. Classroom materials include a variety of information useful in the classroom, including space science lesson plans and activities (all grade levels and many subjects), astronomy information, film/video list, computer programs, career information, computer graphics, and a source list for pictures, posters, and other educational materials.

Elementary and Secondary Programs Branch
Educational Affairs Division
Mail Code XEE
NASA Headquarters
Washington, DC 20546

Aerospace Education Services Program (AESP) specialists conduct workshops for teachers each summer at NASA field centers, elementary and secondary schools, and on college campuses. Workshops cover astronomy, aeronautics, life in space, principles of rocketry, earth sciences, and remote sensing. A typical workshop includes how-to and hands-on activities to help teachers incorporate what they learn into classroom activities and programs to supplement existing curricula.

NATIONAL AIR AND SPACE MUSEUM

Education Division, MRC 305
National Air and Space Museum
Washington, DC 20560 (202) 786-2109

The Education Resource Center (ERC) of the National Air and Space Museum (NASM) is open to teachers of all levels and disciplines. The ERC offers teachers access to educational materials pertaining to aviation, space, and the Museum's collections. These materials are produced by NASM, the National Aeronautics and Space Administration (NASA), and other government agencies, and private organizations. Additional information on the ERC and other NASM educational programs may be obtained by writing to the address above. Educational materials include the following:

Curriculum Packages: Complete units on specific topics are available on request for grades K-12. Write and tell them the subjects and grades you teach, and they will be happy to send you the appropriate packages. Requests must be made by teachers on school letterhead.

Lesson Plans: Hundreds of classroom activities on aerospace-related topics, arranged according to subject and grade levels, are available for duplication when you visit the ERC. This service is not available through the mail.

Public Domain Software: Aerospace-related public domain computer software for use with Apple II series and IBM PC computers is available for duplication when you visit the ERC, as well as through the mail. In both cases, teachers must provide blank diskettes. Contact the ERC for a current catalog and mail-in procedures.

Commercial Software: A growing collection of IBM PC and Apple II series commercial software on aerospace topics is available on a preview-only basis for visiting teachers.

Videodiscs and CD-Roms: Visit the ERC to preview our growing collection of these new audiovisual formats.

Filmstrips: The ERC's large collection of filmstrips is available for preview. NASM-produced filmstrips may be obtained from the National Audiovisual Center, 8700 Edgewood Drive, Capitol Heights, MD 20743, (301) 763-1896.

Videos: Hundreds of videos can be previewed at the ERC. Videos must be rented or purchased from their respective suppliers.

Slide Sets: A variety of slide sets are available for preview in the ERC. The NASM-produced "Milestones of Flight" set is available through NASA CORE.

Other Resources: A variety of resources such as science kits, posters, brochures, and catalogs are available as reference materials.

"Skylines" Newsletter: The Education Division publishes a newsletter for teachers. Please write and ask to be placed on our mailing list.

ERC Workshops: Half-day workshops, to aid educators in utilizing the ERC, are scheduled on request. Participants receive assistance in compiling educational units to meet specific needs.

Other Workshops: Throughout the year, the Education Division offers

aerospace-related teacher workshops that are announced in the Skylines newsletter. Contact the Education Division for more information.

Tours and Group Reservations: Free docent-led tours of the Museum are offered year-round for school groups, on a variety of subjects and grade levels. Reservations must be made by mail at least three weeks in advance but no earlier than eight weeks in advance of visit. School group reservation for the Einstein Planetarium and Langley Theater are also available. Request a current tour brochure and reservation form from the Tour Scheduling Office, MRC 305, National Air and Space Museum, Washington, DC 20560.

NATIONAL ARCHIVES

Education Branch (NEEE)
National Archives and Records Administration
Washington, DC 20408 (202) 724-0454

The National Archives preserves and makes available to the public the permanently valuable records of the U.S. Government. It offers teachers from the upper elementary grades through the secondary levels a workshop called *Primarily Teaching* that introduces them to the holdings and organization of the National Archives. *Primarily Teaching* emphasizes secondary strategies, but educators at all levels adapt them to their particular needs. Participants will learn how to do research in historical records; to create classroom material from records; and to present documents in ways that sharpen students' skills and enthusiasm for history, social studies, and the humanities.

Education Branch (NEEE)
National Archives and Records Administration
Washington, DC 20408 (202) 724-0454

The Education Branch of the National Archives offers teachers of upper elementary through secondary school students publications and teaching units to aid in the teaching of historical documents and eras. They include "Milestone Documents", an ongoing series of booklets which focus on some of the great documents that have shaped the course of U.S. history. (Each booklet includes a historical introduction and transcriptions and facsimiles of the featured documents.) Also available is "Teaching With Documents", an invaluable aid to teachers who wish to enliven their curriculum through the use of primary sources. This collection of articles began as a feature series appearing in Social Education, the journal of the National Council for the Social Studies. Each essay highlights on National Archives document and provides practical suggestions for using the documents in several classroom settings.

NATIONAL GALLERY OF ART

Office of Elementary and Secondary Education
Arts and Industries Building
Room 1163, Smithsonian Institution
Washington, DC 20560 (202) 357-3049

The *Resource Guide for Teachers* contains educational materials available not only from the National Gallery of Art, but the John F. Kennedy Center for the Performing Arts and the Smithsonian Institution as well. The materials include bibliographies, posters, slide sets, films teacher's manuals, videocassettes, and curriculum units. Below are some materials listed in the *Resource Guide.*

NATIONAL MUSEUM OF NATURAL HISTORY

Office of Education, Room 212
Mail Stop 158
National Museum of Natural History
Washington, DC 20560 (202) 357-2747

The National Museum of Natural History offers visiting programs for school children and workshops for teachers. *Old Growth Forests, Animals,* and *Dinosaurs* are a few of the programs for kids, and *Endangered Species and Extinction, Rocks and Minerals,* and *Oceans* are a few of the workshops for teachers. For information on these and other services available, including slide sets, contact the office above.

NEPTUNE

NASA CORE
Lorain County Joint Vocational School
15181 Route 58 South
Oberlin, OH 44074 (216) 774-1051

Voyager Encounters Neptune is a set of color photographs taken when Voyager encountered Neptune in August of 1989. It includes pictures of the Great Dark Spot, Neptune's rings and Triton. Appropriate for children in grades 4-12.

Be patient. If any phone number is incorrect, call (area code) 555-1212 and request the new listing.

The Government Works for Kids, Too

Teaching Resource Center
Jet Propulsion Laboratory
4800 Oak Grove Dr.
Mail Stop CS-530
Pasadena, CA 91109 (818) 354-6916

Voyager Mission to Neptune and *Neptune Computer Graphics, Set 2* are slides sets ($6 each) available from the Teaching Resource Center. Also available is the video *Jupiter, Saturn, Uranus and Neptune* ($25).

NORTH AMERICAN CONTINENT

U.S. Geological Survey
P.O. Box 25425
Denver, CO 80225

Our Changing Continent is a publication that discusses the evidence and techniques scientists use to reconstruct the history of the changing land surface of the North American continent.

NUCLEAR ENERGY

Office of Plans and Evaluations
Office of Nuclear Energy
U.S. Department of Energy
1000 Independence Ave., SW
Washington, DC 20585 (202) 586-9720

Since 1982, nuclear energy has been second only to coal as an energy source for the production of electricity in the United States, surpassing oil, natural gas, and hydroelectric power. The office above has several publications available, some of which are listed below, to more fully understand this valuable source of energy and the role it plays. Teachers can supplement their science curricula with the use of these publications:

Answers to Questions
Approaches to Nuclear Safety
Atoms to Electricity
The First Reactor
High-Level Nuclear Waste: A Safe, Permanent Solution
The History of Nuclear Energy
How Nuclear Energy Plants Work
Light Water Breeder Reactor
Low-Level Nuclear Waste: Safe, Permanent Disposal
Nuclear Energy: Benefit for All Americans
Nuclear Energy Economics
Nuclear Energy Plant Safety
The Nuclear Fuel Cycle
Nuclear Power in Space
Nuclear Powerplant Safety: Design and Planning
Nuclear Powerplant Safety: Operations
Nuclear Powerplant Safety: Source Terms
Radiation in Perspective
Radiosotopes: Today's Applications
Understanding Radiation

National Energy Information Center, EI-231
Energy Information Administration
Forrestal Building
Washington, DC 20585 (202) 586-8800

Information on nuclear power generation is available from the National Energy Information Center. The NEIC offers free of charge *Energy Information Sheets*, which contain information on topics ranging from crude oil production to coal consumption to nuclear power generation.

OCEANS

U.S. Geological Survey
P.O. Box 25425
Denver, CO 80225

The U.S. Geological Survey has two publications available on oceans. *Why is the Ocean Salty?* discusses the origin of the oceans and the sources of their salinity (also available in Spanish) and *The Exclusive Economic Zone: An Exciting New Frontier* describes the geologic processes that form the ocean floors.

Office of Education, Room 212
Mail Stop 158
National Museum of Natural History
Washington, DC 20560 (202) 357-2747

The National Museum of Natural History has several workshops for teachers including one on oceans. In this workshop teachers become familiar with ancient and modern reefs and how ocean populations have changed over time. They also learn the ecology of and strategies for competing in a water environment and survey briefly the problems in today's ocean environments.

OIL

California Energy Extension Service
1400 Tenth St., Room 209
Sacramento, CA 95814 (916) 323-4388

Energy Facts for Classroom Teachers is a publication anyone can use to obtain interesting facts not only on oil, but recycling, natural gas, and other energy conservation-related topics as well.

National Energy Information Center, EI-231
Energy Information Administration
Forrestal Building
Washington, DC 20585 (202) 586-8800

Crude oil production is one of the many topics covered in the National Energy Information Center's *Energy Information Sheets*. Information ranging from the above to coal consumption to nuclear power generation is provided. The information can be used by teachers and upper elementary students to supplement curricula and reports.

Office of Fossil Energy Communications
1000 Independence Ave., SW
Room 4G-085
Washington, DC 20585 (202) 586-6503

The office above provides technical and public education-related information on oil, coal, and natural gas technologies, and the Nation's petroleum reserves. It offers *Dinosaurs and Power Plants*, a 16-page brochure designed for students that relates the story of mining and drilling for coal, gas, and oil; environmental concerns; and modes of transportation.

OPOSSUM

U.S. Fish and Wildlife Service
U.S. Department of the Interior
4401 N. Fairfax Drive
Mail Stop 130
Arlington, VA 22203 (703) 358-1711

Do you know much about this marsupial? Find out more by reading the publication *Opossum*.

OWLS

U.S. Fish and Wildlife Service
U.S. Department of the Interior
4401 N. Fairfax Drive
Mail Stop 130
Arlington, VA 22203 (703) 358-1711

Is your child fascinated with owls? Obtain the publication *Spotted Owl* and *Great Horned Owl* so she can learn more about them.

OZONE

Public Information Center
U.S. Environmental Protection Agency
401 M Street, SW, PM-211B
Washington, DC 20460 (202) 260-2080

Learn about the pollutants ozone and carbon monoxide in the *Environmental Backgrounder: Ozone and Carbon Monoxide*. This six-page publication provides important information on these two major public health concerns and can be used by educators to supplement science curricula.

PALEOANTHROPOLOGY

Office of Education, Room 212
Mail Stop 158
National Museum of Natural History
Washington, DC 20560 (202) 357-2747

What Does It Mean to Be Human? Human Origins is one of several visiting programs offered by the National Museum of Natural History. Here students in grades one and up can learn about the family history of humankind. Students investigate human's place in nature, identify characteristics of our genus and

Be patient. If any phone number is incorrect, call (area code) 555-1212 and request the new listing.

The Government Works For Kids, Too

species, and trace the biological and cultural evolution of humankind to the end of the last Ice Age. By examining real skeletal materials, replicas of fossils, and ancient stone tools, students get a feel for the real stones, bones and methods of paleoanthropology.

PANAMA CANAL

Panama Canal Commission
1825 I Street, NW, Suite 1050
Washington, DC 20006 (202) 634-6441

Would you like to teach your students or children about the Panama Canal? Call the office above to receive a copy of the publications, *Panama Canal: The Vital Link for World Trade* and *The Panama Canal: Pictorial Map*. Both of these publications provide interesting facts and information about the Panama Canal.

PANDAS

U.S. Fish and Wildlife Service
U.S. Department of the Interior
4401 N. Fairfax Drive
Mail Stop 130
Arlington, VA 22203 (703) 358-1711

Pandas are such an interesting animal. Help your child learn more about them by reading the publication *Giant Panda*.

PEDESTRIAN SAFETY

National Highway Traffic Safety Administration
U.S. Department of Transportation
400 Seventh St., SW
Washington, DC 20590 (202) 366-9550

Contact the office above to receive publications on pedestrian safety. Appropriate for elementary children are *Safe Street Crossing for Kids: A Planning Guide* and *Safe Street Crossing for Kids: A Program that Works*.

PEN PALS

U.S. Postal Service Olympic Pen Pal Club
P.O. Box 9419
Gaithersburg, MD 20898-9419

Children six years and older who enjoy writing may be interested in joining Stamper, the U.S. Postal Service Olympic Pen Pal Club. For $5.95 a child receives a pen pal's name and address along with a Stamper sign, a Stamper calendar, an extra-thick note pad, a big world map, a Stamper activity book, an official membership card and button, a Stamper frame, and Stamper stationery. Write to the address above for more information.

PENNSYLVANIA

Office of Environmental Education
Pennsylvania Department of Education
333 Market St.
Harrisburg, PA 17126 (717) 783-6994

Available from the office above is *The Friendly Forest Fun Book*, an activity book designed to help elementary teachers enhance students' awareness and knowledge about Pennsylvania's forest lands, the resources the forest provides to both wildlife and the consumer, and the enjoyment that can be obtained from the proper use of our forests.

PESTICIDES

U.S. Fish and Wildlife Service
U.S. Department of the Interior
4401 N. Fairfax Drive
Mail Stop 130
Arlington, VA 22203 (703) 358-1711

Pesticide Use and Endangered Species is available free from the U.S. Fish and Wildlife Service.

Public Information Center (PM-211B)
401 M St., SW
Washington, DC 20460

Don't Bug Me, for grades K-3, is a pamphlet illustrating the safe use of pesticides and includes pictures and captions.

PESTS

Cooperative Extension Service
University of Nebraska - Lincoln
Department of Entomology
210 Plant Industry Bldg.
Lincoln, NE 68583-0816 (402) 472-2125

Educational materials on the topic of integrated pest management of crops are available from the Institute of Agriculture and Natural Resources at the University of Nebraska. A free catalog which lists environmental films and videotapes for young people's viewing is also available.

PETROLEUM

National Energy Information Center (NEIC)
Energy Information Administration, EI-231
U.S. Department of Energy
1000 Independence Ave., SW
Room 1F-048
Washington, DC 20585 (202) 586-8800

Petroleum is one of several types of energy used today. The National Energy Information Center (NEIC) provides information on petroleum and other energy sources, such as natural gas, coal, electricity and renewable energy. Students can use the information provided on the one-page information sheets for science reports.

PETS

Center for Veterinary Medicine
Food and Drug Administration
Public Health Service
U.S. Department of Health and Human Services
7500 Standish Place
Rockville, MD 20855 (301) 594-1755

There are many factors involved in the care and feeding of a household pet. The office above has several fact sheets which parents can use to teach their children how to care for pets properly.

PETTY, RICHARD

Photographic Services
American History Building
Room CB-054
Smithsonian Institution
Washington, DC 20560 (202) 357-1933

The color poster *American Motor Racing: Richard Petty Car* is available for $10.

PHEASANTS

U.S. Fish and Wildlife Service
U.S. Department of the Interior
4401 N. Fairfax Drive
Mail Stop 130
Arlington, VA 22203 (703) 358-1711

Teach your students about pheasants after reading the *Ring-necked Pheasant* publication.

PHYSICAL FITNESS

Physical Fitness Award Program
President's Council on Physical Fitness and Sports
701 Pennsylvania Ave., NW
Washington, DC 20004 (202) 272-3421

American youth have participated in the Presidential Physical Fitness Award Program or the "President's Challenge" since 1966. The program includes all young people from ages six through 17, including those students with special needs. In addition, two awards have been added to go with the prestigious Presidential Physical Fitness Award for outstanding achievement. The National Physical Fitness Award was introduced in 1987 and is for those who reach a basic yet challenging level of fitness. A new award called the Participant Physical Fitness Award, introduced in the Fall of 1991, is for those who attempt the President's Challenge but don't qualify for a Presidential or National Award. The booklet *Get Fit! A Handbook for Youth Ages 6-17* will help children become as physically fit as they can be.

Be patient. If any phone number is incorrect, call (area code) 555-1212 and request the new listing.

The Government Works for Kids, Too

PLANETS

R. Woods
Consumer Information Center - Y
P.O. Box 100
Pueblo, CO 81002

Full-color photos and descriptions of the planets in the solar system can be found in the publication *A Look at the Planets*. Includes data on space explorations. 8 pp. (1985. NASA) 150X. $1. Write to the above address.

Superintendent of Documents
U.S. Government Printing Office
Washington, DC 20402 (202) 783-3238

Information Summaries: Our Planets At a Glance is a 16-page publication that serves as an excellent source of concise information on the planets. Use it as a supplement to science curricula.

Superintendent of Documents
U.S. Government Printing Office
Washington, DC 20402 (202) 783-3238

The publication *Comparing the Planets* introduces comparative planetology by presenting information gathered from NASA space missions. In addition to showing the size of planets and their distance from the Sun, it describes planets in terms of composition, density, atmosphere, and geology. Printed in color. 32x56 inches. 1979. Stock No. 033-000-00744-2. $3.50.

POCAHONTAS

Attn: Public Inquiries Office
Bureau of Indian Affairs
Mail Stop 2620 (MIB)
U.S. Department of Interior
Washington, DC 20240 (202) 208-3711

The publication *Famous Indians: A Collection of Short Biographies* describes the history and lives, from Pocahontas to Sitting Bull, of twenty famous American Indians. All were leaders in a great struggle to preserve treasured lands and lifeways. With their tribesmen, they are inseparably linked to our country's history from its earliest beginnings through generations of growth. This publication is a wonderful source of information for students and teachers.

POISON

Food and Drug Administration
Consumer Communications HFE-88
Rockville, MD 20857

Most products are made to look attractive so people will buy them -- even products that can be poisonous. But things made attractive for consumers are also attractive to children. Many poisonings that occur involve children who are too young and innocent to "know better." *Dennis the Menace Takes a Poke at Poison* is a comic book that teaches children to "always ask first" before they taste. Write to the office above for a free copy.

POSTERS

Department of Public Programs
Room BB53
National Museum of American History
Smithsonian Institution
Washington, DC 20560 (202) 357-4187

The color poster *A More Perfect Union* is an excellent educational aid to use when teaching students about the Japanese American internment that occurred during World War II. $8.

Photographic Services
American History Building
Room CB-054
Smithsonian Institution
Washington, DC 20560 (202) 357-1933

The color poster *American Motor Racing: Richard Petty Car* is available for $10.

Department of Public Programs
Room CC53
National Museum of American History
Smithsonian Institution
Washington, DC 20560 (202) 357-4187

Get your child the color poster *American Motorcycles, 1900-1940*. $8.

Department of Public Programs
Room CC53
National Museum of American History
Smithsonian Institution
Washington, DC 20560 (202) 357-4187

For Duke Ellington enthusiasts, this office has the poster *Duke Ellington*, available for $6.

Smithsonian Institution Traveling Exhibition Service
1100 Jefferson Drive, SW
Room 3146
Washington, DC 20560

Use the poster *The Frederick Douglass Years: 1817-1895* to help teach your children about Frederick Douglass. The poster includes biographies of abolitionists and black leaders, and a bibliography. Cost is $1.

Photographic Services
American History Building
Room CB-054
Smithsonian Institution
Washington, DC 20560 (202) 357-1933

Sitting Bull is a poster available for $3 from the Smithsonian Institution.

National Crime Prevention Council
1700 K Street, NW, 2nd Floor
Washington, DC 20006 (202) 466-6272

For drug prevention educators there is the poster *To Be What You Want To Be: Be Drug Free*. This poster has people from many professions with the slogan "To be what you want to be, be drug free." The poster has room for the child to draw himself into the picture. $2.50.

National Clearinghouse for Alcohol and Drug Information
P.O. Box 2345 (800) 729-6686
Rockville, MD 20852 (301) 468-2600

The following posters are available from the National Clearinghouse for Alcohol and Drug Information and are appropriate for elementary school children:

The Herschel Walker Poster (1989). Herschel Walker, football star, salutes the drug-free youth of America in a 22 in. by 27 in. color poster. Reference is made to NCADI as a source for more information. AVD45.

Live the Dream, Say No to Alcohol and Drug Abuse (1989). Poster features Dr. Martin Luther King, Jr. Appropriate for all ages, 15 1/2 in. by 22 in. AV165.

McGruff: Say 'No' to Crack and Other Drugs (1989). Bright red and white poster featuring McGruff, the Crime Dog. McGruff tells kids that crack is poison and a very dangerous drug. Tells them to say a big "no" and walk away. Also provides the NIDA hotline number (800-662-HELP) and a cocaine hotline number (800-COCAINE). 64 in. by 88 in. AVD14.

Superintendent of Documents
Dept. 33
Washington, DC 20402 (202) 783-3238

The American Soldier, Set No. 2 is a set of 10 color posters reproducing paintings of American servicemen and women over the 100-year period from 1863 to 1963. (Includes an explanatory booklet). Use these posters to help teach your children about American history. All posters are 9 x 13 inches and are printed on fine white paper suitable for framing. (S/N 008-020-00227-5, $6, 1989, shipped flat).

Office of Fossil Energy, Room 4G 085
U.S. Department of Energy
1000 Independence Ave., SW
Washington, DC 20585 (202) 586-6503

Call the office above to receive *The Clean Coal Path* poster. It traces the route of several new advances in the clean use of coal, America's most abundant fossil energy resource. During the 1990's, many of these improvements will be used for the first time in power plants to generate new supplies of electricity without polluting the nation's air.

U.S. Fish and Wildlife Service
U.S. Department of the Interior
4401 N. Fairfax Drive
Mail Stop 130
Arlington, VA 22203 (703) 358-1711

The U.S. Fish and Wildlife Service has several posters available to be used by educators, 4-H clubs, or Boy Scout organizations. They include:

Be patient. If any phone number is incorrect, call (area code) 555-1212 and request the new listing.

The Government Works For Kids, Too

Raptors - Hunters On the Wing!
Steel Shot - Are You Using the Right Load?
The Difference Between Endangered and Extinct is Forever
Wetlands - We need 'em... - Wildlife needs 'em too.

California Energy Extension Service
1400 Tenth St., Room 209
Sacramento, CA 95814 (916) 323-4388
The *Classroom Energy Poster Puzzle* is a bulletin board-size poster for children in grades K-4. It serves as a great teaching aid to focus on energy use and abuse in the classroom.

Forest Service
U.S. Department of Agriculture
14th and Independence, SW
P.O. Box 96090
Washington, DC 20090-6090 (202) 205-0957
The poster *How a Tree Grows* (FS-8) teaches about photosynthesis, enzymes, and the various parts of a tree. Its colorful illustrations make it a very useful teaching aid. The eight-page publication *How a Tree Grows* supplements the poster and provides more information on how a tree grows.

Forest Service
U.S. Department of Agriculture
14th and Independence, SW
P.O. Box 96090
Washington, DC 20090-6090 (202) 205-0957
Available from this office is the poster *What We Get From Trees* (FS-68). It lists the various products, ranging from chewing gum to mop handles, which come from trees.

Public Information Center
U.S. Environmental Protection Agency
401 M Street, SW, PM-211B
Washington, DC 20460 (202) 260-2080
The poster *Beneficial Use of Sewer Sludge: Land Application* discusses the various uses of sewer sludge. It shows how sewer sludge is a valuable resource that can be used to improve plant growth and soil quality.

United States Fire Administration
National Academy
Federal Emergency Management Agency
16825 S. Seton Avenue
Emmitsburg, MD 21727 (301) 447-1122
A poster is one of many educational aids included in the U.S. Fire Administration public education kit called "Curious Kids Set Fires." The program was developed to help reduce fire deaths by educating and counseling the child setter. Contact the office above to receive the kit, which also includes handouts for the school classroom, lesson plans for teachers, camera-ready print public service announcements, a press release announcing your local program, a sample letter for the local paper, a resource guide with additional materials you may want to get, and descriptions of pre-adolescent fire prevention and counseling programs from other communities.

Superintendent of Documents
U.S. Government Printing Office
Washington, DC 20402 (202) 783-3238
The National Aeronautics and Space Administration (NASA) produces posters for educators, students, and the general public. All are offered for sale by the Superintendent of Documents, U.S. GPO. Prices may change. Contact your regional GPO outlet or call the office above. The posters include:

Space Shuttle. Shows the external configuration, and internal design and construction of the Space Shuttle. Printed in color. 30x42 inches. Folded. 1978. Stock No. 033-000-00743-4. $3.50.

Comparing the Planets. Introduces comparative planetology by presenting information gathered from NASA space missions. In addition to showing the size of planets and their distance from the Sun, it describes planets in terms of composition, density, atmosphere, and geology. Printed in color. 32x56 inches. 1979. Stock No. 033-000-00744-2. $3.50.

Spacelab Wallsheet. Spacelab and Space Shuttle orbiter during a hypothetical mission. Inserts show life cycle of Spacelab from assembly to launch, different Spacelab configurations, and parts of the vehicle. Printed in color. 43x44 inches. 1983. Stock No. 033-000-00903-8. $3.75.

Space Suit Wallsheet. Near-life-sized poster of Bruce McCandless on his first spacewalk using the manned maneuvering unit. The space suit is labeled showing its various components. Printed in color. 36x56 inches. 1990. Stock No. 033-000-01067-2. $5.50.

International Cometary Explorer Wallsheet. Depicts comet and International Cometary Explorer (ICE) spacecraft, and lists mission details. Printed in color. 37x41 inches. 1985. Stock No. 033-000-00958-5. $4.

Superintendent of Documents
U.S. Government Printing Office
Washington, DC 20402 (202) 783-3238
The National Institute of Standards and Technology (formerly the National Bureau of Standards) of the U.S. Department of Commerce has produced a 29"x45" poster called *The Modernized Metric System.* Available from the Superintendent of Documents (special publication 304), it is an excellent visual tool educators can use to teach their students about the metric system.

Education Division
NASA Headquarters
Washington, DC 20546
Are you looking for more posters available from NASA? NASA Spacelink is a collection of NASA information and educational materials stored on a computer at the Marshall Space Flight Center in Huntsville, Alabama. It includes a listing of all the major NASA educational programs. Classroom materials include a variety of information useful in the classroom (in addition to posters) including space science lesson plans and activities (all grade levels and many subjects), astronomy information, film/video list, computer programs, career information, computer graphics, and a source list for pictures, and other educational materials.

Bureau of Mines
U.S. Department of the Interior
Cochrans Mill Road
P.O. Box 18070
Pittsburgh, PA 15236 (412) 892-4338
The Petroleum Tree illustration shows all the dozens of products that are obtainable from crude oil. This illustration serves as an excellent learning tool for students in the upper elementary grades.

Texas Water Development Board
Office of Public Information
P.O. Box 13231
Austin, TX 78711-3231 (512) 463-8028
Land Use and the Water Cycle is a black and white poster which illustrates the water cycle and different uses of land. It can be used by educators as a teaching aid or by students as a component to a report.

U.S. Government Printing Office (GPO)
Superintendent of Documents
Washington, DC 20402-9325
National Park Service posters and charts are colorful commemorative pieces by well-know artists. They can be used to brighten any classroom. Prices vary from $3.75 to $7 a copy. They include the following:

The Alpine Northwest
The Atlantic Barrier Islands
The Canyon Country
The Desert
Edgar Allan Poe
Everglades
George Washington Carver
Glacier Bay
Greater Yellowstone: Panorama
Hawaii Volcanoes
North Cascades Panorama
The Rocky Mountains
The Sierra Range
Statue of Liberty
Yosemite Panorama

Educational Programs Branch, Room 105
National Oceanic and Atmospheric Administration (NOAA)
11400 Rockville Pike
Rockville, MD 20852 (301) 443-8031
Natural Hazard Watch and Warning with Safety Rules for: Tornadoes, Hurricanes, Floods, Flash Floods, Thunderstorms/Lightning, Winter Storms is a mini-poster

Be patient. If any phone number is incorrect, call (area code) 555-1212 and request the new listing.

that provides easy-to-read information on what to do when there is a natural hazard.

U.S. EPA Region 5
Office of Public Affairs
77 West Jackson Blvd., PI-195
Chicago, IL 60604 (312) 353-2000

Welcome to the Wetlands is a coloring poster (for grades k-12) that explains how wetlands help us and what is a threat to wetlands. Included is information on animals, birds, fish and plants that thrive in wetlands. Limited quantities are available for residents in the six-state Region 5 area (Illinois, Indiana, Michigan, Minnesota, Ohio, Wisconsin).

POWELL, JOHN WESLEY

U.S. Geological Survey
P.O. Box 25425
Denver, CO 80225

Do you want to teach your students about John Wesley Powell? Obtain the publication *John Wesley Powell's Exploration of the Colorado River.* It describes Powell's daring voyage in 1869 through the canyons of the Colorado River, starting at Green River Station, Wyoming, and ending at the junction of the Colorado and Virgin Rivers in Arizona.

PRESIDENTS

Bureau of Engraving and Printing
U.S. Department of the Treasury
14th and C St., SW, Room 602-11A
Washington, DC 20228 (202) 874-2778

Presidential portraits and portraits of the Chief Justices can be purchased from the office above. Teachers can hang these portraits in a classroom or students can use them if they need to present a report on a president. Also available are vignettes of federal government buildings.

RACOONS

U.S. Fish and Wildlife Service
U.S. Department of the Interior
4401 N. Fairfax Drive
Mail Stop 130
Arlington, VA 22203 (703) 358-1711

Would you like to learn more about racoons? Get the publication *Racoon.*

RAIN (See also Acid Rain)

U.S. Geological Survey
P.O. Box 25425
Denver, CO 80225

Rain: A Water Resource provides information on the annual precipitation in areas of the United States, with specific data on several major cities. Explains how to express rainfall as quantities of water. Also available in Spanish.

READING

Indiana University
Smith Research Center, Suite 150
2805 East 10th Street
Bloomington, IN 47408-2698 (812) 855-5847

The Educational Resources Information Center (ERIC) is a nationwide information network designed to provide users with ready access to education literature. It has sixteen clearinghouses, including one which makes available literature on reading and communication skills. The Reading and Communication Skills clearinghouse also has information on educational research and instruction development in reading, writing, speaking, and listening; identification, diagnosis, and remediation of reading problem; speech communication (including forensics), mass communication, interpersonal and small group interaction, interpretation, rhetorical and communication theory, speech sciences, and the theater.

R. Woods
Consumer Information Center
Pueblo, CO 81008

The following booklets and pamphlets on reading may be ordered from the Consumer Information Center. Make check or money order payable to Superintendent of Documents. Send your request to the address above and give the item numbers of the publications you want. Prices include postage and handling.

Help Your Child Become a Good Reader, $.50, 449X
Helping Your Child Use the Library, $.50, 455X
Becoming a Nation of Readers: What Parents Can Do, $.50, 447X

Reading is Fundamental
600 Maryland Ave., SW
Suite 600
Washington, DC 20024 (202) 287-3220

Reading is Fundamental has several publications available at a small charge, including:

Building a Family Library
Children Who Can Read, But Don't....
Children's Bookshelf: A Parent's Guide to Choosing Good Books
Choosing Good Books for Your Children
Encouraging Soon-to-Be Readers
Family Storytelling
Helping Your Children Become Readers/Como Ayudar a Que Sus Ninos Sean Buenos Lectores
Magazines and Family Reading
Reading Aloud to Your Children
Reading is Fun!
Reading is Fun! Tips for Parents of Children Age Birth to 8 Years
The RIF Guide to Encouraging Young Readers
Summertime Reading
TV and Reading
Upbeat and Offbeat Activities to Encourage Reading
When We Were Young: Favorite Books of RIF Kids, RIF Volunteers and Readers of Renown

RECYCLING

Bureau of Mines
U.S. Department of the Interior
Cochrans Mill Road
P.O. Box 18070
Pittsburgh, PA 15236 (412) 892-4338

Children in grades K-5 will enjoy watching the video *Call Me Can* (18:20 mins.). Can is a lively aluminum beverage can who calls out one day in a grocery store to a young boy named Dan. Can has new and exciting stories to tell Dan about recycling, and sings a song about how wonderful it is to be made of aluminum, because he can be recycled over and over. There is no charge for borrowing this video. It is available in 3/4" U-Matic and 1/2" VHS formats only.

Public Information Center
U.S. Environmental Protection Agency
401 M Street, SW, PM-211B
Washington, DC 20460 (202) 260-2080

Help children learn about the need for recycling while reading and coloring the publication, *There Lived a Wicked Dragon.* Written by Martha Finan for the Federal solid waste management programs, it provides a creative way to learn about an important issue.

Education Specialist: SSI
Ohio Department of Natural Resources
Division of Litter Prevention and Recycling
1889 Fountain Square Ct. - F-2
Columbus, OH 43224 (614) 265-6333

Are you looking for some activities your students can do to help teach them about recycling? *Super Saver Investigators* is an interdisciplinary environmental studies activity guide book about recycling (in addition to solid waste and natural resources) for grades kindergarten through 8th and was developed by the Ohio Department of Natural Resources in cooperation with the Ohio Department of Education and Ohio teachers actively involved in environmental studies education. *Super Saver Investigators* contains over 65 hands-on learning activities for grades K-8. The activities are related to science and social studies lessons normally taught by elementary teachers. The activities include skill-building handouts in language arts, math, reading comprehension, creative writing, art and design. It is made available to schools and teachers in Ohio at no cost, through workshops or inservice training. For out-of-state requests there is a charge.

Resource Center
Public Education and Risk Communication Division
Environmental and Occupational Health Sciences Institute

The Government Works For Kids, Too

45 Knightsbridge Road
Piscataway, NJ 08854 (908) 932-0110

"Healthy Environment - Healthy Me" is a interdisciplinary, supplementary environmental and occupational health curriculum. As an "environmental health promotion" curriculum, it is designed to provide young people with the knowledge and understanding for creating a safe and healthful environment at home, in their future workplaces and in their communities. The primary audience is schoolchildren in kindergarten through sixth grade. Both lesson plans and videos are available. Those that help teach about the importance of recycling include:

Videos

(VHS 1/2" $85 each, 3/4" $99 each, previews $25 - previews are available for 2 weeks, the fee may be applied to the purchase price).

Alu-Man the Can (15 min., grades K-3)

This video teaches children about recycling through the adventures of Alu-Man the Can, Nettie Newspaper, Benjamin J. Bottle III, and Mr. "G" the garbage can.

What to Do With All Our Garbage? (20 min., grades 4-6)

In this video Kate, Jenny, and Greg explore the garbage crisis and possible solutions. Source reduction, recycling, sanitary landfills and incineration are discussed. The focus is on what we as consumers can do to reduce the amount of garbage we generate.

Lessons

($29 each)

Recycling: A Community Pollution Solution (First Grade)

Children explore the health consequences of living in a polluted environment and specifically the problems of garbage disposal and solid waste management. Children learn about recycling aluminum, glass and newspaper - one positive community solution to the garbage problem.

Garbage, Garbage, Garbage (Sixth Grade)

Students examine technical topics in solid waste management, specifically: source reduction, recycling, sanitary landfills, incineration, hazardous waste, and household hazardous waste.

Forest Service
U.S. Department of Agriculture
14th and Independence, SW
P.O. Box 96090
Washington, DC 20090-6090 (202) 205-0957

To learn more about recycling and the Forest Service's involvement in it, call the office above for a copy of *Expanding Recycling Horizons.*

Public Information Center
U.S. Environmental Protection Agency
401 M Street, SW, PM-211B
Washington, DC 20460 (202) 260-2080
or
Resource Conservation and Recovery Act
Hotline (800) 424-9346

The following recycling materials are available from either office listed below.

Recycle Today! Educational Materials for Grades K-12 (EPA/530-SW-90-025). Presents the goals and objectives of EPA's School Recycling Program, and describes this handbook as well as the following materials.

Let's Reduce and Recycle: Curriculum for Solid Waste Awareness (EPA/530-SW-90-005). Presents lessons and activities to teach students in grades K-12 about solid waste generation and management. Each unit presents a series of related lessons with vocabulary words, discussion questions, and projects. Practical teaching aids, such as handouts, worksheets, clip art, and a short skit are also included, along with a bibliography of additional sources of information.

Adventures of the Garbage Gremlin: Recycle and Combat a Life of Grime (EPA/530-SW-90-024). Introduces students in grades 4-7 to the benefits of book approach. Students are lead on an adventure in which their peers foil the "Garbage Gremlin" and learn about recycling.

Ride the Wave of the Future: Recycle Today! (EPA/530-SW-90-010). Promotes recycling through a colorful poster designed to appeal to all grade levels. Can be displayed in conjunction with recycling activities or used to help foster recycling.

School Recycling Programs: A Handbook for Educators (EPA/530-SW-90-023). Describes a number of school recycling program options, along with step-by-step instructions on how to set one up. It focuses on implementing actual recycling

projects as a way of teaching the importance and benefits of recycling.

Conservation and Renewable Energy
Inquiry and Referral Service (CAREIRS)
P.O. Box 8900
Silver Spring, MD 20907 (800) 523-2929

Available from this office is *Recycling: What You Can Do.* This two page publication discusses the reasons to recycle and what materials can be recycled.

Office of Environmental Education
Pennsylvania Department of Education
333 Market St.
Harrisburg, PA 17126 (717) 783-6994

Recycling is one of several topics covered in Paul E. Beals' publication *The Newspaper: A Tool for Teaching Environmental Awareness,* an activity book for children in grades K-12. It also covers such topics as acid rain, forest preservation, and waste disposal. This activity book contains newspaper articles and uses them to teach about environmental awareness.

Conservation and Renewable Energy
Inquiry and Referral Service (CAREIRS)
P.O. Box 8900
Silver Spring, MD 20907 (800) 523-2929

Recycling Waste to Save Energy is an information sheet available to educators.

Energy Center
Sonoma State University
1801 East Cotati Ave.
Rohnert Park, CA 94928 (707) 664-2577

Conserve and Renew: Energy Activities is a collection in interdisciplinary energy activities for children in grades 4-6 to be used either as a unit on energy, or as individual activities to complement existing curricula. While the main focus is on conservation and renewables, recycling and ethics are also included. Cost is $10.

California Energy Extension Service
1400 Tenth St., Room 209
Sacramento, CA 95814 (916) 323-4388

Energy Facts for Classroom Teachers is a publication anyone can use to obtain interesting facts on recycling, oil and natural gas, and other energy conservation-related topics.

Jan Lingenfelter
Washington State Department of Ecology
4350 150th Ave., NE
Redmond, WA 98052-5301 (206) 867-7043

Available from the office above is *A-Way With Waste,* 3rd Edition, 1990 (grades K-12), a waste management and recycling curriculum and school program. The goal of the program is to reduce waste and increase recycling at home, at school and in the community. It includes a 602 page interdisciplinary guide of 117 activities. Three sections cover concepts in Solid Waste Management, Hazardous Waste, and Waste and Water. Articles, research reports, glossary, bibliography, fact sheets and resources are also included. This book is free to Washington State teachers who take a workshop. Write or call for prices to purchase curriculum.

RIVERS

U.S. Geological Survey
P.O. Box 25425
Denver, CO 80225

The U.S. Geological Survey makes available dozens of publications, two of which are about rivers. Students can use them to supplement special reports and science projects and teachers can use them to enhance their curricula. The publications are:

"The Big Five" - Some Facts and Figures on our Nation's Largest Rivers. Presents statistics for maximum, minimum, and mean flows for the Nation's largest rivers - the Mississippi, St. Lawrence, Columbia, Ohio, and the Missouri.

River Basins of the United States: A Series. Lists basic facts including historical notes, flow characteristics, and physical statistics on selected river basins.

Water Watch
Division of Water
Department for Environmental Protection
Frankfort Office Park
18 Reilly Road

Be patient. If any phone number is incorrect, call (area code) 555-1212 and request the new listing.

The Government Works for Kids, Too

Frankfort, KY 40601 (502) 564-3410

A Field Guide to Kentucky Rivers and Streams was developed for Water Watch, a public participation program that encourages citizens to adopt a stream, lake or wetland, and then gain hands on experience in protecting and enhancing their adopted water resource.

ROCKETS

NASA Education Division
NASA Headquarters
Washington, DC 20546

Rockets: A Teaching Guide for an Elementary Science Unit on Rocketry is a teaching guide which emphasizes hands-on involvement. Background information about the history of rockets and basic science explaining why rockets work can be found within the publication. The unit also includes basic concepts of rocket control and descriptions of different kinds of rockets.

Elementary and Secondary Programs Branch
Educational Affairs Division
Mail Code XEE
NASA Headquarters
Washington, DC 20546

The principles of rocketry is one of many topics covered in the Aerospace Education Services Program (AESP) workshops held each summer for teachers at NASA field centers, elementary and secondary schools, and on college campuses. Workshops also cover astronomy, aeronautics, life in space, earth sciences, and remote sensing. A typical workshop includes how-to and hands-on activities to help teachers incorporate what they learn into classroom activities and programs to supplement existing curricula. Contact the office above for more detailed information.

ROCKS

U.S. Geological Survey
P.O. Box 25425
Denver, CO 80225

Is your child a rock collector? Then get the publication *Collecting Rocks*. It describes the origin of major rock types and how rocks can provide clues to the Earth's history, and includes suggestions for starting a rock collection, identifying specimens, and housing such a collection.

Office of Education, Room 212
Mail Stop 158
National Museum of Natural History
Washington, DC 20560 (202) 357-2747

The National Museum of Natural History has several different programs and activities held throughout the school year for visiting preschool and elementary school children, including a visiting program on rocks and minerals. In this program, students are introduced to rocks and the major rock-forming minerals by examining exhibited specimens in the Earth and Mineral exhibition halls and by participating in a hands-on classroom activity. Students distinguish between rocks and minerals; identify seven common minerals using the physical properties of luster, color, hardness, and streak; classify seven rock specimens according to their origin (igneous, sedimentary, or metamorphic); and explore the relationship between texture and mineral composition of rocks and the processes that form them.

Office of Education, Room 212
Mail Stop 158
National Museum of Natural History
Washington, DC 20560 (202) 357-2747

The National Museum of Natural History also conducts workshops for teachers. In the workshop *Rocks and Minerals*, teachers work with a geologist in developing ways to introduce students to rocks and minerals. Time is spent in the Earth and Mineral exhibition halls, as well as in a classroom. Activities are designed to provide experience in distinguishing between a rock and a mineral, describing minerals by their physical properties, and using rock texture to classify rocks according to their origin.

ROOSEVELT, FRANKLIN D.

Education Branch (NEEE)
National Archives and Records Administration
Washington, DC 20408 (202) 724-0454

The Education Branch of the National Archives offers teachers of upper elementary through secondary school students publications and teaching units to aid in the teaching of historical documents and eras. They include the following two addresses given by Franklin D. Roosevelt, which are part of the "Milestone Documents" series. Each booklet includes a historical introduction and transcriptions and facsimiles of the featured documents. (8 1/2 x 11, approx. 25 pages each, illustrations, 1986, softcover only, $2.50 each). The publications are:

Franklin D. Roosevelt's Inaugural Address of 1933 (#200112, ISBN 0-911333-69-X)

On War Against Japan: Franklin D. Roosevelt's "Day of Infamy" Address of 1941 (#200114, ISBN 0-911333-70-3)

SALMON

U.S. Fish and Wildlife Service
U.S. Department of the Interior
4401 N. Fairfax Drive
Mail Stop 130
Arlington, VA 22203 (703) 358-1711

The publication *Pacific Salmon* may provide you and your child with insights into this fascinating fish.

SATELLITES

NASA CORE
Lorain County Joint Vocational School
15181 Route 58 South
Oberlin, OH 44074 (216) 774-1051

Portrait of Earth: The Story of Satellites is a videocassette that explains what satellites are and how they perform their daily tasks in orbit around our planet. Captioned at the 2nd, 3rd, and 4th grade levels.

SATURN

Superintendent of Documents
U.S. Government Printing Office
Washington, DC 20402 (202) 783-3238

The Voyager Flights to Jupiter and Saturn is a nontechnical guide describing the Voyager flights from the Jupiter and Saturn flybys. Illustrated. 62 pages. 1982. Stock No. 033-000-00854-6. $5.50.

NASA CORE
Lorain County Joint Vocational School
15181 Route 58 South
Oberlin, OH 44074 (216) 774-1051

Voyagers 2 Encounter Saturn is a set of slides that illustrates Voyager's most significant discoveries about Saturn, including incredible rings, erupting volcanoes and cyclonic storms. Appropriate for grades 4-12.

Teaching Resource Center
Jet Propulsion Laboratory
4800 Oak Grove Dr.
Mail Stop CS-530
Pasadena, CA 91109 (818) 354-6916

Saturn: Voyager 1 and *Saturn: Voyager 2* are two separate sets of color slides with cassette narration. ($11 each. Each 40 slide/cassette program listed below contains 40 color slides and an audio cassette narration with audible beep tones).

SCHOOL ACHIEVERS

Superintendent of Documents
Dept. 33
Washington, DC 20402 (202) 783-3238

How to Help Your Children Achieve in School explains how to help your children improve their study skills, both at home and in school. Tips on maintaining interest and attention are given, and techniques for effective notetaking, studying, remembering, and taking tests are explained. 1983. 28 pp. (S/N 065-000-00176-4, $3.75).

SCHOOL IMPROVEMENT

Superintendent of Documents
Dept. 33
Washington, DC 20402 (202) 783-3238

Call the office above to obtain *Experiences in School Improvement: Story of 16 American Districts*. It discusses the experiences and recommendations of selected

Be patient. If any phone number is incorrect, call (area code) 555-1212 and request the new listing.

The Government Works For Kids, Too

high school principals and superintendents. Some of the recommendations include: redesigning schools to create more productive working and learning environments; changing the structure of the teaching career; developing a system to evaluate administrators effectively and accurately; allowing schools to make more of their own decisions, then holding them accountable for results; and much more. 1988. 91 pp. (S/N 065-000-00343-1, $4.50).

SCIENCE

The Ohio State University
1200 Chambers Road, Room 310
Columbus, OH 43212-1792 (614) 292-6717

The Science, Mathematics, and Environmental Education Clearinghouse is part of the Educational Resources Information Center (ERIC), a nationwide information network designed to provide users with ready access to education literature. This particular clearinghouse provides information on science, mathematics, and environmental education at all levels, and within these three broad subject areas, the following topics; development of curriculum and instructional materials; teachers and teacher education; learning theory/outcomes (including the impact of parameters such as interest level, intelligence, values, and concept development upon learning in these fields); educational programs; engineering; research and evaluative studies; medical applications; and computer applications.

R. Woods
Consumer Information Center
Pueblo, CO 81008

Helping Your Child Learn Science (#611X) is a free publication for parents available from the Consumer Information Center. To order write to the address above.

Department 900
Smithsonian Institution Press
Blue Ridge Summit, PA 17294 (717) 794-2148

Are you looking for science projects for your students? Then get the publication *Smithsonian Surprises: An Educational Activity Book* by Sara Toney. Appropriate for students in grades K-12. $7.95; $2.25 postage and handling first book, $1 each additional book.

SEALS

Marine Mammal Commission
1825 Connecticut Ave., NW, #512
Washington, DC 20009 (202) 606-5504

Children of all ages (and even adults!) will enjoy learning how to draw seals, whales, and dolphins. *How to Draw Whales and Seals* shows you how to draw these mammals in four or five easy steps.

SEEGER, PETE

Smithsonian/Folkways Recordings
416 Hungerford Dr., Suite 320
Rockville, MD. 20850

Pete Seeger is one of several artists whose recordings are available for purchase from Folkways Records, which is administered by the Smithsonian Institution's Office of Folklife Programs. Children's songs by Ella Jenkins and Woody Guthrie can also be purchased, along with dozens of recordings by lesser-known yet still very talented artists.

SESAME STREET

Attn: SSFS
FEMA
P.O. Box 70274
Washington, DC 20024

The Sesame Street Fire Safety Project was developed by the Community Education Services division of the Children's Television Workshop (CTW). The first edition of the *Sesame Street Fire Safety Resource Book* is still available in English and Spanish versions. The second edition of the *Sesame Street Fire Safety Book* contains the original Muppet skits and activities that inspired thousands to teach young children fire safety. Each book is accompanied by an audio cassette that contains five songs. Also included is a five page color brochure highlighting the Sesame Street research study on mass media fire education for young children. To order your free copy, write to the office above.

SHARKS

Office of Education, Room 212
Mail Stop 158
National Museum of Natural History
Washington, DC 20560 (202) 357-2747

Shark Tub is an instructional kit produced by the National Museum of Natural History as a classroom enhancement for the temporary exhibit *Sharks! Fact and Fantasy* (1990), and can be used to supplement any science curriculum. Dive gear tub (3x2x2 ft.) contains small shark specimens, dried shark jaws, shark leather, shark vertebrae, an egg case, a fossil tooth, and other hands-on materials. Curriculum and reference materials are included. Reserve kit by calling (202) 357-2811. Teachers must pick up and return tub at the museum, Monday through Saturday, 10:30 to 4, or Sunday, 12-5. If shipping is necessary, shipping fee is required in advance. It is available on loan for a three-week period and may be requested by writing to the office above.

SITTING BULL

Photographic Services
American History Building
Room CB-054
Smithsonian Institution
Washington, DC 20560 (202) 357-1933

The poster, *Sitting Bull*, is available for $3 for educators and parents who would like to expose their students and children to famous American Indians.

Attn: Public Inquiries Office
Bureau of Indian Affairs
Mail Stop 2620 (MIB)
U.S. Department of Interior
Washington, DC 20240 (202) 208-3711

From Pocahontas to Sitting Bull, the publication, *Famous Indians: A Collection of Short Biographies*, describes the history and lives of twenty famous American Indians. All were leaders in a great struggle to preserve treasured lands and lifeways. With their tribesmen, they are inseparably linked to our country's history from its earliest beginnings through generations of growth.

SKYLAB

NASA CORE
Lorain County Joint Vocational School
15181 Route 58 South
Oberlin, OH 44074 (216) 774-1051

The videocassette, "Our Laboratories in Space," examines some of the scientific and medical experiments that were completed on Skylab, the Apollo-SOYUZ Test Project and future experiments to be conducted on the space shuttle. The slides *3 Flights of Skylab* recounts man's first attempt to establish a permanent laboratory in space. Both are appropriate for grades 4 and up.

SLIDES

Education Resource Center
Education Division, MRC 305
National Air and Space Museum
Washington, DC 20560 (202) 786-2109

The National Air and Space Museum offers to teachers of all levels and disciplines educational materials, including slides, pertaining to aviation, space, and the Museum's collections.

Office of Education, Room 212
Mail Stop 158
National Museum of Natural History
Washington, DC 20560 (202) 357-2747

Slide sets are available for a three-week loan free of charge from the National Museum of Natural History. The slides sets are:

Ancient Cultures: 10,000 B.C. - 600 A.D.
Dinosaurs and Other Giants
Glaciers: Geological Evidence
An Introduction to Archaeology
Introduction to the Natural History Museum
Native Peoples of North American

NASA CORE
Lorain County Joint Vocational School
15181 Route 58 South

Be patient. If any phone number is incorrect, call (area code) 555-1212 and request the new listing.

The Government Works for Kids, Too

Oberlin, OH 44074 (216) 774-1051

The NASA Central Operation of Resources for Educators (CORE), established in cooperation with Lorain County Joint Vocational School, serves as the national distribution center for NASA produced education materials. For a minimal charge the NASA CORE will provide a valuable service to educators unable to visit one of the NASA Teacher Resource Centers (TRC), by making NASA educational audiovisual materials available through its mail order service. Slides available include:

Human Space Flight: Living in Space. Explanation of how astronauts live and work in the Space Shuttle environment. Grades 4 -12.

Propulsion: Space Shuttle. Highlights the NASA Space Transportation System, its functions, and possible uses for the future. Grades 4 - 12.

America in Space: The First 25 Years. Details America's long string of successful space accomplishments, culminating in the Apollo 11 moon landing, the Voyager Missions, and the Space Shuttle program. Grades 4 -12.

Moon Landing - Apollo 11. Tells the story of the most famous spaceflight in history, man's first moon landing. Grades 4 - 12.

The Story of the Flight of Apollo-SOYUZ. Highlights the first meeting between America and Russia in space. Three astronauts and two cosmonauts rendezvoused in orbit, docked and entered each other's craft.

Voyagers Encounter Jupiter. Focuses on the flights of Voyagers I and II as one of the most successful and revealing unmanned spaceflights in history. Grades 4 - 12.

Voyagers 2 Encounter Saturn. Illustrates Voyager's most significant discoveries about Saturn, including incredible rings, erupting volcanoes and cyclonic storms. Grades 4 - 12.

Best of the Space Shuttle 1977-1984. Examines shuttle highlights from the first dramatic shuttle flights to the on-going array of spectacular space walks and experiments. Grades 4 - 12.

The Story of Our Universe. This information-packed program explores the Universe and all of its other worldly phenomena. Grades 4 - 12.

The Return of Halley's Comet. Examines an event heralded by man since the beginning of time, Halley's Comet, and discusses its place in the Universe. Grades 4 - 12.

3 Flights of Skylab. Recounts man's first attempt to establish a permanent laboratory in space. Grades 4 - 12.

Transformations of Flight. A series of slides which present the numbers 1-10 being transformed into ten different air and spacecraft in the history of flight. These slides successfully compliment the videotape also found in this catalog. Produced by the Smithsonian Institution. Grades K - 3.

Voyager Encounters Neptune. Color photographs taken when Voyager encountered Neptune in August of 1989. Includes pictures of the Great Dark Spot, Neptune's rings and Triton. Grades 4 - 12.

Department of Extension Programs
National Gallery of Art
Washington, DC 20565

The National Gallery of Art is continually exploring ways to develop awareness in the visual arts and make its collections accessible to everyone, no matter how far away from the Gallery they may live. They now have an Extension Program which loans not only slide programs, but films and videocassettes to educational institutions, community groups, and to individuals throughout the U.S. free of charge. Write to the office above for more information on how you may bring the National Gallery of Art to your students.

Nebraska Energy Office
9th Floor
State Capitol
P.O. Box 95085
Lincoln, NE 68509 (402) 471-2867

Energy-related slides and other instructional materials, (including video tapes, curriculum guides, and resource books and materials) are available to Nebraska educators only from the office above.

Warning and Forecast Branch, W/OM11
National Weather Service
National Oceanic and Atmospheric Administration
SSMCII
1325 East West Highway, Room 14370
Silver Spring, MD 20910

The following slides can be used by educators to teach school children about safety during natural disasters. They include:

Tornado Slides:
A Slide Series Supplement to "Tornado: A Spotter's Guide"
Tornado Preparedness
Tornado Safety in Residence
The Safest Place in Schools
A Look at the Tornado and other Local Storms

Thunderstorm Slides:
Advanced Meteorologist/Spotter Training Slide Series
When Lightning Strikes

Flash Flood/Flood Slides:
Flash Floods: Myths or Realities
Flash Flood Preparedness

Hurricane Slides:
Hurricane Hugo
Hurricane Eloise
Hurricane Preparedness
Hurricane Alicia
Hurricane Frederick

Winter Storm Slides:
Winter Storms, The Deceptive Killers

Teaching Resource Center
Jet Propulsion Laboratory
4800 Oak Grove Dr.
Mail Stop CS-530
Pasadena, CA 91109 (818) 354-6916

Below are selected color slide packages on space and planetary subjects which can be excellent educational aids for classroom use. To receive an order form contact the office above.

Color Slides with Cassette Narration

($11 each. Each 40 slide/cassette program listed below contains 40 color slides and an audio cassette narration with audible beep tones. Each set comes in its own plastic storage box.)
Our Universe
Apollo 11: The First Moon Landing
Apollo 17: The Final Mission
Viking Lands on Mars
Jupiter: Voyagers 1 & 2
Mt. St. Helens Erupts
Saturn: Voyager 1
Saturn: Voyager 2
History of the Universe: Space Art by Don Dixon
America in Space
Best of the Space Shuttle 1977-1984

Slide Sets

($6 each. Each 20-slide set consists of twenty 35 mm slides held in a plastic vue-file sleeve which will fit into a three ring binder. Many sets have a fact sheet included which lists the title of the slides and may have a brief description or topic.)
Voyager Missions, Computer Graphics
Manned Space Flight: Mercury, Gemini, Apollo, Apollo-Soyuz, Skylab
Space Shuttle Mission STS-1
Earth: Views from Moon and Space Shuttle
Galtech/JPL Facilities
JPL Recent Projects 1973-1983
JPL Historical Missions: Jato, Explorer, Ranger, Surveyor, Mariner
Voyager Missions to Jupiter
Vikings Missions to Mars
Mariner 9 Mission to Mars, Black and White
Voyager Mission to Saturn
IRAS, Set 1, Infrared Astronomical Satellite
Halley's Comet

Voyager Mission to Uranus
IRAS, Set 2, Infrared Astronomical Satellite
Future Missions, Set 2
Voyager Mission to Neptune
Magellan Mission to Venus
Neptune Computer Graphics, Set 2

SMITHSONIAN INSTITUTION

Office of Elementary and Secondary Education
Arts and Industries Building
Room 1163
Smithsonian Institution
Washington, DC 20560 (202) 357-3049

The easiest way to find out what educational materials the Smithsonian Institution has available is to obtain the publication *Resource Guide for Teachers*. The materials include bibliographies, posters, slide sets, films, teacher's manuals, videocassettes, and curriculum units. The publication also includes materials available from the National Gallery of Art and the John F. Kennedy Center for the Performing Arts.

SMOKEY BEAR

Forest Service
U.S. Department of Agriculture
14th and Independence, SW
P.O. Box 96090
Washington, DC 20090-6090 (202) 205-0957

Get in touch with the office above to receive Smokey Bear fire prevention materials, including *The True Story of Smokey Bear* comic book.

SNAKES

U.S. Fish and Wildlife Service
U.S. Department of the Interior
4401 N. Fairfax Drive
Mail Stop 130
Arlington, VA 22203 (703) 358-1711

The U.S. Fish and Wildlife Service has publications on snakes including *Conservation Note 6 - Snakes* and *Snakes*.

SOCIAL STUDIES

California Energy Extension Service
1400 Tenth St., Room 209
Sacramento, CA 95814 (916) 323-4388

Through the lessons of social studies, energy awareness can be taught only in classes. *100 Ways to Celebrate NEED* is a guide which promotes energy awareness and links lessons to not only science, but also to social studies, history, economics, fine arts and language arts. This guide contains 100 activities for children in grades K-12, along with a glossary and teacher background information.

Indiana University
Social Studies Development Center
2805 East 10th Street, Suite 120
Bloomington, IN 47408-2698 (812) 855-3838

The Educational Resources Information Center (ERIC) is a nationwide information network designed to provide users with ready access to education literature, including literature on social studies. The Social Studies/Social Science Education (SO) Clearinghouse contains literature on all levels of social studies and social science education; the contributions of history, geography, and other social science disciplines; applications of theory and research to social science education; education as a social science; comparative education (K-12); content and curriculum materials on social topics such as law-related education ethnic studies, bias and discrimination, aging, and women's equity. Music and art education are also covered.

SOLAR ENERGY

Florida's Governor's Energy Office
The Capitol
Tallahassee, FL 32399-0001 (904) 488-2475

Solar and Energy Conservation Projects for Students was produced by the Florida Solar Energy Center and is available from the office above to elementary school teachers. Another publication, *Energy Research Projects Guide*, will assist

students in their selection of an energy topic for science fair projects. Also available is the *Florida Middle School Energy Education Project*. All are free of charge.

Conservation and Renewable Energy
Inquiry and Referral Service (CAREIRS)
P.O. Box 3048
Merrifield, VA 22116 (800) 523-2929

People are trying to find new ways to heat their homes, factories, offices, and schools without using so much expensive oil and gas. *Solar Energy and You* helps teach children about solar energy and solar heat. Call the office above for this four page publication.

SOLAR SYSTEM

NASA CORE
Lorain County Joint Vocational School
15181 Route 58 South
Oberlin, OH 44074 (216) 774-1051

The NASA Central Operation of Resources for Educators (CORE) serves as the national distribution center for NASA produced education materials, including the video *Our Solar System*. This video teaches the names, orbital positions, and characteristics of each planet using the phrase "my very educated mother just served us nine pizza pies". The program is animated, set to music, and appropriate for early elementary grades. Grade 2 - 6.

SOLDIERS

Superintendent of Documents
Dept. 33
Washington, DC 20402 (202) 783-3238

The American Soldier, Set No. 2 is a set of 10 color posters reproducing paintings of American servicemen and women over the 100-year period from 1863 to 1963. (Includes an explanatory booklet). Use these posters to help teach your children about American history. All posters are 9 x 13 inches and printed on fine white paper suitable for framing. (S/N 008-020-00227-5, $6, 1989, shipped flat).

SPACE EXPLORATION

Superintendent of Documents
U.S. Government Printing Office
Washington, DC 20402 (202) 783-3238

The National Aeronautics and Space Administration produces educational publications for educators, students, and the general public. All are offered for sale by the Superintendent of Documents, U.S. GPO. Prices may change.

NASA CORE
Lorain County Joint Vocational School
15181 Route 58 South
Oberlin, OH 44074 (216) 774-1051

The NASA Central Operation of Resources for Educators (CORE), established in cooperation with Lorain County Joint Vocational School, serves as the national distribution center for NASA produced education materials. For a minimal charge the NASA CORE will provide a valuable service to educators unable to visit one of the NASA Teacher Resource Centers (TRC), by making NASA educational audiovisual materials available through its mail order service. Also available are different memorabilia items which can be used by teachers as awards for students. They include a NASA logo patch, pencils, hats, T-shirts, mugs, and astronaut ice cream.

Elementary and Secondary Programs Branch
Educational Affairs Division
Mail Code XEE
NASA Headquarters
Washington, DC 20546

The Aerospace Education Services Program (AESP), previously known as Spacemobile, is the Educational Affairs Division's premier outreach program. AESP specialists, all former teachers themselves, reach millions of students each year. They cross the country from September to June each year, assisting schools so students and teachers can see first-hand what NASA is all about. Visits are scheduled by field center, and because each field center performs a specific service for NASA, each center's program is a little different from the others. All emphasize current NASA programs, such as the Space Shuttle and the Freedom Space Station. Because of this program's popularity, a visit should be requested well in advance. Although field centers make every effort to accommodate the date a school requests, there is currently about a 2-year waiting list.

Be patient. If any phone number is incorrect, call (area code) 555-1212 and request the new listing.

The Government Works for Kids, Too

Education Division
NASA Headquarters
Washington, DC 20546

NASA Spacelink is a collection of NASA information and educational materials stored on a computer at the Marshall Space Flight Center in Huntsville, Alabama. The system may be accessed over regular telephone lines. It is designed to communicate with a wide variety of computers and modems, especially those most commonly found in classrooms and home. NASA Spacelink is free, but you'll owe your phone company for long distance calls. It includes a listing of all the major NASA educational programs. Subjects include the Aerospace Education Services Project, Urban Community Enrichment Program, Summer High School Apprenticeship Research Program, Space Science Student Involvement Project, Teacher Workshops, Educators Mailing List, Telelectures, Teacher Resource Centers, and Science Fair support. Classroom materials include a variety of information useful in the classroom, including space science lesson plans and activities (all grade levels and many subjects), astronomy information, film/video list, computer programs, career information, computer graphics, and a source list for pictures, posters, and other educational materials.

Elementary and Secondary Programs Branch
Educational Affairs Division
Mail Code XEE
NASA Headquarters
Washington, DC 20546

Aerospace Education Services Program (AESP) specialists conduct workshops for teachers each summer at NASA field centers, elementary and secondary schools, and on college campuses. Workshops cover astronomy, aeronautics, life in space, principles of rocketry, earth sciences, and remote sensing. A typical workshop includes how-to and hands-on activities to help teachers incorporate what they learn into classroom activities and programs to supplement existing curricula.

Education Division, MRC 305
National Air and Space Museum
Washington, DC 20560 (202) 786-2109

The Education Resource Center (ERC) of the National Air and Space Museum (NASM) is open to teachers of all levels and disciplines. The ERC offers teachers access to educational materials pertaining to aviation, space, and the Museum's collections. These materials are produced by NASM, the National Aeronautics and Space Administration (NASA), and other government agencies, and private organizations. Additional information on the ERC and other NASM educational programs may be obtained by writing to the address above. Educational materials include the following:

Curriculum Packages: Complete units on specific topics are available on request for grades K-12. Write and tell them the subjects and grades you teach, and they will be happy to send you the appropriate packages. Requests must be made by teachers on school letterhead.

Lesson Plans: Hundreds of classroom activities on aerospace-related topics, arranged according to subject and grade levels, are available for duplication when you visit the ERC. This service is not available through the mail.

Public Domain Software: Aerospace-related public domain computer software for use with Apple II series and IBM PC computers is available for duplication when you visit the ERC, as well as through the mail. In both cases, teachers must provide blank diskettes. Contact the ERC for a current catalog and mail-in procedures.

Commercial Software: A growing collection of IBM PC and Apple II series commercial software on aerospace topics is available on a preview-only basis for visiting teachers.

Videodiscs and CD-Roms: Visit the ERC to preview our growing collection of these new audiovisual formats.

Filmstrips: The ERC's large collection of filmstrips is available for preview. NASM-produced filmstrips may be obtained from the National Audiovisual Center, 8700 Edgewood Drive, Capitol Heights, MD 20743, (301) 763-1896.

Videos: Hundreds of videos can be previewed at the ERC. Videos must be rented or purchased from their respective suppliers.

Slide Sets: A variety of slide sets are available for preview in the ERC. The NASM-produced "Milestones of Flight" set is available through NASA CORE.

Other Resources: A variety of resources such as science kits, posters, brochures, and catalogs are available as reference materials.

"Skylines" Newsletter: The Education Division publishes a newsletter for teachers. Please write and ask to be placed on our mailing list.

ERC Workshops: Half-day workshops, to aid educators in utilizing the ERC, are scheduled on request. Participants receive assistance in compiling educational units to meet specific needs.

Other Workshops: Throughout the year, the Education Division offers aerospace-related teacher workshops that are announced in the *Skylines* newsletter. Contact the Education Division for more information.

Tours and Group Reservations: Free docent-led tours of the Museum are offered year-round for school groups, on a variety of subjects and grade levels. Reservations must be made by mail at least three weeks in advance but no earlier than eight weeks in advance of visit. School group reservation for the Einstein Planetarium and Langley Theater are also available. Request a current tour brochure and reservation form from the Tour Scheduling Office, MRC 305, National Air and Space Museum, Washington, DC 20560.

Superintendent of Documents
U.S. Government Printing Office
Washington, DC 20402 (202) 783-3238

In June 1984 President Reagan announced a new NASA education program, "Operation Liftoff". This program is designed to encourage pupils in the nation's elementary schools to take a greater interest in mathematics and science. NASA responded to this announcement with a plan to reach students in their formative years in the elementary grades. Operation Liftoff complements the widely acclaimed educational programs NASA now offers at the secondary and university levels. *Living in Space - Operation Liftoff Elementary Space Program: A Resource Guide With Activities for Elementary School Teachers*, one of Operation Liftoff's publications, is available for sale from the office above.

Teaching Resource Center
Jet Propulsion Laboratory
4800 Oak Grove Dr.
Mail Stop CS-530
Pasadena, CA 91109 (818) 354-6916

Below are selected video programs and color slide packages on space and planetary subjects which can be excellent educational aids for classroom use. To receive an order form contact the office above.

Videos
($25 each. Available in VHS and Beta formats, PAL VHS format for use in Europe and Australia only where indicated by a **.)
1st Flight of Space Shuttle STS-1 (30 min.)
Universe (30 min.)
Apollo Moon Landings (56 min.)
History of Flight (56 min.)
Mars and Mercury (the planets) (52 min.)
Mercury and Gemini Spacecraft Missions (56 min.)
Eruption of Mt. St. Helens (30 min.)
America in Space: 1st 25 Years (50 min.)
Shuttle Flights STS-1 thru STS-8 (60 min.)
Jupiter, Saturn, Uranus and Neptune (30 min.)
The Dream is Alive, IMAX (40 min.)
Kennedy Space Center Tour (42 min.)
We Remember: Shuttle Pioneers '81-'87 (60 min.)
Voyager Missions Animation Only (30 min.)

Color Slides with Cassette Narration
($11 each. Each 40 slide/cassette program listed below contains 40 color slides and an audio cassette narration with audible beep tones. Each set comes in its own plastic storage box.)
Our Universe
Apollo 11: The First Moon Landing
Apollo 17: The Final Mission
Viking Lands on Mars
Jupiter: Voyagers 1 & 2
Mt. St. Helens Erupts
Saturn: Voyager 1
Saturn: Voyager 2
History of the Universe: Space Art by Don Dixon
America in Space
Best of the Space Shuttle 1977-1984

Be patient. If any phone number is incorrect, call (area code) 555-1212 and request the new listing.

The Government Works For Kids, Too

Slide Sets

($6 each. Each 20-slide set consists of twenty 35mm slides held in a plastic vue-file sleeve which fits into a three ring binder. Many sets include a fact sheet which lists the title of the slides and may have a brief description or topic.)

Voyager Missions, Computer Graphics
Manned Space Flight: Mercury, Gemini, Apollo, Apollo-Soyuz, Skylab
Space Shuttle Mission STS-1
Earth: Views from Moon and Space Shuttle
Galtech/JPL Facilities
JPL Recent Projects 1973-1983
JPL Historical Missions: Jato, Explorer, Ranger, Surveyor, Mariner
Voyager Missions to Jupiter
Vikings Missions to Mars
Mariner 9 Mission to Mars, Black and White
Voyager Mission to Saturn
IRAS, Set 1, Infrared Astronomical Satellite
Halley's Comet
Voyager Mission to Uranus
IRAS, Set 2, Infrared Astronomical Satellite
Future Missions, Set 2
Voyager Mission to Neptune
Magellan Mission to Venus
Neptune Computer Graphics, Set 2

SPACE SHUTTLE

NASA CORE
Lorain County Joint Vocational School
15181 Route 58 South
Oberlin, OH 44074 (216) 774-1051

For a minimal charge the NASA Central Operation of Resources for Educators (CORE) CORE will provide a valuable service to educators unable to visit one of the NASA Teacher Resource Centers (TRC), by making NASA educational audiovisual materials available through its mail order service. Audiovisual materials which contain information on the Space Shuttle and are appropriate for certain elementary grades include the following:

Videocassettes:

Opening New Frontiers: The Orbital Flight Tests of the Space Transportation System. Covers the first four test missions of the Space Shuttle Columbia, STS flights, 1,2,3, and 4. Also includes events leading up to the first launch, President Reagan's speech after the fourth landing, and highlights of the Orbital Flight Test Program. Grade 4 - 10.

Milestones of Flight. This program was produced by the National Air and Space Museum and is based on the museum's "Milestones of Flight" Gallery. It traces the history of flight from Langley's first attempts to the Space Shuttle. Uses live footage from many history making events. Grade 4 - 10.

Shuttle: A Remarkable Flying Machine. Features the first historic flight of the Space Shuttle Columbia. Highlights include the liftoff on April 12, 1981, the onboard activities of Young and Crippen and a spectacular landing on Rogers Dry Lake bed in California. Grade 4 - adult.

We Deliver: Summary of Shuttle Flights 5,6,7,& 8. Covers the first four operational missions of the Space Transportation System, STS flight 5,6,7 & 8. Stresses the operational common denominator of these missions - satellite deployment. Also includes significant secondary achievements such as the first female astronaut, first black astronaut, first night launch and landing, and some of the more important onboard experiments. Grade 4 - adult.

To Dream...To Learn. The first segment of this program documents two Ohio schools who outfitted school buses as Space Shuttles. The school bus "ground shuttles" were sent on "missions" during which students learned a great deal about space travel. The second half of this program shows shuttle astronauts demonstrating toys during space shuttle mission 51-D. Students were asked to speculate as to how the toys would react in the weightless environment of space. Grade 4 - adult.

NASA Images: Episode 1. Several films about the U.S.'s efforts to land a man on the moon are presented. Subjects discussed include: guidance, navigation, footage from the first manned moon landing and research aircraft which led to the Space Shuttle development. Grade 4 - 12.

Slides:

Human Space Flight: Living in Space. Explanation of how astronauts live and work in the Space Shuttle environment. Grade 4 -12.

America in Space: The First 25 Years. Details America's long string of successful space accomplishments, culminating in the Apollo 11 moon landing, the Voyager Missions, and the Space Shuttle program. Grade 4 -12.

Best of the Space Shuttle 1977-1984. Examines shuttle highlights from the first dramatic shuttle flights to the on-going array of spectacular space walks and experiments. Grade 4 - 12.

Filmstrip Program:

Propulsion: Space Shuttle. Highlights the NASA Space Transportation System, its functions, and possible uses for the future. Grade 4 - 12.

Computer Software (5 1/4" diskettes for use on Apple Computers):

Space Shuttle Mission Facts Data Base. A data base that provides information on the first 30 space shuttle missions including: mission number, orbiter, date, commander and pilot. To use this data base you must have the Apple works program. Produced by Oklahoma State University. Grade K - Adult.

Space Shuttle Commander. Side A introduces students to Newton's laws of motion by asking them to imagine that they are the commander of the space shuttle. Takes a nonmathematical approach to this topic and concentrates on concept formation. Side B contains four question banks to use for practice or evaluation. Copyrighted by and reproduced with permission from Lloyd P. Reiber. Grade 4 - 8.

Superintendent of Documents
U.S. Government Printing Office
Washington, DC 20402 (202) 783-3238

Are you looking for more information on the Space Shuttle? The National Aeronautics and Space Administration produces educational publications for educators, students, and the general public, including those listed below on the Space Shuttle. All are offered for sale by the Superintendent of Documents, U.S. GPO. Prices may change. Contact your regional GPO outlet or call the office above. Materials appropriate for the elementary grades include the following:

Aboard the Space Shuttle (publication). Describes what it would be like to travel into space on a typical Space Shuttle mission, including clothing, food, what the various compartments look like, etc. Illustrated in color. 32 pages. 1980. Stock No. 033-00-00806-6. $2.75.

Space Shuttle (poster). Shows the external configuration, and internal design and construction of the Space Shuttle. Printed in color. 30x42 inches. Folded. 1978. Stock No. 033-000-00743-4. $3.50.

Spacelab Wallsheet (poster). Spacelab and Space Shuttle orbiter during a hypothetical mission. Inserts show life cycle of Spacelab from assembly to launch, different Spacelab configurations, and parts of the vehicle. Printed in color. 43x44 inches. 1983. Stock No. 033-000-00903-8. $3.75.

Teaching Resource Center
Jet Propulsion Laboratory
4800 Oak Grove Dr.
Mail Stop CS-530
Pasadena, CA 91109 (818) 354-6916

Below are selected video programs and color slide packages on the Space Shuttle. To receive an order form contact the office above.

Videos

($25 each. Available in VHS and Beta formats, PAL VHS format for use in Europe and Australia only where indicated by a "**".)
1st Flight of Space Shuttle STS-1 (30 min.)
Shuttle Flights STS-1 thru STS-8 (60 min.)
We Remember: Shuttle Pioneers '81-'87 (60 min.)

Color Slides with Cassette Narration

($11 each. Each 40 slide/cassette program listed below contains 40 color slides and an audio cassette narration with audible beep tones. Each set comes in its own plastic storage box.)
Best of the Space Shuttle 1977-1984

Slide Sets

($6 each. Each 20-slide set consists of twenty 35 mm slides held in a plastic vue-file sleeve which will fit into a three ring binder. Many sets have a fact sheet included which lists the title of the slides and may have a brief description or topic.)
Space Shuttle Mission STS-1
Earth: Views from Moon and Space Shuttle

Be patient. If any phone number is incorrect, call (area code) 555-1212 and request the new listing.

The Government Works for Kids, Too

SPEAKING

Indiana University
Smith Research Center, Suite 150
2805 East 10th Street
Bloomington, IN 47408-2698 (812) 855-5847

The Reading and Communication Skills (CS) Clearinghouse is part of the Educational Resources Information Center (ERIC), a nationwide information network designed to provide users with ready access to education literature. Literature is available on reading, english, and communication skills (verbal and nonverbal), preschool through college; educational research and instruction development in reading, writing, speaking, and listening; identification, diagnosis, and remediation of reading problem; speech communication (including forensics), mass communication, interpersonal and small group interaction, interpretation, rhetorical and communication theory, speech sciences, and the theater. Preparation of instructional staff and related personnel in these areas. All aspects of reading behavior with emphasis on physiology, psychology, sociology, and teaching; instructional materials, curricula, tests/measurement, and methodology at all levels of reading; the role of libraries and other agencies in fostering and guiding reading; and diagnostics and remedial reading services in schools and clinical settings.

STAMPS CLUBS

U.S. Postal Service
Ben Franklin Stamp Club Program (BFSC)
Washington, DC 20260-6755

In 1974 the U.S. Postal Service established the Benjamin Franklin Stamp Club Program to create an awareness of stamps and to demonstrate their educational and entertaining benefits to students in the fourth through seventh grades. Stamp collecting is an enjoyable experience that teaches important skills applicable to every day life (for example, organization, appreciation of valuable objects, the value of money and how to manage money). Teachers or administrators interested in starting clubs can call their local postmaster or, for more information on the BFSC Program, write to the office above.

STARS

R. Woods
Consumer Information Center - Y
P.O. Box 100
Pueblo, CO 81002

Stars in Your Eyes: A Guide to the Northern Skies contains helpful hints on how to find the seven best known constellations and an explanation on how they were named. 23 pp. (1988. DOD) 155X. $1.50. Write to the office above to receive a copy.

STEAM

U.S. Geological Survey
P.O. Box 25425
Denver, CO 80225

The publication *Natural Steam for Power* describes the investigation of geothermal steam as a potential source of energy for power needs worldwide. It also discusses the nature and behavior of steam formed underground.

STREAMS

Water Watch
Division of Water
Department for Environmental Protection
Frankfort Office Park
14 Reilly Road
Frankfort, KY 40601 (502) 564-3410

A Field Guide to Kentucky Rivers and Streams was developed for Water Watch, a public participation program that encourages citizens to adopt a stream, lake or wetland, and then gain hands on experience in protecting and enhancing their adopted water resource. *Kentucky Wild Rivers* is also available from the office above.

SWANS

U.S. Fish and Wildlife Service
U.S. Department of the Interior
4401 N. Fairfax Drive
Mail Stop 130
Arlington, VA 22203 (703) 358-1711

Is your child fascinated with swans? Then get the publication *Trumpeter Swan* so he can learn more about them.

TEACHER WORKSHOPS

Education Resource Center
Education Division, MRC 305
National Air and Space Museum
Washington, DC 20560 (202) 786-2109

The Education Resource Center (ERC) of the National Air and Space Museum (NASM) is open to teachers of all levels and disciplines. The ERC offers teachers access to educational materials pertaining to aviation, space, and the Museum's collections. They offer half-day workshops, to aid educators in utilizing the ERC, and are scheduled on request. Participants receive assistance in compiling educational units to meet specific needs.

Office of Education, Room 212
Mail Stop 158
National Museum of Natural History
Washington, DC 20560 (202) 357-2747

The National Museum of Natural History Workshops for Teachers offers the following workshops for elementary and middle school teachers. Contact the office above for specific dates.

Old Growth Forests: Learn about the ecology of old growth forests from a Forest Service ranger. Review materials available for pre- and post-visit activities, including the instructional kit. Join the ranger to explore the temporary exhibit about old growth forests.

Indian Walkaround: The workshop reviews Walkaround logistics, presents background information on Native Americans, and ideas for classroom activities. This year's topic is "Native American Traditional Clothing, Then and Now." Logistical information includes teachers' and parents' roles, storage of coats and lunches, the Walkaround route, and what to expect.

Dinosaurs: A walk through the Dinosaur Hall to help teachers and aides design a visit for their classes, followed by an informal lecture on major dinosaur groups represented in the exhibit hall.

Climate and Endangered Species: A workshop designed to help teachers and aides design a visit or prepare for a guided tour. The identification of all endangered and extinct modern animals on exhibit is followed by an informal talk about why certain groups of animals are more vulnerable than others.

Seeds of Change: Become acquainted with the ideas, issues, and information embodied in the concept of the Columbian Exchange and in the exhibit *Seeds of Change.* Gather suggestions on using the exhibition with social studies, geography, and history classes and projects. Workshop includes activities in the exhibit and in the classroom.

Rocks and Minerals: Work with a geologist in developing ways to introduce students to rocks and minerals. Time is spent in the Earth and Mineral exhibition halls, as well as in a classroom. Activities are designed to provide experience in: 1) distinguishing between a rock and a mineral, 2) describing minerals by their physical properties, and 3) using rock texture to classify rocks according to their origin.

Oceans: Become familiar with ancient and modern reefs and how ocean populations have changed over time. Learn the ecology of and strategies for competing in a water environment. Survey briefly the problems in today's ocean environments.

Understanding Culture: Introducing Culture Into Your Classroom and/or Curricula: Culture is a major concept in social studies, language and literature, history, art, philosophy - and in life. The workshop provides an understanding of culture and how it works, a perspective on world cultures and the concepts of multiculturalism and Eurocentrism. Included are suggestions for resources, learning activities, and strategies for integrating an understanding of culture into social studies, geography, history, biology, language arts, art, sociology, and anthropology. Workshop involves using museum exhibits for teaching.

National Science Teachers Association
Space, Science, and Technology Programs
1742 Connecticut Ave., NW
Washington, DC 20009 (202) 328-5800

The NASA Education Workshop for Elementary School Teachers (NEWEST) gives outstanding elementary teachers a chance to personally experience the U.S.

Be patient. If any phone number is incorrect, call (area code) 555-1212 and request the new listing.

aerospace program. As a NEWEST participant, you will spend two weeks during the summer at one of NASA's research centers learning about the latest in space and aeronautics activities. You will work with NASA experts and elementary curriculum specialists to fit the wealth of materials you will receive into your classroom teaching.

Elementary and Secondary Programs Branch
Educational Affairs Division
Mail Code XEE
NASA Headquarters
Washington, DC 20546

Aerospace Education Services Program (AESP) specialists conduct workshops for teachers each summer at NASA field centers, elementary and secondary schools, and on college campuses. Workshops cover astronomy, aeronautics, life in space, principles of rocketry, earth sciences, and remote sensing. A typical workshop includes how-to and hands-on activities to help teachers incorporate what they learn into classroom activities and programs to supplement existing curricula.

Education Branch (NEEE)
National Archives and Records Administration
Washington, DC 20408
(202) 724-0454

The National Archives preserves and makes available to the public the permanently valuable records of the U.S. Government. It offers teachers from the upper elementary grades through the secondary levels a workshop called *Primarily Teaching* that introduces them to the holdings and organization of the National Archives. *Primarily Teaching* emphasizes secondary strategies, but educators at all levels adapt them to their particular needs. Participants will learn how to do research in historical records; to create classroom material from records; and to present documents in ways that sharpen students' skills and enthusiasm for history, social studies, and the humanities.

Texas Parks and Wildlife Department
Ilo Hiller, Project WILD Coordinator
4200 Smith School Rd.
Austin, TX 78744

Project Wild is an award-winning environmental and conservation education program of instructional workshops and supplementary materials for teachers of kindergarten through high school age youth which prepares students to be responsible decision makers. The *Project Wild* materials are distributed free of charge to teachers and youth group leaders who attend one of the Texas Parks and Wildlife sponsored six-hour instructional workshops. The *Project Wild* guides cannot be purchased or obtained in any other manner.

TEACHING

American Association of
Colleges for Teacher Education
One Dupont Circle NW, Suite 610
Washington, DC 20036-1186
(202) 293-2450

The Educational Resources Information Center (ERIC) is a nationwide information network designed to provide users with ready access to education literature. ERIC collects, analyzes, and distributes information from local, state, federal, and international agencies, as well as private sources. It consists of 16 clearinghouses including the Teacher Education Clearinghouse. The clearinghouse contains information on school personnel at all levels; teacher selection and training, preservice and inservice preparation, and retirement; the theory, philosophy, and practice of teaching; curricula and general education not specifically covered by other Clearinghouses; and all aspects of physical, health, and recreation education.

TELESCOPE, HUBBLE SPACE

NASA CORE
Lorain County Joint Vocational School
15181 Route 58 South
Oberlin, OH 44074
(216) 774-1051

Computer software is available on the Hubble Space Telescope. The *Hubble Space Telescope Educational Software Project* consists of four Apple II disks with reproducible information sheets and reference materials: *Windows to the Universe* chronicles the history of astronomical observations from the unaided eye through the Hubble Space Telescope; *Telescopes* explains the science of optics and the design and characteristics of telescopes; *Introduction to the Hubble Space Telescope* explains the design and operation of the Hubble Space Telescope; *Images From Space* describes the process through which light is captured by the Hubble space Telescope and converted into images on Earth; *Activities Disk*

contains a collection of classroom activities and illustrations relating to telescopes; *Glossary* contains an Appleworks data base of more than 300 astronomy terms. Also includes two Macintosh Applications Software (requires Pagemaker program 3.02 version or higher): *Hubble Space Telescope Model* contains the pattern and instructions for making a detailed model of NASA's Hubble Space Telescope: *Telescope Primer* outline of the basic principles behind the design and operation of telescopes. Includes many diagrams that can be enlarged and used for making transparencies. Grade 5-8.

THUNDERSTORMS

Warning and Forecast Branch, W/OM11
National Weather Service
National Oceanic and Atmospheric Administration
SSMCII
1325 East West Highway, Room 14370
Silver Spring, MD 20910

The office above has the following audiovisuals available which can be used by educators to teach school children about safety during natural disasters:

Thunderstorm Videotape:
Everyday Weather Project: Thunderstorms

Thunderstorm Slides:
Advanced Meteorologist/Spotter Training Slide Series
When Lightning Strikes

TIME, GEOLOGIC

U.S. Geological Survey
P.O. Box 25425
Denver, CO 80225

The publication *Geologic Time* explains relative and radiometric time scales and how geologists measure the age of the Earth. It also illustrates the scientific processes that are used to interpret the Earth's geologic history.

TORNADO

Warning and Forecast Branch, W/OM11
National Weather Service
National Oceanic and Atmospheric Administration
SSMCII
1325 East West Highway, Room 14370
Silver Spring, MD 20910

The office above has the following audiovisuals available which can be used by educators to teach school children about safety during natural disasters.

Tornado 16 mm Films:
Minneapolis Tornado of July 1986 (Copyrighted)
Terrible Tuesday
Day of the Killer Tornadoes
Tornado at Pleasant Hill
Tornado: A Spotter's Guide (Copyrighted)
Tornado: On the Spot Training (silent and with soundtrack)
Neosho

Tornado Videotapes:
Minneapolis Tornado of July 1986 (Copyrighted)
Terrible Tuesday
Day of the Killer Tornadoes
Tornado: A Spotter's Guide (Copyrighted)
Tornado: On the Spot Training (silent and with soundtrack)
Tornado Near Ellis, Kansas
Neosho

Tornado Slides:
A Slide Series Supplement to "Tornado: A Spotter's Guide"
Tornado Preparedness
Tornado Safety in Residence
The Safest Place in Schools
A Look at the Tornado and other Local Storms

TOXICS

Donna Spreitzer
Local Government Commission

Be patient. If any phone number is incorrect, call (area code) 555-1212 and request the new listing.

The Government Works for Kids, Too

909 12th St., #205
Sacramento, CA 95814 (916) 448-1198

Available from this office is *Toxic is My Home? You Bet!*, for grades K-3, 4-6, 7-8, and 9-12 (available in Spanish only). Developed by Golden Empire Health Planning Center as a one-week course of instruction, this school curriculum identifies: toxics in the home environment; methods for reducing exposure to household toxics; unsafe circumstances involving toxic products; and safer alternatives to using such products. Step by step teaching instructions, masters for worksheets, teacher answer guides, and evaluation methods are all included.

TREES

U.S. Geological Survey
P.O. Box 25425
Denver, CO 80225

Tree Rings: Timekeepers of the Past explains how past environmental conditions have been recorded in tree rings and how scientists interpret this information.

Forest Service
U.S. Department of Agriculture
14th and Independence, SW
P.O. Box 96090
Washington, DC 20090-6090 (202) 205-0957

Trees offer many benefits to the environment and play a vital role in reducing water and wind erosion, keeping rivers and streams clean, and counteracting the greenhouse effect. To learn more about trees and how they help the environment, contact the office above to receive a copy of *Trees are the Answer....to America's Growing Environmental Concerns*.

Forest Service
U.S. Department of Agriculture
14th and Independence, SW
P.O. Box 96090
Washington, DC 20090-6090 (202) 205-0957

The publication *Why Leaves Change Color* (FS-12) can be used by adults and upper elementary schoolchildren to learn why leaves change their color. It also contains instructions on how to copy leaves with crayons and how to make leaf prints with a stamp pad.

Forest Service
U.S. Department of Agriculture
14th and Independence, SW
P.O. Box 96090
Washington, DC 20090-6090 (202) 205-0957

The poster *How a Tree Grows* (FS-8) teaches about photosynthesis, enzymes, and the various parts of a tree. Its colorful illustrations make it a very useful teaching aid. The eight-page publication *How a Tree Grows* supplements the poster and provides more information on how a tree grows.

Forest Service
U.S. Department of Agriculture
14th and Independence, SW
P.O. Box 96090
Washington, DC 20090-6090 (202) 205-0957

Available from this office is the poster *What We Get From Trees* (FS-68). It lists the various products, ranging from chewing gum to mop handles, which come from trees.

TROUT

U.S. Fish and Wildlife Service
U.S. Department of the Interior
4401 N. Fairfax Drive
Mail Stop 130
Arlington, VA 22203 (703) 358-1711

Learn more about one of the most popular fish with the publication *Trout*.

TRUMAN

Education Branch (NEEE)
National Archives and Records Administration
Washington, DC 20408 (202) 724-0454

The Truman Years: 1945-1953 is a teaching unit available from the Education Branch of the National Archives. It is published by the National Archives and SIRS, Inc., and is designed to help students of U.S. history, government, and economics understand the process by which history is written and to develop analytical skills. It contains about 50 reproductions of documents - charts, photographs, letters, drawings, and posters - and a detailed teacher's guide. The materials deal with certain key issues of the period, with governmental and political responses to these issues, and with public attitudes.

U.S. CAPITOL

Architect of the Capitol
Washington, DC 20515 (202) 225-1200

The United States Capitol contains a wealth of architectural history. Publications are provided from the office above which can be used to teach schoolchildren about the history of the U.S. Capitol so that they may attain a greater appreciation of U.S. history and architecture. The publications include:

Architects of the Capitol
Flags Over the East and West Central Fronts of the United States Capitol
Cornstalk or Corncob Columns and Capitals
History of the Old Subway Transportation System Connecting the Capitol and the Russell Office Building
Minton Title in the U.S. Capitol
Statuary Hall: Old Hall of the House
Statue of Freedom
The Architecture of the Unites States Capitol
The Canopy in the Rotunda of the U.S. Capitol
The United States Capitol
The United States Capitol: A Brief Architectural History
Those Who Have Lain in State in the Rotunda

Architect of the Capitol
Washington, DC 20515 (202) 225-1200

Photographs and slides of the U.S. Capitol from the Collection of the Architect of the Capitol are available from the National Graphic Center, 205 West Jefferson Street, Falls Church, VA 22046 (703-533-8700). Teachers can use them to supplement a history lesson.

U.S. COAST GUARD

Public Affairs
U.S. Coast Guard
U.S. Department of Transportation
Washington, DC 20593-0001 (202) 267-1587

Our Day with the Coast Guard provides a fun way for children to learn about the U.S. Coast Guard. By providing information in a coloring book format, kids can learn what it's like to be in the Coast Guard. The coloring book includes activities such as a maze and connect-the-dots.

U.S. FISH AND WILDLIFE SERVICE

U.S. Fish and Wildlife Service
U.S. Department of the Interior
4401 N. Fairfax Drive
Mail Stop 130
Arlington, VA 22203 (703) 358-1711

Would you or your child like to learn more about America's sea turtles, diving ducks, or the golden eagle? Or what about endangered species such as the grizzly bear, spotted owl or gray wolf? Or why not decorate your classroom or child's bedroom with some of the 30 portraits of fish they have available? The U.S. Fish and Wildlife Service has dozens of easy-reading brochures and publications which can provide information for school reports, 4-H club assignments, or Boy Scout projects.

UNIVERSE

Teaching Resource Center
Jet Propulsion Laboratory
4800 Oak Grove Dr.
Mail Stop CS-530
Pasadena, CA 91109 (818) 354-6916

Two educational aids are available from the office above. The video *Universe* (30 min.) is available for $25 and the set of color slides with cassette narration *Our Universe* is available for $11.

UNIVERSITIES

The George Washington University
One Dupont Circle, NW, Suite 630

Be patient. If any phone number is incorrect, call (area code) 555-1212 and request the new listing.

The Government Works For Kids, Too

Washington, DC 20036-1183 (202) 296-2597

The Higher Education Clearinghouse has education literature on topics relating to college and university conditions, problems, programs, and students; curricular and instructional programs, and institutional research at the college or university level; federal program, professional education (medicine, law, etc.), professional continuing education, collegiate computer-assisted learning and management, graduate education, university extension programs, teaching-learning, legal issues and legislation, planning, governance, finance, evaluation, inter-institutional arrangements, management of institutions of higher education, and business or industry educational programs leading to a degree.

URANUS

Teaching Resource Center
Jet Propulsion Laboratory
4800 Oak Grove Dr.
Mail Stop CS-530
Pasadena, CA 91109 (818) 354-6916

Are you looking for materials to teach your children about Uranus. Contact the office above for *Jupiter, Saturn, Uranus and Neptune* (30 min.), a video for $25, and the slide set *Voyager Mission to Uranus*, $6.

NASA CORE
Lorain County Joint Vocational School
15181 Route 58 South
Oberlin, OH 44074 (216) 774-1051

Voyager, The Grand Tour is a computer animated video that highlights the significant features discovered by Voyagers 1 and 2 as these spacecraft traveled past the outer planets of Jupiter, Saturn, Uranus and Neptune. Copyrighted and reproduced with permission from Martin Marietta. For educational use only. Grade 4 - 12.

VENUS

Venus Names
Magellan Project Office
Mail Stop 230-201
Jet Propulsion Laboratory
4800 Oak Grove Drive
Pasadena, CA 91109 (818) 354-4321

Scientists of the Magellan Project, in association with the U.S. Geological Survey, are inviting the public to propose names of notable women for the many impact craters and large volcanic vents being discovered on Venus by the Magellan spacecraft's imaging radar. "We want everyone, especially students, to share in the adventure of discovery," said Magellan Project Scientist Dr. Steve Saunders. Names sent to the Magellan Project offices at NASA's Jet Propulsion Laboratory will be compiled for the Working Group of Planetary Systems Nomenclature, a committee of the International Astronomical Union (IAU). The IAU gives final approval to names for bodies in the solar system. Because the IAU meets only every 3 years and its last meeting was in July, 1991, names newly proposed for Venusian features will not be considered until the following meeting in 1994. But names proposed this year, if accepted as provisional by the nomenclature committee, may be used on published maps and in articles, pending final approval by the IAU. For more information, including the criteria for the names submitted, write to the office above.

Teaching Resource Center
Jet Propulsion Laboratory
4800 Oak Grove Dr.
Mail Stop CS-530
Pasadena, CA 91109 (818) 354-6916

The slide set *Magellan Mission to Venus* is available for $6 from the office above.

VIDEOS

Education Division, MRC 305
Education Resource Center
National Air and Space Museum
Washington, DC 20560 (202) 786-2109

Aerospace-related videos are available from the Education Resource Center (ERC) of the National Air and Space Museum (NASM). The ERC offers teachers access to educational materials pertaining to aviation, space, and the Museum's collections. These materials are produced by NASM, the National Aeronautics and Space Administration (NASA), and other government agencies, and private organizations.

Ag in the Classroom
Room 317-A Administration Building
U.S. Department of Agriculture
Washington, DC 20350

Ag in the Classroom produces videos to help students in grades K-12 acquire the knowledge needed to become agriculturally literate. The objective of Ag in the Classroom is to encourage educators to teach more about our food and fiber system and the role of agriculture in our economy and society. The program is primarily carried out in each state by a group composed of educators, government officials, and representatives from agricultural organizations and agribusinesses. Materials available for the program include the following videos for elementary-school educators. The videos are:

1986 Ag in the Classroom shows how Ag in the Classroom works and offers a glimpse of enthusiastic teachers and students involved in Ag in the Classroom around the country. (16 minutes.)

America's Most Crucial Industry helps viewers of all ages understand agriculture's vital role in the American economy. This tape can also be purchased for $12 from: Video Transfer, 4709-B Arundel Avenue, Rockville, MD 20852. (14 minutes.)

Department of Extension Programs
National Gallery of Art
Washington, DC 20565

The National Gallery of Art is continually exploring ways to develop awareness in the visual arts and make its collections accessible to everyone, no matter how far away from the Gallery they may live. They now have an Extension Program which loans not only videocassettes, but also slide programs and films, free of charge to educational institutions, community groups, and to individuals throughout the U.S. Write to the office above for more information on how you may bring the National Gallery of Art to your students.

NASA CORE
Lorain County Joint Vocational School
15181 Route 58 South
Oberlin, OH 44074 (216) 774-1051

The NASA Central Operation of Resources for Educators (CORE), established in cooperation with Lorain County Joint Vocational School, serves as the national distribution center for NASA produced education materials. For a minimal charge the NASA CORE will provide a valuable service to educators unable to visit one of the NASA Teacher Resource Centers (TRC), by making NASA educational audiovisual materials available through its mail order service. Videocassettes appropriate for certain elementary grades include the following:

A Man's Reach Should Exceed His Grasp. Presents the story of flight and man's reach for new freedom through aviation and the exploration of space. From the Wright Brother's flight at Kitty Hawk to the landing on the moon and future missions to the planets, the tape depicts the fulfillment of the ancient dream of flight. Grade 4 - 9.

Opening New Frontiers: The Orbital Flight Tests of the Space Transportation System. Covers the first four test missions of the Space Shuttle Columbia, STS flights, 1,2,3, and 4. Also includes events leading up to the first launch, President Reagan's speech after the fourth landing, and highlights of the Orbital Flight Test Program. Grade 4 - 10.

Milestones of Flight. This program was produced by the National Air and Space Museum and is based on the museum's "Milestones of Flight" Gallery. It traces the history of flight from Langley's first attempts to the Space Shuttle. Uses live footage from many history making events. Grade 4 - 10.

Transformations of Flight. An animated video that presents ten important air and spacecraft in the history of flight. Includes a lesson guide. Produced by the Smithsonian Institution. Grade K - 3.

Portrait of Earth: The Story of Satellites. The film explains what satellites are and how they perform their daily tasks in orbit around our planet. Captioned at the 2nd, 3rd, and 4th grade levels.

Space Station: The Next Logical Step. Chronicles space milestones preceding the proposed Space Station. Focuses on man's desire to spend more time working and living in space and illustrates a possible Space Station design. Grade 4 - 6.

The Time of Apollo. In the year 1961, the President of the U.S. stated, "This nation should commit itself to achieving the goal, before this decade is out, of landing a man on the Moon and returning him safely to Earth." This program

Be patient. If any phone number is incorrect, call (area code) 555-1212 and request the new listing. 1293

The Government Works for Kids, Too

is a tribute to the historical accomplishments of the Apollo missions. Grade 4 - adult.

Shuttle: A Remarkable Flying Machine. Features the first historic flight of the Space Shuttle Columbia. Highlights include the liftoff on April 12, 1981, the onboard activities of Young and Crippen and a spectacular landing on Rogers Dry Lake bed in California. Grade 4 - adult.

We Deliver: Summary of Shuttle Flights 5,6,7 & 8. Covers the first four operational missions of the Space Transportation System, STS flight 5,6,7 & 8. Stresses the operational common denominator of these missions - satellite deployment. Also includes significant secondary achievements such as the first female astronaut, first black astronaut, first night launch and landing, and some of the more important onboard experiments. Grade 4 - adult.

The Dream Is Alive. Narrated by Walter Cronkite, *The Dream Is Alive* gives you a window seat on the shuttle. Share the astronaut's experiences of working, eating and sleeping in zero gravity....look back at our magnificent Earth and witness an exciting satellite repair. Copyrighted by the Smithsonian Institution/Lockhead Corporation. Grade 4 - adult.

To Dream...To Learn. The first segment of this program documents two Ohio schools who outfitted school buses as Space Shuttles. The school bus "ground shuttles" were sent on "missions" during which students learned a great deal about space travel. The second half of this program shows shuttle astronauts demonstrating toys during space shuttle mission 51-D. Students were asked to speculate as to how the toys would react in the weightless environment of space. Grade 4 - adult.

Our Solar System. Teaches the names, orbital positions, and characteristics of each planet using the phrase "my very educated mother just served us nine pizza pies". The program is animated, set to music, and appropriate for early elementary grades. Grade 2 - 6.

Voyager, The Grand Tour. A computer animated video that highlights the significant features discovered by Voyagers 1 and 2 as these spacecraft traveled past the outer planets of Jupiter, Saturn, Uranus and Neptune. Copyrighted and reproduced with permission from Martin Marietta. For educational use only. Grade 4 - 12.

Mars, The Next Step. Depicts a mission to Mars involving three vehicles launched from Earth, six months of interplanetary travel, and the establishment of a base on the martian soil. Grade 4 - 8.

Return To The Moon Videoconference Kit. Taping of an interactive teleconference on January 26, 1990. Students joined Apollo astronaut Michael Collins and NASA guest educator Dr. Lynn Bondurant on a "Return to the Moon", participating in a series of unique problem-solving and hands on activities. Accompanying curriculum material includes: and activity booklet, slides and a moon map. Grade 5 - 8.

Zero-G and Space Suits. Describes the space suit worn by Apollo astronauts. The three major parts of the suit are described. Weightlessness is also examined and explained with animation, and Newton's three laws of motion are presented. Astronauts are shown in zero-gravity and in an extravehicular activity (EVA). Grade 4 - adult.

Project Mercury: An Early Step. Summarizes the project Mercury flights of the 60's. Shows the designing and building of the spacecraft, the training of the seven original astronauts, the MR-2 launch with the chimp HAM, and highlights of Alan Shepard's first flight, as well as the flights of other Mercury astronauts. Grade 4 - adult.

Gemini Science. Scientists explain life science experiments developed for the Gemini missions. Includes a brief synopsis of the missions. Grade 4 - adult.

Our Laboratories in Space. Examines some of the scientific and medical experiments that were completed on Skylab, the Apollo-SOYUZ Test Project and future experiments to be conducted on the space shuttle. Grade 4- adult.

NASA Images: Episode 1. Several films about the U.S.'s efforts to land a man on the moon are presented. Subjects discussed include: guidance, navigation, footage from the first manned moon landing and research aircraft which led to the Space Shuttle development. Grade 4 - 12.

NASA Images: Episode 2. Historic film documenting NASA highlights from 1967 and a 1968 Apollo flight are shown. 1967 highlights include the first unmanned test flight of the Saturn V moon rocket as well as footage showing satellite launches. A second documentary film, "The Flight of Apollo 7" shows the first manned Earth-orbital Apollo mission. Grade 4 - 12.

NASA Images: Episode 3. Three motion picture segments are presented including clips from a 1977 animated film "Space Spider Robot". The Space Spider project, now inactive, was designed to "weave" large structures in space. A historic 1967 film shows step-by-step animation of manned moonflights which were to follow in future years. Finally, a 1979 film shows how jet engines were tested for noise levels. Grade 4 - 12.

NASA Images: Episode 4. Fascinating footage from two 1974 films about weightlessness about Skylab, NASA's first "Space Station". Why weightlessness occurs in spacecraft in low Earth orbit, Newton's laws, and how fluids act in microgravity are described by scientist-pilot Dr. Owen Garriott who was on the crew of the second manned skylab mission. Grade 4 - 12.

Drug Video Program
Office of Public Affairs
U.S. Department of Education
400 Maryland Ave., SW
Washington, DC 20202

Originally designed for schools, these programs are now available for home use. Each program is closed captioned and comes with its own parent's or teacher's guide to help you discuss each program's message and the serious problem of drug abuse with your child. Contact the office above for ordering information. Programs for elementary children include:

The Drug Avenger. ($35, 73 minutes, 16-page Parent's Guide, 1988, VHS Order No. DGA17535). Three children from the future travel back to the 20th Century to take on the life-threatening problem of drug abuse in 10 animated programs.

Fast Forward Future. ($30, 61 minutes, 23-page Teacher's Guide, 1988., VHS Order No. DGA 17532). Actor Richard Kiley as "Mentor" shows three elementary students the future with the Fast Forward machine. The students see the effects of using drugs and staying drug free.

Straight Up. ($40, 90 minutes, 2-page Teacher's Guide, 1988, VHS Order No. DGA17529). Academy award winning actor Lou Gosset, Jr., as Cosmo takes a boy named Ben, played by Chad Allen of NBC's "Our House", on a journey in the "fate" elevator. Ben's travels teach him valuable lessons about why drugs are harmful and how to refuse them.

State Capitol
Nebraska Energy Office
9th Floor
P.O. Box 95085
Lincoln, NE 68509 (402) 471-2867

Energy-related video tapes in addition to curriculum guides, slides, and resource books and materials, are available to Nebraska educators only.

California Energy Extension Service
1400 Tenth St., Room 209
Sacramento, CA 95814 (916) 323-4388

A video of a step-by-step guide called *Energy Patrol* is available from the office above. This video actively involves students in the upper elementary grades in reducing their school's energy consumption.

Public Information Center
U.S. Environmental Protection Agency
401 M Street, SW, PM-211B
Washington, DC 20460 (202) 260-2080

General Motors has produced a video entitled "I Need the Earth and the Earth Needs Me." Initially distributed by the Environmental Protection Agency to 4th graders, it is available from the Public Information Center to children of all ages. Children will enjoy watching this video while learning the importance of keeping our air, water, and soil clean.

Resource Center
Public Education and Risk Communication Division
Environmental and Occupational Health Sciences Institute
45 Knightsbridge Road
Piscataway, NJ 08854 (908) 932-0110

"Healthy Environment - Healthy Me" is a interdisciplinary, supplementary environmental and occupational health curriculum. As an "environmental health promotion" curriculum, it is designed to provide young people with the knowledge and understanding for creating a safe and healthful environment at

Be patient. If any phone number is incorrect, call (area code) 555-1212 and request the new listing.

The Government Works For Kids, Too

home, in their future workplaces and in their communities. The primary audience is schoolchildren in kindergarten through sixth grade. Videos include:

Alexandria's Clean-Up Fix-Up Parade (15 min., grades K-2)
Alexandria decides to get the community involved in a litter pick-up campaign after seeing the harm that litter caused a swan family in the park.

Alu-Man the Can (15 min., grades K-3)
This video teaches children about recycling through the adventures of Alu-Man the Can, Nettie Newspaper, Benjamin J. Bottle III, and Mr. "G" the garbage can.

Safety Sense (14 min., grades K-3)
Jason and Alice are safety detectives as they explore the possible health hazards of using and storing hazardous products incorrectly.

Sam's Safety Star Award (15 min., grades 1-3)
Sam, the TV camera, learns that risks are part of everyday activities like crossing the road, driving a bicycle, swimming and riding in a car. He learns to look and think before he acts.

Down the Drain (22 min., grades 3-5)
As Chris begins to pour some Polish-All down the drain, the sink comes alive. The animated sink explains why certain products can pollute the water supply. Chris learns the proper way to dispose of hazardous waste.

Keeping the Lid on Air Pollution (20 min., grades 4-6)
Terry has a homework assignment to write about two pollution controls. He ends up inside the school library computer and learns about different types of air pollutants (focusing on ozone) and air pollution controls.

The Inside Story on Air Pollution (19 min., grades 4-6)
Danny, Terry's friend, and his sister go into the computer to investigate the sources and health effects of indoor air pollution in the home. They also learn how to reduce and prevent indoor air pollution problems.

What to Do With All Our Garbage? (20 min., grades 4-6)
Kate, Jenny, and Greg explore the garbage crisis and possible solutions. Source reduction, recycling, sanitary landfills and incineration are discussed. The focus is on what we as consumers can do to reduce the amount of garbage we generate.

University of California Extension Media Center
2176 Shattuck Ave.
Berkeley, CA 94704
(415) 642-0460

A free catalog listing environmental films and videos for young people is available upon request from the office above.

Information Services
Great Lakes Regional Office
P.O. Box 32869
Detroit, MI 48232-2869
(313) 226-2170

Video tapes relating to Great Lake Studies are listed in the *Directory of Great Lakes Education Materials*. More than 600 educators were surveyed to produce the publication, a free-for-the-requesting directory that contains information on video tapes, pamphlets, technical reports, booklets, curriculum based and classroom-based materials for classes concentrating on Great Lakes studies.

Warning and Forecast Branch, W/OM11
National Weather Service
National Oceanic and Atmospheric Administration
SSMCII, 1325 East West Highway, Room 14370
Silver Spring, MD 20910

The office above has the following warning and forecast videotapes available which can be used by educators to teach school children about safety during natural disasters. They include:

Tornado Videotapes:
Minneapolis Tornado of July 1986 (Copyrighted)
Terrible Tuesday
Day of the Killer Tornadoes
Tornado: A Spotter's Guide (Copyrighted)
Tornado: On the Spot Training (silent and with soundtrack)
Tornado Near Ellis, Kansas
Neosho

Thunderstorm Videotapes:
Everyday Weather Project: Thunderstorms

Hurricane Videotapes
Hurricane
Before the Hurricane Strikes
Everyday Weather Project: Hurricanes

Cooperative Extension Service
University of Nebraska - Lincoln
Institute of Agriculture and Natural
Resources Nebraska
Department of Entomology
210 Plant Industry Bldg.
Lincoln, NE 68583-0816
(402) 472-2125

The Institute promotes the use of nonchemical control of pests and low uses of pesticides. The Institute has a free brochure which describes educational materials on the topic of integrated pest management of crops. A pamphlet which describes videotapes and a field scout manual can also be purchased from the address above. A free catalog which lists environmental films and videotapes for young people's viewing is available. Programs are available on a rental basis.

Bureau of Mines
U.S. Department of the Interior
Cochrans Mill Road
P.O. Box 18070
Pittsburgh, PA 15236
(412) 892-4338

Children in grades K-5 will enjoy watching the video *Call Me Can* (18:20 mins.). Can is a lively aluminum beverage can who calls out one day in a grocery store to a young boy named Dan. Can has new and exciting stories to tell Dan about recycling, and sings a song about how wonderful it is to be made of aluminum, because he can be recycled over and over. There is no charge for borrowing this video. It is available in 3/4" U-Matic and 1/2" VHS formats only.

Teaching Resource Center
Jet Propulsion Laboratory
4800 Oak Grove Dr.
Mail Stop CS-530
Pasadena, CA 91109
(818) 354-6916

Below are selected video programs on space and planetary subjects which can be excellent educational aids for classroom use. To receive an order form contact the office above. The videos include:

1st Flight of Space Shuttle STS-1 (30 min.)
Universe (30 min.)
Apollo Moon Landings (56 min.)
History of Flight (56 min.)
Mars and Mercury (the planets) (52 min.)
Mercury and Gemini Spacecraft Missions (56 min.)
Eruption of Mt. St. Helens (30 min.)
America in Space: 1st 25 Years (50 min.)
Shuttle Flights STS-1 thru STS-8 (60 min.)
Jupiter, Saturn, Uranus and Neptune (30 min.)
The Dream is Alive, IMAX (40 min.)
Kennedy Space Center Tour (42 min.)
We Remember: Shuttle Pioneers '81-'87 (60 min.)
Voyager Missions Animation Only (30 min.)

VOLCANOES

Geologic Inquiries Group
U.S. Geological Survey
907 National Center
Reston, VA 22092
(703) 648-4383

The *Selected Packet of Geologic Teaching Aids* is prepared for elementary school teachers (and high school teachers) of general science, geography, social studies, environmental education and other earth science-related subjects. It contains leaflets, booklets, reference lists, and an activity sheet entitled "Make Your Own Paper Model of a Volcano". To receive a packet, send a request on school letterhead indicating the subject that is taught and the grade level to the office listed below.

U.S. Geological Survey
P.O. Box 25425
Denver, CO 80225

Volcanic Hazards at Mount Shasta, California describes the kinds of volcanic activity that have occurred in the past, shows areas that could be affected in the future, and suggests ways of reducing the risks.

The Government Works for Kids, Too

WASHINGTON, GEORGE

National Archives Teaching Aids
Education Branch (NEEE)
National Archives and Records Administration
Washington, DC 20408 (202) 724-0454

Washington's Inaugural Address of 1789 (#200101, ISBN 0-911333-39-8) is available as a teaching unit from the National Archives Teaching Aids Education Branch (NEEE). This booklet includes a historical introduction and transcriptions and facsimiles of the featured documents. 8 1/2 x 11, approx. 25 pages each, illustrations, 1986. Softcover only, $2.50 each.

WASTE DISPOSAL

Office of Environmental Education
Pennsylvania Department of Education
333 Market St.
Harrisburg, PA 17126 (717) 783-6994

Paul E. Beals' publication *The Newspaper: A Tool for Teaching Environmental Awareness* is an activity book for children in grades K-12. It covers such topics as acid rain, forest preservation, waste disposal, and recycling. This activity book contains newspaper articles and uses them to teach about environmental awareness.

WATER

U.S. Geological Survey
P.O. Box 25425
Denver, CO 80225

The following publications are an excellent source of information for both upper elementary students and educators. Students can use them to supplement special reports and science projects and teachers can use them to enhance their curricula. To obtain single copies write to the office above.

Ground Water: An Undervalued Resource. Describes the need for using ground water, the role of ground water in the economy, and an analysis of regional aquifer systems. Discusses the ways in which ground water and surface water interact.

Ground Water and the Rural Homeowner. Presents a short description of ground water, some of the problems associated with ground water, and some suggestions for help with problems.

Ground Water Contamination--No "Quick Fix" in Sight. Explains how ground water is contaminated by septic tanks or cesspools, municipal lagoons, sewers, landfills, or tailings piles, and the need for further research in contamination prevention.

How Much Water in a 12-ounce Can? A Perspective on Water-Use Information. Provides information on how water was a free resource but now is considered an expensive commodity. Demonstrates how the ever-increasing use of water by industry and in the home is depleting existing supplies.

The Hydrologic Cycle. Explains the natural process by which water is circulated from the seas to the atmosphere, to the land, and back to the seas in a continuous cycle.

Water Dowsing. Provides a brief history of water dowsing. Explain how hydrologists of the USGS and other agencies use scientific methods to locate ground water.

Water in the Urban Environment: Erosion and Sediment. Explores the dual role that water plays as both as resource and a hazard. Discusses possible actions that minimize erosion and sedimentation.

The Water of the World. Discusses the amount of water contained in the world's atmosphere, on the surface, and underground. Describes the world's water balance.

Water Use in the United States, 1980. Summarizes the use of the Nation's water supply for domestic, industrial, rural, and irrigation purposes.

What is Water?. Describes the basic chemical properties of water and its diverse physical characteristics. Briefly explains the formation of water on Earth. Also available in Spanish.

Why is the Ocean Salty? Discusses the origin of the oceans and the sources of their salinity. Also available in Spanish.

Texas Water Development Board
Office of Public Information
P.O. Box 13231
Austin, TX 78711-3231 (512) 463-8028

Do You Know How to Keep Our Water Clean is a publication written for children which addresses the need for a clean environment. It discusses the "story on water" and recycling. It is a twenty page publication which ends with a crossword puzzle.

Texas Water Development Board
Office of Public Information
P.O. Box 13231
Austin, TX 78711-3231 (512) 463-8028

Land Use and the Water Cycle is a black and white poster which illustrates the water cycle and different uses of land. It can be used by educators as a teaching aid or by students as a component to a report.

Texas Water Development Board
Office of Public Information
P.O. Box 13231
Austin, TX 78711-3231 (512) 463-8028

The Texas Water Education Network Directory is a collection of water education materials suitable for use in public schools.

Texas Water Development Board
Office of Public Information
P.O. Box 13231
Austin, TX 78711-3231 (512) 463-8028

Water Education Teams, or WETs, are groups of young people who work together to understand and preserve the water resources in their local environment. The WET Project is intended as a supplemental or extracurricular activity for schoolchildren, or a special project for youth organizations. WETs select and survey a local surface water body, which may be a creek, lake, stream, reservoir or river. Then, through water testing, local observation and problem solving, WETs work to identify existing or potential sources of pollution. The students conclude by preparing community awareness projects to share what they have learned. Contact the office above to receive a copy of the *WET Project Instruction Handbook* which contains WET student activities, teacher resources and references, and sections on the basics of water quality. There also is a section of indoor/outdoor activities for areas without access to a body of water.

Texas Water Development Board
Office of Public Information
P.O. Box 13231
Austin, TX 78711-3231 (512) 463-8028

Invasion of the Water Hogs is a four page publication on water conservation written for children and describes the various ways in which water conservation can be achieved.

Public Information Center (PM-211B)
U.S. Environmental Protection Agency
401 M Street, SW, PM-211B
Washington, DC 20460

America's Wetlands: Our Vital Link Between Land and Water provides information on the types of wetlands, wetland values, status and trends of wetlands, and wetlands protection. Both educators and students can benefit from the information provided.

Kentucky Natural Resources and
Environmental Protection Cabinet
Department for Environmental Protection
Frankfort Office Park
18 Reilly Road
Frankfort, KY 40601 (502) 564-3410

Free pamphlets available include *Kentucky Wild Rivers* and *10 Ways You Can Help Keep Kentucky Water Resources Clean*. *A Field Guide to Kentucky Rivers and Streams* and *A Field Guide to Kentucky Lakes and Wetlands* are available to teachers. Also available is information on the *Water Watch Program*, a program conducted by the Division of Water with services designed to encourage and support citizen participation in the wise management of community water resources, including streams, lakes, wetlands and groundwater. Any individual, group, family, organization, school or business can become and official "Kentucky Water Watcher".

Be patient. If any phone number is incorrect, call (area code) 555-1212 and request the new listing.

The Government Works For Kids, Too

WEATHER

Superintendent of Documents
Dept. 33
Washington, DC 20402 (202) 783-3238

Use the *Cloud Code Chart* to help teach children about cloud formations. This chart illustrates and describes the 36 cloud formations according to the international system of classification. 1972. Rep. 1988. 31 x 19 ins. Shipped folded. (S/N 003-018-00050-4, $2.25).

Warning and Forecast Branch, W/OM11
National Weather Service
National Oceanic and Atmospheric Administration
SSMCII
1325 East West Highway, Room 14370
Silver Spring, MD 20910

The office above has the following audiovisuals available which can be used by educators to teach school children about safety during natural disasters:

Tornado 16 mm Films
Minneapolis Tornado of July 1986 (Copyrighted)
Terrible Tuesday
Day of the Killer Tornadoes
Tornado at Pleasant Hill
Tornado: A Spotter's Guide (Copyrighted)
Tornado: On the Spot Training (silent and with soundtrack)
Neosho

Tornado Videotapes
Minneapolis Tornado of July 1986 (Copyrighted)
Terrible Tuesday
Day of the Killer Tornadoes
Tornado: A Spotter's Guide (Copyrighted)
Tornado: On the Spot Training (silent and with soundtrack)
Tornado Near Ellis, Kansas
Neosho

Tornado Slides
A Slide Series Supplement to "Tornado: A Spotter's Guide"
Tornado Preparedness
Tornado Safety in Residence
The Safest Place in Schools
A Look at the Tornado and other Local Storms

Thunderstorm Videotapes
Everyday Weather Project: Thunderstorms

Thunderstorm Slides
Advanced Meteorologist/Spotter Training Slide Series
When Lightning Strikes

Flash Flood 16 mm Films
The Awesome Power
Flash Flood
Flood

Flash Flood Videotapes
The Awesome Power

Flash Flood/Flood Slides
Flash Floods: Myths or Realities
Flash Flood Preparedness

Hurricane 16 mm Films
A Lady Named Camille
Hurricane Decision
Hurricane

Hurricane Videotapes
Hurricane
Before the Hurricane Strikes
Everyday Weather Project: Hurricanes

Hurricane Slides
Hurricane Hugo
Hurricane Eloise
Hurricane Preparedness
Hurricane Alicia

Hurricane Frederick

Tsunami Video
1983 Sea of Japan Tsunami

Winter Storm 16 mm film
Survival in the Cold

Winter Storm Videotapes
Survival in the Cold

Winter Storm Slides
Winter Storms, The Deceptive Killers

Additional 16 mm Films
An Ill Wind
Rising Waters
Watch Along the Watershed
Earthwatch
NOAA, A Global View
Galaxy
Before It Hits Home
Hurricane: Before the Storm
Hurricane Aetna: Date with Disaster
Cities Don't Die
Winter Storm

Educational Programs Branch, Room 105
National Oceanic and Atmospheric Administration (NOAA)
11400 Rockville Pike
Rockville, MD 20852 (301) 443-8031

The office above provides educational materials to educators and the public. They can tailor requests for appropriate grade levels and curricula. Some of their weather publications include the following (which are appropriate for grades 3-6):

The Amateur Weather Forecaster. Learn the importance of keeping a weather log, some of the most common weather instruments, and some reliable weather forecasting statements.

Watch Out....Storms Ahead! Owlie Skywarn's Weather Book. Includes weather warnings, tornado facts, flash flood and winter storm instructions.

Natural Hazard Watch and Warning with Safety Rules for: Tornadoes, Hurricanes, Floods, Flash Floods, Thunderstorms/Lightning, Winter Storms. This mini-poster provides easy-to-read information on what to do when there is a natural hazard.

WETLANDS

Public Information Center (PM-211B)
U.S. Environmental Protection Agency
401 M Street, SW, PM-211B
Washington, DC 20460

America's Wetlands: Our Vital Link Between Land and Water provides information on the types of wetlands, wetland values, status and trends of wetlands, and wetlands protection. Both educators and students can benefit from the information provided.

U.S. Fish and Wildlife Service
U.S. Department of the Interior
4401 N. Fairfax Drive
Mail Stop 130
Arlington, VA 22203 (703) 358-1711

For those interested in finding out more about wetlands, obtain the publications *America's Endangered Wetlands* and *Wetlands.*

Water Watch
Division of Water
Department for Environmental Protection
Frankfort Office Park
14 Reilly Road
Frankfort, KY 40601 (502) 564-3410

Contact the office above to obtain a copy of *A Field Guide to Kentucky Lakes and Wetlands.* This booklet offers an illustrated guide and discussion for field observation along and within Kentucky's lakes and wetlands. It can be used by educators and upper elementary schoolchildren.

Be patient. If any phone number is incorrect, call (area code) 555-1212 and request the new listing.

The Government Works for Kids, Too

U.S. EPA Region 5
Office of Public Affairs
77 West Jackson Blvd., PI-195
Chicago, IL 60604 (312) 353-2000

Welcome to the Wetlands (grades K-12) is a coloring poster that explains how wetlands help us and what is a threat to wetlands. Included is information on animals, birds, fish and plants that thrive in wetlands. Limited quantities of the following are available for residents in the six-state Region 5 area (Illinois, Indiana, Michigan, Minnesota, Ohio, Wisconsin).

WHALES

Marine Mammal Commission
1825 Connecticut Ave., NW, #512
Washington, DC 20009 (202) 606-5504

Children of all ages (and even adults!) will enjoy learning how to draw whales, seals and dolphins. *How to Draw Whales and Seals* shows you how to draw these mammals in four or five easy steps.

WHOOPING CRANES

U.S. Fish and Wildlife Service
U.S. Department of the Interior
4401 N. Fairfax Drive
Mail Stop 130
Arlington, VA 22203 (703) 358-1711

The publication *Whooping Crane* will teach you more about this interesting bird.

WILDLIFE CONSERVATION

Texas Parks and Wildlife Department
Ilo Hiller, Project WILD Coordinator
4200 Smith School Rd.
Austin, TX 78744

Project Wild is an award-winning environmental and conservation education program of instructional workshops and supplementary materials for teachers of kindergarten through high school age youth which prepares students to be responsible decision makers. The *Project Wild* materials are distributed free of charge to teachers and youth group leaders who attend one of the Texas Parks and Wildlife sponsored six-hour instructional workshops. The *Project Wild* guides cannot be purchased or obtained in any other manner.

Public Information Center
U.S. Environmental Protection Agency
401 M Street, SW, PM-211B
Washington, DC 20460 (202) 260-2080

Save Our Species: Endangered Species Coloring Book will introduce children to 21 endangered and threatened plants and animals found in the United States. As they color the pages, they will journey to oceans, swamps, deserts, and islands and bring to life a variety of plants and animals.

U.S. Fish and Wildlife Service
U.S. Department of the Interior
4401 N. Fairfax Drive
Mail Stop 130
Arlington, VA 22203 (703) 358-1711

Would you or your child like to learn more about America's sea turtles, diving ducks, or the golden eagle? Or what about endangered species such as the grizzly bear, spotted owl or gray wolf? Or why not decorate your classroom or child's bedroom with some of the 30 portraits of fish they have available? The U.S. Fish and Wildlife Service has dozens of easy-reading brochures and publications which can provide information for school reports, 4-H club assignments, or Boy Scout projects.

WOLVES

U.S. Fish and Wildlife Service
U.S. Department of the Interior
4401 N. Fairfax Drive
Mail Stop 130
Arlington, VA 22203 (703) 358-1711

Two publications are available from the U.S. Fish and Wildlife Service for those interested in wolves, *Red Wolf* and *Gray Wolf* publications.

WOODSY OWL

Forest Service
U.S. Department of Agriculture
14th and Independence, SW
P.O. Box 96090
Washington, DC 20090-6090 (202) 205-0957

Give a hoot! Don't pollute! *Woodsy Owl's 1991-92 Campaign Catalog* is filled with dozens of items children can use (such as bike stickers, bookmarks, name tags, balloons, pens, pencils, lunch bags) that have the Woodsy Owl logo on them. Contact the office above for a catalog or the National Association of State Foresters/Woodsy Owl Campaign at (803) 737-8800.

WORLD WARS

National Archives Teaching Aids
Education Branch (NEEE)
National Archives and Records Administration
Washington, DC 20408 (202) 724-0454

World War I - The Home Front and *World War II - The Home Front* are two teaching units available from the Education Branch of the National Archives. Published by the National Archives and SIRS, Inc., the teaching units are designed to help students of U.S. history, government, and economics understand the process by which history is written and to develop analytical skills. Each unit contains about 50 reproductions of documents - charts, photographs, letters, drawings, and posters - and a detailed teacher's guide. The materials deal with certain key issues of the period, with governmental and political responses to these issues, and with public attitudes. Individual units are $40 each. To order, send a purchase order to: SIRS, Inc., P.O. Box 2348, Boca Raton, FL 33427-2348: or call toll free: (800) 3327-0513 (except AK and FL call collect 407-994-0079). For information on other teaching aids contact the office above.

WRIGHT BROTHERS

NASA CORE
Lorain County Joint Vocational School
15181 Route 58 South
Oberlin, OH 44074 (216) 774-1051

The videocassette *A Man's Reach Should Exceed His Grasp* presents the story of flight and man's reach for new freedom through aviation and the exploration of space. From the Wright Brother's flight at Kitty Hawk to the landing on the moon and future missions to the planets, the tape depicts the fulfillment of the ancient dream of flight. Grade 4 - 9.

Education Office
Federal Aviation Administration
U.S. Department of Transportation
400 7th Street, SW
Washington, DC 20590 (202) 366-7500

Use the publication *How We Made the First Flight* to teach your children about the Wright brothers experiences. Written in Orville Wright's own words, it is a description of his and Wilbur's first flights.

WRITING

Indiana University
Smith Research Center, Suite 150
2805 East 10th Street
Bloomington, IN 47408-2698 (812) 855-5847

Education literature on writing can be obtained from one of the Educational Resources Information Center (ERIC) clearinghouses called Reading and Communication Skills. Literature is available on reading, english, and communication skills (verbal and nonverbal), preschool through college; educational research and instruction development in reading, writing, speaking, and listening; identification, diagnosis, and remediation of reading problem; speech communication (including forensics), mass communication, interpersonal and small group interaction, interpretation, rhetorical and communication theory, speech sciences, and the theater.

Be patient. If any phone number is incorrect, call (area code) 555-1212 and request the new listing.

Current Events and Homework

Whether you are struggling with a school term paper or are eager to impress your boss by obtaining the latest statistics and analysis of practically any subject, help is right at hand. Few people, even those of us living in Washington, DC, are aware of all the studies generated around the clock by a division of the Library of Congress. Approximately 500 PhDs working at the Congressional Research Service (CRS) grind out these reports on almost any topic imaginable and these studies are made available to all 525 Members of Congress.

Your U.S. Representative and Senators have instantaneous access to over 10,000 reports on current events through a computerized on-line network. And a phone call or letter to one of your legislators is all it takes for you to tap into this rich information resource. To get copies of these reports you must go through the office of your U.S. Representative or Senator. There is no charge for these concise reports which are unquestionably the "best information value" because the material contained in these studies are the highlights from materials prepared by other experts in federal government agencies as well as the private sector. Researchers, students of all ages, marketing reps, entrepreneurs, and ordinary citizens should take advantage of this information gold mine.

The Reason Why These Reports Are Constantly Updated

If a congressional committee plans an investigation, for example, on the home health care situation, the CRS specialists will complete a background study and their findings will be available to anyone in the public domain. If a lawmaker is concerned about the situation in Poland, these experts will prepare a complete analysis of the situation and when warranted, will keep it up-to-date every day as events change. If a Congressman is going to address an industry group on a subject like "Captive Off-Shore Insurance Companies", most likely his staff is going to rely on the information generated by CRS. They can tap into this database and out will spew a 10 to 30 page report written by an expert who spends much of his or her career studying this subject.

CRS Reports Are Easy To Understand...They're Written For Congressmen

Although these studies are prepared by PhDs you do not have to worry about being able to understand them. These reports summarize historical context as well as fast breaking developments and are presented in layman's language. Also, the CRS adheres to its non-partisan mission to serve all Members of Congress. One rationale for getting CRS studies is actually to see what material legislators and their staff are using for background, whether it be for speeches or policy decision making. In addition to covering most business or student subject areas, these reports are an easy way to stay current on complex world events and issues of peripheral concern.

How To Get A Report

Getting your hands on a half a dozen reports can be easy. Just remember you cannot get studies directly from CRS but only by contacting a Member's Washington or district office. Sometime problems arise if you don't have the proper title or publication number. If you don't receive copies in a week or two, a follow-up phone call is necessary. Keep in mind that helping constituents in this way is a welcome task, especially when a legislator's reelection is close at hand. If you find one office uncooperative, try another. Remember we each have two Senators and one Representative. You can contact all legislators in Washington, DC by calling the Capitol Hill Switchboard at (202) 224-3121.

Sample Entry

It is next to impossible to get the *CRS Index to Reports and Issues Briefs* which is why we've reproduced it here. In addition to reports, this list includes Issue Briefs, which are summaries of CRS reports. At the end of the chapter you will find two other CRS products, Info Packs and Audio Briefs.

To make sure you understand the way these reports are listed, we have dissected one entry here.

* Polygraph Testing: Employee and Employer Rights: Issue Brief, Gail McCallion IB87126

Polygraph Testing: Employee and Employer Rights = Title
Issue Brief = Issue Brief (rather than a full length CRS report)
Gail McCallion = Congressional Research Service Author
IB87126 = Report Number

Be patient. If any phone number is incorrect, call (area code) 555-1212 and request the new listing.

Current Events and Homework

Although these reports are available through your U.S. Representative or Senator, you may be able to contact the author of the report directly at: Congressional Research Service, Library of Congress, Washington, DC 20540, (202) 707-5700. Also, after reading the reports or issue briefs, you may want to follow up and check with the CRS specialist to track down any of his or her articles which have been published in trade publications. Since the Congressional Research Service is only in the habit of responding to requests from Congress, it is especially important to treat CRS experts with respect.

These thousand or so reports are grouped under several hundred subject categories. It may require browsing through this chapter to find the category heading of interest. You'll notice that certain categories are cross-referenced, for example, under "Labor-Earnings and Benefits" you'll be instructed to "see Labor--Policies and Legislation." If you are unable to find a particular category or have no luck locating a report on a given subject, ask your Member of Congress to send you the most recent CRS list of reports for that particular issue. Of course, new reports are added to the CRS immense portfolio every day to reflect the developments both at home and abroad.

Current Events and Homework

ABM Treaty

* Arms Control: Issues for Congress, Issue Brief, Stanley R. Sloan, IB87002
* The New Interpretation of the ABM Treaty--Salient Issues, Charles R. Cellner, 87-164 S

Abortion

* see Birth Control--Abortion

Acid Rain

* see Air Pollution--Acid Rain Action

Adult Education

* see Federal Aid to Education--Adult and Vocational, Occupational Training--Adult and Vocational Education

Adult Illiteracy

* see Elementary and Secondary Education

Aeronautics

* see also Airline Industry, Aviation Safety and Security, Transportation
* The Airport Improvement Program: Federal Capital Spending and Airport Capacity J.F. Hornbeck 91-180 E
* Aviation Excise Taxes: Their Role in the Deficit Reduction Effort of 1990, Nonna A. Noto 91-309 E
* Commercial High Speed Aircraft Opportunities and Issues, Richard E. Rowberg, etc., 89-163 SPR
* Countries With Smoking Bans on Domestic and International Flights, Law Library of Congress. American-British Law Division. LL90-68
* High Speed commercial Transports: Environmental Issues and NASA's High Speed Research Program, John D. Moteff. 90-547 SPR
* Labor problems at Eastern Air Lines: Archived Issue Brief, Linda LeGrande IB88052
* The National Aero-Space Plane Program: A Brief History, John D. Moteff, 88-146 SPR

Aeronautics -- Airline Industry

* Aircraft Manufacturing: Changing Conditions and Federal Policies, John W. Fischer, 86-76 E
* Airline Industry Expense Components: 1978-1987; An Examination and Analysis of Trends, John W. Fisher, etc., 88-502 E
* Airline Mergers and Labor Protective Provisions: Issue Brief, Linda LeGrande, IB87179
* Airlines under Deregulation at Mid-Decade: Trends and Policy Implications, John W. Fischer, 86-67 E
* Airport and Airway Program Reauthorization: Archived Issue Brief, John W. Fischer, IB87051
* The Airport Improvement Program: Selected Economic, and Legislative Issues, J.F. Hornbeck, 88-683 E
* Civilian and Military Pilots: The Labor Market Relationship, John W. Fischer, etc., 86-28 E
* The Demand for General Aviation Aircraft: Background, Analysis and Outlook, John W. Fischer, etc., 85-1108 E
* Employee Participation in National Mediation Board, Determination of Single Carrier Status, Vincent E. Treacy, 88-433 A
* Employee Protection Legislation: A Comparison of H.R. 1101, H.R. 2828, and H.R. 3332, Mark Jickling, 88-426 E
* Labor Problems at Eastern Air Lines: Issue Brief, Linda LeGrande, IB88052
* The Proposed Airline Passenger Protection Act of 1987: Analysis of the Bankruptcy Transportation Plans With Regard to the Taking Issue, Douglas Reid Weimer, 87-984 A

Aeronautics -- Aviation Safety and Security

* Air Traffic Controllers: Labor Relations Since the Demise of PATCO, Gail McCallion, 87-786 E
* Airlines: Safety and Service Issues; Info Pack, IP386A

* Aviation and the 101st Congress: Safety and Policy Issues; Issue Brief, J. Glen Moore, IB89045
* Aviation Safety and in the 100th Congress: Bills, Hearings and a Summary of Major Actions, J. Glen Moore, 89-18 SPR
* Aviation Safety, Capacity, and Service; Issue Brief, J. Glen Moore, IB87233
* Aviation Safety: Maintaining Safety in a Deregulated Industry Environment; Archived Issue Brief, J. Glen Moore, IB87032
* Aviation Safety: Major Congressional Actions; Archived Issue Brief, J. Glen Moore, IB89018
* Aviation Safety: Policy and Oversight, J. Glen Moore, etc., 86-69 SPR
* Aviation Safety and Industry Concerns in the 101st Congress: Bills, Hearings and a Summary of Major Actions, J. Glen Moore and John W. Fischer 91-392 SPR
* Aviation Safety and Service: A Congressional Users Guide, John W. Gischer and J. Glen Moore 91-272 E
* Aviation Safety: Runway Incursions, J. Glen Moore 91-145 SPR
* Aviation Safety: System Fundamentals and Congressional Actions; Archived Issue Brief, J. Glen Moore, IB88008
* Chronology of Hearings on Aviation Safety and Matters of Related Interest in the 99th Congress, J. Glen Moore, 87-49 SPR
* FAA Proposed Rule to Expand the Use of More C Altitude-Reporting Transponders in the United States, J. Glen Moore, 88-302 SPR
* National Transportation Policy Alternatives: Safety Issues; Proceedings of a CRS Congressional Seminar, J. Glen Moore 90-467 E
* United States Civil Aviation Security, M. Suzanne Cavanagh, 87-931 GOV

AFDC

* see Public Welfare--AFDC

Affirmative Action Programs

* see Equal Employment Opportunity

Afghanistan

* Afghanistan After Five Years: Status of the Conflict, the Afghan Resistance and the U.S. Role, Richard Cronin, 85-20 F
* Afghanistan After the Soviet Withdrawal: Contenders for Power, Richard P. Cronin, 89-146 F
* Afghanistan Peace Talks: An Annotated Chronology and Analysis for the United Nations-Sponsored Negotiations, Richard P. Cronin, 88-149 F
* Afghanistan: Selected References, Sherry B.Shapiro, 88-308 L
* Afghanistan: Status, U.S. Role, and Implications of a Soviet Withdrawal; Archived Issue Brief, Richard P. Cronin and Francis T. Milo. IB88049
* Afghanistan: U.S. Policy Options; Issue Brief, Kenneth Katzman IB91111
* Television Network Evening News Coverage of Afghanistan: A Perspective After Eight Years of War, Denis Steven Rutkus, 88-319 GOV

Africa

* see also Foreign Relations, Politics and Government,Economic Conditions, Individual Countries, Foreign Policy and Assistance Programs
* Africa: Environmental Issues, Brenda Brananman 90-383 F
* AIDS in Africa: Background/Issues for U.S. Policy, Raymond W. Copson, 87-768 F
* Angola: Conflict Assessment and U.S. Policy Options, Raymond W. Copson, 86-189 F
* Angola: Issues for the United States; Archived Issue Brief, Raymond Copson, etc., IB81063
* Angola/Namibia Negotiations; Issue Brief, Brenda M. Branaman, IB87047
* Angola/Namibia Peace Prospects: Background, Current Problems and Chronology, Raymond W. Copson, 88-559 F
* The Effectiveness of Food Aid: Implications of Changes in Farm, Food, Aid and Trade Legislation; Proceedings of a CRS Workshop Held on April 25, 1988, Charles E Hanrahan, 88-493 ENR
* Food Production and Food Policy in Sub-Saharan Africa: A 20 Country Survey, Charles Hanrahan, etc., 85-150 ENR
* Mozambique: Conflict Assessment/U.S. Policy, Raymond W. Copson, 85-150 ENR
* Namibia Chronology: February 1986 Through April 1987, Raymond W.

Be patient. If any phone number is incorrect, call (area code) 555-1212 and request the new listing.

Current Events and Homework

Copson, etc., 87-353 F
* Namibia: United Nations Negotiations for Independence/U.S. Interests; Archived Issue Brief, Brenda Branaman, IB9073
* North African Petroleum, Joseph Riva 84-216 SPR
* Population Growth and Natural Resource Deterioration in Drought-Stricken Africa, Susan Abbasi, 85-1149 ENR
* South Africa: African National Congress, Brenda Branaman, 86-186 F
* South Africa: U.S. Policy Debate Over Sanctions and Assistance; Issue Brief, Brenda M. Branaman. IB90157
* South Africa: Opposition on the Right, Brenda Branaman, 88-628 F
* South Africa: President's Report on Progress Toward Ending Apartheid, Raymond W. Copson, 88-628 F
* South Africa: Recent Developments; Issue Brief, Brenda Branaman, etc., IB85213
* South Africa: The Current Situation; Info Pack, IP340S
* South Africa: The United Democratic Front, Brenda M. Branaman, 86-758 F
* Southern Africa: U.S. Regional Policy at a Crossroads?, Raymond Copson, 85-201 F
* Sudan: U.S. Foreign Assistance Facts: Issue Brief, Ellen Laipson, etc., IB85065
* Tunisia After Bourguiba: Issues for U.S. Policy, Ellen B. Laipson, 88-31 F
* The United States and Southern Africa: A Review of United Nations Resolutions and United States Voting Patterns, 1946-October 1985, Frankie King, 86-21 F
* U.S. Foreign Assistance to the Middle East and North Africa: Fiscal Years 1988, 1989, and 1990, Clyde R. Mark, 89-192 F

Africa -- Economic Conditions

* African Debt: The Official Donor Response and Potential Alternative Strategies, Alan K. Yu, IB5014
* Mozambique: U.S. Foreign Assistance Facts; Archived Issue Brief, Raymond Copson, etc, IB5114
* The Reagan Administration Sanctions Against South Africa: Their Potential Economic Impact, William H. Cooper, 85-955 E
* Sanctions Against South Africa: Activities of the 99th Congress, Brenda M. Branaman, 87-200 F
* Sanctions Against South Africa: Impact on the United States; Issue Brief, William H. Cooper, IB87198
* The South Africa Financial Crisis: The Role of U.S. Banks, Walter W. Eubanks, 86-550 E
* South Africa: International Sanctions; Archived Issue Brief, Jeanne S. Affelder, etc, IB86157
* South Africa: Legislation of the 99th Congress, Brenda M. Branaman, 85-799 F
* South Africa: U.S. Economic Ties; Emerging Issues, Archived Issue Brief, William H. Cooper, IB85117
* South Africa: U.S. Policy After Sanctions; Issue Brief, Brenda Branaman, IB87128
* South Africa: U.S. Policy After Sanctions; Issue Brief, Brenda M. Branaman, IB87128
* Southern Africa: U.S.Foreign Assistance; Issue Brief, Raymond W. Copson, IB87152
* Uranium Hexafluoride Imports from South Africa: Archived Issue Brief, Barbara B. Black, etc., IB88066
* World Bank Activities in Ethiopia, Jonathan E. Sanford, 87-857 F
* The 99th Congress and South African Sanctions, Robert Shepard, 87-942 F
* The 99th Congress and the African Economic Crisis, Carol Lancaster, 87-914 F

Africa -- Foreign Relations

* Africa: Democracy and U.S. Policy; Audio Brief, Ray Copson and Ted Dagne AB50220
* Africa: U.S. Foreign Assistance Issues, Issue Brief, Raymond W. copson, Brenda M. Branaman and Theodore S. Dagne IB91097
* African Famine: The Search for Solutions; Issue Brief, Charles E. Hanrahan and Theodore S. Dagne IB91082
* Africa's Wars 1980-1990: Conditions, Causes and Prospects for the Future; Videoprogram, Raymond W. Copson LTR91-869
* Angola: Issues for the United States; Archived Issue Brief, Raymond Copson and Robert Shepard IB81063
* Angola/Namibia Negotiations: Archived Issue Brief, Brenda M. Branaman IB89047
* Ethiopia: New Thinking in U.S. Policy, Theodore S. Dagne 91-489 F
* Kenya: Political Unrest and U.S. Policy; Issue Brief, Theodore S. Dagne IB90152

* Liberia: Issues for the United States; Issue Brief, Brenda M. Branaman IB91105
* Mozambique: Conflict Assessment/U.S. Policy, Raymond W. Copson 88-516 F
* Namibia: United Nations Negotiations for Independence/U.S. Interests; Archived Issue Brief, Brenda Branaman IB79073
* South Africa: Selected References, Sherry B. Shapiro 89-459 L
* South Africa: U.S. Foreign Assistance: Archived Issue Brief, Raymond W. Copson IB87152
* Sudan: U.S. Foreign Assistance Facts; Issue Brief, Ellen Laipson and Raymond Copson IB87152

Africa -- Politics and Government

* Africa: Status of Democratization, Theodore S. Dagne 91-380 F
* Africa's Wars: Conditions, Causes, and Prospects for the Future; Audio Brief AB50206
* Algeria in Crisis: Democracy, Islamism, and Implications for U.S. Policy 91-591 F
* Angola: War and famine; Issue Brief, Raymond W. Copson IB91030
* Ethiopia: War and Famine; Archived Issue Brief, Raymond W. Copson IB90049
* The Horn of Africa: A Trip Report, Theodore dagne 91-823 F
* The Legal Basis for South Africa's Retention of Walvis Bay, Law Library of Congress. Near Eastern and African Law Division. LL90-5
* Nigeria; Economic and Political Reforms and Issues in U.S. Nigerian Relations, Theodore S. Dagne 89-672 F
* Recent Political Developments in Ethiopia and Somalia, Theodore S. Dagne 91-452 F
* South Africa: African National Congress, Brenda Brananman 86-186 F
* South Africa: Opposition on the Right, Brenda Branaman 88-628 F
* South Africa: Recent Developments: Issue Brief, Brenda Branaman and Frankie King IB85213
* South Africa: The Current Situation; Info Pack IP340S
* Zaire: Political Crisis, Raymond W. Copson 91-721 F

African National Congress

* South African: African National Congress, Brenda Branaman, 86-186 F

Age Discrimination in Employment

* see Equal Employment Opportunity

Aged

* see Old Age

Agent Orange

* see Veterans

Agricultural Credit

* see Agriculture-Farm Income

Agricultural Exports

* see Agriculture--Foreign Trade

Agricultural Price Supports

* see Agriculture-Dairy Industry, Agriculture, Policies and Legislation, and Agriculture-Sugar Industry

Agriculture

* see also Dairy Industry, Drought, Environmental Aspects, Farm Income, Foreign Trade, Livestock, Policies and Legislation, Disasters, Genetics, Pesticides
* Agricultural Research and Extension: Current Issues, Jean M. Rawson 91-717 ENR
* Agricultural Research: Issues for the 1980s, Christine Matthews Rose, 87-430 SPR
* Agriculture and Food: An Alphabetical Microthesaurus of Terms Selected from the Legislative Indexing Vocabulary, Shirley Loo, 89-512 L
* Biotechnology: Bibliography-in-Brief, 1985-1988, B.F. Mangan, 88-566 L
* Counting Migrant and Seasonal Farmworkers: A Persistent Data Void, Dennis M. Roth, 85-797 E
* Energy Inputs and Costs in U.S. Agriculture, Bernard A. Gelb, 85-797 E
* Glossary of Agricultural Terms, Geoffrey S. Becker, 89-321 ENR
* Information Services for Agriculture: The Role of Technology, Robert Lee Chartrand, etc., 88-108 S
* International Fund for Agricultural Development, Susan Epstein, 87-4 ENR

Africa / Agriculture

* Rural Community Development: Selected References, Rebecca Mazur, 88-17 L
* Selected Reports Available on Food and Agricultural, Topics, by Environment and Natural Resources Policy Division, Food and Agriculture Section, 89-244 ENR
* Soviet Agricultural/Food Outlook: 1991/92, Remy Jurenas 91-708 ENR
* Utility Fuel Options: Using Excess Corn Supplies, Duane A. Thompson, 87-541 ENR
* Wheat Classification, Carl Ek, 88-54 ENR

Agriculture -- Dairy Industry

* Background Information on Casein, Geoffrey S. Becker, 87-505 ENR
* Bovine Somatotropin (BST or BGH): A Status Report, Ralph N. Chite 90-576 ENR
* A Brief Look at Federal Milk Marketing Orders, Geoffrey Becker, 84-581 ENR
* Current Dairy Issues: Archived Issue Brief, Jean Rawson, IB86029
* Dairy Issues: Issue Brief, Jasper Womach, IB89063
* The Dairy Markets Without Federal Support, Geoffrey Becker, 86-692 ENR
* Dairy Policy Issues; Issue Brief, Ralph Chite IB90030
* Dairy Production Controls: A Review of the National Commission on Dairy Policy's Recommendations, Jean M. Rawson, 88-355 ENR
* Dairy Provisions of the 1990 Farm Bill, Ralph M. Chite 91-125 ENR
* The Dairy Program: Twenty Questions, Geoffrey S. Becker, 87-848 ENR
* Federal Dairy Policy; The Basics-- A Compendium of Resource Material from the CRS Seminar Series, Ralph M. Chite 90-97 ENR
* Milk Marketing Orders: Background and Current Issues, Ralph M. Chite 90-542 ENR
* Milk Standards: Grade A vs. Grade B, Ralph M. Chite 91-589 ENR
* Nonfat Solids Standards for Milk: Proposed Legislative Changes, Ralph M. Chite 91-772 ENR
* Regional Dairy Trends and Federal Policy, Geoffrey S. Becker, 87-743 ENR
* A Statistical Profile of the Dairy Sector, Jean M. Rawson, 88-99 ENR

Agriculture -- Drought

* Agriculture and the Drought of 1988: Archived Issue Brief, Ralph Chite, IB88073
* Agriculture, Drought, and the Federal Response: Issue Brief, Ralph Chite, I89-89
* Agriculture: Drought of 1988; Info Pack, IP403A
* The Drought of 1988: Bibliography-in-Brief, Ted L. Burch, 88-553 L
* Expected Impact of the Drought on Food Prices and Federal Food Aid, Geoffrey S. Becker, etc., 88-633 ENR
* Legal Issues Related to Diversion of Water from Lake Michigan to the Mississippi River, Pamela Baldwin, 88-585 A
* Monitoring and Forecasting Drought and Famine, Charles Hanrahan, etc., 85-1059 ENR

Agriculture -- Environmental Aspects

* Aflatoxin and Agriculture, Carl Ek 89-525 ENR
* Agricultural Effects on Groundwater Quality, Donald V. Feliciano, 86-891 ENR
* Agricultural Nonpoint Pollution Policy: A Federal Perspective, Claudia Copeland and Jeffrey A. Zinn 86-191 ENR
* Agriculture and the Environment: Archived Issue Brief, Jean Rawson and Jeffrey A. Zinn IB89086
* Agricultural Pollution of Groundwater: Bibliography-in-Brief, 1985-1987, Adrienne C. Grenfell, 88-29 L
* Agricultural Resource Conservation Issues: Archived Issue Brief, Jeffrey A. Zinn, IB87132
* Agriculture and the Environment: Issue Brief, Geoffrey Becker, etc., IB89086
* Compliance Provisions for Resource Conservation: A Status Report, Jeffrey Zinn, 88-662 ENR
* The California Drought: Effects on Agriculture and Related Resources, Betsy A. Cody, Ralph M. Chite and Geoffrey S. Becker 91-208 ENR
* Compliance Provisions for Resource Conservation: A Status Report, Jeffrey Zinn 88-662 ENR
* The Conservation Reserve: A Status Report, Jeffrey Zinn, 88-716 ENR
* The Food Security Act of 1985: Resource Conservation Provisions, Jeffrey Zinn, 86-576 ENR
* Global Climate Change: Issue Brief, Robert E. Morrison, IB89005
* Groundwater Issues and the U.S. Department of Agriculture: An Institutional Perspective, Jeffrey Z. Zinn, 88-322 ENR
* Groundwater Quality: Current Federal Programs and Recent Congressional Activities, Jeffrey Zinn and Mary Tiemann 89-195 ENR

* Ozone and Plants: A Status Report, Jeffrey A. Zinn, etc., 87-496 ENR
* Proposed Senate Amendments to FIFRA, James Aidala, 88-471 ENR
* Regulation U.S. Pesticide Exports: Policy Issues and Proposed Legislation, Jasper Womach 91-568 ENR
* Soil and Water Conservation Issues in the 101st Congress: Issue Brief, Jeffrey A. Zinn, etc., IB89080
* Superbug: Agriculture's Whitefly Problem, Geoffrey S. Becker 91-828 ENR
* Sustainable Agriculture: Archived Issue Brief, Jean M. Rawson IB90081
* Western Irrigation: Background Data on Current Issues, Jeffrey Zinn, etc., 86-696 ENR
* Wetlands Protection: Issues in the 101st Congress;, Issue Brief, Jeffrey Z. Zinn, etc., IB89076

Agriculture -- Farm Income

* Agriculture: The Farm Financial Situation; Info Pack, IB323A
* Agriculture Credit: GSE Reform and Other Issues; Archived Issue Brief, Ralph Chite IB89121
* Agriculture Credit: GSE Reform and Other Issues; Archived Issue Brief, Ralph Chite IB91126
* Agricultural Energy Use and the Iraqi Crisis, Ralph M. Chite 90-397 ENR
* Commercial Farm Banks and Their Borrowers: Legislative Issues; Archived Issue Brief, Remy Jurenas, IB86085
* Family Farmer Reorganization: Summary and Legal Analysis of Chapter 12 of the United States Bankruptcy Code, Robin Jeweler, 88-708 A
* Farm Credit Administration and Federal Depository Institution Supervisory Agencies: Comparison of Enforcement Powers, M. Maureen Murphy, 87-662 A
* Farm Credit Overview: Major Legislation of the 99th Congress, Jean Rawson, etc., 87-28 ENR
* Farm Credit System: Legislative Issues: Archived Issue Brief, Remy Jurenas IB87033
* Farm Credit System Loan Restructuring and Foreclosure Policies, Remy Jurenas, 88-404 ENR
* Farm Income and Debt: Bibliography-in-Brief, 1988, Rebecca Mazur, 88-480 L
* Farmer Mac and the Agricultural Secondary Market, Ralph Chite, 89-246 ENR
* Farmer Transition Programs, Rebecca Mazur, 88-364 L
* Farmers Home Administration: Farm Credit Policies and Issues, Issue Brief, Ralph Chite, IB87215
* Farmers Home Administration Provisions in the Agricultural Credit Act of1987, Jean M. Rawson, 88-210 ENR
* FmHA Losses and the Federal Budget, Ralph Chite, 89-34 ENR
* History and Operation of the Commodity Credit Corporation, Plus a Compilation of Data, Jasper Womach and Susan Epstein 86-151 ENR
* Implementation of the Agricultural Credit Act of 1987; Issue Brief, Ralph Chite, etc., IB88089
* Overview of the Number of Farms Going Out of Business, Jean M. Rawson, 88-228 ENR
* A Review of Farmers Home Administration's New Policy for Delinquent Farm Borrowers, Ralph Chite, 88-715 ENR
* Tax Issues Affecting Family Agriculture: Archived Issue Brief, Jack Taylor, etc., IB88054
* Wheat Price Supports: From Country Loan Rate to Class Loan Rate?, Carl Ek, 88-269 ENR

Agriculture and Food

* Agricultural Export Programs: Current Issues, IB89107
* Agricultural Issues in the 101st Congress, IB89030
* Agricultural Trade, IB88011
* Agriculture and the Budget, IB87032
* Agriculture and the Environment, IB89086
* Agriculture, Drought, and the Federal Response, IB89089
* Agriculture in the GATT: After the Midterm Review, IB89027
* Dairy Issues, IB89063
* Farmers Home Administration: Farm Credit Policies and Issues, IB87215
* Food Labeling, IB80055
* Foreign Food Aid: Reauthorization Issues, IB89097
* Implementation of the Agricultural Credit Act of 1987, IB88089
* Soil and Water Conservation Issues in the 101st Congress, IB89080
* Sugar Policy Issues, IB88091

Agriculture -- Foreign Trade

* Addressing Unfair Trade: Agricultural Cases under Section 301 of the Trade Act of 1974, Donna U. Vogt 89-522 ENR
* Agricultural Exports: Does Administration Effort Match Potential?

Be patient. If any phone number is incorrect, call (area code) 555-1212 and request the new listing.

Current Events and Homework

Summary of Hearings Held February 5, 10, 18, 24, March 18, 25, May 19, and 20, 1987, Susan B. Epstein,. etc., 87-794 ENR

* Agricultural Exports: Overview and Selected Data, Donna U. Vogt, 88-403 ENR

* Agricultural Export Program and Issues; Issue Brief, Susan B. Epstein IB90064

* Agricultural Exports: Federal Assistance and Promotion Programs, Remy Jurenas and Donna U. Vogt 89-351 ENR

* Agricultural Exports: Overview and Selected Data, Donna U. Vogt 90-35 ENR

* Agricultural Imports: What, from Whom, Why, How Much?, Jasper Womach, 88-361 ENR

* Agricultural Trade: Issue Brief, Donna U. Vogt, IB88011

* Agricultural Trade Legislation in the 100th Congress: A Comparison of Selected Provisions of H.R. 3 and S. 1420, Charles E. Hanrahan, etc., 87-677 ENR

* Agricultural Trade: The United States and Selected, Developed and Developing Countries, Susan B. Epstein and Jasper Womach 87-198 ENR

* Agricultural Trade Policy: The 1990 Fram Bill and the GATT Negotiations, Charles E. Hanrahan 90-267 S

* Agriculture in the GATT:: After the Midterm Review, Issue Brief, Charles E. Hanrahan, IB89027

* Agriculture in the GATT: Toward the Next Round of Multilateral Trade Negotiations, Charles Hanrahan, Penelope Cate and Donna Vogt 86-98 ENR

* Agriculture in the U.S.-Canada Free Trade Agreement, Charles E. Hanrahan and Susan B. Epstein 88-363 ENR

* Agriculture in a U.S.-Mexico-Canada Free Trade Agreement, Charles E. Hanrahan 91-252 RCO

* Cargo Preference and Agriculture: Background and Current Issues, Carl Ek, 87-134 ENR

* Cargo Preference and Agriculture, Carl Ek, 89-633 ENR

* China's Most-Favored-Nation Status: U.S. Wheat Exports, Susan B. Epstein 91-447 ENR

* The "Citrus-Pasta Dispute" Between the United States and the European Community, Donna U. Vogt, 87-911 ENR

* The Common Agricultural Policy of the European Community and Implications for U.S. Agricultural Trade, Donna U. Vogt, etc., 86-111 ENR

* Cotton Trade: The United States and Foreign Competition, Susan B. Epstein, 87-557 ENR

* EC Ban on Importing U.S. Pork and Beef, Susan Epstein 91-390 ENR

* The Effectiveness of Food Aid: Implications of Changes in Farm, Food Aid, and Trade Legislation; Proceedings of a CRS Workshop Held on April 25, 1988, Charles E. Hanrahan, 88-493 ENR

* Export of Pesticides, James V. Aidala, 89-73 ENR

* Exports of High-Valued Agricultural Products: Trends and Issues, Susan B. Epstein, etc., 87-636 ENR

* Fruit and Vegetables in a U.S.-Mexico-Canada Free Trade Agreement, Geoffrey S. Becker 91-362 ENR

* Grain Quality Issues: A Status Report, Carl W. Ek, 88-323 ENR

* Import Restrictions on Meat-History and Current Issues, Jean Rawson, 85-956 ENR

* International Coffee Agreement, Donna Vogt, 84-224 ENR

* International Coffee Agreement, A Statue Report, Donna U. Vogt 90-159 ENR

* Kangaroo Management Controversy, Malcolm M. Simmons, 88-468 ENR

* Latin American Debt and U.S. Agricultural Exports: Assessment of a Proposed Approach, Charles E. Hanrahan, 87-402 ENR

* Proceedings of the CRS Workshop on Canada-U.S. Free-Trade Agreement: How Will It Affect the United States?, Arlene Wilson, 88-356 E

* Proposed European Community Consumption Tax on Vegetable Oils: A Status Report, Donna Vogt, 87-407 ENR

* Restricting Lamb Imports: A Policy Issue, Jasper Womach, 87-642 ENR

* Selected Data on U.S. Agricultural High-Valued Product Exports, Susan B. Epstein, 87-471 ENR

* Statutory Authorities Related to Official Foreign Debt, Jeanne J. Grimmett 91-381 A

* Soviet Agriculture: U.S.-U.S.S.R Grain Sales and Prospects for Expanded Agricultural Trade; Archived, Issue Brief, John Hardt, IB86019

* Sugar Policy Issues: Issue Brief, Remy Jurenas IB90036

* Tariffication: Negotiating Reductions in Agricultural Import Barriers in the Uruguay Round, Donna U. Vogt and Charles E. Hanrahan 89-555 ENR

* Tensions in United States-European Community Agricultural Trade, Donna Vogt, etc., 86-112 ENR

* U.S. Agricultural Assistance to the Soviet Union: Policy Issues; Issue Brief, Remy Jurenas IB90139

* U.S. Agricultural Exports to China, Susan B. Epstein and Charles E. Hanrahan 89-391 ENR

* U.S. Agricultural Trade Opportunities with Pacific, Rim Nations, Robert M. Goldstein, 88-755 ENR

* U.S. Agricultural Trade Policy: Selected Readings, Ted L. Burch 90-328 L

* The U.S.-Canada Pork Dispute, Susan Epstein, 89-311 ENR

* U.S.-European Community Trade Dispute Over Meat Containing Growth Hormones, Donna Vogt, 89-6 ENR

* U.S. Farm Trade: Selected References, 1985-1985, Rebecca Mazur, 87-5 L

* U.S. Japanese Agricultural Trade Relations: Selected Information, Donna U. Vogt, 88-655 ENR

* Why U.S. Agricultural Exports Have Declines in the 1980s, Charles Hanrahan, 84-223 ENR

* Will the Export Enhancement Program Survive?, Susan B. Epstein, 89-139 ENR

Agriculture -- Livestock

* Antibiotics: Health Implications of Use in Animal Feed; Archived Issue Brief, Sarah Taylor, IB85076

* Bovine Growth Hormone (Somatotropin) Agricultural and Regularly Issues, Geoffrey S. Becker, etc., 86-1020 ENR

* The Cattle Industry and Federal Programs that Affect It. A Compilation and Analysis, Jack Taylor, etc., 86-160 E

* Federal Grazing Fees on Lands Administered by the Bureau of Land Management and the Forest Service; A History of Legislation and Administrative Policies, Adela Backiel, etc. 85-592 ENR

* Grazing Fees: A Fact Sheet, Adela Backiel 91-265 ENR

* Haying and Grazing on Set-Aside Crop Acreage, Carl W. Ek, 89-9 ENR

* Pork Growth Hormone (Somatotropin): Agricultural and Regulatory Issues, Susan Epstein, etc. 89-661 ENR

* Rangeland Condition: Attempts to Chart Its Progress, Bruce Beard, 84-757 ENR

Agriculture -- Policies and Legislation

* After the Drought: The Next Farm Bill; Audio Brief, Jasper Womach, AB50183

* Agricultural Disaster Assistance: Issue Brief, Ralph Chite IB91099

* Agricultural Domestic and Trade Policy: Economic Conditions and Legislative Issues, Jasper Womach, etc., 88-277 ENR

* Agricultural Issues in the 101st Congress: Issue Brief, Geoffrey Becker, IB89030

* Agricultural Issues in the 102d Congress: Issue Brief, Jean M. Rawson IB91085

* Agricultural Policy for the 1990's: Audio Brief, Charles Hanrahan and Carl Ek AB50217

* Agriculture and the Budget: Issue Brief, Geoffrey Becker, IB87032

* Agricultural and the Budget: Issue Brief, Carl Ek IB91124

* Agriculture and the Gramm-Rudman-Hollings Deficit Control Act, Geoffrey Becker, 86-547 ENR

* Agriculture: The 1990 Farm Bill; Info Pack IP295A

* Agriculture: The 1990 Farm Bill; Selected References, 1989-1991, Lisa B. Dove 91-712 L

* The Cattle Industry and Federal Programs that Affect It: A Compilation and Analysis, Jack Taylor, etc., 86-160 E

* The Conservation Title of the 1990 Farm Bill, Jeffrey A. Zinn 90-562 ENR

* Crop Insurance and Disaster Assistance; Archived Issue Brief, Ralph Chite IB90080

* Crop Insurance Reform: A Review of the Commission Recommendations, Ralph M. Chite 89-624 ENR

* Decoupling Farm Programs, Carl W. Ek, 88-604 ENR

* Farm Commodity Promotion Programs, Geoffrey S. Becker, 91-151 ENR

* Federal Crop Insurance: Background and Current Issues, Ralph Chite 88-739 ENR

* Federal Programs and Policies Affecting the U.S. Fruit and Vegetable Industries, Geoffrey S.Becker 91-637 ENR

* Fruit and Vegetable Issues in the 102nd Congress, Geoffrey S. Becker 91-409 ENR

* Farm Problems: Agricultural Legislation in the 100th Congress; Archived Issue Brief, Penelope Cate, IB87006

* Farm Support Programs: Their Purpose and Evolution, Geoffrey S. Becker, 88-160 ENR

* The Farmer-Owned Reserve Program, Carl W. Ek, 88-534 ENR

* Federal Farm Marketing Programs, Geoffrey Becker, etc., 86-93 ENR

* Federal Poultry Inspection; A Briefing, Geoffrey S. Becker, 87-432 ENR

* Food for Peace, 1954-1986: Major Changes in Legislation, Susan B. Epstein, 87-409 ENR

* Foreign Food Aid Programs: Effectiveness Issues; Archived Issue Brief, Charles E. Hanrahan, IB88057

Agriculture / Air Pollution

* Fundamentals of Domestic Farm Programs, Geoffrey S. Becker, 89-151 ENR
* Grain Stocks and Reserves: A Briefing, 90-168 ENR
* The Heifer Tax: Uniform Capitalization and Farmers, Gregg A. Esenwein, 88-462 E
* Mandatory Programs for Wheat and Feed Grains: A Pro/Con Discussion, Carl Ek, 85-833 ENR
* Migrant and Seasonal Farmworkers: Characteristics and Related Federal Laws, Sharon House, 83-174 EPW
* National Research Initiative of the U.S. Department of Agriculture, Christine M. Matthews 91-435 SPR
* National Standards for Organic Food Production and Labeling, Jean M. Rawson 90-244 ENR
* New Crops and New Farm Products: A Briefing, Jean M. Rawson, 88-771 ENR
* Organized Farming: Legislative Proposals: Archived Issue Brief, Jeffrey Zinn, IB83186
* The Payment-In-Kind (PIK) Program: Archived Issue Brief, Mark McMinimy, IB83021
* The Payment Limitation: Background and Current Issues, Carl W. Ek, 87-12 ENR
* Pesticide Policy Issues: Debating FIFRA in the 102nd Congress; Issue Brief, Jasper Womach IB91055
* Provisions of the 1990 Farm Bill, Geoffrey S. Becker 90-533 ENR
* Rural Development Legislation: Comparative Summaries, Sandra S. Osbourn 90-232 GOV
* Rural Policy in an Era of Change and Diversity, Sandra S. Osbourn, 88-482 GOV
* Small Farms--Current Issues and Alternative Policies, Jeffrey Zinn, 86-23 ENR
* Soil and Water Conservation Issues in the 102nd Congress: Issue Brief, Jeffrey A. Zinn IB91031
* Sunflowers: Background and Current Issues, Carl W. Ek, 87-898 ENR
* Tax Effects of Title V of the Family Farm Act (H.R. 1425, 100th Congress), Marie B. Morris, 87-582 A
* The Tobacco Price Support Program: Arguments for and Against, Jasper Womach, 85-66 ENR
* The Tobacco Price Support Program: Policy issues; Archived Issue Brief, Jasper Womach, IB85163
* Tobacco Programs of the U.S. Department of Agriculture: Their Operation and Cost, Jasper Womach, 91-404 ENR
* The Triple Base Plan, Carl Ek 89-381 ENR
* U.S. Agricultural Policy: Selected Readings, 1987-1990, Ted L. Burch, 90-230 L
* USDA Commodity Certificate Exchanges: The Wheat Auction, Carl W.Ek, 88-645 ENR
* USDA's "Section 32" Fund, Geoffrey S. Becker, 91-391 ENR
* Wheat Classification, Carl Ek 88-54 ENR
* Wheat, Feed Grains, and Soybeans: Domestic Program, Issues; Archived Issue Brief, Carl W. Ek, IB87154
* Wool and Mohair Price Support Program Background and Policy Issues for 1990 Farm Bill, Jasper Womach 89-438 ENR
* The 1985 Farm Bill: A Summary; Archived Issue Brief, Geoffrey Becker, IB86013
* The 1990 Farm Bill: Grains an Oilseeds Issues; Archived Issue Brief, Carl W. Ek IB90007
* The 1990 Farm Bill: Overview; Archived Issue Brief, A. Barry Carr, etc. IB90019
* 1987 Commodity Program Options: A Brief Introduction, Carl Ek, 87-77 ENR
* 1987 Commodity Program Options: Expanding the Marketing Loan, Carl Ek, etc., 87-530 ENR
* The 1990 Farm Bill: Issues Likely to Shape the Policy Debate, Jasper Womach, 88-700 ENR

Agriculture -- Sugar Industry

* see also Agriculture--Foreign Trade
* Drawback of Sugar Duties and Fees: Lengthening the Time Allowance, Jasper Womach, 87-742 ENR
* An Explanation of the European Community's Sugar Regime and Comparison to the U.S. Sugar Program, Jasper Womach, etc. 85-77, ENR
* National Sugar Policies of the Major Sugar Importers and Exporters. Prepared by Landell Mills Commodities Studies edited by Jasper Womach 85-228 ENR
* Sugar Policy: Current Issues; Issue Brief, Jasper Womach IB88091
* World Sugar Trade and U.S. Sugar Policy, Jasper Womach, etc. 85-144 ENR

Aid to Families with Dependent Children

* see Public Welfare--AFDC

AIDS

* see Medicine--Aids, Civil Liberties and Rights--Discrimination and Integration

Air Pollution

* see also Acid Rain, Indoor Air Pollution, Mobile Sources, Ozone, Earth Sciences, and Environmental Protection, Law and Legislation, Clean Air Act
* Agriculture and the Environment; Issue Brief, Geoffrey Becker, etc. IB89086
* Air Pollutant-Induced Stress to Forest Ecosystems--An Overview of Forest Damage, Adela Backiel, etc. 86-560 ENR
* Air Quality; Issue Brief, John E. Blodgett IB87124
* Clean Air Act: An Overview; Archived Issue Brief, Maria Grimes IB86067
* Clean Air Act Provisions to Protect National Parklands, Maria Grimes 85-1013 ENR
* The Clean Air Standards Attainment Act: An Analysis of Welfare Benefits from S. 1894, Larry B. Parker 88-298 ENR
* Controlling Carbon Dioxide Emissions, Amy Abel, etc. 89-157 ENR
* The Environmental Protection Agency's Proposed Strategy for Post-1987 Nonattainment Areas, Mira Courpas 87-980 ENR
* Global Climate Change: Audio Brief, David Gushee, etc. AB50189
* Global Climate Change: Issue Brief, Robert E. Morrison IB89005
* Global Climate Changes and the Green House Effect:, Congressional Activity and Options; Archived Issue Brief, David Gushee IB88077
* Glossary of Air Quality Terms, Mira Courpas 89-247 ENR
* Hazardous Air Pollutants: A Review of the Statutory Requirements and Their Implementation; Archived Issue Brief, Maria Grimes IB85185
* Hazardous Air Pollutants: An Analysis of Title V of S. 1894, James E. McCarthy 88-265 ENR
* Health Benefits of Air Pollution Control: A Discussion, John Blodgett 89-161 ENR
* Impact of Air Pollution on National Park Units: A Summary of Hearings Held by the House Subcommittee, on National Parks and Recreation, May 20-21, 1985, George Siehl, etc. 85-933
* Incinerating Municipal Solid Waste: A Health Benefit Analysis of Controlling Emissions, Environmental & Natural Resources Policy Division 89-260 ENR
* International Environment: Overview of Major Issues; Issue Brief, Mary Tiemann, etc. IB89057
* Municipal Waste Incineration: An Analysis of Section 306 of S. 1894, James E. McCarthy 88-402 ENR
* Protecting Visibility under the Clean Air Act, Joan Hartmann, etc. 85-736 ENR
* Summary Discussion of S. 1894: The Proposed Clean Air Standards Attainment Act, Congressional Research Service 88-378 ENR
* Toxic Air Pollution: Bibliography-in-Brief, 1986-1 987, Adrienne C Grenfell 88-37 L
* Using Incentives for Environmental Protection: An Overview, John L. Moore, Larry Parker, David E. Gushee, John E. Blodgett and James E. McCarthy 89-360 ENR

Air Pollution -- Acid Rain

* Acid Rain, Air Pollution, and Forest Decline; Issue Brief, Adela Backiel IB86031
* Acid Rain: Bibliography-in-Brief, 1986-1987, Adrienne C. Grenfell 87-788 L
* Acid Rain Bills in the 100th Congress: Comparison of the Major Provisions of H.R. 2666, H.R. 4331, S. 316, S. 1894, and the Cuomo-Celeste Proposal Larry Parker, etc. 88-490 ENR
* Acid Rain Control and Clean Coal Technology: An Analysis of Title II of S. 1894, Larry Parker 88-266 ENR
* Acid Rain Control: An Analysis of Title IV of S. 1630, Larry B. Parker 90-63 ENR
* Acid Rain Control: What Is a 10 Million Ton SO_2 Reduction?, Larry B. Parker and John E. Blodgett 89-243 ENR
* Acid Rain, DOE's Clean Coal Technology Program, and the Lewis-Davis Report: Squaring a Circle?, Larry B. Parker 87-60 ENR
* Acid Rain in the 100th Congress: Comparison of the, Major Provisions of S. 95, S. 300, S. 316, S. 321, S. 1123, H.R. 1664, and H.R. 1679 Larry Parker 87-82 ENR
* Acid Rain: Info Pack, IP134A
* Acid Rain: Issues in the 100th Congress: Issue Brief, Larry Parker, etc. IB87045
* Acid Rain Legislation and Midwest Industry: A Mountain or a Molehill?, Larry Parker, etc. 85-1152 ENR

Current Events and Homework

* Acid Rain Legislation and the Domestic Aluminum Industry, Marc Humphries, etc. 89-327 ENR
* Acid Rain Legislation in the 101st Congress: Archived Issue Brief, Mira Courpas and Larry Parker IB89144
* Acid Rain; Scientific Progress and Outlook; Audio Brief, AB50128
* Acid Rain: Selected References, 1989-1001, Lisa B. Dove 91-596 L
* Action and Its Volunteer Programs, Evelyn Howard, etc., 87-716 EPW
* Canada's Progress on Acid Rain Control: Shifting Gears or Stalled in Neutral?, Mira Courpas, etc. 88-353 ENR
* Department of Energy's Clean Technology Program: Demonstrating Better Ways to Use America's Black Gold; Archived Issue Brief, Paul F. Rothberg IB87093
* Distributing the Cost of Acid Rain Control: Cost-Sharing under a Freedom-of-Choice Proposal, Larry Parker 89-536 ENR
* DOE's Clean Coal Technology Program: Demonstrating Better Ways to Use America's Black Gold, Paul Rothberg 87-393 SPR
* DOE's Clean Coal Technology Program: Goals and Funding: Issue Brief, Larry Parker IB88071
* House Acid Rain Bills in the 100th Congress: Comparison of the Major Provision of H.R. 1664, H.R. 16 79, H.R. 2497/H.R. 2498, H.R. 2666, H.R. 3632, etc, Larry Parker, etc. 88-362 ENR
* Implementing Acid Rain Legislation: Issue Brief, Larry Parker IB91035
* Senate Acid Rain Bills in the 100th Congress: Comparison of the Major Provisions of S. 95, S. 300, S. 321 and S. 1123, and S.--- Larry B. Parker, etc. 87-605 ENR

Air Pollution -- Indoor Air Pollution

* Asbestos in Buildings: Activity in the 100th Congress, Claudia Copeland 89-267 ENR
* Asbestos in Buildings: Current Issues; Archived Issue Brief, Claudia Copeland IB86084
* Asbestos in Public Buildings: Comparison of Two Bills, Claudia Copeland 88-368 ENR
* Availability of Trained Persons to Implement the Asbestos Hazard Emergency Response Act, Claudia Copeland 88-259 ENR
* Comparison of Bills to Amend the Asbestos Hazard Emergency Response Act, Claudia Copeland 88-262 ENR
* Indoor Air Pollution: Audio Brief, Michael Simpson etc. AB50188
* Indoor Air Pollution: Cause for Concern?, Mira Courpas 88-745 ENR
* Indoor Air Pollution: Issue Brief, Mira Courpas, etc. IB88902
* Indoor Air Quality Problems: Present and Future; Videoprogram, Michael M. Simpson and Christopher H. Dodge LTR91-858
* Radon: An Overview of Health and Environmental Issues; Info Pack, IP363R
* Radon and Indoor Air Pollution: Bibliography-in-Brief, 1986-1987, Adrienne C. Grenfell 87-853 L
* Radon: Congressional and Federal Concerns: Issue Brief, Christopher H.Dodge and Mira Courpas IB86144

Air Pollution -- Law and Legislation

* Air Pollution--Clean Air Act: Info Pack IP008A
* Air Quality Implementing the Clean Air Act Amendments of 1990; Issue Brief, Susan Mayer IB91022
* Clean Air Act: Permit Provisions in- and Senate-Passed Bills, Claudia Copeland 90-38 ENR
* Coke Oven Emissions: A Case Study of 'Technology-Based' Regulation, Environment and Natural Resources Policy Division 89-533 ENR
* Emission Standards for Coke Ovens in Japan, Law Library of Congress. Far Eastern Law Division LL90-16
* Hazardous Air Pollutants: Revising Section 112 of the Clean Air Act; Archived Issue Brief, James W. McCarthy IB89094
* Potential Benefits of Enacting Clean Air Act Amendments, John E. Blodgett 90-73 ENR

Air Pollution -- Mobile Sources

* Air Pollution: Are Current Standards for Trucks Sufficient? Issue Brief, David E. Gushee IB86140
* Alternative Fuels for Motor Vehicles; Some Environmental Issues, David E. Gushee 88-624 S
* Alternative Fuels and Reformulated Gasoline: Issue Brief, David Gushee IB91008
* Alternative Transportation Fuels: What's at Stake?, David Gushee 90-229 S
* Carbon Dioxide Emissions from Methanol as a Vehicle Fuel, David E. Gushee 88-407 S
* Clean Air Act: Gasoline Vapor Recovery; Archived Issue Brief, David E. Gushee IB87029

* Clean Air Act Issues: Motor Vehicle Emission Standards and Alternative Fuels; Archived Issue Brief, David E. Gushee IB86140
* Emission Controls on Motor Vehicles and Fuels: An Analysis of Title II of S. 1894, David E. Gushee 88-297 A
* Emissions Impact of Oxygenated (Alcohol/Gasoline) Fuels, David E. Gushee 87-436 S
* Ethanol Fuel and Global Warming, Migdon Segal 89-164 SPR
* Methanol Fuel: Economics and Implementation; a Review of Current Studies, David E. Gushee and Robert L. Bamberger 89-562 S
* Mobile Sources of Air Pollution: Policy Trends and Prospects, Maria Grimes, etc. 86-73 ENR
* Oxygenated Fuels: Emissions Impacts and Implementation Issues, David E. Gushee 89-490 S
* Platinum Group Metals Use in the World Auto Industry: Effects of Tougher Tailpipe Emission Standards, Marc Humphries 90-219 ENR
* The Role of Transportation Controls in Urban Air Quality, David E. Gushee, etc. 88-101 S
* Trucking and the Clean Air Act Amendments of 1990: Some Economic Implications, Stephen J. Thompson 91-132 E

Air Pollution -- Ozone

* Ambient Air Quality Standards: An Analysis of Title IV of S. 1896, John E. Blodgett 88-271 ENR
* CFC Phase-Out Bills in the 101st Congress: Comparison of Provisions, David E. Gushee 89-314 ENR
* Clean Air Act Issues: Ozone Nonattainment; Issue Brief, Mira Courpas IB89046
* Controlling Carbon Dioxide Emissions, Amy Abel, etc. 89-157 ENR
* Energy Demand and Carbon Dioxide Production, Richard E. Rowberg 91-170 SPR
* Ethanol Fuel and Global Warming, Migdon Segal 90-441 SPR
* Global Climate Change and Ozone Depletion: Selected References 1989-1991, Karen L. Alderson 91-549 L
* Greenhouse Effect and Ozone Depletion; Info Pack, IP405G
* Near Term Options for Reducing United States Carbon Dioxide Emissions, Environment and Natural Resources Policy Division; Science Policy Research Division 91-133 ENR
* Ozone and Carbon Monoxide Nonattainment: An Analysis of Title I of S. 1894, Mira Courpas 88-316 ENR
* Ozone and Carbon Monoxide Nonattainment: An Analysis of Title I of the Proposed Clean Air Standards Attainment Act, David E. Gushee 87-751 S
* Ozone and Carbon Monoxide Nonattainment: Comparison of the Major House and Senate Bills and the EPA Proposed Policy, Mira Courpas, etc. 88-141 ENR
* Ozone and Plants: A Status Report, Jeffrey A. Zinn, etc. 87-496 ENR
* Ozone/Carbon Monoxide Nonattainment: Is It What It Seems to Be?, David E. Gushee 88-148 S
* Rockets and Ozone: Should Alternative Technologies Be Developed?, John D. Moteff 91-819 SPR
* The Stratospheric Ozone Layer: Regulatory Issues; Issue Brief, David Gushee IB89021
* The Unpredictable Atmosphere: Selected References, Karen L. Alderson, etc. 89-43 L

Airline Industry

* see Aeronautics--Airline Industry

Airplane Crashes

* see Aeronautics--Aviation Safety and Security

Airports

* see Aeronautics--Airline Industry, Aeronautics--Aviation Safety and Security

Alar

* see Pesticides

Alaska National Interest Lands Conservation Act

* see Arctic National Wildlife Refuge

Alcoholism

* see Drug Abuse--Alcoholism

Algeria

* Algeria in Crisis: Democracy, Islamism, and Implications for U. S. Policy, Carol Migdalovitz 91-591 F

All-Terrain Vehicles

* see Recreation

Alternative Energy Sources

* see Power Resources-Alternative Energy Sources

Alzheimer's Disease

* see Medicine

American Samoa

* Territorial Political Development: An Analysis of Puerto Rico, Northern Mariana Islands, Guam, Virgin Islands, American Samoa and Micronesian Compacts, Bette A. Taylor 88-657 GOV

American Telephone and Telegraph Company

* see also Telecommunication-Telephone Industry
* American Telephone and Telegraph Co. Flow-Through of State Gross Receipts Taxes, Angela Gilroy, 87-43 E
* The American Telephone and Telegraph Company Divestiture: Background, Provisions, and Restructuring, Angela A. Gilroy, 84-58 E
* Telephone Industry Deregulation: Selected References, Robert Howe 88-751 L
* Telephone Industry Issues; Info Pack, IB2571

Americans With Disabilities Act

* The Americans With Disabilities Act: An Overview of Major Provisions, Nancy Lee Jones 90-366 A
* The Americans With Disabilities Act: Equal Employment Opportunity Commission Proposed Regulations on Equal Employment Opportunity for Individuals With Disabilities, Nancy Lee Jones 91-291 A
* The Americans With Disabilities Act: Info Pack IP443A
* Americans With Disabilities Act of 1989: Analysis of the Remedies and Enforcement Provisions of S. 933, as Passed by the Senate, Charles V. Dale 90-112 A
* The Possible Applicability of the Americans With Disabilities Act to Indian Tribes, Elizabeth B. Bazan 91-497 A

Amtrak

* see also Transportation--Railroads
* Amtrak: An Overview, Stephen J. Thompson 88-687 E
* AMTRAK and the Future of Intercity Rail Passenger Service: Issue Brief, Stephen J. Thompson IB88041
* Federal Assistance to Amtrak, Lenore Sek 86-77 E

Angola

* Angola: Conflict Assessment and U.S. Policy Options, Raymond W. Copson 86-189 F
* The Angola Food Emergency: Extend of the Problem and Current U.S. Emergency Assistance Policy, Alan K. Yu 89-14 F
* Angola: Issues for the United States; Archived Issue Brief, Raymond W. Copson and Robert Shepard IB81063
* Angola/Namibia Negotiations: Archived Issue Brief, Brenda M. Branaman IB89047
* Angola/Namibia Peace Prospects: Background, Current Problems, and Chronology, Raymond W. Copson 88-559 F
* Angola: War and Famine; Issue Brief, Raymond W. Copson IB91030
* Southern Africa: U.S. Regional Policy at a Crossroads?, Raymond W. Copson 85-201 F

Animal Rights

* see Agriculture, Research and Development and Wildlife

Animal Use in Research

* see Research and Development

Anorexia

* see Medicine

Antarctica

* see Polar Regions

Anti-Drug Abuse Act

* see also Drug Abuse
* Anti-Drug Abuse Act of 1988 (H.R. 5210, 100th Congress): Highlights of

Enacted Bill, Harry Hogan, etc. 88-707 GOV
* The Anti-Drug Abuse Act of 1988 (P.L. 100-690): Reports and Other Executive Branch Actions Required, Suzanne Cavanagh, etc. 89-406 GOV
* Drug Control: Federal Financial Assistance to State and Local Governments, Keith Bea 90-464 GOV
* Drug Control: Highlights of P.L. 99-570, Anti-Drug Abuse Act of 1986 (Drug-Related Provisions Only), Harry Hogan, etc. 86-968 GOV
* Narcotics Control Assistance for State and Local Governments: The Anti-Drug Abuse Act of 1988, William Woldman 89-181 GOV
* National Drug Control Strategy, 1989: Background and Policy Questions, Harry Hogan 89-567 GOV
* National Drug Control Strategy, 1990: Discussion of Selected Priority Highlights; Companion to CRS Report 89-567 GOV (National Drug Control Strategy, 1989), Harry Hogan 90-122 GOV
* State and Local Assistance for Narcotics Control;, The Anti-Drug Abuse Act of 1986, William F. Woldman 87-75 GOV

Antisatellite Weapons

* see Weapons Systems--Space Weapons

Antitrust Law

* see also Corporations--Mergers
* The American Telephone and Telegraph Company Divestiture: Background, Provisions, and Restructuring, Angela Gilroy 84-58 E
* Auto Insurance Markets: Is Federal Regulation Needed to Achieve Efficiency and Competitiveness? Proceedings of a CRS Congressional Seminar, Rawle O. King, Economics Division 90-514 E
* Commercial Banking Competition and Regulation: Public Policy Considerations, William Jackson 85-104 E
* Corporate Mergers: A Look at the Record, Kevin F. Winch, etc. 87-612 E
* Corporate Mergers and Acquisitions: Selected References, 1986-1989, Robert S. Kirk 89-114 L
* Economic Concentration in the United States, 1975-1986: A Selected Bibliography, Edward Knight and Felix Chin 86-82 E
* General Overview of United States Antitrust Law, Janice E. Rubin 90-581 A
* The Impact of U.S. Antitrust Law on Joint Activity, by Corporations: Some Background, Janice E. Rubin 89-291 A
* Insurance Reform: An Analysis of H. R. 1663, Rawle O. King 90-410 E
* Insurance Industry Regulation and Supervision: A Reexamination of the McCarran-Ferguson Act of 1945; Archived Issue Brief, David Whiteman IB86149
* Japan: Resale Price Maintenance, Dick K. Nanto 91-289 E
* Joint Research and Development Ventures; Antitrust Considerations: Archived Issue Brief, Wendy Schacht IB83178
* The McCarren-Ferguson Act's Exemption of the Business of Insurance from Federal Antitrust Law, Henry Cohen 90-212 A
* Merger Guidelines--A Case Study of the LTV and Republic Steel Corporations, Gwenell L. Bass 84-133 E
* Merger Tactics and Public Policy, Carolyn Brancato 82-13 E
* Mergers and Their Impact on Today's Economy: A Survey, Julius Allen 82-118 E
* New Directions in Antitrust Law? Current Proposals for Reform, With Emphasis on Proposals Concerning Mergers and Monetary Damage Awards, Janice E. Rubin 86-1014 A
* Resale Price Maintenance: Does It Help or Harm Consumers? Issue Brief, Bruce K. Mulock IB88103
* Resale Price Maintenance: Recent Supreme Court Decisions (Monsanto Corp. v. Spray-Rite Service Corp; Business Electronics Corp v. Sharp Electronics), Janice E. Rubin 88-639 A

Anzus

* Australia, New Zealand, and the Pacific Islands; Issues for U.S. Policy; Issue Brief, Robert G. Sutter IB86158

Apartheid

* see South Africa

Appropriations

* see Public Finance

Aquaculture

* see Fisheries

Aquino, Corazon

* see also Philippines

Be patient. If any phone number is incorrect, call (area code) 555-1212 and request the new listing.

Current Events and Homework

* Philippines under Aquino; Issue Brief, Larry A. Niksch IB86104

Arctic National Wildlife Refuge

* see also Energy
* Applicability of Alaska State Laws to Oil and Gas Development in the Arctic National Wildlife Refuge, Pamela Baldwin 88-420 A
* Arctic National Wildlife Refuge: A Checklist of CRS Products, Ted L. Burch 92-5 L
* Arctic National Wildlife Refuge: Bibliography-in-Brief, Ted L. Burch 91-633 L
* Arctic National Wildlife Refuge: Major Oil Development of Wilderness? Congressional Research Service. Edited, John E. Blodgett and John L. More, Environment and Natural Resources Policy Division 88-161 ENR
* The Arctic National Wildlife Refuge: Oil, Gas, and, Wildlife; Archived Issue Brief, Lynne Corn, etc. IB87026
* Arctic Oil, Arctic Refuge; Videoprogram, M. Lynne Corn LTR91-1489
* Arctic Resources: Over a Barrel?; Issue Brief, M. Lynne Corn, Claudia Copeland and Pamela Baldwin IB91011
* Arctic Resources Controversy: A Comparison of H.R. 3601 and S. 2214, Environment and Natural Resources Policy Division, 88-380 ENR
* Arctic Resources Controversy: An Overview; Archived Issue Brief, M. Lynne Corn, etc. IB87228
* Arctic Resources Controversy: Issue Brief, M. Lynne Corn, etc. IB89058
* Environmental Effects of Energy Development in the Arctic National Wildlife Refuge: A Critique of the Final Legislative Environment Impact Statement, M. Lynne Corn, etc. 87-490 ENR
* Oil Companies and the Development of the Arctic National Wildlife Refuge, John J. Schanz 88-106 S
* The Outlook for U.S. Energy Supplies and the Arctic National Wildlife Refuge Decision, John J. Schanz 88-73 S

Argentina

* Debt Rescheduling: The Argentine Case, 1982-1988, Glennon J. Harrison 88-505 E

Arias Plan

* Central American Compliance with the August 5, 1987 Peace Agreement as of November 5, 1987, Nina M. Serafino 87-916 F
* Central American Peace Process: Selected References, Robert S. Kirk 88-389 L
* The Central American Peace Prospects: U.S. Interests and Response; Issue Brief, Nina M. Serafino IB87200
* Costa Rica: Country Background Report, Nina M. Serafino 88-577 F

Armenia

* see also U.S.S.R.
* Armenia: Basic Facts, Carol Migdalovitz 91-747F

Arms Control

* see also Conventional Negotiations and Treaties, U.S. Policies, INF, Nuclear Energy-Nuclear Exports and Non-Proliferation, and National Defense and Security
* Arms and Arms Control: An Alphabetical Microthesaurus of Terms Selected from the Legislative Indexing Vocabulary, Shirley Loo 87-961 L
* Arms Control and Intelligence: Bibliography-in-Brief, 1979-1987, Terri Lehto, etc. 87-499 S
* Arms Control and Strategic Weapons in the 99th Congress, Robert C. Gray 87-892 F
* Arms Control: Issues for Congress; Issue Brief, Stanley R. Sloan IB87002
* ASATs: Antisatellite Weapons Systems; Issue Brief, Marcia Smith IB85176
* China's Nuclear Weapons and Arms Control Policies: Implications for the United States, Robert G. Sutter 88-374 F
* Defense Spending: An Introduction to Arms Control, Burdensharing, and Other Key Questions; Archived Issue Brief, Alice C. Maroni IB88043
* The Implications for Strategic Arms Control of Nuclear Armed Sea Launched Cruise Missiles, Alva Bowen, etc. 86-25 F
* International Atomic Energy Agency: Strengthen Verification Authority? Issue Brief, Warren H. Donnelly, etc. IB91109
* Middle East Arms Control and Related Issues, Foreign Affairs and national Defense Division 91-384 F
* NATO Nuclear Modernization and Arms Control: Issue Brief, Stanley R. Sloan IB89049
* Nuclear Weapons in the U.S. Force Structure: Fact Sheet on the President's September 27 Proposals, Amy F. Woolf 91-715 F

Arms Control -- Conventional

* The CFE Treaty and Nuclear Weapons in Europe, Catherine Guicherd 91-207 F
* The CFE Treaty: Verification and Compliance Issues; Issue Brief, Mark M. Lowenthal IB91009
* Chemical and Biological Warfare: Selected references, 1988-1991, Valentin Leskovsek 91-739 L
* Conventional Armed Forces in Europe Treaty: Selected References, 1987-1990, Sherry B. Shapiro 91-134 L
* Conventional Arms control in Europe: Prospects for Accord: Issue Brief, Stanley Sloan IB86064
* Implications of President Bush's September 27th Nuclear Weapons Proposals: Effects on the Nuclear Weapons complex, Jonathan Medalia 91-728 F
* NATO: Conventional Arms Control and Related Political Issues; Info Pack IP425N
* The Treaty on Conventional Armed Forces in Europe: A Chronology, Stanley R. sloan 90-593 F
* Treaty on Conventional Armed Forces in Europe(CFE): A Primer, Catherine Guicherd 91-525 RCO
* Verifying Compliance With a Conventional Arms Control Accord: Considerations for the Congress, Stanley R. Sloan 90-79 F
* West European Attitudes Toward the Treaty on Conventional Armed Forces in Europe, Stanley R. Sloan 90-592 F

Arms Control -- Negotiations and Treaties

* see also INF
* Arms Control: Negotiations to Limit Defense and Space Weapons;Archived Issue Brief, Steven Hildreth IB86073
* Arms Control: Negotiations to Reduce INF Weapons; Archived Issue Brief, Paul Gallis IB86054
* Arms Control: Negotiations to Reduce Strategic Offensive Nuclear Weapons; Archived Issue Brief, Steven A. Hildreth and Amy F. Woolf IB88088
* Arms Control: Overview of the Geneva Talks; Archived Issue Brief, Steven Hildreth IB85157
* Assessing the INF Treaty by Foreign Affairs and National Defense Division, 88-211 F
* Ballistic Missile Forces under START: Critical Issues for Congress in FY1991, Foreign Affairs and National Defense Division 90-228 F
* British and French Strategic Nuclear Force Modernization: Issues for Western Security and Arms Control, Charlotte Phillips Preece, etc. 89-140 F
* Chemical Weapons: A Summary of Proliferation and Arms Control Activities; Issue Brief, Steven R. Bowman IB89042
* The Conference on Disarmament in Europe (CDE): Archived Issue Brief, Charlotte Preece and Steven Bowman IB84060
* Conventional Arms Control in Europe: Prospects for Accord; Issue Brief, Stanley Sloan IB86064
* Cooperative Measures in START Verification, Amy F. Woolf 91-492 F
* East-West Conventional Force Reduction Negotiations: Bibliography-in-Brief, 1980-1987, Valentin Leskovsek 87-313 L
* The Effect of a Comprehensive Test Ban on the Strategic Defense Initiative, Cosmo DiMaggio 85-972 SPR
* Forum: The START Treaty in an Era of Uncertainty?; Congressional Research Service REV 10-91
* The Geneva Negotiations on Space and Nuclear Arms: Soviet Positions and Perspectives, Jeanette Voas 86-512 S
* Implications for NATO Strategy of a Zero-Outcome Intermediate-Range Nuclear Missile Accord, Stanley R. Sloan 87-614 F
* Index to the Treaty on Conventional Armed forces in Europe (CFE Treaty), Mark M. Lowenthal 91-526 RCO
* Monitoring Nuclear Test Bans, David W. Cheney 86-155 SPR
* The Moscow Summit at First Glance: Audio Brief, Stuart Goldman, etc. AB50168
* Naval Arms Control: Issue Brief, Ronald O'Rourke IB89132
* Naval Arms Control: Selected References, 1987-1991, Valentin Leskovsek 91-797 L
* The New Interpretation of the ABM Treaty-Salient Issues, Charles R. Gellner 87-164 S
* Non-Proliferation: A Compilation of Basic Documents on the International, U.S. Statutory, and U.S. Executive Branch Components of Non-Proliferation Policy, Zachary S. Davis and Warren H. Donnelly 91-85 RCO
* Non-Proliferation Regimes: A Comparative Analysis of Policies to Control the Spread of Nuclear, Chemical and Biological Weapons and Missiles, Zachary S. Davis 91-334 ENR
* Nuclear Arms Control: Disposal of Nuclear Warheads and Their Fissile

Arctic National Wildlife Refuge / Asia

Materials; Archived Issue Brief, Warren H. Donnelly, etc. IB88024
* Nuclear Arms Control: The Geneva Talks; Info Pack, IP341N
* Nuclear Weapons Material: Ending U.S.-Soviet Production and Disposing of Inventories; Issue Brief, Warren H. Donnelly and Zachary Davis IB91129
* On-Site Inspections in Arms Control: Verifying Compliance With INF and START, Amy F. Woolf 89-592 F
* The President's Report on Soviet Noncompliance With Arms Control Agreements: A Discussion of the Charges, Jeanette Voas 84-160 F
* Proposals for Ending U.S. and Soviet Production of Fissile Materials for Nuclear Weapons: Issue Brief, David Cheney and Warren H. Donnelly IB89141
* The Resumption of U.S.-Soviet Nuclear Arms Control Talks: The Soviet Point of View, Jeanette Voas 85-605 S
* SALT II Treaty: U.S. and Soviet Interim Observance of Its Terms: Archived Issue Brief, Charles Gellner IB80018
* Soviet Compliance Behavior: The Record of the SALT I and II Agreements on Offensive Arms, Charles Gellner 86-541 S
* Soviet SALT II Compliance Behavior: The SS-25 and Encryption of Telemetry, Jeanette Voas 86-734 S
* Start: Central Limits and Key Provisions, Amy F. Woolf 91-575 F
* Start: Chronology of Major Events, Amy F. Woolf 91-592 F
* Start: Effects on U.S. and Soviet Forces, Amy F. Woolf 91-574 F
* Start Index: An Index to the Strategy Arms Reduction Treaty, Mark M. Lowenthal 91-782 S
* Start Strategic Arms reduction Talks Treaty: Checklist of Public Policy Literature and CRS Products, Sherry B. Shapiro 91-638 L
* START: A Current Assessment of U.S. and Soviet Positions, Steven A. Hildreth, etc. 88-400 F
* Statements by Mikhail Gorbachev Relating to Arms Control, July 1, 1986-June 30, 1987, Terri Lehto, etc. 87-646 S
* The Strategic Arms Reduction Talks: Questions of Concern to the 101st Congress, Amy F. Woolf 89-330 F
* Strategic Arms Reduction Treaty (START): Verification and Compliance Issues; Issue Brief, Mark M. Lowenthal IB91139
* The Threshold Test Ban and Peaceful Nuclear Explosion Treaties: Background Information and Senate Ratification Issues, Steven A. Hildreth, etc. 87-34 F
* The U.N. Conference on a comprehensive Test Ban: Its relation to U.S. Non-Proliferation Policy, Warren H. Donnelly, etc. 91-491 ENR
* Verification and Compliance: Soviet Compliance With Arms Control Agreements; Issue Brief, Amy F. Woolf IB84131
* Verifying Arms Control Agreements: The Soviet View, Jeanette M. Voas, Stuart D. Goldman and Paul E. Gallis 87-316 F.
* Verification and Compliance: Soviet Compliance With Arms Control Agreements; Issue Brief, Stuart Goldman, etc. 87-316 F
* Weapons Nonproliferation Policy and Legislation, Foreign Affairs and National Defense Division 91-536 F

Arms Control -- U.S. Policies

* The Bush Administration's Proposal for ICBM Modernization, SDI, and the B-2 Bomber, Jonathan Medalia 89-281 F
* Nuclear Risk Reduction Centers: Archived Issue Brief, Steven A. Hildreth IB86142
* Statements by President Reagan Relating to Arms Control, April 1, 1986-January 31, 1987, Terri Lehto 87-116 S
* Statements by President Reagan Relating to Arms Control, February 1, 1987-May 31, 1987, Terri Lehto 87-525 S
* Statements by President Reagan Relating to Arms Control: February 2, 1985-December 31, 1985, Jeanette Voas 86-549 F
* Statements by President Reagan Relating to Arms Control: January 1, 1986-March 31, 1986, Jeanette Voas 86-663 S
* Statements by President Reagan Relating to Arms Control: June 1, 1987-December 31, 1987, Terri Lehto 88-69 S
* Statements by President Reagan Relating to the INF Treaty, June 1, 1987-December 31, 1987, Terri Lehto 88-60 S

Arms Sales

* see Military Assistance

Arms Shipments to Iran

* see Iran

Arms Transfers

* see Military Assistance

Arts and Humanities

* Arts and Humanities: FY88-FY89 Funding Issues; Archived Issue Brief, Robert Lyke IB82026
* Arts and Humanities: Funding Issues in the 101st Congress; Archived Issue Brief, Susan Boren IB90050
* Copyright Law: Performance Rights in Musical Compositions and Videocassette Recordings, Douglas Reid Weimer 89-639 A
* Cultural or Arts Policies in Selected Foreign Countries, Law Library of Congress, Far Eastern Law Division LL90-25
* Federal Assistance to Libraries: Background Information and Issues Related to Current Programs, Wayne Riddle 87-647 EPW
* Federal Assistance to Libraries: Current Programs and Issues, Wayne Clifton Riddle 90-220 EPW
* Fundraising Techniques for Groups: Bibliography-in-Brief, 1968-1987, Robert S. Kirk 87-380 L
* Fundraising Techniques for Groups: Selected References, 1987-1991, Robert S. Kirk 91-427 L
* Law Prohibiting the Sale of Historic Artifacts, Law Library of Congress. Near Eastern and African Law Division LL89-54
* Organizations and Associations: A List of Information Sources, Walter S. Albano 91-658 C
* Resale Royalties for Visual Artists: Background Information and Analysis, Julius W. Allen 88-416 E
* Rock Music Lyrics: Selected References, 1985-1990, Tangela G. Roe 90-596 L

Asbestos

* see Air Pollution--Indoor Air Pollution

Asean

* The Association of Southeast Asian Nations (ASEAN): Economic Development Prospects and the Role for the United States, Larry Niksch 84-171 F
* Economic Changes in the Asian Pacific Rim: Policy Prospectus, Congressional Research Service 86-923 S

Asia

* see also Economic Conditions, Foreign Relations, Foreign Trade, National Defense, Nuclear Energy Politics, and Government, individual countries, e.g. Japan
* Chinese Student and Scholar Organizations in the United States, Kerry Dumbaugh 90-558 F
* Comparison of the Achievement of American Elementary and Secondary Pupils With Those Abroad--The Examinations Sponsored by the International Assoc, Wayne Riddle 86-683 EPW
* The Indian Community in the United States, Margaret Siciliano 84-792 F
* Japanese Science and Technology: Some Recent Efforts to Improve U.S. Monitoring, Nancy R. Miller 86-195 SPR
* Space Activities of the United States, Soviet Union and Other Launching Countries/Organizations; 1957-1988, Marcia S. Smith 89-183 SPR
* Space Commercialization in China and Japan, Marcia S. Smith 88-519 SPR
* U.S.-Taiwan Economic Relations: Views of Some Members of the Taiwan Economic Elite, Arlene Wilson 89-21 E

Asia -- Economic Conditions

* The Association of Southeast Asian Nations (ASEAN):, Economic Development Prospects and the Role of the United States Larry Niksch 84-171 F
* China Sanctions: Some Possible Effects, Economics Division; Foreign Affairs and National Defense Division 90-186 E
* Economic Changes in the Asian Pacific Rim: Policy Prospectus, Congressional Research Service 86-923 S
* Hong Kong-U.S. Economic Relations: Some Views from Hong Kong's Economic Elite, Kerry Dumbaugh 89-23 F
* Japan's High Prices: Some Causes and Their Relationship to Trade Policy, Dick K. Nanto 88-243 E
* The Petroleum Endowment of the People's Republic of China, Joseph P. Riva, Jr. 86-102 SPR
* Singapore-U.S. Economic Relations: Some Views from Singapore's Economic Elite, Richard P. Cronin 89-49 F
* The Stock Market in Japan: An Overview and Analysis, Arturo Wiener and Edward Knight 89-306 E
* U.S. Banks and the People's Republic of China, Walter W. Eubanks. 84-840 E
* U.S.-South Korean Economic Relations: Views of Some Members of the Korean Economic Elite, William Cooper 88-656 E

Current Events and Homework

Asia -- Foreign Relations

* Afghanistan Peace Talks: An Annotated Chronology and Analysis of the United Station-Sponsored Negotiations, Richard P. Cronin 88-149 F
* Cambodia: U.S. Foreign Assistance Facts; Archived Issue Brief, Robert Sutter IB85153
* The Cambodian Crisis: Problems of a Settlement and Policy Dilemmas for the United States; Archived Issue Brief, Robert G. Sutter IB89020
* The Cambodian Crisis: Congress Presses for Policy Change, Robert G. Sutter 91-175 F
* The Cambodian Peace Agreement: Issues for U.S. Policy; Issue Brief, Robert G. Sutter IB91146
* China-India Border Friction: Background Information and Possible Implications, Robert G. Sutter, etc. 87-514 F
* China-U.S Relations: Issues for Congress; Issue Brief, Kerry Dumbaugh IB84135
* Chinese Foreign Policy in Asia and the Sino-Soviet Summit: Background, Prospects and Implications for U.S. Policy, Robert G. Sutter 89-298 F
* Japan-U.S. Relations in the 1990s, Larry Niksch 89-264 F
* Japan-U.S. Relations; Archived Issue Brief, Robert Sutter IB81026
* Japan-U.S. Relations: Issues for Congress; Issue Brief, Robert G. Sutter IB89133
* Japanese Government Cooperation With the United States--U.S. Officials' Perspectives, Robert G. Sutter 90-435 F
* Japan's Expanding Role and Influence in the Asia-Pacific Region: Implications for U.S.Interests and Policy, Richard P. Cronin 90-432 F
* Kashmir: Conflict and Crisis; Archived Issue Brief, David E. Lockwood and Barbara Leitch LePoer IB90087
* The Kashmir Dispute: Historical Background to the Current Struggle, Richard P. Cronin and Barbara Leitch LePoer 91-563 F
* Korea and Congress, 1950-1990, Kerry Dumbaugh 85-171 F
* Korea and Congress, 1950-1990, Kerry Dumbaugh 85-171 F
* Korea/U.S. Relations: Issues for Congress; Issue Brief, Robert G. Sutter IB89136
* The Missing-In-Action (MIAs) and Vietnam-U.S. Relations: Issues for the United States, Robert Sutter 87-655 F
* Pakistan After Zia: Implications for Pakistan and U.S. Interests; Archived Issue Brief, Richard Cronin IB88096
* Pakistan's Request for the U.S. AWACS: Archived Issue Brief, Kerry Dumbaugh IB87188
* Philippines: U.S. Foreign Assistance Facts; Issue Brief, Larry Niksch IB85077
* POWS's and MIAs in Indochina and Korea: Status and Accounting Issues, Robert L. Goldich IB88061
* Prisoner of War/Missing in Action in SE Asia: Info Pack, IP127P
* The Rajiv Gandhi Visit: Issues in U.S.-India Relations, Richard Cronin 85-838 F
* Sino-Soviet Relations: Recent Improvements and Implications for the United States; Issue Brief, Robert Sutter IB86138
* South Asia: Current Developments and Issues for U. S. Policy; Report on a Trip to Pakistan and India April 8-30, 1986, Richard P. Cronin 86-741 F
* South Korea and the United States: The Chaning Relationship, Larry Niksch 87-522 F
* Sri Lanka's Gamble for Ethnic Peace; Archived Issue Brief, Stanley J. Heginbothan IB87183
* Taiwan: Recent Developments and Their Implications for the United States; Issue Brief, Robert Sutter IB87092
* The United States, Pakistan and the Soviet Threat to Southern Asia: Options for Congress, Richard Cronin 85-152 F
* United States Policy Toward Vietnam: A Summary Review of Its History, Larry Niksch, etc. 85-16 F
* U.S.-Japan Agreement for Nuclear Cooperations: Monitoring Its Implementation; Archived Issue Brief, Warren H. Donnelly IB88095
* Vietnam in Transition: Implications for U.S. Policy, Robert G. Sutter 89-177 F
* Vietnam: Procedural and Jurisdictional Questions Regarding Possible Normalization of U.S. Diplomatic and Economic relations, Alan K. Yu, Robert G. Sutter and Vladimir N. Pregelj 89-631 F

Asia -- Foreign Trade

* China-U.S. Relation and Most-Favored Nation Status: Issues and Options for Congress, Kerry Dumbaugh 91-524 F
* China's Most-Favored-Nation Status: U.S. Wheat Exports, Susan B. Epstein 91-447 ENR
* China's Trade Patterns, Wayne M. Morrison 91-561 E
* European Community-Japan Trade Relations: A European Perspective, Dick E. Nanto 86-166 E
* Exchange Rate Management in Taiwan, South Korea and Hong Kong, Arlene Wilson 87-401 E
* Forum: Trade Negotiations: Broadening the World Trading System; Also Environmental Concerns for the Year 2000, Congressional Research Service. Congressional Research Service REV 5-90
* Japan Briefing Book., Congressional Research Service 87-323 E
* The Japan Development Bank, Dick Nanto 83-563 E
* Japan: Increasing Investment in the United States, James Jackson 87-747 E
* Japan-South Korea Economic Relations: South Korea's Approach to the "Japan Problem", Dick M. Nanto 87-953 E
* Japan and an East Asian Trading Bloc, Dick K. Nanto 91-840 E
* Japan: Prospects for Greater market Openness, Raymond J. Ahearn 89-390 F
* Japan-United States Economic Relations: Views of Japan's Economic Decisionmakers, Dick Nanto 86-52 E
* Japan-U.S. Economic Relations: Bibliography-in-Brief, 1986-1987, Robert S. Kirk 87-45 L
* Japan-U.S. Trade and Economic Relations; Info Pack, IP201J
* Japan-U.S. Trade Relations; Archived Issue Brief, Raymond J. Ahearn IB81011
* Japan's Automobile Industry and Barriers to Purchases of U.S. Cars, Dick Nanto, etc. 87-793 E
* Japan's Financial Liberalization: Effects on the United States, James K. Jackson 89-102 E
* Japan's Response to the 1988 Omnibus Trade Bill, Dick Nanto 89-133 E
* JETRO: The Japan External Trade Organization, R. Kevin Flaherty 85-1112 E
* Market Access in Japan: The U.S. Experience, Raymond J. Ahearn 85-37 E
* Most-Favored-Nation Status of the People's Republic of China: Issue Brief, Vladimir N., Pregelj IB89119
* The MOSS Talks: Success or Failure?, Patricia A. Wertman 85-1129 E
* Pacific Rim Initiatives; a CRS Trade Team Product 89-405 D
* Sino-Japanese Economic Relations in the Post-Mao Decade, Dick N. Nanto, etc. 86-170 E
* South Korea and Taiwan: Expanding Trade Ties With the United States; Issue Brief, William Cooper IB86151
* Steel Imports of Hot Rolled Sheet from Korea in the Absence of Import Restraint: Hypothetical Effects on West Coast Steel Producers, David J. Cantor 88-678 E
* Super 301 Action Against Japan, Brazil and India: Rationale, Reaction, and Future Implications, Raymond J. Ahearn, etc. 90-25 F
* Taiwan-U.S. Free Trade Area: Economic Effects and Related Issues, William Cooper 89-96 E
* U.S. Agricultural Exports to China, Susan B. Epstein and Charles E. Hanrahan 89-391 ENR
* U.S. Agricultural Trade Opportunities With Pacific Rim Nations, Robert Goldstein 88-755 ENR
* U.S.-Japanese Agricultural Trade Relations: Selected Information, Donna U. Vogt 89-655 ENR
* U.S. Trade Policy Towards Japan: Where Do We Go from Here?, William Cooper 89-307 E
* U.S. Wood Exports to the Pacific Rim, Ross W. Gorte 88-548 ENR

Asia -- National Defense

* Afghanistan After Five years: Status of the Conflict, the Afghan Resistance and the U.S. Role, Richard Cronin 85-20 F
* Afghanistan After the Soviet Withdrawal: Contenders for Power, Richard Cronin 89-146 F
* Afghanistan: Selected References, Sherry B. Shapiro 88-308 L
* Afghanistan: Status, U.S. Role and Implications of a Soviet Withdrawal; Archived Issue Brief, Richard Cronin and Francis T. Miko IB88049
* Chinese Arms Sales to the Persian Gulf: A Fact Sheet, Robert Sutter 88-286 F
* China-U.S. Cooperation: Military Sales, Government Programs, Multilateral Aid, and Private-Sector Activities, Kerry Dumbaugh and Larry Q. Nowels 89-355 F
* FSX Fighter Agreement With Japan: Issue Brief, Richard F. Grimmett IB89060
* FSX Technology: Irs Relative Utility to the United States and Japanese Aerospace Industries, John D. Moteff 89-237 SPR
* Insurgency and Counterinsurgency in the Philippines, Larry Niksch 85-1038 F
* Japan's Military Buildup: Goals and Accomplishments, Gary Reynolds 89-68 F
* The NATO Allies, Japan, and the Persian Gulf, Paul Gallis
* Pakistan's Nuclear Programs: U.S. Foreign Policy Considerations; Issue Brief, Richard Cronin IB87227

Asia / Astronautics

* Philippine Bases: U.S. Redeployment Options, Alva Bowen 86-44 F
* Philippine Bases Negotiations: Archived Issue Brief, Larry A. Niksch IB90142
* Television Network Evening News Coverage of Afghanistan: A Perspective After Eight Years of War, Denis Steven Rutkus 88-319 GOV
* Thai-U.S. Economic Relations: Some Views of Thailand's Economic Elite, Raymond Ahearn 89-60 F
* U.S.-Soviet Military Balance, Book VI Far East, Middle East Assessments, John Collins, etc. 80-166 S

Asia -- Nuclear Energy

* China's Nuclear Weapons and Arms Control Policies:, Implications for the United States, Robert G. Sutter 88-374 F
* Implementation of the U.S.-Chinese Agreement for Nuclear Cooperation: Archived Issue Brief, Warren Donnelly IB86050
* India and Nuclear Weapons: Issue Brief, Warren Donnelly IB86125
* Pakistan and Nuclear Weapons: Issue Brief, Warren Donnelly IB86110
* Plutonium: Department of Energy Approval of Plutonium Shipment from France to Japan: Archived Issue Brief, Warren Donnelly IB84116
* Plutonium Economics and Japan's Nuclear Fuel Cycle Policies, Robert Civiak 88-235 SPR
* The U.S.-China Agreement for Nuclear Cooperation: Congressional Review; Archived Issue Brief, Mark Martel, etc. IB85203

Asia -- Politics and Government

* China in Crisis: Public Dissent and the Power Struggle; Archived Issue Brief, Kerry B. Dumbaugh IB89100
* China's Future; Archived Issue Brief, Kerry Dumbaugh IB85108
* China's Prospects for Continuing Reform: The 13th Party Congress and After, Kerry Dumbaugh 88-638 F
* China's Prospects After Tiananmen Square: Current Conditions, Future Scenarios, and a Survey of Expert Opinion, Kerry Dumbaugh, Shirley Kan and Robert Sutter 91-137 F
* Chinese Leadership Changes: Implications for the United States, Charles Steffens 86-131 F
* Chinese Leadership Stability and Policy Reform: A Report on a Visit to China April 1987, Robert G. Sutter 87-361 F
* Crisis in the Indian Punjab: Evolution, Issues, Competing Positions and Prospects, Richard Cronin 84-152 F
* The Gandhi Assassination: Implications for India and U.S. - Indian Relations, Richard Cronin 84-790 F
* India's Punjab Crisis: Issues, Prospects and Implications, Richard Cronin 87-850 F
* India: Regional Dissidence and Human Rights Problems, Richard P. Cronin and Barbara Leitch Lepoer 91-585 F
* India: The Assassination of Rajiv Gandhi and Implications for U.S. Interests, Richard P. Cronin and Barbara Leitch Lepoer 91-441 F
* India's Internal Security Legislation: Basic Facts and Human Rights Implications, Barbara Leitch LePoer 91-599 F
* India's Sikhs and the Crisis in Punjab State: Summary Brief Points, Richard Cronin 87-509 F
* Justice and Human Rights in China: Criminal Trials of the Leading 1989 Pro-Democracy Activists, Law Library of Congress. Far Eastern Law Division LL91-6
* Korean Political Tensions: Implications for the United States; Archived Issue Brief, Robert Sutter IB86071
* North Korea: Country Background Report, Charles S. Lee 90-475 F
* Philippines under Aquino: Issue Brief, Larry A. Niksch IB86104
* Philippines under Aquino; Issue Brief, Larry Niksch IB86104
* Tibet: Disputed Facts About the Situation in Tibet, Kerry B. Dumbaugh 88-40 F
* Taiwan's Elections: Implications fo4r Taiwan's Development and U.S. Interests, Robert G. Sutter 90-11 F

Aspartame

* see Food--Labeling and Safety

Association of South East Asian Nations

* see Asean

Astronautics

* see also Weapons Systems--Space Weapons, Satellite, Space Commercialization
* American Public Opinion on the Space Program, Rosita M. Thomas 91-90 GOV
* Astronautics and Space: An Alphabetical Microthesaurus of Terms Selected from the Legislative Indexing Vocabulary, Shirley Loo 88-397 L
* Choosing the Future of the Space Program: Audio Brief, Marcia Smith AB50222
* Choosing the Future of the Space Program; Videoprogram, Marcia Smith LTR91-1492
* Civilian Space Policy under the Reagan Administration: Potential Impact of the January 1988 Directive, Patricia E. Humphlette 88-237 SPR
* Commercial High Speed Aircraft Opportunities and Issues and Issues, Richard Rowberg, etc. 89-163 SPR
* Commercial Space Activities in Europe, Patricia E. Humphlette 88-531 SPR
* Commonly Used Acronyms and Program Names in the Space Program, Marcia Smith 87-256 SPR
* Commonly Used Acronyms and Program Names in the Space Program, Marcia S. Smith and David P. Radzanowski 90-624 SPR
* The Future of the Land Remote Sensing Satellite System, Karl A. Rohrer, etc. 89-242 SPR
* Legal and Constitutional Issues Involved in Mediasat Activities, Rita Ann Reimer 87-684 A
* The LIGO (Laser Interferometer Gravitational Observatory) Proposal, Daniel Morgan and Richard E. Rowberg 91-661 SPR
* Major Worldwide Orbital Launch Vehicles, Marcia S. Smith and David P. Radzanowski 90-621 SPR
* Mediasat: The Use of Remote-Sensing Satellites by News Agencies, Patricia E. Humphlett 87-70 SPR
* The Moon/Mars Proposal: President Bush's Space Exploration Initiative (SEI); Issue Brief, Marcia S. Smith IB90112
* NASA under Scrutiny: The Shuttle and Hubble; Archived Issue Brief, David P. Radzanowski IB90114
* National Aero-Space Plane: Archived Issue Brief, John D. Moteff and David P. Radzanowski IB89128
* The National Aero-Space Plane Program: A Brief History, John Moteff 88-146 SPR
* National Aeronautics and Space Administration (NASA) Fiscal Year 1991 Appropriations, David P. Radzanowski 90-613 SPR
* National Aeronautics and Space Administration (NASA) Fiscal Year 1992 Budget Request, David P. Radzanowski 91-214 SPR
* The National Space Council, Patricia E. Humphlett 89-429 SPR
* New Soviet Space Launch Vehicles, Marcia Smith 87-462 SPR
* Radioisotope Thermal Generators (RTGs) as Spacecraft Power Sources, Marcia S. Smith 88-111 SPR
* Rockets and Ozone: Should Alternative Technologies Be Developed?. John D. Moteff 91-819 SPR
* Soviet Space Commercialization Activities, Marcia S. Smith 88-473 SPR
* Space Activities of the United States, Soviet Union and Other Launching Countries/Organizations: 1957-1990, Marcia S. Smith 91-621 SPR
* Space Commercialization in China and Japan, Marcia S. Smith 88-519 SPR
* Space Debris: A Growing Problem, Marcia S. Smith, 91-138 SPR
* Space Facilities: The ISF/CDSF Space Station Controversy: Issue Brief, Marcia S. Smith IB88053
* Space Issues: A Checklist of CRS Products, B.F. Mangan 91-929 L
* Space Issue: Info Pack, IP371S
* Space Issues: Selected References, 1986-1988, B.F. Mangan 88-565 L
* Space Launch Options: Issue Brief, Patricia Humphlette, etc. IB87018
* Space Launch Options: Issue Brief, David P. Radzanowski and Marcia Smith IB86121
* Space Policy: Issue Brief, Patricia Humphlette, etc. IB87018
* Space Policy: Issue Brief, Marcia Smith and David P. Radzanowski IB87018
* Space Policy: Selected References, 1989-1990, B.F. Mangan 90-600 L
* Space Stations:, Issue Brief, Marcia Smith IB85209
* The UFO Enigma, George Havas, etc. 83-205 SPR
* United States Law Applicable in Outer Space, Daniel Hill Zafren 86-881 A
* U.S. Military Satellites and Survivability, Arthur Manfredi 86-581 SPR
* U.S. National Aero-Space Plane: A Comparison With Aero-Space Plane Programs in Other Countries, and Future U.S. Options, Marcia S. Smith, David P. Radzanowski and John D. Moteff 89-629 SPR
* U.S. Space Commercialization Activities, Patricia E. Humphlette 88-518 SPR
* Worldwide Space Launch Sites, Marcia S. Smith 91-514 SPR

Astronautics -- Satellites

* Development Problems of the Next Generation Geostationary Operational Environmental Satellites (GOES-NEXT), David P. Radzanowski 91-634 SPR
* The Future of Land Remote Sensing Satellite System, David P. Radzanowski 91-685 SPR
* Military and Civilian Satellites in Support of the Persian Gulf War, Marcia S. Smith 91-215 SPR
* Mission to Planet Earth, David P. Radzanowski 91-89 Spr

Current Events and Homework

* Mission to Planet Earth and the U.S. Global Change Research Program, Marcia S. Smith and John R. Justus 90-300 SPR
* Satellite technology and world food security, Marcia S. Smith, Susan R. Fletcher, Charles E. Hanrahan and Patricia E. Humphlett 89-566 S
* U.S. Military Satellites and Survivability, Arthur Manfredi 86-581 SPR

Astronautics -- Space Commercialization

* Commercial Space Activities in Europe, Tony Reichhardt 91-835 SPR
* Soviet Space Commercialization: Selling the Mir Space Station, Marcia S. Smith 91-702 SPR
* Space Commercialization Activities in the soviet Union, Marcia S. Smith 90-372 SPR
* Space Commercialization in China and Japan, Karl A. Rohrer and Marcia S. Smith 89-367 SPR
* Space Launch Infrastructure: State Initiatives to Develop Commercial Spaceports, David P. Radzanowski 91-120 SPR
* Space Program "Spinoffs": Secondary Applications and Economic Returns from Civilian Space Technology, David P. Radzanowski 91-190 SPR
* U.S. Space Commercialization Activities, Patricia e. Humphlett 88-518 SPR

Astronomy

* see Astronautics

AT&T Divestiture

* see American Telephone and Telegraph Company, Telecommunication--Telephone Industry

Atomic Energy

* see Nuclear Energy

Atomic Weapons

* see Weapons Systems-- Nuclear Weapons

Australia

* Australia, New Zealand, and the Pacific Islands; Issues for U.S. Policy; Archived Issue Brief, Robert G. Sutter IB86158
* Australia-U.S. Relations:, A Briefing Paper, Robert G. Sutter 87-383 F
* Kangaroo Management Controversy, Malcolm M. Simmons 88-468 ENR

Authorization

* see Public Finance

Automobile Industry

* see Industry-Automobile Industry

Aviation Safety

* see Aeronautics--Aviation Safety and Security

Azerbaijan

* see also U.S.S.R.
* Azerbaijan: Basic Facts, Keith Berner 91-808 F

B-1 Bomber

* see also Weapons Systems--Non-Nuclear Weapons
* B-1B Strategic Bomber: Issue Brief, Dagnija Sterste-Perkins IB87157

Baker Plan

* see also International Finance-Foreign Loans
* The "Baker Plan": A Remedy for the International Debt Crisis?: Issue Brief, Patricia Wertman IB86106
* The Mexican Debt Accords and Their Financial Implications: An Overview, Patricia A. Wertman 86-179 E

Balanced Budget and Emergency Deficit Control Act

* see Gramm-Rudman-Hollings Act

Balanced Budgets

* see Gramm-Rudman-Hollings Act, Public Finance-Deficits, Budget Enforcement Act

Balance of Payments

* see Foreign Trade--Imports and Exports

Balance of Trade

* see Foreign Trade--Imports and Exports

Baltic States

* see also Eastern Europe
* The Baltic Republics: U.S. Policy concerns; Issue Brief, Vita Bite IB90075
* Baltic States: Current Foreign Policy Issues; Bibliography in Brief, Sherry Shapiro 91-483 L

Bank Failures

* see Money and Banking-Failures and Deposit Insurance

Bank of Credit and Commerce International (BCCI)

* see International Finance--Foreign Banks and Banking

Banking

* see Money and Banking, International Finance--Foreign Banks and Banking

Bankruptcy

* see Credit

Base Closing

* see National Defense--Military Bases

Base Rights Countries

* see National Defense-Military Bases

BCCI (Bank of Credit and Commerce International)

* see International Finance--Foreign Banks and Banking

Beach Closings

* see Coastal Areas

Belarus Republic

* see also U.S.S.R.
* Belarus Republic (Formerly belorussia): Basic facts, Keith Berner 91-780 F

Belize

* Belize: Country Background Report, Mark P. Sullivan 88-568 F

Bicentennial of the Congress

* see Congress

Bicentennial of the Constitution

* see Constitution (U.S.)

Biennial Budgeting

* see Public Finance-Budget Process

Bilingual Education

* see Elementary and Secondary Education--Policies and Legislation

Biological Weapons

* see Weapons Systems

Biotechnology

* see Genetics, Research and Development

Birth Control

* see also Abortion
* Advertising Condoms: Legal and Constitutional Consideration, Rita Ann Reimer 87-325 A
* Family Planning: Title X of the Public Health Service Act: Issue Brief, Edward Kiebe IB88005
* Family Planning: Title X of the Public Health Service Act: Issue Brief, Melvina Ford IB91096
* International Population and Family Planning Programs: Issues for Congress; Archived Issue Brief, Vita Bite IV85187
* International Population and Family Planning Programs: Issues for Congress; Issue Brief, Shirley Kan IB85187
* Legal Analysis of the Department of Health and Human Services' Proposed Regulations to Amend Current, Regulations Governing the Use of Federal Funds, Karen J. Lewis 87-840 EPW

Astronautics / Budget Deficits

* Teenage Sexual Activity and Childbearing: An Analysis of the Relationships of Behavior to Family and, Personal Background, Jeanne E. Griffith 87-637 EPW

Birth Control -- Abortion

* Abortion: An Historical Perspective; Selected References, 1973-1988, Charles P. Dove 88-706
* Abortion in World Religions, Charles H. Whittier 88-357 GOV
* Abortion: Info Pack, IP001A
* Abortion: Judicial and Legislative Control: Archived Issue Brief, Charles Dale, etc. IB74019
* Abortion: Judicial Control: Issue Brief, Karen J. Lewis, IB88006
* Abortion Law in the Aftermath of Webster, Karen J. Lewis, 91-573 A
* Abortion Laws in China, Germany and Great Britain, Law Library of Congress LL90-79
* Abortion: Legislative Control: Issue Brief, Thomas P. Carr IB88007
* Abortion: National and State Public Opinion Polls, Rinn-Sup Shinn and Rosita M. Thomas, 89-591 GOV
* A Comparative Survey of the Laws on Abortion of Selected Countries, Law Library of Congress. European Law Division LL90-32
* Fetal Research: A Survey of State Law, Mildred Washington 88-198 A
* Freedom of Speech and Government Funding: Implications of Rust v. Sullivan, Henry Cohen 91-488 A
* The Moral Arguments in the Controversy Over Abortion, With Reference to "Human Life Amendment" Resolutions, Charles H. Whittier 86-802 GOV
* Legal Analysis of Constitutional Issues Raised by the So-Called "Kemp-Hatch" Amendment Restricting Federal Funding of Abortion Counseling and Referral, Charles Dale 85-1142 A
* Legal Analysis of H.R. 1729, the "President's Pro-life Bill of 1987",, Charles V.Dale 87-682 A
* The Moral Arguments in the Controversy Over Abortion, With Reference to "Human Life Amendment" Resolutions, Charles H. Whittier 86-802 GOV
* Webster v Reproductive Health Services: Another Look at the Abortion Issue, Karen Lewis 89-245 A

Black Lung

* see Worker's Compensation

Blacks

* see also Civil Liberties and Rights-Discrimination and Integration, Equal Employment Opportunity
* Black Americans: A Checklist of Selected CRS Products, Tangela g. Roe 91-787 L
* Blacks' Labor Market experiences in the 1980s and 1990s, Linda Levine 90-307 E
* Black Members of the United States Congress 1789-1991, Mildred L. Amer 91-429 GOV
* Blacks and Politics: Selected References, 1987-1990, Tangela G. Roe 90-296 L
* Black Population in the 99th Congress Districts, David Huckabee 85-764 GOV
* Blacks and Tax Reform, 1985-1986; An Assessment of Possible Impacts on Blacks of Selected Proposals, by the President and Provisions of the Tax Reform, William Ellis, etc. 86-117 GOV
* Clarence Thomas: Bibliography-in Brief, 1981-1991, George Walser 91-692 L
* Comparative Quality of Rental Housing Obtained by Whites, Grace Milgram 87-626 E
* Economic Growth and Changing Labor Markets: Those Left Behind; Adult Black Workers: The Progress of Some, Linda LeGrande 84-228 E
* Historically Black Colleges and Universities and African-American Participation in Higher Education, William W. Ellis and James B. Stedman 89-588 S
* Martin Luther King: Selected References, 1978-1989, Jean Bowers 90-586 L
* Speech Material: Martin Luther King's Birthday; Info Pack, IP372M
* The U.S. Black Population, by Census Division, State and Congressional District, Jennifer D. Williams 86-711 GOV
* Underrepresented Minorities and Women in Science, Mathematics, and Engineering: Problems and Issues for the 1990s, Christine M. Matthews 91-26 SPR
* The Voting Rights Act of 1965 as Amended, Paul Downing 84-203 GOV
* Voting Rights act: A Checklist of CRS Products, George Walser 92-15 L

Block Grants

* see State and Local Government--Block Grants, Intergovernmental Fiscal Relations

Board of Governors of the Federal Reserve System (U.S.)

* see also Money and Banking-Monetary Policy
* Budget Deficits and Monetary Policy, Carol Leisenring 81-128 E
* The Economics of Federal Reserve Independence, G. Thomas Woodward 90-118 E
* Federal Reserve: Development and Responsiveness to Government, William Jackson 89-636 E
* The Federal Reserve Discount Rate: Its Significance in Monetary Policy, G. Thomas Woodward 87-17 E
* Federal Reserve Financing, William Jackson 91-746 E
* Federal Reserve System: Accountability and Independence; Issue Brief, F. Jean Wells IB89146
* Federal Reserve System; Info Pack, IP105F
* Membership of the Board of Governors of the Federal Reserve System, December 1913-October 1986, Roger S. White, etc. 86-985 E
* The Targeting of Monetary Policy: Money Supply Growth or Interest Rates?, Gail E. Makinen 86-596 E

Boland Amendment

* see Foreign Relations, Iran-Contra Affair
* The Boland Amendments: A Chronology of Congressional Action, Joseph Maheady 87-833 A
* Contra Aid: Analysis of Whether the National Security Council and the NSC Staff are an Agency or Entity Involved in Intelligence Activities, Larry Eig 87-566 A

Bolivia

* Narcotics Control and the Use of U.S. Military Personnel: Operations in Bolivia and Issues for Congress, Raphael Perl 86-800 F

Bond

* see Corporations--Securities Industry

Bottle Bills

* see Solid Wastes

Brady Handgun Violence Prevention Act

* see Crimes and Offenses--Gun Control

Bradley Plan

* see International Finance-Foreign Loans

Brazil

* Brazilian Petroleum Status, Joseph P. Riva, Jr. 89-328 SPR
* Natural Resources Conservation and Development in Brazil: An Overview and Related Issues, Russell Hawkins 84-802 ENR
* Super 301 Action Against Japan, Brazil and India: Rationale, Reaction, and Future Implications, Raymond J. Ahearn, Richard Cronin and Larry Storrs 90-25 F

Brunei

* The Association of Southeast Asian Nations (ASEAN) : Economic Development Prospects and the Role of the United States, Larry Niksch 84-171 F

Budget and Government Spending

* see Defense Economics, Economic Policy, Local Finance, Procurement, Public Finance, State and Local Government--Intergovernmental Fiscal Relations, Taxation

Budget Deficits

* see also Gramm-Rudman-Hollings Act, Public Finance-Public Debt and Deficits
* Agriculture and the Budget, IB87032
* Budget Action for FY 1990 During 1989, IB89090
* Budget Background for FY 1990, IB89072
* Congressional Budget Process Reform: 101st Congress, IB89022
* The Debt Limit, IB87127
* Deficit Reduction: Spending and Revenue Options, IB89003
* The Federal Budget for Fiscal Year 1989, IB84233
* The Federal Debt: Who Bears Its Burdens, IB84233
* Sequestration Actions for FY 90 Under the Gramm-Rudman-Hollings Act, IB89017

Current Events and Homework

Budget Enforcement Act

* Budget Enforcement Act of 1990: A General Explanation; Videoprogram, Robert Keith LTR91-919
* Budget Enforcement Act of 1990: Brief Summary, Edward Davis and Robert Keith 90-520 GOV
* Budget Enforcement Act of 1990: Contents Listing, Edward Davis and Robert Keith 90-516 GOV
* Budget Enforcement Act of 1990: Cross-References to Laws and Rules Amended, Edward Davis and Robert Keith 90-517 GOV
* Budget Enforcement Act of 1990: Legislative History, Edward Davis and Robert Keith 90-518 GOV
* Budget Enforcement in 1991: A Checklist of CRS Products and Public Policy Literature, Robert S. Kirk 91-338 L
* Discretionary Spending Limits for Fiscal Year 1991: November 1990 Adjustments and "Mini-Sequester", Edward Davis and Robert Keith 90-528 GOV
* Points of Order Under the Congressional Budget Act of 1974, Edward Davis 91-347 GOV

Budget Process

* see Public Finance--Budget Process

Budgets

* see Defense Economics--Defense Budgets Public Finance

Bulgaria

* U.S.-Bulgarian Relations Since World War II, James Voorhees 91-327 F

Burdensharing (National Defense)

* see Defense Economics--Burdensharing

Bush, George

* see also Presidents (U.S.)
* The Forty-First President: George Bush, Selected References, 1972-1988, George Walser 88-699 L

Business, Industry, and Consumer Affairs

* Automobile Insurance Crisis, IB89013
* CFTC Reauthorization and the Futures Trading "Sting", IB89051
* Corporate Mergers, IB87171
* Industrial Innovation: Debate Over Government Policy, IB84004
* Legal Issues of Insider Trading in Securities, IB87052
* Leveraged Buyouts, IB89036
* Products Liability: A Legal Overview, IB77021
* Resale Price Maintenance: Does It Help or Harm Consumers?, IB88103
* U.S. Postal Service, IB88084
* The U.S. Postal Service: Its Treatment in the Federal Budget, IB88035
* The U.S. Uranium Industry: Changing Prospects and the Federal Role, IB89079

Business and Society

* see also Regulation and Deregulation and Corporations
* Cable Television Franchises; Do Franchising Authorities Have Any Recourse If the Franchisee Raises Subscription Rates? Janice E. Rubin 87-448 A
* The Community Reinvestment Act: Its Role in Local Economic Development, J.F. Hornbeck 88-732 E
* Community Reinvestment Act: Legal Analysis, M. Maureen Murphy 89-135 A
* Confidentiality and Secrecy Orders in Civil Cases, Kenneth R. Thomas 89-225 A
* Corporate Governance in America: The Board and Business Leadership; Corporate Boards; Interaction and Functional Relationship with Constituent Groups, Kevin Winch 82-197 E
* Financing Business and Economic Development: Three Private-Sector Initiatives, J.F. Hornbeck 88-598 A
* Foreign Corrupt Practices Act Amendments of 1988, Michael V. Seitzinger 88-589 A

Business and Society-- Regulation and Deregulation

* see also Corporations-Securities Industry, Money and Banking--Law and Regulation
* Airlines under Deregulation at Mid-Decade: Trends and Policy Implications, John Fischer 86-67 E
* Broadcast Regulation in the 100th Congress: A Legislative Overview, Bernevia M. McCalip 89-88 E
* Cable Television Rate Regulation: Issue Brief, Angele L. Gilroy IB91079
* Changing Regulation of Surface Transportation: Development and Implications of Current Policies, Kenneth R. DeJarnette 86-64 E
* Corporate Securities: Laws Enacted in the 101st Congress, Kevin F. Winch 91-179 E
* Cost-Benefit Analysis in Federal Regulation: A Review and Analysis of Developments, 1978-1984, Julius W. Allen 84-74 E
* Costs and Benefits of Federal Regulation: An Overview, Julius Allen 78-152 E
* Depository Financial Institutions: Alternative Regulatory Approaches, F. Jean Wells 86-174 E
* Depository Financial Institutions: Regulatory Restructuring, F. Jean Wells 84-139 E
* Electric Utilities: Deregulation, Diversification, Acid Rain, Tall Stack Regulation, and Electric Demand Issues, Archived Issue Brief, Donald Dulchinos, etc. IB85134
* Estimating the Costs of Federal Regulation: Review of Problems and Accomplishments to Date, Julius Allen 78-205 E
* Federal Regulation--Issues Before the 100th Congress: Archived Issue Brief, Rogelio Garcia IB86163
* Financial Deregulation: A Status Report, F. Jean Wells 87-800 E
* Financial Deregulation in the United States: An Introduction, F. Jean Wells 85-41 E
* Financial Deregulation: Relaxing Ceilings on Deposit Interest Rates, 1978-1980, William Jackson 81-176 E
* Financial Interest and Syndication (FIN-SYN): An Overview of Federal Regulation of Television Network Programming Practices, Kevin B. Greely 91-368 A
* Information Services: What Role for the Bell Operating Companies;, Angele A. Gilroy 90-348 E
* Legislative Approaches to Risk Decision Making, Claudia Copeland 87-945 ENR
* Prohibiting Television Advertising of Alcoholic Beverages: A Constitutional Analysis, Rita Ann Riemer 88-22 A
* Reregulation of Cable Television: A Legal Overview, Janice E. Rubin 91-370 A
* The Report of the Vice President's Task Group on Regulation of Financial Services: A Brief Summary and Evaluation F. Jean Wells 85-693 E
* Shippers by Truck and Rail: Deregulation Effects and Prospects, Kenneth R. DeJarnette 86-66 E
* Should the 'Baby Bells' Be Allowed to Manufacture? Issue Brief, Stephen J. Downs and David B. Hack IB91094
* Surface Transport Carriers: Deregulation Effects and Prospects, Lenore Sek, etc. 86-65 E
* Telephone Industry Deregulation: Selected References, 1984-1988, Robert Howe 88-751 L
* Telephone Industry Issues: Info Pack, IP257T
* United States Regulations: Finding Regulatory Material, Mark Gurevitz 90-590 A
* Wage and Employment Effects of Transport Deregulation: Pending Policy Issues, Richard S. Belous 86-68 E

Business Cycles

* see Economic Conditions--Business Cycles

Business Electronics Corp. V. Sharp Electronics Co

* Resale Price Maintenance: Recent Supreme Court Decisions (Monsanto Co v. Spray-Rite Service Co);, Janice E. Rubin 88-639 A

Business Ethics

* see Business and Society, Corporations--Securities Industry

Business Failures

* see Credit--Bankruptcy

Business, Industry and Consumer Affairs

* see Antitrust Law, Business and Society, Computers, Consumers, Corporations, Credit, Industrial Technology, Industry, Insurance, International Corp, Money and Banking, Small Business

Buy American Act

* 'Buy American' Regulations: Effects on Surface Transportation, John W. Fischer 86-78 E
* Protectionist Legislation in 1985, Raymond J. Ahearn, etc. 86-632 E

Byelorussia
* see Belarus Republic

Cable Television
* see Telecommunication-Television

Cambodia
* Cambodia: U.S. Foreign Assistance Facts: Archived Issue Brief, Robert Sutter IB85153
* The Cambodian Crisis: Congress Presses for Policy change, Robert G. Sutter 91-175 F
* The Cambodian Crisis: Problems of a Settlement and Policy Dilemmas for the United States: Archived Issue Brief Robert G. Sutter IB89020
* The Cambodian Peace Agreement: Issues for U.S. Policy; Issue Brief, Robert G. Sutter

Campaign Financing
* see Politics and Elections--Campaign Funds

Campaign Funds
* see Congress--Apportionment and Elections, Politics and Elections--Campaign Funds

Canada
* Agriculture in a U.S.-Mexico-Canada Free Trade Agreement, Charles E. Hanrahan 91-252 RCO
* Agriculture in the U.S.-Canada Free Trade Agreement, Charles E. Hanrahan and Susan B. Epstein 88-363 ENR
* Automotive Products Trade with Canada and the U.S. Canada Free Trade Area Agreement, Vladimir N. Pregelj 88-122 E
* The Canada-U.S. Free Trade Agreement: A Selected Bibliography, 1985-1988, Felix Chin 88-388 L
* Canada-U.S. Free Trade Agreement: Issue Brief, Arlene Wilson IB87173
* Canada-U.S. Free Trade Area Agreement: Info Pack, IP395C
* Canada-U.S. Free Trade Negotiations; Archived Issue Brief, Raymond J. Ahearn IB85215
* Canada-U.S.-Mexico Free Trade Agreements: Selected References, 1989-1991, Felix Chin 91-331 L
* Canada's Constitutional Crisis: Archived Issue Brief, Steven J. Woehrel and Arlene E. Wilson IB90133
* Canada's Progress on Acid Rain Control: Shifting Gears or Stalled in Neutral?, Mira Courpas, etc. 88-353 ENR
* Canadian Electricity: The U.S. Market and the Free Trade Agreement, Amy Abel 88-427 ENR
* The Canadian Free Trade Agreement and the Textile and Apparel Industries, Edward Rappaport 87-979 E
* The Canadian Health Care System, Beth C. Fuchs and Joan Sokolovsky 90-95 EPW
* Canadian Laws Respecting Donations of Organs from Anencephalic Babies, Law Library of Congress. American-British Law Division LL90-65
* Canadian Nuclear-Powered Attack Submarine Program: Issues for Congress: Archived Issue Brief, Ronald O'Rourke IB88083
* Dispute Settlement Provisions in the United States-Canada Free Trade Agreement, Jeanne Jagelski and Kenneth R. Thomas 88-603 A
* Divorce, Maintenance and Child Support Laws in Australia, Canada, England and New Zealand, Law Library of Congress. American-British Law Division LL90-65
* The Effect of the Canada-U.S. Free Trade Agreement on U. S. Industries, Economics Division 88-506 E
* Exempting Forest Products Shipments from the Jones Act Requirements, Ross W. Gorte 87-887 ENR
* Fruits and Vegetables in a U.S.-Mexico-Canada free Trade Agreement, Geoffrey S. Becker 91-362 ENR
* Government Procurement in Canada: Sourcing Policy, Law Library of Congress. American-British Law Division LL90-8
* Measures Canada Has and Has Not Taken to Protect the Spotted Owl, Law Library of Congress. American-British Law Division LL90-52
* North American Free Trade Agreement: A Checklist of CRS Products and Public Policy Literature, Felix Chin 91-450 L
* North American Free Trade Agreement: Issues for Congress, Congressional Research Service 91-282 E
* Proceedings of the CRS Workshop on Canada-U.S. Free Trade Agreement: How Will It Affect the United States? Arlene Wilson 88-356 E
* Selected Nonferrous Mineral Subsidies and the U.S.-Canada Free Trade Agreement, Marc Humphries 88-774 ENR
* Securities Registration and Disclosure Laws in Canada, Germany, Japan,

the United Kingdom and the United States, Stephen F. Clarke, etc. 91-613 A
* Steel Imports from Canada and the President's Steel Program: Archived Issue Brief, David J. Cantor IB87197
* Trade Legislation in 1988: Conflict and Compromise, George Holliday and Arlene Wilson 89-494 E
* U.S.-Canada free Trade Agreement: Assessment and Implications for a U.S.-Mexico Free Trade Agreement, Arlene Wilson 90-450 E
* U.S.-Canada Free Trade Agreement: International Implications, Raymond J. Ahearn and Francis T. Miko 88-249 F
* U.S. Free Trade Agreements With Canada and Israel: comparison of the major Provisions, Arlene Wilson 91-243 E
* U.S.-Canada Free-Trade Agreement: States Affected by Major Provisions, Lenore Sek 88-347 E
* The U.S.-Canada Pork Dispute, Susan Epstein 89-311 ENR
* U.S.-Canada Trade: An Overview, Lenore Sek 88-331 E
* U.S. Jewelry Manufacturing, International Competitiveness and H.R. 3, Bernard A. Gelb 87-875 E

Canada-U.S. Free Trade Agreement
* see Canada

Capital Budgeting
* see Public Finance--Budget Process

Capital Flight
* see International Finance

Capital Gains Taxation
* see Taxation-Personal Income Tax, Capital Gains Tax

Capital Investments
* see Corporations

Capital Punishment
* see Crimes and Offenses--Capital Punishment

Carbon Dioxide and Global Warming
* see Earth Sciences

Caribbean Area
* Belize: Country Background Report, Mark P. Sullivan 88-568 F
* Caribbean Apparel Exports: Greater Access to the U.S. Market, Edward Rappaport 88-128 E
* Caribbean Area: Bibliography-in-Brief, 1980-1988, Robert S. Kirk 88-152 L
* Caribbean Basin Initiative: Info Pack, IP190C
* The Caribbean: A Primer on the Region's Independent Nations, Foreign Affairs and National Defense Division 90-445 F
* U.S. Bilateral Economic and Military Assistance to Latin American and the Caribbean: Fiscal Years 1 946-1987, K. Larry Storrs 87-694 F

Carl D. Perkins Vocational Education Act
* see also Occupational Training--Adult and Vocational Education, Federal Aid to Education--Adult and Vocational
* Carl D. Perkins Vocational Education Act: Issues for Reauthorization; Archived Issue Brief, Paul M. Irwin and Richard N. Apling IB89069
* The Carl D. Perkins Vocational Education Act (P.L., 98-524): Summary and Compensation With Selected Provisions of the Vocational Education Act, of 1963 Paul Irwin 85-697 EPW
* Federal Policy for Vocational Education: Selected References, Peter Giordano 88-747 L
* Federal Vocational Education Legislation: Recurring Issues During the Last Quarter Century, Richard N. Apling and Paul M. Irwin 88-704 EPW
* Vocational Education Performance Standards, Richard N. Apling 89-440 EPW

Catastrophic Health Insurance
* see Health Insurance

Casualty Insurance
* see Insurance--Property/Casualty

CBI
* see Caribbean Area

Current Events and Homework

Censorship
* see Civil Liberties and Rights

Census
* see Population

Census of Population and Housing (1990)
* see Population--Census
* Adjusting the 1990 Census: Background and a Pro-Con Analysis, Alexander Lurie 88-305 GOV
* The Census Bureau's Plans for Using Computerized Maps in 1990: Fact Sheet, Daniel Melnick 87-206 GOV
* Census Data for Congressional Use: Types and Availability of 1990 Decennial Census Products, Jennifer D. Williams 91-641 GOV
* Census Questions and OMB's Review of the Census Bureau Proposal: A Summary and Brief Analysis, Daniel Melnick, etc. 88-42 GOV
* Census 1990: Selected References, 1987-1990, M. Alexandra Salinas 91-266 L
* Counting Undocumented Aliens in the Decennial Census, Thomas M. Durbin 88-438 A
* House Apportionment Following the 1990 Census: Using the Official Counts, David C. Huckabee 91-130 GOV
* How the Adjusted Census Results Would Be Used to Obtain Block Level Counts, Daniel Melnick 90-56 GOV
* The Proposed Department of Commerce Guidelines for Adjusting the 1990 Census: An Analysis and Review, Daniel Melnick 90-52 GOV
* Proposed Exclusion of Illegal Aliens from the Population Used to Apportion the House of Representatives: A Methodological and Policy Analysis, Jennifer D. Williams, etc. 88-418 GOV
* Reapportionment and Redistricting, Info Pack, Congressional Reference Division IB119R
* Statistical Adjustment of the Decennial Census: A Constitutional Analysis of Statutory Proposals, Thomas Durbin 87-947 A
* Steps in Conducting the 1990 Census, Daniel Melnick 87-205 GOV
* The 1990 Census: Including Foreign Based Military and Civilian Personnel in the State Counts, David C. Huckabee 90-305 GOV
* The 1990 Decennial Census and the Counting of Illegal Aliens, Thomas M. Durbin 88-62 A

Central America
* see also Latin America, Foreign Policy and Assistance Programs, Foreign Relations
* Belize: Country Background Report, Mark P. Sullivan 88-568 F
* Central America and U.S. Foreign Assistance: Issues for Congress; Issue Brief, Jonathan Sanford IB84075
* Central America: U.S. Relations With Costa Rica, Guatemala, and Honduras; Info Pack, IP352C
* Central American Compliance With the August 5, 1987 Peace Agreement as of November 5, 1987, Nina M. Serafino 87-916 F
* Central American Peace Process: Selected References, Robert S. Kirk 88-389 L
* The Central American Peace Prospects: U.S. Interests and Response; Issue Brief, Nina M. Serafino IB87200
* Contra Aid, FY82-FY88: Summary and Chronology of Major Congressional Action on Key Legislation Concerning U.S. Aid to the Anti-Sandinista Guerrillas, Nina M. Serafino 88-563 F
* Costa Rica: Country Background Report, Nina M. Serafino 88-577 F
* El Salvador: Bibliography-in-Brief, 1987-1989, Robert S. Kirk 90-14 L
* El Salvador: Info Pack, IP121E
* El Salvador: U.S. Foreign Assistance Facts: Issue Brief, K. Larry Storrs, etc. IB85113
* Guatemala: Country Background Report, Maureen Taft-Morales 88-586 F
* Guatemala: U.S. Foreign Assistance Facts; Archived Issue Brief, Jonathan Sanford IB85100
* Honduras: U.S. Foreign Assistance Facts: Archived Issue Brief, Robert E. Sanchez IB85080
* Honduras: U.S. Military Activities; Issue Brief, James Wootten IB84134
* International Commission on Central America: Initial Views; Audio Brief, Larry Storrs AB50176
* Kissinger Commission Implementation: Action by the Congress Through 1986 on the Recommendations of the National Bipartisan Commission on Central Amer., K. Larry Storrs 87-291 F
* Major Trends in U.S. Foreign Assistance to Central America: 1978-1986, Jonathan Sanford 86-88 F
* Nicaragua: Conditions and Issues for U.S. Policy: Issue Brief, Nina Serafino IB82115
* Nicaragua: Info Pack, IP073N
* Panama: Bibliography-in-Brief, Robert S. Kirk 90-12 L
* A Summary and Analysis of the Report of the National Bipartisan "Kissinger" Commission on Central America, January 1984, Richard Cronin, etc. 84-39 F
* U.S. Assistance to Nicaragua Guerrillas: Issues for the Congress; Archived Issue Brief, Nina Serafino IB84139
* U.S. Foreign Aid to Central America; 1986-1988, Jonathan E. Sanford 87-465 F

Central America -- Foreign Relations
* Central America and U.S. Foreign Assistance: Issues for Congress; Issue Brief, Mark P. Sullivan IB84075
* Central American Peace Prospects: U.S. Interests and Response; Issue Brief, Nina M. Serafino IB87200
* Congress and Policy Toward Central America in 1989, Mark P. Sullivan, etc. 90-347 F
* El Salvador: U.S. Aid in 1987 and 1988; Archived Issue Brief, K. Larry Storrs IB85113
* Panama-U.S. Relations: Issue for Congress; Issue Brief, Mark P. Sullivan IB90044

Central American Peace Prospects
* see Arias Plan, Central America

CFE Treaty
* The CFE Treaty and Nuclear Weapons in Europe, Catherine Guicherd 91-207 F
* The CFE Treaty: Verification and Compliance Issues; Issue Brief, Mark Lowenthal IB91009
* Conventional Armed Forces in Europe Treaty: Selected References, 1987-1990, Sherry B. Shapiro 91-134 L
* Conventional Arms Control in Europe: Prospects for Accord; Issue Brief, Stanley Sloan IB86064
* The Treaty on Conventional Armed Forces in Europe: A Chronology, Stanley R. Sloan 90-593 F
* Treaty on Conventional Armed Forces in Europe (CFE): A Primer, Catherine Guicherd 91-525 RCO
* West European Attitudes Toward the Treaty on Conventional Armed Forces in Europe, Stanley R. Sloan 90-592 F

Chastain V. Sundquist
* Summary and Analysis of Chastain V. Sundquist, Recent Court of Appeals Decision Concerning Application of the Official Immunity Doctrine to Congress, Jay R. Shampansky 88-120 A

Chemical Warfare
* see Weapons Systems--Chemical Warfare

Chemicals
* see also Solid Wastes
* After Regulation of Industrial Hazardous Waste: What Role for Incineration?, Barbara B. Black, etc. 89-57 S
* CFC Phase-Out Bills in the 101st Congress: Comparison of Provisions, David E. Gushee 89-314 ENR
* Chemicals in the Environment: Audio Brief, James Aidala AB50152
* Chemicals in the Environment: Selected References on Managing Environmental Risks, Rebecca Mazur 87-26 L
* Degradable Plastics; Archived Issue Brief, Martin R. Lee IB88067
* Environmental Impairment Liability Insurance: Overview of Availability Issues, Rawle O. King 89-269 E
* Escaping Superfund Liability: The Innocent Landowner and Lender Exceptions, Robert Meltz 91-91 A
* Hazardous Air Pollutants: Revising Section 112 of the Clean Air Act; Archived Issue Brief, James E. McCarthy IB89094
* Hazardous Chemical Facilities and Community Right to-Know: Current Issues; Archived Issue Brief, James Aidala IB86069
* Hazardous Materials Transportation: Laws, Regulations, and Policy; Archived Issue Brief, Paul Rothberg IB76026
* Hazardous Waste and the Superfund Program: Info Pack, IP094H
* Hazardous Waste Fact Book, James E. McCarthy, etc. 87-56 ENR
* Hazardous Waste Management: RCRA Oversight in the 100th Congress; Issue Brief, James McCarthy IB87087
* Liability of Superfund "Response Action Contractors" and EPA for Injury from Contractor-Conducted Cleanups Robert Meltz 89-292 A
* The Superfund Amendments and Reauthorization Act of 1986: Archived

Issue Brief, Mark Anthony Reisch IB87080
* The Toxic Substances Control Act: Implementation Issues; Archived Issue Brief, Jim Aidala IB83190
* Treatment Technologies at Superfund Sites, Environment and Natural Resources Policy Division 91-713 ENR
* U.S. Chemicals Manufacturing: Status, Issues, and Prospects, Bernard A. Gelb 88-387 E
* U.S. Chemical Manufacturing: World Status and Issues, Bernard A. Gelb 91-807 E
* Waste in the Marine Environment: Selected References, Ted Burch 89-263 L

Chief Financial Officers Act

* The Chief Financial Officers Act of 1990: An Overview, Virginia A. McMurtry 91-184 GOV
* Chief Financial Officers Act of 1990: House Action on Funding Limitations for FY 1992, Kathy Dolan 91-553 GOV

Child Abandonment

* see Families--Domestic Relations

Child Abuse

* see Families--Child Welfare

Child Care

* see Families--Day Care

Child Pornography

* see Civil Liberties and Rights--Pornography and Obscenity

Child Support

* see Families--Domestic Relations, Families--Child Welfare

Child Welfare

* see Families--Child Welfare

Children

* see Families

China

* see also Policies and Domestic Issues, Hong Kong, Taiwan
* China-India Border Friction: Background Information and Possible Implications, Robert G. Sutter, etc. 87-514 F
* China Sanctions: Some Possible Effects, Economics Division 90-186 E
* China-U.S. Cooperation: Military Sales, Government Programs, Multilateral Aid, and Private-Sector Activities, Kerry Dumbaugh, etc. 89-355 F
* China-U.S. Relations and Most-Favored-Nation Status: Issues and Options for Congress, Kerry Dumbaugh 91-524 F
* China-U.S. Relations: Issues for Congress; Issue Brief, Kerry Dumbaugh IB84135
* China-U.S. Trade Issues: Issue Brief, Wayne Morrison IB91121
* China's Most-Favored-Nation Status: U.S. Wheat Exports, Susan B. Epstein 91-447 ENR
* China's Nuclear Weapons and Arms Control Policies: Implications for the United States, Robert G. Sutter 88-374 F
* China's Prospects for Continuing Reform: The 13th Party Congress and After, Kerry Dumbaugh 88-638 F
* China's View of the "New World Order"--Possible Implications for Sino-U.S. Relations, Robert G. Sutter 91-665 F
* Chinese Arms Sales to the Persian Gulf: A Fact Sheet, Robert Sutter 88-286 F
* Chinese Foreign Policy in Asia and the Sino-Soviet Summit: Background, Prospects and Implications for U.S. Policy, Robert G. Sutter 89-298 F
* Chinese Leadership Changes: Implications for the United States, Charles F. Steffens 86-131 F
* Chinese Leadership Stability and Policy Reform: A Report on a Visit to China, April 1987, Robert G. Sutter 87-361 F
* Chinese Student and Scholar Organizations in the United States, Kerry Dumbaugh 90-558 F
* Economic Changes in the Asian Pacific Rim: Policy Prospectus, Prepared by Congressional Research Service 86-923 S
* Gorbachev's Reform Strategy: Comparisons With Hungarian and Chinese Experience, Francis T. Miko, etc. 87-813 F
* Implementation of the U.S.-Chinese Agreement for Nuclear Cooperation; Archived Issue Brief, Warren Donnelly IB86050

* Most-Favored-Nation Status for China and the Soviet Union: Procedure for Extending or Denying the Status, Archived Issue Brief, Vladimir N. Pregelj IB90107
* Most-Favored-Nation Status of the People's Republic of China; Issue Brief, Vladimir N. Pregelj IB89119
* The Petroleum Endowment of the People's Republic of China, Joseph P. Riva 86-102 SPR
* Sino-Japanese Economic Relations in the Post-Mao Decade, Dick N. Nanto, etc. 86-170 E
* Sino-Soviet Relations: Recent Improvements and Implications for the United States; Issue Brief, Robert G. Sutter IB86138
* Space Commercialization in China and Japan, Marcia S. Smith, etc. 89-367 SPR
* Status Report on U.S.-Chinese Science and Technology Relationships, Genevieve J. Knezo 90-8 SPR
* U.S. Agricultural Trade Opportunities with Pacific Rim Nations, Robert M. Goldstein 88-755 ENR
* U.S. Arms Sales to China, Kerry Dumbaugh, etc. 85-138 F
* U.S. Banks and the People's Republic of China, Walter W. Eubanks 84-840 E
* The U.S.-China Agreement for Nuclear Cooperation: Congressional Review; Archived Issue Brief, Mark Martel, etc. IB85203

China -- Policies and Domestic Issues

* China in Crisis: Public Dissent and the Power Struggle; Archived Issue Brief, Kerry B. Dumbaugh IB89100
* China's Military: Roles and Implications for U.S. Policy Toward China, Shirley Kan 91-731 F
* China's Prospects After Tiananmen Square: Current Conditions, Future Scenarios, and a Survey of Expert Opinion, Kerry Dumbaugh, etc. 91-137 F
* Communist Holdout States: China, Cuba, Vietnam, and North Korea; Issue Brief, K. Larry Storrs IB91128
* Freedom of Emigration of Chinese Citizens under Chinese Law and New Policy and Provisions on Overseas Study, Law Library of Congress LL90-40
* Justice and Human Rights in China: Criminal Trials of the Leading 1989 Pro-Democracy Activists, Law Library of congress LL91-6
* The Petroleum Endowment of the People's Republic of China, Joseph P. Riva 86-102 SPR
* Recent Developments in the Chinese Population Control Program, Law Library of Congress LL90-17
* Types of Incarceration and Forced Labor in the People's Republic of China, Law Library of Congress LL90-64

Chloroflurocarbons

* see Air Pollution--Ozone, Chemicals

Church-State Issues

* see Religion

CIS States

* see Eastern Europe, U.S.S.R.

City of Richmond V. J.A. Croson Co.

* Minority Business Set-Asides and the Constitution: A Legal Analysis of the U.S. Supreme Court Ruling in City of Richmond V. J.A. Croson Co., Charles V. Dale 89-124 A

Civil Defense

* see Disasters, National Defense

Civil Liberties and Rights

* see also Discrimination and Integration, Pornography and Obscenity, Privacy, Abortion, International Law
* Censorship and the Abridgment of Freedom of Speech in Nazi Germany, Law Library of Congress LL90-56
* Civil RICO and Protest Activity, Lou Fields 89-320 A
* Constitutional and Statutory Issues Relating to the Use of Behavior Modification on Children in Institutions, Nancy L. Jones 86-100 A
* The Constitutional Rights of Mental Patients, Charles Dale 85-585 A
* The Constitutionality of Excessive Corporal Punishment in the Public Schools, David M. Ackerman, etc. 88-413 A
* Court Cases Involving Governmental Assistance to the Facilities of Sectarian Institutions and the Establishment Clause, David M. Ackerman 88-372 A
* Developments in the Law of Church and State Since 1980, David M.

Current Events and Homework

Ackerman 91-822 A
* Emigration and Human Rights in the U.S.S.R.: Is There a New Approach? Archived Issue Brief, John P. Hardt IB88019
* Emigration: Soviet Compliance With the Helsinki Accords; Archived Issue Brief, John Hardt, etc. IB82080
* Employee Access to Personnel Records and Information: Rights under Federal and State Law, Kirk D. Nemer 89-335 A
* Establishment Clause Jurisprudence and the Display of Religious Symbols, David M. Ackerman 89-614 A
* Extension of the Civil Rights Commission: Archived Issue Brief, Leslie Gladstone IB87166
* Fair Housing Act Amendments: Archived Issue Brief, Paul Downing IB87116
* Federal Authority to Prohibit Prerecorded Commercial Telephone Calls:, A Constitutional Analysis, Rita Ann Reimer 87-10 A
* Flag Desecration and Related Number of People Arrested, Law Library of Congress LL89-51
* Flag Desecration: Info Pack, Congressional Reference Division IP440F
* The Government and the Press, Denis Steven Rutkus 90-589 GOV
* Human Rights in U.S. Foreign Relations: Six Key Questions in the Continuing Policy Debate, Vita Bite 81-257 F
* The Interception of Communications: A Legal Overview of Bugs and Taps, Charles Doyle 88-105 A
* The Judicial and Legislative Treatment of Pregnancy: A Review of Developments from Unprotected Status to Anti-Discrimination-Equal Treatment Charles Dale, etc. 87-277 A
* Overview of Recent Judicial Decisions on the Constitutional Right of Mental Patients to Refuse Treatment, Nancy Jones 85-548 A
* Polygraph Testing: Employee and Employer Rights; Issue Brief, Gail McCallion IB87126
* Polygraph Testing of Employees in Private Industry, Britt Liddicoat 85-929 A
* Press Restrictions in the Persian Gulf War: First Amendment Implications, Henry Cohen 91-316 A
* "Public Figures" and the Intentional Infliction of Emotional Distress: Hustler Magazine v. Falwell, Rita Ann Reimer 88-177 A
* Selected Federal Victim Compensation Systems, Gloria E. Moreno 88-573 EPW
* Some Constitutional Questions Regarding the Federal Income Tax Laws, Howard Zaritsky, etc. 84-168 A
* States Designating English as the Official State Language, Mark Gurevitz 91-104 A
* A Survey of the Statutory Definitions of Death, Mildred Washington 91-635 A
* The United States Flag: Federal Law Relating to Display and Associated Questions, James Hall 90-338 A

Civil Liberties and Rights -- Discrimination and Integration

* see also Blacks, Equal Employment Opportunity, Minorities, Women--Policies and Legislation
* Acquired Immune Deficiency Syndrome (AIDS): A Brief Overview of the Major Legal Issues, Nancy Lee Jones 87-236 A
* AIDS: Acquired Immune Deficiency Syndrome; Selected References, 1988-1991, B.F. Mangan 91-419 L
* AIDS and Discrimination: Legal Limits on Insurance Underwriting Practices, Kirk D. Nemer 88-381 A
* AIDS Discrimination Issues; Legislative and Executive Actions; Archived Issue Brief, Mark Eddy IB89125
* AIDS in the Workplace: Employee V. Employer Interest, Gail McCallion 87-510 E
* American Public Opinion on AIDS: A CRS Major Issue Before the 101st Congress, Rosita M. Thomas 89-85 GOV
* The Americans With Disabilities Act; Info Pack IP443A
* Americans With Disabilities Act of 1989: Analysis of the Remedies and Enforcement Provisions of S. 933, as Passed by the Senate, Charles V. Dale 90-112 A
* Blood Testing for Antibodies to the AIDS Virus: The Legal Issues, Charles Dale, etc. 87-738 A
* Civil Rights: Archived Issue Brief, Charles Dale IB90027
* Civil Rights: Equal Employment Opportunity and Affirmative Action; Info Pack IP424C
* Civil Rights Legislation: Response to Grove City College V. Bell: Archived Issue Brief, Bob Lyke IB87123
* Civil Rights Protection in the United States; Brief Summaries of Constitutional Amendments, Federal Laws and Executive Orders, Leslie W.

Gladstone 91-718 GOV
* Civil Rights Restoration Act: Bibliography-in-Brief, 1984-1988, Charles Dov 88-332 L
* The Civil Rights Restoration Act of 1987: Legal Analysis of P.L. 100-259, Karen J. Lewis, etc. 88-171 A
* Comparative Chart of Unfair Immigration-Related Employment Practices, Title VIII of the Fair Housing Act, Title VII of the Civil Rights Act of 1964 and the Rehabilitation Act of 1973, Larry M. Eig 90-209 A
* Comparative Quality of Rental Housing Obtained by Whites, Blacks and Hispanics, Grace Milgram 87-626 E
* Congressional and State Reapportionment and Redistricting: A Legal Analysis, Thomas M. Durbin, etc. 91-292 A
* Disabled Infants and Toddlers Program (Individuals With Disabilities Education Act): Reauthorization Issues, Steven R. Aleman 91-454 EPW
* The Fair Housing Act: A Legal Overview, Henry Cohen 89-683 A
* Fair Housing Act Amendments: Archived Issue Brief, Paul Downing IB87116
* The Fair Labor Standards Act and Employment of Workers With Disabilities: The Case of the Salvation Army, William G. Whittaker 91-93 E
* Federal Policies and Program Relating to Sex Discrimination and Sex Equity in Education, 1963-1985, Bob Lyke, etc. 85-116 EPW
* Homosexuality and Immigration Law After the Immigration Act of 1990, Larry M. Eig 91-495 A
* Homosexual Rights: Legal Analysis of H.R. 709/S 464, the "Civil Rights Amendments Act of 1987", Charles V. Dale 87-593 A
* Legal Implications of the Contagious Disease or Infections Amendment to the Civil Rights Restoration, Act, S. 557, Nancy Lee Jones 88-214 A
* Metro Broadcasting v. FCC: The Constitutionality of Federally Mandated Minority Preference Policies, Kevin B. Greely 90-479 A
* An Overview of Legal Developments in Homosexual Rights, Charles Dale 85-717 A
* The Potential Liability of Insurance Companies and Self-Insured Businesses for Unauthorized Disclosure of Medical Information Provided in Connection, Kirk D. Nemer 88-509 A
* Prohibiting Discrimination on the Basis of Affectional or Sexual Orientation: Arguments for and Against Proposed Legislation, Mark A. Eddy 87-825 GOV
* Prohibiting Discrimination on the Basis of Sexual Orientation: Arguments for and Against Proposed Legislation, Mark Eddy 89-222 GOV
* Redress for Japanese Americans under the Civil Liberties Act of 1988: Questions and Answers, James Sayler 90-488 GOV
* School Board of Nassau County V. Arline: A Person With the Contagious Disease of Tuberculosis May be Covered under Section 504 of the Rehabilitation Act, Nancy Lee Jones 87-238 A
* Segregation and Discrimination in Housing: A Review of Selected Studies and Legislation, Paul M. Downing, etc. 89-317 GOV
* Sex Discrimination and the United States Supreme Court: Developments in the Law, Karen J. Lewis 89-500 A
* Supreme Court Decisions Interpreting Section 504 of the Rehabilitation Act of 1973, Nancy Jones 85-926 A
* The Voting Rights Act of 1965 as Amended, Paul Downing 84-203 GOV

Civil Liberties and Rights -- Pornography and Obscenity

* Child Pornography: Legal Consideration: Archived Issue Brief, Rita Reimer IB83148
* FCC Regulation of Indecent Radio and Television Broadcasting, Rita Ann Reimer 88-291 A
* Federal Obscenity and Child Pornography Law, Henry Cohen 91-118 A
* Obscenity: A Legal Primer, Rita Ann Reimer 87-665 A
* Regulating Record Lyrics: A Constitutional Analysis, Rita Reimer 87-632 A
* Regulation of Sexually Explicit Commercial Telephone Conversation ("Dial-a-Porn"): Legal and Constitutional Analysis, Rita Ann Reimer 88-150 A
* Rock Music Lyrics: Selected References, 1985-1990, Tangela G. Roe 90-596 L

Civil Liberties and Rights -- Privacy

* Advance Directives and Health Care Facilities, Celinda Franco 91-117 EPW
* Advance Medical Directives, Kenneth R. Thomas 91-27 A
* Birth, Life and Death: Fundamental Life Decisions and the Right to Privacy, Kenneth R. Thomas 90-180 A
* Caller I.D. and Automatic Telephone Number Identification; Issue Brief, David B. Hack IB90085
* Employee Access to Personnel Records and Information: Rights under Federal and State Law, Kirk D. Nemer 89-335 A

Civil Liberties / Clean Water Act

* Federal Authority to Prohibit Prerecorded Commercial Telephone Calls: A Constitutional Analysis, Rita Ann Reimer 87-10 A
* The Fourth Amendment--A Changing Landscape, Elizabeth B. Bazan 91-542 A
* The Interception of Communications: A Legal Overview of Bugs and Taps, Charles Doyle 88-105 A
* The Personal Identification Card in the Federal Republic of Germany, Law Library of Congress LL90-37
* Privacy and Technology: Selected References, 1986-1991, Tangela G. Roe 91-841 L
* The Right to Die: Fundamental Life Decisions After Cruzan v. Director, Missouri Dept. of Health, Kenneth R. Thomas 90-371 A
* Treatment and Appointment Directives: Living Wills, Powers of Attorney, and Other Advance Medical Care Documents, Kenneth R. Thomas 91-87 A

Civil Rico

* see Criminal Procedure

Civil Rights

* see Blacks, Civil Liberties and Rights, Criminal Procedures, Equal Employment Opportunity, Handicapped, Indians, Minorities, Old Age, Religion, Women

Civil Rights Acts

* see Civil Liberties and Rights--Discrimination and Integration

Civil Rights and Liberties

* Abortion: Judicial Control, IB88006
* Abortion: Legislative Control, IB88007
* Equal Rights for Women, IB83077
* Parental Leave: Legislation in the 101st Congress, IB86132
* The School Prayer Controversy: Pro-Con Arguments, IB84081
* Selected Women's Issues in the 101st Congress, IB89104
* Supreme Court: Church-State Cases, October 1988 Term, IB88105

Civil Rights Restoration Act

* see also Civil Liberties and Rights--Discrimination and Integration
* Civil Rights Legislation: Response to Grove City College V.Bell; Archived Issue Brief, Bob Lyke IB87123
* Civil Rights Restoration Act: Bibliography-in-Brief, 1984-1988, Charles Dove 88-332 L
* The Civil Rights Restoration Act of 1987: Legal Analysis of P.L. 100-259, Karen J. Lewis, etc. 88-171 A

Civil Service

* see Government Employees

Civil Service Retirement System

* see Pensions-Civil Service

Classified Information Procedures Act

* Classified Information Procedures Act (CIPA): An Overview, Larry M. Eig 89-172 A

Clayton Act

* see Antitrust Law

Clean Air Act

* see also Air Pollution
* Acid Rain Bills in the 100th Congress: Comparison of the Major Provisions of H.R. 1666, H.R. 4331, S. 316, S. 1894, and the Cuomo-Celeste Proposal, Larry Parker, etc. 88-490 ENR
* Acid Rain Control: An Analysis of Title IV of S. 1630, Larry B. Parker 90-63 ENR
* Acid Rain Control and Clean Coal Technology: An Analysis of Title II of S.1894, Larry Parker 88-266 ENR
* Acid Rain in the 100th Congress: Comparison of the Major Provisions of S. 95, S. 300, S. 316, S. 321, S. 1123, H.R. 1664, and H.R. 1679 Larry B. Parker 87-82 ENR
* Acid Rain Legislation in the 101st Congress; Archived Issue Brief, Mira Courpas, etc. IB89144
* Acid Rain: Selected References, 1989-1991, Lisa B. Dove 91-596 L
* Air Pollution--Clean Air Act: Info Pack IP008A
* Air Quality: Implementing the Clean Air Act Amendments of 1990; Issue Brief, Susan Mayer IB91022
* Air Quality: Issue Brief, John E. Blodgett IB87124
* Alternative Fuels and Reformulated Gasoline; Issue Brief, David Gushee IB91008
* Alternative Transportation Fuels: What's at Stake?, David E. Gushee 90-229 S
* Ambient Air Quality Standards: An Analysis of Title IV of S. 1896, John Blodgett 88-271 ENR
* Clean Air Act: An Overview; Archived Issue Brief, Maria Grimes IB86067
* Clean Air Act: Gasoline Vapor Recovery; Archived Issue Brief, David Gushee IB87029
* The Clean Air Act in the Courts: Significant Cases from 1980 to 1988, Robert Meltz, etc. 88-460 A
* Clean Air Act Issues: Ozone Nonattainment; Issue Brief, Mira Courpas 89064
* Clean Air Act: Permit Provisions in- and Senate-Passed Bills, Claudia Copeland 90-38 ENR
* Clean Air Act Provisions to Protect National Parklands, Maria Grimes 85-1013 ENR
* The Clean Air Standards Attainment Act: An Analysis of Welfare Benefits from S. 1894, Larry B. Parker 88-298 ENR
* Coke Oven Emissions: A Case Study of "Technology-Based" Regulation, Environment and Natural Resources Policy Division 89-533 ENR
* Distributing the Cost of Acid Rain Control: Cost-Sharing under a Freedom-of-Choice Proposal, Larry Parker 89-536 ENR
* Emission Controls on Motor Vehicles and Fuels: An Analysis of Title II of S. 1894, David Gushee 88-297 S
* Environmental Issues: From the 101st to the 102nd Congress, Environment and Natural Resources Policy Division 91-11 ENR
* Environmental Protection Legislation in the 101st Congress; Issue Brief, Environmental and Natural Resources Section IB89033
* Environmental Protection Legislation in the 102nd Congress; Issue Brief, Environmental and Natural Resources Section IB91042
* Hazardous Air Pollutants: A Review of the Statutory Requirements and Their Implementation; Archived Issue Brief, Maria Grimes IB85185
* Hazardous Air Pollutants: An Analysis of Title V of S. 1894, James McCarthy 88-402 ENR
* Hazardous Air Pollutants: Revising Section 112 of the Clean Air Act; Archived Issue Brief, James E. McCarthy IB89094
* Health Benefits of Air Pollution Control: A Discussion, John Blodgett 89-161 ENR
* Implementing Acid Rain Legislation: Issue Brief, Larry Parker IB91035
* Municipal Waste Incineration: An Analysis of Section 306 of S. 1894, James E. McCarthy 88-402 ENR
* Ozone and Carbon Monoxide Nonattainment: Comparison of the Major House and Senate bills and the EPA Proposed Policy Mira Courpas, etc. 88-141 ENR
* Platinum Group Metals Use in the World Auto Industry: Effects of Tougher Tailpipe Emission Standards, Marc Humphries 90-219 ENR
* Potential Benefits of Enacting Clean Air Act Amendments, John E. Blodgett 90-73 ENR
* Protecting Visibility under the Clean Air Act, Joan Hartmann, etc. 85-736 ENR
* The Role of Transportation Controls in Urban Air Quality, David E. Gushee, etc. 88-101 S
* Summary Discussion of S. 1894: The Proposed Clean Air Standards Attainment Act, Congressional Research Service 88-378 ENR
* Trucking and the Clean Air Act Amendments of 1990: Some Economic Implications, Stephen J. Thompson 91-132 E

Clean Coal Technology Program

* see Fossil Fuels--Coal

Clean Water Act

* see also Air Pollution
* Chronology: EPA Regulation of Stormwater Discharge, Claudia Copeland 88-495 ENR
* Clean Water Act Activities: Post-Public Law 100-4, Claudia Copeland 88-768 ENR
* Clean Water Act Reauthorization; Issue Brief, Claudia Copeland IB91052
* Clean Water: EPA Municipal Construction Grants Program; Archived Issue Brief, Claudia Copeland, IB83013
* Clean Water: Section 404 Dredge and Fill Permit Program; Archived Issue Brief, Charles Copeland, IB83011
* Criminal Provisions in Federal Environmental Statutes: A Compilation, Maribel Nicholson 89-652 A
* Environmental Protection Legislation in the 101st Congress; Issue Brief,

Current Events and Homework

Environmental and Natural Resources Policy Div. IB89033
* Environmental Protection Legislation in the 102nd Congress; Issue Brief, Environmental and Natural Resources Policy Div. IB91042
* Municipal Compliance With the Clean Water Act: Is the Glass Half Full or Half Empty?, Claudia Copeland, 88-421 ENR
* Nonpoint Source Provisions of the Clean Water Act Amendments of 1987, John Blodgett, 87-154 ENR
* Reauthorization of the Clean Water Act: A Checklist of CRS Products, Lisa B. Dove 91-913 L
* Water Quality: Addressing the Nonpoint Pollution Problem; Archived Mini Brief, Claudia Copeland, MB83030
* Water Quality: Implementing the Clean Water Act: Archived Issue Brief, Claudia Copeland, IB89102
* Water Quality: 1987 Clean Water Act Amendments: Archived Issue Brief, Claudia Copeland, IB87049
* Wetlands Protection: Issues in the 101st Congress:, Issue Brief, Jeffrey A. Zinn, etc., IB89076

Climate Change (Global Climate Change)
* see Earth Sciences

Coal
* see Fossil Fuels--Coal

Coal Gasification
* see Fossil Fuels--Coal

Coastal Areas
* see also Water Pollution--Oil Spills
* Coastal Resource Issues: Archived Issue Brief, Jeffrey A. Zinn, IB87144
* Comparison of United States and United Kingdom Offshore Oil and Gas Leasing and Development Systems, Malcolm M. Simmons, 86-1011 ENR
* Compliance Provisions for Resource Conservation: A Status Report, Jeffrey Zinn, 88-662 ENR
* Corals and Coral Reef Protection, Eugene H. Buck 91-671 ENR
* Declining Bonus Values in Outer Continental Shelf Oil and Gas Lease Sales, Malcolm Simmons, 85-871 ENR
* Infectious Waste and Beach Closing, Martin R. Lee, 88-596 ENR
* Legislation Which Protects Offshore and Coastal Environments, Malcolm Simmons, 86-593 ENR
* Managing Coastal Development Through the Coastal Zone Management and Flood Insurance Programs: Experience to Date and the Views from Selected States, Gary Kamimura, etc., 88-354 ENR
* OCS Revenue Sharing, Malcolm M. Simmons 91-182 ENR
* Outer Continental Shelf Leasing and Development: Issue Brief, Malcolm M. Simmons, etc. IB89028
* Outer Continental Shelf Leasing and Development, Issues in the 102nd Congress; Issue Brief, Malcolm M. Simmons IB91063
* Preventing Beach Closings: Legislative Options; Issue Brief, Martin R. Lee, B88102I
* Waste in the Marine Environment: Info Pack IP407W
* Waste in the Marine Environment: Selected References, Ted Burch, 89-263 L
* Wetland Issues in the 102nd Congress, Issue Brief, Jeffrey A. Zinn, etc. IB91058
* Wetlands Issues: Info Pack IP423W
* Wetlands Protection: Issues in the 101st Congress; Issue Brief, Jeffrey A. Zinn, etc., IB89076
* Wetlands: Selected References, 1986-1989, Ted Burch 89-453 L

Cobra
* see Public Finance-Budget Programs

Cocaine
* see Drug Abuse

Columbus Day
* Speech Material; Columbus Day; Info Pack IP380C

Commodities
* see Agriculture, Minerals and Materials

Commodity Credit Corporation
* The Farmer-Owned Reserve Program, Carl W. Ek, 88-534 ENR
* Fundamentals of Domestic Farm Programs, Geoffrey S. Becker, 89-151 ENR
* History and Operation of the Commodity Credit Corporation, Plus a Compilation of Data, Jasper Womach, etc., 86-151 ENR

Common Agricultural Policy
* see also European Economic Community
* The Common Agricultural Policy of the European Community and Implications for U.S. Agricultural Trade, Donna U. Vogt, etc., 86-111 ENR
* An Explanation of the European Community's Sugar Regime and Comparison to the U.S. Sugar Program, Jasper Womach, etc. 85-77 ENR
* Proposed European Community Consumption Tax on Vegetable Oils: A Status Report, Donna U. Vogt, 87-407 ENR
* Tensions in United States-European Community Agricultural Trade, Donna U. Vogt, etc., 86-112 ENR

Commonwealth of Independent States
* see Eastern Europe

Communications
* see Postal Service, Press, Public Opinion, Telecommunication

Communist Countries
* see China, Cuba, Eastern Europe, U.S.S.R.

Community Reinvestment Act
* The Community Reinvestment Act: Its Role in Local Economic Development, J.F. Hornbeck, 88-732 E
* Community Reinvestment Act: Legal Analysis, M. Maureen Murphy, 89-135 A

Comparable Worth (Wages)
* see Equal Employment Opportunity

Competition in Contracting Act
* The Competition in Contracting Act: Its Application to the Department of Defense, Andrew Mayer 85-115 F
* Competition in Federal Public--The New Look: Changes and Implementation; the Competition in Contracting Act Title VII of Public Law 98-369, Robert G. Lauck, 85-82 A

Competitive Equality Banking Act
* The Competitive Equality Banking Act of 1987 (P.L. 100-86); Archived Issue Brief, Walter W. Eubanks, etc., IB87187
* Financial Industry Restructuring: Developments in the 100th Congress; Archived Issue Brief, F. Jean Wells, IB87194

Competitiveness
* see Foreign Trade-Competitiveness

Comprehensive Environmental Response, Compensation and Liability Act
* see Superfund

Computer Security
* see Computers

Computers
* Automation and Computers: An Alphabetical Microthesaurus of Terms Selected from the Legislative Indexing Vocabulary, Shirley Loo, 90-376 L
* Automation and Small Business: Technological Development and the Competitiveness of U.S. Industry, Wendy H. Schacht, etc. 88-300 SPR
* Building the National Research and Education Network: Issue Brief, Stephen Gould IB90126
* Computer Crimes and Security: Bibliography-in-Brief 1985-1988, Karen Alderson, 88-654 L
* Computer Security: English Legislation in the Making, Law Library of Congress LL90-22
* Computer Security Enhancement to Prevent Disasters and Crimes, Stephen B. Gould 91-239 SPR
* Computer Security Issues: the Computer Security Act of 1987: Archived Issue Brief, Glenn J. McLoughlin, IB87164
* Computer Software and Copyright Law, Douglas Reid Weimer 91-281 A
* Computer Viruses: Technical Overview and Policy Considerations, Robert Helfant, etc. 88-556 SPR

Climate Change / Congress

* Computers in Elementary and Secondary Schools: An Analysis of Recent Congressional Action, James B. Stedman, 88-419 EPW
* Congress and Information Technology, Jane Bortnick 91-783 SPR
* Forum: Information Technology Revolution, Also, Science and the Budget: 1990 Update, Congressional Research Service REV 7-90
* High-Performance Computing: An Overview, Issue Brief, Stephen Gould IB90015
* Information Policy and Technology Issues: Public Laws of the 95th Through 101st Congresses, Robert Lee Chartrand, etc. 91-569 SPR
* Information Technology for Emergency Operations: Audio Brief, AB50117
* Information Technology in Our Time: Selected References, Robert Chartrand, 88-733 SPR
* Issues in U.S. Advanced Technology Policy: A Review of the National Advisory Committee on Semiconductors Report, a Strategic Industry at Risk, Glenn J. McLoughlin 90-234 SPR
* The Legislator as User of Information Technology, Robert Chartrand, etc. 87-983 S
* SEMATECH: The Semiconductor Manufacturing Technology Initiative, Glenn J. McLoughlin 91-155 SPR
* Semiconductor Devices: The Changing Competitiveness of U.S. Merchant Producers, 1977-1987, Gary Guenther, 88-191 E
* Semiconductor Manufacturing Technology Proposal: SEMATECH; Issue Brief, Glenn J. McLoughlin, IB87212
* Semiconductors: Issues Confronting the Industry: Bibliography-in-Brief, 1985-1988, Karen Alderson, 88-445 L
* Supercomputers and Artificial Intelligence: Federal Initiatives; Archived Issue Brief, Nancy Miller, IB85105
* Telecommunications and Information-Systems Standardization-Is America Ready?, David Hack 87-458 SPR
* The U.S. Semiconductor Industry and the SEMATECH Proposal, Glenn J. McLoughlin, etc., 87-354 SPR
* Video Display Terminals and Problems of Modern Office Health, Safety and Policy: An Update, Christopher H. Dodge 89-684 SPR

Conference on Security and Cooperation in Europe

* Conference on Security and Cooperation in Europe (CSCE): The Vienna Meeting; Issue Brief, Francis T. Miko, IB87220
* Emigration: Soviet Compliance With the Helsinki Accords: Archived Issue Brief, John Hardt, etc., IB82080

Congress

* see also Apportionment and Elections, Budget Process, Executive Relations, Foreign Relations, Legislative Procedure and Operations, Members, Military Policies, Offices, Oversight
* Bicentennial of the Congress; Selected References, 1970-1989, George Walser, 89-90 L
* Bicentennial of the U.S. Congress: Info Pack, IB411C
* Characteristics of Congress: Audio Brief, AB50129
* Charactersitics of Congress, Walter Kravitz LTR91-876
* Congress: A Selected Annotated Bibliography, Mary Cook, etc. 85-49 GOV
* Congress and Congressional Operations: An Alphabetical Microthesaurus of Terms Selected from the Legislative Indexing Vocabulary, Shirley Loo, 91-506 L
* Congress and Information Technology, Jane Bortnick 91-783 SPR
* Congress in the Public Eye: Media and Public Opinion; Videoprogram, Steven Roberts, etc. LTR91-949
* Congress: Info Pack, IP022C
* Congress: Issues for the 101st Congress; Info Pack, Congressional Reference Division, IP410C
* Congress: Issues for the 102nd Congress; Info Pack, Congressional Reference Division, IP444C
* Congressional Gold Medals, Stephen Stathis 84-117 GOV
* Congressional Gold Medals 1776-1989, Stephen W. Stathis 89-586 GOV
* The Congressional Scene: Selected Publications Covering the Congress, Pamela M. Dragovich 89-113 C
* Foreign Interest Lobbying: Issue Brief, Richard C. Sachs IB91101
* Forum: Congress in the Year 2000, Congressional Research Service REV 1-90
* Legal and Congressional Ethics Standards of Relevance to Those Who Lobby Congress, Jack Maskell 91-163 A
* Members Roundtable: What We Ought To Know About Our National Legislature; Videoprogram, Wyche Fowler, etc LTR91-867
* Newspaper and Television Network News Coverage of Congress During the Summers of 1979 and 1989: A Content Analysis, Denis Steven Rutkus, etc. 91-238 GOV
* Selected Bicentennial Celebrations Commemorating the 100th Anniversaries

of the U.S. Constitution and of the U.S. Congress, Roger H. Davidson, etc. 86-171 S
* Time and History on the Hill, David McCullough LTR91-909
* The United States House of Representatives: Selected References, Peter Giordano 89-613 L
* The United States Senate: Selected References, Jean Bowers 89-669 L
* U.S. Government: Info Pack, IP162U
* Washington, DC and the U.S. Capitol Building: Info Pack, IP132W

Congress -- Apportionment and Elections

* Apportioning Seats in the House of Representatives: The Method of Equal Proportions, David C. Huckabee, 88-143 GOV
* The Authority of the Senate to Refuse to Seat Certified Members-Elect, Thomas Durbin, 85-609 A
* Black Population in 99th Congress Districts, David Huckabee 85-764 GOV
* Campaign Activities by Congressional Employees, Jack Maskell 89-574 A
* Campaign Activities by Congressional Staff: Audio Brief, AB50118
* Campaign Finance: Selected References, 1988-1990, Jean Bowers 91-356 L
* Census Data for Congressional Use: Types and Availability of 1990 Decennial Census Products, Jennifer D. Williams 91-641 GOV
* Congressional and State Legislative Redistricting and Racial Vote Dilution under Section 2 of the Voting Rights Act of 1965, Thomas M. Durbin 91-668 A
* Congressional and State Reapportionment and Redistricting: A Legal Analysis, Thomas M. Durbin, etc. 91-292 A
* Congressional Districts: Apportioning Seats and Dividing States into Single Member Districts, David Huckabee 90-573 GOV
* Congressional Districts of the 100th Congress: Rankings by 1980 Population, Land Area, and Population Density, David Huckabee, 87-370 GOV
* Counting Undocumented Aliens in the Decennial Census, Thomas Durbin, 88-438 A
* Expenditures for Campaign Services: A Survey of 1988 Congressional Candidates in Competitive Elections, Joseph E. Cantor, etc. 90-457 GOV
* Hispanic Population in 99th Congress Districts, David Huckabee, 85-763 GOV
* House Apportionment Following the 1990 Census: Using the Official Counts, David Huckabee, 91-130 GOV
* House Campaign Expenditures, Receipts and Sources of Funds: 1980-1990, Joseph E. Cantor, etc. 91-628 GOV
* Interest Groups and Lobbying: Selected References, 1989-1991, Jean Bowers 91-537 L
* Political Action Committees: Selected References, 1989-1991, Jean Bowers 91-382 L
* Procedure for House Contested Election Cases, Thomas Durbin, 84-859 A
* Proposed Exclusion of Illegal Aliens from the Population Used to Apportion the House of Representatives: A Methodological and Policy Analysis, Jennifer D. Williams, etc. 88-418 GOV
* Re-Election Rates of Senate Incumbents: 1790-1988, David C. Huckabee 90-250 GOV
* Reapportionment and Redistricting: Info Pack, Congressional Reference Division, IP199R
* Reelection Rates of House Incumbents: 1790-1988, David Huckabee 89-173 GOV
* Remedies Available to the House of Representatives After an Investigation of a Contested Election Case, Thomas Durbin, 85-658 A
* Senate Campaign Expenditures, Receipts and Sources of Funds: 1980-1990, David C. Huckabee, etc. 91-406 GOV
* Special Elections and Membership Changes in the 100th Congress, Thomas H. Neale, 89-95 GOV
* Special Elections and Membership Changes in the 101st Congress, Second Session, Thomas H. Neale, 91-189 GOV
* Special Elections and Membership Changes in the 101st Congress, 1st Session, Thomas H. Neale, 90-36 GOV
* Summary Data on 1988 Congressional Candidates' Expenditure Survey: Addendum to CRS Report 90-457 GOV, Joseph E. Cantor, etc. 90-526 GOV
* Term Limits; Info Pack IP439T
* 99th Congress Districts Classified by the Proportion of Population Over Age 65 (Ranking All District, by Their Total Population Over 65, etc.), David Huckabee 85-910 GOV

Congress -- Budget Process

* see also Public Finance--Budget Process
* Biennial Budgeting: Background and Congressional Options, James V. Saturno 89-295 GOV
* Budget Making and the Legislative Process: Audio Brief, Robert Keith, etc. AB50164

Current Events and Homework

* Budget Process; Info Pack IP012B
* Budget Process Legislation Introduced in the Senate During the 100th Congress; Comparison of Selected Measures, Edward Davis, etc., 87-611 GOV
* Budget Process Reform Legislation Introduced in the 101st Congress: Selected Listing, James Saturno, 89-304 GOV
* Changes in the Congressional Budget Process Made by the 1985 Balanced Budget Act (P.L. 99-177), Robert Keith, 86-713 GOV
* Congress and a Balanced Budget Amendment to the U.S. Constitution, James Saturno 89-4 GOV
* Congressional Approaches to Biennial Budgeting, Michael D. Margeson, etc. 87-653 GOV
* Congressional Approaches to Regulating Continuing Resolutions: Measures Introduced in the 100th Congress, James Saturno, 88-359 GOV
* Congressional Budget Process Reform; Archived Issue Brief, Edward Davis IB89022
* Continuing Appropriations for Fiscal Year 1988; Conference Initiatives in P.L. 100-202, James Saturno, 88-263 GOV
* The Effects of a Two-Year Defense Budget Authorization, Alice Maroni, 85-940 F
* The Federal Budget Process: Selected References, Robert Howe 88-436 L
* An Introduction to the Spending and Budget Process in Congress, Stanley Bach 86-20 GOV
* Legal Analysis of Proposal to Repeal Deferral Authority under the Impoundment Control Act, Richard Ehlke 86-1024 A
* Legislation, Appropriations, and Budgets: The Development of Spending Decision-Making in Congress, Allen Schick, 84-106 GOV
* Legislative Branch: Budget Authority, FY 1962-FY 1988, Paul Dwyer, 88-290 GOV
* Manual on the Federal Budget Process, Allen Schick, etc. 87-286 GOV
* Omnibus Budget Reconciliation Act of 1987; A Summary of Congressional Action on P.L. 100-203, James Saturno, 88-296 GOV
* The Power of the Purse in Foreign Policy; Process and Problems in Congressional Funding, Ellen Collier 85-182 F
* Presidential Impoundment Authority After City of New Haven V. United States, Richard Ehlke, etc., 87-173 A
* Proposed and Actual Budget Totals for the Fiscal Years 1980 Through 1988, Philip D. Winters 88-544 E
* Reconciliation for Fiscal Year 1987: A Summary of Congressional Action, James Saturno 87-772 GOV
* Regular Appropriations Enacted Separately and in Continuing Appropriations, Fiscal Years 1977-1987, Sandy Streeter 87-826 GOV
* Selected Tables on the Federal Budget Regarding Chronologies of Certain Actions, Aggregate Budget Levels, and Other Information James Saturno, etc. 87-710 GOV
* Senate Consideration of Regular Appropriations Bill is under Waivers of Section 303(A) of the 1974 Budget Act, Robert Keith 89-37 GOV
* Sequestration of Budgetary Resources for Fiscal Year 1986 under the 1985 Balanced Budget Act, Robert Keith 86-872 GOV
* Summary and Analysis of the Ramifications of Bowsher v. Synar, the Gramm-Rudman-Hollings Deficit Reduction Act Case, Morton Rosenbert, etc. 86-788 A
* U.S. House of Representatives and Senate: Budget Authority FY 1962-FY 1988, Paul Dwyer 88-260 GOV
* Waivers of the Congressional Budget Act Granted or Rejected in the Senate During 1986, Edward Davis, etc. 87-78 GOV
* Waivers of the 1974 Budget Act Considered in the Senate During the 100th Congress, Robert Keith 89-76 GOV

Congress -- Executive Relations

* see also Congress--Foreign Relations, Congress--Oversight
* Cabinet and Other High Level Nominations that Failed to Be Confirmed, 1789-1989, Rogelio Garcia, 89-253 GOV
* Congressional Access to Information from the Executive: A Legal Analysis, Richard Ehlke 86-50 A
* Congressional Control of Agency Decision and Decisionmakers: The Unitary Executive Theory and Separation of Powers, Morton Rosenberg, 87-838 A
* Congressional Control of Executive Actions: Alternatives to the Legislative Veto, Frederick Kaiser, 83-227 GOV
* Congressional Intervention in the Administrative Process: Legal andEthical Considerations, Jack H. Maskell, etc. 90-440 A
* Congressional Liaison Offices of Selected Federal Agencies, Barbara J. Hilson 88-58 C
* Executive Agreements Submitted to Congress: Legislative Procedures Used Since 1970, Ellen C. Collier, etc. 90-548 F
* Inspectors General: Resources for Oversight: Audio Brief, AB50109
* Intelligence Reform: Recent History and Proposals, Alfred B. Prados, 88-562 F
* Intelligence Reform: Recent History and Proposals, Alfred B. Prados 88-562 F
* Item Veto: Selected Issues; Archived Issue Brief, Gary Galemore IB84055
* Legal Issues Related to the Possible Release of Classified Information by Senators, Representatives, or Members of Their Staffs, Elizabeth B. Bazan 89-322 A
* The Pocket Veto: A Legal Analysis, Jay R. Shampansky 90-43 A
* The Possible Interaction Between the Impeachment Process and the Double Jeopardy Clause, Elizabeth B. Bazan 89-112 A
* Presidential Nominations and Appointments to Full-Time Positions on Regulatory and Other Collegial Boards and Commissions, 1989-1990, Rogelio Garcia 89-401 GOV
* Presidential Vetoes and Ronald Reagan's Use of the Process in the Second Term: Issue Brief, Gary Galemore IB85093
* Presidential Vetoes During the Bush Administration: Issue Brief, Gary L. Galemore IB89111
* A Question Period for Congress: Proposals to Bring Cabinet Officials Before the Legislature, Paul S. Rundquist 91-305 GOV
* Resolutions of Inquiry in the House of Representatives: A Brief Description, Richard S. Beth 87-365 GOV
* Separate But Equal: Two Hundred Years of Legislative-Executive-Judicial Relations; Videoprogram, Louis Fisher, etc. LTR91-955
* Veto Overrides by Congress, 1969-1988, Gary L. Galemore 89-436 GOV

Congress -- Foreign Relations

* see also Presidents (U.S.)--Foreign Relations
* Bipartisan Foreign Policy and Policymaking Since World War II, Ellen C. Collier 89-612 F
* Congress and Foreign Intelligence Operations: Selected References, Sherry B. Shapiro 91-620 L
* Congress and Foreign Policy: Selected References, Sherry B. Shapiro 91-222 L
* Congress and Foreign Policymaking, Ellen Collier 90-627 F
* Congress and the President in U.S. Foreign Policymaking: A Selected, Annotated Bibliography, Sherry B. Shapiro, 89-318 L
* Examples of Treaties Not Ratified Due to Senate Reservations and/or Amendments, David M. Ackerman, 87-977 A
* Foreign Policy Roles of the President and Congress, Ellen C. Collier, 86-163 F
* The Growing Role of Congress in Soviet Diplomacy and Negotiations, Joseph G. Whelan 88-714 S
* Korea and Congress, 1950-1990, Kerry Dumbaugh, 85-171 F
* The Power of the Purse in Foreign Policy: Process and Problems in Congressional Funding, Ellen Collier 85-182 F
* The Role of Congress in Soviet Diplomacy and Negotiations: Audio Brief, Joseph Whelan AB50175
* Senate Approval of Treaties: A Brief Description With Examples from Arms Control, Ellen C. Collier 91-667 F
* The Senate's Amended Rule for Considering Treaties, Stanley Bach 87-876 GOV
* The U.N. Congress: Legislation Affecting Participation and Contributions (98th, 99th, and 100th Congresses), Vita Bite, etc., 89-223 F
* U.S. Senate Rejection of Treaties: A Brief Survey of Past Instances, Ellen Collier, 87-305 F
* U.S.-Soviet Relations: Audio Brief, John Hardt, etc. AB50178

Congress -- Legislative Procedure and Operations

* Abolition of the House Internal Security Committee, Paul Rundquist 88-203 GOV
* Agriculture in the GATT: After the Midterm Review; Issue Brief, Charles E. Hanrahan IB89027
* The Amending Process in the House of Representatives, Stanley Bach, 91-605 GOV
* The Amending Process in the Senate, Stanley Bach 83-230 GOV
* Arranging the Legislative Agenda of the House of Representatives: The Impact of Legislative Rules and Practices, Stanley Bach, 86-110 GOV
* Bicameralism: The House and Senate, Ilona Nickels 91-800 GOV
* Bills Introduced and Laws Enacted: Selected Legislative Statistics 1947-1990, Rozanne M. Barry 91-646 C
* A Brief Overview of Floor Procedure in the House of Representatives, Stanley Bach, 89-59 S
* Caucuses and Legislative Service Organizations: Responses to Frequently Asked Questions, Sula P. Richardson 89-422 GOV
* Caucuses and Legislative Service Organizations of the 101st Congress: An Information Directory, Sula P. Richardson, 89-277 GOV

Congress / Members

* Chairmen of House Standing Committees Who Relinquished Original Chairmanship in Order to Chair a Different House Standing Committee, Carol Hardy 88-393 GOV
* Commemorative Legislation, Stephen W. Stathis, etc. 91-5 GOV
* Commissions and Boards to Which House Party Leaders Appoint Representatives, as of March 28, 1988, Carol Hardy, 88-276 GOV
* Commissions and Boards to Which Senate Leaders Appoint Senators, as of September 22, 1988, Carol Hardy 88-698 GOV
* Committee of the Whole: An Introduction, Ilona Nickels 85-943 GOV
* Compendium of Precedents Involving Evidentiary Rulings and Applications of Evidentiary Principles from Selected Impeachment Trials, Elizabeth B. Bazan, etc. 89-413 A
* Conducting Committee Hearings: A Guide for Preparation and Procedure, Richard Sachs 82-211 GOV
* Conference Committee and Related Procedures: An Introduction, Stanley Bach 91-576 GOV
* Congress' Contempt Power, Jay Shampansky 86-83 A
* Congressional Adjournment Dates, Targeted and Actual: 95th Through 100th Congress, (1977-1988), Ilona B. Nickels 89-583 GOV
* Congressional Committee Staff and Fundings: Issue Brief, Carol Hardy IB82006
* The Congressional Record, Mildred Amer, 86-152 GOV
* Congressional Reform: Selected Proposals for Institutional Change in the 102nd Congress, James V. Saturno 91-595 GOV
* Congressional Roll Call and Other Recorded Votes: Statistical Summary of 1st Through 101st Congresses (1789-1990), John Pontius 91-571 GOV
* The Congressional Scene: Selected Publications Covering the Congress, Pamela M. Dragovich 91-68 C
* The Congressional Standing Committee System: An Introductory Guide, Judy Schneider, etc. 89-418 GOV
* The Discharge Rule in the House of Representatives: Procedure, History and Statistics, Richard S. Beth 90-84 GOV
* Early Organization Meetings of the Congress, Judy Schneider 90-486 GOV
* Expedited Procedure: A Definition and Brief Discussion, Ilona Nickels 85-945 GOV
* Fast-Track Procedures for Trade Agreements: Implications for Congress of Their Extension, Ilona B. Nickels 91-248 GOV
* The First Day of a New Congress: A Guide to Proceedings on the House Floor, Ilona B. Nickels 91-2 GOV
* Guiding a Bill Through the Legislative Process: Considerations for Legislative Staff, Ilona B. Nickels 87-288 GOV
* House and Senate Committee Assignment Process, Judy Schneider 90-574 GOV
* House and Senate Rules of Procedure: A Brief Comparison, Ilona Nickels 90-50 GOV
* House and Senate Standing Committees and Subcommittees With Jurisdiction Over National Drug Abuse Policy, 100th Congress, Carol Hardy 88-634 GOV
* The House of Representatives and the House of Commons: A Brief Comparison of American and British Parliamentary Procedures, Paul S. Rundquist 91-522 GOV
* How to Follow Current Federal Legislation and Regulations, Carol D. Davis 91-66 C
* Immunity for Witnesses Testifying Before Congressional Committees, Jay R. Shampansky 86-1026 A
* Indicators of House of Representatives Workload and Activity, Roger H. Davidson, etc. 87-492 S
* Indicators of Senate Activity and Workload, Roger Davidson, etc. 85-133 S
* An Introduction to Conference Committee and Related Procedures, Stanley Bach 84-215 GOV
* An Introduction to the Legislative Process on the House Floor, Stanley Bach 86-96 GOV
* An Introductory Guide to the Congressional Standing Committee System, Judy Schneider, etc., 87-211
* Joint Sessions and Joint Meetings of Congress, April 6, 1789-March 20, 1987, Clay H. Wellborn, 87-244 GOV
* Legislative Procedure: An Introduction; Info Pack, IP247L
* Legislative Procedures of the U.S. Congress; Videoprogram, Walter Oleszek LTR91-915
* The Legislative Process on the House Floor: An Introduction, Stanley Bach 91-519 RCO
* The Legislative Process on the Senate Floor: An Introduction, Stanley Bach 91-520 GOV
* Legislative Reorganization Act of 1946: Summary of Provisions, Frederick H. Pauls 91-593 RCO
* Legislative Vetoes Enacted After Chadha, Louis Fisher, etc. 87-389 GOV
* Minority Staffing: A Chronological History, Judy Schneider 90-153 GOV
* The Motion to Recommit in the House: The Minority's Motion, Ilona Nickels, 89-641 GOV
* North American Free Trade Agreement: Issues for Congress, Congressional Research Service 91-282 E
* One-Minute Speeches: House Practice and Procedure, Ilona B. Nickels 90-47 GOV
* Overview of Senate Action on Presidential Appointments During 100th Congress, Rogelio Garcia, 88-78 GOV
* Parliamentary Reference Sources: An Introductory Guide, Ilona Nickels, 89-593 GOV
* Points of Order and Appeals in the Senate, Stanley Bach, 89-69 S
* Preparing Legislative Histories; Videoprogram, David Siddall LTR91-910
* Private Bills: Selected Statistics, 1975-1986, With Special Reference to Private Immigration Bills, Richard S. Beth, 87-650 GOV
* Private Immigration Measures in the House of Representatives: Contemporary Procedure and Its Historical Development, Richard S. Beth, 87-408 GOV
* Questioning Supreme Court Nominees--A Recurring Issue, Denis Steven Rutkus 90-429 GOV
* Resolving Legislative Differences in Congress: Conference Committees and Amendments Between the Houses, Stanley Bach, 91-538 GOV
* Select and Special Committees in the United States Senate; An Historical Analysis, Judy Schneider 91-555 GOV
* Senate Confirmation of Supreme Court Nominees: Selected References, George Walser 91-547 L
* Senate Floor Managers: Functions and Duties, Richard S. Beth 87-328 GOV
* Senate Legislative Floor Procedures: Audio Brief, AB50143
* Senate Legislative Floor Procedures: Videoprogram, Stanley Bach LTR91-920
* Senate Procedure, Rules, and Organizations: Proposals for Change in the 100th Congress; Archived Issue Brief, Ilona B. Nickels, IB87120
* Senate Procedure, Rules, and Organization: Proposals for Change in the 101st Congress; Issue Brief, Ilona B. Nickels IB89074
* Senate Rules and Practices on Committee, Subcommittee, and Chairmanship Assignment Limitations, as of October 5, 1990, Judy Schneider 90-490 GOV
* Some Devices for Post-Closure Delay in the Senate, Stanley Bach 88-592 GOV
* Sources of Legislative History as Aids to Statutory Construction, George Costello 89-86 A
* Sources of Legislative Proposals in the U.S. Congress, Judy Schneider 91-764 GOV
* Special Rules in the House of Representatives, Stanley Bach 91-730 S
* Special Rules Proposing to Limit Floor Amendments, 1981, 1987, Stanley Bach 88-307 GOV
* Staff Depositions in Congressional Investigations, Jay R. Shampansky 91-679 A
* The State of the Senate: Conditions, Proposals, and Prospects for Change, Stanley Bach 88-136 GOV
* Suspension of the Rules in the House of Representatives, Stanley Bach 86-103 GOV
* Toward an Informed Legislator: The Development of the Congressional Research Service; Videoprogram, Charles Mathias, Jr., etc. LTR91-950
* U.S. Free Trade Agreements With Canada and Israel: Comparison of the Major Provisions, Arlene Wilson 91-243 E
* Voting by Proxy in Congressional Committees, Richard Sachs 83-81 GOV
* Words Taken Down: Unparliamentary Language in the House, Ilona B. Nickels 90-114 GOV

Congress -- Members

* see also Political Ethics
* Black Members of the United States Congress, 1789-1991, Mildred L. Amer 91-429 GOV
* Brief Comparison of Retirement Eligibility and Benefits for Members of Congress and Executive Branch Personnel, Carolyn L. Merck 91-664 EPW
* A Brief History of Congressional Action Restricting Members' Outside Earned Income, Mildred Amer 87-416 GOV
* A Brief History of Congressional Pay Legislation, Paul E. Dwyer, etc. 87-685 GOV
* Caucuses and Legislative Service Organizations of the 101st Congress: An Information Directory, Sula P. Richardson 89-277 GOV
* Caucuses and Legislative Service Organizations of the 102nd Congress: An Informational Directory, Sula P. Richardson 91-449 GOV
* Chaplains in congress, Charles H. Whittier 90-54 GOV
* Colleges and Universities Attended by Representatives of the 100th Congress, Mildred Amer 87-348 GOV
* Colleges and Universities Attended by Representatives of the 101st

Current Events and Homework

Congress, Mildred Amer 89-149 GOV

* Colleges and Universities Attended by Representatives of the 102nd Congress, Mildred Amer 91-511 GOV
* Colleges and Universities Attended by Senators of the 100th Congress, Mildred Amer 87-349 GOV
* Colleges and Universities Attended by Senators of the 101st Congress, Mildred L. Amer 89-121 GOV
* Colleges and Universities Attended by Senators of the 102nd Congress, Mildred L. Amer 91-510 GOV
* Commission on Executive, Legislative, and Judicial Salaries: An Historical Overview, Sharon S. Gressle 89-38 GOV
* Comparison of President Bush's Honoraria Reform Act of 1989 With Existing Laws, Orders, and Regulations, Mildred L. Amer 89-481 GOV
* Comparison of the Civil Service Retirement System for Members of Congress and Executive Branch Employees, Carolyn Merck 85-681 EPW
* Congressional Pay, Selected Wages and Pensions, and Social Security: Compared to CPI, 1969-1989, Frederick H. Pauls, etc. 89-63 GOV
* Congressional Tenure: A Review of Efforts to Limit House and Senate Service, Sula P. Richardson 89-537 GOV
* Congressional Votes and Judicial Action on Outside Income and Honoraria Restrictions, 1974-1990, Mildred L. Amer 91-139 GOV
* Congressional Votes on Outside Earned Income and Honoraria, 1974-1987, Mildred Amer 87-982 GOV
* Congressional Workload, Judy Schneider 90-631 GOV
* The Constitutional Amendment to Regulate Congressional Salary Increases: A Slumbering Proposal's New Popularity, David Huckabee 86-889 GOV
* The Duties of a Member of Congress, Ilona B. Nickels 86-666 GOV
* Educational Degrees Attained by Members of Congress, 94th Through 101st Congresses, Mildred Amer 89-92 GOV
* Ethics in Government: Reform of Laws and Regulations; Issue Brief, Mildred L. Amer IB89134
* The Ethics of a Private Law Practice by Members and Employees of Congress, Jack Maskell 85-663 A
* Expulsion and Censure Actions Taken by the Full Senate Against Members, Jack Maskell 90-299 A
* Federal Employees' Retirement System Handbook for Members of Congress: Benefits under the Federal Employees' Retirement System, Educational and Public Welfare Division 87-189 EPW
* Federal Executive, Legislative, and Judicial Compensation: The Situation and Choices for the 101st Congress, James P. McGrath 89-70 GOV
* Federal Tax Law Peculiarly Applicable to Members of Congress, Robert B. Burdette 87-482 A
* Freshmen Members of Congress: 88th-100th Congresses (Number and Percentage for House, Senate, and Combined), Mildred L. Amer 88-328 GOV
* History of the Salary of the Clerk of the House of, Representatives: May 1, 1956-January 1, 1988, Paul Dwyer 87-973 GOV
* Honoraria and Outside Earned Income: Summary of Current Restrictions in the Legislative and Executive Branches, Jack Maskell 89-29 A
* House Discipline of Members After Conviction But Before Final Appeal, Jack Maskell 88-197 A
* Independent Investigations of Allegations of Wrongdoing by Members of Congress, Jack Maskell 88-488 A
* Ineligibility of a Member of Congress for a Civil Office in the Federal Government Which Was Created, or for Which the Salary was Increased, Jack Maskell 87-579 A
* Members of Congress Who Have Served in Both the House and the Senate, 1789-1989, Mildred Amer 89-45 GOV
* Members of the U.S. Congress Who Have Died of Other Than Natural Causes While Still in Office: A Selected List, Mildred Amer 91-480 GOV
* Members of the U.S. Congress Who Have Served Thirty Years or More, Mildred Amer 91-194 GOV
* Membership of the 101st Congress: A Profile, Mildred Amer 90-630 GOV
* Membership of the 102nd Congress: A Profile, Mildred Amer 91-86 GOV
* Organizations that Rate Members of Congress on Their Voting Records, Kathy Doddridge 91-65 C
* Partisan Divisions in Congress, 1927-1987, Kevin Coleman 87-214 GOV
* Party Leaders in Congress, 1789-1991: Vital Statistics, Carol Hardy Vincent, etc. 91-414 GOV
* Pay Raise Proposals for Members of Congress, Top Officials and Federal Judges: Issues and Outlook, James P. McGrath 89-621 GOV
* Prohibition on Members of Congress Contracting with the Federal Government, Jack Maskell 91-815 A
* Qualifications and Eligibility of Members of Congress, Thomas Durbin 84-188 A
* Restrictions on the Outside Earned Income and Honoraria of Members of Congress 1975-1991, Mildred Amer 91-558 GOV
* Retirement for Members of Congress, Carolyn L. Merck 91-96 EPW
* The Role of a Member of Congress, Ilona B. Nickels 90-628 GOV
* Salaries and Allowances: Congress, Archived Issue Brief, Paul Dwyer IB80206
* Salaries for Members of Congress: Issue Brief, Paul Dwyer IB86017
* Salaries of Members of Congress: Congressional Votes, 1967-1990, Paul Dwyer 90-150 GOV
* Security Clearances for Members of Congress and the Judiciary, Frederick M. Kaiser 87-704 GOV
* Selected Courtesies and Privileges Extended to Former Members of the House of Representatives, Mildred L. Amer 90-342 GOV
* Selected Courtesies and Privileges Extended to Former Senators, Mildred L. Amer 90-341 GOV
* Selected Listing of Education-Related Memorials to Former or Current Members of Congress, Christine Tebben, etc. 88-626 EPW
* The Senate Chaplaincy, Charles H. Whittier 86-916 GOV
* Shadow Representatives in Congress: History and Current Developments, Garrine P. Laney 91-64 GOV
* Some Federal Tax Implications of Replacing the Current Limitation on a Senator's Acceptance of Honoraria With an Outright Prohibition Against Acceptance of any Honoraria, Robert B. Burdette 88-599 A
* Speaker of the House (Former); Office Allowances, Staff Assistance, and Franking Privilege, Paul Dwyer 88-304 GOV
* The Speaker of the House: His Powers and Duties, Ilona B. Nickels 87-64 GOV
* Special Tax Rules for Members of Congress, Robert B. Burdette 89-615 A
* Statistical Summary of Congressional Roll Call and, Other Recorded Votes: First Through Ninety-Ninth Congresses (1789-1986), Sula Richardson, etc. 87-126 GOV
* Summary and Analysis of Chastain v. Sundquist, Recent Court of Appeals Decision Concerning Application of the Official Immunity Doctrine to Members of, Jay R. Shampansky 88-120 A
* Summary of Changes in the Ethics Rules for the House of Representatives, Jack Maskell 91-734 A
* Summary of the Effect of New Ethics Laws on the Senate, Jack Maskell 91-723 A
* Survivor Benefits for Families of Members of Congress, Carolyn L. Merck 91-507 EPW
* Voting Records of Members of Congress: A Self-Help Guide to Their Compilation, Peggy Garvin 91-67 C
* Women in the United States Congress, Mildred L. Amer 91-333 GOV

Congress -- Military Policy

* Congress and the Strategic Defense Initiative: A Detailed Overview of Legislative Action, 1984-1987, Robert J. Crawford, etc. 87-749 F
* Congressional Procedure for Considering Legislation Opposing Arms Sales, Richard Grimmett 86-63 F
* Dellums v. Bush: President Bush's Authority to Initiate Offensive Operations in the Persian Gulf Challenged in the Courts by House Members and Law Professors, Raymond J. Celada 90-585 A
* Military Base Closures: A Side by Side Comparison of Current Legislation, Andrew C. Mayer 88-472 F
* Military Base Closures: Congress and the Executive Branch, Andrew Mayer 85-212 F
* Military Base Closures: Issue Brief, Andrew Mayer IB89026
* Sectional Analysis of the "War Powers Resolution" (WPR) as It Would Be Amended by the "War Powers Resolution Amendments of 1988" (S.J. Res. 323, 100th, Raymond J. Celada 88-441 A
* U.S. Defense Planning: A Critique, John Collins, etc. 82-167 S
* The War Powers Resolution: Fifteen Years of Experience, Ellen C. Collier 88-529 F
* War Powers Resolution: Info Pack, IB131W
* War Powers Resolution: Presidential Compliances: Issue Brief, Ellen Collier IB81050
* War Powers Resolution: The Controversial Act's Search for a Successful Litigation Posture, Raymond J. Celada 88-64 A
* The War Powers Resolution (WPR): Some Implications, of S.J. Res. 323 "War Powers Resolution Amendments of 1988" Raymond J. Celada 88-464 A
* War Powers Resolution: Info Pack, IP131W
* War Powers Resolution: Presidential Compliance: Issue Brief, Ellen Collier IB81050
* War Powers: Selected References, Sherry B. Shapiro 89-305 L

Congress -- Offices

* Campaign Activities by Congressional Employees, Jack Maskell 82-165 A
* Conducting Legislative Research in a Congressional Office, Clay H. Wellborn 89-331 GOV

Congress / Constitution

* Congressional Employees: Minimum Wages and Overtime Pay, the Fair Labor Standards Act, William G. Whittaker 89-678 E
* Congressional Liaison Offices of Selected Federal Agencies, Office of Special Programs 91-348 PGM
* Congressional Office Operations: Info Pack, IP151C
* The Congressional Research Service, Evelyn Howard 91-415 PGM
* Constitutionality of Franking Statute Upheld by U. S. District Court in Common Cause v. Bolger, Elizabeth Yadlosky 82-155 S
* Grants Work in a Congressional Office, Rhoda Newman 89-658 C
* Internships and Fellowships: Info Pack, IP0631
* Legislative History: A Guide for Constituents, Mark Gurevitz 89-596 A
* Legislative Research: A Guide to Conducting Legislative Research in a Congressional Office; Info Pack, IP321L
* The Legislator as User of Information Technology, Robert Lee Chartrand, etc. 87-983 S
* Pages of the United States Congress, Mildred L. Amer 90-470 GOV
* Post Employment Restricting on Employees and Members of the House of Representatives, Jack Maskell 87-573 A
* Sexual Harassment Policy: Rules Applicable to Congressional Offices, Leslie W. Gladstone 91-744 GOV
* A Summary of Selected Regulations of the Fair Labor Standards Act, Charles V. Ciccone 90-499 E
* U.S. Congress Official Mail Costs: FY 1972 to FY 1991, John Pontius 90-345 GOV

Congress--Oversight

* see also Congress--Executive Relations
* Conducting Oversight: Legal, Procedural, and Practical Aspects; Audio Brief, Walter Oleszek AB50156
* Conducting Oversight: Legal, Procedural and Practical Aspects; Videoprogram, Steven Ross, etc. LTR91-918
* Congress and Intelligence Policy: Selected References, Sherry Shapiro 88-36 L
* Congressional Oversight, Frederick M. Kaiser 90-632 GOV
* Effective Oversight: Planning for the Future; Audio Brief, Walter Oleszek AB50155
* Effective Oversight: Planning for the Future; Videoprogram, Richard Bolling, etc. LTR91-917
* Executive Perspectives on Oversight: Audio Brief, AB50116
* Executive Perspectives on Oversight; Videoprogram, Eileen Siddman, etc. LTR91-952
* Former Members View Oversight: Audio Brief, AB50111
* Former Members View Oversight; Videoprogram, Gilbert Gude, etc. LTR91-954
* Inspectors General: Resources for Oversight; Videoprogram, Thomas Novotny, etc. LTR91-956
* A Member's Reflections on Oversight: Audio Brief, AB50112
* A Member's Reflections on Oversight; Videoprogram, John Moss LTR91-913
* Outside Perspectives on Oversight: Audio Brief, Walter Oleszek AB50157
* Outside Perspectives on Oversight; Turning the Tables on Congress; Videoprogram, Tom Novotny, LTR91-877
* Oversight and Congressional Policymaking; Videoprogram, John Dingell LTR91-912
* Oversight Authority and Major Procedures: Audio Brief, AB50114
* Oversight Authority and Major Procedures; Videoprogram, Mark Nadel, etc. LTR91-951
* Oversight in Action: A Variety of Experiences; Videoprogram, Morton Rosenberg, etc. LTR91-953
* Oversight in Action: Audio Brief, AB50110
* Oversight Powers and Constraints, Audio Brief, AB50115
* Powers and Constraints of Oversight; Videoprogram, Antonin Scalia, etc. LTR91-911
* The Role of Media in Oversight; Videoprogram, Henry Hubbard, etc. LTR91-914
* The Role of the Media in Oversight: Audio Brief, AB50113

Congress and Foreign Policy

* see Congress--Foreign Relations

Congressional Budget and Impoundment Control Act

* see also Congress-Budget Process, Public Finance--Budget Process
* Changes in the Congressional Budget Process Made by the 1985 Balanced Budget Act (P.L. 99-177), Robert Keith 86-713 GOV
* Legal Analysis of Proposal to Repeal Deferral Authority under the Impoundment Control Act, Richard Ehlke 86-1024 A

* Manual on the Federal budget Process, Allen Schick, etc. 87-286 GOV
* Rescissions by the President Since 1974: Background and Proposals for Change, Virginia A. McMurty 89-271 GOV
* Waivers of the Congressional Budget Act Granted or Rejected in the Senate During 1986, Edward Davis, etc. 87-78 GOV

Congressional Budget Process

* see Congress-Budget Process, Public Finance--Budget Process

Congressional Caucuses

* see Congress-Budget Process, Congress--Members

Congressional Districts

* see Congress-Apportionment and Elections

Congressional Elections

* see Congress-Apportionment and Elections

Congressional Ethics

* see Congress--Members, Political Ethics

Congressional Oversight

* see Congress-Oversight

Congressional Pay

* see Congress--Members

Congressional-Presidential Relations

* see Congress-Executive Relations, Congress-Foreign Relations, Congress-Military Policy, Presidents (U.S.)-Foreign Relations, War Powers Resolution

Congressional Record

* The Congressional Record, Mildred Amer 86-152 GOV

Congressional Research Service

* The Congressional Research Service, Evelyn Howard 91-415 PGM
* Toward an Informed Legislator: The Development of the Congressional Research Service; Videoprogram, Charles Mathias, Jr., etc. LTR91-950

Congressional Veto

* see Congress-Executive Relations

Conrail

* see Transportation--Railroads

Conservation of Wildlife

* see Wildlife--Conservation

Constitution (U.S.)

* American National Government: An Overview, Frederick M. Kaiser 91-302 GOV
* Civil Rights Legislation: Response to Grove City College v. Bell; Archived Issue Brief, Bob Lyke IB87123
* Congress and a Balanced Budget Amendment to the U. S. Constitution, James Saturno 89-4 GOV
* Congressional Control of Agency Decision and Decisionmakers: The Unitary Executive Theory and Separation of Powers, Morton Rosenberg 897-383 A
* Constitution of the United States: Its History, Development and Amending Process; Info Pack, IP339C
* The Constitutional Amendment to Regulate Congressional Salary Increases: A Slumbering Proposal's New, Popularity, David C. Huckabee 86-889 GOV
* Constitutional Amendments to Balance the Budget and Limit Federal Spending in the 100th Congress: A Table of Features, Thomas J. Nicola 87-445 A
* Constitutional Conventions: Political and Legal Questions: Issue Brief, David Huckabee, etc. IB80062
* The Constitutionality of Excessive Corporal Punishment in the Public Schools, David M. Ackerman, etc. 88-413 A
* Impeachment: An Overview of Constitutional Provisions, Procedure and Practice, Elizabeth B. Bazan 88-637 A
* Ineligibility of a Member of Congress for a Civil Office in the Federal Government Which Was Created, or for Which the Salary Was Increased

Current Events and Homework

Jack Maskell 87-579 A
* A Legal Analysis of the Fourteenth Amendment's Equal Protection Clause and the Proposed Equal Rights Amendment, Karen Lewis 85-662 A
* Morrison V. Olson: Constitutionality of the Independent Counsel Law, Jack H. Maskell 88-469 A
* Presidential Signing Statements--Use in Statutory Construction, George A. Costello 87-894 A
* Proposed Amendments to the Constitution of the United States of America Introduced in Congress from the 91st Congress, 1st Session, Through the 98th Congress, 2nd Session, Richard Davis 85-36 GOV
* Selected Bicentennial Celebration Commemorating the 200th Anniversaries of the U.S. Constitution and of the U.S. Congress, Roger H. Davidson, etc. 86-171 S.
* The Separation of Powers Doctrine: An Overview of Its Rationale and Application, Jay Shampansky, 86-1027 A

Constitutional Conventions

* see Constitution (U.S.)

Consumer Credit

* see Credit

Consumer Price Index

* see Economic Conditions--Inflation

Consumer Protection

* see Consumers

Consumers

* Accepting or Rejecting an Executory Contract Governing Intellectual Property in Bankruptcy: Legal Analysis of H.R. 4657, Robin Jeweler, etc. 88-557 A
* All-Terrain Vehicles: The December 1987 Consent Agreement and Related Developments, Migdon Segal 88-275 SPR
* Cigarettes and Other Tobacco Products: Should Congress Ban All Advertising and Promotion? Issue Brief, Bruce Mulock IB86105
* The Cost of Our Food, Geoffrey S. Becker 88-761 ENR
* Digital Audio Recorder Act of 1987--Analysis of H. R. 1384 and S. 506 With Policy Alternatives, David Hack 87-698 SPR
* Environmental Labeling in Canada, Germany, and Japan, Law Library of Congress LL90-63
* Fast Food Restaurant Labeling, Donna V. Porter 87-736 SPR
* H.R. 3030, 102nd Congress, and Fifty-State Surveys on Selected Products Liability Issues, Henry Cohen, etc. 91-735 A
* Income and Expenditures of Selected Consumer Groups, 1973-1985, Marc E. Smyrl 88-318 S
* L-Tryptophan--Health Problems, Production and Regulatory Status, Proceedings of a CRS Seminar, Donna V. Porter 91-758 SPR
* Oil Overcharge Restitution: Background and Data, Bernard Gelb 88-287 E
* Products Liability: A Legal Overview: Archived Issue Brief, Henry Cohen IB77021
* Products Liability Laws in Selected EEC Countries and Japan, Law Library of Congress LL90-38
* Products Liability Reform: Analysis of H.R. 1115, 100th Congress, as Reported by Subcommittees, Henry Cohen 88-53 A
* Products Liability: Some Legal Issues, Henry Cohen 88-677 A
* The Proposed Airline Passenger Protection Act of 1987: Analysis of the Bankruptcy Transportation Plans With Regard to the Taking Issue, Douglas Reid Weimer 87-984 A
* A Survey of Bottled Water Regulations in Selected Countries, Law Library of Congress LL90-61
* The Tort Reform Debate: Pros, Cons, Federal Proposals, State Statutes, Henry Cohen 86-579 A
* Tort Reform: State Statutory Caps on Damages, Henry Cohen, etc. 87-835 A

Consumption Taxes

* see Taxation--Consumption Taxes

Contadora Group

* see Central America, Latin America

Contested Congressional Elections

* see Congress--Apportionment and Elections, Politics and Elections-Election law

Continental Shelf

* see Coastal Areas

Contra Aid and the Reagan Doctrine

* see Contras

Contras

* see also Foreign Policy and Assistance Programs
* Arms Shipments to Iran: Archived Issue Brief, Richard M. Preece IB87022
* Central American Peace Process: Selected References, Robert Kirk 88-389 L
* Chart of Unclassified Legislative Restrictions Regarding Support for Military or Paramilitary Operations in Nicaragua, 1982-1986, Larry Eig, 87-222 A
* Compilation of Selected Laws Relating to the National Security Council Arms, Transfers, Intelligence, Activities, Aid to the Contras and Appropriation, American Law Division 86-1028 A
* Contra Aid, FY82-FY88: Summary and Chronology of Major Congressional Action on Key Legislation Concerning U.S. Aid to the Anti-Sandinista Guerrillas, Nina M. Serafino 88-563 F
* Iran Arms and Contra Funds: Selected Chronology of Events, 1979-1987, Richard M. Preece, etc. 86-190 F
* Iran Arms Sales and Contra Funds: Summaries of Key Legislative Provisions, Clyde R. Mark, etc. 87-13 F
* Kissinger Commission Implementation: Action by the Congress Through 1986 on the Recommendations of the National Bipartisan Commission on Central America, K. Larry Storrs J7-291 F
* Nicaragua: Bibliography-in-Brief, 1986-1987, Valentin Leskovsek 87-382 L
* The Nicaraguan Resistance ("Contras"): Background and Major Concerns of Congress, Veronica R. Clifford 87-943 F
* Nicaragua's "Civic" Opposition: Players, Problems and Prospects, Nina Serafino 87-735 F
* U.S. Assistance to Nicaraguan Guerrillas; Issues for the Congress; Archived Issue Brief, Nina Serafino IB84139

Conventional Force Reduction Talks

* see Arms Control--Negotiations and Treaties, Arms Control--Conventional, CFE Treaty

Conventional Weapons

* see Arms Control--Conventional, Weapons Systems--Non-Nuclear Weapons, Weapons Systems-Weapons Facts

Copyright

* see Patents and Inventions

Corporate Takeovers

* see Corporations-Mergers

Corporation for Public Broadcasting

* see Telecommunication

Corporation Taxes

* see Taxation-Corporation Taxes

Corporations

* see also Mergers, Securities Industry, International Corporations, Taxation--Corporation Taxes, Business, Industry, and Consumer Affairs
* The American Telephone and Telegraph Company Divestiture: Background, Provisions, and Restructuring, Angela A. Gilroy 84-58 E
* Assessing Structural Tax Revision With Macroeconomic Models: The Treasury Tax Proposals and the Allocation of Investment, Jane G. Gravelle 85-645 E
* Capital Sources for U.S.Corporations With Particular Reference to Public Policy Issues, Julius W. Allen 86-165 E
* The Corporate Bond Rating Process: An Assessment of Its Accuracy and Usefulness, Gary W. Shorter 87-96 E
* Corporate Debt: A Profile of Major Indicators, Carolyn Brancato, etc. 86-94 E
* Corporate Debt Financing: An Annotated Bibliography, 1986-1990, Kevin F. Winch, etc. 90-225 E
* Corporate Finance Trends, Kevin F. Winch 89-597 E
* Corporate Governance in America: The Board and Business Leadership; Annotations of Reports in the Series, Kevin F. Winch 83-644 E
* Corporate Governance In America: The Board and Business Leadership:

Constitutional Conventions / Corporations

Corporate Boards: Analysis of Characteristics and Trends, Edward Knight 82-198 E

* Corporate Governance in America: The Board and Business Leadership; Corporate Boards: Interaction and Functional Relationship with Constituent Groups, Kevin Winch 82-197 E
* Domestic Profits of U.S. Corporations, 1968-1988, Marc E. Smyrl, etc. 90-278 S
* An Economic Analysis of the Effects of the Finance Committee Staff Proposal to Revise Subchapter C of Internal Revenue Code on Incentives for Corporations, Donald W. Kiefer 85-1016 E
* Foreign Direct Investment in the U.S.: Identifying the Ultimate Beneficial Owner, James K. Jackson 90-610 E
* Insurance for Directors and Officers: The 1987 Market, Sylvia Morrison 87-545 E
* Japanese Management Practices and Their Implications for U.S. Policy, Dick Nanto 82-114 E
* The Largest Corporations in the United States: Information and Addresses from the Forbes 500, Felicia G. Kolp 91-532 C
* Letter-of-Credit Enhancement of Commercial Paper Issues: A Case Study in the Competitiveness of U.S. Banks, Patricia A. Wertman 91-147 E
* Patterns in the Financing of U.S. Industry: Gross Proceeds of New Security Offerings, Kevin F. Winch 88-616 E
* Public Utilities Holding Company Act of 1935: Is This the Time for Reform: Issue Brief, Amy Abel IB89052

Corporations -- Mergers

* Airline Mergers and Labor Protective Provisions: Issue Brief, Linda LeGrande IB87179
* Corporate Mergers: A Look at the Record, Kevin F. Winch, etc. 87-612 E
* Corporate Mergers: A Snapshot View, Kevin F. Winch, etc. 87-612 E
* Corporate Mergers: An Overview of Major Issues, Carolyn Kay Brancato 87-250 E
* Corporate Mergers and Acquisitions: Selected References, 1986-1989, Robert Kirk 89-114 L
* Corporate Mergers: Issue Brief, Gary Shorter IB87171
* Corporate Ownership of Banks and Savings Institutions, and Interstate Banking: Selected Listings, F. Jean Wells 84-105 E
* Corporate Takeovers: A Survey of Recent Developments and Issues, Julius W. Allen 87-726 E
* Corporate Takeovers: Alternatives for Merger Finance, Kevin F. Winch, etc. 87-254 E
* An Economic Analysis of the Effects of the Finance Committee Staff Proposal to Revise Subchapter C of the Internal Revenue Code on Incentives for Corporate Reorganization, Donald W. Kiefer 85-1016 E
* Employee Protection Legislation: A Comparison of H.R. 1101, H.R. 2828 and H.R. 3332, Mark Jickling 88-426 E
* European Community's New Merger Laws: Overview and Implications for U.S. Firms, Gary W. Shorter 91-240 E
* Foreign Mergers and Acquisitions: Non-U.S. Companies Acquiring U.S. Companies, Kevin F. Winch, etc. 87-711 E
* Greenmail and the Market for Corporate Control: Impact on Shareholders, Issues of Fairness and Recent Developments, Carolyn Brancato 85-181 E
* Greenmail: Corporate Management vs. Corporate Raiders vs. Corporate Shareholders; Archived Issue Brief, Kevin Winch IB87064
* Hostile Corporate Takeovers: Investment Adviser Fees, Kevin Winch 87-217 E
* Impact of Mergers and Related Phenomena on Shareholders, Julius W. Allen 84-199 E
* Insider Trading and Greenmail Payments, Michael V. Seitzinger 87-567
* Legal Analysis of Shareholder Voting Rights During a Corporate Restructuring, Michael V. Seitzinger 89-123 A
* Leveraged Buyouts and the Pot of Gold: Trends, Public Policy, and Case Studies, Carolyn Kay Brancato, etc. 88-156 E
* Leveraged Buyouts; Info Pack, IP414L
* Leveraged Buyouts: Archived Issue Brief, Gary W. Shorter, etc. IB89036
* Leveraged Buyouts: Recent Trends, Gary Shorter 89-101 E
* Leveraged Buyouts: Selected References, 1987-1989, Robert Howe 89-156 L
* Merger Activity and Leveraged Buyouts: Sound Corporate Restructuring or Wall Street Alchemy?, Carolyn Kay Brancato, etc. 84-643 E
* Merger Advisory Fees: Structure and Cost, Gary W. Shorter 91-143 E
* Merger and Acquisition Activity: The Level of Hostile Mergers, Carolyn Kay Brancato, etc. 87-507 E
* Merger Credit: Should It Be Regulated? A Preliminary Review, Kevin F. Winch 84-69 E
* Merger Guidelines--A Case Study of the LTV and Republic Steel Corporations, Gwenell L. Bass 84-133 E
* Merger Legislation in the 100th Congress, Mark Jickling 88-453 E
* Merger Tactics and Public Policy, Carolyn Brancato 82-13 E
* Mergers and Acquisitions: A Glossary of Terms, Mark Jickling, etc. 89-128 E
* Mergers and Acquisitions: The Impact on Labor, Gail McCallion 87-705 E
* Mergers and Their Impact on Today's Economy: A Survey, Julius Allen 82-118 E
* New Directions in Antitrust Law? Current Proposals for Reform With Emphasis on Proposals Concerning Mergers and Monetary Damage Awards, Janice E. Rubin 86-1014 A
* The Role of Secured Bank Credit in Corporate Acquisitions, Kevin Winch 81-186 E
* Securities Law: Background and Recent Developments in Tender Offers and in Insider Trading, Michael V. Seitzinger 88-239 A
* Takeover Bids and Highly Confident Letters, Carolyn Kay Brancato 87-724 A
* Tax Aspects of Leveraged Buyouts, Jane G. Gravelle 89-142 S
* Tender Offer Laws and Regulations, Michael V. Seitzinger 87-15 A
* Tender Offer Reform Legislation: A Comparison of S. 1323 and H.R. 2172, Gary Shorter 87-963 E
* The United States Bankruptcy Code: A Sectional Analysis of Provisions Governing Liquidation and Reorganization, Robin Jeweler 91-727 A

Corporations -- Securities Industry

* Arbitration under Section 10(B) of the Securities Exchange Act of 1934, Michael V. Seitzinger 87-881 A
* Bodies Responsible for the Regulation of Trading in Securities and Trading in Commodity Futures in Various Foreign Countries, Law Library of Congress LL90-19
* Capital Market Changes in the United Kingdom, Japan, West Germany, and Singapore: A Brief Survey, Julius W. Allen 88-49 E
* CFTC and SEC: A Comparison of Regulatory Authorities, Mark Jickling 89-199 E
* CFTC Reauthorization; Issue Brief, Mark Jickling, etc. IB89051
* CFTC Reauthorization and the Futures Trading "Sting": Issue Brief, Mark Jickling, etc. IB89051
* Constitutional Considerations Implicated by a Hypothetical Proposal to Tax the Investment Income of a Tax-Exempt Entity Affiliated With a State or Local, Robert B. Burdette 88-551 A
* The Corporate Bond Rating Process: An Assessment of Its Accuracy and Usefulness, Gary W. Shorter 87-96 E
* Corporate Debt: A Perspective on Leverage, Kevin Winch, etc. 91-554 E
* Corporate Securities; Issue Brief, Kevin F. Winch IB91037
* Corporate Securities: Laws Enacted in the 101st Congress, Kevin F. Winch 91-179 E
* Corporate Securities: Marketplace Introduction, Kevin F. Winch 91-353 E
* Discount Brokerage of Securities: A Status Report, Kevin Winch 84-32 E
* The Dow Jones Industrial Average, Gary Shorter 86-775 E
* Federal Home Loan Mortgage Corporation Preferred Stock Ownership: Lift the Restrictions?: Archived Issue Brief, Barbara L. Miles IB88076
* Financial Markets: A New Framework of Issues, Walter Eubanks 88-485 E
* Futures Markets and the Price of Oil, Mark Jickling 91-324 E
* The Glass-Steagall Act: Bibliography-in-Brief, 1981-1988, Felix Chin 88-98 L
* Globalization of Securities Markets, Kevin F. Winch, etc. 89-363 E
* Globalization of Securities Markets: A Selected Annotated Bibliography, Edward Knight, etc. 89-359 E
* Government Securities Market: Disturbances and Regulation, William Jackson 87-165 E
* Growing Internationalization of Stock Markets: Implications for Financial Regulation: Archived Issue Brief, Edward Knight IB88037
* High Yield Bond Market, Kevin F. Winch 90-349 E
* Insider Trading-Carpenter v. United States, Michael V. Seitzinger 87-946 A
* Institutional Investors and Their Role in Equity Financing and Corporate Governance, Julius W. Allen 85-163 E
* The Internationalization of Securities Trading Markets, Julius Allen 86-14 E
* Issues in the Regulation of Futures and Options Trading, Julius Allen 83-108 E
* Junk Bonds: 1988 Status Report, Kevin F. Winch 89-22 E
* Legal Analysis of the Government Securities Act of 1986 and Its Application to Broker/Dealers Convinced of Insider Trading Violations, Michael V. Seitzinger 87-280 A
* Legal Analysis of What Constitutes Reliance under SEC Rule 10B-5, Michael V. Seitzinger 87-279 A
* Legal Analysis of Whether a Corporation Must Disclose in Public Filings With the Securities and Exchange Commission the Facts of Its Being Investigated, Michael V. Seitzinger 88-334 A
* Legal Issues of Insider Trading in Securities: Issue Brief, Michael V. Seitzinger IB87052

Current Events and Homework

* Limited Partnership Rollups: Congressional, Regulatory, and Investor Concerns; Issue Brief, Gary W. Shorter IB91083
* Margin Credit for Securities: Some Recent Proposals, Kevin Winch 85-2070 E
* Margin Use in Securities and Futures Markets: A Glossary of Terms, Kevin Winch 88-47 E
* Margin Use in Securities and Futures Market: An Annotated Bibliography, Kevin Winch, etc. 88-50 E
* Merchant Banking: Opportunities or Problems for U. S. Banks?, Walter Eubanks, etc. 87-351 E
* Money Market Mutual Funds, William Jackson 83-232 E
* A National Market System for Stock Trading: A Review of Developments and Issues, Julius Allen 85-28 E
* One Share/One Vote and the Issue of Dual Class Common Stock; Shareholder Rights and Regulatory Concerns; Archived Issue Brief, Gary W. Shorter IB87099
* Penny Stocks; Legal Issues, Michael Seitzinger 88-10 A
* Program Trading and Stock Market Reform, Mark Jickling 90-580 E
* Program Trading: Bibliography-in-Brief, 1986-1988, With Introductory Articles, Felix Chin 88-173 L
* Program Trading: Is Computerized Stock Market Trading a Blessing or a Curse: Archived Issue Brief, Kevin F. Winch IB87100
* Regulating International and European Community Securities Trading, Julius W. Allen 90-340 E
* The Role of High Yield Bonds (Junk Bonds) In Capital Markets and Corporate Takeovers: Public Policy Implications, Kevin Winch, etc. 85-694 E
* Salomon Brothers' Violations: Explanation, Consequences, and Options for Reform; Issue Brief, James M. Bickley, etc. IB91134
* Securities and Commodities Fraud, Michael V. Seitzinger 87-84 A
* Securities and Exchange Commission Rule 144A: Resales of Private Placements to Institutional Investors, Michael V. Seitzinger 91-202 A
* Securities Enforcement Remedies and Penny Stock Reform Act of 1990, Michael V. Seitzinger 90-557 A
* Securities Fraud and Civil RICO, Michael Seitzinger 89-462 A
* Securities Investor Protection Corporation (SIPC): Customer Indemnification When a Securities Firm Fails, Kevin Winch 82-125 E
* Securities Law: Analysis of Cases Concerning Insider Trading under Section 10(B) of the Securities Exchange Act of 1934, Michael Seitzinger 87-480 A
* Securities Law: Environmental Disclosures, Michael V. Seitzinger 91-422 A
* Securities Law: Proxy Regulation, Michael V. Seitzinger 91-398 A
* Securities Registration and Disclosure Laws in Canada, Germany, Japan, the United Kingdom, and the United States, Stephen F. Clarke, etc. 91-613 A
* The Securities Transactions Tax: An Overview of the Issues, Donald W. Kiefer 90-350 S
* Should Short-Term Trading in the Stock Market Be Discouraged?, Donald W. Kiefer 87-51 S
* SIPC: Capital Adequacy and Recent Reforms, Gary W. Shorter 91-650 E
* Stock Exchange Specialists: A Review of Their Role in Equities Trading, Julius W. Allen 89-251 E
* The Stock Market "Crash" of 1987: Implications for Public Policy, Edward Knight, etc. 88-410 E
* The Stock Market "Crash" of 1987: Implications for Public Policy; Archived Issue Brief, Edward Knight, etc. IB88020
* The Stock Market Crash of 1987: Selected References, 1987-1988, Felix Chin 88-609 L
* The Stock Market "Crash" of 1987: The Early Response of Regulators, Kevin Winch 87-989 E
* The Stock Market Crash of 1987: The Legislative Response, Mark Jickling 88-543 E
* The Stock Market in Japan: An Overview and Analysis, Arturo Wiener, etc. 89-306 E
* Stock Market "Short-Termism:" Implications for Corporate Planning Horizons, Donald W. Kiefer 91-448 E
* Stock Price Determination: The Efficient Markets Hypothesis and Selected Criticism, Kevin Winch 85-1056 E
* A Stock Transfer Tax: Preliminary Economic Analysis, Donald W. Kiefer 87-278 S
* Taxation of Securities Transactions to Discourage Short-Term Investment: A Selected Bibliography, Louis Alan Talley 90-415 E
* Will the Stock Market "Crash" End the Current Economic Expansion? Economic Prospects for the Year Ahead, Gail E. Makinen 88-51 E

Costa Rica

* Central America: U.S. Relations With Costa Rica, Guatemala, and Honduras: Info Pack, IP352C
* Central American Peace Process: Selected References, Robert Kirk 88-389 L
* Costa Rica: Country Background Report, Nina M. Serafino 88-577F

Covert Actions

* see Intelligence Activities

Crack Babies

* see Drug Abuse

Credit

* see also Bankruptcy, Money and Banking, Public Finance--Credit Programs
* The ABCs of Public Venture Capital Investment, Jan. E. Christopher 88-757 E
* Bank and Thrift Financial Problems, the Credit Crunch, and Lending to the Building Industry, Barbara L. Miles 91-417 E
* Business Failure: A Review of the Concept and Its Significance in the American Economy, Julius Allen, etc. 81-195 E
* Capital, Credit, and Crowding Out: Cycles and Trends in Flows of Funds Over Three Decades, William Jackson 82-142 E
* The Community Reinvestment Act After FIRREA, M. Maureen Murphy 91-754 A
* The Community Reinvestment Act: Its Role in Local Economic Development, J.F. Hornbeck 88-732 E
* Community Reinvestment Act: Legal Analysis, M. Maureen Murphy 89-135 A
* Credit Cards: Selected References, Pauline H. Smale, etc. 86-777 E
* Credit Reform in the Budget Agreement of November 1990, James M. Bickley 91-269 E
* Credit Reform Proposal of the Reagan Administration: Analysis and Policy Issues, James M. Bickley 87-456 E
* Crowding Out? Federal, State and Local Government Borrowing and the Debt Economy, William Jackson 87-274 E
* Debt Cards: Background and Public Policy Issues, Pauline Smale 84-120 E
* Debt Collection by the United States Government: Existing Legal Options, Henry Cohen 88-412 A
* Fair Credit Reporting Act: Comparison of 102nd Congress Bills and Current Law, Henry Cohen 91-364 A
* Fair Credit Reporting Act: Issues of Consumer Protection; Issue Brief, Bruce K. Mulock IB90153
* Family Farmer Reorganizations: Summary and Legal Analysis of Chapter 12 of the United States Bankruptcy Code, Robin Jeweler 88-708 A
* Farmer Mac and the Agricultural Secondary Market, Ralph Chite 89-246 ENR
* FmHA Losses and the Federal Budget, Ralph Chite 89-34 ENR
* Home Equity Loans under the New Tax Reform Act: Possible Benefits and Potential Dangers, Richard Bourdon 87-692 E
* Interest Rates on Consumer and Commercial Loans: Why the Difference?, Helen J. Scott 85-818 E
* Letter-of-Credit Enhancement of Commercial Paper Issues: A Case Study in the Competitiveness of U.S. Banks, Patricia A. Wertman 91-147 E
* Merger Credit: Should It be Regulated?, A Preliminary Review, Kevin F. Winch 84-569 E
* A National Interest Rate Ceiling for the U.S. Economy?, John Henderson, etc. 82-57 E
* Nondischargeability of DWI Judgements in Bankruptcy: Survey of Case Law, Robin Jeweler 90-21 A
* Proposed Federal Taxation of Credit Unions: A Pro-Con Analysis, James M. Bickley 86-84 E
* Recent Developments in Bankruptcy Law, Robin Jeweler 91-152 A
* Reserve Requirements, Capital Standards, and Credit Expansion, G. Thomas Woodward 91-446 E
* Should Credit Unions Be Taxed: Issue Brief, James M. Bickley IB89066
* State and Local Equity, Capital Funds: Selected Case Studies, Jan E. Christopher 88-758 E
* Statutory Authorities Related to Official Foreign Debt, Jeanne J. Grimmett 91-381 A
* The Unbanked Sector: Some Economic Issues, Ngina Chiteji 91-610 E
* The United States Bankruptcy Code: A Sectional Analysis of Provisions Governing Liquidation and Reorganization, Robin Jeweler 91-727 A

Credit -- Bankruptcy

* Accepting or Rejecting an Executory Contract Governing Intellectual Property in Bankruptcy: Legal Analysis of H.R. 4657, Robin Jeweler, etc. 88-557 A
* Bankruptcy Law: Comparison of Two Bills in the 100th Congress, H.R. 2501 and H.R. 2688 to Amend 11 U .S.C. (Section) 547 Dealing with Voidable Preferen, Robin Jeweler 87-822 A

* Business Failure: A Review of the Concept and Its Significance in the American Economy, Julius Allen, etc. 81-195 E
* The United States Bankruptcy Code: A Sectional Analysis of Provisions Governing Liquidation and Reorganization, Robin Jeweler 89-122 A
* The United States Bankruptcy Code: Legal Implications of an Investor-Owned Utility Reorganization under Chapter 11, Robin Jeweler 88-140 A

Credit Unions

* see Money and Banking--Financial Institutions

Crimes and Offenses

* see also Capital Punishment, Gun Control, Terrorism
* Bank of Credit and Commerce International (BCCI): Some Legal Implications, M. Maureen Murphy 91-652 A
* BCCI: Issues for Congress, Issue Brief, Raphael F. Perl IB91125
* Capital Punishment: Archived Issue Brief, Elizabeth Bazan IB73013
* Capital Punishment: Info Pack, IP015C
* Child Abuse and Neglect in the United States: Legislative Issues; Selected References, 1985-1988, Edith Sutterlin 89-13 L
* Civil RICO and Protest Activity, Lou Fields 89-320 A
* Computer Security Issues: The Computer Security Act of 1987; Archived Issue Brief, Glenn J. McLoughlin IB87164
* Crime and Crime Control: National Public Opinion Polls, Rinn-Sup Shinn 90-583 GOV
* Crime and Criminal Justice: An Alphabetical Microthesaurus of Terms Selected from the Legislative Indexing Vocabulary, Shirley Loo 88-437 L
* Crime Control: Criminal Theory; Selected References, 1989-1991, Jean Bowers 91-394 L
* Crime Control: Federal Initiatives; Archived Issue Brief, William Woldman, etc. IB86042
* Crime Control: Federal Initiatives; Info Pack IP310C
* Crime, Drug, and Gun Control: Comparison of Major Bills under Consideration by the House Judiciary Committee, 102nd Congress, Keith Bea, etc. 91-687 GOV
* Crime, Drug, and Gun Control: Comparison of Major Omnibus Bills of the 102nd Congress, American Law Division, Harry Hogan 91-737 GOV
* Crime, Drug, and Gun Control: Summary of S. 1241 (102nd Congress) as Passed by the Senate, Government Division 91-581 GOV
* Criminal Tax Law: A Summary of Cheek v. United States, Thomas B. Ripy 91-187 A
* Elder Abuse: Bibliography-in-Brief, 1980-1988, Edith Sutterlin, etc. 88-221 L
* Juvenile Delinquency in the United States: Bibliography-in-Brief, 1985-1988, Edith Sutterlin 88-554 L
* Organized Crime: Bibliography-in-Brief, 1984-1987, Marsha Cerny 87-534 L
* The Parental Kidnapping Prevention Act of 1980: Background, Analysis and Subsequent Developments, Rita Ann Reimer 88-294 A
* Spouse Abuse: Background and Federal Programs to Address the Problem, Susan Schillmoeller, etc. 86-1035 EPW
* The State's Duty to Child Abuse Victims: DeShaney v. Winnebago County, Department of Social Services, Lou Fields 89-201
* Violent Crimes Committed Against the Elderly, Statistics from 1980-1989, David Teasley 91-580 GOV

Crimes and Offenses -- Capital Punishment

* Capital Punishment, Law Library of Congress, LL89-1
* Capital Punishment: Info Pack IP015C
* Capital Punishment: Mexico and Selected Central American Nations, Law Library of Congress LL90-18
* Capital Punishment: Selected References, 1986-1991, Tangela G. Roe 91-284 L
* Present Civilian Federal Death Penalty Statutes, Elizabeth B. Bazan 91-254 A

Crimes and Offenses -- Gun Control

* Brady Handgun Control Bill: H.R. 7/S. 257, 102nd Congress, Harry L. Hogan 91-399 GOV
* Firearms Regulations in Various Foreign Countries, Law Library of Congress, LL90-80
* Gun Control Act of 1968, as Amended: Digest of Major Provisions, P.L. 90-618, 90th Congress, H.R. 17735, October 22, 1968, Harry Hogan 85-166 GOV
* Gun Control Amendments, 1986 (Firearms Owners' Protection Act P.L. 99-308, as Amended by P.L. 99-360); Brief Summary of Major Provisions, Harry Hogan 86-784 GOV
* Gun Control: Info Pack, IP051G
* Gun Control: Issue Brief, Harry Hogan IB89093
* Gun Control: Selected References, 1982-1988, Elizabeth S. Lane 88-405 L
* Gun Control: S. 747, 101st Congress ("Antidrug, Assault Weapons Limitation Act of 1989"), Compared to Relevant Existing Law, Harry Hogan 89-375 GOV
* Gun Control: Selected References, 1989-1991, Tangela G. Roe 91-471 L
* Guns and Gun Control: National Public Opinion Polls, Rinn-Sup Shinn 90-545 GOV
* Handgun Buyer Background Check Proposals: Comparison of H.R. 7/S.257 and H.R. 1412, 102nd Congress, Harry Hogan 91-351 GOV
* Handgun Buyer Background Checks: Comparison of Bills Passed by the House and Senate, 102nd Congress, Harry Hogan 91-719 GOV
* Semiautomatic Military-Style Firearms: Proposed Statutory Definitions, Keith Bea 89-415 GOV
* Semiautomatic Military-Style Firearms: Statistics and Issues, Keith Bea 91-112 GOV

Criminal Procedure

* Brief Overview of the Political Offense Exception Standard in American Bilateral Extradition Practice, Larry Eig 85-895 A
* Civil RICO: An Overview of Recent Federal Case Law, and Proposed Legislation, Lou Fields 89-74 A
* Classified Information Procedures Act (CIPA): An Overview, Larry Eig 89-172 A
* Crime and Forfeiture, Charles Doyle 90-537 A
* Crime Control Act of 1990 (P.L. 101-647), Harry Hogan 91-69 GOV
* Crime Control: Criminal Theory; Selected References, 1989-1991, Jean Bowers 91-394 L
* Crime Control: Federal Initiatives, Info Pack IP310C
* Crime Control: Federal Response; Selected References, 1990-1991, Jean M. Bowers 91-428 L
* Crime Control: The Federal Response; Issue Brief, Suzanne Cavanagh, IB90078
* Crime, Drug, and Gun Control: Summary of S. 1241 (102nd Congress) as Passed by the Senate, Government Division 91-581 GOV
* Federal Forfeiture Funds, M. Maureen Murphy 86-880 A
* The Federal Grand Jury, Charles Doyle 91-512 A
* Federal Habeas Corpus: Background and Issues, Charles Doyle 91-24 A
* Federal Obscenity and Child Pornography Law, Henry Cohen 91-118 A
* Federal Sentencing Guidelines, Suzanne Cavanagh 91-499 GOV
* The Fourth Amendment--A Changing Landscape, Elizabeth B. Bazan 91-542 A
* How the Federal Sentencing Guidelines Work, Charles Doyle 91-534 A
* Independent Investigations of Allegations of Wrongdoing by Members of Congress, Jack Maskell 88-488 A
* Mandatory Sentencing and the Requirements of the Eighth Amendment After Harmelin v. Michigan, Charles Doyle 91-749 A
* Miranda After 1981: Supreme Court Case Law and the Justice Department Response, Lou Fields 88-517 A
* Morrison v. Olson: Constitutionality of the Independent Counsel Law, Jack Maskell 88-469 A
* Overview of the Independent Counsel Provisions of the Ethics in Government Act, Jack Maskell 88-631 A
* The Possible Interaction Between the Impeachment Process and the Double Jeopardy Clause, Elizabeth, B. Bazan 89-112 A
* RICO: A Brief Sketch, Charles Doyle 91-223 A
* Sentencing Guidelines for Federal Courts: Policy Considerations, Suzanne Cavanagh 87-508 GOV
* United States Sentencing Commission Guidelines: Preliminary Legal Analysis, Charles Doyle 88-13 A
* United States Sentencing Commission: Preliminary Analysis, Charles Doyle 89-308 A

Critical Technologies

* see Industrial Technology, Research and Development, Science Policy, Technology and Civilization

Crude Oil Windfall Profit Tax Act

* see Taxation--Corporation Taxes

Cuba

* Angola/Namibia Peace Prospects: Background, Current Problems, and Chronology, Raymond Copson 88-559 F
* Communist Holdout States: China, Cuba, Vietnam, and North Korea; Issue Brief, K. Larry Storrs IB91128
* Restrictions on U.S. Trade With Cuba: A Chronology of Major Actions and

Present Status, Vladimir N. Pregelj 86-909 E
* The United States and Cuba During the Carter Administration, Margaret Siliciano, etc. 85-988 F
* The United States and Cuba During the Reagan Administration, Judith Levenfeld, etc. 85-989 F

Currency Devaluation

* see International Finance

Cyprus

* British, Greek and Turkish Views on the Interpretation of the Treaty of Guarantee of 1980, Law Library of Congress LL90-42
* Cyprus: Status of U.N. Negotiations; Issue Brief, Ellen B. Laipson IB89140
* Cyprus: Turkish Cypriot "Statehood" and Prospects for Settlement: Archived Issue Brief, Ellen B. Laipson IB84062
* Greece and Turkey: The Seven-Ten Ratio in Military Aid, Ellen Laipson 90-29 F
* Greece and Turkey: U.S. Foreign Assistance Facts: Issue Brief, Carol Migdalovitz IB86065
* Greek-Turkish Relations: Beginning of a New Era?, Ellen Laipson 88-724 F

Dairy Industry

* see Agriculture--Dairy Industry

Davis-Bacon Act

* see also Labor--Policies and Legislation
* Avoiding Urban/Rural Wage Inequities in Determination of Prevailing Wage Rated Under the Davis-Bacon Act, William G. Whittaker 85-631 E
* The Davis-Bacon Act: A Comparison of Selected Provisions of Bills Introduced in the 100th Congress, William G. Whittaker 87-527 E
* The Davis Bacon Act: A Review of the Literature, William G. Whittaker 84-137 E
* The Davis-Bacon Act and Federal Contract Construction Wage Policy: Background Analysis and Recent Legislative Interest, William G. Whittaker 87-563 E
* Davis-Bacon Act: Consideration in the 100th Congress; Archived Issue Brief, William G. Whittaker IB87149
* The Davis-Bacon Act: Consideration in the 101st Congress; Issue Brief, William Whittaker IB89037
* The Davis-Bacon Act Suspension of 1971: The Nixon Administration, Organized Labor and the Prevailing Wage Statute in Federal and Federally Assisted Co, William Whittaker 79-249 E
* Major Repairs or Non-Routine Maintenance: Defining Davis Bacon Coverage under the Comprehensive Improvement Assistance Program, William G. Whittaker 85-887 E

Day Care

* see Families--Day Care

Daylight Savings Time

* see Standards

Death Penalty

* see Crimes and Offenses--Capital Punishment

Debt Crisis

* see International Finance-Foreign Loans

Defense

* see Defense Economics, Military Personnel, National Defense, Weapons Systems

Defense Budgets

* see Defense Economics--Defense Budgets

Defense Burden Sharing

* see Defense Economics

Defense Capability

* see Defense Economics, National Defense

Defense Contracts

* see Defense Economics--Procurement

Defense Economics

* see also Burdensharing, Defense Budgets, Procurement, National Defense, Weapons Systems, Security
* Applying Defense Resources to Environmental Problems; Archived Issue Brief, Congressional Research Service IB90127
* The Defense Spending Dilemma: Audio Brief, Daniel Lockwood, etc. AB50181
* Forum: Economic Conditions and Outlook, Congressional Research Service REB8-91
* Leases of Defense Articles: Legislative Provisions, and Restrictions, Richard F. Grimmett, 87-396 F
* Machine Tools: Imports and the U.S.Industry, Economy and Defense Industrial Base, Gary Guenther 86-762 E
* Military Construction: Current Controversies and Long-Term Issues, Martin Cohen, etc. 91-669 F
* The U.S. Commitment to Europe's Defense: A Review of Cost Issues and Estimates, Alice Maroni, etc. 85-211 F
* Working Capital Funds in the Department of Defense: A Primer, Alice Maroni, etc. 86-91 F

Defense Economics -- Burdensharing

* Allied Burdensharing: Audio Brief, Paul Gallis, etc. AB50182
* Allied Burdensharing in Transition: Status and Implications for the United States, Gary J. Pagliano 91-774 F
* Burdensharing: Selected References, 1979-1988, Sherry B. Shapiro 88-423 L
* Defense Burdensharing: Selected References, 1979-1989, Sherry B. Shapiro, 89-546 L
* Defense Burdensharing: The United States, NATO and Japan: Info Pack, IP399D
* Defense Burdensharing: U.S. Relations With NATO Allies and Japan, Stanley R. Sloan 88-449 F
* Defense Spending: An Introduction to Arms Control, Burdensharing, and Other Key Questions; Archived Issue Brief, Alice C. Maroni IB88043
* Japan's Contributions in Support of the U.S.-Led Multinational Forces in the War Against Iraq, Richard P. Cronin 91-293 F
* NATO Burdensharing: An Analysis of Major Legislation in the 100th Congress, Christopher C. Bolkcom 88-772 F
* Persian Gulf War: U.S. Costs and Allied Financial Contributions; Issue Brief, Stephen Daggett, etc. IB91019

Defense Economics -- Defense Budgets

* B-2 Strategic Bomber; Issue Brief, Dagnija Sterste-Perkins IB9-156
* The Budget Debate: How Much for Defense? Archived Issue Brief, Alice Maroni, etc. IB87117
* Defense and Foreign Aid Budget Analysis and the Use of Constant Dollars, Alice C. Maroni, etc. 86-154 F
* Defense and Highway Spending: Estimates of Their Effects on the U.S. Economy, David J. Cantor 90-237 E
* Defense Budget Cuts and the Economy; Issue Brief, Economics Division IB90012
* Defense Budget for FY 1990: Congressional Action; Archived Issue Brief, Stephen Daggett IB89054
* Defense Budget for FY 1990: Data Summary, Stephen Daggett 89-310 F
* Defense Budget for FY 1991: Authorization and Appropriations; Archived Issue Brief, Stephen Daggett IB90070
* Defense Budget for FY 1991: Data Summary, Stephen Daggett 90-93 F
* Defense Budget for FY 1992: Authorization and Appropriations; Issue Brief, Stephen Daggett IB91044
* Defense Budget for FY 1992, Data Summary, Stephen Daggett 91-181 F
* The Defense Budget Freeze: Why Defense Spending Will Increase, Alice Maroni 85-888 F
* A Defense Budget Primer, Robert E. Foelber 88-349 F
* Defense Spending: An Introduction to Arms Control, Burden Sharing, and Other Key Questions; Issue Brief Alice Maroni IB88043
* Defense Spending Cuts and Employment Adjustments, Linda Levine 90-55 E
* Defense Spending: Info Pack, Congressional Reference Division IP434D
* Defense Spending Priorities: Archived Issue Brief, Robert E. Foelber IB87235
* Defense Spending Priorities: Archived Issue Brief, Robert E. Foelber IB87231
* Defense Spending: Selected References, 1976-1988, Sherry B. Shapiro 88-535 L
* Economic Adjustment Assistance to Communities and Workers Affected by Defense Cutbacks, Congressional Research Service 90-126 CRS
* The Effects of a Two-Year Defense Budget Authorization, Alice Maroni

Currency Devaluation / Developing Countries

85-940 F
* Estimating Funding for Strategic Forces; A Review of the Problems, Alice Maroni 84-652 F
* Federal Economic Aid to Communities, Workers and Businesses Affected by Defense Cuts, Edward Knight 91-54 E
* The Fiscal Year 1989 Defense Budget Request Data Summary, Alice Maroni 88-182 F
* Funding for Selected Defense Programs: FY 1990 Authorization and Appropriation: Archived Issue Brief, Stephen Daggett IB89087
* Funding for Selected Weapons: Authorization and Appropriation: Archived Issue Brief, Robert E. Foelber IB88058
* The FY 1990 Budget Debate: How Much for Defense? Archived Issue Brief, Stephen Daggett, etc. IB89073
* The FY 1991 Budget Debate: How Much for Defense?, Archived Issue Brief, Stephen Daggett IB90061
* The FY 1992 Budget Debate: How Much for Defense?, Issue Brief, Stephen Daggett IB91066
* FY88 Defense Budget: Congressional Action on Defense Authorizations and Appropriations: Archived Issue Brief, Robert E. Foelber IB87129
* The Gramm-Rudman-Hollings Deficit Reduction Process (P.L. 99-177) and the Department of Defense: A Summary Review, Alice Maroni, etc. 86-7 F
* The Gramm-Rudman-Hollings Deficit Reduction Process: The Defense Aspects of the Initial Sequestration Report for Fiscal Year 1987, Alice Maroni, etc. 86-875 F
* The Gramm-Rudman-Hollings Sequestration Process for FY 1986: A Summary of DOD Elements in the OMB/CB O and GAO Sequestration Reports: Policy Alert, Alice Maroni, etc. 86-16 F
* The Impact of Defense Spending on Employment, Carolyn Brancato, etc. 82-182 E
* A Peace Dividend in 1990-91?, Stephen Daggett 90-85 F
* Short-Term Continuing Resolutions: The Department of Defense Experience, Alice C. Maroni 89-579 F
* Special Access Programs and the Defense Budget: Understanding the "Black Budget"; Archived Issue Brief, Alice C. Maroni, etc. IB87201
* Special Access Programs, Confidential Funding, and the Defense Budget: Bibliography-in-Brief, Sherry B. Shapiro 87-802 L
* Suspension of Budget Enforcement Procedures in the Event of a Declaration of War, Robert Keith 91-98 GOV
* Telephone Excise Taxes--Are Revenues Dedicated for Defense Spending?, Louis Alan Talley 90-611 E
* Unobligated and Unexpended Balances in the Department of Defense Budget: A Brief Review, Alice Maroni 86-580 F

Defense Economics -- Procurement

* The Competition in Contracting Act: Its Application to the Department of Defense, Andrew Mayer 85-115 F
* The Defense Acquisition Improvement Act of 1986: An Analysis of Key Provisions, Andrew C. Mayer 87-733 F
* Defense Acquisition: Major Structural Reform Proposals; Archived Issue Brief, David E. Lockwood IB86112
* Defense Acquisition Reform, Andrew Mayer 91-455 F
* Defense Acquisition Reform: Issues for the 100th Congress; Archived Issue Brief, David Lockwood IB87206
* The Defense Procurement Bribery and Fraud Investigation: A Chronology from Press Reports, David P. Fite 88-491 F
* The Defense Procurement Bribery and Fraud Investigation: A Chronology of Press Reports, David P. Fite, etc. 89-218 F
* The Defense Procurement Bribery and Fraud Investigation: Profiles of Persons and Companies Mentioned In Press Reports, David Fite 88-528 F
* The Defense Procurement Improvement Act of 1985, Andrew Mayer 86-115 F
* Defense Procurement Investigation: Archived Issue Brief, Gary J. Pagliano, etc. IB88081
* Defense Procurement Managers and Weapons Acquisition Reform, David Lockwood 86-13 F
* Defense Procurement Reform: Issue Brief, David E. Lockwood IB89015
* Defense Procurement Reform: 1988 Procurement Reform Provisions Included in Four Major Statutes Enacted in 1988, Andrew C. Mayer 89-261 F
* Defense Procurement: The Fraud and Bribery Investigation: Info Pack, IP404D
* LHX and Army Aviation Modernization: Issues for Congress: Issue Brief, Steven R. Bowman IB88086
* Military Alcoholic Beverage Procurement: Issues and Legislation, David F. Burreli 88-411 F
* Military Procurement Procedures of Foreign Governments: Centralization of the Procurement Function, Andrew Mayer 84-229 F
* The National Defense Stockpile: Department of Defense Policy and

Management, Alfred R. Greenwood 91-481 ENR
* The Packard Commission Report and Defense Acquisition Organization, David Lockwood 86-717 F
* Post Employment "Revolving Door" Restrictions on Department of Defense Personnel, Jack Maskell 88-478 A
* Selected Defense Procurement Acquisition Profiles: A Data Base, Alice C. Maroni, etc. 88-234 F
* Statutes and Regulations of Potential Relevance to Allegations of Defense Procurement Fraud, Jack H. Maskell, etc. 88-457 A
* Under Secretary of Defense for Acquisition: Role and Responsibilities; Archived Issue Brief, David E. Lockwood IB88016
* U.S. Defense Acquisition Reform: Major Congressional Initiatives; Archived Issue Brief, David Lockwood IB85103
* U.S. Weapons Procurement: Should a Civilian Agency Be in Charge?, David Lockwood 84-61 F

Defense Industrial Base

* see Defense Economics

Defense Policy

* see National Defense

Defense Procurement

* see Defense Economics--Procurement

Defense Spending

* see Defense Economics

Defense Spending and the Economy

* see Defense Economics--Defense Budgets

Deficit Reduction

* see Public Finance--Deficits

Deflation

* see Economic Conditions--Business Cycles, Economic Conditions--Inflation

Deforestation

* see Forests and Forestry

Democratic National Convention (1988:Atlanta, GA.)

* A Summary of National and State Party Laws Concerning the Election of Delegates to the 1988 Democratic and Republican National Conventions, Kevin Coleman 88-102 GOV

Deposit Insurance

* see Money and Banking--Failures and Deposit Insurance

Depression (Business Cycles)

* see Economic Conditions--Business Cycles

Deregulation

* see Business and Society--Regulation and Deregulation, Money and Banking--Law and Regulation

Desegregation in Education

* see Elementary and Secondary, Education--Policies and Legislation, Higher Education--Integration

Decertification

* see International Environmental Affairs

Developing Countries

* see also Economic Conditions, Foreign Loans
* Capital Flight and Highly Indebted Countries: An Analytical Survey of the Literature, Glennon J. Harrison 91-273 E
* Capital Flight: Problems Associated With Definitions and Estimates, Glennon J. Harrison 91-274 E
* Child Health in the Third World: U.S. and International Initiatives: Archived Issue Brief, Lois McHugh IB85189
* Conventional Arms Transfers to the Third World, 1983-1990, Richard F. Grimmett 91-578 F
* The Effectiveness of Food Aid: Implications of Changes in Farm, Food Aid, and Trade Legislation; Proceedings of a CRS Workshop Held on April 25,

Current Events and Homework

1988, Charles E. Hanrahan 88-493 ENR

* Environment and Development: U.S. Assistance Programs and Congressional Initiatives, Curt Tarnoff 91-548 F
* Environment and International Economic Development: The Role of Cost-Benefit Analysis, John L. Moore, etc. 87-774 ENR
* Environmental Protection in Developing Countries: Selected References, 1983-1987, Rebecca Mazur 87-488 L
* International Environment: Overview of Major Issues: Issue Brief, Mary Tiemann, etc. IB89-57
* Missile Proliferation: Survey of Emerging Missile Forces, Foreign Affairs and National Defense Division 88-642 F
* Tropical Deforestation: International Implications: Issue Brief, Susan Fletcher IB89010
* Tropical Deforestation: Selected References, 1987-1990, Lisa B. Dove 90-578 L
* Tropical Forests: Bibliography-in-Brief, 1985-1988, Adrienne C. Boniface 88-274 L

Developing Countries -- Economic Conditions

* The "Banker Plan": A Remedy for the International Debt Crisis?: Issue Brief, Patricia Wertman IB86106
* The Citicorp Initiative: A Brave New World for the Third World Debt Problem, Patricia Wertman 87-750 E
* Debt-for-Nature Swaps in Developing Countries: An Overview of Recent Conservation Efforts, Betsy Cody 88-647 ENR
* Debt Service Indicators of the Seventeen Most Highly Indebted Developing Countries, 1978-1986, Patricia Wertman, etc. 88-452 E
* The Effectiveness of Food Aid: Implications of Changes in Farm, Food Aid, and Trade Legislation: Proceedings of a CRS Workshop Held on April 25, 1988, Charles E. Hanrahan 88-493 ENR
* Environment and International Economic Development: The Role of Cost-Benefit Analysis, John L. Moore, etc. 87-774 ENR
* Finance and Adjustment: The international Debt Crisis, 1982-1984, Patricia Wertman 84-162 E
* Foreign Food Aid Programs: Effectiveness Issues; Archived Issue Brief, Charles Hanrahan IB88057
* An International Debt Management Authority: A Brief Overview, Patricia Wertman 89-208 E
* International Fund for Agricultural Development, Susan Epstein 87-4 ENR
* International Monetary Fund: Bibliography-in-Brief, 1983-1987, Robert S. Kirk 87-47L
* A Survey of U.S. International Economic Policy and Problems, Alfred Reifman 88-666 S
* Trade of the Seventeen Highly Indebted Countries: A Brief Overview, Patricia Wertman, etc. 88-521 E
* U.S. Agricultural Trade Opportunities With Pacific Rim Nations, Robert M. Goldstein 88-755 ENR
* U.S. Bank Exposure in the Seventeen Highly Indebted Countries: 1982-1987, Patricia Wertman, etc. 88-522 E

Developing Countries -- Foreign Loans

* The "Brady Plan" and the Third World Debt Problem, Patricia A. Wertman 89-425 E
* An International Debt Management Authority: Could It Spell R-E-L-I-E-F?, Economics Division 88-607 E
* The International Debt Problem: Congressional Proposals: Archived Issue Brief, Patricia Wertman IB87177
* Latin American Debt and U.S. Agricultural Exports: Assessment of a Proposed Approach, Charles E. Hanrahan 87-402 ENR
* Statutory Authorities Related to Official Foreign Debt, Jeanne J. Grimmett 91-381 A
* Third World Debt: Selected References, 1988-1990, Robert Howe 90-255 L
* The World Bank: Bibliography-in-Brief of Recent Works, Felix Chin 89-464 L
* World Bank/IMF Adjustment Loans and the Poor in Developing Countries, Foreign Affairs and National Defense Division 91-176 F

Developing Countries' Debts

* see International Finance -- Foreign Loans, Developing Countries--Foreign Loans

Developmental Disabilities

* see Handicapped

Digital Audio Recorder Act

* Digital Audio Recorder Act of 1987-- Analysis of H.R. 184 and S. 506 With

Policy Alternatives, David Hack 87-698 SPR

Disability Insurance

* see Social Security

Disabled

* see Handicapped

Disarmament

* see Arms Control--Negotiations and Treaties

Disasters

* see also Agriculture, Earth Sciences, Food Relief, National Defense, Nuclear Energy, Water Resources, Weapons Systems
* Agricultural Disaster Assistance; Issue Brief, Ralph Chite IB91099
* The California Drought: Effects on Agriculture and Related Resources, Betsy A. Cody, etc. 91-208 ENR
* The Chernobyl Accident: Implications for DOE's Production Reactors: Archived Issue Brief, Robert L. Civiak IB86092
* Civil Defense and the Effects of Nuclear War: Info Pack, IP174C
* Civil Defense: Archived Issue Brief, Gary Reynolds, etc. IB8428
* Civil Liability for Transboundary Damage from a Nuclear Accident: The Joint International Protocol, Barbara B. Black, etc. IB89023
* Crop Insurance and Disaster Assistance; Archived Issue Brief, Ralph Chite IB90080
* Earthquake and Disaster Relief Policies: San Francisco Bay Area Earthquake; Archived Issue Brief, James E. Mielke, etc. IB89149
* Emergency Drought Relief: A Comparison of the House and Senate Versions of H.R. 355, Betsy A. Cody 91-793 ENR
* Ethiopia: U.S. Foreign Assistance Facts: Archived Issue Brief, Raymond Copson, etc. IB85014
* The Evolving National Flood Insurance program, Malcolm M. Simmons 88-641 ENR
* Federal Disaster Relief Legislation and Administration: A Summary, Clark F. Norton 88-386 GOV
* Federal Earthquake Insurance and Reinsurance Legislation in the 102nd Congress, Jean K. Rosales 91-659 E
* International Notification and Assistance for Nuclear Accidents: Congressional Action on Two Conventions; Archived Issue Brief, Warren H. Donnelly IB87082
* Managing Coastal Development Through the Coastal Zone Management and Flood Insurance Programs: Experience to Date and the Views from Selected States, Gary Kamimura, etc. 88-354 ENR
* Monitoring and Forecasting Drought and Famine, Charles Hanrahan, etc. 85-1059 ENR
* The National Earthquake Hazards Reduction Program, David W. Cheney 89-473 SPR
* National Flood Insurance Program; Issue Brief, Malcolm Simmons IB90010
* Nuclear Winter: Bibliography-in-brief, B.F. Mangan 88-325 L
* Population Growth and Natural Resource Deterioration in Drought-Stricken Africa, Susan Abbasi 85-1149 ENR

Discount Brokers

* see Corporation-Securities Industry

Discrimination

* see Blacks, Civil Liberties and Rights-- Discrimination and Integration, Equal Employment Opportunity, Minorities, Women--Policies and Legislation

Discrimination in Employment

* see Equal Employment Opportunity

District of Columbia

* DC Statehood: A Brief Background Report, Bette A. Taylor 87-609 GOV
* DC Statehood: The Historical Context and Recent Congressional Actions, Garrine P. Laney 91-25 GOV
* Inexpensive Hotels and Housing in Washington, DC, Bette A. Alberts 91-425 RCO
* Shadow Representatives in Congress: History and Current Developments, Garrine P. Laney 91-64 GOV
* Washington, DC and the U.S. Capitol Building: Info Pack, IB132W

Dollar Value

* see International Finance--Foreign Exchange Rates

Domestic Violence

* see Crimes and Offenses

Draft

* see Military Personnel

Dropouts

* see Elementary and Secondary Education--Students

Drought

* see Agriculture--Environmental Aspects

Drug Abuse

* see also Alcoholism, Drug Testing, International Narcotics Control, Policies and Legislation, Crime and Justice
* Cocaine and American Society: Selected References, 1985-1990, Tangela G. Roe 90-497 L
* Confronting Students Concerning Suspected Drug Use: Potential Liability of Educators, M. Maureen Murphy 86-952 A
* "Crack" Cocaine, Edward Klebe 89-428 EPW
* Crime and Forfeiture, Charles Doyle 90-537 A
* Drug Abuse and Control: An Alphabetical Microthesaurus of Terms Selected from the Legislative Indexing Vocabulary, Shirley Loo 90-143 L
* Drug Abuse in America: Info Pack, IB303D
* Drug Abuse: Selected References, 1986-1988, Elizabeth S. Lane 88-625 L
* Forum: The Drug Problem, Congressional Research Service, REV 11-89

Drug Abuse -- Alcoholism

* Advertising of Alcoholic Beverages in the Broadcast Media: Archived Issue Brief, Bruce K. Mulock IB85097
* Alcohol Use and Abuse by Women, Edith Fairman Cooper 91-680 SPR
* Drug and Alcohol Abuse: Prevention, Treatment, and Education, Edward Klebe 86-1052 EPW
* Drunk Driving and Raising the Drinking Age: Info Pack, IP186D
* Drunk Driving: Bibliography-in-Brief, 1983-1988, Edith Sutterlin 88-655 L
* Drunk Driving; Issue Brief, Migdon Segal IB83157
* Drunk Driving Laws in Foreign Countries, Law Library of Congress LL89-88
* Legal Analysis of Questions Regarding the National Minimum Drinking Age, Douglas Weimer 85-772 A
* Nondischargeability of DWI Judgements in Bankruptcy: Survey of Case Law, Robin Jeweler 90-21 A
* Prohibiting Television Advertising of Alcoholic Beverages: A Constitutional Analysis, Rita Ann Reimer 88-22 A
* Traynor v. Turnage: The Exclusion of Alcoholics from Certain Veterans' Educational Benefits Does Not Violate Section 504 of the Rehabilitation Act of, Nancy Lee Jones 88-358 A

Drug Abuse -- Drug Testing

* Constitutional Analysis of Proposals to Establish a Mandatory Public Employee Drug Testing Program, Charles V. Dale 88-293 A
* Drug Free Workplace Initiatives: Federal Legislation Affecting the Private Sector, Gail McCallion 88-508 E
* Drug Testing and the Drug-Free Workplace: A Bibliographic Guide and Reader, Peter Giordano 90-6 L
* Drug Testing and Urinalysis in the Workplace: Legal Aspects, M. Maureen Murphy, etc. 86-996 A
* Drug Testing for Illegal Substances, Blanchard Randall IV 87-36 SPR
* Drug Testing in the Workplace: An Overview of Employee and Employer Interests: Archived Issue Brief, Gail McCallion IB87139
* Drug Testing in the Workplace: Federal Programs; Archived Issue Brief, Sharon S. Gressle IB87174
* Drug Testing: Selected References, 1986-1987, Rebecca Mazur 88-33 L
* Drug Testing: The Experience of the Transportation Industry, Gail McCallion 89-26 E
* Drug Testing: The Response to Drugs in the Workplace; Info Pack, IB350D
* Governmentally Mandated Drug Testing of Public Employees: A Survey of Recent Constitutional Developments, Charles V. Dale 90-103 A
* Legal Analysis of Recent Appropriation Riders to Insure a "Drug-Free Workplace", Charles V. Dale 88-450 A
* Transportation Industry Drug Testing, Gail McCallion 90-425 E

Drug Abuse -- International Narcotics Control

* Drug Control, Federal Efforts to Reduce the Supply: Selected References, 1987-1990, Jean Bowers 90-617 L
* Drug Control: International Policy and Options: Issue Brief, Raphael F. Perl, IB88093
* Drugs and Latin America; Audio Brief, Raphael Perl AB50194
* International Aspects of the Drug Trade: The Andean Nations and Cocaine; Selected References, 1988-1990, Tangela G. Roe 91-245 L
* The International Narcotics Trade: An Overview of Its Dimensions, Production Sources, and Organizations, William Roy Surrett 88-643 F
* Major Hong Kong Laws on Illegal Drugs, Law Library of Congress LL90-6
* Punishment for Drug Traffickers in Japan, Law Library of Congress LL89-86
* The Role of the U.S. Military in Narcotics Interdiction; Audio Brief, Raphael Perl AB50171
* The Supply of Prohibited Drugs to Addicts in Britain, Law Library of Congress LL89-46

Drug Abuse -- Policies and Legislation

* AIDS Prevention: State Law Regulating Hypodermic Devices Which Could Affect Needle Exchange Programs, M. Ann Wolfe 89-234 A
* Alcohol, Drug Abuse, and Mental Health Block Grant, and Related Programs: Issue Brief, Edward Klebe IB88009
* Anti-Drug Abuse Act of 1988 (H.R. 5210, 100th Congress): Highlights of Enacted Bill, Harry Hogan, etc. 88-707 GOV
* The Anti-Drug Abuse Act of 1988 (P.L. 199-690): Reports and Other Executive Branch Actions Required., Suzanne Cavanagh, etc. 89-406 GOV
* Anti-Drug Abuse Act of 1988 (P.L. 100-690): Summary of Major Provisions, Harry Hogan, etc. 89-288 GOV
* Crime and Drug Control: Comparison of Pending Senate and House Bills (S. 618 and H.R. 1400/S.635), Government Division, Harry Hogan 91-433 GOV
* Crime Control Act of 1990 (P.L. 101-647): Drug-Related Reports and Other Executive Branch Actions Required, David Teasley 91-654 GOV
* Crime Control Act of 1990 (P.L. 101-647), Harry Hogan 91-69 GOV
* Crime, Drug and Gun Control: Comparison of Major Bills under Consideration by the House Judiciary Committee, 102nd Congress, Keith Bea, etc. 91-687 GOV
* Crime, Drug and Gun Control: Comparison of Major Omnibus Bills of the 102nd Congress, American Law Division 91-737 GOV
* Crime, Drug, and Gun Control: Major Omnibus Legislation Pending; a Checklist of CRS Products, Jean M. Bowers 91-926 L
* Crime, Drug, and Gun Control: Summary of S. 1241 (102nd Congress) as Passed by the Senate, Government Division 91-581 GOV
* Criminal Penalties Regarding Illegal Use and Sale of Drugs, Law Library of Congress LL89-47
* The Defense Department's Drug Law Enforcement and Narcotics Interdiction Responsibilities: A Comparison of House and Senate Amendments in the Defense, Roy Surrett 88-406 F
* Drug Abuse and Control: National Public Opinion Polls, Rinn-Sup Shinn 90-109 GOV
* Drug Abuse: Treatment, Prevention and Education; Info Pack, IP400D
* Drug Abuse Treatment, Prevention and Education: Selected References, 1989-1990, Jean Bowers 90-465 L
* Drug and Alcohol Abuse: Prevention and Treatment: Selected References, 1985-1988, Edith Sutterlin 88-622 L
* Drug and Alcohol Abuse: Prevention, Treatment, and Education, Edward Klebe 86-1052 EPW
* Drug Control at the Federal Level: Coordination and Direction, Harry Hogan 87-780 GOV
* Drug Control: Existing Federal Laws and Pending Legislation, Info Pack IP430D
* Drug Control: Federal Efforts to Reduce the Supply; Info Pack, IP334D
* Drug Control: Federal Financial Assistance to State and Local Governments, Keith Bea 90-464 GOV
* Drug Control: Highlights of P.L. 99-570, Anti Drug Abuse Act of 1986 (Drug Related Provisions Only), Harry Hogan, etc. 86-968 GOV
* Drug Control: International Policy and Options: Issue Brief, Raphael F. Perl IB88093
* Drug Control: Issue Brief, Harry Hogan IB87013
* Drug Control: Legislation in the 101st Congress, Archived Issue Brief, Harry Hogan IB90095
* The Drug Crisis: Federal Aid for Crime Control, Prevention, and Treatment; Selected References, 1986-1989, Tangela G. Roe 90-9 L
* Drug Legalization: Bibliography-in-Brief, Elizabeth S. Lane 88-432 L
* Drug Legalization: Pro and Con, Harry Hogan 88-500 GOV
* Drugs of Abuse: The Legalization Debate; Info Pack, IP401D
* Equitable Distribution and Adoptive Forfeiture, Charles Doyle 90-538 A
* Federal Laws Relating to the Control of Narcotics and Other Dangerous Drugs, Enacted 1961-1985: Brief Summaries, Harry Hogan 86-12 GOV

Current Events and Homework

* Heroin: Legalization for Medical Use, Blanchard Randall 88-86 SPR
* House and Senate Standing Committees and Subcommittees With Jurisdiction Over National Drug Abuse Policy, 100th Congress, Carol Hardy 88-634 GOV
* International Narcotics Control and Foreign Assistance Certification: Requirements, Procedures, Timetables and Guidelines, Raphael F. Perl 88-175 F
* International Narcotics Control: The President's March 1, 1988 Certification for Foreign Assistance Eligibility and Options for Congressional Action; Raphael F. Perl 88-175 F
* The International Narcotics Trade: An Overview of Its Dimensions, Production, Sources, and Organizations, William Roy Surrett 88-643 F
* Money Laundering: Federal Law and Current Legislative Proposals, M. Maureen Murphy 90-157 A
* Narcotic and Illicit Drug Trafficking: Selected References, 1986-1988, Edith Sutterlin 88-579
* Narcotics Control and the Use of U.S. Military Personnel: Operations in Bolivia and Issues for Congress, Raphael Perl 86-800 F
* Narcotics Control Assistance for State and Local Governments: The Anti-Drug Abuse Act of 1988, William Woldman 89-181 GOV
* Narcotics Interdiction and the Use of the Military: Bibliography-in-Brief, 1982, 1988, Sherry B. Shapiro 88-408 L
* National Drug Control Strategy, 1989: Background and Policy Questions, Harry Hogan 89-567 GOV
* National Drug Control Strategy, 1990: Discussion of Selected Priority Highlights; Companion to CRS Report 89-567 GOV (National Drug Control Strategy, 1989), Harry Hogan 90-122 GOV
* Omnibus Drug Initiative Act of 1988: Summary of Major Provisions (H.R. 5210, 100th Congress, as Passed by the House), Harry Hogan 88-640 GOV
* The Role of the U.S. Military in Narcotics Interdiction: Audio Brief, Raphael Perl AB50171
* State and Local Assistance for Narcotics Control: The Anti-Drug Abuse Act of 1986, William Woldman 87-75 GOV
* State and Local Initiatives to Combat Drug Abuse and Drug Abuse-Related Crime: Selected References, 1980-1989, Tangela G. Roe 90-10 L
* Substance Abuse Treatment, Prevention, and Education, Edward R. Klebe 90-412 EPW
* U.S. Sanctions and the State of the Panamanian Economy, Mark P. Sullivan 88-578 F

Drug Abuse Control

* see Drug Abuse--Policies and Legislation

Drug Abuser Rehabilitation

* see Drug Abuse--Policies and Legislation

Drug Free Workplace

* see Drug Abuse--Drug Testing

Drug Legalization

* see Drug Abuse--Policies and Legislation

Drug Rehabilitation

* see Drug Abuse--Policies and Legislation

Drug Testing

* see Drug Abuse--Drug Testing

Drugs

* see also Genetics
* Biotechnology: Bibliography-in-Brief, 1985-1988, B.F. Mangan 88-566 L
* Drug Approval: Access to Experimental Drugs for Severely Ill Patients; Issue Brief, Blanchard Randall, etc. IB89016
* Food and Drug Administration: Selected Funding Data, Donna U. Vogt 91-424 SPR
* Generic Drugs and the Elderly: Issues and Policy Considerations, Samuel Merrill 91-792 SPR
* Medicaid: Reimbursement for Outpatient Prescription Drugs, Melvina Ford 91-235 EPW
* Pharmaceutical Pricing and Patent Law, Sylvia Morrison 91-748 E
* "The Applicability of the Export Proviso of the Federal Food, Drug and Cosmetic Act to "New Drugs", Cathy Gilmore 85-848 A

Drunk Driving

* see Drug Abuse--Alcoholism

Dumping (Foreign Trade)

* see Foreign Trade--Trade Policy

Earth Sciences

* see also Disasters
* Agriculture and the Environment: Issue Brief, Geoffrey Becker, etc. IB89086
* Carbon Dioxide, the Greenhouse Effect, and Climate; A Primer, John Justus 84-594 SPR
* CFC Phase-Out Bills in the 101st Congress; Comparison of Provisions, David E. Gushee 89-314 ENR
* Development Problems of the Next Generation Geostationary Operational Environmental Satellites (GOES-NEXT), David P. Radzanowski 91-634 SPR
* The Drought of 1988: Bibliography-in-Brief, Ted L. Burch 88-553 L
* Earthquake and Disaster Relief Policies: San Francisco Bay Area Earthquake; Archived Issue Brief, James E. Mielke IB89149
* Energy Demand and Carbon Dioxide Production, Richard E. Rowberg 91-170 SPR
* Ethanol Fuel and Global Warming, Migdon Segal 89-164 SPR
* The Federal Cave Resources Protection Act: A Review of a Proposed Bill, George Siehl 85-875 ENR
* The Future of the Land Remote Sensing Satellite System, Karl A. Rohrer, etc. 89-242 SPR
* Global Climate Change and Ozone Depletion: Selected References, 1989-1991, Karen L. Alderson 91-549 L
* Global Climate Change and the Green House Effect: Congressional Activity and Options; Archived Issue Brief, David E. Gushee IB88077
* Global Climate Change and the Green House Effect: Predictions and Uncertainties, Robert E. Morrison 90-179 SPR
* Global Climate Change and the 101st Congress: A Review of Legislation, Wayne A. Morrissey, etc. 91-359 SPR
* Global Climate Change: Audio Brief, David Gushee, etc. AB50189
* Global Climate Change: Issue Brief, Robert E. Morrison IB89005
* Global Climate Change: Policy Issues; Videoprogram LTR91-857
* The Global Environment: Audio Brief, AB50063
* Greenhouse Effect and Ozone Depletion: Info Pack, IP405G
* International Environment: Overview of Major Issues; Issue Brief, Mary Tiemann, etc. IB89057
* Mission to Planet Earth, David P. Radzanowski 91-89 SPR
* Mission to Planet Earth and the U.S. Global Change Research Program, Marcia S. Smith, etc. 90-300 SPR
* Monitoring and Forecasting Drought and Famine, Charles Hanrahan, etc. 85-1059 ENR
* The National Climate Program: Background and Implementation, John R. Justus, etc. 88-289 SPR
* The National Earthquake Hazards Reduction Program, David W. Cheney 89-473 SPR
* Near Term Options for Reducing United States Carbon Dioxide Emissions, Environment and Natural Resources Policy Division 91-133 ENR
* Nuclear Winter: Bibliography-in-Brief, B.F. Mangan 88-325 L
* Potential Improvements in the National Weather Service Through New Technology, Robert Morrison, etc. 85-69 SPR
* The Unpredictable Atmosphere: Selected References, Karen L. Alderson, etc. 89-43 L

East Germany

* see Western Europe

East-West Trade

* see Foreign Trade--East-West

Eastern Air Lines, Inc.

* Labor Problems at Eastern Air Lines: Issue Brief, Linda LeGrande IB88052

Eastern Europe

* see also Economic Conditions, Foreign Relations, Foreign Trade National Defense, Politics and Government, Foreign Policy and Assistance Programs
* American Public Opinion on Eastern Europe, the Soviet Union, and Defense Spending, Rosita M. Thomas 90-444 GOV
* The Chernobyl Accident: Health and Agricultural Effects; Archived Issue Brief, Christopher H. Dodge IB86122
* The Chernobyl Nuclear Accident: Causes, Initial Effects, and Congressional Response; Archived Issue Brief, Warren Donnelly, etc. IB86077
* The Chernobyl Nuclear Accident: Long-Term Political, Economic, and Foreign Policy Implications; Archived Issue Brief, Jean Boone, etc. IB86063
* Eastern Europe; Info Pack IP431E

Drug Abuse Control / Eastern Europe

* Eastern European and Soviet Science and Technology: Capabilities and Needs, William C. Boesman 91-114 SPR
* European Bank for Reconstruction and Development: An Institution of and for the New Europe, Karen Donfried 91-611 F
* Forum: Revolution in Eastern Europe, Congressional Research Service REV 3-90
* Mineral Development in Yugoslavia, Marc Humphries 88-688 ENR
* The New Europe, Audio Brief, Paul Gallis AB50215
* Soviet Space Commercialization Activities, Marcia S. Smith 88-473 SPR
* Space Activities of the United States, Soviet Union and Other Launching Countries/Organizations: 1957-1988, Marcia S. Smith 89-183 SPR
* U.S. Nuclear Cooperation With Hungary and Czechoslovakia: Archived Issue Brief, Warren H. Donnelly, etc. IB91090

Eastern Europe -- Economic Conditions

* Gorbachev's Reform: The Consumer Goods and Services Sector, F. Mike Miles 87-763 F
* Mineral Development in Yugoslavia, Marc Humphries 88-688 ENR
* Oil Price Behavior: Implications for the Soviet Union; Report of the CRS Workshop, June 26, 1986, John P. Hardt, etc. 86-886 S
* The Petroleum Status of Romania, Joseph P. Riva 90-472 SPR
* Poland's Economic Recovery: U.S. Policy Interests; Archived Issue Brief, John Hardt, etc. IB86070
* Poland's Renewal and U.S. Options: A Policy Reconnaissance, Update, John P. Hardt, etc. 87-889 S
* Polish Economic Reform and U.S. Interests, William H. Cooper 91-249 E
* The Polish Official Debt Accord: A Problem of Containment, Patricia A. Wertman 91-474 E
* Reform in Eastern Europe: Implications for Trade, Aid, and Commercial Relations; Archived Issue Brief, John Hardt, etc. IB90017
* Soviet Agricultural/Food Outlook: 1991/92, Remy Jurenas 91-708 ENR
* Soviet Oil Prospects, Joseph Riva 81-91 SPR

Eastern Europe -- Foreign Relations

* Andropov and Reagan as Negotiators: Contexts and Styles in Contrast, Joseph Whelan 83-141 S
* Arms Control: Overview of the Geneva Talks; Archived Issue Brief, Steven Hildreth IB85157
* Baltic States: Current Foreign Policy Issues; Bibliography in Brief, Sherry Shapiro 91-483 L
* A Changing Europe and U.S. Interests; Issue Brief, Stanley R. Sloan IB90062
* Congress and the Transformation of Eastern Europe in 1989, Francis T. Miko 90-503 F
* Eastern Europe: U.S. and International Assistance; Issue Brief, Francis T. Miko, etc. IB90089
* Emigration and Human Rights in the U.S.S.R.: Is There a New Approach? Archived Issue Brief, John P. Hardt IB88019
* Emigration: Soviet Compliance With the Helsinki Accords: Archived Issue Brief, John Hardt, etc. IB82080
* The Moscow Summit at First Glance: Audio Brief, Stuart Goldman, etc. AB50168
* Responses to Changing Europe: Implications for the U.S., Selected References, Valentin Leskovsek 90-5 L
* The Role of Congress in Soviet Diplomacy and Negotiations: Audio Brief, Joseph Whelan AB50175
* Sino-Soviet Relations: Recent Improvements and Implications for the United States; Issue Brief, Robert G. Sutter IB86138
* Soviet-American Relations in 1977: A Chronological Summary and Brief Analysis, William Cooper 79-60 S
* Soviet and American Negotiating Characteristics, Joseph G. Whelan 89-191 S
* Soviet Diplomacy and Negotiating Behavior, 1979-1988: Implications for U.S. Diplomacy in the Soviet-American Future, Joseph G. Whelan 88-674 F
* Soviet Foreign Policy under Gorbachev: Determinants, Developments, Prospects, and Implications, Francis T. Miko 87-39 F
* Soviet Policy in Nordic Europe: New Focus on the Forgotten Flank?, Francis Miko 85-33 F
* Soviet Policy Toward Iran and the Strategic Balance in Southwest Asia, Stuart D. Goldman 87-592 F
* Soviet-U.S. Relations: The Lessons of Past Summit Meetings?, Francis Miko, etc. 85-1037 G
* Soviet-U.S. Summit Meetings Since the 1950s: Selected References, Sherry Shapiro 87-912 L
* Thirty Years of U.S. Soviet Summit Meetings; a Capsule Summary, Stuart Goldman 85-1055 F

* United States and New Europe: Strategy for the Future, Stanley R. Sloan 90-245 S
* U.S.-Bulgarian Relations Since World War II, James Voorhees, 91-327 F
* U.S.-Soviet Relations in a Period of Summitry: Archived Issue Brief, Stuart Goldman IB83066
* U.S.-Soviet Relations: Info Pack, IP233U
* U.S.-Soviet Relations: Selected References, 1986-1988, Elizabeth S. Lane 88-155 L

Eastern Europe -- Foreign Trade

* see also Foreign Trade--East-West
* East-West Trade and the Congress; Proceedings of a CRS Seminar, Glennon J. Harrison 90-529 E
* European Regional Market: A Forgotten Key to Success of European Economies in Transition?, John P. Hardt 91-113 RCO
* Forum: Trade Negotiations: Broadening the World Trading System; Also Environmental Concerns for the Year 2000, Congressional Research Service REV 5-90
* Most Favored National Policy Toward Communist Countries: Archived Issue Brief, Vladimir N. Pregelj IB74139
* Potential Economic Effects of Granting Most Favored Nation Treatment to the Soviet Union, George D. Holliday 85-886 E
* Soviet Agriculture: U.S.-U.S.S.R. Grain Sales and Prospects for Expanded Agricultural Trade: Archived Issue Brief, John Hardt IB86019
* U.S. Export Control Policy and Competitiveness: Proceedings of the CRS Symposium, John P. Hardt, etc. 87-388 S
* U.S.-Soviet Commercial Relations in a Period of Negotiation: Archived Issue Brief, John P. Hardt IB88065
* U.S. Trade Relations With the Soviet Union Since World War II: A Chronology, Vladimir N. Pregelj 89-241 E
* U.S.-U.S.S.R. Commercial Relations: Issues in East-West Trade: Archived Issue Brief, John Hardt, etc. IB86020

Eastern Europe -- National Defense

* Arms Control: Negotiations to Limit Defense and Space Weapons; Issue Brief, Steven Hildreth IB86073
* Arms Control: Negotiations to Reduce INF Weapons: Archived Issue Brief, Paul Gallis IB86054
* The Conference on Disarmament in Europe (CDE): Archived Issue Brief, Charlotte Preece, etc. IB84060
* Conference on Security and Cooperation in Europe (CSCE): The Vienna Meeting; Issue Brief, Francis T. Miko IB87220
* Confidence Building Measures and Force Constraints for Stabilizing East-West Military Relations in Europe, Stanley R. Sloan, etc. 88-591 F
* Conventional Arms Control and Military Stability in Europe, Stanley R. Sloan, etc. 87-831 F
* Conventional Arms Control in Europe: Prospects for Accord; Issue Brief, Stanley Sloan IB86064
* East West Conventional Force Reduction Negotiations: Bibliography-in-Brief, 1980-1987, Valentin Leskovsek 87-313 L
* Essentials of Net Assessment: An Objective Means of Comparing Military Capabilities, John Collins, etc. 80-168 S
* Estimates of Soviet Defense Expenditures: Methodological Issues and Policy Implications, Robert Foelber, etc. 85-131 F
* Monitoring Nuclear Test Bans, David W. Cheney 86-155 SPR
* SALT II Treaty: U.S. and Soviet Interim Observance of Its Terms: Archived Issue Brief, Charles Gellner IB80018
* Strategic Nuclear Forces: Potential U.S./Soviet Trends With or Without SALT: 1985-2000, Jonathan Medalia, etc. 86-135 F
* United States/Soviet Military Balance: Archived Issue Brief, John Collins, etc. IB78029
* U.S. Soviet Military Balance. Book I. Organization, Budgets, Manpower, Technology, John Collins, etc. 80-161 S
* U.S.-Soviet Military Balance. Book II. Strategic Nuclear Trends, John Collins, etc. 80-162 S
* U.S.-Soviet Military Balance. Book III. General Purpose Force Trends, John Collins, etc. 80-163 S
* U.S.-Soviet Military Balance. Book IV. Airlift and Sealift, John Collins, etc. 80-164 S
* U.S. Soviet Military Balance Book V. NATO and the Warsaw Pact, John Collins, etc. 80-165 S
* U.S.-Soviet Military Balance. Book VI. Far East, Middle East Assessments, John Collins, etc. 80-166 S

Eastern Europe -- Politics and Government

* The Baltic Republics: U.S. Policy Concerns; Issue Brief, Vita Bite IB90075

Current Events and Homework

* East European Developments: A Summary of Major Issues and Chronology, January-April 1990, Theodore S. Dagne 90-286 F
* East European Developments: A Summary of Major Issues and Chronology, May-August 1990, Michael D. Scanlan 90-456 F
* East European Trends and U.S. Policy: Issue Brief, Francis T. Miko IB89138
* Eastern Europe: A New Focus; Selected References, 1989-1990, Sherry Shapiro 90-287 L
* Eastern Europe: Summary of a Workshop on Economic and Political Transition, Foreign Affairs and National Defense Division, Julie Kim 91-843 F
* Estonia: Background Information, Larry Silverman 83-64 F
* Estonia: Basic Facts, Vita Bite 91-762 F
* Glasnost and Perestroika under Gorbachev: A Chronology July 1987-December 1988, Charlotte Kea 89-138 F
* Gorbachev's Reform Strategy: Comparisons With the Hungarian and Chinese Experience, Francis T. Miko, etc. 87-813 F
* Latvia: Background Information, Allan Nanes, etc. 83-154 F
* Latvia: Basic Facts, Vita Bite 91-844 F
* Lithuania: Background Information, Dorothy Fontana 83-53 F
* Poland in Transition, Thomas J. Lang 91-704 F
* Romania: Political Crisis and Possible Future Developments, Sergiu Verona 91-751 F
* Soviet Nationalities Problems, Stuart D. Goldman 88-668 F
* Soviet Reforms: Glasnost and Perestroika, Bibliography-in-Brief, 1985-1988, Valentin Leskovsek 88-144 L
* Soviet "Restructuring" under Gorbachev: A Chronology, January 1985-June 1987, F. Mike Miles 87-551 F
* Soviet Union: An Assessment of Recent Republic and Local Elections, Steven J. Woehrel 90-355 F
* Yugoslavia: Crisis in the Federation, Jon W. Western 90-333 F
* Yugoslavia: Issue Brief, Steven J. Woehrel IB91089
* Yugoslavia's Kosovo Crisis: Ethnic Conflict Between Albanians and Serbs, Steven J. Woehrel 89-603 F

Eating Disorders

* see Medicine

Economic Conditions

* see also Business Cycles, Income, Inflation, Saving and Investment
* American In Economic Decline?, Alfred Reifman 89-182 S
* American Public Opinion on the Federal Budget Deficit, Government Taxing and Spending, and the Economy, Rosita M. Thomas 91-403 GOV
* American's Underground Economy, Barry Molefsky 81-181 E
* Catholic Social Teaching and the U.S. Economy: The Pastoral Letter of the American Catholic Bishops, Charles H. Whittier 87-104 GOV
* The Dollar, the Trade Deficit, and the U.S. Economy: Audio Brief, William Cooper, etc. AB50174
* The Economic Dimension of U.S. Power, Audio Brief, Dick Nanto AB50196
* Economic Forecasts and Gramm-Rudman-Hollings, Brian W. Cashell 87-934 E
* Economic Issues Before the 102nd Congress, Congressional Research Service, Edward Knight 91-407 E
* The Economic Outlook: A Comparison of Econometric Forecasts; Issue Brief, Brian Cashell IB83244
* Economic Policy: Selected Issues of Interest to the 101st Congress, Edward Knight 89-209 E
* Economy: Background and Prospects: Info Pack IP393E
* An Evaluation of the Index of Leading Economic Indicators, Barry Molefsky 81-179 E
* Forecast Comparisons: OMB, CBO, and the Blue Chip Economic Indicators; Issue Brief, Brian W. Cashell IB89-35
* Gramm-Rudman-Hollings Budget Adjustments: Sensitivity to Economic Assumption; Archived Issue Brief, Barry Molefsky, etc. IB85217
* The Gramm-Rudman-Hollings Targets: How Might They Affect the Economy, Gail Makinen, etc. 86-1036 E
* The Growing U.S. External Debt: Nature and Implications, Craig Elwell 87-798 E
* Implications of Uncertainty in Economic Forecasting, under Gramm-Rudman-Hollings: Options for Congressional Response, David C. Grinnell 86-829 S
* Iraq-Kuwait Oil Price Rise: U.S. Economic Effects, Bernard A. Gelb 90-434 E
* The Labor Market of the 1980s: Unemployment Omens in a Growing Economy: Archived Issue Brief, Dennis M. Roth IB87110
* The Low U.S. Savings Rate: Perspectives and Policy Options, Gail Makinen, etc. 88-552 E
* National Economic Statistics and Indicators, Barry Molefsky 85-909 E
* Personal Savings in the United States, Barry Molefsky 85-1050 E
* The Philips Curve vs. the Natural Rate of Unemployment: Their Potential as Policymaking Guides in Our Modern Economy, Charles V. Ciccone 86-896 E
* The Reagan Strategy for Economic Revitalization: The Results Thus Far, Edward Knight 83-218 E
* The Rise and Fall of Nations: Is America in Decline? a Bibliography of Points of View, Robert S. Kirk 89-214 L
* Saving and National Wealth: Issue Brief, Brian W. Cashell IB88097
* Saving and Rate of Return Incentives: Estimates of the Interest Elasticity of Personal Saving, William Jackson 81-198 E
* Selected Comparative Economic Statistics for Seven Major Industrial Countries, 1970-1985, Dario Scuka 85-564 E
* Selected Economic Statistics: Definitions, Sources of Information, and Historical Tables, Felicia G. Kolp, etc. 91-720 C
* The Uncertain Economic Expansion: Economic Prospects for the Year Ahead: Archived Issue Brief, Gail Makinen IB86074
* The Underground Economy: Selected References, Barry Molefsky 84-738 E
* The U.S. Economy: Background and Prospects; Selected References, 1987-1988, Robert Howe 88-82 L

Economic Conditions -- Business Cycles

* The Administration's Economic Forecast: An Evaluation; Issue Brief, Brian W. Cashell IB89012
* Business Cycles: What Happens and Why?, Brian Cashell 85-51 E
* Current Economic Conditions and Selected Forecasts: Issue Brief, Gail Makinen IB89044
* Economic Conditions: Archived Issue Brief, Gail Makinen IB87004
* Economy: Conditions and Outlook; Info Pack, Congressional Reference Division IP449E
* The Economy's Performance Since 1981: A Comparative Analysis, Edward Knight 88-336 E
* Forum: Economic Conditions and Outlook, Congressional Research Service REV 8-91
* Impact of the Business Cycle on Productivity Growth in the U.S. Economy, Mary Jane Bole 82-172 E
* Is Faster Growth in Germany and Japan the Key to Faster U.S. Growth?, Gail Makinen 86-836 E
* Is the Current Economic Expansion Consistent With History, Gail Makinen 87-871 E
* Is the Service Sector Recession-Proof?, Linda LeGrande 88-132 E
* Manufacturing Employment by State as a "Recession Vulnerability Indicator", Linda Levine 91-35 E
* Prospects for an Economic Downturn, G. Thomas Woodward 89-105 E
* Prospects for an Economic Downturn (After the Stock Market Plunge), G. Thomas Woodward 88-12 E
* Prospects for Economic Growth in the Long Run, Brian W. Cashell 91-657 E
* Quarterly Economic Briefing, Gail Makinen LTR91-862
* Recession in the United States: Economic Effects and Policy Implications, Economics Division 80-134 E
* Recession in 1982: Economic Risks and Prospects: Policy Responses to Recession and Recovery: A Historical Perspective, Edward Knight 82-4 E
* Rising Interest Rates and the Economic Expansion: Can They Co-Exist?, Craig K. Elwell 84-818 E
* The Slowdown in the Current Economic Expansion: Recession or Soft Landing, Gail Makinen 88-718 E
* The Smoot-Hawley Tariff Act of 1930: Its Effects on U.S. Trade and Its Role in the Great Depression of 1929-1933, George Holliday, etc. 87-993 E
* Unemployment Compensation: Response to the Current Economic Downturn; Issue Brief, Gene Falk, etc. IB91005
* Will the Stock Market "Crash" End the Current Economic Expansion?, Economic Prospects for the Year Ahead, Gail E. Makinen 88-51 E

Economic Conditions -- Income

* American Living Standards, Mary Jane Bolle 90-158 E
* Earnings as a Measure of Regional Economic Performance, Linda LeGrande, etc. 87-377 E
* Economic Status of the Elderly: Archived Issue Brief, Brian W. Cashell IB87095
* Income and Expenditures of Selected Consumer Groups, 1973-1985, Marc E. Smyrl 88-318 S
* Measures of Real Earnings Since 1970, William A. Cox 88-692 S
* Middle Class Decline? Income Distribution Trends: Bibliography-in-Brief,

Eating Disorders / Education of the Handicapped

1983-1987, Robert S. Kirk 87-460 L
* Middle Class Decline? Income Distribution Trends: Selected References, 1987-1991, Robert Howe 91-609 L
* Middle Class Erosion and Growing Income Inequality: Fact or Fiction?, Richard S. Belous, etc. 85-203 E
* Minimum Wage Earnings and the EITC: Making the Connection, Charles Ciccone 88-736 E
* Real Earnings in America: 1947-1985, Richard S. Belous 86-615 E
* Who's Keeping Up in the 1980's? Compensation as an Indicator, Linda LeGrande 87-883 E
* Young vs. Old? Intergenerational Economic Equity: Bibliography-in-Brief, 1978-1987, Saundra Shirley-Reynolds 87-467 L

Economic Conditions -- Inflation

* Anti-Inflation Policy: The Administration's Strategy, Edward Knight 80-37 E
* Are Mandatory Wage and Price Controls Needed to Combat Current Inflation?, Edward Knight 80-64 E
* The Consumer Price Index: A Brief Overview, Brian Cashell 87-651 E
* Consumer Price Index: Background and Current Data; Archived Issue Brief, Pauline H. Smale IB83246
* A Consumer Price Index for the Elderly: Would It Make Any Difference, Brian W. Cashell 87-552 E
* Economic Growth and Inflation, Brian Cashell 88-742 E
* Expectations as a Factor in Contemporary Inflation: Implications for Analysis and Economic Policy, Julius Allen 81-52 E
* A Falling Dollar and Domestic Inflation, Craig K. Elwell 86-127 E
* Inflation: Causes, Costs, and Current Status, Gail Makinen 90-460 E
* Inflation and Economic Capacity, Brian Cashell 85-189 E
* Inflation in 1980: A Survey of Selected Economic Issues, Economics Division 80-59 E
* Inflation: Its Current Status; Issue Brief, Gail Makinen IB90129
* Is Inflation under Control? The Underlying Versus the Actual Rate of Inflation, Gail Makinen 86-774 E
* U.S. Government Price Statistics, Barry Molefsky 81-237 E

Economic Conditions -- Saving and Investment

* Capital Gains Taxes, IRA's and Savings, Jane G. Gravelle 89-543 S
* Federal Tax Policy and Saving, Gregg A. Esenwein 91-178 E
* Foreign Investment: Effects on the U.S. Economy and National Economic Security: Proceedings of a CRS Seminar, Congressional Research Service, James K. Jackson 90-604 E

Economic Growth and Jobs

* see Economic Conditions, Labor

Economic Policy

* see also Foreign Trade--Trade Policy, Money and Banking --Monetary Policy, Public Finance--Deficits, Public Finance-Fiscal Policy, Public Finance--Public Debt and Deficits, Taxation--Tax Reform
* The American Response to Foreign Competition: Audio Brief, Mary Jane Bolle, etc. AB50180
* Are Mandatory Wage and Price Controls Needed to Combat Current Inflation?, Edward Knight 80-64 E
* Budget Deficits and Monetary Policy, Carol Leisenring 81-128 E
* The Dollar and the Trade Deficit: What's to be Done?, Craig Elwell, etc. 88-430 E
* Economic Growth and Inflation, Brian Cashell 88-742 E
* Economic Issues Before the 102nd Congress, Congressional Research Service, Edward Knight 91-407 E
* Economic Policy: Selected Issues of Interest to the 101st Congress, Edward Knight 89-209 E
* Economic Policymaking in U.S. Government: Proceedings of a Congressional Symposium, April 26, 1988, Congressional Research Service 88-461 E
* Economic Policymaking Problems. Part One: Institutions and Processes, Leon M. Cole, etc. 89-299 E
* Economic Policymaking Problems: Part Two: Theories and Forecasts, Leon M. Cole, etc. 89-300 E
* The Economics of Federal Reserve Independence, G. Thomas Woodward 90-118 E
* The Economy's Performance Since 1981: A Comparative Analysis, Edward Knight 88-336 E
* Effectiveness of Mandatory Wage and Price Controls During the Nixon Administration, A Selected Annotated Bibliography, Edward Knight, etc. 80-91 E
* The Employment Act of 1946, as Amended, and the Opportunity for

Economic Planning: The Federal Government's Response, Dennis Roth 82-21 E
* Federal Reserve System Special Anti-Inflation Programs Announced March 14, 1980: A Brief Description, Roger White 80-73 E
* Monetary Policy: Current Policy and Conditions; Issue Brief, Gail Makinen IB91110
* Prospects for an Economic Downturn, G. Thomas Woodward 89-105 E
* The Reagan Economic Strategy: Implications for Small Business, Edward Knight 81-232 E
* The Reagan Strategy for Economic Revitalization: The Results Thus Far, Edward Knight 83-218 E
* Recession in the United States: Economic Effects and Policy Implications, Economics Division 80-134 E
* The Slowdown in the Current Economic Expansion: Recession or Soft Landing?, Gail Makinen 88-718 E
* A Survey of U.S. International Economic Policy and Problems, Alfred Reifman 88-666 S
* U.S. Economic Policy in an International Context: Deficits, Taxes, and Monetary Policy, Jane G. Gravelle, etc. 84-12 E
* U.S. Economic Policy in an International Context: U.S. Wages and Unit Labor Costs in a World Economy, Richard S. Belous 84-172 E

Economic Recovery

* see Economic Conditions--Business Cycles

Economic Statistics

* see Economic Conditions

Ecuador

* The Petroleum Status of Ecuador, Joseph P. Riva 90-211 SPR

Education

* see also Elementary and Secondary Education, Federal Aid to Education, Higher Education, Occupational Training
* Adult Literacy Issues, Programs, and Options, IB85167
* Carl D. Perkins Vocational Education Act: Issues for Reauthorization, IB89069
* Early Childhood Education and Development: Federal Policy Issues, IB88048
* Education: Federal Concerns, IB87151
* Education Funding Issues for FY 90, IB89039
* Guaranteed Student Loans: Defaults, IB88050
* Saving for College, IB89078
* Science, Engineering, and Mathematics Precollege and College Education, IB88068
* Teachers: Issues for the 101st Congress, IB89098

Education Consolidation and Improvement Act

* Education Block Grant Reauthorization: Selected Options, Paul M. Irwin 87-494 EPW
* Education for Disadvantaged Children: Reauthorization Issues: Archived Issue Brief, Wayne Riddle IB87070
* Vouchers for the Education of Disadvantaged Children: Analysis of the Reagan Administration Proposal, Wayne Riddle 85-1022 EPW

Education for all Handicapped Children Act

* Constitutional and Statutory Issues Relating to the Use of Behavior Modification on Children in Institutions, Nancy L. Jones 86-1000 A
* P.L. 94-142, the Education for All Handicapped Children Act: Its Development, Implementation, and Current Issues, Charlotte Fraas 86-552 EPW
* The 'Stay Put' Provision of the Education for All Handicapped Children Act: Honig, California Superintendent of Public Instruction v. Doe Et Al, Meredith A. Yancey 88-494 A

Education Funding

* see Federal Aid to Education, Higher Education--Student Aid

Education of Handicapped Children

* see Handicapped--Children

Education of the Handicapped Act

* Education of the Handicapped Act Discretionary Programs: Background and Current Issues, Margot A. Schenet 89-67 EPW
* Summary of the Education of the Handicapped Act Amendments of 1986,

Current Events and Homework

P.L. 99-457, Charlotte Jones Fraas 86-926 EPW

Education Savings Bond Program
* Saving for College With Education Savings Bonds, Gerald Mayer 89-207 E

Educational Reform
* see Elementary and Secondary Education, Higher Education

Egypt
* Egypt: U.S. Foreign Assistance Facts: Archived Issue Brief, Ellen B. Laipson IB85060
* Egyptian Military Debt Forgiveness: Costs, Implications, and the Role of Congress; Archived Issue Brief, Larry Q. Nowels IB90137
* Egypt's New Foreign Policy Activism: Considerations for the United States, Ellen Laipson 90-188 F

El Salvador
* Central American Peace Proces: Selected References, Robert Kirk 88-389 L
* El Salvador Aid: Congressional Action, 1981-1986 on President Reagan's Request for Economic and Military Assistance for El Salvador, K. Larry Storrs 87-230 F
* El Salvador and U.S. Aid: Congressional Action in 1989; Archived Issue Brief, K. Larry Storrs IB90011
* El Salvador: Bibliography-in-Brief, 1987-1989, Robert S. Kirk 90-14 L
* El Salvador Highlights, 1960-1990: A Summary of Major Turning Points in Salvadoran History and U.S. Policy, K. Larry Storrs 90-149 F
* El Salvador: Info Pack, IP121E
* El Salvador--Legal System, Judicial Reform, and Major Human Rights Cases Involving the Military, K. Larry Storrs 90-177 F
* El Salvador: Status of the War and the Role of U.S. Aid, James P. Wootten 90-193 F
* El Salvador: Status of U.N.-Mediated Government-Guerilla Peace Talks, K. Larry Storrs 91-304 F
* El Salvador under Cristiani: U.S. Foreign Assistance Decisions; Issue Brief, K. Larry Storrs IB89122
* El Salvador: U.S. Aid in 1987 and 1988, Archived Issue Brief, K. Larry Storrs IB85113
* El Salvador: U.S. Foreign Assistance Facts; Issue Brief, K. Larry Storrs, etc. IB85113
* El Salvador, 1982-1984: A Chronology of a Period of Transition Resulting from the 1982 and 1984 Elections, K. Larry Storrs 87-656 F
* A Summary and Analysis of the Report of the National Bipartisan "Kissinger" Commission on Central American, January 1984, Richard Cronin, etc. 84-39 F

Elderly
* see Old Age

Election Law
* see Congress-Apportionment and Elections, Politics and Elections--Election Law

Elections
* see also Congress--Apportionment and Elections, Politics and Elections--Election Law, Presidents (U.S.)
* Campaign Financing, IB87020
* The Fairness Doctrine and the Equal Opportunities Doctrine, IB82087
* Federal Elections Commission, IB81104

Electoral College
* see Politics and Elections--Election Law

Electrification
* see Power Resources--Electric Power

Electronic Funds Transfers
* see Money and Banking--Financial Institutions

Electronics
* SEMATECH Facts, Glenn J. McLoughlin 91-831 SPR

Elementary and Secondary Education
* see also Policies and Legislation, Students, Prayer and Religion, Federal Aid to Education--Elementary and Secondary

* Adult Illiteracy: Selected References, Peter Giordano 89-249 L
* Adult Literacy Issues, Programs, and Options; Issue Brief, Paul Irwin IB85167
* AIDS and the Public Schools: Legal Issues Involved in the Education of Children, Nancy Lee Jones 88-329 A
* Comparative Education: Statistics on Education in the United States and Selected Foreign Nations, Kenneth Redd 88-764 EPW
* Comparison of the Achievement of American Elementary and Secondary Pupils With Those Abroad--The Examinations Sponsored by the Inter. Assoc. for Eval., Wayne Riddle 86-683 EPW
* Computers in Elementary and Secondary Schools: An Analysis of Recent Congressional Action, James Stedman 88-419 EPW
* Confronting Students Concerning Suspected Drug Use: Potential Liability of Educators, M. Maureen Murphy 86-952 A
* Constitutional Rights of High School Students: A Select Overview, Rita Ann Reimer 88-224 A
* The Constitutionality of Excessive Corporal Punishment in the Public Schools, David M. Ackerman, etc. 88-413 A
* Corporal Punishment in the Public Schools: A Fifty State Survey, M. Ann Wolfe 91-798 A
* Dropping Out: The Educational Vulnerability of at-Risk Youth, Congressional Research Service 88-417 EPW
* Early Childhood Education and Development: Federal, Policy Issues; Issue Brief, Wayne Riddle IB88048
* Economic Benefits of Education, Linda LeGrande 88-753 E
* Education: An Alphabetical Microthesaurus of Terms Selected from the Legislative Indexing Vocabulary, Shirley Loo 89-54 L
* The Education of the Handicapped: Selected References, 1984-1987, Marsha K. Cerny 87-529 L
* The Educational Attainment of Select Groups of "At Risk" Children and Youth, James Stedman 87-290 EPW
* A Guide to Print and Non-Print Teaching Aids, Michelle Springer 89-289 C
* High School Dropouts: Archived Issue Brief, Robert F. Lyke IB87167
* High School Dropouts: Bibliography-in-Brief, 1986-1988, Peter Giordano 88-580 L
* Leadership in Educational Administration Development Program: A Summary of Provision, James B. Stedman 87-204 EPW
* Public School Choice: Recent Developments and Analysis of Issues, Wayne Riddle, etc. 89-219 EPW
* State Funding for Education Reform, K. Forbis Jordan 86-735 S
* Teacher Supply and Demand, Forbis Jordan 85-994 EPW
* Teachers: Issues for the 101st Congress: Issue Brief, James Stedman IB89098

Elementary and Secondary Education -- Policies and Legislation
* Adult Education Act Reauthorization: Selected Options, Paul M. Irwin 87-57 EPW
* AMERICA 2000: The President's Education Strategy, James B. Stedman 91-430 EPW
* Background Information on Equal Access Statute, David Ackerman 84-842 A
* Bilingual Education: Recent Evaluations of Local School District Programs and Related Research on Second-Language Learning, Rick Holland 86-611 EPW
* Chapter 1 Concentration Grants: An Analysis of the Concept, and Its Embodiment in Federal Elementary, and Secondary Education Legislation, Wayne Riddle 88-670 EPW
* Child Care and Early Childhood Development: The Federal Role; Selected References, 1988-1991, Edith Sutterlin 91-521 L
* A Comparison of the Education Provisions in the Omnibus Trade Bill, H.R. 3, as Passed by the House by the Senate, Paul M. Irwin, etc. 87-634 EPW
* Computers in Elementary and Secondary Schools: An Analysis of recent Congressional Action, James B. Stedman 88-419 EPW
* The Concept of "Secular Humanism" in the Context of Elementary and Secondary Education: Discussion of the Variety of Meanings, and References in Feder, Wayne Riddle 86-545 EPW
* Conditional Deregulation of Federal Elementary and Secondary Education Programs: The AMERICA 2000 Proposal, Wayne clifton Riddle 91-531 EPW
* Dwight D. Eisenhower Mathematics and Science Education Act: An Analysis of Recent Legislative Action and Program Evaluations, James Stedman 89-24 EPW
* Early Childhood Education and Development: Federal Policy Issues; Issue Brief, Wayne Riddle IB88048
* Education: Federal Concerns; Issue Brief, Angela Evans IB87151
* Education for Disadvantaged Children: Major Themes in the 1988

Education Savings Bond Program / Endangered Species Act

Reauthorization of Chapter 1, Wayne Riddle 89-7 EPW
* Education: Issues of Quality and Reform: Info Pack, IP256E
* Education Legislation in the 100th Congress: A Brief Summary; Archived Issue Brief, Wava Gregory IB87134
* Education of the Handicapped Act Discretionary Programs: Background and Current Issues, Margot A. Schenet 89-67 EPW
* Education Proposals in Trade Competitiveness Legislation: Archived Issue Brief, K. Forbis Jordan, etc. IB87108
* Education Provisions of the Trade Act of 1988, P.L. 100-418, Paul Irwin, etc. 88-750 EPW
* Education Reform Reports: Content and Impact, James Stedman, etc. 86-56 EPW
* Educational Challenges of the Congress: Achieving National Education Goals and Reforming Student Assistance; Videoprogram, James B. Stedman, etc. LTR91-880
* Elementary and Secondary Education: A Summary of the Augustus F. Hawkins-Robert T. Stafford Elementary and Secondary School Improvement Amendments of 1988, Public Law 100-297, Education and Public Welfare Division 88-458 EPW
* Employer Education Assistance: A Brief Discussion of Current Legislation and Issues, Bob Lyle 88-202 EPW
* Expenditures in Public School Districts: Why Do They Differ? Wayne C. Riddle 90-322 EPW
* The Federal Agency for Education: History and Background Information, Angela Evans 81-93 EPW
* Federal Education Policies and Programs: Selected References, 1981-1988, Peter Giordano 89-12 L
* Federal Education Programs Serving Limited English Proficient Students, Ruby Ann M. Esquibel 89-285 EPW
* Federal Policies and Programs Relating to Sex Discrimination and Sex Equity in Education, 1963-1985, Bob Lyke, etc. 85-116 EPW
* Foreign Language and International Education: The Federal Role, Wayne c. Riddle 89-657 EPW
* Head Start Issues in FY 1986: Funding, Administration, and Recent Evaluation, Sharon Stephan 86-554 EPW
* The Head Start Program: Background Information and Issues, Anne C. Stewart, etc. 90-98 EPW
* The Impact Aid Program Under Section 3 of Public Law 81-874, Richard Apling 91-111 EPW
* The Impact Aid Programs (P.L. 81-874 and P.L. 81-815): Modification Resulting from the Augustus F. Hawkins-Robert T. Stafford Elementary and Secondary, Richard N. Apling 88-399 EPW
* Legal Implications for Federal Civil Rights Enforcement of Judge Pratt's Recent Order Dismissing the Action in Adam v. Bennett, Charles V. Dale 88-85 A
* Maintenance of Effort Provisions for Major Federal Elementary and Secondary Education Programs, Education and Public Welfare Division 91-172 EPW
* Merit Grants to Schools Based on Performance: The America 2000 Proposal, Wayne C. Riddle 91-612 EPW
* National Education Goals: Federal Policy Issues; Issue Brief, Wayne Riddle, etc. IB91077
* National Education Goals: Major Legislation Considered by the 101st Congress, Wayne Riddle, etc. 90-555 EPW
* National Education Goals: Where Are We Now?, James B. Stedman, etc. 90-169 EPW
* National Literacy Act of 1991: Major Provisions of P.L. 102-73, Paul M. Irwin 91-811 EPW
* National Teachers' Examination: Background and Issues, Forbis Jordan 85-732 EPW
* The Neighborhood Schools Improvement Act, H.R. 3320: Summary and Analysis, Wayne Riddle, etc. 91-794 EPW
* Prayer and Religion in the Public Schools: What Is, and Is Not, Permitted, David M. Ackerman 90-559 A
* Provisions of the Tax Reform Act of 1986 Pertaining to Education, Robert Lyke 87-67 EPW
* Religion in the Public Schools: Pluralism and Teaching about Religions, Charles H. Whittier 89-104 GOV
* The School Prayer Controversy: Pro-Con Arguments, Archived Issue Brief, Charles Whittier IB84081
* Section 2 of P.L. 81-874, Federal Impact Aid to Local School District: Background, Funding History, and Recent Regulation, Richard N. Apling 88-220 EPW
* The "Stay Put" Provisions of the Education for All Handicapped Children Act: Honig, California Superintendent of Public Instruction V. Doe Et Al Meredith A. Yancey 88-494 A
* Summary and Analysis of the Education Amendments of 1984, P.L. 98-511, Angela Giordano-Evans, etc. 84-769 EPW
* Summary of Adult Education Act, as Amended by the Education Amendments of 1984 (P.L. 98-511), Paul Irwin 84-829 EPW
* Summary of the Education of the Handicapped Act Amendments of 1986, P.L. 99-457, Charlotte Jones Fraas 86-926 EPW
* Teachers: Issues for the 101st Congress, James B. Stedman 90-117 EPW
* Teachers: Issues for the 101st Congress, Archived Issue Brief, James B. Stedman IB89098
* Teachers: Issues for the 102nd Congress; Issue Brief, James B. Stedman IB91024
* Tuition Tax Credits, Bob Lyke 91-230 EPW

Elementary and Secondary Education -- Prayer and Religion

* Prayer and Religion in the Public Schools: What Is and Not Permitted David M. Ackerman 89-25 A
* Prayer and Religion in U.S. Public Schools: Bibliography-in-Brief, 1983-1988, Edith Sutterlin 88-663 L
* Religion in the Public Schools: Judicial Decisions, David M. Ackerman 88-770 A
* Religion in the Public Schools: Pluralism and Teaching About Religions, Charles H. Whittier 89-104 GOV
* The School Prayer Controversy: Pro-Con Arguments; Issue Brief, Charles Whittier IB84081
* School Prayer: The Congressional Response, 1962-1988, David Ackerman 88-676 A

Elementary and Secondary Education -- Students

* Dropping Out: The Educational Vulnerability of At-Risk Youth, Congressional Research Service 88-417 EPW
* The Educational Attainment of Select Groups of "at Risk" Children and Youth, James B. Stedman 87-290 EPW
* Head Start: Percentage of Eligible Children Served and Recent Expansions, Anne Stewart 91-572 EPW
* Head Start Reauthorization Amendments Enacted During the 101st Congress, Anne C. Stewart 90-642 EPW
* High School Dropout Rates, Bob Lyke 91-776 EPW
* High School Dropouts: Archived Issue Brief, Robert F. Lyke IB87167
* High School Dropouts: Current Federal Programs, Bob Lyke 90-144 EPW
* High School Dropouts: New Legislation and Other Federal Programs, Bob Lyke 90-556 EPW
* National Assessment of Educational Progress: Background and Status, Paul M. Irwin, etc. 91-232 EPW
* Underrepresented Minorities and Women in Science, Mathematics, and Engineering: Problems and Issues for the 1990s, Christine M. Matthews 91-26 SPR

Embassies and Diplomatic Corps

* see Foreign Relations

Emigration

* see Immigration

Employee Retirement Income Security Act

* Pension Issues; Info Pack IP428P
* Private Pension Plan Standards: A Summary of ERISA, Ray Schmitt 91-22 EPW
* Retirement Income: Bibliography-in-Brief, 1986-1987, Edith Sutterlin 88-28 L
* Women's Pension Equity: A Summary of the Retirement Equity Act of 1984, Ray Schmitt 84-217 EPW

Employment

* see Labor--Employment and Unemployment

Employment Discrimination

* see Equal Employment Opportunity

Endangered Species Act

* Consideration of Economic Factors under the Endangered Species Act, Pamela Baldwin 89-274 A
* Economic Impacts of Protecting the Northern Spotted Owl, Ross W. Gorte 90-74 ENR
* Endangered Species Act: A Checklist of CRS Products, Lisa B. Dove 91-917 L

Current Events and Homework

* Endangered Species Act Issues: Issue Brief, M. Lynne Corn IB91086
* Endangered Species Act: The Listing and Exemption Processes, M. Lynne Corn, etc. 90-242 ENR
* Endangered Species Act: Reauthorization and Funding: Issue Brief, M. Lynne Corn IB87089
* Endangered Species, Bibliography-in-Brief, 1986-1987, Adrienne C. Grenfell 87-459 L
* Kangaroo Management Controversy, Malcolm M. Simmons 88-468 ENR
* Pacific Salmon and Steelhead: Potential Impacts of Endangered Species Act Listings, Eugene H. Buck, etc. 91-267 ENR
* Salmon and Smelt on the Pacific Coast: Endangered Species Act Listing Proposals and Issues; Issue Brief, Eugene H. Buck, etc. IB91112
* Spotted Owls and Old Growth Forests; Issue Brief, M. Lynne Corn IB90094
* Spotted Owls and the Timber Industry; Issue Brief, M. Lynne Corn IB89077

Energy

* see also Fossil Fuels, Nuclear Energy, Power Resources
* Alcohol Fuels, IB74087
* Arctic Resources Controversy, IB89058
* Civil Liability for Transboundary Damage from a Nuclear Accident: the Joint International Protocol, IB89023
* Coal Slurry Pipeline Issues, IB89105
* DOE's Clean Coal Technology Program: Goals and Funding, IB88071
* Domestic Natural Gas Production, IB89009
* Domestic Oil Production Under Conditions of Continued Low Drilling Activity, IB87068
* Energy Conservation: Technical Efficiency and Program Effectiveness, IB85130
* Energy Security, IB89006
* Nuclear Energy Policy, IB88090
* Nuclear Power Plant Safety and Regulation, IB86130
* Nuclear Power: Technology Overview, Statistics, and Projections, IB81070
* Nuclear Weapons Production Complex: Modernization and Cleanup, IB89062
* Oil Storage Tanks: Construction and Testing Issues Since the Ashland Oil Spill, IB88015
* Outer Continental Shelf Leasing and Development, IB89028
* Public Utilities Holding Company Act of 1935: Is This the Time for Reform?, IB89052
* Renewable Energy: Federal Programs, IB87050
* The Strategic Petroleum Reserve, IB87050
* U.S.-Japan Agreement for Nuclear Cooperation: Monitoring Its Implementation, IB88095

Energy Conservation

* see Power Resources--Energy Conservation

Energy Development on Public Lands

* see Public Lands

Energy Policy

* see Power Resources--Energy Policy

Energy Security

* see Fossil Fuels-Petroleum

Energy Taxes

* see Taxation--Consumption Taxes

England

* see Great Britain

English As the Official U.S. Language

* see Minorities

Enterprise Zones

* see Urban Affairs

Entitlement Programs

* see Pensions, Public Welfare, Social Security

Environment

* Antarctica: Environmental Protection Issues: Summary of a CRS Research Workshop, Susan R. Fletcher 89-272 ENR

* Directory of Environmental and Conservation Organizations in the Washington, DC Metropolitan Area, Mira Courpas 89-99 ENR
* International Environment: Overview of Major Issues: Issue Brief, Mary Tiemann, etc. IB89057
* Nuclear Weapons Production Complex: Modernization and Cleanup; Issue Brief, David W. Cheney, etc. IB89062
* Environmental Economics: The Clean Air Standards Attainment Act: An Analysis of Welfare Benefits from S. 1894, Larry B. Parker 88-298 ENR
* Controlling Carbon Dioxide Emissions, Amy Abel, etc. 89-157 ENR
* Environmental Factors in Benefit-Cost Analyses of Development Activities, Ross Gorte 86-702 ENR
* Ozone and Carbon Monoxide Nonattainment: An Analysis of Title I of S. 1894, Mira Courpas 88-316 ENR

Environmental Economics

* Applying Defense Resources to Environmental Problems: Archived Issue Brief, Congressional Research Service IB90127
* Distributing the Cost of Acid Rain Control: Cost-Sharing under a Freedom-of-Choice Proposal, Larry Parker 89-536 ENR
* Environmental Factors in Benefit-Cost Analyses of Development Activities, Ross Gorte 86-702 ENR
* Green Taxes in Various Countries, Law Library of Congress LL90-49
* The Tax Treatment of Expenditures on Anti-Pollution Equipment in Selected Foreign Countries, Law Library of Congress LL90-10
* Using Incentives for Environmental Protection: An Overview, John L. Moore, etc. 89-360 ENR

Environmental Health

* see also Air Pollution--Indoor Air Pollution, Chemicals, Occupational Health and Safety
* Aflatoxin and Agriculture, Carl Ek 89-525 ENR
* Agent Orange: Veterans' Complaints and Studies of Health Effect; Archived Issue Brief, Sam Merrill, etc. IB83043
* Asbestos in Buildings: Current Issues; Archived Issue Brief, Claudia Copeland IB86084
* Brief Summary of Several Federal Statutes Which Arguably Provide the Federal Government the Authority to Control the Disposal of Infectious Hospital, Cathy Gilmore 87-658 A
* The Chernobyl Accident: Health and Agricultural Effects; Archived Issue Brief, Christopher H. Dodge IB86122
* The Clean Air Standards Attainment Act: An Analysis of Welfare Benefits from S. 1894, Larry Parker 88-298 ENR
* Hazardous Air Pollutants: Revising Section 112 of the Clean Air Act, Archived Issue Brief, James E. McCarthy IB89094
* Hazardous Chemical Facilities and Community Right-to-Know: Current Issues; Archived Issue Brief, James Aidala IB86069
* Health Benefits of Air Pollution Control: A Discussion, John BLodgett 89-161 ENR
* High Speed Commercial Transports: Environmental Issues and NASA's High Speed Research Program, John D. Moteff 90-547 SPR
* Power Lines and Electromagnetic Fields: Issues for Congress; Issue Brief, Christopher H. Dodge IB91051
* Risk Assessment in Health and Environmental Regulation; Archived Issue Brief, David Cheney IB84124
* Summary Discussion of S. 1894: The Proposed Clean Air Standards Attainment Act, Congressional Research Service 88-378 ENR
* Toxic Chemicals: Environmental and Health Issues; Audio Brief, AB50104
* The Toxic Substances Control Act: Implementation Issues; Archived Issue Brief, Jim Aidala IB83190
* Underground Storage of Natural Gas, James E. Mielke, etc. 88-187 SPR

Environmental Law

* see also Air Quality, Hazardous Substances, Law and Legislation, Water Quality
* Antarctica: Environmental Protection Issues; Summary of a CRS Research Workshop, Susan R. Fletcher 89-272 ENR
* Applying Defense Resources to Environmental Problems: Archived Issue Brief, Congressional Research Service IB90127
* Beverage Container Deposit Laws in the States, Mark Gurevitz 89-334 A
* CFC Phase-Out Bills in the 101st Congress: Comparison of Provisions, David E. Gushee 89-314 ENR
* The Clean Air Act in the Courts: Significant Cases from 1980 to 1988, Robert Meltz, etc. 88-460 A
* A Department of Environmental Protection?, Martin R. Lee, etc. 89-587 ENR
* Directory of Environmental and Conservation Organizations in the

Energy / Environmental Law

Washington, DC, Metropolitan Area, Mira Courpas 89-99 ENR
* Environmental Block Grants: A Discussion of Current Issues, Claudia Copeland 86-561 ENR
* Environmental Impairment Liability Insurance: Overview of Availability Issues, Rawle O. King 89-269 E
* Environmental Issues: National Public Opinion Polls, Rinn-Sup Shinn, etc. 90-405 GOV
* Environmental Labeling in Canada, Germany, and Japan, Law Library of Congress LL90-63
* Environmental Legislation and Trade: A Checklist of CRS Products, Ted L. Burch 92-7 L
* The Environmental Protection Agency: Cabinet-Level Status? Issue Brief, Mary E. Tiemann, etc. IB90069
* Environmental Protection Agency: FY 90 Funding: Issue Brief, Martin R. Lee IB88062
* Environmental Protection Agency: FY 1992 Budget; Issue Brief, Martin r. Lee IB91115
* The Environmental Protection Agency's Proposed Strategy for Post-1987 Nonattainment Areas, Mira Courpas 87-980 ENR
* Environmental Protection: An Alphabetical Microthesaurus of Terms Selected from the Legislative Indexing Vocabulary, Shirley Loo 87-792 L
* Environmental Protection Legislation in the 100th Congress: Archived Issue Brief, Environment and Natural Resources Policy Division IB87065
* Environmental Protection Legislation in the 101st Congress; Issue Brief, Environmental and Natural Resources Policy Division IB89033
* Environmental Protection Legislation: Reference Guide, Eugene H. Buck 87-519 ENR
* Export of Pesticides, James Aidala 89-73 ENR
* International Environmental: Overview of Major Issues: Issues Brief, Mary Tiemann, etc. IB89057
* Licensing and Special Use Permit Requirements for Hydroelectric Dam Projects under the Federal Power, Act and the Federal Land Policy and Management Act, Robin Jeweler 88-459 A
* Major International Environmental Issues; A Checklist of CRS Products, Lisa B. Dove 92-13 L
* NEPA Compliance at Department of Energy Defense Production Facilities, Mark Holt, etc. 90-127 ENR
* Outdoor Advertising Control Along Federal-Aid Highways, Malcolm Simmons 86-605 ENR
* RCRA Authorization: Audio Brief, Jim McCarthy, etc. AB50179
* Reauthorization of RCRA: A Checklist of CRS Products, Ted L. Burch 91-911 L
* Reauthorization of the Clean Water Act: A Checklist of CRS Products, Lisa B. Dove 91-913 L
* Recycling: Info Pack, Congressional Reference Division IP437R
* Selected Environmental and Related Industrial Interest Groups: SUmmary Guide, Environment and Natural Resources Policy Division 91-295 ENR
* Setting Priorities for Department of Energy Environmental Activities, mark Holt, etc. 91-150 ENR
* Solid Waste Management: RCRA Reauthorization Issues; Issue Brief, Mark Reisch, etc. IB91069
* Summaries of Federal Environmental Laws Administered by EPA, Environment and Natural Resources Policy Division 87-226 ENR
* U.S. Chemical Manufacturing: World Status and Issues, Bernard A. Gelb 91-807 E
* Using Incentives for Environmental Protection: An Overview, John L. Moore, etc. 89-360 ENR
* Wetlands Protection: Issues in the 101st Congress: Issue Brief, Jeffrey A. Zinn, etc. IB89076

Environmental Law -- Air Quality

* Acid Rain Bills in the 100th Congress; Comparison of the Major Provisions of H.R. 2666, H.R. 4331, S., 316, 1894, and the Cuomo-Celeste Proposal, Larry Parker, etc. 88-490 ENR
* Acid Rain Control: An Analysis of Title IV of S. 1630, Larry B. Parker 90-63 ENR
* Acid Rain Control and Clean Coal Technology: An Analysis of Title II of S. 1894, Larry Parker 88-266 ENR
* Acid Rain Control: What Is a 10 Million Ton S02 Reduction?, Larry B. Parker, etc. 89-243 ENR
* Acid Rain Legislation and the Domestic Aluminum Industry, Marc Humphries, etc. 89-327 ENR
* Acid Rain Legislation in the 101st Congress: Archived Issue Brief, Mira Courpas, etc. IB89144
* Acid Rain: Selected References, 1989-1991, Lisa B. Dove 91-596 L
* Air Quality: Implementing the Clean Air Act Amendments of 1990; Issue Brief, Susan Mayer IB91022
* Alternative Transportation Fuels: What's at Stake?, David E. Gushee 90-229 S
* Ambient Air Quality Standards: An Analysis of Title IV of S. 1896, John E. Blodgett 88-271 ENR
* Asbestos in Public Buildings: Comparison of Two Bills, Claudia Copeland 88-368 ENR
* Availability of Trained Persons To Implement the Asbestos Hazard Emergency Response Act, Claudia Copeland 88-259 ENR
* The Clean Air Act in the Courts: Significant Cases from 1980 to 1988, Robert Meltz, etc. 88-460 A
* Clean Air Act: Permit Provisions in- and Senate-Passed Bills, Claudia Copeland 90-38 ENR
* Coke Oven Emissions: A Case Study of "Technology-Based" Regulation, Environment and Natural Resources Policy Division 89-533 ENR
* Comparison of Bills To Amend the Asbestos Hazard Emergency Response Act, Claudia Copeland 88-262 ENR
* Emission Controls on Motor Vehicles and Fuels: An Analysis of Title II of S. 1894, David E. Gushee 88-297 S
* Global Climate Change and the 101st Congress: A Review of Legislation, Wayne A. Morrissey, etc. 91-359 SPR
* Glossary of Air Quality Terms, Mira Courpas 89-247 ENR
* Hazardous Air Pollutants: An Analysis of Title V of S. 1894, James E. McCarthy 88-265 ENR
* Health Benefits of Air Pollution Control: A Discussion, John Blodgett 89-161 ENR
* House Acid Rain Bills in the 100th Congress: Comparison of the Major Provision of H.R. 1664, H.R. 16 79, H.R. 2497/H.R. 2498, H.R. 2666, H.R. 3632, H.R, Larry Parker, etc. 88-226 ENR
* House Acid Rain Bills in the 101st Congress: Comparison of the Major Provisions of H.R. 144 and H.R. 1470, Larry Parker, etc. 89-226 ENR
* Ozone and Carbon Monoxide Nonattainment: An Analysis of Title I of S. 1894, Mira Courpas 88-316 ENR
* Potential Benefits of Enacting Clean Air Act Amendments, John E. Blodgett 90-73 ENR
* The Stratospheric Ozone Layer: Regulatory Issues; Issue Brief, David Gushee IB89021
* Summary Discussion of S. 1894: The Proposed Clean Air Standards Attainment Act, Congressional Research Service 88-378 ENR
* Trucking and the Clean Air Act Amendments of 1990: Some Economic Implications, Stephen J. Thompson 91-132 E

Environmental Law -- Hazardous Substances

* Chemicals in the Environment: Audio Brief, James Aidala AB50152
* Chemicals in the Environment: Selected References on Managing Environmental Risks, Rebecca Mazur 87-26 L
* Escaping Superfund Liability: The Innocent Landowner and Lender Exceptions, Robert Meltz 91-91 A
* Hazardous Air Pollutants: Revising Section 122 of the Clean Air Act; Archived Issue Brief, James E. McCarthy IB89094
* Incinerating Municipal Solid Waste: A Health Benefit Analysis of Controlling Emissions, Environmental and Natural Resources Policy Division, 89-260 ENR
* Liability of Superfund "Response Action Contractors" and EPA for Injury from Contractor-Conducted Cleanups, Robert Meltz 89-292 A
* Municipal Waste Incineration: An Analysis of Section 3016 of S. 1984, James McCarthy 88-402 ENR
* Solid and Hazardous Waste Management: Issue Brief, James E. McCarthy IB90022
* The Toxic Substances Control Act: Implementation Issues; Archived Issue Brief, Jim Aidala IB83190
* Waste Exports: U.S. and International Efforts to Control Transboundary Movement; Issue Brief, Mary Tiemann IB89123
* Waste Management: Issue Brief, James E. McCarthy IB89007

Environmental Law -- Law and Legislation

* Alternative Fuels and Reformulated Gasoline; Issue Brief, David Gushee IB91008
* Billboard Control Along Federal-Aid Highways: Legislative Proposals in the 101nd; Issue Brief, Malcolm Simmons IB91054
* Billboard Control Along Federal-Aid Highways: Legislative Proposals in the 102nd Congress, Malcolm Simmons 91-283 ENR
* Clean Water Act Reauthorization: Issue Brief, Claudia Copeland IB91052
* Criminal Provisions in Federal Environmental Statutes: A Compilation, Maribel Nicholson 89-652 A
* Enforcement of Environmental Laws at Federal Facilities: Legal Issues, Robert Meltz 90-390 A

Current Events and Homework

* Environmental Issues: From the 101st to the 102nd Congress, Environment and Natural Resources Policy Division 91-11 ENR
* Environmental Protection Laws and Treaties: Reference Guide, Environment and Natural Resources Policy Division 91-136 ENR
* Environmental Protection Legislation in the 102nd Congress; Issue Brief, Environment and Natural Resources Policy Division IB91042
* Environmental Regulation and the GATT, Jeanne J. Grimmett 91-285 A
* Implementing Acid Rain Legislation: Issue Brief, Larry Parker IB91035
* Securities Law: Environmental Disclosures, Michael V. Seitzinger 91-422 A
* Summaries of Environmental Laws Administered by the Environmental Protection Agency, Environment and Natural Resources Division 91-251 ENR
* Wetland Issues in the 102nd Congress; Issue Brief, Jeffrey A. Zinn, etc. IB91058

Environmental Law -- Waste Quality

* Oil Pollution Liability and Compensation, Martin R. Lee 88-611 ENR

Environmental Law -- Water Quality

* After the Exxon Valdez Spill: Oil Pollution Liability and Compensation Legislation, Martin R. Lee 89-266 ENR
* The Alaskan Oil Spill and Gasoline Prices, Lawrence C. Kumins 89-250 ENR
* Chronology: EPA Regulation of Stormwater Discharge, Claudia Copeland 88-495 ENR
* Clean Water Act Activities: Post Public Law 100-4, Claudia Copeland 88-768 ENR
* Clean Water Act Citizen Suits Held Limited to Ongoing Violations: Gwaltney of Smithfield v. Chesapeake Bay Foundation, George A. Costello 88-46 A
* The Exxon Valdez Oil Spill: Issue Brief, Martin R. Lee, etc. IB89075
* Groundwater Quality: Current Federal Programs and Recent Congressional Activities, Jeffrey Zinn, etc. 89-195 ENR
* Groundwater Quality Protection Issues; Archived Issue Brief, Mary Tiemann IB89081
* Groundwater Quality: Current Federal Programs and Recent Congressional Activities, Jeffrey Zinn, etc. 89-195 ENR
* Infectious Waste and Beach Closings, Martin R. Lee 88-596 ENR
* Municipal Compliance With the Clean Water Act: Is the Glass Half Full or Half Empty?, Claudia Copeland 88-421 ENR
* Oil Pollution Liability and Compensation Legislation After the Exxon Valdez Oil Spill: Issue Brief, Martin R. Lee IB89082
* Preventing Beach Closings: Legislative Options; Issue Brief, Martin R. Lee IB88102
* A Review of Oil Pollution Prevention Regulations After the Monongahela River Spill, Martin R. Lee 88-448 ENR
* Waste in the Marine Environment: Selected References, Ted Burch 89-263 L
* Water Quality: Implementing the Clean Water Act: Issue Brief, Claudia Copeland IB89102

Environmental Protection

* see also Air Pollution, Chemicals, Environmental Economics, Environmental Health, Environmental Law, Solid Wastes, Water Pollution
* Acid Rain, Air Pollution, and Forest Decline, IB86031
* Acid Rain: Issues in the 101st Congress, IB87045
* Agriculture and the Environment, IB89086
* Air Quality, IB87124
* Asbestos in Buildings: Current Issues, IB86084
* Clean Air Act Issues: Motor Vehicle Emission Standards and Alternative Fuels, IB86140
* Clean Air Act Issues: Ozone Nonattainment, IB89064
* Degradable Plastics, IB88067
* Environmental Protection Agency: FY 90 Funding, IB89032
* Environmental Protection Legislation in the 101st Congress, IB89033
* The Exxon Valdez Oil Spill, IB89033
* Global Climate Change, IB89005
* Groundwater Quality Protection: Issues in the 101st Congress, IB89081
* Hazardous Air Pollutants: Proposals for Revising Section 112 of the Clean Air Act, IB87087
* Hazardous Waste Management: RCRA Oversight in the 101st Congress, IB87087
* Indoor Air Pollution, IB88092
* International Environment: Overview of Major Issues, IB89057
* Oil Pollution Liability and Compensation Legislation After the Exxon Valdez Oil Spill, IB89082
* Oil Storage Tanks: Construction and Testing Issues Since the Ashland Oil Spill, IB88015
* Preventing Beach Closings: Legislative Options, IB88102
* Solid Waste Management, IB87176
* Stratospheric Ozone Depletion: Regulatory Issues, IB89021
* Tropical Deforestation: International Implications, IB89010
* Waste Management, IB89007
* Water Quality: Implementing the Clean Water Act, IB89102

Equal Access to Justice Act

* see Law

Equal Employment Opportunity

* Affirmative Action in the Employment of Persons With Handicaps under Federal Contracts: Section 503 of the Rehabilitation Act, Mary F. Smith 88-701 EPW
* Affirmative Action: The Debate, the Supreme Court, and Employment; Selected References, 1987-1990, Tangela G. Roe 91-205 L
* Affirmative Action Revisited: A Review of Recent Supreme Court Actions, Charles V. Dale 87-442 A
* Age Discrimination in Employee Benefit Plans: United States Supreme Court Decision in Public Employees Retirement System of Ohio v. Betts, Kathleen S. Swendiman 89-478 A
* Age Discrimination in Employment Act: Recent Enforcement Actions by the Equal Employment Opportunity Commission, Charles V. Dale 87-783 A
* Age Discrimination in Employment: Current Legal Developments, Patricia A. Prochaska 87-681 A
* The Americans With Disabilities Act: Equal Employment Opportunity Commission Proposed Regulations on Equal Employment Opportunity for Individuals With Disabilities, Nancy Lee Jones 91-291 A
* The Americans With Disabilities Act (ADA): Legal Analysis of Proposed Legislation Prohibiting Discrimination on the Basis of Handicap, Nancy Lee Jones 88-621 A
* Attorneys' Fees and Expert Witness Fees under the Civil Rights Act of 1991, Henry Cohen 91-818 A
* Blacks' Labor Market Experiences in the 1980s and 1990s, Linda Levine 90-307 E
* The Civil Rights Act of 1991: A Legal Analysis of Various Proposals to Reform the Federal Equal Employment Opportunity Laws, Charles V. Dale 91-757 A
* Civil Rights: Equal Employment Opportunity and Affirmative Action: Info Pack IP424C
* Comparable Worth/Pay Equity in the Federal Government: Issue Brief, Linda LeGrande IB85116
* Comparative Analysis of Title VII of the 1964 Civil Rights Act, the Age Discrimination in Employment Act, and The Rehabilitation Act of 1973, Charles V. Dale 89-240 A
* Comparative Chart of Unfair Immigration-Related Employment Practices, Title VIII of the Fair Housing Act, Title VII of the Civil Rights Act of 1964, and the Rehabilitation Act of 1973, Larry M. Eig 90-209 A
* Disabled Persons: State Laws Concerning Accessibility and Discrimination, M. Ann Wolfe 89-409 A
* The Economic Equity Act of 1987: Archived Issue Brief, Leslie Gladstone IB87221
* Elimination of the Professional and Administrative Career Examination (PACE) and Proposed Alternative Selection Procedures, Paul Downing 89-315 GOV
* Employment Discrimination Claims under 42 U.S.C. 1981: Judicial Decisions After Patterson v. McLean Credit Union, Kevin B. Greely 91-142 A
* Federal Appeals Court Decisions on Disparate Impact After Wards Cove Packing Co. v. Atonio, Charles V. Dale 91-165 A
* Federal Policies and Programs Relating to Sex Discrimination and Sex Equity in Education, 1963-1985, Bob Lyke, etc. 85-116 EPW
* Federal Programs for Minority and Women-Owned Businesses, Mark Eddy 90-312 GOV
* The "Glass Ceiling:" Access of Women and Minorities to Management Positions, Linda Levine 91-623 E
* Legal Implications of the Contagious Disease or Infections Amendment of the Civil Rights Restoration Act, S. 557, Nancy Lee Jones 88-214 A
* Pay Equity Legislation in the 102nd Congress; Issue Brief, Linda Levine IB91080
* The Results of Affirmative Action under Executive Order 11146: Summaries of Recent Studies, Paul M. Downing 86-672 GOV
* Selected Women's Issues Legislation Enacted Between 1832-1988, Leslie Gladstone 89-514 GOV
* Sex-Based Employment Discrimination: UAW v. Johnson Controls, Inc., Gina M. Stevens 91-323 A

* Sexual Harassment in the Workplace: Selected References, Jean Bowers 91-836 L
* Sexual Harassment Policy: Rules Applicable to Congressional Offices, Leslie Gladstone 91-744 GOV
* Survey of State Statutes Concerning Employment Discrimination of Handicapped Persons, M. Ann Wolfe 87-561 A
* Women's Economic Equity Act: H.R. 3085/S. 1480 and Subtitles Introduced as Separate Legislation, Leslie Gladstone 90-154 GOV
* Women's Economic Equity: H.R. 3085/S. 1480; Archived Issue Brief, Leslie W. Gladstone IB90014

Equal Rights Amendment (Proposed)

* see Women

ERISA

* see Employee Retirement Income Security Act

Espionage

* see Intelligence Activities, Internal Security

Estonia

* The Baltic Republics: U.S. Policy Concerns; Issue Brief, Vita Bite IB90075
* Estonia: Background Information, Larry Silverman 83-64 F
* Estonia: Basic Facts, Vita Bite 91-762 F

Ethanol

* see Power Resources--Alternative Energy Sources

Ethics in Government Act

* see also Government Employees-Ethics, Political Ethics
* Conflicts of Interest: The Department of Defense and the Revolving Door Problem, Andrew C. mayer 86-188 F
* Legislative History and Purposes of Enactment of the Independent Counsel (Special Prosecutor) Provisions of the Ethics in Government Act of 1978 Jack Maskell 87-192 A
* Overview of the Independent Counsel Provisions of the Ethics in Government Act, Jack Maskell 88-631 A
* Summary of Constitutional Issues Raised in Challenges to the Independent Counsel Provisions of Federal Law, Jack Maskell 87-483 A

Ethics Reform Act

* see Political Ethics

Ethiopia

* Ethiopia: New Thinking in U.S. Policy, Theodore S. Dagne 91-489 F
* Ethiopia: U.S. Foreign Assistance Facts: Archived Issue Brief, Raymond Copson, etc. IB85014
* Ethiopia: War and Famine; Archived Issue Brief, Raymond W. Copson IB90049
* Recent Political Developments in Ethiopia and Somalia, Theodore S. Dagne 91-452 F
* World Bank Activities in Ethiopia, Jonathan E. Sanford 87-857 F

Ethnic Groups

* see Blacks, Minorities

Europe 1992

* see European Economic Community, Western Europe--Integration

European Bank for Reconstruction and Development

* see Foreign Aid--Europe

European Economic Community

* Banking in "Europe 1992", William Jackson 89-456 E
* The "Citrus-Pasta Dispute" Between the United States and the European Community, Donna U. Vogt 7-911 ENR
* The Common Agricultural Policy of the European Community and Implications for U.S Agricultural Trade, Donna U. Vogt, etc. 86-111 ENR
* Energy Conservation Policies of the European Community and United States: Comparing Apples and Oranges, Amy Abel 89-604 ENR
* The Europe 1992 Plan: Science and Technology Issues, Science Policy Research Division 89-178 SPR
* The European Central Banking System and Monetary Union, Walter W. Eubanks 90-42 E
* European Community: Issues Raised by 1992 Integration, Congressional Research Service 89-323 E
* The European Community: Its Structure and Development, Martin E. Elling 88-620 F
* European Community-Japan Trade Relations: A European Perspective, Dick Nanto 86-166 E
* European Community: The 1992 Plan: Info Pack, IP408E
* The European Community: 1992 and Reciprocity, Glennon J. Harrison 89-227 E
* European Community: 1992 Plan for Economic Integration: Issue Brief, Glennon Harrison IB89043
* The European Community's 1992 Plan: An Overview of the Proposed "Single Market", Glennon J. Harrison 88-623 E
* The European Community's 1992 Plan: Bibliography-in-Brief, 1986-1988, Robert Howe 88-754 L
* The European Community's 1992 Plan: Effects on American Direct Investment, James K. Jackson 89-339 E
* The European Community;s 1992 Plan: Selected References, 1989-1991, Robert Howe 91-299 L
* European Community's New Merger Laws: Overview and Implications for U.S. Firms, Gary W. Shorter 91-240 E
* An Explanation of the European Community's Sugar Regime and Comparison to the U.S. Sugar Program, Jasper Womach, etc. 85-77 ENR
* Firewalls or Chinese Walls in European Universal Banking, Law Library of Congress LL89-94
* Products Liability Laws in Selected EEC Countries and Japan, Law Library of Congress LL90-38
* Responses to Changing Europe: Implications for the U.S.; Selected References, Valentin Leskovsek 90-5L
* Tensions in the United States-European Community Agricultural Trade, Donna Vogt, etc. 86-112 ENR
* U.S. Commercial Relations With the European Community, George D. Holliday 85-32 E
* U.S.-European Community Trade Dispute Over Meat Containing Growth Hormones, Donna Vogt 89-6 ENR
* U.S. Wood Exports to Europe and the 1992 EC Economic Integration, Ross W. Gorte 89-580 ENR

Exchange Rates

* see International Finance-Foreign Exchange Rates

Excise Taxes

* see Taxation-Consumption Taxes

Executive Organization

* see Presidential Appointments
* Administering Public Functions at the Margin of Government: The Case of Federal Corporations, Ronald Moe 83-236 GOV
* Amendments to the Prompt Payment Act of 1982: Action in the 100th Congress, Thomas Youth 87-558 GOV
* Analysis of the Office of Science and Technology Policy, Genevieve J. Knezo 88-205 SPR
* Awards of Attorneys' Fees by Federal Courts and Federal Agencies, Henry Cohen 91-584 A
* The Central Intelligence Agency: Organizational History, Mark Lowenthal 78-168 F
* The Chief Financial Officers Act of 1990: An Overview, Virginia A. McMurtry 91-184 GOV
* Chief Financial Officers Act of 1990: House Action on Funding Limitations for FY 1992, Kathy Dolan 91-553 GOV
* Commission on Executive, Legislative, and Judicial Salaries: An Historical Overview, Sharon S. Gressle 88-667 GOV
* Conducting Oversight: Legal, Procedural, and Practical Aspects; Videoprogram, Steven Ross LTR91-918
* Congressional Liaison Offices of Selected Federal Agencies, Office of Special Programs Inquiry Section 91-348 PGM
* The Executive Branch of the U.S. Government, Harold C. Relyea 91-698 GOV
* Executive Perspectives on Oversight: Videoprogram, Eileen Siddman, Charles Bingman, Dwight Ink, Chester Newland, Eleanor Chelimsky LTR91-952
* Extension of the Civil Rights Commission: Archived Issue Brief, Paul Downing IB87166
* The Federal Agency for Education: History and Background Information, Angela Evans 81-93 EPW
* Federal Executive Departments: An Overview, Gary L. Galemore 91-716

Current Events and Homework

GOV
* The Federal Executive Establishment: Evolution and Trends, Ronald Moe 79-255 GOV
* A Guide to Using the Federal Register and the Code of Federal Regulations, Rita Reimer 86-57 A
* How to Follow Current Federal Legislation and Regulation, Carol D. Davis 91-66 C
* Inspectors General: Resources for Oversight; Videoprogram, Thomas Novotny, etc. LTR91-956
* Intelligence Reform: Recent History and Proposals, Alfred B. Prados 88-562 F
* The Iran/Contra Affair: Implications for the National Security Adviser and the NSC Staff; Archived Issue Brief, Joel M. Woldman IB87107
* Managing the Government, Ronald C. Moe 90-629 GOV
* National Economic Commission: Equitable Deficit Reduction; Archived Issue Brief, Barry Molefsky IB88032
* The National Security Council: Organizational History, Mark Lowenthal 78-104 F
* Office of Inspector General in the Central Intelligence Agency: Development and Proposals, Frederick M. Kaiser 89-129 GOV
* OMB and Agency Rulemakings: A Description of the Regulatory Review Process under Executive Orders 12 498 and 12291, Morton Rosenberg 85-728 A
* Planning, Managing, and Funding DOD's Technology Base Programs, Michael E. Davey 89-319 SPR
* Presidential Commissions: Their Purpose and Impact, Stephanie Smith 87-668 GOV
* The President's Cabinet, Ronald Moe 86-982 GOV
* Privatization of the National Technical Information Service, Jane Bortnick, etc. 87-492 SPR
* A Question Period for Congress: Proposals to Bring Cabinet Officials Before the Legislature, Paul S. Rundquist, 91-305 GOV
* Separate But Equal: Two Hundred Years of Legislative-Executive-Judicial Relations; Videoprogram, Louis Fisher, Robert Katzmann, James Buckley LTR91-955
* Social Security: The Independent Agency Question: Issue Brief, David Koitz IB86120
* United States Regulations: Finding Regulatory Material, Mark Gurevitz 90-590 A
* The U.S. Customs Service: Recent Issues and Concerns, Frederick M. Kaiser 91-733 GOV
* U.S. Government: Info Pack, IP162U
* What Would It Mean to Make the Social Security Administration an Independent Entity, David Koitz 89-309 EPW

Executive Organization -- Presidential Appointments

* Cabinet and Other High Level Nominations that Failed to Be Confirmed, 1789-1989, Rogelio Garcia 89-253 GOV
* The Forest Service Budget: Trust Funds and Special Accounts, Ross W. Gorte, etc. 89-75 ENR
* Overview of Senate Action on Presidential Appointments During 100th Congress, Rogelio W. Gorte 88-78 GOV
* Presidential Nominations and Appointments to Full-Time Positions in Executive and Legislative Branches, 1987-1988, Rogelio Garcia 89-55 GOV
* Presidential Nominations and Appointments to Full-Time Positions on Regulatory and Other Collegial Boards and Commissions, Rogelio Garcia 89-401 GOV
* Presidential Nominations to Full-Time Positions in Executive Departments During the the 101st Congress, Rogelio Garcia 91-315 GOV
* Presidential Nominations to Full-Time Positions in Independent and Other Agencies, 101st Congress, Rogelio Garcia 91-236 GOV
* Presidential Nominations to Full-Time Positions on Regulatory Boards and Commission, 1987-1988, Rogelio Garcia 89-64 GOV
* Presidential Nominations to Full-Time Positions on Regulatory and Other Collegial Boards and Commissions, Rogelio Garcia, 91-237 GOV
* Women Nominated and Appointed to Full-Time Civilian Positions by President George Bush, Rogelio Garcia 91-314 GOV
* Women Nominated and Appointed to Full-Time Civilian Positions by President Reagan, Rogelio Garcia 89-236 GOV

Executive Organization -- Reorganization

* A Department of Environmental Protection? Martin R. Lee and Mary E. Tiemann 89-587 ENR
* The Environmental Protection Agency: Cabinet-Level Status? Issue Brief, Mary E. Tiemann and Martin R. Lee IB90069
* Extension of the Civil Rights Commission: Archived Issue Brief, Leslie W. Gladstone IB87166
* Intelligence Reform: Recent History and Proposals, Alfred B. Prados 88-562 F
* Social Security: The Independent Agency Question; Issue Brief, David Koitz IB86120
* What Would It Mean to Make the Social Security Administration an Independent Entity?, David Koitz 89-309 EPW

Export Administration Act

* see Foreign Trade--Export Controls
* Export Control Reform in the 100th Congress: A Comparison of Selected Provisions of H.R. 3 and S. 1409, Glennon Harrison 87-529 E
* Export Controls: Issue Brief, George Holliday, etc. IB87122
* U.S. Export Control Policy and Competitiveness: Proceedings of the CRS Symposium, John P. Hardt, etc. 87-388 S

Export Controls

* see Foreign Trade--East-West, Foreign Trade--Export Controls

Export-Import Bank of the United States

* Export-Import Bank Financial Issues: Archived Issue Brief, James Jackson IB88013
* Export-Import Bank: Financing Problems and Issues, James Jackson 88-61 E

Exports

* see Agriculture--Foreign Trade, Foreign Trade--Export Controls, Foreign Trade--Imports and Exports

Fair Housing Act

* The Fair Housing Act: A Legal Overview, Henry Cohen 89-863 A
* Fair Housing Act Amendments: Archived Issue Brief, Paul Downing IB87116
* Fair Housing Amendments Prohibiting Discrimination Against Families With Children Except in Housing for Older Persons, Henry Cohen 89-111 A
* Segregation and Discrimination in Housing: A Review of Selected Studies and Legislation, Paul Downing, etc. 89-317 GOV

Fair Labor Standards Act

* Computer Service Personnel: Overtime Pay under Section 13 (A) (1) of the Fair Labor Standards Act, William G. Whittaker 91-759 E
* Congressional Employees: Minimum Wages and Overtime Pay, the Fair Labor Standards Act, William G. Whittaker 89-678 E
* The Fair Labor Standards Act Amendments of 1977 (P. L. 95-151): Discussion With Historical Background, William Whittaker, etc. 78-171 E
* The Fair Labor Standards Act: Analysis of Economic Issues in the Debates of 1937-1938, William G. Whittaker 89-568 E
* The Fair Labor Standards Act: Consideration During the 102nd Congress: Issue Brief, William G. Whittaker IB91020
* Fair Labor Standards Act: Treatment of State and Local Government: Archived Issue Brief, Dennis M. Roth, etc. IB85195
* The Federal Minimum Wage: Consideration in the 100th Congress; Archived Issue Brief, William G. Whittaker IB87063
* Minimum Wage Issues: Info Pack IP249M
* Minimum Wage: Selected References, 1978-1987, Felix Chin 87-162 L
* Minimum Wage Standards under the Fair Labor Standards Act: Background Analysis and Recent Legislative Interest, William G. Whittaker 87-111 E
* Sheltered Workshops for Persons With Handicaps: Background Information and Recent Legislative Changes, Mary F. Smith 87-362 EPW
* The Small Business Exemption in the Fair Labor Standards Act: Number of Employees Subject to the 1989 Amendments, Charles V. Ciccone 91-307 E
* A Summary of Selected Regulations of the Fair Labor Standards Act, Charles V. Ciccone 90-499 E

Fairness Doctrine

* see Politics and Elections--Election Law, Telecommunication

Families

* see Child Welfare, Day Care, Domestic Relations
* Analysis of Legal and Constitutional Issues Involved in Surrogate Motherhood, Rita Reimer 88-240 A
* Assistance to Families: A Chart Comparing Some Existing Tax Provisions and Pending Proposals, Marie B. Morris 89-279 A
* Benefits for Former Military Spouses: Info Pack IP313B

Executive Organization / Families

* Child Nutrition Program Information and Data, Jean Yavis Jones 88-248 EPW
* Children, Families, and Domestic Relations: An Alphabetical Microthesaurus of Terms Selected from the Legislative Indexing Vocabulary, Shirley Loo 90-40 L
* The Earned Income Tax Credit, Carmen Solomon 86-1031 EPW
* Elder Abuse: Bibliography-in-Brief, 1980-1988, Edith Sutterlin, etc. 88-221 L
* Fair Housing Amendments Prohibiting Discrimination Against Families With Children Except in Housing for Older Persons, Henry Cohen 89-111 A
* Family and Medical Leave Legislation: Summary Comparison of H.R. 2, S. 5, H.R. 319, S 418, and S. 688, Leslie W. Gladstone 91-434 GOV
* Family Law: Authority of Congress to Legislate on Domestic Relations Questions, Lou Fields, etc. 89-152 A
* Family Leave: Bibliography-in-Brief, 1985-1988, Edith Sutterlin 91-586 L
* The Judicial and Legislative Treatment of Pregnancy: A Review of Developments from Unprotected Status to Anti-Discrimination-Equal Treatment and Speci, Charles Dale, etc. 87-277 A
* Legal Overview of Grandparent Visitation Rights, Gina Marie Stevens, etc., 91-684 A
* Maternity and Parental Leave Policies: A Comparative Analysis, Leslie Gladstone, etc. 85-148 GOV
* Military Benefits for Former Spouses: Legislation and Policy Issues, David Burreli 89-187 F
* Parental leave: Info Pack IP367P
* Parental Leave: Legislation in the 100th Congress; Issue Brief, Leslie Gladstone IB86132
* Social Security: The Economic Well-Being of Social Security Families in 1989, Madeleine T. Smith 91-321 EPW
* Surrogate Mothers: Bibliography-in-Brief, 1985-1988, Edith Sutterlin 88-268 L
* Teenage Pregnancy: Selected Reference, 1986-1988, Peter Giordano 89-119 L

Families -- Child Welfare

* Adolescent Pregnancy: Programs and Issues; Issue Brief, Ruth Ellen Wasem IB91118
* Adoption: Federal Programs and Issues, Dale H. Robinson, 91-131 EPW
* Assistance to Families: A Chart Comparing Some Existing Tax Provisions and Pending Proposals, Marie B. Morris 89-279 A
* Cash Welfare Funds and Homeless Families With Children, Carmen D. Solomon 88-394 EPW
* Child Abuse Act and Related Programs: Reauthorization Issues; Issue Brief, Dale H. Robinson IB91027
* Child Abuse and Neglect: Data and Federal Programs, Dale Robinson 89-127 EPW
* Child Abuse and Neglect in the United States: Legislative Issues: Selected References, 1985-1988, Edith Sutterlin 89-13 L
* Child Abuse: Info Pack IP019C
* Child Health in the Third World: U.S. and International Initiatives: Archived Issue Brief, Lois McHugh IB85189
* Child Nutrition: Expiring Provisions and Prospective Issues in the 102nd Congress, Jean Yarvis Jones, 91-110 EPW
* Child Nutrition: Issues in the 101st Congress; Issue Brief, Jean Yavis Jones IB89048
* Child Nutrition: Program Information, Funding, and Participation, FY1980-FY1990, Jean Yavis Jones 91-681 EPW
* Child Nutrition: 1990 Issues and Legislation; Archived Issue Brief, Jean Yavis Jones IB90115
* Child Pornography: Legal Considerations; Archived Issue Brief, Rita Reimer IB83148
* The Child Support Enforcement Program: Policy and Practice, Carmen D. Solomon 89-659 EPW
* Child Welfare and Foster Care Reform: Issues for Congress; Issue Brief, Karen Spar IB90145
* Child Welfare, Foster Care, and Related Programs under Titles IV-B and IV-E of the Social Security Act, Sharon Stephan 87-324 EPW
* Child Welfare in the 102nd Congress: A Comparison of House and Senate Bills, Karen Spar 91-648 EPW
* Children and Youth Social Service Programs: The Administration's FY 1990 Budget Proposals, Sharon Stephan 89-194 EPW
* The Children of Teenage Mothers, Jeanne E. Griffith 87-94 EPW
* Children With Special Needs: Tax Assistance Proposals; Archived Issue Brief, Louis Alan Talley IB89153
* Commercial Television: Should Children's Television Be Regulated? Bernevia M. McCalip 84-663 E
* Demographic and Social Patterns of Infant Mortality, Jeanne Griffith 86-133 EPW
* Developmentally Delayed Children: Prenatal Factors, Nutritional Needs and Services, Donna V. Porter, etc. 87-516 SPR
* Divorce, Maintenance and Child Support Laws in Australia, Canada, England, and New Zealand, Law Library of Congress, American-British Law Division LL90-65
* Early Childhood Education and Development: Federal Policy Issues; Issue Brief, Wayne Riddle IB88048
* The Earned Income Tax Credit: A Growing Form of Aid to Children, James R. Storey 91-402 EPW
* The Educational Attainment of Select Groups of 'at Risk' Children and Youth, James Stedman 87-290 EPW
* The Family Support Act of 1988: How It Changes the Aid to Families With Dependent Children (AFDC) and Child Support Enforcement Programs, Carmen D. Solomon 88-702 EPW
* Federal Obscenity and Child Pornography Law, Henry Cohen 91-118 A
* Federal Programs Affecting Children, Sharon House, etc. 87-306 EPW
* Federal Programs for Children and Their Families, Sharon L. House 90-131 EPW
* Foster Care and Federal Law: Significant Developments and Continuing Issues, Gina M. Stevens 91-539 A
* Foster Care Protections under Titles IV-B and IV-E of the Social Security Act, Sharon Stephan 88-165 EPW
* Health Care for Children: Federal Programs and Policies, Joseph Cislowski 88-217 EPW
* Hispanic Children in Poverty, Vee Burke, etc. 85-170 EPW
* Infant Formula: National Problems; Archived Mini Brief, Donna Porter MB82244
* Media Entertainment Sex and Violence: Impact on Society, Especially Children, Edith Fairman Cooper 86-925 SPR
* Medicare, Medicaid, and Maternal and Child Health Programs: An Overview of Major Legislation Enacted from 1980 Through 1986, Janet Kline, etc. 87-296 EPW
* Minor Children's Income: Effect of the Tax Reform Act of 1986, Marie B. Morris 87-21 A
* Restrictive Rental Practices and Families With Children, Susan Vanhorenbeck 86-746 E
* Right of Minors to Consent to Medical Care, Rita Ann Reimer 86-939 A
* Spouse Abuse: Background and Federal Programs to Address the Problem, Susan Schillmoeller, etc. 86-1035 EPW
* State Statutes Which Consider Race as a Factor in Foster Care Placements and a List of State Agencies Responsible for Regulating Foster Care, Gloria P. Sugars 91-193 A
* The State's Duty to Child Abuse Victims: DeShaney vs. Winnebago County Department of Social Services, Lou Fields 89-201 A
* Statistical and Program Data on Single-Parent Families with Children, Carmen D. Solomon 86-723 EPW
* Teenage Pregnancy and Childbearing: Incidence Data, Sharon Stephan 87-11 EPW
* Teenage Pregnancy: Issues and Legislation: Issue Brief, Sharon Stephan, etc. IB86128
* Teenage Sexual Activity and Childbearing: An Analysis of the Relationships of Behavior to Family and Personal Background, Jeanne E. Griffith 87-637 EPW
* Teenage Suicide: Bibliography-in-Brief, 1981, 1988, Peter Giordano, etc. 88-652 L
* Young Dependent Tax Credit: Analysis of H.R. 3944 and S. 2187 (100th Congress), Marie Morris 88-383 A
* The Youth Sub-Minimum Wage: Proposals of the 98th Congress, William Whittaker 84-185 E
* Youth Suicide: Sudden Adolescent Death, Edith Fairman Cooper 88-428 SPR

Families -- Day Care

* Background Information on Major Child Care Programs and Legislation under the Jurisdiction of the Committee on Finance, Sharon D. Stephan 89-283 EPW
* Child Care: An Analysis of Major Issues and Policy Options Considered by the 100th Congress, Anne C. Steward 89-47 EPW
* Child Care and Early Childhood Development: The Federal Role; Selected References, Edith Sutterlin 91-521 L
* Child Day Care: Advantages and Disadvantages to Providing Federal Support in the Form of Vouchers, Sharon Stephan 87-766 EPW
* Child Day Care: Archived Issue Brief, Anne Stewart IB89011
* Child Day Care: Federal Policy Issues and Legislation; Archived Issue Brief, Sharon Stephan IB87193
* Child Day Care: Funding Under Selected Programs, Susan Schillmoeller, etc. 88-686-EPW

Be patient. If any phone number is incorrect, call (area code) 555-1212 and request the new listing.

Current Events and Homework

* Child Day Care: Info Pack IP306C
* Child Day Care: Issue Brief, Sharon Stephen IB89011
* Child Day Care: Patterns of Use Among Families With Preschool Children, Thomas Gabe, etc. 88-762 EPW
* Child Day Care: Selected References, 1986-1988, Edith Sutterlin 89-31 L
* Choices in Child Care Act of 1988: Analysis of Title I of H.R. 4768 (100th Congress), Marie Morris 88-477 A
* Church-State and Nondiscrimination Aspects of H.R. 3660, the 'Act for Better Child Care Services of 1988', as Approved by the Home Subcommittee on Hum., David M. Ackerman 88-497 A
* Day Care and the Law of Church and State: Constitutional Mandates and Policy Options David M. Ackerman 89-170 A
* Day Care: Effects of Tax Provisions in Welfare Reform Legislation on Selected Bills in 100th Congress, Marie Morris 89-61 A
* Day Care Services: Current Tax Laws, Marie Morris 87-680 A
* Distributional Effects of Selected Proposals to Modify the Earned Income Tax Credit, Thomas Gabe 89-553 EPW
* Parental Choices in Child Care Act of 1989 S. 392, Marie Morris 89-215 A

Families -- Domestic Relations

* Authority of Congress to Legislate on Family Law Questions, Rita Reimer 86-59 A
* Benefits for Former Military Spouses: Info Pack IP313B
* Child Support: Bibliography-in-Brief, 1984-1988, Edith Sutterlin 88-510 L
* The Child Support Enforcement Amendments of 1984, Margaret Malone 84-796 EPW
* Child Support: Issues and Legislation: Info Pack, Congressional Reference Division IP286C
* Family Law: Authority of Congress to Legislate on Domestic Relations Questions, Lou Fields, etc. 89-152 A
* "Forum Shopping" in Divorce Cases, Rita Reimer 87-728 A
* Interstate Modification of Child Support Orders, Rita Ann Reimer 87-817 A
* Legal Analysis of "The International Child Abduction Act" (S.147 and H.R. 2673, 100th Congress) (Implementing the Hague Convention on the Civil Aspects, Rita Ann Reimer 88-121 A
* The Parental Kidnapping Prevention Act of 1980: Background, Analysis and Subsequent Developments, Rita Ann Reimer 88-294 A
* Possible Federal Enforcement of Interstate Child Visitation Orders, Rita Ann Reimer 87-424 A
* Thompson v. Thompson: Federal Courts Are Not Authorized to Resolve State Custody Disputes Arising under the Parental Kidnapping Prevention Act, Rita Ann Reimer 88-63 A

Family Leave

see Families

Family Planning

* see Birth Control

Famine

* see Disasters, Food Relief

Far East

* see Asia

Farm Credit

* see Agriculture--Farm Income, Farm Credit System (U.S.)

Farm Credit System (U.S.)

* see also Agriculture--Farm Income
* Agricultural Credit: GSE Reform and Other Issues: Archived Issue Brief, Ralph Chite IB89121
* Agricultural Credit: GSE Reform and Other Issues; Issue Brief, Ralph Chite IB91126
* Agriculture: The Farm Financial Situation; Info Pack IP323A
* Farm Credit Overview: Major Legislation of the 99th Congress, Jean Rawson, etc. 87-28 ENR
* Farm Credit System: Legislative Issues: Archived Issue Brief, Remy Jurenas IB87033
* Farm Credit System Loan Restructuring and Foreclosure Policies, Remy Jurenas 88-404 ENR
* Farm Income and Debt: Bibliography-in-Brief, 1988, Rebecca Mazur 88-480 L
* Farmer Mac and the Agricultural Secondary Market, Ralph Chite 89-246 ENR

* Farmers Home Administration: Farm Credit Policies and Issues; Issue Brief, Ralph Chite IB87215
* Farmers Home Administration Provisions in the Agricultural Credit Act of 1987 Jean M. Rawson 88-210 ENR
* Implementation of the Agricultural Credit Act of 1987; Issue Brief, Ralph Chite, etc. IB88089

Farm Income Tax

* see Agriculture--Farm Income, Taxation--Business Taxes

Farm Lands

* see Agriculture--Environmental Aspects

Farm Problems

* see Agriculture

FDIC

* see Federal Deposit Insurance Corporation, Money and Banking--Failures and Deposit Insurance

Federal Advisory Bodies

* see Executive Organization

Federal Aid to Education

* see also Adult and Vocational, Elementary, Secondary, and Higher Education
* Adult Illiteracy: Selected References, Peter Giordano 89-249 L
* Analysis of the Constitutionality of the Administration's Chapter 1 Voucher Proposal under the Establishment of Religion Clause of the First Amendment, David Ackerman 85-1143 A
* Block Grant Funding for Federal Education Programs : Background and Pro and Con Discussions, K. Forbis Jordan 86-992 S
* A Comparison of the Education Provisions in the Omnibus Trade Bill, H.R. 3, as Passed by the House and by the Senate, Paul Irwin, etc. 87-634 EPW
* Department of Education Funding Issues: FY1992; Issue Brief, Angela Evans IB91065
* Department of Education Programs for Science and Mathematics Education: Background, Status, Issues, and Options, K. Forbis Jordan 86-739 S
* Education Block Grant Reauthorization: Selected Options, Paul Irwin 87-494 EPW
* Education: Federal Concerns: Issue Brief, Angela Evans IB87151
* Education Funding Issues for FY 89; Archived Issue Brief, Angela Evans IB88036
* Education Funding Issues for FY 90: Archived Issue Brief, Angela Evans IB89039
* Education Funding Issues for FY1991: Archived Issue Brief, Angela Evans IB90046
* Education: Funding Issues; Info Pack IP199E
* Education Legislation in the 100th Congress: A Brief Summary: Archived Issue Brief, Wava Gregory IB87134
* Education of the Handicapped Act Discretionary Programs; Background and Current Issues, Margaret A. Schenet 89-67 EPW
* Educational Challenges for the Congress: Audio Brief, James Stedman, etc. AB50218
* Educational Challenges of the Congress: Achieving National Education Goals and Reforming Student Assistance; Videoprogram, James B. Stedman, etc. LTR91-880
* Federal Assistance to Libraries Current Program and Issues, Wayne Clifton Riddle 89-197 EPW
* Federal Education Policies and Programs; Selected References, 1987-1988, Peter Giordano 89-12 L
* Federal Education Programs Serving Limited English Proficient Students, Ruby Ann M. Esquibel 89-285 EPW
* Federal Impact Aid and State School Finance Equalization Programs, K. Forbis Jordan 87-589 S
* Federal Programs Affecting Children, Sharon House, etc. 87-306 EPW
* Federal Tax Expenditures Related to Education, Bob Lyke 91-461 EPW
* Foreign Language and International Education: The Federal Role, Wayne Clifton Riddle 89-657 EPW
* Gramm-Rudman-Hollings and Department of Education Programs, Angela Evans 86-544 EPW
* National Education Goals: Major Legislation Considered by the 101st Congress, Wayne Riddle, etc. 90-555 EPW
* Office of Educational Research and Improvement, FY 1992 Budget Request, Paul M. Irwin 91-188 EPW

Families / Federal Election Campaign Act

* State Allotments for Education Programs under H.R. 3, the Omnibus Trade Bill of 1987, as Passed by the House and the Senate, Paul M. Irwin, etc. 87-683 EPW
* State Funding for Education Reform, K. Forbis Jordan 86-735 S
* Summary and Analysis of the Education Amendments of 1984, P.L. 98-511, Angela Giordano-Evans, etc. 84-769 EPW
* Summary of the Adult Education Act, as Amended by the Education Amendments of 1984 (P.L. 98-522), Paul Irwin 84-829 EPW
* Teacher Training and Improvement, FY 88 Budget Proposal; Archived Issue Brief, K. Forbis Jordan IB86047
* U.S. Department of Education: Major Program Trends, Fiscal Years 1980-1991, Paul M. Irwin 91-10 EPW
* Vocational Education and Proposals for Trade Competitiveness, Paul M. Irwin 87-340 EPW
* Vouchers for the Education of Disadvantaged Children; Analysis of the Reagan Administration Proposal, Wayne Riddle 85-1022 EPW

Federal Aid to Education -- Adult and Vocational

* Adult Literacy Issues, Programs, and Options; Issue Brief, Paul Irwin IB85167
* Carl D. Perkins Vocational Education Act: Issues for Reauthorization; Issue Brief, Paul Irwin, etc. IB89069
* Education Provisions of the Trade Act of 1988, P.L. 100-418, Paul Irwin, etc. 88-750 EPW
* Federal Vocational Education Legislation: Recurring Issues During the Last Quarter Century, Richard Apling, etc. 88-704 EPW
* Proprietary Schools, Robert Lyke 91-440 EPW
* Proprietary Schools and Student Financial Aid Programs: Background and Policy Issues, Charlotte J. Fraas 90-427 EPW
* Proprietary Schools: The Regulatory Structure, Margot A. Schenet 90-424 EPW
* Tax Provisions Pertaining to Education in Title IX of the Omnibus Budget Reconciliation Act of 1990, Bob Lyke 90-546 EPW

Federal Aid to Education -- Elementary and Secondary

* Chapter 1 Concentration Grants: An Analysis of the Concept, and Its Embodiment in Federal Elementary and Secondary Education Legislation, Wayne Riddle 88-670 EPW
* Computers in Elementary and Secondary Schools: An Analysis of Recent Congressional Action, James Stedman 88-419 EPW
* Conditional Deregulation of Federal Elementary and Secondary Education Programs: The AMERICA 2000 Proposal, Wayne C. Riddle 91-531 EPW
* Dwight D. Eisenhower Mathematics and Science Education Act: An Analysis of Recent Legislative Action and Program Evaluations, James Stedman 89-24 EPW
* Education for Disadvantaged Children: Major Themes in the 1988 Reauthorization of Chapter 1, Wayne C. Riddle 89-7 EPW
* Education for Disadvantaged Children: Reauthorization Issues; Archived Issue Brief, Wayne Riddle IB87070
* Education of the Handicapped Act Discretionary Programs: Background and Current Issues, Margot A. Schenet 89-67 EPW
* Elementary and Secondary Education; A Summary of the Augustus F. Hawkins-Robert T. Stafford Elementary and Secondary School Improvement Amendments of 1988, P.L. 100-297, Education and Public Welfare Division 88-458 EPW
* Federal Aid to Elementary and Secondary Education : A Side-by-Side Comparison of Current Law with H. R. 5, as Passed by the House of Representatives, Education and Public Welfare Division 88-42 EPW
* Federal Assistance for Elementary and Secondary Education; Background Information on Selected Programs Likely to Be Considered for Reauthorization by Education and Public Welfare Division. Education 87-330 EPW
* Federal Elementary and Secondary Education Programs: Reauthorization Issues: Archived Issue Brief, K. Forbis Jordan IB87055
* High School Dropouts: Current Federal programs, Bob Lyke 90-144 EPW
* The Impact Aid Program under Section 3 of the Public Law 81-874, Richard Apling 91-111 EPW
* The Impact Aid Programs (P.L. 81-874 and P.L. 81-8 15): Modification Resulting from the Augustus F. Hawkins-Robert T. Stafford Elementary and Secondary, Richard N. Apling 88-399 EPW
* Maintenance of Effort Provisions for Major Federal Elementary and Secondary Education Programs, Education and Public Welfare Division 91-172 EPW
* The Neighborhood Schools Improvement Act, H.R. 3320: Summary and Analysis, Wayne Riddle, etc. 91-794 EPW
* Public School Choice: Recent Developments and Analysis of Issues, Wayne

Riddle, etc. 89-219 EPW
* School Assistance for Federally Affected Areas (Impact Aid): Background and Reauthorization Options for P.L. 81-874, K. Forbis Jordan 87-606 S
* Section 2 of P.L. 81-874, Federal Impact Aid to Local School Districts: Background, Funding History, and Recent Regulations, Richard Apling 88-220 EPW
* Summary of the Education of the Handicapped Act Amendments of 1986, P.L. 99-457, Charlotte Jones Fraas 86-926 EPW

Federal Aid to Education -- Higher Education

* Appropriations Enacted for Specific Colleges and Universities by the 96th Through 100th Congress, Susan H. Boren 89-82 EPW
* Christa McAuliffe Fellowship Program: Reauthorization by the 102nd Congress, James B. Stedman 91-388 EPW
* Civil Rights Legislation: Response to Grove City College v. Belt; Archived Issue Brief, Bob Lyke IB87123
* The Guaranteed Student Loan Programs: Current Status and Issues, Charlotte J. Fraas 91-556 EPW
* Guides to Financial Aid for Students: A Checklist, M. Alexandra Salinas 91-601 L
* The Higher Education Act: Authorization and Budget Authority from FY 1987 to FY 1991, Margot A. Schenet 91-127 EPW
* The Higher Education Amendments of 1986 (P.L. 99-498): A Summary of Provisions, Education and Public Welfare Division 87-187 EPW
* Higher Education: Reauthorization of Higher Education Act; Issue Brief, Margot A. Schenet IB90028
* "Nontraditional" Students Attending Postsecondary Institutions, Richard N. Apling 91-484 EPW
* Paul Douglas Teacher Scholarships: Reauthorization Issues for the 102nd Congress, James B. Stedman 91-508 EPW
* The Pell Grant Program: Background and Reauthorization Issues, Susan Boren 91-642 EPW
* Revenue Sources for Higher Education Institutions, K. Forbis Jordan 86-956 S
* Saving for College With Education Savings Bonds, Gerald Mayer 89-207 E
* Student Aid Need Analysis Simplification: Issues and Options, Margot A. Schenet 91-567 EPW
* Student Financial Aid: Authorizations of Appropriations, Budget Requests, Enacted Appropriations and Outlays for Federal Student Financial Aid Programs FY1965 through FY1990, Susan H. Boren 89-184 EPW
* Title III, Higher Education Act: Issues for Reauthorization by the 102nd Congress, James B. Stedman 91-566 EPW
* Title V of the Higher Education Act: Programs for Teachers, James B. Stedman 91-377 EPW
* The U.S. Department of Education's Student Loan Default Reduction Initiative: Background and Analysis, Charlotte J. Fraas 89-454 EPW

Federal Aid to Housing

* see Housing--Assistance

Federal Budget

* see Public Finance

Federal Deposit Insurance Corporation

* see Money and Banking--Failures and Deposit Insurance
* Bank Bailouts: Open-Bank Assistance by the Federal Deposit Insurance Corporation, William Jackson 86-1041 E
* Deposit Taking Institutions: Their Federal Regulatory Structure, F. Jean Wells, etc. 91-286 E
* Depository Financial Institution Failures: The 1980s Experience, Pauline H. Smale 88-549 E
* The Economics of Deposit Insurance, G. Thomas Woodward 89-32 E
* Federal Deposit Insurance Funds: An Overview of FDIC and FLIC Finances, William Jackson 87-2 E
* Federal Deposit Insurance Funds and Regulatory Agencies: Merger and Consolidation Issues, F. Jean Wells 88-279 E
* The Federal Deposit Insurance Funds: Their Financial Condition and Public Policy Proposals in the 100th Congress; Archived Issue Brief, F. Jean Wells IB88082
* Financial Institutions: Problems and Restructuring: A CRS Compilation, Walter Eubanks. 87-586 E
* FIRREA: The Financial Institutions Reform, Recovery, and Enforcement Act of 1989: A Summary, M. Maureen Murphy 89-503 A

Federal Election Campaign Act

* see Politics and Elections--Campaign Funds

Be patient. If any phone number is incorrect, call (area code) 555-1212 and request the new listing.

Current Events and Homework

Federal Employees
* see Government Employees

Federal Employees Health Benefits Program
* see Government Employees--Pay and Benefits

Federal Employees' Retirement System
* see also Pensions--Civil Service
* Federal Employees Retirement System Handbook for Members of Congress; Benefits under the Federal Employees Retirement System, Education and Public Welfare Division 87-189 EPW
* A Retirement Plan for Federal Workers Covered by Social Security: An Analysis of the Federal Employees Retirement System (P.L. 99-335), Education and Public Welfare Division. Civil Service, 86-137 EPW

Federal Food, Drug, and Cosmetic Act
* The Applicability of the Export Proviso of the Federal Food, Drug and Cosmetic Act to "New Drugs", Cathy Gilmore 85-848 A

Federal Home Loan Mortgage Corporation
* Federal Home Loan Mortgage Corporation Preferred Stock Ownership: Lift the Restrictions?: Archived Issue Brief, Barbara L. Miles IB88076

Federal Insecticide, Fungicide, and Rodenticide Act
* see Pesticides

Federal Pay
* see Government Employees--Pay and Benefits

Federal Reserve System
* see Board of Governors of the Federal Reserve System (U.S.), Money and Banking--Monetary Practice

Federal Salary Act
* see Government Employees--Pay and Benefits

Federal Savings and Loan Insurance Corporation
* see also Money and Banking--Failures and Deposit Insurance
* Banks and Thrift Institutions: Restructuring and Solvency Issues, F. Jean Wells 88-749 E
* The Competitive Equality Banking Act of 1987 (P.L. 100-86): Archived Issue Brief, Walter W. Eubanks, etc. IB87187
* Depository Financial Institution Failures: The 1980s Experience, Pauline Smale 88-549 E
* The Economics of Deposit Insurance, G. Thomas Woodward 89-32 E
* Federal Deposit Insurance Funds: An Overview of FDIC and FSLIC Finances, William Jackson 87-2 E
* Federal Deposit Insurance Funds and Regulatory Agencies: Merger and Consolidation Issues, F. Jean Wells 88-279 E
* The Federal Deposit Insurance Funds: Their Financial Condition and Public Policy Proposals in the 100th Congress; Archived Issue Brief, F. Jean Wells IB88082
* Federal Savings and Loan Insurance Corporation: Current Estimates of Future Costs of Resolving "Problem-Institution" Cases, F. Jean Wells 86-728 E
* Federal Savings and Loan Insurance Corporation Recapitalization Act of 1986: A Brief Explanation and Analysis, F. Jean Wells 86-728 E
* Federal Savings and Loan Insurance Corporation: Recapitalization and Alternatives: Archived Issue Brief, F. Jean Wells IB87027
* Federal Savings and Loan Insurance Corporation: Studies for the 101st Congress, F. Jean Wells 88-672 E
* Financial Industry Restructuring: Developments in the 100th Congress; Archived Issue Brief, F. Jean Wells IB87194
* The FSLIC Issue: A Status Report, F. Jean Wells 89-77 E
* FSLIC Policy Options, F. Jean Wells 89-56 E
* FSLIC, the Budget, and the Economy, G. Thomas Woodward 89-17 E
* S&L Problems and FLIC; Info Pack, IP415S

Federal Tort Claims Act
* Federal Tort Claims Act: Current Legislative and Judicial Issues, Henry Cohen 88-168 A
* Liability of Superfund "Response Action Contractors" and EPA for Injury from Contractor-Conducted Cleanups Robert Meltz 89-292 A

Federalism
* see State and Local Government--Intergovernmental Fiscal Relations

Federated States of Micronesia
* Territorial Political Development: An Analysis of Puerto Rico, Northern Mariana Islands, Guam, Virgin Islands, American Samoa, and the Micronesian Com, Bette A. Taylor 88-657 GOV

FERS
* see Federal Employees Retirement System, Pensions--Civil Service

Financial Aid to Students
* see Federal Aid to Education, Higher Education--Student Aid

Financial And Fiscal Affairs
* see Credit, Economic Conditions, Economic Policy, Insurance, International Finance, Money and Banking

Financial Deregulation
* see Corporations--Securities Industry, Money and Banking--Law and Regulation

Financial and Fiscal Affairs
* Bank Failures: Recent Trends and Policy Options, IB86148
* Banks and Thrifts: Restructuring and Solvency, IB89002
* Foreign Banking in the United States, IB87104
* Glass-Steagall Act, IB87061
* Multilateral Development Banks: Issues for the 101st Congress, IB87218

Financial Institutions
* see Money and Banking

Financial Institutions Reform, Recovery and Enforcement Act
* The Community Reinvestment Act After FIRREA, M. Maureen Murphy 91-754 A
* FIRREA: The Financial Institutions Reform, Recovery, and Enforcement Act of 1989: A Summary, M. Maureen Murphy 89-503 A
* Forum: Banks and Thrifts--Restructuring and Solvency, Congressional Research Service REV 10-89
* Housing Finance Restructuring: Changes and New Issues Created by FIRREA (P.L. 101-73), William Jackson, etc. 91-296 E
* Resolution Trust Corporation: Its Organization for Management Decision-Making, F. Jean Wells 91-711 E
* Savings Institutions and Their Regulatory Environment under P.L. 101-73, F. Jean Wells 90-136 E

FIRREA
See Financial Institutions Reform, Recovery, and Enforcement Act, Money and Banking--Failures and Deposit Insurance

Fiscal Policy
* see Public Finance

Fisheries
* Aquaculture: Experience of Major Corporations, Eugene H. Buck 86-963 ENR
* Aquaculture: Status of Technology and Future Prospects; Archived Issue Brief, Eugene Buck, etc. IB83004
* Brief Summaries of Federal Animal Protection Statutes, Henry Cohen 88-541 A
* Costs and Revenues of Foreign Fishing in U.S. Waters, Ross Gorte 84-676 ENR
* Dolphin Protection: A Fact Sheet, Eugene H. Buck 90-587 ENR
* Driftnets: A Controversial Fishing Method, Eugene H. Buck 90-311 ENR
* The European Zebra Mussel, Dreissena Polymorpha, Eugene H. Buck 90-116 ENR
* Federal Agency Programs in Living Aquatic Resources and Aquatic Habitat Protection, Eugene Buck 89-53 ENR
* Fisheries Budgets: Federal Expenditures for Fisheries Programs, and Revenue Collections from Fisheries Interests, Eugene H. Buck, etc. 86-850 ENR
* Fisheries Conservation and Management: The Magnuson Act in the 100th Congress, Eugene Buck 89-65 ENR

* Fisheries Issues in the 101st Congress Commercial, Recreational and Aquaculture,; Issue Brief, Eugene H. Buck IB89041
* Fishery Resource Allocation Conflicts, Eugene Buck 87-182 ENR
* Limited Access for Commercial Fishing: Individual State Programs, Eugene Buck 86-698 ENR
* Magnuson Fishery Conservation and Management Act: Ten-Year Perspective; Archived Issue Brief, Eugene Buck IB86028
* Mandatory Federal Seafood Inspection: An Overview, Geoffrey Becker 83-198 ENR
* The National Marine Fisheries Service Budget: A Guide to Special Accounts, Eugene Buck, etc. 86-894 ENR
* North Pacific Fur Seals: Issues and Options, Eugene Buck 85-654 ENR
* Protecting Endangered and Threatened Sea Turtles, Eugene Buck 87-540 ENR
* Salmon and Smelt on the Pacific Coast: Endangered Species Act Listing Proposals and Issues; Issue Brief, Eugene H. Buck, etc. IB91112
* Status of the U.S Commercial Fishing Industry: Summary of Information, Eugene Buck 88-444 ENR
* Turtle Excluder Devices: Sea Turtles and/or Shrimp?, Eugene H. Buck 90-327 ENR
* Waste from Fish Harvesting and Processing: Growing Environmental Concerns, Eugene H. Buck 90-575 ENR
* Whale Conservation, Eugene Buck, etc. 88-391 ENR

Fisheries -- Law and Legislation

* Corals and Coral Reef Protection, Eugene H. Buck 91-671 ENR
* Endangered Species Act Issues: Issue Brief, M. Lynne Corn IB91086
* Living Aquatic Resource Laws and Treaties: Reference Guide, Eugene H. Buck 89-620 ENR
* Marine Mammal Protection Act Reauthorization: Population-Too Large or Too Small? Issue Brief, Eugene Buck IB88038
* Pacific Salmon and Steelhead: Potential Impacts of Endangered Species Act Listings, Eugene H. Buck, etc, 91-267 ENR
* Zebra Mussel Legislation in the 101st Congress, Eugene H. Buck 90-641 ENR

Flags

* see History (U.S.)

Floods

* See Disasters, Water Resources

Fluoride in Drinking Water

* see Public Health

Food

* see also Food Relief
* Agriculture and Food: An Alphabetical Microthesaurus of Terms Selected form the Legislative Indexing Vocabulary, Shirley Loo 89-512 L
* Antibiotics: Health Implications of Use in Animal Feed; Archived Issue Brief, Sarah Taylor IB85076
* Aquaculture: Experience of Major Corporations, Eugene Buck 86-963 ENR
* Aspartame: An Artificial Sweetener, Donna Porter 84-649 SPR
* Biotechnology: Bibliography-in-Brief, 1985-1988, B.F. Mangan 88-566 L
* The Cost of Our Food, Geoffrey S. Becker 88-761 ENR
* Diet, Nutrition, and Health: Selected References, 1986-1990, Bonnie F. Mangan 90-306 L
* Farm Commodity Promotion Programs, Geoffrey S. Becker 91-151 ENR
* Food and Color Additives: "De Minimis" and, Sara Taylor IB85119
* Low-Calorie Sweeteners: Aspartame, Cyclamate, and Saccharin: Archived Issue Brief, Sarah Taylor IB85119
* A National Nutrition Monitoring System: Background and Legislative Mandate, Donna V. Porter 91-785 SPR
* Native Americans: Nutrition and Diet-Related Diseases, Donna V. Porter 87-246 SPR
* Nonfat Solids Standards for Milk: Proposed Legislative Changes, Ralph M. Chite 91-772 ENR
* The Nutrition Education and Training Programs: Programs Operations and Legislative History, Evelyn Howard 85-753 EPW
* Pesticides in Food: A Checklist of CRS Products, Karen L. Alderson 91-918 L
* Preservation of Food by Irradiation, Donna V. Porter 86-1046 SPR
* Satellite Technology and World Food Security, Marcia S. Smith, etc. 89-566 S
* Selected Reports Available on Food and Agricultural Topics, Environmental and Natural Resources Policy Division 89-244 ENR

* Soviet Agricultural/Food Outlook: 1991/92, Remy Jurenas 91-708 ENR
* Sulfites: Food Preservatives, Donna V. Porter 86-887 SPR
* User Fees-- An Issue for the Meat, Poultry and Egg, Industry, Jean Rawson 85-695 ENR

Food -- Labeling and Safety

* Aflatoxin and Agriculture, Carl Ek 89-525 ENR
* Apple Alarm: Public Concern About Pesticide Residues in Fruits and Vegetables, James V. Aidala 89-166 ENR
* Antibiotics: Health Implications of Use in Animal Feed; Archived Issue Brief, Sarah Taylor IB85076
* Fast Food Restaurant Labeling, Donna V. Porter 87-736 SPR
* Federal Poultry Inspection: A Brief, Geoffrey S. Becker 87-432 ENR
* Food and Color Additives: "De Minimis" and, Sarah E. Taylor 87-678 SPR
* Food and Drug Administration: Selected Funding Data, Donna U. Vogt 91-424 SPR
* Food Labeling: Issue Brief, Donna V. Porter IB80055
* Food Safety: Issues in the 101st Congress; Issue Brief, Donna U. Vogt IB90096
* Food Safety Policy: Selected Scientific and Regulatory Issues; Archived Issue Brief, Sarah Taylor, etc. IB83158
* HACCP (Hazard Analysis and Critical Control Point) in Meat, Poultry, and Seafood Inspection, Geoffrey S. Becker 91-832 ENR
* Import Restrictions on Meat-History and Current Issues, Jean Rawson 85-956 ENR
* L-Tryptophan--Health Problems, Production and Regulatory Status: Proceedings of a CRS Seminar, Donna V. Porter 91-758 SPR
* Labeling of Tropical Oils: Legislation, Health, and Trade Issues, Donna Porter, etc. 87-910 SPR
* Low-Calorie Sweeteners: Aspartame, Cyclamate, and Saccharin; Archived Issue Brief, Sarah Taylor IB85119
* Mandatory Federal Seafood Inspection: An Overview, Geoffrey Becker 83-198 ENR
* Meat and Poultry Inspection: Background and Current Issues, Kellie Dworaczyk 89-448 ENR
* Milk Standards: Grade A vs. Grade B, Ralph M. Chite 91-589 ENR
* National Standards for Organic Food Production and Labeling, Jean M. Rawson 90-244 ENR
* Nutrition Labeling and Education Act of 1990: P.L. 101-535, Donna V. Porter 91-146 SPR
* Nutrition Labeling: Status of Reform Efforts; Proceedings of a Seminar, Donna V. Porter 91-579 SPR
* Pesticide Monitoring Program: Developing New Methods to Detect Pesticide Residues in Food, Sara Taylor 87-413 SPR
* Presicide Policy Issues: Debating FIFRA in the 102nd Congress, Issue Brief, Jasper Womach IB91055
* Regulating U.S. Pesticide Exports: Policy Issues and Proposed Legislation, Jasper Womach 91-568 ENR
* The Safety of Imported Foods, Donna U. Vogt 91-644 SPR
* Seafood Inspection Issues; Archived Issue Brief, Geoffrey Becker IB89126

Food, Agriculture, Conservation, and Trade Act

* Agriculture: The 1990 Farm Bill; Selected References 1989-1991, Lisa B. Dove 91-712 L

Food Labeling

* see Food--Labeling and Safety

Food Relief

* see Domestic, Foreign
* Child Nutrition Program Information and Data, Jean Yavis Jones 88-248 EPW
* Selected Reports Available on Food and Agricultural Topics, Environment and Natural Resources Policy Div. 89-244 ENR

Food Relief -- Domestic

* AFDC, Food Stamps, and Work: History, Rules and Research, Emmett Carson, Etc. 87-599 EPW
* Child Nutrition: Expiring Provisions and Prospective Issues in the 102nd Congress, Jean Yarvis Jones 91-110 EPW
* Child Nutrition: Issues in the 101st Congress; Archived Issue Brief, Jean Yavis Jones IB89048
* Child Nutrition: 1990 Issues and Legislation; Archived Issue Brief, Jean Yavis Jones IB90115
* Chronology and Brief Description of Federal Food Assistance Legislation, 1935-1987, Jean Yavis Jones 88-100 EPW

Current Events and Homework

* Commodity Donations for Domestic Food Programs: Archived Issue Brief, Jean Yavis Jones IB89070
* The Commodity Supplemental Food Program: Program Description and Background Information, Jean Yavis Jones, etc 90-101 EPW
* Domestic Food Assistance: Overview of Programs, Issues and Legislation: Archived Issue Brief, Jean Yavis Jones, etc. IB88059
* Deomstic Food Assistance: 1990 Issues and Legislation; Archived Issue Brief, Jean Yavis Jones, etc IB90072
* Expected Impact of the Drought on Food Prices and Federal Food Aid, Geoffrey S. Becker, etc. 88-633 ENR
* Federal Food Assistance Programs and a Brief Bibliography on Hunger in the United States, Virginia MacEwen, etc. 86-719 L
* Federal Regulation of Foods Sold in Competition With the School Lunch Program, Jean Yavis Jones 91-227 EPW
* Food Stamps in the United States: Bibliography-in-Brief, 1986-1988, Edith Sutterlin 88-424 L
* Food Stamps: 1986 Issues; Archived Issue Brief, Joe Richardson IB86038
* Food Stamps: 1987 Issues; Archived Issue Brief, Joe Richardson IB88045
* How the Food Stamp Program Works: 11th Edition, Joe Richardson 89-196 EPW
* Hunger in Brief: Reports and Proposals for Expanded Federal Efforts, Donna V. Porter, etc. 86-703 SPR
* Older Americans Act Nutrition Program, Carol O'Shaughnessy 90-115 EPW
* The President's FY 1992 Budget and Child Nutrition, Jean Yarvis Jones 91-164 EPW
* Special Supplemental Food Program for Women, Infants, and Children (WIC): Description, History and Data, Jean Yavis Jones 86-794 EPW
* Summary of Reports Concerning Hunger in American, 1983-1986, Donna V. Porter, etc. 86-791 SPR
* Temporary Emergency Food Assistance Program (TEFAP): 1987 Issues; Archived Issue Brief, Jean Jones IB87090
* USDA's Commodity Inventory: Food for the Hungry?, Geoffrey S. Becker 87-880 ENR
* USDA's Section 32 Fund, Geoffrey S. Becker 91-391 ENR
* The WIC Program: Issues in the 102nd Congress; Issue Brief, Jean Yavis Jones IB90097

Food Relief -- Foreign

* African Famine: The Search for Solutions; Issue Brief, Charles E. Hanrahan, etc. IB91082
* The Angola Food Emergency: Extent of the Problem and Current U.S. Emergency Assistance Policy, Alan K. Yu 89-14 F
* Cargo Preference and Agriculture, Carl Ek 89-633 ENR
* The Effectiveness of Food Aid: Implications of Changes in Farm, Food Aid, and Trade Legislation; Proceedings of a CRS Workshop Held on April 25, 1988, Charles E. Hanrahan 88-493 ENR
* Ethiopia: War and Famine; Archived Issue Brief, Raymond W. Copson IB90049
* Ethiopia: U.S. Foreign Assistance Facts: Archived Issue Brief, Raymond Copson, etc. IB85014
* Food for Peace, 1954-1986: Major Changes in Legislation, Susan B. Epstein 87-409 ENR
* Food Production and Food Policy in Subsaharan Africa: A 20 Country Survey, Charles Hanrahan, etc. 85-150 ENR
* Foreign Food Aid: Current Policy Issues, Charles E. Hanrahan, etc. 87-923 ENR
* Foreign Food Aid Programs: Effectiveness Issues: Archived Issue Brief, Charles E. Hanrahan IB88057
* International Fund for Agricultural Development, Susan Epstein 87-4 ENR
* Iraq's Food and Agricultural Situation During the Embargo and the War, Susan B. Epstein 91-199 ENR
* Kurdish Refugee Relief and Other Humanitarian Aid Issues in Iraq: Archived Issue Brief, Lois B. McHugh, etc IB91072
* Monitoring and Forecasting Drought and Famine, Charles E. Hanrahan, etc. 85-1059 ENR
* Soviet Humanitarian Aid: Emergency Health Assistance, Lois McHugh 91-725 F
* U.S. Bilateral and Multilateral Food Assistance Programs, Susan Epstein 85-114 ENR
* The World Embargo on Food Exports to Iraq, Susan B. Epstein 90-462 ENR

Food Safety

* see Food--Labeling and Safety

Food Security Act

* see also Agriculture
* Cargo Preference and Agriculture: Background and Current Issues, Carl Ek 89-633 ENR
* Compliance Provisions for Resource Conservation: A Status Report, Jeffrey Zinn 88-662 ENR
* The Conservation Reserve: A Status Report, Jeffrey Zinn 88-716 ENR
* Dairy Issues: Issue Brief, Jasper Womach IB89063
* The Effectiveness of Food Aid: Implications of Changes in Farm, Food Aid, and Trade Legislation: Proceedings of a CRS Workshop Held on April 25, 1988, Charles E. Hanrahan 88-493 ENR
* Soil and Water Conservation Issues in the 101st Congress: Issue Brief, Jeffrey Zinn IB89080
* The 1990 Farm Bill: Issues Likely to Shape the Policy Debate, Jasper Womach 88-700 ENR
* U.S. Agricultural Policy: Selected Readings, 1987-1990, Ted L. Burch 90-230 L

Food Stamp Plan

* see Food Relief--Domestic

Foreign Aid

* see Africa, Asia, Europe, Latin America, Middle East, Foreign Investments, Foreign Trade, Military Assistance
* Child Health in the Third World: U.S. and International Initiatives; Archived Issue Brief, Lois McHugh IB85189
* Current Issues With the "Base-Rights" Countries and Their Implications, Richard Grimmett 88-726 F
* Defense and Foreign Aid Budget Analysis and the Use of Constant Dollars, Alice C. Maroni, etc. 86-154 F
* Department of Defense Humanitarian Aid, Carol R. Kuntz, etc. 87-808 F
* Development Assistance Policy: A Historical Overview, Theodore W. Galdi 88-285 F
* The Effectiveness of Food Aid: Implications of Changes in Farm, Food Aid, and Trade Legislation; Proceedings of a CRS Workshop Held on April 25, 1988, Charles E. Hanrahan 88-493 ENR
* Environment and Development: U.S. Assistance Programs and Congressional Initiatives, Curt Tarnoff 91-548 F
* The Foreign Affairs Funding Debate in 1987, Larry Q. Nowels 89-154 F
* Foreign Aid--A Policy Overview: Archived Issue Brief, Gary J. Pagiliano, etc. IB87016
* Foreign Aid: Budget, Policy, and Reform; Issue Brief, Larry Q. Nowels IB89014
* Foreign Aid: Info Pack, IP044F
* Foreign Aid: Selected References, Sherry Shapiro 89-403 L
* Foreign Assistance and Defense Transactions and Their Direct Effect on the U.S. Balance of Payments: Summary of Statistical Data, 1960-1987, Vladimir N. Pregelj 90-572 E
* Foreign Assistance Budget and Policy Issues for FY 89: Archived Issue Brief, Larry Q. Nowels IB88056
* Foreign Assistance: Congressional Initiatives to Reform U.S. Foreign Aid in 1989, Larry Q. Nowels 90-236 F
* Foreign Policy Budget: Issues and Priorities for the 1990s; Archived Issue Brief, Larry Q. Nowels, etc. IB90037
* International Narcotics Control and Foreign Assistance Certification: Requirements, Procedures, Timetables and Guidelines, Raphael F. Perl 88-130 F
* International Population and Family Planning Programs: Issues for Congress; Issue Brief, Shirley Kan IB85187
* Migration and Refugee Assistance Budget: Problems and Prospects; Issue Brief, Lois McHugh IB89150
* An Overview of the Economic Support Fund, Larry Q. Nowels 88-284 F
* An Overview of U.S. Foreign Aid Programs, Stanley J. Heginbotham, etc. 88-283 F
* Population Programs of AID: Background of Legislation--99th Congress, Vita Blue 86-109 F
* The Power of the Purse in Foreign Policy: Process and Problems in Congressional Funding, Ellen Colier 85-182 F
* Reforming the Foreign Assistance Programs: Audio Brief, Larry Nowels AB50185
* Tied Aid Credits; Issue Brief, James K. Jackson IB89131
* The World Bank: Eighteen Questions and Answers, Jonathan E. Sanford 86-769 F
* World Bank/IMF Adjustment Loans and the Poor in Developing Countries, Foreign Affairs and National Defense Division 91-176 F
* A World Capital Shortage? Will Increased Demand by Germany, Eastern

Food Relief / Foreign Investments

* U.S. Mexico Economic Relations: An Overview, Lenore Sek 87-485 E
* Caribbean Basin Initiative: Info Pack, IB190C

Foreign Aid -- Middle East

* Arab Economic Aid Donors and Recipients: Trends in Aid Flows to the Middle East/North Africa, 1973-1989, Larry Q. Nowels, etc. 91-476 F
* Egypt: U.S. Foreign Assistance Facts: Archived Issue Brief, Ellen B. Laipson IB85060
* Israel: U.S. Foreign Assistance Facts: Issue Brief, Clyde Mark IB85066
* Israel's Request for U.S. Loan Guarantees; Issue Brief, Larry Q. Nowels, etc. IB91103
* Jordan: Persian Gulf Crisis and U.S. Aid, Alfred B. Prados 91-247 F
* Jordan: U.S. Foreign Assistance Facts; Archived Issue Brief, Richard Preece IB85120
* The Middle East and North Africa: U.S. Foreign Assistance in Fiscal Year 1990, 1991, and 1992, Carmen R. Graham Garland 91-834 F
* U.S. Foreign Assistance to the Middle East and North Africa: Fiscal Years 1988, 1989, and 1990, Clyde R. Mark 89-192 F

Foreign Banks and Banking

* see International Finance--Foreign Banks and Banking

Foreign Competition

* see Foreign Trade--Competitiveness

Foreign Debt

* see International Finance--Foreign Loans

Foreign Direct Investment in the U.S.

* see Foreign Investments

Foreign Exchange Rates

* see International Finance--Foreign Exchange Rate

Foreign Investments

* see also Foreign Aid, Foreign Investments--Japan, Foreign Trade
* American Direct Investment Abroad: Effects on Trade, Jobs, and the Balance of Payments, James K. Jackson 88-546 E
* American Direct Investments Abroad: How Much Are They Worth?, James K. Jackson 88-507 E
* The Citicorp Initiative: A Brave New World for the Third World Debt Problem, Patricia A. Wertman 87-750 E
* Corporate Securities: Laws Enacted in the 101st Congress, Kevin F. Winch 91-179 E
* Employment in the United States: Potential Effects of Changing Foreign Economies; Archived Issue Brief, Charles V. Ciccone IB89129
* European Community: Issues Raised by 1992 Integration, Congressional Research Service 89-323 E
* Federal Taxes and Foreign Investment in U.S. Business: An Assessment, David L. Brumbaugh 91-582 E
* Foreign Banking in America, William Jackson 91-472 E
* Foreign Direct Investments in the United States: Data Collection, Disclosure, and Effects, James K. Jackson 88-79 E
* Foreign Direct Investment in the United States: Issue Brief, James Jackson 87226
* Foreign Direct Investment in the U.S.: A Decade of Growth, James K. Jackson 91-349 E
* Foreign Direct Investment in the U.S.: Identifying the Ultimate Beneficial Owner, James K. Jackson 90-610 E
* Foreign Direct Investment: Shaking Up the Established Order? James K. Jackson 90-588 E
* Foreign Direct Investment: The Economics of National Security Issues; Issue Brief, James K. Jackson IB90143
* Foreign Direct Investment: Why Companies Invest Abroad, James K. Jackson 90-569 E
* The Foreign Investment Conundrum, James K. Jackson 89-58 E
* Foreign Investment: Effects on the U.S. Economy and National Economic Security: Proceedings of a CRS Seminar, Congressional Research Service 90-604 E
* Foreign Investment in the United States: Major Federal Restrictions, Michael V. Seitzinger 88-164 A
* Foreign Investment in U.S. Securities in 1990, James K. Jackson 91-486 E
* Foreign Investment: The Exon-Florio National Security Test, James K. Jackson 90-463 E
* Foreign Investments in the United States: Selected References, 1987-1990,

Europe and the Soviet Union Strain World Capital Markets? Alfred Reifman 91-616 RCO

Foreign Aid -- Africa

* Africa: U.S. Foreign Assistance Issues; Issue Brief, Raymond W. Copson, etc IB91097
* Africandebt: The Official Donor Response and Potential Alternative Strategies, Alan K. Yu 89-228 F
* The Angola Food Emergency: Extent of the Problem and Current U.S. Emergency Assistance Policy, Alan K. Yu 89-14 F
* Angola: Issues for the United States; Archived Issue Brief, Raymond Copson, etc. IB81063
* Ethiopia: U.S. Foreign Assistance Facts; Archived Issue Brief, Raymond Copson, etc. IB85014
* Mozambique: U.S. Foreign Assistance Facts; Issue Brief, Ellen Laipson, etc. IB85065
* Sudan: U.S. Foreign Assistance Facts; Issue Brief, Ellen Laipson, etc IB85065
* U.S. Foreign Assistance to the Middle East and North Africa: Fiscal Years 1988, 1989, and 1990, Clyde R. Mark 89-192 F
* The 99th Congress and the African Economic Crisis, Carol Lancaster 87-914 F

Foreign Aid -- Asia

* Cambodia: U.S. Foreign Assistance Facts; Archived Issue Brief, Robert Sutter IB85153
* China-U.S. Cooperation: Military Sales, Government Programs, Multilateral Aid, and Private Sector Activities, Kerry Dumbaugh, etc 89-355F
* Pakistan Aid Cutoff: U.S. Nonproliferation and Foreign Policy Consideration; Issue Brief, Richard P. Cornin IB90149
* Pakistan: U.S. Foreign Assistance Facts; Archived Issue Brief, Richard P. Cronin IB85112
* Philippines: U.S. Foreign Assistance Facts; Issue Brief, Larry Niksch IB85077

Foreign Aid -- Europe

* Belize: Country Background Report, Mark P. Sullivan 88-568 F
* Eastern Europe: U.S. and International Assistance, Issue Brief, Francis T. Miko, etc IB90089
* European Bank for Reconstruction and Development: An Institution of and for the New Europe, Karen Donfried 91-611 F
* Greece and Turkey: U.S. Foreign Assistance Facts; Issue Brief, Carol Migdalovitz IB86065
* Lend-Lease: An Historic Overview and Repayment Issues, Patricia Wertman 85-844 E
* The Marshall Plan: Design, Accomplishments, and Relevance to the Present, Curt Tarnoff 91-3F
* Soviet Humanitarian Aid: Emergency Health Assistance, Lois McHugh 91-725 F
* U.S. and International Assistance to the Former Soviet Union: Issue Brief, Vita Bite IB91050
* Western Aid Report on the Soviet Economy, John P. Hardt 91-16 RCO

Foreign Aid -- Latin America

* see also Contras
* Central America and U.S. Foreign Assistance: Issues for Congress; Issue Brief, Jonathan Sanford IB84075
* Compilation of Selected Laws Relating to the National Security Council, Arms Transfers, Intelligence, Activities, Aid to the Contras, and Appropriation, American Law Division 86-1028
* El Salvador Aid: Congressional Action, 1981-1986, on President Reagan's Requests for Economic and Military Assistance for El Salvador, Larry K. Storrs 87-230 F
* El Salvador: U.S. Foreign Assistance Facts; Issue Brief, K. Larry Storrs, etc. IB85113
* Guatemala: U.S. Foreign Assistance Facts; Archived Issue Brief, Jonathan Sanford IB85100
* Honduras: U.S. Foreign Assistance Facts; Archived Issue Brief, Robert Sanchez IB85080
* International Commission on Central America: Initial Views; Audio Brief, Larry Storrs AB50176
* Major Trends in U.S. Foreign Assistance to Central America: 1978-1986, Jonathan Sanford 86-88 F
* U.S. Bilateral Economic and Military Assistance to Latin America and the Caribbean: Fiscal Years 1946 to 1987, K. Larry Storrs 87-694 F
* U.S. Foreign Aid to Central America: 1986-1988, Jonathan Sanford 87-465 F

Current Events and Homework

Robert Howe 90-512 L
* Foreign Investments in the United States; Trends and Impact, William Cooper 85-932 E
* Foreign Investments in the U.S.: Bibliography-in-Brief, 1990-1991, Robert Howe 91-656 L
* Foreign Investments in the U.S.; Info Pack, IP398F
* Foreign Mergers and Acquisitions: Non-U.S. Companies Acquiring U.S. Companies, Kevin F. Winch, etc. 87-711 E
* Foreign Ownership of U.S. Assets: Past, Present, and Prospects, James K. Jackson, etc. 88-295 E
* Major Federal Tax Provisions that Directly Affect International Trade and Investment, David Brumbaugh 86-764 E
* Mineral Development in Yugoslavia, Marc Humphries 88-688 ENR
* Offshore Manufacturing by U.S. Corporations; Selected Bibliography, With Introductory Readings, Robert S. Kirk 86-834 L
* PACs Sponsored by Corporations Partly or Wholly Owned by Foreign Investors, Roger Walke, etc 89-618 GOV
* Registering Foreign Investment: Proposed Legislation; Issue Brief, James Jackson IB89-92
* Restrictions on Foreign Ownership of Assets in Various Countries, Law Library of Congress LL89-101
* State Regulation of the Purchase of Real Property by Foreign Citizens, Michael V. Seitzinger 88-451 A
* Statutory Restrictions on Trade and Financial Transactions With the Soviet Union, Jeanne J. Grimmett 91-649 A
* A Survey of U.S. International Economic Policy and Problems, Alfred Reifman 88-666 S
* Tariff Items 807.00 and 806.30 and the Mexican Maquiladoras, Patricia Wertman 87-500 E
* Tax Reform and Foreign Investment by U.S. Firms, David Brumbaugh 87-89 E
* Taxation of Foreign Investments in Selected Countries, Law Library of Congress LL91-5
* Taxation of Overseas Investment Subpart F and the Tax Reform Act of 1986, David Brumbaugh 87-167 E
* The United States as a Debtor Nation and International Capital Flows: Bibliography-in-Brief, 1984-1987, Robert S. Kirk 88-11 L
* Unfair Foreign Trade Practices and Extension of Super 301, Dick K. Nanto 91-546 E
* U.S. Foreign Direct Investment Policy: Response to Foreign Government Barriers and Distortions, Raymond Ahearn 82-20 E
* U.S.-Mexico Economic Relations: An Overview, Lenore Sek 87-485 E
* A World Capital Shortage? Will Increased Demand by Germany, Eastern Europe and the Soviet Union Strain World Capital Markets? Alfred Reifman 91-616 RCO

Foreign Investments -- Japan

* Japan-U.S. Economic Issues: Investment, Saving, Technology and Attitudes, Dick K. Nanto 90-78 E
* Japan-U.S. Relations: Selected References, 1986-1991, Robert S. Kirk 91-162 L
* Japan: Increasing Investment in the United States, James Jackson 89-102 E
* Japanese Acquisitions of U.S. Companies, James K. Jackson 90-4 E
* Japanese Investment in the United States, James K. Jackson 90-13 E
* Japan's Financial Liberalization: Effects on the United States, James Jackson 89-102 E
* Japan's Foreign Investment Laws and the T. Boone Pickens Case, Law Library of Congress LL90-36
* The Semi-Gas Systems Sale: Technology and National Security Issues, Glenn J. McLoughlin 91-263 SPR

Foreign Loans

* see International Finance--Foreign Loans

Foreign Policy and Assistance Programs

* see also Arms Control, Foreign Aid, Foreign Relations, Intelligence Activities, International Agencies, International Law, Military Assistance, National Defense, Terrorism
* AIDS: International Problems and Issues, IB87214
* Angola/Namibia Negotiations, IB89047
* Australia, New Zealand, and the Pacific Islands: Issues for U.S. Policy, IB86158
* Cambodian Crisis: Problems of a Settlement and Policy Dilemmas for the United States, IB89020
* Central America and U.S. Foreign Assistance: Issues for Congress, IB84075
* Central American Peace Prospects: U.S. Interests and Response, IB87200
* China in Crisis: Public Dissent and the Power Struggle, IB89100
* China-U.S. Relations: Issues for Congress, IB84135
* Drug Control: International Policy and Options, IB88093
* El Salvador: U.S. Foreign Assistance Facts, IB85113
* Foreign Aid: Budget, Policy, and Reform, IB89014
* Foreign Food Aid: Reauthorization Issues, IB89097
* Greece and Turkey: U.S. Foreign Assistance Facts, IB86065
* Honduras: U.S. Military Activities, IB84134
* Implementation of the U.S.-Chinese Agreement for Nuclear Cooperation, IB86050
* India and Nuclear Weapons, IB86125
* Iran-Iraq War, IB88060
* Israel and Nuclear Weapons, IB87079
* Israel: U.S. Foreign Assistance Facts, IB85066
* Israeli-American Relations, IB82008
* Japan-U.S. Relations, IB81026
* Korean Political Tensions: Implications for the United States, IB86071
* Lebanon: The Remaining U.S. Hostages, IB85183
* Mexico-U.S. Relations: Issues for Congress, IB86111
* Middle East Peace Proposals, IB82127
* Nicaragua: Conditions and Issues for U.S. Policy, IB82115
* Northern Ireland and the Republic of Ireland: U.S. Foreign Assistance Facts, IB87069
* Nuclear Arms Control: Disposal of Nuclear Warheads, IB88024
* Pakistan and Nuclear Weapons, IB86110
* Pakistan's Nuclear Program: U.S. Foreign Policy Considerations, IB87227
* Palestine and the Palestinians, IB76048
* Panama: U.S. Policy After the May 1989 Elections, IB89106
* Panama's Political Crisis: Prospects and U.S. Policy Concerns, IB87230
* Philippines Under Aquino, IB86104
* Philippines: U.S. Foreign Assistance Facts, IB85077
* POWs and MIAs in Indochina and Korea: Status and Accounting Issues, IB88061
* Sino-Soviet Relations: Recent Improvements and Implications for the United States, IB86138
* South Africa: Recent Developments, IB85213
* South Africa, Nuclear Weapons and the IAEA, IB87199
* South Africa: U.S. Policy After Sanctions, IB87128
* Southern Africa: U.S. Foreign Assistance, IB87152
* Soviet Perestroika: Political and Economic Change Under Gorbachev, IB89038
* Sudan: Foreign Assistance Facts, IB85065
* Taiwan: Recent Developments and their Implications for the United States, IB87092
* U.N. System Funding: Congressional Issues, IB86116
* U.S.-Japan Agreement for Nuclear Cooperation: Monitoring Its Implementation, IB88095
* U.S.-Soviet Relations, IB89008
* Vietnam-U.S. Relations: The Missing-in-Action (MIA) and the Problem of Cambodia, IB87210

Foreign Relations

* see Africa, Asia, Eastern Europe, Foreign Policy, Latin America, Middle East, Pacific Area, Reagan Doctrine, Western Europe, Iran-Contra Affair, Terrorism
* Ambassadorial Appointments: The Congressional Debate Over Qualifications and Implications for U.S. Policy, Warren W. Lenhart 91-385 F
* America in Economic Decline?, Alfred Reifman 89-182 S
* Anti-Terrorism Policy: A Pro-Con Discussion of Retaliation and Deterrence Options, James Wooten, etc. 85-832 F
* Case Studies of Counter-Insurgencies, Larry Niksch 85-60 F
* Chart of Diplomatic and Consular Immunities, Larry Eig 88-183 A
* Congress and Foreign Policy: Selected References, Sherry Shapiro 89-318 L
* Congress and the President in U.S. Foreign Policymaking: A Selected Annotated Bibliography, Sherry B. Shapiro 86-183 L
* Countries of the World: Sources of Information, Margaret E. Melun 91-645 C
* Diplomacy and the U.S. Foreign Service: A Glossary of Basic Terms, Joel M. Woldman 86-159 F
* Diplomatic Security: The Marine Security Guard Program at U.S. Missions Abroad, Joel Woldman 87-602 F
* The Economic Dimension of U.S. Power: Audio Brief, Dick Nanto AB50196
* Embassy Demonstrations in the District of Columbia : An Overview of Boos v. Barry, Larry Eig 88-343 A
* Examples of Treaties Not Ratified Due to Senate Reservations and/or Amendments, David M. Ackerman 87-977 A

Foreign Investments / Foreign Relations

* Foreign Interest Lobbying: Issue Brief, Richard C. Sachs IB91101
* Foreign Policy and International Relations: An Alphabetical Microthesaurus of Terms Selected from the Legislative Indexing Vocabulary, Shirley Loo 86-725 L
* Foreign Policy Debate in America: Three Views for the Post Cold War Era, Robert G. Sutter, etc 91-833 F
* Foreign Policy: Info Pack, IP297F
* Foreign Policy Roles of the President and Congress, Ellen C. Collier 86-163 F

* Human Rights in the U.S. Foreign Relations: Six Key Questions in the Continuing Policy Debate, Vita Blue 81-257 F
* The National Endowment for Democracy: Archived Issue Brief, Joel Woldman IB83107
* National Endowment for Democracy: Issue Brief, Paul Graney, etc. IB90093
* National Power in a Changing World: Audio Brief, Alfred Reifman AB50195
* The Power of the Purse in Foreign Policy: Process and Problems in Congressional Funding, Ellen Collier 85-182 F
* President and Foreign Policy: Selected References, Sherry Shapiro 88-219 L
* Privatization in the Conduct of U.S. Foreign Policy: A Survey of Past and Current Practice, Ellen Collier 88-327 F
* The Rise and Fall of Nations: Is America In Decline? A Bibliography of Points of View, Robert S. Kirk 89-214 L
* Sectional Analysis of the "War Powers Resolution" (WPR) As It Would Be Amended by the "War Powers Amendment of 1988" (S.J. Res. 323, 100th Congress), Raymond J. Celada 88-441 A
* The Security of U.S. Embassies and Other Overseas Civilian Installations, Joel Woldman 85-11 F
* Soviet and American Negotiating Characteristics, Joseph G. Whelan 89-191 S

* Terrorism: U.S. Policy Options; Issue Brief, James Wooten IB81141
* The United States Institute of Peace, Joel Woldman 86-15 F
* U.S. Canada Free Trade Agreement: International Implications, Raymond J. Ahearn, etc. 88-249 F
* U.S. International Broadcasting: An Assessment for Reform, David a. Hennes 91-587 F
* U.S. Presidential National Security Advisers: Changing Roles and Relationships, Joel Woldman 87-334 F
* U.S. Senate Rejection of Treaties: A Brief Survey of Past Instances, Ellen Collier 87-305 F
* War Powers Resolution: Info Pack, IP131 W
* War Powers Resolution: Presidential Compliance; Issue Brief, Ellen Collier IB81050
* War Powers Resolution: The Controversial Act's Search for a Successful Litigation Posture, Raymond J. Celada 88-64 A
* The War Powers Resolution (WPR): Some Implications, of S.J. Res. 323, "War Powers Resolution Amendments of 1988", Raymond J. Celada 88-464 A

Foreign Relations -- Africa

* Angola: Conflict Assessment and U.S. Policy Options, Raymond Copson 86-189 F
* Angola: Issues for the United States; Archived Issue Brief, Raymond Copson, etc. IB81063
* Angola/Namibia Peace Prospects: Background, Current Problems, and Chronology, Raymond W. Copson 88-559 F
* Ethiopia: New Thinking in U.S. Policy, Theodore S. Dagne 91-489 F
* Ethiopia: War and Famine: Archived Issue Brief, Raymond W. Copson IB90049
* Kenya: Political Unrest and U.S. Policy; Issue Brief, Theodore S. Dagne IB90152
* Liberia: Issues for the United States; Issue Brief, Brenda M. Branaman IB91105
* Mozambique: Conflict Assessments/U.S. Policy, Raymond Copson 88-516 F
* Recent Political Developments in Ethiopia and Somalia, Theodore s. Dagne 91-452 F
* Sanctions Against South Africa: Impact on the United States; Issue Brief, William Cooper IB87198
* South Africa: International Sanctions; Archived Issue Brief, Jeanne Affelder, etc. IB86157
* South Africa: Legislation of the 99th Congress, Brenda Branaman 85-799 F
* South Africa: President's Report on Progress Toward Ending Apartheid, Raymond Copson 87-829 F
* South Africa: Recent Developments; Issue Brief, Brenda Branaman, etc. IB85213
* South Africa: Selected References, Sherry Shapiro 89-459 L
* South Africa: U.S. Policy After Sanctions; Issue Brief, Brenda Branaman IB87128

* South Africa: U.S. Policy Debate Over Sanctions and Assistance; Issue Brief, Brenda M. Branaman IB90157
* Southern Africa: U.S. Regional Policy at a Crossroads?, Raymond Copson 85-201 F
* The United States and Southern Africa: A Review of United Nations Resolutions and United States Voting Patterns, 1946-October 1985, Frankie King 86-21 F

Foreign Relations -- Asia

* Afghanistan After Five Years: Status of the Conflict, the Afghan Resistance and the U.S. Role, Richard Cronin 85-20 F
* Afghanistan After the Soviet Withdrawal: Contenders for Power, Richard Cronin 89-146 F
* Afghanistan Peace Talks: An Annotated Chronology and Analysis of the United Nations-Sponsored Negotiations, Richard Cronin 88-149 F
* Afghanistan: U.S. Policy Options; Issue Brief, Kenneth Katzman IB91111
* Cambodia: U.S. Foreign Assistance Facts: Archived Issue Brief, Robert Sutter IB85153
* The Cambodia Crisis: Problems of a Settlement and Policy Dilemmas for the United States: Archived Issue Brief, Robert Sutter IB89020
* China-U.S. Relations: Issues for Congress; Issue Brief, Kerry Dumbaugh IB84135
* China's Future: Archived Issue Brief, Kerry Dumbaugh IB85108
* China's Nuclear Weapons and Arms Control Policies; Implications for the United States, Robert. G. Sutter 88-374 F
* Chinese Foreign Policy in Asia and the Sino-Soviet Summit: Background, Prospects and Implications for U.S. Policy, Robert G. Sutter 89-298 F
* Chinese Leadership Changes: Implications for the United States, Charles F. Steffens 86-131 F
* FSX Fighter Agreement With Japan: Archived Issue Brief, Richard F. Grimmett, etc. IB89060
* The Gandhi Assassination: Implications for India and U.S. Indian Relations, Richard Cronin 84-790 F
* Hong Kong-U.S. Economic Relations: Some Views from Hong Kong's Economic Elite, Kerry Dumbaugh 89-23 F
* India: The Assasination of Rajiv Gandhi and Implications for U.S. Interests, Richard P. Cronin, etc 91-441 F
* Japan-U.S. Relations: A Briefing Book, Congressional Research Service 91-401 F
* Japan-U.S. Relations: Archived Issue Brief, Robert Sutter IB81026
* Japan-U.S. Relations in the 1990s, Larry Niksch 89-264 F
* Japan-U.S. Relations: Issues for Congress, Issue Brief, Robert G. Sutter IB89133
* Japan-U.S. Relations: Selected References, 1986-1991, Robert S. Kirk 91-162 L
* Japanese Government Cooperation With the United States--U.S. Officials' Perspectives, Robert G. Sutter 90-435 F
* Korea and Congress, 1950-1990, Kerry Dumbaugh 85-171 F
* Korea-U.S. Relations: Issues for Congress; Issue Brief, Robert G. Sutter IB89136
* Korean Political Tensions: Implications for the United States; Archived Issue Brief, Robert Sutter IB86071
* Lobbying by Foreign Interests, Richard C. Sachs 91-318 GOV
* The Missing-In-Action (MIAs) and Vietnam-U.S. Relations: Issues for the United States, Robert Sutter 87-655 F
* Pakistan After Zia: Implications for Pakistan and U.S. Interest; Archived Issue Brief, Richard P. Cronin IB88096
* The Rajiv Gandhi Visit: Issues in the U.S.-India Relations, Richard Cronin 85-838 F
* Singapore-U.S. Economic Relations: Some Views From Singapore's Economic Elite, Richard Cronin 89-49 F
* South Korea and the United States: The Changing Relationship, Larry Niksch 87-522 F
* Sri Lanka's Gamble for Ethnic Peace: Archived Issue Brief, Stanley J. Heginbotham IB87183
* Taiwan: Recent Developments and Their Implications for the United States Issue Brief, Robert G. Sutter IB87092
* Taiwan's Elections: Implications for Taiwan;s Development and U.S. Interests, Robert G. Sutter 90-11 F
* Thai-U.S. Economic Relations: Some Views of Thailand's Economic Elite, Raymond J. Ahearn 89-60 F
* The United States, Pakistan, the Soviet Threat to Southern Asia: Options for Congress, Richard Cronin 85-152 F
* United States Policy Toward Vietnam: A Summary Review of Its History, Larry Niksch, etc. 85-16 F
* The U.S. China Agreement for Nuclear Cooperation: Congressional Review; Archived Issue Brief, Mark Martel, etc. IB85203

Current Events and Homework

* U.S.-Japan Agreement for Nuclear Cooperation: Monitoring Its Implementation; Archived Issue Brief, Warren H. Donnelly IB88095
* Vietnam in Transition: Implications for U.S. Policy, Robert G. Sutter 89-177 F
* Vietnam: Procedural and Jurisdictional Questions Regarding Possible Normalization of U.S. Diplomatic and Economic Relations, Alan K. Yu, etc 89-631 F
* Vietnam-U.S. Relations: The Debate Over Normalization; Issue Brief, Robert G. Sutter IB87210
* Vietnam-U.S. Relations: The Missing-in-Action (MIAs) and the Impasse Over Cambodia: Issue Brief, Robert G. Sutter IB87210
* Visit to South Korea and Taiwan, September 11-24, 1988 Trip Report, Larry Niksch 88-740 F

Foreign Relations -- Eastern Europe

* A Changing Europe and U.S. Interests; Issue Brief, Stanley R. Sloan IB90062
* Andropov and Reagan as Negotiators: Contexts and Styles in Contrast, Joseph Whelan 83-141 S
* Arms Control: Negotiations to Reduce INF Weapons; Archived Issue Brief, Paul Gallis IB856054
* Congress and the Transformation of Eastern Europe in 1989, Francis T. Miko 90-503 F
* Continuity and Change in Soviet Diplomacy and Negotiations under Gorbachev, Joseph G. Whelan 89-39 F
* East European Trends and U.S. Policy; Issue Brief, Francis T. Miko IB89138
* Embassy Construction Controversies: Moscow and Washington; Issue Brief, Joel Woldman IB87232
* Gorbachev Reform Program After the 1988 Party Conference; Summary of a Roundtable Workshop, Francis T. Miko 89-130 F
* The Gorbachev Speech to the United Nations, New York, Dec. 7, 1988, Foreign Affairs and National Defense Division 88-776 F
* Gorbachev's World View: May 1990; Audio Brief, Joseph Whelan AB50223
* Gorbachev's Worldview under Siege: Perestroika at Risk, June 1990-June 1991, Joseph G. Whelan 91-632 RCO
* The Growing Role of Congress in the Soviet Diplomacy and Negotiations, Joseph G. Whelan 88-714 S
* Implications for U.S. Diplomacy in the U.S. Soviet Future: Audio Brief, Joseph Whelan AB50173
* The Moscow Summit at First Glance: Audio Brief, Stuart Goldman, etc. AB50168
* Nuclear Risk Reduction Centers; Archived Issue Brief, Steven Hildreth IB86142
* Responses to Changing Europe: Implications for the U.S.; Selected References, Valentin Leskovsek 90-5 L
* The Resumption of U.S.-Soviet Nuclear Arms Control Talks: The Soviet Point of View, Jeanette Voas 85-605 S
* The Role of Congress in Soviet Diplomacy and Negotiations: Audio Brief, Joseph Whelan AB50175
* Soviet and American Negotiating Characteristics, Joseph G. Whelan 89-191 S
* Soviet-American Relations in 1977: A Chronological Summary and Brief Analysis, William Cooper 79-60 S
* Soviet Coup Attempt: Background and Implications; Archived Issue Brief, Raymond W. Copson IB91106
* Soviet Diplomacy and Negotiating Behavior, 1979-1988: Implications for U.S. Diplomacy in the Soviet-American Future, Joseph G. Whelan 88-674 F
* Soviet-U.S. Relations: A Briefing Book, Congressional Research Service 89-342 F
* Soviet-U.S. Relations: The Lessons of Past Summit Meetings, Francis T. Miko, etc. 85-1037 F
* Soviet-U.S. Summit Meetings Since the 1950s: Selected References, Sherry Shapiro 87-912 L
* Thirty Years of U.S.-Soviet Summit Meetings; A Capsule Summary, Stuart Goldman 85-1055 F
* United States and New Europe: Strategy for the Future, Stanley R. Sloan 90-245 S
* U.S. Embassy in Moscow: Options for Congress; Issue Brief, David Hennes IB90141
* U.S. Soviet Maritime Boundary Agreement, Stuart D. Goldman 91-443 F
* U.S.-Soviet Relations in a Period of Summitry: Archived Issue Brief, Stuart Goldman IB83066
* U.S.-Soviet Relations in the Gorbachev Era: Selected References, Robert S. Kirk 89-51 L
* U.S.-Soviet Relations: Info Pack, IP233U
* U.S.-Soviet Relations: Selected References, 1986-1988, Elizabeth S. Lane

88-155 L
* Yugoslavia's Kosovo Crisis: Ethnic Conflict Between Albanians and Serbs, Steven J. Woehrel 89-603 F
* The 1987 Reagan-Gorbachev Summit Agenda, Francis T. Miko 87-925 F

Foreign Relations -- Foreign Policy

Bipartisan Foreign Policy and Policymaking Since World War II, Ellen C. Collier 89-612 F
* Congress and Foreign Policy: Selected References, Sherry B. Shapiro 91-222 L
* Congress and Foreign Policymaking, Ellen Collier 90-627 F
* Diplomacy and the U.S. Foreign Service: A Glossary of Basic Terms, Joel M. Woldman 86-159 F
* The Environment as a Foreign Policy Issue: Issue Brief, Curt Tarnoff IB89151
* Foreign Policy Budget: Issues and Priorities for the 1990s; Archived Issue Brief, Larry Q. Nowels, etc IB90037
* Foreign Policy Budget: Priorities for the 102nd Congress; Issue Brief, Larry Q. Nowels, etc IB91014
* Foreign Policy: Info Pack IP297F
* Foreign Policy Roles of the President and Congress, Ellen C. Collier 86-163 F
* Maintaining U.S. Influence in a Changing World: Audio Brief, Stan Sloan AB50197
* National Emergency Powers, Harold C. Relyea 91-383 GOV
* President and Foreign Policy: Selected References, Sherry B. Shapiro 91-157 L
* Searching for Post-Cold War Foreign Policy Budget Priorities, Ellen Collier 91-824 F
* U.S. Presidential National Security Advisers: Changing Roles and Relationships, Joel M. Woldman 87-334 F
* The U.S. Role in a New World Order: Prospects for George Bush's Global Vision, Stanley R. Sloan 91-294 RCO
* War Powers Resolution: Info Pack IP131W
* War Powers Resolution: Presidential Compliance; Issue Brief, Ellen Collier IB81050
* War Powers Resolution: The Controversial Act's Search for a Successful Litigation Posture, Raymond J. Celada 88-64 A

Foreign Relations -- Latin America

* Arms Shipments to Iran: Archived Issue Brief, Richard M. Preece IB87022
* Belize: Country Background Report, Mark P. Sullivan 88-568 F
* The Boland Amendments: A Chronology of Congressional Action, Joseph Maheady 87-833 A
* Central America, Selected References, 1985-1988, Valentin Leskovsek 89-28 L
* Central America: U.S. Relations With Costa Rica, Guatemala, and Honduras: Info Pack, IP352C
* Central American Compliance With the August 5, 1987 Peace Agreement as of November 5, 1987, Nina M. Serafino 87-916 F
* The Central American Peace Prospects: U.S. Interests and Response: Issue Brief, Nina M. Serafino IB87200
* Chart of Unclassified Legislative Restrictions Regarding Support for Military or Paramilitary Operations in Nicaragua, 1982-1986, Larry Eig 87-222 A
* Compilation of Selected Laws Relating to the National Security Council, Arms Transfers, Intelligence Activities, Aid to the Contras, and Appropriations, American Law Division 86-1028 A
* Congress and Policy Toward Central America in 1989, Mark P. Sullivan, etc. 90-347 F
* Congress and U.S. Policy Toward Nicaragua in 1987, Linda Robinson 89-158 F
* Contra Aid: Analysis of Whether the National Security Council (NSC) and the NSC Staff are an 'Agency, or Entity Involved in Intelligence Activities' co, Larry E. Eig 87-566 A
* Contra Aid, FT82-FY88: Summary and Chronology of Major Congressional Action on Key Legislation Concerning U.S. Aid to the Anti-Sandinista Guerrillas, Nina M. Serafino 88-563 F
* Costa Rica: Country Background Report, Nina M. Serafino 88-577 F
* Drugs and Latin America: Audio Brief, Raphael Perl AB50194
* El Salvador Aid: Congressional Action, 1981-1986, on President Reagan's Requests for Economic and Military Assistance for El Salvador, K. Larry Storrs 87-230 F
* El Salvador: Bibliography-in-Brief, 1987-1989, Robert S. Kirk 90-14 L
* El Salvador Highlights, 1960-1990: A Summary of Major Turning Points in Salvadoran History and U.S. Policy, K. Larry Storrs 90-149 F

Foreign Relations / Western Europe

* El Salvador: Info Pack, IP121E
* El Salvador: Status of the War and the Role of U.S. Aid, James P. Wootten 90-193 F
* El Salvador under Cristiani: U.S. Foreign Assistance Decisions; Issue Brief, K. Larry Storrs IB89122
* El Salvador: U.S. Aid in 1987 and 1988; Archived Issue Brief, K. Larry Storrs IB85113
* El Salvador: U.S. Foreign Assistance Facts: Issue Brief, K. Larry Storrs, etc. IB85113
* Grenada: Issues Concerning the Use of U.S. Forces;, Archived Issue Brief, Janice Hanover IB83170
* Guatemala: Country Background Report, Maureen Taft-Morales 88-586 F
* Iran Arms Sales and Contra Funds: Summaries of Key Legislative Provisions, Clyde R. Mark, etc. 87-13 F
* Kissinger Commission Implementation: Action by the Congress Through 1986 on the Recommendations of the National Bipartisan Commission on Central America, K. Larry Storrs 87-291 F
* Mexico-U.S. Relations: Issues for Congress; Issue Brief, K. Larry Storrs, etc. IB86111
* The Monroe Doctrine and U.S. Policy Options for the Western Hemisphere, Raphael Perl 84-225 F
* Narcotics Control and the Use of U.S. Military Personnel: Operations in Bolivia and Issues for Congress, Raphael Perl 86-800 F
* Nicaragua: An Overview of U.S. Policy, 1979-1986, Mark P. Sullivan 87-855 F
* Nicaragua: Bibliography-in-Brief, 1986-1987, Valentin Leskovsek 87-382 L
* Nicaragua: Conditions and Issues for U.S. Policy: Issue Brief, Nina Serafino IB82115
* Nicaragua v. United States: The International Court of Justice Decision, David Hill Zafren 86-748 A
* Nicaraguan Elections and Transition: Issues for U.S. Policy, Nina M. Serafino 90-187 F
* Panama: Bibliography-in-Brief, Robert S. Kirk 90-12 L
* Panama: Trade, Finance, and Proposed Economic Sanctions, Glennon J. Harrison 88-188 E
* Panama: U.S. Policy After the May 1989 Elections; Archived Issue Brief, Mark P. Sullivan IB89106
* Panama's Political Crisis: Prospects and U.S. Policy Concerns: Issue Brief, Mark P. Sullivan IB87230
* Panama-U.S. Relations: Issue for Congress; Issue Brief, Mark P. Sullivan IB90044
* Peru: Country Background Report, Maureen Taft-Morales 90-247 F
* The Reagan Doctrine: U.S. Assistance to Anti-Marxist Guerrillas: Archived Issue Brief, Raymond W. Copson IB87005
* A Summary and Analysis of the Report of the National Bipartisan "Kissinger" Commission on Central America, January 1984, Richard Cronin, etc. 84-39 F
* The United States and Cuba During the Carter Administration, Margaret Siliciano, etc 85-988 F
* The United States and Cuba During the Reagan Administration, Margaret Siliciano, etc. 85-988 F
* The United States and Cuba During the Reagan Administration, Judith Levenfeld, etc. 85-989 F
* U.S. Assistance to Nicaraguan Guerrillas: Issues for the Congress; Archived Issue Brief, Nina Serafino IB84139
* U.S. Sanctions and the State of the Panamanian Economy, Mark Sullivan 88-578 F

Foreign Relations -- Middle East

see also Iraq-Kuwait Crisis

* Arms Shipments to Iran: Archived Issue Brief, Richard M. Preece IB87022
* Compilation of Selected Laws Relating to the National Security Council, Arms Transfers, Intelligence, Activities, Aid to the Contras, and Appropriation, American Law Division 86-1028 A
* Congress and the Iran-Contra Affair, Joel M. Woldman 88-765 F
* Egypt's New Foreign Policy Activism: Considerations for the United States, Ellen Laipson 90-188 F
* Insuring U.S.Interests in the Persian Gulf: Summary and Proceedings of the Workshop Held on October 6, 1987, Congressional Research Service, Gary Pagliano 88-725 F
* Iran After Khomeini: Implications for U.S.-Iranian Relations, Alfred B. Prados 90-132 F
* Iran Arms and Contra Funds: Selected Chronology of Events, 1979-1987, Richard Preece, etc. 86-190 F
* Iran Arms Sales and Contra Funds: Summaries of Key Legislative Provisions, Clyde R. Mark, etc. 87-13 F
* The Iran/Contra Affair: Implications for the National Security Adviser and the NSC Staff; Archived Issue Brief, Joel Woldman IB87107
* Iran-Contra Affair: Organization Profiles, Heather B. Longton 87-625 F
* Iran-Contra Affair: Status of the Recommendations Contained in the Joint Report of the House and Senate Selected Committees, Clyde R. Mark 88-324 F
* Iran-Iraq War: Issue Brief, Richard Preece IB88060
* Israeli-American Relations: Issue Brief, Ellen B. Laipson IB82008
* Israeli-Palestinian Conflict: Bibliography-in-Brief, 1982-1988, Robert Kirk 88-251 L
* Israel's Interest in Nuclear Power: Implications for U.S. Non-Proliferation Policy: Archived Issue Brief, Mark Martel, etc. IB85166
* Israel's Participation in the International Atomic, Energy Agency and the 32nd IAEA General Conference: Archived Issue Brief, Warren Donnelly IB88072
* Issues in the Middle East: Audio Brief, Clyde Mark, etc. AB50177
* Laws Implicated by Shipments of Military Materials to Iran, Raymond J. Celada 86-1005 A
* Lebanon: The Remaining U.S Hostages; Issue Brief, Clyde Mark IB85183
* Libya: U.S. Relations: Archived Issue Brief, Raymond Copson, etc. IB86040
* Middle East Peace Proposals: Issue Brief, Clyde Mark IB82127
* Palestine Liberation Organization Offices in the United States, Clyde Mark IB87207
* Persian Gulf: Iran Air Flight 655: Archived Issue Brief, Ellen Laipson IB88080
* Persian Gulf: Post-War Issues; Info Pack IP452P
* The Persian Gulf War: Preliminary Foreign Policy "Lessons" and Perceptions, Mark M. Lowenthal 91-260 RCP
* Persian Gulf: Selected References, Sherry Shapiro 88-533 L
* Persian Gulf: U.S. Military Operations; Archived Issue Brief, Ronald O'Rourke IB87145
* Saudi Arabia: U.S. Missile Sale, 1986; Archived Issue Brief, Clyde Mark IB86068
* Soviet Policy Toward Iran and the Strategic Balance in Southwest Asia, Stuart Goldman 87-592 F
* United States Interests in Lebanon, John Creed 85-873 F
* United States-Iraqi Relations, Richard Preece 86-142 F
* U.S. Policy Toward Iran: 1979-1986, Richard M. Preece 87-974 F

Foreign Relations -- Pacific Area

* Australia, New Zealand, and the Pacific Islands: Issues for U.S. Policy; Issue Brief, Robert G. Sutter IB86158
* Oceania and the United States: A Primer, Robert Sutter 85-218 F
* Pacific Rim Initiatives; a CRS Trade Team Product 89-405 D
* Palau's Evolving Relationship With the United States: Introduction and Chronology of Developments, Luella S. Christopher 88-442 F
* Philippine Bases Negotiations: Archived Issue Brief, Larry A. Niksch IB90142

Foreign Relations -- Reagandoctrine

* Angola: Issues for the United States; Archived Issue Brief, Raymond Copson, etc. IB81063
* Cambodia: U.S. Foreign Assistance Facts; Archived Issue Brief, Robert Sutter IB85153
* Mozambique: U.S. Foreign Assistance Facts; Archived Issue Brief, Raymond Copson IB85114
* Reagandoctrine: Selected References, 1979-1988, Sherry Shapiro 88-395 L
* The Reagandoctrine: U.S. Assistance to Anti-Marxist Guerrillas; Archived Issue Brief, Raymond W. Copson IB87005

Foreign Relations -- Western Europe

* Cyprus: Status of U.N. Negotiations; Issue Brief, Ellen B. Laipson IB89140
* European Community: Issues Raised by 1992 Integration, Congressional Research Service 89-323 E
* The European Community: Its Structure and Development, Martin E. Elling 88-620 F
* European-U.S. Affairs: Responding to a Changing Relationship; Issue Brief, Karen E. Donfried, etc. IB89127
* German Foreign Policy After the Gulf War: Implications for U.S. Interests, Paul E. Gallis 91-451 F
* Germany's Future and U.S. Interests: Archived Issue Brief, Paul E. Gallis, etc. IB90006
* Greek-Turkish Relations: Beginning of a New Era?, Ellen Laipson 88-724 F
* The INF Treaty and Its Political-Military Implications for Western Europe, Hugh DeSantis 88-57 F
* NATO: Conventional Arms Control and Related Political Issues; Info Pack IP425N

Current Events and Homework

* The Netherlands Elections and the Cruise Missile Issue: Implications for the United States and for NATO, Paul Gallis 86-27 F
* Soviet Policy in Nordic Europe: New Focus on the Forgotten Flank?, Francis Miko 85-33 F
* The Strategic Defense Initiative and United States, Alliance Strategy, Paul Gallis, etc. 85-48 F
* United States Military Installations in Spain, Richard Grimmett 84-149 F
* The U.S. Commitment to Europe's Defense: A Review of Cost Issues and Estimates, Alice Maroni, etc. 85-211 F

Foreign Service (U.S. State Dept.)

* see Foreign Relations

Foreign Trade

* see Competitiveness, East-West, Export Controls, Imports and Exports, Sanctions, Trade Agreements and Negotiations, Trade Policy, Agriculture-Foreign Trade, Foreign Aid, Foreign Investments
* America in Economic Decline?, Alfred Reifman 89-182 S
* Americandirect Investment Abroad: Effects on Trade, Jobs, and the Balance of Payments, James K. Jackson 88-546 E
* American Direct Investments Abroad: How Much are They Worth?, James K. Jackson 88-507 E
* Chronology of Important Events in International Economics, George Holliday 85-512 E
* The Economic Dimension of U.S. Power; Audio Brief, Dick Nanto AB50196
* Environmental Legislation and Trade: A Checklist of CRS Products, Ted L. Burch 92-7L
* The European Community: 1992 and Reciprocity, Glennon J. Harrison 89-227 E
* The European Community's 1992 Plan: Selected References, 1989-1991, Robert Howe 91-299 L
* Foreign Assistance and Defense Transactions and Their Direct Effect on the U.S. Balance of Payments:, Summary of Statistical Data, 1960-1987, Vladimir N. Pregelj 88-545 E
* Foreign Interest Lobbying: Issue Brief, Richard C. Sachs IB91101
* Japan-U.S. Relations: A Briefing Book, Congressional Research Service 91-401 F
* Japan-U.S. Relations: Selected References, 1986-1991, Robert s. Kirk 91-162 L
* Japanese Lobbying and U.S. Automobile Policy, Dick K. Nanto 91-186 E
* Japan's Industrial Groups: The Keiretsu, Dick K. Nanto 90-609 E
* Kuwait Reconstruction: Sources of Information; Info Pack, Congressional Reference Division IP450K
* National Power in a Changing World, Audio Brief, Alfred Reifman AB50195
* Selected Reports Available on Food and Agricultural Topics, Environment and Natural Resources Policy Division 89-244 ENR
* Trade and International Finance: An Alphabetical Microthesaurus of Terms Selected from the Legislative Indexing Vocabulary, Shirley Loo 89-653 L
* Trade: Issue Brief, George Holliday, etc. IB91015
* Trade Topics: Summaries of Selected CRS Products, 1989-1990, Robert Howe 90-554 L
* The United States as a Debtor Nation and International Capital Flows: Bibliography-in-Brief, 1984-1987, Robert Kirk 88-11 L
* U.S. Metric Conversion, Edith Fairman Cooper 91-83 SPR
* Will the Export Enhancement Program Survive?, Susan B. Epstein 89-139 ENR

Foreign Trade -- Competitiveness

* America in Economic Decline?, Alfred Reifman89-182 S
* The American Response to Foreign Competition: Audio Brief, Mary Jane Bolle, etc. AB50180
* Automation and Small Business: Technological Development and the Competitiveness of U.S. Industry, Wendy Schacht, etc. 88-300 SPR
* Balancing the National Interest: U.S. National Security Export Controls and Global Economic Competition: A Summary of the National Academy of Sciences, John P. Hardt, etc. 87-119 S
* Commercialization of Technology and Issues in the Competitiveness of Selected U.S. Industries: Semiconductors, Biotechnology, and Superconductors, Leonard G. Kruger, etc. 88-486 SPR
* A Comparison of the Education Provisions in the Omnibus Trade Bill, H.R. 3, as Passed by the House and by the Senate, Paul Irwin, etc. 87-634 EPW
* Competitiveness: Current Issues and Proposals; Info Pack, IP368C
* Cooperative R&D: Federal Efforts to Promote Industrial Competitiveness: Issue Brief, Wendy Schacht IB89056
* Corporate Tax Reform and International Competitiveness, Jane Gravelle 86-42 E
* Education Proposals in Trade Competitiveness Legislation: Archived Issue Brief, K. Forbis Jordan, etc. IB87108
* Education Provisions of the Trade Act of 1988, P.L. 100-418, Paul Irwin, etc. 88-750 EPW
* Employment in the United States: Potential Effects of Changing Foreign Economies; Archived Issue Brief, Charles V. Ciccone IB89129
* The Export Enhancement Program One Year later, Susan Epstein 86-695 ENR
* Foreign Trade and U.S. Employment: Bibliography-in -Brief, 1983-1987, Robert Kirk 87-344 L
* High-Technology Trade: Bibliography-in-Brief, 1985-1988, Robert Kirk 88-572 L
* International Competitiveness and the Tax Reform Act of 1986, Jane Gravelle 87-428 E
* Japan: Resale Price Maintenance, Dick K. Nanto 91-289 E
* Japan's Steel Industry: Positioning for Survival, James K. Jackson 88-346 E
* Japan-U.S. Trade and Economic Relations: Bibliography-in-Brief, 1990-1991, Robert Howe 91-655 L
* Japanese Companies and Technology: Lessons to Learn?, Wendy H. Schacht 91-375 SPR
* Machine Tools: Imports and the U.S. Industry, Economy and Defense Industrial Base, Gary Guenther 86-762 E
* Maintaining U.S. Influence in a Changing World; Audio Brief, Stan Sloan AB50197
* Major Federal Tax Provisions that Directly Affect International Trade and Investment, David Brumbaugh 86-764 E
* The Omnibus Trade and Competitiveness Act of 1988 (P.L. 100-418); An Analysis of the Major Trade Provisions, Economics Division 88-390 E
* The Omnibus Trade and Competitiveness Act: Technology Development Provisions, Wendy Schacht 89-93 SPR
* Research and Development Funding: FY 1990: Archived Issue Brief, Science Policy Research Division IB89040
* Research and Development Funding: FY 89: Archived Issue Brief, Michael Davey IB88040
* Science, Technology, and the International Competitiveness of American Industry: Selected References, 1985-1988 B. F. Mangan 88-587 L
* The Semi-Gas Systems Sale: Technology and National Security Issues, Glenn J. McLoughlin 91-263 SPR
* Semiconductor Devices: The Changing Competitiveness of U.S. Merchant Producers, 1977-87, Gary Guenther 88-191 E
* Semiconductor Manufacturing Technology Proposal: SEMATECH: Issue Brief, Glenn J. McLoughlin IB87212
* Semiconductors: Issues Confronting the Industry: Bibliography-in-Brief, 1985-1988, Karen Alderman 88-445 L
* Small Business, Technology Development, and Manufacturing: Competitiveness Issues, Wendy H. Schacht 89-685 SPR
* State Allotments for Education Programs under H.R. 3, the Omnibus Trade Bill of 1987, as Passed by the House and The Senate, Paul Irwin, etc. 87-683 EPW
* Steel Imports of Hot Rolled Sheet from Korea in the Absence of Import Restraints: Hypothetical Effects on West Coast Steel Producers, David J. Cantor 88-678 E
* Taxation of U.S. Investment Abroad: Archived Issue Brief, David Brumbaugh IB87060
* Technological Advancement and the Competitiveness of Selected U.S. Industries: Issues for Consideration, Wendy Schacht, etc. 87-345 SPR
* Technological Advancement and U.S. Industrial Competitiveness, Wendy Schacht 88-689 SPR
* Trade, Technology, and Competitiveness: Issue Brief, Wendy Schacht IB87053
* U.S. Economic Policy in an International Context: U.S. Wages and Unit Labor Costs in a World Economy, Richard Belous 84-172 E
* U.S. Export Control Policy and Competitiveness: Proceedings of the CRS Symposium, John P. Hardt, etc. 87-388 S
* The U.S. Intelligence Community: A Role in Supporting Economic Competitiveness?, Richard A. Best 90-571 F
* U.S. Jewelry Manufacturing, International Competitiveness, and H.R. 3, Bernard Gelb 87-875 E
* The U.S. Semiconductor Industry and the SEMATECH Proposal, Glenn McLoughlin, etc. 87-354 SPR
* Vocational Education and Proposals for Trade Competitiveness, Paul Irwin 87-340 EPW
* Wage Rates and Exchange Rates, Linda LeGrande 88-252 E

Foreign Trade -- East-West

* Balancing the National Interest: U.S. National Security Export Controls, and Global Economic Competition: A Summary of the National Academy of Science, John P. Hardt, etc. 87-119 S
* China-U.S. Relations and Most-Favored Nation Status: Issues and Options for Congress, Kerry Dumbaugh 91-524 F
* China-U.S. Trade Issues: Issue Brief, Wayne Morrison IB91121
* China's Most-Favored-Nation Status: U.S. Wheat Exports, Susan B. Epstein 91-447 ENR
* China's Trade Patterns, Wayne M. Morrison 91-561 E
* Commercial Relations With the Soviet Union: Prospects for a Common United States-Japanese Policy, John P. Hardt 91-196 RCO
* A Congressional Guide for Economic Negotiations With the Soviet Union, John P. Hardt, etc. 88-19 S
* East-West Trade and the Congress; Proceedings of a CRS Seminar, Glennon J. Harrison 90-529 E
* Eastern Europe; Info Pack IP431E
* European Regional Market: A Forgotten Key to Success of European Economics in Transition?, John P. Hardt 91-113 RCO
* Export Control Reform in the 100th Congress: A Comparison of Selected Provisions of H.R. 3 and S. 1409, Glennon Harrison 87-529 E
* Export Controls: Issue Brief, George Holliday, etc. IB87122
* Hong Kong-U.S. Economic Relations: Some Views from Hong Kong's Economic Elite, Kerry Dumbaugh 89-23 F
* Most-Favored-Nation Policy Toward Communist Countries: Archived Issue Brief, Vladimir N. Pregelj IB74139
* Most-Favored-Nation Status of the People's Republic of China: Issue Brief, Vladimir N. Pregelj IB89119
* Potential Economic Effects of Granting Most-Favored-National Treatment to the Soviet Union, George Holliday 85-886 E
* Singapore-U.S. Economic Relations: Some Views from Singapore's Economic Elite, Richard Cronin 89-49 F
* Soviet Energy: An Engine or a Brake on Commercial Relations in the 1990s?, John P. Hardt 91-211 RCO
* Soviet Trade and Economic Relations With Western Europe, Glennon J. Harrison, etc. 91-631 E
* Soviet-U.S Trade Relations: The Bilateral Trade Agreement, William H. Cooper 91-662 E
* Thai-U.S. Economic Relations: Some Views of Thailand's Economic Elite, Raymond Ahearn 89-60 F
* The Toshiba/Kongsberg Case: Proposals to Expand U.S. Penalties for Illegal Exports of High Technology Goods, Glennon Harrison 87-988 E
* Toshiba-Kongsberg Technology Diversion: Issues for Congress; Archived Issue Brief, Raymond Ahearn, etc. IB87184
* U.S. Agricultural Assistance to the Soviet Union: Policy Issues, Issue Brief, Remy Jurenas IB90139
* U.S. Export Control Policy and Competitiveness; Proceedings of the CRS Symposium, John P. Hardt, etc. 87-388 S
* U.S.-Soviet Commercial Relations: Archived Issue Brief, John P. Hardt, etc. IB89110
* U.S.-Soviet Commercial Relations in the Age of Perestroika: Selected References, 1985-1990; a CRS Trade Team Product, Robert S. Kirk 90-240 L
* U.S.-Soviet Commercial Relations in a Period of Negotiation: Archived Issue Brief, John Hardt IB88065
* U.S.-Soviet Relations in the Gorbachev Era: Selected References, Robert Kirk 89-51 L
* U.S. Taiwan Economic Relations: Views of Some Members of the Taiwan Economic Elite, Alren Wilson 89-21 E
* U.S. Trade Relations With the Soviet Union Since World War II: A Chronology, Vladimir N. Pregelj 89-241 E
* U.S.-U.S.S.R. Commercial Relations: Issues in East-West Trade: Archived Issue Brief, John Hardt, etc. IB86020

Foreign Trade -- Export Controls

* Austrian Export Control Legislation, Law Library of Congress, LL90-51
* The Commercial Implications of Exporting and Importing Military Technology: A Review of the Issues, John D. Moteff 90-409 SPR
* Export Controls: Archived Issue Brief, George Holliday, etc. IB91064
* Finding Common Ground: U.S. Export Controls in a Changed Global Environment: A Summary of the National Academy of Sciences Study, Glennon J. Harrison 91-161 E
* Regulation of Timber Exports: Legislative Options, Kenneth R. Thomas 89-617 A
* Statutory Restrictions on Trade and Financial Transactions With the Soviet Union, Jeanne J. Grimmett 91-649 A
* Toshiba-Kongsberg Technology Diversion: Issues for Congress; Archived

Issue Brief, Raymond Ahearn, etc. IB87184

Foreign Trade -- Imports and Exports

* Agricultural Export Program and Issues; Issue Brief, Susan B. Epstein IB(0064
* Agricultural Exports: Federal Assistance and Promotion Programs, Remy Jurenas, etc. 89-351 ENR
* Agricultural Exports: Overview and Selected Data, Donna Vogt 90-35 ENR
* Agricultural Imports: What, from Whom, Why, How Much, Jasper Womach 88-361 ENR
* Agricultural Trade Policy: The 1990 Farm Bill and the GATT Negotiations, Charles E. Hanrahan 90-267 S
* Agriculture in the GATT: After the Midterm Review; Issue Brief, Charles Hanrahan IB89027
* Alaskan Oil Exports; Archived Issue Brief, Gary Pagliano IB84085
* America's Steel Industry: Modernizing to Compete, David Cantor 84-786 E
* Brazil: Selected Foreign Trade Data, Rawle O. King 88-320 E
* Canada's Prohibition on the Importation of Goods Produced by Prisoners, Law Library of Congress LL90-15
* Caribbean Apparel Exports: Greater Access to the U.S. Market, Edward B. Rappaport 88-128 E
* Cotton Trade: The United States and Foreign Competition, Susan Epstein 87-557 ENR
* Customs Ruling on Multipurpose Vehicles: Archived Issue Brief, Gwenell Bass IB89053
* Digital Audio Recorder Act of 1987-- Analysis of H.R. 1384 and S. 506 With Policy Alternatives, David Hack 87-698 SPR
* Disposition of Import Relief Cases under Section 201 of the Trade Act of 1974 Since 1981: A Survey, Vladimir Pregelj 88-207 E
* The Dollar and the Trade Deficit: An Updated on Recent Trends, Forecasts; and Policy Options, Craig K. Elwell 88-693 E
* The Dollar and the Trade Deficit: What's to be Done?, Craig Elwell, etc. 88-430 E
* The Dollar, the Trade Deficit, and the Economy, G. Thomas Woodward 88-722 E
* The Dollar, the Trade Deficit, and the U.S. Economy: Audio Brief, William Cooper, etc. AB50174
* Drawback of Sugar Duties and Fees: Lengthening the Time Allowance, Jasper Womach 87-742 ENR
* EC Ban on Importing U.S. Pork and Beef, Susan Epstein 91-390 ENR
* Employment and Output Effects of the Extension of Japan's Voluntary Automobile Export Restraints on the U.S. Automobile and Steel Industries, Gwenell Bass 85-710 E
* Export-Import Bank: Financing Commercial Military Sales; Issue Brief, James K. Jackson, etc. IB91074
* Foreign Prohibitions on the Importation of Goods Produced by Prison Labor, Law Library of Congress, LL90-43
* Foreign Sourcing by the U.S. Automobile Industry, Kevin Flaherty 85-1052 E
* Foreign-Trade Zones and the U.S. Automobile Industry, Gwenell L. Bass, etc 88-659 E
* The "Gephardt Amendment": A Comparison to "Super 301" in the Senate Trade Bill, Lenore Sek 88-206 E
* The Gray Market for Imported Automobiles, R. Kevin Flaherty 85-651 E
* Implementation of the President's Steel Program: Implications for Output and Employment of the Steel and Steel-Related Industries, David J. Cantor 86-518 E
* Import Penetration During the Eighties: Anatomy of the Data, Bernard A. Gelb 86-876 E
* International Coffee Agreement: A Status Report, Donna U. Vogt 90-159 ENR
* Japan's Automobile Industry and Barriers to Purchases of U.S. Cars, Dick K. Nanto, etc. 87-793 E
* Japan-U.S. Economic Issues: Investment, Saving, Technology and Attitudes, Dick K. Nanto 90-78 E
* Kangaroo Management Controversy, Malcolm M. Simmons 88-468 ENR
* Log Export Restrictions, Ross W. Gorte 91-365 ENR
* Machine Tools: Imports and the U.S. Industry, Economy and Defense Industrial Base, Gale Guenther 86-762 E
* Manufactured Exports and Regional Economic Growth in the United States, 1987 to 1983: A Preliminary Assessment Gary Guenther 86-855 E
* Market Access in Japan: The U.S. Experience, Raymond Ahearn 85-37 E
* Mexico's Maquiladora Industry, M. Angeles Villarreal 91-706 E
* Offshore Manufacturing by U.S. Corporations: Selected Bibliography, With Introductory Readings, Robert Kirk 86-834 L
* The "Oil Import Bill" Of the United States, 1945-1987: A Historical Record of U.S Merchandise Trade and Petroleum With Related Balances, Dario

Current Events and Homework

Scuka 88-107 E
* Oil Import Fees (Taxes) for Deficit Reduction: Revenue and Economic Effects: Issue Brief, Salvatore Lazzari IB87189
* Oil Import Tax: Some General Economic Effects, Bernard Gelb 87-259 E
* Oil Import Taxes: An Economic Analysis of S. 694, the Economic Security Act of 1987, Salvatore Lazzari 87-779 E
* Oil Import Taxes: Revenue and Economic Effects, Bernard Gelb, etc. 86-572 E
* Oil Imports from OPEC: Recent and Projected Trends, Bernard Gelb 88-558 E
* Petroleum in the United States: Selected Data Focused on the Oil Import Tax Issue, Bernard Gelb 86-1054 E
* The Safety of Imported Foods, Donna U. Vogt 91-644 SPR
* Selected Data on U.S. Agricultural High-Valued Product Exports, Susan Epstein 87-471 ENR
* South Korea and Taiwan: Expanding Trade Ties With the United States; Issue Brief, William Cooper IB86151
* Status of the U.S. Commercial Fishing Industry: Summary of Information, Eugene Buck 88-444 ENR
* Status Report on U.S.-Chinese Science and Technology Relationships, Genevieve J. Knezo 90-8 SPR
* Steel Imports: Are the VRA Countries Filling Their Quota, David J. Cantor 89-81 E
* Steel Imports: Arguments for and Against Extension of the President's Steel Program: Issue Brief, David J. Cantor IB88109
* Steel Prices and Import Restraints, David Cantor 88-204 E
* Sugar Policy: Current Issues; Issue Brief, Jasper Womach IB88091
* Sugar Policy Issues; Issue Brief, Remy Jurenas IB90036
* Summary of Information About Foreign Trade by States Available from Federal and Non-Federal Sources, Dario Scuka 84-588 E
* Super 301 Action Against Japan, Brazil and India: Rationale, Reaction, and Future Implications, Raymond J. Ahearn, etc. 90-25 F
* Tariff Items 807.00 and 806.30 and the Mexican Maquiladoras, Patricia Wertman 87-500 E
* The Textile Industry in the United States: Conflicting Factual Claims, Edward B. Rappaport 91-373 E
* Textile Trade Controls: A Comparison of Bills in the 99th and 100th Congresses, Edward B. Rappaport 87-607 E
* Tied Aid Credits: Issue Brief, James K. Jackson IB89131
* Timber Export Taxes: Constitutional and International Law Implications, Kennety R. Thomas 91-416 A
* The Applicability of the Export Proviso of the Federal Food, Drug and Cosmetic Act to "New Drugs"*, Cathy Gilmore 85-848 A
* Trade and Current Account Balances: Statistics: Issue Brief, Wayne M. Morrison IB87112
* Trade Deficits and the Dollar: Bibliography-in-Brief, 1984-1987, Robert Kirk 87-888 L
* Trade in Telecommunications Products and Services: Legislation in the 100th Congress, Glennon Harrison 87-844 E
* Trade Issues and Trade Deficits: Background, Statistics, and Proposed Legislation; Info Pack, IP263T
* Trade of the Seventeen Highly Indebted Countries: A Brief Overview, Patricia Wertman, etc. 88-521 E
* United States Merchandise Trade and Balances With Major Trading Partners, 1985, Dario Scuka 88-81 E
* United States Merchandise Trade and Trade Balances With W. Germany, 1960-1987, Dario Scuka 88-117 E
* United States Merchandise Trade and Trade Balances, 1945-1987, Dario Scuka 88-104 E
* U.S. Agricultural Exports to China, Susan B. Epstein, etc. 89-391 ENR
* U.S. Automobile Industry: Issues and Statistics, Gwenell L. Bass 85-792 E
* U.S. Commercial Relations With the European Community, George D. Holliday 85-32 E
* U.S. Economic Policy in an International Context: The U.S. Automobile Industry in International Competition: Voluntary Export Restraints and Domestic, Dick K. Nanto 85-34 E
* U.S. Exports of Solid Wood Products, Ross Gorte 87-208 ENR
* U.S.-Japanese Agricultural Trade Relations: Selected Information, Donna U. Vogt 89-655 ENR
* U.S. Jewelry Manufacturing International Competitiveness and H.R. 3, Bernard A. Gelb 87-875 E
* U.S. Mexico Trade in the Automotive Industry, M. Angeles Villarreal, etc. 91-533 E
* U.S. Petroleum Exports--A Review of Fact and Policy, Lawrence C. Kumins 91-166 ENR
* U.S. Trade and Payments Balances: What Do They Mean?, Arlene Wilson 85-26 E
* The U.S. Trade Deficit: Causes, Consequences and Cures, Craig Elwell, etc. 86-116 E
* U.S. Wood Exports to Europe and the 1992 EC Economic Integration, by Ross W. Gorte 89-580 ENR
* U.S. Wood Exports to the Pacific Rim, Ross Gorte 88-548 ENR
* Venezuelan Petroleum: A Source of Increasing U.S. Imports?, Joseph P. Riva 90-70 SPR
* Wood Export Promotion, Susan B. Epstein, etc. 90-94 ENR

Foreign Trade -- Sanctions

* Ban on Imports from Iran: Economic Effect on the United States, Bernard A. Gelb 88-6 E
* Blockade: Some International and Domestic Legal Implications, Raymond J. Celada 90-386 A
* China Sanctions: Some Possible Effects, Economics Division; 90-186 E
* Iraq, Kuwait, and IEEPA, Raymond J. Celada 90-373 A
* Iraq: U.S. Economic Sanctions; Archived Issue Brief, Clyde R. Mark IB90109
* Iraq's Food and Agricultural Situation During the Embargo and the War, Susan B. Epstein 91-199 ENR
* Naval Restriction of Commerce Against Iraq: Historic Background, Implications and Options, Mark M. Lowenthal 90-388 S
* Panama: Trade, Finance, and Proposed Economic Sanctions, Glennon Harrison 88-188 E
* The Reagan Administration Sanctions Against South Africa: Their Potential Economic Impact, William Cooper 85-955 E
* Restrictions on U.S. Trade With Cuba: A Chronology of Major Actions and Present Status, Vladimir N. Pregelj 86-909 E
* Sanctions Against South Africa: Activities of the 99th Congress, Brenda Branaman 87-200 F
* Sanctions Against South Africa: Impact on the United States: Issue Brief, William Cooper IB87198
* Seizure of Foreign Vessels in United States Ports, Daniel Hill Zafren 87-760 A
* South Africa: International Sanctions; Archived Issue Brief, Jeanne S. Affelder, etc. IB86157
* South Africa: Legislation of the 99th Congress, Brenda Branaman 85-799 F
* South Africa-U.S. Economic Ties: Emerging Issues; Archived Issue Brief, William Cooper IB85117
* South Africa: U.S. Policy After Sanctions; Issue Brief, Brenda Branaman IB87128
* Southern Africa: U.S. Foreign Assistance; Issue Brief, Raymond W. Copson IB87152
* Tax Sanctions and U.S. Investment in South Africa, David Brumbaugh 88-112 E
* U.S. Economic Sanctions Imposed Against Specific Foreign Countries, 1979 to the Present, Theodore W. Galdi, etc. 88-612 F
* U.S.-European Community Trade Dispute Over Meat Containing Growth Hormones, Donna Vogt 89-6 ENR
* U.S. Foreign Trade Sanctions Imposed for Foreign Policy Reasons in Force as of April 10, 1988, Vladimir Pregelj 88-301 E
* U.S. Sanctions and the State of the Panamanian Economy, Mark Sullivan 88-578 F
* The U.S. Trade Embargo Against Nicaragua After Two -and-a-Half Years, Glennon J. Harrison 87-870 E
* The World Embargo on Food Exports to Iraq, Susan B. Epstein 90-462 ENR

Foreign Trade -- Trade Agreements and Negotiations

* Agriculture in a U.S.-Mexico-Canada Free Trade Agreement, Charles E. Hanrahan 91-252 RCO
* Agriculture in the U.S.-Canada Free Trade Agreement, Charles Hanrahan, etc. 88-363 ENR
* Automotive Products Trade With Canada and the U.S.-Canada Free Trade Area Agreement, Vladimir Pregelj 88-122 E
* The Canada-U.S. Free Trade Agreement: A Selected Bibliography, 1985-1988, Felix Chin 88-388 L
* Canada-U.S. Free Trade Agreement; Issue Brief, Arlene Wilson IB87173
* Canada-U.S. Free Trade Area Agreement: Info Pack, IP395C
* Canada-U.S. Free Trade Negotiations: Archived Issue Brief, Raymond Ahearn IB85215
* Canada-U.S.-Mexico Free Trade Agreements: Selected References, 1989-1991, Felix Chin 91-331 L
* Canadian Electricity: The U.S. Market and the Free Trade Agreement, Amy Abel 88-427 ENR
* The Canadian Free Trade Agreement and the Textile and Apparel

Foreign Trade / Trade Policy

Industries, Edward Rappaport 87-979 E

* A Congressional Guide for Economic Negotiations With the Soviet Union, John P. Hardt, etc. 88-19 S
* Dispute Settlement and the General Agreement on Tariffs and Trade, Raymond Ahearn 85-680 E
* Dispute Settlement Provisions in the United States-Canada Free Trade Agreement, Jeanne Jagelski, etc. 88-603 A
* The Effect of the Canada-U.S. Free Trade Agreement on U.S. Industries, Economics Division 88-506 E
* Environmental Regulation and the GATT, Jeanne J. Grimmett 91-285 A
* The Europe 1992 Plan: Science and Technology Issues, Science and Policy Research Division 89-178 SPR
* European Community: Issues Raised by 1992 Integration, Congressional Research Service 89-323 E
* European Community: The 1992 Plan; Info Pack, IP408E
* The European Community: 1992 and Reciprocity, Glennon Harrison 89-227 E
* European Community: 1992 Plan for Economic Integration; Issue Brief, Glennon Harrison IB89043
* The European Community's 1992 Plan: An Overview of the Proposed "Single Market", Glennon Harrison 88-623 E
* The European Community's 1992 Plan: Bibliography-in-Brief, 1986-1988, Robert Howe 88-754 L
* European-U.S. Affairs: Responding to a Changing Relationship; Issue Brief, Karen E. Donfried, etc. IB89127
* Fast-Track Procedures for Trade Agreements: Implications for Congress of Their Extension, Ilona B. Nickels 91-248 GOV
* Forum: Trade Negotiations: Broadening the World Trading System; Also Environmental Concerns for the Year 2000, Congressional Research Service, REV 5-90
* Fruits and Vegetables in a U.S.-Mexico-Canada Free Trade Agreement, Geoffrey S. Becker 91-362 ENR
* The GATT Trade Talks: Prospects for Selected Manufacturing Industries, Edward B. Rappaport 91-821 E
* Government Procurement in Canada: Sourcing Policy, Law Library of Congress LL90-8
* Japan and an East Asian Trading Bloc, Dick K. Nanto 91-840 E
* Japan-U.S. Trade: A Chronology of Major Events, 1980-1990, Wayne M. Morrison, etc. 91-494 E
* Japan-U.S. Trade: The Structural Impediments Initiative, William H. Cooper 90-276 E
* Japanese-U.S. Trade: The Construction Issue, William H. Cooper 91-303 E*
* Japan's Protected Market: Significance, Extent, Outlook, and Challenges for U.S. Policy, Raymond Ahearn 90-326 F
* Japan's Response to the 1988 Omnibus Trade Bill, Dick Nanto 89-133
* Mexico-U.S. Free Trade Agreement; Info Pack, Congressional Reference Division IP445M
* The MOSS Talks: Success or Failure?, Patricia Wertman 85-1129 E
* Negotiating Authority for the Uruguay Round of Multilateral Trade Negotiations, Jeanne Jagelski 87-103 A
* North American Free Trade Agreement: A Checklist of CRS Products and Public Policy Literature, Felix Chin 91-450 L
* A North American Free Trade Agreement: Congressional Concerns; Proceedings of a CRS Seminar, Lenore M. Sek 91-786 E
* North American Free Trade Agreement; Issue Brief, Lenore Sek IB90140
* North American Free Trade Agreement: Issues for Congress, Congressional Research Service 91-282 E
* A North American Free Trade Area? A Brief Review of the Major Issues, Alfred Reifman 91-418 RCO
* Proceedings of the CRS Workshop on Canada-U.S. Free-Trade Agreement: How Will It Affect the United States? Arlene Wilson 88-356 E
* Selected Nonferrous Mineral Subsidies and the U.S.-Canada Free Trade Agreement, Marc Humphries 88-774 ENR
* The Smoot-Hawley Tariff Act of 1930: Its Effects on U.S. Trade and Its Role in the Great Depression of 1929-1933, George Holliday, etc. 87-993 E
* Taiwan-U.S. Free Trade Area: Economic Effects and Related Issues, William Cooper 89-96 E
* Tariffication: Negotiating Reductions in Agricultural Import Barriers in the Uruguay Round, Donna U. Vogt, etc. 89-555 ENR
* Textiles in the World Trade System: Archived Issue Brief, Edward B. Rappaport IB89139
* Trade Legislation in 1988: Conflict and Compromise, George Holliday, etc. 89-494 E
* Trade Negotiations: The Uruguay Round; Issue Brief, Lenore Sek IB86147
* The Uruguay Round of Multilateral Trade Negotiations: Major Issues, Lenore M. Sek 90-496 E
* Uruguay Round of Trade Negotiations and Its Impact on the U.S. Service Sector, Economics Division, Gwenell L. Bass, 91-233 E
* U.S.-Canada Free Trade Agreement: Assessment and Implications for a U.S.-Mexico Free Trade Agreement, Arlene Wilson 90-450 E
* U.S.-Canada Free Trade Agreement: International Implications, Raymond Ahearn, etc. 88-249 F
* U.S.-Canada Free Trade Agreement: States Affected by Major Provisions, Lenore Sek 88-347 E
* U.S.-Canada Trade: An Overview, Lenore Sek 88-331 E
* U.S. Free Trade Agreements With Canada and Israel: Comparison of the Major Provisions, Arlene Wilson 91-243 E
* U.S.-Japan Trade: The Structural Impediments Initiative; Audio Brief, William Cooper AB50207

Foreign Trade -- Trade Policy

* Addressing Unfair Trade: Agricultural Cases under Section 301 of the Trade Act of 1974, Donna U. Vogt 89-522 ENR
* Agricultural Policy for the 1990's; Audio Brief, Charles Hanrahan, etc. AB50217
* Agricultural Trade Legislation in the 100th Congress: A Comparison of Selected Provisions of H.R. 3 and S. 1420, Charles Hanrahan, etc. 87-677 ENR
* Auctioning Import Quotas, Lenore Sek 87-669 E
* Background Information on Casein, Geoffrey S. Becker 87-505 ENR
* "Buy America" Regulations: Effects on Surface Transportation, John Fischer 86-78 E
* Cargo Preference and Agriculture, Carl Ek 89-633 ENR
* A Comparison of the Education Provisions in the Omnibus Trade Bill, H.R. 3, as Passed by the House and by the Senate, Paul Irwin, etc. 87-634 EPW
* Customs Service User Fees, Frederick M. Kaiser 87-676 GOV
* Dispute Settlement Provisions in the United States-Canada Free Trade Agreement, Jeanne Jagelski, etc. 88-603 A
* East Asian Trade Trends: Interpretations of Their Causes and Implications for U.S. Interests and Policy, Raymond J. Ahearn 90-491 F
* Economic Issues Before the 102nd Congress, Congressional Research Service, Edward Knight 91-407 E
* Exports Credits: Proposals to Combat the Use by Foreign Governments of Mixed Credits, George Holliday 85-1061 E
* Export-Import Bank Financial Issues; Archived Issue Brief, James Jackson IB88013
* Export-Import Bank: Financing Problems and Issues, James K. Jackson 88-61 E
* Exports of High Valued Agricultural Products: Trends and Issues, Susan Epstein, etc. 87-636 ENR
* Foreign Trade and U.S. Employment: Bibliography in Brief, 1983-1987, Robert Kirk 87-344 L
* Foreign Trade Barriers and Section 301: Archived Issue Brief, Lenore Sek IB89113
* Free Trade and Protection: Selected Bibliography, 1983-1987, With Introductory Readings, Robert Kirk 87-734 L
* Free Trade Versus Protectionism: An Analysis of the Issue, Raymond Ahearn 78-32 E
* Fruit and Vegetable Issues in the 102nd Congress, Geoffrey S. Becker 91-409 ENR
* The "Gephardt Amendment": A Comparison to "Super 301" in the Senate Trade Bill, Lenore Sek 88-206 E
* Hong Kong-U.S. Economic Relations: Some Views from Hong Kong's Economic Elite, Kerry Dumbaugh 89-23 F
* Import Relief: A Brief Historical Survey of Presidential Discretion in Providing a Remedy in Escape Clause/Import Relief Investigations, Vladimir N. Pregelj 87-542 E
* Japan Briefing Book, Congressional Research Service 87-323 E
* Japan: Prospects for Greater Market Openness, Raymond J. Ahearn 89-390 F
* Japan-South Korea Economic Relations: South Korea's Approach to the "Japan Problem", Dick Nanto 87-953 E
* Japan-United States Economic Relations: Views of Japan's Economic Decisionmakers, Dick Nanto 86-52 E
* Japan-U.S. Economic Relations; Bibliography-in-Brief, 1986-1987, Robert Kirk 87-45 L
* Japan-U.S. Economic Relations: Cooperation or Confrontation? Issue Brief, William Cooper IB87158
* Japan-U.S. Economic Relations: Selected References, 1989-1991, Robert Howe 91-213 L
* Japan-U.S. Relations: Archived Issue Brief, Robert Sutter IB81026
* Japan-U.S. Relations: Issues for Congress, Issue Brief, Robert G. Sutter IB89133

Be patient. If any phone number is incorrect, call (area code) 555-1212 and request the new listing.

Current Events and Homework

* Japan-U.S. Trade: An Overview, William Cooper 88-127 E
* Japan-U.S. Trade and Economic Relations: Info Pack, IP201J
* Japan-U.S. Trade Relations: Archived Issue Brief, Raymond Ahearn IB81011
* Japan's High Prices: Some Causes and Their Relationship to Trade Policy, Dick K. Nanto 88-243 E
* Most-Favored-Nation Treatment of Foreign Trading Partners by the United States: A Summary, Vladimir Pregelj 87-211 E
* Negotiating Authority for the Uruguay Round of Multilateral Trade Negotiations, Jeanne Jagelski 87-103 A
* The Omnibus Trade and Competitiveness Act of 1988 (P.L. 100-418): An Analysis of the Major Trade Provisions, Economics Division 88-390 E
* Pacific Rim Initiatives; a CRS Trade Team Product 89-405 D
* The President's Steel Program: Background and Implementation, David J. Cantor 86-658 E
* Proceedings of the CRS Symposium on U.S. Trade: Policy Issues Confronting the 100th Congress, William Cooper 87-267 E
* Protectionist Legislation in 1985, Raymond Ahearn, etc. 86-632 E
* Protectionist Policies of Major U.S. Trading Partners, Raymond J. Ahearn 86-655 E
* Restricting Lamb Imports: A Policy Issue, Jasper Womach 87-642 ENR
* A Results-Oriented Trade Policy, Alfred Reifman 89-541 S
* Singapore-U.S. Economic Relations: Some Views from Singapore's Economic Elite, Richard P. Cronin 89-49 F
* Steel Imports from Canada and the President's Steel Program: Archived Issue Brief, David Cantor IB87197
* Steel Imports: Is the President's Steel Program Working?; Archived Issue Brief, David J. Cantor IB86141
* A Survey of U.S. International Economic Policy and Problems, Alfred Reifman 88-666 S
* Tax Policy and U.S. Trade Performance, Gregg A. Esenwein, etc. 89-635 E
* Telecommunications Trade: Market Access Legislation; Archived Issue Brief, Raymond Ahearn, etc. IB85206
* Textile and Apparel Trade Protection: Issue Brief, Edward B. Rappaport IB87109
* Textile Trade Controls: A Comparison of Bills in the 99th Congress, Edward Rappaport 87-607 E
* Trade: Issue Brief, Arlene Wilson, etc. IB87003
* Trade Remedies Available to the United States under International Agreements and Corresponding Domestic Laws, Vladimir N. Pregelj 85-1008 E
* Trade Remedy Reform, Raymond J. Ahearn 87-117 E
* Trade, Technology, and Competitiveness: Issue Brief, Wendy Schacht IB87053
* Unfair Foreign Trade Practices and Extension of Super 301, Dick K. Nanto 91-546 E
* Unfair Foreign Trade Practices: Section 301 of the Foreign Trade Act of 1974: Archived Issue Brief, Lenore Sek IB88051
* Unfair Foreign Trade Practices: Section 301 of the Trade Act of 1974, Lenore Sek 87-960 E
* United States-Mexican Trade Relations: Present Problems, Future Prospects, Patricia Wertman 85-139 E
* U.S. Agricultural Trade Opportunities With Pacific Rim Nations, Robert M. Goldstein 88-755 ENR
* U.S. Agricultural Trade Policy: Selected Readings, 1988-90, Ted L. Burch 90-328 L
* The U.S.-Canada Pork Dispute, Susan Epstein 89-311 ENR
* U.S. Export Development Assistance for Manufactured Goods: Alternative Approaches, William Cooper 86-47 E
* U.S. Intellectual Property Rights and Trade, Lenore Sek 86-383 E
* U.S.-Japanese Agricultural Trade Relations: Selected Information, Donna Vogt 88-159 ENR
* U.S.-South Korean Economic Relations: Views of Some Members of the Korean Economic Elite, William H. Cooper 88-656 E
* The U.S. Trade Deficit: Causes, Consequences and Cures, Alfred Reifman, etc. 90-561 E
* U.S. Trade Policy Towards Japan: Where Do We Go from Here?, William Cooper 89-307 E
* Vietnam: Procedural and Jurisdictional Questions Regarding Possible Normalization of U.S. Diplomatic and Economic Relations, Alan K. Yu, etc. 89-631 F
* Vocational Education and Proposals for Trade Competitiveness, Paul Irwin 87-340 EPW

Forests and Forestry

see Timber, Tropical

* Acid Rain, Air Pollution, and Forest Decline: Issue Brief, Adela Backlei IB86031
* Air Pollutant-Induced Stress to Forest Ecosystems- An Overview of Forest Damage, Adela Backlei, etc. 86-560 ENR
* The Alaska National Interest Lands Conservation Act: Legislative History of the Tongass Timber Provisions, Adela Backlei, etc. 87-434 ENR
* Arctic Resources Controversy: Issue Brief, M. Lynne Corn, etc. IB89058
* Arctic Resources: Over a Barrel?, Issue Brief, M. Lynne Corn, etc. IB91011
* Comparison of Pacific Northwest Forest Bills: Part I, by Adela Backiel, etc. 91-626 ENR
* Debt-for-Nature Swaps in Developing Countries: An Overview of Recent Conservation Efforts, Betsy Cody 88-647 ENR
* Dominant Use Management in the National Forest System, Ross Gorte 86-714 ENR
* Exempting Forest Products Shipments from the Jones Act Requirements, Ross W. Gorte 87-887 ENR
* Federal Land Management Transfers Proposed Between Bureau of Land Management and Forest Service: Archived Issue Brief, Ross Gorte, etc. IB85101
* Federal Timber Sales, John Beuter 85-96 ENR
* The Forest Service Budget: Trust Funds and Special Accounts, Ross Gorte, etc. 89-75 ENR
* Forest Service Land and Resource Planning: A Chronology of Laws, Adela Backlei 86-986 ENR
* The Forest Service's 1980 RPA Program: Comparison With Accomplishments, Ross Gorte 86-902 ENR
* Future U.S. Forestry Issues, Ross W. Gorte 87-854 ENR
* History of Release Language in Wilderness Legislation, 1979-1984, Ross Gorte 87-559 ENR
* International Environment: Overview of Major Issues; Issue Brief, Mary Tiemann, etc. IB89057
* The Major Federal Land Management Agencies: Management of Our Nation's Lands and Resources, Environment and Natural Resources Policy Division 90-239 ENR
* Modifying BLM Timber Contracts: An Analysis of a Recent Proposal, Ross Gorte 87-757 ENR
* National Forest Receipts: Sources and Dispositions, Ross Gorte 89-284 ENR
* Natural Resources Conservation and Developments in Brazil: An Overview and Related Issues, Russell Hawkins 84-802 ENR
* An Overview of Federal Tax Policies Encouraging Donations of Conservation Easements to Preserve Natural Areas, Richard Dunford 84-48 ENR
* Ozone and Plants: A Status Report, Jeffrey A. Zinn, etc. 87-496 ENR
* Policy Analysis of the Proposed Revision of the Forest Service Administrative Appeals Regulations: Public Input, Timing, and Delays, Ross W. Gorte 88-483 ENR
* The Renewable Resources Extension Act, Adela Backlei 86-821 ENR
* Special Management Areas in the National Forest System, Ross Gorte 88-571 ENR
* The Sport Hunting Safety and Preservation Act of 1991: Constitutionality of H.R. 371, 102nd Congress, Henry Cohen 91-442 A
* Spotted Owls and the Timber Industry: Issue Brief, M. Lynne Corn IB89077
* Summary of Recent Reports on Forest Service Timber Sale Costs and Revenues, Ross Gorte 84-799 ENR
* Tongass National Forest Issues: Issue Brief, Adela Backeil IB89055
* Tropical Deforestation; Info Pack, IP416T
* Tropical Deforestation: International Implications; Issue Brief, Susan R. Fletcher IB89010
* Tropical Deforestation: The International Tropical Timber Agreement, Ross Gorte 87-795 ENR
* Tropical Forests: Bibliography-in-Brief, 1985-1988, Adrienne C. Boniface 88-274 L
* U.S. Exports of Solid Wood Products, Ross Gorte 87-208 ENR
* U.S. Wood Exports to the Pacific Rim, Ross Gorte 88-548 ENR
* Wilderness: Additions to the National Wilderness Preservation System; Archived Issue Brief, Ross Gorte IB83151
* Wilderness Areas and Federal Water Rights, Pamela Baldwin 89-11 A
* Wilderness Issues in the 102nd Congress: Issue Brief, Betsy A. Cody IB91029
* Wilderness: Overview and Statistics, Ross W. Gorte 89-460 ENR

Forests and Forestry -- Timber

* The Alaska National Interest Lands Conservation Act: Legislative History of the Tongass Timber Provisions, Adela Backiel, etc. 87-434 ENR
* Economic Impacts of Protecting the Northern Spotted Owl, Ross W. Gorte 90-74 ENR
* Endangered Species Act: The Listing and Exemption Processes, M. Lynne

Corn, etc. 90-242 ENR
* Exempting Forest Products Shipments from the Jones Act Requirements, Ross W. Gorte 87-887 ENR
* Federal Timber Sales, John Beuter 85-96 ENR
* Log Export Restrictions, Ross W. Gorte 91-365 ENR
* Modifying BLM Timber Contracts: An Analysis of a Recent Proposal, Ross W. Gorte 87-757 ENR
* National Forest Receipts: Sources and Dispositions, Ross W. Gorte 89-284 ENR
* Old Growth Forests in the Pacific Northwest: Background and Issues; Issue Brief, Adela Backiel IB90111
* Regulation of Timber Exports: Legislative Options, Kenneth R. Thomas 89-617 A
* Spotted Owls and Old Growth Forests; Issue Brief, M. Lynne Corn IB90094
* Timber Export Taxes: Constitutional and International Law Implications, Kenneth R. Thomas 91-416 A
* Tongass National Forest Issues; Archived Issue Brief, Adela Backiel IB89055
* U.S. Exports of Solid Wood Products, Ross W. Gorte 87-208 ENR
* U.S. Wood Exports to Europe and the 1992 EC Economic Integration, Ross W. Gorte 89-580 ENR
* U.S. Wood Exports to the Pacific Rim, Ross W. Gorte 88-548 ENR
* Wood Export Promotion, Susan B. Epstein, etc. 90-94 ENR

Forests and Forestry -- Tropical

* Tropical Deforestation; Info Pack IP416T
* Tropical Deforestation: International Implications; Archived Issue Brief, Susan R. Fletcher IB89010
* Tropical Deforestation: Selected References, 1987-1990, Lisa B. Dove 90-578 L
* Tropical Deforestation: The International Tropical Timber Agreement, Ross W. Gorte 87-795 ENR

Fossil Fuels

* see Coal, Gasoline, Natural Gas, Petroleum, and Energy
* Arctic National Wildlife Refuge: A Checklist of CRS Products, Ted L. Burch 92-5 L
* Controlling Carbon Dioxide Emissions, Amy Abel, etc. 89-157 ENR
* Energy Demand and Carbon Dioxide Production, Richard E. Rowberg 91-170 SPR
* Energy Impacts: Archived Issue Brief, Duane Thompson, etc. IB87021
* Energy Policy: A Checklist of Public Policy Literature and CRS Products, Ted L. Burch 91-55 L
* Forum: Energy Policy; a Post-War Framework, Congressional Research Service REV 3-91
* Public Utilities Holding Company Act of 1935: Is This the Time for Reform: Issue Brief, Amy Abel IB89052
* Royalty Rates for Coal, Oil and Gas Production on Federally Administered Lands, Adela Backiel, etc. 83-595 S

Fossil Fuels -- Coals

* The Abandoned Mine Land Reclamation Program: Too Little, Too Late, to Complete, Duane Thompson 86-730 ENR
* Acid Rain Control and Clean Coal Technology: An Analysis of Title II of S. 1894, Larry Parker 88-266 ENR
* Acid Rain Control: What Is a 10 Million Ton SO_2 Reduction?, Larry B. Parker, etc. 89-243 ENR
* Acid Rain, DOEs Clean Coal Technology Program, and the Lewis-Davis Report: Squaring a Circle?, Larry B. Parker 87-60 ENR
* Coal Slurry Pipelines: Archived Issue Brief, Robert Bamberger IB83008
* Coke Oven Emissions: A Case Study of "Technology-Based" Regulation, Environment and Natural Resources Policy Division 89-533 ENR
* Department of Energy's Clean Coal Technology Program: Demonstrating Better Ways to Use American's Black Gold; Archived Issue Brief, Paul F. Rothberg IB87093
* DOE's Clean Coal Technology Program: Demonstrating Better Ways to Use America's Black Gold, Paul Rothberg 87-393 SPR
* DOE's Clean Coal Technology Program: Goals and Funding; Issue Brief, Larry Parker IB88071
* House Acid Rain Bills in the 101st Congress: Comparison of the Major Provisions of H.R. 144 and H.R. 1470, Larry Parker, etc. 89-226 ENR
* Royalties on Federal Coal: Issues in the Treatment of Royalty Payments and Externally-Related Taxes, Salvatore Lazzari, etc. 88-250 E

Fossil Fuels -- Gasoline

* The Alaskan Oil Spill and Gasoline Prices, Lawrence C. Kumins 89-250 ENR
* Alternative Fuels and Reformulated Gasoline: Issue Brief, David Gushee IB91008
* Automobile Fuel Economy Standards: Another Cup of CAFE? Issue Brief, Robert Bamberger IB90122
* BTU Taxes, Carbon Taxes, and Other Energy Tax Options for Deficit Recuction, Salvatore Lazzari 90-384 E
* Clean Air Act: Gasoline Vapor Recovery; Archived Issue Brief, David E. Gushee IB87029
* Emissions Impact of Oxygenated (Alcohol/Gasoline) Fuels, David Gushee 87-436 S
* Gasoline Excise Tax: Economic Impacts of an Increase; Issue Brief, Bernard A. Gelb, etc. IB87078
* Gasoline: Lead Phasedown: Archived Mini Brief, Robert Bamberger IB83220
* Oil Price Implications: Reshuffling Energy Policy? Archived Issue Brief, Robert Bamberger, etc. IB86146
* Underground Storage Tanks: New Federal Requirements; Archived Issue Brief, Mary E. Tiemann IB90054

Fossil Fuels -- Natural Gas

* Domestic Natural Gas Production: Issue Brief, Joseph Riva IB89009
* The Enigma of Natural Gas, Joseph P. Riva 88-561 SPR
* Natural Gas and the Generation of Electricity, Alvin Kaufman, etc. 90-253 ENR
* Natural Gas: Background, Perspectives, and Issues:, Archived Issue Brief, Larry Kumins, etc. IB86011
* Natural Gas Legislation: Streamlining the Regulatory Process; Issue Brief, Larry Kumins IB91138
* Natural Gas Pipelines: Federal Policy Issues in Contract Carriage, Donald Dulchinos 86-74 S
* Natural Gas Policy: Archived Issue Brief, Lawrence Kumin IB81020
* Underground Storage of Natural Gas, James E. Mielke, etc. 88-187 SPR

Fossil Fuels -- Petroleum

* After the Exxon Valdez Spill: Oil Pollution Liability and Compensation Legislation, Martin R. Lee 89-266 ENR
* Agricultural Energy Use and the Iraqi Crisis, Ralph M. Chite 90-397 ENR
* Alaskan Oil Exports: Archived Issue Brief, Gary Pagliano IB84085
* American Public Opinion on the Iraq-Kuwait Crisis Until January 15, Rosita M. Thomas 91-109 GOV
* Applicability of Alaska State Laws to Oil and Gas Development in the Arctic National Wildlife Refuge, Pamela Baldwin 88-420 A
* Arctic National Wildlife Refuge: Bibliography-in-Brief, Ted L. Burch 91-633 L
* Arctic National Wildlife Refuge: Congressional Consideration Since the 99th Congress, M. Lynne Corn, etc. 91-325 ENR
* The Arctic National Wildlife Refuge: Major Oil Development or Wilderness?, Congressional Research Service 88-161 ENR
* The Arctic National Wildlife Refuge: Oil, Gas, and Wildlife: Archived Issue Brief, Lynne Corn, etc. IB87026
* Arctic Oil, Arctic Refuge, Videoprogram, M. Lynne Corn, LTR 91-1489
* Arctic Resources Controversy: A Comparison of H.R. 3601 and S. 2214, Environment and Natural Resources Policy Division 88-380 ENR
* Arctic Resources Controversy: Issue Brief, M. Lynne Corn, etc. IB89058
* Arctic Resources: Over a Barrel?, Issue Brief, M. Lynne Corn, etc. IB91011
* Aspects of the Mobilization of the Petroleum Industry in World War II and the Korean War, Robert Bamberger 84-773 ENR
* Brazilian Petroleum Status, Joseph P. Riva 89-328 SPR
* Colombian Petroleum Status, Joseph P. Riva 89-437 SPR
* Comparison of United States and United Kingdom Offshore Oil and Gas Leasing and Development Systems, Malcolm M. Simmons 86-1011 ENR
* Declining Bonus Values in Outer Continental Shelf, Oil and Gas Lease Sales, Malcolm Simmons 85-871 ENR
* Disruption of Oil Supply from the Persian Gulf: Near-Term U.S. Vulnerability (Winter 1987/88), Clyde R. Mark, etc. 87-863 ENR
* Domestic Oil Production; Archived Issue Brief, Joseph P. Riva IB87068
* Domestic Oil Production under Conditions of Continued Low Drilling Activity: Issue Brief, Joseph R. Riva, jr. IB87068
* Double-Bottom/Double-Hull Tankers: Pro and Con, James E. Mielke 90-152 SPR
* Energy Security: Issue Brief, Carl E. Behrens IB89006
* Energy Tax Options to Increase Federal Revenue, Salvatore Lazzari 87-539 E
* Enhanced Oil Recovery Methods, Joseph Riva 87-827 SPR
* Environmental Effects of Energy Development in the Arctic National

Current Events and Homework

Wildlife Refuge: A Critique of the Final Legislative Environmental Impact Statement, M. Lynne Corn, etc. 87-490 ENR
* The Exxon Valdez Oil Spill: Archived Issue Brief, Martin R. Lee, etc. IB89075
* Federal Regulation of Used Oil, Mark Reisch 86-747 ENR
* The Financial Impact of Oil Price Behavior on International Development and Trade: Transnational Oil Companies and Persian Gulf Oil Exporters; Report, Clyde R. Mark, etc. 86-903 F
* Futures Markets and the Price of Oil, Mark Jickling 91-324 E
* A History of Federal Energy Tax Policy: Conventional as Compared to Renewable and Nonconventional Energy Resources, Salvatore Lazzari 88-455 E
* Iraq-Kuwait Oil Price Rise: U.S. Economics Effects, Bernard A. Gelb 90-434 E
* Kuwaiti Oil Well Fires, Joseph P. Riva 91-313 SPR
* Mexican Petroleum, Joseph Riva 83-178 SPR
* Mexican Oil: Less Than Meets the Eye, Joseph P. Riva 91-535 SPR
* The NATO Allies, Japan, and the Persian Gulf, Paul Gallis 84-184 F
* North African Petroleum, Joseph Riva 84-216 SPR
* Northwest European Region Petroleum (Including the North Sea), Joseph Riva 85-187 SPR
* OCS Revenue Sharing, Malcolm M. Simmons 91-182 ENR
* The Oil and Gas Leasing System on Federal Lands, Marc Humphries 91-577 ENR
* Oil and Iraq's Invasion of Kuwait: Archived Issue Brief, Carl Behrens, etc. IB90116
* Oil Companies and the Acquisition of Federal Petroleum Leases, John J. Schanz 88-213 S
* Oil Companies and the Development of the Arctic National Wildlife Refuge, John J. Schanz 88-106 S
* Oil from the Persian Gulf: Production, Disposition, and Transportation; Archived Issue Brief, Robert Bamberger, etc. IB88063
* The "Oil Import Bill" of the United States, 1945-1987: A Historical Record of U.S. Merchandise Trade, and Petroleum With Related Balances, Dario Scuka 88-107 E
* Oil Import Fees (Taxes) for Deficit Reduction: Revenue and Economic Effects; Issue Brief, Salvatore Lazzari IB87189
* Oil Import Tax: Some General Economic Effects, Bernard Gelb 87-259 E
* Oil Import Taxes: An Economic Analysis of S. 694, The Economic Security Act of 1987, Salvatore Lazzari 87-779 E
* Oil Import Taxes: Revenue and Economic Effects, Bernard A. Gelb, etc. 86-572 E
* Oil Imports from OPEC: Recent and Project Trends, Bernard Gelb 88-558 E
* Oil Market Overview, Lawrence C. Kumins 90-411 ENR
* Oil Overcharge Restitution: Background and Data, Bernard Gelb 88-287 E
* Oil Pollution Liability and Compensation Legislation After the Exxon Valdez Oil Spill: Issue Brief, Martin R Lee IB89082
* Oil Price Behavior: Implications for the Soviet Union: Report of the CRS Workshop, June 26, 1986, John P. Hardt, etc. 86-886 S
* Oil Price Decreases: Illustrative Effects on U.S. Oil Use, Production, and Imports, Bernard Gelb 86-599 E
* Oil Price Implications: Reshuffling Energy Policy? Archived Issue Brief, Robert Bamberger, etc. IB86146
* Oil Production and Reserves in the Soviet Republics, Joseph P. Riva 91-674 SPR
* Oil Prospect Profitability in the United States: Estimated Expectation in 1972, 1981, 1985, and 1986, Bernard Gelb, etc. 87-38 E
* Oil Royalty Trusts, Carolyn K. Brancato 84-575 E
* Oil Spill Response Technologies, James E. Mielke 90-146 SPR
* Oil Spills: Info Pack IP426O
* Oil Spills: Selected References, Ted L. Burch 90-138 L
* Oil Storage Tanks: Construction and Testing Issues Since the Ashland Oil Spill: Archived Issue Brief, Fred J. Sissine IB88015
* Oil Supply and the Gulf Crisis: Current Status Report, Lawrence Kumins 90-614 ENR
* Onshore Oil and Gas Resources on Federal Lands: Evaluating the Current Leasing System: Archived Issue Brief, Adela Backiel, etc. IB87077
* Outer Continental Shelf Leasing and Development: Issue Brief, Malcolm M. Simmons, etc. IB89028
* Outer Continental Shelf Leasing and Development, Issues in the 102nd Congress; Issue Brief, Malcolm M. Simmons IB91063
* The Outlook for U.S. Energy Supplies and the Arctic National Wildlife Refuge Decision, John Schanz 88-73 S
* An Overview of Soviet Oil and Gas in the World Arena, John P. Hardt, etc. 88-157 S
* Persian Gulf Oil: Its Critical Importance to World Oil Supplies, Joseph P. Riva 91-220 SPR
* The Petroleum Endowment of the People's Republic of China, Joseph P. Riva 86-102 SPR
* Petroleum in the United States: Selected Data Focused on the Oil Import Tax Issue, Bernard Gelb 86-1054 E
* The Petroleum Production Potential of South America, Joseph P. Riva 90-270 SPR
* The Petroleum Status of Ecuador, Joseph P. Riva 90-211 SPR
* The Petroleum Status of Romania, Joseph P. Riva 90-472 SPR
* Petroleum Status of the Western Persian Gulf, Joseph P. Riva 90-378 SPR
* Proceedings of the CRS Workshop on Canada-U.S. Free-Trade Agreement: How Will It Affect the United States? Arlene Wilson 88-356 E
* A Review of Oil Pollution Prevention Regulations After the Monongahela River Spill, Martin R. Lee 88-448 ENR
* Soviet Economic Conditions and Relations: Status and Prospects; Soviet Oil, Joseph Riva 91-639 SPR
* Soviet Oil Prospects, Joseph Riva 81-91 SPR
* The Strategic Petroleum Reserve: Issue Brief, Robert Bamberger IB87050
* The Strategic Petroleum Reserve and the Drawdown Dilemma, Robert L. Bamberger, etc. 90-492 ENR
* Telecommuting: A National Option for Conserving Oil, Fred Sissine 90-524 SPR
* U.S. Petroleum Exports--A Review of Fact and Policy, Lawrence C. Kumins 91-166 ENR
* Venezuelan Petroleum: A Source of Increasing U.S. Imports?, Joseph P. Riva 90-70 SPR
* The World's Conventional Oil Production Capability Projected into the Future by Country, Joseph P. Riva, Jr. 87-414 SPR

Foundations

* see Arts and Humanities

France

* British and French Strategic Nuclear Force Modernization: Issues for Western Security and Arms Control, Charlotte Philips Preece, etc. 89-140 F
* The Clandestine Trade in Heavy Water: A Chronology, Barbara B. Black, etc. 89-66 ENR
* Franco-German Security Cooperation: Implications for the NATO Alliance, Paul Gallis 89-16 F

Franking Privilege

* see Postal Service, Congress--Offices

Freedom of Information Act

* see also Government Information
* Access to Government Information in the United States, Harold C. Relyea 91-697 GOV
* The Administration and Operation of the Freedom of Information Act: An Overview, 1966-1990, Harold C. Relyea 90-508 GOV
* Freedom of Information Act/Privacy Act: A Guide to Their Use; Info Pack, IP047F

FSLIC

* see Federal Savings and Loan Insurance Corporation, Money and Banking--Failures and Deposit Insurance

FSX (Fighter)

* see Weapons Systems--Non-Nuclear Weapons)

Gandhi, Indira

* The Gandhi Assassination: Implications for India and U.S.-Indian Relations, Richard Cronin 84-790 F

Gandhi, Rajiv

* The Rajiv Gandhi Visit: Issues in U.S.-India Relations, Richard Cronin 85-383 F

Gasohol

* see Power Resources--Alternative Energy Sources

Gasoline

* see Fossil Fuels--Gasoline

Gasoline Tax

* see Taxation--Consumption Taxes

Gatt

* see General Agreement on Tariffs and Trade

Gay Rights

* see Civil Liberties and Rights--Discrimination and Integration

Gaza Strip

* Israeli-Palestinian Conflict: Bibliography-in-Brief, 1982-1988, Robert Kirk 88-251 L
* Israeli-Palestinian Conflict: Info Pack, IP397I
* Palestinian Disturbances in the Gaza Strip and West Bank: Policy Issues and Chronology, Ellen Laipson 88-114 F

Gender Gap

* See Women

Gene Therapy

* see Genetics

General Agreement on Tariffs and Trade

* see also Foreign Trade--Trade Agreements and Negotiations
* Addressing Unfair Trade: Agricultural Cases under Section 301 of the Trade Act of 1974, Donna U. Vogt 89-522 ENR
* Agricultural Policy for the 1990's; Audio Brief, Charles Hanrahan, etc. AB50217
* Agricultural Trade: Issue Brief, Donna Vogt IB88011
* Agricultural Trade Policy: The 1990 Farm Bill and the GATT Negotiations, Charles E. Hanrahan 90-267 S
* Agriculture in the GATT: After the Midterm Review; Issue Brief, Charles Hanrahan IB89027
* Agriculture in the GATT: Toward the Next Round of Multilateral Trade Negotiations, Charles Hanrahan, etc. 86-98 ENR
* Auctioning Import Quotas, Lenore Sek 87-669 E
* Decoupling Farm Programs, Carl W. Ek 88-604 ENR
* Dispute Settlement and the General Agreement on Tariffs and Trade, Raymond Ahearn 85-680 E
* Environmental Legislation and Trade: A Checklist of CRS Products, Ted L. Burch 92-7 L
* Environmental Regulation and the GATT, Jeanne J. Grimmett 91-285 A
* The GATT Trade Talks: Prospects for Selected manufacturing Industries, Edward B. Rappaport 91-821 E
* Government Procurement in Canada: Sourcing Policy, Law Library of Congress LL90-8
* Negotiating Authority for the Uruguay Round of Multilateral Trade Negotiations, Jeanne Jagelski 87-103 A
* Regulation of Timber Exports: Legislative Options, Kenneth R. Thomas 89-617 A
* Tariffication: Negotiating Reductions in Agricultural Import Barriers in the Uruguay Round, Donna U. Vogt, etc. 89-555 ENR
* Textile Trade Controls: A Comparison of Bills in the 99th and 100th Congresses, Edward Rappaport 87-607 E
* Trade: Issue Brief, George Holliday, etc. IB91015
* Trade Negotiations: The Uruguay Round: Issue Brief, Lenore Sek IB86147
* Trade Remedies Available to the United States under International Agreements and Corresponding Domestic Laws, Vladimir N. Pregelj 85-1008 E
* The Uruguay Round of Multilateral Trade Negotiations: Major Issues, Lenore M. Sek 90-496 E
* U.S. Agricultural Trade Opportunities With Pacific Rim Nations, Robert M. Goldstein 88-755 ENR
* U.S. Agricultural Trade Policy: Selected Readings, 1988-90, Ted L. Burch 90-328 L
* U.S.-Canada Free Trade Agreement: International Implications, Raymond J. Ahearn, etc. 88-249 F

General Interest

* see History (U.S.) and References Sources
* Additions to the Major Issues File, IB89001
* Archived Issue Brief List, IB89000
* CRS Television Program Schedule Channel 6 Congressional Cable System, IB83145

Genetics

* see also Research and Development
* Agricultural Research: Issues for the 1980s, Christine Matthews Rose 87-430 SPR
* Biotechnology: A Public Policy Primer, Sarah E. Taylor, etc. 89-389 SPR
* Bovine Growth Hormone(Somatotropin): Agricultural and Regulatory Issues, Geoffrey S. Becker, etc. 86-1020 ENR
* Bovine Somatotropin (BST or BGH): A Status Report, Ralph N. Chite 90-576 ENR
* Commercialization of Technology and Issues in the Competitiveness of Selected U.S. Industries; Semiconductors, Biotechnology, and Superconductors, Leonard G. Kruger, etc. 88-486 SPR
* Federal Regulation of Biotechnology: Archived Issue Brief, Judith Johnson, etc. IB89068
* Genetic Screening; Archived Issue Brief, Judith A. Johnson IB90121
* Human Gene Therapy: Archived Issue Brief, Judith Johnson IB84119
* Human Gene Therapy: Issue Brief, Judith Johnson IB87040
* Patenting Life: Issue Brief, Sarah Taylor IB87222
* Proposal to Map and Sequence the Human Genome: Issue Brief, Irene Stith-Coleman IB88012

Genocide

* see International Law--Human Rights

Genocide Convention

* Genocide Convention; Archived Issue Brief, Vita Blue IB74129

Georgian Republic

* Georgian Republic: Basic Facts, Daniel R. Cain 91-790 F

Gephardt Amendment

* see Foreign Trade--Trade Policy

German Reunification

* Forum: Revolution in Eastern Europe, Congressional Research Service, REV 3-90

Germany

* see Eastern Europe, West Germany

Glasnost

* see U.S.S.R. -- Politics and Government

Glass-Steagall Act

* see also Corporations--Securities Industry, Money and Banking--Law and Regulation
* Banking in the United States: An Overview, Info Pack IB429B
* Bank Service Diversification: A Comparative Summary of Major Financial Reform Measures Facing the Congress, William Jackson, etc. 88-84 E
* Bank Soundness in Light of the Tax Reform Act of 1986 and Possible Glass-Steagall Act Repeal, Walter W. Eubanks 88-118 E
* Banker-Broker Competition and the Glass-Steagall Act: The Mutual Funds Example, William Jackson 87-921 E
* Banks and Thrift Institutions: Restructuring and Solvency Issues, F. Jean Wells 88-749 E
* Expansion of Bank Powers Since CEBA, the Competitive Equality Banking Act of 1987, M. Maureen Murphy 89-666 A
* The Glass-Steagall Act: A Legal Overview, Henry Cohen 82-189 A
* The Glass-Steagall Act: Bibliography-in-Brief, 1981-1988, Felix Chin 88-98 L
* Glass-Steagall Act: Issue Brief, William Jackson IB87061
* Glass-Steagall Act: The Legal Landscape of Financial Restructuring, M. Maureen Murphy 88-335 A
* Glass Steagall Act: Should Bankers Be Brokers?, Issue Brief, William D. Jackson IB91038
* The Separation of Banking and Commerce, William Jackson 87-352 E

Global Climatic Changes

* see Earth Sciences

Global Securities Market

* see Corporations--Securities Industry, International Finance

Gorbachev, M.S.

* Continuity and Change in Soviet Diplomacy and Negotiations under Gorbachev, Joseph G. Whelan 89-39 F
* Gorbachev Reform Program After the 1988 Party Conference: Summary of a Roundtable Workshop, Francis T. Miko 89-130 F

Current Events and Homework

* The Gorbachev Speech to the United Nations, New York, Dec. 7, 1988, Foreign Affairs and National Defense Division 88-776 F
* Gorbachev's Reform Strategy: Comparisons With the Hungarian and Chinese Experience, Francis T. Miko, etc. 87-813 F
* Gorbachev's Reform: The Consumer Goods and Services Sector, F. Mike Miles 87-763 F
* Soviet Coup Attempt: Background and Implications, Archived Issue Brief, Raymond W. Copson IB91106
* Soviet Foreign Policy under Gorbachev: Determinants, Developments, Prospects, and Implications, Francis T. Miko 87-39 F
* Soviet "Restructuring" under Gorbachev: A Chronology, January 1985-June 1987, F. Mike Miles 87-551 F
* Statements by Mikhail Gorbachev Relating to Arms Control, July 1, 1986-June 30, 1987, Terri Lehto, etc. 87-646 S

Government and Politics

* see Congress, Constitution (U.S.), Executive Organization, Government Employees, Government Information, History (U.S.), Political Ethics, Politics and Elections, Presidents (U.S.), State and Local Government

Government Contracts

* see Defense Economics--Procurement, Procurement, Ethics, Pay and Benefits, Political Activities, Military Personnel, Military Personnel-Pensions, Pens

Government Employees

* see Ethics, Pay and Benefits, Political Activities, Military Personnel, Military Personnel-Pensions, Pensions-Civil Service
* Brief Summary of Statutory and Regulatory Procedural Rights of Federal Employees in the Event of an Agency Disciplinary Proceeding, Michael V. Seitzinger 86-962 A
* Career Guidance and Federal Job Information: Info Pack, IP016C
* Constitutional Analysis of Proposals to Establish a Mandatory Public Employee Drug Testing Program, Charles V. Dale 88-293 A
* Displaced Employee Assistance: Federal Civilian Programs, Sharon Gressle 86-976 A
* Drug Testing in the Workplace: Federal Programs; Archived Issue Brief, Sharon Gressle IB87174
* Elimination of the Professional and Administrative Career Examination (PACE) and Proposed Alternative Selection Procedures, Paul M. Downing 89-315 GOV
* The "Glass Ceiling:" Access of Women and Minorities to Management Positions, Linda Levine 91-623 E
* Governmentally Mandated Drug Testing of Public Employees: A Survey of Recent Constitutional Developments, Charles V. Dale 90-103 A
* Internships and Fellowships: Info Pack, IP063I
* Legal Analysis of S. 541, 100th Congress, a Bill to Provide that Certain Postal Service Employees Have Procedural and Appeal Rights in the Event of Ad, Michael Seitzinger 87-433 A
* President Reagan's Productivity Improvement Program: Deja Vu, Fresh Start to an Old Story, or Lasting Reform? Peter Benda, etc. 86-89 S
* The Priority Placement Program (PPP) in the Department of Defense, James McGrath 86-977 GOV
* Public Employment in the United States: A Compilation of Statistical Trends, 1950-1983, Barbara Schwemle, etc. 84-91 GOV
* Security Clearances for Congressional and Judicial Employees, Frederick M. Kaiser 87-809 GOV
* The Senior Executive Service (SES): Morale and Staffing Problems--A Brief Overview, James McGrath 87-315 GOV

Government Employees -- Ethics

* The Acceptance of Gifts by Employees in the Executive Branch, Jack Maskell 85-1089 A
* The Appearance of Impropriety as a Standard for Disciplining Federal Employees, Jack Maskell 85-687 A
* Brief Summary of Statutory and Regulatory Procedural Rights of Federal Employees in the Event of an Agency Disciplinary Proceeding, Michael V. Seitzinger 89-962 A
* Conflicts of Interest: The Department of Defense and the Revolving Door Problem, Andrew Mayer 86-188 F
* Constitutional Analysis of "Revolving Door" Proposal Regarding Expansion of Post-Employment Conflicts of Interest Law for Federal Officials, Jack Maskell 88-590 A
* The Defense Procurement Bribery and Fraud Investigation: Profiles of Persons and Companies Mentioned in Press Reports, David P. Fite 88-528 F
* Defense Procurement Investigation: Archived Issue Brief, Gary J. Pagliano, etc. IB88081
* Defense Procurement: The Fraud and Bribery Investigation: Info Pack, IP404D
* Ethics in Government: Reform of Laws and Regulations; Issue Brief, Mildred L. Amer IB89134
* Overview of Ethics and Conflict of Interest Provisions Applicable to Executive Branch Employees, Jack Maskell 85-667 A
* Overview of Whistleblower Protections in Federal Law, Jack Maskell 86-1018 A
* Post Employment "Revolving Door" Restrictions on Department of Defense Personnel, Jack Maskell 88-478 A
* Regulations on the Receipt of Gifts by Spouses of Government Employees, Jack Maskell 85-689 A
* Whistleblower Protections for Federal Employees, L. Paige Whitaker 90-41 A

Government Employees -- Pay and Benefits

* Age Discrimination in Employee Benefit Plans: United States Supreme Court Decision in Public Employees Retirement System of Ohio v. Betts, Kathleen S. Swendiman 89-478 A
* Benefit and Pay Increases in Selected Federal Programs, 1969-1991, Carolyn L. Merck 91-513 EPW
* Benefits to Individuals Based on Previous Employment: Interactions and Offsets in Selected Programs, Carolyn Merck 85-869 EPW
* Civil Service Retirement: Bibliography-in-Brief, 1985-1988, Edith Sutterlin 88-538 L
* Commission on Executive, Legislative, and Judicial Salaries: An Historical Overview, Sharon S. Gressle 89-38 GOV
* Comparable Worth/Pay Equity in the Federal Government: Issue Brief, Linda LeGrande IB85116
* Comparison of President Bush's Honoraria Reform Act of 1989 With Existing Laws, Orders, and Regulations, Mildred L. Amer 89-481 GOV
* Comparison of Retirement Systems for Executive Branch Employees, Members of Congress and Active Duty, Military Personnel, Carolyn Merck, etc. 85-685 EPW
* Congressional Pay, Selected Wages and Pensions, and Social Security: Compared to CPI, 1969-1989, Frederick H. Pauls, etc. 89-63 GOV
* Constitutionality of Delegating Pay-Setting Authority in the Federal Salary Act, Thomas Nicola 87-137 A
* Fair Labor Standards Act: Treatment of State and Local Government; Archived Issue Brief, Dennis Roth, etc. IB85195
* Federal Civil Service Retirement for People With Military Service and Social Security: "Catch 62", Carolyn Merck 84-680 EPW
* Federal Employees and the FY1992 Budget Proposals: Issue Brief, James P. McGrath, IB91108
* The Federal Employees Health Benefits Program: Archived Issue Brief, Janet Lundy IB89124
* Federal Employees Health Benefits Program: Issues and Problems; Archived Issue Brief, Janet Lundy IB83134
* Federal Employees Pay Comparability Act of 1990: A Summary of Provisions, Barbara L. Schwemle, etc. 91-328 GOV
* Federal Executive, Legislative, and Judicial Compensation: The Situation and Choices for the 101st Congress, James McGrath 89-70 GOV
* Federal Government General Schedule Salary Increases Compared With Index Data, Sharon S. Gressle 90-134 GOV
* Federal Salary Systems Implementation Timetable, Sharon S. Gressle 90-535 GOV
* Fiduciary Responsibility Requirements of the Pension and Retirement Plans for State Employees, Joyce A. Thorpe, etc. 88-614 A
* Financing the Federal Civil Service Retirement Programs: Payments Into and Out of the Trust Fund, Carolyn L. Merck 91-464 EPW
* Honoraria and Outside Earned Income: Summary of Current Restrictions in the Legislation and Executive Branches, Jack Maskell 89-29 A
* Medicare Coverage of Employees of State and Local Governments, David Koitz 88-369 EPW
* Overtime and Premium Pay for U.S. Customs Service Inspectors, Barbara L. Schwemle 91-473 GOV
* Pay Raise Proposals for Members of Congress, Top Officials and Federal Judges: Issues and Outlook, James P. McGrath 8621 GOV
* Pay Raises and Honoraria Reform for Members of Congress, Top Officials, Federal Judges: Issues and Outlook, James P. McGrath 90-422 GOV
* Pay Reform for Federal White-Collar Employees: A Conceptual Analysis and Comparison of Two Legislative Proposals, Barbara L. Schwemie 87-828 GOV
* Provisions of the Balanced Budget and Emergency Deficit Control Act of 1985 Affecting Pay and Benefits for Federal Workers and Retirees, Carolyn Merck 86-502 EPW

Government / Gramm-Rudman-Hollings Act

* Provisions of the Tax Reform Act of 1986 Affecting Federal Workers and Retirees, Carolyn Merck 86-928 EPW
* Retirement for Federal Employees: FY1991 Budget Issues; Archived Issue Brief, Carolyn L. Merck IB90041
* Retirement Systems for Federal Employees; Info Pack, IP205R
* Salaries and Allowances: The Executive Branch; Issue Brief, Sharon Gressle IB81263
* Salary Rates and Estimated Costs under the Ethics Reform Act of 1989, Sharon S. Gressle 91-264 GOV
* Social Security and Medicare Coverage of Employees of State and Local Governments, David Koitz, etc. 87-132 EPW
* Social Security and Medicare: Proposals to Cover State and Local Government: Issue Brief, Geoffrey C. Kollmann IB90065
* Survivor Benefits under the Civil Service Retirement System, Carolyn L. Merck 91-204 EPW
* Treatment of Former Spouses under Various Federal Retirement Systems, Marie B. Morris 88-512 A
* The U.S. Postal Service: Adjustment Cost for Retirement COLAs and Health Benefits under the 1990 Budget Act, Bernevia McCalip 91-191 E

Government Employees -- Political Activities

* Campaign Activities by Congressional Employees, Jack Maskell 89-574 A
* A Compilation of State Laws Governing Political Activity of Public Employees, Jack Maskell, etc. 87-904 A
* Hatch Act Amendments: Political Activity and the Civil Service; Archived Issue Brief, Barbara L. Schwemle IB87153
* Hatch Act: Bibliography-in-Brief, 1976-1987, Rebecca Mazur 88-94 L
* The Hatch Act: Existing Statute Compared With House and Senate Proposals, Barbara L. Schwemle 89-282 GOV
* The Hatch Act: Existing Statute Compared With 102nd Congress Proposals, Barbara L. Schwemle 91-544 GOV
* Hatch Act; Info Pack, IP298H
* Legal and Constitutional Framework of "Hatch Act" Restrictions on Political Activities of Federal Employees, Jack Maskell 89-280 A
* State Statutory Provisions Regarding Political Activities by Public Employees, Jack Maskell 87-841 A

Government Information

* Access to Government Information in the United States, Harold C. Relyea 91-697 GOV
* The Administration and Operation of the Freedom of Information Act: An Overview, 1966-1990, Harold c. Relyea 90-508 GOV
* The Anti-Drug Abuse Act of 1988 (P.L. 100-690): Reports and Other Executive Branch Actions Required, Suzanne Cavanagh, etc. 89-406 GOV
* Classified Information Procedures Act (CIPA): An Overview, Larry Eig 89-172 A
* Confidentiality and Secrecy Orders in Civil Cases, Kenneth R. Thomas 89-225 A
* Congressional Access to Information from the Executive: A Legal Analysis, Richard Ehlke 86-50 A
* Form Letters: Tell Your Constituents Where to Get Government Publications; Info Pack, IP222F
* Freedom of Information Act/Privacy Act: A Guide to Their Use; Info Pack, IP047F
* Government Publications--How, What, When, Where, and Why: Info Pack, IP264G
* Information Policy and Technology Issues: Public Laws of the 95th Through 101st Congresses, Robert Lee Chartrand etc. 91-569 SPR
* International Migration Data: Sources and Quality, Jennifer D. Williams 91-466 GOV
* Legal Issues Related to the Possible Release of Classified Information by Senators, Representatives, or Members of Their Staffs, Elizabeth B. Bazan 89-322 A
* Paperwork Management in the Federal Government, Stephanie Smith 89-189 GOV
* Paperwork Reduction and Information Resources Management; Issue Brief, Stephanie Smith IB91107
* The Personal Identification Card in the Federal Republic of Germany, Law Library of Congress LL90-37
* Privatization of the National Technical Information Service, Jane Bortnick, etc. 87-491 SPR
* Protecting Classified Information: A Compilation and Index of Major Findings and Recommendations, 1905-1987, Frederick M. Kaiser, etc. 87-293 GOV
* Security Clearances for Congressional and Judicial Employees, Frederick M. Kaiser 87-809 GOV

* Security Clearances for Members of Congress and the Judiciary, Frederick M. Kaiser 87-704 GOV
* Sources of State Juror Lists, Paul L. Morgan 89-337 A
* United States Regulations: Finding Regulatory Material, Mark Gurevitz 90-590 A
* Where to Get Publications from the Executive and Independent Agencies: A Directory of Sources for Official Documents, Deborah C. Brudno, etc. 91-82 C

Government Paperwork

* see Government Information

Government and Politics

* Congressional Committee Staff and Funding, IB82006
* Constitutional Conventions: Political and Legal Questions, IB80062
* Hatch Act Amendments: Political Activity and the Civil Service, IB87153
* Presidential Nominating Process: Proposed Reforms, IB86117
* Presidential Nominating Process: Proposed Reforms, IB86117
* Puerto Rico: Political Status Options, IB89065
* Retirement for Federal Employees: FY 90 Budget Issues, IB89034
* Salaries and Allowances: The Executive Branch, IB81263
* Salaries for Members of Congress, IB86017
* Senate Procedure, Rules, and Organization: Proposals for Change in the 101st Congress, IB89074

Government Procurement

* see Defense Economics--Procurement, Procurement

Government Regulation

* see Business and Society-Regulation and Deregulation, Money and Banking--Law and Regulation

Government Securities Act

* Legal Analysis of the Government Securities Act of 1986 and Its Application to Broker/Dealers Convicted of Insider Trading Violation, Michael V. Seitzinger 87-280 A

Government Spending

* see Public Finance

Gramm-Rudman-Hollings Act

* see also Public Finance-Deficits
* Agriculture and the Gramm-Rudman-Hollings Deficit Control Act, Geoffrey Becker 86-547 ENR
* Budget Cuts: Updated Projections and Gramm-Rudman-Hollings; Archived Issue Brief, William Cox IB86072
* Budget Enforcement Act of 1990: A General Explanation; Videoproram, Robert Keith LTR91-919
* Budget Enforcement Act of 1990: Brief Summary, Edward Davis, etc. 90-520 GOV
* Budget Enforcement Act of 1990: Contents Listing, Edward Davis, etc. 90-516 GOV
* Budget Enforcement Act of 1990: Cross-References to Laws and Rules Amended, Edward Davis, etc. 90-517 GOV
* Budget Enforcement Act of 1990: Legislative History, Edward Davis, etc. 90-518 GOV
* Budget Sequestration Procedures for Fiscal Year 1987: Summary of Congressional Action, Robert Keith 86-1049 GOV
* Debt-Limit Increase and 1985 Balanced Budget Act Reaffirmation: Summary of Public Law 100-199 (H.J. Res. 324), Edward Davis, etc. 87-865 GOV
* Debt-Limit Increases for Fiscal Year 1987: Summary of Congressional Action in 1986 (Including Proposed Modifications to the 1985 Balanced Budget Act), Robert A. Keith, etc. 86-974 GOV
* Deficit Reduction in 1988: Archived Issue Brief, William Cox IB87023
* Economic Forecasts and Gramm-Rudman-Hollings, Brian Cashell 87-934 E
* Explanation of the Balanced Budget and Emergency Deficit Control Act of 1985-P.L. 99-177 (the Gramm-Rudman-Hollings Act), Allen Schick 85-1130 GOV
* The Federal Budget for Fiscal Year 1988: Archived Issue Brief, Philip D. Winters IB87057
* The Federal Budget For Fiscal Year 1989: Issue Brief, Philip Winters IB88064
* The Federal Budget Process: Selected References, Robert Howe 88-436 L
* The Forest Service Budget: Trust Funds and Special Accounts, Ross Gorte,

Current Events and Homework

etc, 89-75 ENR
* Gramm-Rudman-Hollings and Department of Education Programs, Angela Evans 86-544 EPW
* Gramm-Rudman-Hollings Budget Adjustments: Sensitivity to Economic Assumptions; Archived Issue Brief, Barry Molefsky, etc. IB85217
* The Gramm-Rudman-Hollings Deficit Reduction Plan: The Target of a Balanced Budget and the Risk of Recession, Craig Elwell 86-534 E
* The Gramm-Rudman-Hollings Deficit Reduction Process (P.L. 99-177) and the Department of Defense: A Summary Review, Alice Maroni, etc. 86-7 F
* The Gramm-Rudman-Hollings Deficit Reduction Process: The Defense Aspects of the Initial Sequestration Report for Fiscal Year 1987, Alice Maroni, etc. 86-875 F
* Gramm-Rudman-Hollings: Potential Economic Effects of Meeting Deficit Targets; Archived Issue Brief, Brian W. Cashell IB87059
* The Gramm-Rudman-Hollings Sequestration Process for FY 1986: A Summary of DOD Elements in the OMB/CB O and GAO Sequestration Reports: Policy Alert, Alice Maroni, etc. 86-16 F
* The Gramm-Rudman-Hollings Targets: How Might They Affect the Economy, Gail Makinen, etc. 86-1036 E
* Health Programs and the Gramm-Rudman-Hollings Legislation: The 1986 Sequestration and the President's FY 87 Budget Proposal, James Reuter 86-648 EPW
* Implications of Uncertainty in Economic Forecasting under Gramm-Rudman-Hollings: Options for Congressional Response, David Grinnell 86-829 S
* An Introduction to the Spending and Budget Process in Congress, Stanley Bach 90-288 S
* Manual on the Federal Budget Process, Allen Schick, etc. 87-286 GOV
* Provisions of the Balanced Budget and Emergency Deficit Control Act of 1985 Affecting Pay and Benefits for Federal Workers and Retirees, Carolyn Merck 86-502 EPW
* Selected Federal Research and Development Agencies and Programs and the Gramm-Rudman-Hollings Deficit Reduction Act: An Analysis of the Impact on Them, Michael E. Davey 86-37 SPR
* Sequestration Actions for Fiscal Year 1988 under the Gramm-Rudman-Hollings Act: Archived Issue Brief, Robert Keith IB87224
* Sequestration Actions for FY 89 under the Gramm-Rudman-Hollings Act: Archived Issue Brief, Robert Keith IB88078
* Sequestration Actions for FY 90 under the Gramm-Rudman-Hollings Act: Issue Brief, Robert Keith IB89017
* Sequestration Actions in 1990 under the Gramm-Rudman-Hollings Act: Archived Issue Brief, Robert Keith IB90055
* Sequestration of Budgetary Resources for Fiscal Year 1986 under the 1985 Balanced Budget Act, Robert A. Keith 86-872 GOV
* Summary and Analysis of the Ramifications of Bowsher v. Synar, the Gramm-Rudman-Hollings Deficit Reduction Act Case, Morton Rosenberg, etc. 86-788 A
* Suspension of Budget Enforcement Procedures in the Event of a Declaration of War, Robert Keith 91-98 GOV
* Wastewater Treatment Programs; Impact of Gramm-Rudman-Hollings Act and Prospects for Federal Funding (With Appendix); Archived Issue Brief, Claudia Copeland IB86018

Grants

* see Reference Sources--Grants

Great Britain

* British and French Strategic Nuclear Force Modernization: Issues for Western Security and Arms Control, Charlotte Phillips Preece, etc. 89-140 F
* The British Experience With Indexed Bonds, G. Thomas Woodward 87-926 E
* Comparison of United States and United Kingdom Offshore Oil and Gas Leasing and Development Systems, Malcolm M. Simmons 86-1011 ENR
* U.S. Civilian and Defense Research and Development Funding: Some Trends and Comparisons With Selected Industrialized Nations, William Boesman, etc. 84-195 SPR

Greece

* Current Issues With the "Base-Rights" Countries and Their Implications, Richard F. Grimmett 88-726 F
* Greece: An Assessment of the June 1989 Elections, Ellen Laipson 89-431 F
* Greece and Turkey: The Seven-Ten Ratio in Military Aid, Ellen Laipson 90-29 F
* Greece and Turkey: U.S. Foreign Assistance Facts: Issue Brief, Carol Migdalovitz IB86065
* Greek-Turkish Relations: Beginning of a New Era?, Ellen Laipson 88-724 F
* Greek-U.S. Bases Agreement: Archived Issue Brief, Richard F. Grimmett IB89155
* The Seven-Ten Ratio in Military Aid to Greece and Turkey: A Congressional Tradition, Ellen Laipson 85-79 F
* United States Military Installations in Greece, Richard Grimmett 84-24 F

Greenhouse Effect

* see Air Pollution--Ozone, Earth Sciences

Grenada

* Grenada: Issues Concerning the Use of U.S. Forces; Archived Issue Brief, Janice Hanover IB83170

Ground Wave Emergency Network (GWEN)

* The Ground Wave Emergency Network, Gary K. Reynolds 89-206 F

Groundwater Contamination

* see Water Pollution--Groundwater

Grove City College v. Bell

* Civil Rights Legislation: Response to Grove City College v. Bell; Archived Issue Brief, Bob Lyke IB87123

Guam

* Territorial Political Development: An Analysis of Puerto Rico, Northern Mariana Islands, Guam, Virgin Islands, and American Samoa, and the Micronesian, Bette A. Taylor 88-657 GOV

Guatemala

* Central America: U.S. Relations With Costa Rica, Guatemala, and Honduras: Info Pack, IP352C
* Central American Peace Process: Selected References, Robert Kirk 88-389 L
* Guatemala: Country Background Report, Maureen Taft-Morales 88-586 F
* Guatemala: U.S. Foreign Assistance Facts; Archived Issue Brief, Jonathan Sanford IB85100

Gulf Cooperation Council

* The Gulf Cooperation Council, Richard Preece 85-516 F

Gun Control

* see Crimes and Offenses--Gun Control

Gun Control Act

* Gun Control Act of 1968, as Amended: Digest of Major Provisions, P.L. 90-618, 90th Congress, H.R. 17 735, October 22, 1968, Harry Hogan 85-166 GOV

Haiti

* Haiti: Political Developments and U.S. Policy Concerns: Archived Issue Brief, Maureen Taft-Morales IB88104
* Haiti: Prospects for Democracy and U.S. Policy Concerns: Issue Brief, Maureen Taft-Morales IB91043

Handicapped

* see Americans with Disabilities Act, Children, Employment, Policies and Legislation, Rehabilitation Act, Social Services
* Accessibility for the Handicapped in Federally Funded Buildings: The Law and Its Implementation, Mary Smith 85-613 EPW
* Architectural Barriers and the Physically Handicapped: Selected References, 1974-1988, Charles Dove 89-108 L
* Bibliography of Selected Law Review Articles Concerning Handicapped Persons, M. Ann Wolfe 87-968 A
* Blind Vendors in Federal Facilities: Brief Background and Program Data, mary F. Smith 91-753 EPW
* Community-Based Services for Individuals With Severe Disabilities: Summary and Analysis of S. 1673 and H.R. 3454, Mary F. Smith 88-212 EPW
* Community Services under Medicaid for Persons With Mental Retardation: Archived Issue Brief, Mary f. Smith IB89135
* Comparative Analysis of Title VII of the 1964 Civil Rights Act, the Age Discrimination in Employment Act, and the Rehabilitation Act of 1973, Charles V. Dale 89-240 A
* Developmental Disabilities Programs; FY 1989 Budget Information, Mary F. Smith 88-181 EPW

* Developmental Disabilities Programs; Statutory Authority and Program Operations, Mary F. Smith 88-52 EPW
* Digest of Data on Persons With Disabilities, 84-115 EPW
* Disabled Persons: State Laws Concerning Accessibility and Discrimination, M. Ann Wolfe 89-409 A
* Elderly and Handicapped Housing: Recent Developments in Section 202, Susan M. Vanhorenbeck 89-667 E
* Housing for the Elderly and Handicapped: Section 202; Issue Brief, Susan M. Vanhorenbeck IB84038
* Medicaid Services for Persons With Mental Retardation or Related Conditions, Mary F. Smith 88-759
* Regulations Promulgated Pursuant to Section 504 of the Rehabilitation Act of 1973: A Brief History and Present Status, Nancy Jones, etc. 86-53 A
* Remedies and Standing to Sue under S. 933, the "Americans With Disabilities Act of 1989", Charles V. Dale 89-336 A
* School Board of Nassau County v. Arline: A Person With the Contagious Disease of Tuberculosis May Be Covered under Section 504 of the Rehabilitation, Nancy Lee Jones 87-238 A
* Section 504 of the Rehabilitation Act: Statutory Provisions, Legislative History, and Regulatory Requirement, Mary F. Smith 89-48 EPW
* Selected Legislation Affecting Persons With Handicaps: 100th Congress, Mary F. Smith 89-106 EPW
* Social Security: Re-Examining Eligibility for Disability Benefits; Archived Issue Brief, David Koitz IB82078
* Social Security: The 5-Month Waiting Period for Disability Insurance Benefits, David Koitz 79-239 EPW
* Supreme Court Decisions Interpreting Section 504 of the Rehabilitation Act of 1973, Nancy Jones 85-926 A
* Tax Code Provisions of Interest to the Disabled and Handicapped, Louis Alan Talley 87-721 E
* Telephone Access for the Hearing Impaired: Federal Actions to Increase Availability, Angele A. Gilroy 86-917 E
* Transportation for Elderly and Handicapped People: Programs, Regulations, and Issues, Lenore Sek 85-699 E
* Work Disincentives and Disability Insurance, David Koitz 80-160 EPW

Handicapped -- Children

* Constitutional and Statutory Issues Relating to the Use of Behavior Modification on Children in Institutions, Nancy Jones 86-1000 A
* Education of the Handicapped Act Discretionary Programs: Background and Current Issues, Margot A. Schenet 89-67 EPW
* The Education of the Handicapped: Selected References, 1984-1987, Marsha Cerny 87-520 L
* P.L. 94-142, the Education for All Handicapped Children: Background, Issues, and Federal Policy Options, Charlotte Fraas 86-55 EPW
* Preschool Programs for the Education of Handicapped Children: Background, Issues, and Federal Policy Options Charlotte Fraas 86-55 EPW
* The "Stay Put" Provision of the Education for All Handicapped Children Act: Honig, California Superintendent of Public Instruction v. Doe Et Al, Meredith A. Yancey 88-494 A
* Summary of the Education of the Handicapped Act Amendments of 1986, P.L. 99-457, Charlotte Jones Fraas 86-926 EPW
* Vouchers for the Education of Disadvantaged Children: Analysis of the Reagan Administration Proposal, Wayne Riddle 85-1022 EPW

Handicapped -- Employment

* Affirmative Action in the Employment of Persons With Handicaps under Federal Contracts: Section 503 of the Rehabilitation Act, Mary F. Smith 88-701 EPW
* The Americans With Disabilities Act (ADA): Legal Analysis of Proposed Legislation Prohibiting Discrimination on the Basis of Handicap, Nancy Lee Jones 88-621 A
* Employment of Persons With Handicaps under the Javits-Wagner-O'Day Act: Summary of the Special Procurement Program and Current Issues, Mary F. Smith 88-610 EPW
* Randolph-Sheppard Act: the Blind Vendors Program, Mary F. Smith 85-603 EPW
* Sheltered Workshops for Persons With Handicaps: Background Information and Recent Legislative Change, Mary F. Smith 87-362 EPW
* Survey of State Statutes Concerning Employment Discrimination of Handicapped Persons, M. Ann Wolfe 87-561 A
* Vocational Rehabilitation and Related Programs for Persons With Handicaps: FY 1990 Budget Request, Mary F. Smith 89-176 EPW
* Work Disincentives and Disability Insurance, David Koitz 80-160 EPW
* Work Incentives for Disabled Supplemental Security Income (SSI) Recipients: Section 1619 of the Social Security Act, Carmen D. Solomon 87-427 EPW

Handicapped -- Policies and Legislation

* Affirmative Action in the Employment of Persons With Handicaps under Federal Contracts: Section 503 of the Rehabilitation Act, Mary F. Smith 88-701 EPW
* The Americans With Disabilities Act: An Overview of Major Provisions, Nancy Lee Jones 90-366 A
* The Americans With Disabilities Act: Equal Employment Opportunity Commission Proposed Regulations on Equal Employment Opportunity for Individuals With Disabilities, Nancy Lee Jones 91-291 A
* The Americans With Disabilities Act: Info Pack IP443A
* Americans With Disabilities Act of 1989: Analysis of the Remedies and Enforcement Provisions of S. 933, as Passed by the Senate, Charles V. Dale, 90-112 A
* Business Tax Provisions of Interest to the Handicapped--Including Changes Made under the Revenue Reconciliation Act of 1990, Louis Alan Talley 90-636 E
* Children With Special Needs: Tax Assistance Proposals; Archived Issue Brief, Louis Alan Talley IB89153
* Comparative Analysis of Title VII of the 1964 Civil Rights Act, the Age Discrimination in Employment Act, and the Rehabilitation Act of 1973, Charles V. Dale 89-240 A
* Developmental Disabilities Programs: Statutory Authority and program Operations, Mary F. Smith 88-52 EPW
* Disabled Infants and Toddlers Program (Individuals ith Disabilities Education act): Reauthorization Issues, Steven R. Aleman 91-454 EPW
* Education of the Deaf Act: Background and Reauthorization Issues, Steven R. Aleman 91-509 EPW
* Education of the Handicapped Act Amendments of 1990, P.L. 101-476: A Summary, Steven R. Aleman 91-297 EPW
* Education of the Handicapped Act Discretionary Programs: Background and Current Issues, Margot A. Schenet 89-67 EPW
* The Fair Labor Standards Act and Employment of Workers With Disabilities: The Case of the Salvation Army, William G. Whittaker 91-93 E
* Federal Tax Code Provisions of Interest to the Disabled and Handicapped, Louis Alan Talley, 91-21 E
* Medicaid Services for Persons With Mental Retardation or Related Conditions, Mary F. Smith 88-759
* P.L. 94-142, the Education for All Handicapped Children Act: Its Development, Implementation, and Current Issues, Charlotte Fraas 86-552 EPW
* The Possible Applicability of the Americans With Disabilities Act to Indian Tribes, Elizabeth B. Bazan 91-497 A
* Section 504 of the Rehabilitation Act: Statutory Provisions, Legislative History, and Regulatory Requirements, Mary F. Smith 89-48 EPW
* Summary of the Education of the Handicapped Act Amendments of 1986, P.L. 99-457, Charlotte J. Fraas 86-926 EPW

Hatch Act

* see also Government Employees--Political Activities
* A Compilation of State Laws Governing Political Activity of Public Employees, Jack Maskell, etc. 87-904 A
* Hatch Act Amendments: Political Activity and the Civil Service: Archived Issue Brief, Barbara Schwemle IB87153
* Hatch Act: Bibliography-in-Brief, 1976-1987, Rebecca Mazur 88-94 L
* The Hatch Act: Existing Statute Compared With House and Senate Proposals, Barbara L. Schwemle 89-282 GOV
* The Hatch Act: Existing Statutes Compared 102nd Congress Proposals, Barbara L. Schwemle 91-544 GOV
* Hatch Act: Info Pack, IP298H
* Legal and Constitutional Framework of "Hatch Act" Restrictions on Political Activities of Federal Employees, Jack Maskell 89-280 A

Hazardous Substances

see Chemicals, Solid Wastes

Hazardous Wastes

* see Solid Wastes, Superfund

Head Start Program

* see Elementary and Secondary Education

Health

* see Drug Abuse, Drugs, Environmental Health, Health Facilities, Health Insurance, Medical Economics, Medical Personnel, Medicare and Medicaid,

Current Events and Homework

Medicine, Mental Health, Occupational Health and Safety, Public Health
* Acquired Immune Deficiency Syndrome and Military Manpower Policy, IB87202
* Acquired Immune Deficiency Syndrome (AIDS): Health Care Financing and Services, IB87219
* AIDS: An Overview of Issues, IB87150
* AIDS: International Problems and Issues, IB87214
* Alzheimer's Disease, IB83128
* Catastrophic Health Insurance: Medicare, IB87106
* Drug Approval: Access to Experimental Drugs for Severely Ill Patients, IB89016
* Federal Funding for AIDS Research and Prevention, IB87028
* Health Benefits for Retirees: An Uncertain Future, IB88004
* Health Care, IB87009
* Health Care Expenditures and Prices, IB77066
* Health Professions Education and Nurse Training Programs: Titles VII and VIII of the Public Health Service Act, IB88055
* Human Fetal Research and Tissue Transplantation, IB88100
* Indoor Air Pollution, IB88092
* Long Term Care for the Elderly, IB88098
* Mandated Employer Provided Health Insurance, IB87168
* Medicaid: FY 90 Budget and Child Health Initiatives, IB89031
* Medicare: FY 90 Budget, IB89029
* Medicare: Prospective Payments for Inpatient Hospital Services, IB87180
* Military Medical Care Services: Questions and Answers, IB87155
* Pediatric HIV Infection: Selected Research Issues, IB89099
* Private Health Insurance: Continuation Coverage, IB87182
* Radon: Congressional and Federal Concerns, IB86144

Health Care Costs

* see Medical Economics

Health Facilities

* Advance Directives and Health Care Facilities, Celinda Franco 91-117 EPW
* Brief Summary of Several Federal Statutes Which Arguably Provide the Federal Government the Authority to Control the Disposal of Infectious Hospital, Cathy Gilmore 87-658 A
* Community Health Centers and the Primary Care Block Grant, John Gray 86-899 EPW
* Community Services under Medicaid for Persons With Mental Retardation: Archived Issue Brief, Mary F. Smith IB89135
* Description of Residential Facilities for the Elderly, Evelyn Tager 84-19 EPW
* Financing and Delivery of Long-Term Care Services for the Elderly, Carol O'Shaughnessy, etc. 88-379 EPW
* Hospital Capital Cost Reimbursement under Medicare, Joseph Cislowski, etc. 86-598 EPW
* Hospital Patient Protection: The Consolidated Omnibus Budget Reconciliation Act "anit-Dumping" Law, Beth C. Fuchs, etc. 90-321 EPW
* Medicare: Prospective Payments for Inpatient Hospital Services; Archived Issue Brief, Celinda Franco, etc. IB87180
* Medicare: Recalculating Payment Rates under the Prospective Payment System, Mark Merlis 87-574 EPW
* Rural Hospitals, Mark Merlis 89-296 EPW
* Rural Hospitals under Medicare's Prospective Payment System and the Omnibus Budget Reconciliation Act of 1986 (P.L. 99-509), Joseph Cislowski, etc. 87-816 EPW

Health Insurance

* see also Medicare and Medicaid
* Access to Health Care and Health Insurance: Bibliography-in-Brief, 1986-1987, Edith Sutterlin 88-27 L
* AIDS and Discrimination: Legal Limits on Insurance Underwriting Practices, Kirk D. Nemer 88-381 A
* The Canadian Health Care System, Beth C. Fuchs, etc. 90-95 EPQ
* Catastrophic Health Insurance: Bibliography-in-Brief, 1986-1988, Marsha Cerny, etc. 88-401 L
* Catastrophic Health Insurance: Info Pack, IP370C
* Catastrophic Health Insurance: Medicare; Issue Brief, Jennifer O'Sullivan IB87106
* Employees Group Health Insurance Benefits Continuation under COBRA, Vincent E. Treacy, etc. 91-97 A
* Employer Provided Health Insurance: Comparison of the Major Provisions of the "Minimum Health Benefits for All Workers Act" (S. 1265/H.R. 2508) as Int., Beth C. Fuchs, etc. 88-588 EPW
* Federal Employees Health Benefits Program: Archived Issue Brief, Janet Lundy IB89124
* Financing and Delivery of Long-Term Care Services for the Elderly, Carol O'Shaughnessy, etc. 88-379 EPW
* Financing Catastrophic Health Care: Possible Effects on Marginal and Average Income Tax Rates, Gregg Esenwein 89-132 E
* Financing Long-Term Care for the Elderly: Audio Brief, Richard Price, etc. AB50187
* Health Benefit Plans and the Impact of Section 89: Archived Issue Brief, Beth Fuchs, etc. IB89083
* Health Benefits for Retirees: An Uncertain Future; Archived Issue Brief, Beth C. Fuchs IB88004
* Health Care Access: Federal Policy Issues; Info Pack, IP421H
* Health Care: Archived Issue Brief, Janet Kline IB87009
* Health Care Financing and Health Insurance: A Glossary of Terms, Education and Public Welfare Division. Health Sect 88-539 EPW
* Health Care for Children: Federal Programs and Policies, Joseph A. Cislowski 88-217 EPW
* Health Care: Issue Brief, Janet Kline IB87009
* Health Insurance and the Uninsured: Background Data and Analysis, Education and Public Welfare Division. Health Ins 88-537 EPW
* Health Insurance: Approaches for Universal Coverage, Beth Fuchs, etc. 90-568 EPW
* Health Insurance Continuation Coverage under COBRA: Issue Brief, Beth C. Fuchs IB87182
* Health Insurance Coverage: Characteristics of the Insured and Uninsured Populations, Madeleine Smith, etc. 91-618 EPW
* Health Insurance: Employer Benefits Required under COBRA and Pending Proposals; Info Pack, IP389H
* Health Insurance: Issue Brief, Mark Merlis IB91093
* Health Insurance: Info Pack, IP072H
* Health Insurance Legislation in the 102nd Congress, Beth C. Fuchs, etc. 91-564 EPW
* Health Insurance that Supplements Medicare: Background Material and Data, Jennifer O'Sullivan, etc 89-421 EPW
* Health Maintenance Organizations (HMO) and Employer Group Health Plans, Mark Merlis 91-261 EPW
* Health Maintenance Organizations: Bibliography-in-Brief, 1983-1987, Bonnie Mangan 88-87 L
* Increasing Access to Health Insurance: Audio Brief, AB50166
* The Japanese Health Care System, Joan Sokolovksy, etc. 89-572 EPW
* Legal Analysis of LTV Corporations's Unilateral Termination of Retirees' Health and Life Insurance Benefits on the Date of Filing in Bankruptcy, Vincent Treacy 86-845 A
* Legal Authority of Bankrupt Employer Unilaterally to Terminate Retiree's Benefits under a Collective Bargaining Agreement, Vincent Treacy 86-826 A
* Long Term Care Financing: Selected References, Peter Giordano 89-42 L
* Long-Term Care Legislation: Summary of Selected Bills, Carol O'Shaughnessy, etc. 89-238 EPW
* Mandated Employer Provided Health Insurance: Issue Brief, Beth C. Fuchs IB87168
* Medicare Catastrophic Coverage Act of 1988 (P.L. 100-360), Jennifer Sullivan 89-155 EPW
* Medicare: Risk Contracts With Health Maintenance Organizations and Competitive Medical Plans, Mark Merlis 88-138 EPW
* Medigap and Related Private Health Insurance Legislation in the 101st Congress, Janet Lundy 91-140 EPW
* Military Medical Care Services: Questions and Answers; Archived Issue Brief, David F. Burrelli IB87155
* National Health Expenditures: Trends from 1960-1989, Kathleen M. King, etc. 91-588 EPW
* The Potential Liability of Insurance Companies and Self-Insured Businesses for Unauthorized Disclosure of Medical Information Provided in Connection, Kirk D. Nemer 88-509 A
* Private Health Insurance Continuation Coverage; Issue Brief, Beth Fuchs IB87182
* Private Health Insurance Continuation Coverage: Legislative History of Title X of COBRA, Beth C. Fuchs 87-613 EPW
* Public Opinion on Long-Term Health Care needs, Costs and Financing, Rosita M. Thomas 90-151 GOV
* Tax Expenditures for Health Care, Nonna A. Noto, 92-12 E
* Tax Options for Financing Long-Term Care for the Elderly, Jane G. Gravelle, etc. 89-329 E
* Taxation of Employer-Provided Health Benefits, Beth Fuchs 90-507 EPW

Helsinki Accords

* Emigration: Soviet Compliance With the Helsinki Accords; Archived Issue Brief, John Hardt, etc. IB82080

High Definition Television

* see Telecommunication--Television

High Technology

* see Computers, Industry-High Technology Industries, Research and Development

Higher Education

* see Integration, Law and Legislation, Student Aid, Federal Aid to Education--Higher Education
* Analysis of the Protection of Pupil Rights Amendment--The "Hatch Amendment"--Regarding Student Rights in Federally Funded Educational Research, Experi., Rick Holland 86-801 EPW
* Building the National Research and Education Network: Issue Brief, Stephen Gould IB90126
* Chinese Student and Scholar Organizations in the United States, Kerry Dumbaugh 90-558 F
* Civil Rights Legislation: Response to Grove City College v. Bell; Archived Issue Brief, Bob Lyke IB87123
* Colleges and Universities Attended by Representatives of the 102nd Congress, Mildred L. Amer 91-511 GOV
* Colleges and Universities Attended by Senators of the 102nd Congress, Mildred L. Amer 91-510 GOV
* A Comparison of the Education Provisions in the Omnibus Trade Bill, H.R. 3, as Passed by the House and by the Senate, Paul Irwin, etc. 87-634 EPW
* Early Labor Market Experiences of Proprietary School Students, Robert Lyke, etc. 91-177 EPW
* Economic Benefits of Education, Linda LeGrande 88-753 E
* Education: An Alphabetical Microthesaurus of Terms Selected From the Legislative Indexing Vocabulary, Shirley Loo 89-54 L
* Education: Issues of Quality and Reform: Info Pack, IP256E
* The Education of the Handicapped: Selected References, 1984-1987, Marsha Cerny 87-529 L
* Education Provisions of the Trade Act of 1988, P.L. 100-418, Paul Irwin, etc. 88-750 EPW
* Elderly: State Survey of Statutes or Policy Concerning Fees in Higher Education Institutions, M. Ann Wolfe 91-298 A
* Equity, Excellence, and the Distribution of Federal Research and Development Funds, William Boesman, etc. 88-422 SPR
* The Federal Agency for Education: History and Background Information, Angela Evans 81-93 EPW
* Historically Black Colleges and Universities and African-American Participation in Higher Education, William W. Ellis, etc 89-588 S
* Indirect Costs at Academic Institutions: Background and Controversy; Issue Brief, Genevieve J. Knezo IB91095
* Minority Enrollment Trends in Higher Education, James B. Stedman 91-460 EPW
* National Mean Scores of the Scholastic Aptitude Test and the American College Test, Steven R. Aleman 89-97 EPW
* The National Sea Grant College Program: Issue Brief, Robert Morrison IB87163
* The National Sea Grant Program: Comparisons With Land Grant, Robert Morrison, etc. 85-1148 SPR
* "Nontraditional" Students Attending Postsecondary Institutions, Richard N. Apling 91-484 EPW
* Postsecondary Educational Experiences of High School Graduates, Richard Apling 91-374 EPW
* Proprietary Schools, Robert Lyke 91-440 EPW
* Proprietary Vocational Schools: Selected References, 1965-1991, M. Alexandra Salinas, etc. 91-312 L
* Revenue Sources for Higher Education Institutions, K. Forbis Jordan 86-956 S
* Speech Material: Graduation; Info Pack, IB379G
* Study Abroad: Bibliography-in-Brief, Peter Giordano 88-627 L
* Underrepresented Minorities and Women in Science, Mathematics, and Engineering: Problems and Issues for the 1990s, Christine M. Matthews 91-26 SPR
* Where Postsecondary Students Go to School, Richard Apling 91-322 EPW

Higher Education -- Integration

* Civil Rights Legislation: Response to Grove City College v. Bell; Archived Issue Brief, Bob Lyke IB87123
* Civil Rights Restoration Act: Bibliography-in-Brief, 1984-1988, Charles Dove 88-332 L
* The Civil Rights Restoration Act of 1987: Legal Analysis of P.L. 100-259, Karen J. Lewis, etc. 88-171 A

* Federal Policies and Programs Relating to Sex Discrimination and Sex Equity in Education, 1963-1985, Bob Lyke, etc. 85-116 EPW

Higher Education -- Law and Legislation

* Education Provisions of the Trade Act of 1988, P.L. 100-418, Paul M. Irwin, etc. 88-750 EPW
* Educational Challenges of the Congress: Achieving National Education Goals and Reforming Student Assistance, Videoprogram, James B. Stedman, etc. LTR91-880
* The Higher Education Act: Authorization and Budget Authority from FY 1987 to FY 1991, Margot A. Schenet 91-127 EPW
* Higher Education: Reauthorization of Higher Education Act; Issue Brief, Margot A. Schenet IB90028
* Tax Provisions Pertaining to Education in Title XI of the Omnibus Budget Reconciliation Act of 1990, Bob Lyke 90-546 EPW
* Title III, Higher Education Act: Issues for Reauthorization by the 102nd Congress, James B. Stedman 91-566 EPW

Higher Education -- Student Aid

* The College Assistance Migrant Program and the Migrant High School Equivalency Program, Robert Lyke 86-749 EPW
* College Costs: Analysis of Trends in Costs and Sources of Support, Margot A. Schenet 88-694 EPW
* College Costs and Student Financial Aid: Selected References, Peter Giordano 89-117 L
* Direct Student Loans: A Pro and Con Analysis, Charlotte J. Fraas 91-691 EPW
* Education Savings Bonds: Eligibility for Tax Exclusion, Bob Lyke 89-570 EPW
* Employer Education Assistance: A Brief Discussion of Current Legislation and Issues, Bob Lyke 88-202 EPW
* Employer Education Assistance: A Profile of Recipients, Their Educational Pursuits, and Employers, Steven R. Aleman 89-33 EPW
* Employer Education Assistance: Current Tax Status and Issues, Bob Lyke 89-148 EPW
* Federal Taxation of Student Aid, Bob Lyke 91-487 EPW
* Financial Aid for Students; Info Pack, IP042F
* Financing Postsecondary Education Attendance: Current Issues Involving Access and Choice, James B. Stedman 88-315 EPW
* Guaranteed Student Loan (GSL) Deferments: A Pro/Con Analysis, Charlotte Jones Fraas 87-118 EPW
* The Guaranteed Student Loan Programs: Current Status and Issues, Charlotte Fraas 91-556 EPW
* Guaranteed Student Loans: Defaults; Archived Issue Brief, Charlotte Fraas IB88050
* Guides to Financial Aid for Students: A Checklist, M. Alexandra Salinas 91-601 L
* The Higher Education Amendments of 1986 (P.L. 99-498): A Summary of Provisions, Education and Public Welfare Division 87-187 EPW
* Internships and Fellowships; Info Pack, IP063I
* National Service: Selected References, Peter Giordano 89-165 L
* The New GI Bill: Recruiting and Retention, David Burrelli 87-652 F
* Paul Douglas Teacher Scholarships: Reauthorization Issues for the 102nd Congress, James B. Stedman 91-508 EPW
* The Pell Grant Program: Background and Reauthorization Issues, Susan Boren 91-642 EPW
* The Perkins Loan Program: Background and Issues for Reauthorization, Kenneth Redd 90-272 EPW
* Proprietary Schools and Student Financial Aid Programs: Background and Policy Issues, Charlotte J. Fraas 90-427 EPW
* Proprietary Vocational Schools: Bibliography-in-Brief, Peter Giordano 88-515 E
* Saving for College: Archived Issue Brief, Robert Lyke IB89078
* Saving for College With Education Savings Bonds, Gerald Mayer 89-207 E
* Selected Amendments Enacted Since 1980 to Control Guaranteed Student Loan Defaults, Charlotte J. Fraas 91-246 EPW
* Student Aid Need Analysis Simplification: Issues and Options, Margot A. Schenet 91-567 EPW
* Student Financial Aid: Authorization of Appropriations, Budget Requests, Enacted Appropriations and Outlays for Federal Student Financial Aid Programs FY 1965 Through FY 1990, Susan H. Boren 89-184 EPW
* Student Loans--An Income Contingent Approach Proposed by the Reagan Administration for National Direct Student Loans, Wayne Riddle 86-669 EPW
* Tax Treatment of Interest Payments on Educational Loans, Louis Alan Talley 91-219 E

Current Events and Homework

* The U.S. Department of Education's Student Loan Default Reduction Initiative: Background and Analysis, Charlotte J. Fraas, 89-454 EPW

Higher Education Act

* see Federal Aid to Education--Higher Education, Higher Education
* Educational Challenges of the Congress: Achieving National Education Goals and Reforming Student Assistance, Videoprogram, James B. Stedman, etc. LTR91-880
* The Higher Education Act: Authorization and Budget Authority from FY 1987 to FY 1991, Margot A. Schenet 91-127 EPW
* Higher Education: Reauthorization of Higher Education Act; Issue Brief, Margot A. Schenet IB90028
* Paul Douglas Teacher Scholarships: Reauthorization Issues for the 102nd Congress, James B. Stedman, 91-508 EPW
* Student Aid Need Analysis Simplification: Issues and Options, Margot A. Schenet 91-567 EPW
* Title III, Higher Education Act: Issues for Reauthorization by the 102nd Congress, James B. Stedman 91-566 EPW

Highway Beautification Act

* Outdoor Advertising Control Along Federal-Aid Highways, Malcolm Simmons 86-605 ENR

Highway Safety

* see Highways--Safety Measures

Highway Trust Fund

* Federal Excise Taxes on Gasoline and the Highway Trust Fund--a Short History, Louis Alan Talley 89-174 E

Highway

* see Safety Measures, Infrastructure, Transportation
* Billboard Control Along Federal-Aid Highways: Legislative Proposals in the 102nd Congress, Malcolm M. Simmons 91-283 ENR
* Billboards Along Interstate and Federal-Aid Primary Highways: Why No Reliable Estimates of Their Number Exist, Bruce K. Mulock 91-115 E
* The "Bridge Crisis": An Economic Development Perspective; Issue Brief, J.F. Hornbeck IB88085
* Defense and Highway Spending: Estimates of Their Effects on the U.S. Economy, Daivd J. Cantor 90-237 E
* Federal Excise Taxes on Gasoline and the Highway Trust Fund-A Short History, Louis Alan Talley 91-192 E
* Federal, State, and Local Highway Spending: Update on Trends and Implications, J.F. Hornbeck 90-433 E
* Highway Safety, Highspeed Trains, and Maglev: A Checklist of CRS Products, Karen L. Alderson 92-6 L
* Maintaining Highway and Bridge Investments: What Role for Federal Grant Programs?, J.F. Hornbeck 90-277 E
* Matching Federal Aid for Highways: Rationale from Post Roads to Interstates, J.F. Hornbeck 91-12 E
* Outdoor Advertising Control Along Federal-Aid Highways, Malcolm Simmons 86-605 ENR
* Scenic Byways: Issues and Actions, John O. Spengler, etc. 88-479 ENR
* Surface Transportation Program Reauthorization: Issue Brief, Kenneth DeJarnette IB90032
* Surface Transportation Reauthorization 1991: A Comparison of Current Law With the Bush Administration Bill (H.R. 1351), Economics Division 91-290 E
* Surface Transportation Reauthorization 1991: Major Provisions in Senate, House, and Administration Bills, J.F. Hornbeck, etc. 91-625 E
* Transport Policy Problems: Elements of a National Plan; Proceedings of a CRS Symposium, Leon M. Cole 89-545 E
* Transportation and Public Policy: Longer and Heavier Trucks, Stephen J. Thompson 91-469 E
* Transportation Infrastructure: Issue Brief, Kenneth DeJarnette IB91075
* Transportation Infrastructure: Selected References, Karen L. Alderson 91-502 L
* Transportation Policy Issues: Selected References, Karen L. Alderson 91-501 L
* Transportation Status and Outlook: A Checklist of CRS Products, Karen L. Alderson 91-916 L
* Trucking and Public Policy: Longer and Heavier Trucks, Stephen J. Thompson 91-15 E
* Trucking Issues: Selected References, Karen L. Alderson 91-504 L

Highways -- Safety Measures

* Automobile Crash Protection: Issue Brief, Migdon Segal IB83085
* Drunk Driving and Raising the Drinking Age: Info Pack, IP186D
* Drunk Driving: Bibliography-in-Brief, 1983-1988, Edith Sutterlin 88-665 L
* Drunk Driving: Issue Brief, Migdon Segal IB83157
* Highway Safety, Traffic Congestion, and Innovations for Improvement; Selected References, Karen L. Alderson 91-503 L
* Legal Analysis of Questions Regarding the National Minimum Drinking Age, Douglas Weimer 85-772 A
* Motor Vehicle Safety: Policy Trends and Prospects, Migdon Segal 85-184 SPR
* Motor Vehicle Safety: Research and Development, Migdon Segal 85-184 SPR
* Roadway Safety Issues: The Federal program, Cosmo DiMaggio 85-62 E
* Roadway Safety: National Trends and Policies, Cosmo DiMaggio 86-71 SPR
* Speed Limits for Motor Vehicles: Archived Issue Brief, Migdon R. Segal IB86153
* Three-Wheel All-Terrain Vehicles: Safety Problems, Migdon Segal 85-749 SPR
* Truck and Bus Safety: Archived Issue Brief, Migdon R. Segal IB88022
* Truck Safety: Issue Brief, Migdon R. Segal IB88022
* The 55-MPH National Speed Limit: Issue Brief, Migdon Segal IB86153

Hispanic Americans

* see Minorities

History (U.S.)

* Banking: A Brief Profile of Its History and Structure, F. Jean Wells, etc. 91-259 E
* Bicentennial of the Congress: Selected References, 1970-1989, George Walser 89-90 L
* Bicentennial of the U.S. Congress; Info Pack, IP411C
* Cabinet and Other High Level Nominations that Failed to Be Confirmed, 1789-1989, Rogelio Garcia 89-253 GOV
* Commemorative Legislation, Stephen W. Stathis, etc. 91-5 GOV
* Congressional Gold Medals, 1776-1989, Stephen Stathis 89-586 GOV
* Congressional Roll Call and Other Recorded Votes: Statistical Summary of 1st Through 101st Congresses (1789-1990), John Pontius 91-571 GOV
* Congressional Tenure: A Review of Efforts to Limit House and Senate Service, Sula P. Richardson 89-537 GOV
* Constitution of the United States Including the Bill of Rights: Info Pack IP339C
* Constitution of the United States: Its History, Development and Amending Process; Info Pack, IP339C
* Federal Holiday Legislation, Stephan Stathis 86-759 GOV
* Federal Presidential Libraries, Harold C. Relyea 90-595 GOV
* Federalism: Key Episodes in the History of the American Federal System, Sandra Osborne 82-139 GOV
* The Flag: Info Pack, IP365F
* Flag Desecration: Info Pack, Congressional Reference Division IP440F
* Flag Etiquette: Info Pack IP365 F
* Foreign Ownership Of U.S. Assets: Past, Present, and Prospects, James K. Jackson, etc. 88-295E
* Historic Preservation Program: Structure, History, and Congressional Policies, Malcolm Simmons 87-302 ENR
* Inauguration of the President: Info Pack, IP316I
* Individuals Arrested on Charges of Espionage Against the United States Government: 1966-1989, Suzanne Cavanaugh 89-324 GOV
* The Lives of the Presidents of the United States: An Introductory Biography, James Sayler 91-812 GOV
* Major Acts of Congress and Treaties Approved by the Senate, 1789-1980, Christopher Deli, etc. 82-156 GOV
* Manassas National Battlefield Park: The Battle Continues, John O. Spengler, etc. 88-514 ENR
* Martin Luther King, Jr.: Selected References, 1978-1989, Jean Bowers 90-586 L
* Matching Federal Aid for Highways: Rationale from Post Raods to Interstates, J.F. Hornbeck 91-12 E
* Members of Congress Who Have Served in Both the House and the Senate, 1789-1989, Mildred L. Amer 89-45 GOV
* Members of the U.S. Congress Who Have Died of Other Than Natural Causes While Still in Office: A Selected List, Mildred Amer 91-480 GOV
* Members of the U.S. Congress Who Have Served Thirty Years or More, Mildred L. Amer 91-194 GOV
* National Emergency Powers, Harold C. Relyea 91-383 GOV
* Native American Heritage: Selected References, Tangela G. Roe 91-773 L

* Party Leaders in Congress, 1789-1991: Vital Statistics, Carol Hardy Vincent, etc. 91-414 GOV
* Pearl Harbor 50th Anniversary: Info Pack, Congressional Reference Division IP455P
* The Presidency of the United States: Info Pack, IP409P
* Provisions of Historic and Archaeological Preservation Statutes, Malcolm M. Simmons 88-660 ENR
* Re-election Rates of Senate Incumbents: 1790-1988, David C. Huckabee 90-250 GOV
* Redress for Japanese Americans under the Civil Liberties Act of 1988: Questions and Answers, James Sayler 90-488 GOV
* Re-election Rates of House Incumbents: 1790-1988, David C. Huckabee 89-173 GOV
* Rural Policy in an Era of Change and Diversity, Sandra S. Osborne 88-482 GOV
* Rural Policy in the United States: A History, Sandra S. Osborne 88-487 GOV
* Select and Special Committees in the United States Senate: An Historical Analysis, Judy Schneider 91-555 GOV
* Selected Bicentennial Celebrations Commemorating the 200th Anniversaries of the U.S. Constitution and of the U.S. Congress, Roger Davidson, etc. 86-171
* Selected Women's Issues Legislation Enacted Between 1832-1988, Leslie Gladstone 89-514 GOV
* Shadow Representatives in Congress: History and Current Developments, Garrine P. Laney 91-64 GOV
* Speech Material: Abraham Lincoln's and George Washington's Birthdays; Info Pack, IP373A
* Speech Material: Columbus Day; Info Pack, IP380C
* Speech Material: Fourth of July; Info Pack, IP377F
* Speech Material: Martin Luther King's Birthday; Info Pack, IP372M
* Speech Material: Thanksgiving Day; Info Pack, IP381T
* Time and History on the Hill, David McCullough LTR91-909
* The United States Flag: Federal Law Relating to Display and Associated Questions, James Hall 90-338 A
* Vice Presidents of the United States, 1789-1981: Brief Biographical Notes, Christopher Deli 81-23 GOV
* The Virgin Islands of the United States: A Descriptive and Historical Profile, Bette Taylor 88-429 GOV
* Women in the United States Congress, Mildred Amer 91-333 GOV

H.K. Porter Co, Inc. v. Dade Co, Florida

* United States Supreme Court Actions Regarding Minority Business Set-Asides After City of Richmond v. J.A. Croson Co., Charles V. Dale 89-202 A

Holidays

* see Reference Sources--Speechwriting

Homeless

* see Public Welfare--Homeless

Honduras

* Central America: U.S. Relations With Costa Rica, Guatemala, and Honduras: Info Pack, IP352C
* Central American Peace Process: Selected References, Robert Kirk 88-389 L
* Honduras: U.S. Foreign Assistance Facts, Archived Issue Brief, Robert Sanchez IB85080
* Honduras: U.S. Military Activities: Issue Brief, James Wooten IB84134

Hong Kong

* Exchange Rate Management in Taiwan, South Korea and Hong Kong, Arlene Wilson 87-41 E
* Hong Kong-U.S. Economic Relations: Some Views from Hong Kong's Economic Elite, Kerry Dumbaugh 89-23 F
* Major Hong Kong Laws on Illegal Drugs, Law Library of Congress LL90-6
* U.S. Agricultural Trade Opportunities With Pacific Rim Nations, Robert Goldstein 88-755 ENR

Honoraria

* see Congress--Members, Political Ethics

Hormones in Meat

* see Agriculture--Foreign Trade, Agriculture--Livestock

Hospitals

* see Health Facilities

House of Representatives

* see Congress

Housing

* see Assistance, Finance
* Abstracts of Recommendations of Certain Organizations on National Housing Policy, Economics Division 88-23 E
* Affordability of Moderate Income Housing in the 1980s: Bibliography-in-Brief, 1984-1988, Robert Howe 88-669 L
* Bank Diversification: Into Real Estate?, William Jackson 88-648 E
* Border State "Colonies": Background and Options for Federal Assistance, Claudia Copeland, etc. 87-906 ENR
* Comparative Quality of Rental Housing Obtained by Whites, Blacks, and Hispanics, Grace Milgram 87-626 E
* Comparison of the Departments of Energy and Health and Human Services Weatherization Assistance Programs, Mary Smith, etc. 89-229 EPW
* Existing Housing Resources v. Need, Grace Milgram, etc. 87-81 E
* Expanding Housing Opportunities Through Residential Conversions and Homesharing, Nancy Saltojanes 84-70 S
* The Fair Housing Act: A Legal Overview, Henry Cohen 89-683 A
* Fair Housing Act Amendments: Archived Issue Brief, Paul Downing IB87116
* Fair Housing Amendments Prohibiting Discrimination Against Families With Children Except in Housing for Older Persons, Henry Cohen 89-111 A
* Homeless Housing: HUD's Shelter Programs; Archived Issue Brief, Susan Vanhorenbeck IB87098
* Housing Alternatives: Archived Issue Brief, Morton J. Schussheim IB87024
* Housing and Housing Finance: An Alphabetical Microthesaurus of Terms Selected from the Legislative Indexing Vocabulary, Shirley Loo 86-1033 L
* Housing Conditions of Hispanic Americans, Susan M. Vanhorenbeck 85-952 E
* Housing in Rural Areas, Nancy Saltojanes 85-61 S
* Housing Issues for the 1990s: Selected References, 1988-1990, Robert Howe 90-119 L
* Housing Policy and Implications for Current Programs: Info Pack, IP417H
* Housing Policy: Homeownership Affordability: Issue Brief, Barbara Miles IB88108
* Income Tax Exclusion of Gain from Sale of a Primary Residence, Louis Alan Talley 90-194 E
* Major Repairs of Non-Routine Maintenance: Defining Davis-Bacon Coverage under the Comprehensive Improvement Assistance Program, William G. Whittaker 85-887 E
* Manufactured Housing: Trends and Prospects, Marc E. Smyrl 88-303 S
* The Missions and Management of HUD, Morton J. Schussheim 90-332 S
* Rental Real Estate: Passive Activity Loss Limits; Issue Brief, Richard Bourdon IB900786
* Restrictive Rental Practices and Families With Children, Susan Vanhorenbeck 86-746 E
* Segregation and Discrimination in Housing: A Review of Selected Studies and Legislation, Paul Downing, etc. 89-317 GOV
* Summaries of Papers on U.S. Housing Policy Prepare for the Center for Real Estate Development, the Massachusetts Institute of Technology, Morton J. Schussheim 88-222 S
* The Tax Reform Act of 1986 and Owners of Rental Housing, Richard Bourdon 86-919 E
* The Theory of Rent Control, Barbara Miles 78-109 E
* Homelessness: Issues and Legislation in the 101st Congress, IB88070
* Housing and Community Development, IB89004
* Housing for the Elderly and Handicapped: Section 202, IB84038
* Housing Policy: Homeownership Affordability, IB88108
* Housing Policy: Low- and Moderate- Income, IB88106
* Mortgage Revenue Bonds for First-Time HomeBuyers: Should the Program be Continued Beyond 1989?, IB87181

Housing -- Assistance

* The Assisted Housing Stock: Potential Losses from Prepayment and "Opt-Outs", Grace Milgram 87-879 E
* Congregate Housing: The Federal Programs and Examples of State Programs, Susan Vanhorenbeck 86-918 E
* The Cranston-Gonzalez National Affordable Housing Act; Key Provisions and Analysis, Morton J. Schussheim 91-124 RCO
* Elderly and Handicapped Housing: Recent Developments in Section 202, Susan M. Vanhorenbeck 89-667 E

Current Events and Homework

* Federal Housing Programs Affecting Elderly People, Susan Vanhorenbeck 88-576 E
* Home Buyer Assistance; Tax Deferred Savings for Downpayments, Richard Bourdon 88-576 E
* Homeless Housing: HUD's Shelter Programs; Archived Issue Brief, Susan Vanhorenbeck IB84038
* Housing: Access and Affordability: Audio Brief, Mort Schussheim AB50172
* The Housing and Community Development Act of 1987 and the Steward B. McKinney Homeless Assistance Act: Summary and Analysis, Barbara Miles 88-481 E
* Housing and Community Development: Audio Brief, Morton Schussheim, etc. AB50184
* Housing and Community Development; Issue Brief, Morton J. Schussheim IB89004
* Housing Assistance: A Brief History and Description of Current HUD Programs, Grace Milgram 88-712 E
* Housing for the Elderly and Handicapped: Section 202; Archived Issue Brief, Susan Vanhorenbeck IB84038
* Housing- and Moderate-Income Assistance Programs; Issue Brief, Grace Milgram IB91006
* Housing Low-Income Persons through Use of Existing Housing Stock, Susan Vanhorenbeck 88-584 E
* Housing Policy- and Moderate-Income Assistance; Issue Brief, Grace Milgram IB88106
* Housing: Problems and Policies, Archived Issue Brief, Morton J. Schussheim IB89004
* Housing Programs: Issues in-and Moderate-Income Housing Assistance; Archived Issue Brief, Grace Milgram IB87101
* Housing the Low-Income Family With Children, Morton J. Schussheim 87-518 S
* Rent Control and the Potential Denial of Federal Housing Assistance, Richard Bourdon 88-431 E
* Rural Housing Programs of the Farmers Home Administration: Brief Descriptions and Budget Data, B. Ellington Foote 87-171 E
* Tax Subsidies to Housing, 1953-83, Jane Gravelle 82-178 E
* Trends in Funding and Numbers of Households in HUD-Assisted Housing, Fiscal Years 1975-1991, Grace Milgram 91-369 E
* Urban Housing Assistance Programs in the United States, Grace Milgram 89-137 E

Housing -- Finance

* The Decision to Refinance a High-Rate Mortgage, E. Richard Bourdon 86-85 E
* Federal and Related Agencies Supporting Home Mortgage Markets, William Jackson, etc. 88-360 E
* Federal Home Loan Mortgage Corporation Preferred Stock Ownership: Lift the Restrictions?: Archived Issue Brief, Barbara Miles IB88076
* The Federal Housing Administration: Limits on Insurance Commitments, B. Ellington Foote 88-366 E
* Federal Housing Administration: Raising the Mortgage Limit, B. Ellington Foote 89-252 E
* FHA's Mortgage Insurance Premium Refund Programs, Barbara L. Miles 87-709 E
* Financial Markets: A New Framework of Issues, Walter W. Eubanks 88-485 E
* The Financing of Rental Housing, Keith P. Rasey 86-1045 S
* Home Equity Loans: Bibliography-in-Brief, 1984-1988, Felix Chin 88-511 L
* Home Equity Loans under the New Tax Reform Act: Possible Benefits and Potential Dangers, Richard Bourdon 87-692 E
* The Home Mortgage Interest Deduction for Boats Used as Second Homes, Richard Bourdon 87-366 E
* The Home Mortgage Interest Deduction: Recent Changes in the Tax Laws, Richard Bourdon 88-126 E
* Housing Finance: Development and Evolution in Mortgage Markets, Barbara Miles 83-44 E
* Housing Finance Restructuring: Changes and New Issues Created by FIRREA (P.L. 101-73), William Jackson, etc. 91-296 E
* Housing Programs of VA and FHA: A Comparison, B. Ellington Foote 91-604 E
* A Housing Trust Fund: Some Potential Sources, Barbara L. Miles, etc 88-234 E
* Income Tax Treatment of Rental Housing and Real Estate Investment After the Tax Reform Act of 1986, Jack Taylor 87-603 E
* Mortgage Commitments and Interest Rate "Lock-Ins":, What is the Problem?, Barbara Miles 87-873 E
* Mortgage Revenue Bonds and the Mortgage Interest Deduction: The Option of Reallocating Tax Expenditures for Housing, Dennis Zimmerman 91-597 E
* Mortgage Revenue Bonds for First-Time Home Buyers:, Should the Program Be Continued? Archived Issue Brief, Richard Bourdon IB91119
* The Mortgage Servicing Industry and Issues: Servicing Transfers, Adjustable Mortgage Errors and Escrow Overcharges, Barbara L. Miles 91-583 E
* Recent Developments in the Real Estate Settlement Procedures Act, Richard Bourdon 88-730 E
* REMIC (Real Estate Mortgage Investment Conduit): The New Security for Financing Real Estate, Barbara Miles 87-73 E
* Tax Policy and Rental Housing: An Economic Analysis, Jane Gravelle 87-536 E
* Use of IRA's for a First-Home Purchase: Pro/Con and Alternatives; Issue Brief, Richard Bourdon IB91084
* Veterans Administration Guaranteed Housing Loans: Raising the Funding Fee; Archived Issue Brief, Ellington Foote IB87146
* Veterans Administration Guaranteed Housing Loans: The Rising Cost of VA Mortgages, B. Ellington Foote 87-453 E

Housing and Community Development Act

* The Housing and Community Development Act of 1987 and the Stewart B. McKinney Homeless Assistance Act: Summary and Analysis, Barbara Miles 88-481 E

Housing for the Aged

* see Old Age--Housing

Housing Subsidies

* see Housing--Assistance

Housing Trust Fund

* A Housing Trust Fund: Some Potential Sources, Barbara L. Miles, etc. 88-134 E

Human Rights

* see International Law-- Human Rights

Hungary

* Gorbachev's Reform Strategy: Comparisons With the Hungarian and Chinese Experience, Francis T. Miko, etc. 87-813 F

Hunger

* see Food Relief, Public Welfare

Hydropower

* see Water Resources

Illegal Aliens

* see Immigration

Illiteracy

* see Elementary and Secondary Education

Immigration

* see Law and Legislation, Refugees
* Alien Eligibility Requirements for Major Federal Assistance Programs, Joyce Vialet, etc. 89-435 EPW
* Chinese Students and Other Chinese in the U.S.: Immigration Issues and Options, Ruth Ellen Wasem 89-293 EPW
* Comparison of Legal Immigration Legislation in the 101st Congress, S. 358, H.R. 672, and S. 448, With Existing Law, Joyce C. Vialet 89-190 EPW
* Counting Undocumented Aliens in the Decennial Census, Thomas C. Durbin 88-438 A
* El Salvador: Bibliography-in-Brief, 1986-1989, Robert S. Kirk 89-204 L
* Emigration: Soviet Compliance With the Helsinki Accords; Archived Issue Brief, John Hardt, etc. 85-599 EPW
* Extended Voluntary Departure and Other Grants of Blanket Relief from Deportation, Sharon Stephen 85-599 EPW
* The Immigration and Nationality Act--Questions and Answers, Joyce Vialet 87-917 EPW
* Immigration, Ethnic Groups, and Nationalities: An Alphabetical Microthesaurus of Terms Selected from the Legislative Indexing Vocabulary, Shirley Loo 91-670 L
* International Migration Data: Sources and Quality, Jennifer D. Williams 91-466 GOV

Housing / Indians

* Legal Immigration and Immigrants in the U.S.; Selected References, Peter Giordano 89-297 L
* Mexico-U.S. Relations: Issues for Congress; Issue Brief, K. Larry Storrs, etc. IB86111
* Numerical Limits and the Preference System for Immigrants in the Simpson-Mazzoli Bills, 97th and 98th Congress; Summary and Debate, Joyce Vialet 87-958 EPW
* Overview of Deportation Procedures, Larry Eig 88-743 A
* Private Bills: Selected Statistics, 1975-1986, With Special Reference to Private Immigration Bills, Richard Beth 87-650 GOV
* Proposed Exclusion of Illegal Aliens from the Population Used to Apportion the House of Representatives: A Methodological and Policy Analysis, Jennifer D. Williams, etc. 88-418 GOV
* Refugee Admissions and Resettlement Policy: Issue Brief, Joyce Vialet IB89025
* Social Security: Alien Beneficiaries; Archived Issue Brief, David Koitz IB82001
* The Soviet Emigration and Travel Bill: Assessments and Implications for U.S. Interests, Jim Nichol 91-518 F
* Soviet Jewish Emigration: Issue Brief, Clyde R. Mark IB90083
* 'Sponsored Aliens' and Refugees: Immigrant Status and Eligibility for Selected Benefits and Services, Ruth Ellen Wasem 88-334 EPW
* The 1990 Decennial Census and the Counting of Illegal Aliens, Thomas Durbin 88-62 A
* Immigration: Numerical Limits and the Preference System, IB88018
* Immigration Status of Salvadorans and Nicaraguans, IB87205
* Refugee Admissions and Resettlement Policy, IB89025

Immigration -- Law and Legislation

* Analytic and Policy Perspectives on Legal Immigration, Ruth Ellen Wasem 90-260 EPW
* Asylum and Temporary Protected Status under U.S. Immigration Law, Ruth Ellen Wasem 91-530 EPW
* A Brief History of U.S. Immigration Policy, Joyce Vialet 91-141 EPW
* Citizenship of Foreign-Born Children Through Descent or Adoption: The Law of Australia, Canada, Great Britain, and the United States, Larry M. Eig, etc. 91-565 A
* Comparative Chart of Unfair Immigration-Related Employment Practices, Title VIII of the Fair Housing Act, Title VII of the Civil Rights Act of 1964, and the Rehabilitation Act of 1973, Larry M. Eig 90-209 A
* Freedom of Emigration of Chinese Citizens under Chinese Law and New Policy and Provisions on Overseas Study, Law Library of Congress LL90-40
* Health Exams, Including AIDS Tests, Required of Foreign Students, Law Library of Congress LL90-82
* Homosexuality and Immigration Law After the Immigration Act of 1990, Larry M. Eig 91-495 A
* Immigration Act of 1990 (P.L. 101-649), Joyce C. Vialet, etc. 90-601 EPW
* Immigration Admission of HIV-Positive Aliens; Issue Brief, Joyce C. Vialet IB91062
* Immigration and Refugee Policy: Info Pack, IP1641
* Immigration and Related Legislation Enacted in the 101st Congress, 1989-1990, Joyce C. Vialet 91-262 EPW
* Immigration and Related Legislation Enacted in the 100th Congress, 1987-1988, Joyce Vialet 88-766 EPW
* Immigration: Issues and Legislation in the 100th Congress; Archived Issue Brief, Joyce Vialet IB87014
* Immigration Legislation--Questions and Answers, Joyce C. Vialet 91-493 EPW
* Immigration: Numerical Limits and the Preference System; Archived Issue Brief, Joyce Vialet IB88018
* Immigration of Workers into Australia, Canada, Sweden, and the United Kingdom, Law Library of Congress LL90-2
* Immigration: Status of Undocumented Salvadorans and Nicaraguans: Archived Issue Brief, Ruth Ellen Wasem IB87205
* Political Asylum: New Rules Analyzed, Larry M. Eig 90-487 A
* Private Immigration Measures in the House of Representatives: Contemporary Procedure and Its Historical Development, Richard Beth 87-408 GOV

Immigration -- Refugees

* Immigration and Refugee Policy: Info Pack IP1641
* Immigration and Refugees (101st Congress); Archived Issue Brief, Joyce C. Vialet IB90029
* Migration and Refugee Assistance Budget: Problems and Prospects; Issue Brief, Lois McHugh IB89150
* Refugee Admissions and Resettlement Policy: Issue Brief, Joyce C. Vialet

IB89025
* Refugee Resettlement Assistance Funding, Joyce Vialet 91-683 EPW
* Refugees in U.S. Foreign Policy, Lois McHugh 90-419 F
* 'Sponsored Aliens' and Refugees: Immigrant Status and Eligibility for Selected Benefits and Services, Ruth Ellen Wasem 88-34 EPW
* The World Refugee Problem and International Response: Selected References, 1986-1989, Karen L. Alderson 90-28 L

Import Quotas

* see Foreign Trade--Imports and Exports

Incineration of Wastes

* see Solid Wastes

Income

* see Economic Conditions--Income, Labor--Earnings and Benefits

Income Distribution

* see Economic Conditions--Income, Labor--Earnings and Benefits

Income Maintenance Programs

* see Food Relief--Domestic, Pensions, Public Welfare, Social Security, Workers' Compensation
* Health Benefit Plans and the Impact of Section 89, IB89083
* Health Benefits for Retirees: An Uncertain Future, IB88004
* Individual Retirement Account Issues and Savings Account proposals, IB89085
* Pension Asset Reversions: Whose Money Is it?, IB89091
* Railroad Retirement and Unemployment: Recent Issues, IB84068
* Refundable Tax Credits To Aid Working Poor Families, IB86120
* Social Security: The Independent Agency Question, IB86120
* Welfare, IB87007

Income Tax

* see Taxation--Business Taxes, Taxation--Corporation Taxes, Taxation--Personal Income Tax

Indexing (Economic Policy)

* see Economic Conditions--Inflation, Public Welfare , Social Security, Taxation

India

* China-India Border Friction: Background Information and Possible Implications, Robert Sutter, etc. 87-514 F
* Crisis in the Indian Punjab: Evolution, Issues, Competing Positions and Prospects, Richard Cronin 84-152 F
* The Gandhi Assassination: Implications for India and U.S.-Indian Relations, Richard Cronin 84-790 F
* India and Nuclear Weapons: Issue Brief, Warren Donnelly IB86125
* India: Regional Dissidence and Human Rights Problems, Richard P. Cronin, etc. 91-585 F
* India: Technology Import, Law Library of Congress LL90-21
* India: The Assassination of Rajiv Gandhi and Implications for U.S. Interests, Richard P. Cronin, etc. 91-441 F
* The Indian Community in the United States, Margaret Siciliano 84-792 F
* India's Internal Security Legislation: Basic Facts and Human Rights Implications, Barbara Leitch LePoer 91-599 F
* India's Punjab Crisis: Issues, Prospects and Implications, Richard Cronin 87-850 F
* India's Sikhs and the Crisis in Punjab State: Summary Briefing Points, Richard P. Cronin 87-509 F
* Kashmir: Conflict and Crisis; Archived Issue Brief, David E. Lockwood, etc. IB90087
* The Kashmir Dispute: Historical Background to the Current Struggle, Richard P. Cronin, etc. 91-563 F
* The Rajiv Gandhi Visit: Issues in U.S.-India Relations, Richard Cronin 85-838 F
* South Asia: Current Developments and Issues for U. S. Policy: Report on a Trip to Pakistan and India,, April 8-30, 1986, Richard P. Cronin 86-741 F
* Super 301 Action Against Japan, Brazil and India: Rationale, Reaction, and Future Implications, Raymond J. Ahearn, etc. 90-25 F

Indians

* American Indian Budget Issues: 101st Congress; Issue Brief, Roger Walke IB89046

Current Events and Homework

* American Indian Policy: Background, Nature, History, Current Issues, Future Trends, Richard Jones 87-227 GOV
* American Indian Policy: Selected Budget Issues in the 100th Congress; Archived Issue Brief, Roger Walke IB87103
* American Indian Religious Freedom: The Legal Landscape, M. Maureen Murphy 88-370 A
* The Catawba Indian Tribe's Land Claim: A Legal Analysis, M. Maureen Murphy 89-293 A
* Federal Trust Responsibility to Indian Tribes for Protection of Natural Resources, M. Maureen Murphy 89-379 A
* Gambling on Indian Reservations, M. Maureen Murphy 85-743 A
* Gambling on Indian Reservations: Archived Issue Brief, Roger Walke IB86087
* Indian Affairs Legislation Enacted or Considered by the 98th Congress, Richard Jones 85-90 GOV
* Indian and Indian-Interest Organizations, Richard Jones, etc. 84-131 GOV
* Indian Tribal Government Civil Jurisdiction: Emerging Jurisprudence, M. Maureen Murphy 91-61 A
* Indian Tribal Government Jurisdiction Over Indians Not Enrolled in the Tribe, M. Maureen Murphy 91-707 A
* Indian Tribal Government Zoning Authority, M. Maureen Murphy 88-744 A
* Indians: Land Claims by Eastern Tribes; Archived Issue Brief, Richard Jones IB77040
* Latin American Indigenous Peoples and Considerations for U.S. Assistance, Congressional Research Service 91-663 F
* Native American Heritage: Selected References, Tangela G. Roe 91-773 L
* Native Americans: Nutrition and Diet-Related Diseases, Donna Porter 87-246 SPR
* Navajo-Hopi Relocation: Archived Issue Brief, Roger Walke IB86021
* The Possible Applicability of the Americans With Disabilities Act to Indian Tribes, Elizabeth B. Bazan 91-497 A
* Taxation Within Indian Lands: The Legal Framework, M. Maureen Murphy 87-249 A
* Territorial Extent of Indian Tribal Civil Jurisdiction: Disestablishment of Reservation Status, M. Maureen Murphy 87-976 A

Individual Retirement Accounts

* see Pensions--IRAs

Individuals With Disabilities Education Act

* see Handicapped--Policies and Legislation

Indonesia

* The Association of Southeast Asian Nations (ASEAN) : Economic Development Prospects and the Role of the United States, Larry Niksch 84-171 F
* Economic Changes in the Asian Pacific Rim: Policy Prospectus, Congressional Research Service 86-923 S
* U. S. Agricultural Trade Opportunities With Pacific Rim Nations, Robert M. Goldstein 88-755 ENR

Indoor Air Pollution

* see Air Pollution--Indoor Air Pollution

Industrial Competitiveness

* see Foreign Trade--Competitiveness, Industry

Industrial Policy

* see Foreign Trade--Competitiveness, Industry

Industrial Technology

* America's Steel Industry: Modernizing to Compete, David J. Cantor 84-786 E
* Automation and Small Business: Technological Development and the Competitiveness of U.S. Industry, Wendy Schacht, etc. 88-300 SPR
* Clean Air Act: Gasoline Vapor Recovery; Archived Issue Brief, David E. Gushee IB87029
* Commercialization of Technology and Issues in the Competitiveness of Selected U.S. Industries; Semiconductors, Biotechnology, and Superconductors, Leonard G. Kruger, etc. 88-486 SPR
* Controlling Carbon Dioxide Emissions, Amy Abel, etc. 89-157 ENR
* Direct Federal Support for Technological Innovation: Issues and Options, Christopher Hill, etc. 84-118 S
* The Effect of the Tax Reform Act of 1986 on Technological Innovation, Jane Gravelle 87-124 E
* Enhanced Oil Recovery Methods, Joseph Riva 87-827 SPR
* Industrial Competitiveness and Technological Advancement: Debate Over Government Policy; Issue Brief, Wendy H. Schacht IB91132
* Industrial Design Protection, Law Library of Congress LL90-23
* Industrial Innovation:, The Debate Over Government Policy: Archived Issue Brief, Wendy Schacht IB84004
* Issues in U.S. Advanced Technology Policy: A Review of the National Advisory Committee on Semiconductors Report, a Strategic Industry at Risk, Glenn J. McLoughlin 90-234 SPR
* Japanese Basic Research Policies, Genevieve J. Knezo 90-363 SPR
* Japanese Companies and Technology: Lessons to Learn? Wendy H. Schacht 91-375 SPR
* Japanese Science and Technology: Some Recent Efforts to Improve U.S. Monitoring, Nancy Miller 86-195 SPR
* Japan's Science and Technology Strategies and Policies: Issue Brief, Glenn McLoughlin IB90053
* Science and Technology: Federal Policy and Economic Impact: Bibliography-in-Brief, 1983-1986, Virginia MacEwen 87-79 L
* Science, Technology, and the International Competitiveness of American Industry: Selected References, 1985-1988, B.F. Mangan 88-587 L
* Semiconductor Manufacturing Technology Proposal: SEMATECH; Issue Brief, Glenn J. McLoughlin IB87212
* Small Business, Technology Development, and Manufacturing: Competitiveness Issues, Wendy H. Schacht 89-685 SPR
* Social Science Approaches to Innovation and Productivity, Christine Matthews Rose 86-710 SPR
* Stevenson-Wydler Technology Innovation Act: A Federal Effort to Promote Industrial Innovation: Archived Issue Brief, Wendy Schacht IB85082
* Superconductivity: Bibliography-in-Brief, 1980-1988, B.F. Mangan 88-632 L
* Technological Advancement and the Competitiveness of Selected U.S. Industries: Issues for Consideration, Wendy Schacht, etc. 87-345 SPR
* The Toshiba/Kongsberg Case: Proposals to Expand U.S. Penalties for Illegal Exports of High Technology Goods, Glennon Harrison 87-988 E
* Toshiba-Kongsberg Technology Diversion: Issues for Congress; Archived Issues Brief, Raymond Ahearn, etc. IB87184
* Trade, Technology, and Competitiveness: Issue Brief, Wendy Schacht IB87053
* The U.S. Semiconductor Industry and the SEMATECH Proposal, Glenn J. McLoughlin, etc. 87-354 SPR
* U.S. Space Commercialization Activities, Patricia Humphlett 88-518 SPR

Industry

* see Automobile Industry, High Technology Industries, Steel Industry, Textile Industry, Business and Society, Computers, Corporations, Foreign Trade--Competitiveness, Telecommunication--Telephone Industry
* The American Response to Foreign Competition; Audio Brief, Mary Jane Bolle, etc. AB50180
* The Auto Industry's 1990 Round of Collective Bargaining, Gail McCallion 90-500 E
* Automobile Fuel Economy Standards: Another Cup of CAFE?, Issue Brief, Robert Bamberger IB90122
* Concentration in the U.S Daily Newspaper Industry:, Trends and Issues, R. Kevin Flaherty 84-727 E
* Cooperative R&D: Federal Efforts to Promote Industrial Competitiveness; Issue Brief, Wendy H. Schacht IB89056
* The Effect of the Canada-U.S. Free Trade Agreement on U.S. Industries, Economics Division 88-506 E
* Equity, Excellence, and the Distribution of Federal Research and Development Funds, William C. Boesman, etc. 88-422 SPR
* The GATT Trade Talks: Prospects for Selected Manufacturing Industries, Edward B. Rappaport 91-821 E
* Impact of the Business Cycle on Productivity Growth in the U.S. Economy, Mary Jane Bolle 82-172 E
* The Impact of U.S. Antitrust Law on Joint Activity by Corporations: Some Background, Janice E. Rubin 89-291 A
* Japanese Lobbying and U.S. Automobile Policy, Dick K. Nanto 91-186 E
* Japanese Management Practices and Their Implications for U.S. Policy, Dick Nanto 82-114 E
* Japan's Industrial Groups: The Keiretsu, Dick K. Nanto 90-609 E
* Limiting the Growth of Tax-Exempt Industrial Development Bonds: An Economic Evaluation, Dennis Zimmerman 84-37 E
* Machine Tools: Imports and the U.S. Industry, Economy, and Defense Industrial Base, Gary Guenther 86-762 E
* Manufacturing Employment by State as a "Recession Vulnerability Indicator", Linda Levine 91-35 E
* Mexico's Maquiladora Industry, M. Angeles Villarreal 91-706 E
* Platinum Group Metals Use in the World Auto Industry: Effects of

Individual Retirement Accounts / INF

Tougher Tailpipe Emission Standards, Marc Humphries 90-219 ENR
* The Research and Development Tax Credit: A Comparison of the Arguments For and Against, Office of Senior Specialists 88-333 S
* A Secondary Market for Industrial Mortgages: A New Method for Financing Industrial Development, Edward Knight 84-111 E
* Selected Environmental and Related Industrial Interest Groups: Summary Guide, Environment and Natural Resources Policy Division 91-295 ENR
* Service Sector Productivity in the United States: A Survey, Julius Allen 88-717 E
* Technological Advancement and U.S. Industrial Competitiveness, Wendy Schacht 88-689 SPR
* The Textile Industry in the United States: Conflicting Factual Claims, Edward B. Rappaport 91-373 E
* Textile Trade Controls: A Comparison of Bills in the 99th and 100th Congresses, Edward B. Rappaport 87-607 E
* Textiles in the World Trade System: Archived Issue Brief, Edward B. Rappaport IB89139
* Tourism: Its Contributions to the U.S. Economy, Bernevia M. McCalip 90-502 E
* Uruguay Round of Trade Negotiations and Its Impact on the U.S. Service Sector, Economics Division 91-233 E
* U.S. Chemicals Manufacturing: Status, Issues, and Prospects, Bernard Gelb 88-387 E
* U.S. Jewelry Manufacturing, International Competitiveness, and H.R. 3, Bernard Gelb 87-875 E
* Wage Rates and Exchange Rates, Linda LeGrande 88-252 E

Industry -- Automobile Industry

* Automobile Fleet Incentives or Split-Pricing Practices, Gwenell L. Bass 85-714 E
* Automobile Fuel Economy Standards: Another Roll Back? Archived Issue Brief, Robert Bamberger IB88046
* Customs Ruling on Multipurpose Vehicles; Archived Issue Brief, Gwenell Bass IB89053
* Employment and Output Effects of the Extension of Japan's Voluntary Automobile Export Restraints on the U.S. Automobile and Steel Industries, Gwenell Bass 85-710 E
* Foreign Sourcing by the U.S. Automobile Industry, Kevin Flaherty 85-1052 E
* Foreign Trade Zones and the U.S. Automobile Industry, Gwenell Bass, etc. 88-659 E
* The Gray Market for Imported Automobiles, R. Kevin Flaherty 85-651 E
* Japan's Automobile Industry and Barriers to Purchases of U.S. Cars, Dick Nanto, etc. 87-793 E
* Transport Manufacturing: A Review and Appraisal of Federal Assistance Policies, Gwenell Bass 86-75 E
* U.S. Automobile Industry: Issues and Statistics, Gwenell Bass 85-792 E
* U.S. Economic Policy in an International Context: The U.S. Automobile Industry in International Competition: Voluntary Export Restraints and Domestic, Dick K. Nanto 85-34 E

Industry -- High Technology Industries

* Commercialization of Technology and Issues in the Competitiveness of Selected U.S. Industries: Semiconductors, Biotechnology, and Superconductors, Leonard G. Kruger, etc. 88-486 SPR
* High-Technology Trade: Bibliography-in-Brief, 1985-1988, Robert Kirk 88-572 L
* India: Technology Import, Law Library of Congress LL90-21
* Issues in U.S. Advanced Technology Policy: A Review of the National Advisory Committee on Semiconductors Report, a Strategic Industry at Risk, Glenn J. McLoughlin 90-234 SPR
* Japanese and U.S. Industrial Associations: Their Role in High-Technology Policymaking: A Japan Task Force Report, Dick K. Nanto, etc. 91-477 E
* Semiconductor Devices: The Changing Competitiveness of U.S. Merchant Producers, 1977-87, Gary Guenther 88-191 E
* Semiconductor Manufacturing Technology Proposal: SEMATECH; Issue Brief, Glenn J. McLoughlin IB87212
* Semiconductors: Issues Confronting the Industry: Bibliography-in-Brief, 1985-1988, Karen Alderson 88-445 L
* Technological Advancement and U.S. Industrial Competitiveness, Wendy H. Schacht 88-689 SPR

Industry -- Steel Industry

* America's Steel Industry: Modernizing to Compete, David Cantor 84-786 E
* Compensation in U.S. and Foreign Steel Industries, Linda LeGrande 88-314 E
* Employment and Output Effects of the Extension of Japan's Voluntary Automobile Export Restraints on the US. Automobile and Steel Industries, Gwenell Bass 85-710 E
* An Evaluation of the Reconstruction Finance Corporation With Implications for Current Capital Needs of the Steel Industry, James Bickley 80-43 E
* Federal Taxes, the Steel Industry, and Net Operating Loss Carryforwards, David Burmaugh 88-5 E
* Hypothetical Effects of Lower Interest Rates on the Costs of Production of the Integrated Steel Industry, David Cantor 85-738 E
* Implementation of the President's Steel Program: Implications for Output and Employment of the Steel and Steel-Related Industries, David Cantor 86-518
* The Influence of Labor Costs on the Total Cost of Steel Production in Integrated Steel Mills: Effects of Hypothetical Labor Cost Reductions, David Cantor 85-912 E
* Japan's Steel Industry: Positioning for Survival, James Jackson 88-346 E
* Merger Guidelines--a Case Study of the LTV and Republic Steel Corporations, Gwenell Bass 84-133 E
* New Technology for the U.S. Steel Industry: A Great Leap Forward?, Leonard Kruger 86-636 SPR
* The President's Steel Program: Background and Implementation, David J. Cantor 86-658 E
* Steel Imports: Arguments for and Against Extension of the President's Program: Issue Brief, David Cantor IB88109
* Steel Imports from Canada and the President's Steel Program: Archived Issue Brief, David Cantor IB87197
* Steel Imports: Is the President's Steel Program Working? Archived Issue Brief, David Cantor IB86141
* Steel Imports of Hot Rolled Sheet from Korea in the Absence of Import Restraints: Hypothetical Effects on West Coast Steel Producer, David Cantor 88-678 E
* The Steel Industry's Impact on the Economy in 1988, David Cantor 88-664 E
* Steel Manufacturing in the United States: Can a Smaller Industry Be Profitable?, David Cantor 87-649 E
* Steel Markets in the United States: Where Have All the Buyers Gone?, David Cantor 87-474 E
* Steel Prices and Import Restraints, David Cantor 88-204 E
* Steel Prices in 1987 and 1988: How Have the Small Buyers Fared?, David Cantor 89-230 E
* The U.S. Steel Industry: Factors Influencing Gains in Industry Productivity, David Cantor 87-498 E

Industry -- Textile Industry

* The Canadian Free Trade Agreement and the Textile and Apparel Industries, Edward Rappaport 87-979 E
* Compensation in the Textile and Apparel Industries: International and Domestic Comparisons, Dennis Roth, etc. 85-671 E
* Textile and Apparel Trade Protection: Issue Brief, Edward B. Rappaport IB87109
* Textile Trade Controls: A Comparison of Bills in the 99th and 100th Congress, Edward Rappaport 87-607 E

INF

* see Arms Control, Weapons Systems--Nuclear Weapons
* Arms Control: Negotiations to Reduce INF Weapons: Archived Issue Brief, Paul Gallis IB86054
* Arms Control: Ratification of the INF Treaty; Archived Issue Brief, Paul Gallis IB88003
* Assessing the INF Treaty, Foreign Affairs and National Defense Division 88-211 F
* Chemical Weapons Disarmament Talks: Archived Issue Brief, Steven R. Bowman IB87047
* Implications for NATO Strategy of a Zero-Outcome Intermediate-Range Nuclear Missile Accord, Stanley Sloan 87-614
* INF and the INF Treaty: Bibliography-in-Brief, 1983-1988, Valentin Leskovsek 88-454 L
* The INF Treaty and Its Political-Military Implications for Western Europe, Hugh DeSantis 88-57 F
* INF Treaty: Environmental Issues; Archived Issue Brief, Mary E. Tiemann IB88023
* INF Treaty: Info Pack, IP392I
* Intermediate-Range Nuclear Forces Treaty: Timetable of Elimination and Verification Provisions and Glossary of Key Terms, Joseph M. Freeman 88-153

Current Events and Homework

* Nuclear Arms Control: Disposal of Nuclear Warheads and Their Fissile Materials; Archived Issue Brief, Warren Donnelly, etc. IB88024
* On-Site Inspections in Arms Control: Verifying Compliance with INF and START, Amy F. Woolf 89-592 F
* Statements by President Reagan Relating to the INF Treaty, June 1, 1987-December 31, 1987, Teri Lehto 88-60 S

Inflation

* see Economic Conditions-Inflation

Information

* see Computers, Government Information, Press

Information and Privacy

* see Civil Liberties and Rights, Computers

Infrastructure

* see Highways, Marine Transportation, Procurement, Regional Development, Solid Wastes, Transportation, Urban Affairs, Water Resources, Waterways
* The Airport Improvement Program: Federal Capital Spending and Airport Capacity, J.F. Hornbeck 91-180 E
* Amenity Resources and Rural Economic Growth: Report on a National Policy Symposium, George H. Siehl 90-380 ENR
* The American Infrastructure: Selected References, 1985-1988, Robert Howe 89-41 L
* The "Bridge Crisis": An Economic Development Perspective: Issue Brief, J.F Hornbeck IB88085
* The FY 1989 Federal Budget for Public Works Infrastructure, Claudia Copeland 88-176 ENR
* Infrastructure: A Brief Overview from the National Level, William Ellis, etc. 87-30 S
* Maintaining Highway and Bridge Investments: What Role for Federal Grant Programs?, J.F. Hornbeck 90-277 E
* The Nation's Water Supply: An Overview of Conditions and Prospects, 86-893 ENR
* Navigable Waters: States Required to Keep Them "Forever Free", Marie B. Morris 91-726 A
* Rural Community Development: Selected References, Rebecca Mazur 88-17 L
* Transport Policy Problems: Elements of a National Plan; Proceedings of a CRS Symposium, Leon M. Cole 89-545 E
* Transportation Infrastructure and Economic Development, J.F.Hornbeck 89-109 E
* Transportation Infrastructure: Issue Brief, Kenneth DeJarnette IB91075
* Transportation Infrastructure Reauthorization: Highway and Mass Transit Issues; Info Pack IP453T
* Transportation Infrastructure: Selected References, Karen L. Alderson 91-502 L
* Transportation Status and Outlook: A Checklist of CRS Products, Karen L. Alderson 91-916 L

INS v. Chadha

* see Congress--Executive Relations

Insider Trading

* see Corporations--Securities Industry

Institute for Scientific and Technological Cooperation

* Institute for Scientific and Technological Cooperation: Archived Issue Brief, Genevieve Knezo IB79033

Insurance

* see Liability Issues, Health Insurance, Property/Casualty, Regulation, Solvency Issues
* AIDS and Discrimination: Legal Limits on Insurance Underwriting Practices, Kirk Nemer 88-381 A
* Automobile Insurance Controversy, Rawle King 88-731 E
* Automobile Insurance Crisis: Issue Brief, Rawle King IB89013
* Captive Off-Shore Insurance Companies, David Whiteman 84-507 E
* Environmental Impairment Liability Insurance: Overview of Availability Issues, Rawle O. King 89-269 E
* The Evolving National Flood Insurance Program, Malcolm M. Simmons 88-641 ENR
* Federal Crop Insurance: Background and Current Issues, Ralph Chite 88-739 ENR
* FHA's Mortgage Insurance Premium Refund Programs, Barbara Miles 87-709 E
* Fraternal Association Insurance as a Source of Life and Health Coverage, David Whiteman 87-784 E
* How Life Insurance Policies Generate Investment Income, Jack Taylor 88-326 E
* Insurance: An Alphabetical Microthesaurus of Terms, Selected from the Legislative Indexing Vocabulary, Shirley Loo 88-582 L
* Insurance: An Introduction to the Industry, Jean K. Rosales 89-482 E
* Insurance Company Insolvencies: A Checklist of CRS Products, Felix Chin 92-18 L
* Insurance Industry Regulation and Supervision: A Reexamination of the McDarran-Ferguson Act of 1945;, Archived Issue Brief, David Whiteman IB86149
* Insurance Underwriting and the Insurance Rate Classification Process, David Whiteman 84-550 E
* Life Insurance Tax Issues: Archived Issue Brief, Jack Taylor IB90098
* Managing Coastal Development Through the Coastal Zone Management and Flood Insurance Programs: Experience to Date and the Views from Selected States, Gary Kamimura, etc. 88-354 ENR
* The "Pooling" Process in Insurance and Reinsurance, David Whiteman 84-540 E
* Products Liability: A Legal Overview: Archived Issue Brief, Henry Cohen IB77021
* Property-Casualty Insurance Market Operation, David Whiteman 85-629 E
* Single-Premium Life Insurance Market Operation, Jack Taylor IB88074
* A Summary of the Provisions of the Tax Reform of 1986 Affecting the Treatment of Insurance Companies and Products, Robert Burdette 87-696 A
* Tax Status of Group Legal Services Plans, Louis Alan Talley 90-418 E
* Tax Treatment of Life Insurance: Basic Information, Robert B. Burdette 90-395 A
* The U.S. Insurance Industry and Financial Intermediation, Jean K. Rosales 90-249 E

Insurance -- Liability Issues

* Commercial Insurance and Liability Problems: Legislative Proposals in the 99th Congress, Kevin Flaherty 86-731 E
* Environmental Impairment Liability Insurance: Overview of Availability Issues, Rawle King 89-269 E
* Federal Tort Claims Act: Current Legislative and Judicial Issues, Henry Cohen 88-168 A
* Insurance for Directors and Officers: The 1987 Market, Sylvia Morrison 87-545 E
* Liability Insurance and Tort Liability Reform: Legislative Proposals in the 99th Congress, Edward Rappaport, etc. 87-97 E
* Liability Insurance and Tort Reform: Archive Issue Brief, Henry Cohen, etc. IB87015
* Liability Insurance Availability and Affordability Problems as a Function of Property-Casualty Insurance Market Fluctuations, David Whiteman 85-826 E
* The Liability Insurance Controversy: Archived Issue Brief, David Whiteman IB86154
* Liability Insurance: Selected References, 1986-1988, Felix Chin 88-163 L
* Liability Insurance: The Allocation of Investment Income by Line of Insurance, David Cantor 86-858 E
* Nuclear Liability Legislation: Price-Anderson Act Renewal Issues: Archived Issue Brief, Mark Holt IB88034
* Products Liability: A Legal Overview: Issue Brief, Henry Cohen IB77021
* Products Liability Reform: Analysis of H.R. 1115, 100th Congress, as Reported by Subcommittee, Henry Cohen 88-53 A
* Recent Judicial Expansions of Products Liability and Other Tort Law, Henry Cohen 86-847 A
* State Initiatives Regarding Commercial Liability Insurance: 1986 Efforts to Address the Shortage of Coverage and Its High Price, Sylvia Morrison 86-971 E
* Tort Injury Compensation Reform: Various Approaches, Henry Cohen 87-666 A
* The Tort Reform Debate: Pros, Cons, Federal Proposals, State Statutes, Henry Cohen 86-579 A
* Tort Reform: State Statutory Caps on Damages, Henry Cohen, etc. 87-835 A

Insurance -- Property/Casualty

* Agricultural Disaster Assistance: Issue Brief, Ralph Chite IB91099
* Crop Insurance and Disaster Assistance; Archived Issue Brief, Ralph Chite IB90080
* Crop Insurance Reform: A Review of the Commission Recommendations,

Inflation / International Agencies

Ralph M. Chite 89-624 ENR
* Earthquake and Disaster Relief Policies: San Francisco Bay Area Earthquake; Archived Issue Brief, James E. Mielke, etc. IB89149
* Federal Crop Insurance: Background and Current Issues, Ralph Chite 88-739 ENR
* Federal Earthquake Insurance and Reinsurance Legislation in the 102nd Congress, Jean K. Rosales 91-659 E
* The National Earthquake Hazards Reduction Program, David W. Cheney 89-473 SPR
* National Flood Insurance Program: Issue Brief, Malcolm Simmons IB90010
* Property/Casualty Insurance; Issues and Challenges for the 1990s, Rawle O. King 91-209 E
* Property/Casualty Insurance Market Operation, David Whiteman 85-629 E

Insurance -- Regulation

* Auto Insurance Markets: Is Federal Regulation Needed to Achieve Efficiency and Competitiveness? Proceedings of a CRS Congressional Seminar 90-514 E
* Expansion of Bank Industry Insurance powers Through Bank Subsidiaries of Bank Holding Companies, M. Maureen Murphy 90-130 A
* Insurance Issue Facing Congress: Archived Issue Brief, Jean K. Rosales IB89143
* Insurance Reform: An Analysis of H.R. 1663, Rawle O. King 90-410 E
* Insurance Regulation and the McCarran-Ferguson Act; Issue Brief, Jean K. Rosales IB90102
* Insurance Regulation by the States, Edward B. Rappaport 90-504 E
* The McCarren-Ferguson Act's Exemption of the Business of Insurance from Federal Antitrust Law, Henry Cohen 90-212 A

Insurance -- Solvency Issues

* Financial Condition of Life Insurance Companies: Archived Issue Brief, Rawle O. King IB91091
* Insurance Company Insolvencies and Pension Benefits: Issue Brief, Ray Schmitt, IB91123
* Insurance Company Insolvencies: Are Insurers at Risk? Proceedings of a CRS Congressional Seminar, Rawle O. King 91-795 E
* Insurance Company Solvency, Edward B. Rappaport 89-470 E
* Insurance Failures: An Overview of Recent Trends and Implications, Rawle O. King 91-805 E
* Insurer Insolvency: Federal Proposals and Legislation, Rawle O. King 91-829 E
* Life Insurer Insolvency: Issue Brief, Jean K. Rosales, etc. IB91088

Insurance Sales By Banks

* see Money and Banking--Law and Regulation

Integration

* see Blacks, Civil Liberties and Rights--Discrimination and Integration, Elemenatry and Secondary Education--Policies and Legislation, Equal Employment Opportunity, Higher Education--Integration, Housing

Intelligence Activities

* Arms Control and Intelligence: Bibliography-in-Brief, 1979-1987, Teri Lehto, etc. 87-499 S
* The Central Intelligence Agency: Organizational History, Mark Lowenthal 78-168 F
* Congress and Foreign Intelligence Operations: Selected References, Sherry B. shapiro 91-620 L
* Congress and Intelligence Policy: Selected References, Sherry Shapiro 88-36 L
* Contra Aid: Analysis of Whether the National Security Council (NSC) and the NSC Staff Are an "agency, or Entity Involved in Intelligence Activities" Co, Larry E. Eig 87-566 A
* Covert Actions: Congressional Oversight: Archived Issue Brief, Richard F. Grimmett IB87208
* Individuals Arrested on Charges of Espionage Against the United States Government: 1966-1989, Suzanne Cavanaugh 89-324 GOV
* Inspector General in the CIA Compared to Other Statutory Inspectors General, Frederick M. Kaiser 89-679 GOV
* Intelligence Budgets: Contents and Releasability, Alfred B. Prados 89-465 F
* Intelligence Community Leadership: Development and Debate Since 1947, Alfred B. Prados 89-414 F
* Intelligence Issues for 102nd Congress: Issue Brief, Richard a. Best IB91017
* Intelligence Oversight in Selected Democracies, Alfred B. Prados, etc. 90-483 F
* Intelligence Reform Issues: Archived Issue Brief, Alfred B. Prados IB88029

* Intelligence Reform: Recent History and Proposals, Alfred Prados 88-562 F
* Office of Inspector General in the Central Intelligence Agency: Development and Proposals, Frederick M. Kaiser 89-129 GOV
* Reforming Defense Intelligence, Richard A. Best 91-475 F
* Special Access Programs, Confidential Funding, and the Defense Budget: Bibliography-in-Brief, Sherry Shapiro 87-802 L
* U.S. Defense Planning: A Critique, John Collins, etc. 82-167 S
* The U.S. Intelligence Community: A Role in Suporting Economic Competitiveness?, Richard A. Best 90-571 F

Interest Rates

* see Money and Banking--Interest Rates

Intergovernmental Fiscal Relations

* see State and Local Government--Intergovernmental Fiscal Relations

Internal Security

* Abolition of the House Internal Security Committee, Paul Rundquist 88-203 GOV
* Classified Information Procedures Act (CIPA): An Overview, Larry Eig 89-172 A
* Contra Aid: Analysis of Whether the National Security Council (NSC) and the NSC Staff Are an "agency, or Entity Involved in Intelligence Activities" Co, Larry E. Eig 87-566 A
* Individuals Arrested on Charges of Espionage Against the United States Government: 1966-1989, Suzanne Cavanaugh 89-324 GOV
* Legal Issues Related to the Possible Release of Classified Information by Senators, Representatives, or Members of Their Staffs, Elizabeth B. Bazan 89-322 A
* National Emergency Powers, Harold C. Relyea 91-383 GOV
* Protecting Classified Information: A Compilation and Index of Major Findings and Recommendations, 1905-1987, Frederick M. Kaiser, etc. 87-293 GOV
* Redress for Japanese Americans under the Civil Liberties Act of 1988: Questions and Answers, James Sayler 90-488 GOV
* Scientific Communication and National Security: Bibliography-in-Brief, 1982-1987, Virginia MacEwen, etc. 87-110 L
* Security Clearances for Congressional and Judicial Employees, Frederick Kaiser 87-809 GOV
* Security Clearances for Members of Congress and the Judiciary, Frederick M. Kaiser 87-704 GOV

International Agencies

* Access to World Bank Information, Jonathan E. Sanford 89-89 F
* Answers to Nine Questions on the United Nations, Lois McHugh 84-31 F
* Cyprus: Status of U.N. Negotiations: Issue Brief, Ellen B. Laipson IB89140
* Environmental Activities of Selected International Organizations, Wendy Woods, etc. 90-17 ENR
* The IMF Quota Increase: New Directions for the International Monetary Fund; Issue Brief, Patricia A. Wertman IB91059
* International Atomic Energy Agency: Bibliography-in-Brief, Bonnie F. Mangan 89-259 L
* International Fund for Agricultural Development, Susan Epstein 87-4 ENR
* International Labor Organization: Issues of U.S. Membership: Archived Issue Brief, Lois McHugh IB77073
* International Monetary Fund and World Bank: Info Pack, IP245I
* International Monetary Fund: Bibliography-in-Brief, 1983-1987, Robert Kirk 87-47 L
* International Monetary Fund: Selected Annotated References; 1989-1991, Robert S. Kirk, etc. 91-523 L
* Iraq-Kuwait: The United Nations Response Before the War; Archived Issue Brief, Marjorie Ann Brown IB90147
* Iraq-Kuwait: U.N. Security Council Resolutions: Texts and Votes, Marjorie Ann Browne 91-395 F
* Israel's Participation in the International Atomic, Energy Agency and the 32nd IAEA General Conference: Archived Issue Brief, Warren Donnelly I88072
* Presidential Remarks About the International Atomic Energy Agency: Selected Excerpts, Barbara Black 89-27 ENR
* Soviet Membership in the International Monetary Fund, Patricia A. Wertman 90-216 E
* The Soviet Union and the United Nations: Congressional Issues; Archived Issue Brief, Vita Bite IB88069
* The U.N. and Congress: Legislation Affecting Participation and Contributions (98th, 99th, and 100th Congress), Vita Bite, etc. 89-223 F
* U.N. Funding: Congressional Issues; Issue Brief, Vita Bite IB86116

Current Events and Homework

* UNESCO-U.S. Withdrawal in Perspective: Archived Issue Brief, Lois McHugh IB84086
* United Nations Conference on Environment and Development (UNCED): Brazil 1992, Susan R. Fletcher 91-363 ENR
* United Nations Peacekeeping: Historical Overview and Current Issues, Marjorie Ann Browne 90-96 F
* United Nations Peacekeeping: Issues for Congress; Archived Issue Brief, Marjorie Ann Browne IB90103
* United Nations Reform: Issues for Congress, Marjorie Ann Browne 88-593 F
* United Nations Role in the Iran-Iraq War: Issues and Options, Lois B. McHugh, etc. 88-463 F
* The United States and Southern Africa: A Review of United Nations Resolutions and United States Voting Patterns, 1946-October 1985, Frankie King 86-21
* United States Contributions to UNICEF, Lois McHugh 88-154 F
* U.S. Bilateral and Multilateral Food Assistance Programs, Susan Epstein 85-114 ENR
* U.S. Withdrawal from the International Labor Organization: Successful Precedent for UNESCO?, Lois McHugh 84-202 F
* U.S. Withholding and Arrearages to the United Nations Regular Budget: Issues for Congress, Vita Bite 91-515 F
* The World Bank: Bibliography-in-Brief of Recent Works, Felix Chin 89-464 L
* The World Bank: Eighteen Questions and Answers, Jonathan E. Sanford 86-769 F
* World Health Organization: Effects of Reduced U.S. Contributions, Lois McHugh 87-108 F

International Atomic Energy Agency

* Implementation of the U.S.-Chinese Agreement for Nuclear Cooperation: Archived Issue Brief, Warren Donnelly IB86050
* International Atomic Energy Agency: Bibliography-in-Brief, Bonnie Mangan 89-259 L
* International Atomic Energy Agency: Strengthen Verification Authority? Issue Brief, Warren H. Donnelly, etc. IB91109
* Israel's Participation in the International Atomic, Energy Agency and the 32nd IAEA General Conference: Archived Issue Brief, Warren H. Donnelly IB88072
* Presidential Remarks About the International Atomic Energy Agency: Selected Excerpts, Barbara Black 89-27 ENR

International Banking

see International Finance--Foreign Banks and Banking

International Brotherhood of Teamsters, Chauffeurs, Warehousemen and Helpers of America

* The International Brotherhood of Teamsters; an Historical and Bibliographical Review, William Whittaker 77-71 E

International Coffee Agreement

* International Coffee Agreement, Donna Vogt 84-224 ENR

International Commission on Central American Recovery and Development

* International Commission on Central America: Initial Views; Audio Brief, Larry Storrs AB50176

International Competitiveness

* see Foreign Trade--Competitiveness

International Corporations

* The European Community's New Merger Laws: Overview and Implications for U.S. Firms, Gary W. Shorter 91-240 E
* The European Community's 1992 Plan: Effects on American Direct Investment, James K. Jackson 89-339 E
* The Financial Impact of Oil Price Behavior on International Development and Trade: Transnational Oil, Companies and Persian Gulf Exporters; Report of, Clyde R. Mark, etc. 86-903 F
* Foreign Direct Investment in the U.S.; Identifying the Ultimate Beneficial Owner, James K. Jackson 90-610 E
* Foreign Corrupt Practices Act Amendments of 1988, Michael V. Seitzinger 88-589 A
* Foreign Mergers and Acquisitions: Non-U.S. Companies Acquiring U.S. Companies, Kevin F. Winch, etc. 87-711 E

* Japan-U.S. Economic Issues: Investment, Saving, Technology and Attitudes, Dick K. Nanto 90-78 E
* Japan's Industrial Groups: The Keiretsu, Dick K. Nanto 90-609 E
* Major Federal Tax Provisions that Directly Affect International Trade and Investment, David Brumbaugh 86-764 E
* Offshore Manufacturing by U.S Corporations: Selected Bibliography, With Introductory Readings, Robert Kirk 86-834 L
* Taxation of Foreign-Source Income: A Survey: A Brief Overview of Concepts, Provisions, and Issues in the Federal Taxation of Foreign-Source Income, David L. Brumbaugh 83-636 E
* Taxation of Foreign-Source-Income: A Survey: The U .S. Foreign Tax Credits: Provisions, Effects and Issues, David Brumbaugh 83-222 E
* U.S. Taxation of Overseas Investment: Selected Issues in the 102nd Congress, David L. Brumbaugh 91-682 E

International Debt Crisis

* see International Finance--Foreign Loans

International Economic Relations

* see Foreign Aid, Foreign Investment, Foreign Trade

International Environmental Affairs

* Africa: Environmental Issues, Brenda Branaman, 90-383 F
* Agriculture and the Environment: Archived Issue Brief, Jean Rawson, etc. IB89086
* Antarctica: Environmental Protection Issues: Summary of a CRS Research Workshop, Susan Fletcher 89-272 ENR
* Canada's Progress on Acid Rain Control: Shifting Gears or Stalled in Neutral?, Mira Courpas, etc. 89-272 ENR
* CFC Phase-Out Bills in the 101st Congress: Comparison of Provisions, David Gushee 89-314 ENR
* Congress and International Environmental Issues in 1989, Curt Tarnoff 90-364 F
* Current International Environmental Negotiations, Susan R. Fletcher 91-820 ENR
* Debt-for-Nature Swaps in Developing Countries: An Overview of Recent Conservation Efforts, Betsy Cody 88-647 ENR
* Desertification: Overview of a Global Environmental Problem, Susan Abbasi 84-599 ENR
* Driftnets: A Controversial Fishing Method, Eugene H. Buck 90-311 ENR
* Emission Standards for Coke Ovens in Japan, Law Library of Congress LL90-16
* Environment and Development: U.S. Assistance programs and Congressional Initiatives, Curt Tarnoff 91-548 F
* Environment and International Economic Development: The Role of Cost-Benefit Analysis, John Moore, etc. 87-774 ENR
* The Environment as a Foreign Policy Issue: Issue Brief, Curt Tarnoff IB89151
* Environmental Activities of Selected International Organizations, Wendy Woods, etc. 90-17 ENR
* Environmental Legislation and Trade: A Checklist of CRS Products, Ted L. Burch 92-7 L
* Environmental Protection in Developing Countries: Selected References, 1983-1987, Rebecca Mazur 87-488
* Environmental Protection Laws and Treaties: Reference Guide, Environment and Natural Resources Policy Division 91-136 ENR
* Environmental Regulation and the GATT, Jeanne J. Grimmett 91-285 A
* Export of Pesticides, James V. Aidala 89-73 ENR
* Global Climate Changes and the Green House Effect:, Congressional Activity and Options: Archived Issue Brief, David Gushee IB88077
* Global Climate Change and Ozone Depletion: Selected References, 1989-1991, Karen L. Alderson 91-549 L
* The Global Environment: Audio Brief, AB50063
* International Environment: Major United States Legislation, Congressional Research Service 90-292 ENR
* International Environment: Overview of Major Issues: Issue Brief, Mary Tiemann, etc. IB89057
* International Environment Issues: Overview, Issue Brief, Susan Fletcher IB91047
* Major International Environmental Issues: A Checklist of CRS Products, Lisa B. Dove 92-13 L
* Regulating U.S. Pesticide Exports: Policy Issues and Proposed Legislation, Jasper Womach 91-568 ENR
* The Stratospheric Ozone Layer: Regulatory Issues: Issue Brief, David Gushee IB89021
* Tropical Deforestation: Info Pack, IP416T

International Atomic Energy Agency / International Finance

* Tropical Deforestation: International Implications: Archived Issue Brief, Susan Fletcher IB89010
* Tropical Deforestation: The International Tropical Timber Agreement, Ross W. Gorte 87-795 ENR
* Tropical Deforestation: Selected References, 1987-1990, Lisa B. Dove 90-578 L
* United Nations Conference on Environment and Development (UNCED); Brazil 1992, Susan R. Fletcher 91-363 ENR
* The Unpredictable Atmosphere: Selected References, Karen Alderson, etc. 89-43 L
* Waste Exports: U.S. and International Efforts to Control Transboundary Movement; Issue Brief, Mary Tiemann IB89123
* Waste in the Marine Environment: Selected References, Ted Burch 89-263 L
* Whale Conservation, Eugene H. Buck, etc. 88-391 ENR

International Finance

* see Foreign Banks and Banking, Foreign Exchange Rates, Foreign Loans, Multilateral Development Banks
* The British Experience With Indexed Bonds, G. Thomas Woodward 87-926 E
* Capital Flight and Highly Indebted Countries: An Analytical Survey of the Literature, Glennon J. Harrison 91-273 E
* Capital Flight: Problems Associated With Definitions and Estimates, Glennon J. Harrison 91-274 E
* Capital Market Changes in the United Kingdom, Japan, West Germany, and Singapore: A Brief Survey, Julius W. Allen 88-49 E
* Chronology of Important Events in International Economics, George Holliday 85-512 E
* Domestic and International Monetary-Fiscal Policy Coordination, Thomas F. Dernburg 84-145 E
* Exchange Control Laws in the West Indies, Law Library of Congress LL90-24
* The Financial Impact of Oil Price Behavior on International Development and Trade: Transnational Oil, Companies and Persian Gulf Oil Exporters: Clyde R. Mark, etc. 86-903 F
* Financial Markets: A New Framework of Issues, Walter Eubanks 88-485 E
* Foreign Investment in U.S. Securities in 1990, James K. Jackson 91-486 E
* Globalization of Securities Markets, Kevin F. Winch, etc. 89-363 E
* Globalization of Securities Markets: A Selected Annotated Bibliography, Edward Knight, etc. 89-359 E
* Growing Internationalization of Stock Markets: Implications for Financial Regulation: Archived Issue, Brief Edward Knight IB88037
* International Banking Facilities and the Eurocurrency Market, William Jackson, etc. 82-27 E
* The Internationalization of Securities Trading Markets, Julius W. Allen 86-14 E
* Is Faster Growth in Germany and Japan the Key to Faster U.S. Growth?, Gail E. Makinen 86-836 E
* Japan's Financial Liberalization: Effects on the United States, James K. Jackson 89-102 E
* Merchant Banking: Opportunities or Problems for U.S. Banks?, Walter Eubanks, etc. 87-351
* Progress Against Poverty in the United States (1959 to 1987), Thomas Gabe 89-211 EPW
* Regulating International and European Community Securities Trading, Julius W. Allen 90-340 E
* The Role of Gold in the International Monetary System, Arlene Wilson 80-47 E
* A Survey of U.S. International Economic Policy and Problems, Alfred Reifman 88-666 S
* Trade and Current Account Balances: Statistics; Issue Brief, Wayne M. Morrison IB87112
* Trade and International Finance: An Alphabetical Microthesaurus of Terms Selected from the Legislative Indexing Vocabulary, Shirley Loo 89-653 L
* A World Capital Shortage? Will Increased Demand by Germany, Eastern Europe and the Soviet Union Strain World Capital Markets?, Alfred Reifman 91-616 RCO

International Finance -- Foreign Banks and Banking

* Bank of Credit and Commerce International (BCCI): Some Legal Implications, M. Maureen Murphy 91-652 A
* Banking in "Europe 1992", William Jackson 89-456 E
* Banking Systems in the United States, Japan, and the European Community: Comparative Studies, F. Jean Wells 90-357 E
* BCCI: Bibliography-in-Brief, Karen L. Alderson 91-676 L
* BCCI: Issues for Congress; Issue Brief, Raphael F. Perl IB91125
* BCCI: Key Events, Companies, Individuals, and Selected Articles, Paul Janov 91-640 C
* Deposit Guarantees in Other Countries, G. Thomas Woodward 89-637 E
* Edge Act International Banking Corporations, William Jackson 91-459 E
* The European Central Banking System and Monetary Union, Walter W. Eubanks 90-42 E
* Firewalls or Chinese Walls in European Universal Banking, Law Library of Congress LL89-94
* Foreign Banking in America, William Jackson 91-472 E
* Japan: Regulatory Structure and Delivery of Financial Services, Walter W. Eubanks 90-351 E
* The Soviet Banking Revolution: Its Realization and Implications for Congress, Walter W. Eubanks 91-256 E

International Finance -- Foreign Exchange Rates

* Deficit Reduction and the Foreign Exchange Value of the Dollar, Brian W. Cashell, etc. 87-990 E
* The Dollar and the Trade Deficit: What's to Be Done?, Craig Elwell, etc. 88-430 E
* Domestic and International Monetary-Fiscal Policy Coordination, Thomas F. Dernburg 84-145 E
* Exchange Rate Management in Taiwan, South Korea and Hong Kong, Arlene Wilson 87-401 E
* Exchange Rates: The Dollar in International Markets: Archived Issue Brief, Arlene Wilson IB78033
* A Falling Dollar and Domestic Inflation, Craig K. Elwell 86-127 E
* Foreign Exchange Intervention, Arlene Wilson 86-915 E
* How Much Has the International Exchange Value of the Dollar Declined?, Gail Makinen 87-429 E
* Next Steps in International Monetary Reform: Exchange Rate Targeting?, Alfred Reifman 88-1 S
* Special Drawing Rights in the International Monetary System: Their Nature, Evolution, and Future Role, Craig Elwell 88-348 E
* Trade Deficits and the Dollar: Bibliography-in-Brief, 1984-1987, Robert S. Kirk 87-88 L
* Trade: Issue Brief, Arlene Wilson, etc. IB87003
* Wage Rates and Exchange Rates, Linda LeGrande 88-252 E

International Finance -- Foreign Loans

* African Debt: The Official Donor Response and Potential Alternative Strategies, Alan K. Yu 89-228 F
* The "Baker Plan": A Remedy for the International Debt Crisis?: Issue Brief, Patricia Wertman IB86106
* Bank Lending to the Third World: Risk Considerations, William Jackson 88-525 E
* Beyond the Brady Plan: Toward a Differentiated Debt Strategy?, a CRS Trade Team Product, Patricia A. Wertman 90-181 E
* The "Brady Plan" and the Third World Debt Problem, Patricia A. Wertman 89-425 E
* The Citicorp Initiative: A Brave New World for the Third World Debt Problem, Patricia Wertman 87-750 E
* Debt-for-Nature Swaps in Developing Countries: An Overview of Recent Conservation Efforts, Betsy Cody 88-647 ENR
* Debt Rescheduling Agreements in Latin America, 1980-86, Glennon Harrison 87-360 E
* Debt Rescheduling: The Argentine Case, 1982-1988, Glennon Harrison 88-505 E
* Debt Service Indicators of the Seventeen Most Highly Indebted Developing Countries, 1978-1986, Patricia Wertman, etc.
* Economic Perestroika: Gorbachev at the London Economic Summit, July 17, 1991; Audio Brief, Joseph Whalen AB50227
* Finance and Adjustment: The International Debt Crisis, 1982-84, Patricia Wertman 84-162 E
* The Growing U.S. External Debt: Nature and Implications, Craig Elwell 87-798 E
* An International Debt Management Authority: Could It Spell R-E-L-I-E-F?, Economics Division 88-607 E
* The International Debt Problem: Congressional Proposals: Archived Issue Brief, Patricia Wertman IB87177
* The International Debt Problem: Impact and Response, Glennon Harrison, etc. 88-76 E
* The International Debt Problem: Options for Solution, Patricia Wertman 86-922 E
* International Debt Problems: Background, Statistics, Proposed Solutions: Info Pack, IP234I

Current Events and Homework

* International Lending Patterns of U.S. Banks: Financial and Regulatory Trends, William Jackson 85-124 E
* Latin American Debt and U.S. Agricultural Exports: Assessment of a Proposed Approach, Charles E. Hanrahan 87-304 ENR
* Latin American Debt: Characteristics, Trends, and U.S. Policy, Mark P. Sullivan 91-343 F
* Latin American Debt Crisis: Selected References, 1987-1990, Robert Howe 90-251 L
* The Mexican Debt Accords and Their Financial Implications: An Overview, Patricia Wertman 86-179 E
* The Mexican Debt Swap: The Advent of Debt Relief?, Patricia Wertman 88-145 E
* Poland's Economic Recovery: U.S. Policy Interests:, Archived Issue Brief, John Hardt, etc. IB86070
* Polish Economic Reform and U.S. Interests, William H. Cooper 91-249 E
* The Polish Official Debt Accord: A Problem of Containment, Patricia A. Wertman 91-474 E
* Rescheduling International Debt, Glennon Harrison 89-126 E
* The South Africa Financial Crisis: The Role of U.S. Banks, Walter Eubanks 86-550 E
* Statutory Authorities Related to Official Foreign Debt, Jeanne J. Grimmett 91-381 A
* Third World Debt: Selected References, 1988-1990, Robert Howe 90-255 L
* Trade of the Seventeen Highly Indebted Countries: A Brief Overview, Patricia Wertman, etc. 88-521 E
* U.S. Bank Exposure in the Seventeen Highly Indebted Countries: 1982-1987, Patricia Wertman, etc. 88-522 E
* U.S. Banks and the People's Republic of China, Walter Eubanks 84-840 E
* U.S. Tax Treatment of Bad Foreign Loans, David L. Brumbaugh 89-302 E
* Western Aid Report on the Soviet Economy, John P. Hardt 91-16 RCO
* World Bank/IMF Adjustment Loans and the Poor in Developing Countries, Foreign Affairs and National Defense Division 91-176 F
* Worldwide Bank Exposure in the Seventeen Highly Indebted Countries, 1982-1987, Patricia Wertman 88-527 E

International Finance -- Multilateral Development Banks

* see Banks
* Access to World Bank Information, Jonathan E. Sanford 89-89 F
* European Bank for Reconstruction and Development: An Institution of and for the New Europe, Karen Donfried 91-611 F
* The IMF Quota Increase: New Directions for the International Monetary Fund; Issue Brief, Patricia A. Wertman IB91059
* International Monetary Fund and World Bank: Info Pack, IP2245I
* International Monetary Fund: Bibliography-in-Brief, 1983-1987, Robert Kirk 87-47 L
* International Monetary Fund: Selected Annotated References, 1989-1991, Robert S. Kirk, etc. 91-523 L
* Multilateral Development Banks: Issues for the 101st Congress; Archived Issue Brief, Jonathan E. Sanford IB87218
* Multinational Bank Supervision, Walter W. Eubanks 91-768 E
* Soviet Membership in the International Monetary Fund, Patricia A. Wertman 90-216 E
* Soviet Membership in the International Monetary Fund: Is It Feasible Now? Arlene Wilson 91-686 E
* Soviet Participation in International Financial Institutions; Issue Brief, Shirley A. Kan, etc. IB91133
* World Bank Activities in Ethiopia, Jonathan E. Sanford 87-857 F
* The World Bank: Bibliography-in-Brief of Recent Works, Felix Chin 89-464 L
* The World Bank: Eighteen Questions and Answers, Jonathan E. Sanford 86-769 F

International Fund for Agricultural Development

* International Fund for Agricultural Development, Susan Epstein 87-4 ENR

International Labor Organization

* International Labor Organization: Issues of U.S. Membership: Archived Issue Brief, Lois McHugh IB77073
* U.S. Withdrawal from the International Labor Organization: Successful Precedent for UNESCO?, Lois McHugh 84-202 F

International Law

* see Human Rights
* Blockade: Some International and Domestic Legal Implications, Raymond J. Celada 90-386 A
* Countries With Smoking Bans on Domestic and International Flights, Law Library of Congress LL90-68
* Firearms Regulations in Various Foreign Countries, Law Library of Congress LL90-80
* The Geneva Convention Relative to the Treatment of Prisoners of War, Larry M. Eig 91-122 A
* Genocide Convention: Archived Issue Brief, Vita Bite IB74129
* India: Regional Dissidence and Human Rights Problems, Richard P. Cronin, etc. 91-585 F
* An International Criminal Court, Daniel Hill Zafren 90-385 A
* Jurisdiction under International Law: Some Basics, Raymond J. Celada 90-76 A
* Justice and Human Rights in China: Criminal Trials of the Leading 1989 Pro-Democracy Activists, Law Library of Congress LL91-6
* The Law of the Sea Conference: A U.S. Perspective: Archived Issue Brief, Marjorie Brown IB81153
* Legal Analysis of "The International Child Abduction Act" (S.1347 and H.R. 2673, 100th Congress) (Implementing the Hague Convention on the Civil Aspe.), Rita Ann Reimer 88-121 A
* Legal Status of United States Citizens in Iraq and Kuwait, David M. Ackerman 90-406 A
* Living Aquatic Resource Laws and Treaties: Reference Guide, Eugene H. Buck 89-620 ENR
* Patent Laws in Selected Countries, Law Library of Congress LL90-81
* Political Asylum: New Rules Analyzed, Larry M. Eig 90-487 A
* Regulation of Lobbying in Foreign Countries, Law Library of Congress LL90-85
* Seizure of Foreign Vessels in United States Ports, Daniel Hill Zafren 87-760 A
* The United States and International Human Rights Treaties: A Summary of Provisions and Status in the Ratification Process, Vita Bite 90-308 F
* United States Law Applicable in Outer Space, Daniel Hill Zafren 86-881 A

International Law -- Human Rights

* Emigration and Human Rights in the U.S.S.R.: Is There a New Approach? Archived Issue Brief, John P. Hardt IB88019
* Genocide Convention: Archived Issue Brief, Vita Blue IB74129
* Guatemala: U.S. Foreign Assistance Facts: Archived Issue Brief, Jonathan Sanford IB85100
* Human Rights in U.S. Foreign Relations: Six Key Questions in the Continuing Policy Debate, Vita Blue 81-257 F
* Latvia: Background Information, Allan Nanes, etc. 83-154 F

International Monetary Fund

* see International Finance-Foreign, Exchange Rates, International Finance--Multilateral Development Banks
* Debt Rescheduling Agreements in Latin America, 1980-86, Glennon Harrison 87-360 E
* Finance and Adjustment: the International Debt Crisis, 1982-84, Patricia Wertman 84-162 E
* The IMF Quota Increase: New Directions for the International Monetary Fund; Issue Brief, Patricia A. Wertman IB91059
* International Monetary Fund and World Bank: Info Pack, IP2245I
* International Monetary Fund: Bibliography-in-Brief, 1983-1987, Robert Kirk 87-47 L
* International Monetary Fund: Selected Annotated References; 1989-1991, Robert S. Kirk, etc 91-523 L
* The Mexican Debt Accords and Their Financial Implications: An Overview, Patricia Wertman 86-179 E
* The Polish Official Debt Accord: A Problem of Containment, Patricia A. Wertman 91-474 E
* Soviet Membership in the International Monetary Fund, Patricia A. Wertman 90-216 E
* Soviet Membership in the International Monetary Fund: Is It Feasible Now?, Arlene Wilson 91-686 E
* Soviet Participation in International Financial Institutions; Issue Brief, Shirley A. Kan, etc. IB91133
* Western Aid Report on the Soviet Economy, John P. Hardt 91-16 RCO

International Relations

* see Foreign Relations

International Trade

* see Foreign Trade

Iran

see also Iran Contra Affair

International Finance / Iraq-Kuwait Crisis

* Arms Shipments to Iran: Archived Issue Brief, Richard Preece IB87022
* Arms Transfers to Iran Since 1979: Reports from the Media, Jonathan Medalia 86-187 F
* Ban on Imports from Iran: Economic Effect on the United States, Bernard Gelb 88-6 E
* Compilation of Selected Laws Relating to the National Security Council, Arms Transfers, Intelligence Activities, Aid to the Contras, etc., American Law Division 86-1028 A
* Immunity for Witnesses Testifying Before Congressional Committees, Jay R. Shampansky 86-1026 A
* Iran After Khomeini: Implications for U.S.-Iranian Relations, Alfred B. Prados 90-132 F
* Iran Arms and Contra Funds: Selected Chronology of Events, 1979-1987, Richard Preece, etc. 86-190 F
* Iran Arms Sales and Contra Funds: Summaries of Key Legislative Provisions, Clyde R. Mark, etc. 87-13 F
* The Iran/Contra Affair: Implications for the National Security Adviser and the NSC Staff: Archived Issue Brief, Joel M. Woldman IB87107
* Iran/Contra Affair: Organization Profiles, Heather B. Longton 87-625 F
* Iran/Iraq War: Issue Brief, Richard Preece IB88060
* Laws Implicated by Shipments of Military Materials to Iran, Raymond Celada 86-1005 A
* Lebanon: The Remaining U.S. Hostages: Issue Brief, Clyde Mark IB85183
* Soviet Policy Toward Iran and the Strategic Balance in Southwest Asia, Stuart Goldman 87-592 F
* U.S. Policy Toward Iran: 1979-1986, Richard Preece 87-974 F

Iran-Contra Affair

* see also Foreign Policy and Assistance Programs
* Arms Shipments to Iran: Archived Issue Brief, Richard M. Preece IB87022
* Compilation of Selected Laws Relating to the National Security Council, Arms Transfers, Intelligence Activities, Aid to the Contras, etc., American Law Division 86-1028 A
* Congress and the Iran-Contra Affair, Joel Woldman 88-765 F
* Contra Aid: Analysis of Whether the National Security Council (NSC) and the NSC Staff are an "agency or Entity Involved In Intelligence Activities",etc, Larry E. Eig 87-566 A
* Iran Arms and Contra Funds: Selected Chronology of Events, 1979-1987, Richard Preece, etc. 86-190 F
* Iran Arms Sales and Contra Funds: Summaries of Key Legislative Provisions, Clyde Mark, etc. 87-13 F
* The Iran/Contra Affair: Implications for the National Security Adviser and the NSC Staff: Archived Issue Brief, Joel Woldman IB87107
* Iran Contra Affair: Organization Profiles, Heather Longton 87-625 F
* Iran-Contra Affair: Status of the Recommendations Contained in the Joint Report of the House and Senate Selected Committees, Clyde Mark 88-324 F
* U.S. Presidential National Security Advisers: Changing Roles and Relationships, Joel Woldman 87-334 F

Iran-Iraq War

* see Middle East-Iran - Iraq War, Persian Gulf

Iraq

* see also Iraq-Kuwait Crisis
* Blockade: Some International and Domestic Legal Implications, Raymond J. Celada 90-386 A
* International Atomic Energy Agency: Strengthen Verification Authority?, Issue Brief, Warren H. Donnelly, etc. IB91109
* Iran-Iraq War: Issue Brief, Richard Preece 86-142 F
* Iraq and Kuwait: Economic Profiles, Dario Scuka 90-399 E
* Iraq and Nuclear Weapons: Issue Brief, Warren Donnelly IB90113
* Iraq, Kuwait and IEEPA, Raymond J. Celada 90-373 A
* Iraq/Kuwait Crisis: A Summary of Foreign Support for Multinational Efforts in the Perisna Gulf, Timothy D. Hoyt 90-505 F
* Iraq/Kuwait Crisis: U.S. Policy and Options; Archived Issue Brief, Alfred B. Prados, etc. IB90117
* Iraq/Kuwait: The United Nations Response Before the War; Archived Issue Brief, Marjorie Ann Brown IB90147
* Iraq: U.S. Economic Sanctions; Archived Issue Brief, Clyde R. Mark IB90109
* The Iraqi Crisis: National Public Opinion Polls, Rosita M. Thomas 90-436 GOV
* Iraq's Invasion of Kuwait: A Review of Events, Issue Brief, Renee L Stasio IB90118
* Iraq's Post-War Compliance Record: A Chronology, Kenneth Katzman 91-740 F

* Legal Status of United States Citizens in Iraq and Kuwait, David M. Ackerman 90-406 A
* Naval Restriction of Commerce Against Iraq: Historic Background, Implications and Options, Mark M. Lowenthal 90-388 S
* Oil and Iraq's Invasion of Kuwait: Archived Issue Brief, Carl Behrens, etc. IB90116
* Persian Gulf Conflict: Post-War Issues for Congress; Archived Issue Brief, Raymond W. Copson IB90132
* Persian Gulf War: Key U.S. Military Personnel and Compensation Questions; Archived Issue Brief, Robert L. Goldich IB90124
* Persian Gulf War: U.S. Reserve Callup and Reliance on the Reserves; Issue Brief, Robert L. Goldich IB90144
* The Strategic Petroleum Reserve and the Drawdown Dilemma, Robert L. Bamberger, etc. 90-492 ENR
* United States-Iraqi Relations, Richard M. Preece, 86-142 F
* U.S. and Allied Options Early in the Persian Gulf Crisis, John M. Collins 90-394 S
* The World Embargo on Food Exports to Iraq, Susan B. Epstein 90-462 ENR

Iraq-Kuwait Crisis

* see Middle East--Iraq-Kuwait, Military Assistance, Persian Gulf
* Activation of Selected Reserves under Executive Order 12727 and Executive Order 12733 for Service in the Arabian Peninsula, Robert B. Burdette 90-563 A
* Agricultural Energy Use and the Iraqi Crisis, Ralph M. Chite 90-397 ENR
* American Public Opinion on the Iraq-Kuwait Crisis Until January 15, Rosita M. Thomas 91-109 GOV
* Arms Sales to Saudi Arabia: Current Status; Issue Brief, Richard F. Grimmett IB91007
* Blockade: Some International and Domestic Legal Implications, Raymond J. Celada 90-386 A
* Dellums v. Bush: President Bush's Authority to Initiate Offensive Operations in the Persian Gulf Challenged in the Courts by House Members and Law Professors, Raymond J. Celada 90-585 A
* Desert Shield and Desert Storm: Implications for Future U.S. Force Requirements, John M. Collins 91-361 RCO
* Egyptian Military Debt Forgiveness: Costs, Implications, and the Role of Congress; Archived Issue Brief, Larry Q. Nowels IB90137
* Futures Markets and the Price of Oil, Mark Jickling 91-324 E
* The Geneva Convention Relative to the Treatment of Prisoners of War, Larry M. Eig 91-122 A
* Iraq and Kuwait: Conflicting Historical Claims, Alfred B. Prados 91-34 F
* Iraq and Kuwait: Economic Profiles, Dario Scuka 90-399 E
* Iraq and Nuclear Weapons: Issue Brief, Warren Donnelly IB90113
* Iraq, Kuwait and IEEPA, Raymond J. Celada 90-373 A
* Iraq-Kuwait Crisis: A Chronology of Events, July 17-March 3, 1991, Clyde R. Mark, etc. 91-14 F
* Iraq/Kuwait Crisis: A Summary of Foreign Support for Multinational Efforts in the Perisna Gulf, Timothy D. Hoyt 90-505 F
* Iraq/Kuwait Crisis: Congressional Action Through January 1991, Clyde R. Mark 91-156 F
* Iraq/Kuwait Crisis: Is Water a Weapon?, Carol Migdalovitz 91-105 F
* Iraq/Kuwait Crisis: Selected Administration Statements, August-December 15, 1990, Theodore J. Craig 91-13 F
* Iraq/Kuwait Crisis: The International Response and Burdensharing Issues; Archived Issue Brief, Gary J. Pagliano IB90131
* Iraq/Kuwait Crisis: U.S. Costs and Allied Financial Contributions, Stephen Daggett, etc. 90-640 F
* Iraq/Kuwait Crisis: U.S. Policy and Options; Archived Issue Brief, Alfred B. Prados, etc. IB90117
* Iraq/Kuwait: The United Nations Response Before the War; Archived Issue Brief, Marjorie Ann Brown IB90147
* Iraq-Kuwait: U.N. Security Council Resolutions: Texts and Votes, Marjorie Ann Browne 91-395 F
* Iraq: U.S. Economic Sanctions; Archived Issue Brief, Clyde R. Mark IB90109
* The Iraqi Crisis: National Public Opinion Polls, Rosita M. Thomas 90-436 GOV
* Iraq's Invasion of Kuwait: A Review of Events, Issue Brief, Renee L Stasio IB90118
* Israel and the Persian Gulf Crisis, Clyde R. Mark 91-458 F
* Japan's Contributions in Support of the U.S.-Led Multinational Forces in the War Against Iraq, Richard P. Cronin 91-293 F
* Japan's Response to the Persian Gulf Crisis: Implications for U.S.-Japan Relations, Larry A. Niksch, etc. 91-444 F
* Kurdish Refugee Relief and Other Humanitarian Aid Issues in Iraq;

Current Events and Homework

Archived Issue Brief, Lois B. McHugh, etc IB91072
* Kurdish Separatism in Iraq: Developments and Implications for the United States, Alfred B. Prados 91-397 F
* Kuwait: Background, Restoration, and Questions for the United States, Theodore Craig 91-288 F
* Kuwaiti Oil Well Fires, Joseph P. Riva 91-313 SPR
* Legal Status of United States Citizens in Iraq and Kuwait, David M. Ackerman 90-406 A
* Legislation Would Be Required to Reinstate the Draft, Robert B. Burdette 91-168 A
* Military and Civilian Satellites in Support of the Persian Gulf War, marcia S. Smith 91-215 SPR
* Naval Restriction of Commerce Against Iraq: Historic Background, Implications and Options, Mark M. Lowenthal 90-388 S
* Oil and Iraq's Invasion of Kuwait: Archived Issue Brief, Carl Behrens, etc. IB90116
* The Patriot Air Defense System and the Search for an Anatactical Ballistic Missile Defense, Steven A. Hildreth, etc. 91-456 F
* Persian Gulf Conflict: Post-War Issues for Congress; Archived Issue Brief, Raymond W. Copson IB90132
* The Persian Gulf War and the Draft, Robert L. Goldich 91-103 F
* Persian Gulf War: Defense-Policy Implications for Congress, Congressional Research Service, Ronald O'Rourke 91-421 F
* Persian Gulf War: Info Pack, Congressional Reference Division IP448P
* Persian Gulf War: International Implications; Archived Issue Brief, Alfred B. Prados, etc. IB91025
* Persian Gulf War: Iraqi Scud Ballistic Missile Systems, Warren W. Lenhart, etc. 91-173 F
* Persian Gulf War Region: Basic Maps, Richard F. Grimmett 91-94 F
* Persian Gulf War: U.S. Costs and Allied Financial Contributions; Issue Brief, Stephen Daggett, etc. IB91019
* Persian Gulf War: U.S. Reserve Callup and Reliance on the Reserves; Issue Brief, Robert L. Goldich IB90144
* Persian Gulf War: Water Resources and the War; Selected References, Sherry B. Shapiro 91-169 L
* Press Restrictions in the Persian Gulf War: First Amendment Implications, Henry Cohen 91-316 A
* Reparations, Raymond J. Celada 91-224 A
* The Strategic Petroleum Reserve and the Drawdown Dilemma, Robert L. Bamberger, etc. 90-492 ENR
* A Summary of the Soldiers' and Sailors' Civil Relief Act, as Amended, Robert B. Burdette 91-342 A
* U.S. and Allied Options Early in the Persian Gulf Crisis, John M. Collins 90-394 S

IRAs

* see Pensions

Ireland

* Northern Ireland and the Republic of Ireland: U.S. Foreign Assistance Facts; Issue Brief, Bert Cooper, Jr. IB87069

Israel

* The Holy See and Recognition of Israel, Charles Whittier 86-833 GOV
* Israel and Nuclear Weapons: Archived Issue Brief, Warren H. Donnelly IB87079
* Israel and the Persian Gulf Crisis, Clyde R. Mark 91-458 F
* Israel: U.S. Foreign Assistance Facts; Issue Brief, Clyde Mark IB85066
* Israeli-American Relations: Issue Brief, Ellen B. Laipson IB82008
* The Israeli Economy and Its External Economic Relations: An Overview, Patricia A. Wertman 91-690 E
* The Israeli Economy: Archived Issue Brief, Clyde Mark IB84138
* Israeli-Palestinian Conflict: Bibliography-in-Brief, 1982-1988, Robert Kirk 88-251 L
* Israeli-Palestinian Conflict: Info Pack, IP397I
* Israeli-United States Relations: Issue Brief IB82008
* Israel's Interest in Nuclear Power: Implications for U.S. Non-Proliferation Policy: Archived Issue Brief, Mark Martel, etc. IB85166
* Israel's Participation in the International Atomic Energy Agency and the 32nd IAEA General Conference: Archived Issue Brief, Warren H. Donnelly IB88072
* Israel's Request for U.S. Loan Guarantees: Issue Brief, Larry Q. Nowels, etc. IB91103
* Palestinian Disturbances in the Gaza Strip and West Bank: Policy Issues and Chronology, Ellen Laipson 88-114 F
* U.S. Free Trade Agreements With Canada and Israel: Comparison of the

Major Provisions, Arlene Wilson 91-243 E
* Voting Rights to U.S. Citizens in Israeli elections for Parliament, Law Library of Congress LL90-58

Italy

* Military Bases in Europe: The Crotone Issue; Issue Brief, Richard F. Grimmett IB90138
* United States Military Installation in Italy, Richard Grimmett 84-12 F

Item Veto

* see Congress-Budget Process, Public Finance-Budget Process

Japan

* see Foreign Relations, Foreign Trade, Investment and Finance
* Capital Gains Taxation of Individuals in Japan, Gregg A. Esenwein 89-581 E
* Comparative Corporate Tax Burdens in the United States and Japan and Implications for Relative Economic Growth, Jane Gravelle 83-177 E
* Comparison of the Achievement of American Elementary and Secondary Pupils With Those Abroad--the Examinations Sponsored by the International Assoc., et, Wayne Riddle 86-683 EPW
* Defense Burdensharing: U.S Relations With NATO Allies and Japan, Stanley Sloan 88-449 F
* Economic Changes in the Asian Pacific Rim: Policy Prospectus, Congressional Research Service 86-923 S
* Emission Standards for Coke Ovens in Japan, Law Library of Congress LL90-16
* Employment and Output Effects of the Extension of Japan's Voluntary Automobile Export Restraints on the U.S. Automobile and Steel Industries, Gwenell Bass 85-710 E
* European Community-Japan Trade Relations: A European Perspective, Dick Nanto 86-166 E
* FSX Fighter Agreement With Japan: Archived Issue Brief, Richard F. Grimmett, etc. IB89060
* FSX Fighter Program: Info Pack, IP420F
* FSX Technology: Its Relative Utility to the United States and Japanese Aerospace Industries, John D. Moteff 89-237 SPR
* Is Faster Growth in Germany and Japan the Key to Faster U.S Growth?, Gail E. Makinen 86-836 E
* Japan Briefing Book, Congressional Research Service 87-323 E
* The Japan Development Bank, Dick Nanto 83-563 E
* Japan: Increasing Investment in the United States, James Jackson 87-747 E
* Japan-South Korea Economic Relations: South Korea's Approach to the "Japan Problem", Dick Nanto 87-953 E
* Japan: Summaries of Selected Products, 1989-1990, Robert S. Kirk 90-400 L
* Japan and U.S. Industrial Associations: Their Role in High-Technology Policymaking: a Japan Task Force Report, Dick K. Nant, etc. 91-477 E
* Japan-United States Economic Relations: Views of Japan's Economic Decisionmakers, Dick Nanto 86-52 E
* Japan-U.S. Economic Relations: Bibliography-in-Brief, 1986-1987, Robert Kirk 87-45 L
* Japan-U.S. Trade: An Overview, William H. Cooper 88-127 E
* Japan-U.S. Trade and Economic Relations: Info Pack, IP201J
* Japan-U.S. Trade Relations: Archived Issue Brief, Raymond Ahearn IB81011
* Japanese Basic Research Policies, Genevieve J. Knezo 90-363 SPR
* Japanese FSX Fighter Controversy, Richard Grimmett 90-309 F
* The Japanese Health Care System, Joan Sokolovsky, etc. 89-572 EPW
* Japanese Management Practices and Their Implications for U.S. Policy, Dick Nanto 82-114 E
* Japanese Prison Education System, Law Library of Congress LL90-50
* Japanese Science and Technology: Some Recent Efforts to Improve U.S. Monitoring, Nancy Miller 86-195 SPR
* Japanese Technical Information: Opportunities to Improve U.S. Access, Christopher Hill 87-818 S
* Japan's Automobile Industry and Barriers to Purchases of U.S. Cars, Dick Nanto, etc. 87-793 E
* Japan's Financial Liberalization: Effects on the United States, James Jackson 89-102 E
* Japan's Military Buildup: Goals and Accomplishments, Gary Reynolds 89-68 F
* Japan's Prime Minister: Selection Process, 1991 Candidates and Implications for the United States, Jeffrey D. Young 91-695 F
* Japan's Science and Technology Strategies and Policies; Issue Brief, Glenn McLoughlin IB90053
* Japan's World War II Reparations: A Fact Sheet, Larry A. Niksch 91-216 F

* JETRO: The Japan External Trade Organization, R. Kevin Flaherty 85-1112 E
* Market Access in Japan: The U.S. Experience, Raymond Ahearn 85-37 E
* The MOSS Talks: Success or Failure?, Patricia Wertman 85-1129 E
* The NATO Allies, Japan, and the Persian Gulf, Paul Gallis 84-184 F
* Plutonium Economics and Japan's Nuclear Fuel Cycle Policies, Robert Civiak 88-235 SPR
* Sino-Japanese Economic Relations in the Post Mao Decade., Dick Nanto, etc. 86-170 E
* Space Commercialization in China and Japan, Marcia S. Smith, etc. 89-367 SPR
* The Stock Market in Japan: An Overview and Analysis, Arturo Wiener, etc. 89-306 E
* United States Merchandise Trade and Trade Balances With Japan, 1960-1987, Dario Scuka 88-81 E
* U.S. Agricultural Trade Opportunities With Pacific Rim Nations, Robert Goldstein 88-755 ENR
* U.S. Civilian and Defense Research and Development Funding: Some Trends and Comparisons With Selected Industrialized Nations, William Boesman, etc. 84-195 SPR
* U.S. Japanese Agricultural Trade Relations: Selected Information, Donna Vogt 88-159 ENR

Japan -- Foreign Relations

* Defense Burdensharing: U.S. Relations with NATO Allies and Japan, Stanley R. Sloan 88-449 F
* Japan-U.S. GLobal Partnership: Implications of the Postponement of the President's November 1991 Trip to Japan, Richard P. Cronin 91-796 F
* Japan-U.S. Relations: A Briefing Book, Congressional Research Service 91-401 F
* Japan-U.S. Relations in the 1990s, Larry Niksch 89-264 F
* Japan-U.S. Relations: Archived Issue Brief, Robert Sutter IB81026
* Japan-U.S. Relations: Issues for Congress; Issue Brief, Robert G. Sutter IB89133
* Japan-U.S. Relations: Selected References, 1986-1991, Robert S. Kirk 91-162 L
* Japanese Government Cooperation With the United States--U.S. Officials' Perspectives, Robert G. Sutter 90-435 F
* Japan's Contributions in Support of the U.S.-Led Multinational Forces in the War Against Iraq, Richard P. Cronin 91-293 F
* Japan's Expanding Role and Influence in the Asia-Pacific Region: Implications for U.S. Interests and Policy, Richard P. Cronin 90-432 F
* Japan's Response to the Persian Gulf Crisis: Implications for U.S.-Japan Relations, Larry A. Niksch, etc. 91-444 F
* Lobbying by Foreign Interests, Richard C. Sachs 91-318 GOV

Japan -- Foreign Trade

* Commercial Relations With the Soviet Union: Prospects for a Common United States-Japanese Policy, John P. Hardt 91-196 RCO
* Japan and an East Asian Trading Bloc, Dick K. Nanto 91-840 E
* Japan: Prospects for Greater Market Openness, Raymond J. Ahearn 89-390 F
* Japan: Resale Price Maintenance, Dick K. Nanto 91-289 E
* Japan: Summaries of Selected Products, 1989-1990, Robert S. Kirk 90-400 L
* Japan-U.S. Economic Issues: Investment, Saving, Technology and Attitudes, Dick K. Nanto 90-78 E
* Japan-U.S. Economic Relations: Selected References, 1989-1991, Robert Howe 91-213 L
* Japan-U.S. Trade: A Chronology of Major Events, 1980-1990, Wayne M. Morrison, etc. 91-494 E
* Japan-U.S. Trade and Economic Relations: Bibliography-in-Brief, 1990-1991, Robert Howe 91-655 L
* Japan-U.S. Trade and Economic Relations: Info Pack IP201J
* Japan-U.S. Trade: The Structural Impediments Initiative, William H. Cooper 90-276 E
* Japanese Companies and Technology: Lessons to Learn?, Wendy H. Schacht 91-375 SPR
* Japanese-U.S. Trade: The Construction Issue, William H. Cooper 91-303 E
* Japan's Protected Market: Significance, Extent, Outlook, and Challenges for U.S. Policy, Raymond Ahearn 90-326 F
* Super 301 Action Against Japan, Brazil, and India: Rationale, Reaction, and Future Implications, Raymond J. Ahearn, etc. 90-25 F
* U.S.-Japan Trade: The Structural Impediments Initiative, Audio Brief, William Cooper AB50207
* U.S.-Japanese Agricultural Trade Relations: Selected Information, Donna U. Vogt 89-655 ENR

Japan -- Investment and Finance

* Banking Systems in the United States, Japan, and the European Community: Comparative Studies, F. Jean Wells 90-357 E
* Japan: Regulatory Structure and Delivery of Financial Services, Walter W. Eubanks 90-351 E
* Japanese Acquisitions of U.S. Companies, James K. Jackson 90-4 E
* Japanese Investment in the United States, James K. Jackson 90-13 E
* Japan's Foreign Investment Laws and the T. Boone Pickens Case, Law Library of Congress LL90-36
* Securities Registration and Disclosure Laws in Canada, Germany, Japan, the United Kingdom, and the United States, Stephen F. Clarke, etc. 91-613 A
* The Stock Market in Japan: An Overview and Analysis, Arturo Wiener, etc. 89-306 E

Japanese Reparations

* see Civil Liberties and Rights--Discrimination and Integration, Japan

Job Retraining

* see Occupational Training--Job Training

Job Training Partnership Act

* Job Training: FY 88 Budget and Legislative Issues: Archived Issue Brief, Karen Spar IB87039
* Job Training Partnership Act: Pending Legislation and Budget Issues; Archived Issue Brief, Karen Spar IB89117
* Jobs: Job Training and the Labor Market; Info Pack IP246J
* Training for Dislocated Workers under the Job Training Partnership Act, Karen Spar 89-44 EPW

Joint Ventures

* see Foreign Investments

Jordan

* Jordan: Persian Gulf Crisis and U.S. Aid, Alfred B. Prados 91-247 F
* Jordan: Recent Developments and Implications for U.S. Interests, Ellen Laipson, etc. 90-354 F
* Jordan: U.S. Foreign Assistance Facts: Archived Issue Brief, Richard Preece IB85120

Judiciary

* see also Supreme Court
* An Analysis of S.J. Res. 113, a Proposed Constitutional Amendment Relating to the Removal of Federal Judges, Elizabeth Bazan 87-764 A
* Commission on Executive, Legislative, and Judicial Salaries: An Historical Overview, Sharon Gressle 89-38 GOV
* Comparison of President Bush's Honoraria Reform Act of 1989 With Existing Laws, Orders and Regulations, Mildred L. Amer 89-481 GOV
* Confidentiality and Secrecy Orders in Civil Cases, Kenneth Thompson 89-225 A
* Election of Federal Judges, Paul Morgan 88-179 A
* Establishing Federal Judicial Districts, Paul Morgan 88-344 A
* Ethics in Government: Reform of Laws and Regulations; Issue Brief, Mildred L. Amer IB89134
* Federal, Executive, Legislative and Judicial Compensation: The Situation and Choices for the 101st Congress James McGrath 89-70 GOV
* The Federal Grand Jury, Charles Doyle 91-512 A
* Impeachment of Federal or National Judges, Law Library of congress LL89-71
* Law, Lawyers, and the Judiciary: An Alphabetical Microthesaurus of Terms Selected from the Legislative Indexing Vocabulary, Shirley Loo 90-584 L
* Pay Raise Proposals for Members of Congress, Top Officials and Federal Judges: Issues and Outlook, James P. McGrath 89-621 GOV
* Pay Raises and Honoraria Reform for Members of Congress, Top Officials, Federal Judges: Issues and Outlook, James P. McGrath 90-422 GOV
* President Reagan's Judicial Nominations During the 100th Congress: A Statistical Overview and Listing of Nominees and Dates of Confirmation or other, Denis Stevens Rutkus 89-50 GOV
* Salaries and Allowances: The Judiciary: Issue Brief, Sharon Gressle IB81264
* Separate but Equal: Two Hundred Years of Legislative-Executive-Judicial Relations; Videoprogram, Louis Fisher, etc. LTR91-955
* Sources of Legislative History as Aids to Statutory Construction, George A. Costello 89-86 A
* Sources of State Juror Lists, Paul Morgan 89-337 A
* United States Court System: Finding Federal Case Material, Elizabeth B. Bazan, etc. 90-221 A

Current Events and Homework

* United States Sentencing Commission: Preliminary Analysis, Charles Doyle 89-308 A
* U.S. Government: Info Pack, IP162U

Judiciary -- Supreme Court

* Clarence Thomas: Bibliography-in-Brief, 1981-1991, George Walser 91-692 L
* Forum: Supreme Court Review: 1989-90 Term, Congressional Research Service REV 9-90
* The Judicial Opinions of Supreme Court Nominee Judge Clarence Thomas, Kenneth R. Thomas 91-562 A
* The Next Supreme Court: Return to the Future; Videoprogram, Johnny H. Killian LTR91-1493
* Questioning Supreme Court Nominees--A Recurring Issue, Denis Steven Rutkus 90-429 GOV
* Senate Confirmation of Supreme Court Nominees: Selected References, George Walser 91-547 L
* The Speed With Which Action Has Been Taken on Supreme Court Nominations in the Last 25 Years, Denis Steven Rutkus 87-576 A
* Supreme Court: Bibliography-in-Brief, 1970-1988, Charles P. Dove 88-192 L
* Supreme Court: Church-State Cases, October 1984 Term; Archived Issue Brief, David Ackerman IB84229
* Supreme Court: Church-State Cases, October 1984 Term; Archived Issue Brief, David Ackerman IB85207
* Supreme Court: Church-State Cases, October 1986 Term; Archived Issue Brief, David Ackerman IB86129
* Supreme Court Church-State Cases, October 1987 Term; Archived Brief, David Ackerman IB87217
* Supreme Court: Church-State Cases, October 1988 Term; Issue Brief, David Ackerman IB88105
* Supreme Court: Church-State Cases, 1989-90 Term; Archived Issue Brief, David M. Ackerman IB90040
* Supreme Court: Church-State Cases, 1990-91 Term; Archived Issue Brief, David M. Ackerman IB91056
* Supreme Court: Church-State Cases, 1991-92 Term; Issue Brief, David M. Ackerman IB91136
* Supreme Court Opinions October 1990 Term, George A. Costello 91-551 A

Junk Bonds

* see Corporations-Securities Industry

Juvenile Delinquency

* see Crimes and Offenses

Kashmir

* Kashmir: Conflict and Crisis; Archived Issue Brief, David E. Lockwood, etc. IB90087
* The Kashmir Dispute: Historical Background to the Current Struggle, Richard P. Cronin, etc. 91-563 F

Kazakhstan

* see also U.S.S.R.
* Kazakh Republic: Basic Facts, Jim Nichol 91-743 F

King, Martin Luther

* Martin Luther King, Jr.: Selected References, Jean Bowers 90-586 L
* Speech Material: Martin Luther King's Birthday; Info Pack, IP372M

Kirghizia

* see also U.S.S.R.
* Kirghiz Republic: Basic Facts, Jim Nichol 91-760 F

Kissinger Commission

* Kissinger Commission Implementation: Action by the Congress Through 1986 on the Recommendations of the National Bipartisan Commission on Central America, K. Larry Storrs 87-291 F
* A Summary and Analysis of the Report of the National Bipartisan "Kissinger" Commission on Central America, January 1984, Richard Cronin, etc. 84-39 F

Korea

* see also South Korea
* U.S. Agricultural Trade Opportunities With Pacific Rim Nations, Robert M. Goldstein 88-755 ENR

Kuwait

* see also Iraq-Kuwait Crisis, Middle East--U.S. Concerns
* Iraq and Kuwait: Economic Profiles, Dario Scuka 90-399 E
* Iraq, Kuwait, and IEEPA, Raymond J. Celada 90-373 A
* Iraq/Kuwait Crisis: A Summary of Foreign Support for Multinational Efforts in the Persian Gulf, Timothy D. Hoyt 90-505 F
* Iraq-Kuwait Crisis: U.S. Policy and Options, Archived Issue Brief, Alfred B. Prados, etc. IB90117
* Iraq-Kuwait: The United Nations Response Before the War; Archived Issue Brief, Marjorie Ann Brown IB90147
* The Iraqi Crisis: National Public Opinion Polls, Rosita M. Thomas 90-436 GOV
* Iraq's Invasion of Kuwait: A Review of Events; Issue Brief, Renee L. Stasio IB90118
* Kuwait: Background, Restoration, and Questions for the United States, Theodore Craig 91-288 F
* Kuwaiti Oil Well Fires, Joseph P. Riva 91-313 SPR
* Oil and Iraq's Invasion of Kuwait: Archived Issue Brief, Carl Behrens, etc. IB90116
* Persian Gulf Conflict: Post-War Issues for Congress; Archived Issue Brief, Raymond W. Copson IB(0132
* Persian Gulf War: Key U.S. Military Personnel and Compensation Questions; Archived Issue Brief, Robert L. Goldich IB90124
* Persian Gulf War: U.S. Reserve Callup and Reliance on the Reserves; Issue Brief, Robert L. Goldich IB90144
* The Strategic Petroleum Reserve and the Drawdown Dilemma, Robert L. Bamberger, etc. 90-492 ENR

Labor

* see Earnings and Benefits, Minimum Wages, Policies and Legislation, Productivity, Employment and Unemployment, Unions
* Career Guidance and Federal Job Information: Info Pack, IP016C
* Civilian and Military Pilots: The Labor Market Relationship, John W. Fischer, etc. 86-28 E
* Counting Migrant and Seasonal Farmworkers: A Persistent Data Void, Dennis M. Roth 85-797 E
* A Demographic Portrait of Older Workers, Gail McCallion 88-636 E
* Early Retirement Incentive Plans under the Age Discrimination in Employment Act of 1967, as Amended., Kathleen S. Swendiman 88-608 A
* Economic Conditions: Archived Issue Brief, Gail Makinen IB87004
* Economic Policy: Selected Issues of Interest to the 101st Congress, Edward Knight 89-209 E
* Education and Job Growth, Linda LeGrande 88-476 E
* Employment Abroad: Info Pack, IP065E
* Employment and Labor: An Alphabetical Microthesaurus of Terms Selected from the Legislative Indexing Vocabulary, Shirley Loo 88-748 L
* Employment and Unemployment: Some International Comparisons, Gail McCallion 88-673 E
* Employment Status of the States: Data and Trends: Archived Issue Brief, Linda LeGrande IB82098
* Employment Trends in the 1980s from a National Industrial and Geographic Perspective, Linda LeGrande, etc. 86-130 E
* Employment Trends Through the 1990s: Selected References, 1986-1989, Robert Howe 89-203 L
* Farmer Transition Programs, Rebecca Mazur 88-364 L
* Hours of Work: Historical Trends and Recent Policy Initiative, William G. Whittaker 86-61 E
* The Impact of Defense Spending on Employment, Carolyn Brancato, etc. 82-182 E
* The Influence of Labor Costs on the Total Cost of Steel Production in Integrated Steel Mills: Effects of Hypothetical Labor Cost Reductions, David J. Cantor 85-912 E
* Internships and Fellowships: Info Pack, IP063I
* Older Workers: the Transition to Retirement, Gail McCallion 89-286 E
* Polygraph Testing of Employees in Private Industry, Britt Liddicoat 85-929 A
* Productivity and U.S. Living Standards; Issue Brief, William A. Cox IB88107
* Service Sector Productivity in the United States: A Survey, Julius W. Allen 88-717 E
* Airline Mergers and Labor Protective Provisions, IB87179
* Comparable Worth/Pay Equity in the Federal Government, IB85116
* Construction Industry Collective Bargaining: Prehire Agreement and Double Breasting, IB85177
* The Davis-Bacon Act: Consideration in the 101st Congress, IB89037
* Displaced Homemakers, IB84132

Judiciary / Labor

* Drug Testing in the Workplace: An Overview of Employee and Employer Interests, IB87139
* Drug Testing in the Workplace: Federal Programs, IB87174
* The Federal Minimum Wage: Consideration in the 101st Congress, IB89061
* Labor Problems At Eastern Air Lines, IB88052
* Labor Protection in the Railroad Industry, IB87204
* Occupational Disease Notification Proposals: Is Legislation Necessary, IB86150
* Parental Leave: Legislation in the 101st Congress, IB86132
* Plant Closing Legislation: Worker Adjustment and Retraining Notification Act (WARN), IB87160
* Polygraph Testing: Employee and Employer Rights, IB87126
* Targeted Jobs Tax Credit, IB87142

Labor -- Earnings and Benefits

* see Labor -- Policies and Legislation, for Family Leave, see Families
* Cafeteria Plans for Employee Benefits and the Proposed Dollar Limitation, James R. Storey 87-941 EPW
* Compensation in the Textile and Apparel Industries: International and Domestic Comparisons, Dennis M. Roth, etc. 85-671 E
* Compensation in U.S. and Foreign Steel Industries, Linda LeGrande 88-314 E
* Computer Service Personnel: Overtime Pay under Section 13 (A) (1) of the Fair Labor Standards Act, William G. Whittaker 91-759 E
* Congressional Pay, Selected Wages and Pensions, and Social Security: compared to CPI, 1969-1989, Frederick H. Pauls, etc. 89-63 GOV
* Earnings as a Measure of Regional Economic Performance, Linda LeGrande, etc. 87-377 E
* Economic Benefits of Education, Linda LeGrande 88-753 E
* Employee Stock Ownership Plans: An Overview, Gerald Mayer 89-80 E
* Employee Stock Ownership Plans: Minimum Requirements to Qualify for Tax Advantages, Gerald Mayer 89-36 E
* ESOPs and Corporate Productivity, Gary W. Shorter 91-557 E
* Flexible Benefit Plans: Policies and Issues, James R. Storey 90-54 EPW
* Legal Analysis of LTV Corporation's Unilateral Termination of Retirees' Health and Life Insurance Benefits on the Date of Filing in Bankruptcy, Vincent E. Treacy 86-845 A
* Legal Authority of Bankrupt Employer Unilaterally to Terminate Retirees' Benefits under a Collective Bargaining Agreement, Vincent E. Treacy 86-826 A
* Mandated Employer-Provided Benefits: the Likely Employment Consequences, Linda LeGrande 88-209 E
* Measures of Real Earnings Since 1970, William A. Cox 88-692 S
* Middle Class Decline?, Income Distribution Trends: Bibliography-in-Brief, 1983-1987, Robert S. Kirk 87-460 L
* Middle-Class Decline? Income Distribution Trends: Selected References, 1987-1991, Robert Howe 91-609 L
* Middle Class Erosion and Growing Income Inequality : Fact or Fiction?, Richard S. Belous, etc. 85-203 E
* Pension Portability: What Does It Mean?, How Does it Work?, What Does it Accomplish?, Ray Schmitt 88-498 EPW
* Real Earnings in America: 1947-1985, Richard S. Belous 86-615 E
* Retiree Benefits in the Eastern Air Lines Bankruptcy, Robin Jeweler 91-462 A
* Section 89 Nondiscrimination Rules for Employee Benefits, Ray Schmitt, etc. 88-470 EPW
* The Service Sector: Employment and Earnings in the 1980s, Linda LeGrande 85-167 E
* Tax Status of Group Legal Services Plans, Louis Alan Talley 90-418 E
* Two-Tier Wage Systems in the U.S. Economy, Richard S. Belous 85-165 E
* U.S. Economic Policy in an International Context: U.S. Wages and Unit Labor Costs in a World Economy, Richard S. Belous 84-172 E
* Wage Rates and Exchange Rates, Linda LeGrande 88-252 E
* Who's Keeping Up in the 1980's Compensation as an Indicator, Linda LeGrande 87-883 E

Labor -- Employment and Unemployment

* Adjustment Assistance: Should Congress Create New Programs for Dislocated Workers? Issue Brief, James R. Storey IB91143
* Blacks' Labor Market Experiences in the 1980s and 1990s, Linda Levine 90-307 E
* Career Guidance and Federal Job Information: Info Pack IP016C
* Defense Spending Cuts and Employment Adjustments, Linda Levine 90-55 E
* Economic Adjustment Assistance to Communities and Workers Affected by Defense Cutbacks, Congressional Research Service 90-126 CRS
* Education and Job Growth, Linda LeGrande 88-476 E
* Employer Responses to Workforce Diversity, Linda Levine 91-226 E
* Employment Abroad; Info Pack IP065E
* Employment in the United States: Potential Effects of Changing Foreign Economies; Archived Issue Brief, Charles V. Ciccone IB89129
* Employment Trends Through the 1990s: Selected References, 1987-1990, Robert Howe 90-208 L
* Internships and Fellowships; Info Pack IP063I
* Is the Service Sector Recession-Proof?, Linda LeGrande 88-132 E
* Jobs: Job Training and the Labor Market, Info Pack IP246J
* Labor Shortages: Reality or Myth? Linda LeGrande 89-487E
* A Lagging Unemployment Rate and an Improving Economy, Linda Levine 91-543E
* Manufacturing Employment by State as a "Recession Vulnerability Indicator", Linda Levine 91-35 E
* Plant Closing Legislation: Worker Adjustment and Retirement Notification Act (WARN); Archived Issue Brief, Mary Jane Bolle IB87160
* Targeted Jobs Tax Credit; Archived Issue Brief, Linda Levine IB87142
* The Targeted Jobs Tax Credit, 1978-1987, Linda LeGrande 87-616 E
* Unemployment, Dislocated Workers, and Job Creation; Issue Brief, Linda Levine, IB90154
* Unemployment in the 1980s and the Outlook for the 1990s, Linda Levine 90-501 E
* Workforce Diversity in the 1990s: Bibliography-in-Brief, 1988-1991, Robert Howe 91-387 L

Labor -- Minimum Wages

* The Fair Labor Standards Act: Analysis of Economic Issues in the Debates of 1937-1938, William G. Whittaker 89-568 E
* The Federal Minimum Wage: Changes Made by 101st Congress and Their Implications; Archived Issue Brief, William G. Whittaker IB90082
* The Federal Minimum Wage: Consideration in the 100th Congress; Archived Issue Brief, William G. Whittaker IB87063
* The Federal Minimum Wage: Consideration in the 101st Congress; Issue Brief, William G. Whittaker IB89061
* Minimum Wage: Bibliography-in-Brief, 1985-1990, Felix Chin 90-226 L
* Minimum Wage Earnings and the EITC: Making the Connection, Charles V. Ciccone 88-736 E
* Minimum Wage Issues: Info Pack, IP249M
* Minimum Wage Laws in Selected Countries, Law Library of Congress LL90-234
* Minimum Wage: Selected Reference, 1978-1987, Felix Chin 87-162 L
* Minimum Wage Standards under the Fair Labor Standards Act: Background Analysis and Recent Legislative Interests, William G. Whittaker 87-111 E
* The Small Business Exemption in the Fair Labor Standards Act: Number of Employees Subject to the 1989 Amendments, Charles V. Ciccone 91-307 E
* The Youth Sub-Minimum Wage: Proposals of the 98th Congress, William Whittaker 84-185 E

Labor -- Policies and Legislation

* Administrative Discretion to Set Aside the Eight-Hour Provisions of the Walsh-Healey Public Contracts Act (1936) and the Contract Work Hours Standards, William G. Whittaker 83-500 E
* Avoiding Urban/Rural Wage Inequities in Determination of Prevailing Wage Rates under the Davis-Bacon Act, William G. Whittaker 85-631 E
* Building and Construction Industry Labor Law Amendments of 1987: Comparison of Original and Amended Versions of H.R. 281, Gail McCallion 88-270 E
* Child Labor: Issues for the 102nd Congress; Issue Brief, William G. Whittaker IB91004
* The College Assistance Migrant Program and the Migrant High School Equivalency Program, Robert Lyke 86-749 EPW
* Comparison of State Plant Closing Laws, Mary Jane Bolle, etc. 84-556 E
* Constitutional Questions Concerning Proposed Family Leave Legislation in 99th Congress, Vincent E. Treacy 86-812 A
* The Davis-Bacon Act: A Comparison of Selected Provisions of Bills Introduced in the 100th Congress, William G. Whittaker 87-527 E
* The Davis-Bacon Act: Consideration in the 102nd Congress; Issue Brief, William G. Whittaker IB91012
* The Davis Bacon Act: A Review of the Literature, William G. Whittaker 84-137 E
* The Davis-Bacon Act and Federal Contract Construction Wage Policy: Background Analysis and Recent Legislative Interest, William G. Whittaker 87-563 E
* Davis-Bacon Act: Consideration in the 100th Congress; Archived Issue

Current Events and Homework

Brief, William G. Whittaker IB87149
* The Davis-Bacon Act: Consideration in the 101st Congress; Issue Brief, William G. Whittaker IB89037
* The Davis-Bacon Act Suspension of 1971: The Nixon Administration, Organized Labor and the Prevailing, Wage Statute in Federal and Federally Assisted Co., William Whittaker 79-249 E
* Employee Access to Personnel Records and Information: Rights under Federal and State Law, Kirk D. Nemer 89-335 A
* Employee Participation in National Mediation Board, Determination of Single Carrier Status, Vincent E. Treacy 88-433 A
* Employee Protection Legislation: A Comparison of H.R. 1101, H.R. 2828 and H.R. 3332, Mark Jickling 88-426 E
* Employment and Training Programs and Policies for Older Workers: An International Overview, Dennis M. Roth, etc. 86-639 E
* Employment of Persons With Handicaps under the Javits-Wagner-O'Day Act: Summary of the Special Procurement Program and Current Issues, Mary F. Smith 88-610 EPW
* The Fair Labor Standards Act Amendments of 1977 (P.L. 95-151): Discussion With Historical Background, William Whittaker, etc. 78-171 E
* The Fair Labor Standards Act: Consideration During the 102nd Congress; Issue Brief, William G. Whittaker IB91020
* Fair Labor Standards Act: Treatment of State and Local Government; Archived Issue Brief, Dennis M. Roth, etc. IB85195
* International Labor Organization: Issues of U.S. Membership: Archived Issue Brief, Lois McHugh, IB77073
* Jobs: The Employment Situation and Job Training Programs; Info Pack, IP246J
* Labor Issues in the 100th Congress: The Second Session, by Economics Division, 88-113 E
* Labor Issues in the 102nd Congress: The First Session, Economics Division 91-228 E
* Labor Laws: Exemption or Exclusion of the White House, Supreme Court, and Congress, Economics Division 91-799 E
* Labor Laws in Selected Foreign Countries, Law Library of Congress LL91-3
* Labor Protection in Railroad Industry: Issue Brief, Linda LeGrande IB87204
* Legal Analysis of Recent Appropriation Riders to Insure a "Drug-Free Workplace", Charles V. Dale 88-450 A
* Major Repairs or Non-Routine Maintenance: Defining Davis-Bacon Coverage under the Comprehensive Improvement Assistance Program, William G. Whittaker 85-887 E
* The McNamara-O'Hara Service Contract Act: Discretionary Authority of the Secretary of Labor under Section 4 (B) and the Mandatory Wage Rate Determination, William G. Whittaker 86-533 E
* The McNamara-O'Hara Service Contract Act: Origins and Evolution, 1965-1987, William G. Whittaker 87-42 E
* Migrant and Seasonal Farmworkers: Characteristics and Related Federal Laws, Sharon House 83-174 EPW
* Polygraph Testing: Employee and Employer Rights: Issue Brief, Gail McCallion IB87126
* Sheltered Workshops for Persons With Handicaps: Background Information and Recent Legislative Changes, Mary F. Smith 87-362 EPW
* Survey on Applicability of National Labor Laws to Vessels of Foreign Registry, Law Library of Congress LL90-7
* U.S. Withdrawal from the International Labor Organization: Successful Precedent for UNESCO?, Lois McHugh 84-202 F
* The Walsh-Healey Public Contracts Act of 1936 and the Issue of Overtime Pay: Proposals of the 99th Congress With Background Perspectives, William G. Whittaker 86-33 E
* The Youth Sub-Minimum Wage: Proposals of the 98th Congress, William Whittaker 84-185 E

Labor -- Productivity

* Impact of the Business Cycle on Productivity Growth in the U.S. Economy, Mary Jane Bolle 82-172 E
* Increasing Productivity in the United States: Ways in Which the Private and Public Sectors Can Contribute to Productivity Improvement, Julius Allen 80-44 E
* President Reagan's Productivity Improvement Program: Deja Vu, Fresh Start to an Old Story, or Lasting Reform? Perter Benda, etc. 86-89 S
* Productivity and U.S. Living Standards: Issue Brief, William A. Cox IB88107
* Social Science Approaches to Innovation and Productivity, Christine Matthews 86-710 SPR
* The U.S. Steel Industry: Factors Influencing Gains in Industry Productivity, David J. Cantor 87-498 E

Labor -- Unemployment

* American Direct Investment Abroad: Effects on Trade, Jobs, and the Balance of Payments, James K. Jackson 88-546 E
* Declining Unemployment: Some Observations, Dennis M. Roth 87-679 E
* Economic Growth and Changing Labor Markets: Those Left Behind; Adult Black Workers: the Progress of Some, Linda LeGrande 84-228 E
* Economic Growth and Changing Labor Markets: Those Left Behind; Women Workers (Un)changed Position, Linda LeGrande 84-112 E
* Foreign Trade and U.S. Employment: Bibliography-in-Brief, 1983-1987, Robert S. Kirk 87-344 L
* Is the Service Sector Recession-Proof?, Linda LeGrande 88-132 E
* The Labor Market of the 1980s: Unemployment Omens in a Growing Economy; Archived Issue Brief, Dennis M. Roth IB87110
* Manufacturing Job Trends by Geographic Area, Linda LeGrande 88-55 E
* Mergers and Acquisitions: The Impact on Labor, Gail McCallion 87-705 E
* The Phillips Curve vs. the Natural Rate of Unemployment: Their Potential as Policymaking Guides in Our Modern Economy, Charles V. Ciccone 86-896 E
* Plant Closing Legislation: Economic Dislocation and Worker Adjustment Assistance Act; Issue Brief, Mary Jane Bolle IB87160
* Plant Closings: Selected References, 1984-1988, Felix Chin 88-615 L
* The Relationship Between "Right-to-Work" Laws and Unemployment, Richard S. Belous 84-632 E
* States/Counties of the Lower Mississippi River Valley: Statistics on Per Capita Personal Income and Unemployment Rates, Jan E. Christopher 88-254 E
* Targeted Jobs Tax Credit: Action in the 100th Congress; Issue Brief, Linda LeGrande IB87142
* The Targeted Jobs Tax Credit, 1978-1987, Linda LeGrande 87-616 E
* Unemployment: Why and How It Is Falling, Linda LeGrande 89-78 E

Labor -- Unions

* Air Traffic Controllers: Labor Relation Since the Demise of PATCO, Gail McCallion 87-786 E
* Airline Mergers and Labor Protective Provisions: Issue Brief, Linda LeGrande IB87179
* The Auto Industry's 1990 Round of Collective Bargaining, Gail McCallion 90-500 E
* The Changing Role of Strike Activity in Labor Management Disputes, Gail McCallion 90-281 E
* Collective-Bargaining Trends: the 1980s and Beyond, Gail McCallion 88-208 E
* Construction Industry Collective Bargaining: Prehire Agreements and Double Breasting; Issue Brief, Gail McCallion IB85177
* The International Brotherhood of Teamsters; an Historical and Bibliographical Review, William Whittaker 77-71 E
* Labor Problems at Eastern Air Lines: Archived Issue Brief, Linda LeGrande IB88052
* The New York Daily News Strike, Gail McCallion 91-149 E
* Rail Labor Disputes: Presidential and Congressional Intervention, 1980-1991, Linda Levine 91-100 E
* Strike Activity: Recent Trends, Gail McCallion 88-446 E
* Strike Regulations in Various Countries, Law Library of Congress LL91-4
* Strike Replacements: Archived Issue Brief, Gail McCallion IB90104
* Use of Compulsory Union Dues for Political and Ideological Purposes: An Analysis of Supreme Court Decisions and Federal Legislation Re Such Use, Thomas M. Durbin 86-1056 A
* Use of Compulsory Union Dues for Political and Other Ideological Purposes, Thomas M. Durbin 88-737 A

Labor Shortages

* see Labor

Land Use

* Appeals of Federal Land Management Plans and Activities: A Report on a CRS Research Workshop, Pamela Baldwin 90-104 A
* Compensation for Regulatory "Takings": First English Evangelical Lutheran Church of Glendale v. County of Los Angeles, Joseph Maheady 87-623 A
* Compliance Provisions for Resource Conservation: A Status Report, Jeffrey Zinn 88-662 ENR
* Consideration of Economic Factors under the Endangered Species Act, Pamela Baldwin 89-274 A
* Court Rulings During 1990 on Constitutional Taking Claims Against the United States, Robert Meltz 91-171 A
* The Federal Power of Eminent Domain: A Summary of Principles, Robert Meltz 85-206 A

Labor / Latin America

* Haying and Grazing on Set-Aside Crop Acreage, Carl W. Ek 89-9 ENR
* Indian Tribal Government Zoning Authority, M. Maureen Murphy 88-744 A
* Land and Water Conservation Fund: Information and Status, George H. Siehl 89-159 ENR
* Manassas National Battlefield Park: The Battle Continues, John O. Spengler, etc. 88-514 ENR
* Military and Recreation Interests in American Lands: Selected References, Lisa B. Dove 90-426 L
* Private Property Protection Legislation in the 102nd Congress; Issue Brief, Robert Meltz IB91076
* Revisiting the Law of Regulatory Takings: the Supreme Court's Decisions in Keystone, Nollan, and First English Robert Meltz 87-959 A
* Scenic Landscape Protection, George H. Siehl 90-525 ENR
* Taking Decisions of the Supreme Court: A Chronology, Robert Meltz 90-102 A
* Taking Decisions of the Supreme Court: A Compilation of Holding on Selected Issues, Robert Meltz 87-737 A
* Wetlands Protection: Issue in the 101st Congress; Issue Brief, Jeffrey A. Zinn, etc. IB89076
* When the United States Takes Property: Legal Principles, Robert Meltz 91-339 A
* Wilderness Issues in the 102nd Congress; Issue Brief, Betsy A. Cody IB91029

Laser Interferometer Gravitational Observatory

* The LIGO (Laser Interferometer Gravitational Observatory) Proposal, Daniel Morgan, etc. 91-661 SPR

Latin America

* See Economic Conditions, Foreign Aid, Foreign Relations, Foreign Trade, National Defense, Politics and Government, Central America
* Caribbean Area: Bibliography-in-Brief, 1980-1988, Robert S. Kirk 88-152 L
* The Caribbean: A Primer on the Region's Independent Nations, Foreign Affairs and National Defense Division 90-445 F
* International Commission on Central America: Initial Views; Audio Brief, Larry Storrs AB50176
* Latin American Indigenous Peoples and Considerations for U.S. Assistance, Congressional Research Service, Nina M. Serafino 91-663 F
* Natural Resources Conservation and Development in Brazil: An Overview and Related Issue, Russell Hawkins 84-802 ENR

Latin America -- Economic Conditions

* Beyond the Brady Plan: Toward a Differentiated Debt Strategy? a CRS Trade Team Product, Patricia A. Wertman 90-181 E
* Brazilian Petroleum Status, Joseph P. Riva, Jr. 89-328 SPR
* Colombian Petroleum Status, Joseph P. Riva 89-437 SPR
* Debt Rescheduling Agreements in Latin America, 1980-86, Glennon J. Harrison 87-360 E
* Debt Rescheduling: the Argentine Case, 1982-1988, Glennon J. Harrison 88-505 E
* Debt Service Indicators of the Seventeen Most Highly Indebted Developing Countries, 1978-1986, Patricia A. Wertman, etc. 88-452 E
* The Enterprise for the Americas Initiative: Issues for Congress; Issue Brief, Nina M. Serafino IB90130
* Latin American Debt and U.S. Agricultural Exports: Assessment of a Proposed Approach, Charles E. Hanrahan 87-402 ENR
* Latin American Debt: Characteristics, Trends, and U.S. Policy, Mark P. Sullivan 91-343 F
* Latin American Debt Crisis: Selected References, 1987-1990, Robert Howe 90-251L
* The Mexican Debt Accords and Their Financial Implications: An Overview, Patricia A. Wertman 86-179 E
* The Mexican Debt Swap: The Advent of Debt Relief?, Patricia A. Wertman 88-145 E
* Mexican Oil: Less Than Meets The Eye, Joseph P. Riva 91-535 SPR
* Mexican Petroleum, Joseph Riva 83-178 SPR
* The Petroleum Production Potential of South America, Joseph P. Riva 90-270 SPR
* The Petroleum Status of Ecuador, Joseph P. Riva 90-211 SPR
* Trade of the Seventeen Highly Indebted Countries: A Brief Overview, Patricia A. Wertman, etc. 88-521 E
* U.S. Bank Exposure in the Seventeen Highly Indebted Countries: 1982-1987, Patricia A. Wertman, etc. 88-522 E
* U.S.-Mexico Economic Relations: An Overview, Lenore Sek 87-485 E
* Worldwide Bank Exposure in the Seventeen Highly Indebted Countries, 1982-1987, Patricia A. Wertman, etc. 88-527 E

Latin America -- Foreign Aid

* Caribbean Basin Initiative: Info Pack, IP190C
* Central America and U.S. Foreign Assistance: Issues for Congress; Issue Brief, Mark P. Sullivan IB84075
* El Salvador Aid: Congressional Action, 1981-1986, on President Reagan's Requests for Economic and Military Assistance for El Salvador, K. Larry Storrs 87-230 F
* El Salvador and U.S. Aid: Congressional Action in 1989; Archived Issue Brief, K. Larry Storrs IB90011
* El Salvador under Cristiani: U.S. Foreign Assistance Decisions; Issue Brief, K. Larry Storrs IB89122
* El Salvador: U.S. Aid in 1987 and 1988; Archived Issue Brief, K. Larry Storrs, IB85113
* El Salvador: U.S. Foreign Assistance Facts; Issue Brief, K. Larry Storrs, etc. IB85113
* Guatemala: U.S. Foreign Assistance Facts; Archived Issue Brief, Jonathan Sanford IB85100
* Honduras: U.S. Foreign Assistance Facts; Archived Issue Brief, Robert E. Sanchez IB85080
* Major Trends in U.S. Foreign Assistance to Central America: 1978-1986, Jonathan Sanford 86-88 F
* U.S. Assistance to Nicaraguan Guerrillas: Issues for the Congress: Archived Issue Brief, Nina Serafino IB84139
* U.S. Bilateral Economic and Military Assistance to Latin America and the Caribbean: Fiscal Year 1946 to 1987, K. Larry Storrs 87-694 F
* U.S. Foreign Aid to Central America; 1986-1988, Jonathan E. Sanford 87-465 F

Latin America -- Foreign Relations

* Argentina, Brazil, and Nuclear Proliferation: Archived Issue Brief, Warren H. Donnelly, etc. IB89103
* Arms Shipments to Iran: Archived Issue Brief, Richard M. Preece IB87022
* The Boland Amendments: A Chronology of Congressional Action, Joseph Maheady 87-833 A
* The Central American Peace Prospects: U.S. Interests and Response; Issue Brief, Nina M. Serafino IP352C
* The Central American Peace Prospects: U.S. Interests and Response; Issue Brief, Nina M. Serafino IB87200
* Congress and Policy Toward Central America in 1989, Mark P. Sullivan, etc. 90-347 F
* Congress and Policy Toward Latin America in 1990, Nina M. Serafino, etc. 91-838 F
* Congress and U.S. Policy Toward Nicaragua in 1987, Linda Robinson 89-158 F
* Contra Aid: Analysis of Whether the National Security Council(NSC) and the NSC Staff Are an "Agency or Entity Involved in Intelligence Activities" Cov., Larry E. Eig 87-566 A
* Drugs and Latin America, Audio Brief, Raphael Perl AB50194
* El Salvador: Bibliography-in-Brief, 1987-1989, Robert S. Kirk 90-14 L
* El Salvador Highlights, 1960-1990: A Summary of Major Turning Points in Salvadoran History and U.S. Policy, K. Larry Storrs 90-149 F
* El Salvador: Status of the War and the Role of U.S. Aid, James P. Wootten, 90-193 F
* International Aspects of the Drug Trade: The Andean Nations and Cocaine: Selected References, 1988-1990, Tangela G. Roe 91-245 L
* Iran Arms and Contra Funds: Selected Chronology of Events, 1979-1987, Richard M. Preece, etc. 86-190 F
* Kissinger Commission Implementation: Action by the Congress Through 1986 on the Recommendation of the National Bipartisan Commission on Central America, K. Larry Storrs 87-291 F
* Legislative Histories of Statutory Restrictions on Funding for Covert Assistance for Military or Paramilitary Operations in Nicaragua, FY 1983-FY 1986, Larry M. Eig 87-538 A
* Mexico-U.S. Relations: Issues for Congress; Issue Brief, K. Larry Storrs, etc. IB86111
* Mexico-U.S. Relations in the Salinas Period (1988-1994): Issues for Congress; Issue Brief, K. Larry Storrs IB91061
* Narcotics Control and the Use of U.S. Military Personnel: Operations in Bolivia and Issues for Congress, Raphael Perl 86-800 F
* Nicaragua: An Overview of U.S. Policy, 1979-1986, Mark P. Sullivan 87-855 F
* Nicaragua: Conditions and Issues for U.S. Policy: Issue Brief, Nina Serafino IB82115
* Nicaragua v. United States: The International Court of Justice Decision, Daniel Hill Zafren 86-748 A
* The Nicaraguan Resistance ("Contras"): Background and Major Concerns

Current Events and Homework

of Congress, Veronica R. Clifford 87-943 F
* Panama and the Future of the U.S. Military Bases: An Examination of Panamanian Views, Mark P. Sullivan 91-784 F
* Panama: Bibliography-in-Brief, Robert S. Kirk 90-12 L
* Panama: Trade, Finance, and Proposed Economic Sanctions, Glennon J. Harrison 88-188 E
* Panama's Political Crisis: Prospects and U.S. Policy Concerns; Issue Brief, Mark P. Sullivan IB87230
* Panama: U.S. Policy After the May 1989 Elections; Archived Issue Brief, Mark P. Sullivan IB89106
* Panama-U.S. Relations: Issue for Congress; Issue Brief, Mark P. Sullivan IB90044
* Peru-U.S. Relations under the Fujimori Government, Nicholas Cochrane 91-689 F
* A Summary and Analysis of the Report of the National Bipartisan "Kissinger" Commission on Central America, January 1984, Richard Cronin, etc. 84-39 F
* The United States and Cuba During the Carter Administration, Margaret Siliciano, etc. 85-988 F
* The United States and Cuba During the Reagan Administration, Judith Levenfeld, etc. 85-989 F
* U.S. Sanctions and the State of the Panamanian Economy, Mark P. Sullivan 88-578 F

Latin America -- Foreign Trade

* Agriculture in a U.S.-Mexico-Canada Free Trade Agreement, Charles E. Hanrahan 91-252 RCO
* Brazil: Selected Foreign Trade Data, Rawle O. King 88-320 E
* Canada-U.S.-Mexico Free Trade Agreements: Selected References, 1989-1991, Felix Chin 91-331 L
* Capital Flight: Problems Associated With Definitions and Estimates; Glennon J. Harrison 91-274 E
* Fast-Track Procedures for Trade Agreements: Implications for Congress of Their Extension, Ilona B. Nickels 91-248 GOV
* Fruits and Vegetables in a U.S.-Mexico-Canada Free Trade Agreement, Geoffrey S. Becker 91-362 ENR
* Mexico-U.S. Free Trade Agreement: Info Pack, Congressional Reference Division IP445M
* Mexico Maquiladora Industry, M. Angeles Villarreal 91-706 E
* North American Free Trade Agreement: A Checklist of CRS Products and Public Policy Literature, Felix Chin 91-450 L
* North American Free Trade Agreement; Issue Brief, Lenore Sek IB90140
* North American Free Trade Agreement: Issues for Congress, Congressional Research Service, 91-282 E
* A North American Free Trade Area? A Brief Review of the Major Issues, Alfred Reifman 91-418 RCO
* Restrictions on U.S. Trade With Cuba: A Chronology of Major Actions and Present Status, Vladimir N. Pregelj 86-909 E
* Seizure of Foreign Vessels in United States Ports, Daniel Hill Zafren 87-760 A
* Tariff Items 807.00 and 806.30 and the Mexican Maquiladoras, Patricia Wertman 87-500 E
* United States-Mexican Trade Relations: Present Problems, Future Prospects, Patricia Wertman 85-139 E
* U.S.-Canada Free Trade Agreement: Assessment and Implications for a U.S.-Mexico Free Trade Agreement, Arlene Wilson 90-450 E
* U.S.-Mexico Trade in the Automotive Industry, M. Angeles Villarreal, etc. 91-533 E
* The U.S. Trade Embargo Against Nicaragua After Two-and-a-Half Years, Glennon J. Harrison 87-870 E

Latin America -- National Defense

* Arms Shipments to Iran: Archived Issue Brief, Richard M. Preece IB87022
* Chart of Unclassified Legislative Restrictions Regarding Support for Military or Paramilitary Operations in Nicaragua, 1982-1986, Larry Eig 87-222 A
* Contra Aid FY82-FY88: Summary and Chronology of Major Congressional Action on Key Legislation Concerning U.S. Aid to the Anti-Sandinista Guerrillas, Nina M. Serafino 88-563 F
* Grenada: Issues Concerning the Use of U.S. Forces;, Archived Issue Brief, Janice Hanover IB83170
* Iran Arms and Contra Funds: Selected Chronology of Events, 1979-1987, Richard M. Preece, etc. 86-190 F
* Iran Arms Sales and Contra Funds: Summaries of Key Legislative Provisions, Clyde R. Mark, etc. 87-13 F

Latin America -- Politics and Government

* Belize: Country Background Report, Mark P. Sullivan 88-568 F
* Chile: Country Background Report, Thomas P. Rowan 91-231 F
* Costa Rica: Country Background Report, Nina M. Serafino 88-577 F
* El Salvador: Bibliography-in-Brief, 1986-1989, Robert S. Kirk 89-204 L
* El Salvador: Info Pack, IP121E
* El Salvador, 1982-1984: A Chronology of a Period of Transition Resulting from the 1982 and 1984 Elections, K. Larry Storrs 87-656 F
* El Salvador--Legal System, Judicial Reform, and Major Human Rights Cases Involving the Military, K. Larry Storrs 90-177 F
* El Salvador: Status of U.N.-Mediated Government-Guerrilla Peace Talks, K. Larry Storrs 91-304 F
* Guatemala: Country Background Report, Maureen Taft-Morales 88-586 F
* Haiti: Political Developments and U.S. Policy Concerns: Archived Issue Brief, Maureen Taft-Morales IB88104
* Haiti: Prospects for Democracy and U.S. Policy Concerns; Issue Brief, Maureen Taft-Morales IB91043
* Mexico: Problems and Prospects; Info Pack, IP358M
* Mexico: Selected References, Sherry B. Shapiro 90-369 L
* Nicaragua: Bibliography-in-Brief, 1986-1987, Valentin Leskovsek 87-382 L
* Nicaraguan Elections and Transition: Issues for U.S. Policy, Nina M. Serafino 90-187 F
* Nicaragua: Info Pack, IP073N
* Nicaragua's "Civic" Opposition: Players, Problems and Prospects, Nina M. Serafino 87-735 F
* Peru: Country Background Report, Maureen Taft-Morales 90-247 F
* Puerto Rico: Political Status Options; Issue Brief, Garrine P. Laney IB89065

Latvia

* The Baltic Republics: U.S. Policy Concerns; Issue Brief, Vita Bite IB90075
* Latvia: Background Information, Allan Nanes, etc. 83-154 F
* Latvia: Basic Facts, Vita Bite 91-844 F

Law

* Awards of Attorney's Fees Against the United States: The Equal Access to Justice Act, as Interpreted by the Supreme Court in Pierce v. Underwood Henry Cohen 88-570 A
* Awards of Attorney's Fees by Federal Courts and Federal Agencies, Henry Cohen 91-584 A
* The Constitutionality of Federal Tort Reform, Henry Cohen 86-941 A
* The Ethics of a Private Law Practice by Members and Employees of Congress, Jack Maskell 85-663 A
* Federal Statutory Research, Rita Reimer 85-219 A
* Federal Tort Claims Act: Current Legislative and Judicial Issues, Henry Cohen 91-317 A
* Laws, Lawyers, and the Judiciary: An Alphabetical Microthesaurus of Terms Selected from the Legislative Indexing Vocabulary, Shirley Loo 90-584 L
* Legal Research: An Introduction, Law Library of Congress LL91-1
* Preparing Legislative Histories; Videoprogram, David Siddall LTR91-910
* Reform of the English Legal Profession: Green, White and Pale, Law Library of Congress LL90-74
* Subsequent Legislative History as an Aid to Statutory Construction: Recent Supreme Court Usages, George Costello 85-1081 A
* Tax Status of Group Legal Services Plans, Louis Alan Talley 90-418 E
* Tort Injury Compensation Reform: Various Approaches, Henry Cohen 87-666 A
* The Tort Reform Debate: Pros, Cons, Federal Proposals, State Statutes, Henry Cohen 86-579 A
* Tort Reform: State Statutory Caps on Damages, Henry Cohen, etc. 87-835 A
* United States Law: Finding Statutory Material, Thomas B. Ripy, etc. 90-110 A
* Use of the Military to Enforce Civilian Law: Posse Comitatus Act and Other Considerations, Charles Doyle 88-583 A
* Waiver of Eleventh Amendment Immunity from Suit: State Survey, Kirk D. Nemer 88-465 A

Law, Crime, and Justice

* see Crimes and Offenses, Criminal Procedure, Drug Abuse, Internal Security, Judiciary, Law, Police, Prisons
* Crime Control: Federal Initiatives, IB86042
* Drug Control, IB87013
* Drug Testing in the Workplace: An Overview of Employee and Employer Interests, IB87139
* Gun Control, IB89093
* Legal Issues of Insider Trading in Securities, IB87052

* Prison Conditions: Congressional Response, IB81171
* Supreme Court: Church-State Cases, October 1988 Term, IB88105

Lebanon

* Lebanon: The Current Crisis, Issue Brief, Clyde R. Mark IB89118
* Lebanon: The Remaining U.S. Hostages; a Chronology, 1984-March 19, 1991, Clyde R. Mark 91-410 F
* Lebanon: The Remaining U.S. Hostages; Issue Brief, Clyde Mark IB85183
* United States Interests in Lebanon, John Creed 85-873 F

Legislative Procedure

* see Congress-Legislative Procedure and Operations

Legislative Veto

* see Congress--Executive Relations

Lend-Lease Settlement Agreement

* Lend-Lease: An Historic Overview and Repayment Issues, Patricia Wertman 85-844 E

Leveraged Buyouts

* see Corporations--Mergers

Liability Insurance Crisis

* see Insurance--Liability Issues

Liberia

* Liberia: Issues for the United States; Issue Brief, Brenda M. Branaman IB91105

Libraries

* see Arts and Humanities

Libya

* Libya: U.S. Relations; Archived Issue Brief, Raymond Copson, etc. IB86040
* Libya's Nuclear Energy Situation: Archived Issue Brief, Mark Martel, etc. IB85079

Lifeline Telephone Service Act

* see Telecommunication--Telephone Industry

Lincoln, Abraham

* Speech Material: Abraham Lincoln's and George Washington's Birthdays; Info Pack, IP373A

Literacy

* see Elementary and Secondary Education

Lithuania

* The Baltic Republics: U.S. Policy Concerns, Issue Brief, Vita Bite IB90075
* Lithuania: Background Information, Dorothy Fontana 83-53 F

Living Wills

* see Medicine--Ethical Issues

Lobbying

* see Politics and Elections--Practical Politics

Local Finance

* The ABCs of Public Venture Capital Investment, Jan E. Christopher 88-757 E
* American Telephone and Telegraph Co. Flow-Through of State Gross Receipts Taxes, Angele Gilroy 87-43 E
* Comments Concerning the Supreme Court's Decision in South Carolina v. Baker, Robert B. Burdette 88-443 A
* Compilation of State Laws Pertaining to the Exemptions from State Sales Taxes for Federal Purchases, Mark Gurevitz 89-232 A
* Constitutionality of State Legislation Exempting Property Within the State from Judgments for Failure to Pay Another State's Income Taxes on Pension or Retirement Benefits, Marie B. Morris 91-453 A
* Crowding Out? Federal, State and Local Government Borrowing and the Debt Economy, William Jackson 87-274 E
* Expiring Tax-Exempt Bond Provisions: Small-Issue IDBs and Mortgage Revenue bonds, Dennis Zimmerman 90-417 E
* Federal Budget and Tax Policy and the State-Local Sector: Retrenchments in the 1980s, Lillian Rymarowicz, etc. 88-600 E
* Federal Income Tax Deduction for State and Local Taxes: A Brief History of the Law, Thomas Ripy 85-853 A
* The Judicial Power of Taxation: A Legal Analysis of the U.S. Supreme Court Ruling in Missouri v. Jenkins, Charles V. Dale 90-294 A
* Limiting the Growth of Tax-Exempt Industrial Development Bonds: An Economic Evaluation, Dennis Zimmerman 84-37 E
* Lotteries: Bibliography-in-Brief, 1974-1987, Marsha Cerny 87-392 L
* The Payments in Lieu of Taxes Program: Background and Current Status, Stacey M. Kean 87-321 E
* Selective Local Government Excise Taxes on Hotel, Motel, and Other Transient Lodging as of July 1, 1986, Lillian Rymarowicz 86-793 E
* State Income Taxation of Military Personnel and United States Citizens Residing Outside of the United States, John Luckey 91-590 A
* State Taxation of Nonresidents' Retirement Income, Robert B. Burdette 89-224 A
* Tax-Exempt Bond-Financed Takeover of Investor-Owned Utilities: An Issue of Privatization and Competition, Dennis Zimmerman 88-174 E
* Tax Exempt Bond Legislation, 1968-1990: An Economic Perspective, Dennis Zimmerman 91-143 E
* Tax-Exempt Bond Provisions of the Technical and Miscellaneous Revenue Act of 1988, Dennis Zimmerman 88-741 E
* Tax-Exempt Bonds: A Summary of Changes Made by the Tax Reform Act of 1986, Robert B. Burdette 87-9 A
* Tax-Exempt Bonds and Twenty Years of Tax Reform: Controlling Public Subsidy of Private Activities, Dennis Zimmerman 87-922 E
* Tax Reform: Its Potential Effect on the State and Local Sector, Dennis Zimmerman 87-233 E
* Taxation Within Indian Lands: The Legal Framework, M. Maureen Murphy 87-249 A
* Timber Export Taxes: Constitutional and International Law Implications, Kenneth R. Thomas 91-416 A

Long-Term Care

* see Old Age--Health Issues

LTV Corporation

* Legal Analysis of LTV Corporation's Unilateral Termination of Retirees' Health and Life Insurance Benefits on the Date of Filing in Bankruptcy, Vincent E. Treacy 86-845 A

Luxury Tax

* see Taxation--Consumption Taxes

M-X Missile

* see Weapons Systems--Nuclear Weapons
* Strategic Forced: MX ICBM (Weapons Facts); Archived Issue Brief, Jonathan Medalia, etc. IB84046

Magnuson Fishery Conservation and Management Act

* Fisheries Conservation and Management: The Magnuson Act in the 100th Congress, Eugene H. Buck 89-65 ENR

Malaysia

* The Association of Southeast Asian Nations (ASEAN) : Economic Development Prospects and the Role of the United States, Larry Niksch 84-171 F
* Economic Changes in the Asian Pacific Rim: Policy Prospectus., Congressional Research Service 86-923 S
* U.S. Agricultural Trade Opportunities With Pacific Rim Nations, Robert M. Goldstein 88-755 ENR

Manassas National Battlefield Park

* Manassas National Battlefield Park: The Battle Continues, John O. Spengler, etc. 88-514 ENR

Mandela, Nelson

* South Africa: African National Congress, Brenda Branaman 86-186 F

Manpower Training Programs

* see Occupational Training--Job Training

Current Events and Homework

Marine Mammal Protection Act
* see Fisheries

Marine Transportation
* see Infrastructure
* After the Exxon Valdez Spill: Oil Pollution Liability and Compensation Legislation, Martin R. Lee 89-266 ENR
* Cargo Preference and Agriculture, Carl Ek 89-633 ENR
* Double-Bottom/Double-Hull Tankers: Pro and Con, James E. Mielke 90-152 SPR
* The Exxon Valdez Oil Spill: Archived Issue Brief, Martin R. Lee, etc. IB89075
* Oil Pollution Liability and Compensation Legislation After the Exxon Valdez Oil Spill: Issue Brief, Martin R. Lee IB89082
* Oil Spill Response Technologies, James E. Mielke 90-146 SPR
* Oil Spills: Selected References, Ted L. Burch 90-138 L
* Seizure of Foreign Vessels in United States Ports, Daniel Hill Zafren 87-760 A
* Survey on Applicability of National Labor Laws to Vessels of Foreign Registry, Law Library of Congress LL90-7
* U.S. Merchant Shipping: Federal Assistance and Policy Issues, Lenore Sek 86-79 E

Marine Waste
* see Coastal Areas, Solid Wastes

Marshall Islands
* Territorial Political Development: An Analysis of Puerto Rico, Northern Mariana Islands, Guam, Virgin Islands, and American Samoa, and the Micronesian, Bette A. Taylor 88-657 GOV

Mass Media
* see Press, Telecommunication

MBFR
* see Mutual Balanced Force Reduction Talks

Meat
* see Agriculture--Livestock, Food

Medicaid
* see Medicare and Medicaid--Medicaid

Medical Economics
* AIDS: Acquired Immune Deficiency Syndrome; Selected References, B.F. Mangan 89-333 L
* Appropriations for Selected Health Programs, FY 1980-FY 1991, Edward R. Klebe 91-769 EPW
* Controlling Health Care Costs, Mark Merlis 90-64 EPW
* Elderly Home Care: Tax Incentives and Proposals for Change, Louis Alan Talley 89-662 E
* Generic Drugs and the Elderly; Issues and Policy Considerations, Samuel Merrill 91-792 SPR
* Health Care: Archived Issue Brief, Janet Kline IB87009
* Health Care Costs and Cost Containment, Audio Brief, Kathleen King, etc. AB50216
* Health Care Costs and Cost Containment, Kathleen M. King, etc. LTR91-878
* Health Care Costs at the End of Life, Kathleen M. King 90-368 EPW
* Health Care Cost Containment: Bibliography-in-Brief, 1986-1988, Charles P. Dove 88-376 L
* Health Care Costs: Info Pack, IP223H
* Health Care Expenditures and Prices: Issue Brief, James Reuter IB77066
* Health Care Financing and Health Insurance: A Glossary of Terms, Education and Public Welfare Division. Health Sect 88-539 EPW
* Health Care: Issue Brief, Janet Kline IB87009
* Health Care Issues for the 102nd Congress, Education and Public Welfare Division 91-128 EPW
* Health Insurance and the Uninsured: Background Data and Analysis, Education and Public Welfare Division. Health Insurance, 88-537 EPW
* Health Insurance Coverage: Characteristics of the Insured and Uninsured Populations, Madeleine Smith, etc. 91-618 EPW
* The Japanese Health Care System, Joan Sokolovsky, 89-572 EPW
* Medicare: Geographic Variations in Payments for Physician Services, James A. Reuter 88-775 EPW
* Medicare: Prospective Payments for Inpatient Hospital Services; Issue Brief, Julian Pettingill, etc. IB87180
* Medicare: Recalculating Payment Rates under the Prospective Payment System, Mark Merlis 87-574 EPW
* Medicare Reimbursement: Selected References, 1986-1988, Peter Giordano 88-679 L
* Medicare's Prospective Payment System: An Analysis of the Financial Risk of Outlier Cases, Congressional Research Service 87-877 EPW
* Medicare's Prospective Payment System: The 98th and 99th Congresses, Joseph Cislowski, etc. 87-862 EPW
* National Health Expenditures: Trends from 1960-1989, Kathleen M. King, etc. 91-588 EPW
* National Health Spending, 1989: A Description of Spending by Services and Payers, Kathleen King, etc. 91-527 EPW
* National Health Spending, 1990: A Description of Spending by Services and Payers, Kathleen King, etc. 91-814 EPW
* Patient Outcome Research and Practice Guidelines: A Plan for Research and Policy, Bernice S. Reyes 91-50 SPR
* A Prospective Payment System for Hospital-Based Physician Services under Medicare; a Report Prepared for the Subcommittee on Health, Committee on Ways, Education and Public Welfare Division 87-715 EPW
* Public Health and the Congress: Selected References, Karen Alderson, etc. 89-147 L
* Rationing Health Care, Kathleen King 90-346 EPW
* Rural Hospitals under Medicare's Prospective Payment System and the Omnibus Budget Reconciliation Act of 1986 (P.L. 99-509), Joseph A. Cislowski, etc. 87-816 EPW

Medical Personnel
* Clinical Laboratory Improvement Amendments of 1988 (CLIA), Jennifer O'Sullivan 90-421 EPW
* Health Professions Education and Nurse Training Programs: Titles VI and VIII; Issue Brief, Edward Klebe IB88055
* HIV Infected Health Care Workers: The Legal Issues, Nancy Lee Jones 91-598 A
* HIV Infected Health Care Workers: The Medical and Scientific Issues, Judith A. Johnson 91-622 SPR
* Life-Sustaining Technologies: Medical and Moral issues, Marilyn Littlejohn, etc. 91-45 SPR
* Medicare Payments to Hospitals and Physicians: Info Pack, IP317M
* Medicare Physician Payment Reform, Jennifer O'Sullivan, etc. 91-643 EPW
* Medicare: Physicians Payments, James Reuter 88-658 EPW
* Medicare: Physician Referrals to Clinical Laboratories, Jennifer O'Sullivan 90-439 EPW
* Medicare's Peer Review Organizations, Beth C. Fuchs 90-273 EPW
* National Health Service Corps, Celinda M. Franco 91-729 EPW
* Nurses: Supply and Demand; Bibliography-in-Brief, 1981-1988, Edith Sutterlin 88-729 L

Medicare
* see Medicare and Medicaid--Medicare

Medicare and Medicaid
* see Medicaid, Medicare
* Health Insurance Legislation in the 102nd Congress, Beth C. Fuchs, etc. 91-564 EOW
* Medicare and Medicaid: Bibliography-in-Brief, 1986-1988, Edith Sutterlin 88-560 L
* Medicaid Cost Explosion: A Checklist of CRS Products, Charles Dove 92-11 L
* Medicare, Medicaid, and Maternal and Child Health Programs: An Overview of Major Legislation Enacted from 1980 Through 1986, Janet Kline, etc. 87-296 EPW
* Medicare and Medicaid Nursing Home Reform Provisions in the Omnibus Budget Reconciliation Act of 1987, P.L. 100-203, Richard Price 90-80 EPW
* Medicare-Medicaid: Info Pack, IP067M
* Medicare Physician Payment Reform: A Checklist of CRS Products, Edith Sutterlin 92-10 L
* National Health Expenditures: Trends from 1960-1989, Kathleen M. King, etc. 91-588 EPW

Medicare and Medicaid -- Medicaid
* Community Services under Medicaid for Persons With Mental Retardation: Archived Issue Brief, Mary F. Smith IB89135
* Health Care for Children: Federal Programs and Policies, Joseph A. Cislowski 88-217 EPW

* Medicaid Eligibility for the Elderly in Need of Long Term Care, Edward Neuschler, etc. 87-986 EPW
* Medicaid: FY90 Budget; Issue Brief, Mark Merlis IB89031
* Medicaid: FY 1991 Budget and Child Health Initiatives; Archived Issue Brief, Melvina Ford IB90043
* Medicaid: FY 1992 Budget: Archived Issue Brief, Melvina Ford IB91036
* Medicaid: FY90 Budget and Child Health Initiatives; Archived Issue Brief, Mark Merlis IB89031
* Medicaid: Provider Donations and Provider-Specific Taxes, Mark Merlis 91-722 EPW
* Medicaid: Reimbursement for Outpatient Prescription Drugs, Melvina Ford 91-235 EPW
* Medicaid Services for Persons With Mental Retardation or Related Conditions, Mary F. Smith 88-759
* Medicaid: Spousal Impoverishment, Jennifer O'Sullivan 87-648 EPW
* Medicaid "2176" Waivers for Home and Community-Based Care, Carol O'Shaughnessy, etc. 85-817 GOV

Medicare and Medicaid -- Medicare

* Catastrophic Health Insurance: Bibliography-in-Brief, Edith Sutterlin 89-444 L
* Catastrophic Health Insurance: Comparison of the Major Provision of the "Medicare Catastrophic Protection Act of 1987" (H.R. 2470 as Passed by the House, Jennifer O'Sullivan, etc. 87-948 EPW
* Catastrophic Health Insurance: Medicare; Issue Brief, Jennifer O'Sullivan IB87106
* The Financial Outlook for Medicare, David Koitz 91-357 EPW
* The Financial Outlook for Social Security and Medicare, David Koitz 91-830 EPW
* Financing Catastrophic Health Care: Possible Effects on Marginal and Average Income Tax Rates, Gregg A. Esenwein 89-132 E
* Growth in the Volume of Medicare Physician Services: A Framework for Analysis, Gene Falk 88-466 EPW
* Health Insurance that Supplements Medicare: Background Material and Data, Jennifer O'Sullivan, etc. 89-421 EPW
* Hospital Capital Cost Reimbursement under Medicare, Joseph Cislowski, etc. 86-598 EPW
* Long-Term Care Legislation: Summary of Selected Bills, Carol O'Shaughnessy, etc. 89-238 EPW
* Medicare: Arguments for and Against Continuing Coverage for Disability Insurance Recipients Who Return to Work, David Koitz 87-837 EPW
* Medicare: Arguments for and Against the Medicare 24-Month Waiting Period for the Disabled, David Koitz 87-484 EPW
* Medicare Catastrophic Coverage Act of 1988 (P.L. 100-360), Jennifer O'Sullivan 89-155 EPW
* Medicare Coverage of Employees of State and Local Governments, David Koitz 88-369 EPW
* Medicare Financing, David Koitz 91-517 EPW
* Medicare: FY1991 Budget; Archived Issue Brief, Celinda M. Franco, etc. IB90045
* Medicare: FY1992 Budget; Archived Issue Brief, Celinda M. Franco, etc. IB91032
* Medicare: FY90 Budget; Archived Issue Brief, Kathleen M. King, etc. IB89029
* Medicare: Geographic Variations in Payments for Physician Services, James A. Reuter 88-775 EPW
* Medicare: Its Use, Funding, and Economic Dimensions, David Koitz, etc. 89-134 EPW
* Medicare Part B: The Supplementary Medical Insurance Program, James Reuter, etc. 86-153 EPW
* Medicare: Payment for Hospital Capital Costs; Archived Issue Brief, Mark Merlis IB91028
* Medicare: Payments for Clinical Laboratory Services, Jennifer O'Sullivan 90-416 EPW
* Medicare Payments to Hospitals and Physicians: Info Pack, IP317M
* Medicare Physician Payment Reform, Jennifer O'Sullivan, etc. 91-643 EPW
* Medicare: Physician Payments, James Reuter 88-658 EPW
* Medicare: Physician Referrals to Clinical Laboratories, Jennifer O'Sullivan 90-439 EPW
* Medicare: Proposals to Increase the Amount of Earnings Subject to the Hospital Insurance Tax, David Koitz 90-66 EPW
* Medicare: Prospective Payments for Inpatient Hospital Services; Archived Issue Brief, Celinda Franco, etc. IB87180
* Medicare: Recalculating Payment Rates under the Prospective Payment System, Mark Merlis 87-574 EPW
* Medicare Reimbursement: Selected References, 1986-1988, Peter Giordano 88-679 L
* Medicare: Risk Contracts With Health Maintenance Organizations and Competitive Medical Plans, Mark Merlis 88-138 EPW
* Medicare's Peer Review Organizations, Beth C. Fuchs 90-273 EPW
* Medicare's Physician Fee Schedule; Issue Brief, Kathleen M. King, etc. IB91116
* Medicare's Prospective Payments System: An Analysis of the Financial Risk of Outlier Cases, Congressional Research Service 87-877 EPW
* Medicare's Prospective Payment System: The 98th and 99th Congresses, Joseph Cislowski, etc. 87-862 EPW
* Medigap and Related Private Health Insurance Legislation in the 101st Congress, Janet Lundy 91-140 EPW
* The Peer Review Organization Program, Joseph Cislowski 87-860 EPW
* Physician Payments by Medicare: Bibliography-in-Brief, 1987-1990, Charles P. Dove 91-160 L
* Premium Effect of Proposed Medicare Catastrophic Legislation on Federal Annuitants, Janet P. Lundy 87-801 EPW
* Prospective Budgeting for Medicare's Physician Service, James Reuter, etc. 89-600 EPW
* A Prospective Payment System for Hospital-Based Physician Services under Medicare; a Report Prepared for the Subcommittee on Health, Committee on Ways, Education and Public Welfare Division 87-715 EPW
* Rural Hospitals under Medicare's Prospective Payment System and the Omnibus Budget Reconciliation Act of 1986 (P.L. 99-509), Joseph A. Cislowski, etc. 87-816 EPW
* Social Security Medicare Coverage of Employees of State and Local Governments, David Koitz, etc. 87-132 EPW
* Social Security and Medicare: How Are They Treated in Determining the National Debt?, David Koitz 85-1132 EPW
* Soeical Security and Medicare: Proposals to Cover State and Local Government, Issue Brief, Geoffrey C. Kollmann IB90065

Medicare Catastrophic Coverage Act

* Medicare Catastrophic Coverage Act of 1988 (P.L. 100-360), Jennifer O'Sullivan 89-155 EPW

Medicine

* see Aids, Ethical Issues, Genetics, Public Health
* Alzheimer's Disease: Bibliography-in-Brief, 1982-1987, B.F. Mangan 88-312 L
* Alzheimer's Disease: Archived Issue Brief, Samuel Merrill IB83128
* Biotechnology: Bibliography-in-Brief, 1985-1988, B.F. Mangan 88-566 L
* Breast Implants: Safety and FDA Regulation, Judith Johnson 91-842 SPR
* Brief Summary of Several Federal Statutes Which Arguably Provide the Federal Government the Authority to Control the Disposal of Infectious Hospital Waste, Cathy Gilmore 87-658 A
* Clinical Laboratory Improvement Amendments of 1988 (CLIA), Jennifer O'Sullivan 90-421 EPW
* Consortium to Establish a Registry for Alzheimer's Disease (CERAD): A Federally Funded Research Program, Samuel Merrill 91-352 SPR
* Diet, Nutrition, and Health: Selected References, 1986-1990, Bonnie F. Mangan 90-306 L
* Dioxin and Agent Orange Health Effects: An Update, Samuel Merrill, etc. 91-195 SPR
* Eating Disorders: Anorexia Nervosa and Bulimia, Bernice S. Reyes, etc. 87-630 SPR
* Organ Transplantation in the United States: Analysis of Selected Ethical Issues, Marilyn Littlejohn 89-103 SPR
* Osteoporosis: An Overview of Recent Developments, Bernice S. Reyes, etc. 87-843 SPR
* Patient Outcome Research and Practice Guidelines: A Plan for Research and Policy, Bernice S. Reyes 91-50 SPR
* Personal Medical Communication Technologies, Bernice S. Reyes 91-278 SPR
* Vaccine Injury Compensation; Archived Issue Brief, Pamela W. Smith IB87046
* Women's Health Issues; Selected References, 1986-1991, Bonnie F. Mangan 91-606 L

Medicine -- AIDS

* Acquired Immune Deficiency Syndrome (AIDS): A Brief Overview of the Major Legal Issues, Nancy Lee Jones 87-236 A
* Acquired Immune Deficiency Syndrome and Military Manpower Policy: Issue Brief, David F. Burrelli IB87202
* Acquired Immune Deficiency Syndrome (AIDS): Health Care Financing and Services; Issue Brief, Mark Merlis IB87219
* Advertising Condoms: Legal and Constitutional Considerations, Rita Ann

Current Events and Homework

Reimer 87-325 A
* AIDS--Health Care Costs: Bibliography-in-Brief, 1985-1986, Bonnie Mangan 87-32 L
* AIDS: Acquired Immune Deficiency Syndrome; Info Pack, IP261A
* AIDS: Acquired Immune Deficiency Syndrome: Selected References, 1988-1991, B.F. Mangan 91-419 L
* AIDS: An Overview of Issues: Issue Brief, Judith A. Johnson IB87150
* AIDS and Discrimination: Legal Limits on Insurance Underwriting Practices, Kirk D. Nemer 88-381 A
* AIDS and Other Diseases: Federal Spending and Morbidity and Mortality Statistics, Judith A. Johnson 91-358 SPR
* AIDS and the Public Schools: Legal Issues Involved in the Education of Children, Nancy Lee Jones 88-329 A
* AIDS: Audio Brief, Mark Merlis, etc. AB50186
* AIDS Discrimination Issues: Legislation and Executive Actions; Archived Issue Brief, Mark Eddy IB89125
* AIDS in Africa: Background/Issues for U.S. Policy, Raymond W. Copson 87-768 F
* AIDS in the Workplace: Employee Vs Employer Interest, Gail McCallion 87-510 E
* AIDS: International Problems and Issues; Issue Brief, Lois B. McHugh IB87214
* AIDS Prevention: State Law Regulating Hypodermic Devices Which Could Affect Needle Exchange Programs, M. Ann Wolfe 89-234 A
* AIDS: Progress and Problems, Pamela Smith LTR91-860
* American Public Opinion on AIDS: A CRS Major issue Before the 101st Congress, Rosita M. Thomas 89-85 GOV
* Blood: Collection, Testing, and Processing, Irene Stith-Coleman 87-641 SPR
* Blood Testing for Antibodies to the AIDS Virus: The Legal Issues, Charles Dale, etc. 87-738 A
* Federal Funding for AIDS Research and Prevention: Issue Brief, Judith A. Johnson IB87028
* Fifty State Survey of States Statutes Concerning Venereal Disease as It May Relate to AIDS, M. Ann Wolfe 87-240 A
* Health Exams, Including AIDS Tests, Required of Foreign Students, Law Library of Congress LL90-82
* HIV Infected Health Care Workers: The Legal Issues, Nancy Lee Jones 91-598 A
* HIV Infected Health Care Workers: The Medical and Scientific Issues, Judith A. Johnson 91-622 SPR
* The Potential Liability of Insurance Companies and Self-Insured Businesses for Unauthorized Disclosure of Medical Information Provided in Connection, W Kirk D. Nemer 88-509 A
* Summary of State Statutes Which Specifically Mention Acquired Immune Deficiency Syndrome, M. Ann Wolfe 87-239 A
* Women and AIDS: Selected References, 1986-1991, Bonnie F. Mangan 91-607 L

Medicine -- Ethical Issues

* Advance Directives and Health Care Facilities, Celinda Franco 91-117 EPW
* Advance Medical Directives, Kenneth R. Thomas 91-27 A
* Animal Use in Research: Bibliography-in-Brief, 1985-87, Adrienne C. Grenfell 88-72 L
* Animal Welfare Issues, Info Pack IP360A
* Animals in Biomedical Research: Selected References, 1988-1990, B.F. Mangan 91-6L
* Biomedical Ethics and Congress: History and Current Legislative Activity; Issue Brief, Irene Stith-Coleman IB86078
* Biomedical Ethics: Audio Brief, Science Policy Research Division AB50004
* Biomedical Research: Use of Animals; Issue Brief, Blanchard Randall IB83161
* Canadian Laws Respecting Donations of Organs from Anencephalic Babies, Law Library of Congress LL90-75
* The Federal Role in Bone Marrow Transplantation, Bernice S. Reyes 90-303 SPR
* Fetal Research: A Survey of State Law, Mildred Washington 88-198 A
* Human Fetal Research and Tissue Transportation: Issue Brief, Irene Stith-Coleman IB88100
* Life-Sustaining Technologies: Medical and Moral Issues, Marilyn Littlejohn, etc. 91-45 SPF
* The Right to Die: Fundamental Life Decisions After Cruzan v. Director, Missouri Dept. of Health, Kenneth R. Thomas 90-371 A
* A Survey of the Statutory Definitions of Death, Mildred Washington 91-635 A
* Treatment and Appointment Directives: Living Wills, Powers of Attorney, and Other Advance Medical Care Documents, Kenneth R. Thomas 91-87 A

Members of Congress

* see Congress--Members

Mental Health

* Bethel: A Model Community for Housing and Treating the Mentally Ill, Morton J. Schussheim 90-511 RCP
* Childhood Mental Disorders: Attention-Deficit Hyperactivity Disorder, Autism, and Dyslexia, Edith Fairman Cooper 91-405 SPR
* Community-Based Services for Individuals With Severe Disabilities: Summary and Analysis of S. 1673 and H.R. 3454, Mary F. Smith 88-212 EPW
* Constitutional and Statutory Issues Relating to the Use of Behavior Modification on Children in Institutions, Nancy L. Jones 86-1000 A
* The Constitutional Rights of Mental Patients, Charles Dale 85-585 A
* Eating Disorders: Anorexia Nervosa and Bulimia, Bernice S. Reyes, etc. 87-630 SPR
* Homelessness and Commitment: The Cases of Joyce Brown (a/k/a Billie Boggs), Kirk D. Nemer 88-186 A
* Homeless Mentally Ill Persons: Problems and Programs, Edward r. Klebe 91-344 EPW
* Overview of Recent Judicial Decisions on the Constitutional Right of Mental Patients to Refuse Treatment, Nancy Jones 85-548 A
* Teenage Suicide: Bibliography-in-Brief, 1982-1988, Peter Giordano, etc. 88-652 L
* Youth Suicide: Sudden Adolescent Death, Edith Fairman Cooper 88-428 SPR

Mentally Retarded

* see Handicapped

Mergers

* see Corporations--Mergers

Methanol

* see Power Resources--Alternative Energy Sources

Mexico

* Fast-Track Procedures for Trade Agreements: Implications for Congress of Their Extension, Ilona B. Nickels 91-248 GOV
* Fruits and Vegetables in a U.S.-Mexico-Canada Free Trade Agreement, Geoffrey S. Becker 91-362 ENR
* The Mexican Debt Accords and Their Financial Implications: an Overview, Patricia A. Wertman 86-179 E
* Mexican Oil: Less Than Meets The Eye, Joseph P. Riva 91-535 SPR
* Mexican Petroleum, Joseph Riva 83-178 SPR
* Mexico: Problems and Prospects; Info Pack, IP358M
* Mexico: Selected References, Sherry B. Shapiro 90-369 L
* Mexico-U.S. Relations: Issues for Congress; Issue Brief, K. Larry Storrs, etc. IB86111
* Mexico-U.S. Relations in the Salinas Period (1988-1994): Issues for Congress, Issue Brief K. Larry Storrs IB91061
* Mexico's Maquiladora Industry, M. Angeles Villarreal 91-706 E
* North American Free Trade Agreement: A Checklist of CRS Products and Public Policy Literature, Felix Chin 91-450 L
* North American Free Trade Agreement: Issues for Congress, Congressional Research Service 91-282 E
* Tariff Items 807.00 and 806.30 and the Mexican Maquiladoras, Patricia Wertman 87-500 E
* United States-Mexican Trade Relations: Present Problems, Future Prospects, Patricia Wertman 85-139 E
* U.S.-Mexico Economic Relations: An Overview, Lenore Sek 87-485 E
* U.S.-Mexico Trade in the Automotive Industry, M. Angeles Villarreal, etc. 91-533 E

Mexico-U.S. Free Trade Area

* see Latin America--Foreign Trade

Mias
* see Military Personnel

Microthesauri

* see Reference Sources--Microthesauri

Middle East

* see Arab-Israeli Conflict, Arms Sales and Foreign Assistance, Iran-Iraq War, Iraq-Kuwait, Petroleum, U.S. Concerns, Iran-Contra Affair, Persian Gulf

Medicine / Middle East

* Activation of Selected Reserves under Executive Order 12727 and Executive Order 12733 for Service in the Arabian Peninsula, Robert B. Burdette 90-563 A
* Ethiopian Jews; Archived Issue Brief, Theodore S. Dagne IB90105
* The Gulf Cooperation Council, Richard Preece 85-516 F
* The Holy See and Recognition of Israel, Charles J. Whittier 86-833 GOV
* International Atomic Energy Agency: Strengthen Verification Authority? Issue Brief, Warren H. Donnelly, etc. IB91109
* Iran-Iraq War: Archived Issue Brief, Richard M. Preece IB88060
* The Israeli Economy: Archived Issue Brief, Clyde Mark IB84138
* Israel's Participation in the International Atomic Energy Agency and the 32nd IAEA General Conference: Archived Issue Brief, Warren H. Donnelly IB88072
* Libya's Nuclear Energy Situation: Archived Issue Brief, Mark Martel, etc. IB85079
* Persian Gulf: Iran Air Flight 655; Archived Issue Brief, Ellen Laipson IB88080
* Soviet Policy Toward Iran and the Strategic Balance in Southwest Asia, Stuart D. Goldman 87-592 F
* Syria: Background and Status, Alfred B. Prados 91-468 F

* Voting Rights to U.S. Citizens in Israeli Elections for Parliament, Law Library of Congress LL90-58
* Yemen, Kirk Campbell 91-540 F

Middle East -- Arab-Israeli Conflict

* Israeli-Arab Conflict: A Review of U.S. Policy Statements Regarding U.N. Security Council Resolution 242 and "Land and Peace", Carol Migdalovitz 91-376 F
* Israeli-Palestinian Conflict: Bibliography-in-Brief, 1982-1988, Robert S. Kirk 88-251 L
* Israeli-Palestinian Conflict: Info Pack, IP397I
* Middle East Military Balance, Clyde Mark 85-591 F
* Middle East Peace Proposals: Archived Issue Brief, Clyde Mark IB82127
* Palestine and the Palestinians: Issue Brief, Clyde Mark IB76048
* Palestinian Disturbances in the Gaza Strip and West Bank: Policy Issues and Chronology, Ellen Laipson 88-114 F

Middle East -- Arms Sales and Foreign Assistance

* Arab Economic Aid Donors and Recipients: Trends in Aid Flows to the Middle East/North Africa, 1973-1989, Larry Q. Nowels, etc. 91-476 F
* Arms Sales to Saudi Arabia: Current Status, Issue Brief, Richard F. Grimmett IB91007
* Arms Shipments to Iran: Archived Issue Brief, Richard M. Preece IB87022
* Arms Transfers to Iran Since 1979: Reports from the Media, Jonathan Medalia 86-187 F
* Arms Transfers to Saudi Arabia: Presidential Authority to Waive Legislative Restrictions, Richard F. Grimmett 90-393 F
* Background on Delivery of AWACS Aircraft to Saudi Arabia, Richard F. Grimmett 86-744 F
* Control of Arms Transfers to the Middle East, Audio Brief, Richard Grimmett AB50221
* Egyptian Military Debt Forgiveness: Costs, Implications, and the Role of Congress; Archived Issue Brief, Larry Q. Nowels, IB90137
* Egypt: U.S. Foreign Assistance Facts; Archived Issue Brief, Ellen B. Laipson IB85060
* Iran Arms Sales and Contra Funds: Summaries of Key Legislative Provisions, Clyde R. Mark, etc. 87-13 F
* Israel: U.S. Foreign Assistance Facts; Issue Brief, Clyde Mark IB85066
* Israel's Request for U.S. Loan Guarantees; Issue Brief, Larry Q. Nowels, etc. IB91103
* Jordan: U.S. Foreign Assistance Facts; Archived Issue Brief, Richard Preece IB85120
* Laws Implicated by Shipments of Military Materials to Iran, Raymond C. Celada 86-1005 A
* The Middle East and North Africa: U.S. Foreign Assistance in Fiscal Year 1990, 1991, and 1992, Carmen R. Graham Garland 91-834 F
* Middle East Arms Control and Related Issues, Foreign Affairs and National Defense Division 91-384 F
* Middle East Arms Supply: Recent Control Initiatives; Issue Brief, Alfred b. Prados IB91113
* Saudi Arabia Arms Sales, 1987: Archived Issue Brief, Clyde R. Mark, etc. IB87209
* Saudi Arabia: U.S. Missile Sale, 1986: Archived Issue Brief, Clyde Mark IB86068
* U.S. Foreign Assistance to the Middle East and North Africa: Fiscal Years

1988, 1989, and 1990, Clyde R. Mark 89-192 F

Middle East -- Iran-Iraq War

* Iran-Iraq War: Issue Brief, Richard M. Preece IB88060
* The NATO Allies, Japan, and the Persian Gulf, Paul Gallis 84-184 F
* Persian Gulf and the War Powers Debate: Issue Summary and Review of Events; Archived Issue Brief, Clyde R. Mark IB87207
* Persian Gulf: Iran Air Flight 655: Archived Issue Brief, Ellen Laipson IB88080
* Persian Gulf: Overview of Issue; Archived Issue Brief, Ellen B. Laipson IB87229
* Persian Gulf: Selected References, Sherry B. Shapiro 88-533 L
* United Nations Role in the Iran-Iraq War: Issues and Options, Lois B. McHugh, etc. 88-463 F

Middle-East -- Iraq-Kuwait

* The Army's Roundout Concept After the Persian Gulf War, Robert L. Goldich 91-763 F
* Chemical and Biological Weapons in the Persian Gulf Area: Health Effects and Protections, Michael M. Simpson 91-46 SPR
* Dellums v. Bush: President Bush's Authority to Initiate Offensive Operations in the Persian Gulf Challenged in the Courts by House Members and Law Professors, Raymond J. Celada 90-585 A
* German Foreign Policy After the Gulf War: Implications for U.S. Interests, Paul E. Gallis 91-451 F
* Iraq and Kuwait: Conflicting Historical Claims, Alfred B. Prados 91-34 F
* Iraq and Kuwait: Economic Profiles, Dario Scuka 90-399 E
* Iraq, Kuwait, and IEEPA, Raymond J. Celada 90-373 A
* Iraq-Kuwait Crisis: A Chronology of Events, July 17-March 3, 1991, Clyde R. Mark, etc. 91-14 F
* Iraq/Kuwait Crisis: A Summary of Foreign Support for Multinational Efforts in the Persian Gulf, Timothy D. Hoyt, 90-505 F
* Iraq/Kuwait Crisis: Congressional Action Through January 1991, Clyde R. Mark 91-156 F
* Iraq-Kuwait Crisis: Is Water a Weapon?, Carol Migdalovitz 91-105 F
* Iraq-Kuwait Crisis: Selected Administration Statements, August-December 15, 1990, Theodore J. Craig 91-13 F
* Iraq/Kuwait Crisis: The International Response and Burdensharing Issues; Archived Issue Brief, Gary J. Pagliano IB90131
* Iraq/Kuwait Crisis: U.S. Costs and Allied Financial Contributions, Stephen Daggett, etc. 90-640 F
* Iraq-Kuwait Crisis: U.S. Policy and Options; Archived Issue Brief, Alfred B. Prados, etc. IB90117
* Iraq-Kuwait: The United National Response Before the War, Archived Issue Brief, Marjorie Ann Brown IB90147
* Iraq-Kuwait: U.N. Security Council Resolutions: Texts and Votes, Marjorie Ann Browne 91-395 F
* The Iraqi Crisis: National Public Opinion Polls, Rosita M. Thomas 90-436 GOV
* Iraq's Food and Agricultural Situation During the Embargo and the War, Susan B. Epstein 91-199 ENR
* Iraq's Post-War Compliance Record: A Chronology, Kenneth Katzman 91-740 F
* Israel and the Persian Gulf Crisis, Clyde R. Mark 91-458 F
* Japan's Contributions in Support of the U.S.-Led Multinational Forces in the War Against Iraq, Richard P. Cronin 91-293 F
* Japan's Response to the Persian Gulf Crisis: Implications for U.S.-Japan Relations, Larry A. Niksch, etc. 91-444 F
* Jordan: Persian Gulf Crisis and U.S. Aid, Alfred B. Prados 91-247 F
* Kurdish Refugee Relief and Other Humanitarian Aid Issues in Iraq: Archived Issue Brief, Lois B. McHugh, etc. IB91072
* Kurdish Separatism in Iraq: Developments and Implications for the United States, Alfred B. Prados 91-397 F
* Kuwait: Background, Restoration, and Questions for the United States, Theodore Craig 91-288 F
* Kuwait Reconstruction: Sources of Information, Info Pack, Congressional Reference Division IP450K
* Military Geography of Iraq and Adjacent Arab Territory, John M. Collins 90-431 RCO
* Oil Supply and the Gulf Crisis: Current Status Report, Lawrence kumins 90-614 ENR
* Operation Desert Storm: An Assessment, Robert L. Goldich, etc. LTR91-873
* The Patriot Air Defense System and the Search for an Antitactical Ballistic Missile Defense, Steven A. Hildreth, etc. 91-456 F
* Persian Gulf Conflict: Post-War Issues for Congress, Archived Issue Brief,

Current Events and Homework

Raymond W. Copson IB90132
* Persian Gulf: Post-War Issues, Info Pack IP452P
* The Persian Gulf War and the Draft, Robert L. Goldich, 91-103 F
* Persian Gulf War: Defense-Policy Implications for Congress, Congressional Research Service, Ronald O'Rourke 91-421 F
* Persian Gulf War: Info Pack, Congressional Reference Division IP448P
* Persian Gulf War: International Implications; Archived Issue Brief, Alfred B. Prados, etc. IB91025
* Persian Gulf War: Iraqi Scud Ballistic Missile Systems, Warren W. Lenhart, etc. 91-173 F
* Persian Gulf War: Key U.S. Military Personnel and Compensation Questions, Archived Issue Brief, Robert L. Goldich IB90124
* The Persian Gulf War: Preliminary Foreign Policy "Lessons" and Perceptions, Mark M. Lowenthal 91-260 RCO
* Persian Gulf War Region: Basic Maps, Richard F. Grimmett 91-94 F
* Persian Gulf War: U.S. Costs and Allied Financial Contributions; Issue Brief, Stephen Daggett, etc. IB91019
* Persian Gulf War: U.S. Reserve Callup and Reliance on the Reserves, Issue Brief, Robert L. Goldich IB90144
* Persian Gulf War: Water Resources and the War; Selected References, Sherry B. Shapiro 91-169 L
* The Post-War Middle East: Significant Trends, Audio Brief, Alfred Prados AB50224
* Press Restrictions in the Persian Gulf War: First Amendment Implications, Henry Cohen 91-316 A
* Reparations, Raymond J. Celada 91-224 A

Middle East -- Petroleum

* Energy Security: Issue Brief, Carl E. Behrens IB89006
* The Financial Impact of Oil Price Behavior on International Development and Trade: Transnational Oil Companies and Persian Gulf Oil Exporters; Report, Clyde R. Mark, etc. 86-903 F
* Kuwaiti Oil Well Fires, Joseph P. Riva 91-313 SPR
* Oil from the Persian Gulf: Production, Disposition, and Transportation; Archived Issue Brief, Robert Bamberger, etc. IB88063
* Oil Imports from OPEC: Recent and Projected Trends, Bernard A. Gelb 88-558 E
* Persian Gulf Oil: Its Critical Importance to World Oil Supplies, Joseph P. Riva 91-220 SPR
* The Strategic Petroleum Reserve and the Drawdown Dilemma, Robert L. Bamberger, etc. 90-492 ENR
* The World's Conventional Oil Production Capability Projected into the Future by Country, Joseph P. Riva, Jr. 87-414 SPR

Middle East -- U.S. Concerns

* see also Iraq-Kuwait Crisis
* Agricultural Energy Use and the Iraqi Crisis, Ralph M. Chite 90-397 ENR
* Algeria in Crisis: Democracy, Islamism, and Implications for U.S. Policy, Carol Migdalovitz 91-591 F
* Ban on Imports from Iran: Economic Effect on the United States, Bernard A. Gelb 88-6 E
* Blockade: Some International and Domestic Legal Implications, Raymond J. Celada 90-386 A
* Disruption of Oil Supply from the Persian Gulf: Near-Term U.S. Vulnerability (Winter 1987/88), Clyde R. Mark, etc. 87-863 ENR
* Egypt's New Foreign Policy Activism: Considerations for the United States, Ellen Laipson 90-188 F
* Insuring U.S. Interests in the Persian Gulf: Summary and Proceedings of the Workshop Held on October, 6, 1987 by the Congressional Research Service, Gary J. Pagliano 88-725 F
* Iran After Khomeini: Implications for U.S.-Iranian Relations, Alfred B. Prados 90-132 F
* The Israeli Economy and Its External Economic Relations: An Overview, Patricia A. Wertman 91-690 E
* Israeli-United States Relations: Issue Brief, IB82008
* Israel's Interest in Nuclear Power: Implications for U.S. Non-Proliferation Policy; Archived Issue Brief, Mark Martel, etc. IB85166
* Issues in the Middle East: Audio Brief, Clyde Mark, etc. AB50177
* Jordan: Recent Developments and Implications for U.S. Interests, Ellen Laipson, etc. 90-354 F
* Lebanon: The Current Crisis, Issue Brief, Clyde R. Mark IB89118
* Lebanon: The Remaining U.S. Hostages; a Chronology, 1984-March 19, 1991, Clyde R. Mark 91-410 F
* Lebanon: The Remaining U.S. Hostages; Issue Brief, Clyde Mark IB85183
* Legal Status of United States Citizens in Iraq and Kuwait, David M. Ackerman 90-406 A

* Libya: U.S. Relations; Archived Issue Brief, Raymond Copson, etc. IB86040
* Oil and Iraq's Invasion of Kuwait: Archived Issue Brief, Carl Behrens, etc. IB90116
* Palestine Liberation Organization Offices in the United States, Clyde R. Mark 88-484 F
* Persian Gulf: U.S. Military Operations; Archived Issue Brief, Ronald O'Rourke IB87145
* Petroleum Status of the Western Persian Gulf, Joseph P. Riva 90-378 SPR
* United States Interests in Lebanon, John Creed 85-873 F
* United States-Iraqi Relations, Richard M. Preece 86-142 F
* U.S. and Allied Options Early in the Persian Gulf Crisis, John M. Collins 90-394 S
* U.S. Policy Toward Iran: 1979-1986, Richard M. Preece 87-974 F
* U.S., Soviet, and Western European Naval Forces in the Persian Gulf Region, Robert J. Ciarrocchi 87-956 F
* U.S.-Soviet Military Balance. Book VI. Far East, Middle East Assessments, John Collins, etc. 80-166 S

Midgetman (Missile)

* "Midgetman" Small ICBM (Weapon Acts): Archived Issue Brief, Jonathan Medalia, etc. IB84044

Migrant Labor

* see Labor

Military Assistance

* see Africa, Asia, Latin America, Middle East
* Arms Sales: U.S. Policy: Info Pack, IP214A
* Congressional Procedure for Considering Legislation Opposing Arms Sales, Richard Grimmett 86-63 F
* Conventional Arms Transfers to the Third World, 1983-1990, Richard f. Grimmett 91-578 F
* Current Issues With the "Base-Rights" Countries and Their Implications, Richard F. Grimmett 88-726 F
* Defense Articles and Services Supplied to Foreign Recipients: Legislative Restrictions on Their Use, Richard Grimmett 86-18 F
* Department of Defense Humanitarian Aid, Carol R. Kuntz, etc. 87-808 F
* EC 1992: Potential Implications for Arms Trade and Cooperation, Margaret Berry Edwards, 89-642 F
* Export-Import Bank: Financing Commercial Military Sales; Issue Brief, James K. Jackson, etc. IB91074
* Foreign Assistance and Defense Transactions and Their Direct Effect on the U.S. Balance of Payments: Summary of Statistical Data, 1960-1989, Vladimir N. Pregelj 90-572 E
* Greece and Turkey: The Seven-Ten Ratio in Military Aid, Ellen Laipson 90-29 F
* Leases of Defense Articles: Legislative Provisions and Restrictions, Richard F. Grimmett 90-392 F
* Lend-Lease: An Historic Overview and Repayment Issues, Patricia Wertman 85-844 E
* The Middle East and North Africa: U.S. Foreign Assistance in fiscal Year 1990, 1991, and 1992, Carmen R. Graham Garland 91-834 F
* Missile Proliferation: A Discussion of U.S. Objectives and Policy Options, Robert Shuey 90-120 F
* Missile Proliferation: Survey of Emerging Missile Forces, Foreign Affairs and National Defense Division 88-642 F
* Near East Arms Transfers, August 2, 1990-November 1, 1991, Alfred B. Prados, etc. 91-839 F
* An Overview of United States Military Assistance Programs, Richard F. Grimmett 88-282 F
* Pros and Cons of Military Intervention: Audio Brief, Foreign Affairs and National Defense Division AB50033
* The Seven-Ten Ratio in Military Aid to Greece and Turkey: A Congressional Tradition, Ellen Laipson 85-79 F
* Trends in Conventional Arms Transfers to the Third World by Major Supplier, 1980-1987, Richard F. Grimmett 88-352 F

Military Assistance -- Africa

* Angola: Issues for the United States; Archived Issue Brief, Raymond Copson, etc. IB81063
* Mozambique: U.S. Foreign Assistance Facts; Archived Issue Brief, Raymond Copson IB85114
* Sudan: U.S. Foreign Assistance Facts; Issue Brief, Ellen Laipson, etc. IB85065
* U.S. Foreign Assistance to the Middle East and North Africa: Fiscal Years 1988, 1989, and 1990, Clyde R. Mark 89-192 F

Military Assistance -- Asia

* Cambodia: U.S. Foreign Assistance Facts; Archived Issue Brief, Robert Sutter IB85153
* China-U.S. Cooperation: Military Sales, Government Programs, Multilateral Aid, and Private-Sector Activities, Kerry Dumbaugh, etc. 89-355 F
* Chinese Arms Sales to the Persian Gulf: A Fact Sheet, Robert G. Sutter 88-286 F
* Pakistan: U.S. Foreign Assistance Facts; Archived Issue Brief, Richard P. Cronin IB85112
* Pakistan's Request for the U.S. AWACS: Archived Issue Brief, Kerry B. Dumbaugh IB87188
* Philippines: U.S. Foreign Assistance Facts; Archived Issue Brief, Larry Niksch IB85077
* U.S. Arms Sales to China, Kerry Dumbaugh, etc. 85-138 F

Military Assistance -- Latin America

* Central America and U.S. Foreign Assistance: Issues for Congress; Issue Brief, Mark P. Sullivan IB84075
* Central America: U.S. Relations With Costa Rica, Guatemala, and Honduras; Info Pack, IP352C
* Chart of Unclassified Legislative Restrictions Regarding Support for Military or Paramilitary Operations in Nicaragua, 1982-1986, Larry Eig 87-222 A
* Compilation of Selected Laws Relating to the National Security Council, Arms Transfers, Intelligence Activities, Aid to the Contras, and Appropriations, American Law Division 86-1028 A
* El Salvador Aid: Congressional Action, 1981-1986, on President Reagan's Requests for Economic and Military Assistance for El Salvador, K. Larry Storrs 87-230 F
* El Salvador: U.S. Aid in 1987 and 1988, Archived Issue Brief, K. Larry Storrs IB85113
* El Salvador: U.S. Foreign Assistance Facts; Issue Brief, K. Larry Storrs, etc. IB85113
* Guatemala: Country Background Report, Maureen Taft-Morales 88-586 F
* Guatemala: U.S. Foreign Assistance Facts; Archived Issue Brief, Jonathan Sanford IB85100
* Honduras: U.S. Foreign Assistance Facts; Archived Issue Brief, Robert E. Sanchez IB85080
* Legislative Histories of Statutory Restrictions on Funding for Covert Assistance for Military or Paramilitary Operations in Nicaragua, FY 1983-1986, Larry M. Eig 87-538 A
* The Reagan Doctrine: U.S. Assistance to Anti-Marxist Guerrillas; Archived Issue Brief, Raymond W. Copson IB87005
* U.S. Bilateral Economic and Military Assistance to Latin America and the Caribbean: Fiscal Years 1946 to 1987, K. Larry Storrs 87-694 F

Military Assistance -- Middle East

* Arms Sales to Saudi Arabia: Current Status, Issue Brief, Richard F. Grimmett IB91007
* Arms Shipments to Iran: Archived Issue Brief, Richard M. Preece IB87022
* Arms Transfers to Iran Since 1979: Reports from the Media, Jonathan Medalia 86-187 F
* Arms Transfers to Saudi Arabia: Presidential Authority to Waive Legislative Restrictions, Richard F. Grimmett 90-393 F
* Background on Delivery of AWACS Aircraft to Saudi Arabia, Richard F. Grimmett 86-744 F
* Control of Arms Transfers to the Middle East, Audio Brief, Richard Grimmett AB50221
* Egypt: U.S. Foreign Assistance Facts; Archived Issue Brief, Ellen B. Laipson IB85060
* Egyptian Military Debt Forgiveness: Costs, Implications, and the Role of Congress; Archived Issue Brief, Larry Q. Nowels IB90137
* Iran Arms and Contra Funds: Selected Chronology of Events, 1979-1987, Richard M. Preece, etc. 86-190 F
* Israel: U.S. Foreign Assistance Facts; Issue Brief, Clyde Mark IB85066
* Jordan: U.S. Foreign Assistance Facts; Archived Issue Brief, Richard Preece IB85120
* Laws Implicated by Shipments of Military Material to Iran, Raymond J. Celada 86-1005 A
* Middle East Arms Supply: Recent Control Initiatives; Issue Brief, Alfred B. Prados IB91113
* Persian Gulf: Post-War Issues; Info Pack IP452P
* Saudi Arabia Arms Sales, 1987: Archived Issue Brief, Clyde R. Mark, etc. IB87209
* Saudi Arabia: U.S. Missile Sale, 1986; Archived Issue Brief, Clyde Mark IB86068

* U.S. Foreign Assistance to the Middle East and North Africa: Fiscal Years 1988, 1989, and 1990, Clyde R. Mark 89-192 F

Military Bases

* see National Defense--Military Bases

Military Pensions

* see Military Personnel--Pensions

Military Personnel

* see Pensions
* Acquired Immune Deficiency Syndrome and Military Manpower Policy: Issue Brief, David F. Burrelli IB87202
* Activation of Selected Reserves under Executive Order 12727 and Executive Order 12733 for Service in the Arabian Peninsula, Robert B. Burdette 90-563 A
* Civilian and Military Pilots: The Labor Market Relationship, John W. Fischer, etc. 86-28 E
* The Geneva Convention Relative to the Treatment of Prisoners of War, Larry M. Eig 91-122 A
* Legislation Would Be Required to Reinstate the Draft, Robert B. Burdette 91-168 A
* Military and Recreation Interests in American Lands; Selected References, Lisa B. Dovd 90-426 L
* Military Assignment and Separation Policies Based on Certain Family Considerations, Robert B. Burdette 91-101 A
* Military Health Care/CHAMPUS Management Initiatives, David F. Burrelli 91-420 F
* Military Manpower and Compensation: FY88 Budget Issues; Archived Issue Brief, Robert L. Goldich IB87081
* Military Manpower and Compensation: FY89 Budget Issues; Issue Brief, Robert L. Goldich IB88025
* Military Manpower and Compensation: FY90 Budget Issues; Issue Brief, Robert L. Goldich IB89024
* Military Medical Care Services: Questions and Answers; Issue Brief, David F. Burrelli IB87155
* Military Personnel Overseas Allowances: Issues and Legislation, David F. Burrelli 89-216 F
* Military Recruiting: Controversy Over the Use of Educational Credentials, David F. Burrelli 88-474 F
* National Guard Overseas Training Missions: An Issue for U.S. Military Manpower Policy, David F. Burrelli 86-181 F
* National Services: Info Pack, IP418N
* National Service: Selected References, Peter Giordano 89-165 L
* The New GI Bill: Recruiting and Retention, David F. Burrelli 87-652 F
* The Persian Gulf War and the Draft, Robert L. Goldich 91-103 F
* Persian Gulf War: U.S. Reserve Callup and Reliance on the Reserves; Issue Brief, Robert L. Goldich IB90144
* POWs and MIAs in Indochina and Korea: Status and Accounting Issues, Robert L. Goldich IB88061
* Prisoner of War/Missing in Action in SE Asia: Info Pack, IP127P
* Special Operations Forces: Issues for Congress, James Wooten 84-227 F
* Standby Draft Registration: Archived Issue Brief, David Burrelli IB82101
* State Income Taxation of Military Personnel and United States Citizens Residing Outside of the United States, Joyce Thorpe, etc. 87-706 A
* A Summary of the Military Selective Service Act as It Relates to Conscientious Objector Status, James W. Watson 91-329 A
* United Nations Peacekeeping: Historical Overview and Current Issues, Marjorie Ann Browne 90-96 F
* Vietnam-U.S. Relations: The Debate Over Normalization; Issue Brief, Robert G. Sutter IB87210
* Vietnam-U.S. Relations: The Missing-in-Action (MIAs) and the Impasse Over Cambodia; Issue Brief, Robert G. Sutter IB87210
* Women in the Armed Forces (With Appendix): Archived Issue Brief, Ellen Collier IB79045
* Women in the Military: Bibliography-in-Brief, Sherry B. Shapiro 91-408 L
* The 1990 Census: Including Foreign Based Military and Civilian Personnel in the State Counts, David C. Huckabee 90-305 GOV

Military Personnel -- Compensation and Pensions

* Benefits for Former Military Spouses: Info Pack, IP313B
* COLAs for Military Retirees: Summary of Congressional and Executive Branch Action Since 1982, Robert L. Goldich 91-7 F
* Comparison of Retirement Systems for Executive Branch Employees, Members of Congress and Active Duty Military Personnel, Carolyn Merck, etc. 85-685 EPW

Current Events and Homework

* Congressional Pay, Selected Wages and Pension, and Social Security: Compared to CPI, 1969-1989, Frederick H. Pauls, etc. 89-63 GOV
* Deductibility of Reservists' Transportation Expenses, Robert B. Burdette 91-603 A
* Federal Tax Treatment of Combat Pay, Robert B. Burdette 91-144 A
* Military Benefits for Former Spouses: Legislation and Policy Issues, David F. Burrelli 89-187 F
* Military Deployment and Family Policy: Archived Issue Brief, David F. Burrelli IB91100
* Military Manpower and Compensation: FY 1991 Budget Issues; Archived Issue Brief, Robert L. Goldich IB90039
* Military Manpower and Compensation: FY 1992 Budget Issues; Issue Brief, Robert L. GOldich IB91026
* Military Manpower and Compensation: FY 89 Budget Issues; Archived Issue Brief, Robert L. Goldich IB88025
* Military Manpower and Compensation: FY 90 Budget Issues; Archived Issue Brief, Robert L. Goldich IB89024
* Military Medical Care Services: Questions and Answers; Archived Issue Brief, David F. Burrelli IB87155
* Military Personnel Overseas Allowances: Issues and Legislation, David F. Burrelli 89-216 F
* Military Retirement: Major Legislative Issues; Issue Brief, Robert Goldich IB85159
* The Military Retirement Reform Act of 1986: Issues and Implications, Robert L Goldich 87-702 F
* The Military Survivor Benefit Plan: A Description of Its Provisions, David F. Burrelli 89-186 F
* The New GI Bill: Recruiting and Retention, David F. Burrelli 87-652 F
* Persian Gulf War: Key U.S. Military Personnel and Compensation Questions; Archived Issue Brief, Robert L. Goldich IB90124
* State Income Taxation of Military Personnel and United States Citizens Residing Outside of the United States, John Luckey 91-590 A
* A SUmmary of the Soldiers' and Sailors' Civil Relief Act, as Amended, Robert B. Burdette 91-342 A
* Treatment of Former Spouses under Various Federal Retirement Systems, Marie B. Morris 88-512 A

Military Retirement

* see Military Personnel--Compensation and Pensions

Milliken v. Michigan Road Builders Assn.

* United States Supreme Court Actions Regarding Minority Business Set-Asides After City of Richard v. J.A. Croson Co., Charles V. Dale 89-202 A

Minerals and Materials

* see National Defense--Strategic Stockpiles
* Acid Rain Legislation and the Domestic Aluminum Industry, Marc Humphries, etc. 89-327 ENR
* Antarctic Mineral Resources Regime: Diplomacy and Development; Archived Issue Brief, James E. Mielke, etc. IB88101
* Antarctica: Environmental Protection Issues: Summary of a CRS Research Workshop, Susan R. Fletcher 89-272 ENR
* Asbestos in Buildings: Activity in the 100th Congress, Claudia Copeland 89-267 ENR
* Asbestos in Buildings: Current Issues; Archived Issue Brief, Claudia Copeland IB86084
* Economic Conditions of the U.S. Tungsten Industry, Bernard A. Gelb 86-964 E
* The Federal Royalty and Tax Treatment of the Hard Rock Minerals Industry: An Economic Analysis, Salvatore Lazzari 90-493 E
* Federal Spending on Materials Research and Development: FY 1990-FY 1992, John D. Moteff, etc. 91-389 SPR
* Hard Minerals in the U.S. Exclusive Economic Zone:, Resource Assessments and Expectations. Part I--Sand and Gravel, Placers, and Phosphorite, James E. Mielke 87-885 SPR
* Hard Minerals in the U.S. Exclusive Zone: Resource, Assessments and Expectations. Part II--Ferromanganese Modules, Cobalt-Manganese Crusts, and Polymet, James E. Mielke 87-975 SPR
* International Mineral Market Control and Stabilization: Historical Perspectives, John Schanz, etc. 86-601 S
* Materials Availability: A Cause for Concern?, Leonard Kruger, etc. 83-171 SPR
* Mineral Development in Yugoslavia, Marc Humphries 88-688 ENR
* The National Defense Stockpile: Department of Defense Policy and Management, Alfred R. Greenwood 91-481 ENR

* National Defense Stockpile Requirements: A Review of the Secretary of Defense's Report to Congress, Alfred R. Greenwood
* National Forest Receipts: Sources and Dispositions, Ross W. Gorte 89-284 ENR
* Potential Mineral Resources in Antarctica and the Antarctic Minerals Convention, James E. Mielke 90-72 SPR
* The Rural Abandoned Mine Program: A Brief Background, Duane A. Thompson 87-105 ENR
* Selected Nonferrous Mineral Subsidies and the U.S.-Canada Free Trade Agreement, Mark Humphries 88-774 ENR
* Strategic and Critical Materials Policy: Research and Development: Archived Issue Brief, Leonard Kruger IB74094
* The Subsidization of Non-Fuel Mineral Production at Home and Abroad, John J. Schanz, Jr. 87-62 S
* Uranium Enrichment Issues; Issue Brief, Marc Humphries IB90151
* The U.S. Uranium Industry: Changing Prospects and the Federal Role; Issue Brief, Barbara B. Black IB89079
* The 1872 Mining Law: Time for Reform?, Issue Brief, Marc Humphries IB89130

Minimum Wages

* see Labor--Minimum Wages

Minorities

* see Hispanics, Blacks, Civil Liberties and Rights--Discrimination and Integration, Equal Employment Opportunity, Indians, Women
* Armenian Population by State, 1980, Jennifer D. Williams 86-853 GOV
* Bilingual Education: Recent Evaluations of Local School Districts Programs and Related Research on Second-Language Learning, Rick Holland 86-611 EPW
* Comparative Quality of Rental Housing Obtained by Whites, Blacks, and Hispanics, Grace Milgram 87-626 E
* Czechoslovak Population by State, 1980, Jennifer D. Williams 86-837 GOV
* Federal Education Programs Serving Limited English Proficient Students, Ruby Ann M. Esquibel 89-285 EPW
* .Federal Programs for Minority and Women-Owned Businesses, Mark Eddy 89-278 GOV
* Financing Postsecondary Education Attendance: Current Issues Involving Access and Choice, James B. Stedman 88-315 EPW
* Greek Population by State and Congressional District, Jennifer Williams 85-827 GOV
* Hispanic Children in Poverty, Vee Burke, etc. 85-170 EPW
* Hispanic Population in 99th Congress Districts, David Huckabee 85-763 GOV
* Housing Conditions of Hispanic Americans, Susan M. Vanhorenbeck 85-952 E
* Immigration, Ethnic Groups and Nationalities: An Alphabetical Microthesaurus of Terms Selected from the Legislative Indexing Vocabulary, Shirley Loo 91-670 L
* The Indian Community in the United States, Margaret Siciliano 84-792 F
* Issues in the 100th Congress of Special Interest to Hispanics: An Overview of Major Issues Identified by the Congressional Hispanic Caucus, Jennifer D. Williams 87-755 GOV
* Lithuanian Population by State, 1980, Jennifer Williams 87-71 GOV
* Minority Business Set-Asides and the Constitution:, A Legal Analysis of the U.S. Supreme Court Ruling in City of Richmond v. J.A. Croson Co., Charles V. Dale 89-124 A
* Minority Enrollment Trends in Higher Education, James B. Stedman 91-460 EPW
* Minority Ownership of Broadcast Facilities: A Summary of Federal Communications Commission's Policies and Rules, Bernevia M. McCalip 87-273 E
* Redress for Japanese Americans under the Civil Liberties Act of 1988: Questions and Answers, James Sayler 90-488 GOV
* Selected Demographic Characteristics of the U.S. Hispanic Population and of Hispanic Subgroups, Jennifer Williams 86-536 GOV
* States Designating English as the Official State Language, Mark Gurevitz 91-104 A
* Turkish Population by State, Jennifer Williams 85-1067 GOV
* Underrepresented Minorities and Women in Science, Mathematics, and Engineering: Problems and Issues for the 1990s, Christine M. Matthews 91-26 SPR
* United States Supreme Court Actions Regarding Minority Business Set-Asides After City of Richmond v. J.A. Croson Co., Charles V. Dale 89-202 A
* The U.S. Asian Population, by Census Division, State, and Congressional

District, Jennifer D. Williams 86-771 GOV
* The U.S. Filipino Population, by Congressional District, Jennifer D. Williams 86-760 GOV
* The U.S. Hispanic Population Living in Counties Located Within 100, 150, and 200 Miles of the Mexican Border, Jennifer D. Williams 87-146 GOV
* Voting Rights Act: A Checklist of CRS Products, George Walser 92-15 L
* Workforce Diversity in the 1990s: Bibliography-in-Brief, 1988-1991, Robert Howe 91-387 L
* Yugoslavia's Kosovo Crisis: Ethnic Conflict Between Albanians and Serbs, Steven J. Woehrel 89-603 F

Minorities -- Hispanics

* Hispanic Heritage in the United States: Tradition, Achievement, and Aspiration, Thomas H. Neale 89-532 GOV
* Hispanic Heritage: Selected References, M. Alexandra Salinas 91-615 L
* U.S. Hispanics: A Demographic Profile, Jennifer D. Williams 89-469 GOV

Minority Business Set Asides

* see Minorities

Minority Issues

* American Indian Budget Issues: 101st Congress, IB89046
* Navajo-Hopi Relocation, IB86021
* Selected Women's Issues in the 101st Congress, IB89104

Minority Preference in Telecommunication

* see Minorities

Miranda Decision

* see Criminal Procedure

Missing in Action

* see Military Personnel

Mississippi Power & Light Co. v. Mississippi Ex Re

* State Versus Federal Ratemaking Authority: Mississippi Power & Light Co. v. Mississippi Ex Rel. Moore., Robin Jeweler 88-651 A

Mississippi River

* Legal Issues Related to Diversion of Water from Lake Michigan to the Mississippi River, Pamela Baldwin 88-585 A

Moldova

* see also U.S.S.R.
* Moldova Republic: Basic Facts, Sergiu Verona 91-779 F

Monetary Policy

* see Money and Banking--Monetary Policy

Money and Banking

* see Failures and Deposit Insurance, Financial Institutions, Interest Rates, Law and Regulation, Monetary Policy
* Capital Sources for U.S. Corporations With Particular Reference to Public Issues, Julius W. Allen 86-165 E
* The Citicorp Initiative: A Brave New World for the Third World Debt Problem, Patricia A. Wertman 87-750 E
* Common Legal Questions and Answers Concerning Currency, Legal Tender and Money, 83-150 A
* Debit Cards: Background and Public Policy Issues, Pauline Smale 84-120 E
* Farmer Mac and the Agricultural Secondary Market, Ralph Chite 89-246 ENR
* Foreign Ownership of U.S. Assets: Past, Present, and Prospects, James K. Jackson, etc. 88-295 E
* Gold Use, Production, and Trade: A Profile, Bernard A. Gelb 88-613 E
* Individual Retirement Accounts and Financial Savings: New Evidence, William Jackson 86-125 E
* Money and Banking: An Alphabetical Microthesaurus of Terms Selected from the Legislative Indexing Vocabulary, Shirley Loo 88-530 L
* Money and Near-Monies: A Primer, John B. Henderson 83-125 E
* A New U.S. Dollar Coin, Pauline Smale 88-75 E
* Redesign of the U.S. Currency, Pauline Smale 87-301 E
* The Role of Gold in the International Monetary System, Arlene Wilson 80-47 E
* Tax-Favored Savings: All Savers Certificates and Individual Retirement

Accounts, William Jackson 85-168 E
* U.S. Tax Treatment of Bad Foreign Loans, David L. Brumbaugh 89-302 E

Money and Banking -- Failures and Deposit Insurance

* Bank and Thrift Financial Problems, the Credit Crunch, and Lending to the Building Industry, Barbara L. Miles, etc. 91-417 E
* Bank Bailouts: Open-Bank Assistance by the Federal Deposit Insurance Corporation, William Jackson 86-1041 E
* Bank Failures: Recent Trends and Policy Options; Archived Issue Brief, Pauline Smale IB86148
* Banks and Savings Institutions: Employment Trends, Linda Levine 91-703 E
* Banks and Thrift Institutions: Restructuring and Solvency Issues, F. Jean Wells 88-749 E
* Banks and Thrifts: Restructuring and Solvency; Issue Brief, F. Jean Wells IB89002
* Banks and Thrifts: Restructuring and Solvency 1990; Archived Issue Brief, F. Jean Wells IB90002
* Banks, Savings and Loan Associations, and Their Federal Deposit Insurance Funds: A Financial Analysis, William Jackson 83-82 E
* Deposit Guarantees in Other Countries, G. Thomas Woodward 89-637 E
* Deposit Insurance Reform: Evaluating the Proposals, G. Thomas Woodward 90-403 E
* Depository Financial Institution Failures: The 1980s Experience, Pauline H. Smale 88-549 E
* Depository Institutions: Government Actions Since FIRREA, F. Jean Wells 90-377 E
* The Economics of Deposit Insurance, G. Thomas Woodward 89-32 E
* Federal Bank Regulators' Positions on 1980 Deposit Insurance Increase to $100,000, M. Maureen Murphy 90-447 A
* Federal Deposit Insurance Corporation (FDIC) Pass-Through Insurance for Pension Plans, Ray Schmitt, etc. 91-411 EPW
* Federal Deposit Insurance Coverage of Public Funds, F. Jean Wells 87-517 E
* Federal Deposit Insurance Funds: An Overview of FDIC and FSLIC Finances, William Jackson 87-2 E
* Federal Deposit Insurance Funds and Regulatory Agencies: Merger and Consolidation Issues, F. Jean Wells 88-279 E
* The Federal Deposit Insurance Funds: Their Financial Condition and Public Policy Proposals in the 100th Congress; Archived Issue Brief, F. Jean Wells IB88082
* The Federal Deposit Insurance Mechanism: Recent Economic Literature, F. Jean Wells 85-65 E
* The Federal Regulation of Depository Institutions:, A Brief Overview, Maureen Murphy 87-511 E
* Federal Regulation of the Savings and Loan Industry: Legal Framework, Michael V. Seitzinger 88-734 A
* Federal Savings and Loan Insurance Corporation: Current Estimates of Future Costs of Resolving "Problem-Institution" Cases, Jean Wells 88-520 E
* Federal Savings and Loan Insurance Corporation Recapitalization Act of 1986: A Brief Explanation and Analysis, F. Jean Wells 86-728 E
* Federal Savings and Loan Insurance Corporation: Recapitalization and Alternatives; Archived Issue Brief, F. Jean Wells IB87027
* Federal Savings and Loan Insurance Corporation: Studies for the 101st Congress, F. Jean Wells 88-672 E
* Financial Crises of the 1970s and 1980s: Causes, Developments, and Government Responses, William Jackson, etc. 89-290 E
* The FSLIC Issue: A Status Report, F. Jean Wells 89-77 E
* FSLIC Policy Options, F. Jean Wells 89-56 E
* FSLIC, the Budget, and the Economy, G. Thomas Woodward 89-17 E
* Origins and Development of the Savings and Loan Situation, G. Thomas Woodward 90-522 E
* Public Rescue of Private Liabilities: The Continental Illinois Case, William Jackson 85-172 E
* Resolution Trust Corporation: Its Organization for Management Decision-Making, F. Jean Wells 91-711 E
* Restructuring the Savings and Loan Industry: Bibliography-in-Brief, 1986-1989, Robert Howe 89-162 L
* S&L Problems and FSLIC; Info Pack, IP415S
* The Savings and Loan Cleanup: Background and Progress; Issue Brief, Barbara Miles, etc. IB91070
* The "Savings and Loan Cleanup": Federal Regulatory Arrangements and Proposals for Change, F. Jean Wells 91-810 E

Money and Banking -- Financial Institutions

* Automated Teller Machine (ATM) Security: State and Federal Legislation, LaVonne M. Grabiak, etc. 87-375 A

Current Events and Homework

* Bank Diversification: Into Real Estate?, William Jackson 88-648 E
* Bank Holding Companies, William Jackson 84-76 E
* The Bank Holding Company Act: Background, Summary, and Analysis, William Jackson, etc. 86-26 A
* Bank and Securities: An Overview of Their Workforces, Linda LeGrande 88-35 E
* Banking: A Brief Profile of Its History and Structure, F. Jean Wells, etc. 91-259 E
* Banking Fees and Service Charges, Pauline H. Smale 86-39 E
* Banking in "Europe 1992", William Jackson 89-456 E
* Banking in the United States: An Overview; Info Pack. IP429B
* Banks, Savings and Loan Associations, and Their Federal Deposit Insurance Funds: A Financial Analysis William Jackson 83-82 E
* Banks and Thrifts in Transition: Issue Brief, F. Jean Wells IB91003
* The Conservation Reserve: A Status Report, Jeffrey Zinn 88-716 ENR
* Corporate Ownership of Banks and Savings Institutions, and Interstate Banking: Selected Listings, F. Jean Wells 84-105 E
* Deregulation or Re-Regulation of Financial Services? Activities of the Depository Institutions Deregulation Committee, 1980-82, William Jackson 83-87 E
* Electronic Fund Transfers: Regulation of Paperless-Entry Transactions, Including Automatic Payroll Deposits, M. Maureen Murphy 89-62 A
* Financial Institutions: Problems and Prospects; Info Pack, IP291F
* Foreign Banking in America, William Jackson, 91-472 E
* Foreign Banking in the U.S.: Issue Brief, William Jackson IB87104
* Forum: Banks and Thrifts--Restructuring and Solvency, Congressional Research Service review, REV 10-89
* International Banking Facilities and the Eurocurrency Market, William Jackson, etc. 82-27 E
* International Lending Patterns of U.S. Banks: Financial and Regulatory Trends, William Jackson 85-124 E
* Letter-of-Credit Enhancement of Commercial Paper Issues: A Case Study in the Competitiveness of U.S. Banks, Patricia A. Waterman, 91-147 E
* Merchant Banking: Opportunities of Problems in U.S. Banks?, Walter Eubanks, etc. 87-351 E
* P.L. 97-320, Garn-St. Germain Depository Institutions Act of 1982: A Brief Explanation, F. Jean Wells 82-177 E
* Proposed Federal Taxation of Credit Unions: A Pro/Con Analysis, James M. Bickley 86-84 E
* Should Credit Unions Be Taxed: Issue Brief, James M. Bickley 90-498 E
* The Soviet Banking Revolution: Its Realization and Implications for Congress, Walter W. Eubanks, 91-256 E
* The Unbanked Sector: Some Economic Issues, Ngina Chiteji, 91-610 E
* U.S. Bank Exposure in the Seventeen Highly Indebted Countries: 1982-1987, Patricia A. Wertman, etc. 88-522 E
* U.S. Banks and the People's Republic of China, Walter W. Eubanks 84-840 E
* U.S. Banks in the Global Economy: Effects of Capital, Tax and Regulatory Requirements, Walter W. Eubanks, etc., 90-293 E

Money and Banking -- Interest Rates

* Capital, Credit, and Crowding Out: Cycles and Trends in Flows of Funds Over Three Decades, William Jackson 82-142 E
* Crowding Out? Federal, State and Local Government Borrowing and the Debt Economy, William Jackson 87-274 E
* Do Deficits Influence the Level of Interest Rates?, G. Thomas Woodward 85-14 E
* An Economic Analysis and Brief Legislative Overview of Usury Ceilings, William Anderson 81-172 E
* Financial Deregulation: Relaxing Ceilings on Deposit Interest Rates, 1978-1980, William Jackson 81-176 E
* Government Actions that Affect Interest Rates: Mechanisms and Macroeconomic Repercussions, Craig Elwell 82-128 E
* High Interest Rates: Causes, Consequences, and Issues, Thomas F. Dernburg 84-53 E
* Hypothetical Effects of Lower Interest Rates on the Costs of Production of the Integrated Steel Industry David J. Cantor 85-738 E
* Interests Rates on Consumer and Commercial Loans: Why the Difference?, Helen J. Scott 85-818 E
* A National Interest Rate Ceiling for the U.S. Economy?, Jonathan Henderson, etc. 82-57 E
* Rising Interest Rates and the Economic Expansions:, Can They Co-Exist?, Craig K. Elwell 84-818 E
* Saving and Rate of Return Incentives: Estimates of the Interest Elasticity of Personal Saving, William Jackson 81-198 E

Money and Banking -- Law and Regulation

* see Glass-Steagall Act
* Bank Service Diversification: A Comparative Summary of Major Financial Reform Measures Facing the Congress, William Jackson, etc. 88-84 E
* Bank Soundness in Light of the Tax Reform Act of 1986 and Possible Glass-Steagall Act Repeal, Walter W. Eubanks 88-118 E
* Bank-Broker Competition and the Glass-Steagall Act:, The Mutual Funds Example, William Jackson 87-921 E
* Banking Acts: Major Federal Legislation Since the American Revon Necessary? Issue Brief, Mary Jane Bolle IB86150

Money and Banking -- Law and Regulation

* see also Glass-Steagall Act
* The Bank Holding Company Act: Background, Summary, and Analysis, William Jackson, etc. 86-26 A
* Bank of Credit and Commerce International (BCCI): Some Legal Implications, M. Maureen Murphy, 91-652 A
* Bank Regulatory Agency Restructuring under Expanded Powers: Some Alternatives, F. Jean Wells, 90-552 E
* Bank Sales of Insurance: Issue Brief, Jean K. Rosales, etc., IB89157
* Bank Service Diversification: Policy Issues for the 1990's, William Jackson, 90-534 E
* Banking Acts: Major Federal Legislation Since the American Revolution, William Jackson, 86-4 E
* Banking Systems in the United States, Japan and the European Community: Comparative Studies, F.Jean Wells 90-357 E
* BCCI: Bibliography-in-Brief, Karen L. Alderson, 91-676 L
* BCCI: Key Events, Companies, Individuals, and Selected Articles, Paul Janov 91-640 C
* The Community Reinvestment Act After FIRREA, M. Maureen Murphy, 91-754 A
* Deposit-Taking Institutions: Their Federal Regulatory Structure, F. Jean Wells, etc. 91-286 E
* Edge Act International Banking Corporations, William Jackson, 91-459 E
* Expansion of Bank Industry Insurance Powers Through Bank Subsidiaries of Bank Holding Companies, M. Maureen Murphy, 90-130 A
* Expansion of Bank Powers Since CEBA, the Competitive Equality Banking Act of 1987, M. Maureen Murphy 89-666 A
* Financial Deregulation: A Status Report, F. Jean Wells, 87-800 E
* Financial Services Holding Companies: Diversified Interstate Bankers?, William Jackson 91-470 E
* FIRREA: The Financial Institutions Reform, Recovery, and Enforcement Act of 1989: A Summary, M. Maureen Murphy 89-503 A
* Forum Banks and Thrifts in Transition, by Congressional Research Service, REV 5-91
* Geographic Expansion of Banks: Restricting Bank Growth Across State Lines and Within States, M. Maureen Murphy, 91-119 A
* Glass-Steagall Act: Should Bankers Be Brokers? Issue Brief, William D. Jackson, IB91038
* Glass-Steagall Act: The Legal Landscape of Financial Restructuring, M. Maureen Murphy, 88-335
* Glossary on Banking Reforms: Issues Pending in the 102nd Congress, F. Jean Wells, 91-678 E
* Money Laundering: Federal Law and Current Legislative Proposals, M. Maureen Murphy, 90-157 A
* Multinational Bank Supervision, Walter W. Eubanks, 91-768 E
* Permissible Securities Investments for Banks and Thrifts, M. Maureen Murphy, 87-886 A
* Reserve Requirements, Capital Standards, and Credit Expansion, G. Thomas Woodward, 91-446 E
* Risk Based Bank Capital, Walter W. Eubanks, etc. 91-617 E
* Savings Institutions and Their Regulatory Environment under P.L. 101-73, F. Jean Wells, 90-136 E

Money and Banking -- Monetary Policy

* Budget Deficits and Monetary Policy, Carol Leisenring 81-128 E
* Domestic and International Monetary-Fiscal Policy Coordination, Thomas F. Dernburg 84-145 E
* The Economics of Federal Reserve Independence, G. Thomas Woodward, 90-118 E
* The Federal Advisory Council: Bankers Recommending Policies to the Federal Reserve, William Jackson, 90-625 E
* Federal Reserve: Development and Responsiveness to Government, William Jackson, 89-636 E
* The Federal Reserve Discount Rate: Its Significance in Monetary Policy, G. Thomas Woodward 87-17 E

* Federal Reserve Financing, William Jackson, 91-746 E
* Federal Reserve System: Accountability and Independence, Issue Brief, F. Jean Wells, IB89146
* Federal Reserve System: Info Pack, IP105F
* Membership of the Board of Governors of the Federal Reserve System, December 1913-October 1986, Roger S. White, etc. 86-985 E
* Monetarist and Keynesian Worlds--What's the Difference?, Helen J. Scott 84-181 E
* Monetary Policy: Current Policy and Conditions; Issue Brief, Gail E. Makinen, IB91110
* Monetary Policy: Basic Principles, Current Conditions, and Prospects, G. Thomas Woodward 88-255 E
* Monetary Policy: Current Policy and Conditional; Archived Issue Brief, G. Thomas Woodward IB87113
* The Targeting of Monetary Policy: Money Supply Growth or Interest Rates?, Gail E. Makinen 86-596 E
* Targets for Monetary Policy, G. Thomas Woodward 88-256 E
* U.S. Economic Policy in an International Context: Deficits, Taxes, and Monetary Policy, Jane G. Gravelle, etc. 84-125 E
* U.S. Monetary Policy, the Economy and the Foreign Exchange Value of the Dollar, 1960-1986, Helen J. Scott 86-109 E

Monroe Doctrine

* The Monroe Doctrine and U.S. Policy Options for the Western Hemisphere, Raphael Perl 84-225 F

Mortgages

* see Housing--Finance

Most Favored Nation Trade Policies

* see Foreign Trade--East-West, Foreign Trade--Trade Policy

Mozambique

* Mozambique: Conflict Assessment/U.S. Policy, Raymond W. Copson 88-516 F
* Mozambique: U.S. Foreign Assistance Facts; Archived Issue Brief, Raymond Copson IB85114
* Southern Africa: U.S. Regional Policy at a Crossroads?, Raymond Copson 85-201 F

Multilateral Development Banks

* see International Finance--Multilateral Development Banks

Multinational Corporations

* see International Corporations

Mutual Balanced Force Reduction Talks

* Conventional Arms Control in Europe: Prospects for Accord: Issue Brief, Stanley Sloan IB86064
* East-West Conventional Force Reduction Negotiations: Bibliography-in-Brief, 1980-1987, Valentin Leskovsek 87-313 L

Namibia

* Angola/Namibia Negotiations: Issue Brief, Brenda M. Branaman IB89047
* Angola/Namibia Peace Prospects: Background, Current Problems, and Chronology, Raymond W. Copson 88-559 F
* Namibia Chronology: February 1986 Through April 1987, Raymond W. Copson, etc. 87-353 F
* Namibia: United Nations Negotiations for Independence/U.S. Interests; Archived Issue Brief, Brenda Branaman IB79073
* Southern Africa: U.S. Regional Policy at a Crossroads?, Raymond Copson 85-201 F
* The United States and Southern Africa: A Review of United Nations Resolutions and United States Voting Patterns, 1946-October 1985, Frankie King 86-21 F

Narcotics

* see Drug Abuse, Drugs

National Ambient Air Quality Standards (NAAQS)

* Ozone and Carbon Monoxide Non-attainment: An Analysis of Title I of S. 1894, Mira Courpas 88-316 ENR
* Ozone and Carbon Monoxide Non-attainment: An Analysis of Title I of the Proposed Clean Air Standards Attainment Act, David E. Gushee 87-751 S
* Ozone/Carbon Monoxide Non-attainment: Is It What It Seems to Be?, David E. Gushee 88-148 S

National Credit Union Share Insurance Fund

* see Money and Banking--Failures and Deposit Insurance
* Depository Financial Institution Failures: The 1980s Experience, Pauline H. Smale 88-549 E
* Federal Deposit Insurance Funds and Regulatory Agencies: Merger and Consolidation Issues, F. Jean Wells 88-279 E
* The Federal Deposit Insurance Funds: Their Financial Condition and Public Policy Proposals in the 100th Congress; Archived Issue Brief, F. Jean Wells IB88082

National Debt

* see Public Finance--Deficits

National Defense

* see Military Balance, Military Bases, Strategic Stockpiles, Arms Control, Defense Economics, Internal Security, Military Assistance, Military Personnel, Weapons Systems
* Arms and Arms Control: An Alphabetical Microthesaurus of Terms Selected from the Legislative Indexing Vocabulary, Shirley Loo 87-961 L
* B-2 Strategic Bomber: Issue Brief, Dagnija Sterste-Perkins, IB90156
* The Bush Administration's Proposal for ICBM Modernization, SDI, and the B-2 Bomber, Jonathan Medalia 89-281 F
* Case Studies of Counter-Insurgencies, Larry Niksch 85-60 F
* Chemical-Biological Warfare: Bibliography-in-Brief, 1985-1988, Valentin Leskovsek 88-605 L
* The Clandestine Trade in Heavy Water: A Chronology, Barbara B. Black, etc. 89-66 ENR
* Classified Information Procedures Act (CIPA): An Overview, Larry M. Eig 89-172 A
* The Commercial Implications of Exporting and Importing Military Technology, A Review of the Issues, John D. Moteff, 90-409 SPR
* Countries of the World: Sources of Information, Margaret E. Melun, 91-645 C
* The Defense Department's Drug Law Enforcement and Narcotics Interdiction Responsibilities: A Comparison of House and Senate Amendments in the Defense, Roy Surrett 88-406 F
* Defense Basic Research Priorities: Funding and Policy Issues, Genevieve J. Knezo, 90-506 SPR
* Defense Laboratories: Proposals for Closure and Consolidation, Michael E. Davey, 91-135 SPR
* Defense-Related Independent Research and Development in Industry, Joan Winston 85-205 S
* The Defense Spending Dilemma: Audio Brief, Daniel Lockwood, etc. AB50181
* Defense Technology and Industrial Base: Bibliography-in-Brief, Karen L. Alderson 89-145 L
* DOD's Federally Funded Research and Development Centers, Michael E. Davey, 91-378 SPR
* Department of Defense Organization: Current Legislative Issues; Archived Issue Brief, Robert Goldich IB86036
* FSX Fighter Agreement With Japan: Issue Brief, Richard F. Grimmett IB89060
* FSX Technology: Its Relative Utility to the United States and Japanese Aerospace Industries, John D. Moteff 89-237 SPR
* The Ground Wave Emergency Network, Gary K. Reynolds 89-206 F
* Honduras: U.S. Military Activities; Issue Brief, James Wootten IB84134
* Instances of Use of United States Armed Forces Abroad, 1789-1989, Ellen C. Collier, 89-651 F
* Insurgency and Counterinsurgency in the Philippines, Larry Niksch 85-1038 F
* Leveraging DOD's R&D Investment, Acquiring External Technology, John D. Moteff, 91-102 SPR
* Managing Defense Department Technology Base Programs, Michael E. Davey 88-310 SPR
* Military Research and Development: Implications for Civilian Science and the Economy; Bibliography-in-Brief, 1982-1986, Virginia MacEwen 87-59 L
* Military Strategy: Bibliography-in-Brief, 1983-1986, Valentin Leskovsek 87-40 L
* Narcotics Interdiction and the Use of the Military: Bibliography-in-Brief, 1982-1988, Sherry B. Shapiro 88-408 L
* National Defense and Military Operations: An Alphabetical Microthesaurus of Terms Selected from the Legislative Indexing Vocabulary, Shirley Loo 91-496 L
* National Defense Stockpile Requirements: A Review of the Secretary of

Current Events and Homework

Defense's Report to Congress, Alfred R. Greenwood, 89-474 ENR
* The National Security Council: Organizational History, Mark Lowenthal 78-104 F
* NATO at 40: Bibliography Resources, Sherry B. Shapiro 89-175 L
* NATO Burdensharing: An Analysis of Major Legislation in the 100th Congress, Christopher C. Bolkcom 88-772 F
* Nuclear Escalation, Strategic Anti-Submarine Warfare, and the Navy's Forward Maritime Strategy, Ronald O'Rourke 87-138 F
* Nuclear Weapons Material Production: Options for Meeting Tritium and Plutonium Needs; Archived Issue Brief, David W. Cheney, etc. IB88099
* Planning Managing, and Funding DOD's Technology Base Programs, Michael E. Davey 89-319 SPR
* The President's Powers in Time of War: A Brief Overview, David M. Ackerman, 91-95 A
* Pros and Cons of Military Intervention: Audio Brief, Foreign Affairs and National Defense Division AB50033
* Review of U.S. Research and Development Programs in Ballistic Missile Defense, John D. Moteff 89-150 SPR
* The Rise and Fall of Nations: Is America in Decline?; a Bibliography of Points of View, Robert S. Kirk 89-214 L
* The Role of the U.S. Military in Narcotics Interdiction: Audio Brief, Raphael Perl AB50171
* Science and Engineering Education: The Role of the Department of Defense, Christine M. Matthews 89-256 SPR
* Sectional Analysis of the "War Powers Resolution" (WPR) as It Would Be Amended by the "War Powers Resolution Amendments of 1988" (S.J. Res. 323, 100th, Raymond J. Celada 88-441 A
* Special Operations and Low-Intensity Conflict: U.S. Process and Problem; Archived Issue Brief, Jim Nichol, IB90091
* The Strategic Defense Initiative: Program Description and Major Issues, John D. Moteff 88-721 SPR
* Strategic Policy at a Crossroads: Critical Choices, and Policy Dilemmas Facing the United States Today, Amy F. Woolf, etc. 89-210 F
* Suspension of Budget Enforcement Procedures in the Event of a Declaration of War, Robert Keith, 91-98 GOV
* U.S. Defense Planning: A Critique, John Collins, etc. 82-167 S
* Use of the Military to Enforce Civilian Law: Posse Comitatus Act and Other Considerations, Charles Doyle 88-583 A
* War Powers Resolutions: Presidential Compliance; Issue Brief, Ellen Collier IB81050
* War Powers Resolution: The Controversial Act's Search For a Successful Litigation Posture, Raymond J. Celada 88-64 A

National Defense -- Military Balance

* Allied Burdensharing: Audio Brief, Paul Gallis, etc. AB50182
* Balance of Power; Selected References, 1985-1989, Valentin Leskovsek 89-325 L
* Burdensharing: Selected References, 1979-1988, Sherry B. Shapiro 88-423 L
* Conference on Security and Cooperation in Europe (CSCE): The Vienna Meeting; Issue Brief, Francis T. Miko IB87220
* Confidence Building Measures and Force Constraints for Stabilizing East-West Military Relations in Europe, Stanley R. Sloan, etc. 88-591 F
* Conventional Arms Control in Europe: Prospects for Accord: Issue Brief, Stanley Sloan IB86064
* Defense Capability: Issue for Congress; Archived Issue Brief, Robert E. Foelber IB87012
* Defense Spending: an Introduction to Arms Control, Burden Sharing, and Other Key Questions; Issue Brief, Alice C. Maroni IB88043
* Essentials of Net Assessment: An Objective Means of Comparing Military Capabilities, John Collins, etc. 80-168 S
* Estimates of Soviet Defense Expenditures: Methodological Issues and Policy Implications, Robert Foelber, etc. 85-131 F
* A European Defense Identity: Challenge and Opportunity for NATO, Catherine Guicherd, 91-478 RCO
* European-U.S. Affairs: Responding to a Changing Relationship; Issue Brief, Karen E. Donfried, etc. IB89127
* Japan's Military Buildup: Goals and Accomplishments, Gary K. Reynolds 89-68 F
* Maintaining U.S. Influence in a Changing World: Audio Brief, Stan Sloan, AB50197
* Middle East Military Balance, Clyde Mark 85-591 F
* Military Balance: Info Pack, IP069M
* The NATO Allies, Japan, and the Persian Gulf, Paul Gallis 84-184 F
* NATO Burdensharing: An Analysis of Major Legislation in the 100th Congress, Christopher C. Bolkcom, 88-772 F
* NATO Conventional Arms Control and Related Political Issues; Info Pack, IP425N

* NATO Conventional Arms Control Issues; Selected References, Sherry B. Shapiro 89-479 L
* NATO Conventional Force Structure and Doctrine: Possible Defensive Changes After an INF Treaty, Robert L. Goldich 88-169 F
* The NATO Strategy Review: Negotiating the Future of the North Atlantic Alliance, Stanley R. Sloan, 91-379 RCO
* National Power in a Changing World: Audio Brief, Alfred Reifman, AB50195
* Naval Arms Control: Issue Brief, Ronald O'Rourke, IB89132
* On-Site Inspections in Arms Control: Verifying Compliance With INF and START, Amy F. Woolf, 89-592 F
* Soviet Armed Forces Statistical Trends, 1985-1990, John M. Collins, etc. 91-636 RCO
* Soviet Policy in Nordic Europe: New Focus on the Forgotten Flank?, Francis Miko 85-33 F
* Soviet Policy Toward Iran and the Strategic Balance in Southwest Asia, Stuart D. Goldman 87-592 F
* The Strategic Defense Initiative: Major Changes During the 101st Congress and Potential Issues for the 102nd Congress, John D. Moteff, 91-121 SPR
* Strategic Defense Initiative: Selected References, 1988-1990, Valentin Leskovsek, 91-19 L
* Toshiba-Kongsberg Technology Diversion: Issues for Congress; Archived Issue Brief, Raymond Ahearn, etc. IB87184
* United States and Soviet Special Operations, John M. Collins 87-398 S
* United States/Soviet Military Balance: Archived Issue Brief, John Collins, etc. IB78029
* U.S. Armed Forces Statistical Trends, 1985-1990, John M. Collins, etc., 91-672 RCO
* U.S. Army Combat-to-Support Ratios: A Framework for Analysis, Robert L. Goldich, 89-386 F
* The U.S. Commitment to Europe's Defense: A Review of Cost Issues and Estimates, Alice Maroni, etc. 85-211 F
* U.S., Soviet, and Western European Naval Forces in the Persian Gulf Region, Robert J. Ciarrocchi 87-956 F
* U.S.-Soviet Military Balance. Book I. Organization, Budgets, Manpower, Technology, John Collins, etc. 80-161 S
* U.S.-Soviet Military Balance. Book II. Strategic Nuclear Trends, John Collins, etc. 80-162 S
* U.S.-Soviet Military Balance. Book III. General Purpose Force Trends, John Collins, etc. 80-163 S
* U.S.-Soviet Military Balance. Book IV. Airlift and Sealift, John Collins, etc. 80-164 S
* U.S.-Soviet Military Balance. Book V. NATO and the Warsaw Pact, John Collins, etc. 80-165 S
* U.S.-Soviet Military Balance. Book VI. Far East, Middle East Assessments, John Collins, etc. 80-166 S
* U.S./Soviet Military Balance: Statistical Trends, 1970-1979 (End of Year Figures), John M. Collins, etc. 87-839 S
* U.S./Soviet Military Balance: Statistical Trends, 1980-1987 (as of January 1, 1988), John M. Collins, etc. 88-425 F
* US-Soviet Military Balance, 1980-1985, John Collins 85-89 S

National Defense -- Military Bases

* Current Issues With the "Base-Rights" Countries and Their Implications, Richard F. Grimmett 88-726 F
* Greek-U.S. Bases Agreement: Archived Issue Brief, Richard F. Grimmett, IB89155
* Military Base Closures: A Side by Side Comparison of Current Legislation, Andrew C. Mayer 88-472 F
* Military Base Closures: Congress and the Executive Branch, Andrew Mayer 85-212 F
* Military Base Closures: Issue Brief, Andrew Mayer IB89026
* Military Bases in Europe: The Crotone Issue, Issue Brief, Richard F. Grimmett, IB90138
* Military Base Closures: The 102nd Congress: Issue Brief, Andrew Mayer IB91087
* The Navy's Strategic Homeporting Program: Issue for Congress; Archived Issue Brief, Ronald O'Rourke IB85193
* Philippine Bases Negotiations: Archived Issue Brief, Larry A. Niksch, IB90142
* Philippine Bases: U.S. Redeployment Options, Alva Bowen 86-44 F
* United States Military Installations in Greece, Richard Grimmett 84-24 F
* United States Military Installations in Italy, Richard Grimmett 84-12 F
* United States, Military Installations in Portugal, Richard Grimmett 86-6 F
* United States Military Installations in Spain, Richard Grimmett 84-149 F
* United States Military Installations in Turkey, Richard Grimmett 84-221 F
* U.S.-Spanish Bases Agreement: Issue Brief, Richard F. Grimmett IB88010

National Defense -- Military Policy

* Aircraft Carrier Force Levels and Deployment Patterns: Issues and Options, Ronald O'Rourke, 91-516 F
* AX Aircraft Program: Issues and Options; Issue Brief, Bert H. Cooper, IB91104
* Defense Policy: Threats, Force Structure, and Budget Issues; Issue Brief, Robert L. Goldich, etc. IB90013
* Department of Defense Organization: current Legislative Issues; Archived Issue Brief, Robert Goldich, IB86036
* Navy Seawolf and Centurion Attack Submarine Programs: Issue Brief, Ronald O'Rourke, IB91098
* New Directions for National Defense, John M. Collins, 90-323 S
* The Role of the U.S. Military in Narcotics Interdiction: Audio Brief, Raphael Perl, AB50171

National Defense -- Persian Gulf

* American Public Opinion on the Iraq-Kuwait Crisis Until January 15, Rosita M. Thomas 91-109 GOV
* The Army's Roundout Concept After the Persian Gulf War, Robert L. Goldich, 91-763 F
* Desert Shield and Desert Storm: Implications for Future U.S. Force Requirements, John M. Collins, 91-361 RCO
* Iraq-Kuwait Crisis: U.S. Policy and Options; Archived issue Brief, Alfred B. Prados, etc. IB90117
* Iraq's Food and Agricultural Situation During the Embargo and the War, Susan B. Epstein, 91-199 ENR
* Military and Civilian Satellites in Support of the Persian Gulf War, Marcia S. Smith, 91-215 SPR
* Military Geography of Iraq and Adjacent Arab Territory, John M. Collins, 90-431 RCO
* Operation Desert Storm: An Assessment, Robert L. Goldich, etc. LTR91-873
* Persian Gulf: Post-War Issues; Info Pack, IP452P
* Persian Gulf War: Info Pack, Congressional Reference Division, IP488P
* Persian Gulf War: Iraqi Scud Ballistic Missile Systems, Warren W. Lenhart, etc. 91-173 F
* Persian Gulf War: U.S. Costs and Allied Financial Contributions; Issue Brief, Stephen Daggett, etc. IB91019
* Press Restrictions in the Persian Gulf War: First Amendment Implications, Henry Cohen, 91-316 A
* Reparations, Raymond J. Celada, 91-242 A

National Defense and Security

* A-12 Advanced Tactical Aircraft (ATA) Program Weapons Facts, IB87115
* Acquired Immune Deficiency Syndrome and Military Manpower Policy, IB87202
* Advanced Tactical Fighter (ATF) Aircraft (Weapons Facts), IB87111
* Argentina, Brazil, and Nuclear Proliferation, IB89103
* Arms Control: Issues for Congress, IB87002
* Arms Control: Negotiations to Limit Defense and Space Weapons, IB86073
* Arms Control: Negotiations to Reduce Strategic Offensive Nuclear Weapons, IB88088
* ASATs: Antisatellite Weapon Systems, IB85176
* AV-8B V/STOL Aircraft (Weapons Facts), IB88044
* B-1B Strategic Bomber, IB87157
* B-2 Advanced Technology Bomber, IB87216
* Chemical Weapons: A Summary of Proliferation and Arms Control Activities, IB89042
* Conference on Security and Cooperation in Europe (CSCE): After the Vienna Meeting, IB87220
* Conventional Arms Control in Europe: Prospects for Accord, IB86064
* Defense Budget for FY 1990: Congressional Action, IB89054
* Defense Procurement: Investigation into Alleged Abuses, IB88081
* Defense Procurement Reform, IB89015
* Defense Spending: An Introduction to Arms Control, Burdensharing, and Other Key Questions, IB88043
* Defense Spending Priorities, IB87231
* Embassy Construction Controversies: Moscow and Washington, IB87232
* F-14D Fighter Aircraft (Weapons Facts), IB89101
* FSX Fighter Agreement With Japan, IB89060
* Funding for Selected Defense Programs: FY 1990 Authorization and Appropriation, IB89087
* The FY 1990 Budget Debate: How Much for Defense?, IB89073
* Intelligence Reform Issues, IB88029
* LHX and Army Aviation Modernization: Issues for Congress, IB88086
* Military Base Closures, IB89026

* Military Manpower and Compensation: FY 90 Budget Issues, IB89024
* Military Medical Care Services: Questions and Answers, IB87155
* Military Retirement: Major Legislative Issues, IB85159
* MX, "Midgetman," and Minuteman Missile Programs, IB77080
* NATO Nuclear Modernization and Arms Control, IB89049
* Nuclear Arms Control: Disposal of Nuclear Warheads, IB88024
* Nuclear Nonproliferation Policy in the 101st Congress, IB89084
* Nuclear Weapons Production Complex: Modernization and Cleanup, IB89062
* Seawolf or SSN-21 Nuclear-Powered Attack Submarine, IB85169
* Special Access Programs and the Defense Budget: Understanding the 'Black Budget', IB87201
* The Strategic Defense Initiative: Issues for Congress, IB88033
* Strategic Defense Initiative (SDI): Mission Objectives for Directing the Program, IB88028
* Terrorism: U.S. Policy Options, IB81141
* Terrorist Incidents Involving U.S. Citizens or Property 1981-1989: A Chronology, IB86096
* Trident Program, IB73001
* U.S.-Spanish Bases Agreement, IB88010
* V-22 Osprey Tilt Rotor Aircraft (Weapons Facts), IB86103
* Verification and Compliance: Soviet Compliance With Arms Control Agreements, IB84131
* War Powers Resolution: Presidential Compliance, IB81050

National Defense -- Strategic Stockpiles

* Aspects of the Mobilization of the Petroleum Industry in World War II and the Korean War, Robert Bamberger 84-773 ENR
* Defense Petroleum Reserve: Organizational Options for Meeting DOD's Emergency Fuel Supply Requirements David Lockwood 84-201 F
* National Defense Stockpile Policy--The Congressional Debate, Alfred R. Greenwood 86-863 ENR
* Nuclear Weapons Material Production: Options for Meeting Tritium and Plutonium Needs; Archived Issue Brief, David W. Cheney, etc. IB88099
* The Reagan Administration Proposes Dramatic Changes to National Defense Stockpile Goals, Alfred Greenwood 86-578 ENR
* Strategic and Critical Materials Policy: Research and Development: Archived Issue Brief, Leonard Kruger IB74094

National Defense Student Loan Program

* see Higher Education--Student Aid

National Economic Commission (U.S.)

* Deficit Reduction: The National Economic Commission Options Model, Barry Molefsky, etc. 88-606 E
* National Economic Commission: Equitable Deficit Reduction; Archived Issue Brief, Barry Molefsky IB88032

National Endowment

* see Arts and Humanities

National Flood Insurance Program

* see Water Resources

National Priorities

* Congress: Issue for the 101st Congress; Info Pack, Congressional Reference Division IP410C
* Congress: Issues for the 102nd Congress; Info Pack, Congressional Research Division, IP44
* CRS Major Issues for the 101st Congress, First Session, Congressional Research Service 90-46 CRS
* CRS Major Issues for the 102nd Congress, First Session, Congressional Research Service 91-1 CRS
* Defense Spending: Info Pack, Congressional Reference Division, IP434D
* Economic Policymaking the U.S. Government: Proceedings of a Congressional Symposium, April 26, 1988, Congressional Research Service 88-461 E
* Economic Policymaking Problems. Part One: Institutions and Processes, Leon M. Cole, etc. 89-299 E
* Economic Policymaking Problems. Part Two: Theories and Forecasts, Leon M. Cole, etc. 89-300 E
* Energy Policy: Info Pack, Congressional Reference Division, IP447E
* Federalism in the United States: Toward the Third Century; an Overview of Trends and Issues, Sandra S. Osbourn 89-262 GOV
* Foreign Policy Budget: Issues and Priorities for the 1990s; Archived Issue Brief, Larry Q. Nowels, etc. IB90037

Current Events and Homework

* Forum: Congress in the Year 2000, Congressional Research Service, REV 1-90
* The FY1991 Budget Debate: How Much for Defense: Archived Issue Brief, Stephen Daggett, IB90061
* A Peace Dividend in 1990-91? Stephen Daggett, 90-85 F
* The Persian Gulf War; Preliminary Foreign Policy "Lessons" and Perceptions, Mark M. Lowenthal, 91-260 RCO
* Rural Policy in the United States: A History, Sandra S. Osbourn 88-487 GOV
* Science and Technology Issues for the 102nd Congress, Science Policy Research Division, 90-620 SPR

National Science Foundation (U.S.)

* Federal Support of Basic Research and the Establishment of the National Science Foundation and Other Research Agencies, William C. Boesman 88-456 SPR
* The LIGO (Laser Interferometer Gravitational Observatory) Proposal, Daniel Morgan, etc., 91-661 SPR
* The National Earthquake Hazards Reduction Program, David W. Cheney, 89-473 SPR

National Sea Grant Program

* see Oceanography

National Security Council (U.S.)

* Compilation of Selected Laws Relating to the National Security Council, Arms Transfers, Intelligence, Activities, Aid to the Contras, and Appropriation, American Law Division 86-1028 A
* Contra Aid: Analysis of Whether the National Security Council (NSC) and the NSC Staff Are an "agency, or Entity Involved in Intelligence Activities" Co., Larry E. Eig 87-566 A
* The National Security Council: Organizational History, Mark Lowenthal 78-104 F
* U.S. Presidential National Security Advisers: Changing Roles and Relationships, Joel M. Woldman 87-334 F

National Service

* see Public Welfare

National Space Council (U.S.)

* The National Space Council, Patricia E. Humphlett, 89-429 SPR

National Wilderness Preservation System

* The Major Federal Land Management Agencies: Management of Our Nation's Lands and Resources, by Environment and Natural Resources Policy Division, 90-239 ENR
* Wilderness Areas and Federal Water Rights, Pamela Baldwin 89-11 A
* Wilderness Issues in the 102nd Congress: Issue Brief, Betsy A. Cody, IB91029
* Wilderness Overview and Statistics, Ross W. Gorte, 89-460 ENR

NATO

* see North Atlantic Treaty Organization

Natural Disasters

* see Disasters

Natural Gas

* see Fossil Fuel--Natural Gas

Natural Resources

* see Coastal Area, Fisheries, Forests and Forestry, Fossil Fuels, Land Use, Minerals and Materials, Oceanography, Public Lands, Water Resources
* Agriculture and the Environment: Archived Issue Brief, Jean Rawson, etc. IB89086
* Agricultural Resource Conservation Issues: Archived Issue Brief, Jeffrey A. Zinn IB87132
* Agriculture and the Environment: Issue Brief, Geoffrey Becker, etc. IB89086
* Amenity Resources in Rural Economics: Selected References, Ted L. Burch, etc., 90-218 L
* Antarctic Mineral Resources Regime: Diplomacy and Development; Issue Brief, James E. Mielke, etc. IB88101
* Antarctica: Environmental Protection Issues; Summary of a CRS Research Workshop, Susan R. Fletcher 89-272 ENR
* Arctic Oil, Arctic Refuge; Videoprogram, M. Lynne Corn, LTR91-1489
* Arctic Resources Controversy: Issue Brief, M. Lynne Corn, etc. IB89058
* Arctic Resources Over a Barrel? Issue Brief, M. Lynne Corn, etc. IB91011
* The California Drought, Effects on Agriculture and Related Resources, Betsy A. Cody, etc. 91-208 ENR
* Compliance Provisions for Resource Conservation: A Status Report, Jeffery Zinn, 88-662 ENR
* The Conservation Title of the 1990 Farm Bill, Jeffery A. Zinn, 90-562 ENR
* Criminal Provisions in Federal Environmental Statues: A Compilation, Maribel Nicholson, 89-652 A
* Federal Trust Responsibility to Indian Tribes for Protection of Natural Resources, M. Maureen Murphy, 89-379 A
* International Environmental Issues: Overview; Issue Brief, Susan Fletcher, IB91047
* The Major Federal Land Management Agencies: Management of Our Nation's Lands and Resources, Environment and Natural Resources Policy Division, 90 239 ENR
* Major International Environmental Issues: A Checklist of CRS Products, Lisa B. Dove, 92-13 L
* Natural Resource Issues in National Defense Programs, George H. Siehl, 91-781 ENR
* Policy Analysis of the Proposed Revisions of the Forest Service Administrative Appeals Regulations: Public Input, Timing, and Delays, Ross W. Gorte, 88-483 ENR
* Public Lands and Resources: BLM Management Issues; Issue Brief, Adela Backiel, etc. IB91068
* Scenic Landscape Protection, George H. Siehl, 90-525 ENR
* The Subsidization of natural Resources in the United States, Environment and Natural Resources Policy Division, 86-588 S
* Tropical Deforestation: Selected References, 1987-1990, Lisa B. Dove, 90-578 L
* Wilderness Issues in the 102nd Congress: Issue Brief, Betsy A. Cody, IB91029
* Coastal Resource Issues: Archived Issue Brief, Jeffrey A. Zinn IB87144
* Compliance Provisions for Resource Conservation: A Status Report, Jeffrey Zinn 88-662 ENR
* The Conservation Reserve: A Status Report, Jeffrey Zinn 88-716 ENR
* Consideration of Economic Factors under the Endangered Species Act, Pamela Baldwin 89-274 A
* Debt-for-Nature Swaps in Developing Countries: An Overview of Recent Conservation Efforts, Betsy Cody 88-647 ENR
* Environmental Protection in Developing Countries: Selected References, 1983-1987, Rebecca Mazur 87-488 L
* Federal Agency Programs in Living Aquatic Resources and Aquatic Habitat Protection, Eugene H. Buck 89-53 ENR
* The Major Federal Land Management Agencies: Management of Our Nation's Lands and Resources, Adela Backiel, etc. 87-22 ENR
* Managing Coastal Development Through the Coastal Zone Management and Flood Insurance Programs: Experience to Date and the Views from Selected States, Gary Kamimura, etc. 88-354 ENR
* Natural Resources Conservation and Development in Brazil: An Overview and Related Issues, Russell Hawkins 84-802 ENR
* Policy Analysis of the Proposed Revision of the Forest Service Administrative Appeals Regulations: Public Input, Timing, and Delays, Ross W. Gorte 88-483 ENR
* Population Growth and Natural Resource Deterioration in Drought-Stricken Africa, Susan Abbasi 85-1149 ENR
* Selected Reports Available on Food and Agricultural Topics, Environment and Natural Resources Policy Division 89-244 ENR
* Soil and Water Conservation Issues in the 101st Congress: Issue Brief, Jeffrey A. Zinn IB89080
* Spotted Owls and the Timber Industry: Issue Brief, M. Lynne Corn IB89077
* The Subsidization of Natural Resources in the United States, Environment and Natural Resources Policy Division 86-588 S
* Tongass National Forest Issues Brief, Adela Backiel IB89055
* Wetlands Issues: Info Pack, IP423W
* Wetlands Protection: Issues in the 101st Congress; Issue Brief, Jeffrey A. Zinn, etc. IB89076
* Antarctic Mineral Resources Regime: Diplomacy and Development, IB88101
* Arctic Resources Controversy, IB89058
* Coastal Barrier Protection Issues in the 101st Congress, IB89095
* Endangered Species Act: Reauthorization and Funding, IB87089
* Fisheries Issues in the 101st Congress: Commercial, Recreational, and Aquaculture, IB89041
* Outer Continental Shelf Leasing and Development, IB89028
* Soil and Water Conservation Issues in the 101st Congress, IB89080
* Spotted Owls and the Timber Industry, IB87088

* Tongass National Forest Issues, IB89055
* Tropical Deforestation: International Implications, IB89010
* Water Resources Development Act: Implementing the Omnibus Project Reforms, IB87088
* Wetlands Protection: Issues in the 101st Congress, IB89076

Naval Petroleum Reserves

* see National Defense--Strategic Stockpiles

Netherlands

* The Netherlands Elections and the Cruise Missile Issue: Implications for the United States and for NATO, Paul Gallis 86-27 F

New Zealand

* Australia, New Zealand, and the Pacific Islands: Issue for U.S. Policy; Issue Brief, Robert G. Sutter IB86158

Newspaper Preservation Act

* The Newspaper Preservation Act (15 U.S.C.[Sections] 1801-1804), Janice E. Rubin 89-239 A

Nicaragua

* The Boland Amendments: A Chronology of Congressional Action, Joseph Maheady 87-833 A
* Central American Peace Process: Selected References, Robert Kirk 88-389 L
* Chart of Unclassified Legislative Restrictions Regarding Support for Military or Paramilitary Operations in Nicaragua, 1982-1986, Larry Eig. 87-222 A
* Compilation of Selected Laws Relating to the National Security Council, Arms Transfers, Intelligence, Activities, Aid to the Contras, and Appropriation, American Law Division 86-1028 A
* Congress and U.S. Policy Toward Nicaragua in 1987, Linda Robinson 89-158 F
* Contra Aid: Analysis of Whether the National Security Council (NSC) and the NSC Staff Are an "agency, or Entity Involved in Intelligence Activities" Co., Larry E. Eig 87-566 A
* Contra Aid, FY82-FY88: Summary and Chronology of Major Congressional Action on Key Legislation Concerning U.S. Aid to the Anti-Sandinista Guerrillas, Nina M. Serafino 88-563 F
* Iran Arms and Contra Funds: Selected Chronology of Events, 1979-1987, Richard D. Shuey, etc. 86-190 F
* The Iran/Contra Affair: Implications for the National Security Adviser and the NSC Staff; Archived Issue Brief, Joel M. Woldman IB87107
* Legislative Histories of Statutory Restrictions on Funding for Covert Assistance for Military or Paramilitary Operations in Nicaragua, FY 1983-FY 1986, Larry M. Eig 87-538 A
* Nicaragua: An Overview of U.S. Policy, 1979-1986, Mark P. Sullivan 87-855 F
* Nicaragua: Bibliography-in-Brief, 1986-1987, Valentin Leskovsek 87-382 L
* Nicaragua: Conditions and Issues for U.S. Policy; Issue Brief, Nina Serafino IB82115
* Nicaragua: Info Pack, IP073N
* Nicaragua v. United States: The International Court of Justice Decision, Daniel Hill Zafren 86-748 A
* Nicaraguan Elections and Transition: Issues for U.S. Policy, Nina M. Serafino, 90-187 F
* The Nicaraguan Resistance ("Contras"): Background and Major Concerns of Congress, Veronica R. Clifford 87-943 F
* Nicaragua's "Civic" Opposition: Players, Problems and Prospects, Nina M. Serafino 87-735 F
* A Summary and Analysis of the Report of the National Bipartisan "Kissinger" Commission on Central America, January 1984, Richard Cronin, etc. 84-39 F
* U.S. Assistance to Nicaraguan Guerrillas: Issues for the Congress; Archived Issue Brief, Nina Serafino IB84139
* The U.S. Trade Embargo Against Nicaragua After Two-and-a-Half Years, Glennon J. Harrison 87-870 E

Nobel Prizes

* The Nobel-Prize Awards in Science as a Measure of National Strength in Science, Christopher T. Hill, etc. 86-727 S

North American Free Trade Agreement

* see also Canada, Latin America -- Foreign Trade

* A North American Free Trade Agreement: Congressional Concerns; Proceedings of a CRS Seminar, Lenore M. Sek, 91-786 E

North Atlantic Treaty Organization

* Allied Burdensharing in Transition: Status and Implications for the United States, Gary J. Pagliano, 91-774 F
* Burdensharing: Selected References, 1979-1988, Sherry B. Shapiro 88-423 L
* Confidence Building Measures and Force Constraints for Stabilizing East-West Military Relations in Europe, Stanley R. Sloan, etc. 88-591 F
* Defense Burdensharing: U.S. Relations With NATO Allies and Japan, Stanley R. Sloan 88-449 F
* A European Defense Identity: Challenge and Opportunity for NATO, Catherine Buidherd, 91-478 RCO
* *European-U.S. Affairs: Responding to a Changing Relationship; Issue Brief, Daren E. Donfried, etc. IB89127
* Franco-German Security Cooperation: Implications for the NATO Alliance, Paul E. Gallis 89-16 F
* Implications for NATO Strategies: A Brief Constitutional Analysis, Rita Ann Reimer 87-422 A
* NATO Conventional Arms Control and Related Political Issues; Info Pack, IP425N
* NATO Conventional Arms Control Issues; Selected References, Sherry B. Shapiro, 89-479-L
* The NATO Strategy Review: Negotiating the Future of the North Atlantic Alliance, Stanley R. Sloan, 91-379 RCO
* United States and New Europe: Strategy for the Future, Stanley R. Sloan, 90-245 S
* Television Network Evening News Coverage of Afghanistan: A Perspective After Eight Years of War, Denis Steven Rutkus 88-319 GOV

Northern Ireland

* Northern Ireland and the Republic of Ireland: U.S. Foreign Assistance Facts; Issue Brief. Bert H. Cooper, Jr. IB87069
* Northern Ireland: The Anglo-Irish Agreement and Its Implications for Congress: Policy Alert. Allan Nanes 85-1107 F

Northern Mariana Islands

* Territorial Political Development: An Analysis of Puerto Rico, Northern Mariana Islands, Guam, Virgin Islands, and American Samoa, and the Micronesian, Bette A. Taylor 88-657 GOV

Nuclear Energy

* see Accidents and Safety, Nuclear Exports and Non-Proliferation Power Production, Arms Control, Disasters, Solid Wastes--Radioactive Wastes, Weapons Systems, Nuclear Weapons
* Controlling Carbon Dioxide Emissions. Amy Abel, etc. 89-157 ENR
* International Atomic Energy Agency: Bibliography-in-Brief. Bonnie F. Mangan 89-259 L
* Nuclear Energy: An Alphabetical Microthesaurus of Terms Selected from the Legislative, Indexing Vocabulary, Shirley Loo 87-962 L
* Nuclear Energy: Bibliography-in-Brief, 1989-1990, B.F. Mangan, 90-314 L
* Nuclear Energy Policy: Issue Brief. Mark Holt, etc. IB88090
* Nuclear Energy Policy: Selected References, 1985-1988. Karen L. Alderson 88-763 L
* Nuclear Weapons in the Soviet Union: Issues and Prospects; Issue Brief, Amy F. Woolf, IB91144
* Nuclear Weapons Production Complex: Modernization and Cleanup; Issue Brief. David W. Cheney, etc. IB89062
* Nuclear Winter: Bibliography-in-Brief. B.F. Mangan 88-325 L
* Presidential Remarks About the International Atomic Energy Agency: Selected Excerpts. Barbara Black 89-27 ENR
* Superconducting Super Collider: Issue Brief. William C. Boesman IB87096
* Superconducting Super Collider: Issues; Info Pack. IP384S
* Superconducting Super Collider: Bibliography-in-Brief. Bonnie F. Mangan 88-45 L
* The U.S. Uranium Industry: Changing Prospects and the Federal Role; Issue Brief. Barbara B. Black IB89079
* Uranium Enrichment Issues: Issue Brief, Marc Humphries IB90151
* Uranium Enrichment Unrecovered Costs, Mark Holt, 90-476 ENR

Nuclear Energy -- Accidents and Safety

* The Chernobyl Accident: Health and Agricultural Effects; Archived Issue Brief. Christopher H. Dodge IB86122
* The Chernobyl Accident: Implications for DOE's Production Reactors; Archived Issue Brief. Robert L. Civiak IB86092

Current Events and Homework

* The Chernobyl Nuclear Accident: Causes, Initial Effects, and Congressional Response; Archived Issue Brief, Warren Donnelly, etc. IB86077
* The Chernobyl Nuclear Accident: Long-Term Political, Economic, and Foreign Policy Implications; Archived Issue Brief, Jean Boone, etc. IB86083
* Civil Liability for Transboundary Damage from a Nuclear Accident: The Joint International Protocol. Barbara B. Black, etc. IB89023
* International Notifications and Assistance for Nuclear Accidents: Congressional Action on Two Conventions; Archived Issue Brief, Warren H. Donnelly IB87082
* Nuclear Energy: Safety and Waste Issues; Info Pack, IP074N
* Nuclear Powerplant Safety and Regulation: Issue Brief. Mark Holt, IB86130
* Nuclear Powerplants: Emergency Planning; Archived Issue Brief. Cosmo DiMaggio IB86127

Nuclear Energy -- Nuclear Exports and Non-Proliferation

* Argentina, Brazil, and Nuclear Proliferation: Archived Issue Brief, Warren H. Donnelly, etc. IB89103
* China's Nuclear Weapons and Arms Control Policies: Implications for the United States. Robert G. Sutter 88-374 F
* The Clandestine Trade in Heavy Water: A Chronology. Barbara B. Black, etc. 89-66 ENR
* French Nuclear Deterrence Policy: Issues for Western Security in the Post-Cold War Era, Catherine Guicherd, 91-837 F
* Implementation of the U.S.-Chinese Agreement for Nuclear Cooperation: Archived Issue Brief. Warren Donnelly IB86050
* India and Nuclear Weapons: Issue Brief. Warren Donnelly IB86125
* Israel and Nuclear Weapons: Issue Brief. Warren H. Donnelly IB87079
* International Atomic Energy Agency: Bibliography-in-Brief, Bonnie F. Mangan, 89-259 L
* International Atomic Energy Agency: Strengthen Verification Authority? Issue Brief, Warren H. Donnelly, etc., IB91109
* Iraq and Nuclear Weapons: Issue Brief, Warren Donnelly, IB90113
* Israel and Nuclear Weapons: Archived Issue Brief, Warren H. Donnelly, IB87079
* Israel's Interests in Nuclear Power: Implications for U.S. Non-Proliferation Policy; Archived Issue Brief, Mark Martel, etc. IB85166
* Israel's Participation in the International Atomic Energy Agency and the 32nd IAEA General Conference: Archived Issue Brief, Warren H. Donnelly IB88072
* Libya's Nuclear Energy Situation: Archived Issue Brief, Mark Martel, etc. IB85079
* Non-Proliferation: A Compilation of Basic Documents on the International, U.S. Statutory, and U.S. Executive Branch Components of Non-Proliferation Policy, Zachary S. Davis, etc., 91-85 RCO
* Non-Proliferation Regimes: A Comparative Analysis of Policies to Control the Spread of Nuclear, Chemical and Biological Weapons and Missiles, Zachary S. Davis, 91-334 ENR
* North Korea's Nuclear Weapons Program: Issue Brief, Larry A. Niksch, IB91141
* Nuclear Arms Control: Disposal of Nuclear Warheads; Issue Brief, Warren H. Donnelly IB88024
* Nuclear Material from Dismantled Warheads: What to Do With It and How to Verify Its Disposal: A Preliminary Analysis, Warren H. Donnelly 87-437 S
* Nuclear Nonproliferation Policy in the 101st Congress: Issue Brief, Warren H. Donnelly IB89084
* Nuclear Nonproliferation Policy in the 102nd Congress: Issue Brief, Warren H. Donnelly IB91023
* Nuclear Nonproliferation: Selected References, 1985-1988, B.F. Mangan 88-682 L
* Nuclear Terrorism: Implementation of Title VI of the Omnibus Diplomatic Security and Antiterrorism Act of 1986; Archived Issue Brief, Warren H. Donnelly IB87213
* Nuclear Waste Management: Selected References, 1985-1988, Karen L. Alderson 89-118 L
* Nuclear Weapons Materials: Ending U.S.-Soviet Production and Disposing of Inventories: Issue Brief, Warren H. Donnelly, etc. IB91129
* Pakistan and Nuclear Weapons: Issue Brief, Warren Donnelly IB86110
* Pakistan's Nuclear Program: U.S. Foreign Policy Considerations; Issue Brief, Richard P. Cronin IB87227
* Pakistan's Nuclear Status: Issue Brief, Zachary Davis, etc., IB91142
* Plutonium: Department of Energy Approval of Plutonium Shipment from France to Japan; Archived Issue Brief, Warren H. Donnelly IB84116
* Presidential Remark's About the International Atomic Energy Agency: Selected Excerpts, Barbara Black, 89-27 ENR
* Proposals for Ending U.S. and Soviet Production of Fissile Materials for Nuclear Weapons: Issue Brief, David Cheney, etc., IB89141
* South Africa, Nuclear Weapons and the IAEA: Issue Brief, Warren H. Donnelly IB87199
* South Africa's New Nuclear Status: Archived Issue Brief, Zachary Davis, etc., IB91131
* The U.N. Conference on a Comprehensive Test Ban: Its Relation to U.S. Non-Proliferation Policy, Warren Donnelly, etc., 91-491 ENR
* Uranium Hexafluoride Imports from South Africa: Archived Issue Brief, Barbara B. Black, etc. IB88066
* The U.S.-China Agreement for Nuclear Cooperation: Congressional Review; Archived Issue Brief, Mark Martel, etc. IB85203
* U.S.-Japan Agreement for Nuclear Cooperation: Monitoring Its Implementation; Issue Brief, Warren H. Donnelly IB88095
* U.S.-Japanese Nuclear Cooperations: Revision of the Bilateral Agreement; Archived Issue Brief, Warren Donnelly IB87159
* U.S. Nuclear Cooperation with Hungary and Czechoslovakia: Archived Issue, Warren H. Donnelly, etc., IB91090
* Weapons Nonproliferation Policy and Legislation, Foreign Affairs and National Defense Division, 91-536 F

Nuclear Energy -- Power Production

* Cost Accounting, Pricing, and Cost Recovery in DOE's Uranium Enrichment Program, Robert Civiak 85-1041 SPR
* Economic Analysis of the Tax Treatment of Nuclear Power Plant Decommissioning Costs, Donald W. Kiefer 84-28 E
* Economics of Plutonium Use in Light Water Reactions, Robert Civiak 85-780 SPR
* Federal and State Regulation of Nuclear and Non-Nuclear Electric Utilities and of Nuclear Materials, Michael V. Seitzinger 87-221 A
* High-Level Nuclear Waste Repository: Yucca Mountain Site Characterization Plans, James E. Mielke, 91-185 SPR
* Magnetic Fusion Energy: Issue Brief, Richard E. Rowberg, IB91039
* Nuclear Energy: Enrichment and Reprocessing of Nuclear Fuels: Archived Issue Brief, Robert Civiak IB77126
* Nuclear Energy: Safety and Waste Issues. Info Pack IP074N
* Nuclear Energy: Uranium Enrichment; Archived Issue Brief, Robert Civiak IB84008
* Nuclear Fusion Power: Archived Issue Brief, Robert Civiak, etc. IB76047
* Nuclear Liability Legislation: Price-Anderson Renewal Issues; Archived Issue Brief, Mark Holt IB88034
* Nuclear Material from Dismantled Warheads: What to Do With It and How to Verify Its Disposal: A Preliminary Analysis, Warren H. Donnelly 87-437 S
* Nuclear Material Transportation: Safety Concerns, Governmental Regulations and Activities, and Options to Improve Federal Programs, Paul Rothberg 84-45 SPR
* Nuclear Power: Technology Overview, Statistics and Projections; Issue Brief, Mark Holt IB81070
* Nuclear Powerplant Safety and Regulation: Issue Brief, Robert L. Civiak, etc. IB86130
* The Nuclear Regulatory Commission: Organization History, Robert Civiak 81-147 SPR
* Nuclear Weapons Material Production: Options for Meeting Tritium and Plutonium Needs; Archived Issue Brief, David W. Cheney, etc. IB88099
* Plutonium Economics and Japan's Nuclear Fuel Cycle Policies, Robert Civiak 88-235 SPR
* Uranium Enrichment: Projected Earnings of the Proposed U.S. Enrichment Corporation, Robert L. Civiak 88-232 SPR
* The U.S. Uranium Industry: What Assistance Does It Need? Barbara B. Black, etc. 88-760 ENR

Nuclear Exports

* see Nuclear Energy--Nuclear Exports and Non-Proliferation

Nuclear Non-Proliferation

* see Nuclear Energy--Nuclear Exports and Non-Proliferation

Nuclear Power

* see Nuclear Energy--Power Production

Nuclear Power Plant Accidents

* see Nuclear Energy--Accidents and Safety

Nuclear Waste

* see Solid Wastes--Radioactive Wastes

Nuclear Weapons

* see Arms Control, Nuclear Energy--Nuclear Exports and Non-Proliferation, Weapons Systems--Nuclear Weapons

Nuclear Winter

* see Disasters

Nursing Homes

* see Health Facilities, Old Age -- Health Issues

Nutrition

* see Food, Food Relief

Occupational Health and Safety

* AIDS in the Workplace: Employee Vs Employer Interest, Gail McCallion 87-510 E
* Black Lung Programs: 1987 Issues and Action, Gloria E. Moreno, etc. 88-68 EPW
* Construction Workers: Safety and Health Legislation; Issue Brief, Mary Jane Bolle, IB90150
* Federal Agency Workers: How Safe Are They? Mary Jane Bolle, 91-412 E
* High Risk Occupational Disease Notification and Prevention Act of 1987: Side-by-Side Comparison of H.R. 162 and S. 79, Mary Jane Bolle 88-43 E
* Mine Safety: Recent Trends, Mary Jane Bolle, 90-207 E
* Occupational Disease Notification Proposals: Is Legislation Necessary? Issue Brief, Mary Jane Bolle IB86150
* Occupational Safety and Health Issues: Info Pack, IP456O
* OSHA Safety Inspection Targeting: Causes and Effects, Mary Jane Bolle 88-194 E
* Sex-Based Employment Discrimination: UAW v. Johnson Controls, Inc., Gina M. Stevens, 91-323 A
* Tort Liability of the Federal Government and Its Contractors to Veterans Exposed to Atomic Radiation, Henry Cohen 86-979 A
* Video Display Terminals (VDT's): Health, Safety, and Labor-Management Issues, Christopher H. Dodge, etc. 87-314 SPR
* Video Display Terminals and Problems of Modern Office Health, Safety and Policy: An Update, Christopher H. Dodge, 89-684 SPR

Occupational Training

* see Adult and Vocational Education, Job Training
* Apprenticeship Training: Proposed Department of Labor Regulations, William G. Whittaker, 90-606 E
* A Comparison of the Education Provisions in the Omnibus Trade Bill, H.R. 3, as Passed by the House and by the Senate, Paul M. Irwin, etc. 87-634 EPW
* Education and Job Growth, Linda LeGrande 88-476 E
* Education Proposals in Trade Competitiveness Legislation: Archived Issue Brief, K. Forbis Jordan, etc. IB87108
* Education Provisions of the Trade Act of 1988, P.L. 100-418, Paul M. Irwin, etc. 88-750 EPW
* Education and Training of the Workforce: A Checklist of CRS Products, M. Alexandra Salinas, 92-3L
* Employer Education Assistance: A Brief Discussion of Current Legislation and Issues, Bob Lyke 88-202 EPW
* Farmer Transition Program, Rebecca Mazur 88-364 L
* Job Hunting and Resume Writing: Selected References, B.F. Mangan 88-720 L
* Job Training: FY88 Budget and Legislative Issues; Archived Issue Brief, Karen Spar IB87039
* Job Training: FY89 Budget and Legislative Issues: Archived Issue Brief, Karen Spar IB88027
* Job Training Partnership Act: Background and Description, Karen Spar 83-76 EPW
* Jobs: The Employment Situation and Job Training Programs; Info Pack IP246J
* Labor Issues in the 102nd congress: The First Session, by Economics Division; Education and Public Welfare Division: Government Division, 91-228 E
* The New GI Bill: Recruiting and Retention, David F. Burrelli 87-652 F
* Targeted Jobs Tax Credit: Action in the 100th Congress; Issue Brief, Linda LeGrande IB87142
* The Targeted Jobs Tax Credit, 1978-1987, Linda LeGrande 87-616 E
* Trade Adjustment Assistance: The Program for Workers, Celinda M. Franco 89-265 EPW
* Training for Dislocated Workers under the Job Training Partnership Act, Karen Spar 89-44 EPW
* Vocational Rehabilitation and Related Programs for Persons With Handicaps: FY 1990 Budget Request, Mary F. Smith 89-176 EPW

Occupational Training -- Adults and Vocational Education

* Adult Education Act Reauthorization: Selected Options. Paul M. Irwin 87-57 EPW
* AFDC, Food Stamps, and Work: History, Rules, and Research, Emmett Carson, etc. 87-599 EPW
* Apprenticeship Training in America: the "Fitzgerald Act" (1937-1991), William G. Whittaker IB91092
* Carl D. Perkins Vocational Education Act: Issues for Reauthorization; Issue Brief, Paul M. Irwin, etc. IB89069
* The Carl D. Perkins Vocational Education Act (P.L. 98-524): Summary and Compensation With Selected Provisions of the Vocational Education Act of 1963, Paul Irwin 85-697 EPW
* Early Labor Market Experiences of Proprietary School Students, Robert Lyke, etc., 91-177 EPW
* Education Provisions of the Trade Act of 1988, P.L. 100-418, Paul M. Irwin, etc., 88-750 EPW
* Federal Policy for Vocational Education: Selected References, Peter Giordano 88-747 L
* Federal Vocational Education Legislation: Recurring Issues During the Last Quarter Century, Richard N. Apling, etc. 88-704 EPW
* Proprietary Schools, Robert Lyke, 91-440 EPW
* Proprietary Schools: A Description of Institutions and Students, Steven R. Aleman, etc. 90-428 EPW
* Proprietary Schools: The Regulatory Structure, Margot A. Schenet, 90-424 EPW
* Proprietary Vocational Schools: Bibliography-in-Brief. Peter Giordano 88-515 L
* Proprietary Vocational Schools: Selected References, 1965-1991, M. Alexandra Salinas, etc., 91-312 L
* Summary of the Adult Education Act, as Amended by the Education Amendments of 1984 (P.L. 98-511), Paul Irwin 84-829 EPW
* Vocational Education and Proposals for Trade Competitiveness, Paul M. Irwin 87-340 EPW
* Vocational Education: Major Provisions of the 1990 Amendments (P.L. 101-392), Paul M. Irwin, etc., 91-675 EPW
* Vocational Education Performance Standards, Richard N. Apling 89-440 EPW
* Vocational Education Reauthorization: House and Senate Legislation, 101st Congress, Paul M. Irwin, 90-280 EPW

Occupational Training -- Job Training

* Adjustment Assistance: Should Congress Create New Programs for Dislocated Workers? Issue Brief, James R. Storey IB91143
* Federal Employment and Training Programs: FY 1992 Budget Issues, Karen Spar, 91-257 EPW
* High School Dropouts and the Family Support Act, Vee Burke, 90-532 EPW
* Income Support for Workers Dislocated by Federal Policy Initiatives, James R. Storey, 90-330 EPW
* Job Training: FY88 Budget and Legislative ISSUES: ARCHIVED Issue Brief, Karen Spar IB87039
* Job Training Partnership Act: Legislation and Budget Issues; Issue Brief, Ann Lordeman, etc., IB1117
* Job Training Partnership Act: Pending Legislation and Budget Issues; Archived Issue Brief, Karen Spar, IB89117
* Jobs: Job Training and the Labor Market; Info Pack, IP246J
* Tax Incentives to Train or Retrain the Work Force, Nonna A. Noto, etc., 91-225 E
* Training for Dislocated Workers under the Job Training Partnership Act, Karen Spar, 89-44 EPW

Oceanography

* The Law of the Sea Conference: A U.S. Perspective; Archived Issue Brief, Marjorie Browne IB81153
* Marine Plastics Pollution Control Legislation, Martin R. Lee 88-377 ENR
* National Oceans Policy Commission Proposal: Issue Brief, Robert E. Morrison IB87203
* The National Sea Grant College Program: Issue Brief, Robert E. Morrison IB87163
* The National Sea Grant Program: Comparisons With Land Grant, Robert Morrison, etc. 85-1148 SPR
* Toxic Waste Incineration at Sea: Archived Issue Brief, Martin Lee IB85131
* U.S. Ocean Research and Exploration: Archived Issue Brief, John R. Justus, etc. IB87165
* Waste in the Marine Environment: Selected References, Ted L. Burch

Be patient. If any phone number is incorrect, call (area code) 555-1212 and request the new listing.

Current Events and Homework

89-263 Targeting: Causes and Effects, Mary Jane Bolle 88-194 E

Oil

* see Fossil Fuels--Petroleum, Water Pollution -- Oil Spills

Oil Import Fee

* see Fossil Fuels--Petroleum

Oil Spills

* see Water Pollution--Oil Spills

Old Age

* see Employment, Health Issues, Housing, Medicare and Medicaid, Pensions
* Adult Day Care: Background, Funding, Cost-Effectiveness Issues, and Recent Legislation, Susan Schillmoeller, etc. 86-121 EPW
* Age Discrimination in Employee Benefit Plans: United States Supreme Court Decision in Public Employees Retirement System of Ohio v. Betts, Kathleen S. Swendiman, 89-478 A
* Age Discrimination in Employment: Current Legal Developments, Patricia A. Prochaska, 87-681 A
* The Aged: Bibliography-in-Brief, Edith Sutterlin 89-258 L
* Aged: Info Pack, IP003A
* Aging and the Elderly: An Alphabetical Microthesaurus of Terms Selected from the Legislative Indexing Vocabulary, Shirley Loo 88-752 L
* Comparative Analysis of Title VII of the 1964 Civil Rights Act, the Age Discrimination in Employment Act, and the Rehabilitation Act of 1973, Charles V. Dale 89-240 A
* A Consumer Price Index for the Elderly: Would It Make Any Difference? Brian W. Cashell 87-552 E
* Economics Status of the Elderly: Issue Brief, Brian W. Cashell IB87095
* Economic Status of the Elderly Population, Archived Issue Brief, Brian W. Cashell IB87095
* Elder Abuse: Bibliography-in-Brief, 1980-1988, Edith Sutterlin, etc. 88-221 L
* Elderly: State Survey of Statutes or Policy Concerning Fees in Higher Education Institutions, M. Ann Wolfe, 91-298 A
* Federal Income Tax Treatment of the Elderly, Louis Alan Talley, 91-217 E
* Life Care Communities: Description and Current Issues, Evelyn Howard 85-1127 EPW
* Older Americans Act Amendments of 1987: P.L. 100-175; a Summary of Provisions, Carol O'Shaughnessy 88-233 EPW
* Older Americans Act: Participants in Supportive and Nutrition Services, Carol O'Shaughnessy 86-867 EPW
* Older Americans Act Programs: Brief Summary and Funding Levels, FY 1988-FY 1991 Carol O'Shaughnessy 90-200 EPW
* Older Americans Act: 1991 Reauthorization Issues; Issue Brief, Carol O'Shaughnessy, IB91002
* Older Taxpayers and the Tax Reform Act of 1986, Gerald Mayer 88-547 E
* Paying for the Baby Boom's Retirement, Congressional Research Service 87-905 EPW
* Selected Legislation Affecting the Elderly in the 102nd Congress, Dana Hamilton, 91-624 EPW
* Supplemental Security Income (SSI): Changes Made by the 101st Congress, Carmen D. Solomon, 90-605 EPW
* Transportation for Elderly and Handicapped People: Programs, Regulations, and Issues, Lenore M. Sek 85-699 E
* Various Effects of Raising the Normal Retirement Age for Social Security Benefits, David Koitz 84-677 EPW
* Violent Crimes Committed Against the Elderly, Statistics from 1980-1989, David Teasley, 91-580 GOV
* Working After Normal Retirement Age: Pension Accruals for Post-65 Service, Ray Schmitt 88-618 EPW
* Young vs. Old? Intergenerational Economic Equity: Bibliography-in-Brief, 1978-1987, Saundra Shirley-Reynolds 87-467 L
* 99th Congress Districts Classified by the Proportion of Population Over Age 65 (Ranking All Districts by Their Total Population Over 65 and Percent), David Huckabee 85-910 GOV

Old Age -- Employment

* Age Discrimination in Employment Act: Recent Enforcement Actions by the Equal Employment Opportunity Commission, Charles V. Dale 87-783 A
* Age Discrimination in Employment: Current Legal Developments, Patricia A. Prochaska 87-681 A
* A Demographic Portrait of Older Workers, Gail McCallion 88-636 E
* Early Retirement Incentive Plans under the Age Discrimination in Employment Act of 1967, Kathleen S. Swendiman 88-608 A
* Employment and Training Programs and Policies for Older Workers: An International Overview, Dennis M. Roth, etc. 86-639 E
* Older Workers: the Transition to Retirement, Gail McCallion 89-286 E
* Old Age--Health Issues Aging: Health Effects and Behavior, Samuel Merrill, Jr. 87-404 SPR
* Alzheimer's Disease: Bibliography-in-Brief, 1982-1987, B. F. Mangan 88-312 L
* Alzheimer's Disease: Issue Brief, Samuel Merrill IB83128
* Catastrophic Health Insurance: Medicare; Issue Brief, Jennifer O'Sullivan IB87106
* The Elderly and the Health Care Dilemma: Is an Ounce of Prevention Worth a Pound of Cure? Science Policy Research Division. Life Sciences Se. 85-968 SPR
* Financing and Delivery of Long-Term Care Services for the Elderly, Carol O'Shaughnessy, etc. 88-379 EPW
* Financing Long-Term Care for the Elderly: Audio Brief, Richard Price, etc. AB50187
* Health: Long-Term Care; Info Pack IP402H
* Health Promotion and Disease Prevention for the Elderly, James Reuter, etc. 86-40 EPW
* Long-Term Care Financing: Selected References, Peter Giordano 89-42 L
* Long-Term Care for the Elderly: Issue Brief, Richard J. Price, etc. IB88098
* Medicaid Eligibility for the Elderly in Need of Long Term Care, Edward Neuschler, etc. 87-986 EPW
* Medicare Catastrophic Coverage Act of 1988 (P.L. 100-360), Jennifer O'Sullivan 89-155 EPW
* Osteoporosis: An Overview of Recent Developments, Bernice S. Reyes, etc. 87-843 SPR
* Tax Options for Financing Long-Term Care for the Elderly, Jane G. Gravelle, etc. 89-329

Old Age -- Health Issues

* Alzheimer's Disease: Achieved Issue Brief, Samuel Merrill, IB83128
* Catastrophic Health Insurance: Medicare; Archived Issue Brief, Jennifer O'Sullivan, IB87106
* Characteristics of Nursing Home Residents and Proposals for Reforming Coverage of Nursing Home Care, Richard Price, etc., 90-471 EPW
* Elderly Home Care: Tax Incentives and Proposals for Change, Louis Alan Talley, 89-662 E
* Financing and Delivery of Long-Term Care Services for the Elderly, Carol O;Shaughnessy, etc., 88-379 EPW
* Health Care Costs at the End of Life, Kathleen M. King, 90-368 EPW
* Health: Long-Term Care; Info Pack, IP402H
* Long-Term Care for the Elderly: Issue Brief, Richard J. Price, etc., IB88098
* Older Americans Act Nutrition Program, Carol O'Shaughnessy, 90-115 EPW
* Personal Medical Communication Technologies, Bernice S. Reyes, 91- 278 SPR
* Public Opinion on Long-Term Health Care Needs, Costs and Financing, Rosita M. Thomas, 90-151 GOV
* Tax Options for Financing Long-Term Care for the Elderly, Jane G. Gravelle, etc., 89-329 E

Old Age -- Housing

* Congregate Housing: The Federal Program and Examples of State Programs, Susan Vanhorenbeck 86-918 E
* Description of Residential Facilities for the Elderly, Evelyn Tager 84-19 EPW
* Elderly and Handicapped Housing: Recent Developments in Section 202, Susan M. Vanhorenback, 89-667 E
* Federal Housing Programs Affecting Elderly People, Susan Vanhorenbeck 88-576 E
* Housing for the Elderly and Handicapped: Section 202; Issue Brief, Susan M. Vanhorenbeck IB84038

Older American Act

* Older Americans Act Amendments of 1987: P.L. 100-175; A Summary of Provisions, Carol O'Shaughnessy 88-233 EPW
* Older Americans Act Nutrition Program, Carol O'Shaughnessy, 90-115 EPW
* Older Americans Act: Participants in Supportive and Nutrition Services, Carol O'Shaughnessy 86-867 EPW
* Older Americans Act Programs: Brief Summary and Funding Levels, FY1988-FY 1991, Carol O'Shaughnessy 90-220 EPW
* Older Americans Act: 1991 Reauthorization issues; Issue Brief, Carol O'Shaughnessy, IB91002

Omnibus Budget Reconciliation Act

* Budget Enforcement Act of 1990: Brief Summary, Edward Davis and Robert Keith, 90-520 GOV
* Budget Enforcement Act of 1990: Contents Listing, Edward Davis, etc., 90-516 GOV
* Budget Enforcement Act of 1990: Cross-References to Laws and Rules Amended, Edward Davis, etc., 90-517 GOV
* Budget Enforcement Act of 1990: Legislative History, Edward Davis, etc., 90-518 GOV
* The Estate Freeze Controversy, Salvatore Lazzari 89-125 E
* Individual Income Tax Rates, Gregg A. Esenwein, 91-750 E
* Private Pension Plan Standards: A Summary of ERISA, Ray Schmitt, 91-22 EPW
* The U.S. Postal Service: Adjustment Cost for Retirement COLAs and Health Benefits under the 1990 Budget Act, Bernevia McCalip, 91-191 E

Omnibus Taxpayer Bill of Rights

* The Omnibus Taxpayer Bill of Rights, Marie B. Morris, etc. 89-136 A

Omnibus Trade and Competitiveness Act

* Addressing Unfair Trade: Agricultural Cases under Section 301 of the Trade Act of 1974, Donna U. Vogt, 89-522 ENR
* Education Provisions of the Trade Act of 1988, P.L. 100-418, Paul M. Irwin, etc. 88-750 EPW
* Japan's Response to the 1988 Omnibus Trade Bill, Dick K. Nanto 89-133 E
* The Omnibus Trade and Competitiveness Act. Technology Development Provisions, Wendy H. Schacht 89-93 SPR
* Trade Legislation in 1988: Conflict and Compromise, George Holliday, etc., 89-494 E
* U.S. Metric Conversion, Edith Fairman Cooper, 91-83 SPR

Opec Countries

* see Middle East

Operation Desert Shield

* see Iraq-Kuwait Crisis

Operation Desert Storm

* see Iraq-Kuwait Crisis

OSHA

* see Occupational Health and Safety

Ozone

* see Air Pollution-Ozone

Ozone Layer (Upper Atmosphere)

* see Earth Sciences

Pacific Area

* see Names of Individual Countries
* Australia, New Zealand, and the Pacific Islands: Issue for U.S. Policy; Issue Brief, Robert G. Sutter IB86158
* Australia-U.S. Relations: A Briefing Paper, Robert G. Sutter 87-858 F
* Divorce, Maintenance and Child Support Laws in Australia, Canada, England and New Zealand, by Law Library of Congress, American-British Law Division, LL90-65
* Economic Changes in the Asian Pacific Rim: Policy Prospectus, Congressional Research Service 86-923 S
* Kangaroo Management Controversy, Malcolm M. Simmons 88-468 ENR
* Oceania and the United States: A Primer, Robert Sutter 85-218 F
* Pacific Island Nations and the United States: Developing a Closer Dialogue: Condensed Proceedings of a Workshop, Luella S. Christopher, 90-541 F
* Pacific Island Nations: Overview of Trends and problems in the South and West Pacific, Luella S. Christopher, 90-396 F
* Pacific Rim Initiatives; a CRS Trade Team Product, 89-405 D
* Palau's Evolving Relationship With the United States: Introduction and Chronology of Development, Luella S. Christopher 88-442 F
* Territorial Political Development: An Analysis of Puerto Rico, Northern Mariana Islands, Guam, Virgin Islands, and America Samoa, and the Micronesian, Bette A. Taylor 88-657 GOV
* U.S. Wood Exports to the Pacific Rim, Ross W. Gorte 88-548 ENR

Pacific Rim

* see Asia, Pacific Area

Pakistan

* Kashmir: Conflict and Crisis; Archived Issue Brief, David E. Lockwood, etc., IB90087
* The Kashmir Dispute: Historical Background to the Current Struggle, Richard P. Cronin, etc., 91-563 F
* Pakistan After Zia: Implications for Pakistan and U.S. Interests; Archived Issue Brief, Richard P. Cronin IB88096
* Pakistan Aid Cutoff: U.S. Nonproliferation and Foreign Policy Consideration; Issue Brief, Richard P. Cronin, IB90149
* Pakistan and Nuclear Weapons: Issue Brief, Warren Donnelly IB86110
* Pakistan: U.S. Foreign Assistance Facts; Archived Issue Brief, Richard P. Cronin IB85112
* Pakistan's Nuclear Program: U.S. Foreign Policy Considerations; Issue Brief, Richard P. Cronin IB87227
* Pakistan's Nuclear Status: Issue Brief, Zachary Davis, etc., IB91142
* Pakistan's Request for the U.S. AWACS: Archived Issue Brief, Kerry B. Dumbaugh IB87227
* South Asia: Current Developments and Issues for U. S. Policy; Report on a Trip to Pakistan and India, April 8-30, 1986, Richard P. Cronin 86-741 F
* The United States, Pakistan and the Soviet Threat to Southern Asia: Options for Congress, Richard Cronin 85-152 F

Palau Islands

* Palau's Evolving Relationship With the United States: Introduction and Chronology of Developments, Luella S. Christopher 88-442 F
* Territorial Political Development: An Analysis of Puerto Rico, Northern Mariana Islands, Guam, Virgin Islands, and American Samoa, etc., Bette Taylor 88-657 GOV

Palestine

* Israeli-Palestinian Conflict: Bibliography-in-Brief, 1982-1988, Robert Kirk 88-251 L
* Israeli-Palestinian Conflict: Info Pack IP397I
* Middle East Peace proposals: Issue Brief, Clyde Mark IB82127
* Palestine and the Palestinians: Issue Brief, Clyde Mark IB76048
* Palestinian Disturbances in the Gaza Strip and West Bank: Policy Issues and Chronology, Ellen Laipson 88-114 F

Palestine Liberation Organization

* see Middle East-Arab-Israeli Conflict

Palestinians

* see Middle East-Arab-Israeli Conflict

Panama

* Panama and the Future of the U.S. Military Bases: An Examination of Panamanian Views, Mark P. Sullivan, 91-784 F
* Panama: Bibliography-in-Brief, Robert S. Kirk, 90-12 L
* Panama: Trade, Finance, and Proposed Economic Sanctions, Glennon J. Harrison 88-188 E
* Panama: U.S. Policy After the May 1989 Elections; Archived Issue Brief, Mark P. Sullivan, IB89106
* Panama-U.S. Relations: Issue for Congress; Issue Brief, Mark P. Sullivan, IB90044
* Panama's Political Crisis: Prospects and U.S. Policy Concerns: Issue Brief, Mark Sullivan IB87230
* U.S. Sanctions and the State of the Panamanian Economy, Mark Sullivan 88-578 F

Paperwork Reduction Act

* see also Government Information
* Paperwork Reduction and Information Resources Management: Issue Brief, Stephanie Smith, IB91107

Parental Kidnapping

* see Families--Domestic Relations

Parental Kidnapping Prevention Act

* The Parental Kidnapping Prevention Act of 1980: Background, Analysis and Subsequent Development, Rita Ann Reimer 88-294 A

Current Events and Homework

* Thompson v. Thompson: Federal Courts Are Not Authorized to Resolve State Custody Disputes Arising under the Parental Kidnapping Prevention Act, Rita Ann Reimer 88-63 A

Parental Leave

* see Families

Parks

* Arctic National Wildlife Refuge: Bibliography-in-Brief, Adrienne Grenfell 88-30 L
* The Arctic National Wildlife Refuge: Oil, Gas, and Wildlife: Archived Issue Brief, Lynne Corn, etc. IB87026
* Arctic Resources Controversy: Issue Brief, M. Lynne Corn, etc. IB89058
* Arctic Resources: Over a Barrel?, Issue Brief, M. Lynne Corn, etc., IB91011
* Clean Air Act Provisions to Protect National Parklands, Maria Grimes 85-1013 ENR
* A Comparison of Provisions of Bills Introduced in the 99th Congress to Create A Columbia Gorge National Scenic Area, M. Lynne Corn 86-629 ENR
* Establishment of New National Park System Units: A Brief Review of Procedures, Criteria and Alternatives, George Siehl 91-153 ENR
* The Federal Cave Resources Protection Act: A Review of a Proposed Bill, George Siehl 85-875 ENR
* Impact of Air Pollution on National Park Units: A Summary of Hearings Held by the House Subcommittee on National Parks and Recreation, May 20, 21, 1985, George Siehl, etc. 85-933 ENR
* Issues Surrounding the Greater Yellowstone Ecosystem: A Brief Review, M. Lynne Corn, etc. 85-1146 ENR
* Land and Water Conservation Fund: Information and Status, George Siehl 89-159 ENR
* The Major Federal Land Management Agencies: Management of Our Nation's Lands and Resources, by Environment and Natural Resources Policy Division, 90-239 ENR
* Manassas National Battlefield Park: The Battle Continues, John O. Spengler, etc. 88-514 ENR
* National Park Entrance and Recreation User Fees: Archived Issue Brief, George Siehl IB87121
* National Park Issues in the 100th Congress, George Siehl 87-179 ENR
* National Recreation Areas, George Siehl 88-644 ENR
* Old Growth Forests in the Pacific Northwest: Background and Issues; Issue Brief, Adela Backiel, IB90111
* An Overview of National Park Issues in the 100th Congress: Archived Issue Brief, George Siehl IB87072
* The Sawtooth National Recreation Area: Potential National Park, Ross W. Gorte 87-951 ENR
* Scenic Byways: Issues and Action, John Spengler, etc. 88-479 ENR
* Scenic Landscape Protection, George H. Siehl, 90-525 ENR
* Trails Programs in Federal Agencies: A Data Compilation, George Siehl 89-8 ENR
* Water Rights and the Wild and Scenic Rivers Act, Pamela Baldwin, 90-196 A
* Wilderness Issues in the 102nd Congress: Issue Brief, Betsy A. Cody, IB91029
* Wilderness Overview and Statistics, Ross W. Gorte, 89-460 ENR

Patents and Inventions

* Accepting or Rejecting an Executory Contract Governing Intellectual Property in Bankruptcy: Legal Analysis of H.R. 4657, Robin Jeweler, etc. 88-557 A
* Computer Software and Copyright Law, Douglas Reid Weimer, 91-281 A
* Copyright--Application Procedures: Info Pack IP215C
* Copyright and Compilations of Facts: Feist Publications v. Rural Telephone Service, Co., Douglas Reid Weimer, 91-552 A
* Copyright Law: Fair Use of Unpublished Material, Henry Cohen, 90-304 A
* Copyright Law: Legalizing Home Taping of Audio and Video Recordings: Archived Issue Brief, Paul Wallace IB2075
* Copyright Law: Performance Rights in Musical Compositions and Videocassette Recordings, Douglas Reid Weimer, 89-639 A
* Digital Audio Recorder Act of 1987-- Analysis of H.R. 1384 and S. 506 With Policy Alternatives, David Hack 87-698 SPR
* Digital Audio Tape (DAT) Recording: Issue Brief, David B. Hack, etc., IB90004
* Emerging Electronic Technology and American Copyright Law, Douglas Reid Weimer, 90-310 A
* Industrial Design Protection, by Law Library of Congress. European Law Division, LL90-23
* Legal Analysis of a Memorandum of Understanding Between the United States and the Federal Republic of Germany Concerning Patent Rights Resulting from, Michael V. Seitzinger 87-281 A
* Patenting Life: Issue Brief, Sarah Taylor IB87222
* Patent Laws in Selected Countries, by Law Library of Congress. LL90-81
* Pharmaceutical Pricing and Patent Law, Sylvia Morrison, 91-748 E
* Resale Royalties for Visual Artists: Background Information and Analysis, Julius Allen 88-416 E
* U.S. Intellectual Property Rights and Trade, Lenore Sek 86-383 E
* Videocassette Recorders: Legal Analysis of Home Use, Douglas Reid Weimer 89-30 A

Payment-in-Kind Program

* see Agriculture--Policies and Legislation

Peace Dividend

* see Defense Economics, Defense Budgets

Peaceful Nuclear Explosions Treat

* The Threshold Test Ban and Peaceful Nuclear Explosion Treaties: Background Information and Senate Ratification Issues, Steven A. Hildreth, etc. 87-34 F

Penny Stocks

* see Corporations, Securities Industries

Pension Benefit Guarantee Corporation

* see Pensions

Pensions

* see also Civil Service, Social Security, IRAs
* Benefit and Pay Increases in Selected Federal Programs, 1969-1991 Carolyn L. Merck 91-513 EPW
* Benefits to Individuals Based on Previous Employment: Interactions and Offsets in Selected Programs, Carolyn L. Merck, 91-463 EPW
* Constitutional Considerations Implicated by a Hypothetical Proposal to Tax the Investment Income of a Tax-Exempt Entity Affiliated with a State or Local, Robert B. Burdette 88-551 A
* Early Retirement Incentive Plans under the Age Discrimination in Employment Act of 1967, as Amended, Kathleen S. Swendiman 88-608 A
* Effects of Stock Market Downturn on Pensions, Ray Schmitt 88-15 EPW
* Exempting Pension Benefits in Bankruptcy, Robin Jeweler, 91-724 A
*Explanations for the Trend Away from Defined Benefit Pension Plans, Angela Chang, 91-647 EPW
* Federal Deposit Insurance Corporation (FDIC) Pass-Through Insurance for Pension Plans, Ray Schmitt, etc., 91-411 EPW
* Federal Habeas Corpus: Background and Issues, Charles Doyle, 91-24 A
* Four Questions About National Retirement Income Security, Rich Hobbie, etc. 88-242 EPW
* The Indexation of Federal Programs, Royal Ship 82-103 S
* Individual Retirement Account Issues and Savings Accounts Proposals: Issue Brief, James Storey IB89085
* Individual Retirement Accounts and Financial Savings: New Evidence, William Jackson 86-125 E
* Individual Retirement Accounts (IRAs) After the Tax Reform Act of 1986, Gregg A. Esenwein 87-712 E
* Individual Retirement Accounts: Issues After Enactment of the 1986 Tax Reform: Archived Issue Brief, James Storey, etc. IB87225
* Insurance Company Insolvencies and Pension Benefits: Issue Brief, Ray Schmitt, IB91123
* Legal Analysis of LTV Corporation's Unilateral Termination of Retiree's Health and Life Insurance Benefits on the Date of Filing in Bankruptcy, Vincent Treacy 86-845 A
* Legal Authority of Bankrupt Employer Unilaterally to Terminate Retirees Benefits under a Collective Bargaining Agreement, Vincent Treacy 86-826 A
* Meeting the Pension Obligation: Underfunding and Overfunding Issues: Archived Issue Brief, Ray Schmitt IB87170
* Minimum Universal Pension System, Ray Schmitt 87-197 EPW
* New Vesting Requirements for Private Pension Plans, Ray Schmitt 88-166 EPW
* Paying for the Baby Boom's Retirement, Congressional Research Service 87-905 EPW
* Pension Asset Reversions: Whose Money Is It? Issue Brief, Raymond Schmitt, etc. IB89091
* Pension Issues: Info Pack, IP428P
* Pension Portability: What Does It Mean? How Does It Work? What Does It Accomplish? Ray Schmitt 88-498 EPW

Parental Leave / Persian Gulf

* Private Pension Issues, Ray Schmitt, 91-174 EPW
* Private Pension Plan Standards: A Summary of the Employment Retirement Income Security Act of 1974 (ERISA) as Amended, Ray Schmitt 88-681 EPW
* Private Pension Plan Standards: A Summary of (ERISA), Ray Schmitt 91-22 EPW
* Railroad Retirement and Employment: Recent Issues: Issue Brief, Dennis Snook, etc. IB84068
* Retiree Benefits in the Eastern Air Lines Bankruptcy, Robin Jeweler, 91-462 A
* Retirement Benefits Security Act of 1987: Legal Analysis of S. 548, 100th Congress, Vincent Treacy 87-294 A
* Retirement for Members of Congress, Carolyn L. Merck 91-96 EPW
* Retirement Income: Bibliography-in-Brief, 1986-1987, Edith Sutterlin 88-28 L
* Rules Governing Salary Reduction Retirement Plans, James R. Storey, 90-510 EPW
* Salary Reduction Retirement Plans: How They Work After the 1986 Tax Reform, James Storey 88-226 EPW
* Section 89 Nondiscrimination Rules for Employee Benefits, Ray Schmitt, etc. 88-470 EPW
* Simplification of Pension Rules; Proposals and Issues; Issue Brief, James R. Storey, IB90123
* State Taxation of Nonresidents' Retirement Income, Robert Burdette 89-224 A
* States that Will Award Spouses a Share of Retirement Benefits at the Time of Divorce, Marie Morris, etc. 87-782 A
* Survivor Benefits for Families of Members of Congress, Carolyn L. Merck, 91-507 EPW
* Tax-Favored Savings: All Savers Certificates and Individual Retirement Accounts, William Jackson 85-168 E
* Women's Pension Equity: A Summary of the Retirement Equity Act of 1984, Ray Schmitt 84-217 EPW
* Working After Normal Retirement Age: Pension Accruals for Post-65 Service, Ray Schmitt 88-618 EPW
* Young v. Old? Intergenerational Economic Equity: Bibliography-in-Brief, 10978-1987, Saundra Shirley-Reynolds 87-467 L

Pensions -- Civil Service

* Age Discrimination in Employee Benefit Plans: United States Supreme Court Decision in Public Employees Retirement System of Ohio v Betts, Kathleen S. Swendiman, 89-478 A
* Benefits to Individuals Based on Previous Employment: Interactions and Offsets in Selected Programs, Carolyn Merck 85-869 EPW
* Brief Comparison of Retirement Eligibility and Benefits for Members of Congress and Executive Branch Personnel, Carolyn L. Merck, 91-664 EPW
* Civil Service Retirement: Bibliography-in-Brief, 1985-1988, Edith Sutterlin 88-538 L
* Civil Service Retirement: Withdrawal of Contributions ("Lump-Sum Payments") and Taxation of Benefits, Carolyn L. Merck 87-99 EPW
* Comparison of Retirement Systems for Executive Branch Employees, Members of Congress and Active Duty Military Personnel, Carolyn Merck, etc. 85-685 EPW
* Comparison of the Civil Service Retirement System for Members of Congress and Executive Branch Employees, Carolyn Merck 85-681 EPW
* Criteria and Precedents for Providing Federal Civil Service Retirement Credit for Non-Federal Employment, Carolyn Merck 88-317 EPW
* Federal Civil Service Retirement for People With Military Service and Social Security: "Catch 62", Carolyn Merck 91-431 EPW
* Federal Civil Service Retirement: Withdrawal of Contributions ("Lump-Sum Payments") and Taxation of Benefits, Carolyn L. Merck, 90-313 EPW
* Federal Employees and the FY 1992 Budget Proposals: Issue Brief, James P. McGrath, IB91108
* Federal Employees Retirement System Handbook for Members of Congress: Benefits under the Federal Employees' Retirement System, Education and Public Welfare Division 87-189 EPW
* Fiduciary Responsibility Requirements of the Pension and Retirement Plans for State Employees, Joyce Thorpe, etc. 88-614 A
* Financing the Civil Service Retirement System: Payments Into and Out of the Trust Fund, Carolyn Merck 91-464 EPW
* Post-Retirement Maintenance of Real Benefit Level, Civil Service Retirement Team 85-750 EPW
* Premium Effect of Proposed Medicare Catastrophic Legislation on Federal Annuitants, Janet Lundy 87-801 EPW
* Provisions of the Balanced Budget and Emergency Deficit Control Act of 1985 Affecting Pay and Benefits for Federal Workers and Retirees, Carolyn Merck 86-502 EPW
* Provisions of the Tax Reform Act of 1986 Affecting Federal Workers and

Retirees, Carolyn Merck 86-928 EPW
* Public Pension Plans: The Issues Raised Over Control of Plan Assets, American Law Division; Education Public Welfare Division, 90-319 A
* Retirement for Federal Employees: FY1991 Budget Issues; Archived Issue Brief, Carol L. Merck, IB90041
* Retirement for Federal Employees: FY 90 Budget Issues: Issue Brief, Carolyn Merck IB89034
* A Retirement Plan for Federal Workers Covered by Social Security: An Analysis of the Federal Employees Retirement System (P.L. 99-335), Education and Public Welfare Division 86-137 EPW
* Retirement Systems for Federal Employees: Info Pack IP205R
* Social Security: The Offset of Social Security Spousal Benefits for Government Pensions, Nancy Miller, etc. 86-43 EPW
* State Taxation of Federal Retirement Income: Davis v. Michigan Department of Treasury, Marie B. Morris 89-233 A
* States Affected by the Supreme Courts Ruling on Tax Discrimination Against Federal Retirees, Mark Gurevitz, etc. 89-275 A
* Summary and Analysis of the Civil Service Retirement Spouse Equity Act, as Amended, Rita Ann Reimer 87-781 A
* Treatment of Former Spouses under Various Federal Retirement Systems, Marie Morris 90-256 A
* The U.S. Postal Service: Adjustment Cost for Retirement COLAs and Health Benefits under the 1990 Budget Act, Bernevia McCalip, 91-191 E
* What Amount of a Civil Service Retirement System (CSRS) Pension Is Equivalent to a Social Security Benefit? Geoffrey C. Kollmann, 90-324 EPW

Pensions -- IRAS

* Individual Retirement Account Issues and Savings Accounts Proposals: Issue Brief, James I. Storey, IB89085
* Individual Retirement Accounts: Issues After Enactment of the 1986 Tax Reform; Archived Issue Brief, James R. Storey, etc., IB87225
* IRA Alternatives: A Comparison of Taxpayer Benefits, Donald W. Kiefer, 90-191 E
* Use of IRA's for a Firs-Home Purchase: Pro/Con and Alternatives; Issue Brief, Richard Bourdon, IB91084

People's Republic of China

* see China

Perestroika

* see U.S.S.R. -- Politics and Government, U.S.S.R. -- Economic Conditions

Persian Gulf

* see also National Defense and Security
* Chinese Arms Sales to the Persian Gulf: A Fact Sheet, Robert Sutter 88-286 F
* Disruption of Oil Supply from the Persian Gulf: Near-Term U.S. Vulnerability (Winter 1987/88), Clyde Mark, etc. 87-863 ENR
* Insuring U.S.Interests in the Persian Gulf: Summary and Proceedings of the Workshop Held on October 6, 1987 by the Congressional Research Service, Gary J. Pagliano 88-725 F
* Iran-Iraq War: Archived Issue Brief, Richard M. Preece, IB88060
* Iraq-Kuwait Oil Price Rise: U.S. Economic Effects, Bernard A. Gelb, 90-434 E
* Iraq-Kuwait: The United Nations Response Before the War; Archived Issue Brief, Marjorie Ann Brown, IB90147
* Iraq's Food and Agricultural Situation During the Embargo and the War, Susan B. Epstein, 91-199 ENR
* The NATO Allies, Japan, and the Persian Gulf, Paul Gallis 84-184 F
* Oil from the Persian Gulf: Production, Disposition, and Transportation: Archived Issue Brief, Robert Bamberger, etc. IB88063
* Persian Gulf and the War Powers Debate: Issue Summary and Review of Events: Archived Issue Brief, Clyde Mark IB87207
* Persian Gulf: Iran Air Flight 655: Archived Issue Brief, Ellen Laipson IB88080
* Persian Gulf Oil, Its Critical Importance to World Oil Supplies, Joseph P. Riva, 91-220 SPR
* Persian Gulf: Overview of Issues: Archived Issue Brief, Ellen Laipson IB87220
* Persian Gulf: Selected References, Sherry Shapiro 88-533 L
* Persian Gulf: U.S. Military Operations: Archived Issue Brief, Ronald O'Rourke IB87145
* The Persian Gulf, 1987: A Chronology of Events, Clyde Mark 88-129 F
* Petroleum Status of the Western Persian Gulf, Joseph P. Riva, 90-378 SPR
* United Nations Role in the Iran-Iraq War: Issues and Options, Lois McHugh, etc. 88-463 F

Current Events and Homework

* U.S., Soviet, and Western European Naval Forces in the Persian Gulf Region, Robert J. Ciarrocchi 87-956 F

Persian Gulf War

* see Iraq-Kuwait Crisis

Peru

* Peru-U.S. Relations under the Fujimori Government, Nicholas Cochrane, 91-689 F

Pesticides

* Agent Orange: Veterans' Complaints and Studies of Health Effects: Archived Issue Brief, Sam Merrill, etc. IB83043
* Agricultural Effects on Groundwater Quality, Donald V. Feliciano 86-891 ENR
* Agriculture and the Environment: Issue Brief, Jean Rawson, etc. IB89086
* Apple Alarm: Public Concern About Pesticide Residues in Fruits and Vegetables, James Aidala 89-166 ENR
* Dioxin and Agent Orange Health Effects: An Update, Samuel Merrill, etc. 91-195 SPR
* Export of Pesticides, James Aidala 89-73 ENR
* Food Safety: Issues in the 101st Congress; Issue Brief, Donna Vogt, IB90096
* Fruit and Vegetable Issues in the 102nd Congress, Geoffrey Becker, 91-409 ENR
* Pesticide Monitoring Program: Developing New Methods to Detect Pesticide Residues in Food, Sarah E. Taylor, 87-413 SPR
* Pesticide Policy Issues: Debating FIFRA in the 102nd Congress; Issue Brief, Jasper Womach, IB91055
* Pesticide Regulation: Legislative Debate About FIFRA in 1986, James Aidala 87-417 ENR
* Pesticides in Food: A Checklist of CRS Products, Karen L. Alderson, 91-918 L
* Pesticides Issues: Reauthorization of P.L. 92-516: Issue Brief, James Aidala IB87192
* Predator Control and Compound 1080: Archived Mini Brief, Jim Aidala MB82241
* Proposed Senate Amendments to FIFRA, James Aidala 88-471 ENR
* Regulating U.S. Pesticide Exports: Policy Issues and Proposed Legislation, Jasper Womach, 91-568 ENR
* Superbug: Agriculture's Whitefly Problem, Geoffrey S. Becker, 91-828 ENR

Petroleum

* see Fossil Fuels--Petroleum

Philippines

* The Association of Southeast Asian Nations (ASEAN): Economic Development Prospects and the Role of the United States, Larry Niksch 84-171 F
* Current Issues With the 'Base-Rights' Countries and Their Implications, Richard Grimmett 88-726 F
* Economic Changes in the Asian Pacific Rim: Policy Prospectus, Congressional Research Service 86-923 S
* Insurgency and Counterinsurgency in the Philippines, Larry Niksch 85-1038 F
* Philippine Bases: U.S. Redeployment Options, Alva Bowen 86-44 F
* Philippines under Aquino: Issue Brief, Larry Niksch IB86104
* Philippines: U.S. Foreign Assistance Facts: Issue Brief, Larry Niksch IB85077
* U.S. Agricultural Trade Opportunities with Pacific Rim Nations, Robert M. Goldstein 88-755 ENR

Plant Shutdowns

* see Industry, Labor--Unemployment

Plastics Pollution in the Ocean

* see Water Pollution, Solid Wastes

Plutonium

* see Nuclear Energy

Poland

* Poland's Economic Recovery: U.S. Policy Interests: Archived Issue Brief, John Hardt, etc. IB86070
* Poland in Transition, Thomas J. Lang, 91-704 F
* Poland's Renewal and U.S. Options: A Policy Reconnaissance Update, John Hardt, etc. 87-889 S
* Polish Economic Reform and U.S. Interests, William H. Cooper, 91-249 E
* The Polish Official Debt Accord: A Problem of Containment, Patricia A. Wertman, 91-474 E

Polar Regions

* Antarctic Mineral Resources Regime: Diplomacy and Development: Issue Brief, James Mielke, etc. IB88101
* Antarctica: Environmental Protection Issues: Summary of a CRS Research Workshop, Susan Fletcher, 89-272 ENR
* Arctic National Wildlife Refuge: Congressional Consideration Since the 99th Congress, M. Lynne Corn, etc., 91-325 ENR
* Arctic Resources Controversy: Issue Brief, M. Lynne Corn, etc. IB89058
* Arctic Resources: Over a Barrel? Issue Brief, M. Lynne Corn, etc. IB91011
* Environmental Effects of Recent Activities in Antarctica, James E. Mielke, etc. 88-439 SPR
* Potential Mineral Resources in Antarctica and the Antarctic Minerals Convention, James E. Mielke, 90-71 SPR

Police

* Drug Control, Federal Efforts to Reduce the Supply: Selected References, 1987-1990, Jean Bowers, 90-617 L
* Equitable Distribution and Adoptive Forfeiture, Charles Doyle, 90-538 A
* Miranda After 1981: Supreme Court Case Law and the Justice Department Response, Lou Fields 88-517 A
* Narcotics Control Assistance for State and Local Governments: The Anti-Drug Abuse Act of 1988, William Woldman 89-181 GOV
* U.S. Assistance for Foreign Police Forces, Alan K. Yu, 89-419 F
* Use of the Military to Enforce Civilian Law: Posse Comitatus Act and Other Considerations, Charles Doyle 88-583 A

Political Action Committees

* see Politics and Elections--Campaign Funds

Political Conventions

* see Politics and Elections--Election Law

Political Ethics

* see also Ethics in Government Act, Government Employees--Ethics, Congress--Members
* An Analysis of S.J. Res. 113, a Proposed Constitutional Amendment Relating to the Removal of Federal Judges, Elizabeth Bazan 87-764 A
* Arms Shipments to Iran: Archived Issue Brief, Richard Preece IB87022
* Comparison of President Bush's Honoraria Reform Act of 1989 With Existing Laws, Orders, and Regulations, Mildred L. Amer, 89-481 GOV
* Compendium of Precedents Involving Evidentiary Rulings and Applications of Evidentiary Principles from Selected Impeachment Trials, Elizabeth B. Bazan, etc., 89-413 A
* Conflicts of Interest: The Department of Defense and the Revolving Door Problem, Andrew Mayer 86-188 F
* Congress and the Iran-Contra Affair, Joel Woldman 88-765 F
* Congressional Hearings on a Matter for Which an Independent Counsel Has Been Named, Jack H. Maskell 86-1043 A
* Congressional Votes and Judicial Action on Outside Income and Honoraria Restrictions, 1974-1990, Mildred L. Amer, 91-139 GOV
* Constitutional Analysis of 'Revolving Door' Proposal Regarding Expansion of Post-Employment Conflicts of Interest Law, Jack Maskell 88-590 A
* Disqualification or Refusal of Federal Official from Government Matters Involving Former Clients or Employers, Jack Maskell 86-948 A
* Ethics in Government: Reform of Laws and Regulations; Issue Brief, Mildred L. Amer, IB89134
* The Ethics of a Private Law Practice by Members and Employees of Congress, Jack Maskell 85-663 A
* Expulsion and Censure Actions Taken by the Full Senate Against Members, Jack Maskell, 90-299 A
* House Discipline of Members After Conviction but after Final Appeal, Jack H. Maskell 88-197 A
* Immunity for Witnesses Testifying Before Congressional Committees, Jay R. Shampansky 86-1026 A
* Impeachment: An Overview of Constitutional Provisions, Procedure and Practice, Elizabeth Bazan 88-637 A
* Independent Investigation of Allegations of Wrongdoing by Members of Congress, Jack Maskell 88-488 A
* Iran-Contra Affair: Organization Profiles, Heather Longton 87-625 F
* Japanese Lobbying and U.S. Automobile Policy, Dick K. Nanto, 91-186
* Legislative History and Purposes of Enactment of the Independent Counsel

Be patient. If any phone number is incorrect, call (area code) 555-1212 and request the new listing.

(Special Prosecutor) Provisions of the Ethics in Government Act of 1978, Jack Maskell 87-192 A
* Morrison v. Olson: Constitutionality of the Independent Counsel Law, Jack Maskell 88-469 A
* Overview of Ethics and Conflict of Interest Provisions Applicable to Executive Branch Employees, Jack Maskell 85-667 A
* Overview of the Independent Counsel Provisions of the Ethics in Government Act, Jack Maskell 88-631 A
* The Possible Interaction Between the Impeachment Process and the Double Jeopardy Clause, Elizabeth B. Bazan 89-10 A
* Post Employment ("Revolving Door") Ethics Bill of the 100th Congress Vetoed by the President, Jack Maskell 89-10 A
* Post Employment "Revolving Door" Restrictions on Department of Defense Personnel, Jack Maskell 88-478 A
* Prohibition on Members of Congress Contracting With the Federal Government, Jack Maskell 91-815 A
* Regulations on the Receipt of Gifts by Spouses of Government Employees, Jack Maskell 85-689 A
* Restrictions on the Outside Earned Income and Honoraria of Members of Congress 1975-1991, Mildred Amer, 91-588 GOV
* Summary of Constitutional Issues Raised in Challenges to the Independent Counsel Provisions of Federal Law, Jack Maskell 87-483 A

Political Parties

* see Politics and Elections--Practical Politics

Politics

* see Politics and Elections

Politics and Elections

* see Campaign Funds, Election Law, Practical Politics
* American national Government and Politics: Selected Introductory References, Tangela G. Roe, 90-231 L
* Blacks and Politics: Selected References, 1987-1990, Tangela G. Roe, 90-296 L
* Campaign Finance Reform: A Checklist of CRS Products, Jean Bowers, 91-912 L
* Census: A Checklist of CRS Products, Tangela G. Roe, 91-914 L
* The Forty-First President: George Bush, Selected References, 1972-1988, George Walser 88-699 L
* The Hatch Act: Existing Statute Compared With House and Senate Proposals, Barbara L. Schwemie 89-282 GOV
* Political Action Committees: Selected References, 1987-1989, Jean Bowers 89-276 L
* Political Campaigns and Elections: An Alphabetical Microthesaurus of Terms Selected from the Legislative Indexing Vocabulary, Shirley Loo 88-671 L
* U.S. Political party System, Thomas H. Neale, 90-633 GOV
* Voting Rights Act: A Checklist of CRS Products, George Walser, 92-15 L

Politics and Elections -- Campaign Funds

* Analysis of Proposed Federal Legislation to Limit PACS and to Encourage Individual Contributions, Thomas Durbin 87-583 A
* Analysis of the Provision in S. 1806 (Sen. Boren, 99th Congress) Making the Definition of "Independent Expenditure" More Precise, Thomas Durbin 86-1016 A
* Campaign Activities by Congressional Employees, Jack Maskell 82-165 A
* Campaign Finance: Info Pack, IP014C
* Campaign Finance Legislation in the 101st Congress, Joseph E. Cantor, 90-113 GOV
* Campaign Finance Reform: A Summary and Analysis of Legislative Proposals in the 98th and 99th Congresses, Joseph Cantor 87-1 GOV
* Campaign Finance: Selected References, 1986-1989, Jean Bowers 89-231 L
* Campaign Finance: Selected References, 1988-1990, Jean Bowers 91-356 L
* Campaign Financing and Corporate Expenditures: An Analysis of Austin v. Michigan Chamber of Commerce, L. Paige Whitaker, 90-199 A
* Campaign Financing in Federal Elections: A Guide to the Law and Its Operations, Joseph Cantor 91-770 GOV
* Campaign Financing: Issue Brief, Joseph E. Cantor, etc., IB87020
* Campaign Financing: National Public Opinion Polls, by Rinn-Sup Shinn, 91-346 GOV
* Campaign Financing of National Elections in Foreign Countries, Law Library of Congress, LL91-8
* Campaign Financing/Public Financing: Archived Issue Brief, Thomas Durbin IB73017
* Congressional Districts: Apportioning Seats and Dividing States into Single Member Districts, David Huckabee, 90-573 GOV
* Constitutional Analysis of S. 2 (100th Congress), Senatorial Election Campaign Act of 1987, Thomas Durbin 87-326 A
* Constitutionality of Legislation Prohibiting Lobbyists from Soliciting Contributions for Federal Elections, Thomas Durbin 87-555 A
* Constitutionality of Proposals Prohibiting All Independent Expenditures in Federal Elections, Thomas Durbin 87-570 A
* The Constitutionality of the Limitation on the Amount of Contributions a Publicly-Funded Candidate Can Receive from Out-of-State Contributors, Thomas M. Durbin, 87-547 A
* Expenditures for Campaign Services: A Survey of 1988 Congressional Candidates in Competitive Elections, by Joseph E. Cantor, etc., 90-457 GOV
* Federal Election Commission: Issue Brief, Thomas Durbin IB81104
* First Amendment Issues and Major Supreme Court Decisions Relating to Campaign Finance Reform Legislation, Thomas Durbin 87-80 A
* Foreign Participation in Federal Elections: A Legal Analysis, Thomas Durbin 87-554 A
* House Campaign Expenditures: 1980-1986, David C. Huckabee, etc. 87-451 GOV
* House Campaign Expenditures, Receipts and Sources of Funds: 1980-1990 by Joseph E. Cantor, etc., 91-628 GOV
* Legal Analysis of Specialized Multicandidate PACs and Private Tax-Exempt Foundations of Potential Federal Office Candidates, Thomas Durbin 86-844 A
* Limits on Lobbying and Political Activity by Tax-Exempt Organizations: Historical Background and Continuing Issues, Marie Morris 87-821 A
* Lobbying by Foreign Interests, Richard C. Sachs, 91-318 GOV
* PACs Sponsored by Corporations Partly or Wholly Owned by Foreign Investors, Roger Walke, etc., 89-618 GOV
* Political Action Committee Contributions Received by House Candidates: 1980-1986, David Huckabee, etc. 87-550 GOV
* Political Action Committees (PACs): Info Pack IP196P
* Political Action Committees: Selected References, 1989-1991, Jean Bowers, 91-382 L
* The Presidential Election Campaign Fund and Tax Checkoff, Joseph Cantor 85-180 GOV
* Prohibiting All PAC Contributions to Federal Office Candidates: A Constitutional Analysis, Thomas Durbin 87-549 A
* Senate Campaign Expenditures, Receipts and Sources of Funds: 1980-1990, David Huckabee, etc. 91-406 GOV
* "Soft Money" in Federal Elections: A Legal Analysis, Thomas Durbin 88-492 A
* Summary Data on 1988 Congressional Candidates' Expenditure Survey: Addendum to CRS Report 90-457 GOV, Joseph E. Cantor, etc., 90-526 GOV
* Use of Compulsory Union Dues for Political and Ideological Purposes: An Analysis of Supreme Court Decisions and Federal Legislation Re Such Use, Thomas Durbin 86-1056 A
* Whether or Not Senatorial Public Financing Proposals Impose Unconstitutional Monetary Sanctions, Thomas Durbin 87-660 A
* Whether Senatorial Public Financing Proposals Violate the Constitutional Rights of Contributors, Thomas Durbin 87-459 A

Politics and Elections -- Election Law

* The American Electoral College: Origins, Development, Proposals for Reform or Abolition, Thomas Neale 79-72 GOV
* Campaign Financing/Public Financing: Archived Issue Brief, Thomas Durbin IB73017
* Congressional and State Legislative Redistricting and Racial Vote Dilution under Section 2 of the Voting Rights Act of 1965, Thomas Durbin, 91-668 A
* Constitutionality of Legislation Providing for Mail Registration and Election Day Registration for Federal Elections, Thomas Durbin 87-247 A
* The Eighteen Years Old Vote: the Twenty-Sixth Amendment and Subsequent Voting Rates of Newly Enfranchised Age Groups, Thomas Neale 83-103 GOV
* The Election Process in the United States, Kevin J. Coleman, etc., 90-205 GOV
* Election Reform in the United States: Major Current Issues, Government Division, 90-210 GOV
* Electoral College: Bibliography-in-Brief, 1958-1988, George Walser 88-680L
* Electoral College: Info Pack IP031E
* The Electoral College Method of Electing the President and Vice President and Proposals for Reform, Thomas Durbin 88-555 A
* Electoral Votes Based on the 1990 Census, David C. Huckabee, 91-809 GOV
* Extending the Fairness Doctrine to the Print Media, Thomas Durbin 87-584 A
* The Fairness Doctrine and the Equal Opportunities Doctrine: Archived Issue Brief, L. Paige Whitaker, IB82087

Current Events and Homework

* The Fairness Doctrine: Selected References, 1979-1987, Rebecca Mazur 88-24 L
* The Hatch Act: Existing Statute Compared With House and Senate Proposals, Barbara L. Schwemle, 89-282 GOV
* The Hatch Act: Existing Statues Compared with 102nd Congress Proposals, Barbara L. Schwemle, 91-544 GOV
* Hatch Act: Info Pack IP298H
* A Legal Analysis of the Equal Time Rule After the FCC's Abolition of the Fairness Doctrine, Thomas Durbin 87-754 A
* A Legal Analysis of the FCC's Abolition of the Fairness Doctrine, Thomas M. Durbin, 87-754 A
* Legal and Constitutional Framework of "Hatch Act" Restrictions on Political Activities of Federal Employees, Jack Maskell 89-280 A
* Making the General Election Day a Holiday or Changing the General Election Day to Sunday, Thomas M. Durbin 87-596 A
* Presidential Elections in the United States, Thomas H. Neale, 91-467 GOV
* Proposals to Reform Our Presidential Electoral System: A Survey of the Historical Background and Development of the Electoral College, A Compilation, Thomas Durbin 84-150 A
* Re-Election Rates of Senate Incumbents: 1790-1988, David C. Huckabee, 90-250 GOV
* Remedies Available to the House of Representatives After an Investigation of a Contested Election Case, Thomas Durbin 85-658 A
* Special Elections and Membership Changes in the 100th Congress, Thomas Neale 89-95 GOV
* Special Elections and Membership Changes in the 101st Congress, Second Session, Thomas Neale 91-189 GOV
* Special Elections and Membership Changes in the 101st Congress, First Session, Thomas Neale 90-36 GOV
* State Statutory Provisions Regarding the Political Activities by Public Employees, Jack Maskell 87-841 A
* A Summary of National and State Party Laws Concerning the Election of Delegates to the 1988 Democratic and Republican National Conventions, Kevin Coleman 88-102 GOV
* The U.S. Election Process, Thomas H. Neale, 91-803 GOV
* Use of Compulsory Union Dues for Political and Other Ideological Purposes, Thomas Durbin 88-737 A
* Voter Registration and Turnout: 1948-1988, Royce Crocker 89-179 GOV
* Voter Registration and Turnout in the States With Mail and Motor-Voter Registration Systems, Royce Crocker 90-105 GOV
* The Voting Rights Act of 1965: A Legal Overview, L. Paige Whitaker, 91-736 A
* The Voting Rights Act of 1965 as Amended, Paul Downing 84-203 GOV

Politics and Elections -- Practical Politics

* Brief Histories of Major and Minor Political Parties in the United States--A Compilation of Extracts 1789-1979 Frederick Paula, etc. 80-169 GOV
* Campaign Activities by Congressional Employees, Jack Maskell, 89-574
* Changes in the Presidential Nomination Process: Looking to 1988: Issue Brief, Kevin Coleman IB86117
* The Fairness Doctrine and the Equal Opportunities Doctrine: Issue Brief, Thomas Durbin 82087
* Final Delegate Totals and Dates for Presidential Primaries and Caucuses, 1988, Kevin J. Coleman 89-180 GOV
* Foreign Interest Lobbying: Issue Brief, Richard C. Sachs, IB91101
* "The Gender Gap": Differences Between Men and Women in Political Attitudes and Voting Behavior in the 1980's, Jennifer D. Williams, 89-547 GOV
* A Guide to the Presidential Election Process, Joseph Cantor, etc. 88-629 GOV
* Initiative Referendum, and Recall: Direct Democracy in the United States, Thomas H. Neale, 91-752 GOV
* Interest Groups and Lobbying: Selected References, 1987-1989, Jean Bowers 89-257 L
* Interest Groups and Lobbying: Selected References, 1989-1991, Jean Bowers 91-537 L
* Legal and Congressional Ethics Standards of Relevance to Those Who Lobby Congress, Jack Maskell, 91-163 A
* Lobbying: Info Pack IP066L
* Lobbying in the United States, Richard Sachs, 91-765 GOV
* Lobbyists and Interest Groups: A List of Information Sources, Barbara Hillson, 91-660 C
* Negative Campaigning in National Politics: An Overview, Thomas Neale 91-775 GOV
* The New Religious Right: Background, Current Agenda, Future Prospects, Charles Whittier 87-615 GOV
* Political Campaigns and Elections: An Alphabetical Microthesaurus of

Terms Selected from the Legislative Indexing Vocabulary, Shirley Loo, 88-671 L
* Presidential Nominating Process: Proposed Reforms; Archived Issue Brief, Kevin J. Coleman, IB86117
* Reelection Rates of House Incumbents: 1790-1988, David Huckabee 89-173 GOV
* Regulation of Lobbying in Foreign Countries, Law Library of Congress, LL90-85
* Speechwriting and Delivery: Info Pack IP139S
* Speechwriting in Perspective: A Brief Guide to Effective and Persuasive Communication, Charles Whittier 86-1034 GOV
* The 1984 Presidential Election: The Platforms Presented by the Democratic Party (Mondale/Ferraro) and the Republican Party (Reagan/Bush), Kevin Coleman 84-182 GOV

Polygraph Testing of Employees

* see Labor

Poor

* see Public Welfare

Population

* see Census, Census of Population and Housing (1990)
* Adjusting the 1990 Census: Background and a Pro-Con Analysis, Alexander Luri 88-305 GOV
* The Census Bureau's Plans for Using Computerized Maps in 1990: Fact Sheet, Daniel Melnick 87-206 GOV
* Census: A Checklist of CRS Products, Tangela G. Roe, 91-914 L
* Census Questions and OMB's Review of the Census Bureau Proposal: A Summary and Brief Analysis, Daniel Melnick, etc. 88-42 GOV
* Counting Undocumented Aliens in the Decennial Census, Thomas Durbin 88-438 A
* House Apportionment Following the 1990 Census: Preliminary Projections, David Huckabee 88-567 GOV
* International Population and Family Planning Programs: Issues for Congress: Issue Brief, Shirley Kan IB85187
* Population Growth and Natural Resource Deterioration in Drought-Stricken Africa, Susan Abbasi 85-1149 ENR
* Population Programs of AID: Background of Legislation--99th Congress, Vita Blue 86-1009 F
* Proposed Exclusion of Illegal Aliens from the Population Used to Apportion the House of Representatives: A Methodological and Policy Analysis, Jennifer D. Williams, etc. 88-418 GOV
* Reapportionment and Redistricting: Info Pack, Congressional Reference Division, IP119R
* Statistical Adjustment of the Decennial Census: Constitutional Analysis of Statutory Proposals, Thomas Durbin 87-947 A
* Steps in Conducting the 1990 Census, Daniel Melnick 87-205 GOV
* The U.S. White Population, by Census Division, State, and Congressional District, Jennifer Williams 86-860 GOV
* The 1990 Decennial Census and the Counting of Illegal Aliens, Thomas Durbin 88-62 A
* 99th Congress Districts Classified by the Proportion of Population Over Age 65 (Ranking all Districts by Their Total Population over 65 and Percent over), David Huckabee 89-910 GOV

Population -- Census

* Adjusting the 1990 Census: Background and a Pro-Con Analysis, Alexander Lurie, 88-305 GOV
*Census Data for Congressional Use: Types and Availability of 1990 Decennial Census Products, Jennifer D. Williams, 91-641 GOV
* Census 1990: Selected References, 1987-1990, M. Alexandra Salinas, 91-266 L
* Counting Undocumented Aliens in the Decennial Census, Thomas M. Durbin, 88-438 A
* House Apportionment Following the 1990 Census: Using the Official Counts, David C. Huckabee, 91-130 GOV
* How the Adjusted Census Results Would Be Used to Obtain Block Level Counts, Daniel Melnick, 90-56 GOV
* The Proposed Department of Commerce Guidelines for Adjusting the 1990 Census: An Analysis and Review, Daniel Melnick, 90-51 GOV
Proposed Exclusion of Illegal Aliens from the Population Used to Apportion the House of Representative: A Methodological and Policy Analysis, Jennifer D. Williams, etc., 88-418 GOV
* Statistical Adjustment of the Decennial Census: A constitutional Analysis of Statutory Proposals, Thomas Durbin, 87-947 A

Politics and Elections / Power Resources

* The 1990 Census: Including Foreign Based Military and Civilian Personnel in the State Counts, David C. Huckabee, 90-305 GOV
* The 1990 Decennial Census and the Counting of Illegal Aliens, Thomas M. Durbin 88-62 A

Pornography and Obscenity

* see Civil Liberties and Rights--Pornography and Obscenity

Portugal

* Current Issues With the "Base-Rights" Countries and Their Implications, Richard Grimmett 88-726 F
* United States Military Installations in Portugal, Richard Grimmett 86-6 F

Posse Comitatus Act

* Use of the Military to Enforce Civilian Law: Posse Comitatus Act and Other Considerations, Charles Doyle 88-583 A

Postal Service

* Commemorative Postage Stamps: History, Selection, Criteria, and Revenue Raising Potential, Bernevia M. McCalip 88-575 E
* Constitutionality of Franking Statute Upheld by U.S. District Court in Common Cause v. Bolger, Elizabeth Yadlosky 82-155 S
* Legal Analysis of S. 541, 100th Congress, a Bill to Provide that Certain Postal Service Employees Have Procedural and Appeal Rights in the Event of Ad, Michael Seitzinger 87-433 A
* Postal Service's Mail Monopoly: Issue Brief, by Bernevia M. McCalip, IB91045
* The Postal Service: Its Treatment in the Federal Budget: Issue Brief, Bernevia McCalip IB88035
* Postal Workers Negotiations: The 1987 Contract, Gail McCallion 87-851 E
* The U.S. Postal Service: A Public or Private Enterprise?: Issue Brief, Bernevia M. McCalip IB88084
* U.S. Congress Official Mail Costs: FY 1972 to FY 1991, by John Pontius, 90-345 GOV
* The U.S. Postal Service: Adjustment Cost for Retirement COLAs and Health Benefits under the 1990 Budget Act, by Bernevia McCalip, 91-191 E
* U.S. Postal Service Appropriations: History and Current Status, Bernevia M. McCalip, 91-227 E
* The U.S. Postal Service Monopoly: Should It Be Repealed? : Archived Issue Brief, Bernevia McCalip IB85182

Poverty

* see Public Welfare

Power Resources

* see Alternative Energy Sources, Electric Power, Energy Conservation, Energy Policy, Fossil Fuels, and Nuclear Energy
* Controlling Carbon Dioxide Emissions, Amy Abel, etc. 89-157 ENR
* Energy Conservation and Renewables: A Checklist of CRS Products, Karen L. Alderson, 91-919 L
* Energy Tax Policy Issues: A Checklist of CRS Products, Karen L. Alderson, 92-8 L
* The Europe 1992 Plan: Science and Technology Issues, Science Policy Research Division 89-178 SPR
* Soviet Energy: An Engine or a Brake on Commercial Relations in the 1990s?, John P. Hardt, 91-211 RCO
* The Strategic Petroleum Reserve and the Drawdown Dilemma, Robert L. Bamberger, etc. 90-492 ENR

Power Resources -- Alternative Energy Sources

* Alcohol Fuels: Bibliography-in-Brief, Karen Alderson 88-415 L
* Alcohol Fuels: Issue Brief, Migdon Segal IB74087
* Alcohol Fuels Tax Incentives: Current Law and Proposed Option to Expand Current Law, Salvatore Lazzari 89-343 E
* Alternative Fuels and Reformulated Gasoline: Issue Brief, David Gushee, IB91008
* Alternative Fuels for Motor Vehicles: Some Environmental Issues, David Gushee 88-624 S
* Alternative Transportation Fuels: What's at Stake? David E. Gushee, 90-229 S
* Analysis of Possible Effects of H.R. 2031, Legislation Mandating Use of Ethanol and Methanol in Gasoline, Congressional Research Service 88-71 SPR
* Analysis of Possible Effects of H.R. 2052, Legislation Mandating Use of Ethanol in Gasoline, Migdon Segal, etc. 87-819 SPR
* Ethanol Fuel and Global Warming, Migdon Segal 90-441 SPR
* Geothermal Energy: Renewable or Depletable? James E. Mielke, 90-599 SPR
* Handbook of Alternative Energy Technology Development and Policy, Science Policy Research Division 83-43 SPR
* Methanol Fuel: Economics and Implementation: a Review of Current Studies, David E. Gushee, etc. 89-562 S
* Near Term Options for Reducing United States Carbon Dioxide Emissions, by Environment and Natural Resources Policy Division, Science Policy Research Division, 91-133 ENR
* Renewable Energy: A New National Commitment? Issue Brief, Fred J. Sissine, IB90110
* Renewable Energy: Federal Program: Issue Brief, Fred Sissine IB87140
* Renewable Energy Technology: A Review of Legislation, Research, and Trade, Fred Sissine, etc. 87-318 SPR
* Trucking and the Clean Air Act Amendments of 1990: Some Economic Implications, Stephen J. Thompson, 91-132 E
* Utility Fuel Options: Using Excess Corn Supplies, Duane A. Thompson 87-541 ENR
* Wind Energy: Archived Issue Brief, Fred Sissine IB80091
* Wind Energy Development and Utility Capacity Credits: A Review of Research, Implementation and Policy Issues under the Public Utility Regulatory Act, Fred Sissine 84-101 SPR

Power Resources

* Accelerated Depreciation, the Investment Tax Credit, and Their Required Ratemaking Treatment in the Public Utility Industry: A Background Report, Donald W. Kiefer 87-312 S
* Acid Rain Legislation and Midwest Industry: A Mountain or a Mole Hill? Larry Parker, etc. 85-1152 ENR
* The Bonneville Power Administration: To Sell or Not to Sell, Alvin Kaufman, etc. 86-176 E
* Canadian Electricity: The U.S. Market and the Free Trade Agreement, Amy Abel 88-427 ENR
* The Effect of Alternative Depreciation Systems on Marginal Effective Tax Rates on Public Utility Property, Donald Keifer 86-506 E
* Electric Rate Effects of Cogeneration and Wheeling : Should PURPA Be Amended? Archived Issue Brief, Sylvia Morrison IB87119
* Electric Utilities: Deregulation, Diversification, Acid Rain, Tall Stack Regulation, and Electric Demand Issues: Archived Issue Brief, Donald Dulchinos, etc. IB85134
* Electric Utility Regulation in the Brave New World, Alvin Kaufman 88-135 ENR
* Federal and State Regulation of Nuclear and Non-Nuclear Electric Utilities and of Nuclear Materials, Michael Seitzinger 87-221 A
* Federal Hydropower: Repaying the Debt: Archived Issue Brief, John Moore IB85125
* Federal Hydropower: The Administration's Proposal to Sell Government Assets: Archived Issue Brief, John Moore IB86057
* The Federal Power Marketing Administrations: To Privatize or Not to Privatize, Alvin Kaufman, etc. 86-90 S
* Licensing and Special Use Permit Requirements for Hydroelectric Dam Projects under the Federal Power Act and the Federal Land Policy and Management Act, Robin Jeweler 88-459 A
* Public Utilities Holding Company Act of 1935: Is This the Time for Reform: Issue Brief, Amy Abel IB89052
* PURPA: Should It Be Amended to Facilitate the Sale of Bulk Power by Bid?: Archived Issue Brief, Sylvia Morrison IB88014
* Rural Electric Cooperative Defaults: Origins, Current Status, and Legislative Implications, Sylvia Morrison 88-665 E
* State Versus Federal Ratemaking Authority: Mississippi Power & Light Co. v. Mississippi Ex Rel. Moore, Robin Jeweler 88-651 A
* Superconductivity: An Overview: Issue Brief, Richard Rowberg, etc. IB87191
* Superconductivity: Bibliography-in-Brief, 1980-1988, B.F. Mangan 88-632 L
* Superconductors: Info Pack IB390S
* The Tax Reform Act of 1986: The Effects on Public Utilities, Donald Kiefer 84-211 E
* The United States Bankruptcy Code: Legal Implications of an Investor-Owned Utility Reorganization under Chapter, Robin Jeweler 88-140 A
* Wheeling in the Electric Utility Industry, Environment and Natural Resources Policy Division 87-289 ENR

Power Resources - Electric Power

* Acid Rain Legislation and Midwest Industry: A Mountain or a Mole Hill?

Current Events and Homework

Larry Parker, etc. 85-1152 ENR
* Canadian Electricity: The U.S. Market and the Free Trade Agreement, Amy Abel, 88-427 ENR
* Controlling Carbon Dioxide Emissions, Amy Abel, 89-157 ENR
* Electromagnetic Fields: Health Effects; Bibliography-in-Brief, 1988-1991, Karen L. Alderson 91-701 L
* Federal and State Regulation of Nuclear and Non-Nuclear Electric Utilities and of Nuclear Materials, Michael V. Seitzinger, 77-221 A
* Natural Gas and the Generation of Electricity, Alvin Kaufman, etc., 90-253 ENR
* Power Lines and Electromagnetic Fields; Issues for Congress; Issue Brief, Christopher H. Dodge, IB91051
* Public Utilities Holding Company Act of 1935: Is this the Time for Reform? Issue Brief, by Amy Abel, IB89052
* Rural Electric Cooperative Defaults: Origins, Current Status, and Legislative Implications, Sylvia Morrison, 88-665 E
* The Rural Electrification Administration: Background and Current Issues, Carl Ek, etc. 91-614 ENR

Power Resources -- Energy Conservation

* Comparison of the Departments of Energy and Health and Human Services Weatherization Assistance Programs, Mary Smith, etc. 89-229 EPW
* DOE Energy Conservation Budget Trends: A Review With Comparisons to Other DOE Programs, Fred Sissine 87-486 SPR
* Energy Conservation and Electric Utilities: Developments and Issues in Regulating Program Profitability, Fred Sissine, 90-275 SPR
* Energy Conservation Policies of the European Community and United States: Comparing Apples and Oranges, Amy Abel, 89-604 ENR
* Energy Conservation: Prospects for Cogeneration Technology: Archived Issue Brief, Fred Sissine IB83068
* Energy Conservation: Technical Efficiency and Program Effectiveness: Archived Issue Brief, Fred Sissine IB85130
* Energy Efficiency and Renewable Energy Provisions of House and Senate national Energy Strategy Legislation: A Side-by-Side Comparison, Fred Sissine, etc., 91-709 SPR
* The Low-Income Home Energy Assistance Program, Joe Richardson, 91-465 EPW
* Weatherization Assistance Programs of the Departments of Energy and Health and Human Services, Mary F. Smith, etc., 90-285 EPW

Power Resources -- Energy Policy

* Defense Laboratories: PROPOSALS FOR Closure and Consolidation, Michael E. Davey, 91-135 SPR
* DOE's FY1992 Budget: Issue Brief, Marc Humphries, IB91060
* Energy Excise Taxes for Deficit Reduction: Archived Issue Brief, Salvatore Lazzari IB87172
* Energy Impacts: Archived Issue Brief, Duane Thompson, etc. IB87021
* Energy Policy: A Checklist of Public Policy Literature and CRS Products, Ted L. Burch, 91-55 L
* Energy Policy: Info Pack, Congressional Reference Division, IP447E
* Energy Policy: Issue Brief, Robert Bamberger, IB90021
* Energy Security: Issue Brief, Carl Behrens IB89006
* Forum: Energy Policy; A Post-War Framework, Congressional Research Service review, v.12, Mar.-Apr. 1991, REV 3-91
* A History of Federal Energy Tax Policy: Conventional as Compared to Renewable and Nonconventional Energy Resources, Salvatore Lazzari 88-455 E
* The National Energy Strategy: Summary and Analysis, Robert L. Bamberger, 91-204 ENR
* Setting Priorities for Department of Energy Environmental Activities, Mark Holt, etc., 91-150 ENR

Practical Politics

* see Congress--Apportionment and Elections, Politics and Elections--Practical Politics

Prayer in the Public Schools

* see Elementary and Secondary Education--Prayer and Religion

Presidential Appointments

* see Executive Organization--Presidential Appointments, Presidents (U.S.)

Presidential-Congressional Relations

* see Congress--Executive Relations, Congress--Foreign Relations, Congress--Military Policy, Presidents (U.S.)--Foreign Relations, War Powers Resolution

Presidents (U.S.)

* see also Foreign Relations, Veto
* Benefits to Former Presidents, Stephanie Smith, 91-229 GOV
* The Examined Life: Writing Congressional Biographies; Videoprogram, Robert Caro, etc., LTR91-866
* Executive Agreements Submitted to Congress: Legislative Procedures Used Since 1970, Ellen C. Collier, etc., 90-548 F
* Federal Benefits to Former Presidents and Their Widows, Stephanie Smith 85-173 GOV
* Federal Expenditures for Former Presidents: Archived Issue Brief, Stephanie Smith IB85129
* Federal Presidential Libraries, Harold C. Relyea, 90-595 GOV
* The Forty-First President: George Bush, Selected References, 1972-1988, George Walser 88-699 L
* Inauguration of the President: Info Pack IP316I
* The Lives of the Presidents of the United States: An Introductory Bibliography, James Sayler, 91-812 GOV
* National Emergency Powers, Harold C. Relyea, 91-383 GOV
* The Presidency of the United States: Info Pack IP409P
* The Presidency: Selected References, 1985-1988, Elizabeth Lane 89-84 L
* Presidential Commissions: Their Purpose and Impact, Stephanie Smith 87-668 GOV
* Presidential Elections in the United States, Thomas H. Neale, 91-467 GOV
* Presidential Emergency Powers Over Domestic Affairs: Executive Order No. 211490 and P.R.M. No. 32: Archived Issue Brief, Raymond Nattern IB80087
* Presidential Remarks About the International Atomic Energy Agency: Selected Excerpts, Barbara Black 89-27 ENR
* Presidential Signing Statements--Use in Statutory Construction, George Costello 87-894 A
* Presidential Succession: A Short History, Ronald Moe 78-244 GOV
* Presidential Tenure: A History and Analysis of the President's Term of Office, Stephen Stathis 81-129 GOV
* Presidential Transition: Selected References, 1960-1988, George Walser 88-691 L
* Presidential Vetoes and Ronald Reagan's Use of the Process in the Second Term: Issue Brief, Gary Galemore IB85093
* Presidential Vetos and Ronald Reagan's Use of the Process in His First Term: Archived Issue Brief, Gary Galemore IB81174
* Recess Appointment: Legal Overview, Richard C. Ehlke 87-832 A
* Salary of the President of the United States Compared with that of Other High-Level Government Officials, Sharon Gressle 90-89 GOV
* The U.S. Presidency; Office and Powers, Harold C. Relyea, 91-699 GOV
* U.S. Presidents: An Alphabetical Microthesaurus of Terms Selected from the Legislative Indexing Vocabulary , Shirley Loo 89-131 L
* Vetoes During President Reagan's First Term, 1981-1984, Gary Galemore 86-681 GOV
* Vice Presidents of the United States, 1789-1981: Brief Bibliographical Notes, Christopher Dell 81-23 GOV

Presidents (U.S.) -- Foreign Relations

* Andropov and Reagan as Negotiators: Context and Styles in Contrast, Joseph Whelan 83-141 S
* Central American Peace Process: Selected References, Robert Kirk 88-389 L
* Congress and the President in U.S. Foreign Policymaking: A Selected, Annotated Bibliography, Sherry Shapiro 86-183 L
* Foreign Policy Roles of the President and Congress, Ellen C. Collier 86-163 F
* The Iran/Contra Affair: Implications for the National Security Adviser and the NSC Staff: Archived Issue Brief, Joel Woldman IB87107
* Iraq-Kuwait Crisis: Selected Administration Statements, August-December 15, 1990, Theodore J. Craig, 91-13 F
* President and Foreign Policy: Selected References, Sherry Shapiro 91-157 L
* The President's Powers in Time of War: A Brief Overview, David M. Ackerman, 91-95 A
* Sectional Analysis of the "War Powers Resolution" (WPR) as It Would Be Amended by the "War Powers Resolution Amendments of 1988" (S.J. Res. 323, 100th), Raymond J. Celada 88-441 A
* Statements by President Reagan Relating to Arms Control, April 1, 1986-January 31, 1987, Teri Lehto 87-116 S
* Statements by President Reagan Relating to Arms Control, February 1, 1987-May 31, 1987, Teri Lehto 87-525 S
* Statements by President Reagan Relating to Arms Control: February 2, 1985-December 31, 1985, Jeanette Voas 86-549 F
* Statements by President Reagan Relating to Arms Control, January 1, 1984-March 31, 1984, Lynn Rusten 84-616 F

* Statements by President Reagan Relating to Arms Control: January 1, 1986-March 31, 1986, Jeanette Voas 86-663 S
* Statements by President Reagan Relating to Arms Control: June 1, 1987-December 31, 1987, Teri Lehto 88-69 S
* Statements by President Reagan Relating to the INF Treaty, June 1, 1987-December 31, 1987, Teri Lehto 88-60 S
* U.S. Presidential National Security Advisers: Changing Roles and Relationships, Joel Woldman 87-334 F
* The War Powers Resolution: Fifteen Years of Experience, Ellen Collier 88-529 F
* War Powers Resolution: Info Pack IP131W
* War Powers Resolution: Presidential Compliance: Issue Brief, Ellen Collier IB81050
* War Powers Resolution: The Controversial Act's Search for a Successful Litigation Posture, Raymond J. Celada 88-64 A
* The War Powers Resolution (WPR): Some Implications of S.J. Res. 323, "War Powers Resolution Amendments of 1988", Raymond J. Celada 88-464 A
* War Powers: Selected References, Sherry Shapiro 89-305 L

Presidents (U.S.) -- Veto

* The Pocket Veto: A Legal Analysis, Jay R. Shampansky, 90-43 A
* The President and the Budget Process: Expanded Impoundment and Item Veto Proposals; Issue Brief, Virginia A. McMurty, IB89148
* Presidential Vetoes During the Bush Administration: Issue Brief, Gary L. Galemore, IB89111
* Veto Overrides by Congress 1969-1988, Gary L. Alemore, 89-436 GOV

Press

* Concentration in the U.S. Daily Newspaper Industry: Trends and Issues, R. Kevin Flaherty 84-727 E
* Confidentiality and Secrecy Orders in Civil Cases, Kenneth Thomas 89-225 A
* Copyright and Compilations of Facts: Feist Publications v. Rural Telephone Service, Co. Douglas Reid Weimer, 91-552 A
* Crime and Crime Control: National Public Opinion Polls, Rinn-Sup Shinn, 90-583 GOV
* Extending the Fairness Doctrine to the Print Media, Thomas Durbin 87-584 A
* The Government and the Press, Denis Steven Rutkus, 90-589 GOV
* High School Student Press Rights: Hazelwood School District v. Kuhlmeier, Rita Ann Reimer 88-167 A
* Mediasat: The Use of Remote Sensing Satellites by News Agencies, Patricia E. Humphlett 87-70 SPR
* The Newspaper Preservation Act (15 U.S.C. (Sections) 1801-1804), Janice E. Rubin 89-239 A
* Newspaper and Television NETWORK News Coverage of Congress During the Summers of 1979 and 1989: A Content Analysis, Denis Steven Rutkus, etc. 91-238 GOV
* The New York Daily News Strike, Gail McCallion, 91-149 E
* Press Restrictions in the Persian Gulf War: First Amendment Implications, Henry Cohen, 91-316 A
* "Public Figures" and the Intentional Infliction of Emotional Distress: Hustler Magazine v. Falwell, Rita Ann Reimer 88-177 A
* Research Journal Prices--Trends and Problems, Richard Rowberg 88-264 SPR
* Taxation of the Press: A Brief Constitutional Analysis, Rita Ann Reimer 87-422 A
* Television Network Evening News Coverage of Afghanistan: A Perspective After Eight Years of War, Denis Stevens Rutkus 88-319 GOV

Price-Anderson Insurance and Indemnity Act

* see also Nuclear Energy--Accidents and Safety
* Nuclear Liability Legislation: Price-Anderson Act Renewal Issues: Archived Issue Brief, Mark Holt IB88034

Prisoners of War in Southeast Asia

* see Military Personnel

Prisons

* Canada's Prohibition on the Importation of Goods Produced by Prisoners, Law Library of Congress, American-British Law Division, LL90-15
* Foreign Prohibitions on the Importation of Goods Produced by Prison Labor, Law Library of Congress. American-British Law Division, LL90-43
* Japanese Prison Education System, Law Library of Congress. Far Eastern Law Division, LL90-50
* Prison Conditions: The Congressional Response-Issue Brief, William Woldman IB81171
* Prison Reform: Federal Role: Archived Issue Brief, Barbara McClure IB75077
* Prison and Prisoners: Federal Role; Issue Brief, Keith Bea, IB81171
* Social Security Benefits for Prisoners: Archived Issue Brief, David Koitz IB81163

Privacy

* see Civil Liberties and Rights

Privatization

* see Public Finance--Privatization

Procurement

* see also Defense Economics--Procurement, Infrastructure, * For new products from CRS, scan the current CRS Update under Budget and Government Spending
* Administrative Discretion to Set Aside the Eight-Hour Provisions of the Walsh-Healey Public Contracts Act (1936) and the Contract Work Hours Standards, William G. Whittaker 83-500 E
* Amendments to the Prompt Payment Act of 1982: Action in the 100th Congress, Thomas Youth 87-558 GOV
* Asbestos in Buildings: Activity in the 100th Congress, Claudia Copeland 89-267 ENR
* Avoiding Urban/Rural Wage Inequities in Determination of Prevailing Wage Rates under the Davis-Bacon Act, William Whittaker 85-631 E
* Business: Doing Business with the Federal Government: Info Pack, IP305B
* Competition in Federal Public Contracting--the New Look: Changes and Implementation: the Competition Contracting Act Title VII of Public Law 98-369, Robert G. Lauck 85-82 A
* Compilation of State Laws Pertaining to the Exemptions from State Sales Taxes for Federal Purchases, Mark Gurevitz 89-232 A
* The Davis Bacon Act: A Review of the Literature, William Whittaker 84-137 E
* The Davis-Bacon Act and Federal Contract Construction Wage Policy: Background Analysis and Recent Legislative Interest, William Whittaker 87-563 E
* Federal Civilian Procurement Reform Initiatives: Archived Issue Brief, Stephanie Smith IB86126
* Federal Programs for Minority and Women-Owned Businesses, Mark Eddy 89-278 GOV
* Federal Property Sales and Auctions: Sources of Information, Felicia G. Kolp, 90-622 C
* Government Procurement in Canada: Sourcing Policy, Law Library of Congress. American-British Law Division, LL90-8
* Liability of Superfund "Response Action Contractors" and EPA for Injury from Contractor-Conducted Cleanups, Robert Meltz 89-292 A
* The McNamara-O'Hara Service Contract Act: Discretionary Authority of the Secretary of Labor under Section 4(B) and the Mandatory Wage Rate Determination, William G. Whittaker 86-533 E
* Minority Business Set-Asides and the Constitution: A Legal Analysis of the U.S. Supreme Court Ruling in City of Richmond v. J.A. Croson Co., Charles V. Dale 89-124 A
* Private Property Protection Legislation in the 102nd Congress: Issue Brief, Robert Meltz, IB91076
* Productivity in Public Works Construction--Options for Improvement, Russell Vakharia 88-97 SPR
* The Prompt Payment Act, John R. Luckey, 90-167
* The Service Contract Act of 1965, Robert Lauck 86-779 A
* Short-Term Continuing Resolutions: The Department of Defense Experience, Alice C. Maroni, 89-579 F
* United States Supreme Court Actions Regarding Minority Business Set-Asides After City of Richmond v. J.A. Croson, Charles V. Dale 89-202 A
* When the United States Takes Property: Legal Principles, Robert Meltz, 91-339 A

Productivity

* see Labor-Productivity

Products Liability

* see Consumers, Insurance--Liability Issues

Professional and Administrative Career Examination

* Elimination of the Professional and Administrative Career Examination (PACE) and Proposed Alternative Selection Procedures, Paul Downing 89-315 GOV

Current Events and Homework

Program Trading
* see Corporations--Securities Industry

Property Insurance
*see Insurance--Property/Casualty

Proprietary Schools
* see Occupational Training--Adult and Vocational Education

Protectionism
* see Foreign Trade--Imports and Exports, Foreign Trade--Trade Policy

Public Administration
* Privatization from a Public Management Perspective, Ronald Moe 89-160 GOV

Public Broadcasting
* see Telecommunication

Public Finance
* see Budget Process, Budget Programs, Credit Programs, Deficits, Fiscal Policy, Privatization, Congress-Budget Process, Local Finance, Public Debt and Deficits, for new products from CRS, scan the current CRS Update under Budget and Government Spending, for Defense Budgets see Defense Economics--Defense Budgets
* Budget Background for FY 1990: Issue Brief, Philip D. Winters IB89072
* Budget for Fiscal Year 1989: Info Pack, IP394B
* Budget for Fiscal Year 1990: Info Pack, IP413B
* Budget for Fiscal Year 1991: Info Brief, Phillip Winters IB90067
* Budget for Fiscal Year 1992: Info Pack, Congressional Reference Division IB446B
* Budget for Fiscal Year 1992: Info Brief, Phillip Winters IB91046
* The Capital Gains Response to a Tax Rate Change: Is It Overestimated?, Donald Kiefer 88-216 S
* The Chief Financial Officers Act of 1990: An Overview, Virginia A. McMurty, 91-184 GOV
* Chief Financial Officers Act of 1990: House Action on Funding Limitations for FY 1992, Kathy Dolan, 91-553 GOV
* Economic Policymaking Problems, Part One: Institutions and Processes, Leon M. Cole, etc. 89-299 E
* Economic Policymaking Problems: Part Two: Theories and Forecasts, Leon M. Cole, etc. 89-300 E
* The Effect of Federal Tax and Budget Policies in the 1980s on the State-Local Sector, Lillian Rymarowicz, etc. 86-2 E
* Federal Budget and Tax Policy and the State-Local Sector: Retrenchment in the 1980s, Lillian Rymarowicz, etc. 88-600 E
* The Federal Budget for Fiscal Year 1988: Archived Issue Brief, Philip Winters IB87057
* The Federal Budget for Fiscal Year 1989: Issue Brief, Philip Winters IB88064
* Federal Employees and the FY 1992 Budget Proposals: Issue Brief, James P. McGrath, IB91108
* Federal Government Spending: An Alphabetical Microthesaurus of Terms Selected from the Legislative Indexing Vocabulary, Shirley Loo, 88-467 L
* The Federal Money Trail: Data Sources on Federal Aid, Grants, Loans, and Procurement in States and Local Areas, James R. Riehl, 91-550 C
* Federal User Fees: An Overview, Julius W. Allen, 89-625 E
* The Fiscal Position of Selected OECD Nations, Gregg A. Esenwein, 91-490 E
* Fiscal Year 1992 Budget: Data in Brief, J. Michael Anderson, 91-255 C
* Privatization from a Public Management Perspective, Ronald C. Moe, 89-160 GOV

Procurement
* Compilation of State Laws Pertaining to the Exemptions from State Sales Taxes for Federal Purchases, Mark Gurevitz 89-232 A
* The Davis Bacon Act: A Review of the Literature, William Whittaker 84-137 E
* The Davis-Bacon Act and Federal Contract Construction Wage Policy: Background Analysis and Recent Legislative Interest, William Whittaker 87-563 E
* Federal Civilian Procurement Reform Initiatives: Archived Issue Brief, Stephanie Smith IB86126
* Federal Programs for Minority and Women-Owned Business, Mark Eddy 89-278 GOV

* Liability of Superfund "Response Action Contractors" and EPA for Injury From Contractor-Conducted Cleanups, Robert Meltz 89-292 A
* Major Repairs of Non-Routine Maintenance: Defining Davis-Bacon Coverage under the Comprehensive Improvement Assistance Program, William G. Whittaker 85-887 E
* The McNamara-O'Hara Service Contract Act; Discretionary Authority of the Secretary of Labor under Section 4(B) and the Mandatory Wage Rate Determination, William G. Whittaker 86-533 E
* Minority Business Set-Asides and the Constitution:, A Legal Analysis of the U.S. Supreme Court Ruling, in City of Richmond v. J.A. Croson Co., Charles V. Dale 89-124 A
* Productivity in Public Works Construction-Options Improvement, Russell Vakharia 88-97 SPR
* The Service Contract Act of 1965, Robert G. Lauck 86-779 A
* United States Supreme Court Actions Regarding Minority Business Set-Asides After City of Richmond v. J.A. Croson, Charles V. Dale 89-202 A

Productivity
* see Labor--Productivity

Products Liability
* see Consumers, Insurance--Liability Issues

Professional and Administrative Career Examination
* Elimination of the Professional and Administrative Career Examination (PACE) and Proposed Alternative Selection Procedures, Paul M. Downing 89-315 GOV

Program Trading
* see Corporations--Securities Industry

Protectionism
* see Foreign Trade--Imports and Exports, Foreign Trade--Trade Policy

Public Administration
* Privatization from a Public Management Perspective, Ronald C. Moe 89-160 GOV

Public Broadcasting
* see Telecommunication

Public Finance
* see Budget Process, Budget Programs, Credit Programs, Deficits, Fiscal Policy Privatization, Congress--Budget Process, Local Finance
* The Authorization/Appropriation Process, Walter Kravitz, LTR91-875
* Biennial Budgeting: Background and Congressional Options, James V. Saturno, 89-295 GOV
* Budget Background for FY1990: Issue Brief, Philip D. Winters IB89072
* Budget Enforcement Act of 1990: A General Explanation; Videoprogram, Robert Keith, LTR91-919
* Budget Enforcement in 1991: Issue Brief, Robert Keith, IB91013
* Budget for Fiscal Year 1989: Info Pack, IP394B
* Budget for Fiscal Year 1990: Info Pack, IP413B
* Budget Process: Info Pack. IP012B
* The Capital Gains Response to a Tax Rate Change: Is it Overestimated?, Donald W. Kiefer 88-216 S
* Congress and a Balanced Budget Amendment to the U.S. Constitution, James V. Saturno, 89-4 GOV
* Congressional Budget Process Reform: Archived Issue Brief, Edward Davis. IB87196
* Congressional Budget Process Reform: 101st Congress; Archived Issue Brief, Edward Davis, IB89022
* Contents Listing for P.L. 101-239, Omnibus Budget Reconciliation Act of 1989, James V. Saturno, 90-90 GOV
* Credit Reform in the Budget Agreement of November 1990, James M. Bickley, 91-269 E
* Debt Limit Increase and 1985 Balanced Budget Act Reaffirmation: Summary of Public Law 100-119 (H.J. Res. 324), Edward Davis, etc. 87-865 GOV
* Discretionary Spending Limits for Fiscal year 1991: November 1990 Adjustments and "Mini-Sequester", Edward Davis, etc., 90-528 GOV
* Discretionary Spending Limits for Fiscal year 1991: "Mini-Sequester" of April 25, 1991, Robert Keith, 91-413 GOV
* Economic Policymaking Problems. Part One: Institutions and Processes, Leon M. Cole, etc. 89-299 E

Program Trading / Public Finance

* Economic Policymaking Problems. Part Two: Theories and Forecasts, Leon M. Cole, etc. 89-300 E
* The Effects of Federal Tax and Budget Policies in the 1980s on the State-Local Sector, Lillian Rymarkowicz, etc. 89-2 E
* Federal Budget and Tax Policy and the State-Local Sector: Retrenchment in the 1980s, Lillian Rymarowicz, etc. 88-600 E
* The Federal Budget for Fiscal Year 1988; Archived Issue Brief, Philip D. Winters IB87057
* The Federal Budget for Fiscal Year 1989: Issue Brief, Philip D. Winters IB88064
* Federal Budget Issues: Summaries of Selected CRS Products, 1990-1991, Robert S. Kirk, 91-766 L
* Financial Crises of the 1970s and 1980s: Causes, Developments, and Government Responses, William Jackson, etc. 89-290 E
* Government Securities Market: Disturbances and Regulation, William Jackson 87-165 E
* Head Start Reauthorization Amendments Enacted During the 101st Congress, Anne C. Steward, 90-642 EPW
* An Introduction to the Spending and Budget Process in Congress, Stanley Bach, 90-288 S
* Legislation Appropriations, and Budgets: The Development of Spending Decision-Making in Congress, Allen Shick, 84-106 GOV
* A National Lottery: Overview and Economic Analysis, Gregg A. Esenwein, etc. 87-811 E
* "Pass-As-You-Go" Budget Enforcement Procedures in 1991: Issue Brief, Edward Davis, IB91127
* Points of Order under the Congressional Budget Act of 1974, Edward Davis, 91-347 GOV
* The President and the Budget Process: Expanded Impoundment and Item Veto Proposals; Issue Brief, Virginia A. McMurty, IB89148
* The President's Budget Submission: Format, Deadlines, and Transition Years, Virginia A. McMurty, etc., 88-661 GOV
* Proposed and Actual Budget Totals for the Fiscal Years 1980 Through 1988, Philip D. Winters 88-544 E
* Senate Consideration of Regular Appropriations Bills under Waivers of Section 303 (A) of the 1974 Budget Act, Robert Keith, 89-37 GOV
* Should the Treasury Issue Indexed Bonds?, G. Thomas Woodward 88-4 E
* Sequestration Actions for Fiscal Year 1988 under the Gramm-Rudman-Hollings Act: Archived Issue Brief, Robert Keith, IB87224
* Sequestration Actions for Fiscal Year 1989 under the Gramm-Rudman-Hollings Act: Archived Issue Brief, Robert Keith, IB88078
* Sequestration Actions for Fiscal Year 1990 under the Gramm-Rudman-Hollings Act: Archived Issue Brief, Robert Keith, IB89017
* Social Security Financing, David Koitz, etc. LTR91-879
* Summary and Legislative History of Public Law 98-473: Continuing Appropriations for Fiscal Year 1985, (H.J. Res. 648), Edward Davis, etc. 85-12 GOV
* Suspension of Budget Enforcement Procedures in the Event of a Declaration of War, Robert Keith, 91-98 GOV
* Suspension of Budget Enforcement Procedures in the Event of Low Economic Growth, Robert Keith, 91-99 GOV
* U.S. Savings Bonds; Benefits and Costs of Variable Rates, James M. Bickley 86-924 E
* Waivers of the Congressional Budget Act of 1974 Considered by the Senate in 1991, Edward Davis, 91-696 GOV
* Waivers of the 1974 Budget Act Considered in the House During the 100th Congress, Edward M. Davis, 89-535 GOV
* Waivers of the 1974 Budget Act Considered in the Senate During the 100th Congress, Robert Keith, 89-76 GOV

Introduced in the 100th Congress, James Saturno 88-350 GOV
* Congressional Budget Process Reform: Archived Issue Brief, Edward Davis IB87196
* The Effects of a Two-Year Defense Budget Authorization, Alice Maroni 85-940 F
* The Federal Budget Process: Selected References, Robert Howe 88-436 L
* An Introduction to the Spending and Budget Process in Congress, Stanley Bach 86-20 GOV
* Item Veto Bills Introduced in the House of Representatives During the 100th Congress, Gary Galemore 87-468 GOV
* Legal Analysis of Proposal to Repeal Deferral Authority under the Impoundment Control Act, Richard Ehlke 86-1024 A
* Legal Analysis of the Government Securities Act of 1986 and Its Application to Broker/Dealers Convicted of Insider Trading Violations Michael V. Seitzinger 87-280 A
* Legislation, Appropriations, and Budgets: The Development of Spending Decision-Making in Congress, Allen Schick 84-106 GOV
* Legislative Branch: Budget Authority, FY 1962-FY 1988, Paul Dwyer 88-290 GOV
* Manual on the Federal Budget Process, Allen Schick, etc. 87-286 GOV
* Omnibus Budget Reconciliation Act of 1987: A Summary of Congressional Action on P.L. 100-203, James Saturno 88-296 GOV
* The Power of the Purse in Foreign Policy: Process and Problems in Congressional Funding, Ellen Collier 85-182 F
* Presidential Impoundment Authority After City of New Haven v. United States, Richard Ehlke, etc. 87-173 A
* The President's Budget Submission: Format, Deadlines, and Transition Years, Virginia A. McMurtry, etc. 88-661 GOV
* Reconciliation for Fiscal Year 1987: A Summary of Congressional Action, James Saturno 87-772 GOV
* Regular Appropriations Enacted Separately and in Continuing Appropriations, Fiscal Years 1977-1987, Sandy Streeter 87-826 GOV
* Rescissions by the President Since 1974: Background and Proposals for Change, Virginia A. McMurtry 89-271 GOV
* Selected Tables on the Federal Budget Regarding Chronologies of Certain Actions, Aggregate Budget Levels, and Other Information, James Saturno, etc. 87-710 GOV
* Senate Consideration of Regular Appropriations Bills under Waivers of Section 303(A) of the 1974 Budget Act, Robert Keith 89-37 GOV
* Sequestration Actions for FY 90 under the Gramm-Rudman-Hollings Act: Issue Brief, Robert Keith IB89071
* Sequestration of Budgetary Resources for Fiscal Year 1986 under the 1985 Balanced Budget Act, Robert A. Keith 86-872 GOV
* Summary and Analysis of the Ramifications of Bowsher v. Synar, the Gramm-Rudman-Hollings Deficit Reduction Act Case, Morton Rosenberg, etc. 86-788 A
* Waivers of the 1974 Budget Act Considered in the Senate During the 100th Congress, Robert Keith 89-76 GOV

Public Finance -- Budget Process

* Biennial Budgeting: Background and Congressional Options, James V. Saturno 89-295 GOV
* Budget Making and the Legislative Process: Audio Brief, Robert Keith, etc. AB50164
* Budget Process: Info Pack, IP012B
* Budget Process Legislation Introduced in the Senate During the 100th Congress: Comparison of Selected Measures, Edward Davis, etc. 87-611 GOV
* Budget Process Reform Legislation Introduced in the 101st Congress: Selected Listing, James V. Saturno 89-304 GOV
* Budget Sequestration Procedures for Fiscal Year 1987: Summary of Congressional Action, Robert Keith 86-1049 GOV
* Changes in the Congressional Budget Process made by the 1985 Balanced Budget Act (P.L. 99-177), Robert Keith 86-713 GOV
* Congressional Approaches to Biennial Budgeting, Michael D. Margeson, etc. 87-653 GOV
* Congressional Approaches to Regulating Continuing Resolutions: Measures

Public Finance -- Budget Programs

* Acid Rain Legislation in the 101st Congress: Archived Issue Brief, Mira Courpas, etc. IB89144
* Adult Education Act Reauthorization: Selected Options, Paul Irwin 87-57 EPW
* Agricultural Disaster Assistance: issue Brief, Ralph Chite, IB91099
* Agriculture and the Budget: Issue Brief, Carl Ek IB91124
* Airport and Airway Program Reauthorization; Archived Issue Brief, John Fischer IB87051
* Appropriations Enacted for Specific Colleges and Universities by the 96th Through 100th Congresses, Susan H. Boren, 89-82 EPW
* Appropriations for Selected Health Programs, FY 1980-FY 1991, Edward R. Klebe, 91-769 EPW
* Arts and Humanities: FY88-FY89 Funding Issues; Archived Issue Brief, Robert Lyke IB82026
* Arts and Humanities: Funding Issues in the 101st Congress: Archived Issue Brief, Susan Boren, IB90050
* Cash and Noncash Benefits for Persons With Limited Income: Eligibility Rules, Recipient and Expenditure Data, FY 1986-88, Vee Burke, 89-595 EPW
* Cash and Noncash Benefits for Persons With Limited Income: Eligibility Rules, Recipient and Expenditure Data, FY 1988-90, Vee Burke, 91-741 EPW
Child Nutrition: Program Information, Funding, and Participation, FY 1980-FY 1990, Jean Yavis Jones, 91-681 EPW
* Child Welfare and Foster Care Reform: Issues for Congress: Issue Brief, Karen Spar, IB90145
* Defense and Foreign Aid Budget Analysis and the Use of Constant Dollars, Alice C. Maroni, etc. 86-154 F
* Department of Education Funding Issues: FY1992; Issue Brief, Angela

Current Events and Homework

Evans, IB91065
DOE's FY 1992 Budget: Issue Brief, Marc Humphries, IB91060
* Developmental Disabilities Programs: FY 1989 Budget Information, Mary F. Smith 88-181 EPW
* Energy Conservation: Technical Efficiency and Program Effectiveness; Issue Brief, Fred Sissine, IB85130
* Education for Disadvantaged Children: Reauthorization Issues: Archived Issue Brief, Wayne Riddle IB87070
* Education Funding Issues for FY 89: Archived Issue Brief, Angela Evans IB88036
* Education Legislation in the 100th Congress: A Brief Summary; Archived Issue Brief, Wava Gregory IB87134
* Entitlements and Other Mandatory Spending Accounts in the Federal Budget, Gene Falk 87-920 EPW
* Environmental Protection Agency: FY 1992 Budget; Issue Brief, Martin R. Lee IB91115
* Environmental Protection Agency: FY 90 Funding: Issue Brief, Martin R. Lee IB89032
* The Environmental Protection Agency's FY89 Budget; Archived Issue Brief, Martin R. Lee IB88062
* Federal Aid to Domestic Transportation: A Brief History from the 1800s to the 1980s, Nancy Heiser 88-574 E
* Federal Budget and Tax Policy and the State-Local Sector: Retrenchment in the 1980s, Lillian Rymarovicz, etc., 88-600 E
* Federal Budget Policies and the State-Local Sector; 1980-1986, Lillian Rymarovicz, etc. 87-234 E
* Federal Programs Affecting Children, Sharon House, etc. 87-306 EPW
* Federal Spending Proposed in the Fiscal Year 1989 Budget for Selected Major Income Maintenance Programs, Vee Burke 88-227 EPW
* The Financial Outlook for Medicare, David Koitz, 91-357 EPW
* The Financial Outlook for Social Security and Medicare, David Koitz, 91-830 EPW
* Financing Solid Waste Management Programs: A Survey of the States, David S. Loughran, etc., 89-656 ENR
* Financing the Federal Civil Service Retirement Programs; Payments into and Out of the Trust Fund, Carolyn L. Merck, 91-464 EPW
* Fish and Wildlife Service: Compensation to Local Governments, M. Lynne Corn, 90-192 ENR
* Foreign Aid: Budget, Policy, and Reform; Issue Brief, Larry Q. Nowels, IB89014
* Foreign Policy Budget: Priorities for the 102nd Congress; Issue Brief, Larry Q. Nowels, etc., IB91014
* The Forest Service Budget: Trust Funds and Special Accounts, Ross W. Gorte, etc. 89-75 ENR
* The FY 1989 Federal Budget for Public Works Infrastructure, Claudia Copeland 88-176 ENR
* The Gramm-Rudman-Hollings Deficit Reduction Process: The Defense Aspects of the Initial Sequestration Report for FY 1987, Alice Maroni,. etc. 86-875 F
* A Guide to Trust Funds, Special Accounts, and Foundations in the Fish and Wildlife Service Budget, M. Lynne Corn 86-722 ENR
* Health Programs and the Gramm-Rudman-Hollings Legislation: The 1986 Sequestrations and the President's FY 87 Budget Proposal, James Reuter 86-648 EPW
* Health Programs Appropriations: FY 1980-FT 1989, Edward Klebe 89-79 EPW
* The Higher Education Act: Authorization and Budget Authority from FY 1987 to FY 1991, Margot A. Schenet, 91-127 EPW
* Job Training: FT 88 Budget and Legislative Issues:, Archived Issue Brief, Karen Spar IB87039
* Land and Water Conservation Fund: Information and Status, George Siehl 89-159 ENR
* Medicaid: FY 1992 Budget; Archived Issue Brief, Melvina Ford, IB91036
* Medicare Financing, David Koitz, 91-517 EPW
* Medicare FY 1992 Budget; Archived Issue Brief, Celinda M. Franco, etc. IB91032
* Medicare Physician Payment Reform, Jennifer O'Sullivan, etc., 91-643 EPW
* Migration and Refugee Assistance Budget: Problems and Prospects; Issue Brief, Lois McHugh, IB89150
* Military Manpower and Compensation: FY 88 Budget Issues: Archived Issue Brief, Robert L. Goldich IB87081
* National Aeronautics and Space Administration (NASA) Fiscal year 1992 Budget Request, David P. Radzanowski, 91-214 SPR
* National Forest Receipts: Sources and Dispositions, Ross W. Gorte 89-284 ENR
* National Health Expenditures: Trends from 1960-1989, Kathleen M. King, etc. 91-588 EPW
* National Health Spending, 1989: A Description of Spending by Services and Payers, Kathleen King, etc., 91-527 EPW
* The National Marine Fisheries Service Budget: A Guide to Special Accounts, Eugene Buck, etc. 86-894 ENR
* OCS Revenue Sharing, Malcolm M. Simmons, 91-182 ENR
* The Oil and Gas Leasing System on Federal Lands, Marc Humphries, 91-577 ENR
* Outer Continental Shelf Leasing and Development, Issues in the 102nd Congress: Issue Brief, Malcolm M. Simmons, IB91063
* An Overview of National Park Issues in the 100th Congress: Archived Issue Brief, George H. Siehl IB87072
* The Pell Grant Program: Background and Reauthorization Issues, Susan Boren, 91-642 EPW
* Provisions of the 1990 Farm Bill, Geoffrey S. Becker, 90-553 ENR
* Refugee Admissions and Resettlement Policy: Issue Brief, Joyce C. Vialet, IB89025
* Refugee Resettlement Assistance Funding, Joyce Vialet, 91-683 EPW
* Repayment of Corps of Engineers Construction Costs, Malcolm M. Simmons 87-262 ENR
* Research and Development Funding: FY 86 and FY 87: Issue Brief, Science Policy Research Div, Genevieve Kenzo IB86062
* Research and Development Funding: FY 88: Archived Issue Brief, Research and Development Team, Science Policy Res IB87083
* Research and Development Funding: FY 89: Archived Issue Brief, Michael E. Davey IB88040
* Rural Areas and Clean Water: Impacts of the Water Quality Act of 1987, Claudia Copeland 87-257 ENR
* The Rural Electrification Administration: Background and Current Issues, Carl Ek, etc., 91-614 ENR
* Selected Federal Research and Development Agencies and Programs and the Gramm-Rudman-Hollings Deficit Reduction Act: An Analysis of the Impact on FY 8, Michael E. Davey, etc. 86-37 SPR
* Social Security: Its Removal from the Budget and New Procedures for Considering Changes to the Program, David Koitz, 91-9 EPW
* Social Security: The Effect of National Debt Limitations in 1985, David Koitz 85-1118 EPW
* Soil and Water Conservation Issues in the 102nd Congress: Issue Brief, Jeffrey A. Zinn, IB91031
* Student Financial Aid: Authorizations of Appropriations, Budget Requests, Enacted Appropriations and Outlays for Federal Student Financial Aid Programs FY 1965 Through FY 1990, Susan H. Boren, 89-184 EPW
* The Superfund Amendments and Reauthorization Act of 1986: Archived Issue Brief, Mark E. Anthony Reisch IB87080
* Tobacco Programs of the U.S. Department of Agriculture: Their Operation and Cost, Jasper Womach, 91-404 ENR
* Transportation Trust Funds: Economic and Policy Issues; Issue brief, J. F. Hornbeck, IB90057
* Trust Funds and the Federal Deficit, David Koitz, etc., 90-106 EPW
* Understanding U.S. Transportation Program Finances, Stephen J. Thompson, 91-745 E
* U.S. Department of Education: Major Program Trends, Fiscal Years 1980-1990, Education and Public Welfare Division 89-144 EPW
* U.S. Department of Education: Major Program Trends, Fiscal Years 1980-1991, Paul M. Irwin, 91-10 EPW
* The U.S. Postal Service: Its Treatment in the Federal Budget; Issue Brief, Bernevia M. McCalip IB88035
* USDA's Section 32 Fund, Geoffrey S. Becker, 91-391 ENR
* Veterans Programs: FY 89 Budget; Archived Issue Brief, Anne C. Steward IB88047
* Veterans' Program: Major Legislation and Issues in the 102nd Congress; Issue Brief, Anne Steward, etc., IB91053
* Waste Management: Issue Brief, James McCarthy IB89007
* Wastewater Treatment Programs; Impact of Gramm-Rudman-Hollings Act and Prospects for Federal Funding (With Appendix); Archived Issue Brief, Claudia Copeland IB86018
* Welfare: Issue Brief, Vee Burke, IB87007
* 1989 Budget Perspectives: Federal Spending for the Human Resource Programs: Tables and Figures Portraying the President's 1989 Budget Plan in the Cont., Gene Falk 88-351 EPW
* 1990 Budget Perspective: Federal Spending for the Human Resource Programs, 1965-1988, Gene Falk, etc. 89-87 EPW
* 1992 Budget Perspectives: Federal Spending for the Social Welfare Programs, Gene Falk, etc., 91-280 EPW

Public Finance -- Credit Programs

* Credit Reform: Chiles-Comenici Proposal Contrasted With Reagan Proposal, James Bickley 87-939 E

Public Finance / Public Debt

* Credit Reform Proposal of the Reagan Administration: Analysis and Policy Issues, James Bickley 87-456 E
* Debt Collection by the United States Government: Existing Legal Options, Henry Cohen 88-412 A
* An Evaluation of the Reconstruction Finance Corporation With Implications for Current Capital Needs of the Steel Industry, James Bickley 80-43 E
* Federal Credit Policies and Credit Allocation by Economic Objectives, James Bickley 86-3
* Transport Manufacturing: A Review and Appraisal of Federal Assistance Policies, Gwenell L. Bass 86-75 E

Public Finance -- Deficits

* see also Budget and Government Spending
* Agriculture and the Gramm-Rudman-Hollings Deficit Control Act, Geoffrey Becker 86-547 ENR
* Budget Action for FY 1990 During 1989: Issue Brief, Philip D. Winters IB89090
* Budget Action in the 100th Congress, 1st Session (1987): Archived Issue Brief, William Cox IB88030
* Budget Cuts: Updated Projections and Gramm-Rudman-Hollings; Archived Issue Brief, William Cox IB86072
* Budget Deficits and Monetary Policy, Carol Leisenring 81-128 E
* Congress and a Balanced Budget Amendment to the U. S. Constitution, James Saturno 89-4 GOV
* Constitutional Amendments to Balance the Budget and Limit Federal Spending in the 100th Congress: A Table of Features, Thomas Nicola 87-445 A
* Crowding Out? Federal, State and Local Government Borrowing and the Debt Economy, William Jackson 87-274 E
* The Debt Limit in 1987: Issue Brief, Philip Winters IB87127
* Debt-Limit Increase and 1985 Balanced Budget Act Reaffirmation: Summary of Public Law 100-119 (H.J. Res. 324), Edward Davis, etc. 87-865 GOV
* Debt-Limit Increases for FY 1987: Summary of Congressional Action in 1986 (Including Proposed Modifications to the 1985 Balanced Budget Act), Robert Keith, etc. 86-974 GOV
* Deficit Reduction and Economic Growth, Brian W. Cashell 89-349 E
* Deficit Reduction in 1988: Archived Issue Brief, William A. Cox IB87023
* Deficit Reduction Issues: Info Pack, IP274D
* Deficit Reduction: Spending and Revenue Options: Issue Brief, Donald W. Kiefer IB89003
* Deficit Reduction: The National Economic Commission Options Model, Barry Molefsky, etc. 88-606 E
* Deficit Targets, National Savings, and Social Security, Jane Gravelle 88-513 S
* Do Deficits Influence the Level of Interest Rates?, G. Thomas Woodward 85-14 E
* Energy Excise Taxes for Deficit Reduction: Archived Issue Brief, Salvatore Lazzari IB87172
* Explanation of the Balanced Budget and Emergency Deficit Control Act of 1985--Public Law 99-177 (the Gramm-Rudman-Hollings Act), Allen Schick 85-1130 GOV
* Federal Debt and Interest Measures Used in the Federal Budget, Philip D. Winters 83-158 E
* The Federal Debt: Who Bears Its Burdens? Issue Brief, William Cox IB84233
* Gramm-Rudman-Hollings and Department of Education Programs, Angela Evans 86-544 EPW
* Gramm-Rudman-Hollings Budget Adjustments: Sensitivity to Economic Assumptions; Archived Issue Brief, Barry Molefsky, etc. IB85217
* The Gramm-Rudman-Hollings Deficit Reduction Plan: The Target of a Balanced Budget and the Risk of Recession Review, Craig K. Elwell 86-534 E
* The Gramm-Rudman-Hollings Deficit Reduction Process (P.L. 99-177) and the Department of Defense: A Summary Review, Alice Maroni, etc. 86-7 F
* Gramm-Rudman-Hollings: Potential Economic Effects of Meeting Deficit Targets; Archived Issue Brief, Brian W. Cashell IB87059
* The Gramm-Rudman-Hollings Sequestration Process for FY 1986: A Summary of DOD Elements in the OMB/CB O and GAO Sequestration Reports; Policy Alert, Alice Maroni, etc. 86-16 F
* The Gramm-Rudman-Hollings Targets: How Might They Affect the Economy, Gail Makinen, etc. 86-1036 E
* House and Senate Action on Legislation Increasing the Debt Limit for Fiscal Year 1987 (H.J. Res. 668 and H.R. 5395) (Including Modifications to the 1985), Robert A. Keith, etc. 86-871 GOV
* How the Government Borrows: A Primer, Thomas Woodward 85-762 E
* Implications of Uncertainty in Economic Forecasting under

Gramm-Rudman-Hollings: Options for Congressional Response, David Grinnell 86-829 S
* Is the National Debt a Burden on Future Generation ?, Gail Makinen 86-682 E
* Major Revenue Raising Options: An Overview, Gregg A. Esenwein 88-756 E
* Management of the Federal Loan Portfolio: Recent Developments in Debt Collection and Sale of Loan As Sets, Virginia A. McMurtry 87-140 GOV
* National Economic Commission: Equitable Deficit Reduction: Archived Issue Brief, Barry Molefsky IB88032
* A Proposal for Raising Revenue by Reducing Capital Gains Taxes, Jane G. Gravelle 87-562 E
* Reducing the Deficit With Energy Taxes, Craig K. Elwell 86-653 E
* Revenue-Raising Options: Archived Issue Brief, Gregg A. Esenwein IB87169
* Rural Electric Cooperative Defaults: Origins, Current Status, and Legislative Implications, Sylvia Morrison 88-665 E
* Sequestration Actions for Fiscal Year 1988 under the Gramm-Rudman-Hollings Act: Archived Issue Brief, Robert Keith IB88078
* Social Security and Medicare: How Are They in Determining the National Debt?, David Koitz 85-1132 EPW
* Social Security: Issues in Taxing Benefits under Current Law and under Proposals to Tax a Greater Share of Benefits, Geoffrey Kollmann 89-40 EPW
* Social Security: Its Impact on the Federal Budget Deficit, David Koitz 88-218 EPW
* Value-Added Tax for Deficit Reduction: Issue Brief, James Bickley IB87097
* What Large Deficits Will Do If They Continue (and What Will Happen If They are Reduced), G. Thomas Woodward 85-102 E

Public Finance -- Fiscal Policy

* Capital, Credit, and Crowding Out: Cycles and Trends in Flows of Funds Over Three Decades, William Jackson 82-142 E
* Domestic and International Monetary-Fiscal Policy Coordination, Thomas F. Dernburg 84-145 E
* Government Actions that Affect Interest Rates: Mechanisms and Macroeconomic Repercussions, Craig Elwell 82-128 E
* Monetarist and Keyensian Worlds-What's the Difference?, Helen J. Scott 84-181 E
* Prospects for an Economic Downturn, G. Thomas Woodward 89-105 E
* Tax Policy and Spillover Effects: The Use of Tax Provisions to Induce Socially Desirable Activities, Jane Gravelle 80-186 E
* Tax Policy Prospects in the Bush Administration: Issue Brief, Salvatore Lazzari IB89019
* U.S. Economic Policy in an International Context: Deficits, Taxes, and Monetary Policy, Jane Gravelle, etc. 84-125 E

Public Finance -- Privatization

* The Bonneville Power Administration: To Sell or Not to Sell, Alvin Kaufman, etc. 86-176 E
* Conrail: An Analysis of the Federal Assistance Policy and Proposed Sale, Kenneth R. DeJarnette 86-51 E
* Customs Service User Fees, Frederick M. Kaiser 87-676 GOV
* Federal Hydropower: The Administration's Proposal to Sell Government Assets; Archived Issue Brief, John Moore IB86057
* The Federal Power Marketing Administrations: To Privatize or Not to Privatize, Alvin Kaufman, etc. 86-90 S
* Privatization from a Public Management Perspective, Ronald C. Moe 89-160 GOV
* Privatization of the National Technical Information Service, Jane Bortnick, etc. 87-491 SPR
* Tax-Exempt Bond-Financed Takeover of Investor-Owned Utilities: An Issue of Privatization and Competition, Dennis Zimmerman 88-174 E
* The U.S. Postal Service: A Public or Private Enterprise? Issue Brief, Bernevia M. McCalip IB88084

Public Finance -- Public Debt and Deficits

* see Budget and Government Spending
* American Public Opinion on the Federal Deficit, Rosita M. Thomas, 89-419 GOV
* Aviation Excise Taxes: Their Role in the Deficit Reduction Effort of 1990, Nonna A. Noto, 91-309 E
* Budget Deficit Reduction: Spending and Revenue Options; Archived Issue Brief, Donald W. Wiefer, IB90023
* Congress and a Balanced Budget Amendment to the U.S. Constitution, James V. Saturno, 89-4 GOV
* Debt-Limit Increase and 1985 Balanced Budget Act Reaffirmation:

Current Events and Homework

Summary of Public Law 100-119 (H.J. Res. 324), Edward Davis, etc. 87-865 GOV
* The Federal Debt: Who Bears Its Burdens? Issue Brief, William Cox, IB84233
* A Proposal for Raising Revenue by Reducing Capital Gains Taxes?, Jane G. Gravelle, 87-562 E
* Public Debt Reduction Fund, Louis Alan Talley, 91-268 E
* Rural Electric Cooperative Defaults: Origins, Current Status, and Legislative Implications, Sylvia Morrison, 88-665-E
* Sequestration Actions for Fiscal Year 1988 under the Gramm-Rudman-Hollings Act: Archived Issue Brief, Robert Keith, IB7224
* Sequestration Actions for FY 1989 under the Gramm-Rudman-Hollings Act: Archived Issue Brief, Robert Keith, IB88078
* Sequestration Actions in 1990 under the Gramm-Rudman-Hollings Act: Archived Issue Brief, Robert Keith, IB90055
* Social Security: Issues in Taxing Benefits under Current Law and under Proposals to Tax a greater Share of Benefits, Geoffrey Killmann, 89-40 EPW
* Social Security: Its Impact on the Federal Budget Deficit, David Koitz, 88-218 EPW
* Transportation Trust Funds: Economic and Policy Issues; Issue Brief, J.F. Hornbeck, IB90057
* Value-Added Tax: Concepts, Policy Issues, and OECD Experiences, James M. Bickley, 91-559 E
* Value-Added Tax for Deficit Reduction: Issue Brief, James M. Bickley, IB91078

Public Health

* Antibiotics: Health Implications of Use in Animal Feed; Archived Issue Brief, Sarah Taylor IB85076
* Blood: Collection, Testing, and Processing, Irene Stich-Coleman 87-641 SPR
* Child Health in the Third World: U.S. and International Initiatives; Archived Issue Brief, Lois McHugh IB85189
* Cigarettes and Other Tobacco Products; Should Congress Bank All Advertising and Promotion?, Bruce K. Mulock IB86105
* Cigarettes and Other Tobacco Products: Should Congress Ban All Advertising and Promotion? Archived Issue Brief, Bruce Mulock IB86105
* The Constitutionality of Banning Cigarette Advertising, Henry Cohen, 90-82 A
* Countries With Smoking Bans on Domestic and International Flights, Law Library of Congress, American-British Law Division, LL90-68
* Demographic and Social Patterns of Infant Mortality, Jeanne Griffith 86-133 EPW
* The Elderly and the Health Care Dilemma: Is an Ounce of Prevention Worth a Pound of Cure?, Science Policy Research Division-Life Sciences Sec 85-968 SPR
* Environment Regulation and the GATT, Jeanne J. Grimmett, 91-285 A
* Fluoride in Drinking Water: Should the National Standard Be Made Less Stringent? Archived Issue Brief, Donald Feliciano IB86014
* Food and Drug Administration: Selected Funding Data, Donna U. Vogt, 91-424 SPR
* Health Benefits of Air Pollution Control: A Discussion, John Blodgett 89-161 ENR
* Health Care for Children: Federal Programs and Policies, Joseph A. Cislowski 88-217 EPW
* Health Care: Issue Brief, Janet Kline IB87009
* Health Exams, Including AIDS Tests, Required of Foreign Students, Law Library of Congress, LL90-82
* Health Programs and the Gramm-Rudman-Hollings Legislation: The 1986 Sequestration and the President's FY 87 Budget Proposal, James Reuter 86-648 EPW
* Health Programs Appropriations: FY 1980-FY 1989, Edward Klebe 89-79 EPW
* Health Promotion and Disease Prevention for the Elderly, James Reuter, etc. 86-40 EPW
* Maternal and Child Health Initiatives: Archived Issue Brief, Melvina Ford, IB91057
* Milk Standards: Grade A vs. Grade B, Ralph M. Chite, 91-589 ENR
* National Health Service Corps, Celinda M. France, 91-729 EPW
* Native Americans: Nutrition and Diet-Related Diseases, Donna V. Porter 87-246 SPR
* The Proposed Prohibition on Advertising Tobacco Products: A Constitutional Analysis, Rita Ann Reimer 87-3 A
* Public Health Policy and the Congress: Selected References, Karen Alderson, etc. 89-147 L
* Right of Minors to Consent to Medical Care, Rita Ann Reimer 86-939 A
* Smokeless Tobacco: Health Concerns Spark Advertising and Labeling Controversy, Bruce K. Mulock 86-519 E
* Smokeless Tobacco: Snuff and Chewing Tobacco; Bibliography-in-Brief, 1983-1987, Edith Sutterlin 88-115 L
* Smoking and Tobacco Issues: Info Pack, IP356S
* Survey of the Fifty States and the District of Columbia Statutes Generally Concerning the Quarantine and Isolation of Persons Having A Contagious or, M. Ann Wolfe 87-765 A
* The U.S. Public Health Service: Health Care Services and Resources, Edward R. Klebe, 91-279 EPW
* World Health Organization: Effects Reduced U.S. Contributions, Lois B. McHugh 87-108 F

Public Lands

* see also Forests and Forestry, Parks
* A Report of Federal Land Management Plans and Activities: A Report on a CRS Research Workshop, Pamela Baldwin, 90-104 A
* Arctic National Wildlife Refuge: Bibliography-in-Brief- Ted L. Burch, 91-633 L
* Arctic National Wildlife Refuge: Congressional Consideration Since the 99th Congress, M. Lynne Corn, etc., 91-325 ENR
* Arctic Oil, Arctic Refuge; Videoprogram, M. Lynne Corn, LTR91-1489
* Arctic Resources: Over a Barrel? Issue Brief, M. Lynne Corn, etc, IB910011
* The Catawba Indian Tribe's Land Claim: A Legal Analysis, M. Maureen Murphy 89-293 A
* Comparison of Pacific Northwest Forest Bills: Part I, Adela Backiel, etc., 91-626 ENR
* Dominant Use Management in the National Forest System, Ross Gorte 86-714 ENR
* Establishment of New National Park System Units: A Brief Review of Procedures, Criteria and Alternatives, George H. Siehl, 91-153 ENR
* Federal Grazing Fees on Lands Administered by the Bureau of Land Management and the Forest Service: A History of Legislation and Administration Policy, Adela Backiel, etc. 85-592 ENR
* Federal Land Management Transfers Proposed Between Bureau of Land Management and Forest Service: Archived Issue Brief, Ross Gorte, etc. IB85101
* The Federal Power of Eminent Domain: A Primer, Robert Meltz 85-1086 A
* Federal Property Sales and Auctions: Sources of Information, Felicia G. Kolp, 90-622 C
* The Federal Royalty and Tax Treatment of the hard Rock Minerals Industry: An Economic Analysis, Salvatore Lazzari, 90-493 E
* Forest Service Land and Resource Planning: A Chronology of Laws, Adela Backiel 86-986 ENR
* Grazing Fees: A Fact Sheet, Adela Backiel, 91-265 ENR
* History of Release Language in Wilderness Legislation, 1979-1984, Ross Gorte 87-559 ENR
* Licensing and Special Use Permit Requirements for Hydroelectric Dam Projects under the Federal Power Act and the Federal Land Policy and Management Act, Robin Jeweler 88-459 A
* Log Export Restrictions, Ross W. Gorte, 91-365 ENR
* The Major Federal Land Management Agencies: Management of Our Nation's Lands and Resources, Adela Backiel, etc. 87-22 ENR
* The Major Federal Land Management Agencies: Management of Our Nation's Lands and Resources, Environment and Natural Resources Policy Division, 90-239 ENR
* Military and Recreation Interests in American Lands: Selected References, Lisa B. Dove, 90-426 L
* National Recreation Areas, George Siehl 88-644 ENR
* Oil Companies and the Acquisition of Federal Petroleum Leases, John J. Schanz 88-213 S
* Oil and Gas Leasing System on Federal Lands, Marc Humphries, 91-57 ENR
* Onshore Oil and Gas Resources on Federal Lands: Evaluating the Current Leasing System: Archived Issue Brief, Adela Backiel, etc. IB87077
* Public Access Across Private Lands to Federal Lands, Adela Backiel, etc. 86-650 A
* Public Land Management: Issues in the Bureau of Land Management; Archived Issue Brief, Adela Backiel, etc. IB87076
* Public Land and Resources: BLM Management Issues; Issue Brief, Adela Backiel, etc., IB91068
* Rangeland Condition: Attempts to Chart Its Progress, Bruce Beard 84-757 ENR
* The "Right to Roam": English Law on Public Rights-of-Way and Access to the Countryside, Law Library of Congress, American-British Law Division LL90-48
* Royalty Rates for Coal, Oil and Gas Production on Federally Administered Lands, Adela Backiel, etc. 83-595 S

Public Health / Public Welfare

* Summary of Recent Reports on Forest Service Timber, Sale Costs and Revenues, Ross Gorte 84-799 ENR
* Wilderness Areas and Federal Water Rights, Pamela Baldwin 89-11 A
* Wilderness Issues in the 102nd Congress: Issue Brief, Betsy A. Cody, IB91029
* Wilderness Overview and Statistics, Ross W. Gorte, 89-460 ENR

Public Opinion

* Abortion: National and State Public Opinion Polls, Rinn-Sup Shinn, etc., 89-591 GOV
* American Public Opinion on AIDS: A CRS Major Issue Before the 101st Congress, Rosita M. Thomas 89-85 GOV
* American Public Opinion on Eastern Europe, the Soviet Union, and Defense Spending, Rosita M. Thomas, 90-444 GOV
* American Public Opinion on the Federal Budget Deficit, Government Taxing and Spending, and the Economy, Rosita M. Thomas, 91-403 GOV
* American Public Opinion on the Federal Deficit, Rosita M. Thomas, 89-410 GOV
* American Public Opinion on the Iraq-Kuwait Crisis Until January 15, Rosita M. Thomas, 91-109 GOV
* American Public Opinion on the Space Program, Rosita M. Thomas, 91-90 GOV
* Campaign Financing: National Public Opinion Polls, Rinn-Sup Shinn, 91-346 GOV
* Crime and Crime Control: National Public Opinion Polls, Rinn-Sup Shinn, 90-583 GOV
* Drug Abuse and Control: National Public Opinion Polls, Rinn-Sup Shinn, 90-109 GOV
* Environmental Issues: National Public Opinion Polls, Rinn-Sup Shinn, etc., 90-405 GOV
* The "Gender Gap": Differences Between Men and Women in Political Attitudes and Voting Behavior in the 1980s. Jennifer D. Williams, 89-547 GOV
* A Guide to the Survey Polls File on SCORPIO, Office of Automated Information Services. Informat 86-138 AU
* Hong Kong-U.S. Economic Relations: Some Views from Hong Kong's Economic Elite, Kerry Dumbaugh 89-23 F
* The Iraqi Crisis: National Public Opinion Polls, Rosita M. Thomas, 90-436 GOV
* Public Opinion and Tax Reform: What Do the Polls Mean?, Wayne M. Morrison 85-878 E

Public Utility Regulatory Policies Act

* Electric Rate Effects of Cogeneration and Wheeling : Should PURPA Be Amended?; Archived Issue Brief, Sylvia Morrison IB87119
* PURPA: Should It be Amended to Facilitate the Sale of Bulk Power by Bid? Archived Issue Brief, Sylvia Morrison IB88014
* Wind Energy Development and Utility Capacity Credits: A Review of Research, Implementation and Policy Issues under the Public Utility Regulatory Policy, Fred Sissine 84-101 SPR

Public Welfare

* see AFDC, Homeless, Income Maintenance or Social Services
* The ACTION Agency Volunteer Programs, Dale H. Robinson, 90-452 EPW
* ACTION and Its Volunteer Program, Evelyn Howard, etc. 87-716 EPW
* Alien Eligibility Requirements for Major Federal Assistance Programs, Joyce Vialet, etc., 89-435 EPW
* Cash and Noncash Benefits for Persons With Limited Income: Eligibility Rules, Recipient and Expenditure Data, FY 1985-87, Vee Burke 88-595 EPW
* Cash and Noncash Benefits for Persons With Limited Income: Eligibility Rules, Recipient and Expenditure Data, FY 1988-90, Vee Burke 91-741 EPW
* Community Services Block Grants: FY 89 Budget Issues, Karen Spar 88-193 EPW
* Community Services Block Grants: History, Funding, Program Data, Karen Spar, etc. 87-739 EPW
* Community Services Block Grants and Related Programs, Karen Spar, 90-60 EPW
* Comparison of the Departments of Energy and Health and Human Services Weatherization Assistance Programs, Mary Smith, etc. 89-229 EPW
* Distributional Effects of Selected Proposals to Modify the Earned Income Tax Credit, Thomas Bage, 89-553 EPW
* Federal Programs Affecting Children, Sharon House, etc. 87-306 EPW
* Federal Spending for Social Welfare Programs in Fiscal year 1990, Gene Falk, 90-550 EPW
* Federal Spending Proposed in the Fiscal Year 1989 Budget for Selected Major Income Maintenance Programs, Vee Burke 88-227 EPW
* Head Start Issues in FY 1986: Funding, Administration, and Recent Evaluations, Sharon Stephan 86-554 EPW
* Head Start Reauthorization Amendments Enacted During the 101st Congress, Anne C. Stewart, 90-642 EPW
* Hispanic Children in Poverty, Vee Burke, etc. 85-170 EPW
* Housing the Low-Income Family With Children, Morton J. Schussheim 87-518 S
* Income Support Programs: Changes in Spending, Distribution and Impact on Poverty of Government Benefit Programs, Gene Falk 86-141 EPW
* The Indexation of Federal Programs, Royal Shipp 82-103 S
* Inventory of Federally Indexed Programs, Vee Burke 81-168 EPW
* The Low-Income Home Energy Assistance Program, Joe Richardson, 91-465 EPW
* Migration and Refugee Assistance Budget:: Problems and Prospects; Issue Brief, Lois McHugh, IB89150
* National Service: Info Pack, IP418N
* National Service: Issues and Proposals in the 101st Congress; Issue Brief, Karen Spar IB89071
* National Service Proposals: The Implications for Federal Student Aid, Steven Aleman, etc. 89-254 EPW
* National Service: Selected References, Peter Giordano 89-165 L
* Poverty in the United States, Thomas P. Gabe, etc., 91-742 EPW
* Progress Against Poverty in the United States (1959 to 1989), Thomas Gabe 91-355 EPW
* Public Welfare: An Alphabetical Microthesaurus of Terms Selected from the Legislative Indexing Vocabulary, Shirley Loo 91-629 L
* Refunded Tax Credits to Aid Working Poor Families: Archived issue Brief, James R. Storey, IB89109
* Social Security Benefits, Cash Relief, and Food Aid: A Short History, Vee Burke 86-45 EPW
* The Social Services Block Grant Program: History, Description, and Current Trends, Evelyn Howard 86-145 EPW
* Solicitation of Charitable Contributions: A Survey of State Statutes, John Luckey, etc. 87-950 A
* Statehood for Puerto Rico: The Effect on Social Welfare Programs, Carol L. Merck, 91-47 EPW
* Supplemental Security Income (SSI) Legislation in the 101st Congress; Archived Issue Brief, Carmen D. Solomon, IB89112
* Welfare and Poverty: Info Pack, IP098W
* Welfare and Poverty: Selected References, 1990-1991, M. Alexandra Salinas, 91-619 L
* Welfare: Issue Brief, Vee Burke IB87007
* Welfare Reform: Archived Issue Brief, Vee Burke IB77069
* Welfare Reform: Bibliography-in-Brief, 1986-1987, Edith Sutterlin 88-25 L
* Welfare Reform: Brief Summaries of Selected Major Proposals, Vee Burke, etc. 88-223 EPW
* Work Disincentives in Income-Tested Programs, Vee Burke 80-158 EPW
* Work Incentives for Disabled Supplemental Security Income (SSI) Recipients: Section 1619 of the Social Security Act, Carmen Solomon 87-427 EPW
* 1992 Budget Perspectives: Federal spending for the Social Welfare Programs, Gene Falk, etc., 91-280 EPW

Public Welfare -- AFDC

* AFDC, Food Stamps, and Work: History, Rules, and Research, Emmett Carson, etc. 87-599 EPW
* Aid to Families with Dependent Children (AFDC) and Postsecondary Education, Carmen D. Solomon, 90-549 EPW
* Aid to Families With Dependent Children (AFDC) and Work: Tables Summarizing Treatment of Earnings, Vee Burke 87-74 EPW
* Aid to Families With Dependent Children (AFDC): Need Standards, Payment Standards, and Maximum Benefits for Families With No Countable Income, Carmen Solomon 88-602 EPW
* Aid to Families With Dependent Children (AFDC): Work and Training Issues: Archived Issue Brief, Carmen Solomon IB86094
* Aid to Families With Dependent Children (AFDC), Work Programs, and Child Support: A Comparison of H. R. 3100/S. 1655 With Current Policy, Carmen Solomon 87-907 EPW
* Analysis of Federal-State Cost-Sharing in the Aid to Families With Dependent Children Program, Education and Public Welfare Division 82-62 EPW
* Child Support: Bibliography-in-Brief, 1984-1988, Edith Sutterlin 88-510 L
* The Child Support Enforcement Program: Policy and Practice, Carmen D. Solomon, 89-659 EPW
* Child Welfare in the 102nd Congress: A Comparison of House and Senate Bills, Karen Spar, 91-648 EPW
* The Family Support Act of 1988: How It Changes the Aid to Families With

Current Events and Homework

Dependent Children (AFDC) and Child Support Enforcement Programs, Carmen D. Solomon 88-702 EPW
* High-School Dropouts and the Family Support Act, Vee Burke, 90-532 EPW
* State Use of the Aid to Families With Dependent Children-Unemployed Parent (AFDC-UP) Program: An Overview, Celinda M. Franco, etc. 87-969 EPW
* Statistical and Program Data on Single-Parent Families With Children, Carmen Solomon 86-723 EPW

Public Welfare -- Homeless

* Cash Welfare Funds and Homeless Families With Children, Carmen Solomon 88-394 EPW
* Constitutional Analysis of Proposed Regulations Issued by the Department of Housing and Urban Development Regarding the Participation of Religious Or, David M. Ackerman 87-444 A
* Homeless Housing: HUD's Shelter Programs; Archived Issue Brief, Susan Vanhorenbeck IB87098
* Homeless in America: Info Pack, IP314H
* The Homeless: Overview of the Problem and the Federal Response, Susan Schillmoeller, etc. 87-927 EPW
* Homelessness and Commitment: The Cases of Joyce Brown (AKA Billie Boggs), Kirk D. Nemer 88-186 A
* Homelessness in the U.S.: Bibliography-in-Brief, 1986-1988, Edith Sutterlin 88-396 L
* Homelessness: Issues and legislation in 1988: Issue Brief, Ruth Ellen Wasem IB88070
* Homelessness: Medical Conditions, Edith Fairman Cooper, 91-201 SPR
* Homelessness and the Federal Response, 1987-1991, Ruth Ellen Wasem, 91-500 EPW
* The Homelessness Problem: Background and Legislation: Archived Issue Brief, David Koitz IB87143
* The Housing and Community Development Act of 1987 and the Stewart B. McKinney Homeless Assistance Act Summary and Analysis, Barbara Miles 88-481 E
* Programs Benefiting the Homeless: FY 87-FY89 Appropriations Trends, Ruth Ellen Wasem 89-20 EPW

Public Works

* see Infrastructure, Procurement

Puerto Rico

* Puerto Rico: Political Status Options: Issue Brief, Bette Taylor IB89065
* Puerto Rico's Status Options and Federal Taxes: Issue Brief, David L. Brumbaugh, IB90086
* Statehood for Puerto Rico: The Effect on Social Welfare Programs, Carolyn L. Merck, 91-47 EPW
* Territorial Political Development: An Analysis of Puerto Rico, Northern Mariana Islands, Guam, Virgin Islands, and American Samoa, and the Micronesian, Bette A. Taylor 88-657 GOV

Punjab

* India's Punjab Crisis: Issues, Prospects, and Implications, Richard P. Cronin 87-850 F
* India's Sikhs and the Crisis in Punjab State: Summary Briefing Points, Richard Cronin 87-509 F

Purpa

* see Public Utility Regulatory Policies Act

Racketeer Influenced and Corrupt Organizations Act

* see Criminal Procedure

Radioactive Wastes

* see Solid Wastes--Radioactive Wastes

Radon

* see Air Pollution--Indoor Air Pollution

Railroads

* see Transportation--Railroads

Rangeland

* see Agriculture-Livestock

Reagan Doctrine

* see Foreign Relations--Reagan Doctrine

Reagan, Ronald

* Andropov and Reagan as Negotiators: Contexts and Styles in Contrast, Joseph Whelan 83-141 S
* Presidential Vetoes and Ronald Reagan's Use of the Process in the Second Term: Issue Brief, Gary Galemore IB85093
* Statements by President Reagan Relating to Arms Control April 1, 1986-January 31, 1987, Teri Lehto 87-116 S
* Statements by President Reagan Relating to Arms Control; February 2, 1985-December 31, 1985, Jeanette Voas 86-549 F
* Statements by President Reagan Relating to Arms Control, January 1, 1984-March 31, 1984, Lynne Rusten 84-616 F
* Statements by President Reagan Relating to Arms Control, January 1, 1986-March 31, 1986, Jeanette Voas 86-663 S
* Statements by President Reagan Relating to Arms Control: June 1, 1987-December 31, 1987, Teri Lehto 88-60 S
* Statements by President Reagan Relating to the INF Treaty, June 1, 1987-December 31, 1987, Teri Lehto 88-60 S
* Vetoes During President Reagan's First Term, 1981-1984, Gary Galemore 86-681 GOV

Real Estate Settlement Procedures Act

* Recent Developments in the Real Estate Settlement Procedures Act, Richard Bourdon 88-730 E

RCRA

* see Resource Conservation and Recovery Act

Recession

* see Economic Conditions--Business Cycles

Recombinant DNA

* see Genetics

Recreation

* All-Terrain Vehicles: The December 1987 Consent Agreement and Related Developments, Migdon Segal 88-275 SPR
* Land and Water Conservation Fund: Information and Status, George H. Siehl 89-159 ENR
* Military and Recreation Interests in American Lands: Selected References, Lisa B. Dove, 90-426 L
* National Forest Receipts: Sources and Disposition, Ross W. Gorte 89-284 ENR
* National Recreation Areas, George Siehl 88-644 ENR
* Outdoor Recreation: A Comparison of Two Federal Commissions, George Siehl 87-61 ENR
* Outdoor Recreation: A New Commission Is Created: Archived Issue Brief, George Siehl IB83223
* Scenic Byways: Issues and Action, John Spengler, etc. 88-479 ENR
* Special Management Areas in the National Forest System, Ross Gorte 88-571 ENR
* The Sport Hunting Safety and Preservation Act of 1991: Constitutionality of H.R. 371, 102nd Congress, Henry Cohen, 91-442 A
* Tourism: Its Contributions to the U.S. Economy, Bernevia M. McCalip, 90-501 E
* Trails Programs in Federal Agencies: A Data Compilation, George Siehl 89-8 ENR

Recycling

* see Solid Wastes

Reference Sources

* see Directories, Microthesauri, Scorpio, Speechwriting
* Bills Introduced and Laws Enacted: Selected Legislative Statistics, 1947-1990, Rozanne M. Barry, 1991-646 C
* Conducting Legislative Research in a Congressional Office, Clay H. Wellborn 89-331 GOV
* Form Letters: Tell Your Constituents Where to Get Government Publications; Info Pack, IP222F
* Government Publications--How, What, When, Where, and Why: Info Pack, IP264G
* A Guide to Print and Non-Print Teaching Aids, Winfield Swanson, etc. 83-184 C

Public Welfare / Reference Sources

* How to Find Information About Your Subject: A Guide to Reference Materials in Local Libraries, Merete Gerli 88-299 C
* How to Follow Current Legislation and Regulations:, Info Pack, IP122H
* Legislative Research: A Guide to Conducting Legislative Research in a Congressional Office: Info Pack, IP321L
* Public Speaking and Speechwriting: Selected References, Jean Bowers, 91-817 L
* Washington, DC and the U.S. Capitol Building: Info Pack, IP132W

Reference Sources -- Directories

* Conducting Legislative Research in a Congressional Office, Clay H. Wellborn, 89-331 GOV
* Congressional Liaison Offices of Selected Federal Agencies, Barbara Hillson 88-58C
* Congressional Liaison Offices of Selected Federal Agencies, by Office of Special Programs. Inquiry Section. 91-348 PGM
* The Congressional Scene: Selected Publications Covering the Congress, Pamela Dragovich 91-68 C
* Countries of the World: Sources of Information, Margaret E. Melun, 91-645 C
* CRS TV and Audio Products for Congress: Issue Brief, Gary Levine, IB83145
* Directory of Environmental and Conservation Organizations in the Washington, DC Metropolitan Area, Mira Courpas 89-99 ENR
* The Federal Money Trail: Data Sources of Federal Aid, Grants, Loans, and Procurement in States and Local Areas, James R. Riehl, 91-550 C
* From Letters: Tell Your Constituents Where to Get Government Publications; Info Pack: IP222F
* Government Publications--How, What, When, Where, and Why: Info Pack, IP264G
* A Guide to Print and Non-Print Teaching Aids, Michelle Springer, 89-289 C
* Hotlines and Other Useful Government Telephone Numbers: Info Pack, IP106H
* How to Find Information About a Subject: A Guide to Reference Materials in Local Libraries, Merete Gerli, 90-155 C
* How to Follow Current Federal Legislation and Regulations, Carol D. Davis, 91-66 C
* How to Follow Current Federal Legislations and Regulations: Info Pack, IP122H
* Indian and Indian-Interest Organizations, Richard Jones, etc. 84-131 GOV
* Inexpensive Hotels and Housing in Washington, DC, Bette A. Alberts, 91-425 RCO
* Internships and Fellowships: Congressional, Federal and Other Work Experience Opportunities, Betsy Reifsnyder 90-148 C
* The Largest Corporations in the United States: Information and Addresses from the Forbes 500, Felicia G. Kolp, 91-532 C
* Legislative History: A Guide for Constituents, Mark Gurevitz, 89-596 A
* Legislative Research: A Guide to Conducting Legislative Research in a Congressional Office; Info Pack, IP321L
* Lobbyists and Interest Groups: A List of Information Sources, Barbara Hillson, 91-600 C
* Organizations and Associations: A List of Information Sources, Walter S. Albano, 91-658 C
* Organizations that Rate Members of Congress on Their Voting Records, Kathy Doddridge, 91-65 C
* Parliamentary Reference Sources: An Introductory Guide, Ilona B. Nickels, 89-593 GOV
* Pictures of Government Officials, Treva Turner 88-59 C
* Small Business Assistance Programs: Sources of Information; Info Pack, IP422S
* United States Court System: Finding Federal Case Material, Elizabeth B. Bazan, etc., 90-221 A
* United States Law: Finding Statutory Material. Thomas B. Ripy, etc., 90-110 A
* Voting Records of Members of Congress: A Self-Help Guide to Their Compilation, Peggy Garvin, 91-67 C
* Where to Get Publications from the Executive and Independent Agencies: A Directory of Sources for Official Documents, Deborah C. Brudno, etc. 91-82 C

Reference Sources -- Grants

* Fundraising Techniques for Groups: Bibliography-in-Brief, 1968-1987, Robert Kirk 87-380 L
* Fundraising Techniques for Groups: Bibliography-in-Brief, 1987-1991, Robert Kirk 91-427 L
* Grant Proposal Development, Rhoda Newman, 90-430 C
* Grants and Foundation Support: Info Pack, IP050G
* Grants and Foundation Support: Selected Sources of Information, Lynne Kennedy, etc., 90-262 C
* Grants Work in a Congressional Office, Rhoda Newman, 89-658 C
* Writing the Grant Proposal, Lee Decker 85-8C

Reference Sources -- Microthesauri

* Aging and the Elderly: An Alphabetical Microthesaurus of Terms Selected from the Legislative Indexing Vocabulary, Shirley Loo 88-752 L
* Agriculture and Food: An Alphabetical Microthesaurus of Terms Selected from the Legislative Indexing, Vocabulary, Shirley Loo 89-512 L
* Arms and Arms Control: An Alphabetical Microthesaurus of Terms Selected from the Legislative Indexing Vocabulary, Shirley Loo 87-961 L
* Astronautics and Space: An Alphabetical Microthesaurus of Terms Selected from the Legislative Indexing Vocabulary, Shirley Loo 88-397 L
* Automation and Computers: An Alphabetical Microthesaurus of Terms Selected from the Legislative Indexing Vocabulary, Shirley Loo 90-376 L
* Children, Families and Domestic Relations: An Alphabetical Microthesaurus of Terms Selected from the Legislative Indexing Vocabulary, Shirley Loo 90-40 L
* Congress and Congressional Operation: An Alphabetical Microthesaurus of Terms Selected from the Legislative Indexing Vocabulary, Shirley Loo 91-506 L
* Crime and Criminal Justice: An Alphabetical Microthesaurus of Terms Selected from the Legislative Indexing Vocabulary, Shirley Loo 88-437 L
* Drug Abuse and Control: An Alphabetical Microthesaurus of Terms Selected from the Legislative Indexing Vocabulary, Shirley Loo, 90-143 L
* Education: An Alphabetical Microthesaurus of Terms Selected from the Legislative Indexing Vocabulary, Shirley Loo 89-54 L
* Employment and Labor: An Alphabetical Microthesaurus of Terms Selected from the Legislative Indexing Vocabulary, Shirley Loo 88-748 L
* Environmental Protection: An Alphabetical Microthesaurus of Terms Selected from the Legislative Indexing Vocabulary, Shirley Loo 87-792 L
* Federal Government Spending: An Alphabetical Microthesaurus of Terms Selected from the Legislative Indexing Vocabulary, Shirley Lee, 88-467 L
* Foreign Policy and International Relations: An Alphabetical Microthesaurus of Terms Selected from the Legislative Indexing Vocabulary, Shirley Loo 90-367 L
* Housing and Housing Finance: An Alphabetical Microthesaurus of Terms Selected from the Legislative Indexing Vocabulary, Shirley Loo 86-1033 L
* Immigration, Ethnic Groups, and Nationalities: An Alphabetical Microthesaurus of Terms Selected from the Legislative Indexing Vocabulary, Shirley Loo, 91-670 L
* Insurance: An Alphabetical Microthesaurus of Terms Selected from the legislative Indexing Vocabulary, Shirley Loo 88-582 L
* Law, Lawyers, and the Judiciary: An Alphabetical Microthesaurus of Terms Selected from the Legislative Indexing Vocabulary, Shirley Loo, 90-584 L
* Money and Banking: An Alphabetical Microthesaurus of Terms Selected from the Legislative Indexing Vocabulary, Shirley Loo 88-530 L
* National Defense and Military Operations: An Alphabetical Microthesaurus of Terms Selected from the Legislative Indexing Vocabulary, Shirley Loo 91-496 L
* Nuclear Energy: An Alphabetical Microthesaurus of Terms Selected from the Legislative Indexing Vocabulary, Shirley Loo 87-962 L
* Political Campaigns and Elections: An Alphabetical Microthesaurus of Terms Selected from the Legislative Indexing Vocabulary, Shirley Loo 88-671 L
* Political Campaigns and Elections: An Alphabetical Microthesaurus of Terms Selected from the Legislative Indexing Vocabulary, Shirley Loo, 88-671 L
* Public Welfare: An Alphabetical Microthesaurus of Terms Selected from the Legislative Indexing Vocabulary, Shirley Loo 87-390 L
* Taxes and Taxation: An Alphabetical Microthesaurus of Terms Selected from the Legislative Indexing Vocabulary, Shirley Loo 89-646 L
* Trade and International Finance: An Alphabetical Microthesaurus of Terms Selected from the Legislative Indexing Vocabulary, Shirley Loo 89-653 L
* Transportation: An Alphabetical Microthesaurus of Terms Selected from the Legislative Indexing Vocabulary, Shirley Loo 88-524 L
* U.S. Presidents: An Alphabetical Microthesaurus of Terms Selected from the Legislative Indexing Vocabulary, Shirley Loo 89-131 L
* Water and Water Resources Development: An Alphabetical Microthesaurus of Terms Selected form the Legislative Indexing Vocabulary, Shirley Loo 90-544 L
* Women: An Alphabetical Microthesaurus of Terms Selected from the Legislative Indexing Vocabulary, Shirley Loo 88-710 L

Current Events and Homework

Reference Sources -- SCORPIO

* A Guide to the Survey Polls File on SCORPIO, Office of Automated Information Services 86-138 AU
* SCORPIO Reference Manual, Congressional Research Service Automation Office 91-366 AU

Reference Sources -- Speechwriting

* Public Speaking: Bibliography-in-Brief, 1983-1987, Adrienne C. Grenfell 87-790 L
* Speech Material: Abraham Lincoln's and George Washington's Birthdays: Info Pack, IP373A
* Speech Material: Columbus Day; Info Pack, IP380C
* Speech Material: Fourth of July; Info Pack, IP377F
* Speech Material: Graduation; Info Pack, IP379G
* Speech Material: Martin Luther King's Birthday; Info Pack, IP372M
* Speech Material: Thanksgiving Day; Info Pack, IP381T
* Speech Material: Veterans Day; Info Pack, IP378V
* Speechwriting and Delivery: Info Pack, IP139S
* Speechwriting in Perspective: A Brief Guide to Effective and Persuasive Communication, Charles H. Whittier 86-1034 GOV

Refugees

* see Immigration--Refugees

Regional Development

* see also Infrastructure
* The ABCs of Public Venture Capital Investment, Jan Christopher 88-757 E
* The "Bridge Crisis": An Economic Development Perspective; Issue Brief, J.F. Hornbeck IB88085
* Community Development Issues in the 102nd Congress: Issue Brief, Eugene Boyd, IB91067
* The Community Reinvestment Act: Its Role in Local Economic Development, J.F. Hornbeck 88-732 E
* Community Reinvestment Act: Legal Analysis, Maureen Murphy 89-135 A
* Earnings as a Measure of Regional Economic Performance, Linda LeGrande, etc. 87-377 E
* Economic Development: A Listing of Federal Programs, Jan E. Christopher 88-536 E
* The Economic Health of the Lower Mississippi River Valley, Jan Christopher 88-253 E
* Economic Policy: Selected Issues of Interest of the 101st Congress, Edward Knight 88-703 E
* Economic Redevelopment in the Cities, Jan E. Christopher 88-703 E
* Enterprise Zones: Bibliography-in-Brief, 1984-1989, Felix Chin, 90-39 L
* Expiring Tax-Exempt Bond Provisions: Small-Issue IDBs and Mortgage Revenue Bonds, Dennis Zimmerman, 90-417 E
* Federal Enterprise Zone: The Prospect for Economic Development: Issue Brief, J.F. Hornbeck IB89050
* Federal Tax Incentives for Enterprise Zones: Analysis of Economic Effects and Rationales, Dennis Zimmerman, 89-371 E
* Financing Business and Economic Development: Three Private-Sector Initiatives, J. F. Hornbeck 88-598 E
* Infrastructure: A Brief Overview from the National Level, William W. Ellis, etc. 87-30 S
* Manufactured Exports and Regional Economic Growth in the United States, 1977 to 1983: A Preliminary Assessment, Gary L. Guenther 86-855 E
* Regional Economic Development Programs of the Federal Government, Jan E. Christopher 88-309 E
* Rural Community Development: Selected References, Rebecca Mazur 88-17 L
* Rural Policy in an Era of Change and Diversity, Sandra Osborne 88-482 GOV
* Rural Policy in the United States: A History, Sandra S. Osborne 88-487 GOV
* Selected Options for Federal Support of State and Local Technology Development Programs, Wendy H. Schacht 87-201 SPR
* State and Local Equity Capital Funds: Selected Case Studies, Jan E. Christopher 88-758 E
* States/Counties of the Lower Mississippi River Valley: Statistics on Per Capita Personal Income and Unemployment Rates, Jan Christopher 88-254 E
* Transportation Infrastructure and Economic Development, J.F. Hornbeck 89-109 E

Regional Development -- Rural

* Amenity Resources and Rural Economic Growth: Report on a National Policy Symposium, George H. Siehl, 90-380 ENR

* Rural Areas and Clean Water: Impacts of the Water Quality Act of 1987, Claudia Copeland, 87-257 ENR
* Rural Development Legislation: Comparative Summaries, Sandra S. Osbourn, 90-232 GOV
* Rural Economic Development: Selected References, 1988-1989, Jean Bowers, 90-16 L
* The Rural Electrification Administration: Background and Current Issues, Carl Ek, etc., 91-614 ENR
* Rural Policy in an Era of Change and Diversity, Sandra S. Osbourn, 88-482 GOV
* Rural Policy in the United States: A History, Sandra S. Osbourn, 88-487 GOV

Regulatory Reform

* see Business and Society-Regulation and Deregulation,Aeronautics, Telecommunication

Rehabilitation Act

* see also Handicapped
* Affirmative Action in the Employment of Persons With Handicaps under Federal Contracts: Section 503 of the Rehabilitation Act, Mary Smith 88-701 EPW
* Regulations Promulgated Pursuant to Section 404 of the Rehabilitation Act of 1973: A Brief History and Present Status, Nancy Jones, etc. 86-53 A
* Section 504 of the Rehabilitation Act: Statutory Provisions, Legislative History, and Regulatory Requirements, Mary F. Smith, 89-48 EPW
* School Board of Nassau County v. Arline: A Person With the Contagious Disease of Tuberculosis May be Covered under Section 504 of the Rehabilitation Act, Nancy Lee Jones 87-238 A
* Section 504 of the Rehabilitation Act: Statutory Provisions, Legislative History, and Regulatory Requirements, Mary F. Smith 89-48 EPW
* Supreme Court Decisions Interpreting Section 504 of the Rehabilitation Act of 1973, Nancy Jones 85-926 A

Religion

* Abortion in World Religions, Charles H. Whittier 88-357 GOV
* American Indian Religious Freedom: The Legal Landscape, M. Maureen Murphy 88-370 A
* Background Information on Equal Access Statute, David Ackerman 84-842 A
* Catholic Social Teaching and the U.S. Economy: The Pastoral Letter of the American Catholic Bishops, Charles Whittier 87-104 GOV
* Chaplains in Congress, Charles H. Whittier, 90-65 GOV
* Court Cases Involving Governmental Assistance to the Facilities of Sectarian Institutions and the Establishment Clause, David M. Ackerman, 88-372 A
* Church-State and Nondiscrimination Aspects of H.R. 36670, the "Act for Better Child Care Services of 1988", as Approved by the House Subcommittee on, David M. Ackerman 88-497 A
* The Concept of "Secular Humanism" in the Context of Elementary and Secondary Education: Discussion of the Variety of Meanings, and References, Wayne Riddle 86-545 EPW
* Court Cases Involving Governmental Assistance to the Facilities of Sectarian Institutions and the Establishment Clause, David Ackerman 88-372 A
* Creationism in the Public Schools: Summary and Analysis of Edwards v. Aguillard, David Ackerman 89-170 A
* Day Care and the Law of Church and State: Constitutional Mandates and Policy Options, David Ackerman 89-170 A
* Developments in the Law of Church and State Since 1980, David M. Ackerman, 91-822 A
* Establishment Clause Jurisprudence and the Display of Religious Symbols, David M. Ackerman, 89-614 A
* Exempt Status of Religious Groups, Marie B. Morris 87-846 A
* Forum: Supreme Court Review: 1989-90 Term, Congressional Research Service Review, REV 9-90
* The Holy See and Recognition of Israel, Charles H. Whittier 86-833 GOV
* India's Sikhs and the Crisis in Punjab State: Summary Briefing Points, Richard P. Cronin 87-509 F
* The Just War in Certain Religious Traditions: Christianity; Judaism; Islam, and Buddhism, Charles A. Whittier 87-915 GOV
* The Law of Blasphemy in England and Wales, Law Library of Congress, American-British Law Division, LL90-70
* Life Sustaining Technologies: Medical and Moral Issues, Marilyn Littlejohn and Irene Stith-Coleman, 91-45 SPR
* The New Religious Right: Background, Current Agenda, Future Prospects,

Charles Whittier 87-615 GOV
* Prayer and Religion in the Public Schools: What Is, and Is Not, Permitted, David Ackerman 89-25 A
* Prayer and Religion in U.S. Public Schools: Bibliography-in-Brief, 1983-1988, Edith Sutterlin 88-663 L
* Religion and Public Policy: Background and Issues in the 80's, Charles Whittier 84-104 GOV
* Religion in the Public Schools: Judicial Decisions, David Ackerman 88-770 A
* Religion in the Public Schools: Pluralism and Teaching About Religions, Charles Whittier 89-104 GOV
* The Right to Die: Fundamental Life Decisions After Cruzan v. Director, Missouri Dept. of Health, Kenneth R. Thomas, 90-371 A
* The School Prayer Controversy: Pro-Con Arguments; Issue Brief, Charles Whittier IB84081
* School Prayer: The Congressional Response, 1962-1988, David Ackerman 88-676 A
* Science and Religion: Conflict and Accommodations in the Darwinian Controversy, Charles Whittier 87-395 GOV
* The Senate Chaplaincy, Charles Whittier 86-916 GOV
* Silent Prayer and Mediation in World Religions, Charles Whittier 88-18 GOV
* Supreme Court: Church-State Cases, October 1984 Term; Archived Issue Brief, David Ackerman IB84229
* Supreme Court: Church-State Cases: October 1985 Term; Archived Issue brief, David Ackerman IB85207
* Supreme Court: Church-State Cases, October 1986 Term; Archived Issue Brief, David Ackerman IB86129
* Supreme Court: Church-State Cases, October 1987 Term; Archived Brief, David Ackerman IB88105
* Supreme Court: Church-State Cases, 1990-1991 Term; Archived Brief, David Ackerman IB91056
* Supreme Court: Church-State Cases, 1991-92 Term; Issue Brief, David M. Ackerman, IB91136

Republican National Convention (1988: New Orleans)

* A Summary of National and State Party Laws Concerning the Election of Delegates to the 1988 Democratic and Republican National Conventions, Kevin Coleman 88-102 GOV

Research and Development

* see also Defense, Funding and Genetics
* Agricultural Research: Issues for the 1980s, Christine Matthews Rose 87-430 SPR
* Allocation of Research and Development Costs and the U.S. Foreign Tax Credit, David Brumbaugh 89-220 E
* American Science at a Critical Crossroads: A Checklist of CRS Products, Karen L. Alderson, 91-927 L
* Analysis of the Office of Science and Technology Policy, Genevieve J. Knezo 88-205 SPR
* Animal Use in Research: Bibliography-in-Brief, 1985-87, Adrienne C. Grenfell 88-72 L
* Animal Welfare Issues: Info Pack, IP360A
* Biomedical Ethics and Congress: History and Current Legislative Activity; Issue Brief, Irene Stith-Coleman IB86078
* Biomedical Research: Use of Animals; Issue Brief, Blanchard Randall IB83161
* Biotechnology: A Public Policy Primer, Sarah E. Taylor, etc., 89-389 SPR
* Brief Summaries of Federal Animal Protection Statutes, Henry Cohen 91-791 A
* Commercialization of Technology and Issues in the Competitiveness of Selected U.S. Industries: Semiconductors, Biotechnology, and Superconductors Leonard G. Kruger, etc. 88-486 SPR
* Cooperative R&D: Federal Efforts to Promote Industrial Competitiveness: Issue Brief, Wendy Schacht IB89056
* Defense-Related Independent Research and Development in Industry, Joan Winston 85-205 S
* Defense Technology and Industrial Base: Bibliography-in-Brief, Karen Alderson 89-145 L
* Desalination Research and Development; Issue Brief, James E. Mielke, IB91048
* Economic Policy: Selected Issues of Interest to the 101st Congress, Edward Knight 89-209 E
* The Federal Research Internet and the National Research and Education Network: Prospects for the 1990s, Stephen Gould, 90-362 SPR
* Globalization of Research and Development; Selected References, Karen L.

Alderson, 91-801 L
* The Impact of U.S. Antitrust Law on Joint Activity by Corporations: Some Background, Janice E. Rubin 89-291 A
* Industrial Competitiveness and Technological Advancement: Debate Over Government Policy; Issue Brief, Wendy H. Schacht, IB91132
* Industrial Innovation: The Debate Over Government Policy: Issue Brief, Wendy Schacht IB84004
* Japanese Basic Research Policies, Genevieve J. Knezo, 90-363 SPR
* Japanese Science and Technology: Some Recent Efforts to Improve U.S. Monitoring, Nancy R. Miller 86-195 SPR
* Japanese Technical Information: Opportunities to Improve U.S. Access, Christopher T. Hill 87-818 S
* Japanese Technical Information: Opportunities to Improve U.S. Access, Christopher T. Hill, 87-818 S
* Japan's Science and Technology Strategies and Policies: Issue Brief, Glenn McLouglin, IB90053
* Joint Research and Development Ventures: Antitrust, Considerations; Archived Issue Brief, Wendy Schacht IB83178
* Managing Defense Department Technology Base Programs, Michael Davey 88-310 SPR
* Measuring the Economic Benefits of Federally Supported Research: A Bibliography, Genevieve J. Knezo, etc., 91-335 SPR
* Military Research and Development: Implications for Civilian Science and the Economy; Bibliography-in-Brief, 1982-1986, Virginia MacEwen 87-59 L
* National Research Initiative of the U.S. Department of Agriculture, Christine M. Matthews, 91-435 SPR
* Planning, Managing, and Funding DOD's Technology Base, Michael Davey 89-319 SPR
* Productivity and U.S. Living Standards; Issue Brief, William A. Cox IB88107
* Renewable Energy: A New National Commitment? Issue Brief, Fred J. Sissine IB90110
* Research Journal Prices-Trends and Problems, Richard Rowberg 88-264 SPR
* Review of U.S. Research and Development Programs in Ballistic Missile Defense, John D. Moteff 89-150 SPR
* Science and Technology: Federal Policy and Economic Impact: Bibliography-in-Brief, 1983-1986, Virginia MacEwen 87-79 L
* Science and Technology Policies and Practices in Industrialized Countries Other Than the U.S.: Bibliography-in-Brief, Karen L. Alderson 89-46 L
* Scientific Communication and National Security: Bibliography-in-Brief, 1982-1987, Virginia MacEwen, etc. 87-110 L
* Small Business Innovation Development Act: H.R. 4260 Amendments to P.L. 97-219; Archived Issue Brief, Wendy Schacht IB86118
* Small Business, Technology Development, and Manufacturing: Competitiveness Issues, Wendy H. Schacht, 89-685 SPR
* Soviet Civilian Research and Development Facilities and Funding, William C. Boesman, etc. 91-778 SPR
* Superconducting Super Collider: Current Issues and Legislation: Issue Brief, William C. Boesman, IB87096
* Superconducting Super Collider: Science, Costs, and Benefits, William C. Boesman, 90-178 SPR
* Technological Advancement and U.S. Industrial Competitiveness, Wendy Schacht 88-689 SPR
* Technology Policy: The Challenges of R& D Collaboration, Christopher T. Hill, 90-92 RCO
* Technology Transfer: Utilization of Federally Funded Research and Development; Issue Brief, Wendy Schacht IB85031
* World Inventory of 'Big Science' Research Instruments and Facilities, William C. Boesman 88-38 SPR

Research and Development -- Defense

* The Commercial Implications of Exporting and Importing Military Technology: A Review of the Issues, John D. Moteff, 90-409 SPR
* Cooperative R&D: Federal Efforts to Promote Industrial Competitiveness; Issue Brief, Wendy H. Schacht. IB89056
* Defense Basic Research Priorities: Funding and Policy Issues, Genevieve J. Knezo, 90-506 SPR
* DOD's Federally Funded Research and Development Centers, Michael E. Davey, 91-378 SPR
* Leveraging DOD's R& D Investment: Acquiring External Technology, John D. Moteff, 91-102 SPR
* Managing Defense Department Technology Base Programs, Michael E. Davey, 88-310 SPR
* Planning, Managing, and Funding DOD's Technology Base Programs, Michael E. Davey, 89-319 SPR

Current Events and Homework

Research and Development -- Funding

* Direct Federal Support for Technological Innovation: Issues and Options, Christopher Hill, etc. 84-118 S
* Equity, Excellence, and the Distribution of Federal Research and Development Funds, William C. Boesman, etc. 88-422 SPR
* The Federal Contribution to Basic Research: Background Material for 1987 Hearings, Michael Davey, etc. 87-633 SPR
* Federal Spending on Materials Research and Development: FY1990-FY1992, John D. Moteff, 91-389 SPR
* Federal Support of Basic Research and the Establishment of the National Science Foundation and Other Research Agencies, William C. Boesman 88-456 SPR
* The "Grace" Report on R&D (The President's Private Sector Survey on Cost Control in the Federal Government: Task Force Report on Research and Develop), William Boesman 84-65 SPR
* Indirect Costs at Academic Institutions: Background and Controversy: Issue Brief, Genevieve J. Knezo, IB91095
* Research and Development Funding: FY 1992; Archived Issue Brief, Science Policy Research Division IB90048
* Research and Development Funding: FY 1991; Archived Issue Brief, Science Policy Research Division IB91003
* Research and Development Funding: FY 1990; Issue Brief, Science Policy Research Division IB89040
* Research and Development Funding: FY 86 and FY 87: Issue Brief, Science Policy Research Division. Genevieve Knezo IB86062
* Research and Development Funding: FY 88; Archived Issue Brief, Research and Development Team. Michael Davey IB87083
* Research and Development Funding: FY 89; Archived Issue Brief, Michael Davey IB88040
* The Research and Development Tax Credit: A Comparison of the Arguments For and Against, Office of Senior Specialists 88-333 S
* The Research and Experimentation Tax Credit: Archived Issue Brief, David L. Brumbaugh, IB90008
* Science and Technology Policy and Funding: Reagan Administration; Archived Issue Brief, Genevieve Knezo IB82108
* Selected Federal Research and Development Agencies, and Programs and the Gramm-Rudman-Hollings Deficit Reduction Act: An Analysis of the Impact on Them, Michael Davey 86-37 SPR
* The Tax Credit for Research and Development: An Analysis, Jane G. Gravelle 85-6 E
* Technology Transfer: Utilization of Federally Funded Research and Development: Issue Brief, Wendy Schacht, IB85031
* U.S. Civilian and Defense Research and Development Funding: Some Trends and Comparisons With Selected Industrialized Nations, William Boesman, etc. 84-195 SPR

Resource Conservation and Recovery Act

* see also Solid Waste
* Environmental Impairment Liability Insurance: Overview of Availability Issues, Rawle O. King 89-269 E
* Environmental Issues: From the 101st to the 102nd Congress, Environment and Natural Resources Policy Division, 91-11 ENR
* Environmental Protection Legislation in the 102nd Congress; Issue Brief, Environmental and Natural Resources Policy Div. IB91042
* Environmental Protection Legislation in the 101st Congress; Issue Brief, Environmental and Natural Resources Policy Div. IB89033
* Hazardous Waste Fact Book, James E. McCarthy, etc. 87-56 ENR
* Hazardous Waste Management: RCRA Oversight in the 100th Congress; Issue Brief, James E. McCarthy IB87087
* Preventing Beach Closings: Legislative Options; Issue Brief, Martin R. Lee IB88102
* RCRA Authorization: Audio Brief, Jim McCarthy, etc. AB50179
* Reauthorization of RCRA: A Checklist of CRS Products, Ted L. Burch, 91-911 L
* Solid Waste Management: RCRA Reauthorization Issues; Issue Brief, Mark Reisch, etc., IB91069
* Waste Exports: U.S. and International Efforts to Control Transboundary Movement; Issue Brief, Mary Tiemann, IB89123
* Waste Management: Issue Brief, James McCarthy IB89007

Retirement

* see Military Personnel--Compensation and Pensions, Old Age, Pensions, Social Security, Women

Retirement Equity Act

* Women's Pension Equity: A Summary of the Retirement Equity Act of 1984, Ray Schmitt 84-217 EPW

Revenue Sharing

* see State and Local Government

Revolving Door (Post Federal Employment Ethics)

* see Government Employees--Ethics, Political Ethics

Rico

* see Criminal Procedure

Right to Die

* see Medicine--Ethical Issues

Rock Music Lyrics

* see Arts and Humanities

Roe v. Wade

* see Abortion

Romania

* Romania: Political Crisis and Possible Future Developments, Sergiu Verona, 91-751 F

Rural Areas and Policy

* see Regional Development-Rural

Rural Electrification

* see Power Resources--Electric Power

Safe Drinking Water Act

* see also Water Pollution
* Safe Drinking Water; Archived Issue Brief, Mary E. Tiemann IB86080

Sales Tax

* see Taxation--Consumption Taxes

Salomon Brothers, Inc.

* Salomon Brothers' Violations: Explanation, Consequences, and Options for Reform; Issue Brief, James M. Bickley, etc., IB91134

Salt Talks

* see Strategic Arms Limitation Talks

Salvation Army

* The Fair Labor Standards Act and Employment of Workers With Disabilities: The Case of the Salvation Army, William G. Whittaker, 91-93 E

Sanctions

* see Foreign Trade-Sanctions

Satellites

* see Astronautics--Satellites

SAT Tests

* see Higher Education

Saudi Arabia

* see also Iraq-Kuwait Crisis
* Arms Sales to Saudi Arabia: Current Status; Issue Brief, Richard F. Grimmett, IB91007
* Arms Transfers to Saudi Arabia: Presidential Authority to Waive Legislative Restrictions, Richard F. Grimmett, 90-393 F
* Background on Delivery of AWACS Aircraft to Saudi Arabia, Richard F. Grimmett 86-744 F
* Saudi Arabia: U.S. Missile Sale, 1986; Archived Issue Brief, Clyde Mark., IB86068

Savings

* see Economic Conditions, Saving and Investment

Savings and Loan Institutions

* see Money and Banking--Failures and Deposit Insurance, Money and Banking--Financial Institutions

School Integration

* see Elementary and Secondary Education--Policies and Legislation, Higher Education

School Lunch Program

* see Food Relief--Domestic

School Prayer

* see Elementary and Secondary Education--Policies and Legislation

Schools

* see Elementary and Secondary Education, Federal Aid to Education, Higher Education

Science and Technology

* see Astronautics, Chemicals, Computers, Earth Sciences, Genetics, Industrial Technology, Medicine, Minerals and Materials, Oceanography, Patents and Inventions, Research and Development, Science Manpower, Science Policy, Standards, Technology and Civilization, Telecommunication
* Biomedical Ethics and Congress: History and Current Legislative Activity, IB86078
* Biomedical Research: Use of Animals, IB83161
* Drug Approval: Access to Experimental Drugs For Severely Ill Patients, IB89016
* Federal Regulation of Biotechnology, IB89068
* Global Climate Change, IB89005
* Human Fetal Research and Tissue Transplantation, IB88100
* Human Gene Therapy, IB87040
* National Oceans Policy Commission Proposal, IB87203
* National Sea Grant College Program, IB87163
* Patenting Life, IB87222
* Proposal to Map and Sequence the Human Genome, IB88012
* Research and Development Funding: FY 1990, IB89040
* Science, Engineering, and Mathematics Precollege and College Education, IB88068
* Semiconductor Manufacturing Technology Proposal: SEMATECH, IB87212
* Space Facilities: The ISF/CDSF/Space Station Controversy, IB88053
* Space Launch Options, IB86121
* Space Policy, IB87018
* Space Stations, IB85209
* Superconducting Super Collider, IB87096
* Superconductivity: An Overview, IB87191
* Technology Transfer: Utilization of Federally Funded Research and Development, IB85031

Science Manpower

* Building the National Research and Education Network: Issue Brief, Stephen Gould, IB90126
* Department of Education Programs for Science and Mathematics Education: Background, Status, Issues, and Options, K. Forbis Jordan., 86-739 S
* Dwight D. Eisenhower Mathematics and Science Education Act: An Analysis of Recent Legislative Action and Program Evaluations, James B. Stedman. 89-24 EPW
* The Nobel-Prize Awards in Science as a Measure of National Strength in Science, Christopher T. Hill and Joan D. Winston., 86-727 S
* Science and Engineering Education: The Role of the Department of Defense, Christine M. Matthews. 89-256 SPR
* Science, Engineering, and Mathematics Precollege and College Education: Issue Brief, Christine Matthews Rose., IB88068
* Scientific Education: Selected References, 1985-1990. B.F. Mangan, 90-263 L
* Scientific Misconduct in Academia: Efforts to Address the Issue, Marilyn J. Littlejohn, etc., 89-392 SPR
* Underrepresented Minorities and Women in Science, Mathematics, and Engineering: Problems and Issues for the 1990s, Christine M. Matthews, 91-26 SPR

Science Policy

* American Science at a Critical Crossroads: A Checklist of CRS Products, Karen L. Alderson, 91-927 L
* Analysis of the Office of Science and Technology Policy, Genevieve J. Knezo. 88-205 SPR

* Building the National Research and Education Network: Issue Brief, Stephen Gould, IB90126
* Eastern European and Soviet Science and Technology: Capabilities and Needs, William C. Boesman, 91-114 SPR
* Establishing a Department of Science and Technology: An Analysis of the, Proposal of the President's Commission on Industrial Competitiveness, Michael Davey, Christopher Hill and Wendy Schacht., 85-122 SPR
* The Federal Contribution to Basic Research: Background Material for 1987 Hearings, Michael E. Davey and Genevieve Knezo., 87-633 SPR
* Federal Support of Basic Research and the Establishment of the National Science Foundation and Other Research Agencies, William C. Boesman. 88-456 SPR
* Forum Information: Technology Revolution; Also, Science and the Budget: 1990 Update, Congressional Research Service review, v. 11, July-Aug. 1990, REV 7-90
* Indirect Costs at Academic Institutions: Background and Controversy; Issue Brief, Genevieve J. Knezo, IB91095
* Industrial Competitiveness and Technological Advancement: Debate Over Government Policy; Issue Brief, Wendy H. Schacht, IB91132
* Information Policy and Technology Issues: Public Laws of the 95th Through 101st Congresses, Robert Lee Chartrand, etc., 91-569 SPR
* Institute for Scientific and Technological Cooperation: Archived Issue Brief, Genevieve Knezo. IB79033
* Issues in U.S. Advanced Technology Policy: A Review of the National Advisory Committee on Semiconductors Report, a Strategic Industry at Risk, Glenn J. McLoughlin, 90-234 SPR
* Japanese and U.S. Industrial Associations: Their Role in High-Technology Policymaking; a Japan Task Force Report, Dick K, Nanto, etc., 91-477 E
* The Nobel-Prize Awards in Science as a Measure of National Strength in Science, Christopher T. Hill and Joan D. Winston., 86-727 S
* Public Health Policy and the Congress: Selected References, Karen Alderson, Charles Dove, Peter Giordano, Bonnie Mangan and Edith Sutterlin., 89-147 L
* Science and Engineering Education: The Role of the Department of Defense, Christine M. Matthews. 89-256 SPR
* Science and Technology Issues for the 102nd Congress, Science Policy Research Division, 90-620 SPR
* Science and Technology Policies and Practices in Industrialized Countries Other Than the U.S.: Bibliography-in-Brief, Karen L. Alderson., 89-46 L
* Science and Technology Policy and Funding: Reagan Administration; Archived Issue Brief, Genevieve Knezo. IB82108
* Scientific Misconduct in Academia: Efforts to Address the Issue, Marilyn J. Littlejohn, etc., 89-392 SPR
* Status Report on U.S.-Chinese Science and Technology Relationships, Genevieve J. Knezo, 90-8 SPR
* Technology Development and Regionalization: A Checklist of CRS Products, Bonnie F. Mangan, 92-9 L
* White House Office of Science and Technology Policy: An Analysis, Genevieve J. Knezo, 89-689 SPR

Scorpio

* see Reference Sources--Scorpio

SDI

* see Strategic Defense Initiative

Secondary Market for Industrial Mortgages

* see Industry

Securities Exchange Act

* see also Corporations--Securities Industry
* Arbitration under Section 10 (B) of the Securities Exchange Act of 1934, Michael V. Seitzinger., 87-881 A
* Insider Trading and Greenmail Payments, Michael V. Seitzinger. 87-567 A
* Legal Analysis of What Constitutes Reliance under SEC Rule 10b-5, Michael V. Seitzinger. 87-279 A
* Securities Law: Analysis of Cases Concerning Insider Trading under Section 10 (B) of the Securities Exchange Act of 1934, Michael V. Seitzinger. 87-480 A
* The Stock Market 'Crash' of 1987: The Early Response of Regulators, Kevin F. Winch. 87-989 E
* Tender Offer Laws and Regulations, Michael V. Seitzinger., 87-15 A

Securities Fraud

* see Corporations--Securities Industry

Current Events and Homework

Securities Industry
* see Corporations--Securities Industry

Securities Investor Protection Corporation
* Securities Investor Protection Corporation (SIPC): Customer Indemnification When a Securities Firm Fails, Kevin Winch., 82-125 E

Securities Transfer Tax
* see Taxation--Business Taxes

Sematech
* see Computers

Semiconductors
* see Computers

Semitech
* see Computers

Senate
* see Congress

Sentencing Reform Act
* see also Criminal Procedure
* United States Sentencing Commission Guidelines: Preliminary Legal Analysis, Charles Doyle. 88-13 A

Sex Discrimination
* see Women

Sherman Act
* see Antitrust Law

Shipping
* see Marine Transportation, Transportation

Singapore
* The Association of Southeast Asian Nations (ASEAN): Economic Development Prospects and the Role of the United States, Larry Niksch. 84-171 F
* Singapore-U.S. Economic Relations: Some Views from Singapore's Economic Elite, Richard P. Cronin. 89-49 F
* U.S. Agricultural Trade Opportunities With Pacific Rim Nations, Robert M. Goldstein. 88-755 ENR

Small Business
* The ABCs of Public Venture Capital Investment, Jan E. Christopher. 88-757 E
* Automation and Small Business: Technological Development and the Competitiveness of U.S. Industry, Wendy H. Schacht and Glenn J. McLoughlin. 88-300 SPR
* Business: Doing Business With the Federal Government; Info Pack, IP305B
* Federal Programs for Minority and Women-Owned Business, Mark Eddy, 90-312 GOV
* Cable Television Franchises: Do Franchising Authorities Have Any Recourse If the Franchisee Raises Subscription Rates?, Janice E. Rubin., 87-448 A
* Economic Effects of a VAT on Small Business, James M. Bickley., 88-288 E
* Federal Programs for Minority and Women-Owned Businesses, Mark Eddy. 89-278 GOV
* Financing Business and Economic Development: Three Private-Sector Initiatives, J. F. Hombeck. 88-598 E
* Measuring the Economic Benefits of Federally Supported Research: A Bibliography, Genevieve J. Knezo, etc., 91-335 SPR
* Metro Broadcasting v. FCC: The Constitutionality of Federally Mandated Minority Preference Policies, Kevin B. Greely, 90-479 A
* Microenterprises: Opportunities for Self-Sufficiency, Bruce K. Mulock, 91-688 E
* Minority Business Set-Asides and the Constitution: A Legal Analysis of the U.S. Supreme Court Ruling in City of Richmond v. J.A. Croson Co, Charles V. Dale. 89-124A
* Minority Ownership of Broadcast Facilities: A Summary of Federal Communications Commission's Policies and Rules, Bernevia M. McCalip. 87-273 E
* The Reagan Economic Strategy: Implications for Small Business, Edward Knight. 81-232E
* Small Business Assistance Programs Sources of Information: Info Pack, IP422S
* Small Business Exemption in the Fair Labor Standards Act: Number of Employees Subject to the 1989 Amendments, Charles V. Ciccone, 91-307 E
* Small Business Innovation Development Act: H.R. 4260 Amendments to P.L. 97-219; Archived Issue Brief, Wendy H. Schacht., IB86118
* Small Business in the U.S. Economy: Selected Congressional Oversight and Initiatives: Archived Issue Brief, Bruce K. Mulock, IB89145
* Small Business, Technology Development, and Manufacturing: Competitiveness Issues, Wendy H. Schacht, 89-685 SPR
* State and Local Equity Capital Funds: Selected Case Studies, Jan E. Christopher. 88-758E
* United States Supreme Court Actions Regarding Minority Business Set-Asides After City of Richmond v. J.A. Croson Co, Charles V. Dale. 89-202A

Smoking
* see Public Health

Smoot-Hawley Tariff Act
* The Smoot-Hawley Tariff Act of 1930: Its Effects on U.S. Trade and Its Role in the Great Depression of 1929-1933, George Holliday and Gail Makinen. 87-993 E

Social Security
* see Benefits, Finance, Income Maintenance
* Changing Progressivity of the Federal Individual Income Tax and Social Security Tax, Donald W. Kiefer., 87-723 E
* A Consumer Price Index for the Elderly: Would It Make Any Difference? Brian W. Cashell., 87-552 E
* Deficit Targets, National Savings, and Social Security, Jane G. Gravelle., 88-513 S
* How Long Does It Take for New Retirees to Recover the Value of Their Social Security Taxes?, Geoffrey Kollman, etc., 88-384 EPW
* Income Support Programs: Changing in Spending, Distribution, and Impact on Poverty of Government Benefit Programs, Gene Falk., 86-141 EPW.
* The Indexation of Federal Programs, Royal Shipp, 82-103 S.
* Major Decisions in the House and Senate Chambers on Social Security: 1935-1985, Carmen D. Solomon, 86-193 EPW
* Social Security: A Checklist of CRS Products, M. Alexandra Salinas, 92-4 L
* The Social Security Amendments of 1983:, Archived Issue Brief, Geoffrey Kollman. IB83070
* Social Security: An Introduction; Selected References, 1989-1991, Charles Dove, 91-777 L
* Social Security: An Overview of President Reagan's 1981 Proposals:, Archived Issue Brief, David Koitz, etc. IB81036.
* Social Security and Medicare Coverage of Employees of State and Local Government, David Koitz, etc. 87-132 EPW.
* Social Security and Medicare: How Are They Treated in Determining the National Debt? David Koitz, 85-1132 EPW
* Social Security and Medicare: Proposals to Cover State and Local Government: Issue Brief, Geoffrey C. Kollmann, IB90065
* Social Security: How Is It Treated in Determining the Federal Budget? David Koitz. 87-978 EPW
* Social Security: National Committee to Preserve Social Security and Medicare; Info Pack, IP345S
* The Social Security Notch, David Koitz, etc. 83-565 EPW
* The Social Security Number: Chronology of Federal Developments Affecting Its Use, Kathleen S. Swendiman, 91-825 A
* The Social Security Number:, Its Historical Development and Legal Restrictions on Its Use, Joseph Maheady, etc. 85-655 A
* Social Security:, The Earnings Test, Geoffrey Kollman, 88-89 EPW.
* Social Security:, The Effect of National Debt Limitations in 1985, David Koitz, 85-1118 EPW.
* Social Security:, The Independent Agency Questions; Issue Brief, David Koitz, IB86120.
* What Would It Mean to Make the Social Security Administration an Independent Entity? David Koitz, 89-309 EPW
* Work Disincentives and Disability Insurance, David Koitz, 80-160 EPW.

Social Security -- Benefits
* An Analysis of a Proposal to Authorize "Super IRA's" as an Alternative to Social Security Benefits, David Koitz, 87-14 EPW.
* The Automatic Benefit Increase in Social Security, David Koitz, etc. 83-22

Securities Industry / Solid Wastes

EPW.
* Benefit and Pay Increases in Selected Federal Programs, 1969-1991, Carolyn L. Merck, 91-513 EPW
* Social Security: Alien Beneficiaries; Archived Issue Brief, David Koitz, IB82001.
* Social Security and Tax-Free Fringe Benefits: Background and Issues, Geoffrey Kollman, 85-124 EPW.
* Social Security Benefits, Cash Relief, and Food Aid: A Short History, Vee Burke, 86-45 EPW.
* Social Security Benefits for Prisoners: Archived Issue Brief, David Koitz, IB81163.
* Social Security: Current Issues, Benefits and Financing; Info Pack, IP153S
* Social Security:, Illustrations of Current Benefit Levels for Persons Born from 1895 to 1935, Geoffrey Kollman, etc. 88-248 EPW.
* Social Security:, Issues in Taxing Benefits under Current Law and under Proposals to Tax a Greater Share of Benefits, Geoffrey Kollman, 89-40 EPW.
* The Social Security Notch, David Koitz, etc. 83-565 EPW.
* The Social Security "Notch": Info Pack, IP266S
* The Social Security Notch Issue: Examples of Benefit Levels for People Born from 1895 to 1940, David Koitz, etc., 91-804 L
* Social Security Notch: Selected References, 1983-1991, M. Alexandra Salinas, 91-804 L
* Social Security: Proposed Modifications to the Earnings Test; Issue Brief, Geoffrey Kollman, IB89114
* Social Security: Re-Examining Eligibility for Disability Benefits: Archived Issue Brief, David Koitz, IB82078.
* Social Security: Technical Comparison of Various "Notch" Bills Introduced in the 100th Congress, David Koitz., 88-257 EPW
* Social Security: The Cost-of-Living Adjustment (COLA) in January 1989, David Koitz and Geoffrey Kollmann. 88-675 EPW
* Social Security: The Cost-of-Living Adjustment (COLA) in January 1992, David Koitz and Geoffrey Kollmann. 91-756 EPW
* Social Security: The Earnings Test, Geoffrey Kollmann, 88-89 EPW
* Social Security: The Economic Well-Being of Social Security Families in 1989, Madeleine T. Smith, 91-321 EPW
* Social Security: The Offset of Social Security Spousal Benefits for Government Pensions, Nancy Miller and Geoffrey Kollman. 86-43 EPW
* Social Security: The Relationship of Taxes and Benefits for Future Retirees, Geoffrey Kollmann., 87-203 EPW
* Social Security: The Windfall Benefit Provision; Archived Issue Brief, Geoffrey Kollmann. IB87211
* Social Security: The 5-Month Waiting Period for Disability Insurance Benefits, David Koitz. 79-239 EPW
* Summary of Major Changes in the Social Security Cash Benefits Program: 1935-1990, Geoffrey Kollmann. 90-582 EPW
* Supplemental Security Income (SSI): Changes Made by the 101st Congress, Carmen D. Solomon, 90-605 EPW
* Taxing Social Security Benefits: Background and Programmatic Issues, Geoffrey Kollman., 83-152 EPW
* Treatment of Former Spouses under Various Federal Retirement Systems, Marie B. Morris., 88-512 A
* Various Effects of Raising the Normal Retirement Age for Social Security Benefits, David Koitz., 84-677 EPW
* What Amount of a Civil Service Retirement System (CSRS) Pension Is Equivalent to a Social Security Benefit? Geoffrey C. Kollmann, 90-324 EPW
* Work Disincentives and Disability Insurance, David Koitz, 80-160 EPW

Social Security -- Finance

* see also Taxation--Social Security Taxes
* The Financial Outlook for Social Security and Medicare, David Koitz, 91-830 EPW
* How Long Does It Take New Retirees to Recover the Value of Their Social Security Taxes? Geoffrey Kollmann, 91-4 EPW
* Paying for the Baby Boom's Retirement, Congressional Research Service. 87-905 EPW
* Social Security and 1990 Legislation to Increase the Federal Debt Ceiling: Archived Issue Brief, David Koitz, IB90125
* Social Security: Changes in the Self-Employment Tax for 1990, David Koitz, 90-24 EPW
* **Social Security Financing: Bibliography-in-Brief, 1985-1988,** Charles P. Dove., 88-434 L
* Social Security Financing and Taxation: Recent Issues; Info Pack, Congressional Reference Division, IP435S
* Social Security Financing: Selected References, 1988-1991, Edith Sutterlin, 91-206 L
* Social Security Financing, David Koitz, etc., LTR91-879
* Social Security: Investing the Surplus, Geoffrey Kollmann, 91-129 EPW

* Social Security: Its Funding Outlook and Significance for Government Finance, David Koitz., 86-674 EPW
* Social Security: Its Impact on the Federal Budget Deficit, David Koitz., 88-218 EPW
* Social Security: Its Removal from the BUdget and New Procedures for Considering Changes to the Program, David Koitz, 91-9 EPW
* The Social Security Surplus: A Discussion of Some of the Issues, David S. Koitz. 88-709 EPW
* Social Security: Surplus Receipts Trigger New Financing Debate; Issue Brief, David Koitz, etc., IB90033
* Social Security: The Effect of the Baby Boom, Geoffrey Kollmann., 87-981 EPW
* Social Security: The Effect of National Debt Limitations in 1985, David Koit, 85-1118 EPW
* Social Security: The Macroeconomic Effects of Cutting Payroll Taxes, Brian W. Cashell, 91-345 E
* Would a Social Security Tax Cut Increase Progressivity? Donald W. Kiefer, 90-235 S

Social Security Notch

* see Social Security--Benefits

Social Security Taxes

* see Social Security--Finance, Taxation--Social Security Taxes

Social Services

* see Families, Federal Aid to Education, Food Relief, Handicapped, Housing, Medicare and Medicaid, Occupational Training, Old Age, Pensions, Public Welfare, Veterans
* Alcohol, Drug Abuse, and Mental Health Block Grant, and Related Programs, IB88009
* Child Day Care, IB89011
* Child Nutrition: Issues in the 101st Congress, IB89048
* Commodity Donations for Domestic Food Programs, IB89070
* Economic Status of the Elderly, IB87095
* Family Planning: Title X of the Public Health Service Act, IB88005
* Homelessness: Issues and Legislation in the 101st Congress, IB88070
* Long-Term Care for the Elderly, IB88098
* National Service: Issues and Proposals in the 101st Congress, IB89071
* Teenage Pregnancy: Issues and Legislation, IB86128

Solid Wastes

* see also Radioactive Wastes, Infrastructure, Superfund, Environmental Protection
* After Regulation of Industrial Hazardous Waste: What Role for Incineration?, Barbara B. Black and David E. Gushee., 89-57 S
* Beverage Container Deposit Laws in the States, Mark Gurevitz., 89-334 A
* Degradable Plastics: Issue Brief, Martin R. Lee. Updated regularly., IB88067
* Desalination: Environmental Considerations, James E. Mielke, 91-426 SPR
* Environmental Impairment Liability Insurance: Overview of Availability Issues, Rawley O. King., 89-269 E
* Federal Regulation of Used Oil, Mark Reisch. 86-747 ENR
* Financing Solid Waste Management Programs: A Survey of the States, David S. Loughran, etc., 89-656 ENR
* Hazardous Waste and the Superfund Program: Info Pack IP094H
* Hazardous Waste Fact Book, James E. McCarthy and Mark E. Anthony Reisch. 87-56 ENR
* Hazardous Waste Management and the Superfund Program: Info Pack, IP094H
* Hazardous Waste Management: RCRA Oversight in the 100th Congress; Issue Brief, James E. McCarthy. IB87087
* Hazardous Wastes: Selected References, 1986-1987, Adrienne C. Grenfell. 87-874 L
* Incinerating Municipal Solid Waste: A Health Benefit Analysis of Controlling Emissions, Environmental and Natural Resources Policy Division. 89-260 ENR
* International Environment: Overview of Major Issues; Issue Brief, Mary Tiemann and Susan R. Fletcher. IB89057
* Interstate Shipment of Municipal Solid Waste, James E. McCarthy, etc., 90-413 ENR
* Liability of Superfund "Response Action Contractors" and EPA for Injury from Contractor-Conducted Cleanups, Robert Meltz., 89-292 A
* Marine Plastics Pollution Control Legislation, Martin R.Lee. 88-377 ENR
* Municipal Waste Incineration: An Analysis of Section 306 of S. 1894, James E. McCarthy. 88-402 ENR
* Preventing Beach Closings: Legislative Options; Issue Brief, Martin R. Lee.

Current Events and Homework

IB88102
* RCRA Authorization: Audio Brief, Jim McCarthy, etc. AB50179
* Reauthorization of RCRA: A Checklist of CRS Products, Ted L. Burch, 91-911 L
* Recycling and Reducing Packaging Waste: How the United States Compares to Other Countries, James E. McCarthy, 91-802 ENR
* Recycling, Info Pack, Congressional REference Division, IP437R
* Solid and Hazardous Waste Management: Issue Brief, James E. Mc Carthy, IB90022
* Solid Waste Management: Info Pack IP396S.
* Solid Waste Management: Issue Brief, Renee E. Pannebaker, etc. IB87176.
* Solid Waste Management: RCRA Reauthorization Issues; Issue Brief, Renee E. Pannebaker, etc., IB87176
* Solid Waste Management: Selected References, Rebecca Mazur, 89-273 L.
* State and Local Burdens on Imported Waste: Constitutional Issues, Robert Meltz, 91-771 A
* The Superfund Amendments and Reauthorization Act of 1986: Archived Issue Brief, Mark E. Anthony Reisch, IB87080.
* Toxic Waste Incineration at Sea: Archived Issue Brief, Martin lee IB85131.
* Treatment Technologies at Superfund Sites, Environment and Natural Resources Policy Division, 91-713 ENR
* Using Incentives for Environmental Protection: An Overview, John L. Moore, etc., 89-360 ENR
* Waste Exports: U.S. and International Efforts to Control Transboundary Movement; Issue Brief, Mary Tiemann, IB89123
* Wastes from Fish Harvesting and Processing: Growing Environmental Concerns, Eugene H. Buck, 90-575 ENR
* Waste in the Marine Environment; Info Pack, IP407W
* Waste in the Marine Environment: Selected References, Ted L. Burch, 89-263 L
* Waste Management: Issue Brief, James E. McCarthy, IB89007.

Solid Wastes -- Radioactive Wastes

* see Environmental Protection
* The Administration's Proposed Hazardous Materials Transportation Safety Bill: Selected Comments and Analysis, Paul Rothberg, 87-693 SPR
* Hazardous Materials Transportation: Laws, Regulations, and Policy: Archived Issue Brief, Paul Rothberg, IB76026.
* High Level Nuclear Waste Repository: Yucca Mountain Site Characterization Plans, James E. Mielke, 91-185 SPR
* Legal Analysis of Whether a State Can Exclude Low-Level Radioactive Waste Generated Outside the State from Disposal Within the State, Michael V. Seitzinger, 86-957 A.
* Nuclear Material from Dismantled Warheads: What to Do With It and How to Verify Its Disposal: A Preliminary Analysis, Warren H. Donnelly, 87-437 S.
* Nuclear Waste Disposal: Archived Issue Brief, Carl E. Behrens, IB87178.
* Nuclear Waste: Low-Level Disposal Facilities; Archived Issue Brief, Carl Behrens, IB85214.
* Nuclear Waste Management: Selected References, 1985-1988, Karen L. Alderson, 89-118 L.

Somalia

* Recent Political Developments in Ethiopia and Somalia, Theodore S. Dagne, 91-452 F

South Africa

* see Foreign Policy and Assistance Programs
* Angola/Namibia Peace Prospects: Background, Current Problems, and Chronology, Raymond W. Copson, 88-559 F.
* The Legal Basis for South Africa's Retention of Walvis Bay, Law Library of Congress, Near Eastern and African Law Division, LL90-5
* The Reagan Administration Sanctions Against South Africa: Their Potential Economic Impact, William H. Cooper, 85-955 E.
* Sanctions Against South Africa: Activities of the 99th Congress, Brenda M. Branaman, 87-200 F.
* Sanctions Against South Africa: Impact on the United States; Issue Brief, William Cooper, IB87198.
* South Africa: African National Congress, Brenda Branaman, 86-186 F
* South Africa and Nuclear Weapons: Archived Issue Brief, Warren H. Donnelly, IB87199
* The South Africa Financial Crisis: The Role of U.S. Banks, Walter Eubanks, 86-550 E.
* South Africa: International Sanctions; Archived Issue Brief, Jeanne S. Affelder, etc. IB86157.
* South Africa: Legislation of the 99th Congress, Brenda Branaman, 85-799 F.
* South Africa, Nuclear Weapons and the IAEA: Issue Brief, Warren H.

Donnelly, IB87199.
* South Africa: Opposition on the Right, Brenda Branaman, 88-628 F
* South Africa: President's Report on Progress Toward Ending Apartheid, Raymond W. Copson, 87-829 F
* South Africa: Recent Developments: Issue Brief, Brenda Branaman, etc. IB85213
* South Africa: Selected References, Sherry Shapiro, 89-459 L
* South Africa: The Current Situation; Info Pack, IP340S
* South Africa: The United Democratic Front, Brenda M. Branaman, 86-758 F.
* South Africa-U.S. Economic Ties: Emerging Issues; Archived Issue Brief, William H. Cooper, IB87128.
* South Africa: U.S. Policy After Sanctions; Issue Brief, Brenda M. Branaman, IB87128
* South Africa: U.S. Policy Debate Over Sanctions and Assistance; Issue Brief, Brenda M. Branaman, IB90157
* Southern Africa: U.S. Regional Policy at a Crossroads, Raymond Copson, 85-201 F.
* South Africa's Future: Toward a Negotiated Settlement? Raymond W. Copson, 90-302 F
* South Africa's New Nuclear Status: Archived Issue Brief, Zachary Davis, etc., IB91131
* The United States and Southern Africa: A Review of United Nations Resolutions and United States Voting Patterns, 1946-October 1985, Frankie King, 86-21.
The 99th Congress and South Africa Sanctions, Robert Shepard. 87-942 F

South Korea

* Exchange Rate Management in Taiwan, South Korea and Hong Kong, Arlene Wilson. 87-401E
* Japan-South Korea Economic Relations: South Korea's Approach to the "Japan Problem", Dick M. Nanto. 87-953 E
* Korea and Congress, 1950-1990, Kerry Dumbaugh. 85-171 F
* Korean Political Tensions: Implications for the United States; Issue Brief, Robert Sutter. IB86071
* Korea-U.S. Relations: Issues for congress: Issue Brief, Robert G. Sutter, IB89136
* Korean Political Tensions: Implications for the United States; Archived Issue Brief, Robert Sutter, IB86071
* South Korea and Taiwan: Expanding Trade Ties With the United States; Issue Brief, William H. Cooper., IB86151
* South Korea and the United States: The Changing Relationship, Larry A. Niksch. 87-522 F
* Visit to South Korea and Taiwan, Larry A. Niksch. 88-740 F

South West Africa People's Organization

* Angola/Namibia Peace Prospects: Background, Current Problems, and Chronology, Raymond W. Copson. 88-559 F
* Namibia Chronology: February 1986 Through April 1987, Raymond W. Copson and Lynn Thomas., 87-353 F

Soviet Disintegration

* see U.S.S.R.--Republics

Soviet Union

* see U.S.S.R

Space Policy

* see Astronautics

Space Shuttle

* see Astronautics

Space Weapons

* see Weapons Systems--Space Weapons

Spain

* Current Issues With the "Base-Rights" Countries and Their Implications, Richard F. Grimmett., 88-726 F
* United States Military Installations in Spain, Richard Grimmett., 84-149 F
* U.S.-Spanish Bases Agreement: Issue Brief, Richard F. Grimmett. IB88010

Spanish Americans (U.S.)

* see Minorities

Solid Wastes / Stock Market Crash

Speechwriting

* see Reference Sources--Speechwriting

Spetsnaz

* United States and Soviet Special Operations, John M. Collins., 87-398 S

Sports

* see Recreation

Spotted Owl

* see Wildlife--Conservation

Spying

* see Intelligence Activities

Staggers Rail Act

* see also Transportation--Railroads
* The Rail Captive Shipper Question, Kenneth R. DeJarnette., 88-649 E
* Railroad Economic Regulation: Issue Brief, Stephen J. Thompson and Rick Holland. IB85017
* Summary of the Staggers Rail Act of 1980, Stephen J.Thompson. 85-9 E

Standards

* Daylight Saving Time, Heidi G. Yacker, 91-386 C
* Daylight Saving Time: Archived Issue Brief, David Hack. IB77020.
* Telecommunications and Information-Systems Standardization--Is America Ready?, David Hack. 87-458 SPR
* U.S. Metric Conversions, Edith Fairman Cooper, 91-83 SPR

Star Wars Weapons

* see International Law, Weapons Systems--Space Weapons

Start Talks

* see Arms Control--Negotiations and Treaties, Strategic Arms Reduction Talks

State and Local Government

* see Block Grants, Intergovernmental Fiscal Relations, State Governments
* Amenity Resources and Rural Economic Growth: Report on a National Policy Symposium, George H. Siehl, 90-380 ENR
* Congressional and State Reapportionment and Redistricting: A Legal Analysis, Thomas M. Durbin, etc., 91-292 A
* Space Launch Infrastructure: State Initiatives to Develop Commercial Spaceports, David P. Radzanowski, 91-120 SPR
* State and Local Burdens on Imported Waste: Constitutional Issues, Robert Meltz, 91-771 A

State and Local Government -- Block Grants

* Alcohol, Drug Abuse, and Mental Health Block Grant and Related Programs: Issue Brief, Edward Klebe., IB88009
* Block Grant Funding for Federal Education Programs: Background and Pro and Con Discussion, K. Forbis Jordan., 86-992 S
* Block Grants: Inventory and Funding History, Sandra S. Osbourne. 87-845 GOV
* Community Health Centers and the Primary Care Block Grant, John Gray. 86-899 EPW
* Community Services Block Grants: FY89 Budget Issues, Karen Spar., 88-193 EPW
* Community Services Block Grants: History, Funding, Program Data, Karen Spar and Kimberly T. Henderson. 87-739 EPW
* Education Block Grant Reauthorization: Selected Options, Paul M. Irwin. 87-494 EPW
* Environmental Block Grants: A Discussion of Current Issues, Claudia Copeland. 86-561 ENR
* The Social Services Block Grant Program: History, Description, and Current Trends, Evelyn Howard. 86-145 EPW

State and Local Government -- Intergovernmental Fiscal Relations

* Alcohol, Drug Abuse, and Mental Health Block Grant and Related Programs: Issue Brief, Edward Klebe, IB88009
* Community Development Block Grants: Summary of the Law and Its Implementation, Eugene Boyd, 90-420 GOV
* Community Services Block Grants and Related Programs, Karen Spar, 90-60 EPW
* Constitutional Considerations Implicated, a Hypothetical Proposal to Tax the Investment Income of a Tax-Exempt Entity Affiliated With a State or Local Government, Robert B. Burdette., 88-551 A
* Drug Control: Federal Financial Assistance to State and Local Governments, Keith Bea, 90-464 GOV
* Economic Development: A Listing of Federal Programs, Jan E. Christopher. 88-536 E
* Economic Development and Community Revitalization Programs: Sources of Information; Info Pack, IP412E
* The Effect of Federal Tax and Budget Policies in the 1980s on the State-Local Sector, Lillian Rymarowicz and Dennis Zimmerman., 86-2 E
* Federal Budget and Tax Policy and the State-Local Sector: Retrenchment in the 1980s, Lillian Rymarowicz and Dennis Zimmerman., 88-600 E
* Federal Budget Policies and the State-Local Sector: 1980-1986, Lillian Rymarowicz and Dennis Zimmerman., 87-234 E
* Federal Tax Payments, State Residents and Federal Expenditures in Individual States, Fiscal Year 1988, Lillian Rymarowicz., 90-57 E
* Federal Tax Payments, State Residents and Federal Expenditures in Individual States, Fiscal Year 1986, Lillian Rymarowicz., 88-398 E
* Federal Tax Payments, State Residents and Federal Expenditures in Individual States, Fiscal Year 1987, Lillian Rymarowicz., 88-409 E
* Federalism in the United States: Toward the Third Century; an Overview of Trends and Issues, Sandra S. Osbourne. 89-262 GOV
* Grants Work in a Congressional Office, Rhoda Newman., 82-22 C
* Medicare, Medicaid, and Maternal and Child Health Programs: An Overview of Major Legislation Enacted from 1980 Through 1986, Janet Kline, Jennifer O'Sullivan and Joseph A. Cislowski. 87-296 EPW
* The Payments in Lieu of Taxes Program: Background and Current Status, Stacey M. Kean. 87-321 E
* Regional Economic Development Programs of the Federal Government, Jan E. Christopher., 88-309 E
* Rural Economic Development: Selected References, 1988-1989, Jean Bowers, 90-16 L
* Targeted Fiscal Assistance, Stacey M. Kean. 87-347 E
* Tax Reform: Its Potential Effect on the State and Local Sector, Dennis Zimmerman. 87-233 E

State and Local Government -- State Governments

* The Governors and Lieutenant Governors of the States and Other Jurisdictions, Isabelle Malloy., 89-270 C
* Partisan Divisions in State Legislatures; Combined Upper and Lower House Totals, 1927-1987, Kevin Coleman. 87-213 GOV
* Summary of State Statutes Which Specifically Mention Acquired Immune Deficiency Syndrome, M. Ann Wolfe. 87-239 A
* Waiver of Eleventh Amendment Immunity from Suit: State Survey, Kirk D. Nemer. 88-465 A

State Taxation

* see Local Finance

Steel Industry

* see Industry--Steel Industry

Stevenson-Wydler Technology Innovation Act

* Direct Federal Support for Technological Innovation: Issues, and Options, Christopher Hill and Wendy Schacht. 84-118 S
* Stevenson-Wydler Technology Innovation Act: A Federal Effort to Promote Industrial Innovation; Archived Issue Brief, Wendy Schacht. IB85082

Stewart B. McKinney Homeless Assistance Act

* see Public Welfare--Homeless
* Homelessness in the U.S.: Bibliography-in-Brief, 1986-1988, Edith Sutterlin, 88-396 L
* The Housing and Community Development Act of 1987 and the Steward B. McKinney Homeless Assistance Act: Summary and Analysis, Barbara Miles, 88-481 E
* Programs Benefiting the Homeless: FY87-FY89 Appropriations Trends, Ruth Ellen Wasem, 89-20 EPW.

Stock Market

* see Corporations--Securities Industry

Stock Market Crash

* see Corporations--Securities Industry

Be patient. If any phone number is incorrect, call (area code) 555-1212 and request the new listing.

Current Events and Homework

Stock Transfer Tax
* see Taxation--Business Taxes

Strategic Arms Limitation Talks
* see also Arms Control--Negotiations and Treaties
* Arms Control: Issues for Congress; Issue Brief, Stanley R. Sloan, IB87002.
* SALT II Treaty: U.S. and Soviet Interim Observance of Its Terms: Archived Issue Brief, Charles Gellner, IB80018.
* Soviet Compliance Behavior: The Record of the SALT I and II Agreements on Offensive Arms, Charles Gellner., 86-541 S
* Soviet SALT II Compliance Behavior: The SS-25 and Encryption of Telemetry, Jeanette Voas. 86-734 S
* Verification and Compliance: Soviet Compliance With Arms Control Agreements; Issue Brief, Stuart Goldman., IB84131

Strategic Arms Reduction Talks
* see also Arms Control--Negotiations and Treaties
* Arms Control: Negotiations to Reduce Strategic Offensive Nuclear Weapons; Issue Brief, Steven A. Hildreth and Amy F. Woolf. IB88088
* Forum: The START Treat in an Era of Uncertainty?, Congressional Research Service Review, v. 12, Oct.-Nov. 1991, REV 10-91
* On Site Inspections in Arms Control: Verifying Compliance With INF and START, Amy F. Woolf, 89-592 F
* START: Central Limits and Key Provisions, AMy F. Woolf, 91-575 F
* START: Chronology of Major Events, Amy F. Woolf, 91-592 F
* START: A Current Assessment of U.S. and Soviet Positions, Steven A. Hildreth, Al Tinajero and Amy Woolf. 88-400 F
* START: Effects on U.S. and Soviet Forces, Amy F. Woolf, 91-574 F
START Index: An Index to the Strategy Arms Reduction Treaty, Mark M. Lowenthal, 91-782 L
START: Strategic Arms Reduction Talks Treaty: Checklist of Public Policy Literature and CRS Products, Sherry B. Shapiro, 91-638 L
* Strategic Arms Reduction Treaty (START): Verification and Compliance Issues; Issue Brief, Mark M. Lowenthal, IB91139
* The Strategic Arms Reduction Talks: Questions of Concern to the 101st Congress, Amy F. Woolf. 89-330 F

Strategic Defense Initiative
* see National Defense and Security
* Arms Control and Strategic Weapons in the 99th Congress, Robert C. Gray., 87-892 F
* Arms Control: Issues for Congress; Issue Brief, Stanley R.Sloan. IB87002
* Arms Control: Negotiations to Limit Defense and Space Weapons; Issue Brief, Steven Hildreth. IB86073
* Arms Control: Overview of the Geneva Talks; Archived Issue Brief, Steven Hildreth. IB85157
* Brilliant Pebbles: Implications for the Strategic Defense Initiative, John D. Moteff, 90-291 S{R
* Congress and the Strategic Defense Initiative: A Detailed Overview of Legislative Action, 1984-1987, Robert J. Crawford and Steven A. Hildreth. 87-749 F
* Directed Energy Weapons Research: Status and Outlook, Cosmo DiMaggio. 85-183 SPR
* The Effect of a Comprehensive Test Ban on the Strategic Defense Initiative, Cosmo DiMaggio. 85-972 SPR
* Ethical and Religious Aspects of SDI: Pro and Con, Charles H. Whittier., 87-535 GOV
* The Geneva Negotiations on Space and Nuclear Arms: Soviet Positions and Perspectives, Jeanette Voas. 86-512 S
* Legal Analysis of a Memorandum of Understanding Between the United States and the Federal Republic of Germany Concerning Patent Rights Resulting from Strategic Defense Initiative Research, Michael V. Seitzinger. 87-281 A
* The New Interpretation of the ABM Treaty--Salient Issues, Charles R. Gellner., 87-164 S
* Potential Offensive Capabilities of SDI Space Weapons, Cosmo DiMaggio., 87-807 SPR
* The Strategic Defense Initiative: Major Changes During the 101st Congress and Potential issues for the 102nd Congress by John D. Moteff, 91-121 SPR
* The Strategic Defense Initiative: A Model for Estimating Launch Costs, Cosmo DiMaggio and Robert L. Civiak. 87-475 SPR
* Strategic Defense Initiative (SDI): Near-Term Mission objectives; Archived Issue Brief, Cosmo DiMaggio, etc., IB88028
* Strategic Defense Initiative: Selected References, 1988-1990, Valentin Leskovsek, 91-19 L
* The Strategic Defense Initiative and United States Alliance Strategy, Paul Gallis, Mark Lowenthal and Marcia Smith. 85-48 F
* Strategic Defense Initiative: Info Pack, IP346S
* The Strategic Defense Initiative: Is the Software Feasible? Audio Brief, AB50141
* The Strategic Defense Initiative: Issues for Congress; Issue Brief, Steven Hildreth., IB85170
* The Strategic Defense Initiative: Issues for Phase I Deployment; Issue Brief, Steven A. Hildreth, IB88033
* The Strategic Defense Initiative : Program Description and Major Issues, Cosmo DiMaggio, Arthur Manfredi, and Steven Hildreth, 86-8 SPR
* Strategic Defense Initiative (SDI): Mission Objectives for Directing the Program; Issue Brief, Cosmo DiMaggio and Jack Moteff, IB88028.
* Strategic Defense Initiative: Selected References, 1986-1988, Valentin Leskovsek, 88-184 L.

Strategic Defense Stockpiles
* see National Defense--Strategic Stockpiles

Strategic Petroleum Reserve Program
* Defense Petroleum Reserve: Organizational Options for Meeting DOD's Emergency Fuel Supply Requirements, David Lockwood, 84-201 F.
* The Strategic Petroleum Reserve: Issue Brief, Robert Bamberger, IB87050.

Stratospheric Ozone Layer
* see Earth Sciences

Student Aid
* see Higher Education-Student Aid

Student Loans
* see Higher Education--Student Aid

Sudan
* Sudan: U.S. Foreign Assistance Facts; Issue Brief, Ellen Laipson and Raymond Copson, IB85065

Sugar Industry
* see Agriculture--Sugar Industry, Agriculture--Foreign Trade

Summit Meetings (U.S.-U.S.S.R.)
* see U.S.S.R.--Foreign Relations

Superconducting Super Collider
* see Nuclear Energy
* Superconducting Super Collider: Current Issues and Legislation; Issue Brief, William C. Boesman IB87096
* The Superconducting Super collider Project in 1991: Revised Costs; Magnets; and Foreign Participation, William C. Boesman, 91-308 SPR
* Superconducting Super Collider: Science, Costs, and Benefits, William C. Boesman, 90-178 SPR

Superconductivity
* see Power Resources--Electric Power

Superconductors
* see Power Resources--Electric Power

Superfund
* see also Solid Wastes
* Chemicals in the Environment: Audio Brief, James Aidala. AB50152
* Criminal Provisions in Federal Environmental Statutes: A Compilation, Maribel Nicholson, 89-269 E
* Environmental Impairment Liability Insurance: Overview of Availability Issues, Rawle O. King. 89-269 E
* Environmental Issues: From the 101st to the 102nd Congress, Environment and Natural Resources Policy Division, 91-11 ENR
* Environmental Protection Legislation in the 102nd Congress; Issue Brief, Environmental and Natural Resources Policy Division. Environmental Protection Section. IB91042
* Environmental Protection Legislation in the 101st Congress; Issue Brief, Environmental and Natural Resources Policy Division. Environmental Protection Section. IB89033
* Escaping Superfund Liability: The Innocent Landowner and Lender

Stock Transfer Tax / Taxation

Exceptions, Robert Meltz, 91-91 A
* Hazardous Waste Fact Book, James E. McCarthy and Mark E. Anthony Reisch. 87-56 ENR
* Hazardous Waste Management and the Superfund Program: Info Pack, IP094H
* Indoor Air Pollution: Issue Brief, Mira Courpas, Christopher H. Dodge and Fred J. Sissine. IB88092
* Liability of Superfund "Response Action Contractors" and EPA for Injury from Contractor-Conducted Cleanups, Robert Meltz., 89-292 A
* Solid and Hazardous Waste Management: Issue Brief, James E. McCarthy, IB90022
* The Superfund Amendments and Reauthorization Act of 1986: Archived Issue Brief, Mark E. Anthony Reisch. IB87080
* Treatment Technologies at Superfund Sites, Environment and Natural Resources Policy Division, 91-713 ENR
* Waste Management: Issue Brief, James E. McCarthy. IB89007

Supplemental Security Income Program

* see Public Welfare

Support of Dependents

* see Families

Supreme Court

* see Judiciary--Supreme Court

Surrogate Motherhood

* see Families

Synthetic Fuels

* see Fossil Fuels--Coal

Syria

* Syria: Background and Status, Alfred B. Prados, 91-468 F

Taiwan

* Exchange Rate Management in Taiwan, South Korea and Hong Kong, Arlene Wilson. 87-401 E
* Taiwan: Recent Developments and Their Implications for the United States; Issue Brief, Robert G. Sutter, IB87092
* Taiwan's Elections Implications for Taiwan's Development and U.S. Interests, Robert G. Sutter, 90-11 F
* South Korea and Taiwan: Expanding Trade Ties With the United States; Issue Brief, William H. Cooper., IB86151
* Taiwan: Recent Developments and Their Implications for the United States; Issue Brief, Robert G. Sutter. IB87092
* U.S. Agricultural Trade Opportunities With Pacific Rim Nations, Robert M. Goldstein. 88-755 ENR
* U.S.-Taiwan Economic Relations: Views of Some Members of the Taiwan Economic Elite, Arlene Wilson. 89-21 E
* Visit to South Korea and Taiwan, Trip Report, Larry A. Niksch. 88-740 F

Tajikistan

* see also U.S.S.R.
* Tajikistan: Basic Facts, Liam Wasley, 91-806 F

Tariffs

* see Foreign Trade--Imports and Exports, Foreign Trade--Trade Agreements and Negotiations, Foreign Trade--Trade Policy

Tax Reform

* see Taxation--Tax Reform

Tax Reform Act of 1986

* The Heifer Tax: Uniform Capitalization and Farmers, Gregg A. Esenwein. 88-462 E
* The Home Office Deduction under the Tax Reform Act of 1986, John Luckey. 86-973 A

Taxation

* see Business Taxes, Capital Gains Tax, Consumption Taxes, Corporation Taxes, Personal Income Tax, Tax Reform, Local Finance, Social Security Taxes

* Alcohol Fuels Tax Incentives: Current Law and Proposed Options to Expand Current Law, Salvatore Lazzari. 89-343 E
* American Public Opinion on the Federal Budget Deficit, Rosita M. Thomas, 91-403 GOV
* The Anti-Injunction Act: A Brief Legislative and Judicial History of Section 7421 of the Internal Revenue Code of 1986, John R. Luckey. 87-597 A
* Comparative Tax Burdens: The United States and Seven OECD Countries, Gregg A. Esenwein, 90-206 E
* A Concise History of U.S. Federal Taxation, Louis Alan Talley, 90-295 E
* Constitutional Considerations Implicated, a Hypothetical Proposal to Tax the Investment Income of a Tax-Exempt Entity Affiliated With a State or Local Government, Robert B. Burdette., 88-551 A
* Criminal Tax Law: A Summary of Cheek V. United States, Thomas B. Ripy, 91-187 A
* The Effect of Federal Tax and Budget Policies in the 1980s on the State-Local Sector, Lillian Rymarowicz and Dennis Zimmerman., 86-2 E
* Employee Stock Ownership Plans: An Overview, Gerald Mayer. 89-80 E
* Employee Stock Ownership Plans: Minimum Requirements to Qualify for Tax Advantages, Gerald Mayer., 89-36 E
* Exempt Status of Religious Groups, Marie B. Morris. 87-846 A
* Federal Budget and Tax Policy and the State-Local Sector: Retrenchment in the 1980s, Lillian Rymarowicz and Dennis Zimmerman., 88-600 E
* Federal Tax Payments, State Residents and Federal Expenditures in Individual States, Fiscal Year 1986, Lillian Rymarowicz., 88-398 E
* Federal Tax Payments State Residents and Federal Expenditures in Individual States, Fiscal Year 1987, Lillian Rymarowicz., 88-409 E
* Federal Tax Policy and Saving, Gregg A. Esenwein, 91-178 E
* A Financial Transactions Tax? The Proposed Federal Par User's Fee, William Jackson and Jack Taylor., 88-103 E
* The Gramm-Rudman-Hollings Targets: How Might They Affect the Economy, Gail Makinen and Brian Cashell. 86-1036 E
* The Heifer Tax: Uniform Capitalization and Farmers, Gregg A. Esenwein., 88-462 E
* The Judicial Power of Taxation: A Legal Analysis of the U.S. Supreme Court Ruling in Missouri v. Jenkins, Charles V. Dale, 90-294 A
* Life Insurance Tax Issues: Archived Issue Brief, Jack Taylor, IB90098
* Limits on Lobbying and Political Activity, Tax-Exempt Organizations: Historical Background and Continuing Issues, Marie B. Morris. 88-821 A
* Major Revenue Raising Options: An Overview, Gregg A. Esenwein. 88-756 E
* The OECD Multilateral Convention on Mutual Administrative Assistance in Tax Matters, Harry G. Bourevitch, 89-377 A
* Overview of Internal Revenue Code Changes Affecting Tax-Exempt Organizations in Years 1986-1988, Marie B. Morris., 88-738 A
* The Progressivity Effects of the Individual Income Tax Revisions in the Tax Reform Act of 1986: The Conference Bill Compared to Current Law, the House Bill, and the Senate Bill, Donald W. Kiefer, 86-892 E
* A Proposal for Raising Revenue Reducing Capital Gains Taxes?, Jane G. Gravelle. 87-562 E
* **Proposed Federal Taxation of Credit Unions: A Pro/Con Analysis, James M. Bickley. 86-84E**
* Provisions of the Tax Reform Act of 1986 Pertaining to Education, Robert Lyke, 87-67 EPW
* Puerto Rico's Status Options and Federal Taxes: Issue Brief, David L. Brumbaugh, IB90086
* Revenue-Raising Options: Archived Issue Brief, Gregg A. Esenwein. IB87169
* Should Credit Unions Be Taxed: Issue Brief, James M. Bickley. IB89066
* Significant Federal Tax Acts: 1954-1986, Louis Alan Talley. 87-727 E
* Significant Federal Tax Legislation, 1960-1969, Louis Talley. 79-232 E
* Significant Federal Tax Legislation, 1970-1978, Louis Talley. 79-207 E
* Some Constitutional Questions Regarding the Federal Income Tax Laws, Howard Zaritsky and John R. Luckey., 84-168 A
* A Stock Transfer Tax: Preliminary Economic Analysis, Donald W. Kiefer., 87-278 S
* A Summary of the Provisions of the Tax Reform of 1986 Affecting the Treatment of Insurance Companies and Products, Robert B. Burdette, 87-696 A
* The Targeted Jobs Tax Credit, 1978-1987, Linda LeGrande. 87-616 E
* Tax Effects of Title V of the Family Farm Act (H.R. 1425, 100th Congress), Marie B., Morris. 87-582 A
* Tax-Exempt Bonds: A Summary of Changes Made, the Tax Reform Act of 1986, Robert B. Burdette. 87-9 A
* Tax Expenditures for Health Care, Nonna A. Noto, 92-12 E
* Tax Issues Affecting Family Agriculture: Archived Issue Brief, Jack Taylor and Gregg A. Esenwein. IB88054
* Tax Policy and Spillover Effects: The Use of Tax Provisions to Induce Socially Desirable Activities, Jane Gravelle., 80-186 E

Current Events and Homework

* Tax Policy and U.S. Trade Performance, Gregg A. Esenwein, etc., 89-635 E
* Tax Subsidies to Housing, 1953-83, Jane Gravelle. 82-178 E
* Taxation Within Indian Lands: The Legal Framework, M. Maureen Murphy., 87-249 A
* Taxes and Taxation: An Alphabetical Microthesaurus of Terms Selected from the Legislative Indexing Vocabulary, Shirley Loo. 89-646 L
* Taxes: Significant Federal Tax Acts, 1954-1990, Louis Alan Talley, 91-234 E
* The Underground Economy: Selected References, Barry Molefsky. 84-738 E
* U.S. Economic Policy in an International Context: The U.S. Tax Structure: Its Level, Composition and Progressivity Compared to Seven Other Nations, Donald W. Kiefer and Gregg A. Esenwein. 84-233 E
* U.S. Tax Treatment of Bad Foreign Loans, David L. Brumbaugh. 89-302 E
* Gasoline Excise Tax: Economic Impacts of an Increase, IB87078
* Oil Import Fees (Taxes) For Deficit Reduction: Revenue and Economic Effects, IB87189
* Should Credit Unions Be Taxed, IB89066
* Tax Policy Prospects in the Bush Administration, IB89019
* Taxation of Capital Gains, IB89108
* A Value-Added Tax contrasted with a National Sales Tax, IB87156
* Value-Added Tax for Deficit Reduction, IB87097

Taxation -- Business Taxes

* Antitrust, Capital Gains, and Research and Development Tax Benefits in Several Industrialized Nations, Law Library of Congress, European Law Division, LL90-26
* Business Tax Provisions of Interest to the HANDICAPPED Including Changes Made under the Revenue Reconciliation Act of 1990, Louis Alan Talley, 90-636 E
* Comparative Corporate Tax Burdens in the United States and Japan and Implications for Relative Economic Growth, Jane Gravelle, 83-177 E
* Corporate Tax Integration: Issues and Options, Jane G. Gravelle, 91-482 RCO
* Corporate Tax Reform and International Competitiveness, Jane G. Gravelle, 86-42 E
* An Economic Analysis of the Effects of the Finance Committee Staff Proposal to Revise Subchapter C of the Internal Revenue Code on Incentives for Corporate Reorganization, Donald W. Kiefer, 85-1016 E
* Economic Analysis of the Tax Treatment of Nuclear Power Plant Decommissioning Costs, Donald W. Keifer, 84-28 E
* The Federal Royalty and Tax Treatment of the Hard Rock Minerals Industry: An Economic Analysis, Salvatore Lazzari, 90-493 E
Federal Taxes and Foreign Investment in U.S. Business: An Assessment, David L. Brumbaugh, 91-582 E
* Merger Activity and Leveraged Buyouts: Sound Corporate Restructuring or Wall Street Alchemy? Carolyn Kay Brancato, etc., 84-643 E
* Rental Real Estate: Passive Activity Loss Limits; Issue Brief, Richard Bourdon, IB90076
* The Research and Development Tax Credit: A Comparison of the Arguments for and Against, Office of Senior Specialists, 88-333 S
* The Research and Experimentation Tax Credit: Archived Issue Brief, David L. Brumbaugh, IB90008
* The Securities Transactions Tax: An OVerview of the Issues, Donald W. Kiefer, 90-350 S
Should Credit Unions Be Taxed? James M. Bickley, 90-498 E
* The Targeted Jobs Tax Credit, 1978-1987, Linda LeGrande, 87-616 E
*The Tax Credit for Research and Development: An Analysis, Jane G. Gravelle, 85-6 E
* Tax Incentives to Train or Retrain the Work Force, Nonna A. Noto, etc., 91-225 E
Tax Policy and Rental Housing: An Economic Analysis, Jane G. Gravelle, 87-536 E
* The Tax Treatment of Expenditures on Anti-Pollution Equipment in Selected Foreign Countries, Law Library of Congress, American-British Law Division, LL90-10
* Taxation of Foreign Investments in Selected Countries, Law Library of Congress, LL91-5
* Taxation of Securities Transactions to Discourage Short-Term Investment: A Selected Bibliography, Louis Alan Talley, 90-415 E
* Taxing Intangibles: An Economic Analysis, Jane G. Gravelle, etc., 91-744 E
* U.S. Taxation of Overseas Investment: Selected Issues in the 102nd Congress, David L. Brumbaugh, 91-682 E

Taxation -- Capital Gains Tax

* Can a Capital Gains Tax Cut Pay for Itself? Jane G. Gravelle, 90-161 S
* Capital Gains Tax Issues, Jane G. Gravelle, 88-80 E
* Capital Gains Taxation: An Analysis of the Recent Debate; Archived Issue Brief, Gregg A. Esenwein, IB88042
* Capital Gains of Individuals in Japan, Gregg A. Esenwein, 89-581 E
* Capital Gains Taxes, IRA's, and Savings, Jane G. Gravelle, 89-543 S
* A History of Taxation of Individual Capital Gains Income, Gregg A. Esenwein, 91-594 E
* Income Tax Exclusion of Gain from Sale of a Primary Residence, Louis Alan Talley, 90-194 E
* Limits to Capital Gains Feedback Effects, Jane G. Gravelle, 91-250 E
* A Proposal for Raising Revenue by Reducing Capital Gains Taxes?, Jane G. Gravelle, 87-562 E

Taxation -- Consumption Taxes

* Alcohol Excise Taxes on Beverages: archived Issue Brief, Louis Alan Talley, IB90059
* Alcohol Occupational Taxes for Distilled Spirits, Beer, and Wine: Archived Issue Brief, Louis Alan Talley, IB90056
* Alcohol, Tobacco, and Gasoline Excise Tax Rates Adjusted for Inflation, Louis Alan Talley, etc., 91-210 E
* Aviation Excise Taxes: Their Role in the Deficit Reduction Effort of 1990, Nonna A. Noto, 91-309 E
* Broad-Based Federal Consumption Taxation: A Value-Added Tax Contrasted With a National Sales Tax, James M. Bickley., 87-787 E
* BTU Taxes, Carbon Taxes, and Other Energy Tax options for Deficit Reduction, Salvatore Lazzari, 90-384 E
* Economic Effects of a VAT on Small Business, James M. Bickley. 88-288 E
* Effects of a Value Added Tax on Capital Formation, Jane G. Gravelle., 88-697 S
* Federal Excise Taxes on Alcoholic Beverages: A Summary of Present Law and a Brief History, Thomas B. Ripy. 91-310 A
* Federal Excise Taxes on Gasoline and the Highway Trust Fund--A Short History, Louis Alan Talley., 91-192 E
* Gasoline Excise Tax: Economic Impacts of an Increase; Issue Brief, Bernard A. Gelb and Salvatore Lazzari. IB87078
* History and Economics of U.S. Excise Taxation of Luxury Goods, Louis Alan Talley, Jack Taylor and Dennis Zimmerman., 91-306 E
* A History of Federal Energy Tax Policy: Conventional as Compared to Renewable and Nonconventional Energy Resources, Salvatore Lazzari. 88-455 E
* National Sales Tax: Selected Policy Issues, James M. Bickley. 84-141 E
* Oil Import Fees (Taxes) for Deficit Reduction: Revenue and Economic Effects; Issue Brief, Salvatore Lazzari. IB87189
* Oil Import Taxes: Revenue and Economic Effects, Bernard A. Gelb and Salvatore Lazzari. 86-572 E
* On the Significance of Gasoline Tax Regressivity, Salvatore Lazzari, 91-816 E
* Reducing the Deficit With Energy Taxes, Craig K. Elwell. 86-653 E
* Taxes on Alcohol Products--Increases under the Revenue Reconciliation Act of 1990, Louis Alan Talley, 90-597 E
* Taxes on Tobacco Products--Increases under the Revenue Reconciliation Act of 1990, Louis Alan Talley, 90-637 E
* Telephone Excise Tax: Archived Issue Brief, Louis Alan Talley. IB87185
* Telephone Excise Taxes--Are Revenues Dedicated for Defense Spending? Louis Alan Talley, 90-611 E
* Tobacco Excise Taxes: Archived Issue Brief, Louis Allen Talley, IB90101
* Tobacco Taxes: A Selected Bibliography, Louis Alan Talley, etc., 90-398 E
* Value-Added Tax: Concepts, Policy Issues, and OECD Experiences, James M. Bickley, 91-559 E
* A Value-Added Tax Contrasted With a National Sales Tax: Issue Brief, James M. Bickley. IB87156
* Value-Added Tax for Deficit Reduction: Issue Brief, James M. Bickley., IB91708
* Value-Added Tax: A Selected Bibliography, 1980-1989, Felix Chin, 90-163 L
* Value Added Tax: Tax Bases and Revenue Yields, James M. Bickley. 91-271 E

Taxation -- Corporation Taxes

* Accelerated Depreciation, the Investment Tax Credit, and Their Required Rate-making Treatment in the Public Utility Industry: A Background Report, Donald W. Kiefer. 87-312 S * Allocation of Research and Development Costs and the U.S. Foreign Tax Credit, David L. Brumbaugh. 89-220 E
* Assessing Structural Tax Revision With Macroeconomic Models: The Treasury Tax Proposals and the Allocation of Investment, Jane G. Gravelle. 85-645 E
* Business Taxes and Inflation Following the Tax Reform Act of 1986, David L. Brumbaugh. 88-719 E
* Captive Off-Shore Insurance Companies, David Whiteman., 84-507 E

Taxation / Personal Income Tax

* Comparative Corporate Tax Burdens in the United States and Japan and Implications for Relative Economic Growth, Jane Gravelle. 83-177 E
* The Corporate Income Tax and the U.S. Economy, David L. Brumbaugh and Jane G. Gravelle. 84-143 E
* The Corporate Minimum Tax: Rationale, Effects, and Issues, David L. Brumbaugh. 89-213 E
* An Economic Analysis of the Effects of the Finance Committee Staff Proposal to Revise Subchapter C of the Internal Revenue Code on Incentives for Corporate Reorganization, Donald W. Kiefer. 85-1016 E
* Economic Analysis of the Tax Treatment of Nuclear Power Plant Decommissioning Costs, Donald W. Kiefer. 84-28 E
* The Effect of Alternative Depreciation Systems on Marginal Effective Tax Rates on Public Utility Property, Donald W. Kiefer. 86-506 E
* Energy Tax Options to Increase Federal Revenue, Salvatore Lazzari. 87-539 E
* Federal Income Taxation of Corporate Farms, Jack Taylor. 87-940 E
* Federal Taxes, the Steel Industry, and Net Operating Loss Carryforwards, David L. Brumbaugh. 88-5 E
* History and Continuing Issues on Unrelated Trade or Business Income Tax: Sections 511-513 of the Internal Revenue Code, Thomas B. Ripy, Marie B. Morris and Carmen Pomares., 87-248 A
* How Are Windfall Profit Tax Revenues Used?, Bernard A. Gelb. 84-651 E
* Leveraged Buyouts: Selected References, 1987-1989, Robert Howe. 89-156 L
* Major Federal Tax Provisions that Directly Affect International Trade and Investment, David L. Brumbaugh., 86-764 E
* Merger Activity and Leveraged Buyouts: Sound Corporate Restructuring or Wall Street Alchemy?, Carolyn Kay Brancato and Kevin F. Winch. 84-643 E
* Oil Import Tax: Some General Economic Effects, Bernard A. Gelb. 87-259 E
* Oil Royalty Trusts, Carolyn Kay Brancato. 84-575 E
* The Possessions Tax Credit (IRC Section 936): Background and Issues, David L. Brumbaugh. 88-200 E
* The Research and Development Tax Credit: A Comparison of the Arguments for and Against, Office of Senior Specialists. 88-333 S
* Royalties on Federal Coal: Issues in the Treatment of Royalty Payments and Externality-Related Taxes, Salvatore Lazzari, Duane Thompson and Dennis Zimmerman., 88-250 E.
* Tax Aspects of Leveraged Buyouts, Jane G. Gravelle. 89-142 S
* The Tax Credit for Research and Development: An Analysis, Jane G. Gravelle. 85-6E
* Tax Sanctions and U.S. Investment in South Africa, David L. Brumbaugh., 88-112 E
* Taxation of Foreign-Source Income: A Survey; A Brief Overview of Concepts, Provisions, and Issues in the Federal Taxation of Foreign-Source Income, David L. Brumbaugh., 83-636 E
* Taxation of Foreign-Source Income: A Survey; The U.S. Foreign Tax Credit: Provisions, Effects and Issues, David L. Brumbaugh., 83-222 E
* Taxation of Overseas Investment: Subpart F and the Tax Reform Act of 1986, David L. Brumbaugh. 87-167 E
* Taxation of the Press: A Brief Constitutional Analysis, Rita Ann Reimer., 87-422 A
* Taxation of U.S. Investment Abroad: Archived Issue Brief, David L. Brumbaugh. IB87060
* Taxes in Public Utility Rates: Phantom Taxes or Real Tax Benefits?, Donald W. Kiefer. 84-21 1 E
* Why Some Corporations Don't Pay Taxes, David L. Brumbaugh and Wayne M. Morrison. 85-75 E
* Wind Energy Development and Utility Capacity Credits: A Review of Research, Implementation and Policy Issues under the Public Utility Regulatory Policies Act, Fred Sissine., 84-101 SPR

Taxation -- Personal Income Tax

* *antitrust, Capital Gains, and Research and Development Tax Benefits in Several Industrialized Nations, Law Library of Congress, European Law Division, LL90-26
* Assistance to Families: A Chart Comparing Some Existing Tax Provisions and Pending Proposals, Marie B. Morris. 89-279 A
* The Bush Capital Gains Tax Proposal, Donald W. Kiefer. 89-341 S
* The Capital Gains Response to a Tax Rate Change: Is It Overestimated?, Donald W. Kiefer. 88-216 S
* Capital Gains Tax Issues, Jane G. Gravelle. 88-80 E
* Capital Gains Taxation: An Analysis of the Recent Debate; Archived Issue Brief, Gregg A. Esenwein., IB88042
* Changing Progressivity of the Federal Individual Income Tax and Social Security Tax, Donald W. Kiefer. 87-723 E
* Charitable Contributions of Appreciated Assets, Louis Alan Talley, 90-579 E
* Charitable Contributions: Pros and Cons of Deductibility, Louis Alan Talley, 90-449 E
* Children With Special Needs: Tax Assistance Proposals; Archived Issue Brief, Louis Alan Talley, IB89153
* Comments Concerning the Supreme Court's Decision in South Carolina v. Baker, Robert B. Burdette. 88-443 A
* Day Care: Effect of Tax Provisions in Welfare Reform Legislation on Selected Bills in 100th Congress, Marie B. Morris. 89-61 A
* Day Care Services: Current Tax Laws, Marie B. Moms. 87-680 A
* Deductibility of Reservists' Transportation Expenses, Robert B. Burdette, 91-603 A
* Distributional Effects of Selected Proposals to Modify the Earned Income Tax Credit, Thomas Gabe, 89-553 EPW
* The Earned Income Tax Credit, Carmen Solomon. 86-1031 EPW
* The Earned Income Tax Credit: A Growing Form of Aid to Children, James R. Storey, 91-402 EPW
* Education Savings Bonds: Eligibility for Tax Exclusion, Bob Lyke, 89-570 EPW
* The Effects of Indexation on Tax Revenues and Distributional Effects of the U.S. Individual Income Tax System: A Historical Simulation, Donald W. Kiefer. 83-115 E
* Elderly Home Care: Tax Incentives and Proposals for Change, Louis Alan Talley, 89-662 E
* Employer Education Assistance: A Brief Discussion of Current Legislation and Issues, Bob Lyke. 88-202 EPW
* Employer Education Assistance: Current Tax Status and Issues, Bob Lyke. 89-148 EPW
* Employer Education Assistance: Current Tax Status and Reauthorization Issues, Bob Lyke. 90-195 EPW
* The Estate Freeze Controversy, Salvatore Lazzari. 89-125 E
* Federal Estate, Gift, and Generation-Skipping Taxes: A Legislative History and Description of Current Law, John R. Luckey. 90-635 A
* Federal Income Tax Deduction for State and Local Taxes: A Brief History of the Law, Thomas Ripy. 85-853 A
* Federal Income Tax Treatment of the Elderly, Louis Alan Talley, 91-217 E
* Federal Income Tax Treatment of the Family, Jane G. Gravelle, 91-694 RCO
* Federal Individual Income Tax Terms: An Explanation, Louis Alan Talley, 90-213 E
* Federal Tax Code Provisions of Interest to the Disabled and Handicapped, Louis Alan Talley, 91-21 E
* Federal Tax Expenditures Related to Education, Bob Lyke, 91-461 EPW
* Federal Tax Law Peculiarly Applicable to Members of Congress, Robert B. Burdette. 87-482 A
* Federal Tax Treatment of Combat Pay, Robert B. Burdette, 91-144 A
* Federal Taxation of Americans Who Work Abroad, David L. Brumbaugh. 87-452 E
* Federal Taxation of Student Aid, Bob Lyke, 91-EPW
* "Feedback" Effects of Tax Policy: Distributional Implications, Donald W. Kiefer. 89-94 S
* Financing Catastrophic Health Care: Possible Effects on Marginal and Average Income Tax Rates, Gregg A. Esenwein. 89-132 E
* Frequently Asked Questions Concerning the Federal Income Tax, John R. Luckey, 89-623 A
* Home Buyer Assistance: Tax-Deferred Savings for Downpayments, Richard Bourdon. 88-773 E
* How Life Insurance Policies Generate Investment Income, Jack Taylor., 88-326 E
* Income Tax Averaging: Background and Analysis, Gregg A. Esenwein. 88-601 E
* The Individual Income Tax and Marriage Neutrality, Gregg A. Esenwein., 88-8 E
* Individual Income Tax Rates, Gregg A. Esenwein. 90-619 E
* Individual Income Tax Rates, Gregg A. Esenwein. 90-750 E
* Individual Income Tax Rates for 1988: Archived Issue Brief, Gregg A. Esenwein. IB88017
* Individual Retirement Accounts (IRAs) After the Tax Reform Act of 1986, Gregg A. Esenwein. 87-712 E
* Older Taxpayers and the Tax Reform Act of 1986, Gerald Mayer. 88-547 E
* The Omnibus Taxpayer Bill of Rights, Marie B. Morris, John R. Luckey and Thomas B. Ripy. 89-136 A
* The Omnibus Trade and Competitiveness Act: Technology Development Provisions, Wendy H. Schacht. 89-93 SPR
* An Overview of Federal Tax Policies Encouraging Donations of Conservation Easements to Preserve Natural Areas, Richard Dunford. 84-48 ENR
* Parental Choices in Child Care Act of 1989: S. 392, Marie Morris. 89-215 A

Current Events and Homework

* Pension Issues: Info Pack, IP428P
* Proceedings of the CRS Symposium on U.S. Trade: Policy Issues Confronting the 100th Congress, William Cooper. 87-267 E
* Refundable Tax Credits for Families With Children: Issue Brief, James R. Storey, IB91120
* Refundable Tax Credits to Aid Working Poor Families: Archived Issue Brief, James R. Storey, IB89109
* Risk Assessment in Health and Environmental Regulation; Archived Issue Brief, David Cheney. IB84124
* Rules Governing Salary Reduction Retirement Plans, James R. Storey, 90-510 EPW
* Saving for College: Issue Brief, Robert F. Lyke. IB89078
* Saving for College With Education Savings Bonds, Gerald Mayer. 89-207 E
* Science and Technology: Federal Policy and Economic Impact; Bibliography-in-Brief, 1983-1986, Virginia MacEwen. 87-79 L
* Section 89 Nondiscrimination Rules for Employee Benefits, Ray Schmitt and Beth C. Fuchs. 88-470 EPW
* Single-Premium Life Insurance: Archived Issue Brief, Jack Taylor. IB88074
* Social Security and Tax-Free Fringe Benefits: Background and Issues, Geoffrey Kollmann. 85-123 EPW
* Social Security: Issues in Taxing Benefits under Current Law and under Proposals to Tax a Greater Share of Benefits, Geoffrey Kollmann. 89-40 EPW
* Some Federal Tax Implications of Replacing the Current Limitation on a Senator's Acceptance of Honoraria With an Outright Prohibition Against Acceptance of Any Honoraria, Robert B. Burdette, 88-599 A
* Special Tax Rules for Members of Congress, Robert B. Burdette, 89-615 A
* State Income Taxation of Military Personnel and United States Citizens Residing Outside of the United States, John Luckey, 91-590 A
* States Affected by the Supreme Court's Ruling on Tax Discrimination Against Federal Retirees, Mark Gurevitz, etc., 89-275 A
* Stevenson-Wydler Technology Innovation Act: A Federal Effort to Promote Industrial Innovation; Archived Issue Brief, Wendy Schacht. IB85082
* Student Personal/Dependency Exemption and Standard Deduction, Louis Alan Talley, 90-172 E
* Tax Amnesty: A Selected Bibliography, Louis Alan Talley, etc., 90-530 E
* Tax Cut Proposals: Info Pack, IP457T
* Tax-Favored Savings: All Savers Certificates and Individual Retirement Accounts, William Jackson., 85-168 E
* Tax Options for Financing Long-Term Care for the Elderly, Jane G. Gravelle and Jack Taylor. 89-329 E
* Tax provisions Pertaining to Education in Title XI of the Omnibus Budget Reconciliation Act of 1990, Bob Lyke, 90-546 EPW
* Tax Provisions Which Benefit Employed Parents With Children, Marie B. Morris. 89-169 A
* Taxing Social Security Benefits: Background and Programmatic Issues, Geoffrey Kollman. 83-152 EPW
* Tax Status of Group Legal Services Plans, Louis Alan Talley, 90-418 E
* Tax Treatment of Interest Payments on Educational Loans, Louis Alan Talley, 91-219 E
* Taxation of Employer-Provided Health Benefits, Beth Fuchs, etc., 90-507 EPW
* Taxation of Interest Earnings on Pre-Need Funeral Trusts, Louis Alan Talley, 90-602 E
* Taxation of Interest on Personal Savings, Law Library of Congress, LL90-83
* Tuition Tax Credits, Bob Lyke, 91-230 EPW
* Young Dependent Tax Credit: Analysis of H.R. 3944 and S. 2187 (100th Congress), Marie B. Morris. 88-383 A

Taxation -- Social Security Taxes

* How long does it Take New Retirees to Recover the Value of Their Social Security Taxes? Geoffrey Kollmann, 91-4 EPW
* Social Security: Changes in the Self-Employment Tax for 1990, David Koitz, 90-24 EPW
* Social Security: Issues in Taxing Benefits under Current Law and under Proposals to Tax a Greater Share of Benefits, Geoffrey Kollmann, 89-40 EPW
* Social Security: The Macroeconomic Effects of Cutting Payroll Taxes, Brian W. Cashell, 91-345 E
* Would a Social Security Tax Cut Increase Progressivity?, Donald W. Kiefer, 90-235 S

Taxation -- Tax Reform

* Assessing Structural Tax Revision With Macroeconomic Models: The Treasury Tax Proposals and the Allocation of Investment, Jane G. Gravelle. 85-645 E
* Bank Soundness in Light of the Tax Reform Act of 1986 and Possible Glass-Stegall Act Repeal, Walter W. Eubanks. 88-1 18 E
* Blacks and Tax Reform, 1985-1986: An Assessment of Possible Impacts on Blacks of Selected Proposals, the President and Provisions of the Tax Reform Act of 1985 (H.R. 3838), William Ellis and Darlene Colbert. 86-117 GOV
* Corporate Tax Reform and International Competitiveness, Jane G. Gravelle, 86-42 E
* Depreciation and the Tax Reform Act of 1986 (P.L. 99-514), David L. Brumbaugh. 87-342 E
* The Effect of the Tax Reform Act of 1986 on Technological Innovation, Jane G. Gravelle. 87-124 E
* Effective Corporate Tax Rates in the Major Revision Plans: A Comparison of the House, Senate, and Conference Committee Versions, Jane G. Gravelle., 86-854 E
* The Home Mortgage Interest Deduction for Boats Used as Second Homes, Richard Bourdon. 87-366 E
* The Home Mortgage Interest Deduction: Recent Changes in the Tax Laws, Richard Bourdon. 88-126 E
* The Home Office Deduction under the Tax Reform Act of 1986, John Luckey, 86-973 A
* Income Tax Treatment of Rental Housing and Real Estate Investment After the Tax Reform Act of 1986, Jack Taylor. 87-603 E
* International Competitiveness and the Tax Reform Act of 1986, Jane G. Gravelle. 87-428 E
* Minor Children's Income: Effect of the Tax Reform Act of 1986, Marie B. Morris. 87-21 A
* The Progressivity Effects of the Individual Income Tax Revisions in the Tax Reform Act of 1986: The Conference Bill Compared to Current Law, the House Bill, and the Senate Bill, Donald W. Kiefer. 86-892 E
* Provisions of the Tax Reform Act of 1986 Affecting Federal Workers and Retirees, Carolyn Merck. 86-928 EPW
* Provisions of the Tax Reform Act of 1986 Pertaining to Education, Robert Lyke. 87-67 EPW
* Public Opinion and Tax Reform: What Do the Polls Mean?, Wayne M. Morrison. 85-878 E
* A Summary of the Provisions of the Tax Reform of 1986 Affecting the Treatment of Insurance Companies and Products, Robert Burdette. 87-696 A
* Tax Code Provisions of Interest to the Disabled and Handicapped. Louis Alan Talley. 87-721 E
* Tax Issues: Archived Issue Brief, Nonna A. Noto. IB87186
* Tax Policy and Rental Housing: An Economic Analysis, Jane G. Gravelle., 87-536 E
* Tax Policy Prospects in the Bush Administration: Issue Brief, Salvatore Lazzari. IB89019
* The Tax Reform Act of 1986 and Owners of Rental Housing, Richard Bourdon. 86-919 E
* The Tax Reform Act of 1986 (H.R. 3838): Effective Versus Statutory Marginal Tax Rates, Gregg A. Esenwein. 86-912 E
* Tax Reform Act of 1986: Independent Contractors and Section 1706; Archived Issue Brief, Marie B. Morris. IB87073
* Tax Reform Act of 1986 (P.L. 99-514): Comparison of New With Prior Tax Law, Stacey M. Kean and David L. Brumbaugh. 87-231 E
* The Tax Reform Act of 1986 (P.L. 99-514): Proposed Changes; Archived Issue Brief, David L. Brumbaugh and Wayne M. Morrison. IB87091
* The Tax Reform Act of 1986: The Effects on Public Utilities, Donald W. Kiefer. 87-224 E
* Tax Reform and Foreign Investment, U.S. Firms, David L. Brumbaugh. 87-89 E
* Tax Reform Effects: Archived Issue Brief, Congressional Research Service. IB87010
* Tax Reform: Its Potential Effect on the State and Local Sector, Dennis Zimmerman. 87-233 E
* Taxation of Commercial Banks in the Tax Reform Act of 1986 (Conference Agreement), James M. Bickley. 86-933 E
* The 1986 Tax Reform Act: Constitutionality of the Retroactive Application of Certain Provisions, Thomas B. Ripy and Marie B. Morris. 87-440 A

Taxpayer Rights

* see Taxation--Personal Income Tax

Teachers

* see Elementary and Secondary Education

Technological Innovation

* see Research and Development

Technology and Civilization

* Balancing the National Interest: U.S. National Security Export Controls and

Taxation / Telecommunication

Global Economic Competition: A Summary of the National Academy of Sciences Study, John P. Hardt and Jean F. Boone. 87-119S

* Critical Technologies Lists: A Comparison, Genevieve J. Knezo, 91-367 SPR
* Controlling Carbon Dioxide Emissions, Amy Abel, Mark E. Holt and Larry B. Parker. 89-157 ENR
* Direct Federal Support for Technological Innovation: Issues and Options, Christopher Hill and Wendy Schacht. 84-118 S
* The Europe 1992 Plan: Science and Technology Issues, Science Policy Research Division. 89-178 SPR
* European Community: Issues Raised by 1992 Integration, Congressional Research Service. .89-323 E
* Export Controls: Issue Brief, George Holliday and Glennon J. Harrison. IB87122
* High-Technology Trade: Bibliography-in-Brief, 1985-1988, Robert S. Kirk. 88-572L
* Industrial Competitiveness and Technological Advancement: Debate Over Government Policy; Issue Brief, Wendy H. Schacht, IB91132
* Institute for Scientific and Technological Cooperation: Archived Issue Brief, Genevieve Knezo. IB79033
* Japan: Summaries of Selected Products, 1989-1990, Robert S. Kirk, 90-400 L
* Japanese and U.S. Industrial Associations: Their Role in High-Technology Policymaking; a Japan Task Force Report, Dick K. Nanto, etc., 91-477 E
* Japanese Technical Information: Opportunities to Improve U.S. Access, Christopher T. Hill. 87-818 S
* New Crops and New Farm Products: A Briefing, Jean M.Rawson. 88-771 ENR
* The Omnibus Trade and Competitiveness Act: Technology Development Provisions, Wendy H. Schacht, 89-93 SPR* * * Privacy and Technology: Selected References, 1986-1991, Tangela G. Roe, 91-841 L
* Proceedings of the CRS Symposium on U.S. Trade; Policy Issues Confronting the 10th Congress, William Cooper, 87-267 E.
* Risk Assessment in Health and Environmental Regulation; Archived Issue Brief, David Cheney IB84124.
* Science and Technology: Federal Policy and Economic Impact: Bibliography-in-Brief, 1983-1986, Virginia MacEwen, 87-79 L
* Stevenson-Wydler Technology Innovation Act: A Federal Effort to Promote Industrial Innovation: Archived Issue Brief, Wendy Schacht, IB85082.
* Technology Development and Regionalization: A Checklist of CRS Products, Bonnie F. Mangan, 92-9 L
* Technology Transfer: Utilization of Federally Funded Research and Development; Issue Brief, Wendy Schacht, IB85031
* U.S. Export Control Policy and Competitiveness; Proceedings of the CRS Symposium, John P. Hardt, and Jean F. Boone, 87-388 S.

Technology Transfer

* see Technology and Civilization

Teenage Pregnancy

* see Families

Teenage Suicide

* see Families

Telecommunication

* see Telephone Industry, Television, Communications
* Advertising of Alcoholic Beverages in the Broadcast Media: Archived Issue Brief, Bruce K. Mulock, IB85097
* Congress and Information Technology, Jane Bortnick, 91-783 SPR
* Constitutional Issues Relevant to Consideration of FCC Policy on Minority "Preferences" or "Merits" in Broadcast Licensing Proceedings, Charles V. Dale, 87-8 A.
* Copyright Law: Legalizing Home Taping of Audio and Video Recordings: Archived Issue Brief, Paul Wallace, IB82075.
* Extending the Fairness Doctrine to the Print Media, Thomas M. Durbin, 87-584 A.
* The Fairness Doctrine and the Equal Opportunities Doctrine; Issue Brief, Thomas Durbin IB82087.
* FCC Regulation of Indecent Radio and Television Broadcasting, Rita Ann Reimer, 88-291 A
* Forum; Information Technology Revolution; Also, Science and the Budget: 1990 Update, Congressional Research Service Review, v. 11, July-Aug. 1990, REV 7-90
* The Ground Wave Emergency Network, Gary K. Reynolds, 89-206 F.
* Information Policy and Technology Issues: Public Laws of the 95th Through 101st Congresses, Robert Lee Chartrand. 91-569 SPR.
* Information Technology in Our Time: Selected References, Robert L.

Chartrand, 88-733 SPR.
* Information Technology Utilization in Emergency Management, Robert Chartrand, and Trudie Punaro, 85-74 S.
* The Interception of Communications: A Legal Overview of Bugs and Taps, Charles Doyle, 88-105 A.
* Issues in U.S. Advanced Technology Policy: A Review of the National Advisory Committee on Semiconductors Report, a Strategic Industry at Risk, Glenn J. McLouglin, 90-234 SPR
* A Legal Analysis of the FCC's Abolition of the Fairness Doctrine, Thomas M. Durbin, 87-754 A.
* Media Entertainment Sex and Violence: Impact on Society, Especially Children, Edith Fairman Cooper, 86-925 SPR.
* Mediasat:The Use of Remote Sensing Satellites by News Agencies, Patricia E. Humphlett, 87-70 SPR.
* Metro Broadcasting v. FCC: The Constitutionality of Federally Mandated Minority Preference Policies, Kevin B. Greely, 90-479 A
* Minority Ownership of Broadcast Facilities: A Summary of Federal Communications Commission's Policies and Rules, Bernevia McCalip, 87-273 E.
* Multiple Ownership of Radio and Television Stations; History, Background and Recent Rule Changes, Bernevia McCalip, 85-153 E.
* Newspaper and Television Network News coverage of Congress During the Summers of 1979 and 1989: A Content Analysis, Denis Steven Rutkus, etc., 91-238 GOV
* Space Commercialization in China and Japan, Karl A. Rohrer, etc., 89-367 SPR.
* Telecommunications and Information Systems Standardization--Is America Ready?, David Hack, 87-458 SPR.
* Telecommunications Trade: Market Access Legislation; Archived Issue Brief, Raymond Ahearn and Donald Dulchinos, IB85206
* Trade in Telecommunications Products and Services; Legislation in the 100th Congress, Glennon J. Harrison, 87-844 E.
* U.S. International Broadcasting: An Assessment for Reform, David A. Hennes, 91-587 F
* U.S. Space Commercialization Activities, Patricia E. Humphlett, 88-518 SPR.
* Videocassette Recorder: Legal Analysis of Home Use, Douglas Reid Weimer, 89-30 A.

Telecommunication -- Telephone Industry

* Access Charges for Enhanced Service Providers: FCC Proposal to Eliminate Exemption Provides Controversy: Archived Issue Brief, Brucke K. Mulock, IB87223.
* American Telephone and Telegraph Co. Flow-Through of State Gross Receipts Taxes, Angela Gilroy, 87-43 E.
* The American Telephone and Telegraph Company Divestiture: Background, Provisions, and Restructuring, Angela A. Gilroy, 84-58 E.
* Caller I.D. and Automatic Telephone Number Identification; Issue Brief, David B. Hack, IB90085
* Federal Authority to Prohibit Prerecorded Commercial Telephone Calls: A Constitutional Analysis, Rita Ann Reimer, 87-10 A.
* Information Services: What Role for the Bell Operating Companies?, Angela A. Gilroy, 90-348 E
* Lifeline Telephone Service: Federal Activity and Controversies, Angela Gilroy, 88-90 E.
* The Rural Electrification Administration: Background and Current Issues, Carl Ek, etc., 91-614 ENR
* Should the "Baby Bells" Be Allowed to Manufacture? Issue Brief, Stephen J. Downs, etc., IB91094
* Telephone Access for the Hearing Impaired: Federal Actions to Increase Availability, Angela A. Gilroy. 86-917 E.
* Telephone Excise Tax: Archived Issue Brief, Louis Alan Talley. IB87185
* Telephone Excise Taxes--Are Revenues Dedicated for Defense Spending?, Louis Alan Talley, 90-611 E
* Telephone Industry Deregulation: Selected References, 1984-1988, Robert Howe. 88-751 L
* Telephone Industry Issues: Bibliography-in-Brief, 1990-1991; Robert Howe, 91-608 L
* Telephone Industry Issues: Info Pack, IP257T
* Telephone Industry Residential Subscriber Line Charges and the Lifeline Options; Issue Brief, Angela A. Gilroy. IB85152

Telecommunication -- Television

* Broadcast Regulation in the 100th Congress: A Legislative Overview, Bernevia M. McCalip. 89-88E
* Cable Television Franchises: Do Franchising Authorities Have Any

Recourse If the Franchisee Raises Subscription Rates?, Janice E. Rubin., 87-448 A

* Cable Television Rate Regulation: Issue Brief, Angele L. Gilroy, IB91079
* Cable Television Rate Reregulation: Background and Status, Angele A. Gilroy, 91-400 E
* Cable Television: Selected References, 1986-1989, Felix Chin. 89-212 L
* Cable TV: Info Pack, IP104C
* Children's Programming Requirements: The Slow pace of Change, Bernevia McCalip, 91-673 E
* Commercial Television: Should Children's Television Be Regulated?, Bernevia M. McCalip. 84-663 E
* Financial Interest and Syndication (FIN-SYN): An Overview of Federal Regulation of Television Network Programming Practices, Kevin B. Greely, 91-368 A
* High-Definition Television (HDTV) in the United States--What Does an "Even Playing-Field" Look Like? (With Policy Options), David B. Hack. 88-365 SPR
* High-Definition Television: Issue Brief, David Hack. IB89088
* The Home Dish Market: H.R. 2848 (100th Congress) and the Copyright Liability of Satellite Carriers, Angela A. Gilroy. 88-728 E
* Release of Government-Held Spectrum for Non-Government Use: Issue Brief, David B. Hack, IB91114
* Regulation of Cable Television: A Legal Overview, Janice E. Rubin, 91-370 A
* The Scrambling of Cable Satellite Programming and the Backyard Satellite Dish Market: Archived Issue Brief, Angela A. Gilroy., IB86123
* The Scrambling of Satellite Signals and the Backyard Satellite Dish Market: Background, Controversies and Congressional Activity, Angela A. Gilroy. 86-120 E
* Television Network Evening News Coverage of Afghanistan: A Perspective After Eight Years of War, Denis Steven Rutkus. 88-319 GOV
* Videocassette Recorders: Legal Analysis of Home Use, Douglas Reid Weimer., 89-30 A

Telephone Industry

* see Telecommunication --Telephone Industry

Television

* see Telecommunication --Television

Temporary Emergency Food Assistance Program

* Temporary Emergency Food Assistance Program (TEFAP): 1987 Issues; Archived Issue Brief, Jean Jones. IB87090

Tender Offers

* see Corporations --Mergers

Territories

* The Governors and Lieutenant Governors of the States and Other Jurisdictions, Isabelle Malloy. .89-270 C
* Palau's Evolving Relationship With the United States: Introduction and Chronology of Developments, Luella S. Christopher. 88-442 F
* The Possessions Tax Credit (IRC Section 936): Background and Issues, David L. Brumbaugh. 88-200 E
* Puerto Rico: Political Status Considerations; Selected References, 1972-1990, Jean Bowers, 91-18 L
* Puerto Rico: Political Status; Info Pack, IP419P
* Puerto Rico: Political Status Options; Issue Brief, Bette A. Taylor. IB89065
* Puerto Rico's Status Options and Federal Taxes: Issue Brief, David L. Brumbaugh, IB90086
* Shadow Representatives in Congress: History and Current Developments, Garrine P. Laney, 91-64 GOV
* Statehood for Puerto Rico: The Effect on Social Welfare Programs, Carolyn Merck, 91-47 EPW
* Territorial Political Development: An Analysis of Puerto Rico, Northern Mariana Islands, Guam, Virgin Islands, and American Samoa, and the Micronesian Compacts of Free Association, Bette A. Taylor., 88-657 GOV
* The Virgin Islands of the United States: A Descriptive and Historical Profile, Bette A. Taylor. .88-429 GOV

Terrorism

* The Anti-Terrorism Act of 1987: Constitutional and Statutory Issues Which May Be Raised in Relation to Its Interpretation and Enforcement, Kenneth R. Thomas. 88-382 A
* Anti-Terrorism Policy: A Pro-Con Discussion of Retaliation and Deterrence Options, James Wootten and Raphael Perl. 85-832 F
* The Changing Nature of International Terrorism, Allan Nanes. 85-625 F
* Combatting International Terrorism: Audio Brief, James P. Wootten. AB50151
* Combatting State-Supported Terrorism: Differing U.S. and West European Perspectives, Paul E. Gallis and James P. Wootten., 88-313 F
* Crime and Drug Control: Comparison of Pending Senate and House Bills (S. 618 and H.R. 1400/S. 635), Government Division. Harry Hogan, 91-433 GOV
* The Guilford Four, Law Library of Congress, American-British Law Division, LL89-106
* Lebanon: The Remaining U.S. Hostages; a Chronology, 1984-1987, Clyde R. Mark. 88-499 F
* Lebanon: The Remaining U.S. Hostages; Issue Brief, Clyde Mark., IB85183
* Nuclear Terrorism: Implementation of Title VI of the Omnibus Diplomatic Security and Anti-terrorism Act of 1986; Archived Issue Brief, Warren H. Donnelly. IB87213
* The Security of U.S. Embassies and Other Overseas Civilian Installations, Joel Woldman. 85-11 F
* Statutes Authorizing Sanctions Against Countries Supporting International Terrorism, Jeanne Jagelski. 87-327
* A Terrorism Chronology: 1981-1986: Incidents Involving U.S. Citizens or Property, Richard Dulaney. 86-531 F
* Terrorism: Info Pack, IP299T
* Terrorism: U.S. Policy Options; Issue Brief, James Wootten., IB81141
* Terrorist Incidents Involving U.S. Citizens or Property 1981-1986: A Chronology; Issue Brief, James P. Wootten. IB86096
* U.S. Assistance for Foreign Police Forces, Alan K. Yu, 89-419 F
* The 99th Congress and the Response to International Terrorism, Richard W. Boyd and Martha Crenshaw. 87-893 F

Textile Industry

* see Industry--Textile Industry

Thailand

* The Association of Southeast Asian Nations (ASEAN): Economic Development Prospects and the Role of the United States, Larry Niksch. 84-171 F
* Economic Changes in the Asian Pacific Rim: Policy Prospectus. Prepared by the Congressional Research Service., 86-923 S
* Thai-U.S. Economic Relations: Some Views of Thailand's Economic Elite, Raymond J. Ahearn. 89-60 F

Third World

* see Developing Countries

Thomas, Clarence

* Clarence Thomas: Bibliography-in-Brief, 1981-1991, George Walser, 91-692 L
* The Judicial Opinions of Supreme Court Nominee Judge Clarence Thomas, Kenneth R. Thomas, 91-562 A

Tibet

* Tibet: Disputed Facts About the Situation in Tibet, Kerry B. Dumbaugh. 88-40F

Timber Industry

* see Forests and Forestry-Timber

Tobacco Industry

* see Agriculture--Policies and Legislation

Tokyo Stock Exchange

* The Stock Market in Japan: An Overview and Analysis, Arturo Wiener and Edward Knight. 89-306 E

Torts

* see Law

Toshiba/Kongsberg Illegal Exports Affair

* see Foreign Trade--East-West

Toxic Substances

* see Chemicals, Pesticides, Solid Wastes

Toxic Substances Control Act

* Environmental Protection Legislation in the 101st Congress; Issue Brief, Environmental and Natural Resources Policy Division. Environmental Protection Section. IB89033
* The Toxic Substances Control Act: Implementation Issues; Archived Issue Brief, Jim Aidala. IB83190

Toxic Wastes

* see Solid Wastes, Superfund

Trade

* see Agriculture--Foreign Trade, Foreign Trade, International Finance

Trade Act

* see Foreign Trade--Trade Policy

Trade Deficit

* see Foreign Trade--Imports and Exports, Foreign Trade--Trade Policy

Trade and International Finance

* The "Baker Plan": A Remedy for the International Debt Crisis, IB86106
* Canada-U.S. Free Trade Agreement, IB87173
* CBI II: Expanding the Caribbean Basin Economic Recovery Act, IB89096
* Cooperative R&D: Federal Efforts to Promote Industrial Competitiveness, IB89056
* European Community: 1992 Plan for Economic Integration, IB89043
* Export Controls, IB87122
* Export-Import Bank Financial Issues, IB88013
* Foreign Direct Investment in the United States, IB87226
* Japan-U.S. Economic Relations: Cooperation or Confrontation?, IB87158
* Multilateral Development Banks: Issues for the 101st Congress, IB87218
* Registering Foreign Investment: Proposed Legislation, IB89092
* Sanctions Against South Africa: Impact on the United States, IB87198
* South Korea and Taiwan: Expanding Trade Ties with the United States, IB86151
* Steel Imports: Arguments For and Against Extension of the President's Steel Program, IB88109
* Trade, IB87003
* Trade Negotiations: The Uruguay Round, IB86147
* Trade, Technology, and Competitiveness, IB87053
* U.S.-Soviet Commercial Relations, IB89110

Trade Legislation

* see Foreign Trade--Trade Policy

Trade Negotiations

* see Foreign Trade--Trade Agreements and Negotiations

Transportation

* see Railroads, Aeronautics, Highways, Infrastructure, Marine Transportation
* The Administration's Proposed Hazardous Materials Transportation Safety Bill: Selected Comments and Analysis, Paul F. Rothberg., 87-693 SPR
* Airline Mergers and Labor Protective Provisions, IB87179
* Air Pollution: Are Current Standards for Trucks Sufficient?; Issue Brief, David E. Gushee. IB86140
* Alternative Fuels for Motor Vehicles: Some Environmental Issues, David E. Gushee. 88-624S
* Amtrak: Can It Save $100 Million a Year on Workers' Compensation and Employee Retirement?, IB88041
* AMTRAK: 1991 Legislative Issues; Archived Issue Brief, Stephen J. Thompson, IB88041
* Automobile Crash Protection, IB83085
* Aviation and the 101st Congress: Safety and Policy Issues, IB89045
* "Buy American" Regulations: Effects on Surface Transportation, John W. Fischer. 86-78E
* The Bridge "Crisis": An Economic Development Perspective, IB88085
* Drunk Driving, IB83157
* Changing Regulation of Surface Transportation: Development and Implications of Current Policies, Kenneth R. DeJarnette., 86-64 E
* Federal Aid to Domestic Transportation: A Brief History from the 1800s to the 1980s, Nancy Heiser. 88-574 E
* Hazardous Materials Transportation: Laws, Regulations, and Policy; Archived Issue Brief, Paul Rothberg. IB76026
* High Speed Ground Transportation; Issue Brief, Stephen J. Thompson, IB91049
* Highway Safety, Highspeed Trains, and Maglev: A Checklist of CRS Products, Karen L. Alderson, 92-6 L
* Highway Safety, Traffic Congestion, and Innovations for Improvement; Selected References, Karen L. Alderson, 91-503 L
* Interstate Shipment of Municipal solid Waste, James E. McCarthy, etc., 90413 ENR
* National Transportation Policy Alternatives: Environmental Issues, Leon M. Cole, 90-289 E
* National Transportation Policy Alternatives: Safety Issues; Proceedings of a CRS Congressional Seminar, J. Glen Moore, 90-467 E
* Rail Labor Disputes: Presidential and Congressional Intervention, 1980-1991, Linda Levine, 91-100 E
* Railroad Economic Issues in the 101st Congress, IB85017
* Railroad Retirement and Unemployment: Recent Issues; Archived Issue Brief, Dennis Snook, IB84068
* Railroads: Legislative Issues: Selected References, Karen L. Alderson, 91-505 L
* Shippers by Truck and Rail: Deregulation Effects and Prospects, Kenneth R. DeJarnette. 86-66E
* Speed Limits for Motor Vehicles, IB86153
* Surface Transport Carriers: Deregulation Effects and Prospects, Lenore Sek and Stephen J. Thompson. 86-65 E
* Surface Transportation Program Reauthorization: Issue Brief, Kenneth DeJarnette, IB90032
* Surface Transportation Reauthorization 1991: A Comparison of Current Law With the Bush Administration Bill (H.R. 1351), Economics Division. J.F. Hornbeck, 91-290 E
* Surface Transportation Reauthorization 1991: Major Provisions in Senate, House, and Administration Bills, J.F. Hornbeck, etc., 91-625 E
* Transport Manufacturing: A Review and Appraisal of Federal Assistance Policies, Gwenell L. Bass. 86-75 E
* Transport Policy Problems: Elements of a National Plan; Proceedings of a CRS Symposium, Leon M. Cole, 89-545 E
* Transportation: An Alphabetical Microthesaurus of Terms Selected from the Legislative Indexing Vocabulary, Shirley Loo., 88-524 L
* Transportation for Elderly and Handicapped People: Programs, Regulations, and Issues, Lenore M. Sek. 85-699 E
* Transportation and Public Policy: Longer and Heavier Trucks, Stephen J. Thompson, 91-469 E
* Transportation in the United States: Perspectives on Federal Policies, Congressional Research Service., 89-100 E
* Transportation Industry Drug Testing, Gail McCallion, 90-425 E
* Transportation Infrastructure: Issue Brief, Kenneth DeJarnette, IB91075
* Transportation Infrastructure Reauthorization: Highway and Mass Transit Issues; Info Pack, IP453T
* Transportation Infrastructure: Selected References, Karen L. Alderson, 91-502 L
* Transportation: National Plans and Policies: Proceedings of a CRS Congressional Seminar, 89-559 E
* Transportation Policy Issues: Selected References, Karen L. Alderson, 91-501 L
* Transportation Status and Outlook: A Checklist of CRS Products, Karen L. Alderson, 91-916 L
* Transportation Trust Funds: Economic and Policy Issues; Issue Brief, J.F. Hornbeck, IB90057
* Truck and Bus Safety, IB88022
* Trucking Economic Issues in the 101st Congress, IB76019
* Trucking Economic Regulation: Issue Brief, Stephen J. Thompson. IB76019
* Trucking and Public Policy: Longer and Heavier Trucks, Stephen J. Thompson, 91-15 E
* Trucking and Clean Air Act Amendments of 1990: Some Economic Implications, Stephen J. Thompson, 91-132 E
* Trucking Economic Issues in the 101st Congress: Archived Issue Brief, Stephen J. Thompson, IB76019
* Trucking Issues: Selected References, Karen L. Alderson, 91-504 L
* Understanding U.S. Transportation Program Finances, Stephen J. Thompson, 91-745 E
* U.S. Mexico Trade in the Automotive Industry, M. Angeles Villareal, etc., 91-533 E
* Wage and Employment Effects of Transport Deregulation: Pending Policy Issues, Richard S. Belous. 86-68 E

Transportation -- Railroads

* Amtrak: An Overview, Stephen J. Thompson. 88-687 E
* AMTRAK and the Future of Intercity Rail Passenger Service: Issue Brief, Stephen J. Thompson., IB88041
* Conrail: An Analysis of the Federal Assistance Policy and Proposed Sale,

Current Events and Homework

Kenneth R. DeJarnette., 86-51 E

* Federal Assistance to AMTRAK, Lenore Sek., 86-77 E
* High Speed Ground Transportation (HSGT): Prospects and Public Policy., Stephen J. Thompson., 89-221 E
* High Speed Passenger Trains: Foreign Experience and U.S. Prospects, John Fischer and Lenore Sek., 82-157 E
* Labor Protection in Railroad Industry: Issue Brief, Linda LeGrande. IB87204
* The Rail Captive Shipper Question, Kenneth R. DeJarnette., 88-649 E
* Railroad Economic Regulation: Issue Brief, Stephen J. Thompson and Rick Holland. IB85017
* Railroad Economic Trends, Stephen J. Thompson. 87-521 E
* Railroad Retirement and Employment: Recent Issues; Issue Brief, Dennis Snook, Richard Hobbie and Emmett Carson. IB84068
* Railroad Safety: Selected Options That Might Promote Safety; Archived Issue Brief, Paul F. Rothberg. IB87138
* Summary of the Staggers Rail Act of 1980, Stephen J.Thompson. 85-9 E

Treaties

* see Arms Control--Negotiations and Treaties, Congress, Foreign Relations, Foreign Trade--Trade Agreements and Negotiations, International Law

Treaty on the Non-Proliferation of Nuclear Weapons

* Nuclear Non-proliferation: Selected References, 1985-1988, B. F. Mangan., 88-682 L
* South Africa, Nuclear Weapons and the IAEA: Issue Brief, Warren H. Donnelly., IB87199

Tropical Forests

* see Forests and Forestry--Tropical

Trucking

* see Transportation

Trust Territory of the Pacific Islands

* Territorial Political Development: An Analysis of Puerto Rico, Northern Mariana Islands, Guam, Virgin Islands, and American Samoa, and the Micronesian Compacts of Free Association, Bette A. Taylor., 88-657 GOV

Tuition Tax Credits

* see Elementary and Secondary Education--Policies and Legislation

Tunisia

* Tunisia After Bourguiba: Issues for U.S. Policy, Ellen B. Laipson. 88-31 F

Turkey

* Current Issues With the "Base-Rights" Countries and Their Implications, Richard F. Grimmett. 88-726 F
* Greece and Turkey: The Seven-Ten Ratio in Military Aid, Ellen Laipson, 90-29 F
* Greece and Turkey: U.S. Foreign Assistance Facts; Issue Brief, Ellen B. Laipson. IB86065
* Greek-Turkish Relations: Beginning of a New Era?, Ellen Laipson., 88-724 F
* The Seven-Ten Ratio in Military Aid to Greece and Turkey: A Congressional Tradition, Ellen Laipson., 85-79 F
* United States Military Installations in Turkey, Richard Grimmett., 84-221 F

Turkmenistan

* see U.S.S.R.
* Turkmen Republic: Basic Facts, Jim Nichol, 91-767 F

UFOS

* see Astronautics

Ukraine

* Ukraine: Basic Facts, Carmen R. Garland, 91-789 F

Unemployment

* see Labor--Employment and Unemployment

Unemployment Compensation

see Workers' Compensation

UNESCO

* UNESCO-U.S. Withdrawal in Perspective: Archived Issue Brief, Lois McHugh. IB84086
* U.S. Withdrawal from the International Labor Organization: Successful Precedent for UNESCO?, Lois McHugh. 84-202 F

UNICEF

* United States Contributions to UNICEF, Lois McHugh. 88-154 F

Uniformed Services Former Spouses Protection Act

* Military Benefits for Former Spouses: Legislation and Policy Issues, David F. Burrelli. 89-187 F

UNITA

* Angola: Conflict Assessment and U.S. Policy Options, Raymond W. Copson., 86-189 F
* Angola: Issues for the United States; Archived Issue Brief, Raymond Copson and Robert Shepard. IB81063
* Angola/Namibia Peace Prospects: Background, Current Problems, and Chronology, Raymond W. Copson. 88-559 F

United Nations

* Answers to Nine Questions on the United Nations, Lois McHugh. 84-31 F
* Cyprus: Status of U.N. Negotiations; Issue Brief, Ellen B. Laipson, IB89140
* Iraq-Kuwait: The United Nations Response Before the War; Archived Issue Brief, Marjorie Ann Brown, IB90147
* Iraq-Kuwait: U.N. Security Council Resolutions: Texts and Votes, Marjorie Ann Browne, 91-395 F
* Namibia: United Nations Negotiations for Independence/U.S. Interests; Archived Issue Brief, Brenda Branaman. IB79073
* Palestine Liberation Organization Offices in the United States, Clyde R. Mark. 88-484 F
* U. N. Funding: Congressional Issues; Issue Brief, Vita Bite. IB86116
* United Nations Peacekeeping: Historical Overview and Current Issues, Marjorie Ann Browne, 90-96 F
* United Nations Peacekeeping: Issues for Congress; Archived Issue Brief, Marjorie Ann Browne, IB90103
* United Nations Reform: Issues for Congress, Marjorie Ann Browne. 88-593 F
* United Nations Role in the Iran-Iraq War: Issues and Options, Lois B. McHugh and Gary J. Pagliano., 88-463 F
* The United States and Southern Africa: A Review of United Nations Resolutions and United States Voting Patterns, 1946-October 1985, Frankie King., 86-21 F
* U.S. Withholding and Arrearages to the United Nations Regular Budget: Issues for Congress, Vita Bite, 91-515 F

United Nations Conference on the Law of the Sea

* The Law of the Sea Conference: A U.S. Perspective; Archived Issue Brief, Marjorie Browne. IB881153

United States Postal Service

* see Postal Service

United States Sentencing Commission

* Federal Sentencing Guidelines, Suzanne Cavanagh, 91-499 GOV
* United States Sentencing Commission: Preliminary Analysis, Charles Doyle. 89-308 A

Uranium

* see Nuclear Energy

Urban Affairs

* see also Infrastructure
* The ABCs of Public Venture Capital Investment, Jan E. Christopher. 88-757 E
* Border State "Colonias": Background and Options for Federal Assistance, Claudia Copeland and Mira Courpas. 87-906 ENR
* Community Development Block Grants: Summary of the Law and Its Implementation, Eugene Boyd, 90-420 GOV
* Community Development Issues in the 102nd Congress: Issue Brief, Eugene Boyd, IB91067
* Economic Development and Community Revitalization Programs: Sources of Information; Info Pack IP412E
* Economic Redevelopment in the Cities, Jan E. Christopher., 88-703 E

Be patient. If any phone number is incorrect, call (area code) 555-1212 and request the new listing.

Treaties / U.S. Food and Drug Administration

* Enterprise Zone and Alternative Area Redevelopment Legislation: Archived Issue Brief, Dennis M. Roth and Jan E. Christopher., IB85135
* Enterprise Zones: Bibliography-in-Brief, 1984-1989, Felix Chin, 90-39 L
* Federal Enterprise Zones: The Prospect for Economic Development; Issue Brief, J. F. Hombeck. IB89050
* Federal Tax Incentives for Enterprise Zones: Analysis of Economic Effects and Rationales, Dennis Zimmerman, 89-371 E
* Municipal Compliance With the Clean Water Act: Is the Glass Half Full or Half Empty?, Claudia Copeland. 88-421 ENR
* Transportation Infrastructure and Economic Development, J. F. Hombeck. 89-109 E

Urban and Regional Development

* see Infrastructure, Land Use, Regional Development, Urban Affairs
* Federal Enterprise Zones: The Prospect for Economic Development, IB89050

Urban Transit

* see Transportation

Uruguay Round of Multilateral Trade Negotiations

* see also Foreign Trade--Trade Agreements and Negotiations
* Agriculture in the GATT: After the Midterm Review; Issue Brief, Charles E. Hanrahan. IB89027
* Forum: Trade Negotiations: Broadening the World Trading System; Also Environmental Concerns for the Year 2000, Congressional Research Service review, v.11, May-June 1990, REV 5-90
* Negotiating Authority for the Uruguay Round of Multilateral Trade Negotiations, Jeanne Jagelski. 87-103 A
* Trade Negotiations: The Uruguay Round; Issue Brief, Lenore Sek., IB86147
* The Uruguay Round of Multilateral Trade Negotiations: Major Issues, Lenore M. Sek, 90-496 E
* Uruguay Round of Trade Negotiations and Its Impact on the U.S. Service Sector, Gwenell L. Bass, 91-233 E

U.S. Air Force

* see National Defense

U.S. Army

* see National Defense

U.S. Bureau of Land Management

* Public Lands and Resources: BLM Management Issues; Issue Brief, Adela Backiel, etc.,IB91068
* Wilderness Issues in the 102nd Congress: issue Brief, Betsy A. Cody, IB91029

U.S. Bureau of the Census

* see Population

U.S. Central Intelligence Agency

* see Intelligence Activities

U.S. Central Intelligence Agency, Office of Inspector General

* Office of Inspector General in the Central Intelligence Agency: Development and Proposals, Frederick M. Kaiser. 89-129 GOV

U.S. Commission on Executive, Legislative, and Judicial Salaries

* Commission on Executive, Legislative, and Judicial Salaries: An Historical Overview, Sharon S. Gressle. 89-38 GOV

U.S. Commodity Futures Trading Commission

* CFTC and SEC: A Comparison of Regulatory Authorities, Mark Jickling., 89-199 E
* CFTC Reauthorization and the Futures Trading "Sting": Issue Brief, Mark Jickling and Kevin F. Winch. IB89051
* CFTC Reauthorization: Issue Brief, Mark Jickling, etc., IB89051

U.S. Congress, House, Committee on Internal Security

* Abolition of the House Internal Security Committee, Paul Rundquist., 88-203 GOV

U.S. Congress. House. Committee on Un-American Activities

* Abolition of the House Internal Security Committee, Paul Rundquist., 88-203 GOV

U.S. Customs Service

* Overtime and Premium Pay for Customs Service Inspectors, Barbara L. Schwemle, 91-473 GOV
* The U.S. Customs Service: Recent Issues and Concerns, Frederick M. Kaiser, 91-733 GOV

U.S. Dept. of Agriculture

* see Agriculture
* Agriculture and the Budget: Issue Brief, Carl Ek, IB91124

U.S. Dept. of Defense

* see National Defense

U.S. Dept. of Education

* see Elementary and Secondary Education, Federal Aid to Education, Higher Education

U.S. Dept. of Energy

* see Fossil Fuels, Nuclear Energy, Power Resources

U.S. Dept. of Housing and Urban Development

* see Housing

U.S. Embassy (U.S.S.R.)

* U.S. Embassy in Moscow: Options for Congress; Issue Brief, David Hennes, IB90141

U.S. Environmental Protection Agency

* see also Environmental Law
* Apple Alarm: Public Concern About Pesticide Residues in Fruits and Vegetables, James V. Aidala. 89-166 ENR

U.S. Executive Office of the President

* The U.S. Presidency: Office and Powers, Harold C. Relyea, 91-699 GOV

U.S. Farmers Home Administration

* Farm Income and Debt: Bibliography-in-Brief, 1988, Rebecca Mazur. 88-480 L
* Farmers Home Administration: Farm Credit Policies and Issues; Issue Brief, Ralph Chite. IB87215
* FMHA Losses and the Federal Budget, Ralph Chite. 89-34 ENR
* Implementation of the Agricultural Credit Act of 1987: Issue Brief, Ralph Chite and Remy Jurenas. IB88089
* A Review of Farmers Home Administration's New Policy for Delinquent Farm Borrowers, Ralph Chite. 88-715 ENR

U.S. Federal Aviation Administration

* Aviation Safety and the 100th Congress: Bills, Hearings and a Summary of Major Action, J. Glen Moore. 89-18 SPR
* Aviation Safety, Capacity, and Service: Issue Brief, Glen Moore. IB87233
* Aviation Safety: Major Congressional Actions; Archived Issue Brief, J. Glen Moore. IB89018
* FAA Proposed Rule to Expand the Use of More C Altitude-Reporting Transponders in the United States, J. Glen Moore., 88-302 SPR

U.S. Federal Election Commission

* see Politics and Elections--Campaign Funds

U.S. Federal Emergency Management Agency

* see Disasters

U.S. Federal Housing Administration

* see Housing--Finance

U.S. Food and Drug Administration

* see also Drugs Food Medicine
* Breast Implants: Safety and FDA Regulation, Judith Johnson

Current Events and Homework

U.S Forest Service
* see Forests and Forestry

U.S. National Aeronautics and Space Administration
* see also Aeronautics, Astronautics
* Civilian Space Policy under the Reagan Administration: Potential Impact of the January 1988 Directive, Patricia E. Humphlett. 88-237 SPR
* Commercial High Speed Aircraft Opportunities and Issues, Richard E. Rowberg, Kathleen Hancock and Christopher T. Hill., 89-163 SPR
* Space Facilities: The ISF/CDSF Space Station Controversy; Issue Brief, Marcia S. Smith. IB88053
* Space Issues: Info Pack, IP371S
* Space Issues: Selected References, 1986-1988, B. F.Mangan. 88-565 L
* Soviet Space Commercialization: Selling the Mir Space Station, Marcia S. Smith, 91-702 SPR

U.S. National Mediation Board
* Employee Participation in National Mediation Board Determination of Single Carrier Status, Vincent E. Treacy. 88-433 A

U.S. National Park Service
* see Parks

U.S. Nuclear Regulatory Commission
* see Nuclear Energy

U.S. Occupational Safety and Health Administration
* Occupational Safety and Health Issues: Info Pack, IP456O

U.S. Office of Educational Research and Improvement
* Office of Educational Research and Improvement, FY 1992 Budget Request, Paul M. Irwin, 91-188 EPW

U.S. Office of National Drug Control Policy
* see Drug Abuse--Policies and Legislation

U.S. Office of Science and Technology Policy
* White House Office of Science and Technology Policy: An analysis, Genevieve J. Knezo, 89-689 SPR

U.S. Postal Service
* see Postal Service

U.S. Public Health Service
* The U.S. Public Health Service: Health Care Services and Resources, Edward R. Klebe, 91-279 EPW

U.S. Securities and Exchange Commission
* CFTC and SEC: A Comparison of Regulatory Authorities, Mark Jickling., 89-199 E

U.S. Selective Service System. National Service System
* see Military Personnel

U.S. Special Operations Forces
* United States and Soviet Special Operations, John M. Collins. 87-398 S

U.S. Strategic Petroleum Reserve
* see National Defense--Strategic Stockpiles

U.S. Supreme Court
* see Judiciary--Supreme Court

U.S. Veterans Administration
* see Veterans
* Traynor v. Turnage: The Exclusion of Alcoholics from Certain Veterans' Educational Benefits Does Not Violate Section 504 of the Rehabilitation Act of 1973, Nancy Lee Jones. 88-358 A

U.S. as a Debtor Nation
* see Foreign Investments, International Finance

U.S.-Canada Free Trade Agreement
* see Canada

U.S. Farmers Home Administration
* see Agriculture--Farm Income

U.S. Federal Aviation Administration
* see Aeronautics

U.S. Government
* see Executive Organization

U.S.-Mexico Free-Trade Agreement
* see Latin America-Foreign Trade

U.S. Navy
* see National Defense

U.S.-U.S.S.R. Summit Meetings
* see U.S.S.R.--Foreign Relations

User Charges
* see Public Finance

U.S.S.R
* see Economic Conditions, Foreign Assistance, Foreign Relations, Foreign Trade, National Defense, Politics and Government, Space Exploration
* American Public Opinion on Eastern Europe, the Soviet Union, and Defense Spending, Rosita M. Thomas, 90-444 GOV
* The Chernobyl Accident: Health and Agricultural Effects; Archived Issue Brief, Christopher H. Dodge. IB86122
* The Chernobyl Nuclear Accident: Causes, Initial Effects, and Congressional Response; Archived Issue Brief, Warren Donnelly, Carl Behrens, Mark Martel, Robert Civiak and Christopher Dodge. IB86077
* The Chernobyl Nuclear Accident: Long-Term Political, Economic, and Foreign Policy Implications; Archived Issue Brief, Jean Boone, Stuart Goldman, John Hardt, Francis Miko and Charlotte Preece. IB86083
* Eastern European and Soviet Science and Technology: Capabilities and Needs, William C. Boesman, 91-114 SPR
* Glasnost and Perestroika under Gorbachev: A Chronology July 1987-December 1988, Charlotte Kea. 89-138 F
* Soviet Civilian Research and Development Facilities and Funding, William C. Boesman, etc, 91-778 SPR
* Soviet Participation in International Financial Institutions; Issue Brief, Shirley A. Kan, etc., IB91133
* Soviet Space Commercialization: Selling the Mir Space Station, Marcia S. Smith, 91-702 SPR
* Space Activities of the United States, Soviet Union and Other Launching Countries/Organizations: 1957-1990, Marcia S. Smith 91-621 SPR
* Space Commercialization Activities in the Soviet Union, Marcia S. Smith, 90-372 SPR
* Statutory Restrictions on Trade and Financial Transactions With the Soviet Union, Jeanne J. Grimmett. 91-649 A

U.S.S.R. -- Economic Conditions
* Gorbachev's Reform: The Consumer Goods and Services Sector, F. Mike Miles. 87-763 F
* Oil Price Behavior: Implications for the Soviet Union; Report of the CRS Workshop, John P. Hardt and Jean F. Boone., 86-886 S
* The Soviet Banking Revolution: Its Realization and Implications for Congress, Walter W. Eubanks, 91-256 E
* Soviet Economic Conditions and Relations: Status and Prospects; Soviet Oil, 91-639 SPR
* Soviet Economic Conditions: Monetary and Structural Problems and Prospects, William H. Cooper, 91-630 E
* Soviet Membership in the International Monetary Fund: Is It Feasible Now?. Arlene Wilson, 91-686 E
* Soviet Oil Prospects, Joseph Riva. 81-91 SPR
* Soviet Reforms: Glasnost and Perestroika, Bibliography-in-Brief, 1985-1988, Valentin Leskovsek. 88-144 L
* Soviet "Restructuring" under Gorbachev: A Chronology, January 1985-June 1987, F. Mike Miles. 87-551 F
* Soviet Transition to a Market Economy: Archived Issue Brief, John P. Hardt IB90148

U.S.S.R. -- Foreign Assistance

* European Bank for Reconstruction and Development: An Institution of and for the New Europe, Karen Donfried, 91-611 F
* Soviet MEMBERSHIP IN THE International Monetary Fund, Patricia A. Wertman, 90-216 E
* U.S. Agricultural Assistance to the Soviet Union: Policy Issues; Issue Brief, Remy Jurenas, IB90139
* U.S. and International Assistance to the Former Soviet Union: Issue Brief, Vita Bite, IB91050
* Western Aid Report on the Soviet Economy, John P. Hardt, 91-16 RCO

U.S.S.R. -- Foreign Relations

* Afghanistan Peace Talks: An Annotated Chronology and Analysis of the United Nations-Sponsored Negotiations, Richard P. Cronin., 88-149 F
* Afghanistan: Status, U.S. Role, and Implications of a Soviet Withdrawal; Archived Issue Brief, Richard P. Cronin, etc., IB88049
* Andropov and Reagan as Negotiators: Contexts and Styles in Contrast, Joseph Whelan. 83-141 S
* Continuity and Change in Soviet Diplomacy and Negotiations under Gorbachev, Joseph G. Whelan. 89-39 F
* Embassy Construction Controversies: Moscow and Washington; Issue Brief, Joel M. Woldman. IB87232
* Emigration and Human Rights in the U.S.S.R.: Is There a New Approach? Archived Issue Brief, John P. Hardt. IB88019
* Emigration: Soviet Compliance With the Helsinki Accords; Archived Issue Brief, John Hardt and Jean Boone. IB82080
* The Gorbachev Speech to the United Nations, New York, Dec. 7, 1988, Foreign Affairs and National Defense Division. 88-776 F
* Gorbachev's Worldview on the Eve of the Washington II Summit, May 1990, Joseph G. Whelan, 91-439 RCO
* Implications for U.S. Diplomacy in the U.S.-Soviet Future: Audio Brief, Joseph Whelan. AB50173
* The Moscow Summit at First Glance: Audio Brief, Stuart Goldman, John Hardt, Francis Miko and Steve Hildreth., AB50168
* Sino-Soviet Relations: Recent Improvements and Implications for the United States: Issue Brief, Robert G. Sutter., IB86138
* Soviet-American Relations in 1977: A Chronological Summary and Brief Analysis, William Cooper., 79-60 S
* Soviet and American Negotiating Characteristics, Joseph Whelan. 89-191 S
* Soviet Diplomacy and Negotiating Behavior, 1979-1988: Implications for U.S. Diplomacy in the Soviet-American Future, Joseph G. Whelan. 88-674F
* The Soviet Emigration and Travel Bill: Assessments and Implications for U.S. Interests, Jim Nichol, 91-518 F
* Soviet Jewish Emigration: Issue Brief, Clyde R. Mark, IB90083
* Soviet Foreign Policy under Gorbachev: Determinants, Developments, Prospects, and Implications, Francis T. Miko. 87-39 F
* Soviet Policy in Nordic Europe: New Focus on the Forgotten Flank?, Francis Miko. 85-33F
* The Soviet Union and the United Nations: Congressional Issues; Archived Issue Brief, Vita Bite. IB88069
* Soviet-U.S. Relations: A Briefing Book, Congressional Research Service. 91-270 F
* Soviet-U.S. Relations: The Lessons of Past Summit Meetings, Francis T. Miko and Linda Krueger. .85-1037 F
* Soviet-U.S. Summit Meetings Since the 1950s: Selected References, Sherry B. Shapiro., 87-912 L
* Thirty Years of U.S.-Soviet Summit Meetings; a Capsule Summary, Stuart Goldman. 85-1055 F
* The United States, Pakistan and the Soviet Threat to Southern Asia: Options for Congress, Richard Cronin., 85-152 F
* U.S. Embassy in Moscow: Options for Congress; Issue Brief, David Hennes, IB90141
* U.S.-Soviet Maritime Boundary Agreement, Stuart D. Goldman, 91-443 F
* U.S.-Soviet Relations: Audio Brief, John Hardt, Stuart Goldman and Francis Miko., AB50178
* U.S.-Soviet Relations in a Period of Summitry: Archived Issue Brief, Stuart Goldman. IB83066
* U.S.-Soviet Relations in the Gorbachev Era: Selected References, Robert S. Kirk. 89-51L
* U.S.-Soviet Relations: Info Pack, IP233U
* U.S.-Soviet Relations: Issue Brief, Stuart D. Goldman IB89008
* U.S.-Soviet Relations: Selected References, 1986-1988, Elizabeth S. Lane. 88-155 L

U.S.S.R. -- Foreign Trade

* A Congressional Guide for Economic Negotiations With the Soviet Union, John P. Hardt and Jean F. Boone. 88-19 S
* Commercial Relations With the Soviet Union: Prospects for a Common United States-Japanese Policy, John P. Hardt, 91-196 RCO
* East-West Trade and the congress; Proceedings of a CRS Seminar, Glennon J. Harrison, 90-529 E
* European Regional Market: A Forgotten Key to Success of European Economies in Transition?, John P. Hardt, 91-113 RCO
* Most-Favored-Nation Status for China and the Soviet Union: Procedure for Extending or Denying the Status; Archived issue Brief, Vladimir N. Prefelj, IB90107
* Oil Price Behavior: Implications for the Soviet Union; Report of the CRS Workshop, John P. Hardt and Jean F. Boone., 86-886 S
* An Overview of Soviet Oil and Gas in the World Arena, John P. Hardt and Jean F. Boone. 88-157 S
* Potential Economic Effects of Granting Most-Favored-Nation Treatment to the Soviet Union, George D. Holliday., 85-886 E
* Soviet Energy: An Engine or a Brake on Commercial Relations in the 1990s? John P. Hardt, 91-211 RCO
* Soviet Trade and Economic Relations With Western Europe, Glennon J. Harrison, etc., 91-631 E
* Soviet-U.S. Trade Relations: The Bilateral Trade Agreement, William H. Cooper, 91-662
* Statutory Restrictions on Trade and Financial Transactions With the Soviet Union, Jeanne J. Grimmett, 91-649 A
* U.S. Soviet Commercial Relations: Archived Issue Brief, John P. Hardt, etc., IB89110
* U.S.-Soviet Commercial Relations in the Age of Perestroika: Selected References, 1985-1990, a CRS Trade Team Product, by Robert S. Kirk, 90-240 L
* Soviet Agriculture: U.S.-U.S.S.R. Grain Sales and Prospects for Expanded Agricultural Trade: Archived Issue Brief, John Hardt. IB86019
* U.S.-U.S.S.R. Commercial Relations: Issues in Issues-West Trade: Archived Issue Brief, John Hardt and Jean Boone.

U.S.S.R. -- National Defense

* Arms Control: Negotiations to Limit Defense and Space Weapons; Issue Brief, Steven Hildreth. IB86073
* Arms Control: Negotiations to Reduce INF Weapons; Archived Issue Brief, Paul Gallis. IB86054
* Arms Control: Overview of the Geneva Talks; Archived Issue Brief, Steven Hildreth. IB85157
* Arms Control: Ratification of the INF Treaty; Archived Issue Brief, Paul E. Gallis. IB88003
* Estimates of Soviet Defense Expenditures: Methodological Issues and Policy Implications, Robert Foelber and Stephen Donahue. 85-131 F
* The INF Treaty and Its Political-Military Implications for Western Europe, Hugh DeSantis. 88-57 F
* INF Treaty: Environmental Issues; Archived Issue Brief, Mary E. Tiemann. IB88023
* Intermediate-Range Nuclear Forces Treaty: Timetable of Elimination and Verification Provisions and Glossary of Key Terms, Joseph M. Freeman., 88-153 F
* Military Balance: Info Pack IP069M
* Military Strategy: Bibliography-in-Brief, 1983-1986, Valentin Leskovsek. 87-40 L
* Monitoring Nuclear Test Bans, David W. Cheney. 86-155 SPR
* Nuclear Risk Reduction Centers: Archived Issue Brief, Steven A. Hildreth. IB86142
* Nuclear Weapons in the Soviet Union: Issues and Prospects; Issue Brief, Amy F. Woolf, IB91144
* The President's Report on Soviet Noncompliance With Arms Control Agreements: A Discussion of the Charges, Jeanette Voas., 84-160 F
* The Resumption of U.S.-Soviet Nuclear Arms Control Talks: The Soviet Point of View, Jeanette Voas. 85-605 S
* SALT II Treaty: U.S. and Soviet Interim Observance of Its Terms: Archived Issue Brief, Charles Gellner. IB80018
* Soviet Armed Forces Statistical Trends, 1985-1990 (as of January 1, 1991), John M. Collins, etc., 91-636 RCO
* Soviet Armed Forces Status and Prospects in September 1991, John M. Collins, 91-653 RCO
* Soviet Compliance Behavior: The Record of the SALT I and II Agreements on Offensive Arms, Charles Gellner. 86-541 S
* Soviet SALT II Compliance Behavior: The SS-25 and Encryption of Telemetry, Jeanette Voas. 86-734 S
* Soviet Tank Improvements vs. U.S. Army Antitank Weapons: Addressing the Imbalance, Floyd Mike Miles. 89-71 F
* Statements by President Reagan Relating to the INF Treaty, June 1,

Current Events and Homework

1987-December 31, 1987, Teri Lehto., 88-60 S
* Strategic Nuclear Forces: Potential U.S./Soviet Trends With or Without SALT: 1985-2000, Jonathan Medalia, Al Tinajero and Paul Zinsmeister. 86-135 F
* United States/Soviet Military Balance: Archived Issue Brief, John Collins and Thomas Glakas., IB78029
* U.S., Soviet, and Western European Naval Forces in the Persian Gulf Region, Robert J. Ciarrocchi. 87-956 F
* U.S.-Soviet Military Balance. Book I. Organization, Budgets, Manpower, Technology, John Collins and Elizabeth Severns., 80-161 S
* U.S.-Soviet Military Balance. Book II. Strategic Nuclear Trends, John Collins and Elizabeth Severns. 80-162 S
* U.S.-Soviet Military Balance. Book III. General Purpose Force Trends, John Collins and Elizabeth Severns. 80-163 S
* U.S.-Soviet Military Balance. Book IV. Airlift and Sealift, John Collins and Elizabeth Severns. 80-164 S
* U.S.-Soviet Military Balance. Book VI. Far East, Middle East Assessments, John Collins and Elizabeth Severns. 80-166 S
* U.S./Soviet Military Balance: Statistical Trends, 1970-1979 (End of Year Figures), John M. Collins and Bernard C. Victory., 87-839 S
* US-Soviet Military Balance, 1980-1985, John Collins. 85-89 S
* Verification and Compliance: Soviet Compliance With Arms Control Agreements; Issue Brief, Stuart Goldman. IB84131
* Verifying Arms Control Agreements: The Soviet View, Jeanette M. Voas, Stuart D. Goldman and Paul E. Gallis. 87-316 F

U.S.S.R. -- Politics and Government

* Chronology of Key Soviet Events in the Period Before the coup: March 1990-July 1991, Ana Goshko, 91-732 F
* Economic Perestroika: Gorbachev at the London Economic Summit, July 17, 1991; Audio Brief, Joseph Whalen AB50227
* The Former Soviet Union: Prospects and Implications; Viedoprogram, John Hardt, etc, LTR91-1495
* Gorbachev Reform Program After the 1988 Party Conference: Summary of a Roundtable Workshop, Francis T. Miko., 89-130 F
* Gorbachev's Reform Strategy: Comparisons With the Hungarian and Chinese Experience, Francis T. Miko and Kerry Dumbaugh., 87-813 F
* Gorbachev's World View: May 1990, Audio Brief, Joseph Whelan, AB50223
* Gorbachev's World View Under Siege: Perestroika at Risk; Audio Brief, Joseph Whelan, AB50226
* Gorbachev's World View under Siege: Perestroika at Risk; June 1990-June 1991, Joseph G. Whelan, 91-632 RCO
* The New Soviet Legislature, Stuart D. Goldman, 90-478 F
* Post Soviet Transition: Issue Brief, Stuart D. Goldman, IB91135
* Soviet Coup Attempt: Background and Implications; Archived Issue Brief, Raymond W. Copson, IB91106
* The Soviet Emigration and Travel Bill: Assessments and Implications for U.S. Interests, Jim Nichol, 91-518 F
* Soviet Federal Crisis, Steve J. Woehrel, 91-600 F
* Soviet Foreign Policy under Gorbachev: Determinants, Developments, Prospects, and Implications, Francis T. Miko. 87-39 F
* Soviet Nationalities Issues: Bibliography-in-Brief, 1980-1988, Sherry B. Shapiro., 88-746 L
* Soviet Nationalities Issues: Selected References, Sherry B. Shapiro, 91-545 L
* Soviet Nationalities Problems, Stuart D. Goldman. 88-668 F
* Soviet Perestroika: Political and Economic Change under Gorbachev; Issue Brief, Stuart D. Goldman., IB89038
* Soviet Referendum Implications for U.S. Interests, Steven J. Woehrel, 91-275 F
* Soviet Reforms: Glasnost and Perestroika, Bibliography-in-Brief, 1985-1988, Valentin Leskovsek. 88-144 L
* Soviet Reforms: Glasnost and Perestroika, Selected References, 1988-1990, Valentin Leskovsek, 90-264 L
* Soviet "Restructuring" under Gorbachev:, A Chronology, January 1985-June 1987, F. Mike Miles, 87-551 F
* Soviet Union: A Chronology of Events Surrounding the coup Attempt August 1-September 15, 1991, Sergiu Verona, 91-705 F
* Soviet Union: An Assessment of Recent Republic and Local Elections, Steven J. Woehrel, 90-355 F
* The Soviet Union in Crisis: Before the Coup; Archived Issue Brief, Stuart D. Goldman, IB91040
* Soviet Union in the 1990s: Selected References, 1989-1991, Sherry B. Shapiro, 91-354 L
* U.S.S.R. Supreme Soviet: Major Legislation, Julie Kim, 90-459 F
* The 28th Soviet Communist Party Congress: Outcomes and Implications, Jim Nichol, 90-365 F

U.S.S.R. -- Republics

* Armenia: Basic Facts, Carol Migdalovitz, 91-747 F
* Azerbaijan: Basic Facts, Keith Berner, 91-808 F
* Belarus Republic (Formerly Belorussia): Basic Facts, Keith Berner, 91-780 F
* Georgian Republic: Basic Facts, Daniel R. Cain, 91-790 F
* Kazakh Republic: Basic Facts, Jim Nichol, 91-743 F
* Kirghiz Republic: Basic Facts, Jim Nichol, 91-760 F
* Moldova Republic: Basic Facts, Sergiu Verona, 91-779 F
* Oil Production and Reserves in the Soviet Republics, Joseph P. Riva, 91-674 SPR
* Russian Republic: Basic Facts, Jim Nichol, 910710 F
* Soviet Union in Transition: Basic Maps, Richard F. Grimmett, 91-677 F
* Tajikistan: Basic Facts, Liam Wasley, 91-806 F
* Turkmen Republic: Basic Facts, Jim Nichol, 91-767 F
* Ukraine: Basic Facts, Carmen R. Garland, 91-789 F
* Uzbek Republic: Basic Facts, Jim Nichol, 91-761 F

U.S.S.R. -- Space Exploration

* New Soviet Space Launch Vehicles, Marcia S. Smith. 87-462 SPR
* Soviet Space Commercialization Activities, Marcia S. Smith. .88-473 SPR

Uzbekistan

* see U.S.S.R.
* Uzbek Republic: Basic Facts, Jim Nichol, 91-761 F

Value-Added Tax

* see Taxation--Consumption Taxes

Vatican City

* The Holy See and Recognition of Israel, Charles H. Whittier. 86-833 GOV

Venezuela

* Venezuelan Petroleum: A Source of Increasing U.S. Imports?, Joseph P. Riva, 90-70 SPR

Venture Capital

* see Corporations, Small Business

Veterans

* Agent Orange: Veterans' Complaints and Studies of Health Effects; Archived Issue Brief, Sam Merrill and Michael Simpson. IB83043
* Attorneys' Fees for the Representation of Veterans Benefits Claimants, James Hall. 88-225 A
* Benefits for Former Military Spouses: Info Pack IP313B
* Dioxin and Agent Orange Health Effects: An Update, Samuel Merrill, etc., 91-195 SPR
* The New GI Bill: Recruiting and Retention, David F. Burrelli. 87-652 F
* Speech Material: Veterans Day; Info Pack. IP378V
* State Veterans' Affairs Administrators as Executive Officers in the Various States, David Turner. 87-872 A
* Statutory Preclusion of Veterans' Claims from Judicial Review under 38 U.S.C. 21 1, Charles V. Dale. 88-373 A
* Tort Liability of the Federal Government and Its Contractors to Veterans Exposed to Atomic Radiation, Henry Cohen. 86-979 A
* Traynor v. Turnage: The Exclusion of Alcoholics from Certain Veterans' Educational Benefits Does Not Violate Section 504 of the Rehabilitation Act of 1973, Nancy Lee Jones., 88-358 A
* Use of Veterans' Disability Benefits for Child Support: Rose v. Rose, Rita Ann Reimer. 87-376 A
* Veterans Administration Guaranteed Housing Loans: Raising the Funding Fee; Archived Issue Brief, Ellington Foote. IB87146
* Veterans Administration Guaranteed Housing Loans: The Rising Cost of VA Mortgages, B. Ellington Foote. 87-453 E
* Veterans' Benefits for Filipino Veterans, Mary Smith, 91-788 EPW
* Veterans' Compensation for Service-Connected Disability: Program Description, Relevant Data, and Current Issues, Mary F. Smith. 87-628 EPW
* Veterans' Educational Assistance Programs, Mary F. Smith, 90-69 EPW
* The Veterans' Pension Program, Barbara McClure. 84-122 EPW
* Veterans' Program: Major Legislation and Issues in the 102nd Congress; Issue Brief, Anne Stewart, etc., IB91053
* Veteran's Program: The FY1990 Budget and Major Legislation; Archived Issue Brief, Mary F. Smith and Anne C. Stewart. IB89059
* Veterans' Programs: FY89 Budget; Archived Issue Brief, Anne C. Stewart., IB88047
* Veterans' Programs: Major Legislation and Current Issues; Archived Issue

Brief, Mary F. Smith, etc., IB90134
* Veterans' Reemployment Rights: Brief Summary, Robert B. Burdette, 91-244 A

Veterans' Benefits and Services

* Veterans' Programs:, The FY 1990 Budget, IB89059

Veto

* see Presidents (U.S.)--Veto

Vice Presidents

* see Presidents (U.S.)

Vietnam

* Communist Holdout States: China, Cuba, Vietnam, and North Korea; Issue Brief, K. Larry Storrs, IB91128
* The Missing-In-Action (MIAs) and Vietnam-U.S. Relations: Issues for the United States, Robert Sutter. 87-655 F
* Prisoners of War/Missing in Action in SE Asia: Info Pack IP127P
* United States Policy Toward Vietnam: A Summary Review of Its History, Larry Niksch, Ellen Collier and M. T. Haggard., 85-16 F
* Vietnam in Transition: Implications for U.S. Policy, Robert G. Sutter., 89-177 F
* Vietnam: Procedural and Jurisdictional Questions REgarding Possible Normalization of U.S. Diplomatic and Economic Relations, Alan K. Yu, etc., 89-631

Violence

* see Terrorism

Virgin Islands

* Territorial Political Development: An Analysis of Puerto Rico, Northern Mariana Islands, Guam, Virgin Islands, and American Samoa, and the Micronesian Compacts of Free Association, Bette A. Taylor., 88-657 GOV
* The Virgin Islands of the United States: A Descriptive and Historical Profile, Bette A. Taylor. 88-429 GOV

Vocational Education

* see Federal Aid to Education--Adult and Vocational, Occupational Training--Adult and Vocational Education

Volunteers and Volunteer Program

* see Public Welfare

Volunteer Workers

* see Public Welfare

Voting

* see Politics and Elections--Practical Politics

Voting Rights Act

* Voting Rights Act: A Checklist of CRS Products, George Walser, 92-15 L
* The Voting Rights Act of 1965 as Amended., Paul Downing. 84-203 GOV
* The Voting Rights Act of 1965: A Legal Overview, L. Paige Whitaker, 91-736 A

Walsh-Healey Public Contracts Act

* see Procurement

War and Peace

* see Foreign Relations, National Defense, Terrorism, War Powers Resolution

War Powers Resolution

* Congress and Foreign Policymaking, Ellen Collier 90-627 F
* Grenada: Issues Concerning the Use of U.S. Forces; Archived Issue Brief, Janice Hanover. IB83170
* Honduras: U.S. Military Activities; Issue Brief, James Wootten. IB84134
* Persian Gulf and the War Powers Debate: Issue Summary and Review of Events; Archived Issue Brief, Clyde R.Mark. IB87207
* Sectional Analysis of the "War Powers Resolution" (WPR) as It Would Be Amended, the "War Powers Resolution Amendments of 1988" (S.J. Res. 323, 100th Congress, 2nd Sess.), Raymond J. Celada. 88-441 A
* The War Powers Resolution: Fifteen Years of Experience, Ellen C. Collier. 88-529F

* War Powers Resolution: Info Pack, IP131W
* War Powers Resolution: Presidential Compliance; Issue Brief, Ellen Collier. IB81050
* War Powers Resolution: The Controversial Act's Search for a Successful Litigation Posture, Raymond J. Celada. 88-64 A
* The War Powers Resolution (WPR): Some Implications of S.J. Res. 323, "War Powers Resolution Amendments of 1988", Raymond J. Celada. 88-464 A
* War Powers: Selected References, Sherry B. Shapiro. 89-305 L

Washington, DC

* see District of Columbia

Washington, George

* Speech Material: Abraham Lincoln's and George Washington's Birthdays; Info Pack, IP373A

Waste Management

* see Solid Wastes

Water Pollution

* see Groundwater, Oil Spills, Clean Water Act, Environmental Protection
* Agricultural Nonpoint Pollution Policy: A Federal Perspective, Claudia Copeland and Jeffrey A. Zinn. 86-191 ENR
* Agriculture and the Environment: Issue Brief, Geoffrey Becker and Jeffrey A. Zinn. IB89086
* Chronology: EPA Regulation of Stormwater Discharge, Claudia Copeland. 88-495 ENR
* Clean Water Act Activities: Post-Public Law 100-4, Claudia Copeland. 88-768 ENR
* Clean Water Act Reauthorization: Issue Brief, Claudia Copeland, IB91052
* Clean Water: EPA Municipal Construction Grants Program; Archived Issue Brief, Claudia Copeland. IB83013
* Clean Water: Section 404 Dredge and Fill Permit Program; Archived Issue Brief, Claudia Copeland. IB83011
* Forum Water Quality and Resources, CRS Review, v. 12, Dec. 1991, REV 12-91
* Infectious Waste and Beach Closings, Martin R. Lee. 88-596 ENR
* International Environment: Overview of Major Issues; Issue Brief, Mary Tiemann and Susan R. Fletcher. IB89057
* Marine Plastics Pollution Control Legislation, Martin R. Lee. 88-377 ENR
* Municipal Compliance With the Clean Water Act: Is the Glass Half Full or Half Empty?, Claudia Copeland. 88-421 ENR
* The Nation's Water Supply: An Overview of Conditions and Prospects., 86-893 ENR
* Nonpoint Source Provisions of the Clean Water Act Amendments of 1987, John Blodgett. 87-154 ENR
* Preventing Beach Closings: Legislative Options; Issue Brief, Martin R. Lee., IB88102
* Reauthorization of the Clean Water Act: A Checklist of CRS Products, Lisa B. Dove, 91-913 L
* Rural Areas and Clean Water: Impacts of the Water Quality Act of 1987, Claudia Copeland. 87-257 ENR
* Using Incentives for Environmental Protection: An Overview, John L. More, etc., 89-360 ENR
* Waste from Fish Harvesting and Processing: Growing Environmental Concerns, Eugene H. Buck, 90-575 ENR
* Waste in the Marine Environment: Info Pack, IP407W
* Waste in the Marine Environment: Selected References, Ted L. Burch. 89-263 L
* Waste Management: Issue Brief, James E. McCarthy.IB89007
* Wastewater Treatment Programs; Impact of Gramm-Rudman-Hollings Act and Prospects for Federal Funding (With Appendix); Archived Issue Brief, Claudia Copeland. IB86018
* Water and Water Resources Development: An Alphabetical Microthesaurus of Terms Selected from the Legislative Indexing Vocabulary, Shirley Loo. 90-544 L
* Water Quality: Addressing the Nonpoint Pollution Problem; Archived Mini Brief, Claudia Copeland. MB83241
* Water Quality: Implementing the Clean Water Act; Archived Issue Brief, Claudia Copeland., IB89102
* Water Quality: 1987 Clean Water Act Amendments: Archived Issue Brief, Claudia Copeland. IB87049
* Water Resources: Quality and Quantity; Info Pack, IP369W
* Zebra Mussel Legislation in the 101st Congress, Eugene H. Buck, 90-641 ENR

Current Events and Homework

Water Pollution -- Groundwater

* Agricultural Effects on Groundwater Quality, Donald V. Feliciano. 86-891 ENR
* Agricultural Nonpoint Pollution Policy: A Federal Perspective, Claudia Copeland, etc.,86-191 ENR
* Agricultural Pollution of Groundwater: Bibliography-in-Brief, 1985-1987, Adrienne C. Grenfell., 88-29 L
* Groundwater Contamination and Protection: Archived Issue Brief, Mary E. Tiemann. IB86079
* Groundwater Issues and the U.S. Department of Agriculture: An Institutional Perspective, Jeffrey A. Zinn. 88-322 ENR
* Groundwater Quality: Current Federal Programs and Recent Congressional Activities, Jeffrey Zinn and Mary Tiemann. 89-195 ENR
* Groundwater Quality Protection: Issues in the 101st Congress; Archived Issue Brief, Mary Tiemann. IB89081
* Groundwater: What It Is, and How It Is Being Protected., Donald Feliciano. 85-191 ENR
* The Nation's Water Supply: An Overview of Conditions and Prospects, 86-893 ENR
* Nonpoint Source Provisions of the Clean Water Act Amendments of 1987, John Blodgett, 87-154 ENR
* Proposed Senate Amendments to FIFRA, James Aidala. 88-471 ENR
* Safe Drinking Water Act: Implementing the 1986 Amendments; Issue Brief, Mary E. Tiemann, IB91041
* Status of Ogallala Aquifer Research and Development under Water Resources Development Act (Section 1 l21), H. Steve Hughes., 87-506 ENR
* Underground Storage Tanks: New Federal Requirements; Archived Issue Brief; Mary E. Tiemann, IB90054

Water Pollution -- Oil Spills

* After the Exxon Valdez Spill: Oil Pollution Liability and Compensation Legislation, Martin R. Lee. 89-266 ENR
* The Alaskan Oil Spill and Gasoline Prices, Lawrence C. Kumins. 89-250 ENR
* Double-Bottom/Double-Hull Tankers: Pro and Con, James E. Mielke, 90-152 SPR
* The Exxon Valdez Oil Spill: Issue Brief, Martin R. Lee and Robert Bamberger. IB89075
* Federal Statutes and Regulations Relating to Oil Spills: A Brief Summary, George A. Costello. 86-958 A
* Oil in the Ocean: The Short and Long-Term Impacts of a Spill, James E. Mielke, 90-356 SPR
* Oil Pollution Liability and Compensation, Martin R. Lee. 88-611 ENR
* Oil Pollution Liability and Compensation Legislation After the Exxon Valdez Oil Spill: Issue Brief, Martin R. Lee., IB89082
* Oil Spill Response Technologies, James E. Mielke, 90-146 SPR
* Oil Spills: Info Pack, IP426O
* Oil Spills: Selected References, Ted L. Burch, 90-138 L
* A Review of Oil Pollution Prevention Regulations After the Monongahela River Spill, Martin P.. Lee. 88-448 ENR

Water Resources

* see Disasters, Infrastructure, Water Pollution--Groundwater
* Agriculture and the Environment: Issue Brief, Geoffrey Becker and Jeffrey A. Zinn. IB89086
* Brief History of the U.S. Water Resources Council [1965-1984], H. Steve Hughes. 87-643 ENR
* The California Drought: Effects on Agriculture and Related Resources, Betsy A. Cody, etc., 91-208 ENR
* Canadian Electricity: The U.S. Market and the Free Trade Agreement, Amy Abel. 88-427 ENR
* Desalination: Environmental Considerations, James E. Mielke, 91-426 SPR
* Desalination Research and Development; Issue Brief, James E. Mielke, IB91048
* Emergency Drought Relief: A Comparison of the House and Senate Versions of H.R. 355, Betsy A. Cody, 91-793 ENR
* The Evolving National Flood Insurance Program, Malcolm M. Simmons. 88-641 ENR
* Express Language on Federal Water Rights in the 100th Congress, Pamela Baldwin. 89-91 A
* Federal Hydropower: Repaying the Debt; Archived Issue Brief, John Moore. IB85125
* Federal Hydropower: The Administration's Proposal to Sell Government Assets; Archived Issue Brief, John Moore. IB86057
* The Federal Water Resources Research Effort: Background and Status under the Reagan Administration, Malcolm Simmons. 84-600 ENR
* Fluoride in Drinking Water: Should the National Standard Be Made Less Stringent?; Archived Issue Brief, Donald Feliciano., IB86014
* Forum: Water Quality and Resources, CRS review, v. 12, REV 12-91
* Groundwater Quality: Current Federal Programs and Recent Congressional Activities, Jeffrey Zinn and Mary Tiemann., 89-195 ENR
* Groundwater Quality Protection: Issues in the 101st Congress; Issue Brief, Mary Tiemann. IB89081
* Legal Issues Related to Diversion of Water from Lake Michigan to the Mississippi River, Pamela Baldwin. 88-585 A
* Licensing and Special Use Permit Requirements for Hydroelectric Dam Projects under the Federal Power Act and the Federal Land Policy and Management Act, Robin Jeweler., 88-459 A
* Major Federal Water Resources Agencies: History and Functions of the Army Corps of Engineers and the Bureau of Reclamation, Steve Hughes. 86-770 ENR
* Managing Coastal Development Through the Coastal Zone Management and Flood Insurance Programs: Experience to Date and the Views from Selected States, Gary Kamimura, Jeffrey A. Zinn and Malcolm Simmons. 88-354 ENR
* The Nation's Water Supply: An Overview of Conditions and Prospects., 86-893 ENR
* Persian Gulf War: Water Resources and the War; Selected References, Sherry Shapiro, 91-169 L
* Repayment of Corps of Engineers Construction Costs, Malcolm M. Simmons. 87-262 ENR
* Safe Drinking Water Act: Implementing the 1986 Amendments; Issue Brief, Mary E. Tiemann, IB91041
* Safe Drinking Water: Archived Issue Brief, Mary E. Tiemann. IB86080
* Status of Ogallala Aquifer Research and Development under Water Resources Development Act (Section 1 121), H. Steve Hughes. 87-506 ENR
* A Survey of Bottled Water Regulations in Selected Countries, Law Library of Congress, European Law Division, LL90=61
* Water and Water Resources Development: An Alphabetical Microthesaurus of Terms Selected from the Legislative Indexing Vocabulary, Shirley Loo., 90-544 L
* Water Conservation: Options for the Residential Sector, Claudia Copeland, 89-548 ENR
* Water Resources Development Act: Implementing the Omnibus Project Reforms; Issue Brief, Steve Hughes. 1B87088
* Water Resources: Quality and Quantity; Info Pack, IP369W
* Water Rights and the Wild and Scenic Rivers Act, Pamela Baldwin, 90-196 A
* Western Irrigation: Background Data on Current Issues, Jeffrey Zinn and Elizabeth Turner. 86-696 ENR
* Western Water Supplies: Issues in the 102nd Congress; Issue Brief, Betsy A. Cody, IB91102
* Wetlands: Selected References, 1986-1989, Ted Burch, 89-453 L
* Wilderness Areas and Federal Water Rights, Pamela Baldwin. 89-11 A

Waterways

* see Infrastructure
* Navigable Waters: States Required to Keep Them "Forever Free", Marie B. Morris, 91-726 A

Weapons

* see Weapons Systems

Weapons Facts

* see Weapons Systems-- Weapons Facts

Weapons Systems

* see also Chemical Warfare, Non-Nuclear Weapons, Nuclear Weapons, Space Weapons, Weapons Facts, Disasters, National Defense, National Defense and Security
* Binary Chemical Weapons Production: Issues for Congress; Archived Issue Brief, Steven Bowman. IB85212
* Chemical Weapons: A Summary of Proliferation and Arms Control Activities; issue Brief, Steven R. Bowman, IB89042
* Chemical Weapons Proliferation: Issues for Congress; Issue Brief, Steven R. Bowman, IB90084
* Funding for Selected Weapons: Authorization and Appropriation: Archived Issue Brief, Robert E. Foelber. IB88058
* Missile Proliferation: Survey of Emerging Missile Forces, Foreign Affairs and National Defense Division., 88-642 F
* Review of U.S. Research and Development Programs in Ballistic Missile Defense, John D. Moteff. 89-150 SPR

Water Pollution / Weapons Systems

* Strategic Policy at a Crossroads: Critical Choices and Policy Dilemmas Facing the United States Today, Amy F. Woolf, Jonathan Medalia and Steven A. Hildreth., 89-210 F

Weapons Systems -- Non-Nuclear Weapons

* see also Weapons Systems--Chemical Warfare, Weapons Systems--Nuclear Weapons, Weapons Systems--Weapons Facts
* A-12 Advanced Tactical Aircraft (ATA) Program (Weapons Facts:) Archived Issue Brief, Bert H. Cooper, IB87115
* Advanced Tactical Fighter (ATF) Aircrafts (Weapons Facts:) Issue Brief, Bert H. Cooper, IB87111
* Advanced Technology Bomber: Issue Brief, Dagnija Sterste-Perkins. IB87216
* Aircraft Carriers (Weapons Facts): Archived Issue Brief, Ronald O'Rourke., IB87043
* AMRAAM Air-to-Air Missile (Weapons Facts); Archived Issue Brief, Bert H. Cooper IB86041
* Anti-Tank Guided Missile: Status of the U.S. Army's Man-Portable System; Archived Issue Brief, Michael D. Scanlan, IB90063
* Army Aviation Modernization and the RAH-66 Program: Issues for Congress; Archived Issue Brief, Steven R. Bowman, IB88086
* Army Forward Area Air Defense System: Weapons Facts: Archived Issue Brief, Steven R. Bowman. IB87136
* Army Issues: Bradley Fighting Vehicle (Weapons Facts): Archived Issue Brief, Steven Bowman. IB86061
* B-1B Strategic Bomber: Issue Brief, Dagnija Sterste-Perkins, IB87157
* The C-17 Cargo Plane and the Airlift Shortfall: Archived Issue Brief, James Wootten. IB84099
* Canadian Nuclear-Powered Attack Submarine Program: Issues for Congress; Archived Issue Brief, Ronald O'Rourke. IB88083
* Chemical-Biological Warfare: Bibliography-in-Brief,1985-1988, Valentin Leskovsek. 88-605 L
* Chemical and Biological Warfare: Selected References, 1988-1991, Valentin Leskovsek, 91-739 L
* Chemical Weapons: A Summary of Proliferation and Arms Control Activities; Issue Brief, Steven R. Bowman.IB89042
* Conventional Arms Control and Military Stability in Europe, Stanley R. Sloan, Steven R. Bowman, Paul E. Gallis and Stuart D. Goldman. 87-831 F
* The Cost of a U.S. Navy Aircraft Carrier Battlegroup, Ronald O'Rourke. 87-532 F
* East-West Conventional Force Reduction Negotiations: Bibliography-in-Brief, 1980-1987, Valentin Leskovsek. 87-313 L
* FSX Fighter Agreement With Japan: Archived Issue Brief, Richard F. Grimmett, etc., IB89060
* FSX Fighter Program: Info Pack, IP420F
* FSX Technology: Its Relative Utility to the United States and Japanese Aerospace Industries, John D. Moteff, 89-237 SPR
* Japanese FSX Fighter Controversy, Richard Grimmett, 90-309 F
* LHX and Army Aviation Modernization: Issues for Congress; Issue Brief, Steven R. Bowman. IB88086
* LHX Helicopter Program (Weapons Facts): Archived Issue Brief, Steve Bowman., IB86095
* Nuclear Escalation, Strategic Anti-Submarine Warfare, and the Navy's Forward Maritime Strategy, Ronald O'Rourke. 87-138 F
* Soviet Tank Improvements vs. U.S. Army Antitank Weapons: Addressing the Imbalance, Floyd Mike Miles. 89-71 F
* Stinger Air Defense Missiles: Characteristics and Distribution, Steven R. Bowman. 87-824 F
* V-22 Osprey Tilt-Rotor Aircraft (Weapons Facts:) Issue Brief, Bert H. Cooper, IB86103

Weapons Systems -- Nuclear Weapons

* see INF, Nuclear Energy--Nuclear Exports and Non-Proliferation
* An Accidental Launch Protection System (ALPS): Requirements and Proposed Concepts; Archived Issue Brief, Amy F. Woolf. IB88079
* Ballistic Missile Forces under START: Critical Issues for Congress in FY1991, Foreign Affairs and National Defense Division, 90-228 F
* British and French Strategic Nuclear Force Modernization: Issues for Western Security and Arms Control, Charlotte Phillips Preece and Joseph M. Freeman., 89-140 F
* The Bush Administration's Proposal for ICBM Modernization, SDI, and the B-2 Bomber, Jonathan Medalia. 89-281 F
* The Chernobyl Accident: Implications for DOE's Production Reactors; Archived Issue Brief, Robert L. Civiak. IB86092
* China's Nuclear Weapons and Arms Control Policies: Implications for the United States, Robert G. Sutter. 88-374 F
* Civil Defense and the Effects of Nuclear War: Info Pack IP174C
* Civil Defense: Archived Issue Brief, Gary Reynolds and Dagnija Sterste-Perkins., IB84128
* Estimating Funding for Strategic Forces; a Review of the Problems, Alice Maroni. 84-652 F
* The Geneva Negotiations on Space and Nuclear Arms: Soviet Positions and Perspectives, Jeanette Voas., 86-512 S
* Implications for NATO Strategy of a Zero-Outcome Intermediate-Range Nuclear Missile Accord, Stanley R. Sloan. 87-614 F
* The Implications for Strategic Arms Control of Nuclear Armed Sea Launched Cruise Missiles, Alva Bowen, Stanley Sloan and Ronald O'Rourke. 86-25 F
* International Atomic Energy Agency: Strengthen Verification Authority? Issue Brief, Warren H. Donnelly, etc., IB91109
* Israel and Nuclear Weapons: Issue Brief, Warren H. Donnelly. IB87079
* "Midgetman" Small ICBM: Issues Facing Congress in 1986, Jonathan Medalia., 86-58 F
* "Midgetman" Small ICBM (Weapon Acts): Archived Issue Brief, Jonathan Medalia and Alice Maroni. IB84044
* Missile Proliferation: A Discussion of U.S. Objectives and Policy Options, Robert Shuey, 90-120 F
* MX, "Midgetman," and Minuteman Missile Programs: Issue Brief, Jonathan Medalia. IB77080
* NATO Nuclear Modernization and Arms Control: Issue Brief, Stanley R. Sloan. 1B89049
* The Netherlands Elections and the Cruise Missile Issue: Implications for the United States and for NATO, Paul Gallis., 86-27 F
* Nuclear Escalation, Strategic Anti-Submarine Warfare, and the Navy's Forward Maritime Strategy, Ronald O'Rourke., 87-138 F
* Nuclear Explosions in Space: The Threat of EMP (Electromagnetic Pulse); Archived Mini Brief, Robert Civiak. MB82221
* Nuclear Material from Dismantled Warheads: What to Do With It and How to Verify Its Disposal: A Preliminary Analysis, Warren H. Donnelly. 87-437 S
* Nuclear Nonproliferation: Selected References, 1985-1988, B. F. Mangan. 88-682 L
* Nuclear Risk Reduction Centers: Archived Issue Brief, Steven A. Hildreth., IB86142
* Nuclear Weapons Production Complex: Environmental Compliance and Waste; Issue Brief, Mark Holt, IB90074
* Nuclear Weapons Production Complex: Modernization and Cleanup; Issue Brief, David W. Cheney and Mark Holt., IB89062
* Nuclear Weapons Production Complex: Modernization and Safety; Issue Brief, William Boesman, etc., IB90052
* Nuclear Weapons Use: International Law and the United States Position, Ellen Collier., 84-109 F
* Nuclear Winter: Bibliography-in-Brief, B. F. Mangan. 88-325 L
* Rocky Flats and U.S. Nuclear Weapons Programs: Alternatives for the Future, Congressional Research Service, 91-276 F
* Seawolf or SSN-21 Nuclear-Powered Attack Submarine: Issue Brief, Ronald O'Rourke. IB85169
* Strategic Forces: MX ICBM (Weapons Facts); Archived Issue Brief, Jonathan Medalia and Alice Maroni. IB84046
* Strategic Nuclear Forces: Potential U.S./Soviet Trends With or Without SALT: 1985-2000, Jonathan Medalia, Al Tinajero and Paul Zinsmeister. 86-135F
* Tort Liability of the Federal Government and Its Contractors to Veterans Exposed to Atomic Radiation, Henry Cohen. 86-979 A
* Trident II Missile (Weapons Facts); Archived Issue Brief, Jonathan Medalia and Alice Maroni. IB84045
* Trident Program: Issue Brief, Jonathan Medalia. IB73001

Weapons Systems -- Space Weapons

* see National Defense and Security
* Arms Control: Negotiations to Limit Defense and Space Weapons; Issue Brief, Steven Hildreth., IB86073
* Arms Control: Overview of the Geneva Talks; Archived Issue Brief, Steven Hildreth. IB85157
* ASATs: Antisatellite Weapons Systems; Issue Brief, Marcia Smith., IB85176
* Brilliant Pebbles: Implications for the Strategic Defense Initiative, John D. Moteff, 90-291 SPR
* Congress and the Strategic Defense Initiative: A Detailed Overview of Legislative Action, 1984-1987, Robert J. Crawford and Steven A. Hildreth. 87-749F
* Directed Energy Weapons Research: Status and Outlook, Cosmo DiMaggio. 85-183 SPR
* The Effect of a Comprehensive Test Ban on the Strategic Defense Initiative, Cosmo DiMaggio. 85-972 SPR
* Ethical and Religious Aspects of SDI: Pro and Con, Charles H. Whittier.

Current Events and Homework

87-535 GOV
* Legal Analysis of a Memorandum of Understanding Between the United States and the Federal Republic of Germany Concerning Patent Rights Resulting from Strategic Defense Initiative Research, Michael V. Seitzinger., 87-281 A
* Potential Offensive Capabilities of SDI Space Weapons, Cosmo DiMaggio. 87-807 SPR
* Project Defender., Prepared, the Office of Senior Specialists. 87-689 S
* The Strategic Defense Initiative: A Model for Estimating Launch Costs, Cosmo DiMaggio and Robert L. Civiak. 87-475 SPR
* The Strategic Defense Initiative and United States Alliance Strategy, Paul Gallis, Mark Lowenthal and Marcia Smith. 85-48 F
* Strategic Defense Initiative: Info Pack, IP346S
* The Strategic Defense Initiative: Is the Software Feasible? Audio Brief, AB50141
* The Strategic Defense Initiative: Issues for Congress; Issue Brief, Steven Hildreth. IB85170
* The Strategic Defense Initiative: Issues for Phase I Deployment; Issue Brief, Steven A. Hildreth. IB88033
* The Strategic Defense Initiative: Major Changes During the 101st Congress and Potential Issues for the 102nd Congress, John D. Moteff, 91-121 SPR
* The Strategic Defense Initiative: Program Description and Major Issues, Cosmo DiMaggio, Arthur Manfredi and Steven Hildreth. 86-8 SPR
* Strategic Defense Initiative (SDI): Near-Term Mission Objectives: Archived Issue Brief, Cosmo DiMaggio, etc., IB88028
* Strategic Defense Initiative: Selected References, 1986-1988, Valentin Leskovsek. 88-184L
* U.S. Military Satellites and Survivability, Arthur Manfredi. 86-581 SPR

Weapons Systems -- Weapons Facts

* A-12 Advanced Tactical Aircraft (ATA) Program (Weapons Facts): Issue Brief, Bert H. Cooper. IB87115
* A-12 Contract Cancellation: Alternative Paths for Naval Aviation, Ronald O'Rourke, 91-88 F
* Advanced Tactical Fighter (ATF) Aircraft (Weapons Facts): Issue Brief, Bert H. Cooper. IB87111
* Advanced Technology Bomber: Issue Brief, Dagnija Sterste-Perkins., IB87216
* Aircraft Carrier Force Levels and Deployment Patterns: Issues and Options, Ronald O'Rourke, 91-516 F
* Aircraft Carriers (Weapons Facts): Archived Issue Brief, Ronald O'Rourke. IB87043
* AMRAAM Air-to-Air Missile (Weapons Facts); Archived Issue Brief, Bert H. Cooper. IB86041
* Antitank Guided Missile: U.S. Army's Non-Portable Medium System; Issue Brief, Edward F. Bruner, IB91130
* Army Forward Area Air Defense System: Weapons Facts: Archived Issue Brief, Steven R. Bowman. IB87136
* Army Issues: Bradley Fighting Vehicle (Weapons Facts): Archived Issue Brief, Steven Bowman. IB86061
* ASATs: Antisatellite Weapons Systems; Issue Brief, Marcia Smith. IB85176
* Attack Submarines and Aircraft Carrier Battlegroups: A New Mix for the U.S. Navy?, Ronald O'Rourke. 88-635 F
* AV-8B V/STOL Aircraft (Weapons Facts); Issue Brief, Bert H. Cooper. IB88044
* AX Aircraft Program: Issues and Options; Issue Brief, Bert H. Cooper, IB91104
* B-2 Strategic Bomber: Issue Brief, Dagnija Sterste-Perkins, IB90156
* The C-17 Cargo Plane Production Status Issue Brief, James P. Wooten, IB90090
* F-14D Fighter Aircraft (Weapons Facts:) Archived Issue Brief, Bert H. Cooper, IB89101
* LHX Helicopter Program (Weapons Facts): Archived Issue Brief, Steve Bowman., IB86095
* "Midgetman" Small ICBM (Weapon Acts): Archived Issue Brief, Jonathan Medalia and Alice Maroni. IB84044
* MX, "Midgetman," and Minuteman Missile Programs: Issue Brief, Jonathan Medalia. IB77080
* Navy Carrier Aircraft: Issues and Options; issue Brief, Bert H. Cooper, IB89156
* Navy Seawolf and Centurion Attack Submarine Programs: Issue Brief, Ronald O'Rourke, IB91098
* The Patriot Air Defense System and the Search for an Antitactical Ballistic Missile Defense, Steven A. Hildreth, etc., 91-456 F
* Seawolf or SSN-21 Nuclear-Powered Attack Submarine: Archived Issue Brief, Ronald O'Rourke. IB90051
* The Strategic Defense Initiative: issues for Congress; Issue Brief, Steven

Hildreth, IB85170
* Stinger Air Defense Missiles: Characteristics and Distribution, Steven R. Bowman. 87-824F
* The Strategic Defense Initiative: Issues for Congress; Issue Brief, Steven Hildreth. IB85170
* Strategic Forced: MX ICBM (Weapons Facts); Archived Issue Brief, Jonathan Medalia and Alice Maroni. IB84046
* Trident II Missile (Weapons Facts); Archived Issue Brief, Jonathan Medalia and Alice Maroni. IB84045
* Trident Program: Issue Brief, Jonathan Medalia. IB73001
* V-22 Osprey Tilt-Rotor Aircraft (Weapons Facts): Issue Brief, Bert H. Cooper. 86103

Weather

* see Earth Sciences

Weatherization Assistance

* see Power Resources-- Energy, Conversation

Welfare

* see Public Welfare

West Bank

* Israeli-Palestinian Conflict: Bibliography-in-Brief, 1982-1988, Robert S. Kirk. 88-251 L
* Israeli-Palestinian Conflict: Info Pack IP397I
* Palestinian Disturbances in the Gaza Strip and West Bank: Policy Issues and Chronology, Ellen Laipson. 88-114 F

West Germany

* see German Reunification
* European-U.S. Affairs: Responding to a Changing Relationship; Issue Brief, Karen E. Donfried, etc., IB89127
* Franco-German Security Cooperation: Implications for the NATO Alliance, Paul E. Gallis. 89-16F
* Is Faster Growth in Germany and Japan the Key to Faster U.S. Growth?, Gail E. Makinen. 86-836E
* Legal Analysis of a Memorandum of Understanding Between the United States and the Federal Republic of Germany Concerning Patent Rights Resulting from Strategic Defense Initiative Research, Michael V. Seitzinger. 87-281 A
* United States Merchandise Trade and Trade Balances With W. Germany, 1960-1987, Dario Scuka. 88-117 E

Western Europe

* see Integration, National Defense, European Economic Community, Foreign Policy and Assistance Programs, national Defense and Security, Trade and International Finance
* The "Citrus-Pasta Dispute" Between the United States and the European Community, Donna U. Vogt. 33 p.87-911 ENR
* Commercial Space Activities in Europe, Patricia E. Humphlett. 88-531 SPR
* The Common Agricultural Policy of the European Community and Implications for U.S. Agricultural Trade, Donna U. Vogt, Jasper Womach and Rebecca Mazur. 86-111 ENR
* Cyprus: Status of U.N. Negotiations; Issue Brief; Ellen B. Laipson, IB89140
* Cyprus: Turkish Cypriot "Statehood" and Prospects for Settlement: Archived Issue Brief, Ellen B. Laipson. 1B84062
* Divorce, Maintenance and Child Support Laws in Australia, Canada, England and New Zealand, Law Library of Congress, American-British Division, LL90-65
* Employment and Unemployment: Some International Comparisons, Gail McCallion. 88-673 E
* European Community: Issues Raised, 1992 Integration, Congressional Research Service., 89-323 E
* The European Community: Its Structure and Development, Martin E. Elling. 88-620 F
* European Community-Japan Trade Relations: A European Perspective, Dick K. Nanto. 86-166 E
* European Community: The 1992 Plan; Info Pack IP408E
* European Community: 1992 Plan for Economic Integration; Issue Brief, Glennon J. Harrison. IB89043
* The European Community's 1992 Plan: Bibliography-in-Brief, 1986-1988, Robert Howe. 88-754 L
* The European Community's 1992 Plan: Effects on American Direct Investment, James K. Jackson. 89-339 E
* An Explanation of the European Community's Sugar Regime and

Weapons Systems / Wildlife

Comparison to the U.S. Sugar Program, Jasper Womach and Donna Vogt. 85-77 ENR

* Greece: An Assessment of the June 1989 Elections, Ellen Laipson, 89-431 F
* Greece and Turkey: U.S. Foreign Assistance Facts; Issue Brief, Ellen B. Laipson. IB86065
* Greek-Turkish Relations: Beginning of a New Era?, Ellen Laipson. 88-724 F
* The Holy See and Recognition of Israel, Charles H. Whittier. 86-833 GOV
* The House of Representatives and the House of Commons: A Brief Comparison of American and British Parliamentary Procedures, Paul S. Rundquist, 91-522 GOV
* Labor Laws in Selected Foreign Countries, Law Library of Congress, LL91-3
* Northern Ireland and the Republic of Ireland: U.S. Foreign Assistance Facts; Issue Brief, Bert H. Cooper, Jr. IB87069
* Northern Ireland: The Anglo-Irish Agreement and Its Implications for Congress: Policy Alert, Allan Nanes. 85-1107 F
* Northwest European Region Petroleum (Including the North Sea), Joseph Riva. 85-187 SPR
* Plutonium: Department of Energy Approval of Plutonium Shipment from France to Japan; Archived Issue Brief, Warren H. Donnelly. IB84116
* Proposed European Community Consumption Tax on Vegetable Oils: A Status Report, Donna U. Vogt.87-407 ENR
* Reform of the English Legal Profession: Green, White and Pale, Law Library of Congress, AMerican-British Law Division, LL90-74
* Securities Registration and Disclosure Laws in Canada, Germany, Japan, the United Kingdom, and the United States, Stephen F. Clarke, etc., 91-613 A
* Space Activities of the United States, Soviet Union and Other Launching Countries/Organizations: 1957-1988, Marcia S. Smith. 89-183 SPR
* Soviet Trade and Economic Relations With Western Europe, Glannon J. Harrison, etc., 91-631 E
* A Survey of Bottled Water Regulations in Selected Countries, Law Library of Congress, European Law Division, LL90-61
* Taxation of Interest in Personal Savings, Law Library of Congress, LL90-83
* Tensions in United States-European Community Agricultural Trade, Donna U. Vogt and Jasper Womach. 86-112 ENR
* United States Merchandise Trade and Trade Balances With W. Germany, 1960-1987, Dario Scuka. 88-117 E
* U.S. Commercial Relations With the European Community, George D. Holliday. 85-32 E

Western Europe -- Integration

* Banking in "Europe 1992" William Jackson, 89-456 E
* A Changing Europe and U.S. Interests: Issue Brief, Stanley R. Sloan, IB90062
* EC Ban on Importing U.S. Pork and Beef, Susan Epstein, 91-390 ENR
* EC 1992: Potential Implications for Arms Trade and Cooperation, MArgaret Berry Edwards, 89-642 F
* Energy Conservation Policies of the European Community and United States: Comparing Apples and Oranges, Amy Abel, 89-604 ENR
* European community: Issues Raised by 1992 Integration, Congressional Research Service, 89-323 E
* The European Community: Its STructure and Development, Martin E. Elling, 88-620 F
* European Community: The 1992 Plan; Info Pack, IP408E
* European Community: 1992 Plan for Economic Integration; Issue Brief, Glannon J. Harrison, IB89043
* European Community's New Merger Laws: Overview and Implications for U.S. Firms, Gary W. Shorter, 91-240 E
* The European Community's 1992 Plan: Effects on American Direct Investment, James K. Jackson, 89-339 E
* The European Community's 1992 Plan: Selected References, 1989-1991, Robert Howe, 91-299 L
* European-U.S. Affairs: Responding to a Changing Relationship; Issue Brief, Karen E. Donfried, etc., IB89127
* German-American Relations in the New Europe: Issue Brief, Steven J. Woehrel, etc., IB91018
* German Unification, Paul E. Gallis, etc., 90-523 F
* Germany's Future and U.S. Interests: archived Issue Brief, Paul E. Gallis, etc., IB90006
* The New Europe, Audio Brief, Paul Gallis, etc., AB50215
* Responses to Changing Europe: Implications for the U.S.; Selected References, Valentin Leskovsek, 90-5 L
* U.S. Wood Exports to Europe and the 1992 EC Economic Integration, Ross W. Gorte, 89-580 ENR

Western Europe -- National Defense

* British and French Strategic Nuclear Force Modernization: Issues for Western Security and Arms Control, Charlotte Phillips Preece and Joseph M. Freeman. 89-140 F
* The Conference on Disarmament in Europe (CDE): Archived Issue Brief, Charlotte Preece and Steven Bowman. IB84060
* Conference on Security and Cooperation in Europe (CSCE): The Vienna Meeting; Issue Brief, Francis T. Miko. IB87220
* Confidence Building Measures and Force Constraints for Stabilizing East-West Military Relations in Europe, Stanley R. Sloan and Mikaela Sawtelle., 88-591 F
* Conventional Arms Control and Military Stability in Europe, Stanley R. Sloan, Steven R. Bowman, Paul E. Gallis and Stuart D. Goldman. 87-831 F
* Defense Burden Sharing: The United States, NATO and Japan; Info Pack, IP399D
* A European Defense Identity: Challenge and Opportunity for NATO, Catherine Guicherd, 91-478 RCO
* Franco-German Security Cooperation: Implications for the NATO Alliance, Paul E. Gallis. 89-16F
* Greek-U.S. Bases Agreement: Archived Issue Brief, Richard F. Grimmett, IB89155
* Implications for NATO Strategy of a Zero-Outcome Intermediate-Range Nuclear Missile Accord, Stanley R.Sloan. 87-614 F
* Military Bases in Europe: The Crotone Issue; Issue Brief, Richard F. Grimmett, IB90138
* The NATO Allies, Japan, and the Persian Gulf, Paul Gallis. 84-184 F
* NATO at 40: Bibliographic Resources, Sherry B. Shapiro. 89-175 L
* NATO Burdensharing: An Analysis of Major Legislation in the 100th Congress, Christopher C. Bolkcom. 88-772 F
* NATO: Conventional Arms Control and Related Political Issues; Info Pack, IP425N
* NATO Conventional Arms Control Issues: Selected References, Sherry B. Shapiro, 89-479 L
* NATO Conventional Force Structure and Doctrine: Possible Defensive Changes After an INF Treaty, Robert L. Goldich. 88-169 F
* NATO Nuclear Modernization and Arms Control: Issue Brief, Stanley R. Sloan. IB89049
* The NATO Strategy Review: Negotiating the Future of the North Atlantic Alliance, Stanley R. Sloan, 91-379 RCO
* The Netherlands Elections and the Cruise Missile Issue: Implications for the United States and for NATO, Paul Gallis. 86-27 F
* The Seven-Ten Ratio in Military Aid to Greece and Turkey: A Congressional Tradition, Ellen Laipson. 85-79 F
* The Strategic Defense Initiative and United States Alliance Strategy, Paul Gallis, Mark Lowenthal and Marcia Smith. 85-48 F
* United States Military Installations in Greece, Richard Grimmett. 84-24 F
* United States Military Installations in Italy, Richard Grimmett. 84-12 F
* United States Military Installations in Portugal, Richard Grimmett. 86-6 F
* United States Military Installations in Spain, Richard Grimmett. 84-149 F
* United States Military Installations in Turkey, Richard Grimmett. 84-221 F
* United States and New Europe: Strategy for the Future, Stanley R. Sloan, 90-245 S
* The U.S. Commitment to Europe's Defense: A Review of Cost Issues and Estimates, Alice Maroni and John Ulrich. 85-211 F

Wetlands

* see Coastal Areas

Whistleblowers

* see Government Employees-Ethics

Wilderness Areas

* see Forests and Forestry--Timber

Wildlife

* see Conservation
* Animals in Biomedical Research: Selected References, 1988-1990, B.F. Mangan,, 91-6 L
* Applicability of Alaska State Laws to Oil and Gas Development in the Arctic National Wildlife Refuge, Pamela Baldwin., 88-420 A
* Arctic National Wildlife Refuge: Bibliography-in-Brief, Ted L. Burch, 91-633 L
* Arctic National Wildlife Refuge: A Checklist of CRS Products, Ted L. Burch, 92-5 L
* The Arctic National Wildlife Refuge: Major Oil Development or Wilderness?, Congressional Research Service. Edited by John E. Blodgett and

Current Events and Homework

John L. Moore, Environment and Natural Resources Policy Division., 88-161 ENR

* The Arctic National Wildlife Refuge: Oil, Gas, and Wildlife; Archived Issue Brief, Lynne Corn and John Schanz. IB87026
* Arctic Resources Controversy: A Comparison of H.R. 3601 and S. 2214, Environment and Natural Resources Policy Division., 88-380 ENR
* Arctic Resources Controversy; an Overview; Archived Issue Brief, M. Lynne Corn, John E. Blodgett and Pamela Baldwin. IB87228
* Arctic Resources Controversy: Issue Brief, M. Lynne Corn, Claudia Copeland and Pamela Baldwin. IB89058
* Brief Summaries of Federal Animal Protection Statutes, Henry Cohen. 91-791 A
* Consideration of Economic Factors under the Endangered Species Act, Pamela Baldwin. 89-274 A
* Debt-for-Nature Swaps in Developing Countries: An Overview of Recent Conservation Efforts, Betsy Cody. 88-647 ENR
* Endangered Species Act: Reauthorization and Funding; Issue Brief, M. Lynne Corn. IB87089
* Endangered Species, Bibliography-in-Brief, 1986-1987, Adrienne C. Grenfell., 87-450 L
* Endangered Species, A Checklist of CRS Products, Lisa B. Dove, 91-917 L
* Endangered Species: Info Pack, IP192E
* Environmental Effects of Energy Development in the Arctic National Wildlife Refuge: A Critique of the Final Legislative Environmental Impact Statement, M. Lynne Corn, John Blodgett, Eugene H. Buck, Claudia Copeland and Mark R. Dillenbeck. 87-490 ENR
* The Exxon Valdez Oil Spill: Issue Brief, Martin R. Lee and Robert Bamberger. IB89075
* Fish and Wildlife Service: Compensation to Local Governments, M. Lynne Corn, 90-192 ENR
* A Guide to Trust Funds, Special Accounts, and Foundations in the Fish and Wildlife Service Budget, M. Lynne Corn., 86-722 ENR
* Kangaroo Management Controversy, Malcolm M. Simmons. 88-468 ENR
* The Major Federal Land Management Agencies: Management of Our Nation's Lands and Resources, Environment and Natural Resources Policy Division, 90-239 ENR
* Marine Mammal Protection Act Reauthorization: Population--Too Large or Too Small? Issue Brief, Eugene H. Buck. IB88038
* North Pacific Fur Seals: Issues and Options, Eugene Buck., 85-654 ENR
* Oil Companies and the Development of the Arctic National Wildlife Refuge, John J. Schanz. 88-106 S
* Old Growth Forests in the Pacific Northwest: Background and Issues; Issue Brief, Adela Backiel, IB90111
* The Outlook for U.S. Energy Supplies and the Arctic National Wildlife Refuge Decision, John J. Schanz. 88-73 S
* An Overview of Federal Tax Policies Encouraging Donations of Conservation Easements to Preserve Natural Areas, Richard Dunford. 84-48 ENR
* Predator Control and Compound 1080: Archived Mini Brief, Jim Aidala. MB82241
* Protecting Endangered and Threatened Sea Turtles, Eugene H. Buck. 87-540 ENR
* Special Management Areas in the National Forest System, Ross W. Gorte., 88-571 ENR
* Spotted Owls and the Timber Industry: Issue Brief, M. Lynne Corn. IB89077
* Wetlands Protection: Issues in the 101st Congress; Issue Brief, Jeffrey A. Zinn, M. Lynne Corn and Claudia L. Copeland. IB89076
* Whale Conservation, Eugene H. Buck and Jennifer A. Heck. 88-391 ENR
* Wild Horses and Burros: Federal Management Issues; Archived Issue Brief, Adela Backiel and Alison Holt. IB85138
* Wilderness: Overview and Statistics, Ross W. Gorte. 88-16 ENR

Wildlife -- Conservation

* Applicability of Alaska State Laws to Oil and Gas Development in the Arctic National Wildlife Refuge, Pamela Baldwin, 88-420 A
* Arctic National Wildlife Refuge: Bibliography-in-Brief, Ted L. Burch, 91-633 L
* Arctic National Wildlife Refuge: Congressional Consideration Since the 99th Congress, M. Lynne Corn, etc., 91-325 ENR
* The Arctic National Wildlife Refuge: Major Oil Development or Wilderness?, Congressional Research Service, Edited: John E. Blodgett, etc., 88-161 ENR
* Arctic Resources: Over a Barrel? Issue Brief, M. Lynne Corn, etc., IB91011
* Dolphin Protection: A Fact Sheet, Eugene H. Buck, 90587 ENR
* Economic Impacts of Protecting the Northern Spotted Owl, Ross W. Gorte, 90-74 ENR
* Endangered Species Act Issues: Issue Brief, M. Lynne Corn, IB91-86
* Endangered Species Act: The Listing and Exemption Processes, M. Lynne Corn, etc., 90-242 ENR
* Endangered Species: Info Pack, IP192 E
* Kangaroo Management Controversy, Malcolm M. Simmons, 88-468 ENR
* Living Aquatic Resource Laws and Treaties: Reference Guide, Eugene H. Buck, 89-620 ENR
* Marine Mammal Protection Act Reauthorization: Population--Too Large or Too Small? Archived Issue Brief, Eugene H. Buck, IB88038
* Measures Canada Has and Has Not Taken to Protect the Spotted Owl, Law Library of Congress, American-British Law Division, LL90-52
* Oil Companies and the Development of the Arctic National Wildlife Refuge, John H. Schanz, 88-106 S
* The Outlook for U.S. Energy Supplies and the Arctic National Wildlife Refuge Decision, John J. Schanz, 88-73 S
* Pacific Salmon and Steelhead: Potential Impacts of Endangered Species Act Listings, Eugene H. Buck, etc., 91-267 ENR
* Special Management Areas in the National Forest System, Ross W. Gorte, 88-571 ENR
* Spotted Owls and Old Growth Forests: issue Brief, M. Lynne Corn, IB90094
* Turtle Excluder Devices: Sea Turtles and/or Shrimp? Eugene H. Buck, 90-327 ENR
* Whale Conservation, Eugene H. Buck, 90-283 ENR

Windfall Profits Tax

* see Taxation--Corporation Taxes

Women

* see also Policies and Legislation, Civil Liberties and Rights--Discrimination and Integration, Equal Employment Opportunity, Pensions, Minority Issues
* Alcohol Use and Abuse by Women, Edith Fairman Cooper, 91-680 SPR
* Breast Implants: Safety and FDA Regulation, Judith Johnson, 91-842 SPR
* Economic Growth and Changing Labor Markets: Those Left Behind; Women Workers (Un)changed Position, Linda LeGrande. 84-112 E
* The "Gender Gap": Differences Between Men and Women in Political Attitudes and Voting Behavior in the 1980s, Jennifer D. Williams, 89-547 GOV
* The "Glass Ceiling:" Access of Women and Minorities to Management Positions, Linda Levine, 91-623 E
* Surrogate Mothers: Bibliography-in-Brief 1985-1988, Edith Sutterlin. 88-268 L
* Women: An Alphabetical Microthesaurus of Terms Selected from the Legislative Indexing Vocabulary, Shirley Loo. 88-710L
* Women and AIDS: Selected References: 1986-1991, Bonnie F. Mangan, 91-607 L
* Women in the Armed Forces (With Appendix): Archived Issue Brief, Ellen Collier. IB79045
* Women in the United States Congress, Mildred L. Amer. 91-333 GOV
* Women Nominated and Appointed to Full-Time Civilian Positions, President Reagan, Rogelio Garcia. 89-236 GOV
* Women and Politics: Bibliography-in-Brief, 1985-1989, Michelle Cadoree, 90-176 L
* Women Nominated and Appointed to Full-Time Civilian Positions by President George Bush, Rogelio Garcia, 91-314 GOV
* Women's Health Issues: Selected References, 1986-1991, Bonnie F. Mangan, 91-606 L
* Women's Pension Equity: A Summary of the Retirement Equity Act of 1984, Ray Schmitt. 84-217 EPW

Women -- Policies and Legislation

* Comparable Worth/Pay Equity in the Federal Government: Issue Brief, Linda LeGrande. IB85116
* Displaced Homemakers: Issue Brief, Leslie Gladstone. IB84132
* The Economic Equity Act of 1987: Archived Issue Brief, Leslie Gladstone. IB87221
* Equal Rights for Women: Issue Brief, Leslie Gladstone..IB83077
* Federal Councils on the Status of Women, Established Executive Order: Summary and Analysis, Leslie Gladstone. 85-1121 GOV
* Federal Policies and Programs Relating to Sex Discrimination and Sex Equity in Education, 1963-1985, Bob Lyke and Rick Holland. 85-116 EPW
* Federal Programs for Minority and Women-Owned Businesses, Mark Eddy. 89-278 GOV
* A Legal Analysis of the Fourteenth Amendment's Equal Protection Clause and the Proposed Equal Rights Amendment, Karen Lewis. 85-662A
* Maternity and Parental Leave Policies: A Comparative Analysis, Leslie Gladstone, Jennifer Williams and Richard S.Belous., 85-148 GOV

Wildlife / Zimbabwe

* Parental Leave: Info Pack, IP367P
* Pay Equity Legislation in the 102nd Congress: Issue Brief, Linda Levine, IB91080
* The Proposed Equal Rights Amendment, Leslie Gladstone. 85-154 GOV
* Selected Women's Issues in the 100th Congress: Archived Issue Brief, Leslie W. Gladstone. IB87133
* Selected Women's Issues in the 101st Congress: Archived Issue Brief, Leslie W. Gladstone, IB 89104
* Selected Women's Issues Legislation Enacted Between 1832-1988, Leslie Gladstone. 89-514 GOV
* Sex-Based Employment Discrimination: UAW v. Johnson Controls, Inc., Gina M. Stevens, 91-323 A
* Sex Discrimination and the United States Supreme Court: Developments in the Law, Karen J. Lewis. 89-500 A
* Sexual Harassment in the Workplace: Selected References, Jean Bowers, 91-836 L
* Women's Economic Equity Act: H.R. 3085/S. 1480 and Subtitles Introduced as Separate Legislation, Leslie Gladstone, 90-154 GOV
* Women's Economic Equity: H.R. 3085/S 1489; Archived Issue Brief, Leslie W. Gladstone, IB90014
* Women's issues in the 102nd Congress: Selected Legislation; Issue Brief, Leslie W. Gladstone, IB91034

Workers' Compensation

* see Unemployment Compensation
* Benefits to Individuals Based on Previous Employment: Interactions and Offsets in Selected Programs, Carolyn L. Merck, 91-463 EPW
* Black Lung Programs: 1987 Issues and Action, Gloria E. Moreno and Joe Richardson. 88-68 EPW
* Federal Black Lung Disability Benefits Program, Barbara McClure., 81-239 EPW
* How the Unemployment Compensation System Works, Celinda M. Franco. 89-326EPW
* Income support for Workers Dislocated by Federal Policy Initiatives, James R. Storey, 90-330 EPW
* Railroad Retirement and Employment: Recent Issues; Issue Brief, Dennis Snook, Richard Hobbie and Emmett Carson. IB84068
* Selected Federal Victim Compensation Systems, Gloria E.Moreno. 88-573 EPW
* Summary and Legislative History of P.L. 97-1 19, "Black Lung Benefits Revenue Act of 1981", Barbara McClure. 88-59 EPW
* Unemployment Compensation: Problems and Issues, Education and Public Welfare Division. Unemployment Compensation Team. 88-597 EPW
* Unemployment Insurance: Changes Made by the 98th Congress, Emmett Carson. 85-230 EPW
* Work Disincentives in the Unemployment Insurance (UI) System, Richard Hobbie. 80-159 EPW
* Workers' Compensation, 91-396 EPW

Workers' Compensation -- Unemployment Compensation

* The Uncompensated Unemployed: An Analysis of Unemployed Workers Who Do Not Receive Unemployment Compensation, Gene Falk, 90-565 EPW
* Unemployed Workers Who Do Not Receive Unemployment Compensation: Impact and Incidence, Gene Falk, 90-566 EPW
* Unemployment Compensation: A History of Extended Benefits for the Long-Term Unemployed, Gene Falk, 91-738 EPW
* Unemployment Compensation: Info Pack, IP451U
* Unemployment Compensation: Problems and Issues, Education and Public Welfare Division, Unemployment Compensation Team, 88-597 EPW
* Unemployment compensation: Response to the Current Economic Downturn; Issue Brief, Gene Falk, etc., IB91005
* Unemployment compensation: Selected References, 1988-1991, M. Alexandra Salinas, 91-221 L
* Unemployment Compensation: The Unemployment Trust Fund and the FEDERAL Budget, Gene Falk, 91-529 EPW

World Bank

* International Monetary Fund and World Bank: Info Pack IP245I
* Multilateral Development Banks: Issues for the 101st Congress; Archived Issue Brief, Jonathan E. Sanford, IB87218
* Soviet Participation in International Financial Institutions; Issue Brief, Shirley A. Kan, etc., IB91133
* Western Aid Report on the Soviet Economy, John P. Hardt, 91-16 RCO
* World Bank Activities in Ethiopia, Jonathan Sanford, 87-857 F.

* The World Bank: Bibliography-in-Brief, of Recent Works, Felix Chin, 89-464 L
* The World Bank: Eighteen Questions and Answers, Jonathan E. Sanford, 86-769 F

World Health Organization

* World Health Organization: Effects of Reduced U.S. Contributions, Lois McHugh, 87-108 F

Yellowstone National Park

* Issues Surrounding the Greater Yellowstone Ecosystem: A Brief Review, M. Lynne Corn, Ross W. Gorte and George Siehl, 85-1146 ENR

Yemen

* Yemen, Kirk Campbell, 91-540 F

Youth Employment

* see Labor

Yugoslavia

* Mineral Development in Yugoslavia, Marc Humphries, 88-688 ENR
* Some Basic Features of the Judicial System of Yugoslavia, Law Library of Congress, European Law Division, LL90-39
* Yugoslavia: Crisis in the Federation, Jon W. Western, 90-333 F
* Yugoslavia: Issue Brief, Steven J. Woehrel, IB91089

Zaire

* Zaire: Political Crisis, Raymond W. Copson, 91-721 F

Zimbabwe

* The United States and Southern Africa: A Review of the United Nations Resolutions and United States Voting Patterns, 1946-October 1985, Frankie King

Audio Brief List

Acid Rain; Scientific Progress and Outlook: Audio Brief, AB50128
Africa: Democracy and U.S. Policy; Audio Brief, AB50220
Africa's Wars: Conditions, Causes, and Prospects for the Future; Audio Brief AB50206
After the Drought: The Next Farm Bill; Audio Brief, AB50183
Agricultural Policy for the 1990's: Audio Brief, AB50217
AIDS: Audio Brief, AB50186
Allied Burdensharing: Audio Brief, AB50182
The American Response to Foreign Competition: Audio Brief, AB50180
Biomedical Ethics: Audio Brief, AB50004
Budget Making and the Legislative Process: Audio Brief, AB50164
Campaign Activities By Congressional Staff: Audio Brief, AB50118
Characteristics of Congress: Audio Brief, AB50129
Chemicals in the Environment: Audio Brief, AB50152
Choosing the Future of the Space Program: Audio Brief, AB50222
Combatting International Terrorism: Audio Brief, AB50151
Conducting Oversight: Legal, Procedural, and Practical Aspects; Audio Brief, AB50156
Control of Arms Transfers to the Middle East, Audio Brief, AB50221
The Defense Spending Dilemma: Audio Brief, AB50181
The Dollar, the Trade Deficit, and the U.S. Economy: Audio Brief, AB50174
Drugs and Latin America; Audio Brief, AB50194
The Economic Dimension of U.S. Power, Audio Brief, AB50196
Economic Perestroika: Gorbachev at the London Economic Summit, July 17, 1991; Audio Brief, AB50227
Educational Challenges for the Congress: Audio Brief, AB50218
Effective Oversight: Planning for the Future; Audio Brief, AB50155
Executive Perspectives on Oversight: Audio Brief, AB50116
Financing Long-Term Care for the Elderly: Audio Brief, AB50187
Former Members View Oversight: Audio Brief, AB50111
Global Climate Change: Audio Brief, AB50189
The Global Environment: Audio Brief, AB50063
Gorbachev's World View: May 1990; Audio Brief, AB50223
Gorbachev's World View Under Siege: Perestroika at Risk; Audio Brief, AB50226
Health Care Costs and Cost Containment, Audio Brief, AB50216
Housing: Access and Affordability; Audio Brief, AB50172
Housing and Community Development: Audio Brief, Ab50184
Implications for U.S. Diplomacy in the U.S.-Soviet Future: Audio Brief,

Be patient. If any phone number is incorrect, call (area code) 555-1212 and request the new listing.

Current Events and Homework

AB50173
Increasing Access to Health Insurance: Audio Brief, AB50166
Indoor Air Pollution: Audio Brief, AB50188
Information Technology for Emergency Operations: Audio Brief, AB50117
Inspectors General: Resources for Oversight; Audio Brief, AB50109
International Commission on Central America: Initial Views; Audio Brief, AB50176
Issues in the Middle East: Audio Brief, AB50177
Maintaining U.S. Influence in a Changing World: Audio Brief, AB50197
A Member's Reflections on Oversight: Audio Brief, AB50112
The Moscow Summit at First Glance: Audio Brief, AB50168
National Power in a Changing World: Audio Brief, AB50195
The New Europe, Audio Brief, AB50215
Outside Perspectives on Oversight: Audio Brief, AB50157
Oversight Authority and Major Procedures: Audio Brief, AB50114
Oversight in Action: Audio Brief, AB50110
Oversight Powers and Constraints: Audio Brief, AB50115
The Post-War Middle East: Significant Trends, Audio Brief, AB50224
Pros and Cons of Military Intervention: Audio Brief, AB50033
RCRA Authorization: Audio Brief, AB50179
Reforming the Foreign Assistance Program: Audio Brief, AB50185
The Role of Congress in Soviet Diplomacy and Negotiations: Audio Brief, AB50175
The Role of the Media in Oversight: Audio Brief, AB50113
The Role of the U.S. Military in Narcotics Interdiction: Audio Brief, AB50171
Senate Legislative Floor Procedures: Audio Brief, AB50143
Soviet Diplomacy under Gorbachev: Continuity and Change; Audio Brief, AB50190
The Strategic Defense Initiative: Is the Software Feasible?; Audio Brief, AB50141
Strategic Policy Issues: The Bush Administration's ICBM Modernization Program; Audio Brief, AB50191
Toxic Chemicals: Environmental and Health Issues; Audio Brief, AB50104
U.S.-Japan Trade: The Structural Impediments Initiative; Audio Brief, AB50207
U.S.-Soviet Relations: Audio Brief, AB50178

Info Pack Listing

Abortion: Info Pack, IP001A
Acid Rain: Info Pack, IP134A
Affirmative Action: Info Pack, IP424A
Aged: Info Pack, IP003A
Agriculture: Drought of 1988; Info Pack, IP403A
Agriculture: The Farm Financial Situation; Info Pack, IP323A
Agriculture: The 1990 Farm Bill; Info Pack, IP295A
AIDS: Acquired Immune Deficiency Syndrome; Info Pack, IP261A
Air Pollution-Clean Air Act: Info Pack, IP008A
Airlines: Safety and Service Issues: Info Pack, IP386A
The Americans With Disabilities Act: Info Pack, IP443A
Animal Welfare Issues, Info Pack, IP360A
Arms Sales: U.S. Policy: Info Pack, IP214A
Banking in the United States: An Overview, Info Pack IB429B
Benefits for Former Military Spouses: Info Pack, IP313B
Bicentennial of the U.S. Congress: Info Pack, IP411C
Budget for Fiscal Year 1989: Info Pack, IP394B
Budget for Fiscal Year 1990; Info Pack, IP413B
Budget for Fiscal Year 1992: Info Pack, IB446B
Budget Process: Info Pack, IP012B
Business: Doing Business With the Federal Government; Info Pack, IP305B
Cable TV: Info Pack, IP104C
Campaign Finance: Info Pack, IP014C
Canada-U.S. Free Trade Area Agreement; Info Pack, IP395C
Capital Punishment: Info Pack, IP015C
Career Guidance and Federal Job Information: Info Pack, IP016C
Caribbean Basin Initiative: Info Pack, IP190C
Catastrophic Health Insurance: Info Pack, IP370C
Central America: U.S. Relations With Costa Rica, Guatemala, and Honduras; Info Pack, IP352C
Child Abuse; Info Pack, IP019C
Child Day Care: Info Pack, IP306C
Child Support: Issues and Legislation; Info Pack, IP286C
Civil Defense and the Effects of Nuclear War; Info Pack, IP174C
Civil Rights: Equal Employment Opportunity and Affirmative Action; Info Pack IP424C
Competitiveness: Current Issues and Proposals; Info Pack, IP368C
Congress: Info Pack, IP022C
Congress: Issues for the 101st Congress; Info Pack, IP410C
Congress: Issues for the 102nd Congress; Info Pack, IP444C
Congressional Office Operations: Info Pack, IP151C
Constitution of the United States: Its History, Development, and Amending Process; Info Pack, IP339C
Copyright-Applications Procedures: Info Pack, IP215C
Crime Control: Federal Initiatives; Info Pack IP310C
Defense Burdensharing: The United States, NATO and Japan; Info Pack, IP399D
Defense Procurement: The Fraud and Bribery Investigation; Info Pack, IP404D
Defense Spending: Info Pack, IP434D
Deficit Reduction Issues: Info Pack, IP274D
Drug Abuse in America: Info Pack, IP303D
Drug Abuse: Treatment, Prevention and Education: Info Pack, IP400D
Drug Control: Existing Federal Laws and Pending Legislation, Info Pack IP430D
Drug Control: Federal Efforts to Reduce the Supply; Info Pack, IP334D
Drug Testing: The Response to Drugs in the Workplace; Info Pack, IP350D
Drugs of Abuse: The Legalization Debate; Info Pack, IP401D
Drunk Driving and Raising the Drinking Age: Info Pack, IP186D
Eastern Europe; Info Pack IP431E
Economic Development and Community Revitalization Programs; Sources of Information; Info Pack, IP412E
Economy: Background and Prospects; Info Pack, IP393E
Economy: Conditions and Outlook; Info Pack, IP449E
Education: Funding Issues: Info Pack, IP199E
Education: Issues of Quality and Reform; Info Pack IP256E
El Salvador: Info Pack, IP121E
Electoral College: Info Pack, IP031E
Employment Abroad: Info Pack, IP065E
Endangered Species: Info Pack, IP192E
Energy Policy: Info Pack, IP447E
European Community: The 1992 Plan; Info Pack, IP408E
Federal Reserve System: Info Pack, IP105F
Financial Aid for Students; Info Pack, IP042F
Financial Institutions: Problems and Prospects: Info Pack, IP291F
The Flag: Info Pack, IP365F
Flag Desecration: Info Pack, IP440F
Flag Etiquette: Info Pack IP365 F
Foreign Aid: Info Pack, IP044F
Foreign Investments in the U.S.: Info Pack, IP398F
Foreign Policy: Info Pack, IP297F
Form Letters: Tell Your Constituents Where to Get Government Publications; Info Pack, IP222F
Freedom of Information Act/Privacy Act: A Guide to Their Use; Info Pack, IP047F
FSX Fighter Program: Info Pack, IP420F
Government Publications--How, What, When, Where, and Why: Info Pack, IP264G
Grants and Foundation Support: Info Pack, IP050G
Greenhouse Effect and Ozone Depletion: Info Pack, IP405G
Gun Control: Info Pack, IP051G
Hatch Act: Info Pack, IP298H
Hazardous Waste and the Superfund Program; Info Pack, IP094H
Health Care Access: Federal Policy Issues: Info Pack, IP421H
Health Care Costs: Info Pack, IP223H
Health Insurance: Employer Benefits Required under COBRA and Pending Proposals: Info Pack, IP389H
Health Insurance: Info Pack, IP072H
Health: Long-Term Care: Info Pack, IP402H
Homeless in America: Info Pack, IP314H
Hotlines and Other Useful Government Telephone Numbers: Info Pack, IP106H
Housing Policy and Implications for Current Programs; Info Pack, IP417H
How to Follow Current Federal Legislation and Regulations: Info Pack, IP122H
Immigration and Refugee Policy: Info Pack, IP164I
Inauguration of the President: Info Pack, IP316I
INF Treaty: Info Pack, IP392I
International Debt Problems: Background, Statistics, Proposed Solutions; Info Pack, IP234I
International Monetary Fund and World Bank: Info Pack, IP245I
Internships and Fellowships: Info Pack, IP063I
Israeli-Palestinian Conflict: Info Pack, IP397I
Japan-U.S. Trade and Economic Relations: Info Pack, IP201J

Info Pack Listings

Jobs: The Employment Situation and Job Training Programs: Info Pack, IP246J

Kuwait Reconstruction: Sources of Information; Info Pack, IP450K

Legislative Procedure: An Introduction; Info Pack, IP247L

Legislative Research: A Guide to Conducting Legislative Research in a Congressional Office; Info Pack, IP321L

Leveraged Buyouts: Info Pack, IP414L

Lobbying: Info Pack, IP066L

Medicare-Medicaid: Info Pack, IP067M

Medicare Payments to Hospitals and Physicians: Info Pack, IP317M

Mexico: Problems and Prospects: Info Pack, IP358M

Mexico-U.S. Free Trade Agreement; Info Pack, IP445M

Military Balance: Info Pack, IP069M

Minimum Wage Issues: Info Pack, IP249M

National Services: Info Pack, IP418N

NATO: Conventional Arms Control and Related Political Issues: Info Pack, IP425N

Nicaragua: Info Pack, IP073N

Nuclear Arms Control: The Geneva Talks: Info Pack, IP341N

Nuclear Energy: Safety and Waste Issues; Info Pack, IP074N

Occupational Safety and Health Issues: Info Pack, IP456O

Oil Spills: Info Pack, IP426O

Parental Leave: Info Pack, IP367P

Pearl Harbor 50th Anniversary: Info Pack, IP455P

Pension Issues; Info Pack IP428P

Persian Gulf: Post-War Issues; Info Pack IP452P

Persian Gulf War: Info Pack, IP448P

Political Action Committees (PACs): Info Pack, IP196P

The Presidency of the United States; Info Pack, IP409P

Prisoner of War/Missing in Action in SE Asia; Info Pack, IP127P

Puerto Rico: Political Status: Info Pack, IP419P

Radon: An Overview of Health and Environmental Issues; Info Pack, IP363R

Reapportionment and Redistricting, Info Pack, IB119R

Recycling: Info Pack, IP437R

Retirement Systems for Federal Employees: Info Pack, IP205R

S&L Problems and FSLIC: Info Pack, IP415S

Small Business Assistance Programs Sources of Information: Info Pack, IP422S

Smoking and Tobacco Issues; Info Pack, IP356S

Social Security: Current Issues, Benefits and Financing: Info Pack, IP153S

Social Security Financing and Taxation: Recent Issues; Info Pack, IP435S

Social Security: National Committee to Preserve Social Security and Medicare; Info Pack, IP345S

The Social Security "Notch": Info Pack, IP266S

Solid Waste Management: Info Pack, IP396S

South Africa: The Current Situation: Info Pack, IP340S

Space Issues: Info Pack, IP371S

Speech Material: Abraham Lincoln's and George Washington's Birthdays; Info Pack, IP373A

Speech Material: Captive Nations Week: Info Pack, IP375C

Speech Material; Columbus Day; Info Pack IP380C

Speech Material: Fourth of July; Info Pack, IP377F

Speech Material: Graduation; Info Pack, IB379G

Speech Material: Labor Day; Info Pack, IP374L

Speech Material: Martin Luther King's Birthday; Info Pack, IP372M

Speech Material: Thanksgiving Day; Info Pack, IP381T

Speech Material: Veterans Day; Info Pack, IP378V

Speechwriting and Delivery: Info Pack, IP139S

Strategic Defense Initiative: Info Pack, IP346S

Superconducting Super Collider: Issues; Info Pack, IP384S

Superconductors: Info Pack, IP390S

Tax Cut Proposals: Info Pack, IP457T

Telephone Industry Issues: Info Pack, IP257T

Term Limits; Info Pack IP439T

Terrorism: Info Pack, IP299T

Trade Issues and Trade Deficits: Background, Statistics, and proposed Legislation: Info Pack, IP263T

Transportation Infrastructure Reauthorization: Highway and Mass Transit Issues; Info Pack IP453T

Tropical Deforestation: Info Pack, IP416T

Unemployment Compensation: Info Pack, IP451U

U.S. Government: Info Pack, IP162U

U.S.-Soviet Relations: Info Pack, IP233U

War Powers Resolution: Info Pack, IP131W

Washington, DC and the U.S. Capitol Building: Info Pack, IP132W

Waste in the Marine Environment: Info Pack, IP407W

Water Resources: Quality and Quantity: Info Pack, IP369W

Welfare and Poverty: Info Pack, IP098W

Wetlands Issues: Info Pack, IP423W

Be patient. If any phone number is incorrect, call (area code) 555-1212 and request the new listing.

Experts

8,000 Free Experts

You may have heard of the "seven-phone call rule" for tracking down an expert who will help you for free. Well, now you can throw that phrase out the window. With this handy list of 8,000 government experts you are likely to find the right subject specialist in only ONE phone call.

Do you have a new idea to revolutionize the crayon market? Shetty Sundar at the U.S. International Trade Commission has spent her career analyzing this market. Want to know how many women-owned businesses there are in the United States? Contact Leonel Miranda at the Bureau of Census and she will give you the official data. You'll find sixty bureaucrats listed in this chapter who are experts in computers and the computer industry. You will also find experts on sewing machines, eggs, fish nets, and robots. Remember each of these professionals has devoted his or her life work to studying a specific area and will share their knowledge without charging a penny **just as long as you treat them right.** (Refer to the *Tips on Finding Information* chapter, specifically "The Art of Getting a Bureaucrat to Talk" and "Case Study: Jelly Beans", for guidance on how to deal with bureaucrats.)

The abbreviations for the federal agency which precede an expert's telephone number are spelled out below. If you have trouble with a telephone number, after all, numbers change all the time, simply contact the agency directly.

ACYF = Administration for Children and Youth and Families, HHS, 901 D St., SW, Washington, DC 20447

ADAMHA = Alcohol, Drug Abuse, and Mental Health Administration, HHS, 5600 Fishers Lane, Room 13C05, Rockville, MD 20857

AGRI = National Agriculture Statistics Service, U.S. Department of Agriculture, 14th and Independence Avenue, SW, Washington, DC 20250

AHCPR = Agency for Health Care Policy and Research, HHS, 2101 East Jefferson St., Ste. 501, Rockville, MD 20852

AOA = Administration on Aging, HHS, 330 Independence Avenue, Washington, DC 20201

ASH = Assistant Secretary for Health, HHS, 200 Independence Avenue, SW, Room 719-H, Hubert Humphrey Bldg., Washington, DC 20201

ATSDR = Agency for Toxic Substances and Disease Registry, HHS, 1600 Clifton Rd., NE, Mail Stop 828, Atlanta, GA 30333

BEIB = Biomedical Engineering and Instrumentation Branch, NIH, 9000 Rockville Pike, Bldg. 13, Bethesda, MD 20892

BHCDA = Bureau of Health Care Delivery and Assistance, HHS, 5600 Fishers Lane, Room 7-05, Rockville, MD 20857

BJSCONTA = U.S. Department of Justice, 10th and Constitution Avenue, NW, Washington, DC 20530

CC = Clinical Center, NIH, 9000 Rockville Pike, Bldg. 10, Bethesda, MD 20892

CDC = Centers for Disease Control, HHS, Room 2067, Bldg. 1, Atlanta, GA 30333

CENSUS = Data Users Service Division, Customer Service, Bureau of Census, U.S. Department of Commerce, Washington, DC 20233

CNTYCOM = Country Desk Officers, International Trade Administration, U.S. Department of Commerce, Washington, DC 20230

CNTYMINE = Bureau of Mines, U.S. Department of Interior, 810 7th St., NW, Washington, DC 20241

CNTY STATE = United States Department of State, 2201 C St., NW, Washington, DC 20520

COMMERCE = Industry Experts, Public Affairs, International Trade Administration, U.S. Department of Commerce, Washington, DC 20230

CPSC = Consumer Product Safety Commission, 5401 Westbard Avenue, N.W., Washington, DC 20816

CUSTOMS = U.S Customs Service, Department of the Treasury, Customs Information Exchange, U.S. Customhouse, Code 20437, 6 World Trade Center, New York, NY 10048

DAS = Division of Administrative Services, NIH, Building 1, 9000 Rockville Pike, Bethesda, MD 20892

DC = District of Columbia

DCRT = Division of Computer Research and Technology, NIH, 9000 Rockville Pike, Bethesda, MD 20892

DEO = Division of Equal Opportunity, NIH, 9000 Rockville Pike, Bldg. 31, Bethesda, MD 20892

DMCH = Division of Maternal and Child Health, HHS, 5600 Fishers Lane, Rockville, MD 20857

DN = Division of Nursing, HHS, 5600 Fishers Lane, Rockville, MD 20857

DPCS = Division of Primary Care Services, HHS, 5600 Fishers Lane, Rockville, MD 20857

DPM = Division of Personnel Management, NIH, 9000 Rockville Pike, Bldg. 1, Bethesda, MD 20892

DRG = Division of Research Resources, NIH, 9000 Rockville Pike, Bldg. 31, Bethesda, MD 20892

DRR = Division of Research Resources, NIH, 9000 Rockville Pike, Bldg. 31, Bethesda, MD 20892

DRS = Division of Research Services, NIH, 9000 Rockville Pike, Bldg. 12, Room 4007, Bethesda, MD 20892

ECONOMICS = Bureau of Economic Analysis, U.S. Department of Commerce, Washington, DC 20230

EPA = Environmental Protection Agency, 401 M St., Washington, DC 20460

FAES = Foundation for Advanced Education in the Sciences, Inc., NIH, One Cloister Court, Building 60, Suite 230, Bethesda, MD 20814-1460

FCC = Federal Communications Commission, 1919 M St., NW, Room 734, Washington, DC 20554-0001

FDA = Food and Drug Administration, HHS, 5600 Fishers Lane, Room 1505 Parklawn Bldg., Rockville, MD 20857

FIC = Fogarty International Center, NIH, 9000 Rockville Pike, Bldg. 38, Bethesda, MD 20892

FS = Forest Service, U.S. Department of Agriculture, Auditors Building, 201 14th Street, S.W., Washington, DC 20250

FWS = Fish and Wildlife Service, Department of the Interior, 1849 C Street, N.W., Washington, DC 20240

FTC = Federal Trade Commission, 6th St. and Pennsylvania Avenue, NW, Washington, DC 20580

HCFA = Health Care Financing Administration, HHS, 200 Independence Avenue, SW, Room 435-H, Hubert Humphrey Bldg., Washington, DC 20201

Be patient. If any phone number is incorrect, call (area code) 555-1212 and request the new listing.

Experts

HHS = Regional Directors, Health and Human Services, Room 638-E, Hubert Humphrey Bldg., 200 Independence Avenue, SW, Washington, DC 20201

HHSREG = Regional Directors, Health and Human Services, Room 638-E, Hubert Humphrey Bldg., 200 Independence Avenue, SW, Washington, DC 20201

HRSA = Health Resources and Services Administration, HHS, 5600 Fisher Lane, Room 1443, Parklawn Bldg., Rockville, MD 20857

IHS = Indian Health Service, HHS, Room 6-35, Parklawn Bldg., Rockville, MD 20857

IG = Inspector General, Office of, HHS, 330 Independence Avenue, SW, Room 5259, HHS Cohen Bldg., Washington, DC 20201

LABOR = Bureau of Labor Statistics, U.S. Department of Labor, 2 Massachusetts Avenue, NE, Washington, DC 20212

MAPB = Medical Arts and Photography Branch, 9000 Rockville Pike, Bldg. 10, Bethesda, MD 20892

MD = Maryland

MINES = Division of Mineral Commodities, U.S. Department of Interior, 810 7th St., NW, Washington, DC 20241

NASA = National Aeronautics and Space Administration, Washington, DC 20546

NCDB = National Center for Drugs and Biolgics, NIH, 9000 Rockville Pike, Bldg. 29, Bethesda, MD 20892

NCHS = National Center for Health Statistics, HHS, 6525 Belcrest Rd., Hyattsville, MD 20782

NCI = National Cancer Institute, NIH, 9000 Rockville Pike, Bldg. 31, Bethesda, MD 20892

NCNR = National Center for Nursing Research, NIH, 9000 Rockville Pike, Bldg. 31, Bethesda, MD 20892

NEA = National Endowment for the Arts, 1100 Pennsylvania Avenue, N.W., Washington DC 20506

NEH = National Endowment for the Humanities, 1100 Pennsylvania Avenue, N.W., Washington, DC 20506

NEI = National Eye Institute, NIH, 9000 Rockville Pike, Bldg. 31, Bethesda, MD 20892

NEIC = National Energy Information Center, Energy Information Administration, U.S. Department of Energy, E1-231, Forrestal Building, Washington, DC 20585

NHLBI = National Heart, Lung, and Blood Institute, NIH, 9000 Rockville Pike, Bldg. 31, Bethesda, MD 20892

NIA = National Institute on Aging, NIH, 9000 Rockville Pike, Bldg. 31, Bethesda, MD 20892

NIAID = National Institute of Allergy and Infectious Diseases, NIH, 9000 Rockville Pike, Bldg. 31, Bethesda, MD 20892

NIAMS = National Institute of Arthritis and Musculoskeletal and Skin Diseases, 9000 Rockville Pike, Bldg. 31, Bethesda, MD 20892

NICHD = National Institute of Child Health and Human Development, NIH, 9000 Rockville Pike, Bldg. 31, Bethesda, MD 20892

NIDA = National Institute on Drug Abuse, HHS, 5600 Fishers Lane, Rockville, MD 20857

NIDDK = National Institute of Diabetes and Digestive and Kidney Diseases, NIH, 9000 Rockville Pike, Bldg. 31, Bethesda, MD 20892

NIDR = National Institute of Dental Research, NIH, 9000 Rockville Pike, Bldg. 31, Bethesda, MD 20892

NIEHS = National Institute of Environmental Health Sciences, NIH, Research Triangle Park, NC 27709

NIGMS = National Institute of General Medical Sciences, NIH, 5333 Westbard Avenue, Room 926, Bethesda, MD 20892

NIH = National Institutes for Health, 9000 Rockville Pike, Bldg 1, Room 126, Bethesda, MD 20892

NIMH = National Institute of Mental Health, NIH, 5600 Fishers Lane, Rockville, MD 20857

NINDS = National Institute of Neurological Disorders and Stroke, 9000 Rockville Pike, Bldg. 31, Bethesda, MD 20892

NLM = National Library of Medicine, 8600 Rockville Pike, Bethesda, MD 20894

OB = Office of Biologics, NIH, 9000 Rockville Pike, Bldg. 29, Bethesda, MD 20892

OCA = Office of Consumer Affairs, HHS, 1620 L St., NW, Ste. 700, Washington, DC 20036

OC = Office of Communications, NIH, 9000 Rockville Pike, Bldg. 1, Bethesda, MD 20892

OCR = Office for Civil Rights, HHS, 300 Independence Avenue, SW, Room 5044, HHS Cohen Bldg., Washington, DC 20201

OD = Office of the Director, NIH, 9000 Rockville Pike, Bldg. 1, Bethesda, MD 20892

OERT = Office of Extramural Research and Training, NIH, P.O. Box 12233, Research Triangle Park, NC 27709

OHDS = Office of Human Development Services, HHS, 200 Independence Avenue, SW, Washington DC 20201

OPRR = Office for Protection from Research Risks, NIH, 9000 Rockville Pike, Bldg. 31, Bethesda, MD 20892

ORS = Office of Research Services, NIH, 9000 Rockville Pike, Bldg. 1, Bethesda, MD 20892

PEC = Peace Corps, 1990 K St., NW, Washington, DC 20526

PHS = Public Health Service, HHS, Office of Communication, 200 Independence Avenue, SW, Washington, DC 20201

SSA = Social Security Administration, HHS, 6401 Security Blvd., Room 932, Altmeyer Bldg., Baltimore, MD 21235

SSAREG = Public Information Contacts, Social Security Administration, HHS, 6401 Security Blvd., Room 932, Altmeyer Bldg., Baltimore, MD 21235

TRADREP = Office of the U.S. Trade Representative, 600 17th St., NW, Washington, DC 20506

USITC = Office of Industries, U.S. International Trade Commission, 500 E. St., SW, Washington, DC 20436

UMD = University of Maryland, University of Maryland-College Park, College Park, MD 20742

UVA = University of Virginia, Office of Television News, Booker House, PO Box 9018, Charlottesville, VA 22906-9018

VA = Virginia

VIC = Visitor Information Center, NIH, 9000 Rockville Pike, Bldg.10, Bethesda, MD 20892

VRP = Veterinary Resources Program, NIH, 9000 Rockville Pike, Bldg. 14, Bethesda, MD 20892

Be patient. If any phone number is incorrect, call (area code) 555-1212 and request the new listing.

Experts

A

ABS resins....Misurelli, Denby USITC 202-205-3362
ABS resins....Taylor, Ed USITC 202-205-3362
ACTH, Excessive Secretion....Staff NHLBI 301-496-4236
AG Indexes with options....Fichert, David CFT 312-353-3181
AIDS....Staff PHS Hotline 800-342-2437
AIDS....Staff NIAID 301-496-5717
AIDS....Staff NCI 301-496-5583
AIDS (Acquired Immune Deficiency Syndrome)....Kytle, Rayford PHS 202-690-6867
AIDS - PHS....Staff PHS 800-843-9388
AIDS Dementia....Staff NINDS 301-496-5751
AIDS, Neurological Symptoms or Effects of....Staff NINDS 301-496-5751
AIDS, Neurological Symptoms or Effects of....Staff NIDCD 301-496-7243
AIDS, Pediatric....Staff NICHD 301-496-5133
AIDS, Research Facilities....Staff NCRR 301-496-5545
AIDS/HIV....Jaffe, Harold W. CDC 404-639-2000
AM Intercity Relays--FCC....Staff FCC 202-634-6307
AM Radio Advertising....Staff FCC 202-632-7551
AM Radio Assignment & Transfer Applications....Staff FCC 202-254-9470
AM Radio Construction Permit Applications....Staff FCC 202-254-9570
AM Radio--Radio Programming....Staff FCC 202-632-7048
AM Radio Station--New....Staff FCC 202-254-9570
AM Radio Stations....Staff FCC 202-632-7010
AM Remote Pickups....Staff FCC 202-634-6307
ARC (AIDS-Related Complex)....Staff NIAID 301-496-5717
ASEAN....Paine, George Cnty Commerce 202-482-3875
Abaca....Cook, Lee USITC 202-205-3471
Abetalipoproteinemia....Staff NHLBI 301-496-4236
Abortion (Research Relating to)....Staff NCHS 301-436-8500
Abortion (Research Relating to)....Staff CDC 404-639-3286
Abortion (Research Relating to)....Staff NICHD 301-496-5133
Abortion/Surveillance Data....Berreth, Don CDC 404-639-3286
Above Ground Storage Tanks....Staff EPA 202-260-1130
Abrasion (Corneal)....Staff NEI 301-496-5248
Abrasive....White, Linda USITC 202-205-3427
Abrasive Products....Presbury, Graylin COMMERCE 202-482-5158
Abrasives, Manmade....Austin, Gordon MINES 202-501-9388
Abrasives, Natural....Austin, Gordon MINES 202-501-9388
Absences from Work, Empl/Unempl Statistics....Staff LABOR 202-606-6378
Access Charge Rules and Policies....Staff FCC 202-632-9342
Access Charge Tariff....Staff FCC 202-632-6387
Accessories....Schiazzano, Patricia CUSTOMS 212-466-5881
Accident Prevention and the Elderly....Staff NIA 301-496-1752
Accident Statistics....Staff NCHS 301-496-8500
Accident Statistics....Staff CDC 404-329-3286
Accounting....Chittum, J. Marc COMMERCE 202-482-0345
Accounting and Related Issues....Lee, Ronald CENSUS 301-763-4270
Accreditation (Health Professions)....Staff HRSA/BHPr 301-443-3376
Accreditation (Nurse Training)....Staff HRSA/BHPr 301-443-5786
Acetal resins....Misurelli, Denby USITC 202-205-3362
Acetates....Michels, David USITC 202-205-3352
Acetic acid....Michels, David USITC 202-205-3352
Acetone....Michels, David USITC 202-205-3352
Acetoricinoleic acid ester....Johnson, Larry USITC 202-205-3351
Achondroplasia....Staff NICHD 301-496-5133
Achondroplasia....Staff NIAMS 301-496-8188
Acid Rain....Staff EPA 202-233-9150
Acid Rain....Swink, Denise NEIC 202-586-9680
Acid, oleic....Randall, Rob USITC 202-205-3366
Acid, stearic....Randall, Rob USITC 202-205-3366
Acidosis....Staff NICHD 301-496-5133
Acids, inorganic....Trainor, Cynthia USITC 202-205-3354
Acne....Staff NIAMS 301-496-8188
Acne (Cystic)....Staff NIAMS 301-496-8188
Acoustic Neuroma....Staff NINDS 301-496-5751
Acoustic Neuroma....Staff NIDCD 301-296-7243
Acquired Immune Deficiency Syndrome (AIDS)....Staff NIAID 301-496-5717
Acquired Immune Deficiency Syndrome (AIDS)....Staff NCI 301-496-5583
Acquired Immune Deficiency Syndrome (AIDS)....Staff PHS 800-342-2437
Acquisitions, Land....Staff FWS 202-358-2200
Acromegaly....Staff NIDDK 301-496-3583
Acrylates....Michels, David USITC 202-205-3352
Acrylic resins....Misurelli, Denby USITC 202-205-3362
Acrylonitrile....Michels, David USITC 202-205-3352
Actinide Chemistry....Marianelli, Robert NEIC 301-903-5804
Activated carbon....Randall, Bob USITC 202-205-3366
Acupuncture....Staff NINDS 301-496-5751
Acute Hemorrhagic Conjunctivitis....Staff NEI 301-496-5248
Acute Leukemia....Staff NCI 301-496-5583
Acyclic plasticizers....Johnson, Larry USITC 202-205-3351
Adding Machines....Baker, Scott USITC 202-205-3386
Addison's Disease....Staff NIDDK 301-496-3583
Addressing Machines....Taylor, Kayla USITC 202-205-3390
Addressing machines....Baker, Scott USITC 202-205-3386
Adenoma of the Thyroid....Staff NIDDK 301-496-3583
Adherence to Therapeutic Regimens....Staff NCNR 301-496-0526
Adhesives....Jonnard, Aimison USITC 202-205-3350
Adhesives/Sealants....Prat, Raimundo COMMERCE 202-482-0128
Adipic acid esters....Johnson, Larry USITC 202-205-3351
Adjudication....Langan, Patrick Justice Stat 202-616-3490
Adjudication....Gaskins, Carla Justice Stat 202-508-8850
Administration, Director, Office of....Carney, Kenneth G. NLM 301-496-6491
Administrative Law Judges....Cabell, Henry B. FTC 202-326-3642
Administrative Law Judges....Harriger, Patricia A. FTC 202-326-3626
Administrative Law Judges....Jones, Shirley J. FTC 202-326-3634
Administrative Law Judges....Parker, Lewis, F. FTC 202-326-3632
Administrative Law Judges....Timony, James P. FTC 202-326-3635
Admission (Health Professions Schools)....Staff BHPr 301-443-3376
Admission Procedures (Patient)....Staff CC 301-496-4891
Admissions (Patient)....Staff CC 301-496-3315
Adolescence....Staff NIMH 301-443-4515
Adolescence....Staff NICHD 301-496-5133
Adolescent Drug Use....Brown, Mona ADAMHA 301-443-6245
Adolescent Pregnancy....Staff NICHD 301-496-5133
Adoption....Long, Susan ACF 202-401-9215
Adrenal Gland....Staff NIDDK 301-496-3583
Adrenal Insufficiency....Staff NICHD 301-496-5133
Adrenoleukodystrophy....Staff NINDS 301-496-5751
Adult Education....Staff FAES 301-496-7976
Advanced Industrial Concepts....Gunn, Marvin NEIC 202-586-5377
Advanced Solid Rocket Motor....Staff NASA 205-544-7061
Advanced Space Transportation Systems....Staff NASA 814-864-6170
Advanced Studies....Staff FIC 301-496-2516
Advanced Training (Registered Nurse)....Staff BHPr 301-443-5786
Advertising....Chittum, J. Marc COMMERCE 202-482-0345
Advertising....Zanot, Eric J. UMD 301-405-2429
Advertising services....Sweet, Mary Elizabeth USITC 202-205-3455
Adynamia....Staff NINDS 301-496-5751
Aerial Cable....Staff FCC 202-634-1800
Aerodynamic Research....Staff NASA 804-864-3305
Aeroelasticity Research....Staff NASA 804-864-6120
Aeronautics....Andersen, Drucella NASA 202-453-8613
Aeronautics....Ellis, Linda NASA 216-433-2900
Aeronautics....Koehler, Keith NASA 804-824-1579
Aeronautics Research....Schauer, Catherine NASA 804-864-3314
Aerospace - Space Marketing Support....Vacant COMMERCE 202-482-1228
Aerospace - Space Programs....Pajor, Peter LABOR 202-482-2122
Aerospace Financing Issues....Bender, Juliet COMMERCE 202-482-4222
Aerospace Industry Analysis....Walsh, Hugh COMMERCE 202-482-4222
Aerospace Industry Data....Walsh, Hugh COMMERCE 202-482-4222
Aerospace Information and Analysis....Walsh, Hugh COMMERCE 202-482-4222
Aerospace Market Development....Vacant COMMERCE 202-482-1228
Aerospace Market Promo.....Vacant COMMERCE 202-482-1228

ABS Resins / Air Compressors

Aerospace Policy and Analysis....Bath, Sally H. COMMERCE 202-482-4222
Aerospace Technology....Ellis, Linda NASA 216-433-2900
Aerospace Trade Policy Issues....Bath, Sally COMMERCE 202-482-2124
Aerospace Trade Promo.....Vacant COMMERCE 202-482-1228
Aerospace- Marketing Support....Driscoll, George COMMERCE 202-482-1228
Afghanistan....Gilman, Timothy Cnty Commerce 202-482-2954
Afghanistan (Kabul)....Staff Cnty State 202-647-9552
Afghanistan/Minerals....Kuo, Chin Cnty Mines 202-501-9693
Africa/trade matters....Frechette, Myles US Trade Rep 202-395-6135
Agammaglobulinemia....Staff NIAID 301-496-5717
Agar agar....Jonnard, Aimison USITC 202-205-3350
Age Search (Access to Personal Census Records)....Staff CENSUS 301-763-7936
Age and Sex (U.S.)....Staff CENSUS 301-763-7950
Ageism....Staff NIA 301-496-1752
Agent Orange....Berreth, Don CDC 404-639-3286
Agglomerating machinery....Greene, William USITC 202-205-3405
Aging...Staff NIA 301-496-1752
Aging...Sprott, Richard L. FAES 301-496-4996
Aging (Mental Health)....Staff NIMH 301-443-4515
Aging, Administration on....McCarthy, Jack AOA 202-619-0556
Aging, National Institute on....Shure, Jane AOA 301-496-1752
Aging-Related Maculopathy....Staff NEI 301-496-5248
Agreements--Collective Bargaining/Public File....Cimini, Michael LABOR 202-606-6275
Agribusiness, Major Proj.....Bell, Richard COMMERCE 202-482-2460
Agricultural Affairs/trade matters....Early, Suzanne US Trade Rep 202-395-6127
Agricultural Chemicals....Maxey, Francis P. COMMERCE 202-482-0128
Agricultural Finances....Morehart, Mitch Agri 202-219-0801
Agricultural Finances....Hacklander, Duane Agri 202-219-0798
Agricultural Finances - Cash Receipts....Williams, Roberts Agri 202-219-0804
Agricultural Finances - Cash Receipts....Dixon, Connie Agri 202-219-0804
Agricultural Finances - Costs & Returns....Morehart, Mitch Agri 202-219-0801
Agricultural Finances - Costs & Returns....Dismukes, Robert Agri 202-219-0801
Agricultural Finances - Credit & Fin. Mrkts- World....Baxter, Tim Agri 202-219-0706
Agricultural Finances - Credit & Financial Markets....Stam, Jerry Agri 202-219-0892
Agricultural Finances - Credit & Financial Markets....Ryan, Jim Agri 202-219-0798
Agricultural Finances - Credit & Financial Markets....Sullivan, Pat Agri 202-219-0719
Agricultural Finances - Farm Household....Ahearn, Mary Agri 202-219-0807
Agricultural Finances - Farm Real Estate Taxes....DeBraal, Peter Agri 202-219-0425
Agricultural Finances - Farm, Annual....Strickland, Roger Agri 202-219-0804
Agricultural Finances - Future Markets....Heifner, Richard Agri 202-219-0868
Agricultural Finances - Futures Markets - Crops....Evans, Sam Agri 202-219-0841
Agricultural Finances - Futures Markets-Livestock....Jessee, W.B. Agri 202-219-0767
Agricultural Finances - Income - Farm Forecast....McElroy, Bob Agri 202-219-0800
Agricultural Finances - Prices, Parity & Indexes....Milton, Bob Agri 202-720-3570
Agricultural Finances - Prices, Parity & Indexes-Recev'd....Vanderberry, Herb Agri 202-720-5446
Agricultural Finances - Prices, Parity & Indexes - Paid....Kleweno, Doug Agri 202-720-4214
Agricultural Finances - Production Costs- Tob/Sweeteners....Clauson, Annette Agri 202-219-0890
Agricultural Finances - Production Costs....Kleweno, Doug Agri 202-720-4214
Agricultural Finances - Production Costs - Crops....Dismukes, Robert Agri 202-219-0801
Agricultural Finances - Production Costs - Dairy....Matthews, Ken Agri 202-219-0770
Agricultural Finances - Subsidies....Mabbs-Zeno, Carl Agri 202-219-0631
Agricultural Finances - Subsidies....Nelson, Fred Agri 202-219-0896
Agricultural Finances - Taxes....Durst, Ron Agri 202-219-0896
Agricultural Finances - Wages & Labor....Kurtz, Tom Agri 202-690-3228
Agricultural Finances - Wages & Labor....Duffield, James Agri 202-219-0033
Agricultural Finances - Wages & Labor....Oliveira, Victor Agri 202-219-0033
Agricultural Finances - Production Costs - Livestock....Shapouri, H. Agri 202-219-0770
Agricultural Finances - Production Costs - Sweeteners....Lord, Ronald Agri 202-219-0888
Agricultural Lands....Staff FWS 703-358-1713
Agricultural Machinery....Weining, Mary COMMERCE 202-482-4708
Agricultural machinery....Vacant USITC 202-205-3380
Agriculture - State - Delaware, Dover....Feurer, T.W. Agri 302-736-4811
Agriculture, Crop Statistics....Jahnke, Donald CENSUS 301-763-8567
Agriculture, Data Requirements and Outreach....Miller, Donald CENSUS 301-763-8561
Agriculture, Farm Economics....Liefer, James A. CENSUS 301-763-8566
Agriculture, General Information....Manning, Tom CENSUS 301-763-1113
Agriculture, Guam....Hoover, Kent CENSUS 301-763-8564
Agriculture, Livestock Statistics....Hutton, Linda CENSUS 301-763-8569
Agriculture, No. Marianas....Hoover, Kent CENSUS 301-763-8564
Agriculture, Puerto Rico....Hoover, Kent CENSUS 301-763-8564
Agriculture, State - Alabama, Montgomery....Kleweno, Dave Agri 205-223-7263
Agriculture, State - Alaska, Palmer....Brown, D.A. Agri 907-745-4272
Agriculture, State - Arizona, Phoenix....Bloyd, B. L. Agri 602-640-2573
Agriculture, State - Arkansas, Little Rock....Klugh, B.F. Agri 501-324-5145
Agriculture, State - California, Sacramento....Tippett, H.J. Agri 916-551-1533
Agriculture, State - Colorado, Lakewood....Hudson, C.A. Agri 303-236-2300
Agriculture, State - Florida, Orlando....Freie, R.L. Agri 407-648-6013
Agriculture, State - Georgia, Athens....Snipes, L.E. Agri 404-546-2236
Agriculture, State - Hawaii, Honolulu....Rowley, H.K. Agri 808-973-9588
Agriculture, State - Idaho, Boise....Gerhardt, D.G. Agri 208-334-1507
Agriculture, State - Illinois, Springfield....Clampet, J.L. Agri 217-492-4295
Agriculture, State - Indiana, West Lafayette....Gann, R.W. Agri 317-494-8371
Agriculture, State - Iowa, Des Moines....Skow, D.M. Agri 515-284-4340
Agriculture, State - Kansas, Topeka....Bryam, T.J. Agri 913-233-2230
Agriculture, State - Kentucky, Louisville....Williamson, D. D. Agri 502-582-5293
Agriculture, State - Louisiana, Baton Rouge....Frank, A.D. Agri 504-922-1362
Agriculture, State - Maryland, Annapolis....West, M.B. Agri 301-841-5740
Agriculture, State - Michigan, Lansing....Fedewa, D.J. Agri 517-377-1831
Agriculture, State - Minnesota, St. Paul....Rock, C.C. Agri 612-296-2230
Agriculture, State - Mississippi, Jackson....Knight, G.R. Agri 601-965-4575
Agriculture, State - Missouri, Columbia....Walsh, P.A. Agri 314-876-0950
Agriculture, State - Montana, Helena....Sands, J. Agri 406-449-5303
Agriculture, State - Nebraska, Lincoln....Aschwege, J.L. Agri 402-437-5541
Agriculture, State - Nevada, Reno....Lies, C. R. Agri 702-784-5584
Agriculture, State - New England - Concord, NH....Davis, A.R. Agri 603-224-9639
Agriculture, State - New Jersey, Trenton....Battaglia, R.J. Agri 609-292-6385
Agriculture, State - New Mexico, Las Cruces....Gore, C.E. Agri 505-522-6023
Agriculture, State - New York, Albany....Schooley, R.E. Agri 518-457-5570
Agriculture, State - North Carolina, Raleigh....Murphy, R.M. Agri 919-856-4394
Agriculture, State - North Dakota, Fargo....Wiyatt, S.D. Agri 701-239-5306
Agriculture, State - Ohio, Columbus....Ramey, J.E. Agri 614-469-5590
Agriculture, State - Oklahoma, Oklahoma City....Bellinghausen, R. P. Agri 405-525-9226
Agriculture, State - Oregon, Portland....Williamson, P. M. Agri 503-326-2131
Agriculture, State - Pennsylvania, Harrisburg....Evans, W.C. Agri 717-787-3904
Agriculture, State - South Carolina, Columbia....Power, H.J. Agri 803-765-5333
Agriculture, State - South Dakota, Sioux Falls....Ranek, J.C. Agri 605-330-4235
Agriculture, State - Tennessee, Nashville....Brantner, C.R. Agri 615-781-5300
Agriculture, State - Texas, Austin....Findley, D. S. Agri 512-482-5581
Agriculture, State - Utah, Salt Lake City....Gneiting, D.J. Agri 801-524-5003
Agriculture, State - Virginia, Richmond....Bass, R. Agri 804-786-3500
Agriculture, State - Washington, Tumwater....Hasslen, D.A. Agri 206-586-8919
Agriculture, State - West Virginia, Charleston....Loos, Dave Agri 304-558-2217
Agriculture, State - Wisconsin, Madison....Pratt, L.H. Agri 608-264-5317
Agriculture, State - Wyoming, Cheyenne....Coulter, R.W. Agri 307-772-2181
Agriculture, Virgin Islands....Hoover, Kent CENSUS 301-763-8564
Agroforestry....Huke, Susan FS 202-205-1589
Aid to Families with Dependent Children (AFDC)....Long, Susan ACF 202-401-9215
Aids and IV drug abuse....Brown, Mona ADAMHA 301-443-6245
Air Compressors, Gas....McDonald, Edward COMMERCE 202-482-2107

Be patient. If any phone number is incorrect, call (area code) 555-1212 and request the new listing.

Experts

Air Conditioners....Rocks, Michael CUSTOMS 212-466-5669
Air Conditioning Equipment....Vacant COMMERCE 202-482-3509
Air Enforcement Division....Staff EPA 202-26-=2820
Air Environmental Laws....Wallo, Andrew NEIC 202-586-4996
Air Gas Compressors, Trade Promo.....Heimowitz, Leonard COMMERCE 202-482-0558
Air Pollution....Staff EPA 301-382-7645
Air Pollution....Staff EPA 301-382-5575
Air Pollution Control Equipment....Jonkers, Loretta COMMERCE 202-482-0564
Air Pollution and Respiratory Health....Etzel, Ruth CDC 404-488-7320
Air Quality (Outdoor Cities)....Staff EPA 202-26-=5575
Air Quality Management Division....Staff EPA 202-541-5621
Air Quality Planning and Standards....Staff EPA 202-541-5616
Air Risc Hotline....Staff EPA 919-541-0888
Air Traffic Control Equipment (Market Support)....Driscoll, George COMMERCE 202-482-1228
Air Transportation Services....Lahey, Kathleen USITC 202-205-3409
Air and Energy Policy Division....Staff EPA 202-260-5490
Air and Radiation....Staff EPA 202-260-7400
Air conditioners....Mata, Ruben USITC 202-205-3403
Air transportation services....Lahey, Kathleen USITC 202-205-3409
Airborne Science and Applications....Staff NASA 415-604-3934
Aircraft....Dicerbo, Mario CUSTOMS 212-466-5672
Aircraft....Andersen, Peder USITC 202-205-3409
Aircraft & Aircraft Engines, Market Support....Driscoll, George COMMERCE 202-482-1228
Aircraft Auxiliary Equipment, Market Support....Driscoll, George COMMERCE 202-482-1228
Aircraft Engines, Trade Promo.....Vacant COMMERCE 202-482-1228
Aircraft Fuel Economy Research....Ellis, Linda NASA 216-433-2900
Aircraft Noise Abatement Research....Ellis, Linda NASA 216-433-2900
Aircraft Operating Problems Research....Koehler, Keith NASA 804-824-1579
Aircraft Parts, Market Support....Driscoll, George COMMERCE 202-482-1228
Aircraft Parts, Trade Promo/Aux Equipment....Vacant COMMERCE 202-482-1228
Aircraft Propulsion....Ellis, Linda NASA 216-433-2900
Aircraft Reliability Research....Peto, Mary Ann NASA 216-433-2902
Aircraft Testing....Staff NASA 804-864-3314
Aircraft and Aircraft Engines, Trade Promo.....Vacant COMMERCE 202-482-1228
Airlines....Johnson, C William COMMERCE 202-482-5012
Airport Equipment, Market Support....Driscoll, George COMMERCE 202-482-1228
Airport Equipment, Trade Promo.....Vacant COMMERCE 202-482-1228
Airports, Ports, Harbors, Major Projects....Piggot, Deborne COMMERCE 202-482-3352
Alarms, burglar and fire....Scott, Baker USITC 202-205-3386
Alaska Natural Gas Transportation System (ANGTS)....Bayer, Michael NEIC 202-586-4669
Albania....Fabrizo, Lynn Cnty Commerce 202-482-4915
Albania....Becker, Margaret Peace Corps 202-606-3547
Albania....Sowry, Jenny Peace Corps 202-606-3547
Albania....Staff Cnty State 202-647-3187
Albania\Minerals....Plachy, Josef Cnty Mines 202-501-9673
Albinism (Eyes)....Staff NEI 301-496-5248
Albright's Syndrome....Staff NIAMS 301-496-8188
Albright's Syndrome....Staff NICHD 301-496-5133
Albums (autograph, photograph)....Stahmer, Carsten USITC 202-205-3321
Alcohol....Staff ADAMHA 301-443-4883
Alcohol....Staff NCALI 301-468-2600
Alcohol (and Cancer)....Staff NCI 301-496-5583
Alcohol Abuse and Alcoholism, National Institute on....Miller, Diane ADAMHA 301-443-3860
Alcohol Fuels....Staff NEIC 202-586-9920
Alcohol Fuels....Russell, John NEIC 202-536-8053
Alcohol Fuels....Detchon, Reid NEIC 202-586-4220
Alcohol and Aging....Staff NIA 301-496-1752
Alcohol and Aging....Staff NCALI 301-468-2600
Alcohol and Aging....Staff ADAMHA 301-443-4883
Alcohol, Drug Abuse, & Mental Health Block Grants....Hurley, Joan ADAMHA 301-443-6549
Alcohol, oleyl....Randall, Rob USITC 202-205-3366
Alcoholic Beverages....Kenney, Cornelius COMMERCE 202-482-2428
Alcoholism....Staff ADAMHA 301-443-4883
Alcoholism....Staff NCALI 301-468-2600
Alcohols....Michels, David USITC 202-205-3352
Alcohols, polyhydric, fatty acids....Land, Eric USITC 202-205-3349
Aldehydes....DiMaria, Joseph CUSTOMS 212-466-4769
Aldehydes....Michels, David USITC 202-205-3352
Aldosteronism....Staff NHLBI 301-496-4236
Alexander's Syndrome....Staff NINDS 301-496-5751
Algeria....Johnson, Jeffrey/Clement, Claude/Cerone, Chris Cnty Commerce 202-482-1870
Algeria (Algiers)....Staff Cnty State 202-647-4680
Algeria/Minerals....Michalski, Bernadette Cnty Mines 202-501-9699
Alien Restricted Permits....Staff FCC 202-632-7240
Alkali metals....Connant, Kenneth USITC 202-205-3346
Alkaloids....Nesbitt, Elizabeth USITC 202-205-3355
Alkaptonuria....Staff NHLBI 301-496-4236
Alkylating Agents....Staff NCI 301-496-5583
Allergic Diseases....Kaliner, Michael A. FAES 301-496-9314
Allergies....Staff NIAID 301-496-5717
Allergies (Eyes)....Staff NEI 301-496-5248
Allergy & Infectious Diseases, National Inst. of....Randall, Patricia NIH 301-496-5717
Allied Health Professions....Staff HRSA/BHPr 301-443-3376
Almonds....Burket, Stephen USITC 202-205-3318
Alopecia....Staff NIAMS 301-496-8188
Alpaca....Shelton, Linda USITC 202-205-3457
Alpers Syndrome....Staff NINDS 301-496-5751
Alpha-1-antitrypsin Deficiency (liver)....Staff NIDDK 301-496-3583
Alpha-1-antitrypsin Deficiency (lung)....Staff NHLBI 301-496-4236
Alternate Fuels Statistics....Geidl, John NEIC 202-254-5570
Alternate energy....Foreso, Cynthia USITC 202-205-3348
Alternative Fuels....Allsup, Jerry NEIC 202-586-9118
Alternative Fuels Data Center....Eberhardt, James NEIC 202-586-9837
Alternative Motor Fuels....Bower, Marc NEIC 202-586-3891
Alum. Forgings, Electro....Cammarota, David COMMERCE 202-482-0575
Alum. Sheet, Plate/Foil....Cammarota, David COMMERCE 202-482-0575
Alumina....Conant, Kenneth USITC 202-205-3346
Aluminum....Plunkert, Patricia MINES 202-501-9419
Aluminum....McNay, Deborah USITC 202-205-3425
Aluminum Extrud. Alum Rolling....Cammarota, David COMMERCE 202-482-0575
Aluminum compounds....Greenblatt, Jack USITC 202-205-3353
Alveolar Bone (Regeneration/Resorption)....Staff NIDR 301-496-4261
Alveolar Microlithiasis....Staff NHLBI 301-496-4236
Alveolar Proteinosis....Staff NHLBI 301-496-4236
Alzheimer's Disease....Staff NIA 301-496-1752
Alzheimer's Disease....Staff NINDS 301-496-5751
Alzheimer's Disease....Staff NIMH 301-443-4515
Alzheimer's Disease....Staff NIDCD 301-496-7243
Alzheimer's Disease....Baldwin, Elaine ADAMHA 301-443-4536
Amateur Licenses....Staff FCC 717-337-1212
Amaurotic Idiocy....Staff NINDS 301-496-5751
Ambergris....Land, Eric USITC 202-205-3349
Ambiguous Genitalia....Staff NICHD 301-496-5133
Amblyopia....Staff NEI 301-496-5248
Ambulance & Rescue Squads....Staff FCC 717-337-1212
Ambulatory Patient Centers....Staff CC 301-496-3141
Amebiasis....Staff NIAID 301-496-5717
American Nurses' Association....Staff NIH 816-474-5720
American fisheries products....Corey, Roger USITC 202-205-3327
Amides....Michels, David USITC 202-205-3352
Amides, fatty acids of (surface-active agents)....Land, Eric USITC 202-205-3349
Amines....Michels, David USITC 202-205-3352
Amines, fatty acids of (surface-active agents)....Land, Eric USITC 202-205-3349
Amino Acid Disorders....Staff NICHD 301-496-5133
Amino acids....Michels, David USITC 202-205-3352
Ammonia....Trainor, Cynthia USITC 202-205-3354
Ammonium nitrate, fuel-sensitized....Johnson, Larry USITC 202-205-3351
Ammonium nitrate, non-explosive or non-fertilizer....Greenblatt, Jack USITC 202-205-3353
Ammonium phosphate....Greenblatt, Jack USITC 202-205-3353
Ammonium sulfate....Greenblatt, Jack USITC 202-205-3353
Ammunition....Robinson, Hazel USITC 202-205-3496
Amniocentesis....Staff NICHD 301-496-5133
Ammonium nitrate, fertilizer....Trainor, Cynthia USITC 202-205-3354
Amplifiers....Sherman, Thomas USITC 202-205-3389
Amplifiers....Taylor, Kayla USITC 202-205-3390

Air Conditioners / Arteriosclerosis

Amyloid Polyneuropathy....Staff NINDS 301-496-5751
Amyloidosis....Staff NIDDK 301-496-3583
Amyloidosis....Staff NIAMS 301-496-8188
Amyloidosis....Staff NEI 301-496-5248
Amyotonia Congenita....Staff NINDS 301-496-5751
Amyotrophic Lateral Sclerosis....Staff NIDCD 301-496-7243
Amyotrophic Lateral Sclerosis....Staff NINDS 301-496-5751
Analgesic-Associated Nephropathy....Staff NIDDK 301-496-3583
Analgesics....Nesbitt, Elizabeth USITC 202-205-3355
Analysis and Data, Producer Price Indexes....Howell, Craig LABOR 202-606-7705
Analytical Chemistry....Staff NIGMS 301-496-7301
Analytical Instrument (Trade Promo)....Manzolino, Frank COMMERCE 202-482-2991
Analytical Instruments....Nealon, Marquarite COMMERCE 202-482-2991
Anaplasia....Staff NCI 301-496-5583
Andalusite....DeSapio, Vincent USITC 202-205-3435
Andorra....Staff Cnty State 202-647-1412
Anemia....Staff NIDDK 301-496-3583
Anemia (Hemolytic and Aplastic)....Staff NCI 301-496-5583
Anemia (Hemolytic and Aplastic)....Staff NHLBI 301-496-4236
Anencephaly....Staff NINDS 301-496-5751
Anesthesiology....Staff NIGMS 301-496-7301
Anesthesiology (Dental)....Staff NIDR 301-496-4261
Aneurysm....Staff NHLBI 301-496-4236
Aneurysm (Brain or Spinal)....Staff NINDS 301-496-5751
Angelman's Disease....Staff NINDS 301-496-5751
Angina Pectoris....Staff NHLBI 301-496-4236
Angioedema....Staff NIAID 301-496-5717
Angiography....Staff NHLBI 301-496-4236
Angioplasty....Staff NHLBI 301-496-4236
Angles, shapes, and sections (steel)....Vacant USITC 202-205-3419
Angola....Holm-Olsen, Finn Cnty Commerce 202-482-4228
Angola (Luanda)....Staff Cnty State 202-647-8252
Angola/Minerals....King, Audie L. Cnty Mines 202-501-9674
Angora....Shelton, Linda USITC 202-205-3467
Anguilla....Brooks, Michelle Cnty Commerce 202-482-2527
Aniline Dyes (and Cancer)....Staff NCI 301-496-5583
Animal (Caging, Housing, Watering)....Staff NCRR 301-496-5175
Animal Bedding....Staff OD/DL 301-496-1160
Animal Colonies and Models (Special)....Staff DRR 301-496-5175
Animal Feeds....Janis, William V. COMMERCE 202-482-2250
Animal Feeds....Conte, Ralph CUSTOMS 212-466-5759
Animal Food....Staff OD/DL 301-496-1160
Animal Genetics....Staff NCRR/VRP 301-496-5255
Animal Health....Staff NCRR/VRP 301-496-4463
Animal Husbandry....Staff NCRR/VRP 301-496-2527
Animal Models for Aging Research....Staff NIA 301-496-1752
Animal Nutrition....Staff NCRR/VRP 301-496-4481
Animal Research....Staff NCRR 301-496-5545
Animal Research....Staff OD/DC 301-496-8740
Animal Research (Intramural)....Staff NCRR 301-496-5795
Animal Research (Intramural)....Staff OD/DC 301-496-8740
Animal Resources Program....Staff NCRR 301-496-5175
Animal Sanitation....Staff OD/ORS 301-496-2960
Animal Welfare....Staff NCRR 301-496-5545
Animal Welfare....Staff OD/DC 301-496-8740
Animal Welfare Policy....Staff OPRR 301-496-7163
Animal feeds....Pierre-Benoist, John USITC 202-205-3320
Animal oil, fats, greases....Reeder, John USITC 202-205-3319
Animals: Guide for the Care and Use of Lab Animals....Staff NCRR 301-496-5545
Aniridia....Staff NEI 301-496-5248
Ankylosing Spondylitis....Staff NIAMS 301-496-8188
Anorexia Nervosa....Staff NICHD 301-496-5133
Anorexia Nervosa....Staff NIMH 301-496-4515
Anosmia....Staff NINDS 301-496-5751
Anosmia....Staff NIDCD 301-496-7243
Anoxia....Staff NHLBI 301-496-4236
Antarctica/Minerals....Doan, David Cnty Mines 202-501-9678
Antenatal Diagnosis....Staff NICHD 301-496-5133
Antenna....Kitzmiller, John USITC 202-205-3387
Antenna Structures & Towers....Staff FCC 202-634-7521
Anthracite....Foreso, Cynthia USITC 202-205-3348
Anthrax....Staff NIAID 301-496-5717
Anti-infective agents....Nesbitt, Elizabeth USITC 202-205-3355
Anti-inflammatory agents....Nesbitt, Elizabeth USITC 202-205-3355

Antialphatrypsin....Staff NIDDK 301-496-3583
Antibiotics....Staff NIAID 301-496-5717
Anticoagulant Drugs....Staff NHLBI 301-496-4236
Anticonvulsants....Nesbitt, Elizabeth USITC 202-205-3355
Antidiuretic Hormone....Staff NIDDK 301-496-3583
Antidiuretic Hormone....Staff NHLBI 301-496-4236
Antigua and Barbuda (St. John's)....Staff Cnty State 202-647-2621
Antigua/Barbuda....Brooks, Michelle Cnty Commerce 202-482-2527
Antigua/Minerals....Torres, Ivette Cnty Mines 202-501-9680
Antihistamines....Nesbitt, Elizabeth USITC 202-205-3355
Antimetabolites....Staff NCI 301-496-5583
Antimony....Llewellyn, Thomas MINES 202-501-9395
Antimony....Lundy, David USITC 202-205-3439
Antimony compounds....Greenblatt, Jack USITC 202-205-3353
Antipyretics....Nesbitt, Elizabeth USITC 202-205-3355
Antiques....Mushinske, Larry CUSTOMS 212-466-5739
Antiques....Spalding, Josephine USITC 202-205-3498
Antisocial Behavior....Staff NIMH 301-496-4515
Antiviral Substances....Staff NIAID 301-496-5717
Aorta....Staff NHLBI 301-496-4236
Aortic Insufficiency/Stenosis....Staff NHLBI 301-496-4236
Aortic Valve....Staff NHLBI 301-496-4236
Aortitis....Staff NHLBI 301-496-4236
Apes and Monkeys (Medical Research)....Staff NCRR 301-496-5545
Aphakia....Staff NEI 301-496-5248
Aphasia....Staff NINDS 301-496-5751
Aphasia (due to Stroke)....Staff NINDS 301-496-5751
Aphthous Stomatitis-Recurrent....Staff NIDR 301-496-4261
Aplastic Anemia....Staff NHLBI 301-496-4236
Apparatus, Filtering/Purifying....Rocks, Michael CUSTOMS 212-466-5669
Apparel....Dulka, William COMMERCE 202-482-4058
Apparel, Body Supporting....Burtnik, Brian CUSTOMS 212-466-5880
Apparel, Food and Raw Materials, Intl. Price Ind....Frumkin, Rob LABOR 202-606-7106
Apparel, Knit Wearing: Boys'....Ryan, Mary CUSTOMS 212-466-5877
Apparel, Knit Wearing: Men's....Ryan, Mary CUSTOMS 212-466-5877
Apparel, Leather....Schiazzano, Patricia CUSTOMS 212-466-5881
Apparel, Miscellaneous....DeGaetano, Angela CUSTOMS 212-466-5540
Apparel, Plastic Wearing....Schiazzano, Patricia CUSTOMS 212-466-5881
Apparel, Women's Woven Wearing....Crowley, Eileen CUSTOMS 212-466-5866
Apparel, Woven Wearing: Boys'....Shea, Gerard CUSTOMS 212-466-5878
Apparel, Woven Wearing: Men's....Shea, Gerard CUSTOMS 212-466-5878
Appliances, Small....Smyth, James CUSTOMS 212-466-2084
Appraisals, Land....Staff FWS 703-358-1713
Apraxia....Staff NINDS 301-496-5751
Aquaculture....Little, Robert Agri 202-720-6147
Aquaculture....Moore, Joel Agri 202-720-3244
Aquaculture....Harvey, Dave Agri 202-219-0890
Aquaculture....Staff FWS 703-358-1715
Aquatic Resource Education....Staff FWS 703-358-2156
Aquatic Species Management....Staff FWS 703-358-1710
Arachnoiditis....Staff NINDS 301-496-5751
Aran Duchenne Spinal Muscular Dystrophy....Staff NINDS 301-496-5751
Arch Glazing Petition....Giles, Ken CPSC 301-504-0580
Archaeology Research....Staff NEH 202-606-8210
Archeology....Staff FWS 703-358-2043
Architecture....Harris, William M. UVA 701-924-6450
Architecture Services....Stonitsch, Laura USITC 202-205-3408
Architecture, Urban Planning....Beatley, Timothy UVA 701-924-6459
Area Measurement....Hirschfeld, Don CENSUS 301-763-3827
Argentina....Mye, Randolph Cnty Commerce 202-482-1548
Argentina....Eschelman, Michael Peace Corps 202-606-3376
Argentina....Lustumbo, Julie Peace Corps 202-606-3575
Argentina (Buenos Aires)....Staff Cnty State 202-647-2401
Argentina/Minerals....Velasco, Pablo Cnty Mines 202-501-9677
Argon....Conant, Kenneth USITC 202-205-3346
Armenia....Staff Cnty State 202-647-8671
Arms....Robinson, Hazel USITC 202-205-3496
Arnold-Chiari Malformations....Staff NINDS 301-496-5751
Arrhythmias....Staff NHLBI 301-496-4236
Arsenic....Loebenstein, Roger MINES 202-501-9416
Arsenic....Conant, Kenneth USITC 202-205-3346
Arsenic compounds....Greenblatt, Jack USITC 202-205-3353
Art, works of....Spalding, Josephine USITC 202-205-3498
Arteriosclerosis....Staff NHLBI 301-496-4236
Arteriosclerosis (Cerebral)....Staff NINDS 301-496-5751

Be patient. If any phone number is incorrect, call (area code) 555-1212 and request the new listing.

Experts

Arteriovenous Malformations (Cerebral & Spinal)....Staff NINDS 301-496-5751
Arteritis (eyes)....Staff NEI 301-496-5248
Arthritis....Staff NIAMS 301-496-8188
Arthritis....Staff NIA 301-496-1752
Arthritis & Musculoskeletal & Skin Dis., Nat'l Ins....Raab, Connie NIH 301-496-8118
Arthritis Information Clearinghouse....Staff NIAMS 301-495-4484
Arthrogryposis Multiplex Congenita....Staff NIAMS 301-496-8188
Arthrogryposis Multiplex Congenita....Staff NICHD 301-496-5133
Artificial Blood Vessels....Staff NHLBI 301-496-4236
Artificial Heart....Staff NHLBI 301-496-4236
Artificial Heart Valves....Staff NHLBI 301-496-4236
Artificial Insemination....Staff NICHD 301-496-5133
Artificial Intelligence....Staff NLM 301-496-9300
Artificial Intelligence....Kader, Victoria COMMERCE 202-482-0571
Artificial Intelligence Research....Staff NASA 713-483-5111
Artificial Joints....Staff NIAMS 301-496-8188
Artificial Lung....Staff NHLBI 301-496-4236
Artificial Skin....Staff NIGMS 301-496-7301
Artificial flowers....Spalding, Josephine USITC 202-205-3498
Artificial flowers of man-made fibers....Cook, Lee USITC 202-205-3471
Artificial mixtures of fatty substances....Randall, Rob USITC 202-205-3366
Aruba....Brooks, Michelle Cnty Commerce 202-482-2527
Aruba/Minerals....Torres, Ivette Cnty Mines 202-501-9680
Asbestos....Virta, Robert MINES 202-501-9384
Asbestos....White, Linda USITC 202-205-3427
Asbestos & the Workplace....Berreth, Don CDC 404-639-3286
Asbestos (and Cancer)....Staff NCI 301-496-5583
Asbestos Action Program (Technical Questions)....Staff EPA 202-260-3949
Asbestos Clearinghouse....Staff EPA 800-368-5838
Asbestos Ombudsman & Small Business Clearinghouse....Staff EPA 202-305-5938
Asbestos Ombudsman Clearinghouse/Hotline....Staff EPA 800-368-5888
Asbestos Publications....Staff EPA 202-554-1404
Asbestos/Cement Products....Pitcher, Charles COMMERCE 202-482-0132
Asbestosis....Staff NHLBI 301-496-4236
Asbestosis....Staff CDC/NIOSH 404-639-3286
Asia/trade matters....Lake, Charles US Trade Rep 202-395-3900
Asparagus....Nunis, Kelly USITC 202-205-3324
Aspartame, Neurological Effects of....Staff NINDS 301-496-5751
Asperger's Syndrome....Staff NINDS 301-496-5751
Aspergillosis....Staff NIAID 301-496-5717
Asphalt....White, Linda USITC 202-205-3427
Asphalt, Natural....Solomon, Cheryl C. MINES 202-501-9393
Asphyxia....Staff NINDS 301-496-5751
Aspirin Allergy....Staff NIAID 301-496-5717
Aspirin-Myocardial Infarction Study (AMIS)....Staff NHLBI 301-496-4236
Assembly Equipment....Abrahams, Edward COMMERCE 202-482-0312
Assist. Commissioner, Consumer Prices & Price Index....Armknecht, Paul LABOR 202-606-6952
Assistant Commis., Empl/Unempl. Stats, Curr. Empl. An....Bregger, John E. LABOR 202-606-6388
Assistant Commiss., Empl/Unempl. Stats, Fed/State....Ziegler, Martin LABOR 202-606-6500
Assistant Commissioner, Compensation Levels & Trnd....MacDonald, Kathleen M. LABOR 202-606-6302
Assistant Commissioner, Industry Prices & Pr. Index....Tibbetts, Thomas LABOR 202-606-7700
Assistant Commissioner, Intl. Price Indexes....Reut, Katrina LABOR 202-606-7100
Assistant Commissioner, Safety, Health & Work. Cond....Eisenberg, William M. LABOR 202-606-6304
Associate Commissioner, Compensation & Work. Cond.....Stelluto, George LABOR 202-606-6300
Associate Commissioner, Empl/Unempl Stats....Plewes, Thomas J. LABOR 202-606-6400
Associate Commissioner, Employment Projections....Kutscher, Ronald LABOR 202-606-5700
Associate Commissioner, Prices & Living Cond.....Dalton, Kenneth LABOR 202-606-6960
Associate Commissioner, Productivity & Technology.....Dean, Edwin R. LABOR 202-606-5600
Asthma....Staff NIAID 301-496-5717
Asthma....Staff NHLBI 301-496-4236
Astigmatism....Staff NEI 301-496-5248
Astronaut Training....Staff NASA 713-483-5111
Astronomy....Chevalier, Roger A. UVA 701-924-7494
Astronomy Research....Gundy, Cheryl NASA 301-338-4707
Astrophysical Research....Katz, Jessie NASA 301-286-5566
Asymmetric Septal Hypertrophy (ASH)....Staff NHLBI 301-496-4236
Ataxia....Staff NINDS 301-496-5751
Ataxia Telangiectasia....Staff NCI 301-496-5583
Ataxia Telangiectasia....Staff NINDS 301-496-5751
Atelectasis....Staff NHLBI 301-496-4236
Atherosclerosis....Staff NHLBI 301-496-4236
Atherosclerosis (Cerebral)....Staff NINDS 301-496-5751
Atherosclerosis (Effect on Vision)....Staff NEI 301-496-5248
Athetosis....Staff NINDS 301-496-5751
Athletic equipment....Robinson, Hazel USITC 202-205-3496
Atmospheric Science Research....Staff NASA 804-864-6122
Atmospheric and Indoor Air Programs....Staff EPA 202-233-9140
Atomic Vapor Laser Isotope Separation Plant....Forsythe, Larry NEIC 301-903-4610
Atopic Dermatitis....Staff NIAMS 301-496-8188
Atrial Fibrillation....Staff NHLBI 301-496-4236
Atrophy....Staff NINDS 301-496-5751
Attention Deficit Disorder....Staff NINDS 301-496-5751
Attention Deficit Disorder....Staff NICHD 301-496-5133
Attention Deficit Disorder....Staff NIMH 301-443-4515
Auctions....Staff FCC 202-633-5940
Audio Visual Services....Siegmund, John COMMERCE 202-482-4781
Audio components....Taylor, Kayla USITC 202-205-3390
Audiology (Clinical Center patients)....Staff CC 301-496-5368
Audiovisual Material (For Health Prof. Education)....Staff NLM 301-496-6095
Audiovisual Materials (Nursing)....Staff HRSA/BHPr 301-443-5786
Australia....Bouck, Gary (Bus.)/Golike, William (Policy) Cnty Commerce 202-482-3646
Australia....Lyday, Travis Cnty Mines 202-501-9695
Australia (Canberra)....Staff Cnty State 202-647-9691
Austria....Combs, Philip Cnty Commerce 202-482-2920
Austria (Vienna)....Staff Cnty State 202-647-1484
Austria/Minerals....Buck, Donald E. Cnty Mines 202-501-9670
Autism....Staff NINDS 301-496-5751
Autism....Staff NICHD 301-443-5133
Autism....Staff NIMH 301-443-4515
Auto Ind. Affairs Parts/Suppliers....Reck, Robert O. COMMERCE 202-482-1419
Auto Industry Affairs....Keitz, Stuart COMMERCE 202-482-0554
Auto Parts/Suppliers (Trade Promotions)....White, John C. COMMERCE 202-482-0671
Autoimmune Disease....Staff NIAID 301-496-5717
Autoimmune Disease....Staff NIAMS 301-496-8188
Automatic Teller Machine Theft....Kaplan, Carol Justice Stat 202-307-0759
Automation (Laboratory Apparatus and Processes)....Staff NCRR/BEIB 301-496-4426
Automobile - Catalytic Converters....Staff EPA 202-233-9090
Automobile - Imports....Staff EPA 202-233-9660
Automobile Emissions....Staff EPA 202-260-7647
Automobile Emissions- Recalls....Staff EPA 202-233-9260
Automobile Parts....Topolansky, Adam USITC 202-205-3394
Automobile Warranty Information....Staff EPA 202-233-9100
Automobiles....Desoucey, Robert CUSTOMS 212-466-5667
Automobiles....Hagey, Michael USITC 202-205-3392
Autonomic drugs....Nesbitt, Elizabeth USITC 202-205-3355
Average Retail Food Prices--Monthly, CPI....Cook, William LABOR 202-606-6988
Average Retail Prices & Indexes of Fuels & Utls.....Adkins, Robert LABOR 202-606-6985
Average Retail Prices & Indexes, Motor Fuels Only....Chelena, Joseph LABOR 202-606-6982
Aversives....Giles, Ken CPSC 301-504-0580
Aviation Licenses....Staff FCC 717-337-1212
Aviation Rules & Hearings....Staff FCC 202-632-7175
Aviation Services (Rules)....Staff FCC 202-632-7175
Aviation and Helicopter Services....Johnson, William C. COMMERCE 202-482-5012
Avionics Marketing....Driscoll, George COMMERCE 202-482-1228
Avionics Testing....Deason, Billie A. NASA 713-483-5111
Azides....Johnson, Larry USITC 202-205-3351

Arthritis / Bicycles

B

B-19 Infection (Human Parvovirus)....Staff NICHD 301-496-5133
BCG (Bacillus Calmette-Guerin)....Staff NCI 301-496-5583
Baby Bottle Tooth Decay....Staff NIDR 301-496-4261
Baby Walkers....Tyrrell, Elaine CPSC 301-504-0580
Baby carriages, strollers, and parts....Seastrum, Carl USITC 202-205-3493
Baccalaureate Nursing Schools....Staff HRSA/BHPr 301-443-2134
Back Problems....Staff NINDS 301-496-5751
Back Problems....Staff NIAMS 301-496-8188
Bacterial Meningitis....Staff NIAID 301-496-5717
Bacterial Meningitis....Staff NIDCD 301-496-7243
Bacteriologic Media....Staff OD/ORS 301-496-6017
Bacteriology....Staff NIAID 301-496-5717
Bags....Gorman, Kevin CUSTOMS 212-466-5893
Bags or sacks....Cook, Lee USITC 202-205-3471
Bahamas....Soto, Rodrigo Cnty Commerce 202-482-2527
Bahamas (Nassau)....Staff Cnty State 202-647-2621
Bahamas/Minerals....Torres, Ivette Cnty Mines 202-501-9680
Bahrain....Clement, Claude Cnty Commerce 202-482-5545
Bahrain (Manama)....Staff Cnty State 202-647-6572
Bahrain/Minerals....Michalski, Bernadette Cnty Mines 202-501-9699
Bail (Federal)....Kaplan, Carol Justice Stat 202-307-0759
Bakery Products....Janis, William V. COMMERCE 202-482-2250
Balance of Payments, Chief....Bach, Christopher L., ECONOMIC 202-523-0620
Ball Bearings....Reise, Richard COMMERCE 202-482-3489
Balls, sports and play....Robinson, Hazel USITC 202-205-3496
Baltic States....Staff Cnty State 202-647-3187
Baltics....Taylor, Jeff Peace Corps 202-606-5519
Baltics Republic Desk....Green, Pam/Lewens, Susan Cnty Commerce 202-482-3952
Baltimore Longitudinal Study of Aging....Staff NIA 301-496-1752
Baltimore Longitudinal Study of Aging....Staff NIA 301-550-1766
Bamboo....Vacant USITC 202-205-3306
Bandages, impregnated w/ medicinals....Randall, Rob USITC 202-205-3366
Banding, Bird....Staff FWS 703-358-1714
Bangladesh....McQueen, Cheryl Cnty Commerce 202-482-2954
Bangladesh (Dhaka)....Staff Cnty State 202-647-9552
Bangladesh/Minerals....Vacant Cnty Mines 202-501-9694
Banking....Candilis, Wray O. COMMERCE 202-482-0339
Banking services....Brown, Richard USITC 202-205-3438
Banking services....Holoyda, Olha USITC 202-205-3436
Barbados....Brooks, Michelle Cnty Commerce 202-482-2527
Barbados....Staff Cnty State 202-647-2621
Barbados/Minerals....Torres, Ivette Cnty Mines 202-501-9680
Barbasco....Wanser, Stephen USITC 202-205-3363
Barbiturates....Nesbitt, Elizabeth USITC 202-205-3355
Barbuda/Minerals....Torres, Ivette Cnty Mines 202-501-9680
Barge Freight Index....Sepsey, Judy CFT 312-353-9025
Barite....Searls, James, P. MINES 202-501-9407
Barite....Johnson, Larry USITC 202-205-3351
Barium....Lundy, David USITC 202-205-3439
Barium carbonate....Johnson, Larry USITC 202-205-3351
Barium compounds....Greenblatt, Jack USITC 202-205-3353
Barium pigments....Johnson, Larry USITC 202-205-3351
Barium sulfate....Johnson, Larry USITC 202-205-3351
Barlow's Syndrome (Mitral Valve Prolapse)....Staff NHLBI 301-496-4236
Barrettes....Burns, Gail USITC 202-205-3501
Bars (steel)....Vacant USITC 202-205-3419
Bartter's Syndrome....Staff NHLBI 301-496-4236
Basal Cell....Staff NCI 301-496-5583
Basic Energy Sciences....Stull, Diane NEIC 301-903-5565
Basic Paper & Board Mfg....Smith, Len COMMERCE 202-482-0375
Basic Research....Staff NIGMS 301-496-7301
Basketwork, wickerwork, related products....Ruggles, Fred USITC 202-205-3325
Bathing caps....Jones, Jackie USITC 202-205-3466
Bathing caps....Hamey, Amy USITC 202-205-3465
Batten's Disease....Staff NINDS 301-496-5751
Battered Spouses....Staff NIMH 301-443-4515
Battered Spouses....Staff Hot-Line 301-654-1881
Batteries....Miller, Julius CUSTOMS 212-466-4680
Batteries....Eaton, Russell NEIC 202-586-0205
Batteries....Kolberg, Mary USITC 202-205-3401
Batteries, Storage....Larrabee, David COMMERCE 202-377-0575
Battery-Driven Vehicles....Alpaugh, Richard NEIC 202-586-1477

Bauxite....Sehnke, Errol D. MINES 202-501-9421
Bauxite (for metal)....McNay, Deborah USITC 202-205-3425
Bauxite calcined....White, Linda USITC 202-205-3427
Bauxite, Alumina, Prim Alum....Cammarota, David COMMERCE 202-482-0575
Bay rum or bay water....Land, Eric USITC 202-205-3349
Beads....Witherspoon, Ricardo USITC 202-205-3489
Beads, articles of....Witherspoon, Ricardo USITC 202-205-3489
Beans, ex oilseed....McCarty, Timothy USITC 202-205-3324
Bearings....Riedl, Karl CUSTOMS 212-466-5493
Bearings, ball and roller....Stonitsch, Laura USITC 202-205-3408
Bed Wetting....Staff NICHD 301-443-5133
Bedding....Hansen, John CUSTOMS 212-466-5854
Bedspreads....Sweet, Mary Elizabeth USITC 202-205-3455
Beef....Ludwick, David USITC 202-205-3329
Beer....Salin, Victoria USITC 202-205-3331
Behavioral and Social Sciences....Staff NICHD 301-496-6832
Behcet's Disease (Neurological Effects of)....Staff NINDS 301-496-5751
Behcet's Disease (Systemic)....Staff NIDR 301-496-4261
Behcet's Disease (Systemic)....Staff NIAMS 301-496-8188
Belarus....Staff Cnty State 202-647-6764
Belgium....Bensimon, Simon Cnty Commerce 202-482-5041
Belgium (Brussels)....Staff Cnty State 202-647-6071
Belgium/Minerals....Newman, Harold R. Cnty Mines 202-501-9669
Belize....Brooks, Michelle Cnty Commerce 202-482-2527
Belize....Brown, Brenda L. Peace Corps 202-606-3624
Belize (Belize City)....Staff Cnty State 202-647-4980
Belize/Minerals....Mobbs, Philip Cnty Mines 202-501-9679
Bell's Palsy....Staff NINDS 301-496-5751
Belting and Hose....Prat, Raimundo COMMERCE 202-482-0128
Belting of rubber or plastics (for machinery)....Johnson, Larry USITC 202-205-3351
Belting, industrial....Cook, Lee USITC 202-205-3471
Belts, apparel: Leather....Jones, Jackie USITC 202-205-3466
Belts, apparel: Other mens and boys....Linkins, Linda USITC 202-205-3469
Belts, apparel: Other womens and girls....Linkins, Linda USITC 202-205-3467
Bemiconductor Prod. Equipment & Materials....Finn, Erin COMMERCE 202-482-2795
Benign Congenital Hypotonia....Staff NINDS 301-496-5751
Benign Mucosal Pemphigoid....Staff NIAMS 301-496-8188
Benign Prostatic Hyperplasia....Staff NIDDK 301-496-3583
Benin....Henke, Debra Cnty Commerce 202-482-4228
Benin....Olson, Susan Peace Corps 202-606-3136
Benin....Sanchez, Patricia Peace Corps 202-606-3237
Benin (Cotonou)....Staff Cnty State 202-647-2865
Benin/Minerals....van Oss, Hendrik Cnty Mines 202-501-9687
Bensenoid intermediates, miscellaneous....Matusik, Ed USITC 202-205-3356
Bentonite....Lukes, James USITC 202-205-3426
Benzene....Raftery, Jim USITC 202-205-3365
Benzenoid paints....Johnson, Larry USITC 202-205-3351
Benzenoid plasticizers....Johnson, Larry USITC 202-205-3351
Benzenoid plastics....Misurelli, Denby USITC 202-205-3362
Benzenoid varnishes....Johnson, Larry USITC 202-205-3351
Benzo(a)pyrene....Staff NCI 301-496-5583
Benzoic acid....Matusik, Ed USITC 202-205-3356
Berger's Disease....Staff NIDDK 301-496-3583
Beriberi (Neurological)....Staff NINDS 301-496-5751
Beriberi (Nutritional)....Staff NIDDK 301-496-3583
Bermuda....Brooks, Michelle Cnty Commerce 202-482-2527
Bermuda (Hamilton)....Staff Cnty State 202-647-8027
Bermuda/Minerals....Torres, Ivette Cnty Mines 202-501-9680
Bernard-Soulier Syndrome....Staff NIDDK 301-496-3583
Beryllium....Duggan Brian COMMERCE 202-482-0575
Beryllium....Kramer, Deborah A. MINES 202-501-9394
Beryllium....Lundy, David USITC 202-205-3439
Beryllium compounds....Greenblatt, Jack USITC 202-205-3353
Beta-thalassemia (Cooley's Anemia)....Staff NHLBI 301-496-4236
Betatron....Staff NCI 301-496-5583
Beverages....Kenney, Cornelius COMMERCE 202-482-2428
Beverages, Alcoholic....Maria, John CUSTOMS 212-466-5730
Beverages, Alcoholic....Salin, Victoria USITC 202-205-3331
Beverages, Non-alcoholic....Dennis, Alfred USITC 202-205-3316
Bhutan....Gilman, Timothy Cnty Commerce 202-482-2954
Bhutan....Staff Cnty State 202-647-2141
Bhutan/Minerals....Vacant Cnty Mines 202-501-9694
Bicycles....Vanderwolf, John COMMERCE 202-482-0348

Experts

Bicycles....Tyrrell, Elaine CPSC 301-504-0580
Bicycles....Desoucey, Robert CUSTOMS 212-466-5667
Bicycles and parts....Seastrum, Carl USITC 202-205-3493
Bilateral Agreements....Staff FIC 301-496-5903
Biliary Cirrhosis....Staff NIDDK 301-496-3583
Bilirubinemia....Staff NICHD 301-496-5133
Billfolds....Seastrum, Carl USITC 202-205-3493
Billiard cloth....Cook, Lee USITC 202-205-3471
Binocular Vision....Staff NEI 301-496-5248
Binswanger's Disease....Staff NINDS 301-496-5751
Bio-related Chemistry....Staff NIGMS 301-496-7301
Biochemistry Instrumentation....Staff DRR 301-496-5545
Biodegradable Plastics....Staff EPA 202-260-5649
Bioethics....Bonkovsky, Frederick O. FAES 301-496-2429
Biofeedback....Staff NIMH 301-443-4515
Biofeedback....Staff NHLBI 301-496-4236
Biofuels....Morrer, Richard NEIC 202-586-8072
Biogasoline....Moorer, Richard NEIC 202-586-8072
Biohazard Control....Staff OD/ORS 301-496-2960
Biohazard Identification....Staff OD/ORS 301-496-2960
Biohazards (Cancer Research)....Staff NCI 301-496-5583
Biological Community Profiles....Staff FWS 703-358-1710
Biological Information Services....Goshorn, Jeanne C. NLM 301-496-1131
Biological Models & Materials Resources Program....Staff NCRR 301-402-0630
Biology....Block, Gene D. UVA 701-982-5255
Biomedical Communications....Staff NLM 301-496-6308
Biomedical Computer Centers....Staff NCRR 301-496-5411
Biomedical Engineering....Staff NIGMS 301-496-7301
Biomedical Engineering....Staff NCRR/BEIB 301-496-4741
Biomedical Information Services....Spann, Melvin L. NLM 301-496-1131
Biomedical Research Development Grant Programs....Staff NCRR 301-496-6743
Biomedical Research Support Program....Staff NCRR 301-496-5411
Biomedical Research Support Program....Staff DRR 301-496-6743
Biomedical Research Training and Fellowships....Staff NIGMS 301-496-7301
Biomedical Research Training and Fellowships....Staff DRG 301-496-7441
Bioorganic Chemistry....Kirk, Kenneth L. FAES 301-496-2619
Biophysics....Staff NIGMS 301-496-7301
Biopsy....Staff NCI 301-496-5583
Biotechnology....Arakaki, Emily COMMERCE 202-482-3888
Biotechnology Information....Staff NLM 301-496-4441
Biotechnology, Trade Promo....Gwaltney, G. P. COMMERCE 202-482-3090
Bird meat....Newman, Douglas USITC 202-205-3328
Birth....Staff NICHD 301-496-5133
Birth Defects (Developmental)....Staff NICHD 301-496-5133
Birth Defects (Neurological)....Staff NINDS 301-496-5751
Birth Defects and Developmental Disabilities....Oakley, Godfrey P. CDC 404-488-7150
Birth Defects and Genetic Diseases....Erickson, David J. CDC 404-488-7160
Birth Place....Hansen, Kristin CENSUS 301-763-3850
Birth Weight....Staff NICHD 301-496-5133
Bismuth....Jasinski, Stephen MINES 202-501-9418
Bismuth....Lundy, David USITC 202-205-3439
Bismuth compounds....Greenblatt, Jack USITC 202-205-3353
Bituminous coal....Foreso, Cynthia USITC 202-205-3348
Black Holes....Staff NASA 205-544-0034
Black Lung Disease....Berreth, Don CDC 404-639-3286
Black Lung Disease....Gambino, Phil SSA 410-965-8904
Black powder....Johnson, Larry USITC 202-205-3351
Blankets....Sweet, Mary Elizabeth USITC 202-205-3455
Blasting caps....Johnson, Larry 202-205-3351
Blastomycosis....Staff NIAID 301-496-5717
Bleaching machines....Greene, William USITC 202-205-3405
Blepharitis....Staff NEI 301-496-5248
Blepharospasm....Staff NINDS 301-496-5751
Blepharospasm....Staff NEI 301-496-5248
Blind (Rehabilitation and Research)....Staff NEI 301-496-5248
Bloch-Sulzberger Syndrome (Neurological Effects)....Staff NINDS 301-496-5751
Blood Brain Barrier....Staff NINDS 301-496-5751
Blood Cells....Staff NHLBI 301-496-4236
Blood Coagulation....Staff NHLBI 301-496-4236
Blood Diseases....Staff NHLBI 301-496-4236
Blood Donations....Staff CC 301-496-1048
Blood Fractions....Staff NHLBI 301-496-4236
Blood Groups....Staff NHLBI 301-496-4236

Blood Plasma....Staff FDA/NCDB/OB 301-496-4396
Blood Plasma....Staff NHLBI 301-496-4236
Blood Pressure....Staff NHLBI 301-496-4236
Blood Resources (National)....Staff NHLBI 301-496-4236
Blood Substitutes....Staff NHLBI 301-496-4236
Blood Vessels....Staff NHLBI 301-496-4236
Blouses....Holoyda, Olha USITC 202-205-3467
Blowers....Riedl, Karl CUSTOMS 212-466-5493
Blowers and Fans....Jonkers, Loretta COMMERCE 202-482-0564
Boat Building, Major Proj.....Piggot, Deborne COMMERCE 202-482-3352
Boats....Wholey, Patrick CUSTOMS 212-466-5668
Boats, Craft....Vanderwolf, John COMMERCE 202-482-0348
Boats, Pleasure....Vanderwolf, John COMMERCE 202-482-0348
Boats, Pleasure....Lahey, Kathleen USITC 202-205-3409
Body Weight....Staff NIDDK 301-496-3583
Body-supporting garments, includes corset/brassieres....Linkins, Linda USITC 202-205-3469
Boilers....Rocks, Michael CUSTOMS 212-466-5669
Boilers....Vacant USITC 202-205-3380
Bolivia....Lindow, Herbert Cnty Commerce 202-482-2521
Bolivia....Godbey, Maria Elena Peace Corps 202-606-3198
Bolivia....Erlandson, Barbara Peace Corps 202-606-3499
Bolivia (La Paz)....Staff Cnty State 202-647-3076
Bolivia/Minerals....Velasco, Pablo Cnty Mines 202-501-9677
Bolivian Hemorrhagic Fever....Staff NIAID 301-496-5717
Bolting cloth....Cook, Lee USITC 202-205-3471
Bolts....Brandon, James USITC 202-205-3433
Bone Disorders....Staff NIAMS 301-496-8188
Bone Marrow Failure....Staff NHLBI 301-496-4236
Bone Marrow Transplantation....Staff NCI 301-496-5583
Bone Marrow Transplantation....Staff NIAID 301-496-5717
Bone Marrow Transplantation....Staff NHLBI 301-496-4236
Bone black....Johnson, Larry USITC 202-205-3351
Bone char....Randall, Rob USITC 202-205-3366
Bone, articles of....Spalding, Josephine USITC 202-205-3498
Book Store (Clinical Center)....Staff FAES 301-496-5274
Bookbinding machinery....Slingerland, David USITC 202-205-3400
Books....Lofquist, William S. COMMERCE 202-482-0379
Books....Abramowitz, Carl CUSTOMS 212-466-5733
Books....Stahmer, Carsten USITC 202-205-3321
Books (Export Promo)....Kimmel, Edward COMMERCE 202-482-3640
Books-Information-NIH Library....Staff NCRR 301-496-2184
Books-Information-NIH Library....Staff NLM 301-496-6095
Borax....Greenblatt, Jack USITC 202-205-3353
Boric acid....Trainor, Cynthia USITC 202-205-3354
Boron....Lyday, Phyllis A. MINES 202-501-9405
Boron....Lundy, David USITC 202-205-3439
Boron compounds....Greenblatt, Jack USITC 202-205-3353
Botswana....Holm-Olsen, Finn Cnty Commerce 202-482-4228
Botswana....Grimmett, Michael Peace Corps 202-606-3246
Botswana....Woodfork, Jacqueline Peace Corps 202-606-3247
Botswana (Gaborone)....Staff Cnty State 202-647-8252
Botswana/Minerals....Antonides, Lloyd Cnty Mines 202-501-9686
Bottles, pails and dishes, of rubber of plastics....Raftery, Jim USITC 202-205-3365
Botulism....Staff NIAID 301-496-5717
Boundaries of Legal Areas, Boundary Changes....Goodman, Nancy CENSUS 301-763-3827
Boundaries of Legal Areas, State Boundary Certifica....Stewart, Louise CENSUS 301-763-3827
Bowel Diseases, Inflammatory....Staff NIDDK 301-496-3583
Bowen's Disease....Staff NCI 301-496-5583
Brachial Plexus Injuries....Staff NINDS 301-496-5751
Bradycardia....Staff NHLBI 301-496-4236
Braids, other....Shelton, Linda USITC 202-205-3457
Brain....Staff NINDS 301-496-5751
Brain Banks....Staff NINDS 301-496-5751
Brain Injury....Staff NINDS 301-496-5751
Brain Tumor....Staff NCI 301-496-5583
Brain Tumor....Staff NINDS 301-496-5751
Brain Tumor....Staff NIDCD 301-496-7243
Brass....Lundy, David USITC 202-205-3439
Brazil....Farris, Larry Cnty Commerce 202-482-3871
Brazil (Brasilia)....Staff Cnty State 202-647-8252
Brazil/Minerals....Gurmendi, Alfredo Cnty Mines 202-501-9681
Bread and other baked goods....Schneider, Greg USITC 202-205-3326
Breast Cancer....Staff NCI 301-496-5583

Be patient. If any phone number is incorrect, call (area code) 555-1212 and request the new listing.

Billfolds / Bureau of Competition (FTC)

Breast Milk....Staff NICHD 301-496-5133
Breeder reactor....Greenblatt, Jack USITC 202-205-3353
Brick, ceramic....White, Linda USITC 202-205-3427
British Indian Ocean Territories (BIOT)....Staff Cnty State 202-647-8913
British Pound with options....Lang, Dawn M. CFT 312-35-39018
Broadcast Allocation....Staff FCC 202-634-6530
Broadcast Call Letters....Staff FCC 202-634-1923
Broadcast News....Barkin, Steve UMD 301-405-2412
Broadcast Station Inspections....Staff FCC 202-632-7014
Broadcasting services....R-Archila, Laura USITC 202-205-3411
Broiler with options....Fichert, David CFT 312-353-3181
Bromine....Lyday, Phyllis A. MINES 202-501-9405
Bromine....Conant, Kenneth USITC 202-205-3346
Bronchiectasis....Staff NHLBI 301-496-4236
Bronchitis (Chronic)....Staff NHLBI 301-496-4236
Brooms....Burns, Gail USITC 202-205-3501
Brucellosis....Staff NIAID 301-496-5717
Brunei....Cung, Raphael Cnty Commerce 202-482-3875
Brunei (Bandar Seri Begawan)....Staff Cnty State 202-647-3276
Brunei/Minerals....Vacant Cnty Mines 202-501-9694
Brushes....Brownchweig, Gilbert CUSTOMS 212-466-5744
Brushes....Burns, Gail USITC 202-205-3501
Bruxism....Staff NIDR 301-496-4261
Bubonic Plague....Staff NIAID 301-496-5717
Buckets....Kaplan, Kathy CPSC 301-504-0580
Buckles....Shildneck, Ann USITC 202-205-3499
Buerger's Disease (Thromboangiitis Obliterans)....Staff NHLBI 301-496-4236
Builders Hardware....Williams, Franklin COMMERCE 202-482-0132
Builders' Wares....Mazzola, Joan CUSTOMS 212-466-5880
Building Materials and Construction....Pitcher, Charles B. COMMERCE 202-482-0132
Building Materials, Trade Policy....Smith, Mary Ann COMMERCE 202-482-0132
Building boards....Ruggles, Fred USITC 202-205-3325
Building components (wood)....Ruggles, Fred USITC 202-205-3325
Buildings, Energy Efficient....Kapus, Theodore NEIC 202-586-9123
Bulbar Palsy....Staff NINDS 301-496-5751
Bulgaria....Sowry, Jenny Peace Corps 202-606-3547
Bulbs (lamps)....Cutchin, John USITC 202-205-3396
Bulgaria....Fabrizio, Lynn Cnty Commerce 202-482-4915
Bulgaria....Becker, Margaret Peace Corps 202-606-3547
Bulgaria (Sofia)....Staff Cnty State 202-647-3188
Bulgaria/Minerals....Plachy, Joseph Cnty Mines 202-501-9673
Bulimia....Staff NIMH 301-443-4513
Bulimia....Staff NICHD 301-496-5133
Bulletin Board....Staff CENSUS 301-763-1580
Bullous Pemphigoid....Staff NIAMS 301-496-8188
Bunker "C" fuel oil....Foreso, Cynthia USITC 202-205-3348
Bureau of Competition - Accounting....Broberg, Evelyn S. FTC 202-326-2569
Bureau of Competition - Accounting....Painter, David T. FTC 202-326-2574
Bureau of Competition - Accounting....Rowe, Ronald Baylor FTC 202-326-2610
Bureau of Competition - Accounting....Steffen, Boris J. FTC 202-326-2573
Bureau of Competition - Administration....Baumgartner, Phillip A. FTC 202-326-2546
Bureau of Competition - Administration....Foster, Patricia A. FTC 202-326-2852
Bureau of Competition - Administration....Kennedy, Chandra FTC 202-326-2547
Bureau of Competition - Administration....Kereszturi, Joyce A. FTC 202-326-2541
Bureau of Competition - Administration....McGraw, Jeanne M. FTC 202-326-2565
Bureau of Competition - Administration....Onley, Essie FTC 202-326-2544
Bureau of Competition - Administration....Salters, Willie FTC 202-326-2561
Bureau of Competition - Administration....Saltzman, Harold E. FTC 202-326-3459
Bureau of Competition - Administration....Shelton, Joyce A. FTC 202-326-2856
Bureau of Competition - Compliance....Baruch, Roberta S. FTC 202-326-2861
Bureau of Competition - Compliance....Brown, Renee FTC 202-326-2687
Bureau of Competition - Compliance....Chosid, Robin S. FTC 202-326-2031
Bureau of Competition - Compliance....Davidson, Kenneth FTC 202-326-2863
Bureau of Competition - Compliance....Dietrich, Diana L. FTC 202-326-3512
Bureau of Competition - Compliance....Ducore, Daniel P. FTC 202-326-2526
Bureau of Competition - Compliance....Eckhaus, Joseph FTC 202-326-2687
Bureau of Competition - Compliance....Gill, Pamela A. FTC 202-326-2765
Bureau of Competition - Compliance....Lawler, Stewart FTC 202-326-3181
Bureau of Competition - Compliance....Libby, Kenneth A. FTC 202-326-2694
Bureau of Competition - Compliance....Lippincott, Holly FTC 202-326-3237
Bureau of Competition - Compliance....Miller, Joseph FTC 202-326-3361
Bureau of Competition - Compliance....Ortiz, Rafael A. FTC 202-326-2687
Bureau of Competition - Compliance....Piotrowski, Elizabeth A. FTC 202-326-2623
Bureau of Competition - Compliance....Pozen, Sharis Arnold FTC 202-326-2937
Bureau of Competition - Compliance....Randall, Raymond L. FTC 202-326-2768
Bureau of Competition - Compliance....Rohlck, Eric C. FTC 202-326-2681
Bureau of Competition - Compliance....Scott, Pauline FTC 202-326-2670
Bureau of Competition - Compliance....Seymour, Jane R. FTC 202-326-2687
Bureau of Competition - Compliance....Von Nirschel, David FTC 202-326-3213
Bureau of Competition - Compliance....Youngwood, Gordon FTC 202-326-2682
Bureau of Competition - Gen. Lit. (Assoc & Business)....Banks, Jonathan FTC 202-326-2773
Bureau of Competition - Gen. Lit. (Assoc & Business)....Boynton, Evelyn B. FTC 202-326-2737
Bureau of Competition - Gen. Lit. (Assoc & Business)....Brandon, Jeff FTC 202-326-2929
Bureau of Competition - Gen. Lit. (Assoc & Business)....Catt, Malcolm L. FTC 202-326-2911
Bureau of Competition - Gen. Lit. (Assoc & Business)....Cox, Kent FTC 202-326-2058
Bureau of Competition - Gen. Lit. (Assoc & Business)....Draluck, Jonathan FTC 202-326-2564
Bureau of Competition - Gen. Lit. (Assoc.& Business)....Harcketts, J. Dennis FTC 202-326-2783
Bureau of Competition - Gen. Lit. (Assoc & Business)....Hoagland, John R. FTC 202-326-2893
Bureau of Competition - Gen. Lit. (Assoc & Business).....Leviton, Lenore FTC 202-326-2779
Bureau of Competition - Gen. Lit. (Assoc & Business).....Lomax, Joan C. FTC 202-326-2901
Bureau of Competition - Gen. Lit. (Assoc & Business).....Marks, Randall FTC 202-326-2571
Bureau of Competition - Gen. Lit. (Assoc & Business)....McCartney, P. Abbott FTC 202-326-2695
Bureau of Competition - Gen. Lit. (Assoc & Business)....McNeely, Michael FTC 202-326-2904
Bureau of Competition - Gen. Lit. (Assoc & Business)....Middleton, Judith A. FTC 202-326-2915
Bureau of Competition - Gen. Lit. (Assoc & Business)....Oppenheim, Martha H. FTC 202-326-2941
Bureau of Competition - Gen. Lit. (Assoc & Business).....Sesnowitz, Douglas K. FTC 202-326-2901
Bureau of Competition - Gen. Lit. (Assoc & Business).....Veney, Wanda M. FTC 202-326-2895
Bureau of Competition - Gen. Lit. (Assoc & Business)....Zimmerman, Seth B. FTC 202-326-2800
Bureau of Competition - Gen. Lit. (Energy & Food)....Carrington, Daveene FTC 202-326-2619
Bureau of Competition - Gen. Lit. (Energy & Food)....Casey, Christopher FTC 202-326-2652
Bureau of Competition - Gen. Lit. (Energy & Food)....Chung, Cecil FTC 202-326-3204
Bureau of Competition - Gen. Lit. (Energy & Food)....Dodson, Beverly A. FTC 202-326-2939
Bureau of Competition - Gen. Lit. (Energy & Food)....Fishkin, James FTC 202-326-2663
Bureau of Competition - Gen. Lit. (Energy & Food)....Frumin, Jill M. FTC 202-326-2758
Bureau of Competition - Gen. Lit. (Energy & Food)....Henning, Renee S. FTC 202-326-2621
Bureau of Competition - Gen. Lit. (Energy & Food)....Hershey, Micheline FTC 202-326-2191
Bureau of Competition - Gen. Lit. (Energy & Food)....Hevener, Carl D. FTC 202-326-2843
Bureau of Competition - Gen. Lit. (Energy & Food)....Johnson, Dennis F. FTC 202-326-2712

Experts

Bureau of Competition - Gen. Lit. (Energy & Food)....Jones, Robert FTC 202-326-2740

Bureau of Competition - Gen. Lit. (Energy & Food)....Joseph, Anthony Low FTC 202-326-2910

Bureau of Competition - Gen. Lit. (Energy & Food)....Krulla, Rhett R. FTC 202-326-2608

Bureau of Competition - Gen. Lit. (Energy & Food)....Lawrence, Jo Ann FTC 202-326-2642

Bureau of Competition - Gen. Lit. (Energy & Food)....Licker, Naomi FTC 202-326-2851

Bureau of Competition - Gen. Lit. (Energy & Food)....Liedquist-Scott, Philo FTC 202-326-2631

Bureau of Competition - Gen. Lit. (Energy & Food)....Lipson, Frank FTC 202-326-2617

Bureau of Competition - Gen. Lit. (Energy & Food)....McDonald, Carol E. FTC 202-326-2616

Bureau of Competition - Gen. Lit. (Energy & Food)....Nolan, Arthur J. FTC 202-326-2770

Bureau of Competition - Gen. Lit. (Energy & Food)....Petrizzi, Maribeth FTC 202-326-2646

Bureau of Competition - Gen. Lit. (Energy & Food)....Proctor, Barbara FTC 202-326-2630

Bureau of Competition - Gen. Lit. (Energy & Food)....Richman, Peter FTC 202-326-2563

Bureau of Competition - Gen. Lit. (Energy & Food)....Robinson, Emily K. FTC 202-326-2640

Bureau of Competition - Gen. Lit. (Energy & Food)....Salemi, Constance M. FTC 202-326-2643

Bureau of Competition - Gen. Lit. (Energy & Food)....Schildkraut, Marc G. FTC 202-326-2622

Bureau of Competition - Gen. Lit. (Energy & Food)....Schneider, Marc FTC 202-326-2062

Bureau of Competition - Gen. Lit. (Energy & Food)....Shapiro, Barbara K. FTC 202-326-2633

Bureau of Competition - Gen. Lit. (Energy & Food)....Silver, Daniel FTC 202-326-3102

Bureau of Competition - Gen. Lit. (Energy & Food)....Skubel, Marmichael O. FTC 202-326-2611

Bureau of Competition - Gen. Lit. (Energy & Food)....Tovsky, Robert S. FTC 202-326-2634

Bureau of Competition - Gen. Lit. (Energy & Food)....Villavicencio, Alice M. FTC 202-326-3155

Bureau of Competition - Gen. Lit. (Energy & Food)....Washington, Norris FTC 202-326-2606

Bureau of Competition - Gen. Lit. (Energy & Food)....Wilensky, Steven FTC 202-326-2650

Bureau of Competition - Gen. Lit. (Health Care)....Bellack, George R. FTC 202-326-2763

Bureau of Competition - Gen. Lit. (Health Care)....Blumenreich, Linda FTC 202-326-2751

Bureau of Competition - Gen. Lit. (Health Care)....Brownman, Joseph S. FTC 202-326-2605

Bureau of Competition - Gen. Lit. (Health Care)....Bruno, Marian FTC 202-326-2846

Bureau of Competition - Gen. Lit. (Health Care)....Clark-Coleman, Sheila FTC 202-326-2759

Bureau of Competition - Gen. Lit. (Health Care)....Connelly-Draper, Molly FTC 202-326-2760

Bureau of Competition - Gen. Lit. (Health Care)....Davis, Rendell A., Jr. FTC 202-326-2894

Bureau of Competition - Gen. Lit. (Health Care)....Day, Robert FTC 202-326-2772

Bureau of Competition - Gen. Lit. (Health Care)....Friedman, Alan J. FTC 202-326-2742

Bureau of Competition - Gen. Lit. (Health Care)....Gibbs, Garry FTC 202-326-2767

Bureau of Competition - Gen. Lit. (Health Care)....Greene, Stephanie FTC , 203-326-2925

Bureau of Competition - Gen. Lit. (Health Care)....Hilder, Elizabeth FTC 202-326-2545

Bureau of Competition - Gen. Lit. (Health Care)....Holmes, Deborah A. FTC 202-326-2752

Bureau of Competition - Gen. Lit. (Health Care)....Horoschak, Mark J. FTC 202-326-2756

Bureau of Competition - Gen. Lit. (Health Care)....Jones, Patricia Y. FTC 202-326-2942

Bureau of Competition - Gen. Lit. (Health Care)....Kenyon, Kathleen FTC 202-326-2429

Bureau of Competition - Gen. Lit. (Health Care)....Maxwell, Sally L. FTC 202-326-2674

Bureau of Competition - Gen. Lit. (Health Care)....McDuffie, Lourine FTC 202-326-2735

Bureau of Competition - Gen. Lit. (Health Care)....Meier, Markus FTC 202-326-2781

Bureau of Competition - Gen. Lit. (Health Care)....Moreland, Judith A. FTC 202-326-2776

Bureau of Competition - Gen. Lit. (Health Care)....Narrow, David M. FTC 202-326-2744

Bureau of Competition - Gen. Lit. (Health Care)....Osnowitz, Steve FTC 202-326-2746

Bureau of Competition - Gen. Lit. (Health Care)....Ostheimer, Michael FTC 202-326-2699

Bureau of Competition - Gen. Lit. (Health Care)....Pender, David FTC 202-326-2549

Bureau of Competition - Gen. Lit. (Health Care)....Porter, Dora L. FTC 202-326-2752

Bureau of Competition - Gen. Lit. (Health Care)....Schorr, Gary FTC 202-326-3063

Bureau of Competition - Gen. Lit. (Health Care)....Soudakoff, Alan FTC 202-326-2747

Bureau of Competition - Gen. Lit. (Health Care)....Tucker, Deborah FTC 202-326-2766

Bureau of Competition - Gen. Lit. (Health Care)....Voss, Oscar M. FTC 202-326-2750

Bureau of Competition - Gen. Lit. (Non-Mergers)....Antalics, Michael FTC 202-326-4821

Bureau of Competition - Gen. Lit. (Non-Mergers)....Arthridge, Thomas FTC 202-326-4824

Bureau of Competition - Gen. Lit. (Non-Mergers)....Barnes, Rosenna FTC 202-326-2796

Bureau of Competition - Gen. Lit. (Non-Mergers)....Bauer, Mark, D. FTC 202-326-2723

Bureau of Competition - Gen. Lit. (Non-Mergers)....Bloom, Morris A. FTC 202-326-2707

Bureau of Competition - Gen. Lit. (Non-Mergers)....Cole, Judith A. FTC 202-326-2693

Bureau of Competition - Gen. Lit. (Non-Mergers)....Cook, Robert FTC 202-326-2771

Bureau of Competition - Gen. Lit. (Non-Mergers)....Constantini, Amie M. FTC 202-326-3186

Bureau of Competition - Gen. Lit. (Non-Mergers)....Costilo, L. Barry FTC 202-326-2748

Bureau of Competition - Gen. Lit. (Non-Mergers)....Cunningham, Linda FTC 202-326-2638

Bureau of Competition - Gen. Lit. (Non-Mergers)....Dagen, Richard FTC 202-326-2628

Bureau of Competition - Gen. Lit. (Non-Mergers)....Doyle, Robert W., Jr. FTC 202-326-2819

Bureau of Competition - Gen. Lit. (Non-Mergers)....Dugan, John, F. FTC 202-326-2715

Bureau of Competition - Gen. Lit. (Non-Mergers)....Easterling, Wallace W. FTC 202-326-2936

Bureau of Competition - Gen. Lit. (Non-Mergers)....Gray, Jessica FTC 202-326-3342

Bureau of Competition - Gen. Lit. (Non-Mergers)....Hackley, Jacqueline FTC 202-326-2729

Bureau of Competition - Gen. Lit. (Non-Mergers)....Horwitz, Reid B. FTC 202-326-2053

Bureau of Competition - Gen. Lit. (Non-Mergers)....Inglefield, David L. FTC 202-326-2637

Bureau of Competition - Gen. Lit. (Non-Mergers)....Johnson, Joyce FTC 202-326-2576

Bureau of Competition - Gen. Lit. (Non-Mergers)....Klein, Deborah E. FTC 202-326-2813

Bureau of Competition - Gen. Lit. (Non-Mergers)....Menna, Mark FTC 202-326-2722

Bureau of Competition - Gen. Lit. (Non-Mergers)....Mills, Karen FTC 202-326-2052

Bureau of Competition - Gen. Lit. (Non-Mergers)....Moscatelli, Catharine FTC 202-326-2749

Bureau of Competition - Gen. Lit. (Non-Mergers)....Nagata, Ernest A. FTC 202-326-2714

Bureau of Competition - Gen. Lit. (Non-Mergers)....Nolan, Paul FTC 202-326-2770

Be patient. If any phone number is incorrect, call (area code) 555-1212 and request the new listing.

Bureau of Competition / FTC

Bureau of Competition - Gen. Lit. (Non-Mergers)....Oxenham, Sarah FTC 202-326-2226

Bureau of Competition - Gen. Lit. (Non-Mergers)....Parker, Patrice FTC 202-326-2837

Bureau of Competition - Gen. Lit. (Non-Mergers)....Potts, Agnes FTC 202-326-3186

Bureau of Competition - Gen. Lit. (Non-Mergers)....Ragano, James M. FTC 202-326-3186

Bureau of Competition - Gen. Lit. (Non-Mergers)....Ramadhan, Allee A. FTC 202-326-2716

Bureau of Competition - Gen. Lit. (Non-Mergers)....Riddell, Stephen FTC 202-326-2721

Bureau of Competition - Gen. Lit. (Non-Mergers)....Schultheiss, Patricia FTC 202-326-2877

Bureau of Competition - Gen. Lit. (Non-Mergers)....Seesel, John H. FTC 202-326-2702

Bureau of Competition - Gen. Lit. (Non-Mergers)....Stone, David J. FTC 202-326-3186

Bureau of Competition - Gen. Lit. (Non-Mergers)....Sockwell, Stephen W., Jr. FTC 202-326-2950

Bureau of Competition - Gen. Lit. (Non-Mergers)....Spriggs, Valicia A. FTC 202-326-2839

Bureau of Competition - Gen. Lit. (Non-Mergers)....Stevens, Peer L. FTC 202-326-3154

Bureau of Competition - Gen. Lit. (Non-Mergers)....Waldeck, Cecelia FTC 202-326-3669

Bureau of Competition - Gen. Lit. (Non-Mergers)....Weber, John C. FTC 202-326-2682

Bureau of Competition - Gen. Lit. (Non-Mergers)....Williams, Tonya FTC 202-326-2752

Bureau of Competition - Gen. Lit. (Non-Mergers)....Woodard, Carolyn FTC 202-326-2706

Bureau of Competition - General Litigation....Berg, Karen E. FTC 202-326-2960

Bureau of Competition - General Litigation....Bernstein, Steven K. FTC 202-326-2423

Bureau of Competition - General Litigation....Brooks, Sylvia M. FTC 202-326-5916

Bureau of Competition - General Litigation....Dadoun, David FTC 202-326-3103

Bureau of Competition - General Litigation....Elmore, Ernest FTC 202-326-3109

Bureau of Competition - General Litigation....Heydenreich, Melissa FTC 202-326-2543

Bureau of Competition - General Litigation....Higgins, Claudia R. FTC 202-326-2682

Bureau of Competition - General Litigation....Holden, James FTC 202-326-2963

Bureau of Competition - General Litigation....Jex, Elizabeth FTC 202-326-3273

Bureau of Competition - General Litigation....Levy, Richard A. FTC 202-326-2682

Bureau of Competition - General Litigation....Lingos, Annthalia FTC 202-326-2682

Bureau of Competition - General Litigation....Malester, Ann B. FTC 202-326-2682

Bureau of Competition - General Litigation....Mendel, Jacqueline FTC 202-326-2603

Bureau of Competition - General Litigation....Moiseyev, Michael FTC 202-326-3106

Bureau of Competition - General Litigation....Paige, Margaret C. FTC 202-326-2682

Bureau of Competition - General Litigation....Person, Brenda W. FTC 202-326-2682

Bureau of Competition - General Litigation....Pettee, Susan P. FTC 202-326-2682

Bureau of Competition - General Litigation....Pickett, Robert FTC 202-326-2682

Bureau of Competition - General Litigation....Piercy, Carey FTC 202-326-2962

Bureau of Competition - General Litigation....Tahyar, Benjamin FTC 202-326-2889

Bureau of Competition - General Litigation....Triggs, Casey FTC 202-326-2804

Bureau of Competition - General Litigation....Yahia, Terri FTC 202-326-2602

Bureau of Competition - General Litigation....Wilkinson, Laura FTC 202-326-2830

Bureau of Competition - General Litigation....Wilmer, Bobbie J. FTC 202-326-2836

Bureau of Competition - International Antitrust....Briseno, Liliana O. FTC 202-326-2731

Bureau of Competition - International Antitrust....Crise, Cameron J. FTC 202-326-2731

Bureau of Competition - International Antitrust....Feuillan, Jacques C. FTC 202-326-2379

Bureau of Competition - International Antitrust....Karlsson, Paul FTC 202-326-2566

Bureau of Competition - International Antitrust....Lindstrom, Talbot S. FTC 202-326-2717

Bureau of Competition - International Antitrust....Parisi, John J. FTC 202-326-2133

Bureau of Competition - International Antitrust....Schimpff, Kirsten M. FTC 202-326-2731

Bureau of Competition - International Antitrust....Shanahan, Deirdre E. FTC 202-326-2951

Bureau of Competition - International Antitrust....White, Roxanne FTC 202-326-2954

Bureau of Competition - Office of the Director....Arquit, Kevin J. FTC 202-326-2556

Bureau of Competition - Office of the Director....Clark, Barbara A. FTC 202-326-2562

Bureau of Competition - Office of the Director....Egan, James C., Jr. FTC 202-326-2886

Bureau of Competition - Office of the Director....Forster, Mary C. FTC 202-326-2551

Bureau of Competition - Office of the Director....Green, Geoffrey FTC 202-326-2641

Bureau of Competition - Office of the Director....Greenbaum, Joan S. FTC 202-326-2629

Bureau of Competition - Office of the Director....Rowe, Ronald A. FTC 202-326-2575

Bureau of Competition - Office of the Director....Snider, Virginia L. FTC 202-326-2682

Bureau of Competition - Office of the Director....Steptoe, Mary Lou FTC 202-326-2584

Bureau of Competition - Office of the Director....Taylor, Mildred E. FTC 202-326-2553

Bureau of Competition - Office of the Director....Whitener, Mark D. FTC 202-326-2845

Bureau of Competition - Office of the Director....Winslow, Walter T., Jr. FTC 202-326-2560

Bureau of Competition - Policy & Evaluation....Averitt, Neil W. FTC 202-326-2885

Bureau of Competition - Policy & Evaluation....Cariaga, Frances P. FTC 202-326-2882

Bureau of Competition - Policy and Evaluation....Kattan, Joseph FTC 202-326-2884

Bureau of Competition - Policy & Evaluation....Mongoven, James F. FTC 202-326-2879

Bureau of Competition - Policy & Evaluation....Morse, Howard FTC 202-326-2949

Bureau of Competition - Policy and Evaluation....Doying, William A.E. FTC 202-326-2582

Bureau of Competition - Premerger Notification....Bellamy, Lottie FTC 202-326-3100

Bureau of Competition - Premerger Notification....Cohen, Victor FTC 202-326-2849

Bureau of Competition - Premerger Notification....Colding, Dollie FTC 202-326-2866

Bureau of Competition - Premerger Notification....Crouse, Lynda M. FTC 202-326-2880

Bureau of Competition - Premerger Notification....Epps, Melea R.C. FTC 202-326-2705

Bureau of Competition - Premerger Notification....Hancock, Thomas F. FTC 202-326-2946

Bureau of Competition - Premerger Notification....Horton, Renee A. FTC 202-326-2842

Bureau of Competition - Premerger Notification....Kaplan, Jeffrey FTC 202-326-2943

Bureau of Competition - Premerger Notification....Owen, Deborah K. FTC 202-326-2151

Bureau of Competition - Premerger Notification....Rubenstein, Hy David FTC 202-326-2887

Be patient. If any phone number is incorrect, call (area code) 555-1212 and request the new listing.

Experts

Bureau of Competition - Premerger Notification....Schechter, William I. FTC 202-326-3119
Bureau of Competition - Premerger Notification....Sharpe, Patrick FTC 202-326-2848
Bureau of Competition - Premerger Notification....Sipple, John M., Jr. FTC 202-326-2862
Bureau of Competition - Premerger Notification....Smith, Richard B. FTC 202-326-2850
Bureau of Competition - Premerger Notification....Speed, Bernice L. FTC 202-326-2280
Bureau of Competition - Premerger Notification....Wolfe, Mary E. FTC 202-326-2880
Bureau of Competition - Premerger Notification....Peay, Sandra M. FTC 202-326-2844
Bureau of Consumer Affairs - Advertising Practices....Bloom, Jeffrey I. FTC 202-326-3327
Bureau of Economics - Antitrust....Ferguson, James M. FTC 202-326-3386
Bureau of Economics - Office of the Director....Painter, Susan FTC 202-326-3370
Burkina Faso....Michelini, Philip Cnty Commerce 202-482-4388
Burkina Faso (Ouagadougou)....Staff Cnty State 202-647-3066
Burkina Faso/Minerals....Van Oss, Hendrik Cnty Mines 202-501-9687
Burkitt's Lymphoma....Staff NCI 301-496-5583
Burma (Myanmar)....Paine, George Cnty Commerce 202-482-3875
Burma (Rangoon)....Staff Cnty State 202-647-7108
Burma/Minerals....Vacant Cnty Mines 202-501-9694
Burn Research....Staff NIGMS 301-496-7301
Burning Mouth Syndrome....Staff 301-496-4261
Bursitis....Staff NIAMS 301-496-8188
Burundi....Michelini, Philip Cnty Commerce 202-482-4388
Burundi (Bujumbura)....Staff Cnty State 202-647-3139
Burundi/Minerals....Antonides, Lloyd Cnty Mines 202-501-9686
Buses....Hagey, Michael USITC 202-205-3392
Business Administration....Allen, Brandt R. UVA 701-924-4842
Business Cycle Indicators....Statistical Indicators Staff ECONOMIC 202-523-0500
Business Data Centers....Rowe, John CENSUS 301-763-1580
Business Establishment List, Empl/Unempl. Stats....Searson, Michael LABOR 202-606-6469
Business Forms....Bratland, Rose Marie COMMERCE 202-492-0380
Business Licenses....Staff FCC 717-337-1212
Business Opportunities, Small and Woman-Owned....Staff HUD 202-708-1428
Business Outlook, Chief....Green, George R. ECONOMIC 202-523-0701
Business Radio....Staff FCC 717-337-1212
Business Statistics, Business Owners' Characterist....McCutcheon, Donna CENSUS 301-763-5517
Business Statistics, Minority Businesses....McCutcheon, Donna CENSUS 301-763-5517
Business, Statistics, County Business Patterns....Decker, Zigmund CENSUS 301-763-5430
Business/Industry Data Centers....Rowe, John CENSUS 301-763-1580
Businesses, Disadvantaged....Miranda, Leonel NEIC 202-254-5583
Businesses, Minority-Owned....Miranda, Leonel NEIC 202-254-5583
Businesses, Women-Owned....Miranda, Leonel NEIC 202-254-5583
Butadiene....Raftery, Jim USITC 202-205-3365
Butane....Land, Eric USITC 202-205-3349
Butter....Warren, J Fred USITC 202-205-3311
Buttons....Shildneck, Ann USITC 202-205-3499
Butyl alcohol....Michels, David USITC 202-205-3352
Butyl benzyl phthalate....Johnson, Larry USITC 202-205-3351
Butyl oleate....Johnson, Larry USITC 202-205-3351
Butyl rubber....Misurelli, Denby USITC 202-205-3362
Butyl stearate....Johnson, Larry USITC 202-205-3351
Butylene....Raftery, Jim USITC 202-205-3365
Byssinosis (Brown Lung Disease)....Staff NHLBI 301-496-4236

C

CAD/CAM/CAE Software....Swann, Vera A. COMMERCE 202-482-0396
CD Players....Dicerbo, Mario CUSTOMS 212-466-5672
CD-ROM....Staff CENSUS 301-763-4673
CDC Information Center....Kennedy, Joan U. CDC 404-639-1601
CDC Information Center (Library).... CDC 404-639-3396
CEA (Carcinoembryonic Antigen)....Staff NCI 301-496-5583
CENDATA....Staff CENSUS 301-763-2074

CO/Fuel Gas Detectors....Mesa, Stacey Reuben CPSC 301-504-0580
Cable Access Policy....Staff FCC 202-632-7480
Cable Broadcasting....Siegmund, John COMMERCE 202-482-4781
Cable Pole Attachments....Staff FCC 202-632-1861
Cable Telephone....Staff FCC 202-634-1830
Cable Television Complaints....Staff FCC 202-632-7048
Cable Television Cross Ownership....Staff FCC 202-634-1830
Cable Television Franchising....Staff FCC 202-632-7076
Cablegrams....Staff FCC 202-632-7265
Cadastral Surveys....Staff FWS 703-358-1713
Cadmium....Llewellyn, Thomas MINES 202-501-9395
Cadmium....Lundy, David USITC 202-205-3439
Caffeine and its compounds....Nesbitt, Elizabeth USITC 202-205-3355
Calcium....Miller, Michael MINES 202-501-9409
Calcium....Lundy, David USITC 202-205-3439
Calcium carbonate....Tepordei, Valentin V. MINES 202-501-9392
Calcium carbonate....Johnson, Larry USITC 202-205-3351
Calcium compounds....Greenblatt, Jack USITC 202-205-3353
Calcium pigments....Johnson, Larry USITC 202-205-3351
Calcium sulfate....Johnson, Larry USITC 202-205-3351
Calculators....Baker, Scott USITC 202-205-3386
Calculus....Staff NIDR 301-496-4261
Calendaring machines....Slingerland, David USITC 202-205-3400
Call Sign Block Allocation....Staff FCC 202-653-8126
Call Signs Allocation....Staff FCC 202-634-1923
Calligraphy....Staff FWS 202-208-4111
Cambodia....Pho, Hong-Phong B. Cnty Commerce 202-482-3875
Cambodia (Phom Penh)....Staff Cnty State 202-647-3133
Cambodia/Minerals....Vacant Cnty Mines 202-501-9694
Cameos....Witherspoon, Ricardo USITC 202-205-3489
Cameras....Kiefer, Barbara CUSTOMS 212-466-5685
Cameroon....Henke, Debra Cnty Commerce 204-482-5149
Cameroon....Blackwell, Gloria Peace Corps 202-606-3998
Cameroon....Swezy, Virginia Peace Corps 202-606-3998
Cameroon (Yaounde)....Staff Cnty State 202-647-1707
Cameroon/Minerals....Dolley, Thomas Cnty Mines 202-501-9690
Camphor....Randall, Rob USITC 202-205-3366
Campus Radio Stations....Staff FCC 202-653-6288
Canada....Don, Jonathan Cnty Commerce 202-482-3101
Canada (Ottawa)....Staff Cnty State 202-647-2170
Canada/Minerals....Doan, David Cnty Mines 202-501-9678
Canada/trade matters....Weiss, David US Trade Rep 202-395-5663
Canadian Dollar with options....Bice, David CFT 312-353-7880
Canavan's Disease....Staff NINDS 301-496-5751
Cancer (Reproductive Tract)....Staff NCI 301-496-5583
Cancer (Reproductive Tract)....Staff NICHD 301-496-5133
Cancer Control Program....Staff NCI 301-496-5583
Cancer Institute, National....Nealon, Eleanor NIH 301-496-6631
Cancer Institute, National....Newman, Patricia NIH 301-496-6641
Cancer Prevention....Wyatt, Stephen W. CDC 404-488-5496
Cancer Research....Staff NCI 301-496-5583
Cancer and Aging....Staff NIA 301-496-1752
Candida....Staff NIAID 301-496-5717
Candida....Staff NIDR 301-496-4261
Candidiasis....Staff NIAID 301-496-5717
Candidiasis....Staff NIDR 301-496-4261
Candles....Brownchweig, Gilbert CUSTOMS 212-466-5744
Candles....Randall, Rob USITC 202-205-3366
Candy....Maria, John CUSTOMS 212-466-5730
Canes....Burns, Gail USITC 202-205-3501
Canker Sores....Staff NIDR 301-496-4261
Canned Goods....Hodgen, Donald A. COMMERCE 202-482-3346
Canoes....Lahey, Kathleen USITC 202-205-3409
Capacitors....Josephs, Irwin CUSTOMS 212-466-5673
Capacitors....Malison, Andrew USITC 202-205-3391
Cape Verde....Michelini, Philip Cnty Commerce 202-482-4388
Cape Verde....Fossum, Linnea Peace Corps 202-606-3708
Cape Verde (Praia)....Staff Cnty State 202-647-3391
Cape Verde Islands/Minerals....King, Audie L. Cnty Mines 202-501-9674
Capital Goods (Trade Prom)....Brandis, Jay COMMERCE 202-482-0560
Capital Measurement, Productivity Research....Harper, Michael LABOR 202-606-5603
Capital Punishment....Greenfeld, Lawrence Justice Stat 202-616-3281
Capitation Grants for Health Professions Schools....Staff HRSA/BHPr 301-443-5794
Capitation Grants for Nurse Training....Staff HRSA/BHPr 301-443-5786
Caprolactam monomer....Matusik, Ed USITC 202-205-3356

Burma / Chad

Caps....Jones, Jackie USITC 202-205-3466
Caps....Hamey, Amy USITC 202-205-3465
Carbon....Johnson, Larry USITC 202-205-3351
Carbon Black....Prat, Raimundo COMMERCE 202-482-0128
Carbon Products....Brownchweig, Gilbert CUSTOMS 212-466-5744
Carbon activated....Randall, Bob USITC 202-205-3366
Carbon and graphite electrodes....Cutchin, John USITC 202-205-3396
Carbon black....Johnson, Larry USITC 202-205-3351
Carbon dioxide....Conant, Kenneth USITC 202-205-3346
Carbon disulfide....Conant, Kenneth USITC 202-205-3346
Carbon tetrachloride....Michels, David USITC 202-205-3352
Carboxylic acids....Michels, David USITC 202-205-3352
Carboxymethyl cellulose salts (surface active)....Land, Eric USITC 202-205-3349
Carcalon (Krebiozen)....Staff NCI 301-496-5583
Carcinogen....Staff NCI 301-496-5583
Carcinogen Assessment....Staff EPA 202-260-5898
Carcinoma....Staff NCI 301-496-5583
Card cases....Seastrum, Carl USITC 202-205-3493
Cardiac Disease....Staff NHLBI 301-496-4236
Cardiac Pacemakers....Staff NHLBI 301-496-4236
Cardiomegaly....Staff NHLBI 301-496-4236
Cardiomyopathy (Hypertrophic, Dilated)....Staff NHLBI 301-496-4236
Cardiopulmonary Resuscitation (CPR)....Staff NHLBI 301-496-4236
Cardiovascular Disease....Staff NHLBI 301-496-4236
Cardiovascular drugs....Nesbitt, Elizabeth USITC 202-205-3355
Carditis....Staff NHLBI 301-496-4236
Career Criminals....Langan, Patrick Justice Stat 202-616-3490
Career Criminals....Greenfeld, Lawrence Justice Stat 202-616-3281
Careers in Nursing....Staff DRR 301-443-5786
Caribbean....Frechette, Myles US Trade Rep 202-395-6135
Caribbean Basin....Dowling, Jay Cnty Commerce 202-482-1648
Caribbean Primate Research Center....Staff NCRR 301-496-5411
Caries....Staff NIDR 301-496-4261
Carpal Tunnel Syndrome....Staff NINDS 301-496-5751
Carpal Tunnel Syndrome....Staff NIAMS 301-496-8188
Carpets....Sweet, Mary Elizabeth USITC 202-205-3455
Carrier Equipment....Staff FCC 202-634-1800
Carrots....McCarty, Timothy USITC 202-205-3324
Carrying Cases....Gorman, Kevin CUSTOMS 212-466-5893
Cartography....Staff FWS 703-358-1713
Case....Swann, Vera COMMERCE 202-482-4936
Casein....Randall, Rob USITC 202-205-3366
Cash registers....Baker, Scott USITC 202-205-3386
Castile soap....Land, Eric USITC 202-205-3349
Casting machines....Greene, William USITC 202-205-3405
Cat Cry Syndrome (Cri Du Chat)....Staff NICHD 301-496-5133
Cat Scratch Fever....Staff NIAID 301-496-5717
Catalytic Converters....Staff EPA 202-233-9090
Cataplexy....Staff NINDS 301-496-5751
Cataract....Staff NEI 301-496-5248
Catheterization (Cardiac or Heart)....Staff NHLBI 301-496-4236
Cathode-Ray tubes....Kitzmiller, John USITC 202-205-3351
Cattle (Feeder) with options....Fichert, David CFT 312-353-3181
Cattle with options....Fichert, David CFT 312-353-3181
Caulking compounds....Johnson, Larry USITC 202-205-3351
Caulks....Johnson, Larry USITC 202-205-3351
Caustic potash....Conant, Kenneth USITC 202-205-3346
Caustic soda....Conant, Kenneth USITC 202-205-3346
Caymans....Brooks, Michelle Cnty Commerce 202-482-2527
Cedar leaf....Land, Eric USITC 202-205-3349
Celiac Disease....Staff NIDDK 301-496-3583
Celiac Disease....Staff NIAID 301-496-5717
Cell Aging....Staff NIA 301-496-1752
Cell Bank....Staff NIGMS 301-496-7301
Cell Biology....Staff NIGMS 301-496-7301
Cellular Function....Staff NIGMS 301-496-7301
Cellular Immunology....Finerty, John FAES 301-496-7815
Cellular Mobile Radio....Staff FCC 202-653-6400
Cellular Structure....Staff NIGMS 301-496-7301
Cement....Pitcher, Charles COMMERCE 202-482-0132
Cement....Solomon, Cheryl C. MINES 202-501-9393
Cement Plants, Major Proj.....White, Barbara COMMERCE 202-482-4160
Cement, hydraulic....White, Linda USITC 202-205-3427
Cements of rubber, vinyl, etc.....Jonnard, Aimison USITC 202-205-3350
Cements, dental....Randall, Rob USITC 202-205-3366
Census Awareness (Regional Offices)....Staff CENSUS 301-763-4683
Census Catalog....McCall, John CENSUS 301-763-1584
Census Customer Service Fax Number....Staff CENSUS 301-763-4794
Census Geographic Concepts....Staff CENSUS 301-763-5720
Census History....Bohme, Frederick CENSUS 301-763-7936
Census Personnel Locator....Staff CENSUS 301-763-7662
Census and You (Monthly Newsletter)....Morton, Jackson CENSUS 301-763-1584
Census and You (Monthly Newsletter)....Tillman, Neil CENSUS 301-763-1584
Census of Retail Trade, Guam....Larson, Odell CENSUS 301-763-8226
Census of Retail Trade, Guam....Hoover, Kent CENSUS 301-763-8564
Census of Retail Trade, Puerto Rico....Larson, Odell CENSUS 301-763-8226
Census of Retail Trade, Puerto Rico....Hoover, Kent CENSUS 301-763-8564
Census of Retail Trade, Virgin Islands....Larson, Odell CENSUS 301-763-8226
Census of Retail Trade, Virgin Islands....Hoover, Kent CENSUS 301-763-8564
Census of Selected Service Industries, Guam....Larson, Odell CENSUS 301-763-8226
Census of Selected Service Industries, Guam....Hoover, Kent CENSUS 301-763-8564
Census of Selected Service Industries, Puerto Rico....Larson, Odell CENSUS 301-763-8226
Census of Selected Service Industries, Puerto Rico....Hoover, Kent CENSUS 301-763-8564
Census of Selected Service Industries, Virgin Isl....Larson, Odell CENSUS 301-763-8226
Census of Selected Service Industries, Virgin Isl....Hoover, Kent CENSUS 301-763-8564
Census of Wholesale Trade, Guam....Larson, Odell CENSUS 301-763-8226
Census of Wholesale Trade, Guam....Hoover, Kent CENSUS 301-763-8564
Census of Wholesale Trade, Puerto Rico....Larson, Odell CENSUS 301-763-8226
Census of Wholesale Trade, Puerto Rico....Hoover, Kent CENSUS 301-763-8564
Census of Wholesale Trade, Virgin Islands....Larson, Odell CENSUS 301-763-8226
Census of Wholesale Trade, Virgin Islands....Hoover, Kent CENSUS 301-763-8564
Centenarians....Staff NIA 301-496-1752
Center for Hazardous Materials Hotline....Staff EPA 800-334-2467
Centers for Disease Control....Staff CDC 404-329-3291
Centers of Population....Hirschfeld, Don CENSUS 301-763-3827
Central Africa Republic....Michelini, Philip Cnty Commerce 202-482-4388
Central African Republic (Bangui)....Staff Cnty State 202-647-3139
Central African Republic/Minerals....Dolley, Thomas Cnty Mines 202-501-9690
Central Core Disease....Staff NINDS 301-496-5751
Central Storeroom....Staff OD/DL 301-496-9156
Centrifuges....Slingerland, David USITC 202-205-3400
Ceramic Gas Turbines....Alpaugh, Richard NEIC 202-586-8012
Ceramic construction articles....White, Linda USITC 202-205-3427
Ceramic sanitary fixtures....Fulcher, Nancy USITC 202-205-3434
Ceramic table, kitchen articles....McNay, Deborah USITC 202-205-3425
Ceramics....Kalkines, George CUSTOMS 212-466-5794
Ceramics (Advanced)....Shea, Moira COMMERCE 202-482-0128
Ceramics Machinery....Shaw, Eugene COMMERCE 202-482-3494
Cereal breakfast foods....Schneider, Greg USITC 202-205-3326
Cereal grains....Pierre-Benoist, John USITC 202-205-3320
Cereals....Janis, William V. COMMERCE 202-482-2250
Cerebellar Arteriosclerosis....Staff NINDS 301-496-5751
Cerebellar Arteriovenous Malformations....Staff NINDS 301-496-5751
Cerebellar Ataxia....Staff NINDS 301-496-5751
Cerebellar Lesions....Staff NINDS 301-496-5751
Cerebral Death....Staff NINDS 301-496-5751
Cerebral Degeneration....Staff NINDS 301-496-5751
Cerebral Palsy....Staff NINDS 301-496-5751
Cerebral Palsy....Staff NIDCD 301-496-7243
Cerebrotendious Xanthomatosis....Staff NINDS 301-496-5751
Cerebrovascular Disease....Staff NINDS 301-496-5751
Cerium....DeSapio, Vincent USITC 202-205-3435
Cerium compounds....Greenblatt, Jack USITC 202-205-3353
Ceroid Lipofuscinosis....Staff NINDS 301-496-5751
Cesium....Reese, Robert G., Jr. MINES 202-501-9413
Cesium compounds....Greenblatt, Jack USITC 202-205-3353
Chad....Michelini, Philip Cnty Commerce 202-482-4388
Chad....Hanson, Julie Peace Corps 202-606-3004

Experts

Chad (N'Djamena)....Staff Cnty State 202-647-1707
Chad/Minerals....Dolley, Thomas Cnty Mines 202-501-9690
Chagas' Disease....Staff NIAID 301-496-5717
Chain, of base metal....Vacant USITC 202-205-3419
Chairs....Spalding, Josephine USITC 202-205-3498
Chalazion....Staff NEI 301-496-5248
Chalk (pigment grade)....Johnson, Larry USITC 202-205-3351
Chalks....Shetty, Sundar USITC 202-205-3486
Channel black....Johnson, Larry USITC 202-205-3351
Chaparral Tea....Staff NCI 301-496-5583
Characteristics of Injuries and Illnesses, Comp. Wk....Biddle, Elyce LABOR 202-606-6170
Charcoal Broiling of Meat....Staff NCI 301-496-5583
Charcot-Marie-Tooth Disease....Staff NINDS 301-496-5751
Charge Syndrome....Staff NICHD 301-496-5133
Check-writing machines....Scott, Baker USITC 202-205-3386
Chediak-Higashi Syndrome....Staff NIAID 301-496-5717
Cheese....Warren, J Fred USITC 202-205-3311
Chelation Therapy (For Arterios., Hemosiderosis)....Staff NHLBI 301-496-4236
Chemical Elements....DiMaria, Joseph CUSTOMS 212-466-4769
Chemical Emergency Preparedness and Prevention....Staff EPA 202-260-8600
Chemical Hazards....Staff OD/ORS 301-496-2960
Chemical Information Services....Hazard, George F. NLM 301-496-1131
Chemical Measurement Techniques....Patrinus, Aristides NEIC 301-903-5348
Chemical Plants, Major Proj.....Haraguchi, Wally COMMERCE 202-482-4877
Chemical Sciences....Marianelli, Robert NEIC 301-903-5804
Chemical Spills....Staff FWS 703-358-1713
Chemical Spills National Response Center....Staff EPA 202-426-2675
Chemical and Petroleum Branch....Staff EPA 919-541-5874
Chemical and Physical Hazards....Kapolka, Robert J. CDC 404-639-3147
Chemical elements....Conant, Kenneth USITC 202-205-3346
Chemicals....Kelly, William J. COMMERCE 202-482-0128
Chemicals (Technical and Non-Technical Questions)....Staff EPA 202-554-1404
Chemicals and Allied Products....Siesseger, Frederic COMMERCE 202-482-0128
Chemotherapy (Cancer)....Staff NCI 301-496-5583
Chemotherapy (Effect on Teeth)....Staff NIDR 301-496-4261
Chesapeake Bay Program....Staff EPA 301-267-0061
Chicken pox....Staff NIAID 301-496-5717
Chief Economist, BEA....Triplett, Jack E. ECONOMIC 202-523-0759
Child Abuse....Staff OHDS/ACYF 301-245-2859
Child Abuse & Neglect....Long, Susan ACF 202-401-9215
Child Care, Population....O'Connell, Martin CENSUS 301-763-5303
Child Care, Population....Bachu, Amara CENSUS 301-763-5303
Child Development....Staff OHDS/ACYF 301-775-7782
Child Rearing....Staff NIMH 301-443-4515
Child Welfare....Staff OHDS/ACYF 301-775-8888
Childbirth....Staff NICHD 301-496-5133
Childbirth....Staff HRSA/BHCDA/DMCH 301-443-2170
Childhood Malignancies....Staff NCI 301-496-5583
Childhood Mental Illness....Staff NIMH 301-443-4515
Childhood Progressive Dementia....Staff NINDS 301-496-5751
Children (Gifted)....Staff NIMH 301-443-4515
Children's Attitudes Towards Aging....Staff NIA 301-496-1752
Chile....Turner, Randy Cnty Commerce 202-482-1495
Chile....Eschelman, Michael Peace Corps 202-606-3376
Chile....Lustumbo, Julie Peace Corps 202-606-3575
Chile....Staff Cnty State 202-647-2407
Chile/Minerals....Velasco, Pablo Cnty Mines 202-501-9677
China, People's Republic of (Beijing)....Staff Cnty State 202-647-6300
China/Minerals....Tse, Pui-Kwan Cnty Mines 202-501-9696
China/trade matters....Lake, Charles US Trade Rep 202-395-3900
Chinaware....Harris, John COMMERCE 202-482-1178
Chinaware....Kalkines, George CUSTOMS 212-466-5794
Chinaware articles....McNay, Deborah USITC 202-205-3425
Chlamydial Infections....Staff NIAID 301-496-5717
Chlorides, nonmetallic....Conant, Kenneth USITC 202-205-3346
Chlorine....Conant, Kenneth USITC 202-205-3346
Chlorofluorocarbons....Michels, David USITC 202-205-3352
Chlorofluorocarbons (CFC)....Staff EPA 202-233-9190
Chloroform....Michels, David USITC 202-205-3352
Chocolate....Maria, John CUSTOMS 212-466-5730
Chocolate....Gallagher, Joan USITC 202-205-3317
Cholera....Staff NIAID 301-496-5717
Cholesterol....Staff NHLBI/IC 301-951-3260
Chondrocalcinosis....Staff NIAMS 301-496-8188
Chondrosarcoma....Staff NCI 301-496-5583
Chordoma....Staff NCI 301-496-5583
Choriocarcinoma....Staff NCI 301-496-5583
Chorionic Villus Sampling (CVS)....Staff 301-496-5133
Choroiditis....Staff NEI 301-496-5248
Christmas Decorations....Rauch, Theodore CUSTOMS 212-466-5892
Christmas Island/Minerals....Lyday, Travis Cnty Mines 202-501-9695
Chrome pigments....Johnson, Larry USITC 202-205-3351
Chromium....Presbury, Graylin COMMERCE 202-482-5158
Chromium....Papp, John F. MINES 202-501-9438
Chromium....Vacant USITC 202-205-3419
Chromium compounds....Greenblatt, Jack USITC 202-205-3353
Chronic Bronchitis....Staff NHLBI 301-496-4236
Chronic Disease Nutrition....Byers, Tim E. CDC 404-488-5121
Chronic Disease Prevention....Koplan, Jeffrey P. CDC 404-488-5401
Chronic EBV....Staff NIAID 301-496-5717
Chronic Fatigue Syndrome....Staff NIAID 301-496-5717
Chronic Granulomatous Disease....Staff NIAID 301-496-5717
Chronic Hepatitis with Rheumatic Disease....Staff NIAMS 301-496-8188
Chronic Infections....Staff NIAID 301-496-5717
Chronic Myelogenous Leukemia....Staff NCI 301-496-5583
Chronic Obstructive Lung Disease (COPD)....Staff NCNR 301-496-0526
Chronic Obstructive Lung Disease (COPD)....Staff NHLBI 301-496-4236
Cicatricial Pemphigoid....Staff NEI 301-496-5248
Cigarette Lighters....Maruggi, Al CPSC 301-504-0580
Cigarette Safety....Kaplan, Kathy CPSC 301-504-0580
Cigarettes (Research)....Staff NCI 301-496-5583
Cigars and cigarettes....Salin, Victoria USITC 202-205-3331
Cigars and cigarettes holders....Burns, Gail USITC 202-205-3501
Cigars and cigarettes lighters....Burns, Gail USITC 202-205-3501
Cinchona bark alkaloids and their salts....Nesbitt, Elizabeth USITC 202-205-3355
Cinnamon oil (essential oil)....Land, Eric USITC 202-205-3349
Circulation/Circulatory System....Staff NHLBI 301-496-4236
Circumcision....Staff NICHD 301-496-5133
Cirrhosis....Staff NIDDK 301-496-3583
Citizenship....Staff CENSUS 301-763-7955
Citral....Land, Eric USITC 202-205-3349
Citrates....Michels, David USITC 202-205-3352
Citric acid....Michels, David USITC 202-205-3352
Citrus fruits....Dennis, Alfred USITC 202-205-3316
Civet....Land, Eric USITC 202-205-3349
Civil Air Patrol (Rules)....Staff FCC 202-632-7175
Civil Aircraft Agreement....Bender, Juliet COMMERCE 202-482-1228
Civil Aviation....Johnson, C William COMMERCE 202-482-5012
Civil Cases (Federal)....Kaplan, Carol Justice Stat 202-307-0759
Civil Engineering....Demetsky, Michael J. UVA 701-924-6362
Civil Money Penalties....Holtz, Judy IG 202-619-1142
Clackerballs....Tyrell, Elaine CPSC 301-504-0850
Classification....Hartman, Frank CENSUS 301-763-2474
Classification System, Standard Industrial, Em/Un....Bennott, William LABOR 202-606-6464
Claudication....Staff NHLBI 301-496-4236
Clays....Virta, Robert MINES 202-501-9384
Clays....DeSapio, Vincent USITC 202-205-3435
Clean LAN/Waste Lan Hotline....Staff EPA 202-260-0056
Clean Lakes Program....Staff EPA 202-260-7840
Cleaners, under 10 lbs each....Randall, Rob USITC 202-205-3366
Cleaning....Bedore, James USITC 202-205-3424
Cleaning machinery....Slingerland, David USITC 202-205-3400
Cleaning machines (textile)....Greene, William USITC 202-205-3405
Cleanwater Act....Staff EPA 202-260-5882
Clearances (News Releases)....Staff OD/OC 301-496-2535
Clearinghouse for Census Data Services....Staff CENSUS 301-763-1580
Cleft Lip....Staff NIDR 301-496-4261
Cleft Palate....Staff NIDR 301-496-4261
Climate Change Division....Staff EPA 202-260-8825
Clocks....Piropato, Louis CUSTOMS 212-466-5895
Clocks....Luther, Dennis USITC 202-205-3497
Closures, stoppers, seals, lids, caps, rubber or plastic....Trainor, Cynthia USITC 202-205-3354
Clotting Disorders....Staff NHLBI 301-496-4236
Clove oil (essential oil)....Land, Eric USITC 202-205-3349
Coal....Biggerstaff, Margie NEIC 202-586-3867
Coal....Karsteter, Dorothy NEI~C 202-586-8800

Chairs / Commissioner's Office (FTC)

Coal....Foreso, Cynthia USITC 202-205-3348
Coal Exports....Oddenino, Charles COMMERCE 202-482-1466
Coal Exports....Yancik, Joseph J. COMMERCE 202-482-1466
Coal Statistics....Geidl, John NEIC 202-254-5570
Coal Technology Export Program....Swink, Denise NEIC 202-586-9680
Coal Workers' Pneumoconiosis (Black Lung Disease)....Staff NHLBI 301-496-4236
Coal and Electricity....Como, Anthony NEIC 202-586-5935
Coal and Minerals....Staff FWS 703-358-2183
Coal tar, crude....Foreso, Cynthia USITC 202-205-3348
Coal, Technology....Siegel, Jack NEIC 202-586-1650
Coal-tar pitch....Foreso, Cynthia USITC 202-205-3348
Coarctation of the Aorta....Staff NHLBI 301-496-4236
Coast Station Licenses....Staff FCC 717-337-1212
Coast Station Rules & Hearings....Staff FCC 202-632-7175
Coastal Anadromous Fish....Staff FWS 703-358-1718
Coastal Barrier Coordination....Staff FWS 703-358-2183
Coastal Barrier Research....Staff FWS 703-358-1710
Coated Garments: Boys'....Raftery, William CUSTOMS 212-466-5851
Coated Garments: Men's....Raftery, William CUSTOMS 212-466-5851
Coated Garments: Women's....Raftery, William CUSTOMS 212-466-5851
Coated fabric apparel....Jones, Jackie USITC 202-205-3466
Coating machines....Greene, William USITC 202-205-3405
Coats' Disease....Staff NEI 301-496-5248
Coats, Women's Knit....Crowley, Michael CUSTOMS 212-466-5852
Coaxial/Underground Cable....Staff FCC 202-634-1800
Cobalt....Staff NCI 301-496-5583
Cobalt....Cammmarota, David COMMERCE 202-482-0575
Cobalt....Shedd, Kim B. MINES 202-501-9420
Cobalt....Lundy, David USITC 202-205-3439
Cobalt compounds....Greenblatt, Jack USITC 202-205-3353
Cockayne's Syndrome....Staff NIA 301-496-1752
Cocks and valves....Mata, Ruben USITC 202-205-3403
Cocoa....Gallagher, Joan USITC 202-205-3317
Coffee....Maria, John CUSTOMS 212-466-5730
Coffee....Schneider, Greg USITC 202-205-3326
Coffee & Tea....Gray, Fred Agri 202-219-0888
Cogan's Syndrome....Staff NEI 301-496-5248
Cogeneration Energy Systems....Eustis, John NEIC 202-586-2098
Cognition....Staff NIMH 301-496-5133
Cognition....Staff NIMH 301-443-4515
Coin purses....Seastrum, Carl USITC 202-205-3493
Coke for fuel....Foreso, Cynthia USITC 202-205-3348
Coke, calcined (non-fuel)....White, Linda USITC 202-205-3427
Cold Storage....Lange, John Agri 202-720-0585
Coley's Mixed Toxins....Staff NCI 301-496-5583
Colitis....Staff NIDDK 301-496-3583
Collagen Disease....Staff NIAMS 301-496-8188
Collagen/Collagenase....Staff NIDR 301-496-4261
Collapsed Lung....Staff NHLBI 301-496-4236
Collective Bargaining Agreements Analysis....Cimini, Michael LABOR 202-606-6275
Collective Bargaining Settlements, Major, Comp/Wk....Devine, Janice M. LABOR 202-606-6276
Collective Bargaining--Public File, Agreements....Cimini, Michael LABOR 202-606-6275
Colombia (Bogota)....Staff Cnty State 202-647-3023
Colombia/Minerals....Mobbs, Philip Cnty Mines 202-501-9679
Color Blindness (Deficiency)....Staff NEI 301-496-5248
Colorectal Neoplasms....Staff NCI 301-496-5583
Coloring Matter....Joseph, Stephanie CUSTOMS 212-466-5768
Colostomy....Staff NIDDK 301-496-3583
Columbia....MacNamara, Laura Cnty Commerce 202-482-1659
Columbium....Presbury, Graylinn, C. COMMERCE 202-482-5158
Columbium....Cunningham, Larry D. MINES 202-501-9443
Columbium....Lundy, David USITC 202-205-3439
Coma....Staff NINDS 301-496-5751
Combs....Brownchweig, Gilbert CUSTOMS 212-466-5744
Combs....Burns, Gail USITC 202-205-3501
Commerce....DeMong, Richard F. UVA 701-924-3227
Commercial Development of Space....Selby, Barbara NASA 703-557-5609
Commercial Lighting Fixtures....Whitley, Richard A. COMMERCIAL 202-482-0682
Commercial Operator Licenses....Staff FCC 202-632-7240
Commercial Operators....Staff FCC 202-632-7240
Commercial Printing....Lofquist, William COMMERCE 202-482-0379
Commercial Space Ventures....Selby, Barbara NASA 703-556-5609

Commercial/Indus Refrig....Bodson, John COMMERCIAL 202-482-3509
Commercial Aircraft (Trade Policy)....Bath, Sally COMMERCE 202-482-4222
Commissioner's Office....Starek, Roscoe B., III FTC 202-326-2150
Commissioner's Office....Steiger, Janet D. FTC 202-326-2100
Commissioner's Office....Yao, Dennis A. FTC 202-326-2171
Commissioner's Office - Azcuenaga, Mary L.....Blumenthal, Don M. FTC 202-326-3797
Commissioner's Office - Azcuenaga, Mary L.....Blunt, Deborah M. FTC 202-326-2145
Commissioner's Office - Azcuenaga, Mary L.....Bokat, Karen G. FTC 202-326-2912
Commissioner's Office - Azcuenaga, Mary L.....Buek, Alexandra P. FTC 202-326-2145
Commissioner's Office - Azcuenaga, Mary L.....Heim, Joan L. FTC 202-326-2145
Commissioner's Office - Azcuenaga, Mary L.....Jeter, LaJuan J. FTC 202-326-2145
Commissioner's Office - Azcuenaga, Mary L.....Parrish, Pearl D. FTC 202-326-2145
Commissioner's Office - Azcuenaga, Mary L.....Warden, John B. FTC 202-326-2145
Commissioner's Office - Owen, Deborah K.....Clayborne, Delores M. FTC 202-326-2152
Commissioner's Office - Owen, Deborah K.....Eisenstat, Philip FTC 202-326-2157
Commissioner's Office - Owen, Deborah K.....Felder, Clayrine K. FTC 202-326-2153
Commissioner's Office - Owen, Deborah K.....Hogue, Cynthia A. FTC 202-326-2158
Commissioner's Office - Owen, Deborah K.....Plyler, Joyce FTC 202-326-2155
Commissioner's Office - Starek, Roscoe B., III....Cook, Barbara A. FTC 202-326-2150
Commissioner's Office - Starek, Roscoe B., III....Evans, Janet M. FTC 202-326-2125
Commissioner's Office - Starek, Roscoe B., III....Hobson, Paula Ann FTC 202-326-2124
Commissioner's Office - Starek, Roscoe B., III....Krauss, Joseph FTC 202-326-2713
Commissioner's Office - Starek, Roscoe B., III....Norris, Catherine FTC 202-326-2123
Commissioner's Office - Starek, Roscoe B., III....Samter, Nadine S. FTC 202-326-2129
Commissioner's Office - Starek, Roscoe B., III....Stockum, Steve FTC 202-326-3376
Commissioner's Office - Steiger, Janet D.....Anderson, Emily FTC 202-326-2109
Commissioner's Office - Steiger, Janet D.....Armstrong, Katherine FTC 202-326-3250
Commissioner's Office - Steiger, Janet D.....Cohen, William E. FTC 202-326-2110
Commissioner's Office - Steiger, Janet D.....Cohn, Susan FTC 202-326-3053
Commissioner's Office - Steiger, Janet D.....Conn, David FTC 202-326-2114
Commissioner's Office - Steiger, Janet D.....Crist, Sandy FTC 202-326-2105
Commissioner's Office - Steiger, Janet D.....Ewing, Faye FTC 202-326-2111
Commissioner's Office - Steiger, Janet D.....Hamill, James C., Jr. FTC 202-326-2107
Commissioner's Office - Steiger, Janet D.....Miles, Elizabeth D. FTC 202-326-2108
Commissioner's Office - Steiger, Janet D.....Oas, Julia FTC 202-326-2483
Commissioner's Office - Steiger, Janet D.....Washington, Monica FTC 202-326-2111
Commissioner's Office - Steiger, Janet D.....White, Robert S. FTC 202-326-2102
Commissioner's Office - Yao, Dennis A.....Corley, Derry L. FTC 202-326-2168
Commissioner's Office - Yao, Dennis A.....Dahdouh, Thomas FTC 202-326-2263
Commissioner's Office - Yao, Dennis A.....DeSanti, Susan S. FTC 202-326-2167
Commissioner's Office - Yao, Dennis A.....Harris, LaVerne H. FTC 202-326-2170
Commissioner's Office - Yao, Dennis A.....Murphy, R. Dennis FTC 202-326-3524
Commissioner's Office - Yao, Dennis A.....Thompson, Patricia V. FTC 202-326-2169

Experts

Commissioner's Office - Yao, Dennis A.....Vecchi, Christa Van Anh FTC 202-326-3166

Commissioner, Special Assistant to Office of....Barkume, Anthony J. LABOR 202-606-7808

Commissioner, Special Assistant to Office of....Parks, William LABOR 202-606-7807

Commodity and Programs & Policies - Crops....Evans, Sam Agri 202-219-0840

Common Carrier Development Stations....Staff FCC 202-634-1706

Common Carrier Radio Microwave Services....Staff FCC 202-634-1706

Common Carrier Radio Mobile Services....Staff FCC 202-632-6400

Common Carrier Statistics....Staff FCC 202-632-0745

Common Cold....Staff NIAID 301-496-5717

Commonwealth of Independent States....Levine, Richard Cnty Mines 202-501-9685

Commonwealth of Independent States....Lester, Toby Peace Corps 202-606-3973

Commonwealth of Independent States....Hirsch, Roderick Peace Corps 202-606-3973

Commonwealth of Independent States....Staff Cnty State 202-647-9559

Communicable and Infectious Diseases....Staff CDC 404-639-3286

Communicable and Infectious Diseases....Staff NIAID 401-496-5717

Communication Human (Disorders)....Staff NINDS 401-496-5751

Communication Human (Disorders)....Staff NIMH 401-443-4515

Communication Human (Disorders)....Staff NIDCD 401-496-7243

Communication Human (Normal)....Staff NICHD 301-496-5133

Community Corrections and Detention....Clark, John R. Justice Stat 202-514-8585

Community Energy Systems....Klunder, Kurt NEIC 202-586-2826

Community Health Centers....Mehuron, Charlotte HRSA 301-443-3376

Community Planning and Development....Staff HUD 202-708-0270

Community Services Program....Long, Susan ACF 202-401-9215

Commuting, Population....Boertein, Celia CENSUS 301-763-3850

Commuting....Salopek, Phil CENSUS 301-763-3850

Comoros....Walkins, Chandra Cnty Commerce 202-482-3317

Comoros....Schmitz, Virginia Peace Corps 202-606-3334

Comoros (Moroni)....Staff Cnty State 202-647-5684

Comoros/Minerals....King, Audie L. Cnty Mines 202-501-9674

Compensation and Working Conditions, Asst. Commis.....Stelluto, George LABOR 202-606-6300

Compensation and Working Conditions, Employee Ben.....Staff LABOR 202-606-6222

Compensation and Working Conditions, Employer Costs....Rogers, Brenda LABOR 202-606-6199

Compensation and Working Conditions, Industry injuries & illness....Staff LABOR 202-606-6180

Compensation and Working Conditions, Recorded Message....24-hour hotline LABOR 202-606-7828

Compensation and Working Conditions, Supp. Data....Biddle, Elyce LABOR 202-606-6275

Compensation and Working Conditions, Supp. Data....Biddle, Elyce LABOR 202-606-6170

Compensation and Working Conditions, Work Injury Report Surveys....Jackson, Ethel LABOR 202-606-6180

Compensation Levels & Trends, Asst. Commis.....MacDonald, Kathleen M. LABOR 202-606-6302

Composites, Advanced....Manion, James COMMERCE 202-482-5157

Composting (Yardwaste and Municipal Solid Waste)....Staff EPA 202-262-4745

Computational Aerodynamics....Farrar, Diane NASA 415-604-3934

Computational Molecular Biology....Staff DRCT 301-496-1141

Computer Consulting....Adkins, Robert COMMERCE 202-482-4781

Computer Crime....Kaplan, Carol Justice Stat 202-307-0759

Computer Networks....Spathopoulos, Vivian COMMERCE 202-482-0572

Computer Professional Services....Atkins, Robert COMMERCE 202-482-4781

Computer Systems and Services, Chief....Doyle, James P. ECONOMIC 202-523-0978

Computer and Communication Systems, Director of....Bennett, Harry D. NLM 301-496-1351

Computer and DP Services....Inoussa, Mary COMMERCE 202-482-5820

Computer and DP Services....Atkins, Robert G. COMMERCE 202-482-4781

Computer, Midrange....Hoffman, Heidi M. COMMERCE 202-482-2053

Computer, Personal....Woods, R. Clay COMMERCE 202-482-3013

Computer, Personal....Miles, Timothy O. COMMERCIAL 202-482-2990

Computer, Portable....Hoffman, Heidi M. COMMERCE 202-482-2053

Computer, Super....Streete, Jonathan P. COMMERCE 202-482-0572

Computer/data processing services....Xavier, Neil USITC 202-205-3450

Computers & Business Equipment, Office of....McPhee, John E. COMMERCE 202-482-0572

Computers in Medical Research....Staff DCRT 301-496-6203

Computers in Medical Research....Staff NCRR 301-496-5411

Computers, Midrange....Hoffman, Heidi M. COMMERCE 202-482-2053

Computers, Trade Promo.....Fogg, Judy A. COMMERCE 202-482-4936

Computing Device Emission Standards....Staff FCC 202-653-6288

Consumer Protection Bureau - Enforcement....Ecklund, Stephen C. FTC 202-326-3034

Concrete and products....White, Linda USITC 202-205-3427

Condensate, lease....Foreso, Cynthia USITC 202-205-3348

Conductors....Cutchin, John USITC 202-205-3396

Conduit....Cutchin, John USITC 202-205-3396

Conduits....Miller, Julius CUSTOMS 212-466-4680

Confectionery....Gallagher, Joan USITC 202-205-3317

Confectionery Products....Kenney, Cornelius COMMERCE 202-482-2428

Confidentiality of Data....Kaplan, Carol Justice Stat 202-307-0759

Confidentiality and Privacy Issues....Gates, Jerry CENSUS 301-763-5062

Congenital Abnormalities....Staff NICHD 301-496-5133

Congenital Abnormalities....Staff NINDS 301-496-5751

Congenital Abnormalities....Staff NEI 301-496-5248

Congenital Adrenal Hyperplasia....Staff NIDDK 301-496-3583

Congenital Adrenal Hyperplasia....Staff NICHD 301-496-5133

Congenital Heart Disease....Staff NHLBI 301-496-4236

Congenital Infections....Staff NIAID 301-496-5717

Congestive Heart Failure....Staff NHLBI 301-496-4236

Congo....Henke, Debra Cnty Commerce 202-482-5149

Congo (Brazzaville)....Staff Cnty State 202-647-3139

Congo/Minerals....Dolley, Thomas Cnty Mines 202-501-9690

Congressional Affairs....Staff CENSUS 301-763-2446

Congressional Districts, Address Locations....Swapshur, Ernie CENSUS 301-763-5692

Congressional Districts, Boundaries....Hammill, Robert CENSUS 301-763-5720

Congressional Districts, Component Areas....Hamill, Robert CENSUS 301-763-5720

Congressional Relations Office....Drummy, Maureen FTC 202-326-2149

Conjunctivitis....Staff NEI 301-496-5248

Connective Tissue Diseases....Staff NIAMS 301-496-8188

Conservation....King, Marion NEIC 202-586-8800

Constipation....Staff NIDDK 301-496-3583

Constipation and Aging....Staff NIA 301-496-1752

Construction Machinery....Heimowitz, L. COMMERCE 202-482-0558

Construction Statistics, Census/Industry Surveys....Visnansky, Bill CENSUS 301-763-7546

Construction Statistics, Constr Authorzd by Bldg Permit....Hoyle, Linda CENSUS 301-763-7244

Construction Statistics, New Residential, Charact....Berman, Steve CENSUS 301-763-7842

Construction Statistics, New Residential, House Complet....Fondelier, David CENSUS 301-763-5731

Construction Statistics, New Residential, Housing Start....Fondelier, David CENSUS 301-763-5731

Construction Statistics, New Residential, In Select MSA....Jacobson, Dale CENSUS 301-763-7842

Construction Statistics, New Residential, Sales....Berman, Steve CENSUS 301-763-7842

Construction Statistics, Residential Alterations....Roff, George CENSUS 301-763-5705

Construction Statistics, Residential Repairs....Roff, George CENSUS 301-763-5705

Construction Statistics, Value New Constr Put in Place....Meyer, Allan CENSUS 301-763-5717

Construction and Forestry, PPI, Prices/Lv. Cond....Davies, Wanda LABOR 202-606-7713

Construction paper....Rhodes, Richard USITC 202-205-3322

Construction services....Stonitsch, Laura USITC 202-205-3408

Construction, Domestic....MacAuley, Patrick COMMERCE 202-482-0132

Construction, Machinery....Heimowitz, L. COMMERCE 202-482-0558

Consulting services....SeSapio, Vincent USITC 202-205-3435

Consumer Affairs (all press inquiries)....Shaw Crouse, Janice OCA 202-634-4310

Consumer Affairs, Energy Affairs....Buchan, Douglas NEIC 202-586-5373

Consumer Expenditure Survey....Hoff, Gail CENSUS 301-763-2063

Consumer Expenditure Survey, Prices, Data Tapes....Passero, William LABOR 202-606-6900

Commodity / Consumer Protection Bureau

Consumer Expenditure Survey, Prices & Liv. Cond....Jacobs, Eva LABOR 202-606-6900

Consumer Expenditure Survey, Surv. Data & Tapes....Passero, William LABOR 202-606-6900

Consumer Expenditure Survey, Surv. Oper., Pr/Lv.....Dietz, Richard LABOR 202-606-6872

Consumer Goods....Bodansky, Harry COMMERCE 202-482-4783

Consumer Price Index, Prices & Liv. Cond.....Jackman, Patrick LABOR 202-606-6952

Consumer Price Indexes, Avg. Retail Food Pr--Mo.....Cook, William LABOR 202-606-6988

Consumer Price Indexes, Pr/Lv. Con, Data Diskettes....Gibson, Sharon LABOR 202-606-6968

Consumer Price Indexes, Prices & Living Cond.....Jackman, Patrick LABOR 202-606-6952

Consumer Price Indexes, Prices & Living Conditions....Staff LABOR 202-606-7000

Consumer Price Indexes, Recorded CPI Detail....24-Hour Hotline LABOR 202-606-7828

Consumer Price Indexes, Avg. Ret. Pr., Fuels & Util.....Adkins, Robert LABOR 202-606-6985

Consumer Prices and Price Indexes, Asst. Comm....Armknecht, Paul LABOR 202-606-6952

Consumer Protection Bureau - Service Industry....Jones-Thompson, Gwendolyn L. FTC 202-326-3305

Consumer Protection Bureau - Service Industry Practices....Bash, Eric FTC 202-326-2892

Consumer Protection Bureau - Service Industry Practices.....Daynard, Matthew FTC 202-326-3291

Consumer Protection Bureau....Blickman, Neil J. FTC 202-326-3038

Consumer Protection Bureau....George, Jeanne FTC 202-326-3226

Consumer Protection Bureau....Hanson, Jean R. FTC 202-326-3236

Consumer Protection Bureau....Jackson, Howard R. FTC 202-326-3170

Consumer Protection Bureau....Lefevre, John F. FTC 202-326-3209

Consumer Protection Bureau....Vickers, Kate FTC 202-326-3670

Consumer Protection Bureau - Advertising....Amundsen, Jeri FTC 202-326-3180

Consumer Protection Bureau - Advertising Practices....Andrews, John C. FTC 202-326-2613

Consumer Protection Bureau - Advertising Practices....Bank, Kevin M. FTC 202-326-2675

Consumer Protection Bureau - Advertising Practices....Cheek, Robert C. FTC 202-326-3045

Consumer Protection Bureau - Advertising Practices....Cleland, Richard FTC 202-326-3088

Consumer Protection Bureau - Advertising Practices....Colbert, Lynne J. FTC 202-326-3571

Consumer Protection Bureau - Advertising Practices....Dahl, Brian A. FTC 202-326-3182

Consumer Protection Bureau - Advertising Practices....Del Borello, Michael FTC 202-326-3051

Consumer Protection Bureau - Advertising Practices....Dershowitz, Michael FTC 202-326-3158

Consumer Protection Bureau - Advertising Practices....Downs, Linda S. FTC 202-326-3147

Consumer Protection Bureau - Advertising Practices....Embrack, Kenneth A. FTC 202-326-3247

Consumer Protection Bureau - Advertising Practices....Engle, Mary Koelbel FTC 202-326-3161

Consumer Protection Bureau - Advertising Practices....Fair, Lesley A. FTC 202-326-3081

Consumer Protection Bureau - Advertising Practices....Fink, Duane E. FTC 202-326-3145

Consumer Protection Bureau - Advertising Practices....Forbes, Dean C. FTC 202-326-2831

Consumer Protection Bureau - Advertising Practices....Forbes, Georgianna A. FTC 202-326-3183

Consumer Protection Bureau - Advertising Practices....Fremont, Laura FTC 202-326-2649

Consumer Protection Bureau - Advertising Practices....Greisman, Lois C. FTC 202-326-3404

Consumer Protection Bureau - Advertising Practices....Guelzow, Lynn F. FTC 202-326-2386

Consumer Protection Bureau - Advertising Practices....Hoppock, Theodore H. FTC 202-326-3087

Consumer Protection Bureau - Advertising Practices....Johnson, Barbara J. FTC 202-326-3149

Consumer Protection Bureau - Advertising Practices....Kando, Carol A. FTC 202-326-3152

Consumer Protection Bureau - Advertising Practices....Kastriner, Marianne FTC 202-326-3165

Consumer Protection Bureau - Advertising Practices....Knight, Sydney FTC 202-326-2162

Consumer Protection Bureau - Advertising Practices....Koff, Karen J. FTC 202-326-2687

Consumer Protection Bureau - Advertising Practices....Kolish, Elaine D. FTC 202-326-3042

Consumer Protection Bureau - Advertising Practices....Kopchik, Lisa B. FTC 202-326-3139

Consumer Protection Bureau - Advertising Practices....Kull, Michael D. FTC 202-326-3467

Consumer Protection Bureau - Advertising Practices....Levin, Toby M. FTC 202-326-3156

Consumer Protection Bureau - Advertising Practices....Maher, Anne FTC 202-326-2987

Consumer Protection Bureau - Advertising Practices....Matthews, Cynthia I. FTC 202-326-3151

Consumer Protection Bureau - Advertising Practices....Murray, Joanna C. FTC 202-326-3256

Consumer Protection Bureau - Advertising Practices....Peeler, C. Lee FTC 202-326-3090

Consumer Protection Bureau - Advertising Practices....Pillsbury, Harold C. FTC 202-326-3194

Consumer Protection Bureau - Advertising Practices....Priesman, Phillip FTC 202-326-2484

Consumer Protection Bureau - Advertising Practices....Robinson, Henrietta FTC 202-326-3043

Consumer Protection Bureau - Advertising Practices....Rosso, Rosemary FTC 202-326-2174

Consumer Protection Bureau - Advertising Practices....Rusk, Michelle K. FTC 202-326-3148

Consumer Protection Bureau - Advertising Practices....Skidmore, Patricia A. FTC 202-326-3050

Consumer Protection Bureau - Advertising Practices....Sneed, Devenette FTC 202-326-3360

Consumer Protection Bureau - Advertising Practices....Thomas, Sheri FTC 202-326-3398

Consumer Protection Bureau - Advertising Practices....Warder, Nancy S. FTC 202-326-3048

Consumer Protection Bureau - Advertising Practices....Washington, Janice C. FTC 202-326-3332

Consumer Protection Bureau - Advertising Practices....Watts, Marianne R. FTC 202-326-3074

Consumer Protection Bureau - Advertising Practices....Weinstein, Loren FTC 202-326-2687

Consumer Protection Bureau - Advertising Practices....Wilkenfeld, Judith D. FTC 202-326-3150

Consumer Protection Bureau - Advertising Practices....Winston, Joel FTC 202-326-3153

Consumer Protection Bureau - Consumer & Bus. Educ....Andrean, Michael D. FTC 202-326-3650

Consumer Protection Bureau - Consumer & Bus. Educ.....Carter, Joanne B. FTC 202-326-2446

Consumer Protection Bureau - Consumer & Bus. Educ.....Moss, Betty W. FTC 202-326-3650

Consumer Protection Bureau - Consumer & Bus. Educ.....Sachs, Nancy L. FTC 202-326-3270

Consumer Protection Bureau - Consumer & Bus. Educ.....Tressler, Colleen P. FTC 202-326-2368

Consumer Protection Bureau - Consumer & Bus. Educ.....Vawter, Irene FTC 202-326-3268

Consumer Protection Bureau - Credit Practices....Baheri, Leila M. FTC 202-326-5610

Consumer Protection Bureau - Credit Practices....Berrelez, Rolando FTC 202-326-3211

Consumer Protection Bureau - Credit Practices....Brinckerhoff, Clarke FTC 202-326-3208

Consumer Protection Bureau - Credit Practices....Brown, Connie FTC 202-326-3212

Consumer Protection Bureau - Credit Practices....Carroll, Millicent FTC 202-326-2696

Consumer Protection Bureau - Credit Practices....Childs, Beverly R. FTC 202-326-3174

Consumer Protection Bureau - Credit Practices....Cohen, Stephen FTC

Experts

202-326-3222
Consumer Protection Bureau - Credit Practices....Credle, Lillie R. FTC 202-326-2975
Consumer Protection Bureau - Credit Practices....D'Entremont, Donald FTC 202-326-2736
Consumer Protection Bureau - Credit Practices....Fitzpatrick, Roger J. FTC 202-326-3172
Consumer Protection Bureau - Credit Practices....Flanigan, Stephanie P. FTC 202-326-2382
Consumer Protection Bureau - Credit Practices....Grimes, David G. FTC 202-326-3171
Consumer Protection Bureau - Credit Practices....Grissett, Heide FTC 202-326-3008
Consumer Protection Bureau - Credit Practices....Isaac, Ronald G. FTC 202-326-3231
Consumer Protection Bureau - Credit Practices....Kane, Thomas E. FTC 202-326-2304
Consumer Protection Bureau - Credit Practices....Keller, Christopher W. FTC 202-326-3159
Consumer Protection Bureau - Credit Practices....Lamb, Cynthia S. FTC 202-326-3001
Consumer Protection Bureau - Credit Practices....Levin, Arthur, B. FTC 202-326-3040
Consumer Protection Bureau - Credit Practices....Medine, David FTC 202-326-3224
Consumer Protection Bureau - Credit Practices....Morris, Lucy Eggersten FTC 202-326-3295
Consumer Protection Bureau - Credit Practices....Nixon, Judith M. FTC 202-326-3173
Consumer Protection Bureau - Credit Practices....Reynolds, Carole L. FTC 202-326-3230
Consumer Protection Bureau - Credit Practices....Sheelor, Margaret A. FTC 202-326-3007
Consumer Protection Bureau - Credit Practices....Szurgot, Charles F. FTC 202-326-3229
Consumer Protection Bureau - Credit Practices....Taylor, Brenda A. FTC 202-326-3125
Consumer Protection Bureau - Credit Practices....Twohig, Peggy FTC 202-326-3210
Consumer Protection Bureau - Credit Practices....Wahl, Hughes E. FTC 202-326-2999
Consumer Protection Bureau - Credit Practices....Wilmore, Sandra FTC 202-326-3169
Consumer Protection Bureau - Credit Practices....Wilson, Laura FTC 202-326-3236
Consumer Protection Bureau - Enforcement....Boyle, Terrence J. FTC 202-326-3016
Consumer Protection Bureau - Enforcement....Brewer, Joel N. FTC 202-326-2967
Consumer Protection Bureau - Enforcement....Dingfelder, Justin FTC 202-326-3017
Consumer Protection Bureau - Enforcement....Dublin, Brenda J. FTC 202-326-2976
Consumer Protection Bureau - Enforcement....Easton, Robert E. FTC 202-326-3029
Consumer Protection Bureau - Enforcement....Feinstein, Jeffrey E. FTC 202-326-2372
Consumer Protection Bureau - Enforcement....Frankle, Janice Podoll FTC 202-326-3022
Consumer Protection Bureau - Enforcement....Frisby, Robert FTC 202-326-2098
Consumer Protection Bureau - Enforcement....Graybill, Dean C. FTC 202-326-3284
Consumer Protection Bureau - Enforcement....Koman, Joseph J., Jr. FTC 202-326-3014
Consumer Protection Bureau - Enforcement....Lewis, Ronald D. FTC 202-326-2985
Consumer Protection Bureau - Enforcement....Martin, Vada L. FTC 202-326-3002
Consumer Protection Bureau - Enforcement....Massie, Thomas D. FTC 202-326-2982
Consumer Protection Bureau - Enforcement....McDonald, Jerry R. FTC 202-326-2971
Consumer Protection Bureau - Enforcement....Metrinko, Peter FTC 202-326-2104
Consumer Protection Bureau - Enforcement....Mickum, George B. FTC 202-326-3132
Consumer Protection Bureau - Enforcement....Mills, James G. FTC 202-326-3035
Consumer Protection Bureau - Enforcement....O'Brien, George T. FTC 202-326-2972
Consumer Protection Bureau - Enforcement....Patch, Susanne S. FTC 202-326-2981
Consumer Protection Bureau - Enforcement....Phillips, Joyce D. FTC 202-326-3041
Consumer Protection Bureau - Enforcement....Proctor, Deloris FTC 202-326-2349
Consumer Protection Bureau - Enforcement....Sacks, Ruth S. FTC 202-326-3033
Consumer Protection Bureau - Enforcement....Simpson, Robert M. FTC 202-326-2974
Consumer Protection Bureau - Enforcement....Sizemore, Diana H. FTC 202-326-3027
Consumer Protection Bureau - Enforcement....Tatum, Barbara FTC 202-326-2978
Consumer Protection Bureau - Enforcement....Thomas, Beverly J. FTC 202-326-2938
Consumer Protection Bureau - Enforcement....Toufexis, Rose FTC 202-326-3011
Consumer Protection Bureau - Enforcement....Vecellio, Constance M. FTC 202-326-2966
Consumer Protection Bureau - Enforcement....Witkowski, Wallace A. FTC 202-326-3015
Consumer Protection Bureau - Enforcement....Wright, Janet FTC 202-326-2980
Consumer Protection Bureau - Enforcement....Wilenzick, Marc B. FTC 202-326-2442
Consumer Protection Bureau - Marketing Practices....Bresnahan, Linda Jean FTC 202-326-3129
Consumer Protection Bureau - Marketing Practices....Cohn, Thomas A. FTC 202-326-3352
Consumer Protection Bureau - Marketing Practices....Cook, John M. FTC 202-326-2056
Consumer Protection Bureau - Marketing Practices....Danielson, Carole I. FTC 202-326-3115
Consumer Protection Bureau - Marketing Practices....Donohue, Richard C. FTC 202-326-3112
Consumer Protection Bureau - Marketing Practices....Feinstein, Mary S. FTC 202-326-3064
Consumer Protection Bureau - Marketing Practices....Grant, Elizabeth FTC 202-326-3299
Consumer Protection Bureau - Marketing Practices....Guerard, Collot FTC 202-326-3338
Consumer Protection Bureau - Marketing Practices....Harrington, Eileen FTC 202-326-3127
Consumer Protection Bureau - Marketing Practices....Haynes, William L. FTC 202-326-3107
Consumer Protection Bureau - Marketing Practices....Hile, Allen FTC 202-326-3122
Consumer Protection Bureau - Marketing Practices....Hodapp, Lawrence FTC 202-326-3105
Consumer Protection Bureau - Marketing Practices....Howard, Patricia S. FTC 202-326-2321
Consumer Protection Bureau - Marketing Practices....Howerton, Kent C. FTC 202-326-3013
Consumer Protection Bureau - Marketing Practices....Ireland, Robert S. FTC 202-326-3114
Consumer Protection Bureau - Marketing Practices....Jennings, Carol FTC 202-326-3010
Consumer Protection Bureau - Marketing Practices....Johnson, Delores M. FTC 220-326-3124
Consumer Protection Bureau - Marketing Practices....Jones, Cotie W. FTC 202-326-2047
Consumer Protection Bureau - Marketing Practices....Kresses, Mamie FTC 202-326-2070
Consumer Protection Bureau - Marketing Practices....Laden, Gary M. FTC 202-326-3118
Consumer Protection Bureau - Marketing Practices....Modell, Shira D. FTC 202-326-3116
Consumer Protection Bureau - Marketing Practices....Pitofsky, Sally Forman FTC 202-326-3318
Consumer Protection Bureau - Marketing Practices....Quaresima, Richard A. FTC 202-326-3130
Consumer Protection Bureau - Marketing Practices....Reznek, Sarah FTC

Consumer Protection Bureau / Control Devices

202-326-2213
Consumer Protection Bureau - Marketing Practices....Salsburg, Daniel FTC 202-326-3032
Consumer Protection Bureau - Marketing Practices....Samley, Deborah FTC 202-326-2709
Consumer Protection Bureau - Marketing Practices....Shikiar, Robert FTC 202-326-3009
Consumer Protection Bureau - Marketing Practices....Smith, Arlene FTC 202-326-2390
Consumer Protection Bureau - Marketing Practices....Stamps, Shirley L. FTC 202-326-3099
Consumer Protection Bureau - Marketing Practices....Stone, Christopher FTC 202-326-3138
Consumer Protection Bureau - Marketing Practices....Toporoff, Steven FTC 202-326-3135
Consumer Protection Bureau - Marketing Practices....Torok, David FTC 202-326-3075
Consumer Protection Bureau - Marketing Practices....Tregillus, Craig FTC 202-326-2970
Consumer Protection Bureau - Marketing Practices....Vera, Martha W. FTC 202-326-3096
Consumer Protection Bureau - Office of Director....Betts, Raymond L. FTC 202-326-3163
Consumer Protection Bureau - Office of Director....Broder, Betsy FTC 202-326-3968
Consumer Protection Bureau - Office of Director....Brown, Gloria FTC 202-326-3047
Consumer Protection Bureau - Office of Director....Chung, Jock K. FTC 202-326-2984
Consumer Protection Bureau - Office of Director....Cutler, Barry J. FTC 202-326-3238
Consumer Protection Bureau - Office of Director....Damtoft, Russel W. FTC 202-326-3312
Consumer Protection Bureau - Office of Director....Enright, Maureen FTC 202-326-3160
Consumer Protection Bureau - Office of Director....Gorss, Janel A. FTC 202-326-3246
Consumer Protection Bureau - Office of Director....Hutchins, Clovia FTC 202-326-3215
Consumer Protection Bureau - Office of Director....Jung, Louise R. FTC 202-326-2989
Consumer Protection Bureau - Office of Director....Legal, Sharon V. FTC 202-326-3240
Consumer Protection Bureau - Office of Director....Maronick, Thomas J. FTC 202-326-2291
Consumer Protection Bureau - Office of Director....McDowell, Heather FTC 202-326-3356
Consumer Protection Bureau - Office of Director....Parnes, Lydia B. FTC 202-326-2676
Consumer Protection Bureau - Operations....Allen, Theodoshia FTC 202-326-3251
Consumer Protection Bureau - Operations....Burruss, James S., Jr. FTC 202-326-3261
Consumer Protection Bureau - Operations....Clayborne, Leroy, Jr. FTC 202-326-3252
Consumer Protection Bureau - Operations....Comtois, Joseph D. FTC 202-326-3255
Consumer Protection Bureau - Operations....Cossette, Darlene M. FTC 202-326-3255
Consumer Protection Bureau - Operations....Miller, Sylvia FTC 202-326-3258
Consumer Protection Bureau - Operations....Milton, Kathleen FTC 202-326-3253
Consumer Protection Bureau - Operations....Peterson, Mark D. FTC 202-326-3731
Consumer Protection Bureau - Operations....Ross, Michelle FTC 202-326-3260
Consumer Protection Bureau - Operations....Shapr, Kanili FTC 202-326-6196
Consumer Protection Bureau - Operations....Soranno, Donatos S. FTC 202-326-3255
Consumer Protection Bureau - Service Industry Pract....Crowley, John A. FTC 202-326-3280
Consumer Protection Bureau - Service Industry....Chambers, Sylvia J. FTC 202-326-3286
Consumer Protection Bureau - Service Industry....Dolan, James Reilly FTC 202-326-3292
Consumer Protection Bureau - Service Industry....Feinberg, Melissa FTC 202-326-3315
Consumer Protection Bureau - Service Industry....Fields, Mary C. FTC 202-326-3098
Consumer Protection Bureau - Service Industry....Fix, David FTC 202-326-3298
Consumer Protection Bureau - Service Industry....Frankel, David P. FTC 202-326-2166
Consumer Protection Bureau - Service Industry....Friedman, Robert D. FTC 202-326-3297
Consumer Protection Bureau - Service Industry....Gordimer, Douglas FTC 202-326-3003
Consumer Protection Bureau - Service Industry....Gross, Walter, III FTC 202-326-3319
Consumer Protection Bureau - Service Industry....Gurwitz, Stephen FTC 202-326-3272
Consumer Protection Bureau - Service Industry....Hippsley, Heather FTC 202-326-3285
Consumer Protection Bureau - Service Industry....Jones, Elaine FTC 202-326-3622
Consumer Protection Bureau - Service Industry....Katz, Michael A. FTC 202-326-3123
Consumer Protection Bureau - Service Industry....Kelly, Deborah H. FTC 202-326-3004
Consumer Protection Bureau - Service Industry....Kelly, Richard F. FTC 202-326-3304
Consumer Protection Bureau - Service Industry....Kinscheck, Renate FTC 202-326-3283
Consumer Protection Bureau - Service Industry....Lamberton, Peter W. FTC 202-326-3274
Consumer Protection Bureau - Service Industry....McCarey, Michael C. FTC 202-326-3303
Consumer Protection Bureau - Service Industry....Mereu, Richard FTC 202-326-3245
Consumer Protection Bureau - Service Industry....Osinbajo, Deborah A. FTC 202-326-3316
Consumer Protection Bureau - Service Industry....Owens, Denise FTC 202-326-3277
Consumer Protection Bureau - Service Industry....Rich, Jessica FTC 202-326-2148
Consumer Protection Bureau - Service Industry....Rosenfeld, Dana FTC 202-326-2113
Consumer Protection Bureau - Service Industry....Rothchild, John FTC 202-326-3307
Consumer Protection Bureau - Service Industry....Rushkoff, Bennett FTC 202-326-3439
Consumer Protection Bureau - Service Industry....Sheer, Alain FTC 202-326-3321
Consumer Protection Bureau - Service Industry....Spiegel, David R. FTC 202-326-3281
Consumer Protection Bureau - Service Industry....Spiro, Daniel A. FTC 202-326-3288
Consumer Protection Bureau - Service Industry....Stevenson, Hugh FTC 202-326-3511
Consumer Protection Bureau - Service Industry....Tait, Monica FTC 202-326-3505
Consumer Protection Bureau - Service Industry....Toone, Cassandra L. FTC 202-326-3276
Consumer Protection Bureau - Service Industry....Vidas, Sandra M. FTC 202-326-2456
Consumer Protection Bureau - Service Industry....Wagner, Connie FTC 202-326-3309
Consumer Protection Bureau - Service Industry....Williams, Gwendolyn C. FTC 202-326-3311
Consumer Protection Bureau - Service Industry Prac....Buckley, John D. FTC 202-326-3317
Consumer Protection Bureau - Service Industry Prac....Curtin, Theodore C. FTC 202-326-2311
Contact Lenses....Staff NEI 301-496-5248
Containers (of wood)....Ruggles, Fred USITC 202-205-3325
Containers, of base metal....Fulcher, Nancy USITC 202-205-3434
Contaminants, Environmental....Staff FWS 703-358-2148
Continental Shelf, Outer....Staff FWS 202-358-2183
Continuous Ambulatory Peritoneal Dialysis (CAPD)....Staff NIDDK 301-496-3583
Contraception....Staff NICHD 301-496-5133
Contraceptives....Staff NICHD 301-496-5133
Contraceptives....Cruzan, Susan FDA 301-443-3285
Control Devices (non-licenses)....Staff FCC 202-653-6288

Be patient. If any phone number is incorrect, call (area code) 555-1212 and request the new listing.

Experts

Conventional Fossil Fuel Power (Major Projects)....Dollison, Robert COMMERCE 202-482-2733
Conventions, Exhibits....Dickinson, Joanne CENSUS 301-763-2370
Converted Paper Prod....Stanley, Gary COMMERCE 202-482-0375
Converters....Greene, William USITC 202-205-3405
Cook Islands....Lagoy, Michele Peace Corps 202-606-3227
Cook Islands....Staff Cnty State 202-647-3546
Cooley's Anemia....Staff NHLBI 301-496-4236
Cooperative Forestry....Liu, Karen FS 202-205-1378
Copper....Jolly, Janice L. MINES 202-501-9414
Copper....Edelstein, Daniel MINES 202-501-9415
Copper....Lundy, David USITC 202-205-3439
Copper Wire Mills....Duggan, Brain COMMERCE 202-482-0575
Copper compounds....Greenblatt, Jack USITC 202-205-3353
Copper/Brass Mills....Duggan, Brian COMMERCE 202-482-0575
Copra and coconut oil....Reeder, John USITC 202-205-3319
Cor Pulmonale....Staff NHLBI 301-496-4236
Cordage....Konzet, Jeffrey CUSTOMS 212-466-5885
Cordage machines....Greene, William USITC 202-205-3405
Cordless Telephone....Staff FCC 202-653-6288
Cork and cork products....Ruggles, Fred USITC 202-205-3325
Corn Products....Janis, William V. COMMERCE 202-482-2250
Corn with options....Gore, Philip CFT 312-886-3044
Corn, field....Pierre-Benoist, John USITC 202-205-3320
Corneal Disorders....Staff NEI 301-496-5248
Corneal Transplantation....Staff NEI 301-496-5248
Cornelia deLange Syndrome....Staff NICHD 301-496-5133
Coronary Angioplasty....Staff NHLBI 301-496-4236
Coronary Artery Surgery Study (CASS)....Staff NHLBI 301-496-4236
Coronary Bypass....Staff NHLBI 301-496-4236
Coronary Disease....Staff NHLBI 301-496-4236
Corrections....Innes, Christopher Justice Stat 202-724-3121
Corrections....Beck, Allen Justice Stat 202-616-3277
Corrections....Greenfeld, Lawrence Justice Stat 202-616-3281
Corrections....Huggins, Wayne M. Justice Stat 202-307-3106
Corrections....Baunach, Phyllis Jo Justice Stat 202-307-0361
Corrections - Community....Baunach, Phyllis Jo Justice Stat 202-307-0361
Corrections - General....Greenfeld, Lawrence Justice Stat 202-616-3281
Corrections - General....Baunach, Phyllis Jo Justice Stat 202-307-0361
Corrections - General....Beck, Allen Justice Stat 202-616-3277
Corrections - General....Stephan, James Justice Stat 202-616-7273
Corrections - General....Innes, Christopher Justice Stat 202-724-3121
Corrections - General....Kline, Susan Justice Stat 202-724-3118
Corrections - General....Kane, Patrick R. Justice Stat 202-307-3226
Corrections - State....Shipley, Bernard Justice Stat 202-307-7703
Corundum-Emery....Austin, Gordon MINES 202-501-9388
Cosmetic Allergy....Staff FDA 301-245-1061
Cosmetic and Toiletry Preparations....Joseph, Stephanie CUSTOMS 212-466-5768
Cosmetic creams....Land, Eric USITC 202-205-3349
Cosmetics....Hurt, William COMMERCE 202-482-0128
Cosmetics....Lecos, Chris FDA 202-205-4144
Cosmetics (Export Promo)....Kimmel, Ed COMMERCE 202-482-3460
Cosmetics, perfumery, toilet preparations....Land, Eric USITC 202-205-3349
Cost Rica....Stanton, Dan Peace Corps 202-606-3620
Cost of Crime - General....Lindgren, Sue Justice Stat 202-307-0760
Cost of Crime - General....Rand, Michael Justice Stat 202-616-3494
Cost of Crime - To Government....Lindgren, Sue Justice Stat 202-307-0760
Cost of Crime - To Victims....Klaus, Patsy Justice Stat 202-307-0776
Cost-of-Living Abroad, Productivity & Technology....Capdevielle, Patricia LABOR 202-606-5654
Costa Rica....Subrin, Laura Cnty Commerce 202-482-2527
Costa Rica....Tumaylle, Carol Peace Corps 202-606-3321
Costa Rica (San Jose)....Staff Cnty State 202-647-3381
Costa Rica/Minerals....Mobbs, Richard Cnty Mines 202-501-9679
Costochondritis....Staff NIAMS 301-496-8188
Costume Jewelry, Trade Promo....Beckham, R. COMMERCE 202-482-5478
Cote d'Ivoire....Strozier, Maisha Peace Corps 202-606-3185
Cote d'Ivoire (Abidjan)....Staff Cnty State 202-647-2865
Cote d'Ivoire (Ivory Coast)....van Oss, Hendrik Cnty Mines 202-501-9687
Cotton....Latham, Roger Agri 202-720-5944
Cotton....Skinner, Robert Agri 202-219-0841
Cotton....Meyer, Leslie Agri 202-219-0840
Cotton....Sweet, Mary Elizabeth USITC 202-205-3455
Cotton - World....Whitton, Carolyn Agri 202-219-0826
Cotton Seed Oil....Janis, William V. COMMERCE 202-482-2250
Cottonseed and cottonseed oil....Reeder, John USITC 202-205-3319

Council of Europe....Staff Cnty State 202-647-1708
County Business Patterns....Decker, Zigmund CENSUS 301-763-5430
County and City Data Books....Cevis, Wanda CENSUS 301-763-1034
Courier Services....Elliot, Fred COMMERCE 202-482-1134
Court Appeals....Gaskins, Carla Justice Stat 202-508-8550
Court Appeals....Langan, Patrick Justice Stat 202-616-3490
Court Appeals....Lindgren, Sue Justice Stat 202-307-0760
Court Case Processing Time....Gaskins, Carla Justice Stat 202-508-8550
Court Case Processing Time - Federal....Kaplan, Carol Justice Stat 202-307-0759
Court Caseload....Gaskins, Carla Justice Stat 202-508-8550
Court Caseload....Langan, Patrick Justice Stat 202-616-3490
Court Organization....Gaskins, Carla Justice Stat 202-508-8550
Court Organization....Langan, Patrick Justice Stat 202-616-3490
Courts....Langan, Patrick Justice Stat 202-616-3490
Courts....Gaskins, Carla Justice Stat 202-508-8550
Coxsackie Virus (Hand-Food & Mouth Disease)....Staff NIAID 301-496-5717
Coxsackie Virus (Hand-Foot & Mouth Disease)....Staff NICHD 301-496-5133
Cranes....Greene, William USITC 202-205-3405
Craniofacial Malformations....Staff NIDR 301-496-4261
Crayons....Sundar, Shetty USITC 202-205-3486
Creams, cosmetic....Land, Eric USITC 202-205-3349
Cretinism....Staff NIDDK 301-496-3583
Creutzfeldt-Jakob Disease....Staff NINDS 301-496-5751
Cri Du Chat (Cat Cry Syndrome)....Staff NICHD 301-496-5133
Crib Death (SIDS)....Staff NICHD 301-496-5133
Crib Toys....Tyrrell, Elaine CPSC 301-504-0580
Crigler-Najar Syndrome....Staff NIDDK 301-496-3583
Crime Incidence, Rates, and Trends....Dillingham, Steven Justice Stat 202-307-0765
Crime Incidence, Rates, and Trends....Klaus, Patsy Justice Stat 202-307-0776
Crime Incidence, Rates, and Trends....Taylor, Bruce Justice Stat 202-616-3498
Crime Measurement Methods....Dodge, Richard Justice Stat 202-616-3485
Crime Measurement Methods....Taylor, Bruce Justice Stat 202-616-3498
Crime Measurement Methods....Rand, Michael Justice Stat 202-616-3494
Crime Prevention Measures....Shields, Stephanie Justice Stat 202-466-6272
Crime Seasonality....Dodge, Richard Justice Stat 202-616-3485
Crime Severity....Klaus, Patsy Justice Stat 202-307-0776
Crime Types: Homicide....Zawitz, Marianne Justice Stat 202-616-3499
Crime Types: Homicide....White, Paul Justice Stat 202-307-0771
Crime Types: Federal, Bank Robbery, Computer....Kaplan, Carol Justice Stat 202-307-0759
Crime Types: Rape, Robbery, Assault, Theft....Klaus, Patsy Justice Stat 202-307-0776
Crime Types: Rape, Robbery, Assault, Theft....Rand, Michael Justice Stat 202-616-3494
Crime Types: Rape, Robbery, Assault, Theft....Harlow, Catherine Justice Stat 202-307-0757
Crime and the Elderly....Staff NIA 301-496-1752
Crime, Incidence, Rates, and Trends....Rand, Michael Justice Stat 202-616-3494
Crime, Location of....Dodge, Richard Justice Stat 202-616-3485
Crime, Population....McGinn, Larry CENSUS 301-763-1735
Criminal Defendants....Gaskins, Carla Justice Stat 202-508-8550
Criminal Defendants....Langan, Patrick Justice Stat 202-616-3490
Criminal Defendants - Federal....Kaplan, Carol Justice Stat 202-307-0759
Criminal History Data Quality....Kaplan, Carol Justice Stat 202-307-0759
Criminal Justice Agencies....Lindgren, Sue Justice Stat 202-307-0760
Criminal Justice Expenditure and Employment....Lindgren, Sue Justice Stat 202-307-0760
Critical Care Medicine Department....Staff CC 301-496-9565
Crohn's Disease....Staff NIDDK 301-496-3583
Crohn's Disease....Staff NIAID 301-496-5717
Crop Protection....Staff FWS 703-358-2043
Cross-Eye....Staff NEI 301-496-5248
Crude Oil....Heath, Charles NEIC 202-586-6860
Crude Oil Markets....Cook, John NEIC 202-586-5214
Crude cresylic acid....Foreso, Cynthia USITC 202-205-3348
Crude petroleum....Foreso, Cynthia USITC 202-205-3348
Crushing machines....Greene, William USITC 202-205-3405
Cryolite....White, Linda USITC 202-205-3427
Cryosurgery (Eyes)....Staff NEI 301-496-5248
Cryptococcosis....Staff NIAID 301-496-5717
Cryptosporidiosis....Staff NIAID 301-496-5717
Cuba....Soto, Rodrigo Cnty Commerce 202-482-2527

Conventions / Demography

Cuba (Havana)....Staff Cnty State 202-647-9272
Cuba/Minerals....Gurmendi, Alfredo Cnty Mines 202-501-9681
Cucumbers....McCarty, Timothy USITC 202-205-3324
Culm....Foreso, Cynthia USITC 202-205-3348
Cupric oxide....Conant, Kenneth USITC 202-205-3346
Cuprous oxide....Conant, Kenneth USITC 202-205-3346
Current Analysis of U.S. Export & Import Price Ind....Vachris, Michelle LABOR 202-606-7155
Current Business Analysis, (Acting Chief)....Fox, Douglas R. ECONOMIC 202-523-0697
Current Business Statistics....Statistical Series Staff ECONOMIC 202-523-6336
Current Employment Analysis, Assist. Comm. Empl/Unempl....Bregger, John E. LABOR 202-606-6378
Current Wage Developments, Comp. & Working Cond....Cimini, Michael LABOR 202-606-6275
Current-Carrying Wiring Devices....Whitley, Richard A. COMMERCE 202-482-0682
Curtains....Sweet, Mary Elizabeth USITC 202-205-3455
Cushing's Syndrome....Staff NIDDK 301-496-3583
Cushing's Syndrome....Staff NINDS 301-496-5751
Cushing's Syndrome....Staff NICHD 301-496-5133
Cushions....Spalding, Josephine USITC 202-205-3498
Customer Service....Staff CENSUS 301-763-4100
Cut Flowers....Conte, Ralph CUSTOMS 212-466-5759
Cut flowers....Burket, Stephen USITC 202-205-3318
Cutis Laxa....Staff NHLBI 301-496-4236
Cutlery....Harris, John COMMERCE 202-482-1178
Cutlery....Preston, Jacques CUSTOMS 212-466-5488
Cutlery....MacKnight, Peggy USITC 202-205-3431
Cutting machines textile....Greene, William USITC 202-205-3405
Cyclic Idiopathic Edema....Staff NHLBI 301-496-4236
Cyclitis....Staff NEI 301-496-5248
Cyprus....Corro, Ann Cnty Commerce 202-482-3945
Cyprus (Nicosia)....Staff Cnty State 202-647-6113
Cyprus/Minerals....King, Audie L. Cnty Mines 202-501-9674
Cystic Acne....Staff NIAMS 301-496-8188
Cystic Fibrosis (Pancreas)....Staff NIDDK 301-496-3583
Cystinosis....Staff NICHD 301-496-5133
Cystinuria....Staff NIDDK 301-496-3583
Cystitis....Staff NIDDK 301-496-3583
Cytology....Staff NCI 301-496-5583
Cytomegalic Inclusion Disease....Staff NINDS 301-496-5751
Cytomegalic Inclusion Disease....Staff NIDCD 301-496-7243
Cytomegalovirus (Congenital)....Staff NHLBI 301-496-4236
Cytomegalovirus (Congenital)....Staff NICHD 301-496-5133
Cytomegalovirus (Congenital)....Staff NIAID 301-496-5717
Czechoslovakia....Mowrey, Mark Cnty Commerce 202-482-2645
Czechoslovakia (Prague)....Staff Cnty State 202-647-3298
Czechoslovakia/Minerals....Plachy, Josef Cnty Mines 202-501-9673

D

D'Jibouti....Watkins, Chandra Cnty Commerce 202-482-4564
D-Mark with options....Bice, David CFT 312-35-37880
DES (Diethylstilbestrol)....Staff NCI 301-496-5583
DES (Diethylstilbestrol)....Staff NICHD 301-496-5133
DES (Diethylstilbestrol)....Staff FDA 301-443-3170
DMSO (Dimethylsulfoxide)....Staff NCI 301-496-5583
DMSO (Dimethylsulfoxide)....Staff FDA/NCDB 301-443-1016
DNA....Staff NCI 301-496-5583
DNA....Staff NIGMS 301-496-7301
Dairy Products....Janis, William V. COMMERCE 202-482-2250
Dairy Products - Milk, Ice Cream, etc.....Buckner, Dan Agri 202-720-4448
Dairy Products - Milk, Ice Cream, etc.....Miller, Jim Agri 202-219-0770
Dairy Products - Milk, Ice Cream, etc.....Short, Sara Agri 202-219-0769
Dairy products....Warren, J Fred USITC 202-205-3311
Dam Safety....Staff FWS 703-35801719
Dance....Butler, Jeanne NEA 202-682-5435
Dandy-Walker Syndrome....Staff NINDS 301-496-5751
Darier's Disease....Staff NIAMS 301-496-8188
Data Acquisition Systems....Brown, Dwayne NASA 202-543-8956
Data Base Services....Inoussa, Mary COMMERCE 202-482-5820
Data Diskettes & Tapes, State & Area Labor Force....Marcus, Jessie LABOR 202-606-6392
Data Diskettes and Tapes, Empl. & Wages, Empl/Unempl....Buso, Michael LABOR 202-606-6378
Data Diskettes, Consumer Price Indexes, Pr/Lv. Con....Gibson, Sharon LABOR 202-606-6968
Data Diskettes, Employment Projections....Bowman, Charles LABOR 202-606-5702
Data Diskettes, Prices and Living Conditions....Rosenberg, Elliott LABOR 202-606-7728
Data Processing Services....Atkins, Robert G. COMMERCE 202-482-4781
Data Tapes, Industry-Occup. Matrix, Empl. Proj.....Turner, Delores LABOR 202-606-5730
Data Tapes, Productivity & Technology....Kriebel, Bertram LABOR 202-606-5606
Data and Tapes, Consumer Expend. Survey, Prices....Passero, William LABOR 202-606-6900
Data processing machines....Bringe, Julie USITC 202-205-3390
Data processing services....Xavier, Neil USITC 202-205-3450
Day Care....Long, Susan ACF 202-401-9215
Deafness....Staff NIDCD 301-496-7243
Deafness, National Institute of....Allen, Marin NIH 301-496-7243
Death and Dying....Staff NIMH 301-443-4515
Death and Dying....Staff NIA 301-443-1752
Decalcomanias (decals)....Stahmer, Carsten USITC 202-205-3321
Decennial Census, 1990 Counts f/Current Boundaries....Miller, Joel CENSUS 301-763-5720
Decennial Census, Content & Tabula, Program Design....Berman, Patricia CENSUS 301-763-7094
Decennial Census, Content, General....Paez, Al CENSUS 301-763-4251
Decennial Census, Content, General....Lichtman-Panzer, Paulette CENSUS 301-763-5270
Decennial Census, Count Information....Staff CENSUS 301-763-5002
Decennial Census, Count Information....Staff CENSUS 301-763-5020
Decennial Census, Count Questions, 1990 Census....Kobilarcik, Ed CENSUS 301-763-4894
Decennial Census, Demographic Analysis....Robinson, Gregg CENSUS 301-763-5590
Decennial Census, Housing Data, Special Tabuls. of....Downs, Bill CENSUS 301-763-8553
Decennial Census, Litigation....Gregg, Valerie CENSUS 301-763-7787
Decennial Census, Population Data, Special Tab. of....Cowan, Rosemarie CENSUS 301-763-7947
Decennial Census, Post-Enumeration Surveys....Hogan, Howard CENSUS 301-763-1794
Decennial Census, Publications, General....Landman, Cheryl CENSUS 301-763-3938
Decennial Census, Publications, General....Porter, Gloria CENSUS 301-763-4908
Decennial Census, Reapportionment....Turner, Marshall CENSUS 301-763-5820
Decennial Census, Redistricting....Talbert, Cathy CENSUS 301-763-4070
Decennial Census, Sampling Methods....Woltman, Henry CENSUS 301-763-5987
Decennial Census, Tabulations, General...Landman, Cheryl CENSUS 301-763-3938
Decennial Census, Tabulations, General....Porter, Gloria CENSUS 301-763-4908
Decennial Census, User-Defined Area Program....Quasney, Adrienne CENSUS 301-763-4282
Decennial Management....Walsh, Thomas CENSUS 301-763-2682
Decennial Planning Division....Vacant CENSUS 301-763-7670
Decontamination....Staff OD/ORS 301-496-2960
Decontamination (Radioactive Spills)....Staff OD/ORS 301-496-2254
Decubitus Ulcers....Staff NIA 301-496-1752
Deep Space Communications Complex....Wood, Alan S. NASA 818-354-5011
Defense Energy Projects....Carroll, Wade NEIC 301-903-3321
Degenerative Basal Ganglia Disease....Staff NINDS 301-496-5751
Degenerative Joint Disease....Staff NIAMS 301-496-8188
Deglutition....Staff NIDR 301-496-4261
Dejerine-Sottas Disease....Staff NINDS 301-496-5751
Delivery of Nursing Care....Staff NCNR 301-496-0526
Dementia....Staff NINDS 301-496-5751
Dementia....Staff NIA 301-496-1752
Demographic Programs, Statistical Research....Ernst, Lawrence CENSUS 301-763-7880
Demographic Studies, Center for....Wetzel, James R. CENSUS 301-763-7720
Demography....Staff NICHD 301-496-5133
Demography of Aging....Staff NIA 301-496-1752
Demyelinating Diseases....Staff NINDS 301-496-5751

Experts

Dengue....Staff NIAID 301-496-5717
Denmark....Lyons, Maryanne Cnty Commerce 202-482-3254
Denmark (Copenhagen)....Staff Cnty State 202-647-5669
Denmark/Minerals....Rabchevsky, George Cnty Mines 202-501-9672
Dental Assistants (Education)....Staff HRSA/BHPr 301-443-6837
Dental Care Programs (Aged, Handicapped, Prepaid)....Staff HRSA 301-443-6853
Dental Diseases/Disorders....Staff NIDR 301-496-4261
Dental Research, National Institute of....Jacquet, Brent NIH 301-496-4261
Dental Restorative Materials....Staff NIDR 301-496-4261
Dental cements....Randall, Rob USITC 202-205-3366
Dentobacterial Plaque Infection....Staff NIDR 301-496-4261
Dentures....Staff NIDR 301-496-4261
Depreciation Rules....Staff FCC 202-632-7500
Depression....Staff NIMH 301-443-4515
Depression and Aging....Staff NIMH 301-443-1185
Depression and Aging....Staff NIA 301-496-1752
Depth Perception....Staff NEI 301-496-5248
Deputy Commissioner, Office of....Barron, William G. LABOR 202-606-7802
Deputy Director (Acting), BEA....Young, Allan H. ECONOMIC 202-523-0693
Dermatitis Herpetiformis....Staff NIAMS 301-496-8188
Dermatological agents....Nesbitt, Elizabeth USITC 202-205-3355
Dermatology....Staff NIAMS 301-496-8188
Dermatology....Staff NCI 301-496-5583
Dermatomyositis....Staff NIAMS 301-496-8188
Dermatomyositis....Staff NINDS 301-496-5751
Dermographism....Staff NIAID 301-496-5717
Desalination/Water Reuse....Wheeler, Frederica COMMERCE 202-482-3502
Design Arts....Kriegsman, Sali Ann NEA 202-682-5435
Detergents....Joseph, Stephanie CUSTOMS 212-466-5768
Detergents....Land, Eric USITC 202-205-3349
Developmental Disabilities....Long, Susan ACF 202-401-9215
Developmental Disabilities and Birth Defects....Oakley, Godfrey P. CDC 404-488-7150
Developmental Disorders....Staff NINDS 301-496-5751
Developmental Disorders....Staff NIDCD 301-496-7243
Developmental Disorders....Staff NICHD 301-496-5133
Developmental Endocrinology....Chrousos, George P. FAES 301-496-5800
Developmental Endocrinology....Vamvakopoulos, Nicholas FAES 301-496-6994
Devic's Syndrome....Staff NINDS 301-496-5751
Dextrine....Randall, Rob USITC 202-205-3366
Di(2-ethylhexyl) adipate....Johnson, Larry USITC 202-205-3351
Di(2-ethylhexyl) phthalate....Johnson, Larry USITC 202-205-3351
Diabetes....Taylor, Simeon FAES 301-496-2596
Diabetes (And Arteriosclerosis)....Staff NHLBI 301-496-4236
Diabetes (Juvenile)....Staff NIDDK 301-496-3583
Diabetes Clearinghouse....Staff NIDDK 301-468-2162
Diabetes Insipidus....Staff NIDDK 301-496-3583
Diabetes Mellitus....Staff NIDDK 301-496-3583
Diabetes and Aging (Type 1 and Type 2)....Staff NIDDK 301-496-3583
Diabetes and Aging (Type 1 and Type 2)....Staff NIA 301-496-1752
Diabetes and Pregnancy....Staff NICHD 301-496-5133
Diabetes with Insulin Allergy or Resistance....Staff NIAID 301-496-5717
Diabetes with Insulin Allergy or Resistance....Staff NIDDK 301-496-3583
Diabetes, Digestive & Kidney Disorders, Nat'l Inst....Singer, Betsy NIH 301-496-3583
Diabetic Neuropathy....Staff NINDS 301-496-5751
Diabetic Retinopathy....Staff NEI 301-496-5248
Diagnostic Laboratories for Animal Disease....Staff NCRR 301-496-5175
Diagnostic Radiology....Staff CC 301-496-7700
Dial-a-Porn Complaints....Staff FCC 202-632-7553
Dialysis, Kidney....Staff NIDDK 301-496-3583
Diamond....Austin, Gordon MINES 202-501-9388
Diamond, Industrial....Prebury, Graylin COMMERCE 202-482-5158
Diamonds....DeSapio, Vincent USITC 202-205-3435
Diarrheal Illnesses....Staff NIDDK 301-496-3583
Diarrheal Illnesses....Staff NIAID 301-496-5717
Diathermy Approval....Staff FCC 301-725-1585
Diatomite....Davis, Lawrence L. MINES 202-501-9386
Diatomite....White, Linda USITC 202-205-3427
Dictation machines....Sherman, Thomas USITC 202-205-3389
Diego Garcia....Staff Cnty State 202-647-8913
Diethylstilbestrol (DES)....Staff NCI 301-496-5583
Diethylstilbestrol (DES)....Staff FDA 301-443-3170
Diethylstilbestrol (DES)....Staff NICHD 301-496-5133
Diffuse Sclerosis....Staff NINDS 301-496-5751
Digestive Diseases....Staff NIDDK 301-496-3583
Digestive Diseases Clearinghouse....Staff NIDDK 301-468-6344
Digital Electronic Message Service....Staff FCC 202-634-1706
Digital Terminations Systems....Staff FCC 202-634-1706
Dilsobutylene....Raftery, Jim USITC 202-205-3365
Dilsodecyl phthalate....Johnson, Larry USITC 202-205-3351
Dinnerware of ceramic....McNay, Deborah USITC 202-205-3425
Dioctyl phthalates....Johnson, Larry USITC 202-205-3351
Diphtheria....Staff NIAID 301-496-5717
Diploma Schools of Nursing....Staff HRSA/BHPr 301-443-2134
Direct Broadcasting Satellites....Staff FCC 202-632-9356
Direct Distance Dialing....Staff FCC 202-632-5550
Direct Mail....Elliot, Fred COMMERCE 202-482-3574
Director, BEA....Carson, Carol S. ECONOMIC 202-523-0707
Director, Office of the....Lindberg, Donald A. NLM 301-496-6221
Disability Benefits, Social Security....Gambino, Phil SSA 410-965-8904
Disc Drives, Diskettes....Kader, Victoria COMMERCE 202-482-0571
Discoid Lupus Erythematosus....Staff NIAMS 301-496-8188
Discouraged Workers, Empl./Unempl. Stats....Hamel, Harvey LABOR 202-606-6378
Discouraged Workers, Employment Statistics....Hamel, Harvey LABOR 202-606-6378
Disease Information Hotline.... CDC 404-322-4555
Disease Prevention....Staff NCNR 301-496-0526
Disinfection....Staff OD/ORS 301-496-2960
Displaced Workers, Empl/Unempl Statistics....Gardner, Jennifer LABOR 202-606-6378
Disposal (Animal Waste, Dead Animal, Infect. Materials)....Staff OD/ORS 301-496-2960
Distillate fuel oil....Foreso, Cynthia USITC 202-205-3348
Distilled Water....Staff OD/ORS 301-496-2960
Distribution services....Xavier, Neil USITC 202-205-3450
Diuretics....Staff NHLBI 301-496-4236
Diurnaldystonia....Staff NINDS 301-496-5751
Diverticulitis....Staff NIDDK 301-496-3583
Divorce Statistics....Heuser, Robert CDC 301-436-8954
Dizziness....Staff NINDS 301-496-5751
Dizziness....Staff NIDCD 301-496-7243
Djibouti, Republic of (Djibouti)....Staff Cnty State 202-647-8852
Djibouti/Minerals....Antonides, Lloyd Cnty Mines 202-501-9686
Doll carriages, stroller, and parts....Seastrum, Carl USITC 202-205-3493
Dolls....Vacant COMMERCE 202-482-0338
Dolls....Wong, Alice CUSTOMS 212-466-5538
Dolls....Luther, Dennis USITC 202-205-3497
Dolomite, dead burned....DeSapio, Vincent USITC 202-205-3435
Domestic Oil Reserves Statistics....Lique, Diane Q. NEIC 202-586-6090
Domestic Satellite Licenses....Staff FCC 202-634-1624
Domestic Violence....Klaus, Patsy Justice Stat 202-307-0776
Domestic Violence....Rand, Michael Justice Stat 202-616-3494
Domestic Violence....Langan, Patrick Justice Stat 202-616-3490
Dominica....Brooks, Michelle Cnty Commerce 202-482-2527
Dominica (Roseau)....Staff Cnty State 202-647-2621
Dominica/Minerals....Torres, Ivette Cnty Mines 202-501-9680
Dominican Republic....Soto, Rodrigo Cnty Commerce 202-482-2527
Dominican Republic....Pauk, Jennifer L. Peace Corps 202-606-3323
Dominican Republic (Santo Domingo)....Staff Cnty State 202-647-2620
Dominican Republic/Minerals....Doan, David Cnty Mines 202-501-9678
Down Syndrome....Staff NICHD 301-496-5133
Down apparel....Jones, Jackie USITC 202-205-3466
Draperies....Sweet, Mary Elizabeth USITC 202-205-3455
Drawing instruments....Shetty, Sundar USITC 202-205-3486
Dresses....Crowley, Michael CUSTOMS 212-466-5852
Dresses....Holoyda, Olha USITC 202-205-3467
Dressing machines (textile)....Greene, William USITC 202-205-3405
Drilling Mus/Soft Compounds....Vacant COMMERCE 202-482-0564
Drink-preparing machines....Jackson, Georgia USITC 202-205-3399
Drinking Water Branch....Staff EPA 202-260-5526
Drinking Water Standards....Staff EPA 202-260-7575
Drinking and Cancer....Staff NCI 301-496-5583
Drug Abuse Treatment....Hurley, Joan ADAMHA 301-443-6549
Drug Abuse, National Institute on....Brown, Mona ADAMHA 301-443-6245
Drug Abuse, Prenatal....Brown, Mona ADAMHA 301-443-6549
Drug Abuse, Treatment....Hurley, Joan ADAMHA 301-443-6549
Drug Abuse, in Workplace....Brown, Mona ADAMHA 301-443-6245
Drug Allergy....Staff NIAID 301-496-5717
Drug Enforcement Administration....Staff EPA 202-307-1000

Denmark / Economics Bureau

Drug Hemolytic Anemia....Staff NIDDK 301-496-3583
Drug Purpura....Staff NIDDK 301-496-3583
Drug Resistance....Staff NIAID 301-496-5717
Drug Test Guidelines....Brown, Mona ADAMHA 301-443-6245
Drugs....Hurt, William COMMERCE 202-482-0128
Drugs & Drug Labeling....Lecos, Chris FDA 202-205-4144
Drugs & Drug Labeling: AIDS Drugs....Peterson, Faye FDA 301-443-3285
Drugs & Drug Labeling: Generic....Shaffer, Michael FDA 301-443-3285
Drugs & Drug Labeling: Orphan Drugs....Cruzan, Susan FDA 301-443-3285
Drugs & Drug Labeling: Over-the Counter....Snider, Sharon FDA 301-443-3285
Drugs & Drug Labeling: Women's Issues (Drugs)....Cruzan, Susan FDA 301-443-3285
Drugs & Drug Labeling:Prescription Drugs, Biologic....Peterson, Faye FDA 301-443-3285
Drugs (Cancer)....Staff NCI 301-496-5583
Drugs (Cardiac)....Staff NHLBI 301-496-4236
Drugs (Eyes)....Staff NEI 301-496-5248
Drugs (Use and Abuse)....Staff NIDA 301-443-6500
Drugs - General....Lindgren, Sue Justice Stat 202-307-0760
Drugs and Aging....Staff NIA 301-496-1752
Drugs and Prisoners....Baunach, Phyllis Jo Justice Stat 202-307-0361
Drugs and Prisoners....Stephan, James Justice Stat 202-616-7273
Drugs, natural....Nesbitt, Elizabeth USITC 202-205-3355
Drugs, synthetic....Nesbitt, Elizabeth USITC 202-205-3355
Drunk Driving....Zawitz, Marianne Justice Stat 202-616-3499
Dry Edible Beans....Budge, Arvin Agri 202-720-4285
Dry Edible Beans....Lucier, Gary Agri 202-219-0884
Dry Edible Beans....Greene, Catherine Agri 202-219-0886
Dry Eyes....Staff NEI 301-496-5248
Dry-cleaning machines....Jackson, Georgia USITC 202-205-3399
Drying machines....Jackson, Georgia USITC 202-205-3399
Duchenne Muscular Dystrophy....Staff NINDS 301-496-5751
Duchenne Muscular Dystrophy....Staff NIAMS 301-496-8188
Duck Stamps....Staff FWS 202-208-4354
Dumping Toxic Waste....Staff EPA 202-260-4627
Dupuytren's Contracture....Staff NIAMS 301-496-8188
Dupuytren's Contracture....Staff NINDS 301-496-5751
Durable Consumer Goods....Ellis, Kevin M. COMMERCE 202-482-1176
Dust Inhalation Diseases (Pneumonoconioses)....Staff NHLBI 301-496-4236
Dust Inhalation Diseases (Pneumonoconioses)....Staff FDA 301-443-3170
Dust Inhalation Diseases (Pneumonoconioses)....Staff CDCW/NIOSH 404-639-3286
Dwarfism....Staff NICHD 301-496-5133
Dyeing machines....Greene, William USITC 202-205-3405
Dyes....Wanser, Stephen USITC 202-205-3363
Dynamite....Johnson, Larry USITC 202-205-3351
Dysautonomia....Staff NINDS 301-496-5751
Dysentery....Staff NIAID 301-496-5717
Dyskinesia....Staff NINDS 301-496-5751
Dyslexia....Staff NICHD 301-496-5133
Dyslexia....Staff NINDS 301-496-5751
Dyslexia....Staff NIMH 301-443-4513
Dyslexia....Staff NIDCD 301-496-7243
Dysmenorrhea....Staff NICHD 301-496-5133
Dystonia....Staff NINDS 301-496-5751
Dystonia Musculorum Deformans (Torsion Dystonia)....Staff NINDS 301-496-5751

E

E. Caribbean....Brooks, Michelle Cnty Commerce 202-482-2527
ECG....Staff NHLBI 301-496-4236
EKG....Staff NHLBI 301-496-4236
EPA Action Line....Staff EPA 800-223-0425
EPA Journal....Staff EPA 202-260-4359
EPA Recycling Program....Staff EPA 202-260-6980
ERIP (Energy-Related Inventions Program)....Staff NEIC 202-586-1479
Ear Infection....Staff NDCD NINDS 301-496-7243
Earnings Publication....Green, Gloria LABOR 202-606-6373
Earnings, Employment and Earnings Publication....Green, Gloria LABOR 202-606-6373
Earnings, Foreign Countries, Productivity & Tech.....Capdevielle, Patricia LABOR 202-606-5654
Earnings, Population Survey....Mellor, Earl LABOR 202-606-6378
Earnings, Real--News Release, Empl/Unempl. Stats....Hiles, David LABOR

202-606-6547
Earth Observing System (EOS)....Staff NASA 301-286-5566
Earth-moving machines....Stonitsch, Laura USITC 202-205-3408
Earthenware....Harris, John COMMERCE 202-482-1178
Earthenware....Kalkines, George CUSTOMS 212-466-5794
Earthenware, articles of....McNay, Deborah USITC 202-205-3425
East Caribbean....Almaguer, Antoinette Peace Corps 202-606-3322
Eastern European Health Scientist Exchange Program....Staff FIC 301-496-4784
Eaton-Lambert Myasthenic Syndrome....Staff NINDS 301-496-5751
Echocardiography....Staff NHLBI 301-496-4236
Eclampsia/Preeclampsia....Staff NICHD 301-496-5133
Ecological Effects Branch....Staff EPA 202-305-7347
Econometrics, Assistant to Director....Hirsch, Albert A. ECONOMIC 202-523-0729
Economic Accounts, Associate Director for National....Parker, Robert P. ECONOMIC 202-523-0517
Economic Bureau - Antitrust....Boner, Roger FTC 202-326-3455
Economic Bureau - Antitrust....Creswell, Jay S., Jr. FTC 202-326-3519
Economic Bureau - Consumer Protection....Cox, Carolyn FTC 202-326-3434
Economic Bureau - Office of the Director....Brown,Mary FTC 202-326-3429
Economic Bureau - Office of the Director....Deyak, Timothy FTC 202-326-3379
Economic Census Products....Zeisset, Paul CENSUS 301-763-1792
Economic Growth/Empl Proj, Occupational Outlook Quarterly....Fountain, Melvin LABOR 202-606-5707
Economic Growth/Empl Proj, Associate Commissioner....Kutscher, Ronald LABOR 202-606-5700
Economic Growth/Empl Proj, Data Diskettes....Bowman, Charles LABOR 202-606-5702
Economic Growth/Empl Proj, Economic Growth Proj....Saunders, Norman LABOR 202-606-5723
Economic Growth/Empl Proj, Ind-Occpl Empl Matrix....Turner, Delores LABOR 202-606-5730
Economic Growth/Empl Proj, Labor Force Projection....Fullerton, Howard LABOR 202-606-5711
Economic Growth/Empl Proj, Occupational Outlook Hand....Pilot, Michael LABOR 202-606-5703
Economic Growth/Empl Proj, Occupational Projections....Rosenthal, Neal LABOR 202-606-5701
Economic Programs, Statistical Research....Monsour, Nash J. CENSUS 301-763-5702
Economic Projections, Employment Projections....Saunders, Norman LABOR 202-606-5723
Economics....Elzinga, Kenneth G. UVA 701-924-6752
Economics Bureau....Cahill, Patricia FTC 202-326-3346
Economics Bureau....Duke, Richard M. FTC 202-326-3453
Economics Bureau....Schumann, Lawrence FTC 202-326-3359
Economics Bureau....Ward, Michael R. FTC 202-326-2096
Economics Bureau - Antitrust....Brashears, Nicole K. FTC 202-326-2455
Economics Bureau - Antitrust....Breen, Denis A. FTC 202-326-3447
Economics Bureau - Antitrust....Brogan, Robert D. FTC 202-326-3508
Economics Bureau - Antitrust....Bustamante, Rene FTC 202-326-3396
Economics Bureau - Antitrust....Callison, Elizabeth FTC 202-326-3521
Economics Bureau - Antitrust....Coate, Malcolm FTC 202-326-3351
Economics Bureau - Antitrust....Coleman, Mary FTC 202-326-3617
Economics Bureau - Antitrust....Cucinelli, Ieva P. FTC 202-326-3450
Economics Bureau - Antitrust....Dobson, Douglas C. FTC 202-326-3465
Economics Bureau - Antitrust....Fisher, Alan A. FTC 202-326-3516
Economics Bureau - Antitrust....Freeman, Barry FTC 202-326-3372
Economics Bureau - Antitrust....Gessler, Geary A. FTC 202-326-3463
Economics Bureau - Antitrust....Gessler, Kevin O. FTC 202-326-2306
Economics Bureau - Antitrust....Glasner, David FTC 202-326-3345
Economics Bureau - Antitrust....Grinshteyn, Ilona FTC 202-326-3355
Economics Bureau - Antitrust....Gulyn, Peter FTC 202-326-2194
Economics Bureau - Antitrust....Harmon, Bernadette D. FTC 202-326-3449
Economics Bureau - Antitrust....Howell, John M. FTC 202-326-3456
Economics Bureau - Antitrust....Iosso, Thomas FTC 202-326-2720
Economics Bureau - Antitrust....Jaynes, Philip W. FTC 202-326-3507
Economics Bureau - Antitrust....John, Tammy FTC 202-326-3462
Economics Bureau - Antitrust....Kneuper, Robert FTC 202-326-3469
Economics Bureau - Antitrust....Layher, William N. FTC 202-326-3515
Economics Bureau - Antitrust....Levinson, Robert FTC 202-326-3517
Economics Bureau - Antitrust....Levy, Roy FTC 202-326-3353
Economics Bureau - Antitrust....Martin, Fred FTC 202-326-3514
Economics Bureau - Antitrust....Megna, Pamela FTC 202-326-3491
Economics Bureau - Antitrust....Nelson, Steven R. FTC 202-326-3523

Experts

Economics Bureau - Antitrust....Patterson, Margaret A. FTC 202-326-3472
Economics Bureau - Antitrust....Pegram, William M. FTC 202-326-3336
Economics Bureau - Antitrust....Pidano, Charles FTC 202-326-3454
Economics Bureau - Antitrust....Rodriguez, Armando FTC 202-326-3616
Economics Bureau - Antitrust....Sacher, Seth B. FTC 202-326-3612
Economics Bureau - Antitrust....Silvia, Louis FTC 202-326-3471
Economics Bureau - Antitrust....Simpson, John D. FTC 202-326-3451
Economics Bureau - Antitrust....Tatem, Lewis FTC 202-326-3373
Economics Bureau - Antitrust....Wadbrook, Clare FTC 202-326-3420
Economics Bureau - Antitrust....Wagner, Curtis FTC 202-326-3348
Economics Bureau - Antitrust....Zichterman, Elizabeth C. FTC 202-326-3410
Economics Bureau - Antitrust....Williams, Mark FTC 202-326-3374
Economics Bureau - Consumer Protection....Butters, Gerald R. FTC 220-326-3393
Economics Bureau - Consumer Protection....Daniel, Lisa M. FTC 202-326-3394
Economics Bureau - Consumer Protection....Dulisse, Brian FTC 202-326-3614
Economics Bureau - Consumer Protection....Fahnline, Kathryn FTC 202-326-3611
Economics Bureau - Consumer Protection....Foster, Susan W. FTC 202-326-3482
Economics Bureau - Consumer Protection....Lacko, James FTC 202-326-3387
Economics Bureau - Consumer Protection....Lean, David F. FTC 202-326-3480
Economics Bureau - Consumer Protection....Mulholland, Joseph FTC 202-326-3378
Economics Bureau - Consumer Protection....Pappalardo, Janis K. FTC 202-326-3380
Economics Bureau - Consumer Protection....Porter, Russell FTC 202-326-3460
Economics Bureau - Consumer Protection....Sciolli, Stefano FTC 202-326-3388
Economics Bureau - Consumer Protection....Silversin, Louis FTC 202-326-3385
Economics Bureau - Consumer Protection....Small, Helen W. FTC 202-326-3375
Economics Bureau - Consumer Protection....VanderNat, Peter FTC 202-326-3518
Economics Bureau - Consumer Protection....Wells, Pamela L. FTC 202-326-3371
Economics Bureau - Economic Policy Analysis....Chase, Vera FTC 202-326-3354
Economics Bureau - Economic Policy Analysis....Daniel, Tim FTC 202-326-3520
Economics Bureau - Economic Policy Analysis....Fitzpatrick, M.E. (Keety) FTC 202-326-3427
Economics Bureau - Economic Policy Analysis....Grawe, Oliver FTC 202-326-3445
Economics Bureau - Economic Policy Analysis....Hilke, John C. FTC 202-326-3483
Economics Bureau - Economic Policy Analysis....Howarth, Dolly A. FTC 202-326-3382
Economics Bureau - Economic Policy Analysis....Ippolito, Pauline M. FTC 202-326-3477
Economics Bureau - Economic Policy Analysis....Kelly, Kenneth H. FTC 202-326-3358
Economics Bureau - Economic Policy Analysis....Kleit, Andrew FTC 202-326-3481
Economics Bureau - Economic Policy Analysis....Kobayashi, Bruce FTC 202-326-3363
Economics Bureau - Economic Policy Analysis....Metzger, Michael FTC 202-326-3367
Economics Bureau - Economic Policy Analysis....Morkre, Morris E. FTC 202-326-3365
Economics Bureau - Economic Policy Analysis....Reiffen, David FTC 202-326-2027
Economics Bureau - Economic Policy Analysis....Reitzes, James FTC 202-326-3349
Economics Bureau - Economic Policy Analysis....Vita, Mike FTC 202-326-3493
Economics Bureau - Economic Policy Analysis....Wellford, Charissa FTC 202-326-3020
Economics Bureau - Economics Policy Analysis....Rogers, Robert FTC 202-326-3368
Economics Bureau - Office of the Director....Altrogge, Phyllis D. FTC 202-326-3464
Economics Bureau - Office of the Director....Anderson, Keith B. FTC 202-326-3428
Economics Bureau - Office of the Director....Bond, Ronald S. FTC 202-326-3424
Economics Bureau - Office of the Director....Carpenter, Lynn J. FTC 202-326-3390
Economics Bureau - Office of the Director....Langenfeld, James FTC 202-326-3423
Economics Bureau - Office of the Director....Meadows, Chrystal E. FTC 202-326-3489
Economics Bureau - Office of the Director....Munson, Delores A. FTC 202-326-3613
Economics Bureau - Office of the Director....Pautler, Paul A. FTC 202-326-3357
Economics Bureau - Office of the Director....Peterman, John L. FTC 202-326-3431
Economics Bureau - Office of the Director....Richards, Karin F. FTC 202-326-2601
Economics Bureau - Office of the Director....Rosano, William V. FTC 202-326-3422
Economics Bureau - Office of the Director....Samuels, Carolyn FTC 202-326-3412
Economics Bureau - Office of the Director....Simmons, Gwendolynn FTC 202-326-3395
Economics Bureau - Office of the Director....Williams, Cheryl G. FTC 202-326-3418
Economics Bureau- Office of the Director....Farber, Leslie FTC 202-326-3510
Economizers.... USITC 202-205-3380
Ectodermal Dysplasias....Staff NIAMS 301-496-8188
Ectodermal Dysplasias....Staff NIDR 301-496-4261
Ectopic Hormones....Staff NIDDK 301-496-3583
Ecuador....MacNamara, Laura Cnty Commerce 202-482-1659
Ecuador....Godbey, Maria Elena Peace Corps 202-606-3198
Ecuador....Erlandson, Barbara Peace Corps 202-606-3499
Ecuador (Quito)....Staff Cnty State 202-647-3338
Ecuador/Minerals....Velasco, Pablo Cnty Mines 202-501-9677
Eczema....Staff NIAID 301-496-5717
Eczema....Staff NIAMS 301-496-8188
Edema....Staff NHLBI 301-496-4236
Edible gelatin....Jonnard, Aimison USITC 202-205-3350
Edible preparations....Schneider, Greg USITC 202-205-3326
Education....Bunker, Linda K. UVA 701-924-0740
Education....Gibbs, Anette UVA 701-924-3880
Education (Nursing)....Staff HRSA/BHPr/DN 301-443-5786
Education Facilities, Major Proj....White, Barbara COMMERCE 202-482-4160
Education Services....Reeder, John USITC 202-205-3319
Education and Curriculum Support Projects....Staff CENSUS 301-763-1510
Education, Energy Management....Duane, Jerry NEIC 202-586-2366
Education, Environmental....Staff FWS 703-358-2029
Educational Attainment, Empl/Unempl. Stats....Staff LABOR 202-606-6378
Educational Attainment, Employment Statistics....Staff LABOR 202-606-6378
Educational Programs....Sindelar, Terri NASA 202-453-8400
Educational Television....Staff FCC 202-632-6908
Educational Television....Staff FCC 202-632-6357
Educational/Training....Francis, Simon COMMERCE 202-482-0345
Eggs....Newman, Douglas USITC 202-205-3328
Egypt....Sams, Thomas/Wright, Corey Cnty Commerce 202-482-4441
Egypt, Arab Republic of (Cairo)....Staff Cnty State 202-647-1228
Egypt/Minerals....Dolley, Thomas Cnty Mines 202-501-9690
Ehlers-Danlos Syndrome....Staff NIAMS 301-496-8188
Eisenmenger's Syndrome....Staff NHLBI 301-496-4236
El Salvador....Lee, Helen Cnty Commerce 202-482-2527
El Salvador (San Salvador)....Staff Cnty State 202-647-4961
El Salvador/Minerals....Mobbs, Philip Cnty Mines 202-501-9679
Elastic fabrics....Shelton, Linda USITC 202-205-3457
Elastomers....Misurelli, Denby USITC 202-205-3362
Elderly Victims....Klaus, Patsy Justice Stat 202-307-0776
Elec/Power Gen/Transmission & Dist Eqt (Trade Pro)....Brandes, Jay COMMERCE 202-482-0560
Electric Energy Statistics....Geidl, John NEIC 202-254-5570
Electric Industrial Apparatus Nec....Whitley, Richard A. COMMERCE 202-482-0682
Electric Machinery & Trans., Producer Price Index....Yatsko, Ralph LABOR 202-606-7745

Be patient. If any phone number is incorrect, call (area code) 555-1212 and request the new listing.

Economics Bureau / Employment

Electric Networks....Brewer, Robert H. NEIC 202-586-2828
Electric Vehicles....Barber, Kenneth NEIC 202-586-2198
Electric Vehicles....Alpaugh, Richard NEIC 202-586-8012
Electric and Hybrid Propulsion Systems....Barber, Kenneth NEIC 202-586-2198
Electric and Nuclear Power....Welch, Thomas NEIC 202-586-8800
Electric and Nuclear Power....Jeffers, William NEIC 202-586-8800
Electric sound and visual signalling apparatus....Baker, Scott USITC 202-205-3386
Electric-Magnetic Field Technical Questions....Staff EPA 301-260-9640
Electrical Articles....Miller, Julius CUSTOMS 212-466-4680
Electrical Engineering....Papantoni-Kazakos, Panayota UVA 701-924-6102
Electrical Power Plants, Major Proj.....Dollison, Robert COMMERCE 202-482-2733
Electrical Structures....Miller, Julius CUSTOMS 212-466-4680
Electrical Vol Standards....Mesa, Stacey Reuben CPSC 301-504-0580
Electricity....Sugg, William COMMERCE 202-482-1466
Electricity Transmission....Brewer, Robert NEIC 202-586-2828
Electricity Transmission, Health Effects of....Brewer, Robert NEIC 202-586-2828
ElectroOptical Instruments, Trade Promo.....Gwaltney, G. P. COMMERCE 202-482-2991
Electrocardiogram....Staff NHLBI 301-496-4236
Electromechanical appliances....Jackson, Georgia USITC 202-205-3399
Electron Microscopy....Staff NCRR 301-496-5545
Electron Microscopy....Staff NIDR 301-496-4261
Electron Microscopy....Staff DRS/BEIB 301-496-2599
Electronic Components/Prod & Test Eqt, Trade Promo....Burke, Joseph J. COMMERCE 202-482-5014
Electronic Database Services....Inoussa, Mary COMMERCE 202-482-5820
Electronic Eavesdropping....Staff FCC 202-632-7260
Electronic Fund Transfer Crime....Kaplan, Carol Justice Stat 202-307-0759
Electronic Prod. and Test.....Finn, Erin COMMERCE 202-482-3360
Electronic Prod. and Test (Export Promo)....Ruffin, Marlene COMMERCE 202-482-0570
Electronic Telephone Switching....Staff FCC 202-634-1800
Electronic technology....Puffert, Douglas USITC 202-205-3402
Electronic tubes....Malison, Andrew USITC 202-205-3391
Electronic, (Legislation)....Donnelly, Margaret COMMERCE 202-482-5466
Electrothermic appliances....Jackson, Georgia USITC 202-205-3399
Elementary and Secondary Education Programs....Staff NEH 202-606-8377
Elements, chemical...Conant, Kenneth USITC 202-205-3346
Elephantiasis....Staff NIAID 301-496-5717
Elevators....Greene, William USITC 202-205-3405
Elevators, Moving Stairways....Weining, Mary COMMERCE 202-482-4708
Eligibility Criteria (Grants)....Staff DRG 301-496-7441
Embolism....Staff NHLBI 301-496-4236
Embroidery machines....Greene, William USITC 202-205-3405
Emergency Broadcasting System....Staff FCC 202-632-3906
Emergency Medical Services....Staff FCC 717-337-1212
Emergency Plan. & Community Right-to-Know Hotline....Staff EPA 800-535-0202
Emigration....Woodrow, Karen CENSUS 301-763-5990
Emission Standards....Staff EPA 202-541-5571
Emissions Standards Division....Staff EPA 919-541-5544
Emphysema....Staff NHLBI 301-496-4236
Empl.& Wages, Empl/Unempl, Data Diskettes and Tapes....Buso, Michael LABOR 202-606-6567
Empl/Unempl Stats, (ES202), Empl/Wgs Ind....Bush, Joseph LABOR 202-606-6373
Empl/Unempl Stats, Assistant Commis.....Plewes, Thomas J. LABOR 202-606-6400
Empl/Unempl Stats, Occl Empl/Unempl, Occpl Empl Sv....Johnson, Lawrence LABOR 202-606-6569
Empl/Unempl Stats, State Data, Demographic Charact....Biederman, Edna LABOR 202-606-6392
Empl/Unempl Stats, Std Industrial Classification....Bennott, William LABOR 202-606-6474
Empl/Unempl Stats, Std Occupational Classification....McElroy, Michael LABOR 202-606-6516
Empl/Unempl Stats, Unempl Ins Stats, Claimant Data....Terwilliger, Yvonne LABOR 202-606-6392
Empl/Unempl Stats, Unempl Ins Stats, Establ Record....Cimini, Michael LABOR 202-606-6275
Empl/Unempl Stats., Benchmarks....Getz, Patricia LABOR 202-606-6521
Empl/Unempl, National Data, Data Diskettes....Singleton, Christopher LABOR 202-606-6551
Empl/Unempl. Stats, Business Establishment List....Searson, Michael LABOR 202-606-6479
Empl/Unempl.Stats, Curr. Empl. An, Assistant Commis.....Bregger, John E. LABOR 202-606-6388
Employee Benefit Survey, General Info., Comp./Wk. Con....Staff LABOR 202-606-6222
Employee Benefit Survey, Health & Life Insur.....Blostin, Allan LABOR 202-606-6240
Employee Benefit Survey, Retirement & Capital Acc....Houff, James LABOR 202-606-6238
Employee Benefits,Compensation & Working Condition....Staff LABOR 202-606-6199
Employer Costs for Employee Comp, Comp & Working....Rogers, Brenda LABOR 202-606-6199
Employment....Palumbo, Thomas CENSUS 301-763-8574
Employment & Unempl. Statistics, Flexitime & Shift....Mellor, Earl LABOR 202-606-6378
Employment & Unempl. Statistics, Older Workers....Rones, Philip LABOR 202-606-6378
Employment & Unempl. Statistics, Part-time Workers....Nardone, Thomas LABOR 202-606-6378
Employment & Unempl. Statistics, Working Poor....Herz, Diane LABOR 202-606-6378
Employment & Unempl. Stats, Labor Force Data Disk....Marcus, Jessie LABOR 202-606-6392
Employment & Unempl. Stats, Longitud. Data/Gr.Flow....Horvath, Francis LABOR 202-606-6345
Employment & Unempl. Stats, States Est. Surv. Data....Podgornik, Guy LABOR 202-606-6559
Employment & Unempl. Stats. Earnings, Pop. Survey....Mellor, Earl LABOR 202-606-6378
Employment & Unempl. Stats., Mass Layoff Stats.....Siegel, Lewis LABOR 202-606-6404
Employment & Unempl. Stats., Minimum Wage Data....Haugen, Steve LABOR 202-606-6378
Employment & Unempl. Stats., Multiple Jobholders....Stinson, John LABOR 202-606-6373
Employment & Unempl. Stats., States Est. Surv.....Shipp, Kenneth LABOR 202-606-6559
Employment Analysis, Current, Assist. Comm. Empl/Unempl....Bregger, John E. LABOR 202-606-6388
Employment Cost Index, Comp. & Working Cond.....Shelly, Wayne LABOR 202-606-6199
Employment Projections, Assistant Commis.....Kutscher, Ronald LABOR 202-606-5700
Employment Projections, Data Diskettes....Bowman, Charles LABOR 202-606-5702
Employment Projections, Economic Growth....Saunders, Norman LABOR 202-606-5723
Employment Projections, Productivity & Technology....Fullerton, Howard LABOR 202-606-5711
Employment Projections, Productivity & Technology....Franklin, James LABOR 202-606-5709
Employment Requirements Tables, Productivity & Tech....Franklin, James LABOR 202-606-5709
Employment Statistics....Palumbo, Thomas CENSUS 301-763-8574
Employment Stats, Area Data, Demog Charact....Biederman, Edna LABOR 202-606-6392
Employment Stats, Area Data, Employment....Shipp, Kenneth LABOR 202-606-6559
Employment Stats, Curr Empl Anal., Assist. Commis.....Bregger, John E. LABOR 202-606-6388
Employment Stats, Discouraged Workers....Hamel, Harvey LABOR 202-606-6378
Employment Stats, Displaced Workers....Horvath, Francis LABOR 202-606-6345
Employment Stats, Dropouts....Cohany, Sharon LABOR 202-606-6378
Employment Stats, Earn Stats, Qrtly Empl and Wage....Bush, Joseph LABOR 202-606-6567
Employment Stats, Earnings Publication....Green, Gloria LABOR 202-606-6373
Employment Stats, Educational Attainment....Staff LABOR 202-606-6378
Employment Stats, Employment Publication....Green, Gloria LABOR 202-606-6373
Employment Stats, Family Charactr of Labor Force....Hayghe, Howard LABOR 202-606-6378
Employment Stats, Ind Earn Stats, Mthly Payr Surv....Seifert, Mary Lee

Experts

LABOR 202-606-6552
Employment Stats, Ind Empl Stats, Mthly Payr Surv....Seifert, Mary Lee LABOR 202-606-6552
Employment and Earnings Period. Empl/Unempl. Stats....Green, Gloria LABOR 202-606-6373
Employment and Unemployment Statistics, Est. Surv.....Seifert, Mary Lee LABOR 202-606-6552
Employment, Area Data....Shipp, Kenneth LABOR 202-606-6559
Employment/Unempl Stats, Minorities....Cattan, Peter LABOR 202-606-6378
Employment/Unempl Stats, Permanent Plant Closings....Siegel, Lewis LABOR 202-606-6404
Employment/Unempl Stats, State Data, Employment....Shipp, Kenneth LABOR 202-606-6559
Employment/Unempl Stats, Students....Cohany, Sharon LABOR 202-606-6378
Employment/Unempl Stats, Veterans....Cohany, Sharon LABOR 202-606-6378
Employment/Unempl Stats, Women....Hayghe, Howard LABOR 202-606-6378
Employment/Unempl Stats, Work-life Estimates....Horvath, Francis LABOR 202-606-6345
Employment/Unempl Stats, Permanent Mass Layoffs....Siegel, Lewis LABOR 202-606-6404
Employment/Unemployment Stats, Older Workers....Rones, Philip LABOR 202-606-6378
Employment/Unempl Stats, Machine Readable Data....Green, Gloria LABOR 202-606-6373
Employment/Unempl Stats, Associate Commissioner....Plewes, Thomas J. LABOR 202-606-6400
Employment/Unempl Stats, Real Earnings, News Release....Hiles, David LABOR 202-606-6547
Employment/Unempl Statistics, Trends....Staff LABOR 202-606-6378
Enamel....Staff NIDR 301-496-4261
Enamels....Johnson, Larry USITC 202-205-3351
Encephalitides....Staff NINDS 301-496-5751
Encephalitis....Staff NIAID 301-496-5717
Encephalitis....Staff NINDS 301-496-5751
Encephalitis Lethargica....Staff NINDS 301-496-5751
Encephalomyelitis....Staff NINDS 301-496-5751
Encopresis....Staff NICHD 301-496-5133
Endangered Species Bulletins, Tech.....Staff FWS 703-358-2166
Endangered Species Permits....Staff FWS 703-358-2104
Endangered Species Recovery Plans....Staff FWS 703-358-2171
Endangered Species Research....Staff FWS 703-358-1710
Endangered Species Listing....Staff FWS 703-358-2171
Endocarditis....Staff NHLBI 301-496-4236
Endocardium....Staff NHLBI 301-496-4236
Endocrine Gland....Staff NICHD 301-496-5133
Endocrinologic Muscle Disease....Staff NINDS 301-496-5751
Endocrinology....Staff NIDDK 301-496-3583
Endocrinology (Sexual Development)....Staff NICHD 301-496-5133
Endocrinology of Aging....Staff NIA 301-496-1752
Endodontics....Staff NIDR 301-496-4261
Endometriosis....Staff NICHD 301-496-5133
Energy & Environ. Sys.....Greer, Damon COMMERCE 202-482-5456
Energy Assist. Block Grant/For Low Income Families....Long, Susan ACF 202-401-9215
Energy Assist. Block Grant/For Low Income Families....Long, Susan ACF 202-401-9215
Energy Biosciences Research....Rabson, Robert NEIC 301-903-2873
Energy Conservation....Davis, Michael J. NEIC 202-586-9220
Energy Conservation....Freedman, Karen NEIC 202-586-8800
Energy Conservation Programs....Staff FWS 703-358-1719
Energy Consumption Surveys....Carlson, Lynda NEIC 202-586-1112
Energy Demand Forecasts....Rodekohr, Mark NEIC 202-586-1130
Energy Efficient Buildings....Oliver, Robert NEIC 202-586-9190
Energy Efficient Buildings....Kapus, Theodore NEIC 202-586-9123
Energy Information Statistical Standards....Bishop, Yvonne NEIC 202-254-5419
Energy Information Statistics....Bishop, Yvonne NEIC 202-254-5419
Energy Inventions....Staff NEIC 202-586-1479
Energy Management Education....Duane, Jerry NEIC 202-586-2366
Energy Markets Short-Term Forecasting....Staff NEIC 202-586-1441
Energy Pollutant Research....Smith, David NEIC 301-903-5468
Energy Supply and Conversion Forecasts....Hutzler, Mary J. NEIC 202-586-2222
Energy Technical Assistance....Bowes, Ronald NEIC 202-586-5517

Energy, Commodities....Yancik, Joseph J. COMMERCE 202-482-1466
Energy, Commodities....Oddenino, Charles L. COMMERCE 202-482-1466
Energy, Producer Price Index....Caswell, Maria LABOR 202-606-7722
Energy, Renewable....Rasmussen, John COMMERCE 202-482-1466
Energy, Renewable....Davis, Michael J. NEIC 202-586-9220
Energy, Solar....San Martin, Robert NEIC 202-586-9275
Energy-Related Business Assistance....Lane, Harry NEIC 202-586-9104
Energy-Related Inventions Program (ERIP)....Staff NEIC 202-586-1479
Energy-Related Inventions and Innovations....Staff NEIC 202-586-1479
Engine Design....Eberhardt, James NEIC 202-586-9387
Engineering (Biomedical)....Staff NCRR/BEIP 301-496-4426
Engineering (Biomedical)....Staff DCRT 301-496-1111
Engineering (Biomedical)....Staff NIGMS 301-496-7301
Engineering Surveys--Field Strength....Staff FCC 202-632-7040
Engineering resins....Misurelli, Denby USITC 202-205-3362
Engineering services....Stonitsch, Laura USITC 202-205-3408
Engineering/Construction Services, Trade Promo.....Ruan, Robert COMMERCE 202-482-0359
Engines....Josephs, Irwin CUSTOMS 212-466-5673
Engines....Anderson, Peder USITC 202-205-3388
Enterprise Statistics....Monaco, Johnny CENSUS 301-763-1758
Enterprise Statistics....Staff CENSUS 301-763-1758
Entertainment Industries....Siegmund, John COMMERCE 202-482-4781
Entertainment services....R-Archila, Laura USITC 202-205-3488
Environment services....DeSapio, Vincent USITC 202-205-3435
Environment, Safety and Health Concerns....Ziemer, Paul NEIC 202-586-6151
Environmental Carcinogens....Staff NCI 301-496-5583
Environmental Contaminants....Staff FWS 703-358-2148
Environmental Control....Staff OD/ORS 301-496-3537
Environmental Economics, Chief....Rutledge, Gary L. ECONOMIC 202-523-0687
Environmental Education....Staff EPA 202-260-4958
Environmental Education....Staff FWS 703-358-2029
Environmental Hazards and Health Effects....Falk, Henry CDC 404-488-7300
Environmental Health....Staff NIEHS 919-541-3345
Environmental Health Sciences, Nat'l Institute of....Lee, Hugh NIH 919-541-3345
Environmental Health, National Center for....Houk, Vernon N. CDC 404-488-7000
Environmental Issues - General Information Hotline....Staff EPA 800-759-4372
Environmental Law....Staff FCC 202-632-6990
Environmental Mutagenesis....Staff NIEHS 919-541-3345
Environmental Requirements for Laboratory Animals....Staff OD 301-496-1357
Environmental Safety....Staff OD/ORS 301-496-3537
Environmental Sciences....Allen, Ralph O. UVA 701-982-4922
Environmental Statistics and Information....Staff EPA 202-260-2680
Environmental Teratology....Staff NIEHS 919-541-3345
Environmental Toxicology....Zeeman, Maurice G. FAES 202-260-1237
Environmental Toxicology....Staff FWS 703-358-1710
Enzymes....Nesbitt, Elizabeth USITC 202-205-3355
Eosinophilic Granuloma of the Lung....Staff NHLBI 301-496-4236
Eosinophilic Syndrome....Staff NIAID 301-496-5717
Epidemic Aid/Disease Outbreaks....Berreth, Don CDC 404-639-3286
Epidemiology....Friedman, Lawrence M. FAES 301-496-2533
Epidemiology/Biostatistics....Hirsch, Robert FAES 202-994-7778
Epidemiology....Thacker, Stephen B. CDC 404-639-3661
Epidemiology of Aging....Staff NIA 301-496-1752
Epidermodysplasis Verruciformis....Staff NIAMS 301-496-8188
Epidermolysis Bullosa....Staff NIAMS 301-496-8188
Epikeratophakia....Staff NEI 301-496-5248
Epilepsy....Staff NINDS 301-496-5751
Epilepsy....Chandler, Jerry L. FAES 301-496-1846
Epistaxis (Nosebleed)....Staff NHLBI 301-496-4236
Epoxides....Michels, David USITC 202-205-3352
Epoxidized ester....Johnson, Larry USITC 202-205-3351
Epoxidized linseed oils....Johnson, Larry USITC 202-205-3351
Epoxidized soya oils....Johnson, Larry USITC 202-205-3351
Epoxy resins....Misurelli, Denby USITC 202-205-3362
Epstein-Barr Syndrome....Staff NIAID 301-496-5717
Epstein-Barr Virus....Staff NIAID 301-496-5717
Equal Employment Opportunity....Staff OD/DEO 301-496-6301
Equatorial Guinea....Henke, Debra Cnty Commerce 202-482-4228
Equatorial Guinea (Malabo)....Staff Cnty State 202-647-3139
Equatorial Guinea/Minerals....Dolley, Thomas Cnty Mines 202-501-9690

Be patient. If any phone number is incorrect, call (area code) 555-1212 and request the new listing.

Employment / Executive Director's Office (FTC)

Equipment Measurement Authorization....Staff FCC 301-725-1585
Equipment leasing....Bedore, James USITC 202-205-3424
Equatorial Guinea....Blackwell, Gloria Peace Corps 202-606-3998
Equatorial Guinea....Swezey, Virginia Peace Corps 202-606-3998
Erythema Elevatum Diutinum....Staff NIAMS 301-496-8188
Erythema Nodosum....Staff NIAID 301-496-5717
Erythroblastosis Fetalis....Staff NICHD 301-496-5133
Erythrocytes (Red Blood Cells)....Staff NHLBI 301-496-4236
Erythrocytes (Red Blood Cells)....Staff FDA/NCDB 301-496-3556
Esophagus, Carcinoma....Staff NCI 301-496-5583
Esotropia....Staff NEI 301-496-5248
Essential Hypertension....Staff NHLBI 301-496-4236
Essential oils....Land, Eric USITC 202-205-3349
Establishment Survey, Data Disk....Podgornik, Guy LABOR 202-606-6559
Establishment Survey, Emp/Unemp....Shipp, Kenneth LABOR 202-606-6559
Establishment Survey, National, Empl/Unempl.....Seifert, Mary Lee LABOR 202-606-6552
Establishment Survey, Natl., Indus. Classif. Empl/Unempl....Getz, Patricia LABOR 202-606-6521
Establishment Survey, States & Areas, Data Diskette....Podgornik, Guy LABOR 202-606-6559
Establishment Survey, States & Areas, Empl/Unemp....Shipp, Kenneth LABOR 202-606-6559
Esters, fatty-acid, of polyhydric alcohols....Land, Eric USITC 202-205-3349
Estimates & Incidence/Industry Injuries & Illness....Staff LABOR 202-606-6180
Estonia....Staff Cnty State 202-647-3187
Estrogen Replacement Therapy....Staff NICHD 301-496-5133
Estrogen Replacement Therapy....Staff NCI 301-496-5583
Estrogen Replacement Therapy....Staff FDA 301-443-3170
Estrogen Replacement Therapy....Staff NIAMS 301-496-8188
Estrogen Replacement Therapy....Staff NIA 301-496-1752
Estrogen Therapy....Staff NIA 301-496-1752
Ethane....Land, Eric USITC 202-205-3349
Ethanol....DiMaria, Joseph CUSTOMS 212-466-4769
Ethanolamines....Michels, David USITC 202-205-3352
Ethers....DiMaria, Joseph CUSTOMS 212-466-4769
Ethers....Michels, David USITC 202-205-3352
Ethers, fatty-acid, of polyhydric alcohols....Land, Eric USITC 202-205-3349
Ethiopia....Watkins, Chandra Cnty Commerce 202-482-4564
Ethiopia (Addis Ababa)....Staff Cnty State 202-647-8852
Ethiopia/Minerals....Antonides, Lloyd Cnty Mines 202-501-9686
Ethyl alcohol (ethanol) for nonbeverage use....Michels, David USITC 202-205-3352
Ethylene....Raftery, Jim USITC 202-205-3365
Ethylene dibromide....Michels, David USITC 202-205-3352
Ethylene glycol....Michels, David USITC 202-205-3352
Ethylene oxide....Michels, David USITC 202-205-3352
Ethylene-propylene rubber....Misurelli, Denby USITC 202-205-3362
Eurodollars with options....SIA Manasses CFT 312-353-9027
Europe/trade matters....Marcich, Christopher US Trade Rep 202-395-4620
European Assistance....Balfour, Michele FTC 202-326-2371
European Community....Ludolph, Charles Cnty Commerce 202-482-5276
European Economic Community (EEC)....Staff Cnty State 202-647-1708
Ewing's Sarcoma....Staff NCI 301-496-5583
Ex Parte Rules....Staff FCC 202-632-6990
Exec. Director's Office - Procurement & Gen. Services....Bussard, Clyde FTC 202-326-2266
Exec. Director's Bureau - Procurement & Gen. Services....Rice, Melvin L. FTC 202-326-2297
Exec. Director's Office - Procurement & Gen. Services.....Stokes, Akyva L. FTC 202-326-2278
Exec. Director's Office - Procurement & Gen. Services.....Wells, Ernest L. FTC 202-326-2248
Exec. Director's Office - Procurement & Gen. Services....Duncan, Mary A. FTC 202-326-2248
Exec. Director's Office - Procurement & Gen. Services....Fuehrerh, Carl E., Jr. FTC 202-326-2270
Exec. Director's Office - Procurement & Gen. Services....Wilson, Ricardo M. FTC 202-326-2261
Exec. Director's Office - Procurement & Gen. Services.....Meritt, Claude O., Jr. FTC 202-326-2286
Exec. Director's Office - Procurement & Gen. Services.....Simpson, Flossie I. FTC 202-326-2297
Exec. Director's Office - Procurement & Gen Services....Royster, Lawrence D., Sr. FTC 202-326-2251
Exec. Director's Office - Procurement & Gen. Services.....Sefchick, Jean FTC 202-326-2258
Exec. Director's Office - Procurement & Gen. Services....Felder, J. Allen FTC 202-326-2269
Exec. Director's Office - Procurement & Gen. Services....Short, Francis G. FTC 202-326-2251
Exec. Director's Office - Procurement & Gen. Services.....Goines, Russell E. FTC 202-326-2267
Exec. Director's Office - Procurement & Gen. Services....Cox, Donald W. FTC 202-326-2274
Exec. Director's Office - Procurement & Gen. Services....Dickerson, William F. FTC 202-326-3735
Exec. Director's Office - Procurement & Gen. Services....Hayes, Ronald FTC 202-326-3734
Exec. Director's Office - Procurement & Gen. Services....Thornton, Kristy FTC 202-326-2533
Exec. Director's Office - Procurement & Gen. Services....Vasser, Robert M. FTC 202-326-2245
Exec. Director's Office - Procurement & Gen. Services.....Scott, John T. FTC 202-326-2297
Exec. Director's Office - Procurement & Gen. Services....Armstead, Gloria FTC 202-326-2262
Executive Director's Office....Baugh, Elaine H. FTC 202-326-2196
Executive Director's Office....Giffin, James M. FTC 202-326-2209
Executive Director's Office....Holland, Peggy FTC 202-326-3426
Executive Director's Office....Hunter, Nancy L. FTC 202-326-2202
Executive Director's Office....Kelsey, Teresa J. FTC 202-326-2196
Executive Director's Office....Letalik, Kitsie E. FTC 202-326-2259
Executive Director's Office....Lewis, Andrea FTC 202-326-2647
Executive Director's Office....Manley, Bernita L. FTC 202-326-3533
Executive Director's Office....Proctor, Alan FTC 202-326-2204
Executive Director's Office....Straight, Rosemarie FTC 202-326-2207
Executive Director's Office....Stultz, Rachel FTC 202-326-2199
Executive Director's Office....Walton, Robert, III FTC 202-326-2205
Executive Director's Office....Zytnick, Joseph FTC 202-326-2224
Executive Director's Office....Wiggs, Barbara B. FTC 202-326-2196
Executive Director's Office - Automated Systems....Chambers, Michael D. FTC 202-326-2379
Executive Director's Office - Automated Systems....Chmielewski, Richard FTC 202-326-2402
Executive Director's Office - Automated Systems....Clark, Randal S. FTC 202-326-3500
Executive Director's Office - Automated Systems....Condor, Karen FTC 202-326-3402
Executive Director's Office - Automated Systems....DeVaughn, Willetta FTC 202-326-2233
Executive Director's Office - Automated Systems....Donovan, Tammy M. FTC 202-326-2588
Executive Director's Office - Automated Systems....Edwards, Kathleen N. FTC 202-326-2240
Executive Director's Office - Automated Systems....Feldmann, Lester A. FTC 202-326-2216
Executive Director's Office - Automated Systems....Frank, F. Michael FTC 202-326-2217
Executive Director's Office - Automated Systems....Gabriel, Jack FTC 202-326-2250
Executive Director's Office - Automated Systems....Hales, Gregory E. FTC 202-326-2795
Executive Director's Office - Automated Systems....Haley, Brian FTC 202-326-2226
Executive Director's Office - Automated Systems....Hines, David C. FTC 202-326-3527
Executive Director's Office - Automated Systems....Horne, Dawn R. FTC 202-326-2281
Executive Director's Office - Automated Systems....Jaye, Jeffrey A. FTC 202-326-3136
Executive Director's Office - Automated Systems....Johnson, Gracie E. FTC 202-326-2211
Executive Director's Office - Automated Systems....Johnson, Loretta FTC 202-326-3624
Executive Director's Office - Automated Systems....Krim, Mead Ann FTC 202-326-3407
Executive Director's Office - Automated Systems....Krupinski, Robert FTC 202-326-2231
Executive Director's Office - Automated Systems....Lewis, Matthew FTC 202-326-2791
Executive Director's Office - Automated Systems....Lynch, Dennis FTC 202-326-2840

Be patient. If any phone number is incorrect, call (area code) 555-1212 and request the new listing.

Experts

Executive Director's Office - Automated Systems....Mills, Mark C. FTC 202-326-3214
Executive Director's Office - Automated Systems....Momeni, Ali FTC 202-326-2232
Executive Director's Office - Automated Systems....Morris, Derrick FTC 202-326-2235
Executive Director's Office - Automated Systems....Moser, William E. FTC 202-326-2227
Executive Director's Office - Automated Systems....Nguyen, Kim FTC 202-326-2283
Executive Director's Office - Automated Systems....Overholt, Roberta FTC 202-326-2228
Executive Director's Office - Automated Systems....Pascoe, George FTC 202-326-3405
Executive Director's Office - Automated Systems....Passarelli, Joseph FTC 202-326-2394
Executive Director's Office - Automated Systems....Pinegar, Timothy S. FTC 202-326-2570
Executive Director's Office - Automated Systems....Pitt, Julia K. FTC 202-326-2369
Executive Director's Office - Automated Systems....Robertson, Diana FTC 202-326-2230
Executive Director's Office - Automated Systems....Russo, Jim FTC 202-326-2218
Executive Director's Office - Automated Systems....Seelinger, Douglas A. FTC 202-326-2237
Executive Director's Office - Automated Systems....Smith, Susan D. FTC 202-326-2220
Executive Director's Office - Automated Systems....Snyder, I. Michael FTC 202-326-2298
Executive Director's Office - Automated Systems....Travis, Robin FTC 202-326-3539
Executive Director's Office - Automated Systems....Vaughn, Brooks FTC 202-326-2215
Executive Director's Office - Automated Systems....Veneroso, Carmela FTC 202-326-2254
Executive Director's Office - Automated Systems....Wu, John FTC 202-326-2238
Executive Director's Office - Automated Systems....West, Harold D. FTC 202-326-2011
Executive Director's Office - Automated Systems....Williams, Ken FTC 202-326-2082
Executive Director's Office - Budget & Finance....Arnold, Richard D., II FTC 202-326-2314
Executive Director's Office - Budget & Finance....Farmer, Melissa S. FTC 202-326-2244
Executive Director's Office - Budget & Finance....Fielding, Parcellena FTC 202-326-2312
Executive Director's Office - Budget & Finance....Gates, Dawn M. FTC 202-326-2314
Executive Director's Office - Budget & Finance....Gee, Jennifer C. FTC 202-326-2433
Executive Director's Office - Budget & Finance....Graham, Otto C. FTC 202-326-2315
Executive Director's Office - Budget & Finance....Hailes, Gail E. FTC 202-326-2318
Executive Director's Office - Budget & Finance....Hendershot, Alec R. FTC 202-326-3334
Executive Director's Office - Budget & Finance....Hodge, Denise D. FTC 202-326-2324
Executive Director's Office - Budget & Finance....Jefferson, Betty A. FTC 202-326-2327
Executive Director's Office - Budget & Finance....King, Linda G. FTC 202-326-2323
Executive Director's Office - Budget & Finance....Lancaster, Dorothy M. FTC 202-326-2488
Executive Director's Office - Budget & Finance....Mason, Dorothy T. FTC 202-326-2329
Executive Director's Office - Budget & Finance....Simms, Anthony FTC 202-326-2325
Executive Director's Office - Budget & Finance....Smith, Deona J. FTC 202-326-2330
Executive Director's Office - Budget & Finance....Smith, Virginia FTC 202-326-2339
Executive Director's Office - Budget & Finance....Spyres, Julie K. FTC 202-326-3301
Executive Director's Office - Budget & Finance....Squalls, Cora L. FTC 202-326-2322
Executive Director's Office - Budget & Finance....Savell, Toby Sunshine FTC 202-326-2422
Executive Director's Office - Budget & Finance....Thompson, Carl M. FTC 202-326-2337
Executive Director's Office - Budget & Finance....Thorpe, Wilhelmina FTC 202-326-2219
Executive Director's Office - Information Services....Bolden, Sandra B. FTC 202-326-2406
Executive Director's Office - Information Services....Booker, Lance FTC 202-326-2523
Executive Director's Office - Information Services....Bush, Edgar A. FTC 202-326-2421
Executive Director's Office - Information Services....Carter-Johnson, Jean FTC 202-326-2405
Executive Director's Office - Information Services....Chambers, Dewayne W. FTC 202-326-2222
Executive Director's Office - Information Services....Coleman, Kwame S. FTC 202-326-2528
Executive Director's Office - Information Services....Eperson, Patricia C. FTC 202-326-2420
Executive Director's Office - Information Services....Golden, Keith G. FTC 202-326-2410
Executive Director's Office - Information Services....Harewood, Stanley M. FTC 202-326-2222
Executive Director's Office - Information Services....Harris, Diane FTC 202-326-2528
Executive Director's Office - Information Services....Johnson, Dana FTC 202-326-2431
Executive Director's Office - Information Services....Johnson, Phyllis A. FTC 202-326-2507
Executive Director's Office - Information Services....Jones, Deborah A. FTC 202-326-2222
Executive Director's Office - Information Services....Jones, Michael J. FTC 202-326-2660
Executive Director's Office - Information Services....Kelly, Eldora FTC 202-326-2404
Executive Director's Office - Information Services....Long, Marcus D. FTC 202-326-2660
Executive Director's Office - Information Services....Maisel, Theodore A. FTC 202-326-2415
Executive Director's Office - Information Services....Moore, Joyce M. FTC 202-326-2872
Executive Director's Office - Information Services....Musser, Franklin L. FTC 202-326-2411
Executive Director's Office - Information Services....Pearson, Drake A. FTC 202-326-2412
Executive Director's Office - Information Services....Pierce, Marilyn S. FTC 202-326-2659
Executive Director's Office - Information Services....Proctor, Jerusha E. FTC 202-326-2408
Executive Director's Office - Information Services....Reese, Genevieve E. FTC 202-326-2409
Executive Director's Office - Information Services....Titzer, Kristine L. FTC 202-326-2407
Executive Director's Office - Information Services....Tucker, Francenia FTC 202-326-2430
Executive Director's Office - Information Services....Verter, DeShonda L. FTC 202-326-2013
Executive Director's Office - Information Services....Wise, Taleiha FTC 202-326-2508
Executive Director's Office - Information Services....Woodson, Margaret B. FTC 202-326-2417
Executive Director's Office - Information Services....Wiley, Bessie M. FTC 202-326-2416
Executive Director's Office - Library....Anderson, Rita D. FTC 202-326-2834
Executive Director's Office - Library....Bacon, Geraldine G. FTC 202-326-2380
Executive Director's Office - Library....Blades, Donna L. FTC 202-326-3005
Executive Director's Office - Library....Conrad, Jean FTC 202-326-2378
Executive Director's Office - Library....Cunningham, Jack FTC 202-326-2387
Executive Director's Office - Library....Curtin, Frank FTC 202-326-2280
Executive Director's Office - Library....Douglass, Franklin S. FTC 202-326-2376
Executive Director's Office - Library....Dowdle, Walter D. FTC 202-326-2505
Executive Director's Office - Library....Hammonds, Estelle FTC 202-326-2388

Be patient. If any phone number is incorrect, call (area code) 555-1212 and request the new listing.

Executive Director's Office (FTC) / Families

Executive Director's Office - Library....Hynes, Barbara A. FTC 202-326-2389
Executive Director's Office - Library....Jennings, Bruce FTC 202-326-2383
Executive Director's Office - Library....Knott, Margie FTC 202-326-2395
Executive Director's Office - Library....Ottie, Denise B. FTC 202-326-2381
Executive Director's Office - Library....Sims, Shirlene FTC 202-326-2395
Executive Director's Office - Library....Smith, Ayanna FTC 202-326-2390
Executive Director's Office - Library....Sullivan, R. Elaine FTC 202-326-2385
Executive Director's Office - Library....Watts, David V. FTC 202-326-2241
Executive Director's Office - Personnel....Allen, Gelinda A. FTC 202-326-2658
Executive Director's Office - Personnel....Axelrod, Harold FTC 202-326-2790
Executive Director's Office - Personnel....Berry, Chrishania R. FTC 202-326-2363
Executive Director's Office - Personnel....Brooks, Judy FTC 202-326-2347
Executive Director's Office - Personnel....Carter, Carole A. FTC 202-326-2550
Executive Director's Office - Personnel....Caton, Kathleen FTC 202-326-2342
Executive Director's Office - Personnel....Clark, Vivian Renee FTC 202-326-2365
Executive Director's Office - Personnel....Cooper, Erica FTC 202-326-2021
Executive Director's Office - Personnel....Coote, Sharon FTC 202-326-2348
Executive Director's Office - Personnel....Crayton, Erika L. FTC 202-326-2022
Executive Director's Office - Personnel....Davis, Elliot FTC 202-326-2022
Executive Director's Office - Personnel....Harris, Barbara A. FTC 202-326-2428
Executive Director's Office - Personnel....Holmes, Ann FTC 202-326-2345
Executive Director's Office - Personnel....La Veille, Monica FTC 202-326-2361
Executive Director's Office - Personnel....McCoy, Catherine M. FTC 202-326-2358
Executive Director's Office - Personnel....Schwarz, Mae FTC 202-326-2341
Executive Director's Office - Personnel....Smith, Del FTC 202-326-2357
Executive Director's Office - Personnel....Steinberg, Sharon FTC 202-326-2364
Executive Director's Office - Personnel....Hines, Calvin FTC 202-326-2273
Executive Director's Office - Proc. & Gen. Services....Clayborne, Charles FTC 202-326-2272
Executive Director's Office - Proc. & Gen. Services....Lorette, Barbara D. FTC 202-326-2260
Executive Director's Office - Proc. & Gen. Services.....Haines, John, P. FTC 202-326-2252
Executive Director's Office - Proc. & Gen. Services.....Hymon, James F. FTC 202-326-3736
Executive Director's Office - Proc. & Gen. Services.....Justice, Julius FTC 202-326-2275
Executive Director's Office - Proc. & Gen. Services.....Moore, David L. FTC 202-326-2277
Executive Director's Office - Proc. & Gen. Services.....Moore, Francenia K. FTC 202-326-2872
Executive Director's Office - Proc. & Gen. Services.....Hutcherson, Willie S. FTC 202-326-2297
Executive Director's Office - Proc. & Gen. Services....Greulich, Sherron FTC 202-326-2271
Executive Director's Office - Starek, Roscoe B. III....Riley, Katherine E. FTC 202-326-2127
Exercise and Aging....Staff NIA 301-496-1752
Exercise and the Heart....Staff NHLBI 301-496-4236
Exhibits and Publications (Printing)....Charuhas, Joseph NLM 301-496-6308
Exhibits, Conventions....Dickinson, Joanne CENSUS 301-763-2370
Exotic Fish....Staff FWS 703-358-1718
Exotic Species....Staff FWS 703-358-1718
Exotropia....Staff NEI 301-496-5248
Experimental Aerodynamics....Mewhinney, Michael NASA 415-604-3937
Experimental Aerodynamics....Hutchison, Jane NASA 415-604-4698
Experimental Allergic Encephalomyelitis (EAE)....Staff NINDS 301-496-5751
Experimental Development Stations....Staff FCC 202-653-8141
Experimental Immunology....O'Shea, John FAES 301-846-1330
Explosives....Maxey, Francis P. COMMERCE 202-482-0128
Explosives....Preston, Jacques CUSTOMS 212-466-5488
Explosives....Cantrell, Raymond L. MINES 202-501-9581
Explosives....Johnson, Larry USITC 202-205-3351
Export & Import Price Indexes, Curr. Anal.....Vachris, Michelle LABOR 202-606-7155
Export Trading Company Affairs....Muller, George COMMERCE 202-482-5131
Exposure Evaluation Division....Staff EPA 202-260-1866

Express Delivery Service....Elliott, Fred COMMERCE 202-482-1134
Extramural Associates Program....Staff OD/OERT 301-496-9728
Extrapyramidal Disorders....Staff NINDS 301-496-5751
Eye (Radiation and Ultra Violet Effect)....Staff FDA/NCDRH 301-443-4690
Eye (Statistics)....Staff NCHS 301-436-8500
Eye Banks....Staff NEI 301-496-5248
Eye Care....Staff NEI 301-496-5248
Eye Diseases....Staff NEI 301-496-5248
Eye Exercises....Staff NEI 301-496-5248
Eye Institute, National....Stein, Judith NIH 301-496-5248
Eye Strain....Staff NEI 301-496-5248
Eye glasses....Johnson, Christopher USITC 202-205-3488
Eyeglasses....Staff NEI 301-496-5248

F

FAES (Foundation for Adv. Educa. in the Sciences)....Staff FAES 301-496-7976
FM Radio Advertising....Staff FCC 202-632-7551
FM Radio Intercity Relays....Staff FCC 202-634-6307
FM Radio Remote Pickup....Staff FCC 202-634-6307
FM Radio Stations....Staff FCC 202-632-6908
FM Radio Stations--New....Staff FCC 202-632-6908
FM Translators/Boosters....Staff FCC 202-634-6307
Fabric folding machines....Greene, William USITC 202-205-3405
Fabricated Metal Construction Materials....Williams, Franklin COMMERCE 202-482-0132
Fabrics, Coated or Laminated....Barth, George CUSTOMS 212-466-5884
Fabrics, Embroidered....Konzet, Jeffrey CUSTOMS 212-466-5885
Fabrics, Knit....Konzet, Jeffrey CUSTOMS 212-466-5885
Fabrics, Non-Woven....Barth, George CUSTOMS 212-466-5884
Fabrics, Technical....Barth, George CUSTOMS 212-466-5884
Fabrics, Woven....Tytelman, Alan CUSTOMS 212-466-5896
Fabrics, woven: cotton....Freund, Kimberlie USITC 202-205-3456
Fabrics, woven: glass....McNay, Deborah USITC 202-205-3425
Fabrics, woven: jute....Cook, Lee USITC 202-205-3471
Fabrics, woven: manmade fibers....Freund, Kimberlie USITC 202-205-3456
Fabrics, woven: pile....Freund, Kimberlie USITC 202-205-3456
Fabrics, woven: silk....Freund, Kimberlie USITC 202-205-3456
Fabrics: Tufted....Freund, Kimberlie USITC 202-205-3456
Fabrics: billiard cloth....Cook, Lee USITC 202-205-3471
Fabrics: bolting cloth....Cook, Lee USITC 202-205-3471
Fabrics: coated....Cook, Lee USITC 202-205-3471
Fabrics: elastic....Freund, Kimberlie USITC 202-205-3456
Fabrics: impression....Freund, Kimberlie USITC 202-205-3456
Fabrics: knit....Freund, Kimberlie USITC 202-205-3456
Fabrics: narrow....Freund, Kimberlie USITC 202-205-3456
Fabrics: nonwoven....Sussman, Donald USITC 202-205-3470
Fabrics: oil cloths....Cook, Lee USITC 202-205-3471
Fabrics: tapestry, woven....Freund, Kimberlie USITC 202-205-3456
Fabrics: tire....Cook, Lee USITC 202-205-3471
Fabrics: tracing cloth....Cook, Lee USITC 202-205-3471
Fabrics: embroidered....Freund, Kimberlie USITC 202-205-3456
Fabrics: woven, wool....Fruend, Kimberlie USITC 202-205-3456
Fabry's Disease....Staff NINDS 301-496-5751
Fabry's Disease....Staff NICHD 301-496-5133
Facial Neuralgia (Tic Douloureux)....Staff NINDS 301-496-5751
Facilities Management....Bass, Robert C. FTC 202-326-2265
Facilities Management....Glisson, Thomas A. FTC 202-326-2308
Facilities Management....Lampkins, Gladys M. FTC 202-326-2307
Facilities Management....Morris, J. Wayne FTC 202-326-2310
Facilities Management....Morris, Patrick A. FTC 202-326-2309
Facilities Management....Singleton, Frieda FTC 202-326-2580
Facsimile (FAX)--Wire....Staff FCC 202-634-1800
Fainting (Syncope)....Staff NHLBI 301-496-4236
Fair Housing and Equal Opportunity....Staff HUD 202-708-3735
Falconry....Staff FWS 703-358-1821
Falls and Frailty....Staff NIA 301-496-1752
Familial Ataxia Telangiectasia....Staff NCI 301-496-5583
Familial Ataxia Telangiectasia....Staff NINDS 301-496-5751
Familial Dysautonomia (Riley-Day Syndrome)....Staff NINDS 301-496-5751
Familial Hypertension....Staff NHLBI 301-496-4236
Familial Periodic Paralysis....Staff NINDS 301-496-5751
Familial Spastic Paraparesis....Staff NINDS 301-496-5751
Families....Staff CENSUS 301-763-7987
Family Characteristics of Labor Force....Hayghe, Howard LABOR

Experts

202-606-6378
Family Issues....Long, Susan ACF 202-401-9215
Family Medicine Training....Staff HRSA/BHPr 301-443-6837
Family Nursing Practitioner....Staff HRSA/BHPr 301-443-6333
Family Planning....Staff NCNR 301-496-0526
Family Planning....Eddinger, Lucy ASH 202-690-8335
Family Planning (Research)....Staff NICHD 301-496-5133
Family Size....Staff NICHD 301-496-5133
Family and Aging....Staff NIA 301-496-1752
Fanconi's Anemia....Staff NHLBI 301-496-4236
Fans....Mata, Ruben USITC 202-205-3403
Farm Bill....Staff FWS 703-358-2043
Farm Machinery....Weining, Mary COMMERCE 202-482-4708
Farm Population....Dahmann, Don CENSUS 301-763-5158
Farmlands....Staff FWS 703-358-2043
Farms & Land - Corporate & Family Farms....Reimund, Donn Agri 202-219-0522
Farms & Land - Farm Numbers....Ledbury, Dan Agri 202-720-1790
Farms & Land - Farm Output & Productivity....Douvelis, George Agri 202-219-0432
Farms & Land - Farm Real Estate....Hexem, Roger Agri 202-219-0419
Farms & Land - Foreign Land Ownership....DeBraal, Peter Agri 202-219-0425
Farms & Land - Land Ownership & Tenure....Wunderlich, Gene Agri 202-219-0425
Farms & Land - Land Use....Daugherty, Arthur Agri 202-219-0424
Farms & Land - World....Urban, Francis Agri 202-219-0717
Farsightedness....Staff NEI 301-496-5248
Fasteners (Industrial)....Reise, Richard COMMERCE 202-482-3489
Fasteners (Nails, Screws, Etc.)....Fitzgerald, John CUSTOMS 212-466-5492
Fats and Oils....Janis, William V. COMMERCE 202-482-2250
Fats and vegetable oils and their products....Reeder, John USITC 202-205-3319
Fatty acids....Randall, Rob USITC 202-205-3366
Fatty alcohols of animal or vegetable origin....Randall, Rob USITC 202-205-3366
Fatty and Aromatic Substances....Joseph, Stephanie CUSTOMS 212-466-5768
Fatty ethers of animal or vegetable origin....Randall, Rob USITC 202-205-3366
Fatty substances derived from animal, marine, veg....Randall, Rob USITC 202-205-3366
Fatty-acid amides....Land, Eric USITC 202-205-3349
Fatty-acid esters of polyhydric alcohols....Land, Eric USITC 202-205-3349
Fatty-acid quaternary ammonium salts (surface act)....Land, Eric USITC 202-205-3349
Fear of Crime....Lindgren, Sue Justice Stat 202-307-0760
Fear of Crime....Klaus, Patsy Justice Stat 202-307-0776
Fear of Crime....Rand, Michael Justice Stat 202-616-3494
Feather products....Spalding, Josephine USITC 202-205-3498
Feathers....Steller, Rose USITC 202-205-3323
Febrile Convulsions....Staff NINDS 301-496-5751
Febrile Seizures....Staff NICHD 301-496-5133
Federal Justice....Kaplan, Carol Justice Stat 202-307-0759
Feed Grains - Corn, Sorghum, Barley, Oats....Van Lahr, Charles Agri 202-720-7369
Feed Grains - Corn, Sorghum, Barley, Oats....Tice, Thomas Agri 202-219-0840
Feed Grains - Corn, Sorghum, Barley, Oats....Cole, James Agri 202-219-0840
Feed Grains - Corn, Sorghum, Barley, Oats - World....Riley, Peter Agri 202-219-0824
Feeds, animal....Pierre-Benoist, John USITC 202-205-3320
Feldspar....Potter, Michael J. MINES 202-501-9387
Feldspar....White, Linda USITC 202-205-3427
Female Offenders....Conley, Joyce Justice Stat 202-633-2214
Female Offenders - Federal....Kaplan, Carol Justice Stat 202-307-0759
Female Victims....Klaus, Patsy Justice Stat 202-307-0776
Fencing, Metal....Shaw, Robert COMMERCE 202-482-0132
Ferments....Nesbitt, Elizabeth USITC 202-205-3355
Ferricyanide blue....Johnson, Larry USITC 202-205-3351
Ferrites....Cutchin, John USITC 202-205-3396
Ferroalloys.... USITC 202-205-3419
Ferroalloys Products....Presbury Greylin COMMERCE 202-482-0609
Ferrocerium....Johnson, Larry USITC 202-205-3351
Ferrocyanide blue....Johnson, Larry USITC 202-205-3351
Ferrous Scrap....Sharkey, Robert COMMERCE 202-482-0606
Fertility....Staff NICHD 301-496-5133
Fertility Drugs....Staff NICHD 301-496-5133
Fertility/Births....Bachu, Amara CENSUS 301-763-5303
Fertility/Births....O'Connell, Martin CENSUS 301-763-5303
Fertilizers....Maxey, Francis P. COMMERCE 202-482-0128
Fertilizers....Brownchweig, Gilbert CUSTOMS 212-466-5744
Fertilizers....Trainor, Cynthia USITC 202-205-3354
Fetal Alcohol Syndrome....Staff NICHD 301-496-5133
Fetal Alcohol Syndrome Prevention....Floyd, Louise CDC 404-488-7370
Fetal Monitoring....Staff NICHD 301-496-5133
Fetus....Staff NICHD 301-496-5133
Fever....Staff NIAID 301-496-5717
Fever Blisters....Staff NIDR 301-496-4261
Fibers....Konzet, Jeffrey CUSTOMS 212-466-5885
Fibers: abaca....Cook, Lee USITC 202-205-3471
Fibers: alpaca....Warlick, William USITC 202-205-3459
Fibers: camel hair....Warlick, William USITC 202-205-3459
Fibers: cashmere....Warlick, William USITC 202-205-3459
Fibers: cotton....Sweet, Mary Elizabeth USITC 202-205-3455
Fibers: flax....Cook, Lee USITC 202-205-3471
Fibers: jute....Cook, Lee USITC 202-205-3471
Fibers: wool....Warlick, William USITC 202-205-3459
Fibers: angora....Warlick, William USITC 202-205-3459
Fibers: manmade....Warlick, William USITC 202-205-3459
Fibers: silk....Warlick, William USITC 202-205-3459
Fibers: sisal and henequen....Cook, Lee USITC 202-205-3471
Fibrillation....Staff NHLBI 301-496-4236
Fibrin....Randall, Rob USITC 202-205-3366
Fibrinolysis....Staff NHLBI 301-496-4236
Fibroid Tumors....Staff NICHD 301-496-5133
Fibromuscular Hyperplasia....Staff NHLBI 301-496-4236
Fibromuscular Hyperplasia....Staff NIAMS 301-496-8188
Fibromyalgia....Staff NIAMS 301-496-8188
Fibrositis....Staff NIAMS 301-496-8188
Fibrotic Lung Diseases....Staff NHLBI 301-496-4236
Field Disturbance....Staff FCC 202-653-7313
Fifth Disease....Staff NIAID 301-496-5717
Fiji....Lagoy, Michele Peace Corps 202-606-3227
Fiji (Suva)....Staff Cnty State 202-647-3546
Fiji/Minerals....Lyday, Travis Cnty Mines 202-501-9695
Filariasis....Staff NIAID 301-496-5717
Filberts....Burket, Stephen USITC 202-205-3318
Film....Brownchweig, Gilbert CUSTOMS 212-466-5744
Film (photographic)....Bishop, Kate USITC 202-205-3494
Film, plastics....Misurelli, Denby USITC 202-205-3362
Films, Wildlife Video....Staff FWS 202-205-5611
Filters/Purifying Equipment....Jonkers, Loretta COMMERCE 202-482-0564
Finance and Management Ind.....Candilis, Wray O. COMMERCE 202-482-0339
Financial services....Brown, Richard USITC 202-205-3438
Finland....Lyons, Maryanne Cnty Commerce 202-482-3254
Finland (Helsinki)....Staff Cnty State 202-647-6071
Finland/Minerals....Buck, Donald E. Cnty Mines 202-501-9670
Fire....Staff FCC 717-337-1212
Fire Management....Staff FWS 703-358-2043
Fire Safety....Cowart, Everett CDC 404-639-3148
Firearms....Preston, Jacques CUSTOMS 212-466-5488
Firearms....Robinson, Hazel USITC 202-205-3496
Firewood....Ruggles, Fred USITC 202-205-3325
Fireworks....Glover, Stephanie CPSC 301-504-0580
Fireworks....Johnson, Larry USITC 202-205-3351
First aid kits....Randall, Rob USITC 202-205-3366
Fish....Brady, Thomas CUSTOMS 212-466-5790
Fish....Corey, Roger USITC 202-205-3327
Fish & Wildlife Law Enforcement....Staff FWS 703-358-1949
Fish Broodstock Program....Staff FWS 703-358-1715
Fish Conservation and Management Act....Staff 703-358-1715
Fish Control Chemicals....Staff FWS 703-358-1715
Fish Culture Information....Staff FWS 703-358-1715
Fish Disease Diagnosis/Control....Staff FWS 703-358-1715
Fish Diseases/Research....Staff FWS 703-358-1715
Fish Ecology....Staff FWS 703-358-1710
Fish Habitat Research....Lennartz, Michael R. FS 202-205-1524
Fish Hatcheries....Staff FWS 703-358-1715
Fish Health Inspections....Staff FWS 703-358-1715
Fish Husbandry....Staff FWS 703-358-1718
Fish Law Enforcement....Staff FWS 703-358-1949
Fish Nets and Nettings....Barth, George CUSTOMS 212-466-5884
Fish Propagation....Staff FWS 703-358-1715

Family Issues / Forfeiture

Fish and Wildlife News....Staff FWS 202-208-5634
Fish and Wildlife Reference Service....Staff FWS 703-358-2156
Fish and Wildlife Service....Staff EPA 703-208-4111
Fish nets and netting....Cook, Lee USITC 202-205-3471
Fish oils....Reeder, John USITC 202-205-3319
Fish, Exotic....Staff FWS 703-358-1718
Fisheries, Major Proj.....Bell, Richard COMMERCE 202-482-2460
Fishery Information Systems....Staff FWS 703-558-1861
Fishing on Refuges....Staff FWS 703-358-1718
Fishing tackle....Robinson, Hazel USITC 202-205-3496
Flags....Cook, Lee USITC 202-205-3471
Flares....Johnson, Larry USITC 202-205-3351
Flashlights....Cutchin, John USITC 202-205-3396
Flat glass and products....Lukes, James USITC 202-205-3426
Flat goods....Seastrum, Carl USITC 202-205-3493
Flat panel displays....Malison, Andrew USITC 202-205-3391
Flatgoods....Gorman, Kevin CUSTOMS 212-466-5893
Flaxseed and linseed oil....Reeder, John USITC 202-205-3319
Flight Control Research....Witherspoon, John NASA 804-864-6170
Flight Research Programs....Lovato, Nancy NASA 805-258-3448
Flight Simulation Research....Hutchison, Jane NASA 415-604-4968
Flight simulating machines....Andersen, Peder USITC 202-205-3388
Floaters....Staff NEI 301-496-5248
Floating structures....Lahey, Kathleen USITC 202-205-3409
Floor Coverings....Hansen, John CUSTOMS 212-466-5854
Floor coverings, textile....Sweet, Mary Elizabeth USITC 202-205-3465
Flooring (wood)....Ruggles, Fred USITC 202-205-3325
Floppy Baby (Nemaline Myopathy)....Staff NINDS 301-496-5751
Floral waters....Land, Eric USITC 202-205-3349
Floriculture....Brewster, Jim Agri 202-720-7688
Floriculture....Johnson, Doyle Agri 202-219-0884
Flour....Janis, William V. COMMERCE 202-482-2250
Flour (grain)....Pierre-Benoist, John USITC 202-205-3320
Flower and foliage: artificial, other....Spalding, Josephine USITC 202-205-3498
Flower and foliage: preserved, other....Spalding, Josephine USITC 202-205-3498
Flowers....Janis, William V. COMMERCE 202-482-2250
Flowers, Artificial....Rauch, Theodore CUSTOMS 212-466-5892
Fluid Power....McDonald, Edward COMMERCE 202-482-0680
Fluorescein Angiography....Staff NEI 301-496-5248
Fluoridation....Staff CDC 404-639-3286
Fluoridation....Staff NIDR 301-496-4261
Fluoridation....Berreth, Don CDC 404-639-3286
Fluoride Research....Staff NIDR 301-496-4261
Fluorine....Conant, Kenneth USITC 202-205-3346
Fluorocarbons....Michels, David USITC 202-205-3352
Fluorosis....Staff NIDR 301-496-4261
Fluorspar....Miller, Michael MINES 202-501-9409
Fluorspar....DeSapio, Vincent USITC 202-205-3435
Fluxes....White, Linda USITC 202-205-3427
Fogarty Publications....Staff FIC 301-496-2075
Fogarty Scholars....Staff FIC 301-496-4161
Foil, metal: aluminum....Yost, Charles USITC 202-205-3432
Foil, metal: other....Lundy, David USITC 202-205-3439
Folk Arts....Sheehy, Daniel NEA 202-682-5449
Food - Food Assistance and Nutrition....Smallwood, Dave Agri 202-219-0864
Food - Food Assistance and Nutrition....Smallwood, Dave Agri 202-219-0867
Food - Food Away From Home....Price, Charlene Agri 202-219-0866
Food - Food Consumption....Putnam, Judy Agri 202-219-0870
Food - Food Demand & Expenditures....Blaylock, James Agri 202-219-0862
Food - Food Demand & Expenditures....Haidacher, Richard Agri 202-219-0870
Food - Food Demand & Expenditures (World)....Stallings, Dave Agri 202-219-0708
Food - Food Manufacturing....Gallo, Tony Agri 202-219-0866
Food - Food Manufacturing & Retailing....Handy, Charles Agri 202-219-0866
Food - Food Policy....Myers, Les Agri 202-219-0860
Food - Food Policy....Smallwood, Dave Agri 202-219-0864
Food - Food Policy (World)....Westcott, Paul Agri 202-219-0840
Food - Food Policy - World....Lynch, Loretta Agri 202-219-0689
Food - Food Safety & Quality....Roberts, Tanya Agri 202-219-0864
Food - Food Safety & Quality....Lin, Bina-Hwah Agri 202-219-0459
Food - Food Wholesaling....Epps, Walter Agri 202-219-0866
Food - Marketing Margins & Statistics....Haidacher, Richard Agri 202-219-0870
Food - Marketing Margins & Statistics....Dunham, Denis Agri 202-219-0870
Food - Marketing Margins & Statistics....Elitzak, Howard Agri 202-219-0870
Food - Marketing Margins & Statistics....Handy, Charles Agri 202-219-0866
Food - Price Spreads (Meat)....Duewer, Larry Agri 202-219-0712
Food - Retailing....Kaufman, Phil Agri 202-219-0866
Food Additives....Staff FDA 301-472-4750
Food Additives/Dyes....Corwin, Emil FDA 202-205-4144
Food Grains - Rice....Owens, Marty Agri 202-720-2157
Food Grains - Wheat....Siegenthaler, Vaughn Agri 202-720-8068
Food Grains - Wheat....Allen, Ed Agri 202-219-0841
Food Labeling....Staff FDA 301-472-4750
Food Labeling....Lecos, Chris FDA 202-205-4144
Food Prices & Consumer Index....Parlett, Ralph Agri 202-219-0870
Food Prices & Consumer Price Index....Dunham, Denis Agri 202-219-0870
Food Prices Retail, Consumer Expenditure Survey....Cook, William LABOR 202-606-6988
Food Products Machinery....Shaw, Gene COMMERCE 202-482-3494
Food Retailing....Kenney, Cornelius COMMERCE 202-482-2428
Food and Chemicals, Prices/Lv. Cond....Hippen, Roger LABOR 202-606-7723
Food, Apparel, & Raw Materials, Intl. Price Ind.....Frumkin, Rob LABOR 202-606-7106
Food, Raw Materials, and Apparel, Intl. Price Ind....Frumkin, Rob LABOR 202-606-7106
Food-preparing machines....Jackson, Georgia USITC 202-205-3399
Footwear with Uppers of Rubber, Plastic or Leather....Francke, Eric CUSTOMS 212-466-5890
Footwear....Byron, James E. COMMERCE 202-482-4034
Footwear....Shildneck, Ann USITC 202-205-3499
Forecasting Prison Populations....Shipley, Bernard Justice Stat 202-307-7703
Foreign Born Population....Staff CENSUS 301-763-7955
Foreign Countries, Labor Force & Unemployment....Sorrentino, Constance LABOR 202-606-5654
Foreign Countries--Hourly Compensation Costs....Capdevielle, Patricia LABOR 202-606-5654
Foreign Countries--Prices, Prod. & Tech.....Godbout, Todd LABOR 202-606-5654
Foreign Countries--Productivity, Unit Labor Costs....Neef, Arthur LABOR 202-606-5654
Foreign Language Education....Staff NEH 202-606-8373
Foreign Medical Students....Mehuron, Charlotte HRSA 301-443-3376
Foreign Scientists Assistance....Staff FIC 301-472-6166
Foreign Trade Data Services....Mearkle, Hayden CENSUS 301-763-7754
Foreign Trade Data Services....Staff CENSUS 301-763-5140
Foreign Trade, Shippers Export Declaration....Blyweiss, Hal CENSUS 301-763-5310
Foreign trade zones....Burns, Gail USITC 202-205-2501
Forest Diseases....Smith Richard S. FS 202-205-1532
Forest Fire Sciences....Donoghue, Linda R. FS 202-205-1561
Forest Insects....Lyon, Robert L. FS 202-205-1532
Forest Products....Smith, Len COMMERCE 202-482-0375
Forest Products....Fitzgerald, Richard O. FS 202-205-1753
Forest Products, Domestic Construction....Kristensen, Chris COMMERCE 202-482-0384
Forest Products, Trade Policy....Hicks, Michael COMMERCE 202-482-0375
Forest Protection....Staff FWS 703-358-2043
Forest Radio Service....Staff FCC 717-337-1212
Forest Recreation and Urban Forestry....Ewert, Alan FS 202-205-1092
Forestry & Construction, Prices and Living Cond.....Davies, Wanda LABOR 202-606-7713
Forestry Atmospheric Deposition Research....Dunn, Paul H. FS 202-205-1524
Forestry Ecosystem Research....Szaro, Robert FS 202-205-1524
Forestry Wetlands Research....Bartuska, Ann M. FS 202-205-1524
Forestry and Construction, Prices/Lv. Cond....Davies, Wanda LABOR 202-606-7713
Forestry, Global Change Research....Niebla, Elvia E. FS 202-205-1561
Forestry, Land Reclamation....Duscher, Karl FS 202-205-1224
Forestry, Lands and Resource Information....Holmes, Chris FS 202-205-1006
Forestry, Mineral Materials....Marshall, Steve FS 202-205-1242
Forestry, Oil and Gas Analysis....Holm, Melody FS 303-236-9376
Forestry, Pesticide Use....Staff FS 202-205-1600
Forestry, Soils Program....Avers, Peter FS 202-205-1473
Forestry, Solid Leasable Minerals....Kurcaba FS 202-205-1243
Forestry, Water Rights....Glasser, Steve FS 202-205-1473
Forestry, Water Rights Program....Glasser, Steve FS 202-205-1473
Forfeiture....Zawitz, Marianne Justice Stat 202-616-3499
Forged-steel grinding balls....Stonitsch, Laura USITC 202-205-3408
Forgings Semifinished Steel....Bell, Charles COMMERCE 202-482-0609

Experts

Fork-lift trucks....Murphy, Mary USITC 202-205-3401
Formaldehyde....Michels, David USITC 202-205-3352
Fossil Energy....Stuntz, Linda NEIC 202-586-6660
Fossil Fuel Power Generation, Major Proj.....Dollison, Robert COMMERCE 202-482-2733
Foster Care....Long, Susan ACF 202-401-9215
Foundry Equipment....Kemper, Alexis COMMERCE 202-482-5956
Foundry Industry....Bell, Charles COMMERCE 202-482-0609
Foundry products....Vacant USITC 202-205-3419
Fracture Healing....Staff NIAMS 301-496-8188
Fragile X Syndrome....Staff NICHD 301-496-5133
France....Mikalis, Elana Cnty Commerce 202-482-6008
France (Paris)....Staff Cnty State 202-647-2633
France/Minerals....Newman, Harold R. Cnty Mines 202-501-9669
Franchising....Staff FCC 202-254-3407
Franchising services....Bedore, James USITC 202-205-3424
Fraud (Scientific)....Staff OD/OSI 301-496-2624
Fraud Hotline, HUD....Staff HUD 800-347-3735
Fraud, Waste & Abuse-Investigations, Audits....Holtz, Judy IG 202-619-1149
Freedom of Information....Staff OD/DC 301-496-5633
Freedom of Information Office....Coleman, Gary PHS 202-690-7453
Freedom of Information, Office of....Leathers, Laura CDC 404-639-2388
French Antilles....Staff Cnty State 202-647-2620
French Guinea/Minerals....Mobbs, Philip Cnty Mines 202-501-9679
French Polynesia....Staff Cnty State 202-647-3546
Freon (chlorofluorocarbons)....Michels, David USITC 202-205-3352
Frequencies Allocations, Government....Staff FCC 202-653-8141
Frequencies Allocations, International....Staff FCC 202-653-8126
Frequencies Allocations, Non-Government....Staff FCC 202-653-8108
Friedreich's Ataxia....Staff NINDS 301-496-5751
Frohlich's Syndrome (Adiposogenital Dystrophy)....Staff NINDS 301-496-5751
Frohlich's Syndrome (Adiposogenital Dystrophy)....Staff NIDDK 301-496-3583
Frohlich's Syndrome (Adiposogenital Dystrophy)....Staff NICHD 301-496-5133
Frozen Fruits, Vegetables & Specialties....Hodgen, Donald A. COMMERCE 202-482-3346
Fructose....Randall, Rob USITC 202-205-3366
Fruit, edible, ex citrus....Vacant USITC 202-205-3306
Fruits and Tree Nuts....Hintzman, Kevin Agri 202-720-5412
Fruits and Tree Nuts - Tree Nuts....Johnson, Doyle Agri 202-219-0884
Fruits and Tree Nuts....Shields, Dennis Agri 202-219-0884
Fruits and Tree Nuts....Bertelsen, Diane Agri 202-219-0884
Fruits and Vegetables....Hopartd, Stanley CUSTOMS 212-466-5760
Fuchs' Dystrophy....Staff NEI 301-496-5248
Fuel oil (nos. 1, 2, 3, 4, 5, 6)....Foreso, Cynthia USITC 202-205-3348
Fuel oil, bunker "C"....Foreso, Cynthia USITC 202-205-3348
Fuel oil, navy special....Foreso, Cynthia USITC 202-205-3348
Fuel, jet....Foreso, Cynthia USITC 202-205-3348
Fuels and Utls. Retail Prices, Consumer Price Index....Adkins, Robert LABOR 202-606-6985
Fuels and Chemical Analysis....Staff EPA 313-668-4245
Fuels and Utilities Index, Monthly....Adkins, Robert LABOR 202-606-6985
Fulminates....Johnson, Larry USITC 202-205-3351
Fumes (Hazardous)....Staff OD/ORS 301-496-2960
Fungal Diseases (Eyes)....Staff NEI 301-496-5248
Fungal Infections....Staff NIAID 301-496-5717
Funnel Chest (Pectus Excavatum)....Staff NHLBI 301-496-4236
Fur Goods....Byron, James E. COMMERCE 202-482-4034
Fur and furlike apparel....Jones, Jackie USITC 202-205-3466
Fur and furlike apparel....Hamey, Amy USITC 202-205-3465
Furfural....Michels, David USITC 202-205-3352
Furnace black....Johnson, Larry USITC 202-205-3351
Furnaces....Mesa, Stacey Reuben CPSC 301-504-0580
Furnaces....Rocks, Michael CUSTOMS 212-466-5669
Furnaces....Mata, Ruben USITC 202-205-3403
Furnishings....Hansen, John CUSTOMS 212-466-5854
Furniture....Vacant COMMERCE 202-482-0338
Furniture....Mushinske, Larry CUSTOMS 212-466-5739
Furniture....Spalding, Josephine USITC 202-205-3498
Furskins....Steller, Rose USITC 202-205-3323
Fuse/Burn....Glover, Stephanie CPSC 301-504-0580
Fused Alumina, (Abrasive)....Austin, Gordon MINES 202-501-9388
Fuses: Blasting....Vacant USITC 202-205-3343
Fuses: electrical....Malison, Andrew USITC 202-205-3391
Fusion Energy....Davies, Anne NEIC 301-903-4941
Fusion Energy....Greenblatt, Jack USITC 202-205-3353
Fusion Plasma....Crandall, David NEIC 301-903-4596
Fuzzy Logic,...Kader, Victoria COMMERCE 202-482-0571

G

G. Bissaue....Fossum, Linnea Peace Corps 202-606-3708
G6PD Deficiency....Staff NHLBI 301-496-4236
GBF/DIME System....Staff CENSUS 301-763-1580
Gabon....Henke, Debra Cnty Commerce 202-482-5149
Gabon....Blackwell, Gloria Peace Corps 202-606-3998
Gabon....Swezey, Virginia Peace Corps 202-606-3998
Gabon (Libreville)....Staff Cnty State 202-647-1707
Gabon/Minerals....King, Audie L. Cnty Mines 202-501-9674
Galactorrhea....Staff NIDDK 301-496-3583
Galactosemia....Staff NIDDK 301-496-3583
Galactosemia....Staff NICHD 301-496-5133
Galactosemia....Staff NINDS 301-496-5751
Galileo Flight Project....Wilson, James NASA 818-354-5011
Gallbladder....Staff NIDDK 301-496-3583
Gallium....Kramer, Deborah A. MINES 202-501-9394
Gallium....Lundy, David USITC 202-205-3439
Gallstones....Staff NIDDK 301-496-3583
Gambia....Michelin, Philip Cnty Commerce 202-482-4388
Gambia....McCormick, Michael L. Peace Corps 202-606-3644
Gambia....Herring, Debra Peace Corps 202-606-3644
Gambia, The (Banjul)....Staff Cnty State 202-647-3395
Gambia/Minerals....van Oss, Hendrick Cnty Mines 202-501-9687
Game animals....Steller, Rose USITC 202-205-3323
Games....McKenna, Thomas CUSTOMS 212-466-5475
Games....Robinson, Hazel USITC 202-205-3496
Games and Childrens' Vehicles....Vanderwolf, John COMMERCE 202-482-0348
Gamma Ray Observatory....Beasley, Dolores NASA 301-286-2806
Gamma Ray Observatory....Staff NASA 301-286-5565
Garage Door Openers--Licenses....Staff FCC 717-337-1212
Garage Door Openers--Not Licensed....Staff FCC 202-653-6288
Garage Door Operators....Mesa, Stacey Reuben CPSC 301-504-0580
Garnet....Austin, Gordon MINES 202-501-9388
Garters and suspenders....Linkins, Linda USITC 202-205-3469
Gas Reserves Statistics....Lique, Diane NEIC 202-586-6090
Gas Vol Standards....Mesa, Stacey Reuben CPSC 301-504-0580
Gas generators....Vacant USITC 202-205-3380
Gas oil....Foreso, Cynthia USITC 202-205-3348
Gas-operated metalworking appliances....Vacant USITC 202-205-3380
Gaseous Diffusion Plants (GDP)....Bennett, John NEIC 301-903-5832
Gases, Greenhouse....Patrinus, Aristides NEIC 301-903-5348
Gaskets/Gasketing Materials....Reiss, Richard COMMERCE 202-482-3489
Gasoline....Foreso, Cynthia USITC 202-205-3348
Gasoline, Retail Prices....Chelena, Joseph LABOR 202-606-6982
Gastric Hypersecretion....Staff NIDDK 301-496-3583
Gastrinoma....Staff NIDDK 301-496-3583
Gastrointestinal Disorders....Staff NIDDK 301-496-3583
Gastrointestinal Tract Diseases....Staff NIDDK 301-496-3583
Gaucher's Disease....Staff NINDS 301-496-5751
Gauze, impregnated with medicinals....Randall, Rob USITC 202-205-3366
Gears....Riedl, Karl CUSTOMS 212-466-5493
Gelatin....Brownchweig, Gilbert CUSTOMS 212-466-5744
Gelatin, articles of....Spalding, Josephine USITC 202-205-3498
Gelatin, edible....Jonnard, Aimison USITC 202-205-3350
Gelatin, inedible....Jonnard, Aimison USITC 202-205-3350
Gelatin, photographic....Jonnard, Aimison USITC 202-205-3350
Gem Stones....Austin, Gordon MINES 202-501-9388
Gems....DeSapio, Vincent USITC 202-205-3435
Gemstones, imitation....Witherspoon, Ricardo USITC 202-205-3489
Gen. Indus. Mach. Nec, Exc 35691....Shaw, Eugene COMMERCE 202-482-2204
GenBank (Genetic Sequence Data Bank)....Staff NIGMS 301-496-7301
General Agreement on Trade and Tariffs (GATT)....Klein, Cecelia US Trade Rep 202-395-3063
General Aviation Aircraft (Market Support)....Driscoll, George COMMERCE 202-482-1228
General Clinical Research Centers Program....Staff DRR 301-496-6595
General Counsel's Office....Ballard, Sonia D. FTC 202-326-2669
General Information....Staff CENSUS 301-763-4100
General Information - Environmental Issues Hotline....Staff EPA

Fork-lift Trucks / Greenhouse Gases

800-759-4372
General Litigation (Assoc. & Business Practices)....Abrahamsen, Dana FTC 202-326-2906
General Litigation (Assoc. and Business Practices)....Alexander, Janice FTC 202-326-2891
General Litigation (Health Care)....Allen, Patricia A. FTC 202-326-3176
General Mobile Licenses....Staff FCC 717-337-1212
General Mobile Radio Service....Staff FCC 717-337-1212
General, Medical Sciences, National Institute of....Dieffenbach, Ann NIH 301-496-7301
Generator Sets/Turbines (Major Proj)....Dollison, Robert COMMERCE 202-482-2733
Generators....Cutchin, John USITC 202-205-3396
Genetic Pancrea. Involv. not due to Cystic Fibrosis....Staff NIDDK 301-496-3583
Genetics....Staff NINDS 301-496-5751
Genetics....Staff NIGMS 301-496-7301
Genetics....Staff NIDR 301-496-4261
Genetics....Staff NICHD 301-496-5133
Genetics....Parry, Dilys M. FAES 301-496-4947
Genetics (Animal Monitoring)....Staff NCRR/VRP 301-496-9188
Genetics of Aging....Staff NIA 301-496-1752
Genetics, Developmental....Adhya, Sankar L. FAES 301-496-2495
Genital Herpes....Staff NIAID 301-496-5717
Genital Warts....Staff NIAID 301-496-5717
Geothermal Energy....Mock, John E. NEIC 202-586-5340
Geology....Goodell, Grant UVA 701-924-0559
Geophysical Phenomena Research....Staff NASA 415-604-3937
Geophysical Research....Beasley, Dolores NASA 301-286-2806
Georgia....Staff 202-647-8671
Geoscience Research....Coleman, James NEIC 301-903-5822
Geothermal Loan Guarantee Program....Staff NEIC 202-586-1539
Geriatric Medicine....Staff NIA 301-496-1752
Geriatric Medicine....Roth, Jesse FAES 301-558-8198
Geriatric Psychiatry....Staff NIMH 301-443-4515
Geriatric Psychiatry....Staff NIA 301-496-1752
Geriatrics....Staff NIA 301-496-1752
German Measles (Rubella)....Staff NIAID 301-496-5717
Germanium....Llewellyn, Thomas O. MINES 202-501-9395
Germanium....Lundy, David USITC 202-205-3439
Germanium oxides....Conant, Kenneth USITC 202-205-3346
Germany....Fisher, Brenda Cnty Commerce 202-482-2434
Germany....Kloepfer, Joan Cnty Commerce 202-482-2841
Germany....Staff Cnty State 202-647-2005
Germany, East/Minerals....Rabchevsky, George Cnty Mines 202-501-9672
Germfree Rodents....Staff NCRR/VRP 301-496-5255
Gerontology....Staff NIA 301-496-1752
Gerson Method....Staff NCI 301-496-5583
Gerstmann's Syndrome....Staff NICHD 301-496-5133
Gestation....Staff NICHD 301-496-5133
Ghana....Henke, Debra Cnty Commerce 202-482-5149
Ghana....McCormick, Michael L. Peace Corps 202-606-3644
Ghana....Herring, Debra Peace Corps 202-606-3644
Ghana (Accra)....Staff Cnty State 202-647-4567
Ghana/Minerals....van Oss, Hendrik Cnty Mines 202-501-9687
Giardiasis....Staff NIAID 301-496-5717
Gibraltar....Staff Cnty State 202-647-8027
Giftware (Export Promo)....Beckham, Reginald COMMERCE 202-482-5478
Gigantism....Staff NIDDK 301-496-3583
Gilbert's Syndrome....Staff NIDDK 301-496-3583
Gilles de la Tourette's Disease....Staff NINDS 301-496-5751
Gingivitis....Staff NIDR 301-496-4261
Glace fruit and vegetable substances....Frankel, Lee USITC 202-205-3315
Glands....Staff NIDDK 301-496-3583
Glass....Bunin, Jacob CUSTOMS 212-566-5796
Glass (flat)....Lukes, James USITC 202-205-3426
Glass articles, nspf....Lukes, James USITC 202-205-3426
Glass containers....Lukes, James USITC 202-205-3426
Glass fiber....Lukes, James USITC 202-205-3426
Glass yarn....Lukes, James USITC 202-205-3426
Glass, Flat....Williams, Franklin COMMERCE 202-482-0132
Glassblowing....Staff NCRR/BEIP 301-496-5195
Glassware....Harris, John COMMERCE 202-482-0348
Glassware....McNay, Deborah USITC 202-205-3425
Glassware (Issue and Washing)....Staff OD/ORS 301-496-4595
Glassworking machines....Vacant USITC 202-205-3380
Glaucoma....Staff NEI 301-496-5248

Glazing compounds....Johnson, Larry USITC 202-205-3351
Gliomas....Staff NINDS 301-496-5751
Global Change Division....Staff EPA 202-233-9190
Global Climate Change....Galas, David J. NEIC 301-903-3251
Globoid Cell Leukodystrophy....Staff NINDS 301-496-5751
Glomerulonephritis....Staff NIDDK 301-496-3583
Gloves....Burtnik, Brian CUSTOMS 212-466-5880
Gloves....Jones, Jackie USITC 202-205-3466
Gloves (Work)....Byron, James E. COMMERCE 202-482-3459
Glucose Intolerance....Staff NIDDK 301-496-3583
Glue....Brownchweig, Gilbert CUSTOMS 212-466-5744
Glue size....Jonnard, Aimison USITC 202-205-3350
Glue, articles of....Spalding, Josephine USITC 202-205-3498
Glue, of animal or vegetable origin....Jonnard, Aimison USITC 202-205-3350
Gluten Intolerance....Staff NIDDK 301-496-3583
Glycerine....Michels, David USITC 202-205-3352
Glycogen Storage Disease....Staff NIDDK 301-496-3583
Glycogen Storage Disease....Staff NICHD 301-496-5133
Glycols....Michels, David USITC 202-205-3352
Goats....Steller, Rose USITC 202-205-3323
Goiter....Staff NIDDK 301-496-3583
Gold....Lucus, John M. MINES 202-501-9417
Gold....McNay, Deborah USITC 202-205-3425
Gold compounds....Greenblatt, Jack USITC 202-205-3353
Gold with options....Rosenfeld, David CFT 312-353-9026
Golf equipment....Robinson, Hazel USITC 202-205-3496
Gonads....Staff NICHD 301-496-5133
Gonorrhea....Staff NIAID 301-496-5717
Goodpasture's Syndrome....Staff NHLBI 301-496-4236
Goodpasture's Syndrome....Staff NIDDK 301-496-3583
Gout....Staff NIAMS 301-496-8188
Government and Foreign Affairs....Abraham, Henry J. UVA 701-924-3958
Government and Foreign Affairs....Cooper, Alice H. UVA 701-924-4660
Government and Foreign Affairs....Jordan, David C. UVA 701-924-3298
Government, (Acting Chief)....Ziemer, Richard C. ECONOMIC 202-523-0715
Government, Productivity in, Prod. & Tech.....Forte, Darlene J. LABOR 202-606-5621
Government-Press Relations, Broadcast Journalism....Holman, Ben UMD 301-405-2420
Government-Press relations....Hiebert, Ray E. UMD 301-405-2419
Governments, Criminal Justice Statistics....Cull, Diana CENSUS 301-763-7789
Governments, Employment....Stevens, Alan CENSUS 301-763-5086
Governments, Federal Expenditure Data....Kellerman, David CENSUS 301-763-5276
Governments, Finance....Wulf, Henry CENSUS 301-763-7664
Governments, Governmental Organization....Cull, Diana CENSUS 301-763-7789
Governments, Operations Support and Analysis....Fanning, William CENSUS 301-763-4403
Governments, Survey Operations....Speight, Genevieve CENSUS 301-763-7783
Governments, Taxation....Keffer, Gerard CENSUS 301-763-5356
Graduate Courses....Staff FAES 301-496-7976
Grain....Conte, Ralph CUSTOMS 212-466-5759
Grain Mill Products....Janis, William V. COMMERCE 202-482-2250
Grain products, milled....Pierre-Benoist, John USITC 202-205-3320
Grains....Pierre-Benoist, John 202-205-3320
Granite....White, Linda USITC 202-205-3427
Granulocytopenia....Staff NIDDK 301-496-3583
Granulomatous Diseases....Staff NIAID 301-496-5717
Grape Cure....Staff NCI 301-496-5583
Grapefruit oil (essential oil)....Land, Eric USITC 202-205-3349
Graphite....Taylor, Harold A. MINES 202-501-9754
Graphite....White, Linda USITC 202-205-3427
Grasslands....Staff FWS 703-358-2043
Grateful Med (Software for Information Retrieval)....Staff NLM 301-496-3583
Grave's Disease (Eye Complications)....Staff NEI 301-496-5248
Grave's Disease (General Information)....Staff NIDDK 301-496-3583
Grease, lubricating....Foreso, Cynthia USITC 202-205-3348
Great Lakes Fisheries....Staff FWS 703-358-1718
Greece....Corro, Ann Cnty Commerce 202-482-3945
Greece (Athens)....Staff Cnty State 202-647-6113
Greece/Minerals....Rabchevsky, George Cnty Mines 202-501-9672
Greenhouse Gases....Patrinus, Aristides NEIC 301-903-5348

Be patient. If any phone number is incorrect, call (area code) 555-1212 and request the new listing.

Experts

Greenland....Staff Cnty State 202-647-5669
Greenland/Minerals....Rabchevsky, George Cnty Mines 202-501-9672
Greensand....Searls, James P. MINES 202-501-9407
Greeting Cards....Bratland, Rose Marie COMMERCE 202-482-0380
Grenada....Brooks, Michelle Cnty Commerce 202-482-2527
Grenada (St. George's)....Staff Cnty State 202-647-2621
Grinding machines....Greene, William USITC 202-205-3405
Ground Water Exploration and Development....Wheeler, Frederica COMMERCE 202-482-3509
Ground Water Protection....Staff EPA 202-260-7077
Ground Water and Drinking Water....Staff EPA 202-250-5543
Ground fish....Corey, Roger USITC 202-205-3327
Group Quarters, Population....Smith, Denise CENSUS 301-763-7883
Growth Hormone Deficiency....Staff NIDDK 301-496-3583
Growth and Development....Staff NICHD 301-496-5133
Guadeloupe/Minerals....Torres, Ivette Cnty Mines 202-501-9680
Guadeloupe....Brooks, Michelle Cnty Commerce 202-482-2527
Guadeloupe (Basse-Terre)....Staff Cnty State 202-647-2620
Guatemala....Lee, Helen Cnty Commerce 202-482-2527
Guatemala....Brown, Brenda L. Peace Corps 202-606-3624
Guatemala (Guatemala City)....Staff Cnty State 202-647-4980
Guatemala/Minerals....Mobbs, Philip Cnty Mines 202-501-9679
Guatemalan Rain Forest....Bauer, Gerald FS 703-235-1676
Guide for the Care and Use of Laboratory Animals....Staff NCI 301-496-5545
Guides....Young, Gary CENSUS 301-763-1584
Guillain-Barre Syndrome (Polyneuritis)....Staff NINDS 301-496-5751
Guinea....Michelin, Philip Cnty Commerce 202-482-4388
Guinea....Strozier, Maisha Peace Corps 202-606-3185
Guinea (Conakry)....Staff Cnty State 202-647-2865
Guinea-Bissau....Michelin, Philip Cnty Commerce 202-482-4388
Guinea-Bissau (Bissau)....Staff Cnty State 202-647-4567
Guinea-Bissau/Minerals....Izon, David Cnty Mines 202-501-9692
Guinea/Minerals....Izon, David Cnty Mines 202-501-9692
Gum Disease....Staff NIDR 301-496-4261
Gums and resins....Reeder, John USITC 202-205-3319
Gun cotton....Johnson, Larry USITC 202-205-3351
Gunpowder....Johnson, Larry USITC 202-205-3351
Guns and Ammunition....Vanderwolf, John COMMERCE 202-482-0348
Gut, articles of....Spalding, Josephine USITC 202-205-3498
Gut; catgut, whip gut, oriental gut, and wormgut....Ludwick, David USITC 202-205-3329
Guyana....Brooks, Michelle Cnty Commerce 202-482-2527
Guyana (Georgetown)....Staff Cnty State 202-647-4195
Guyana/Minerals....Mobbs, Philip Cnty Mines 202-501-9679
Gynecological Research....Nelson, Lawrence FAES 301-496-4686
Gynecology....Staff NICHD 301-496-5133
Gynecomastia....Staff NICHD 301-496-5133
Gynecomastia....Staff NIDDK 301-496-3583
Gypsum....Davis, Lawrence L. MINES 202-501-9386
Gypsum....White, Linda USITC 202-205-3427
Gypsum board....Ruggles, Fred USITC 202-205-3325
Gyrate Atrophy....Staff NEI 301-496-5248

H

HIV Infection....Staff NIAID 301-496-5717
HIV Infection....Staff NCI 301-496-5583
HIV/AIDS....Jaffe, Harold W. CDC 404-639-2000
HIV: Oral Complications....Staff NIDR 301-496-4261
HUD Fraud Hotline....Staff HUD 800-347-3735
Habeas Corpus....Kaplan, Carol Justice Stat 202-307-0759
Habitat Management....Staff FWS 703-358-1718
Habitat Models....Staff FWS 703-358-1710
Habitat Resources Research....Staff FWS 703-358-1710
Hafnium....Templeton, David A. MINES 202-501-9391
Hafnium....Lundy, David USITC 202-205-3439
Hailey's Disease....Staff NIDDK 301-496-3583
Hair....Steller, Rose USITC 202-205-3323
Hair Loss....Staff NIAMS 301-496-8188
Hair Ornaments....Brownchweig, Gilbert CUSTOMS 212-466-5744
Hair Spray....Staff FDA 301-245-1061
Hair curlers, nonelectric....Burns, Gail USITC 202-205-3501
Hair ornaments....Burns, Gail USITC 202-205-3501
Hair, articles of....Burns, Gail USITC 202-205-3501
Haiti....Soto, Rodrigo Cnty Commerce 204-482-2527
Haiti....Almaguer, Antoinette Peace Corps 202-606-3322
Haiti (Port-au-Prince)....Staff Cnty State 202-647-4195
Haiti/Minerals....Torres, Ivette Cnty Mines 202-501-9680
Halides, nonmetallic....Conant, Kenneth USITC 202-205-3346
Hallervorden-Spatz Disease....Staff NINDS 301-496-5751
Halogenated hydrocarbons....Michels, David USITC 202-205-3352
Halogens....Conant, Kenneth USITC 202-205-3346
Hand Saws, Saw Blades....Shaw, Eugene COMMERCE 202-482-3494
Hand Tools....Schulberg, Martin CUSTOMS 212-466-5487
Hand tools with self-contained motor....Cutchin, John USITC 202-205-3396
Hand tools: household....Brandon, James USITC 202-205-3433
Hand tools: other....Brandon, James USITC 202-205-3433
Hand, Foot, and Mouth Disease....Staff NIAID 301-496-5717
Hand/Edge Tools Ex Mach Tl/Saws....Shaw, Eugene COMMERCE 202-482-3494
Handbags....Byron, James E. COMMERCE 202-482-4034
Handbags....Gorman, Kevin CUSTOMS 212-466-5893
Handbags....Seastrum, Carl USITC 202-205-3493
Handbook, Occupational Outlook, Empl. Projections....Pilot, Michael LABOR 202-606-5703
Handicapped Discrimination....Haynes, Marcella OCR 202-619-0671
Handkerchiefs....Jones, Jackie USITC 202-205-3466
Handkerchiefs....Hamey, Amy USITC 202-205-3465
Handwork yarns: cotton....Warlick, William USITC 202-205-3459
Handwork yarns: manmade fibers....Warlick, William USITC 202-205-3459
Handwork yarns: wool....Shelton, Linda USITC 202-205-3457
Hansen's Disease....Staff NIAID 301-496-5717
Happy Puppet Syndrome....Staff NINDS 301-496-5751
Harada's Disease....Staff NEI 301-496-5248
Hard Surfaced Floor Coverings....Shaw, Robert COMMERCE 202-482-0132
Hardboard....Ruggles, Fred USITC 202-205-3325
Hardening of the Arteries....Staff NHLBI 301-496-4236
Harassing Telephone Calls....Staff FCC 202-632-7553
Hashimoto's Disease....Staff NIDDK 301-496-3583
Hats....Jones, Jackie USITC 202-205-3466
Hats....Hamey, Amy USITC 202-205-3465
Hay....Eldridge, Herb Agri 202-720-7621
Hay....Tice, Thomas Agri 202-219-0840
Hay Fever....Staff NIAID 301-496-5717
Hazard Screening....Giles, Ken CPSC 301-504-0580
Hazard Waste Publications....Staff EPA 202-260-8864
Hazardous Chemical Spills....Staff FWS 703-358-2148
Hazardous Site Evaluation Division....Staff EPA 202-603-8800
Hazardous Substances Information....Staff NLM 301-496-1131
Hazardous Substances Information Office....Siegel, Sidney NLM 301-496-5022
Hazardous Waste - Superfund....Staff EPA 202-920-9810
Hazardous Waste Cleanups....Staff EPA 202-260-8864
Hazardous Waste Disposal....Lytle, Jill NEIC 202-586-0370
Hazardous Waste Disposal Unit....Staff EPA 202-307-8833
Hazardous Waste Enforcement - General....Staff EPA 202-260-9810
Hazardous Waste Ombudsman Hotline....Staff EPA 800-262-7937
Hazardous Waste Spills - Emergency Response....Staff EPA 202-260-8720
Hazardous Waste Transporting Generating or Permits....Staff EPA 202-260-4627
Hazardous Wastes....Berreth, Don CDC 404-639-3286
Head Injury....Staff NINDS 301-496-5751
Head Injury....Staff NIDCD 301-496-7243
Head Lice (Pediculosis)....Staff NIAID 301-496-5717
Head Start....Long, Susan ACF 202-401-9215
Headache....Staff NINDS 301-496-5751
Headwear....Schiazzano, Patricia CUSTOMS 212-466-5881
Headwear....Hamey, Amy USITC 202-205-3465
Headwear....Jones, Jackie USITC 202-205-3466
Health....Francis, Simon COMMERCE 202-482-2697
Health & Life Insurance, Comp. & Working Condition....Blostin, Allan LABOR 202-606-6240
Health Care - Nurse....Brooke, Joan FTC 202-326-2120
Health Care Policy & Research, Agency for....Isquith, Bob AHCPR 301-227-8364
Health Care Policy & Research, Agency for....Isquith, Bob AHCPR 301-227-8364
Health Care Resources....Mehuron, Charlotte HRSA 301-443-3376
Health Care Technology....Isquith, Bob AHCPR 301-227-8674
Health Effects Division....Staff EPA 202-305-7351
Health Effects of Electricity Transmission....Brewer, Robert NEIC 202-586-2828
Health Expenditures (U.S. Totals)....Hardy, Robert HCFA 202-690-6145

Greenland / Hormones

Health Information Programs Development, Dir. of....Siegel, Elliot R. NLM 301-496-8834
Health Maintenance Organizations (HMOs)....Hardy, Robert HCFA 202-690-6145
Health Manpower Education....Staff HRSA/BHPr 301-443-2060
Health Professionals....Staff HRSA/BHPr 301-443-2060
Health Professions and Health Profession Loans....Mehuron, Charlotte HRSA 301-443-3376
Health Promotion and Disease Prevention....Harris, Linda ASH 202-205-9370
Health Promotion and Disease Prevention....Berreth, Don CDC 404-639-3286
Health Research, Office of....Staff EPA 202-260-5900
Health Services Research Information....Cahn, Marjorie NLM 301-496-0176
Health Start....Mehuron, Charlotte HRSA 301-443-3376
Health Statistics, National Center for....Sandra, Smith NCHS/CDC 301-436-7551
Health Surveys....Mangold, Robert CENSUS 301-763-5508
Health and Environmental Research....Galas, David J. NEIC 301-903-3251
Health and medical services....R-Archila, Laura USITC 202-205-3411
Hearing Disorders....Staff NINDS 301-496-5751
Hearing Disorders....Staff NIDCD 301-496-7243
Hearing Loss and Aging....Staff NINDS 301-496-5751
Hearing Loss and Aging....Staff NIA 301-496-1752
Hearing Loss and Aging....Staff CC 301-496-5368
Heart Attacks....Staff NHLBI 301-496-4236
Heart Block....Staff NHLBI 301-496-4236
Heart Disease....Staff NHLBI 301-496-4236
Heart Pacemaker....Staff NHLBI 301-496-4236
Heart Transplantation....Staff NHLBI 301-496-4236
Heart Valves....Staff NHLBI 301-496-4236
Heart, Lung and Blood Inst.....Bellicha, Terry NIH 301-496-4236
Heart-Lung Machines....Staff NHLBI 301-496-4236
Heat Stroke and Aging....Staff NIA 301-496-1752
Heat Tapes....Mesa, Stacey Reuben CPSC 301-504-0580
Heat Treating Equipment....Kemper, Alexis COMMERCE 202-482-5956
Heat process equipment....Slingerland, David USITC 202-205-3400
Heat-Resistant Materials....Staff NASA 804-864-6120
Heat-insulating articles....DeSapio, Vincent USITC 202-205-3435
Heating Equipment Ex. Furnaces....Bodson, John COMMERCE 202-482-3509
Heavy Metals (Cadmium, Zinc, Mercury)....Staff NIEHS 919-541-3345
Helicopter Services....Johnson, C. William COMMERCE 202-482-5012
Helicopters....Walsh, Hugh COMMERCE 202-482-4222
Helicopters (Trade Promo)....Vacant COMMERCE 202-482-1228
Helicopters, Market Support....Driscoll, George COMMERCE 202-482-1228
Heliotropin....Land, Eric USITC 202-205-3349
Helium....Conant, Kenneth USITC 202-205-3346
Helium, Division of Helium Field Operations....Leachman, William D. MINES 806-376-2604
Hematology....Finlayson, John FAES 301-496-5544
Hemiplegia....Staff NINDS 301-496-5751
Hemodialysis....Staff NIDDK 301-496-3583
Hemoglobin Genetics....Staff NIDDK 301-496-3583
Hemoglobinopathies....Staff NIDDK 301-496-3583
Hemolytic Anemia....Staff NIDDK 301-496-3583
Hemolytic Disease (Newborn)....Staff NICHD 301-496-5133
Hemolytic Disease (Newborn)....Staff NHLBI 301-496-4236
Hemophilia....Staff NHLBI 301-496-4236
Hemophilus Influenzae....Staff NIAID 301-496-5717
Hemorrhagic Diseases....Staff NIDDK 301-496-3583
Hemorrhagic Diseases....Staff NHLBI 301-496-4236
Hemorrhoids....Staff NHLBI 301-496-4236
Hemorrhoids....Staff NIDDK 301-496-3583
Hemosiderosis....Staff NHLBI 301-496-4236
Henoch-Schonlein Purpura....Staff NIAID 301-496-5717
Henoch-Schonlein Purpura....Staff NICHD 301-496-5133
Hepatitis....Staff NIAID 301-496-5717
Hepatitis....Staff NIDDK 301-496-3583
Hepatitis....Herrmann, Kenneth L. CDC 404-639-2339
Hepatitis (Treatment of Acute or Chronic)....Staff NIDDK 301-496-3583
Hepatitis (Treatment of Acute or Chronic)....Staff NIAID 301-496-5717
Herbicide-Fungicides....Staff EPA 202-305-6250
Hereditary Angioedema....Staff NIAID 301-496-5717
Hereditary Cerebellar Ataxia....Staff NINDS 301-496-5751
Hereditary Emphysema....Staff NHLBI 301-496-4236
Hereditary Movement Disorders....Staff NINDS 301-496-5751
Hereditary Nervous System Tumors....Staff NINDS 301-496-5751
Heredity and Cancer....Staff NCI 301-496-5583
Heritable Disorders of Connective Tissue....Staff NHLBI 301-496-4236
Heritable Disorders of Connective Tissue....Staff NIAMS 301-496-8188
Hernias (Abdominal, Bladder)....Staff NIDDK 301-496-3583
Herniated Disc....Staff NIAMS 301-496-8188
Herpes (Nervous System Involvement)....Staff NINDS 301-496-5751
Herpes Simplex (Eye Effects)....Staff NEI 301-496-5248
Herpes Simplex Virus (Oral Lesions)....Staff NIDR 301-496-4261
Herpes Simplex Virus (Type II)....Staff NIAID 301-496-5717
Herpes Zoster (Shingles)....Staff NINDS 301-496-5751
Herpes Zoster-Varicella Infections....Staff NIAID 301-496-5717
Heterocyclic Compounds....Winters, William CUSTOMS 212-466-5747
Hiatal Hernia....Staff NIDDK 301-496-3583
Hiccups....Staff NHLBI 301-496-4236
Hide cuttings....Trainor, Cynthia USITC 202-205-3354
Hides....Steller, Rose USITC 202-205-3323
High Alpha Technology....Nolan, Donald NASA 805-258-3447
High Blood Pressure....Staff NHLBI 301-496-4236
High Blood Pressure....Staff NIA 301-496-1752
High Blood Pressure....Staff NHLBI/IC 301-951-3260
High Energy Fuel Research....Ellis, Linda NASA 216-443-2900
High Tech Trade, U.S. Competitiveness....Hatter, Victoria L. COMMERCE 202-482-3913
High Voltage Electron Microscopy....Staff NCRR 301-496-5411
High Voltage Transmission Lines....Klunder, Kurt NEIC 202-586-2826
High-Density Lipoproteins (HDL)....Staff NHLBI 301-496-4236
Hill-Burton Health Facilities....Mehuron, Charlotte HRSA 301-443-3376
Hirsutism....Staff NIAMS 301-496-8188
Hispanic and Other Ethnic Population Statistics....Staff CENSUS 301-763-7955
Histiocytosis....Staff NCI 301-496-5583
Histiocytosis....Staff NHLBI 301-496-4236
Histoplasmosis....Staff NIAID 301-496-5717
Histoplasmosis (Eye)....Staff NEI 301-496-5248
Historical Medical Prints and Photographs....Staff NLM 301-496-5961
Historical Prints and Photographs....Keister, Lucinda NLM 301-496-5961
Historical Statistics....Staff CENSUS 301-763-7936
History....Braun, Herbert UVA 701-924-6397
History of Medicine....Staff NLM 301-496-5405
History of Medicine....Teigen, Philip NLM 301-496-5405
Hives....Staff NIAID 301-496-5717
Hodgkin's Disease....Staff NCI 301-496-5583
Hogs....Ludwick, David USITC 202-205-3329
Hogs (live) with options....Prentice, Jon CFT 312-353-8647
Hoists/Overhead Cranes....Wiening, Mary COMMERCE 202-482-4708
Home & Community Based Care (Medicaid)....Hardy, Robert HCFA 202-690-6145
Home Care, Nursing Home Care, Hospital Care....Staff NCNR 301-496-0526
Home Health Care....Hardy, Robert HCFA 202-690-6145
Home furnishings....Sweet, Mary Elizabeth USITC 202-205-3455
Homeless....Long, Susan ACF 202-401-9215
Homeless....Staff HUD 202-708-1480
Homeless Population....Taeuber, Cynthia CENSUS 301-763-7883
Homocystinuria....Staff NICHD 301-496-5133
Homocystinuria....Staff NHLBI 301-496-4236
Honduras....Lee, Helen Cnty Commerce 202-482-2527
Honduras....Stanton, Dan Peace Corps 202-606-3620
Honduras....Tumaylle, Carol Peace Corps 202-606-3321
Honduras (Tegucigalpa)....Staff Cnty State 202-647-3381
Honduras/Minerals....Mobbs, Philip Cnty Mines 202-501-9679
Honey....Hoff, Fred Agri 202-219-0883
Honey - Prices....Schuchardt, Rick Agri 220-690-3236
Honey - Prod.....Kruchten, Tom Agri 202-690-4870
Hong Kong....Bakar, Sheila Cnty Commerce 202-482-3932
Hong Kong....Staff Cnty State 202-647-6300
Hong Kong/Minerals....Tse, Pui-Kwan Cnty Mines 202-501-9696
Hoof, articles of....Spalding, Josephine USITC 202-205-3498
Hoofs, crude....Ludwick, David USITC 202-205-3329
Hooks and eyes....Shildneck, Ann USITC 202-205-3499
Hormone Distribution....Staff NIDDK 301-496-3583
Hormones....Staff NIDDK 301-496-3583
Hormones....Nesbitt, Elizabeth USITC 202-205-3355
Hormones (Sex)....Staff NICHD 301-496-5133
Hormones and Cancer....Staff NCI 301-496-5583
Horn, articles of....Spalding, Josephine USITC 202-205-3498
Horn, crude....Ludwick, David USITC 202-205-3329

Experts

Horse Racing Programming and Advertising....Staff FCC 202-632-7048
Horses....Steller, Rose USITC 202-205-3323
Horticultural machinery....Vacant USITC 202-205-3380
Hose and Belting....Prat, Raimundo COMMERCE 202-482-0128
Hose, industrial....Cook, Lee USITC 202-205-3471
Hose, of rubber or plastics....Johnson, Larry USITC 202-205-3351
Hoses....Mazzola, Joan CUSTOMS 212-466-5880
Hosiery....Linkins, Linda USITC 202-205-3469
Hospice....Hardy, Robert HCFA 202-690-6145
Hospice Care....Staff NIA 301-496-1752
Hospital Administrators....Staff HRSA/BHPr 301-443-2134
Hospital Care Statistics....Pokras, Robert CDC 301-436-7125
Hospital Infections....Staff NIAID 301-496-5717
Hospital-Based Schools of Nursing....Staff HRSA/BHPr 301-443-2134
Hotel & Restaurant Eq., Export Promo.....Kimmel, Edward K. COMMERCE 202-482-3640
Hotels and Motels....Sousane, J. Richard COMMERCE 202-482-4582
Hotline (Fraud & Abuse)....Holtz, Judy IG 202-619-1142
Hourly Compensation Costs, Foreign Countries....Capdevielle, Patricia LABOR 202-606-5654
Household Appliances....Harris, John M. COMMERCE 202-482-0348
Household Articles Plastic....Rauch, Theodore CUSTOMS 212-466-5892
Household Articles, Metal....Smyth, James CUSTOMS 212-466-2084
Household Estimates for States and Counties....Staff CENSUS 301-763-5221
Household Furniture....Vacant COMMERCE 202-482-0338
Household Hazardous Waste....Staff EPA 202-260-5649
Household Wealth....Lamas, Enrique CENSUS 301-763-8578
Households Touched by Crime....Rand, Michael Justice Stat 202-616-3494
Housewares....Harris, John COMMERCE 202-482-1178
Housing Construction....Cosslett, Patrick COMMERCE 202-482-0132
Housing and Urban Development. Major Proj.....White, Barbara COMMERCE 202-482-4160
Housing, American Housing Survey....Montfort, Edward CENSUS 301-763-8551
Housing, Components of Inventory Change Survey....Maynard, Jane CENSUS 301-763-8551
Housing, Decennial Census....Downs, Bill CENSUS 301-763-8553
Housing, Income Statistics....Staff CENSUS 301-763-8576
Housing, Indian....Staff HUD 202-708-0950
Housing, Information....Downs, Bill CENSUS 301-763-8553
Housing, Market Absorption....Smoler, Anne CENSUS 301-763-8552
Housing, Multifamily....Staff HUD 202-708-2495
Housing, New York City Housing & Vacancy Survey....Harper, Margaret CENSUS 301-763-8552
Housing, Public....Staff HUD 202-708-0950
Housing, Single Family....Staff HUD 202-708-3175
Housing, Vacancy Data....Fraser, Wallace CENSUS 301-763-8165
Hubble Space Telescope....Villard, Ray NASA 301-338-4514
Hubble Space Telescope (HST)....Katz, Jesse NASA 301-286-5566
Human Development....Staff NICHD 301-443-5133
Human Genetic Mutant Cell Repository....Staff NIGMS 301-496-7301
Human Papilloma Virus (HPV)....Staff NCI 301-496-5583
Human Papilloma Virus (HPV)....Staff NIAID 301-496-5717
Humane Transport of Fish and Wildlife....Staff FWS 703-358-2095
Hungary....Touhey, Brian Cnty Commerce 202-482-2645
Hungary....Becker, Margaret Peace Corps 202-606-3547
Hungary....Sowry, Jenny Peace Corps 202-606-3547
Hungary (Budapest)....Staff Cnty State 202-647-3298
Hungary/Minerals....Steblez, Walter Cnty Mines 202-501-9671
Hunt's Disease....Staff NINDS 301-496-5751
Hunter Education Programs....Staff FWS 703-358-2156
Hunter's Syndrome....Staff NIDDK 301-496-3583
Hunting and Fishing Survey, National....Staff FWS 703-358-2156
Hunting, Refuges....Staff FWS 703-358-2043
Huntington's Disease....Staff NINDS 301-496-5751
Hurler's Syndrome....Staff NICHD 301-496-5133
Hurler's Syndrome....Staff NIDDK 301-496-3583
Hyaline Membrane Disease....Staff NICHD 301-496-5133
Hyaline Membrane Disease....Staff NHLBI 301-496-4236
Hydraulics....Riedl, Karl CUSTOMS 212-466-5493
Hydrazine....Conant, Kenneth USITC 202-205-3346
Hydro Power Plants, Major Proj.....Healey, Mary Alice COMMERCE 202-482-4333
Hydrocarbon Geoscience Research....Juckett, Donald NEIC 202-586-5600
Hydrocarbons....Winters, William CUSTOMS 212-466-5747
Hydrocarbons....Raftery, Jim USITC 202-205-3365
Hydrocephalus....Staff NINDS 301-496-5751
Hydrocephalus....Staff NICHD 301-496-5133
Hydrochloric acid....Trainor, Cynthia USITC 202-205-3354
Hydroelectric Energy....Loose, Ronald NEIC 202-586-8086
Hydroelectric Power....Loose, Ronald NEIC 202-586-8066
Hydroelectric Power Projects....Staff FWS 703-358-2183
Hydrofluoric acid....Trainor, Cynthia USITC 202-205-3354
Hydrogen....Conant, Kenneth USITC 202-205-3346
Hydroxides, inorganic....Conant, Kenneth USITC 202-205-3346
Hygienists (Education)....Staff HRSA/BHPr 301-443-6837
Hyperactivity....Staff NIMH 301-443-4515
Hyperactivity....Staff NICHD 301-496-5133
Hyperactivity....Staff NINDS 301-496-5751
Hyperbaric Chamber - UMD Shock Trauma Center....Staff 301-528-6294
Hyperbaric Oxygenation....Staff NHLBI 301-496-4236
Hyperbilirubinemia....Staff NICHD 301-496-5133
Hyperbilirubinemia....Staff NIDDK 301-496-3583
Hypercalcemia....Staff NIDDK 301-496-3583
Hypercalciuria....Staff NIDDK 301-496-3583
Hypercholesterolemia....Staff NHLBI 301-496-4236
Hyperglycemia....Staff NIDDK 301-496-3583
Hyperkinesis....Staff NIMH 301-443-4515
Hyperlipidemia....Staff NHLBI 301-496-4236
Hyperlipoproteinemia....Staff NHLBI 301-496-4236
Hyperparathyroidism....Staff NIDDK 301-496-3583
Hyperpyrexia (heat stroke/heat exhaustion)....Staff NIA 301-496-1752
Hypersensitivity Pneumonitis....Staff NIAID 301-496-5717
Hypersonic Aircraft....James, Donald G. NASA 415-604-3935
Hypersonic Engines....Staff NASA 804-864-3305
Hypertension....Staff NHLBI/IC 301-951-3260
Hypertension....Staff NCNR 301-496-0526
Hyperthermia....Staff NCI 301-496-5583
Hyperthermia (heat stroke/heat exhaustion)....Staff NIA 301-496-1752
Hyperthyroidism....Staff NIDDK 301-496-3583
Hypertriglyceridemia....Staff NHLBI 301-496-4236
Hyperuricemia....Staff NIDDK 301-496-3583
Hyperventilation....Staff NHLBI 301-496-4236
Hypnotics....Nesbitt, Elizabeth USITC 202-205-3355
Hypobetalipoproteinemia....Staff NHLBI 301-496-4236
Hypocomplementemic Glomerulonephritis....Staff NIAID 301-496-5717
Hypoglycemia....Staff NHLBI 301-496-4236
Hypoglycemia....Staff NIDDK 301-496-3583
Hypogonadism....Staff NIDDK 301-496-3583
Hypogonadism....Staff NICHD 301-496-5133
Hypokalemia....Staff NHLBI 301-496-4236
Hypokalemic Periodic Paralysis....Staff NINDS 301-496-5751
Hypolipoproteinemia....Staff NIDDK 301-496-3583
Hypoparathyroidism....Staff NIDDK 301-496-3583
Hypopituitarism....Staff NIDDK 301-496-3583
Hypospadias....Staff NICHD 301-496-5133
Hypotension....Staff NHLBI 301-496-4236
Hypothalamus....Staff NIDDK 301-496-3583
Hypothalamus....Staff NICHD 301-496-5133
Hypothermia (Accidental)....Staff NIA 301-496-1752
Hypothyroidism, Goitrous....Staff NIA 301-496-3583
Hypotonia....Staff NINDS 301-496-5751
Hypoventilation....Staff NHLBI 301-496-4236
Hypoxia....Staff NHLBI 301-496-4236
Hypsarrhythmia....Staff NINDS 301-496-5751

I

IGE....Staff NIAID 301-496-5717
Iceland....Lyons, Maryanne Cnty Commerce 202-482-3254
Iceland (Reykjavik)....Staff Cnty State 202-647-5669
Iceland Disease....Staff NINDS 301-496-5751
Iceland/Minerals....Buck, Donald E. Cnty Mines 202-501-9670
Ichthyosis....Staff NIAMS 301-496-8188
Idiopathic Hypertrophic Subaortic Stenosis (IHSS)....Staff NHLBI 301-496-4236
Idiopathic Inflammatory Myopathy....Staff NINDS 301-496-5751
Idiopathic Osteoporosis....Staff NIAMS 301-496-8188
Idiopathic Thrombocytopenic Purpura (ITP)....Staff NHLBI 301-496-4236
Idiopathic Thrombocytopenic Purpura (ITP)....Staff NIDDK 301-496-3583
IgE....Staff 301-496-5717
Ignition equipment....Kolberg, Mary USITC 202-205-3401
Ileitis....Staff NIDDK 301-496-3583

Horses / Insect Stings

Image Processing....Staff DCRT 301-496-2250
Image Processing....Staff DCRT 301-496-7963
Immigration....Dye, Larry ACF 202-401-9215
Immigration (Legal/Undocumented)....Woodrow, Karen CENSUS 301-763-5590
Immune Deficiency Diseases....Staff NIAID 301-496-5717
Immunization....Berreth, Don CDC 404-639-3286
Immunization, Disease....Orenstein, Walter A. CDC 404-639-180
Immunizations (Foreign Travel)....Staff CDC 404-639-3286
Immunology....Staff NIAID 301-496-5717
Immunology (Cancer)....Staff NCI 301-496-5583
Immunotherapy (Cancer)....Staff NCI 301-496-5583
Implantable Defibrillator....Staff NHLBI 301-496-4236
Implants, Lens....Staff NEI 301-496-5248
Impotence....Staff NIMH 301-443-4515
Impotence....Staff NIDDK 301-496-3583
In Vitro Fertilization....Staff NICHD 301-496-5133
Inactive Waste Site Management....Duffy, Leo P. NEIC 202-586-7710
Inactive Waste Site Cleanup....Duffy, Leo P. NEIC 202-586-7710
Inappropriate Antidiuretic Hormone Syndrome....Staff NHLBI 301-496-4236
Inborn Errors of Metabolism....Staff NICHD 301-496-5133
Inborn Errors of Metabolism....Staff NINDS 301-496-5751
Inborn Errors of Metabolism....Staff NHLBI 301-496-4236
Inborn Errors of Metabolism....Staff NICHD 301-496-5133
Inborn Heart Defects....Staff NHLBI 301-496-4236
Incapacitation....Langan, Patrick Justice Stat 202-616-3490
Incapacitation....Greenfeld, Lawrence Justice Stat 202-616-3281
Incidental Radiation Devices....Staff FCC 202-653-6288
Incinerators....Staff EPA 202-308-8461
Incontinence....Staff NIA 301-496-1752
Indexes of Fuels and Utilities, Monthly....Adkins, Robert LABOR 202-606-6985
India....Simmons, John/Crown, John/Gilman, Tim Cnty Commerce 202-482-2954
India (New Delhi)....Staff Cnty State 202-647-2351
India/Minerals....Vacant Cnty Mines 202-501-9694
Indian Fisheries Resources/Treaties....Staff FWS 703-358-1718
Indian Health....DeAsis, Patricia IHS 301-44-3593
Indian Health....Stone, Hardy IHS 301-443-3593
Indian Housing....Staff HUD 202-708-0950
Indian Hunting, Migratory Birds....Staff FWS 703-358-1773
Indian Wildlife Assistance....Staff FWS 703-358-1718
Indians - Administration for Native Americans....Long, Susan ACF 202-401-9215
Indigent Defense....Gaskins, Carla Justice Stat 202-508-8550
Indium....Jasinski, Stephen M. MINES 202-501-9418
Indium....Lundy, David USITC 202-205-3439
Indonesia....Goddin, Karen Cnty Commerce 202-482-3875
Indonesia (Jakarata)....Staff Cnty State 202-647-3276
Indonesia/Minerals....Kuo, Chin Cnty Mines 202-501-9693
Indoor Air Division....Staff EPA 202-233-9030
Indoor Air Division, National Program....Staff EPA 202-233-9030
Induced Movement Disorders....Staff NINDS 301-496-5751
Industrial Chemicals....Whitley, Richard A. COMMERCE 202-482-0682
Industrial Chemicals (Effects on Human Health)....Staff NIEHS 919-541-3345
Industrial Chemicals and Cancer....Staff NCI 301-496-5583
Industrial Classification, Est. Surv, Natl. Emp/Unemp....Getz, Patricia LABOR 202-606-6521
Industrial Drives/Gears....Reiss, Richard COMMERCE 202-482-3489
Industrial Gases....Kostalas, Antonios COMMERCE 202-482-0128
Industrial Heating Equipment....Staff FCC 202-653-6288
Industrial Hygiene....Staff OD/ORS 301-496-2960
Industrial Hygiene....Gaunce, Jean A. CDC 404-639-3415
Industrial Minerals, Assistant Branch Chief....Morse, D. MINES 202-501-9402
Industrial Minerals, Assistant Branch Chief....Mozian, Z. MINES 202-501-9396
Industrial Minerals, Chief, Branch of....Barsotti, Aldo F. MINES 202-501-9399
Industrial Organic Chemicals....Hurt, William COMMERCE 202-482-4333
Industrial Prices & Price Indexes, Asst. Commis.....Tibbetts, Thomas LABOR 202-606-7700
Industrial Process Controls....Nealon, Marguerite COMMERCE 202-482-0411
Industrial Process Controls (Export Promo)....Manzolilo, Frank COMMERCE 202-482-2991
Industrial Productivity....Streb, Alan NEIC 202-586-9232
Industrial Solid (Non Hazardous) Waste....Staff EPA 202-260-4807
Industrial Structure....Davis, Lester A. COMMERCE 202-482-4924
Industrial Technology Transfer....Duane, Jerry NEIC 202-586-2366
Industrial Trucks....Wiening, Mary COMMERCE 202-482-4608
Industrial ceramics....DeSapio, Vincent USITC 202-205-3435
Industrial diamonds....DeSapio, Vincent USITC 202-205-3435
Industrial gases....Conant, Kenneth USITC 202-205-3346
Industrial licenses....Staff FCC 717-337-1212
Industrial, Scientific, & Medical Equipment....Staff FCC 202-653-6288
Industry Data Centers....Rowe, John CENSUS 301-763-1580
Industry Projections and Economic Growth, Empl. Pro....Bowman, Charles LABOR 202-606-5702
Industry Wage Surveys, Comp. & Work. Conditions....Kellinson, Jonathan LABOR 202-606-6245
Industry and Commodity Classification....Venning, Alvin CENSUS 301-763-1935
Industry-Occupational Employment Matrix....Turner, Delores LABOR 202-606-5730
Industry/trade matters....Phillips, Don 202-385-5656
Inedible gelatin....Jonnard, Aimison USITC 202-205-3350
Inertial Confinement Fusion....Kahalas, Sheldon NEIC 301-903-5491
Infant Formula....Corwin, Emil FDA 202-205-4144
Infant Mortality....Staff NICHD 301-496-5133
Infant Mortality....Staff NCHS 301-436-8500
Infant Mortality....Staff CDC 404-639-3286
Infant Mortality/"Health Start"....Smith, Sandra CDC 301-436-7135
Infant Mortality/"Healthy Start"....Mehuron, Charlotte HRSA 301-443-3376
Infant Nutrition....Staff NICHD 301-496-5133
Infant Suffocation....Tyrrell, Elaine CPSC 301-504-0580
Infantile Muscular Atrophy....Staff NINDS 301-496-5751
Infantile Muscular Atrophy....Staff NIAMS 301-496-8188
Infantile Spinal Muscular Atrophy....Staff NINDS 301-496-5751
Infants (Care)....Staff HRSA 301-443-2086
Infants' accessories or apparel....Holoyda, Olha USITC 202-205-3469
Infections....Staff NIAID 301-496-5717
Infectious Arthritis....Staff NIAMS 301-496-8188
Infectious Eye Disease....Staff NEI 301-496-5248
Infectious Materials (Disposal)....Staff OD/ORS 301-496-2960
Infectious Mononucleosis....Staff NIAID 301-496-5717
Infectious Wastes....Staff EPA 202-260-8551
Infertility....Staff NICHD 301-496-5133
Inflammatory Bowel Disease....Staff NIDDK 301-496-3583
Inflammatory Bowel Disease....Staff NIAID 301-496-5717
Inflatable Articles....McKenna, Thomas CUSTOMS 212-466-5475
Influenza....Staff NIAID 301-496-5717
Influenza....Berreth, Don CDC 404-639-3286
Information Industries....Inoussa, Mary C. COMMERCE 202-482-5820
Information Services, Chief,....DiCesare, Constance LABOR 202-606-5886
Information Specialists, Publ. & Special Studies....Staff LABOR 202-606-7828
Information services....Xavier, Neil USITC 202-205-3450
Infraction Reports--International....Staff FCC 202-653-8138
Infrared Astronomy....Hutchison, Jane NASA 415-604-4968
Ingot molds....Greene, William USITC 202-205-3405
Inherited Blood Abnormalities....Staff NHLBI 301-496-4236
Inherited Blood Abnormalities....Staff NIDDK 301-496-3583
Inherited Metabolic Disorders....Staff NIDDK 301-496-3583
Inherited Neurologic Abnormalities....Staff NINDS 301-496-5751
Injunctions....Staff FCC 202-632-7112
Injuries (Eye)....Staff NEI 301-496-5248
Injury Prevention and Control....Broome, Claire V. CDC 404-488-4690
Ink....Brownchweig, Gilbert CUSTOMS 212-466-5744
Ink powders....Johnson, Larry USITC 202-205-3351
Inks....Johnson, Larry USITC 202-205-3351
Inland Fish and Reservoirs....Staff FWS 703-358-1710
Innovative Energy Research....Polansky, Walter NEIC 301-903-5995
Inorganic Chemicals....Kostallas, Anthony COMMERCE 202-482-0128
Inorganic Compounds & Mixtures....DiMaria, Joseph CUSTOMS 212-466-4769
Inorganic Pigments....Kostallas, Anthony COMMERCE 202-482-0128
Inorganic acids....Trainor, Cynthia USITC 202-205-3354
Inorganic compounds and mixtures....Greenblatt, Jack USITC 202-205-3353
Inorganic hydroxides....Conant, Kenneth USITC 202-205-3346
Inorganic oxides....Conant, Kenneth USITC 202-205-3346
Insanity Defense....Baunach, Phyllis Jo Justice Stat 202-307-0361
Insect Stings Allergy....Staff NIAID 301-496-5717

Experts

Insecticide-Rodenticides....Staff EPA 202-305-5200
Insects, Forest....Lyon, Robert FS 202-205-1532
Insomnia....Staff NIMH 301-443-4515
Inspector General Whistle Blower Hotline....Staff EPA 800-424-4000
Institutional Conservation Methods....Volk, Robert NEIC 202-586-8034
Instrument Development....Staff DRS/BEIB 301-496-4741
Instrument Development....Staff NCRR/BEIP 301-496-4741
Instruments, Drafting....Losche, Robert CUSTOMS 212-466-5670
Instruments, Measuring and Controlling....Riedl, Karl CUSTOMS 212-466-5493
Instruments, Navigational....Losche, Robert CUSTOMS 212-466-5670
Instruments: controlling....Moller, Ruben USITC 202-205-3495
Instruments: dental....Johnson, Christopher USITC 202-205-3488
Instruments: drawing....Shetty, Sundar USITC 202-205-3486
Instruments: mathematical calculating....Shetty, Sundar USITC 202-205-3486
Instruments: measuring or checking....Moller, Ruben USITC 202-205-3495
Instruments: medical....Johnson, Christopher USITC 202-205-3488
Instruments: musical....Witherspoon, Ricardo USITC 202-205-3489
Instruments: navigational....Shetty, Sundar USITC 202-205-3486
Instruments: surgical....Johnson, Christopher USITC 202-205-3488
Instruments: surveying....Shetty, Sundar USITC 202-205-3486
Instruments: testing....Moller, Ruben USITC 202-205-3495
Insulation....Shaw, Robert COMMERCE 202-482-0132
Insulators, ceramic....Cutchin, John USITC 202-205-3396
Insulinomas....Staff NIDDK 301-496-3583
Insurance....McAdam, Bruce COMMERCE 202-482-0346
Insurance....Bedore, James USITC 202-205-3424
Insurance Claimants (Unempl). Empl/Unempl.Stats.....Terwilliger, Yvonne LABOR 202-606-6392
Int'l Economics, Balance of Payments....Bach, Christopher L. ECONOMIC 202-523-0620
Int'l Economics, Current Account Analysis....DiLullo, Anthony J. ECONOMIC 202-523-0621
Int'l Economics, Current Account Estimates....Kealy, Walter G. ECONOMIC 202-523-0625
Int'l Economics, Special Analysis....Lawson, Ann ECONOMIC 202-523-0628
Int'l, Capital Expend. of Major-Owned Foreign Affil.....Fahim-Nadir, Mahnaz ECONOMIC 202-523-0640
Int'l, For. Dir US Invest. - New Investment Surv.....Cherry, Joseph ECONOMIC 202-523-0654
Int'l, For. Dir US Invest. New Investment Surv Anal....Fahim-Nadir, Mahnaz ECONOMIC 202-523-0640
Int'l, Quarterly & Annual Balance of Payments Anal....Bezirganian, Steve D. ECONOMIC 202-523-0641
Int'l, Quarterly & Annual Balance of Payments Data....Fouch, Gregory G. ECONOMIC 202-523-0547
Int'l, US Direct Investment Abroad, Analysis....Mataloni, Raymond J. ECONOMIC 202-523-3451
Int'l, Analysis of US Transact-Unaffiliated Foreigner....Whichard, Obie G. ECONOMIC 202-523-0646
Int'l, Analysis-US Transact's w/Unaffil Foreigners....DiLullo, Anthony J. ECONOMIC 202-523-0632
Int'l, Annual Surveys-US Transact's w/Unaffil Foreigners....Emond, Christopher J. ECONOMIC 202-523-0632
Int'l, Benchmark Survey-US Transact's w/Unaffil For.....Kozlow, Ralph ECONOMIC 202-523-0632
Int'l, Foreign Dir. US Invest, Benchmark & Annual Anal....Bezirganian, Steve D. ECONOMIC 202-523-0641
Int'l, Foreign Dir. US Invest, Benchmark & Annual Surv....Bomkamp, James L. ECONOMIC 202-523-0559
Int'l, US Direct Invest. Abroad, Payments Data Bal.....New, Mark W. ECONOMIC 202-523-0612
Int'l, US Direct Invest. Abroad, Benchmark & Annual Sur....Walker, Patricia G. ECONOMIC 202-523-0612
Integrated Data Processing, Transmission of....Staff FCC 202-632-5550
Intellectual Development....Staff NICHD 301-496-5133
Intellectual Property Rights, Services....Siegmund, John E. COMMERCE 202-482-4781
Inter'l, Multinat'l Corps, Analysis of Activities....Mataloni, Raymond J. ECONOMIC 202-523-3451
Interception of Radio Communications....Staff FCC 202-632-6990
Interconnection of Telephone Equipment....Staff FCC 202-634-1800
Interferon....Staff NIAID 301-496-5717
Interferon....Staff NCI 301-496-5583
Interindustry Economics, (Acting Chief)....Maley, Leo C. ECONOMIC 202-523-0683
Interlocking Directors....Staff FCC 202-632-4887
International, Merchandise Trade....Murad, Howard ECONOMIC 202-523-0668
International Activities....Glickman, Marianne NEA 202-682-5422
International Activities, Fish and Wildlife....Staff FWS 703-358-1754
International Affairs, NASA....Rahn, Debra NASA 202-453-8455
International Allocation Agreements....Staff FCC 202-653-8108
International Allocation Treaties....Staff FCC 202-653-8126
International Commodities....Siesseger, Fred COMMERCE 202-482-5124
International Crime Data....Kalish, Carol Justice Stat 202-307-0235
International Economics, Associate Director....Landefeld, Steven J. ECONOMIC 202-523-0695
International Energy Analysis....Brodman, John NEIC 202-586-5893
International Forestry....Sirmon, Jeff M. FS 202-205-1650
International Health....Davis, Joe H. CDC 404-639-2101
International Health Activities....Simmons, Paul B. PHS 202-690-6867
International Investment, Chief....Barker, Betty L. ECONOMIC 202-523-0659
International Major Projects....Thibeault, Robert COMMERCE 202-482-5225
International Price Indexes, Assist. Commiss.....Reut, Katrina LABOR 202-606-7100
International Price Indexes, Food, Raw Matls, Appl....Frumkin, Rob LABOR 202-606-7106
International Price Indexes, Machinery....Costello, Brian LABOR 202-606-7107
International Price Indexes, Revision, Pr/Lv.Cond.....Reut, Katrina LABOR 202-606-7100
International Programs, Director....Hsieh, Richard C. NLM 301-496-6481
International Research....Staff NEH 202-606-8204
International Statistics, Africa....Hobbs, Frank CENSUS 301-763-4221
International Statistics, Asia....Hobbs, Frank CENSUS 301-763-4221
International Statistics, China, People's Republic....Banister, Judith CENSUS 301-763-4012
International Statistics, Europe....Balswin, Godfrey CENSUS 301-763-4022
International Statistics, International Data Base....Johnson, Peter CENSUS 301-763-4811
International Statistics, Latin America....Hobbs, Frank CENSUS 301-763-4221
International Statistics, North America....Hobbs, Frank CENSUS 301-763-4221
International Statistics, Oceania....Hobbs, Frank CENSUS 301-763-4221
International Statistics, Soviet Union....Kostinsky, Barry CENSUS 301-763-4022
International Statistics, Women in Development....Jamison, Ellen CENSUS 301-763-4086
International Thermonuclear Experimental Reactor....Dowling, Robert J. NEIC 301-903-5378
International Transportation....Watts, Patricia ECONOMIC 202-523-0611
International Travel....Bolyard, Joan E. ECONOMIC 202-523-0609
International Visitors Program....Pane Pinto, Nina CENSUS 301-763-2839
International Visitors Program....Vandrovec, Gene CENSUS 301-763-2829
International, Foreign Military Sales....McCormick, William O. ECONOMIC 202-523-0619
International, Government Transactions....Thomas, Gregory ECONOMIC 202-523-0615
International, Private Capital Transactions....Scholl, Russell B. ECONOMIC 202-523-0603
Interplanetary Space Probes....Brown, Dwayne C. NASA 202-453-8956
Interstate Land Sales Registration....Staff HUD 202-708-0502
Interstitial Cystitis....Staff NIDDK 301-496-2583
Interstitial Lung Diseases....Staff NHLBI 301-496-4236
Interstitial Nephritis....Staff NIDDK 301-496-3583
Intestinal Malabsorption Syndrome....Staff NIDDK 301-496-3583
Intracranial Aneurysm....Staff NINDS 301-496-5751
Intraocular Lenses....Staff NEI 301-496-5248
Intrauterine Growth Retardation....Staff NICHD 301-496-5133
Introduced Species, Fish and Wildlife....Staff FWS 703-358-1718
Intrusion Alarms....Staff FCC 202-653-6288
Inventions, Energy-Related....Staff NEIC 202-586-1479
Investment Management....Muir, S. Cassin COMMERCE 202-482-0346
Investment in Plant and Equipment....Gates, John CENSUS 301-763-5596
Iodine....Lyday, Phillis A. MINES 202-501-9405
Iodine....Conant, Kenneth USITC 202-205-3346
Ionosphere....Staff FCC 202-653-8166
Iran....Fitzgerald-Wilks, Kate/Thanos, Paul Cnty Commerce 202-482-1860
Iran....Staff Cnty State 202-647-6111
Iran/Minerals....Antonides, Lloyd Cnty Mines 202-501-9686

Insecticide / Labor Force

Iraq....Sams, Thomas/Wright, Corey Cnty Commerce 202-482-4441
Iraq (Baghdad)....Staff Cnty State 202-647-5692
Iraq/Minerals....Heydari, Michael Cnty Mines 202-501-9688
Ireland....Fitzpatrick, Boyce Cnty Commerce 202-482-2177
Ireland (Dublin)....Staff Cnty State 202-647-5669
Ireland/Minerals....Newman, Harold R. Cnty Mines 202-501-9669
Iridocyclitis....Staff NEI 301-496-5248
Iritis....Staff NEI 301-496-5248
Iron & Steel....Houck, Gerald MINES 202-501-9439
Iron & Steel Scrap....Brown, Raymond E. MINES 202-501-9427
Iron & Steel Slag....Solomon, Cheryl S. MINES 202-501-9393
Iron Deficiency Anemia....Staff NIDDK 301-496-3583
Iron Ore....Kirk, William S. MINES 202-501-9430
Iron blues....Johnson, Larry USITC 202-205-3351
Iron compounds....Greenblatt, Jack USITC 202-205-3353
Iron ore....Vacant USITC 202-205-3419
Irrigation, Major Proj.....Bell, Richard COMMERCE 202-482-2460
Irritable Bowel Syndrome....Staff NIDDK 301-496-3583
Isador....Staff NCI 301-496-5583
Ischemia....Staff NHLBI 301-496-4236
Ischemic Heart Disease....Staff NHLBI 301-496-4236
Isinglass....Jonnard, Aimison USITC 202-205-3350
Islet Cell Hyperplasia....Staff NIDDK 301-496-3583
Islet Cell Transplants....Staff NIDDK 301-496-3583
Isobutane....Raftery, Jim USITC 202-205-3365
Isobutylene....Raftery, Jim USITC 202-205-3365
Isoprene....Raftery, Jim USITC 202-205-3365
Isopropyl myristate....Johnson, Larry USITC 202-205-3351
Isotope Production....Erb, Donald NEIC 301-903-2593
Isotopes....Staff NCI 301-496-5583
Israel....Fitzgerald-Wilkes, Kate/Thanos, Paul Cnty Commerce 202-482-1870
Israel (Tel Aviv)....Staff Cnty State 202-647-3672
Israel/Minerals....King, Audie L. Cnty Mines 202-501-9674
Italy....Fitzpatrick, Boyce Cnty Commerce 202-482-2177
Italy (Rome)....Staff Cnty State 202-647-2453
Italy/Minerals....Rabchevsky, George Cnty Mines 202-501-9672
Ivory Coast....Michelini, Paul Cnty Commerce 202-482-4388
Ivory Coast/Minerals....van Oss, Hendrik Cnty Mines 202-501-9687
Ivory, articles of....Spalding, Josephine USITC 202-205-3498
Ivory, tusks....Ludwick, David USITC 202-205-3329

J

Jackets: mens and boys....Linkins, Linda USITC 202-205-3469
Jackets: womens and girls....Holoyda, Olha USITC 202-205-3467
Jails, Inmates, and Crowding....Baunach, Phyllis Jo Justice Stat 202-307-0361
Jails, Inmates, and Crowding....Stephan, James Justice Stat 202-616-7273
Jails, Inmates, and Crowding....Greenfeld, Lawrence Justice Stat 202-616-3281
Jails, Inmates, and Crowding....DeWitt, Charles Justice Stat 202-307-2942
Jakob-Creutzfeldt Disease....Staff NINDS 301-496-5751
Jamaica....Soto, Rodrigo Cnty Commerce 202-482-2527
Jamaica....Almaguer, Antoinette Peace Corps 202-606-3322
Jamaica (Kingston)....Staff Cnty State 202-647-2620
Jamaica/Minerals....Torres, Ivette Cnty Mines 202-501-9680
Jams and Jellies....Hodgen, Donald A. COMMERCE 202-482-3346
Jams, jellies, and marmalades....Vacant USITC 202-205-3306
Japan....Cantall, W./Leslie, E./Kennedy, E./Christian, A. Cnty Commerce 202-482-2425
Japan (Tokyo)....Staff Cnty State 202-647-3152
Japan/Minerals....Wu, John Cnty Mines 202-501-9697
Japan/trade matters....Lake, Charles US Trade Rep 202-395-3900
Japanese Yen with options....Bice, David CFT 312-353-7880
Jet fuel....Foreso, Cynthia USITC 202-205-3348
Jewelry, Export Promo.....Beckham, Reginald COMMERCE 202-482-5478
Jewelry....Harris, John M. COMMERCE 202-482-1178
Jewelry....Piropato, Louis CUSTOMS 212-466-5895
Jewelry....Witherspoon, Ricardo USITC 202-205-3489
Job Vacancy Stats, Employment Statistics....Devens, Richard LABOR 202-606-6402
Jordan....Fitzgerald-Wilkes, Kate/Thanos, Paul Cnty Commerce 202-482-1857
Jordan (Amman)....Staff Cnty State 202-647-1022
Jordan/Minerals....Dolley, Thomas Cnty Mines 202-501-9690
Joseph's Disease....Staff NINDS 301-496-5751
Journal, EPA....Staff EPA 202-260-4659

Journalism research methods....Newhagan, John D. UMD 301-405-2417
Judges....Gaskins, Carla Justice Stat 202-508-8550
Judges....Langan, Patrick Justice Stat 202-616-3490
Judiciary....Gaskins, Carla Justice Stat 202-508-8550
Judiciary....Langan, Patrick Justice Stat 202-616-3490
Juices....Maria, John CUSTOMS 212-466-5730
Juices, fruit....Dennis, Alfred USITC 202-205-3316
Juices, vegetable....Dennis, Alfred USITC 202-205-3316
Juvenile Corrections....Baunach, Phyllis Jo Justice Stat 202-307-0361
Juvenile Corrections....Kline, Susan Justice Stat 202-724-3118
Juvenile Delinquency....Staff NIMH 301-443-4515
Juvenile Diabetes....Staff NIDDK 301-443-3583
Juvenile Rheumatoid Arthritis....Staff NIAMS 301-496-8188
Juvenile Spin. Musc. Atrophy (Kug.-Wel. Disease)....Staff NINDS 301-496-5751
Juveniles - General....Lindgren, Sue Justice Stat 202-307-0760
Juxtaglomerular Hyperplasia (Bartter's Syndrome)....Staff NHLBI 301-496-4236

K

Kanner's Syndrome....Staff NINDS 301-496-5751
Kaolin....Lukes, James USITC 202-205-3426
Kaposi's Sarcoma....Staff NCI 301-496-5583
Kawasaki Disease....Staff NIAID 301-496-5717
Kawasaki Disease....Staff CDC 401-639-3286
Kearns-Sayre Syndrome....Staff NINDS 301-496-5751
Kenya....Watkins, Chandra Cnty Commerce 202-482-4564
Kenya....Schmitz, Virginia Peace Corps 202-606-3334
Kenya (Nairobi)....Staff Cnty State 202-647-5684
Kenya/Minerals....Izon, David Cnty Mines 202-501-9692
Keratitis....Staff NEI 301-496-5248
Keratoconus....Staff NEI 301-496-5248
Keratomileusis....Staff NEI 301-496-5248
Keratoplasty....Staff NEI 301-496-5248
Kerosene....Foreso, Cynthia USITC 202-205-3348
Ketones....Michels, David USITC 202-205-3352
Key cases....Seastrum, Carl USITC 202-205-3493
Kidney....Staff NIDDK 301-496-3583
Kidney Dialysis....Hardy, Robert HCFA 220-690-6145
Kidney Stones....Staff NIDDK 301-496-3583
Kidney, Urology Clearinghouse....Staff NIDDK 301-468-6345
Kiribati (Tarawa)....Staff Cnty State 202-647-3546
Kiribati (Gilbert Islands)/Minerals....Lyday, Travis Cnty Mines 202-501-9695
Kitchen Cabinets....Auerbach, Mitchel COMMERCE 202-482-0375
Kleine-Levin Syndrome....Staff NINDS 301-496-5751
Klinefelter's Syndrome....Staff NICHD 301-496-5133
Knitting machines....Greene, William USITC 202-205-3405
Knotted Netting....Konzet, Jeffrey CUSTOMS 212-466-5885
Koch Antitoxins....Staff NCI 301-496-5583
Korea....Donius, Jeffrey/ Amador, Ranato/ Duvall, Dan Cnty Commerce 202-482-4957
Korea, North and South....Staff Cnty State 202-647-7717
Korea, North/Minerals....Kuo, Chin Cnty Mines 202-501-9693
Korea, South/Minerals....Kuo, Chin Cnty Mines 202-501-9693
Krabbe's Disease....Staff NINDS 301-496-5751
Krebiezen (Carcalon)....Staff NCI 301-496-5583
Kugelberg-Welander Disease (Juv. Spi. Mus. Atoph.)....Staff NINDS 301-496-5751
Kuru....Staff NINDS 301-496-5751
Kuwait....Wright, Corey/Sams, Thomas Cnty Commerce 202-482-1680
Kuwait (Kuwait)....Staff Cnty State 202-647-6562
Kuwait/Minerals....Michalski, Bernadette Cnty Mines 202-501-9699
Kyanite....DeSapio, Vincent USITC 202-205-3435
Kyanite-Mullite....Potter, Michael J. MINES 202-501-9387
Kyrgyzstan....Staff Cnty State 202-647-6859

L

LNG Plants (Major Proj)....Thomas, Janet COMMERCE 202-482-4146
Labels....Cook, Lee USITC 202-205-3471
Labor Composition, Multifactor Productivity, Hrs.....Rosenblum, Larry LABOR 202-606-5606
Labor Force Data, Data Disk & Tapes....Marcus, Jessie LABOR 202-606-6392

Be patient. If any phone number is incorrect, call (area code) 555-1212 and request the new listing.

Experts

Labor Force Data, Machine-readable data, Empl/Un....Green, Gloria LABOR 202-606-6373
Labor Force Projections....Fullerton, Howard LABOR 202-606-5711
Labor Force and Unemployment, Foreign Countries....Sorrentino, Constance LABOR 202-606-5654
Labor Force, State and Area Tapes and Diskettes....Marcus, Jessie LABOR 202-606-6392
Laboratory Animals....Staff NCRR 301-496-5545
Laboratory Animals....Staff NCRR 301-496-2527
Laboratory Glassware....Staff OD/ORS 301-496-4595
Laboratory Instruments....Nealon, Marguerite COMMERCE 202-482-3411
Laboratory Instruments, Trade Promo.....Gwaltney, G.P. COMMERCE 202-482-3090
Labyrinthitis....Staff NINDS 301-496-5751
Labyrinthitis....Staff NIDCD 301-496-7243
Lace....Konzet, Jeffrey CUSTOMS 212-466-5885
Lace....Sweet, Mary Elizabeth USITC 202-205-3455
Lacemaking machines....Greene, William USITC 202-205-3405
Lacings....Cook, Lee USITC 202-205-3471
Lacquers....Johnson, Larry USITC 202-205-3351
Lacrimal Glands....Staff NEI 301-496-5248
Lactation....Staff NIDDK 301-496-3583
Lactose....Randall, Rob USITC 202-205-3366
Lactose Intolerance....Staff NIDDK 301-496-3583
Laetrile....Staff NCI 301-496-5583
Lakes....Wanser, Stephen USITC 202-205-3363
Lamb....Steller, Rose USITC 202-205-3323
Laminar Flow Rooms....Staff OD/ORS 301-496-2960
Lamp black....Johnson, Larry USITC 202-205-3351
Lamps....Kalkines, George CUSTOMS 212-466-5794
Lamps (bulbs)....Cutchin, John USITC 202-205-3396
Land Disposal....Staff EPA 202-260-4687
Land Disposition, Fish and Wildlife....Staff FWS 703-358-1713
Land Fields....Staff EPA 202-260-4687
Land Mobile Common Carrier....Staff FCC 202-653-0914
Land Mobile Frequent Assignment Techniques....Staff FCC 717-337-1411
Land Mobile Operational Review of Radio....Staff FCC 202-632-6497
Land Resource Usage and Analysis....Staff FWS 703-358-1706
Land Transportation....Staff FCC 717-337-1212
Land and Space Based Remote Sensing Instruments....Staff NASA 804-864-6170
Land and Water Conservation Fund....Staff FWS 703-358-1713
Language....Staff NINDS 301-496-5751
Language....Staff NIDCD 301-496-7243
Language....Staff CENSUS 301-763-1154
Language Development....Staff NICHD 301-496-5133
Language and journalism....McAdams, Katherine C. UMD 301-405-2423
Laos....Pho, Hong-Phong B. Cnty Commerce 202-482-3875
Laos (Vientiane)....Staff Cnty State 202-647-3133
Laos/Minerals....Vacant Cnty Mines 202-501-9694
Laser (Cancer Surgery)....Staff NCI 301-496-5583
Laser (Tatoo Removal/Dermatology)....Staff 301-496-8188
Laser Angioplasty....Staff NHLBI 301-496-4236
Laser Energy Conversion Techniques....Staff NASA 804-864-6122
Laser Treatment (Eyes)....Staff NEI 301-496-5248
Lasers, Trade Promo.....Manzolilo, Frank COMMERCE 202-482-2991
Lassa Fever....Staff NIAID 301-496-5717
Latin America/trade matters....Frechette, Myles US Trade Rep 202-395-6135
Latvia....Staff Cnty State 202-647-3187
Launch Vehicles....Brown, Dwayne C. NASA 202-453-8956
Laundry machines....Jackson, Georgia USITC 202-205-3399
Laurence-Moon-Bardet-Biedl Syndrome....Staff NINDS 301-496-5751
Law Enforcement, Prosecution & Courts - State....Manson, Donald Justice Stat 202-616-3491
Law Suits Litigation....Staff FCC 202-632-7112
Lawn & Garden Equipment....Vanderwof, John COMMERCE 202-482-0348
Layoff Statistics, Empl/ Unempl. Stats.....Siegel, Lewis LABOR 202-606-6404
Lead....Woodbury, William D. MINES 202-501-9444
Lead....White, Linda USITC 202-205-3427
Lead Based Paints....Staff CDC 404-639-3286
Lead Encephalopathy....Staff NINDS 301-496-5751
Lead Poisoning....Staff CDC 404-639-3286
Lead Poisoning....Staff NIEHS 919-541-3345
Lead Poisoning....Grigg, Bill PHS 202-690-6867
Lead Poisoning Prevention....Binder, Suzanne CDC 404-488-7330
Lead Poisoning Prevention....Giles, Ken CPSC 301-504-0580
Lead Products....Larrabee, David COMMERCE 202-482-0575
Lead compounds....Greenblatt, Jack USITC 202-205-3353
Lead for pencils....Shetty, Sundar USITC 202-205-3486
Lead pigments....Johnson, Larry USITC 202-205-3351
Lead-Poisoning Anemia....Staff NHLBI 301-496-4236
Learning Center for Interactive Technology....Staff NLM 301-496-6280
Learning Disabilities....Staff NINDS 301-496-5751
Learning Disabilities....Staff NICHD 301-496-5133
Learning Disabilities....Staff NIMH 301-443-4515
Learning Disabilities....Staff NIDCD 301-496-7243
Lease condensate....Foreso, Cynthia USITC 202-205-3348
Leasing Equipment and Vehicles....Shuman, John COMMERCE 202-482-3050
Leather....Steller, Rose USITC 202-205-3323
Leather Products....Byron, James E. COMMERCE 202-482-4034
Leather Tanning....Byron, James E. COMMERCE 202-482-4034
Leather apparel....Jones, Jackie USITC 202-205-3466
Leather apparel....Hamey, Amy USITC 202-205-3465
Leather footwear parts....Shildneck, Ann USITC 202-205-3499
Leather, Producer Price Index....Paik, Soon LABOR 202-606-7714
Lebanon....Wright, Corey/Sams, Thomas Cnty Commerce 202-482-4441
Lebanon (Beirut)....Staff Cnty State 202-647-1030
Lebanon/Minerals....Michalski, Bernadette Cnty Mines 202-501-9699
Leber's Disease....Staff NEI 301-496-5248
Left Ventricular Assist Device (LVAD)....Staff NHLBI 301-496-4236
Legal Services....Chittum, J. Marc. COMMERCE 202-482-0345
Legal Services....Posey, Melanie USITC 202-205-3303
Legg-Perthes Disease....Staff NIAMS 301-496-8188
Legionella Pneumophila....Staff NIAID 301-496-5717
Legionella Pneumophila....Staff CDC 404-639-3286
Legionnaire's Disease....Staff NIAID 301-496-5717
Legionnaire's Disease....Staff CDC 404-639-3286
Legislation....Gregg, Valerie CENSUS 301-763-7787
Legislation....Lacy, Velma CENSUS 301-763-4001
Legislative Information....Staff OD/DIA 301-496-3471
Leigh's Disease (Subacute Necrotizing Encephal.)....Staff NINDS 301-496-5751
Leishmaniasis....Staff NIAID 301-496-5717
Lemon oil (essential oil)....Land, Eric USITC 202-205-3349
Lennox-Gastaut Syndrome....Staff NINDS 301-496-5751
Lens....Staff NEI 301-496-5248
Lens Implants....Staff NEI 301-496-5248
Lenses....Johnson, Christopher USITC 202-205-3488
Leprosy....Staff NIAID 301-496-5717
Lesch-Nyhan Disease....Staff NIDDK 301-496-3583
Lesch-Nyhan Disease....Staff NINDS 301-496-5751
Lesch-Nyhan Disease....Staff NIMH 301-443-4515
Lesotho....Holm-Olsen, Finn Cnty Commerce 202-482-4228
Lesotho....Grimmett, Michael Peace Corps 202-606-3246
Lesotho....Woodfork, Jacqueline Peace Corps 202-606-3247
Lesotho (Maseru)....Staff Cnty State 202-647-8252
Lesotho/Minerals....King, Audie L. Cnty Mines 202-501-9674
Leukemia....Staff NCI 301-496-5583
Leukoaraiosis....Staff NINDS 301-496-5751
Leukodystrophy....Staff NINDS 301-496-5751
Leukoencephalopathy....Staff NINDS 301-496-5751
Leukoplakia....Staff NIDR 301-496-4261
Levulose....Randall, Rob USITC 202-205-3366
Liberia....Michelini, Philip/Cerone, Chris Cnty Commerce 202-482-4388
Liberia (Monrovia)....Staff Cnty State 202-647-3391
Liberia/Minerals....van Oss, Hendrik Cnty Mines 202-501-9687
Librarians Office....Staff DRS 301-496-2447
Library....Staff CENSUS 301-763-5042
Library (National Library of Medicine)....Staff NLM 301-496-6095
Library - Toxic Substances....Staff EPA 202-260-3944
Libya....Clement, Claude Cnty Commerce 202-482-5545
Libya (Tripoli)....Staff Cnty State 202-647-4674
Libya/Minerals....Dolley, Thomas Cnty Mines 202-501-9690
Lice....Staff NIAID 301-496-5717
Licenses, Federal Permits....Staff FWS 703-358-2183
Lichen Planus....Staff NIDR 301-496-4261
Lichen Planus....Staff NIAMS 301-496-8188
Liechtenstein....Staff Cnty State 202-647-1484
Life Cycle....Staff NIA 301-496-1752
Life Expectancy....Staff NIA 301-496-1752
Life Extension....Staff NIA 301-496-1752
Life Insurance and Health, Comp. & Working Cond.....Blostin, Allan LABOR 202-606-6240

Be patient. If any phone number is incorrect, call (area code) 555-1212 and request the new listing.

Laboratory Animals / Machines

Life Review....Staff NIA 301-496-1752
Life Sciences Research....Staff NASA 713-438-5111
Life on Other Planets....Staff NASA 415-604-3934
Light Water Reactor Safety....Giessing, Daniel NEIC 301-903-3456
Light oil....Foreso, Cynthia USITC 202-205-3348
Lighting Devices....Staff FCC 202-653-6288
Lighting Fixtures....Kalkines, George CUSTOMS 212-466-5794
Lighting equipment....Kolberg, Mary USITC 202-205-3401
Ligninsulfonic acid and its salts....Land, Eric USITC 202-205-3349
Lignite....Foreso, Cynthia USITC 202-205-3348
Lime....Miller, Michael MINES 202-501-9409
Lime....White, Linda USITC 202-205-3427
Limestone....White, Linda USITC 202-205-3427
Linear Accelerator....Staff NCI 301-496-5583
Lipid Research Clinics....Staff NHLBI 301-496-4236
Lipid Storage Diseases....Staff NINDS 301-496-5751
Lipid Transport Disorders....Staff NHLBI 301-496-4236
Lipidemia....Staff NHLBI 301-496-4236
Lipidosis....Staff NINDS 301-496-5751
Lipoproteins....Staff NHLBI 301-496-4236
Liquefied natural gas (LNG)....Land, Eric USITC 202-205-3349
Liquefied petroleum gas (LPG)....Land, Eric USITC 202-205-3349
Liquefied refinery gas (LRG)....Land, Eric USITC 202-205-3349
Liquid Metal Reactors (LMR)....Rosen, Sol NEIC 301-903-3218
Liquid Waste....Staff OD/ORS 301-496-2960
Liquid Waste (Radioactive)....Staff OD/ORS 301-496-2254
Listeriosis....Staff NIAID 301-496-5717
Literature....Bradford, Gigi NEA 202-682-5451
Literature of journalism....Paterson, Judith UMD 301-405-2425
Lithium....Ober, Joyce A. MINES 202-501-9406
Lithium....Conant, Kenneth USITC 202-205-3346
Lithium compounds....Greenblatt, Jack USITC 202-205-3353
Lithium stearate....Randall, Rob USITC 202-205-3366
Lithuania....Staff Cnty State 202-647-3187
Liver....Staff NIDDK 301-496-3583
Livestock - Cattle....Shepler, Glenda Agri 202-720-3040
Livestock - Cattle & Sheep....Gustafson, Ron Agri 202-219-1286
Livestock - Hogs....Hamer, Hubert Agri 202-720-3106
Livestock - Hogs....Southard, Leland Agri 202-219-0767
Livestock - Sheep....Simpson, Linda Agri 202-720-3578
Livestock - World....Bailey, Linda Agri 202-219-1286
Livestock - World....Shagam, Shayle Agri 202-219-0767
Livestock Damage Control....Staff FWS 703-358-1718
Living Arrangements, Population....Saluter, Arlene CENSUS 301-763-7987
Local Government Radio....Staff FCC 717-337-1212
Local Television Transmission....Staff FCC 202-634-1706
Locked-In Syndrome....Staff NINDS 301-496-5751
Locks....Smyth, James CUSTOMS 212-466-2084
Locks and Keys....Staff OD/ORS/Locksmith 301-496-3507
Loeffler's Syndrome....Staff NIAID 301-496-5717
Logs, Wood....Hicks, Michael COMMERCE 202-482-0375
Logs, rough....Ruggles, Fred USITC 202-205-3325
Long-Term Care & Alternatives....Hardy, Robert HCFA 202-690-6145
Longevity (Statistics)....Staff NCHS 301-436-8500
Longevity (Statistics)....Staff NIA 301-496-1752
Longitudinal Data/Gross Flows, Empl/Unempl. Stats.....Horvath, Francis LABOR 202-606-6345
Lotteries....Staff FCC 202-632-6990
Lou Gehrig's Disease....Staff NINDS 301-496-5751
Loudspeakers....Sherman, Thomas USITC 202-205-3389
Low Back Pain....Staff NIAMS 301-496-8188
Low Back Pain (Sciatica)....Staff NINDS 301-496-5751
Low Birth Weight....Staff NICHD 301-496-5133
Low Blood Pressure....Staff NHLBI 301-496-4236
Low Energy Nuclear Research....Hendrie, David NEIC 301-902-3610
Low Power Television Stations....Staff FCC 202-632-7426
Low Power Transmitters....Staff FCC 202-653-6288
Low Vision Aids....Staff NEI 301-496-5248
Low fuming brazing rods....Lundy, David USITC 202-205-3439
Low-Density Lipoproteins (LDL)....Staff NHLBI 301-496-4236
Low-Income Weatherization Assistance....Staff NEIC 202-586-2204
Lowe Syndrome (Oculocerebrorenal)....Staff NICHD 301-496-5133
Lowe's Syndrome....Staff NEI 301-496-5248
Lube fittings....Fravel, Dennis USITC 202-205-3404
Lubricating grease....Foreso, Cynthia USITC 202-205-3348
Lubricating oil....Foreso, Cynthia USITC 202-205-3348
Luggage....Byron, James E. COMMERCE 202-482-3034
Luggage....Gorman, Kevin CUSTOMS 212-466-5893
Luggage....Seastrum, Carl USITC 202-205-3493
Lumber....Wise, Barbara COMMERCE 202-482-0375
Lumber....Ruggles, Fred USITC 202-205-3325
Lumber with options....Rosenfeld, Donald CFT 312-353-9026
Lunar Landing Research Vehicle....Haley, Donald E. NASA 805-258-3456
Lunar Landing Research Vehicle....Nolan, Donald A. NASA 805-358-3447
Lunar Samples Research....Staff NASA 713-483-5111
Lung Cancer....Staff NCI 301-496-5583
Lung Disease (Asbestosis)....Staff NIEHS 919-541-3345
Lung Disease (Infectious/Allergenic)....Staff NIAID 301-496-5717
Lung Disease (Non-infec., Non-aller., Non-tumor.)....Staff NHLBI 301-496-4236
Lung Disease (Tumorous/Cancerous)....Staff NCI 301-496-5583
Lupus Erythematosus....Staff NIAMS 301-496-8188
Lupus Erythematosus....Staff NINDS 301-496-5751
Lupus Erythematosus....Staff NIAID 301-496-5717
Luxembourg....Bensimon, Simon Cnty Commerce 202-482-5401
Luxembourg (Luxembourg)....Staff Cnty State 202-647-6664
Luxembourg/Minerals....Newman, Harold R. Cnty Mines 202-501-9699
Lyme Arthritis/Lyme Disease....Staff NIAID 301-496-5717
Lyme Arthritis/Lyme Disease....Staff NIAMS 301-496-8188
Lymphadenopathy Syndrome (LAD)....Staff NIAID 301-496-5717
Lymphedema....Staff NCI 301-496-5583
Lymphoblastic Lymphosarcoma....Staff NCI 301-496-5583
Lymphoma....Staff NCI 301-496-5583
Lymphosarcoma....Staff NCI 301-496-5583

M

MARC (Minority Access to Research Careers)....Staff NIGMS 301-496-7301
MBS resins....Misurelli, Denby USITC 202-205-3362
Macao....Matheson, JeNelle Cnty Commerce 202-482-2462
Macaroni and other alimentary pastes....Schneider, Greg USITC 202-205-3326
Macau....Staff Cnty State 202-647-6300
Machine Belts and Clothing....Barth, George CUSTOMS 212-466-5884
Machine Tool Accessories....McGibbon, Patrick COMMERCE 202-482-0314
Machine-readable Data, Labor Force Data, Empl/Unempl....Green, Gloria LABOR 202-606-6373
Machinery, Agricultural....Wholey, Patrick CUSTOMS 212-466-5668
Machinery, Excavating....Wholey, Patrick CUSTOMS 212-466-5668
Machinery, Heavy Industrial....Horowitz, Alan CUSTOMS 212-466-5494
Machinery, International Price Indexes....Costello, Brian LABOR 202-606-7107
Machinery, Intl. Price Ind., Prices & Liv. Cond....Costello, Brian LABOR 202-606-7107
Machinery, Office and Textile....Brodbeck, Arthur CUSTOMS 212-466-5490
Machinery, Prices and Living Conditions....Alterman, William LABOR 202-606-7108
Machinery, Printing....Rocks, Michael CUSTOMS 212-466-5669
Machines & machinery: agricultural or horticultural....Vacant USITC 202-205-3380
Machines and machinery: adding....Baker, Scott USITC 202-205-3386
Machines and machinery: addressing....Baker, Scott USITC 202-205-3386
Machines and machinery: agglomerating....Greene, William USITC 202-205-3405
Machines rolling (textile)....Greene, William USITC 202-205-3405
Machines, spraying: agricultural/horticultural....Vacant USITC 202-205-3380
Machines, spraying: other....Slingerland, David USITC 202-205-3400
Machines, textile: bleaching....Greene, William USITC 202-205-3405
Machines, textile: calendaring and rolling....Greene, William USITC 202-205-3405
Machines, textile: cleaning....Greene, William USITC 202-205-3405
Machines, textile: coating....Greene, William USITC 202-205-3405
Machines, textile: drying....Greene, William USITC 202-205-3405
Machines, textile: dyeing....Greene, William USITC 202-205-3405
Machines, textile: embroidery....Greene, William USITC 202-205-3405
Machines, textile: knitting....Greene, William USITC 202-205-3405
Machines, textile: lacemaking....Greene, William USITC 202-205-3405
Machines, textile: printing....Greene, William USITC 202-205-3405
Machines, textile: spinning....Greene, William USITC 202-205-3405
Machines, textile: tobacco....Jackson, Georgia USITC 202-205-3399
Machines, textile: tools, machine....Fravel, Dennis USITC 202-205-3404
Machines, textile: vending....Jackson, Georgia USITC 202-205-3399
Machines, textile: washing....Greene, William USITC 202-205-3405

Experts

Machines, textile: weaving....Greene, William USITC 202-205-3405
Machines, textile: weighing....Slingerland, David USITC 202-205-3400
Machines: agricultural or horticultural....McCarty, Timothy USITC 202-205-3398
Machines: bookbinding....Slingerland, David USITC 202-205-3400
Machines: calculators....Baker, Scott USITC 202-205-3386
Machines: cash registers....Baker, Scott USITC 202-205-3386
Machines: casting machines....Greene, William USITC 202-205-3405
Machines: checkwriting....Baker, Scott USITC 202-205-3386
Machines: cleaning (heat process equipment)....Slingerland, David USITC 202-205-3400
Machines: cleaning (textiles)....Greene, William USITC 202-205-3405
Machines: coating....Greene, William USITC 202-205-3405
Machines: converters....Greene, William USITC 202-205-3405
Machines: cordage....Greene, William USITC 202-205-3405
Machines: crushing....Greene, William USITC 202-205-3405
Machines: cutting....Greene, William USITC 202-205-3405
Machines: data processing....Bringe, Julie USITC 202-205-3390
Machines: dressing....Greene, William USITC 202-205-3405
Machines: drink preparing....Jackson, Georgia USITC 202-205-3399
Machines: dry cleaning....Jackson, Georgia USITC 202-205-3399
Machines: drying....Jackson, Georgia USITC 202-205-3399
Machines: dyeing....Greene, William USITC 202-205-3405
Machines: earth moving....Stonitsch, Laura USITC 202-205-3408
Machines: embroidery....Greene, William USITC 202-205-3405
Machines: fabric folding....Greene, William USITC 202-205-3405
Machines: farm....Vacant USITC 202-205-3380
Machines: flight simulators....Anderson, Peder USITC 202-205-3388
Machines: food preparing....Jackson, Georgia USITC 202-205-3399
Machines: horticultural....Vacant USITC 202-205-3380
Machines: mining....Stonitsch, Laura USITC 202-205-3408
Machines: office copying....Baker, Scott USITC 202-205-3386
Machines: packaging....Slingerland, David USITC 202-205-3400
Machines: paper....Slingerland, David USITC 202-205-3400
Machines: paperboard....Slingerland, David USITC 202-205-3400
Machines: postage franking....Baker, Scott USITC 202-205-3386
Machines: printing....Slingerland, David USITC 202-205-3400
Machines: pulp....Slingerland, David USITC 202-205-3400
Machines: reeling....Greene, William USITC 202-205-3405
Machines: rolling (metal)....Fravel, Dennis USITC 202-205-3404
Machines: rolling nes....Slingerland, David USITC 202-205-3400
Machines: screening....Greene, William USITC 202-205-3405
Machines: sealing....Slingerland, David USITC 202-205-3400
Machines: sewing....Greene, William USITC 202-205-3405
Machines: shoe....Vacant USITC 202-205-3380
Machines: sorting....Greene, William USITC 202-205-3405
Machines: stone processing....Greene, William USITC 202-205-3405
Machines: stoneworking....Vacant USITC 202-205-3380
Machines: Rolling (textile)....Greene, William USITC 202-205-3405
Macroglobulinemia and Myeloma....Staff NCI 301-496-5583
Macular Degeneration....Staff NEI 301-496-5248
Madagascar....Watkins, Chandra Cnty Commerce 202-482-4564
Madagascar, Republic of (Antananarivo)....Staff Cnty State 202-647-5684
Madagascar/Minerals....Dolley, Thomas Cnty Mines 202-501-9690
Magazines....Bratland, Rose Marie COMMERCE 202-482-0380
Magnesite: crude....White, Linda USITC 202-205-3427
Magnesite: dead burned....DeSapio, Vincent USITC 202-205-3435
Magnesium....Cammarota, David COMMERCE 202-482-0575
Magnesium....DeSapio, Vincent USITC 202-205-3435
Magnesium & Mg Comps....Kramer, Deborah A. MINES 202-501-9394
Magnesium compounds....Greenblatt, Jack USITC 202-205-3353
Magnetic Confinement....Willis, John NEIC 301-903-4095
Magnetic Fusion....Finn, Thomas G. NEIC 202-586-5444
Magnetic Resonance Imaging....Staff NINDS 301-496-5751
Magnetic devices....Cutchin, John USITC 202-205-3396
Mailing services....Xavier, Neil USITC 202-205-3450
Mainframes....Miles, Tim COMMERCE 202-482-2990
Maintenance services....Bedore, James USITC 202-205-3424
Major Industries, Technological Trends in....Riche, Richard LABOR 202-606-5626
Major Market Index with options....Fedinets, Robert P. CFT 312-353-9016
Major Projects....Thiebeault, Robert COMMERCE 202-482-5225
Malabsorptive Diseases....Staff NIDDK 301-496-3583
Malaria....Staff NIAID 301-496-5717
Malaria....Campbell, Carlos C. CDC 404-488-4046
Malawi....Holm-Olsen, Finn Cnty Commerce 202-482-4228
Malawi....Brill, Terry Peace Corps 202-606-3535
Malawi (Lilongwe)....Staff Cnty State 202-647-8433
Malawi/Minerals....King, Audie L. Cnty Mines 202-501-9690
Malaysia....Cung, Raphael Cnty Commerce 202-482-3875
Malaysia (Kuala Lumpur)....Staff Cnty State 202-647-3276
Malaysia/Minerals....Wu, John Cnty Mines 202-501-9697
Maldives....Simmons, John Cnty Commerce 202-482-2954
Maldives....Staff Cnty State 202-647-2351
Mali....Michelini, Philip Cnty Commerce 202-482-4388
Mali....Hanson, Julie Peace Corps 202-606-3004
Mali Republic (Bamako)....Staff Cnty State 202-647-3066
Mali/Minerals....van Oss, Hendrik Cnty Mines 202-501-9687
Malignancy....Staff NCI 301-496-5583
Malnutrition....Staff NIDDK 301-496-3583
Malnutrition....Staff NICHD 301-496-5133
Malocclusion....Staff NIDR 301-496-4261
Malpractice (Medical)....Mehuron, Charlotte HRSA 301-443-3376
Malta....McLaughlin, Robert Cnty Commerce 202-482-3748
Malta....DiMeo, Pam Peace Corps 202-606-3196
Malta....Schildwachter, Christy Peace Corps 202-606-3196
Malta (Valletta)....Staff Cnty State 202-647-2453
Malta/Minerals....Plachy, Josef Cnty Mines 202-501-9673
Malts....Pierre-Benoist, John USITC 202-205-3320
Mammals, Marine....Staff FWS 703-358-1718
Mammography....Staff NCI 301-496-5583
Management Consulting....Chittum, J. Marc COMMERCE 202-482-0345
Management consulting services....DeSapio, Vincent USITC 202-205-3435
Manganese....Presbury, Graylin COMMERCE 202-482-5158
Manganese....Jones, Thomas S. MINES 202-501-9428
Manganese....Vacant USITC 202-205-3419
Manganese compounds....Greenblatt, Jack USITC 202-205-3353
Mania....Staff NIMH 301-443-4515
Manifold Business Forms....Bratland, Rose Marie COMMERCE 202-482-0380
Manmade Fiber....Dulka, William COMMERCE 202-482-4058
Manmade fibers....Freund, Kimberlie USITC 202-205-3456
Manmade fibers....Shelton, Linda USITC 202-205-3457
Manmade fibers....Warlick, William USITC 202-205-3459
Manned Flight....Phelps, Patti NASA 407-867-4444
Mantles....Vacant USITC 202-205-3343
Manufacturers Operations Division....Staff EPA 202-233-9240
Manufacturers, Prod Data, Durables, Census/Annl Svy....Hansen, Kenneth CENSUS 301-763-7304
Manufacturers, Prod Data, Nondurables, Cur Indrl Rp....Flood, Thomas CENSUS 301-763-5911
Manufacturers, Special Topics, Concentration....Goldhirsch, Bruce CENSUS 301-763-1503
Manufacturers, Special Topics, Inventories....Runyan, Ruth CENSUS 301-763-2502
Manufacturers, Special Topics, Pollution Abatement....Champion, Elinor CENSUS 301-763-5616
Manufactures, Nondurables....Zampogna, Michael CENSUS 301-763-2510
Manufactures, Special Topics, Monthly Shipments....Runyan, Ruth CENSUS 301-763-2502
Manufactures, Special Topics, Orders....Runyan, Ruth CENSUS 301-763-2502
Manufactures, Special Topics, Research/Develop Capa....Champion, Elinor CENSUS 301-763-5616
Manufactures, Prod Data, Nondurables, Census/Annual Svy....Zampogna, Michael CENSUS 301-763-2510
Manufacturing, Durables (Census/Annual Survey)....Hansen, Kenneth CENSUS 301-763-7304
Maple Syrup Urine Disease....Staff NIDDK 301-496-3583
Maps, 1980 Census Map Orders....Baxter, Leila CENSUS 812-288-3192
Maps, 1990 Census....Staff CENSUS 301-763-4100
Maps, Cartographic Operations....Staff CENSUS 301-763-3973
Maps, Computer Mapping....Broome, Fred CENSUS 301-763-3973
Marble, breccia, and onyx....White, Linda USITC 202-205-3427
Marfan's Syndrome....Staff NIAMS 301-496-8188
Marfan's Syndrome....Staff NHLBI 301-496-4236
Margarine....Janis, William V. COMMERCE 202-482-2250
Marijuana (Effect on Glaucoma)....Staff NEI 301-496-5248
Marijuana (In Urine)....Staff NIDA 301-443-6245
Marine Insurance....Johnson, C. William COMMERCE 202-482-5012
Marine Mammal Research....Staff FWS 703-358-1710
Marine Mammals....Staff FWS 703-358-1718
Marine Recreational Equipment, Export Promo.....Beckham, Reginald COMMERCE 202-482-5478

Machines / Methyl Alcohol

Marine Services....Staff FCC 717-337-1212
Marine and Estuarine Protection....Staff EPA 202-260-7166
Marital Characteristics of Labor Force....Hayghe, Howard LABOR 202-606-6378
Marital Status....Saluter, Arlene CENSUS 301-763-7987
Maritime Services....Lahey, Kathleen USITC 202-205-3409
Maritime Shipping....Johnson, C. William COMMERCE 202-482-5012
Marker (Cancer)....Staff NCI 301-496-5583
Marketing....Morin, Bernard A. UVA 701-924-3477
Marketing Promo., Basic Ind.....Trafton, Donald R. COMMERCE 202-482-2493
Marriage Statistics....Heuser, Robert CDC 301-436-8954
Mars Exploration....Keegan, Sarah NASA 703-271-5591
Marsh Land....Staff FWS 703-358-2043
Marshall Islands (Majuro)....Staff Cnty State 202-647-0108
Martinique....Brooks, Michelle Cnty Commerce 202-482-2527
Martinique (Fort-de-France)....Staff Cnty State 202-647-2620
Martinique/Minerals....Torres, Ivette Cnty Mines 202-501-9680
Mass Layoff Statistics, Empl/Unempl. Stats.....Siegel, Lewis LABOR 202-606-6404
Mass Layoff Statistics, Employment/Unemployment....Siegel, Lewis LABOR 202-606-6404
Mass Layoffs, Employment Statistics....Siegel, Lewis LABOR 202-606-6404
Mass Spectrometers....Staff NCRR 301-496-5411
Mass media and society....Stepp, Jr., Carl UMD 301-405-2428
Mastectomy....Staff NCI 301-496-5583
Mastication....Staff NIDR 301-496-4261
Matches....Johnson, Larry USITC 202-205-3351
Materials, Advanced....Cammarota, David COMMERCE 202-482-0575
Maternal & Child Health....Mehuron, Charlotte. HRSA 301-443-3376
Maternal and Child Nutrition....Wong, Faye L. CDC 404-488-5099
Mattresses....Spalding, Josephine USITC 202-205-3498
Mauritania....Michelini, Philip Cnty Commerce 202-482-4388
Mauritania....Hanson, Julie Peace Corps 202-606-3004
Mauritania (Nouakchott)....Staff Cnty State 202-647-2865
Mauritania/Minerals....Michalski, Bernadette Cnty Mines 202-501-9699
Mauritius....Watkins, Chandra Cnty Commerce 202-482-4564
Mauritius (Port Louis)....Staff Cnty State 202-647-5684
Mauritius/Minerals....Antonides, Lloyd Cnty Mines 202-501-9686
McArdle's Disease....Staff NINDS 301-496-5751
Measles....Staff NIAID 301-496-5717
Measles Encephalitis....Staff NINDS 301-496-5751
Measles Immunization....Staff CDC 404-329-3534
Meat Products....Hodgen, Donald A. COMMERCE 202-482-3346
Meat and Dairy Products....Brady, Thomas CUSTOMS 212-466-5790
Meat, inedible....Ludwick, David USITC 202-205-3329
Mech. Power Transmission Eqmt. Nec.....Reise, Richard COMMERCE 202-482-3489
Mechanical and Aerospace Engineering....Jacobson, Ira D. UVA 701-924-6217
Meconium Aspiration Syndrome....Staff NICHD 301-496-5133
Media (Bacteriologic)....Staff OD/ORS 301-496-6017
Media Arts....O'Doherty, Brian NEA 202-682-5452
Medicaid....Hardy, Robert HCFA 202-690-6145
Medical Care for Aged....Staff NIA 301-496-1752
Medical Devices....Cruzan, Susan FDA 301-443-3285
Medical Equipment....Staff FCC 202-653-6288
Medical Facilities, Major Proj.....White, Barbara COMMERCE 202-482-4160
Medical Fraud/Quackery....Adams, Betsy FDA 301-443-4177
Medical Information System (MIS)....Staff CC 301-496-7946
Medical Instruments....Fuchs, Michael COMMERCE 202-482-0550
Medical Instruments....Preston, Jacques CUSTOMS 212-466-5488
Medical Instruments, Trade Promo.....Keen, George B. COMMERCE 202-482-2010
Medical Monitoring Program....Staff EPA 202-260-1640
Medical Photography....Staff NCRR/MAPB 301-496-5995
Medical School Grants....Mehuron, Charlotte HRSA 301-443-3376
Medical Scientist Training Program....Staff NIGMS 301-496-7301
Medical Staff Fellowship Training Program....Staff CC 301-496-2427
Medical Statistics....Flegal, Katherine CDC 301-436-7075
Medical Subject Headings.....Schuyler, Peri L. NLM 301-496-1495
Medical Waste....Staff EPA 202-260-8551
Medical apparatus....Johnson, Christopher USITC 202-205-3488
Medically Underserved Areas....Mehuron, Charlotte HRSA 301-443-3376
Medicare....Hardy, Robert HCFA 202-690-6145
Medicine for the Public (Lect., Videos, Booklets)....Staff CC 301-496-2563
Medicine, National Library of....Baldwin, Elaine ADAMHA 301-443-4536
Mediterranean Fever....Staff NIAID 301-496-5717
Mediterranean Fever....Staff NIAMS 301-496-8188
Mediterranean/trade matters....Marcich, Christopher US Trade Rep 202-395-4620
Medlars/Medline....Staff NLM 301-496-6193
Meige's Syndrome (Facial Dystonia)....Staff NINDS 301-496-5751
Meige's Syndrome (Facial Dystonia)....Staff NIDCD 301-496-7243
Melamine....Michels, David USITC 202-205-3352
Melamine resins....Misurelli, Denby USITC 202-205-3362
Melanoma....Staff NCI 301-496-5583
Melanoma....Staff NEI 301-496-5248
Melkerson's Syndrome....Staff NINDS 301-496-5751
Memory....Staff NINDS 301-496-5751
Memory....Staff NIMH 301-443-4515
Memory Loss....Staff NIA 301-496-1752
Meniere's Disease....Staff NINDS 301-496-5751
Meniere's Disease....Staff NIDCD 301-496-7243
Meningitis....Staff NIAID 301-496-5717
Meningitis....Staff NINDS 301-496-5751
Meningitis....Wenger, Jay d. CDC 404-639-2215
Meningocele....Staff NINDS 301-496-5751
Meningocele....Staff NICHD 301-496-5133
Meningococcal Meningitis....Staff NIAID 301-496-5717
Menkes' Disease....Staff NINDS 301-496-5751
Menopause....Staff NIA 301-496-1752
Menstruation....Staff NICHD 301-496-5133
Mental Health and Aging....Staff NIMH 301-443-4515
Mental Health and Aging....Staff NIA 301-496-1752
Mental Retardation....Staff NICHD 301-496-5133
Mental Retardation (PCMR)....Long, Susan ACF 202-401-9215
Menthol....Land, Eric USITC 202-205-3349
Mercury....Reese, Jr., Robert MINES 202-501-9413
Mercury....Conant, Kenneth USITC 202-205-3346
Mercury Poisoning....Staff NINDS 301-496-5751
Mercury compounds....Greenblatt, Jack USITC 202-205-3353
Mercury in Fish....Staff EPA 301-755-0100
Mercury, Fluorspar....Manion, James J. COMMERCE 202-482-5157
Mergers and Acquisitions....Staff FCC 202-632-4887
Metabolic (Nervous System)....Staff NINDS 301-496-5751
Metabolic Disorders....Staff NIDDK 301-496-3583
Metabolism (Inborn Errors)....Staff NICHD 301-496-5133
Metabolism (Inborn Errors)....Staff NINDS 301-496-5751
Metachromatic Leukodystrophy....Staff NINDS 301-496-5751
Metal Articles....Schulberg, Martin CUSTOMS 212-466-5487
Metal Building Products....Williams, Franklin COMMERCE 202-482-0132
Metal Cookware....Harris, John COMMERCE 202-482-0348
Metal Cutting Machine Tools....Vacant COMMERCE
Metal Cutting Tools Fr Mach Tools....Vacant COMMERCE
Metal Foils....Fitzgerald, John CUSTOMS 212-466-5492
Metal Forming Machine Tools....Vacant COMMERCE
Metal Metabolism....Staff NIDDK 301-496-3583
Metal Powders....Duggan, Brian COMMERCE 202-482-0575
Metal rolling mills....Fravel, Dennis USITC 202-205-3404
Metal working machines....Fravel, Dennis USITC 202-205-3404
Metallurgy Research....Thomas, Iran NEIC 301-903-3426
Metals....Fitzgerald, John CUSTOMS 212-466-5492
Metals, Assistant Branch Chief....Butterman, W. MINES 202-501-9425
Metals, Assistant Branch Chief....Sibley, S.F. MINES 202-501-9344
Metals, Chief, Branch of....Makar, Harry MINES 202-501-9432
Metals, Prices & Living Conditions....Kazanowski, Edward LABOR 202-606-7735
Metals, Secondary....Manion, James J. COMMERCE 202-482-5157
Metalworking....Mearman, John COMMERCE 202-482-0315
Metalworking Equipment Nec.....McGibbon, Patrick COMMERCE 202-482-0314
Metastases....Staff NCI 301-496-3583
Metastic Tumors (Central Nervous System)....Staff NINDS 301-496-5751
Meteorological Research....Loughlin, John NASA 301-286-5565
Meteorological instruments....Shetty, Sundar USITC 202-205-3486
Metered Service--Message Units....Staff FCC 202-632-7553
Methacrylates....Michels, David USITC 202-205-3352
Methane....Moorer, Richard NEIC 202-586-8072
Methane....Land, Eric USITC 202-205-3349
Methanol....DiMaria, Joseph CUSTOMS 212-466-4769
Methodology, Prices and Living Conditions....Rosenberg, Elliott LABOR 202-606-7728
Methyl alcohol (methanol)....Michels, David USITC 202-205-3352

Experts

Methyl ethyl ketone....Michels, David USITC 202-205-3352
Methyl oleate....Johnson, Larry USITC 202-205-3351
Methylene Chloride....Giles, Ken CPSC 301-504-0580
Metropolitan Areas....Forstall, Richard/Fitzsimmons, James CENSUS 301-763-5158
Metropolitan Areas (MSA's), Population....Forstall, Richard CENSUS 301-763-5158
Mexico....Bannister, Rebeccaw Lowry/Ingrid Mohn Cnty Commerce 202-482-0300
Mexico (Mexico, D.F.)....Staff Cnty State 202-647-9894
Mexico/Minerals....Torres, Ivette Cnty Mines 202-501-9680
Mexico/trade matters....Roh, Charles US Trade Rep 202-395-5663
Mica....Presbury, Graylin COMMERCE 202-482-5158
Mica....Davis, Lawrence L. MINES 202-501-9386
Mica....White, Linda USITC 202-205-3427
Miscellaneous Reimbursable....Godoy, Francisco FTC 202-326-3757
Microbiological Monitoring....Staff OD/ORS 301-496-2960
Microbiology....Garges, Susan FAES 301-496-2095
Microcephaly....Staff NINDS 301-496-5751
Microcephaly....Staff NICHD 301-496-5133
Microorganisms Control....Staff OD/ORS 301-496-2960
Microphones....Sherman, Thomas USITC 202-205-3389
Microscopes....Johnson, Christopher USITC 202-205-3488
Microtropia....Staff NEI 301-496-5248
Microvascular Surgery....Staff NINDS 301-496-5751
Microwave Auxiliary--Common Carrier....Staff FCC 202-634-1706
Microwave Auxiliary--Mass Media....Staff FCC 202-634-6307
Microwave Cable Television Relay Service....Staff FCC 202-254-3420
Microwave Closed Loop....Staff FCC 202-634-1706
Microwave Common Carrier Licenses....Staff FCC 202-634-1706
Microwave Licenses....Staff FCC 202-634-1706
Microwave Monitoring Stations....Staff FCC 202-632-7593
Microwave Multipoint Distribution....Staff FCC 202-634-1706
Microwave Ovens....Staff FCC 202-653-6288
Microwave Radio Relay....Staff FCC 202-634-1706
Microwave Television--Pickup....Staff FCC 202-634-1706
Microwave, Protection from Interference....Staff FCC 202-632-7593
Middle Ear Infections....Staff NINDS 301-496-5751
Middle Ear Infections....Staff NIDCD 301-496-7243
Migraine (Headache)....Staff NINDS 301-496-5751
Migrant Health....Mehuron, Charlotte HRSA 301-44303376
Migration, Current Statistics....DeAre, Diana CENSUS 301-763-3850
Migratory Bird Research....Staff FWS 703-358-1710
Mild Retardation Prevention.... CDC 404-488-7370
Military Lands, Wildlife....Staff FWS 703-358-1718
Military Stations....Staff FCC 202-653-8141
Milk....Warren, J Fred USITC 202-205-3311
Milk Intolerance....Staff NIDDK 301-496-3583
Millinery ornaments....Spalding, Josephine USITC 202-205-3498
Millwork....Wise, Barbara COMMERCE 202-482-0375
Minamata Disease (Mercury Poisoning)....Staff NINDS 301-496-5751
Mineral Based Cons. Materials, Asphalt....Pitcher, Charles B. COMMERCE 202-482-0132
Mineral Based Cons. Mats., Gypsum....Pitcher, Charles B. COMMERCE 202-482-0132
Mineral Based Cons. Mats., Stone....Pitcher, Charles B. COMMERCE 202-482-0132
Mineral Based Const. Mats., Clay....Pitcher, Charles B. COMMERCE 202-482-0132
Mineral Based Const. Mats., Concrete....Pitcher, Charles B. COMMERCE 202-482-0132
Mineral Industries....McNamee, John CENSUS 301-763-5938
Mineral Metabolism....Staff NIDDK 301-496-3583
Mineral oil....Foreso, Cynthia USITC 202-205-3348
Mineral salts....Randall, Rob USITC 202-205-3366
Mineral substances, miscellaneous....Lundy, David USITC 202-205-3439
Mineral wool....White, Linda USITC 202-205-3427
Minerals in the World Economy/Minerals....Kimbell, Charles Cnty Mines 202-501-9659
Minerals, Non-Metallic....Bunin, Jacob CUSTOMS 212-566-5796
Minimal Brain Dysfunction....Staff NINDS 301-496-5751
Minimal Brain Dysfunction....Staff NIMH 301-443-4515
Minimum Wage Data, Empl/Unempl. Stats.....Haugen, Steve LABOR 202-606-6378
Minimum Wage Data, Employment/Unemployment....Haugen, Steve LABOR 202-606-6378
Mining....Staff FCC 717-337-1212
Mining....Stonitsch, Laura USITC 202-205-3408
Mining Machinery....McDonald, Edward COMMERCE 202-482-0680
Mining Machinery, Trade Promo....Zanetakos, George COMMERCE 202-482-0552
Mining machines....Stonitsch, Laura USITC 202-205-3408
Mink....Kruchten, Tom Agri 202-690-4870
Minorities, Empl./ Unempl. Stats.....Cattan, Peter LABOR 202-606-6378
Minority Access to Research Careers (MARC)....Staff NIGMS 301-496-7301
Minority Aging....Staff NIA 301-496-1752
Minority Biomedical Research Support (MBRS)....Staff NIGMS 301-496-7301
Minority Health....Crawford, Blake ASH 301-443-5224
Minority High School Student Research Apprentices....Staff NCRR 301-496-6743
Mirror Fusion Systems....Brewer, Robert NEIC 202-586-2828
Misc. Textile and Related Articles....Falcone, Anthony CUSTOMS 212-466-5886
Miscellaneous animal products....Ludwick, David USITC 202-205-3329
Miscellaneous articles of pulp and paper....Rhodes, Richard USITC 202-205-3322
Miscellaneous benzenoid intermediates....Matusik, Ed USITC 202-205-3356
Miscellaneous fish products....Corey, Roger USITC 202-205-3327
Miscellaneous products....Spalding, Josephine USITC 202-205-3498
Miscellaneous vegetable products....Pierre-Benoist, John USITC 202-205-3320
Miscellaneous wood products....Ruggles, Fred USITC 202-205-3325
Mitochondrial Myopathies....Staff NINDS 301-496-5751
Mitral Valve....Staff NHLBI 301-496-4236
Mixed Connective Tissue Disease....Staff NIAMS 301-496-8188
Mixtures (artificial) of fatty substances....Randall, Rob USITC 202-205-3366
Mixtures of inorganic compounds....Greenblatt, Jack USITC 202-205-3353
Mixtures of organic compounds....Michels, David USITC 202-205-3352
Mobile Homes....Cosslett, Patrick COMMERCE 202-482-0132
Mobile Services Licenses....Staff FCC 202-632-6400
Mobile Telephone Services....Staff FCC 202-653-5560
Mobilization Planning....Staff FCC 202-632-7025
Moccasins....Shildneck, Ann USITC 202-205-3499
Model Airplanes....Staff FCC 717-337-1212
Model Rocket Motors....Tyrrell, Elaine CPSC 301-504-0580
Models....Luther, Dennis USITC 202-205-3497
Models (Mathematical)....Staff NCRS/BEIB 301-496-5771
Modular High Temperature Reactors....Rosen, Sol NEIC 301-903-3218
Molasses....Williams, Joan USITC 202-205-3313
Molders' boxes, forms, and patterns....Greene, William USITC 202-205-3405
Molding....Rocks, Michael CUSTOMS 212-466-5669
Moldings, wooden....Ruggles, Fred USITC 202-205-3325
Molecular Biology....Staff NIGMS 301-496-7301
Molecular Biology....Davies, David R. FAES 301-496-4295
Molecular Genetics....Staff NIGMS 301-496-7301
Molecular Hematology....Anderson, W. French FAES 301-496-5844
Molecular Immunogenetics and Vaccine Research....Berzofsky, Jay A. FAES 301-496-6874
Molecular Pharmacology....Kohn, Kurt W. FAES 301-496-1924
Molybdenum....Cammarota, David COMMERCE 202-482-0575
Molybdenum....Blossom, John MINES 202-501-9435
Molybdenum....DeSapio, Vincent USITC 202-205-3435
Molybdenum compounds....Greenblatt, Jack USITC 202-205-3353
Monaco....Staff Cnty State 202-647-2633
Mongolia....Matheson, Jenell Cnty Commerce 202-482-2462
Mongolia....Swanson, Alan Peace Corps 202-606-3040
Mongolia....Huston, Christine Peace Corps 202-606-3040
Mongolia....Staff Cnty State 202-647-6300
Mongolia/Minerals....Wu, John Cnty Mines 202-501-9697
Mongolism (Down Syndrome)....Staff NICHD 301-496-5133
Monitoring Stations, Protection from Interference....Staff FCC 202-632-7593
Monitoring Telephone Service....Staff FCC 202-632-5550
Monofilaments, manmade....Sweet, Mary Elizabeth USITC 202-205-3455
Mononucleosis....Staff NIAID 301-496-5717
Monorails....Wiening, Mary COMMERCE 202-482-4708
Monserrat/Minerals....Torres, Ivette Cnty Mines 202-501-9680
Monosodium glutamate....Land, Eric USITC 202-205-3349
Monthly Labor Review,Exec. Ed., Public & Spec Stud....Fisher, Robert W. LABOR 202-606-5903
Monthly Product Announcement....Baker, Bernice L. CENSUS 301-763-1584
Montserrat....Brooks, Michelle Cnty Commerce 202-482-2527
Moon Exploration....Keegan, Sarah NASA 703-271-5591
Morocco....Clement, Claude/Cerone, Chris Cnty Commerce 202-482-2527

Metropolitan Areas / National Crime Survey

Morocco....DiMeo, Pam Peace Corps 202-606-3196
Morocco....Schildwachter, Christy Peace Corps 202-606-3196
Morocco (Rabat)....Staff Cnty State 202-647-4675
Morocco/Minerals....Dolley, Thomas Cnty Mines 202-501-9690
Mortality Rates (Cancer)....Staff NCI 301-496-5583
Mortality Statistics....Rosenbery, Harry CDC 301-436-8884
Mortgage Backed Securities....Lang, Dawn M. CFT 312-353-9018
Motion Pictures....Seigmund, John COMMERCE 202-482-4781
Motion pictures....R-Archila, Laura USITC 202-205-3411
Motor Carrier....Staff FCC 717-337-1212
Motor Fuels, Only, Avg. Ret. Prices and Indexes....Chelena, Joseph LABOR 202-606-6982
Motor Neuron Disease....Staff NINDS 301-496-5751
Motor Vehicles....Warner, Albert T. COMMERCE 202-482-0669
Motor Vehicles Auto Ind. Affairs....Gaines, Robin COMMERCE 202-482-0669
Motor oil....Foreso, Cynthia USITC 202-205-3348
Motor transportation services....Lahey, Kathleen USITC 202-205-3409
Motor vehicles: armored vehicles....Kolberg, Mary USITC 202-205-3401
Motor vehicles: buses....Hagey, Michael USITC 202-205-3392
Motor vehicles: fork-lift/self-propelled trucks....Hagey, Michael USITC 202-205-3392
Motor vehicles: passenger autos....Hagey, Michael USITC 202-205-3392
Motor vehicles: snowmobiles....Kolberg, Mary USITC 202-205-3401
Motor vehicles: tractors, extruck tractors....Vacant USITC 202-205-3380
Motor vehicles: trucks (includes truck tractors)....Hagey, Michael USITC 202-205-3392
Motorcycles....Vanderwolf, John COMMERCE 202-482-0348
Motorcycles....Desoucey, Robert CUSTOMS 212-466-5667
Motorcycles....Murphy, Mary USITC 202-205-3401
Motors....Smyth, James CUSTOMS 212-466-2084
Motors, Elect....Whitley, Richard A. COMMERCE 202-482-0682
Motors: electric....Cutchin, John USITC 202-205-3396
Motors: non-electric....Andersen, Peder USITC 202-205-3388
Moya-Moya Disease....Staff NINDS 301-496-5751
Mozambique....Holm-Olsen, Finn Cnty Commerce 202-482-5148
Mozambique (Maputo)....Staff Cnty State 202-647-8252
Mozambique/Minerals....van Oss, Hendrik Cnty Mines 202-501-9687
Mucopolysaccharidosis....Staff NIAMS 301-496-8188
Mufflers (apparel)....Jones, Jackie USITC 202-205-3466
Mufflers (apparel)....Hamey, Amy USITC 202-205-3465
Multi-Infarct Dementia....Staff NIA 301-496-1752
Multi-Infarct Dementia....Staff NINDS 301-496-5751
Multifactor Productivity, Labor Composition, Hrs.....Rosenblum, Larry LABOR 202-606-5606
Multifamily Housing....Staff HUD 202-708-2495
Multilateral trade negotiations....Lavoral, Warren US Trade Rep 202-395-3324
Multiple Basal Cell Carcinoma....Staff NCI 301-496-5583
Multiple Myeloma....Staff NCI 301-496-5583
Multiple Risk Factor Intervention Trial....Staff NHLBI 301-496-4236
Multiple Sclerosis....Staff NINDS 301-496-5751
Multiple Sclerosis....Staff NIDCD 301-496-7243
Multiple Warts....Staff NCI 301-496-5583
Multipoint Distribution Service....Staff FCC 202-634-1706
Mumps....Staff NIAID 301-496-5717
Muni Bonds with options....SIA Manasses CFT 312-35-39027
Municipal Solid Waste Management....Staff EPA 202-260-9872
Municipal Solid Waste Management - Combustion....Staff EPA 202-260-4745
Municipal Waste....Gross, Thomas J. NEIC 202-586-9497
Murmurs (Heart)....Staff NHLBI 301-496-4236
Muscle Disease....Staff NINDS 301-496-5751
Muscle Disease....Staff NIAMS 301-496-8188
Muscle Wasting....Staff NINDS 301-496-5751
Muscle Wasting....Staff NIAMS 301-496-8188
Muscular Dystrophy....Staff NINDS 301-496-5751
Muscular Fatigue....Staff NINDS 301-496-5751
Musculoskeletal Fitness....Staff NIAMS 301-496-8188
Museums and Historic Orgns. Projects....Staff NEH 202-606-8284
Mushrooms....McCarty, Timothy USITC 202-205-3324
Music....Siegmund, John COMMERCE 202-482-4781
Music....Handy, D. Antoinette NEA 202-682-5445
Musical Instruments....Harris, John COMMERCE 202-482-0348
Musical Instruments....Kalkines, George CUSTOMS 212-466-5794
Musical instruments, accessories....Witherspoon, Ricardo USITC 202-205-3489
Musical instruments, parts....Witherspoon, Ricardo USITC 202-205-3489

Musk, grained or in pods....Land, Eric USITC 202-205-3349
Mutual Funds....Muir, S. Cassin COMMERCE 202-482-0343
Myasthenia Gravis....Staff NINDS 301-496-5751
Mycoplasma....Staff NIAID 301-496-5717
Mycosis Fungoides....Staff NCI 301-496-5583
Mycotoxins....Staff NIEHS 919-541-3345
Myelodysplastic Syndromes....Staff NHLBI 301-496-4236
Myelofibrosis....Staff NHLBI 301-496-4236
Myelofibrosis....Staff NCI 301-496-5583
Myeloma....Staff NCI 301-496-5583
Myocardial Infarction....Staff NHLBI 301-496-4236
Myocardium....Staff NHLBI 301-496-4236
Myoclonus....Staff NINDS 301-496-5751
Myofascial Pain Syndrome....Staff NIAMS 301-496-8188
Myopia....Staff NEI 301-496-5248
Myositis....Staff NIAMS 301-496-8188
Myositis....Staff NINDS 301-496-5751
Myositis Ossificans....Staff NIAMS 301-496-8188
Myotonia Atrophica....Staff NINDS 301-496-5751
Myotonia Atrophica....Staff NIAMS 301-496-8188
Myotonia Congenita....Staff NINDS 301-496-5751
Myotonia Congenita....Staff NIAMS 301-496-8188
Myotonia Congenita....Staff NICHD 301-496-5133
Myotonia Dystrophica....Staff NINDS 301-496-5751
Myths on Aging....Staff NIA 301-496-1752

N

NASA Engineering....Peto, Mary Ann NASA 216-433-2902
NASA Industrial Applications Centers....Selby, Barbar NASA 703-557-5609
NASA Mission Safety....Brown, Dwayne C. NASA 202-453-8956
NASA Science and Engineering Labs....Sahli, Jim NASA 205-544-6528
NASA Scientific Balloon Program....Koehler, Keith NASA 804-824-1579
NASA Sounding Rocket Program....Koehler, Keigh NASA 804-824-1579
NASA Tethered Satellite....Berg, Jerry NASA 205-544-6540
NATO (North Atlantic Treaty Organization)....Staff Cnty State 202-647-1622
Nails....Yost, Charles USITC 202-205-3442
Namibia....Holm-Olsen, Finn Cnty Commerce 202-482-4228
Namibia....Grimmett, Michael Peace Corps 202-606-3246
Namibia....Woodfork, Jacqueline Peace Corps 202-606-3247
Namibia....Staff Cnty State 202-647-8252
Namibia/Minerals....Heydari, Michael Cnty Mines 202-501-9688
Naphtha....Foreso, Cynthia USITC 202-205-3348
Naphthalene (refined)....Matusik, Ed USITC 202-205-3356
Napkins, cloth....Sweet, Mary Elizabeth USITC 202-205-3455
Narcolepsy....Staff NINDS 301-496-5751
Narrow fabrics....Shelton, Linda USITC 202-205-3457
Nat'l, Input-Output Tables, Computer Tapes, Disks & Print....Carter, Esther M. ECONOMIC 202-523-0792
Nat'l, Fed. Govt Defense Purchases of Goods & Services....Galbraith, Karl D. ECONOMIC 202-523-3472
Nat'l, State & Local Govt, Purchases of Goods & Services.....Peters, Donald L. ECONOMIC 202-523-0726
Nat'l, Fed. Govt Nondefense Purchases-Goods & Services....Mangan, Robert ECONOMIC 202-523-5017
Nat'l, Input-Output Tables, Goods-Producing Industry....Bonds, Belinda ECONOMIC 202-523-0843
Nat'l, Input-Output Tables, Services Producing Industry....Horowitz, Karen ECONOMIC 202-523-3505
Natality Statistics....Heuser, Robert CDC 301-436-8954
Natality, Marriage and Divorce Statistics....Heuser, Robert CDC 301-436-8954
National Air Data Branch....Staff EPA 919-541-5583
National Air Toxic Information Clearinghouse....Staff EPA 919-541-0850
National Cancer Program....Staff NCI 301-496-5583
National Cholesterol Education Program....Staff NHLBI 301-496-0554
National Crime Survey....DeBarry, Marshall Justice Stat 202-307-0775
National Crime Survey....Rand, Michael Justice Stat 202-616-3494
National Crime Survey....Taylor, Bruce Justice Stat 202-616-3498
National Crime Survey - Data Tapes....DeBerry, Marshall Justice Stat 202-307-0775
National Crime Survey - Data Tapes....Rand, Michael Justice Stat 202-616-3494
National Crime Survey - Data Tapes....Taylor, Bruce Justice Stat 202-616-3498
National Crime Survey - General....Klaus, Patsy Justice Stat 202-307-0776

Experts

National Crime Survey - General....Rand, Michael Justice Stat 202-616-3494
National Crime Survey - General....Taylor, Bruce Justice Stat 202-616-3498
National Crime Survey - General....DeBerry, Marshall Justice Stat 202-307-0775
National Crime Survey - General....Dodge, Richard Justice Stat 202-616-3485
National Crime Survey - General....Harlow, Caroline Justice Stat 202-307-0757
National Crime Survey - Redesign....Taylor, Bruce Justice Stat 202-616-3498
National Crime Survey - Redesign....Dodge, Richard Justice Stat 202-616-3485
National Crime Survey - Supplements....Kindermann, Charles Justice Stat 202-616-3489
National Environmental Policy Act....Staff FCC 202-632-6990
National Environmental Policy Act (NEPA)....Borgstrom, Carol NEIC 202-586-4600
National Establishment Survey, Empl/Unempl....Seifert, Mary Lee LABOR 202-606-6552
National Establishment Survey, Indust. Classif. E/Un....Getz, Patricia LABOR 202-606-6521
National Fish Hatchery System....Staff FWS 703-358-1715
National Health Service Corps....Mehuron, Charlotte HRSA 201-443-3376
National High Blood Pressure Education Program....Staff NHLBI 301-496-0554
National Hunting and Fishing Survey....Staff FWS 703-358-2156
National Income and Wealth, Auto Output....McCully, Clint ECONOMIC 202-523-0819
National Income and Wealth, Chief....Donahoe, Gerald F. ECONOMIC 202-523-0669
National Pesticides Survey....Staff EPA 202-260-7176
National Pesticides Telecommunications Network....Staff EPA 800-858-7378
National Pollutant Discharge Elimination System....Staff EPA 703-821-4660
National Projections, States & Metro. Areas....Johnson, Kenneth P. ECONOMIC 202-523-0971
National Radon Hotline....Staff EPA 800-767-7236
National Services Information Centers....Johnson, Sam CENSUS 301-763-1384
National, Business Cycle Indicators....Green, George R. ECONOMIC 202-523-0800
National, Capital Consumption....John C. Musgrave ECONOMIC 202-523-0837
National, Capital Expenditures....Cartwright, David W. ECONOMIC 202-523-0791
National, Capital Stock....Musgrave, John C. NATIONAL 101-523-0837
National, Composite Indexes....Robinson, Charles S. ECONOMIC 202-523-0800
National, Computer Price Index....Won, Gregory U. ECONOMIC 202-523-5421
National, Construction....Robinson, Brooks B. ECONOMIC 202-523-0592
National, Corporate Profits and Taxes....Petrick, Kenneth A. ECONOMIC 202-523-0888
National, Cyclically-Adjusted Budget....Michael Well ECONOMIC 202-523-3470
National, Depreciation....Musgrave, John W. ECONOMIC 202-523-0837
National, Disposable Personal Income....Cybert, Pauline M. ECONOMIC 202-523-0832
National, Dividends....Petrick, Kenneth A. ECONOMIC 202-523-0888
National, Employee Benefit Plans....Sensenig, Arthur L. ECONOMIC 202-523-0809
National, Employee Compensation....Sensenig, Arthur L. ECONOMIC 202-523-0809
National, Environmental Studies....Rugledge, Gary L. ECONOMIC 202-523-0687
National, Farm Output, Product, and Income....Smith, George ECONOMIC 202-523-0821
National, Federal Govt., Contributions & Transfers....Tsehaye, Benyam ECONOMIC 202-523-0885
National, Federal Govt., Receipts and Expenditures....Dobbs, David T. ECONOMIC 202-523-0744
National, GNP by Industry....Mohr, Michael W. ECONOMIC 202-523-0795
National, GNP, Computer Tapes, Disks and Printouts....Blue, Eunice V. ECONOMIC 202-523-0804
National, GNP, Current Estimates....Mannering, Virginia H. ECONOMIC 202-523-0824
National, Gross Private Domestic Investment....Cartwright, David W. ECONOMIC 202-523-0791
National, Input-Output Annual Tables....Planting, Mark A. ECONOMIC 202-523-0867
National, Input-Output, Benchmark Tables....Maley, Leo C. ECONOMIC 202-523-0683
National, Interest Income and Payments....Weadock, Teresa L. ECONOMIC 202-523-0833
National, Inventories....Baldwin, Steven ECONOMIC 202-523-0784
National, Inventory/Sales Ratios....Stiller, Jean M. ECONOMIC 202-523-6585
National, Methodology....Beckman, Barry A. ECONOMIC 202-523-0800
National, National Income....Seskin, Eugene P. ECONOMIC 202-523-0848
National, Net Exports....Ehemann, Christian ECONOMIC 202-523-0699
National, Output Measures....Ehemann, Christian ECONOMIC 202-523-0669
National, Personal Consumpt. Expenditures, Prices....McCully, Clint ECONOMIC 202-523-0819
National, Personal Consumption Expend, Other Goods....Key, Greg ECONOMIC 202-523-0778
National, Personal Consumption Expend., Services....McCully, Clint ECONOMIC 202-523-0819
National, Personal Consumption Expenditures....McCully, Cling ECONOMIC 202-523-0819
National, Personal Consumption Expenditures, Autos....Johnson, Everette P. ECONOMIC 202-523-0807
National, Personal Income....Cypert, Pauline M. ECONOMIC 202-523-0832
National, Plant and Equipment Expenditures....Crawford, Jeffrey W. ECONOMIC 202-523-0782
National, Pollution Abatement & Control Spending....Rutledge, Gary L. ECONOMIC 202-523-0687
National, Price Measures (Fixed-Weighted)....Herman, Shelby A. ECONOMIC 202-523-0828
National, Producers' Durable Equipment....Crawford, Jeffrey W. ECONOMIC 202-523-0782
National, Proprietors' Income, Nonfarm....Abney, Willie J. ECONOMIC 202-523-0811
National, Rental Income....Smith, George ECONOMIC 202-523-0821
National, Residential Construction....Robinson, Brooks, B. ECONOMIC 202-523-0592
National, Savings....Donahoe, Gerald F. ECONOMIC 202-523-0669
National, State & Local Govt., Receipts & Expend.....Sullivan, David F. ECONOMIC 202-523-0725
National, Statistical Series....Young, Mary D. ECONOMIC 202-523-0500
National, Structures....Robinson, Brooks B. ECONOMIC 202-523-0592
National, UN and OCED System of National Accounts....Honsa, Jeanette M. ECONOMIC 202-523-0839
National, Wages and Salaries....Sensenig, Arthur L. ECONOMIC 202-523-0809
National, Wealth Estimates....Musgrave, John C. ECONOMIC 202-523-0837
Natural Gas....Gillett, Tom COMMERCE 202-482-1466
Natural Gas....Tomaszewski, Clifford NEIC 202-586-9482
Natural Gas....Altman, Paula NEIC 202-586-8800
Natural Gas....Cogan, Jonathan NEIC 202-586-8800
Natural gas....Land, Eric USITC 202-205-3349
Natural gas liquids (NGL)....Land, Eric USITC 202-205-3349
Natural pearls....Witherspoon, Ricardo USITC 202-205-3489
Natural rubber....Misurelli, Denby USITC 202-205-3362
Natural, Synthetic Rubber....Hurt, William COMMERCE 202-482-0128
Nauru....Staff Cnty State 202-647-3546
Nauru/Minerals....Lyday, Travis Cnty Mines 202-501-9695
Naval Reactor Propulsion....Staff NEIC 301-903-3465
Navigation, Air or Water....Staff FCC 202-632-7175
Navigational instruments....Shetty, Sundar USITC 202-205-3486
Navy special fuel oil....Foreso, Cynthia USITC 202-205-3348
Nearsightedness....Staff NEI 301-496-5248
Neckties....Linkins, Linda USITC 202-205-3469
Nemaline Myopathy (Floppy Baby)....Staff NINDS 301-496-5751
Neonatal Adaptation....Staff NICHD 301-496-5133
Neonatal Asphyxia....Staff NINDS 301-496-5751
Neoplasms (Trophoblastic)....Staff NCI 301-496-5583
Nepal....Gilman, Timothy Cnty Commerce 202-482-2954
Nepal....Ordonez, Miguel Peace Corps 202-606-3118
Nepal (Kathmandu)....Staff Cnty State 202-647-1450
Nepal/Minerals....Vacant Cnty Mines 202-501-9694
Nepheline Syenite....Potter, Michael J. MINES 202-501-9387
Nephritis....Staff NIDDK 301-496-3583
Nephrocalcinosis....Staff NIDDK 301-496-3583
Nephrolithiasis....Staff NIDDK 301-496-3583
Nephrotic Syndrome....Staff NIDDK 301-496-3583
Nerve Damage....Staff NINDS 301-496-5751
Netherlands....Bensimon, Simon Cnty Commerce 202-482-5401

National Environment Policy Act / Nuts

Netherlands (The Hague)....Staff Cnty State 202-647-6664
Netherlands Antilles....Brooks, Michelle Cnty Commerce 202-482-2527
Netherlands Antilles (Curacao)....Staff Cnty State 202-647-2620
Netherlands Antilles/Minerals....Torres, Ivette Cnty Mines 202-501-9680
Netherlands/Minerals....Rabchevsky, George Cnty Mines 202-501-9672
Nettings: fish....Cook, Lee USITC 202-205-3471
Nettings: other....Sweet, Mary Elizabeth USITC 202-205-3455
Neural Stimulation....Staff NINDS 301-496-5751
Neural Stimulation....Staff NIDCD 301-496-7243
Neural Tube Defects....Staff NINDS 301-496-5751
Neural Tube Defects....Staff NICHD 301-496-5133
Neuralgia....Staff NINDS 301-496-5751
Neuritis (Peripheral Neuropathy)....Staff NINDS 301-496-5751
Neuro-Ophthalmology....Staff NEI 301-496-5248
Neuroaxonal Dystrophy....Staff NINDS 301-496-5751
Neuroblastoma....Staff NEI 301-496-5248
Neuroendocrinology....Bondy, Caroline FAES 301-496-6664
Neurofibromatosis (von Recklinghausen's)....Staff NINDS 301-496-5751
Neurofibromatosis (von Recklinghausen's)....Staff NIDCD 301-496-7243
Neurogenic Arthropathy....Staff NINDS 301-496-5751
Neurogenic Disability (Mouth and Pharynx)....Staff NIDR 301-496-4261
Neuroimaging....Alger, Jeffry R. FAES 301-496-6801
Neurologic Disease....Staff NINDS 301-496-5751
Neurological Disorders & Stroke, Nat'l Inst. of....Emr, Marian NIH 301-496-5924
Neurology....Grafman, Jordan FAES 301-496-0220
Neuromuscular Disease....Staff NINDS 301-496-5751
Neuromyopathies....Staff NINDS 301-496-5751
Neuromyositis....Staff NINDS 301-496-5751
Neuronal Ceroid Lupofuscinoses....Staff NINDS 301-496-5751
Neuropathies....Staff NINDS 301-496-5751
Neuropharmacology....Staff NINDS 301-496-5751
Neurosclerosis....Staff NINDS 301-496-5751
Neurosyphilis....Staff NINDS 301-496-5751
New Caledonia....Staff Cnty State 202-647-3546
New Caledonia/Minerals....Lyday, Travis Cnty Mines 202-501-9695
New Zealand....Bouck, Gary (Bus.)/Golike, William (Policy) Cnty Commerce 202-482-3647
New Zealand (Wellington)....Staff Cnty State 202-647-9691
New Zealand/Minerals....Lyday, Travis Cnty Mines 202-501-9695
Newborn....Staff NICHD 301-496-5133
News Gathering and Publishing....Staff FCC 717-337-1212
Newspaper management....Smith, Michael V. UMD 301-405-2427
Newspapers....Bratland, Rose Marie COMMERCE 202-482-0380
Newsprint....Stahmer, Carsten USITC 202-205-3321
Nicaragua....Subrin, Laura Cnty Commerce 202-482-2527
Nicaragua....Brown, Brenda L. Peace Corps 202-606-3624
Nicaragua (Managua)....Staff Cnty State 202-647-4975
Nicaragua/Minerals....Mobbs, Philip Cnty Mines 202-501-9679
Nickel....Kuck, Peter H. MINES 202-501-9436
Nickel....Lundy, David USITC 202-205-3439
Nickel Products....Presbury, Graylin COMMERCE 202-482-0575
Nickel compounds....Greenblatt, Jack USITC 202-205-3353
Niemann-Pick Disease....Staff NINDS 301-496-5751
Niemann-Pick Disease....Staff NEI 301-496-5248
Niger....Michelini, Philip Cnty Commerce 202-482-4388
Niger....Hanson, Julie Peace Corps 202-606-3004
Niger (Niamey)....Staff Cnty State 202-647-3066
Niger/Minerals....Izon, David Cnty Mines 202-501-9692
Nigeria....Henke, Degra Cnty Commerce 202-482-4228
Nigeria....McCormick, Michael L. Peace Corps 202-606-3644
Nigeria....Herring, Debra Peace Corps 202-606-3644
Nigeria (Abuja)....Staff Cnty State 202-647-3395
Nigeria/Minerals....Izon, David Cnty Mines 202-501-9692
Night Blindness....Staff NEI 301-496-5248
Nightwear....DeGaetano, Angela CUSTOMS 212-466-5540
Nikkei with options....Fedinets, Robert P. CFT 312-353-9016
Nitric acid....Trainor, Cynthia USITC 202-205-3354
Nitrites....Michels, David USITC 202-205-3352
Nitrogen....Cantrell, Raymond MINES 202-501-9581
Nitrogen....Conant, Kenneth USITC 202-205-3346
Nitrogen Compounds....Joseph, Stephanie CUSTOMS 212-466-5768
Nitrogenous fertilizers....Trainor, Cynthia USITC 202-205-3354
Nitrosamines....Staff NCI 301-496-5583
Nobel Prize....Staff NIGMS 301-496-7301
Noise....Staff NIDCD 301-496-7243
Noise....Staff NINDS 301-496-5751

Noise Information....Staff EPA 202-260-1089
Non-Game Wildlife....Staff FWS 703-358-1718
Non-Hodgkins Malignant Lymphoma....Staff NCI 301-496-5583
Non-Toxic Shot....Staff FWS 703-358-1773
Non-alcoholic Beverages....Kenney, Cornelius COMMERCE 202-482-2428
Non-benzenoid resins....Misurelli, Denby USITC 202-205-3362
Non-electric Machinery, Prices and Living Cond....Dickerson, Bryandt LABOR 202-606-7734
Non-electric motors and engines....Andersen, Peder USITC 202-205-3388
NonFarm Proprietors' Income & Employment....Levine, Bruce ECONOMIC 202-254-6634
Noncurrent Carrying Wiring Devices....Whitley, Richard A. COMMERCE 202-482-0682
Nondurable Goods....Simon, Leslie B. COMMERCE 202-482-0341
Nonenumerated products....Spalding, Josephine USITC 202-205-3498
Nonferrous Foundries....Duggan, Brian COMMERCE 202-482-0610
Nonferrous Metals....Marion, James J. COMMERCE 202-482-0575
Noninfectious Chemical Agents (Eff. on Human Hea.)....Staff NIEHS 919-541-3345
Nonmetallic Minerals Nec....Manion, James J. COMMERCE 202-482-0575
Nonresidential Constr (Domestic)....MacAuley, Patrick COMMERCE 202-482-0132
Norwalk Agent....Staff NIAID 301-496-5717
Norway....Devlin, James Cnty Commerce 202-482-4414
Norway (Oslo)....Staff Cnty State 202-647-5669
Norway/Minerals....Buck, Donald E. Cnty Mines 202-501-9670
Nosebleed (Epistaxis)....Staff NHLBI 301-496-4236
Nuclear (Heart Pacemaker)....Staff NHLBI 301-496-4236
Nuclear Energy....Greenblatt, Jack USITC 202-205-3353
Nuclear Energy....Staff NEIC 301-903-5447
Nuclear Energy Statistics....Geidl, John NEIC 202-254-5570
Nuclear Facility Safety....Kornack, Wallace NEIC 202-586-4400
Nuclear Fusion....Davies, Anne NEIC 301-903-4941
Nuclear Magnetic Resonance....Becker, Edwin D. FAES 301-496-1024
Nuclear Magnetic Resonance Spectrometers....Staff NCRR 301-496-5411
Nuclear Medicine Department....Staff CC 301-496-6455
Nuclear Physics....Hess, Wilmot NEIC 301-903-3713
Nuclear Power Plants....Werner, Thomas NEIC 301-903-3773
Nuclear Power Plants, Major Proj....Dollison, Robert COMMERCE 202-482-2733
Nuclear Power Projects....Staff FWS 703-358-2183
Nuclear Safety Issues....Staff NEIC 301-903-3465
Nuclear Safety Regulations....Blush, Steven NEIC 202-586-2407
Nuclear Weapons Stockpiles....Mistretta, Michael J. NEIC 301-903-6699
Number Research, Price and Index, Pr/Lv. Cond....Zieschang, Kimberly LABOR 202-606-6573
Numerical Contrls. Fr. Mach. Tools....McGibbon, Patrick COMMERCE 202-482-0314
Numerical controls....Malison, Andrew USITC 202-205-3391
Nursing Homes....Staff NIA 301-496-1752
Nursing Homes....Hardy, Robert HCFA 202-690-6145
Nursing Homes and Care....Staff HRSA/DPCS 301-443-2270
Nursing Interventions....Staff NCNR 301-496-0526
Nursing Research, National Center for....Pollin, Geraldine NIH 301-496-0207
Nursing Research, National Center for....McBride, Esther NIH 301-496-0207
Nursing Systems....Staff NCNR 301-496-0526
Nutrition....Staff NICHD 301-496-5133
Nutrition....Staff HRSA/DMCH 301-443-4026
Nutrition....Staff NIDDK 301-496-3583
Nutrition....Meyers, Linda ASH 202-205-9907
Nutrition....Trowbridge, Frederick L. CDC 404-488-5090
Nutrition....Hubbard, Van S. FAES 301-496-7823
Nutrition....Meyers, Linda ASH 202-205-9907
Nutrition Research Coordination....Staff OD 301-496-9281
Nutrition and Aging....Staff NIA 301-496-1752
Nutrition, Maternal and Child....Wong, Faye L. CDC 404-488-5099
Nutritional Statistics....Looker, Ann CDC 301-436-7072
Nuts....Conte, Ralph CUSTOMS 212-466-5759
Nuts, Bolts, Washers....Reise, Richard COMMERCE 202-482-3489
Nuts, Edible....Janis, William V. COMMERCE 202-482-2250
Nuts, Edible....Burket, Stephen USITC 202-205-3318
Nystagmus....Staff NEI 301-496-5248

Be patient. If any phone number is incorrect, call (area code) 555-1212 and request the new listing.

Experts

O

Oakum....Cook, Lee USITC 202-205-3471
Oats with options....Gore, Philip CFT 312-886-3044
Obesity....Staff NIDDK 301-496-3583
Obesity....Staff NIMH 301-496-4515
Obesity in Children....Staff NICHD 301-496-5133
Obstruction Markings--Antenna....Staff FCC 202-632-7521
Occupation Statistics....Priebe, John/Masumura, Wilfred CENSUS 301-763-8574
Occupational Data/Current Survey, Empl/Unempl.St.....Staff LABOR 202-606-6378
Occupational Diseases....Staff CDC/NIOSH 404-639-3286
Occupational Lung Disease....Staff NHLBI 301-496-4236
Occupational Medicine....Pettengill, Harry NEIC 301-903-7030
Occupational Mobility, Occup. Data, Empl/Unempl. Data....Rones, Philip LABOR 202-606-6378
Occupational Outlook Handbook, Employment Proj.....Pilot, Michael LABOR 202-606-5703
Occupational Outlook Quarterly, Empl. Proj.....Fountain, Melvin LABOR 202-606-5707
Occupational Projections....Rosenthal, Neal LABOR 202-606-5701
Occupational Safety....Gibbs, Roy NEIC 301-903-4343
Occupational Safety & Health, National Institute for....Berreth, Don CDC 404-639-3286
Occupational Safety and Health....Millar, J. Donald CDC 404-639-3771
Ocean Biological Experiments....Koehler, Keith NASA 802-824-1579
Ocean Energy....Loose, Ronald NEIC 202-586-8086
Ocean Physics Research....Koehler, Keith NASA 804-824-1579
Ocean Shipping....Johnson, William C. COMMERCE 202-482-5012
Ocean Thermal Energy....Loose, Ronald NEIC 202-586-8086
Oceans and Coastal Protection Division....Staff EPA 202-260-1952
Oceans and Watersheds....Staff EPA 202-260-7166
Ocular Hypertension....Staff NEI 301-496-5248
Oculocraniosomatic Neuromuscular Disease....Staff NINDS 301-496-5751
Odor....Staff NINDS 301-496-5751
Odor....Staff NIDCD 301-496-7243
Odoriferous Compounds....Joseph, Stephanie CUSTOMS 212-466-5768
Odoriferous or aromatic substances....Land, Eric USITC 202-205-3349
Off-Track Betting....Staff FCC 202-632-7048
Off-the-Air Pickup....Staff FCC 202-634-1706
Offal....Ludwick, David USITC 202-205-3329
Offender-based Transaction Statistics....Manson, Donald Justice Stat 202-616-3491
Offender-based Transaction Statistics....Langan, Patrick Justice Stat 202-616-3490
Offenders....Baunach, Phyllis Jo Justice Stat 202-307-0361
Offenders....Greenfeld, Lawrence Justice Stat 202-616-3281
Offenders....Stephan, James Justice Stat 202-616-7273
Offenders....Beck, Allen Justice Stat 202-616-3277
Offenders - Federal....Kaplan, Carol Justice Stat 202-307-0759
Offenders, Female....Baunach, Phyllis Jo Justice Stat 202-307-0361
Offenders, Female - Federal....Kaplan, Carol Justice Stat 202-307-0759
Office copying machines....Baker, Scott USITC 202-205-3386
Office machines....Baker, Scott USITC 202-205-3386
Office of Congressional Relations....Hall, Dorian J. FTC 202-326-2186
Office of Congressional Relations....Leslie, Louise M. FTC 202-326-2195
Office of Congressional Relations....Prendergast, William B. FTC 202-326-2195
Office of Consumer and Competition Advocacy....Laney, Veronica FTC 202-326-2249
Office of Consumer and Competition Advocacy....Wise, Michael O. FTC 202-326-3444
Office of Inspector General....Treitsch, Dennis R. FTC 202-326-2581
Office of Inspector General....Trzeciak, Adam R. FTC 202-326-2435
Office of Inspector General....Zirkel, Frederick J. FTC 202-326-2800
Office of Inspector General....Williams, Joyce E. FTC 202-326-2313
Office of Public Affairs....Elder, Donald FTC 202-326-2181
Office of Public Affairs....Jansen, Bonnie FTC 202-326-2161
Office of Public Affairs....Leslie, John T. FTC 202-326-2178
Office of Public Affairs....Mack, Brenda A. FTC 202-326-2182
Office of Public Affairs....Shaipro, Howard FTC 202-326-2176
Office of the Commissioner....Azcuenaga, Mary L. FTC 202-326-2145
Office of the General Counsel....Coleman, Jill E. FTC 202-326-2414
Office of the General Counsel....Cox, John H. FTC 202-326-2568
Office of the General Counsel....Crockett, Elaine FTC 202-326-2453
Office of the General Counsel....Cummins, Jerold D. FTC 202-326-2471
Office of the General Counsel....Dawson, Rachel Miller FTC 202-326-2463
Office of the General Counsel....DeLuca, Nancy F. FCC 202-326-2440
Office of the General Counsel....DeMille-Wagman, Lawrence FTC 202-326-2448
Office of the General Counsel....Dooley, Frederick E. FTC 202-326-2443
Office of the General Counsel....DuPree, Scott E. FTC 202-326-2479
Office of the General Counsel....Etheridge, Monica M. FTC 202-326-2666
Office of the General Counsel....Fields, Kwasi A. FTC 202-326-2452
Office of the General Counsel....Freedman, Bruce G. FTC 202-326-2464
Office of the General Counsel....Golden, William P. FTC 202-326-2494
Office of the General Counsel....Goosby, Consuella M. FTC 202-326-2486
Office of the General Counsel....Greenfield, Gary M. FTC 202-326-2753
Office of the General Counsel....Hurwitz, James D. FTC 202-326-2847
Office of the General Counsel....Isenstadt, Ernest J. FTC 202-326-2473
Office of the General Counsel....Kane, Maryanne S. FTC 202-326-2450
Office of the General Counsel....Kaye, Ira S. FTC 202-326-2426
Office of the General Counsel....Levine, Joanne L. FTC 202-326-2474
Office of the General Counsel....Lewis, Tina M. FTC 202-326-2465
Office of the General Counsel....Melman, Leslie R. FTC 202-326-2478
Office of the General Counsel....Miller, Rachel Dawson FTC 202-326-2463
Office of the General Counsel....Murphy, John T. FTC 202-326-2457
Office of the General Counsel....Neal, Valary FTC 202-326-2066
Office of the General Counsel....Orlans, Melvin H. FTC 202-326-2475
Office of the General Counsel....Pahl, Thomas B. FTC 202-326-2115
Office of the General Counsel....Polydor, Cheryl L. FTC 202-326-2279
Office of the General Counsel....Pressley, Doris P. FTC 202-326-2916
Office of the General Counsel....Rittner, Kathleen FTC 202-326-2498
Office of the General Counsel....Shaffer, Jay C. FTC 202-326-2557
Office of the General Counsel....Shonka, David C. FTC 202-326-2436
Office of the General Counsel....Spears, James M. FTC 202-326-2480
Office of the General Counsel....Tang, Alexander FTC 202-326-2447
Office of the General Counsel....Wagman, Lawrence FTC 202-326-2448
Office of the General Counsel....Worthy, Betty J. FTC 202-326-2459
Office of the General Counsel....White, Christian S. FTC 202-326-2476
Office of the General Counsel....Winerman, Marc L. FTC 202-326-2451
Office of the Secretary....Ashe, Maurice FTC 202-326-2516
Office of the Secretary....Berman, Benjamin I. FTC 202-326-2960
Office of the Secretary....Carson, Diane B. FTC 202-326-2501
Office of the Secretary....Clark, Donald S. FTC 202-326-2514
Office of the Secretary....Dickerson, Eunice L. FTC 202-326-3347
Office of the Secretary....Foster, Elizabeth M. FTC 202-326-2187
Office of the Secretary....Liebman, Marvin FTC 202-326-2069
Office of the Secretary....Lofty, Bernita V. FTC 202-326-3117
Office of the Secretary....Parker, Shalena FTC 202-326-2512
Office of the Secretary....Pierce, Diane E. FTC 202-326-2519
Office of the Secretary....Plummer, C. Landis FTC 202-326-2520
Office of the Secretary....Reynolds, Ronald H. FTC 202-326-2521
Office of the Secretary....Tanner, Trina A. FTC 202-326-2517
Office of the Secretary....Thielen, John J. FTC 202-326-2506
Office of the Secretary....Tinker, Wallace FTC 202-326-2192
Office of the Secretary....Wood, Dolores A. FTC 202-326-2518
Office of the Secretary....Williams, Linda A. FTC 202-326-2515
Offshore Radio Telecommunications Service....Staff FCC 202-653-5560
Oil & Gas (Fuels Only)....Gillett, Tom COMMERCE 202-482-1466
Oil & Gas Development & Refining, Maj. Proj.....Bell, Richard COMMERCE 202-482-2460
Oil Field Machinery....McDonald, Edward COMMERCE 202-482-0680
Oil Field Machinery, Trade Promo.....Zanetakos, George COMMERCE 202-482-0552
Oil Pollution....Staff EPA 202-260-6862
Oil Shale Reserves Management....Furiga, Richard NEIC 202-586-4410
Oil Shale, Major Proj.....Bell, Richard COMMERCE 202-482-2460
Oil Spills....Staff FWS 703-358-2148
Oil Spills - Emergency Response Division....Staff EPA 202-260-6862
Oil and Gas Leasing on Fish and Wildlife Refuges....Staff FWS 703-358-2043
Oil and Gas Statistics....Peterson, Jimmie NEIC 202-586-6401
Oil and Hazardous Material Spills....Staff EPA 202-267-2675
Oil and Hazardous Material Spills Response Hotline....Staff EPA 800-424-8802
Oil, Used....Staff EPA 202-260-6261
Oil, lubricating....Foreso, Cynthia USITC 202-205-3348
Oilcloth....Cook, Lee USITC 202-205-3471
Oils, Animal and Vegetable....Maria, John CUSTOMS 212-466-5730
Oils, essential....Land, Eric USITC 202-205-3349
Oilseeds....Reeder, John USITC 202-205-3319
Oilseeds - Soybeans, Sunflowers....Kerestes, Dan Agri 202-270-9526
Oilseeds - Soybeans, Sunflowers....Hoskin, Roger Agri 202-219-0840

Oakum / Paper

Oilseeds - Soybeans, Sunflowers....McCormick, Ian Agri 202-219-0840
Oilseeds - Soybeans, Sunflowers - World....Morgan, Nancy Agri 202-219-0826
Older Women....Staff NIA 301-496-1752
Older Workers, Empl/Unempl. Stats.....Rones, Philip LABOR 202-606-6378
Oleic acid....Randall, Rob USITC 202-205-3366
Oleic acid ester....Johnson, Larry USITC 202-205-3351
Oleyl alcohols....Randall, Rob USITC 202-205-3366
Olivopontocerebellar Atrophy....Staff NINDS 301-496-5751
Oman....Fitzgerald-Wilks, Kate/Thanos, Paul Cnty Commerce 202-482-2039
Oman (Muscat)....Staff Cnty State 202-647-6558
Oman/Minerals....Michalski, Bernadette Cnty Mines 202-501-9699
On Site Contractor Employees....Baxter, Robert L., II FTC 202-326-2243
On Site Contractor Employees....Cassagnol, Pascale FTC 202-326-2088
On Site Contractor Employees....Gardner, Kevin P. FTC 202-326-2243
On Site Contractor Employees....Hallman, Kevin J. FTC 202-326-2243
On Site Contractor Employees....Lathern, Ronald C. FTC 202-326-2290
On Site Contractor Employees....Saunders, Paristina FTC 202-326-2243
Onchocerciasis....Staff NEI 301-496-5248
Oncology....Staff NCI 301-496-5583
One-Way Paging and Signaling....Staff FCC 202-653-5560
Ophthalmia Neonatorum....Staff NEI 301-496-5248
Ophthalmic....Johnson, Christopher USITC 202-205-3488
Ophthalmic Congenital and Genetic Disease....Staff NEI 301-496-5248
Ophthalmology Research....Staff NEI 301-496-5248
Oppenheim's Disease (Amyotonia Congenita)....Staff NINDS 301-496-5751
Optic Atrophy....Staff NEI 301-496-5248
Optic Neuritis....Staff NEI 301-496-5248
Optical Equipment....Kiefer, Barbara CUSTOMS 212-466-5685
Optical elements....Johnson, Christopher USITC 202-205-3488
Optical goods....Johnson, Christopher USITC 202-205-3488
Optometry Research....Staff NEI 301-496-5248
Oral Cancer....Staff NIDR 301-496-4261
Oral Contraceptives....Staff NICHD 301-496-5133
Oral Health....Marianos, Donald W. CDC 404-488-4452
Oral Surgery-Intravenous Sedation....Staff NIDR 301-496-4261
Orange oil (essential oil)....Land, Eric USITC 202-205-3349
Ordering Info (Computer Software, Publications)....Customer Services Staff CENSUS 301-763-4100
Ores....Fitzgerald, John CUSTOMS 212-466-5492
Organ Donations (Eyes)....Staff NEI 301-496-5248
Organ Transplants....Mehuron, Charlotte HRSA 301-443-3376
Organ Transplants/Medicare, Medicaid Funding....Hardy, Robert HCFA 202-690-6145
Organic Chemicals....Hurt, William COMMERCE 202-482-0128
Organic acids....Michels, David USITC 202-205-3352
Organization for Economic Cooperation & Develop.....Staff Cnty State 202-647-2469
Organo-Sulfur Compounds....Winters, William CUSTOMS 212-466-5747
Organo-metallic compounds....Michels, David USITC 202-205-3352
Original Telephone & Telephone Plant Cost....Staff FCC 202-632-3772
Orotic Aciduria....Staff NIDDK 301-496-3583
Orphan Drugs....Staff NINDS 301-496-5751
Orphan Drugs....Staff OD 301-496-1454
Orphan Drugs....Staff FDA 301-443-4903
Orphan Drugs....Cruzan, Susan FDA 301-443-3285
Orthodontics....Staff NIDR 301-496-4261
Orthognathic Surgery....Staff NIDR 301-496-4261
Orthokeratology....Staff NEI 301-496-5248
Orthopedic Implants....Staff NIAMS 301-496-8188
Orthostatic Hypotension....Staff NHLBI 301-496-4236
Orthostatic Hypotension....Staff NINDS 301-496-5751
Orthotics....Staff NIAMS 301-496-8188
Ossein....Jonnard, Aimison USITC 202-205-3350
Osteitis Deformans....Staff NIAMS 301-496-8188
Osteoarthritis....Staff NIAMS 301-496-8188
Osteoarthritis....Staff NIA 301-496-1752
Osteoarthritis with Age....Staff NIA 301-496-1752
Osteogenesis....Staff NIAMS 301-496-8188
Osteogenesis Imperfecta....Staff NIAMS 301-496-8188
Osteogenesis Imperfecta....Staff NICHD 301-496-5133
Osteogenic Sarcoma....Staff NCI 301-496-5583
Osteomalacia....Staff NIAMS 301-496-8188
Osteomyelitis....Staff NIAMS 301-496-8188
Osteoporosis....Staff NIAMS 301-496-8188
Osteoporosis....Staff NICHD 301-496-5133
Osteoporosis with Age....Staff NIAMS 301-496-8188
Osteosclerosis (Osteopetrosis)....Staff NIAMS 301-496-8188

Osteosclerosis (Osteopetrosis)....Staff NICHD 301-496-5133
Ostomy....Staff NIDDK 301-496-3583
Otitis Media....Staff NINDS 301-496-5751
Otitis Media....Staff NIAD 301-496-5717
Otitis Media....Staff NIDCD 301-496-7243
Otosclerosis....Staff NINDS 301-496-5751
Otosclerosis....Staff NIDCD 301-496-7243
Outdoor Air - Cities....Staff EPA 202-260-5575
Outdoor Lightning Fixtures....Whitley, Richard A. COMMERCE 202-482-0682
Outdoor Power (Export Promo)....Beckham, Reginald COMMERCE 202-482-5478
Outer Continental Shelf....Staff FWS 703-358-2183
Ovarian Cancer....Staff NCI 301-496-5583
Ovens....Mata, Ruben USITC 202-205-3403
Oviduct....Staff NICHD 301-496-5133
Ovulation....Staff NICHD 301-496-5133
Ovum....Staff NICHD 301-496-5133
Oxalosis & Hyperoxaluria....Staff NIDDK 301-496-3583
Oxides, inorganic....Conant, Kenneth USITC 202-205-3346
Oxygen....Conant, Kenneth USITC 202-205-3346
Oxygenators (Artificial Lungs)....Staff NHLBI 301-496-4236
Ozone - Stratospheric....Staff EPA 292-233-9190

P

PCB's (Polychlorinated Biphenyl) Chem. Regulations....Staff EPA 202-260-3933
PHS Commissioned Corps....Simmons, Paul B. ASH 202-690-6867
PKU (Phenylketonuria)....Staff NICHD 301-496-5133
PMS (Premenstrual Syndrome)....Staff NICHD 301-496-5133
PMS (Premenstrual Syndrome)....Staff NIMH 301-443-4515
Pacemaker (Cardiac/Heart)....Staff NHLBI 301-496-4236
Pacemakers....Cruzan, Susan FDA 301-443-3285
Pacific Islands....Bouck, Gary (Bus.)/Golike, William (Policy) Cnty Commerce 202-482-3647
Pacific Islands (General)....Staff Cnty State 202-647-3546
Pacific/trade matters....Lake, Charles US Trade Rep 202-395-3900
Packaging Machinery....Shaw, Gene COMMERCE 202-482-3494
Packaging machines....Slingerland, David USITC 202-205-3400
Paget's Disease of Bone (Osteitis Deformans)....Staff NIAMS 301-496-8188
Paging--Common Carrier....Staff FCC 202-652-0914
Paging--One Way....Staff FCC 717-337-1212
Pain....Staff NIDR 301-496-1752
Pain....Staff NINDS 301-496-5751
Pain (Cancer Related)....Staff NCI 301-496-5583
Pain (Oral-Facial)....Staff NIDR 301-496-4261
Pain and the Elderly....Staff NIA 301-496-1752
Paint....Brownchweig, Gilbert CUSTOMS 212-466-5744
Paint rollers....Burns, Gail USITC 202-205-3501
Paint sets, artist's....Johnson, Larry USITC 202-205-3351
Paintings....Mushinske, Larry CUSTOMS 212-466-5739
Paintings....Johnson, Larry USITC 202-205-3351
Paints/Coatings....Prat, Raimundo COMMERCE 202-482-0128
Pajamas....Linkins, Linda USITC 202-205-3469
Pakistan....McQueen, Cheryl Cnty Commerce 202-482-2954
Pakistan....Ordonez, Miguel Peace Corps 202-606-3118
Pakistan (Islamabad)....Staff Cnty State 202-647-9823
Pakistan/Minerals....Kuo, Chin Cnty Mines 202-501-9693
Palau (Koror)....Staff Cnty State 202-647-0108
Palm oil....Reeder, John USITC 202-205-3319
Palmitic acid esters....Johnson, Larry USITC 202-205-3351
Palpitation....Staff NHLBI 301-496-4236
Palsy, Cerebral....Staff NINDS 301-496-5751
Panama....Subrin, Laura Cnty Commerce 202-482-2527
Panama....Stanton, Dan Peace Corps 202-606-3620
Panama....Tumaylle, Carol Peace Corps 202-606-3321
Panama (Panama City)....Staff Cnty State 202-647-4986
Panama/Minerals....Mobbs, Philip Cnty Mines 202-501-9679
Pancreatic Diseases....Staff NIDDK 301-496-3583
Panencephalitis....Staff NINDS 301-496-5751
Panty hose....Linkins, Linda USITC 202-205-3469
Pantyhose....DeGaetano, Angela CUSTOMS 212-466-5540
Pap Smear....Staff NCI 301-496-5583
Paper....Stanley, Gary COMMERCE 202-482-0375
Paper....Rhodes, Richard USITC 202-205-3322

Be patient. If any phone number is incorrect, call (area code) 555-1212 and request the new listing.

Experts

Paper & Board Packaging....Smith, Leonard S. COMMERCE 202-482-0375
Paper Industries Machinery....Abrahams, Edward COMMERCE 202-482-0312
Paper and Paper Products....Abromowitz, Carl CUSTOMS 212-466-5733
Paper machines....Slingerland, David USITC 202-205-3400
Paper, products of....Stahmer, Carsten USITC 202-205-3321
Paperboard....Rhodes, Richard USITC 202-205-3322
Paperboard machines....Slingerland, David USITC 202-205-3400
Paperboard, products of....Stahmer, Carsten USITC 202-205-3321
Papermakers' felts....Cook, Lee USITC 202-205-3471
Papermaking materials....Rhodes, Richard USITC 202-205-3322
Papilloma Virus and Cancer....Staff NCI 301-496-5583
Papua New Guinea....Nagle, Douglas Peace Corps 202-606-3290
Papua New Guinea....Jefferson, Mary Peace Corps 202-606-3231
Papua New Guinea....Schell, Russell Peace Corps 202-606-3231
Papua New Guinea (Port Moresby)....Staff Cnty State 202-647-3546
Papua New Guinea/Minerals....Lyday, Travis Cnty Mines 202-501-9695
Paraguay....Mye, Randolph Cnty Commerce 202-482-1548
Paraguay....Godbey, Maria Elena Peace Corps 202-606-3198
Paraguay....Erlandson, Barbara Peace Corps 202-606-3499
Paraguay (Asuncion)....Staff Cnty State 202-647-2296
Paraguay/Minerals....Gurmendi, Alfredo Cnty Mines 202-501-9681
Paralysis Agitans....Staff NINDS 301-496-5751
Paralysis, Periodic....Staff NINDS 301-496-5751
Paramedical Training....Staff HRSA/BHPr 301-443-5794
Paramyotonia Congenita....Staff NINDS 301-496-5751
Paraplegia....Staff NINDS 301-496-5751
Parasitic Disease....Staff NIAID 301-496-5717
Parasitic Diseases....Collery, Daniel G. CDC 404-488-4050
Parasitology....Staff NIAID 301-496-5717
Parathyroid Disorders....Staff NIDDK 301-496-3583
Parachutes....Andersen, Peder USITC 202-205-3388
Parkinson's Disease....Staff NINDS 301-496-5751
Parkinson's Disease....Staff NIDCD 301-496-7243
Parkinsonism-Dementia....Staff NINDS 301-496-5751
Parole and Parolees....Huggins, M. Wayne Justice Stat 202-307-3106
Parole and Parolees....Greenfeld, Lawrence Justice Stat 202-616-3281
Paroxysmal Atrial Tachycardia (PAT)....Staff NHLBI 301-496-4236
Paroxysmal Nocturnal Hemoglobinuria....Staff NHLBI 301-496-4236
Paroxysmal Nocturnal Hemoglobinuria....Staff NIAID 301-496-5717
Pars Planitis....Staff NEI 301-496-5248
Part-time Workers, Employment/Employment....Nardone, Thomas LABOR 202-606-6378
Particle Beams....Wood, Robert NEIC 301-903-5535
Particle board....Ruggles, Fred USITC 202-205-3325
Party favors....Luther, Dennis USITC 202-205-3497
Parvovirus Infections....Staff NIAID 301-496-5717
Passenger autos, trucks, and buses....Hagey, Michael USITC 202-205-3392
Pasta....Janis, William V. COMMERCE 202-482-2250
Patents, Fish and Wildlife....Staff FWS 703-358-1730
Pathogen-Free Mice and Rats....Staff DRS/VRB 301-496-5255
Patient Dumping....Holtz, Judy IG 202-619-1142
Paving Materials, Asphalt....Pitcher, Charles COMMERCE 202-482-0132
Paving Materials, Concrete....Pitcher, Charles COMMERCE 202-482-0132
Pay Cable Television....Staff FCC 202-632-7480
Peanuts....Latham, Roger Agri 202-720-5944
Peanuts....Sanford, Scott Agri 202-219-0840
Peanuts....Burket, Stephen USITC 202-205-3318
Peanuts - World....McCormick, Ian Agri 202-219-0840
Pearl essence....Johnson, Larry USITC 202-205-3351
Pearls....Witherspoon, Ricardo USITC 202-205-3489
Peat....Cantrell, Raymond MINES 202-501-9581
Peat moss....Trainor, Cynthia USITC 202-205-3354
Pectin....Janis, William V. COMMERCE 202-482-2250
Pectin....Jonnard, Aimison USITC 202-205-3350
Pectus Excavatum (Funnel Chest)....Staff NHLBI 301-496-4236
Pedodontics....Staff NIDR 301-496-4261
Peer Review Organizations (PROs)....Hardy, Robert HCFA 202-690-6145
Peer Review Orgs./Sanctions....Holtz, Judy IG 202-619-1142
Pelizaceous-Merzbacher Disease....Staff NINDS 301-496-5751
Pelvic Inflammatory Disease....Staff NIAID 301-496-5717
Pemphigus Vulgaris....Staff NIAMS 301-496-8188
Pemphigoid....Staff NIAMS 301-496-8188
Pencils....Smyth, James CUSTOMS 212-466-2084
Pencils....Shetty, Sundar USITC 202-205-3486
Pencils/Pens, etc.....Vacant COMMERCE 202-482-0338
Penicillin....Nesbitt, Elizabeth USITC 202-205-3355
Pens....Smyth, James CUSTOMS 212-466-2084
People/China....Chu, Robert Cnty Commerce 202-482-2462
People/China....McCall, Laura Cnty Commerce 202-482-3583
Peptic Ulcers....Staff NIDDK 301-496-3583
Perchloroethylene....Michels, David USITC 202-205-3352
Perfumery, cosmetics, and toilet preps....Land, Eric USITC 202-205-3349
Periarteritis Nodosa....Staff NHLBI 301-496-4236
Periarteritis Nodosa....Staff NIAID 301-496-5717
Pericardial Tamponade....Staff NHLBI 301-496-4236
Pericarditis....Staff NHLBI 301-496-4236
Pericardium....Staff NHLBI 301-496-4236
Perinatal Biology....Staff NICHD 301-496-5133
Periodic Paralysis....Staff NINDS 301-496-5751
Periodicals....Bratland, Rose Marie COMMERCE 202-482-0380
Periodontal Diseases....Staff NIDR 301-496-4261
Peripheral Nerve Tumor....Staff NINDS 301-496-5751
Peripheral Neuropathy (Neuritis)....Staff NINDS 301-496-5751
Peripheral Vascular Disease....Staff NHLBI 301-496-4236
Perlite....Bolen, Wallace P. MINES 202-501-9389
Permit Information, Fish and Wildlife....Staff FWS 703-358-2104
Pernicious Anemia....Staff NIDDK 301-496-3583
Peroneal Muscular Atrophy....Staff NINDS 301-496-5751
Peroxides and Acetals....DiMaria, Joseph CUSTOMS 212-466-4769
Peroxides, inorganic....Conant, Kenneth USITC 202-205-3346
Personal leather goods....Seastrum, Carl USITC 202-205-3493
Personality....Staff NIMH 301-443-4515
Pertussis....Staff NIAID 301-496-5717
Peru....Lindow, Herbert Cnty Commerce 202-482-2521
Peru (Lima)....Staff Cnty State 202-647-3360
Peru/Minerals....Mobbs, Philip Cnty Mines 202-501-9679
Pesticide Hotline....Staff EPA 806-743-3095
Pesticide Information....Staff EPA 202-305-5919
Pesticide Monitoring....Staff FWS 703-358-2148
Pesticide Monitoring Programs, National....Staff FWS 703-358-2148
Pesticides....Staff NIEHS 919-541-3345
Pesticides....Wanser, Stephen USITC 202-205-3363
Pesticides Information Center....Staff EPA 202-305-5805
Pesticides and Toxic Enforcement....Staff EPA 202-260-8690
Pesticides and Toxic Substances....Staff EPA 202-235-5300
Pesticides....Reilly, Cornelius CUSTOMS 212-466-5770
Pet Food....Janis, William V. COMMERCE 202-482-2250
Pet Products (Export Promo)....Kimmel, Edward K. COMMERCE 202-482-3640
Pet animals (live)....Steller, Rose USITC 202-205-3323
Petrochemicals....Hurt, William COMMERCE 202-482-0128
Petrochemicals Plants, Major Proj....Haraguchi, Wally COMMERCE 202-482-4877
Petrochemicals, Cyclic Crudes....Hurt, William COMMERCE 202-482-0128
Petroleum....Winters, William CUSTOMS 212-466-5747
Petroleum....Withrow, Leola NEIC 202-586-8800
Petroleum....Christian, Trisha NEIC 202-586-8800
Petroleum....Foreso, Cynthia USITC 202-205-3348
Petroleum (Ground Level)....Staff EPA 919-541-5526
Petroleum Offshore Drilling....Staff FCC 717-337-1212
Petroleum Products Markets....Cook, John NEIC 202-586-5214
Petroleum Statistics....Heath, Charles NEIC 202-586-6860
Petroleum, Crude and Refined Products....Gillett, Tom COMMERCE 202-482-1466
Peyronie's Disease....Staff NIDDK 301-496-3583
Phacoemulsification....Staff NEI 301-496-5248
Pharmaceuticals....Hurt, William COMMERCE 202-482-0128
Pharmaceuticals....Reilly, Cornelius CUSTOMS 212-466-5770
Pharmacology Information System (PROPHET)....Staff DRR 301-496-5411
Pharmacology Research Associate Training Program....Staff NIGMS 301-496-7301
Pharmacology/Toxicology....Staff NIGMS 301-496-7301
Pharmacology/Toxicology....Staff NIEHS 919-541-3345
Pharynx....Staff NIDR 301-496-4261
Phenol....Matusik, Ed USITC 202-205-3356
Phenolic resins....Misurelli, Denby USITC 202-205-3362
Phenylketonuria (PKU)....Staff NICHD 301-496-5133
Pheochromocytema....Staff NHLBI 301-496-4236
Philippines....Paine, George Cnty Commerce 202-482-3875
Philippines (Manila)....Staff Cnty State 202-647-1221
Philippines/Minerals....Lyday, Travis Cnty Mines 202-501-9695
Phlebitis....Staff NHLBI 301-496-4236
Phlebothrombosis....Staff NHLBI 301-496-4236

Be patient. If any phone number is incorrect, call (area code) 555-1212 and request the new listing.

Paperboard / Pompe's Disease

Phobias....Staff NIMH 301-496-4513
Phonograph and parts....Sherman, Thomas USITC 202-205-3389
Phonograph records....Sherman, Thomas USITC 202-205-3389
Phonographic equipment....Sherman, Thomas USITC 202-205-3389
Phonographs....Sherman, Thomas USITC 202-205-3389
Phosphate Rock....Stowasser, William F. MINES 202-501-9408
Phosphatic fertilizers....Trainor, Cynthia USITC 202-205-3354
Phosphoric acid....Trainor, Cynthia USITC 202-205-3354
Phosphoric acid esters....Johnson, Larry USITC 202-205-3351
Phosphorus....Trainor, Cynthia USITC 202-205-3354
Phosphorus compounds....Conant, Kenneth USITC 202-205-3346
Photocells....Malison, Andrew USITC 202-205-3391
Photocoagulation....Staff NEI 301-496-5248
Photocopy Services....Staff NIH Library/DRS 301-496-2983
Photocopying apparatus....Baker, Scott USITC 202-205-3386
Photographic Equipment & Supplies....Watson, Joyce COMMERCE 202-482-0574
Photographic chemicals....Wanser, Stephen USITC 202-205-3363
Photographic film: scrap....Bishop, Kathryn USITC 202-205-3494
Photographic film: waste....Bishop, Kathryn USITC 202-205-3494
Photographic gelatin....Jonnard, Aimison USITC 202-205-3350
Photographic supplies....Bishop, Kathryn USITC 202-205-3494
Photographs....Stahmer, Carsten USITC 202-205-3321
Photographs (Historical)....Staff NLM 301-496-5961
Photography....Staff NCRRR/MAPB 301-496-5995
Photovoltaics....Rannels, James E. NEIC 202-586-1720
Phthalic acid esters....Johnson, Larry USITC 202-205-3351
Phthalic anhydride....Matusik, Ed USITC 202-205-3356
Physical Environment. Agents (Effect on Hum. Hea.)....Staff NIEHS 919-541-3345
Physical Fitness & Sports, President's Council on....Guback, Steve ASH 202-272-3430
Physician's Assistant....Staff HRSA/BHPr 301-443-5794
Physicians Radio--Private....Staff FCC 202-632-1212
Physics....McCarthy, James UVA 701-924-6783
Physiology....Staff NIGMS 301-496-7301
Pi-Mesons (Cancer Treatment)....Staff NCI 301-496-5583
Pick's Disease....Staff NINDS 301-496-5751
Pick's Disease....Staff NIA 301-496-1752
Pig iron....Vacant USITC 202-205-3419
Pigments....Brownchweig, Gilbert CUSTOMS 212-466-5744
Pigments, inorganic....Johnson, Larry USITC 202-205-3351
Pigments, organic....Wanser, Stephen USITC 202-205-3363
Pillow blocks....Fravel, Dennis USITC 202-205-3404
Pillowcases....Sweet, Mary Elizabeth USITC 202-205-3455
Pillows....Spalding, Josephine USITC 202-205-3498
PinWorms....Staff NIAID 301-496-5717
Pinball machines....Robinson, Hazel USITC 202-205-3496
Pinene....Michels, David USITC 202-205-3352
Pink Eye....Staff NEI 301-496-5248
Pipe, of rubber or plastics....Johnson, Larry USITC 202-205-3351
Pipelines (Major Promo)....Bell, Richard COMMERCE 202-482-2460
Pipes, tobacco....Johnson, Christopher USITC 202-205-3488
Pitch from wood....Randall, Rob USITC 202-205-3366
Pituitary Tumors....Staff NINDS 301-496-5751
Pituitary Tumors....Staff NIDDK 301-496-3583
Pituitary Tumors....Staff NICHD 301-496-5133
Pityriasis Rosea....Staff NIAMS 301-496-8188
Pityriasis Rubra Pilaris....Staff NIAMS 301-496-8188
Placenta....Staff NICHD 301-496-5133
Plant Closings Statistics....Siegel, Lewis LABOR 202-606-6404
Plants....Conte, Ralph CUSTOMS 212-466-5759
Plants, live....Burket, Stephen USITC 202-205-3318
Plaque (Dental)....Staff NIDR 301-496-4261
Plasma Cell Cancer....Staff NCI 301-496-5583
Plaster products....White, Linda USITC 202-205-3427
Plastic Construction Products, Most....Williams, Franklin COMMERCE 202-482-0132
Plastic Materials....Shea, Moira COMMERCE 202-482-0128
Plastic Products....Prat, Raimundo COMMERCE 202-482-0128
Plastic Products Machinery....Shaw, Eugene COMMERCE 202-482-3494
Plastic Sheet....Mazzola, Joan CUSTOMS 212-466-5880
Plastic wood....Johnson, Larry USITC 202-205-3351
Plasticizers....Johnson, Larry USITC 202-205-3351
Plastics....Misurelli, Denby USITC 202-205-3362
Plastics products....Raftery, Jim USITC 202-205-3365
Plastics, Biodegradable....Staff EPA 202-260-5649

Platelet Abnormalities....Staff NIDDK 301-496-3583
Platelet Requests....Staff NHLBI 301-496-4236
Platelet Requests....Staff NCI 301-496-5583
Platelet Requests....Staff CC 301-496-3608
Plateletpheresis Center....Staff CC 301-496-4321
Platinum....Rosenfeld, David CFT 312-353-9026
Platinum Group Metals....Loebenstein, J. Roger MINES 202-501-9416
Platinum compounds....Greenblatt, Jack USITC 202-205-3353
Platinum group metals....McNay, Deborah USITC 202-205-3425
Pleasure boats....Lahey, Kathleen USITC 202-205-3409
Pleurisy....Staff NHLBI 301-496-4236
Plumbing Fixtures....Shaw, Robert COMMERCE 202-482-0132
Plumbing Fixtures and Fittings....Shaw, Robert COMMERCE 202-482-0132
Plutonium....Greenblatt, Jack USITC 202-205-3353
Plywood....Ruggles, Fred USITC 202-205-3325
Plywood/Panel Products....Wise, Barbara COMMERCE 202-482-0375
Pneumococcal Infections....Staff NIAID 301-496-5717
Pneumoconioses (Dust Inhalation Disease)....Staff NHLBI 301-496-4236
Pneumocystis Carinii....Staff NIAID 301-496-5717
Pneumothorax....Staff NHLBI 301-496-4236
Point-of-Use Water Treatment....Vacant COMMERCE 202-482-0564
Point-to-Point Microwave Common Carrier....Staff FCC 202-634-1706
Poison Control Ctrs....Staff DC 202-835-4080
Poison Control Ctrs....Staff MD 301-530-3880
Poison Control Ctrs....Staff VA 703-379-3700
Poison Ivy....Staff NIAID 301-496-5717
Poland....Zuck, Audrey Cnty Commerce 202-482-2645
Poland (Warsaw)....Staff Cnty State 202-647-1070
Poland/Minerals....Steblez, Walter Cnty Mines 202-501-9671
Pole Attachments....Staff FCC 202-634-1861
Police Statistics....White, Paul Justice Stat 202-307-0771
Police Statistics....Manson, Donald Justice Stat 202-616-3491
Polioencephalitis (Cerebral Poliomyelitis)....Staff NINDS 301-496-5751
Poliomyelitis....Staff NIAID 301-496-5717
Polishes under 10 lbs each....Randall, Rob USITC 202-205-3366
Political Broadcasting....Staff FCC 202-632-7586
Political Broadcasts on Television....Staff FCC 202-632-7586
Political campaign agendas in US and Britain....Gurevitch, Michael UMD 301-405-2418
Pollen Allergy....Staff NIAID 301-496-5717
Pollution (Air, Waste, Water)....Staff EPA 301-382-5508
Pollution Abatement Reporting....Staff FWS 703-358-1719
Pollution Control Equipment....Jonkers, Loretta COMMERCE 202-482-0564
Pollution Prevention Division....Staff EPA 202-260-3557
Pollution Prevention Policy....Staff EPA 202-260-3557
Polyarteritis....Staff NHLBI 301-496-4236
Polycarbonate resins....Misurelli, Denby USITC 202-205-3362
Polycystic Kidney Disease....Staff NIDDK 301-496-3583
Polycythemia (Secondary)....Staff NHLBI 301-496-4236
Polycythemia (Vera)....Staff NCI 301-496-5583
Polyester resins....Misurelli, Denby USITC 202-205-3362
Polyethylene....Misurelli, Denby USITC 202-205-3362
Polyethylene terephthalate (PET) resins....Misurelli, Denby USITC 202-205-3362
Polyhydric alcohol....Michels, David USITC 202-205-3352
Polyhydric alcohols of polysaccharides and rare....Randall, Rob USITC 202-205-3366
Polyhydric alcohols, fatty acids of, animal/veg....Land, Eric USITC 202-205-3349
Polyisoprene rubber....Misurelli, Denby USITC 202-205-3362
Polymers....Misurelli, Denby USITC 202-205-3362
Polymyalgia Rheumatica....Staff NIAMS 301-496-8188
Polymyositis....Staff NIAMS 301-496-8188
Polymyositis....Staff NINDS 301-496-5751
Polyneuritis (Guillain-Barre Syndrome)....Staff NINDS 301-496-5751
Polyostotic Fibrous Dysplasia (Albright's Syndr.)....Staff NIAMS 301-496-8188
Polypropylene....Misurelli, Denby USITC 202-205-3362
Polyps and Cancer....Staff NCI 301-496-5583
Polyps, Colon....Staff NIDDK 301-496-3583
Polyps, Colon....Staff NCI 301-496-5583
Polysaccharides....Randall, Rob USITC 202-205-3366
Polystyrene resins....Misurelli, Denby USITC 202-205-3362
Polyurethane resins....Misurelli, Denby USITC 202-205-3362
Polyvinyl alcohol resins....Misurelli, Denby USITC 202-205-3362
Polyvinyl chloride....Misurelli, Denby USITC 202-205-3362
Pompe's Disease....Staff NINDS 301-496-5751

Be patient. If any phone number is incorrect, call (area code) 555-1212 and request the new listing.

Experts

Pompe's Disease....Staff NIDDK 301-496-3583
Poor, Working, Employment/Unemployment Statistics....Herz, Diane LABOR 202-606-6378
Population Dynamics and Problems....Staff NICHD 301-496-5133
Population Ecology, Fish and Wildlife....Staff FWS 703-358-1710
Population Health Studies....Goldsmith, Robert NEIC 301-903-5926
Population Information....Staff CENSUS 301-763-5002
Population Survey (Current), Earnings, Empl/Unempl.....Mellor, Earl LABOR 202-606-6378
Population, Age and Sex (States, Counties)....Staff CENSUS 301-763-5072
Population, Aging....Goldstein, Arnold CENSUS 301-763-7883
Population, Apportionment....Speaker, Robert CENSUS 301-763-7962
Population, Citizenship....Staff CENSUS 301-763-7955
Population, Commuting....Boertein, Celia CENSUS 301-763-3850
Population, Consumer Expenditure Survey....Hoff, Gail CENSUS 301-763-2063
Population, Crime....McGinn, Larry CENSUS 301-763-1735
Population, Disability....McNeil, Jack CENSUS 301-763-8300
Population, Education....Staff CENSUS 301-763-1154
Population, Estimates....Staff CENSUS 301-763-7722
Population, General Information....Staff CENSUS 301-763-5002
Population, Group Quarters....Smith, Denise CENSUS 301-763-7883
Population, Homeless....Tauber, Cynthia CENSUS 301-763-7883
Population, Language....Staff CENSUS 301-763-1154
Population, Longitudinal Surveys....Dopkowski, Ronald CENSUS 301-763-2767
Population, National Estimates....Staff CENSUS 301-763-7950
Population, National Surveys....Staff CENSUS 301-763-7950
Population, Outlying Areas....Levin, Michael CENSUS 301-763-5134
Population, Place of Birth...Hansen, Kristin CENSUS 301-763-3850
Population, School District Data....Ingold, Jane CENSUS 301-763-3476
Population, State & Outlying Areas Estimates....Staff CENSUS 301-763-5072
Population, State Projections....Staff CENSUS 301-763-1902
Porcelain Electrical Supplies, Part....Whitley, Richard A. COMMERCE 202-482-2213
Pork....Ludwick, David USITC 202-205-3329
Pork bellies with options....Prentice, Jon CFT 312-353-8647
Porphyria....Staff NIAMS 301-496-8188
Porphyria....Staff NIDDK 301-496-3583
Portugal....Double, Mary Beth Cnty Commerce 202-482-4508
Portugal (Lisbon)....Staff Cnty State 202-647-1412
Portugal/Minerals....Newman, Harold R. Cnty Mines 202-501-9669
Position Emission Tomography....Wood, Robert NEIC 301-903-5355
Positron Emission Tomography....Staff NINDS 301-496-5751
Postage-franking machines....Baker, Scott USITC 202-205-3386
Postal Services....Staff OD/DAS (Mailroom) 301-496-5651
Postdoctoral Fellowships....Staff OD/OERT 301-496-1963
Postdoctoral Fellowships....Staff DRG 301-496-7441
Postherpetic Neuralgia....Staff NINDS 301-496-5751
Postnatal Care....Staff NICHD 301-496-5133
Postpolio Myelitis Atrophy....Staff NINDS 301-496-5751
Postpolio Syndrome....Staff NINDS 301-496-5751
Postural Hypotension....Staff NHLBI 301-496-4236
Potash....Searls, James P. MINES 202-501-9407
Potash....Trainor, Cynthia USITC 202-205-3354
Potassic fertilizers....Trainor, Cynthia USITC 202-205-3354
Potassium & sodium salts from coconut & other oils....Land, Eric USITC 202-205-3349
Potassium (Content of Foods)....Staff NHLBI 301-496-4236
Potassium chloride....Trainor, Cynthia USITC 202-205-3354
Potassium compounds....Greenblatt, Jack USITC 202-205-3353
Potatoes....Budge, Arvin Agri 202-720-4285
Potatoes....Lucier, Gary Agri 202-219-0884
Potatoes....Zepp, Glenn Agri 202-219-0883
Potatoes....McCarty, Timothy USITC 202-205-3324
Pottery....Harris, John M. COMMERCE 202-482-0348
Pottery....McNay, Deborah USITC 202-205-3425
Poultry....Newman, Douglas USITC 202-205-3328
Poultry - Broilers, Turkeys and Eggs....Moore, Joel Agri 202-720-3244
Poultry - Broilers, Turkeys and Eggs....Little, Robert Agri 202-720-6147
Poultry - Broilers, Turkeys, Eggs....Krutchen, Tom Agri 202-690-4870
Poultry - Broilers, Turkeys, Eggs....Christensen, Lee Agri 202-219-0714
Poultry - Broilers, Turkeys, Eggs....Perez, Agnes Agri 202-219-0714
Poultry - Broilers, Turkeys, Eggs - World....Witucki, Larry Agri 202-219-0766
Poultry Products....Hodgen, Donald A. COMMERCE 202-482-3346
Poverty Statistics, Current Surveys....Staff CENSUS 301-763-8578
Powder, smokeless....Johnson, Larry USITC 202-205-3351
Powered-Lift Technology....Waller, Peter NASA 415-604-3938
Prader-Willi Syndrome....Staff NICHD 301-496-5133
Precious Metal Jewelry....Harris, John M. COMMERCE 202-482-1178
Precious stones....White, Linda USITC 202-205-3427
Precocious Puberty....Staff NICHD 301-496-5133
Predator Control, Fish and Wildlife....Staff FWS 703-358-1718
Prefabricated Buildings, Metal....Williams, Franklin COMMERCE 202-482-0132
Prefabricated Buildings, Wood....Cosslett, Patrick COMMERCE 202-482-0132
Pregnancy....Staff NICHD 301-496-5133
Pregnancy....Staff NCNR 301-496-0526
Pregnancy and Infant Health....Atrash, Hani K. CDC 404-488-5147
Prematurity....Staff NICHD 301-496-5133
Prenatal Care....Staff NICHD 301-496-5133
Prenatal Nutrition....Staff NICHD 301-496-5133
Prepared Meats....Hodgen, Donald A. COMMERCE 202-482-3346
Presbycusis....Staff NINDS 301-496-5751
Presbycusis....Staff NIDCD 301-496-7243
Presbycusis/Hearing and Aging....Staff NINDS 301-496-5751
Presbycusis/Hearing and Aging....Staff NIA 301-496-1752
Presbycusis/Hearing and Aging....Staff NIDCD 301-496-7243
Presbyopia....Staff NEI 301-496-5248
Presenile Dementia....Staff NIA 301-496-1752
Presenile Dementia....Staff NINDS 301-496-5751
Presenile Dementia....Staff NIMH 301-443-4515
Press Information....Staff CENSUS 301-763-4040
Pretrial Release and Crime - Federal....Kaplan, Carol Justice Stat 202-307-0759
Preventive Health Block Grant....Berreth, Don CDC 404-639-3286
Price Indexes (Consumer) Prices & Liv. Cond.....Jackman, Patrick LABOR 202-606-6952
Price Indexes, International, Assist. Commiss.....Reut, Katrina LABOR 202-606-7100
Price and Index Number Research, Prices/Lv. Cond....Zieschang, Kimberly LABOR 202-606-6573
Prices & Liv. Cond, Consumer Expenditure Survey....Jacobs, Eva LABOR 202-606-6900
Prices & Living Conditions, Assist. Commis.....Dalton, Kenneth LABOR 202-606-6960
Prices & Living Conditions, Consumer Price Indexes....Staff LABOR 202-606-7000
Prices & Living Conditions, Food, Raw Matls, Apprl....Frumkin, Rob LABOR 202-606-7106
Prices & Living Conditions, Intl. Prices, Revision....Reut, Katrina LABOR 202-606-7100
Prices & Living Conditions, Intl. Pr., Machinery....Costello, Brian LABOR 202-606-7107
Prices and Living Conditions, Data Diskettes....Rosenberg, Elliott LABOR 202-606-7728
Prices and Living Conditions, Non-electric mach.....Dickerson, Bryandt LABOR 202-606-7734
Prices and Living Conditions, Services....Gerduk, Irwin LABOR 202-606-7748
Prices and Living Conditions, Statistical Methods....Hedges, Brian LABOR 202-606-6897
Prices, Foreign Countries, Prod. & Technol.....Godbout, Todd LABOR 202-606-5654
Prices/Living Cond, Asst Commr, Consumer Price Index....Armknecht, Paul LABOR 202-606-6952
Prices/Living Cond., Recorded PPI Detail....24-hour hotline LABOR 202-606-7828
Prices/Living Conditions, Dept. Store Inventory....Gibson, Sharon LABOR 202-606-6968
Prices/Living Conds, Associate Commissioner....Dalton, Kenneth LABOR 202-606-6960
Prices/Living Conds, Asst Commr, Consumer Prices....Armknecht, Paul LABOR 202-606-6952
Prices/Living Conds, CPI Recorded Detail....24-Hour Hotline LABOR 202-606-7828
Prices/Living Conds, CPI, Data Diskettes....Gibson, Sharon LABOR 202-606-6968
Prices/Living Conds, Consumer Expend Survey....Jacobs, Eva LABOR 202-606-6900
Prices/Living Conds, Consumer Expend Survey Data....Passero, William LABOR 202-606-6900
Prices/Living Conds, Consumer Expend Survey Operations....Dietz, Richard

Population / Progeria

LABOR 202-606-6872
Prices/Living Conds, Consumer Expend Survey Tapes....Passero, William LABOR 202-606-6900
Prices/Living Conds, Consumer Price Indexes....Jackman, Patrick LABOR 202-606-6952
Prices/Living Conds, Data Diskettes....Rosenberg, Elliott LABOR 202-606-7728
Prices/Living Conds, Electric machinery & Transpor....Yatsko, Ralph LABOR 202-606-7745
Prices/Living Conds, Estd Retail Food Price, Mthly....Cook, William LABOR 202-606-6988
Prices/Living Conds, Forestry and Construction....Davies, Wanda LABOR 202-606-7713
Prices/Living Conds, Index Number Research Studies....Zieschang, Kimberly LABOR 202-606-6573
Prices/Living Conds, Indexes, Fuels, Mthly....Adkins, Robert LABOR 202-606-6985
Prices/Living Conds, Indexes, Utils, Mthly....Adkins, Robert LABOR 202-606-6985
Prices/Living Conds, Intl Price Indexes....Reut, Katrina LABOR 202-606-7100
Prices/Living Conds, Leather....Paik, Soon LABOR 202-606-7714
Prices/Living Conds, Machinery....Alterman, William LABOR 202-606-7108
Prices/Living Conds, Metals....Kazanowski, Edward LABOR 202-606-7735
Prices/Living Conds, Non-electric Machinery....Dickerson, Bryandt LABOR 202-606-7734
Prices/Living Conds, PPI, Current Analysis....Howell, Craig LABOR 202-606-7705
Prices/Living Conds, PPI, Forestry....Davies, Wanda LABOR 202-606-7713
Prices/Living Conds, Price Research Studies....Zieschang, Kimberly LABOR 202-606-6753
Prices/Living Conds, Producer Price Indexes....Tibbetts, Thomas LABOR 202-606-7700
Prices/Living Conds, Recorded CPI Summary...24-Hour quickline LABOR 202-606-6994
Prices/Living Conds, Retail Prices, Fuels, Mthly....Adkins, Robert LABOR 202-606-6985
Prices/Living Conds, Retail Prices, Gasoline....Chelena, Joseph LABOR 202-606-6982
Prices/Living Conds, Retail Prices, Utils, Mthly....Adkins, Robert LABOR 202-606-6985
Prices/Living Conds, Textiles....Paik, Soon LABOR 202-606-7714
Prices/Living Conds, Transportation Equipment....Yatsko, Ralph LABOR 202-606-7745
Primary Lateral Sclerosis....Staff NINDS 301-496-5751
Primary Plastics....Reilly, Cornelius CUSTOMS 212-466-5770
Primate Research....Staff NCRR 301-496-5545
Primate Research Centers Program....Staff NCRR 301-496-5175
Principe....Blackwell, Gloria Peace Corps 202-606-3998
Principe....Swezey, Virginia Peace Corps 202-606-3998
Printed Matter....Abramowitz, Carl CUSTOMS 212-466-5733
Printed circuit boards....Malison, Andrew USITC 202-205-3391
Printed matter....Stahmer, Carsten USITC 202-205-3321
Printing & Publishing....Lofquist, William COMMERCE 202-482-0379
Printing Trade Services....Bratland, Rose Marie COMMERCE 202-482-0380
Printing Trades Machines/Equipment....Kemper, Alexis COMMERCE 202-482-5956
Printing ink....Johnson, Larry USITC 202-205-3351
Printing machines....Slingerland, David USITC 202-205-3400
Printing machines (textiles)....Greene, William USITC 202-205-3405
Prisoner Surveys, National Prisoner Statistics....McGinn, Larry CENSUS 301-763-1735
Prisons, Prisoners, and Crowding....Beck, Allen Justice Stat 202-616-3277
Prisons, Prisoners, and Crowding....Innes, Christopher Justice Stat 202-724-3121
Prisons, Prisoners, and Crowding....Baunach, Phyllis Jo Justice Stat 202-307-0361
Prisons, Prisoners, and Crowding....Greenfeld, Lawrence Justice Stat 202-616-3281
Prisons, Prisoners, and Crowding....Huggins, Wayne M. Justice Stat 202-307-3106
Prisons, Prisoners, and Crowding....Stephan, James Justice Stat 202-616-7273
Privacy and Security of Data....Kaplan, Carol Justice Stat 202-307-0759
Private Carriers Communications....Staff FCC 717-337-1212
Private Operational Fixed Services....Staff FCC 717-337-1212
Private Security....Zawitz, Marianne Justice Stat 202-616-3499
Private Wire Systems--Telephone & Telegraph....Staff FCC 202-634-1800

Privatization of Corrections....Lindgren, Sue Justice Stat 202-307-0760
Probation and Probationers....Greenfeld, Lawrence Justice Stat 202-616-3281
Procaine....Staff NIA 301-496-1752
Process Control Instruments....Nealon, Margaret COMMERCE 202-482-3411
Process Control Instruments, Trade Promo.....Manzolilo, Frank COMMERCE 202-482-2991
Producer Price Indexes Prices/Living Cond.....Tibbetts, Thomas LABOR 202-606-7700
Producer Price Indexes, Analysis and Data....Howell, Craig LABOR 202-606-7705
Producer Price Indexes, Analysis and Data....Howell, Craig LABOR 202-606-7705
Producer Price Indexes, Electric Machinery & Trans....Yatsko, Ralph LABOR 202-606-7745
Producer Price Indexes, Forestry & Construction....Davies, Wanda LABOR 202-606-7713
Producer Price Indexes, Metals....Kazanowski, Edward LABOR 202-606-7735
Producer Price Indexes, Textiles & Leather....Paik, Soon LABOR 202-606-7714
Productivity & Technology, Assist. Commis.....Dean, Edwin R. LABOR 202-606-5600
Productivity & Technology, Data Diskettes....Fulco, Lawrence J. LABOR 202-606-5604
Productivity & Technology, Data Tapes....Kriebel, Bertram LABOR 202-606-5606
Productivity & Technology, Employment Projections....Franklin, James LABOR 202-606-5709
Productivity & Technology, Employment Requirement Tbls....Franklin, James LABOR 202-606-5709
Productivity/Techlgy, Compensation, For. Countries....Capdevielle, Patricia LABOR 202-606-5654
Productivity/Techlgy, Data Tapes....Kriebel, Bertram LABOR 202-606-5606
Productivity/Techlgy, Earnings, Foreign Countries....Capdevielle, Patricia LABOR 202-606-5654
Productivity/Techlgy, For Countries, Other Econ In....Neef, Arthur LABOR 202-606-5654
Productivity/Techlgy, Foreign Countries, Labor For....Sorrentino, Constance LABOR 202-606-5654
Productivity/Techlgy, Foreign Countries, Productivity....Neef, Arthur LABOR 202-606-5654
Productivity/Techlgy, Foreign Countries, Unemployment....Sorrentino, Constance LABOR 202-606-5654
Productivity/Techlgy, Productivity Research....Harper, Michael LABOR 202-606-5603
Productivity/Techlgy, Productivity in Government....Forte, Darlene J. LABOR 202-606-5621
Productivity/Techlgy, Productivity & Costs-News Release....Fulco, Lawrence J. LABOR 202-606-5604
Productivity/Techlgy, Productivity Trends Federal Govt....Ardolini, Charles W. LABOR 202-606-5618
Productivity/Technlgy, Associate Commissioner....Dean, Edwin R. LABOR 202-606-5600
Productivity/Technlgy, Cost-of-Living Abroad....Capdevielle, Patricia LABOR 202-606-5654
Productivity/Technlgy, Tech Trends, Major Ind....Riche, Richard LABOR 202-606-5626
Productivity Research, Capital Measurement, Pr/Tch....Harper, Michael LABOR 202-606-5603
Productivity Trends Selected Industries....Ardolini, Charles W. LABOR 202-606-5618
Productivity Trends in Selected Ind. & Fed. Gov't....Ardolini, Charles W. LABOR 202-606-5618
Productivity in Government, Productivity & Tech....Forte, Darlene J. LABOR 202-606-5621
Productivity, Multifactor, Labor Composition, Hrs.....Rosenblum, Larry LABOR 202-606-5606
Productivity, Unit Labor Costs, Foreign Countries....Neef, Arthur LABOR 202-606-5654
Professional services....Xavier, Neil USITC 202-205-3450
Progeria....Staff NIA 301-496-1752
Progestins and Progesterone....Staff NICHD 301-496-5133
Progestins and Progesterone....Staff HRSA/DMCH 301-443-4026
Progressive Cerebral Degeneration....Staff NINDS 301-496-5751
Progressive Dementia in Children....Staff NINDS 301-496-5751
Progressive Infantile Spinal Muscular Atrophy....Staff NINDS 301-496-5751
Progressive Leukodystrophy....Staff NINDS 301-496-5751
Progressive Multifocal Leukoencephalopathy....Staff NINDS 301-496-5751

Be patient. If any phone number is incorrect, call (area code) 555-1212 and request the new listing.

Experts

Progressive Muscular Atrophy....Staff NINDS 301-496-5751
Progressive Supranuclear Palsy....Staff NINDS 301-496-5751
Progressive Systemic Sclerosis....Staff NINDS 301-496-5751
Progressive Systemic Sclerosis....Staff NIAMS 301-496-8188
Project LASER Discovery Lab....Armstrong, Pat NASA 205-544-1798
Project LASER Volunteer Programs....Widenhofer, Karen NASA 205-544-3234
Projections, Labor Force, Employment Projections....Fullerton, Howard LABOR 202-606-5711
Projections, Occupational, Empl. Proj.....Rosenthal, Neal LABOR 202-606-5701
Projectors (photographic)....Bishop, Kathryn USITC 202-205-3494
Propagation Research, Fish and Wildlife....Staff FWS 703-358-1710
Propagation--Radio Waves....Staff FCC 202-632-7025
Propane....Land, Eric USITC 202-205-3349
Property Records--Common Carrier....Staff FCC 202-634-1861
Propulsion Systems....Brogan, John NEIC 202-586-1477
Propylene....Raftery, Jim USITC 202-205-3365
Propylene glycol....Michels, David USITC 202-205-3352
Propylene oxide....Michels, David USITC 202-205-3352
Prosecution....Gaskins, Carla Justice Stat 202-508-8550
Prosecution....Langan, Patrick Justice Stat 202-616-3490
Prostaglandins....Staff NICHD 301-496-5133
Prostaglandins....Staff NHLBI 301-496-4236
Prostate Enlargement....Staff NIDDK 301-496-3583
Prostate/Hyperplasia of the Prostate....Staff NIA 301-496-1752
Prostate/Hyperplasia of the Prostate....Staff NIDDK 301-496-3583
Prostatitis....Staff NIDDK 301-496-3583
Prostheses (Heart and Blood Vessel)....Staff NHLBI 301-496-4236
Prostheses (Orthotics)....Staff NIAMS 301-496-8188
Prosthodontics....Staff NIDR 301-496-4261
Protein Abnormalities with Neurologic Disease....Staff NINDS 301-496-5751
Protein Engineering....Staff DCRT 301-496-1100
Prurigo Nodularis....Staff NIAMS 301-496-8188
Pseudogout....Staff NIAMS 301-496-8188
Pseudohypoparathyroidism....Staff NIDDK 301-496-3583
Pseudosenility....Staff NIA 301-496-1752
Pseudotumor Cerebri....Staff NEI 301-496-5248
Pseudotumor Cerebri....Staff NINDS 301-496-5751
Pseudoxanthoma Elasticum....Staff NHLBI 301-496-4236
Psittacosis....Staff NIAID 301-496-5717
Psoriasis....Staff NIAMS 301-496-8188
Psoriatic Arthritis....Staff NIAMS 301-496-8188
Psychology....Allen, Joseph P. UVA 701-982-4727
Psychology....McCarty, Richard UVA 701-924-4730
Psychoneuroimmunomodulation....Staff NINDS 301-496-5751
Psychopharmacology....Staff NIMH 301-443-4515
Psychotherapeutic agents....Nesbitt, Elizabeth USITC 202-205-3355
Psychotic Episodes....Staff NIMH 301-443-4515
Pterygium....Staff NEI 301-496-5248
Ptosis....Staff NEI 301-496-5248
Public Affairs Office....Banks, Valarie FTC 202-326-2177
Public Affairs, Office of....Berreth, Donald CDC 404-639-3286
Public Cellular Radio....Staff FCC 202-632-6400
Public Defense....Gaskins, Carla Justice Stat 202-508-8550
Public Health Practice Program....Baker, Edward L. CDC 404-639-1900
Public Health and Safety....Ziemer, Paul NEIC 202-586-6151
Public Housing....Staff HUD 202-708-0950
Public Information Center....Staff EPA 202-260-7751
Public Information Office....Dye, Larry ACF 202-401-9215
Public Information Office....Miller, James ADAMHA 301-443-8956
Public Information Office....Isquith, Bob AHCPR 301-227-8364
Public Information Office....Grigg, Bill ASH 202-690-6867
Public Information Office....Fendler, Gary FDA 301-443-1130
Public Information Office....Erbe, Kevin L. HCFA 202-690-8390
Public Information Office....Mehuron, Charlotte HRSA 301-443-3376
Public Information Office....Holtz, Judy IG 202-619-1142
Public Information Office....DeAsis, Patricia IHS 301-443-3593
Public Information Office....Velez, Larry OCR 202-619-1587
Public Information Office....Gambino, Phil SSA 410-965-8904
Public Information Office - Atlanta....Mull, Daryl SSAREG 404-331-0612
Public Information Office - Boston....Czarnowski, Kurt SSAREG 617-565-2881
Public Information Office - Chicago....Mahler, Mary SSAREG 312-353-7092
Public Information Office - Dallas....O'Neil, Dee SSAREG 214-767-4191
Public Information Office - Denver....Shellhamer, Janice SSAREG 303-844-4441
Public Information Office - Kansas City....Bischof, Ken SSAREG 816-426-6191
Public Information Office - New York....Clark, John SSAREG 212-264-2500
Public Information Office - Philadelphia....Edward, Dana SSAREG 215-596-6981
Public Information Office - San Francisco....Walker, Leslie SSAREG 415-744-4664
Public Information Office - Seattle....Farrell, Dan SSAREG 206-399-4256
Public Information Office, Chief....Howenstine, Barbara W. ECONOMIC 202-523-0777
Public Information, Director, Office of....Mehnert, Robert NLM 301-496-6308
Public Information, Fish and Wildlife Service....Staff FWS 202-208-5634
Public Land Mobile Radio Service....Staff FCC 202-653-5560
Public Microwave....Staff FCC 202-634-1706
Public Opinion About Crime....Lindgren, Sue Justice Stat 202-307-0760
Public Opinion About Crime....Zawitz, Marianne Justice Stat 202-616-3499
Public Relations....Grunig, James E. UMD 301-405-2416
Public Rural Radio....Staff FCC 202-653-5560
Public Services Division....Lacroix, Eve-Marie NLM 301-496-5501
Public Surveys, Fish and Wildlife Service....Staff FWS 703-358-1730
Public Use, Fish and Wildlife Hatcheries....Staff FWS 703-358-1715
Public Use, Fish and Wildlife Refuges....Staff FWS 703-358-2029
Public relations....R-Archila, Laura USITC 202-205-3411
Public relations theory and techniques....Zerbinos, Eugenia UMD 301-405-2430
Public relations, magazine journalism....Grunig, Larissa A. UMD 301-405-2431
Public-Use Microdata Samples....Campbell, Carmen CENSUS 301-763-2005
Publications (Inquiries) and NLM Photos/Slides....Beckwith, Frances NLM 301-496-6308
Publications Information, Public. & Spec. Studies....Staff LABOR 202-606-7828
Publications Office, Press Officer....Hoyle, Kathryn LABOR 202-606-5902
Publications Office, Recorded Current....24-Hour Hotline LABOR 202-606-7828
Publications Office, TDD (Telecom. Device for Deaf)....TDD LABOR 202-606-5897
Publications and Special Studies, Assoc. Com....Klein, Deborah P. LABOR 202-606-5900
Publishing....Lofquist, William COMMERCE 202-482-0379
Puerto Rico....Soto, Rodrigo Cnty Commerce 202-482-2527
Pulleys....Vacant USITC 202-205-3380
Pulmonary Alveolar Proteinosis....Staff NHLBI 301-496-4236
Pulmonary Angiomyomatosis....Staff NHLBI 301-496-4236
Pulmonary Diseases (Infectious/Allergenic)....Staff NIAID 301-496-5717
Pulmonary Diseases (Non-Inf., Non-All., Non-Tum.)....Staff NHLBI 301-496-4236
Pulmonary Diseases (Tumorous/Cancerous)....Staff NCI 301-496-5583
Pulmonary Edema....Staff NHLBI 301-496-4236
Pulmonary Embolism....Staff NHLBI 301-496-4236
Pulmonary Emphysema....Staff NHLBI 301-496-4236
Pulmonary Fibrosis....Staff NHLBI 301-496-4236
Pulp Mills, Major Proj.....White, Barbara COMMERCE 202-482-4160
Pulp machines....Slingerland, David USITC 202-205-3400
Pulp, articles of....Rhodes, Richard USITC 202-205-3322
Pulpmills....Stanley, Gary COMMERCE 202-482-0375
Pulpwood....Ruggles, Fred USITC 202-205-3325
Pumice....Bolen, Wallace P. MINES 202-501-9389
Pumice....White, Linda USITC 202-205-3427
Pumps....Riedl, Karl CUSTOMS 212-466-5493
Pumps, Pumping Eqmt....McDonald, Edward COMMERCE 202-482-0680
Pumps, Valves, Comp (Trade Promo.)....Heimowitz, Leonard COMMERCE 202-482-0558
Pumps, air and vacuum....Mata, Ruben USITC 202-205-3403
Pumps, liquid....Mata, Ruben USITC 202-205-3403
Pure Red Cell Aplasia....Staff NHLBI 301-496-4236
Purpura....Staff NIAMS 301-496-8188
Purpura....Staff NIDDK 301-496-3583
Putty....Johnson, Larry USITC 202-205-3351
Puzzles....Luther, Dennis USITC 202-205-3497
Pyelonephritis....Staff NIDDK 301-496-3583
Pyorrhea....Staff NIDR 301-496-4261
Pyrethrum....Wanser, Stephen USITC 202-205-3363
Pyridine....Foreso, Cynthia USITC 202-205-3348

Q

Qatar....Fitzgerald-Wilks, Kate/Thanos, Paul Cnty Commerce 202-482-1870
Qatar (Doha)....Staff Cnty State 202-647-6572
Qatar/Minerals....Izon, David Cnty Mines 202-501-9692
Quadriplegia....Staff NINDS 301-496-5751
Quality Control--Common Carrier....Staff FCC 202-634-1800
Quarantine, Disease....McCance, Charles R. CDC 404-639-1455
Quarterly Financial Report....Zarrett, Paul CENSUS 301-763-2718
Quarterly, Occupational Outlook, Empl. Proj.....Fountain, Melvin LABOR 202-606-5707
Quartz Crystal....Ober, Joyce A. MINES 202-501-9406
Quartzite....White, Linda USITC 202-205-3427
Quasars....Staff NASA 205-544-0034
Quaternary ammonium salts, fatty acids....Land, Eric USITC 202-205-3349
Quebracho....Wanser, Stephen USITC 202-205-3363
Quill, articles of....Spalding, Josephine USITC 202-205-3498
Quilts....Sweet, Mary Elizabeth USITC 202-205-3455

R

RCRA Information Hotline....Staff EPA 415-744-2074
RCRA/Superfund (OUST Hotline)....Staff EPA 800-424-9346
Rabies....Staff NIAID 301-496-5717
Race Statistics....Staff CENSUS 301-763-2607
Racing shells....Hagey, Michael USITC 202-205-3392
Radar Intrusion Alarms (unlicensed)....Staff 202-653-6288
Radar apparatus....Kitzmiller, John USITC 202-205-3387
Radial Keratotomy....Staff NEI 301-496-5248
Radiation....Staff NCI 301-496-5583
Radiation (Effect on Eyes)....Staff NEI 301-496-5248
Radiation (Effect on Teeth)....Staff NIDR 301-496-4261
Radiation (Nervous System)....Staff NINDS 301-496-5751
Radiation (Nonionizing)....Staff OD/ORS 301-496-2960
Radiation (Nonionizing)....Staff NIEHS 919-541-3345
Radiation (X-ray) Effects on Fetus....Staff FDA 301-443-2356
Radiation Environmental Laws....Wallo, Andrew NEIC 202-586-4996
Radiation Hazards....Staff FCC 202-653-8169
Radiation Programs, Office of....Staff EPA 202-233-9320
Radiation Protection....Simpson, Paul D. CDC 404-639-3145
Radiation Questions....Staff EPA 202-233-9280
Radiation Safety....Cruzan, Susan FDA 301-443-3285
Radiation Safety (Radio. Spills, Lab. Surveys)....Staff OD/ORS 301-496-5774
Radiation Safety Badges....Staff OD/ORS 301-496-2254
Radiation Safety Officer....Staff NIH 301-496-2254
Radiation Studies....Smith, James M. CDC 404-488-7040
Radiation Studies Division....Staff EPA 202-233-9340
Radio & TV Broadcast Eqpmt....Rettig, Theresa COMMERCE 202-482-4466
Radio Broadcasting Advisory Committee....Staff FCC 202-632-6485
Radio Control Devices (licensed)....Staff FCC 202-632-4964
Radio Control Devices (non-licensed)....Staff FCC 202-653-6288
Radio Frequency Devices....Staff FCC 202-653-6288
Radio Noise....Staff FCC 301-725-1585
Radio Propagation....Staff FCC 202-632-7025
Radio apparatus and parts....Kitzmiller, John USITC 202-205-3387
Radio navigational apparatus....Kitzmiller, John USITC 202-205-3387
Radio receivers....Kitzmiller, John USITC 202-205-3387
Radioactive Materials (Shipping & Receiving)....Staff OD/ORS 301-496-2254
Radioactive Waste Disposal....Lytle, Jill NEIC 202-586-0370
Radioactive Waste Disposal at NIH (Solid & Liquid)....Staff OD/ORS 301-496-2254
Radiograms....Staff FCC 202-632-7265
Radiolocation--Industrial....Staff FCC 717-337-1212
Radionuclide Techniques in CV Diagnosis....Staff NHLBI 301-496-4236
Radios....Dicerbo, Mario CUSTOMS 212-466-5672
Radioscope Power Systems....Lane, Robert NEIC 301-903-4362
Radiotelegraph Common Carrier....Staff FCC 202-632-7265
Radiotelegraph Operator License....Staff FCC 202-632-7240
Radiotelephone Common Carrier Services....Staff FCC 202-652-6400
Radiotelephone Equipment....Staff FCC 301-725-1585
Radiotherapy (Cancer)....Staff NCI 301-496-5583
Radium....Staff NCI 301-496-5583
Radon Division....Staff EPA 202-233-9370
Radon Information....Staff EPA 202-233-9370
Radon Publications....Staff EPA 202-260-8366
Rags....Cook, Lee USITC 202-205-3471

Rail, locomotives....Lahey, Kathleen USITC 202-205-3409
Railroad Equipment....Wholey, Patrick CUSTOMS 212-466-5668
Railroad Services....Sousane, J. Richard COMMERCE 202-482-4582
Railroads....Staff FCC 717-337-1212
Railroads (Major Proj)....Smith, Jay L COMMERCE 202-482-4642
Railway rolling stock....Lahey, Kathleen USITC 202-205-3409
Rain Forests....Martin, R. Michael FS 703-235-1676
Rainwear....Shetty, Sundar USITC 202-205-3457
Ramsey Hunt Syndrome....Staff NINDS 301-496-5751
Ramsey Hunt Syndrome....Staff NIDCD 301-496-7243
Range Research....Lennartz, Michael R. FS 202-205-1524
Rape....Baldwin, Elaine ADAMHA 301-443-4536
Rare Disorders (Neurological)....Staff NINDS 301-496-5751
Rare Earths....Hedrick, James B. MINES 202-501-9412
Rare saccharides....Randall, Rob USITC 202-205-3366
Rare-earth compounds....Greenblatt, Jack USITC 202-205-3353
Rare-earth metals....Conant, Kenneth USITC 202-205-3346
Rate Base (International, Telegraph & Telephone)....Staff FCC 202-632-3772
Rate Level (International, Telegraph & Telephone)....Staff FCC 202-632-5550
Rate Structure (International, Telegraph & Telephone....Staff FCC 202-632-5550
Rate of Return (International, Telegraph & Telephone....Staff FCC 202-632-3772
Rattan....Ruggles, Fred USITC 202-205-3325
Raw Materials, Food, & Apparel, Intl. Price Ind.....Frumkin, Rob LABOR 202-606-7106
Raynaud's Disease....Staff NHLBI 301-496-4236
Raynaud's Disease....Staff NIAMS 301-496-8188
Reading Development....Staff NINDS 301-496-5751
Reading Development....Staff NICHD 301-496-5133
Reading Disorders....Staff NICHD 301-496-5133
Reading Disorders....Staff NINDS 301-496-5751
Reading Disorders....Staff Dept. of Education 202-245-8707
Reading Disorders....Staff NIDCD 301-496-7243
Real Earnings--News Release, Empl/Unempl. Stats....Hiles, David LABOR 202-606-6547
Recalls (Automobile Emissions)....Staff EPA 202-233-9260
Recalls (drugs)....Adams, Betsy FDA 301-443-3285
Recalls (food)....Corwin, Emil FDA 202-205-4144
Recidivism....Beck, Allen Justice Stat 202-616-3277
Recidivism....Greenfeld, Lawrence Justice Stat 202-616-3281
Recidivism....Shipley, Bernard Justice Stat 202-307-7703
Recombinant DNA....Staff NIAID 301-496-5717
Recombinant DNA....Staff NIGMS 301-496-7301
Recombinant DNA Activity....Staff OD 301-770-0131
Reconstituted crude petroleum....Foreso, Cynthia USITC 202-205-3348
Recorded CPI Detail, Prices & Living Cond.....24-Hour Hotline LABOR 202-606-7828
Recorded Messages, Compensation & Working Condition....24-hour hotline LABOR 202-606-7828
Records, tapes and recording media....Sherman, Thomas USITC 202-205-3389
Recovery Plans, Endangered Species....Staff FWS 703-358-2183
Recreation, Fish and Wildlife Recreation....Staff FWS 703-358-1715
Recreation, Refuges....Staff FWS 703-358-2029
Recreational Equipment, Export Promo.....Beckham, Reginald COMMERCE 202-482-5478
Rectifiers....Josephs, Irwin CUSTOMS 212-466-5673
Recurrent Fever....Staff NIAID 301-496-5717
Recurrent Pyogenic Infections....Staff NIAID 301-496-5717
Recycling (General Issues)....Staff EPA 202-260-6261
Recycling Program (EPA)....Staff EPA 202-260-6980
Red Blood Cells (Erythrocytes)....Staff FDA/NCDB 301-496-3556
Red Blood Cells (Erythrocytes)....Staff NHLBI 301-496-4236
Reduction of Carrier Service....Staff FCC 202-632-7553
Reeling machines....Greene, William USITC 202-205-3405
Reflex Sympathetic Dystrophy Syndrome....Staff NIAMS 301-496-8188
Reflux Nephropathy....Staff NIDDK 301-496-3583
Refractive Errors....Staff NEI 301-496-5248
Refractories....DeSapio, Vincent USITC 202-205-3435
Refractory Anemia....Staff NHLBI 301-496-4236
Refractory Products....Duggan, Brian COMMERCE 202-482-0610
Refrigeration....Rocks, Michael CUSTOMS 212-466-5669
Refrigeration equipment....Mata, Ruben USITC 202-205-3403
Refsum's Disease....Staff NINDS 301-496-5751
Refugee Resettlement....Long, Susan ACF 202-401-9215

Experts

Regional Director - Atlanta....Williams, Thomas T. HHSREG 404-331-2442
Regional Director - Boston....Davenport, Sue Winthrop HHSREG 617-565-1500
Regional Director - Chicago....Brummet-Flaum, Delilah HHSREG 312-353-5160
Regional Director - Dallas....Standefer, Paulette HHSREG 214-767-3301
Regional Director - Denver....Artist, Jane HHSREG 303-844-4545
Regional Director - Kansas City....Petrowsky, Dana HHSREG 816-426-2821
Regional Director - New York....Johnson, Jr., Cleveland HHSREG 212-264-4600
Regional Director - Philadelphia....Jacobs, Alma HHSREG 215-596-6492
Regional Director - San Francisco....Phelon, Ronald W. FTC 415-744-7920
Regional Director - San Francisco....Dana, III, Deane HHSREG 415-556-6746
Regional Director - Seattle....Kelly, Bernard E. HHSREG 206-553-0420
Regional Economic Analysis, Chief....Kort, John R. ECONOMIC 202-523-0946
Regional Economic Measurement, Chief....Hazen, Linnea ECONOMIC 202-254-6642
Regional Economics, Associate Director....Knox, Hugh W. ECONOMIC 202-523-0751
Regional Economics, Associate Director....Knox, Hugh W. ECONOMIC 202-523-0751
Regional Enteritis....Staff NIDDK 301-496-3583
Regional Medical Libraries....Staff NLM 301-496-4777
Regional Office - Atlanta....Staff CENSUS 404-347-2274
Regional Office - Atlanta....Alphin, Katherine B. FTC 404-347-7520
Regional Office - Atlanta....Bolen, Ida FTC 404-347-7046
Regional Office - Atlanta....Brennan, Virginia FTC 404-347-7540
Regional Office - Atlanta....Couillou, Chris M. FTC 404-347-7517
Regional Office - Atlanta....Davis, Paul K. FTC 404-347-4836
Regional Office - Atlanta....Dowdy, Lemuel W. FTC 404-347-7538
Regional Office - Atlanta....Foster, Andrea FTC 404-347-7516
Regional Office - Atlanta....House, Nicole L. FTC 404-347-7541
Regional Office - Atlanta....Kirtz, Harold E. FTC 404-347-7522
Regional Office - Atlanta....Laitsch, Ronald E. FTC 404-347-7535
Regional Office - Atlanta....Liebes, Cinday A. FTC 404-347-7514
Regional Office - Atlanta....Ozburn, Chris Edmonds FTC 404-347-7515
Regional Office - Atlanta....Powell, Saundra FTC 404-347-4836
Regional Office - Atlanta....Rohrer, James T. FTC 404-347-7534
Regional Office - Atlanta....Schanker, Barbara S. FTC 404-347-7518
Regional Office - Atlanta....Taylor, Mark FTC 404-347-7512
Regional Office - Atlanta....Wallace, Cheryl J. FTC 404-347-7521
Regional Office - Atlanta....Walton, Doris P. FTC 404-347-7532
Regional Office - Atlanta....Whittaker, Ingrid FTC 404-347-7536
Regional Office - Atlanta....Williams, Addie L. FTC 404-347-7510
Regional Office - Boston....Staff CENSUS 617-565-7078
Regional Office - Boston....Block, Paul G. FTC 617-565-7240
Regional Office - Boston....Bolton, Barbara E. FTC 617-565-7240
Regional Office - Boston....Caverly, Andrew FTC 617-565-7240
Regional Office - Boston....Cooper, Joanne FTC 617-565-7240
Regional Office - Boston....Cooper, Gary S. FTC 617-565-7240
Regional Office - Boston....Greenberg, Sara FTC 617-565-7240
Regional Office - Boston....Haley, Mary G. FTC 617-565-7240
Regional Office - Boston....Harrington, Diane J. FTC 617-565-7240
Regional Office - Boston....Keniry, David I., Jr. FTC 617-565-7240
Regional Office - Boston....La Due, Charles M. FTC 617-565-7240
Regional Office - Boston....McDonough, William P. FTC 617-565-7240
Regional Office - Boston....Morse, Phoebe D. FTC 617-565-7240
Regional Office - Boston....Robertson, Terry L. FTC 617-565-7240
Regional Office - Boston....Schultz, Cornelia FTC 617-565-7240
Regional Office - Boston....Sexton, Colleen FTC 617-565-7240
Regional Office - Boston....Sica, Joseph P. FTC 617-565-7240
Regional Office - Boston....Wood, Kristie FTC 617-565-7240
Regional Office - Boston....Wood, Pamela J. FTC 617-565-7240
Regional Office - Chicago....Staff CENSUS 312-353-0980
Regional Office - Chicago....Baker, Steven C. FTC 312-353-8156
Regional Office - Chicago....Daniels, Janice A. FTC 312-353-1156
Regional Office - Chicago....DiGiulio, Barbara A. FTC 312-353-4445
Regional Office - Chicago....Dodge, Karen D. FTC 312-353-4448
Regional Office - Chicago....Franczyk, Nicholas J. FTC 312-353-7957
Regional Office - Chicago....Fuller, Catherine R. FTC 312-353-5576
Regional Office - Chicago....Genda, Christine M. FTC 312-353-5261
Regional Office - Chicago....Hallerud, John C. FTC 312-353-5575
Regional Office - Chicago....Hughes, Timothy T. FTC 312-353-4431
Regional Office - Chicago....Krause, Alan E. FTC 312-353-4441
Regional Office - Chicago....McGrew, Theresa M. FTC 312-353-5532
Regional Office - Chicago....Miller, Michael T. FTC 312-353-5260
Regional Office - Chicago....Olson, Mary E. FTC 312-353-4427
Regional Office - Chicago....Owen, Nathan P. FTC 312-353-4435
Regional Office - Chicago....Russell, Thomas J. FTC 312-353-4523
Regional Office - Chicago....Smith, Michele FTC 312-353-5045
Regional Office - Chicago....Wronka, Kathleen F. FTC 312-353-4442
Regional Office - Chicago....Williams, Vassoria L. FTC 312-353-4426
Regional Office - Cleveland....Amdur, Ilene FTC 216-522-4210
Regional Office - Cleveland....Balster, Steven W. FTC 216-522-4210
Regional Office - Cleveland....Broyles, Phillip FTC 216-522-4210
Regional Office - Cleveland....Doubrava, Brenda W. FTC 216-522-4210
Regional Office - Cleveland....Greene, Willie L. FTC 216-522-4210
Regional Office - Cleveland....Griffiths, Stephanie M. FTC 216-522-4210
Regional Office - Cleveland....Hessoun, Bonnie T. FTC 216-522-4210
Regional Office - Cleveland....King, Michael L. FTC 216-522-4210
Regional Office - Cleveland....Lerner, Louis L. FTC 312-353-5528
Regional Office - Cleveland....Mendenhall, John M. FTC 216-522-4210
Regional Office - Cleveland....Milgrom, Michael FTC 216-522-4210
Regional Office - Cleveland....Pirrone, Jaclyn S. FTC 216-522-4210
Regional Office - Cleveland....Plottner, David V. FTC 216-522-4210
Regional Office - Cleveland....Powell, Catherine F. FTC 216-522-4210
Regional Office - Cleveland....Rose, Michael B. FTC 216-522-4210
Regional Office - Cleveland....Sternlicht, Melissa FTC 216-522-4210
Regional Office - Cleveland....Vantusko, Mary Jo. FTC 216-522-4210
Regional Office - Cleveland....Zeman, Gerald C. FTC 216-522-4210
Regional Office - Cleveland....Williams, Brinley H. FTC 216-522-4210
Regional Office - Dallas....Staff CENSUS 214-767-7105
Regional Office - Dallas....Arthur, Susan E. FTC 214-767-5503
Regional Office - Dallas....Black, Michael R. FTC 202-326-3457
Regional Office - Dallas....Blackman, Claire R. FTC 214-767-5503
Regional Office - Dallas....Donsky, Robin L. FTC 214-767-5503
Regional Office - Dallas....Elliott, James E. FTC 214-767-5503
Regional Office - Dallas....Garcia, Ernestina FTC 214-767-5503
Regional Office - Dallas....Golder, James R. FTC 214-767-5503
Regional Office - Dallas....Gosha-Nelson, Jannette FTC 214-767-5503
Regional Office - Dallas....Griggs, W. David FTC 214-767-5503
Regional Office - Dallas....Kennedy, Gary D. FTC 214-767-5503
Regional Office - Dallas....Lenamond, Leslee A. FTC 214-767-5503
Regional Office - Dallas....Malmberg, Kristin L. FTC 214-767-5503
Regional Office - Dallas....McCowan, Curtistene S. FTC 214-767-5503
Regional Office - Dallas....Morgan, Maridel S. FTC 214-767-5503
Regional Office - Dallas....Shepherd, Judith A. FTC 214-767-5503
Regional Office - Dallas....Spears, Debby H. FTC 214-767-5503
Regional Office - Dallas....Weart, Steven E. FTC 214-767-5503
Regional Office - Denver....Staff CENSUS 303-969-7750
Regional Office - Denver....Burns, Michael D. FTC 303-844-3565
Regional Office - Denver....Carter, Thomas B. FTC 214-767-5503
Regional Office - Denver....Charter, Janice FTC 303-844-2868
Regional Office - Denver....Cole, Pamela M. FTC 303-844-2255
Regional Office - Denver....Cramer, Norman FTC 303-844-2275
Regional Office - Denver....Dahnke, Jeffrey FTC 303-844-2254
Regional Office - Denver....Farrand, Kelli A. FTC 303-844-2253
Regional Office - Denver....Gomez, Cynthia FTC 303-844-3082
Regional Office - Denver....Keese, Deborah C. FTC 303-844-2271
Regional Office - Denver....Kessler, Jonathan FTC 303-844-2276
Regional Office - Denver....Kraus, Loretta FTC 303-844-2273
Regional Office - Denver....Mooers, Elizabeth FTC 303-844-2274
Regional Office - Denver....Naylor, Sharon L. FTC 303-844-3576
Regional Office - Denver....Redd, Patricia R. FTC 303-844-3590
Regional Office - Denver....Wild, Claude C., III FTC 303-844-3571
Regional Office - Detroit....Staff CENSUS 313-354-4654
Regional Office - Kansas City....Staff CENSUS 816-891-7562
Regional Office - Los Angeles....Dawson, Darlene FTC 310-575-7974
Regional Office - Los Angeles....Deitch, Russell S. FTC 310-575-7965
Regional Office - Los Angeles....Donaldson, Nancy D. FTC 310-575-7890
Regional Office - Los Angeles....Frauens, Sue L. FTC 310-575-7890
Regional Office - Los Angeles....French, Kathy S. FTC 310-575-6138
Regional Office - Los Angeles....Guler, Ann M. FTC 310-575-7966
Regional Office - Los Angeles....Jacobs, John D. FTC 310-575-6602
Regional Office - Los Angeles....McKown, Raymond E. FTC 310-575-7962
Regional Office - Los Angeles....Roark, Paul R. FTC 310-575-7870
Regional Office - Los Angeles....Sekovich, Dale S. FTC 310-575-7572
Regional Office - Los Angeles....Smart, Bret S. FTC 310-575-7975
Regional Office - Los Angeles....Staples, Greg FTC 310-575-7990
Regional Office - Los Angeles....Stock, Linda M. FTC 310-575-7896
Regional Office - Los Angeles....Syta, Thomas J. FTC 310-575-7879
Regional Office - Los Angeles....Updegrove, Paul M. FTC 310-575-2420

Be patient. If any phone number is incorrect, call (area code) 555-1212 and request the new listing.

Regional Director (HHS) / Retirement

Regional Office - Los Angeles....Watenmaker Dorothy N. FTC 310-575-7890
Regional Office - Los Angeles....Williams, Daylan M. FTC 310-575-7890
Regional Office - Los Angeles....Willis, Elizabeth M. FTC 310-575-7971
Regional Office - Los Angles....Staff CENSUS 818-904-6339
Regional Office - New York....Staff CENSUS 212-264-4730
Regional Office - New York....Au, Alice FTC 212-264-1210
Regional Office - New York....Bloom, Michael J. FTC 212-264-1201
Regional Office - New York....D'Amato, Donald G. FTC 212-264-1223
Regional Office - New York....Eichen, Robin E. FTC 212-264-1250
Regional Office - New York....Fischman, Ethel B. FTC 212-264-4688
Regional Office - New York....Freeman, Debra A. FTC 212-264-1229
Regional Office - New York....Goldsmith, Harriet S. FTC 212-264-1208
Regional Office - New York....Lipkowitz, Eugene FTC 212-264-1230
Regional Office - New York....Loughnan, Alan FTC 212-264-1232
Regional Office - New York....McLean, Rhonda J. FTC 212-264-1211
Regional Office - New York....Oteri, Patricia FTC 212-264-9804
Regional Office - New York....Presti, Angelo M. FTC 212-264-1220
Regional Office - New York....Roth, Marc S. FTC 212-264-8855
Regional Office - New York....Thompson, Luvennia H. FTC 212-264-0287
Regional Office - New York....Waldman, Ronald FTC 212-264-1242
Regional Office - San Francisco....Badger, Linda K. FTC 415-744-7920
Regional Office - San Francisco....Davis, Venita L. FTC 415-744-7920
Regional Office - San Francisco....Dominguez-Aldama, Rosa FTC 415-744-7920
Regional Office - San Francisco....Ehrenreich, Eric FTC 415-744-7920
Regional Office - San Francisco....Gold, Matthew FTC 415-744-7920
Regional Office - San Francisco....Kauffman, Craig D. FTC 415-744-7920
Regional Office - San Francisco....Klurfeld, Jeffrey A. FTC 415-744-7920
Regional Office - San Francisco....Kundig, Sylvia J. FTC 415-744-7920
Regional Office - San Francisco....Newmann, David M. FTC 415-744-7920
Regional Office - San Francisco....O'Brien, Kerry FTC 415-744-7920
Regional Office - San Francisco....Sodergren, Harold G. FTC 415-744-7920
Regional Office - San Francisco....Steiner, Jerome M., Jr. FTC 415-744-7920
Regional Office - San Francisco....Steinitz, Sidney FTC 202-326-3282
Regional Office - San Francisco....Stone, Ralph E. FTC 415-744-7920
Regional Office - San Francisco....Wodinsky, Erika R. FTC 415-744-7920
Regional Office - San Francisco....Wright, Gerald E. FTC 415-744-7920
Regional Office - San Francisco....Weigand, John FTC 415-744-7920
Regional Office - Seattle....Staff CENSUS 206-728-5314
Regional Office - Seattle....Benfield, Mary T. FTC 206-553-4656
Regional Office - Seattle....Brook, Randall H. FTC 206-553-4656
Regional Office - Seattle....Durham, Eleanor FTC 206-553-4656
Regional Office - Seattle....Fournier, Dean A. FTC 206-553-4656
Regional Office - Seattle....France, Laureen FTC 206-553-4656
Regional Office - Seattle....Harwood, Charles A. FTC 206-553-4656
Regional Office - Seattle....Hensley, Patricia A. FTC 202-553-4656
Regional Office - Seattle....Kirkwood, John B. FTC 206-553-4646
Regional Office - Seattle....Koester, Brian J. FTC 206-553-4656
Regional Office - Seattle....Leigh, Patricia FTC 206-553-4656
Regional Office - Seattle....McPeek, Zhenin FTC 206-553-4656
Regional Office - Seattle....Nielsen, Kathryn C. FTC 206-553-5656
Regional Office - Seattle....Schroeder, Robert J. FTC 206-553-4656
Regional Office - Seattle....Schuller, Stella A. FTC 206-553-4656
Regional Office - Seattle....Stansell, Maxine FTC 206-553-4656
Regional Office - Seattle....Thorleifson, Tracy S. FTC 206-553-4656
Regional Office - Seattle....Woods, K. Shane FTC 206-553-4656
Regional Office - Seattle....Zerbe, Richard O. FTC 206-553-4656
Regional Office - Seattle....Zweibel, George J. FTC 206-553-4656
Regional Office -Charlotte....Staff CENSUS 704-371-6142
Regional Office- Dallas....Hickman, Joseph L. FTC 214-767-5503
Regional, BEA Economic Areas....Trott, Jr., Edward A. ECONOMIC 202-523-0973
Regional, Disposable Personal Income....Brown, Robert ECONOMIC 202-254-6632
Regional, Dividends, Interest & Rental Income....Jolley, Charles A. ECONOMIC 202-254-6637
Regional, Economic Situation, Current....Friedenberg, Howard L. ECONOMIC 202-523-0979
Regional, Farm Proprietors' Income & Employment....Zavrel, James M. ECONOMIC 202-254-6638
Regional, Gross State Product Estimates....Dunbar Ann E. ECONOMIC 202-523-9180
Regional, Methodology....Bailey, Wallace K. ECONOMIC 202-254-6635
Regional, Personal Income & Employment, Metro Area....Hazan, Linnea ECONOMIC 202-254-6642
Regional, Personal Income and Employment, States....Hazan, Linnea ECONOMIC 202-254-6642
Regional, Personal Income and Employment, Counties....Hazan, Linnea ECONOMIC 202-254-6642
Regional, Projections-States & Metropolitan Areas....Pigler, Carmen C. ECONOMIC 202-523-0586
Regional, Shift-Share Analysis....Kort, John R. ECONOMIC 202-523-0946
Regional, State Ecometric Modeling....Lienesch, C. Thomas ECONOMIC 202-523-0943
Regional, State Quarterly Personal Income....Whiston, Isabelle B. ECONOMIC 202-254-6672
Regional, Transfer Payments....Levine, Bruce ECONOMIC 202-254-6634
Regional, Wage & Salary Income & Employment....Carnevale, Sharon ECONOMIC 202-254-7703
Regional, Requests for Pers. Income & Employment Data....Information System Staff ECONOMIC 202-254-6630
Regulators....Vacant USITC 202-205-3380
Rehabilitation....Staff NIA 301-496-1752
Reiter's Syndrome....Staff NIAMS 301-496-8188
Relays....Miller, Julius CUSTOMS 212-466-4680
Religious Studies....Childress, James F. UVA 701-924-3741
Remission....Staff NCI 301-496-5583
Remote Sensing Techniques....Sullivan, Nancy NASA 601-688-3341
Remote Sensor Systems....Koehler, Keith NASA 804-824-1579
Renal Disorders in Children....Staff NIDDK 301-496-3583
Renal Glycosuria....Staff NIDDK 301-496-3583
Renal Hypertension....Staff NHLBI 301-496-4236
Renal Tubular Acidosis....Staff NHLBI 301-496-4236
Renal Vascular Disease....Staff NHLBI 301-496-4236
Renewable Energy....Davis, Michael J. NEIC 202-586-9220
Renewable Energy Conversion....Kessler, Roland NEIC 202-586-8089
Renewable Energy Eqpmt....Garden, Les COMMERCE 202-482-0556
Renewable Energy Resources....King, Marion NEIC 202-586-8800
Renewable Energy Resources....Freedman, Karen NEIC 202-586-8800
Renovascular Hypertension....Staff NHLBI 301-496-4236
Rental (Scientific)....Staff DRS 301-496-4131
Reporting Crime to Police....Harlow, Caroline Justice Stat 202-307-0757
Reproductive Disorders....Staff NICHD 301-496-5133
Rescue Squads....Staff FCC 717-337-1212
Research & Development....Price, James B. COMMERCE 202-482-4781
Research (ethical issues)....Staff OD/OERT 301-496-7005
Research Aircraft....Brown, Dwayne C. NASA 202-453-8956
Research Career Development....Staff DRG 301-496-7441
Research Grants....Staff DRG 301-496-7441
Research Training....Staff DRG 301-496-7441
Research Training....Staff NIGMS 301-496-7301
Residence Adjustment....Zabronsky, Daniel ECONOMIC 202-254-6639
Residential Lighting Fixtures....Whitley, Richard A. COMMERCE 202-482-0682
Residual fuel oil....Foreso, Cynthia USITC 202-205-3348
Resistors....Josephs, Irwin CUSTOMS 212-466-5673
Resistors....Malison, Andrew USITC 202-205-3391
Resource Conservation and Reclamation Act (RCRA)....Traceski, Thomas NEIC 202-586-2481
Respiratory Diseases....Good, Robert C. CDC 404-639-3052
Respiratory Diseases (Infectious/Allergenic)....Staff NIAID 301-496-5717
Respiratory Diseases (Non-In., Non-All., Non-Tum.)....Staff NHLBI 301-496-4236
Respiratory Diseases (Tumorous/Cancerous)....Staff NCI 301-496-5583
Respiratory Syncytial Virus....Staff NIAID 301-496-5717
Restless Leg Syndrome....Staff NINDS 301-496-5751
Restricted Radiation Devices....Staff FCC 202-653-6288
Retail Trade....Margulies, Marvin J. COMMERCE 202-482-5086
Retail Trade, Advance Monthly Sales....Piencykoski, Ronald CENSUS 301-763-5294
Retail Trade, Annual Sales....Piencykoski, Ronald CENSUS 301-763-5294
Retail Trade, Census....Russell, Anne CENSUS 301-763-7038
Retail Trade, Monthly Inventories....Piencykoski, Ronald CENSUS 301-763-5294
Retail Trade, Monthly Trade Report....True, Irving CENSUS 301-763-7128
Retinal Degeneration....Staff NEI 301-496-5248
Retinal Detachment....Staff NEI 301-496-5248
Retinal Diseases....Staff NEI 301-496-5248
Retinal Diseases....Dudley, Peter A. FAES 301-496-5884
Retinal Vascular Disease....Staff NEI 301-496-5248
Retinitis Pigmentosa....Staff NEI 301-496-5248
Retinoblastoma....Staff NEI 301-496-5248
Retinopathies....Staff NEI 301-496-5248
Retirement....Staff NIA 301-496-1752

Experts

Retirement & Capital Acc, Employee Benefit Survey....Houff, James LABOR 202-606-6238
Retirement of Telephone Plants....Staff FCC 202-634-1861
Rett's Syndrome....Staff NINDS 301-496-5751
Reunion....Staff Cnty State 202-647-2453
Reunion/Minerals....Antonides, Lloyd Cnty Mines 202-501-9686
Reye's Syndrome....Staff NINDS 301-496-5751
Rh Factor....Staff NHLBI 301-496-4236
Rhabdomyosarcoma and Undifferentiated Sarcomas....Staff NCI 301-496-5583
Rhenium....Blossom, John W. MINES 202-501-9435
Rhenium....Lundy, David USITC 202-205-3439
Rheumatic Fever....Staff NIAID 301-496-5717
Rheumatic Heart....Staff NHLBI 301-496-4236
Rheumatoid Arthritis....Staff NIAMS 301-496-8188
Rhinitis....Staff NIAID 301-496-5717
Rhodium compounds....Greenblatt, Jack USITC 202-205-3353
Ribbons: inked....Cook, Lee USITC 202-205-3471
Ribbons: other....Shelton, Linda USITC 202-205-3457
Ribbons: typewriter....Shelton, Linda USITC 202-205-3457
Rice....Pierre-Benoist, John USITC 202-205-3320
Rice Milling....Janis, William V. COMMERCE 202-482-2250
Rice with options....Sepsey, Judy CFT 312-353-9025
Ricinoleic acid esters....Johnson, Larry USITC 202-205-3351
Rickets, Vitamin-D Resistant....Staff NIDDK 301-496-3583
Rickettsial Diseases....Staff NIAID 301-496-5717
Riding Mowers....Mesa, Stacey Reuben CPSC 301-504-0580
Riding crops....Burns, Gail USITC 202-205-3501
Rifles....Robinson, Hazel USITC 202-205-3496
Riley-Day Syndrome....Staff NINDS 301-496-5751
Ringworm....Staff NIAID 301-496-5717
River Blindness....Staff NEI 301-496-5248
River Blindness....Staff NIAID 301-496-5717
Roads, Railroads, Mass Trans (Major Proj)....Smith, Jay L. COMMERCE 202-482-4642
Robotics Research....Staff NASA 713-483-5111
Robots....Vacant COMMERCE 202-482-0314
Rocky Mountain Spotted Fever....Staff NIAID 301-496-5717
Rods, plastics....Misurelli, Denby USITC 202-205-3362
Roller Bearings....Reise, Richard COMMERCE 202-482-3489
Rolling Mill Machinery....Abrahams, Edward COMMERCE 202-482-0312
Rolling machines, except metal....Slingerland, David USITC 202-205-3400
Rollings mills, metal....Fravel, Dennis USITC 202-205-3401
Romania....Fabrizio, Lynn Cnty Commerce 202-482-2645
Romania....Becker, Margaret Peace Corps 202-606-3547
Romania....Sowry, Jenny Peace Corps 202-606-3547
Romania (Bucharest)....Staff Cnty State 202-647-3187
Romania/Minerals....Steblez, Walter Cnty Mines 202-501-9671
Roofing, Asphalt....Pitcher, Charles COMMERCE 202-482-0132
Root Caries....Staff NIDR 301-496-4261
Rope....Cook, Lee USITC 202-205-3471
Rosemary oil (essential oil)....Land, Eric USITC 202-205-3349
Rotavirus....Staff NIAID 301-496-5717
Rouges....Land, Eric USITC 202-205-3349
Rubber....Prat, Raimundo COMMERCE 202-482-0128
Rubber Products....Prat, Raimundo COMMERCE 202-482-0128
Rubber Sheet....Mazzola, Joan CUSTOMS 212-466-5880
Rubber and Plastic Articles....Mazzola, Joan CUSTOMS 212-466-5880
Rubber, Synthetic and Natural....Joseph, Stephanie CUSTOMS 212-466-5768
Rubber, natural....Misurelli, Denby USITC 202-205-3362
Rubber, synthetic....Misurelli, Denby USITC 202-205-3362
Rubella....Staff NIAID 301-496-5717
Rubeola....Staff NIAID 301-496-5717
Rubidium....Reese, Jr., Robert MINES 202-501-9413
Rugs....Hansen, John CUSTOMS 212-466-5854
Rugs....Sweet, Mary Elizabeth USITC 202-205-3455
Runaway Youth/Homeless....Long, Susan ACF 202-401-9215
Rural Aged....Staff NIA 301-496-1752
Rural Development....Mazie, Sara Agri 202-219-0530
Rural Development....McGranahan, David Agri 202-219-0532
Rural Development - Agric. & Community Linkages....Hines, Fred Agri 202-219-0525
Rural Development - Business & Industry....Bernat, Andrew Agri 202-219-0540
Rural Development - Community Development....Sears, David Agri 202-219-0544
Rural Development - Credit & Financial Markets....Sullivan, Pat Agri 202-219-0719
Rural Development - Employment....Swaim, Paul Agri 202-219-0552
Rural Development - Employment....Parker, Tim Agri 202-219-0541
Rural Development - Local Government Finance....Reeder, Richard Agri 202-219-0542
Rural Development - Local Government Finance....Jansen, Anicca Agri 202-219-0542
Rural Health....Mehuron, Charlotte HRSA 301-443-3376
Rural Residence....Staff CENSUS 301-763-7962
Russia....Brougher, J./Lewens, S./Smith, T./Johnson, P. Cnty Commerce 202-482-0354
Russia....Staff Cnty State 202-647-9806
Rwanda....Michelini, Philip Cnty Commerce 202-482-4388
Rwanda (Kigali)....Staff Cnty State 202-647-3139
Rwanda/Minerals....Antonides, Lloyd Cnty Mines 202-501-9686

S

S&P 500 Index with options....Fedinets, Robert P. CFT 312-353-9016
S&P MidCap400 Index with options....Fedinets, Robert P. CFT 312-353-9016
S-Franc with options....Bice, David CFT 312-35-37880
SAN resins....Misurelli, Denby USITC 202-205-3362
SCOR (Specialized Centers of Research)....Staff NHLBI 301-496-4236
Saccharin....Land, Eric USITC 202-205-3349
Saddlery & Harness Products....Byron, James COMMERCE 202-482-3034
Safe Drinking Water Hotline....Staff EPA 800-426-4791
Safety Equipment, Trade Promo.....Umstead, Dwight COMMERCE 202-482-2410
Safety, Health & Work. Cond, Asst. Commiss.....Eisenberg, William M. LABOR 202-606-6304
Salicin....Randall, Rob USITC 202-205-3366
Saliva....Staff NIDR 301-496-4261
Salivary System Diseases....Staff NIDR 301-496-4261
Salmonella Infections....Staff NIAID 301-496-5717
Salmonellosis and Turtles....Staff CDC 404-639-3286
Salt....Kostick, Dennis S. MINES 202-501-9410
Salt....Greenblatt, Jack USITC 202-205-3353
Salts, inorganic....Greenblatt, Jack USITC 202-205-3353
Salts, organic....Michels, David USITC 202-205-3352
Sampling Methods, Current Programs....Waite, Preston J. CENSUS 301-763-2672
San Marino....Staff Cnty State 202-647-2453
Sanction of Health Providers....Holtz, Judy IG 202-619-1142
Sand....White, Linda USITC 202-205-3427
Sand & Gravel, Construction....Tepordei, Valentin V. MINES 202-501-9392
Sandals....Shildneck, Ann USITC 202-205-3499
Sanitation....Staff OD/ORS 301-496-2960
Santavuori Disease....Staff NINDS 301-496-5751
Sao Tome....Blackwell, Gloria Peace Corps 202-606-3998
Sao Tome....Swezey, Virginia Peace Corps 202-606-3998
Sao Tome and Principe....Michelini, Philip Cnty Commerce 202-482-3318
Sao Tome and Principe....Staff Cnty State 202-647-1707
Sao Tome and Principe/Minerals....Dolley, Thomas Cnty Mines 202-501-9690
Saphenous Vein Bypass Grafts....Staff NHLBI 301-496-4236
Saran....Misurelli, Denby USITC 202-205-3362
Sarcoidosis....Staff NIAID 301-496-5717
Sarcoidosis....Staff NHLBI 301-496-4236
Sarcoidosis....Staff NEI 301-496-5248
Sarcoma....Staff NCI 301-496-5583
Sarcoma of Bone and Soft Tissue....Staff NCI 301-496-5583
Sardines....Corey, Roger USITC 202-205-3327
Satellite Communications....Peto, Mary Ann NASA 216-433-2902
Satellite Coordination & Interference....Staff FCC 202-653-8153
Satellite Design....Staff NASA 301-286-5566
Satellite Rates....Staff FCC 202-632-5550
Satellite Spread Spectrum....Staff FCC 301-725-1585
Satellite Systems....Staff FCC 202-634-1624
Satellite Systems Coordination....Staff FCC 202-653-8153
Satellite Testing....Staff NASA 301-286-5565
Satellite Tracking....Staff NASA 301-286-2806
Satellite, Domestic Facilities....Staff FCC 202-634-1624
Satellite, International Coordination....Staff FCC 202-653-8144
Satellite, International Facilities....Staff FCC 202-632-7265
Satellite, Maritime....Staff FCC 202-632-7175
Satellites, Communications....Cooper, Patricia COMMERCE 202-482-4466

Reunion / Sickle Cell Anemia

Satin white....Johnson, Larry USITC 202-205-3351
Saudi Arabia....Johnson, Jeffrey/Clement, Claude Cnty Commerce 202-482-4652
Saudi Arabia (Riyadh)....Staff Cnty State 202-647-7550
Saudi Arabia/Minerals....Michalski, Bernadette Cnty Mines 202-501-9699
Sausages....Ludwick, David USITC 202-205-3329
Scabies....Staff NIAID 301-496-5717
Scales....Slingerland, David USITC 202-205-3400
Scandium....Hedrick, James B. MINES 202-501-9412
Scarves....Jones, Jackie USITC 202-205-3466
Scarves....Hamey, Amy USITC 202-205-3465
Schilder's Disease....Staff NINDS 301-496-5751
Schistosomiasis....Staff NIAID 301-496-5717
Schizophrenia....Staff NIMH 301-443-4515
Scholars-in-Residence....Staff FIC 301-496-4161
School District Data....Ingold, Jane CENSUS 301-763-3476
Schwanoma....Staff NCI 301-496-5583
Sciatica....Staff NINDS 301-496-5751
Science and Technology Research Programs....Staff NEH 202-606-8210
Scientific Instruments, Trade Promo.....Manzolilo, Frank COMMERCE 202-482-2991
Scientific Measurement/Control Equipment....Nealon, Marguerite COMMERCE 202-482-3411
Scleroderma....Staff NIAMS 301-496-8188
Sclerosis....Staff NINDS 301-496-5751
Sclerosis, Multiple....Staff NINDS 301-496-5751
Scoliosis....Staff NIAMS 301-496-8188
Scrap cordage....Cook, Lee USITC 202-205-3471
Screening machines....Greene, William USITC 202-205-3405
Screw Machine Products....Reise, Richard COMMERCE 202-482-3489
Screws....Brandon, James USITC 202-205-3433
Screws, Washers....Reise, Richard COMMERCE 202-482-3489
Sculptures....Mushinske, Larry CUSTOMS 212-466-5739
Sea Lamprey Control....Staff FWS 703-358-1710
Sealing machinery....Slingerland, David USITC 202-205-3400
Seasonal Adjustment Methodology, Empl/Unempl. Stats....McIntire, Robert LABOR 202-606-6345
Seat belts....Cook, Lee USITC 202-205-3471
Sebacic acid esters....Johnson, Larry USITC 202-205-3351
Securities industries....Brown, Richard USITC 202-205-3438
Security & Commodity Brokers....Muir, S. Cassin COMMERCE 202-482-0347
Sedatives....Nesbitt, Elizabeth USITC 202-205-3355
Seeds....Conte, Ralph CUSTOMS 212-466-5759
Seeds, field and garden....Pierre-Benoist, John USITC 202-205-3320
Seeds, oil-bearing....Reeder, John USITC 202-205-3319
Seeds, spice....Ruggles, Fred USITC 202-205-3325
Segawa's Dystonia....Staff NINDS 301-496-5751
Selenium....Edelstein, Daniel MINES 202-501-9415
Selenium....Conant, Kenneth USITC 202-205-3346
Selenium compounds....Greenblatt, Jack USITC 202-205-3353
Self Protection, Justifiable Use of Force....Zawitz, Marianne Justice Stat 202-616-3499
Semiconductors....Mussehl-Aziz, Judee COMMERCE 202-482-2846
Semiconductors....Josephs, Irwin CUSTOMS 212-466-5673
Semiconductors....Malison, Andrew USITC 202-205-3391
Senegal....Michelini, Philip Cnty Commerce 202-482-4388
Senegal....Strozier, Maisha Peace Corps 202-606-3185
Senegal (Dakar)....Staff Cnty State 202-647-2865
Senegal/Minerals....van Oss, Hendrik Cnty Mines 202-501-9687
Senile Dementia....Staff NIA 301-496-1752
Senile Dementia....Staff NINDS 301-496-5751
Senile Dementia....Staff NIMH 301-443-1185
Senile Macular Degeneration....Staff NEI 301-496-5248
Sensorimotor Research....Zoltick, Brad J. FAES 301-496-9375
Sentencing....Gaskins, Carla Justice Stat 202-508-8550
Sentencing....Kane, Patrick R. Justice Stat 202-307-3226
Sentencing....Baunach, Phyllis Jo Justice Stat 202-307-0361
Sentencing - Federal....Kaplan, Carol Justice Stat 202-307-0759
Septal Defects....Staff NHLBI 301-496-4236
Service Industries, Census....Moody, Jack CENSUS 301-763-7039
Service Industries, Communication....Shoemaker, Dennis CENSUS 301-763-2662
Service Industries, Finance....Marcus, Sidney CENSUS 301-763-1386
Service Industries, Insurance....Marcus, Sidney CENSUS 301-763-1386
Service Industries, Real Estate....Marcus, Sidney CENSUS 301-763-1386
Service Industries, Transportation....Shoemaker, Dennis CENSUS 301-763-2662
Service Industries, Utilities....Shoemaker, Dennis CENSUS 301-763-2662
Service Industries, Current Selected Service Report....Zabelsky, Thomas CENSUS 301-763-1725
Service Industry Practices....Abdullah, Raouf M. FTC 202-326-3024
Service Industry Practices....Alcock, Jane FTC 404-347-7537
Service Industry Practices....Aliza, Ben FTC 202-326-2905
Services, DAS....Powers, Linda F. COMMERCE 202-482-5261
Services, Data Base....Inoussa, Mary C. COMMERCE 202-482-5820
Services, Data Processing....Atkins, Robert G. COMMERCE 202-482-4781
Services, Prices/Lv. Cond....Gerduk, Irwin LABOR 202-606-7748
Services/trade matters....Broadman, Harry US Trade Rep 202-395-3606
Sewage Sludge - Beneficial Use/Technology Transfer....Staff EPA 202-260-9525
Sewage Treatment - Industrial Pretreatment Program....Staff EPA 202-260-9525
Sewing Notions....Rauch, Theodore CUSTOMS 212-466-5892
Sewing and knitting needles....Laney-Cummings, Karen USITC 202-205-3431
Sewing machine needles....Greene, William USITC 202-205-3405
Sewing machines....Greene, William USITC 202-205-3405
Sewing thread: cotton....Warlick, William USITC 202-205-3459
Sewing thread: manmade fibers....Warlick, William USITC 202-205-3459
Sewing thread: silk....Shelton, Linda USITC 202-205-3457
Sewing thread: wool....Shelton, Linda USITC 202-205-3457
Sex Change....Staff NICHD 301-496-5133
Sex Determination....Staff NICHD 301-496-5133
Sex Hormones....Staff NICHD 301-496-5133
Sex and Aging....Staff NIA 301-496-1752
Sexual Development....Staff NICHD 301-496-5133
Sexually Transmitted Diseases....Staff NIAID 301-496-5717
Sexually Transmitted Diseases and HIV Prevention....Wasserheit, Judith N. CDC 404-639-2552
Seychelles....Watkins, Chandra Cnty Commerce 202-482-4564
Seychelles....Schmitz, Virginia Peace Corps 202-606-3334
Seychelles (Victoria)....Staff Cnty State 202-647-5684
Seychelles/Minerals....Antonides, Lloyd Cnty Mines 202-501-9686
Sezary Syndrome....Staff NIAMS 301-496-8188
Shale oil....Foreso, Cynthia USITC 202-205-3348
Shared Energy Cooperatives....Klunder, Kurt NEIC 202-586-2826
Shared Instrumentation Grant....Staff NCRR 301-496-6743
Shawls....Jones, Jackie USITC 202-205-3466
Sheep....Steller, Rose USITC 202-205-3323
Sheet, plastics....Misurelli, Denby USITC 202-205-3362
Sheets, bed....Sweet, Mary Elizabeth USITC 202-205-3455
Shell, articles of....Spalding, Josephine USITC 202-205-3498
Shellac and other lacs....Reeder, John USITC 202-205-3319
Shellac, varnish....Johnson, Larry USITC 201-205-3351
Shellfish....Brady, Thomas CUSTOMS 212-466-5790
Shellfish....Newman, Douglas USITC 202-205-3328
Shells, crude....Steller, Rose USITC 202-205-3323
Shingles (Herpes Zoster)....Staff NINDS 301-496-5751
Shingles (Herpes Zoster)....Staff NIAID 301-496-5717
Shingles and shakes (wood)....Ruggles, Fred USITC 202-205-3325
Shingles, Wood....Wise, Barbara COMMERCE 202-482-0375
Shingles, asphalt....Rhodes, Richard USITC 202-205-3322
Ship Earth Stations....Staff FCC 202-632-7175
Ship Inspections....Staff FCC 202-632-7014
Ship Licensing....Staff FCC 717-337-1212
Ship Rules/Exemptions....Staff FCC 202-632-7175
Shirts....Holoyda, Olha USITC 202-205-3467
Shock (Cardiogenic)....Staff NHLBI 301-496-4236
Shock (Hemorrhagic)....Staff NHLBI 301-496-4236
Shock Trauma Center....Staff UMD 301-528-6294
Shoe machinery....Vacant USITC 202-205-3380
Shoe parts....Shildneck, Ann USITC 202-205-3499
Shoes....Shildneck, Ann USITC 202-205-3499
Short-Term Forecasts of Energy Markets....Kilgore, Calvin NEIC 202-586-1617
Shorts....DeGaetano, Angela CUSTOMS 212-466-5540
Shorts: mens and boys....Linkins, Linda USITC 202-205-3469
Shorts: womens and girls....Holoyda, Olha USITC 202-205-3467
Shotguns....Robinson, Hazel USITC 202-205-3496
Shrimp....Newman, Douglas USITC 202-205-3328
Shy-Drager Syndrome....Staff NINDS 301-496-5751
Shy-Drager Syndrome....Staff NIMH 301-443-4515
Sickle Cell Anemia....Staff NHLBI 301-496-4236
Sideroblastic Anemia....Staff NHLBI 301-496-4236

Be patient. If any phone number is incorrect, call (area code) 555-1212 and request the new listing.

Experts

Siding (wood)....Ruggles, Fred USITC 202-205-3325
Sierra Leone....Michelini, Philip Cnty Commerce 202-482-4388
Sierra Leone....McCormick, Michael L. Peace Corps 202-606-3644
Sierra Leone....Herring, Debra Peace Corps 202-606-3644
Sierra Leone (Freetown)....Staff Cnty State 202-647-3395
Sierra Leone/Minerals....Michalski, Bernadette Cnty Mines 202-501-9699
Sight Substitution Systems....Staff NEI 301-496-5248
Silica....White, Linda USITC 202-205-3427
Silicon....Cunningham, Larry D. MINES 202-501-9443
Silicon....Conant, Kenneth USITC 202-205-3346
Silicon Carbide Abrasive....Austin, Gordon MINES 202-501-9388
Silicone resins....Misurelli, Denby USITC 202-205-3362
Silicones....Michels, David USITC 202-205-3352
Silk....Freund, Kimberlie USITC 202-205-3456
Silk....Shelton, Linda USITC 202-205-3457
Silk....Warlick, William USITC 202-205-3459
Sillimanite....DeSapio, Vincent USITC 202-205-3435
Silver....Reese, Jr., Robert G. MINES 202-501-9413
Silver....McNay, Deborah USITC 202-205-3425
Silver compounds....Greenblatt, Jack USITC 202-205-3353
Silver with options....Rosenfeld, David CFT 312-353-9026
Silverware....Harris, John COMMERCE 202-482-1178
Singapore....Cung, Raphael Cnty Commerce 202-482-3875
Singapore (Singapore)....Staff Cnty State 202-647-3278
Singapore/Minerals....Tse, Pui-Kwan Cnty Mines 202-501-9696
Single Family Housing....Staff HUD 202-708-3175
Single Side Band--Standards....Staff FCC 202-653-6288
Sinusitis....Staff NIAID 301-496-5717
Sirups....Williams, Joan USITC 202-205-3313
Sjogren's Syndrome....Staff NIAMS 301-496-8188
Sjogren's Syndrome....Staff NIAID 301-496-5717
Sjogren's Syndrome....Staff NINDS 301-496-5751
Sjogren's Syndrome....Staff NEI 301-496-5248
Sjogren's Syndrome....Staff NIDR 301-496-4261
Ski equipment....Robinson, Hazel USITC 202-205-3496
Skin Cancer....Staff NCI 301-496-5583
Skin Diseases....Staff NIAMS 301-496-8188
Skin and Aging....Staff NIA 301-496-1752
Skin and Aging....Staff NIAMS 301-496-8188
Skin and Sunlight....Staff NIAMS 301-496-8188
Skin and Sunlight....Staff NCI 301-496-5583
Skins (animal)....Steller, Rose USITC 202-205-3323
Skirts....Holoyda, Olha USITC 202-205-3467
Skirts, Knit and Woven....DeGaetano, Angela CUSTOMS 212-466-5540
Slack....Foreso, Cynthia USITC 202-205-3348
Slacks, mens and boys....Linkins, Linda USITC 202-205-3467
Slacks, womens and girls....Holoyda, Olha USITC 202-205-3467
Slate....White, Linda USITC 202-205-3427
Sleep Disorders....Staff NINDS 301-496-5751
Sleep Disorders....Staff NIMH 301-443-4515
Sleep Disturbances....Staff NIMH 301-443-4515
Sleep and Aging....Staff NIA 301-496-1752
Sleep and Aging....Staff NIMH 301-443-1185
Sleepwear....Kaplan, Kathy CPSC 301-504-0580
Slide fasteners....Shildneck, Ann USITC 202-205-3499
Slippers....Shildneck, Ann USITC 202-205-3499
Slow Viruses....Staff NINDS 301-496-5751
Small Business Innovation Research Program....Selby, Barbara NASA 703-557-5609
Small Business Trade Policy....Burroughs, Helen COMMERCE 202-482-4806
Small Cell Carcinoma....Staff NCI 301-496-5583
Small and Woman-Owned Business Opportunities....Staff HUD 202-708-1428
Smallpox....Staff NIAID 301-496-5717
Smell (Disorders)....Staff NINDS 301-496-5751
Smell (Disorders)....Staff NIDCD 301-496-7243
Smoke Detectors....Glover, Stephanie CPSC 301-504-0580
Smokeless Tobacco (Oral Complications)....Staff NIDR 301-496-4251
Smokeless powder....Johnson, Larry USITC 202-205-3351
Smokers' Articles....Conte, Ralph CUSTOMS 212-466-5759
Smokers' articles....Burns, Gail USITC 202-205-3501
Smoking & Health....Hensley, Timothy CDC 404-488-5705
Smoking (Cancer related)....Staff NCI 301-496-5583
Smoking and Health....Staff Off. on Smok. and Health 301-443-1575
Smoking and Health....Eriksen, Michael P. CDC 404-488-5701
Smoking and Health, Public Information....McKenna, Jeffrey P. CDC 404-488-5705
Smoking and Heart Disease....Staff NHLBI 301-496-4236

Snackfood....Janis, William V. COMMERCE 202-482-2250
Snap fasteners....Shildneck, Anna USITC 202-205-3499
Soap, castile....Land, Eric USITC 202-205-3349
Soap, surface-active agents, synthetic detergent....Land, Eric USITC 202-205-3349
Soap, toilet....Land, Eric USITC 202-205-3349
Soaps....Joseph, Stephanie CUSTOMS 212-466-5768
Soaps, Detergents, Cleansers....Hurt, William COMMERCE 202-482-0128
Soapstone....White, Linda USITC 202-205-3427
Social Services Block Grant....Long, Susan ACF 202-401-9215
Social Work Department....Staff CC 301-496-2381
Social and Behavioral Research on Aging....Staff NIA 301-496-1752
Social and Behavioral Sciences....Staff NICHD 301-496-6832
Sociology....Caplow, Theodore UVA 703-924-6397
Sociology of Journalism....Levy, Mark R. UMD 301-405-2389
Soda ash....Conant, Kenneth USITC 202-205-3346
Sodium....Lecos, Chris FDA 202-205-4144
Sodium....Conant, Kenneth USITC 202-205-3346
Sodium Compounds....Kostick, Dennis S. MINES 202-501-9410
Sodium and potassium salts of oils, greases, fat....Land, Eric USITC 202-205-3349
Sodium benzoate....Matusik, Ed USITC 202-205-3356
Sodium bicarbonate....Conant, Kenneth USITC 202-205-3346
Sodium carbonate....Conant, Kenneth USITC 202-205-3346
Sodium compounds....Greenblatt, Jack USITC 202-205-3353
Sodium hydroxide....Conant, Kenneth USITC 202-205-3346
Soft Drink....Kenney, Cornelius COMMERCE 202-482-2428
Software....Smolenskni, Mary COMMERCE 202-482-2053
Software....Hijikata, Heidi C. COMMERCE 202-482-0571
Software services....Xavier, Neil USITC 202-205-3450
Software, Export Promo....Fogg, Judy COMMERCE 202-482-4936
Solar Burns (Eye Effects)....Staff NEI 301-496-5248
Solar Cells/Photovoltaic Devices/Small Hydro....Garden, Les COMMERCE 202-482-0556
Solar Energy Conversion....San Martin, Robert NEIS 202-586-9275
Solar Energy Conversion....Annan, Robert H. NEIC 202-586-1720
Solar Eqmt. Ocean/Biomass....Garden, Les COMMERCE 202-482-0556
Solar Equipment, Geoth....Garden, Les COMMERCE 202-482-0556
Solar Phenomena Research....Staff NASA 415-604-3937
Solar System Exploration....Farrar, Diane NASA 415-604-3934
Solar Thermal and Biomass Power....Burch, Gary NEIC 202-586-8121
Solar energy....Foreso, Cynthia USITC 202-205-3348
Solid Waste Disposal....Staff OD/ORS 301-496-3537
Solid Waste Disposal (Radioactive)....Staff OD/ORS 301-496-2254
Solid Waste Information Clearinghouse Hotline....Staff EPA 800-677-9424
Solid Waste Management (Municipal)....Staff EPA 202-260-9872
Solid Waste Office of....Staff EPA 202-260-4627
Solomon Islands....Nagle, Douglas Peace Corps 202-606-3290
Solomon Islands....Jefferson, Mary Peace Corps 202-606-3231
Solomon Islands....Schell, Russell Peace Corps 202-606-3231
Solomon Islands (Honiara)....Staff Cnty State 202-647-3546
Solomon Islands/Minerals....Lyday, Travis Cnty Mines 202-501-9695
Somalia....Watkins, Chandra Cnty Commerce 202-482-4564
Somalia (Mogadishu)....Staff Cnty State 202-647-8852
Somalia/Minerals....Antonides, Lloyd Cnty Mines 202-501-9686
Sorbitol....Randall, Rob USITC 202-205-3366
Sorting machines....Greene, William USITC 202-205-3405
Sound signaling apparatus....Baker, Scott USITC 202-205-3386
Sounding Rocket Program....Koehler, Keith NASA 804-824-1579
Sounding Rockets....Brown, Dwayne C. NASA 202-453-8956
South Africa....Solomon, Emily Cnty Commerce 202-482-5148
South Africa, Republic of (Pretoria)....Staff Cnty State 202-647-8432
South Africa/Minerals....Heydari, Michael Cnty Mines 202-501-9688
South Pacific Commission....Staff Cnty State 202-647-3546
Soy Products....Janis, William V. COMMERCE 202-482-2250
Soybean Meal with options....Sweet, Margie CFT 312-353-3288
Soybean oil with options....Sweet, Margie CFT 312-353-3288
Soybeans and soybean oil....Reeder, John USITC 202-205-3319
Soybeans with options....Sweet, Margie CFT 312-353-3288
Space Communications....Brown, Dwayne C. NASA 202-453-8956
Space Derived Technology....Dunbar, Brian NASA 202-453-1547
Space Exploration....Keegan, Sarah NASA 703-271-5591
Space Flight....Cast, Jim NASA 202-453-1142
Space Flight....Campion, Edward S. NASA 202-453-1134
Space Flight Systems....Peto, Mary Ann NASA 216-433-2902
Space Industry Machinery, Nec....Shaw, Eugene COMMERCE 202-482-3494
Space Policy Development....Pajor, Pete COMMERCE 202-482-4222

Be patient. If any phone number is incorrect, call (area code) 555-1212 and request the new listing.

Siding / Starches

Space Propulsion....Ellis, Linda NASA 216-433-2900
Space Remote Sensing Commercialization....Sullivan, Nancy NASA 601-688-3341
Space Science and Applications....Cleggett-Haleim, Paula NASA 202-453-1547
Space Science and Applications....Braukus, Michael NASA 202-453-1549
Space Shuttle....James, Donald G. NASA 415-604-3935
Space Shuttle....Malone, June NASA 205-544-7061
Space Shuttle Engine Testing....Sullivan, Nancy NASA 601-688-3341
Space Shuttle Program....Staff NASA 713-483-5111
Space Shuttle Propulsion Testing....Sullivan, Nancy NASA 601-688-3341
Space Shuttle Research....Staff NASA 804-864-6122
Space Station Freedom....Peto, Mary Ann NASA 216-433-2902
Space Station Freedom....Simmons, Mike NASA 205-544-6537
Space Technology....Staff NASA 205-544-6538
Space Vehicle Testing....Buckingham, Bruce NASA 407-867-2468
Space technology....Anderen, Drucella NASA 202-453-8613
Spacecraft....Anderson, Peder USITC 202-205-3388
Spacelab....Hess, Mark NASA 202-453-4164
Spacelab Missions Operations....Drachlis, David NASA 205-544-6538
Spain....Double, Mary Beth Cnty Commerce 202-482-4508
Spain (Madrid)....Staff Cnty State 202-647-1412
Spain/Minerals....Newman, Harold R. Cnty Mines 202-501-9669
Spanish, Italian and Portuguese languages....Opere, Fernando UVA 701-924-7159
Spasmodic Dysphonia....Staff NINDS 301-496-5751
Spasmodic Torticollis....Staff NINDS 301-496-5751
Spastic Hemiplegia....Staff NINDS 301-496-5751
Spastic Paraplegia....Staff NINDS 301-496-5751
Spastic Quadriplegia....Staff NINDS 301-496-5751
Spasticity....Staff NINDS 301-496-5751
Special Industry Machinery, Nec....Shaw, Eugene COMMERCE 202-482-3494
Special Population Censuses....Dopkowski, Ronald CENSUS 301-763-2767
Special Topics - Agricultural History....Bowers, Douglas Agri 202-219-0787
Special Topics - Alternative Crops....Glaser, Lewrene Agri 202-219-0888
Special Topics - Biotechnology....Reilly, John Agri 202-219-0450
Special Topics - Biotechnology (Dairy)....Fallert, Richard Agri 202-219-0712
Special Topics - Commodity Programs & Policies....Harwood, Joy Agri 202-219-0840
Special Topics - Commodity Programs & Policies-Honey....Hoff, Fred Agri 202-219-0883
Special Topics - Commodity Programs & Policies-Tobacco....Grise, Verner Agri 202-219-0890
Special Topics - Commodity Programs & Policies-Crops....Westcott, Paul Agri 202-219-0840
Special Topics - Commodity Programs & Policies-Dairy....Fallert, Richard Agri 202-219-0712
Special Topics - Commodity Programs & Policies-Sugar....Lord, Ron Agri 202-219-0888
Special Topics - Commodity Programs & Policies-World....Dixit, Praveen Agri 202-219-0632
Special Topics - Economic Linkages to Agriculture....Edmondson, William Agri 202-219-0785
Special Topics - Energy....Gill, Mohinder Agri 202-219-0464
Special Topics - Farm Labor Laws....Runyan, Jack Agri 202-219-0932
Special Topics - Farm Labor Market....Whitener, Leslie Agri 202-219-0932
Special Topics - Farm Machinery....Vesterby, Marlow Agri 202-219-0422
Special Topics - Farm Structure....Reimund, Donn Agri 202-219-0522
Special Topics - Fertilizer....Taylor, Harold Agri 202-219-0464
Special Topics - Fertilizer....Rives, Sam Agri 202-720-2324
Special Topics - Macroeconomic Conditions....Monaco, Ralph Agri 202-219-0872
Special Topics - Macroeconomic Conditions (World)....Baxter, Tim Agri 202-219-0706
Special Topics - Natural Resource Policy....Osborn, Tim Agri 202-219-0401
Special Topics - Natural Resource Policy....Ribaudo, Marc Agri 202-219-0444
Special Topics - Natural Resource Policy (World)....Urban, Francis Agri 202-219-0717
Special Topics - Pesticides....Padgitt, Merritt Agri 202-219-0433
Special Topics - Pesticides....Vandeman, Ann Agri 202-219-0433
Special Topics - Pesticides....Delvo, Herman Agri 202-219-0456
Special Topics - Pesticides....Love, John Agri 202-219-0886
Special Topics - Pesticides....Rives, Sam Agri 202-720-2324
Special Topics - Population....Beale, Calvin Agri 202-219-0535
Special Topics - Population....Swanson, Linda Agri 202-219-0535
Special Topics - Population - World....Urban, Francis Agri 202-219-0705
Special Topics - Seeds....Gill, Mohinder Agri 202-219-0464
Special Topics - Soil Conservation....Osborn, Tim Agri 202-219-0405
Special Topics - Soil Conservation....Magleby, Richard Agri 202-219-0435
Special Topics - Sustainable Agriculture....Gajewski, Greg Agri 202-219-0883
Special Topics - Sustainable Agriculture....Vandeman, Ann Agri 202-219-0433
Special Topics - Transportation....Hutchinson, T.Q. Agri 202-219-0840
Special Topics - Water & Irrigation....Gollehon, Noel Agri 202-219-0410
Special Topics - Water & Irrigation....Hostetler, John Agri 202-219-0410
Special Topics - Water Quality....Ribaudo, Marc Agri 202-219-0444
Special Topics - Water Quality....Crutchfield, Steve Agri 202-219-0444
Special Topics - Water Quality....Rives, Sam Agri 202-720-2324
Special Topics - Weather....Owens, Marty Agri 202-720-2157
Special Topics - Weather....Teigan, Lloyd Agri 202-219-0705
Special classification provisions....Shetty, Sundar USITC 202-205-3486
Species Profiles, Fish and Wildlife....Staff FWS 703-358-1710
Spectacles....Johnson, Christopher USITC 202-205-3488
Speech....Staff NIDR 301-496-4261
Speech and Language Disorders....Staff NINDS 301-496-5751
Speech and Language Disorders....Staff NICHD 301-496-5133
Speech and Language Disorders....Staff NIDCD 301-496-7243
Speed Changers....Reise, Richard COMMERCE 202-482-3489
Speed changers....Fravel, Dennis USITC 202-205-3404
Sphingolipidoses....Staff NINDS 301-496-5751
Sphingolipidoses Mucopolysaccaridoses & Stor. Dis.....Staff NINDS 301-496-5751
Spices....Conte, Ralph CUSTOMS 212-466-5759
Spices....Schneider, Greg USITC 202-205-3326
Spielmeyer-Sjogren's Disease....Staff NINDS 301-496-5751
Spina Bifida....Staff NINDS 301-496-5751
Spina Bifida....Staff NICHD 301-496-5133
Spina Bifida....Staff NIDCD 301-496-7243
Spinal Arachnoiditis....Staff NINDS 301-496-5751
Spinal Cord Injury....Staff NINDS 301-496-5751
Spinal Cord Lesions....Staff NINDS 301-496-5751
Spinal Cord Tumors....Staff NINDS 301-496-5751
Spinal Muscular Atrophy....Staff NINDS 301-496-5751
Spinning machines....Greene, William USITC 202-205-3405
Spinocerebellar Degeneration....Staff NINDS 301-496-5751
Split Channel Operations....Staff FCC 202-653-5560
Sponge, articles of....Spalding, Josephine USITC 202-205-3498
Sponges, marine....Ludwick, David USITC 202-205-3329
Sporting Goods....McKenna, Thomas CUSTOMS 212-466-5475
Sporting Goods and Athletic....Vanderwolf, John COMMERCE 202-482-0348
Sporting Goods, Export Promo.....Beckham, Reginald COMMERCE 202-482-5478
Sporting goods....Robinson, Hazel USITC 202-205-3496
Sports Blackouts....Staff FCC 202-632-7048
Sports Medicine....Staff NIAMS 301-496-8188
Spraying machinery: agricultural/horticultural....Vacant USITC 202-205-3380
Spraying machinery: other....Slingerland, David USITC 202-205-3400
Squamous Cell....Staff NCI 301-496-5583
Sri Lanka....Simmons, John Cnty Commerce 202-482-2954
Sri Lanka....Ordonez, Miguel Peace Corps 202-606-3118
Sri Lanka (Colombo)....Staff Cnty State 202-647-2351
Sri Lanka/Minerals....Vacant Cnty Mines 202-501-9694
St. Bartholomey....Brooks, Michelle Cnty Commerce 202-482-2527
St. Kitts-Nevis....Brooks, Michelle Cnty Commerce 202-482-2527
St. Lucia....Brooks, Michelle Cnty Commerce 202-482-2527
St. Martin....Brooks, Michelle Cnty Commerce 202-482-2527
St. Vincent Grenadines....Brooks, Michelle Cnty Commerce 202-482-2527
Stained Teeth (Tetracycline)....Staff NIDR 301-496-4261
Stains....Johnson, Larry USITC 202-205-3351
Standard Industrial Classification, Empl/Unempl....Bennott, William LABOR 202-606-6474
Standard Occupational Classification, Empl/Unempl....McElroy, Michael LABOR 202-606-6516
Staphylococcal Infections....Staff NIAID 301-496-5717
Staple fibers, manmade....Sweet, Mary Elizabeth USITC 202-205-3455
Starches....Pierre-Benoist, John USITC 202-205-3320
Starches, chemically treated....Randall, Rob USITC 202-205-3366
State Data Center Program....Carbaugh, Larry CENSUS 301-763-1580
State Energy Programs....Demetrops, James NEIC 202-586-9187
State Projections....Staff CENSUS 301-763-1902
State and Area Labor Force Data, Data Disk & Tapes....Marcus, Jessie LABOR 202-606-6392
State and Area Labor Force Data, Demog. Char. E/Un....Biederman, Edna LABOR 202-606-6392

Experts

State and Metropolitan Area Data Books....Cevis, Wanda CENSUS 301-763-1034
State and Outlying Area Estimates....Staff CENSUS 301-763-5072
States & Areas Establishment Survey, Data Disk.....Podgornik, Guy LABOR 202-606-6559
States & Areas Establishment Survey, Empl/Unempl....Shipp, Kenneth LABOR 202-606-6559
Statistical Abstract....King, Glenn CENSUS 301-763-5299
Statistical Areas....Staff CENSUS 301-763-3827
Statistical Briefs....Bernstein, Robert CENSUS 301-763-1584
Statistical Methods, Prices & Living Cond.....Hedges, Brian LABOR 202-606-6897
Statistical Research for Demographic Programs....Ernst, Lawrence CENSUS 301-763-7880
Statistical Research for Economic Programs....Monsour, Nash J. CENSUS 301-763-5702
Statistical Surveys, National Fish and Wildlife....Staff FWS 703-358-1730
Statistician, Chief....Young, Allan H. ECONOMIC 202-523-0693
Statistics....Dillingham, Steven Justice Stat 202-307-0765
Statistics (Blindness and Visual Disorders)....Staff NEI 301-496-5248
Statistics (Health)....Staff NCHS 301-496-8500
Statistics (Health)....Staff CDC 404-639-3286
Staurolite....Austin, Gordon MINES 202-501-9388
Stearic acid....Randall, Rob USITC 202-205-3366
Stearic acid esters....Randall, Rob USITC 202-205-3366
Steatite....White, Linda USITC 202-205-3427
Steel Industry Products....Bell, Charles COMMERCE 202-482-0608
Steel, Basic Shapes and Forms....Ilardi, Paula CUSTOMS 212-466-5476
Steel: Ingots, blooms, and billets....Mascola, Robert USITC 202-205-3428
Steel: angles, shapes, and sections....Vacant USITC 202-205-3419
Steel: bars....Vacant USITC 202-205-3419
Steel: pipe and tube and fittings....MacKnight, Peggy USITC 202-205-3431
Steel: plate....Mascola, Robert USITC 202-205-3428
Steel: rails....Yost, Charles USITC 202-205-3432
Steel: sheet....Mascola, Robert USITC 202-205-3428
Steel: strip....Mascola, Robert USITC 202-205-3428
Steel: tubes....Laney-Cummings, Karen USITC 202-205-3431
Steel: waste and scrap....Vacant USITC 202-205-3419
Steel: wire....Yost, Charles USITC 202-205-3442
Steel: wire rods....Yost, Charles USITC 202-205-3442
Steel: Pipes....MacKnight, Peggy USITC 202-205-3431
Steele-Richardson Disease....Staff NINDS 301-496-5751
Stereo apparatus....Sherman, Thomas USITC 202-205-3389
Sterilization....Staff NICHD 301-496-5133
Steroid Contraceptives....Staff NICHD 301-496-5133
Steroid Hormones....Stoney, Simons S. FAES 301-496-6797
Steroid Hypertension....Staff NHLBI 301-496-4236
Stevens-Johnson Syndrome....Staff NIAID 301-496-5717
Stiff Man Syndrome....Staff NINDS 301-496-5751
Still's Disease....Staff NIAMS 301-496-8188
Stomach Cancer....Staff NCI 301-496-5583
Stone....Bunin, Jacob CUSTOMS 212-566-5796
Stone and products....White, Linda USITC 202-205-3427
Stone, Crushed....Tepordei, Valentin V. MINES 202-501-9392
Stone, Dimension....Taylor, Harold A. MINES 202-501-9754
Stone-processing machines....Greene, William USITC 202-205-3405
Stoneware articles....McNay, Deborah USITC 202-205-3425
Stoneworking machines....Vacant USITC 202-205-3380
Storage Batteries....Larrabee, David COMMERCE 202-482-0575
Storm Water....Staff EPA 703-821-4823
Storm Water Hotline....Staff EPA 703-821-4823
Stoves/Woodburning....Staff EPA 919-541-2821
Strabismus....Staff NEI 301-496-5248
Stranger-to-Stranger Crime....Rand, Michael Justice Stat 202-616-3494
Streptococcal Infections....Staff NIAID 301-496-5717
Streptokinase....Staff NHLBI 301-496-4236
Stress....Staff NIMH 301-496-4513
Stress (EKG)....Staff NHLBI 301-496-4236
Stress and Aging....Staff NIA 301-496-1752
Striatonigral Degeneration....Staff NINDS 301-496-5751
Stroke....Staff NINDS 301-496-5751
Stroke (Hypertension)....Staff NHLBI 301-496-4236
Strontium....Ober, Joyce A. MINES 202-501-9406
Strontium....Lundy, David USITC 202-205-3439
Strontium compounds....Greenblatt, Jack USITC 202-205-3353
Strontium pigments....Johnson, Larry USITC 202-205-3351
Structures of base metals....Yost, Charles USITC 202-205-3442
Student Conservation Programs, Fish and Wildlife....Staff FWS 703-358-2029
Students, Youth, and Dropouts, Empl/Unempl. Stats.....Cohany, Sharon LABOR 202-606-6378
Studio Transmitter Links, Common Carrier....Staff FCC 202-634-1706
Studio Transmitter Links, Mass Media....Staff FCC 202-634-6307
Sturge-Weber Syndrome....Staff NINDS 301-496-5751
Stuttering....Staff NINDS 301-496-5751
Stuttering....Staff NIDCD 301-496-7243
Sty....Staff NEI 301-496-5248
Styrene (monomer)....Matusik, Ed USITC 202-205-3356
Styrene resins....Misurelli, Denby USITC 202-205-3362
Subacute Necrotizing Encephalomyelopathy (Leighs')....Staff NINDS 301-496-5751
Subacute Sclerosing Panencephalitis....Staff NINDS 301-496-5751
Subarachnoid Hemorrhage....Staff NINDS 301-496-5751
Submarine Cable....Staff FCC 202-632-7265
Subscription Television....Staff FCC 202-632-6357
Subseabed Disposal Research....Warnick, Walter NEIC 301-903-3122
Substance Abuse Prevention, Office of....Setal, Mel ADAMHA 301-443-9936
Sudan....Watkins, Chandra Cnty Commerce 202-482-4564
Sudan (Khartoum)....Staff Cnty State 202-647-9742
Sudan/Minerals....Antonides, Lloyd Cnty Mines 202-501-9686
Sudanophilic Leukodystrophy....Staff NINDS 301-496-5751
Sudden Cardiac Death....Staff NHLBI 301-496-4236
Sudden Infant Death Syndrome....Staff NICHD 301-496-5133
Sugar....Maria, John CUSTOMS 212-466-5730
Sugar....Williams, Joan USITC 202-205-3313
Sugar and Sweeteners....Eldridge, Herb Agri 202-720-7621
Sugar and Sweeteners....Lord, Ronald Agri 202-219-0888
Sugar and Sweeteners....Buzzanell, Peter Agri 202-219-0888
Suicide....Staff NIMH 301-443-4513
Suicide....Baldwin, Elaine ADAMHA 301-443-4536
Suit-Jackets....Crowley, Michael CUSTOMS 212-466-5852
Suits....Crowley, Michael CUSTOMS 212-466-5852
Suits: men's and boys'....Linkins, Linda USITC 202-205-3469
Suits: women's and girls'....Holoyda, Olha USITC 202-205-3467
Sulfides, nonmetallic....Conant, Kenneth USITC 202-205-3346
Sulfiting Agents....Lecos, Chris FDA 202-205-1144
Sulfur....Ober, Joyce MINES 202-501-9406
Sulfur....Trainor, Cynthia USITC 202-205-3354
Sulfur dioxide....Conant, Kenneth USITC 202-205-3346
Sulfuric acid....Trainor, Cynthia USITC 202-205-3354
Sulfuryl chloride....Conant, Kenneth USITC 202-205-3346
Summer Research Fellowship Program....Staff CC 301-496-2427
Sunlight and Skin Cancer....Staff NCI 301-496-5583
Sunspot Cycle....Staff FCC 202-653-8166
Supercomputers....Streeter, Jonathan COMMERCE 202-482-0572
Superconducting Super Collider Project....Cipriano, Joseph NEIC 214-708-2521
Superconductivity....Eaton, Russell NEIC 202-586-0205
Superconductors....Chiarado, Roger COMMERCE 202-482-0402
Superfund....Staff EPA 202-260-2180
Superfund....Berreth, Don CDC 404-639-3286
Superfund Hazardous Waste....Staff EPA 800-346-5009
Superphosphates....Trainor, Cynthia USITC 202-205-3354
Supersonic (Mach 1-5) Engine Testing....Staff NASA 804-864-6125
Supplemental Security Income (SSI)....Gambino, Phil SSA 410-965-8904
Supplies (Central Storeroom)....Staff OD/DAS 301-496-9156
Surface Active Agents....Joseph, Stephanie CUSTOMS 212-466-5768
Surface-active agents....Land, Eric USITC 202-205-3349
Surgeon General....Fingland, Mary Jane PHS 202-690-7163
Surgery (Cancer)....Staff NCI 301-496-5583
Surgery (Oral)....Staff NIDR 301-496-4261
Surgical Treatment of Heart Disease....Staff NHLBI 301-496-4236
Surgical apparatus....Johnson, Christopher USITC 202-205-3488
Suriname....Brooks, Michelle Cnty Commerce 202-482-2527
Suriname (Paramaribo)....Staff Cnty State 202-647-4195
Suriname/Minerals....Mobbs, Philip Cnty Mines 202-501-9679
Survey Data and Tapes, Consumer Expend. Surv.....Passero, William LABOR 202-606-6900
Survey Operations, Consumer Expend. Survey. Pr/Lv....Dietz, Richard LABOR 202-606-6872
Survey of Income and Program Participation (SIPP)....Staff CENSUS 301-763-2764
Surveys, Migratory Birds....Staff FWS 703-358-1714
Surveys, National Fish and Wildlife....Staff FWS 703-358-1730
Surveys, Waterfowl Harvest....Staff FWS 703-358-1714

Statistical Areas / Television

Surveys, Waterfowls Population....Staff FWS 703-358-1714
Sutures, surgical....Randall, Rob USITC 202-205-3366
Swaziland....Holm-Olsen, Finn Cnty Commerce 202-482-5148
Swaziland....Brill, Terry Peace Corps 202-606-3535
Swaziland (Mbabane)....Staff Cnty State 202-647-8252
Swaziland/Minerals....van Oss, Hendrik Cnty Mines 202-501-9687
Sweat Gland Disorders....Staff NIAMS 301-496-8188
Sweaters....Crowley, Michael CUSTOMS 212-466-5852
Sweaters....Holoyda, Olha USITC 202-205-3467
Sweatshirts....Crowley, Michael CUSTOMS 212-466-5852
Sweatshirts....Holoyda, Olha USITC 202-205-3467
Sweden....Devlin, James Cnty Commerce 202-482-4414
Sweden (Stockholm)....Staff Cnty State 202-647-6071
Sweden/Minerals....Buck, Donald E. Cnty Mines 202-501-9670
Swimwear....Jones, Jackie USITC 202-205-3466
Swimwear....Hamey, Amy USITC 202-205-3465
Swimwear, Adult....Shea, Gerard CUSTOMS 212-466-5878
Swimwear, Childrens'....Kirschner, Bruce CUSTOMS 212-566-5865
Swimwear: womens and girls....Linkins, Linda USITC 202-205-3469
Swine Flu....Staff NIAID 301-496-5717
Switches, Electric....Malison, Andrew USITC 202-205-3391
Switches, telephone....Bien, William USITC 202-205-3398
Switchgear & Switchboard Apparatus....Whitley, Richard A. COMMERCE 202-482-0682
Switzerland....Combs, Philip/Wright, Corey Cnty Commerce 202-482-2920
Switzerland (Bern)....Staff Cnty State 202-647-1484
Switzerland/Minerals....Buck, Donald E. Cnty Mines 202-501-9670
Sydenham's Chorea....Staff NINDS 301-496-5751
Syncope (Fainting)....Staff NHLBI 301-496-4236
Synfuel Plants....Frye, Keith NEIC 301-903-2098
Synovitis....Staff NIAMS 301-496-8188
Synthesis Gas....Der, Victor NEIC 301-903-2877
Synthetic detergents....Land, Eric USITC 202-205-3349
Synthetic iron oxides and hydroxides....Johnson, Larry USITC 202-205-3351
Synthetic natural gas (SNG)....Land, Eric USITC 202-205-3349
Synthetic rubber....Misurelli, Denby USITC 202-205-3362
Syphilis....Staff NIAID 301-496-5717
Syria....Wright, Corey/Sams, Thomas Cnty Commerce 202-482-4441
Syria/Minerals....Michalski, Bernadette Cnty Mines 202-501-9699
Syrian Arab Republic (Damascus)....Staff Cnty State 202-647-1131
Syringomyelia....Staff NINDS 301-496-5751
System Integration....Atkins, Robert COMMERCE 202-482-4781
Systemic Lupus Erythematosus....Staff NIAMS 301-496-8188
Systolic Hypertension in the Elderly (SHEP)....Staff NHLBI 301-496-4236
Systolic Hypertension in the Elderly (SHEP)....Staff NIA 301-496-1752

T

T-Bills with options....SIA Manasses CFT 312-353-9027
T-Bonds with options....Redheffer, Nancy L. CFT 312-353-9015
T-Cell Deficiency....Staff NIAID 301-496-5717
T-Notes (2,5, 6-10) with options....Redheffer, Nancy L. CFT 312-353-9015
T-Notes/Bonds (Zeros) with options....Redheffer, Nancy L. CFT 312-353-9015
T-Shirts....Holoyda, Olha USITC 202-205-3467
T-Shirts, Knit....DeGaetano, Angela CUSTOMS 212-466-5540
TELEX, International & Domestic....Staff FCC 202-632-7265
TIGER System Products....Staff CENSUS 301-763-4100
TIGER, Applications....Carbaugh, Larry CENSUS 301-763-1580
TIGER, Future Plans....Staff CENSUS 301-763-4664
TSH, Excessive Secretion....Staff NIDDK 301-496-3583
TTY - Population Information....Staff CENSUS 301-763-5020
TV Broadcasting....Siegmund, John COMMERCE 202-482-4781
TV Communications Eqmt....Gossack, Linda COMMERCE 202-482-4466
TV Violence....Baldwin, Elaine ADAMHA 301-443-4536
Tablecloths....Sweet, Mary Elizabeth USITC 202-205-3455
Tachycardia....Staff NHLBI 301-496-4236
Taiwan....Davis, Ian/Carroll, Paul/Duvall, Dan Cnty Commerce 202-482-4957
Taiwan Coordination....Staff Cnty State 202-647-7711
Taiwan/Minerals....Tse, Pui-Kwan Cnty Mines 202-501-9696
Tajikistan....Staff Cnty State 202-647-8671
Takayasu's Arteritis....Staff NIAID 301-496-5717
Take Pride in America Program, Fish and Wildlife....Staff FWS 703-358-2156
Talc....Virta, Robert MINES 202-501-9384
Talc....White, Linda USITC 202-205-3427

Tall oil....Randall, Rob USITC 202-205-3366
Tangier Disease....Staff NHLBI 301-496-4236
Tangier Disease....Staff NINDS 301-496-5751
Tanning products and agents....Wanser, Stephen USITC 202-205-3363
Tantalum....Presbury, Graylin COMMERCe 202-482-5158
Tantalum....Cunningham, Larry D. MINES 202-501-9443
Tantalum....Lundy, David USITC 202-205-3439
Tanzania....Holm-Olsen, Finn Cnty Commerce 202-482-4228
Tanzania....Hohman, Eric Peace Corps 202-606-3709
Tanzania (Dar es Salaam)....Staff Cnty State 202-647-5684
Tanzania/Minerals....Izon, David Cnty Mines 202-501-9692
Tape Players....Dicerbo, Mario CUSTOMS 212-466-5672
Tape players....Sherman, Thomas USITC 202-205-3389
Tape recorders and players, audio....Sherman, Thomas USITC 202-205-3389
Tape recordings....Sherman, Thomas USITC 202-205-3389
Tapestries....Hansen, John CUSTOMS 212-466-5854
Tapestries....Sweet, Mary Elizabeth USITC 202-205-3455
Taping of Telephone Calls....Staff FCC 202-632-7260
Taps....Mata, Ruben USITC 202-205-3403
Tar Sands....Der, Victor NEIC 301-903-2877
Tar sands oil....Foreso, Cynthia USITC 202-205-3348
Tardive Dyskinesia....Staff NIMH 301-443-4515
Tardive Dyskinesia....Staff NINDS 301-496-5751
Tarsal Tunnel Syndrome....Staff NINDS 301-496-5751
Taste....Staff NIDR 301-496-4261
Taste and Smell Dysfunction....Staff NINDS 301-496-5751
Taste and Smell Dysfunction....Staff NIDCD 301-496-7243
Tay-Sach's Disease....Staff NINDS 301-496-5751
Tea....Janis, William V. COMMERCE 202-482-2250
Tea....Maria, John CUSTOMS 212-466-5730
Tea....Schneider, Greg USITC 202-205-3326
Technological Developments and Nursing Care....Staff NCNR 301-496-0526
Technology Centers, Fish....Staff FWS 703-358-1714
Technology Transfer, Office of....Adler, Reid FAES 301-496-0750
Technology Trends In Major Industries....Riche, Richard LABOR 202-606-5626
Teenage Pregnancy....Eddinger, Lucy ASH 202-690-8335
Teenage Pregnancy....Staff NICHD 301-496-5133
Teeth....Staff NIDR 301-496-4261
Telangiectasis (Rendu-Osler-Weber Dis., Syndrome)....Staff NHLBI 301-496-4236
Telecommunications for Deaf, Public & Spec. Studies....TDD LABOR 202-606-5897
Telecommunication Devices for the Deaf....Staff FCC 202-632-6999
Telecommunications....Stechschulte, Roger COMMERCE 202-482-4466
Telecommunications (Network Eqpt)....Henry, John COMMERCE 202-482-4466
Telecommunications (TV Broadcast Equip.)....Rettig, Thersa E. COMMERCE 202-482-4466
Telecommunications Services....Shefrin, Ivan COMMERCE 202-48244661
Telecommunications, CPE....Edwards, Dan COMMERCE 202-482-4466
Telecommunications, Cellular....Gossack, Linda COMMERCE 202-482-4466
Telecommunications, Fiber Optics....Judge, Paulames COMMERCE 202-482-4466
Telecommunications, Major Projects....Paddock, Rick COMMERCE 202-482-4466
Telecommunications, Network Equipment....Henry, John COMMERCE 202-482-4466
Telecommunications, Radio....Gossack, Linda COMMERCE 202-482-4466
Telecommunications, Satellites....Cooper, Patricia COMMERCE 202-482-4466
Telecommunications, Services....Shefrin, Ivan COMMERCE 202-482-4466
Telecommunications, Trade Promo.....Rettig, Theresa E. COMMERCE 202-482-4466
Telegraph Service....Staff FCC 202-632-7876
Telegraph and Telephone Rates....Staff FCC 202-632-5550
Telegraph and telephone apparatus....Bien, William USITC 202-205-3398
Telephone Equipment Interconnection....Staff FCC 202-634-1800
Telephone Lines....Staff FCC 202-632-1800
Telephone Telegraph Rates....Staff FCC 202-632-5550
Telephone services....Posey, Melanie USITC 202-205-3303
Telephones....Josephs, Irwin CUSTOMS 212-466-5673
Telephones, Wireless....Dicerbo, Mario CUSTOMS 212-466-5672
Teleprinter (Telephone, Telegraph)....Staff FCC 202-634-1800
Telescopes....Johnson, Christopher USITC 202-205-3488
Teletext Services....Inoussa, Mary COMMERCE 202-482-5820
Television Advertising....Staff FCC 202-632-7551

Experts

Television Advertising Intercity Relays....Staff FCC 202-634-6307
Television Political Broadcasting Fairness....Staff FCC 202-632-7586
Television Programming....Staff FCC 202-632-7048
Television Religious Petition....Staff FCC 202-632-7000
Television Remote Pickups....Staff FCC 202-634-6307
Television Stations--New....Staff FCC 202-632-6495
Television Translators....Staff FCC 202-632-7698
Television equipment....Kitzmiller, John USITC 202-205-3387
Television programming....Staff FCC 202-632-7551
Televisions....Dicerbo, Mario CUSTOMS 212-466-5672
Tellurium....Edelstein, Daniel MINES 202-501-9415
Tellurium compounds....Greenblatt, Jack USITC 202-205-3353
Temporal Arteritis (Eyes)....Staff NEI 301-496-5248
Temporal Arteritis (Neurological Aspects of)....Staff NINDS #01-496-5751
Temporomandibular Joint Disorders....Staff NIDR 301-496-4261
Tendonitis....Staff NIAMS 301-496-8188
Tennis equipment....Robinson, Hazel USITC 202-205-3496
Tents and tarpaulins....Freund, Kimberlie USITC 202-205-3456
Test Tube Babies....Staff NICHD 301-496-5133
Testicular Cancer....Staff NCI 301-496-5583
Tetanus....Staff NIAID 301-496-5717
Tetraethyl lead....Michels, David USITC 202-205-3352
Tetralogy of Fallot....Staff NHLBI 301-496-4236
Tetramer of proplyene....Raftery, Jim USITC 202-205-3365
Tetramethyl lead....Michels, David USITC 202-205-3352
Tetrapropylene....Raftery, Jim USITC 202-205-3365
Textile Machinery....Vacant COMMERCE 202-482-0679
Textile calendaring and rolling machines....Greene, William USITC 202-205-3405
Textile finishing agents....Land, Eric USITC 202-205-3349
Textile machines....Greene, William USITC 202-205-3405
Textile washing, bleaching, dyeing, machines....Greene, William USITC 202-205-3405
Textiles....Dulka, William A. COMMERCE 202-482-4058
Textiles and Leather, Prices and Living Conditions....Paik, Soon LABOR 202-606-7714
Textiles, Trade Promo....Molnar, Ferenc COMMERCE 202-482-2043
Thailand....Kelly, Jean Cnty Commerce 202-482-3875
Thailand....Swanson, Alan Peace Corps 202-606-3040
Thailand....Huston, Christine Peace Corps 202-606-3040
Thailand....Hower, Mark Peace Corps 202-606-5517
Thailand (Bangkok)....Staff Cnty State 202-647-7108
Thailand/Minerals....Vacant Cnty Mines 202-501-9694
Thalassemia....Staff NHLBI 301-496-4236
Thalassemia....Staff NIDDK 301-496-3583
Thallium....Llewellyn, Thomas MINES 202-501-9395
Thallium compounds....Greenblatt, Jack USITC 202-205-3353
Theater....McCord, Karyl NEA 202-682-5425
Theories of Aging....Staff NIA 301-496-1752
Thoracic-Outlet Syndrome....Staff NINDS 301-496-5751
Thorium....Hedrick, James B. MINES 202-501-9412
Thorium....DeSapio, Vincent USITC 202-205-3435
Thorium compounds....Greenblatt, Jack USITC 202-205-3353
Thread: cotton....Warlick, William USITC 202-205-3459
Thread: manmade fibers....Warlick, William USITC 202-205-3459
Thread: silk....Shelton, Linda USITC 202-205-3467
Threatened Species Permits, Fish and Wildlife....Staff FWS 703-358-2104
Thrombasthenia....Staff NIDDK 301-496-3583
Thrombocytopenia....Staff NIDDK 301-496-3583
Thromboembolism....Staff NHLBI 301-496-4236
Thrombolysis....Staff NHLBI 301-496-4236
Thrombophlebitis....Staff NHLBI 301-496-4236
Thrombosis....Staff NHLBI 301-496-4236
Thyroid (Adenoma of)....Staff NIDDK 301-496-3583
Thyroiditis....Staff NIDDK 301-496-3583
Thyroma....Staff NCI 301-496-5583
Thyroxine-iodine....Staff NIDDK 301-496-3583
Tic Douloureux (Trigeminal Neuralgia)....Staff NINDS 301-496-5751
Ticks....Staff NIAID 301-496-5717
Tie-line--Telegraph Telephone....Staff FCC 202-632-5550
Tiger, Products....Staff CENSUS 301-763-4100
Tights....DeGaetano, Angela CUSTOMS 212-466-5540
Tiles, ceramic....McNay, Deborah USITC 202-205-3425
Timber Management....Staff FS 303-498-1803
Timber Management, Fish and Wildlife....Staff FWS 703-358-2043
Time Served in Prison....Beck, Allen Justice Stat 202-616-3277
Time Served in Prison....Innes, Christopher Justice Stat 202-724-3121
Time Served in Prison....Greenfeld, Lawrence Justice Stat 202-616-3281
Time Served in Prison - Federal....Kaplan, Carol Justice Stat 202-307-0759
Time switches....Luther, Dennis USITC 202-205-3497
Timing apparatus....Luther, Dennis USITC 202-205-3497
Tin....Carlin, Jr., James F. MINES 202-501-9411
Tin....DeSapio, Vincent USITC 202-205-3435
Tin Products....Presbury, Graylin COMMERCE 202-482-5158
Tin compounds....Greenblatt, Jack USITC 202-205-3353
Tinnitus....Staff NINDS 301-496-5751
Tinnitus....Staff NIDCD 301-496-7243
Tires....Prat, Raimundo COMMERCE 202-482-0128
Tires....Rauch, Theodore CUSTOMS 212-466-5892
Tires and tubes, of rubber of plastics....Raftery, Jim USITC 202-205-3365
Tissue Culture Cells (Freezing and Storage)....Staff OD/ORS 301-496-2960
Tissue Culture Media....Staff OD/ORS 301-496-6017
Tissue Plasminogen Activator (TPA)....Staff NHLBI 301-496-4236
Tissue Typing....Staff NIAID 301-496-5717
Titanium....Gambogi, Joseph MINES 202-501-9390
Titanium....DeSapio, Vincent USITC 202-205-3435
Titanium compounds....Greenblatt, Jack USITC 202-205-3353
Titanium dioxide....Johnson, Larry USITC 202-205-3351
Titanium pigments....Johnson, Larry USITC 202-205-3351
Tobacco....Eldridge, Herb Agri 202-720-7621
Tobacco....Grise, Verner Agri 202-219-0890
Tobacco....Capehart, Tom Agri 202-219-0890
Tobacco....Conte, Ralph CUSTOMS 212-466-5759
Tobacco Products....Kenney, Cornelius COMMERCE 202-482-2428
Tobacco and tobacco products....Salin, Victoria USITC 202-205-3351
Tobacco machines....Jackson, Georgia USITC 202-205-3399
Tobacco pipes....Burns, Gail USITC 202-205-3501
Togo....Henke, Debra Cnty Commerce 202-482-5149
Togo....Sanchez, Patricia Peace Corps 202-606-3237
Togo (Lome)....Staff Cnty State 202-647-2865
Togo/Minerals....King, Audie L. Cnty Mines 202-501-9674
Toilet preps, cosmetics, and perfumery....Land, Eric USITC 202-205-3349
Toilet soaps....Land, Eric USITC 202-205-3349
Toll Charges....Staff FCC 202-632-5550
Toluene....Raftery, Tim USITC 202-205-3365
Tomatoes....McCarty, Timothy USITC 202-205-3324
Toners....Wanser, Stephen USITC 202-205-3363
Tonga....Lagoy, Michele Peace Corps 202-606-3227
Tonga (Nuku'alofa)....Staff Cnty State 202-647-3546
Tonga/Minerals....Lyday, Travis Cnty Mines 202-501-9695
Tongue....Staff NIDR 301-496-4261
Tools, Machine....Losche, Robert CUSTOMS 212-466-5670
Tools/Dies/Jigs/Fixtures....Vacant COMMERCE
Topographic Map (USGS) Indexes, Fish and Wildlife....Staff FWS 703-358-1713
Topped crude petroleum....Foreso, Cynthia USITC 202-205-3348
Torsion Dystonia (Dystonia Musculorum Deformans)....Staff NINDS 301-496-5751
Torticollis (Wryneck)....Staff NINDS 301-496-5751
Toto....Olson, Susan Peace Corps 202-606-3136
Tourette Syndrome....Staff NINDS 301-496-5751
Tourette Syndrome....Staff NIMH 301-443-4515
Tourette Syndrome....Staff NIDCD 301-496-7243
Tourism (Major Proj)....White, Barbara COMMERCE 202-482-4160
Tourism services....Burns, Gail USITC 202-205-3501
Tourism services....Sousane, J. Richard COMMERCE 202-482-4582
Tow, manmade....Sweet, Mary Elizabeth USITC 202-205-3455
Towels....Hansen, John CUSTOMS 212-466-5854
Towels....Sweet, Mary Elizabeth USITC 202-205-3455
Towers--Painting and Lighting of....Staff FCC 202-632-7521
Toxic Effects Branch....Staff EPA 202-260-3430
Toxic Shock Syndrome....Staff NIMH 301-496-5717
Toxic Shock Syndrome....Staff NICHD 301-496-5133
Toxic Shock Syndrome....Staff CDC 401-639-3286
Toxic Substances & Disease Registry, Agency for....Greenwell, Mike ATSDR 404-639-0727
Toxic Substances Library....Staff EPA 202-260-3944
Toxicology....DeRosa, Christopher CDC 404-639-6300
Toxicology....Davis, Barbara D. FAES 202-260-9493
Toxicology Branch....Staff EPA 202-305-8711
Toxicology Program, National....Stopinski, Helen NIEHS/NIH 919-541-3991
Toxicology Programs/Special. Information Services....Staff NLM 301-496-1131
Toxicology/Pharmacology....Staff NIEHS 919-541-3345

Tellurium / U.S. Trade

Toxicology/Pharmacology....Staff NIGMS 301-496-7707
Toxocariasis....Staff NEI 301-496-5248
Toxoplasmosis....Staff NIAID 301-496-5717
Toxoplasmosis....Staff NEI 301-496-5248
Toys....Vanderworlf, John COMMERCE 202-482-0348
Toys....Wong, Alice CUSTOMS 212-466-5538
Toys....Luther, Dennis USITC 202-205-3497
Toys and Games (Export Promo)....Beckham, Reginald COMMERCE 202-482-5478
Toys for pets, christmans deco, figurines, etc.....Raftery, Jim USITC 202-205-3365
Trace Metals (and CVD)....Staff NHLBI 301-496-4236
Trachoma....Staff NEI 301-496-5248
Track Suits....Crowley, Michael CUSTOMS 212-466-5852
Tractors....Wholey, Patrick CUSTOMS 212-466-5668
Tractors (except truck tractors)....Vacant USITC 202-205-3380
Trade Related Employment....Teske, Gary R.A. COMMERCE 202-482-2056
Traffic Safety....Zawitz, Marianne Justice Stat 202-616-3499
Trailers and other vehicles not self-propelled....Kolberg, Mary USITC 202-205-3401
Training Courses....Staff CENSUS 301-763-1510
Transceivers....Kitzmiller, John USITC 202-205-3387
Transformation (Cell)....Staff NCI 301-496-5583
Transformers....Whitley, Richard A. COMMERCE 202-482-0682
Transformers....Josephs, Irwin CUSTOMS 212-466-5673
Transformers....Cutchin, John USITC 202-205-3396
Transfusional Hemosiderosis....Staff NHLBI 301-496-4236
Transient Ischemic Attacks....Staff NINDS 301-496-5751
Transplantation (Cornea)....Staff NEI 301-496-5248
Transplantation Immunology....Staff NIAID 301-496-5717
Transplants (He, Valv, Lung, Blo, Vess, Vei, Ar)....Staff NHLBI 301-496-4236
Transplants (Liver, Pancreas, Kidney)....Staff NIDDK 301-496-3583
Transplants (Organ Procurement)....Staff HRSA 301-443-7577
Transportation....Staff OD/Motor Pool 301-496-3426
Transportation Equipment, Producer Price Index....Yatsko, Ralph LABOR 202-606-7745
Transportation Industries....Alexander, Albert COMMERCE 202-482-4581
Transportation, Truck Inventory and Use....Bostic, William CENSUS 301-763-2735
Transposition of the Great Vessels....Staff NHLBI 301-496-4236
Transsexuality....Staff NICHD 301-496-5133
Transverse Myelitis....Staff NINDS 301-496-5751
Trapping, Hatcheries....Staff FWS 703-358-1715
Trapping, Refuges....Staff FWS 703-358-2043
Trauma Research....Staff NIGMS 301-496-7301
Trauma Research (Cent. Ner. Sys., Head, Spin. Cr.)....Staff NINDS 301-496-5751
Travel & Tourism....Sousane, J. Richard COMMERCE 202-482-4582
Travel Surveys....Cannon, John CENSUS 301-763-5468
Travel goods....Seastrum, Carl USITC 202-205-3493
Treaties, Indian Fisheries....Staff FWS 703-358-1718
Treatment Improvement, Office for....Hurley, Joan ADAMHA 301-443-6549
Tremors....Staff NINDS 301-496-5751
Tremors....Staff NIDCD 301-496-7243
Trench Mouth....Staff NIDR 301-496-4261
Trichinosis....Staff NIAID 301-496-5717
Trichloroethylene....Michels, David USITC 202-205-3352
Trichomoniasis....Staff NIAID 301-496-5717
Tricks....Luther, Dennis USITC 202-205-3497
Tricuspid Valve....Staff NHLBI 301-496-4236
Tricycles....Seastrum, Carl USITC 202-205-3493
Trigeminal Neuralgia (Tic Douloureux)....Staff NINDS 301-496-5751
Triglycerides....Staff NHLBI 301-496-4236
Trimellitic acid esters....Johnson, Larry USITC 202-205-3351
Trinidad and Tobago (Port-of-Spain)....Staff Cnty State 202-647-2621
Trinidad and Tobago....Brooks, Michelle Cnty Commerce 202-482-2527
Trinidad and Tobago/Minerals....Torres, Ivette Cnty Mines 202-501-9680
Trinitrotoluene....Johnson, Larry USITC 202-205-3351
Tripoli....Austin, Gordon MINES 202-501-9388
Tropical Diseases....Staff NIAID 301-496-5717
Tropical Forestry....Martin, Michael R. FS 703-235-1676
Tropical Spastic Paraparesis....Staff NINDS 301-496-5751
Troposphere Interference....Staff FCC 202-632-7025
Troposphere, Interference to Wash, DC Area....Staff FCC 301-962-2729
Trousers....DeGaetano, Angela CUSTOMS 212-466-5540
Trousers: mens and boys....Linkins, Linda USITC 202-205-3469
Trousers: women's and girls'....Holoyda, Olha USITC 202-205-3467
Truck tractors....Hagey, Michael USITC 202-205-3392
Trucking Services....Sousane, J. Richard COMMERCE 202-482-4581
Trucks....Hagey, Michael USITC 202-205-3392
Truncus Arteriosus....Staff NHLBI 301-496-4236
Trypanosomiasis....Staff NIAID 301-496-5717
Trypsinogen Deficiency....Staff NIDDK 301-496-3583
Tuberculosis....Staff NIAID 301-496-5717
Tuberculosis....Staff CDC 404-639-3286
Tuberculosis.... CDC 404-639-2501
Tuberous Sclerosis....Staff NINDS 301-496-5751
Tubes....Josephs, Irwin CUSTOMS 212-466-5673
Tubes for pneumatic tires....Raftery, Jim USITC 202-205-3365
Tubing, of rubber or plastics....Johnson, Larry USITC 202-205-3351
Tularemia....Staff NIAID 301-496-5717
Tumor....Staff NCI 301-496-5583
Tumor Immunology....Staff NCI 301-496-5583
Tumors (Eye)....Staff NEI 301-496-5248
Tumors with Endocrine Function....Staff NIDDK 301-496-3583
Tuna....Corey, Roger USITC 202-205-3327
Tungsten....Smith, Gerald R. MINES 202-501-9431
Tungsten....Lundy, David USITC 202-205-3439
Tungsten compounds....Greenblatt, Jack USITC 202-205-3353
Tunisia....Wright, Corey/Sams, Thomas Cnty Commerce 202-482-1860
Tunisia....DiMeo, Pam Peace Corps 202-606-3196
Tunisia....Schildwachter, Christy Peace Corps 202-606-3196
Tunisia (Tunis)....Staff Cnty State 202-647-3614
Tunisia/Minerals....Dolley, Thomas Cnty Mines 202-501-9690
Turkey....Lamb, Heidi Cnty Commerce 202-482-5373
Turkey (Ankara)....Staff Cnty State 202-647-6114
Turkey/Minerals....van Oss, Hendrik Cnty Mines 202-501-9687
Turkmenistan....Staff Cnty State 202-647-8671
Turks & Caicos Islands....Soto, Rodrigo Cnty Commerce 202-482-2527
Turner Syndrome....Staff NICHD 301-496-5133
Turntables....Sherman, Thomas USITC 202-205-3389
Turpentine....Reeder, John USITC 202-205-3319
Turtles (Salmonellosis)....Staff CDC 404-639-3286
Tuvalu....Lagoy, Michele Peace Corps 202-606-3227
Tuvalu (Funafuti)....Staff Cnty State 202-647-3546
Twine....Cook, Lee USITC 202-205-3471
Typewriters....Baker, Scott USITC 202-205-3386
Typhoid Fever....Staff NIAID 301-496-5717

U

US Trade & Foreign Agriculture....Baxter, Tim Agri 202-219-0706
US Trade & Foreign Agriculture....Stallings, David Agri 202-219-0688
US Trade & Foreign Agriculture - Africa & Mideast....Kurtzig, Mike Agri 202-219-0680
US Trade & Foreign Agriculture - Asia - East....Coyle, William Agri 202-219-0610
US Trade & Foreign Agriculture - Asia - South....Landes, Rip Agri 202-219-0664
US Trade & Foreign Agriculture - Canada....Simone, Mark Agric 202-219-0610
US Trade & Foreign Agriculture - China....Tuan, Francis Agri 202-219-0626
US Trade & Foreign Agriculture - Developing Economies....Mathia, Gene Agri 202-219-0680
US Trade & Foreign Agriculture - Eastern Europe....Koopman, Robert Agri 202-219-0621
US Trade & Foreign Agriculture - Eastern Europe....Cochrane, Nancy Agri 202-219-0621
US Trade & Foreign Agriculture - Exports....MacDonald, Steve Agri 202-219-0822
US Trade & Foreign Agriculture - Exports & Imports....Warden, Thomas Agri 202-219-0822
US Trade & Foreign Agriculture - Food Aid....Kurtzig, Mike Agri 202-219-0680
US Trade & Foreign Agriculture - Food Aid Programs....Suarez, Nydia Agri 202-219-0821
US Trade & Foreign Agriculture - Latin America....Link, John Agri 202-219-0660
US Trade & Foreign Agriculture - Pacific Rim....Coyle, William Agri 202-219-0610
US Trade & Foreign Agriculture - Programs....Ackerman, Karen Agri 202-219-0821

Be patient. If any phone number is incorrect, call (area code) 555-1212 and request the new listing.

Experts

US Trade & Foreign Agriculture - Trade & Finance....Magiera, Steve Agri 202-219-0633

US Trade & Foreign Agriculture - Trade & Finance....Roningen, Vern Agri 202-219-0631

US Trade & Foreign Agriculture - USSR....Zeimetz, Kathryn Agri 202-219-0624

US Trade & Foreign Agriculture - Western Europe....Coyle, William Agri 202-219-0610

USSR (Moscow)....Staff Cnty State 202-647-8671

Uganda....Watkins, Chandra Cnty Commerce 202-482-4564

Uganda....Fossum, Linnea Peace Corps 202-606-3708

Uganda (Kampala)....Staff Cnty State 202-647-5684

Uganda/Minerals....Izon, David Cnty Mines 202-501-9692

Ukraine....Hower, Mark Peace Corps 202-606-5517

Ukraine....Taylor, Jeff Peace Corps 202-606-5519

Ulcerative Colitis....Staff NIDDK 301-496-3583

Ulcerative Lesions (Oral)....Staff NIDR 301-496-4261

Ulcers....Staff NIDDK 301-496-3583

Ultrasonics Equipment....Staff FCC 202-653-8247

Umbrellas....Burns, Gail USITC 202-205-3501

Underground Nuclear Testing....Williams, Irvin NEIC 301-903-5341

Underwear....Burtnik, Brian CUSTOMS 212-466-5880

Underwear....Linkins, Linda USITC 202-205-3469

Unemployment Statistics....Palumbo, Thomas CENSUS 301-763-8574

Unemployment and Labor Force, Foreign Countries....Sorrentino, Constance LABOR 202-606-5654

Unfinished oils....Foreso, Cynthia USITC 202-205-3348

Uniform Crime Reports - Redesign Implementation....White, Paul Justice Stat 202-307-0771

Uniform Crime Reports - Redesign Implementation....Manson, Donald Justice Stat 202-616-3491

Unions, Employee Associations, Membership, Comp/Wk....Cimini, Michael LABOR 202-606-6275

Unit Labor Costs, Productivity....Neef, Arthur LABOR 202-606-5654

United Arab Emirates....Clement, Claude Cnty Commerce 202-482-5545

United Arab Emirates (Abu Dhabi)....Staff Cnty State 202-647-6558

United Arab Emirates/Minerals....King, Audie L. Cnty Mines 202-501-9674

United Kingdom....McLaughlin, Robert Cnty Commerce 202-482-3748

United Kingdom (London)....Staff Cnty State 202-647-8027

United Kingdom/Minerals....Newman, Harold R. Cnty Mines 202-501-9669

Universal joints....Topolansky, Adam USITC 202-205-3394

Unresectable Chrondosarcoma or Osteogenic Sarcoma....Staff NCI 301-496-5583

Upholstery fabrics....Freund, Kimberlie USITC 202-205-3456

Upper Atmosphere Research Satellite....Loughlin, John NASA 301-286-5565

Upper Atmosphere Research Satellite....Staff NASA 301-286-2806

Uranium....Sugg, William COMMERCE 202-482-1466

Uranium....DeSapio, Vincent USITC 202-205-3435

Uranium Enrichment....Swell, Philip NEIC 301-903-4321

Uranium compounds....Greenblatt, Jack USITC 202-205-3353

Uranium oxide....Greenblatt, Jack USITC 202-205-3353

Urban Residence....Staff CENSUS 301-763-7962

Urban and Community Forestry Programs....Conrad Robert FS 202-205-0823

Urban/Rural Residence....Staff CENSUS 301-763-7962

Urea....Trainor, Cynthia USITC 202-205-3354

Urea resins....Misurelli, Denby USITC 202-205-3362

Uremia....Staff NIDDK 301-496-3583

Uric Acid Kidney Stones....Staff NIDDK 301-496-3583

Urinary Incontinence....Staff NIA 301-496-1752

Urinary Tract Diseases....Staff NIDDK 301-496-3583

Urinary Tract Infections....Staff NIDDK 301-496-3583

Urinary Tract Tumors....Staff NIDDK 301-496-3583

Urine Volume....Staff NIDDK 301-496-3583

Urokinase....Staff NHLBI 301-496-4236

Urolithiasis....Staff NIDDK 301-496-3583

Urticaria....Staff NIAID 301-496-5717

Uruguay....Turner, Roger Cnty Commerce 202-482-1495

Uruguay....Eschelman, Michael Peace Corps 202-606-3376

Uruguay....Lustumbo, Julie Peace Corps 202-606-3575

Uruguay (Montevideo)....Staff Cnty State 202-647-2296

Uruguay/Minerals....Gurmendi, Alfredo Cnty Mines 202-501-9681

Uterus....Staff NICHD 301-496-5133

Utility, Retail Prices....Adkins, Robert LABOR 202-606-6985

Uveitis....Staff NEI 301-496-5248

Uzbekistan....Staff Cnty State 202-647-6731

V

VCR's....Dicerbo, Mario CUSTOMS 212-466-5672

VD....Staff NIAID 301-496-5717

VD (Control and Treatment)....Staff CDC 404-639-3286

Vacancies, NIH Recording....Staff NIH 301-496-1209

Vaccine Licensing....Peterson, Faye FDA 301-443-3285

Vaccines....Staff FDA/NCDB/OB 301-496-3556

Vaccines....Staff NIAID 301-496-5717

Vaccines....Nesbitt, Elizabeth USITC 202-205-3355

Vacuum cleaners....Jackson, Georgia USITC 202-205-3399

Vaginitis....Staff NIAID 301-496-5717

Valves....Riedl, Karl CUSTOMS 212-466-5493

Valves (Heart)....Staff NHLBI 301-496-4236

Valves and cocks....Mata, Ruben USITC 202-205-3403

Valves, Pipefittings Ex Brass....Reise, Richard COMMERCE 202-482-3489

Valvular Heart Disease....Staff NHLBI 301-496-4236

Vanadium....Hilliard, Henry E. MINES 202-501-9429

Vanadium....Lundy, David USITC 202-205-3439

Vanadium compounds....Greenblatt, Jack USITC 202-205-3353

Vanatu (Port Vila)....Staff Cnty State 202-647-3546

Vanillin....Land, Eric USITC 202-205-3349

Vanuatu....Nagle, Douglas Peace Corps 202-606-3290

Vanuatu....Jefferson, Mary Peace Corps 202-606-3231

Vanuatu....Schell, Russell Peace Corps 202-606-3231

Vanuatu/Minerals....Lyday, Travis Cnty Mines 202-501-9695

Varicella, Congenital....Staff NINDS 301-496-5751

Varicose Veins....Staff NHLBI 301-496-4236

Varnish....Brownchweig, Gilbert CUSTOMS 212-466-5744

Varnishes....Johnson, Larry USITC 202-205-3351

Vascular Collapse....Staff NHLBI 301-496-4236

Vasculitis....Staff NHLBI 301-496-4236

Vasculitis....Staff NIAID 301-496-5717

Vasculitis....Staff NHLBI 301-496-4236

Vasectomy....Staff NICHD 301-496-5133

Vatican....Staff Cnty State 202-647-2453

Vector-Borne Infectious Diseases....Gubler, Duane J. CDC 303-221-6428

Vegetable fibers (except cotton)....Cook, Lee USITC 202-205-3471

Vegetable glue....Jonnard, Aimison USITC 202-205-3350

Vegetables....Hintzman, Kevin Agri 202-720-5412

Vegetables....Lucier, Gary Agri 202-219-0884

Vegetables....Greene, Catherine Agri 202-219-0886

Vegetables....Hamm, Shannon Agri 202-219-0886

Vegetables....Hodgen, Donald A. COMMERCE 202-482-3346

Vegetables....Nunis, Kelly USITC 202-205-3324

Vegetables - Fresh....Brewster, Jim Agri 202-720-7688

Vegetables - Proc.....Budge, Arvin Agri 202-720-4285

Vehicle Propulsion Systems....Allsup, Jerry NEIC 202-586-9118

Vehicles, Special Purpose....Desoucey, Robert CUSTOMS 212-466-5667

Veiling....Sweet, Mary Elizabeth USITC 202-205-3455

Vending machines....Jackson, Georgia USITC 202-205-3399

Venereal Disease....Staff NIAID 301-496-5717

Venereal Disease (Control and Treatment)....Staff CDC 404-639-3286

Venezuela....Lindow, Herbert Cnty Commerce 202-482-4303

Venezuela (Caracas)....Staff Cnty State 202-647-3338

Venezuela/Minerals....Torres, Ivette Cnty Mines 202-501-9680

Ventilation....Staff OD/ORS 301-496-2960

Vermiculite....Potter, Michael J. MINES 202-501-9387

Vertigo....Staff NINDS 301-496-5751

Vertigo....Staff NIDCD 301-496-7243

Vests, mens'....Jones, Jackie USITC 202-205-3466

Veterans Status....Palumbo, Thomas CENSUS 301-763-8574

Veterans Status....Jones, Selwyn CENSUS 301-763-8574

Veterans, Employment Statistics....Cohany, Sharon LABOR 202-606-6378

Veterinary Medicine....Snider, Sharon FDA 301-443-3285

Veterinary instruments....Johnson, Christopher USITC 202-205-3488

Victim and Witness Assistance Programs....Kaplan, Carol Justice Stat 202-307-0759

Victim and Witness Assistance Programs....Zawitz, Marianne Justice Stat 202-616-3499

Victims of Crime....Meister, Brenda G. Justice Stat 202-307-5983

Victims of Crime....Rand, Michael Justice Stat 202-616-3494

Victims of Crime....Klaus, Patsy Justice Stat 202-307-0776

Victims of Crime....Taylor, Bruce Justice Stat 202-616-3498

Video Services....Plock, Ernest COMMERCE 202-482-4781

Video Transmission--Common Carrier....Staff FCC 202-634-1706

Video games....Robinson, Hazel USITC 202-205-3496

U.S.S.R. / Whips

Videotex Services....Inoussa, Mary C. COMMERCE 202-482-5820
Vietnam....Pho, Hong-Phong B. Cnty Commerce 202-482-3875
Vietnam....Staff Cnty State 202-647-3132
Vietnam/Minerals....Vacant Cnty Mines 202-501-9694
Vincent's Infection....Staff NIDR 301-496-4261
Vinyl chloride monomer....Michels, David USITC 202-205-3352
Vinyl resins or plastics....Taylor, Ed USITC 202-205-3362
Violations, Fish and Wildlife Laws....Staff FWS 703-358-1949
Virgin Islands (UK)....Brooks, Michelle Cnty Commerce 202-482-2527
Virgin Islands (US)....Soto, Rodrigo Cnty Commerce 202-482-2527
Virology....Staff NIAID 301-496-5717
Virus (Cancer Related)....Staff NCI 301-496-5583
Virus Tumor Biology....Brady, John FAES 301-496-0988
Vision Care (Statistics)....Staff NCHS 301-436-8500
Vision and Aging....Staff NEI 301-496-5248
Vision and Aging....Staff NIA 301-496-1752
Visitor Centers, Hatcheries....Staff FWS 703-358-1715
Visual Arts....Staff NEA 202-682-5448
Visual communications....Roche, James M. UMD 301-405-2408
Visual signaling apparatus....Baker, Scott USITC 202-205-3386
Vital Statistics, Division of....Patterson, John E. CDC 301-436-8951
Vital Statistics, Family Growth Survey.... CDC 301-436-8731
Vitamin E (and Cardiovascular Disease)....Staff NHLBI 301-496-4236
Vitamin Supplements and Aging....Staff NIA 301-496-1752
Vitamins....Nesbitt, Elizabeth USITC 202-205-3355
Vitamins C,D,E, (and CVD)....Staff NHLBI 301-496-4236
Vitamins/Minerals....Corwin, Emil FDA 202-205-4144
Vitiligo....Staff NIAMS 301-496-8188
Vitrectomy....Staff NEI 301-496-5248
Vocal Cord Paralysis....Staff NINDS 301-496-5751
Vocal Cord Paralysis....Staff NIDCD 301-496-7243
Vogt-Koyanagi Disease....Staff NEI 301-496-5248
Volunteerism....Long, Susan ACF 202-401-9215
Von Recklinghausen's Disease....Staff NINDS 301-496-5751
Von Willebrand's Disease....Staff NHLBI 301-496-4236
Voting Districts....McCully, Cathy CENSUS 301-763-3827
Voting and Registration....Jennings, Jerry CENSUS 301-763-4547
Voyager Flight Project....Doyle, Jim NASA 818-354-5011

W

WARC Frequency Allocations....Staff FCC 202-632-7025
WARC Frequency Coordination....Staff FCC 202-653-8126
WARC Frequency lists, Notification & Registration....Staff FCC 202-653-8126
WARC Interference....Staff FCC 202-653-8126
Wage Developments, Current, Comp. & Working Cond....Cimini, Michael LABOR 202-606-6275
Wages/Indl Rels, Collect Barg Agreements Analysis....Cimini, Michael LABOR 202-606-6275
Wages/Indl Rels, Collect Barg Settlements, Major....Devine, Janice M. LABOR 202-606-6276
Wages/Indl Rels, Empl Benefit Surv, Other Benefits....Houff, James LABOR 202-606-6238
Wages/Indl Rels, Empl Benefit Surv, Pension Plans....Houff, James LABOR 202-606-6238
Wages/Indl Rels, Employment Cost Index....Shelly, Wayne LABOR 202-606-6199
Wages/Indl Rels, Health Studies....Webber, William LABOR 202-606-6161
Wages/Industrial Relations, Current Wage Developments....Cimini, Michael LABOR 202-606-6275
Wages/Industrial Relations, Special Projects....Webber, William LABOR 202-606-6162
Wages/Industrial Relations, Unions, Membership....Cimini, Michael LABOR 202-606-6275
Wages/Industrial Relations, Work Stoppages....Cimini, Michael LABOR 202-606-6275
Waldenstroms Macroglobulinemia....Staff NCI 301-496-5583
Walkie-Talkies (unlicensed)....Staff FCC 202-653-6288
Walking sticks....Burns, Gail USITC 202-205-3501
Wall coverings, of rubber or plastics....Raftery, Jim USITC 202-205-3365
Wallets....Seastrum, Carl USITC 202-205-3493
Wallets, Billfolds, Flatgoods....Byron, James E. COMMERCE 202-482-4034
Walleye....Staff NEI 301-496-5248
Wallpaper....Stahmer, Carsten USITC 202-205-3321
Warm Air Heating Eqmt....Vacant COMMERCE 202-482-3509

Warts....Staff NIAID 301-496-5717
Washington issues....Callahan, Christopher UMD 301-405-2432
Waste Detoxification....Gross, Thomas J. NEIC 202-586-9497
Waste Heat Recovery....Gross, Thomas J. NEIC 202-586-9497
Waste Material Management....Walter, Donald K. NEIC 202-586-6750
Waste Products Utilization....Gross, Thomas J. NEIC 202-586-9497
Waste Reduction Technologies....Gross, Thomas J. NEIC 202-586-9497
Waste Treatment and Disposal....Staff EPA 301-382-4627
Waste and Chemical Policy Division....Staff EPA 202-26--2747
Waste and scrap (metals)....Lundy, David USITC 202-205-3439
Waste or scrap....Spalding, Josephine USITC 202-205-3498
Waste, textile: cotton....Sweet, Mary Elizabeth USITC 202-205-3455
Waste, textile: manmade fiber....Sweet, Mary Elizabeth USITC 202-205-3455
Waste, textile: silk....Shelton, Linda USITC 202-205-3457
Waste, textile: wool....Shelton, Linda USITC 202-205-3457
Wastepaper....Stanley, Gary COMMERCE 202-482-0375
Watches....Harris, John COMMERCE 202-482-1178
Watches....Piropato, Louis CUSTOMS 212-466-5895
Watches....Luther, Dennis USITC 202-205-3497
Water Division....Staff EPA 202-260-7700
Water Enforcement Division....Staff EPA 202-260-8180
Water Environmental Laws....Staff NEIC 202-586-4996
Water Hardness (and CVD)....Staff NHLBI 301-496-4236
Water Pollution....Staff EPA 301-382-5508
Water Projects, Federal....Staff FWS 703-358-1719
Water Resource Equipment....Vacant COMMERCE 202-482-3509
Water Resource Usage and Analysis....Staff FWS 703-358-1710
Water Rights Agreements, Fish and Wildlife....Staff FWS 703-358-1719
Water Supply....Staff OD/ORS 301-496-3537
Water and Sewage Treatment Plants....Vacant COMMERCE 202-482-4643
Wave Energy....Loose, Ronald NEIC 202-586-8086
Wax, articles of....Spalding, Josephine USITC 202-205-3498
Waxes....Brownchweig, Gilbert CUSTOMS 212-466-5744
Waxes....Randall, Rob USITC 202-205-3366
Weapons Testing....Staff NEIC 301-903-3441
Weapons and Crime....Rand, Michael Justice Stat 202-616-3494
Weapons and Crime....Taylor, Bruce Justice Stat 202-616-3498
Wearing Apparel: Boys (sizes 2-7 only)....Kirschner, Bruce CUSTOMS 212-466-5865
Wearing Apparel: Girls (sizes 2-7 only)....Kirschner, Bruce CUSTOMS 212-466-5865
Wearing Apparel: Infants....Kirschner, Bruce CUSTOMS 212-466-5865
Weatherization Assistance....Staff NEIC 202-586-2204
Weatherization Assistance - Elderly....Staff NEIC 202-586-2204
Weatherization Assistance - Handicapped....Staff NEIC 202-586-2204
Weatherization Assistance - Low Income Individuals....Staff NEIC 202-586-2204
Weaving machines....Greene, William USITC 202-205-3405
Weber-Christian Disease....Staff NIAMS 301-496-8188
Weber-Christian Disease....Staff NIAID 301-496-5717
Weekly and Annual Earnings--Current Pop. Survey....Mellor, Earl LABOR 202-606-6378
Wegener's Granulomatosis....Staff NIAMS 301-496-8188
Wegener's Granulomatosis....Staff NIAID 301-496-5717
Wegener's Granulomatosis....Staff NIAMS 301-496-8188
Weighing machinery....Slingerland, David USITC 202-205-3400
Welding apparatus....Mata, Ruben USITC 202-205-3403
Welding/Cutting Apparatus....Kemper, Alexis COMMERCE 202-482-5956
Welfare and AFDC JOBS Programs....Long, Susan ACF 202-401-9215
Werdnig-Hoffmann Disease....Staff NINDS 301-496-5751
Werner's Syndrome....Staff NIDDK 301-496-3583
Wernicke's Disease....Staff NINDS 301-496-5751
Western European Union (WEU)....Staff Cnty State 202-647-8050
Western Hemisphere Programs, Fish and Wildlife....Staff FWS 703-358-1767
Western Sahara....Dolley, Thomas Cnty Mines 202-501-9690
Western Samoa....Lagoy, Michele Peace Corps 202-606-3227
Western Samoa (Apia)....Staff Cnty State 202-647-3546
Wetlands Division....Staff EPA 202-260-9916
Wetlands Inventory, National....Staff FWS 703-358-1744
Wetlands Protection Hotline....Staff EPA 800-832-7828
Whalebone, articles of....Spalding, Josephine USITC 202-205-3498
Wheat....Pierre-Benoist, John USITC 202-205-3320
Wheat with options....Sepsey, Judy CFT 312-353-9025
Wheel goods: motorized....Hagey, Michael USITC 202-205-3392
Wheel goods: non-motorized....Seastrum, Carl USITC 202-205-3493
Whiplash....Staff NINDS 301-496-5751
Whips....Burns, Gail USITC 202-205-3501

Be patient. If any phone number is incorrect, call (area code) 555-1212 and request the new listing.

Experts

Whiskey....Salin, Victoria USITC 202-205-3331
Whistleblower Hotline....Staff EPA 800-424-4000
White Collar Crime....Kaplan, Carol Justice Stat 202-307-0759
Wholesale Trade....Margulies, Marvin COMMERCE 202-482-5086
Wholesale Trade, Census....Trimble, John CENSUS 301-763-5281
Wholesale Trade, Current Sales and Inventories....Gordon, Dale CENSUS 301-763-3916
Wholesale services....Bedore, James USITC 202-205-3424
Whooping Cough....Staff NIAID 301-496-5717
Wilderness Planning....Twiss, John FS 202-205-1404
Wilderness Planning, Fish and Wildlife....Staff FWS 703-358-2043
Wildlife Assistance....Staff FWS 703-358-1713
Wildlife Ecology....Staff FWS 703-358-1710
Wildlife Health Research....Staff FWS 703-358-1710
Wildlife Management, Refuges....Staff FWS 703-358-2043
Wildlife Permits....Staff FWS 703-358-1744
Wildlife Research....Lennartz, Michael R. FS 202-205-1524
Wildlife, Exotic....Staff FWS 703-358-1718
Wildlife, Injurious....Staff FWS 703-358-1718
Wildlife, Law Enforcement....Staff FWS 703-358-1949
Wildlife, Non-Game....Staff FWS 703-358-1718
Wildlife, Range and Fish Habitat Research....Lennartz, Michael R. FS 202-205-1424
Wilms' Tumor....Staff NCI 301-496-5583
Wilson Disease....Staff NIDDK 301-496-3583
Wilson Disease....Staff NINDS 301-496-5751
Wind Energy....Loose, Ronald NEIC 202-586-8086
Windmill Components....Garden, Les COMMERCE 202-482-0556
Wines....Salin, Victoria USITC 202-205-3331
Wire....Fitzgerald, John CUSTOMS 212-466-5492
Wire....Yost, Charles USITC 202-205-3442
Wire Cloth....Williams, Franklin COMMERCE 202-482-0132
Wire Cloth, Industrial....Reise, Richard COMMERCE 202-482-3489
Wire Facilities....Staff FCC 202-634-1800
Wire Rods....Fitzgerald, John CUSTOMS 212-466-5492
Wire and Wire Products....Vacant COMMERCE 202-482-0606
Wire or Cable Licenses....Staff FCC 202-634-1800
Wire rods....Yost, Charles USITC 202-205-3442
Wireless Microphones (licensed)....Staff FCC 717-337-1212
Wireless Microphones (non-licensed)....Staff FCC 202-653-6288
Wiretapping....Staff FCC 202-632-7260
Wiring sets....Cutchin, John USITC 202-205-3396
Wiskott-Aldrich Syndrome....Staff NCI 301-496-5583
Wolff-Parkinson-White Syndrome (WPW)....Staff NHLBI 301-496-4236
Wollastonite....Potter, Michael J. MINES 202-501-9387
Women in journalism....Beasley, Maurine UMD 301-405-2413
Women's Health Issues....Staff OD 301-496-5787
Women's Health and Fertility....Peterson, Herbert B. CDC 404-488-5250
Women, Employment/Unemployment Statistics....Hayghe, Howard LABOR 202-606-6378
Women, Population....Smith, Denise CENSUS 301-763-7883
Wood (densified)....Ruggles, Fred USITC 202-205-3325
Wood Containers....Hicks, Michael COMMERCE 202-482-0375
Wood Preserving....Hicks, Michael COMMERCE 202-482-0375
Wood Products....Stanley, Gary COMMERCE 202-482-0375
Wood Products....Garretto, Paul CUSTOMS 212-466-5779
Wood Products, Misc.....Stanley, Gary COMMERCE 202-482-0375
Wood Technology....Staff FS 202-205-1565
Wood Working Machinery....McDonald, Edward COMMERCE 202-482-0680
Wood products, rough primary....Ruggles, Fred USITC 202-205-3325
Wood pulp....Rhodes, Richard USITC 202-205-3322
Wood veneers....Ruggles, Fred USITC 202-205-3325
Wool....Freund, Kimberlie USITC 202-205-3456
Wool....Shelton, Linda USITC 202-205-3457
Wool....Warlick, William USITC 202-205-3459
Wool and Mohair....Lawler, John Agri 202-219-0840
Wool and Mohair....Skinner, Robert Agri 202-219-0841
Wool and Mohair....Simpson, Linda Agri 202-720-3578
Wool grease, sulfonated or sulfated....Land, Eric USITC 202-205-3349
Word processors....Baker, Scott USITC 202-205-3386
Work Experience, Employment/Unemployment Stats....Mellor, Earl LABOR 202-606-6378
Work Injuries, Reports & Surveys of, Comp. & Work....Jackson, Ethel LABOR 202-606-6180
Work Injury, Report Surveys, Comp & Working Cond.....Jackson, Ethel LABOR 202-606-6180

Work Stoppages, Compensation & Working Conditions....Cimini, Michael LABOR 202-606-6275
Work-life Estimates, Employment Statistics....Horvath, Francis LABOR 202-606-6345
Workers, Older, Empl/Unempl. Stats.....Rones, Philip LABOR 202-606-6378
Working Conditions....Cimini, Michael LABOR 202-606-6275
Working Conditions, Employment Cost Data....Shelly, Wayne LABOR 202-606-6199
Working Conditions, Safety & Health, Asst.Comm.....Eisenberg, William M. LABOR 202-606-6304
Working Poor, Employment/Unemployment Statistics....Herz, Diane LABOR 202-606-6378
Works of Art....Mushinske, Larry CUSTOMS 212-466-5739
Wound Healing (LDBA)....Staff NIDR 301-496-4261
Woven Outerwear: Boys'....Raftery, William CUSTOMS 212-466-5851
Woven Outerwear: Men's....Raftery, William CUSTOMS 212-466-5851
Woven Outerwear: Women's....Raftery, William CUSTOMS 212-466-5851
Wryneck (Torticollis)....Staff NINDS 301-496-5751

X

X-ray (Radiation Effects on Fetus)....Staff FDA 301-443-2356
X-ray Technician....Staff HRSA/BHPr 301-443-5794
X-ray apparatus....Johnson, Christopher USITC 202-205-3488
Xanthinuria....Staff NIDDK 301-496-3583
Xanthomatosis....Staff NHLBI 301-496-4236
Xeroderma Pigmentosum....Staff NCI 301-496-5583
Xerophthalmia....Staff NEI 301-496-5248
Xeroradiography....Staff NCI 301-496-5583
Xerostomia (Dry Mouth)....Staff NIDR 301-496-4261
Xylene....Raftery, Jim USITC 202-205-3365
Xylenol....Matusik, Ed USITC 202-205-3356

Y

YAG Laser....Staff NEI 301-496-5248
Yarns....Konzet, Jeffrey CUSTOMS 212-466-5885
Yarns....Shelton, Linda USITC 202-205-3457
Year 2000 Research and Development....Staff CENSUS 301-763-8601
Yeast....Janis, William V. COMMERCE 202-482-2250
Yeast Infections....Staff NIAID 301-496-5717
Yellow Fever....Staff NIAID 301-496-5717
Yellow Page Advertising....Staff FCC 202-632-7553
Yellowcake....Greenblatt, Jack USITC 202-205-3353
Yemen....DiMeo, Pam Peace Corps 202-606-3196
Yemen....Schildwachter, Christy Peace Corps 202-606-3196
Yemen (Aden)/Minerals....Michalski, Bernadette Cnty Mines 202-501-9699
Yemen (Sana)/Minerals....Michalski, Bernadette Cnty Mines 202-501-9699
Yemen Arab Republic (Sanaa)....Staff Cnty State 202-647-6571
Yemen, Republic of....Fitzgerald-Wilkes, Kate/Thanos, Paul Cnty Commerce 202-482-1870
Youth Conservation Corps, Fish and Wildlife....Staff FWS 703-358-2029
Youth, Employment Statistics....Cohany, Sharon LABOR 202-606-6378
Youth, Students, and Dropouts, Empl./Unempl. Stats....Cohany, Sharon LABOR 202-606-6378
Yttrium....Hedrick, James B. MINES 202-501-9412
Yugoslavia....Keller, Jeremy Cnty Commerce 202-482-2645
Yugoslavia (Belgrade)....Staff Cnty State 202-647-4138
Yugoslavia/Minerals....Steblez, Walter Cnty Mines 202-501-9671

Z

Zaire....Henke, Debra Cnty Commerce 202-482-5149
Zaire, Republic of (Kinshasa)....Staff Cnty State 202-647-2080
Zaire/Minerals....Heydari, Michael Cnty Mines 202-501-9688
Zambia....Holm-Olsen, Finn Cnty Commerce 202-482-4228
Zambia (Lusaka)....Staff Cnty State 202-647-8433
Zambia/Minerals....Antonides, Lloyd Cnty Mines 202-501-9686
Zeolites....Virta, Robert MINES 202-501-9384
Zimbabwe....Holm-Olsen, Finn Cnty Commerce 202-482-4228
Zimbabwe....Brill, Terry Peace Corps 202-606-3535
Zimbabwe (Harare)....Staff Cnty State 202-647-9429
Zimbabwe/Minerals....Izon, David Cnty Mines 202-501-9692
Zinc....Jolly, James H. MINES 202-501-9422

Whiskey / Zoris

Zinc....White, Linda USITC 202-205-3427
Zinc compounds....Greenblatt, Jack USITC 202-205-3353
Zip Codes, Demographic Data....Staff CENSUS 301-763-4100
Zip Codes, Economic Data....Russell, Anne CENSUS 301-763-7038
Zip Codes, Geographic Relationships....Quarato, Rose CENSUS 301-763-4667
Zippers....Shildneck, Ann USITC 202-205-3499

Zirconium....Templeton, David A. MINES 202-501-9391
Zirconium....DeSapio, Vincent USITC 202-205-3435
Zirconium compounds....Greenblatt, Jack USITC 202-205-3353
Zollinger-Ellison Syndrome....Staff NIDDK 301-496-3583
Zoonoses....Staff NIAID 301-496-5717
Zoris....Shildneck, Ann USITC 202-205-3499

Be patient. If any phone number is incorrect, call (area code) 555-1212 and request the new listing.

Index

A

A Home of Your Own, 697
ABC's of Exporting, 855
ABC's of Income Tax, 492
Aberdeen Proving Ground, 941
Abortions, 575, 576
Accidents
aviation, 782, 783, 818, 819
driving-while-intoxicated, 579
drug-related, 579
elderly, 559
hazardous materials, 357, 820, 826, 1144
highway, 352-53, 818, 827
identifying victims, 614
investigation, 818
marine, 818
motorboats, 1216
National Transportation Safety Board, 818
pipeline, 818
product investigation reports, 109
public hearings, 821
railroad, 818
traffic, 579, 895, 1220, 1225
Accountants, 635
Accounting, 435
Acid drainage in mines, 812, 1118, 1142
Acid rain, 800, 970, 977, 999, 1083
Acid Rain: The Student's First Sourcebook, 1261
activity book, 1264, 1283, 1296
assessment program, 1108
environmental lab, 1101
greenhouse effect, 1084
prevention research, 1030
research, 1103
student's sourcebook, 1267
tracer bullets, 1203
U.S. foreign policy, 1100
wall chart, 1132
Acne, 537, 539
Acoustics, 1011
Acousto-elasticity, 1003
Acquired Immune Deficiency Syndrome
see AIDS
ACTION, 383
drug abuse prevention office, 588
drug abuse prevention, 589
public information office, 62
Actuaries
Enrollment Board, 453
registration, 453
Acupuncture, 515, 977, 1203
chronic pain, 545
tracer bullets, 515
Addiction
see drugs, 349, 578
Adhesives, 955, 976, 1228
Adjustable rate mortgages, 105, 120, 867
Administration on Aging, 556
Administrative Conference of the
United States, 63
Adolescents, 526
drugs and peer pressure, 588
family-based drug treatment, 595
health, 516, 962
Adopt-A-Horse program, 26
Adoption, 527, 532, 1186
adolescent family program grants, 369
community grants, 366
Family Life Information Exchange, 526
grants, 386
international, 419
program grants, 366
research grants, 286
services, 532
Advertising
alcohol, 774
deceptive claims or practices, 94
history, 303, 304
solar products, 94
tourism, 421
Advocacy
handicapped legal rights, 619
Aerial Photos Of Your Neighborhood, 26
Aerodynamics, 982, 1225
Aeromedical research, 261, 784, 939
Aeronautics, 939, 981, 987, 1225
charts, 1088
educational videoconferences, 163
flight simulation, 986
human factors, 982
hypersonic aircraft, 982
military research, 940, 982
rotorcraft and powered-lift technology, 982
supermaneuverability, 990
systems, 940, 982
teacher workshops, 1257, 1277, 1284, 1288, 1291
Aerosols, 1083, 1109
Aerospace
aerospace-related software, 161
Airspace System, National, 971
Ames Research Center, 990
astronaut training, 986
astronautical research and
development, 1184
automated space flight, 982
commercial opportunities, 981
congressional caucus, 1186, 1187
computer software, 1253, 1277, 1288
education programs, 26, 161, 984
Education Services Program, 1276, 1287
educational materials, 1253, 1268, 1277, 1288, 1290, 1293
exploration, 989
flight research, 982
Goddard Space Flight Center, 990
Jet Propulsion Laboratory, 990
John F. Kennedy Space Center, 990
Langley Research Center, 990
legislation, 986
Lewis Research Center, 990
library, 308
Lyndon B. Johnson Space Center, 990
Marshall Space Flight Center, 990
materials research, 1006
medical experiments, 986
National Space Technology
Laboratories, 990
peaceful uses of, 1187
research and technology development, 989
Senate committee, 1181
solar system exploration, 982
Space Shuttle, 986
Space Station, 971, 989
spacecraft, 989
Spacelab, 989
statistics, 990
structures research, 939, 982
technology and exploration, 303
technology licensing, 982
U.S. Space Foundation, 163
Vandenberg Air Force Base, 989
Affirmative Action, 268, 627, 863, 885-888
Labor Market Data, 884
Afghanistan, 1186
Africa, 792, 922, 1181, 1184
African Development Foundation, 922, 970, 1031
agriculture, 931, 970, 1031
art, 294, 313
foreign aid, U.S., 931, 970, 1031
studies, 306
technology, 931, 970, 1031
African Development Foundation, 63, 922
Afro-Americans
Black congressional caucus, 1186
health care, 348
migration, 1275
historical and cultural research, 313
Age discrimination, 26
Agency for International Development, 848, 913, 924
investments in developing countries, 853
statistics, 872
Agent Orange, 390, 968
Aggravated assault, 610
Aging and the elderly
Baltimore Longitudinal Study of
Aging, 557
career training in aging, 557
education, 153
elder abuse, 503, 535, 557
employment, 246
Federal Council on the Aging, 558
foster grandparent volunteers, 383
gerontology research, 557
Healthy Older People Program, 518, 558
home buying guide, 96
House Select Committee, 1185
humanities activities, 317
innovative programs, 556
Long-term care, 558
National Institute on Aging, 557
Native American program grants, 366
nutrition, 525
postal carrier alert program, 113
preventive services, 973
program grants, 366
research grants, 184, 286, 557, 768
Senate committees, 1182
Senior Companions Volunteers, 384
statistics, 868, 874
travel abroad, 418
victims of crime, 611
Agrichemical contamination, 962
Agricultural employer's tax, 493
Agricultural Research Service, 851
Agriculture
acreage data, 1042
Africa, 931, 970, 1031
AgExport Action Kit, 851

The thousands of studies in the Current Events Chapter and Experts Chapter are not included in this Index.

Index

Agriculture (continued)
alternative farming practices, 140, 1023
Bulletin board, 1233
cash value of farm products, 1027
commodity reports, 873, 1024
congressional caucus, 1186
consumer pricing research, 1036
container equipment regulations, 1036
cooperatives, 929, 1026
Country Market Profiles, 851
crop prices, 1042
daily news hotline, 1023
databases, 1215, 1219
development program, 360, 1042
directories, 1042
disease databases, 1021
district farm economy, 105, 867
domestic marketing, 1183
donation of animal feed, 357, 1027
economic reports, 105, 867, 1037
educational and technical assistance, 158, 1030, 1253, 1293
employment, 1042
energy issues, 1183
engineering, 1022
equipment, 1042
exports and imports, 1038, 1039, 1042
Extension Services, 344, 1025, 1240
Farm Credit System, 428, 1026
Farmer's Tax Guide, 493
feasibility studies, 1030
finance, 1037
Food and Security Act of 1986, 630
food assistance grants, 360
foreign, 1038, 1041, 1183, 1231
Foreign Agriculture Service (FAS), 850
foreign investment in U.S., 121
Foreign Market Information, 851
foreign specialists, 846
foreign trade, 1037, 1038
grading, 1034, 1042
grants, 182, 360
history, 142, 976, 1203
House committee, 1183
income surveys, 1042
inspection, 1033, 1034, 1042
international development, 912, 926
literature searches, 1021
loans, 125, 359, 630
low-input, 140, 1023
management, 1027
market analysis reports, 1030
Market News Service, 1042
marketing, 1022, 1027, 1035, 1042
mine program, 360
natural disaster grants, 360
natural disaster loans, 359
new crops development, 1028
Office Space for Agricultural Exporters, 850
OSHA rules, 266
patents, 724, 1028
post-harvest processing, 1030
postharvest technology, 970, 1031
production projections, 1022, 1042
publications, 1042, 1043
recorded message, 93
regulation offices, 1033
relending program, 359
reports, 1042, 1043
research, 282, 1033, 1042
resource grants, 360
Senate Committee, 1180
services, 1043
Special Programs For Agricultural Products, 850
specialization, 1027
state agencies, 1042
statistics, 862, 863, 1042
surpluses, 522
taxation, 1181
technology, 965, 970, 1025, 1031
trade shows, 1042
trade, 1042, 1223
training grants, 359
transportation facilities, 1031
unfair trading practices, 1035
water and wetlands, 125

Agriculture, U.S. Department of
AGRICOLA, 1021
Agricultural Conservation Program, 1027, 1129
Agricultural Marketing Service, 1029, 1035
Agricultural State Conservation Service, 1025, 1026, 1124, 1129, 1130
Beltsville Agricultural Research Center, 1033
Commodity Credit Corporation, 356, 1033
Conservation Reserve Program, 1025, 1026, 1124
Cooperative Extension Service, 1030
disaster assistance programs, 357, 1027
Economic Research Service databases, 1041
Foreign Agricultural Service, 1038
Forest Service, 351, 409, 1107, 1242
general information, 1031
Graduate School, 156
Higher Education Program, 157
Human Nutrition Information Service, 523
Land-Grant Institutions, 155
National Agricultural Library, 1028
National Arboretum Library, 141
Packers and Stockyards Administration, 1035
Public information office, 41
Quarterly Report to Congress, 1030
Rural Electrification Administration, 790
Soil Conservation Service, 1027, 1126
State Agricultural Experiment Stations, 1030
Transportation Services, 1031
Veterinary Services, 1024
volunteer programs, 383
water resource programs, 1032, 1113, 1115, 1118, 1121

Agronomy, 1024

Aid, international
child health, 916
disaster assistance, 920
economic development, 918
education, 918
energy development, 919
environmental issues, 926
Food for Peace, 919
nutrition, 927
private and voluntary organizations, 934, 929
project databases, 918
Sahel development, 930

AIDS, 515, 764, 973, 977
AIDSLINE database, 504
azidothymidine (AZT) research, 540
Centers for Disease Control, 538
children's programs, 364
community programs grants, 364
contraception research, 527
databases, 501, 538
drug reimbursements grants, 363
economics, 972
education programs, 151, 973
Federal response to, 972
grants, 363
health insurance, 972
HIV operation plan, 538
HIV/AIDS federal employees, 595
hotline, 26, 537
in the workplace, 501, 538
insect transmission, 972
international statistics, 872
intravenous drug users, 579
IV drug users, 588
law enforcement, 609
National AIDS Information Clearinghouse, 501, 538
precautions for professionals, 538
program grants, 363
research grants, 183, 284, 538
Surgeon General's report, 501, 538

Air, 976
Clean Air Act, 1110
climatic analysis, 1085, 1092
indoor pollution, 515
pollution, 1085, 1092, 1095, 1098

Air bags, 94, 96, 420, 818, 825

Air conditioning, 776

Air Force
procurement, 941

Air pollution
coloring books, 1252
control program grants, 376
research grants, 377

Air Services, Essential, 762

Air shows, 348, 350

Air traffic controllers, 782, 788 976
Job Bank, 26

Aircraft, 1225
accident data, 781, 819
air taxis, 352, 785
cabin fires, 1011
civil, 783
commuter, 352, 785
drug smugglers, 599
flight data, 782
highjacking, 788, 941
jets, 779, 976, 1203
maintenance data, 782
noise levels, 348, 782, 1095
ownership database, 782, 788
registration, 783, 1215
repair stations, 782, 788
statistics, 784
structures, 1007
testing, 940

Airline Passenger Complaint Center, 26

Airlines
antitrust violations, 782
consumer rights, 94, 420, 781
displaced workers, 243
employment data, 786
essential service, 96, 352, 785
financial information, 781
mergers, 782
passenger safety, 420, 782
scheduled flights, 1216
traffic statistics, 781

Airports, 788, 941
air traffic control, 976
bearing and distance information, 787
bomb threats, 788, 941
civilian, 787
construction standards, 783
databases, 784
development projects, 787
displaced persons program, 787
environmental impact, 787
flight planning information, 787
gross receipts, 777, 819
Improvement Program, 761
records of hazards to air navigation, 787
runways, 787

The thousands of studies in the Current Events Chapter and Experts Chapter are not listed in this Index.

Index

security issues, 788, 941
security, 783, 941
statistics, 784, 787
tours, 161, 243, 268, 396, 785
walk-through detection devices, 783, 941
weapon detection devices, 788, 941
Air traffic, 781, 785
Alabama
Affirmative Action, 884
Automated Tax Refund Information, 466
company directories, 664
corporation information, 658
Department of Public Safety, Drivers License Division, 641
Downpayment Assistance Program, 130
Housing Finance Authority, 130
IRS hotline, 464
Labor Market, 884
licensed professionals, 636
Low-Income Housing Tax Credit Program, 130
Mortgage Credit Certificate Program, 130
Mortgage Revenue Bond Program, 130
Multi-Family Bond Program, 130
Securities Commission, 668
Small Business Administration Office, 837
state data centers, 899
state information, 36
State International Trade Offices, 858
State Labor Office, 884
State Occupational Information Coordinating Community, 636
State Planning Office, 908
state procurement office, 841
state tax assistance, 498
Surplus property, 705
Tax form distribution center, 470
Tax forms and publications, 491
Trends in Employment and Unemployment, 884
unclaimed property, 711
Uniform Commercial Code Office, 630
U.S. International Trade Administration Office, 855
Alaska
Akcens Quarterly Newsletter, 884
Automated Tax Refund Information, 466
Bureau of Land Management office, 695
Career Guide, 884
Center for International Business, 664
company directories, 664
Condo Association Loan Program, 131
Condominium Projects, 130
corporation information, 658
Directory of Licensed Occupations, 885
Division of Banking, Securities and Corporations, 668
Division of Occupational Licensing, Department of Commerce, 636
Economic Trends, 884
Employment Insurance, 885
Home Ownership Assistance Program, 130
Housing Finance Corp., 130
IRS hotline, 464
licensed professionals, 636
Mobile Home Loan Program, 130
Mobile Home Park Loans, 130
mobile home parks, 130
Mortgage Guaranty Insurance Corporation, 131
Non-Conforming Property Program, 130
Refinance Program, 130
Refinance Program of a Non-AHFC Loan, 130
Second Mortgage Program, 130
Second Mortgage Program for Health and Safety Repairs, 131

Small Business Administration Office, 837
state data centers, 899
state information, 36
State International Trade Offices, 858
State Labor Office, 884
State Planning Office, 908
state procurement office, 841
State Salary Survey, 885
state tax assistance (corporation), 498
Statistical Quarterly, 905
surplus property, 705
Tax Exempt Mortgage Program, 130
Tax form distribution center, 470
Tax forms and publications, 491
Taxable Mortgage Program, 130
Triplex/Fourplex Mortgage Program, 130
unclaimed property, 711
Uniform Commercial Code Division, 630
U.S. International Trade Administration Office, 855
Veterans Mortgage Program, 130
Wage Rates, 884
Alaskan Natives
substance abuse treatment, 595
Alaskan oil spill, 942
Alaskan pipeline, 818, 1067
Alcohol
advertising, 774
bottling, 774
bulk sales, 774
denatured, 775
fuel, 764, 1049
labeling, 774
manufacturing, 775
regulations, 775
tax classification, 774
tax credit (fuel use), 486
trade laws, 774
emergency preparedness program, 357, 533
Alcoholism, 346, 515, 576, 976
abuse program grants, 363
automobile safety, 352, 826
cirrhosis of the liver, 546
clearinghouse, 593
community programs, 364
education grants, 179, 183
elderly, 533
health insurance coverage, 577
National Clearinghouse for Alcohol and Drug Information, 527, 578, 588-590, 594
prevention and treatment programs, 577, 1025, 1230, 1240
program grants, 364, 369
research grants, 284, 285, 287
research results, 588
Senate subcommittee, 1182
technical support to organizations, 588
treatment costs, 972
Algae, 977, 1203
Alien residents
Certificate, 478
Income Tax Statement, 480
All terrain vehicles, 109
Allergies, 515, 538, 977, 1203
food, 520
research grants, 286
Alloys, 997, 1005, 1224
Alpacas, Peru, 924
Aluminum, 1006
Alzheimer's, 514, 515, 539, 556, 970
tracer bullet, 1203
American Depository Receipts, 435
American Indians, 1272
See also Native Americans
arts and crafts, 1267
Enterprise Development, 837

languages, 1273
programs, 759
slides, 1285
American motor racing, 1276, 1279, 1280
American Samoa
Exclusion of Income, 482
Wage and Tax Statement, 472
Ames-Dryden Flight Research Facility, 985
Ames Research Center, 990
AMTRAK, 70
Amyotrophic lateral sclerosis, 539
Ancient cultures, 1255
slides, 1285
Andrew W. Mellon Lectures in the Fine Arts, 317
Anesthesia research, 566
Anger
National Institute of Mental Health, 532
Spanish publications, 532
Angiography, 972
Animal Poison Control Center, National, 1142, 1239
Animal research, 574
educational lesson plans, 1255, 1274
Animals, 1241
biomedical research, 574
disease diagnosis, 141
diseases, foreign, 1028
drug toxicology testing, 1023, 1241
drugs and medicated feeds, 1241
endangered species, 976, 1137, 1203
ethical issues, 1023, 1241
experimental, 1223
livestock and veterinary services, 1028
parasitology, 1023
patents, 514, 970
poison control, 1142, 1239
research alternatives, 514, 970
research grants, 282
transgenic, 515, 970
travel by air, 1241
Annuities tax, 472
Anorexia nervosa, 515, 977, 1203
Ansel Adams prints, 26
Antarctica, 988
geologic maps, 1090
research expeditions, 292, 401, 415
science stations, 914, 1095, 1132
Antennas, 1010
Anthropology, 309, 320
education, 153
Anti-takeover amendments, 868
Anti-toxins, 944
Antitrust
airlines, 782
business reviews, 611
consumers, 609
investigations, 609
joint research ventures, 610
nuclear industry, 1072
Senate committee, 1182
Apheresis, 973
Apnea
see Sudden Infant Death Syndrome, 530
Apollo missions
Apollo-SOYUZ, 1286
moon landings video, 1276, 1288, 1295
videos, 276, 1294
Appalachia
economic development, 344
grants, 388
Apparel industry, 910
Appliances
energy standards, 1049, 1054
household, 1049
Appraisals
health risk appraisals, 517

The thousands of studies in the Current Events Chapter and Experts Chapter are not included in this Index.

Index

Aquaculture, 757, 1023, 800, 976, 1203
- emergency loans, 125

Aquarium, National, 400

Aquatic weed control, 1133

Arc-welding, 1011

Archaeology, 304, 314, 942, 1008, 1095, 1121, 1285
- grants, 303
- import controls, 318
- slides, 1285
- underwater, 972
- preservation technology, 972

Architects, 635
- tax reform, 120

Architecture, 304, 762
- drawings archives, 294, 304, 314, 1088
- photographs, 296, 297
- transportation, 292, 403, 822, 826, 1107
- U.S. Capitol, 307, 1292

Archives
- archival training course, 247, 308
- Archives of American Art, 313, 315
- art photographs, 296
- directory of National Archives, 308
- economic data, 866
- educational research, 166
- Eliot Elisofon Photographic Archives, 294, 313
- federal laws, 615, 1191
- federal motion pictures, 294, 295
- Folkways Records, 305, 317
- genealogy research, 647
- German Army records, 312
- Human Studies Film, 296, 297
- legislative, 1191
- maps, 294
- military data files, 307, 312
- military service records, 646
- Moses and Frances Asch Collection, 295, 317
- National Air and Space Archives, 303
- National Anthropological Archives, 308, 313
- prisoner-of-war records, 648
- records management, 305
- Security and Exchange Commission records, 442
- security-classified records, 304
- ship passenger arrival records, 648
- sound recordings, 294, 295
- State historical records, 311
- vice-presidential papers, 311
- Vietnam War, 311
- Watergate tapes and transcripts, 312

Archives and Records Administration, National
- Center for Electronic Records, 305
- documentary editions, 647
- genealogical workshops, 647
- Institute for the Editing of Historical Documents, 306
- Legislative Archives Center, 1191
- Modern Archives Institute, 247, 308
- Motion Picture, Sound, and Video Branch, 294, 295
- National Audiovisual Center, 294
- National Personnel Records Center, 272, 273, 647
- Nixon Presidential Materials Project, 311
- Records Administration Information Center, 305
- State Historical Records Advisory Board, 311
- Still Pictures Branch, 296
- volunteer programs, 383

Arctic, 988
- foreign policy issues, 914, 1095, 1132
- oil and gas exploration, 972
- research expeditions, 292, 401, 415

Artificial intelligence, 977, 1203

Arizona
- *Aerospace in Arizona -- An Assessment of Market Opportunities,* 907
- Affirmative Action, 885
- Agribusiness Profiles, 908
- Automated Tax Refund Information, 466
- Bureau of Land Management office, 695
- Community Profiles, 907
- company directories, 664
- Corporation information, 658
- Department of Commerce, 131
- Department of Revenue, 636
- *Directory of High Technology Companies,* 908
- Directory of International Services, 908
- Employer Wage Survey, 885
- Energy Data Report, 908
- Exporters Directory, 908
- Government Jobs, 885
- Housing Trust Fund, 131
- Indian Profiles, 908
- Industrial Profiles, 908
- IRS hotline, 464
- Labor Market Information-Annual Planning Information, 905
- Labor Market Newsletter, 885
- Licensed Occupation Requirements, 885
- licensed professionals, 636
- Low Interest Mortgage Programs, 131
- Low-Income Housing Tax Credits, 131
- Major Employers, 885
- Motor Vehicles Division, 641
- Occupational Employment Forecasts, 885
- Rental Rehabilitation Program, 131
- *Rural Economic Development Resource Directory,* 908
- Securities Division, Arizona Corporation Commission, 668
- Small Business Administration Office, 837
- state data centers, 899
- state information, 36
- State International Trade Offices, 858
- State Labor Office, 885
- State Planning Office, 908
- state procurement office, 841
- state tax assistance, 498
- Summer Jobs For Students, 885
- surplus property, 705
- Tax form distribution center, 470
- Tax forms and publications, 491
- unclaimed property office, 712
- Uniform Commercial Code Department, 630
- U.S. International Trade Administration Office, 855
- World Trade Review Quarterly Newsletter, 908

Arizona Annual Economic Profile, 908

Arkansas
- Affordable Housing Program, 131
- Automated Tax Refund Information, 466
- company directories, 664
- corporation information, 658
- Current Employment Developments, 885
- Directory of Licensed Occupations, 885
- Home Energy Loan Program, 131
- IRS hotline, 464
- Labor Force Statistics, 885
- licensed professionals, 636
- Licensing boards and professions, 636
- Low-Income Housing Tax Credit Program, 131
- Occupational Trends, 885
- Office of Motor Vehicle Registration, 641
- Securities Department, 668
- Single-Family housing, 131
- Small Business Administration Office, 837
- Small Business Development Center, 731
- state data centers, 900
- state information, 36
- State International Trade Offices, 858
- State Labor Office, 885
- State Planning Office, 908
- state procurement office, 841
- state tax assistance, 498
- surplus property, 705
- Tax form distribution center, 470
- Tax forms and publications, 491
- unclaimed property office, 712
- Uniform Commercial Code, 631
- U.S. International Trade Administration Office, 855

Arlington National Cemetery, 944

Armaments, 939

Armed forces
- *see also Military*
- drug testing, 606-07

Arms control and disarmament, 936, 937, 1186
- arms transfers, 937
- chemical weapons, 936
- computer simulated warfare, 937
- congressional relations, 937
- crisis stability issues, 937
- economic impact of treaties, 935
- Europe, 936
- House Committee on, 1184
- INF Treaty, 936
- international relations, 936
- legal issues, 936
- media coverage, 937
- military expenditure statistics, 938
- Missile Technology Control Regime, 937
- multilateral arms control, 936
- national agenda, 938
- news releases, 937
- nuclear export control issues, 936
- nuclear safeguards, 937
- nuclear test ban monitoring, 937
- policy statements, 936
- public diplomacy activities, 935
- public perceptions of U.S. policy, 937
- research, 938
- Soviet compliance, 938
- space, 970
- speakers, 938
- treaty compliance, 937, 938
- weapons systems impact statements, 935

Arms transfer, 937

Army Corps of Engineers, 942
- aquatic pest control, 414, 1109

Army, U.S.
- aircraft, 941
- budget, 942
- Center of Military History, 950
- Materiel Command, 957
- personnel locator, 646, 942
- procurement, 943
- research labs, 943, 982
- Reserve band, 348

Arson, 610, 1005
- community program grants, 379
- database, 610
- forensic studies, 774
- victims, 354, 610

Art
- African, 313
- Air Force collection, 313
- American Indian, 318
- Andrew W. Mellon Lectures in the Fine Arts, 317
- Army collection, 315
- Asian and Near Eastern, 316

The thousands of studies in the Current Events Chapter and Experts Chapter are not listed in this index.

Index

Congress, 315
donations to embassies, 315
duck stamp design competition, 291, 1133
education literature, 1287
educational grants, 172
educational materials, 173
eighteenth and nineteenth century, 310
films, 28
folk, 319, 375
fraud, 95
history, 315
grants, 173
insurance, 762
lectures, 28
minority grants, 375
modern and contemporary, 317
Naval history, 953
Pentagon collection, 401
publications, 316
shows, traveling, 702
slides, films, and videos, 26, 1286, 1293
Smithsonian Institute Traveling Exhibition Service, 702
South and Southeast Asian, 316
state program grants, 375
stolen, 610
student fellowships, 186
U.S. Capitol collection, 315
Arthritis, 538-39
children, 539
Chinese elderly, 557
diet, 539
employment, 539
exercise, 516, 539
information clearinghouse, 502
Multipurpose Arthritis Centers, 539
National Institute of Arthritis and Musculoskeletal and Skin Diseases, 537, 539
research, 286, 767
videotape, 539
Artifacts, analysis techniques, 1008
Artificial insemination, 514, 970
Artificial intelligence, 573
Artists
free money, 26
freelance, 29
polar expeditions, 292, 401, 415
traveling abroad, 293, 315
Arts, 762
arts education grants, 144, 290, 315
challenge grants, 375
congressional caucus, 1186
cross discipline grants, 292
energy awareness, 1259, 1260, 1269, 1272, 1273, 1287
experts abroad program, 291, 309, 415, 913
folk arts funding programs, 290, 314
international festivals, 292
library, 311, 321
local programs grants, 375
performing arts, 314, 316
Senate subcommittee, 1182
source materials, 306, 1094
Arts America, 859
Asbestos, 111, 119, 515, 977, 1095, 1203
community grants, 377
Asia, 922
Aspartame, 525
Asset Acquisition Statement, 488
Assets
Tax Guide for Basis of Property, 495
Tax Guide on Sales and Other Dispositions, 494
Asthma, 515, 538, 539, 977, 1203
Astrogeology, 1092, 1240
Astronautics, 987

Astronauts, 163
applications to be, 982
educator programs, 161
slides, 1286, 1289
Astronomy, 992, 1277, 1281, 1288
computer software, 1253
hotline, 32
Hubble Space Telescope, 986
infrared, 982
Naval Observatory, 953
Space Telescope Science Institute, 986
teacher workshops, 1257, 1277, 1284, 1288, 1291
X-ray astrophysics, 990
Athletes
drug prevention, 594
Atmosphere, 1086
chemical processes, 1083
fluid dynamics, 1050
research grants, 283
satellite research, 990
Atmospheric research, 1083, 1109
Atomic clock, 960, 1239
Atomic mapping, 997
Atomic vapor laser isotope separation, 1072, 1077
Auctions, 695
real estate, 123, 124
U.S. Postal Service, 26
Audiovisual Center, National, 294
Audiovisual materials
drug prevention, 589, 1252
hurricanes, 1995
National Library of Medicine, 504
weather warning, 1268, 1270, 1272, 1286, 1291
information for kids, 1297
NASA, 1252, 1253, 1255, 1268, 1274-1277,
film list, 1281
Gemini, 1271
Hubble Space Telescope, 1272, 1291
Skylab, 1285
space exploration, 1287
space shuttle, 1289
Uranus, 1293
Audits, 641
federal agencies, 871
foreign fellowships, 158
government standards, 870
Autism, 509, 551
Auto safety hotline, 26
Automated manufacturing, 1005
Automation, 241, 248, 971
Automobiles
accident costs, 1227
air bags, 94, 420, 818
air pollution, 1113
alternative alcohol fuels, 1113
automatic transmission repair, 96
child safety seats, 94, 420, 818
consumer complaints, 1227
crash test results, 94, 420, 818
damage statistics, 1227
defects, 94, 420, 818
door locks, 96, 825
drivers' licenses, 641
engine emissions, 1068
engineering, 1113
frontal crashworthiness, 94, 420, 818
fuel alternatives, 971
general motors protection, 96
grants for veterans, 390
importation, 100
industry, 974
insurance costs, 1227
leasing, 96
maintenance and repairs, 99, 976
mandatory passive restraints, 973

market regulation, 94
materials research, 1006
odometer tampering, 94, 98, 420, 615, 818
owner registration, 641
rearview mirrors, 96, 825
recalls, 94, 420, 818
repairability, 1227
safety, 94, 420, 818, 1227
seat belts, 94, 420, 818
tire treadwear, 1227
tires, 94, 420, 818
used-cars, 1227
Volkswagen protection program, 96
Aviation
accident investigations, 781
accident prevention, 781
accidents, 782, 783, 786, 818
air traffic control system, 781
aircraft design, 986
airports, 787
audiovisual materials, 294
bird strikes, 785, 1132
civil, 1181, 1184
civil, U.S., 245, 786
commuter and air taxi operators, 352, 785
congressional forum, 1186
consumer complaints, 785
educational grants, 172
equipment specifications, 784
FAA facilities, 782, 788
films, 786
financial operations, 774, 782
forecasts, 784
fuel consumption, 784
fuel trends, 786
fuels, 1227
grants for airports, 373
highjacking, 788, 941
history, 944
international, 786
international policy, 786, 925
load requirements, 986
medical certification, 261, 787
military, 944
national airspace system, 787
near mid-air collisions, 782
overseas markets, 786
pilot training schools, 248, 787
registration records, 783
safety, 100, 261, 787, 821, 831, 974
safety bulletin board, 1238
schools, 782, 788
security, 786
statistics, 785
voice recorders, 782
weather forecasts, 1086
Avionics, 953, 986, 988
Awards program
environmental, 1263, 1267
physical fitness, 1279
AZT grants, 363

B

Babysitters, 615
Background Notes on the Countries of the World, 860
Bacteriology, 1103, 1118, 1148, 1151
Bald eagles, 945, 1132, 1142
Ballistic missiles, 970
Ballistics, 944, 963
Balloons, high altitude, 983
Baltic States, 1186
Baltimore Longitudinal Study of Aging, 557

The thousands of studies in the Current Events Chapter and Experts Chapter are not included in this Index.

Index

Banking, State
Alabama, 447
Alaska, 447
Arizona, 447
Arkansas, 448
bulletin board, 1235
California, 448
Colorado, 448
complaint action, 27
Connecticut, 448
Delaware, 448
District of Columbia, 448
Florida, 448
Georgia, 448
Hawaii, 448
Idaho, 448
Illinois, 448
Indiana, 448
Iowa, 448
Kansas, 448
Kentucky, 448
Louisiana, 448
Maine, 448
Maryland, 449
Massachusetts, 449
Michigan, 449
Minnesota, 449
Mississippi, 449
Missouri, 449
Montana, 449
Nebraska, 449
Nevada, 449
New Hampshire, 449
New Jersey, 449
New Mexico, 449
New York, 449
North Carolina, 449
North Dakota, 449
Ohio, 449
Oklahoma, 449
Oregon, 450
Pennsylvania, 450
Rhode Island, 450
South Carolina, 450
South Dakota, 450
State offices, 447
State regulations, 447
Tennessee, 450
Texas, 450
Utah, 450
Vermont, 450
Virginia, 450
Washington, 450
West Virginia, 450
Wisconsin, 450
Wyoming, 450
Banking and finance
African Development Bank, 426
agricultural credit economy, 105, 867
annual percentage rates, 427
Asian Development Bank, 426
asset quality, 430
Call Reports, 427
capital adequacy, 430
cease-and-desist orders, 428
community reinvestment programs, 345, 349, 427
competition, 973
complaint reporting system, 105, 427, 867
consolidations, 427
consumer credit regulations, 105, 426-27, 867
deposit summaries, 428
developing countries, 426
discount rate changes, 427
domestic securities markets, 431
earnings, 430
education programs, 426
examinations, 427
FDIC regulations, 428
federal cash system, 428
Federal Open Market Committee, 431
Federal Reserve Banks, 105-06, 432, 867-68
Federal Savings and Loan Insurance Corporation, 430
foreign banking organizations, 427
foreign exchange markets, 431
holding companies, 426, 430
House committee, 1183
Inter-American Development Bank, 426
international, 872, 873
international FDIC approval, 429
law, 426, 427
legislation, 426
liquidation litigation, 426, 430
Lockbox Network, 428
management/administration, 430
margin requirements, 427
merger decisions, 426, 427, 429
money supply, 431
national banks, creation of, 427
new banks, 427
open market operations, 432
purchases, 427
ratings, 430
registration and reporting, 430
regulation, 427, 429
Report of Condition and Income Statements of Banks, 427
research, 426
reserve requirements, 427
Senate committee, 1181
treasury securities, 106, 444, 867
trust assets, 428
Truth-in-Lending Act, 427
Uniform Interagency Bank Rating System, 430
World Bank, 426
Bankruptcy, 436, 610, 619
tax guide, 496
Barbers, 635
Barley, 1220
Barney Studio House, 313
Base closures, 346, 944
Beautification projects, 353
Bed and breakfast facilities, 671
Beef, 1186, 1229
production, 1028
Beekeeping, 926, 1024, 1029, 1239
Beer production, 774
Begonias, 140
Bell, Alexander Graham, 303
Beneficiary's Share of Income, 477
Benefit plan, 482
Benefits
coal miners, 251
direct deposit, 107
disabilities, 255
electronic delivery, 424
employment, 251, 1184
federal employees, 268
food stamps, 522
Job Training Partnership Act, 249
longshore and harbor workers, 253
maritime workers, 253
pension equity, 254
pensions and retirement funds, 254
railroad unemployment, 274
unemployment insurance, 249
veterans, 143, 390
Bibliographies, 1199, 1212
technical, 979
Bicycles
safety, 353, 829

Big Bang theory, 982
Bilingualism
education literature, 1274
Bioaccumulation, 1009
Biofeedback, 515, 976, 1203
Biofuels, 1050, 1061
Biologics, 573
biological agents, 944
biological weapons, 944
Biology, 309, 320, 1103, 1109
clearinghouses, 1118, 1148
toxicology databases, 1151
Biomass feedstocks, 1050
Biomass Programs, 763
Biomedical research
at National Institutes of Health, 573
bimolecular and cellular structure, 573
BIOETHICSLINE database, 505
biologics, 573
Biomedical Research Technology Program, 573
blood disease, 506
computing technology, 573
databases, 504
engineering, 528, 574
ethics, 1216
grants and contracts, 573, 574
health risk appraisals, 517
House Committee on, 1183
Human Specimen Bank, 573
international health science development, 574
kidney transplants, 550
medical devices, 568, 570
military solicitations, 942, 982
minority institutions, 573
minority professional opportunities, 247
National Institute of General Medical Sciences, 528, 574
National Institutes of Health, 574
National Library of Medicine, 501
technology transfer, 568
veterans, 968
Biophysics, 767
Biotechnology, 779, 976, 997, 1055, 1103
agricultural applications, 965, 1025
clearinghouses, 1118, 1148
commercial, international, 970, 1031
commercialization, 963
engineered organisms testing, 970
foreign policy issues, 1100
global economics, 963
international development, 930
investment in, 974
joint U.S./Japanese projects, 963
legislation, 1024
ownership issues, 970
patents, 970
toxicology databases, 1151
tracer bullets, 1203
Birds
aviation accidents, 785, 1132
banding, 1216
bibliography, 1132
captive propagation research, 1133
ducks, 1133
geese, 1133
Hawaiian, 1133
lead poisoning, 1138
mallards, 1218
migration, 1216
migratory game, 1135
mourning doves, 1225
North American Waterfowl Management Plan, 1133
waterfowl, 1137, 1218
Bird strikes, 785, 1132

The thousands of studies in the Current Events Chapter and Experts Chapter are not listed in this Index.

Index

Births, 575, 576, 1232
Birth control
see contraception, 527
Birthday Greetings from the President, 27
Births, 1232
Black banks, 106, 867
Black holes, 983
Black Lung Benefit Trusts, 251
Return of Excise Tax on Excess Contributions, 485
Tax related forms, 475
Blindness, 504, 540
American Printing House for the Blind, 563
braille books, 563
free library services, 564
clinical trials, 547
computer hardware and software, 563
prevention, 540
tax information, 461
Blood
alcohol analysis, 1005
disease research grants, 286, 767
national blood data system, 566
products, 573
resource education program, 566
technology, 972
Blue Sky laws, 668
BMWs, 641
Boat auctions, 28
Boating, 1139
chart updates, 414, 808
commercial vessels, 798
correspondence course, 410, 797
customs regulations, 417
drawbridge operations, 414, 808
education, 410, 414, 798
free inspections, 410
grants, 372
hotline, 27, 414
lessons, 27
navigation rules, 412
port safety, 410, 611, 967, 1096
radionavigation, 410, 797
safety, 413, 808
search and rescue service, 410, 798
St. Lawrence River, 413
Bolivia
cooperatives, 924
Bomb threats, 775
Bond guarantees, 755
Bond markets, 106, 867
Bone disease, 559
Bonsai trees, 140, 141, 1027
Book auctions, Library of Congress, 702
Books
braille, 1201
Center for the Book, 145, 1199
children's, 145, 1199
North American, 304, 1199
preservation, 974
rare, 292, 311, 1203
science and technology, 962, 1200
surplus, 1204
Borders, 1186
Borides, 1224
Botanic Garden, U.S., 140
Botany, 309, 320
economic, 140, 141, 1027
educational programs, 140
tropical and subtropical plants, 140
Bowel disorders, 540
Braille, 1201
Tax Guide for Small Business, 461
Your Federal Income Tax, 461
Brain
Tissue Bank, 573

transplants, 550
tumors, 540
Breast cancer, 540
Breastfeeding
nutrition, 527
Breath testers, 1005
Breeding
animals and plants, 1033
Bridges, 797, 825, 1003, 1184
Broadcasting, 290, 292, 294, 308, 1202
foreign media, 934
foreign, 792
Radio Free Europe, 929
Radio Liberty, 929
Voice of America, 933
Brokers, 436
barter exchange transactions, 478
broker-dealer registration, 441
revocations, 435
suspensions, 437
brokers, 436
Broker-dealers, 442
Budget, 1181, 1213
balanced, 1186
defense, 1183
Buffalo, 396, 1132
Building and construction
blueprint catalog, 119
building rehabilitation standards, 119
cost reduction in housing, 120
earthquake design, 119
education facilities, 143, 152
energy cost reduction, 119
energy efficiency research, 119
energy-efficient housing designs, 119
fair housing activities, 121
finishing wood exteriors, 120
funding for handicapped housing, 121
handicap access planning, 119
health care facilities, 567
historic, 306
indoor environmental hazards, 119
interstate land sales, 123
lead based paint abatement, 119
materials research, 998
multifamily property standards, 123
rehabilitation technology, 120
research, 998
safety guidelines, 266
seismic design, 1010
solar access, 119
solar energy, 1062
tax reform effects, 120
technology, 998
Bulimia, 515, 977, 1203
Bullet-resistant equipment, 1005
Bulletin boards, electronic
agriculture, 1233
aviation safety, 1238
banking, 1235
computer security, 1233
Computerized Information Delivery Service (CIDS), 1233
ecology, 1236
economic information, 1235
economy, 1235
Energy, 1234, 1237
environment, 1233, 1234, 1236-1238
Federal Reserve Economic Data (FRED), 1235
geomagnetic and solar activity, 1238
hazardous materials, 1235
interest rates, 1235
job information, 1233, 1235, 1238
marine advisories, 1236
medical, 1236
NASA Johnson Space Center, 1235

pesticides, 1236
Space Environment Lab, 1238
taxes, 1235
United States Courts, 1238
Bumpers, 96, 825
Bureau of Economic Analysis, 862
Bureau of Labor Statistics
Productivity and Technology Statistics, 853
Bureau of the Census, 899
Bureau of the Public Debt, 1233
Burglary, 610
Burros, adoption, 695, 1138, 1215, 1242
Buses, 821, 1181
Business
aerospace activities, 981
aerospace, 983
agriculture competitiveness, 1026
airlines, 782
antitrust reviews, 611
antitrust, 1182
Business Assistance Service, 775
Business Reply Mailgram, 113
child care programs, 239, 779
consumer affairs, 776
consumer complaints, 102
consumer rule guides, 776
customer relations, 776
development grants and loans, 361
drug-free helpline, 590
economic activity, 862
education grants, 178, 181, 189
energy conservation, 1051
expenses tax guide, 494
foreign industrial development, 916, 1199
franchise law, state, 722, 772
grants, 376, 727
hiring incentives, 777
home-based, 26, 297
hotlines, 727
industrial directory, 1223
international development programs, 915
labor market data, 884
loans, 754
loans for teens, 27
management consulting, 717
minority-owned, 723, 1228
Native Americans, 722
property sales, 483
research grants, 283
safety consultation, 266
Start-Up Money, 27
state money, 727
statistics, 862
tax credits for employment policies, 780
taxation, 460
Technology Assistance Centers, 729
technology development, 1014
U.S. Chamber of Commerce, 775
venture capital, 729
Business America, 855
Business, International
document authentication, 415
overseas security, 417
seminars, 416
terrorism guidelines, 418
Bus lines, 777, 827

C

C-SPAN, 1192
Cable television, 796
Calcium dietary guidelines, 520
Calibration, 998
California
Doing Business in California, 908

The thousands of studies in the Current Events Chapter and Experts Chapter are not included in this Index.

Index

California (continued)
Affirmative Action, 885
Automated Tax Refund Information, 466
Bureau of Land Management office, 695
California Statistical Abstract, 905
CHFA Resale Program, 131
company directories, 664
Compensating Balance Program, 131
corporation information, 658
Department of Housing and Community Development, 131
Department of Motor Vehicles, 641
Development Loan Program, 131
educational boardgame, 1260
Emergency Shelter Program, 131
Employment and Payrolls, 885
Energy Conservation Rehabilitation Program, 131
environmental education material, 1266
Family Housing Demonstration Program, 131
Farmworker Housing Grant Program, 131
Federal Emergency Shelter Grant Program, 131
Franchises, 771
Highway Patrol, Used Vehicle Sales Office, 705
Home Ownership Assistance Program, 131
Home Purchase Assistance Program, 131
Housing Finance Agency, 131
Housing Rehabilitation Program-Owner Component, 131
International Trade Policy, 908
IRS hotlines, 464
Labor Market Bulletin, 885
licensed professionals, 636
Licensing boards professions, 636
Matching Downpayment Program, 131
Mobile Home Park Assistance Program, 131
Multi-Family Program, 131
Natural Disaster Assistance Program, 131
Occupational Guides, 885
Office of Migrant Services, 131
Permanent Housing for the Handicapped Homeless Program, 131
PLP Natural Disaster Component, 131
Pre-Development Loan Program, 131
Projections of Employment, 885
Rental Housing Construction Program, 131
Rental Security Deposit Guarantee Demonstration Program, 131
Rural Communities Facilities Technical Assistance Program, 131
Section 8 Housing Assistance Program, 131
Securities Regulation Division, 668
Self-Help Builder Assistance Program, 131
Self-Help Housing Program, 131
Senior Citizen Shared Housing Program, 131
Small Business Administration Offices, 837
state data centers, 900
state information, 36
State International Trade Offices, 858
State Labor Office, 885
State Planning Office, 908
state procurement office, 841
State Rental Rehabilitation Program, 131
state tax assistance, 498
surplus property auctions, 705
Tax form distribution center, 470
Tax forms and publications, 491
unclaimed property office, 712
Uniform Commercial Code Division, 631
U.S. International Trade Administration Offices, 855

Campaigns
federal, 1185
Senate committee, 1182
Camping, 403, 404, 942, 1095, 1121, 1135
reservations at national forests, 403
TVA lands, 408
Canada
environmental issues, 1103, 1118, 1148,
Cancer
Annual Report on Carcinogens, 542
awareness education, 541
breast cancer programs, 545
breast cancer, 540
Cancer Information Service, 502
CANCERLIT, 541
carcinogenesis, 541
carcinogens, 540
cervical, 972
chemical carcinogenesis, 541
clinical oncology, 541
CLINPROT, 541
colorectal, 972
community resources, 502
current research, 502, 541
detection, 502, 766
diagnosis and treatment, 541
diet and cancer, 520
drugs treatment research, 567
environmental risks, 514, 541, 970
experimental drugs, 567
financial assistance, 502
Frederick Cancer Research Facility, 541
grants and fellowships, 541
Hotline, 502
International Cancer Information Center, 541
International Cancer Research Databank, 540
mammography, 545
physician referrals, 502
prevention, 516
publications, 541
radiation therapy, 541
radon and lung cancer, 540
research grants, 170, 184, 285
research, 766-67, 950
research, diagnosis, and treatment, 541
saccharin, 975
smoking, tobacco use, 554
speakers, 541
testicular, 516
unconventional treatments, 33, 541
virology, 541
Cape Canaveral, 989
Capital Construction Fund, 489
Capital formation,
hospitals, 566
Capital Gains and Losses
Form 1040, sch. D., 476
Form 1041, sch. D., 477
Form 1120, Sch. D, 479
Capital stock, 657
Capitol Hill guided tours, 27
Capitol, U.S., 1292
Captioning, 764
Car rental, 96
Carbides, 1224
Carbon monoxide
educational publication, 1264
Carcinogens
regulation, 973
Cardio-pulmonary resuscitation, 527
CARE, 1036
Care Provider's Identification and Certification Tax Forms, 473
Careers, 655
aerospace, 161

agriculture sciences, 157
air traffic controller, 244, 819
art museums, 243
aviation, 161, 243, 268, 396, 785
business, 243, 246
carpentry, 246
communications, 243
computer science, 248, 805, 1112, 1114
computers, 243
construction, 243
corrections and rehabilitation, 244
corrections management, 611
counseling, 1025, 1240
criminal justice, 244
dental practitioners, 243
design, 243
dietetics, 243
education and development programs, 155, 160
education, 243
electronics maintenance technicians, 244, 819
engineering, 243, 244, 248, 805, 819, 1112, 1114
Environmental Protection Agency, 269
environmental protection, 245
FBI, 612
finance, 245, 247
Foreign Service, 245, 921
forest rangers, 270, 1124
health technologists, 243
Job Information Centers, Federal, 269
job placement, 239, 244
law enforcement, 244
legal occupations, 243
management, 243
matching skills with job, 247
mathematics, 243, 248, 805, 1112, 1114
mechanics, 243
medical practitioners, 243
metalworking, 243
military, 951
mining, 245, 247
museum practices, 243, 319
NASA scientists and engineers, 150, 164
National Health Service Corps, 345, 350, 576
nursing, 243, 246
occupational reference guide, 248
painting, 246
performing arts, 243
pharmacy, 243
projected occupational employment, 234
protective services, 243
rangers, 1123
sales, 243
science and technology, 977
science, 248, 805, 1112, 1114
scientific, 243
Secret Service agents, 616
service occupations, 243
social service, 243
state labor data, 884
stress management, 535
transportation, 243
woodworking, 243
zoos, 243
Cargo, 970
Caribbean, 922
Economic Recovery Act of 1983, 849
Cars
auctions, 28
Cartography, 306, 1094, 1088-1090, 1200, 1090
cadastral, 1088
census maps, 876
digital, 1089

The thousands of studies in the Current Events Chapter and Experts Chapter are not listed in this Index.

Index

National Mapping Division Historical Archives, 1090

Cartoons
nutrition and weight loss, 523

Cash Payments
Reporting payments over $10,000, 497
Tax Reporting form for payments over $10,000, 487

Casinos
Currency transaction, 488
Currency Transactions Reports, 488

Casualty reporting, 940, 944

Casualties and thefts, 482

Catalog of Federal Domestic Assistance, 754, 1213

Catalysts, 1007

Caulking, 1061

Caustics, 1144

CD-Roms, aerospace-related, 1277, 1288

Census
American Indian reservations, 876
CD-ROM format, 863
custom data products, 861
custom projects, 899
data workshops, 878
depository libraries, 863
geography, 870
informational seminars, 875
international visitors, 872
mapping algorithms, 872
maps, 861, 862
National Clearinghouse for Census Data Services, 864
online services, 863
questionnaire content, 861
sample design, 861
teaching materials, 876
tract/block numbering area maps, 864

Center for Exposure Assessment Modeling Bulletin Board, 1233

Centers for Disease Control, 504, 538

Central Intelligence Agency
declassified reports, 915, 1199
public information office, 63

Ceramics, 813, 944, 963, 968, 971
information center, 1224
low-temperature electronics, 1005
neutron-scattering experiments, 1007
production, 999

Cerebral palsy, 509, 544, 551

Cerebrovascular disease, 972

Certified Development Company Loans, 755

Cesarean childbirth, 526
medical technologies, 568

Chamber of Commerce of the United States, 775

Charitable Contributions
noncash, 487
Tax Guide, 494

Cheap office space overseas, 851

Check forgery, 432

Checking accounts, 105, 867

Chemical propulsion, 945, 984

Chemical weapons, 936-37, 945

Chemicals
agricultural, 1022
composition measurements, 999
defense technologies, 945
extraction from plants, 970, 1031
fishery, 1134, 1143
industrial process, 1151
industrial residues, 1223
international control, 1151
pesticide hotline, 572, 1029, 1145
thermodynamic properties, 1015
toxic effects registry, 571, 572
toxicity, 1229

Chemistry, 987, 1012, 1014, 1103, 1109
analytical, 999, 1095, 1110

atmospheric, 1084, 1103
Center for Analytical Chemistry, 999
clearinghouses, 1118, 1148
compositional mapping, 999
depth profiling, 999
environmental research grants, 283
fires, 1002
metrological calibrations, 999
process metrology, 999
separation concepts, 1001
toxicology databases, 1151
ultra-trace analysis, 999

Chemotherapy, 1228

Certificate of need regulation, 94

Chesapeake Bay, 945, 1085, 1095, 1101, 1110, 1132, 1142

coloring book, 1252, 1262

Chicago River, coloring book, 1252, 1262

Chicken, 1229

Child abuse and neglect
anger, 532
foster care, 532
foster grandparent volunteers, 383
hotline, 587
information clearinghouse, 532
legal issues, 610
National Center for Child Abuse and Neglect, 532
National Resource Center on Child Sexual Abuse, 533
national resource center, 532
prevention and treatment, 532
program grants, 366, 367
prosecution of, 610
research, 532
research grants, 286, 367
runaway hotline, 535
runaway youth shelters, 535
sexual abuse, 533

Child and Dependent Care Expenses
Tax Guide, 493
Tax related forms, 481

Child care, 234, 239, 241, 779, 876
business loans, 728
community grants, 367
energy activities, 1260
food program, 385
grants, 386
handicapped programs, 386

Child custody, 419

Child development grants, 374

Child health, 528
adoption services, 532
baby-bottle tooth decay, 551
child care programs, 148
child welfare services, 532
fetal development, 528
foster grandparent volunteers, 383
hyperactivity, 146
infant development and disorders, 529
infant formula, 522
international assistance programs, 916
mental retardation, 528, 535
National Institute of Child Health and Human Development, 526
National Resource Center on Child Sexual Abuse, 533
nutrition, 524
prenatal development and care, 148
publications, 505, 528, 575
research, 528
Reye's syndrome, 568
safety resources, 527
sudden infant death syndrome, 530

Child labor laws, 235, 239, 251

Child molesters, 614

Child safety restraints, 96, 825

Child safety seats, 94, 420, 818

Child support, 28
enforcement grants, 367
enforcement research grants, 368

Childbirth
see pregnancy, 529

Children's issues, 1212
alcoholic parents, 578
automobile safety seats, 94, 420, 818
child care, 234
congressional caucus, 1186
development center grants, 367
exploited and missing, 614
fire safety, 350
foster care and adoption, 148
House Select Committee on, 1185
juvenile delinquency, 614
labor laws, 234, 251
Limit on Alternative Minimum Tax, 489
literature, 145, 1199
mental health, 972
nutrition education for low-income, 523
pornography, 614
President's physical fitness awards, 518
professional education, 532
protection, 614
risk factors, 516
runaways, 615
Senate committee, 584
Senate subcommittee, 1182
sexual abuse, 533
third world, 916
toys for tots, 351
victimization and the law, 610
victimization, 533

China
broadcasts, 792
consumer markets, 876
medicines, 567
science and technology, 977, 1203
technology transfer, 971
trade with, 1186
transportation technology, 932, 979

Chlorofluorocarbons, 1006

Cholesterol, 521
database, 553
education programs, 544
Info-Line, 27
screening, 346, 576, 972

Christmas
Bureau of Land Management, 1239
Toys for Tots, 351
trees, 27, 140, 350, 695, 1124
tree bibliography, 1130
tree fires, 349

Chromium, 815, 952

Chronic disease prevention, 545

Chronic pain
abatement techniques, 545
acupuncture, 545

Cigarettes
pregnancy, 527
safety, 97, 1124

Cities, 1225
National League of, 346

Citizens arrested overseas, 860

Citizens Emergency Center, 860
shipping and seamen, 860
welfare and whereabouts, 860

Citizenship education, 623, 916, 1227

Civics/Govt Structure
medical libraries, 505

Civil Air Patrol, 945

Civil defense, 355
grants, 380

Civil liberties, 974
international, 923

The thousands of studies in the Current Events Chapter and Experts Chapter are not included in this Index.

Index

Civil rights, 610
Asian Americans, 626
banking laws, 107
case history, 627
Commission on, U.S., 627
complaints, 627
discrimination on the job, 628
enforcement history, 627
fair housing law, 628
farm workers, 624
government hearings, 627
grants, 174
highway construction contracts, 777, 826
housing discrimination, 121, 122
legislation, 627
medicine, 974
migrant workers, 252
minority and female workers, 629
police practices, 627
religious discrimination, 629
school desegregation, 629
Senate committee, 1182
sex discrimination, 629
Voting Rights Act, 629
Civil Rights, U.S. Commission on, 627
Civil service, 275, 1184
studies, 271
taped message, 93
Civil War teaching unit, 1251
Claim for Tax Refund Forms, 474
Claims on federal lands, 811, 1127
Clergy and religious workers
Social Security information, 494
Climate, 1085, 1101
crime correlatives, 879
database, 1217
greenhouse effect, 977, 1098
historical information, 1083
pollution impact, 1083, 1109
research grants, 283
short-term conditions, 1217
solar radiation averages, 1062, 1086
solar radiation, 1083, 1109
statistics, 865
wind, 1062, 1086
Cloud formations, 1251, 1297
Cloud seeding, 1114
Coal, 1053, 1186
clean-coal technology, 1064
combustion research, 1067
combustion, 971, 1067
consumption, 1217, 1261, 1278
distribution, 1067
education-related material, 1270, 1278
educational material, 1259, 1270
exporting, 1068
exports, 971
flue gas cleanup, 1067
leases, federal, 971
legislation, 1067
liquefaction, 1067
methane recovery from, 812, 816, 1070, 1129
poster, 1251, 1260, 1271, 1278
preparation, 1067
prices, 1067, 1229
products, 1260
research grants, 288
reserves, 1067
slurries, 1067
slurry pipelines, 777, 827, 972
small producers, 718, 1071
sulfur dioxide control, 1067
supply and demand, 1067, 1229
technology, 1067
Technology Program, 764
TVA contracts, 718, 1071
Coast Guard, 1181
coloring book, 1252, 1292
drug smuggling, 606
House Committee on, 1184
Reserve, 798, 945
Coast lines, 798, 1096
Coastal awareness, 1113
films, 1262, 1268
teacher's resource guide, 1262
Cobalt, 815, 952
Cocaine
pharmacology, 578
public service announcements, 593
Coins
congressional, 431
gold and silver bullion, 432
recorded message, 93
Coinsurance mortgage, 128
Cold environments research, 945, 963
Cold neutrons, 1011
Collective bargaining agreements, 256, 260, 619
College
drug-free network, 589
education literature, 1252, 1293
College graduates, 875
Colon disorders, 546
Colorado
Affirmative Action, 885
Automated Tax Refund Information, 466
Bureau of Land Management office, 695
Commercial Division Programs, 131
company directories, 664
Construction Loan Fund, 131
corporation information, 658
Deferred-5 (D-5) Program, 131
Directory of Services, 908
Division of Securities, Department of Regulatory Agencies, 668
Economic Perspective, 905
Employment and Wages, 885
Housing and Finance Authority, 130, 131
Housing Development Loan Fund, 131
IRS hotlines, 464
licensed professionals, 636
Licensing Board/Professions, 636
Low-Income Housing Tax Credit Program, 131
Mortgage Credit Certificate, 131
Motor Vehicle Division, Traffic Records, 642
Occupational Employment Outlook Projection, 885
Rental Acquisition Program, 131
Rural Development Loan Program, 131
Section 8 Moderate Rehabilitation Program, 131
Shelter Housing Assistance Program, 131
Single-Family Program, 131
Small Business Development Center, 732
Special Needs Housing Fund, 131
Special Projects Program, 131
state data centers, 900
state information, 36
State International Trade Offices, 858
State Labor Office, 885
State Planning Office, 908
state procurement office, 841
state tax assistance, 498
surplus property auctions, 705
Tax form distribution center, 470
Tax forms and publications, 491
Tax-Exempt Bond Program, 131
unclaimed property office, 712
Uniform Commercial Code Division, 631
U.S. International Trade Administration Office, 855
Colorectal cancer, 972
Coloring books
air pollution, 1252, 1261
Chesapeake Bay, 1252, 1262
Chicago River, 1252, 1262
drug abuse, 590
endangered species, 1252, 1298
environment, 1252, 1267
environmental, 1262, 1267, 1282
Happy Earth Day, 1252, 1263
Mark Trail, 1252, 1264
U.S. Coast Guard, 1252, 1292
woodstoves, 1252
Combustion, 1067
Comet, Halley's
slides, 1252, 1272, 1286
Comic books, 304
alcohol prevention, 1253
drug prevention, 1253
environmental education, 1266
fire prevention, 1269, 1287
poison, 1253, 1280
Commerce
grants and loans, 361
Commerce Business Daily, 836
Commerce Clearing House Blue Sky Law Reports, 668
Commerce, U.S. Department of
Bureau of the Census, 862
Franchise Opportunities Handbook, 772
fraud hotline, 251, 276
International Economics, Bureau of Economic Analysis, 853
library, 775
National Telecommunications and Information Administration, 778, 794
Office of Business Analysis, 848
public information offices, 42
World Trade Reference Room, 843
Commercial News USA, 854
Commission on Civil Rights, 63
Commodities
agricultural, 1013, 1030, 1037, 1231
agricultural imports, 1039
agricultural regulations, 1037
agricultural wholesalers, 1036
cocoa, 1037
coffee, 1037
commercial uses, 1030
Commodity Credit Corporation, 356, 1033
corn, 356, 1033
cotton, 873, 1024, 1183
dairy, 873, 1024
databases, 1221
dry milk, 356, 1033
feed grains, 1183
fishery, 799
foreign trade reports, 1038
fruits, 873, 1024
grading services, 1034
grain, 873, 1024
international agreements, 1183
international trade statistics, 1038
jute, 1037
livestock, 873, 1024
marketing assistance, 1034
minerals, 452, 813, 946, 1224
movements, 1217
peanuts, 1183
pesticide content, 525, 1029, 1142
poultry, 873, 1024
price indexes, 874
prices, 1223
pricing indexes, 872
rice, 356, 1033
rice, 1183
soybeans, 1183
strategic, 814

The thousands of studies in the Current Events Chapter and Experts Chapter are not listed in this Index.

Index

sugar, 1183
surplus donations, 345, 523, 1034
tobacco, 873, 1024, 1031, 1034, 1183
vegetables, 873, 1024
wheat, 356, 1033, 1183
Commodity Futures Trading Commission, 63
Common carriers, 776, 790
insurance, 825
Communications
engineering, 573
FCC recorded message, 93
systems, 945
Communism, 914, 929
combatting in U.S., 933
Communities
agricultural processing plant, 346
banking reinvestment, 349
child abuse prevention grants, 532
development grants, 185, 370
dropout programs, 349, 611
drug free schools program grants, 382
economic development, 349
employment development, 350
equipment loans, 350, 953
ethnic disputes, 349, 612, 616
facilities loans, 359
fire prevention, 349
flood damage prevention, 356
grants and loans, 359
health services, 344-46, 518, 575-76
health planning, 504
housing rehabilitation, 120
juvenile justice assistance, 613
Marine Corps, 348, 350
military impact, 346, 944
minority health care, 348, 362-63
National Guard, 350, 952
neighborhood watch programs, 612
nuclear plant construction, 1079
Planned Approach to Community Health Program, 346, 576
planning grants, 370
post office closings, 114
program grants, 380
racial conflicts, 349, 612, 615, 616
rural development assistance, 347, 1027
statistics, 868
tourism development, 420
toxic spills hotline, 355, 1143
urban development grants, 728
volunteer programs, 384
volunteer anti-drug program, 590
wastewater treatment, 1118
youth shelters, 535
Community Property and the Federal Income Tax Tax Guide, 495
Company case studies
Directory of Harvard Business School Cases and Related Course M, 655
Government and Commercial Databases, 655
Company case studies for as little as $2.00, 654
Company information, 907
labor market data, 884
US Securities and Exchange Commission Filings, 649
Complete financials on franchising companies, 655
Composite materials, 142, 977, 1005, 1203
Compost, 140, 1024
Computers, 107, 424, 1013, 1059
applications portability, 997
CAD/CAM, 977, 1010, 1203
CD-ROM, 1012
compatibility standards, 1000
Computer Systems Laboratory, National, 1000

digital cartography, 1089
education programs, 167
European technology, 966
federal agencies, 1000
fraud, 107, 424, 610
geodetic applications, 992
grants, 762
graphics, 1004, 1010
graphics, NASA, 1277, 1281, 1288
image processing programs, 574
information science, 762
integrated manufacturing systems, 1010
microcomputers, 779, 977, 1203
military, 400, 950
neurochemistry research, 574
neurogenetics research, 574
neurophysiology research, 574
protection standards, 1009
reliability characteristics, 1229
research and applications, 982
research grants, 288
robotics applications, 1012
security, 971, 976, 1000, 1203
security bulletin board, 1233
simulated conventional warfare, 937
site evaluation software, 898
software interface standards, 1000
speech recognition, 1013
super, 961, 974
tapes, 899
telecommunications technology, 1000
useage statistics, 876
Computer software, 985, 1289
aerospace-related, 1253, 1277, 1288
astronomy, 1253
COSMIC, 985
Hubble Space Telescope, 1253, 1272, 1291
Space Shuttle, 1253, 1255, 1289
technology, 958
technology exchange, 1059
Computer tapes and diskettes of professionals, 635
Computerized Information Delivery Service (CIDS), 1233
Concerts
National Gallery of Art, 291
Navy Band, 350, 954
Condom testing, 27
Condominiums
mortgage insurance, 126, 127
Condors, California, 1254
Congress
aviation, 1181
biographies of members, 646, 1188
budget, federal, 1181
committee hearings, 402
Congressional Record, 1189, 1213
consumer issues, 1181
consumers, 1181
daily digest, 1189
General Accounting Office assistance, 1190
hearings, 1192
historical documents, 1189, 1199
leadership, 1190
legislation documents, 1188
Merchant Marine, 1181
minority leader, 1192
ocean policy, 1181
Pages, 149
photographs of members, 648, 1191
political appointment, 648, 1191
public bills and resolutions, 1188, 1202
radio coverage, 1192
records archives, 1191
salaries and expenses, 27, 648, 1192
science, technology, and space, 1181
securities, 1181

Sergeant at Arms, 1190, 1192
telecommunications, 1181
telephone directories, 1189
television coverage, 1191
tourism issues, 1181
treaty ratification, 1193
Vice President, 1189
Congressional Research Service, 1199
Congressmen
Federal Procurement help, 836
Connecticut
Apartment Conversion for the Elderly, 132
Automated Tax Refund Information, 466
company directories, 664
corporation information, 659
Economic Report of the Governor, 905
Home Mortgage Program, 131
Housing Finance Authority, 131
IRS hotlines, 464
Labor Force Data, 885
licensed professionals, 636
Low-Income Housing Tax Credit Program, 132
Manufacturing Firms, 885
Market Rate Multi-Family Program, 132
Occupational Licensing Division, Dept. of Consumer Product, 636
Private Rental Investment Mortgage and Equity Program, 132
Rehabilitation Mortgages, 131
Reverse Annuity Mortgages (RAM), 131
Securities and Business Investments Division, 669
Single-Family Mortgage Program, 132
Small Business Development Center, 732
state data centers, 900
State Department of Motor Vehicles, 642
state information, 36
State International Trade Offices, 858
State Labor Office, 885
State Planning Office, 908
state procurement office, 841
state tax assistance, 498
surplus property auctions, 705
Tax form distribution center, 470
Tax forms and publications, 491
unclaimed property office, 712
Uniform Commercial Code Division, 631
U.S. International Trade Administration Office, 855
Conscientious objectors, 648, 945, 956
Conservation, 755
biological diversity, 970, 1031
duck stamps, 1133
energy research grants, 288
energy, institutional, 1056
farmlands, 1025, 1026, 1124, 1129, 1130
fish and wildlife development, 1121
flood management, 1121
grants, 360
Great Plains conservation assistance, 1027, 1126
greenhouse effect, 977, 1098
ground water quality, 344, 1025, 1032, 1240
groundwater, 1112
international assistance, 929
international policies, 1100
landscaping assistance, 141
loans, 359
migratory waterfowl, 1130
renewable energy, 1061
research and development, 763
research grants, 289
salinity reduction, 1122
Senate Subcommittee, 1181
soil and water, 1027
soil erosion, 1027, 1129

The thousands of studies in the Current Events Chapter and Experts Chapter are not included in this Index.

Index

Conservation (continued)
soil surveys, 1030, 1129
solar energy, 971
State-level programs, 1118
summer jobs, 32
water pollution, 1130
water, 1109, 1121
watershed management, 1126
watershed protection, 1121
Youth Corps, 250, 1141
youth job programs, 246

Conventional forces, 1181

Conspiracy, 610

Constellations
Northern Skies, 1254, 1290

Constitution, 1254, 619, 623
amendments, 1182, 1184
educational grants, 181
teaching units, 1254

Construction, 760, 762, 946
census, 866
energy conservation, 1050
fatalities, 1216
grant program, 377
grants, 381
highways, 352, 826, 998
nuclear facilities, 1072, 1074
nuclear fallout shelters, 354
nuclear reactors, 1080
offshore, 803, 1113, 1135
OSHA rules, 266
prisons, 616
quality assurance, 1009
residential, 974
standards research, 998
standards, 1010
state housing programs, 131
statistics, 862, 868, 870

Consultants, for the government, 27, 29

Consumer Cooperative Exemption Application, 481

Consumer Price Index, 106, 865, 1224

Consumer Product Safety Commission
consumer deputy program, 109
library, 109
National Injury Information Clearinghouse, 109
public information office, 63
safety standard changes, 112

Consumer products and safety
accident investigations, 109
airlines, 94, 420, 781
antitrust violations, 609
appliance labeling, 100
automobiles, 94, 96, 420, 818
banking education, 426
banking laws, 427
blenders, 111
boating safety, 414
business relations, 776
Buyer Beware List, 102
care labeling, 95
chemical content information, 109
children poisoning, 109
clothes dryers, 111
consumer and producer prices, 873
Consumer Information Catalog, 95
Consumer Information Center, 95
Consumer Price Index, 240
counterfeit goods, 98
defective products, 109
data files, 103
diet, 1218
drugs, 504, 523, 525, 569
education programs, 95, 102, 176
electronic banking, 96
energy, 1051

equal credit opportunity, 106, 867
expenditures and income, 106, 865
eye care, 96
Federal Trade Commission, 95
flammable fabrics, 111, 146
food budget, 520
food pricing, 1036
food safety, 523
fruit and vegetable picking, 525, 1035
funerals, 97
get-rich-quick schemes, 437
health care information, 503
health remedy fraud, 97
health spas, 97
highway safety, 352, 827
hotline, 102
House Committee on, 1183
illegal telephone solicitors, 95
injury and illness data, 109, 506
international affairs, 95
Jewelry, 95
laser surgery, 506
lawn mower-related injuries, 109
layaway purchase plans, 96
legal services, 100
litigation, 611
mail fraud, 98, 115
mail service, 113
meat and poultry hotline, 98, 1034, 1035
media assistance, 95
medical care, 973
medical devices, 569
mobile homes, 123
moving company regulations, 98
Office of Consumer Affairs, 95
organic and natural foods, 525
pharmaceuticals, 566, 569
press releases, 102
product standards, 1007
publications, 95, 102
pyramid sales schemes, 98
radon, 99, 1102
range/oven fires, 109
rare coins, 96
recalls, 1228
recorded message, 93
reducing food costs, 1030
regulation impact studies, 94
reports, 102
resource handbook, 109
safety investigations, 111
scams, 104
shopping by mail, 96
smoke detectors, 111
solar energy, 1061
state offices, 102
tampons and toxic shock syndrome, 551
telephone investment fraud, 96
unordered merchandise, 96
warranties, 96
work-at-home schemes, 101

Contact lenses, 972

Continent, North American, 1258, 1278

Continental Congress, 304

Contraception
International Committee for Contraceptive Research, 573
Population Council, 573
reproductive disorders, 529
research, 573
risks and effectiveness, 526
safety and effectiveness, 527
sex steroids, 573
sexually transmitted diseases, 527
World Health Organization, 573

Contraception effectiveness, 526

Contractors, 755

Contracts
labor surplus areas, 238

Controlled substances, 606, 616

Convenience food markets, 522

Cooley's anemia, 546

Cooperative Education Program
Certification of Youth Participation, 486

Cooperative housing, 759
low-income rental housing, 126

Cooper-Hewitt Museum, 304

Cooperative research, 1000

Copper, 971

Copyright Office, 1020

Copyrights, 292, 295, 308, 1017, 1200
examining practices, 1200
home copying, 973
maps, 295, 1200
motion pictures and filmstrips, 292, 295, 1200
nondramatic literary works, 292, 308, 1200
performing arts, 292, 1200
registration procedures, 1200
renewals, 295, 1200
research assistance, 1200
serials and periodicals, 292, 308, 1200
sound recordings, 295, 1200
The Right Way to Get a Copyright, 1020
visual arts, 292, 295, 1200

Corn, 1186, 1220

Corporate Dissolution or Liquidation
Tax forms, 475

Corporate Qualified Stock Purchase
Election, 486

Corporation information, state
Alabama, 658
Alaska, 658
Arizona, 658
Arkansas, 658
California, 658
Colorado, 658
Computer Tape Files, 658
Connecticut, 659
Custom Services, 658
Delaware, 659
District of Columbia, 659
Georgia, 659
Hawaii, 659
Idaho, 659
Illinois, 659
Indiana, 659
Iowa, 660
Kentucky, 660
Louisiana, 660
Mailing Labels, 658
Maine, 660
Maryland, 660
Massachusetts, 660
Michigan, 660
Microfiche and Microfilm, 658
Minnesota, 660
Mississippi, 660
Missouri, 660
Montana, 661
Nebraska, 661
Nevada, 661
New Companies, 658
New Hampshire, 661
New Jersey, 661
New Mexico, 661
New York, 661
North Carolina, 661
Ohio, 661
Oklahoma, 661
Online Access, 658
Oregon, 662
Pennsylvania, 662
Rhode Island, 662

The thousands of studies in the Current Events Chapter and Experts Chapter are not listed in this Index.

Index

South Dakota, 662
Telephone, Mail, and Walk-In Services, 657
Tennessee, 662
Texas, 662
Utah, 662
Vermont, 662
Virginia, 662
Washington, 663
West Virginia, 663
Wisconsin, 663
Wyoming, 663
Corporation Source Book, 1987, 453
Corporations
8K reports, 442, 649
Affiliations Schedule for Taxes, 474
Annual Report to Stockholders, 435, 649
antitrust violations, 609
Application for Quick Refund of Est. Tax Overpayment, 482
Application for Tentative Refund, 480
Articles of Incorporation, 657
assets of noninsured pension funds, 442
balance sheets, 435
business operations, 435
CEO, 664
changes in securities, 437
computer systems, 664
consumer complaints, 102
databases, 664
defaults upon senior securities, 437
disclosure obligations, 443, 725
employment figures, 664
export market, 664
Extension of Time for Payment of Taxes, 480
Federal Income Tax Forms - Package 1120, 479
financial data, 435
financial policy directives, 436
Financial Statements, 649
foreign, 437
Form 10-K, 435
Form 10-Q, 437
going public, 443, 725
import market, 664
income statements, 435
industrial directory, 1223
industry trends, 664
Information Statement by United Kingdom Withholding Agents, 481
key personnel, 664
legal proceedings involving, 435
mailing lists, 664
management security ownership, 435
manufacturing, 664
market segment information, 435
marketing information, 664
new product plans, 435
origin of funds, 435
Ownership Certificate (tax related forms), 476
parents, 435
products, 664
properties, 435
prospectus, 440
reorganization proceedings, 436
research and development activities, 435
Rule 144 filings, 442
SEC directory of companies, 436
securities filings, 442
SIC codes, 664
state directories, 664
subsidiaries, 435
tax information, 480, 486, 494
tax statistics, 453
unaudited financial statements, 437

Underpayment of Estimated Tax, 480
working capital, 442
Correctional institutions, 615-16
community grants, 372
training program grants, 371
Cosmetic surgery, 453
Cosmetics, 504, 522, 523, 525, 569
Cosmetologists, 635
Cost sharing or profit split, 485
Cotton, 755
Counseling
education literature, 1254
drug prevention, 594
substance abuse training, 593
Counterfeiting statistics, 431
Country home loans, 27
Country information studies, 860
Country trade statistics, 849
County and local information
Chambers of Commerce, 652
courts, 653
development authority, 652
newspapers: business editors, 652
County subdivision censuses, 865
Court of Appeals, U.S.
records and briefs, 618, 925, 1193, 1201
Courts
Administrative Office of the U.S. Courts, 619
appellate procedure, 619
bankruptcy, 619
civil procedure, 619, 620
criminal procedure, 620
Extraditions, 600
federal judiciary, 620
federal magistrates, 620
federal, 620, 1182
judicial proceedings, 619
judicial research, 621
management, 620
organization and process, 620
rules of evidence, 619
Supreme Court of the U.S., 622
tax, 622
U.S. District, 619
CPSC
see Consumer Product Safety Commission
Crafts artists, 762
grants, 762
Crane, Whooping, 1254, 1298
Crash test results, 94, 420, 818
Crashworthiness, 96, 825
Craters, 1254, 1293
Creative thinking, 1254
Credit
billing errors, 107
building better credit, 96
card billing errors, 108
card fraud, 96
consumer credit laws, 105, 867
cosigning loans, 96
credit repair clinics, 107
fair credit reporting, 96, 108
fair reporting, 107
histories, 106, 867
home equity, 96
state mortgages, 130
women and credit, 96
women, 108
Credit card fraud, 107, 424
Credit Counseling for Home Buyers, 28
Credit for the elderly or the disabled, 461
Credit plans, 96
Credit repair help, 28
Credit unions
asset quality, 433
CAMEL ratings, 433

capital adequacy, 433
Central Liquidity Facility, 433
complaints, 433
creditor safeguards, 433
earnings, 433
examiner training, 433
federal credit union charters, 433
federal listings, 434
financial performance, 433
financial trends, 433
insurance fund, 433
liquidations, 433
loan program, 375
management, 433
operations monitoring, 433
organizing, 433
share insurance, 433
Crib death, 539
Crime, 1231
age makeup, 879
antitrust, 610
armed robberies, 879
automated teller machine fraud, 107, 424
burglary, 610
child abuse, 610
civil aviation, 788, 941
civil rights violations, 627
Clearinghouse on Family Violence, 557
computer fraud, 107, 424
congressional caucus, 1186
credit card fraud, 107, 424
criminal histories, 611
criminal justice, 582
data center, 600
database, 1226
DNA fingerprinting, 612
drug offenders, 608
drug thefts, 616
drug use forecasting, 608
drug use survey, 583
drug trafficking, 613, 800, 923, 949
drunk driving, 611
DWI, 612
economic cost, 611
elderly, 559
families, 612
firearms tracing, 613
forensic evidence, 613
gambling, 610
grants, 387
history, 974
insurance, 349, 611
international criminal justice center, 583
international drug fugitives, 606
international fugitives, 606
juvenile, 879
library, 612
Mafia, 606
mental disorder, 612
Native Americans program grants, 371
neighborhoods, 350, 615
nuclear incidents, 1072
organized crime and drugs, 606
police officers killed, 614
polluting, 613, 800, 923, 949
prevention, 351, 615
prostitution, 610
public lands, 1123
rape, 611
Recidivism and drug offenders, 607
risk of violence, 611
schools, 612
securities fraud, 437
State-level, 610
statistics, state, 879
stolen property, 611
technology, 974

The thousands of studies in the Current Events Chapter and Experts Chapter are not included in this Index.

Index

Crime (continued)
tire tracks, 613
U.S., 610
victim/offender relationships, 610
victims assistance program grants, 371
Victims of Crime Resource Center, 607
victims, 1226
violent, 611
wanted persons, 611
weapons used in, 610
white-collar, 879
wildlife protection, 611, 1133
Crime insurance, 28
Crime lab scientists, 774
Crime victims assistance, 28
Criminal justice grants, 371
Criminal justice, 611, 612
Crops
insurance program, 758, 1025
narcotics, 599, 603
payment subsidies, 357, 1027
pollination, 1029
production research, 1027
rotation, 140, 1023
Crude oil production, 1261, 1278
Cryogenic wind tunnel, 990
Cryogenics, 1009
Cuba
missile crisis, 1254, 1273
Cuban entrants, mental health, 765
Cultivation practices, 140, 1023
Cultural exchanges, Russian, 917, 933
Culture, understanding of
teacher workshops, 1254, 1290
Cumulative List of Organizations, 461
Currency
counterfeiting statistics, 431
damaged redemption, 107, 431
production, 431
research, 309
Smithsonian numismatic collection, 320
Transaction Report, 483
Customer relations, 776
Customs, 860
drug interdiction, 599
drug sniffing dogs, 600
foreign visitors, 416
living abroad, 416
pleasure boats, 417
private flyers rules, 416
returning U.S. residents, 418
rules for travelers, 416
vessel owners and masters, 418
Customs Service, U.S.
auctions, 698
Miscellaneous Property, 698
Cyclamates, 525

D

Dairy Indemnity Program, 755
Dairy production, 1028
Dams, 1184
design, 961
safety, 354, 1110, 1121
Dance, 292, 1202
Data
centers, 899
formats, 899
prices, 899
Database Publishing Company, 667
Databases
(DIRLINE), 507, 1207
abandoned mines, 1215
accident investigations, 109

Ada Information Clearinghouse, 947
AGRICOLA, 520, 1021
agricultural diseases, 1021
agriculture, 1215
AIDS, 501, 538
AIDSLINE, 504
air carrier market data, 781
aircraft registrations, 1215
airports, 787
all terrain vehicle deaths, 109
alternative fuels, 1068
American art, 319
American paintings, 314
American sculpture, 314
archeology, 304
arson cases, 610
Art Exhibition, 314
aviation, 782, 784, 788
AVLINE, 504
bilingual education, 145
BIOETHICSLINE, 505
bird banding, 1216
cancer, 502, 541
CATLINE, 504
census maps, 876
chemical propulsion, 945, 984
chemicals in consumer products, 109
chemicals, 1226
CHEMLINE, 357, 571
child abuse and neglect, 532
cholesterol and smoking, 553
CLINPROT, 504
coal use technology, 1067
Combined Health Information Database (CHID), 502, 549
commercial vessel inspections, 798
commodities, 1221
Computer Retrieval of Information on Scientific Projects, 574
consumer product defects, 109
cooperative data projects, 1000
corporations, 664
criminal justice, 599
crude oil analyses, 1068
driver licenses revoked, 352, 647, 829
drug abuse prevention, 590
economics, 866
education, 1255
education research (ERIC), 166, 169
emergency preparedness, 356
energy, 1063
Energy, U.S. Department of, 1056
enhanced oil recovery, 1068
environmental satellite data, 1086
environmental, 1085, 1101, 1135
ERIC, 147, 166
explosives, 955, 976
family violence, 503, 535, 557
financial disclosure on federal candidates, 647, 1190
fire research, 1002
fire, 356
FIREBASE, 1130
foreign agricultural trade, 1041
foreign agriculture investment, 121
gas extraction technologies, 1070
geographic names, 345, 1090, 1222
government/industry technical exchange, 959
grain exports, 1220
groundwater, 1099
hazardous waste, 1103, 1118, 1148, 1151
health education programs, 524, 530
HEALTH, 504
health status files, 505
highway traffic safety, 352, 827
HISTLINE, 504

historic preservation, 309, 345
horse/burro adoption, 1215
hydrocarbon engineering, 1003
Inter-American Foundation funded projects, 926
interactive technologies, 295
international development, 918
International Development, U.S. Agency for, 920
labor-management issues, 256
legal briefs, 621
legal, 1220
medical devices, 567
medical ethics, 1216
Medical Literature Analysis and Retrieval System (MEDLARS), 501
medical literature, 504
MEDLINE, 504
mental health, 534
microcomputers, 951, 968
military R&D, 946
military research, 1218
mining and minerals, 451, 813, 946
National Agricultural Library, 1033
National Coal Resources Data System, 812, 1053, 1068
National Electronic Injury Surveillance System, 109, 506
National Occupational Hazard Survey, 263
non-nuclear survivability/vulnerability data, 950
nuclear facilities, 1073
Nutrient Data Bank, 524
nutrition, 520
occupational health, 508
oceanography, 805, 1085
overseas security information, 417
pacemakers, 1217
patents, U.S., 979
pesticides, 1145
Peter A. Juley and Son Collection, 294, 314
phase diagram, 1008
pipeline safety, 820, 1070, 1102, 1146
poisoning incidents, 109
polymers, 955, 976
procurement, 1220
railroads, 830
Registry of Toxic Effects of Chemical Substances (RTECS), 571, 572
research referrals, 947, 964
residential energy consumption, 1062
Rural Electrification Administration, 790
science and technology, 163, 1203, 1204
Securities and Exchange Commission, 442
securities sales, 442
securities transactions, 442
semiconductors, 951, 968
SERLINE, 504
small business, 718
Smithsonian Art Index, 314
Smithsonian Permanent Collection, 314
Smithsonian Slide and Photograph Archives, 294, 314
smoking and health, 554
Space Shuttle, 1253, 1255, 1289
standard reference data, 1014
stolen art, 610
swimming pool-related deaths of children, 109
tactical weapons, 959
thermochemical tables, 1015
toxicology, 1103, 1118, 1148, 1151
TOXLINE, 357, 571
traffic accidents, 895
traffic fatalities, 1220
transportation research, 353, 823

The thousands of studies in the Current Events Chapter and Experts Chapter are not listed in this Index.

Index

Treasury securities, 446
unemployment insurance, 255
union contracts, 240, 260
veterans medical data, 393
weather, 1083
world agricultural economics, 1041
world population, 878

Deafness
education materials, 145, 563
grants for interpreters, 178
research grants, 284

Deafness and communicative disorders, 503, 563, 766

Death
alcohol and drug use, 579
children and grieving, 533
consumer products, 506
grieving process, 533
hospice, 506
minorities and Blacks, 507
organ or tissue donation, 506
preparation for, 506

Deaths, 1232
highway fatalities, 579
national statistics, 575
overseas, 860
pregnancy-related, 529

Debates, high school, 149, 1200

Debentures, 444

Debt
collateral, 630
collection, 96
federal, 107, 445, 1241
international, 1181
online search access, 630
personal or corporate, 630
states offer online access to debt files, 630

Deductibility of payments to charities, 454

Deep seabed mining, 812, 1051, 1111

Deep space tracking, 985, 986

Deer, 1255

Defense Language Institute Foreign Language Center, 860

Defense Logistics Agency, 836

Defense Mapping Agency, 947, 1089

Defense Nuclear Facilities Safety Board, 63

Defense Reutilization and Marketing sales, 699

Defense, U.S. Department of
budget statistics, 946, 955
contracts, 959, 990
fraud hotline, 947
How to Buy Surplus Personal Property, 698
industry, 1181
Miscellaneous Property auction, 698
organizational information, 947
prime contractors, 958
public information offices, 43
research solicitations, 943
Selling to the Military, 834
Small Business and Economic Utilization, 840
spending, 936
surplus property, 959

Deferred Vested Benefits
Annual registration statement, 485

Delaware, 641
Automated Tax Refund Information, 466
Business Research Section, 908
Community Development Block Grants, 132
company directories, 664
corporation information, 659
Division of Professional Regulation, 636
Division of Securities, Department of Justice, 669
Emergency Shelter Grants Program, 132
Food Processors, Banking, and Automotive Just-In-Time Suppliers, 907
Housing Development Funds, 132
Housing Rehabilitation Loan Program, 132
IRS hotlines, 464
Labor Supply and Demand, 885
licensed professionals, 636
Low-Income Housing Tax Credit Program, 132
Motor Vehicles Division, 642
Multi-Family Mortgage Revenue Bonds, 132
Procurement Guide, 908
Public Housing Home Ownership Program, 132
Rent Subsidy Programs, 132
Rental Rehabilitation Program, 132
Small Business Administration Office, 837
Small Business Start-Up Guide, 908
state data centers, 900
State Housing Authority, 132
state information, 36
State International Trade Offices, 858
State Labor Office, 885
State Planning Office, 908
state procurement office, 841
state tax assistance, 498
surplus property auctions, 705
Tax form distribution center, 470
Tax forms and publications, 491
unclaimed property office, 712
Uniform Commercial Code Section, 631
U.S. International Trade Administration Office, 855

Delaware Data Book, 908

Dementia, 514, 539, 970
brain aging, 557
causes and treatment, 539
experimental therapies, 546

Demographic maps, 898

Demographics, 764, 907
Center for Population Research, 529
crime, 879
developing nations, 1223
Inter-agency Committee on Population Research, 529
international, 1223
research grants, 289
science work force, 971
students, 230

Dennis the Menace comic book, 1253, 1280

Dental care, free and low-cost, 28

Dental health and dentistry
audiovisual materials, 294
baby-bottle tooth decay, 551
dentists, 96
disease, 518
education and practice, 244
educational grants, 171, 185
Epidemiology and Oral Disease Prevention Program, 517
fluoridation, 517, 551
military research, 954
oral disease research, 517
periodontal disease, 550, 551
records, 614
research grants, 284, 286, 517, 1218
tooth decay, 517

Dental implants, 28

Denver geology, 1252, 1258

Department of ____
See rest of Name

Depreciation tax guide, 482, 494

Depression, recognition and treatment, 533

Desalination, 975

Design, 304, 314, 316
computer aided, 977, 1203

fellowships, 291

Detroit Service Center Bulletin Board Service, 1233

Developmental disabilities legal protection, 619

Diabetes, 146, 515, 977, 1203, 1226
Chinese, 557
control programs, 546
eye disease, 546
information clearinghouse, 504, 546
prevention programs, 545
program grants, 387
research grants, 286
research, 504, 546, 767

Diagnostic imaging, 541

Diagnostic Related Groups, 972

Dial-A-Museum, 93

Dialysis, peritoneal, ambulatory, 972

Diesel fuel daily price, 825, 1051

Diet, 1218
guidelines, 520
heart disease, 548
medications, 569
nutrient data analysis, 521
nutrition guidelines, 523
nutrition survey, 522
nutritional factors, 344, 1025, 1240
nutritional strategies, 524
supplements, elderly, 521

Diets
diet books, 522
fad diets, 522
nutrition value, 524
weight reduction products, 522

Digestive diseases, 504, 547, 767

Digital cartography, 1089

Digital spatial data applications, 965, 1089

Dinosaurs
slides, 1285
Smithsonian visiting program, 1255
teacher workshops, 1255, 1290

Dioxin, 972

Direct payments, 754

Direct sellers
Tax information, 496

Directory of Harvard Business School Cases and Related Course, 655

Disabilities and the disabled, 767, 1227
developmental disabilities, 517
drug and alcohol treatment, 595
education of, 764
grants for veterans, 394
legal services, 619
mental retardation prevention, 517
national health survey, 575
rehabilitation resource center, 509
research grants, 289
services grants, 366
social security grants, 387
veterans housing loans, 128

Disabled, Housing Assistance
California Energy Conservation Rehabilitation Program, 131
California Housing Rehabilitation Program, 131
California Permanent Housing for the Handicapped Homeless, 131
D.C. Housing Finance for Elderly, Dependent and Disabled, 132
District of Columbia Home Improvements for Handicapped, 132
Hawaii Public Housing Projects, 132
Idaho Stewart B. McKinney Permanent Housing Program, 133
Kansas Permanent Housing for Handicapped Homeless, 133
Kentucky Permanent Housing for Homeless Handicapped, 133

The thousands of studies in the Current Events Chapter and Experts Chapter are not included in this Index.

Index

Disabled, Housing Assistance (continued)
Maine MSHA 202 Start Program, 133
Massachusetts Multi-Family Bond Program, 134
Michigan Housing for the Handicapped, 134
Michigan Special Housing Program, 135
Michigan Supported Independent Living Program, 135
Minnesota Accessibility Deferred Loan Program, 135
Minnesota Intermediate Care Facilities, 135
New Hampshire Rental Assistance, 136
New Mexico State Housing Rehabilitation Program, 136
Ohio Home Ownership Incentive Programs, 137
Oregon Elderly and Disabled Housing Program, 137
Pennsylvania Lower-Income Home Ownership Program, 137
Tennessee Veterans housing finance, 138
Vermont ENABLE Program, 138
Washington Multi-Family Program, 139
Wisconsin Community Housing Alternatives Program, 139
Wisconsin Rental Housing Programs, 139
Disasters, natural, etc.
assistance program grants, 380, 929
crisis counseling, 533
grants, 380
HSDB database on toxics, 505
international assistance, 920
legal services, 357, 620
loans, 754
mental health programs, 357, 533
mortgage insurance, 126
relief, 354
state preparedness grants, 380
temporary housing, 357
toxic chemicals, 357, 571
weather, 357
Disclosure Inc., 649
Disclosure Statement
Commissioner of Patents and Trademarks, 1017
Discovery Theater, 313
Discrimination
age, 26
banking credit, 107
employment program grants, 375
employment, 517, 628
government contractors, 236
housing, 629
sex and marital status in credit, 107
workplace, 627
Disease
See also Health
community prevention grants, 365
livestock and poultry, 1021
research grants, 282-87, 768
District of Columbia
Affirmative Action, 885
Automated Tax Refund Information, 466
Census Tract Map, 908
Citizen's Guide to Zoning, 908
Corporation information, 659
data centers, 900
Delinquent Home Mortgage Payments Program, 132
Department of Consumer and Regulatory Affairs, 637
Department of Housing and Community Development, 132
Department of Public Works Information Office, 642

Direct Loan Rehabilitation Program, 132
Directory of 200 Major Employers, 885
Distressed Properties Program, 132
District Labor Office, 885
District Planning Office, 908
Division of Securities, DC Public Service Commission, 669
First Right Purchase Assistance Program, 132
Home Improvements for the Handicapped, 132
Home Purchase Assistance Program, 132
Homestead Housing Preservation Program, 132
House Committee on, 1183
Housing Finance Agency, 132
Housing Finance for Elderly, Dependent, and Disabled, 132
Housing Monographs by Ward, 907
Indices, 905
information, 37
International Trade Offices, 858
IRS hotline, 464
Labor Market Information, 885
licensed professionals, 637
Low-Income Housing Tax Credit Program, 132
Market Assessment for Downtown Washington, 908
Multi-Family Housing Rehabilitation Loan Program, 132
Multi-Family Program, 132
Occupational Employment, 885
Office of Property Control, 706
Population Monograph by Ward, 908
procurement office, 841
Recorder of Deeds, 631
Rental Rehabilitation Program, 132
Section 8 Moderate Rehabilitation Program, 132
Single-Family Housing Rehabilitation Program, 132
Single-Family Purchase Program, 132
State of the Wards Report, 909
surplus property auctions, 705
Tax form distribution center, 470
Tax forms and publications, 491
unclaimed property office, 712
U.S. International Trade Administration Office, 855
Weatherization Assistance Program, 132
Dividends
Statement for Receipts, 478
Divorce
release of claims for children, 487
statistics, 575-76
DNA fingerprinting, 612
Dockets
Securities and Exchange Commission, 441
Doctors
pregnancy-related deaths, 529
DOD
see Defense, U.S. Department of
DOE
see Energy, U.S. Department of
Dogs, 1255
drug sniffing, 600
Dolphins, 1255
drawing, 1255, 1274, 1285, 1298
Domestic companies, 657
Domestic International Sales Corporations, 479, 483
Computation of interest charge, 488
Donations
donee information return, 487
energy-related lab equipment, 1052
tax guide for determining value, 495

to non-profit organizations, 702
Doppler data, 992
Dosimeters, 1009
DOT
see Transportation, U.S. Department of
Douglass, Frederick, 1255, 1280
Drainage, 1011, 1030, 1129
Dredging permits, 345, 948
Drinking
videos, 591
Driver licenses, 352, 648, 829
Driver's license database, 641
Drivers, drunk, 599, 612
Driving research, 353, 825
Dropouts, 349, 610
Droughts, 97, 1143
Drug abuse
anti-drug volunteer programs, 383
children, 152
Cocaine Anonymous, 593, 595
community program grants, 364, 379, 590
Drug Abuse Warning Network, 349, 612
drug-free workplace, 590
education campaign, 147
employee assistance programs, 591
heroin, 613
highway accidents, 579
House Narcotics Committee, 582, 1185
information and treatment hotline, 595
local rehab centers, 583
Narcotics Anonymous, 593, 595
narcotics identification, 606
pregnancy, 364
prevention programs, 363-69, 1025, 1240
prevention videos, 147, 589
research programs, 766, 283-85
school program grants, 382
senior companion volunteers, 384
treatment programs, 593, 595, 1230
waiting list reduction grants, 365
workplace programs, 262
Drug czar, 584
Drug dealers
asset seizures, 600
border war, 971
counternarcotics intelligence, 599
high-level, 603
money laundering, 606
Narcotics Border Indiction System, National, 613, 801, 923, 949
paroles, 608
property auctions, 700
sentencing, 608
smuggling hotline, 600
theft of, 616
trafficking, 613, 800, 923, 949
Drug Enforcement Agency
Drug prevention and rehabilitation
Little League program, 1274
Medicare coverage, 595
poster, 1280
video, 1294
Drug testing, 612
high-risk youth, 579
military, 606
video, 592
videos, 607
Drugs (medications)
see also Pharmaceuticals
brand names, 566
database and clearinghouse, 583
generic equivalents, 566, 568
free programs, 31
hazards, 764
labeling, 972
Medicaid coverage, 595
registration, 616

Index

video on medicines and elderly, 569
Drugs (prescription) for free, 31
Drunk driving, 94, 420, 611, 818
Ducks, 1257
Duke Ellington, 1259, 1280
Dun & Bradstreet, 649, 1229
Dyslexia, 509, 551

E

8-K filings, 442
Eagles, 1257
Earned income tax credit, 453, 496
Earnings, 873
Earth Observing System, 985
Earth sciences
- interior, 1257, 1258
- slides, 1257, 1286, 1289
- teacher workshops, 1257, 1277, 1284, 1288, 1291

Earthquakes, 97, 991-994, 1257-1259, 1271, 1275
- construction standards, 1001, 1010
- environmental hazards, 1143
- hazard reduction, 354, 761
- maps, 1092
- program grants, 380
- publications, 1240
- safety, 28, 354
- San Andreas Fault, 1258, 1259
- small business, 354
- survival, 1258, 1259
- tracer bullets, 977, 996, 1203

East Asia, 306
Eastern Europe, 930
- Business Information Center, 849

Eating disorders
- anorexia nervosa, 520
- bulimia, 520, 521

Ecology, 309, 320, 800
- bulletin board, 1236
- coastal, 961
- marine, 1099
- Mississippi River, 1137
- research, 1096, 1133
- wetlands, 1098, 1137

Economic Analysis
- State Labor Data, 884

Economic indicators
- recorded message, 93
- bulletin board, 1235

Economics
- 7th Federal Reserve District, 105, 867
- agriculture, 970, 1031, 1215, 1037
- AIDS, 972
- American forecasts, 869
- and energy awareness, 1259, 1260, 1269, 1272, 1273, 1287
- arms control programs, 935
- budget deficit, 869
- Bureau of the Census, 866
- business conditions, 869
- community development, 345
- competition investigations, 99
- Congressional Budget Office, 869, 1186
- Consumer Price Index, 107, 865
- correctional facilities, 615
- crime statistics, 611, 879
- defense spending, 935
- demand and income composition of GNP, 868
- developing countries, 429
- development grants and loans, 361
- direct investment estimates, 869
- education, 153
- electronic bulletin board, 866

energy industry, 105, 867, 1052, 1057
- environmental, 1098
- experts abroad program, 291, 309, 415, 913
- experts, government, 868
- federal archives, 866
- federal policy, 869
- Federal Reserve System, 424
- fishing industry, 413, 798, 1136
- foreign countries, 916, 1199
- foreign developments and U.S. employment, 236, 921
- foreign trade, 610
- government finances, 868, 869, 870
- Gross National Product, 866, 869
- Gross State Product, 862, 874
- growth, 866, 869
- hours and earnings survey, 237, 871
- household, 871
- income assets, 874
- industries, U.S., 866
- inflation rates, 866, 869
- interest rates, 869
- interindustry, 871
- international policy, 1181, 1184
- international productivity comparisons, 871
- international transactions accounts, 869
- international, 106, 868
- labor statistics, 235, 865-66
- Labor Statistics, Bureau of, 238, 872
- leading indicators, 866
- legislation, 869
- merchandise trade, 866
- mineral industry, 814
- New England states, 105, 867
- Panama Canal, 806, 928
- personal income and outlays, 866
- policy, 867
- Presidential spending proposals, 869
- productivity trends, 874
- public grants, 361
- regional development, 866, 874
- retail prices, 874
- rural development, 347
- securities and exchanges, 866, 868
- small business, 717
- southeast U.S., 105, 867
- spending policies, 869
- stockpiling, defense, 970
- supply and demand for strategic materials, 867
- surplus of deficit, 870
- tax analysis, 460, 869
- technology, impact of new, 240, 874, 970, 1031
- telecommunications industry, 776, 790
- tourism development, 420
- transportation policy, 819
- underdeveloped countries, 918
- unemployment, 869
- wage rates and earnings trends, 235, 866
- wages and prices, 869
- weapons technology, 935

Ecosystems management, 1025, 1031
Editing seminars, 306
Education
- academic advising, 157
- academic knowledge base, 167
- administration, 143, 152, 166, 382
- adolescent achievement, 152
- adult and continuing, 152, 155, 159-60, 187
- adult grants, 187
- aeronautics, 147
- aerospace, 161, 319, 945, 1276
- Afro-American, 313
- agricultural sciences, 158
- alternative schools, 152
- American history, 314, 317

art, 153, 166, 290, 292, 317
Arts-In-Education Program, 144, 290, 315
at risk students, 152
aviation, 161, 243, 261, 268, 396, 785, 787
bilingual, 145, 149, 167, 179, 1216
Center for the Book, 145, 1199
Challenger Center for Space Science Education, 161
child care programs, 148
childhood, 148
children: risk factors, 516
Civil Air Patrol, 161
class size, 147
classroom productivity, 168
comparative, 153
computers, 153, 163, 167
Congressional Pages, 149
congressional study group, 1186
contemporary design, 314, 316
counseling and personnel services, 146
critical and creative thinking, 146
curricula research, 146, 159, 166, 167
dance, 153, 166, 292
databases, 230
Department of Education Offices, 231
disadvantaged children, 151
discipline, 152, 168
dropouts, 147, 168, 180, 349, 611
educational management, 143, 152
Educational Testing Service, 153
elementary curriculum, 147-48
engineering, 163
English as a second language, 149, 167
environmental, 148, 161-163, 406, 1096, 1103
ERIC Document Reproduction Service, 147
ERIC Service Providers, 166
evaluation systems, 148
facility planning, 143, 152, 179
family formation, 168
finances, 147, 230
foreign exchange programs, 155-57, 305, 913, 922
foreign language, 149, 156, 167, 921, 949
Fulbright program, 174, 187
geophysics, 994
gifted persons, 148, 153
graduate and professional, 157
grants, 174, 176, 177, 180, 181, 182, 187, 188, 189, 282, 380
grants for handicapped, 179
grants for instructors, 189
grants for teachers, 170, 172
grants for veterans, 186
handicapped, 147, 148, 153, 179
health, 153, 524, 528, 530, 545
hearing impaired, 145, 563
high school debate topics, 149, 1200
high school equivalency examination, 246
higher education, 147, 157
history program grants, 181
home and school relationships, 148
homework, 168
horticulture, 140
humanities, 153, 172
inner city, 152
interactive technologies, 295
international assistance, 918
international science fair, 163
international volunteers, 931
job training, 166
junior colleges, 158
labor market impacts, 166
language grants, 174
languages and language sciences, 149, 167
law, 153, 178

The thousands of studies in the Current Events Chapter and Experts Chapter are not included in this Index.

Index

Education (continued)
leadership skills, 167, 168
learning disabilities, 973
learning skills, 147, 167
learning theory, 153
legal contexts, 143, 152
library and information science, 147, 167
limited English proficient, 144, 145
linguistics, 167
literature, 153
loans and grants, 188
loans for health care professionals, 250
lunar rocks on loan, 162
magnet programs, 152, 381
marketing, 230
mass communication, 151
MATHCOUNTS, 162
mathematics, 147, 153, 162, 163, 167
medical grants, 171, 183
medical school student assistance, 247
medical scientist training program, 247
metric system, 778
Mexican Americans, 152
microcomputers, 167
migrants, 152
minorities, 154
music, 153
NASA report to educators, 162
National Air and Space Museum, 163
National Archives teaching kits, 152
national educational longitudinal study, 168
National Gallery of Art, 317
National Peace Essay Contests, 916, 929
Native Americans, 149, 168
Natural history, 151, 320
outdoor, 152
phonics, 152
physical education, 153
political science, 153
postsecondary, 159, 1183
Presidential Scholars, 151
private schools, 168
professional continuing, 157
psycholinguistics, 149, 167
reading and communication skills, 151
Reading Is Fundamental (RIF), 151
reading, 147, 151-153
regional laboratories, 168
remedial, 151
research and development centers, 168
research archives, 166
research clearinghouse (ERIC), 166
research grants for minority faculty, 573
research grants, 178, 289
Resources in Education, 147, 166
rhetoric, 151
rural, 152
savings bonds, 147, 445
school finances, 230
school reform, 148
school workplace conditions, 152
science, 153, 163, 167
Sea-Grant Colleges, 159, 808, 1103, 1115
secondary schools, 147
Selective Service, 153
Senate committee, 1182
social sciences, 153
social studies, 153, 167
sociolinguistics, 149, 167
sociology, 153
Space Camp, 163
space science, 984
special needs, 168
speech communication, 151
staff information, 230
state centers, 230
state reform, 152
statistics, 147, 152, 169, 230, 868
student grants, 185, 189
student loans, 380
student populations, 230
study abroad, 149, 167
study of America, 921
tax paying programs, 461
teacher information, 153, 230
teaching grants, 178, 181
technical institutes, 158
technology and children, 148
technology, 167, 169, 574, 965, 971
test taking skills, 151
tests and measurement devices, 153
theater, 151, 166, 292
TV's influence, 152
U.S. Space Foundation, 163
urban schools, 154
USDA programs, 156, 157
veterans, 143
vocational and technical, 155, 160, 168
vocational grants, 176, 180, 289, 382
writing, 151, 153
Education teams (WETS), 1265, 1296
Education, U.S. Department of
financial assistance programs, 147
Office of Educational Research and Development, 167
public information offices, 46
Small Business procurement, 840
Educational Resources Information Center (ERIC), 166
EEOC
see Equal Employment Opportunity Commission
Eisenhower, Dwight D., 1259
Elderly, 760
housing finance assistance, 130
housing loans, 369
legal protection, 619
program grants, 171, 366
rental housing mortgage insurance, 127
research grants, 184
tax counseling, 374
tax credit information, 494
Elderly, Housing Assistance
California Energy Conservation Rehabilitation Program, 131
California Multi-Family Program, 131
California Senior Citizen Shared Housing Program, 131
Colorado Special Needs Housing Fund, 131
Connecticut Apartment Conversion for the Elderly, 132
Connecticut Reverse Annuity Mortgages, 131
D.C. Housing Finance for Elderly, 132
Elderly Housing Program Fund, 139
Elderly Rural Rehabilitation Program, 133
FmHA Supplemental Subsidy Program, 135
Hawaii Public Housing Projects, 132
Illinois Homebuyer Program, 133
Kentucky Grants to the Elderly for Energy Repairs, 133
Maine Home Equity Conversion Mortgage, 133
Maryland Elderly Rental Housing Program, 134
Maryland Reverse Equity Program, 134
Massachusetts Supportive Services in Elderly Housing, 134
Minnesota Elderly Home Sharing Program, 135
New Hampshire Rental Assistance, 136
New Jersey Continuing Care Retirement Communities, 136
New Jersey Services for Independent Living Program, 136
New Mexico State Housing Rehabilitation Program, 136
New York Housing Opportunities Program for Elderly, 136
New York State Housing Authority, 136
North Carolina Governor's NCHFA/ FmHA Elderly Subsidy Program, 137
Ohio Multi-Family Rental Development Program, 137
Oregon Elderly and Disabled Housing Program, 137
Pennsylvania Supportive Services Program, 137
Vermont ENABLE Program, 138
Wisconsin Rental Housing Programs, 139
Elections
campaign finance activity, 647, 1190
campaign finance records, 1188
contribution limitations, 647, 1190
database, 1224
federal campaign finance law, 646, 1189
federal rules and administration, 1182
finance, federal, 1221
labor political activity, 646, 1190
National Clearinghouse on Election Administration, 646, 1190
online computer information system, 1191
political action committees, 1189
political committees, 647, 1190
returns, 1224
State election finance records, 648, 1192
technical assistance programs, 345, 1189
U.S. presidential funding, 1189
Elective surgery hotline, 509
Electricity, 971, 973, 1052, 1059, 1063
consumer cost reduction, 1060
consumer power demand, 1057
consumer rate statistics, 1052
consumption research, 1058
educational material, 1259, 1270
exporting, 1059
generation control, 1060
load management, 1060
remote controlled cycling, 1057
rural electric companies, 1052
rural, 1229
Electrodynamic phenomena, 990
Electromagnetic fields, 948, 965, 974, 977, 1203
Electronic bulletin boards
agricultural trade reports, 1038
bilingual education, 145
economic indicators, 866
education data and announcements, 146
fire research, 1002
labor statistics, 873
NASA programs and activities, 163
Electronic fund transfers, 107
Electronic Publishing System (EPUB), 1234
Electronic tax filing, 454, 488
Electronics, 951, 968, 1225
automotive, 779, 976
competition, international, 973
industry, 974
Elementary schools
curriculum, 1255
drug abuse videos, 591
substance abuse prevention, 591
Eliot Elisofon Photographic Archives, 294, 313
Elk, 1259
Ellington, Duke, 1259, 1280
Emancipation Proclamation, 1259
Embassies art program, 315
Embassies, U.S., fax numbers, 846

The thousands of studies in the Current Events Chapter and Experts Chapter are not listed in this Index.

Index

Emergencies
see also Disasters
disasters, international, 920
Emergency Broadcast System, 355
enemy attack, 356
management, 355
medical services, 355
mental health programs, 357, 533
program grants, 380
temporary housing, 357
toxic chemicals, 357, 571
training grants, 379
Emergency rooms
consumer product-related injuries, 109
Employees
hazards detection, 572
Public Schools and Tax-Exempt Organizations, 495
Emission levels, 1113
Employment
agency grants, 372
agriculture, 248, 1042
air traffic controllers, 243
apprenticeship programs, 243, 245
corporate statistics, 664
development grants, 361
disabled workers, 234
discrimination, 375
dislocated workers, 239, 248
displaced homemakers, 244, 245
elderly, 234, 245, 246
Eskimos, 248
Federal Job Information Centers, 93, 268, 269
grants for senior citizens, 389
grants for Veterans, 388
grants, 173, 386, 388
handicapped, 179, 237, 245, 251, 626
House Committee on, 1183
income maintenance, 249
Interstate Job Bank, 247
Job Corps, 246
job prospects, 243
job service offices, 247
job training grants, 386, 388
Job Training Partnership Act, 246, 249
limited English language proficiency, 245
longitudinal surveys, 238, 872
Native Americans, 248, 388
pensions and retirement funds, 254
placement program grants, 372
polygraph testing, 253
project grants, 287
reemployment services, 248
requirements by industry, 236, 249
resume preparation, 247
retraining services, 248
single parents, 245
statistical data, 372
summer, 275
tax credits for employers, 780
trade adjustment grants, 388
training program grants, 372
veterans, 234, 244
welfare recipients, 245, 249
women in highway construction, 249
women, 245
youth programs, 186, 245, 246
Employment opportunities
accountants, 246
attorneys, 246
commodity and industry specialists, 246
economists, 246
engineering, 273
finance, 273
International Trade Commission, U.S., 246
management, 273
mathematicians, 273
physicists, 273
Postal Service, U.S., 273
Employment, federal
civil service law violations, 272
complaints, 272
discrimination, 272
employee attitudes, 269
grievance filings, 268
personnel records, 272
political abuses, 271
prohibited personnel practices, 272
Encyclopedia of Associations, 654
Endangered species, 1133, 1259
Smithsonian visiting program, 1259
teacher workshops, 1259, 1290
Energy, 1057, 1261, 1278
activities, 1259, 1260, 1277, 1287
alcohol fuel loans, 1049
alternative fuels, 1027, 1081
appliance standards, 1049
audits, 729, 1055
bulletin board, 1234, 1237
collection technology, 1063
conservation, 288, 379, 567, 776, 1053
hot water heaters, 1065
House Energy and Commerce Committee, 1183
information for kids, 1260
NTIS, 1056
consumption, 1059
consumption video, 1260, 1281, 1294
conversion technology, 1063
dams and steam plants, 1064
education materials, 1260-61, 1266, 1270, 1278
efficient buildings, 1050
emergencies, 1051, 1052
end use, 1058
energy-saving advertising claims, 94
environmental policy, 1054
fossil, 289, 1068
fusion, 972, 1057, 1073
geothermal, 812, 976, 1068, 1203
development, 1055
publications, 1061
tracer bullets, 1050
grants for inventions, 288, 368
home insulation labeling, 100
home weatherization, 129-30
housing efficiency, 119
hydroelectric power, 1055, 1112
industrial use, 971, 1056
international, 919, 1051, 1057
international economic research, 872
Lawrence Berkeley Laboratory, 992, 1054
legislation, 1057
management, 1054
markets, 1058
municipal waste, 971
National Energy Information Center, 1059
National outlook, 980, 1064
national policy, 1183
nuclear, 1072, 1080, 1261
ocean thermal, 971, 976, 1050, 1059, 1061, 1084
offshore resources, 971, 1184
passive solar homes, 119
photovoltaic power, 1059, 1061
prices, 1059, 1183
production, 1059
regulation, 1054, 1061, 1181
renewable and nonrenewable, 1061, 1260
research and development, 173, 187, 288, 1184
residential consumption, 972, 1062, 1229
resource development, 1098
Russian, 972
seminar grants, 173
Senate committee, 1181
small business loans, 726
software, 1059
solar, 971, 976, 1050, 1061, 1063, 1064
State conservation programs, 1063
steam, 1258, 1261, 1290
storage, 1061
supplies, 1059
supply and demand, international, 1057
supply disruptions, 1069
systems vulnerability, 966, 1063
taxation, 1181
transmission, 1183
transportation consumption, 819, 1062
water heater program, 1064
water heating, 776
weatherization grants, 389, 1065
wind power, 976, 1050, 1061, 1203
Energy Conservation Financing
Agricultural Conservation Program, 756
Basic Energy Sciences--University and Science, 763
Business and Industrial Loans, 757
Business Energy Fund Program, 139
California Energy Conservation Rehabilitation Program, 131
Clean Coal Technology Program, 764
Conservation Research and Development, 763
DEER Program, 139
Energy Conservation and Housing Rehabilitation Incentive Program, 137
Energy Conservation Revolving Loan Fund, 135
Energy Efficiency Program - New Construction, 138
Energy Extension Service, 763
Energy Improvements Program, 136
Energy-Efficient Homes Program, 137
Energy-Efficient Housing Production Program, 137
Energy-Rated Homes of Vermont Mortgage Program, 138
Energy-Related Inventions, 763
Fossil Energy Research and Development, 764
Georgia Energy Fund, 132
Grants to the Elderly for Energy Repairs (GEER), 133
Home Energy Loan Program, 131, 134, 135, 139
Home Energy/Improvement Loan Program, 138
Home Improvement Loan Program, 139
Home Improvements/Weatherization Loan Program, 135
Indoor Plumbing Program, 134
Industrial Energy Conservation, 763
Multi-Family Home and Energy Loan Program, 134
Nuclear Energy, Reactor Systems, Development, 764
Regional Biomass Programs, 763
Rehabilitation Mortgages, 131
Renewable Energy Research and Development, 763
Rental Housing Energy Conservation Program, 137
Rental Property Energy Efficiency Loan Fund, 139
Rural Clean Water Program (RCWP), 756
Vermont Housing and Conservation Board, 138
Weatherization Assistance Program, 132

The thousands of studies in the Current Events Chapter and Experts Chapter are not included in this Index.

Index

Energy conservation technology grants, 763
Energy Related Invention Assistance Program, 30
Energy, U.S. Department of
freedom of information, 1060
libraries, 1057
public information offices, 46
Small Business Innovative Research Program, 840
Engineering, 987, 1012, 1057
adhesives, 955
agricultural, 1022
air traffic control, 245, 786
apprenticeships, 956
Army Corps of Engineers, 949, 967
automotive, 1113
bridge, 797, 825
cadastral, 1126
ceramics, 999
chemical, 999, 1011
coastal, 410, 801
construction, 950
demographics, 971
education, 971
electrical, 1001
electronics, 1001
Engineering Laboratory, National, 1006
environmental, 1100, 1103, 1118, 1148, 1151
evaluation, 951, 968
fire protection, 1002
genetic, 1099, 1101
historic, 306
hydrocarbons, 1003
hydrology, 1121
information systems, 1000, 1004
information technology, 967
manufacturing, 1010
marine, 804
materials scarcity, 971
mining, 778, 813
oceanographic, 1086, 1113
research grants, 186, 283, 287
standards, 1005
statistical, 1014
structural, 1014
systems, 959, 980
Engines, jet, 779, 976, 1203
English-Spanish Glossary of Words and Phrases, 454
Enterprise zones, 120
Entomology, 309, 320
Environment, 972
acid rain, 1054, 1101
activity book, 1262, 1263
agricultural research, 1030
air and water protection, 1107
air pollution control, 376
bulletin board, 1233, 1234, 1236-1238
Coast Guard, U.S., 801, 926, 1100
complaints, 1144
congressional study conference, 1186
Council on Environmental Quality, 1102
curriculum, 1263, 1283, 1294
database, 1223
Earth-space, 1086, 1104
education, 162, 1103, 1253, 1262, 1264
Clearinghouse, 1274
Helping Your Child Learn Science, 1285
Solid Waste Environmental Education programs, 1266
engineering, 1100, 1109, 1118
films, 1267, 1268, 1294, 1295
Florida educational material, 1266, 1270
fraud hotline, 1100
Great Lakes, 1098, 1267, 1271
greenhouse effect, 977, 1098

impact statements, 1054, 1097, 1098
international, 926, 929, 1054, 1100
legal issues, 1103, 1118, 1148, 1151
legislation, 347, 1101, 1194
litigation, 610
marine protection, 412, 803, 1086, 1102, 1113, 1114, 1135, 1145
natural hazards, 97, 1143
New England, 1097
Oceanic and Atmospheric Administration, National, 1086
pesticides, 1029, 1030, 1129
President's Youth Awards, 1267
recycling, 351, 1147
Resource Conservation and Recovery Act, 1103, 1147
RTECS database, 505
Senate committee, 1181
Senior Employment Program, 389
speakers, 943
standards, 1109
Superfund, 1151
terms and acronyms, 1262
tropical deforestation, 1100
TVA programs, 1106
U.S. foreign policy, 1100
videos, 1263, 1283, 1294
water quality, 344, 377, 1025, 1032, 1240
Environmental barriers
handicapped or disabled, 564
Environmental Protection Agency, U.S., 63, 162, 1096
Environmental Question Line, 28
Enzyme aspartate aminotransferase, 1014
EPA
see Environmental Protection Agency
Epidemiology, 245
Epilepsy, 509, 515, 551, 976, 1203
therapies, 547
Equal Employment Opportunity Commission, 64, 883-84
Erosion, 755, 942, 1095, 1121, 1226
Escrow accounts, 96
Eskimos
arts and crafts, 1267
Inuit arts, 1267
Smithsonian visiting program, 1273
Estate and gift taxes, 454, 473
Estrogen and osteoporosis, 520, 559
Estuaries, 1113, 1217, 1267
Ethanol production, 910, 1027, 1061
Ethics
medical research, 1216
Senate committee, 1182
Ethiopian jewry, 1186
Ethnic disputes, 349, 612, 616
Ethnomusicology, 305, 1200
Eurodollar bonds, 868
Europe, 306, 792
foreign affairs, 1184
European Commission, 966
European Community Information Service, 853
European Space Agency, 989
Exchange rates, 1221
Excise taxes, 493, 488, 489
Executive Branch, 40
Exempt (tax) organizations
Public request for tax form inspection, 482
Tax on Unrelated Business Income, 496
Exemptions to the Blue Sky laws, 668
Exercise
arthritis, 516
elderly, 516, 558
heart disease, 516
obesity, 524
orthopedic research, 509
President's Council on Physical

Fitness, 516
President's physical fitness awards, 518
swimming, 516
walking, 516
Expenditures to influence legislation, 485
Experimental homes, 760
Exploding galaxies, 983
Explosives, 955, 971, 976
commerce, 777
forensic studies, 774
hotline, 96, 110
identification, 612
storage, 777
tracing, 612
Exporting, 755
advice hotline, 28
business directory of resources, 855
Export-Import Bank, 429, 848
Export Trading Company (ETC) Guidebook, 855
regulations and product standards, 851
tax exemption certificate, 480
Export-Import Bank of the United States, 64
Extraditions, drugs, 600
Extraterrestrial life, 976, 982, 1203
Eyes
elderly, 559
free library services, 564
macular degeneration, 559
National Eye Institute, 504, 540
research, 504, 539

F

F-18 fighter jet, 990
FAA
see Federal Aviation Administration
FACS Info Service, Inc., 650
Fallout shelters, 357
Family issues
action against addiction, 349
adjustment and crisis, 534
adjustment to change, 504
childbearing, 517, 1240
economics, 517, 1240
educational program grants, 180
family violence hotline, 587
farms, 125, 1026
financial management assistance, 1025, 1240
genetics, 526
home care chronically ill, 506
home care terminally ill, 506
home economics, 504
home ownership loans, 126
information center, 534
marital relationships, 517, 1240
planning program grants, 365
research grants, 283
Schools Without Drugs manual, 590
Senate caucus, 1186
violence prevention, 367
Family farms, 125
Family Life Research Grants, 765
Family planning, 505, 527
adolescent pregnancy, 527, 531
adoption, 527
contraception, 526
developing countries, 929
research grants, 287
sterilization, 526
Family violence, 503, 535, 612
Fannie Mae, 121
Farm cooperatives, 1026
Farm Credit Administration, 428

The thousands of studies in the Current Events Chapter and Experts Chapter are not listed in this Index.

Index

freedom of information, 1026
public information office, 64

Farming
credit, 1183
crop insurance, 1025, 1183
dairy, 1183
data, 1042
family, 1182
income, 1226, 1230
livestock, 1183
loans, 630, 728, 757
natural disaster assistance, 357, 1027
poultry, 1183
production expenses, 1226
production techniques, 1042
rental income, 483
research grants, 282
soil conservation, 1183
taxes, 476, 480, 493
workers, 388, 624

Fast foods dietary guide, 522

Fatalities
job-related, 1216
traffic accidents, 1225
traffic, 1220

Fax Directory Of Overseas Commercial Counselors, 846

FBI
see Federal Bureau of Investigation

FCC
see Federal Communication Commission

FDIC
see Federal Deposit Insurance Corporation

Fed Flash Bulletin Board, 1235

Federal AIDS/HIV employees, 595

Federal Aviation Administration, 64, 161

Federal Bureau of Investigation
career information, 612
drug abuse education, 590
public information office, 54
Special Agent Drug Coordinator, 591
substance abuse education, 591
tours, 614

Federal Communications Commission, 64

Federal Council on the Aging, 558

Federal Data Base Finder, 655

Federal Deposit Insurance Corporation
auctions, 695
Liquidation Book, 696
public information, 64
rules and regulations, 429
Uniform Interagency Bank Rating System, 430

Federal depository libraries, 1213

Federal Document Retrieval, Inc., 650

Federal Election Commission, 646, 1189
campaign finance law complaints, 646, 1189
library, 646, 1190
public information, 65

Federal Emergency Management Agency, 65

Federal Emergency Shelter Grant Program, 131

Federal government jobs, 30

Federal Housing Administration (FHA), 696

Federal Housing Finance Board, 65

Federal Information Sources, 653
Airlines, Air Freight Carriers, and Air Taxis, 653
Airports, 653
Bank Holding Companies and State Members of the Federal Reserve, 653
Banks, National Communications Division, 653
Barge and Vessel Operators, 653
Cable Television System Operators, 653
Colleges, Universities, Vocational Schools, and Public Schools, 653
Commodity Trading Advisors, 653
Consumer Products Corrective Actions Division, 653
Electric and Gas Utilities and Gas Pipeline Companies, 653
Exporting Companies, 653
Federal Land Bank and Production Credit Associations, 653
Foreign Corporations World Traders Data Report, 653
Government Contractors Federal Procurement Data Center, 653
Hospitals and Nursing Homes National Center for Health Statistics, 653
Land Developers Office of Interstate Land Registration, 653
Mining Companies Mine Safety and Health Administration, 653
Non-Profit Institutions US Internal Revenue Service, 654
Nuclear Power Plants Director, Office of Nuclear Reactor Regulations, 654
Pension Plans, 654
Pesticide and Chemical Manufacturers, 654
Pharmaceutical, Cosmetic and Food Companies, 654
Radio and Television Stations, 654
Railroads, Trucking Companies, Bus Lines, Freight Forwarders, 654
Savings and Loan Associations, 654
Telephone Co.'s, Overseas Telegraph Co.'s, Microwave C, 654

Federal Insurance Contributions Act, 473

Federal Jobs Bulletin Board, 1235

Federal Labor Relations Authority, 65, 257, 271

Federal Laboratory Consortium, 960, 980

Federal Maritime Commission, 65

Federal Mediation and Conciliation Service, 65, 256, 257, 259, 619

Federal Mine Safety and Health Review Commission, 65, 264

Federal National Mortgage Association, 121

Federal Procurement Data Center, 833, 836

Federal Property available to the homeless, 702

Federal Register
list of foreign gifts, 702

Federal Reserve Banks, 428

Federal Reserve Economic Data (FRED), 1235

Federal Reserve System
Board of Governors, 427
Community Affairs Officers, 106, 867
public information office, 65
resource materials, 424

Federal Retirement Thrift Investment Board, 66

Federal Savings and Loan Insurance Corporation, 430

Federal tax
see Tax, federal

Federal Tax Deposit Coupon, 486

Federal Trade Commission, 770
consumer complaints, 95
Franchise and Business Opportunities Rule, 770
Franchise Rule Information Hotline, 771
public information office, 66
trade regulation enforcement, 100
Uniform Franchise Offering Circular (UFOC), 771

Feed grain, 755

Fellowships
agricultural sciences, 157
architecture, 290, 291, 311, 321
biomedical sciences, 247
cancer research, 541
choreographers, 290
composers, 291
creative writers, 244, 246, 304, 308
cultural anthropology, 303
dancers, 290
dentistry research, 517
design arts, 290, 291
Distinguished Designer Fellowships, 290
documentary editing, 305
educational exchanges, 157, 305, 922
environmental education, 156, 1096
fashion design, 290, 291
film and video, 295
foreign auditors, 158
foreign scientists, 574
Fulbright scholarships, 157, 305, 922
graphic design, 290, 291
historic preservation, 290, 291
history of art, 311, 321
industrial design, 290, 291
interior design, 290, 291
international peace, 307, 937
jazz performance and composition, 291
Latin America and Caribbean research, 156
literature translators, 244, 247, 304, 308
master folk artists, 290, 314
media arts, 295
mimes, 290, 292
minority faculty--biomedical science, 247
minority health research, 574
minority visiting scientists, 247
music, 291
NASA graduate research, 159, 162
neurological research, 509, 551
opera and musical theater, 291
pharmacology research, 574
pharmacology, 566, 569
playwrights, 290, 292
Presidential library research, 310
reproductive sciences, 529
science and technology policy issues, 166, 964
Smithsonian Institution, 308, 320, 321
Smithsonian International Scholars Program, 305
solo performance artists, 290, 292
solo recitalists, 291
study art in France, 292
study art in Japan, 292
theater, 290, 292
urban design, 290, 291
urban planning, 290, 291
visual arts, 311, 321
visual media, 293, 348
White House, 160

FEMA
see Federal Emergency Management Agency

Ferns, 140

Ferrets, 1268

Ferries, 827

Fertility, 515, 529, 970

Fertilizers, 1027
chemical and organic, 1027
environmental impact, 1031
production, 1031
research, 1027

Fiduciaries, taxes, 477, 484

Films, 33, 762
American Indians, 318
archives, 295, 1202
Army Corps recreational facilities, 410, 1056
art, 144, 294, 315, 317, 1286, 1293
aviation, 786
close-captioned for deaf, 175, 764
citizenship education, 623
combat, 294, 295
documentaries, 294, 295
drug prevention, 147, 589

The thousands of studies in the Current Events Chapter and Experts Chapter are not included in this Index.

Index

Films (continued)
- earth-science, 1089
- employment cooperative programs, 256
- environment, 1267, 1268, 1294
- ethnographic, 296, 297
- federal motion picture archives, 294, 295
- flash flood, 1268, 1270, 1297
- floods, 1084
- historical, 303, 304
- hurricanes, 1268, 1297
- IRS, 462
- marine issues, 411, 801
- military, 948
- mineral resources, 814
- mining industry, 812
- Museum-related careers, 243, 319
- National Audio-Visual Center, 949
- National Parks, 407
- Natural history, 320, 406, 1136
- newsreels, 294, 295
- Oceanic and Atmospheric Administration, National, 808
- Panama Canal, 806, 928
- pests, 1268, 1279, 1295
- Postal Service, U.S., 117
- research and development tests, 294, 295
- small business, 722
- Smithsonian collection, 306
- tornados, 1268, 1291, 1297

Filmstrips
- aerospace-related, 1277, 1288
- NASA, 1268, 1289
- Space Shuttle, 1268, 1289

Finance
- African Development Bank, 429
- Asian Development Bank, 429
- capital movements, 877
- Chemical Bank, 121
- domestic monetary policy, 1183
- education savings bonds, 147, 445
- electronic funds transfer system, 424
- Fannie Mae, 121
- federal deposits, 428
- foreign debts, 873
- foreign investment in U.S., 869
- foreign money markets, 869
- forgery, 432
- health care, 575
- InterAmerican Bank, 429
- interest rates, 869
- International Monetary System, 873
- junk bonds, 436
- legislation, 430
- leverage buyouts, 436
- monetary policy, 1181
- national housing finance system, 122
- retirement bonds, 445
- savings bonds, 445, 446
- Treasury checks, 431
- Treasury security investments, 428
- Uniform Commercial Code, 630

Financial assistance overseas, 860

Finders of unclaimed property, 711

Finding SEC filings
- FACS Info Service, Inc., 650
- Federal Document Retrieval, Inc., 650
- Meredith Hurt & Associates, 650
- Prentice Hall Legal and Financial Services, 650
- Research Information Services, 650
- Vickers Stock Research Corp., 650
- Washington Document Service, 650
- Washington Service Bureau, 650

Fine arts, energy awareness, 1259, 1260, 1269
- information for kids, 1272-73, 1287

Fingerprints, 614

Fires
- christmas trees, 349
- cigarettes, 1002
- combustion products, 1002
- computer simulation, 1002-03
- congressional caucus, 1186
- consumer product-related, 109
- databases, 356
- firefighting, 356, 379
- flammable furnishings, 1002
- management, 1124
- marine, 412, 804, 1113
- mass transportation vehicles, 1002
- physics, 1002
- predictions, 1002
- prevention, 1006
- protection, 1124
- Research Information Service, 1011
- research, 1002, 1011
- residential sprinklers, 349, 351
- safety, 97, 349, 1011, 1124
- smoke control, 1003
- smoke detectors, 349
- wildfire suppression, 1124
- wildland fire detection, 1130

Fire prevention
- educational programs, 1269, 1270
- poster, 1269, 1281
- publications, 1269
- Sesame Street fire safety, 1269, 1285
- Smokey Bear prevention materials, 1269, 1287

Firearms
- curios and relics, 775
- drugs, 603
- forensic studies, 774
- hotline, 94
- importation, 775
- identification, 110
- licensees, 775
- state laws and ordinances, 613
- statistics, 774
- tracing services, 613

Firefighters, 356

Firewood, 27, 696, 1240

Fireworks safety, 111, 777

FIRST Program grants, 181

Fish
- Alaskan, 1132
- conservation, 1221
- diseases, 1134, 1143
- ecology, 1136
- exotic, 1133
- health research, 245, 1134
- husbandry, 1133
- nuisance fish control, 1135
- photographs, 295, 1134
- salmon, 1136
- steelhead, 1136
- warm water, 1133

Fish and Wildlife Service, U.S., 383, 1137
- general interest publications, 1292, 1298

Fisheries, 413, 798, 929, 975, 1086, 1133, 1136
- biology, 1101, 1113
- chemicals, 1135
- conservation research grants, 282
- contaminant research, 1134
- development research, 245, 1134
- foreign, 800
- grants, 361
- international assistance, 914
- management, 245, 1134
- Pacific Coast, 1136
- pesticides, 1134, 1143
- products, 110, 799
- regulation and protection, 1184
- research grants, 283, 800, 1107

Fishermen's Contingency Fund, 758

Fishermen's Guaranty Fund, 761

Fishermen's Protection Act, 761

Fish exports, 799

Fishing
- commercial, 410, 801
- Fishermen's Protective Act, 800, 807, 919
- foreign policy, 926
- industry competition, 800
- international, 800, 919
- Vessel and Gear Damage Compensation Fund, 758

Fish husbandry, 245, 1134

Flags, 28, 1192, 1239

Flaxseed, 1220

Flight
- research, 985
- supersonic, 986

Floods, 97, 755, 1084, 1087, 1143
- control, 1184
- flash, 1268, 1270, 1286, 1297
- hazard map, 356
- insurance, 129
- plain management, 356
- prevention programs, 356

Flood-prone areas, 356

Floriculture, 140, 141, 1027

Florida
- Affirmative Action, 885
- Affordable Housing Loan Program, 132
- Automated Tax Refund Information, 466
- company directories, 665
- corporation information, 659
- County Comparisons, 909
- Department of Professional Regulation, 637
- Division of Securities and Investor Protection, 669
- Employment Statistics, 885
- environmental education material, 1266, 1270
- Finance, Insurance and Real Estate Industry, 885
- First-Time Homebuyer Mortgage Revenue Bond Program, 132
- *Florida Statistical Abstract,* 905
- *Guide to Florida Environmental Permitting,* 909
- Highway Safety and Motor Vehicles Department, 642
- Home Ownership Assistance Program, 132
- Housing Finance Agency, 132
- IRS hotlines, 464
- Labor Market Trends, 885
- licensed professionals, 637
- Low-Income Housing Tax Credit Program, 132
- Market-Rate Multi-Family Bond Loan Program, 132
- Monthly Tourist Surveys, 907, 909
- Occupational Employment in Hospitals, 885
- Section 8 Program, 132
- Services Industry, 885
- Small Business Administration Office, 837
- State Apartment Incentive Loan Program, 132
- state data centers, 900
- state information, 37
- State International Trade Offices, 858
- State Labor Office, 885
- State Planning Office, 909
- state procurement office, 841
- state tax assistance, 498
- surplus property auctions, 706
- Tax form distribution center, 470
- Tax forms and publications, 491
- unclaimed property office, 712

Index

Uniform Commercial Code Division, 631
U.S. International Trade Administration Office, 855

Flowers
Botanic Garden shows, 141

Fluidized bed combustion, 1067

Fluids, 999, 1003

Fluorocarbons, 988

FmHA loans, 28

Folk arts, grants, 762

Folklife and folklore
activities and programs, 305, 1200
African, 313
archive, 305, 308, 317, 1202
culture, 305, 1200
Festival of American Folklife, 291, 317
grass-roots oral history, 305, 1200
music, 305, 1200
recordings, 305, 1200
research, 291, 317

Folkways Records, 305, 317

Food

see also Nutrition, 521

additives, 515, 522, 523, 976, 1203
allergies, 520
alternative agricultural opportunities, 1023, 1031
assistance programs, 522
astronauts, for, 989
calories, 523, 525
cartoons, 523
Child Nutrition Program, 522
composition information, 344, 1025, 1240
consumer complaints, 523
consumer information, 504, 523, 525, 569
consumption, 522, 1217
contaminants, environmental, 970
dietary analysis software, 521
distribution volunteers, 384
domestic food programs, 356, 1033
economics, 1034
elderly and diet, 521
embargos, 522
expenditures, 522
fat and sodium content, 522
Food Distribution Program, 522
Food For Peace, 1036
Food Stamp Program, 522
grading, retail, 970, 1036
grants, 385
inexpensive recipes, 523
information systems, 970, 1036
irradiation, 1034
labeling, 522, 1034
labels, 523
low acid canned products, 1224
marketing studies, 1033
meat poisoning/complaint hotline, 98, 1034, 1035
nutrition labels, 520, 524
organic foods, 525
organisms, 522
packaging, 1033
pesticide residues, 970, 1031, 1036
preparation and refrigeration, 523
production, 970, 1036
radiation, 522
research, 283, 970, 1022, 1031
safety and inspection, 522, 523, 1034
seafood inspection, 110, 799
shelf-life dating, 970, 1036
sweetener additives, 525
tampering hotline, 523
transportation, 1033
vitamin content, 1015
weight loss, 523
wholesaling, 1033

Women, Infants, and Children Program, 522

Food and Agriculture Organization, 1041

Food and Drug Administration, 504, 520-525, 569, 570
animal and pet products, 1241
research, 764
small business assistance, 722

Food and Security Act of 1986, 630

Food For Peace, 920, 1036, 1183

Food marketing, 970, 1031

Food stamps
budget, 520
grants for state agencies, 385
grants, 385
Puerto Rico, 385
Senate Committee, 1180

Footwear, 1186

Forage crops, 1029

Forecasting data, markets, 898, 908

Foreign addresses taxes, 492

Foreign affairs

see also Foreign policy

Asia and the Pacific, 1184
Australia, 918
Brunei, 918
Burma, 918
Cambodia, 918
Canada, 919
Center for the Study of, 915
China, 918
Country Background Notes, 416, 917
East Asia and the Pacific, 918
ecology, 1100
energy producing countries, 1060
Europe, 919
fishing agreements, 800, 919
human rights, 923
Indonesia, 918
Japan, 918
Laos, 918
Malaysia, 918
New Zealand, 918
Philippines, 918
publications, 914
Singapore, 918
Soviet Union, 919
Sub-Sahara Africa, 912
Taiwan, 918
Thailand, 918
the Koreas, 918
Vietnam, 918
Western Hemisphere, 1184

Foreign Agricultural Service, 850
help with selling commodities abroad, 852

Foreign agriculture experts
Animal and Plant Health Inspection Service, 846
Economic Research Service, Agriculture and Trade Analysis, 846
Food Safety and Inspection Service, 846
Food Transportation, International Transportation Branch, 846

Foreign companies, 657
Acquisitions and Dispositions of stock, 484
Information, 484
U.S. Income Tax Return, 479

Foreign death tax, 473

Foreign demographic profiles, 851

Foreign earned income, 481

Foreign energy experts, 846

Foreign experts
Agriculture, 846
Economic Assistance to Foreign Countries, 846
Energy resources, 846
Fisheries, 846

Information Programs and Cultural Exchange, 846
Metric, 846
Mineral Resources, 845
Seafood Certificates, 846
Telecommunications Information, 846

Foreign gifts, 702

Foreign investment, 869
investment loans, 763

Foreign labor trends, 855

Foreign Language Assistance in Tax Preparation, 454

Foreign Language Training, 156, 860, 921, 949
Foreign Service Institute, 860

Foreign markets, 609, 843

Foreign moving expenses, 481

Foreign owned corporations, 484

Foreign personal holding company, 484

Foreign policy
Afghanistan, 1186
arms control and disarmament research, 938
Arms Transfer, 937
briefings to special groups, 921
democracy, 924
disinformation issues, 933
economic issues at U..N, 918
economic policy, 924
energy issues, 1057
environmental issues, 1100
european affairs, 1181
food aid, 1037
geographic concerns, 922, 1089
global climate, 1100
human rights, 924
INF Treaty, 936
intelligence research, 917
international aviation, 786
international business, 416, 429
international conflict management, 916, 929
International Monetary System, 873
international treaties, 932
labor issues, 237
Law of the Sea Treaty, 926
marine environment, 926, 1100
maritime affairs, 804, 931
narcotics issues, 918, 1181
Near East and South Asia, 927
nuclear risk reduction, 936
nuclear technology, 1079
Organization of American States, 927
polar affairs, 914, 1095, 1132
politico-military issues, 937
public participation, 921
refugees, 930
research, 915
Senate committee, 1181
telecommunications, 793
U.S. commercial interests, 924
U.S., history of, 923
UNESCO, 932
United Nations, 933
western hemisphere, 924
wildlife conservation, 1100
Wireless File, 933
WORLDNET, 934

Foreign relations
House Committee on, 1183
research, 309

Foreign Sales Corporation, 479, 487

Foreign Service, 915
career opportunities, 245, 921
officer examinations, 246, 925

Foreign Specialists At Other Government Agencies, 845

Foreign Tax Credit, 454, 457, 478, 493

The thousands of studies in the Current Events Chapter and Experts Chapter are not included in this Index.

Index

Foreign Trusts
- U.S. Information Return-Creation, 481
- with U.S. Beneficiaries, 481

Forensic genetic testing, 966

Forensics
- hypnosis uses, 613
- labs, 774

Forest fires, 1124

Forest preservation
- activity book, 1264, 1283, 1296

Forest rangers, 270, 1124

Forest Service, U.S.
- atmosphere sciences, 1125
- biodiversity, 1125
- camping areas, 408
- fire, 1125
- insect and disease reduction, 1027, 1124
- resource economics, 1125
- Smokey Bear, 1129
- volunteer programs, 383
- wood chemistry, 1125

Forestry Incentives Program, 756

Forests
- congressional task force, 1186
- educational material, 1270
- fire control, 1124, 1125
- grants, 360
- harvesting, 1130
- international assistance, 922, 1124
- management, 1125
- marijuana eradication, 607
- Pennsylvania, 1264, 1270, 1279
- protection programs, 1107
- reforestation, 1125
- research grants, 282
- resource management, 1126
- school curricula, 1264, 1270
- Senate Committee, 1180
- Teacher workshops, 1290
- tropical, 931, 970, 1031

Forfeiture, drug cases, 608

Forgery fraud, 432, 610

Formaldehyde hazards, 119

Forms, Inc., 630

Fortune magazine, 905

Fossil energy research, 764

Fossil fuel, 1068

Foster care
- community grants, 366
- grandparent program, 28, 378, 579
- program grants, 367

Foxes, 1270

Fractures, 1003

Franchises, 96, 770
- audiocassettes, videotapes, computer diskettes, 772
- buying assistance, 28, 772
- complaint line, 770
- Federal Trade Commission, 770
- International Franchise Assc., 772
- legal information, 772
- reference material, 772
- rule information hotline, 770, 771
- U.S. Small Business Administration, 773

Franchising information, state
- California, 655
- Hawaii, 655
- Illinois, 655
- Indiana, 656
- Maryland, 656
- Minnesota, 656
- New York, 656
- North Dakota, 656
- Oregon, 656
- Rhode Island, 656
- South Dakota, 656
- Virginia, 656

Washington, 656

Wisconsin, 656

Free booklets for travelers, 860

Free courses on how to prepare taxes, 454, 492

Free legal assistance, 854

Free legal help if you get audited, 455

Free tax help, 453

Freedom of Information
- accessible records, 1154
- administrative appeal procedures, 1159, 1164
- administrative review, 1154
- agency requirements, 1156, 1162
- agency responses, 1164
- books, 1153
- business transactions, 1153
- citizen's guide, 1153
- disclosure, 1153, 1154, 1156, 1160, 1162, 1164, 1165
- drug companies, 569
- Environmental Protection Agency, 1097
- exemptions, 1153, 1157, 1158, 1162
- Farm Credit Administration, 1026
- Federal Labor Relations Authority, 257, 270
- Federal Mediation and Conciliation Service, 258
- fees, 1155, 1162
- Interior, U.S. Department of the, 1100
- judicial appeal, 1160, 1165
- limitations, 1154
- maps, 1153
- medical devices, 570
- Nuclear Regulatory Commission, 1073
- Occupational Safety and Health Review Commission, 265
- Pension Benefit Guaranty Corporation, 252
- photographs, 1153
- Postal Rate Commission, 114
- Privacy Act, 1153, 1160-1162, 1164, 1165
- radiation, 567
- Railroad Retirement Board, 274
- regulations, 1162
- requests, 1153-1156
- sample request letters, 1166
- scope of, 1154
- Securities and Exchange Commission, 441
- state offices, 1154-1156, 1159
- state open records laws, 1153
- Transportation, U.S. Department of, 819
- violations, 1154

Freedom of speech, 923

Freer Gallery of Art, 316

Free treatment programs, 567

FTC
- *see Federal Trade Commission*

Fuel cell, 971

Fuel economy, 94, 818, 1050

Fuels
- alcohol plants permits, 1049
- alcohol, 1057, 1186
- alternatives from farm crops, 1027
- alternative, 818, 1067
- aviation, 1227
- biofuels, 1061
- biomass, 1050
- compressed natural gas, 818
- diesel pricing, 825, 1051
- distilled spirits, 775
- economy standards in motor vehicles, 94, 818, 1050
- efficiency, 101, 823, 1055
- ethanol, 818
- hardwood trees, 1027
- inventories and sales, 489
- methanol, 818

- motor vehicle usage, 827
- oil shale conversion, 1070
- synthetic, 976, 1050
- tax credits, 493, 827
- thermodynamic properties, 1015
- unleaded, 1064, 1117
- wood, 976, 1050, 1203

Fugitives, drug charges, 603

Fulbright scholarships, 157, 174, 305, 922

Fulbright-Hays
- seminars, 175
- training grants, 175

Funerals, 96-7

Fusion, 972, 1057, 1073

Fish and Wildlife Service, U.S.
- general interest publications, 1292, 1298

Forest Service, U.S.
- Alaskan Region, 696
- Eastern Region, 696
- Intermountain Region, 696
- Northern Region, 696
- Pacific Northwest Region, 696
- Pacific Southwest Region, 696
- Rocky Mountain Region, 696
- Southern Region, 696
- Southwestern Region, 696

G

Gale Research, Inc
- Encyclopedia of Associations, 654

Gallstones surgery, 547

Gambling winnings, tax on, 472, 485

Gambling, 610

Games of chance, 100

Gamma Ray Observatory, 983

Gardening, 140, 142, 976, 1023
- assistance, free, 140
- classes, 141
- county education programs, 1240
- disease diagnosis assistance, 141
- herb, 142, 976, 1203
- insects and bugs, 141, 1028
- landscape, 142, 976, 1203
- rose culture, 142, 515, 977, 1203
- tracer bullets, 1203
- weed control, 1029
- workshops, 140

Gas guzzler tax, 486

Gas, natural, 1261, 1270, 1278, 1283
- education-related material, 1270, 1278
- educational material, 1259, 1270
- exploration, 803, 1113, 1135
- liquefied natural, 971
- natural, 972

Gases, 1011

Gasohol, 971, 1224

Gasoline, 1227
- bond, 474
- consumption, 1224
- octane posting, 100
- sales, 827
- tax credit, 482

GATT
- *see General Agreement on Tariffs and Trade*

GATT standards, 1003

Gemini missions video, 1271, 1294

Gemstones, 100

Genealogical workshops, 29

Genealogy, 307, 308, 647, 1202
- child education, 1240
- military service records, 646, 647, 949, 955
- research guides, 647
- workshops, 29, 647

General Accounting Office, 869, 1190

The thousands of studies in the Current Events Chapter and Experts Chapter are not listed in this Index.

Index

General Agreement on Tariffs and Trade, 1003
General Services Administration
- *Doing Business With GSA,* 834
- Foreign Gifts, 702
- *GSA's Annual Report,* 834
- Miscellaneous Property, 699
- National Capitol Region, 700
- Office of Design and Construction, 834
- public information office, 66
- regional offices, 700

Generation-Skipping transfer tax, 473
Genetic diseases, 528, 574
Genetics, 526, 528, 529, 574, 1055
- animal, 1033
- applied, 970, 1031
- Cooley's anemia, 546
- disorder testing, 514, 970
- engineering, 1024
- engineering, 1099
- fish, 245, 1134
- forensic uses, 966
- heritable mutations, 515, 970
- international development, 930
- mapping, 514, 970
- plants, 1029
- research, 286, 768
- screening in workplace, 517
- spina bifida, 551
- testing, 514, 970
- therapy, 514, 970
- toxicology, 571
- transgenic animals, 974
- workplace screening, 517

Geodesy, 1086
Geographic Names Information Database, 29
Geography, 308, 1085, 1088-1090, 1101, 1202
- aerial photographs, U.S., 348, 1089, 1239
- census maps, 876
- database, 1217
- education, 153
- foreign policy issues, 922, 1089
- foreign, 1221
- maps, U.S., 1093
- names, 1222
- naming information, 345, 1089
- publication for parents, 1271
- world, 1232

Geological Survey, U.S., 296, 761, 1094
Geology, 309, 320, 1085, 1090, 1101, 1222, 1257, 1259, 1271, 1275
- Antarctic, 994, 1240
- caves, 994, 1085, 1240
- continental margins, 815, 1069
- cores, 991
- earthquakes, 993, 1092
- energy resources, 993, 1092
- environmental, 992
- Exclusive Economic Zone of the United States, 815, 1069
- hazards, 97, 1143
- international, 994
- landslides, 994
- maps, 992, 993, 1092, 1258
- marine, 992, 994, 1085, 1240
- mineral resources, 993, 1092
- naming and classification, 993, 1090
- offshore drilling, 815, 1069
- scientific publications, 993
- teaching aids, 1257, 1271, 1295
- teaching materials, 165, 991
- time, 1258, 1291
- volcanoes, 993, 1092

Geomagnetic and solar activity, 1238
Geophysics, 982, 992, 1085, 1101
George D. Hall Publishing Company, 665
Georgia
- Appalachian: grants and loans for site

development, 132
- Automated Tax Refund Information, 466
- Business Services and Regulations, 669
- Clerk of Superior Court at the County level, 631
- Clerk of the Superior Court, 630
- company directories, 665
- corporation information, 659
- Development Advances for Non-Profit Sponsors, 132
- Employment and Wages, 885
- Energy Fund, 132
- *Georgia Descriptions and Data - A Statistical Abstract,* 905
- Governor's Policy Statement, 909
- Homeless Shelter Programs, 132
- IRS hotlines, 464
- licensed professionals, 637
- Licensing boards and professions, 637
- Low-Income Housing Credit Program, 132
- Mortgage Credit Certificate Program, 132
- Motor Vehicle Records, 642
- Multi-family Bond Program, 132
- Occupational Employment, 885
- Rental Rehabilitation Program, 132
- Residential Finance Authority, 132
- Section 8 Existing Housing Assistance, 132
- Single-Family Home Ownership Loan Program, 132
- Small Business Administration Offices, 837
- state data centers, 900
- state information, 37
- State International Trade Offices, 858
- State Labor Office, 885
- State Planning Office, 909
- state procurement office, 841
- state tax assistance, 498
- surplus property auctions, 706
- Tax form distribution center, 470
- Tax forms and publications, 491
- unclaimed property office, 712
- U.S. International Trade Administration Office, 855

Geosciences research and grants, 288, 987
Geothermal energy, 764
Geriatrics
- *see also Aging,* 557
- educational grants, 170, 171, 185
- grants for veterans, 391

German Army records, 312
Gerontology, 557
Get-rich-quick schemes, 437
Geysers, 994, 1085, 1240
Ghettos, 876
Gift tax, 474
Ginnie Mae mortgage-backed, 121
Glaciers, 1085, 1111, 1240, 1258
- *Glaciers: A Water Resource,* 1271
- slides, 1285

Glaciology, 992
Glass, 1224
Glaucoma, 557, 973
Global climate change, 1054, 1125
Global demographics, 853
Goats, 1271
Goddard Space Flight Center, 990
Gold, 1258, 1085, 1240
- prospecting, 31, 1258, 1271

Gold Hill Publishing Company, 666
Government
- auctions, 695
- claims settlement, 616
- debt donations, 107, 1241
- federal payments, 432
- financial management, 431
- monthly income and expenses, 870
- program evaluation, 874

state and local grants, 375
Government contracts, 833
- bid and contract protests, 834
- Free Local Help, 836
- publications, 834
- Small Business Administration's 8(a) Program, 834
- small business set-asides, 836
- State Procurement Offices, 841
- subcontracting directory, 833, 834
- surety bond, 834
- U.S. Government purchasing and sales directory, 834
- women, 834

Government National Mortgage Association, 121
Government operations, 1184
Government Printing Office, U.S., 1019, 1212, 1213
Government procurement
- *Commerce Business Daily,* 833, 836
- Defense Logistics Agency, 836
- *Doing Business With the Department of ____,* 833
- Federal Procurement Data Center, 833
- *Guide to Specifications and Standards,* 834
- minority and labor surplus areas, 836
- Office of Small and Disadvantaged Business Utilization, 833
- small business set-asides, 836
- small business specialists, 834
- *Small Business Subcontracting Directory,* 834
- veterans, 836
- woman-owned businesses, 834, 836

Government-funded research, 840
Governmental affairs, 1182
Governmental bond issues, 486
Governor's Association, National, 346
Grain, 755, 931, 970, 1031
- exports, 1220
- grain storage, 929
- inspections, 1034
- small grains, 1029

Grants, 754
- Acquired Immunodeficiency Syndrome (AIDS), 765
- advanced study research, 307
- African development, 922
- aging research, 557, 768
- Agricultural Conservation Program, 756
- AIDS prevention programs, 538
- Air Force research, 941, 962
- Airport Improvement Program, 761
- American Indian Program, 759
- Anterior Segment Diseases, 768
- archival research projects, 305
- Army research, 943
- Arthritis, 767
- Biological Response to Environmental Health Hazards, 765
- Biomass Programs, 763
- biomedical research, 573
- Biophysics, 767
- Blood diseases, 767
- cancer, 541, 766, 767
- Capital Construction Fund, 761
- captioning for people with disabilities, 764
- cellular and molecular basis of disease research, 768
- coal technology, 764
- Colorado River Basin Salinity Control Program, 756
- commodity loans and purchases, 755
- community block development, 728
- community health programs, 344, 575
- computer and information science and engineering, 762

The thousands of studies in the Current Events Chapter and Experts Chapter are not included in this Index.

Index

Grants (continued)
conservation, 756, 763
Construction Reserve Fund, 761
cotton production stabilization, 755
criminal justice research, 613
cross discipline art, 292
Dairy Indemnity Program, 755
dance, 290, 762
deafness and communication, 766
demographics, 764
design arts, 762
diabetes, 767
diagnostic imaging research, 541
digestive diseases, 767
disabled--innovation and development, 764
disaster assistance, 354
document preservation, 308
drug abuse, 590, 766
Earthquake Hazards Reduction Program, 761
education for disabled children, 764
educational media and materials, 764
Emergency Conservation Program, 755
Emergency Livestock Assistance, 756
energy conservation, 763
Energy Extension Service, 763
energy sciences, 763
energy-related inventions, 763
essential air services, 762
family life research, 765
family planning services, 531
farms, 757
feed grain, 755
film/radio/television, 762
fire research, 1002
Fishermen's Contingency Fund, 758
Fishing Vessel and Gear Damage Compensation Fund, 758
folk arts, 762
food and drug research, 764
foreign agricultural market development and promotion, 758
foreign relations research, 310, 927
Forestry Incentives Program, 756
fossil energy, 764
genetics, 768
geology, 761
Grain Reserve Program, 756
Great Plains Conservation, 758
health care financing research, 767
health risks, 765
health-related research, 574
heart diseases, 767
human genome research, 766
industrial development, 757
injury prevention, 765
Interest Rate Reduction Program, 757, 759
international research, 307
jazz organizations, 291
kidney diseases, 767
literature, 762
lung diseases, 767
Market Promotion Program, 758
mental health research, 765, 766
minority AIDS education, 766
Minority Business and Industry Association, 759
Minority Business Development Centers, 758
minority health projects, 348
museum professionals, 319
music festivals, 291
music theater, 291
National Institutes of Health, 573
neurological research, 509, 551, 768
nuclear energy, 764
nursing research, 248

occupational safety and health, 766
opera-musical theater, 762
operating assistance for troubled multifamily housing, 760
operating-differential subsidies, 761
oral diseases, 765
pediatric AIDS, 765
pharmacology, 768
population research, 768
procurement technical assistance, 759
publication of scholarly texts, 307
publishing, 244, 247, 304, 308
renewable energy, 763
rental housing for lower income families, 760
reproductive disorders, 529
research for mothers and children, 768
retinal and choroidal diseases, 768
rice production, 756
runaway youth shelters, 535
rural clean water, 756
rural economic development, 758
rural health, 766
rural rental assistance, 757
science research, 957, 978
Service Corps of Retired Executives, 755
Small Business Innovation Research (SBIR), 756, 765
social services, 767
state historical records, 311
strabismus, amblyopia and visual processing, 769
Superfund technology, 762, 763
sustainable agriculture research, 757
technology integration, 764
theater, 290, 292, 762
toxicology, 765
Trade Adjustment Assistance, 758
transportation research, 823
veterans' homes, 393
visual arts, 762
Water Bank Program, 756, 761, 1118
Wheat production, 756
women's business ownership assistance, 755
Wool Act payments, 756
Graphic design, 762
Graphite, 1224
Gravity, 992
Grazing, 1028, 1126
Great Depression, 1271
Great Lakes, 1098
conservation grants, 361
education services, 159, 807, 1103, 1115
educational material, 1267, 1295
fish research, 1135
fisheries research, 1135
nautical charts, 805, 1093
pollution, 803, 1113, 1135
research grants, 282
videocassettes, 1267, 1295
Great Plains conservation, 360, 758
Greenhouse effect, 977, 1083, 1084, 1098, 1103
Greenhouses, 1061
Gross National Product, 93, 873
Ground water, 972, 1098, 1112, 1258, 1271, 1296
contamination, 962
GSA
see General Services Administration
Guam
data centers, 900
taxes, 472, 483
Guided weapons systems, 953
Guns, drugs, 603
Guthrie, Woody, recordings, 1271, 1273, 1276, 1285
Gynecology, 528
Gypsy moths, 140, 1027

H

Haiti, development, 924
Halfway houses, veterans drug abusers, 596
Halley's Comet, 1252, 1272, 1286, 1289
Halocarbons, 1083, 1109
Handguns, ammunition, 1005
Handicapped, 176
access to buildings, 121
affirmative action, 146
arts activities, 317
assistance loans, 146
books for the blind, 1201
construction grants, 381
drug rehabilitation, 595
education and development, 148, 153
educational grants, 174, 175, 177, 187
educational research grants, 175
employment, federal, 268, 389
employment laws, 237, 251, 626
employment program grants, 179
employment with government contracts, 236
employment with Postal Service, 273
foster grandparent volunteers, 383
grants for blind elderly, 389
grants for instructors, 189
grants for media, 179
grants for teachers, 175
grants, 178, 381, 386, 389
guide to the Smithsonian, 316
housing access, 119
housing loans, 369
infant/toddler grants, 179
instructional materials, 175
legal services, 619
loans, 755
mail programs, 115
mass transit access problems, 352, 820
preschool grants, 382
rehabilitation programs, 564, 1227
research grants, 289
SEC information on audio cassette, 442
Senate subcommittee, 1182
Social Security insurance, 387
speech, 563
statistics, 146
tax information, 465, 496
teaching grants, 178
technology, 971
transportation, 819
travel information, 421
visitors to U.S., 420
Harbors, 1184
Harris Publishing Company, 665-667
Hawaii
Affirmative Action, 885
Automated Tax Refund Information, 466
Business Registration Division, 669
Communication Industry, 885
company directories, 665
corporation information, 659
Drivers and Owners: Division of Motor Vehicles and Licenses, 642
education grants, 181
Franchises, 771
Housing Authority, 132
Housing Finance Revolving Fund, 132
Hula Mae Single-Family Program, 132
IRS hotlines, 464
Job Hunters's Guide, 885
Labor Shortages in Agriculture, 885
Licensing boards and professions, 637
Modernization and Maintenance, 132
Occupational Employment Statistics, 885
professionals, 637

The thousands of studies in the Current Events Chapter and Experts Chapter are not listed in this Index.

Index

Public Housing Projects, 132
Section 8 Certificate/Voucher Programs, 132
Small Business Administration Offices, 837
state data centers, 900
state information, 37
State International Trade Offices, 858
State Labor Office, 885
State of Hawaii Statistical Abstract, 905
State Planning Office, 909
state procurement office, 841
State Rent Supplement Program, 132
state tax assistance, 498
surplus property auctions, 706
Tax form distribution center, 470
Tax forms and publications, 491
Tax Reform: Multi-Family Program, 132
unclaimed property office, 712
Uniform Commercial Code, 631
U.S. International Trade Administration Office, 856
Wage Rate, 885
Workers Compensation, 885
Hawaiian Natives drug abuse, 592
Hazardous chemicals, 505
Hazardous materials
bulletin board, 1235
House Subcommittee on, 1183
transportation accidents, 357, 820-21, 826, 1144
Hazardous substances, occupational, 508
Hazardous waste, 359, 972, 1098, 1144
detoxifying, 1063
management program grants, 378
Head injuries, 509, 540, 547
prevention, 547
rehabilitation, 547
Head Start research grants, 285
Head-on collisions, 96, 825
Health
ambulatory care, 508
bibliography, 508
Centers for Disease Control, 504
certification grants, 367
clinical nutrition research, 521
Combined Health Information Database, 549
community centers, 365
disease prevention goals, 518
ethics, 1216
Federation Information Catalog, 517
financing research, 767
grants, 363, 364
grants for facilities, 368
grants for instructors, 170
Health Professionals Training, 171
health sciences databases, 504
home health care, 364
House Committee on Health Care, 1183
information service, 504
international programs, 571, 1100
loans for hospitals, 369
migrant worker health, 344, 345, 350, 575, 576
minorities, health, 348
Minority Health Education, 170
National Center for Health Statistics, 575
National Health and Nutrition Examination Survey, 575
National Health Information Center, 507, 1207
National Health Interview Survey, 575
National Health Service Corps Program, 345, 350, 576
National Hospital Discharge Survey, 575
National Nursing Home Survey, 575
Native Americans, 507
Nurse Anesthetist Traineeships, 182
Nurse Practitioner Traineeships, 183
policy and research evaluations, 576
prevention project grants, 517
preventive services, 518
programs for refugees, 387
Project Share, 1228
promotion grants, 369
promotion programs, 263, 517, 523
Public Health Traineeships, 185
research grants, 171, 183, 185, 282-288, 364
resource database, 1216
risk assessment, 517, 572
rural areas, 518, 1187
screening tests, 518
statistics, 575, 576
student grants, 182
student loans, 183
Surgeon General, 502, 518
technology, 566, 972
training for veterans, 157
urban and rural areas, 346, 576
volunteers, 383
women, 505
workplace evaluations, 262
World Health Organization, 576
Health and Human Services, U.S. Department of
public information offices, 47
Small Business Innovative Research Program, 840
Health care facilities
construction guidelines, 567
energy conservation, 566
financing, 566, 767
Health care profession
credentialing, 270
disease control training, 244
education, 244
Epidemic Intelligence Service, 245
epidemiology training, 245
gerontology career training, 557
gynecologists, 529
industrial hygiene courses, 248, 262
international health sciences, 574
medical scientist training, 247
National Health Service Corps, 250
nursing research, 248
obstetricians, 529
Practitioner Reporting System, 569
program research, 244
publications, 505, 528, 575
resource development, 270
scholarships, 29
selecting physicians, 96
Health centers grants, 362
Health foods, 525
Health hazards, environmental, 765
Health Information Center, National, 507, 1207
Health Information Hotline, 29
Health risks, environmental exposures, 765
Health spas, 96
Health, National Institutes of
Computer Retrieval of Information on Scientific Projects, 574
grants information, 574
National Cancer Institute, 502, 540, 541
National Eye Institute, 504, 547
National Heart, Lung, and Blood Institute, 506, 574
National Institute for Occupational Safety and Health, 262, 263, 531, 571, 572
National Institute of Allergy and Infectious Diseases, 538, 539, 548, 549
National Institute of Arthritis and Musculoskeletal and Skin Diseases, 509, 537, 539, 540, 547
National Institute of Child Health and Human Development, 526-530, 535
National Institute of Dental Research, 517
National Institute of Environmental Health Sciences, 571
National Institute of General Medical Sciences, 528, 574
National Institute of Mental Health, 507, 533, 535, 546, 573
National Institute of Neurological Disorders and Stroke, 509
National Institute of Occupation Safety and Health, 262
National Institute on Aging, 557
National Institute on Alcohol Abuse and Alcoholism, 577
National Institute on Deafness and Other Communicative Disorder, 509, 565
publications bibliography, 508
technology assessment and transfer, 568
homeless care, 344, 345, 350, 575, 576
Hearing aid dealers, 635
Hearing aids, 558
Hearing impairment, 514, 970, 973
Heart attacks, 1014
risk factors, 548
Heart disease, 506
balloon dilation, 548
cholesterol, 544
diagnosis and treatment, 548
diet, 523
mitral valve prolapse, 550
research, 767
research grants, 286
risk factors, 523
transplantation, 574
videos, 548
Heat pumps, 1061
Heat, solar, 1261, 1272, 1287
Heavy Vehicle Use Tax Return, 480
Helium, 948
Help In Selling To Developing Nations, 851
Help With Selling Commodities Abroad, 852
Hemodialysis, 973
Henry, Joseph, 303
Herbicides
narcotic plants, 603
Herbicides, 414, 1109
Herbs, 140, 141, 142, 1027, 1203
Heroin, 608, 613
Herpes, 549
HHS

see Health and Human Services, U.S. Department of

High blood pressure, 521, 548
smoking, 553
Spanish publications, 548
High risk youth, 579
drugs, 588
High-technology
research and development, 983
Highways, 777, 819, 822, 932, 979
accidents, 818, 895
assistance to foreign governments, 824, 914
beautification, 292, 822, 826, 1107
bicycle paths, 403
construction contracts, 777, 826
construction grants, 373
construction safety, 352, 826
drunk drivers, 599, 603
environmental impact, 292, 822, 826, 1107
fatal accidents, 353
grants, 374
impact of, 826
Junkyards, the Highway, and Visual Quality, 353
noise abatement, 826
relocation assistance, 353, 829

The thousands of studies in the Current Events Chapter and Experts Chapter are not included in this Index.

Index

Highways (continued)
speed limit, 98, 352, 614, 828
statistics, 827
Hijacking, 788, 941
Hill-Burton Hospital Free Care, 567, 568
Hiring incentives, 777
Hirshorn Museum and Sculpture Garden, 317
Hispanics
congressional caucus, 1186
drug abuse hotline, 593
Historic home renovation loans, 29
Historic preservation
environmental issues, 292, 822, 826, 1107
Historic Sites of the U.S., 307, 401
Housing Rehab: Programs, Techniques and Resources, 120
ideas, 29
List of Classified Structures, 403
National Historic Landmarks Program, 306
National Parks, 304, 317, 403
tax incentives, 306, 350
Historical landmarks, 306, 397
History, 1212
Air Force aviation, 940
American, 317
American agriculture, 142, 976, 1203
American war memorials, 396
arms control and disarmament, 935
Army medicine, 942
audiovisual materials, 294
aviation, 161, 944
Capitol, U.S., 1241
census records, 864
civil rights enforcement, 627
criminal, 974
federal laws, 616
legal, 609
legislation, 1188
local, 308, 647, 1202
Marine Corps, 950
Maryland, 310
medical, 951
military test flights, 960
military, 303, 314, 940-942, 950
National Parks, 407
personal, 1227
Philadelphia, 310
prisons, 616
rural post offices, 114
science and technology, 303, 314
Senate, U.S., 1190
technology, 977, 1203
U.S. Capitol, 307
U.S. foreign policy, 923
United States, 314
visual arts in America, 315
Washington, D.C., 1241
HIV
see AIDS
Holding companies, 438
Homes
asbestos, 111
crime insurance, 349, 611
economics workshops, 29
energy audits, 1055
flood hazards, 356
historic renovation loans, 29
home equity credit lines, 96
indoor air quality, 111
insulation safety, 111
low-income repair loans, 125
mortgage interest deduction tax, 497
neighborhood crime, 610
property title, 126
radon levels, 1103
solar heat conversion, 1061
tax information, 494

Home sales
Tax Information, 494
Tax related forms for people over 55, 480
Home-based business tips, 29
Home-based industries, 237
Homeless
alcohol program grants, 364
assistance program, 363
community support, 362
drug program grants, 364
education grants, 179
emergency services grants, 368
grants, 360
program grants, 363
shelters, 124
surplus property for shelters, 124
Homeless, housing assistance
California Emergency Shelter Program, 131
California Federal Emergency Shelter Grant Program, 131
California Permanent Housing for the Handicapped Homeless Program, 131
California Rental Security Deposit Guarantee Demonstration Program, 131
Delaware Emergency Shelter Grants Program, 132
Georgia Homeless Shelter Programs, 132
Idaho Stewart B. McKinney Permanent Housing Program, 133
Iowa Homeless-Shelter Assistance, 133
Kansas Permanent Housing for Handicapped, 133
Kentucky Permanent Housing for Homeless Handicapped Persons, 133
Maine Homeless Shelter Assistance, 133
Massachusetts Chapter 707 Transitional Housing Program, 134
Michigan Emergency Housing Apartment Program, 134
Michigan Homeless Children's Fund, 134
Michigan Housing for the Handicapped, 134
Minnesota $1.00 Home Set-Aside Program, 135
Missouri Operation Homeless, 135
New Jersey Transitional Housing Program, 136
Oklahoma Homeless Program, 137
South Dakota Emergency Shelter Grants Program, 138
Homemakers, 971
Homeowners Associations
U.S. Income Tax Return, 479
Homes, financing
adjustable rate mortgages, 120
Department of Housing and Urban Development, 697
Farmers Home Administration, 696
H.O.P.E., 697
mortgage lock-ins, 120
mortgage refinancing, 120
Veterans Administration, 698
Homesteading program assistance, 370
Homicide, 612
Honey, 1029
Horses, adoption, 1138, 1215, 1242
Horticulture, 140, 141, 1027
classes, free, 141
therapy, 141
Hospitals, 759
construction, 566
cost controls, 566
emergency room injury data, 506
energy conservation, 1056
insurance (Medicare) tax, 474

loans to, 369, 566
national survey, 576
state mental health institutions, 535
stay length, 973
veterans drug abuse research, 596
Hotlines
agriculture news, 1023
AIDS, 537
air toxics, 1109, 1111
alcohol, tobacco, and firearms, 94
arson, 96, 110
automobile safety, 94, 420, 818, 1227
banking consumer complaints, 105, 427
boating safety, 414
business, state, 727
Consumer Product Safety Commission, 1108
consumer product-related injuries, 109
criminal statistics, 879
drug abuse, 593, 595
drug smuggling, 600
drug-free workplace helpline, 590
employment discrimination, 627
energy conservation, 1062
environmental, 1099
EPA employment, 269
equal employment, 627
explosives, 96, 110
Forest Service Drug Reporting, 603
free medical care, 567, 568
hazardous waste regulations, 1103
hazardous waste, 1144
inmate locator, 614, 647
meats and poultry complaints, 98, 1034, 1035
oil spills, 806, 1114, 1145
plant care, 141
recorded message, 93
renewable energy, 1061
retirement plans tax, 455
runaways, 535
safe drinking water, 1103, 1115
savings bonds, 445
second surgical opinions, 509, 570
sexually transmitted diseases, 537
small business and EPA regulation, 718, 1104
small business, 717
Spanish drug abuse hotline, 593
taxes on retirement plans, 456
technology commercialization, 1050
toll-free drug abuse, 586
toxic spills, 355, 1143, 1145
transportation of hazardous materials, 1144
travel and tourism, state, 422
unleaded fuels, 1064, 1117
veterans exposed to radiation, 943
veterans insurance, 392
waste minimization, 1152
Houdini, Harry, 292, 311, 1203
House of Representatives
administration and management, 1184
Clerk, 1190
Code of Official Conduct, 1185
committee listing, 1190
Doorkeeper, 1190
governing rules, 1184
legislative process, 1184
library, 1190
recorded message, 93
Speaker, 1189
tours, 397
Ways and Means committee, 1185
Household employers employment tax, 475, 497
Housing, 757
access for the handicapped, 119
Agricultural finance programs, 131, 135,

The thousands of studies in the Current Events Chapter and Experts Chapter are not listed in this Index.

Index

American Housing Survey, 119, 861
community loans, 369
community reinvestment programs, 348
developing countries, 923
development grants, 370
disabled persons, 119
disabled veterans, 394
discrimination, 121, 122, 629
discrimination hotline, 29
earth-sheltered, 1061
economic and policy analyses, 122
energy audits, 1055
energy consumption, 1062, 1229
environmental hazard removal, 130, 133
escrow accounts, 96
fair housing plans, 121
FHA-insured mortgage programs, 123
finance agencies (HFAs), 130
first time financing, 122
free counseling, 120
grants, 359, 371
homeless citizens, 119
House Committee on, 1183
housing discrimination agencies, 122
HUD anti-drug efforts, 607
HUD-approved counseling agencies, 122
loan financing, 120
low-income household assistance, 123
manufactured homes, 120, 123
military relocation assistance, 956
minority assistance, 131, 134
mobile home manufacturing, 123
multifamily properties, 123
Native Americans, 123, 150, 626, 629, 1127
outlying areas mortgages, 126
program grants, 369
public, 120, 584, 599, 607,
rehabilitation grants, 370
rental rate survey, 123
repair loans, 347, 1027
research, 123
settlement costs, 123
single-family home auctions, 124
statistics, 863, 868, 873, 876, 877
temporary, 357
urban homesteading, 120, 124
Housing and Urban Development, U.S. Department of
counseling services, 122
Indian Programs Office, 697
Programs of HUD, 697, 702
Property Disposition facilities, 697
public information offices, 51
regional offices, 697
repossessed homes, 695
Urban Homesteading Program, 697
Housing coops, mortgage insurance, 126
Hubble Space Telescope, 986, 989, 1253, 1272, 1291
HUD
see Housing and Urban Development, U.S. Department of
Human genome research, 766
Human rights, 923
congressional caucus, 1186
foreign policy, 924
House Subcommittee on, 1184
international complaints, 237
U.S. violations, 930
Humanities
educational grants, 172
grants, 186
preservation research grants, 287
research grants, 172, 186, 287
student grants, 186
Human Specimen Bank, 573
Hunger, 913

House Select Committee on, 1185
Hunting, waterfowl, 1137
Huntington's Disease, 509
family roster, 549
Hurricane Hugo, 942
Hurricanes, 755, 358, 1087
films, 1268, 1297
preparedness grants, 380
safety, 357
slides, 1272, 1286, 1297
videos, 1272, 1295, 1297
Hydrobiology, 1103, 1118, 1148, 1151
Hydrocarbons, 1003, 1216
Hydrogeology, 962
Hydrology
maps, 1090
National Environmental Data Clearinghouse, 1085, 1101
regional hydrologists, 1115
soil conservation, 1030, 1129
Water Resources Activities of the Geological Survey in (State), 1119
Hydroponics, 1028
Hydropower energy, 1062
Hydrothermal processes, 1084
Hypnosis, forensic uses, 613
Hypothermia, elderly, 556

I

ICC
see Interstate Commerce Commission
Ice
Coast Guard, 410, 611, 1096
Marines Weather Log, 412, 803
National Ocean Service, 1113
Navigational Weather Log, 967
Ice breaker expeditions, 29, 292, 401, 415
Ice technology, 412, 803, 1113
Idaho
Affirmative Action, 885
Area Employment Newsletter, 885
Automated Tax Refund Information, 466
Bureau of Land Management Offices, 695
company directories, 665
corporation information, 659
Department of Self-Governing Agencies, Bureau of Occupational, 637
Economic Development Agenda, 909
Employment and Wages by Industry, 885
Housing Agency, 132
Idaho Blue Book, 905
IRS hotlines, 464
licensed professionals, 637
Low-Income Housing Tax Credit Program, 133
Mortgage Credit Certificates, 132
Multi-Family Housing Financing, 133
Rental Rehabilitation Program, 133
Section 8 Existing Certificate and Voucher Program, 133
Section 8 Moderate Rehabilitation Program, 132
Section 8 New Construction/Substantial Rehabilitation Program, 132
Securities Bureau, Department of Finance, 669
Single Family Mortgage Purchase Program, 132
Small Business Administration Offices, 837
state data centers, 900
state information, 37
State International Trade Offices, 858
State Labor Office, 885

State Planning Office, 909
state procurement office, 841
state tax assistance, 498
Stewart B. McKinney Permanent Housing Program for Handicapped, 133
surplus property auctions, 706
Tax form distribution center, 470
Tax forms and publications, 491
Transportation Department, Economics and Research Section, 642
unclaimed property office, 712
Uniform Commercial Code Division, 631
U.S. International Trade Administration Office, 856
Identifying overseas opportunities, 852
Iguanas, 926
Illinois
Affirmative Action, 885
Affordable Housing Trust Fund, 133
Annual Report, 909
Automated Tax Refund Information, 466
company directories, 665
Congregate Housing Finance Program, 133
corporation information, 659
Department of Professional Regulations, 637
Drivers Services Division, 642
Employment Industrial Summary, 885
Franchises, 771
Homebuyer Program, 133
Housing Development Authority, 133
IRS hotlines, 464
Labor Market Review, 885
licensed professionals, 637
Moderate Rehabilitation Program, 133
Occupational Employment Statistics, 885
Securities Department, 669
Small Business Administration Office, 837
state data centers, 901
state information, 37
State International Trade Offices, 858
State Labor Office, 885
State Planning Office, 909
state procurement office, 841
state tax assistance, 498
Statistical Abstract, 905
surplus property auctions, 706
Tax form distribution center, 470
Tax forms and publications, 491
unclaimed property office, 713
Uniform Commercial Code Division, 631
U.S. International Trade Administration Office, 856
wild mammals, 1266, 1274
wildlife conservation activities, 1272
Immigration and naturalization
"green" cards, 623, 913
alien registration cards, 623, 913
asylum, 924
drugs, 605
emergency travel requests, 623, 930
Immigration and Naturalization Service, 623
orphan petitions, 924
permanent resident status, 623, 924
political asylum, 625, 929
Senate committee, 1182
student visas, 623, 931
temporary visas, 623, 927
work visas, 623, 931
Immigration and Naturalization Service, 623
Immune system, 538
Immunization
community grants, 365
goals, 518
vaccines, 517

The thousands of studies in the Current Events Chapter and Experts Chapter are not included in this Index.

Index

Importing-exporting, 972
agriculture, 1038, 1041, 1221
agriculture pricing alerts, 1220
archeological materials, 318
arms and ammunition, 110, 1225
coal, 971
databases, 1222, 1228
developing countries, 417
distilled spirits, wines, and beer, 775
electricity, 1059
farm products, 1039
fish products, 799
foreign buyers, 1221
foreign policy issues, 610, 933
grain, 1034, 1220
international food shows, 1039
military equipment, 936, 938
natural gas, 1059
nuclear materials, 1073
oil and gas, 1060
pharmaceutics, 569
plant and animal certification, 1037, 1040
pleasure boats, 417
price changes, 1223
price indexes, 241, 877
U.S. agriculture, 1039
vehicles, 100
wildlife and pets, 418
Incineration, ocean, 975
Income tax, 496
indebtedness, 475
individual tax model, 456
preparation services, 96
retirement trust account, 483-84
statistics, 456
tax practitioners, 456
tax return preparers credit, 485
estate tax, 473
Incubators, small business, 722
Indians, American, 1272
see also Native Americans
arts, 1267, 1272
corporation loans, 757
drug abuse, 595
drug education, 592
health services, 507
land areas, 1273
languages, 1273
legal services, 621, 629
Smithsonian visiting program, 1273
tribal school drug education, 592
Indiana
Automated Tax Refund Information, 466
company directories, 665
corporation information, 659
Drivers and Owners: Indiana Bureau of Motor Vehicles, 642
Franchises, 771
Housing Finance Authority, 133
Indiana: Its Economy, Its People, 905
Infrastructure, 909
IRS hotlines, 464
licensed professionals, 637
Low-Income Housing Tax Credit, 133
Low-Income Housing Trust Fund, 133
Multi-Family Program, 133
Occupational Wage Surveys, 885
Professional Licensing Agency, 637
Property Tax Abatement, 909
Securities Division, 669
Single-Family Program, 133
Small Business Administration Office, 837
Small Business Development Centers, 736
Some Aspects of Demographic Change in Indiana from 1980 to 2000, 907
state data centers, 901
state information, 37

State International Trade Offices, 858
State Labor Office, 885
State Planning Office, 909
state procurement office, 841
state tax assistance, 498
Strategic Economic Development Plan, 909
surplus property auctions, 706
Tax form distribution center, 470
Tax forms and publications, 491
unclaimed property office, 713
Uniform Commercial Code Division, 631
U.S. International Trade Administration Office, 856
Vocational Education, 909
Indian Health Service, 507
Indian reservations, 865
Indoor air quality, 998
Indoor tanning, 96
Industrial development grants, 757
Industrial hygiene, 263
health hazard evaluation, 262
Industries
drug-free helpline, 590
maritime, 974
service, 870
steel, U.S., 971
Industry directories, 907
INF Treaty, 936
Infectious diseases, 538
immune system, 549
Rocky Mountain Spotted Fever, 549
schistosomiasis, 549
Infertility, 514, 970, 973
treatments, 529
Inflation, 866
Information
companies, 649, 657
franchising companies, 655
on demand, 29
research techniques, 8
return trust allocation of an accumulation, 477
Information Agency, U.S.
Arts America, 859
Information USA, 649
Infrared, 976
Injuries
clearinghouse, 506
hospital emergency room data, 506
Injury Information Clearinghouse, National, 110
prevention, 765
Inland waterways, 822, 932, 979
Inmate locator line, 29, 614, 647
Insanity, criminal defense, 612
Insect control, 806, 928, 1225
Insects
control, 142, 976, 1203
transmission of AIDS, 972
Insider trading, 438
Installment sale income, 486, 494
Institute of Standards and Technology, National
cooperative research, 1000
research and testing facilities, 1009
tours, 397, 1015
Insular Islands, 1100
Insulation, 111, 1061
Insurance, 754
AIDS, 972
alcoholism treatment coverage, 577
Arts and Artifacts Indemnity, 762
Bond Guarantees for Surety Companies, 755
common carriers, 825
complaints, 29
congressional caucus, 1186
crime, 28, 349, 611

Crop Insurance, 758
federal credit unions, 433
financial institutions, 1183
Fishermen's Guaranty Fund, 761
flood, 356
Foreign Investment Insurance, 763
hazard, 356
health, 973
Maritime War Risk Insurance, 761
Medicare, 972
pension plans, 253
prescription drugs, 566
Protection of Ships from Foreign Seizure, 761
questions, 29
railroad unemployment, 274
regulation studies, 94
tax related forms, 484
unemployment, 1230
veterans, 392
war risk for ships, 809, 934
Insurance agents, 635
Insurance companies, 490, 761
Intellectual property, 973
Intensive care units, 973
Inter-American Development Bank, 853
Inter-American Foundation, 67
Inter-Arts Program, 292
Inter-company Transfer Price or Commission, 479
Interagency Council on the Homeless, 702
Interest and dividend income, 476
Interest expense tax guide, 495
Interest rates
bulletin board, 1235
reduction program, 757
Interior design, 762
Interior, U.S. Department of the, 1100
Bureau of Indian Affairs, 1099
Bureau of Land Management, 695
Bureau of Mines, 810-812, 814-816
Bureau of Reclamation, 1055
Bureau of Reclamation, 811, 1123
Earth Science Information Office, 991
Minerals Management Service, 810, 815, 1126
National Park Service, 407, 1127
Office of Surface Mining Reclamation and Enforcement, 810, 816, 1129
public information offices, 51
Youth Conservation Corps, 250, 1130
Internal Revenue Service, 457
appeals, 460
assistance through the media, 457
automated refunds, 466
Bulletin Index - Digest System, 461
delinquent child support payments, 457
community outreach, 457
corporation tax statistics, 453
criminal investigations, 457
electronic tax filing, 454
foreign language assistance, 454
free courses on tax preparation, 454
free legal help if you get audited, 455
free publications, 491
future tax legislation, 455
historian, 455
retirement plans, 455
in-house IRS audit manuals, 456
international taxes, 457
money laundering, 606
obtaining prior year tax returns, 459
penalties and interest, 459
problem resolution staff, 462
regional offices, 458
Service Centers, 458
Small Business Tax Education Course, 459

The thousands of studies in the Current Events Chapter and Experts Chapter are not listed in this index.

Index

speakers and customized seminars, 458
Special Enrollment Agents, 458
tax audits, 460
tax counseling for the elderly, 460
Tax Forms Distribution Centers, 470
unclaimed refunds, 459
videos and films, 462
Wage Reporting, 462
International assistance
agriculture development, 919
health policy, 576
Peace Corps, 919
International boycott, 485
International business
ABC's of exporting, 855
Agency For International Development (AID), 848
Agent Distributor Service, 849, 850
agricultural products, 850
Alaska Trade Directory, 664
Basic Guide to Exporting, 854
Business America, 855
Caribbean Basin opportunities, 849
catalog exhibitions, 850
Commercial News USA, 854
company and industry directories, 857
customized export mailing lists, 849
customized market studies, 849
ex-communist countries, 849
export marketing seminars, 857
Export Programs: A Business Directory of U.S. Government Resources, 855
export regulations and product standards, 851
export tax exemption certificate, 480
Export Trading Company (ETC) Guidebook, 855
export-import bank financing, 848
Exporter's Guide to Federal Resources for Small Business, 854
exporter's hotline, 843
foreign buyer program, 850
foreign demographic profiles, 851
foreign labor trends, 855
foreign service posts, 855
free newsletters, 857
Gold Key Service, 850
help in selling to developing nations, 851
help with selling commodities abroad, 852
identifying overseas opportunities, 852
International Trade Administration field offices, 843
investment missions, 850
investments, 853
export loans, 848
marketing research and company intelligence, 847, 857
matchmaker trade delegations, 850
National Trade Data Bank, 853
New Product Information Service, 849
Office Space for Agricultural Exporters, 850
overseas contacts, 857
Overseas Private Investment Corporation (OPIC), 848
Persian Gulf development opportunities, 849
planning services for exporters, 852
Small Business Administration Export Loans, 848
state government money and assistance, 848, 857
state International Trade Offices, 858
trade fairs, 850
trade leads databases, 857
trade missions, 850
Trade Opportunities Program (TOP), 850
Trade Promotion Coordinating Committee, 843
Trade Remedy Assistance Center, 853
travel and tourism, 850
U.S. International Trade Administration Field Offices, 855
U.S. Seminar Missions, 850
U.S. Specialized Trade Missions, 850
videos, 850
world import/export statistics, 851
world traders data reports, 849
International development
agriculture, 912
child health, 916
child survival, 916
International drug trafficking, 599
International Energy Agency, 1051
International Energy Data Base, 853
International Expertise, 853
International Franchise Association, 772
International Franchising Association (IFA), 773
International Labor Organization, 237, 933
International Monetary Fund, 853
International Prices, 852
International Relations
global ecology, 931, 938
human rights, 931, 938
United States Institute of Peace, 931, 938
Internships, 32
building technology, 1003
dietetic, 391
management, public, 273
military history, 950
Native Americans, 308, 320
Smithsonian Institution, 321
space technology research, 958, 989
Interpol drug cases, 608
Interstate Commerce Commission, 777, 827
decisions and notices, 827
legal documents, 828
library, 778
public information office, 67
speakers, 828
Interstate holding companies, 438
Interstate land sales fraud-line, 30
Invention financing
aging research, 768
agriculture research and education, 757
arthritis, 767
blood diseases, 767
cancer, 766, 767
cellular and molecular basis of disease, 768
deafness and communication, 766
diabetes, 767
digestive diseases, 767
disabled--innovation and development, 764
drug abuse research, 766
educational research, 764
energy-related inventions, 763
family life research grants, 765
food and drug administration research, 764
genetics, 768
government purchases of inventions, 840
health care financing, 767
heart and vascular diseases, 767
human genome, 766
injury prevention, 765
kidney diseases, 767
lung diseases, 767
mental health, 766
mortgage insurance--experimental projects, 760
mothers and children research, 768
neurological disorders, 768
neurosciences, 768
nutrition research, 767
occupational safety, 766
oral diseases, 765
population research, 768
retinal and choroidal diseases, 768
Small Business Innovation Research (SBIR), 756, 765
social services research, 767
Inventions, 729, 977, 1203
commercialization, 1015
development grants, 1008
energy-related, 1002
evaluation assistance, 1008
grants, 288
marketing, 1008
patents, trademarks and copyrights, 1017
workshops, 1007
Investment credit
computation forms, 481
general business credit tax, 481
recapture, 482
Investment guaranties, foreign, 763
Investment income and expenses, 495
Investment loans, 763
Investment missions, 850
Investments
abroad, 869
adviser registration, 438
biotechnology, 970
company prospectus, 440
consumer guide, 106, 436
foreign investment in U.S., 869, 1223
fraudulent schemes, 440
residential mortgage market, 121
telephone investment fraud, 96
Treasury securities, 428
unit investment trust, 441
variable annuity, 441
Iowa
A Statistical Profile of Iowa, 907
Affirmative Action, 886
Automated Tax Refund Information, 466
Bureau of Professional Licensing, 637
Closing Cost Assistance, 133
company directories, 665
corporation information, 660
Department of Transportation, Drivers Services, 642
Economic Development Loan Program, 133
Employment and Unemployment Information, 886
Finance Authority, 133
Homeless Shelter Assistance, 133
Housing Assistance Fund Program, 133
Industry/Occupational Projections, 886
IRS hotlines, 464
Labor Market Information Directory, 886
licensed professionals, 637
Low-Income Housing Tax Credit Program, 133
Mortgage Credit Certificate Program, 133
Securities Bureau, Office of Commissioner of Insurance, 669
Single-Family Mortgage Loans, 133
Small Business Administration Office, 837
Small Business Loan Program, 133
state data centers, 901
state information, 37
State International Trade Offices, 858
State Labor Office, 886
State Planning Office, 909
state procurement office, 841
state tax assistance, 499
Statistical Profile, 909
Statistical Profile of Iowa, 905
surplus property auctions, 706
Targeted Area Assistance Program, 133
Tax form distribution center, 470

The thousands of studies in the Current Events Chapter and Experts Chapter are not included in this Index.

Index

Iowa (continued)
Tax forms and publications, 491
Title Guaranty Program, 133
unclaimed property office, 713
Uniform Commercial Code Division, 631
U.S. International Trade Administration Offices, 856
Wage Surveys, 886
Iraq, 453
Ireland, 1186
Irrigation, 1030, 1129, 1184
IRS
see Internal Revenue Service
ITA
See United States International Trade Administration

J

Jails, 1224
Jamaica, unemployed women, 924
Japan
science and technology, 979
technical resources, 968
technology, 977, 1203
Japanese war relocation, 647, 951
Jelly beans, 8
Jenkins, Ella
recordings, 1271, 1273, 1276, 1285
Jennings Randolph Program for International Peace, 307, 937
Jet Propulsion Laboratory, 990
Jewelry, consumer laws, 777
Job counseling fraud, 237, 252
Jobs
see also Employment and Workplace
air traffic controllers, 26
bulletin board, 1233, 1235, 1238
federal government, 30
retraining, 30
safety Inspections On-Site, 30
Securities and Exchange Commission, 248
summer, 275
tax credit, 485
trends, 30
Youth Conservation Corps, 250, 1141
John F. Kennedy Center for the Performing Arts, 1273, 1277, 1287
John F. Kennedy Space Center, 990
Johnson Space Center Bulletin Board, 1235
Joint Chiefs of Staff, 950
Joseph Henry Papers, 303
Journalism
foreign press centers, 921
polar expeditions, 292, 401, 415
Judicial Branch, 40, 620
Judiciary
House Committee on, 1184
Junk bonds, 436
Jupiter, 1273, 1284
slides, 1273, 1286, 1288, 1289
videos, 1273, 1278, 1288, 1293, 1295
Justice, U.S. Department of
anti-drug coordination, 606
public information offices, 54
Juveniles
clearinghouse, 583
delinquency data, 606, 614
drug users, 584
offenders, 599
professional training, 606
respect for laws, 593

K

Kansas, 668
Affirmative Action, 886
Association Directory, 909
Automated Tax Refund Information, 466
company directories, 665
corporation information, 660
Directory of Kansas Warehouse and Distribution Centers, 908
Drivers: Topeka Drivers Licenses Bureau, 642
Economic Development Statutes, 909
Emergency Shelter Grant Program, 133
IRS hotline, 464
Job Shops, 909
Labor Force Estimates, 886
Labor Market Summary, 886
licensed professionals, 637
Licensing boards, 637
Manufacturers and Products, 909
Manufacturing Firms in Exports, 909
Occupational Staffing Patterns, 886
Office of Housing, 133
Office of Securities Commissioner, 669
Permanent Housing for Handicapped Homeless, 133
Rental Rehabilitation Loan Program, 133
Small Business Administration Office, 837
state data centers, 901
state information, 37
State International Trade Offices, 858
State Labor Office, 886
State Planning Office, 909
state procurement office, 841
state tax assistance, 499
surplus property auctions, 706
Tax Credits for Low-Income Housing, 133
Tax form distribution center, 470
Tax forms and publications, 491
Titles and Registration Bureau, 642
unclaimed property office, 713
Unemployment Insurance Claims, 886
Uniform Commercial Code Division, 631
U.S. International Trade Administration Office, 856
Wage Surveys, 886
Warehouse and Distribution Centers, 909
Kennedy Space Center video, 1273, 1288, 1295
Kennedy, John F.
Cuban missile crisis address to the Nation, 1254, 1273
inaugural address of 1961, 1273
Kentucky
Affirmative Action, 886
Annual Economic Report, 909
Appalachian Housing Program, 133
Automated Tax Refund Information, 466
Career Outlook and Opportunities, 886
company directories, 665
corporation information, 660
Country Home Program, 133
Division of Securities, Department of Financial Institutions, 669
Elderly Rural Rehabilitation Program, 133
EPIC (Equity Partners Investing in the Commonwealth) Program, 133
Field Services/Special Population Needs Emergency Fund, 133
Grants to the Elderly for Energy Repairs (GEER), 133
Housing Corporation, 133
Housing Trust, 133
IRS hotline, 464
Kentucky Economic Statistics, 905
KHC Rural Program, 133

KHC Urban Program, 133
Labor Force Estimates, 886
Labor Market Newsletter, 886
lakes and wetlands, 1264, 1297
licensed professionals, 637
Licensing boards and professions, 637
Low-Income Housing Tax Credits, 133
Non-Agricultural Wage and Salary Employment, 886
Occupational Outlook, 886
Occupational Profiles, 886
Permanent Housing for Homeless Handicapped Persons, 133
Rental Deposits Surety Program, 133
Rental Housing Finance Program, 133
Residential Investment Program, 133
rivers and streams, 1264, 1290
Section 8 Programs, 133
Single-Family Home Ownership, 133
Small Business Administration Office, 837
state data centers, 901
state information, 37
State International Trade Offices, 858
State Labor Office, 886
State Planning Office, 909
state procurement office, 841
state tax assistance, 499
surplus property auctions, 706
Tax form distribution center, 470
Tax forms and publications, 491
Total Wages by Industrial Division, 886
Transportation Cabinet, Division of Driver Licensing, 642
unclaimed property office, 713
Uniform Commercial Code Division, 632
U.S. International Trade Administration Office, 856
Water Watch Program, 1266, 1273, 1296
Kerosene, 1227
Key Officers of Foreign Service Posts, 855
Kidneys
disease, 549
extracorporeal shock wave, 550
grants, 286
research, 767
stones, treatment, 550
transplants, 550
Kimberley Bulletin Board System, 1235
King, Jr., Martin Luther
drug prevention poster, 1273, 1280
Korean War Memorial, 400

L

L.L. Bean, 898
Labeling regulation, 1034
Labor
Federal Labor Relations Authority, 257, 271
health manpower, 504
international policy, 237
recorded message, 93
unfair practices, 257, 271
Labor issues
benefit plans, 251
biological rhythms and shift work, 550
Bureau of Labor Statistics, 873
Caribbean basin, 234, 915
child labor laws, 235, 239, 251
collective bargaining agreements, 256, 260
compensation for federal employees, 255
contract negotiations, 260
drug abuse programs, 262
Federal Mediation and Conciliation Service, 256, 619

The thousands of studies in the Current Events Chapter and Experts Chapter are not listed in this Index.

Index

federal wage-hour standards, 252
federally-assisted programs, 236
foreign labor, 236, 241, 252, 625, 934
formal complaints, 252
health hazard evaluation, 262-63, 267
home-based industries, 237
international issues, 236, 872, 921
job loss due to imports, 249
labor practices, 259
labor surplus areas, 238
market developments, 238
migrant and farm workers, 252
minimum wages, 239
National Institute for Occupational Safety and Health, 262, 263, 531, 572
National Labor Relations Board, 258
National Occupational Hazard Survey Databases I & II, 263
Occupational Safety and Health Administration, 262
overtime pay, 239
pension and retirement audits, 253, 272
plant closings or major lay-offs, 239, 248
postal workers, 273
practice lawsuit statistics, 258
productivity and federal employees, 273
safety, 262, 266, 267
Senate committee, 1182
statistics online, 873
statistics, 237, 871
strikes and work stoppages, 242
tax policies, 236
technology, impact of, 237, 924
transit system employees, 255
unemployment insurance, 255
wage and earnings survey, 241, 877
wage and hour investigations, 240
wage garnishments, 251
white-collar occupations, 241
women, 241, 877
women's employment patterns, 234
women-families-welfare, 242, 246
work and family responsibilities, 234
workforce education research, 239
workforce projections, 234
workplace literacy, 242, 246
youth, 242, 246
Labor market data
business location, 884
company information, 884
employee development, 884
marketing, 883
wage and benefit information, 884
Labor unions
bargaining unit, 256
Certification of Representative (RC), 258
drug abuse programs, 590
elections, 258
Employer Petition (RM), 258
representation elections, 258
Unit Clarification (UC), 258
Withdrawal of Union-Shop Authority (UD), 258
Labor, U.S. Department of
Labor Historian, 237
library, 238
public information offices, 55
Labor-management, 271
Federal Mediation and Conciliation Service, 258, 259
federal, 271
mediation cases, 257, 621
Lakes, 1217
Kentucky, 1264, 1297
restoration, 1112
Lamb, 1229
Land

cadastral surveys, 1124
public management, 1134
public, 1184
reclamation, 1184
Landmarks, historic, 306
LANDSAT images, 1090, 1093, 1200
Landscape architecture, 762, 1030, 1129
Landscaping, 142, 976, 1061, 1203
assistance, 141
Landslides, 97, 994, 1143
Langley Research Center, 990
Language, 149, 167
attrition, 167
disorders, 509
educational grants, 174
foreign research grants, 175
grants for teachers, 177
minority programs, 167
student grants, 187
Larceny, 610
Laser surgery, 568
Lasers, 779, 954, 958-59, 969, 976-78, 989-90, 1009
free-electron, 1011
interferometer, 1010
Latest News On Foreign Opportunities, 852
Latin America, 792, 922
Caribbean affairs, 306
field research fellowships, 156
health activities, 924
Peru, 924
research project histories, 915
small and micro enterprises, 924
Law
African, 618, 925, 1193, 1201
American-British, 618, 925, 1193, 1201
Americans arrested abroad, 415
ancient, 618, 925, 1193, 1201
banking and finance, 426, 427
campaign finance, 646, 1189
canon, 618, 925, 1193, 1201
Chinese, 618, 925, 1193, 1201
civil, 618, 925, 1193, 1201
Coast Guard, U.S., 611
constitutional, 620
education grants, 178, 188
education organizations, 143, 152
environmental, 1097, 1098, 1100
European, 618, 925, 1193, 1201
Far Eastern, 618, 925, 1193, 1201
FDIC liquidation litigation, 430
Freedom of Information, 1153-1166
Hispanic, 618, 925, 1193, 1201
history of, 609
insanity defense, 612
international arms control, 936
Islamic, 618, 925, 1193, 1201
Jewish, 618, 925, 1193, 1201
judicial research, 621
Law School Clinic Program, 621
legal assistance for the poor, 621
legal services, 621, 622
legal suits abroad, 419
medieval, 618, 925, 1193, 1201
mining, 812, 816, 1129
Near Eastern, 618, 925, 1193, 1201
poverty law, 621
Privacy Act, 1153
Roman, 618, 925, 1193, 1201
tax, 462
water resources, 1121
Law enforcement
grants, 371
program grants, 371
Law-related education
juvenile justice, 593
Lawrence Livermore National Laboratory, 950
Lawn care, 31, 141

Lawyers, 635
Layaways, 777
Lead, 1112
paint poisoning, 119, 506, 550, 571
Leadership, Surgeon General, 502
Learning disabilities, 973
Leasing
gas, 1069, 1071, 1128
mineral, oil, gas, 1126
oil shale, 971
oil, 1069, 1071, 1128
outer continental shelf, 816, 1069, 1124
Leaves, 1264, 1274, 1292
Legal Assistance Network, 854
Legal Services Corporation, 621
Legalization grants, 386
Legislation
aerospace, 986
animal welfare, 1023, 1241
arms control and disarmament, 937, 1179
asbestos, 1095
banking and finance, 426, 430
biotechnology, 1024
child protection, 614
children's rights, 614
civil rights, 627
coal, 1067
consumer protection, 95
cost estimates of, 869
crime victims, 1226
currency issues, 1183
document rooms, 1188
education issues, 1183
energy, 1057
environmental, 1097, 1101, 1102
european common market, 1002
federal elections, 1184, 1189
fiscal consequences, 1186
higher education, 157
history of, 1188, 1191, 1201
House Select Committee, 1185
Internal Revenue Service, 456
internal revenue, 457
labor, 1183
legal assistance to the poor, 621
minimum wage, 1183
petroleum industry, 1069
public attendance at hearings, 402
publications, 1213
public lands, 1126
school lunch programs, 1183
State-level, 347, 1194
taxes, 460
telecommunications, 776, 790
transportation, 100, 819
women's issues, 241
Legislative Branch, 40
Legislative process, 149, 1191
Leprosy, 550
Lewis Research Center, 990
Librarian grants, 188
Libraries
Agency for International Development, U.S., 912, 913
Army Center of Military History, 315
Army Corps of Engineers, 942
Army Materials and Mechanics Research Center, 945, 963
Army Materiel Command, 959, 979
Army Medical Library, 942
Arson Resource Center, 354, 610
art slides, 296, 320
Bell-Henry Library, 303
binational centers, 415, 915, 1205
Botanic Garden, U.S., 140
Bureau of Land Management, 1126
Bureau of Mines, 815

The thousands of studies in the Current Events Chapter and Experts Chapter are not included in this Index.

Index

Libraries (continued)
Bureau of the Census, 776
catalog cards, 1200, 1202
Census Bureau, 863
children's useage, 152
Coast Guard law, 611
Commerce Department, U.S., 775, 776
Consumer Product Safety Commission, 109
Doris and Henry Dreyfuss Study Center and Library, 304
Edwards Air Force Base, 960
energy research, 1057
Environmental Protection Agency, 1097
Environmental Research Laboratory, 1099
environmental research, 1103, 1118, 1148, 1151
Farm Credit Administration, 1026
Federal Depository Libraries, 1213
Federal Election Commission, 646, 1190
Fire Research Information Service, 1011
House of Representatives, 1190
inter-library loans, 1201
Interstate Commerce Commission, 777
Labor, U.S. Department of, 238
Lawrence Livermore National Lab, 950
library and information science, 167
Marine Corps Historical Center, 950
marine research, 412, 804, 1113
military history, 942
military logistics, 950
museum operations, 316
Museum Support Center Library, 319
National Agricultural Library, 1028
National Air and Space Museum Branch Library, 308
National Arboretum Library, 141
National Endowment for the Humanities, 1201, 1205
National Fisheries Research Center, 1135
National Gallery of Art, 320
National Institute of Standards and Technology, 776
National Library of Medicine, 501
National Museum of African Art Library, 313
National Museum of American History Branch Library, 303, 314
National Museum of Natural History Library, 309, 320
National Oceanic and Atmospheric Administration, 776
National Sea Grant Depository, 808
National Victims Resource Center, 612
Natural Resources Library, 1101
Naval Historical Center, 953
Naval Observatory, 953
Nuclear Regulatory Commission, 1080
Occupational Safety and Health Administration, 263
Oceanic and Atmospheric Administration, National, 1083
Office of Personnel Management, 272
overseas, 415, 915, 1205
Patent and Trademark Office, 776
Performing Arts Library, 290, 292, 294
Postal Service, U.S., 114
Presidential, U.S., 310
Radio Free Europe/Radio Liberty, 930
Radiobiology Research Institute, 956
Smithsonian Institution, 311, 321
Strughold Aeromedical, 939
Supreme Court of the U.S., 616
Transportation, U.S. Department of, 822
U.S. Geological Survey Photographs, 296, 1094
United States Information Agency, 933
USGS Drilling Core Library, 991

water resources, 1121
Library
career training grants, 176
construction grants, 381
grants, 176, 180
literacy programs, 381
research grants, 176, 289
Senate, 1192
Library of Congress, 1020
catalog databases, 1199
Catalog of Copyright Entries, 1020
collections, 1201
copy service, 1203
database, 1226
gifts, 1240
guide to, 1201
House Committee on, 1184
information services, 307, 1201
private research desks, 310, 1202
procurement, 1204
reading rooms, 307, 647, 1201
rules and administration, 1182
telephone reference service, 311, 1204
tours, 1201
Tracer Bullets, 99, 121, 141, 515, 779, 962, 976, 996, 1050, 1200, 1203
Licensing
boards, state, 635, 636
drivers, 1218
nuclear power plants, 1072
Lie detector reliability, 30, 31, 253, 614, 971
Life insurance
income Tax Return, 479
information return, 488
Information Return for Determination, 488
tax related form, 474
Life-sustaining technology, 514, 970
Lifestyle
cancer prevention, 516
drug-free teens, 593
eating habits survey, 521
health risk appraisal, 517
risk factors, 516
Lighting, energy efficient, 1061
Limnology, 1085, 1101
Linguistics, education literature, 1274
Liquid Metal Fast Breeder Reactor, 1074
Liquor regulations, 775
Literacy, 152
grants, 179, 180
program grants, 181, 381
TVA programs, 346
volunteers, 384
workplace, in the, 242, 246
Literature
education, 1255, 1272, 1274, 1282, 1285
experts abroad program, 291, 309, 415, 913
Science Education Clearinghouse, 1287
sound recordings, 295, 1201
teacher workshops, 1290
Lithology, 1222
Lithotripsy, 972
Litigation
child abuse, 610
consumer issues, 611
liability and worklife, 234
securities, 441, 442
Little League drug education program, 1274
Livestock, 1028, 1126
assistance, 756
diseases, 1033
feed drugs, 970, 1031
production, 1042
vaccinations, 1035
veterinary services, 1028
Loan guarantees, 754
Loans, 754

African development, 923
alcohol fuel production facilities, 1049
Business and Industrial Loans, 757
Business Loans for 8(a) Program Participants, 755
business, 727
Certified Development Company Loans, 755
child care businesses, 728
children and teenagers, 1024
Commodity Loans and Purchases, 755
Construction or Substantial Rehabilitation of Condominium Projects, 759
Cooperative Projects, 759
Direct Investment Loans, 763
disaster assistance, 354
Economic Injury Disaster Loans, 754
emergency disasters, 728
Emergency Loans, 757
Experimental Homes, 760
Experimental Projects Other Than Housing, 760
Experimental Rental Housing, 761
Farm Labor Housing Loans and Grants, 757
Farm Operating Loans, 757
Farm Ownership Loans, 757
Federal Ship Financing Guarantees, 761
Foreign Investment Guaranties, 763
Handicapped Assistance Loans, 755
Hospitals, 759
Housing for the Elderly or Disabled, 760
Indian Tribes and Tribal Corporation Loans, 757
Intermediary Relending Program, 757
Loans for Small Business, 754
Local Development Company Loans, 754
Manufactured Home Parks, 759
Minority Economic Impact Loans, 763
Mortgage Insurance - Homes, 759
Mortgage Insurance-Two Year Operating Loss Loans, 760
Multifamily Rental Housing, 760
National Health Service Corps, 769
Nursing Homes, 759
Physical Disaster Loans, 754
Property Improvement Loan, 760
Purchase of Sales-Type Cooperative Housing Units, 759
Purchase of Units in Condominiums, 759
Purchase or Refinancing of Existing Multifamily Housing Project, 760
Rental Housing, 760
Rental Housing for the Elderly, 760
Rental Housing in Urban Renewal Areas, 760
rural, 27
Rural Economic Development Loans and Grants, 758
Rural Electrification Loans and Loan Guarantees, 758
Rural Rental Housing Loans, 757
Rural Telephone Bank Loans, 758
Rural Telephone Loans and Loan Guarantees, 758
small business, 32
Small Business Investment Companies, 754
Small Business Loans (Regular Business Loans), 754
small business, 717
Soil and Water Loans, 757
student defaults, 1222
transportation business, 722, 820
Veterans Loan Program, 755
Youth Project Loans, 347, 1027
Lock-in interest rates, 120
Long-term care, 558

The thousands of studies in the Current Events Chapter and Experts Chapter are not listed in this Index.

Index

Louisiana
- Affirmative Action, 886
- Automated Tax Refund Information, 467
- company directories, 665
- corporation information, 660
- Department of Public Safety and Corrections, 643
- Employment and Wages, 886
- Housing Development Action Grants, 133
- Housing Finance Agency, 133
- IRS hotline, 464
- Labor Market Information, 886
- licensed professionals, 637
- Licensing boards and professions, 637
- Multi-Family, 133
- Occupational Employment Statistics, 886
- Securities Commission, 669
- Single-Family, 133
- Small Business Administration Office, 837
- state data centers, 901
- state information, 37
- State International Trade Offices, 858
- State Labor Office, 886
- State Planning Office, 909
- state procurement office, 841
- state tax assistance, 499
- surplus property auctions, 706
- Tax Credit Program, 133
- Tax form distribution center, 470
- Tax forms and publications, 491
- unclaimed property office, 713
- Uniform Commercial Code, 630, 632
- U.S. International Trade Administration Office, 856

Louisiana Purchase, 1274

Love Canal, 972

Low-Income Housing Credit, 488

Low input agriculture, 965, 1025

Low-level radioactive waste, 964, 1143

Lung disease research, 286, 767

Lungs, 506

Lyme disease, 539

Lyndon B. Johnson Space Center, 990

M

M. Lee Smith Publishers & Printers, 666

MacRAE's Industrial Directories, 664, 666

Mafia, 606

Magnetic resonance imaging, 973

Magnet schools grants, 381

Magnetohydrodynamics, 1067

Mail
- air, 1217
- automation, 974
- businesses, 113
- classification, 115
- customs duty, 114
- domestic postal services, 114
- elderly watch program, 113
- fraudulent schemes, 98, 115
- handicapped, 115
- hazardous material, 114
- high-speed automated mail sorting equipment, 113
- highway contract route, 118
- international services, 114
- pornography, 115
- post office closings, 117
- postage stamp designs, 114
- postal law violations, 98, 115
- rate complaints, 117
- rates and fees, 114
- rural post offices, 114
- service changes, 117
- third-class bulk rates, 118
- ZIP Code information, 115

Mailing Lists, 635, 641, 682, 1214
- brokers, 668
- Name Authority File database, 505

Maine, 130
- Automated Tax Refund Information, 467
- Careers In Maine Woods, 886
- company directories, 665
- corporation information, 660
- Department of Professional and Financial Regulation, 638
- Disabled Persons housing, 130
- Environmental Access Grants and Loans (EAGL), 133
- Environmental Hazard removal, 130
- Home Equity Conversion Mortgage, 133
- Home Improvement Program, 133
- Home Preservation Grant Program, 133
- Home Purchase Program, 133
- Home Start Program, 133
- Homeless Shelter Assistance, 133
- IRS hotline, 464
- Land Acquisition Program, 133
- licensed professionals, 638
- Low-Income Housing Tax Credit, 134
- Maine Statistical Summary, 905
- Manufacturing Directory, 665
- Mental Health Facilities Fund, 133
- Motor Vehicle Division, 643
- MSHA 202 Start Program, 133
- New Housing Initiatives Program, 133
- Occupational Staffing Patterns in Hospitals, 886
- Purchase Plus Improvement, 133
- Rental Loan Program, 133
- Rental Rehabilitation Program, 133
- Section 8 Certificates and Vouchers, 134
- Section 8 Moderate Rehabilitation, 134
- Section 8 New Construction, 134
- Securities Division, Bureau of Banking, 669
- Small Business Administration Office, 837
- state data centers, 901
- State Housing Authority, 133
- state information, 37
- State International Trade Offices, 858
- State Labor Office, 886
- State Planning Office, 909
- state procurement office, 841
- state tax assistance, 499
- Supportive Housing Initiative Program (SHIP), 133
- surplus property auctions, 707
- Tax form distribution center, 470
- Tax forms and publications, 491
- unclaimed property office, 713
- Underground Oil Storage Tank Removal Program, 133
- Uniform Commercial Code Division, 632
- U.S. International Trade Administration Office, 856
- Women and Minority housing, 130

Mammals, 1086
- drawing, 1255, 1274, 1285, 1298
- Illinois, 1266, 1274
- marine, 408, 803, 1135, 1138

Mammography, 545

Management and technical assistance, 754

Manganese, 815, 952

Manufactured homes, 120, 123 759

Manufacturing
- automated, 1010
- automation, 999
- awards, 1005
- chemical, 997
- computerized automation, 971
- computers, 1000
- control technology, 999
- data communications systems, 998
- discrete parts, 999
- drugs, 1221
- durable goods, 870
- emerging technologies, 1001
- engineering, 1005, 1010
- environmental issues, 778
- fatalities, 1216
- flexible computer-integrated, 979
- metal fabrication, 1013
- nondurable goods, 870
- process sensors, 1005
- quality control, 1015
- robotics, 999
- semiconductors, 1013
- statistics, 863
- technology transfer, 1015
- trade deficit, 974

Manure, 1240

Manuscripts
- archive, 308, 1202
- preservation, 310, 1202
- rare American, 305, 1202
- rare, 292, 311, 1203

Maps, 1214, 1257
- aerodiometric, 1088
- aeromagnetic, 1088
- aeronautical charts, 1090, 1200
- American Indian reservations, 865
- Antarctic, 1088, 1090
- Army exploration, 942
- astrogeology, 1092, 1240
- bathymetric, 805, 1093
- cadastral survey, 1124
- cadastral, 1088
- census, 861, 862
- copyrights, 1020
- county subdivision censuses, 865
- Defense Mapping Agency, 947, 1089
- digital cartography, 1089
- flood-prone areas, 356
- geodetic, 992
- geographic names, 346, 1093
- geologic, 1090, 1200, 1222, 1258
- geophysical, 1090
- hazardous material spills, 822
- hydrologic, 1090
- Indian reservations, 123, 150, 626, 629, 1127
- land cover, 1090, 1126
- land use, 1090, 1126, 1222
- LANDSAT, 1090, 1093, 1200
- mines, 813, 1093
- minerals, 1090, 1200
- mines, 778, 813, 1093
- moon, 1092, 1240
- National Archives, 294, 304, 314, 1088
- National Atlas of U.S., 1093, 1241
- National Mapping System, 1093
- National Parks, 1094
- nautical charts, 805, 1090, 1093, 1200
- oil, gas, and coal, 1090
- photoimage, 1093
- soil, 1090, 1200
- State topographic, 1094
- statistical, 876
- Tennessee Valley Authority, 413
- topographic, 1090, 1093, 1200
- topographic-bathymetric, 1094
- U.S., 1093
- voting districts, 877
- weather, daily, 1087, 1094

Margin trading, 439

Mariculture, 976, 1203

Mariel-Cubans, grants, 371

Marijuana, 599, 607, 1014
- eradication, 600

The thousands of studies in the Current Events Chapter and Experts Chapter are not included in this Index.

Index

Marine
advisories bulletin board, 1236
construction, 945
drug smuggling, 606
economics, 410, 801
foreign policy, 1100
OSHA rules, 266
research, 1113
unions, 804
war risk insurance, 761
Market information and franchising trends, 655, 899, 907
Marketing
agricultural commodities, 873, 970, 1024, 1030-31, 1037
center, 1037
development programs, 1042
House Committee on Agriculture, 1183
reports, 1038
Agricultural Information and Marketing Service, 1038
airlines, passenger, 781
corporations, 664
deceptive practices, 98
education data, 230
electricity, 1058
energy, 1058
fish exports, 799
fishing industry, 800
food, 970, 1031
foreign agriculture, 1037
international travel, 421
inventions, 1008
Labor Market Data, 883
Motor Vehicle Offices, State, 641
overseas with U.S. government help, 854
petroleum industry, 1069, 1070
power generated at Federal facilities, 1058
prescription drugs, 973
Public Utility Commissions, 677
recreation survey, 408, 413
regional economic forecasts, 874
research, 876
shipbuilding, 808
tourism, 420, 421
transportation industry, 777, 819
uranium, 1077
wheelchairs, 973
Market News Service, 1042
Marriage statistics, 576
Mars, 977, 1092, 1203, 1240
slides, 1274, 1286, 1288, 1289
video, 1274, 1288, 1294, 1295
Marshall Space Flight Center, 990
Marshals Service, U.S., seized property, 1225
Martin, August
learning activities, 1244, 1274
Maryland, 130
Accessory, Shared and Sheltered Housing Program, 134
Affirmative Action, 886
Automated Tax Refund Information, 467
Chesapeake Bay, 909
Civilian Labor Force Employment and Unemployment, 886
Commercial Fishing Industry, 909
company directories, 665
Construction Loan Program, 134
corporation information, 660
Current Employment Statistics, 886
Department of Housing and Community Development, 134
Division of Maryland Occupational and Professional Licensing, 638
Division of Securities, 669
Elderly Rental Housing Program, 134
Emergency Mortgage Assistance, 134
Energy Bank Program, 134
Franchises, 771
Group Home Financing Program, 134
Home and Energy Loan Program, 134
Housing Rehabilitation Program, 134
Housing Rehabilitation Program-Single Family, 134
Impact of Professional Sports on the Maryland Economy, 907
Indoor Plumbing Program, 134
Industries, 886
IRS hotline, 465
licensed professionals, 638
Low-Income Housing Tax Credit Program, 134
Mortgage Program, 134
Motor Vehicle Administration, 643
Multi-Family Bond Program, 134
Multi-Family Home and Energy Loan Program, 134
Non-Profit Rehabilitation Program, 134
Occupational Industrial Outlook, 886
Occupational Wage Information, 886
Partnership Rental Housing Program, 134
Population Projections, 886
Preakness, 909
Professional Sports, 909
Rental Housing Allowance Pilot Program, 134
Rental Housing Production Program, 134
Residential Lead Paint Abatement Program, 134
Reverse Equity Program, 134
Section 8 Existing Certificate/Voucher Program, 134
Section 8 Moderate Rehabilitation Program, 134
Section 8 Rental Rehabilitation Program, 134
Services Industry, 886
Settlement Expense Loan Program, 134
Shelter One, 134
Small Business Administration Office, 837
state data centers, 901
state information, 37
State International Trade Offices, 858
State Labor Office, 886
state procurement office, 841
State Statistical Abstract, 907
state tax assistance, 499
Statistical Abstract, 906, 909
surplus property auctions, 707
Tax form distribution center, 470
Tax forms and publications, 491
Telecommunications, 909
unclaimed property office, 713
Uniform Commercial Code Division, 632
U.S. International Trade Administration Office, 856
Workers' Compensation, 909
Mass transit, 352, 353, 779, 820
House Committee, 1184
Senate Committee, 1181
Urban Mass Transit Administration, 829
Massachusetts
80/20 Program, 134
Acquisition Set-Aside Program, 134
Automated Tax Refund Information, 467
Careers and Training in Allied Health, 886
Chapter 707 Residential Services Programs, 134
Chapter 707 Scattered Site Certificate Program, 134
Chapter 707 Transitional Housing Program, 134
company directories, 665
corporation information, 660
Employment and Wages, 886
Executive Office of Communities and Development, 134
General Lending, 134
Home Improvement Program, 134
Home Ownership Opportunity Program, 134
Housing Finance Agency, 134
IRS hotline, 465
licensed professionals, 638
Licensing boards and professions, 638
Low-Income Housing Tax Credit Program, 134
Manufacturing Industries, 886
Mortgage Credit Certificate Program, 134
Mortgage Insurance Program, 134
Neighborhood Rehabilitation Programs, 134
New Construction Set-Aside, 134
Project TAP (Tenant Assistance Program), 134
Registry of Motor Vehicles, 643
Rental Acquisition Development Initiative, 134
Section 8 Certificate/Voucher Programs, 134
Securities Division, 669
Small Business Development Centers, 739
state data centers, 901
State Housing Assistance for Rental Productions (SHARP), 134
state information, 37
State International Trade Offices, 858
State Labor Office, 886
State Planning Office, 909
state procurement office, 841
state tax assistance, 499
Supportive Services in Elderly Housing, 134
surplus property auctions, 707
Tax form distribution center, 470
Tax forms and publications, 491
unclaimed property office, 713
Uniform Commercial Code Division, 632
U.S. International Trade Administration Office, 856
Materials, 975, 1003, 1005, 1014, 1015
chemical properties, 1007
Mathematics, 987, 997, 1007, 1012
education literature, 1274, 1285
energy educational materials, 1260, 1274
grants, 179
publication for parents, 1274
research grants, 186, 288
teaching grants, 178, 189
Mayors, U.S. Conference of, 346
McGruff crime prevention campaign, 583
McKinney Act, 702
Meals on Wheels, 384
Measurements
air, 1011
heat, 1011
high voltage, 1010
linearity, 1010
methodology, 1012
moisture transfer, 1011
noise, 1010
sound, 1010
technology, 1006
time, 1010
tools, 1005
Measuring devices, 682
Meat and poultry hotline, 33
Meats, 1229
Mechanics
composite materials, 1003

The thousands of studies in the Current Events Chapter and Experts Chapter are not listed in this Index.

Index

nonlinear fractures, 1003

Media

reaction to U.S., 920

Mediation Board, National, 259

Medicaid

costs, 575

fraud control program grants, 367

state grants, 386

Medical issues

animal research laboratories, 1255, 1274

bulletin board, 1236

care, free, 30

care quality, 973

devices, 972

education, 972

grants, 386

information systems, 973

quackery, 567

tax guide, 493

technologies, 972

waste, 972, 973

Medical devices, 567, 764, 970

approval assistance, 568, 723

Medical professionals, 635

emergency medical personnel, 357, 533

Medical quackery, 567

Medical school, 960

Medical technologies, 567, 568, 723

Medical treatment database, 1227

Medical waste, 1144

technology, 1145

Medicare

claims, 558

costs, 575

Excess Tax Credit, 482

prepaid health, 576

prescription drug benefits, 569, 968

prescription drugs, 569

Senate committee, 1181

Senate subcommittee, 1181

videotapes, 558

Medicare, 146, 972

Medications

see Pharmaceuticals

food interactions, 521

over-the-counter drugs, 569

Medicine

audiovisual materials, 294

civil rights, 974

ethics, 1216

grants and loans, 182

humanities research, 306

nuclear, 1055

Mediterranean fruit fly, 1022

Memorial, Korean War veterans, 400

Meningitis, 540

Mental health, 507

biochemical bases, 550

community program grants, 362, 364

computer-aided research, 574

crisis counseling, 357, 533

emergency mental health, 357, 533

emergency preparedness, 357, 533

legal services, 619

Mental Retardation Research Centers, 535

President's Committee on Mental Retardation, 535

program grants, 369

Project D/ART (Depression/Awareness, Recognition, Treatment, 533, 546

rehabilitation, 507, 533, 546

research, 507, 533, 546

research grants, 363, 766

training grants, 365

Mental retardation, 507, 515, 976, 1203

President's Committee on Mental Retardation, 517

research centers, 535

Mentors, small business, 32

Mercedes, 641

Merchant Marine, 1181, 1184

Merchant vessels, 1224

Mercury

video, 1274, 1275, 1288, 1295

Mercury (planet), 1092, 1240

Mercury flights, 1275, 1294

Meredith Hurt & Associates, 650

Merit Systems Protection Board, 68

Metallic alloys, 1005

Metallurgy, 976, 1203, 1228

Metal fabrication, 1013

Metals, 944, 963, 1224

fabrication technology, 1013

manufacturing, 999

quality research, 1006

Meteorology, 1085

National Meteorological Center, 1085

satellites, 1086

Methadone, 595

Metrics

conversions, 778

system, 778

transition program, 778

Metrology, 1010

Mexico, migrant workers, 924

Michigan, 130

70/30 Rental Housing Program, 134

80/20 Direct Lending Program, 134

Affirmative Action, 886

Automated Systems Manufacturing, 909

Automated Tax Refund Information, 467

Business Incorporations, 909

Business Reference Sources, 909

Chemical Industry, 909

Community Development Block Grant (Small Cities) Program, 134

company directories, 665

Comprehensive Neighborhood Rehabilitation Competition, 134

Corporation and Securities Bureau, 669

corporation information, 660

Department of License and Regulation, 638

Drivers: Michigan Systems Programming Division, 643

Emergency Housing Apartment Program (EHAP), 134

Employment and Unemployment Estimates, 886

Employment Trends, 886

Export Assistance, 909

Food Processing, 909

Forest Products, 909

Fortune 500 Companies Headquarters, 909

Franchises, 771

Freddie Mac/MSHDA Housing Initiative, 135

High Risk Home Improvement Program, 134

Home and Neighborhood Improvement Loans, 134

Home Improvement Loan Program (HIP/CHIP), 134

Homeless Children's Fund, 134

HOPE (Housing Opportunities Providing Equity), 134

Housing Assistance Program, 134

Housing for the Handicapped, 134

Housing for the Homeless, 134

Industrial Construction Trends, 909

IRS hotline, 465

Labor Force, 909

Labor Market Review, 886

Labor Training, 909

licensed professionals, 638

Loans to Non-Profits, 135

Low-Income Housing Tax Credit Program, 134

Machine Tool Industry, 909

Machine Tool Industry Update, 907

Metal Fabricating Industry, 909

Michigan Private 100, 908

Moderate Rehabilitation Loans to Landlords, 134

Mortgage Credit Certificates, 134

Neighborhood Builders Alliance, 135

Neighborhood Housing Grant Program, 135

Neighborhood Preservation Program (NPP), 135

New Capital Expenditures, 909

Occupation/Industry Outlook 1995, 886

Occupations in Education, 886

Pass Through Program, 135

Plastics Industry, 909

Population Projections for Michigan to the Year 2010, 907

Property Tax, 909

Sales and Use Tax, 909

Section 8 Existing Rental Allowance Program, 134

Service Industry, 909

Set-Asides for Non-Profits, 135

Single-Family Home Mortgage, 134

Small Business Administration Office, 837

Small Business Centers, 909

Special Housing Program, 135

state data centers, 901

State Financial Assistance, 909

State Housing Development Authority, 134

state information, 37

State International Trade Offices, 858

State Labor Office, 886

State Planning Office, 909

state procurement office, 841

state tax assistance, 499

Supported Independent Living Program and Respite Program, 135

surplus property auctions, 707

Tax form distribution center, 470

Tax forms and publications, 491

Tax Review, 909

Taxable Bond Program, 135

Top Privately Held Companies, 909

unclaimed property office, 713

Unemployment Insurance Program Statistics, 886

Uniform Commercial Code Section, 632

Urban Development Initiative, 135

U.S. International Trade Administration Office, 856

Women Employment Trends 1982 to Present, 886

Microanalysis, 1009

Microbiology, 1099, 1103, 1109, 1118, 1148, 1151

research grants, 286

Microcircuits, 951, 968

Microelectronics, 974

Microgravity research, 981

Microwave ovens, 567

Middle East

foreign affairs, 1184

technology transfer, 971

Midlife crisis, 534

Migrant workers

educational grants, 152, 174, 180, 189, 381

employment program grants, 152, 372

health, 344, 345, 350, 575, 576

health centers grants, 365

rights, 252

student grants, 178

The thousands of studies in the Current Events Chapter and Experts Chapter are not included in this Index.

Index

Migrant workers (continued)
transportation, 821
Migration, Afro-American, 1275
Migratory birds, 1135
Military
Air Force band, 348
Air Force history, 940
Air Force, 348, 350, 940
aircraft testing, 940
alliance defense, 1181
arms transfers, 937
Army aircraft, 941
Army budget, 942
Army Materiel Command, 957
Army personnel locator, 646, 942
Army research labs, 943, 982
Army Reserve band, 348
aviation, 944
bands, 348
base closures, 346, 944
bases in foreign countries, 944
budget, 946
career officers, 951
casualty reporting, 940, 944
cemeteries, 1184
Civil Air Patrol, 945
communications, 945
community services, 143, 348
contractors, largest, 950
conventional forces, 1181
current research, 1218
Defense Intelligence Agency, 949
defense spending, 936, 938
Edwards Air Force Base, 949
energy consumption, 947, 1067
films, 948
foreign sales, 936, 949, 959
fuel supply, 949, 1068
historical records, 647, 940, 942, 951
installations and facilities, 950, 1183
intelligence, 1183
Joint Chiefs of Staff, 950
land use plans, 362
laundry and food services, 940
Lawrence Livermore National Laboratory, 950
logistics, 950
manpower and personnel, 1181, 1183
Marine Corps, 950
medical research, 954
medical scholarships, 951
missiles, 400, 952
National Guard, 953
Navy budget, 954
nuclear energy, 1183
nuclear weapons, 954
personnel locator, 940
personnel records, 647, 951
photographic archives, 941, 955
procurement, 936, 940, 948, 956, 1183
projection forces, 1181
public works facilities, 950
readiness, 1181, 1183
records corrections, 946
recruitment, 943
regional defense, 1181
registration status, 648, 957
research and development clearinghouse, 946, 1183
Reserve Officers Training Corps (ROTC), 956
retirement home, 956
rocket launching, 949
Seabees, 953
seapower, 1183
Senate Committee, 1181
service classification, 958
service record archives, 646
Soviet weapons systems, 943
star wars, 975
super computer, 961
tactical weapons, 959
target survivability, 950
tax information, 492
technology transfer, 943, 982, 1181
terminology, 948
training and organization, 362, 960
transportation, 952
underwater warfare, 960
Vietnam casualties, 648, 960
war records archives, 307, 312
weapons museum, 961
weapons systems, 943, 1183
weapons tracking systems, 958
Military base closures, mortgage insurance, 128
Military relocation assistance, 956
Milk, 755
Mineral resources, 1257, 1259, 1271, 1275
Mineral sciences, 309, 320
Minerals, 814, 971, 1224, 1275
chromium, 815, 952
claims on federal lands, 811, 1127
cobalt, 815, 952
consumption, 452, 814
corrosion, 813, 968
critical, 814, 952
experts, 451, 813
exploration, 971
films, 814
foreign countries, 451, 812
historical information, 1275
industry surveys, 452, 778, 814
manganese, 815, 952
marine, 971
platinum, 815, 952
production, 452, 814
Smithsonian visiting program, 1275
statistics, 870
stratigraphic nomenclature, 993, 1090
teacher workshops, 1275, 1284, 1290
yearbooks, 452, 815
Mining, 814
abandoned, 1215
acid drainage reduction, 812, 1118, 1142
Bureau of Mines, 811
closure orders, 264
coal, 812, 816, 1129
company information, 778, 813, 1093
congressional caucus, 1186
deep seabed, 812, 1051, 1111
disability grants, 388
economic policy, 814
emergency procedures, 264
engineering, 778, 813
environmental regulations, 814
equipment and machinery, 264
exploration leasing, 816, 1069, 1124
Federal Mine Safety and Health Review Commission, 264
House Subcommittee on, 1184
injuries and illnesses, 264
interest groups, 778, 813
library, 815
management theory, 264
map repositories, 813, 1093
mineral experts, 451, 813
mineral processing, 814
program grants, 372
reclamation, 718, 810, 812, 816, 1071, 1123, 1129
research, 815
robotics research, 815
roof support or ventilation systems, 264
safety, 263, 264, 815
Senate committee, 1181
staking claims on federal lands, 811, 1127
surface, 972
technology, 264, 452
uranium, 1082
waste facilities, 264
Minnesota, 130
$1.00 Home Set-Aside Program, 135
Accessibility Deferred Loan Program, 135
Automated Tax Refund Information, 467
Careers, 886
company directories, 665
Compare Minnesota, 906
corporation information, 660
Deferred Loan Program, 135
Department of Public Safety, Driver/Vehicle Services Division, 643
Elderly Home Sharing Program, 135
Employment and Wage Data, 886
Employment Outlook to 1993, 886
Franchises, 771
Great Minnesota Fix-Up Fund, 135
Home Energy Loan Program, 135
Home Ownership Assistance Fund, 135
Housing Finance Agency, 135
Housing Trust Fund, 135
Indian Housing Programs, 135
Innovative Housing Loan Program, 135
Intermediate Care Facilities for the Developmentally Disabled, 135
IRS hotline, 465
Labor Market Review, 886
licensed professionals, 638
Licensing boards and professions, 638
Low-Income Housing Tax Credit Program, 135
Low-Income Individuals and Small Family Rental Housing Program, 135
Low-Income Large Family Rental Housing Program, 135
Mental Health Commission, 909
Migrant Housing Program, 135
Mortgage Program, 135
Neighborhood Preservation Loan Program, 135
New Construction Tax Credit Mortgage/Bridge Loan Program, 135
Purchase Plus Program, 135
Registration and Licensing Division, 669
Rental Rehabilitation Grant Program, 135
Rental Rehabilitation Loan Program, 135
Revolving Loan Program, 135
Section 8 Housing Assistance, 135
Small Business Administration Office, 838
state data centers, 901
State Hospital Facilities, 909
state information, 38
State International Trade Offices, 858
State Labor Office, 886
State Planning Offices, 909
state procurement office, 841
state tax assistance, 499
surplus property auctions, 707
Tax form distribution center, 470
Tax forms and publications, 491
unclaimed property office, 713
Uniform Commercial Code Division, 632
Urban and Rural Homesteading Program, 135
Urban Indian Housing Program, 135
U.S. International Trade Administration Office, 856
Minorities, 309
alcoholism, 591
arts grants, 375
biomedical research, 573
biomedical science fellowships, 247

The thousands of studies in the Current Events Chapter and Experts Chapter are not listed in this Index.

Index

business development, 283, 723
business loans, 728
business, 717, 1228
community health projects, 348
drug prevention grants, 583
economic impact loans, 763
education, 154
educational grants, 187, 190
energy programs, 1058
energy research grants, 173
entrepreneurs, 723
Faculty Fellowships, 308, 320
government procurement, 836
grants for scientists, 573
health grants, 363
health research, 348, 574
language education, 144
Minority Business Development Centers, 723
NASA education programs, 154, 165
research grants, 170, 182, 184, 282, 285
research travel funds, 288
science grants, 178
small business assistance, 724, 1182
Smithsonian participation, 316
teaching grants, 171, 182, 282
Minority Business Development Agency, 723
Minority Business Development Centers, 758
Mint, U.S, 1240
Misinformation, 6
Missiles, 400, 952, 958
ballistic, 970
MX, 971
Missile Technology Control Regime, 937
Missing in action (MIAs),
Korean War memorial, 400
Missing people, 30, 611
Mississippi
Affirmative Action, 886
Automated Tax Refund Information, 467
Business Services, 910
company directories, 665
corporation information, 660
Department of Public Safety/Data Processing, 643
Downpayment Assistance Program, 135
Employment and Job Openings 1995, 886
Energy Conservation Revolving Loan Fund, 135
Farm Income and Expenditures, 886
Home Corporation, 135
Industrial Incentives, 910
IRS hotline, 465
Labor Force Averages, 886
Labor Market Data, 886
licensed professionals, 638
Licensing boards and professions, 638
Low-Income Housing Tax Credit Program, 135
Manufacturers, 910
Manufacturers Directory, 910
Mississippi Statistical Abstract, 906
New Manufacturers, 909
Occupational Employment and Job Openings, 886
Population Projections, 910
Rental Rehabilitation Program, 135
Securities Division, 669
Single-Family Home Ownership Program, 135
Small Business Administration Office, 838
state data centers, 902
state information, 38
State International Trade Offices, 858
State Labor Office, 886
State Planning Office, 909
state procurement office, 841
state tax assistance, 499
surplus property auctions, 707
Tax form distribution center, 470
Tax forms and publications, 491
Transfer Payments, 886
unclaimed property office, 714
Uniform Commercial Code Division, 632
U.S. International Trade Administration Office, 856
Mississippi River, 1137
Missouri
Affirmative Action, 886
Agribusiness Sector, 910
Automated Tax Refund Information, 467
Blended Multi-Family Program, 135
company directories, 665
corporation information, 660
Data Sources Directory, 910
Demographic and Economic Profile, 910
Department of Revenue, Information Services Bureau, 643
Division of Professional Registration, 638
earthquakes, 1257, 1259, 1275
Employment Outlook, 886
Export Trade, 910
FmHA Supplemental Subsidy Program, 135
Home Health Care, 910
Home Health Care and the Homemaker, 907
Home Improvements/Weatherization Loan Program, 135
Housing Development Commission, 135
Housing Inventory Recycling Program, 135
Housing Program Utilization, 910
Housing Trust Fund Program, 135
HUD Repo Properties, 135
IRS hotline, 465
Labor Area Trends, 886
licensed professionals, 638
Low-Income Housing Tax Credit Program, 135
Multi-Family Program, 135
Neighborhood Loan Program, 135
Office of Secretary of State, 669
Operation Homeless, 135
RTC Home Purchase Program, 135
Section 8 Programs, 135
Single-Family Housing, 135
Small Business Administration Office, 838
Small Business Development Centers, 741
state data centers, 902
state information, 38
State International Trade Offices, 858
State Labor Office, 886
State Planning Office, 910
state procurement office, 841
state tax assistance, 499
Statistical Abstract, 906
surplus property auctions, 707
Tax form distribution center, 470
Tax forms and publications, 491
Transportation System, 910
unclaimed property office, 714
Uniform Commercial Code Division, 632
U.S. International Trade Administration Office, 856
Mitral valve prolapse, 528
MOAA MASC Library Bulletin Board, 1235
Mobile home
construction and safety standards, 123
safety, 112
state loans, 130
Mohair, 756
Molecular structure, 1009
Molten salt heat transfer, 1063
Monetary policy, 432

Money
counterfeit, 431
educational information, 1281
foreign exchange rates, 1221
foreign money markets, 869
laundering, 606
programs, 30
selling overseas, 848
unclaimed, 711
uncut currency, 1275
Money markets, 106, 867
Money orders, 711
Money supply, 431
Monitoring investments in developing countries, 853
Montana
Apprenticeable Occupations, 886
Automated Tax Refund Information, 467
Board of Housing, 135
Bureau of Land Management office, 695
company directories, 665
Consumer Products Buyer's Directory, 908
corporation information, 661
County Profiles, 907
Drivers Services, 643
Employment and Labor Force, 886
IRS hotline, 465
licensed professionals, 638
Low-Income Housing Tax Credit Program, 135
Manufacturers and Products Directory, 910
Montana Statistical Abstract, 906
Mortgage Credit Certificate Program, 135
Multi-Family Program, 135
Professional and Occupational Licensing, Business Regulation, 638
Recycled Mortgage Purchase Program, 135
Reverse Annuity Mortgage Loans, 135
Securities Department, State Auditor's Office, 669
Single-Family Programs, 135
Small Business Administration Offices, 838
state data centers, 902
state information, 38
State International Trade Offices, 859
State Labor Office, 886
State Planning Office, 910
state procurement office, 842
State Summary Volume, 906
state tax assistance, 499
Statistical Abstract, 910
surplus property auctions, 707
Tax form distribution center, 470
Tax forms and publications, 491
unclaimed property office, 714
Uniform Commercial Code Bureau, 632
U.S. International Trade Administration Office, 856
Moon
landing, 1276
rocks, 30
slides, 1276, 1286, 1288
videos, 1289, 1294
Moonshine seizures, 774
Mopeds, 353, 826
Mortgages
adjustable rate, 96, 105, 120, 867
closing process, 105, 867
credit certificates, 487
escrow accounts, 96
Fannie Mae, 121
federally-insured loans, 123
FHA insurance, 123
graduated payment program, 127
growing equity mortgages, 128
health care facilities, 568
insurance, 759

The thousands of studies in the Current Events Chapter and Experts Chapter are not included in this Index.

Index

Mortgages (continued)
interest credit, 488
lender's information return, 487
lock-in interest rates, 105, 120, 867
redlining, 121
refinancing, 105, 120, 127, 867
rehabilitation mortgage insurance, 126
second, 96
state housing help, 130
Moses and Frances Asch Collection, 295, 317
Mothers and children research, 369, 768
Motion Pictures and Filmstrips, 295, 1128
copyrights, 1020
Motor Vehicle Records, 30, 641
Motor vehicles
fuel efficiency, 101, 823, 1055
racing, 1276, 1279, 1280
taxes, 827
Motorcycle helmets, 96, 825
Motorcycles, 353, 826
importation, 100
poster, 1276, 1280
Mourning doves, 1225
Moving expenses tax, 494, 481
Mt. St. Helens
slides, 1276, 1286, 1288
video, 1276, 1288, 1295
Multifamily housing, 759, 760
Multiple sclerosis, 509, 551
Multiple support declaration, 480
Municipal waste recycling programs, 1027
Munitions, 1225
trade, 936
Murder, 612
Musculoskeletal and skin disease, 502, 509, 540
Museology, 311, 316, 321
conservation science, 319
Museums, 762
African Art, 313
Air and Space Museum, 319
American Art and Portrait Gallery, 315
American Indian, 318, 397
American Indians, 318
Anacostia Neighborhood Museum, 313
Army Center of Military History, 950
Barney Studio House, 313
conservation grants, 291, 318
conservation research, 316
Cooper-Hewitt Museum, 304
Dial-A-Museum, 93
educational program funding, 291, 318
Freer Gallery of Art, 316
Hirshhorn Museum and Sculpture Garden, 317
insurance for international exhibitions, 315
Interior, U.S. Department of the, 319, 400
military weapons, 961
Museum of Natural History, 320
museum training programs, 291, 318
National Air and Space Museum, 939, 981
National Lending Service, 321
National Museum Act, 319
National Museum of American Art, 319
National Museum of American History, 313
National Museum of Health and Medicine, 952
National Museum of Natural History, 303, 308
National Parks, 319
National Portrait Gallery, 303, 314, 317
operation and management, 316
Renwick Gallery, 313
research services, 319
Sackler Gallery, 316
shops, 321
Music, 292, 1202

children's, 1271, 1273, 1276
Congress, 400
education literature, 1287
Julliard String Quartet, 290
Musical theater, 762
Musicians, overseas tours, 291
Muskrats, 1276
Mutual fund distributions, 495
Mutual funds, 442

N

Names, geographic, 1258, 1271
Narcotics, 606, 610
see also Drugs
discretionary grant program, 371
drug sniffing dogs, 600
foreign affairs, 918
foreign policy, 924
NASA
see National Aeronautics and Space Administration
National Aeronautics and Space Administration
Ames-Dryden Flight Research Facility, 985
Central Operation of Resources for Educators, 164
educational publications, 1253, 1289
Johnson Space Center Bulletin Board, 1235
memorabilia, 1276, 1287
minority participation programs, 150, 164
Operation Liftoff, 1288
patented inventions, 987
procurement report, 987
public information office, 68
Small Business Innovative Research Grants, 840
Spacelink, 163, 1253, 1276, 1281, 1288
Teacher Resource Network, 164
videos, 30
National Air and Space Museum, 319
educational materials, 1253, 1268, 1277, 1288, 1290, 1293
National Arboretum, 141, 400
National Archives and Records Administration, 68
educational units, 1254, 1259, 1271, 1273, 1274, 1277, 1284, 1292, 1296, 1298
teachers workshop, 1277, 1291
National Association of Abandoned Property Administrators, 711
National Association of Securities Dealers' Central Registration, 668
National Audio-Visual Center, 949
National Capital Planning Commission, 69
National Clearinghouse on Legal Services, 621
National Credit Union Administration, 69
National Ecology Research Center (NERC) Bulletin Board, 1236
National Endowment for the Arts, 144, 290, 315
American Film Institute Independent Filmmaker, 295
artists abroad program, 293, 315
dance program, 290
design arts program, 290, 291
Folk Arts Program, 290, 314
Inter-Arts Program, 292
international activities, 292
library, 1205
Literature Program, 244, 246, 304, 308
media arts, 295
museum program, 291, 318
music program, 291
opera and musical theater, 291
special constituencies, 316

theater program, 290, 292
visual arts program, 293, 348
National Endowment for the Humanities
document preservation grants, 308
events and grants, 305
humanities projects in museums, 317
interpretative research, 303
library, 1201
science and technology research, 306
television and radio support, 297
text programs, 307
National Eye Institute, 504, 539
National forests, camping and recreation, 403
National Foundation on the Arts and the Humanities, 69
National Gallery of Art
Center for Advanced Study in the Visual Arts, 311, 321
concerts, 291
donations to, 315
educational materials, 1273, 1277, 1287
films, 317
library, 320
National Lending Service, 321
photographic services, 296, 320
slide loans, 296, 320
National Guard, 953
grants, 182
National Health Service Corps Members, 769
National Information Systems, 665
National Institute for the Conservation of Cultural Property, 316, 320
National Institute of Standards and Technology, 851
National Institutes of Health, 502
National Labor Relations Board
public information office, 70, 258
public meetings, 258
speakers, 258
National Mediation Board, 70
National Museum of African Art, 313
National Museum of American Art, 319
National Museum of American History, 314
National Museum of Natural History, 296, 297
instructional kits, 1270, 1272, 1285
slide sets, 1255, 1285
visiting programs, 1255, 1259, 1267, 1273, 1275, 1277, 1279, 1284
National Museum of History
teacher workshops, 1254, 1255, 1259, 1275, 1284, 1290
National Oceanic and Atmospheric Administration, 43, 1113
National Park Service, 406, 1093, 1102
National Parks, 406, 1128
National Pesticide Information Retrieval System, 1236
National Portrait Gallery, 303, 314
National Railroad Passenger Corporation (AMTRAK), 70
National Science Foundation, 762
public information office, 70
Small Business Innovative Research Grants, 840
National Security Council, 956
National Sudden Infant Death Syndrome Clearinghouse, 530
National Technical Information Service, 852
National Trade Data Bank, 843, 853
National Transportation Safety Board, 70
Native Americans, 1101
American Indians Enterprise Development, 837
ancestry census, 30
arts and crafts, 318
Bureau of Indian Affairs, 1099
business development, 722

The thousands of studies in the Current Events Chapter and Experts Chapter are not listed in this Index.

Index

census count, 626
children's programs, 371
community program grants, 36, 370
drug abuse treatment, 595
education grants, 176, 381
education programs, 152, 626
employment discrimination project grants, 375
employment grants, 388
employment training, 248
food programs, 386
genealogical research, 307
Government Procurement Assistance, 836
health care, 973
health grants, 183, 364, 365
health services, 123, 150, 626, 629, 1127
historical manuscripts, 303, 306, 308, 309
House Subcommittee on, 1184
housing, 246, 622, 626
HUD Indian Programs Office, 697
Indian Health Service, 507
job training grants, 372
land trust, 812, 1126
library services, 381
medical grants and scholarships, 182
Minnesota Indian Housing Programs, 135
Minnesota programs for urban indians, 130
program grants for elderly, 366
publications, 309, 318, 626
research grants, 283, 286
reservations, 865, 1217
Senate Select Committee, 1182
slides, 1285
Smithsonian training program, 319
social services, 246, 622
student grants, 188
tribal membership, 307, 626
VISTA volunteers, 384
NATO, 919, 971
Natural disasters
energy systems, 966, 1063
grants, 380
small business loans, 718
Natural gas
educational material, 1259, 1270, 1278
extraction, 1070
Natural History Museum, slides, 1285
Natural landmarks, 309, 400, 1101
Natural resources sales, 700, 1226
Naturalization, 916
see also Immigration and Naturalization
Nautical charts, 805, 1093
Naval Academy, 93
Naval systems research, 952
Navigation, 414, 808, 1086
aids, 787
instrumentation, 412, 804, 1113
river, 961
Navinfonet, 1236
Navy, U.S., 954
concert band, 350, 954
Reserve, 954
ship plans, 954
Near East and South Asia foreign policy, 927
Nebraska
Affirmative Action, 887
Agricultural Finance Programs, 135
Automated Tax Refund Information, 467
Bureau of Securities, Department of Banking and Finance, 669
Communications Industry, 910
company directories, 666
corporation information, 661
Department of Motor Vehicles, 644
Economic Indicators, 910
Employment and Earnings Report, 887
Ethanol Distilling Industry, 910
First-Time Farmer Loan, 135
Hazardous Waste, 910
Home Improvement Loan Program, 135
Investment Finance Authority, 135
IRS hotline, 465
Job Prospects, 887
licensed professionals, 638
Licensing boards and professions, 638
Low-Income Housing Tax Credit Program, 136
Manufacturers, 910
Multi-Family Loan Program, 135
Nebraska Industry -- A Survey of Concerns, Needs and Future Plans, 907
Nebraska Statistical Handbook, 906
Occupational Newsletter, 887
Pet Food, 910
Pharmaceuticals, 910
Profit Opportunities in Nebraska for Manufacturers of Pet Food, 907
Scientific, Measuring and Controlling Instruments, 910
Single-Family Mortgage Program, 135
Small Business Administration Office, 838
state data centers, 902
state information, 38
State International Trade Offices, 859
State Labor Office, 886
State Planning Office, 910
state procurement office, 842
state tax assistance, 499
surplus property auctions, 707
Tax form distribution center, 470
Tax forms and publications, 492
unclaimed property office, 714
Uniform Commercial Code Division, 632
U.S. International Trade Administration Office, 856
Vegetable Production, 910
Visitors Survey, 910
Nehemiah housing, 128, 370
Neighborhood Watch Programs, 30, 351, 612, 615
Neighborhoods
statistics, 870
Nematodes, 1225
Neonatal care, 973
Neptune
slides, 1277, 1278, 1286, 1287, 1289
video, 1273, 1278, 1288, 1293, 1295
NERC Habitat Model Reference Library, 1236
Nerve regeneration, 550
Neurological disorders, 509, 551, 768
Neuroscience, 514, 550, 768, 970
Neutrons, 1011
activation, 1009
defraction, 1007
radiography, 1007
scattering research, 1007
Nevada
Automated Tax Refund Information, 467
Bureau of Land Management office, 695
Community Profiles -- Demographic Facts, 907
company directories, 666
corporation information, 661
Department of Commerce, Housing Division, 136
Department of Motor Vehicles, 644
Economic Update, 887
Industrial Development Bonds, 136
Industrial Directory, 910
IRS hotline, 465
Job Finding Techniques, 887
licensed professionals, 638
Licensing boards and professions, 638
Occupational Projections, 887
Rural Area Housing Program, 136
Rural Housing Authority, 136
Securities Division, 669
Single Family Mortgage Purchase Program, 136
Small Business Administration Office, 838
state data centers, 902
state information, 38
State International Trade Offices, 859
State Labor Office, 887
State Planning Office, 910
state procurement office, 842
Statistical Abstract, 906
surplus property auctions, 707
Tax form distribution center, 470
Tax forms and publications, 492
unclaimed property office, 714
Uniform Commercial Code Division, 632
U.S. International Trade Administration Office, 856
Wage Survey, 887
New business for suppliers, 655
New England economic indicators, 886
New Hampshire
Affordable Home Ownership Program, 136
Affordable Housing Fund, 136
Automated Tax Refund Information, 467
Changes in Households and Households Size for Towns and Cities, 907
company directories, 666
Corporation information, 661
Department of Safety, Data Processing, 644
Department of State, Bureau of Securities Regulation, 669
Downpayment/Closing Cost Assistance Program, 136
Economic Characteristics, 910
Employment and Wages by County, 887
Energy Improvements Program, 136
Home Equity Conversion Program, 136
Housing Finance Authority, 136
Housing Supply, 910
IRS hotline, 465
licensed professionals, 638
Licensing boards and professions, 638
Low-Income Housing Tax Credit Program, 136
Mixed Income Rental Programs, 136
Mortgage Credit Certificate Program, 136
Multi-Family Housing Program, 136
Occupational Outlook 1995, 887
Planning Information, 887
Population Projections, 910
Rental Assistance, 136
Section 8 Housing Programs, 136
Single-Family Mortgage Program, 136
Small Business Administration Office, 838
Special Needs Fund, 136
state data centers, 902
state information, 38
State International Trade Offices, 859
State Labor Office, 887
State Planning Office, 910
state procurement office, 842
Supportive Services Program, 136
surplus property auctions, 708
Tax form distribution center, 471
Tax forms and publications, 492
unclaimed property office, 714
Uniform Commercial Code Division, 632
U.S. International Trade Administration Office, 856
Users Guide to Labor Market Information, 887
New Jersey, 906
Annual Economic Forecast, 907
Automated Tax Refund Information, 467

The thousands of studies in the Current Events Chapter and Experts Chapter are not included in this Index.

Index

New Jersey (continued)
Boarding House Life Safety Improvement Loan Program, 136
Bureau of Securities, Division of Consumer Affairs, 669
Centralized Licensing for the Licensing Boards, 639
company directories, 666
Continuing Care Retirement Communities, 136
Corporation information, 661
Development Set-Aside Program, 136
Division of Motor Vehicles, 644
Employment and Economy Newsletter, 887
Home Buyers 100% Financing Program, 136
Home Buyers Program, 136
Home Ownership for Performing Employees (HOPE) Program, 136
Housing Agency, 136
IRS hotline, 465
licensed professionals, 639
Low-Income Housing Tax Credit Program, 136
Multi-Family Rental Housing Program, 136
Regional Labor Market Reviews, 887
Rental Repair Loan Program, 136
Revolving Loan Program, 136
Seed Money Loan Program, 136
Services for Independent Living Program, 136
Small Business Administration Offices, 838
state data centers, 902
state income tax, 499
state information, 38
State International Trade Offices, 859
State Labor Office, 887
State Planning Office, 910
state procurement office, 842
surplus property auctions, 708
Tax form distribution centers, 471
Tax forms and publications, 492
Transitional Housing Program, 136
unclaimed property office, 714
Uniform Commercial Code Division, 633
U.S. International Trade Administration Office, 856

New Mexico
Automated Tax Refund Information, 467
Bureau of Land Management office, 695
company directories, 666
Corporation information, 661
Financial Resources, 910
Hours and Earnings Estimates, 887
HUD Rental Rehabilitation Program, 136
International Trade, 910
IRS hotline, 465
Labor Market Review, 887
licensed professionals, 639
Licensing boards and professions, 639
Low-Income Housing Tax Credit Program, 136
Manufacturing Directory, 910
Mortgage Finance Authority, 136
Multi-Family Programs, 136
Nonagricultural Wage and Salary Employment, 887
Regulation and Licensing Department, 639
Rio Grande Research Corridor, 910
Section 8 Housing Assistance Payments Program (Voucher), 136
Securities Division, Regulation and Licensing Department, 669
Single-Family Program, 136
Small Business Administration Offices, 838
state data centers, 902
State Housing Authority, 136
State Housing Rehabilitation Program, 136
state income tax, 499
state information, 38
State International Trade Offices, 859
State Labor Office, 887
State Planning Office, 910
state procurement office, 842
surplus property auctions, 708
Tax form distribution center, 471
Tax forms and publications, 492
Taxation and Revenue Department, Motor Vehicle Division, 644
unclaimed property office, 714
Uniform Commercial Code Division, 633
U.S. International Trade Administration Offices, 856

New York, 130
Alpine Ski Industry, 910
Apparel Industry, 910
Apprentice Training Hours and Earnings, 887
Automated Tax Refund Information, 467
Bureau of Investor Protection and Securities, 669
Business Fact Book Supplement, 910
Business Statistics, 910
Business Trends, 910
Careers Exploration and Job Seeking, 887
Clinton Preservation Program, 136
Collective Bargaining Settlements, 887
company directories, 666
corporation information, 661
Demographic Groups, 887
Department of Motor Vehicles, Data Preparation, 644
Directory of Labor Unions and Employee Organizations, 887
Disabled Persons housing programs, 130
Division of Housing and Community Renewal, 136
Division of Professional Licensing, Cultural Education Center, 639
Environmental Hazard removal, 130
Franchises, 771
Guide to Career Opportunities, 887
Housing Development Fund, 136
Housing Opportunities Program for the Elderly-RESTORE, 136
Industrial Development Bond report, 910
Infrastructure Development Demonstration Program, 136
IRS hotline, 465
Job Openings, 887
Jobs and Housing, 910
Labor Area Summary, 887
licensed professionals, 639
Low-Income Housing Tax Credit Program, 136
Low-Income Housing Trust Fund, 136
Neighborhood Preservation Program, 136
Neighborhood Redevelopment Demonstration Program, 136
New York Statistical Yearbook, 906
Non-Agricultural Wage and Salary Employment, 887
Occupational Guide, 887
Occupational Supply and Demand, 887
Printing and Publishing Industry, 910
Rental Rehabilitation Program, 136
Rural Area Revitalization Program, 136
Rural Home Ownership Assistance Program, 136
Rural Preservation Program, 136
Rural Rental Assistance Program, 136
Section 8 Existing Housing Program, 136
Section 8 Moderate Rehabilitation Program, 136
Senior Citizen Rent Increase Exemption, 136
Shared Housing Development Program, 136
Small Business Administration Office, 838
Special Needs Housing Program, 136
state data centers, 902
State Housing Authority, 136
state income tax, 499
state information, 38
State International Trade Offices, 859
State Labor Office, 887
State Planning Office, 910
state procurement office, 842
State Unemployment Insurance, 887
Statistical Profile of the Printing and Publishing Industry, 907
surplus property auctions, 708
Tax form distribution center, 471
Tax forms and publications, 492
Tax Structure, 910
Turn Key/Enhanced Housing Trust Fund, 136
unclaimed property office, 714
Uniform Commercial Code Division, 633
Urban Initiative Program, 136
U.S. International Trade Administration Offices, 856
Women and Minority Housing Programs, 130

Newspapers, 308, 309, 927, 1202
NIDDKUH Electronic Bulletin Board, 1236
Night vision, 954, 969
Nitrides, 1224
Nixon Presidential Materials Project, 311
Nobel laureates, 502
NOAA

see National Oceanic and Atmospheric Administration

Noise, 348, 782, 977, 1095, 1098, 1181, 1203
abatement, 1097
assessment, 119
measurements, 1010
Noise Control Act, 1102
prevention, 264

Non-profits
drug prevention, 603
educational organization credit, 481
elderly and handicapped housing, 127
Noncash charitable contributions, 487
Nonfood products, 1034
Nonresident aliens tax, 477, 494
Nontaxable energy grants, 486
North American continent, 1258, 1278

North Carolina
Automated Tax Refund Information, 467
Business Directory, 666
Catalyst Loan Program, 137
company directories, 666
Corporation information, 661
Driver information, 644
Energy Conservation and Housing Rehab Incentive Program, 137
Energy-Efficient Housing Production Program, 137
Governor's NCHFA/FmHA Elderly Subsidy Program, 137
Home Improvement Loan Program, 137
Home Ownership Challenge Fund, 137
Housing Finance Agency, 137
IRS hotline, 465
licensed professionals, 639
Licensing boards and professions, 639
Low-Income Housing Tax Credit Program, 137
Manufacturing Firms, 887
Maxwell/Fuller Self-Help Housing

The thousands of studies in the Current Events Chapter and Experts Chapter are not listed in this Index.

Index

Program, 137
Mortgage Credit Certificate Program, 137
Multi-Family Loan Program, 137
Multi-Family subsidized Program, 137
Non-Profit Development Program, 137
North Carolina State Statistical Abstract, 906
Rental Rehabilitation Program, 137
Resolution Trust Corporation Clearinghouse, 137
Securities Division, 669
Single-Family Mortgage Loan Program, 137
Small Business Administration Office, 838
state data centers, 902
state income tax, 499
state information, 38
State International Trade Offices, 859
State Labor Office, 887
State Planning Office, 910
state procurement office, 842
surplus property auctions, 708
Tax form distribution center, 471
Tax forms and publications, 492
unclaimed property office, 714
Uniform Commercial Code Division, 633
U.S. International Trade Administration Office, 856
Wage Rates in Selected Occupations, 887
North Dakota
Automated Tax Refund Information, 467
company directories, 666
Corporation information, 661
Drivers License and Traffic Safety Division, 644
Economic Development Commission, 910
Economic Indicators, 910
Employment Surveys, 887
Franchises, 771
Housing Assistance, 137
Housing Assistance Program, 137
Housing Finance Agency, 137
IRS hotline, 465
licensed professionals, 639
Licensing boards and professions, 639
Low-Income Housing Tax Credit Program, 137
Manufacturers, 910
Moderate Rehabilitation Program, 137
North Dakota Statistical Abstract, 906
Occupational Projections, 887
Office of Securities Commissioner, 669
Prairie Scans, 910
Resources, 910
Single Family Program, 137
Small Business Administration Office, 838
state data centers, 903
state income tax, 500
state information, 38
State International Trade Offices, 859
State Labor Office, 887
State Planning Office, 910
state procurement office, 842
surplus property auctions, 708
Tax form distribution center, 471
Tax forms and publications, 492
unclaimed property office, 714
Uniform Commercial Code Division, 633
U.S. International Trade Administration Office, 856
Wage Surveys and Benefits, 887
Northern Mariana Islands tax, 472, 493
Nuclear
abnormal occurrences, 1072
accelerators, 1057
accidents, 1072
atmospheric testing, 943

attack preparation, 357
energy, 1072, 1080
exports and imports, 1073
extortion, 1073
facilities, 1073
fallout shelters, 357
fines, 1080
fuel supply and demand, 1081
fusion, 1057, 1073
licensing, 1074, 1079, 1080
light water reactors, 971
Liquid Metal Fast Breeder Reactor, 1074
magnetic resonance imaging, 973
medicine, 1055
nonproliferation, 1073
physics, 1057
proliferation, 971
reactor inspections, 1074, 1081
reactors, 1079, 1080
safeguards, 1080, 1081
State programs, 1081
testing treaties, 971
violations, 1080
war, 971
waste management, 1082
waste, 1074
weapons, 954, 958, 989
Nuclear attack, 380
Nuclear decommissioning funds, 479
Nuclear energy, 764, 1261
international trade policy, 1073
Nuclear Non-Proliferation Treaty, 936, 1073
nuclear power, 1079
nuclear testing, 937
reactor accidents, 1079
Nuclear fallout shelter plans, 30
Nuclear magnetic resonance, 974
Nuclear physics
foreign policy, 1100
research grants, 288
Nuclear power, 1064
generation, 1261, 1278
safety and reliability, 1082
Tennessee Valley Authority plants, 1082
Nuclear reactors, 1080
Nuclear regulation, 1181
Nuclear Regulatory Commission
importing and exporting, 1073
public information office, 71
Small Business Innovative Research Grants, 840
Nuclear war survival guide, 31
Nuclear waste, 964, 965, 1143, 1145
management, 965, 1143
program grants, 379
Nuclear weapons, 936
nonproliferation issues, 936
nuclear fuel cycles, 937
risk reduction, 936
safeguard systems, 937
Senate subcommittee, 1181
Nursing, 973
grants, 170, 182, 183
research grants, 285
student loans, 184
Nursing homes, 124, 635, 759
grants, 376
loans, 369
Nutrition, 263, 517, 521, 523, 541, 1034
and the aging process, 525
Centers for Disease Control assistance, 524
child care food program, 385
children, 385, 524
chronic diseases, 524
clinical research, 521
community programs, 346, 545, 576

consumer attitudes, 522
consumption, 1217
education and training grants, 359, 520
elderly individuals, 518, 558
energy metabolism, 524
food assistance programs, 522
food stamps, 385
grants, 359
House committee, 1183
infants, 385
international development, 927
literature, 1033
malnutrition research, 523
microcomputer software, 1033
nutrient retention in foods, 523
pregnant and lactating women, 524
Recommended Daily Allowances, 524
research grants, 286, 522, 767, 970, 1030, 1036
school, 1180
senior citizens, 386
summer food service program, 385
women, 385

O

OAQPS Technology Transfer Network, 1237
Oats, 1220
Obesity, 524
Obtaining Copies of SEC Documents, 650
Occupational safety and health
research grants, 766
Occupational Safety and Health Administration, 56, 267
Occupational Safety and Health Review Commission, 71, 266
Ocean energy, 1059
Ocean dumping, 410, 611, 967, 1096
Oceanography, 805, 988, 1085, 1095, 1110, 1113, 1184
atmospheric interactions, 1084
energy exchanges, 1084
library, 1083
research, 283, 805, 1085
satellites, 1084
Sea Grant publications, 808
technology, 972
waste disposal, 1084
Oceans, 975, 1086, 1113, 1181, 1258, 1278, 1296
chemical properties, 805, 1085
coastal programs grants, 361
coastal waters, 798, 805, 1085, 1096
dumping, 412, 804, 1113, 1145
energy, 764, 1059, 1061
floors, 1258, 1278
incineration, 972
margin drilling, 975
marine weather, 412, 803, 1084
nautical charts, 805, 1093
Oceanographic Data Center, National, 805, 1085
physics, 982
Senate committee, 1181
teacher workshops, 1278, 1290
technology, 1084, 1103
thermal energy conversion, 971
undersea research, 1086, 1107, 1122
Odd lot and round lot transactions, 442
Odometers, 98, 615
Office automation, 973
Office of Corporations, 630
Office of Fuels Programs Management Information System (MIS), 1237
Office of Government Ethics, 71
Office of Personnel Management, 71

The thousands of studies in the Current Events Chapter and Experts Chapter are not included in this Index.

Index

Office of Research and Development Electronic Bulletin Board, 1238
Office of Special Counsel, 71
Office of Technology Assessment, 514
Office of Technology Assessment and Forecast (OTAF), 1018
Office of Uniform Commercial Code, 630
Offshore structures, 798
Ohio
403 Rental Housing Gap Financing Program, 137
Annual Report, 910
Automated Tax Refund Information, 467
Bureau of Motor Vehicles, 644
company directories, 666
Corporation information, 661
County Profiles, 906
Development Loan Program, 137
Division of Securities, 669
First-Time Homebuyer Program, 137
Home Ownership Incentive Programs, 137
Housing Finance Agency, 137
IRS hotline, 465
Labor Market Review, 887
Licensed professionals, 639
Low-Income Housing Tax Credit Program, 137
Multi-Family Rental Development Program, 137
Occupational Projections 1995, 887
Rental Housing Energy Conservation Program, 137
Section 8 Rental Assistance Program, 137
Seed Money Loan Program, 137
Small Business Administration Office, 838
state data centers, 903
state income tax, 500
state information, 38
State International Trade Offices, 859
State Labor Office, 887
State Planning Office, 910
state procurement office, 842
surplus property auctions, 708
Tax form distribution center, 471
Tax forms and publications, 492
unclaimed property office, 715
Uniform Commercial Code Division, 633
U.S. International Trade Administration Offices, 856
Worker Training Program Activities, 887
Oil, 1261, 1270, 1278, 1283
Arctic, 972
crude production, 1225, 1261, 1278
education-related material, 1270, 1278
exploration, 803, 1113, 1135
Fee Deposit for Outer Continental Shelf Oil, 485
grants, 764
leasing agreements, 1069, 1070, 1101
leasing of public lands, 1069, 1071, 1128
naval petroleum reserves, 1183
oil shale, 812, 1053, 1068
policy, 1069
production, 972
recovery, 971
recycling, 1070
shale conversion, 971, 1070
tankers, 971
Oil spills, 412, 803, 806, 926, 1100, 1114, 1135
Oklahoma
Affirmative Action, 887
Automated Tax Refund Information, 467
company directories, 666
corporation information, 661
County Employment and Wage Data, 887
Department of Securities, 669
Employment Statistics, 887

Homeless Program, 137
Housing Finance Agency, 137
IRS hotline, 465
licensed professionals, 639
Licensing board and professions, 639
Multi-Family Mortgage Revenue Bond Program, 137
Occupational Wage Surveys, 887
Section 8 Existing Housing Assistance Program, 137
Section 8 Rental Rehabilitation Program, 137
Section 8 Voucher Assistance Program, 137
Single-Family Mortgage Revenue Bond Program, 137
Small Business Administration Offices, 838
state data centers, 903
state income tax, 500
state information, 38
State International Trade Offices, 859
State Labor Office, 887
State Planning Office, 910
state procurement office, 842
Statistical Abstract, 906
surplus property auctions, 708
Tax Commission, Motor Vehicle Division, 644
Tax form distribution center, 471
Tax forms and publications, 492
unclaimed property office, 715
Uniform Commercial Code Office, 633
U.S. International Trade Administration Office, 856
Older Americans
see Aging and Elderly
Olympics, congressional caucus, 1187
On-line economic bulletin board, 853
On-line Library System (OLS), 1238
On-the-Job drug testing, 607
One-Participant Owners and Their Spouses Pension Benefit Plan, 485
OPEC, 1060
Open-end investment company, 441
Open systems interconnection, 1008
Opera grants, 762
Operation Desert Shield, 453
Tax information for those affected, 497
Operation Liftoff, 1288
OPM Atlanta Region Bulletin Boards System, 1238
Optical communications equipment, 1006
Optical disc, 779, 977, 1203
Optical diseases
research grants, 287
Optical disk media, 1008
Optical emission, 1005
Optics, 958, 989
fiber, 977, 1203
Optometry, 244
Oral diseases, 765
Orchids, 140
Oregon
Licensing boards and professions, 639
Affirmative Action, 887
Agricultural Employment, 887
Asia Representatives Office, 910
Automated Tax Refund Information, 467
Bureau of Land Management office, 695
Business and Employment Outlook, 887
Business Expansion, 910
Community Development Corporation Program, 137
company directories, 666
corporation information, 662
Department of Transportation, Motor Vehicles Division, 644
Directory of Oregon Electronic

Products, 908
Division of Finance and Corporate Securities, 669
Economic Trends, 910
Elderly and Disabled Housing Program, 137
Electronic Products, 910
Exporter's Handbook, 910
Family Rental Housing Program, 137
Forest Products, 910
Franchises, 771
Housing Agency, 137
Industrial Equipment and Supplies, 910
International Trade Directory, 910
IRS hotlines, 465
Lenders' Tax Credit Program, 137
licensed professionals, 639
Low-Income Housing Tax Credit, 137
Low-Income Rental Housing Fund, 137
Manufacturers, 910
Manufacturing Plants, 910
Mobile Home Park Purchase Program, 137
mobile home parks, 130
Mortgage Credit Certificate Program, 137
Occupational Program Planning System, 887
Oregon Economic Profile, 906
Partnership Housing Team, 137
Seed Money Advance Program, 137
Single-Family Mortgage Program, 137
Small Business Administration Offices, 839
state data centers, 903
state income tax, 500
state information, 38
State International Trade Offices, 859
State Labor Office, 887
State Planning Office, 910
state procurement office, 842
surplus property auctions, 709
Tax form distribution center, 471
Tax forms and publications, 492
Taxes, 910
unclaimed property office, 715
Uniform Commercial Code Division, 633
U.S. International Trade Administration Office, 856
Wage Information, 887
Organ procurement grants, 363
Organ rejection, 574
Organic analysis, 1009
Organic wastes, 1030, 1129
Organization of American States (OAS), 927
Organization of Licensing Boards, 636
Organizations
Exempt Business Income Tax Return, 476
Income Tax Exemptions, 475
Organized crime, 606
FBI, 600
Original Discount Instruments, 497
Orphan drugs, 551, 569
Orthographics, 1010
Orthopedics, 509, 540, 547
OSHA
see Occupational Safety and Health Administration
Osteoporosis, 515, 977, 1203
elderly, 557
older women, 559
OTA
see Office of Technology Assessment
Other industry experts and sources
100 Industry Analysts--Commerce Dept., 654
industry observers, 654
suppliers, 654
trade associations, 654
trade magazines, 654

The thousands of studies in the Current Events Chapter and Experts Chapter are not listed in this index.

Index

Overseas Private Investment Corporation (OPIC), 848
Overseas travel, 31, 859
Over-the-counter drugs, 525
Overtime pay, 239
Owls, 1278
Oxidant pollution, 1109
Oxides, 1224
Ozone, 977, 1054, 1084, 1098, 1109
educational publication, 1264, 1278
holes, 988
stratospheric, 1083
tropospheric, 1083
urban, 972

P

Pacemakers, 1217
Pacific Basin
development grants, 370
health program grants, 364
Paget's bone disease, 559
Painters, 31, 762
Paleoanthropology, 1279
Paleobiology, 320
Pan American Games, 345
Panama Canal, 806, 807, 928, 929, 1279
House Committee on, 1184
Panama Canal Commission, 71
Pandas, 1279
Paper, 779
dioxin reduction, 972
Paraplegic housing, 128
Parasitology, 1023
Parental kidnapping, 614
Parents
drug abuse prevention skills, 580
drug alliance groups, 592
drug-free schools manual, 590
family-based drug treatment, 595
Foster Grandparents, 579
Guide to Drug Abuse Prevention, 592
Parkinson's disease, 509, 550
Parks, National, 400, 406, 408, 1128 1184
cultural resources, 304, 317, 403
reservations, 407
Senate committee, 1181
Parole, drug offenders, 607
Partnerships
capital gains and losses tax forms, 477
federal income tax forms package, 477
interests report of sale, 487
tax information, 494
tax returns, 1978-1982, 453
Passive energy conserving homes, 119
Passive solar homes, 119
Passports, 417, 419, 860
Patent and Trademark Office, 1017
Patent searches, 1018
CompuServe, 1019
Derwent, 1019
Manual and Index to U.S. Patent Classifications, 1019
Mead Data Central, 1019
Rapid Patent, 1019
search fee, 1018
Patents, 1017
agricultural research, 724, 1028
Air Force, 940
animal, 514, 970
Army, 942
attorneys, 1018
biotechnology, 963, 970
CD-Rom discs, 1018
conducting your own patent search, 1018

database, 979
depository libraries, 1018, 1019
disclosure statement, 1017
electronic information, 1020
general information concerning
patents, 1018
government-owned, 942, 953, 955
intellectual property, 973
interference proceeding, 1018
House Committee on, 1184
Navy, U.S., 953
Patent Attorneys and Agents Registered to Practice, 1018
seeds, 141, 1029
Senate subcommittee, 1182
specifications, 1018
statistics, 979
Voucher Affidavit, 1017
Pathobiology, 1099
PCBs, 1145
Peace, high school essay contests, 929
Peace Corps, 31
agriculture programs, 926
business development programs, 915
foreign policy, 1181
public information office, 71
Peale Family Papers, 310
Pedestrians, 825
safety, 353, 829, 1279
Pennsylvania
Annual Report, 910
Automated Tax Refund Information, 467
Bureau of Drivers Licenses
Information, 644
Bureau of Professional and Occupational Affairs, 639
Career Guide, 887
company directories, 666
corporation information, 662
Current Trends in Employment and Wages, 887
Directory of Licensed Occupational Information Systems, 887
Directory of Occupational Wage Information, 887
forest lands, 1264, 1279
Home Owners Emergency Mortgage Assistance Program, 137
HomeStart Program, 137
Hospital Occupational Staffing Patterns, 887
Housing Finance Agency, 137
Industry Trends and Outlook 1995, 887
IRS hotline, 465
Labor Force Data, 887
Labor Market Job Guides, 887
licensed professionals, 639
Low-Income Housing Tax Credit Program, 137
Lower-Income Home Ownership Program, 137
Microcomputer Occupational Information System, 887
Non-Profit Seed Fund Program, 137
Occupational Trends and Outlook, 887
Rental Housing Development Program, 137
Rental Rehabilitation Program, 137
Securities Commission, 669
Small Business Administration Offices, 839
state data centers, 903
state income tax, 500
state information, 39
State International Trade Offices, 859
State Labor Office, 887
State Planning Office, 910
state procurement office, 842

Statewide Home Ownership Program, 137
Statistical Abstract, 906
Supportive Services Program, 137
surplus property auctions, 709
Tax form distribution center, 471
Tax forms and publications, 492
unclaimed property office, 715
Unemployment Fact Sheet, 887
Uniform Commercial Code Division, 633
U.S. International Trade Administration Offices, 856
Pennsylvania Avenue Development Corporation, 71
Pension Benefit Guaranty Corporation, 72, 239
Pensions, 31, 252, 272, 876
federal employees, 275
financial statements, 253
insurance, 253
interest rates, 93
liabilities, 254
military genealogy, 647, 955
protection and retirement equity, 254
recorded message, 93
statistics, 871
summary plan description (SPD), 253
tax guide, 495, 497
trusteeships, 254
Pentagon, drug policy, 607
People's Republic of China, 415
Peregrine falcons, 945, 1132, 1142
Performing arts, 292, 308, 1202
copyrights, 1020
Kennedy Center, 308, 1202
traveling abroad programs, 293, 315
Perimatology, 529
Periodontal disease, 551
Perkins student loans, 188, 380
Permafrost, 994, 1085, 1240, 1258
Personnel management, 272
Peru, alpacas and economic development, 924
Pest control, 1030
equipment, 1029
Pesticide, 525, 929, 1029, 1097, 1098
bulletin board, 1236
database, 1118
hotline, 31, 572, 1029, 1145
information for kids, 1259, 1267, 1279
database, 1145
food, 970, 1031, 1036
health hazards, 571
narcotic plants, 603
products inventory, 1142
program grants, 377
registration, 1145
research, 1134
residues in food, 1230
science, 1099
spraying, 785, 1029
water quality, 1109
Pests and diseases, 1022
Petroleum, 295, 1128, 1227
Alaskan exports, 1069
consumption, 1069
discovery, 1069
educational material, 1259, 1270
extraction methods, 1068
interest group, 1070
marketing, 1069
naval reserves, 1069
overcharges/refunds, 1059, 1070
potential, U.S., 1070
product prices, 1070
production, 1069
refining, 1069
research, 1003
statistics, 1070, 1227
strategic reserves, 1069, 1071

The thousands of studies in the Current Events Chapter and Experts Chapter are not included in this Index.

Index

Petroleum (continued)
supply, 972
tax reform, 1069
windfall profits tax, 1069
world prices, 1071
Pets, 99, 976, 1203
caring for, 1255, 1279
films and videos, 1268, 1279, 1295
importation, 418
Petty, Richard, 1276, 1279, 1280
Pharmaceuticals, 567
adverse reactions to, 1215
Center for Drug Evaluation and Research, 566, 569
drug establishments, 569
drug reactions, 566
drug registration directory, 566
generic drugs, 96
import products, 569
labeling, 566, 569
labeling, 972
latest developments, 566
metal-containing, 1009
orphan drugs, 569
over-the-counter drugs, 566, 569
patent-terms, 974
pharmacology fellowships, 574
prescription drug establishments, 569
prescription drugs, 568
private label distributors, 569
problem reporting, 569
research and development, 569, 976
research on human subjects, 976
safety standards, 566, 569
sales to developing countries, 569, 965
tampering hotline, 523
Pharmacists, 96
Pharmacology, 528, 566, 569, 768, 574
Pharmacy, 244
Pheasants, 1279
Phenomenon, Dial-A, 93
Photographers, 762
grants, 762
polar expeditions, 292, 401, 415
Photographs
aerial, U.S., 348, 1089, 1239
agriculture, 1122
air and space, 308
Air Force aircraft, 941
Air Force art collection, 313
Air Force test flights, 949
American art, 319
American history, 296, 303, 1202
American Indians, 303, 308
American war memorials, 396
architecture, 294, 304, 314, 1088
architecture, Washington, D.C., 297
archive, 308, 1202
Army and Air Force, 315
Army art collection, 315
art, 294, 314
fish and wildlife, 295, 1134
forestry, 296, 1128
geological surveys, 1090
historic American figures, 303, 314
historic engineering projects, 306
historical, 303, 304
labor and employment-related, 237
landslides, 994
Matthew Brady Civil War collection, 941
members of Congress, 648, 1191
military history, 318, 951, 955
minerals, 296, 1128
National Archives, 296
National Gallery of Art collection, 296, 320
National Parks, 296
National Portrait Gallery, 320

Naval history, 953
Panama Canal, 296, 806, 928
President, U.S., 1239
rangeland subjects, 296, 1128
rare, 292, 311, 1203
realty, 296, 1128
reservoirs, 1122
Senate history, 1190
Smithsonian's collections, 296, 321
space, 32, 297, 1094, 1241
sub-Saharan African Art, 294, 313
Tennessee Valley Authority land, 413
U.S. Air Force Pre-1954 Still Photograph Collection, 303
U.S. and foreign aircraft, 294
U.S. Capitol, 296
U.S. Geological Survey, 296, 1094
water resources, 1122
Word War II, 941
Photovoltaics, 764, 1059, 1061
Physical disasters loans, 376
Physical fitness
Amateur Athletic Union, 518
award program, 1279
Presidential Sports Award, 518
Physical sciences grants, 288
Physicians, 972, 973
educational grants, 184
grants, 182
training grants, 171
Physics, 987, 1012, 1014, 1103, 1118, 1148, 1151
arc, 1003
earth and ocean, 990
solar-terrestrial, 994
Pilots
customs rules, 416
examiner bulletin board, 1238
training schools, 248, 787
Pipelines, 820, 1070, 1102, 1146, 1181
accidents, 818
safety, 374, 820, 1070, 1102, 1146
Planets, 1280
posters, 1280, 1281
Planning services for U.S. exporters, 852
Plant closings, 971
Plants
answer line, 31
breeding, 140
care hotline, 141
care information, 141
chemical extraction, 970, 1031
diseases, 1225
edible wild, 976, 1203
endangered species, 977, 1203
jojoba, 142, 977, 1203
medicinal, 141, 976
narcotic, 603, 606
oilseed, 142, 977, 1203
propagation, 140
protection and rescue, 141
rare or endangered, 140
workshops, 31
Plant pathology, 1029
Plant pests and diseases, 1029
Plastics, 955, 976, 1008, 1228
Planting genetics, 1029
Platinum, 815, 952
Plumbing fixtures, 1011
Pocahontas, 1272, 1280, 1285
Poets, 762
grants, 762
Poison
Animal Poison Control Center, National, 1142, 1239
control, 764
Dennis the Menace comic book, 1253, 1280
lead in drinking water, 1112

prevention, 111, 146
Poisonings, 109
Polar expeditions for civilians, 31
Police, 614, 879
drug abuse education, 590
drugs training, 605
equipment testing, 1005
foreign drug seizures, 600
grants, 387
law enforcement center, 606
law enforcement explorer, 606
marijuana plants, 607
radar, 1005
speakers bureau, 592
use of deadly force, 615
Political asylum, 625, 929
Politics, candidate finances, 1221
Pollution
acidic deposition, 1109
aerospace research, 982
agricultural, 1097, 1098
air quality, 1109
air toxics hotline, 1109, 1111
air, 1085, 1092, 1098, 1225
Clean Air Act, 972
Clean Water Act, 1111
climate change, 1109
emission levels, 1113
fertilizers, 1027
fisheries research, 1134
human mortality, 1099
indoor air quality, 1109
indoor air, 515, 977, 1203
international issues, 926
metals contamination, 812, 1118, 1142
monitoring, 1101, 1102
noise prevention, 264
noise, 348, 782, 977, 1095, 1181, 1203
oceans, 805, 1114
oil spills, 806, 1114, 1145
oil, 806, 928
ozone, 1083, 1109
research grants, 288
seafloor mining, 803, 1113, 1135
solid waste disposal, 812, 1118, 1142
standards, 1109
water, 1098, 1101, 1103, 1118, 1148, 1151, 1225
Western water supplies, 1122
Polygraph testing rights, 31
Polygraphs, 614, 971
Polymers, 955, 976, 1005, 1011
composites, 1008
Ponzi schemes, 437
Pools, 112
Poor, 767
Population
aging and the elderly, 874
birth statistics, 576, 878
congressional coalition, 1187
database, 1223
death rates, 878
foreign countries, 863
growth rates, 878, 1232
House Subcommittee on, 1184
international assistance, 929
migratory rates, 878, 1232
patterns, charting of, 907
POPLINE database, 505
projections, 878, 1232
research grants, 286, 768
statistics, 863, 873, 876, 877
world, 878, 1232
Populism, congressional caucus, 1187
Pork, 1229
Pornography
child, 614

The thousands of studies in the Current Events Chapter and Experts Chapter are not listed in this Index.

Index

postal laws, 115
Portland MMEL Bulletin Board, 1238
Ports, 807, 822, 932, 979
Postage rate changes, 117
Postage stamp designs, 114
Postage stamps collection, 320
Postal Rate Commission, 72, 117
Postal Service, U.S.
- closings, 117
- customer complaints, 113
- customer service representatives, 114
- employment opportunities, 273
- House Subcommittee on, 1184
- library, 114
- pen pals, 1279
- post office closings, 118
- Postal Inspection Service, 98, 115
- procurement opportunities, 117

Poster
- alcohol abuse, 589
- A More Perfect Union, 1280
- American motorcycles, 1276, 1280
- American soldier, 1287
- coal, 1251, 1260, 1271, 1278
- drug abuse, 590
- drug prevention, 1280
- Duke Ellington, 1259, 1280
- endangered species, 1281
- energy consumption, 1260, 1281, 1294
- environment, 1265
- fire prevention, 1269, 1281
- Herschel Walker drug prevention, 1280
- International Cometary Explorer, 1281
- Martin Luther King drug prevention, 1273, 1280
- NASA, 1277, 1281, 1288
- National Park Service, 407
- petroleum products illustration, 1261, 1281
- planets, 1280, 1281
- Richard Petty car, 1276, 1279, 1280
- Sewage sludge, 1265, 1281
- Sitting Bull, 1280, 1285
- smoking, 554
- Space Shuttle, 1281, 1289
- Spacelab, 1281, 1289
- Space suit, 1281
- trees, 1265, 1281, 1292
- water cycle, 1265, 1292
- weather watch, 1281, 1297
- wetlands, 1267, 1281, 1282, 1298

Poultry, 863, 1229
- production and diseases, 1028

Poverty, 873

Powell, John Wesley, 1258, 1282

Power
- atmospheric fluidized bed
- combustion, 1067
- commercial cogeneration, 973
- electric, 1052, 1059
- generated at Federal facilities, 1058
- hydroelectric, 1056, 1112

Power of Attorney, 459, 481

Pre-fab housing mortgage insurance, 126

Pregnancy, 528, 545
- adolescents, 526
- AIDS grants, 364
- diabetic, 546
- drug abuse program grants, 364
- food supplements, 522
- premature birth, 530
- smoking, 527
- sonograms, 530
- Spanish publications, 530
- supplemental food program, 385
- teenage, 531

Prentice Hall Legal and Financial Services, 650

Preschool

handicapped program grants, 382
Prescription drugs for free, 31
Prescription drugs, 568, 968
Preservation
- books, 974
- manuscripts, 310, 1202
- research grants, 287
- rural housing grants, 125

President, U.S.
- annual budget, 869
- daily schedule, 93, 1241
- document status, 311
- financial statements, 273
- medals depicting, 1240
- photographs, 1239
- portraits, 1241, 1282
- protection of, 616
- succession rules and administration, 1182
- voice on current issues, 93

President, Vice, senate leader, 1189

President's Committee on Mental Retardation, 535

President's Council on Physical Fitness and Sports, 516, 518

Presidential management intern program, 375

Presidential scholars, 151

Presidents, U.S.
- documents, 310
- libraries, 310
- Lincoln, Abraham, 952
- Nixon White House tapes, 312
- public funding of elections, 1189

Press, foreign centers, 921

Price supports, 755

Primate research, 574

Printing and publishing industry
- New York, 910
- Virginia, 911

Printmakers grants, 762

Prisoners, drug charges, 608

Prisoners-of-war, 648, 945, 956

Prisons
- corrections research grants, 287
- drug-free, 599
- economic impact of, 615
- inmate locator line, 614, 647
- program grants, 371
- recidivism, 616
- reforms, 616

Privacy, 974

Private company information, 649

Private schools
- annual certification of racial nondiscrimination, 485

Pro-life, congressional caucus, 1187

Probation, 621

Procurement
- Agency for International Development, 931
- Air Force, 940
- aviation, 782, 788
- contract loans, 718
- database, 1220
- Defense contractors, largest, 950
- Defense contracts, 945, 946, 958-59, 1183
- Defense Logistics Agency, 946
- Education Department contracts, 167
- Federal Aviation Administration, 788
- Federal Retirement Thrift Investment Board, 276
- health care products, 392
- ink contracts, 1214
- Library of Congress, 1204
- medical devices, 973
- military base exchanges, 941
- military commodity commands, 957
- military computer systems, 942
- military exchanges, 960

minority-owned business, 717
NASA, 987
Navy, 953-54, 988
Panama Canal Commission, 806, 928
paper contracts, 1214
Postal Service, U.S., 117
printing contracts, 1214
Smithsonian Institution, 319
specifications and standards, 959
subcontracting opportunities, 948

Procurement Automated Source System (PASS), 837

Procurement technical assistance, 759

Producer Price Index, 1224

Producer's loans, 479

Product info on 25 world markets, 853

Professional and personal relocation, 898

Project Share, 1228

Propane, 1227

Property improvement loan insurance, 127

Propulsion, 1225
- research, 988

Prosecutors
- drug trafficking, 603
- federal coordination, 603

Prospecting for gold, 31

Prospecting, 811, 812, 1126, 1127, 1240

Prostitution, 610
- child, 614

Proxy filings, 440

Psychology
- chemical dependence research, 578
- history of, 976

Psychotherapy, 972

Psychotropic substances
- *see drugs,* 583

Public corporations, 649

Public corruption and fraud, 610

Public debt, 93

Public housing, 120
- anti-drug effort, 584
- database, 584
- drug abuse, 607
- drug dealers, 599
- drug eradication, 607
- environmental hazards, 124
- evictions, 599

Public information offices
- Action, 62
- Administrative Conference of the United States, 63
- African Development Foundation, 63
- Central Intelligence Agency, 63
- Commission on Civil Rights, 63
- Commodity Futures Trading Commission, 63
- Consumer Product Safety Commission, 63
- Defense Nuclear Facilities Safety Board, 63
- Environmental Protection Agency, 63
- Equal Employment Opportunity Commission, 64
- Executive Branch, 40
- Export-Import Bank of the United States, 64
- Farm Credit Administration, 64
- Federal Communications Commission, 64
- Federal Deposit Insurance Corporation, 64
- Federal Election Commission, 65
- Federal Emergency Management Agency, 65
- Federal Housing Finance Board, 65
- Federal Labor Relations Authority, 65
- Federal Maritime Commission, 65
- Federal Mediation and Conciliation Service, 65
- Federal Mine Safety and Health Review Commission, 65

The thousands of studies in the Current Events Chapter and Experts Chapter are not included in this Index.

Index

Public information offices (continued)
Federal Reserve System, 65
Federal Retirement Thrift Investment Board, 66
Federal Trade Commission, 66
General Services Administration, 66
Inter-American Foundation, 67
Interstate Commerce Commission, 67
Judicial Branch, 40
Legislative Branch, 40
Merit Systems Protection Board, 68
National Aeronautics and Space Administration, 68
National Archives and Records Administration, 68
National Capital Planning Commission, 69
National Credit Union Administration, 69
National Foundation on the Arts and the Humanities, 69
National Labor Relations Board, 70
National Mediation Board, 70
National Railroad Passenger Corporation (AMTRAK), 70
National Science Foundation, 70
National Transportation Safety Board, 70
Nuclear Regulatory Commission, 71
Occupational Safety and Health Review Commission, 71
Office of Government Ethics, 71
Office of Personnel Management, 71
Office of Special Counsel, 71
Panama Canal Commission, 71
Peace Corps, 71
Pennsylvania Avenue Development Corporation, 71
Pension Benefit Guaranty Corporation, 72
Postal Rate Commission, 72
Railroad Retirement Board, 72
Resolution Trust Corporation, 72
Securities and Exchange Commission, 72
Selective Service System, 72
Small Business Administration, 72
Tennessee Valley Authority, 73
Thrift Depositor Protection Oversight Board, 74
U.S. Arms Control and Disarmament Agency, 74
U.S. Department of Agriculture, 41
U.S. Department of Commerce, 42
U.S. Department of Defense, 43
U.S. Department of Education, 46
U.S. Department of Energy, 46
U.S. Department of Health and Human Services, 47
U.S. Department of Housing and Urban Development, 51
U.S. Department of Justice, 54
U.S. Department of Labor, 55
U.S. Department of State, 56
U.S. Department of the Interior, 51
U.S. Department of Transportation, 58
U.S. Department of Treasury, 60
U.S. Department of Veterans Affairs, 62
U.S. Information Agency, 74
U.S. International Development Cooperation Agency, 74
U.S. International Trade Commission, 74
U.S. Postal Service, 75
Public lands, 295, 1128
drug agents, 607
drug labs, 600
revenue generated by, 875, 1128
Public policy, 274
Public service announcements, drug abuse, 593
Public trading, 436
Public works, 346
infrastructure, 777, 967

Publications
government, 1201
state government, 1191, 1204
Publishing
American books overseas, 304, 913
electronic, 1001
government bookstores, 1212
government contracts, 1214
Government Printing Office, 1212
ink contracts, 1214
Puerto Rico
Automated Tax Refund Information, 467
data centers, 903
Form 1040-ES (spanish), 477
IRS hotline, 465
Small Business Administration Office, 839
State International Trade Offices, 859
Tax form distribution center, 471
Tax forms and publications, 492
U.S. International Trade Administration Office, 856
VISTA volunteers, 31
Withholding Statement, 472
Pyramid schemes, 437

Q

Quality control, 1004
Quarantines, agricultural, 1035
Quarks, 976, 1203
Quasars, 983

R

Rabies, 549
Raccoons, 1282
Race and ethnicity, 868
Racial conflict resolution, 349, 612, 616
Radar, police
reports, 31
systems, 952
Radiation, 566, 971, 1009, 1079, 1097, 1098, 1102, 1147
food processing, 1034
measurement, 1009
risks, 540
safety, 569, 570
Radio, 762
cellular, 977, 1203
federal usage, 792
frequency compatibility, 787
Voice of America, 933
Radiobiology, 956, 1055
Radio Free Europe, 929
Radio Liberty, 929
Radiological Defense grants, 380
Radon, 99, 119, 1102, 1103
see also cancer, 540
state housing agencies, 130
gas leaks, 31
Railroad Retirement
Tax Forms, 472
Tax information, 496
Railroad Retirement Board, 72
Railroad workers grants, 389
Railroads
abandoned, 829
accidents, 818, 830
accounting systems, 830
coal rates, 830
congressional caucus, 1187
contract summaries, 825
crossing hazards, 352, 826

customer complaints, 420, 824
derailments, 1003
employee grievances, 259
employee service records, 274
equipment inspections, 830
financial systems, 830
freight statistics, 830
grain transportation, 830
House Committee on, 1183
job placement service, 269
mergers, 830
Northeast Corridor, 829
Passenger Services, 420, 824, 976
Railroad Adjustment Board, National, 259
research and development, 830
safety, 100, 821, 830, 831, 976
safety program grants, 373
Senate committee, 1181
statistics, 779
ticket and travel information, 420, 824
Rain, 1258, 1282
Rain, acid

see also acid rain
activity book, 1264, 1283, 1296
student's sourcebook, 1267
Ranchers, 757, 1042
emergency loans, 125
Range and wildlife ecology, 1125
Rape, 611, 612
Rapid transit, 976
Rare diseases, 551, 569
Rare earth, 1228
Reactors, 1079, 1080
Reading
education literature, 1282, 1290, 1298
publication for parents, 1282
Reading is Fundamental, 1282
Reading Is Fundamental, 151
Real estate, 29
agents and brokers, 635
auctions, 124
brokers, 96
consumer protection laws, 123
crime statistics, 879
discriminatory practices, 121
General Services Administration Property Sales, 700
interstate land sales, 123
investment Trusts, 479
land sale fraud, 123
military relocation assistance, 956
mortgage investment tax, 490
multifamily properties, 123
Small Business Administration (SBA), 701
surplus property, 124
transactions tax, 497
Rearview mirrors, 96, 825
Recalls, 352, 827, 1228
Recapture of Low-Income Housing Credit, 488
Recidivism, 616
drug offenders, 607
Recommended Daily Allowances, 524
Recordkeeping for Individuals Tax Guide, 495
Records management, 246
Recreation, 408, 1134
boating, 414
coastal areas, 413
fishing, 413, 798, 1136
Land Between the Lakes, 403
market study, 408, 413
public lands, 408, 413, 1128
safety, 571
Tennessee Valley Authority, 413
water-related areas, 414
wilderness areas, 403, 408, 414
Recreational vehicles, 641
Recycling, 351, 1147, 1260-1265, 1270, 1278, 1282,

The thousands of studies in the Current Events Chapter and Experts Chapter are not listed in this Index.

Index

1283, 1296
activity book, 1264, 1265, 1283, 1296
coloring book, 1252, 1262, 1282
educational activities, 1260, 1283
educational material, 1264, 1265, 1267, 1283
farm nutrients, 1027
Forest Service's involvement, 1265, 1283
grants, 763
oil, 1070
video, 1262, 1263, 1282, 1283, 1295
waste lubricating oil, 1068
Redlining, 121
Refinancing, 105, 120, 127, 867
Refugees
assistance, 368
asylum, 930
grants, 387
House Subcommittee on, 1184
program grants, 381
resettlement grants, 368
Senate subcommittee, 1182
Registry of Toxic Effects of Chemical Substances, 571, 572
Regulation
airports, 788, 941
alcohol sales and production, 774
alcohol, 94
asbestos, 1095
banking, 427
bottling plants, 671
bridges over navigable waterways, 797, 825
building and construction, 1006
carcinogens, 973
Coast Guard, U.S., 798
consumer credit, 106, 867
credit unions, 433
crude oil pricing, 1059
Customs Service, U.S., 416
drinking water, 1115
economic impact studies, 94
energy, 1061
environmental, 1097, 1102
federal elections, 1189
Federal Reserve System, 105
financial institutions, 1183
firearms, 94, 110
fireworks, 777
fisheries and wildlife, 1184
fishery chemicals, 1134, 1143
food processing, 671
franchise buying and selling, 722
interstate commerce, 777, 827
interstate holding companies, 438
maritime, 1229
migrant workers, 821
natural gas companies, 438
navigation, 412
nuclear energy industry, 1184
nuclear power, 1080
nuclear, 1081, 1181
pilot licenses, 787
ports of call, 807
public holding companies, 441
railroads, 830
seabed mining, 812, 1051, 1111
securities, 441
sewerage, 351
tobacco, 94
transportation safety, 821
utility companies, 677
waterfowl hunting, 1137
wetlands, 970, 1031
wildlife importation, 418
Regulator, 1061
Rehab Centers
drug rehab, 579
Rehabilitation

clearinghouse, 509
community loans, 370
drug abuse, 595
drug services, 579
Health Care Financing, 595
Rehabilitation Agencies
program grants, 381
Religious Organizations
Application for Exemption from
Self-Employment Tax, 482
Exemption from employer social security taxes, 487
Social Security Taxes Exemption, 487
Remedy and device fraud, 97
REMIC
Quarterly Notice to Residual Interest, 478
remote sensing, 971, 981
systems, 990
Renewable energy, 1062
Rental Assistance, 757
Rental Housing
elderly mortgage insurance, 127
grants, 128
middle income, 127
Rental housing, 126
supplemental loan insurance, 127
Rental Rates Across the U.S., 31
Renwick Gallery, 313
Reports
agriculture, 1042, 1043
consumer, 102
education, 230
Reproduction, 974
Reproductive science, 528-29
Request for Copy of Tax Form, 459
Research
agriculture, 1042
child support, 368
educational grants, 179
Fulbright, 187
graduate fellowships, 186
grants, 170, 171, 173, 175, 177, 183, 185, 282-286, 288, 289, 361
health grants, 184
medical fellowships, 185
minority grants, 182, 184
Research Activities
Credit for Increasing Research Activities, 486
Research Information Services, 650
Reserve Officers Training Corps (ROTC), 956
Reserves
grants, 182
Reservoirs, 1217
Residential Rental Project, 489
Residential Rental Property
Tax Guide, 494
Resolution Trust Corporation, 704
Affordable Housing Disposition Program, 704
Houses and Other Property From Failed S&Ls, 704
Housing for the Homeless, 704
public information office, 72
Real Estate and General Merchandise Anyone Can Buy, 704
Tenant Programs, 704
Resources
community, 1253
Restaurants
sanitation, 671
Rescue operations, 988
Resumes, 247
Retail trade, 870
Retinal and Choroidal Diseases Research, 768
Retirement, 517, 1240
bonds, 445

Federal employees, 275
grants, 387
plans, 1181
railroad workers, 274
senior program grants, 378
Revision de las Declaraciones de Impuesto, 454
Rewards,
Forest Service, 603
Reye's Syndrome
see Child Health, 568
Rheumatic Diseases
geriatric medicine, 551
Rhode Island
Occupational Information Coordinating Commission, 639
Accessory Apartments, 137
Affirmative Action, 888
Annual Economic Trend Series, 906
Automated Tax Refund Information, 467
Buy-It/Fix-It Program, 138
Coastal Resources, 911
company directories, 666
Construction Loan Program, 138
Cooperative Housing Demonstration Program, 138
corporation information, 662
Department of Motor Vehicles, 644
Emergency Housing Assistance Program, 138
Employer Assisted Housing, 138
Employment and Wages by City and Industry, 888
Employment Newsletter, 888
Energy-Efficient Homes Program, 137
First Homes Program, 137
Forensic Services, 910
Franchises, 771
Ground Transportation Plan, 910
Home Equity Conversion Mortgage Program, 138
Home Owner's Notes Program, 138
Home Repair, 137
Hospitals, 888
Housing, 910
Housing and Mortgage Finance Corporation, 137
IRS hotline, 465
Land Bank Program, 138
Lease-Purchase Program, 138
licensed professionals, 639
Low-Income Housing Tax Credit Program, 138
Mortgage Credit Certificates, 138
Nuclear Waste Repositories, 911
Outdoors-Recreation and Conservation, 910
Pre-Development Loan Program, 138
Preservation Loan Fund, 138
Rental Housing, 911
Rental Housing Production and Rehabilitation, 137
Securities Division, Department of Business Regulation, 669
Small Business Administration Office, 839
state data centers, 903
state income tax, 500
state information, 39
State International Trade Offices, 859
State Labor Office, 887
State Planning Office, 910
state procurement office, 842
Supportive Services/Robert Wood Johnston Foundation, 138
surplus property auctions, 709
Tax form distribution center, 471
Tax forms and publications, 492
unclaimed property office, 715

The thousands of studies in the Current Events Chapter and Experts Chapter are not included in this Index.

Index

Rhode Island (continued)
Uniform Commercial Code Division, 633
U.S. International Trade Administration Office, 856
Water Resources, 911
Rice, 755
River basins, 1258, 1283
Rivers, 1184, 1258, 1283
Kentucky, 1264, 1284, 1290
scenic river study, 413
Wild and Scenic River System, 409, 1122
Roads, 1184
statistics, 827
Robotics, 264, 815, 999, 1012, 1015
Robots
industrial, 779, 976
Rockefeller Foundation, 292
Rocketry
teacher workshops, 1257, 1277, 1288, 1291
Rockets, 990
teaching guide, 1284
Rocks, 1258
collecting, 1258, 1284
Smithsonian visiting program, 1275, 1284
teacher workshops, 1275, 1284, 1290
Rocky Mountain Spotted Fever
National Institute of Allergy and Infectious Diseases, 549
Roosevelt, Franklin D.
"Day of Infamy" address of 1941, 1284
inaugural address, 1284
Roses, 140
Rotorcraft and powered-lift technology, 982
ROTC, 956
RTC
see Resolution Trust Corporation
Runaway Youth program grants, 366
Runaways, 535, 615
Rural
Clean Water Program, 1115
communities, 347
congressional caucus, 1187
economic development, 344, 1025, 1240
education, 166
electrification, 1183
health care service corps, 250
health care, 518, 575
housing site loans, 125
low income housing loans, 125
low-income housing repair, 125
mail service, 118
rental assistance aid, 125
rental housing loans, 125
small business, 1182
Rural areas
drug rehab services, 595
nutrition education, 524
Rural Communities
health services, 518
Rural Economic Development Loans, 758
Rural Electrification Loans, 758
Rural Health Research, 766
Rural Telephone Bank Loans, 758
Rural Telephone Loans, 758
Russian/Soviet Studies, 306
Rye, 1220

S

S Corporations
capital gains and losses, 480
federal income tax, 479, 480, 496
Saccharin, 972
consumer information, 525
Sackler Gallery, 316

Safe deposit boxes, 711
Safety
airline, 420, 782
alcohol, 588
antennas, 111
aviation, 784, 785, 974
bicycles, 111, 353, 826, 829
boating, 410
building, 1014
chain saws, 111
children, 527
children's furniture, 111
consumer product hazards, 109
dam, 354
drunk driving, 588
earthquakes, 354
fire, 97, 349, 350, 1124
firefighters, 356
fireplaces, 111
fireworks, 111
hazard measurement equipment, 262
highway drivers, 603
home insulation, 111
House Committee on, 1183
job-related injury and illness, 263
kerosene heaters, 111
kitchen knives, 112
lawn mowers, 111
methylene chloride, 111
mini bikes, 111
mining, 264, 815
motor carrier, 973
navigation, 412
nuclear reactors, 1074, 1080
nuclear, 1072, 1080
occupational health, 508
Occupational Safety and Health Administration, 267
occupational, 264, 1227
pedestrian, 353, 829
playground equipment, 111
pools, 112
product, 776
railroads, 830, 976
skateboards, 111
space heaters, 111
standard evaluations, 261
standards, 112
swimming pool-related deaths, 109
television fire and shock, 111
toys, 112
Transportation Safety Board, National, 822
transportation, 100, 819, 821, 831, 1229
trucking, 821
winter storms, 358
wood burning stoves, 111
workplace, 266
Safety and Health Research Grants, 766
Sahel, 930, 931, 970, 1031
Saint Lawrence Seaway, 412, 807
Salad bars, 671
Salaries, federal, 275
Salmon, 1284
Salt, dietary, 525
Sandwich generation, 559
Sanitation, 671, 806, 928
developing countries, 929
Satellites, 986, 1086
anti-drug abuse broadcasting, 593
correlative measurements, 990
Doppler data, 992
global climate changes, 1084
LANDSAT images, 1090, 1200
maps, 1093
meteorology, 1084
oceanographic research, 988
remotely sensed data, 1085, 1101

repair in space, 988
search and rescue, 988
solar power, 972
upper atmosphere research, 990
videocassette, 1284, 1293
Saturn, 1273, 1284
slides, 1284, 1286, 1288, 1289
video, 1273, 1278, 1288, 1293, 1295
Savings bonds
hotline, 445
marketing, 445
recorded message, 93
statistics, 445
tax status, 445
SBA
see Small Business Administration
SBIR
see Small Business Innovative Research
Schizophrenia, 535
Scholarships, 32
Fulbright-Hays, 174
health professions, 951
Native Americans, 149
recorded message, 93
talented students, 243
veteran health care, 157
tax guide, 494
School busses, 96, 825
Schools
see also Education
action against addiction, 349
breakfast program, 385
crime, 612
drug-free awards, 590
drug-free grants, 593
drug-free schools/community, 590
effective drug prevention, 591
energy conservation, 1056
fluoride programs, 551
high school attitudes, 592
junior high drug prevention video, 592
lunch program, 385
milk program, 385
President's physical fitness awards, 518
Schools Without Drugs manual, 590
violence, 349, 610
Science
apprenticeships, 956
education literature, 1274, 1285
educational grants, 173, 178
grants, 179
international cooperation, 1184
pharmacological research grants, 286
publication for parents, 1285
research and development, 1184
research grants, 173, 287
teaching grants, 178, 189
Science and technology, 308, 1202
education, 163
experts abroad program, 291, 309, 415, 913
foreign policy issues, 1100
information database, 163, 1203, 1204
research grants, 186
SCORE
see Service Corps of Retired Executives Association
Sculptors, grants, 31, 762
SDI, 958, 971, 989
Seabees, 953
Seafloor mining, 803, 1113, 1135
Sea, foreign policy issues, 931
Sea Grant publications, 808
Seafood technology, 410, 801
Seafood, 799, 800
Sealants, 955
Seals
drawing, 1255, 1274, 1285, 1298

The thousands of studies in the Current Events Chapter and Experts Chapter are not listed in this Index.

Index

Search and rescue missions, 410, 412, 611, 804, 967, 1096, 1113
Seat belts, 94, 96, 420, 818, 825
SEC
see Securities and Exchange Commission
SEC Document Rooms, 650
Second Surgical Opinion Line, 32, 509, 570
Secret Service, 616
drugs, 608
Secured property, 478
Securities
13F, 441
8-K filings, 442
accounting regulations, 441
acquisition, 442
annual reports to shareholders, 435
anti-takeover amendments, 868
applications, 442
arbitration procedures, 435
auditing standards, 435
bankrupt securities businesses, 444
banks, 440
block distributions, 442
bonds, 444
charitable institutions, 440
civil injunctions, 443
consumer complaints, 444
consumer guide, 106, 436
counterfeit, 439
criminal prosecution, 437
dealers, 436
electronic processing, 437
equity, 438
exchange registration, 437
exemptive relief, 441
federal laws, 443
federal ownership, 877
financial condition of industry, 442
foreign corporations, 437
foreign issuers, 440
fraud, 437, 439
Ginnie Mae mortgage-backed, 121
government, 275, 445
holding companies, 438
hypothecating customers' funds, 444
information technology, 442
international capital markets, 438
investment adviser registrations, 438, 441
investment assistance, 437
investment companies, 439, 441
law enforcement, 437, 439, 442, 443
lost and stolen, 442
lost or stolen, 439, 442, 445
manipulating market prices, 444
market investigations, 439
new rules, 439
notes, 444
October 1987 market break, 444
opening an account with a broker, 439
over-the-counter markets, 439
ownership reporting, 440
proxy material, 440, 442
public trading, 436
pyramid schemes, 437
quarterly and annual reports, 442
registration exemptions, 440, 441, 442, 443
retirement bonds, 445
rulemaking procedures, 441
rules and regulations, 442
sales inquiries, 442
Securities Information Center, 439
Securities Investor Protection
Corporation, 439
small business assistance, 443, 725
state law requirements, 443, 725
State offices, 668
stop orders, 443

tender offers, 443, 868
transaction violations, 444
violations, 443
working capital of U.S. corporations, 442
Securities and Exchange Commission, 649
annual reports, 441
directory of companies, 436
enforcement activities, 437
jobs, 248
organization information, 441
public information office, 72
public meetings, 436
publications on audio cassette, 442
records archives, 442
Seeds
contamination testing, 141, 1030, 1036
patents, 141, 1029
Seeger, Pete
recordings, 1271, 1273, 1276, 1285
Seized property, 1225
Seizure
drug dealer assets, 608
Selective Service System, 957
Americans overseas, 419
public information office, 72
Self-Employed Retirement Plans, 494, 495
Self-help housing, 130
Semiconductors, 951, 968, 1006, 1010, 1013
Seminars
energy, 173
Fulbright-Hays, 175
humanities, 173
Senate
agriculture committee, 1181
appropriations committee, 1181
Chaplain, 1192
committee listing, 1192
forestry committee, 1181
history, 1190
library, 1192
majority leader, 1189
military committee, 1181
nutrition committee, 1181
recorded message, 93
rules and administration, 1182
science and technology committee, 1181
Secretary of, 1192
Senility, 556
Senior citizens
see also Aging
employment grants, 389
food program, 386
grants for the blind, 389
grants, 388
traveling abroad, 415
Service academies, 159
Service Center Offices, 458
Service Corps of Retired Executives Association (SCORE), 755
Sesame Street
fire prevention materials, 1269, 1285
Set-asides, government contracts, 836
Sewerage, 351
Sexuality
adolescents, 765
alcohol effects, 588
elderly, 556, 559
Sexually transmitted diseases, 518, 537
research grants, 287
Shareholder taxes, 475
Sharks, 976, 1203
exhibit, 1285
Sheep and fur-bearing animals, 1028
Shelter
emergency program grants, 380
grants program, 371
Sherman Act, 609

Ship financing guarantees, 761
Shipboard firefighting, 761
Shipbuilding, 808
Shipping, 761, 798, 1181
building, 808
Coast Guard boardings, 613, 800, 923, 949
customs laws, 418
dry bulk, 1231
federally funded companies, 804, 926
foreign seizure protection, 800, 807, 919
general cargo, 1231
international legal protection, 419
merchant vessels, 1224
regulation database, 1229
regulations, 804
rights of passage, 804
Saint Lawrence Seaway, 807
search and rescue missions, 410, 798
tankers, 1231
traffic monitoring, 809, 832
unions, 804
U.S. Department of Transportation, 701
war insurance, 809, 934
Shoe prints, 613
Shotguns, 1005
SIC codes, 657, 667, 1230
Sickle cell anemia, 515, 551, 976, 1203
Silicides, 1224
Sinusitis, 539
Site location software, 898
SITES Updates, 702
Sitting Bull, 1272, 1280, 1285
Skateboards, 111
Skin
diseases, 551
elderly, 559
information clearinghouse, 551
research grants, 286, 767
Skylab, 1294
slides, 1285, 1286
videos, 1285, 1294
Slaughterhouses, 671
Slides
aerospace-related, 1277, 1288
ancient cultures, 1255
Apollo-SOYUZ, 1286
archaeology, 1285
art, 1268, 1286, 1293
astronauts, 1286, 1286, 1289
dinosaurs, 1285
energy-related, 1261, 1286, 1294
flash flood, 1270, 1286, 1297
glaciers, 1285
Halley's Comet, 1252, 1272, 1286
hurricanes, 1272, 1286, 1297
moon landing, 1276, 1286
Natural History Museum, 1285
Neptune, 1277, 1286
Saturn, 1284, 1286
Skylab, 1285, 1286
space exploration, 1286, 1288, 1289, 1292
Space Shuttle, 1286, 1289
Space Transportation System, 1286
thunderstorms, 1286, 1291, 1297
tornados, 1286, 1291, 1297
Voyager, 1286
Small business
advocates, 727
agriculture, 1042
assistance, 725
capital formation, 435, 443, 718, 724-25
crime prevention, 724
database, 718
Defense Department procurement, 958
deregulation, impact of, 1185
development centers, 376, 725
development company loans, 718

The thousands of studies in the Current Events Chapter and Experts Chapter are not included in this Index.

Index

Small business (continued)
disaster loans, 718
earthquake preparedness, 354
economic trends, 717
economics, 725
energy audits, 729
EPA regulations, 718, 1101, 1104
export assistance, 729, 1039
export expansion, 1182
export opportunities, 724
exports, 1185
FDA regulation assistance, 722
federal securities laws, 443, 725
films, 722
financial management, 722
government contracting, 1182
grants, 376
handicapped assistance loans, 718
high technology, 725
home-based business, 724, 726
hotline, 717
incubators, 722
Institutes, 729
international seminars, 722
international trade assistance, 719
inventors, 729
investment companies, 728
job creation, 725
legislation, 1185
loans, 32, 717, 719
management counseling services, 723
managerial assistance, 725
marketing, 724
mentors, 32
military procurement, 956
minority-owned, 719, 724, 1182
Native Americans, 722
new products, 724
occupational safety and health, 266
personnel management, 724
Procurement Automated Source System, 1228
procurement, 725
product pricing, 724
research and development funding, 724, 725
research studies, 725
rural economy, 1182
seasonal line of credit, 725
securities legal assistance, 442
Senate committee, 1182
Small Business Innovation Research (SBIR), 725
solar energy loans, 726
subcontracting opportunities, 957
surety bonds, 726
tax workshops, 462
taxation, 717, 725
technology transfer, 1013, 1182
timber sales, 701
tourism, 1185
transportation loans, 722, 726, 820
venture capital, 726, 729
veterans, 726
women-owned, 726
Small Business Administration
8(a) program, 834, 836
Business Opportunity Specialist, 834
Legal Assistance Network, 854
Office of Innovation, Research and Technology, 840
Pre-Solicitation Announcement (PSA), 840
Procurement Automated Source System (PASS), 834, 837
public information office, 72
regional offices, 701
Small Business Development Centers, 729, 836

Small Business Innovation Research (SBIR), 719, 725, 840
Small Business Investment Companies, 754
Small Business Tax Education Course, 459
Smithsonian Institution
American graduate studies, 303
Archives, 310, 320
Archives Center, 303, 304
Conservation-Analytical Laboratory, 316
Copper-Hewitt Museum, 314, 316
Discovery Theater, 313
educational materials, 1273, 1277
exhibits and events, 316
Joseph Henry Papers, 303
Museum of Natural History, 320
Museum Reference Center, 316
National Demonstration Laboratory, 295
National Institute for the Conservation of Cultural Property, 316, 320
National Museum of American History, 314
National Museum of Design, 304
National Portrait Gallery, 317
Naturalist Center, 151, 320
Numismatic Collection, 320
Office of Exhibits Central, 320
Office of Folklife Programs, 305, 317
Office of Museum Programs, 319
Office of Research Support, 294, 314
Peale Family Papers, 310
Philatelic Collection, 320
publications, 321
Research Expeditions Program, 384
Sackler Gallery, 316
services for the handicapped, 316
Smithsonian Institution Press, 321
Special Foreign Currency Program, 309
Traveling Exhibition Service (SITES), 702
Woodrow Wilson International Center for Scholars, 305
Smoke detectors, 349, 350
Smoke, 1011
Smokey Bear, 1129
fire prevention material, 1253, 1269, 1287
Smoking, 502, 554, 559
adolescents, 554
carcinogenesis, 554
cessation, 553
community intervention programs, 346, 554, 576
education programs, 554
elderly, 518, 558
free help to quit, 32
mass media, 554
parent guide, 553
passive, 972
pregnancy, 527
prevention programs, 545, 554
research, 554
tobacco use, 554
Smuggling, 613, 800, 923, 949
Snakes, 1287
Snow, 1230
Snuff, health risks, 554
Social sciences, 987
Social Security
cards, 473
coal miner grants, 387
congressional caucus, 1187
disability grants, 387
grants, 387
research grants, 286
self-employment tax, 476
Senate subcommittee, 1181
statistics, 865
survivor's insurance, 387
Social Services community grants, 366, 367

Social studies education literature, 1287
Social workers, 635
Socioeconomic and demographic research, 764
Software, 1253, 1272, 1289
aerospace-related, 161
CD-ROM, 863
competition, 973
data administration, 1004
development, 1010
digital cartography, 1089
digital spatial data, 964, 1089
environmental education, 148, 1096
federally-owned, 969
graphics, 1010
mapping, 964, 1089
mathematical, 1006
National Technical Information Service, 964
portability, 997
SDI, 971
speech recognition, 1013
Soil, 1226, 1230
soil conservation, 1112, 1265
conservation plan certification, 488
erosion, 142, 977, 1203
fertility, 1030, 1129
loans, 757
maps, 1030, 1129
microbes, 140, 1024
water resources, 1030
Solar, 767, 971
buildings, 1062
disturbances, 1086, 1104
energy, 1011, 1062, 1063, 1086
educational materials, 1261
heat, 1261, 1272, 1287
radiation, 1083, 1109
Solar system, 1225
video, 1287, 1294
Soldiers, posters, 1287
Sole proprietorships, 453
Solid earth geophysics, 994
Sorghum, 1220
production, 1029
Sound, 1010
Sound recordings
copyrights, 1020
historical, 295, 1200
South Africa, 415
South Asian studies, 306
South Carolina
Automated Tax Refund Information, 467
Commission on the Future, 907
Community Home Ownership Opportunity Partnership (CHOP), 138
company directories, 666
corporation information, 662
Employment and Wages, 888
Employment Trends, 888
Highway Department, Public Transportation, 645
Home Ownership Mortgage Purchase Program, 138
IRS hotline, 465
Labor Market Review, 888
licensed professionals, 639
Licensing boards and professions, 639
Low-Income Housing Tax Credit Program, 138
Moderate Rehabilitation Program, 138
Multi-Family Development Programs, 138
Occupational Projections 1990, 888
Section 8 Certificates and Vouchers, 138
Section 8 Moderate Rehabilitation Program, 138
Securities Division, 669
Small Business Administration Office, 839

The thousands of studies in the Current Events Chapter and Experts Chapter are not listed in this Index.

Index

South Carolina Statistical Abstract, 906
state data centers, 903
State Housing Financing and Development Authority, 138
state income tax, 500
state information, 39
State International Trade Offices, 859
State Labor Office, 888
State Planning Office, 911
state procurement office, 842
surplus property auctions, 709
Tax form distribution center, 471
Tax forms and publications, 492
unclaimed property office, 715
Uniform Commercial Code Division, 633
U.S. International Trade Administration Offices, 856

South Dakota
Affirmative Action, 888
Automated Tax Refund Information, 467
Central Filing System, 633
company directories, 666
corporation information, 662
Division of Motor Vehicles, 645
Division of Securities, 669
Economic Development Programs, 911
Emergency Shelter Grants Program, 138
Employment and Earnings, 888
Energy Efficiency Program - New Construction, 138
Existing Housing Assistance Payments Program, 138
Franchises, 771
Home Ownership Mortgage Program, 138
Housing Development Authority, 138
IRS hotline, 465
Labor Bulletin, 888
licensed professionals, 639
Licensing boards and professions, 639
Low-Income Housing Tax Credit Program, 138
Manufacturers and Processors, 911
Multi-Family Housing Trust Fund, 138
Occupational Wage Information, 888
Rental Rehab Program, 138
Small Business Administration Office, 839
South Dakota Community Abstract, 906
state data centers, 903
state information, 39
State International Trade Offices, 859
State Labor Office, 888
State Planning Office, 911
state procurement office, 842
Statewide Job Listings, 888
surplus property auctions, 709
Tax form distribution center, 471
Tax forms and publications, 492
unclaimed property office, 715
U.S. International Trade Administration Offices, 856

Southern Africa, 1187

Soviet Union (Russia)
aerospace cooperation, 971
arms control compliance, 938
broadcasts, 792
cultural exchanges with U.S., 933
jewry, 1187
mail to and from, 115
military weapons, 943
propaganda, 933
research, 930
search and rescue program, 988
space programs, 975
transportation technology, 932, 979
U.S./Soviet arms control negotiations, 937
weapons systems, 943

Soybeans, 1187, 1220

Space
arms control, 970
commercial development of, 983
deep space tracking, 985, 986
electrodynamic phenomena, 990
environment lab bulletin board, 1238
European Space Agency, 989
exploration, 989
Galileo, 986
Gamma Ray Observatory, 983
House Committee on, 1184
Hubble Space Telescope, 986, 989
launch options, 971
Magellan, 986
manned flight, 976, 986, 1203
Mars Observer, 986
newsgathering, 971
photos, 32
remote sensor systems, 990
rocket launches, 990
sounding rockets, 990
Soviet programs, 975
Space Network, 990
Space Shuttle, 986, 987, 989
Space Station Freedom, 984
Space Station, 986, 987
Spacelab, 984
Star wars, 975
stations, 971
Tracking and Data Relay Satellite System, 990
transportation, 970, 971
U.S.-Soviet cooperation, 971
vehicle launches, 989
videos, 30
Voyager, 986

Space Camp, 32, 163

Space exploration, 1276, 1287
educational aids, 1253, 1268, 1277, 1288, 1290, 1293
slides, 1257, 1272, 1273, 1275, 1276, 1278, 1284, 1288, 1289, 1292, 1293, 1295
videos, 1257, 1272, 1273, 1275, 1276, 1278, 1284, 1288, 1289, 1292, 1293, 1295

Space heaters, 111

Spacelink, 163, 1253, 1276, 1281, 1288

Space management research, 779

Space Shuttle, 1289
data base, 1253, 1255, 1289
external tank, 986
filmstrip, 1268, 1289
poster, 1281, 1289
slides, 1286, 1288, 1289
video, 1288, 1289, 1295

Space Shuttle Columbia, 1289, 1294
videos, 1289, 1293, 1294

Space Station, 985, 986, 988
videos, 1293

Space suits
poster, 1281
videocassette, 1294

Space Telescope Science Institute, 986

Space Transportation System, 1289, 1294

Spacelab poster, 1281, 1289

Spacemobile, 1276, 1287

Speakers, public service, 275

Speakers
Agency for International Development, 913
agriculture, 913
arms control and disarmament, 938
Army research, 943, 982
Army, 943
astronauts, 161
aviation accident prevention, 781
cancer, 541
cold environments research, 945, 963
Commerce Department, U.S., 775
conservation, 943
consumer affairs, 95
Defense issues, 350, 953
disaster relief, 913
drug experts, 590
economic policy, 913
Employment of the Handicapped Speakers Bureau, 564
Interstate Commerce Commission, 828
law enforcement, 592
Marine Corps, 348, 350
military training and organization, 960
National Endowment for the Arts, 315
naval research and development, 952
occupational safety and health, 266
Overseas travel for artists, 293, 315
Postal Service, 117
public transportation, 821
science and technology, 958
space technology, 958, 989
technology, 944
transportation safety, 822
transportation, 821
U.S. Capitol Historical Society, 1241
wildlife, 943
women's issues, 913
world hunger, 913

Species, endangered
Smithsonian visiting program, 1259
teacher workshops, 1259, 1290

Specimen bank, 1009

Spectrometers, 1009

Speech
computer recognition, 1013
disorders, 509
impairments, 972
speech recognition technology, 1004
rehabilitation, 504, 563

Speed limits, 98, 352, 614, 828

Spinal cord
birth defect, 551
injury, 551

Sports, 518
drug abuse video, 592
experts abroad program, 291, 309, 415, 913
mental health, 535

Sports medicine, 509, 540, 547

St. Lawrence Seaway
recorded message, 93

Stamp clubs, 1290

Stamp tax, 473

Stamps
collecting, 116
design copyrights, 114
duck stamps, 291, 1133
production, 431

Standards, 1007

Star Gazer Hotline, 32

Star Wars (SDI), 959, 971, 975, 990

Stars
Northern Skies, 1254, 1290

Start-up money, rural economic development, 28

State Chamber of Commerce, 664

State data centers, 875, 898, 899

State Department
Center for the Study of Foreign Affairs, 915
Citizens Emergency Center, 415
Country Desk Officers, 845, 917
diplomatic archives, 918
diplomatic missions, 934
diplomatic reception room tours, 397
diplomatic security analysts, 418
embassies, 418, 932
Emergency Medical and Dietary Assistance Program, 415
Foreign Service, 934

The thousands of studies in the Current Events Chapter and Experts Chapter are not included in this Index.

Index

State Department (continued)
historian, 923
intelligence research, 917
international conferences, 925
organizational publication, 927
Overseas Citizens Services, 417
Overseas Security Advisory Council, 417
passport services, 417
public information offices, 56
treaty negotiations, 932
United Nations issues, 932
United States Nuclear Risk Reduction Center, 936
State documents, 657
State government auctions, 705
State information
Capitol Library, 651
Department of Commerce, 651
Directories, 651
Government Operator, 651
State licensing boards, 635
State tax assistance, 498
Statistical Abstract of the United States, 905
Statistical engineering, 1014
Statistics
abortions, 575, 576
accidents involving hazardous material, 357, 820, 826, 1144
aging-related, 868
agriculture, 868, 1042, 1037-38
aid, international, 925
AIDS, 873
air pollution, 1109
air traffic, 781, 785
aircraft accidents, 781
aircraft maintenance, 782
airports, 784
alcohol products, 774
ambulatory care, 567
AMTRAK operations and finance, 824
armed forces, 938
aviation accidents, 782
aviation finances, 786
aviation, 782, 784, 788
banking deposits, 428
banking, 427
banks, failed and problem, 429
beer production, 774
births, 575, 576, 1232
boating accidents, 1216
bond forgery, 431
Bureau of Labor Statistics, 237
Bureau of the Census, 876
business, 862, 1229
campaign finance, 1188
cartographic, 1088, 1089
check forgery, 431
chemical weapons research, 958
child care, 234
cities, 865, 1225
civilian workforce, federal, 276
climate, 1087
coal useage, 1052
collective bargaining, 873
college graduates, 875
commodity pricing, 872, 1217
company health inspections, 262
consumer expenditures, 873
Consumer Price Index, 240
corporate tax, 453
correctional facilities, 616
counterfeiting, 431
county, 865
county-to-county migration, 866
crime, 610, 873, 879
deaths, 575, 576, 1232
Defense Department, 950
demographics, 872
disabilities, 146
divorces, 575, 576
driver licenses, 827
drug abuse, 349, 612
drug crimes, 610
earnings, 873
economic trends, 105, 867
economic, 866, 870, 1219, 1230
education, 147, 152, 168, 230, 868
education, American Indian, 149
educational attainment, 238
elderly, the, 868
electric and telephone borrowers, 791
electric bills, 865
electricity consumption, 1052, 1058
employment and foreign economics, 236, 921
employment and unemployment, 235, 238, 873
employment benefits, 251
employment by industry, 237, 871
Employment Cost Index, 240, 873
energy consumption, residential, 1062
energy supply and demand,
international, 1057
energy, 1062, 1063
excise tax rates, federal, 774
explosive incidents, 110
fatal highway accidents, 353, 831
fatalities, job-related, 1216
federal elections, 1189
Federal government, 1184
federal magistrates, 620
firearms, 774
fish consumption, 799
fisheries, 800
fishing, commercial, 800
fishing, recreational, 800
foreign military sales, 936, 949
foreign trade, 868, 1221
foreign visitors to U.S., 421
fraud, 431
fringe benefits, 876
gasoline, 827
government employment, 865
grants, 372
gross national product, 868
handicapped, 1227
health care personnel, 270
health care, 575
health care, military, 947
health, 973
highway, 827, 1223
household goods carriers, 780
housing finance, 122
housing, 119, 873
Huntington's Disease, 549
hydrocarbon, 1216
hydrologic, 1113
import and export price indexes, 873
income, 871
industrial relations, 238
industries, 866
industry productivity, 871
international development, 872
international travel, 421
international, 863
Job Corps, 237
job training, 873
job-related injuries and illnesses, 263
labor lawsuits, 256
labor practice lawsuits, 258
labor relations, 257, 271
large class I motor carriers, 779
lawn mower-related injuries, 109
marine pollutants, 803, 1113, 1135
maritime trade, 804, 926
marriages, 575, 576
meats, 1229
Medicaid and Medicare, 575
migratory birds, 1135
military arms exports and imports, 938
military expenditures, 938
military fuel consumption, 949, 1068
military manpower, 947
mine map repositories, 813, 1093
mineral commodities, 451, 813
mining injuries and illnesses, 264
minority businesses, 724
minority labor, 238
missile systems research, 941
motor carriers of passengers, 779
motor carriers, 780, 831
National Airport System, 787
National Guard, 953
National Park Service, 407
Native Americans, 123, 150, 626, 629, 1127
New England economics, 105, 867
nuclear operating units, 1079
nutrition in the U.S., 521, 575
occupational analyses, 238
occupational mobility, 238
occupational pay surveys, 240
occupational trends, 245
occupations, nationwide, 871
ocean pollution, 805, 1114
oil spills, 412, 803, 1114, 1135
outdoor recreation, 1129
patents, 979
petroleum industry, 1070, 1225
pilots, 785
population, 529, 868, 878
poultry, 863
pregnancy-related deaths, 529
prices, 869
product-related injuries and deaths, 109
productivity, multifactor, 869, 871, 873
protective intelligence, 431
public lands, 1128
race and ethnicity, 868
rail freight, 830
railroad accidents, 830
railroad benefits, 274
railroad employment, 780
railroads, 779, 780, 831
recidivism, 616
recreational activity, 408, 413
registered securities issues, 442
Saint Lawrence Seaway, 807
savings bonds, U.S., 445
school enrollment, 238
securities industry, 442
shoplifting, 879
small business, 717
smoking, 554
State Data Centers, 875
Statistical Abstract of the United States, 875
strikes and lock outs, 242
student loans, 1222
taxes, 240, 457
technology and the economy, 240, 874
technology transfer, 236, 921, 990
technology trends, 980
tobacco production, 774
tobacco use, 554
toll bridges, 827
tourism, U.S., 420
traffic trends, 827
traffic, 779
transportation, 353, 779, 823, 827, 868
trust assets, 428, 429
tunnels, 827

The thousands of studies in the Current Events Chapter and Experts Chapter are not listed in this Index.

Index

unemployment insurance, 240, 255
uranium, 1074
USDA economic research, 1037
veterans affairs, 862, 871
victims of crime, 617
wages, 869
water, 1118
white-collar crime, 879
white-collar salaries, 241
wildland fire, 1130
wind, 1062, 1086
wine production, 774
women in the workforce, 241, 877
women in the workplace, 234
work stoppages, 235, 865
workers compensation, 235, 865
Statue of liberty, 401
Steam energy, 1258, 1261, 1290
Steel, 1006, 1187
industry, 974
Sterilization
Spanish consent form, 530
vasectomies, 530
Steroids, 586
prevention, 586, 592
Stirling engines, 1063
Stock, 668
Stock broker complaint line, 32
Stolen property, 611
Storms, 358
Strategic Defense Initiative, 975
Strategic materials, 867
Stratigraphic nomenclature, 993, 1090
Streams, 1217
Kentucky, 1264, 1284, 1290
Stress, 515, 977, 1203
Stroke, 509, 551, 573
Structures, 1010
nondestructive evaluations, 1007
Student loan hotline, 32
Students
data, 230
educational grants, 180, 184
foreign student support services, 157
grants and loans, 182, 183, 185, 187, 188
grants, 176, 188, 189
income tax, 493
loans, 380
statistics, 230
volunteer programs, 384
Sub-Saharan African Art, 294, 313
Subsidiary corporation tax, 480
Subsidized energy financing, 486
Substance abuse
legal issues, 590
prevention, 590
Sudden Infant Death Syndrome (SIDS), 530, 533
Sugar
crops, 1029
substitutes, 525
Sulfides, 1224
Summer jobs, 32
Sun, solar activity, 992
Sunbelt, 1187
Sunflower seeds, 1220
Sunshine, 1062, 1086
Supercomputers, 974
Superconducting Super Collider, 761
Superconductors, 971, 1007
Superfund, 972, 1103, 1181
technical assistance, 762
Supreme Court of the U.S., 616, 622
records and briefs, 618, 925, 1193, 1201
Surety companies, 755
Surgeon General, 502
health promotion report, 518
Surplus property, 695

books, 1204
dairy products, 345, 523, 1034
Defense Department, 959
E.G.& G. Dynatrend, Property
auctions, 698
grain for wildlife, 1135
grain oil, 345, 523, 1034
Indianapolis Star, surplus property auction
announcements, 706
manure, 1240
peanuts, 345, 523, 1034
small business, 700
Washington Times, DC surplus property
auctions, 705
Surveying, 1124
Surveys, 875
agriculture, 1042, 1043
Swans, 1290
Swine production, 1028
State, U.S. Department of
public information offices, 56

T

Tactical weapons, 959
Tampons, toxic shock syndrome, 551
Target market identification, 898
Target survivability, 950
Tariffs
common carrier filings, 830
interstate commerce, 829
Senate committee, 1181
Taxes
audits, 460
Automated Refund Information, 466
braille tax information, 461
bulletin board, 1235
changing federal laws, 462
commercial Fishermen, 493
counselling for the Elderly, 460
court, 461
credits for employers, 780
drug traffickers, 608
education for High School Students, 461
elderly assistance, 460
electronic federal deposit system, 424
employment of disabled, 564
estate and gift, 454
exempt organizations, 461, 1231
federal pensions, 275
foreign tax credit, 454
free assistance, 457
hearing impaired services, 461
hotlines, 464
incentives for historical preservation, 306, 350
international, 460
laws, 459
legislation, 869
military personnel, 492
motor vehicle, 827
Operation Desert Shield, 453
petroleum industry, 1069
preparation courses, 32
publications, 491
railroad retirement benefits, 274
rate structure, 456
refunds, 477
rewards, 608
representation before IRS, 458
retirement plans, 456
revenue yields, 456
Senate committee, 1181
shelter registration, 487
small business, 462, 493

state mortgage loans, 130
statistics, 460
wage reporting, 462
workshops for small businesses, 462
Taxpayer Education Coordinators, 455
Teacher Resource Network, 164
Teacher workshops
aerospace-related, 1277, 1288
National Aeronautics and Space
Administration, 1257, 1276, 1277,
1281, 1284, 1288, 1290
National Air and Space Museum, 1277,
1288, 1290
National Archives, 1277, 1291
wildlife conservation, 1291, 1298
Teachers
aeronautics, 164
aerospace workshops, 26
astronomy, 164
education information, 153
educational grants, 179, 181
education literature, 1291
English, 143, 155, 914, 929
foreign education, 143, 914
geology, 165, 992
grants, 170-81, 189
international exchange programs, 155, 913
listing of, 230
math and science, 162
minority grants, 182, 282
research grants, 172
seminar grants, 173
space-related courses, 163
space-related education, 161
special education, 175
statistics, 230, 868
study abroad programs, 155, 913
supply and demand, 868
technology,new, 971
Tear gas devices, 1005
Technical training, 30
Technological innovation, 840
Technology, 1015
Africa, 931, 970, 1031
agriculture, 965, 970, 1025, 1031
anti-pollution, 812, 1118, 1142
assistance centers, 729
ballistic missiles, 970
biofuels, 1050
building, 998, 1003
commercialization, 979, 980, 1000
communications, 347, 790, 964
congressional caucus, 1187
defense, 971
education, 167, 965, 971
energy, 872, 969, 1059, 1063
environmental, 1067, 1084, 1103
European programs, 966
extension services, 1015
federal resources, 948
government developed, 969
grants for handicapped, 179
handicapped, 971
health care, 973
highways, 822, 932, 979
history, 977, 1203
House Subcommittee on, 1184
industrial process, 1056
information, 965, 967, 971, 973, 1004, 1025
international agreements, 980
international competition, 979
international development, 930
Japanese, 976, 977, 979, 1203
legal issues, 1182
measurement, 1006
policy, 980
productivity, 980

The thousands of studies in the Current Events Chapter and Experts Chapter are not included in this Index.

Index

Technology (continued)
research grants, 287
research referral database, 947, 964
Reynolds number research, 990
small business, 725, 1013, 1182
software, 1000
State development, 1014
telecommunications, 1000, 1004
Third World development, 931
water resources, 1118
wind, 1065
workplace, 244
Technology Evaluation Program, 763
Technology in Education, 764
Technology transfer
aerospace, 981, 982
agricultural research, 724, 1028, 1030
Army technology, 943, 982
Army, U.S., 943
biofuels, 1050
biomass energy, 1050
biomedical research, 568
China, 971
coal-based technologies, 1067
energy information services, 1051
Environmental Protection Agency, 966, 1103
Federal Laboratory Consortium, 960, 980
foreign policy, 937
fossil energy, 1068
geothermal energy, 1055
government patents, 969
government/industry data exchange, 959
hotline, 1049
Institute of Standards and Technology, National, 1012
international development, 918
manufacturing, 1015
medical technology, 568
Middle East, 971
military, 960, 980
NASA Industrial Applications Centers, 984
NASA, 985, 990
National Institutes of Health, 973
Navy, U.S., 954
solar energy, 1062
statistics, 990
veterans rehabilitation, 394
Technology Transfer Bulletin Board, 1238
Technology transfer, 980, 1015
Technology-based firms, 840
Teenage
cigarette smoking test, 555
entrepreneurs loans, 757
pregnancy, 1025, 1240
Telecommunications
abroad, 347, 790, 964
computer-related, 796
domestic competition, 796
education, 167
foreign trade opportunities, 796
grants, 283
House Subcommittee on, 1183
Institute for Telecommunication Sciences, 796
integrated services digital networks, 1004
International Maritime Satellite Organization, 793
international policy, 793
International Telecommunication Union, 793
International Telecommunications Satellite Organization, 793
national security issues, 793
National Telecommunications and Information Administration, 778, 794
Organization for Economic Cooperation

and Development, 793
policies and standards, 796
public service groups, 347, 351, 796
radio frequency spectrum, 796
research and development, 796
rural telephone companies, 796
Senate committee, 1181
technology, 966, 1000
Telephone bank loans, 758
Telescope, Hubble Space, 1253, 1272, 1291
Teletax topics numbers and subjects, 468
Television, 762
archive, 295, 1202
cable, 99, 779, 976, 1203
high-definition, 796
violence, 612
WORLDNET, 934
Tennessee
Automated Tax Refund Information, 467
company directories, 666
corporation information, 662
Division of Securities, 670
Drivers: Department of Safety Information System, 645
Economic Statistics, 911
Employment Projections 1990, 888
Home Ownership Program, 138
HOUSE Program, 138
Housing Development Agency, 138
IRS hotline, 465
Labor Force Summary, 888
licensed professionals, 640
Licensing boards and professions, 640
Low-Income Housing Tax Credit, 138
Moderate Rehabilitation Program, 138
Owner-Built Homes, 138
Population, 911
Rental Rehabilitation, 138
Section 8 Rental Assistance Program, 138
Small Business Administration Office, 839
state data centers, 903
state income tax, 500
state information, 39
State International Trade Offices, 859
State Labor Office, 888
State Planning Office, 911
state procurement office, 842
surplus property auctions, 709
Tax form distribution center, 471
Tax forms and publications, 492
Technical Assistance Program, 138
Tennessee State Statistical Abstract, 906
Turn Key III, 138
unclaimed property office, 715
Uniform Commercial Code Section, 633
U.S. International Trade Administration Offices, 856
Veterans, 888
Veterans financing, 138
Women in the Labor Force, 888
Tennessee Valley congressional caucus, 1187
Tennessee Valley Authority
Air Pollution Control, 1109
Computer Systems Section, 1050
heat pump program, 1055
Land Between The Lakes, 410
Power System Control Center, 1060
public information office, 73
Terminal care, 976
Term Papers, 32
Terrorism, 355, 853, 1181, 1186
against energy systems, 966, 1063
international business, 418
overseas missions, 418
preparation and survival, 417
Tethered Satellite System, 990
Texas, 906

Affirmative Action, 888
Agricultural Employment Estimates, 888
Automated Tax Refund Information, 467
Civilian Work Force Estimates, 888
company directories, 666
corporation information, 662
Current Population Survey, 888
Department of Public Safety, 645
Employment and Wages by Industry, 888
Hazardous Waste, 911
Higher Education, 911
Housing Agency, 138
IRS hotlines, 465
licensed professionals, 640
Licensing boards and professions, 640
Low-Income Rental Housing Tax Credit, 138
Mortgage Credit Certificate Program, 138
Natural Gas, 911
Occupational Employment Statistics, 888
Petroleum Industry, 911
Sales and Franchise Tax Exemptions, 911
Sales Tax, 911
Section 8 Housing Assistance Program, 138
Single-Family Bond Program, 138
Small Business Administration Offices, 839
state data centers, 903
state information, 39
State International Trade Offices, 859
State Labor Office, 888
State Planning Office, 911
state procurement office, 842
State Securities Board, 670
surplus property auctions, 709
Tax form distribution center, 471
Tax forms and publications, 492
Taxes, 911
unclaimed property office, 716
Uniform Commercial Code, 633
U.S. International Trade Administration Offices, 856
Textiles, 974
care labeling, 95
congressional caucus, 1187
Theater, 762
education, 151
Thermal Energy, 764
Third World
child survival, 916
debt, 1187
economics, 918
private voluntary organizations, 929
Three Mile Island, 1081
Thrift Depositor Protection Oversight Board, 74
Thrift industry, 430
Thrift supervision, 93
Thunderstorms, 1087
slides, 1286, 1291, 1297
videocassettes, 1291, 1295, 1297
Tides, 1231
Timber
industry, 1130
sales to small business, 701
tax forms, 471
Time
atomic clock, 960, 1239
geologic time, 1258, 1291
Naval Observatory recorded message, 93
Tip income tax, 486
Tires, 96, 825
treadwear, 1227
Tobacco
advertising, 94
chewing, 553
smoking clearinghouse, 553
tax classification, 774
tobacco production, 774

The thousands of studies in the Current Events Chapter and Experts Chapter are not listed in this Index.

Index

tobacco use, 554
Toll bridges, 827
Tomography, 973
Tooth decay, 517
Tornadoes, 358, 1087
films, 1268, 1291, 1297
slides, 1286, 1291, 1297
videocassettes, 1291, 1295, 1297
Tourism
advertising, 421
business development, 729
Canadian to U.S., 421
hotlines, state, 422
National Wildlife Refuge System, 1138
National Wildlife Refuges, 1135
public lands, 408, 413, 1128
small business, 1185
trip planning information, 421
Tours
Air Force bases, 396
Army facilities, 396
Beltsville Agricultural Research Center, 396
Botanic Garden, U.S., 396
Bureau of Engraving and Printing, 397
Capitol, U.S., 397
computer facilities, 400, 950
diplomatic reception rooms, 397
FBI Headquarters, 614
Federal Reserve Board, 397
Government Printing Office, 1214
House of Representatives, U.S., 397
Institute of Standards and Technology, National, 397, 1015
Library of Congress, 1201
military test flight center, 396
missile testing center, 400, 952
National Aquarium, 400
National Arboretum, 141, 400
Naval Coastal Systems Center, 952
Naval Observatory, 943
Panama Canal Administration Building, 401, 417
Panama Canal, 400, 417
Pentagon art collection, 401
robotics demonstrations, 1012
TVA dams and reservoirs, 1110
White House, 402
Toxic agent control, 571
Toxic shock syndrome, 551
Toxic waste
chemical emergency response, 357, 571
disposal, 502
international policies, 1054
Toxicology, 1097, 1098, 1103, 1118, 1148, 1151
aquatic, 1099, 1109, 1113, 1118
biophysics, 571
carcinogens, 540
educational material, 1266, 1292
employee exposure, 264
environmental factors, 571
Hazardous Substances Data Bank, 357, 571
National Center for Toxicological Research, 572
National Toxicology Program, 571
neurotoxicity testing, 550, 571
Registry of Toxic Effects of Chemical Substances (RTECS), 571, 572
research, 571, 765
Toxicology Information Program, 357, 571
Toxicology Information Response Center, 357, 571
TOXNET, 357, 571
wildlife, 1101
TOXLINE database, 504
TOXNET database, 505
Toxoplasmosis, 531

Toys, 112
Trace elements, 1009, 1015
Tracking company information in other states
Attorneys General, 652
Department of Commerce/Economic Development, 652
environment regulators, 652
financial institutions, 651
Food and Drug Companies, 652
minority and small business, 652
state government contractors, 652
utility and cable TV regulators, 651
Trade
adjustment assistance, 758, 971
agreements with developed countries, 931
agricultural, 1037, 1038, 1039, 1223, 1231
China, 1186
database, 1231
deficit, 974
employment in U.S., impact on, 240, 931
fairs, 850
General Agreement on Tariffs and Trade (GATT), 1003, 1037
grain, 931, 970, 1031
immigration policy, impact on, 240, 931
leads databases, 857
maritime, 804, 926
missions, 850
overseas leads, 1231
Panama Canal, 806, 928
policy, 609
Remedy Assistance Center, 853
remedy assistance laws, 726
retail, 870
Senate subcommittee, 1181
shows, 1042
statistics, 862
technology, 971
U.S. agriculture, 1041
wholesale, 870
Trade fairs and missions, 849
Trade Opportunities Program (TOP), 850
Trade Promotion Coordinating Committee, 843
Trademarks, 1017, 1019-20, 1184
attorneys, 1019
Official Gazette, 1019
registration, 1020
search library, 1019
Trademark searches
Bell Atlantic Gateway, 1020
CompuServe, 1020
Derwent, 1020
Trademark Scan, 1020
Trademark Search Library, 1020
Traffic accidents, 373, 895, 1225
Traffic control devices, 353, 830
Traffic safety grants, 374
Training
air traffic controllers, 245, 786
antiterrorism, 613
Census Bureau, 875
child social workers, 614
Coast Guard, U.S., 244
conservation law enforcement, 611, 1133
crime lab scientists, 774
emergency planning, 355
environmental, 1106
Federal executives, 269
fish husbandry, 245, 1134
health care, 157
historical preservation, 306, 350
job, youths, 246
judicial, 621
law enforcement, 613, 614
maritime, 761
Merchant Marines, 249, 809
Native Americans, 245, 622

nuclear regulation, 1080
pilot schools, 248, 787
public policy, 274
racial conflict resolution, 349, 612, 616
trial advocacy, 610
veterans, 143
white collar crime, 613
wildfire investigation, 613
Tranquilizer warnings, 570
Translation of American books, 304, 913
Translators grants, 762
Transportation
accident investigations, 818
agribusiness, 1031
airline archive records, 783
appealing licensing decisions, 818
architecture, 292, 403, 822, 826, 1107
bus lines, 777, 827
coal slurry pipeline, 777, 827
common carrier insurance, 825
database, 353, 823
diesel fuel daily price, 825, 1051
elderly grants, 374
energy, 822
environmental issues, 292, 403, 822, 826, 1107
essential air service, 96, 785
foreign technology, 822, 932, 979
freight forwarders, 777, 827
grants, 373
handicapped grants, 374
hazardous materials, 822, 831, 971, 1152, 1222, 1225
House Committee on, 1184
House Subcommittee on, 1183
information referrals, 822
international policy, 786, 925
Interstate Commerce Commission, 777, 827
interstate, Senate committee, 1181
legal process agents, 828
loss and damage claims, 98
marketing studies, 777, 819
mass transit, 352, 820, 821
mergers, 777, 819
motor carrier applications, 824
national issues, 822, 827
oil tankers, 971
Panama Canal, 806, 928
policy, 100, 819
public, 353, 823
railroad abandonment, 829
railroad contract summaries, 825
railroads, 777, 827
rate reductions/increases, 831
research grants, 287, 822-23, 932, 979
Safety Institute, 100, 821, 831
safety, 822, 1229
security, 822
small business assistance, 726
space, 970
speakers, 821
speed limits, highway, 98, 352, 614, 828
statistics, 779, 823, 827, 868, 870
tariffs, 829
traffic safety projects, 352, 826
training grants, 185
transportation brokers, 777, 827
trucking companies, 777, 827
urban, 1225
water carriers, 777, 827
Transportation Safety Board, National, 820
Transportation, U.S. Department of
freedom of information, 819
libraries, 822
public information offices, 58
Small Business Innovative Research Program, 840

The thousands of studies in the Current Events Chapter and Experts Chapter are not included in this index.

Index

Transportation, U.S. Department of (continued)
Urban Mass Transit Administration, 823
Travel
abroad, 415, 860
advisories, 416, 417
air travel rights, 420, 785
Americans arrested abroad, 415
AMTRAK, 420
Apostle Islands, 403
Caribbean, 415
congressional caucus, 1187
country background notes, 416, 917
customs declarations, 416
customs duty, 417
customs regulations, 417
deaths, 416
document authentication, 415
dutiable articles, 416
Eastern Europe and Yugoslavia, 415
endangered species, 1138
financial assistance, 416
handicapped individuals, 421
highway conditions, 422
highway, 1223
hotel/motel rates, 422
hotlines, state, 422
immunization information, 417
importing agricultural products, 415
maps, 422
marketing, 421
medical assistance, 416
National Wildlife Refuges, 408
overseas advisories, 418
Overseas Citizens Services, 417
Panama Canal, 416
Panama Railroad, 417
passport applications, 415
People's Republic of China, 415
recreation on public lands, 403, 408, 414
senior citizens, 418
South Africa, 415
terrorism abroad, 418
visas, 415
Washington, D.C., 402
weather advice, 422
welfare/whereabouts, 416
Travel Emergency Center, 32
Travel overseas on government expense, 859
Travelers checks, 711
Treasury bills, 93
Treasury securities info-line, 33
bills and notes, 446
Treasury, U.S. Department of, 877
information line, 446
public information offices, 60
Treaties
arms control and disarmament, 936
congressional ratification, 1193
INF Treaty, 936
nuclear testing, 971
Panama Canal, 928
U.S. international agreements, 932
Tree rings, 1258, 1292
Trees, 140, 1130, 1265, 1292
genetic research, 1030
leaves, 1264, 1274, 1292
memorial and historic, 401
poster, 1265, 1281, 1292
products, 1281, 1292
tropical, 140, 1130
urban development, 124
Tribal Government Institute, 839
Tribology, 977, 1203
Trident Program community assistance, 362
Triticale, 1220
Tropical deforestation, 1100
Tropical diseases, 514, 970
Tropical forests, 927, 931, 970, 1031
Tropical rain forests, 927
Trout, 1292
Trucking, 1181
congressional caucus, 1187
importation, 100
Truman years teaching unit, 1292
Trust assets, 428, 429
Trust indentures, 444
Truth-in-Lending Act, 427
Tuberculosis, 518
National Institute of Allergy and Infectious Diseases, 539
research grants, 284
Tunnels, 827
Turkey, 1229
Turkey cooking hotline, 33
TVA
see Tennessee Valley Authority

U

UCC
see Uniform Commercial Code
UCC request forms, 630
Ukraine, 1186
Ulcers, 552
Ultrasound imaging, 530
Unclaimed property, 711
finders, 711
forgotten bank accounts, 711
uncashed stock dividends, 711
Unconventional cancer treatments, 33
Underground storage tanks, 1071, 1152
Underwater warfare, 960
Unemployment, 873, 1230
elderly, 388
grants, 387
insurance, 1181
loans, 758
Uniform Commercial Code (UCC), 630
Uniform Franchise Offering Circular (UFOC), 771
Uniform Interagency Bank Rating System, 430
Unions
collective bargaining agreements, 260
contract database, 240, 260
drug-free helpline, 590
financial disclosure, 259
investigations, 260
labor-management database, 256
labor-management negotiations, 257
members' Bill of Rights, 260
regulation compliance and enforcement, 257
veterans employment, 249
United Nations
agricultural trade data, 1041
Educational Scientific and Cultural Organization, 932
human rights issues, 930
international women's programs, 927
military expenditures, 936
Senate committee, 1181
State Department matters, 932
U.S. economic policy, 918
U.S. mission to, 933
U.S. policy toward, 932
United States Arms Control and Disarmament Agency, 74
United States Information Agency, 74
United States Development Cooperation Agency, 74
United States Geological Survey, 54
United States International Trade Commission, 74
Uranium, 1074
Urban Mass Transit Administration, 829
USDA
see Agriculture, U.S. Department of
USGS
see United States Geological Survey
USIA
see United States Information Agency
Used-cars, 1227

V

VA
see Veterans Affairs, U.S. Department of
Vacations, 1212
Vaccines, 944, 973
Federal policies, 973
influenza, 972
injuries, 972
pneumococcal, 973
Vandenberg Air Force Base, 989
Veal, 1229
Vehicles
crashworthiness, 96, 825
electric and hybrid, 976, 1050
inspections, 100, 822, 1055, 1108
safety standards, 101, 823
traffic fatalities, 1220
Vending machines, 671
Venture capital, 717, 729
Small Business Investment Companies, 754
Venus, 1092, 1240
craters, 1254, 1293
slides, 1287, 1289
Vermont
Affirmative Action, 888
Automated Tax Refund Information, 467
company directories, 667
corporation information, 662
Department of Motor Vehicles, 645
Directory of Labor Market Information, 888
Division of Licensing and Registration, 640
ENABLE Program, 138
Energy-Rated Homes of Vermont Mortgage Program, 138
Home Energy/Improvement Loan Program, 138
Home Mortgage Guarantee Board (VHMGB), 138
Housing and Conservation Board, 138
Housing Finance Agency, 138
Housing Foundation, Inc., 138
Housing Ventures, 138
Housing Vermont, 138
Industrial Projections to 2000, 888
IRS hotline, 465
Labor Market, 888
licensed professionals, 640
Low-Income Housing Tax Credit Program, 138
Mining and Quarrying, 888
Mobile Home Financing, 138
mobile home parks, 130
Mortgage Plus, 138
Mortgages for Vermonters, 138
Multi-Family Financing, 138
New Home Financing, 138
Occupational Projections to 2000, 888
Perpetually Affordable Housing Program, 138
Rural Vermont Mortgage, 138
Securities Division, 670
Small Business Administration Office, 839

The thousands of studies in the Current Events Chapter and Experts Chapter are not listed in this Index.

Index

state data centers, 904
State Housing Authority, 138
state information, 39
State International Trade Offices, 859
State Labor Office, 888
State Planning Office, 911
state procurement office, 842
state tax assistance, 500
surplus property auctions, 710
Tax form distribution center, 471
Tax forms and publications, 492
unclaimed property office, 716
Uniform Commercial Code, 634
U.S. International Trade Administration Office, 856
Vermont Selected Statistics, 906
Wage and Fringe Benefit Survey, 888
Vertebrates, 1137
Vessels
certificate of documentation, 798
crew certification, 798
inspections, 798
Veterans
Agent Orange exposure, 390
Alaska Veterans Mortgage Program, 130
alcohol or drug treatment, 390, 595
ambulatory self-care, 391
appealing benefit claims, 390, 395
Arlington National Cemetery, 391
benefits assistance, 390, 392
burials, 390-93, 944
chemical dependence outpatient help, 596
community program grants, 372
dental services, 391
dependents educational grants, 394
disability payments, 391, 395
disabled and employment, 564
driver training, 391
drug and alcohol treatment, 395, 596
education, 160, 392, 395, 1182
educational grants, 177, 186
employment and training, 249, 372, 388
employment with government contractors, 236
foreign education, 157
Government Procurement Assistance, 836
grants for dependents, 389, 391, 394
grants for homes, 393
grants, 372, 376, 392
health care scholarships, 157
health care, 392
health services research, 967
high school training, 149, 392
hiring incentives, 777
home buying, 122, 392
House Committee on, 1185
housing for disabled, 394
housing guaranteed loans, 128
indemnity grants, 395
insurance, 392, 393
job assistance, 392
job matching service, 244
job training grants, 391
life insurance, 1182
loans, 393
manufactured home loans, 129
Massachusetts General Lending, 134
medical benefits, 392, 393
medical care, 1182
medical grants, 395
medical research, 968
memorial affairs, 1185
nuclear radiation exposure, 390
nursing homes, 393
nutritional care, 391
paraplegic housing, 128
Pennsylvania Homestart Program, 137

pensions, 394, 1182
Presidential Memorial Certificates, 394
prosthetic appliances, 394
radiation exposure, 943
readjustment counseling, 394
recreation, 394
reemployment rights, 249, 255
rehabilitation, 394, 1182
religious services, 391
Senate committee, 1182
small business assistance, 726
small business loans, 719
social work, 394
statistics, 871
survivors educational grants, 394
Tennessee, 138, 888
training, 392
Vietnam, 1187
Virginia, 888
vocational rehabilitation grants, 395
voluntary service, 395
West Virginia, 888
Veterans Affairs, U.S. Department of, 698
public information offices, 62
Veterans Loan Program, 755
Veterinarians, 635
Veterinary drugs, 764, 1024
Veterinary medicine, 244, 1241
Vice-President, U.S.
records archive, 311
Vickers Stock Research Corp., 650
Victims
crime compensation, 599
database, 607
mortgage insurance, 126
resource center, 607
robbery, 611
Videodiscs
aerospace-related, 1277, 1288
Videos, 33, 1289, 1294
aerospace commercial uses, 985
aerospace-related, 1277, 1288
American Vision, 1293
Apollo missions, 1293
art, 1286, 1293
astronauts, 1289, 1294
CANCER, 542
drinking, 591
drug abuse prevention, 589, 590, 591, 1294
drug-free workplace, 590
drug testing, 592, 607
drunk driving, 591
elementary school drug prevention, 591
Employee Assistance Programs, 591
energy consumption, 1260, 1281, 1294
energy-related, 1261, 1286
environmental, 1263, 1267, 1283, 1294-95
flash floods 1270, 1297
franchising, 772
Gemini missions, 1271, 1294
Great Lakes, 1267, 1295
hearing impaired drug abuse, 589
high school drug abuse, 592
hurricanes, 1272, 1295, 1297
junior high school drug abuse, 592
Mars, 1274, 1294
Mercury flights, 1275, 1294
moon landing, 1289, 1294
NASA, 1271, 1289
pests, 1268, 1295
satellites, 1284, 1293
Skylab, 1285, 1294
smoking, 554
solar system, 1287, 1294
space exploration, 30, 1273, 1288, 1289
Space Shuttle Columbia, 1289, 1293, 1294
Space Station, 1293

space suits, 1294
Space Transportation System, 1289, 1294
thunderstorms, 1291, 1295, 1297
tornado, 1291, 1295, 1297
Voyager, 1293, 1294
recycling, 1262-1264, 1282, 1283, 1295
workplace drug abuse, 589
Wright brothers, 1293, 1298
Vietnam War
casualty lists, 648, 960
prisoners-of-war archives, 648
record archives, 311
veterans housing, 130
Violence
adolescent depression, 532
elder abuse, 557
stress, 532
Virgin Islands
Allocation of Individual Income Tax, 489
data centers, 904
Tax form distribution center, 471, 474
Tax forms and publications, 492, 477, 493
Virginia
Automated Tax Refund Information, 467
Business Resource Directory, 888
Business Services Directory, 911
company directories, 667
corporation information, 662
Division of Securities and Retail Franchising, 670
Economic Development Report, 911
Economic Developments, 911
Economic Indicators, 888
Employment and Training Indicators, 888
Employment and Wages in Establishments, 888
Export Management/Trading Companies, 911
Foreign Investment, 911
Franchises, 771
High Technology Communications, 911
High Technology Communications in Virginia, 907
High Technology-Biomedical, 911
Home Mortgage Loan Program, 139
Home Rehabilitation Loan Program, 139
Housing Development Authority, 139
Housing Fund, 139
Industrial Development, 911
IRS hotline, 465
Joint Program for Housing Persons with Mental Disabilities, 139
Labor Force by Sex and Minority Status, 888
Labor Market Review, 888
licensed professionals, 640
Licensed professions, 640
List of Employers By Size, 888
Low-Income Housing Tax Credit Program, 139
Manufacturing, 911
Metalworking Industries, 911
Multi-Family Loan Program, 139
Owners: Dealer and Information, 645
Printing Industry, 911
Public Schools, 888
Rental Rehabilitation Program, 139
Section 8 Rent Subsidy Programs, 139
Small Business Administration Office, 839
state data centers, 904
state information, 39
State Labor Office, 888
State Planning Office, 911
state procurement office, 842
state tax assistance, 500
surplus property auctions, 710
Targeted Area Program, 139

The thousands of studies in the Current Events Chapter and Experts Chapter are not included in this Index.

Index

Virginia (continued)
Tax form distribution center, 471
Tax forms and publications, 492
unclaimed property office, 716
Uniform Commercial Code Division, 634
U.S. International Trade Administration Office, 856
Wage Survey Selected Manufacturers Occupation, 888
Visas, 418, 623 932, 933
requirements of foreign governments, 860
Volunteers In Service To America (VISTA), 31-33, 384
drug prevention, 579
Visual arts
copyrights, 1020
Visual processing, 769
VITA centers, 454
Vitamins, 1015
recommended dietary allowances, 525
Viticulture, 774
Vocational training, 30, 245, 249
auto repair, 246
Voice of America, 401, 933
Volcanoes, 97, 976, 991, 993, 994
environmental hazards, 1143
information for kids, 1257-58, 1271, 1295
maps, 1092
publications, 1240
tracet bullets, 996, 1203
Volkswagen protection program, 96
Voltage, 1010
Volunteer Income Tax Assistance (VITA), 454, 461
Volunteering
consumer product safety, 109
drug alliance, 578
educators, 931
employment training, 384
engineers, 932
Fish and Wildlife Service, 383, 1137
Forest Service, 383
foster grandparents, 28, 383
Geological Survey, 93
grants, 378
health care clinical research, 383
health-care, 927
homelessness, 384
Indian reservations, 384
legal services, 357, 620
National Archives, 383
National Park Service, 383
National Volunteer Week, 383
pharmacology research, 566
program fundraising, 383
program grants, 181, 378
recreation on public lands, 408, 413, 1128
Retired Senior Volunteers Program, 384
senior companion volunteers, 384
Smithsonian research, 384
student community service projects, 384
tax assistance, 455
tax help to the elderly, 461
Veterans Affairs, Department of, 395
Volunteers in Service to America (VISTA), 384
youth treatment programs, 344, 1025, 1240
Voting
Americans overseas, 419
districts, 877
Voyager, 1273, 1284
slides, 1277, 1286, 1289
video, 1288, 1295
videocassette, 1293, 1294

W

Wagering taxes, 474
Wages, 1220
benefit information, 884
garnishments, 251
reporting, 462
Walking
see Exercise, 518
Warfare
biological, 976
chemical, 976
nuclear, 971
risk insurance, 761
Warranties, 96, 101
Washington State
Affirmative Action, 888
Aquaculture, 911
Area Wage Survey, 888
Automated Tax Refund Information, 467
company directories, 667
corporation information, 663
Demographic Information, 888
Department of Licensing, Highways/ Licensing, 645
Economic and Revenue Forecast for Washington State, 906
Foreign Exports, 911
Franchises, 771
IRS hotline, 465
Labor Market Monthly, 888
licensed professionals, 640
Licensed professions, 640
Low-Income Housing Tax Credit Program, 139
Mortgage Credit Certificate Program, 139
Multi-Family Program, 139
Multi-Family Tax Exempt Bond Financing Program, 139
Non-Profit Owners Program, 139
Occupational Profiles and Projections, 888
Securities Division, Department of Licensing, 670
Single Family Mortgage Revenue Bond Program, 139
Small Business Administration Offices, 839
state data centers, 904
State Housing Finance Commission, 139
state information, 39
State International Trade Offices, 859
State Labor Office, 888
State Planning Office, 911
state procurement office, 842
surplus property auctions, 710
Tax form distribution center, 471
Tax forms and publications, 492
unclaimed property office, 716
Uniform Commercial Code Division, 634
U.S. International Trade Administration Offices, 856
Washington, D.C., 402
see also District of Columbia
Washington Document Service, 650
Washington Service Bureau, 650
Washington, George
inaugural address, 1296
tomb, 314
Waste
disposal, 997
exchange network, 1145
hazardous, 976, 1097, 1103, 1118, 1148, 1151, 1203
high-level nuclear, 1074
low-level nuclear, 1077
management, 1142
medical, 972

minimization, 1152
municipal management, 977, 1203
nuclear, 1077
program grants, 288
radioactive, 972, 1079, 1102, 1147
solid, 1097, 1103, 1118, 1148, 1151
water treatment, 1097
Waste disposal, 997
activity book, 1264, 1283, 1296
grants and loans, 359
research grants, 288
Water, 975, 1111, 1258, 1296
acidification, 1118
agricultural water bank loans, 125
chemical contamination, 1118
chemical properties, 1258, 1296
clean, 1262, 1296
Clean Water Act, 1102
conservation, 934, 1265, 1296
cycle poster, 1265, 1292
database, 1217
desalination, 975
drinking, 1111
education materials, 1265, 1296
eutrophication, 1118
federal laws, 1121
fire extinguishing, 1003
flow technology, 1012
groundwater, 1099, 1112, 1258, 1271, 1296
hydrologic cycle, 1258, 1296
industrial water supply, 1121
National Stream Quality Accounting Network, 1118
pollution control grants, 376
pollution, 1098, 1103, 1109, 1118, 1122, 1148, 1151
quality, 1097, 1103, 1118, 1148, 1151
radiation, 1079, 1102, 1147
radionuclide transport, 1145
rain, 1258, 1282
reclamation and preservation, 1032, 1113, 1115
research grants, 1118
resources, national, 1121
rural clean water grants, 125
safety drinking water hotline, 1103, 1115
salinity, 1118
sedimentation, 1118
Senate committee, 1181
siltation, 1125
State programs, 1119
supply, 1097
Water Bank Program, 756
Water dowsing, 1258, 1296
Water pollution
protection grants, 377
research grants, 288
Watershed and aquatic habitat, 1125
Water Watch Program, 1266, 1273, 1296
Waterfowl, 1218
Watergate tapes and trial transcripts, 33, 311
Watershed development, 1184
Weapons
anti-satellite, 970
detection devices, 788, 941
museum, 961
Navy, U.S., 952
nuclear, 954, 958, 989
rifling characteristics, 613
systems, 943, 1183
tracking systems, 958
used in crimes, 610
Weather
aerospace research, 982
Climate Data Center, National, 1083
cloud seeding, 1114
daily maps, 1087, 1094

The thousands of studies in the Current Events Chapter and Experts Chapter are not listed in this Index.

Index

disasters, 357
flash floods, 1083
forecasting, 1297
forecasts, 1085, 1087
hurricanes, 1084
marine, 412, 803, 1084
national, 1086
publications, 1282, 1297
satellites, 1084
short-term predictions, 1083
state-by-state, 1084
tornado forecasting, 1086
tropical cyclones, 412, 803, 1084
tropical research, 1084
winter storms, 358
world-wide, 1087
Weatherization grants, 129, 389
Weatherization, 1061, 1065
Weeds, 1225
control, 1030, 1129
Weights and Measures Offices, State, 682
Welfare
program grants, 366
research grants, 285
training grants, 171
work incentive programs, 249
West Virginia, 906
Affirmative Action, 888
ARC Program, 139
Automated Tax Refund Information, 467
Building Revitalization/Reutilization Program, 139
Community Provider Financing Program, 139
company directories, 667
corporation information, 663
Department of Motor Vehicles, 645
Economic Summary, 888
Emergency Shelters Program, 139
Employment and Earnings Trends, 888
Home Rehab Program, 139
Housing Development fund, 139
Housing Development Fund/Army Corps of Engineers Flood Mitigation, 139
IRS hotline, 465
Land Development Program, 139
licensed professionals, 640
Licensing boards and professions, 640
Low-Income Housing Tax Credit Program, 139
Mortgage Credit Certificate Program, 139
Multi-Family Construction Loan Incentive Program, 139
Occupational Projections, 888
Rental Rehab Program, 139
Securities Division, State Auditor's Office, 670
Single Family Mortgage Program, 139
Small Business Administration Offices, 839
state data centers, 904
state information, 39
State International Trade Offices, 859
State Labor Office, 888
State Planning Office, 911
state procurement office, 842
state tax assistance, 500
surplus property auctions, 710
Tax form distribution center, 471
Tax forms and publications, 492
unclaimed property office, 716
Uniform Commercial Code Division, 634
U.S. International Trade Administration Office, 856
Veterans Report, 888
Wage Survey, 888
Women in the Labor Force, 888
Youth Report, 888

Wetlands, 970, 1031, 1098, 1101, 1122, 1137, 1265, 1296, 1297
Kentucky, 1264, 1297
poster, 1267, 1281, 1282, 1298
Whales
drawing, 1255, 1274, 1285, 1298
foreign policy issues, 914, 1095, 1132
protection, 926, 1100
Wheat, 756, 1220
Wheelchairs, 973
Whistleblower
hotlines, 251, 276
White House, 402
fellowships, 160
historical documents, 923
tours, 402
White-collar crime, 610
White-collar occupations, 241
White-collar salaries, 241
Wholesaling
agriculture, 1036
trade, 870
Whooping cranes, 1254, 1298
WIC (Women, Infants, and Children)
nutrition education, 523
Wild and Scenic River System, 409, 1122
Wildland fire, 1130
Wildlife
Alaskan, 1132
birds, 1135
contaminant research, 1138
database, 1221
disease prevention, 1138
emergency grain assistance, 1135
endangered and threatened, 1132-33
enhancement programs, 1122
federal protection laws, 1138
habitats, 1138
importation, 418
law enforcement, 611, 1133
management, 1134
National Wildlife Refuge System, 1138
Patuxent Wildlife Research Center, 1136
photographs, 295, 1134
publications, 1134
refuges, 396, 408, 1132
regulation and protection, 1184
research, 1134
speakers, 943
technology, 970, 1031
toxicology, 1101
waterfowl, 1137
Wildlife conservation, 945, 1132, 1142
education program, 1291, 1298
general interest publications, 1292, 1298
teacher workshops, 1291, 1298
Wildlife Refuges, 33
Wind
energy, 764, 1061
tunnels, 988
turbines, 1050
Wine, 1187
labeling, 97
production, 774
wineries, 671, 775
Wisconsin, 130
Affirmative Action, 888
Automated Tax Refund Information, 467
Blueprint Loan Program, 139
Business Development Bond Program, 139
Business Energy Fund Program, 139
Career Connection, 888
Career Opportunities Guide, 888
Civilian Labor Force Estimates, 888
Community Housing Alternatives Program, 139
company directories, 667

corporation information, 663
Credit Relief Outreach Program, 139
DEER Program, 139
Department of Regulation and Licensing, 640
Disabled persons housing programs, 130
Elderly Housing Program Fund, 139
Employment, 888
Employment and Business Ownership, 911
Employment and Wages, 888
Entrepreneurial Development Programs, 911
environmental hazard removal, 130
Franchises, 771
Home Energy Loan Program, 139
Home Improvement Loan Program, 139
HOME Program, 139
Housing and Economic Development Authority, 139
Housing Development Authority, 911
Investment Board Investments, 911
IRS hotline, 465
Labor Management Cooperation, 911
licensed professionals, 640
Linked Deposit Loan Program, 139
Low-Income Housing Tax Credits, 139
Management Assistance, 911
Minority Businesses, 911
Neighborhood Housing Program Fund, 139
New Industries, 911
Office of Commissioner of Securities, 670
Ozone Air Quality Management, 911
Partnership for Housing Development, 139
Persons-in-Crisis Housing Program Fund, 139
Plant Expansions, 911
Population Survey, 888
Rental Housing Programs, 139
Rental Property Energy Efficiency Loan Fund, 139
Rental Rehabilitation Program, 139
Section 8 Rent Subsidy Program, 139
Small Business Administration Offices, 839
Small Business Loan Guarantee Program, 139
state data centers, 904
state information, 39
State International Trade Offices, 859
State Labor Office, 888
State Planning Office, 911
state procurement office, 842
state tax assistance, 500
surplus property auctions, 710
Tax form distribution center, 471
Tax forms and publications, 492
Tax Incremental Financing, 911
Tourism, 911
unclaimed property office, 716
Uniform Commercial Code Division, 634
U.S. International Trade Administration Office, 856
Wage Survey, 888
WHEDA Foundation Grants, 139
Women and Minority housing programs, 130
Youth Unemployment, 911
Witnesses
Forest Service and drugs, 603
security protection, 608, 610
WMC Service Corporation, 667
Women
alcoholism, 594
business assistance, 836
business loans, 728
Congress, in, 1188
congressional caucus for, 1187
developing countries, 918, 927, 934

The thousands of studies in the Current Events Chapter and Experts Chapter are not included in this Index.

Index

Women (continued)
- dietary needs, 520
- education grants, 177, 187
- employment in non-traditional fields, 249
- health resources, 515
- highway construction jobs, 249
- Inter-American Foundation, 924
- labor force trends, 234
- legislation affecting, 241
- low-income and nutrition ideas, 523
- National Association of Commissions for Women, 235
- procurement assistance, government, 834, 836, 755
- science careers, 976
- shelters, 612
- small business, 726
- Third World, 912
- workforce, history, 241
- working mothers, 234

Wood, 970, 1031
- insects and diseases, 142, 1032
- processors, 1124
- products, 1124

Woodrow Wilson International Center for Scholars, 306, 1094

Woodsy Owl, 33, 351, 409, 1107, 1242, 1266, 1298

Wool, 756

Workplace
- allergies, 538
- anti-drug program, 589
- automation, 971
- drug abuse hotline, 590
- drug-free helpline, 590
- drugs, 600
- federal employee drug abuse, 592
- health hazards detection, 262, 517, 531, 572, 970
- health promotion, 262, 517, 523
- high blood pressure control programs, 548
- inspection disputes, 266
- passive smoking, 972
- technology, 244
- toxic hazards, 571-72

Workshops, 899
- home economics, 29
- plant and lawn, 31

Workshops, teacher
- National Aeronautics and Space Administration, 1257, 1276, 1277, 1281, 1284, 1288
- National Air and Space Museum, 1277, 1288, 1290
- National Archives, 1277, 1291

World Bank, 429, 853

World Food Program, 1036

World Health Organization, 576

World import/export statistics, 851

World Traders Data Reports, 849

World War I, teaching unit, 1298

World War II, teaching unit, 1298

Wright brothers, 962, 1200, 1293, 1298
- video, 1293, 1298
- Orville, first flights, 1298

Writers, 762
- free money, 26, 33
- freelance, 29
- grants, 762

Writing education, 1282, 1290, 1298

Wyoming
- Affirmative Action, 888
- Automated Tax Refund Information, 467
- Bureau of Land Management office, 695
- Business Development Kit, 911
- Community Development Authority, 139
- company directories, 667
- corporation information, 663
- Department of Transportation, 645
- IRS hotline, 465
- Labor Force Trends, 888
- licensed professionals, 640
- Licensing boards and professions, 640
- Low-Income Tax Credit Program, 139
- Manufacturing and Hospitals, 888
- Manufacturing and Mining, 911
- *Mineral Yearbook*, 911
- Occupational Employment Statistics, 888
- Rental Rehab Program, 139
- Section 8 Rental Assistance Program, 139
- Securities Division, 670
- Single Family Mortgage Program, 139
- state data centers, 904
- state information, 39
- State International Trade Offices, 859
- State Labor Office, 888
- State Planning Office, 911
- state procurement office, 842
- state property auctions, 710
- Tax form distribution center, 471
- Tax forms and publications, 492
- *The Wyoming Data Handbook*, 906
- unclaimed property office, 716
- Uniform Commercial Code, 634
- Urban Homesteading Program, 139
- U.S. International Trade Administration Office, 857
- WCDA CDBG Revolving Loan Fund, 139

X

X-Rays, 972, 1011, 1005, 1226

Y

Your rights as a taxpayer, 492

Youth
- drug-free athletes, 594
- drug testing high-risk, 579
- high risk drug abuse, 588
- Indians and chemical dependence, 592
- positive peer prevention, 593

Youth Conservation Corps, 250, 1141

Z

Zero-gravity drop tower, 988

Zip codes, 636, 899

Zoology
- invertebrate, 320
- vertebrate, 320

The thousands of studies in the Current Events Chapter and Experts Chapter are not listed in this Index.